前　言
Introduction

值此世纪交替之际，《新时代汉英大词典》终于和广大读者见面了。这部词典收词十二万条，另有附录二十余种。它兼顾学习与参考两个目的，以广大英语学习者、使用者为服务对象，也可供外国读者学习汉语、了解中国之用。本书编者不避寒暑，历时十载，三易其稿，反复修改、增删，所刻意追求的目标，可以概括为六个字：求新、求确、求实。

近二十年来，随着我国社会飞速发展，世界科技突飞猛进，汉语新词层出不穷。为了反映这种时代特点，满足读者的需要，本书以求新为宗旨，对那些在社会上得到广泛承认和使用的词语，尽量搜求，并提供确切的英语释义。

在基本语词方面，本书收集了相当一部分近年来涌现的新词语，以及新近进入普通话的方言（含港台词语）和外来语，如“价位”、“低迷”、“误区”、“大款”、“大腕”、“资深”、“发烧友”、“国脚”、“迷你”、“唱衰”、“素质教育”、“应试教育”等。求新的另一重要方面，就是对旧词所形成的新义着力辨析和诠释，因此本书在词义方面多有增益。如“包装”的对象由商品扩展到人和其他事物，“驱动”由“施加外力使动起来”引申为“驱使行动”（受金钱的驱动/在暴利的驱动下）等。

本书不拘泥于一般语词工具书不收或少收百科词条的惯例，在这方面广为搜录。在经贸、金融等社科领域，即收词一万余条，包括不少新词，例如，“知识经济”、“可持续发展”、“期权”、“投资组合”、“对冲基金”、“风险资本”、“物业”、“按揭”等等。

随着各学科的相互渗透，许多自然科学词汇，特别是高科技词汇，已逐渐进入一般人的工作和生活领域。为此，本书对自然科学方面的词语也收录了一万余条，并特别注意收集将对新世纪产生长远影响的新词，例如：“信息高速公路”、“数字地球”、“因特网”、“主页”、“电子邮件”、“网上交易”、“下载”、“黑客”、“千年虫”、“防火墙”、“朊毒”、“克隆”、“仿真技术”、“智能机器人”、“禽流感”、“二恶英”、“隐形飞机”、“灵巧炸弹”、“战区导弹防御系统”等。

所谓求确，首先是力争英语释义切合汉语原意，避免望文生义、以讹传讹、“貌合神离”。例如“文韬武略”，原指《六韬》、《三略》，均属兵书，后引申为用兵的谋略。有的英译为“civil and military skills”，显属望文生义，我们改译为“military expertise; military strategy”。再如“特异功能”，如果译成“extraordinary powers”则形似实非，应译为“extra-sensory perception (ESP)”。关于我国文化的词语，往往更难确切地给以英语释义。例如“节气”一词的传统译法是“solar term”（太阳运行的某一阶段），其解释则往往只指特定的一天及其后的一个阶段。实际上，“节气”首先指太阳到达黄经某一度的时刻，其次指那一天，再次指从这一时刻到太阳抵达下一个黄经度之前的时期。因此，我们对“节气”首先释义为“seasonal division point”，然后给以比较完整的解释。由于反映中国文化的用语，在英语里往往找不到相同或相似的说法，一般词书就语焉不详，甚至予以回避。我们对其中比较常用的或属于“国粹”的，都本着对读者负责的态度，努力予以介绍，如关于线装书的“版口”、“黑口”、“白口”等，

在本书中都有比较详细的解释。

在立条方面，以基本语词而论，我们参考了《现代汉语词典》和其他权威词典，收入了大量的词、词组、惯用语、成语、俗语、谚语等。为了避免随意性，本书努力坚持收词必须符合以下标准：1.经过一定时间考验已站住脚的新词语；2.常见或仍有某种用处的古旧词语；3.比较通用的方言词语（主要是北京或北方方言，以及港台词语）；4.常见的、结构比较固定、已经产生某种转义的词组。

考虑到汉英两种语言在词形变化上一无一有，在义项的划分上我们坚持按意义差别区分词义，以“立足汉语，兼顾英语”的原则来规范义项。一般实词条目不生硬地标示词类，只是在难以用对应词语释义的虚词（助词、介词、连词）和某些实词（量词、叹词、象声词和个别副词）条目中才标明词类，说明用法。而对于汉英两种语言的某些共通之处，如某些植物与其果实同名，某些词的本义可以作同样的引申，或者一个词的某些义项在英语里无区别或区别甚微，我们就不墨守汉语辞书所划分的义项，而是根据英语特点灵活处理（比如合并义项），并举例来说明。

本书注意根据国家的有关标准及权威机构或权威辞书的定译来规范外来词译名。比如 Internet，我们采用“因特网”而不是“英特网”。但为了方便读者，仍列出某些常见的别译、旧译，并用“参见”（*see also*）方式引导查阅有关的定译。至于汉字的字形和读音，也根据权威部门或权威辞书认真予以规范。

至于例证，本书尽力做到三点：1.选例恰当，能说明问题；2.英译准确、地道，符合英语习惯；3.通过不同的例证，引导读者跳出单纯寻求对应说法的窠臼。

总之，无论是英语释义，还是例证翻译，为了对读者负责，我们不仅组织全体编写人员反复推敲，在某些难点上与英美专家切磋，拿出译文来征求他们的意见，还专门聘请经验丰富的英美专家认真审读全书，以保证英语的质量。

所谓求实，就是注重实用性。这表现为：

一、为满足读者在知识面上的多种需求，本书力求收词广泛，仅基本语词就收录近九万五千条。另外，如上所述，本书注意搜集社科和科技等方面的词语，共两万五千余条。

二、注意例证的多样和实用。本书举例尽量做到既有各种常用短语，又有体现不同用法的句子，并注意长短搭配，直译意译结合。通过例证，引导读者进一步理解词义，体会词语在不同语境下使用上的差异，注意运用上的灵活性，以及遣词造句中的种种微妙之处。

三、为读者在使用上提供种种方便。在释义上，本书尽量少用“互见”（cross reference），尤其避免让读者为了一个简单的对应词去“见”（*see*）另一相隔甚远的词条。对重要人物、地名、团体、企业、事件等，除提供对应词外，还附有简释。在某些常用字中，特意选用一些有用的“逆引”例证，如“花”字下列举了“牡丹花”、“荷花”、“菊花”、“梅花”等四大国花和“杜鹃花”等常用花名，以免读者一一查找。对于专名的译文，一般人名以汉语拼音为主，必要时附以旧译；而对近现代的一些重要人物，则一般采用通用的译名，附以汉语拼音。另外，本书还搜集了我国少数民族和港澳台地区的非汉语拼音的常见专名，以及使用汉字或曾经使用汉字但读音迥异的日本、新加坡、朝鲜、韩国、越南等国的重要专名。书后附有二十多种各有特点、比较实用的附录，内中不少颇具中国文化特色，如“亲属关系”、“二十四节气”、“天干地支”、“甲子纪年”等。

本词典在为期十年的编写过程中得到外交学院和商务印书馆领导的大力支持。部分词条的修改稿经英国专家 David Crook 和美籍专家 Jane Su 的校改。附录中有些问题曾经外交部有关同志协助解决。吴岫光、曹燕萍、庄南滨、张良谦、杨莉等参加了部分词条的编写工作。特别是本书篇幅浩

大、涉及面广，在最后的编辑工作中，商务印书馆外语工具书编辑室薛琪、周欣、胡龙彪、王良碧、卢艳丽、许江天、孙亮、张月中、杨冀、周治淮、周陵生、黄家宁等全力以赴，加班加点，认真复核，对保证本书的出版质量起了重要作用。在此，编者谨对上述单位和人员一并表示衷心的谢意。

十年来，我们虽然尽了最大努力以编纂一部能在时代性、科学性和实用性上适应21世纪读者实际需要的新型汉英词典，然而直到完成本书之后才真正体会这一任务的艰巨，并深感仍然存在不少力不从心、有待改进之处。现在我们把这本《新时代汉英大词典》奉献给广大读者和同行专家，请大家在使用中比较、批评，以便进一步补充它、完善它，使它更好地为大家服务。这正是我们编写这部词典的目的所在。

编　者

1999年8月于北京

凡　例

A Guide to the Use of the Dictionary

一　条目安排

1. 本书收词以现代汉语词语为主，酌收古旧语和方言词语，所收条目分单字条目和多字条目。单字条目有繁体、异体的，加括号附于正体之后；异体字只适用于个别义项时，在其左上角加所适用的义项数码，如："眷(❷睠)"、"搜(❶蒐)"。

2. 单字条目按汉语拼音字母顺序排列。同音异调的按声调顺序排列。同音同调的按起笔笔形"点(丶)、横(一)、直(丨)、撇(丿)、折(乛)"的顺序排列，同声旁的字则排在一起。如 chā 音节共收"差、艖、碴、喳、馇、嚓、臿、插、锸、叉、杈、扠"等字，其中"差"、"碴"、"嚓"、"臿"、"叉"按起笔笔顺排列，其他字按声旁分列于这几个字的后面。

3. 单字条目中，形同而音、义不同的，分立条目，如："奔"bēn 和"奔"bèn，"奇"jī 和"奇"qí。形、义相同而音不相同，各有适用范围的，也分立条目，如："露"lù 和"露"lòu，"绿"lǜ 和"绿"lù 。这两类条目用 *see also*（"另见"）相互关联。形、音相同而因词源、词性等原因需要分别处理的，亦分立条目，如："角^1"、"角^2"、"角^3"、"角^4"、"角^5"。轻声字一般排在轻声音节中，如："呗"bei、"得"de、"啰"luo、"们"men 等；但也有为了释义的方便紧接在同形的非轻声后面的，如："头"tou 排在"头"tóu 后面。

4. 多字条目按字头列于所属的单字条目之下。凡多字条目不止一条的，依第二字的拼音顺序排列；第二字相同的，依第三字排列，以下类推。同一字头下音同而字不同的多字条目，按笔画排列。如"年历"排在"年利"的前面。

5. 形同而音、义不同的多字条目，分别立条，如："同行"tóngháng 和"同行"tóngxíng。这类条目也用 *see also*（"另见"）相互关联。

6. 多字条目意义相同而有不同说法的，本书择其最常见的立条，而酌列其他说法于后。如：

　　糟蹋 zāota　*also*"糟踏"❶... ❷...

　　草体 cǎotǐ　❶... ❷ *also*"手写体"...

7. 有些多字条目意义相关而需参见，在英文释义后以 *see also*（"另见"）引出。如："大寒" dàhán ❶... ❷... ❸... *see also*"节气" jiéqi；"二十四节气" èrshísì jiéqì。

8. 以西文字母开始的词语，如："B 超"、"F-1 赛车"…，一律置于词典正文之后。含有西文字母的其他词语，仍按其所属汉字排列，如："阿 Q"…。

二　注音

1. 本书条目均以汉语拼音字母注音。声调一般只注原调，不标变调。儿化音只在原词拼音后

加“r”,不标读音的实际变化。多音节词的音节界线有可能混淆的,用隔音符号(')隔开,如:“堤岸” dī'àn。

2. 多字条目的注音,原则上按词分写。其中四字熟语,凡可以分为两节来读的,中间加短横连写,如:“劳苦功高”láokǔ-gōnggāo;凡不能分成两段读的,直接连写,如:“平心而论”píngxīn'érlùn。

3. 专名和姓氏的注音,第一个字母大写,如:“郗” Xī、“联合国”Liánhéguó、“马六甲海峡” Mǎliùjiǎ Hǎixiá。但某些已转化为普通名词的,不大写,如:“广柑”guǎnggān、“哥特式” gētèshì。

三 释义

1. 本书释义以词语的现代普通话用法为主,酌收某些古旧义和方言义。

2. 汉语字、词的英语释义,一般使用词性相同的对应词;有两个以上对应词的,用分号“;”分开。如:

熬 āo cook in water; boil

有直译和意译的,则通常先直译,后意译。为使二者区分开来,有时还在意译之前,加上〈比喻〉这一门类词。如:

蝼蚁 lóuyǐ mole crickets and ants; nobodies; nonentities

春宵 chūnxiāo spring night;〈比喻〉night of sexual bliss

有时则在二者之间加破折号,以示后者为前者的解释。如:

驴唇不对马嘴 lǘchún bùduì mǎzuǐ donkeys' lips don't match horses' jaws—beside the point

3. 当汉语和英语对应词的词义或用法不完全一致时,加圆括号用英语对释义加以限定或补充。如:

馈赠 kuìzèng present (a gift)

攒三聚五 cuánsān-jùwǔ (of people) gather in threes and fours

英文说明需要夹用汉语的,也放在圆括号内。如:(short for 毛泽东选集)、(shortened as 安)、(popularly known as 艾滋病)。

4. 有些字、词无英语对应词,则采用说明的方式处理。如:

袄 ǎo short Chinese-style coat or jacket

有些社科或科技方面的词语在英语对应词之后附有简短的说明;有的说明属于引申性质,则用圆括弧放在对应词后。如:

安妥 āntuǒ ❶... ❷ ANTU or antu, a rat poison

辛亥革命 Xīnhài Gémìng Revolution of 1911 (led by Dr. Sun Yat-sen, which overthrew the Qing Dynasty)

叹词、助词、象声词等以斜体说明其用法。如:

啊 (呵) á 〈叹词〉 *used to ask a further question or request repetition of what was said*: ...

5. 一词多义的条目,以❶❷❸等数码分列义项。如:

角[1] jué *also* “脚”jué ❶ role; part: ... ❷ 〈戏曲〉type of role: ... ❸ actor or actress: ...

6. 不能单独使用的字,作如下处理:

a) 后面有词条的,不作说明。如:

裤 jiè

裤子 jièzi 〈方言〉 diaper

b) 只能作为某词的词素的,用 *see* (“见”)引出该词。如:

孓 jué *see* “孑孓” jiéjué

猡 luó *see* “猪猡” zhūluó

c) 只用于地名或其他专名中的,用英文说明(斜体)加举例的方式处理。如:

堡 pù *used in place names in lieu of* 铺:十里~ Ten-*li* Pu

7. 同音节或同字头的等义或同义条目中,往往只有主要的条目有释义,而在非主要条目下用 *see* (“见”)引出主条。如:

饧 táng *see* “糖” táng

拉拉蛄 làlàgǔ *see* “蝲蝲蛄” làlàgǔ

8. 需要用门类词时用尖括号标明,放在所适用的词条或义项的释义之前。如:

阿拉 ālā 〈方言〉 ❶ I; me; my: . . . ❷ we; us; our

暗 àn ❶ dark; dim; dull: . . . ❷ hidden; secret: . . . ❸ 〈书面〉 hazy; unclear: . . .

9. 音译的外来语在释义前用圆括号内的 transliteration(“音译”)标明;需要解释的,则用英文注明:

体恤衫 tǐxùshān (transliteration) T-shirt

腊克 làkè (transliteration, same as 清喷漆) lacquer

10. 关于释义的其他说明:

a) 有些条目为某国或某地区的特定制度、事物或说法,本书在释义前加简略英语说明,放在圆括号内。如:

议会 yìhuì. . . (UK) Parliament; (US) Congress; (France) National Assembly; (Japan) Diet; (Germany) Reichstag; (Russia) Duma; (Israel) Knesset: . . .

b) 释义使用非英语外来语时,一般用斜体;如已有英文对应词,则视情况在斜体的外来语名称外加圆括号或径与对应词并列。如:

柜柳 jǔliǔ *also* “元宝枫”. . . *Pterocarya stenoptera*

锯齿草 jùchǐcǎo. . . alpine yarrow (*Achillea alpina*)

阿訇 āhōng *ahung*; imam

c) 释义中的英文缩略语如用于全称后,则用圆括号标出;如直接用于释义,则在其后用圆括号标明全称。如:

锇 é 〈化学〉 osmium (Os)

到岸价格 dào'àn jiàgé cost, insurance and freight (CIF)

托福 tuōfú. . . TOEFL (Test of English as a Foreign Language)

四 例证

1. 本书在条目释义后,用冒号“:”引出例证,例证中用“~”替代本条目,例证之间用“/”隔开。

同一例证有不止一种英译时,如果是词或词组,用“;”隔开,如果是句子则用 *or* 隔开。如:

暗暗 àn'àn secretly; inwardly; to oneself:~起誓 swear to oneself /~思忖 turn sth. over in one's mind; think to oneself / ...

黯然销魂 ànrán-xiāohún extremely sad and depressed; dejected:~者,唯别而已矣! Parting is such sad sorrow. *or* There is no sorrow like sorrow at parting.

2. 为简便起见,有些单字条目的义项以其后的多字条目为例证。本书用 *see*(“见”)引出作为例证的多字条目,并用“~”代替条目单字。如:

判 pàn ❶ distinguish; differentiate; separate: *see* “~别”; “~明” ❷ obviously (different): *see* “~然”; “~若两人” ❸ ... ❹ ...

3. 例证英译的可替换部分放在圆括号内,前面加 *or*,如:

惹 rě ❶ ...:招~是非 bring trouble on (*or* to) oneself; invite trouble ... ❷ ...:此人是个烈性子,~不得。The chap has a fiery temper and is not to be provoked (*or* trifled with)... ❸ ...: 尽量不要~人注意。Try as best as you can not to attract (*or* draw) attention ...

4. 例证按“先短语,后句子;先直译,后意译”的顺序安排。如:

偏[1]piān ❶ inclined or leaning to one side; slanting; diverging:~过身去 turn sideways /正南~东 south by east /中间~右 right of centre /这一处理~宽。The verdict erred on the lenient side. /太阳~西了。The sun slanted to the west. /他打~了。He overshot the mark.

5. 本书例证中的引文不注出处。引用诗词不分行,以英语大写字母表示一行的开始。如:

心潮 xīncháo ...: ... 把酒酹滔滔,~逐浪高! I pledge my wine to the surging torrent, The tide of my heart swells with the waves.

五 其他说明

1. 本书英文一概以英国拼法为准,不列其他拼法;有几种写法的,取规范写法或常见写法,不列变体。

2. 专名作为条目时,本书视必要列出不同译法并加说明,如:

毛泽东 Máo Zédōng Mao Zedong (formerly translated as Mao Tse-tung, 1893 - 1976): ...

珠穆朗玛峰 Zhūmùlǎngmǎfēng Mount Qomolangma (known in the West as Mount Everest): ...

行文中的专名(包括中国不同地区和其他国家使用的汉字专名或汉字译名)一般按“名从主人”的原则处理:毛泽东 Mao Zedong (不用 Mao Tse-tung); 北京 Beijing (不用 Peking);珠穆朗玛峰 Mount Qomolangma; 李光耀 Lee Kuan Yew。

少量长期以来已为英文读者接受的习惯译法,仍予保留。如:

孔子 Confucius; 孟子 Mencius; 长江 Yangtze River; 黄河 Yellow River; 澳门 Macao; 道教 Taoism; 《论语》*Analects*。

3. 释义和例证中的词、词组凡为名词的,开始的冠词均省去,以节省篇幅:

鞍 ān saddle

长江 Chángjiāng Changjiang River; Yangtze River

爱好者 àihàozhě lover (of art, sports, etc.); enthusiast: . . . 足球～ football enthusiast; football fan /文学～ devotee of literature /集邮～ stamp collector; philatelist

如果释义不是对应词,而是一种解释,或者例证中有量词,则英文保留不定冠词。如:

艾[1] ài ❶ . . . ❷ (Ài) a surname

批[2] pī ❶ . . . ❷〈量词〉batch; lot; group:刚到的一～货 a new lot of goods/ . . .

4. 本书引用的资料(包括附录)一般截至1998年年底,少数截至1999年年底。

附:门类词总表

一、词类:

〈副词〉〈介词〉〈连词〉〈量词〉〈叹词〉〈象声〉〈助词〉

二、修辞:

〈褒义〉〈比喻〉〈贬义〉〈粗话〉〈方言〉〈讽刺〉〈古语〉〈敬词〉〈旧语〉〈口语〉〈谦词〉〈书面〉〈俗语〉〈套语〉〈婉词〉〈戏谑〉〈修辞〉〈谚语〉

三、百科:

〈测绘〉〈船舶〉〈道教〉〈地理〉〈地质〉〈电工〉〈电学〉〈电子〉〈动物〉〈法律〉〈纺织〉〈佛教〉〈工美〉〈航海〉〈航空〉〈航天〉〈核物理〉〈化工〉〈化学〉〈环保〉〈机械〉〈基督教〉〈计算机〉〈建筑〉〈交通〉〈金融〉〈经济〉〈军事〉〈考古〉〈会计〉〈矿业〉〈历史〉〈林业〉〈逻辑〉〈美术〉〈迷信〉〈农业〉〈皮革〉〈气象〉〈汽车〉〈商业〉〈摄影〉〈生化〉〈生理〉〈生物〉〈石油〉〈兽医〉〈数学〉〈水利〉〈体育〉〈天文〉〈铁路〉〈通信〉〈统计〉〈外交〉〈外贸〉〈微生物〉〈文学〉〈无线电〉〈舞蹈〉〈物理〉〈戏剧〉〈戏曲〉〈心理〉〈信息〉〈畜牧〉〈药学〉〈冶金〉〈医学〉〈伊斯兰〉〈音乐〉〈印刷〉〈影视〉〈语言〉〈乐器〉〈杂技〉〈哲学〉〈政治〉〈植物〉〈中药〉〈中医〉〈自控〉〈宗教〉

新旧字形对照表

（字形后圆圈内的数字表示字形的笔画数）

Old and New Forms of Characters

(Numbers in circles indicate number of strokes)

旧字形	新字形	新字举例	旧字形	新字形	新字举例
⺿④	艹③	花草	耳⑧	耳⑦	敢嚴
⻍④	⻌③	连速	者⑨	者⑧	都著
幵⑥	开④	型形	直⑧	直⑧	值植
丰④	丰④	艳沣	黾⑧	黾⑧	绳鼋
巨⑤	巨④	苣渠	咼⑨	呙⑧	過蜗
屯④	屯④	纯顿	垂⑨	垂⑧	睡郵
瓦⑤	瓦④	瓶瓷	食⑨	食⑧	飲飽
反④	反④	板饭	郎⑨	郎⑧	廊螂
丑④	丑④	纽杻	彔⑧	录⑧	渌箓
比⑤	比④	昆毕	昷⑩	昷⑨	温瘟
犮⑤	犮⑤	拔茇	骨⑩	骨⑨	滑骼
印⑥	印⑤	茚	鬼⑩	鬼⑨	槐嵬
耒⑥	耒⑥	耕耘	旣⑪	既⑨	溉厩
吕⑦	吕⑥	侣营	蚤⑩	蚤⑨	搔骚
攸⑦	攸⑥	修倏	敖⑪	敖⑩	傲骜
爭⑧	争⑥	净静	莽⑫	莽⑩	漭蟒
产⑥	产⑥	彦産	眞⑩	真⑩	慎填
𦍌⑦	𦍌⑥	差养	䍃⑩	䍃⑩	摇遥
杀⑦	杀⑥	殺摋	黃⑫	黄⑪	廣横
幷⑧	并⑥	屏拼	虛⑫	虚⑪	墟歔
吳⑦	吴⑦	蜈虞	異⑫	異⑪	冀戴
角⑦	角⑦	解确	象⑫	象⑪	像橡
奐⑨	奂⑦	换痪	奧⑬	奥⑫	澳襖
㡀⑧	㡀⑦	敝弊	普⑬	普⑫	谱氆

部首检字表
Radical Index

说　明

部首次序按笔画多少排列，同画数的，按起笔丶一丨丿乛的顺序排列。有些字分别收入几个部首内，如“古”收入“十”部和“口”部；分不清部首的字，按起笔分列丶一丨丿乙五个单笔部首内。

（一）部首目录

（部首右边的号码指检字表的页码）

（二）检字表

1. 字右边的号码指词典正文的页码。
2. 带圆括弧的字是繁体字或异体字。

宀部

辶部

工部

土部

口部

子(孑)部

纟(糸)部

马(馬)部

皿部

钅(金)部

矢部

禾部

ā

吖 ā

吖啶 ādìng 〈化学〉acridine:～黄〈药学〉acriflavine /～染料 acridine dye

吖嗪 āqín 〈化学〉azine

阿

ā 〈方言〉❶ *prefix used to form a term of endearment with a pet name, monosyllabic surname, or number denoting order of seniority in a family*: ～方 A Fang /～财 A Cai /～洪 A Hong /～大 A Da — the eldest (son in a family) ❷ *prefix used before a kinship term*: ～妈 mom/～爸 dad
see also à;ē

阿贝 Ābèi Ernst Abbe (1840-1905), German physicist:～理论〈物理〉Abbe's theory /～聚光镜 Abbe condenser /～折射计 Abbe refractometer

阿鼻地狱 ābí dìyù 〈佛教〉*avici*, infernal region where souls of those who have committed grave sins on earth are consigned

阿比让 Ābǐràng Abidjan, capital of Cote d'Ivoire (formerly Ivory Coast)

阿比西尼亚 Ābǐxīníyà Abyssinia (now called Ethiopia):～人 Abyssinian

阿波罗 Ābōluó Apollo, Greek and Roman god of the sun

阿波罗飞船 Ābōluó fēichuán 〈航天〉Apollo (spaceship)

阿波罗计划 Ābōluó jìhuà 〈航天〉Apollo programme (moon-landing programme launched by NASA of the US in the 1960's and 1970's)

阿布扎比 Ābùzhābǐ Abu Dhabi, capital of the United Arab Emirates

阿昌族 Āchāngzú Achang nationality (living in Yunnan Province)

阿的平 ādìpíng 〈药学〉Atabrine

阿爹 ādiē 〈方言〉❶ dad ❷ (paternal) granddad; grampa

阿斗 Ādǒu ❶ infant name of Liu Shan (刘禅, 207-271), last emperor of Shu Han (蜀汉, 221-263), known for incompetence and weakness of character ❷ weak-minded person; fool: 扶不起的～ good-for-nothing (*or* ne'er-do-well) who is beyond help /他简直是个～。He is simply hopeless. /你如果把他看作～,那你就大错特错了。You are sadly mistaken if you take him for a fool.

阿尔巴尼亚 Ā'ěrbāníyà Albania:～人 Albanian /～语 Albanian (language)

阿尔卑斯山 Ā'ěrbēisīshān the Alps

阿尔茨海默症 Ā'ěrcíhǎimòzhèng *also* "老年痴呆症" lǎonián chīdāizhèng Alzheimer's disease

阿尔法版本 ā'ěrfǎ bǎnběn 〈信息〉alpha

阿尔法粒子 ā'ěrfǎ lìzǐ 〈物理〉alpha particle

阿尔法射线 ā'ěrfǎ shèxiàn 〈物理〉alpha ray

阿尔及尔 Ā'ěrjí'ěr Algiers, capital of Algeria

阿尔及利亚 Ā'ěrjílìyà Algeria:～人 Algerian

阿尔泰山 Ā'ěrtàishān Altai Mountains (in central Asia)

阿飞 āfēi young hooligan or street rowdy, usually in outlandish dress: 这帮～,如不加管束,不久就会成为青少年犯罪分子。These teenage hooligans, if not taken in hand, will soon become juvenile delinquents.

阿伏伽德罗定律 Āfújiādéluó dìnglǜ 〈化学〉Avogadro's law

阿芙蓉 āfúróng 〈旧语〉opium

阿富汗 Āfùhàn Afghanistan:～人 Afghan

阿哥 āgē 〈方言〉❶ elder brother: 大～ eldest brother; Number One ❷ intimate form of address for a man of about one's same age; bro
see also àge

阿根廷 Āgēntíng Argentina:～人 Argentine

阿公 āgōng 〈方言〉❶ (woman's) father-in-law ❷ dad; papa ❸ grandpa ❹ polite form of address for an old man

阿家阿翁 āgū-āwēng *also* "阿家翁"(家 same as 姑) ❶ woman's father-in-law and mother-in-law: 不痴不聋,难作～。It would be difficult to play the role of father- or mother-in-law if you were neither stupid nor deaf. ❷ head of a family

阿訇 āhōng *ahung*; imam

阿混 āhùn 〈方言〉one who always tries to muddle along; Mr. Muddler: 千万不能有～的思想。One must in no case try to muddle along in life. /机关里有些～式的干部。Some government employees simply idle away their time in their office.

阿基米德 Ājīmǐdé Archimedes (c. 287-212 BC), Greek mathematician and inventor of many devices such as the helical screw (still known as Archimedean screw):～原理〈物理〉Archimedes' principle

阿克拉 Ākèlā Accra, capital of Ghana

阿肯 ākěn 〈方言〉folk singer or balladeer of the Kazak nationality

阿Q Ā Kiū *see* "阿 Q" Ā Qiū

阿拉 ālā 〈方言〉❶ I; me; my:～姆妈 my mom ❷ we; us; our

阿拉伯 Ālābó Arab; Arabia:～商人 Arab merchant /～世界 Arab World /～问题专家 Arabist

阿拉伯半岛 Ālābó Bàndǎo Arabian Peninsula; Arabia

阿拉伯共同市场 Ālābó Gòngtóng Shìchǎng Arab Common Market

阿拉伯国家 Ālābó guójiā Arab state or country:～首脑会议 Arab Summit Conference

阿拉伯国家联盟 Ālābó Guójiā Liánméng League of Arab States; Arab League:～公约 Pact of the League of Arab States

阿拉伯海 Ālābóhǎi Arabian Sea

阿拉伯联合酋长国 Ālābó Liánhé Qiúzhǎngguó United Arab Emirates (UAE)

阿拉伯马 ālābómǎ Arabian horse

阿拉伯人 Ālābórén Arab

阿拉伯沙漠 Ālābó Shāmò Arabian Desert

阿拉伯石油输出国组织 Ālābó Shíyóu Shūchūguó Zǔzhī Organization of Arab Petroleum Exporting Countries (OAPEC)

阿拉伯树胶 Ālābó shùjiāo 〈化工〉Arabic gum; gum acacia

阿拉伯数字 Ālābó shùzì *also* "阿拉伯数码" Arabic numerals

阿拉伯也门共和国 Ālābó Yěmén Gònghéguó Yemen Arab Republic

阿拉伯语 Ālābóyǔ Arabic (language)

阿拉伯字母 Ālābó zìmǔ *also* "阿拉伯字母表" Arabic alphabet

阿拉法特 Ālāfǎtè Yasser Arafat (1929-), Palestinian leader

阿拉木图 Ālāmùtú Alma-Ata, former capital of Kazakhstan

阿拉斯加 Ālāsījiā Alaska:～半岛 Alaska Peninsula /～湾 Gulf of Alaska /～山脉 Alaska Mountains /～拖橇狗 Alaskan malamute

阿兰若 ālánrě *also* "兰若" *Aranyakah*; temple

阿里山 Ālǐshān Mount Ali (in Taiwan Province)

阿丽亚娜火箭 Ālìyànà huǒjiàn (Western Europe) Ariane rocket

阿留申群岛 Āliúshēn Qúndǎo Aleutian Islands (southwest of Alaska)

阿留申人 Āliúshēnrén Aleut; Aleutian

A

阿留申语 Āliúshēnyǔ Aleut (language)
阿鲁巴 Ālǔbā Aruba, island in the West Indies
阿罗汉 Āluóhàn *also*“罗汉”Arhat
阿妈 āmā 〈方言〉❶ mom; mum ❷ polite form of address for an elderly woman ❸ female servant; amah
see also àma
阿曼 Āmàn Oman:～人 Omani /～湾 Gulf of Oman /～苏丹国 Sultanate of Oman
阿芒拿 āmángná 〈化学〉ammonal
阿猫阿狗 āmāo-āgǒu 〈方言〉people of any description; people of little importance; Tom, Dick, and Harry; every man jack:哼! ～都来责怪我! Humph! Even these despicable creatures are picking on me!
阿美族 Āměizú largest tribe of the Gaoshan (高山) nationality living in the hilly regions of eastern Taiwan
阿门 āmén 〈基督教〉amen
阿盟 Āméng (short for 阿拉伯国家联盟) Arab League; League of Arab States
阿米巴 āmǐbā amoeba:～脓肿〈医学〉amoebic abscess
阿米巴变形虫 āmǐbā biànxíngchóng 〈计算机〉Maltese Amoeba, a computer virus
阿米巴病 āmǐbābìng 〈医学〉amoebiasis
阿米巴肝炎 āmǐbā gānyán 〈医学〉hepatic amoebiasis
阿米巴痢疾 āmǐbā lìji 〈医学〉amoebic dysentery
阿米妥 āmǐtuǒ 〈药学〉amytal
阿摩尼亚 āmóníyà 〈化学〉ammonia
阿姆哈拉语 Āmǔhālāyǔ Amharic (language in Ethiopia)
阿姆斯特朗 Āmǔsītèlǎng Neil Alden Armstrong (1930-), US astronaut who became the first man on earth to set foot on the moon
阿木林 āmùlín 〈方言〉credulous fool; gullible simpleton; sucker; idiot
阿奶 ānǎi 〈方言〉❶ grandma ❷ polite form of address for an elderly woman
阿尼林 ānílín 〈化学〉aniline:～油 aniline oil
阿帕网 āpàwǎng 〈信息〉Arpanet
阿沛·阿旺晋美 Āpèi Āwàngjìnměi Ngapoi Ngawang Jigme (1910-), Tibetan statesman, Vice-Chairman of the Chinese People's Political Consultative Conference (1993-)
阿皮亚 Āpíyà Apia, capital of Western Samoa
阿片 āpiàn 〈药学〉opium:～制剂 opiate
see also“鸦片”yāpiàn
阿婆 āpó 〈方言〉❶ (a woman's) mother-in-law; mother of one's husband ❷ grandma ❸ polite form of address for an elderly woman
阿朴吗啡 āpǔ mǎfēi 〈药学〉apomorphine
阿Q Ā Qiū *also* Ā Kiū Ah Q, main character in Lu Xun's novella *The True Story of Ah Q* (《阿Q正传》, 1921-1922), a backward peasant who interprets his defeats as moral victories:～精神 Ah Q spirit /一副～相 a complete likeness of Ah Q
阿醛 āquán 〈化学〉(short for 阿拉伯醛) arabinal
阿塞拜疆 Āsàibàijiāng Azerbaijan:～人 Azerbaijani /～共和国 Republic of Azerbaijan
阿是穴 āshìxué 〈中医〉*ashi* point, any nerve point on the affected part of the body (i.e. other than those specified for acupuncture and moxibustion)
阿司匹林 āsīpǐlín 〈药学〉aspirin
阿斯旺 Āsīwàng (Egypt) Aswan:～高坝 Aswan High Dam
阿嚏 ātì 〈象声〉(sound of sneezing) atishoo; ahchoo
阿托品 ātuōpǐn 〈药学〉atropine:～中毒 atropinism
阿伊马拉 Āyīmǎlā Aymara (indigenous tribe in Peru and Bolivia):～语 Aymara (language)
阿姨 āyí ❶〈方言〉mother's sister; auntie ❷ term of address for any woman of one's mother's generation; auntie:刘～ Auntie Liu /谢谢～给我让坐。Thank Auntie for giving me your seat. ❸ nurse; nanny; housemaid:幼儿园的～真好。The teachers in the nursery are very kind. /～领你去买冰棍。Nanny will take you there to get some ice lollies.
阿以战争 Ā-Yǐ zhànzhēng Arab-Israeli wars (1948-1949, 1956, 1967, 1973)
阿月浑子 āyuèhúnzi *also*“开心果”kāixīnguǒ pistachio
阿扎尼亚 Āzāníyà Azania (African name for South Africa):～泛非主义者大会 Pan-African Congress of Azania (PAC)

啊(呵) ā 〈叹词〉*expressing astonishment or admiration*:～,太阳出来了! Oh, the sun has come out! /～,黄河! 你是中华民族的摇篮! O Yellow River! You are the cradle of the Chinese nation.
啊哈 āhā 〈叹词〉❶ *indicating surprise*:～,原来是你呀! Aha, so it is you! ❷ *indicating praise or admiration*:～,这活做的真不错呀! Aha, this job is really well done! ❸ *indicating awareness of the situation*:～,你又在捉弄人,我才不上当呢! Humph! You're pulling my leg again! I won't be taken in this time. ❹ *indicating a feeling of triumph*:～,这下子你输了。Aha, you're defeated.
啊呀 āyā 〈叹词〉❶ *indicating displeasure*:～,怎么满地都是水! Oh no! The floor is flooded! ❷ *indicating surprise or astonishment*:～,我忘带钥匙了! Oh hell! I forgot to take keys with me. /～,这东西怎么这么重! Oh dear, this is real heavy! ❸ *indicating embarrassment or resignation*:～,这事不好办哪! Ah, this is too difficult to handle! *or* This is a hard nut to crack!
啊哟 āyō 〈叹词〉*also*“啊唷”*indicating surprise, pain, etc.*:～,下雪了! Oh dear, it's snowing! /～,你踩着我的脚了! Ouch! You're stepping on my foot (*or* toe)!

锕 ā 〈化学〉actinium (Ac)
锕铅 āqiān 〈化学〉actinium lead (AcD)
锕系元素 āxì yuánsù 〈化学〉actinides
锕铀 āyóu 〈化学〉actinium-uranium (AcU)

腌 ā
see also yān
腌臜 āza ❶〈方言〉filthy; dirty:看你这身油,真～! How dirty you look with grease all over your clothes! /这水实在太～。The water is really too filthy. ❷ uncomfortable; displeased; resentful:在他手下工作时,我受了不少～气。When working under him, I had plenty of pent-up grievances (*or* I often had to bottle up my feelings). ❸ embarrass; make look foolish; insult:行了,你就别～他了。That's enough. Don't make him look foolish any more.

á

嗄 á *see*“啊”á
see also shà

啊(呵) á 〈叹词〉*used to ask a further question or request repetition of what was said*:～? 到底出什么事了? Pardon, what on earth has happened? /～? 明天考不考试呀? Well, is there going to be an examination tomorrow? *or* Shall we sit for the exam tomorrow?

ǎ

啊(呵) ǎ 〈叹词〉*expressing doubt*:～? 今天是你的生日? What! It's your birthday today? /～? 这是怎么回事儿呀? O my, what the dickens is all this about?

à

阿 à
see also ā; ē
阿哥 àge ❶ Manchu form of address of parents for their son ❷ form of address of the Qing royal family for an adolescent prince
see also āgē
阿妈 àma *also*“阿嘛”Manchu form of address for father
see also āmā

啊(呵) à ❶ *expressing consent or agreement*:～,那就走吧。All right, let's go then. ❷ *expressing understanding*:～,我明白了! Oh, I see. ❸ *expressing surprise or admiration*:～,伟大的长城! O magnificent Great Wall! /～,这里怎么有一摊血! Why! There's a pool of blood here!

a

啊(阿、呵) a 〈助词〉❶ *used at the end of a sentence to express admiration*：好漂亮的花儿～！What beautiful flowers! ❷ *used at the end of a sentence as a sign of confirmation or defence*：这种作法很好～！This way of doing things is wonderful indeed! /我没去是因为我有事情～。I didn't go, because I was busy. ❸ *used at the end of a sentence to express doubt*：他们哥俩儿像不像～？Do the two brothers look like each other, eh? ❹ *used in the middle of a sentence indicating a short pause to draw attention to what is to be said next*：今天开这个会～，是想听听各方面的意见。Look! We are holding this meeting today to make sure that different opinions are aired freely. /你～，真傻！Look! How silly you are! ❺ *used after things enumerated*：书～、报纸～、笔～、摆了一桌子。The desk is littered with books, newspapers, pens and whatnot.

āi

哀 āi ❶ grief; sorrow：节～ restrain one's grief /悲～ grieved (*or* sorrowful) ❷ mourning; condolences：致～ express one's condolences /默～三分钟 observe a three-minute silence ❸ pity; compassion：～其不幸 have pity on sb. for his misfortune

哀哀 āi'āi in deep grief：～欲绝 be overwhelmed with grief

哀兵必胜 āibīng-bìshèng an army burning with righteous indignation is bound to win

哀愁 āichóu lamentation; sorrow：过分～就会伤身体。Excessive sorrow harms one's health.

哀怆 āichuàng 〈书面〉grieve

哀辞 āicí 〈书面〉writing in mourning of the deceased, often in rhyme; elegy

哀悼 āidào grieve or mourn over sb.'s death; lament sb.'s death：规定全国～三天 decree three days of national mourning /对他的逝世，我们表示沉痛的～。We express our profound condolences over his death.

哀的美敦书 āidìměidūnshū *also* "最后通牒" zuìhòu tōngdié ultimatum：下～ serve an ultimatum

哀吊 āidiào ❶ grieve over sb.'s death ❷ express deep sympathy for：树上的乌鸦不停地叫着，好像在～他漂泊无依的苦楚。The rooks on the trees kept cawing as if to commiserate with him on his wandering life.

哀而不伤 āi'érbùshāng ❶ grieve with restraint ❷ (of behaviour) moderate; restrained：先生之诗，～。A gentle sadness pervades his poems.

哀感 āigǎn sadness; grief：生离死别的～涌上心头。The grief of separation in life and parting at death welled up in his heart.

哀感顽艳 āigǎn-wányàn 〈书面〉(often used to describe the tone of language) the plaintive notes touch the hearts of the slow-witted as well as the sensitive：这封信写得～。This letter is couched in most moving terms.

哀告 āigào beg piteously; supplicate; implore：四处～ implore everybody's commiserations /苦苦～ present one's case beseechingly

哀歌 āigē ❶ mournful song; dirge; elegy：一曲～ a mournful song/沉浸在一片～声中 be plunged into a sea of mournful dirge ❷ sing mournfully

哀号 āiháo cry piteously; wail; bemoan：他为失去爱子而～。He wailed over the death of his dear son.

哀嚎 āiháo ❶ howl woefully：远处饿狼在～。Hungry wolves were howling in the distance. /受伤的狗在～。The wounded dog was moaning piteously. ❷ *see* "哀号"

哀鸿遍野 āihóng-biànyě victims of the disaster can be found everywhere; the land is swarming with famished refugees：要是旧社会，遇上这样大的水灾，早已是～了。If a flood of such magnitude had hit the land in the old days, the stricken area would have been a scene of desolation and despair.

哀呼 āihū cry piteously; wail：～呻吟 wail and moan

哀毁骨立 āihuǐ-gǔlì 〈书面〉emaciation resulting from grief at the death of one's parent; mere shadow of one's former self

哀家 āijiā 〈旧语〉(usu. used by widowed empress or imperial concubine in old novels and traditional operas) I; me

哀叫 āijiào cry sadly：嘶声～ wail sadly

哀矜 āijīn sympathize; commiserate; feel compassion for：～其不幸 commiserate with sb. /脸上显出一～的神色。There was a compassionate look on his face.

哀恳 āikěn *see* "哀求"

哀苦 āikǔ grieved and miserable：～无依的妇女 helpless woman worn down by grief and misery

哀厉 āilì (of a sound) sad：窗外风声～。Outside the window, the wind was wailing. /歌声清越而～。The song was supremely clear and plaintive.

哀怜 āilián feel compassion for; pity：他心头涌起一种激愤、～的复杂情感。A feeling of indignation and pity welled up in his heart.

哀凉 āiliáng sad; mournful; desolate：～的歌声 mournful tunes of a song

哀悯 āimǐn *see* "哀怜"

哀鸣 āimíng plaintive whine; wail; lament：孤雁～ sad cries of a lone wild goose /我仿佛听到有人在～。I seemed to hear somebody wailing.

哀莫大于心死 āi mòdàyú xīnsǐ nothing causes greater sorrow than despair; no sorrow is greater than despair

哀凄 āiqī sad; melancholy; mournful：～的哭声 heart-rending cry

哀戚 āiqī 〈书面〉be overcome with sorrow：满目荒凉，令人～。One feels very sad at heart at the scene of desolation.

哀启 āiqǐ 〈旧语〉biographical sketch of the deceased, often attached to the obituary notice

哀泣 āiqì sob：低头～ lower one's head and begin to sob

哀切 āiqiè (often used to describe a sound, look, etc.) sad, plaintive; mournful：寒蝉～地叫着。The cicadas shivering in cold weather were singing mournfully. /她用～的眼睛望着他。She looked at him with sad eyes.

哀求 āiqiú entreat; implore; plead piteously：面对歹徒，～是没有用的。It is no use pleading for mercy when one is accosted by a gangster.

哀劝 āiquàn advise in a tearful voice：百般～ advise strongly and almost tearfully

哀荣 āiróng 〈书面〉posthumous honours

哀伤 āishāng grieved; distressed; sad：心情万分～ feel deeply grieved /人死不能复生，大家也不必过于～。As no one can bring the dead back to life, it's no use indulging ourselves in sorrow.

哀思 āisī sad memories (of the deceased); grief; sorrow：在烈士墓前献上一个花圈，以寄托我们的～。We laid a wreath before the martyr's tomb as a token of our remembrance.

哀诉 āisù unbosom oneself in grief：～冤情 pour out one's grievances; sadly recount the gross injustice one has suffered

哀叹 āitàn sigh in sorrow; lament; bemoan; bewail：令人～的失败 lamentable failure /～世间不平之事 bewail the injustices of the world

哀恸 āitòng extreme sorrow or grief：举国～。The entire nation was overwhelmed by sorrow.

哀痛 āitòng grief; sorrow：无限～ boundless grief /万分～ immense sorrow /母亲离我而去了，我的～是无法形容的。Words could not describe how sad I was after mother's death.

哀婉 āiwǎn sad and moving; pathetic：歌声～动人。The song was sad and touching. *or* The song had a pathetic appeal.

哀艳 āiyàn 〈书面〉(of writing, etc.) sad and beautiful：这首诗～动人。The poem is moving in its sad sentiment and beautiful style.

哀怨 āiyuàn plaintive; sad; aggrieved：乐曲缠绵～。The tune is sentimental and plaintive.

哀乐 āiyuè funeral music

哀子 āizǐ son bereaved of his mother
see also "孤哀子" gū'āizǐ

锿 āi 〈化学〉einsteinium (Es)

哎 āi 〈叹词〉❶ *used to convey surprise or dissatisfaction*：～！是老王啊！Why, it's Lao Wang! /～，怎么不早说呢？But why didn't you tell me sooner? ❷ *used as a reminder or warning*：～，大伙儿来歇歇吧！Hey, come and have a break, everyone! /～，别把盘子碰掉了！Look out! Don't knock off the plate!

哎呀 āiyā 〈叹词〉❶ *used to express surprise or dissatisfaction*：～！真没想到他会辞职不干了。Why, I never imagined that he would throw up his job. /～！我忘带眼镜了。My, I forgot to bring my glasses! /～！我们有二十年没见了。Well, it's twenty years since we

A

met last. ❷ *used to express complaints or impatience*：～，丢了太可惜了。Ah, it is a pity to part with it.
哎哟 āiyō 〈叹词〉 *used to show astonishment or pain*：～！玻璃碎啦！Hey, the glass is broken. /～！好疼！Ouch! It hurts!

埃[1] āi dust

埃[2] āi 〈物理〉 angstrom (A)
埃博拉 āibólā 〈医学〉 Ebola, deadly epidemic newly found in Africa
埃尔尼诺 āi'ěrnínuò 〈气象〉 El Nino (Spanish meaning "holy child"), warm but nutrient-deficient Pacific current：～现象 El Nino Phenomenon
埃菲尔铁塔 Āifēi'ěr Tiětǎ Eiffel Tower (in Paris); *la tour Eiffel*
埃及 Āijí Egypt：上～ Upper Egypt /下～ Lower Egypt /～人 Egyptian
埃居 āijū ECU (European Currency Unit, replaced by euro from Jan. 1999)
埃克森公司 Āikèsēn Gōngsī Exxon Corporation (US oil corporation)
埃米尔 āimǐ'ěr emir (title of Muslim ruler, or formerly, male descendant of Muhammad)
埃塞俄比亚 Āisài'ébǐyà Ethiopia：～人 Ethiopian

挨 āi ❶ in the order of; one after another：～人通知 inform one person after another /还没有～到他呢。It's not his turn yet. ❷ near; close to; next to：～肩坐着 sit shoulder to shoulder /～墙站着 stand against the wall /人～人 people packed like sardines /树一棵～一棵。Trees are planted close to one another. /他家紧～着工厂。His house is next to the factory.
see also ái
挨班儿 āibānr 〈口语〉 in turn; one by one：一年级四个班～打扫教室。The four classes of Grade I shall take turns to clean the classroom.
挨边 āibiān ❶ keep to the side：马路上行人要～儿走。Pedestrians must keep to the side of the road. ❷ (used after a number) be close to：我六十～儿了。I'm getting on for sixty. ❸ close to fact; relevant：你说的一点也不～儿！What you said is wide of the mark!
挨次 āicì one by one; in turn; one after another：～领取 get sth. in turn
挨个儿 āigèr 〈口语〉 one by one; in turn：～审问 interrogate them one by one /～买 queue (*or* line) up for sth.
挨光 āiguāng (often used in the early vernacular) carry on a clandestine love affair
挨黑 āihēi 〈方言〉 towards evening; at dusk：～儿才收工 not knock off until dusk /这孩子怎么～儿还不回家? Why isn't the child back yet now it's almost dark?
挨户 āihù from door to door; from house to house：挨门～搜查 carry out a house-to-house search
挨挤 āijǐ crowd together：大家～在一起。We were crowded together. /来宾们挨挨挤挤地站了一屋子。The room was packed with visitors.
see also áijǐ
挨家 āijiā from house to house：～逐户 from door to door/～打听 make enquiries from door to door /你得～去通知。You'll have to notify them from house to house.
挨肩擦背 āijiān-cābèi *also* "挨肩擦膀" rub shoulders; be crowded together
挨肩儿 āijiānr 〈口语〉 (of brothers or sisters) be close in age：他们兄弟三人～，每一个只大一岁。The three brothers are close in age; one is only a year older than another.
挨近 āijìn get close to; be near to：寺庙～深山。The monastery is situated near a range of mountains. /他家～我家。He lives next-door to me. *or* He is my next-door neighbour. /请挨我近一点。Please come a bit closer.
挨靠 āikào ❶ lean against; lean on：她～在他的肩头上。She leaned on his arm. /那两个孩子～着坐在街角。The two children huddled together on the street corner. ❷ depend on：他从小没了父母，没个～。He lost his parents as a child, and has had nobody to rely on.
挨门 āimén from door to door：她～去访问，帮助解决困难。She visited each household to help solve any difficulty that might exist.
挨门逐户 āimén-zhúhù *also* "挨门挨户" go from house to house or door to door
挨排儿 āipáir 〈方言〉 in proper sequence; one by one; methodically：把今天发生的事儿～想一遍，看有没有什么问题。Consider carefully what happened today to see if anything went wrong.
挨晚 āiwǎn 〈方言〉 towards evening; at nightfall

唉 āi 〈叹词〉 ❶ *sound indicating response*：～，来了！All right. I'm coming! ❷ *sound of sighing sadly*：～，我真倒霉！Ah! how unlucky I am! *or* What bad luck!
see also ài
唉声叹气 āishēng-tànqì heave deep sighs; sigh in despair; moan and groan：近来他情绪不高，总是～的。Lately he has been in low spirits, moaning and groaning all the time.
唉呀 āiyā 〈叹词〉 *used to express surprise or dissatisfaction, complaints or impatience*
see also "哎呀" āiyā

欸 āi *see* "唉" āi
see also ǎi; ê

娭 āi
see also xī
娭毑 āijiě 〈方言〉 ❶ father's mother; grandmother; grandma ❷ polite form of address for elderly women

嗳(噯) āi *see* "哎" āi
see also ǎi; ài

ái

癌 ái (formerly pronounced yán) cancer; carcinoma：致～物 carcinogen /原位～ preinvasive cancer /原发～ primary cancer /转移性～ metastatic carcinoma /结肠～ colon cancer /直肠～ carcinoma (*or* cancer) of the rectum /肺～ lung cancer /肝～ liver cancer /子宫～ cancer of the uterus /骨～ cancer in the bones /胃～ cancer of the stomach; stomach cancer /乳腺～ breast cancer /血～ leukaemia /食道～ cancer of the esophagus /皮肤～ cancer of the skin; skin cancer
癌变 áibiàn 〈医学〉 canceration; cancerization
癌病 áibìng 〈医学〉 carcinomatosis; carcinosis
癌恐怖 áikǒngbù 〈心理〉 cancerphobia
癌扩散 áikuòsàn *also* "癌转移" 〈医学〉 metastasis (of cancer); spread of cancer
癌魔 áimó 〈比喻〉 demon of cancer：他顽强地同～作斗争。He fights tenaciously against cancer, the demon that's haunting him.
癌前期病变 áiqiánqī bìngbiàn 〈医学〉 precancerous lesion
癌切除术 áiqiēchúshù 〈医学〉 carcinectomy; carcinomectomy
癌细胞 áixìbāo 〈医学〉 cancer cell
癌细胞溶解 áixìbāo róngjiě 〈医学〉 carcinolysis
癌学 áixué carcinology
癌症 áizhèng 〈医学〉 cancer; carcinoma
癌转移 áizhuǎnyí 〈医学〉 metastasis of cancer

皑(皚) ái 〈书面〉 pure white; snow white
皑皑 ái'ái 〈书面〉 snow white：～积雪 vast expanse of white snow
皑白 áibái pure white; dazzling white：～的梨花遍布山谷。The valley is dotted all over with white pear blossoms.

挨(捱) ái ❶ suffer; endure：～冻 endure (*or* suffer from) cold /～饿 go hungry; be starved /～骂 be given a telling off; get a scolding /～了一记耳光 get a box on the ear ❷ drag out：～了一年又一年 drag out a miserable existence year after year /生了一场大病，终于～过来了。I've been very ill, but finally managed to pull through. ❸ delay; put off：今天能解决的事，为什么要～到明天? Why should we put off till tomorrow sth. we can settle today?
see also āi
挨呲儿 áicīr 〈方言〉 be reproached or reprimanded; get a scolding; get a dressing-down：这孩子太淘气，～活该！He is such a naughty boy that he deserves a dressing-down.

挨打 áidǎ get a beating; get a thrashing; come under attack:～受骂 get both a scolding and a beating /～受气 be bullied and beaten / 处于～的境地 be vulnerable to attacks
挨斗 áidòu be denounced (at a public meeting); be struggled against:他被打成"右派",每天～。He was branded a "Rightist" and was denounced at public meetings every day.
挨挤 áijǐ get pushed or shoved around; get buffeted about in a crowd:那儿的人太多,何必去～! There are so many people over there. Why should you go and get pushed around? /我们挨了半天挤,什么热闹也没看到。We were pushed and elbowed in the crowd and did not even have a glimpse of the fun.
see also āijǐ
挨浇 áijiāo 〈口语〉be caught in a pouring rain
挨剋 áikēi 〈口语〉❶ take a beating or spanking:当年小学生犯小错误也～。In the old days schoolchildren were often beaten for petty faults. ❷ get a talking-to; get a dressing-down; be told off:小陈又迟到,非～不可。Xiao Chen is late again. I'm sure he will get a dressing-down.
挨磨 áimó ❶ be pestered; be annoyed:她是不会罢休的,你就准备～吧。She will not give in. You'd better be prepared for her pestering. /挨骂的是你,～的是你,你图个什么呢? You take a full share of the blame and endure a good deal of the annoyance. What for? ❷ hang about; hover around; linger:他在茶馆附近～了好一阵子,仍不见她的影子。He hung around the tea-house for quite a while but she was still not in sight. /又～了一会,他就搭讪着走了。He hovered round for a while, then joked about something and left.
挨批 áipī be criticized; be denounced:那十年动乱,多少好人～挨斗。During those ten years of turmoil, many good people were criticized and denounced.
挨受 áishòu suffer:～虐待 suffer cruel treatment; be maltreated / 房子已经修好了,不再～风雨的威胁了。The house is well repaired and will be able to withstand the onslaught of wind and rain.
挨延 áiyán put off; delay; procrastinate:按原计划我们已经晚了一个星期了,不能再～了。We are already one week behind schedule and simply cannot afford any further delay.
挨整 áizhěng be in for criticism and denunciation:我那几年老～,吃了不少苦头。I suffered a great deal those years, as I was always made the target of criticism.
挨揍 áizòu 〈口语〉*see* "挨打"

骙 ái 〈书面〉stupid; idiotic:痴～ idiotic

ǎi

霭 ǎi 〈书面〉mist; haze:烟～ mist /晨～ morning haze

蔼[1] ǎi 〈书面〉friendly; affable; amiable:和～ amiable

蔼[2] ǎi 〈书面〉lush; luxuriant
蔼蔼 ǎi'ǎi ❶ lush; luxuriant:草木～ lush vegetation ❷ dim; dark; hazy:暮云～～ hazy evening clouds
蔼然 ǎirán kind-hearted; amiable; genial:～可亲 affable /神色～ look amiable

嗳(噯) ǎi 〈叹词〉*used to show dissent or displeasure*:～,你还是休息吧。Well, you'd better take a short rest. /～,别开玩笑了。Come on, stop kidding, please. /～,不是这样的。No, no, that's not true.
see also āi; ài
嗳腐 ǎifǔ 〈中医〉foul breath
嗳气 ǎiqì belch; eructation
嗳酸 ǎisuān acid rising up from the stomach; having too much hydrochloric acid; hyperacidity

矮 ǎi ❶ short (of stature):我比他～两公分。I'm shorter than he by two centimetres. ❷ low (in height):几棵小～树 a few clumps of bushes /屋檐低～ low rafters ❸ be lower than (in rank or status); be inferior to:我的工资比他～一级。My salary is one grade lower than his. /他自觉比人～半截儿。He always feels inferior to others. *or* He always feels he's second-rate.
矮矮实实 ǎi'ǎi-shíshí short and sturdy; thickset
矮矬 ǎicuó short; low:～个儿 be of short stature; be short/骑着～的战马 ride on a small and sturdy steed
矮矬子 ǎicuózi short person; dwarf
矮凳 ǎidèng low stool
矮笃笃 ǎidūdū (of physical stature) short:～、胖乎乎的身材 of dumpy (*or* stumpy) build
矮墩墩 ǎidūndūn pudgy; dumpy; stocky:～的小伙子 dumpy lad; short and thickset young fellow /这棵小树～的。This young tree is sturdy.
矮秆品种 ǎigǎn pǐnzhǒng 〈农业〉short-stalked variety; short-straw variety
矮个儿 ǎigèr *also* "矮个子" person of short stature; short person
矮化 ǎihuà stunt:食物不足会使人体～。Lack of food may stunt the body.
矮化病 ǎihuàbìng 〈植物〉dwarf disease
矮糠 ǎikāng 〈植物〉(general term for 罗勒) sweet basil
矮林 ǎilín low woods; brush
矮趴趴 ǎipāpā 〈方言〉(of houses, buildings, etc.) very low:眼前只见几座～的土坯房。There were but a few low adobe houses in sight.
矮胖 ǎipàng short and stout; dumpy:这个人～～的。This chap is short and stout.
矮人 ǎirén ❶ dwarf ❷ pigmy or pygmy (a race of people of short stature, usu. under 1.5 metres, to be found in some African and Asian countries)
矮小 ǎixiǎo short and small; undersized:～的个头 short and small / 这匹马过于～了。The horse is much too small in build.
矮小综合征 ǎixiǎo zōnghézhēng 〈医学〉short stature syndrome
矮星 ǎixīng 〈天文〉dwarf (star)
矮种马 ǎizhǒngmǎ pony
矮壮素 ǎizhuàngsù 〈农业〉cycocel; chlormequat chloride
矮子 ǎizi short person; dwarf:言语的巨人,行动的～ a giant in words, a dwarf in deeds
矮子里拔将军 ǎizili bá jiāngjun 〈俗语〉choose a general from among the dwarfs — pick the best of the mediocrities; the one-eyed man is chosen king in the kingdom of the blind

欸 ǎi
see also āi; ê
欸乃 ǎinǎi 〈书面〉〈象声〉❶ creak of an oar being rowed:船儿在水面上滑行,只听得～桨声,更增加了湖面的幽静。While the boat was gliding on the water, nothing but the creaking of the oars could be heard, which added to the quietness of the lake. ❷ sound of a boat song

ài

隘 ài ❶ pass:险～ strategic pass ❷ narrow:林深路～ narrow path in the depth of a forest
隘谷 àigǔ ravine
隘口 àikǒu (mountain) pass
隘路 àilù defile; narrow passage

艾[1] ài ❶ Chinese mugwort (*Artemisia argyi*); moxa ❷ (Ài) a surname

艾[2] ài 〈书面〉❶ old; elderly; aged ❷ the aged; the elderly

艾[3] ài 〈书面〉halt; end:方兴未～ be fast unfolding; be in the ascendant /～～难言 stutter and speak with difficulty; speak haltingly (from embarrassment, etc.)

艾[4] ài 〈书面〉pretty; beautiful:少～ young handsome person
see also yì
艾蒿 àihāo Chinese mugwort; moxa
艾虎 àihǔ ❶〈动物〉fitch ❷ cloth tiger filled with moxa (worn by some people on the head in the belief that it can ward off evils)
艾灸 àijiǔ 〈中医〉moxibustion

A

艾绒 àiróng crushed dry moxa (used in traditional moxibustion)

艾森豪威尔 Àisēnháowēi'ěr Dwight David Eisenhower (1890-1969), five-star general and 34th US President (1953-1961):～主义 Eisenhower Doctrine (foreign policy statement by President Eisenhower in his address to the Congress on 5 Jan. 1957)

艾绳 àishéng rope made of moxa (to be burnt to keep off mosquitoes)

艾窝窝 àiwōwo *also* "爱窝窝" àiwōwo steamed cone-shaped cake made of glutinous rice or millet with sweet filling

艾鼬 àiyòu 〈动物〉 polecat

艾炷 àizhù moxa cone:～灸 moxa-cone moxibustion

艾滋病 àizībìng *also* "爱滋病" àizībìng (popular term for 获得性免疫缺损综合征) AIDS (Acquired Immune Deficiency Syndrome); Aids:～患者 AIDS patient (*or* victim)

艾滋病病毒 àizībìng bìngdú 〈医学〉 HIV; human immunodeficiency virus:传染～ transmit HIV (to sb.)/染上～ be HIV-infected/～携带者 HIV carrier /～阳性反应 test positive for HIV; test (*or* be) HIV-positive

砹

ài 〈化学〉 astatine (At)

硋

ài 〈书面〉 *see* "碍" ài

碍(礙)

ài hinder; obstruct; be in the way of:有～健康 be harmful (*or* detrimental) to health /有～观瞻 be an eyesore; be repugnant to the eye /～于情面 for fear of hurting sb.'s feelings; out of consideration for sb.'s sensibilities /我这样做～着你吗? Am I in your way by so doing?

碍口 àikǒu be too embarrassing to mention:这话有点～。It is rather difficult to bring the matter up.

碍面子 ài miànzi for fear of hurting sb.'s feelings; afraid to wound sb.'s sensibilities:碍着你爸爸的面子,我不好多说什么。I don't want to say any more about it for fear that I should offend your father's feelings. /碍着老朋友的面子,她只好默不作声。For the sake of old acquaintanceship, she had to keep quiet.

碍目 àimù 〈方言〉 *see* "碍眼"

碍难 àinán 〈书面〉 find it difficult to do sth:～从命 find it hard to comply with your wish

碍事 àishì ❶ be in the way; be inconvenient:这些东西摆不好反倒～。These things would be a hindrance if you couldn't arrange them properly. /我怕他～,设法把他支走了。I thought he might be in the way, so I sent him off on some pretext. ❷ (often used in the negative) be of consequence; matter:误了这趟火车不～,还可以乘下一趟的。It doesn't matter if I miss the train, because I can take the next. /她的病不～。She has only a minor complaint.

碍手 àishǒu be in the way; be a hindrance; be a drag:打字机放在这儿太～,得把它挪开。The typewriter gets in the way here. It has to be moved away.

碍手碍脚 àishǒu-àijiǎo be in the way; be a hindrance:我正忙着呢,你别在这儿～的。Please stop hanging around here for I am busy with my work.

碍眼 àiyǎn ❶ be unpleasant to look at; be offensive to the eye; be an eyesore:屋子里唯有这书柜最～。Of all the things in the room, the bookcase is the ugliest. /那座高大的建筑物有点～。That tall building is something of an eyesore. ❷ be out of place:他有事,我们在这儿～。Since he is busy working, we might be a hindrance here.

恧

ài 〈书面〉 *see* 爱 ài

嗳

ài 〈叹词〉 *used to express sadness or regret*:～,真可惜! Oh, what a shame! /～,工作给耽误了! Well, the work is bound to suffer.

see also ǎi

爱(愛)

ài ❶ have profound affection for; love:～人民 love the people /全世界人民都～和平。People all over the world love peace. /他们～上了纯朴的农村生活。They came to appreciate simple rural life. ❷ be fond of; like:～打乒乓球 like playing table tennis /～看书 be fond of reading /～听音乐 be keen on music /～说长道短 delight in gossip ❸ treasure; cherish; hold dear; take good care of:珍～自己的名誉 treasure one's good reputation ❹ be apt to; be in the habit of:～感冒 be liable to colds /～发急 easily get into a temper /～走极端 often go to extremes

爱…不… ài…bù… *used before the same verb to express free choice*:爱信不信 believe it or not /爱要不要 take it or leave it

爱不释手 àibùshìshǒu be so fond of sth. that one can hardly put it down; cannot tear oneself away from sth.; can scarcely take one's eye off sth.:偶然在旧书店里发现了这本书,～,就高价买来了。When I found the book in a second-hand bookshop, I liked it so much that I bought it at a high price.

爱才如命 àicái-rúmìng cherish talent as much as one cherishes one's life; have a great passion for talent:求贤若渴,～ have a great passion for men of virtue and talent

爱财如命 àicái-rúmìng *also* "爱钱如命" love money as if it were one's own life; love nothing better than money; be greedy for money:～的吝啬鬼 miser who values nothing but money

爱巢 àicháo love nest:他们有了一个幸福的～。They've now built their own love nest.

爱称 àichēng term of endearment; pet name; diminutive:"小机灵"是人们对小家伙儿的～。"Little Smartie" is a term of endearment for the kid.

爱宠 àichǒng *also* "宠爱" dote on; make a pet of:为了受到统治者的～,他竭尽阿谀奉承之能事。He stopped at nothing in currying favour with the rulers.

爱答不理 àidā-bùlǐ *also* "爱理不理" show indifference; be cool; be standoffish:别人同她说话,她总是～的。She is always standoffish even when people talk to her.

爱戴 àidài adore; love; hold in high esteem:这位历史教授深受大家～。This professor of history is held in high esteem by us all.

爱迪生 Àidíshēng Thomas Alva Edison (1847-1931), American inventor

爱迪生留声机 Àidíshēng liúshēngjī Edison phonograph

爱迪生蓄电池 Àidíshēng xùdiànchí Edison battery; Edison accumulator

爱尔兰 Ài'ěrlán Ireland; Eire:～人 Irish; Irishman /～语 Irish (language)

爱尔兰共和国 Ài'ěrlán Gònghéguó Republic of Ireland; Eire

爱尔兰共和军 Ài'ěrlán Gònghéjūn Irish Republican Army (secret armed force fighting formerly for Irish independence, now to merge Northern Ireland with Eire)

爱抚 àifǔ have tender affection for:～的眼光 look at sb. affectionately /她～地摸着孩子的头。She fondly caressed the child's head.

爱国 àiguó love one's country; be patriotic:～组织 patriotic organization /～人士 patriotic personage /～志士 dedicated patriot /～心 patriotic sentiment /～热情 patriotic enthusiasm /～学生运动 patriotic student movement /～华侨 patriotic overseas Chinese national /～不分先后 anyone who loves his country is a patriot, whether he rallies to the common cause early or late /～一家 all patriots belong to one family

爱国统一战线 àiguó tǒngyī zhànxiàn patriotic united front

爱国卫生运动 àiguó wèishēng yùndòng patriotic sanitation campaign

爱国主义 àiguózhǔyì patriotism

爱国者 àiguózhě patriot

爱国者导弹 àiguózhě dǎodàn (US) "Patriot" missile

爱好 àihǎo 〈方言〉 ❶ care much about one's looks; be particular about one's dress; pay great attention to one's appearance:她从小就～,总是穿得整整齐齐的。She had cared much about her looks since childhood, and was always neatly dressed. ❷ be on good terms:住的时间长了,村里人都和她很～。The villagers came to be on friendly terms with her after she had lived there for some time.

爱好 àihào ❶ love; be keen on; be fond of:～体育运动 be keen on sports /～文学 be fond of literature /她特别～穿戴,什么时髦穿什么。She always wears the latest fashion because she is fond of fine clothes. ❷ activity one enjoys; hobby:你有什么～? What's your hobby? /我的～是集邮。My hobby is collecting stamps. /人各有～,不要强求一律。As tastes differ, no uniformity should be imposed.

爱好者 àihàozhě lover (of art, sports, etc.); enthusiast:音乐～ lover of music /足球～ football enthusiast; football fan /文学～ devotee of literature /集邮～ stamp collector; philatelist

爱河 àihé 〈比喻〉 river of love (according to Buddhist doctrine, love is like a river from which one can hardly extricate oneself once

A

one has fallen into it)：堕入～ fall head over heels in love
爱护 àihù cherish；treasure；take good care of：～国家财产 take good care of state property /～国家文物 treasure the nation's archaeological artifacts /像～自己眼睛一样～各族人民的团结 cherish the unity among the various nationalities as the apple of one's eye
爱见 àijian 〈方言〉 be fond of；like：老人很～孩子。The old man is fond of children. /年青人～鲜艳的颜色。Young people like bright colours.
爱克斯光 àikèsīguāng X-ray；Roentgen ray：～透视 fluoroscopy；X-ray examination /～诊断 X-ray diagnosis；Roentgen diagnosis /～照片 X-ray film；radiograph /照～ have an X-ray taken
爱克斯光机 àikèsīguāngjī X-ray apparatus
爱克斯射线 àikèsī shèxiàn 〈物理〉 X-ray
爱克斯射线探伤法 àikèsī shèxiàn tànshāngfǎ 〈机械〉 X-ray defectoscopy
爱克斯射线探伤器 àikèsī shèxiàn tànshāngqì 〈机械〉 X-ray flaw detector
爱克斯射线微量分析仪 àikèsī shèxiàn wēiliàng fēnxīyí X-ray microanalyzer
爱理不理 àilǐ-bùlǐ *see* “爱答不理”
爱丽舍宫 Àilìshěgōng (France) Élysée Palace
爱怜 àilián tender affection；compassion：惹人～ arouse one's compassion (*or* tender feelings)
爱恋 àiliàn be in love with；feel deeply attached to：对亲人的～ be attached to one's kith and kin /深深～着妻子 be very much in love with one's wife /姐姐给她的信中充满～之情。Her sister wrote her a very affectionate letter.
爱侣 àilǚ sweethearts
爱美 àiměi ❶ like to be well groomed；like to look smart；be fond of fine clothes：这么小的孩子也知道～！Even such a small child likes to be well groomed. ❷〈书面〉 be on very friendly terms：交往数年，甚相～。They became good friends after they had known each other for several years.
爱美的 àiměide (transliteration) amateur
爱美族 àiměizú 〈方言〉 dressy or fashion-pursuing people (esp. women)
爱面子 ài miànzi have a strong sense of “face”；care too much about one's “face”：这老头儿人不错，就是胆子小，～。The old man is quite nice. His only defect is that he is overcautious and too sensitive about the “face” problem.
爱莫能助 àimònéngzhù would like to help, but not be in a position to do so；be willing to help, but one's hands are tied：很抱歉，我实在是～。I'm awfully sorry, but I am really in no position to help you.
爱慕 àimù ❶ yearn for；long for；envy：～虚荣 be vain ❷ admire；adore：～之情 feeling of adoration (*or* love) /表示对这位伟大诗人的～ express one's admiration for the great poet
爱昵 àinì intimate；affectionate：报以～而羞涩的一笑 respond with bashful yet loving smile
爱琴海 Àiqínhǎi Aegean Sea (part of the Mediterranean between Greece and Anatolia)
爱情 àiqíng love (between man and woman)：纯洁的～ pure love /柏拉图式的～ Platonic love /～专一 be constant in love /处理好～和事业的关系 properly handle the relationship between love and career /～是幸福的，但有时也会给人带来烦恼。Love is happiness, but it may sometimes bring worries.
爱情片 àiqíngpiàn love film
爱人 àirén ❶ husband or wife ❷ sweetheart
爱人以德 àirényǐdé care for people in accordance with the code of ethics：君子～。A gentleman cares for others according to moral principles.
爱沙尼亚 Àishāníyà Estonia：～共和国 Republic of Estonia/～人 Estonian /～语 Estonian (language)
爱神 àishén God of Love；Cupid；Eros；Amor
爱神星 Àishénxīng 〈天文〉 Eros
爱斯基摩狗 àisījīmógǒu Eskimo dog
爱斯基摩人 Àisījīmórén Eskimo
爱委会 àiwěihuì *also* “爱卫会” (short for 爱国卫生运动委员会) Patriotic Sanitation Campaign Committee
爱窝窝 àiwōwo *also* “艾窝窝” àiwōwo steamed cone-shaped cake made of glutinous rice or millet with sweet filling
爱屋及乌 àiwū-jíwū 〈书面〉 love for a person extends even to the crows on his roof；love for a person extends to everything associated with her or him；love me, love my dog：他赏识我哥哥的才华，～，对于我也另眼相待。He admires my brother for his talent and for this reason treats me fairly well.
爱惜 àixī cherish；treasure；use sparingly：～劳动成果 cherish the fruits of labour /～光阴 cherish time；make the best use of time /～青春年华 treasure one's youthful years /～金钱 use money sparingly /～人才 value men of talent
爱小 àixiǎo 〈方言〉 be greedy for petty gains：～的人最后会吃大亏。Those who crave petty gains will end up sustaining huge losses.
爱心 àixīn love；sympathy；compassion：让世界充满～。Fill the world with love. /人人献出一片～。Everybody offered his or her loving care.
爱新觉罗 Àixīnjuéluó Aisin Gioro, family name of Manchu royalty, e.g. Aisin Gioro Puyi (1906-1967), the last emperor (1909-1911) of the Qing Dynasty
爱因斯坦 Àiyīnsītǎn Albert Einstein (1879-1955), noted scientist of theoretical physics
爱因斯坦方程 Àiyīnsītǎn fāngchéng 〈物理〉 Einstein equation：爱因斯坦比热方程 Einstein's equation for specific heat /爱因斯坦引力方程 Einstein's equation for the field of gravity
爱因斯坦统一场论 Àiyīnsītǎn tǒngyīchǎnglùn 〈物理〉 Einstein's united field theories
爱因斯坦相对论 Àiyīnsītǎn xiāngduìlùn 〈物理〉 Einstein's principle of relativity
爱因斯坦宇宙 Àiyīnsītǎn yǔzhòu Einstein universe
爱悦 àiyuè be fond of；love：表现男女互相～的旧体诗 classical poem which describes man and woman in love (*or* the mutual affection between man and woman)
爱憎 ài-zēng love and hate：～分明 know what to love and what to hate；be clear whom to love and whom to hate
爱知 Àizhī Aichi, prefecture in Japan：～县知事 prefect of Aichi
爱重 àizhòng love and respect：他为人正直，很受大家的～。He is loved and respected for his integrity (*or* because he is upright).
爱滋病 àizībìng *see* “艾滋病” àizībìng

瑷(璦) ài

瑷珲 Àihuī (now written as 爱辉) county in Heilongjiang Province
瑷珲条约 Àihuī Tiáoyuē (short for 中俄瑷珲条约) Treaty of Aigun (unequal treaty imposed on the Qing Dynasty by Tsarist Russia, 1858)

叆(靉) ài

叆叇 àidài 〈书面〉 overcast；covered with clouds：朝云～。The morning sky is overcast.

薆(薆) ài 〈书面〉 ❶ cover；shelter ❷ lush vegetation

嗳(噯) ài 〈叹词〉 *used to express regret, etc.*：～，我早怎么没想到！My goodness, why didn't I think of that earlier? /～，当时买下来就好了！Oh! If only I had bought it then.
see also āi；ǎi

暧(曖) ài 〈书面〉 (of daylight) dim

暧暧 ài'ài 〈书面〉 dark；dusk：～远人村。The distant village is shrouded in the deepening shadows of dusk.
暧昧 àimèi ❶ (of attitude, intention, etc.) ambiguous；equivocal：态度～ assume (*or* adopt) an ambiguous attitude/他在这件事上显得有些～。He seems equivocal towards this matter. /文字上～，原因之一是思想上朦胧不清。Linguistic ambiguity arises, among other things, from lack of clarity in thinking. ❷ (of behaviour) shady；dubious；questionable：他们的关系有些～。Their relationship is somewhat dubious.

僾(僾) ài 〈书面〉 ❶ seem：～然。It seems so. *or* It seems as if it were so. ❷ breathing with difficulty

僾尼 Àiní name used by some of the Hanis (哈尼族) for themselves

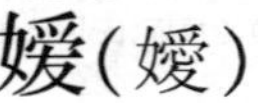 ài *see* “令嫒” lìng'ài

A

ān

安[1] ān ❶ peaceful; quiet; tranquil; calm:～坐 sit quietly /国泰民～。The country is prosperous and the people live in happiness. ❷ stabilize; calm; set at ease:使他～下心来 calm him down; set his mind at ease ❸ be content; be satisfied:～常处顺 be content with the status quo; enjoy a tranquil and stable life ❹ safe; secure; in good health:～抵上海 arrive in Shanghai safe and sound /转危为～ turn danger into safety; pull through (a critical disease, etc.) /居～思危 think of danger in time of security ❺ place in a suitable position; find a place for:这个车间需要～两个技术员。This workshop needs two technicians. /应把他～到重要岗位上。He ought to be placed in a responsible position. ❻ install; fix; fit:～电话 install a telephone /～天线 fix an antenna /～炉子 put in place a stove /门上～个铜把手 have a bronze handle fitted to the door /许多人家～不起空调。Many people can ill afford to have air-conditioners installed in their homes. ❼ bring a charge against; give a nickname; claim credit for sth.:不要把功劳都～在自己身上。You shouldn't claim all the credit for yourself. /给小方～这个罪名是很不公平的。It is unfair to bring such a charge against Xiao Fang. ❽ be up to; harbour:你到底～的是什么心? What on earth are your intentions? /他大概没～好心。He is probably up to no good. ❾ (Ān) a surname

安[2] ān 〈书面〉❶ where:而今～在? Where is it? *or* Where are they? ❷ (often used in a rhetorical sentence) how:～能如此? How could you behave like that? /饱汉～知饿汉饥。The well-fed cannot possibly appreciate how the starving feel.

安[3] ān (short for 安培)〈电学〉ampere

安邦定国 ānbāng-dìngguó bring peace and stability to the country; make the state stable and safe from disturbances

安邦治国 ānbāng-zhìguó effect good administration and stability for the country

安边 ānbiān 〈书面〉maintain stability on the frontiers; bring security to the border areas:～良策 sound policy to ensure security and tranquility in the border areas

安不忘危 ānbùwàngwēi be aware of possible danger in time of peace:我写这首诗有～的意思。I wrote this poem to remind people of possible danger in peace time.

安步当车 ānbù-dàngchē walk over leisurely instead of riding in a carriage; go on foot rather than by car:每日下班返家,～,也算一种锻炼,一种乐趣。Walking back from work every day is a pleasure as well as an exercise.

安瓿 ānbù 〈药学〉ampoule

安插 ānchā ❶ place in a certain position; assign to a job:把自己的亲信～在重要岗位上 plant one's trusted followers in key positions ❷ insert (in a play, story, article, programme, etc.); interpose:在故事中～一段回忆 insert a flashback in the story /晚会上～了一段相声。An item of comic dialogue was interposed in the evening's programme.

安厝 āncuò keep a coffin in a temporary shelter pending burial; lay a coffin in a temporary burial place to be reburied permanently later

安达曼海 Āndámànhǎi Andaman Sea, northeastern part of the Indian Ocean

安道尔 Āndào'ěr Andorra:～公国 Principality of Andorra /～人 Andorran

安的列斯群岛 Āndìlièsī Qúndǎo Antilles Islands

安第斯集团 Āndìsī Jítuán Andean Group (member states: Peru, Ecuador, Bolivia, Colombia, and Venezuela)

安第斯山脉 Āndìsī Shānmài the Andes (Mountains)

安钉子 ān dīngzi drive in a nail — place an obstacle for sb.; place one's agent or trusted follower in a key position

安定 āndìng ❶ (of life, political situation, etc.) stable; quiet; calm; settled:政治～ political stability /社会秩序～ good public order /工作～ job security ❷ maintain; stabilize:～人心 maintain public morale; reassure the public ❸〈药学〉valium; diazepam

安定团结 āndìng-tuánjié stability and unity:～的政治局面 political stability and unity

安定药 āndìngyào tranquilizer; sedative

安定镇痛 āndìng-zhèntòng 〈医学〉neuroleptoanalgesia

安堵 āndǔ 〈书面〉live in peace and security:大灾之年,百姓～如故。Though the country has been hit by a serious natural calamity this year, the people are living in peace and contentment.

安顿 āndùn ❶ find a place for; arrange for; settle in:把孩子～在幼儿园里 put (*or* place) the child in a kindergarten/他们已经～下来了。They have settled in. ❷ tranquil; peaceful:不要吵闹,让老人睡得～一些。Make no noise and let the old man sleep peacefully.

安放 ānfàng place; lay; put in a certain position:把家具～妥帖 put the furniture in place /老人的灵柩～在殡仪馆里。The old man's coffin was placed at the undertaker's. /纪念碑前～着很多花圈。Many wreaths were laid in front of the monument.

安非他明 ānfēitāmíng 〈医学〉amphetamine; Benzedrine:合成～ synthetic amphetamine /～衍化物 dexamphetamine

安分 ānfèn keep one's place; not go beyond one's bounds; be law-abiding:他在村子里是一个不～的人。He was a disaffected element in the village. /你还是～一点儿为好。You'd better behave yourself.

安分守己 ānfèn-shǒujǐ know and keep one's place; abide by the law and behave properly; be law-abiding and god-fearing:～的好人 honest man who knows his place /一家人～地过日子。The whole family lived quietly and contentedly.

安福国会 Ānfú Guóhuì Anfu Parliament, knocked together by the Northern Warlords in 1918 in opposition to Dr. Sun Yat-sen's Parliament in Guangzhou

安抚 ānfǔ appease; placate; pacify:～死者家属 console the family of the deceased /～愤怒的人群 placate an angry crowd /～哭泣的妇女 pacify the sobbing woman

安咐 ānfù 〈方言〉enjoin; exhort

安富尊荣 ānfù-zūnróng be content with one's wealth and high rank; live a peaceful and prosperous life

安哥拉 Āngēlā Angola:～人 Angolan /～人民解放阵线 (shortened as 解阵) Angolan National Liberation Front (FNLA) /～人民解放运动 (shortened as 人运) People's Movement for the Liberation of Angola (MPLA) /争取～彻底独立全国联盟 (shortened as 安盟) National Union for the Total Independence of Angola (UNITA)

安哥拉兔 āngēlātù Angora rabbit

安哥拉羊 āngēlāyáng Angora goat:～毛 Angora; mohair

安圭拉 Āngguīlā Anguilla, an island in the West Indies

安好 ānhǎo in good health; safe and sound; well:不知老母近来～否? I wonder how mother has been keeping? /家中～如常,请勿挂念。Everything is fine in the family as usual. Please set your mind at ease.

安家 ānjiā ❶ settle down:他们要在山区～。They'll settle down in the mountainous region. ❷ set up a home; get married:～立户 set up a home; set up housekeeping /他的儿子已经参加工作,在广州安了家。His son has got a job, married and made a home in Guangzhou.

安家费 ānjiāfèi ❶ allowance for setting up a new home; settling-in allowance ❷ family allowance

安家立业 ānjiā-lìyè settle down and embark on a career:他在海外飘流多年,现在准备回故乡～。After wandering overseas for years, he is now prepared to return home and settle there for good.

安家落户 ānjiā-luòhù make one's home in a place; settle:他俩五十年代去新疆,随后便在那里～。The two of them went to Xinjiang in the fifties and subsequently settled there.

安检 ānjiǎn (short for 安全检查) security check:乘客必须通过～才能登机。Passengers are requested to go through a security check before boarding the plane.

安靖 ānjìng ❶ peaceful and stable:社会～ peace and stability in society ❷〈书面〉bring peace and stability (to a place); stabilize; pacify:～社会秩序 ensure law and order

安静 ānjìng ❶ quiet; noiseless:阅览室里保持～。Keep silence in the reading room. /这房子靠近大街,不～。The house is not quiet for it is near a busy street. ❷ peaceful; calm:孩子们睡得很～。The children slept soundly. /你需要～下来仔细考虑问题。You must calm down so that you may consider the problems carefully. /心绪总也～不下来。I can hardly set my mind at rest.

安居 ānjū settle down (in a place):他用这笔钱买了一小块土地,总算在这儿～下来了。With the money, he bought a small piece of land and settled down here.

安居工程 ānjū gōngchéng housing project for low-income urban

residents; low-cost housing project; affordable housing project

安居乐业 ānjū-lèyè live and work in peace and contentment:推行经济改革,发展生产,使人民~。Carry through economic reform and develop production so that the people may live in peace and plenty.

安卡拉 Ānkălā Ankara, capital of Turkey

安康 ānkāng good health:祝您身体~。I wish you the best of health.

安拉 Ānlā 〈伊斯兰〉Allah

安澜 ānlán 〈书面〉❶ (of a river, etc.) flow calmly in its natural course:江河~。Rivers have been quiet. *or* Rivers have not been in flood. ❷ peaceful; tranquil:天下~。Peace prevails on earth.

安乐 ānlè peace and happiness:生于忧患,死于~。Hardships and trials lead to survival; comforts and pleasure end up in death.

安乐死 ānlèsǐ mercy killing; painless death; euthanasia

安乐窝 ānlèwō cosy nest:夫妇俩一直梦想着为自己建立一个~。The couple always dreamed of building a cosy nest for themselves. /他终于找到了一个~。这工作轻松,又舒服,工资又高。He finally found himself the right niche — a well-paid armchair job (*or* a cushy job).

安乐椅 ānlèyǐ arm chair; easy chair

安理会 Ānlǐhuì (short for 安全理事会) Security Council (of the United Nations)

安曼 Ānmàn Amman, capital of Jordan

安谧 ānmì 〈书面〉tranquil; serene; peaceful:~如常 be peaceful as usual /环境~ tranquil environment /这小山村格外~。The small village is a picture of exceptional tranquility.

安眠 ānmián sleep peacefully:彻夜不得~ cannot sleep soundly the whole night; remain awake all night; have a sleepless night

安眠酮 ānmiántóng 〈药学〉methaqualone; hyminal

安眠药 ānmiányào sleeping pill or tablet; soporific

安秒 ānmiǎo 〈电学〉ampere-second

安民 ānmín reassure the people or public; pacify the public or people:出榜~ put up a notice to reassure the public /保境~ keep the borders (*or* locality) secure and enable the people to live in peace

安民告示 ānmín gàoshì ❶ notice to reassure the public:速出~,令店铺照常开业。Put up a notice immediately to reassure the public and order all the stores and shops to resume business. ❷ advance notice or information:开会前先出个~ keep people informed about a meeting before it is held

安那其主义 ānnàqízhǔyì anarchism
see also "无政府主义" wúzhèngfǔzhǔyì

安乃近 ānnǎijìn 〈药学〉analgin

安南 Ānnán ❶〈地理〉Annam (a former kingdom, now part of Vietnam) ❷〈旧语〉Vietnam

安内攘外 ānnèi-rǎngwài pacify the country and resist foreign aggression:先安内后攘外 pacify the country before resisting foreign aggression (Chiang Kai-shek's excuse for suppressing the Chinese Communists before the Anti-Japanese War broke out in 1937)

安宁 ānníng ❶ tranquil; peaceful; free from disturbance:社会~ social tranquility /生活~ tranquil life /边境~ peace on the borders /采取有力措施,使局势~下来。Effective measures were taken to get the situation in hand. ❷ calm; composed; free from worry:心境~ feel free from worry /这件事搅得我不得~。The problem has upset me greatly. ❸ *also* "眠尔通" mián'ěrtōng 〈药学〉meprobamate; Miltown

安排 ānpái ❶ arrange; deal with in an orderly manner:~一次个别采访 arrange for a personal interview /~食宿 make arrangements for board and lodging /~活动日程 work out a schedule /把客人~在招待所 put the guests up at the guest house /~某人参加会议 arrange for sb. to attend a meeting /座位~ seating arrangement /人事重新~ personnel reshuffling /精心~ thoughtful (*or* meticulous, *or* elaborate) arrangements /长计划、短~ set up a long-term plan with short-term arrangements /根据早先的~ according to a previous schedule /打乱了某人的~ dislocate (*or* disturb) sb.'s arrangements; upset sb.'s apple cart /报纸的版面比过去~得更好了。The layout of the newspaper is much better than before. ❷ remodel; reshape; plan (for reconstruction):重新~延安的山山水水。Reshape the mountains and rivers in the Yan'an area.

安培 ānpéi 〈电学〉(shortened as 安) ampere

安培计 ānpéijì 〈电学〉ammeter; amperemeter

安培数 ānpéishù 〈电学〉amperage

安培小时 ānpéi xiǎoshí 〈电学〉ampere-hour

安贫乐道 ānpín-lèdào find contentment in poverty and joy in one's principle; happy to lead a simple and virtuous life:多年来他~,潜心著述。For years he was content with his lot and devoted himself heart and soul to writing.

安琪儿 ānqí'ér angel

安寝 ānqǐn be asleep

安全 ānquán safe; secure:确保生产~ ensure safety in production /保证人身~ guarantee personal safety /交通~条例 road safety rules /~起飞 safe take-off /~降落 safe landing /~措施 security (*or* safety) measures /~正点 safe and punctual running (of a train, etc.) /~设施 safety devices (*or* equipment, *or* installations) /~操作 safe operation /~规程 safety regulations (*or* rules, *or* code) /~第一 (put) safety first /~停车距离 safe stopping distance

安全棒 ānquánbàng 〈核物理〉safety rod; scram rod

安全保证 ānquán bǎozhèng security assurances

安全玻璃 ānquán bōli safety glass

安全打 ānquándǎ 〈体育〉base hit

安全带 ānquándài safety belt

安全岛 ānquándǎo 〈交通〉safety or pedestrian island; safety strip

安全灯 ānquándēng ❶〈矿业〉safety lamp ❷〈摄影〉safelight

安全电压 ānquán diànyā safe voltage

安全阀 ānquánfá 〈电学〉safety valve; overload valve; protection valve

安全感 ānquángǎn sense of security; public feeling of safety:缺少~ lack a sense of security

安全高度 ānquán gāodù 〈航空〉safe altitude

安全工作区 ānquán gōngzuòqū area of safe operation (ASO)

安全火柴 ānquán huǒchái safety match

安全胶片 ānquán jiāopiàn 〈影视〉safety film; nonflammable film

安全角 ānquánjiǎo 〈军事〉safety angle

安全界 ānquánjiè 〈军事〉safety limit

安全理事会 Ānquán Lǐshìhuì Security Council (of the United Nations):~常任理事国 permanent member of the Security Council /~非常任理事国 non-permanent member of the Security Council

安全链 ānquánliàn 〈矿业〉safety chain

安全帽 ānquánmào safety helmet

安全门 ānquánmén emergency exit

安全期 ānquánqī 〈医学〉safe period:~避孕法 rhythm method

安全梯 ānquántī fire escape; emergency staircase; ladder escape

安全剃刀 ānquán tìdāo safety razor

安全通行证 ānquán tōngxíngzhèng safe-conduct

安全网 ānquánwǎng 〈建筑〉safety netting

安全系数 ānquán xìshù ❶ safety coefficient or factor ❷ something to fall back on:我们必须有个~,以防万一发生意外。We must have something to fall back upon just in case something unexpected happens.

安全销 ānquánxiāo safety pin

安全柱 ānquánzhù 〈矿业〉safety post; safety prop

安全装置 ānquán zhuāngzhì safety gear or apparatus

安然 ānrán ❶ safe:~无事 pass without mishap /~渡过难关 get through unscathed; tide over the difficulties ❷ free from worry; at ease:心里~ feel at ease /~入睡 fall asleep peacefully

安然无恙 ānrán-wúyàng escape unscathed; be safe and sound:别人都受伤了,只有他~。He alone escaped unscathed while the rest were all injured. /飞行十分危险,但他们终于~地返回了地面。They finally returned safe and sound from a dangerous flight.

安忍 ānrěn ❶〈书面〉not bat an eyelid in perpetrating acts of cruelty:志怀~,性挟猜疑 be cruel by temperament and suspicious by nature ❷〈佛教〉patiently endure

安如磐石 ānrúpánshí as solid as a rock:国家的政治基础~。The political foundation of the state is as firm as a rock. *or* The state's political base is rock-solid.

安如泰山 ānrútàishān *also* "稳如泰山" wěnrútàishān as solid as Mount Tai; as firm as a rock:甲队配合默契,球门~。Team A's goal was as secure as Mount Tai thanks to well-coordinated teamwork.

安莎通讯社 Ānshā Tōngxùnshè (shortened as 安莎社) *Agenzia Nazionale Stampa Associata* (ANSA)

安山岩 ānshānyán 〈地质〉andesite

安设 ānshè install; set up:展厅~了报警装置。A warning system is installed in the exhibition hall.

安身 ānshēn make one's home; have a roof over one's head; take shelter:~之处 place to call home /暂时在这间草屋里~吧。Let's take

A

shelter in this hut for the time being.

安身立命 ānshēn-lìmìng settle down in one's life and career; settle down to a quiet life and get on with one's work:他把教育事业作为自己~之所。He has chosen the teaching profession as his lifelong pursuit.

安神 ānshén ❶ soothe the nerves:养心~ tone up the heart and calm the nerves ❷〈中医〉relieve uneasiness of body and mind

安神药 ānshényào 〈中医〉sedative; tranquilizer

安生 ānshēng ❶ peaceful; restful:那年头,局势不平静,人们无法~。No one could live a peaceful life in those turbulent years. ❷ (often of children) quiet; still:你能不能~一会儿? Can you keep quiet just for one moment? /这孩子怕是病了,这几天总也睡不~。I'm afraid the child is ill, for he has not slept well for several nights.

安石榴 ānshíliu *also*"石榴" pomegranate

安史之乱 Ān-Shǐ Zhī Luàn armed rebellion led by An Lushan and Shi Siming in 755, aimed at toppling the Tang Dynasty but later quelled by Tang generals

安适 ānshì serene and comfortable; contented:生活在~环境中 live in ease and comfort /生活虽然清苦一点儿,但日子过得却很~。Their life was spartan but they were quite contented.

安舒 ānshū at ease and relaxed; in peace and comfort:身心~ feel at ease and rested /度一个~的晚年 enjoy the evening of life in peace; spend one's remaining years in peace and comfort

安睡 ānshuì be sound asleep; sleep soundly:很晚了,大家都已~。It's very late at night. Everybody is sound asleep.

安泰 āntài in good health; safe and sound:身心~ enjoy physical and mental health; be sound both in body and mind /祝您全家~。I wish good health to your whole family

安提瓜岛 Āntíguādǎo Antigua (Island)

安提瓜和巴布达 Āntíguā hé Bābùdá Antigua and Barbuda, island country in the Caribbean Sea

安替比林 āntìbǐlín 〈药学〉antipyrine

安恬 āntián easy and comfortable; relaxed and content; gentle and soothing:~地睡了一觉 have a refreshing sleep; sleep a restful sleep /她的声音轻柔~,宛若习习春风拂过草原。Her voice was as gentle and soft as the soothing spring breeze brushing over the grasslands.

安帖 āntiē feel at ease; set one's heart at rest:所有的事都要再检查一遍,她心里才算~。She has to double-check everything before she can set her heart at rest.

安徒生 Āntúshēng Hans Christian Andersen (1805-1875), Danish author celebrated for his fairy tales

安土重迁 āntǔ-zhòngqiān be used to living in one's homeland and feel disinclined to move elsewhere; be attached to one's native land and reluctant to leave it:这里的人们正在改变~的习惯。People here are beginning to change the custom of staying put where they've always been.

安妥 āntuǒ ❶ be relieved; feel secure:找到这么一个好姑娘来照料母亲,他心里觉着~了。He was greatly relieved to have found such a nice girl to look after his mother. ❷ ANTU or antu, a rat poison

安危 ān-wēi safety and danger; safety:把个人的~置之度外 have no thought for one's own safety

安慰 ānwèi ❶ be comforted; find solace; feel happy:孩子们考试成绩好,母亲感到~。Mother felt happy at the good examination results of her children. /大家理解我的心情,这使我感到极大~。It is no small consolation to know that everybody understands how I feel at this moment. ❷ console; give solace to:~病人 extend sympathy to the patient/~死者的家属 console the dependents of the deceased

安慰奖 ānwèijiǎng consolation prize

安慰赛 ānwèisài 〈体育〉consolation event or match

安慰药 ānwèiyào *also*"安慰剂"〈药学〉placebo

安稳 ānwěn ❶ smooth and steady:航天飞机安安稳稳地着陆。The space shuttle landed smoothly. ❷ peaceful; settled; calm:睡不~ cannot sleep in peace /不除掉这个祸根,咱们休想过~日子。We cannot expect to live a peaceful life unless the root cause of the trouble is removed. /这会儿她止住了哭泣,似乎~多了。She has stopped crying and seems to have calmed down a good deal. ❸ (of one's behaviour, etc.) quiet and calm; poised; composed:这孩子一点~劲儿都没有。The child is restless. /老许总是那么~。Lao Xu is always level-headed (*or* calm and poised).

安息 ānxī ❶ rest; go to sleep:你也够累的了,就早点儿~吧。You are so tired. You'd better go and get straight into bed. ❷ rest in peace:老朋友,~吧! May you rest in peace, my old friend! /教授生前的心愿了却了,他可以~了。The professor may now rest in peace, for all his wishes have been realized. ❸ (Ānxī) Parthia, ancient country in central Asia

安息浸信会 Ānxī Jìnxìnhuì 〈宗教〉Seventh Day Baptists

安息日 ānxīrì 〈宗教〉Sabbath

安息香 ānxīxiāng benzoin (plant, resin, or perfume):~酸 benzoic acid

安闲 ānxián peaceful and carefree; leisurely:~自得 carefree and content /他~地住在别墅里。He lived in a villa free from worldly care. /太~了,我又觉得不自在。I was beginning to feel a bit uncomfortable, life had been so uneventful. /退休以后,有些人种花养鸟,~度日。After retirement, some people enjoy life by growing flowers and keeping birds.

安详 ānxiáng serene; composed; unruffled:神态~ look unruffled /老人坚毅~的神色和生前一样。The old man's resolute and serene expression remained the same as when he was alive.

安歇 ānxiē ❶ go to bed; retire for the night:忙了一整天了,马上~吧。You've been working hard the whole day, and should get into bed straight away. ❷ rest:我已经~了几天,可以上班了。I am fit enough to go back to work now I have had a few days' rest.

安心 ānxīn ❶ intend; mean:~不善 harbour evil intentions/不安好心的人没有好报。Evil intentions will be attended by evil consequences. ❷ be at ease; set one's mind at rest:~养病 recuperate patiently /~本职工作 devote oneself to one's work single-mindedly /你有这样的认识,我也就~了。I feel relieved now that you've come to see the matter in a proper light.

安心落意 ānxīn-luòyì feel reassured; have peace of mind:政策不变,大家就会~。A consistent policy will engender a feeling of security among the people.

安逸 ānyì *also*"安佚" easy and comfortable:~的生活 easy, comfortable life /一味贪图~ be bent on seeking comfort and ease /让老人~地度过余年。Old people should be able to spend the remainder of their years in peace and comfort. /这样一来,我也不得~了。As things stand now, I can have no peace of mind.

安营 ānyíng pitch a camp; camp:部队就地~。The troops pitched camp on the spot.

安营扎寨 ānyíng-zhāzhài pitch a camp; camp:地质钻探队在深山里~。The geological prospecting team camped deep in the mountain.

安于 ānyú be content with; be accustomed to:不能~落后。One must not resign oneself to backwardness.

安于现状 ānyú xiànzhuàng take the world as one finds it; be content with the status quo; rest on one's laurels:有的人~,不求进步。Some people are quite content with things as they are, unwilling to move a step forward.

安葬 ānzàng bury (the dead):人们怀着极为悲痛的心情~烈士。People buried the martyr with profound grief.

安扎 ānzhā settle down; camp:全连~在树林里。The whole company camped in the woods.

安枕 ānzhěn put the pillow in place in order to sleep; sleep soundly:战争迫在眉睫,谁能~而卧? Who could sleep soundly on a soft pillow when the war was imminent? /祸根不除,大家不得~。Nobody could set his mind at rest unless the root of the trouble was removed.

安之若素 ānzhī-ruòsù ❶ bear (hardship, etc.) with equanimity ❷ regard (wrongdoing, etc.) with indifference:对这些不良现象,有人开始很痛恨,不久也就~了。At first some people hated these evil practices, but soon came to live with them.

安置 ānzhì find a place for; arrange for:~失业人员 find work for unemployed people /~难民 resettle refugees /退伍军人得到了妥善的~。Proper arrangements have been made for the demobbed soldiers. /那些要用的东西,都已~妥当。All the things needed are ready.

安置办 ānzhìbàn (short for 安置办公室) resettlement office (for ex-servicemen, etc.)

安置费 ānzhìfèi settlement allowance; placement allowance

安装 ānzhuāng install; erect; fix; mount:~玻璃 fix window panes /~自来水管 lay water pipes /机械~公司 machine installation company /饭店的空调设备~好了。The air-conditioning equipment has been installed in the hotel.

安装队 ānzhuāngduì installation or fitting up gang

安装工 ānzhuānggōng installer; mounter

安装图 ānzhuāngtú 〈机械〉installation diagram or drawing

鞍 ān saddle：马～ saddle

鞍鼻 ānbí 〈医学〉saddle nose

鞍部 ānbù saddle (of a hill or mountain)

鞍韂 ānchàn saddle with saddle blanket

鞍钢 Āngāng (short for 鞍山钢铁公司) Anshan Iron and Steel Complex：～宪法 Charter of the Anshan Iron and Steel Complex (a set of guiding principles approved by Mao Zedong in the 1960's for running large industrial enterprises)

鞍架 ānjià saddle-tree

鞍鞯 ānjiān 〈书面〉*see* "鞍韂"

鞍马 ānmǎ ❶〈体育〉pommelled horse; side horse ❷〈书面〉saddle and horse：～生涯 life on horseback — soldiering

鞍马劳顿 ānmǎ-láodùn fatigued by a long journey; travel-worn：您一路～，且在我这里歇息一两天。As you are quite travel-worn, you'd better rest at my house for a couple of days.

鞍皮 ānpí saddle leather

鞍前马后 ānqián-mǎhòu run before or behind the master's horse; act as a faithful attendant：他～地跟你跑，倒落得一身不是。He has been very faithful to you, yet has got nothing but blame.

鞍桥 ānqiáo *also* "鞍桥" pommel or horn and cantle; saddle bow and hind bow; cantle

鞍屉 āntì ❶ saddle blanket; horse blanket; girth ❷ saddle

鞍形山 ānxíngshān 〈地质〉saddleback

鞍子 ānzi saddle

鞍座毯 ānzuòtǎn saddle or horse blanket

桉 ān 〈植物〉eucalyptus

桉树 ānshù eucalyptus

桉油 ānyóu eucalyptus oil

桉油精 ānyóujīng cajeputol

氨 ān 〈化学〉ammonia; hydrogen nitride; NH_3：合成～ synthetic ammonia

氨苯磺胺 ānběn huáng'àn 〈药学〉sulphanilamide

氨草酸 āncǎosuān 〈药学〉ammoniac

氨茶碱 ānchájiǎn 〈药学〉aminophylline

氨合 ānhé 〈化学〉ammoniate：～物 ammoniate

氨合成法 ānhéchéngfǎ ammonia synthesis

氨化 ānhuà ammoniate：～作用 ammoniation; ammonization; ammonification

氨化过磷酸钙 ānhuà guòlínsuāngài 〈农业〉ammoniated superphosphate

氨基 ānjī 〈化学〉amino; amino-group：～苯 aminobenzene /～醇 amino-alcohol /～硫酸 aminosulfuric acid /～脂 aminolipid /～糖 amino sugar /～酸 amino acid /～塑料 aminoplastic /～树脂 amino (*or* amine) resin /～纤维素 aminocellulose

氨基比林 ānjībǐlín 〈药学〉aminopyrine

氨基吡啶 ānjībǐdìng aminopyridine

氨基二苯胺 ānjī èrběn'àn aminodiphenylamine

氨基多肽酶 ānjī duōtàiméi 〈生化〉aminopolypeptidase

氨基合成酶 ānjī héchéngméi 〈生化〉amino-ligase

氨基噻唑 ānjīsāizuò aminothiazole

氨基酸 ānjīsuān amino acid：～型糖尿病〈医学〉amino diabetes /～尿(症)〈医学〉aminoacidurea /～定年术〈考古〉aminoacid dating

氨基酮 ānjītóng aminoketone

氨碱法 ānjiǎnfǎ 〈化学〉ammonia soda process

氨解 ānjiě 〈化学〉aminolysis; ammonolysis

氨冷冻 ānlěngdòng ammonia cooling

氨冷冻机 ānlěngdòngjī 〈机械〉ammonia refrigerating machine

氨硫脲 ānliúniào 〈药学〉thiacetazone

氨伦 ānlún spandex

氨络 ānluò *also* "氨络物"〈化学〉ammine：～物 ammino-complex; ammino-compound

氨气 ānqì 〈化学〉ammonia：～压缩机〈机械〉ammonia compressor /～压缩冷冻机〈机械〉ammonia compression refrigerating machine

氨水 ānshuǐ 〈化学〉ammonia water; aqua ammoniae

氨转化器 ānzhuǎnhuàqì 〈化工〉ammonia convertor

鮟 ān

鮟鱇 ānkāng 〈动物〉angler; goosefish; angler-fish

谙 ān 〈书面〉know well; be well-versed：不～医术 know little about medicine /熟～当地情况 be well acquainted with local conditions /江南好，风景旧曾～。Beautiful is Jiangnan, whose scenery I knew so well once.

谙达 āndá be familiar; be well-versed; be conversant：～世情 be familiar with the ways of the world; be worldly-wise

谙练 ānliàn 〈书面〉be conversant; be skilful; be proficient：这位新上任的教练，对篮球的各种技、战术都非常～。The new coach is conversant with all the techniques and tactics of basketball.

谙事 ānshì 〈方言〉have sense; be sensible：小伙子不～，随便乱说。The young chap is a little callow and liable to blurt out any rubbish.

谙熟 ānshú be familiar; be versed：～古诗 be well-versed in classical poetry

腤 ān 〈书面〉stew; boil (meat, fish, etc.)

庵(菴) ān ❶〈书面〉hut：茅～ thatched hut ❷ nunnery; Buddhist convent：尼～ nunnery

庵堂 āntáng nunnery; Buddhist convent

庵子 ānzi 〈方言〉❶ thatched hut ❷ nunnery

鹌 ān

鹌鹑 ānchun quail

唵 ān *also* "咹"〈叹词〉❶ *used to signal agreement*："你回家吗？""～，是的。""Are you going home now?" "Oh yes." ❷ *used to convey a mild reminder, suggestion or comment*：你们时间很紧，要抓紧啊，～！You are pressed for time and have to speed up. Right? *see also* ǎn

咹 ān *see* "唵" ān *see also* ǎn

媕 ān

媕娿 ān'ē 〈书面〉look irresolute; be hesitant

ǎn

咹 ǎn *see* "唵³" ǎn *see also* ān

铵 ǎn 〈化学〉ammonium：～矾 ammonium alum /硫酸～ ammonium sulphate /碳酸氢～ ammonium bicarbonate

铵离子 ǎnlízǐ ammonium ion

铵盐 ǎnyán ammonium salt

揞 ǎn apply (medicinal powder to a wound)：手破了最好～上一些消炎粉。When you've got a cut in your hand, you'd better apply some medicinal powder to it.

埯(垵) ǎn ❶ hole for planting seeds ❷ dig holes to plant seeds in; dibble ❸〈量词〉一～儿玉米 a cluster of corn seedlings

埯子 ǎnzi 〈方言〉small hole (for dibbling)：挖个～ dig a hole in the earth; dibble

唵¹ ǎn 〈口语〉put (sth. powdery or granular held in one's hand) into the mouth：～了两口雪 swallow two mouthfuls of snow

唵² ǎn *see* "俺" ǎn

唵³ ǎn 〈叹词〉*used to convey interrogation or doubt*：～，你把东西都准备好了吗？You have got everything ready, haven't you? /怎么一直没看见你呀，～？How come, I haven't seen you for ages?

唵⁴ ǎn word used in Buddhist incantations

see also ān

A

俺 ǎn 〈方言〉❶ we (excluding those addressed)：～那里庄稼长得可好了！The crops in our village are growing real well！❷ my；I：～兄弟 my brother

俺家 ǎnjia 〈方言〉❶ I ❷ my family or home；our family or home：这是～的。This is ours.

俺们 ǎnmen 〈方言〉we

àn

案[1] àn ❶ old-fashioned long narrow table：香～ table for offering incense (to gods or ancestors) ❷ long board serving as a table or counter：肉～ board for selling meat；meat counter

案[2] àn ❶ law case；case：命～ case of murder /破～ crack a criminal case /作～ commit a crime ❷ record；file：记录在～ be on record /档～ archive(s) ❸ plan submitted for approval；proposal：议～ draft resolution /方～ proposal；scheme ❹ *see* "按[2]" àn

案板 ànbǎn kneading or chopping board

案秤 ànchèng counter scale；platform scale；platform balance *see also* "台秤" táichèng

案底 àndǐ file or record of previous offences：有～ with a record of previous offences /查阅这个嫌疑犯的～ look through the file of previous offences concerning the suspect

案牍 àndú 〈书面〉office documents and correspondence

案犯 ànfàn 〈法律〉the accused；offender；suspect

案几 ànjī *also* "条几" tiáojī teapoy

案件 ànjiàn law case；case：民事～ civil law case；lawsuit /国际毒品走私～ case of international drug trafficking

案酒 ànjiǔ *also* "按酒" ànjiǔ meat dish to go with wine

案卷 ànjuàn ❶ file folder ❷ records；files；archives：把有关的～调出来查看一下 retrieve the relevant files (from the archives) for review

案例 ànlì case：研究～ case study /～摘要 digest of a case /经济～ economic case /～分析法 case-study method

案目 ànmù 〈旧语〉usher (in a theatre, etc.)

案情 ànqíng details of a case；case：调查～ investigate a case/～复杂 complicated case

案头 àntóu on the desk；on the table：～摆着几件精巧的工艺品。On the desk are a few fine pieces of handicraft.

案头调研 àntóu diàoyán desk research

案头工作 àntóu gōngzuò 〈戏剧〉notes written by a director or actor in preparing for a performance

案头剧 àntóujù 〈戏剧〉closet play；closet drama

案头日历 àntóu rìlì desk calendar

案文 ànwén text：审核～ examine the text /协商～ negotiate the text

案验 ànyàn *also* "按验" ànyàn 〈书面〉investigate the evidence of a case：对罪证一一～ carefully investigate the evidence of the criminal case

案由 ànyóu main points of a case；brief；summary：这份～没有写清楚。The summary (*or* résumé) of this case is not well written.

案语 ànyǔ note；comment *see also* "按语" ànyǔ

案证 ànzhèng evidence relating to a case

案桌 ànzhuō long narrow table

案子 ànzi ❶ old-fashioned long, narrow table ❷ long board serving as a table or counter：面～ kneading board /台球～ billiard table ❸〈口语〉case：应该将～尽快搞清楚。The case should be cleared up as soon as possible.

按[1] àn ❶ press；push down：～键 press a key /～图钉 push down a drawing pin /～电铃 ring an electric bell ❷ leave aside；shelve：～下不表。Let's put the matter aside for the moment. ❸ restrain；control：强～住性子 try hard to control one's temper /你先～下这口气。You'll have to hold back your anger for the time being. ❹ keep one's hand on；keep a tight grip on：～剑 keep one's hand on the sword /手～战刀 keep a tight grip on the sabre ❺ according to；in accordance with：～成 according to percentage；proportionately /～日 per day；per diem /～次进入 enter in due order /～制度办事 act according to the rules /～比例的协调发展 proportionate and co-ordinated growth /～比例削减供给 cut the supply pro rata /～比例复制 reproduce to scale /～资历排列 arrange in order of seniority /～此说法 as the reasoning goes /～每人两张票发 distribute the tickets to everybody, two to each

按[2]**(案)** àn ❶〈书面〉check；refer to：有底本可～。There is the original text to refer to. ❷ note；comment (by the editor, author, etc.)：编者～ editor's note

按兵不动 ànbīng-bùdòng ❶ hold one's troops where they are；refuse to throw one's troops into battle：我军团浴血奋战，你为何～？My army group is fighting a bloody battle. Why are you holding back your troops? ❷ take no action：人人争着干起来了，我们怎能～？Everyone has pitched in, how can we sit idle doing nothing?

按部就班 ànbù-jiùbān follow the prescribed order；keep to the conventional way of doing things：像这样～地干，恐怕难出成果。It seems unlikely for us to achieve anything if we stick to the same old rut.

按察使 àncháshǐ 〈旧语〉❶ general inspector of the civil service from the Tang Dynasty onwards ❷ provincial chief justice in the Ming and Qing dynasties

按分计费 ànfēn-jìfèi 〈通信〉per minute billing

按件计工 ànjiàn-jìgōng pay according to the quantity of work done；piece work pay or reckoning

按键 ànjiàn key (on a keyboard)；push button：暂停～ pause button /倒带～ rewind button

按键式电话机 ànjiànshì diànhuàjī push-button telephone；push phone

按揭 ànjiē 〈方言〉(used usu. in real estate) mortgage：～购房 take out a mortgage to buy a house；buy a house on time /～贷款 mortgage loan /～利率 mortgage (interest) rate /首期～ down-payment /从事～业务 be in the house-mortgaging business

按金 ànjīn 〈方言〉deposit；rent：交纳～ pay a deposit；pay rent

按酒 ànjiǔ meat dishes to go with wine

按扣儿 ànkòur 〈口语〉snap fastener

按劳分配 ànláo-fēnpèi distribution according to work；to each according to his work

按劳计酬 ànláo-jìchóu performance-related pay

按理 ànlǐ according to reason or principle；in the normal course of things；normally：～说，他不会不同意。In the normal course of things, he wouldn't turn down our request. /～冬天是最冷的季节，但去冬有好几天却出现了少有的暖天气。Normally, winter is the coldest season of the year. But the weather was unusually warm for quite a few days last winter.

按例 ànlì as a rule；according to regulations；according to custom or precedent：生活困难的，～可以申请补助。According to regulations those who are in financial difficulty may apply for government subsidy.

按脉 ànmài feel or take the pulse

按摩 ànmó 〈医学〉massage：～疗法 massotherapy /～院 massage parlour

按摩器 ànmóqì massager；masseur

按摩员 ànmóyuán massager；masseur：女～ masseuse

按捺 ànnà *also* "按纳" restrain；check；control：～不住内心的兴奋 cannot restrain one's excitement /～着自己的感情 keep one's feelings in check

按耐 ànnài restrain；control；suppress (anger, excitement, etc.)：她竭力～着怒火。She was trying hard to contain (*or* control) her anger.

按钮 ànniǔ push button：按～ push a button /这是这套设备的总～。This is the push-button control of the entire equipment.

按钮开关 ànniǔ kāiguān push-button switch

按钮控制 ànniǔ kòngzhì push-button control；dash control

按钮战争 ànniǔ zhànzhēng push-button warfare

按期 ànqī on schedule；on time：～完成 finish on schedule/～归还 return on time /～举行会议 hold the meeting as scheduled

按人口平均 ànrénkǒu píngjūn per capita：～收入 per capita income /～国民生产总值 per capita GNP

按时 ànshí on time；on schedule：～投产 go into operation on schedule /～报到 report for work at the appointed time/电影～开演。The film started on time.

A

按说 ànshuō ordinarily; normally; in the ordinary course of events:这电视机刚买了半年,～应该保修。The TV set should normally be serviced free for it was bought only six months ago. /都是国家工作人员,～应该讲理。As government officials, they are supposed to abide by reason.

按图索骥 àntú-suǒjì look for a fine horse with the aid of its picture — try to locate sth. by following up a clue; do sth. mechanically:说明书上写着规格式样,咱们～,何愁找不准。Since specifications and model figures are given in the manual, we are sure to locate everything following up the instructions.

按蚊 ànwén anopheles; malarial mosquito

按下葫芦浮起瓢 ànxià húlu fúqǐ piáo hardly has one gourd been pushed under water when another bobs up — solve one problem only to find another cropping up:他承担的工作太多,～,哪一件也没做好。He has taken on so many jobs that he is always falling short in achieving anything satisfactory.

按需分配 ànxū-fēnpèi distribution according to need; to each according to his need

按压 ànyā suppress; restrain:～住火爆的脾气 suppress one's hot temper

按验 ànyàn investigate the evidence of a case
see also "案验" ànyàn

按语 ànyǔ *also* "案语" ànyǔ note; comment: 编者～ editor's note

按月 ànyuè by the month; monthly; *per mensem*:～付款 pay by the month

按照 ànzhào according to; in accordance with; in the light of; in keeping with:～预订计划完成任务 fulfil the task according to plan / ～新的情况提出新的建议 make new recommendations in the light of the new circumstances /～经济发展给科技部门拨更多资金 allocate more funds for science and technology in keeping with economic development /～实际情况决定工作方针 decide on the policy in line with the actual situation /～广大群众的要求,创办了消费者协会。In response to public demand, a consumers' association was founded. / ～每本一元伍角计算,共四十五元。It added up to 45 *yuan* counting 1.5 *yuan* per copy. /～你的馊主意,这件事只会弄糟。If we acted on your ill-conceived advice, we would only make a mess of the whole thing.

按质论价 ànzhì-lùnjià pricing by quality

胺

àn 〈化学〉amine

胺化 ànhuà amination:～剂 aminating agent /～氧 amine oxide

胺醛树脂 ànquán shùzhī 〈化工〉amine aldehyde resin

胺酸 ànsuān 〈化学〉amino acid

胺盐 ànyán amine salt

黯

àn dim; obscure; gloomy

黯黯 àn'àn dim; gloomy:黄昏时天色～的,使人感到沉闷。I became moody at the deepening gloom of dusk.

黯淡 àndàn *also* "暗淡" àndàn dim; gloomy; bleak:寺庙年久失修,佛像的金身更显得～了。The Buddhist statues have no lustre of gold, for the temple has been in disrepair for years. /古城去掉旧日～的容颜,显得娇丽多姿。The ancient city has rid itself of its former bleak appearance and recovered its youth and grace.

黯黑 ànhēi *also* "暗黑" ànhēi ❶ dark; swarthy:脸色～ have a swarthy complexion ❷ dark; dim:～的夜晚 dark night /天色已经～了。It is already dark.

黯然 ànrán ❶ dim; faint:夜色～。The night was getting darker and darker. ❷ dejected; low-spirited; downcast:～神伤 feel dejected (*or* depressed) /想到伤心的地方,她不禁～泪下。She could not refrain from tears when she brooded over her heart-breaking experience.

黯然失色 ànrán-shīsè be overshadowed; be eclipsed; pale into insignificance:和这幅画比,展室里所有的绘画都～。All the other paintings in the gallery paled by comparison with this one.

黯然销魂 ànrán-xiāohún extremely sad and depressed; dejected: ～者,唯别而已矣! Parting is such sad sorrow. *or* There is no sorrow like sorrow at parting.

暗(❶❸闇)

àn ❶ dark; dim; dull:～红 dark red /～青 dull black /～灰色 dull grey /这间屋子太～。It is too dark in the room. ❷ hidden; secret:心中～喜 feel a surge of inmost joy ❸〈书面〉hazy; unclear:若明若～ have a hazy (*or* unclear) picture (of sth.) /偏听则～。Listen to one side, and you'll be benighted.

暗暗 àn'àn secretly; inwardly; to oneself:～起誓 swear to oneself /～思忖 turn sth. over in one's mind; think to oneself /读了他的文章,我不禁～赞叹。After reading his article, I could not help admiring him secretly. /她听了这一番议论,～吃了一惊。She gasped inwardly to hear the argument.

暗坝 ànbà submerged dam

暗伴星 ànbànxīng 〈天文〉dark companion

暗堡 ànbǎo bunker

暗病 ànbìng *see* "暗疾"

暗补 ànbǔ invisible subsidy (financed by the government); hidden subsidy:改～为明补 replace invisible subsidies (in terms of artificially low prices) with open subsidies (issued to consumers as part of their salaries or benefits)

暗藏 àncáng hide; conceal:～的特务分子 hidden spy (*or* special agent) /～古籍真本 conceal authentic texts of ancient classics /～枪支弹药 illegally possess firearms and ammunition; have a secret cache of firearms and ammunition

暗娼 ànchāng unlicensed or unregistered prostitute

暗场 ànchǎng 〈戏剧〉developments of a drama to be understood by the audience from the actor's lines instead of being acted out on the stage

暗潮 àncháo undercurrent

暗沉沉 ànchēnchēn (of sky) dark:在～的夜里,什么也看不见。Nothing was discernible on such a dark night.

暗处 ànchù ❶ dark place:猫头鹰白天躲在～。The owl hides itself in a dark place during the day. ❷ hideout; cover:你在明处,他在～,你可得小心呵! You must be on your guard as you are in the open while he is hidden in the dark.

暗袋 àndài 〈摄影〉camera bag (for changing film)

暗淡 àndàn dim; faint; dismal; gloomy:色彩～ dull colour /星光～ dim starlight /天色～ overcast sky /前景～ bleak prospect /心情～ dismal mood /～的画面 gloomy picture /脸色显得十分阴沉～ appear very gloomy and sullen

暗道 àndào secret path, passage, or tunnel:据说,当年两处有～可通。It is said that these two places were linked up by a secret passage.

暗地里 àndìli secretly; inwardly; on the sly:～计算 inwardly calculate /～捣鬼 secretly make trouble /～提防着 be inwardly on guard against sb. (*or* sth.) /～给走私者通风报信 tip the smugglers off on the sly

暗渡陈仓 àndù-Chéncāng engage in sth. covertly while making a feint in the open, esp. carry on an illicit love affair
see also "明修栈道,暗渡陈仓" míng xiū zhàndào, àn dù Chéncāng

暗发射体 ànfāshètǐ dark emitter

暗房 ànfáng dark room

暗辐射 ànfúshè dark radiation

暗沟 àngōu covered sewerage; underground drain

暗光灯 ànguāngdēng dim light

暗害 ànhài stab in the back; kill secretly:设圈套对人进行～ lay traps for sb. on the sly /他因反战而被～。He was murdered secretly for his anti-war activities.

暗含 ànhán imply; be implicit:他的话里～着威胁。There is a veiled threat in what he said. /这番话～着极大的挖苦。Those are galling ironical remarks. /这篇短文～的思想很丰富。The short essay is pregnant with meaning.

暗号 ànhào secret signal or sign; countersign; cipher:联络～ contact signal /对～ check the signals

暗合 ànhé agree without prior consultation; coincide:如何处理这件事,他和我的意见不过～而已。We happened to see eye to eye on how to solve this problem.

暗河 ànhé underground river

暗盒 ànhé 〈摄影〉magazine; cassette

暗黑 ànhēi pitch-dark

暗红热 ànhóngrè dark red heat

暗花儿 ànhuār veiled design incised in porcelain or woven in fabric

暗话 ànhuà ❶ code word ❷ comments made behind sb.'s back; gossip:明人不说～。Those who are open and above-board will not speak ill of anybody behind his back.

A

暗火 ànhuǒ smouldering fire
暗疾 ànjí unmentionable disease; disease one is ashamed of
暗记儿 ànjìr secret mark: 在孩子的衣服上做了个～ make a secret mark in the child's clothes
暗间儿 ànjiānr inner room (often serving as a bedroom or storeroom)
暗箭 ànjiàn arrow shot from hiding; attack by a hidden enemy; stab in the back: 放～ attack by underhand means/谨防～ be on guard against stabs in the back /～难防 difficult to ward off an arrow shot from hiding; hard to guard against attacks by a hidden enemy
暗箭伤人 ànjiàn-shāngrén stab sb. in the back; injure sb. by underhand means: 这个人心不正, 惯于～, 不可不防。This man is so evil-minded that he would always try to harm others by underhand means. We must be on our guard.
暗礁 ànjiāo ❶ submerged reef or rock: 我国南海多～。There are lots of submerged reefs in the South China Sea. ❷ latent difficulty; concealed obstacle: 我不知道, 在前进的路上会遇到多少险滩和～。I wonder how many risks and obstacles we'll run into on our way forward.
暗接 ànjiē 〈机械〉secret joint
暗井 ànjǐng 〈矿业〉blind shaft; winze
暗扣 ànkòu ❶ veiled or covered button (on clothing) ❷〈商业〉hidden or disguised commission
暗里 ànli *see*"暗中"
暗流 ànliú ❶ undercurrent ❷ latent trend or tendency
暗楼子 ànlóuzi attic storeroom accessible through an opening in the ceiling by using a ladder
暗码 ànmǎ ❶ secret code: 发～电报 send a telegram in secret code ❷〈旧语〉with no clearly marked price: ～售货 put goods on sale without price tags
暗昧 ànmèi ❶ underhand; stealthy; disgraceful: 做了件～之事 have done something disgraceful /这钱怎么到你手里的? 其中必有～。How did you get hold of the money? There must be something shady about it. /除了十分～地淡淡一笑外, 他再也没有任何表示。Except for a very faint smile, he did not utter even a word. ❷ stupid; dull; silly: ～无知 stupid and ignorant
暗门子 ànménzi 〈方言〉unregistered or unlicensed prostitute
暗盘 ànpán secretly negotiated price between the seller and buyer; under-the-counter price or terms
暗器 ànqì concealed weapon (such as a hidden arrow or darts): 放～ release (*or* launch, *or* shoot) a concealed arrow (*or* dart) /～伤人 kill (*or* injure) sb. by a hidden weapon
暗枪 ànqiāng sniper's shot: 打他的～ snipe at sb. /虽然基本上已经停火, 但不时还有人打～。Although the ceasefire holds, there are snipers' shots from time to time.
暗渠 ànqú ❶ underground stream; underground canal or watercourse ❷〈建筑〉culvert
暗弱 ànruò ❶ (of light) dim; faint: 灯光～ dim light /一束～的光 faint beam of light ❷〈书面〉weak; feeble: 为人～ be stupid and weak-willed; be a weakling
暗杀 ànshā assassinate: 被～的人不下数百。No fewer than hundreds of people were assassinated.
暗杀者 ànshāzhě assassin
暗沙 ànshā *also*"暗砂" submerged coral islet; shoal: 曾母～ Zengmu Shoals (at the southernmost tip of China's Nansha Islands in the South China Sea)
暗伤 ànshāng ❶ internal or invisible injury: 受～ suffer (*or* sustain) an invisible injury ❷ internal or invisible damage: 瓷瓶上有一～。There is an invisible flaw in the porcelain vase. ❸ harm or injure others by underhand means
暗哨 ànshào ❶ hidden post: 放～ post a secret sentry; be on hidden sentry duty ❷ whistle as a secret signal
暗射 ànshè hint at; make veiled reference to; insinuate; attack by innuendo: 你这话是不是有所～? Are you insinuating something by that?
暗射地图 ànshè dìtú outline map (as teaching aid to help students identify places on the map)
暗示 ànshì ❶ drop a hint; hint; suggest: 他作手势～我别说下去。He gestured to me to stop talking. /经理站起来, ～面试到此结束了。The manager stood up, showing that the interview was over. /这段话虽然是针对你说的, 但其中也有些是对我的～。Although these remarks were directed at you, there were some digs at me too. ❷〈心理〉suggestion: ～疗法 suggestion therapy /～感受性 suggestibility
暗事 ànshì shady affair: 明人不做～。A person who is above-board does nothing on the sly.
暗室 ànshì 〈摄影〉darkroom: ～滤光器 darkroom filter /～显影机 darkroom processor
暗适应 ànshìyìng 〈心理〉dark adaption
暗送秋波 ànsòng-qiūbō make (sheep's) eyes at sb. while others are not watching; slyly give sb. the glad eye; make secret overtures to sb.
暗算 ànsuàn plot against: 他父亲几乎遭到一伙人的～。His father narrowly escaped the plot of a gang.
暗榫接合 ànsǔn jiēhé secret heading joint
暗锁 ànsuǒ built-in lock
暗滩 àntān hidden shoal
暗探 àntàn ❶ secret agent; spy ❷ make out on the sly; pry; spy: ～其意 find out sb.'s intention tactfully /～军情 spy on military disposition
暗无天日 ànwútiānrì complete darkness; total absence of justice: ～的社会 society that is an abyss of total darkness; dark society /当年, ～的事情多得很呢! In those days cases of gross injustice were simply too numerous to count!
暗物质 ànwùzhì 〈天文〉dark matter or substance: 宇宙中的～ cosmic dark matter
暗喜 ànxǐ be secretly pleased; feel pleased but not show it
暗匣 ànxiá *see*"暗箱"
暗下 ànxià secretly; on the sly; surreptitiously: 明里不露声色, ～却加紧活动。Nothing seems unusual on the surface, but a conspiracy is brewing.
暗线 ànxiàn foreshadowing
暗线光谱 ànxiàn guāngpǔ 〈物理〉dark-line spectrum
暗箱 ànxiāng 〈摄影〉camera bellows; camera obscura
暗香疏影 ànxiāng-shūyǐng secret fragrance and dappled shadows — a descriptive epithet for plum flowers
暗笑 ànxiào ❶ secret glee: 听了这个消息, 她只是抿着嘴, 低头～。At the news, she tried to suppress her smile in secret glee. ❷ laugh in or up one's sleeve; sneer secretly; snigger: 人们～他干了一件蠢事, 他却认为自己做得对。People laughed secretly at him for his great stupidity, but he thought he had done the right thing.
暗星 ànxīng 〈天文〉dark star: ～云 dark nebula
暗夜 ànyè dark night: 大风刮起一阵尘埃, 白日如同～。As a gust of wind whipped up clouds of dust, day darkened like night.
暗影 ànyǐng ❶ shadow: 草坪印着竹篱的～。The shadows of the bamboo fence were reflected on the lawn. /他们的话给我喜悦的心情投下了忧虑的～。Their words cast a shadow over my joyful mood. ❷〈天文〉umbra
暗语 ànyǔ code word: 传递～ pass on the code word
暗喻 ànyù *also*"隐喻" yǐnyù metaphor
暗中 ànzhōng ❶ in the dark: 躲在～张望 hide in the dark and keep watch ❷ in secret; on the sly; surreptitiously: ～打听 gather information in secret /～活动 carry on surreptitious activities /～帮助他人 give covert assistance to others
暗中摸索 ànzhōng mōsuǒ grope in the dark; explore by oneself: 小刘经过两天的～, 终于找出这台机器的毛病所在。After two days' painstaking exploration by himself, Xiao Liu at last found out what was wrong with the machine. /既有前人的经验可借鉴, 你又何苦～呢? Since there is ready experience to draw on, why do you have to start it all over by yourself (*or* why do you want to reinvent the wheel yourself)?
暗转 ànzhuǎn 〈戏剧〉blackout in the middle of a scene (either to indicate a change in time or for a quick change of setting)
暗自 ànzì inwardly; to oneself; secretly: ～喜欢 keep the joy to oneself /～盘算 secretly calculate /～诧异 feel bewildered in one's mind /～思量 turn over in one's mind /心里～好笑 feel very much amused
暗自庆幸 ànzì qìngxìng secretly congratulate oneself; consider oneself lucky

晻

àn *see*"暗" àn
see also yǎn

岸[1]

àn land along a river, lake, sea, etc.: 湖～ lakeside/ 江～

边 on the bank of a river / 海～边 on the coast / 河两～绿柳成荫。Green willow trees line both sides of the river. / 船靠～了。The ship has come ashore.

岸[2] àn ❶〈书面〉tall; high: 伟～ man of tall and sturdy build ❷〈书面〉haughty; arrogant: 傲～ haughty; supercilious

岸标 ànbiāo shore beacon

岸冰 ànbīng ice that has formed along the banks of a river or lake

岸炮 ànpào coastal artillery

岸然 ànrán 〈书面〉in a solemn manner: 老人站在人群面前，像青松一样挺拔～。Before a big crowd stood the old man, tall and upright like a pine tree.

岸滩平原 àntān píngyuán beach plain

岸信介 Ànxìnjiè Kishi Nobusuke (1896-1987), war criminal during World War II and Japanese Prime Minister from 1957 to 1960

犴 àn *see* "狴犴" bì'àn

āng

肮(骯) āng

肮脏 āngzang ❶ dirty; filthy: ～的街道 dirty street / ～的下水道 filthy sewerage pipe ❷ foul; mean; despicable; sinister: ～的思想 dirty mind / 灵魂～ sinister soul / ～话 dirty (*or* filthy) words

áng

卬 áng 〈书面〉❶ I; me ❷ *see* "昂" áng ❸ (Áng) a surname

昂 áng ❶ hold (one's head) high: 把头～起来! Hold up your head! *or* Chin up! ❷ high; soaring; expensive: 激～ excited and indignant / 物少价～。Prices soar while commodities are in short supply.

昂昂 áng'áng high-spirited; noble; heroic: ～自若 look exalted and composed / ～正气 air of nobility and righteousness / 雄赳赳，气～ valiant and spirited

昂藏 ángcáng 〈书面〉(of people) towering and proud in appearance

昂奋 ángfèn in high spirits; buoyant: ～的心情 buoyant spirit / 情绪～ be full of enthusiasm

昂贵 ángguì expensive; costly; exorbitant: ～的时装 expensive fashions / 价格～。The price is high.

昂然 ángrán upright and dauntless; chin up and chest out: ～挺胸 throw out one's chest proudly / 神态～ dignified and impressive / ～而入 walk in proudly

昂首 ángshǒu hold one's head high

昂首阔步 ángshǒu-kuòbù stride along with one's chin up; stride proudly ahead

昂首望天 ángshǒu-wàngtiān hold one's head up and look into the sky

昂扬 ángyáng spirited; elated; excited: ～欢快的调子 spirited (*or* militant) and joyous tune / 激奋～的音乐 inspiring and spirited music / 群情～。Public feeling runs high.

àng

盎[1] àng ancient vessel with a big belly and a small mouth

盎[2] àng 〈书面〉brimming; abundant

盎格鲁撒克逊 Anggélǔ-Sākèxùn Anglo-Saxon: ～人 Anglo-Saxon / ～后裔白人新教徒 white Anglo-Saxon protestant (WASP, one who belongs to the group of middle- and upper-class Americans descended from British or Northern European settlers, generally regarded as the traditionally dominant or privileged group in the US)

盎然 àngrán abundant; overflowing; exuberant: 生气～ full of vigour / 诗意～ rich in poetic flavour

盎司 àngsī *also* "盎斯" ounce

枊 àng 〈书面〉post for hitching or tethering a horse

āo

爊(熝) āo ❶〈书面〉simmer (sth.) over a low fire ❷〈方言〉cook with many spices: ～鸭 duck cooked with spices ❸〈书面〉*see* "熬" āo

熬 āo cook in water; boil: ～豆腐 stewed bean curd
see also áo

熬心 āoxīn 〈方言〉filled with anxiety; extremely worried: 事儿没办好，真让人～。It is most worrisome that the matter has not been properly handled.

凹 āo concave; hollow; sunken; dented: ～下 depress / ～进 cave in / ～凸不平 uneven; full of bumps and holes
see also wā

凹岸 āo'àn 〈地理〉cutbank; concave bank

凹版 āobǎn 〈印刷〉intaglio; gravure: 手工雕刻～ hand-engraved plate / 照相～ photogravure

凹版腐蚀制版法 āobǎn fǔshí zhìbǎnfǎ 〈印刷〉aquatint

凹版印刷 āobǎn yìnshuā intaglio or gravure printing: ～机 intaglio (*or* gravure) press / ～品 intaglio printed material

凹版照相 āobǎn zhàoxiàng heliogravure

凹版制版 āobǎn zhìbǎn gravure plate-making

凹度 āodù concavity

凹镜 āojìng *see* "凹面镜"

凹脸蝠 āoliǎnfú 〈动物〉slit-faced bat; hollow-faced bat

凹面镜 āomiànjìng *also* "凹镜"; "会聚镜" huìjùjìng concave mirror

凹室 āoshì alcove

凹透镜 āotòujìng concave lens

凹凸镜 āotūjìng concave-convex lens

凹凸轧花 āotū yàhuā 〈纺织〉embossing

凹凸印刷 āotū yìnshuā embossing; die stamping: ～法 die stamping method / ～机 embossing (*or* die stamping) press

凹纹 āowén design in intaglio

凹陷 āoxiàn hollow; depressed: 眼眶～ sunken eyes / ～骨折 depressed fracture / 地形～。The ground caved in.

áo

鏖 áo 〈书面〉engage in fierce battle

鏖兵 áobīng 〈书面〉engage in fierce fighting

鏖战 áozhàn fight hard; engage in fierce battle: 半个世纪前，这里曾是两军～的战场。Fifty years ago, the place was the battleground of two opposing armies.

敖 áo ❶ *see* "遨" áo ❷ (Áo) a surname

敖包 áobāo *aobao*, heap of sand, stone or earth laid out as a road marker or boundary sign by Mongolians, formerly also worshipped as habitation of spirits

熬 áo ❶ cook into gruel, gravy or thick soup; boil; stew: ～粥 make gruel; cook porridge / ～鱼汤 cook fish stew / ～肉冻 boil meat into jelly / ～豆浆 boil soya-bean milk / 用文火～ simmer ❷ decoct sth. by boiling; boil down: ～药 decoct Chinese medicine by boiling medicinal herbs / ～盐 make salt by boiling sea water ❸ endure (pain or a hard life): ～日子 drag out a miserable existence / ～更守夜 keep night-long vigil / ～过难关 struggle through hard times; tide over difficulties / ～白了头发 suffer so much that one's hair has turned grey prematurely / 苦日子总算～过去了。Days of bitter hardship have at long last come to an end. / 他开夜车把眼睛都～红了。He's got bloodshot eyes by burning the midnight oil.
see also āo

熬煎 áojiān suffering; torture; torment: 把病人从病魔的～下解救出来 rescue the patient from the torment of disease

熬炼 áoliàn temper or steel oneself; go through the mill: 她在艰难

A

困苦中～得更坚强了。Hardship steeled her to be a tougher woman. *or* Tempered in adversity, she became tougher than ever.
熬磨 áomó 〈方言〉❶ go through painfully; endure:～时间 find time dragging ❷ pester; try:这孩子真～人。What a trying child!
熬审 áoshěn 〈旧语〉interrogate (a suspect) with torture
熬头儿 áotour hope for a better life after years of suffering; bright future to look forward to:他觉得日子没个～,就自杀了。He committed suicide as he had nothing to look forward to in life. /现在虽说苦点儿,但有～了。Though life is still somewhat hard, there is light at the end of the tunnel.
熬刑 áoxíng (of a suspect or convict) suffer torture rather than plead guilty
熬夜 áoyè stay up late or all night; burn the midnight oil:最近赶写讲稿,天天～。Recently I have stayed up late for nights on end, preparing lecture notes.

謷 áo 〈书面〉slander; defamation; calumny

廒(厫) áo 〈书面〉storehouse for grain, etc.; granary; barn:仓～ storehouse; granary; barn

遨 áo stroll; saunter
遨游 áoyóu roam; travel:～太空 travel in space /～海上 go cruising in the sea /我们乘坐游艇～西湖。We were boating on the West Lake.

聱 áo *see*"佶屈聱牙" jíqū-áoyá

獒 áo 〈动物〉mastiff

嗷 áo
嗷嗷 áo'áo 〈象声〉*used to indicate cries of pain or suffering*:疼得～叫 howl with pain /孤雁～哀鸣。A stray wild goose cried plaintively. /远处狗在～叫。Dogs were yelping in the distance.
嗷嗷待哺 áo'áo-dàibǔ cry piteously for food:一窝小鸟～。A nestful of young birds are crying for food. /大批饥民～。Large numbers of famine victims are moaning for food.
嗷嘈 áocáo 〈书面〉loud and dissonant:笙管～。There was loud and discordant music from flutes and pipes.

螯 áo chela; pincers (of crustaceans)
螯合 áohé 〈化学〉chelate:～作用 chelation
螯合测定法 áohé cèdìngfǎ 〈化学〉chelatometry
螯合剂 áohéjì 〈化学〉chelating agent; chelator
螯合树脂 áohé shùzhī 〈化工〉chelating resin
螯合物 áohéwù 〈化学〉chelate compound /～激光器 chelate laser
螯虾 áoxiā crayfish; crawfish

鳌(鼇) áo huge legendary sea-turtle
鳌山 áoshān hill of lanterns piled in the shape of a huge legendary turtle during the Lantern Festival (the 15th day of the first lunar month)
鳌头 áotóu head of a carved legendary turtle on the stone steps leading to the main hall of the Imperial Palace, steps which the best successful scholar at the palace examination was permitted to ascend:独占～ come out first; be the champion; win first prize

隞 Áo *also*"敖" Áo;"嚣" Áo capital of the Shang Dynasty, situated to the northwest of present Zhengzhou (郑州), Henan Province

翱(翶) áo 〈书面〉take wing
翱翔 áoxiáng soar; hover:展翅～ spread its wings and begin to soar /动力～ dynamic soaring /雄鹰在空中自由～。Eagles are flying freely high in the sky.
翱翔机 áoxiángjī sail plane; soaring glider

ǎo

袄(襖) ǎo short Chinese-style coat or jacket:夹～ lined jacket /花～ flowery coat /棉～ cotton-padded jacket/ 皮～ fur(-lined) coat

拗(抝) ǎo 〈方言〉bend; twist and break:～铁丝 break an iron wire into segments /把竹竿～断 bend and break a bamboo pole
see also ào; niù
拗陷 ǎoxiàn 〈地理〉depression

鹦 ǎo *see*"鹩鹦" láo'ǎo

媪 ǎo 〈书面〉old woman:翁～ old man and woman

ào

傲 ào 〈书面〉*see*"傲" ào

鏊 ào
鏊子 àozi griddle

傲 ào proud; unyielding; haughty; arrogant:心高气～ ambitious and proud; aspiring and haughty /居功自～ be arrogant (*or* haughty) on account of one's achievements/ 青松～雪。The evergreen pines stand unyielding amidst the heavy snow. /这个人太～。This fellow is extremely conceited.
傲岸 ào'àn 〈书面〉proud; haughty:～不群 proud and aloof/ ～平生 maintain one's pride and dignity throughout one's life
傲骨 àogǔ lofty and unyielding character; innate pride:李白具有不向权贵低头的～。Li Bai had the unyielding spirit never to bow to the powers that be.
傲慢 àomàn haughty; arrogant; impudent:表情～ look arrogant / ～自得 haughty and complacent /～无礼 arrogant and insolent
傲睨 àonì 〈书面〉regard superciliously; look down upon; turn up one's nose at:～群雄 look down upon other men of valour; regard the other warriors superciliously /～自若 look immensely proud and complacent; look supercilious
傲气 àoqì air of arrogance; haughtiness:这个人有一股～。The man exudes arrogance.
傲然 àorán proud; unyielding; lofty:他～屹立在敌人面前。He stood defiant and proud before the enemy.
傲世 àoshì despise the world and its people; be extremely proud: ～怨谤之作 work of overweening pride and deep-seated grievances
傲视 àoshì turn up one's nose at; show disdain for; regard superciliously:～权势 hold power and authority in disdain
傲物 àowù 〈书面〉be arrogant and contemptuous; look down upon others:恃才～ be proud of one's (literary) talent and contemptuous of one's peers

骜 ào 〈书面〉❶ fine horse; steed ❷ arrogant; haughty:桀～不驯 overweening and intractable
骜放 àofàng 〈书面〉proud and unconventional; capricious

奡 ào ❶〈书面〉strong and vigorous:排～ (of writing) vigorous and powerful ❷ *see*"傲" ào

岙(嶴) ào (used usu. in place names in coastal Zhejiang and Fujian provinces) level land in a mountain:珠～ Zhu'ao /儒～ Ru'ao

奥[1] ào ❶ profound; abstruse; difficult to comprehend:深～ abstruse; unfathomable /古～ archaic and abstruse ❷ southwest corner of a house; innermost recess of a building:堂～ innermost recess of a hall; hinterland; profundities ❸ (Ào) (short for 奥地利) Austria:普～战争 Austro-Prussian War (1866)

奥[2] ào 〈物理〉(short for 奥斯特) oersted (Oe)
奥博 àobó 〈书面〉❶ profound:蕴意～ profound in implication /文辞～ abstruse in language ❷ erudite; highly learned:知识～ have great learning; be erudite

奥得河 Àodéhé Oder River
奥得-尼斯线 Àodé-Nísīxiàn Oder-Neisse Line (border delimitation line between Poland and Germany after World War II)
奥德赛 Àodésài *Odyssey*, Greek hexameter epic poem in 24 books attributed to Homer
奥地利 Àodìlì Austria:～人 Austrian
奥林匹克村 Àolínpǐkècūn 〈体育〉Olympic Village (for participants in Olympiad)
奥林匹克运动会 Àolínpǐkè Yùndònghuì Olympic Games; Olympiad
奥林匹斯山 Àolínpǐsīshān Mount Olympus (in northeastern Greece, legendary habitation of Greek gods)
奥林匹亚 Àolínpǐyà Olympia (religious centre of ancient Greece, scene of the Olympic Games on the banks of the Alpheus)
奥纶 àolún orlon
奥米伽器 àomǐjiāqì 〈物理〉omegatron
奥秘 àomì profound mystery:探索海底的～ explore (*or* probe) the secrets of the seabed /窥探人生的～ snatch a glimpse of the mysteries of human life /科学打开了太空～的大门。Science has unveiled the mystery of outer space.
奥妙 àomiào profundity; subtlety; secrecy:～精深 profound and abstruse /不解其中之～ fail to understand the subtlety of the situation /看出了其中的～ have got at the secret behind sth.
奥氏体 àoshìtǐ 〈冶金〉austenite:～合金钢 austenitic alloy steel /～不锈钢 austenitic stainless steel /～回火 austemper/～时效处理 austenaging /～退火 austennealing
奥斯卡金像奖 Àosīkǎ jīnxiàngjiǎng "Oscar" — popular term for the Academy Award
奥斯陆 Àosīlù Oslo, capital of Norway
奥斯曼帝国 Àosīmàn Dìguó Ottoman Empire (1290-1922)
奥斯特 àosītè 〈物理〉oersted (Oe), unit of magnetic field strength
奥斯威辛 Àosīwēixīn Oswiecim (Polish town, site of Nazi concentration camp during World War II. German name:Auschwitz): ～集中营 Oswiecim (*or* Auschwitz) concentration camp
奥陶纪 Àotáojì 〈地质〉Ordovician period
奥陶系 Àotáoxì Ordovician system
奥托循环 àotuō xúnhuán 〈机械〉Otto cycle:～发动机 Otto-cycle engine
奥委会 Àowěihuì (short for 奥林匹克委员会) Olympic Committee:国际～ International Olympic Committee (IOC)
奥匈帝国 Ào-Xiōng Dìguó Austro-Hungarian Empire; Austria-Hungary (1867-1918)
奥义 àoyì profound or abstruse ideas:论述《易经》～ enunciate the profound meanings of *The Book of Changes*
奥义书 Àoyìshū *Upanishad*, speculative classic of Hinduism, composed from c.900 BC onwards
奥援 àoyuán 〈书面〉ally; moral or material support:结成～ form an alliance
奥运会 Àoyùnhuì (short for 奥林匹克运动会) Olympiad; Olympic Games
奥旨 àozhǐ profound implication:深得其中～ be capable of appreciating the subtleties of sth. /采撷～ glean the essence of sth.

澳[1] ào ❶ (mostly used in names of places) inlet of the sea; bay:三都～ Sandu Bay ❷ (Ào) (short for 澳门) Macao:港～同胞 compatriots in Hong Kong and Macao

澳[2] Ào (short for 澳大利亚) Australia:～新美 Anzus; ANZUS (Australia, New Zealand and USA)
澳大利亚 Àodàlìyà Australia:～联邦 Commonwealth of Australia /～广播委员会 Australian Broadcasting Commission (ABC) /～人 Australian
澳大利亚抗原 Àodàlìyà kàngyuán Australia antigen; hepatitis-associated antigen (HAA)
澳抗 àokàng (short for 澳大利亚抗原) Australia antigen; hepatitis-associated antigen:～阳性 test positive for HAA
澳门 Àomén Macao
澳门特别行政区 Àomén Tèbié Xíngzhèngqū Macao Special Administrative Region
澳门元 àoményuán (Macao) *Pataca*
澳新美安全条约 Ào-Xīn-Měi Ānquán Tiáoyuē Security Treaty Between Australia, New Zealand and USA; ANZUS Pact (1951)
澳新美理事会 Ào-Xīn-Měi Lǐshìhuì ANZUS Council
澳洲 Àozhōu ❶ Australia ❷ *also* "大洋洲" Oceania; Oceanica

懊 ào regretful; remorseful; annoyed; vexed
懊恨 àohèn regretful; remorseful:～不已 (know) no end of regret (*or* remorse)
懊悔 àohuǐ feel remorseful; repent; regret:小邱因虚度光阴而～。Xiao Qiu was filled with remorse over the wasted time. /我对自己的莽撞很～。I very much regret my rash behaviour.
懊侬 àonóng 〈书面〉displeased; dissatisfied; annoyed
懊恼 àonǎo annoyed; vexed; upset:一脸的～气色 wear an annoyed look /实验失败了,他很～。He was very much upset at the failure of his experiment. /她～地把纸揉成一团,掷到窗外。Out of vexation, she crumpled the paper into a ball and threw it out of the window.
懊丧 àosàng upset; dejected; depressed:事情没办成,他～得吃不下饭。He was so depressed (*or* upset) by his unsuccessful attempt that he could not eat any meal.
懊糟 àozao 〈方言〉upset; vexed:心里挺～ feel quite upset/这点儿小事何必～。Don't be vexed over such a trifle.

坳(㘭、岰) ào depression in a mountain range; col:山～ hollow in the hill /珠峰北～ North Col of Mount Qomolangma
坳口 àokǒu flat land or lowland between mountains or hills

拗(抝) ào ❶ *see* "拗口" ❷ disobedient; intractable; refractory
see also ǎo; niù
拗强 àojiàng (of a person's character or temperament) obstinate; stubborn; refractory; intractable
拗口 àokǒu hard to pronounce; awkward-sounding:句子太长,念起来～。The sentence is too long to read smoothly. *or* The sentence is quite a mouthful.
拗口令 àokǒulìng tongue twister

B

B

bā

捌 bā (used for the numeral 八 on cheques, receipts, etc. to avoid mistakes or alterations) eight

峇 bā

峇厘 Bālí (now translated as 巴厘) Bali, island and tourist resort in Indonesia

八 bā eight (Note that 八 is pronounced with tone 2 when used before words with the 4th tone, e.g. 八岁 básuì eight years old, 八次 bácì eight times. For convenience's sake, however, all the following entries with 八 are marked with tone 1.)

八百年 bābǎinián eight hundred years; long period; long time; ages: 我早～就把书还他了。I returned the book to him ages ago.

八拜之交 bābàizhījiāo sworn brothers; ties of sworn brothers; sworn brotherhood

八宝 bābǎo eight kinds of precious ingredients; eight treasures (choice ingredients of certain special dishes); name given to things made of excellent ingredients

八宝菜 bābǎocài eight-treasure pickles; assorted soy sauce pickles

八宝冬瓜盅 bābǎo dōngguāzhōng steamed whole white gourd containing soup with various delicacies

八宝饭 bābǎofàn eight-treasure rice pudding (rice pudding with eight kinds of ingredients such as red bean paste, raisins, various nuts and seeds, and preserved fruits)

八宝鸡 bābǎojī steamed chicken stuffed with eight delicacies

八宝儿 bābǎor 〈植物〉(general term for 景天) red-spotted stonecrop

八宝山 Bābǎoshān Eight-Treasure Mountain or Babaoshan, place in western Beijing, known for its cemetery: 上～ go to Babaoshan (Cemetery); 〈婉词〉die

八宝箱 bābǎoxiāng *also* "百宝箱" bǎibǎoxiāng treasure chest: 那是他的～。That's the box that holds his precious belongings. *or* That's his treasure chest.

八宝印泥 bābǎo yìnní red seal ink containing cinnabar and oil

八倍体 bābèitǐ 〈生物〉octoploid

八辈子 bābèizi 〈口语〉of long standing; of the worst kind: 我倒了～霉了。I couldn't have worse luck. *or* I'm up to my neck in trouble.

八边形 bābiānxíng octogan

八表 bābiǎo 〈书面〉outlying areas beyond the eight points of the compass; remote corners of the earth

八成 bāchéng ❶ eighty per cent: ～新 mostly new; practically new / ～熟 not quite well-done; not quite ripe ❷ most probably; most likely: ～他病了。Most probably he is ill.

八重唱 bāchóngchàng octet(te)

八重奏 bāchóngzòu octet(te)

八大 Bādà (short for 中国共产党第八次全国代表大会) Eighth National Congress of the Communist Party of China (15-27 Sept. 1956)

八大山人 Bādàshānrén literary name of Zhu Da (朱耷, 1624-1705), a Chinese brush painter

八大员 bādàyuán eight kinds of workers in service trades, namely shop-assistants, ticket sellers, attendants, nurses, street cleaners, cooks, barbers, and postmen

八带鱼 bādàiyú octopus

八斗才 bādǒucái 〈旧语〉very gifted person; person of extraordinary talent

八度 bādù *also* "八度音"〈音乐〉octave: ～笛 octave flute / 他的嗓门一下子降了～。His voice fell one octave all of a sudden.

八段锦 bāduànjǐn eight trigram boxing

八方 bāfāng eight points of the compass; numerous directions; all quarters or sides: ～支援 help comes from all directions; succour arrives from all quarters / ～响应 enthusiastic response from all quarters (*or* sides)

八分书 bāfēnshū (commonly known as 汉隶) style of script (of Han Dynasty), balanced right and left

八分仪 bāfēnyí 〈航海〉〈航空〉octant: ～误差 octantal error

八分音符 bāfēn yīnfú 〈音乐〉eighth note; quaver

八竿子打不着 bā gānzi dǎbuzháo *also* "八杆子打不着" not related in any way; have nothing whatsoever to do (with sb. or sth.): 一门～的亲戚 far-distant relation; third cousin thrice removed / 我跟这件事～。I have nothing whatsoever to do with this. *or* I'm not involved in this at all.

八纲 bāgāng 〈中医〉eight principal syndromes or categories of symptoms, namely *yin* and *yang* (阴阳), exterior and interior (表里), cold and heat (寒热), hypofunction and hyperfunction (虚实)

八纲辨证 bāgāng biànzhèng 〈中医〉differentiation and classification of symptoms and signs based on the eight principal syndromes; analysis and differentiation of pathological conditions in accordance with the eight principal syndromes

八哥儿 bāger *also* "鸲鹆" qúyù 〈动物〉myna(h); crested myna(h)

八股 bāgǔ ❶ eight-part essay prescribed for the imperial civil service examinations (known for its rigidity of form and paucity of ideas) ❷ stereotyped writing: 党～ Party stereotyped writing (rampant in the Communist Party of China in the 1930's)

八卦 bāguà ❶ Eight Trigrams (eight combinations of three whole or broken lines formerly used in divination) ❷ 〈方言〉be meddlesome; be a busybody: 他这个人有点儿～。He likes to poke his nose into other people's business. ❸ 〈方言〉be superstitious; be ignorant: 你怎么还这么～, 信这一套? How could you be so superstitious as to believe it?

八卦教 Bāguàjiào Eight Trigram Society (organized in late 18th century as successor to the White Lotus Society)
see also "天理教" Tiānlǐjiào

八卦炉 bāguàlú (of Taoism) oven for making pills of immortality or elixir of life

八卦婆 bāguàpó 〈方言〉meddlesome woman; busybody

八卦掌 bāguàzhǎng eight-trigram boxing (a kind of Chinese shadow boxing characterized by varied fist techniques and agile movement of feet and legs and by a combination of soft and hard boxing tactics)

八卦阵 bāguàzhèn eight-trigram battle array—supposed by the ancients to have power of confusing invading enemy troops: 摆～ apply mystifying tactics / 他们的～我们心里明白。We are fully aware of their mystifying tactics.

八关会 Bāguānhuì P'alkwanhoe, one of the major traditional festivals in Korea

八国集团 Bāguó Jítuán Group of Seven (US, UK, France, Germany, Italy, Canada and Japan—a group devoted to discussion of world economic issues) plus Russia, a group devoted to discussion of world political issues

八国联军 Bāguó Liánjūn eight-power allied forces, aggressive troops sent by Britain, the United States, Germany, France, tsarist Russia, Japan, Italy, and Austria in 1900, to suppress the anti-imperialist *Yihetuan* Movement (义和团运动)

八行诗 bāhángshī octonary; ottava rima

八行书 bāhángshū *also* "八行"〈旧语〉eight-line letter

八行纸 bāhángzhǐ (traditional-style, ruled) letter paper having eight vertical lines

八荒 bāhuāng outlying areas on all sides; remote areas of the earth:有并吞~之心 be bent on the conquest of the world

八会穴 bāhuìxué 〈中医〉eight strategic nerve points

八极 bājí 〈书面〉farthest corners of the earth; remotest areas of the earth

八级风 bājífēng force 8 wind; fresh gale

八级工 bājígōng eighth-grade worker (highest on the eight-grade wage scale); top-grade worker

八级工资制 bājí gōngzīzhì eight-grade wage scale or system

八极管 bājíguǎn 〈无线电〉octode

八价 bājià 〈化学〉octavalent:~物 octad

八角 bājiǎo ❶〈植物〉anise; star anise ❷ aniseed ❸ octagonal:~风筝 octagonal kite

八角枫 bājiǎofēng 〈植物〉alangium

八角鼓 bājiǎogǔ ❶〈乐器〉octagonal drum with copper clappers attached to its sides (of the Manchu nationality) ❷〈戏曲〉monologue story-telling in rhythmic language and singing accompanied by such a drum and a fiddle

八角帽 bājiǎomào octagonal cap

八角形 bājiǎoxíng octagon; octagonal

八节 bājié eight solar terms containing the Beginning of Spring (立春), Vernal Equinox (春分), Beginning of Summer (立夏), Summer Solstice (夏至), Beginning of Autumn (立秋), Autumnal Equinox (秋分), Beginning of Winter (立冬) and Winter Solstice (冬至):四时~ four seasons and eight solar terms

八进制 bājìnzhì *also* "八进位制"〈数学〉octonary number system; octal:~数 octal number / ~记数法 octal notation / ~计数器〈计算机〉octal counter / ~译码器〈计算机〉octal decoder / ~调试程序 octal debugger / ~装入程序 octal loading program

八九不离十 bā-jiǔ bùlí shí 〈口语〉pretty close; very near; about right:猜个~ make a very close guess / 这件事他估计得~。He almost guessed right. *or* He's not far off the mark.

八开本 bākāiběn octavo; 8vo; 8°

八路 Bālù ❶ *see* "八路军" ❷ Eighth Route Army man; revolutionary:老~ experienced Eighth Route Army soldier; veteran revolutionary /土~ irregular guerrilla (working for the Eighth Route Army); rustic revolutionary

八路军 Bālùjūn Eighth Route Army (led by the Chinese Communist Party during the War of Resistance Against Japan)

八面锋 bāmiànfēng ❶〈贬义〉be smooth and slick; talk glibly trying to please everybody:算命先生言谈犹如~,专门蒙骗老实的乡下人。The fortune-teller talked glibly and unctuously in a bid to fool simple country folks. ❷〈书面〉sharp; incisive:他的言辞~,无往而不胜。His incisive words never failed to serve his purposes.

八面光 bāmiànguāng 〈贬义〉worldly wise; smooth and slick all around:他是这样~,谁也不得罪! He is such a slick guy that he'll offend nobody.

八面玲珑 bāmiàn-línglóng 〈比喻〉be able to get along well with everybody; make oneself pleasant to people all around; be smooth and slick:那时候,~的人到处吃香。In those days, slick people were welcome everywhere.

八面体 bāmiàntǐ octahedron:正~ regular octahedron

八面威风 bāmiàn-wēifēng commanding presence; aura of awesome might

八旗 bāqí "Eight Banners" (Manchu military-administrative system established in the early 1600's and kept throughout the Qing Dynasty):~蒙古 *also* "蒙古~" Mongolian tribes reorganized under the Manchu Eight Banner system

八旗制度 bāqí zhìdù Banner System (of the Qing Dynasty)

八旗子弟 bāqí zǐdì ❶ descendants of the privileged families under the Banner System in the Qing Dynasty ❷ profligate children of privileged families

八扇屏风 bāshàn píngfēng eight-leaf big screen; floor screen

八思巴 Bāsībā Phags-pa (1235-1280), leader of Tibetan lamaism, who created new Mongolian characters

八抬大轿 bātái-dàjiào *also* "八人大轿" big sedan chair (for high officials) carried by eight men:你~请他也请不来。He wouldn't come even if you sent a limousine for him.

八王之乱 Bā Wáng Zhī Luàn Internecine Wars Among Eight Princes (291-306) of the Western Jin Dynasty (265-316) in their scramble for state power

"八五"计划 Bā-Wǔ Jìhuà (short for 第八个五年计划) Eighth Five-Year Plan

八下里 bāxiàli 〈方言〉high and low; everywhere; everybody:为了组织演讲会,他得~求人帮助。To organize a series of lectures, he had to solicit help from all quarters.

八仙 bāxiān ❶ hydrangea; sevenbark (*Hydrangea hortensia*):~花 hydrangea / ~化苷 hydrangin ❷ the Eight Celestials or Immortals (who are, according to legend, Li Tieguai 李铁拐, Han Zhongli 汉钟离, Zhang Guolao 张果老, He Xiangu 何仙姑, Lan Caihe 蓝采和, Lü Dongbin 吕洞宾, Han Xiangzi 韩湘子 and Cao Guojiu 曹国舅) ❸〈方言〉*see* "八仙桌"

八仙过海 bāxiān-guòhǎi 〈谚语〉like the Eight Immortals going across the sea; each in his or her own way:~,各显神通 the Eight Immortals go across the sea, each showing his own skill; like the Eight Celestials crossing the sea, each displays his or her special prowess; each relies on his or her own resource and proves his or her worth

八仙桌 bāxiānzhuō "Eight Immortals" table—big square table around which two people can sit at each side; table large enough to seat eight people

八弦琴 bāxiánqín octachord

八小时工作制 bā xiǎoshí gōngzuòzhì eight-hour day

八言 bāyán poem of eight-character lines

八一建军节 Bā-Yī Jiànjūnjié Army Day (August 1, anniversary of the founding of the Chinese People's Liberation Army)

八一南昌起义 Bā-Yī Nánchāng Qǐyì August 1 Nanchang Uprising (1927)

八一三事变 Bā-Yīsān Shìbiàn August 13 Incident of 1937 (On that day, Japanese aggressor troops launched a large-scale offensive against Shanghai, after which the KMT government was forced to declare a war of resistance against Japanese aggression.)

八音 bāyīn musical sounds made by ancient instruments of eight categories of materials (metal, stone, string, bamboo, gourd, clay, leather, and wood)

八音盒 bāyīnhé *see* "八音匣子"

八音匣子 bāyīn xiázi ❶ *also* "八音盒"; "八音琴" music box; musical box ❷〈方言〉phonograph; gramophone

八月 bāyuè ❶ August ❷ eighth month of the lunar year

八月节 bāyuèjié Mid-Autumn Festival (15th day of the 8th lunar month)

see also "中秋节" Zhōngqiūjié

八折 bāzhé 20 per cent discount:打~ give 20 per cent discount; charge 80 per cent of the original price /这是~买的。This was bought at 20 per cent discount.

八珍 bāzhēn eight delicacies:~蛇羹 snake potage with eight delicacies

八正道 bāzhèngdào 〈宗教〉eightfold way or path

八柱式 bāzhùshì 〈建筑〉octastyle:~门廊 octastyle /~建筑物 octastylos

八字 bāzì ❶ character "八" ❷ Eight Character (in four pairs of two characters each corresponding to one Heavenly Stem and one Earthly Branch, and representing respectively the year, month, day and hour of a person's birth, used as basis for fortune-telling); horoscope:问~ consult a fortune-teller

八字步 bāzìbù measured gait with the toes pointing outwards:踱~ walk in a splayed manner

八字方针 bāzì fāngzhēn policy of readjustment, restructuring, consolidation and improvement (formally adopted by the Ninth Plenary Session of the Eighth Central Committee of the CPC)

八字还没一撇 bā zì hái méi yī piě *also* "八字没一撇" not even the first stroke of the character "八" has appeared — nothing tangible is in sight; there's no sign of anything happening yet:他出国学习的事~呢。Nothing tangible has been forthcoming about his studies abroad. *or* His proposed studies abroad are still up in the air.

八字胡 bāzìhú with a moustache shaped like the Chinese charac-

ter 八; splay-moustached; with a long moustache: 捋～ stroke one's long moustache / 留两撇～ grow a long moustache

八字脚 bāzìjiǎo splayfoot

八字眉 bāzìméi with eyebrows shaped like the Chinese character "八"; splay-eyebrowed; slanted eyebrows

八字帖儿 bāzìtiěr *also* "八字儿" 〈旧语〉 card stating one's birth data (the year, the month, the day and the hour) and used as basis for assessing compatibility of proposed marriage

see also "八字 ❷"

B

八字宪法 Bāzì Xiànfǎ (short for 农业八字宪法) Eight-Point Charter for Agriculture (formulated in the early 1960's as key factors for increasing agricultural production: 土 soil improvement, 肥 rational application of fertilizer, 水 water conservancy, 种 improved seed strains, 密 rational close planting, 保 plant protection, 管 field management, and 工 improvement of farm implements)

八字形拱 bāzìxínggǒng splayed arch

机

bā 〈书面〉 a kind of toothless rake

扒

bā ❶ hold on to; stick to; cling to: ～锅 (of cooked food) stick to the pot / ～窗台 hold on to the window sill / ～墙顶 climb up to the top of the wall ❷ dig up; rake; pull down: ～土 rake earth / ～房 pull down a house ❸ push aside: ～开草棵 push aside the grass ❹ strip off; take off; peel off; skin: ～下湿衣服 strip (*or* peel) off one's wet clothes / ～羊皮 skin a sheep / ～香蕉皮 peel a banana

see also pá

扒车 bāchē jump onto a slow-moving train or bus (usu. stealthily): ～偷煤 jump onto a freight car and steal the coal

扒钉 bādīng cramp

扒拉 bāla push lightly; remove: ～开人群 push one's way through a crowd / ～算盘(珠子) click the beads of an abacus; calculate (with the help of an abacus or figuratively) / 他把钟摆～了一下。He pushed lightly the pendulum of the clock. / 有事儿好好说，别～我! Speak politely if you want anything, and keep your hands off me.

see also pála

扒皮 bāpí strip the skin off (sb. or sth.); exploit harshly: 拦路设卡，遇车～ set up a barrier on the road and extort fees from passing vehicles / 那县令在当地扒了一层皮。The magistrate exploited the local people ruthlessly.

扒头儿 bātour 〈口语〉 handhold; foothold: 这个峭壁连个～都没有，怎么往上爬呀? How can we climb the cliff since it gives no foothold?

叭

bā *see* "吧" bā

叭儿狗 bārgǒu ❶ pekingese ❷ sycophant; toady

see also "巴儿狗" bārgǒu

叭咂 bāza ❶ smack one's lips ❷ 〈方言〉 draw (on a pipe, etc.)

巴[1]

bā ❶ hope earnestly; wait anxiously: ～望 hope in real earnest / 朝～夜望 wait (*or* hope) for sth. to happen day and night ❷ cling to; stick to: 一条壁虎～在玻璃窗上。A house lizard is clinging to the window pane. ❸ get stuck to: 粥～锅了。The porridge got stuck to the bottom of the pot. ❹ thing stuck to sth. else; crust: 锅～ rice crust ❺ 〈方言〉 be close to; be next to: 前不～村，后不着店 with no village ahead and no inn behind / 他家～着一家小客栈。His house was close to a small inn. ❻ 〈方言〉 open: ～着眼瞧 look at sth. with eyes wide open / 桌子上～了一道缝。There is a crack in the desk.

巴[2]

Bā ❶ name of a principality of the Zhou Dynasty (in the eastern part of today's Sichuan Province, now largely under Chongqing Municipality) ❷ eastern part of Sichuan Province (before 1997) ❸ a surname

巴[3]

bā 〈物理〉 bar: 毫～ millibar / 微～ microbar

巴[4]

bā bus: 大～ bus / 小～ minibus

巴巴 bābā *used after an adjective or a similar word for emphasis*: 急～ quite impatient; in too much of a hurry / 紧～ rather tight; straitened / 干～ dry as dust / 可怜～ very piteous

巴巴多斯 Bābāduōsī Barbados, island state in the Caribbean: ～人 Barbadian

巴巴结结 bāba-jiējiē 〈方言〉 ❶ do sth. after a fashion; can barely do sth.: 简易英文小说他～能看懂。He can barely read simplified English novels. ❷ speak haltingly; stammer: 他德语说得～的。He speaks in halting German.

巴巴儿地 bābārde 〈方言〉 ❶ eagerly; anxiously: 他～等了她半天。He has been anxiously waiting for her for quite a while. ❷ deliberately; specially: 他～从老远赶来，满头是汗。He hurried here from a long way off, covered in sweat.

巴贝奇 Bābèiqí Charles Babbage (1792-1871), English mathematician and inventor, generally recognized as pioneer of machine computing

巴比伦 Bābǐlún Babylon (ancient city on the Euphrates, capital of the Babylonian kingdoms, about 1894-1595 and 626-538 BC)

巴比特合金 bābǐtè héjīn babbitt (metal)

巴比妥 bābǐtuǒ 〈药学〉 barbitone; barbital: ～中毒 barbitalism; barbituism

巴别塔 Bābiétǎ Tower of Babel (biblical tower intended to reach from earth to heaven, the building of which was frustrated when Jehovah confused the language of the builders)

巴布教 Bābùjiào 〈宗教〉 Babism

巴布亚新几内亚 Bābùyà Xīnjǐnèiyà Papua New Guinea, island state in the South Pacific: ～人 Papua New Guinean

巴不得 bābude 〈口语〉 be only too anxious (to do sth.); earnestly wish; be eager (to do sth.): 我～不去。I would be only too glad to be spared the trip. / 我～立刻见到他。I wish I could see him right now. / 这正是我～的事。This is exactly what I have been looking for.

巴不能够 bābunénggòu 〈方言〉 *see* "巴不得"

巴丹 Bādān Bataan, a province on Luzon Island of the Philippines: ～死亡行军 Bataan Death March

巴丹吉林沙漠 Bādān Jílín Shāmò Badain Jaran Desert (China's third largest desert in the west of Inner Mongolia)

巴旦杏 bādànxìng ❶ almond tree ❷ almond; amygdala

巴斗 bādǒu round-bottomed basket

see also "笆斗" bādǒu

巴豆 bādòu 〈植物〉 (purging) croton: ～霜 〈中药〉 defatted croton seed powder / ～中毒 crotonism; croton oil poisoning

巴尔的摩 Bā'ěrdìmó Baltimore, major city and port of eastern United States

巴尔干 Bā'ěrgàn the Balkans: ～半岛 the Balkan Peninsula / ～国家 Balkan states; the Balkans / ～同盟 Balkan League (1912-1913) / ～协约 Balkan Entente (formed in 1934) / ～山脉 Balkan Mountains

巴尔扎克 Bā'ěrzhākè Honore de Balzac (1799-1850), French novelist

巴伐利亚 Bāfálìyà Bavaria (in Germany): ～人 Bavarian

巴甫洛夫 Bāfǔluòfū Ivan Petrovich Pavlov (1849-1936), Russian physiologist: ～学说 Pavlovian theory

巴格达 Bāgédá Baghdad, capital of Iraq

巴根草 bāgēncǎo *also* "结缕草" jiélǚcǎo Korea lawn grass

巴哈马 Bāhāmǎ the Bahamas, island state in the western Atlantic: ～人 Bahamian / ～联邦 Commonwealth of the Bahamas

巴赫 Bāhè Johann Sebastian Bach (1685-1750), German composer

巴基斯坦 Bājīsītǎn Pakistan: ～人 Pakistani / ～联合通讯社 Associated Press of Pakistan (APP)

巴戟天 bājǐtiān 〈植物〉 *Morinda officinalis*

巴结 bājie ❶ fawn on; flatter; curry favour with; toady to: 他一辈子不肯去～任何人。He has never tried to curry favour with anybody in all his life. / 他～了半天，什么也没捞到。He fawned on people for all he was worth, but got nothing for his pains. ❷ 〈方言〉 work hard: 工作很～ work very hard

巴克莱银行 Bākèlái Yínháng (UK) Barclays Bank Ltd.

巴克夏猪 bākèxiàzhū Berkshire (swine)

巴枯宁 Bākūníng Mikhail Aleksandrovich Bakunin (1814-1876), Russian revolutionary and exponent of anarchism: ～主义 Bakunism

巴库 Bākù Baku, port city on the Caspian Sea and capital of Azerbaijan

巴拉顿湖 Bālādùnhú Lake Balaton (largest lake in central Europe)

巴拉圭 Bālāguī Paraguay: ～人 Paraguayan

巴勒斯坦 Bālèsītǎn Palestine：～人 Palestinian / ～解放组织 Palestine Liberation Organization (PLO) / ～全国委员会 Palestine National Council
巴厘 Bālí Bali, mountainous island of Indonesia：～人 Balinese / ～语 Balinese
巴黎 Bālí Paris, capital of France：～人 Parisian / ～风格 Parisianism
巴黎公社 Bālí Gōngshè Paris Commune (established by French workers in 1871)：～社员 Communard
巴黎和会 Bālí Héhuì ❶ Paris Peace Conference of 1919 (Jan. 18-June 28) ❷ Paris Conference of 1946 (July 29-Oct. 15)
巴黎绿 bālílǜ 〈化学〉Paris green
巴黎圣母院 Bālí Shèngmǔyuàn Notre-Dame de Paris
巴黎统筹委员会 Bālí Tǒngchóu Wěiyuánhuì (shortened as 巴统) Coordinating Committee (COCOM, for controlling export of strategic materials and equipment to communist countries, established in Paris in November 1949)：～对华禁运货单 Chincon list (amendments on control of exports to China)
巴里纱 bālǐshā *also* "玻璃纱" bōlishā 〈纺织〉voile
巴列 bāliè 〈物理〉barye
巴列维王朝 Bālièwéi Wángcháo Pahlavi Dynasty (1925-1979), last dynasty in Iran
巴林 Bālín Bahrain or Bahrein, state in the Persian Gulf：～人 Bahraini
巴龙霉素 bālóngméisù 〈药学〉paromomycin
巴伦支海 Bālúnzhīhǎi Barents Sea (part of the Arctic Ocean north of Eastern Russia)
巴罗克 Bāluókè baroque (a highly ornate and extravagant style of European art, architecture, and music of the 17th and 18th centuries)：～风格 baroque style
巴马科 Bāmǎkē Bamako, capital of Mali
巴拿马 Bānámǎ Panama：～人 Panamanian / ～地峡 Isthmus of Panama / ～帽 Panama hat
巴拿马运河 Bānámǎ Yùnhé Panama Canal：～区 Panama Canal Zone / ～条约 Treaty of the Panama Canal (1977)
巴纳德 Bānàdé Christiaan Neethling Barnard (1922-), South African surgeon who performed the first human heart transplant in 1967
巴婆 bāpó 〈植物〉pawpaw; papaw (*Asimina triloba*)
巴棋游戏 bāqí yóuxì parcheesi
巴儿狗 bārgǒu ❶ pekinese (a breed of small pet dog) ❷ lapdog; sycophant; toady
see also "哈巴狗" hǎbagǒu
巴塞罗那 Bāsàiluónà Barcelona, city and province of Catalonia in NE Spain
巴山蜀水 Bāshān-Shǔshuǐ mountains and rivers of Ba and Shu — Sichuan：远在天涯，难忘那～故乡情。Though I am at the other end of the world, I can not leave behind sentimental memories of my native province Sichuan.
巴士 bāshì 〈方言〉bus：小～ minibus; minivan / ～站 bus stop
巴士底狱 Bāshìdǐyù the Bastille, citadel and prison in Paris, built in 1369-1383
巴士杀菌法 bāshì shājūnfǎ pasteurization
巴蜀 Bā-Shǔ another name for Sichuan Province
巴斯海峡 Bāsī Hǎixiá Bass Strait (channel separating the island of Tasmania from the mainland of Australia)
巴松管 bāsōngguǎn 〈音乐〉(popular name for 低音管 or 大管) bassoon：～手 bassoonist
巴苏 Bāsū Bejoy Kumar Basu (1912-), Indian doctor who arrived in Yan'an in 1939 as member of an Indian medical team together with Dr. Dwarkanath S. Kotnis (柯棣华)
巴特寮 Bātèliáo Pathet Lao (leftwing nationalist group established in Laos in 1950)
巴统 Bātǒng (short for 巴黎统筹委员会) COCOM
巴头探脑儿 bātóu-tànnǎor pop one's head in and take a stealthy look; pry about：这些小顽童在街拐角～的，不知干什么？What are the urchins at the corner of the street for?
巴图鲁 bātúlǔ warrior (a title conferred on military officers in the Qing Dynasty for meritorious services)
巴望 bāwàng 〈方言〉❶ look forward to; hope：我们～你能来。We hope you will be able to come. ❷ sth. to hope for：有～。Now there is something to look forward to.

巴乌 bāwū a kind of bamboo flute (musical instrument in certain minority nationality areas in Yunnan)
巴西 Bāxī Brazil：～人 Brazilian
巴西果 bāxīguǒ Brazil nut (*Bertholletia excelsa*)
巴西利亚 Bāxīlìyà Brasilia, capital of Brazil
巴西木 bāxīmù *also* "巴西苏木"〈植物〉brazilwood：～素 brasilin / 氧化～素〈化学〉brasilein
巴眨 bāzha 〈方言〉blink; wink：他～着眼睛蹲在角落里不说话。He squatted in the corner, blinking his eyes and saying nothing.
巴掌 bāzhang palm; hand：拍～ clap one's hands / ～大块地 tiniest lot (of land) / 他气得打了孩子一～。He was so angry that he gave the child a slap in the face.

疤

bā ❶ scar; cicatrix：伤～ scar / 牛痘～ vaccination scar / 结～ cicatrisation ❷ sth. like a scar：茶壶上的～ mark on the teapot
疤痕 bāhén cicatrix; scar：树上有块巴掌大的～。The tree bears a cicatrix as big as a man's hand. / 他左眼角下有一个很深的～。He has a deep scar under the corner of his left eye.
疤瘌 bāla *also* "疤拉" scar：～脸 scarred face
疤瘌眼儿 bālayǎnr *also* "疤拉眼儿"〈口语〉❶ eye with a scar on the eyelid ❷ person who has such an eye

粑

bā 〈方言〉cake
粑粑 bābā 〈方言〉cake：玉米～ corn cake
粑粑头 bābātóu *also* "粑粑髻"〈方言〉 hair worn in a bun or coil at the back of the head

芭

bā a kind of fragrant grass mentioned in ancient books
芭蕉 bājiāo 〈植物〉*bajiao* banana (*Musa basjoo*); plantain：～科 *Musaceae*
芭蕉扇 bājiāoshàn palm-leaf fan
芭蕉芋 bājiāoyù *Canna edulis*
see also "姜芋" jiāngyù
芭乐 bālè 〈方言〉guava
芭蕾舞 bālěiwǔ ballet：～演员 ballet dancer / ～女演员 ballerina / ～组曲 ballet suite / ～裙 ballet skirt; tutu

豝(犯)

bā 〈书面〉〈动物〉sow

吧

bā ❶〈象声〉：～的一声，树枝断了。The twig broke off with a snapping sound. / ～～，他们听到两声枪响。Crack! Crack! They heard two shots. ❷〈方言〉draw on or pull at one's pipe, etc.：你也～一口吧。Have a drag, please. ❸ (short for 酒吧) bar
see also ba
吧嗒 bādā 〈象声〉patter; splatter：雨点～～地打在玻璃窗上。Big raindrops pattered on the windows.
吧嗒 bāda ❶ smack one's lips：她～了一下嘴，好像要说点啥。She smacked her lips as if she were going to say something. ❷〈方言〉pull at; suck at：他～了一口烟袋，就出去了。He took a puff at his pipe and went out.
吧唧 bājī 〈象声〉他～～地在泥路上走。He squelched along the muddy road.
吧唧 bāji ❶ smack one's lips：他～着嘴，迟迟不肯说出来。He smacked his lips and hesitated to give an opinion. ❷〈方言〉draw on (a pipe, etc.)：他又点上了一支烟，～了两口。He lit up another cigarette and took a couple of puffs.
吧女 bānǚ barmaid; bar girl

岜

bā stony hill：～关岭 Baguanling, place in the Guangxi Zhuang Autonomous Region

笆

bā basketry; basket：竹～ bamboo basket
笆斗 bādǒu round-bottomed basket; wicker basket
笆篱 bālí 〈方言〉hedge; fence
笆篱子 bālízi 〈方言〉jail; prison
笆篓 bālǒu wicker basket

鲃

bā 〈动物〉barbel
鲃鱼 bāyú barbel

B

bá

茇 bá 〈书面〉❶ roots of grass ❷ live in the grass

拔 bá ❶ pull out; pull up: ～草 pull up weeds / ～软木塞 draw a cork (out of a bottle) / ～钉子 pull out a nail / ～剑 draw one's sword ❷ suck out; draw: ～火 (put a chimney on the stove to) make the fire draw; draw the fire ❸ choose; select; pick: 他是从几百名运动员中～出来的。He was selected from among hundreds of athletes ❹ lift; raise: ～高嗓门 raise one's voice ❺ stand out; surpass ❻ capture; seize: ～掉敌人据点 capture an enemy stronghold ❼ 〈方言〉 cool in water: 把汽水放在冰水里～一～ put a soda bottle in ice water to cool ❽ 〈机械〉 drawing: 冷～ cold drawing / 热～ hot drawing

拔白 bábái 〈方言〉 daybreak

拔本塞源 báběn-sèyuán extirpate the root of (an evil); root out (evil)

拔步 bábù take to one's heels

拔不出腿 bábuchūtuǐ unable to pull one's legs out (of a mire, etc.)—be bogged down in the mire of routine work; be tied down with chores of all kinds: 这事你只要一掺和,准～来。Once you get involved in the matter, you won't be able to extricate yourself from it.

拔除 báchú remove; pull out; eradicate: ～杂草 weed out the rank grass; pull out the weeds / ～敌军哨所 wipe out an enemy sentry post / ～祸根 eradicate the root of trouble

拔萃 bácuì 〈书面〉 pre-eminent; outstanding: 出类～ be out of the common run; be the best and the brightest / ～出群 stand out among one's fellows; be the best of all

拔刀相向 bádāo-xiāngxiàng draw or unsheathe one's sword against sb.

拔刀相助 bádāo-xiāngzhù unsheathe one's sword and go to the rescue of another (for the sake of justice); take up the cudgels against an injustice: 路见不平,～。When a man sees somebody being wantonly attacked on the road, he will immediately go to his rescue.

拔地 bádì (of a mountain, tree, building, etc.) stand tall and erect; rise straight from the ground: ～孤峰 solitary cliff soaring into the air / ～而起的高楼 towering building (*or* high-rise)

拔钉锤 bádīngchuí claw hammer

拔钉斧 bádīngfǔ claw hatchet

拔钉钳 bádīngqián *also* "拔钉器" nail drawer or puller

拔顶 bádǐng ❶ 〈石油〉 topping: ～装置 topping plant ❷ 〈方言〉 go bald: 他已经～,光秃秃的。He is as bald as a coot.

拔毒 bádú 〈中医〉 draw out pus (by applying a plaster to the affected part); draw out poison

拔份儿 báfènr 〈方言〉 push oneself forward and claim superiority over the rest; be pushy

拔缝 báfèng (of glued-up joints) crack: 这里的天花板～了。There is a crack in the ceiling.

拔付 báfù pay for sth. by installments

拔高 bágāo ❶ raise: 他～嗓子喊叫。He shouted at the top of his voice. ❷ deliberately boost (sb. or sth.); play up: ～人物 make a character (in a novel, etc.) larger than life; make a person better than he or she actually is / 对这部电视系列片的评价,显然有故意～的倾向。There is apparently a tendency to overrate this TV series.

拔贡 bágòng ❶ title given to selected candidates from counties and prefectures, who were then sent to take part in the imperial examinations in the national capital ❷ person with such a title

拔管 báguǎn 〈机械〉〈冶金〉 tube drawing; whole drawn tube

拔管机 báguǎnjī pulling machine

拔罐子 bá guànzi 〈中医〉 cupping
see also "拔火罐儿 ❶"

拔海 báhǎi height above sea level
see also "海拔"

拔河 báhé 〈体育〉 tug-of-war

拔火罐儿 bá huǒguànr ❶ 〈方言〉 cup: 她每隔一天去医院拔一次火罐。She goes every other day to the hospital for cupping treatment. ❷ *also* "拔火筒" detachable stove chimney; small funnel over casserole to help draw charcoal fire

拔尖 bájiān ❶ 〈口语〉 top-notch; tiptop: ～人才 top-notch talent; outstanding person / 这孩子门门功课都～儿。The child is at the top of his class in every subject. ❷ push oneself to the front; be pushy: 她这个人处处想～儿,对人往往不够谦虚礼貌。In her effort to outshine others, she often betrays a lack of modesty and courtesy.

拔脚 bájiǎo takes to one's heels

拔节 bájié 〈农业〉 jointing: ～期 jointing stage

拔举 bájǔ select and recommend: ～人才 select qualified personnel (*or* talented people) and recommend them for office

拔锚 bámáo weigh anchor
see also "起锚" qǐmáo

拔苗助长 bámiáo-zhùzhǎng *also* "揠苗助长" yàmiáo-zhùzhǎng attempt to hasten the growth of the shoots by pulling them upward only to find them withered on the very day; pull up seedlings to help them grow — spoil things by a desire for quick success

拔脓 bánóng 〈中医〉 draw out the pus

拔取 báqǔ choose; select: 公司只打算从众多的应聘人员中～十名。The company plans to choose ten from among a large number of applicants.

拔群 báqún be out of the common run; stand head and shoulders above the others: 论才智,他可谓～出类。He is head and shoulders above the others in intelligence.

拔染 bárǎn 〈纺织〉 discharge: ～剂 discharging agent; discharge

拔身 báshēn get away (from pressing duties); extricate oneself: 他工作繁重,实在无法～。He is so tied up at work that he simply can't get away.

拔丝 básī ❶ 〈机械〉 *also* "拉丝" lāsī wire drawing: ～机 wire drawing machine ❷ candied floss: ～山药 fried yam when the sugar can be drawn out in threads; hot candied yam

拔腿 bátuǐ ❶ take to one's heels: ～就跑 take to one's heels at once; start running away immediately / ～就追 give instant chase / 我正要追问,他～竟自走了。Before I could question him, he swung abruptly around on his heels and stalked off. ❷ get away from; extricate oneself from: 工作太忙,我拔不开腿。I am tied up at work and simply can't get away.

拔牙 báyá extract teeth: 我拔去两颗牙。I had two teeth pulled out.

拔牙钳 báyáqián dental or extracting forceps

拔秧 báyāng 〈农业〉 pull up seedlings (for transplanting)

拔营 báyíng 〈军事〉 strike camp; break camp: 部队拂晓～而去。The troops broke camp and left at dawn.

拔招 bázhāo 〈口语〉 *also* "悔棋" huǐqí retract a false move (in a chess game)

拔桩机 bázhuāngjī pile-drawing machine; pile extractor; pile puller

拔擢 bázhuó 〈书面〉 select and promote: ～到领导岗位 be promoted to a position of responsibility

菝 bá

菝葜 báqiā 〈植物〉 chinaroot greenbrier

跋[1] bá cross mountains

跋[2] bá postscript (to a book, article, painting, etc., mostly as appraisal, commentary or textual criticism)

跋扈 báhù domineering; bossy: 他仗着谁的势力,如此～? Whose backing has he got to be so domineering?

跋前踬后 báqián-zhìhòu can neither go ahead nor beat a retreat; be caught in a dilemma; be betwixt and between: ～,动辄得咎 be caught in a dilemma and bound to suffer either way

跋山涉水 báshān-shèshuǐ scale mountains and ford streams; travel across mountains and rivers amid difficulties; travel over land and water: 老中医～,采集中草药。The old doctor of traditional Chinese medicine trudged across mountains and rivers to collect medicinal herbs.

跋涉 báshè trudge; trek: 长途～ trek over a long distance; make a long arduous journey / 他终日～在崎岖的山路上。He trekked on the rugged mountain path all day.

跋文 báwén postscript; epilogue: 书后的～不长,但写得十分精辟、中肯。The epilogue, though short, was very succinct and appropriate.

跋语 báyǔ postscript; epilogue

皻

bá *see*"鮀皻" tuóbá

魃

bá demon (of drought)
see also"旱魃" hànbá

胈

bá 〈书面〉 hair on the leg

八

bá *see* bā

bǎ

靶

bǎ target: 打～ shooting (*or* target) practice /中～ hit the target /环～ round target /碟～ clay pigeon /人像～ silhouette (target) /移动～ moving target /～理论 〈生物〉 target theory /打～用步枪 target rifle

靶标 bǎbiāo target (erected for shooting practice)
靶场 bǎchǎng shooting or firing range: ～警戒旗 range flag
靶船 bǎchuán target ship
靶壕 bǎháo marking pit (in a shooting range)
靶火箭 bǎhuǒjiàn target rocket
靶机 bǎjī target drone
靶器官 bǎqìguān 〈生物〉 target organ
靶台 bǎtái shooting platform
靶细胞 bǎxìbāo 〈生物〉 target cell; target corpusele
靶心 bǎxīn bull's eye
靶纸 bǎzhǐ target sheet
靶子 bǎzi target
靶组织 bǎzǔzhī 〈生物〉 target tissue

把[1]

bǎ ❶ hold; grip; grasp: ～杯 hold a cup (*or* glass) in hand /～着手 hold sb. by the hand; hold sb.'s hand /紧紧～着冲锋枪 hold fast (*or* grasp, *or* grip) one's tommygun /～犁 handle a plough ❷ hold (a baby for it to relieve itself): 给孩子～尿 hold a baby out to piss ❸ control; monopolize: 不要把本部门全部工作～住不放。Don't monopolize every kind of work in your department. ❹ 〈口语〉 guard; watch: ～大门的 goalkeeper ❺ 〈口语〉 keep close to: ～墙角站着 standing in the corner /～着胡同口有一家理发店。Close by the entrance of the lane there is a barber's shop. ❻ hold sth. together: 用铁丝～住裂缝 tie up the cracked part with iron wire ❼ 〈方言〉 give; offer: 这支笔是叔叔～给我的。This pen is a gift from my uncle. ❽ handlebar: 扶～ hold the handlebar /自行车～ handlebar of a bicycle ❾ bundle; bunch: 秫秸～ bundle of sorghum stalks /干草～ bundle of hay ❿ 〈量词〉 (a) *used of a tool with a handle*: 一～钥匙 a bunch of keys /一～剪刀 a pair of scissors /一～雨伞 an umbrella (b) *used of sth. one can pick up with one hand*: 一～干草 a bundle of hay /一～泥土 a handful of earth /一～儿花 a bunch of flowers (c) *used of certain abstract things*: 再加一～劲 put in an extra effort /一～好手 competent person; past master /我这么大～年纪还能说瞎话? Is a man of my age likely to tell a lie? (d) *used of the movement of a hand or an arm*: 擦一～脸 go and wash one's face /帮我一～。Lend me a hand, please! /我一～抓住了小王。I seized hold of Xiao Wang.

把[2]

bǎ 〈介词〉 ❶ *used when the object is the receiver of the action of the ensuing verb*: ～头一扭 turn around /～花浇一浇 water the flowers /～技术学到手 master the skills; learn the trade /～房子收拾一下。Tidy up the room. /～这封信贴上邮票寄出去。Stamp and mail the letter. ❷ *used to indicate the receiver of the action when the verb is* 忙, 累, 急, 气 *etc., followed by a complement*: ～我吓坏了。I was scared stiff. /～我累坏了。I'm really tired out. ❸ *used to show that sth. undesirable has happened*: 正在节骨眼上偏偏～老张累病了。Of all people Lao Zhang fell ill at this juncture.

把[3]

bǎ *added to such measure words as* 百, 千, 万 *or* 里, 丈, 顷, 斤, 个 *to indicate the approximate number*: 个～月 a month or so / 百～块钱 around a hundred *yuan*

把[4]

bǎ *used to refer to a relationship of sworn brotherhood*: 拜～子 become sworn brothers
see also bà

把柄 bǎbǐng handle; excuse; ground: 给人～ give sb. a handle /你到底拿住他什么～? What evidence on earth have you got against him? /她品行端庄, 是不会有什么～落在人家手里的。As a woman of impeccable character, she would give nobody any ground for gossip.

把场 bǎchǎng 〈戏曲〉 give final reminders to, or attend to the final details of an actor or actress before he or she goes on stage

把持 bǎchí ❶ dominate; monopolize: ～权力 monopolize power /～一切 keep everything under one's control; dominate everything /～一个部门 control (*or* dominate) a department ❷ check; control (feelings or emotions): 她一时～不住内心的激动。For a moment she could not check her excitement.

把舵 bǎduò hold the rudder; hold the helm; steer

把风 bǎfēng keep watch (for one's partners in a clandestine activity); be on the lookout

把关 bǎguān ❶ guard a pass: 重兵～ guard a pass with a strong force ❷ check on: 层层～ make checks at all levels /严格～ check stringently; maintain a strict standard /把好质量关 guarantee the quality (of products); do a good job of quality control /把好政治关 ensure political soundness; ensure conformity to political criteria /这件事最后你来～。You should give the final check against the result.

把家 bǎjiā 〈方言〉 run the household

把角儿 bǎjiǎor street corner

把酒 bǎjiǔ raise the wine cup: 明月几时有, ～问青天。When can we enjoy a bright moon? Raising the wine cup to my lips, I ask heaven.

把口儿 bǎkǒur at the street corner: 小街～有一家酒店。There is a wineshop (*or* public house) right at the street corner.

把揽 bǎlan take sole possession of; seize control of; monopolize: ～大权 monopolize all power; keep all power in one's own hands

把牢 bǎláo 〈方言〉 (usu. used in the negative) solid; dependable: 碎砖砌的墙, 不～。Walls built of broken bricks are not solid enough. / 这个人做事不～。He is not reliable.

把理 bǎlǐ 〈方言〉 reasonable; sensible; right: 那小妞说话～。What the little girl said is right.

把脉 bǎmài 〈方言〉 feel the pulse

把门 bǎmén ❶ guard the entrance; keep guard at the door or gate: 这里守卫～很严, 不能随便进去。The gate is under close guard, and no outsiders can go in without permission. /这人嘴上缺个～的。The man has got a big mouth. ❷ 〈体育〉 be a goalkeeper: ～的 〈口语〉 goalkeeper

把弄 bǎnòng 〈方言〉 ❶ fiddle with: 他正～闹钟呢! He is fiddling with the alarm clock. ❷ control and manipulate (power): ～大权 wield power

把势 bǎshi *also* "把式" ❶ 〈口语〉 *wushu*; martial arts: 练～ practise *wushu* (*or* martial arts) ❷ 〈口语〉 person skilled in *wushu* or in a trade: 车～ carter /拾掇牲口的老～ old hand in handling draught animals ❸ 〈方言〉 skill; technique: 学会排字印刷全套～ master the whole series of printing techniques

把守 bǎshǒu guard; defend: ～城门 guard a city gate /～边关 defend a border pass; guard the frontiers /分兵～ divide one's forces for defence

把手 bǎshou 〈方言〉 handle; grip; knob; handlebar: 铜～ copper knob (*or* handle)

把头 bǎtou labour contractor; gangmaster; foreman

把玩 bǎwán 〈书面〉 fondle: ～玉器 fondle jadewares appreciatively/ 展卷～, 不忍释手 unfold the scroll and look at it appreciatively, feeling reluctant to part with it

把稳 bǎwěn 〈方言〉 trustworthy; reliable; dependable: 他这个人老成～。He is both experienced and trustworthy.

把握 bǎwò ❶ hold; keep: 他浑身无力, 自行车也～不稳了。He felt so weak that he couldn't keep his bike steady. ❷ grasp; seize: ～时机 grasp an opportunity; seize the right time /～自己的命运 hold one's fate (*or* destiny) in one's own hands; be master of one's own destiny ❸ (usu. used after 有 or 无) assurance; certainty: 对此很有～ be very positive about (*or* of) that /不打无～之仗 fight no battle one is not sure of winning /有绝对～ be absolutely certain about sth.; be dead sure of sth. /假若～不大, 我就不会把这件事应承下来。If I had been less confident, I would not have taken the work on.

把晤 bǎwù 〈书面〉 meet and shake hands; meet: 兄妹天各一方, ～

无从。As the brother and sister live far apart, they have little chance of seeing each other.

把戏 bǎxì ❶ acrobatics; circus; conjury; jugglery: 变～ play a (jugglery) trick; juggle; conjure /看～ watch an acrobatic show ❷ trick; gambit; ploy; game: 看穿～ see through sb's trick (*or* game)/戳穿～ show up (*or* expose) sb.'s trick (*or* gambit, *or* ploy) /谁知他要要什么鬼～? Who knows what tricks he has up his sleeve?

B

把细 bǎxì 〈方言〉careful; cautious; mindful: 他这个人做事很～。He is careful in everything he does. /凡事～一点儿好, 切不要粗心大意。You can't be too careful in whatever you do.

把兄弟 bǎxiōngdì *also* "盟兄弟" méngxiōngdì sworn brothers

把斋 bǎzhāi observe a day of fasting
see also "封斋" fēngzhāi

把斋节 Bǎzhāijié 〈伊斯兰〉Ramadan, the ninth month of the Moslem year, during which strict fasting is observed from dawn until sunset

把盏 bǎzhǎn 〈书面〉raise a wine cup: 两人～相饮。They raised their wine cups, urging each other to drink.

把捉 bǎzhuō grasp: ～事物的本质 grasp the essence of things

把子 bǎzi ❶ bunch; bundle: 秫秸～ bundle of sorghum stalks ❷ 〈量词〉: (a) 〈贬义〉*used with people*: 一～强盗 a bunch of bandits; a gang of robbers (b) *used with sth. long and slender*: 一～葱 a handful of scallions (c) *used with some abstract ideas*: 加～劲儿 make some extra effort ❸ imitation arms or weapons used in traditional operas ❹ fighting and acrobatics in traditional operas: 练～ practise fighting and acrobatics ❺ *see* "拜把子" bàibǎzi
see also bàzi

把总 bǎzǒng title of military officers in the Ming and Qing dynasties, corresponding to that of a battalion commander

钯 bǎ

〈化学〉palladium (Pd)

钯金合金 bǎjīn héjīn 〈冶金〉palladium gold

钯铜合金 bǎtóng héjīn 〈冶金〉palladium copper

㞎 bǎ

〈方言〉urine; piss; stool

㞎㞎 bǎba (baby talk) piss; stool

bà

霸(覇) bà

❶ chief of feudal princes; overlord: 春秋五～ five overlords of the Spring and Autumn Period ❷ tyrant; despot; bully: 恶～ local tyrant (*or* despot) ❸ hegemonistic power; hegemon: 称～ pronounce oneself overlord; seek hegemony /争～ contend for hegemony; vie for supremacy ❹ dominate; lord it over: 各～一方 each lording it over his locality ❺ (Bà) a surname

霸持 bàchí occupy or hold by force; seize: ～文坛 hold sway in literary circles (by dint of one's influence, power, etc.)

霸道 bàdào ❶ the way of might; rule by force; despotic rule or government: 王道与～ rule by virtue and rule by force; benevolent rule and despotic rule ❷ overbearing; domineering; high-handed: 横行～ ride roughshod over; trample on; tyrannize over

霸道 bàdao (of liquor, medicine, etc.) strong; potent: 这种酒很～, 容易上头。This brand of liquor is fairly strong and easily goes to one's head.

霸蛮 bàmán 〈方言〉❶ arbitrary; wilful: ～要提前下种 want wilfully to sow the seeds ahead of time ❷ rude and unreasonable; arbitrary; peremptory: 他太不讲理, ～要我去。He insisted on my going there; he was so unreasonable. ❸ manage with an effort; do one's best despite difficulty: 那老人的口～张了张, 叹了一口气。With a great effort the old man opened his mouth and heaved a sigh.

霸气 bàqì ❶ rude and unreasonable; arbitrary; domineering: 他说话太～。He's too arbitrary in what he says. ❷ arbitrary or peremptory air; domineering manner: 这个人浑身有一股子～。There is a peremptory air about the man.

霸权 bàquán hegemony; supremacy: 争夺世界～ struggle (*or* vie, *or* contend) for world supremacy /中国决不谋求～, 也不屈服于任何～。China will never seek hegemony, nor will it yield to any hegemonist(ic) pressure.

霸权主义 bàquánzhǔyì hegemonism: ～者 hegemonist /～政策 hegemonist(ic) policy /～行动 act of hegemonism /超级大国～ superpower hegemony (*or* hegemonism) /地区～ regional hegemony (*or* hegemonism)

霸头 bàtou ❶ labour contractor; foreman; gangmaster ❷ local villain or bully; despot

霸王 bàwáng ❶ (Bàwáng) the Conqueror — title for Xiang Yu (项羽, 232-202 BC): ～别姬 the Conqueror bidding farewell to his favorite concubine ❷ local tyrant; despot

霸王鞭 bàwángbiān ❶ rattle stick used in folk dancing ❷ *also* "花棍舞" huāgùnwǔ; "打连厢" dǎ liánxiāng rattle stick dance (form of Han folk dancing with a bamboo or wooden stick studded with coins at each end) ❸ 〈植物〉crab cactus (*Zygocatus truncatus*)

霸业 bàyè achievement or maintenance of overlordship or supremacy; conquest; hegemony: 重整～ try to regain one's former position of supremacy

霸占 bàzhàn forcibly occupy; seize: 非法～ illegally occupy /强行～ occupy by force /～他人财产 come into unlawful possession of sb.'s property /～他人土地 encroach upon sb.'s land

霸主 bàzhǔ ❶ powerful chief of the princes of the Spring and Autumn Period ❷ overlord; hegemon: 海上～ maritime overlord

灞 Bà

灞水 Bàshuǐ Bashui River (east of Xi'an, Shaanxi Province)

坝(壩) bà

❶ dam: ～面 dam face /修～ build a dam ❷ dike; embankment ❸ 〈方言〉sandbar; shoal ❹ (usu. used in place names) flatland; plain: 留～ Liuba or Liu Plain (in Shaanxi)

坝地 bàdì 〈方言〉fields (flanked by embankments) inundated by water drawn from a river

坝顶 bàdǐng dam crest

坝基 bàjī base of a dam; foundations of a dam: ～渗漏 leakage of dam foundations

坝埽 bàsào 〈旧语〉cylindrical buffers made of branches, sorghum stalks and rocks tied up with rope, and placed along Yellow River dikes against floodwaters

坝塘 bàtáng 〈方言〉*also* "塘坝" small reservoir or pond in hilly areas

坝田 bàtián strath

坝址 bàzhǐ damsite

坝子 bàzi ❶ dam; dike ❷ 〈方言〉flatland or plains in southwest China: 川西～ West Sichuan Plain

罢(罷) bà

❶ stop; cease: 作～ give up; call it off /善～甘休 leave the matter at that; let it go at that; take it lying down /欲～不能 find it hard to stop ❷ dismiss; relieve; remove from office ❸ 〈方言〉complete; finish: 吃～饭 after eating one's meal; after the meal

罢笔 bàbǐ stop writing: 就此～。I will stop here.

罢斥 bàchì remove from office; dismiss: ～功臣 dismiss officials of outstanding achievements

罢黜 bàchù 〈书面〉❶ dismiss from office ❷ ban; banish; reject: ～百家, 独尊儒术 pay supreme tribute to Confucianism while banning all other schools of thought

罢工 bàgōng strike; go or be on strike: 总～ general strike /破坏～ break up a strike /发动～ call a strike /停止～ call off a strike /镇压～ put down a strike /抵制～ resist a strike /静坐～ sit-down strike; sit-in strike /非法～ illegal strike /自发～ wildcat strike /闪电式～ lightning strike /零星～ sporadic strikes /声援～ sympathetic strike /～纠察(线) picket (line) /破坏～者 strike-breaker; blackleg; scab

罢工者 bàgōngzhě striker

罢官 bàguān dismiss or remove from office; strip sb. of his office: 《海瑞～》*Hai Rui Dismissed from Office* /在封建时代, 帝王可以不说任何理由就罢任何人的官。In feudal times, the emperor could remove anybody from office without any explanation.

罢教 bàjiào (of teachers) strike; teachers' strike

罢课 bàkè (of students) boycott classes; students' strike

罢了 bàle 〈助词〉just; merely; only: 我只是说说～, 你可不要当真。It was just a casual remark and you mustn't take it so seriously. /你就是不想好好读书～。You just don't want to study hard. That's all there is to it.

罢了 bàliǎo (indicating tolerance) let it pass; it's all right that... but...:他不跟我好也～，何至在街上见了也不理睬。It is perfectly all right if he does not want to be friends with me, but he has gone so far as to cut me dead when we meet in a street.
罢论 bàlùn abandoned idea:此事已作～。The idea has been dropped. *or* We have decided to let the matter drop.
罢免 bàmiǎn recall; remove; dismiss:省人民代表大会有权～省长和副省长。The Provincial People's Congress has the power to dismiss the provincial governor and his deputies.
罢免权 bàmiǎnquán ❶ right of recall; recall ❷ right (of the higher authorities) to remove or dismiss (sb.) from office
罢赛 bàsài refuse to participate in a competition; (of athletes) go on strike:部分球员～，足球联赛前景暗淡。The soccer league matches are under a cloud as some of the players are on strike.
罢市 bàshì (of business people) suspend business as a protest; shopkeepers' strike
罢手 bàshǒu call it quits; give up; stop:就此～ call it quits then and there /不查个水落石出，决不～。We will never stop (*or* give up) until the truth is out.
罢讼 bàsòng *see* "罢诉"
罢诉 bàsù withdraw a lawsuit; abandon or revoke a prosecution:经过调解，原告同意～。After mediation, the plaintiff agreed to withdraw the lawsuit.
罢休 bàxiū give up; stop:你要是惹急了他，他是不会跟你～的。If he is provoked, he will have it out with you.
罢演 bàyǎn refuse to participate in a performance; (of actors or actresses) go on strike:虽是名演员，也不可任意撕毁合同～。Even famous actors and actresses have no right to go back on a contract and refuse to participate in performances.
罢业 bàyè shopkeepers' strike
罢战 bàzhàn end fighting or hostilities; cease fire:双方同意～言和。The two sides agreed to cease hostilities and negotiate peace.
罢职 bàzhí dismiss from office; remove from a position

鲅(鲌) bà Spanish mackerel

鲅鱼 bàyú *also* "蓝点鲅" lándiǎnbà; "马鲛鱼" mǎjiāoyú; "燕鱼" yànyú Spanish mackerel

耙(耚) bà ❶ harrow:圆盘～ disc harrow /钉齿～ spike-tooth harrow ❷ draw a harrow over (a field); harrow:～地 harrow a field
see also pá

耙土机 bàtǔjī 〈农业〉 harrower

把(欛) bà ❶ grip; handle:缸子～儿 handle of a mug /刀～儿 handle of a knife /门～儿 door handle /枪～儿 rifle butt ❷ stem; peduncle; petiole:花～儿 flower stem /梨～儿 petiole of a pear
see also bǎ

把子 bàzi handle:刀～ handle of a knife; military power /印～ (handle of) an official seal; political power
see also bǎzi

鲃 bà 〈方言〉 sticking out of a tooth; bucktooth

弝 bà ❶ middle of a bow (for the hand to grasp) ❷ 〈方言〉 *see* "把子" bàzi

爸 bà 〈口语〉 pa; dad; father:老～ 〈方言〉 pa; dad; daddy

爸爸 bàba 〈口语〉 pa; dad; daddy

ba

吧(罢、罷) ba 〈助词〉 ❶ *used at the end of a sentence to indicate consultation, suggestion, request, or command*:快点儿～。Hurry up, will you? /别说了～。Stop, please. ❷ *used at the end of a sentence to indicate agreement or approval*:好～，我答应你了。OK, you have my word. ❸ *used at the end of a sentence to indicate doubt or surmise*:他在这里是一个陌生人～? He is a stranger here, isn't he? /你就是李先生～? You are Mr. Li, I suppose. ❹ *used at the end of a sentence to indicate probability*:我们会在开会时见到他～。Perhaps we'll see him at the meeting. ❺ *used in a sentence to indicate a pause after suppositions, concessions, or conditions*:比如你～，你普通话就比他讲得好。For example, you speak better standard Chinese than he does. /就算你完全正确～，也该谦虚点儿。Even if you are entirely correct, you should be a bit more modest.
see also bā

bāi

刉 bāi

刉划 bāihuai 〈方言〉 ❶ deal with; handle; arrange:这事儿可不好～。It's a hard nut to crack. ❷ repair; mend; fix

踫 bāi 〈方言〉 lame:脚～手残 disabled in the limbs; crippled

踫子 bāizi 〈方言〉 person with a disabled limb (hand or foot); lame person; cripple

掰(擘) bāi ❶ break off with the fingers and thumb:～两半儿 break sth. into halves (*or* in two) /～着手指算 count on one's fingers /一分钱～成两半花 use every penny for its fullest value; be extremely frugal with one's money ❷ 〈方言〉 break up (relationship); fall apart; fall out:他俩就这么～了。So they've fallen out. *or* So they've broken with each other. ❸ 〈方言〉 *also* "掰哧" analyse; study; examine:我跟他把这个问题～了半天。I spent quite some time going over the problem with him.

掰扯 bāiche 〈方言〉 sort out:这事儿，咱们得～清楚。We'd better sort out the problem together.
掰腕子 bāi wànzi wrist wrestling:你敢跟我～吗? Do you dare to have a wrist-wrestling contest with me?

bái

白[1] bái ❶ white:雪～ snow white /几根～发 a few white (*or* grey) hairs /皮肤～ have a fair complexion /～布 white cloth; calico ❷ bright; light:大天～日 in broad daylight /东方发～。It dawns in the east. ❸ clear:真相大～。Everything is clear now. *or* The whole truth is out. /沉冤莫～。The long-standing injustice has not been redressed. ❹ pure; plain; blank:～纸一张 a piece of white paper; a blank sheet of paper /补～ filler (in a newspaper or magazine) ❺ in vain; for nothing:～说 speak in vain; waste one's breath; words have fallen on deaf ears /～跑了一趟 make a fruitless trip ❻ free of charge; gratis:～吃 get a free meal /～给 offer sth. free of charge ❼ White (as a symbol of counter-revolution or unsound political orientation):～匪 White bandit; White soldier ❽ funeral:红～喜事 weddings and funerals ❾ give a supercilious or unfriendly look:他～了我一眼。He gave me a cold stare. ❿ (Bái) a surname

白[2] bái (of Chinese characters) wrongly written or mispronounced:把字念～了 mispronounce a word

白[3] bái ❶ state; explain:表～ vindicate /辩～ offer an explanation; plead innocence; try to defend oneself /坦～ make a clean breast of; confess ❷ spoken part (in opera, etc.):独～ soliloquy; monologue /对～ dialogue /旁～ aside ❸ dialect:苏～ Suzhou dialect ❹ vernacular; spoken language:文～交杂 with classical and vernacular language mixed together /半文半～ (of style) half classical, half vernacular

白皑皑 bái'ái'ái (of snow, frost, etc.) pure white:～的雪覆盖着大地。The vast land is carpeted with pure white snow.
白矮星 bái'ǎixīng 〈天文〉 white dwarf star
白氨酸 bái'ānsuān *also* "亮氨酸" liàng'ānsuān 〈生化〉 leucine
白案 bái'àn white (kneading) board—cooking that deals with flour or rice (as opposite to meat cooking):他是我店的～师傅。He's our pastry chef in the restaurant.
白澳政策 Bái'ào Zhèngcè White Australia Policy (formerly pursued by Australian governments to restrict the entry of coloured people into the country)
白白 báibái in vain; to no purpose; for nothing:我～浪费了精力。I made my effort in vain. /不要～放过大好时机。Don't let a golden op-

portunity slip through your fingers. /他～忙了一阵子。He busied himself for quite some time for nothing. /水果运不出来,～地烂在山里,真可惜! What a shame it is to have all the fruit go to waste (*or* rot away) in the mountainous area for lack of transport!

白柏 báibǎi 〈植物〉white cedar

白班儿 báibānr 〈口语〉day shift:我这个星期上～。I am on day shift this week.

白斑病 báibānbìng *see*“白癜风”

白板 báibǎn ❶ white bulletin board ❷〈哲学〉*tabula rasa* (the human mind viewed as having no innate ideas)

白版 báibǎn blank (in a sheet of printed matter); blank sheet (in printed matter):一本杂志八页～。There are eight blank pages in the magazine.

白报纸 báibàozhǐ newsprint

白鼻子 báibízi *also*“白鼻头”〈方言〉❶ crafty person ❷ traitor; turncoat

白璧微瑕 báibì-wēixiá speck in white jade—slight blemish on an otherwise perfect character; minor flaw in an otherwise perfect thing:这点小毛病只是～。This insignificant flaw is but a speck in a piece of pure jade.

白璧无瑕 báibì-wúxiá flawless (white) jade; impeccable (moral) integrity:再杰出的人物也不可能十全十美,～。Even the most outstanding people are not as perfect as flawless jade.

白扁柏 báibiǎnbǎi 〈植物〉white cedar (*Chamaecyparis thyroides*)

白醭 báibú mould (on the surface of vinegar, soya sauce, etc.)

白卜鲔 báibǔwěi 〈动物〉wavyback skipjack

白不呲咧 báibucīliē 〈方言〉whitish; faded; tasteless:太阳把窗帘晒得～的。Sunlight has faded the curtains. /菜里酱油放少了,～的,不好吃。I'm afraid the dish is a little bland; it needs a bit more soya sauce.

白不拉几 báibulājī 〈方言〉*see*“白不呲咧”

白菜 báicài Chinese cabbage

白茬 báichá ❶ unsown (field) after the harvest of a crop:～地 unsown field after the harvest of the previous crop ❷ (of a fur coat or jacket) without a cloth or silk covering:～老羊皮袄 sheep skin jacket without a cloth covering

白茶 báichá a kind of unfermented or unbaked and unrolled tea, made by a special process

白碴 báichá *also*“白槎”;“白楂”unpainted or unvarnished wooden furniture:～大门 unpainted wooden gate /屋里的桌椅,都未经油漆,还是～。The desks and chairs in the room are all unpainted; they are still of natural colour.

白痴 báichī ❶ idiocy ❷ idiot

白炽 báichì white heat; incandescence

白炽灯 báichìdēng incandescent lamp:～照明 incandescent lighting

白唇鹿 báichúnlù white-lipped deer

白醋 báicù light-coloured vinegar

白搭 báidā 〈口语〉no use; no good; in vain:功夫全～了。Everything was in vain. *or* Our efforts were all wasted.

白大褂 báidàguà white gown (worn by medical personnel):穿～的 doctor or nurse

白带 báidài 〈生理〉whites; leucorrhea:～过多 leukorrhagia

白蛋白 báidànbái 〈生化〉albumin:～球蛋白比例 albumin-globulin ratio; A-G ratio

白党 báidǎng (of counter-revolutionaries after the October 1917 revolution in Russia) White gang; Whites

白刀子进,红刀子出 báidāozi jìn, hóngdāozi chū 〈口语〉the knife'll go in clean and come out red; knife sb. to death:匪徒叫嚷说:“你要说个‘不’字,我就叫你～。”The bandit yelled: “If you say ‘no’, I'll run this knife through your heart.”

白道 báidào ❶〈天文〉moon's path ❷ (in contrast with 黑道) normal society; law-abiding citizenry:～人物 law-abiding citizen; straight-arrow

白瞪 báideng show the white of one's eye; turn the whites of one's eyes upon; stare angrily; stare with disdain:王大妈～了她一眼。Aunt Wang gave her an angry (*or* a supercilious) stare.

白瞪眼 báidengyǎn be anxious but unable to do anything

白地 báidì ❶ field not sown to crops; uncultivated land ❷ barren and uninhabited land ❸ white ground (for patterns, etc.):～儿兰花儿 blue flowers on a white ground

白癜风 báidiànfēng *also*“白斑病”〈医学〉vitiligo; leucodermia

白貂 báidiāo ermine

白丁 báidīng ❶ person without a degree or an official post in feudal society; commoner ❷ man with no political party affiliations

白洞 báidòng 〈天文〉white hole; region where matter spontaneously appears (hypothetical reverse of a black hole)

白俄 Bái É White Russian (one who fled Russia after 1917); expatriate Russian

白俄罗斯 Bái'éluósī (formerly known as Byelorussia) Belarus:～人 Belarussian /～共和国 Republic of Belarus /～岭 Belarussian Ridge /～公教会 Belarussian Catholic Church

白垩 bái'è chalk (a white soft earthy limestone):～层 chalk bed /～矿场 chalk pit /～质黏土 chalky clay /～粉 whiting

白垩纪 Bái'èjì 〈地质〉Cretaceous period

白垩系 Bái'èxì 〈地质〉Cretaceous system

白发苍苍 báifà-cāngcāng greyhaired; hoary-haired:当年的小伙子,如今已经～。The young men of those days are now hoary-haired.

白发症 báifàzhèng 〈医学〉poliosis

白番杏 báifānxìng *also*“番杏”fānxìng 〈植物〉*Tetragonia expansa*

白矾 báifán 〈化学〉white alum

白饭 báifàn plain cooked rice; cooked rice with nothing to go with it:吃～的 one who eats a meal without paying or working for it; sb. not worth his salt; good-for-nothing /要五个盒饭,外加一份～。Give us five box lunches plus one box of plain cooked rice.

白费 báifèi waste; be of no avail:～唇舌 waste one's breath /～时间 waste one's time /～心思 rack one's brains for nothing

白费蜡 báifèilà useless; in vain; for nothing:我帮你复习半天算是～了。All my efforts to help you with your lessons turned out to be useless.

白粉 báifěn ❶ face powder:她脸上擦了厚厚的一层～。She is thickly powdered. ❷〈方言〉chalk (for whitewashing walls); whitewash ❸ *also*“白面儿”〈方言〉heroin:吸～ take heroin /吸～者 heroin addict

白粉病 báifěnbìng 〈农业〉powdery mildew

白干儿 báigānr cheap, strong liquor distilled from sorghum or maize:老～ good strong white liquor

白宫 Báigōng White House, official residence of the US president in Washington, DC

白姑鱼 báigūyú white Chinese croaker

白骨 báigǔ bones of the dead; white bones; bleached bones:～红颜。A beauty today, a bleached skeleton tomorrow. *or* Beauty is but transient.

白骨顶 báigǔdǐng 〈动物〉coot

白骨精 báigǔjīng ❶ White Bone Demon (in the novel *Pilgrimage to the West*《西游记》) ❷ sinister and ruthless woman

白瓜子 báiguāzǐ pumpkin seed

白冠病 báiguānbìng 〈兽医〉whitecomb

白鹳 báiguàn white crane

白光 báiguāng 〈物理〉white light

白圭微瑕 báiguī-wēixiá *see*“白璧微瑕”

白圭之玷 báiguīzhīdiàn speck or flaw in white jade — slight blemish on an otherwise perfect character; minor blemish in a thing of beauty

白鲑 báiguī 〈动物〉whitefish (*Coregonus*)

白果 báiguǒ 〈植物〉ginkgo; gingko (*Gingko bilboa*)

白果儿 báiguǒr 〈方言〉boiled egg

白果松 báiguǒsōng *see*“白皮松”

白海 Báihǎi White Sea, an inlet of the Barents Sea on the NW coast of Russia

白河车 báihéchē 〈中药〉root of *Rohdea japonica*

白鹤 báihè 〈动物〉white crane (*Grus leucogeranus*)

白喉 báihóu 〈医学〉diphtheria:～抗菌素 diphtheria antitoxin; DAT

白糊糊 báihūhū *also*“白乎乎”;“白胡胡”whitish; milky:天空笼罩着～的雾气。The sky is covered with a whitish mist.

白狐 báihú 〈动物〉arctic fox

白虎 báihǔ ❶ White Tiger, collective name for the western group of seven of the 28 Constellations (二十八宿) ❷ White Tiger, Taoist guardian spirit of the West

白虎星 báihǔxīng 〈迷信〉White Tiger Star—woman whose horoscope is supposed to jinx her family, esp. her husband; jinx; ban-

shee
白花 báihuā 〈纺织〉lap waste
白花花 báihuāhuā shining white:～的胡子 silky white beard; hoary beard /～的盐碱地 whitish alkaline land /～的银子 gleaming silver (coins) /～的水浪 foaming waves
白花蛇 báihuāshé 〈动物〉long-nosed pit viper (*Agkistrodon acutus*)
白化 báihuà albinic; albinotic
白化病 báihuàbìng 〈医学〉albinism:～人 albino
白化体 báihuàtǐ 〈植物〉albino
白话 báihuà ❶ unrealizable or unfounded statement:空口说～ make empty promises; pay lip service ❷〈方言〉gossip; chitchat:她俩一边干活,一边说～。They chitchatted while working. ❸ vernacular:～小说 novel written in the vernacular
白话诗 báihuàshī free verse in vernacular Chinese
白话文 báihuàwén vernacular Chinese; writing in vernacular Chinese:～运动 Vernacular Movement (1917-1919)
白桦 báihuà 〈植物〉white birch
白晃晃 báihuǎnghuǎng white and bright; gleaming:～的刺刀 shining bayonet
白灰 báihuī ❶ (common name for 石灰) lime ❷〈方言〉whitewash
白货 báihuò 〈旧语〉❶ untaxed goods ❷ heroin
白芨 báijī 〈中药〉tuber of hyacinth bletilla (*Bletilla striata*)
白鳖豚 báijìtún *also*"白鳍豚" white-flag dolphin
白碱土 báijiǎntǔ 〈地质〉white alkali soil
白僵病 báijiāngbìng white muscardine
白僵蚕 báijiāngcán 〈中药〉larva of a silkworm with white muscardine
白教 Báijiào (of Lamaism) White Hat Sect
白芥子 báijièzǐ 〈中药〉dried seeds of *Brassica alba*
白金 báijīn ❶ platinum:～坩埚 platinum crucible ❷〈旧语〉silver
白金汉宫 Báijīnhàngōng ❶ Buckingham Palace, London residence of the British sovereign from 1837 ❷ British royal family
白晶晶 báijīngjīng sparkling white:～的盐霜 sparkling white salt efflorescence
白鲸 báijīng 〈动物〉beluga; white whale:《～》*Moby Dick* (novel by Herman Melville, 1851)
白净 báijing (of skin) fair and clear:脸皮～ fair complexion
白酒 báijiǔ liquor usually distilled from sorghum or maize; spirit
白驹过隙 báijū-guòxì time passes as quickly as a white pony flashing past a chink; time flies — life is short
白居易 Bái Jūyì Bai Juyi (772-846), poet of the Tang Dynasty
白剧 báijù local opera of the Bai or Pai nationality in Yunnan Province
白卷 báijuàn unanswered examination paper:交～ hand in an unanswered examination paper; fail to do one's job; "lay an egg"
白军 báijūn *also*"白匪" White army (during the Civil War of 1927-1937, or in Russia, 1918-1920)
白开水 báikāishuǐ plain boiled water
白口 báikǒu ❶ blank-border format (of a traditional thread-bound book)— a format with a blank middle margin between the two pages of a block-printed sheet, presenting a blank edge when the sheet is folded up into the two pages and bound at the opposite edges *see also*"黑口" hēikǒu ❷ spoken part (in an opera)
白口铁 báikǒutiě white (pig) iron
白矿脂 báikuàngzhī 〈化工〉white petrolatum; white vaseline
白蜡 báilà white wax; insect wax:～虫 wax insect
白蜡树 báilàshù Chinese ash
白镴 báilà ❶ solder ❷ pewter:～制品 pewter work
白兰 báilán 〈植物〉gardenia
白兰地 báilándì brandy:～加苏打水 brandy and soda /～黄油 brandy butter /～酒味糖 brandyball
白兰瓜 báilánguā honeydew melon; Lanzhou melon; Wallace melon
白冷杉 báilěngshān 〈林业〉white fir (*Abies concolor*)
白楞 báileng *also*"白愣" turn the white of one's eyes upon; stare angrily or with disdain; cast a supercilious look:～眼 supercilious look; contemptuous look /几句话把他顶得～～的,不吭气了。A few words from me set him staring into space, his mouth shut.
白梨 báilí *also*"罐梨" guànlí white pear (*Pyrus bretschneideri*):京～ Beijing white pear
白栎 báilì *also*"栭栎" érlì white oak
白痢 báilì ❶〈中医〉dysentery with white mucous stool ❷〈兽医〉white diarrhoea
白莲教 Báiliánjiào White Lotus Society (a secret religious society active during the Yuan, Ming and Qing dynasties, which was often used as a cover of peasant rebellions)
白鲢 báilián 〈动物〉silver carp (*Cyprinus carpio*)
白脸 báiliǎn ❶ white face (face painting in Beijing opera usu. for the villain):唱～ play the villain; play the bad cop ❷ fair complexion:小～ handsome but effeminate young man
白蔹 báiliǎn 〈植物〉*Ampelopsis japonica*, whose tuber is used as medicine:～属 Ampelopsis
白亮 báiliàng white and shining; glittering:～的刺刀 glittering bayonet /电灯照得屋里～～的。The electric light lit up the whole room.
白亮亮 báiliàngliàng shining white:～的浪花 white, sparkling spray; white-crested waves /她一笑露出了～的牙齿。She smiled (*or* grinned), revealing her white teeth.
白亮葡萄 báiliàng pútao 〈植物〉mustang grape
白磷 báilín 〈化学〉white phosphorus
白鳞鱼 báilínyú Chinese herring
白蛉 báilíng *also*"白蛉子" sandfly
白蛉热 báilíngrè 〈医学〉sandfly fever
白领 báilǐng white-collar:～工人 white-collar worker /～工作 white-collar job /～阶层 white-collar employees
白令海 Báilìnghǎi Bering Sea
白令海峡 Báilìng Hǎixiá Bering Strait (joining the Arctic and the Pacific)
白榴石 báiliúshí leucite
白柳 báiliǔ 〈植物〉white willow (*Salix alba*)
白鹿 báilù white deer
白鹿洞书院 Báilùdòng Shūyuàn White Deer Cave Academy at Lushan (庐山), Jiangxi Province, one of the oldest academies of ancient China
白鹭 báilù 〈动物〉egret
白露 Báilù ❶ White Dew, 15th seasonal division point, marking the sun's position at 165° on the ecliptic ❷ day marking such a seasonal division point, usu. falling on the 7th or 8th of September ❸ period lasting from such a seasonal division point till the next one (Autumnal Equinox 秋分)
see also"节气" jiéqi;"二十四节气" èrshísì jiéqì
白马非马 báimǎ-fēimǎ "a white horse is not a horse"— a seemingly paradoxical thesis advanced by *Gongsun Long* (公孙龙, 320-250 BC), stressing the difference between the individual and the generic or between the particular and the general
白马王子 báimǎ-wángzǐ prince riding a white horse—Prince Charming
白鳗 báimán *also*"鳗鲡" mánlí 〈动物〉eel
白茫茫 báimángmáng (of mist, snow, floodwater, etc.) vast expanse of whiteness:他眼前是～一片汪洋,早已分不清哪里是道路,哪里是沟塘。Stretching before him was a foamy sea of floodwater, and it was no longer possible to say where the roads or ditches or ponds were.
白猫黑猫论 báimāo-hēimāolùn theory that it doesn't matter if a cat is black or white as long as it catches mice
白毛风 báimáofēng 〈方言〉snowstorm
白毛女 Báimáonǚ *White-Haired Girl*, a popular modern Chinese opera, first produced in 1945
白茅 báimáo 〈植物〉cogon; cogon grass (*Imperata cylindrica*):～根〈中药〉cogon rhizome
白帽子 báimàozi 〈方言〉layman; smatterer; dabbler:半路出家的～ layman who switched to a profession in the middle of his career (*or* switched to a job which he was not trained for)
白煤 báiméi ❶〈方言〉anthracite; hard coal ❷ "white coal"— waterpower
白霉素 báiméisù 〈药学〉albomycin
白蒙蒙 báiméngméng (of mist, smoke, vapour, etc.) whitish and indistinct:～的大雾布满江上。A pall of whitish mist hung over the river.
白米 báimǐ (polished) rice:～饭 cooked rice
白棉纸 báimiánzhǐ stencil tissue paper
白面 báimiàn flour

B

白面儿 báimiànr heroin
白面书生 báimiàn-shūshēng pale-looking, inexperienced young scholar; greenhorn:不谙世事的～ pale-faced scholar inexperienced in the ways of the world
白描 báimiáo ❶〈美术〉line drawing in the traditional ink and brush style ❷ simple, straightforward style of writing
白膜炎 báimóyán 〈医学〉albuginitis
白沫 báimò foam; frothy saliva:他得了羊角风,口吐～。He had an attack of epilepsy, foaming at the mouth.
白木耳 báimù'ěr tremella; (edible) white fungus
白内障 báinèizhàng 〈医学〉cataract:～摘除术 cataract extraction /～冷冻摘除术 cataract cryo-extraction /他双目～,几乎完全失明了。He had cataracts in both eyes and was almost totally blind.
白嫩 báinèn (of complexion) fair and delicate:她有张～的脸庞。She has a fair and delicate complexion.
白尼罗河 Báiníluóhé White Nile River (on the border between Uganda and Sudan)
白砒 báipī 〈化学〉white arsenic; arsenic trioxide
白皮书 báipíshū white paper; white book:《美中关系～》*White Paper on US Relations with China*
白皮松 báipísōng *also* "白果松" lacebark pine
白票 báipiào blank ballot:一百零五张选票中有三张～。There were three blank ballots among the 105 votes cast.
白扑扑 báipūpū whitish:小麦已经开始扬花了,麦穗～的,好像上过粉似的。The wheat has begun flowering, and the ears look as if they were sprinkled with powder.
白旗 báiqí white flag (a sign of surrender or for crossing the fronts):敌军摇着～投降。The enemy troops waved the white flag and surrendered. /敌军联络官打着～走过来送信。An enemy liaison officer walked over holding a white flag to deliver a letter.
白鳍豚 báiqítún 〈动物〉white-flag dolphin
白契 báiqì 〈旧语〉real estate contract without an official seal
白铅 báiqiān ❶ (popular name for 锌) zinc ❷〈冶金〉white lead:～矿 white lead ore; cerussite /～油漆〈化工〉white lead paint
白前 báiqián 〈植物〉*Cynanchum glaucescens*, whose root is used as medicine
白前车叶草 báiqián chēyècǎo 〈植物〉squinancy
白钱 báiqián ❶ coin-shaped steel tool used by a pickpocket to cut into people's bags or pockets ❷ paper money for the dead
白镪 báiqiǎng silver (as currency)
白切 báiqiē *also* "白斩" white cut:～鸡 white cut chicken (slices of boiled chicken served cold with soy sauce and other condiments)
白求恩 Báiqiú'ēn Henry Norman Bethune (1890-1939), Canadian surgeon who came to Yan'an in 1938 to assist the Chinese struggle against Japanese aggression
白区 báiqū White area (Kuomintang-controlled area during the Second Revolutionary Civil War, 1927-1937)
白屈菜 báiqūcài 〈植物〉celandine
白饶 báiráo ❶ give sth. extra free of charge:买一套组合音响,～一个放大器。Buy a hi-fi set and you'll get an amplifier free. ❷〈方言〉no use; no good; in vain:过去的辛苦全算～,得打头儿重来。All our past efforts are in vain, and we have to start all over again.
白热 báirè *also* "白炽" white heat; incandescence:～灯 tungsten lamp
白热化 báirèhuà turn white-hot; reach a crisis or climax:冲突～。The conflict reached a boiling point. /斗争进入～阶段。The struggle was at fever pitch.
白人 báirén ❶ white person; white population; Caucasian:这座城里～比黑人多。There are more whites in the city than blacks. ❷〈方言〉*see* "白丁"
白刃 báirèn naked sword or knife; bayonet:～格斗 bayonet fighting
白刃战 báirènzhàn bayonet charge; hand-to-hand fighting
白日 báirì ❶ sun:～依山尽,黄河入海流。The sun behind the western hills glows, And towards the sea the Yellow River flows. ❷ daytime:洞中不辨～黑夜。It was pitch-dark inside the cave and no one could tell whether it was day or night.
白日见鬼 báirì-jiànguǐ see ghosts and apparitions in broad daylight—indulge in pure fantasy; hallucinate; be the height of absurdity:他们说自己见到了外星人,那不是～吗? They claimed to have seen extraterrestrials, but wasn't it just a figment of their imagination?
白日撞 báirìzhuàng 〈方言〉"daylight burglar"—thief who sneaks into homes in broad daylight while people are away
白日做梦 báirì-zuòmèng daydream; indulge in wishful thinking:你以为他会回心转意,那是～。You think he will come round, but that is daydreaming.
白肉 báiròu *also* "白切肉" plain boiled pork
白润 báirùn (of skin) fair; fair and chubby:～的婴儿 fair, chubby baby
白三叶草 báisānyècǎo 〈植物〉white clover (*Trifolium repens*)
白色 báisè ❶ white:一座三层～小楼 white three-storeyed house ❷ White (as a symbol of reaction):～政权 White regime
白色大陆 báisè dàlù white continent — Antarctica
白色金属 báisè jīnshǔ white metal; silvery alloy
白色恐怖 báisè kǒngbù White terror
白色偏光镜 báisè piānguāngjìng leuccscope
白色人种 báisè rénzhǒng White race; Caucasian race
白色商品 báisè shāngpǐn white goods
白色体 báisètǐ 〈植物〉leucoplast
白森森 báisēnsēn white; pale:～的光 pale light /～的骷髅 bleached human skeleton (*or* skull) /看你那双手～的,会像个木匠吗? Do you think you can pass for a carpenter with those delicate hands of yours?
白沙糖 báishātáng refined white (granulated) sugar
白山黑水 báishān-hēishuǐ Changbai Mountains and Heilongjiang River — northeast China:女真族的故乡,在那～之间。The Nüzhens originated in the Changbai Mountains and along the Heilongjiang River.
白闪闪 báishǎnshǎn shining white; flashing white; glittering white:～的劈刀 shining chopper
白鳝 báishàn *also* "鳗鲡" mánlí 〈动物〉eel
白芍 báisháo 〈中药〉(peeled) root of herbaceous peony (*Paeonia lactiflora*)
白生生 báishēngshēng very white:一簇簇～的菊花 clusters of white chrysanthemums /～的桌布上绣着几朵红玫瑰。The white table-cloth is embroidered with red roses.
白食 báishí free food; free meal:我不喜欢那些吃～的人。I don't like those who are prone to live off other people.
白事 báishì funeral
白手 báishǒu with bare hands:～夺刀 seize the opponent's sword with bare hands
白手起家 báishǒu-qǐjiā *also* "白手成家" start from scratch; be self-made:～的大亨 self-made tycoon /这所学校几乎是～的。This school almost started from scratch. /他开办这家工厂完全是～。He built up his factory literally from nothing.
白首 báishǒu 〈书面〉white-haired; hoary headed; aged:～无成 have achieved nothing even though one is hoary-headed /～穷经 still plod away at ancient classics in old age /～之盟 nuptial vow to be together until death
白鼠 báishǔ 〈动物〉white rat; albino rat
白薯 báishǔ (popular term for 甘薯) sweet potato:烤～ baked sweet potato
白刷刷 báishuāshuā extremely white:漫天飞雪,～的一片。The snowflakes drifting and swirling all around made an infinite mass of whiteness. /照明弹～的光,一下子照到他们脸上。The dazzling light of the tracers suddenly lit up their faces.
白霜 báishuāng white frost; hoarfrost
白水 báishuǐ ❶ plain boiled water ❷〈书面〉clear water
白水泥 báishuǐní 〈建筑〉white cement
白苏 báisū 〈植物〉common perilla
白汤 báitāng meat or vegetable soup without soy sauce; clear soup; consommé
白糖 báitáng (refined) white sugar
白陶 báitáo 〈考古〉white pottery (of the Shang Dynasty):～土 porcelain clay; kaolin
白藤 báiténg rattan:～器皿 rattan ware /～椅子 rattan chair
白体 báitǐ 〈印刷〉lean type:～与黑体不同,笔划较细。Unlike the boldfaced type, the lean type has thin strokes.
白田 báitián land or paddy fields not sown to crops; uncultivated land
白天 báitian daytime; day:～黑夜 day and night /大～抢银行的事也屡见不鲜。Bank robberies carried out in broad daylight are no rare occurrences.
白条 báitiáo ❶ unofficial receipt (in financial transactions);

IOU:打～ give an IOU (instead of paying cash) ❷ slaughtered poultry or animal, stripped of hairs or feathers, or with head, feet and entrails removed:～猪 pig carcass

白铁 báitiě *also*"白铁皮" tin plate:这个桶是用～做的。This bucket is made of tin.

白铁工 báitiěgōng cold metal work; tinman; tinner

白铁矿 báitiěkuàng marcasite

白厅 Báitīng Whitehall (street in Westminster, London, in which many important government offices are located); British government

白铜 báitóng white copper; copper-nickel alloy

白头 báitóu ❶ hoary-headed; white-haired ❷ unsigned:～帖子 anonymous poster (denouncing sb., etc.) /～材料 unsigned document

白头翁 báitóuwēng ❶〈中药〉root of Chinese pulsatilla ❷〈动物〉Chinese bulbul

白头偕老 báitóu-xiélǎo *also*"白头到老" live together to a ripe old age:百年好合,～ live to a ripe old age in conjugal felicity (*or* in matrimonial bliss)

白土子 báitǔzi (common name for 白垩) chalk; whiting

白兔 báitù ❶ white rabbit ❷ legendary rabbit in the moon; moon

白脱 báituō *also*"白脱油";"白塔油" butter

白玩儿 báiwánr ❶ have a good time free; enjoy oneself for free:今儿老张请客,我是～。It's on Lao Zhang today. I'm just having a good time free. ❷ effortless; as easy as pie:那点事儿要我去管,～! It would be as easy as pie if I were asked to take charge of that.

白薇 báiwēi ❶〈植物〉*Cynanchum atratum*:蔓生～ *Cynanchum versicolor* ❷〈中药〉radix cynanchi atrati

白卫军 Báiwèijūn White Guard (defending Tsarist Russia in 1918-1920)

白文 báiwén ❶ text of an annotated book ❷ unannotated edition of a book ❸ intagliated characters (on a seal):一方图章是～,另一方是朱文。One seal has intagliated characters, while the other is in relief.

白钨矿 báiwūkuàng scheelite

白屋 báiwū〈书面〉thatched cottage; unpainted roughly built hut inhabited by the poor

白皙 báixī〈书面〉fair (complexion):他的皮肤天生～。His complexion is naturally fair.

白细胞 báixìbāo〈生理〉white blood cell; white blood corpuscle; leucocyte:～计数 leukocyte count /～减少〈医学〉leukocytopenia /～增多〈医学〉leukocytosis

白细胞瘤 báixìbāoliú〈医学〉leukocytoma

白细胞缺乏症 báixìbāo quēfázhèng〈医学〉aleukaemia; aleukemia

白鲜 báixiān〈植物〉shaggy-fruited dittany (*Dictamnus dasycarpus* or *Dictamnus albus*):～皮 root bark of shaggy-fruited dittany

白鹇 báixián〈动物〉silver pheasant

白鲞 báixiǎng preserved yellow croaker

白相 báixiàng〈方言〉play; have fun; visit:在大树底下～ play under a big tree /到杭州去～～ visit Hangzhou on a sight-seeing trip /这地方真好～。This place is really fun.

白相人 báixiàngrén〈方言〉thug; hooligan; gangster

白熊 báixióng polar bear; white bear

白锈病 báixiùbìng〈植物〉white rust

白絮 báixù ❶ cotton wadding:他的棉衣露出了～。The cotton wadding showed through the torn part of his padded coat. ❷ snowflakes:雪压冬云～飞。Winter clouds are snow-laden with flakes flying all round.

白癣 báixuǎn *also*"白秃风"〈医学〉tinea; ringworm

白雪公主 Báixuě Gōngzhǔ Snow White:《～和七个矮人》*Snow White and the Seven Dwarfs*

白血病 báixuèbìng leukaemia; leucaemia:～患者 leukaemic

白血球 báixuèqiú *also*"白细胞"〈生理〉white blood cell; white blood corpuscle; leucocyte

白鲟 báixún〈动物〉Chinese paddle-fish

白眼 báiyǎn supercilious or scornful look:～看人 look upon sb. with scorn; show disdain towards sb. /老太太不喜欢儿媳妇,过门当天就给她个大～。The old lady who did not like her daughter-in-law cold-shouldered her the very day she moved in after the wedding.

白眼儿狼 báiyǎnrláng one who bites the hand that feeds him; ungrateful, heartless villain

白眼珠 báiyǎnzhū white of the eye

白羊座 Báiyángzuò *also*"白羊宫"〈天文〉Aries

白杨 báiyáng〈植物〉white poplar; *Populus balsamifera*

白洋 báiyáng silver dollar

白药 báiyào〈中药〉*baiyao*, white medicinal powder for treating hemorrhage, wounds, bruises, etc.

白夜 báiyè white night

白衣 báiyī ❶ white frock (doctor's uniform):～战士 medical worker; doctor or nurse ❷〈书面〉man without a degree or official post (who was supposed to wear white or undyed clothes in dynastic times); commoner:～秀士 scholar who never passed any imperial civil examination; untitled scholar

白衣苍狗 báiyī-cānggǒu clouds are so changeable in shape that they look now like white garments and now like grey hounds—changes in human affairs often take freakish forms; vicissitudes of life are like changing cloud formations:～刹那间。Changes may take place in the twinkling of an eye. *or* Events are fast-changing.

白衣天使 báiyī tiānshǐ nurse

白衣修士 Báiyī xiūshì White Friar; Carmelite

白蚁 báiyǐ〈动物〉termite; white ant:～巢 termitary

白翳 báiyì〈中医〉slight corneal opacity; nebula

白银 báiyín (common name for 银) silver

白鼬 báiyòu〈动物〉ermine; stoat

白鱼 báiyú〈动物〉whitefish

白玉草 báiyùcǎo〈植物〉bladder campion

白玉兰 báiyùlán *see*"白兰"

白云苍狗 báiyún-cānggǒu *see*"白衣苍狗"

白云母 báiyúnmǔ〈地质〉muscovite; white mica

白云杉 báiyúnshān〈植物〉white spruce (*Picea alba*)

白云石 báiyúnshí〈地质〉dolomite:～砖 dolomite brick /～石灰岩 dolomite limestone

白灾 báizāi calamity caused by snowstorm (usu. in pastureland)

白斩鸡 báizhǎnjī tender boiled chicken with soy sauce

白芷 báizhǐ〈中药〉root of *Dahurian angelica*

白纸黑字 báizhǐ-hēizì (written) in black and white:～难以抵赖。What is in black and white can hardly be denied.

白质 báizhì〈生理〉white matter (in brain or marrow)

白种 báizhǒng white race; Caucasian race:～人 white (person); Caucasian

白粥 báizhōu plain gruel or porridge

白昼 báizhòu daytime; daylight; day:厅内灯火辉煌,如同～。The hall was so brilliantly illuminated that it looked as if it were broad daylight.

白术 báizhú〈中药〉rhizome of large-headed atractylodes (*Atractylodes macrocephala*)

白专 báizhuān〈贬义〉be professionally competent but politically insensitive; be expert but apolitical:～道路 pursue professional competence to the neglect of political orientation

白撞雨 báizhuàngyǔ〈方言〉shower:下了一场～。There was a passing shower.

白浊 báizhuó〈医学〉gonorrhoea; gonorrhea

白字 báizì wrongly written (*or* mispronounced) character:尽念～ tend to mispronounce characters /～连篇 (of an essay, etc.) teem with wrongly written characters

白族 Báizú Bai nationality; the Bais (living mostly in Yunnan Province):～姑娘 Bai girl /他是～。He is a Bai.

白族吹吹腔 Báizú chuīchuīqiāng ethnic opera of the Bais, popular in western Yunnan

白嘴儿 báizuǐr〈方言〉enjoy dishes without eating rice; eat rice without enjoying dishes:～吃饭 eat rice without touching dishes /这小子真馋,光～吃菜。This chap is a real glutton, wolfing down every dish without taking a morsel of rice.

bǎi

百 bǎi ❶ hundred:几～个人 several hundred people /数以～计 hundreds of /一～五十 one hundred and fifty ❷ numerous; all kinds of:～草 all kinds of herbs /精神～倍 be filled with enormous enthusiasm /千方～计 by every conceivable means /～问不厌,～拿不烦 (of a shop assistant) patiently reply to customers' every question and be ready to show them the goods for the hundredth time; offer

excellent service /～花盛开。All flowers are in full bloom.

百般 bǎibān ❶ in a hundred or thousand and one ways; in every possible way; by every means: ～庇护 take all possible steps to shelter (*or* shield) sb. /～劝解 try in a hundred and one ways to help sb. to get over his worries; do one's best to appease (*or* pacify); try one's best to mediate /～阻挠 try to put a spoke in sb.'s wheel whenever possible /～照顾 show sb. every possible consideration /～挑剔 be extremely picky (*or* fault-finding, *or* nit-picking) /～温柔 be as tender as tender can be; be all tenderness /～讨好 try one's best to flatter; shine up to /～无奈 have no other way out; cannot help it; have no alternative whatsoever ❷ all kinds of; numerous: ～花色 all varieties; numerous colours and patterns /～痛苦 all kinds of suffering (*or* pain)

B

百宝箱 bǎibǎoxiāng *also* "八宝箱" bābǎoxiāng treasure box; treasure trove

百倍 bǎibèi hundred-fold; hundred times: 身价～ one's importance increases a hundredfold; rise dramatically in social status /～努力 work a hundred times harder; make redoubled efforts /展望未来,信心～。Our confidence increases a hundredfold when we think of the bright prospect ahead of us.

百弊 bǎibì all kinds of maladies or malpractices: 有～而无一利 unwise move without a single redeeming feature /～丛生。All kinds of social evils cropped up (*or* crept in). *or* All sorts of evil surfaced.

百病 bǎibìng all kinds of diseases and ailments: ～不生 be immune from disease /包治～ cure all; guarantee to put right all troubles /～丛生。All kinds of diseases and ailments break out.

百不怎么的 bǎi bù zěnmede *also* "百不怎的"; "百不咋" 〈方言〉 not serious; not matter: 这事说了～,不说倒是个事儿。It won't be much of a problem if you make a clean breast of it. Otherwise it might get you into trouble.

百步穿杨 bǎibù-chuānyáng shoot an arrow through a willow leaf from a hundred paces away; shoot with infallible precision: 有～之能 can shoot an arrow with infallible precision; be a crack (*or* dead) shot

百部 bǎibù 〈中药〉 tuber of stemona (*Stemona japonica* or *Stemona sessilifolia*)

百尺竿头,更进一步 bǎi chǐ gāntóu, gèng jìn yī bù even if you have climbed a hundred feet up a pole, go still higher; make still better progress; forge further ahead: 希望大家～,取得更好的成绩。I wish you still better success.

百尺高楼平地起 bǎi chǐ gāolóu píngdì qǐ high buildings rise from the ground — everything starts from scratch; from little acorns big oaks do grow

百出 bǎichū full of; innumerable: 错误～ full of errors /漏洞～ plenty of loopholes /洋相～ make a terrible spectacle (*or* fool) of oneself

百川归海 bǎichuān-guīhǎi all rivers empty into the sea; all roads lead to Rome; all trends tend in one direction; everyone turns to sb. for guidance: 犹如～,各方英才都汇聚到了这座城市。Like rivers emptying into the sea, talented people from all quarters are assembled in this city.

百读不厌 bǎidú-bùyàn one never gets bored even if one reads sth. for the hundredth time; be worth reading a hundred times: 这真是本～的好书。This is a wonderful book you'll never tire of reading.

百端 bǎiduān ❶ various; multifarious: 变幻～ multifarious changes ❷ undertakings or feelings of all kinds: ～交集。A multitude of feelings (*or* thoughts) crowd in upon one. *or* All sorts of sentiments (*or* feelings) well up in one's mind. /～待举。A thousand things remain to be done. *or* Numerous tasks have yet to be undertaken.

百儿八十 bǎi'er-bāshí 〈口语〉 about a hundred; some one hundred; a hundred or so

百发百中 bǎifā-bǎizhòng ❶ every shot hits the bull's-eye; shoot with unfailing precision ❷ act with absolute certainty; do without fail: 他料事如神,～。His predictions are always accurate.

百方 bǎifāng ❶ all quarters: 一人有难,～支援。When one is in trouble, help comes from all sides (*or* quarters). ❷ a hundred and one ways; various means: ～调治,终未奏效。Various ways have been tried to restore his health, but to no avail.

百废待举 bǎifèi-dàijǔ a host of neglected tasks cries out for attention; a thousand and one things wait to be done

百废俱兴 bǎifèi-jùxīng *also* "百废具举" all neglected tasks are being undertaken; do a hundred and one things at the same time

百分 bǎifēn per cent; percent: ～之十 ten percent /～之一 one percent; one hundredth /～误差〈数学〉 percentage error

百分比 bǎifēnbǐ percentage: 按～计算,教育经费绝不算高。In terms of percentage, the appropriation for education is by no means high. / 学外语的女生所占的～较高。There is a higher percentage of girl students majoring in foreign languages.

百分表 bǎifēnbiǎo dial gauge (to the precision of 0.01 millimetre)

百分尺 bǎifēnchǐ *also* "分厘卡" fēnlíkǎ; "千分尺" qiānfēnchǐ micrometre

百分点 bǎifēndiǎn percentage point: 力争通货膨胀率下降五个～ strive for a drop of five percentage points in the inflation rate

百分号 bǎifēnhào percentage symbol (%); percent sign

百分率 bǎifēnlǜ percentage; percent: 命中目标～ percentage of hits /最大～ highest percentage /反对票～是多少? What's the percentage of the dissenting votes? *or* How large is the dissenting vote percentage-wise?

百分数 bǎifēnshù percentage

百分位 bǎifēnwèi 〈统计〉 percentile

百分之百 bǎifēnzhībǎi hundred percent; entirely; out and out; absolutely: 有～的把握 be a hundred percent sure; be absolutely certain /这是～的捏造。This is sheer fabrication.

百分制 bǎifēnzhì hundred-point or percentage system: 五分制与～ five-grade system and hundred-point system

百感交集 bǎigǎn-jiāojí a multitude of feelings surge up; all sorts of feelings well up in one's heart

百合 bǎihé 〈植物〉 lily; lily bulb

百花奖 Bǎihuājiǎng Hundred Flowers Award (for movies, initiated by the film magazine *Popular Movies* 《大众电影》 in 1962 and conferred on the basis of votes of fans)

百花齐放 bǎihuā-qífàng ❶ a hundred flowers blossom at the same time — free development of different varieties and styles of art and literature ❷ flourishing art and literature

百花齐放,百家争鸣 bǎihuā qífàng, bǎijiā zhēngmíng let a hundred flowers blossom and a hundred schools of thought contend — a policy designed in 1956 to promote the sciences and culture

百花齐放,推陈出新 bǎihuā qífàng, tuīchén chūxīn let a hundred flowers blossom and weed through the old to bring forth the new — a policy formulated in the early 1960's to develop theatrical art in socialist society

百花争妍 bǎihuā-zhēngyán all flowers vie for beauty or glamour; the flowers are a riot of colours

百喙莫辩 bǎihuì-mòbiàn *see* "百口莫辩"

百货 bǎihuò general merchandise: 日用～ articles of everyday use /～商店 department store; general store

百计 bǎijì a hundred and one strategems; all sorts of ways and means: ～阻挠 try to obstruct sth. by every possible means

百家 bǎijiā ❶ hundred schools of thought (in ancient times): 诸子～ the various schools of thought and their exponents (during the period from pre-Qin times to the early years of the Han Dynasty) ❷ many households; many families

百家饭 bǎijiāfàn ❶ 〈旧语〉 meal prepared with rice and flour collected from many families (superstition has it that such a meal can rid the family of misfortunes) ❷ *used in the following phrase*: 吃～ go begging (for a living)

百家锁 bǎijiāsuǒ ornament in the shape of an old-fashioned padlock, bought with money donated by relatives and friends, worn by a baby as a symbol of long life

百家姓 Bǎijiāxìng Book of (China's) Family Names

百家言 bǎijiāyán views of a hundred schools

百家衣 bǎijiāyī ❶ dress made of odd bits of cloth donated by many families, worn by a baby as a symbol of long life ❷ patchwork outer vestment worn by a Buddhist monk

百家争鸣 bǎijiā-zhēngmíng ❶ contention of numerous schools of thought in the period of the Spring and Autumn Annals (春秋), and of the Warring States (战国) ❷ *see* "百花齐放,百家争鸣"

百脚 bǎijiǎo 〈方言〉〈动物〉 centipede

百洁布 bǎijiébù scouring pad

百科全书 bǎikē quánshū encyclopaedia: 《不列颠～》 *also* 《大英～》 *Encyclopaedia Britannica*

百科全书派 Bǎikē Quánshūpài Encyclopaedists (headed by Denis Diderot, François de Voltaire and others in 18th century France)
百孔千疮 bǎikǒng-qiānchuāng *also* "千疮百孔" honeycombed with gaping wounds; afflicted with all disorders
百口莫辩 bǎikǒu-mòbiàn even a hundred mouths can't clear things up—find it impossible to justify oneself whatever arguments one may put forward; be very difficult to clarify the matter under the present circumstances: 你这么说,我可是~呀。If you insist on saying so, I just couldn't explain myself even if I had a hundred tongues.
百老汇 Bǎilǎohuì Broadway: ~大街 Broadway Street (running northwest and southeast through New York City) / ~剧院 Broadway Theater (in New York City)
百里才 bǎilǐcái 〈书面〉 man of small talent, capable only of running a county: 此人非~,将来必有大用。He is not a man of small talent but one destined to play a major role in the country.
百里挑一 bǎilǐ-tiāoyī one in a hundred; cream of the crop; pick: 他的手艺真是~。He is indeed one in a hundred in workmanship. /这姑娘是本地~的美人。The girl is a rare beauty locally.
百里香 bǎilǐxiāng 〈植物〉 thyme
百炼成钢 bǎiliàn-chénggāng be tempered into steel: 在极端艰苦的环境中~ be tempered in the crucible of great hardships
百炼千锤 bǎiliàn-qiānchuí *also* "千锤百炼" thoroughly tempered; tempered through repeated trials
百灵 bǎilíng 〈动物〉 lark: ~之歌 song of the lark
百伶百俐 bǎilíng-bǎilì very clever; very bright: ~的姑娘 very bright girl
百米赛跑 bǎimǐ sàipǎo 100-metre dash or sprint
百慕大 Bǎimùdà Bermuda: ~人 Bermudan / ~三角区 Bermuda Triangle (known as the Devil's Triangle for the mysterious disappearance of many ships and aircraft) / ~高气压 〈气象〉 Bermuda high
百衲本 bǎinàběn book containing selections from various texts or editions
百衲衣 bǎinàyī ❶ *kasaa*, a patchwork outer vestment worn by a Buddhist monk ❷ heavily patched garment
百乃定 bǎinǎidìng 〈药学〉 panadin
百年 bǎinián ❶ hundred years; century; many years: ~大业 cause that lasts a hundred years; task (*or* project) of enduring significance ❷ lifetime; human span: 〈婉词〉 ~之后 after sb. is gone; when sb. passes away; after sb.'s death
百年不遇 bǎinián-bùyù not likely to happen once in a century: 这可是~的好机会。This is really a rare opportunity.
百年大计 bǎinián-dàjì (a project) of vital and lasting importance: 建立这座核电站是~。The setting up of the nuclear power plant is a project of enduring importance. /~,质量第一。Projects of enduring importance call for good quality above all else.
百年纪念 bǎinián jìniàn centenary; centennial
百年树人 bǎinián-shùrén it takes a hundred years to make education bear fruit: 十年树木,~。It takes ten years to grow trees but a hundred years to rear people.
百年偕老 bǎinián-xiélǎo be happily married and reach a ripe old age together
百鸟朝凤 bǎiniǎo-cháofèng all birds pay homage to the phoenix — peace and prosperity reign under a sagacious sovereign; all girls rotate round a supreme beauty
百犬吠声 bǎiquǎn-fèishēng one single bark sets all dogs in the neighourhood yapping; follow the herd or the herd instinct
百人百姓,百人百心 bǎirén bǎixìng, bǎirén bǎixīn as people have different names, so they have different natures; people differ in mind and character
百日咳 bǎirìké whooping cough; pertussis: ~疫苗 pertussis vaccine
百日维新 Bǎirì Wéixīn "Hundred Days Reform"—Reform movement of 1898
see also "戊戌变法" Wùxū Biànfǎ
百十 bǎi-shí a hundred or so; some hundred: ~来人 some hundred people
百世 bǎishì hundred generations; long period of time; through the ages: 流芳~ leave a good name for generations; hand down one's good name to posterity
百事可乐 Bǎishì Kělè Pepsi Cola: ~公司 (US) Pepsi Co. Inc.
百事通 bǎishìtōng person who behaves as if he knew everything; Mr. Know-all or Know-it-all
百兽之王 bǎishòuzhīwáng king of all animals — the lion
百思不解 bǎisī-bùjiě fail to understand sth. after thinking it over a hundred times; not have a clue though one has pondered long over the matter: 这个问题我真有点~。The problem remains a mystery to me though I have spent a good deal of time pondering over it.
百岁老人 bǎisuì lǎorén centenarian
百听不厌 bǎitīng-bùyàn (of a story, etc.) be worth hearing a hundred times; (of people) never get bored even if one hears it for the hundredth time
百团大战 Bǎituán Dàzhàn Hundred-Regiment Campaign, large-scale offensive launched by the Eighth Route Army against Japanese aggressors from 20 Aug. to 5 Dec. 1940 in which over 100 regiments of the former took part
百万 bǎiwàn million: ~富翁 millionaire / ~雄师 million bold warriors; mighty army (of one million) / ~分之一 part per million; ppm
百万吨 bǎiwàndūn megaton: ~级 〈船舶〉 megatonnage / ~梯恩梯当量 megaton TNT equivalent
百万伏特 bǎiwàn fútè 〈电学〉 megavolt
百万买宅,千万买邻 bǎiwàn mǎi zhái, qiānwàn mǎi lín 〈俗语〉 a good neighbour is more precious than a house worth a million
百闻不如一见 bǎi wén bùrú yī jiàn it is better to see once than hear a hundred times; seeing is believing
百无禁忌 bǎiwújìnjì all taboos are in abeyance; nothing is taboo; no restrictions of any kind are imposed: 姜太公在此,~。When Patriarch Jiang (legendary character with magic power) is present, all taboos are in abeyance. *or* When somebody (I, you, he, etc.) is around, all can play without restraint. /此人口直心快,说话做事~。This chap is frank and straightforward, and he speaks or acts without fear.
百无聊赖 bǎiwúliáolài not know what to do with oneself; languish in boredom: 我~地开了电视,看了一会儿。I turned on the TV out of sheer boredom and watched for a while. /他~地在街上漫步。Having nothing better to do, he took a stroll in the street.
百无是处 bǎiwúshìchù *also* "百无一是" absolutely nothing is right; nothing is quite gratifying or satisfactory: 有些人看别人~,看自己则毫无缺点。Some people can never find anything positive in others or anything wrong with themselves.
百无一失 bǎiwúyīshī nothing can possibly go wrong; there's no risk at all: 请放心,保你~。You may set your mind at ease; there is no risk at all.
百物 bǎiwù all kinds of commodities or goods; general merchandise: ~昂贵 Things are very expensive.
百响 bǎixiǎng 〈方言〉 hundred fire crackers woven into one long braid; firecrackers
百姓 bǎixìng common people; ordinary people; civilians; the populace: ~足,君孰与不足。When the people are well off, how can the monarch not be?
百业 bǎiyè various trades; all industries: ~凋敝。All business languishes. *or* There is a general slump in the market. /~萧条。Business is slack in all trades. /~兴旺。A scene of prosperity prevails in all sectors of the economy.
百叶 bǎiyè 〈方言〉 ❶ dried thin pieces of bean cream: ~裹肉 minced meat wrapped in *baiye* pieces ❷ cow's or sheep's tripe: 牛~ cow's tripe
百叶窗 bǎiyèchuāng *also* "百页窗" ❶ shutter; (Venetian) blind; jalousie; louvre: ~板 louvre board ❷ 〈机械〉 device resembling a Venetian blind: ~炉 louvre-type oven / ~式倍增系统 venetian-blind dynode system
百叶箱 bǎiyèxiāng 〈气象〉 thermometer screen
百依百顺 bǎiyī-bǎishùn obedient in everything; docile; all obedience: 对某人~ comply with every whim of sb. /她要求儿子~,殊不知,这最终会害了他。She wanted her son to be all obedience and docility, not realizing that this would eventually do him great harm.
百战百胜 bǎizhàn-bǎishèng fight a hundred battles and always emerge the victor; be ever-victorious
百战不殆 bǎizhàn-bùdài fight a hundred battles with no danger of defeat: 知己知彼,~。Know the enemy and know yourself, and

you can fight a hundred battles with no danger of defeat.
百折不挠 bǎizhé-bùnáo *also* "百折不回" show no sign of weakness despite repeated setbacks; be indomitable: ～的战士 dauntless fighter / 在困难面前表现～的精神 display an indomitable spirit in the face of adversity
百褶裙 bǎizhěqún pleated skirt
百足 bǎizú 〈动物〉❶ (another name for 马陆) julid (*Orthomorpha pekuensis*), a millipede of the family *Julidae* ❷ (popular name for 蜈蚣) centipede
百足之虫,死而不僵 bǎi zú zhī chóng, sǐ ér bù jiāng a julid wriggles even after being cut dead; traditional forces die hard; an established family, regime, etc. lingers on though bankrupt

B

佰

bǎi hundred (used for the number 百 on cheques, receipts, etc. to avoid mistakes or alterations)

柏(栢)

bǎi ❶ cypress; cedar; tree of cypress family: 侧～ oriental arborvitae / 刺～ Chinese juniper ❷ (Bǎi) a surname
see also bó; bò
柏树 bǎishù cypress
柏松 bǎisōng cypress pine
柏油 bǎiyóu asphalt; tar; pitch: ～路 asphalt road; tarmac road / ～碎石 tarmacadam / ～混凝土 tar concrete / ～喷洒机 tar sprayer / 铺路～ road tar
柏油纸 bǎiyóuzhǐ a kind of wrapping paper made of two sheets of paper with tar in between to keep things dry
柏子仁 bǎizǐrén 〈中药〉seed of Oriental arborvitae

伯

bǎi *used in* "大伯子" (husband's elder brother; brother-in-law)
see also bó

摆[1](擺)

bǎi ❶ put; lay; place; set in order: ～碗筷 lay (*or* set) the table / 把花盆～在窗台上 put a flowerpot on the windowsill / ～正个人与集体和国家之间的关系 put oneself in a correct relationship with the collective and the state / 水面上一字儿～开十几条渔船。A dozen or so fishing boats were afloat in a row. ❷ put on; assume; show off: ～威风 give oneself airs; put on airs / ～老资格 strike the pose of an elder; flaunt one's seniority / ～出一副傲慢的面孔 assume an air of arrogance / ～出一副可怜相 pretend to be pitiable ❸ sway; swing; wave: 大摇大～ strut; swagger / 鱼尾巴在水中～来～去。The tail of the fish swayed in the water. ❹〈物理〉pendulum: 单～ simple pendulum / 复～ compound pendulum ❺ set forth; state; speak: ～条件 lay down terms; offer conditions / ～出充分理由 give adequate reasons for doing sth.; make a well-reasoned statement; argue one's case well / 把问题～到桌面上来 place the cards on the table; bring the issue out into the open / ～困难, ～利害 list the difficulties and discuss the advantages and disadvantages of the matter involved / 咱们来～一～。Let's have a chat.

摆[2](擺、襬)

bǎi lower hem of a jacket, skirt or gown

摆[3](擺)

bǎi *bai*, Buddhist service or mass gathering to celebrate a festival etc. in China's Dai areas
摆臂 bǎibì oscillation or swing arm
摆布 bǎibu ❶ arrange; decorate; furnish: 这屋子～得十分雅致。The room is furnished in excellent taste. *or* The room is elegantly appointed. ❷ order about; manipulate; have at one's mercy: 任意～别人的命运 wilfully manipulate the fate of sb. else / 任人～ allow oneself to be dictated to; be at sb.'s mercy / 喜欢～人 like to boss others about; be bossy
摆锤 bǎichuí 〈机械〉pendulum bob: ～式冲击试验 pendulum impact test
摆荡 bǎidàng sway; wave: 风起浪涌,船身～。The rising wind and waves rocked the boat. / 柳枝随风轻盈～。The branches of the willow are waving gracefully in the wind.
摆档 bǎidàng 〈方言〉set up a stall: ～卖小吃 set up a stall to sell snacks
摆地摊 bǎi dìtān set up a temporary stall or simply lay out various articles for sale on a newspaper, cloth, etc. spread out on the ground
摆动 bǎidòng sway; oscillate; wave: ～轴 oscillating axle / ～装置 pendulous gadget / 闹钟上的猫眼随着秒针的走动而来回～着。The cat's eyes on the alarm clock's dial plate flickered as the second hand ticked around.
摆动角 bǎidòngjiǎo angle of oscillation; swinging angle
摆动疗法 bǎidòng liáofǎ 〈医学〉pendulum therapy
摆动轮 bǎidònglún wobble wheel
摆动式喷灌机 bǎidòngshì pēnguànjī oscillating sprinkler
摆度 bǎidù swing
摆渡 bǎidù ❶ ferry (sb. or sth.) across a river: 先～物资。Ferry the essential goods across first. / 将这么多人～过去要三个来回。It will take three trips to ferry so many people across. ❷ ferry across; go across by ferry: 我不会游泳,只能～过去。As I'm no swimmer, I can only go across the river by ferry. ❸ ferry boat: 乘～过江 cross the river by ferry
摆饭 bǎifàn lay the table
摆放 bǎifàng lay; place; put in a certain place: 屋里～着新家具。The room is furnished with new furniture.
摆份儿 bǎifènr 〈方言〉go in for ostentation and extravagance; put on airs; throw one's weight about: 在新媳妇面前摆婆婆的份儿 put on the airs of a mother-in-law before the son's bride / 书架上插着几本精装书摆摆份儿。A few de luxe editions were put on the shelves for show.
摆幅 bǎifú range or amplitude of oscillation
摆富 bǎifù parade or flaunt one's wealth; be ostentatious and extravagant
摆杆 bǎigān *see* "摆轴"
摆格 bǎigé 〈方言〉put on airs
摆供 bǎigòng present offerings; offer sacrifices
摆古 bǎigǔ 〈方言〉tell stories: 老爷爷给孩子们～。Grandpa is telling the children stories.
摆咕 bǎigu 〈方言〉❶ fiddle with: 这小孩喜欢～他的小木枪。The kid likes to fiddle with his toy pistol. ❷ repair; fix: 这个闹钟,他～了半天也没修好。He has spent a long time trying in vain to fix the alarm clock. ❸ treat; cure: 老王那么顽固的气管炎都让大夫～好了,真不简单。It's remarkable that the doctor has cured Lao Wang of his chronic bronchitis.
摆好 bǎihǎo enumerate sb.'s merits; commend; praise: 评功～ enumerate sb.'s merits; speak of sb. in glowing terms / 你怎么老是给他～? Why are you singing his praises all the time?
摆划 bǎihua 〈方言〉❶ move back and forth again and again; keep on fiddling with; meddle with: 你别瞎～。Don't meddle with it. ❷ deal with; arrange: 这件事真不好～。The matter is difficult to deal with. *or* This is really a hard nut to crack. ❸ put in order; repair; fix: ～好了,就能把这些废渣变成宝贝。The waste can be turned into treasure if treated properly.
摆簧 bǎihuáng pendulum spring
摆晃 bǎihuàng sway; rock; totter; dodder: 他突然感到有些头晕,眼一阵黑,身子向两边～。Suddenly he felt giddy, and everything went black, and he began to sway from side to side.
摆架子 bǎi jiàzi put on airs; assume great airs: 他不受欢迎的原因是爱～。He is unpopular because he likes to put on airs.
摆件 bǎijiàn ornaments; furnishings
摆脚 bǎijiǎo 〈方言〉ferry: ～船 ferry-boat; ferry / 咱们要～了。Now we are ferrying across.
摆酒 bǎijiǔ spread or give a feast (in sb.'s honour)
摆锯 bǎijù 〈机械〉pendulum saw
摆款儿 bǎikuǎnr put on airs; assume great airs: 白吃我的饭不领情,还想～! He had the cheek to put on airs with me after enjoying a meal at my expense.
摆阔 bǎikuò flaunt or show off one's wealth; show a desire for pomp and extravagance
摆擂台 bǎi lèitái set up a stage for contest and invite challengers; take on challengers or comers one by one
see also "擂台"
摆列 bǎiliè arrange; display; place: 屋里桌椅板凳～得整整齐齐。Tables, chairs, and benches are neatly arranged in the room.
摆龙门阵 bǎi lóngménzhèn 〈方言〉chat; spin a yarn; chew the fat: 他们一有空就～。They love to spin yarns whenever they have time to spare. / ～,他本领不小。He has the gift of gab. *or* He's quite a conversationalist.

摆轮 bǎilún balance wheel (of a mechanical watch or clock); balance:～游丝系统 balance and hair spring system
摆卖 bǎimài ❶ *see* "摆档" ❷ display goods for sale:地摊上～的差不多都是日用品。Almost all the things on street stalls are daily necessities.
摆门面 bǎi ménmian keep up appearances:家道衰落了,他仍然拼命～。Though his family was on the decline, he still made a desperate effort to keep up appearances.
摆门子 bǎi ménzi 〈方言〉chat; chitchat
摆弄 bǎinòng ❶ move back and forth; fiddle with:不停地～铅笔 fiddle with a pencil /你在那儿～什么呢? What are you twiddling with there? ❷ order about; manipulate:你如果愿意任人～,你就这样干下去。You can go on like this if you are willing to allow yourself to be ordered about. /她分明是在～你。She is evidently making a fool of you (*or* twisting you round her little finger). ❸〈方言〉do; manage; handle:～牲口 handle draught animals /～文字,他可是行家了。He is an expert in juggling with words. *or* He is a skilful writer.
摆平 bǎipíng ❶ treat equally; strike a balance; be even-handed or impartial:两边要～ be fair to both sides; be even-handed /必须～学习和体育锻炼的关系。It's necessary to pay equal attention to both study and physical training. ❷〈方言〉punish; mete out punishment to:找个人将他～ have him punished
摆谱儿 bǎipǔr 〈方言〉❶ keep up appearances; show off:爱～的人 showy person /她经济本来不宽裕,可是硬要～。Though she is not well-off, she tries to keep up appearances. ❷ put on airs; throw one's weight about:提升以后,他就跟原来的同事们～了。After his promotion, he began to throw his weight about (*or* put on airs) before his former colleagues.
摆设 bǎishè furnish and decorate:新房里～得既豪华又大方。The bridal chamber is luxuriously and tastefully furnished. /聋子的耳朵——～而已。Like a deaf person's ears, it's of no practical use (*or* purely ornamental).
摆设儿 bǎisher ❶ ornaments; furnishings; decorations:小～ knickknacks /会客室里的～朴素大方。The sitting room is adorned simply and in good taste. ❷ purely ornamental object; figurehead:他这个主席是个～,事情都是秘书长在做。As chairman, he is only a figure head; all business is conducted by the secretary-general. /这些精密仪器没有什么用处,搁在实验室里成了～。These precision instruments are of no use in the laboratory; they are only placed there for show.
摆式打桩机 bǎishì dǎzhuāngjī pendulum pile driver
摆式地震仪 bǎishì dìzhènyí pendulum seismograph
摆式吊车 bǎishì diàochē pendulum crane
摆式风速机 bǎishì fēngsùjī pendulum anemometer
摆式锯 bǎishìjù swinging saw
摆式破碎机 bǎishì pòsuìjī pendulum crusher
摆矢 bǎishǐ 〈物理〉pendulum vector
摆事实,讲道理 bǎi shìshí, jiǎng dàoli present the facts and reason things out:只有～,才能使人心服口服。You can convince people completely and truly only when you base your argument on facts and reason things out.
摆手 bǎishǒu ❶ shake one's hand in disapproval:～让大家走开 signal all of them to leave; wave all of them away ❷ wave one's hand; beckon:两人不知道说什么好,只是互相摆了摆手。Not knowing what to say, they merely waved to each other.
摆手舞 bǎishǒuwǔ folk dance of Tujia (土家) nationality characterized by hand-waving movement before one's chest
摆台 bǎitái lay the table for a (usu. western-style) meal
摆摊子 bǎi tānzi *also* "摆摊儿" ❶ set up a stall:小贩只能在规定的路段～。Vendors are only allowed to set up their stalls at assigned road sections. ❷ set things out for work; get ready for work:他刚摆开摊子,就碰到许多问题。No sooner had he started work than he found himself facing many problems. ❸ go in for ostentation or the grand style:他干的一切都是为了～。All he has done is just for show./ 制定计划时不要～,追求形式。Go in neither for quantitative gains nor for outward impressiveness in planning.
摆谈 bǎitán 〈方言〉❶ narrate; relate; recount:他们在那里围着篝火～故事。Around the campfire they were relating tales to each other. ❷ chat; have a talk:小张最近好像有心事,我想跟他个别～～。It seems Xiao Zhang has something on his mind and I'll have a talk with him alone.
摆脱 bǎituō shake off; break away from; free or extricate oneself from:～追兵 shake off the pursuing enemy /～贫困 shake off (*or* get rid of) poverty /～困境 extricate oneself from a predicament; resolve a dilemma /～战争危险 avert the danger of war /～有害的影响 overcome a harmful influence /～封建观念的束缚 cast off the yoke of the feudal ethical code /～错误思想 rid oneself of erroneous thinking /～繁琐杂事 release oneself from the tangle of trivial matters /～精神负担 be relieved of mental burdens /～旧思想、旧习惯 shed old ideas and ways
摆尾 bǎiwěi wag the tail:～行驶 (of a vehicle) fishtailing /摇头～ wagging one's head complacently; with smug complacency /小狗摆着尾巴迎了上来。The little dog greeted us with a wag of its tail.
摆乌龙 bǎi wūlóng 〈方言〉be confused; be bewildered; misunderstand
摆舞 bǎiwǔ swing; sway; flutter:柳枝随风～。The willow twigs are swaying in the wind.
摆线 bǎixiàn 〈数学〉cycloid:～轨迹 cycloid path /～运动 cycloid motion /～曲线 cycloid curve
摆宴 bǎiyàn host a banquet; feast:～饯行 give (sb.) a farewell dinner party /城里到处～欢庆胜利。There was much feasting in the city to celebrate the victory.
摆样子 bǎi yàngzi do for show:他不读书,桌上堆着书只是为了～。He rarely reads, and the books piled up on his desk are meant to give false impressions. /他满脸诚恳,但那是～。He seemed to be all sincerity, but that was only for show.
摆针 bǎizhēn pointer (on a meter, etc.)
摆阵 bǎizhèn arrange a battle formation; draw up a battle line:摆出一字长蛇阵 deploy troops in a single-line battle array /～是古代的一种战术。To deploy troops in a battle formation was a tactical art in ancient war.
摆振 bǎizhèn 〈航空〉hunt
摆置 bǎizhi put; place; arrange:建筑工地上砖瓦木料都～得整整齐齐。Bricks, tiles and timber are all stacked in good order at the construction site.
摆治 bǎizhi 〈方言〉❶ attend; look after:这块地他～得不错。He has done a good job in cultivating this plot of land. /小马驹病了,他～了一夜。He spent the whole night tending the sick colt. ❷ torture; punish:他把我～得好苦。He caused me a great deal of suffering. ❸ order about; manipulate; dominate; control:他既然上了圈套,就不得不听人家～。Having fallen into the trap prepared for him, he had to do what he was told.
摆钟 bǎizhōng pendulum clock
摆轴 bǎizhóu *also* "摆杆" pendulum shaft or rod; balance staff
摆桌 bǎizhuō throw a dinner party; give a feast:今日请朋友,在家里～。I'm going to invite some friends to dinner at home today.
摆子 bǎizi 〈方言〉malaria:打～ suffer from malaria

捭

bǎi 〈书面〉open; separate
捭阖 bǎihé 〈书面〉open and close—use various means or ways to separate or combine (different forces, factions, etc.):～之术 art of strategic separation and combination
see also "纵横捭阖" zònghéng-bǎihé

bài

鞴(韛)

bài 〈方言〉bellows:风～ bellows /～拐子 bellow's handle

呗

bài *see* "梵呗" fànbài
see also bei

败

bài ❶ be defeated; lose:～下阵来 lose a battle (*or* contest) /转～为胜 turn defeat into victory; snatch a victory out of defeat /一～涂地 suffer a crushing defeat /立于不～之地 remain invincible; be in an impregnable position /骄兵必～。Pride goes before a fall. /兵～如山倒。A rout is like a landslide. /主队以零比三～于客队。The host team lost to the visiting team nil to 3. ❷ defeat; beat:大～对手 thoroughly trounce the opponent /击～入侵者 beat back (*or* repulse) the invaders /挫～了敌人的谍报活动 frustrate the activities of enemy espionage ❸ fail:成～ success or failure /此事难成易～。

The matter is difficult of success but liable to failure. ❹ spoil; ruin: ～胃口 spoil one's appetite / 成事不足, ～事有余 can accomplish nothing but may spoil the show; never make, but always mar; be worse than useless / 事情就～在他手里。It was he who bungled the whole business. ❺ counteract: see "～毒" ❻ decay; wither: 腐～ corrupt; rotten; decayed / 衰～ decline; be on the decline; fall into decay / 破～ ruined; dilapidated / 枯枝～叶 dead twigs and withered leaves / 没有久开不～的花。No flowers remain fresh all the time. or All blooms fade sooner or later. ❼ cause the decline of; ruin

B

败北 bàiběi 〈书面〉 suffer defeat; lose a battle or war: 这个队在最近的比赛中接连～。This team suffered one defeat after another recently.

败笔 bàibǐ faulty stroke in calligraphy or painting; faulty expression in writing; flaw or fault in an otherwise perfect work: 文章写得不错, 但有一处～。The essay is well written except for one fault (or flaw). / 名家的作品也免不了有～。Even the work of a master may not be free from faults (or flawless)

败兵 bàibīng defeated army; routed troops

败草 bàicǎo withered grass: ～残花 withered grass and fallen flowers

败毒 bàidú ❶ 〈医学〉 counteract or neutralize a toxin; detoxify; detoxicate ❷〈中医〉 relieve internal heat or fever

败坏 bàihuài ❶ ruin; undermine; corrupt: ～声誉 discredit; defame / ～学校的纪律 undermine school discipline / 她用流言蜚语～别人的名誉。She ruined others' good names by malicious gossip. ❷ degenerate; dissipate; corrupt: 道德～ morally degenerate / 纪律～ lax discipline / 社会风气～ corrupt social values; depraved social morals; degenerate mores

败坏门楣 bàihuài-ménméi bring discredit on one's family; disgrace one's family

败火 bàihuǒ 〈中医〉 relieve internal heat (or inflammation)

败绩 bàijì 〈书面〉 be utterly defeated; be routed: 敌军～, 我军乘胜追击。The enemy were thoroughly trounced and we pursued on the crest of victory.

败家 bàijiā cause the decline of a family (in wealth and position); dissipate a family fortune: 由投机起家的, 也会因投机而～。Those who make their fortune by speculation will ruin it the same way.

败家子 bàijiāzǐ spendthrift; wastrel; prodigal: 慷公家之慨的～ wastrel who spends public money like water (or is generous at public expense) / 他是个～, 一分钱都攒不起来。He's a spendthrift, incapable of saving a single penny.

败将 bàijiàng defeated general; loser (in a match or game): 手下～ one's defeated opponent; one's vanquished foe

败酱 bàijiàng 〈植物〉 *Patrinia scabiosaefolia*: ～草科 *Valerianaceae* / 白花～ *Patrinia villosa*

败局 bàijú lost game; losing battle: 挽回～ reverse a defeat; retrieve a bad situation / ～已定。The game is lost. or The fate of defeat is as good as sealed.

败军 bàijūn ❶ bring about the defeat of the troops: ～亡国 cause military defeat and national subjugation ❷ defeated army: ～之将, 不足以言勇。The general of a defeated army is in no position to claim bravery. or A defeated general should not boast of his valour.

败类 bàilèi scum of a community; degenerate: 民族～ national traitors; dregs (or scum) of a nation / 一小撮～ a handful of degenerates

败鳞残甲 bàilín-cánjiǎ swirling snowflakes

败柳残花 bàiliǔ-cánhuā also "残花败柳" withered willows and faded flowers—fallen woman; girl who is no longer a virgin

败露 bàilù (of a plot, conspiracy, etc.) fall through and stand exposed; be brought to light: 阴谋终于～。In the end, the conspiracy was exposed. / 政变计划～后, 策划者们均已转入地下。After the aborted coup, the plotters went underground.

败落 bàiluò decline (in wealth and position): 描写一个封建大家族的～ describe the disintegration of a feudal clan / 家道～。The family is on the decline.

败衄 bàinǜ 〈书面〉 suffer defeat; be put to rout: 屡遭～ suffer one defeat after another

败色 bàishǎi ❶ fade: 他穿着一件～的旧衬衣。He is wearing a faded old shirt. ❷ symptom or anger of defeat: 中途岛战役后, 日本～已浓。After the Midway Battle, Japan had betrayed clear symptoms of defeat.

败诉 bàisù lose a lawsuit: ～人 loser of a lawsuit / ～方 the party losing a lawsuit

败退 bàituì retreat in defeat; evacuate after defeat: 节节～ retreat again and again in defeat / 经过几次较量, 敌军纷纷～。After several major trials of strength, the enemy finally retreated helter-skelter.

败亡 bàiwáng be defeated and perish: 好战者一定～。Warmongers are bound to perish in utter defeat.

败胃 bàiwèi spoil one's appetite: 我服了这副中药后有些～。I began to have a jaded appetite after taking a dose of this Chinese herbal medicine.

败谢 bàixiè wither and fall: 青春常在, 永不～。May youth always be with you and never fade.

败行 bàixíng bad conduct; misdemeanour

败兴 bàixìng ❶ dampen (sb.'s) enthusiasm; spoil (sb.'s) pleasure or interest; disappoint: ～而归 come back disappointed / 让人～的事 sth. that spoils sb.'s pleasure / 让人～的家伙 spoilsport / 这家商店常让顾客～而去。Customers often turn away dissatisfied from the shop. ❷〈方言〉 unlucky; unfortunate

败絮 bàixù cotton waste: 利用～生产再生棉或造纸。Cotton waste may be used to produce regenerated cotton or paper. / 金玉其外, 未必不是～其中。All is not gold that glitters.

败血病 bàixuèbìng 〈医学〉 septicaemia

败血性鼠疫 bàixuèxìng shǔyì 〈医学〉 septicemic plague

败叶 bàiyè fallen leaf; withered leaf: 枯枝～ dead twigs and withered leaves / 庭院里覆盖着一层～。The courtyard is covered with a layer of fallen leaves.

败意 bàiyì 〈书面〉 have one's spirits dampened; feel disappointed: 此事令人～。This is disappointing (or depressing) indeed.

败仗 bàizhàng lost battle; defeat: 打～ be defeated in battle; suffer a defeat / 连吃～ suffer defeats in rapid succession / 他在这次考试中又吃了～。He failed again in the recent exam.

败阵 bàizhèn be defeated on the battlefield; be beaten in a contest: ～而逃 lose the field and take to flight / ～而归 return defeated

败子 bàizǐ see "败家子"

败子回头 bàizǐ-huítóu also "浪子回头" làngzǐ-huítóu return or repentance of the prodigal son

败走 bàizǒu be routed; flee in defeat: ～麦城 suffer a major (or critical) defeat; have one's Waterloo / 入侵之敌遭到猛烈抵抗, 终于～。The invaders met with powerful resistance and finally fled in defeat.

拜 bài ❶ do obeisance (to sb.): ～神 worship a deity / 参～ pay respects to (a revered person or the portrait of a deceased revered person) / 朝～ worship; pay (religious) homage to; pay respects (to a monarch) / 跪～ prostrate oneself before (sb.); worship on bended knees; kowtow / 叩～ kowtow / 膜～ prostrate oneself before; worship ❷ extend greetings (on meeting people); congratulate: 团～ gather together and extend greetings to one another on New Year's Eve ❸ make a courtesy call; visit: 回～ pay a return call / ～街坊 visit one's neighbours (on moving into a neighbourhood) ❹ perform a ceremony when an official title is conferred by the emperor; (of a monarch, etc.) appoint: ～相 be made chief minister by the emperor / ～帅 be appointed supreme commander ❺ acknowledge sb. as one's master, teacher, etc.; formally establish a relationship: ～老艺人为师 acknowledge a veteran handicraftsman as one's master / ～为义父 acknowledge sb. as godfather / 结～ become sworn brothers (or sisters) ❻ 〈敬词〉 *used before some verbs*: ～谢 express one's sincere thanks / ～领 accept with thanks ❼ (Bài) a surname

拜把子 bài bǎzi become sworn brothers: 磕头～ become sworn brothers after performing the kowtow ritual

拜拜 bàibai ❶ (say) bye-bye: 对阿姨说～。Say bye-bye to Auntie. / 等钱一到手, 他就跟你～了。As soon as he gets hold of your money, he'll walk out on you. ❷〈旧语〉 (of a woman) curtsy ❸〈方言〉 offer sacrifices to gods or ancestors: 这一天是一年中最大～的日子。This is the day for the biggest memorial ceremony in the year.

拜别 bàibié 〈敬词〉 take leave of sb.: ～师友 bid farewell to one's teachers and friends / 洒泪～ part in tears

拜忏 bàichàn (of Buddhist monks or Taoist priests) pray for people's redemption; say mass for people

拜辞 bàicí 〈敬词〉 take leave of sb.: ～师长, 奔赴边疆 bid farewell to one's teachers and set out for the border area

拜赐 bàicì 〈敬词〉gratefully acknowledge the receipt of a gift
拜倒 bàidǎo 〈贬义〉prostrate oneself; fall on one's knees; grovel: ～在某人脚下 lie prostrate at sb.'s feet / ～于金钱面前 worship at the shrine of Mammon / ～在石榴裙下 be infatuated with a woman
拜祷 bàidǎo kneel and pray; implore
拜垫 bàidiàn cushion for kneeling; hassock
拜读 bàidú 〈敬词〉have the pleasure of reading; peruse with reverence: ～大作，获益不浅。I've had the pleasure of perusing your work and found it very enlightening. *or* I was very much enlightened after reading your celebrated work.
拜耳法 bài'ěrfǎ 〈冶金〉Bayer process
拜耳体 bài'ěrtǐ 〈冶金〉Bayerite
拜访 bàifǎng pay a visit; call on: 正式～ formal (*or* official) visit / 专程～ make a special (*or* exclusive) visit / 顺便～ drop in (on sb.) / ～亲朋好友 call on one's close relatives and friends / 登门～ call at sb.'s house
拜佛 bàifó kneel down or prostrate oneself before the image of Buddha; worship Buddha: 烧香～ burn joss sticks (*or* incense) before the image of Buddha and kneel in prayer
拜伏 bàifú lie prostrate: ～在地 prostrate oneself on the ground (with reverence)
拜服 bàifú 〈敬词〉admire highly: 老兄高见，令人～。I have great admiration for your brilliant ideas.
拜盒 bàihé 〈方言〉*also* "拜匣" small box holding gifts, invitations, etc., for friends when one calls on them; gift box
拜贺 bàihè 〈敬词〉send or offer greetings; extend congratulations: ～新年 wish sb. a Happy New Year; offer New Year greetings
拜候 bàihòu 〈敬词〉pay one's respects to; call to offer one's greetings: 登门～ call at sb.'s house to pay one's respects
拜会 bàihuì (often used on diplomatic occasions) pay a call on sb.; call on: 正式～ pay an official call on sb. / 礼节性～ courtesy call / 告别～ farewell call / 私人～ personal visit / 私下～ private call / 事务性～ business call / ～人 caller; visitor
拜火教 Bàihuǒjiào Zoroastrianism; Mazdaism
拜见 bàijiàn pay a formal visit; call to pay one's respects: ～总统 call on the president to pay respects / 要求～国王陛下 request an audience with his majesty the king / ～师傅 pay one's respects to one's master (*or* teacher); visit one's master
拜节 bàijié extend one's greetings on festive occasions: 去爷爷家～ visit grandpa to offer festival greetings / 春节期间，亲朋相互～。During the Spring Festival, relatives and friends meet each other to exchange festive greetings.
拜金 bàijīn worship of money
拜金主义 bàijīnzhǔyì money worship; Mammonism: ～者 Mammonist
拜爵 bàijué confer a title of nobility (at a special ceremony)
拜客 bàikè call on sb.; pay a call to sb.; pay visits: 这几个月他常出门～。For the last few months, he has been going round to make social calls.
拜恳 bàikěn 〈敬词〉respectfully implore or request: ～驾临。Your gracious presence is cordially requested.
拜聆 bàilíng 〈敬词〉listen respectfully: ～高论 listen respectfully to your enlightening remarks
拜领 bàilǐng 〈敬词〉accept with gratitude: 你的心意我～了，但礼物不能收。I appreciate your kindness but cannot accept the gift. / ～厚赐，不胜感激。I accept your generous gift with boundless gratitude. *or* I wish to extend my deep gratitude to you for your generous gift.
拜伦 Bàilún George Gordon Byron (1788-1824), English poet
拜门 bàimén ❶ call (at sb.'s house) to extend thanks ❷ (of newlyweds) pay a visit to the bride's parents ❸ formally acknowledge sb. as one's master or teacher; take sb. as one's teacher: ～弟子 formally acknowledged pupil; initiated disciple
拜盟 bàiméng become sworn brothers
拜命 bàimìng receive orders from the sovereign
拜年 bàinián pay a New Year call; send New Year greetings; wish a Happy New Year: 电话～ send New Year greetings over the phone; wish (sb.) a Happy New Year over the phone / 每年春节，来老教授家～的学生特别多。During the Spring Festival, many pupils came to the old professor's home to extend New Year greetings (*or* to wish him a Happy New Year).
拜请 bàiqǐng respectfully request or invite sb. (to do sth.)
拜认 bàirèn hold a special ceremony to formally acknowledge sb. as one's master (adoptive father, adoptive mother, etc.)
拜扫 bàisǎo hold a memorial service for a deceased person before the tomb: ～烈士陵墓 hold a memorial service and pay respects to the martyrs before their tombs
拜上帝会 Bài Shàngdì Huì God Worshipping Society, a peasant revolutionary organization founded in 1843 by Hong Xiuquan (洪秀全), leader of the Taiping Revolution
拜师 bàishī acknowledge sb. as master or teacher: ～学艺 be formally apprenticed to a master worker to learn a skill
拜识 bàishí ❶〈敬词〉get acquainted with; make sb.'s acquaintance: ～尊颜，十分荣幸。I am very much honoured to make your acquaintance. ❷〈方言〉sworn brother; bosom friend: 他是我的～。He is my sworn brother (*or* one of my best friends).
拜寿 bàishòu congratulate (usu. an elderly person) on his or her birthday; offer birthday felicitations
拜堂 bàitáng (of bride and groom) make formal bows to the groom's parents at the traditional wedding ceremony; perform the wedding ceremony: ～成亲 perform the wedding ceremony and become husband and wife; be wed
拜天地 bài tiāndì (bride and groom) bow to heaven and earth as part of the traditional wedding ceremony
拜托 bàituō 〈敬词〉ask a favour of; entrust; request: ～您为他找个差使。May I ask (*or* request) you to find a job for him? / 这件事就～给你了。I would like to leave this matter with you. / ～你捎个信儿给她。Would you be kind enough to take a message to her? / ～了。(after sb. has agreed to do sth. for one) Thank you for your help.
拜望 bàiwàng 〈敬词〉call to pay one's respects; call on: 专程去～一位老前辈 make a special trip to call on a respected senior person
拜物教 bàiwùjiào fetishism: 商品～ commodity fetishism
拜匣 bàixiá *see* "拜盒"
拜谢 bàixiè bow one's thanks; thank: ～恩人 thank one's benefactor / 登门～ call on sb. to thank him or her
拜洋 bàiyáng 〈方言〉worship everything foreign
拜谒 bàiyè ❶ pay a formal visit; call to pay respects: ～内阁总理 pay an official visit to the prime minister ❷ pay homage (at a monument, mausoleum, etc.): ～中山陵 pay one's homage at Dr. Sun Yat-sen's Mausoleum
拜占庭 Bàizhàntíng Byzantium: ～帝国 Byzantine Empire (also known as Eastern Roman Empire, 395-1453)

稗 bài ❶ barnyard grass: 敌～ Stam F-34 (*dichloro-propionanilide*) ❷〈书面〉insignificant; unofficial
稗草 bàicǎo *see* "稗子"
稗贩 bàifàn 〈书面〉❶ pedlar; vendor ❷〈贬义〉apply indiscriminately; copy mechanically (sth. trite or sb. else's idea): 辗转～ be indiscriminately applied again and again
稗官野史 bàiguān-yěshǐ unofficial history; book of anecdotes: 此事出于～。The story is an anecdote from unofficial history.
稗记 bàijì account of anecdotes; unofficial history: 浏览诸家～ read various books of anecdotes
稗史 bàishǐ book containing anecdotes; unofficial history; private record of events
稗子 bàizi 〈植物〉barnyard grass; barnyard millet

bai

唄 bai 〈助词〉*see* "呗" bei

bān

猵 bān
猵斓 bānlán gorgeous; bright, coloured; multi-coloured
see also "斑斓" bānlán

斑 bān ❶ spot; speck; speckle; stripe: 黑～ black spot; freckle / 汗～ sweat stain / 油～ oil stains; grease spots / 寿～ black speckle (on the face of aged people) / 雀～ freckle / 红～〈医学〉ery-

thema /瘀～〈医学〉ecchymosis /光～〈天文〉facula ❷ spotted; striped: ～鹟 spotted flycatcher /条～石鲈 striped bass /～驴 zebrass / ～猫 tabby

斑白 bānbái *also*"班白" bānbái grizzled; greying: 须发～ have hoary hair and beard

斑斑 bānbān full of stains or spots: 油迹～ covered with gravy stains /血迹～ blood-stained; full of bloodstains /身上泥土～ stained with mud all over one's body /脸上泪迹～ tear-stained face

B

斑斑可考 bānbān-kěkǎo every spot is a record in itself; there is clear evidence

斑鬓 bānbìn grey-templed; grey-haired

斑驳 bānbó *also*"班驳" bānbó 〈书面〉mottled; motley; patched: 苔痕～的石桥 stone bridge covered with patches of moss /渍痕～的墙壁 wall splashed with water stains /午后的阳光照得窗影斑斑驳驳。Shining through the windows, the afternoon sun cast shadows of motley shapes on the wall. /墙上的标语由于风雨的侵蚀而～了。The weather-beaten slogans on the wall have faded into a patch of mottled inscriptions.

斑驳陆离 bānbó-lùlí variegated; of different colours; multicoloured; many-hued: ～的古瓶 ancient vase of variegated colours /屋里乱放着～的什物。The room was littered with all sorts of junk. /她往下一看,整个山谷～,开满了鲜花。Looking down, she marvelled at the valley sparkling with flowers in all the colours of the rainbow.

斑翅山鹑 bānchì shānchún partridge

斑臭鼬 bānchòuyòu little spotted skunk

斑点 bāndiǎn spot; speckle; dot; macula: ～钝口螈〈动物〉spotted salamander /～砂岩 spotted sandstone /一条有红色～的黄彩带 a yellow ribbon sprinkled with red spots (*or* dots)

斑点病 bāndiǎnbìng 〈农业〉spot disease

斑豆 bāndòu pinto bean

斑蛾 bān'é tabby moth

斑痕 bānhén stain; mark: 霞光射向这一带山头,给它们抹上了黄一道红一道的～。The rays of the morning sun flooded the hilltops, making huge stripes of red and yellow.

斑鸠 bānjiū turtledove

斑枯病 bānkūbìng 〈农业〉spot blight

斑块 bānkuài 〈医学〉plaque (substance that forms on teeth in which bacteria can live and breed)

斑斓 bānlán gorgeous; bright-coloured; multicoloured: ～猛虎 fierce multi-coloured tiger /五彩～ riot of colour /纹彩～的水石 multicoloured pebbles /彩霞～绚丽。The rosy clouds were a spectrum of gorgeous colours.

斑丽鱼 bānlìyú chanchito

斑羚 bānlíng goral

斑鹿 bānlù spotted deer

斑马 bānmǎ zebra: ～纹 zebra stripe

斑马线 bānmǎxiàn 〈交通〉zebra crossing; pedestrian crossing; crosswalk

斑蝥 bānmáo 〈动物〉Chinese blister beetle; cantharis

斑木 bānmù 〈植物〉zebrawood

斑丘疹 bānqiūzhěn 〈医学〉maculopapule

斑铜矿 bāntóngkuàng bornite

斑头雁 bāntóuyàn bar-headed or barhead goose

斑秃 bāntū 〈医学〉alopecia areata

斑尾鸽 bānwěigē band-tailed pigeon

斑纹 bānwén stripe; streak; scaling: 大理石上的～ streaks in marble /斑马身上有美丽的～。The zebra has beautiful stripes all over its body.

斑纹玻璃 bānwén bōli marble glass

斑纹干涉仪 bānwén gānshèyí speckle interferometer

斑鸭 bānyā mottled duck

斑岩 bānyán 〈地质〉porphyry: ～螺 porphyry shell

斑蝇 bānyíng 〈动物〉otitid: ～科 otitidae

斑釉 bānyòu 〈医学〉mottled enamel; fluorosis

斑疹 bānzhěn 〈医学〉macula

斑疹热 bānzhěnrè 〈医学〉spotted fever

斑疹伤寒 bānzhěn shānghán 〈医学〉typhus fever; typhus

斑痣 bānzhì 〈地质〉macle

斑竹 bānzhú mottled bamboo

瘢 bān abnormal pigmentary deposit on the skin; fleck

班 bān ❶ class; grade; team: 升～ go up to the higher grade in school /跳～ skip a grade in school /同～ be in the same class; classmate /学习～ study course; training class /作业～ work team /进修～ class for advanced training /短训～ short-term training course /插～ join a class in the middle of a course /〈口语〉留～ (of pupils) fail to go up to the next grade; stay down /我们虽是同学,他却比我低一个～。Though we studied at the same school, he was my junior by one grade (*or* one grade below me). ❷ shift; duty: 日～ day shift /夜～ night shift /上～ go to work; start work; be on duty/ 下～ come or go off work; be off duty/ 值～ be on duty /倒～ work in shifts; change shifts /换～ change shifts; relieve a person on duty /替～ take over sb.'s shift /轮～ be on duty by turns /接～ take one's turn on duty; take over from; succeed /交～ hand over to the next shift /歇～ be off duty; have time off /加～ work overtime; work an extra shift ❸〈军事〉squad: 加强～ reinforced squad /尖刀～ dagger squad (who lead an attack or who pierce the enemy line to carry out some special mission) /通讯～ signal squad ❹ (formerly also used in names of theatrical troupes) troupe: 戏～ theatrical troupe /掌～ manager of a theatrical troupe /搭～ (of performers) join a troupe temporarily to give performances ❺〈量词〉(a) *referring to a group of people*: 一～坏家伙 a gang of scoundrels /一～很有前途的青年 a group of promising youths /这～老学者是国家的宝贵财富。These old scholars are all valuable assets to our country. (b) *used to indicate the number of runs in transport*: 每天四点发头～车。The first bus starts at 4 a.m. every day. /我通常搭末～车回家。I usually take the last bus of the day back home. /明天有一～飞机去巴黎。There is a passenger flight to Paris tomorrow. ❻ regularly-run; scheduled ❼ (of troops) withdraw or redeploy ❽ (Bān) a surname

班巴拉语 Bānbālāyǔ Bambara (language in west Africa)

班白 bānbái *see*"斑白" bānbái

班辈 bānbèi 〈方言〉generation: 我们几个是一个～。All of us are of the same age group (*or* the same generation).

班驳 bānbó *see*"斑驳" bānbó

班禅额尔德尼·却吉坚赞 Bānchán'é'ěrdéní Quèjíjiānzàn Bainqen Erdini Qoigyi Gyaincain (1938-1989), 9th Panchen Lama

班禅喇嘛 Bānchán lǎma 〈佛教〉Panchen Lama: ～转世 reincarnation of the Panchen Lama

班超 Bān Chāo Ban Chao (32-102), a famous general of the Eastern Han Dynasty, and Ban Gu's younger brother sent to the Western Territories (西域) as Han commissioner

班车 bānchē regular or scheduled bus service; shuttle service: 她每天上下班都坐部里的～。She took the ministry's shuttle bus to and from work every day.

班次 bāncì ❶ order of classes or grades at school: 她比我高两个～。She was two grades my senior. ❷ number of runs or flights: 减少～ reduce the number of runs or flights /这路公共汽车的～很少。This bus route has only a few runs per day. /去秦皇岛的火车临时增加一个～。As a temporary measure, they have provided an extra (number for the) train to Qinhuangdao.

班底 bāndǐ ❶〈旧语〉ordinary members of a theatrical troupe: 当时,那个戏班不仅增加了角儿,～也有变化。By that time, the troupe had not only recruited some leading actors and actresses but had had a general reshuffle of its membership. ❷ key members of an organization; cast: 这届内阁大体上仍然是老～。The present cabinet has by and large retained the old set-up (*or* cast).

班房 bānfáng ❶ duty office of a *yamen* in feudal China; *yamen*-runners ❷〈口语〉jail; prison: 蹲了几天～ be detained or imprisoned for a few days /因犯罪而进了～ be imprisoned for a criminal offence

班固 Bān Gù Ban Gu (32-92), a historian and man of letters of the Eastern Han Dynasty, who wrote *History of Han* (汉书)

班机 bānjī airliner; flight; regular air service: 中国国际航空公司～ Air China flight /干线的～都已改用大型喷气客机。They have changed to jumbo jets for passenger service on all trunk routes. /到昆明每周有两趟～。There are two regular flights to Kunming every week.

班吉 Bānjí Bangui, capital of the Central African Republic

班级 bānjí classes and grades in school

班荆道故 bānjīng-dàogù old friends meet on the way and talk about the old days

班轮 bānlún regular passenger or cargo ship; regular steamship service: ～业务 liner service

半导体结 bàndǎotǐjié semiconductor junction
半导体晶体 bàndǎotǐ jīngtǐ semiconducting crystal
半导体器件 bàndǎotǐ qìjiàn 〈无线电〉semiconductor device
半导体热电偶 bàndǎotǐ rèdiàn'ǒu 〈冶金〉semiconductor thermocouple
半导体三极管 bàndǎotǐ sānjíguǎn transistor
半导体收音机 bàndǎotǐ shōuyīnjī transistor radio or receiver
半导体陶瓷 bàndǎotǐ táocí semi-conductor ceramic
半导体闸流管 bàndǎotǐ zháliúguǎn thyristor
半导体振荡器 bàndǎotǐ zhèndàngqì oscillistor
半导体整流器 bàndǎotǐ zhěngliúqì semiconductor rectifier
半导体装置 bàndǎotǐ zhuāngzhì semiconductor device
半导性 bàndǎoxìng semiconductivity
半岛 bàndǎo peninsula：朝鲜～ Korean Peninsula
半道儿 bàndàor halfway; midway; on the way：～出了岔子。Something went wrong on the way. /走到～上下起雨了。We were only halfway when it began to rain.
半地下室 bàndìxiàshì semi-basement
半点 bàndiǎn least bit：一星～ tiny bit; just a little /他这个人～儿实话也没有。There isn't a jot of truth in what he says.
半吊子 bàndiàozi ❶ person who is not sensible or steady：这个人是个～，说话一点儿正形都没有。There's absolutely no sense in the guy; he is always talking rubbish. ❷ dabbler; smatterer：这个～医生，谁敢信他？Who can really trust this smatterer of a doctor? ❸ trifler; dawdler; careless person who often leaves much to be finished：这个～，总是要别人帮他擦屁股。He always does things by halves, and someone has to clear up the mess for him. *or* He always leaves a lot of loose ends behind for someone to tie up.
半独立 bàndúlì semi-independent：～国家 semi-independent state
半对称 bànduìchèn hemihedral; hemi-symmetrical：～性 hemihedrism; hemisymmetry; hemihedry /～晶体 hemihedron
半发达 bànfādá semi-developed：～国家 semi-developed nation
半费 bànfèi half the fee or price
半封闭式电动机 bànfēngbìshì diàndòngjī 〈机械〉semienclosed or semiclosed motor
半封闭循环 bànfēngbì xúnhuán 〈机械〉semiclosed cycle
半封建 bànfēngjiàn semi-feudal：～社会 semi-feudal society
半疯儿 bànfēngr *also* "半疯子" ❶ half-mad; neurotic：他气了个～，一病就一年。He was almost driven insane with rage and was laid up for a whole year. /她是个～，一会儿哭、一会儿笑的，你们不要认真了。She's quite neurotic, crying one moment and laughing the next. Please pay no attention to her. ❷ anyone who speaks and acts in an illogical, frivolous manner
半复赛 bànfùsài 〈体育〉eighth-finals
半干旱 bàngānhàn semi-arid：～气候 semi-arid climate /～地区 semi-arid region
半钢手表 bàngāng shǒubiǎo wrist watch with a stainless steel back
半耕半读 bàngēng-bàndú part-time farmwork and part-time study
半工半读 bàngōng-bàndú part work, part study; work-study programme：～学校 part-work, part-study school /～上完大学 work one's way through college
半工人阶级 bàngōngrénjiējí quasi-proletarian class
半公开 bàngōngkāi semi-overt; semi-open; more or less open：这时，他的身分已经～了。By then, his status (as a communist, etc.) had become more or less public.
半固态 bàngùtài *also* "半固体" 〈物理〉semisolid：～润滑剂 semisolid lubricant
半官方 bànguānfāng semi-official：～人士 semi-official source /～机构 semi-official organ
半规管 bànguīguǎn 〈生理〉semicircular canal
半酣 bànhān half way through the drinks; under the spell of liquor; half-drunk：酒到～，彼此越说越投机。Getting squiffy, they found each other's company more and more congenial as they talked.
半喉切除术 bànhóu qiēchúshù 〈医学〉hemilaryngectomy
半化石 bànhuàshí semi-fossil：～树脂 semi-fossil resin
半昏迷 bànhūnmí 〈医学〉semicoma; semiconsciousness
半机械化 bànjīxièhuà semi-mechanization
半棘肌 bànjíjī 〈生理〉semi-spinalis
半价 bànjià ❶ half price：～出售 sell at half price /～车票 ticket with a fifty per cent discount; half-price ticket; half fare /～门票 entrance ticket at half price; half-price ticket ❷ 〈化学〉semivalence or semivalency
半腱肌 bànjiànjī 〈生理〉semi-tendinosus
半截 bànjié half or a section of sth.：这铅笔只剩～，不好再削尖了。The pencil is only a stub, and cannot be sharpened. /她的话说了～就打住了。She stopped when she had only finished half of what she had to say. *or* She left half of her words unsaid. /一听这话，他心里就凉了～儿。His heart sank at those words.
半截入土 bànjié-rùtǔ with one foot in the grave：我是个～的人了。I'm a man with one foot in the grave. *or* I am living on borrowed time.
半截子革命 bànjiézi gémìng half-hearted revolutionary; one who gives up the cause of revolution halfway
半斤八两 bànjīn-bāliǎng six of one and half a dozen of the other; tweedledum and tweedledee; much of a muchness; the pot calling the kettle black：这两个人真是～，一丘之貉。The two are people of the same ilk. /他胆小，你的胆子也不见得大，正是～。You are as chicken-hearted as he is, so it's really six of one and half a dozen of the other.
半金属 bànjīnshǔ semimetal：～光泽 semimetallic lustre /～元素 semimetal element
半晶体 bànjīngtǐ 〈物理〉semi-crystal
半径 bànjìng radius：活动～〈军事〉radius of operation /飞行～ flying radius /收敛～〈数学〉radius of convergence /曲率～〈数学〉radius of curvature /在一百公里～之内 within a radius of one hundred kilometres
半径规 bànjìngguī radius gauge
半决赛 bànjuésài 〈体育〉semifinals
半绝缘体 bànjuéyuántǐ 〈物理〉semi-insulator
半开门儿 bànkāiménr 〈方言〉unlicensed or unregistered prostitute
半抗原 bànkàngyuán *also* "不全抗原" bùquánkàngyuán 〈医学〉hapten：～基团 haptenic group
半空 bànkōng ❶ in mid-air; in the air：云彩在～里飞。Clouds are floating in mid-air. ❷ half-empty; not full：～着肚子 feel a little hungry /～着肚子喝酒行吗？Is it all right to drink on a half-empty stomach? ❸ 〈方言〉blighted peanuts
半空中 bànkōngzhōng 〈口语〉in mid air; in the air：两架飞机在～相撞。Two airplanes collided in mid air. /一条美丽的彩虹挂在～。A beautiful rainbow hung across the sky. /～飘着许多彩色气球。Many colourful balloons floated up in the sky. /大楼高耸在～。This high-rise building soars into the air.
半拉 bànlǎ 〈口语〉half：～钟头 half an hour /～馒头 half a steamed bun
半拉子 bànlǎzi 〈方言〉❶ half：房子盖了～，还没完工。The house is only half finished. ❷ 〈旧语〉underage farm labourer
半劳动力 bànláodònglì *also* "半劳力" semi-able-bodied (farm) worker; one able to do light manual labour only
半老徐娘 bànlǎo-xúniáng *also* "徐娘半老" woman of fading charms (from Lady Xu, a concubine of Emperor Yuan of the Liang Dynasty)：徐娘半老，风韵犹存。Though a middle-aged woman, she was not without (her) charms.
半立法条约 bànlìfǎ tiáoyuē semi-legislative treaty
半流体 bànliútǐ *also* "半流质" semifluid; semi-liquid：～饮食 semi-fluid diet
半路 bànlù *also* "半道儿" ❶ halfway; midway; on the way：车到～抛锚了。The car broke down halfway. ❷ in midcourse; halfway through：想好了再干，可别～变卦。Think twice before you take a plunge and don't change your mind midway. /～杀出个程咬金。〈俗语〉There appeared an unexpected intruder halfway. *or* Someone popped out of the blue to interfere.
半路出家 bànlù-chūjiā turn a Buddhist late in life — change to a new profession or speciality for which one has received no previous training：你原来是一个～的和尚！So you only became a monk in middle life. /我教体育是～。I am a PE (*or* PT) teacher though I was not trained for it.
半路夫妻 bànlù-fūqī couple married halfway through life (usu. after a previous marriage)：他俩虽是～，倒也相亲相爱，和和睦睦。Though they had married halfway through life (*or* after a previous marriage), they loved each other and got along well.
半履带 bànlǚdài 〈机械〉half-track

半履带式联合收割机 bànlǚdàishì liánhé shōugējī 〈农业〉half-track combine
半履带拖拉机 bànlǚdài tuōlājī 〈农业〉half-track tractor
半履带载重车 bànlǚdài zàizhòngchē 〈交通〉half-track truck
半履带战车 bànlǚdài zhànchē 〈军事〉half-track tank
半裸体 bànluǒtǐ half naked; topless
半麻醉 bànmázuì 〈医学〉twilight sleep
半面之交 bànmiànzhījiāo casual acquaintance; nodding acquaintance
半膜肌 bànmójī 〈生理〉semi-membranosus
半牧半耕制 bànmù-bàngēngzhì 〈农业〉semi-ranching system
半恼半笑 bànnǎo-bànxiào mixture of amusement and vexation: 她没言语,~地瞪了她女儿一眼。With a mixture of amusement and vexation, she gave her daughter a silent stare.
半内陆国家 bànnèilù guójiā semi-landlocked state
半农半牧区 bànnóng-bànmùqū agricultural-pastoral area
半爿天 bànpántiān 〈方言〉*see* "半边天"
半票 bànpiào half-price ticket; half fare
半瓶醋 bànpíngcù person who has only a little learning but not much; smatterer; dabbler: 此人夸夸其谈,其实只是个~。This chap can hold forth at great length, but he is, at bottom, a smatterer. / 你这些问题,我这个~可回答不了。As I'm only little better than a layman, I'm in no position to answer these questions.
半坡遗址 Bànpō yízhǐ 〈考古〉Banpo site (of the Yangshao neolithic culture near Xi'an, Shaanxi Province)
半破产状态 bànpòchǎn zhuàngtài semi-bankruptcy
半旗 bànqí half-mast: 下~ fly a flag at half-mast
半潜式 bànqiánshì semisubmersible: ~船 semisubmersive vessel
半潜式平台 bànqiánshì píngtái 〈石油〉semisubmersible platform
半潜式钻机 bànqiánshì zuànjī 〈石油〉semisubmersible rigs
半球 bànqiú hemisphere: 东~ Eastern Hemisphere / 南~ Southern Hemisphere / ~地图 hemisphere map / ~体 *also* "~形" hemispheroid
半人马座 Bànrénmǎzuò 〈天文〉Centaurus: ~比邻星〈天文〉*Proxima Centauri*
半日花 bànrìhuā 〈植物〉sun rose; rock rose (*Helianthemum*)
半日制学校 bànrìzhì xuéxiào half-day or double-shift school
半乳糖 bànrǔtáng 〈化学〉galactose
半乳糖胺 bànrǔtáng'àn 〈化学〉galactosamine
半乳糖二酸 bànrǔtáng èrsuān 〈化学〉mucic acid
半乳糖苷酶 bànrǔtáng gānméi 〈化学〉galactosidase
半乳糖酸 bànrǔtángsuān 〈化学〉galactonic acid
半乳糖脂 bànrǔtángzhī 〈化学〉galactolipid
半沙漠 bànshāmò semidesert
半晌 bànshǎng 〈方言〉half a day; for a long time; quite a while: 前~ morning / 后~ afternoon / 晚~ evening / 沉吟了~ hesitate for quite a while; murmur to oneself for a few moments / 气得~说不出话来 be choked with rage / 他走了有~工夫了。He left quite a while ago. *or* It's quite a while since he left.
半晌午 bànshǎngwǔ 〈口语〉about noon; towards high noon; almost noon
半社会主义 bànshèhuìzhǔyì semi-socialism: ~所有制 semi-socialist ownership
半身不遂 bànshēn-bùsuí 〈医学〉hemiplegia; hemiparalysis: ~者 hemiplegic
半身像 bànshēnxiàng ❶ half-length photo or portrait ❷ bust
半深海带 bànshēnhǎidài 〈地理〉bathyal zone
半生 bànshēng half a lifetime: 前~ first half of one's life / 大~ greater (*or* better) part of one's life / ~飘零 wander about homeless for the greater part of one's life
半生不熟 bànshēng-bùshú ❶ underdone; half-cooked: 这肉煮得~,没法吃。The meat is only half-cooked and not fit to eat. ❷ half digested; not well assimilated: 这篇文章他还只弄了个~。He has merely half digested the essay. ❸ not skilled; not practised; half-baked: 他能用~的英语跟外宾谈话。He can communicate with foreign visitors in broken English.
半失业 bànshīyè semi-employed; partly employed
半实心轮胎 bànshíxīn lúntāi cushion tyre; semi-pneumatic tyre
半世 bànshì half a lifetime: 辛劳~,一事无成。I have accomplished nothing though I have worked hard for half my lifetime.
半熟练 bànshúliàn semi-skilled: ~工人 semi-skilled worker / ~劳动 semi-skilled labour
半熟土 bànshútǔ semi-mature soil
半数 bànshù half the number; half: 不到~ less than half / 超过~ more than half / 过~通过 be adopted by a simple majority
半数致死剂量 bànshù zhìsǐ jìliàng 〈医学〉lethal dose of 50% (LD_{50})
半数致死浓度 bànshù zhìsǐ nóngdù 〈医学〉lethal concentration of 50% (LCP_{50})
半数致死时间 bànshù zhìsǐ shíjiān 〈医学〉lethal time of 50% (LT_{50})
半衰期 bànshuāiqī 〈物理〉half-life
半双联法 bànshuāngliánfǎ 〈冶金〉semi-duplex process
半死 bànsǐ half dead; almost dead: 打个~ beat sb. half dead; beat sb. brutally / 气得~ be mad with anger / 庄稼旱得~。Crops are dying from the dry spell.
半死不活 bànsǐ-bùhuó more dead than alive; half dead: 公司已经是~,效率从何谈起! The company is merely dragging along, not to say efficiency!
半速齿轮 bànsù chǐlún half-time gear
半随机存取存储器 bànsuíjī cúnqǔ cúnchǔqì 〈计算机〉semirandom access memory or storage
半天 bàntiān ❶ half a day; half day: 干这点活儿有~时间足够了。We can easily get this much work done in half a day. ❷ long time; quite a long time: 妹妹哭了老~了。My younger sister has been crying for a long time.
半天空 bàntiānkōng in the sky; in the air; in mid-air: ~里响起一声霹雳。A clap of thunder broke in the sky.
半天抓云 bàntiān-zhuāyún ❶ difficult to handle; troublesome; knotty ❷ not to the point; wide of the mark
半头 bàntóu ❶ half a head: 高~ half a head taller ❷ half: ~砖 half a brick ❸〈方言〉teenage; adolescent: ~小子 teenage boy; lad
半透明 bàntòumíng translucent; semitransparent: ~表面 translucent surface / ~反射镜 translucent reflector / ~陶瓷 semitransparent ceramic
半透明度 bàntòumíngdù translucency; translucence
半透明体 bàntòumíngtǐ translucent body
半途 bàntú 〈书面〉halfway; midway: ~拆伙 part company halfway / ~而返 return when one is only halfway through a journey; turn back halfway on one's journey / ~抛弃 leave sb. in the lurch halfway
半途而废 bàntú'érfèi leave off a task unfinished; give up halfway: 坚持到底,决不~。One should persist to the end and never stop (*or* quit) halfway.
半推半就 bàntuī-bànjiù yield with seeming reluctance: 李先生~地把礼物接了。Mr. Li accepted the gift with a show of reluctance.
半退 bàntuì *also* "半退休" semi-retired
半托 bàntuō day care (for children): 你的孩子是~还是全托? Does your child go to a day-care centre or a full-time kindergarten?
半脱产 bàntuōchǎn partly excused from work; partly relieved of one's duties: 他~去参加一个培训班。Partly relieved of his duties he joined a training course. *or* He attended the training course half the day while working the other half.
半拖车 bàntuōchē 〈交通〉semitrailer (STLR)
半脱位 bàntuōwèi 〈医学〉subluxation
半椭圆体 bàntuǒyuántǐ 〈数学〉semiellipsoid
半外交关系 bànwàijiāo guānxi semi-diplomatic relations
半微观世界 bànwēiguān shìjiè 〈物理〉semi-microscopic world
半胃切除术 bànwèi qiēchúshù 〈医学〉hemigastrectomy
半文不白 bànwén-bùbái semi-literary and semi-vernacular
半文盲 bànwénmáng semiliterate
半无产阶级 bànwúchǎnjiējí semi-proletariat
半夏 bànxià 〈中医〉tuber of pinellia (*Pinellia ternata*)
半纤维素 bànxiānwéisù 〈化学〉hemicellulose
半咸水 bànxiánshuǐ brackish water: ~湖 brackish-water lake / ~养殖 brackish-water acquaculture
半显性遗传 bànxiǎnxìng yíchuán 〈医学〉semidominant inheritance
半歇 bànxiē 〈方言〉long time; quite a while
半新不旧 bànxīn-bùjiù not new though not wornout
半信半疑 bànxìn-bànyí half-believing, half-doubting; not quite convinced; doubtful: 这广告吹得太玄,使人不免~。The advertisement sounds too boastful to be convincing. / 他说的虽然有道理,但我仍然~。I was not quite convinced though what he said sounded plausi-

ble.
半星儿 bànxīngr (usu. used in the negative) in the least; tiny bit:他这话并没有~不满的意思。There is not a tinge of displeasure in his words. *or* There is no trace of resentment in his remarks.
半休 bànxiū work half days (because of poor health); be on half-day rest:~一周 work half days for a week; take a week's half-day rest /医生要她~一月。The doctor prescribed half-day rest for a month for her.
半悬挂式割草机 bànxuánguàshì gēcǎojī 〈农业〉 semi-mounted mower
半悬挂式铧式犁 bànxuánguàshì huáshìlí 〈农业〉 semi-mounted mouldboard plough
半血亲 bànxuèqīn half-blood:~关系 of half-blood relationship
半掩门儿 bànyǎnménr *see* "半开门儿"
半腰 bànyāo middle; halfway:山~ halfway up a mountain
半遥控 bànyáokòng 〈无线电〉 semiremote control; semiremote handling
半夜 bànyè ❶ half of a night:前~ *also* "上~" before midnight; first half of the night /后~ *also* "下~" after midnight; second half of the night; wee hours or small hours of the morning /大~ for most of the night; until late at night ❷ midnight; in the middle of the night; late at night:深更~ in the dead of night /工作到~ work until midnight /为人不作亏心事,~敲门心不惊。A person who has done nothing wrong will remain calm if he hears knocks on the door at midnight. *or* A quiet conscience sleeps in thunder.
半夜三更 bànyè-sāngēng in the depth of night; in the middle of night; late at night:~的,你想去哪儿? Where are you going at this time of night?
半音 bànyīn 〈音乐〉 semitone:~音阶 chromatic scale
半影 bànyǐng 〈物理〉 penumbra; half image; half shadow:~效应 penumbral effect /~月食 penumbral lunar eclipse
半影波 bànyǐngbō 〈物理〉 penumbral wave
半语子 bànyǔzi one who cannot enunciate words clearly (because of defective vocal organs)
半元音 bànyuányīn 〈语言〉 semivowel
半圆 bànyuán semicircle:画个~ draw a semicircle /~测角仪 semi-circumferentor
半圆锉 bànyuáncuò half-round file
半圆屋顶 bànyuán wūdǐng 〈建筑〉 semidome
半圆凿 bànyuánzáo half-round chisel
半圆柱体 bànyuánzhùtǐ semicylinder
半月 bànyuè half-moon:~形 lune; semilunar
半月板 bànyuèbǎn meniscus: ~切除术 meniscectomy /~炎 meniscitis
半月瓣 bànyuèbàn 〈生理〉 semilunar valve
半月潮 bànyuècháo fortnightly tide
半月刊 bànyuèkān semimonthly; fortnightly
半沼泽 bànzhǎozé half-bog; semi-bog: ~土 〈农业〉 semiboggy soil
半支莲 bànzhīlián 〈植物〉 ❶ sun plant ❷ Mexican rose
半殖民地 bànzhímíndì semi-colony:~半封建社会 semi-colonial, semi-feudal society
半制品 bànzhìpǐn *see* "半成品"
半中间 bànzhōngjiān middle; halfway:他一口气游到河的~。He swam to the middle of the river at one go. /不料这事~又出了岔儿。Who would have thought that something would go wrong with the matter halfway!
半中腰 bànzhōngyāo 〈口语〉 middle; halfway:把木头从~锯开 saw a log at the middle /他上房上到~,脚忽地打起颤来。His feet started to tremble when he climbed halfway to the roof. /他不等她说完,就~插嘴说开了。He chipped in without waiting for her to finish.
半周期 bànzhōuqī half cycle; half-period
半轴齿轮 bànzhóu chǐlún half axle gear
半主动寻的 bànzhǔdòng xúndì 〈军事〉 semiactive homing: ~导弹 semi-active homer
半主权 bànzhǔquán 〈法律〉 semi-sovereignty: ~国 semi-sovereign state
半桩 bànzhuāng 〈方言〉 ❶ half (of the capacity of a sack): ~口袋 half-filled sack; half a sackful (of grain) ❷ teenage; adolescent: ~小孩 teenager; lad
半子 bànzǐ 〈书面〉 son-in-law
半自动 bànzìdòng semi-automatic; automanual
半自动变速器 bànzìdòng biànsùqì semi-automatic transmission
半自动步枪 bànzìdòng bùqiāng semi-automatic rifle
半自动跟踪 bànzìdòng gēnzōng aided tracking; semi-automatic tracking
半自动化 bànzìdònghuà semi-automation; partial automation
半自动交换台 bànzìdòng jiāohuàntái 〈通信〉 automanual or semi-automatic exchange
半自动系统 bànzìdòng xìtǒng 〈铁路〉 automanual system
半自耕农 bànzìgēngnóng semi-tenant peasant; semi-owner peasant or farmer
半自治 bànzìzhì 〈法律〉 semi-autonomous: ~区域 semi-autonomous region

坢

bàn 〈方言〉 manure; muck; dung:猪栏~ pigpen manure/牛栏~ cattleshed dung

靽

bàn 〈书面〉 croup strap

柈

bàn
柈子 bànzi 〈方言〉 big piece of firewood

拌

bàn ❶ mix;搅~ stir; mix /~草喂牛 prepare fodder for cattle (by mixing hay with bran, etc.) /把糖~进去 add sugar and mix well /凉~菜 cold dishes seasoned with sauce and other condiments /~黄瓜丝 shredded cucumber salad /杂~儿 assorted preserved fruits; mixed sweetmeats; hotchpotch ❷ quarrel; bicker:他俩~了几句,就走了。They had some words with each other before they left.
拌合式封层 bànhéshì fēngcéng mix seal
拌和 bànhuo mix; blend:把菜叶和粗粮~在一起喂鸡。Mix minced vegetable leaves and coarse grain as fodder for chickens.
拌和机 bànhuojī mixing machine
拌浆机 bànjiǎngjī grout mixer
拌面 bànmiàn noodles served with soy sauce and other condiments:芝麻酱~ noodles served with soy sauce, sesame butter, and other condiments
拌蒜 bànsuàn 〈方言〉 walk with faltering steps; stagger:他醉眼朦胧,脚底下~,好不容易才走到家。Sleepy-eyed from drink, he staggered home with difficulty.
拌种 bànzhǒng 〈农业〉 seed dressing:~机 seed dresser
拌嘴 bànzuǐ 〈方言〉 bicker; squabble; quarrel:小两口容易~,也容易和好。The young couple fall out as easily as they make up. /看来他是成心要跟我~。It seems that he is set on picking a quarrel with me.

伴

bàn ❶ companion; partner:搭个~儿 travel together; join sb. on a trip /结~同行 travel together; go together /舞~ dance partner /老~儿 (of an old married couple) husband or wife /伙~儿 partner; companion ❷ accompany:陪~ keep sb. company /老李,~我走一趟吧。Hi, Lao Li, would you like to come with me?
伴唱 bànchàng vocal accompaniment:她随着木偶的舞蹈动作,抑扬顿挫地~着。She sang rhythmically to accompany the dance of the puppets. /川剧里的~是很独特的。Vocal accompaniment in Sichuan opera is quite unique.
伴当 bàndāng 〈旧语〉 (domestic) servant
伴读 bàndú 〈旧语〉 ❶ official tutor who instructs children of a prince ❷ person hired by a rich family to keep the children company in learning
伴和 bànhè accompanied by; in unison with:悲壮的歌声~着她的深沉表演,真是感人肺腑。It touched one to the heart to watch her deeply emotional performance accompanied by a melancholy and stirring song.
伴酒 bànjiǔ (usu. of a girl at a bar or restaurant) accompany sb. while drinking; keep sb. company at a drinking party
伴君如伴虎 bàn jūn rú bàn hǔ to accompany the emperor is to be in the company of the tiger; nearest the king, nearest the widdie or gallows
伴郎 bànláng best man (at a wedding)
伴离子 bànlízǐ 〈物理〉 co-ion
伴流 bànliú 〈航海〉 wake:~测定 determination of wake
伴流系数 bànliú xìshù wake factor

伴流增量 bànliú zēngliàng wake gain
伴侣 bànlǚ companion; mate; partner:结为终身～ become lifelong partners; become man and wife
伴娘 bànniáng bridesmaid
伴陪 bànpéi accompany; keep company:他时刻～着我。He kept me company all the time.
伴生 bànshēng co-exist; accompany; associate

B

伴生发射 bànshēng fāshè 〈电子〉associated emission
伴生金属 bànshēng jīnshǔ 〈冶金〉associated metal:锌的～ associated metal of zinc; associate of zinc
伴生矿物 bànshēng kuàngwù 〈矿业〉accompanying mineral; associated mineral
伴生气 bànshēngqì 〈石油〉associated gas
伴生树 bànshēngshù 〈林业〉associated or accompanying tree; complementary tree:橡树最好的～是椴树和椴树。The maple or the Chinese linden is the most complementary tree for the oak.
伴生元素 bànshēng yuánsù co-existing element; accompanying element; associated element
伴生种 bànshēngzhǒng accompanying species; auxiliary species
伴送 bànsòng accompany (sb. to a place); escort:他～我到火车站。He saw me to the railway station.
伴宿 bànsù 〈方言〉keep vigil before a funeral service; hold a wake over a corpse; wake a corpse
伴随 bànsuí ❶ accompany; follow:～着欢快的乐曲,大家跳起了民间舞蹈。Everyone joined the folk dance to the accompaniment of lively music. /这部词典,～他从年轻到年老。This dictionary has been with him from youth to advanced age. ❷〈数学〉adjoint; conjugate:～问题 adjoint problem
伴随变量 bànsuí biànliàng 〈物理〉adjoint variable
伴随函数 bànsuí hánshù adjoint function
伴随免疫 bànsuí miǎnyì 〈医学〉concomitant immunity
伴随群 bànsuíqún 〈数学〉adjoint group
伴随数 bànsuíshù 〈数学〉adjoint number
伴随细菌 bànsuí xìjūn 〈生物〉satellite microbe
伴体 bàntǐ 〈航天〉companion body
伴同 bàntóng accompany; go together:蒸发和溶解的过程常有温度下降的现象～发生。Evaporation and dissolution are usually accompanied by a drop in temperature. /～前往的还有他的妻子。Accompanying him on the trip was also his wife.
伴舞 bànwǔ ❶ be a dancing partner:邀她去舞会上～ invite her to be a dancing partner at the ball ❷ accompany a singer with dance
伴细胞 bànxìbāo 〈植物〉companion cell
伴星 bànxīng 〈天文〉companion (star)
伴星系 bànxīngxì 〈天文〉companion galaxy
伴性 bànxìng sex-linked:～基因 sex-linked gene /～性状 sex-linked character
伴性遗传 bànxìng yíchuán 〈生物〉sex linkage (inheritance)
伴音 bànyīn sound accompaniment; audio:～剪辑 sound cutting /～通道 sound channel /～信号 audio signal; aural signal; sound signal /～解调器〈通信〉audio demodulator /～信号调制器 aural modulator
伴游 bànyóu ❶ accompany on a sightseeing or pleasure trip ❷ companion on a sightseeing or pleasure trip
伴奏 bànzòu accompany (with musical instruments):吉他～ guitar accompaniment /～者 accompanist /用钢琴为她的独唱～ play a piano accompaniment to her solo; accompany her solo on the piano /他的诗歌朗诵常有音乐～。His poetry recitation was often accompanied by music.

绊

bàn (cause to) stumble; trip; trip over:使～ trip (sb.) up /让砖头～了一跤。I stumbled over a brick. /别让零七碎八的事给～住了。Don't get bogged down in trifles.
绊绊磕磕 bànban-kēkē *also* "磕磕绊绊" ❶ (of a road, etc.) bumpy; rough ❷ (of a person) limping; stumbling
绊创膏 bànchuānggāo adhesive plaster
绊脚石 bànjiǎoshí stumbling block; obstacle:必须搬掉这块～。It is necessary to remove this stumbling block. /骄傲自满是进步的～。Conceit is an obstacle to progress.
绊马坑 bànmǎkēng horse trap
绊马索 bànmǎsuǒ rope for tripping an enemy's horse
绊儿 bànr trip:他一使～就把我摔倒了。He tripped me up and I fell.
绊手绊脚 bànshǒu-bànjiǎo cumbersome; in the way:桌子放得不是地方,～的。The table is in the way; it should be moved. /这人～的,真讨厌。What a nuisance the man is, always getting in the way.
绊子 bànzi ❶ trip:使～ trip ❷ restraining rope; hobble; fetter:如果给马上了～,你还能要求它日行千里吗? How can you expect a horse with a restraining rope to cover a thousand *li* a day?

扮

bàn ❶ play the part of; disguise oneself as:打～ make up; dress up /假～ disguise oneself as; dress up as /装～成公司的经理行骗 pose as a company manager in order to carry out a swindle /他在戏里～一位老渔翁。In the opera, he played the part of an old fisherman. ❷ put on (an expression) ❸〈方言〉thresh; beat; knock:～稻 thresh rice
扮故事 bàn gùshi 〈方言〉take part in folk recreation activities such as walking on stilts, lion dancing, etc.
扮鬼脸 bàn guǐliǎn make grimaces; make faces:他向我扮了个鬼脸。He made faces at me.
扮桶 bàntǒng *also* "扮禾桶"〈方言〉wooden container (usu. square) used for threshing rice
扮戏 bànxì ❶ (of Chinese traditional opera singers) make up:此刻演员们正在后台～。The actors and actresses are making up right now in the dressing rooms. ❷〈旧语〉put on a play; act in a play
扮相 bànxiàng ❶ how an actor or actress looks in costume and makeup; stage appearance:她的～和唱功都很好。Both her stage appearance and singing are excellent. /他的～和长相可不一样了。Made up, he looks quite different from real life. ❷ how one looks in makeup:我这副～如何? How do I look in this makeup?
扮演 bànyǎn play the part of; act:他常在戏里～反面人物。He often plays the part of a villain in opera.
扮装 bànzhuāng make-up:马上就要开演了,他还没有～完。He had not finished his make-up when the performance was to begin soon.

办(辦)

bàn ❶ do; handle; manage; attend to:包～ take personal charge of the job; monopolize everything /承～ undertake; agree to do /代～ do (sth.) for sb.; act on sb.'s behalf /督～ supervise and handle /缓～ postpone; defer /～私事 attend to private affairs /～护照 apply for a passport /～移交手续 go through the hand-over formalities /怎么～? What is to be done? /这件事由他～。He will handle this matter. /他把好事～成了坏事。He has turned a good thing into a bad one. *or* He has made a mess of what might be a good thing. ❷ carry out; set up; run:筹～ make preparations; make arrangements /创～ establish; set up /开～ open; set up; start /民～ run by the community /官～ government-run /～教育 undertake educational work /～福利事业 do welfare work /没有经费,什么也～不成。One can hardly achieve anything without sufficient funding. ❸ purchase; get sth. ready:采～ place an order for sth.; purchase /～酒席 prepare a feast; cater /他要到那儿～些土特产。He is going there to purchase some local specialities. ❹ punish (by law); bring (an offender) to justice:惩～ punish /法～ punish by law; bring (an offender) to justice (*or* book) /查～ investigate and deal with accordingly /依法严～ punish severely according to law /撤职查～ be dismissed from office and duly punished /首恶必～。The chief culprit (*or* arch-criminal) shall be punished severely.
办案 bàn'àn ❶ handle a case:依法～ handle a case according to law /秉公～ be impartial in handling all cases ❷ bring (an offender) to justice; apprehend (a criminal)
办报 bànbào run a newspaper
办差 bànchāi 〈旧语〉perform missions or do errands for the government
办到 bàndào get done; accomplish; fulfill:别人能～的事情,我们也能～。Whatever others can do, we can do too. /好不容易～了一张证明。It was not without some difficulty that we managed to get a certificate. /要我让步,那可办不到。It would be impossible to make me give in.
办法 bànfǎ way; means; measure; approach:解决问题的～ way to solve a problem /提高生产的～ measure (*or* way) to raise production /时间不多了,我们得想个～。As time is short, we must think of a way out. /只要能让她回心转意,用什么～都可以。You may employ whatever means you can to bring her around.
办稿 bàngǎo draft a document; prepare a draft
办公 bàngōng handle official business; work (usu. in an office):～费 administrative (*or* running) expenses /～大楼 office building /

many times
谤讪 bàngshàn 〈书面〉slander; vilify; defame
谤书 bàngshū scurrilous letter; letter of slander
谤议 bàngyì 〈书面〉calumny; slanderous comment: 动遭～ be invariably spoken ill of; be often made an object of slander

塝

bàng 〈方言〉edge of a ditch, ridge, etc., in field (usu. used to form place names): 张家～ Zhangjiabang (in Hubei Province)

蒡

bàng *see* "牛蒡" niúbàng

磅[1]

bàng ❶ pound (about 0.4536 kilogramme): 两～肉 two pounds of meat ❷ scales: 过～ weigh (on the scales) /搁在～上称一称 put sth. on the scales and see how much it weighs ❸ weigh: 把东西～一～ weigh sth. on the scales

磅[2]

bàng 〈印刷〉point: 六～字对我们来说是太小了。The 6-point type is too small for our purposes.
see also páng
磅秤 bàngchèng platform scale; platform balance: ～针盘 weighing dial
磅秤车 bàngchèngchē scale car
磅达 bàngdá 〈物理〉poundal (=13825.4 dynes)
磅卡 bàngkǎ pound-calorie

搒(榜)

bàng 〈书面〉paddle or row a boat: ～船 row a boat
see also péng
搒歌 bànggē boatman's song; boating song

镑

bàng pound (as currency unit): 英～ pound sterling /埃及～ Egyptian pound

傍

bàng ❶ draw near; be close to: 依～ rely on; depend upon; imitate /偎～ lean close to; nestle against /依山～水 situated at the foot of a hill near a stream ❷ (of time) towards; nearly ❸〈方言〉follow; lean on: ～大款 (of a girl) lean on (*or* leech on to) a moneybags; find a sugar daddy; be a mistress for a rich man /～上他,别让他跑了。Follow him and don't let him get away.
傍边儿 bàngbiānr 〈方言〉be close to; near: 村子在小河～。The village is located near a stream.
傍黑儿 bànghēir 〈方言〉at evening; at dusk: ～村西头演电影。There will be a film show at the west end of the village this evening.
傍近 bàngjìn near; draw close to: ～身边 close at hand /～晌午 shortly before noon
傍角儿 bàngjuér 〈方言〉❶ play a supporting role; accompany (the leading actor or actress) with music: 演了～ play a supporting role ❷ minor actor or actress; accompanist: 戏班子的～ minor actors and accompanists of a theatrical troupe
傍亮儿 bàngliàngr 〈方言〉at daybreak; at dawn: ～出发 set out at dawn
傍人门户 bàngrén-ménhù rely on sb. for a living; be unable to stand on one's own feet
傍晌 bàngshǎng 〈方言〉about midday; towards noon: 我们在～的时候歇工吃饭。We stopped for lunch towards noon.
傍晚 bàngwǎn towards evening; at nightfall; at dusk: 他有～散步的习惯。He is in the habit of taking an evening stroll. /～时分,风势更猛了。The wind was blowing even harder towards evening.
傍午 bàngwǔ towards noon: ～,火车到了终点站。The train pulled into the terminus just before noon.
傍依 bàngyī be close to; be near: 小湖～青山。The lakelet is situated close to a green hill.

艕

bàng ❶ (of ships, boats, etc.) draw close and moor with each other: 海湾里船很多,要把船～好。As there are many boats anchored in the bay, make sure our boat is securely moored. ❷ *see* "搒" bàng

膀

bàng *see* "吊膀子" diàobàngzi
see also bǎng; pāng; páng

棓

bàng
棓头 bàngtóu *also* "棒头" bàngtóu 〈方言〉maize; corn

棒

bàng ❶ stick; club; cudgel: 大～ big stick; means of threat /磁～ magnetic rod /电～ electric torch; flashlight /指挥～ baton /接力～ relay baton /当头一～ head-on blow ❷〈口语〉terrific; topping; superb; strong: 画得真～。It's a superb picture. /他身体真～。He is in wonderful health. /你们干得～极了。You did a terrific (*or* swell) job.
棒棒衫 bàngbàngshān a kind of coarsely knitted sweater
棒冰 bàngbīng 〈方言〉ice-lolly; popsicle; ice-sucker; frozen sucker
棒材 bàngcái 〈冶金〉bar; bar stock: ～剪切机 bar shearing machine /～轧机 bar mill
棒操 bàngcāo 〈体育〉club exercise
棒疮 bàngchuāng wounds or scars from being beaten with a club
棒槌 bàngchui ❶ wooden club (used to beat clothes in washing); battledore ❷〈方言〉clumsy; awkward; incompetent: 干这种事我可～了,您多照应。I may need your help since I'm not very good at this.
棒打不回头 bàng dǎ bù huítóu 〈口语〉stubborn; pigheaded: 他这个人～,你不必劝他。Don't try to dissuade him; he's so pigheaded.
棒钢 bànggāng 〈冶金〉bar steel
棒喝 bànghè deal a blow on the head to bring sb. to his senses: 给他当头～ give him a shout and a blow to bring him to his senses; serve a severe warning to sb.
棒客 bàngkè *also* "棒老二"〈方言〉thug; bandit
棒料 bàngliào 〈冶金〉bar stock: ～架 bar stand
棒料车床 bàngliào chēchuáng bar lathe
棒料剪床 bàngliào jiǎnchuáng bar shear
棒硫 bàngliú 〈化学〉roll sulphur
棒磨机 bàngmójī 〈矿业〉rod mill
棒球 bàngqiú baseball
棒球棒 bàngqiúbàng baseball bat
棒球场 bàngqiúchǎng baseball field; diamond
棒球击球手 bàngqiú jīqiúshǒu batter
棒球投手 bàngqiú tóushǒu pitcher
棒儿香 bàngrxiāng incense with thin bamboo or wooden wick
棒杀 bàngshā "kill with the club" — cause sb. to fail by open attack: 对于年轻有为的作家,既不要"～",也不要"捧杀"。It is essential to prevent the suppression of promising young writers by harsh criticism, as well as their corruption by flattery.
棒糖 bàngtáng lollipop; lollypop; sucker
棒头 bàngtóu *also* "棓头" bàngtóu 〈方言〉maize; corn
棒线 bàngxiàn coarse knitting wool
棒针 bàngzhēn thick knitting needle
棒状杆菌 bàngzhuàng gǎnjūn corynebacteria: ～科 corynebacteriaceae /～属 corynebacterium
棒子 bàngzi ❶ stick; club; cudgel ❷〈方言〉maize; corn ❸〈方言〉ear of maize or corn; corncob
棒子面 bàngzimiàn 〈方言〉corn-meal; corn flour: ～粥 cornmeal porridge or mush
棒子手 bàngzishǒu 〈方言〉robber

蚌

bàng freshwater mussel; clam
see also bèng

bāo

褒(襃)

bāo ❶ praise; commend; extol; honour: ～善贬恶 praise virtue and censure vice /此事论者见仁见智,或～或贬。Different people have different views on this matter. They either praise or censure it. ❷〈书面〉(of garment) loose; large: ～衣博带 loose robe with a broad waistband
褒贬 bāobiǎn comment; pass judgment on; appraise: ～是非 pass judgment on the rights and wrongs (of a case) /妄加～ make improper comments; make presumptuous observations /一字～ praise or censure in just one word of comment /他的评论有褒有贬。His

comments are a mixture of praise and stricture.

褒贬 bāobian criticize; condemn; speak ill of:他把这些作品～得一文不值。He condemned these works as worthless as dirt.

褒词 bāocí *also* "褒义词" complimentary word

褒奖 bāojiǎng praise and honour; commend and award:因表现突出多次受到～。He was commended and awarded several times for his exemplary service.

褒美 bāoměi 〈书面〉honour with praise; laud; pay glowing tribute to:～之情,溢于言表 overflow with praise in one's words

褒恤 bāoxù 〈书面〉commend and commiserate; praise and compensate:～遗属 praise and compensate the bereaved family (of a martyr, etc.)

褒扬 bāoyáng praise; commend:～之词 commendatory remarks; laudatory comments/他的劳动热情受到大家～。He was praised by all for his enthusiasm for manual labour.

褒义 bāoyì commendatory sense; laudatory or complimentary meaning:～词 commendatory term/他的这个说法含有～。His comments tend to be laudatory.

煲 bāo 〈方言〉❶ cooking pot; boiler; cooker:瓦～ crock pot/沙～ earthen pot; casserole/铜～ bronze boiler/电饭～ electric(rice) cooker ❷ cook with boiler or cooker:～粥 cook porridge in a boiler

包 bāo ❶ wrap:～书 wrap up a book in a piece of paper; put a jacket (*or* cover) on a book/用头巾～头 wrap up one's hair in a kerchief/～包子 make stuffed buns/她给病人～伤口。She is dressing the wound for the patient. ❷ bundle; parcel; package; pack:邮～ postal parcel/行李～ luggage pack/背着一个大～ carry a big bundle on one's back ❸ bag; sack:提～ handbag; shopping bag; valise/背～ knapsack; field pack; blanket roll; backpack/帆布～ canvas bag; kit bag/草～ straw bag; straw sack;〈比喻〉bungler; good-for-nothing/挎～ satchel/蒲～儿 cattail bag; rush bag/皮～ leather handbag; briefcase; portfolio/腰～ purse; pocket/钱～ wallet; purse/书～ satchel; schoolbag; backpack/针线～ sewing kit/急救～ first-aid kit ❹〈量词〉*used of bundled or packaged things*:一～火柴 a pack of matches; a box of matches/一～纸烟 a packet of cigarettes/两～面粉 two bags (*or* sacks) of flour/一～棉花 a bale of cotton/一～炸药 a pack of dynamite ❺ swelling; protuberance; lump:山～ hill; low hill/沙～ sand dune/脓～ pustule;〈比喻〉worthless fellow; good-for-nothing/背上起了个～ have a swelling in the back ❻ yurt:蒙古～ Mongolian yurt ❼ surround; encircle; envelop:浓烟～住了整个建筑物。The whole building was enveloped in dense smoke./敌人从四面八方～了上来。Enemy troops closed in on us from all sides. ❽ include; contain:无所不～ all-inclusive; all-embracing/这只表价格五百元,不～进口附加税。The price of the watch is 500 *yuan*, not counting the import surcharge. ❾ undertake to fulfil an assignment; be responsible for the whole job:～产量 undertake responsibility for fulfilment of production quota/～得过多 take on too much responsibility and exercise too rigid a control; undertake more than one can do/门前三～ (undertake) three responsibilities for the area in front of one's workplace — cleanliness, care of trees and lawn, and public order/任务～给你了。The job now is entirely your responsibility. ❿ guarantee; assure:～退还洋 guarantee refunding on return of faulty goods/～退～换 guarantee return or change of faulty goods/～你满意。I bet you'll like it. *or* We guarantee satisfaction./这棵树～活。This sapling will survive, I assure you./那没有问题,～在我身上。Don't worry. You can count on me. ⓫ hire; charter:～一架飞机 charter a plane/～一桌酒席 order a feast/～两场电影 make two block bookings in a cinema; order two movie shows/这一层客房我们全～了。We'll book all the rooms on the floor. ⓬ (Bāo) a surname

包办 bāobàn ❶ take sole charge of:这件事你～了吧。You may as well take charge of this all by yourself./本店～宴席。This restaurant offers catering service./他们的结婚酒席将由一家饭馆～。A restaurant will be catering at their wedding. ❷ monopolize:把持～ have exclusive control; monopolize/～代替 push others aside and boss the show; do sth. over the head of sb. (who should be doing it)

包办婚姻 bāobàn hūnyīn arranged marriage or match

包背装 bāobèizhuāng 〈印刷〉wrapped-ridge binding

包庇 bāobì shield; cover up:～罪犯 shield criminal (from punishment)/～违法行为 cover up offences against the law

包藏 bāocáng contain; harbour; conceal:此人～着一肚子坏水。This man is full of evil designs (*or* tricks)./她感到那些话里～着智慧和勇气。She felt that those words were the embodiment of wisdom and courage.

包藏祸心 bāocáng-huòxīn harbour evil intentions or malicious intent; plot mischief:看他嘴上说得娓娓动听,实际上～。Despite his fine-sounding words, in actual fact, he harbours evil intentions at heart.

包层光纤 bāocéng guāngxiān clad-fibre:包层石英光纤 clad silica fibre

包产 bāochǎn (of an owner) fix farm output quotas for a contractor; (of a contractor) undertake full responsibility for contracted production quotas; make a production contract:～指标 production targets set for a contractor/～林 wood contracted to an individual or group with fixed output quotas

包产到户 bāochǎn dàohù contracting output quotas to each farm household

包产到组 bāochǎn dàozǔ contracting output quotas to each work group

包产合同 bāochǎn hétong contract in which production quotas are fixed for contractors; production contract

包产田 bāochǎntián plot of land contracted to either an individual household or group with fixed production output; contracted land

包场 bāochǎng make a block booking; book all the seats in a theatre or cinema; book all or part of the tickets for a film show or play

包抄 bāochāo outflank; envelop:分三路向敌人～过去 outflank the enemy in three directions; close in on the enemy in a three-pronged attack

包车 bāochē ❶ vehicle hired by an individual or institution for a certain period of time; chartered car or bus:拉～ pull a rickshaw exclusively for sb./～夫 rickshaw coolie in sb.'s employ/门前挤满了各公司的～。Lines of cars or buses chartered by companies are parked in front of the door. ❷ be responsible for the use and maintenance of a locomotive, bus or trolley:～组 team responsible for such a vehicle; responsible crew ❸ hire a car for a period of time; charter:包一辆车 charter a car

包乘 bāochéng ❶ charter a boat, car or plane for a period of time ❷ (of a group of crew members) undertake responsibility for service to passengers and for maintenance of a train or boat within a designated section of rail or water transport

包乘制 bāochéngzhì 〈交通〉crew responsibility system

包乘组 bāochéngzǔ 〈交通〉crew responsible for service and maintenance under the crew responsibility system; responsible crew

包虫病 bāochóngbìng 〈医学〉echinococcosis; hydatid disease

包虫囊 bāochóngnáng 〈医学〉hydatid

包船 bāochuán ❶ charter a boat or ship:包了一只船 hire a boat ❷ chartered boat or ship:我们是坐～去武汉的。We went to Wuhan by chartered boat.

包打天下 bāodǎ-tiānxià boss the show; run the business or affair all by oneself; monopolize:～的人,往往以失败而告终。Those who take on every job themselves often end up in failure.

包打听 bāodǎtīng 〈方言〉❶ *see* "包探" ❷ officious inquirer; Nosy Parker; snoop ❸ well-informed guy; Mr. Know-It-All

包单 bāodān 〈方言〉❶ wrapping; wrapper ❷ cover of a padded quilt

包饭 bāofàn ❶ get or supply meals at a mutually agreed monthly rate; board:包午饭 lunch (*or* supply lunch) at a fixed monthly rate/我儿子在一个邻居家～。My son boards with a neighbour. ❷ meals thus supplied:吃～ have meals at a mutually agreed monthly rate/本店提供～。This restaurant provides meals at fixed monthly rates.

包房 bāofáng ❶ rent a hotel room for a period of time ❷ hotel room thus rented

包封 bāofēng wrap up and seal; envelop

包袱 bāofu ❶ cloth-wrapper:把这些零星东西用～包起来。Please wrap up these odds and ends in a cloth-wrapper (*or* bundle). ❷ bundle wrapped in a cloth:把～放在行李架上。Place the bundle on the luggage rack. ❸ load (on one's mind); (mental) burden; hindrance:背上～ assume a burden/背上沉重的思想～ have a heavy load (*or* weight) on one's mind; be weighed down by a mental burden; have a millstone round one's necks/表扬应该是前进的动力,而不应该

是～。Praise should be seen as an encouragement; it should not become a hindrance to progress. ❹ joke or laughing-stock in Chinese comic dialogue, quick-patter, etc.: 抖～ crack jokes (in Chinese comic dialogue)

包袱底儿 bāofudǐr 〈方言〉 ❶ family valuables kept as a nest egg ❷ skeleton in the cupboard or closet; unseemly secret: 抖～ bring sb.'s secret into the open ❸ one's speciality or unique skill: 抖搂～ show one's unique skills

包袱皮儿 bāofupír wrapping cloth

包干儿 bāogānr undertake to do a job until it is completed: 分片～ divide a task into different portions and assign each to an individual or group / 大～ all-round contract system / 财务～ be responsible for one's own finances; assure full responsibility for the balance of one's budget / 划分收支,分级～ apportion revenues and expenditures between the central and local authorities while holding the latter responsible for their own finances at each level / 经费～ take responsibility for one's funding needs after receiving fixed allocations / ～运费 lump sum freight / 扫尾的活由你们几位～。The rounding-off of this job is left entirely to you.

包干制 bāogānzhì (as practised in the liberated areas and the PRC from the 1940's to the early 1950's) overall rationing system; scheme of payment partly in kind and partly in cash
see also "供给制" gōngjǐzhì

包钢 Bāogāng (short for 包头钢铁公司) Baotou Iron and Steel Complex

包工 bāogōng ❶ undertake to perform work within a time limit and according to specifications; contract for a job; job work: ～合同 contract for a job (*or* project); labour contract / ～包料 contract for labour and materials / ～到组,按定额计酬 contracting work quotas to groups with corresponding remuneration / 这项工程由第三队～。This project is now contracted to Team No. 3. ❷ contractor

包工队 bāogōngduì contracting team

包工头 bāogōngtóu labour contractor

包工制 bāogōngzhì labour contract system

包公 Bāogōng (reverential term of address for 包拯 Bao Zheng, 999-1062), legendary upright official of the Northern Song Dynasty who championed the cause of the down-trodden in defiance of the powerful; archetypical honest official

包购包销 bāogòu-bāoxiāo exclusive right to purchase and sell

包谷 bāogǔ *also* "苞谷" bāogǔ 〈方言〉 maize; corn

包管 bāoguǎn assure; guarantee: ～退换。Refunding and exchanges (for faulty goods) are guaranteed. / ～你马到成功。You'll win immediate success, I assure you.

包裹 bāoguǒ ❶ wrap up; bind up: 用纱布～伤口 dress a wound / 把一摞书用牛皮纸～好。Wrap up a pile of books with kraft paper. ❷ bundle; package; parcel: 邮政～ postal parcel

包裹单 bāoguǒdān postal parcel form; postal parcel notification

包含 bāohán contain; include; imply; embody: ～各种因素 include manifold factors / ～几层意思 have several implications / ～着某种倾向 point to certain trends / 这句朴素的话里～了许多深刻的道理。This simple statement embodies profound truth. *or* There is profound truth in this simple statement.

包涵 bāohan 〈套语〉 excuse; forgive: 我的话很直率,请多多～。Excuse me for my blunt remarks. / 照顾不周,您多～。Please forgive me for my inadequate hospitality.

包伙 bāohuǒ *see* "包饭"

包机 bāojī ❶ charter (a plane) ❷ chartered plane; chartered flight: 成都至香港的～已起飞了。The chartered plane from Chengdu to Hong Kong has taken off.

包价 bāojià package price

包价旅游 bāojià lǚyóu inclusive tour; package tour

包剿 bāojiǎo attack from all sides; surround and annihilate

包巾 bāojīn head towel; head gear; turban

包金 bāojīn ❶ gild; cover with gold foil: ～手表 gold-plated wrist watch ❷ *see* "包银"

包茎 bāojīng 〈医学〉 phimosis

包举 bāojǔ cover all; include all: ～无遗 having everything included without exception; all-inclusive; all-embracing / ～宇内 exercise sovereignty over the whole land

包括 bāokuò include; consist of; comprise; embrace: 东北地区～辽宁、吉林、黑龙江三省。northeast China consists of (*or* comprises) Liaoning, Jilin and Heilongjiang provinces. / 办公室里的人, ～我在内都得了感冒。All the people in the office came down with flu, including myself. / 你们的大多数建议都已～在本计划内。This plan has incorporated most of your suggestions. / 所索款项是～邮资在内的全部费用。The money charged covers the entire cost, postage included.

包揽 bāolǎn take on entirely; monopolize (all work): ～一切 put all under one's charge; take on everything; monopolize all / ～词讼 (of a shyster lawyer) monopolize law disputes; engage in legal pettifoggery / 春游的事由老柳一手～,早已办妥。Lao Liu, who is in exclusive charge of the spring outing, has got everything ready.

包罗 bāoluó cover (usu. a wide range); embrace (usu. many or all aspects); include: ～甚广 cover a wide range of things / ～无遗 embrace all; be all-inclusive / 这本词典～了社会科学各个门类的词汇。The dictionary includes terms from all branches of the social sciences.

包罗万象 bāoluó-wànxiàng all-embracing; all-inclusive: ～的百科全书 all-inclusive encyclopedia / ～的世界 kaleidoscopic world / 展品～,美不胜收。The exhibits, a multifarious array, are simply fascinating.

包络 bāoluò 〈通信〉〈数学〉 envelope: ～线 envelope / ～曲线 envelope curve / ～函数 envelope function / ～检测 *also* "～检波" envelope detection

包瞒 bāomán 〈方言〉 hide; conceal; cover up

包米 bāomǐ *also* "苞米" bāomǐ 〈方言〉 maize; corn

包囊 bāonáng ❶ 〈方言〉 bag: ～里装着零碎的绸子。The bag is filled with scraps of silk. ❷ 〈生理〉 cyst: ～细胞 cystocyte / ～干细胞 cystoblast / ～生殖 cystic reproduction

包赔 bāopéi guarantee to compensate: 损坏～ guarantee to compensate for any damage

包皮 bāopí ❶ wrapping; wrapper; casing ❷ 〈生理〉 prepuce; foreskin: ～环切(术) circumcision / ～过长 redundant prepuce

包皮垢 bāopígòu 〈医学〉 smegma

包皮炎 bāopíyán 〈医学〉 posthitis

包票 bāopiào *also* "保票" bǎopiào ❶ 〈旧语〉 warranty ❷ guarantee: 他一定能及时完成这项工作,我敢打～。I can say for certain that he'll be able to finish the job in time.

包容 bāoróng ❶ tolerant; magnanimous: 大度～ magnanimous / 技艺不佳,务望～。We hope that you will forgive us if our performance is not as good as it should be. ❷ contain; hold: 楼上的餐厅可～十桌左右。The dining room upstairs can hold about ten tables.

包身工 bāoshēngōng indentured labourer

包粟 bāosù *also* "苞粟" bāosù 〈方言〉 corn; maize

包弹 bāotán 〈方言〉 speak ill of; criticize: 我还没听到有人～过她一个字。I have never heard anybody speak ill of her in anyway.

包探 bāotàn 〈旧语〉 detective

包头 bāotóu ❶ head makeup (in traditional operas) ❷ (Bāotóu) major city in Inner Mongolia

包头 bāotou ❶ headpiece for decoration (as used by some minority nationalities): 青～ blue headpiece ❷ (of shoes or boots) toecap: 打～ put a toecap on a shoe

包网际搜索程序 bāowǎngjì sōusuǒ chéngxù 〈计算机〉 Packet Internet Groper (PING)

包围 bāowéi ❶ surround; encircle; hem in: 亭子被茂密的树林～着。The pavilion is surrounded by a dense forest. / 外宾刚走出贵宾室,就被记者们团团～起来。The foreign guests were surrounded by reporters as soon as they walked out of the VIP room. / 恐怖分子被小分队四面～。The terrorists were hemmed in on all sides by the detachment. ❷ outflank: 正面进攻与侧翼～相结合 combine a frontal attack with an outflanking movement ❸ *see* "包围圈"

包围圈 bāowéiquān ring of encirclement: 冲出～ break through the ring of encirclement / 缩小～ tighten (*or* close) the ring of encirclement

包席 bāoxí *also* "包桌" table d'hôte dinner: 在馆子里订两桌～ reserve two tables at a restaurant for table d'hôte dinner

包厢 bāoxiāng box (in a theatre or concert hall)

包销 bāoxiāo ❶ have exclusive selling rights: ～权 exclusive selling rights / ～协定 exclusive sales agreement ❷ be the sole sales agent (for a production unit) ❸ underwrite (bonds, etc.): ～本期国库券 underwrite the current issue of treasury bonds

包心菜 bāoxīncài 〈方言〉 cabbage

包修、包换、包赔 bāoxiū bāohuàn bāopéi *also* "三包" sānbāo (three) guarantees for repair, replacement, or compensation for faulty product

包衣 bāoyī ❶ capsule; coating of a tablet or pill ❷ corn husk ❸〈旧语〉family servant
包银 bāoyín 〈旧语〉monthly payment to a troupe or a leading actor or actress by theatre house
包游 bāoyóu all-inclusive tour; package tour
包玉刚 Bāo Yùgāng Sir Yue-kong Pao (1918-1991), Hong Kong shipping tycoon, main sponsor of Ningbo University in Zhejiang Province
包圆儿 bāoyuánr 〈口语〉❶ buy the whole or the remaining lot:～可以便宜点儿。I'll give you a discount if you buy the whole lot. ❷ finish up or off:这儿的清扫工作由你俩～。You two will finish off the cleaning here, won't you?
包月 bāoyuè monthly payment
包孕 bāoyùn 〈书面〉be pregnant with; conceive; contain:局势～着严重的危机。The situation is pregnant with grave danger.
包蕴 bāoyùn include; contain; embody:她简短的话语～着深深的友谊与热情。The few remarks she made embodied profound friendship and enthusiasm.
包扎 bāozā dress; wrap up; bind up:～伤口 dress a wound /他把信件分分类,然后把它们～起来。He sorted out the letters and tied them up separately.
包扎所 bāozāsuǒ dressing station; first-aid station
包拯 Bāo Zhěng *see*“包公”
包治百病 bāozhì-bǎibìng *also*“包医百病”guarantee to cure all diseases:～的药方 panacea; cure-all; remedy for all ills /没有包治社会百病的灵丹妙药。There is no panacea (*or* miracle remedy) for all social evils.
包装 bāozhuāng ❶ pack; package:～车间 packing workshop /～清单 packing list /～设计 packing design /已～好的货物正在往火车上运。The packed cargo is being shifted onto a train wagon. ❷ packing materials:这香皂的～很别致。The packing of the toilet soap is quite unique. ❸ (actor's) makeup, costume, etc.; beautification and marketing (of a singer, politician, etc.); packaging:～与推销一位新歌星 packaging and marketing of a new pop star /歌唱演员总得讲点～。Singers should keep up appropriate appearances.
包装板 bāozhuāngbǎn packing plate; packing board
包装材料 bāozhuāng cáiliào packaging; wrapping
包装机 bāozhuāngjī packager or packaging machine; packer or packing machine; bale press
包装设备 bāozhuāng shèbèi packaging equipment; packing facility
包装箱 bāozhuāngxiāng packing box; packing case or crate
包装业 bāozhuāngyè packing industry
包装纸 bāozhuāngzhǐ packing paper; wrapping paper
包装作业线 bāozhuāng zuòyèxiàn packaging conveyor line
包准 bāozhǔn guarantee; assure:我～按时到达。I assure you I'll arrive on time.
包子 bāozi ❶ steamed stuffed bun ❷〈冶金〉ladle
包租 bāozū ❶ rent (sth.) for subletting ❷ fixed rent for farmland irrespective of the harvest ❸ hire (sth.) for a period of time; charter

炮 bāo ❶ quick-fry; sauté:～羊肉 quick-fried mutton ❷ dry by heat:把湿衣服～干 dry wet clothes by heat
see also páo; pào

苞[1] bāo bud:花～ unopened bud /打～ (of wheat, sorghum) form ears /含～待放 flower in bud;〈比喻〉girl in her puberty; pubescent girl

苞[2] bāo 〈书面〉luxuriant; profuse:竹～松茂 bamboos and pines growing in profusion
苞谷 bāogǔ 〈方言〉corn; maize
苞苴 bāojū 〈书面〉❶ basket woven with cattail leaves ❷ gift; present ❸ bribe:～公行。Bribery was a common practice.
苞鳞 bāolín 〈植物〉bract scale
苞萝 bāoluó 〈方言〉maize; corn
苞米 bāomǐ 〈方言〉corn; maize
苞膜 bāomó indusium
苞片 bāopiàn 〈植物〉bract:小～ bracteole
苞粟 bāosù 〈方言〉corn; maize
苞笋 bāosǔn 〈方言〉winter bamboo shoot
苞叶 bāoyè 〈植物〉bracteal leaf

枹 bāo 〈植物〉*Quercus glandulifera*

龅 bāo
龅牙 bāoyá bucktooth

胞 bāo ❶ afterbirth; placenta:双～胎 twins ❷ born of the same parents:同～ born of the same parents; fellow countryman; compatriot /侨～ countryman (*or* nationals) residing abroad ❸ (short for 细胞) cell; cyto-:～壁 cell wall
胞波 bāobō Paukphaw (Burmese word meaning "kins" or "relatives" often used by the Burmese in addressing the Chinese to express their cordiality); compatriot; relative:～情谊 brotherly friendship
胞弟 bāodì full (younger) brother
胞苷 bāogān 〈生化〉cytidine:～酸 cytidylic acid
胞果 bāoguǒ *also*“包囊”bāonáng 〈生理〉utricle
胞姐 bāojiě full (elder) sister
胞妹 bāomèi full (younger) sister
胞内酶 bāonèiméi 〈生理〉endocellular enzyme
胞外酶 bāowàiméi 〈生理〉ecto-enzyme; exo-enzyme
胞兄 bāoxiōng full (elder) brother
胞芽 bāoyá 〈植物〉gemma
胞液 bāoyè 〈医学〉cytosol
胞衣 bāoyī 〈中医〉afterbirth; secundines
胞蚴 bāoyòu sporocyst
胞子 bāozǐ *also*“孢子”bāozǐ spore
胞族 bāozú phratry

孢 bāo spore:芽～ *also*“胞芽”bāoyá〈植物〉gemma (of a fungus)
孢粉 bāofěn spore and pollen
孢粉学 bāofěnxué palynology
孢苗 bāomiáo 〈生物〉sporeling
孢原 bāoyuán *also*“原孢子”yuánbāozǐ 〈植物〉archespore; archesporium
孢子 bāozǐ spore:～形成 *also*“～生殖”sporogenesis; sporulation /杀～剂 sporicide
孢子虫 bāozǐchóng 〈生物〉sporozoan
孢子果 bāozǐguǒ 〈植物〉sporocarp
孢子囊 bāozǐnáng *also*“孢囊”sporangium:～孢子 sporangiospore
孢子体 bāozǐtǐ sporophore; sporophyte; sporozoite
孢子植物 bāozǐ zhíwù cryptogam

剥 bāo peel; shell; skin:～橘子 peel an orange /～豆 shell beans /～葡萄皮 peel grapes /～蕉抽茧 like peeling a banana or unwinding a cocoon—press on an inquiry step by step
see also bō
剥皮 bāopí peel; skin; shell; ross (of tree bark):剥头皮 scalp

báo

雹 báo hail; hailstone:冰～ hail; hailstone /～害 damage caused by hail
雹暴 báobào hailstorm
雹灾 báozāi disaster caused by hail; hailstorm
雹子 báozi hail; hailstone

薄 báo ❶ thin; flimsy:～片 thin piece (*or* sheet) /～被 light (*or* thin) cotton-wadded quilt /脸上～～地抹了一层粉 apply a thin coat of face powder /擦脸用的～纸 facial tissue ❷ without warmth or depth; coldly; shabbily:我待他的情分不～。I treat him quite generously. ❸ weak; thin; light:酒味太～。The wine tastes insipid (*or* too thin). ❹ infertile; poor:～地 poor land; infertile land
see also bó; bò
薄板 báobǎn 〈冶金〉sheet metal; sheet:～坯 sheet billet /～厂 sheet steel mill /不锈钢～ stainless sheet steel
薄板轧机 báobǎn zhájī 〈冶金〉sheet mill; sheet rolling mill

薄饼 báobǐng thin pancake; wafer
薄绸 báochóu chiffon; ninon
薄脆 báocuì crisp fritter
薄脆饼 báocuìbǐng wafer; waffle; snap
薄钢板 báogāngbǎn 〈冶金〉sheet-metal; sheet steel; sheet stock; thin-gage plate:～厂 sheet steel mill /～矫直机 sheet steel straightening unit /～压延机 sheet steel rolling mill
薄钢片 báogāngpiàn stalloy
薄毛呢 báomáoní 〈纺织〉cassimere
薄壳结构 báoqiào jiégòu 〈建筑〉shell structure
薄壳穹顶 báoqiào qióngdǐng 〈建筑〉shell dome
薄田 báotián infertile soil or land
薄铁皮 báotiěpí 〈冶金〉sheet iron
薄页纸 báoyèzhǐ *also* "薄纸" ❶ tissue paper ❷ (for typing or carbon copies) flimsy

瓝 báo ❶〈书面〉small melon ❷ *see* "马瓝儿" mǎbáor

bǎo

宝(寶、寶) bǎo ❶ treasure; valuables; riches:财～ money and valuables /国～ national treasure /墨～ treasured scroll of calligraphy or painting /元～ shoe-shaped gold or silver ingot used as money in dynastic China /珠～ pearls and jewels; jewelry /无价之～ priceless treasure /文房四～ four treasured items of the study—four treasured writing materials (writing brush, ink stick, ink stone, and paper) /传家～ family heirloom; cherished tradition ❷ precious; treasured:～盒 jewel casket; treasure box; magical box ❸〈旧语〉a kind of gambling device ❹〈敬词〉your: *see* "～眷"; "～号"

宝爱 bǎo'ài 〈书面〉value and like; treasure:这是他～的几部书。These are the books he treasures most.
宝宝 bǎobao (term of endearment for babies) darling; baby; dear:好～ darling baby; good baby /小～们 little babies
宝宝装 bǎobaozhuāng infant clothes
宝贝 bǎobèi ❶ treasure; treasured object:这些山货可是～。These mountain products are everybody's cherished rarities. /他那件～,从来不轻易拿出来给人看。He rarely showed his object d'art to anybody. ❷ darling; dear; baby:好～儿,听话。Darling, be a good child. ❸〈方言〉cherish; treasure; love:老人可～小孙女了。The old man treasured his little granddaughter like the apple of his eye. ❹〈讽刺〉queer fish; crank; good-for-nothing:这个～,不知道又要出什么洋相。No one knows what this crank will be up to again. /你那个～兄弟又喝醉了。That good-for-nothing brother of yours is drunk again. /这个老头真是个～。This old man is quite a character. ❺ cowrie (brightly coloured smooth shell of a tropical mollusk, once used as money in some parts of Africa and Asia):虎斑～ tiger cowrie
宝贝疙瘩 bǎobèi gēda 〈方言〉darling child
宝刹 bǎochà ❶ pagoda of a Buddhist temple ❷〈敬词〉your temple
宝钞 bǎochāo paper currency issued by the governments of the Yuan, Ming, or Qing dynasties
宝城 bǎochéng wall built around an imperial tomb (in the Ming and Qing dynasties)
宝刀 bǎodāo treasured sword; fine sword
宝刀不老 bǎodāo-bùlǎo the man may be old, but not his sword — one maintains one's strength and skills even when advanced in age
宝刀鱼 bǎodāoyú wolf herring (*Chirocentrus dorab*)
宝地 bǎodì ❶ well-situated place or one which abounds in natural resources:这可是块风水～呀! What a treasured place (*or* location) this is! ❷〈敬词〉your place:借贵方一块～暂住几天。I'd be honoured if you would kindly allow me to stay at your place for a few days.
宝典 bǎodiǎn treasured book
宝顶 bǎodǐng top of an emperor's mausoleum
宝幡 bǎofān long narrow banner with Buddhist inscriptions, hung in a monastery
宝盖 bǎogài canopy of an imperial carriage
宝盖儿 bǎogàir *also* "宝盖头儿" the top radical "宀"
宝钢 Bǎogāng (short for 上海宝山钢铁总厂) Shanghai Baoshan Iron and Steel Corporation
宝贵 bǎoguì ❶ valuable; precious:提出了～的意见 put forward valuable suggestions /做出了～的贡献 make significant contributions /献出了～的生命 sacrifice (*or* lay down) one's life /知识分子是国家的～财富。Intellectuals are priceless assets of the country. /这些文物是～的历史遗产。These cultural relics are part of our treasured historic heritage. ❷ value; treasure; set store by:这是中国人民最可～的性格。This constitutes the most valued part of the Chinese national character.
宝号 bǎohào ❶〈敬词〉your shop; your company or firm ❷〈敬词〉your name
宝货 bǎohuò ❶〈旧语〉currency; money ❷ treasured article; precious object ❸ funny guy; sth. of a clown; good-for-nothing
宝剑 bǎojiàn double-edged treasured sword; double-edged sword:青铜～ double-edged bronze sword
宝眷 bǎojuàn 〈敬词〉your wife and children; your family
宝库 bǎokù treasure-house; treasury:知识的～ treasury of knowledge /敦煌石窟是一座中国古代艺术～。Dunhuang Grottoes are a treasure-house of China's ancient art.
宝蓝 bǎolán sapphire blue; azure; bright blue
宝瓶座 Bǎopíngzuò 〈天文〉*also* "宝瓶星座"; "宝瓶宫" Aquarius
宝器 bǎoqì valuable article
宝山 bǎoshān treasure mountain (often used figuratively):许多荒山变成了～。Many barren hills have been turned into treasure hills. /琳琅满目,如入～。As if in a treasure mountain, one is dazzled by the endless array of beautiful objects.
宝山空回 bǎoshān-kōnghuí return empty-handed from a treasure mountain; fail to benefit from a visit to a great master or a seat of learning:如人无手,虽至宝山,亦能空回。Like a man without arms, you can pick up nothing even if you find yourself in a mountain of treasures.
宝石 bǎoshí precious stone; gem; jewel:～镶嵌 gem mounting /～商 jeweller /～琢磨 gem cutting /～轴承 jewel bearing /红～ ruby/蓝～ sapphire /海蓝～ aquamarine /绿～胸针 emerald brooch
宝石学 bǎoshíxué gemmology
宝书 bǎoshū treasured book
宝塔 bǎotǎ pagoda; dagoba
宝塔菜 bǎotǎcài 〈植物〉Chinese artichoke
宝塔诗 bǎotǎshī pyramidal poem; pyramid (verse in which the succeeding lines increase in length)
宝塔筒子 bǎotǎtǒngzi 〈纺织〉cone
宝玩 bǎowán jewels and ancient curios
宝物 bǎowù treasure:故宫的每件陈列品都是～。Every exhibit in the Palace Museum is a treasure.
宝相花 bǎoxiànghuā "happy flower pattern", traditional decorative flower pattern featuring the lotus
宝藏 bǎozàng precious (mineral) deposit; treasure:地下～ underground mineral resources /发掘民间艺术的～ explore the treasure-house of folk arts
宝重 bǎozhòng treasure; value:～先人遗物 treasure one's ancestral heritage /他的字画为收藏家所～。His calligraphy and paintings are treasured by collectors.
宝座 bǎozuò throne:故宫里保存着明清两代皇帝的～。The thrones of the Ming and Qing emperors are kept in the Palace Museum. /他爬上了总督的～。He climbed to the high post of governorship.

保 bǎo ❶ protect; defend; safeguard:劳～ labour protection; labour insurance /～国安民 defend the country and ensure a peaceful life for the people /舍车～帅 sacrifice the rook to preserve the king /明哲～身 be worldly-wise and play safe; keep out of harm's way by discretion ❷ keep; maintain; preserve:他也许能够～住总经理的职位。He may be able to keep his position as general manager. /如果大堤决口,那堤下的农田就都～不住了。Should the dam burst, all the farmland beneath would be ruined. ❸ guarantee; ensure:～熟～甜 ripeness and sweetness (of watermelons) guaranteed /旱涝～收 ensure stable yields despite drought or waterlogging /朝不～夕 not knowing in the morning what may happen in the evening; hang by a thread; live from hand to mouth /～你没问题。You can rest assured that nothing will happen to you. ❹ go bail for; bail:取～ get sb. to go bail for one ❺ guarantor; guarantee:作～ stand guarantor for; sponsor /铺～ guarantee (for sb.) given by a shopkeeper /具～ (get sb. to) sign a guarantee ❻ division under

former household registration system：连环～ administrative system organized on the basis of households to hold each responsible for the other, formerly enforced by the KMT government at the grass roots level ❼ (Bǎo) a surname

保安 bǎo'ān ❶ ensure public security：～措施 security measure /～人员 security personnel /～科 (HK) Security Branch /做好社会～工作 do a good job in maintaining law and order ❷ (ensure) safety (for personnel engaged in production, etc.)：～章程 safety regulations /～制度 safety rules /～装置 protective device

保安刀 bǎo'āndāo ❶ safty razor ❷ sword made by the Bonan nationality (保安族)

保安队 bǎo'ānduì peace preservation corps (local militia corps under warlord and Kuomintang rule)

保安机构 bǎo'ān jīgòu security department; security：～及时获得了这一暗杀阴谋的情报。Security was duly informed of the assassination plot.

保安司 Bǎo'ānsī (HK before 1 July 1997) Secretary for Security

保安族 Bǎo'ānzú Bonan nationality (living mainly in Gansu Province)

保本 bǎoběn protect any investment or deposit against possible loss; keep the capital intact：～保值 protect (bank deposits, etc.) from declining in value (as a result of inflation) /这笔生意仅仅～而已。I only broke even on the deal.

保膘 bǎobiāo keep (livestock) fat and sturdy：～办法 ways to keep the livestock from losing weight

保镖 bǎobiāo ❶ (of armed guards) escort; serve as armed escort：他曾为我店的货物保过镖。He once undertook to escort our goods (to a certain place). ❷ bodyguard; armed escort：便衣～ plainclothes bodyguard /这位司令出行,后面跟了一大群～。Wherever he went, the commander was escorted by a large group of armed guards.

保不定 bǎobudìng *see* "保不住 ❶"

保不齐 bǎobuqí 〈方言〉 *see* "保不住 ❶"

保不住 bǎobuzhù ❶ most likely; more likely than not; may well：他～会反对这事。He is very likely to oppose it. /家乡变化太大,你～认不出来了。Your hometown has changed so much that you may not recognize it any more. /街里街坊地住着,谁也～不触犯谁点儿。In a crowded neighbourhood people can hardly avoid getting in each other's way at one time or another. ❷ impossible to maintain or preserve：他的买卖到最后连老本儿也～了。His business was in such a bad way that in the end he found it impossible even to save his capital. /遇上这样的大旱,这块地的收成就～了。In such a severe drought, you can hardly expect a normal harvest for this plot of land.

保藏 bǎocáng keep in store; preserve：食品～ food preservation /～良种要有一套技术。It requires a set of techniques to preserve the improved seeds. /家里的贵重首饰由女主人～着。Valuable jewelry of the family is in the safekeeping of the mistress.

保持 bǎochí keep; maintain; preserve：～安静 keep quiet /～镇静 keep one's head; keep cool /～健康 keep fit /～干燥 keep dry /～警惕 maintain vigilance; stay alert; be on one's guard /～一定距离 keep at a distance /～生态平衡 maintain ecological balance /～缄默 keep silence; hold one's tongue /与朋友～通讯联系 keep up a steady correspondence with one's friend /～职位 hold down a job (*or* position) /～边界现状 maintain the status quo of the border /～中立 maintain a neutral position; remain neutral; sit on the fence /～晚节 maintain one's integrity in later years; remain a man of integrity to the very end of one's life /～优良传统 carry on (*or* keep up) a fine tradition /水土～ water and soil conservation /～世界记录 hold a world record /～和进一步发展两国的友好合作关系 maintain and further develop the friendly relations and cooperation between the two countries /～全国安定团结的局面 sustain nationwide stability and unity /～小城的古老风貌 preserve the architectural features of the ancient town

保持电键 bǎochí diànjiàn holding key

保持电路 bǎochí diànlù 〈电子〉 retaining circuit; holding circuit

保持系 bǎochíxì 〈农业〉 maintenance line：雄性不育～ male sterile maintenance line

保持系数 bǎochí xìshù retention coefficient

保持状态 bǎochí zhuàngtài hold mode

保存 bǎocún preserve; conserve; keep; save：～精力 preserve one's strength /～活力 conserve one's vitality (*or* energy) /水果～ fruit preservation /当作纪念品～起来 keep (*or* save) sth. as a memento /所有的文件都要～完整。All the documents should be kept intact.

保存程序 bǎocún chéngxù save routine

保存国 bǎocúnguó depositary：～政府 depositary government

保存期 bǎocúnqī retention period

保存序列 bǎocún xùliè saving sequence

保大 Bǎodà Bao Dai (1913-), last emperor of Vietnam (1926-1955)

保单 bǎodān ❶〈旧语〉 written guarantee for sb.'s character and conduct, or solvency ❷ warrant; insurance policy; warranty：人寿～ life insurance policy /这种吸尘器附有五年的～。The vacuum cleaner has a 5-year warranty.

保得住 bǎodezhù keep; maintain：不断地革新技术,精益求精,产品的荣誉才能～。The reputation of a product relies entirely on continued technological innovation and constant improvement of quality.

保底 bǎodǐ ❶ protect an investment or deposit against currency depreciation ❷ guarantee a minimum sum; ensure a basic figure：上不封顶,下不～ set no maximum or minimum; impose no ceiling or floor figure

保丁 bǎodīng man at the beck and call of the headman of a *Bao* *see also* "保甲制度"

保定 bǎodìng ❶ be sure or certain：谁都不能～会发生什么情况。No one knows for certain what is in store. ❷〈兽医〉 immobilize an animal for diagnosis or operation ❸ (Bǎodìng) city in Hebei Province

保兑 bǎoduì 〈商业〉 confirm：～信用证 confirmed letter of credit; confirmed L/C /～公司 confirming house /～银行 confirming bank

保付 bǎofù guaranteed for payment：～支票 certified check /～银行 certified bank /～商行 confirming house /～书 confirming order

保干器 bǎogānqì desiccator

保固 bǎogù (of contractors) guarantee that the construction remains in good shape within a certain time limit

保管 bǎoguǎn ❶ take care of; maintain; store; manage：～业务 storage service; custodian service /请各位旅客～好自己的行李物品。All passengers are kindly requested to take good care of their luggage and other belongings. /这笔遗产现由律师代为～。This legacy is now being managed by the lawyer on behalf of the inheritor. ❷ storekeeper; storeman：老～ old storekeeper /老张在仓库当～。Lao Zhang was the keeper of a warehouse. ❸ certainly; surely：这个牌子的皮鞋你就放心买吧,～没错。You can rest assured that you will get your money's worth if you buy shoes of this brand. /大胆地干吧,～你能马到成功。Act boldly and you will achieve instant success.

保管费 bǎoguǎnfèi storage charges or fees

保管室 bǎoguǎnshì storeroom

保管银行 bǎoguǎn yínháng depositary bank; custodial bank

保管员 bǎoguǎnyuán store keeper; storeman; keeper

保国会 Bǎoguóhuì Society to Preserve the Nation (political organization of the reform movement launched by Kang Youwei 康有为 and others in 1898)

保函 bǎohán 〈商业〉 letter of guarantee (L/G)

保户 bǎohù insured household; insurance policy holder

保护 bǎohù protect; safeguard; preserve; take care of：～国家利益 protect the national interests /～森林 protect (*or* preserve) forests /～身体健康 take care of one's health; keep fit /～视力 preserve one's eyesight /环境～ environmental protection /劳动～ labour protection /受到法律～ under the protection of the law /被～国 protected state; protectorate /～性贸易 protective trade /～条约 treaty of protection /～人民群众的积极性 cherish the initiative of the masses /《～人权与基本自由公约》*Convention for the Protection of Human Rights and Fundamental Freedoms* (Rome, 1950) /《～世界共同遗产公约》*Convention on Conservation of the World Heritage*

保护层 bǎohùcéng protective layer; protective coating

保护地 bǎohùdì protectorate; dependent territory

保护断路器 bǎohù duànlùqì 〈电学〉 protective circuit breaker

保护阀 bǎohùfá maintaining valve

保护关税 bǎohù guānshuì protective duty or tariff

保护关系 bǎohù guānxi protectorate：～条约 treaty of protectorate

保护国 bǎohùguó protectorate

保护价 bǎohùjià protective pricing; price set to protect the manufacturers or producers

保护继电器 bǎohù jìdiànqì 〈电工〉 protective relay; safety relay

保护接地 bǎohù jiēdì 〈电工〉 protective earthing：～装置 protec-

tive earthing device
保护林 bǎohùlín *also* "防护林" fánghùlín protective forest (shelter):~带 shelter belt
保护贸易政策 bǎohù màoyì zhèngcè policy for the protection of trade; protectionist (trade) policy
保护膜 bǎohùmó protective film
保护鸟 bǎohùniǎo protected bird
保护人 bǎohùrén *also* "监护人" jiānhùrén guardian; custodian; patron:未成年人的~ guardian (*or* custodian) of a minor / 文学艺术的~ patron of art and literature
保护伞 bǎohùsǎn 〈贬义〉protective umbrella; shield; cover:核~ nuclear umbrella /拉关系,找~ curry favour with sb. so as to seek protection /官僚主义者往往是经济犯罪的~。Bureaucrats often provide the protective shield for economic crimes.
保护色 bǎohùsè 〈动物〉protective coloration
保护网 bǎohùwǎng 〈建筑〉safety net; protection network; protective net
保护性拘留 bǎohùxìng jūliú 〈法律〉protective custody; protective detention
保护性免疫 bǎohùxìng miǎnyì 〈医学〉protective immunity
保护性涂剂 bǎohùxìng tújì protective coating
保护性抑制 bǎohùxìng yìzhì 〈医学〉protective inhibition
保护罩 bǎohùzhào 〈电工〉safety cover; boot cap; boot
保护主义 bǎohùzhǔyì protectionism:~政策 protectionist policy / 贸易~ trade protectionism
保皇 bǎohuáng defend the emperor or king; be loyal to conservative forces:~派 royalist
保皇党 bǎohuángdǎng royalists; monarchist party:~人 royalist; monarchist
保皇主义 bǎohuángzhǔyì royalism
保加利亚 Bǎojiālìyà Bulgaria:~人 Bulgarian /~语 Bulgarian (language)
保甲制度 bǎojiǎ zhìdù *Bao-jia* system (former administrative system organized on the basis of households, with each *jia* made up of 10 households, and each *bao* of 10 *jias*, and all the *baos* and *jias* responsible for public security, tax-collection and control of the people within their jurisdiction)
保价 bǎojià value insured:~包裹 insured parcel
保价信 bǎojiàxìn insured letter
保驾 bǎojià (often used jocularly) escort or guard the emperor:如果有老李给你~,你就没有什么可怕的了。If you can get Lao Li to escort (*or* help) you, you will have nothing to fear.
保荐 bǎojiàn recommend; speak well of:他~老刘出任理事。He recommended Lao Liu for membership in the council. /她出任行长助理,是由于王先生的大力~。It was on Mr. Wang's strong recommendation that she was appointed Assistant President of the Bank.
保健 bǎojiàn health protection; health care:劳动~ health protection in labour /卫生~ sanitation and health service /妇幼~ health care for women and children; mother and child care /~组织 health care organization /人民~事业 work of protecting the people's health; health care for the people
保健按摩 bǎojiàn ànmó keep-fit massage; therapeutic massage
保健操 bǎojiàncāo setting-up exercises; fitness exercises
保健费 bǎojiànfèi health subsidies; health care cost
保健粉笔 bǎojiàn fěnbǐ non-toxic chalk
保健球 bǎojiànqiú knuckle-relaxers, pair of small iron or small jade or stone balls held in one's palm and kept moving about to exercise the knuckles
保健食品 bǎojiàn shípǐn health food
保健所 bǎojiànsuǒ clinic
保健网 bǎojiànwǎng health care network
保健物理 bǎojiàn wùlǐ health physics
保健箱 bǎojiànxiāng medical kit; health valise
保健员 bǎojiànyuán health worker:社区~ community health worker
保健站 bǎojiànzhàn health centre; community clinic
保教 bǎojiào child care and education:~人员 nursery staff /~工作 child care and education work
保洁 bǎojié keep the environment clean; do sanitation work:加强公园的~工作 step up the sanitation work in parks
保洁箱 bǎojiéxiāng litter-bin
保结 bǎojié 〈旧语〉written pledge or guarantee (for sb.'s legal status and law-abiding behaviour)
保举 bǎojǔ recommend for promotion or appointment by standing guarantor personally:有人向朝廷极力~他。He was strongly recommended to the emperor for promotion.
保靠 bǎokào 〈方言〉sure; reliable; safe:这样做不~。This is not a safe measure to take.
保理 bǎolǐ 〈经济〉factoring:~公司 factoring company
保龄球 bǎolíngqiú *also* "地滚球" dìgǔnqiú ❶ bowling:~场 bowling alley / 玩~ have a game of bowls; go bowling / ~手 bowler ❷ bowling ball
保留 bǎoliú ❶ retain; keep; maintain:他仍然~着年轻时的朝气。He is still as vigorous as when he was young. *or* He still retains his youthful vigour. /老树还~着旺盛的生命力。The old tree is flourishing as ever before. *or* The old tree still maintains its exuberant vitality. /这一传统从解放战争时代一直~到今天。This is a tradition we have kept from the days of the Liberation War. ❷ keep for later; hold back:如果你不同意,你可~自己的观点。If you don't agree, you may keep your own views. ❸ hold a dissenting view; have reservations (about sth.):对决议持~态度 hold dissenting views about the resolution; have reservations about the resolution /有~地赞同 agree with some reservations ❹ reserve; save:~进一步交涉的权利 reserve one's right to make further representations /~学籍 keep sb.'s name on the admission list; grant sb a deferral (*or* deferment) to admission /~原文 stet; let it stand /请给我~一个位子好吗? Will you please save a seat for me? /他毫无~地向乡亲们传授技术。He passed on the technical know-how to the villagers without any reservation. /前三排座位是给外宾~的。The first three rows are reserved for foreign guests.
保留地 bǎoliúdì reservation:印第安~ (US) Indian reservation
保留工资 bǎoliú gōngzī retain one's (previous higher) salary:转业军官的~ retained salaries of demobilized officers
保留剧目 bǎoliú jùmù repertory; repertoire; repertory item
保留利润 bǎoliú lìrùn reserved profit (of a state-owned enterprise after handing over a fixed amount of profit to the state)
保留权限 bǎoliú quánxiàn reserved authority
保留条款 bǎoliú tiáokuǎn reservation clause
保路运动 Bǎolù Yùndòng Movement to Protect Railway Projects (people's movement in southern China in 1911 against the nationalization of locally funded railways and sale of railway rights to foreign imperialist powers by the Qing government)
保媒 bǎoméi serve as a go-between (for marriage)
保密 bǎomì keep confidential; maintain secrecy:~文件 classified (*or* confidential) document /~级别:秘密、机密、绝密 security classification:confidential; secret; top secret /~条例 security regulation / ~电话 secure telephone /~观念强 be security-conscious /~宣誓 vow of silence /这件事要绝对~。We must maintain absolute secrecy about this. /你放心好了,我一定为你~。You can set your mind at rest. I will keep my mouth shut. /大家都知道的事,你还保什么密! You don't have to keep it secret as this is public knowledge. /这个计划暂时要~。The project must be kept under wraps for the time being.
保密局 Bǎomìjú (US) National Security Agency; (KMT government) National Security Bureau
保苗 bǎomiáo 〈农业〉keep or ensure a full stand of seedlings
保命 bǎomìng survive; keep oneself going:这是一家五口的~粮食。This is the grain to keep the family of five from starvation.
保姆 bǎomǔ ❶ domestic child-care nurse; dry nurse; baby sitter:住家~ live-in baby-sitter ❷ housemaid; housekeeper; maid ❸ 〈旧语〉nursery or kindergarten worker
保暖 bǎonuǎn keep warm:冬季~ keeping warm in winter; winter heating /~衣服 warm clothes; warms
保赔保险 bǎopéi bǎoxiǎn 〈商业〉*also* "保赔险" P & I (protection and indemnity) insurance
保赔协会 bǎopéi xiéhuì 〈商业〉protection and indemnity association
保票 bǎopiào *also* "包票" bāopiào ❶〈商业〉warranty; certificate of guarantee ❷ written guarantee; guarantee:我不能为他的安全打~。I cannot vouch for (*or* guarantee) his safety. /你敢打~,她一定会来参加晚会? Are you sure that she'll come to the party?
保全 bǎoquán ❶ save from damage; preserve:~性命 save one's life; save one's bacon /~面子 save face /~名誉 preserve one's reputation /情况危急,阵地无法~。The situation was desperate, and it

was impossible to defend the position. ❷ maintain; repair; keep in good condition: ～工 maintenance worker /～措施 conservatory measure
保人 bǎorén see "保证人"
保山 bǎoshān 〈旧语〉guarantor or matchmaker
保墒 bǎoshāng 〈农业〉preservation of soil moisture: 中耕～ inter-till the field to preserve soil moisture
保释 bǎoshì 〈法律〉release on bail; bail: ～保证书 bail bond /准予～ accept (*or* allow) bail /不准～ refuse bail /在～期间逃跑 jump bail /在～中 be out on bail /把他～出来 bail him out /犯人获准～。The prisoner was granted bail. *or* The prisoner was allowed out on bail.
保释人 bǎoshìrén 〈法律〉bailsman: 为他做～ stand (*or* go) bail for sb.
保收 bǎoshōu ensure the harvest of the crops: 保种～ make sure that both the sowing and harvesting are done in good time
保守 bǎoshǒu ❶ guard; keep safe; secure: ～国家机密 guard (*or* keep) state secrets /～中立 maintain neutrality /我军能够～或夺取的地方,必须～或夺取之。Our troops should capture or hold the places wherever they can. ❷ conservative: ～势力 conservative forces /～思想 conservative ideas; conservative ideology /因循～,不求进取 be an old stick-in-the-mud and devoid of ambition /青年人最有朝气,最少～。Young people are the most active and the least conservative in their thinking.
保守党 Bǎoshǒudǎng (UK) Conservative Party; Tory Party
保守疗法 bǎoshǒu liáofǎ 〈医学〉conservative treatment; non-operative treatment
保守派 bǎoshǒupài conservative
保守主义 bǎoshǒuzhǔyì conservatism
保税 bǎoshuì 〈外贸〉keep in bond: ～制度 bonded system /～仓库 bonded warehouse /～货物 bonded goods; goods in bond /～工厂 bonded factory
保税区 bǎoshuìqū bonded zone; bonded area
保送 bǎosòng recommend for admission to a higher level school: ～优秀毕业生到大学学习 recommend outstanding school graduates for study in college /他被部队～到军事院校深造。He was sent to a military academy for advanced study on the recommendation of his military unit.
保送上垒 bǎosòng shànglěi 〈体育〉(of baseball) walk; receive bases on balls
保胎 bǎotāi prevent miscarriage; help retain the fetus
保泰松 bǎotàisōng 〈药学〉phenylbutazone
保外就医 bǎowài-jiùyī receive medical treatment on bail
保外执行 bǎowài-zhíxíng serve part of one's prison term outside prison on bail
保卫 bǎowèi defend; safeguard; protect: ～国家主权和领土完整 safeguard state sovereignty and territorial integrity /～和平反对战争 oppose war in defence of peace /～边境地区的安宁 maintain the tranquillity of the border region /为～国家财产而献出了生命 give one's life to protect state property /～部门 public security organ (*or* department) /～工作 security work /～科 security section
保温 bǎowēn keeping warm; heat protection: ～温度 holding temperature /～集装箱 insulated container /食堂到冬天要注意饭菜～。Efforts must be made to keep the food warm in the canteen during wintertime.
保温杯 bǎowēnbēi miniature thermos flask; thermos mug
保温材料 bǎowēn cáiliào thermal insulation material
保温层 bǎowēncéng 〈建筑〉(thermal) insulating layer
保温车 bǎowēnchē 〈铁路〉refrigerator wagon or car
保温管道 bǎowēn guǎndào utilidor
保温炉 bǎowēnlú 〈冶金〉holding furnace; maintaining furnace
保温瓶 bǎowēnpíng vacuum flask or bottle; thermos
保温箱 bǎowēnxiāng insulation can; incubator (for a premature baby, etc.)
保鲜 bǎoxiān keep (vegetables, fruits, meat, etc.) fresh: 改进水产品～技术 improve the technique of keeping aquatic products fresh
保鲜剂 bǎoxiānjì antistaling agent
保鲜膜 bǎoxiānmó clingfilm; plastic wrap
保鲜纸 bǎoxiānzhǐ handi-wrap
保险 bǎoxiǎn ❶ insurance: 人身～ personal insurance /人寿～ life insurance /医疗～ medical insurance /健康～ health insurance /养老～ endowment insurance /意外～ accident insurance /财产～ property insurance /火灾～ fire insurance /运输～ transport(ation) insurance /航空～ aviation insurance /海上～ marine insurance /集体～ collective insurance /集团～ group insurance /共同～ co-insurance /强制～ compulsory (*or* obligatory) insurance /社会～ social insurance; social security /失业～ unemployment insurance /再～ re-insurance /双重～ double insurance /不动产～ immovable insurance /动产～ movable insurance /预约～ open policy insurance /原～ original insurance /追加～ supplementary insurance /～赔偿 insurance indemnity /～推销员 insurance canvasser /～凭证 insurance certificate /～合同 insurance contract /～市场 insurance market /～回扣 insurance rebate /～信托 insurance trust /～值 insurance value ❷ safe; secure; reliable: 坐这条旧船过河～吗? Is it safe to cross the river in this shabby old boat? /这是个～的办法。This is a safe (*or* surefire) approach. /为了～起见,你三点以后再来电话。You'd better ring up again after 3 p.m., to be on the safe side. ❸ guarantee; be sure to: 他要老是这样,谁能～他不耽误工作。Nobody can guarantee that he will not neglect his work if he goes on like that. /她～能得第一名。She is bound to come out first. *or* She is sure to win first place. /是他,～没错儿! I swear it's he!
保险代理人 bǎoxiǎn dàilǐrén insurance agent
保险带 bǎoxiǎndài safety belt
保险单 bǎoxiǎndān insurance policy; insurance policy form: ～持有人 policy holder /保险副单 alternate
保险刀 bǎoxiǎndāo safety razor
保险灯 bǎoxiǎndēng safety lamp; gas lamp
保险阀 bǎoxiǎnfá 〈电工〉safety valve
保险法 bǎoxiǎnfǎ insurance law
保险范围 bǎoxiǎn fànwéi insurance coverage
保险费 bǎoxiǎnfèi insurance premium; insurance expense
保险粉 bǎoxiǎnfěn 〈纺织〉sodium hydrosulphite
保险杠 bǎoxiǎngàng (of an automobile) bumper
保险公司 bǎoxiǎn gōngsī insurance company
保险柜 bǎoxiǎnguì safe
保险盒 bǎoxiǎnhé fuse box or block
保险机 bǎoxiǎnjī *also* "保险栓"; "保险" safety catch (on a gun or cannon); safety
保险经纪人 bǎoxiǎn jīngjìrén insurance broker
保险开关 bǎoxiǎn kāiguān 〈电工〉safety switch
保险库 bǎoxiǎnkù vault; safe vault
保险人 bǎoxiǎnrén insurer: 被～ insurant; the insured
保险税 bǎoxiǎnshuì insurance tax
保险丝 bǎoxiǎnsī 〈电工〉fuse; fuse-wire: ～断了,室内一片漆黑。The fuse burned out (*or* was blown), and the room was plunged into total darkness.
保险索赔 bǎoxiǎn suǒpéi insurance claim
保险箱 bǎoxiǎnxiāng safe; strongbox
保险佣金 bǎoxiǎn yòngjīn insurance commission
保险装置 bǎoxiǎn zhuāngzhì safety device
保修 bǎoxiū ❶ guarantee repair service for a commodity sold: 本店所售钟表～一年。There is a year's guarantee with the watches and clocks sold at this shop. ❷ repair; maintenance: 超额完成车辆～任务 over-fulfil the quota of vehicle maintenance
保修单 bǎoxiūdān warranty
保许 bǎoxǔ surely; certainly: 这西瓜～熟了。This watermelon is ripe for sure.
保养 bǎoyǎng ❶ take good care of (one's health); preserve: ～得宜 well-preserved /他平日很注意～身体。He takes very good care of his health. *or* He always takes care to keep himself fit. /你身子单薄,应当好好～。As you have a weak constitution, you'd better take good care of yourself. ❷ service; maintenance; upkeep: 定期～ regular servicing (*or* maintenance); routine checkup /汽车～中心 car service centre /～周期 maintenance period /这段公路～得很差。This section of the road is poorly maintained.
保养费用 bǎoyǎng fèiyòng maintenance or upkeep cost
保养工 bǎoyǎnggōng service or maintenance worker
保养鉴定 bǎoyǎng jiàndìng maintenance evaluation
保养手册 bǎoyǎng shǒucè maintenance manual
保有 bǎoyǒu own; possess; hold: ～大片土地和牧场 own large tracts of land and ranches
保佑 bǎoyòu bless and protect: 上帝～你。May God bless you. /他大难不死,真是菩萨～了。With Buddha's blessing, he made a narrow escape from disaster. /农民们现在靠科技种田,再不靠老天～了。

Today, farmers rely on science and technology. They no longer rely on blessings from heaven.

保育 bǎoyù child care; child welfare

保育率 bǎoyùlǜ 〈畜牧〉survival rate of grown animals

保育员 bǎoyùyuán child care worker; nurse

保育院 bǎoyùyuàn nursery school

保长 bǎozhǎng 〈旧语〉headman of a *bao*

保障 bǎozhàng ❶ ensure; guarantee; safeguard: ～安全 ensure safety /～条款 safeguard clause /充分～人民的言论自由 fully guarantee freedom of speech for the people /依法～人身自由 ensure freedom of the person according to law /～人民的身体健康 protect people's health /发展经济，～供给。Develop the economy and ensure the supplies. ❷ guarantee; assurance: ～制度 safeguard system /缺少必要的～ lack necessary assurance (*or* guarantees) /强大的人民军队是祖国安全的～。A powerful people's army is the guarantee of the country's security.

保真 bǎozhēn 〈电子〉fidelity: ～度 fidelity /高～ high fidelity; hi-fi /～音响设备 hi-fi set

保正 bǎozhèng *see* "保长"

保证 bǎozhèng ❶ ensure; pledge; assure: ～正常的工作秩序 ensure a normal work schedule /～卫星发射的圆满成功 ensure complete success of the launching of a satellite into orbit /～不再发生类似事件 guarantee against recurrence of similar incidents /我敢～你弄错了。I can assure you that you're mistaken. /我～以后再不这么干了。I swear (*or* pledge) that I will not act the way I did. ❷ guarantee: 安全～ security guarantee; safeguard /～重点，统筹兼顾 give priority to key areas while making overall plans with due consideration for other factors /团结是胜利的基本～。Unity is the fundamental guarantee for victory. /一家人的生活有了～。The livelihood of the family is assured. *or* The family is now able to make both ends meet.

保证基金 bǎozhèng jījīn guarantee fund

保证金 bǎozhèngjīn ❶ earnest money; cash deposit; margin: 信托～ trust deposit ❷ 〈法律〉bail

保证汽耗 bǎozhèng qìhào guaranteed steam consumption; steam rate guarantee

保证人 bǎozhèngrén ❶ 〈法律〉bail ❷ 〈商业〉guarantor; bondsman; surety

保证书 bǎozhèngshū guarantee; written pledge; guaranty; letter of guarantee

保证性能 bǎozhèng xìngnéng guaranteed performance

保值 bǎozhí value insured or guaranteed against loss: ～储蓄 savings deposit at inflation-adjusted interests; inflation-adjusted savings deposit

保质 bǎozhì ensure or guarantee the quality of a product: ～期 date stamping

保种 bǎozhòng guaranteed sowing: ～保收 sow in good time to ensure a good harvest; ensure timely sowing and harvesting

保重 bǎozhòng look after oneself; take care of oneself: 寒冬季节，多多～。Take good care of yourself in this severe winter.

保状 bǎozhuàng 〈旧语〉written guarantee: 法官令保人出具～。The judge ordered the guarantor to deposit a written guarantee with the court.

保准 bǎozhǔn ❶ dependable; trustworthy: 他说话不～。What he says may not be true. *or* His words are no guarantee. /这片洼地年年没有收成，改成稻田，收成就～了。The low-lying land failed to yield anything year after year, but a good harvest can be expected once it is turned into paddy fields. ❷ pledge; guarantee; make sure: ～办到。It will surely be done. /这是我的缺点，我～改。This is my shortcoming and I vow to overcome it.

褓(緥) bǎo *see* "襁褓" qiǎngbǎo

堡 bǎo fort; fortress: 碉～ pillbox; fortification /地～ bunker /城～ castle /桥头～ bridgehead; bridge tower /滩头～ beachhead

see also bǔ; pù

堡礁 bǎojiāo coral reef parallel to the coast, which emerge on the ebb tide; barrier reef

堡垒 bǎolěi fortress; stronghold; fort; blockhouse: ～战 blockhouse warfare /科学～ fortress of science /顽固～ stronghold of reaction (*or* conservatism); stubborn fellow; stick-in-the-mud /～最容易从内部攻破。The easiest way to conquer (*or* capture) a fortress is from within.

堡坞 bǎowù 〈旧词〉❶ citadel built by powerful local families against attacks ❷ manorial organization centred upon feudal clans

堡寨 bǎozhài walled or stockaded village

葆[1] bǎo ❶ 〈书面〉preserve; maintain; nurture: 永～青春 maintain one's youth (*or* youthful look); keep alive the youthful spirit ❷ (Bǎo) a surname

葆[2] bǎo 〈书面〉luxuriant growth (usu. of grass): 头如蓬～ shaggy (*or* unkempt) hair

饱 bǎo ❶ have eaten one's fill; be full; be replete: 酒足饭～ eat and drink one's fill /～食暖衣 be well-fed and well-clad /解决人民的温～问题 solve the problem of providing sufficient food and clothing for the people /我只吃了个半～。I'm only half full. ❷ full; plump: 颗颗花生长得那么～。Each and every peanut is grown so plump. ❸ fully; to the full: ～受惊恐 be badly shaken ❹ satisfy: 一～眼福 feast one's eyes (on sth.); enjoy a feast for the eyes ❺ fatten (one's purse); embezzle: 中～私囊 fatten one's purse; line one's pocket

饱餐 bǎocān eat one's full; feast one's eyes on: ～了一顿狍子肉 eat roe deer meat to one's heart's content /～秀色 feast one's eyes on beautiful scenery (*or* the beauty of a girl); enjoy the beautiful scenery very much

饱尝 bǎocháng ❶ enjoy to the full: ～美味 have one's fill of delicate dishes ❷ experience or suffer: ～艰辛 endure all hardships /～人世的痛苦 experience all the agonies of life /～铁窗风味 have a full taste of life behind bars

饱读 bǎodú read extensively; be well-read: ～经书 be well-read (*or* well-versed) in the classics

饱嗝儿 bǎogér belch; burp: 打～ belch

饱含 bǎohán be full of; be filled with: 眼里～着热泪 eyes brimming with tears /胸中～着对大好河山的热爱 be filled with ardent love for one's dear country

饱汉不知饿汉饥 bǎohàn bù zhī èhàn jī 〈谚语〉the well-fed don't know how the starving suffer; you can't feel for the starving with a full belly; little does the fat sow know what the lean means

饱和 bǎohé saturation: ～溶液 saturated solution /～湿度 saturated humidity /～温度 saturation temperature /～压力 saturation pressure /气体～ gas saturation /市场～ saturated market /车厢里已经达到～状态，再也挤不进一个人去。The carriage is filled to capacity and there is not even standing room for another passenger.

饱和差 bǎohéchā 〈气象〉saturation deficit or deficiency

饱和点 bǎohédiǎn saturation point

饱和电抗 bǎohé diànkàng 〈电学〉saturation reactance

饱和电压 bǎohé diànyā 〈电学〉saturation voltage

饱和度 bǎohédù saturation degree: ～控制 saturation control /～数值 saturation value

饱和沸腾 bǎohé fèiténg saturation boiling

饱和轰炸 bǎohé hōngzhà 〈军事〉saturation bombing

饱和剂 bǎohéjì saturant

饱和价格 bǎohé jiàgé satiety price

饱和气体 bǎohé qìtǐ saturated gas

饱和器 bǎohéqì saturator

饱和色 bǎohésè saturated colour

饱和岩 bǎohéyán 〈地质〉saturated rock

饱和液体 bǎohé yètǐ saturated liquid

饱和脂肪酸 bǎohé zhīfángsuān saturated fatty acid: 非～ unsaturated fatty acid

饱和值 bǎohézhí saturation value

饱和指数 bǎohé zhǐshù saturation index

饱经沧桑 bǎojīng-cāngsāng have witnessed or experienced many changes in life; have been through the vicissitudes of life: ～的一生 a life full of ups and downs /他虽然～，仍然童心未泯。Though he has gone through a good deal in life, he is still a child at heart.

饱经风霜 bǎojīng-fēngshuāng having experienced the hardships of life; weather-beaten: ～的面孔 weather-beaten face /～的海员 seasoned sailor /院里的银杏树，～，活了数百年，依然郁郁葱葱。The ginkgo tree in the courtyard has weathered wind and frost for centuries and is still lush and luxuriant.

饱经世故 bǎojīng-shìgù well-versed in the ways of society; worldly-wise：这人年龄不大，却～。Though young, he is quite experienced in the ways of society. /我常向这位～的老人请教。I often solicit advice from the old man who is full of worldly wisdom.
饱经忧患 bǎojīng-yōuhuàn have had one's fill of trials and tribulations; have undergone great hardships in life：～的国家终于站起来了。The long-suffering country is finally up on her own feet.
饱览 bǎolǎn feast one's eyes on; take in fully：～名山胜迹 tour famous mountains and historic sites /他在航天旅行中，～了天外奇观。During his space travel, he has taken in the spectacular sights of outer space.
饱满 bǎomǎn ❶ plump; rounded：颗粒～的稻子 plump-eared rice /颧骨隆起，天庭～ with protruding cheek-bones and a broad forehead/ ～丰腴的字迹 characters written (*or* inscribed) in vigorous, well-rounded strokes ❷ full of; be filled with：精力～ full of vim and vigour /～的工作热情 whole-hearted devotion to one's work /他的情绪～极了。He is overflowing with enthusiasm.
饱满度 bǎomǎndù 〈农业〉plumpness (of seeds)
饱暖 bǎonuǎn be well fed and clad; be in easy circumstances：～勿忘饥寒日。Don't forget the hard times when you live in comfort. /～思淫欲，饥寒起盗心。Easy circumstances tend to breed lewd desires, whereas hunger and cold may drive one to theft.
饱食终日，无所用心 bǎo shí zhōngrì, wú suǒ yòng xīn eat three square meals a day without doing any useful work — live like a parasite; be well-fed and carefree：他～，难怪他发胖了。He is well-fed and cares about nothing else. No wonder he is putting on weight.
饱受 bǎoshòu have a full measure of：～虐待 be maltreated in every way possible /～凌辱 suffer untold humiliations and insults /从小～慈亲的疼爱 be brought up with loving care by one's parents
饱学 bǎoxué learned; scholarly; erudite：～之士 man of learning; learned scholar /～鸿儒 scholar of great erudition
饱以老拳 bǎoyǐlǎoquán deal sb. blow after blow on the face; give sb. a sound beating
饱雨 bǎoyǔ 〈方言〉thorough rain; soaking rain; soaker
饱饫 bǎoyù 〈书面〉❶ eat well; be well fed：十余万人，皆得～。Over one hundred thousand people were all well fed. ❷ fully appreciate：～宏论 hear out sb.'s brilliant views with a deep sense of appreciation
饱孕 bǎoyùn be full of; be filled with; be replete with：空气中～着鲜花的芳香。The air is permeated with the fragrance of flowers.
饱绽 bǎozhàn plump; full：他～的肌肉充满了活力。His strong muscles flex with vigour.
饱胀 bǎozhàng *also*"饱涨" ❶ full; bursting：～的书包 bag bursting with books /花骨朵儿～得像要裂开似的。The bulbs of the flowers are so full that they look as though they will be bursting the next minute. ❷〈比喻〉be full of; be immersed in
饱足 bǎozú be content; be satisfied：侵略者的胃口永远不知道～。The aggressor's appetite is insatiable.

鸨 bǎo ❶〈动物〉bustard：硕～ *also*"大～" great bustard ❷ procuress; madam：老～ procuress; brothel keeper
鸨母 bǎomǔ *also*"鸨儿" procuress; brothel keeper; bawd

bào

报(報) bào ❶ tell; report; announce：谎～军情 give false information about the military situation /漏～ neglect to report/ ～火警 raise the fire alarm/ 将计划～学术委员会审核 submit the plan to the academic council for approval /嫩芽～春到。The new buds are a harbinger of spring. /归来的燕子预～春天的来临。Returning swallows herald spring. ❷ reciprocate; respond; reply：～友人书 reply to a friend /～以热烈的掌声 respond with warm applause; applaud warmly /～以一笑 respond with a smile (*or* laugh) /～以白眼 give sb. a supercilious (*or* disdainful) look /～以嘘声 hiss sb.; greet sb. with boos and catcalls ❸ recompense; requite：投桃～李 give a plum in return for a peach — return a favour with a favour ❹ retaliate; revenge：睚眦必～ seek revenge for every petty grievance ❺ retribution：来世～ retribution in the next life /现世～ retribution in this life /善有善～，恶有恶～。Good will be rewarded with good and evil with evil. ❻ newspaper; paper：办～ run a newspaper /登～ publish in a newspaper /机关～ official newspaper of a party, government, etc. /日～ daily newspaper; daily /晚～ evening paper /这条新闻明天见～。This piece (*or* item) of news will appear in tomorrow's press. ❼ periodical; journal：画～ pictorial; illustrated magazine /学～ journal; academic journal /年～ annuals (of an academic society) /季～ quarterly /月～ monthly /周～ weekly ❽ reportage; bulletin; report：情～ information; intelligence report /墙～ wall newspaper /简～ bulletin; brief report /喜～ bulletin of glad (*or* happy) tidings; piece of good news /战～ battlefield report; war communique; war report /公～ communique; bulletin /快～ bulletin of the latest news; stop press /捷～ news of victory; report of success /海～ poster (for a show or a public activity); bill ❾ telegram; cable：发～ send a telegram; transmit a message (by radio); telegraph
报案 bào'àn report a case (to the security authorities)：向派出所～ report a criminal offence to a sub-police station /从～到破案不过二十四小时。It took only 24 hours to crack the criminal case after it was reported.
报靶 bàobǎ report the result of a shot (in shooting practice)：～手 man who reports the result of shooting practice on the spot
报表 bàobiǎo forms or tables for reporting statistics; report forms：年终～ annual report forms /预算～ budget report forms /资产负债～ balance sheet /损益～〈经济〉profit-and-loss report /财务～ accounting report; financial report /日～ daily report /有些部门～成灾。Some departments are inundated (*or* deluged) with statistical tables.
报偿 bàocháng repay; recompense; reward：老师对我的培养是无法～的。I can never do enough to repay my teachers for their kind instruction. *or* I shall be eternally indebted to my teachers. /她在精神上的创伤你～得了吗？Can you repair the trauma she has sustained?
报呈 bàochéng submit a report (to higher authorities)：～上级备案 submit a report to the higher authorities for the record
报仇 bàochóu revenge; avenge：向敌人～ revenge (*or* avenge) oneself on the enemy; take vengeance on the enemy /为亲人们～ avenge one's dear ones /报私仇 wage a private vendetta against sb.; settle personal scores with /心中燃烧着～的烈火 be burning with a desire for revenge /君子～，十年不晚。A gentleman can afford to wait for as long as ten years to avenge himself.
报仇雪耻 bàochóu-xuěchǐ take revenge and wipe out a humiliation：空怀～之心 cherish the vain hope of wreaking vengeance
报仇雪恨 bàochóu-xuěhèn avenge or wipe out a grievance; revenge or avenge oneself; pay off old scores：为死难烈士～ avenge the fallen heroes
报酬 bàochou reward; remuneration; pay：找到一项～不菲的工作 have found a remunerative job /努力工作不计～ work hard and never bother about pay /经济～ financial reward /物质～ material reward
报酬递减率 bàochou dìjiǎnlǜ 〈经济〉law of diminishing return
报酬率 bàochoulǜ 〈经济〉rate of return
报春 bàochūn be a harbinger of spring：红梅～。The wintersweet heralds the advent of spring.
报春花 bàochūnhuā 〈植物〉primrose; primula
报答 bàodá repay; requite：～知遇之恩 repay sb. for his generous estimate of one's talent /我要一心一意地～祖国的培养。I will devote my life to requiting the care of my country for me.
报单 bàodān ❶ customs declaration; entry; tax declaration：出口～ declaration for exportation /进口～ declaration for importation /海运～ declaration for sea transport /免税货物～ entry for duty-free goods ❷ *see*"报条"
报到 bàodào report for duty; check in; register：向大会秘书处～ check in at the secretariat of the conference /到工作单位～ report for duty at one's work unit /学校在九月初办理新生～手续。The university starts registration of freshmen in early September.
报道 bàodào *also*"报导" report; cover：据新华社～ as is reported by Xinhua News Agency; according to a dispatch by Xinhua News Agency /据官方的～ according to official sources /补充～ follow-up report /有关这件事的零星～ tidbits of information about this incident/ 带偏见的～ biased report /现场～比赛情况 live coverage of a game /各方记者云集北京，～第十一届亚运会。Reporters from all quarters came to Beijing to cover the 11th Asian Games. /各报都以头版头条～了这一事件。The event became the banner headline on the front page in all the newspapers. *or* The event made frontpage news. /我从广播中听了有关这事的全部～。I learned the whole story

(of the event) from a news broadcast. *or* I heard the story on the radio.

报德 bàodé repay sb.'s kindness: 以德~ return good for good / 以怨~ requite kindness with ingratitude

报端 bàoduān part of a newspaper page: 征稿启事已见~。The notice soliciting contributions has appeared in the newspapers.

报恩 bào'ēn pay a debt of gratitude; repay sb. for his or her kindness: ~思想 perpetual desire to repay a person for his or her kindness; obsession with repayment for sb.'s kindness / 以恩~, 以怨报怨 requite like for like

报废 bàofèi discard (as useless or worn out, or defective); scrap: ~零件 faulty parts; scrapped parts / ~器材 scrap equipment / ~油井 abandoned well / ~资产 dead assets / 将旧车~ report an old car as worn out (so as to replace it with a new one); put an old car out to pasture; scrap an old car / 这些次品必须~。These defective (*or* inferior, *or* sub-standard) goods must be scrapped.

报分 bàofēn 〈体育〉 call the score

报复 bàofu retaliate; pay sb. back in his or her own coin; make reprisal: ~关税 retaliatory tariff / ~措施 retaliatory measure / ~行为 vindictive act; act of reprisal / ~性袭击 reprisal raid / ~性惩罚 retributive punishment / ~性很强 be revengeful (*or* vindictive) / 他发誓要~欺骗过他的人。He swore he would get his own back on those who had cheated him.

报复主义 bàofuzhǔyì ❶ principle of an-eye-for-an-eye retaliation (formerly esp. in meting out legal punishment) ❷ vindictiveness; strong desire for revenge

报告 bàogào ❶ report; announce; make known: ~最新科研成果 report on the latest achievements in scientific research / ~出席会议的人数 announce the attendance at a meeting / 详细~事件的经过 give a detailed account of the event from beginning to end / 国务院对全国人民代表大会负责并~工作。The State Council is responsible and accountable to the National People's Congress. ❷ speech; talk; lecture; report: 年度~ annual report / 项目鉴定~ project evaluation report / 考绩~ performance evaluation / 学术~会 academic lecture / 时事~会 lecture (*or* talk) on current affairs / 成绩~单 school report / 化验~单 laboratory test report / 总结~ summing-up report; summary report / 去调查一下, 然后写个~。Go and investigate the matter and then submit your findings.

报告人 bàogàorén lecturer; speaker; reporter; rapporteur (as at a conference or meeting)

报告文学 bàogào wénxué reportage

报告小说 bàogào xiǎoshuō documentary novel

报功 bàogōng ❶ report sb.'s meritorious deeds to the higher authorities or to his or her unit: ~单 written citation (of merit) ❷ 〈书面〉 reward for meritorious service: 崇德~ praise sb. for his (*or* her) integrity and award him (*or* her) for meritorious deeds

报关 bàoguān declare at customs; make a customs declaration: ~行 *also* "~代理人" customs agent (*or* broker) / 有东西要~吗? Anything to declare? / 你们下飞机后第一件事就是~。The first thing after you disembark from the plane is to go through customs.

报关表 bàoguānbiǎo *also* "报关单" customs debenture or declaration; declaration form: 进口~ customs declaration for import

报官 bàoguān report to the authorities

报馆 bàoguǎn (popular term for 报社) newspaper office

报国 bàoguó dedicate oneself to the service of one's country: 以身~ lay down one's life for one's country / ~无门 be denied a chance to serve the country / 精忠~ serve one's country with staunch loyalty

报户口 bào hùkǒu apply for permanent residence; register one's domicile: 给新生婴儿~ register the birth of a newborn baby / 报临时户口 apply for a temporary residence permit

报话 bàohuà ❶ radio communication: ~员 radio operator ❷ message sent over the radio: 他一上午收发了二十份~。He despatched and received a total of 20 radio messages this morning.

报话机 bàohuàjī transmitter-receiver set; handie-talkie; walkie-talkie

报夹 bàojiā newspaper clip

报价 bàojià 〈经济〉 quoted price; quotation: ~单 quotation of prices / ~者 quoter / 初次~ first offer/报优惠价 quote favourable terms

报架 bàojià newspaper holder or rack

报奖 bàojiǎng recommend to the higher authorities for a prize: 做好农业增产~工作。Duly recommend farmers for rewards for increased output.

报捷 bàojié report a success; announce a victory: ~的锣鼓响彻云霄。The beatings of gongs and drums heralding the victory resounded through the skies. / 工厂将超产喜讯向市政府~。The factory reported the overfulfilment of its production plan to the municipal government.

报界 bàojiè the press; the media; journalistic or press circles; journalists: 向~宣布会议日程 announce the agenda of a conference to the press / 引起~的重视 arouse the attention of the press; attract much attention in the media / ~人士 people from the press; press circles / 此事~反应强烈。The press reacted strongly to this matter.

报禁 bàojìn press censorship; (government) control of the press: 开~ lift press censorship; de-regulate the press

报警 bàojǐng report to the police or public security authorities; call the police; give an alarm: 鸣钟~ sound the alarm bell / ~装置 warning device / ~系统 warning system / 报火警 report a fire / 报匪警 report a robbery

报警码 bàojǐngmǎ alarm code

报警器 bàojǐngqì alarm; warner; warning device

报警信号 bàojǐng xìnhào alarm signal; alerting signal: ~继电器 alarm relay

报刊 bàokān newspapers and periodicals; the press: ~杂志 newspapers and magazines / ~发行 distribution of newspapers and periodicals / ~橱窗 glass-fronted billboards for newspapers (for public reading) / ~零售亭 newsstand; kiosk selling newspapers and magazines

报考 bàokǎo enter oneself for an examination: ~大学 register for university entrance exams; offer oneself as a candidate for admission to a university / 个人~志愿 personal options for academic disciplines

报矿 bàokuàng inform the relevant authorities of the location of the mineral ores or reserves one has discovered

报栏 bàolán glass-fronted billboards on which newspapers are put up for public reading

报廊 bàoláng long row of glass-fronted newspaper billboards

报领 bàolǐng request the higher authorities for supplies: ~十万套军服 make (*or* submit) a request for 100,000 army uniforms

报录 bàolù 〈旧语〉 report the results of the imperial examination (to the successful candidates): ~人 messenger who reports such results

报密 bàomì inform against sb.

报名 bàomíng enter one's name; sign; sign up: ~单 entry form / ~参军 sign up to join the army / 愿意春游的同志, 请先到工会~。Those who wish to go on a spring outing please sign at the trade union office. / 他已经~参加这个会议。He has put his name down for the conference.

报命 bàomìng 〈书面〉 report back on the completion of a mission

报幕 bàomù announce items of a (theatrical) programme: 今晚的演出将用中文和英文~。Show items will be announced both in Chinese and English in this evening's soirée.

报幕员 bàomùyuán announcer

报盘 bàopán 〈经济〉 offer: ~人 offerer / 投标~ offer by tender / 附带条件的~ offer with a string attached

报批 bàopī submit to a higher authority for approval: 履行~手续 go through the formalities to secure approval / 层层~ report to the higher authorities at different levels for examination and approval

报屁股 bàopìgu 〈戏谑〉 bottom of page of least importance in a newspaper; inconspicuous spot in a newspaper: ~文章 insignificant newspaper articles

报聘 bàopìn 〈旧语〉 return an official visit

报请 bàoqǐng submit a written report for instruction or approval: ~上级批准 report to the higher authorities for approval / ~最高法院审判 submit (a case) to the supreme court for judgment / ~国务院审处 report (a matter) to the State Council for review and decision / ~人大审议 submit (a report or findings, etc.) to the National People's Congress (NPC) for deliberation

报人 bàorén journalist; pressman

报丧 bàosāng announce sb.'s death; give obituary notice: 派人向死者亲友~ send a messenger to inform relatives and friends of sb.'s death / 不少乡里人仍相信乌鸦~, 喜鹊报喜的说法。Many country folk still believe that crows announce misfortune while magpies bring

good luck.
报社 bàoshè newspaper office; general office of a newspaper; headquarters of a newspaper
报审 bàoshěn submit a written report to the higher authorities for examination
报失 bàoshī report the loss of sth. (to the authorities concerned)
报施 bàoshī 〈书面〉 repay sb.'s kindness; reward
报时 bàoshí give the correct time: ~器 chronopher /~信号 time signal /~台 (telephone) time inquiry service
报数 bàoshù number off: ~! Count off! /一二~! Count off by twos!
报税 bàoshuì declare dutiable goods; make a statement of taxable goods: ~单 taxation (*or* duty declaration) form
报摊 bàotān news-stand; news stall: 无人~ self-service news-stand/ 我在街头~上买了一份《中国电视报》。I bought a "CCTV Weekly" from a street news-stand.
报坛 bàotán the press; journalistic circles: ~巨匠 giant in the journalistic circles; great journalist
报条 bàotiáo 〈旧语〉 written announcement of sb.'s appointment, promotion, or success in the imperial examinations, usu. delivered for a tip
报亭 bàotíng kiosk selling newspapers and periodicals; news-stand
报童 bàotóng 〈旧语〉 street newsboy; newsboy
报头 bàotóu masthead (of a newspaper, etc.); nameplate: ~设计 masthead designing /~和版面 flag and format
报文 bàowén *also* "电文" diànwén text of a telegram or cable
报务 bàowù work of sending and receiving telegraphic messages; radio transmission and receiving operation: 他搞~工作已有二十多年了。He has been a telegraph (*or* radio) operator for over 20 years.
报务员 bàowùyuán radio operator; telegraph operator; radioman
报喜 bàoxǐ announce good news or glad tidings; report success
报喜不报忧 bàoxǐ bù bàoyōu report only what is good while withholding what is unpleasant: ~的作风,害人匪浅。It is a downright harmful practice to report only what is good while withholding what is unpleasant.
报系 bàoxì newspaper chain; syndicate: 赫斯特~ (US) Hurst chain (of newspapers)
报销 bàoxiāo ❶ submit an expense account; ask for reimbursement; reimburse: 向财务处要求~差旅费 ask for reimbursement of one's travelling expenses from the financial division /凭票~ obtain a refund on handing in the receipts /~单据 bill for reimbursement /这笔花费可以~。You'll be reimbursed for the expenses. ❷ submit a list of expended articles; put out to pasture; discard: 这几辆旧的机车该~了。These outmoded locomotives should be discarded (*or* put out to pasture). ❸ wipe out; write off: 他买了些家具,把这个月的工资全~了。The furniture he bought cost him the whole month's pay. /一个上午的时间全给~了。The whole morning was wasted. /我昨天从楼梯上滚下来,差点儿~了。I fell down the stairs yesterday and nearly killed myself (*or* kicked the bucket).
报晓 bàoxiǎo herald the break of day; be a harbinger of dawn: ~的钟声 chimes of the bell heralding the break of day /晨鸡~。The rooster is a harbinger of dawn.
报效 bàoxiào render service to repay kindness: ~祖国 serve one's country /他对我恩重如山,当尽力~。I will do whatever I can to repay him for his great kindness.
报谢 bàoxiè express thanks or appreciation (for sb.'s help or kindness); do in return; acknowledge
报信 bàoxìn notify; inform: 及时~ notify (*or* inform) sb. in time / 通风~ provide sb. with inside information; tip sb. off
报修 bàoxiū report or notify for repairs: 水龙头坏了,赶紧向有关部门~。Notify the relevant department immediately when you find any water tap out of order.
报应 bàoying 〈宗教〉 divine retribution; judgment: 因果~ karma; retribution for sin; punitive justice /这是对你的~。This is a judgment on you for what you have done. *or* It serves you right. /如有天理,必有~。If there's any justice in heaven, retribution is bound to follow. /他们这样作恶,总有一天会得到~的。The evils they do will come home to roost some day. /她深信做坏事总没好~。She is convinced that evil-doing will never pay.
报忧 bàoyōu report unpleasant or disappointing news
报怨 bàoyuàn respond to a grievance: 以德~ return good for evil; requite ingratitude with kindness
报站 bàozhàn announce the next station (for the bus or train to stop at); announce the next stop: 售票员应提前~。The conductor should announce the next stop in plenty of time.
报章 bàozhāng newspapers: ~杂志 newspapers and magazines
报账 bàozhàng submit an expense account for refunding; render an account for reimbursement: 凭单据~。You can get a refund by producing your receipts. /差旅费按有关规定~。Travel expenses may be refunded (*or* reimbursed) according to relevant regulations.
报纸 bàozhǐ ❶ newspaper: 订~ subscribe to a newspaper ❷ newsprint: 白~ newsprint
报子 bàozi ❶ 〈旧语〉 (army) scout ❷ those who come to announce one's promotion or examination success for some fee ❸ *see* "报条" ❹ bill; billboard: 新戏的~刚贴出来,全城就轰动了。The posting of the bill for the new play set the whole city astir.

暴[1] bào ❶ sudden and fierce: 狂风~雨 fierce storm; hurricane ❷ cruel; savage; violent; tyrannical: *see* "~徒"; "~乱" ❸ the cruel and ruthless: 除~安良 get rid of the cruel and ruthless so that the people may live in peace /以~易~ replace violence with violence; substitute tyranny for tyranny; exchange outrage for outrage ❹ hot-tempered; short-tempered: 粗~ rude; rough /脾气真~! What a hot (*or* fiery) temper! ❺ (Bào) a surname

暴[2] bào ❶ stick out; protrude; stand out; bulge: 他额上~满了青筋。Veins stood on his forehead. ❷ expose; reveal

暴[3] bào 〈书面〉 spoil; ruin: 自~自弃 give oneself up for lost

暴病 bàobìng sudden attack of disease: 得了一场~ fall gravely ill all of a sudden /~而死 die of a sudden illness
暴跌 bàodiē fall steeply; drop; slump: 谷价~ sharp fall in grain prices /声价~。His reputation plummeted. /这两天美元汇价连续~,金价坚挺。These days there has been a continuous slump in the exchange rate of the US dollar, while the gold price has been strong.
暴动 bàodòng insurrection; rebellion; uprising: 举行武装~ stage (*or* raise) an armed rebellion (*or* insurrection)
暴发 bàofā ❶ have suddenly become rich or risen to an important position: 这个人在交易所搞投机而~,成为亿万富翁。He started as a speculator at the stock exchange and shortly became a billionaire. ❷ break out: 山洪~。The mountain flood rushed down.
暴发户 bàofāhù nouveau riche; upstart: 他因彩票中奖而成了~。He became an overnight millionaire by winning a prize in a lottery.
暴发性 bàofāxìng fulminant; fulminating: ~感染 fulminating infection /~青光眼 fulminant glaucoma
暴风 bàofēng ❶ windstorm; storm wind; tempest ❷ 〈气象〉 storm (force 11 wind); hurricane
暴风部队 Bàofēng Bùduì (Palestine) "Al-Assifa" Commandos (the Tempest)
暴风雪 bàofēngxuě snowstorm; blizzard: 为~所困 be snowed up in a blizzard
暴风雨 bàofēngyǔ rainstorm; storm; tempest: 遇上~ be caught in a storm /~后的宁静 calm after a storm /~般的掌声 thunderous applause; tumultuous applause /一场权力斗争的~即将来临。A stormy power struggle was imminent.
暴风骤雨 bàofēng-zhòuyǔ violent storm; hurricane; tempest: 掀起了~般的革命斗争。There arose a storm of revolutionary struggle. /三千农民起义者,犹如~长驱直入。Three thousand peasant rebels swept forward with the force of a hurricane.
暴富 bàofù become suddenly rich; strike it rich; rise suddenly in fortune: 一个偶然的机会使他~起来。An unexpected chance made him instantly rich.
暴光 bàoguāng *also* "曝光" bàoguāng ❶ 〈摄影〉 exposure: ~表 exposure meter ❷ lay bare: 让不正之风通过报纸电台~。Lay bare unhealthy trends both in the press and on the radio.
暴喝 bàohè shout suddenly and violently; give a sudden and violent shout
暴横 bàohèng violent and peremptory; high-handed
暴洪 bàohóng flash flood
暴吼 bàohǒu roar; howl: 人群中发出一阵~。A great roar erupted from the crowd.
暴虎冯河 bàohǔ-pínghé kill a tiger with bare hands and cross a

river on foot — act with reckless courage:～,死而无悔者,吾不与也。I shall not work with any harum-scarum who acts with reckless courage and cares not a bit about his own death.

暴举 bàojǔ cruel act; cruelty

暴君 bàojūn tyrant; despot:封建～ tyrant of the feudal age; feudal tyrant /臭名昭著的～ notorious despot

暴客 bàokè 〈书面〉robber; bandit:重门击柝,以待～ have the gates reinforced and make night watchmen patrol the courtyard so as to keep off robbers

暴库 bàokù (of unsold goods) over-pack the warehouse; be very much in surplus:目前产品严重～,必须马上采取促销、减产措施。The products are very much in surplus. It is essential to take immediate measures to promote sales and cut the production.

暴雷 bàoléi abrupt and deafening thunder

暴冷 bàolěng 〈气象〉steep or sharp drop in temperature

暴力 bàolì ❶ violence; force:～行动 act of violence /充满着色情和～ full of sex and violence /诉诸～ resort to violence; appeal to brute force /～侵入〈法律〉forcible entry /～行为受害人 victim of violence /～工具 means of violence ❷ force or violence as exercised by the state:～机器 apparatus of violence /～机构 organ of violence / 军队和警察对于敌对阶级是一种～。The armed forces and police are organs of violence to the opposition classes.

暴力革命 bàolì gémìng violent revolution

暴力镜头 bàolì jìngtóu 〈影视〉carnography

暴力团 bàolìtuán (Japan) *yakuza*, a kind of underworld gangster organization

暴厉 bàolì fierce and stern:声色～ be stern in tone and countenance

暴利 bàolì exorbitant profits; sudden, huge profits; windfall; bonanza:～税 windfall tax /以不正当手段牟取～ reap colossal profits by illegitimate means; profiteering

暴戾 bàolì 〈书面〉ruthless and tyrannical; savage; cruel and fierce:一伙～的匪徒 a gang of ruthless bandits

暴戾恣睢 bàolì-zìsuī 〈书面〉savage and despotic:此人横行不法,～。This man was a lawless despot riding roughshod over the people.

暴敛 bàoliǎn forcible collection of (taxes):横征～ extort excessive taxes and levies; levy exorbitant taxes

暴烈 bàoliè violent; fierce:性情～ be hot-tempered; have a fiery temper /一匹～的黑驹 a fiery black stallion /～的行动 acts of violence and brutality

暴露 bàolù expose; reveal; lay bare; bring to light:～身分 reveal one's identity /～野心 lay bare one's ambition /～意图 disclose one's intention /～原形 unmask one's true colours; expose sth. for what it is /～底蕴 let the cat out of the bag; give away the show /～矛盾 expose a contradiction /～丑恶的嘴脸 expose one's ugly features /～敌军的实力 betray the military strength of the enemy /～了社会上形形色色的黑暗现象 bring the seamy side of society to light; bring to light social evils of all descriptions /一个人本来面目的～要有个过程。It takes time to see a person for what he is. /时间一长,他的弱点就～出来了。With the passage of time, all his weaknesses stood exposed.

暴露面 bàolùmiàn 〈矿业〉free end; free face:～取样 face sampling

暴露文学 bàolù wénxué literature of exposure; muck-raking literature

暴露无遗 bàolù-wúyí be thoroughly exposed; be completely unmasked:短短的一句话,使他的意图～。This short casual remark gave him away completely.

暴乱 bàoluàn riot; rebellion; revolt:平息～ put down a riot; suppress (*or* put down, *or* quell) a rebellion /策划～ plot a rebellion

暴民 bàomín rioters; mob

暴怒 bàonù violent rage; fury:切忌～。Never lose your temper. *or* Guard against sudden fury. /你～起来时,怕人得很。You're terrifying when you're in a rage. /他～了,他拍桌,打椅,捶墙壁。He blew his top, pounding the table, chairs, and partition.

暴虐 bàonüè ❶ brutal; tyrannical; despotic:～行动 act of brutality /～统治 tyrannical rule ❷〈书面〉treat savagely; ride roughshod over:～无辜 handle innocent people savagely /～百姓 ride roughshod over the people

暴弃 bàoqì 〈书面〉give oneself up as hopeless:自甘～ be resigned to one's fate

暴热 bàorè sudden rise in temperature:暴冷～ sudden rise and fall in temperature

暴晒 bàoshài be exposed to the sun:经过～的棉被显得格外松软。After being aired, the cotton-padded quilt feels extremely soft and spongy. /他们不顾烈日～,勘察矿区。In defiance of the scorching sun, they went prospecting the mining area.

暴尸 bàoshī exhibit a corpse; leave a dead body unburied:～街头 leave one's dead body in the street; die unburied /～于市 exhibit sb.'s corpse in the market (as a warning to others)

暴死 bàosǐ die of a violent illness; die a sudden or violent death

暴殄天物 bàotiǎn-tiānwù recklessly waste things (such as grain) that Mother Nature has offered; be recklessly wasteful of Nature's bounties:浪费粮食这种～的行为应该受到谴责。The reckless waste of food should be condemned (*or* severely criticized). /如此～,实在令人痛心。It pains one to see so much of Nature's bounties running to waste.

暴跳 bàotiào ❶ stamp with fury:他太任性,稍不如意,就～起来。He is so self-willed that he will fly into a rage at the slightest provocation. ❷ (of muscles, sparks, etc.) move violently:青筋～ blue veins swelling up /～的火花 sparks flying about

暴跳如雷 bàotiào-rúléi stamp with fury; fly into a violent temper; be in a towering rage:动不动就～ burst into anger for no reason at all /这句话使他气得～。The words made him leap around with fury.

暴突 bàotū protruding; bulging:青筋～ bulging blue veins

暴徒 bàotú rioter; ruffian; thug:一伙作恶多端的～ a horde of thugs who have committed numerous crimes; a band of ruffians guilty of innumerable crimes /狠狠打击这伙～的气焰 deal relentless blows at the hooligans to deflate their arrogance

暴行 bàoxíng atrocity; outrage; ferocity:种族主义政权犯下的种种～ atrocities committed by the racist regime /残害善良的～ act of brutality against innocent people /占领军的～激起了市民的义愤。The outrages committed by the occupation troops aroused great indignation among the citizens.

暴刑 bàoxíng cruel punishment; inhuman penalty; torture

暴性子 bàoxìngzi violent temper; fiery or impetuous temperament:他是个～,你要多担待些。Please be tolerant with him, for he has such a fiery temper.

暴饮暴食 bàoyǐn-bàoshí immoderate eating and drinking

暴雨 bàoyǔ ❶〈气象〉rain that reaches 50-100 millimetres of precipitation in 24 hours ❷ torrential rain; downpour; rainstorm:下～ rain with a vengeance /～成灾 tremendous damage caused by torrential rain /一场～ a heavy downpour of rain /连日～,把这个地区变成了泽国。Several days of torrential rain had turned the entire region into a vast expanse of water.

暴躁 bàozào irascible; irritable:性情～ hot-tempered; irascible by nature /考试砸了,她一整天都～不安。She was irritable (*or* edgy) for the rest of the day after she failed (in) her exam.

暴涨 bàozhǎng (of flood, prices, etc.) rise suddenly and sharply:河水～。The river rose suddenly. /物价～。Prices soared (*or* skyrocketed).

暴涨潮 bàozhǎngcháo (tidal) bore

暴胀 bàozhàng swell suddenly:青筋～ blue veins bulge out

暴政 bàozhèng tyranny; despotic rule:施行～ enforce despotic rule; practise tyranny

暴卒 bàozú 〈书面〉die suddenly; die of a sudden illness:战友～,痛伤我心。I was deeply grieved to learn of the sudden death of a comrade-in-arms.

爆

bào ❶ explode; burst:引～ ignite; detonate /音～ sonic boom /～出点点火星 send sparks flying about /豆荚熟得都～了。Pods are so ripe that they are burst open. /附近林子里～出一阵枪声。There was a burst of gunfire from the wood nearby. ❷ appear or occur unexpectedly; crop up:～出特大新闻 sensational news crops up ❸ quick-fry; quick-boil; pop:～炒 quick-fry and stir /大葱～羊肉 quick-fried mutton slices with scallion /～鱿鱼卷 quick-fried squid rolls

爆豆 bàodòu ❶〈比喻〉pop beans:前面响起一阵～似的枪声。There was a burst of gunfire in the distance. ❷ popped beans

爆肚 bàodǔ 〈口语〉speak too freely; talk irresponsibly

爆肚儿 bàodǔr quick-boiled tripe:油～ quick-fried tripe

爆发 bàofā ❶ (of a volcano) erupt:火山～了。The volcano erupted. ❷ break out:～起义。An uprising broke out. ❸ (of force, feeling, incident, etc.) erupt; break out:1919年～了伟大的"五四"运动。The great May Fourth Movement broke out in 1919. /说着,姑娘们

又～出一阵阵爽朗的笑声。Talking cheerfully, the girls burst into peals of laughter again.
爆发变星 bàofā biànxīng 〈天文〉eruptive variable (star)
爆发点 bàofādiǎn flash point
爆发力 bàofālì 〈体育〉explosive force:这位举重运动员具有很大的～。This weightlifter is known for his great explosive force.
爆发星 bàofāxīng 〈天文〉eruptive or exploding star:～系 eruptive or exploding galaxy
爆发音 bàofāyīn *also* "爆破音";"塞音" sèyīn 〈语言〉explosive; plosive
爆管 bàoguǎn 〈军事〉cartridge igniter; squib
爆花 bàohuā ❶ snuff (of a wick) ❷ popcorn
爆聚 bàojù 〈物理〉implosion
爆冷门 bào lěngmén unexpected turn of events; surprise:本届锦标赛大～,有九名种子选手被淘汰。There were many upsets (*or* surprises) during the current World Championships:nine seeded players were eliminated. /女子单打这次爆出冷门,卫冕冠军被一名新手击败。There is a surprise hit in women's singles: the reigning champion was upset by an unknown player. /今年女子国际象棋比赛有～的可能。There may be an unexpected winner (*or* a dark horse) in this year's women chess game.
爆裂 bàoliè crack; burst; split:这种杯子倒进开水就会～。This kind of glass will crack when boiling water is poured into it. /嘭地一声,一个暖水瓶～在地上。With a bang, a thermos flask burst into pieces on the ground.
爆裂试验 bàoliè shìyàn burst test
爆满 bàomǎn (of a theatre, cinema, stadium, or gymnasium) be filled to capacity:剧院～,盛况空前。The theatre was filled to capacity and it was really a gala occasion. /他们的精彩表演吸引了北京成千上万的观众,场场～。Their excellent performance attracted tens of thousands in Beijing, and the crowd overflowed at each show (*or* the show had a full house for every performance).
爆米花 bàomǐhuā pop rice
爆鸣 bàomíng sound of a blast made by an explosion
爆内幕 bào nèimù make public or reveal the inside story or information
爆棚 bàopéng 〈方言〉*see* "爆满"
爆破 bàopò blow up; demolish; blast; dynamite:～敌人的碉堡 blow up an enemy pillbox /定向～ guided demolition (*or* blast) /～器材〈军事〉demolitions /～小组 demolition squad /～专家 explosives expert
爆破弹 bàopòdàn 〈军事〉demolition bomb; blasting cartridge
爆破雷管 bàopò léiguǎn blasting detonator
爆破手 bàopòshǒu demolition man; dynamiter
爆破筒 bàopòtǒng bangalore (torpedo)
爆破音 bàopòyīn 〈语言〉plosive; explosive
爆破炸弹 bàopò zhàdàn 〈军事〉demolition bomb
爆破作业 bàopò zuòyè 〈建筑〉blasting or demolition operation
爆燃 bàorán 〈机械〉detonation:～式内燃机 explosion engine /～式燃气轮机 explosion gas turbine
爆腾 bàoteng 〈口语〉raise; kick up (dust, ashes, etc.):一刮风,路上就～连天。Whenever the wind blows, dust would be raised (*or* flying) all over the street.
爆响 bàoxiǎng ❶ loud sound of explosion:巨型炸弹顷刻～了。The huge bomb exploded instantly with an ear-deafening sound. ❷ win an overnight reputation:这部电影～全国,获得巨大成功。The film made an instantaneous hit all over the country.
爆音 bàoyīn 〈航空〉sonic boom; shock-wave noise
爆玉米花 bào yùmǐhuā popcorn
爆炸 bàozhà explode; detonate; dynamite; blast:核～ nuclear explosion /～化合物 explosive compound /～装置 explosive device /～螺栓 (of rocket) explosive bolt /～气浪 blast wave /感应～〈军事〉detonation by influence /防～掩蔽所 blast shelter /信息～ information explosion /控制人口～ contain the population explosion (*or* baby boom) /～性的局势 explosive situation /～了一枚原子弹 detonate an atomic bomb /违反操作规程,引起了煤气罐的～。Violation of the operating instructions caused the explosion of the gas tank. /这次～没有造成人畜伤亡。This blast did not cause any loss of human or animal life.
爆炸波 bàozhàbō 〈物理〉blast or burst wave; explosion wave
爆炸成形 bàozhà chéngxíng explosive formation
爆炸地震学 bàozhà dìzhènxué explosion seismology
爆炸锻造 bàozhà duànzào explosive forging
爆炸焊接 bàozhà hànjiē explosive welding or bonding
爆炸极限 bàozhà jíxiàn explosive limit
爆炸减震器 bàozhà jiǎnzhènqì blast damper
爆炸军械处理 bàozhà jūnxiè chǔlǐ 〈军事〉EOD (explosive ordnance disposal)
爆炸力 bàozhàlì explosive force
爆炸铆 bàozhàmǎo explosive riveting
爆炸球 bàozhàqiú 〈体育〉(of golf) explosion shot
爆炸物 bàozhàwù explosive
爆炸性 bàozhàxìng unexpected and sensational; explosive:本县昨天出了一条～新闻。There was a piece of sensational news in this county yesterday.
爆仗 bàozhang firecrackers
爆震 bàozhèn 〈机械〉knock:～燃烧 knocking combustion; knocking behavior
爆震波 bàozhènbō detonation wave
爆震计 bàozhènjì knock-meter
爆震强度 bàozhèn qiángdù knock intensity
爆竹 bàozhú firecracker:放～ let off firecrackers /～迎新。Firecrackers are let off to usher in the new year.

曝 bào

see also pù
曝光 bàoguāng *also* "暴光" ❶〈摄影〉exposure ❷ lay bare
曝光表 bàoguāngbiǎo exposure meter

趵 bào

〈方言〉spring forth; bounce:～突泉 Baotu Spring (a famous spring in Jinan, Shandong Province)
see also bō

豹 bào

❶ leopard; panther:金钱～ leopard (with ring-like spots) /雪～ snow leopard /猎～ cheetah /海～ seal /土～ buzzard /未窥全～〈比喻〉be unable to obtain a complete picture of the overall situation ❷ (Bào) a surname
豹变 bàobiàn 〈比喻〉sudden change in one's behaviour or status
豹略 bàolüè 〈书面〉military strategy
豹猫 bàomāo *also* "山猫" shānmāo leopard cat
豹死留皮 bàosǐ-liúpí 〈比喻〉when a leopard dies, it leaves its skin behind:～,人死留名。Just as a leopard leaves his skin at death, a man leaves his reputation when he dies.
豹头环眼 bàotóu-huányǎn have a head like a leopard's and big, round eyes; well-formed forehead and round eyes:好一个～的魁梧汉子! What a big, tall man with a head like a leopard's and big, round eyes!
豹子 bàozi leopard; panther

抱[1] bào

❶ hold or carry in the arms; clasp in the arms; embrace; hug:怀～ carry in the arms; embrace; cherish /合～的大树 tree which is so big that one can just get one's arms around it /小村三面～水。The village is surrounded by water on three sides. ❷ have one's first child or grandchild:听说你快～孙子了。I hear that you will soon be a grandmother (*or* grandfather). ❸ adopt (a child):她从医院里～了个孩子。She adopted a baby from a hospital. ❹〈方言〉hang together:他们～得很紧。They hang together closely. ❺〈方言〉(of shoes, clothing, etc.) fit well: *see* "～身儿" ❻ cherish; harbour:～有幻想 cherish an illusion /～着同一志愿 harbour the same ambition /～敌对的态度 adopt a hostile attitude /不～成见 have no prejudice; not be prejudiced /不要～住错误观点不放。Don't stick to your wrong views. /我们是～着寻求和平、友谊与合作的目的来的。We have come with the purpose of seeking peace, friendship and cooperation. ❼〈量词〉armful:一～柴禾 an armful of firewood

抱[2](菢) bào

hatch (eggs); brood:～小鸡儿 hatch (out) chickens
抱病 bàobìng be ill; be in poor health:～坚持工作 go on working despite poor health /长期～ have been a victim of a lingering disease; have been ill for a long time
抱不平 bào bùpíng be ready to intervene on behalf of the injured party:打～ champion the cause of a person who has suffered wrong/他心里很替老王～。He felt indignant at the gross injustice done to

compassion /诗人以～的心情谴责了军阀混战。Deeply concerned about the fate of the country and the people, the poet denounced the civil strife among the warlords.

悲恸 bēitòng be extremely grieved; be grief-stricken: ～欲绝 abandon oneself to grief; be overcome with grief

悲痛 bēitòng grieved; sorrowful: 深感～ be deeply grieved; be filled with deep sorrow /～万分 be in extreme grief

悲惜 bēixī deeply regret; sadly lament: 挚友早逝,不胜～。My sorrow knows no bounds at the premature death of my bosom friend.

悲喜交集 bēixǐ-jiāojí mixed feelings of grief and joy; grief mingled with joy: 一朝相见,～。Joy and sorrow mingled at the sudden reunion.

悲喜剧 bēixǐjù tragicomedy

悲辛 bēixīn 〈书面〉sad; sorrowful; bitter: 一生心血,毁于一旦,又何其～。What bitter sorrow to have one's lifelong work wrecked all at once!

悲咽 bēiyè sad and choked with sobs

悲抑 bēiyì 〈书面〉feel sad and gloomy: 噩耗传来,心中～。The sad news plunged him into deep sorrow.

悲吟 bēiyín sing or recite mournfully: 清夜～ sing sadly at night

悲郁 bēiyù sad; melancholy; low-spirited

悲咤 bēizhà 〈书面〉sigh mournfully; lament

悲壮 bēizhuàng solemn and stirring; moving and tragic: ～场面 tragic and stirring scene /～的歌曲 solemn and heroic song

背(揹) bēi ❶ carry on the back: ～行李 carry a bed roll on one's back /～书包 carry a school satchel ❷ bear; shoulder: ～不起责任 can't shoulder a responsibility /我不好插手这种事,我可不愿～恶名。I won't intervene in such matters because I might earn a bad name for my pains. ❸〈方言〉〈量词〉*used to indicate what can be borne by one person on the back*: 一～柴火 a bundle of firewood (for a person to carry on the back)

see also bèi

背榜 bēibǎng 〈旧语〉come out at the bottom of a list of successful candidates

背包 bēibāo ❶ backpack; knapsack; rucksack; field pack: ～徒步旅行 backpacking /～徒步旅行者 backpacker ❷〈军事〉blanket roll: 打～ tie up a blanket roll

背包电台 bēibāo diàntái 〈无线电〉pack unit; walkie-talkie

see also "步谈机" bùtánjī

背包袱 bēi bāofu have a weight or load on one's mind; take on a mental burden: 这类事算不了什么,别在思想上～。It's really nothing. Don't let it weigh on your mind.

背带 bēidài ❶ braces; suspenders: 系～ fasten braces /解～ undo braces ❷ (of a rifle) sling; (of a knapsack) straps

背篼 bēidōu *also* "背斗"〈方言〉basket carried on the back: 他～里装着随身衣物。He carried his clothes in a basket on his back.

背负 bēifù ❶ carry on the back: ～着大麻包 carry a gunnysack on one's back ❷ bear; have on one's shoulder: ～着人民的希望 carry in one's heart the expectations of the people; bear in mind the aspirations of the people

背负式喷粉器 bēifùshì pēnfěnqì 〈农业〉knapsack duster

背负式喷雾器 bēifùshì pēnwùqì 〈农业〉knapsack sprayer: 背负式杠杆喷雾器 knapsack lever type sprayer

背黑锅 bēi hēiguō 〈口语〉be made a scapegoat; be unjustly blamed; take the blame for others: 你何苦替他～呢? Why should you take the blame for him?

背饥荒 bēi jīhuang 〈方言〉be in debt: 最近他背上了不少饥荒。Recently he has run head over heels into debt.

背筐 bēikuāng basket carried on the back

背篓 bēilǒu basket carried on the back

背篓商店 bēilǒu shāngdiàn mobile shop with goods in baskets carried on assistants' backs to sell in mountainous or out-of-the-way areas

背囊 bēináng travelling bag carried on the back; knapsack

背头 bēitóu swept-back hair

背债 bēizhài be saddled with debts: 背了一身债 be saddled with debts; be heavily in debt

背子 bēizi back basket — long and narrow basket for carrying things on the back (common in mountainous areas)

卑 bēi ❶〈书面〉low-lying; low: 地势～湿 low-lying and damp terrain ❷ low; of low rank: 尊～ (of people) high and low /居尊若～ remain humble though in a position of importance ❸ of low character; inferior in quality: *see* "～劣"; "～下" ❹〈书面〉humble; modest: 自～ feel inferior; be diffident

卑鄙 bēibǐ ❶ base; mean; contemptible; despicable: ～手段 contemptible means; dirty tricks /～勾当 dirty deal /～无耻 mean and shameless; base and brazen /～龌龊 sordid; foul ❷〈书面〉inferior and ignorant; shallow; worthless: 先帝不以臣为～,三顾臣于茅庐之中。The late emperor did not regard me as lowly and worthless and called on me three times in my thatched cottage.

卑不足道 bēibùzúdào not worth mentioning; of little consequence; negligible; insignificant: ～的人 nobody; nonentity; man of no consequence

卑辞 bēicí *also* "卑词" humble words; obsequious terms: ～厚礼 humble words and generous gifts

卑恭 bēigōng humble and respectful: 他一看到顶头上司,那张凶狠的脸陡地换成～的笑脸。At the sight of his immediate superior, he abruptly changed his fierce look into a fawning smile.

卑躬屈膝 bēigōng-qūxī *also* "卑躬屈节" bow and scrape; cringe; act servilely or obsequiously: ～事权贵 bow and scrape before the high and mighty; fawn servilely upon the rich and powerful

卑贱 bēijiàn ❶ of lowly or humble origin or status: 出身～ be of lowly origin /～者最聪明,高贵者最愚蠢。The lowly are most intelligent; the elite are most ignorant. ❷ lowly; menial: 把体力劳动看作～的事是完全错误的。It is entirely wrong to regard manual work as being menial.

卑劣 bēiliè base; mean; despicable: ～的伎俩 mean (*or* despicable) trick /～无耻的行为 down-right shameless act

卑陋 bēilòu ❶ humble; mean; lowly: ～的小屋 lowly (*or* mean) hut ❷ base; degrading

卑怯 bēiqiè base and cowardly: 他在危急时擅离职守,真是～。It was indeed base and cowardly of him to leave his post when danger was imminent.

卑屈 bēiqū obedient and docile; cringing: ～的神色 abjectly beseeching look

卑弱 bēiruò 〈书面〉❶ diminishing; decline; waning: 王室～。The royal family is on the decline. ❷ docile and meek: ～以自持 be meek and docile in behaviour; behave meekly

卑视 bēishì despise; look down upon; think little of: 谁～人民群众,谁就犯了极大的错误。He who looks down upon the common people is making a big mistake.

卑琐 bēisuǒ mean and trifling: 渺小～ despicable and mean

卑微 bēiwēi petty and low: 出身～ come from a lowly family

卑猥 bēiwěi ❶ humble; lowly: 身世～ of lowly origin ❷ obsequious; mean: ～的笑容 obsequious smile

卑污 bēiwū despicable in character; evil-minded

卑下 bēixià ❶ (of character, etc.) base; lowly: 品格～ base character ❷ (of status) low; humble: 地位～ low status (*or* station)

卑之无甚高论 bēi zhī wú shèn gāolùn nothing remarkable or outstanding about the view or idea; quite commonplace

卑职 bēizhí ❶〈书面〉humble position; lowly post ❷〈旧语〉〈谦词〉(used by a subordinate official in addressing superiors) your humble subordinate; I

碑 bēi upright stone tablet; stele: 墓～ tombstone /里程～ milestone /人民英雄纪念～ Monument to the People's Heroes /～帽 stone sculpture on top of a stele /～身 body of a stele (usu. inscribed)

碑额 bēi'é top part of a tablet

碑记 bēijì record of events inscribed on a stone tablet

碑碣 bēijié 〈书面〉upright stone tablet; stele

碑刻 bēikè engraving or inscription on a tablet

碑林 bēilín forest of steles; collection of ancient stone tablets: 西安～ Forest of Steles in Xi'an

碑铭 bēimíng inscription on a tablet

碑拓 bēità rubbings from ancient tablets

碑帖 bēitiè rubbings from a stone inscription (usu. used as a model for calligraphy)

碑亭 bēitíng pavilion for sheltering stone tablets

碑文 bēiwén inscription on a tablet

碑阴 bēiyīn back or reverse side of a tablet

碑志 bēizhì record of events inscribed on a tablet

B

碑座 bēizuò stand of a tablet

鹎
bēi 〈动物〉bulbul

箄
bēi 〈书面〉small bamboo cage for fishing
see also pái

B

陂
bēi 〈书面〉❶ pond:～池 pond ❷ waterside; bank ❸ mountain slope
see also pō

陂塘 bēitáng 〈书面〉pond

běi

北[1]
běi ❶ north:城～ north of the city /华～ north China /由此往～ go north from here /坐～朝南 (of a building) with a southern exposure; (of a posture) facing south ❷ North standing for the developed countries:～南对话 North-South dialogue

北[2]
běi 〈书面〉be defeated:三战皆～ lose three battles in succession /败～ suffer defeat

北爱尔兰 Běi'ài'ěrlán Northern Ireland; Ulster:～志愿军 Ulster Volunteer Force (UVF) /～皇家警察 Royal Ulster Constabulary

北半球 běibànqiú Northern Hemisphere

北边 běibiān northern part; north regions:城的～ northern part of the city; north of the city /来自～的威胁 threat from the north; northern threat

北冰洋 Běibīngyáng the Arctic (Ocean)

北部湾 Běibùwān Beibu Gulf (called Gulf of Tonkin in the West)

北朝 Běicháo Northern Dynasties (386-581), namely, the Northern Wei Dynasty (北魏, 386-534), the Eastern Wei Dynasty (东魏, 534-550), the Western Wei Dynasty (西魏, 535-556), the Northern Qi Dynasty (北齐, 550-577) and the Northern Zhou Dynasty (北周, 557-581)

北辰 běichén (used in ancient books) North Star

北达科他 Běidákētā North Dakota, a state in the USA

北大荒 Běidàhuāng Great Northern Wilderness (in northeast China)

北大西洋公约组织 Běi Dàxīyáng Gōngyuē Zǔzhī North Atlantic Treaty Organization (NATO)

北岛 Běidǎo North Island (of New Zealand)

北点 běidiǎn 〈天文〉north point

北斗星 Běidǒuxīng Big Dipper; Plough

北豆腐 běidòufu northern-style beancurd — firm beancurd; firm tofu

北伐军 Běifájūn Northern Expeditionary Army (1926-1927)

北伐战争 Běifá Zhànzhēng (shortened as 北伐) Northern Expedition (1926-1927)
see also "第一次国内革命战争" Dì-Yī Cì Guónèi Gémìng Zhànzhēng

北方 běifāng ❶ north ❷ northern part of the country, esp. the area north of the Yellow River:～人 northerner

北方话 běifānghuà northern dialect, the most important dialect of the Chinese language, which serves as the basis of *putonghua* (普通话, the common speech of the modern Hans)

北方领土 Běifāng Lǐngtǔ Northern Territory, an administrative region in north Australia

北方四岛 Běifāng Sìdǎo (also called 千岛群岛 Kurile Islands) four northern islands (disputed by Russia and Japan)— Habomai Islands (齿舞岛), Kunashiri Islands (国后岛), Shikotan Islands (色丹岛) and Etorofu Islands (择捉岛)

北非 Běi Fēi North Africa

北风 běifēng north wind; Boreas:～呼啸。The north wind is howling.

北瓜 běiguā 〈方言〉pumpkin

北国 běiguó 〈书面〉northern part of the country:～江南 south-like area in the north; Riviera in the north /好一派～风光! What magnificent northern scenery!

北海 Běihǎi North Sea:～油田 North Sea oilfields

北海道 Běihǎidào (Japan) Hokkaido

北海公园 Běihǎi Gōngyuán Beihai Park (former Imperial Winter Palace in Beijing)

北寒带 běihándài north frigid zone

北河二 Běihé'èr 〈天文〉Castor; D Geminorum

北河三 Běihésān 〈天文〉B Geminorum

北回归线 běihuíguīxiàn 〈地理〉Tropic of Cancer

北货 běihuò northern food products (such as red dates, walnuts and preserved persimmons)

北极 běijí ❶ North Pole; Arctic Pole:～探险 Arctic exploration /～海盆 North Polar Basin /～地区 the Arctic ❷ north magnetic pole

北极高云 běijí gāoyún 〈气象〉Arctic high; Arctic anticyclone

北极光 běijíguāng 〈天文〉northern lights; aurora borealis

北极狐 běijíhú Arctic fox (*Alopex lagopus*)

北极霾 běijímái 〈气象〉arctic haze

北极圈 běijíquān Arctic circle

北极犬 běijíquǎn Eskimo dog

北极人种 Běijí rénzhǒng Arctic race

北极星 Běijíxīng Polaris; North star; Polestar

北极星导弹 Běijíxīng dǎodàn (US) Polaris missile

北极熊 běijíxióng Polar bear (*Thalarctos maritimus*)

北京 Běijīng Beijing, capital of the People's Republic of China:～展览馆 Beijing Exhibition Centre /～动物园 Beijing Zoo /～天文馆 Beijing Planetarium /～人 native of Beijing /～居民 resident (*or* inhabitant) of Beijing /～古观象台 Old Beijing Observatory

北京大学 Běijīng Dàxué Peking University or Beijing University, established in 1898 as Capital University (京师大学堂), assuming its present name in 1912

北京时间 Běijīng Shíjiān Beijing Time (standard time in China)

北京条约 Běijīng Tiáoyuē Convention of Peking (Oct. 1860)

北京鸭 běijīngyā Peking duck:北京烤鸭 roast Peking duck /北京填鸭 forcefed Peking duck

北京猿人 Běijīng yuánrén 〈考古〉Peking Man (*Sinanthropus Pekinensis*)

北马里亚纳 Běimǎlǐyànà Northern Mariana Islands (in the west Pacific)

北煤南调 běiméi nándiào supply coal to the south from the north

北美 Běi Měi (short for 北美洲) North America

北美洲 Běi Měizhōu North America

北美自由贸易区 Běi Měi Zìyóu Màoyìqū North America Free Trade Area (NAFTA, including Canada, the USA and Mexico, established in 1994)

北面 běimiàn ❶ north; northern side ❷ face north:～称臣 face north and acknowledge one's allegiance; submit oneself to a foreign power and become its subject or vassal

北欧 Běi Ōu Northern Europe (comprising Norway, Sweden, Finland, Iceland and Denmark); Nordic:～国家 Nordic country /～理事会 Nordic Council (Feb. 1953)

北齐 Běi Qí Northern Qi Dynasty (550-577), one of the Northern Dynasties

北曲 běiqǔ northern operas of Yuan Dynasty and their derivatives
see also "杂剧" zájù

北沙参 běishāshēn 〈植物〉northern lady bell, the root of which is used as herbal medicine

北山羊 běishānyáng *also* "羱羊" yuányáng 〈动物〉ibex

北上 běishàng go up north:明日首途～。We'll set out for the north tomorrow.

北十字 běishízì 〈天文〉Northern Cross

北宋 Běi Sòng Northern Song Dynasty (960-1127)

北苏门答腊 Běi Sūméndálà (Indonesia) Sumata Utara

北梭鱼 běisuōyú bonefish (*Albula vulpes*)

北太平洋高压 Běi Tàipíngyáng gāoyā 〈气象〉Pacific high; Pacific anticyclone

北天极 běitiānjí 〈天文〉north pole; north celestial pole

北图 Běitú (short for 北京图书馆) Beijing National Library

北纬 běiwěi north or northern latitude:～38 度 38th parallel of north latitude

北魏 Běi Wèi Northern Wei Dynasty (386-534), one of the Northern Dynasties

北温带 běiwēndài north temperate zone

北洋 Běiyáng name for the coastal provinces of Liaoning, Hebei and Shandong in the Qing Dynasty:～水师 Northern Fleet of the Qing Dynasty

北洋军阀 Běiyáng Jūnfá Northern Warlords (1912-1927)

北岳 Běiyuè Northern Sacred Mountain (i. e. Mount Heng 恒山 in Shanxi Province)
see also "五岳" Wǔyuè

北周 Běi Zhōu Northern Zhou Dynasty (557-581), one of the Northern Dynasties

bèi

焙 bèi bake over a slow fire:～茶 prepare and cure tea (by baking it over a slow fire) /～干研碎 dry sth. over a fire and grind it into powder /～药 make herb medicine by drying it in the sun (*or* over a fire)

焙粉 bèifěn *also* "发粉" fāfěn; "起子" qǐzi baking-powder

焙燃反应 bèirán fǎnyìng 〈化学〉 roast-reaction

焙烧 bèishāo bake (raw materials such as ores, to such a degree that changes take place in their chemical composition or physical property); roast:～炉 roasting furnace; roaster

焙烧窑 bèishāoyáo 〈化学〉 burning-in kiln

棓 bèi

棓花青 bèihuāqīng 〈化学〉 gallocyanine

棓酸 bèisuān 〈化学〉 gallic acid

棓子 bèizǐ *also* "五棓子" wǔbèizǐ; "五倍子" wǔbèizǐ gall

碚 bèi *used in names of places*: 北～ Beibei, a place in Chongqing Municipality

倍 bèi ❶ times; -fold: 四～ four times; fourfold /大一～ twice as big; twice the size /增长了四～ increase by 400%; register a 400% increase; be five times as much /二的三～是六。Three times two is six. /八是四的两～。Eight is twice as much as four. ❷ double; redouble: 加～努力 with redoubled efforts /独在异乡为异客，每逢佳节～思亲。All alone in a foreign land, I am twice as homesick on a festive occasion.

倍倍尔 Bèibèi'ěr August Bebel (1840-1913), leader of the socialist movement in West Europe

倍道 bèidào 〈书面〉 travel at double speed:～兼行 travel day and night at double speed

倍加 bèijiā all the more:～小心 be all the more careful; be doubly careful /～爱护 take extra care of /～努力 redouble one's efforts /雨后的空气～清新。After the rain, the air is all the fresher.

倍加器 bèijiāqì 〈计算机〉 multiplier

倍率 bèilǜ magnifying power (ratio between the focuses of the object lens and the sight lens of a telescope or microscope

倍频器 bèipínqì 〈电子〉 frequency multiplier

倍儿 bèir 〈方言〉 very; terribly:～棒 very good; terrific /～亮 awfully bright /～精神 very energetic; full of vim and vigour

倍式 bèishì 〈数学〉 multiple formula

倍数 bèishù ❶〈数学〉 multiple: 十五是三和五的～。15 is a multiple of 3 or 5. ❷ quotient of one number divided by another; times

倍他米松 bèitāmǐsōng 〈药学〉 betamethasone

倍蓰 bèixǐ 〈书面〉 many times; multiple

倍压器 bèiyāqì 〈无线电〉 voltage doubler; doubler

倍增 bèizēng double; redouble; multiply:～电压 multiple circuit; doubling circuit /噪声～。The noise redoubled.

倍增器 bèizēngqì 〈电子〉 multiplier: 光电～ photoelectric multiplier

蓓 bèi

蓓蕾 bèilěi bud:～初放。The new buds begin to appear. *or* The flowers are in bud.

孛 bèi (used in ancient books) comet
see also bó

悖(誖) bèi 〈书面〉 ❶ be contrary to; go against:～德 against moral values; immoral /有～常理 contrary to common sense/ 并行不～ parallel and not contrary to each other; not mutually exclusive ❷ perverse; erroneous ❸ puzzled; confused; muddle-headed

悖晦 bèihui *also* "背晦" bèihui 〈方言〉 (often said of old people) confused; muddle-headed; senile

悖理 bèilǐ 〈书面〉 contrary to reason

悖论 bèilùn paradox

悖慢 bèimàn 〈书面〉 insolent and recalcitrant

悖谬 bèimiù 〈书面〉 *also* "背谬" bèimiù absurd; preposterous

悖逆 bèinì 〈书面〉 rebellious; insurrectional; subversive of established rules and values

悖入悖出 bèirù-bèichū ill-gotten, ill-spent; ill-gotten wealth never thrives; easy come, easy go

悖时 bèishí *also* "背时" bèishí ❶ behind the times; outmoded ❷ down on one's luck; unlucky

糒 bèi 〈书面〉 cooked rice

鞴[1] bèi put saddle, etc. on a horse

鞴[2] bèi *see* "鞲鞴" gōubèi

鞴马 bèimǎ put a saddle and a bridle on a horse

备(備、俻) bèi ❶ be equipped with; possess; have: 德才兼～ have (*or* possess) both ability and moral integrity /各种医疗器械无不完～ be equipped with all sorts of medical instruments ❷ prepare; get ready: 我已经把节目～好了。I've got the programme ready. /万事俱～，只欠东风。Everything is ready, but the opportune moment has not come. ❸ provide or prepare against; take precautions against: 以～万一 prepare against all eventualities / 防旱～荒 provide against drought and crop failure ❹ equipment: 军～ military equipment; armaments; arms /装～ equipment ❺ fully; in every possible way:～受拥戴 enjoy full support /～受欺凌 be browbeaten and bullied in every way /关怀～至 show every concern; take every care /～尝艰辛 experience untold hardships and difficulties

备案 bèi'àn put on record or on file; enter (a case) in the records: 此件抄送有关单位～。Send a copy of the document to the departments concerned for the record.

备办 bèibàn get (what is necessary) ready; prepare:～婚事 prepare for the wedding /一切都～好了。Everything needed is ready. *or* All formalities have been completed.

备不住 bèibuzhù 〈方言〉 *also* "背不住" bèibuzhù perhaps; maybe; for all one knows:～他一会儿来。Maybe he will be here in a minute. /咱们在这里瞎找，孩子～已回家了。For all our efforts to look for him around here, the child may be already at home.

备查 bèichá keep for future reference: 所有机密文件都要存档～。All confidential documents should be kept on file for reference.

备查录音 bèichá lùyīn reference recording

备而不用 bèi'érbùyòng have ready just in case; keep for possible future use: 这些东西都是～的。All these things are kept just in case they may be needed in an eventuality.

备份 bèifèn ❶〈方言〉 fill a nominal post; serve as a figurehead: 他这个副部长可是有职有权，绝不是～的。He has full responsibilities and powers as vice-minister, and is no figurehead (*or* decoration). ❷ spare (part):～伞 spare parachute ❸〈信息〉 back-up

备付金 bèifùjīn 〈金融〉 cover

备耕 bèigēng make preparations for ploughing and sowing

备荒 bèihuāng prepare against crop failure or famine

备货 bèihuò stock (a store or shop); (of a shop, etc.) get in a supply of goods: 采购员们正忙于为新年～。The buyers are busy stocking their stores against New Year shopping.

备件 bèijiàn spare part

备降机场 bèijiàng jīchǎng alternate airport

备考 bèikǎo (an appendix, note, etc.) for reference

备课 bèikè (of a teacher or student) prepare one's lessons

备料 bèiliào ❶ get the materials ready (for production or construction) ❷ prepare feed (for livestock)

备轮架 bèilúnjià spare wheel carrier

备品 bèipǐn machine parts or tools kept in reserve; spare parts or tools

备勤 bèiqín get ready for a job; stand by (for service); be on call: 司机～期间严禁饮酒。Drivers are strictly forbidden to drink when on call.

备取 bèiqǔ be on the waiting list (for admission to a school)
备述 bèishù narrate in detail:个中艰辛,难以～。It is difficult to detail all the hardships involved.
备忘录 bèiwànglù ❶〈外交〉memorandum; aide-memoire ❷ memorandum book; filofax
备位 bèiwèi 〈书面〉〈谦词〉merely occupy the post:我只是～而已,无何建树。I'm merely occupying the post and have no achievement to speak of.
备细 bèixì ❶〈书面〉in detail:～地解释一番 explain in detail ❷ (often used in the early vernacular literature) details; particulars:此中～,无人知晓。Nobody knows the detailed (inside) story.
备选 bèixuǎn be an alternative; be on the short list (for further screening):～案文 alternative text /～方案 alternative proposal (*or* scheme)
备用 bèiyòng reserve; alternate; standby; spare:～款项 reserve funds /～泵 emergency (*or* reserve) pump /～断路器 back-up break/ ～机器 standby machine /总统的(波音)707～座机 Presidential backup 707 /～方案 alternative scheme
备用航空站 bèiyòng hángkōngzhàn alternate airport
备用轮胎 bèiyòng lúntāi spare tyre
备用燃油箱 bèiyòng rányóuxiāng reserve fuel tank
备用数据块 bèiyòng shùjùkuài 〈自控〉block standby
备战 bèizhàn prepare for war; be prepared against war:扩军～ arms expansion and war preparations
备至 bèizhì to the utmost; take every care (of sb.); in every possible way:关怀～ be very considerate; show meticulous care /颂扬～ praise sb. profusely; bestow lavish praise on sb. /恭维～ pay high compliments to sb. /仰慕～ show great admiration for sb.
备置 bèizhì prepare and purchase; acquire:他明年要盖房子,正在～砖瓦木料。He is purchasing tiles, bricks and timber for a new house to be built next year.
备注 bèizhù remarks:～栏 remarks column

惫(憊) bèi (formerly pronounced bài) exhausted; fatigued:疲～不堪 be dog-tired (*or* exhausted)
惫乏 bèifá 〈书面〉be tired; be exhausted; be fatigued:奔波数日,他感到异常～。He feels done in (*or* dog-tired) as he has been rushed off his feet these few days.
惫倦 bèijuàn 〈书面〉be tired and drowsy:酒后～,昏昏欲睡 be overcome with fatigue and drowsiness under the influence of wine
惫赖 bèilài cunning and rude; unreasonable and obstreperous; rascally
惫懒 bèilǎn be tired and sluggish:他走不动了,～地坐在路旁。Unable to walk any farther, he sat down wearily by the roadside.
惫累 bèilèi be exhausted:～不堪 be quite worn out
惫色 bèisè tired look:面有～ look fatigued; wear a tired look

辈 bèi ❶ rank or position in a (family or clan) generational hierarchy; generation; seniority:长～ member of a higher (*or* elder, *or* senior) generation in the family (*or* clan) hierarchy; elder; senior /小～ member of a lower (*or* younger, *or* junior) generation in the family (*or* clan) hierarchy; junior /同～ of the same generation /先～ elder generation; forebears; ancestors /他虽然年轻,～儿可大了。Young as he is, he has a high rank in the family (*or* clan) hierarchy. ❷〈书面〉people of a certain kind; the like:无能之～ incompetents; people without ability ❸ lifetime:后半～儿 latter part of one's life
辈出 bèichū come forth in large numbers:人材～。A large number of talented people are coming to the fore. /当时延安人材～。There was a galaxy of talent in Yan'an in those days. /那是英雄～的时代。It was an age of heroes.
辈分 bèifen seniority in the family or clan generational hierarchy; position in the family hierarchy:她的～比我小。She is lower than I in the family generational hierarchy. /论～,我该叫他叔叔。I should call him uncle by his seniority.
辈行 bèiháng seniority in the family or clan hierarchy:他～大。He belongs to a senior generation in the clan.
辈数儿 bèishùr seniority in the family or clan hierarchy; position in the family hierarchy
辈子 bèizi all one's life; lifetime:半～ half a lifetime /他干了一～厨师。He worked as a chef all his life. /这些本事够学一～的了。It will take a lifetime to learn the skills. /学习是一～的事儿。Learning is a lifelong affair.

背[1] bèi ❶ back of the body; dorsum:～疼 backache /搓～ scrub one's back with a towel ❷ back of an object:手～ back of the hand /刀～儿 back of a knife /脚～ instep

背[2] bèi ❶ with the back towards:～着人群站着 stand with one's back to the crowd /～山面海 with hills behind and the sea in front ❷ turn away:把脸～过去 turn one's face away ❸ leave; go away:见～ depart; pass away ❹ hide sth. from; do sth. behind sb.'s back:～着人说话 talk behind sb.'s back /我没什么～人的事。I have nothing to hide from anyone. ❺ recite from memory; learn by heart or by rote:～诗 learn a poem by heart; recite a poem /～台词 learn one's lines (by heart); recite (*or* speak) one's lines ❻ act contrary to; violate; break:不～原文 not deviate from the original meaning of a text /与原则相～ go against the principle ❼ out-of-the-way:～街 back street; side street ❽〈口语〉unlucky:手气～ have bad luck (in gambling) /这两天～透了。I've been down on my luck (in gambling) these days. ❾ hard of hearing:耳～ be hard of hearing
see also bēi
背部 bèibù back of the body; dorsum:～受伤 be wounded (*or* injured) in the back
背部凹陷 bèibù āoxiàn 〈医学〉swayback
背不住 bèibuzhù *also* "备不住" bèibuzhù 〈方言〉perhaps; maybe; for all you know
背场儿 bèichǎngr 〈口语〉quiet or secluded place:咱们找个～谈谈吧。Let's find a quiet place and have a chat.
背城借一 bèichéng-jièyī *also* "背城一战" make a last-ditch stand before the city wall; fight to the last ditch; put up a stubborn resistance:棋下到这个地步,他只有～,与对方作最后一搏了。Driven into a tight corner in the chess game, he had no alternative but to make a risky move as a last resort.
背驰 bèichí run in the opposite direction; run counter to:这两个人的主张正相～。These two men have diametrically opposite views.
背搭子 bèidāzi cloth bag for carrying one's bedding
背褡 bèidā 〈方言〉waistcoat; vest
背道而驰 bèidào'érchí run in the opposite direction; run counter to:同我们的愿望～ run counter to our wish
背道儿 bèidàor back path; deserted trail:他们常去那条～散步。They frequently stroll on that back path.
背地里 bèidìli *also* "背地" behind sb.'s back; privately; on the sly:～瞎议论 gossip behind sb.'s back
背对背 bèiduìbèi *see* "背靠背"
背对背信用证 bèiduìbèi xìnyòngzhèng 〈金融〉back-to-back
背飞 bèifēi 〈体育〉make a backward flight; fly to the sitter's back:打一个漂亮的～,得了一分 (in volleyball) make a smart backward flight and score a point
背风 bèifēng out of the wind; on the lee side; leeward:停泊于～处 be anchored leeside; be berthed on the sheltered side
背旮旯儿 bèigālár 〈方言〉remote corner; out-of-the-way place; hide-out:你们俩躲在这～说什么悄悄话呢? What secret are you two talking about in this hideout?
背躬 bèigōng aside (in traditional operas):打～ utter an aside
背光 bèiguāng ❶ do sth. with one's back to the light; stand in one's own light:这儿～,照相请到别的地方。You are in poor light here. You'd better take your photos somewhere else. ❷ aphototropism; apheliotropism:～性 aphototropism; apheliotropism /～植物 apheliotropic (*or* aphototropic) plant
背后 bèihòu ❶ behind; at the back; in the rear:大树～ behind a big tree /健身房～ at the back of a gymnasium /从～袭击敌人 attack the enemy from the rear ❷ behind sb.'s back:～捣鬼 plot (*or* scheme) behind the scenes; engage in intrigue /～下毒手 stab sb. in the back /不要～说人坏话。Don't speak ill of anybody behind his or her back.
背晦 bèihui confused; befuddled; senile
see also "悖晦" bèihui
背锪孔钻床 bèihuōkǒng zuànchuáng 〈机械〉back spotfacing machine
背货 bèihuò outdated goods which find a poor market
背肌 bèijī dorsal muscle

背集 bèijí 〈方言〉non-marketing days; days on which no fair is held nearby (in a rural area)
背脊 bèijǐ back of the human body
背架 bèijià *also* "背夹" ladder-shaped wooden or bamboo frame for carrying things on one's back
背剪 bèijiǎn ❶ with hands behind one's back:他~起双手,来回走着。He was pacing to and fro with his hands folded behind his back. ❷ with hands tied or clasped on the back:小偷的双手被~着,等候发落。Trussed, the pickpocket was waiting for the verdict of the magistrate.
背角 bèijiǎo unnoticed corner; quiet place:~处站着一个人。A man was standing in an unnoticed corner. /我们找个~处说话。We found a quiet place for our conversation.
背井离乡 bèijǐng-líxiāng leave one's native place (esp. against one's will):父亲十三岁时~,到上海当学徒。Father left home at the age of 13 to become an apprentice in Shanghai.
背景 bèijǐng ❶ stage setting; backdrop; scenery:这场戏的~是波涛汹涌的大海。The scene is set against a roaring sea. /那张照片的~是秋高气爽的蓝天。That picture has the blue autumn sky as its background. ❷ background; backdrop:政治~ political background /时代~ background of the age /这个人的~如何? What is this man's background?
背景亮度 bèijǐng liàngdù background luminance
背景音乐 bèijǐng yīnyuè background music; environment music; muzak
背景噪声 bèijǐng zàoshēng background noise
背静 bèijing quiet and secluded:~地方 secluded place (*or* spot)
背靠背 bèikàobèi ❶ back to back:~地站着 stand back to back ❷ through an intermediary; not to sb.'s face:~批评 criticism through an intermediary; back-to-back criticism /为避免矛盾激化,先~给他提些意见。We'd better first criticize him through an intermediary so as not to sharpen any antagonism.
背阔肌 bèikuòjī 〈生理〉latissimus dorsi
背累 bèilei bear the burden of maintaining a household; burden
背离 bèilí ❶ leave for another place:在这种情况下,我不得不~故土,飘零他乡。Under the circumstances, I had to leave my homeland and drift along. ❷ deviate from; depart from:~人民利益的歪风邪气 evil trends that go against the interests of the people /~联合公报的协议 deviate (*or* depart) from the agreement in the joint communique /不应~已经发表的文件。The document already published should not be contradicted.
背理 bèilǐ unreasonable; irrational:这件事他做得有点儿~。It was somewhat unreasonable of him to act like that.
背梁 bèiliáng 〈方言〉back of the body; dorsum
背令 bèilìng 〈方言〉out of season:~商品 out-of-season goods
背面 bèimiàn back; reverse side; wrong side:照片的~ back of a photo /唱片的~ reverse side of a record /请阅~ please turn over (PTO); see overleaf
背谬 bèimiù *also* "悖谬" bèimiù absurd; preposterous
背年 bèinián 〈方言〉lean year (for fruit trees, bamboo, etc.)
背叛 bèipàn betray; forsake:他宁肯坐牢终生,也决不~自己的祖国。He'd rather spend the rest of his life behind bars than betray his country.
背鳍 bèiqí 〈动物〉dorsal fin
背气 bèiqì 〈口语〉temporarily stop breathing out of illness, fright or other reasons:吓得差点没背过气去。He was nearly out of his wits with fright.
背弃 bèiqì abandon; desert; renounce:~原来的信仰 abandon one's original belief; renounce one's faith (in religion) /~自己的诺言 go back on one's word
背人 bèirén ❶ concealed from the public; unmentionable:~的病 unmentionable disease /他们鬼鬼祟祟地干了不少~的事。They have done quite a few shady deals on the sly. ❷ out of the way; out of sight:~的地方 secluded place
背日性 bèirìxìng 〈植物〉negative heliotropism:植物的根是有~的。The roots of plants are negatively heliotropic.
背射天线 bèishè tiānxiàn backfire antenna
背生 bèisheng 〈方言〉be born posthumously:~儿 posthumous son
背时 bèishí 〈方言〉❶ behind the times; out-of-date ❷ unlucky:~鬼 one who brings ill luck
背视图 bèishìtú back elevation; dorsal view
背书 bèishū ❶ recite a lesson from memory; repeat a lesson ❷ 〈经济〉endorsement (on a cheque):记名~ endorsement in full
背水一战 bèishuǐ-yīzhàn fight with one's back to the river or wall — fight to win or die; fight a last-ditch battle:他们知道,眼下的情势,只有~了。They were fully aware that the only way out under such circumstances was to put up a desperate fight.
背水阵 bèishuǐzhèn battle array with a river at the back; desperate situation where one could only fight to survive
背诵 bèisòng recite; repeat from memory
背向 bèixiàng *also* "向背" support or opposition:中农的~,是土改成败的关键。The success or failure of the land reform depended on the attitude of the middle peasants.
背销 bèixiāo (of commodities) no longer sell well:这种门锁已趋向~。This kind of padlock is no longer in great demand.
背斜 bèixié 〈地质〉anticline:~层 anticlinal stratum /~油气储藏 oil-gas anticlinal deposit
背心 bèixīn sleeveless garment; waistcoat; vest:西服~ waistcoat; vest /汗~ singlet; running (*or* gym) vest /毛~ woolen vest /棉~ cotton-padded waistcoat /羽绒~ down-padded waistcoat /皮~ leather waistcoat
背信弃义 bèixìn-qìyì faithless; perfidious:~的行径 breach of faith; perfidy
背信弃约 bèixìn-qìyuē go back or renege on one's commitment or promise and renounce a treaty or scrap an agreement
背兴 bèixìng 〈方言〉unlucky; down on one's luck:这两天真~,摔了个骨折,又丢了钱。I've been down on my luck the last couple of days. I had a fracture through a fall, and had some money stolen.
背压式汽轮机 bèiyāshì qìlúnjī 〈机械〉back pressure (steam) turbine
背眼 bèiyǎn (of places) hidden; concealed:~的角落里 in a hidden (*or* dark) corner
背阴 bèiyīn in the shade; shady:街道~的一边 shady side of the street /今天的气温在~处也有摄氏 32 度。Today's temperature is as high as 32℃ centigrade in the shade.
背影 bèiyǐng view of sb.'s back; figure viewed from behind:父亲逐渐走远的~ father's receding figure
背约 bèiyuē break an agreement; go back on one's word; fail to honour one's pledge or promise:违心~ break one's promise against one's will
背越式 bèiyuèshì (in the high jump) Fosbury flop; back style:他是跳~的。He uses the (Fosbury) flop in the high jump.
背运 bèiyùn unlucky; unfortunate:~的赌徒 unlucky gambler /走~ have a run of bad luck; be out of luck
背着手 bèizheshǒu with one's hands clasped behind one's back:~来回踱步 walk to and fro with one's hands behind one's back
背主动脉 bèizhǔdòngmài 〈生理〉dorsal aorta
背字儿 bèizìr 〈口语〉*see* "背运"

褙

bèi stick cloth or paper one piece on top of another with paste or glue:裱~字画 mount a picture or calligraphy
褙壳 bèiké *see* "褙子"
褙子 bèizi *also* "袼褙" gēbei;"褙壳" pieces of cloth stuck together with paste:打~ glue pieces of cloth together, mainly used to make the sole of cotton shoes

偝

bèi 〈书面〉❶ desert; betray ❷ with one's back towards

邶

Bèi name of an ancient kingdom in what is now Henan Province

贝(貝)

bèi ❶ (generic term for 软体动物) mollusk; shellfish; scallop:~介 shellfish /珍珠~ pearl shell /干~ dry scallop /鲜~ fresh scallop ❷ cowrie:虎斑~ tiger cowrie ❸ (Bèi) a surname
贝茨 Bèicí Herbert Ernest Bates (1905-1974), English novelist and writer of short stories including *Love for Lydia* (1952) and *The Darling Buds of May* (1958)
贝雕 bèidiāo shell carving:~画 shell carving picture; shell mosaic
贝多 bèiduō *also* "枧多" bèiduō 〈植物〉pattra; talipot
贝多芬 Bèiduōfēn Ludwig van Beethoven (1770-1827), great German composer

贝尔 bèi'ěr ❶〈物理〉bel(B) ❷ (Bèi'ěr) Alexander Graham Bell (1847-1922), Scottish-American scientist and inventor: ~实验室 (US) Bell Telephone Laboratory
贝尔法斯特 Bèi'ěrfǎsītè Belfast, capital of Northern Ireland
贝尔格莱德 Bèi'ěrgéláidé Belgrade, capital of Yugoslavia
贝尔函数 Bèi'ěr hánshù 〈数学〉Baire function
贝尔湖 Bèi'ěrhú Buir Lake (between China and Mongolia)
贝加尔湖 Bèijiā'ěrhú Lake Baikal (in eastern Siberia)
贝壳 bèiké shell: ~类 shellfish / ~工艺品 shellwork / 玉石~浮雕 cameo / ~学 conchology / ~状断口〈地质〉conchoidal fracture
贝壳币 bèikébì shells used as money; wampum; cowrie
贝劳 Bèiláo Belau, a republic comprising a group of islands (Palau Islands, etc.) in the West Pacific
贝勒 bèile *beile*, hereditary title of Manchu nobility below prince (亲王 or 郡王)
贝雷帽 bèiléimào beret: 绿色~ the Green Berets (US special troops)
贝类 bèilèi shellfish; molluscs: ~养殖 shellfish culture / ~学 conchology; malacology
贝利尼 Bèilìní Bellini, family of Venetian Renaissance painters i.e. Jacopo Bellini (1400-1470) and his sons Gentile Bellini (1429-1507) and Giovanni Bellini (1430-1516)
贝鲁特 Bèilǔtè Beirut, capital of Lebanon
贝母 bèimǔ 〈中药〉bulb of fritillary (*Fritilaria thunbergii*)
贝尼特 Bèinítè Stephen Vincent Benet (1898-1943), American poet and novelist best known for his poem *John Brown's Body*
贝宁 Bèiníng Benin (formerly known as Dahomey): ~城 Benin City / ~王国 Kingdom of Benin / ~湾 Bight of Benin / ~人 Beninian
贝丘 bèiqiū 〈考古〉shell mound found in archaeological excavation sites in coastal areas
贝氏体 bèishìtǐ 〈冶金〉bainite: ~淬火 bainite hardening / ~球铁 bainite ductile iron
贝书 bèishū *also* "贝叶书" Buddhist scripture (originally written on pattra leaves)
贝塔版本 bèitǎ bǎnběn 〈信息〉beta
贝塔粒子 bèitǎ lìzǐ 〈物理〉beta particle
贝塔射线 bèitǎ shèxiàn 〈物理〉beta ray
贝叶 bèiyè pattra leaf
贝叶树 bèiyèshù *also* "贝多"〈植物〉pattra
贝聿铭 Bèi Yùmíng Ieoh Ming Pei (1917-), Chinese American architect
贝子 bèizǐ hereditary title of Manchu nobility below *beile* (贝勒)

棂 bèi

棂多 bèiduō *also* "贝叶树" bèiyèshù; "贝多" bèiduō pattra

钡 bèi

barium (Ba): ~中毒 barium poisoning / 氧化~ barium oxide
钡餐 bèicān 〈医学〉barium meal: ~检查 barium meal examination
钡放电器 bèifàngdiànqì 〈电工〉barium discharger
钡基润滑脂 bèijī rùnhuázhī 〈机械〉barium-base grease; Ba-grease
钡铀矿 bèiyóukuàng 〈矿业〉bauranoite

狈 bèi

see "狼狈" lángbèi

被[1] bèi

quilt: 棉~ cotton-padded quilt / 毛巾~ towelling coverlet

被[2] bèi

〈书面〉❶ cover: 凝霜~野草。The grass is covered with a sheet of frost. ❷ meet with; encounter: ~灾 suffer (*or* be hit by) disaster

被[3] bèi

❶〈介词〉*used in a passive sentence to introduce the agent or doer*: 我~雷声惊醒。I was woken up by a thunder-clap. / 那本书~小王拿走了。The book has been taken away by Xiao Wang. ❷〈助词〉*used to form a passive verbal phrase*: ~捕 be arrested; be under arrest / 他~选为小组长。He was elected group leader. / 那棵树~砍倒了。The tree was cut down.
被保护国 bèibǎohùguó protectorate
被保护人 bèibǎohùrén protégé; protégée; ward
被保险人 bèibǎoxiǎnrén insurant; the insured; insured person
被剥削阶级 bèibōxuējiējí exploited class
被剥削者 bèibōxuēzhě the exploited
被捕者 bèibǔzhě 〈法律〉arrestee; captive
被乘数 bèichéngshù 〈数学〉multiplicand
被除数 bèichúshù 〈数学〉dividend
被褡子 bèidāzi *also* "背搭子" bèidāzi cloth bag for carrying one's bedding while travelling
被袋 bèidài bedding bag
被单 bèidān *also* "被单子" ❶ (bed) sheet: ~布 sheeting ❷ quilt cover
被担保人 bèidānbǎorén guaranteed person
被动 bèidòng passive: ~挨打 be in a passive position where one has to take a beating / 变~为主动 regain the initiative / 他若不抓住时机就~了。If he does not seize the chance, he will find himself in a passive (*or* an awkward) position.
被动传感器 bèidòng chuángǎnqì 〈机械〉passive sensor
被动免疫 bèidòng miǎnyì 〈医学〉passive immunity: ~接种 passive immunization
被动溶血 bèidòng róngxuè 〈医学〉passive hemolysis
被动式 bèidòngshì 〈语言〉passive form; passive construction
被动吸烟 bèidòng xīyān passive smoking
被动寻的制导 bèidòng xúndì zhìdǎo 〈航空〉passive homing guidance
被动语态 bèidòng yǔtài 〈语言〉passive voice
被动轴 bèidòngzhóu driven shaft
被诽谤者 bèifěibàngzhě libel(l)ee
被服 bèifú bedding and clothing (esp. for army use): ~厂 clothing factory
被俘 bèifú be captured; be taken prisoner: ~人员 captured personnel
被覆 bèifù ❶ cover ❷ vegetable cover; plant cover: 滥伐森林, 破坏了地面~。Careless and excessive felling of trees has damaged vegetation cover on the ground.
被覆光纤 bèifù guāngxiān coated fiber
被盖 bèigài 〈方言〉quilt: ~卷儿 bundle of bedding
被告 bèigào *also* "被告人"〈法律〉defendant; the accused: ~席 defendant's seat; dock
被格 bèigé *also* "被格子" wooden case (for storing quilts) at one end of *kang*
被管制分子 bèiguǎnzhìfènzǐ 〈法律〉person under public surveillance
被害人 bèihàirén 〈法律〉injured party; victim
被加数 bèijiāshù 〈数学〉summand
被监护人 bèijiānhùrén person under guardianship; ward
被减数 bèijiǎnshù 〈数学〉minuend
被劫持者 bèijiéchízhě hijack victim; hijackee
被拘留者 bèijūliúzhě 〈法律〉detainee; internee
被开方数 bèikāifāngshù 〈数学〉radicand
被里 bèilǐ underneath side of a quilt
被面 bèimiàn facing or outside cover of a quilt: 软缎~ silk quilt cover
被难 bèinàn ❶ be killed in a disaster: 出了车祸, 三人~。Three people were killed in a car accident. ❷ suffer from a disaster: ~的村民纷纷挤进车站。The disaster-stricken villagers swarmed into the station.
被虐待狂 bèinüèdàikuáng 〈心理〉masochism
被迫 bèipò be compelled; be forced; be constrained: ~进行还击 be compelled to fight back / 出于~ under coercion / 她辍学是~的。She discontinued her studies against her own will.
被铺 bèipù 〈方言〉bedding; bed clothes
被侵略者 bèiqīnlüèzhě victim of aggression
被侵权人 bèiqīnquánrén 〈法律〉the infringed
被驱逐出境者 bèiqūzhú chūjìngzhě expellee; deportee
被褥 bèirù bedding; bedclothes: 晒~ air bedding
被上诉人 bèishàngsùrén 〈法律〉appellee
被诉 bèisù be sued: 主权国家通常不能在外国法院~。Sovereign states cannot as a rule be sued in foreign courts.
被套 bèitào ❶ bedding bag ❷ (bag-shaped) quilt case; quilt slip ❸ cotton wadding for a quilt
被提名人 bèitímíngrén nominee
被天席地 bèitiān-xídì 〈比喻〉sleep in the open
被条 bèitiáo 〈方言〉quilt

被统治者 bèitǒngzhìzhě the ruled
被头 bèitóu ❶ piece of cloth sewed on the upper end of a quilt to keep it clean ❷〈方言〉quilt
被窝儿 bèiwōr quilt folded to form sth. like a sleeping bag
被卧 bèiwo quilt
被絮 bèixù cotton padding of a quilt
被选举权 bèixuǎnjǔquán right to be elected
被选举人 bèixuǎnjǔrén the elected
被压迫民族 bèiyāpò mínzú oppressed nation
被遗弃者 bèiyíqìzhě 〈法律〉abandoned or deserted person
被灾 bèizāi disaster-stricken; disaster-devastated
被罩 bèizhào quilt slip; quilt case
被子植物 bèizǐ zhíwù angiosperm
被子 bèizi quilt：叠～ fold up a quilt; make the bed／铺～ unroll a quilt; make the bed／盖好～ cover sb. (*or* oneself) up with a quilt／缝～ stitch a quilt; make a quilt

鞁 bèi ❶ saddle and bridle ❷ saddle (a horse)

㪍 bèi *see* "㪍㪍" wěibèi

鞴 bèi sharpen (a knife on a piece of cloth, leather or a stone); whet; strop
鞴刀 bèidāo sharpen or whet a knife; strop a knife
鞴刀布 bèidāobù piece of cloth on which a knife is sharpened

bei

呗 bei 〈助词〉❶ *used to show that sth. is self-evident*：学生的任务就是学习～。The task for the students is of course to study. ❷ *used to express reluctant agreement or concession*：去就去～。Well, if I must (go), I must.
see also bài

臂 bei *see* "胳臂" gēbei
see also bì

bēn

奔 bēn ❶ run quickly; dash; (of a horse) gallop：狂～ run like mad; dash (*or* tear) along／～马 galloping horse／汽车在山路上飞～。The truck tore along the mountain road. ❷ hurry; hasten; rush：～赴前线 hurry to the front ❸ run away; flee：夜～ run away under the cover of night／东～西窜 flee in all directions
see also bèn
奔巴岛 Bēnbādǎo Pemba Island (off the east coast of Tanzania)
奔北 bēnběi 〈书面〉flee in defeat
奔波 bēnbō dash about; rush about; hurry back and forth：终日～ dash about all day; be on the go all day／四处～ dash around; rush about／～于北京与上海之间 shuttle back and forth between Beijing and Shanghai／为推销产品而～劳顿 bustle about promoting product sales／～了一天，累坏了。I'm played out after running about all day.
奔驰 bēnchí speed; run fast; dash：日夜～ run day and night／列车～而过。A train sped by.
奔驰汽车 Bēnchí qìchē (Germany) Mercedes-Benz car
奔凑 bēncòu converge; crowd together：万千思绪，～脑际。A myriad thoughts welled up in my mind.
奔窜 bēncuàn flee; run away; stampede：枪响了，野兔吓得～到树林里去了。The hare was frightened at the shot and scampered into the woods.
奔放 bēnfàng (of thoughts, feelings, style of writing, etc.) bold and unrestrained; uninhibited：文笔～ write in a vigorous and racy style／热情～ overflowing with enthusiasm; brimming with ardent emotion／豪爽～的性格 bold and dynamic personality
奔赴 bēnfù hurry; hasten; rush：～地震灾区 hasten to the earthquake-stricken area
奔集 bēnjí converge; rally：潮涌般的人群～到高音喇叭下。Large crowds of people converged quickly under the loud-speaker.
奔竞 bēnjìng 〈书面〉bustle about seeking fame or position：～仕途 hustle and bustle on the long crawl in officialdom; jockey for position in the political arena
奔劳 bēnláo bustle about; dash around：长年～ bustle about (*or* toil) all the year round
奔雷 bēnléi thunderbolt：势如～ like a thunderbolt flashing across the sky
奔流 bēnliú ❶ flow at great speed; pour：山洪～而下。Torrents of water rushed down the mountain.／江水向东～入海。The river flows east into the sea.／浩浩长江，～不息。The mighty waters of the Yangtze roll on incessantly. ❷ flowing stream; racing current
奔马痨 bēnmǎláo 〈医学〉galloping consumption; acute consumption
奔马律 bēnmǎlǜ 〈医学〉gallop rhythm; Traube's murmur
奔忙 bēnmáng bustle or dash about：为筹办研讨会而～ dash about getting things ready for the seminar
奔命 bēnmìng rush about on business; be kept on the run; be rushed off one's feet：疲于～ be worn-out running about every day; be kept constantly on the run; be rushed off one's feet
see also bènmìng
奔跑 bēnpǎo run; race：小鹿儿在野生动物园里自由地～。The fawns run about freely in the safari park.／他为找工作的事四处～。He went job-hunting everywhere.
奔泉 bēnquán gushing spring：泪如～ tears stream down one's cheeks
奔丧 bēnsāng hasten home for the funeral of a parent or grandparent
奔驶 bēnshǐ move with great speed; speed：小汽车在高速公路上全速～。The car drove at full speed on the super-highway. *or* The car sped along the expressway.
奔逝 bēnshì (time, water, etc.) pass away rapidly：～的河水 rushing stream／岁月～。Time passes quickly.
奔淌 bēntǎng (of water) flow swiftly; surge forward：江水～。The river surges ahead.
奔逃 bēntáo flee; run away：四处～ flee helter-skelter; run away (*or* scurry off) in all directions／～他乡 flee one's hometown／敌人狼狈～。The enemy scurried off in disarray.
奔腾 bēnténg ❶ gallop：如万马～ as if a thousand horses were galloping ahead ❷ surge forward; roll on in waves：～不息 roll on (*or* surge forward) ceaselessly／黄河～呼啸而来。The roaring waves of the Yellow River roll on and on.
奔腾处理器 Bēnténg chǔlǐqì 〈计算机〉Pentium CPU (central processing unit)
奔腾芯片 Bēnténg xìnpiàn 〈计算机〉Pentium chip
奔突 bēntū dash about; run wildly：犹如野兽～ run about desperately like wild animals／一股强烈的激情在他心中～着。A strong feeling of excitement raced through his mind.
奔湍 bēntuān ❶ swift current; rapid stream; torrent; rapids ❷ (of a river, stream, etc.) swift; rapid; torrential：一股山水从半山腰～而下。A torrent runs rapidly down the mountain.
奔袭 bēnxí 〈军事〉long-range raid：～敌人的据点 make a long march to attack an enemy stronghold
奔向 bēnxiàng march on towards：～光明的未来 stride ahead towards a bright future
奔泻 bēnxiè (of torrents) pour down; rush down：滔滔江水，自三峡～而下。The surging waves roll down the Three Gorges.
奔涌 bēnyǒng gush out; flow rapidly：泉水～ gushing spring／江河～ rivers rushing past／热泪～ hot tears gushing out (*or* streaming down)／激情～ overflow with ardent fervour
奔逐 bēnzhú chase after：孩子们在田野里～着。The children are scampering in the fields.
奔注 bēnzhù (of water) empty swiftly into：万壑～，汇成巨流。A myriad streams rush down to converge into a great river.
奔走 bēnzǒu run around; rush about; bustle about：～相告 run around passing on the message; rush about spreading the (exciting) news／经多方～，他终于恢复了名誉。After seeking help from various quarters, he was rehabilitated.／这位老政治家为了调解纠纷，～于各方之间。The senior politician approached all the parties concerned trying to mediate their differences.
奔走呼号 bēnzǒu-hūháo go about compaigning (for a cause); canvass support：为改善人类的生存环境而～ go about canvassing support for an improved environment for humanity

锛

bēn ❶ adze ❷ cut with an adze：～木头 cut wood with an adze ❸〈方言〉dent（edge of a knife, etc.）：刀使～了。The knife's edge was dented through use.

锛得儿木 bēndermù 〈方言〉woodpecker

锛子 bēnzi adze

B

贲

bēn ❶ *see*“虎贲”hǔbēn ❷（Bēn）a surname

see also bì

贲门 bēnmén 〈生理〉cardia（of the stomach）：～溃疡 ulcer in the cardia /～括约肌 cardiac sphincter

贲门痉挛 bēnmén jìngluán 〈医学〉cardiopasm

贲门扩张术 bēnmén kuòzhāngshù 〈医学〉cardiodiosis

贲门切除术 bēnmén qiēchúshù 〈医学〉cardiectomy

犇

bēn *same as*“奔”bēn

běn

本[1]

běn ❶ root or stem of a plant：无～之木 tree without roots /伐木不自其～，必复生。If you do not tear up（*or* out）a tree by the root, it will grow again. ❷ foundation; basis; origin：教育是立国之～。Education is fundamental to national development. *or* Education is the foundation of a state. ❸ capital; principal：赔～生意 losing business /够～ gain enough to cover the cost /赔了大～ sustain huge losses in business /～小利大 have a small investment but big earnings ❹ main; chief; central：～题 central theme ❺ original; initial：我～以为他会来的。At first, I thought he would come. ❻ one's own; native：～校 this school /～国 one's native country; this country /他～人不同意。He himself didn't agree. ❼ current; this; present：～年 this year; current year /～世纪 this century; present century ❽ according to; based on; in line with：希～上述精神，妥为处理。You are requested to handle the matter in the light（*or* spirit）of the above-mentioned principle. /这篇小说的情节是有所～的。The plot of this novel is based on an actual event. ❾〈书面〉〈量词〉*used of flowering plants*：牡丹十～ ten peony bulbs（*or* plants）

本[2]

běn ❶ book：书～ book /户口～ residence book /练习～ exercise-book /账～ account book; ledger /照相～ photo album /日记～ diary ❷ version; edition：刻～ block-printed edition /精装～ deluxe edition /选～ selected works; anthology /抄～ scribe's copy /译～ translation /善～ valuable edition; excellent edition /影印～ photocopy ❸ script：台～ playscript with stage directions /戏～ opera script /剧～ script /唱～ ballad-singer's songbook ❹ memorial presented to the emperor：奏～ memorial to the throne ❺〈量词〉（a）*used of books of various kinds*：五～书 five books（*or* copies）/两～账 two account books（one for actual, day-to-day use and the other for tax examiners）（b）*used of traditional operas or their scripts*：头～《西游记》first part of the dramatized *Pilgrimage to the West*（c）*used of films*：这部电影有十～。This is a 10-reel film.

本巴人 Běnbārén Bemba, ethnic community in southern Africa

本白布 běnbáibù unbleached cloth

本本 běnběn book：各种～装了一箱子。Books of various kinds filled the box.

本本主义 běnběnzhǔyì book worship（indicating a blind faith in dogma or punctilious adherence to written rules and directives）; dogmatism

本币 běnbì （short for 本位货币）basic unit of a national currency

本部 běnbù main or central part; headquarters：学院～ major campus of the college

本埠 běnbù this town or city：～邮件 local mail

本草 běncǎo （used in general reference to）Chinese（herbal）medicine; Chinese *materia medica*：～方儿 prescription of herbal medicine /《～纲目》*Compendium of Materia Medica*（written by Li Shizhen in 1578）

本朝 běncháo present dynasty; this court; the court（used by the monarch to refer to his or her court）

本初佛 Běnchūfó 〈佛教〉Adi-Buddha

本初子午线 běnchū zǐwǔxiàn first meridian; prime meridian：本初横子午线 prime transverse meridian /本初斜子午线 prime oblique meridian

本茨 Běncí Friedrich Karl Benz（1844-1929）, German engineer who built the first car driven by an internal-combustion engine in Germany in 1885

本大利宽 běndà-lìkuān large capital and huge profit — big business; big capital yielding large profit

本岛 běndǎo main island; island proper

本等 běnděng 〈方言〉duty; responsibility：安分～的人 honest, law-abiding person /做这些事是你我的～。It is your duty as well as mine to attend to these things. *or* This is what we are here for.

本底 běndǐ 〈物理〉background：放射性～ radioactive background /～噪音 background noise /～测定 background determination

本地 běndì local：～特产 local speciality /～风光 local sights; local scene /～干部 local officials /～剧团 local theatrical troupe /～人 native; local inhabitant

本地环路 běndì huánlù 〈信息〉local loop

本地载波 běndì zàibō 〈通信〉local carrier

本动 běndòng 〈天文〉peculiar motion（as of an individual star relative to a group of neighbouring stars）：～速度 peculiar velocity

本笃会 Běndǔhuì 〈天主教〉Benedictine Order（established around 529 AD）

本分 běnfèn ❶ one's job; one's duty：教好书是教师的～。A teacher's job is to give efficient instruction. ❷ contented and law-abiding; decent：守～ keep one's place; never go beyond what is proper /这人很～。He is a decent guy.

本干 běngàn （of a tree, etc.）trunk

本根 běngēn root; origin; source：探其～ trace sth. to its origin（*or* source）

本工 běngōng 〈戏曲〉one's own line or speciality

本固枝荣 běngù-zhīróng when the roots are firm, the branches and leaves flourish — things will develop only when the foundation is sound

本贯 běnguàn native place; ancestral home：～杭州。Hangzhou is one's native place.

本国 běnguó one's own country：～政府 government of this country; this government /～资源 national resources /～含量 domestic content /～经济 domestic economy /～资本 indigenous capital /～产品 home（*or* domestic）product /～注册 home registration

本国法 běnguófǎ national law; *Lex patriae*

本国语 běnguóyǔ native language; mother tongue

本行 běnháng ❶ profession one has always engaged in or been trained for; field of study; special line：我原先就是教师，干了几年翻译工作又回到了老～。I was originally a teacher, and after an interval of a few years' working as a translator, returned to my old profession. / 词典学不是他的～。Lexicography is not his line. ❷ one's current profession or work：熟悉～业务 be well-versed in one's line of work/ 三句话不离～ can never say three sentences without talking shop; can hardly open one's mouth without talking shop

本号 běnhào this shop

本怀 běnhuái 〈书面〉original intention：此举非由～。This is not my original intention. *or* I did not mean to do this.

本籍 běnjí native place; ancestral home：～河南许昌。Xuchang of Henan Province is his native place.

本纪 běnjì 〈历史〉primary chronicle（listing major events of a dynasty centred around the life of the reigning emperor）; emperor's biography：《项羽～》*Biography of Xiang Yu*

本家 běnjiā member of the same family; relative with the same surname

本家儿 běnjiār 〈方言〉person or party concerned：～不来，啥事儿也办不成。Nothing can be done without the participation of the party concerned.

本届 běnjiè current; this year's：～人代会 current session of the National People's Congress /～奥运会 Olympic Games（to be）held this year /～新生的录取工作 this year's enrolment

本金 běnjīn ❶ principal：这笔存款只支取利息，～继续存一年。I want to draw the interest on this account but deposit the principal for another year. ❷ capital：～太少，生意总是做不大。With such limited capital, we can never do business on a larger scale.

本科 běnkē regular undergraduate course（as distinct from junior college *or* correspondence course）：大学～ regular college programme /～生 college student; undergraduate /～毕业 graduate from a regular college or university

坌[1] bèn 〈方言〉dig; turn up:～地 dig the ground; turn up the soil

坌[2] bèn 〈书面〉❶ dust:微～ fine dust ❷ gather; collect ❸ crude and inferior; shoddy ❹ spread with powder

坌集 bènjí 〈书面〉gather together; converge:游行队伍～城区。The demonstrators converged in the downtown area.

坌涌 bènyǒng 〈书面〉well up; surge:心潮～。All kinds of thoughts flash across one's mind. /许多感想～心头。A host of feelings surge in one's heart.

bēng

伻 bēng 〈书面〉envoy

崩 bēng ❶ collapse:山～地裂。Mountains collapse and the ground cracks. ❷ burst; crack; split:豆荚～开了。The pods cracked open. /他们谈～了。Their negotiations broke down. /他们性格不合,早就～了。They were temperamentally incompatible and parted company long ago. ❸ be hit by sth. bursting; hit and smash:小心,别让爆竹～着你! Take care! Don't get hurt by the firecrackers. /弹子～碎了玻璃。The window was smashed by a catapult shot. ❹ 〈口语〉shoot:昨天～了两名杀人犯。Two murderers were executed (*or* shot) yesterday. ❺ (of an emperor) die:驾～了。The emperor passed away.

崩摧 bēngcuī fall apart; collapse; break down:纲纪～。Law and order broke down completely.

崩坏 bēnghuài crack and fall; crumble:茅屋四下里～了。The thatched hut was crumbling on all sides. /农业生产开始商品化,那种自给自足的自然经济开始～了。With the commercialization of farming, the natural economy characterized by self-sufficiency has begun to crumble.

崩毁 bēnghuǐ collapse; cave in:墓室～。The tomb chamber caved in.

崩积层 bēngjīcéng 〈地质〉colluvium

崩解 bēngjiě ❶ disintegrate; crumble; fall apart; collapse:宗法制度终于～。The feudal clan system eventually fell apart. ❷ (of rocks) break into small pieces as a result of erosion

崩决 bēngjué (of dams and dykes) collapse; give way:这场洪水使沿江大堤数处～。The dyke gave way to the floodwater at several places.

崩溃 bēngkuì collapse; crumble; fall apart:经济～ collapse of the economy /全军～ rout of the entire army /处于～边缘 on the verge of collapse /反动统治的～ downfall (*or* collapse) of the reactionary regime

崩裂 bēngliè burst or break apart; crack:炸药轰隆一声,山石～。The dynamite boomed, sending the rocks flying.

崩龙族 Bēnglóngzú Benglong (formerly translated as Penglung) nationality (in Yunnan Province)

崩漏 bēnglòu 〈中医〉uterine bleeding (in menstual period)

崩落 bēngluò collapse and roll down:山石～。Mountain rocks were rolling down.

崩松 bēngsōng *also*"杜松"dùsōng 〈植物〉needle juniper

崩塌 bēngtā collapse; crumble:他因炭窑～而牺牲。He was killed in a charcoal kiln collapse. /强烈的地震把山崖给～了。The cliff collapsed in a strong earthquake.

崩塌压强 bēngtā yāqiáng collapsing pressure

崩坍 bēngtān (of a cliff or slope) crumble and fall; collapse:山崖～。The cliff collapsed.

崩颓 bēngtuí *see*"崩塌"

崩陷 bēngxiàn fall in; cave in

崩症 bēngzhèng *also*"血崩"xuèbēng 〈中医〉metrorrhagia

崩坠 bēngzhuì *see*"崩落"

嘣 bēng 〈象声〉sound of sth. beating, snapping, or bursting:～的一声,提琴弦断了。The violin's string snapped. /我心里～～直跳。My heart was pounding (*or* thumping) incessantly. /爆竹～地一响。Bang, went the firecracker.

嘣豆儿 bēngdòur 〈方言〉roasted broad beans

绷[1]**(繃)** bēng ❶ stretch tight; strain:弓～得很紧。The bowstring is stretched taut. /把绳子～直了。Straighten the rope. /别把弦～得太紧了。Don't overstrain yourself. ❷ (of a dress, a piece of cloth, etc.) tight; taut:衬衫太小,～在身上不舒服。The shirt is so tight that I feel a little uncomfortable in it. ❸ spring; bounce:盒子一打开,弹簧就～出来。When the box was opened, the spring bounced out. ❹ baste; tack; pin:～被头 sew a cover on to the head of a quilt /把花样先～好再绣。Baste the pattern (onto a piece of silk) before embroidering it. ❺ 〈方言〉be barely able to subsist; manage with difficulty:看你还能～多久! I wonder how much longer you can go on like this. ❻ frame matting (for a bed):棕～ frame matting made of palm fibre ❼ embroidery frame

绷[2]**(繃)** bēng 〈方言〉swindle; cheat:坑～拐骗 use all possible means of swindling

see also běng; bèng

绷场面 bēng chǎngmiàn be barely able to keep the appearance of respectability; keep up appearances

绷床 bēngchuáng trampolin:～游戏 trampolining

绷带 bēngdài bandage:～包扎 bandaging /～剪 bandage scissors

绷弓子 bēnggōngzi ❶ door-closing spring or bamboo bow ❷ 〈方言〉catapult

绷簧 bēnghuáng 〈方言〉spring

绷子 bēngzi ❶ embroidery frame; hoop; tambour ❷ frame matting (for a bed):藤～ frame matting made of rattan /～床 bed with frame matting

béng

甭 béng 〈方言〉don't need to:你～管。Don't you bother. *or* Keep off. /～惦记着他。Don't worry about him.

běng

菶 běng

菶菶 běngběng 〈书面〉lush or luxuriant (vegetation)

绷(繃) běng ❶ pull (a long face) ❷ strain oneself:他～不住笑了。He could not but burst out laughing. *or* He could not stifle a laugh.

see also bēng; bèng

绷劲 běngjìn strain one's muscles with bated breath; strain oneself:咬住牙,绷住劲 clench one's teeth and strain one's muscles / 他一～,裤腰带给绷断了。When he strained hard, his belt snapped.

绷脸 běngliǎn pull a long face; be sullen:他一天到晚绷着脸儿,跟谁都生气似的。He pulls a long face (*or* looks displeased) all day as if he were angry with everybody.

bèng

迸 bèng ❶ spout; spurt; burst forth; blurt out:铁水奔流,钢花飞～。Molten iron flows and steel sparks fly all around. /礁石上～起一层浪花。Waves lashed the rocks, shooting up sprays of water. /半天他才～出一句话来。It was quite a while before he was able to blurt out a few words. ❷ break to pieces suddenly:～碎 burst suddenly into fragments; break to pieces all of a sudden

迸脆 bèngcuì ❶ (of food) crisp:麻花吃起来～。The deep-fried flour doughnuts are crisp. ❷ (of voice) clear and sharp; crisp:他答应得～。He made a crisp reply.

迸发 bèngfā burst forth; burst out:大厅里～出一阵掌声。There was an outburst of applause in the hall./冶铁炉里～出熊熊火焰。Tongues of roaring flames shot up from the furnace. /他的愤怒一下子都～出来。The anger smouldering in his bosom exploded.

迸飞 bèngfēi fly in every direction:乱石～。A hailstorm of stones were flying about.

迸溅 bèngjiàn splash (in all directions); burst forth:火花～ sparks flying about /激流冲击着岩石,～起无数飞沫。The rapids dashed

against the rocks spitting foam into the air.

迸裂 bèngliè split; burst (open):～出来的火花飞向四处。Sparks flew in all directions. /他从台架上跌下来,顿时脑浆～。He fell from a scaffold and had his brains dashed out.

迸流 bèngliú gush out:鲜血～。Blood gushed forth.

迸散 bèngsàn dash out in all directions:节日夜空里～着五彩六色的火花。Colourful sparks of the firework display danced across the sky during the festive night.

迸射 bèngshè spew; spout; squirt:子弹从暗堡里～出来。Bullets were spewing out from the hidden bulwork. *or* The hidden bulwork was spewing bullets.

迸涌 bèngyǒng burst; rush:热泪～ burst into tears /他内心～出青春的热情。Youthful enthusiasm swelled his heart.

迸跃 bèngyuè dance; burst forth:怒火～ fly into a rage; explode in anger /火花～。Sparks are flying.

甏

bèng 〈方言〉jar; vat:酒～ vats of wine

泵

bèng pump:离心～ centrifugal pump /高扬程～ high lift pump /～油 pump oil /～出洼地积水 pump out water gathered in a low-lying place

泵阀 bèngfá pump valve

泵房 bèngfáng pump house

泵排量 bèngpáiliàng pumpage; pump delivery

泵室 bèngshì pump chamber

泵推力 bèngtuīlì thrust of pump

泵压 bèngyā pumping pressure

泵站 bèngzhàn 〈水利〉pump plant; pumping station

蚌

bèng

see also bàng

蚌埠 Bèngbù Bengbu, major city in Anhui Province

蹦

bèng leap; jump; spring:用力一～ by one powerful leap/欢～乱跳 alive and kicking / 皮球～得老高。The ball bounced very high. /老人家关心时事,嘴里常～出些新词儿来。The old man was interested in current affairs, and would come out with a couple of new terms every now and then.

蹦蹦儿车 bèngbèngrchē noisy motorized tricycle

蹦蹦儿戏 bèngbèngrxì predecessor for *pingju* 评剧, a local opera of north and northeast China

蹦蹦跳跳 bèngbeng-tiàotiào bouncing and vivacious; lively:孩子们从院子里～地跑进来。Prancing from the courtyard, the children scampered into the room.

蹦跶 bèngda bounce or jump about at last gasp:敌军就像秋后的蚂蚱,～不了几天了。Like grasshoppers after autumn, the enemy troops were on their last legs.

蹦豆儿 bèngdòur 〈方言〉❶ roasted broad beans ❷ little child:这是大的,家里还有个小～。This is the older one; there's a little one at home.

蹦高儿 bènggāor jump; leap:乐得直～ jump with joy

蹦极跳 bèngjítiào 〈体育〉bungee-jumping:我们昨天去玩～了,真够刺激的。We went bungee-jumping yesterday; it was thrilling.

蹦儿 bèngr 〈方言〉❶ jump; hop:他气得直打～。He was jumping about in a rage. *or* He was hopping mad. ❷ capability; trick:看他一个人能有什么～! Let's see what he is capable of all by himself.

蹦跳 bèngtiào jump; prance

蹦子 bèngzi 〈方言〉leap; jump:一个～蹿上了台 land on the platform at one leap

镚

bèng small coin

镚子儿 bèngzǐr 〈方言〉least bit of money; penny:一个～也不给 not even give sb. a penny

镚子 bèngzi *also* "镚儿" small coin:请给我几个钢～。Please give me some coins.

绷(綳)

bèng ❶ split open; crack:瓷杯～了一道缝儿。The china cup has a crack in it. ❷〈口语〉*used before adjectives like* 硬,直,亮, *etc.*, *as an intensifier*:～直 very straight /～亮 exceedingly bright /～硬 hard as rock

see also bēng; běng

绷瓷 bèngcí porcelain with a crackled finish; crackleware

bī

逼(偪)

bī ❶ force; compel; drive; press:～其下野 force (*or* compel) sb. to give up power /～到了难以忍受的程度 be driven (*or* pressed) beyond the limit of one's patience; stretch one's patience to the limit /官～民反。It was the rulers who drove the people into rebellion. /他父母～他学医。His parents are pushing (*or* pressing) him to study medicine. /他～他爸爸给他买吉他。He pestered his father to buy him a guitar. ❷ press for; extort:～交学费 press for payment of tuition ❸ press on towards; advance on; close in on:部队直～县城。The army advanced straight on the county town. ❹〈书面〉narrow:两崖石壁甚～。There is only a narrow opening between the two sharp-cut cliffs.

逼促 bīcù ❶ hasten; hurry:～上路 hasten sb.'s departure ❷ narrow; small:这个地方倒很方便,就是～一点儿。The place is convenient; only it is a bit too small.

逼宫 bīgōng (of ministers, etc.) force the king or emperor to abdicate

逼供 bīgòng extort a confession; try to force sb. to confess:严刑～ extort a confession by atrocious (*or* cruel) torture

逼供信 bī-gòng-xìn obtain confessions by extortion and establish them as evidence; give credence to confessions obtained under duress:严禁～ It is strictly forbidden to obtain confessions by extortion and give them credence.

逼和 bīhé (in chess and some ball games) force the opponent to a draw or tie:主队在终场前一分钟被客队～。The visiting team forced the home team to a draw in the last minute of the game.

逼婚 bīhūn force a girl or woman to marry:～在有些偏远地区仍时而发生。Forced marriages occur from time to time in some remote areas.

逼近 bījìn press on towards; close in on; approach:年关～。The end of the lunar year is drawing near. /天色～黄昏。Dusk is approaching. /土匪已～村子。The bandits were pressing on towards the village.

逼近函数 bījìn hánshù 〈数学〉approximating function

逼掯 bīken 〈口语〉force; press; push:别～他太厉害了,他会翻脸的。Don't push him too hard; he may turn on you.

逼勒 bīlè force; press; coerce

逼良为娼 bīliáng-wéichāng force a girl of good family or woman of virtue to engage in prostitution; force an honest person to do sth. dishonest

逼命 bīmìng ❶ threaten sb. with violence ❷ press sb. to do sth. difficult to accomplish:真～! 这么大的任务,三天内怎么完成! It's little short of murder to ask people to fulfil such a difficult task in three days!

逼迫 bīpò force; compel; coerce:在环境的～下,他不得不变得通融一些了。He had to be more flexible under the circumstances.

逼人 bīrén pressing; threatening:～的眼光 threatening (*or* scrutinizing, *or* piercing) eyes /寒气～。There is a nip in the air. /情势～。The situation is pressing. /你说他们～太甚,可是他们还说让步过多呢。You may say you are being pressed too hard, but they think they are making too many concessions as it is.

逼上梁山 bīshàng-Liángshān have no alternative but to join the Liangshan Marsh rebels — be driven to rebel; be compelled to act desperately:对我来说,走上经商的道路是～的结果。So far as I was concerned, I had no alternative but to become a businessman at the time.

逼使 bīshǐ force sb. to do sth.:敌人严刑审讯,～他供出情报。The enemy tortured him to obtain information. /浑身的疼痛～他不停地哼哼。He groaned with pain, for he was aching all over.

逼视 bīshì look at from close-up; gaze fixedly at; stare intently at:光彩夺目,不可～ shine in all its dazzling splendour /他们二人～着她。The two of them looked her squarely in the eye.

逼熟 bīshú 〈农业〉forced ripening (of crops)

逼死 bīsǐ hound sb. to death:老人是给～的。The old man was driven to commit suicide.

逼问 bīwèn press sb. for an answer; interrogate:他被人们～得无言答对。Though pressed hard for an answer, he couldn't say a word. /这件事无论你怎么～,他也不会说。No matter how hard you try to in-

terrogate him, he won't let on.
逼狭 bīxiá narrow:路径～。The path is narrow.
逼肖 bīxiào 〈书面〉bear a close resemblance to; be the very image of:容貌性格,～乃父。He resembled his father not only in appearance but also in character. *or* He was a chip off the old block.
逼仄 bīzè 〈书面〉narrow; cramped:住房～ cramped living quarters
逼窄 bīzhǎi (of space) narrow:路面～。The road is very narrow./我们这里的办公室～。We are cramped for space in this office.
逼债 bīzhài press for debt repayment; dun:登门～ visit sb. to press for repayment of debt; collect debt at one's doorstep
逼真 bīzhēn ❶ lifelike; true to life:这幅肖像画得～。The portrait is lifelike./他演的角色～。The part he plays is really true to life./这只猫绣得很～。This embroidered cat looks like a live one. ❷ distinctly; clearly:他俩在隔壁说话,我听得～。I heard clearly what they were talking about in the next room.
逼真度 bīzhēndù 〈电子〉fidelity:～准则 fidelity criterion
逼租 bīzū press for rent payment

蝠 bī 〈动物〉slipmouth (*Leiognathus*)

锃 bī 〈书面〉❶ hairpin ❷ finecomb
see also pī

屄(屄) bī 〈粗话〉vaginal orifice; vulva

bí

荸 bí
荸荠 bíqi water chestnut (*Eleocharis tuberosa*)

鼻 bí ❶ nose:鹰钩～ aquiline (*or* Roman) nose/狮子～ pug (*or* snub) nose/酒糟～ brandy nose; acne rosacea/刺～ irritate the nose/扑～ assail the nostrils/～吸避孕剂 sniffing contraceptive ❷ 〈书面〉pioneer; originate
鼻癌 bí'ái 〈医学〉rhino-carcinoma
鼻病 bíbìng 〈医学〉rhinopathy
鼻成形术 bíchéngxíngshù 〈医学〉rhinoplasty
鼻翅儿 bíchìr (common name for 鼻翼) wing of nose; *ala nasi*
鼻出血 bíchūxiě 〈医学〉nosebleed; rhinorrhagia; epistaxis
鼻丁 bíding 〈方言〉nasal mucus
鼻窦 bídòu 〈生理〉(common name for 鼻旁窦) paranasal sinus
鼻窦炎 bídòuyán nasosinusitis
鼻骨 bígǔ nasal bone:～骨折 fracture of the nasal bone
鼻观 bíguān 〈书面〉nostril
鼻管 bíguǎn 〈医学〉nasal tube
鼻化元音 bíhuà yuányīn 〈语言〉nasalized vowel
鼻环 bíhuán nose ring
鼻甲 bíjiǎ turbinate; turbinated bones:～切除术 turbinectomy
鼻甲炎 bíjiǎyán 〈医学〉conchitis
鼻尖 bíjiān *also* "鼻子尖儿" tip of the nose
鼻镜 bíjìng 〈医学〉rhinoscope:电光～ nasoscope/～检查 rhinoscopy
鼻疽 bíjū *also* "马鼻疽" mǎbíjū 〈畜牧〉glanders
鼻科学 bíkēxué rhinology
鼻孔 bíkǒng nostril:～狭窄 stenomycteria/～朝天〈比喻〉look down one's nose at people; be haughty/一个～出气 be hand in glove (with one another)
鼻梁 bíliáng bridge of the nose:高～儿 steep bridge of the nose
鼻毛 bímáo vibrissae
鼻黏膜 bíniánmó nasal mucosa
鼻牛儿 bíniúr 〈方言〉hardened mucus in nostrils; booger
鼻衄 bínǜ 〈医学〉nosebleed; rhinorrhagia; epistaxis
鼻旁窦 bípángdòu *also* "鼻窦" paranasal sinus:～炎 nasosinusitis; paranasal sinusitis
鼻腔 bíqiāng 〈生理〉nasal cavity
鼻青脸肿 bíqīng-liǎnzhǒng bloody nose and swollen face:被打得～ be badly battered; be beaten black and blue
鼻儿 bír ❶ hole in an implement, utensil, etc. for sth. to be inserted into; eye:针～ eye of a needle/门～ bolt staple ❷〈方言〉whistle:这布娃娃上的～一响跟孩子哭似的。If you press the whistle on the doll, it sounds like a baby wailing./火车响着～飞驰而过。The train whistled past.
鼻塞 bísè have a stuffy nose
鼻饰 bíshì nasal ornament
鼻饲 bísì 〈医学〉nasal feeding
鼻酸 bísuān feel a lump in one's throat:见着伤心事就～ feel a lump in one's throat at any painful memory
鼻涕 bítì nasal mucus; snivel:流～ have a running rose
鼻涕虫 bítìchóng *also* "蛞蝓" kuòyú slug
鼻头 bítou 〈方言〉*see* "鼻子"
鼻洼子 bíwāzi *also* "鼻洼" furrow beside the nose
鼻息 bíxī breath:～均匀 regular and even breathing/～不畅 have a stuffy nose/～如雷 snore like thunder/仰人～〈比喻〉be dependent on others; be at sb.'s beck and call
鼻息肉 bíxīròu 〈医学〉rhinopolypus; nasal polypus
鼻咽 bíyān 〈生理〉nasopharynx; rhinopharynx/～瘤〈医学〉rhinopharyngocele/～炎〈医学〉nasopharyngitis; rhinopharyngitis/～癌〈医学〉nasopharyngeal carcinoma/～镜〈医学〉nasopharyngeal mirror
鼻烟 bíyān snuff:～盒 snuffbox/～壶 snuff bottle
鼻炎 bíyán 〈医学〉rhinitis
鼻眼净 bíyǎnjìng 〈药学〉naphazoline
鼻翼 bíyì wing of nose; *ala nasi*
鼻音 bíyīn 〈语言〉nasal sound:说话带～ speak with a twang/～化 nasalization
鼻渊 bíyuān 〈中医〉nasosinusitis
鼻韵母 bíyùnmǔ 〈语言〉(of Chinese pronunciation) vowel followed by a nasal consonant
鼻针疗法 bízhēn liáofǎ 〈中医〉nose-acupuncture therapy
鼻痔 bízhì 〈中医〉nasal polyp; nasal tumour
鼻中隔 bízhōnggé 〈生理〉nasal septum:～炎〈医学〉nasoseptitis
鼻赘 bízhuì 〈医学〉rhinophyma
鼻准 bízhǔn 〈书面〉tip of the nose; bridge of the nose
鼻子 bízi nose:高～ high nose; high-bridged nose/塌～ flat nose; pug nose/鹰钩～ crooked nose; aquiline nose; Roman nose/蒜头～ snub nose/不能光顾～底下那一点小事。We shouldn't merely attend to small matters under our nose./不能让对手牵着我们的～走。We shouldn't allow our opponents to lead us by the nose./她听了这话不禁～一酸。A lump came into her throat upon hearing this.
鼻子眼儿 bíziyǎnr 〈口语〉nostril
鼻祖 bízǔ earliest ancestor; originator (of a tradition, school of thought, etc.); founder:这一学派的～ founder of the school/传说中木匠的～是鲁班。According to legend, Lu Ban is the father of carpenters.

bǐ

鄙 bǐ ❶ low; mean; vulgar:芜～ (of a piece of writing) vulgar and muddled/卑～ mean; base; despicable/粗～ coarse; vulgar; boorish ❷〈谦词〉my ❸〈书面〉despise; disdain; scorn:可～ contemptible ❹〈书面〉out-of-the-way place:边～ remote area
鄙薄 bǐbó ❶〈书面〉look down on; despise; scorn:～书面知识的倾向 tendency to despise book knowledge/～唯利是图的人 have great contempt for self-seekers ❷〈谦词〉shallow and meagre:学生学识～,贻笑大方。Your humble student (I) will but amuse the experts with my shallow and meagre knowledge.
鄙称 bǐchēng ❶ call derogatorily; label contemptuously ❷ derogatory term; pejorative appellation:寄生虫是对不劳而食者的～。"Parasites" is a derogatory term for those who live on other people's labour.
鄙夫 bǐfū 〈书面〉❶ boorish and rustic person ❷〈谦词〉your servant; I:～寡识。This is due to my ignorance. *or* I am ill-informed.
鄙见 bǐjiàn 〈谦词〉my humble opinion:～以为不如置之不理。In my humble opinion, we may as well ignore it.
鄙贱 bǐjiàn 〈书面〉❶ humble; lowly ❷ disdain; look down upon; despise
鄙俚 bǐlǐ 〈书面〉vulgar; uncouth; philistine:文辞～ in coarse language/粗糙～,不值一读 too crude to be worth reading
鄙吝 bǐlìn 〈书面〉❶ vulgar:～之风复萌 re-emergence of vulgar fashions (*or* philistinism) ❷ stingy; miserly; mean

B

鄙陋 bǐlòu shallow; ignorant: ~无知 ignorant and shallow; superficial and poorly informed / ~平庸之辈 ignorant and mediocre person

鄙弃 bǐqì disdain; spurn; loathe: 他那些不正派的作法,遭到了同行们的~。He is spurned by his colleagues for his dishonest practices.

鄙人 bǐrén ❶〈书面〉uneducated or ignorant person ❷〈谦词〉your humble servant; I

鄙视 bǐshì despise; disdain; belittle; look down upon: 我~那些坐享其成的人。I despise those who live off the fruits of others' labour.

鄙俗 bǐsú vulgar; philistine: 思想~ philistine ideas / 举止~不堪 coarse manners

鄙屑 bǐxiè scorn; despise; be contemptuous of: ~的神情 contemptuous look

鄙夷 bǐyí〈书面〉disdain; despise: 我们绝不应该~服务行业的工作人员。We should never look down on people in the service trades. / 他脸上显出~的神气。His face wore a scornful expression.

鄙意 bǐyì〈谦词〉in my opinion; I beg to observe

笔（筆）

bǐ ❶ pen: 蜡~ (wax) crayon / 铱金~ iridium-point pen / 圆珠~ ball-point pen; ball pen / 自来水~ fountain pen / 铅~ pencil / 粉~ chalk / 毛~ writing brush / 钢~ pen / 测电~ test pencil / 朱~ Chinese writing brush dipped in red ink / 铁~ cutting tool used in carving seals, etc.; stencil pen ❷ technique of writing, calligraphy or drawing: 文~ style of writing / 败~ flaw in a good piece of writing; fly in the ointment / 曲~ devious way of recording history adopted by the feudal historiographers to conceal the truth of an event from their contemporaries; devious way of writing; oblique reference ❸ write; pen: 亲~ in one's own hand-writing; in one's own hand ❹ handwriting: 遗~ handwriting of a deceased person ❺〈量词〉*used to indicate sums of money or business*: 几~收入 several items of income / 做了一~生意 do or make a deal (in business) / 我借给他一~钱。I lent him a sum of money. / 还有两~账没记。Two accounts have yet to be entered. ❻〈量词〉*stroke in Chinese painting or calligraphy*: 能画几~山水画 can do a few strokes in landscape painting; be a landscape painter of sorts / "长"字有四~。The character "长" has four strokes. / 字要一~一~地写。Characters should be written stroke by stroke. / 你这一~字比我强。Your handwriting is much better than mine. / 他写得一~好字。He writes a good hand. / 这里再添上几~,就更好了。It would look even better if a few touches could be added here.

笔触 bǐchù brush stroke in Chinese painting and calligraphy; brushwork; style of drawing or writing: 简练而鲜明的~ succinct style / 锋利的~ incisive style of writing

笔床 bǐchuáng stack for holding writing or painting brushes

笔答 bǐdá give a written answer; answer in writing: 最后一道题必须~。The final question should be answered in writing.

笔单 bǐdān list showing an author's or artist's rates of remuneration

笔胆 bǐdǎn rubber tube inside a fountain pen

笔刀 bǐdāo carving knife; graver; burin

笔道儿 bǐdàor stroke: 字形~ shape and strokes of Chinese characters

笔底生花 bǐdǐ-shēnghuā *also* "笔下生花" have an elegant style of writing; write beautifully or brilliantly

笔底下 bǐdǐxia ability to write: ~来得快 write with facility; be a facile writer / ~有功夫 write very well; be versed in the art of writing

笔调 bǐdiào (of writing) tone; style: 嘲弄的~ tone of raillery; cynical tone / ~明快 lucid and lively style

笔陡 bǐdǒu steep; sheer: ~的山崖 sheer cliff

笔端 bǐduān〈书面〉wielding of the pen or brush; style or scope of writing, calligraphy or painting: ~奇趣横生。He writes in a most witty and pleasant manner. / 太湖胜景,尽入~。The painting catches all the charms of the Taihu Lake.

笔伐 bǐfá denounce or condemn in writing: 口诛~ denounce in both speech and writing

笔法 bǐfǎ technique of writing, calligraphy or drawing: 此文~细腻。This is a most exquisite piece of writing.

笔锋 bǐfēng ❶ tip of a writing brush ❷ vigour of style in writing or painting; stroke; touch: ~犀利 wield a pointed pen; write in a pungent style

笔杆子 bǐgǎnzi *also* "笔杆儿" ❶ shaft of a pen or writing brush; pen-holder ❷ ability to write; ability to wield the pen: ~和枪杆子 the pen and the gun / 耍~ wield the pen; write for one's living ❸ effective writer: 他是一个~。He writes effectively.

笔耕 bǐgēng make a living by writing; engage in writing: 年逾古稀,~不辍。He never gave up writing even when he was over seventy.

笔供 bǐgòng written confession

笔管 bǐguǎn handle of a writing brush

笔管条直 bǐguǎn-tiáozhí straight; bolt upright: 这棵松树长得~。This pine stands tall and erect. / 人们都~地坐在那里。People were all sitting bolt upright there.

笔画 bǐhuà *also* "笔划" ❶ strokes of a Chinese character; number of strokes ❷〈计算机〉stroke: ~宽度 stroke width / ~分析 stroke analysis

笔会 bǐhuì ❶ forum in writing: 文艺评论~ written forum on literary criticism ❷ association or club of writers: 国际~ PEN (International Association of Poets, Editors, Essayists, and Novelists)

笔记 bǐjì ❶ take down (in writing): 你口授,我来~。You dictate, and I'll take notes. ❷ note-taking; notes: 记~ take notes / 对~ check notes ❸ pen jottings — a type of literature consisting mainly of short sketches; sketch

笔记本 bǐjìběn notebook: 活叶~ loose-leaf notebook

笔记本电脑 bǐjìběn diànnǎo notebook computer; laptop

笔记小说 bǐjì xiǎoshuō literary sketches; sketchbook: 唐宋~ sketches of the Tang and Song dynasties, precursors of the Chinese novel

笔迹 bǐjì handwriting; chirography; writing: 对~ identify sb.'s hand (*or* handwriting) / ~证据〈法律〉proof of handwriting / ~鉴定〈法律〉handwriting verification; bibliotics / ~鉴定专家 bibliotist

笔迹学 bǐjìxué *also* "笔体学" graphology

笔夹 bǐjiā pocket clip (of a fountain pen or ball pen)

笔架 bǐjià pen rack; penholder

笔尖 bǐjiān ❶ nib; pen point: 铱金~ iridium point (of a fountain pen) ❷ tip of a writing brush or pencil

笔据 bǐjù written pledge (such as receipt, IOU, contract, etc.)

笔力 bǐlì vigour of strokes in calligraphy or drawing; vigour of style in literary composition: ~雄健 powerful strokes; vigorous style / 他的字很工整,但~不够。His calligraphy is neat but lacks vigour. / 文虽短小,~深厚。It is a short but forceful article.

笔立 bǐlì stand erect; rise straight up: ~的山峰 towering mountain peak

笔录 bǐlù ❶ put down (in writing) ❷ notes; records: 口供~ transcript of testimony or confession

笔路 bǐlù ❶ *see* "笔法" ❷ train of thought in writing; organization; composition: 行文先要理清~。Careful organization precedes actual writing.

笔螺 bǐluó mitre shell

笔帽 bǐmào *see* "笔套"

笔名 bǐmíng pen name; pseudonym

笔墨 bǐmò pen and ink; words; writing: 难以用~形容 words cannot describe sth.; sth. is beyond words / 这篇小说在人物心理刻画上很费了一番~。This novel devotes a lot of space to the psychological analysis of the characters. / 作者在这些问题上费了不少~。The author gives a lot of ink to these problems.

笔墨官司 bǐmò-guānsi written polemics; battle of words: 打~ fight a battle of words / 他俩的~没完没了。There seems to be no end to their polemics.

笔墨生涯 bǐmò-shēngyá writing career; literary career; writer's life: 操~ take to the pen as a profession; live by one's pen

笔墨之交 bǐmòzhījiāo literary friend

笔囊 bǐnáng *see* "笔胆"

笔铅 bǐqiān pencil lead

笔峭 bǐqiào precipitous: ~的山崖 precipitous cliff

笔润 bǐrùn "brush moistener" — remuneration or fee for writing, painting or calligraphic work

笔石 bǐshí graptolite

笔试 bǐshì written examination

笔势 bǐshì ❶ style of writing or painting: ~自然朴素 in a natural and simple style ❷ vigour of style in writing: 他的散文~奔放。His prose is written in a bold and powerful style.

笔受 bǐshòu〈书面〉write down what is dictated

笔顺 bǐshùn order of strokes observed in calligraphy

笔诉 bǐsù written accusation or charge
笔算 bǐsuàn ❶ do a sum in writing ❷ written calculation
笔谈 bǐtán ❶ dialogue or conversation in writing ❷ written statement ❸ (often used in names of books) sketches; notes
笔谈电话机 bǐtán diànhuàjī tapewriting telephone (for the deaf)
笔套 bǐtào *also* "笔帽" ❶ cap of a pen, pencil or writing brush ❷ sheath of a pen (often made of cloth, silk, or thread)
笔体 bǐtǐ writing style; calligraphy; handwriting; hand: 我认得出他的～。I can identify his handwriting.
笔铁矿 bǐtiěkuàng 〈地质〉 pencil ore
笔挺 bǐtǐng ❶ (standing) very straight; straight as a ramrod; bolt upright: 营门外～地站着两个卫兵。At the entrance to the barracks two sentries were standing bolt upright. ❷ well-ironed; trim; stiff: 穿一身～的西装 be dressed in an immaculate Western-style suit
笔筒 bǐtǒng pen container; brush pot
笔头儿 bǐtóur ❶ nib; pen point ❷ ability to write; writing skill: 他～还可以。He writes fairly well. /我～慢,他～快,还是请他写决议草案吧。You'd better ask him to draft the resolution, for he writes much faster than I do.
笔误 bǐwù ❶ make a slip of the pen ❷ words written wrong due to carelessness: 这篇文章颇有～。The article contains quite a few wrongly written words.
笔洗 bǐxǐ dish for washing the writing brush
笔下 bǐxià ❶ *see* "笔底下" ❷ wording and purport of what one writes: ～超生 (of a judge or magistrate) save a life by a stroke of the brush; refrain from meting out a capital punishment; let people off /～春风 spring breeze under the brush — (of calligraphy, painting, etc.) lively; vivid /～留情。Don't be too harsh in your critical writings. *or* Be charitable (*or* sparing) in your written criticisms.
笔心 bǐxīn *also* "笔芯" ❶ pencil lead ❷ refill (for a ball-point pen)
笔形 bǐxíng (of Chinese characters) forms of strokes and their combinations
笔形波束 bǐxíng bōshù 〈电学〉 pencil beam: ～天线 pencil-beam antenna
笔削 bǐxuē 〈敬词〉 revise; polish (a piece of writing): 谢谢您的～之功。Thank you for revising my writing.
笔译 bǐyì written translation
笔意 bǐyì author's feeling or mood as conveyed in his calligraphy, painting, or literary work
笔友 bǐyǒu pen-friend; pen pal
笔札 bǐzhá ❶ stationery; writing materials ❷ writing
笔债 bǐzhài commitment to fulfil as a writer, calligrapher or painter: 眼前还有一笔～要还。I still owe sb. an article to write right now.
笔战 bǐzhàn written polemics or controversy
笔者 bǐzhě the author; this writer
笔政 bǐzhèng (in journalism) writing of editorials and important commentaries: 在一家大报主持～ be in charge of editorials and commentaries for a major newspaper
笔直 bǐzhí perfectly straight; straight as a ramrod; bolt upright: 裤线熨得～ well-ironed trousers /～的桅杆 upright mast /沿着小河～走去。Go straight along the stream. /校园里有一条～的大道。A wide road runs right through the campus.
笔致 bǐzhì style of painting, calligraphy or writing
笔资 bǐzī remuneration for writing, calligraphy or painting
笔走龙蛇 bǐzǒu-lóngshé make vigorous and graceful strokes in calligraphy: 文如锦绣,～。The writing is splendid and the calligraphy is vigorous and graceful.

俾 bǐ 〈书面〉 in order to; so as to; so that: ～众周知 so as to make sth. known to all; for the information of all /何不让他们从教,～得发挥所长。They should be encouraged to take on teaching jobs so that they may give full play to their talents.
俾路支人 Bǐlùzhīrén Baluchis
俾路支斯坦 Bǐlùzhīsītǎn Baluchistan (area extending across Pakistan, Iran, and Afghanistan inhabited by Baluchis)
俾斯麦 Bǐsīmài Otto Eduard Leopold Bismarck (1815-1898), Prime Minister of Prussia (1862-1890) and first Chancellor of the German Reich (1871-1890)
俾斯麦海 Bǐsīmàihǎi Bismarck Sea (a part of the SW Pacific stretching 800 km. between the Bismarck Archipelago and New Guinea)
俾斯麦群岛 Bǐsīmài Qúndǎo Bismarck Archipelago, north of Papua New Guinea
俾昼作夜 bǐzhòu-zuòyè make the day serve as night; be idle during the day, but busy at night

匕 bǐ ❶ a type of ancient spoon ❷ 〈书面〉 dagger
匕鬯不惊 bǐchàng-bùjīng (of an army) maintain strict discipline so that there is not the slightest violation of the people's interests
匕首 bǐshǒu dagger

比[1] bǐ ❶ compare; contrast; emulate; compete: ～作风 emulate each other in work style /～工作效率 vie with each other in efficiency /～本事 have a contest of skill /论智力,很少有人～得过他。Few people can compare with him in intelligence. *or* Intellectually, few people can surpass him. ❷ be like; be similar to; match: 寿～南山 live as long as the hills — wish sb. longevity /坚～金石 hard as rock or metal ❸ gesture; gesticulate: 用手～了～ make a gesture with one's hand /用手～了一个"V"字 make a sign of "V" with one's fingers /他～着手势叫我进去。He gestured to me to go in. ❹ 〈方言〉 aim at; direct towards: 恐怖分子用枪～着她。The terrorist pointed his gun at her. ❺ do according to; model after; copy: ～着房间大小买张写字台 buy a writing desk according to the size of the room ❻ draw an analogy; liken to; compare to: 把祖国～作母亲 compare one's country to one's mother /用松柏～节操 liken the pine and cypress to a person's integrity ❼ ratio; proportion: 教员和学生的人数为一～十。The ratio of faculty members to students is one to ten. /这所学校很受人欢迎,考生与录取人数是十～一。The school is so popular that there are ten applicants for every student placement. ❽ to (in a score): 天津队以 90～95 负于上海队。The Tianjin team lost to the Shanghai team by a score of ninety to ninety-five. /甲队与乙队以二～二战平。Team A and Team B tied at two all. ❾ 〈介词〉 than; (superior or inferior) to: 我考得～他好。I did better in the examination than he. /他住的时间～我预料的长。He stayed longer than I had expected. /战斗一次～一次激烈。Each battle was fiercer than the last.

比[2] bǐ (formerly pronounced bì) 〈书面〉 ❶ close together; next to: ～肩而立 stand shoulder to shoulder ❷ depend on; collude with; gang up with: 朋～为奸 gang up to do evil ❸ recently; of late: *see* "比来" ❹ by (then); by the time
比比 bǐbǐ 〈书面〉 ❶ frequently; repeatedly: 邻国～地震。There have been frequent earthquakes in the neighbouring countries. ❷ everywhere; all over
比比皆是 bǐbǐ-jiēshì can be seen everywhere or here, there and everywhere: 这种贝壳海滩上～。These shells can be found everywhere on the seashore.
比并 bǐbìng 〈书面〉 compare: 他俩～起来,倒是各有千秋呢。If you compare one with the other, you'll find each has his strong points.
比才 Bǐcái Georges Bizet (1838-1875), French composer, composer of *Carmen* (1875)
比对 bǐduì compare and verify; compare: 今年虽有旱灾,但与去年～,年景还是很不错的。Despite the drought, this year's harvest is quite good as compared with last year's.
比尔定律 Bǐ'ěr dìnglǜ 〈物理〉 Beer's law
比方 bǐfang ❶ compare to; liken to; draw an analogy between: 我们常用荷花～那些生活在不良环境里而不沾恶习的人。We often draw an analogy between the lotus flowers and those who live uncontaminated by an unhealthy environment. /打个～,时间就是金钱,效率就是生命。By way of analogy, time is gold and efficiency is life. ❷ take for instance or example: 万事开头难,～小孩学步,开头免不了要跌跤。Everything is difficult in the beginning. A child learning to walk, for instance, trips and falls. ❸ if; suppose: 他的字写得真好,～我求他写幅对联,他不会拒绝吧? He is a calligrapher. He won't refuse, will he, if I ask him to write a couplet for me?
比分 bǐfēn 〈体育〉 score: 最后一场的～是三比二。The score of the final game was 3 to 2. /双方～十分接近。It was a close game.
比夫拉 Bǐfūlā Biafra (area in eastern Nigeria proclaimed independent 1967 to 1970)
比夫拉湾 Bǐfūlāwān Bight of Biafra
比附 bǐfù 〈书面〉 draw a forced analogy; make a farfetched comparison: 两国国情不同,不可随意～。As the two countries are different

in circumstances, we cannot draw an analogy between them at random.
比高 bǐgāo relative height; difference in height
比号 bǐhào 〈数学〉 sign of ratio; colon (as in 3:9, which reads three to nine)
比荷卢经济联盟 Bǐ-Hé-Lú Jīngjì Liánméng Benelux (Belgium, the Netherlands, and Luxemburg) Economic Union
比葫芦画瓢 bǐ húlu huà piáo draw a dipper with a gourd as a model; copy; imitate
比画 bǐhua *also* "比划" ❶ gesture; gesticulate:他边说边～着。He was gesticulating as he spoke. ❷ (as in martial arts) have a contest; practise:咱俩～一下,看你进展如何。Let's have a contest and see how much progress you have made.
比基尼岛 Bǐjīnídǎo Bikini (atoll in the Marshall Islands in the Pacific where nuclear tests were conducted by the US from 1946 to 1958)
比基尼泳装 bǐjīní yǒngzhuāng *also* "比基尼";"三点式" sāndiǎnshì (transliteration) bikini
比及 bǐjí 〈书面〉 when; at the time when; by the time:～敌人发觉,我们已冲过了火线。We had already crossed the frontline before the enemy realized what had happened.
比价 bǐjià ❶ price ratio or price comparison; parity; rate of exchange:工农业产品的～ price parities between industrial and agricultural products /日元与美元的～ rate of exchange between the Japanese yen and the US dollar /粮油～ price ratios between grain and oil ❷ cost comparison; comparison of offers (as in bidding)
比肩 bǐjiān 〈书面〉 ❶ shoulder to shoulder; side by side; together:～前进 stride ahead shoulder to shoulder ❷ be as good as; match:她虽是业余歌手,却可与专业歌手～。Amateur as she is, she sings as well as a professional singer.
比肩继踵 bǐjiān-jìzhǒng *also* "摩肩继踵" mójiān-jìzhǒng be packed with people; (people) jostle each other in a crowd
比降 bǐjiàng 〈地理〉 gradient
比较 bǐjiào ❶ compare; contrast:～异同 make a comparison to find out the similarities and differences /～起来 by comparison; in contrast /与原文～ check against the original /无法～ be incomparable /没有～就不能鉴别事物。Only by comparison can things be distinguished. *or* We cannot distinguish one thing from another without making comparisons. /两台电视机一～就分出了高低。Put these two TV sets together and you will find which is better. ❷ than:学生的学习积极性～前一个时期有了明显的提高。The students are showing greater enthusiasm for study now than in the previous period. ❸ comparatively; relatively; fairly; rather:～短 relatively (*or* comparatively) short /～好 fairly good /～方便 quite convenient /今冬的天气～温和。We have had a relatively mild winter this year.
比较成本 bǐjiào chéngběn comparative cost:～说 doctrine of comparative cost
比较法 bǐjiàofǎ 〈法律〉 comparative law:～研究 study of comparative law /比较刑法 comparative penal law
比较法学 bǐjiào fǎxué 〈法律〉 comparative jurisprudence:～派 school of comparative jurisprudence
比较级 bǐjiàojí 〈语言〉 comparative degree; comparative:～形容词 comparative adjective
比较价格 bǐjiào jiàgé *also* "不变价格" bùbiàn jiàgé fixed price or cost; constant price
比较教育学 bǐjiào jiàoyùxué comparative education
比较经济学 bǐjiào jīngjìxué comparative economics:比较静态经济学 comparative static economics
比较利益 bǐjiào lìyì comparative advantage:～学说 theory of comparative advantage
比较伦理学 bǐjiào lúnlǐxué comparative ethics
比较千分尺 bǐjiào qiānfēnchǐ 〈测绘〉 comparator micrometer
比较社会学 bǐjiào shèhuìxué comparative sociology
比较文学 bǐjiào wénxué comparative literature
比较效用 bǐjiào xiàoyòng comparative utility
比较心理学 bǐjiào xīnlǐxué comparative psychology
比较新闻学 bǐjiào xīnwénxué comparative journalism
比较星 bǐjiàoxīng 〈天文〉 comparison star
比较研究 bǐjiào yánjiū comparative studies:中西文化～ comparative studies in Chinese and Western cultures
比较医学 bǐjiào yīxué comparative medicine
比较仪 bǐjiàoyí 〈测绘〉 comparator; comparer
比较语言学 bǐjiào yǔyánxué comparative linguistics
比较哲学 bǐjiào zhéxué comparative philosophy
比较政治学 bǐjiào zhèngzhìxué comparative politics
比较指数 bǐjiào zhǐshù comparison index
比来 bǐlái 〈书面〉 recently; of late:～身体不适 be out of sorts lately
比兰德拉 Bǐlándélā Birendra Bir Bickram Shah Dev (1945-), King of Nepal since 1972
比勒陀利亚 Bǐlètuólìyà Pretoria, administrative capital of South Africa
比利时 Bǐlìshí Belgium:～人 Belgian /～法郎 Belgian franc (BF)
比例 bǐlì ❶ proportion; scale:正～ direct proportion /反～ inverse proportion; inverse ratio /～失调 be out of proportion /按～发展 develop in proportion /拌水泥时要逐渐增加水的～。The proportion of water should be gradually increased in mixing cement. ❷ ratio:这个班男女学生的～大约是 3 比 1。The ratio between boys and girls in this class is roughly 3 to 1. /厂内技术员的～逐渐上升。The ratio of technicians in the factory is on the increase.
比例常数 bǐlì chángshù 〈数学〉 proportionality constant; proportional constant
比例尺 bǐlìchǐ ❶ 〈测绘〉 scale:这张地图的～是一百万分之一。The scale of the map is 1:1,000,000. ❷ architect's scale; engineer's scale
比例代表制 bǐlì dàibiǎozhì proportional representation (PR)
比例税 bǐlìshuì proportional tax:～制 proportional taxation
比例图 bǐlìtú scale map
比例系数 bǐlì xìshù scale factor
比例选举制 bǐlì xuǎnjǔzhì *see* "比例代表制"
比例因数 bǐlì yīnshù 〈数学〉 proportionality factor
比例中项 bǐlì zhōngxiàng 〈数学〉 mean proportional
比量 bǐliang ❶ take rough measurements (with the hand, a stick, etc.):左右两边的书架,我用眼睛～,大概一般高。As far as I can see, the bookshelves on both sides are probably of equal height. ❷ *see* "比试❷"
比邻 bǐlín ❶ neighbour; next-door neighbour:～而居 live as next-door neighbours /海内存知己,天涯若～。A bosom friend afar brings a distant land near. ❷ be in the neighbourhood of; be located close to:他家～百货大楼。His home is in the vicinity of the department store.
比邻星 bǐlínxīng 〈天文〉 self-luminous star nearest to the sun
比率 bǐlǜ ratio; rate:～计 ratio meter
比美 bǐměi compare favourably with; rival:这里的风景可与西湖～。The scenery here is no less beautiful than that of the West Lake. *or* The scenic splendour of this place can certainly compare with that of the West Lake.
比目鱼 bǐmùyú flatfish; flounder
比拟 bǐnǐ ❶ compare; draw a parallel; match:不可～ beyond compare; matchless /难以～ hardly comparable /这种高贵品德是无可～的。This nobility of character is without parallel. ❷ analogy; metaphor; comparison:～的手法在童话和寓言中用得最多。Analogy is used most frequently in fairy tales and fables.
比年 bǐnián *also* "比岁" 〈书面〉 ❶ in recent years:～不登 reap poor harvests for years running ❷ each passing year
比偶 bǐ'ǒu 〈语言〉 antithesis:两句～的文字 two antithetical sentences
比配 bǐpèi match; be compatible:互不～ mutually incompatible
比强度 bǐqiángdù (of material) ratio of strength to specific gravity; specific strength
比丘 bǐqiū 〈宗教〉 (transliteration from the Sanskrit *Bhiksu*) Buddhist monk
比丘尼 bǐqiūní 〈宗教〉 (transliteration from the Sanskrit *Bhiksuni*) Buddhist nun
比热 bǐrè 〈物理〉 specific heat
比容 bǐróng 〈物理〉 specific volume
比如 bǐrú for example; for instance; such as:～他,就是因为勤学苦练,才掌握这门技术的。He, for example, is one of those who have acquired the skill through hard work.
比萨斜塔 Bǐsà Xiétǎ Leaning Tower of Pisa, Italy
比赛 bǐsài match; contest; competition:篮球～ basketball match/射击～ shooting contest /田径～项目 field and track events /～规则 rules of the game; rules of a match /～在激烈地进行着。A fierce competition is going on. /晚上七点半～足球。There will be a football

match at 7:00 p.m. /咱们～～吧，看谁算得快。Let's compete to see who calculates faster.
比色分析 bǐsè fēnxī 〈化学〉colorimetric analysis
比色计 bǐsèjì *also* "色度计" sèdùjì 〈化学〉colorimeter
比上不足，比下有余 bǐ shàng bù zú, bǐ xià yǒu yú better than some, though not as good as others; fair to middling; can pass muster
比绍 Bǐshào Bissau, capital of Guinea-Bissau
比湿 bǐshī 〈气象〉specific humidity
比试 bǐshi ❶ have a competition or contest：谁高谁低，咱们～～吧。Let's have a competition and see who is better. ❷ measure with one's hand or arm; make a gesture of measuring：他先用剑～～一下，接着就一招一式地练了起来。With a flourish of his sword, he started the exercise step by step.
比手画脚 bǐshǒu-huàjiǎo gesticulate as one talks
比速 bǐsù 〈物理〉specific speed; (of a hydroturbine) unit speed
比岁 bǐsuì 〈书面〉❶ (in) recent years ❷ every year; each year; year after year
比索 bǐsuǒ peso (former monetary unit of Spain, currently in use in the Philippines and some Latin American countries)
比特 bǐtè 〈计算机〉bit (basic unit of information in a computing system, expressed in binary notation)：～/秒 bps; bit/s (bits per second)
比武 bǐwǔ martial arts competition; competition in military skills：～招亲 (formerly of a girl versed in *wushu*) marry whoever can defeat one in a martial arts contest
比先 bǐxiān (often used in the early vernacular) formerly; long time ago
比学赶帮超 bǐ-xué-gǎn-bāng-chāo (used in the 1960's) emulate, learn from, catch up with, help and in turn surpass each other
比压 bǐyā 〈物理〉specific pressure
比翼 bǐyì fly wing to wing：～连枝 like birds that pair off wing to wing or trees that have their branches intertwined — deep affection of a devoted couple
比翼鸟 bǐyìniǎo legendary birds with one wing that have to fly in pairs; pair of love birds; devoted couple：在天愿作～，在地愿为连理枝。On high, we'd be two love-birds flying wing towing; On earth, two trees with branches twined from spring to spring.
比翼齐飞 bǐyì-qífēi *also* "比翼双飞"〈比喻〉pair off wing to wing; fly side by side; (of loving husband and wife) keep each other company all the time; help each other to make progress：愿一对新人百年长好，～。We wish the happy couple lasting love and shared progress!
比喻 bǐyù metaphor; analogy; simile; figure of speech：寿比南山只是一种～的说法。To live as long as the hills is only a figure of speech.
比照 bǐzhào ❶ according to; in the light of：～着实物绘图 draw a picture after a model ❷ contrast：两者～，谁优谁劣便很清楚。Put the two side by side and you will see which is superior.
比值 bǐzhí specific value; ratio; rate
比重 bǐzhòng ❶〈物理〉specific gravity：～选种〈农业〉specific gravity selection (of seeds) ❷ proportion：外贸收入占很大～的国家 country whose foreign trade earnings account for the bulk of its national income /第三产业在我国国民经济中的～正在增大。The proportion of tertiary industries is growing in our country's national economy as a whole.
比重计 bǐzhòngjì gravimeter：液体～ hydrometer

吡 bǐ

see also pǐ
吡啶 bǐdìng 〈化学〉pyridine：～甲醛 pyridine carboxaldehyde /～霉素 pyridomycin
吡哆醇 bǐduōchún 〈化学〉pyridoxin
吡咯 bǐluò 〈化学〉pyrrole
吡喃 bǐnán 〈化学〉pyran
吡嗪 bǐqín 〈化学〉pyrazine
吡唑 bǐzuò 〈化学〉pyrazole

秕(粃) bǐ

(of grain) not plump; blighted
秕谷 bǐgǔ *also* "秕谷子" blighted grains
秕糠 bǐkāng ❶ chaff ❷ worthless stuff
秕粒 bǐlì blighted seeds
秕谬 bǐmiù 〈书面〉error; mistake; fallacy
秕政 bǐzhèng 〈书面〉bad government policy
秕子 bǐzi blighted grain

舭 bǐ

bilge
舭舭 bǐdá a kind of ancient ship

妣 bǐ

〈书面〉deceased mother：先～ my deceased (*or* late) mother

佊 bǐ

〈书面〉evil

彼 bǐ

❶ that; those; the other; another：到达桥之～端 reach the other end of the bridge /朝代更迭，此兴～衰。Dynasties changed; one rose when another declined. *or* One rose when another fell — such was the pattern of dynastic changes. ❷ other party; one's opponent：知己知～ know both one's opponent and oneself
彼岸 bǐ'àn ❶〈书面〉(of a river, lake, sea, etc.) other bank; other side：大洋～ on the other side of the ocean ❷〈佛教〉the other shore; Faramita ❸ ideal state of mind that one yearns for：只要坚持不懈，我们一定能够达到胜利的～。With persistence we will get onto the path of victory.
彼此 bǐcǐ ❶ each other; one another：～了解 know each other well /～互相关心 care for each other /～犬牙交错 be locked together; be intersected each with the other /～互致问候 exchange cordial greetings /～配合得很密切 work (*or* act) in close cooperation/ 不分～ share everything they have /～和睦相处 live in peace and amity together ❷〈套语〉*used usu. in reduplication to indicate that all concerned are about the same*：我的本事也不比你强，咱俩～～。I cannot do any better than you. Maybe, we are on the same plane./ 这件事你我都出了力，要论功劳，大家～～。We have both put a good deal of effort into the matter, and our contributions are practically the same.
彼得大帝 Bǐdé Dàdì Peter I (Peter Alexeyevich Romanov, 1672-1725), known as Peter the Great, Tsar (1682-1725) and Emperor (1721-1725) of Russia
彼特拉克 Bǐtèlākè Francesco de Petrarch (1304-1347), Italian poet and scholar, one of the first men of the Renaissance
彼一时，此一时 bǐ yīshí, cǐ yīshí times have changed; the situation is different now：～。当时很时髦的，现在不作兴了。Times have clanged. What was quite fashionable is no longer in vogue now.

bì

滗(潷) bì

decant; strain; drain：把浮油～掉 drain off the fat /请把汤～出去。Decant the soup away, please. /菠菜要～干。Strain the water from spinach.

愎 bì

wilful; self-willed：刚～ obdurate; recalcitrant
愎谏 bìjiàn 〈书面〉intransigent; obstinate; stubborn; opinionated

闭 bì

❶ shut; close：～住眼睛 close one's eyes /～门 shut the door /～口无言 be tongue-tied /～上嘴! Shut up! ❷ stop up; obstruct ❸ stop; end ❹ (Bì) a surname
闭包运算 bìbāo yùnsuàn 〈数学〉closure operation
闭藏 bìcáng 〈书面〉❶ winter freeze; hybernation ❷ store; collect
闭关 bìguān ❶ close a city gate; block a pass; close the country to the outside world ❷〈佛教〉(of a monk) stay secluded meditating and studying scriptures for a fixed period; be in seclusion
闭关锁国 bìguān-suǒguó close the country to the rest of the world; shut one's door to the international community
闭关政策 bìguān zhèngcè policy of closing the country to international communication; closed-door policy
闭关自守 bìguān-zìshǒu close the country to the outside world; seclude oneself from the outside world：自力更生决不是～，孤立奋斗。Self-reliance in no way means self-seclusion or working in isolation.
闭海 bìhǎi closed sea; enclosed sea
闭合 bìhé ❶ closed：～曲线 closed curve /～循环系统 closed circulatory system /～力 closing force /～线 closed line ❷ circularize：～电门，开动机器。Switch on and start up.

B

闭合电路 bìhé diànlù closed-circuit
闭合度 bìhédù 〈地理〉closure
闭合回路 bìhé huílù 〈机械〉closed loop circuit
闭合生态 bìhé shēngtài closed ecology：～系统 closed ecological system
闭合式风洞 bìhéshì fēngdòng 〈航空〉closed-jet wind tunnel
闭合天线 bìhé tiānxiàn closed antenna
闭合性气胸 bìhéxìng qìxiōng 〈医学〉closed pneumothorax
闭会 bìhuì close a meeting; end or adjourn a meeting：现在正是委员会～期间。The committee is not in session at present.
闭架式 bìjiàshì closed stacks (a system of library management which denies readers open access to bookshelves)：～图书馆 closed stacks library
闭经 bìjīng 〈医学〉amenorrhoea
闭卷 bìjuàn closed-book：～考试 closed-book examination (during which examinees are not allowed to use any reference)
闭孔疝 bìkǒngshàn 〈医学〉obturator hernia
闭口 bìkǒu keep one's mouth shut; not speak up：～不语 clam up; keep quiet; remain speechless /你给我～! You shut up!
闭口韵 bìkǒuyùn 〈语言〉syllabic final ending in bilabilas "m" or "b"
闭链烃 bìliàntīng closed chain hydrocarbon
闭路 bìlù closed circuit：～录音 closed circuit recording /～报警装置 closed circuit alarm device /～电流 closed current
闭路电视 bìlù diànshì closed-circuit television
闭路器 bìlùqì 〈电工〉circuit closer
闭路式电视录像机 bìlùshì diànshì lùxiàngjī closed-circuit TV camera
闭门羹 bìméngēng (often used in 吃闭门羹) deny or be denied entrance：叫他吃个～。Deny him admittance. *or* Let him know that he is not welcome.
闭门思过 bìmén-sīguò shut oneself up and ponder over one's mistakes; do re-thinking behind closed doors
闭门谢客 bìmén-xièkè close one's door to visitors; refuse to receive any guest
闭门造车 bìmén-zàochē make a cart behind closed doors; work all alone without reference to actual need; shut oneself off from reality
闭目塞听 bìmù-sètīng shut one's eyes and stop one's ears — be out of touch with reality
闭幕 bìmù ❶ the curtain falls; lower the curtain：演出在一片掌声中～。The curtain falls amidst thunderous applause. ❷ close; conclude：～词 closing address (*or* speech) /～会 closing session /会议是昨天～的。The conference closed yesterday.
闭幕式 bìmùshì closing ceremony
闭气 bìqì ❶ breathe one's last; be dying：我赶到医院时，他正闭过气去。When I got to the hospital, he was breathing his last. ❷ hold one's breath：～，别出声儿！ Hold your breath! Don't make any noise!
闭塞 bìsè ❶ stop up; block：鼻孔～ stuffy nose /～系统 block system /管道～ blocked pipe ❷ difficult of access; out-of-the-way; inaccessible; backward：这地方以前很～。This used to be a backward and out-of-the-way place. ❸ unenlightened：这是个偏僻的小村，消息～。This is a remote mountain village where only a trickle of information comes from the outside world. ❹〈语言〉〈医学〉occlusion
闭塞空间 bìsè kōngjiān dead-air space
闭塞信号 bìsè xìnhào 〈铁路〉block signal
闭塞性动脉硬化 bìsèxìng dòngmài yìnghuà 〈医学〉arteriosclerosis
闭塞眼睛捉麻雀 bìsè yǎnjing zhuō máquè try to catch sparrows with one's eyes blind-folded — act blindly
闭市 bìshì close shop; suspend business：商店于黄昏时提早～。The store closed at dusk, earlier than usual.
闭式冷却系统 bìshì lěngquè xìtǒng closed cooling system
闭式流槽 bìshì liúcáo 〈冶金〉enclosed launder
闭式循环 bìshì xúnhuán 〈机械〉closed cycle：～发动机 closed-cycle engine /～水反应堆 closed-cycle water reactor /～致冷 closed-circuit refrigeration
闭锁 bìsuǒ ❶ (of a system) closed; block：整性～ integrally closed/简单～ simply closed /～元件 blocking element ❷〈医学〉valvular sufficiency：心瓣～不全 valvular insufficiency /二尖瓣～不全 insufficiency of valvula(e) bicuspidalis ❸〈生理〉imperforation
闭锁型风洞 bìsuǒxíng fēngdòng closed-throat tunnel
闭庭 bìtíng 〈法律〉court closed
闭音节 bìyīnjié 〈语言〉closed syllable
闭元音 bìyuányīn 〈语言〉closed vowel
闭月羞花 bìyuè-xiūhuā 〈书面〉(of a woman) one's beauty outshines the moon and puts the flowers to shame; be exceedingly beautiful

敝

bì ❶〈书面〉shabby; worn-out; ragged：～衣恶食 wear shabby clothes and eat poor food; lead a hard life /舌～唇焦 with a weary tongue and parched lips (as from talking too much) ❷〈谦词〉my; our; this：～同乡 my fellow townsman /～厂 our factory; this factory /～姓张。My surname is Zhang. ❸〈书面〉decline; worsen：凋～ destitute; depressed
敝旧 bìjiù old; shabby; worn-out; dilapidated：衣服～ shabby clothes /～的茅屋 old, dilapidated thatched cottage
敝人 bìrén 〈谦词〉your humble servant; I：～对此一无所知。I'm totally ignorant of this.
敝俗 bìsú undesirable custom; objectionable practice
敝屣 bìxǐ 〈书面〉worn-out shoes; worthless thing：弃之如～ cast sth. away like a pair of old shoes
敝帚自珍 bìzhǒu-zìzhēn *also* "敝帚千金" value one's own old broom — cherish sth. of little value simply because it is one's own

蔽

bì cover; shelter; hide：～风雨 shelter from wind and rain/ 衣不～体 be dressed in rags; have nothing but rags on one's back /黄沙～天。The dust covered the sky. /浮云～日。The sun was hidden behind a floating cloud.
蔽芾 bìfèi 〈书面〉(of a tree or plant) small of trunk and leaf：～甘棠，勿剪勿伐。Trim not and cut not the small birchleaf pear trees.
蔽光云 bìguāngyún 〈气象〉opacus：～量 opaque sky cover
蔽匿 bìnì 〈书面〉hide：～罪证 cover up the evidence of a crime /畏罪～ go into hiding for fear of punishment for one's crime; abscond
蔽塞 bìsè ill-informed; out of the way
see also "闭塞" bìsè
蔽障 bìzhàng shelter; obstacle

獘

bì 〈书面〉*see* "毙" bì

弊

bì ❶ fraud; abuse; malpractice：作～ cheat (as in an examination) /舞～ practise fraud; engage in corrupt practices /清查积～ clean up all the malpractices accumulated over the years ❷ disadvantage; harm：～少利多。The advantages outweigh the disadvantages. /有一利必有一～。Advantages are always accompanied by disadvantages.
弊病 bìbìng ❶ malady; ill; malpractice：社会～ social ills ❷ drawback; disadvantage：由于制度不健全，～较多。Many loopholes exist because of inadequate rules and regulations. /干部脱离群众是个大～。It is a big drawback for cadres to be divorced from the people. *or* Great harm is done when our cadres are alienated from the people.
弊窦 bìdòu 〈书面〉irregularity; malpractice; abuse; corrupt practice：严防～滋生 strictly guard against the growth of corrupt practice
弊端 bìduān malpractice; abuse; corrupt practice：社会～ evil social practices; social ills /管理不善，造成诸多～。Mismanagement has caused many problems.
弊害 bìhài disadvantage; harm; drawback
弊绝风清 bìjué-fēngqīng have evil practices eliminated and public morals perfected; clean up social morals：以为采取一两项措施，就可以～，那是幻想。It's a sheer illusion that we can clear up social morality by simply adopting one or two measures.
弊漏 bìlòu disadvantage; flaw; error; shortcoming：补救～ rectify a shortcoming
弊政 bìzhèng 〈书面〉harmful or pernicious policies or political measures：改革～ rectify harmful policies; abolish corrupt politics

币（幣）

bì money; currency：外～ foreign currency /纸～ paper currency; note /硬～ coin /银～ silver coin /金～ gold coin/镍～ nickel coin; nickel /人民～ RMB /本～ standard money /法～ legal tender;〈旧语〉paper currency issued by the former KMT government after 1935 /辅～ fractional currency or money; subsidiary coin /港～ HK dollar /伪～ counterfeit money; forged banknotes;

money issued by a puppet government /～重言甘 much money and sweet words

币帛 bìbó 〈书面〉 wealth; money

币值 bìzhí currency value: ～稳定的货币 stable currency /～波动 currency fluctuation /～调整 currency realignment; currency adjustment /～附加费 currency surcharge

币制 bìzhì currency or monetary system: ～改革 currency (*or* monetary) reform

必 bì ❶ certainly; surely; necessarily: 坚持下去,～有所成。If you persevere you are sure to succeed. /骄～败。Pride goes before a fall. ❷ must; ought to; have to: 事～躬亲 attend to every detail in person; do everything oneself /有法～依,执法～严。Laws must be observed and strictly enforced.

必报点 bìbàodiǎn 〈航空〉 compulsory reporting point

必不可少 bìbùkěshǎo absolutely necessary; indispensable; essential: 毅力是事业成功～的条件。Will power is indispensable to success. /我父亲吃面,蒜是～的。For my father, garlic is a must to go with noodles.

必得 bìděi must; have to: 此事～你办,方可成功。Only you can handle this case with success.

必定 bìdìng ❶ be bound to; be sure to; must: 这消息你听了～高兴。You will surely be delighted at the news. /坚持锻炼～对身体有益处。Continued physical training will definitely benefit your health. /这些话～是他讲的。He must be the person who made such comments. *or* It must be he who said this. ❷ be resolved to; be certain to: 好,我明天～来。I'll be there tomorrow. /你放心,东西我～托人带到。Don't worry. I'll have your package duly delivered. /这病我拖了又拖,现在～得去医院看看了。I have been neglecting my illness far too long and must go and see the doctor now.

必恭必敬 bìgōng-bìjìng *also* "毕恭毕敬" bìgōng-bìjìng reverent and respectful; extremely deferential: 在领导面前,他是～的。He is all reverence before his leaders. /他们～地听她的演讲。They listened to her lecture with extreme deference.

必然 bìrán ❶ inevitable; certain: 长期战争的～结果 inevitable outcome of a prolonged war /事物发展的～趋势 inexorable trend of the development of events /～的道理 logic of things /～胜利 bound (*or* certain) to succeed /为群众做好事,～受到群众的尊敬和信赖。Those who work for the public good will certainly enjoy public respect and trust. ❷ 〈哲学〉 necessity: 自由与～ freedom and necessity

必然规律 bìrán guīlǜ inexorable law

必然王国 bìrán wángguó 〈哲学〉 realm of necessity

必然性 bìránxìng necessity; inevitability; certainty

必修 bìxiū (of a course, lesson, etc.) required; obligatory; mandatory: ～科目 required course

必须 bìxū must; necessary: 理论～联系实际。Theory must be integrated with practice. /～踏踏实实地工作。It is necessary to work in a practical manner. /～谦虚谨慎。It is imperative to remain modest and prudent.

必需 bìxū essential; indispensable; necessary: ～费用 necessary expense /～氨基酸 essential amino-acid /～脂肪酸 essential fatty acid/空气和水是生命所～的。Air and water are essential to life. /生产上所～的设备要及时安装。Equipment needed in (*or* necessary for) production should be installed in time.

必需品 bìxūpǐn daily necessities; necessaries; articles for daily consumption

必要 bìyào necessary; essential; indispensable: ～的规章制度 necessary rules and regulations /～前提 prerequisite; precondition /～条件 essential condition; prerequisite /～性 necessity /在当前的情况下,采取预防措施是十分～的。It is imperative to adopt precautionary measures under the present circumstances. /～的时候,我会亲自去拜访。I'll call on him in person if necessary. /事已至此,我没有在这里呆下去的～了。As it is, I see no point in staying here any longer.

必要产品 bìyào chǎnpǐn 〈经济〉 necessary product

必要价值规律 bìyào jiàzhí guīlǜ law of necessary value

必要劳动 bìyào láodòng 〈经济〉 necessary labour

必要器官 bìyào qìguān 〈生物〉 essential organs

必由之路 bìyóuzhīlù road or route that one must take; only way: 理论联系实际是通向成功的～。Integration of theory with practice is the road to success. /改革开放是强国利民的～。Reform and opening to the outside world are the prerequisites for the prosperity of our nation.

闷 bì 〈书面〉 ❶ close (the door) ❷ prudent

珌(琿) bì 〈书面〉 ornament for the end of a sheath

柲 bì 〈书面〉 handle of a spear or halbert

苾 bì 〈书面〉 fragrant; aromatic

毖 bì 〈书面〉 caution: 惩前～后 punish past wrongdoing to caution those to come; learn from past errors to avoid future mistakes

铋 bì 〈化学〉 bismuth (Bi): ～合金常用于做保险丝。Bismuth alloys are often used to make fuses.

铋酸 bìsuān 〈化学〉 bismuthic acid

铋中毒 bìzhòngdú 〈医学〉 bismuthosis

秘(祕) bì

see also mì

秘鲁 Bìlǔ Peru: ～人 Peruvian

馝 bì

馝馞 bìbó 〈书面〉 strong scent or aroma

駜 bì 〈书面〉 (of horses) stout and strong

碧 bì ❶ 〈书面〉 green jade ❷ bluish green; blue: ～瓦 green glazed tile /～海青天 blue sea merging with the azure sky /～草如茵 carpet of green grass /金发～眼 (of a Caucasian) golden-haired and blue-eyed

碧波 bìbō blue waves: 湖面上～荡漾,白帆点点。White sails dotted the rippling blue lake. /船队劈破万顷～。The fleet ploughed through a vast ocean of blue waves.

碧澄 bìchéng (of water or sky) blue and clear; azure: ～的天空 clear blue sky; azure sky /河水清湛～。The river is crystal clear and bluish green.

碧空 bìkōng pale blue sky; azure sky: ～万里 vast clear skies /～如洗 cloudless blue sky

碧蓝 bìlán bluish green; blue; turquoise: 白云朵朵的天空覆盖着～的海面。A sky of fleecy clouds arches over the blue sea. /湖水～,一清如镜。The dark blue waters of the lake look as clear as a mirror.

碧绿 bìlǜ dark green: ～的河水 green waters of the river /～的田野 expanse of green fields /在～的草坪上,一群孩子在歌舞。A group of children were singing and dancing on the lush lawn.

碧螺春 bìluóchūn *also* "碧萝春" green tea originally produced in the Taihu Lake area

碧落 bìluò 〈书面〉 green void; sky; heaven: ～黄泉 from heaven to the nether world; high and low

碧血 bìxuè blood shed in a just cause: ～黄沙 drench the desert sand with one's loyal blood

碧血丹心 bìxuè-dānxīn absolute loyalty; boundless loyalty

碧油油 bìyōuyōu green and lush: ～的麦苗 green and lush wheat seedlings

碧玉 bìyù jasper — a kind of greenish jade: 小家～ pretty girl of a humble family

碧云寺 Bìyúnsì Temple of the Azure Clouds, or Biyun Monastery, at Fragrant Hill to the west of Beijing

贲 bì 〈书面〉 beautifully adorned

see also bēn

贲临 bìlín 〈书面〉 (of distinguished guests) honour us with your gracious presence

湢 bì 〈书面〉 bathroom

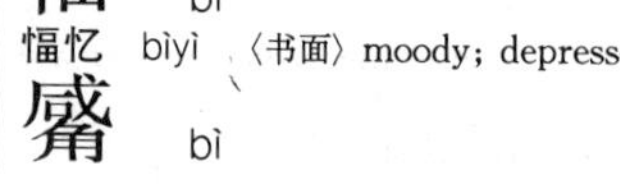

愊 bì

愊忆 bìyì 〈书面〉 moody; depressed

觱 bì

篳篥 bìlì 〈音乐〉 ancient bamboo pipe with a reed mouth piece

皕 bì 〈书面〉 two hundred

庇 bì shelter; protect; shield; screen: 包～ shelter

庇护 bìhù ❶ shelter; shield; put under one's protection; take under one's wing: ～自己的短处 conceal one's shortcomings ❷ 〈法律〉 asylum: 政治～ political asylum / 领土～ territorial asylum / 外交～ diplomatic asylum / 寻求～ seek asylum / 给予～ grant (*or* give) asylum

庇护权 bìhùquán right of asylum

庇护所 bìhùsuǒ sanctuary; asylum: ～的滥用 abuse of asylum

庇荫 bìyīn 〈书面〉 ❶ (of a tree, etc.) give shade ❷ shield; shelter

庇佑 bìyòu 〈书面〉 bless; prosper: 靠祖先～ thanks to the blessings of one's ancestors

毕(畢) bì ❶ finish; complete; conclude: 礼～ after the completion of the ceremony/ ～其功于一役 accomplish the whole task at one stroke ❷ 〈书面〉 fully; altogether; completely: 真相～露 show one's true colours; reveal one's true features ❸ nineteenth of the twenty-eight constellations into which the celestial sphere was divided in ancient Chinese astronomy ❹ (Bì) a surname

毕恭毕敬 bìgōng-bìjìng *also* "必恭必敬" bìgōng-bìjìng reverent and respectful; fully deferential

毕加索 Bìjiāsuǒ Pablo Picasso (1881-1973), Spanish painter and representative of School of Paris painting

毕竟 bìjìng after all; when all is said and done; in the final analysis; all in all: 科学～是科学,容不得半点虚假。In the final analysis, science is science and brooks no falsehood whatsoever. / ～是年轻人,再累,好好睡一觉就没事了。After all, they are young and can overcome any fatigue after a good night's sleep. / 这书～是名著,大家都爱读。The book is a masterpiece, you know, and everybody enjoys reading it.

毕力 bìlì do one's best; exert oneself; use all one's strength; try one's utmost: ～以赴 try one's best; go all out; spare no effort

毕露 bìlù reveal completely; be completely exposed: 原形～ reveal one's true features completely; be shown for what one is; show one's true colours

毕命 bìmìng die (usu. a sudden or violent death): ～疆场 die on the battlefield

毕升 Bì Shēng Bisheng (? -c. 1051), inventor of typography in the Song Dynasty

毕生 bìshēng all one's life; lifetime: ～的研究成果 result of one's lifelong study / ～为之奋斗的事业 cause to which one has devoted all one's life / 他以～的辛劳,换得了科研的可喜成果。As a result of the persevering work of a lifetime, he achieved gratifying results in scientific research.

毕肖 bìxiào 〈书面〉 resemble closely; be the very image of; be true to life: 神态～的画像 lifelike portrait / ～其父 very image of his father

毕星团 Bìxīngtuán Hyades, a group of stars in Taurus near the Pleiades

毕业 bìyè graduate; finish school: 今年五十名学生～。Fifty students have graduated this year. / 他今年本科～。He will complete his undergraduate course this year. / 他有两门课不及格,怎么毕得了业? How could he graduate since he failed in two subjects?

毕业班 bìyèbān graduating class

毕业典礼 bìyè diǎnlǐ graduation (ceremony); commencement

毕业分配 bìyè fēnpèi job assignment on graduation

毕业论文 bìyè lùnwén graduation thesis or dissertation

毕业设计 bìyè shèjì graduation project

毕业生 bìyèshēng graduate

毕业实习 bìyè shíxí graduation field work

毕业证书 bìyè zhèngshū diploma; graduation certificate

荜¹(蓽) bì *see* "筚" bì

荜²(蓽) bì *see* "荜拨"

荜拨 bìbō 〈植物〉 *Piper longum*, whose dried fruit and ear are used as herbal medicine

荜路蓝缕 bìlù-lánlǚ *see* "筚路蓝缕" bìlù-lánlǚ

哔(嗶) bì

哔叽 bìjī 〈纺织〉 serge

跸(蹕) bì 〈书面〉 *see* "驻跸" zhùbì

筚(篳) bì *also* "荜" 〈书面〉 bamboo or wicker fence: ～门 bamboo (*or* wicker) door — poor man's hut / 蓬门～户 thatched hut with a door made of wicker and straw — humble abode

筚篥 bìlì *see* "篳篥" bìlì

筚路蓝缕 bìlù-lánlǚ *also* "荜路蓝蒌" bìlù-lánlǚ 〈书面〉 drive a faggot cart in threadbare clothes to reclaim a mountain wilderness — endure great hardships in pioneer work

筚门圭窦 bìmén-guīdòu faggot cave-like door — impoverished family

饆(饆) bì

饆饠 bìluó a kind of food

毙(斃) bì ❶ (derogatory when used with people) die; get killed: 击～ shoot dead / 束手待～ wait helplessly for one's doom/ 牲口倒～。The animal fell dead. ❷ 〈口语〉 execute; shoot dead; shoot: 昨天～了一名强奸杀人犯。A rapist and murderer was shot yesterday. ❸ 〈书面〉 fall; drop; collapse: 多行不义必自～。An inveterate evil-doer is bound to meet his own doom.

毙命 bìmìng meet violent death; get killed: 一声枪响,匪徒当场～。Bang, bang! The bandit was killed on the spot.

毙伤 bìshāng inflict casualties: ～甚重 suffer exceedingly heavy casualties / ～敌军五千余人 kill and wound over five thousand enemy troops

狴 bì

狴犴 bì'àn 〈书面〉 ❶ legendary beast often painted on prison doors in ancient times ❷ gaol; prison

陛 bì 〈书面〉 flight of steps leading to a palace hall: 丹～ vermillion-painted stone steps leading to a palace hall

陛辞 bìcí 〈书面〉 (of court officials) bid farewell to the emperor

陛见 bìjiàn 〈书面〉 have an audience with the emperor

陛下 bìxià 〈敬词〉 Your Majesty; His or Her Majesty: 国王～ His Majesty the King / 女王～ Her Majesty the Queen / 天皇～ (Japan) His Imperial Majesty / 两位～ Their Majesties / 女王～政府 Her Majesty's Government

畀 bì 〈书面〉 give: ～以重任 entrust sb. with a heavy responsibility

痹(痺) bì 〈中医〉 pain or numbness caused by cold, dampness, etc.; rheumatism

痹症 bìzhèng 〈中医〉 illness caused by wind, cold or dampness, characterized by aching and numbness in the limbs or all over the body

箅 bì

箅子 bìzi grate; grating; grid: 炉～ fire grate / 竹～ bamboo grid (to be put in a pot for steaming food) / 铁～ metal grille; grating

奰 bì 〈书面〉 ❶ angry ❷ big and tall

赑 bì

赑屃 bìxì 〈书面〉 ❶ straining hard ❷ legendary giant turtle (formerly used as a motif for the base of a heavy stone tablet)

庳 bì 〈书面〉 low; low-lying: 宫室卑～ low houses

裨 bì 〈书面〉 benefit; advantage: 于事无～。It won't help matters. *or* It won't do any good.

see also pí

裨补 bìbǔ 〈书面〉 ❶ make up; remedy; make good: ～缺漏 make up what is lacking (*or* missing); remedy shortcomings or defects ❷

benefit; be conducive to: 有所～ be of some benefit (*or* use); be helpful
裨益 bìyì 〈书面〉 benefit; advantage; profit: 对工作大有～ be of great help to one's work; be beneficial to one's work

髀
bì 〈书面〉 thigh; thigh-bone
髀肉复生 bìròu-fùshēng become flabby in one's thighs for lack of riding exercise — accomplish nothing in a life of comfort and ease; idle away one's life: 有～之叹 regret having achieved nothing (*or* wasted one's time) in life

婢
bì slave girl; servant girl: 奴～ slave girls; maidservants
婢女 bìnǚ slave girl; servant girl
婢子 bìzǐ ❶ housemaid; slave girl ❷ 〈谦词〉 (used by a woman in ancient China in reference to herself) I; me

蓖
bì
蓖麻 bìmá *also* "大麻子" dàmázǐ 〈植物〉 castor-oil plant; ricinus: ～子 castor bean
蓖麻蚕 bìmácán castor silkworm
蓖麻毒 bìmádú *also* "蓖麻蛋白" 〈生化〉 ricin
蓖麻油 bìmáyóu ricinus oil; castor oil: ～酸 〈化学〉 ricinoleic acid
蓖麻子中毒 bìmázǐ zhòngdú ricinism

篦
bì comb with a double-edged fine-toothed comb: ～头 comb one's hair
篦式过滤器 bìshì guòlǜqì slotted strainer
篦子 bìzi double-edged, fine-toothed comb
篦子筛 bìzishāi 〈机械〉 bar screen

辟[1]
bì 〈书面〉 monarch; sovereign: 复～ restore a monarchy; restoration

辟[2]
bì 〈书面〉 ❶ ward off; keep away; remove ❷ *see* "避" bì

辟[3]
bì 〈书面〉 (of a sovereign) summon sb. and confer on him an official post
see also pī; pì
辟谷 bìgǔ refrain from eating grain; live without eating grain — ancient Taoist practice of asceticism for the purpose of becoming an immortal
辟邪 bìxié exorcise evil spirits; ward off baneful influences
辟易 bìyì 〈书面〉 beat a retreat; back away

躄
bì ❶ 〈书面〉 gathering or fold (in clothes); crease: 皱～ wrinkles (in crumpled clothes) ❷ folds (of an internal organ such as the stomach or intestines)

避
bì ❶ avoid; evade; shun: ～而不见 avoid meeting (sb.); steer clear of (sb.) / ～开问题 shun a subject; avoid an issue; steer clear of a problem / 不～艰险 be undaunted by danger and hardships; face the danger and hardships squarely ❷ prevent; keep away; repel: ～瘟散 〈中药〉 fever-preventing powder
避车道 bìchēdào 〈交通〉 turn-out
避弹坑 bìdànkēng 〈军事〉 foxhole
避弹衣 bìdànyī flak jacket
避风 bìfēng ❶ take shelter from the wind: 在～处休息一下 take a rest in the lee ❷ *also* "避风头" lie low; stay away from trouble: 先到乡下避避风再说。Stay away in the countryside until the trouble blows over. *or* Go and lie low in the country and see what will happen.
避风港 bìfēnggǎng haven; harbour; shelter: 这个小渔村简直成了走私分子的～。The small fishing village has become a haven (*or* shelter) for smugglers.
避光生物 bìguāng shēngwù photophobe
避光性 bìguāngxìng 〈植物〉 photopathy
避讳 bìhuì avoid a taboo (usu. on the given names of emperors or one's elders)
避讳 bìhui *also* "避忌" ❶ word or phrase to be avoided as taboo; taboo ❷ evade; dodge: 他～提起往事。He deliberately avoids touching on his past experience.
避忌 bìjì *see* "避讳"
避坑落井 bìkēng-luòjǐng dodge a pit only to fall into a well; out of the frying pan into the fire
避雷开关 bìléi kāiguān lightning switch
避雷器 bìléiqì lightning arrester: ～接地装置 grounding of lightning arrester
避雷针 bìléizhēn lightning rod
避免 bìmiǎn avoid; refrain from; avert: ～损失 avoid losses / ～暴露 avert exposure / ～主观片面 never be subjective and one-sided; guard against subjectivity and one-sidedness / ～再次发生意外事件 prevent the recurrence of similar accidents
避难就易 bìnán-jiùyì leave the difficult for the easy; choose the easier, lighter tasks while shunning the more difficult ones; take the easier way out
避难 bìnàn take refuge; seek asylum: ～港 port of refuge / 要求政治～ ask for (*or* seek) political asylum
避难国 bìnànguó 〈法律〉 country of refuge
避难所 bìnànsuǒ refuge; sanctuary; asylum; haven
避匿 bìnì 〈书面〉 go into hiding: ～山中 hide oneself in the mountains
避其锐气，击其惰归 bì qí ruìqì, jī qí duò guī avoid the enemy when he is fresh and full of vigour, and attack him when he is exhausted and in retreat
避让 bìràng avoid; make way for: 他性情粗暴，蛮不讲理，人们都有意～他。Knowing him for a rude and unreasonable man, people all shun him. / 消防车赶赴失火现场时，其它车辆必须～。When a fire engine rushes towards the scene of a fire, all other vehicles must make way.
避实击虚 bìshí-jīxū *also* "避实就虚" ❶ steer clear of the enemy's main strength and strike him where he is weak ❷ avoid the essential and concrete, and deal only with the trivial and abstract
避世 bìshì escape from the bustling world; live the life of a recluse
避暑 bìshǔ ❶ be away for the summer holidays; spend a holiday at a summer resort: ～胜地 summer resort ❷ prevent sunstroke: ～药 medicine for preventing sunstroke; preventive against sunstroke
避税地 bìshuìdì 〈经济〉 tax haven
避蚊胺 bìwén'àn 〈药学〉 deet
避席 bìxí 〈书面〉 stand up (as at a dinner or meeting) to show one's respect for the latecomer
避嫌 bìxián avoid doing anything that may arouse suspicion; avoid suspicion: 这件事牵涉到他的家属，他最好～，不发表意见。As the matter involves his family, he'd better keep his mouth shut to avoid suspicion. / 我应该～，不参加我儿子提升职务的讨论。I'd better stay away from discussions about my son's promotion.
避邪 bìxié 〈迷信〉 ward off evil spirits (with talismans, incantations, etc.)
避役 bìyì 〈动物〉 chameleon
避孕 bìyùn contraception: ～药膏 contraceptive jelly / ～用品 contraceptives
避孕栓 bìyùnshuān contraceptive suppository
避孕套 bìyùntào condom
避孕丸 bìyùnwán contraceptive pill; the pill
避重就轻 bìzhòng-jiùqīng avoid the important and dwell on the trivial; keep silent about major charges while admitting minor ones

璧
bì round flat piece of jade with a hole in the middle (used for ceremonial purposes in ancient China)
璧还 bìhuán 〈敬词〉 ❶ return (a borrowed object) with thanks ❷ decline (a gift) with thanks
璧谢 bìxiè 〈敬词〉 decline (a gift) with thanks
璧赵 bìzhào 〈书面〉 *see* "璧还 ❶"

壁
bì ❶ wall: 铜墙铁～ (like an) iron wall; bastion of iron; impregnable fortress ❷ sth. resembling a wall: 胃～ stomach wall / 锅炉～ wall of a boiler / ～细胞 parietal cell ❸ cliff: 绝～ cliff; precipice ❹ rampart; breastwork: 坚～清野 strengthen the defences and clear the fields ❺ fourteenth of the twenty-eight constellations into which the celestial sphere was divided in ancient Chinese astronomy
壁报 bìbào wall newspaper

B

壁橱 bìchú built-in wardrobe or cupboard; closet
壁单 bìdān poster
壁灯 bìdēng wall lamp; bracket light
壁挂 bìguà (wall) hangings; tapestry:毛织～ wool tapestry /印染～ printed and dyed hangings /刺绣～ embroidered hangings /棉织～ cotton-print hangings /蜡染～ wax-print hangings
壁柜 bìguì built-in wardrobe
壁虎 bìhǔ 〈动物〉gecko; house lizard
壁画 bìhuà mural (painting); fresco:敦煌～ Dunhuang frescoes (*or* murals)
壁角 bìjiǎo corner (as in a room) made by two perpendicular walls:立～ be made to stand in the corner (as punishment)
壁脚 bìjiǎo 〈方言〉❶ foot of a wall ❷ private conversation:他不是存心听～的。It was by sheer chance that he overheard the private conversation.
壁街 bìjiē lane; alley
壁龛 bìkān niche (esp. that in the central hall of a mosque); shrine (in a wall)
壁垒 bìlěi ❶ rampart; barrier:关税～ tariff wall /贸易～ trade barrier ❷ line of demarcation or division:～分明 be diametrically opposed; be sharply divided /哲学中的两大～ two rival camps in philosophy; two diametrically opposed philosophical theories
壁垒森严 bìlěi-sēnyán ❶ closely guarded; strongly fortified ❷ sharply divided
壁立 bìlì (of cliffs, etc.) stand like a wall; rise steeply:～千仞 sheer rise of eight thousand feet /～的山峰 bold cliff
壁炉 bìlú fireplace
壁炉架 bìlújià chimneypiece
壁炉台 bìlútái mantel; mantel shelf
壁球 bìqiú squash; squash rackets
壁上观 bìshàngguān watch the fighting from the ramparts — be an onlooker
壁虱 bìshī ❶ *also* "蜱" pí tick:～感染 tick infestation ❷〈方言〉bedbug
壁饰 bìshì wall decorations or ornaments:堂皇的～ magnificent wall ornaments
壁毯 bìtǎn tapestry:丝织～ silk tapestry
壁厢 bìxiāng (often used in the early vernacular) side:这～ this side /那～ that side
壁障 bìzhàng barrier; obstacle:消除他们之间的无形～ remove the invisible barrier between them
壁纸 bìzhǐ wallpaper:塑料～ plastic print wallpaper
壁钟 bìzhōng wall clock; bracket clock; wag-on-the-wall (clock)
壁柱 bìzhù 〈建筑〉pilaster
壁装起重机 bìzhuāng qǐzhòngjī 〈机械〉wall crane

薜 bì
薜荔 bìlì 〈植物〉climbing fig

躄 bì *see* "躃" bì

躃 bì 〈书面〉❶ fall down ❷ limp

臂 bì ❶ arm:左～ left arm /助一～之力 give sb. a hand; give support to sb. ❷ upper arm
see also bei
臂板信号 bìbǎn xìnhào 〈铁路〉semaphore
臂膀 bìbǎng arm:～粗大 have muscular arms
臂膊 bìbó 〈方言〉arm
臂钏 bìchuàn armlet
臂力 bìlì strength of the arm
臂纱 bìshā black armband (as a sign of mourning)
臂式升降机 bìshì shēngjiàngjī 〈机械〉arm elevator
臂弯 bìwān bend or crook of the arm:他把衣服夹在～里。He took his jacket in his arm.
臂腕 bìwàn wrist
臂章 bìzhāng armband (used to indicate one's rank or position)
臂肘 bìzhǒu elbow
臂助 bìzhù 〈书面〉❶ help; aid ❷ assistant; right hand

嬖 bì 〈书面〉❶ dote on ❷ be in favour (with sb.); win sb.'s favour ❸ favourite
嬖人 bìrén 〈书面〉monarch's favourite (courtier or concubine)
嬖幸 bìxìng 〈书面〉❶ (of an emperor) dote on ❷ monarch's favourite

诐 bì 〈书面〉❶ argue; debate ❷ evil; sinister:～辞 sinister or evil words

髲 bì 〈书面〉wig

弼（弻） bì 〈书面〉assist:辅～ help as an assistant; assist

biān

煸 biān stir-fry before stewing

萹 biān
see also biǎn
萹蓄 biānxù 〈中药〉*Polygonum avaculars*

蝙 biān
蝙蝠 biānfú 〈动物〉bat:吸血～ vampire (bat)
蝙蝠蛾 biānfú'é swift; ghost moth (*Hepialidae*)
蝙蝠衫 biānfúshān blouse or jacket with batwing sleeves (i.e. with narrow cuffs and sleeves widened towards the armpit)
蝙蝠袖 biānfúxiù (as of a blouse, etc.) batwing sleeve
蝙蝠鱼 biānfúyú batfish

鳊（鯿） biān 〈动物〉bream
鳊鱼 biānyú bream

编 biān ❶ weave; plait:～草席 weave a straw mat /～竹筐 weave a bamboo basket /～辫子 plait one's hair ❷ organize; group; arrange:～班 group (*or* organize) into classes /二十个球员～为两个队。The 20 players are organized into two teams. /他被～入了强化班。He was enrolled in an intensive course. /这部小说已～入了当代文学丛书。This novel is included in the contemporary literature series. ❸ edit; compile:～词典 compile a dictionary /他～过两种期刊。He has edited two periodicals. ❹ write; compose:～一首歌词 compose a song /～相声 write a comic dialogue ❺ fabricate; invent; make up; cook up:瞎～ sheer fabrication /这个人爱～瞎话。This chap is prone to tell lies. /她～了一个理由不去开会了。She made (*or* cooked up) an excuse for not attending the meeting. ❻ (often used in book titles) copy; book:人手一～ a copy each /续～ continuation (of a book); sequel /《中国通史简～》*A Concise History of China* ❼ part of a book; book; volume:上～ Book I; Volume I; Part I ❽ authorized or stipulated strength or size; establishment:在～ permanent staff; on the regular payroll /超～ exceed the authorized strength or size; be redundant
编巴 biānba 〈口语〉weave; plait:湖里有的是芦苇,足够咱们～的。There're plenty of reeds in the lake for us to weave (into mats and other wares).
编贝 biānbèi (usu. used to describe people's teeth) shells arranged in neat order:齿如～ have teeth as white and regular as a string of pearls
编程 biānchéng 〈计算机〉program
编次 biāncì order of arrangement
编凑 biāncòu fabricate; invent; concoct; cook up:你可真会瞎～! What a yarn you've spun! /歌词是几个人～起来的。The lyrics of the song were knocked together by several people. /剧本作者精心～了这段情节。The playwright took great pains to weave the story of this episode.
编导 biāndǎo ❶ write and direct (a film, play, etc.):这三部电视剧都是由一位女作家～的。The three TV plays were all written and directed by a woman author. ❷〈戏剧〉playwright-director;〈舞蹈〉choreographer-director;〈影视〉scenarist-director
编订 biāndìng *also* "编定" compile and edit:～《唐宋传奇集》compile and edit *Short Stories of the Tang and Song Dynasties*
编队 biānduì ❶ form into columns; organize into teams ❷〈军事〉

formation (of ships or aircraft): ~飞行 formation flight (*or* flying)/~轰炸 formation bombing

编发 biānfā edit and release (manuscript, news, etc.):新华社~了大会消息。The Xinhua News Agency released dispatches about the conference. /这篇稿子是小王~的。It was Xiao Wang who edited and dispatched this article.

编法儿 biānfǎr try to find ways and means; try by hook or by crook:他老是编着法儿算计人。He was always scheming to do others in.

编挂 biānguà link a trailer to a motor vehicle or coaches to a locomotive

编号 biānhào ❶ number:给本队的车辆~ number the cars in the motorcade ❷ serial number:这辆车的~是十八。The number of this car is 18. *or* This car is No.18.

编后 biānhòu *also* "编后记" (editorial) afterword

编击乐器 biānjī yuèqì chimes

编辑 biānjí ❶ edit; compile:~人员 editorial staff /~委员会 editorial board /他们最近~了一套中学生丛书。They recently compiled a series of books for secondary school students. ❷ editor; compiler:总~ editor-in-chief; chief editor /他是文学副刊的~。He is editor of the literary supplement.

编辑部 biānjíbù editorial department

编辑宏指令 biānjí hóngzhǐlìng 〈信息〉editing macros (EMACS)

编校 biānjiào ❶ edit and revise ❷ editor-reviser

编结 biānjié braid; plait; weave: ~辫子 braid (*or* plait) one's hair/~鱼网 weave a fishing net /~艺术 braiding arts /~品 braidings

编剧 biānjù ❶ write a play, scenario, etc.:这个电视剧由他~。He wrote the TV scenario. ❷〈戏剧〉playwright;〈影视〉screenwriter; scenarist

编练 biānliàn 〈书面〉organize and train:~乡勇 organize and drill a country militia

编列 biānliè ❶ edit; compile:~成书 edit (*or* compile) a book ❷ work out (regulations, rules or plans); make arrangements for (specified projects):国家预备费~十六亿元。The national reserve fund is fixed at 1.6 billion *yuan* (in the budget). ❸〈书面〉compile a household registration book; put (households) in a registration book

编录 biānlù excerpt and edit:~国际问题资料 excerpt and edit materials on international issues

编码 biānmǎ 〈计算机〉code; encode:~方案 code scheme /~规则 code rule /~人 coder; encoder /~机 code machine /~理论 coding theory /~数据 coded (*or* encoded) data

编码变换器 biānmǎ biànhuànqì code converter

编码程序 biānmǎ chéngxù code program

编码磁鼓 biānmǎ cígǔ code drum

编码解码器 biānmǎ jiěmǎqì CODEC (coder/decoder)

编码器 biānmǎqì coder; encoder

编码信号 biānmǎ xìnhào code signal

编目 biānmù ❶ make a catalogue; catalogue:文件~ file cataloguing /为录像带~ catalogue the videotapes /~部 cataloguing department /~人员 cataloguer ❷ catalogue; list:这是新购图书~,请过目。This is a catalogue of newly acquired books. Please look it over.

编目计算机 biānmù jìsuànjī file computer

编拟 biānnǐ write; compile; draft:~提纲 draft (*or* work out) an outline

编年 biānnián annalistic; chronological: ~文集 chronologically collected works

编年史 biānniánshǐ annals; chronicle

编年体 biānniántǐ annalistic style (in historiography); chronological style

编排 biānpái ❶ arrange; lay out:杂志的~ layout of a magazine /~本周课外活动日程 work out a programme for this week's extracurricular activities /本词典的条目按汉语拼音音序~。The entries in this dictionary are arranged in the Chinese phonetic alphabetical order. ❷ write (a play, etc.) and rehearse:~戏剧小品 write and rehearse a skit

编派 biānpai 〈方言〉exaggerate (people's defects); fabricate; cook up:他就会给人~不是。He is quite capable of painting anybody black. /这些驴唇不对马嘴的事我知道是谁~出来的。I know for certain who cooked up these idle tales.

编配 biānpèi arrange and classify:刚~到部队里的士兵 new recruits assigned to the unit /他将~好的文集送交出版社。He sent to the publishing house the collected work he had edited.

编遣 biānqiǎn reorganize (troops, etc.) and discharge surplus personnel

编磬 biānqìng 〈音乐〉series of L-shaped stone or jade plates — a kind of ancient Chinese percussion instrument; stone or jade chimes

编摄 biānshè photographic editing (of movies)

编审 biānshěn ❶ edit and finalize; read and edit:他最近~了两部小说稿。He edited two novels recently. ❷ senior editor

编述 biānshù compile and write: ~讲义 write lecture notes (*or* texts)

编算 biānsuàn 〈方言〉play tricks upon; plot against:他诡计多端,总是~别人。Cunning and crafty, he was always hatching plots against others.

编外 biānwài not on the regular payroll; not on the permanent staff:列入~ take off the regular payroll; treat as an irregular

编外人员 biānwài rényuán employees not on regular payroll; personnel not on the permanent staff; irregular or temporary staff; irregulars

编舞 biānwǔ ❶ choreography ❷ choreographer

编写 biānxiě ❶ compile:~参考书目 compile a bibliography ❷ write; compose:~独幕剧 write a one-act play

编修 biānxiū ❶〈书面〉compile; edit; revise:唐代和宋代都重新~过《本草》。*Materia Medica* was revised twice in the Tang and Song dynasties respectively. ❷〈旧语〉imperial compiler (charged with the task of writing the national history and court conference summaries in the Song Dynasty, but reduced to a titular official attached to the Imperial Academy during the Ming and Qing dynasties)

编选 biānxuǎn select and edit; compile:~教材 compile teaching materials /~漫画作品 select and compile cartoons

编演 biānyǎn write and produce; create and perform (operas, ballads, dances, etc.):~文艺节目 create and put on a performance (*or* show)

编译 biānyì ❶ edit and translate:~人员 editor-translator ❷ editor-translator

编译程序 biānyì chéngxù 〈计算机〉compiling program or routine:~语言 BCY language

编译计算机 biānyì jìsuànjī 〈计算机〉compiling computer

编译器 biānyìqì 〈信息〉compiler

编印 biānyìn edit and print; publish:~小册子 edit and print a pamphlet

编余 biānyú (of personnel) redundant after reorganization (of troops, government units, etc.):安置~人员 relocate redundant staff

编扎 biānzā weave; plait; braid:用竹枝~篱笆 weave (*or* make) a bamboo fence

编造 biānzào ❶ compile; draw up; work out:~预算 draw up a budget /~科研成果统计表 compile a statistical table of achievements in scientific research ❷ create out of imagination:老人给孩子们~了很多有趣的故事。The old man invented many interesting tales for the children. ❸ fabricate; invent; make up:~谎言 fabricate (*or* concoct) lies /他为自己的缺席~了一个理由。He made up a story as an excuse for his absence.

编者 biānzhě editor; compiler

编者按 biānzhě'àn *also* "编者案" editor's note; editorial note

编织 biānzhī weave; knit; plait; braid:~地毯 weave a carpet /~围巾 knit a scarf /~发网 crochet a hairnet

编织机 biānzhījī 〈纺织〉knitter or knitting-machine

编制 biānzhì ❶ weave; plait; braid:~柳条筐 weave wicker baskets ❷ work out; draw up: ~教学方案 draw up a teaching programme /~工程计划 work out a plan for a project ❸ authorized strength or size; establishment:部队~ establishment (for army units) /战时~ wartime establishment /政府机关~ authorized size of a government body /缩小~ reduce (*or* cut down) the staff /扩大~ augment the staff /超过~ overstaffing

编钟 biānzhōng 〈音乐〉chime bells; serial bells; carillon

编著 biānzhù compile; write:在许多份调查报告的基础上,他~了《四川植被》一书。He wrote *Vegetation in Sichuan* on the basis of many field surveys (*or* findings). /这部中国文化史是王教授~的。This history of Chinese culture is compiled by Professor Wang.

编撰 biānzhuàn compile; write:~当代英国小说史 compile a histo-

ry of contemporary English fiction

编缀 biānzhuì ❶ weave:～花环 wreathe flowers into a garland ❷ edit:～成书 edit sth. into a book

编组 biānzǔ organize (people, vehicles, etc.) into groupings; marshal; group

编组场 biānzǔchǎng 〈铁路〉marshalling yard

编纂 biānzuǎn compile:～百科全书 compile an encyclopaedia

B

鞭 biān ❶ whip; lash:马～ horsewhip /皮～ leather-thonged whip /策马扬～ urge one's horse onward with whip and spur ❷ iron nodular staff used as a weapon in ancient China ❸ sth. resembling a whip:教～ (teacher's) pointer ❹ penis of certain male animals used as medicine or cooked as food:牛～ ox's penis ❺ string of small firecrackers:放一挂～ set off a string of firecrackers ❻ 〈书面〉flog; whip; lash:驶马不劳～。One does not have to whip a steed to make it gallop.

鞭把势 biānbǎshi *also* "鞭把式"〈方言〉cart driver; carter

鞭爆 biānbào 〈方言〉firecracker:放～ let off firecrackers

鞭策 biāncè spur on; urge on; encourage:这些批评对我们是一种～。These criticisms will urge us to greater efforts. /有了远大的志向,才能不断～自己上进。Only with lofty aspirations, can you constantly spur yourself on.

鞭长莫及 biāncháng-mòjí be beyond the reach of one's power; be too far away for one to be of help:此事我们～,爱莫能助。This is beyond the reach of our power, eager as we are to be of help. *or* We are in no position to help as the matter is not within our jurisdiction.

鞭笞 biānchī 〈书面〉flog; lash; castigate:作者对损人利己者进行了无情的～。The author lashes out mercilessly at those who seek profits at the expense of others.

鞭虫 biānchóng whipworm

鞭楚 biānchǔ 〈书面〉flog; lash; whip

鞭箠 biānchuí *also* "鞭棰"〈书面〉*see* "鞭打"

鞭打 biāndǎ whip; lash; flog; thrash

鞭打快牛 biāndǎ-kuàiniú whip the ox that works fast — make the diligent work even faster while letting the lazy alone; spur the willing horse

鞭痕 biānhén welt; whip scar; lash mark

鞭花 biānhuā whipcrack; sound made by the tip of a whip when it is wielded:打了几声响亮的～ crack one's whip loud a couple of times

鞭毛 biānmáo 〈生物〉flagellum:～运动 flagellar motility /～生物 flagellatae /～蛋白 flagellin

鞭毛虫 biānmáochóng flagellate:～病 flagellosis /～纲 *Flagellata*

鞭毛藻 biānmáozǎo 〈生物〉flagellate

鞭炮 biānpào ❶ firecrackers ❷ string of small firecrackers

鞭辟入里 biānpì-rùlǐ *also* "鞭辟近里" penetrating; trenchant; incisive:他对问题的分析～。He made a penetrating analysis of the issue.

鞭扑 biānpū 〈书面〉*see* "鞭打"

鞭蛇 biānshé coachwhip (snake)

鞭挞 biāntà 〈书面〉lash; castigate:作者用杂文的形式来讽刺和～社会上的腐败落后现象。The author uses his essays to satirize and castigate the corrupt and backward practices in society. /这出戏无情地～虐待老人的恶劣行为。The play lashes out at the wicked act of ill-treating the aged.

鞭责 biānzé 〈书面〉lash and interrogate

鞭子 biānzi whip

砭 biān ❶ 〈中医〉stone needle used in acupuncture in ancient China ❷ use stone needles in acupuncture (as in ancient China); pierce; castigate:针～ perform acupuncture (on sb.); criticize and help /痛～时弊 castigate the social abuses (*or* ills) of the time

砭骨 biāngǔ chill one to the marrow; cut one to the bone:朔风～。The icy wind cuts one to the marrow.

砭石 biānshí stone acupuncture needle

砭顽起懦 biānwán-qǐnuò awaken or arouse the obtuse and the weak

边(邊) biān ❶ side:正方形的一～ one side of a square ❷ margin; side; edge; brim:宽～草帽 straw hat with a broad brim/在桌～上 on the edge of a table /天～ horizon; end of the earth ❸ hem; border; edge (as an ornament):衬衣的～ hem of a shirt /花～儿 decorative border; lace /金～奖状 gilt-edged certificate of honour ❹ frontier; boundary; border:戍～ garrison the frontiers or the border regions /靖～ pacify the border regions ❺ limit; bound:无～无际的海洋 boundless ocean; vast expanse of ocean ❻ by the side of; close by:坐在窗～ sit by the window /老人把全家人叫到身～。The old man summoned the whole family to his side. /我身～没有零钱 I haven't got any change on me. ❼ part; side:双～条约 bipartite treaty ❽ (used after words indicating time or numerals) close to; near:活到六十～上,还没有坐过飞机呢。Though I'm close to (*or* getting on for) sixty, I've never travelled in a plane yet. ❾ (Biān) a surname

边(邊) bian *suffix of a noun of locality*:这～ here/东～ in the east /左～ on the left /前～ in front /里～ inside /上～ above; over; on top of

边隘 biān'ài 〈书面〉strategic frontier pass or defile

边岸 biān'àn bank; shore:江水浩荡,看不见～。The river is a vast expanse of waves, mighty and boundless.

边鄙 biānbǐ 〈书面〉remote border region

边币 biānbì border region currency (currency notes issued by various border region governments during the War of Resistance Against Japanese Aggression and the War of Liberation)

边…边… biān…biān… *used before two verbs respectively to indicate simultaneous actions*:边听边记 take notes while listening /边干边学 learn while working; train on the job /边吃边谈 talk while eating; talk over dinner /边学边忘 no sooner does one learn sth. than one forgets it; forget sth. as soon as one learns it

边材 biāncái sapwood:～百分率 sapwood percentage

边侧 biāncè beside; by the side of:校园～松柏成林。Flanking the campus are rows of pines and cypresses.

边茶 biānchá *also* "边销茶" tea earmarked for use by China's ethnic minorities in border regions

边城 biānchéng frontier city; border town

边虫病 biānchóngbìng 〈兽医〉anaplasmosis; gall-sickness

边陲 biānchuí 〈书面〉border area; frontier:～小镇 frontier town /多年来他一直守卫在南国～。He has been serving as a frontier guard on the southern border of our country for many years.

边地 biāndì border district; border land

边防 biānfáng frontier or border defence:～部队 frontier guards /～哨 border sentry; border post /～要塞 frontier stronghold

边防检查 biānfáng jiǎnchá frontier inspection; border check:～站 frontier inspection station; border checkpost (*or* checkpoint) /～条例 frontier inspection regulations

边防军 biānfángjūn frontier guards; border guards

边防战士 biānfáng zhànshì frontier guard

边防站 biānfángzhàn frontier station

边锋 biānfēng 〈体育〉wing; wing forward:右～ right wing

边幅 biānfú one's dress or appearance:不修～ not care for one's appearances; be careless about one's dress; be slovenly

边沟 biāngōu drainage ditch on either side of a road or roadbed

边关 biānguān strategic pass at the border

边焊 biānhàn side weld

边患 biānhuàn 〈书面〉external encroachment on the frontier:～频仍。There were frequent external encroachments on the borders.

边际 biānjì limit; bound; boundary; margin:茫无～的草原 boundless (*or* limitless) grasslands /～收益 marginal revenue /～活动 marginal activities /～消费者 marginal consumer /～投资 marginal investment /～储蓄倾向 marginal propensity to save/他说话不着～,谁也没兴趣去听。His remarks were neither here nor there, and nobody cared to listen.

边际比率 biānjì bǐlǜ marginal rate

边际产量 biānjì chǎnliàng marginal product

边际成本 biānjì chéngběn marginal cost:～法 marginal costing

边际分析 biānjì fēnxī marginal analysis

边际幅度 biānjì fúdù margin

边际价值 biānjì jiàzhí marginal value

边际利润 biānjì lìrùn marginal profit;profit margin

边际利益 biānjì lìyì marginal advantage

边际贸易 biānjì màoyì marginal trading

边际生产率论 biānjì shēngchǎnlǜlùn marginal productivity theory
边际税率 biānjì shuìlǜ marginal tax rate
边际效率 biānjì xiàolǜ marginal efficiency：资本～ marginal efficiency of capital
边际效用 biānjì xiàoyòng marginal utility：～论〈经济〉theory of marginal utility／～递减 diminishing marginal utility／边际负效用 marginal disutility
边际信用 biānjì xìnyòng marginal credit
边际需求 biānjì xūqiú marginal demand
边际主义 biānjìzhǔyì marginalism
边疆 biānjiāng border area；frontier；frontier region：保卫～ guard the frontier／支援～建设 aid（*or* support）the construction of the border areas
边角 biānjiǎo edge；periphery；fringe；margin：煤田～资源常年沉睡，无人开采。Marginal coal resources lie unexploited all year round.
边角料 biānjiǎoliào leftover bits and pieces（of industrial material）
边界 biānjiè boundary；border：划定～ demarcate boundaries／越过～ cross a boundary；cross the border／国家～ national boundary／未定～ undefined（*or* undemarcated）boundary／人为～ artificial boundary／～海峡 boundary strait／～委员会 boundary commission／～事件 border incident／～问题 boundary question（*or* issue）／～现状 *status quo* on the border／～争端 boundary dispute／两国～上的人民一向友好，相互往来。The people of the two countries living on the borders have always been on friendly terms and exchanged visits from time to time.
边界标志 biānjiè biāozhì boundary sign or marker
边界层 biānjiècéng〈物理〉boundary layer：～光电池 boundary-layer photocell／～理论 boundary layer theory
边界实际控制线 biānjiè shíjì kòngzhìxiàn line of actual control on the border
边界谈判 biānjiè tánpàn boundary negotiations
边界条约 biānjiè tiáoyuē boundary treaty
边界线 biānjièxiàn boundary line：陆地～ boundary line on land／无形的～ invisible boundary line
边界协定 biānjiè xiédìng boundary agreement
边界协定书 biānjiè xiédìngshū boundary protocol
边界元 biānjièyuán〈物理〉boundary element：～法 boundary element method
边界走向 biānjiè zǒuxiàng alignment of the boundary line
边境 biānjìng border；border area；frontier：～冲突 border clash（*or* conflict）／～地区 border area／～管制 border control／～事件 border incident／～争端 border dispute／封锁～ close the frontier；seal off the borders／开放～ open the border／增加～的不安 aggravate the unrest along the border／令人不安的～状况 disquieting situation on the border／我国政府的建议为缓和两国～紧张局势铺平了道路。The proposal put forward by our government has paved the way for the relaxation of tension on the borders of the two countries.
边境贸易 biānjìng màoyì（shortened as 边贸）frontier trade；border trade
边境制度协定 biānjìng zhìdù xiédìng agreement on the regime of the frontier or border
边款 biānkuǎn inscriptions or patterns carved on the sides or top of a seal
边框 biānkuàng frame；rim：镜子的～ rim of a mirror
边贸 biānmào *see*“边境贸易”
边门 biānmén sidedoor；wicket door；postern door or gate：他从大厅的～走进去。He went into the hall by the sidedoor.
边民 biānmín people living on the frontiers；border inhabitants；frontiersmen
边坡 biānpō slope of the embankment（of a highway or railway）
边卡 biānqiǎ border checkpoint or checkpost
边区 biānqū border area or region：晋察冀～ Shanxi-Chahar-Hebei Border Region
边人 biānrén〈书面〉❶ frontiersmen；people living in border regions ❷ men on active service in border regions
边塞 biānsài frontier fortress：～要地 strategic pass on the frontier
边事 biānshì〈书面〉border affairs
边式 biānshi ❶〈方言〉(of one's dress or figure) smart；sexy ❷〈戏曲〉(of acting) smart and graceful
边庭 biāntíng〈书面〉❶ border administrative office ❷ border region：～吃紧。The situation is rather tense on the borders.
边头 biāntóu ❶ side；edge；bank：江～ on the river bank ❷〈书面〉border；frontier ❸〈方言〉time before a certain event：夜饭～，你来聊聊。Come and have a chat before supper.
边务 biānwù frontier affairs；frontier defence
边线 biānxiàn〈体育〉❶ sideline ❷（as in baseball）foul line；（as in cricket）boundary line
边厢 biānxiāng ❶ side；by the side of ❷〈方言〉aspect；side：他们各讲了一～的道理。They stated their respective views. ❸〈方言〉wing；wingroom
边心距 biānxīnjù〈数学〉apothem
边衅 biānxìn border dispute：挑起～ stir up（*or* provoke）border disputes
边沿 biānyán edge；fringe：池塘～ edge of a pond／昨夜下了大雨，马路～还积着雨水。It rained heavily last night and there are still puddles of water on either side of the road.
边裔 biānyì〈书面〉remote border area
边音 biānyīn〈语言〉lateral（sound）
边圉 biānyǔ〈书面〉frontier；border region
边缘 biānyuán ❶ edge；fringe；verge；brink：战争～政策 brink-of-war policy；brinkmanship／柴达木盆地的～ edge of the Qaidam Basin／有些工厂已到了破产的～。Some factories are on the verge of bankruptcy.／他们挣扎在死亡的～。They are putting up a desperate struggle. ❷ marginal；borderline：～海 marginal sea／～地区 border district；border／～学科 borderline discipline／～地带 periphery／～国家 peripheral state／～战争 peripheral war／～生产者 marginal producer
边缘对接 biānyuán duìjiē edge butt joint
边缘科学 biānyuán kēxué frontier science
边远 biānyuǎn far from the centre；remote；outlying：～山区 outlying mountain area／～县份 remote border counties
边寨 biānzhài stockaded village or mountain stronghold on the border area
边注 biānzhù marginal note
边子 biānzi ❶ side；edge；border：地界～ edge of a lot；border of a plot ❷〈方言〉*see*“边头 ❸”

biǎn

扁 biǎn flat：～鼻子 flat nose／～盒子 flat case；shallow box／面包压～了。The loaf was pressed flat.／别把人看～了。Don't underestimate people's ability. *or* Don't belittle people.
see also piān
扁柏 biǎnbǎi false cypress；*Chamaecyparis*：白～ cypress；white cedar／日本～ Japanese cypress
扁铲 biǎnchǎn flat chisel
扁虫 biǎnchóng flatworm
扁蝽 biǎnchūn flat bug
扁锉 biǎncuò flat file
扁担 biǎndan carrying pole；shoulder pole：～没扎，两头打塌〈谚语〉when the carrying pole is not secured at both ends，its loads slip off — try to grab both but end up getting neither；fall between two stools
扁担星 Biǎndanxīng〈天文〉〈俗语〉Altair
扁豆 biǎndòu ❶ hyacinth bean：小～ lentil ❷〈方言〉kidney bean
扁钢 biǎngāng〈冶金〉flat bar；flat or flat-rolled steel：～锭 flat-shaped ingot；slab ingot／～轧机 flat-rolling mill
扁钢坯轧机 biǎngāngpī zhájī〈冶金〉slabber；slab mill
扁骨 biǎngǔ〈生理〉flat bone
扁卷螺 biǎnjuǎnluó *also*“扁螺”〈动物〉*Planorbis*
扁率 biǎnlǜ〈天文〉oblateness：地球的～是 1/298.257。The oblateness of the earth is 1/298.257.
扁坯 biǎnpī〈冶金〉slab
扁平 biǎnpíng flat：～包装 flat pack（*or* package）／～胸 flat chest／～发动机 pancake engine
扁平湿疣 biǎnpíng shīyóu〈医学〉condyloma latum
扁平足 biǎnpíngzú〈生理〉flatfoot；*pes planus*
扁鹊 Biǎn Què Bian Que（c.407-c.310 BC），whose real name was Qin Yueren（秦越人），China's ancient medical scientist and founder of pulse diagnosis
扁鲨 biǎnshā〈动物〉squatinia
扁食 biǎnshi *also*“饺子”jiǎozi〈方言〉dumpling（with meat and

vegetable stuffing)
扁桃 biǎntáo ❶ almond tree ❷ almond ❸〈方言〉flat peach
扁桃体 biǎntáotǐ 〈生理〉*also*“扁桃腺”tonsil
扁桃体肥大 biǎntáotǐ féidà 〈医学〉hypertrophy of tonsils
扁桃体切除术 biǎntáotǐ qiēchúshù tonsillectomy
扁桃腺炎 biǎntáoxiànyán tonsillitis
扁体字 biǎntǐzì squat-shaped handwriting
扁形动物 biǎnxíng dòngwù flatworm; platyhelminth
扁蝇 biǎnyíng seaweed fly; kelp fly (*Coelopidae*)
扁圆 biǎnyuán ❶〈口语〉oval; oblate:～形 of oval shape ❷ round and flat or shallow:～食品盒 flat round food case
扁嘴 biǎnzuǐ 〈方言〉❶ purse one's lips; pout:他扁起嘴,一句话不说。He pursed his lips and remained silent (*or* did not utter a word). ❷ *also*“扁嘴子”duck
扁嘴雀 biǎnzuǐquè flatbill (*Ramphotrigon*)

惼 biǎn 〈书面〉narrow (of mind)
惼心 biǎnxīn narrow-minded

褊 biǎn 〈书面〉narrow; cramped
褊急 biǎnjí 〈书面〉narrow-minded and short-tempered
褊狭 biǎnxiá 〈书面〉narrow; cramped:居处～ cramped living quarters /气量～ narrow-minded; small-minded
褊小 biǎnxiǎo narrow and small; narrow:土地～ narrow strip of land
褊窄 biǎnzhǎi ❶ narrow:～小路 narrow path ❷ (of mind) petty; narrow:心胸～ narrow-minded; petty-minded

萹 biǎn
see also biān
萹豆 biǎndòu broad beans

碥 biǎn ❶ crag hanging over water ❷ stone steps along dangerous parts of a cliff

匾 biǎn ❶ horizontal inscribed board:门上挂着一块～。An inscribed board hung above the door. ❷ silk banner embroidered with words of praise:绣金～ embroider a silk banner with golden thread ❸ big round shallow basket made from bamboo strips (for raising silkworms or holding grain)
匾额 biǎn'é horizontal inscribed board
匾文 biǎnwén inscription on a horizontal board

窆 biǎn 〈书面〉inter; bury

贬 biǎn ❶ demote; relegate:被～官 be demoted /～为庶民 be degraded to the status of a commoner ❷ devalue; reduce; depreciate:～了值的货币 depreciated currency ❸ censure; belittle; play down:褒～ praise and censure /他们把他的成就～得很低。They deliberately played down his achievements. /有人把他的论文～得一钱不值。Some people rate his research paper as worthless.
贬斥 biǎnchì ❶〈书面〉demote:几经～,他最终以一个小小的县令死于任所。Demoted again and again, he died at his post as a petty county magistrate. ❷ belittle and exclude; discriminate against:他受到同事们的～,心里感到很不是滋味。He was discriminated against by his colleagues, and he felt very bad about it.
贬黜 biǎnchù 〈书面〉demote; dismiss:他原为朝贵,后遭～。He used to be a high official in the royal court, but was demoted later.
贬词 biǎncí derogatory term; expression of censure
贬低 biǎndī deliberately underestimate; belittle; play down:他们极力～她在这项工作中所起的作用。They did their best to play down her role in the task. /我们决不能～实践的重要性。We should never underestimate the importance of practice.
贬官 biǎnguān ❶ demote:将无能之辈通通～ demote all the incompetent officials ❷ demoted official
贬毁 biǎnhuǐ belittle and slander:任人～ allow oneself to be disparaged /他们严厉批评她毫无根据地～别人。They severely criticized her for slandering others so groundlessly.
贬价 biǎnjià lower the price:～出售 sell at a reduced price
贬损 biǎnsǔn speak ill of:他常常背后～他的同事。He often speaks ill of his colleagues behind their backs.
贬义 biǎnyì derogatory sense; pejorative meaning:这话实际含有～。This word is, in fact, derogatory.
贬义词 biǎnyìcí *see*“贬词”
贬抑 biǎnyì belittle; depreciate:他从不～别人的意见。He never tries to underrate other people's views.
贬责 biǎnzé blame; reproach; reprimand:他因失职被～了一顿。He was reproached for dereliction of duty. /对孩子不要因为一点小事就没完没了地～。We shouldn't blame a child endlessly for a petty mistake.
贬谪 biǎnzhé banish from the court; relegate to a border area:几度～,他已心如死灰。The repeated demotions and exiles made him totally apathetic.
贬值 biǎnzhí ❶ (of a currency) depreciate:通货～。The currency has been depreciated. ❷〈经济〉devalue:美元～ devaluation of the US dollar ❸ diminish in value; depreciate:这些过时商品已大大～了。These outdated goods have diminished greatly in value.
贬职 biǎnzhí 〈书面〉demote

biàn

辨 biàn differentiate; distinguish; discriminate:明～是非 discriminate between right and wrong; distinguish right from wrong /不～真伪 fail to distinguish between truth and falsehood; be unable to tell the true from the false
辨白 biànbái try to justify oneself
see also“辩白”biànbái
辨别 biànbié differentiate; distinguish; discriminate; tell apart:～美丑 differentiate between the beautiful and the ugly /～方向 take one's bearings /～古董和复制品 distinguish (*or* tell) a genuine antique from a reproduction /他没有～好坏文风的能力。He is not capable of distinguishing between a good and a bad style.
辨尝 biàncháng taste and judge; sample:～佳肴 savour genuine delicacies
辨风向 biàn fēngxiàng 〈比喻〉try to find out which way the wind blows
辨惑 biànhuò analyse and resolve doubts:质疑～ analyse subtle queries and resolve doubts; raise questions and propose answers /《～篇》〈基督教〉*Apologeticum*
辨明 biànmíng clearly distinguish; strictly discriminate:～方向 take one's bearings
辨认 biànrèn identify; recognize:～指纹 identify a fingerprint /字迹已经模糊,几乎不能～。The inscription is so blurred that it is almost beyond recognition. /在听众里我还能～几个熟悉的面孔。I could still recognize a few familiar faces among the audience.
辨识 biànshí identify; recognize; distinguish:～足迹 identify footprints /～不清 unrecognizable; beyond recognition
辨析 biànxī differentiate and analyse; discriminate:同义词～ synonym discrimination /词义的～ semantic discrimination and analysis
辨喜 Biànxǐ Narendranath Datta Vivekananda (1863-1902), Indian spiritual leader
辨向 biànxiàng sensing:～器 sense finder
辨向天线 biànxiàng tiānxiàn sense antenna; sensing antenna
辨正 biànzhèng *also*“辩正”biànzhèng differentiate (between right and wrong) and rectify (the error)
辨证 biànzhèng *also*“辩证”biànzhèng textual research and discrimination
辨证论治 biànzhèng lùnzhì *also*“辨证施治”〈中医〉diagnosis and treatment based on an overall analysis of the illness and the patient's condition

辩(辯) biàn argue; debate; dispute:能言善～ have the gift of (the) gab; be eloquent and persuasive /～个水落石出 argue a matter out /事情愈～愈明白。The more you argue about the matter, the clearer it becomes. /我～不过他。I am no match for him in argument. *or* I cannot outargue him.
辩白 biànbái *also*“辨白”biànbái offer an explanation of the actual situation so as to remove misunderstanding or censure; try to justify oneself; defend oneself against a charge:他～说,他缺席是因为生病。His absence, he explained, was due to his illness. /我要替他～一下。I'd like to put in a few words for him.
辩驳 biànbó dispute; refute; rebut:无可～ beyond all dispute; ir-

refutable

辩才 biàncái 〈书面〉 eloquence; oratory: 此人颇有～。He is versed in the art of persuasion. *or* He is quite eloquent.

辩辞 biàncí *also* "辩词" biàncí explanation; argument; justification: ～犀利 sharp argument

辩答 biàndá defend one's position; defend oneself (orally)

辩护 biànhù ❶ defend; argue in favour of: 他极力为朋友的所作所为～。He vigorously defended his friend's conduct. ❷ 〈法律〉 defend; plead: 出庭～ (of a lawyer) defend a case in court / 为被告人～ plead for the accused

辩护律师 biànhù lǜshī 〈法律〉 counsel for the defence; defence counsel

辩护权 biànhùquán 〈法律〉 right to defence: 被告人有～。The accused has the right to defence.

辩护人 biànhùrén 〈法律〉 defender; counsel

辩护士 biànhùshì advocate; apologist

辩护制度 biànhù zhìdù 〈法律〉 system of advocacy

辩解 biànjiě make an explanation; try to defend oneself; make excuses; explain away: 人们同声谴责, 他无以～。He could not offer any plausible explanation in the face of unanimous condemnation. / 事情很清楚, 无需～了。Everything is clear, and it's futile trying to explain it away.

辩论 biànlùn argue; debate: 一般性～ general debate (as of the UN General Assembly) / 两位总统候选人将公开～他们的外交政策。The two presidential candidates are going to debate their foreign policies in public. / 谁在～中最先发言? Who opened the debate? *or* Who was the first to take the floor at the debate? / 他们进行了激烈的～。They had quite a heated argument.

辩论会 biànlùnhuì debate: 议会～ parliamentary debate / ～主席 moderator

辩明 biànmíng argue; justify: ～事理 reason (*or* argue) things out

辩难 biànnàn 〈书面〉 retort with challenging questions; try to embarrass or rebut in debate: 互相～ make taunting retorts to each other; challenge each other with disapproving remarks

辩士 biànshì orator; sophist

辩说 biànshuō debate; argue; explain

辩诉 biànsù defend oneself (in a law court)

辩诬 biànwū defend oneself against false charges; plead innocence

辩学 biànxué ❶ branch of learning concerned with debate ❷ 〈旧语〉 logic

辩争 biànzhēng argue; debate; contend: 据理～ argue vigorously on just grounds; contend by reasoning things out

辩正 biànzhèng *also* "辨正" biànzhèng differentiate (between right and wrong) and rectify (errors); distinguish right from wrong: 对一些不实的传说加以～。Sift the truth from what is false in the circulating stories.

辩证 biànzhèng ❶ textual research and discrimination: 专家们经过认真～, 对这批文物的年代有了一致的看法。The experts reached a consensus on the dates of these relics after careful textual research. ❷ dialectical: ～的统一 dialectical unity / ～的方法 dialectical method (*or* approach) / 事物发展的～规律 dialectical law of the development of things

辩证法 biànzhèngfǎ ❶ dialectics: 黑格尔～ Hegelian dialectics / 唯物～ materialistic dialectics ❷ materialistic dialectics: ～的世界观 dialectical world outlook

辩证逻辑 biànzhèng luóji dialectical logic

辩证唯物主义 biànzhèng wéiwùzhǔyì dialectical materialism: ～的认识论 dialectical materialist theory of knowledge / ～观点 dialectical materialist point of view / ～者 dialectical materialist

辩嘴 biànzuǐ 〈方言〉 ❶ squabble; bicker; quarrel: 他常跟同伴～。He often bickers with his pals. ❷ defend oneself (against a charge); offer an explanation: 你闯下了大祸, ～是没有用的。You've got into dreadful trouble and it's no use trying to offer excuses.

辫(辮) biàn

❶ plait; braid; pigtail: 发～ braid; plait / 梳小～儿 wear pigtails ❷ sth. resembling a braid: 蒜～ braid of garlic ❸ 〈方言〉 plait (into a braid): ～辫子 plait one's hair

辫绳 biànshéng ❶ braided rope ❷ lace for tying a pigtail or ponytail

辫子 biànzi ❶ plait; braid; pigtail: 梳～ wear one's hair in braids / 把问题梳梳～ sort out the problems to be tackled ❷ sth. resembling a plait: 草帽～ plaited straw (for making hats, baskets, etc.) ❸ mistake or shortcoming that may be exploited by an opponent; handle: 揪～ seize on sb.'s mistake or shortcoming; capitalize on sb.'s vulnerable point

卞 biàn

❶ 〈书面〉 impetuous: ～急而好洁 be an impetuous but clean fellow ❷ (Biàn) a surname

汴 Biàn

another name for Kaifeng (开封), major city in Henan Province

汴京 Biànjīng another name for Kaifeng (开封) as capital for Liang (梁), Jin (晋), Han (汉), and Zhou (周) of the Five Dynasties, as well as for Northern Song (北宋) and early Jin (金)

忭 biàn

〈书面〉 glad; happy: 不胜欣～ be overjoyed

苄 biàn

〈化学〉 benzyl: ～醇 benzyl alcohol / ～胺 benzylamine; aminotoluene

苄基 biànjī 〈化学〉 benzyl: ～丙酮 benzylacetone / ～氯 benzyl chloride

抃 biàn

〈书面〉 clap (one's hands); applaud

抃舞 biànwǔ clap hands and dance for joy

抃踊 biànyǒng clap hands and jump for joy

变(變) biàn

❶ change; become different: 她主意～了。She changed her mind. / 几年不见, 你～多了。You have changed such a lot since we met a few years ago. / 食堂主食每天～花样。The canteen provides new varieties of staple food every day. ❷ change into; turn into; become: 后进～先进。The backward has become the advanced. / 荒山～良田。The barren hills have turned into cultivated land. / 他脾气～急躁了。He has grown irritable. ❸ change; transform; turn: ～废为宝 change waste material into things of value; recycle waste material / ～农业国为工业国 turn an agricultural country into an industrialized one ❹ changeable; changed ❺ sell off (one's property) ❻ flexible: 通权达～ follow a flexible course of action; be flexible as the occasion requires; adapt oneself to circumstances ❼ unexpected turn of events: 哗～ mutiny / 政～ *coup d'etat* / 事～ incident ❽ short for 变文

变把戏 biàn bǎxì perform conjuring tricks; conjure; juggle: ～的 magician; conjurer; juggler / 我变个把戏给你瞧。Let me perform a conjuring trick for you. / 那个～的从袖子里变出五只兔子和一缸金鱼来。The conjurer, as if by magic, produced five rabbits and a bowlful of goldfish from his sleeves.

变本加厉 biànběn-jiālì worsen; intensify; become aggravated: 形形色色的敌对派别～地互相攻击。The rival factions of all hues are intensifying their efforts to attack each other. / 贸易保护主义不但没有减少, 而且正在～。Protectionism is on the rise rather than on the decline.

变兵 biànbīng mutinous troops; mutineers; rebels

变产 biànchǎn ❶ sell off one's property: ～兴学 sell off one's property to set up schools ❷ realize one's assets: ～利益 gain on realization of assets / ～清算 realization and liquidation

变成 biànchéng change into; turn into; become: 这事～了一个相当严重的问题。This has become a pretty serious problem. / 不到十年功夫, 小镇～了一个工业城市。In less than ten years, the small town has been transformed into an industrial city. / 经过长期战争, 这座城市已～了废墟。Long years of war have reduced the city to ruins.

变磁性 biàncíxìng 〈物理〉 metamagnetism

变蛋 biàndàn (another name for 松花 sōnghuā) preserved egg

变电站 biàndiànzhàn transformer substation

变调 biàndiào ❶ 〈语言〉 tonal modification (referring to a character's change of tone in a specific context, e.g. when two characters of the falling-rising tone are joined together, the first one is pronounced with a rising tone) ❷ *also* "转调" zhuǎndiào 〈音乐〉 modulation; change to another tune: F调太高, 请～。Note F is too high; please change to another note. / 他这次讲话～了。〈比喻〉 He sang a different tune this time.

变动 biàndòng ❶ (usu. of social phenomena) change: 人事～ personnel changes / 近来国际形势发生了很大～。The world situation has undergone a great change recently. ❷ change; alter; modify: 文字上作一些～ make some changes (*or* alterations) in the wording / 任务

~了。We've got a different task now. *or* Our assignment has changed.

变动成本 biàndòng chéngběn variable costs

变法 biànfǎ 〈历史〉political reform; institutional reform: 王安石~ reforms initiated by Wang Anshi of the Song Dynasty / ~维新 constitutional reform and modernization (1898) / ~自强 initiate political reform and self-strengthening; build up strength through political reform

B

变法儿 biànfǎr try different ways; try in a thousand and one ways: 食堂总是~把伙食搞得好一些。The cooks at the canteen try various ways to provide better food. / 只要动脑筋,不会变不出法儿来。If you think seriously about it, you'll be able to find a way out. / 他变着法儿挑她的毛病。He is always trying one way or another to find fault with her.

变分 biànfēn 〈数学〉variation: ~方程 variation equation / ~法 variational method; calculus of variations

变幅 biànfú range of variation: 光~ range of light-variation / 这里雨量~很大,往往在两年相差七百毫米以上。The yearly rainfall registered here varies greatly. The difference can be as much as over 700mm.

变革 biàngé ❶ change; transform: 社会~ social change / ~社会制度 change (*or* transform) the social system / ~自然 transform nature / 这是我国发生伟大~的一年。This is a year of great historic change for our country. ❷〈地质〉revolution

变格 biàngé 〈语言〉declension

变更 biàngēng change; alter; modify: ~作息时间 alter the daily timetable / 今年的年度计划要作一些~。We have to modify our plan for this year. / 修订版的内容有些~。Some changes have been made in the contents of the revised edition.

变工 biàngōng exchange work or labour: ~队 work-exchange team (an agricultural producers' mutual-aid organization)

变宫 biàngōng 〈音乐〉7th of the 7-tone scale in ancient Chinese music, lower by a half tone than *gong* (宫)

变故 biàngù unforeseen event; catastrophe; misfortune: 突遭~ be overtaken by misfortune / 发生了~。Something quite unexpected has happened.

变卦 biànguà change one's mind; go back on one's word; break one's promise: 昨天他同意来的,可他今天~了。Yesterday he agreed to come, but he changed his mind today. / 说好的事,怎么可以~呢? How could you go back on what you've agreed to?

变化 biànhuà change; vary: 化学~ chemical change / 天气~无常 changeable (*or* capricious) weather / 他的战术~多端。His tactics are varied. / 此人情绪~无常。He is moody and unpredictable.

变幻 biànhuàn change irregularly; fluctuate: ~不定的天气 fickle (*or* changeable) weather / 在风云~中,不要迷失方向。You must not lose your bearings in the fast-changing (*or* volatile) situation. / 谈判前途~莫测。The prospect of the negotiations is full of uncertainties.

变换 biànhuàn ❶ vary; alternate: ~速度 vary the speed / ~手法 change one's tactics / ~位置 shift one's position / 季节~ alternation of the seasons / 你应该~一下食谱。You should alter your diet. ❷〈数学〉transform: ~系数 transformation coefficient

变计 biànjì ❶ change the plan; alter tactics ❷〈书面〉emergency plan

变加速度 biànjiāsùdù 〈物理〉varying acceleration: ~运动 varying accelerated motion

变价 biànjià appraise at the current rate: 这些冰箱将~出售。These refrigerators will be sold at the current price.

变焦距 biànjiāojù *also* "变焦"〈摄影〉zoom; varifocal: ~镜头 zoom lens; varifocal lens / ~摄影 zoom shot / ~摄像机 zoom camera

变节 biànjié betray one's country; recant one's faith; turn one's coat: ~行为 act of betrayal; treachery / ~分子 recanter; traitor; renegade; turncoat

变晶 biànjīng 〈物理〉metacryst

变局 biànjú fluid situation; changing or volatile situation; sudden turn of events; emergency: 应付~ cope with the changing situation (*or* sudden turn of events)

变口 biànkǒu 〈戏曲〉(in northern folk art) variant tone; use of various dialects

变例 biànlì departure from a normal course; variant; aberration

变脸 biànliǎn ❶ turn hostile: 我要他信守自己的诺言,他当即~了。As I tried to hold him to his promise, his face darkened instantly. / 两兄弟为了父亲遗产~了。The two brothers fell out over their father's legacy. ❷〈戏曲〉change facial expression rapidly (to show extreme anger, fear, etc.)

变量 biànliàng 〈数学〉variable: ~分析 variable analysis / ~空间 variable space

变量泵 biànliàngbèng 〈机械〉variable displacement pump

变量函数 biànliàng hánshù 〈数学〉variable function

变流器 biànliúqì 〈电工〉converter

变率 biànlǜ variation ratio

变乱 biànluàn ❶ turmoil; social upheaval: 他们都是政治~的牺牲品。They were all victims of the political turmoil. ❷〈书面〉plunge into chaos; create disturbance: 他们的意图是~局势,以求一逞。Their intention was to plunge the land into chaos so as to further their own interests.

变卖 biànmài sell off (one's property): 他需要现金,便~了房产。He sold off his estate for he was in need of cash.

变频 biànpín 〈电子〉frequency conversion: ~管 converter tube

变频器 biànpínqì 〈电工〉frequency converter

变迁 biànqiān changes; vicissitudes: 时代~ changes of the times / 人生~ vicissitudes of life

变色 biànsè ❶ change colour; discolour: 这种漆不会~。This kind of paint will not change colour. / 这个窗帘晒得~了。The curtain has been discoloured by long exposure to sunlight. ❷ change countenance; show signs of displeasure or anger: 勃然~ suddenly change countenance / 他脸上突然~,发起火来。His face suddenly changed colour and he flew into a rage. *or* He went purple with rage.

变色镜 biànsèjìng sun sensitive glasses

变色龙 biànsèlóng ❶〈动物〉chameleon ❷ person who switches loyalty frequently; chameleon: 他是个毫无主见的~。He is a chameleon with no definite convictions of his own.

变色漆 biànsèqī paint which changes colour with the change of temperature

变生肘腋 biànshēng-zhǒuyè incident occurring close at hand: 这种乱子,往往~,无从预防。It is difficult to guard against those troubles which often occur suddenly at close quarters.

变声 biànshēng adolescent change of voice

变石 biànshí alexandrite

变数 biànshù ❶〈数学〉variable: 常数与~ constants and variables ❷ variable factor; variable: 新的~ new variable

变速 biànsù 〈机械〉speed change; gearshift: ~图解 gear shifting diagram / ~扫描 variable-speed scanning

变速比 biànsùbǐ 〈汽车〉gear ratio

变速杆 biànsùgǎn gear shift bar or lever

变速轮 biànsùlún change wheel; variable-speed wheel gear

变速器 biànsùqì change gear

变速系数 biànsù xìshù coefficient of variation in speed

变速箱 biànsùxiāng gear box

变速运动 biànsù yùndòng 〈物理〉variable motion

变态 biàntài ❶〈生物〉metamorphosis: 完全~ complete metamorphosis ❷〈生物〉deformation; anomaly ❸ abnormal; anomalous; aberrant: ~心理 aberrant personality / ~行为 abnormal act

变态反应 biàntài fǎnyìng 〈医学〉allergy: 她患气喘病,对花粉有~。She is a victim of asthma and is allergic to pollen.

变态心理学 biàntài xīnlǐxué abnormal psychology

变体 biàntǐ ❶ variant: 字的~ variant of a character ❷〈天主教〉transubstantiation

变天 biàntiān ❶ change of weather: 我感到要~了。I smell a change in the weather. ❷〈比喻〉restoration of reactionary rule; comeback: 梦想~ dream of staging a comeback

变天账 biàntiānzhàng accounts of confiscated properties, abolished usurious debts, etc., kept secretly for recovery after a comeback

变通 biàntong be flexible; make changes according to specific conditions; stretch a point: ~办法 accommodation; modus vivendi / 根据情况对规定作些~ accommodate one's regulations to specific conditions / 你不能为我~一下吗? Can't you stretch a point (*or* stretch it a bit) in my case?

变为 biànwéi become; turn into; change into: 把荒漠~绿色的原野 turn a desert into an oasis

变位 biànwèi 〈地质〉shift; dislocation; 〈语言〉conjugation; 〈数学〉deflection

变味 biànwèi (as of food) go bad: 昨天做的菜~了。The dish cooked yesterday has gone bad.

变温层 biànwēncéng *also* "对流层" duìliúcéng 〈气象〉tropo-

sphere

变温动物 biànwēn dòngwù poikilothermal or cold-blooded animal

变文 biànwén popular form of narrative literature flourishing in the Tang Dynasty, with alternate prose and rhymed lines for recitation and singing (often on Buddhist themes)

变戏法 biàn xìfǎ perform conjuring tricks; conjure; juggle; do by sleight of hand:～的瞒不了敲锣的〈谚语〉the magician can fool the audience but not the gong-beater standing behind him — people in the know are not to be fooled

变现 biànxiàn 〈商业〉realization:～价值 cash realization value /～能力 cashability; marketability

变相 biànxiàng in disguised form; covert:～贪污 disguised form of corruption /～体罚 corporal punishment in disguise /～剥削行为 covert act of exploitation /～贸易壁垒 covert trade barrier

变心 biànxīn transfer one's affection to another person; break faith:也许他的女朋友～了。Maybe, his girlfriend has jilted (*or* ditched) him.

变星 biànxīng 〈天文〉variable star

变形 biànxíng ❶ be out of shape; become deformed:她的身材～了。She has lost her shape. /我的新帽子被坐得～了。My new hat was sat on and has been crushed out of shape. /病人的脊椎骨已经～。The patient's spine is deformed. ❷〈物理〉deformation; distortion:～观测 deformation observation /～纠正 rectification of distortion ❸ change from human into nonhuman shape and vice versa; metamorphosis

变形虫 biànxíngchóng amoeba:～痢疾 amoebic dysentry

变形动物 biànxíng dòngwù amoebula

变形金刚 biànxíng jīngāng anamorphic king kong, a kind of plastic or metal toy

变形体 biànxíngtǐ 〈动物〉plasmodium

变形温度 biànxíng wēndù distortion temperature

变形仪 biànxíngyí deformeter

变型 biànxíng change category or type; change into a different type or category:这么大个工厂,转轨～谈何容易! It is easier said than done to change the management and category of such a big factory totally.

变性 biànxìng ❶〈化学〉denaturation:～蛋白质 denatured protein ❷ change sex by surgical means

变性酒精 biànxìng jiǔjīng denatured alcohol

变性人 biànxìngrén transsexual

变性手术 biànxìng shǒushù transsexual operation

变性土 biànxìngtǔ 〈地质〉vertisol

变压 biànyā 〈电工〉voltage transformation:～比 transformation ratio /～发电机 varying-voltage generator

变压器 biànyāqì 〈电工〉transformer:电源～ main transformer /降压～ step-down transformer /升压～ step-up transformer /输出～ output transformer /输入～ input transformer /～容量 transformer capacity /～进线套管 transformer bushing /～空载损耗 transformer no-load losses

变样 biànyàng change in appearance or shape; become different:几年没见,他还没～。He hasn't changed a bit since we met a few years ago.

变叶木 biànyèmù 〈植物〉croton (*Codiaeum variegatum*)

变异 biànyì 〈生物〉variation:～性 variability /～系数 coefficient of variation

变易 biànyì change; alter; modify:这些规章制度不可随意～。These regulations must not be changed at will.

变造 biànzào forge; falsify; tamper with (documents, certificates, etc.):～记录 tamper with records /使用～过的身分证 use a forged identity card.

变址存取 biànzhǐ cúnqǔ 〈计算机〉indexed access

变徵 biànzhǐ 〈音乐〉4th of the 7-tone scale in ancient Chinese music, lower by a half tone than *zhi* (徵) which is a note of the ancient Chinese five-tone scale

变质 biànzhì ❶ go bad; deteriorate:这罐头～了。The canned food has gone bad. /牛奶～了。The milk has turned sour. /他已蜕化～了。He has become morally degenerate. ❷〈地质〉metamorphism:～岩 metamorphic rock /～地质学 metamorphic geology

变质处理 biànzhì chǔlǐ 〈冶金〉modification

变种 biànzhǒng ❶〈生物〉mutation; variety:鸽子的各种～ variant types of pigeon ❷ variant; variety:机会主义的～ variety of opportunism /变石是金绿宝石的～。Alexandrite is a variant of chrysoberyl.

变子 biànzǐ 〈物理〉varitron

变奏 biànzòu 〈音乐〉variation

变奏曲 biànzòuqǔ 〈音乐〉variation

变阻器 biànzǔqì 〈电工〉rheostat

遍(徧)

biàn ❶ all over; everywhere:朋友～天下 have friends all over the world /喜讯传～全村。The good news spread throughout the village. ❷〈量词〉(denoting an action from beginning to end) time:这本书我仔细读过两～。I've carefully read the book twice through. /他一～又一～地修改这篇文章。He polished the article again and again.

遍布 biànbù spread all over; be located or found everywhere:通讯网～全国。Communication networks are spread all over the country. /图书馆～全省。Libraries can be found everywhere in the province.

遍地 biàndì everywhere; all around; all over the place:～冰雪。The ground was covered with snow and ice. /牧场上～是牛羊。There are cattle and sheep all over the ranch.

遍地开花 biàndì-kāihuā blossom everywhere; bloom everywhere:乡镇工业～。Township industries have sprung up like mushrooms.

遍及 biànjí spread all over; reach everywhere:～世界各个角落 reach all corners of the world; extend to all quarters of the earth /这一事件的影响～全球。The impact of this incident is felt worldwide.

遍历 biànlì visit all places:～祖国各少数民族地区 visit all the major areas inhabited by ethnic minority groups of China

遍体鳞伤 biàntǐ-línshāng be covered all over with cuts and bruises; be beaten black and blue; be a mass of bruises:他被打得～。He was beaten black and blue.

遍野 biànyě all over the fields; everywhere in the fields; all around the fields:漫山～ all over the hills and fields /庄稼～,一望无际。There is an endless stretch of crops growing all over the fields.

遍于 biànyú everywhere; all over; all around:～全国 all over the country /练太极拳者～城乡。Everywhere in the country, whether in the city or in the countryside, you find people who practise *taijiquan*

艑

biàn 〈书面〉boat; ship

便[1]

biàn ❶ convenient; handy:日夜服务,顾客称～。Customers consider the round-the-clock service very convenient. /这箱子～于携带。The suitcase is easy to carry. /手续简～。The formalities required are simple. ❷ when an opportunity arises; when it is convenient:悉听尊～ suit your own convenience; act at your own discretion; do as you please /得～请来一叙。Drop round and have a chat whenever it's convenient. /你去邮局时就～给我买点邮票来。Please get me some stamps when you go to the post office. /他一时手头不～。He is running short of money (*or* cash) for the moment. ❸ informal; plain; ordinary:～酌候教。I request your gracious presence at an informal dinner. *or* I'll give an informal dinner in your honour. ❹ piss or shit; urine or stool:粪～ excrement; night soil ❺ excrete; relieve oneself:小～ piss; urinate /大～ shit; defecate; evacuate bowels

便[2]

biàn ❶〈副词〉*used in the same way as* 就 *but more formal*:早在50年代我们～认识了。We got acquainted as early as the 50's. /火车开出不久,天～亮了。It dawned soon after the train left the station. /一点～通。He understands the moment you drop a hint. /只要经常锻炼,身体～会强健。You'll keep fit so long as you keep on exercising. ❷〈连词〉*indicating a hypothetical concession*:你～不说,我们也知道。We know everything even though you don't tell us. /～是我输了,也不会介意的。Even if I lose the game, I won't mind.

see also pián

便步 biànbù walk at ease; stroll:我抬头一看,只见王教授正向我～走来。Raising my head, I saw Professor Wang strolling towards me.

便步走 biànbùzǒu 〈军事〉march at ease; route step:～! At ease, march! *or* Route step, march!

便菜 biàncài homely or simple dishes

便餐 biàncān ❶ potluck; simple meal; informal dinner:家常～

simple home meal /今晚在我们这儿吃顿～吧。Please stay and have potluck with us tonight if you don't mind. ❷ have an informal dinner:我们昨晚在饭馆～。We had an informal dinner at a restaurant yesterday evening.

便车 biànchē car in which one can have a free ride:搭乘～去某地 hitchhike one's way to a place; get a lift to a place

便池 biànchí urinal; toilet bowl

便当 biàndang convenient; handy; easy:我家附近商店多,买东西很～。My home is quite handy (*or* convenient) for the shops. /折叠桌用起来很～。A folding table is very convenient.

便道 biàndào ❶ shortcut:抄～走 take a shortcut ❷ pavement; sidewalk:行人走～。Pedestrians walk on the pavement. ❸ makeshift road

便地 biàndì 〈书面〉favourable terrain:敌军已先据～。The enemy has already occupied the favourable terrain of the area.

便殿 biàndiàn palace for emperor's rest or feasting

便毒 biàndú 〈中医〉bubo (in the groin)

便饭 biànfàn ❶ daily food; simple meal:家常～ home-style food; homely meal ❷ have informal dinner:明天请来我家～。Please come and have potluck with us tomorrow.

便服 biànfú ❶ everyday clothes; informal dress ❷ civilian clothes; civvies; mufti:穿～的士兵 soldier in mufti (*or* civvies) /他星期日不穿军装,穿～。He wears civilian clothes instead of an army uniform on Sundays.

便函 biànhán short non-official letter

便壶 biànhú bed urinal; chamber pot

便家 biànjiā 〈旧语〉wealthy family

便笺 biànjiān ❶ note ❷ notepaper:一张～ sheet of notepaper /～本 notepad; memo pad

便捷 biànjié ❶ direct and simple; convenient; easy:机构一精简,办事～多了。With the administrative structure streamlined, it's easier to get business done. ❷ nimble; agile:穿运动服,行动～。It's easier to move about in sportswear. *or* Sportswear allows freedom of movement.

便坑 biànkēng stool pit

便览 biànlǎn brief guide:旅游～ tourist guide /交通～ roadbook

便利 biànlì ❶ convenient; easy:交通～ have good transport facilities; boast good transport service; be conveniently located or situated /为乘客提供～ offer good service to passengers /在这里办工厂有许多～条件。There are many advantages in setting up a factory here. *or* Conditions are favourable for setting up a factory here. ❷ facilitate; render service to:为了～居民,这里新盖了一个百货商店。A new department store has been built here for the convenience of the residents. /日夜商店～群众。A shop that is open round the clock is very convenient for the public.

便了 biànliǎo 〈助词〉(often used in the early vernacular) *used at the end of a sentence to indicate determination, promise or concession*:如有损失,由我承担～。I'll bear any loss all right.

便路 biànlù ❶ shortcut:走～ take a shortcut ❷ convenient route:我上班～送你回家。I'll drive you home on my way to work.

便帽 biànmào (informal) cap

便门 biànmén side door; wicket door:请走～。Go through the side door, please.

便秘 biànmì *also* "便闭"〈医学〉constipation

便民 biànmín for the benefit of the people:～措施 measures benefiting the people /～商店 general store catering to the needs of the community (*or* neighbourhood); convenience store

便溺 biànniào ❶ relieve oneself; answer the call of nature ❷ excrement

便盆 biànpén bedpan

便器 biànqì (bed) urinal; chamber pot; bedpan; water closet or lavatory pan

便签 biànqiān ❶ written message; brief note; memo ❷ notepaper; memo pad; note pad; scribble pad

便桥 biànqiáo temporary or makeshift bridge:小河上搭了个～。A makeshift bridge was put up on the river.

便人 biànrén sb. who can conveniently do a job for sb. else:如有～,我会给你捎点水果去。I'll send you some fruit by someone who goes your way.

便士 biànshì penny:一百～为一英镑。A hundred pence makes a pound.

便所 biànsuǒ lavatory; toilet

便条 biàntiáo (informal) note:她走时留下～说一星期后才能回来。She left a note saying that she would be away for a week.

便桶 biàntǒng commode; chamber pot

便席 biànxí homely meal; simple dinner

便携式 biànxiéshì portable:～打字机 portable typewriter /～电视机 portable TV set /～电台 portable radio station /～穿孔机 port-a-punch /～退休金 portable pension

便携式充气房屋 biànxiéshì chōngqì fángwū portable aerated house

便携式电视摄像机 biànxiéshì diànshì shèxiàngjī portable television camera; walkie-lookie; creepie-peepie

便携式电源 biànxiéshì diànyuán portable power supply unit

便携式计算机 biànxiéshì jìsuànjī portable computer; laptop

便携式雷达 biànxiéshì léidá 〈军事〉portable radar

便携式收发两用机 biànxiéshì shōu-fā liǎngyòngjī 〈无线电〉hand transmitter-receiver

便鞋 biànxié cloth shoes; slippers

便血 biànxiě 〈医学〉have or pass blood in one's stool; hematochezia

便宴 biànyàn informal dinner:设～招待 give a dinner for sb.

便衣 biànyī ❶ civilian clothes; plainclothes:～警察 plainclothes detective ❷ plainclothesman

便宜 biànyí convenient; handy

see also piányi

便宜行事 biànyí-xíngshì act at one's discretion; act as one sees fit:这次采购,你可～。You can make purchases at your discretion this time.

便于 biànyú be easy to; be convenient for:～计算 be easy to calculate; be easily calculable /把数据输入电脑,以～查找。Input the data to facilitate their retrieval.

便纸 biànzhǐ toilet tissue; toilet paper

便中 biànzhōng at one's convenience; when it's convenient:～请告知。Please let me know at your convenience. /我替你捎来一个包裹,望～来取。I've brought you a parcel. Please collect it when it's convenient for you.

便装 biànzhuāng *see* "便服"

便酌 biànzhuó informal dinner:聊备～,恭候光临。Your gracious presence is requested at an informal dinner to be given in your honour.

缏

biàn *used in* "草帽缏" cǎomàobiàn (plaited straw)

see also pián

弁

biàn ❶ man's cap worn in ancient times ❷〈旧语〉low-ranking military officer:马～ (officer's) bodyguard

弁髦 biànmáo 〈书面〉❶ worthless stuff; dirt:有法不依,～而已。The law is worthless if it is not followed. ❷ despise; scorn:～法令 contempt of law /～荣华 spurn worldly honours and comfort

弁言 biànyán 〈书面〉foreword; preface

昪

biàn 〈书面〉❶ bright ❷ joyful; merry

biāo

瀌

biāo

瀌瀌 biāobiāo 〈书面〉heavy (rain or snow)

藨

biāo

藨草 biāocǎo meadowrush; bulrush; scirpus

镳[1]

biāo 〈书面〉bit (of a bridle); curb bit:分道扬～ separate and go different ways

镳[2]

biāo *see* "镖" biāo

穮(穮)

biāo 〈书面〉weeding

标(標)

biāo ❶〈书面〉tip or top of a tree; treetop:松～ tip of a pine tree ❷ outward sign; symptom; superficiality:治～

不如治本 seek a permanent cure rather than temporary relief (*or* a temporary solution) ❸ mark; sign:商～ trade mark /航～ navigation mark /路～ road sign /浮～ buoy /风向～ or 风～ weathercock; weather vane; wind vane /岸～ shore beacon /水位～ water level stake (*or* marking) /草～儿 wisp of straw marking sth. for sale /音～ phonetic symbol; phonetic transcription /立旗为～ set up a flag as a mark ❹ standard; requirement; quota:达～ reach the standard; meet the requirement; fulfil the quota ❺ put a mark, tag or label on; mark; label:～界 delimit a boundary /在那一页～了几个记号 make several marks on that page /在地图上把这个地方～出来。Mark the place on the map. /这些货物还没～价钱。These goods have not been priced yet. *or* We haven't put price tags on these goods. /瓶子上～着"有毒"字样。The bottle was labelled "poison". ❻ prize; award:夺～ compete for first prize; win the championship /足球锦～赛 football championships ❼ tender; bid:开～ open sealed tenders /该公司决定投～修这个体育馆。The firm decided to bid (*or* make a tender) for the new stadium. /一家美国公司中～。An American company won the contract through bidding. ❽〈军事〉regiment in the Qing Dynasty ❾〈量词〉*used only with the numeral* 一:一～人马 a detachment of troops; a group of soldiers

标榜 biāobǎng ❶ brag about; parade; flaunt; advertise:～学术自由 brag about academic freedom /～自由平等 flaunt the banner of liberty and equality ❷ boost; excessively praise:互相～ boost each other; exchange excessive praise; practise logrolling; scratch each other's back /自我～ blow one's own trumpet; sing one's own praises /～自己是一位慈善家 advertise oneself as a philanthropist

标本 biāoběn ❶ root cause and symptoms:～兼治 treat a disease by looking into both its root cause and symptoms; seek both a temporary solution and a permanent cure ❷ specimen; sample:昆虫～ insect specimen /动物～ zoological specimen /植物～ botanical specimen /血液～〈医学〉sample of sb.'s blood /取～ take a sample (of sth.)/他采集各种岩石和矿物～。He collects specimens of various kinds of rocks and minerals. ❸ representative; sample:苏州园林是中国园林的一个～。Suzhou gardens are representative of Chinese gardening.

标本虫 biāoběnchóng 〈动物〉spider beetle

标兵 biāobīng ❶ parade guard (usu. spaced out along a parade route) ❷ example; role model; pacesetter:被树为～ be cited as a pacesetter

标兵线 biāobīngxiàn line of markers

标称 biāochēng specifications written on a product

标尺 biāochǐ ❶〈测量〉surveyor's rod; staff ❷〈水利〉staff gauge ❸ (common name for 表尺)〈军事〉rear sight

标灯 biāodēng signal light; beacon light; beacon:船尾有一盏讯号～。There is a signal light at the stern of the ship. /邮局门口安了一盏玻璃～,上有"夜间电报"四个字。At the gate of the post office there is a glass lamp marked "Night Cable".

标底 biāodǐ bottom price of a bid

标的 biāodì ❶ target ❷ aim; purpose ❸ common objectives of both parties to a commercial contract with regard to their rights and duties in the execution of the project

标点 biāodiǎn ❶ punctuation:这篇文章的～有错误。There are misuses of punctuation in this article. *or* There is something wrong with the punctuation of the essay. ❷ punctuate:请给这篇古文～。Please punctuate this piece of classical writing.

标点符号 biāodiǎn fúhào punctuation (mark)

标定 biāodìng ❶ fix (a certain number or type) as standard; calibrate ❷ standard testing:车间成立了技术小组,对装置进行了～。A technical team was set up in the workshop to conduct standard testing of the device. ❸ fix by given criteria or agreement; demarcate:～边界线 demarcate a boundary by setting up boundary markers (done jointly by the two countries concerned) ❹ standard; normal:～型自行车 standard (type) bicycle

标定曲线 biāodìng qūxiàn rating curve

标定数据 biāodìng shùjù rating or nominal data

标度 biāodù 〈数学〉scale

标度比 biāodùbǐ scale ratio

标度变数 biāodù biànshù scale variable

标度点 biāodùdiǎn scale point

标度方程 biāodù fāngchéng scale equation

标度盘 biāodùpán scaleplate; dial (plate)

标度值 biāodùzhí scale value

标杆 biāogān ❶〈测量〉surveyor's pole ❷ example for others to follow; model:这个石油钻探队是全国著名的～队。This oil drilling team is a pacesetter, well-known throughout the country.

标高 biāogāo 〈测量〉elevation; level:～测量 level measurement

标格 biāogé 〈书面〉character; style:～甚高 noble in character

标号 biāohào ❶ grade:水泥～ grade of cement /高～水泥 high-grade cement ❷ marks and symbols

标徽 biāohuī sign; mark; insignia

标会 biāohuì *also* "合会" héhuì mutual aid society whose members contribute money to help each other in turn

标绘 biāohuì mark; indicate:在军用地图上～双方兵力部署 indicate on a military map the troop dispositions of both sides

标记 biāojì sign; mark; symbol:在树上作个～,以免我们回来时迷路。Make a mark on the tree so that we won't get lost on our way back. /他臂上缠的那条红布是纠察队员的～。The red armband he wears is the symbol of a picket.

标记基因 biāojì jīyīn marker gene

标记原子 biāojì yuánzǐ *also* "示踪原子" shìzōng yuánzǐ labelled atom; tracer

标记阅读器 biāojì yuèdúqì 〈计算机〉badge reader

标价 biāojià mark a price; price:明码～ at a marked price /毛衣还没～。The woollen sweaters remain to be priced. /这件大衣的～是100 元。The coat is priced at 100 *yuan*.

标金 biāojīn ❶ deposit or bond for a bid ❷ gold bar on which the weight and the percentage of gold are marked

标举 biāojǔ 〈书面〉❶ indicate; reveal; show ❷ superb; great

标量 biāoliàng 〈物理〉scalar (quantity):～场〈数学〉scalar field /～流 scalar current /～电导 scalar conductivity

标卖 biāomài ❶ put on sale at a marked price ❷ sell by auction

标明 biāomíng mark; indicate:军长用红铅笔在地图上～了行军路线。The army commander marked the trail route of the march in red pencil on a map.

标牌 biāopái trade mark; logo

标盘 biāopán 〈商业〉bidding quotation

标旗 biāoqí guide flag; marking flag

标签 biāoqiān label; tag:价目～ price tag /在磁盘上贴～ stick a label on the floppy disk

标枪 biāoqiāng javelin:掷～ javelin throw /～运动员 javelin-thrower

标石 biāoshí markstone; marker

标示 biāoshì mark; indicate:～牌 sign post; marker /他用笔在地图上划出了一道红线,～队伍可以从这里通过。He drew a red line on the map, indicating where the troops could pass through.

标售 biāoshòu sell by tender; put a price-tag on sth. for sale

标书 biāoshū ❶ (papers for) invitation to bidding ❷ bidding papers

标题 biāotí title; heading; headline; caption:通栏大字～ banner headline; banner /小～ subheading; crosshead /醒目的～ bold headlines

标题关键词 biāotí guānjiàncí key word out of title

标题音乐 biāotí yīnyuè programme music

标统 biāotǒng 〈军事〉〈旧语〉commander of a *biao* (corresponding to a regiment) in the Qing army

标图 biāotú make marks on a military map, nautical chart or synoptic chart, etc.; plot

标图器 biāotúqì plotter

标图员 biāotúyuán plotter

标下 biāoxià 〈军事〉〈旧语〉❶ my men or troops (used by Qing commanders of governor's rank) ❷ your subordinate (used by a Qing army officer in reference to himself while speaking or writing to his superior)

标箱 biāoxiāng box of specified size for transport of commodities; standardized box:两～建筑材料 two standard-sized boxes of building materials

标新立异 biāoxīn-lìyì put forward novel ideas to show one is different from the ordinary run; do sth. unconventional or unorthodox; create sth. new and original; start sth. new in order to be different:他故意要～,受到了批评。He came in for a lot of criticism for straining after novelty.

标样 biāoyàng sample:服装～ garment sample

标音 biāoyīn mark with phonetic symbols; transcribe:宽式～ broad transcription /严式～ narrow transcription

B

标语 biāoyǔ slogan; poster: 张贴～ put up slogans (*or* posters)
标语牌 biāoyǔpái placard
标语塔 biāoyǔtǎ slogan pylon
标志 biāozhì *also* "标识" ❶ sign; mark; symbol; hallmark: 地图上的～ mark (*or* sign) on a map / 公路沿线竖立着各种交通～。Various traffic signs stand along the highway. ❷ indicate; mark; symbolize: 这个纪念碑～着人们对先烈的怀念。This monument indicates that the people cherish the memory of the martyrs. / 中华人民共和国的成立～着中国一个历史新阶段的开始。The founding of the People's Republic of China marked the beginning of a new historical period in China.
标志层 biāozhìcéng marker bed
标志服 biāozhìfú uniform
标志基因 biāozhì jīyīn 〈生物〉 marker gene
标致 biāozhì (usu. of women) beautiful; pretty: 新娘子长得很～。The bride is very pretty. / 她～的面孔微微一红。Her handsome face flushed slightly.
标桩 biāozhuāng marker; marker pile; stake: 栽～ plant a marker pile
标准 biāozhǔn ❶ standard; criterion: 合乎～ up to standard / 按照国际～ by international standards / 实践是检验真理的惟一～。Practice is the sole criterion of truth. ❷ standard; standardized: ～部件 standardized component; standard part / ～产品 standardized product / ～合同 standard contract; form contract; model contract / ～条款 standard terms / ～制 metric system
标准层 biāozhǔncéng index bed; marker bed; key bed
标准产业贸易分类 biāozhǔn chǎngyè màoyì fēnlèi *also* "标准工业贸易等级" Standard Industrial Trade Classification (SITC)
标准大气压 biāozhǔn dàqìyā 〈物理〉 standard atmosphere
标准大气压力 biāozhǔn dàqì yālì 〈物理〉 normal atmospheric pressure
标准电阻 biāozhǔn diànzǔ 〈电学〉 standard resistance
标准度量衡 biāozhǔn dùliánghéng standard weights and measures
标准粉 biāozhǔnfěn standard wheat flour (about 85% of dry wheat grain)
标准工资 biāozhǔn gōngzī standard wage
标准公顷 biāozhǔn gōngqǐng standard hectare (basic unit for measuring work done by a farming machine, e. g. a tractor)
标准化 biāozhǔnhuà standardize: ～程序 standardization programme / 汽车零件是～了的。The parts of an automobile are standardized.
标准件 biāozhǔnjiàn 〈机械〉 standard part; standard component
标准局 biāozhǔnjú bureau of standards
标准空间发射系统 biāozhǔn kōngjiān fāshè xìtǒng SSLS (standardized space launch system)
标准亩 biāozhǔnmǔ ❶ unit of cultivated land for agricultural taxation ❷ basic unit for measuring the work load of a tractor or combine
标准气压 biāozhǔn qìyā 〈气象〉 standard pressure
标准生成标示语言 biāozhǔn shēngchéng biāoshì yǔyán 〈信息〉 standard generalized mark-up language (SGML)
标准时 biāozhǔnshí standard time
标准时区 biāozhǔn shíqū *also* "时区" shíqū time zone
标准台 biāozhǔntái 〈农机〉 standard unit of tractor (i. e. 15 horsepower): 他们拥有二十～拖拉机。The tractors they own amount to 20 standard units. *or* They have tractors totalling 300 horsepower.
标准特许银行 Biāozhǔn Tèxǔ Yínháng (UK) Standard Chartered Bank
标准像 biāozhǔnxiàng official portrait
标准型 biāozhǔnxíng standard pattern or type
标准音 biāozhǔnyīn standard pronunciation
标准语 biāozhǔnyǔ standard speech
标注 biāozhù mark

瘭 biāo

瘭疽 biāojū 〈中医〉 pyogenic infection of the pad of a finger or toe

熛 biāo 〈书面〉 flame

摽 biāo 〈书面〉 ❶ wave off ❷ abandon

see also biào

摽榜 biāobǎng 〈书面〉 brag about; boast
see also "标榜" biāobǎng

幖 biāo 〈书面〉 flag

镖 biāo dartlike weapon: 飞～ flying dart / 梭～ spear / 保～ bodyguard / 走～ 〈旧语〉 serve as a bodyguard on a journey

镖局 biāojú 〈旧语〉 commercial firm for providing armed escort or bodyguards
镖客 biāokè *also* "镖师" 〈旧语〉 armed escort (of travellers or merchants' caravans)
镖鲈 biāolú 〈动物〉 darter
镖师 biāoshī *see* "镖客"
镖头 biāotóu head of escort; chief bodyguard

膘(臕) biāo fat (of an animal): 长～ get fat; put on flesh; flesh out / 落～ (of livestock) become thin / 蹲～ (of livestock, etc.) fatten up in the shed / ～厚 thick layer of fat (in an animal carcas)

膘膘楞楞 biāobiao-lēnglēng 〈方言〉 ❶ (of the human body) sturdy; brawny; strong: 这个～的小伙子，是地里干活的好把式。This sturdy young chap works like a horse in the fields. ❷ rash and impetuous; blunt: 他说话～，就是不长心眼儿。He always speaks bluntly and without thinking.
膘肥 biāoféi (of animals) brawny and sturdy: 车上拴着三头～粗壮的骡子。Harnessed to the cart were three brawny, sturdy mules.
膘情 biāoqíng how an animal is, esp. with regard to its brawn or fat: 雪灾后，牛群～不好。The cattle got thinner after the snowstorm.
膘实 biāoshi (of an animal) sturdy: 这匹马很～，跑起来像飞似的。This horse is strong and sturdy and gallops like the wind.
膘壮 biāozhuàng *see* "膘肥"

骠 biāo *see* "黄骠马" huángbiāomǎ

see also piào

骠实 biāoshi *see* "膘实" biāoshi

猋 biāo 〈书面〉 ❶ rapid ❷ *see* "飙" biāo

飙(飇、飈) biāo 〈书面〉 very strong wind; hurricane; whirlwind: 狂～ hurricane

飙车 biāochē 〈方言〉 drive a car at top speed; speed
飙风 biāofēng 〈书面〉 strong wind; gale: ～暴雨 tempest; rainstorm; hurricane

彪 biāo ❶ 〈书面〉 young tiger: 虎～～ strapping; full of vigour ❷ 〈书面〉 stripes of a tiger; 〈比喻〉 literary talent ❸ 〈量词〉 *used only with the numeral* 一: 一～人马 a detachment of troops ❹ (Biāo) a surname

彪炳 biāobǐng 〈书面〉 shining; splendid: ～显赫的历史功绩 splendid historic achievement
彪炳千古 biāobǐng-qiāngǔ shine through the ages
彪悍 biāohàn intrepid; doughty; valiant: 粗犷～ rough and intrepid
彪形大汉 biāoxíng dàhàn tall and strong man; burly chap; husky fellow: 门口站着一个～。Standing at the gate was a burly fellow.
彪壮 biāozhuàng tall and strong: 身材～ of sturdy build

滮 biāo 〈书面〉 flow of water

飑 biāo squall: 乌云～ black squall

飑线 biāoxiàn 〈气象〉 squall line
飑云 biāoyún 〈气象〉 squall cloud

驫 biāo 〈书面〉 galloping horses

biǎo

褾 biǎo 〈书面〉 ❶ cuff ❷ trimming; braid; hemming

表(❿**錶**) biǎo ❶ surface; outside; external; outward appearance:地~ earth's surface /由~及里 proceed from the outside to the inside; penetrate the surface to get at the essence /虚有其~ look impressive but lack real worth /~壮不如里壮。Inner strength counts more than outward prowess. ❷ relationship between the children or grand-children of a brother and a sister or of sisters:~姨 female cousin of one's mother /~叔伯 male cousins of one's father ❸ show; express; demonstrate:~决心 express one's determination /~一~心意 express one's appreciation /深~同情 show deep sympathy /按下不~。(in traditional story-telling) Let's suspend the narration for a while. ❹〈中医〉administer medicine to draw out the cold:~汗 induce perspiration (by medication); bring about perspiration ❺ model; example ❻ memorial to an emperor usually on an important event or matter:《出师~》(诸葛亮) *Memorial to the Emperor for a Northern Expedition* (by Zhuge Liang) ❼ table; form; list:时间~ timetable; schedule /课~ school timetable /乘法~ multiplication table /登记~ registration form /履历~ curriculum vitae; résumé /价目~ price list /调查~ questionnaire /日程~ schedule /演员~ cast /工资~ payroll /勘误~ errata; corrigenda /略语~ abbreviations ❽〈旧语〉pole used as a sun dial ❾ meter; gauge:温度~ thermometer /湿度~ humidometer /速度~ speedometer /电度~ kilowatt-hour meter; electric meter /水~ water meter /液压~ hydraulic pressure gauge /油压~ oil pressure gauge ❿ watch; clock:手~(wrist) watch /怀~ pocket watch /跑~ stopwatch /马蹄~ hoof-shaped desk clock (*or* alarm clock) /钟~ clocks and watches; time-pieces

表白 biǎobái vindicate; explain oneself; profess:~诚意 vindicate (*or* assert) one's sincerity /发生了这一切之后,就无需~了。After all that (has happened), there's no need for explanation. /他~自己不了解情况。He professed ignorance of the situation. *or* He alleged that he knew nothing about the situation.

表报 biǎobào statistical tables and reports

表笔 biǎobǐ *also* "表棒" test pencil

表册 biǎocè collected statistical forms; book of tables or forms:公文报告~ documents, written reports and statistical forms

表层 biǎocéng surface layer:~结构 surface structure

表尺 biǎochǐ 〈军事〉rear sight:定~ set the rear sight /~座 rear sight base

表处理语言 biǎochǔlǐ yǔyán *also* "LISP 语言"〈信息〉list processing (LISP)

表达 biǎodá express; convey; show; voice:~自己的感情 give expression (*or* voice) to one's feelings /~力 expressiveness; power of expression /~方式 mode of presentation; way of expression; formulation /无法~ be beyond description; words can hardly express (*or* describe) /我真不知道如何~我的感激心情。I hardly know how to express my gratitude. /他的语调比他的语言更能~他的真实感情。His tone conveyed his real feelings better than his words.

表带 biǎodài watchband; watch strap

表弟 biǎodì son of father's sister, or of mother's brother or sister, who is younger than one; younger male cousin

表兜 biǎodōu watch pocket; fob

表高 biǎogāo 〈航空〉indicated altitude

表哥 biǎogē son of father's sister, or of mother's brother or sister, who is older than one; older male cousin

表格 biǎogé form; table:填写~ fill in a form

表功 biǎogōng ❶〈贬义〉boast of one's meritorious service; claim merit for oneself; claim credit for sth.:丑~ brag unabashedly about one's own deeds ❷〈书面〉commend; cite; honour

表观 biǎoguān 〈物理〉apparent:~运动 apparent motion /~质量 apparent mass

表汗 biǎohàn (make) perspire:~药 perspiratory medicine

表号 biǎohào *see* "表字"

表记 biǎojì sth. given as a token; souvenir

表姐 biǎojiě daughter of father's sister, or of mother's brother or sister, who is older than one; older female cousin

表决 biǎojué decide by vote; vote:交付~ put to the vote; take a vote /用无记名投票方式~ vote by secret ballot /举手~ vote by a show of hands /唱名~ vote by roll call; roll-call vote /口头~ voice vote; vote by "yes" and "no" /起立~ vote by sitting and standing (*or* rising) /鼓掌~ vote by acclamation /~机器 voting machine /~指示牌 vote indicator /~通过 adopt by a vote /不经~通过 adopt without a vote /分段~ vote separately on parts of a proposal /~无结果 inconclusive vote /该议案已~通过。The bill has been voted through. /我们将~决定这一问题。We shall vote on the matter.

表决权 biǎojuéquán right to vote; vote:行使~ exercise the right to vote /无~的列席代表 delegate without the right to vote

表壳 biǎoké watchcase

表礼 biǎolǐ 〈旧语〉present given at the first meeting

表里 biǎolǐ ❶ outside and inside; one's outward show and inner thoughts:~不一 think in one way and behave in another; be hypocritical ❷〈中医〉exterior and interior:表热里寒 exterior heat and interior cold

表里如一 biǎolǐ-rúyī think and act in one and the same way; be exactly what one professes to be; say what one means; be honest and straightforward:这个人言行一致,~。The man thinks and acts in the same way, and always practises what he says.

表链 biǎoliàn watch chain

表列部族 biǎoliè bùzú scheduled tribes (of India)

表列种族 biǎoliè zhǒngzú scheduled castes (of India)

表露 biǎolù show; reveal:他一生气,就~在脸上。Whenever he is angry, he shows it on his face. /字里行间,~着作者对生活的热爱。The author reveals his ardent love for life between the lines. /她内心的悲痛一点也没有~出来。She betrayed nothing of the grief that she felt deep down in her heart.

表妹 biǎomèi daughter of aunt or of maternal uncle, younger than one; younger female cousin

表蒙子 biǎoméngzi watch glass; crystal (glass)

表面 biǎomiàn ❶ surface; face:~光洁度 surface finish (quality) /~淬火 surface hardening /地球的~ surface (*or* face) of the earth /桌子~很光滑。The table has a smooth surface. ❷ appearance; superficiality:就~迹象而论 as far as the appearances go /~是人,暗中是鬼 appear an angel but be a demon at heart /我们不能~看问题。We should not take a superficial view of the matter. /她~上对他很客气,实际上意见可大呢。She was on her best behaviour, but in fact she bore many grudges against him. ❸〈方言〉dial plate; dial ❹〈方言〉*see* "表蒙子"

表面波 biǎomiànbō *also* "地波" dìbō 〈无线电〉ground wave; surface wave

表面处理 biǎomiàn chǔlǐ surface treatment

表面光 biǎomiànguāng good in appearance only:产品不能只求~,还要有高质量。We should require not merely good packaging but high product quality as well.

表面化 biǎomiànhuà come to the surface; become apparent; come to a head:矛盾~了。The contradiction has become apparent. *or* The contradiction is coming to a head.

表面活性剂 biǎomiàn huóxìngjì surface active agent

表面积 biǎomiànjī surface area:~渗透率〈冶金〉permeability surface area

表面价值 biǎomiàn jiàzhí face value

表面麻醉 biǎomiàn mázuì 〈医学〉surface anaesthesia

表面图 biǎomiàntú exterior view

表面文章 biǎomiàn wénzhāng mere show; ostentation:要办实事,不要做~。Do something practical instead of caring for mere show (*or* ostentation). /他那番话不过是~。He was merely paying lip service. *or* His remarks were all rhetoric.

表面现象 biǎomiàn xiànxiàng superficial phenomenon:透过~认识事物的本质 discern the essence of things by looking below the superficial phenomenon

表面硬化 biǎomiàn yìnghuà 〈冶金〉case-hardening

表面张力 biǎomiàn zhānglì 〈物理〉surface tension

表明 biǎomíng make known; make clear; indicate:~立场 make known one's position /~态度 make clear one's attitude /~身分 reveal one's identity /~决心 declare one's determination /~意图 disclose one's intention; show one's hand /有迹象~,两国关系即将正常化。There are indications (*or* signs) that the two countries will normalize their relations soon.

表盘 biǎopán dial plate; dial

表皮 biǎopí 〈生物〉epidermis; cuticle

表皮层 biǎopícéng cuticular layer; stratum epidermis

表皮寄生菌 biǎopí jìshēngjūn dermatophyte

表皮炎 biǎopíyán epidermitis

表曝 biǎopù expose; lay bare:阴谋已~在光天化日之下。The plot has been exposed in broad daylight.

B

表亲 biǎoqīn ❶ cousin ❷ cousinship
表情 biǎoqíng ❶ express one's feelings by facial expression or posture:富于～ expressive /他很会～。He knows how to act. ❷ expression; countenance; look:面部～ facial expression /～不自然 look awkward (*or* unnatural, *or* affected); look not quite oneself /他脸上流露出兴奋的～。He looked very excited.
表施 biǎoshī 〈农业〉top application (of fertilizer)
表示 biǎoshì ❶ express; show:～遗憾 express one's regret /～衷心的感谢 express one's sincere thanks; extend one's heartfelt gratitude /～关切 show concern; be deeply concerned /～慰问 convey one's sympathy (*or* solicitude) /～异议 take exception to /点头～同意 nod one's agreement /他迟到了,向我～歉意。He apologized to me for being late. /这只不过～他们对自己缺乏信心。This merely serves to indicate their lack of confidence in themselves. ❷ indication; manifestation:友好的～ manifestation of friendship; friendly gesture / 他没有任何悔改的～。He has shown no sign of repentance. *or* There's no indication that he is mending his ways. /商标上的头骷髅～巨毒。The skeleton on the trade mark indicates deadly poison.
表示层 biǎoshìcéng 〈信息〉presentation layer
表述 biǎoshù present; convey; explain; state:～已见 state one's views; speak one's mind
表率 biǎoshuài example; model:他是全心全意为人民服务的～。He sets an example of wholehearted service to the people.
表速 biǎosù 〈航空〉indicated airspeed
表态 biǎotài make known one's position; declare where one stands:明确～ take a clear-cut stand /作～性发言 make a statement of one's position /他没有～。He does not commit himself. *or* He is non-committal. /发言人的～有保留。The speaker made the statement with some reservations.
表土 biǎotǔ 〈农业〉surface soil; topsoil
表文 biǎowén memorial to the throne
表现 biǎoxiàn ❶ show; display; manifest:～出非凡的勇敢和机智 display extraordinary courage and resourcefulness /～了高度的责任感 manifest a high sense of responsibility /政治是经济的集中～。Politics is the concentrated expression (*or* manifestation) of economics. /我们需要更多的～农村生活的文学作品。We need more literary works depicting country life. ❷ behaviour; performance:～很好 acquit oneself very well ❸ show off:好～自己 like to show off
表现手法 biǎoxiàn shǒufǎ technique of expression
表现形式 biǎoxiàn xíngshì form or mode of expression; manifestation
表现型 biǎoxiànxíng 〈生物〉phenotype
表现主义 biǎoxiànzhǔyì 〈文学〉expressionism
表象 biǎoxiàng 〈心理〉idea; image; presentation
表象论 biǎoxiànglùn 〈哲学〉representationism
表形文字 biǎoxíng wénzì pictograph; hieroglyph
表兄 biǎoxiōng *see* "表哥"
表兄弟 biǎoxiōngdì ❶ (male) distaff cousin ❷ *see* "表弟"
表演 biǎoyǎn ❶ perform; act; play:～节目 give a performance /～过火 overdo one's part; overact /体育～体操 perform gymnastics /～ sports exhibition /航空模型～ model planes exhibition /今天下午我们都观看了精彩的杂技～。We all watched the superb acrobatic performance this afternoon. ❷ demonstrate:～新操作方法 demonstrate new techniques of operation
表演唱 biǎoyǎnchàng singing with action
表演赛 biǎoyǎnsài 〈体育〉exhibition match
表扬 biǎoyáng praise; commend:～好人好事 praise good people and good deeds /～先进集体 commend advanced units /～信 commendatory letter /这种自我牺牲精神是值得～的。This spirit of self-sacrifice is praiseworthy (*or* highly commendable).
表意文字 biǎoyì wénzì 〈语言〉ideograph; ideogram
表音文字 biǎoyīn wénzì 〈语言〉phonography
表语 biǎoyǔ 〈语言〉predicative
表章 biǎozhāng ❶ memorial to the emperor ❷ *see* "表彰"
表彰 biǎozhāng cite (in dispatches); commend:省政府召开大会,～在科技领域里取得突出成就的集体和个人。The provincial government held a rally to commend those units and individuals that had scored outstanding achievements in the field of science and technology. /为了～他的英勇事迹,人们为他树了一座纪念碑。A monument was erected in recognition of his brave deeds.
表针 biǎozhēn (watch) hand; indicator; pointer
表征 biǎozhēng ❶ symptom; sign; characteristic:他右手托着下巴,这是他陷入沉思的～。He cupped his chin with his right hand, which showed that he was lost in thought. ❷〈物理〉characterization
表证 biǎozhèng 〈中医〉illness that has not attacked the vital organs of the human body
表侄 biǎozhí son of a male cousin on the distaff side; nephew
表侄女 biǎozhínǚ daughter of a male cousin on the distaff side; niece
表字 biǎozì *also* "表号" (usu. related to one's official name in meaning, and used by others as a courtesy name — a common practice in the early vernacular) secondary name:润之是毛泽东的～。Runzhi is the secondary name of Mao Zedong (润之 being related to 泽 in meaning).

裱 biǎo

❶ mount (a picture, etc.):把画～一下 have the painting mounted ❷ paste paper on (a wall, ceiling, etc.); paper
裱褙 biǎobèi mount (a picture, etc.)
裱糊 biǎohú paper (a wall, ceiling, etc.)
裱贴 biǎotiē mount (a picture, scroll, etc.)
裱装 biǎozhuāng mount:～字画 mount calligraphic works and paintings

婊 biǎo

婊子 biǎozi whore; prostitute:小～〈粗话〉whore of a girl /～养的〈粗话〉son of a bitch; bastard

biào

摽[1] biào

❶ fasten together; tie fast:桌子腿活动了,用铁丝～住它吧。The legs of the table have come loose; let's make them fast with a wire. ❷ be arm in arm:～着胳膊走 walk arm in arm ❸ *see* "摽劲儿" ❹〈贬义〉cling to one another:他们俩老～在一块儿。The two of them hang together all the time.

摽[2] biào

〈书面〉❶ fall ❷ hit; strike
see also biāo
摽劲儿 biàojìnr ❶ (of competitors, etc.) strain every muscle; exert oneself to emulate or excel:大伙儿摽着劲儿干。Everybody worked hard with a silent resolve to excel. /他们摽着劲儿地讲排场。They rival each other for extravagance. ❷ be at odds with:她正和男朋友～,一直不理他。She's been in a pique with her boyfriend and wouldn't speak to him.

鳔 biào

❶ swim bladder; air bladder:鱼～ air bladder (of fish) ❷ fish glue ❸〈方言〉glue (with fish glue):这盒子是～上的,没用钉子。The box is glued together without using any nails.
鳔胶 biàojiāo isinglass; fish glue

俵 biào

俵分 biàofēn 〈方言〉distribute according to the number of portions or of persons
俵散 biàosàn divide into portions:分赃～ divide the spoils

biē

瘪(癟) biē

see also biě
瘪三 biēsān 〈方言〉wretched-looking tramp who lives by begging or stealing; bum

憋 biē

❶ suppress; hold back; bottle up:～了一肚子火 bottle up one's anger; be filled with pent-up anger /～了一肚子气要出 itch to air one's pent-up grievances /～足了劲,要好好干一场 be bursting with energy and ready to go all out in one's work /她什么话也～不住。She simply cannot contain herself (*or* hold herself back). /那些年人人～着一股邪气。Everyone had a knot of foul anger in those years. ❷ suffocate; stifle:屋子里～得很。It's very close in

here. /我心里～得慌。I'm suffocating (*or* stifling). ❸〈方言〉force: ～他喝下去。Make him drink it. ❹〈方言〉〈贬义〉mull over; brew: 他心里～什么坏主意呢? What scheme (*or* trick) is he mulling over (*or* brewing) in his mind? ❺〈方言〉be on the lookout for; keep watch on: 猫～耗子。The cat watched for the mouse. /我哪知道他一直～着整我呢。How could I have expected him to be looking for a chance to give me trouble? ❻〈方言〉(of snow or rain) brew; threaten: ～雪 threaten to snow /天这么热,早晚得～一场大雨来。A storm must be brewing; it's so sultry. ❼〈方言〉snap; break: 保险丝～了。The fuse has blown.

憋闷 biēmen be depressed; be dejected: 他心里有点～。He felt somewhat dejected. /这事真叫人～。This is downright depressing. /这姑娘什么事都爱～在心里。The girl is always keeping everything to herself.

憋气 biēqì ❶ feel suffocated or depressed: 大厅里挤满了人,她觉得很～。She felt it was suffocating in the crowded hall. ❷ bottle up one's resentment; feel injured and resentful: 这么不公平还得忍着,有比这还～的吗? Can there be any greater suffering than to have to endure what is obviously unjust?

憋屈 biēqu feel depressed; be dejected; be down-hearted: 你有什么～的事儿跟我说说吧。Tell me what you feel so dejected about. *or* Tell me why you are so unhappy.

憋躁 biēzào choke with resentment; feel injured and resentful: 我心里那个～就甭提了。You can well imagine how resentful I felt.

鳖(鼈) biē soft-shelled turtle

鳖甲 biējiǎ 〈中药〉turtle shell

鳖裙 biēqún *also* "鳖边" calipash

bié

蹩 bié 〈方言〉sprain (one's ankle or wrist)

蹩脚 biéjiǎo 〈方言〉inferior; shoddy; poor: ～的导演 incompetent director /～货 substandard goods; shoddy work; poor stuff /文章写得很～。The article is poorly written.

别[1] bié ❶ leave; part: ～了故乡 leave one's native place /久～重逢 meet again after a long separation /临～赠言 parting advice /话～ bid farewell (to each other) ❷ other; another: ～处 another place; elsewhere /～无出路。There is no other way out. /～有所指。There is an implication here. /又当～论。That's another cup of tea. *or* That's a different matter altogether. ❸〈方言〉turn round; change: 他把头～了过去。He turned his head. /这个人的脾气一时～不过来。His temper is difficult to change in a short time. ❹ (Bié) a surname

别[2] bié ❶ differentiate; distinguish: ～其真伪 determine whether it's true or false /分门～类 classify; put into different categories ❷ difference; distinction: 千差万～ differ in thousands of ways /天渊之～ world of difference; poles apart ❸ classification; category: 派～ faction; group; school of thought /职～ official rank /性～ sex distinction; sex /国～ nationality

别[3] bié ❶ fasten with a pin or clip: 把表格～在一起 pin (*or* clip) the forms together /发卡～在头发上 fasten a hair-pin onto one's hair /他把校徽～在胸前。He pinned a school badge on his breast. ❷ stick in; insert in order to hinder the movement of sth. or sb.: 他腰里～着旱烟袋。He has a long-stemmed Chinese pipe stuck in his belt. /把门～上。Put something under the door to keep it from closing. ❸ cause to stumble by a swinging movement of one's leg; trip up: ～腿 stick one's leg out to trip sb. up ❹ deliberately hinder the advance of a bike or car with one's own: ～车 stop an advancing bike (*or* car) with one's own

别[4] bié ❶ don't: ～客气。Don't stand on ceremony. *or* Make yourself at home. /～愣着。Don't stand there gawking. /～得意太早。Don't count your chickens before they are hatched. /～惹麻烦。Let the sleeping dog lie. ❷ *usu. followed by* 是, *indicating conjecture of sth. against one's own wish*: 你怎么情绪不高,～是没考好吧? Why, you look depressed. Is it because you didn't do well in the exam?

see also biè

别白 biébái 〈书面〉distinguish; differentiate: ～是非 distinguish right from wrong; distinguish between right and wrong

别本 biéběn ❶ duplicate; spare copy; transcript ❷ different version; another version

别才 biécái 〈书面〉*also* "别材" special talent or ability

别裁 biécái ❶ (often used in titles of collected poems) appraise and select: 《唐诗～集》*Selected Tang Poems* ❷ special type or genre of literature

别称 biéchēng another name; alternative name: 滇是云南的～。Dian is another name for Yunnan.

别出机杼 biéchū-jīzhù weave on a different loom — break fresh ground; offer original ideas (in writing or craftsmanship): 他的散文在构思上往往～。He is often fairly original in the presentation of his ideas in writing.

别出心裁 biéchū-xīncái start sth. unique or original; deliberately adopt a different approach; try to be different: 老杨的设计～,受到行家们的好评。Lao Yang's design is quite original; it is highly regarded by experts. /他这个人总爱～,与众不同。He is always trying to be different from everyone.

别处 biéchù other places; elsewhere: 咱们到～看看。Let's take a look at other places. *or* Let's take a look around elsewhere.

别邸 biédǐ high official's villa

别动队 biédòngduì special detachment; commando; fifth column: ～员 ranger; commando /敌人的～ fifth column of the enemy

别风淮雨 biéfēng-huáiyǔ 〈书面〉corruption of the phrase "列风淫雨" (strong wind and incessant rain); textual corruption; error in copying or writing

别个 biégè ❶ others; other people: 这票是给老李而不是给～的。The ticket is for Lao Li and not for anybody else. ❷ other: 这件事～同事都不愿接手。No other colleague is ready to take it over.

别馆 biéguǎn 〈书面〉❶ temporary imperial residence ❷ villa ❸ guest house

别管 biéguǎn ❶〈连词〉no matter (who, what, etc.): ～干什么,都要全力以赴。You must do your best no matter what you do (*or* whatever you do). ❷ leave (sb. or sth.) alone; never mind: ～我,我工作没干完呢。Leave me alone, I haven't finished my job yet. /～闲事。Mind your own business.

别号 biéhào another name (in addition to one's official and courtesy names); informal name; sobriquet: 苏轼,字子瞻,～东坡居士。Su Shi, whose courtesy name was Zizhan, also called himself Dong Po Jushi (Hermit of the Eastern Slope).

别集 biéjí (in contrast with 总集) collected works of an individual author; individual collection of works

别家 biéjiā other stores, shops, factories, etc.: 你要的型号已售完,请到～去看看吧。The goods of your specifications are all sold out. Please try (your luck in) some other stores.

别价 biéjia 〈方言〉*indicating an attempt to prevent or forbid*: ～,您多呆一会儿吧。Don't go. Please stay a bit longer.

别具肺肠 biéjù-fèicháng harbour an ulterior motive; entertain evil designs

别具匠心 biéjù-jiàngxīn possess or show distinctive ingenuity: ～的版面 remarkably ingenious layout (as of a newspaper or magazine)

别具一格 biéjù-yīgé have a unique or distinctive style: 这种建筑～,颇有韵味。This kind of architecture has a peculiar charm, for it has a style of its own. /这种民间舞蹈的表演～。There is something unique about the folk dance.

别具只眼 biéjù-zhīyǎn see what others fail to see; have a special or unique insight: 他对当代政治问题～。He has a remarkably keen insight into contemporary politics. /只有～的人才能罗致人才。It takes a person of special insight to scout talent.

别开生面 biékāi-shēngmiàn develop a new style; break fresh ground; be out of the common run: 这是一次～的农民运动会。It was an entirely new sort of sports meet of the farmers.

别开蹊径 biékāi-xījìng open up a new path; blaze a fresh trail: 在国画上,他～,自成一家。He blazed a fresh trail in traditional Chinese painting and developed a style of his own.

别来无恙 biélái-wúyàng 〈书面〉I believe you've been in good health since we parted; I trust all has been well with you since we

last saw each other
别离 biélí take leave of; leave:～家乡,踏上征途 leave one's native place to start on a long journey /二人洒泪～。The two parted in tears.
别流 biéliú tributary
别论 biélùn another matter; different story:又当～ be otherwise treated; be viewed differently /如果他确因有事不能前来,则当～。It would be a different story if he were really detained by urgent business.
别名 biémíng another name; sobriquet; alias:使用～ use another name (*or* a sobriquet, *or* an alias) /史密斯～辛普森 Smith alias Simpson /过去飞机有个～叫"铁鸟"。In the old days people often called airplanes "iron birds".
别情 biéqíng sentiment felt at parting:惆怅的～ sorrow of parting
别趣 biéqù special interest; peculiar charm
别饶风致 biéráo-fēngzhì of peculiar elegance and charm; have a charm of its own:这幅画生动超脱,～。Lifelike and unconventional, this painting has a rare charm and beauty of its own.
别人 biérén someone else:这里只有我们俩,没有～。There are only the two of us here, and no one else. /这件事只能你我知道,不可对～说。This is strictly between you and me. Don't tell anyone else.
别人 biéren other people; others:为什么不吸收～的意见呢? Why not incorporate other people's views? /～都去了,你怎么不去呢? They have all left. Why didn't you go?
别生枝节 biéshēng-zhījié raise irrelevant issues; be unexpectedly complicated; have new complications:我以为此事可以一帆风顺,谁知又～,殊非始料所及。I thought that it might be plain sailing, but it turned out to be far more complicated than I had expected. /他们先是爽快地表示同意,而后又～。They agreed readily at first, but then raised irrelevant issues.
see also "节外生枝" jiéwài-shēngzhī
别史 biéshǐ history books other than those written in a biographical or annalistic style; unofficial history
别是 biéshì 〈副词〉 *used to indicate anxiety about sth. untoward*:他这会儿还未到,～路上出了什么事儿。Why isn't he here yet? I hope nothing has happened on the way. /～光线不好,没有看明白吧? Perhaps you didn't see clearly because the light was poor?
别树一帜 biéshù-yīzhì set up a new banner; found a new school of thought; have a style of one's own
别墅 biéshù villa
别说 biéshuō let alone; to say nothing of:我见都没见过榴莲,～吃了。I've never seen any durian, let alone eat it.
别提 biétí 〈口语〉 you can well imagine:当时物价之高,就～了。You can well imagine how high the prices were at the time. *or* Commodities were terribly expensive. /那里风景就～多美了。The beauty of the scenery is simply wonderful.
别体 biétǐ ❶ (of Chinese calligraphy) new style evolved from the old ❷ (of Chinese characters) varied form; variant (in form)
别无长物 biéwúchángwù be in possession of nothing other than (is absolutely necessary); be in reduced circumstances:一身之外,～。I have nothing on earth but my own self.
别无二致 biéwú'èrzhì exactly the same; not in the least different:两个人的思想～。They are no different in their thinking. /这两台机器,除了颜色不同外,其他～。The two machines are exactly the same except for the colour.
别无所有 biéwúsuǒyǒu that's all one has:除了一间茅屋和半亩田外,他～。He has no personal possessions other than a thatched hut and half a *mu* of land.
别无他法 biéwútāfǎ have no other way out:除辞职外,我～。I have no alternative but to hand in my resignation.
别无他图 biéwútātú have no other intentions:他说他除了要把事情搞得更好外～。He said he had no other aim than to do a better job of it.
别绪 biéxù surge of sentimental feeling at parting:～依依 reveal a feeling of sentimental attachment at parting
别筵 biéyán farewell banquet or dinner
别样 biéyàng ❶ other:菜市上除了黄瓜、豆荚,～的青菜也很多。There are many other kinds of greens besides cucumbers and beans in the greengrocery market. ❷ different style; sth. different:这毛衣不好看,换个～的。This sweater doesn't look nice. Show me something different.
别业 biéyè 〈书面〉 villa
别异 biéyì ❶ extraordinary; peculiar:风光～ landscape of extraordinary beauty ❷ difference; distinction:二者并无～。There is practically no difference between the two.
别有洞天 biéyǒu-dòngtiān place of unique charm and beauty:越过这重山,风景如画,真是～。Across the mountain the picturesque landscape will present you with a wonderland.
别有风味 biéyǒu-fēngwèi have a distinctive flavour
别有所图 biéyǒu-suǒtú have an ulterior motive; have an axe to grind
别有天地 biéyǒu-tiāndì place of unique beauty; scenery of exceptional charm:～非人间。The place has a unique beauty characteristic of fairyland.
别有用心 biéyǒu-yòngxīn have ulterior motives; have an axe to grind:如果他不是出于无知,就是～。If he is not acting out of sheer ignorance, he must have ulterior motives.
别余 biéyú 〈方言〉 others; the rest:我～的可都不管,就管质量检查。I'll take care of quality control and nothing else.
别择 biézé ❶ appraise and select ❷ make a different choice
别针 biézhēn ❶ safety pin; pin ❷ brooch:钻石～ diamond brooch
别致 biézhì original; novel; exquisite:这别针很～。The brooch is exquisite. /文章结构新颖,体现了作者构思上的～。The novelty of the plot embodies the author's original craftsmanship.
别转 biézhuǎn 〈方言〉 turn away; turn round:他远远地望见我就～了脸。When he saw me from at a distance, he turned his head away.
别传 biézhuàn informal biography; anecdotal biography; anecdotage
别庄 biézhuāng villa:消夏～ summer residence
别子 biézǐ 〈旧语〉 younger son (of an emperor or lord); son by a concubine
别子 biézi ❶ pin (usu. made of bone) for holding fast an old-fashioned hard-covered book, or a scroll of painting or calligraphy ❷ pendant of a pipe pouch
别字 biézì ❶ *also* "白字" báizì incorrectly written or mispronounced character; malapropism:读～ mispronounce a character /写～ write a character wrongly /～连篇 be riddled with wrongly written characters (*or* spelling errors) ❷ *see* "别号"

biě

瘪(癟) biě ❶ shrivelled; shrunken; deflated:干～ dry and shrivelled; wizened /～花生 blighted peanuts /气球～了。The balloon is deflated. /车胎～了。The tyre is flat. ❷〈方言〉 be on a spot; be or put in difficulty:作～ be on a spot; be in a dilemma
see also biē
瘪螺痧 biěluóshā 〈中医〉 chloera (with dehydration)
瘪瘦 biěshòu shrivelled and bony; emaciated:～的脸颊 sunken cheeks
瘪塌塌 biětātā sunken; deflated; emaciated:这只球～的,一点气也没有了。The ball is totally deflated. / 这只橘子～的,水份都跑光了。The orange has dried up and shrivelled. /他久病之后～的,行动都困难了。After a lingering illness, he was reduced to a skeleton and moved about with difficulty.
瘪陷 biěxiàn (of human body) shrivelled; sunken:他眼窝～。He had sunken eyes.
瘪窳 biěyu 〈方言〉 ❶ shrivelled; sunken; deflated:皮球用针一扎就～了。If you pierce the ball with a needle, it will soon shrivel up. ❷ depression; hollow:铁球把地上砸了个大～。The iron ball made a big hole in the ground.
瘪子 biězi 〈方言〉 ❶ dilemma; setback:作～ find oneself in a dilemma; be on a hot spot ❷ blighted grain

biè

别(彆) biè 〈方言〉 sway; bring round:她想干什么就得干什么,谁也～不过她。She always has her own way, and nobody can make her change her mind.
see also bié
别扭 bièniu ❶ awkward; contrary; difficult to deal with:心里～ feel awkward and uncomfortable; feel bad /天气～ unpredictable

(*or* disagreeable) weather /脾气～ be of uncertain temper; be contrary /这衣服她穿着真～。The dress looks so wrong on her. /这趟差出得真～,什么事都没办好。The whole trip was a nuisance. Nothing got done. ❷ not see eye to eye; not get on well: 闹～ be at odds; fall out /两个人素来有些别别扭扭的。The two of them are often at loggerheads with each other. ❸ (of speech or writing) unnatural; awkward: 这句话听起来有点～。This sentence doesn't sound quite right (*or* natural).

别嘴 bièzuǐ 〈方言〉 a bit of a mouthful; tongue-twister: 这个词念起来有点～。This word is a bit of mouthful (*or* a tongue-twister).

bīn

濒 bīn ❶ be close to (the sea, a river, etc.); border on: 东～大海 overlook the sea on the east /～河之郡 prefectural city located on the river ❷ on the point of; on the brink of: ～灭 on the verge of extinction /～别 on the eve of parting

濒近 bīnjìn on the brink of; close to; near: ～绝粮 run short of supplies; be on the verge of starvation /宾馆～东湖。The guesthouse is located near the East Lake.

濒绝 bīnjué on the verge or brink of extinction; dying out: 这里几种稀有植物现已～。A few species of rare plants here are on the verge of extinction.

濒临 bīnlín be close to; border on; be on the verge of: ～黄海 border on the Yellow Sea /～崩溃 on the verge of collapse /～死亡 be at death's door

濒死 bīnsǐ moribund; dying; at one's last gasp; on one's last legs: ～之躯,忽有转机。Unexpectedly there came a turn for the better for the dying man. *or* The person who seemed to be breathing his last took an unexpected turn for the better.

濒死期血栓 bīnsǐqī xuèshuān 〈医学〉 agonal thrombus; agony thrombus

濒危 bīnwēi ❶ be in imminent danger: ～动物 endangered species ❷ be critically ill: ～病人 critically ill person; dying patient

濒行 bīnxíng before setting out; on the eve of departure

濒于 bīnyú be on the brink of: ～破产 teeter on the brink (*or* edge) of bankruptcy /～崩溃 verge on collapse /～绝境 face an impasse /～灭亡 be near extinction

宾(賓、賔) bīn ❶ guest: 外～ foreign guest /国～ state guest /贵～ distinguished guest /待为上～ treat sb. as a guest of honour /相敬如～ (of a married couple) treat each other with respect and courtesy (as if they were host and guest) /喧～夺主 presumptuous guest usurping the host's role; minor issue taking precedence over a major one ❷ (Bīn) a surname

宾白 bīnbái spoken parts in a Chinese opera

宾词 bīncí 〈逻辑〉 predicate

宾从 bīncóng 〈书面〉 ❶ obey; submit to ❷ guest and his attendants ❸ retinue of a guest

宾东 bīndōng host and guest; ranking official and his staff; private tutor and his employer; shopkeeper and shop assistant

宾服 bīnfú 〈书面〉 obey; submit to; be subordinated to

宾服 bīnfu 〈方言〉 admire; be convinced: 你说的那一套,俺不～。I'm not convinced of what you said.

宾附 bīnfù 〈书面〉 join as a vassal state or junior partner; proclaim allegiance to; submit to

宾戈 bīngē (transliteration) bingo, a game popular in the West, in which random drawn numbers are called out and players having all or a set of these numbers win a prize

宾格 bīngé 〈语言〉 objective case

宾馆 bīnguǎn guesthouse: 来访的客人将下榻～。The visitors will stay in the guesthouse.

宾客 bīnkè guests; visitors: ～盈门。One's house is filled with guests.

宾礼 bīnlǐ protocol or courtesy due to a guest: 以～相待 treat as a guest

宾朋 bīnpéng guests and friends: 大宴～ fête one's guests and friends /～满座。The room (*or* house) is packed with guests and friends. *or* No seat is left vacant in the room.

宾天 bīntiān 〈书面〉〈婉词〉 demise of a sovereign or an elder

宾铁 bīntiě *also* "镔铁" bīntiě wrought iron

宾语 bīnyǔ 〈语言〉 object: 直接～ direct object /间接～ indirect object /～补足语 objective complement

宾至如归 bīnzhì-rúguī (of a hotel, guest-house, etc.) where guests feel as comfortable as if they were at home; home away from home

宾主 bīnzhǔ host and guest: ～互致问候。Host and guest exchanged greetings.

滨(濱) bīn ❶ water's edge; bank; shore: 海～ seashore /湖～ lakeshore; lakeside /湘江之～ on the banks of the Xiangjiang River /大连位于黄海之～。Dalian is situated along the coast of the Yellow Sea. ❷ be close to (the sea, a river, etc.); border on: ～海 border on the sea /～海地区 coastal region /～江公园 riverside park /～江大道 boulevard along the bank of a river

滨岸带 bīn'àndài littoral zone

滨藜 bīnlí 〈植物〉 saltbush

滨螺 bīnluó 〈动物〉 periwinkle (*Littorina*)

滨鸟 bīnniǎo shorebird

滨水区 bīnshuǐqū waterfront

槟(檳、梹) bīn

see also bīng

槟树 bīnshù *also* "枫香" fēngxiāng 〈植物〉 sweetgum

槟子 bīnzi 〈植物〉 *binzi*, a species of apple which is slightly sour and astringent

镔(鑌) bīn

镔铁 bīntiě wrought iron

傧(儐) bīn

傧相 bīnxiàng ❶ 〈古语〉 usher (for guests); master of ceremony ❷ attendant of the bride or bridegroom at a wedding: 男～ best man /女～ bridesmaid

缤(繽) bīn

缤纷 bīnfēn 〈书面〉 in riotous profusion: 五彩～ riot of colours; multi-coloured /落英～ profusion of falling petals

缤乱 bīnluàn in confusion: 头发～ dishevelled hair

斌 bīn *see* "彬" bīn

彬 bīn

彬彬 bīnbīn 〈书面〉 urbane; refined: ～然有君子风 have the refined manners of a gentleman

彬彬君子 bīnbīn-jūnzǐ refined gentleman

彬彬有礼 bīnbīn-yǒulǐ affable and courteous; urbane; polite: 此人总是～,给人印象很好。He always impresses people with his friendly and polite manners.

玢 bīn 〈书面〉 a kind of jade

see also fēn

bìn

鬓(鬢、髩) bìn temples; hair over the temples: 两～斑白 have grey temples /霜～ hoary temples

鬓发 bìnfà hair over the temples: ～灰白 be greying at the temples; have greying temples /～已白 have hoary temples

鬓脚 bìnjiǎo *also* "鬓角" ❶ temples ❷ hair over the temples; (UK) sideboards; (US) sideburns: 修～ trim the sideboards

殡(殯) bìn ❶ lay a coffin in a memorial hall ❷ carry a coffin to the burial place: 送～的人很多。Many people took part in the funeral procession.

殡车 bìnchē hearse

殡殓 bìnliàn encoffin a corpse and carry it to the grave

殡仪馆 bìnyíguǎn the undertaker's; funeral parlour or home

殡葬 bìnzàng funeral and interment

摈(擯) bìn 〈书面〉 discard; reject: 恃才倨傲,为人所～ be

rejected by many people for one's overweening pride
摈斥 bìnchì keep out; exclude; reject:～异己 exclude those who hold different opinions; get rid of those who differ from one /他被～在研究小组之外。He was barred from the research group.
摈除 bìnchú discard; get rid of; dispense with:～障碍 get rid of (*or* remove) obstacles /～繁文缛节 dispense with unnecessary formalities /～糟粕 discard the dross
摈黜 bìnchù 〈书面〉dismiss (from office) and banish
摈绝 bìnjué remove; get rid of:～杂念 get rid of (*or* discard) all distracting or selfish considerations
摈弃 bìnqì abandon; discard; cast away (esp. of ideas):～旧习 abolish outmoded customs /形式主义的东西,应坚决～。We should resolutely break with all formalist conceptions.

髌(髕) bìn ❶ kneecap; patella ❷ chop off the kneecaps (a cruel punishment in ancient China)
髌骨 bìngǔ kneecap; patella
髌固定术 bìngùdìngshù patellapexy
髌切除术 bìnqiēchúshù patellectomy

膑(臏) bìn *see* "髌" bìn

bīng

冰(氷) bīng ❶ ice:滴水成～。Drips of water instantly become ice. ❷ feel cold:冷水～脚。The feet feel very cold in the icy water. ❸ put in a place packed with ice; ice:把啤酒～一～。Have the beer iced. ❹ sth. resembling ice
冰坝 bīngbà ice dam
冰棒 bīngbàng 〈方言〉popsicle; ice lolly
冰雹 bīngbáo (commonly known as 雹子) hail; hailstone:一场～ a hailstorm /下～了! It is hailing!
冰崩 bīngbēng 〈地理〉glacier avalanche; ice-fall
冰草 bīngcǎo 〈植物〉wheatgrass
冰场 bīngchǎng skating rink; ice stadium; ice arena
冰碴儿 bīngchár 〈方言〉❶ ice chip ❷ thin coat of ice on water surface
冰川 bīngchuān glacier:～补给 alimentation of glaciers /～地貌 glacial landform /～周期 glacial cycle
冰川沉积 bīngchuān chénjī 〈地质〉ice laid deposit; glacial deposit:～物 glacial sediment
冰川冲积层 bīngchuān chōngjīcéng glacial alluvium
冰川湖 bīngchuānhú glacial lake
冰川平原 bīngchuān píngyuán glacier plain
冰川期 bīngchuānqī glacial period or epoch; ice age (IA)
冰川舌 bīngchuānshé glacier tongue
冰川学 bīngchuānxué glaciology
冰川作用 bīngchuān zuòyòng glaciation
冰船 bīngchuán 〈方言〉*see* "冰床"
冰床 bīngchuáng horse-drawn vehicle like a sleigh as a means of transport on ice; sledge; sled
冰醋酸 bīngcùsuān 〈化学〉glacial acetic acid
冰镩 bīngcuān ice chisel
冰袋 bīngdài 〈医学〉ice bag
冰蛋 bīngdàn frozen egg
冰刀 bīngdāo 〈体育〉(ice) skates
冰岛 Bīngdǎo Iceland:～人 Icelander /～语 Icelandic (language) /～克朗 Icelandic Krona (Ikr)
冰道 bīngdào frozen road (built in winter by stamping piled snow or by utilizing the frozen surface of the water)
冰灯 bīngdēng coloured ice of various shapes with lights inside; ice lantern
冰点 bīngdiǎn 〈物理〉freezing point:～测定器 cryoscope
冰店 bīngdiàn *see* "冰果店"
冰雕 bīngdiāo ice sculpture; ice carving:～艺术 art of ice carving; ice sculpture /～比赛 contest in ice carving
冰冻 bīngdòng ❶ freeze:～季节 freezing season /～地区 frost zone /～处理 cold quenching; deep freezing /～食物 frozen food ❷ 〈方言〉ice
冰冻疗法 bīngdòng liáofǎ ice therapy
冰冻切片 bīngdòng qiēpiàn frozen section
冰冻三尺,非一日之寒 bīng dòng sān chǐ, fēi yī rì zhī hán it takes more than one cold day to freeze three feet of ice; the trouble is deep-rooted; Rome was not built in a day:～,不能旦夕除其患。The trouble has been brewing for quite some time and it is impossible to get rid of it overnight. /～,他的这身功夫可是一生心血的结晶啊。As Rome was not built in a day, his wonderful skill was the crystallization of a lifetime's hard work and dedication.
冰冻蚀刻 bīngdòng shíkè freeze-etching
冰斗 bīngdǒu 〈地质〉cirque
冰毒 bīngdú "ice", popular name for methamphetamine hydrochloride, a deadly addictive stimulant drug
冰帆 bīngfān ice boat; ice-yacht; (US) scooter:～运动 ice-sailing; ice-boating
冰封 bīngfēng be ice-bound; be covered with ice:～雪冻 be ice-bound and snow-covered; be covered with snow and ice /千里～ a hundred leagues are sealed with ice /昆明湖～之后,游人可在上面行走、滑冰。After the Kunming Lake is frozen, visitors can walk and skate on it.
冰峰 bīngfēng ice-covered peak; ice-capped mountain
冰盖 bīnggài 〈地质〉ice-sheet; icecap
冰糕 bīnggāo 〈方言〉❶ ice cream ❷ ice-lolly; popsicle
冰镐 bīnggǎo ice axe
冰挂 bīngguà (common name for 雨凇) verglas; (US) glaze; (UK) glazed frost
冰挂儿 bīngguàr icicle
冰柜 bīngguì freezer; refrigerator
冰棍儿 bīnggùnr ice-lolly; popsicle; frozen sucker; ice-sucker
冰果店 bīngguǒdiàn *also* "冰店" 〈方言〉ice-cream parlour
冰海 bīnghǎi ice-jammed ocean water
冰寒于水 bīnghányúshuǐ ice is colder than water — students surpass their teacher
冰河 bīnghé *see* "冰川"
冰河时代 bīnghé shídài *see* "冰川期"
冰壶秋月 bīnghú-qiūyuè ice in a jade bottle and moon in mid-autumn — person of noble and flawless character
冰花 bīnghuā ❶ ice-flower (as on a window pane in winter):玻璃窗上已经结上了～。The window-panes were covered with ice-flowers. ❷ iced object of art (such as iced fruit, flowers, fish, etc. as ornaments) ❸ frost flower; frost; rime:老头儿的胡子上结了一层～儿。The old man's beard became stiffened with frost.
冰肌玉骨 bīngjī-yùgǔ ❶ flesh of ice and bones of jade — (of a beautiful woman) delicate pale skin ❷ plum blossoms which proudly defy cold weather and display infinite charms; pure and noble
冰激凌 bīngjīlíng *also* "冰淇淋" ice-cream
冰架 bīngjià *also* "陆缘冰" lùyuánbīng ice-shelf (ice floe frozen to the shore)
冰建筑 bīngjiànzhù ❶ architecture involving the use of ice blocks as building material and of water as cement ❷ ice building
冰鉴 bīngjiàn ❶ 〈古语〉box for containing ice ❷ 〈书面〉〈比喻〉bright mirror — ability to differentiate right and wrong ❸ 〈书面〉〈比喻〉the moon
冰窖 bīngjiào icehouse
冰晶 bīngjīng ice crystal
冰晶石 bīngjīngshí cryolite
冰景 bīngjǐng ice scenery, such as ice sculpture, ice lanterns, potted ice landscape, etc.
冰库 bīngkù ice storage
冰块儿 bīngkuàir lump of ice; ice cube
冰冷 bīnglěng ❶ ice-cold:才入冬,河水就那么～。It is only early winter, and yet the water of the river has become icy-cold. ❷ cold and unfriendly; icy; frosty:～的神情 frosty look; icy look
冰凉 bīngliáng ❶ icy-cold:你的脚～。Your feet are icy-cold. ❷ disheartened; in despair:听了他这番话,我的心都～了。My heart sank after I heard what he said. /他的冷笑使我感到全身～。His sneer sent cold shivers down my spine.
冰裂缝 bīnglièfèng *also* "冰隙" 〈地质〉crevasse
冰凌 bīnglíng ice
冰溜子 bīngliūzi *also* "冰溜" icicle
冰轮 bīnglún 〈书面〉ice disc — the moon
冰帽 bīngmào 〈医学〉ice cap
冰凝器 bīngníngqì 〈物理〉cryophorus

冰排 bīngpái ice raft; ice floe

冰排子 bīngpáizi 〈方言〉 see "冰床"

冰盆景 bīngpénjǐng (a kind of ice sculpture) potted ice landscape

冰片 bīngpiàn 〈中药〉 borneol

冰瓶 bīngpíng vacuum bottle or flask for keeping ice, popsicles, etc.

冰瀑 bīngpù 〈地理〉 icefall; glacial cascade; glacial fall

冰期 bīngqī ❶ see "冰川期" ❷ active period of a glacial epoch

冰淇淋 bīngqílín ice cream: 蛋卷~ ice cream cone / 香草~ vanilla icecream / 三色~ icecream with three flavours / ~蛋糕 icecream cake

冰碛 bīngqì 〈地质〉 moraine: ~湖 moraine lake / ~物 (glacial) till/ ~岩 tillite

冰橇 bīngqiāo *also* "雪橇" xuěqiāo sleigh; sledge; sled

冰清玉洁 bīngqīng-yùjié pure as ice and spotless as jade; noble or impeccable in character: 这位先生~，堪为人表。Noble and pure, the gentleman sets a good example to all.

冰情 bīngqíng 〈气象〉 ice condition: ~警报 ice-warning

冰丘 bīngqiū pingo

冰球 bīngqiú 〈体育〉 ❶ ice hockey: ~场 rink / ~队 ice hockey team / ~棍 ice stick ❷ puck

冰染染料 bīngrǎn rǎnliào azoic dyes

冰人 bīngrén 〈书面〉 matchmaker; go-between

冰山 bīngshān ❶ ice-covered mountain: 《~上的来客》 *Visitors from Ice-Covered Mountains* ❷ iceberg: ~的一角 tip of the iceberg ❸ 〈比喻〉 supporter or protector one cannot long rely on

冰上表演 bīngshàng biǎoyǎn ice show

冰上曲棍球 bīngshàng qūgùnqiú 〈体育〉 bandy

冰上舞蹈 bīngshàng wǔdǎo ice dancing

冰上运动 bīngshàng yùndòng ice sports: ~会 ice-sports meet

冰舌 bīngshé glacial tongue; ice tongue

冰蚀谷 bīngshígǔ 〈地质〉 glacial valley

冰释 bīngshì 〈书面〉 (of misgivings, misunderstandings, etc.) disappear; vanish; be dispelled: 他俩的误会已涣然~。Their misunderstanding has vanished (*or* has been dispelled).

冰霜 bīngshuāng ❶ moral integrity: 他刚正不阿，有如~。A man of moral integrity, he is upright and incorruptible. ❷ austere manner; stern countenance: 凛若~ be awe-inspiring / 冷若~ look frosty and stern

冰塑 bīngsù see "冰雕"

冰塔 bīngtǎ 〈地质〉 serac

冰坛 bīngtán ice-sports circles: 世界~ ice-sports circles in the world / ~新秀 new star of ice sports

冰炭 bīng-tàn ice and burning coals; mutually exclusive: 犹如~ just like ice and burning coals

冰炭不相容 bīng-tàn bù xiāngróng as incompatible as ice and burning coals; mutually exclusive: 想不到他们二人的见解竟是~。I didn't realize that their views were so diametrically opposed.

冰糖 bīngtáng crystal sugar; rock candy

冰糖葫芦 bīngtáng húlu candied haws or sometimes other fruit on a stick

冰天雪地 bīngtiān-xuědì world of ice and snow; wide tracts of ice-bound and snow-covered country: 我们这里已是~。Here, we are already in a world of ice and snow.

冰天雪窖 bīngtiān-xuějiào *also* "雪窖冰天" land of ice and snow

冰坨 bīngtuó lump of ice; block of ice: 这冻鸡肚子里有个大~。There's a big lump of ice in the belly of the frozen chicken.

冰雾 bīngwù 〈气象〉 frost fog; ice fog; rime fog

冰隙 bīngxì 〈地质〉 crevasse

冰箱 bīngxiāng ❶ icebox ❷ refrigerator; fridge; frig

冰消瓦解 bīngxiāo-wǎjiě melt like ice and break like tiles; disintegrate; dissolve; collapse: 他们谈心之后，隔阂已经~。After a tête-à-tête, their misunderstanding disappeared like melting ice.

冰绡 bīngxiāo 〈书面〉 very thin and transparent silk fabric

冰鞋 bīngxié skating boots; skates: 旱~ roller skates

冰心 bīngxīn 〈书面〉 pure and innocent soul; loyal heart: 洛阳亲友如相问，一片~在玉壶。Should Luoyang friends and loved ones ask you how I am; My heart's a piece of ice in a chalice carved of jade.

冰穴 bīngxué ice cave

冰雪聪明 bīngxuě-cōngmíng extremely intelligent; extraordinarily bright

冰雪植物 bīngxuě zhíwù cryophyte

冰崖 bīngyá glacial cliff

冰幽幽 bīngyōuyōu *also* "冰丝丝的" a bit chilly

冰浴 bīngyù ice-bath

冰盏儿 bīngzhǎnr 〈旧语〉 small cups made of copper (used as bells by vendors selling cold drinks)

冰镇 bīngzhèn ice; iced: ~汽水 iced soda water or lemonade

冰洲石 bīngzhōushí Iceland spar

冰柱 bīngzhù icicle

冰爪 bīngzhuǎ 〈体育〉 crampon

冰砖 bīngzhuān ice cream in the shape of a brick; ice-cream brick

冰锥 bīngzhuī *also* "冰锥子"; "冰柱"; "冰溜" icicle

并 Bīng
another name for Taiyuan (太原), Shanxi Province
see also bìng

屏 bīng
see also bǐng; píng

屏营 bīngyíng 〈书面〉 (often used in memorials to the throne, letters, etc.) in fear and trepidation; trembling with fear: 不胜~待命之至 awaiting your Majesty's edict with fear and trepidation; anxiously await your instructions

栟 bīng

栟柑 bīnggān a variety of mandarin orange

栟榈 bīnglú 〈古语〉 palm

槟(檳、梹) bīng
see also bīn

槟榔 bīnglang ❶ areca; betel palm ❷ areca nut; betel nut

槟榔屿 Bīnglangyǔ Pinang (of Malaysia)

槟榔子 bīnglangzǐ 〈中药〉 betel nut; areca nut

兵 bīng
❶ weapons; arms: 坚甲利~ strong armour and sharp weapons / 短~相接 fight at close quarters ❷ soldier; serviceman: 当~ join the army; be a soldier / 征~ conscription / 招~ recruit (soldiers) / 新~ recruit / 老~ veteran / 当~的 soldier; armyman; serviceman ❸ army; troops: 炮~ artillery / 骑~ cavalry / 装甲~ armoured corps; armoured force / 精~ crack troops / 散~ stray (*or* disbanded) troops/ ~贵勇不贵多。The strength of an army lies in its morale, not its numbers. ❹ rank-and-file soldier; private: 士~ private / 普通一~ ordinary soldier; rank-and-file soldier / 官~一致 unity between men and officers ❺ about war or military affairs: 纸上谈~ theorize abstractly without referring to reality ❻ (in chess) pawn

兵败如山倒 bīng bài rú shān dǎo a routed army collapses like a landslide; be completely routed

兵变 bīngbiàn mutiny

兵柄 bīngbǐng 〈书面〉 military power; control of armed forces

兵不血刃 bīngbùxuèrèn no swords are stained with blood — win victory without firing a shot: ~就把叛乱平定了。The rebellion was quelled without bloodshed.

兵不厌诈 bīngbùyànzhà in war nothing is too deceitful; in war there can be no objection to deceit; all's fair in war

兵部 Bīngbù 〈历史〉 Ministry of War

兵操 bīngcāo 〈旧语〉 military training; military drill

兵差 bīngchāi 〈旧语〉 conscript labour; army corvée

兵车 bīngchē ❶ ancient war chariot ❷ troop vehicle; troop train

兵船 bīngchuán warship; naval vessel; man-of-war

兵丁 bīngdīng 〈旧语〉 private; rank-and-file soldier

兵端 bīngduān 〈书面〉 hostilities; war: 猝启~。Hostilities broke out abruptly.

兵多将广 bīngduō-jiàngguǎng have numerous troops and many generals; have vast military forces

兵法 bīngfǎ art of war; military strategy and tactics: 《孙子~》 *Sun-tzu's Art of War*

兵符 bīngfú ❶ 〈古语〉 commander's tally (used as authorization for mustering, deploying or commanding an army): 盗取~ steal the commander's tally ❷ see "兵书"

兵戈 bīnggē 〈书面〉 weapons; arms; war; warfare: 不动~ without resorting to war / ~扰攘 war-torn

兵革 bīnggé 〈书面〉 weapons and armour; war: ~未息 the war is

still on; hostilities have not ceased
兵工 bīnggōng war industry:～生产 war (*or* military) production
兵工厂 bīnggōngchǎng munitions factory; arsenal; ordnance
兵贵神速 bīngguìshénsù speed is vital in war; it's speed that counts in war:～,岂可拖延? As swift movement is the best tactic, how can we afford any delay?
兵荒马乱 bīnghuāng-mǎluàn troops on the rampage; chaos of war; turmoil of war:～的年月 turbulent years of war / 那时～, 动荡不安。In those days of lawlessness and disorder, life was chaotic.

B

兵火 bīnghuǒ soldiers and gunfire — war:～连年。There was war for years on end.
兵祸 bīnghuò scourge of war:连遭～ repeatedly ravaged by war; scourges of war coming in succession
兵机 bīngjī ❶ military affairs; military strategies; military plans ❷ military secret
兵家 bīngjiā ❶〈古语〉military strategist ❷ military commander:～所忌 be what a military commander would try to avoid by all means / ～必争之地 place of strategic importance; strategic point / 胜败乃～常事。For a military commander, winning or losing a battle is a common occurrence.
兵舰 bīngjiàn warship
兵谏 bīngjiàn coerce the ruler by force of arms into accepting one's exhortations; exhortations backed up by force of arms
兵精粮足 bīngjīng-liángzú crack or picked troops and abundant provisions
兵来将挡,水来土掩 bīng lái jiàng dǎng, shuǐ lái tǔ yǎn stop an advancing army with troops and on-rushing water with earth (dikes) — counter move for move; counter measure for measure:～,何惧之有? As one move can always be countered by another, what is there to be afraid of?
兵力 bīnglì military strength; armed forces:集中～ concentrate one's forces (*or* troops) / 分散～ deploy one's troops thinly; spread one's forces too thin / ～部署 battle array; troop dispositions / ～强大 formidable military strength / ～优势 numerical superiority / 三个团的～ troops which are three regiments strong; a force of three regiments
兵连祸结 bīnglián-huòjié scourges of war come in quick succession; be war-torn; be war-ridden:～三十余年 be ravaged by successive wars for more than thirty years / 该地区～,百姓苦不堪言。In the war-torn region, the suffering of the inhabitants was beyond description.
兵临城下 bīnglínchéngxià enemy troops are at the city gate; the city is under siege:等到～,他们才签定停战协定。They did not sign the armistice until the enemy troops arrived at the city walls.
兵乱 bīngluàn scourge of war:～之后又发生了瘟疫。In the wake of war came a plague.
兵马 bīngmǎ troops and horses; military forces:～未动,粮草先行。Food and fodder should go before troops start — spadework claims primary importance in any project.
兵马俑 bīngmǎyǒng 〈考古〉terra cotta warriors and horses:秦朝～展览 exhibition of Qin Dynasty terra cotta warriors and horses
兵痞 bīngpǐ army riffraff; wicked seasoned soldier
兵器 bīngqì weaponry; weapons; arms:～车 weapons carrier / ～知识 ABC of military arms
兵强马壮 bīngqiáng-mǎzhuàng well-trained soldiers with sturdy horses — well-equipped and powerful army:他们依仗～,不时侵犯邻国。Backed by superior military strength, they never ceased to invade their neighbouring countries.
兵权 bīngquán control of the armed forces; military power:争～ struggle for control of the army / 杯酒释～ relieve the generals of their control of the armed forces at a feast
兵刃 bīngrèn 〈书面〉weaponry; weapons; arms:～相接 come into armed conflict; cross swords with
兵戎 bīngróng arms; weapons:～相见 resort (*or* appeal) to arms
兵士 bīngshì rank-and-file soldier; private
兵事 bīngshì 〈书面〉military affairs
兵势 bīngshì military strength:～日蹙 gradual weakening of one's military strength
兵书 bīngshū book or treatise on the art of war:熟读～ be well-acquainted with books on the art of war
兵团 bīngtuán ❶ large military unit consisting of several armies or divisions; army group:野战～ field army / ～司令 commander of an army group ❷ army units above the regimental level; troop formation; armed force:主力～ main force / 地方～ local armed forces / 生产建设～ production and construction corps of the army
兵团战士 bīngtuán zhànshì educated youth from cities who went to work in production and construction corps; member of a production and construction corps
兵燹 bīngxiǎn destruction caused by war; ravages of war:～之余,农村一片凄凉。After the war the countryside was a scene of desolation.
兵饷 bīngxiǎng soldier's pay and provisions
兵械 bīngxiè arms and weapons; armament; weaponry
兵衅 bīngxìn war provocation:挑起～ provoke a war (*or* an armed conflict)
兵蚁 bīngyǐ 〈动物〉soldier ant; dinergate
兵役 bīngyì military service:服～ be conscripted for military service; serve in the armed forces
兵役法 bīngyìfǎ military service law
兵役制 bīngyìzhì system of military service
兵营 bīngyíng military camp; barracks
兵勇 bīngyǒng 〈旧语〉rank-and-file soldier; armyman
兵油子 bīngyóuzi 〈旧语〉oily sergeant; army ruffian
兵员 bīngyuán soldiers; troops:～十万 100,000 soldiers; an army 100,000 strong
兵源 bīngyuán human resources (for combat troops); manpower resources (for military service):～充足 abundant sources of troops; ample (*or* plentiful) manpower resources (for combat troops) / ～枯竭。Sources of troops are exhausted.
兵灾 bīngzāi scourge of war:～连年 repeatedly ravaged by war; war-torn; war-ridden
兵站 bīngzhàn military depot; army service station
兵仗 bīngzhàng 〈旧语〉weaponry:～作坊 ordnance workshop
兵制 bīngzhì military system
兵种 bīngzhǒng branch of one of the services:陆军下分步兵、炮兵、装甲兵等～。The army is subdivided into various branches, such as the infantry, the artillery, the armoured force, etc.
兵卒 bīngzú 〈旧语〉soldier

bǐng

禀(稟) bǐng ❶〈书面〉report; petition:～知上级 bring (a matter) to the attention of the leadership / 回～ report back (to one's superior) ❷〈旧语〉petition; written report to one's superior ❸ receive (orders, commands, etc.); be endowed with:天～聪颖 be endowed with natural intelligence
禀白 bǐngbái 〈书面〉beg to report; report (to one's superior)
禀报 bǐngbào report (to one's superior):如实～上级 give a full account (*or* make a detailed report) to the higher authorities
禀呈 bǐngchéng 〈书面〉respectfully submit:～统帅定夺 respectfully submit (*or* present) sth. to the commander-in-chief for final decision
禀承 bǐngchéng *also* "秉承" bǐngchéng 〈书面〉take orders from; act in accordance with
禀复 bǐngfù 〈书面〉report back (to one's superior):垂询之事,不日～。We will report back in a few days about the inquiry.
禀赋 bǐngfù natural endowment; gift:～甚高 be gifted with rare intelligence; be endowed with unusual intelligence
禀告 bǐnggào 〈旧语〉report:此事已～父母。My parents have been informed of what has happened.
禀见 bǐngjiàn 〈书面〉seek an audience (with one's superior); pay respects (to the higher-ups)
禀明 bǐngmíng explain (to one's superior); clarify:向父母～原委 explain the facts to one's parents; tell one's parents the whole story
禀受 bǐngshòu be endowed with; inherit (work, style, temperament, character etc.):他～了他父亲的学者气质。He inherited the scholarly temperament of his father.
禀帖 bǐngtiě 〈旧语〉petition:呈上～ present a petition to the higher-ups
禀性 bǐngxìng nature; disposition:～笃实 be honest and sincere by nature / ～难改 difficult to change one's nature (*or* temper)
禀奏 bǐngzòu submit or present a proposal or memorial to the throne

病逝 bìngshì die of illness; pass away
病死 bìngsǐ die of illness
病榻 bìngtà 〈书面〉sickbed:辗转～ toss and turn in a sickbed /～呻吟 moan and groan in a sickbed
病态 bìngtài ❶ sickly appearance:故作～ pretend to be ill; try to look ill ❷ morbid state; pathosis:～心理 morbid psychology (*or* mentality) /～经济 morbid economy ❸〈数学〉ill condition:～方程 ill-conditioned equation
病体 bìngtǐ ailing health:～有所好转。One's ailing health is improving.
病痛 bìngtòng indisposition; disorder; ailment:两位老人有个～什么的,都由邻居轮流照看。When the two elderly people fell ill, their neighbours took turns to look after them.
病退 bìngtuì retire for health reasons:申请～ apply for retirement for health reasons
病歪歪 bìngwāiwāi *see* "病病歪歪"
病危 bìngwēi be dangerously ill; be terminally ill:～通知 (of a patient) critical condition notice
病位 bìngwèi 〈中医〉seat of disease (in the human body); affected part
病象 bìngxiàng symptom (of an illness)
病休 bìngxiū sick leave:他正在～。He is on sick leave. /医生建议我～一周。The doctor prescribed a week's rest for me.
病恹恹 bìngyānyān sickly-looking:她一年到头都是那么～的提不起精神来。She looked ill and listless all year round.
病殃殃 bìngyāngyāng *see* "病病殃殃"
病秧子 bìngyāngzi 〈口语〉person who is chronically ill; chronic invalid; valetudinarian
病因 bìngyīn cause of illness; pathogeny
病友 bìngyǒu friend made while one is in hospital; ward mate:住院期间结识了几位～。While I was in hospital I made friends with several inmates of the ward.
病愈 bìngyù 〈书面〉get over one's illness; recover from an illness; be recovered:愿你早日～。We wish you a speedy recovery.
病员 bìngyuán person on the sick list; patient
病原 bìngyuán ❶ cause of disease; pathogeny ❷ *see* "病原体"
病原虫 bìngyuánchóng *also* "原虫" protozoon
病原菌 bìngyuánjūn *also* "病菌" pathogenic bacterium
病原体 bìngyuántǐ pathogen
病原学 bìngyuánxué aetiology
病源 bìngyuán cause of a disease; root trouble; aetiology:查明～ investigate the cause of a disease /公式化、概念化的～在于脱离生活实际。A basic weakness in the tendency to stereotypes and generalities lies in detachment from real life.
病院 bìngyuàn specialized hospital:传染～ infectious diseases hospital; isolation hospital /精神～ mental hospital /心脏～ heart hospital
病灾 bìngzāi ❶ poor health and ill luck; illness and misfortune ❷ plague of insects
病灶 bìngzào focus (of infection)
病征 bìngzhēng symptom (of a disease)
病症 bìngzhèng disease; illness:疑难～ difficult and complicated cases (of illness)
病重 bìngzhòng 〈口语〉very ill; seriously ill; in a critical condition
病株 bìngzhū diseased or infected plant
病状 bìngzhuàng symptom (of a disease)

并[1](併) bìng combine; merge; incorporate:两个办公室要～成一个。The two offices will merge (into one). /该公司已于去年～入联想集团。The company was incorporated into Legend Group last year.

并[2](並、竝) bìng ❶ side by side:肩～肩 shoulder to shoulder ❷ simultaneously; equally:两者～重 lay equal stress on both; attach equal importance to both /两法～施 adopt or carry out both measures simultaneously ❸〈副词〉*used before a negative for emphasis, usu. as a retort*:他的法文～不好。His French is not good at all. /我～不想伤害她。I didn't mean to hurt her. /他～没有什么了不起。He is not really that remarkable. ❹ and:他迅速～准确地回答了这个问题。He answered the question promptly and correctly. /会议讨论～通过了这个计划。The meeting discussed and adopted the plan. ❺〈书面〉*used in the same way as* 连:～此浅近道理亦不能明,可谓糊涂之至。One must be terribly muddleheaded if he can not understand a simple truth like that.
see also Bīng
并案 bìng'àn combine related cases:～处理 combine related cases and deal with them as a package
并摆儿 bìngbǎir 〈方言〉in a row; abreast:～停放着五辆桑塔纳。There are five Santanas parked in a row.
并产 bìngchǎn joint production (by different enterprises)
并串联 bìng-chuànlián *also* "并联"〈电工〉parallel series:～接线法 parallel-series connection
并存 bìngcún coexist:两种观点～的局面 situation where two views coexist /二者不能～。The two are mutually exclusive.
并蒂莲 bìngdìlián twin lotus flowers on one stalk — a devoted married couple
并发 bìngfā be complicated by; erupt simultaneously:他的心脏病与肺炎～。His heart trouble is complicated by pneumonia.
并发感染 bìngfā gǎnrǎn 〈医学〉accompanying infection
并发症 bìngfāzhèng 〈医学〉complication
并股 bìnggǔ 〈商业〉split-down
并骨 bìnggǔ burial of husband and wife in the same tomb
并伙 bìnghuǒ form a partnership; go into partnership
并激 bìngjī 〈电工〉shunt excitation:～电动机 shunt motor /～绕组 shunt winding
并驾齐驱 bìngjià-qíqū run neck and neck; drive abreast; be on a par with:两辆车～,向机场驶去。The two cars drove abreast to the airport. /和时代～的人永远年轻。He who keeps abreast with the times feels young always.
并肩 bìngjiān ❶ shoulder to shoulder; side by side; abreast:～前进 advance shoulder to shoulder ❷〈比喻〉take unified action; make joint efforts:～努力 work hard in concert; make concerted efforts /～作战 fight side by side
并进 bìngjìn progress abreast; run parallel:齐头～ advance side by side; go forward together; do two or more things at the same time
并举 bìngjǔ develop simultaneously:农、林、牧、副、渔～ simultaneous (*or* all-round) development of agriculture, forestry, animal husbandry, sidelines and fishery
并卷机 bìngjuǎnjī 〈纺织〉ribbon lap machine
并力 bìnglì 〈书面〉make joint efforts; join forces:～坚守 join forces in defending (a position); jointly hold fast (to the position)
并立 bìnglì stand side by side; exist simultaneously:这两种观点可以～。Both views are equally tenable.
并励 bìnglì 〈电工〉shunt excitation:～电机 shunt-excited machine /～发电机 shunt generator
并联 bìnglián ❶ join together in a parallel manner ❷〈电工〉parallel connection:～电路 parallel circuit /～馈电 parallel feed
并联电弧炉 bìnglián diànhúlú 〈冶金〉parallel-arc furnace
并列 bìngliè stand side by side; be juxtaposed:～榜首 appear side by side at the top of the list of successful candidates /两种产品将～展出。These two products will be on show side by side. /这部小说可以同世界文学名著～。This novel can be placed on a par with literary masterpieces of the world.
并列分句 bìngliè fēnjù 〈语言〉coordinate clause
并列句 bìnglièjù 〈语言〉compound sentence
并流 bìngliú 〈物理〉parallel-flow:～汽轮机〈机械〉parallel-flow turbine
并拢 bìnglǒng put together:～双翅 (of a bird) fold its wings
并茂 bìngmào match each other (in quantity as well as quality); be both excellent:图文～。The illustrations (of a book) match the text in quality.
并排 bìngpái side by side; abreast:三人～走来。Three people walked over abreast.
并辔 bìngpèi ride side by side (on horseback)
并且 bìngqiě ❶ and; also; as well as:同情～支持各国人民的正义斗争 sympathize and support the just struggles of the people of all countries ❷ furthermore; moreover; in addition:这个电影娱乐性很强,～也有教育意义。This movie is not only very entertaining, but instructive as well. /他完成了工作,～完成得很好。He did his job and did it well.
并日 bìngrì 〈书面〉❶ on the same day ❷ for days on end:～趱程 pursue one's journey for days on end
并日而食 bìngrì'érshí 〈书面〉eat one or two meals in every two or

three days — live in poverty or live an extremely busy life

并入 bìngrù merge into; incorporate in:第三章可以～第二章。The third chapter can be incorporated into the second.

并纱 bìngshā 〈纺织〉doubling:～机 doubling winder

并生 bìngshēng 〈生物〉intercrescence

并世 bìngshì in the present world; in contemporary society:～无第二人 unrivalled in contemporary society; peerless

B

并条 bìngtiáo 〈纺织〉drawing:～机 drawing frame

并吞 bìngtūn swallow up; annex; merge:～别国领土 annex the territory of another country /这个公司～了几家小企业。The firm has swallowed up several small enterprises.

并网 bìngwǎng merge and synchronize two or more power grids

并行 bìngxíng ❶ walk side by side:携手～ walk together hand in hand ❷ do two or more things at the same time:打针与吃药～ take both medicine and injections ❸〈计算机〉parallel:～处理 parallel processing /～存取 parallel access; simultaneous access /～输入 parallel entry /～存储 parallel storage

并行不悖 bìngxíng-bùbèi run parallel; not be mutually exclusive; not be contradictory to each other:～的利益 parallel interests /这两种想法完全不同,但是可以～。These two ideas are entirely different but they need not be mutually exclusive.

并行处理机 bìngxíng chǔlǐjī 〈计算机〉parallel processor

并行计算机 bìngxíng jìsuànjī 〈计算机〉parallel computer

并行进化 bìngxíng jìnhuà 〈生物〉parallel evolution

并行通信 bìngxíng tōngxìn 〈信息〉parallel communication

并用 bìngyòng apply (methods) simultaneously:威胁、利诱～ combine threat with cajolery

并指 bìngzhǐ 〈生理〉syndactyl:～畸形 syndactylism

并重 bìngzhòng lay equal stress on; pay equal attention to:理论与实践～ lay equal stress on theory and practice /预防和治疗～。Prevention and cure should be given equal emphasis.

摒

bìng get rid of; dismiss; brush aside:～之门外 keep sb. away

摒除 bìngchú get rid of; renounce:～万难 surmount all difficulties

摒挡 bìngdàng 〈书面〉arrange; put in order:～行李 get one's luggage ready; pack one's things up /～一切 put everything in order

摒绝 bìngjué put a stop to; dismiss for good and all:～一切应酬 stop (*or* cut out) all social engagements /～妄念 resolutely dismiss all unrealistic notions from one's mind; rid one's mind of all illusions

摒弃 bìngqì discard; get rid of; abandon:～前嫌 dispense with all previous ill will /～杂务 get rid of sundry duties

bō

饽

bō bun; cake

饽饽 bōbo 〈方言〉❶ pastry ❷ steamed bun; cake:玉米～ maize cake

拨(撥)

bō ❶ (usu. with hand, foot or stick) stir; poke; turn:～火 poke the fire /～灰 stir ashes /～弦 pluck the strings /～钟 set a clock /～电话号码 dial a telephone number /～算盘 tick off the beads on an abacus /把分针往后～一点。Move the minute hand backward a little. /转轴～弦三两声,未成曲调先有情。A few sweeps on the strings formed no complete air, But one could have a foretaste of feeling there. ❷ allocate; assign; appropriate:～出一笔款子作为教育经费 allocate a sum for education; make an appropriation for education /～十辆卡车运粮 dispatch ten trucks to carry grain /～五个人做这个工作 assign five people for the job ❸ turn round:～头便往回跑 turn round and run back ❹〈量词〉group; batch:轮～休息 take rest by turns /我们分成两～走。We will go in two groups. /来了三～学生。Three batches of students have arrived.

拨兵 bōbīng despatch troops

拨发 bōfā transfer; deliver; set aside; appropriate:～救济粮 set aside relief grains for delivery

拨付 bōfù appropriate (a sum of money); make payments as earmarked:按月～ make monthly appropriations (*or* payments)

拨工 bōgōng 〈方言〉exchange work or labour

拨号 bōhào 〈通信〉dial a number; dial:～系统 dial system

拨号电话 bōhào diànhuà dial telephone

拨号盘 bōhàopán telephone dial; dial plate

拨火棍 bōhuǒgùn poker

拨开 bōkāi push aside:～人群 push through the crowd /～云雾见青天 part the clouds and mist to see the clear skies — restore justice

拨款 bōkuǎn ❶ allocate funds:给基本建设～ allocate funds for capital construction ❷ allocated funds; appropriation:军事～ military appropriation /财政～ financial allocation /～委员会 appropriations committee /～法案 appropriation bill

拨拉 bōla stir; turn; move:～算盘子儿 tick off (*or* move) the beads on an abacus /你当我是谁?把我随意～过来～过去的? What do you take me for that you can order me about?

拨剌 bōlà 〈象声〉*indicating sound of fish splashing in water*:船尾跳鱼～鸣。The fish were splashing about at the stern.

拨浪鼓 bōlanggǔ *also* "波浪鼓" bōlanggǔ rattle-drum (used by pedlars or as a toy)

拨楞 bōleng 〈方言〉wave; shake:他～了一下脑袋,表示不同意。He shook his head in disagreement.

拨乱反正 bōluàn-fǎnzhèng bring order out of chaos; set things to rights; set things right:此正～之时。This is the time when things have to be set to rights.

拨弄 bōnong ❶ move to and fro; fiddle with:～炭火 poke the charcoal fire /用手不停地～铅笔 fiddle with a pencil /小猫用前爪～毛线球。The kitten played with the knitting wool ball with its front paws. ❷ order about; manipulate:命运的～使这两人成了夫妻。It was by a trick of fate that they became husband and wife. /这些人你能～得了吗? Do you think you can handle these people? ❸ stir up; incite:～是非 sow discord; stir up trouble by gossip

拨冗 bōrǒng 〈套语〉find time in the midst of pressing affairs:请～一阅。Please find time to read it.

拨弦乐器 bōxián yuèqì plucked string instrument

拨鱼儿 bōyúr 〈方言〉❶ boiled dough chips (shaped like fish) ❷ jelly chips (shaped like fish) made from bean or sometimes sweet potato; starch:芝麻酱拌～ jelly chips mixed with sesame sauce

拨云见日 bōyún-jiànrì dispel the clouds and see the sun shining through — restore justice; enlighten:先生的教诲,有如～,终身不忘。My master enlightened me as if parting the clouds to reveal the sun, and his instruction will remain for ever green in my memory.

拨正 bōzhèng set right; correct:～航向 correct the course (of a ship, etc.)

拨转 bōzhuǎn turn round:～马头 turn the horse round /～身就走 turn round and walk away

拨准 bōzhǔn put in a correct position:～时钟 set the clock

拨子 bōzi ❶〈乐器〉plectrum ❷ *also* "高拨子" gāobōzi one of the main tunes in Chinese operas ❸〈量词〉batch; group:刚才有一～队伍从这里走过。A group of soldiers passed by just now.

拨奏 bōzòu 〈音乐〉pizzicato

鲅(鱍)

bō

鲅鲅 bōbō 〈书面〉leaping of fish

趵

bō 〈书面〉kick

see also bào

趵趵 bōbō 〈象声〉sound of feet stepping on ground; footfall

播

bō ❶ spread; broadcast:传～ spread (idea, news, etc.)/广～ broadcast /新闻联～ national news on TV (relayed by many stations all over the country) /音乐会正在实况转～。The concert is being broadcast live. ❷ sow (seeds):春～ spring sowing /撒～ broadcast sowing /～小麦 sow wheat ❸〈书面〉migrate; exile

播唱 bōchàng sing over the radio:～京剧唱段 broadcast arias from Beijing opera

播出 bōchū broadcast; transmit; be on the air:～时间 airtime

播传 bōchuán spread; propagate:～科学真理 spread (*or* propagate) scientific truth

播荡 bōdàng ❶ shake; rock; toss:船在巨浪中～着。The boat rocked in the rough sea. ❷〈书面〉drift apart and become homeless; be displaced

播发 bōfā broadcast (news, etc.) on the air:～新闻 broadcast news

播放 bōfàng ❶ transmit by radio; go on the air:～录音讲话 relay

a recorded speech ❷ broadcast：～电视节目 broadcast a TV programme
播幅 bōfú 〈农业〉(row) seeding breadth
播火 bōhuǒ ❶ spread revolution (a term often used before the 1980's) ❷ disseminate the knowledge of science and technology
播讲 bōjiǎng teach or narrate by radio or TV; broadcast：～商业英语 teach business English over the radio
播控中心 bōkòng zhōngxīn broadcasting centre
播弄 bōnong ❶ order about; manipulate：我们新来乍到的，只好由他～。We are new here and have to put up with his manipulations. ❷ instigate; incite; sow discord：～是非的新闻 news that foments discord
播迁 bōqiān 〈书面〉wander about and move from place to place; drift from place to place
播撒 bōsǎ scatter; broadcast：～树种 broadcast tree seeds
播散 bōsàn exude; give off; disseminate; broadcast：田野里～着野花的香气。The scent of wild flowers wafted all over the fields.
播送 bōsòng broadcast; transmit：～国际新闻 broadcast international news /～文艺节目 transmit an entertainment programme
播扬 bōyáng ❶ propagate; spread：～他的劣迹 give publicity to his notorious conduct ❷〈书面〉start; arouse
播音 bōyīn transmit; broadcast：～室 broadcasting studio /～员 announcer /开始～ go on the air /～结束 go off the air /这次～到此结束。That concludes our programme for this transmission.
播映 bōyìng televise; show on television; transmit by television：今晚～英国故事片。A British feature film will be on television tonight.
播种 bōzhǒng sow seeds; sow; seed
播种机 bōzhǒngjī seeder; planter; grain drill
播种 bōzhòng grow by sowing seeds：～玉米 plant corn /～季节 sowing season /按时～ timely sowing /～面积 sown area; seeded area /～期 sowing time

钵（缽） bō

❶ earthen bowl：饭～ rice bowl ❷ alms bowl (of a Buddhist monk)：沿门托～ beg alms from door to door /托～僧 alms-begging monk
钵头 bōtóu 〈方言〉earthen bowl：他捧着一～米饭。He was holding an earthen bowl of cooked rice in both hands.
钵盂 bōyú Buddhist monk's alms bowl
钵子 bōzi 〈方言〉earthen bowl

般 bō

see also bān; pán
般若 bōrě 〈佛教〉(transliteration from the Sanskrit *prajñā*) highest wisdom

波 bō

❶ wave：微～ ripples /海～ sea wave ❷〈物理〉wave：电～ electric wave /声～ sound wave /光～ light wave /电磁～ electromagnetic wave /短～ short wave /中～ medium wave /长～ long wave /纵～ longitudinal wave /横～ transverse wave /微～ microwave ❸ unexpected turn of events：风～ storm; disturbance; turmoil /一～未平，一～又起。Hardly has one upheaval quieted down than another comes up. ❹〈方言〉run; rush：东奔西～ run hither and thither; rush about ❺〈方言〉(transliteration) ball：打～ play ball
波长 bōcháng wavelength：～计 wavemeter; cymometer
波茨坦公告 Bōcítǎn Gōnggào Potsdam Proclamation (26 July 1945)
波茨坦会议 Bōcítǎn Huìyì Potsdam Conference (17 July-2 Aug. 1945) at Potsdam, Germany
波荡 bōdàng rise and fall gently：秋风徐来，湖水～。The lake ripples as the autumn breeze gently blows over it.
波导 bōdǎo 〈物理〉wave guide：～光 optical waveguide
波导管 bōdǎoguǎn wave guide (tube)
波导激光器 bōdǎo jīguāngqì waveguide laser
波导理论 bōdǎo lǐlùn 〈物理〉waveguide theory
波导通信 bōdǎo tōngxìn waveguide communication
波道 bōdào radio frequency channel：～开关 channel switch /～转换开关 channel selector
波动 bōdòng ❶ undulate; fluctuate; rise and fall：情绪～ be in an unsettled state of mind /物价～ price fluctuation /生产～ fluctuation in production /周期性～ cyclical fluctuation /～汇率 fluctuating exchange rate /～幅度 fluctuation margin /他一上台，立即引起了全场一阵～。The moment he appeared on the stage, there rose a buzz of excitement through the audience. ❷〈物理〉wave：～力学 wave mechanics /～学 wave theory
波段 bōduàn wave band：八～的收音机 radio with eight wave bands /～开关 band switch; waver
波段选择器 bōduàn xuǎnzéqì 〈电子〉band selector
波多黎各 Bōduōlígè Puerto Rico：～人 Puerto Rican
波恩 Bō'ēn Bonn (formerly capital of West Germany)
波尔布特 Bō'ěrbùtè Pol Pot (1925? 1928? -1998), leader of Khmer Rouge, and Prime Minister of Cambodia from 1976-1979
波尔多葡萄酒 Bō'ěrduō pútaojiǔ Bordeaux wine
波尔多液 bō'ěrduōyè 〈农药〉Bordeaux mixture
波尔卡 bō'ěrkǎ 〈舞蹈〉polka, a Czech folk dance
波发生器 bōfāshēngqì wave generator
波峰 bōfēng 〈物理〉wave crest
波幅 bōfú 〈物理〉*also*"振幅" zhènfú amplitude：～失真 amplitude distortion /～调制 amplitude modulation /～共振 amplitude resonance
波腹 bōfù 〈物理〉wave loop
波干扰 bōgānrǎo wave interference
波哥大 Bōgēdà Bogota, capital of Colombia
波谷 bōgǔ 〈物理〉trough
波光 bōguāng shimmering of the waves：～鸟影，交相辉映。The shimmering waves and the flitting shadows of birds set off each other.
波函数 bōhánshù 〈物理〉wave function
波焊 bōhàn 〈机械〉wave soldering
波黑共和国 Bō-Hēi Gònghéguó Republic of Bosnia-Herzegovena
波及 bōjí spread to; involve; affect：这次地震～到整个西南地区。The earthquake affected the whole southwestern area. /此案～了好几个政界人物。This case involved quite a few political dignitaries. /该事件的影响～到全国。The impact of the incident spread across the whole country.
波节 bōjié *also*"驻波" zhùbō 〈物理〉standing wave
波谲云诡 bōjué-yúnguǐ *also*"云谲波诡"(of affairs of human life) unpredictable and ever-changing
波裤 bōkù 〈方言〉sports pants
波兰 Bōlán Poland：～人 Pole /～语 Polish (language) /～正教会 Polish Orthodox Church
波澜 bōlán big waves; billows：他的话在她心里激起了阵阵～。His words stirred up billows of emotion deep down in her heart. /～迭起。The sea surged wave upon wave. *or* Incidents occurred one after another.
波澜老成 bōlán-lǎochéng (of a poem or an essay) powerful and masterly
波澜起伏 bōlán-qǐfú ❶ waves rise and fall ❷ (of a piece of writing) one incident comes on top of another; unfolds one climax after another：故事情节～。The plot of the story consists of a series of incidents leading to a climax and dénouement.
波澜壮阔 bōlán-zhuàngkuò enormous expanse of roaring waves; scene unfolding on a magnificent scale：～的民族解放运动 surging tide of the national liberation movement /一首～的史诗 epic of magnificent sweep /～的一生 glorious life
波浪 bōlàng wave：～式 wavy style (of hair) /～起伏 waves rising and falling /～滔天 billows surging sky-high /一道道～不断涌来，撞在岩石上。Wave after wave kept rolling in, dashing over the rocks. /斗争将是长期的、艰巨的，发展是～式的。The struggle will be protracted and arduous, and will have ups and downs in its development.
波浪热 bōlàngrè *see*"波状热"
波浪鼓 bōlanggǔ *also*"拨浪鼓" bōlanggǔ rattle-drum
波累 bōlěi involve; implicate
波棱盖 bōlenggài 〈方言〉kneecap：我摔了一跤，磕破了～。I fell and hurt my knee.
波力发电 bōlì fādiàn wave power generation：～机 wave-powered generator /～厂 wave power station
波利尼西亚 Bōlìníxīyà Polynesia：～人 Polynesian /～语 Polynesian (language) /～群岛 Polynesian Island Group
波粒共振效应 bōlì gòngzhèn xiàoyìng 〈物理〉Cerenkov resonant effect; wave-particle resonant effect
波粒子 bōlìzǐ 〈物理〉wavicle

波罗的海 Bōluódìhǎi Baltic Sea：～诸国 Baltic states (Lithuania, Estonia and Latvia)
波罗的海人 Bōluódìhǎirén Balt (a native or inhabitant of the Baltic region)
波罗蜜 bōluómì ❶〈佛教〉Paramita (arrival on the other shore) ❷ *also* "木菠萝" mùbōluó jackfruit
波罗乃兹 bōluónǎizī *also* "波罗乃兹舞曲" polonaise, music for a Polish dance of the same name

B

波美比重计 Bōměi bǐzhòngjì Baume hydrometer
波美度 bōměidù 〈物理〉degree Baume；〈化学〉Baume degree
波迷 bōmí 〈方言〉(ball game) fan
波面 bōmiàn wave surface
波能 bōnéng wave energy：～发电 generate electricity by using wave energy
波平浪静 bōpíng-làngjìng (of lake, sea, etc.) calm
波剖面 bōpōumiàn wave profile
波普文化 bōpǔ wénhuà culture characterized by pop art; pop culture
波普艺术 bōpǔ yìshù pop art (an art form that uses everyday objects, especially popular mass-produced articles, as its subject matter)
波谱 bōpǔ 〈物理〉spectrum
波谱学 bōpǔxué spectroscopy
波俏 bōqiào beautiful; graceful：白塔在淡灰色天幕的衬托下显得既庄严又～。The White Dagoba, set off by the pale canopy of the sky, looks stately and graceful.
波矢 bōshǐ 〈物理〉wave vector：～空间 wave vector space
波士 bōshì 〈方言〉boss
波束 bōshù 〈物理〉(wave) beam：～发射机 beam transmitter / ～发射器 beam reflector / ～宽度 beam width
波束面 bōshùmiàn 〈通信〉ground area covered by the beams of a communication satellite; footprint
波束指向精度 bōshù zhǐxiàng jīngdù beam-pointing accuracy
波束制导 bōshù zhìdǎo beam rider guidance; beam homing
波数 bōshù 〈物理〉wave number
波斯 Bōsī (former name for 伊朗) Persia：～人 Persian / ～语 Persian (language) / ～湾 Persian Gulf / ～文学 Persian literature / ～御道 Persian Royal Road / ～猫 Persian cat / ～地毯 Persian carpet (*or* rug)
波斯帝国 Bōsī Dìguó Persian Empire (6th c.-4th c.BC)
波斯菊 bōsījú 〈植物〉coreopsis
波斯尼亚 Bōsīníyà Bosnia：～黑塞哥维那 Bosnia-Herzegovena
波速 bōsù wave speed; wave velocity
波涛 bōtāo great waves; billows：万顷～ limitless expanse of surging waves / ～汹涌 rolling waves / ～滚滚的大海 roaring sea
波特 bōtè 〈通信〉baud, unit used to measure the speed of electronic code transmissions
波纹 bōwén ❶ ripple：微风吹来，湖面泛起层层～。A myriad of ripples appear on the lake when a gentle wind blows. ❷ corrugation：～纸板 corrugated cardboard / ～管 corrugated pipe / ～瓦 corrugated tile / ～铁 corrugated iron
波仙 bōxiān 〈方言〉percentage
波形 bōxíng ❶ wave pattern; wave form：～曲线 wave curve / ～花纹 wave pattern ❷〈物理〉waveform; waveshape：～监视器 waveform monitor / ～转换器 waver
波形图 bōxíngtú oscillogram; oscillograph
波音 bōyīn ❶〈音乐〉mordent：逆～ inverted mordent ❷ Boeing (name of an airplane company)：～747 飞机 Boeing 747
波音公司 Bōyīn Gōngsī Boeing Company (US airplane company founded in July 1961 by W. E. Boeing)
波源 bōyuán wave source
波折 bōzhé twists and turns：农业生产曾屡经～，现在终于发展起来了。Agriculture is finally picking up after many twists and turns. / 他的事业曾几经～。His career has witnessed several ups and downs. *or* He has a chequered career.
波磔 bōzhé left-falling and right-falling strokes (in Chinese characters)
波状热 bōzhuàngrè 〈医学〉*also* "波浪热" undulant fever; brucellosis
波状体 bōzhuàngtǐ unduloid
波状纹理 bōzhuàng wénlǐ 〈地质〉current lamination
波状叶 bōzhuàngyè 〈植物〉sinuate leaves
波状云 bōzhuàngyún undulatus
波状运动 bōzhuàng yùndòng wave-like motion
波子 bōzi 〈方言〉bullet
波阻 bōzǔ 〈物理〉wave-drag

菠 bō

菠菜 bōcài spinach
菠薐菜 bōléngcài 〈方言〉spinach
菠萝 bōluó *also* "凤梨" fènglí pineapple
菠萝蜜 bōluómì *also* "波萝蜜" bōluómì jackfruit

啵 bō

see also bo
啵啵 bōbō 〈象声〉*indicating boiling of water*：～响的滚水 burbling boiling water

玻 bō

玻甲鱼 bōjiǎyú shrimpfish; razor fish
玻利维亚 Bōlìwéiyà Bolivia：～人 Bolivian
玻璃 bōli ❶ glass：～杯 glass / ～窗 window pane / ～器皿 glassware; glass vessel / ～刀 glass-cutter / ～工厂 glass works / 彩色～ tinted glass / 彩色拼花～ stained glass / 雕花～ cut glass / 毛～ rough-cast (*or* ground) glass; frosted glass / 导电～ conductive glass / 防弹～ bullet-resisting glass / 钢化～ tempered (*or* toughened) glass / 光学～ optical glass / 耐火～ refractory (*or* fireproof) glass ❷〈口语〉transparent plastic; things that look like glass：有机～ organic glass; plexiglass; perspex
玻璃板 bōlibǎn plate glass; glass top (as of a desk)
玻璃半导体 bōli bàndǎotǐ 〈无线电〉glass or glassy semiconductor
玻璃布 bōlibù glass fabric
玻璃吹制 bōli chuīzhì glassblowing
玻璃电容器 bōli diànróngqì 〈电工〉glass-plate capacitor
玻璃粉 bōlifěn ❶ glass dust ❷ *also* "洋粉" yángfěn; "冻粉" dòngfěn; "燕菜精" yàncàijīng agar-agar powder
玻璃钢 bōligāng glass-fibre reinforced plastic
玻璃合金 bōli héjīn 〈冶金〉glass alloy
玻璃激光器 bōli jīguāngqì glass laser
玻璃胶 bōlijiāo glass cement
玻璃绝缘子 bōli juéyuánzǐ 〈电工〉glass insulator
玻璃棉 bōlimián glass wool
玻璃磨光机 bōli móguāngjī 〈化工〉glass grinder or grinding machine
玻璃熔炉 bōli rónglú 〈化工〉glass furnace
玻璃纱 bōlishā *also* "巴里纱" bālǐshā 〈纺织〉voile
玻璃蚀刻 bōli shíkè hyalography：～器 hyalography
玻璃丝 bōlisī glass silk; spun glass：～纺织品 glass textile
玻璃陶瓷 bōli táocí glass-ceramic
玻璃体 bōlitǐ 〈医学〉crystalline lens
玻璃退火炉 bōli tuìhuǒlú 〈化工〉glass oven
玻璃纤维 bōli xiānwéi glass fibre; fibre glass
玻璃釉 bōliyòu 〈化工〉glass-glaze
玻璃纸 bōlizhǐ cellophane; glassine
玻璃制品 bōli zhìpǐn 〈化工〉glasswork
玻璃砖 bōlizhuān ❶ heavy sheet glass ❷ glass brick
玻璃钻 bōlizuàn 〈化工〉glass drill
玻意耳 Bōyì'ěr Robert Boyle (1627-1691), Irish-born natural philosopher：～定律 Boyle's law
玻鱼 bōyú glassfish; glass perch
玻陨石 bōyǔnshí 〈地质〉tektite

剥 bō

used only in compounds
see also bāo
剥采比 bōcǎibǐ 〈矿业〉stripping-to-ore ratio; stripping ratio
剥夺 bōduó ❶ expropriate; strip (by force)：被～的阶级 expropriated classes ❷ deprive (by law)：～政治权利终身 deprive sb. of his or her political rights for life / ～公民权 deprive sb. of all civil rights; deprive sb. of his or her citizenship; disfranchise sb.
剥肤椎髓 bōfū-chuísuǐ 〈书面〉peel sb.'s skin and break his marrowbones — cruel exploitation; ruthless plunder
剥茧抽丝 bōjiǎn-chōusī reel silk from a cocoon — seek out a clue from a confused or chaotic situation

剥离 bōlí (of tissue, skin, covering, etc.) peel off; come off; be stripped:～矿石 strip ore /匣子上的漆已开始～。The garnish of the box has begun to peel off.
剥离区 bōlíqū 〈矿业〉stripping area
剥离术 bōlíshù 〈医学〉decollement
剥落 bōluò ❶ peel off:墙上的油漆已经～。The paint on the wall has peeled off. /经过多年的风雨侵蚀,石碑有些地方已经～。Parts of the tablet have come off after years of erosion. ❷〈地质〉exfoliation
剥麻机 bōmájī decorticator
剥棉籽绒机 bōmiánzǐróngjī delinter
剥皮机 bōpíjī 〈林业〉barker
剥蚀 bōshí ❶ erode; wear away; corrode; denude:风雨的～ erosion by wind and rain /冰川～ glacial erosion /～土壤 denuded soil /～作用 erosion; denudation ❷ embezzle or seize little by little
剥脱 bōtuō ❶ strip off; tear down:～他的面具,他不过是个没有骨气的奴才。Stripped of his mask, he is nothing but a spineless flunkey. ❷ peel off; come off:柱子上的油漆已经～。The paint on the pillar has come off.
剥脱性皮炎 bōtuōxìng píyán exfoliative dermatitis
剥削 bōxuē exploit:～制度 exploitation system /受到残酷的～ be cruelly exploited /～和压迫 exploitation and oppression /～者 exploiter /被～者 the exploited
剥削阶级 bōxuējiējí exploiting class
剥啄 bōzhuó 〈书面〉〈象声〉tap (on a door or window):～声 sound of tapping

bó

襮 bó 〈书面〉❶ reveal; show:表～ expose; show up ❷ surface; outward look

孛 bó 〈书面〉see "勃" bó
see also bèi

浡 bó 〈书面〉brace up; rise again

鹁 bó
鹁鸽 bógē also "家鸽" jiāgē pigeon
鹁鸪 bógū (commonly known as 水鸪鸪) wood-pigeon

脖 bó ❶ neck ❷ sth. shaped like a neck:长～儿水罐 long-necked jar for carrying water
脖颈儿 bógěngr also "脖颈子" back of the neck; nape
脖梗子 bógěngzi also "脖颈儿" back of the neck; nape
脖领儿 bólǐngr also "脖领子"〈方言〉collar of a garment; collar:抓住他的～不放 seize him by the collar
脖儿掴 bórguāi also "脖儿拐"〈方言〉box sb.'s ears:打他一个～。Give him a box on the ears.
脖子 bózi neck:卡～ clutch at sb.'s throat /割断～ cut sb.'s throat

勃(敦) bó 〈书面〉prosperous; thriving:蓬～ vigorous; thriving
勃勃 bóbó thriving; vigorous; exuberant:朝气～ youthful and vigorous; full of youthful vitality /精神～ very enthusiastic; in exuberant spirits /雄心～ very ambitious
勃发 bófā 〈书面〉❶ thrive; prosper:英姿～ beam with youth and vigour /生机～ be full of vitality (*or* life) ❷ break out; erupt:游兴～ be seized with a desire to go sight-seeing /战争～。The war broke out.
勃朗宁 Bólángníng ❶ Elizabeth Barrett Browning (1806-1861), English poet and critic ❷ Robert Browning (1812-1889), English poet and Elizabeth Browning's husband ❸ John Moses Browning (1855-1926), designer of many automatic weapons:～手枪 Browning pistol /～自动步枪 Browning automatic rifle ❹ Browning (pistol)
勃列日涅夫 Bólièrìnièfū Leonid Ilyich Brezhnev (1906-1982), Soviet statesman:～主义 Brezhnev Doctrine (1977)
勃起 bóqǐ 〈生理〉erection
勃然 bórán ❶ vigorously:～而起 rise spectacularly out of nowhere; thrive with fresh vigour ❷ suddenly:～大怒 fly into a rage /～变色 change colour all at once; turn pale with anger all of a sudden
勃谿 bóxī also "勃豀"〈书面〉domestic bickering as between husband and wife:姑嫂～ bickerings between sisters-in-laws
勃豀 bóxī see "勃谿"
勃兴 bóxīng 〈书面〉rise suddenly; grow vigorously:新文艺运动的～ rise of the new literary movement

渤 bó
渤海 Bóhǎi Bohai Sea

馞 bó see "馝馞" bìbó

博[1] bó ❶ rich; abundant; plentiful:地大物～ vast in territory and rich in natural resources ❷ be knowledgeable and well informed:通今～古 be conversant with things past and present ❸〈书面〉big; wide:宽衣～带 loose gown and wide sash

博[2](**❷簙**) bó ❶ win; gain:以～欢心 win sb.'s favour/聊～一笑 just for your entertainment ❷ gamble:～徒 gambler
博爱 bó'ài universal love; universal fraternity or brotherhood:自由、平等、～ liberty, equality and fraternity
博采 bócǎi collect extensively:～众论 gather (*or* adopt) advice from all quarters
博茨瓦纳 Bócíwǎnà Botswana:～人 Botswanian; Botswanan
博达 bódá 〈书面〉learned; erudite; well-read:才识～ be erudite and insightful
博大 bódà extensive; rich:～精深 be both extensive and profound (in learning)/～的胸怀 broad-minded; large-minded
博得 bódé win; gain:～好评 enjoy a favourable reception; be favourably received /～信任 win sb.'s confidence /～全场喝彩 draw loud applause from the audience; bring the house down
博而不精 bó'érbùjīng know sth. of everything but not a lot about anything; Jack of all trades (and master of none):对英国文学,他～。He had an extensive knowledge of English literature, but did not go very deeply into it.
博古 bógǔ ❶ have an extensive knowledge of the past:～之士 scholar with an extensive knowledge of the past ❷ ancient article; antique ❸ Chinese traditional painting with ancient articles as objects ❹ imitation antique:～瓶 imitation antique vase (*or* bottle)
博古通今 bógǔ-tōngjīn have extensive knowledge of both past and present; be learned and well-informed:他是个～的人。He was a man of learning, both ancient and modern.
博览 bólǎn read extensively:～群书 read widely /～兼收 read widely and absorb extensively
博览会 bólǎnhuì fair; exposition:国际～ international fair /哥伦比亚世界～ World's Columbian Exposition (Chicago, 1894)
博洽 bóqià 〈书面〉broad in learning:～多闻 learned and well-informed
博取 bóqǔ try to gain; court:～欢心 curry favour /～同情 seek sympathy /～美誉 try to win a good name
博施济众 bóshī-jìzhòng provide liberal relief to the poor; bring relief to destitute people extensively; be interested in charities:他是个～的人,经常组织义演,救济灾民。He is a philanthropist and often helps organize benefit performances to relieve disaster victims.
博识 bóshí knowledgeable:多闻～ well-informed and knowledgeable /～之士 knowledgeable man
博识洽闻 bóshí-qiàwén be learned and well-informed
博士 bóshì ❶ doctor (an academic degree):哲学～ Doctor of Philosophy (Ph. D.) /～学位 doctor's degree; doctorate /名誉～学位 honorary doctorate /授与～学位 confer a Ph. D. degree on sb. /～生 Ph. D. candidate; doctorate student /～论文 Ph. D. thesis; Ph. D. dissertation ❷〈古语〉person specialized in a skill or trade:茶～ tea house waiter (who also makes the tea) ❸〈古语〉official title of a specialist (usu. in one of the Confucian classics) in charge of the dissemination of learning
博士后 bóshìhòu ❶ post-doctoral research; post-doctoral studies ❷ one who is engaged in such research or studies
博士买驴 bóshì-mǎilǘ act like the scholar who wrote at length about the purchase of a donkey without even mentioning the animal — write profusely but irrelevantly

博斯普鲁斯海峡 Bósīpǔlǔsī Hǎixiá Bosporus or Bosphorus Strait connecting the Black Sea and the Sea of Marmara
博闻广识 bówén-guǎngshí extensive information and knowledge
博闻强记 bówén-qiángjì *also* "博文强志"; "博文强识" have both wide learning and a retentive memory; have encyclopaedic knowledge: 他～, 人皆不及。Nobody can compare with him in extensive knowledge and retentive memory.
博物 bówù (general name for zoology, botany, mineralogy, physiology, etc.) natural science
博物馆 bówùguǎn museum: 中国历史～ Museum of Chinese History /～学 museology /～馆长 curator
博物学 bówùxué natural history; natural science: ～家 naturalist
博物院 bówùyuàn museum: 故宫～ Palace Museum
博学 bóxué learned; erudite: ～之士 learned scholar /～鸿儒 scholar of great learning /～多才 have both extensive knowledge and ability; be knowledgeable and talented
博雅 bóyǎ erudite; learned; well-educated: ～之士 erudite scholar; well-educated gentleman
博弈 bóyì 〈书面〉 play a game of *go*; play chess: ～规则 rules of the game
博弈论 bóyìlùn game theory
博引 bóyǐn quote extensively: 旁征～ well-provided with a wide range of authoritative quotations; well-documented

薄[1] bó ❶ slight; meagre; small: ～酬 small reward; token (*or* meagre) remuneration /空气稀～ thin air /感情淡～ cherish no deep affection (for sb.); remain indifferent (to each other) /～识〈谦词〉 my humble opinion ❷ not strong or solid; frail: 单～ thin and weak ❸ unkind; ungenerous; mean; frivolous: 刻～ unkind; harsh; mean /轻～ frivolous; flighty /待我不～ treat me generously (*or* kindly) ❹ despise; belittle: 菲～ belittle /鄙～ despise /厚此～彼 favour one and slight the other ❺ (Bó) a surname

薄[2] bó 〈书面〉 approach; near: 日～西山。The sun is setting behind the western hills. /～海同欢。All within the four seas (*or* People all over the country) will rejoice together.
see also báo; bò

薄暗 bó'àn dusk; twilight: ～之中看不清远处。You can't see very far in the twilight.
薄产 bóchǎn small property: 家有～。The family has some property.
薄惩 bóchéng mild punishment: 稍示～, 以视后效。The mild punishment merely serves as a warning for the future.
薄待 bódài treat ungenerously; treat rather badly: 我何尝～于你! When did I ever treat you ungenerously?
薄地 bódì thin soil; infertile land
薄伽丘 Bógāqiū Giovanni Boccaccio (1313-1375), Italian novelist, poet and humanist, author of *Decameron* (《十日谈》, 1348-1353)
薄厚 bóhòu *also* "厚薄" (treat) casually or with kindness: 亲戚有远近, 相待难免有～。There are close and distant relatives, and it's natural some are treated with more cordiality than others.
薄瘠 bójí (of land) lean; thin; unproductive
薄技 bójì 〈谦词〉 slight skill: 愿献～ would like to show my slight skill (for your entertainment) /良田千顷, 不如～随身。A thousand hectares of fertile land is not as good as a slight skill one has learned.
薄浆 bójiāng 〈建筑〉 grout; larry: ～砌筑法 larrying
薄近 bójìn 〈书面〉 come close to; approach; draw near: ～边地 approach the border region
薄敬 bójìng modest present: 区区～, 不足挂齿。It's but a modest present, which is not worth mentioning.
薄酒 bójiǔ 〈谦词〉 light wine: 敬备～, 恭候光临。I will have some wine ready and respectfully await your gracious presence.
薄礼 bólǐ 〈谦词〉 modest gift; small present: 奉上～, 敬希笑纳。I am sending you a small present, and hope you will like it.
薄利 bólì small profit: 可获～ can gain a small profit
薄利多销 bólì-duōxiāo small profits but quick returns; small profits and good sales: 生意人真的做到～, 那倒也会赚钱。If a businessman can really carry out the principle of "small profits and good sales", he will stand to gain.
薄面 bómiàn 〈谦词〉 on my humble account: 我的小儿子太没有礼貌, 希望看在我的～上原谅他。My little son behaved rudely. I hope you will forgive him on my account.
薄明 bómíng at early dawn; at the crack of dawn: ～时分, 我们开始上路。We started out at the crack of dawn.
薄命 bómìng (usu. of women) born under an unlucky star; ill-fated: ～女子 woman of unhappy fate /自古红颜多～。The lot of beautiful women has often been unfortunate since time immemorial.
薄膜 bómó ❶ membrane ❷ (thin) film: 透明～ transparent film /塑料～ plastic film
薄膜半导体 bómó bàndǎotǐ 〈无线电〉 thin-film semiconductor
薄膜材料 bómó cáiliào thin-film material
薄膜存储器 bómó cúnchǔqì 〈计算机〉 film memory or storage
薄膜存储式计算机 bómó cúnchǔshì jìsuànjī 〈计算机〉 thin-film memory computer
薄膜电阻 bómó diànzǔ film resistor
薄膜工艺 bómó gōngyì thin-film technology or process
薄膜集成电路 bómó jíchéng diànlù 〈无线电〉 thin-film integrated circuit
薄膜技术 bómó jìshù 〈物理〉 thin-film technique
薄膜物理学 bómó wùlǐxué thin-film physics
薄膜纤维 bómó xiānwéi film fibre
薄膜阴极 bómó yīnjí film cathode
薄暮 bómù 〈书面〉 dusk; twilight: 日出离家, ～而归 leave home at sunrise and come back at dusk /借着～的残光, 可以看见她在哭泣。In the twilight she could be seen sobbing.
薄片 bópiàn thin slice; thin section: 切成～ cut into thin slices /～分析 thin section analysis
薄情 bóqíng inconstant in love; fickle: ～人 fickle lover
薄弱 bóruò weak; frail: 意志～ weak-willed /基础～ weak-based /技术力量～ lack qualified technical personnel /兵力～ insufficient troop strength /责任心～ have little sense of responsibility /思想工作～ weak in ideological work /～环节 weak link; vulnerable spot
薄胎瓷器 bótāi cíqì 〈工美〉 eggshell china; eggshell porcelain
薄田 bótián infertile land; poor land
薄物细故 bówù-xìgù 〈书面〉 insignificant matters; trifles
薄雾 bówù (thin) mist; haze: 湖面泛起一片～。Above the lake rose a thin mist.
薄晓 bóxiǎo daybreak; dawn
薄行 bóxíng ❶ faithless conduct or behaviour; frivolity; immoral behaviour: 如此～, 岂能容忍! How can we tolerate such frivolous behaviour! ❷ frivolous: 为人～ be frivolous
薄幸 bóxìng 〈书面〉 fickle: ～男儿 fickle man; fickle lover
薄油层 bóyóucéng 〈石油〉 oil sheet
薄葬 bózàng simple burial: 提倡厚养～ advocate good care of one's parents (while they are alive) and simple burials for them (when they are dead)

礴 bó *see* "磅礴" pángbó

搏 bó ❶ wrestle; fight; struggle: 肉～ hand-to-hand fight /最后一～ make a last effort /人生能有几回～! How few are the real challenges of life! ❷ jump upon; pounce on: 狮子～兔。A lion pounced on a rabbit. ❸ beat; throb: 脉～ pulse
搏动 bódòng beat rhythmically; throb; pulsate: 心脏～ throbbing of the heart /～性疼痛 throbbing pain
搏斗 bódòu wrestle; fight; struggle: 近距离～ fight at close quarters /生死～ life-and-death struggle /与歹徒～ grapple with a gangster /和洪水～ battle with the flood
搏击 bójī strike; fight with: 苍鹰～长空 eagles cleave the lofty air/与风浪～ defy storms and waves
搏杀 bóshā fight and kill; combat: 徒手～恶狼 fight and kill a vicious wolf with bare hands /两位棋手正在拼力～。The two chess players are locked in a spirited contest.
搏噬 bóshì (of an animal) pounce on (another animal), clawing and biting
搏战 bózhàn wrestle; struggle

髆 bó 〈书面〉 shoulder

镈 bó ❶ 〈乐器〉 large ancient bell ❷ ancient hoe

捕头 bǔtóu 〈旧语〉head constable; sheriff
捕役 bǔyì *see* "捕快"
捕蝇草 bǔyíngcǎo 〈植物〉Venus's flytrap (*Dionaea muscipula*); flytrap
捕蝇器 bǔyíngqì flytrap
捕蝇纸 bǔyíngzhǐ flypaper
捕鱼 bǔyú catch fish; fish:下海～ go fishing on the sea /～度日 make a living by fishing
捕鱼法 bǔyúfǎ 〈法律〉fishery law
捕鱼权 bǔyúquán 〈法律〉fishery; piscary
捕捉 bǔzhuō catch; seize:～害虫 catch harmful insects /～逃犯 catch an escaped criminal; catch an escapee /～镜头 capture a scene (to take a picture); seize the right moment for a good shot; catch a good shot /～战机 seize a good opportunity for battle; seize the right moment to strike

哺 bǔ ❶ feed (a baby); nurse:嗷嗷待～ cry piteously for food ❷〈书面〉food in one's mouth:一饭三吐～ be unable to eat at leisure (indicating, for instance, a statesman's preoccupation with public affairs)
哺乳 bǔrǔ breast-feed; suckle; nurse:～时间 nursing hours /～期的母亲 nursing mother
哺乳动物 bǔrǔ dòngwù mammal
哺乳瓶 bǔrǔpíng feeding bottle
哺乳室 bǔrǔshì nursing room
哺乳仔畜 bǔrǔ zǐchù suckling
哺喂 bǔwèi feed; give suck to; rear
哺养 bǔyǎng feed; rear:以人乳～ feed with human milk /～成人 raise sb. to adulthood
哺育 bǔyù ❶ feed:～幼儿 feed a baby ❷ nurture; foster:在古老文化的～下,他成为当时著名诗人。Nurtured by the ancient culture he became a well-konwn poet of his day. /黄河、长江～了中华民族。The Yellow River and the Yangtze River have nurtured the Chinese nation.

鵏 bǔ *see* "地鵏" dìbǔ

卜 bǔ ❶ divination; fortune-telling:卖～先生 fortune-teller /求神问～ pray to gods and consult the oracle ❷〈书面〉foretell; predict:前途未～ hard to predict what lies ahead /凶吉未～ hard to tell whether this bodes ill or well /未～先知 be gifted with a second sight ❸〈书面〉select; choose:行期未～。The date of departure is still uncertain. ❹ (Bǔ) a surname
see also bo
卜辞 bǔcí oracle inscriptions of the Shang Dynasty on tortoise-shells or animal bones
卜骨 bǔgǔ oracle bone
卜卦 bǔguà divine by the Eight Trigrams
卜居 bǔjū 〈书面〉select a place to live; make one's home
卜课 bǔkè have a session of divination
卜邻 bǔlín choose a good neighbourhood
卜筮 bǔshì divination by tortoise shell or straw; fortune-telling
卜问 bǔwèn pray and consult the oracle
卜宅 bǔzhái ❶〈古语〉decide on the location of the capital by geomancy ❷〈书面〉decide on the location of a house or tomb by geomancy
卜昼卜夜 bǔzhòu-bǔyè ❶ wine and dine without restraint:～地寻欢作乐 seek sensual pleasure day and night ❷ work day and night:～地努力工作 work hard day and night

补(補) bǔ ❶ mend; patch; repair:缝～ mend and sew/～鱼网 repair a fishing net /～衣 mend (*or* patch) clothes /～靴子 repair boots /～袜子 darn socks /～车胎 patch up a puncture (in a tyre) ❷ fill; make up for:～漏洞 fill (*or* plug) the leak /～空缺 fill up a vacancy /～漏字 supply missing words /取长～短 overcome one's shortcomings by learning strong points from others /～其不足 make up a deficiency /这里再～两句。Add two more sentences here. ❸ nourish:～身体 tone up one's body /这鸡汤很～。The chicken soup is very nourishing. /多吃点肉～一～。Eat more meat to build up your health. ❹〈书面〉benefit; help; use:无～于事 not help matters /不无小～ not be without some advantage; be of some help
补白 bǔbái ❶ filler (in a newspaper or magazine) ❷ additional explanation or remarks:关于这份报告,容我～几句。Allow me to make a few additional remarks concerning the report.
补版 bǔbǎn 〈印刷〉mending
补办 bǔbàn ❶ do sth. after the time it should have been done:～工作许可证 apply for a work permit after one has already been working /～报到手续 report (for work, etc.) after ❷ repay a kindness or favour
补报 bǔbào ❶ make a report after the event; make a supplementary report:其他材料,容后～。Other materials shall be sent in afterwards. ❷ repay (a kindness):先生恩德,无以～。Nothing that I can do shall be enough to repay your generosity and kindness.
补编 bǔbiān supplement:《现代汉语词典～》*Supplement to A Dictionary of the Modern Chinese Language*
补差 bǔchā make up the difference or disparity between one's original salary and pension:他退休以后常常来帮助工作,都从不拿～。Since his retirement, he has often lent a hand in our work without asking for extra pay.
补偿 bǔcháng compensate; make up:照原价～ compensate according to the cost /～损失 compensate for a loss; cover the damage /～差额 make up a deficiency /～保险 insurance by way of indemnity; indemnity insurance /～措施 indemnity (*or* compensatory) measure /～贷款 compensatory financing /～性资金流通 compensatory financial flow /～性金融政策 compensatory monetary policy /～金 compensation; compensatory amount /～性贷款 compensatory credit /～教育 compensational education /这种损失无法～。This loss is irretrievable (*or* beyond retrieval).
补偿电容器 bǔcháng diànróngqì compensation condenser
补偿基金 bǔcháng jījīn compensation fund
补偿贸易 bǔcháng màoyì compensatory trade; compensation trade; counter trade
补偿式串绕电动机 bǔchángshì chuànrào diàndòngjī compensated series motor
补偿式感应电动机 bǔchángshì gǎnyìng diàndòngjī compensated induction motor
补偿式推斥电动机 bǔchángshì tuīchì diàndòngjī compensated repulsion motor
补充 bǔchōng ❶ replenish; supplement; complement; add:～师资力量 replenish the teaching staff /互相～ complement each other; be mutually complementary/～给养 replenish the supply /～两条意见 have two points to add /～新鲜血液 instil new blood /给车间～两台机器 send two more machines to the workshop ❷ additional; complementary; supplementary:～读物 supplementary reading material /～发言 additional remarks /～题 additional questions /～条款 subsidiary; supplementary (*or* additional) provisions
补丁 bǔding patch:打～ put a patch on; patch up
补发 bǔfā supply again; reissue; pay retroactively:～工资 pay wages retroactively /～丢失的身分证 reissue a lost ID card /～办公用品 supply more stationery
补法 bǔfǎ 〈中医〉❶ treatment involving the use of tonics to restore the patient's health ❷ reinforcing method (in acupuncture)
补服 bǔfú ceremonial gown worn by officials in the Ming and Qing dynasties, stitched on the front and back with a special pattern indicating civil or military office and rank
补付 bǔfù ❶ make a deferred payment ❷ reward; repay:您待我真好,我怎样～您才好呢? I don't know how I shall repay you for your kindness.
补骨脂 bǔgǔzhī (commonly known as 破故纸)〈植物〉*Psoralea corylifolia*
补锅匠 bǔguōjiàng tinker
补锅鸟 bǔguōniǎo tinkerbird (*Pogonialus*)
补过 bǔguò make up for one's mistake:将功～ atone (*or* make amends) for one's mistake by meritorious deeds
补焊 bǔhàn 〈机械〉patch weld
补花 bǔhuā 〈工美〉appliqué
补给 bǔjǐ 〈军事〉supply; provision:～品 supplies /～站 depot /～点 supply point /缺乏～ run short of supplies
补给线 bǔjǐxiàn 〈军事〉supply line
补剂 bǔjì tonic:人参～ ginseng tonic
补济 bǔjì replenish; supply:海河缺水时,由滦河～。When the Haihe River is low, water is drawn from the Luanhe River to supply it.
补假 bǔjià ❶ take a deferred vacation or holiday ❷ obtain official

leave of absence after one has been absent (in an emergency, etc.) without it
补角 bǔjiǎo 〈数学〉supplementary angle
补酒 bǔjiǔ tonic wine
补救 bǔjiù remedy:～措施 remedial measure; remedy /不可～ beyond (*or* past) remedy; irremediable /想办法～一下。See what you can do to remedy the situation.

B

补苴 bǔjū 〈书面〉❶ mend; darn; patch ❷ make up (a deficiency); remedy
补苴罅漏 bǔjū-xiàlòu make up a deficiency (esp. in an article or theory)
补考 bǔkǎo make-up examination:因病未参加期末考试的人,下学期初可以～。Those who missed the final exams on account of illness can take make-up exams at the beginning of the next semester.
补课 bǔkè ❶ make up a missed lesson:缺了课的人明天来～。Those who missed the class are required to come tomorrow to make it up. ❷ do remedial work in one's studies; remedy the weak areas in one's work:我们在改变作风方面须补补课。We should take serious measures to catch up and improve our work style.
补漏 bǔlòu ❶ stop leaks; repair (leaky house, etc.):雨季前抓紧修缮～。It is important to repair leaky houses in good time for the rainy season. ❷ plus loopholes (in work); make up deficiencies:纠偏～ remedy deviations and plus loopholes
补炉 bǔlú 〈冶金〉fettling:～材料 fettling (material)
补码 bǔmǎ 〈数学〉complement; complemental code:～法 complementation
补码电路 bǔmǎ diànlù complementary circuit
补苗 bǔmiáo 〈农业〉fill the gaps with seedlings
补偏救弊 bǔpiān-jiùbì remedy defects and rectify errors; rectify abuses
补票 bǔpiào buy a ticket (e.g. on the train) which one failed to get at the booking office
补品 bǔpǐn tonic
补葺 bǔqì repair:楼宇～一新。The buildings look brand new after repair.
补情 bǔqíng repay a kindness
补缺 bǔquē ❶ fill up a vacancy:～选举 by-election ❷ supply a deficiency:～堵漏 make up deficiencies and plug loopholes ❸〈旧语〉(of a candidate) get an official post
补色 bǔsè *also* "余色" yúsè complementary colour
补税 bǔshuì pay the dodged tax or duty; pay an overdue tax; pay a delinquent tax
补胎胶 bǔtāijiāo tyre cement
补台 bǔtái help sb. strengthen his position; boost sb.:同事之间,要相互～,不要拆台。Colleagues should support, not sabotage, each other.
补体 bǔtǐ 〈医学〉complement (in blood serum):～结合试验 complement fixation test
补贴 bǔtiē ❶ subsidize:～信贷 subsidized credit /由政府给予～ be subsidized by the government /此项亏损由总厂～。The head factory will cover the loss incurred. ❷ subsidy; allowance:生活～ living allowances /住房～ housing subsidy /粮食～ grain subsidy /物价～ inflation subsidy /地区～ allowance for people working in certain geographical areas; weighting /出口～ subsidies for export /加班～ overtime pay
补习 bǔxí attend make-up lessons; take lessons after school or work:～班 class (*or* course) of continuing education /～学校 continuation school
补泻 bǔxiè 〈中医〉reinforcing and reducing methods (in acupuncture)
补休 bǔxiū take a deferred leave or holiday
补修 bǔxiū repeat a course one has failed
补选 bǔxuǎn by-election:～党代会代表 hold a by-election for deputies to the Party's Congress
补血 bǔxuè enrich the blood
补血药 bǔxuèyào 〈药学〉blood tonic; haematinic; haematic tonic
补牙 bǔyá 〈医学〉have a tooth filled or stopped; tooth filling
补养 bǔyǎng take a tonic or nourishing food to build up one's health:吃些营养品～一下身体 take sth. to tone up the body
补药 bǔyào tonic
补液 bǔyè ❶〈医学〉fluid infusion ❷ (liquid) tonic:营养～ nutritious drink; tonic
补遗 bǔyí addendum:《全唐诗～》*Addendum to Complete Tang Poems*
补益 bǔyì 〈书面〉❶ be of benefit or help:不无～ be of some benefit (*or* help) ❷ benefit; help:～工作 help the work /～身体 make one stronger; improve one's health
补语 bǔyǔ 〈语言〉complement
补元气 bǔ yuánqì 〈中医〉tonify primordial *qi*
补针 bǔzhēn tonic injection
补正 bǔzhèng add and correct:如有疏漏,敬请～。Please feel free to make any necessary correction or improvement.
补中 bǔzhōng 〈中医〉treatment of asthenia and functional deterioration of the organs with tonics
补种 bǔzhòng reseed; resow; replant
补重系统 bǔzhòng xìtǒng compensating water system (of a submarine)
补助 bǔzhù subsidy; allowance:～金 subsidy /生活～ living allowance (given to people who have financial difficulty) /～票证 extra ration coupons as a subsidy
补助货币 bǔzhù huòbì *also* "辅币" fǔbì fractional money or currency
补助器 bǔzhùqì 〈计算机〉complementer
补缀 bǔzhuì ❶ mend; patch (of clothes):～旧衣 mend (*or* patch) old clothes /缝连～ mend and darn /～成文 patch up an article; write an essay ❷〈工美〉patchwork:～被面 patchwork quilt
补子 bǔzi rank patch (on both front and back of an official gown indicating civilian or military rank in Ming and Qing dynasties)
补足 bǔzú bring up to full strength; make up a deficiency; fill (a vacancy, gap, etc.):如果经常性费用不够,可由县政府～。If the running expense is not sufficient, the county government will supply the deficiency.

卟 bǔ

卟吩 bǔfēn 〈化学〉porphin
卟啉 bǔlín 〈生化〉porphyrin:～症〈医学〉porphyria

堡 bǔ

bourg or village (often used to form place names):吴～ Wubu (in Shaanxi Province)
see also bǎo; pù
堡子 bǔzi 〈方言〉❶ walled-in bourg or hamlet ❷ village

bù

瓿 bù

〈书面〉urn; earthen jar

部 bù

❶ part; section:东～ eastern part /内～ inside; internal /胸～ chest; breast /局～ local; partial /分为两～ divide into two parts ❷ unit; ministry; department:编辑～ editorial board /外交～ ministry of foreign affairs /门市～ business department; business section; shop; store /～级 of ministerial level ❸ headquarters (of military forces):总参谋～ (Headquarters of the) General Staff /连～ company headquarters /前沿指挥～ advance command post /空军司令～ Headquarters of the Air Force ❹ troops; armed forces:奉命率～火速前来增援 receive orders to lead reinforcements to the rescue at once ❺〈书面〉command:所～ troops under one's command ❻〈量词〉*of movies, books, etc.*:一～电影 a film /两～字典 two dictionaries ❼〈量词〉*of machines or vehicles*:五～机床 five lathes /三～汽车 three cars ❽ (Bù) a surname
部队 bùduì ❶ army; armed forces:我三个儿子都在～。My three sons are all on active service. ❷ troop; unit:通讯兵～ signal troops/边防～ frontier troops (*or* guards) /野战～ field army units /～代号 code designation of a military unit /人民解放军北京军区～ PLA units under the Beijing Command
部分 bùfen part; section; portion:～地区 some areas; part of the area /主要～ main part /次要～ parts of secondary importance /大～ majority; most parts /～禁止核试验条约 Partial Nuclear Test Ban Treaty /～解决 partial solution /～出售,～贮存。Part for sale, part to be kept in stock. /原计划有了～改变。There has been some alteration in the original plan.
部件 bùjiàn part; component:从外国进口～ import parts and components from abroad

部件分解图 bùjiàn fēnjiětú exploded view
部将 bùjiàng military officer under one's command
部类 bùlèi category; division: 社会生产有两大~: 生产资料的生产和消费资料的生产。Social production consists of two types — that of the means of production and that of the means of subsistence.
部落 bùluò tribe: ~社会 tribal society / ~首领 tribal chief / ~酋长 chieftain of a tribe
部门 bùmén department; branch: 政府各~ various government departments / 交通~ transport departments / 工业~ departments of industries / ~经济学 departmental economics / 主管~ competent departments (*or* authorities) / 有关~ departments concerned / ~林立、机构臃肿 overlapping and overstaffed departments (*or* administrations) / ~性或~间的经济研究 sectorial or intersectorial economic studies
部曲 bùqū ❶〈古语〉army unit in feudal China ❷〈古语〉private troops (of powerful clans) ❸〈书面〉domestic servant
部首 bùshǒu radicals by which characters are arranged in traditional Chinese dictionaries
部属 bùshǔ ❶ subordinate ❷ affiliated to a ministry: ~机构 organizations affiliated to a ministry / ~院校 universities and colleges under the jurisdiction of various ministries
部署 bùshǔ arrange; map out; lay out; deploy: 作战~ operational plan; battle dispositions / ~兵力 deploy troops / ~明年的工作 make plans for next year's work / ~适宜 be properly planned; be well planned / 快速~部队 rapid deployment forces
部头 bùtóu size (of a book): 大~著作 monumental work; voluminous work
部委 bù-wěi ministries and commissions: 国务院各~ ministries and commissions under the State Council
部位 bùwèi (particularly of the human body) position; location; place: 受伤~ location of an injury / 发音~ positions of organs of speech
部伍 bùwǔ file; formation: ~严整。The troops file in neat formation.
部下 bùxià ❶ troops under one's command: 军长对~要求很严。The army commander was very strict with his men. ❷ subordinate: 他在单位是妻子的~。He was his wife's subordinate in their work unit.
部优 bùyōu ministry-recognized quality product
部长 bùzhǎng minister: ~级会议 conference at ministerial level / ~助理 assistant minister / 联络部~ Minister in charge of the International Liaison Department / 财政~ minister of finance; (US) Secretary of Treasury / 司法~ minister of justice; (US) Attorney General
部长会议 bùzhǎng huìyì Council of Ministers

蔀

bù 〈书面〉❶ cover; shelter ❷ (unit of time in ancient calendar) seventy-six years

篰

bù 〈方言〉bamboo basket

餔

bù

餔子 bùzi baby paste; baby food

簿

bù book: 账~ account book / 户口登记~ household register / 记录~ register
簿册 bùcè notebook; account book
簿籍 bùjí account books, registers, records, etc.
簿记 bùjì ❶ bookkeeping: 复式~ double-entry bookkeeping ❷ standard account book
簿记员 bùjìyuán bookkeeper
簿录 bùlù 〈书面〉❶ record; catalogue; list ❷ check and register (confiscated property)
簿子 bùzi notebook; book

埠

bù ❶ wharf; pier; town or city with a port: 船已抵~。The ship has come into port. ❷〈旧语〉trading port; port city: 开~ open a port for foreign trade (as under the unequal treaties) ❸ city; metropolis: 本~ this city / 外~ other cities / 商~ commercial (*or* trading) city
埠头 bùtóu 〈方言〉wharf; pier: 轮船~ landing pier; landing stage; wharf; dock

不

bù 〈副词〉❶ not; no: ~甚满意 not very pleased / ~再有效 no longer valid / ~买 refuse to buy ❷ *used as a negative prefix before a noun or noun-equivalent to form an adjective*: ~法 illegal; lawless / ~自在 ill at ease / ~道德 immoral / ~利 disadvantageous / ~科学 unscientific ❸ *used as a negative reply to a question*: "他去吗?" "~,他~去。" "Is he going?" "No, he isn't." / "他不爱喝酒吗?" "~,他爱喝酒。" "He doesn't like wine, does he?" "Yes, he does." ❹〈方言〉*used as a question tag*: 你对他的工作满意~? You are pleased with his work, aren't you? / 你喝茶~? Would you care for some tea? ❺ *used in between a verb and its complement to indicate negation*: 拿~动 cannot carry it / 说~清楚 cannot say for certain; cannot explain / 做~好 unable to do a good job of it / 吃~了 difficult to eat all this food ❻ *as part of a structure that expresses indifference, irrelevance, etc.*: 什么困难~困难,再难也得办妥。No matter what difficulty there may be, you have to get things done properly. ❼ either (... or): ~是你去,就是我去。Either you or I have to go there. / 天气坏透了,~是刮风,就是下雨。The weather can't be worse. If it's not windy then it's raining. ❽〈方言〉(used in certain ceremonial expressions) needn't; don't: ~谢。Don't mention it. / ~送。Don't bother to come out. / ~客气。Don't mention it. *or* You are welcome.
不碍 bù'ài ❶ not matter; not affect: ~大局 not affect the overall situation ❷〈方言〉it doesn't matter; that's all right: 我常感到腰酸背痛,医生说~的。I often have aches and pains all over, but the doctor says there's nothing serious. / 这点小事~的,您别放在心上。It's a mere trifle. Don't you worry about it.
不安 bù'ān ❶ not tranquil or peaceful; unstable; unrest: 社会秩序~ social unrest / 坐立~ be restless; be on pins and needles / 这里笼罩着~的气氛。The prevailing atmosphere is one of anxiety (*or* uncertainty) here. / 局势动荡~。The situation is characterized by turbulence and intranquillity. ❷ uneasy; disturbed; restless: 于心~ feel uneasy about sth.; have a guilty conscience / 神色~ look troubled / 消息使他~。He was disturbed by the news. ❸〈套语〉*used to express regret or gratitude*: 给你添了许多麻烦,我深感~。I am very sorry to have caused you so much trouble.
不安本分 bù'ān-běnfèn discontented with one's lot: 此人吃亏在于~。This chap comes out the loser for not resting content with what was his due. *or* He does not know his place. That is why he is always in for trouble.
不安于室 bù'ānyúshì *also* "不安其室" (of a married woman) have extramarital affairs
不安于位 bù'ānyúwèi not be content with one's (official) position; not discharge one's (official) duties conscientiously
不谙世故 bù'ān-shìgù *also* "不谙世事" unsophisticated; not worldly-wise
不白之冤 bùbáizhīyuān unrighted wrong; unredressed injustice: 蒙受~ suffer a gross injustice / 平雪~ right a wrong; redress an injustice
不败之地 bùbàizhīdì invincible position: 立于~ be in an invincible position
不饱和 bùbǎohé 〈化学〉unsaturated: ~化合物 unsaturated compound
不饱和脂肪 bùbǎohé zhīfáng unsaturated fat
不饱和脂肪酸 bùbǎohé zhīfángsuān unsaturated fatty acid
不饱满籽粒 bùbǎomǎn zǐlì 〈农业〉imperfect grain
不卑不亢 bùbēi-bùkàng *also* "不亢不卑" neither haughty nor humble; neither overbearing nor servile; neither supercilious nor obsequious: 采取~的态度 assume an attitude that is neither overbearing nor servile; behave with propriety / 他给人的印象是~。He always gives people the impression that he is modest but confident.
不备 bùbèi ❶ not ready; unprepared; off guard: 乘其~ catch sb. off guard / 伺其~ watch for a chance to take sb. by surprise / 攻其~ launch a surprise attack upon sb. ❷〈旧语〉(used at the end of a letter) that's all for now; so much for now
不悖 bùbèi not mutually exclusive; parallel: 并行~ both can be implemented without coming into conflict with each other; run parallel
不比 bùbǐ no match for; inferior to; unlike: 我校规模~其他院校。Our college cannot compare in scope with many other colleges. / 今冬~往年,天气特别暖和。Unlike past winters, this winter has been

especially mild. /～不知道，一比吓一跳。If you don't compare, you don't know; you jump up with a start when you do.

不必 bùbì need not; not have to; not be necessary: ～客气 need not stand on ceremony /～认真 not have to take it seriously; take it easy /为这点小事想不开，我看大可～。I do not think it wise of you to be troubled by such trifles. /慢慢来，～着急。Take your time. There is no need to worry (*or* There is no tearing hurry).

B

不必要 bùbìyào unnecessary; uncalled-for: ～的忧虑 uncalled-for worries /～的牺牲 unnecessary sacrifice

不避艰险 bùbì-jiānxiǎn shrink or flinch from no difficulty or danger; face hardships and perils squarely

不变 bùbiàn unchanged; constant: ～购买力 constant purchasing power /～美元价值 real dollar value; constant dollar value /以～应万变 make the same unchanged response to a myriad of changes; remain unchanged despite all outside changes

不变规模 bùbiàn guīmó 〈经济〉constant scale

不变价格 bùbiàn jiàgé 〈经济〉fixed price; constant price

不变式 bùbiànshì 〈数学〉invariant

不变形合金 bùbiànxíng héjīn non-deforming alloy

不变性 bùbiànxìng invariance; constancy: ～原理 invariance principle

不变资本 bùbiàn zīběn 〈经济〉constant capital

不便 bùbiàn ❶ inconvenient; inappropriate; unsuitable: 诸多～ quite a lot of inconveniences /交通～ be difficult of access; have poor transport facilities; not be conveniently located /行动～ have difficulty in moving about /给调查带来～ hamper the investigation /此处谈话～。This is not a convenient place to talk. /这包太大，～随身带。This bag is too big to carry with you on the trip. ❷ short of cash; hard up: 手头～ have no (*or* little) money at hand; be short of money (*or* cash)

不辨是非 bùbiàn-shìfēi fail to make a distinction between right and wrong

不辨菽麦 bùbiàn-shūmài be unable to tell beans from wheat — have no knowledge of practical matters

不…不… bù…bù… ❶ *used with two synonyms or analogues as a somewhat emphatic form of "not"*: 不明不白 rather ambiguous; murky /不骄不躁 not conceited (*or* rash); free from arrogance and rashness /不理不睬 ignore; remain indifferent; take no notice of /不知不觉 unconsciously; unawares /不伦不类 nondescript; neither fish nor fowl /不痛不痒 not quite to the point; perfunctory /不闻不问 unconcerned; indifferent /不屈不挠 undaunted /不说不笑 neither speak nor smile — look sullen /不吃不喝 refuse to eat or drink /不言不语 remain silent (*or* speechless) /不折不扣 completely; totally; out and out; thoroughly /不声不响地就把事儿办了 get sth. done without much ado ❷ (used with two antonyms) neither... nor...; not...not... (a) *to indicate "just right"*: 不大不小 neither too big nor too small; just the right size /不多不少 not too much and not too little; just the right amount or number /不早不晚 just on time /不盈不亏 break even /这件大衣不肥不瘦。This coat fits nicely. (b) *to indicate a dilemma*: 不死不活 neither dead nor alive; half-dead; lifeless /不上不下 suspended in mid air; in a (pretty) fix /不中不西 not distinctively Chinese or Western in style ❸ not... without; not... unless: 不见不散 not leave till we meet /不止不行 no motion without rest /生命不息，战斗不止。Fight on until one has shed the last drop of blood. *or* Go on fighting until one breathes one's last.

不才 bùcái 〈书面〉〈谦词〉❶ talentless; worthless: 在下～，不胜其任。As I am without talent, I'm afraid I am not qualified for the job. ❷ your humble servant; I: ～愿闻一二。Your humble servant hopes to benefit from your enlightenment.

不测 bùcè accident; mishap; contingency: ～风云 unforeseen storms /～之祸 unexpected misfortune /倘有～ if anything untoward should happen /险遭～ have a narrow escape /以防～ be prepared for any contingency

不曾 bùcéng never: 我～见过此人。I've never met the man. /此事万万～料到。This is beyond the wildest dream of my imagination.

不差累黍 bùchā-lěishǔ be without the slightest difference; not err by a hair's breadth; tally in every detail; be just right: 两相比较，～。The two are very much the same when you put them side by side. *or* They are no different when you compare one with the other.

不差什么 bùchā shénme ❶ not short of anything; in want of nothing: 要的东西～了。Nearly everything we need is ready. ❷〈方言〉almost: 该找的地方～都找过了。I've searched high and low for it. ❸〈方言〉common; ordinary: 这东西太沉，～的人根本搬不动。The thing is just too heavy for ordinary people to move around.

不称 bùchèn fail to suit; be incompatible; be unworthy of: ～职 incompetent; unfit (*or* unqualified) for the job

不成 bùchéng ❶ won't do: 光想占小便宜可～。It just won't do looking for petty gains at every turn. /别让我参加彩排，我这嗓子可～。Please excuse me from the dress rehearsal for my poor voice's sake. ❷ *used as a tag indicating interrogation, conjecture, surmise, etc.*: 他今天没来，莫非病了～? He didn't show up today. Could it be that he is ill? /难道非向他道歉～? Do I have to apologize to him? /难道就这样算了～? How can we let it go at that?

不成比例 bùchéng bǐlì disproportionate; out of proportion: 学生很多，教员太少，二者～。The number of students is out of proportion to that of teachers. *or* The small number of teachers is disproportionate to the many students.

不成材 bùchéngcái *also* "不成器" good-for-nothing; worthless; ne'er-do-well: ～的儿子 worthless son (of the family) /他尝试了好几种工作，但终～。He tried his hand at different jobs, but just got nowhere.

不成层矿床 bùchéngcéng kuàngchuáng ataxic or unstratified deposit

不成对电子 bùchéngduì diànzǐ unpaired electron

不成话 bùchénghuà *also* "不像话" absurd; ridiculous: 你闹得太～了。You have made such a dreadful scene. *or* You've gone too far.

不成敬意 bùchéng-jìngyì serve merely as a token of respect: 这点东西～，请笑纳。This serves merely as a token of our respect, I hope you'll like it.

不成器 bùchéngqì *see* "不成材"

不成人 bùchéngrén ❶〈古语〉the handicapped ❷ person of bad character

不成体统 bùchéng-tǐtǒng be downright outrageous; speak or behave badly or atrociously: 这里乱哄哄的，简直～! There is sheer pandemonium here. It's simply outrageous! /他们如此闹法太～! They are terribly rowdy, turning everything upside down!

不成文 bùchéngwén unwritten; customary: ～的规定 unwritten rule /～的作法 customary practice

不成文法 bùchéngwénfǎ 〈法律〉unwritten law; customary law; common law

不承认主义 bùchéngrènzhǔyì policy of non-recognition

不逞 bùchěng fail (in one's plans, ambition, etc.): 其谋～。His plot failed.

不逞之徒 bùchěngzhītú unruly person; desperado: 结交～ associate with desperadoes

不齿 bùchǐ 〈书面〉despise; hold in contempt: 为人所～ be held in contempt by all people

不耻下问 bùchǐ-xiàwèn not feel ashamed to seek advice from one's subordinates: 在学习上应当～。In study, one should not feel ashamed to ask and learn from people below.

不啻 bùchì 〈书面〉❶ not less than: 转运过程的亏损～数十万元。The loss caused by the damage in transit amounted to several hundred thousand *yuan*. ❷ as; like; as good as: 七十年人生～一瞬。Seventy years of human life is as short as a wink. /～霄壤之别。There is practically a world of difference.

不充分燃烧 bùchōngfèn ránshāo 〈物理〉insufficient combustion

不充分证据 bùchōngfèn zhèngjù 〈法律〉insufficient evidence

不出所料 bùchū-suǒliào as expected: ～，此事果真泄漏出去了。As had been expected, the matter leaked out.

不出庭 bùchūtíng 〈法律〉default of court appearance; non-appearance: ～者 defaulter /～证书 non-appearance certificate

不揣 bùchuǎi 〈谦词〉(used when one is going to put forward one's view, or to make a request) regardless of; despite: 本人～浅陋，提出一点不同看法。Regardless of my ignorance, I will venture to air a different idea.

不揣冒昧 bùchuǎi-màomèi venture to; presume to; take the liberty of: 我～，请问大名。May I take the liberty of asking your name? / 我～，建议立即召开会议讨论这个问题。If I may venture an opinion, I'd suggest that a meeting be convened at once to look into the matter.

不传导 bùchuándǎo 〈物理〉non-conduction: ～物质 non-conductor

不辞 bùcí ❶ without saying good-bye ❷ not refuse or shirk: 万死

～ shrink from no sacrifice; not recoil from certain death

不辞而别 bùcí'érbié leave without saying good-bye; leave suddenly without a word:我不懂他为什么～。I didn't know why he had gone without a good-bye.

不辞辛苦 bùcí-xīnkǔ make light of hardships; take pains:为了让孩子们吃好,这位老炊事员从来～。The old chef did all he could to prepare good dishes for the children. *or* The old cook worked hard to improve the diet for the kids.

不存芥蒂 bùcún-jièdì bear no grudge; cherish no ill will

不错 bùcuò ❶ correct; right:一点儿也～ perfectly correct; quite right /你估计得～。Your estimate has proved right. *or* You have made a correct estimate. /～, 他是这样说的。Yes, that's what he said. ❷〈口语〉not bad; pretty good:庄稼长得挺～。The crops are growing quite well. /"这部电影怎么样?" "还～。" "How do you like the movie?" "Not bad." /这台计算机挺～。This computer is quite good.

不错眼 bùcuòyǎn 〈方言〉gaze fixedly; stare without batting an eyelid

不打不成器 bù dǎ bù chéngqì 〈俗语〉spare the rod, spoil the child

不打不成相识 bù dǎ bù chéng xiāngshí out of blows friendship grows; no discord, no concord

不打紧 bùdǎjǐn 〈方言〉unimportant; of no consequence (at all):累点～,我明天可以休息。It doesn't matter that I am a bit overworked, for I can have a day off tomorrow. /他的病好多了,～了。Don't worry. He is much better now.

不打眼 bùdǎyǎn 〈方言〉attract no notice; be inconspicuous:～的老头子 old man who attracts no notice

不打自招 bùdǎ-zìzhāo make a confession of one's own accord; disclose unintentionally; give oneself away:这个家伙～。The chap said everything without duress. /你这可是～,不是我逼你啊! This is your own confession for I have never put any pressure on you. /他～泄露了秘密。He let the cat out of the bag unwittingly.

不大 bùdà 〈口语〉❶ not very; not too:～谦虚 not quite modest ❷ not often:他星期天～待在家里。He doesn't often stay at home on Sundays.

不大离 bùdàlí 〈方言〉❶ pretty close; very much alike:这两个孩子样子长得～儿。The two kids resemble each other. ❷ just about right; not bad; just fine:事情解决得～儿了。The matter is as good as settled. /他这个人搞音乐倒是～儿。He's probably the right sort of person to go in for music. /"考得怎么样?" "～儿。" "How did you do in the exam?" "Not too bad."

不待 bùdài ❶ before; not till:～我到家,她就走了。She had left before I came home. ❷ it goes without saying:～言 needless to say /～说 it is certain that; no doubt; naturally ❸〈方言〉must not; will not:有理由好好说,～骂人的。If you believe you are right, you can state your reasons with a civil tongue. /你说破嘴皮子,他也～理你的。You may talk yourself hoarse, but he will not listen.

不待见 bùdàijian 〈方言〉dislike; hate:他～这个孩子。He has a dislike for the child. *or* He is fed up with the child.

不带音 bùdàiyīn 〈语言〉unvoiced
see also "带音" dàiyīn

不逮 bùdài 〈书面〉beyond one's reach:以匡～ help sb. to achieve what he himself cannot possibly accomplish

不戴帽子 bùdài-màozi without being labelled; without being branded (for what one says or does)

不丹 Bùdān Bhutan:～人 Bhutanese /～语 Bhutanese (language)/～王国 Kingdom of Bhutan

不单 bùdān ❶ not the only:那天我邀请的客人有好几位,～是她。She was not the only guest that day. In fact, I invited several. /组织排球队,这～是我个人的意见。I am not the only person that supports the idea of organizing a volley-ball team. ❷ not merely; not simply; not only:这种钢笔～式样美观,而且书写流畅。This kind of pen not only looks nice but also writes smoothly.

不但 bùdàn not only:这座桥～造型美观,而且结构坚固。This bridge is not only nice in layout but also solid in structure.

不惮 bùdàn not be afraid; not fear:～其烦 not mind taking all the trouble; be very patient

不当 bùdàng unsuitable; improper; inappropriate:处理～ not properly dealt with; mishandled /用人～ employ a wrong person for the job /时机～ not an opportune moment /使用～ be put to wrong use /措辞～ wrong choice of words; inappropriate wording /～裁决 unfair verdict /～干涉 unwarranted intervention /～判决 unjust judgment /～行为 improper act or behaviour /～延误 undue delay

不倒翁 bùdǎowēng *also* "扳不倒儿" bānbùdǎor tumbler; roly-poly; "survivor":你要是学会了这一条,就能在社会上成一个～! Once you've learned this trick, you will always be a survivor.

不到黄河心不死 bù dào huánghé xīn bù sǐ 〈谚语〉one does not stop until one reaches the Yellow River — not stop until one reaches one's goal; refuse to give up until all hope is lost:看来这件事你是～,非干到底不可喽。So it seems that you will not give this up until you see it through. /他呀,～。As for him, he will not stop until he comes to a dead end.

不到家 bùdàojiā 〈口语〉lack in skill at sth.; be incompetent:他修车的本事～。He is not very good at fixing bikes. /我的计算机知识～,经不起你一问。I have only a smattering knowledge of computer. I can't really answer your question.

不道德 bù dàodé immoral:～的行为 unethical conduct /他认为乘人之危是～的。He considers it immoral to cash in on somebody's trouble.

不得 bùdé must not; should not; not be allowed:～怠慢 must not be neglected (*or* slighted) /～喧哗 be quiet; keep quiet /坚决执行,～有误 must be carried out without fail /～据为己有。No one is entitled to appropriate it.

不得 bude 〈口语〉(used after a verb) can't; mustn't:马虎～ can't afford to be careless /奈何～ nothing can be done about it /记～ can't remember /批评～ not to be subjected to criticism; be too sensitive to criticism /叫你哭笑～。You don't know whether to laugh or to cry.

不得不 bùdébù have no choice or option but to; cannot but; have to:～有所表示 have to make some gestures /他在事实面前～招认。Confronted with the facts, he had no choice but to confess.

不得而知 bùdé'érzhī unknown; unable to find out:虽经多方面查访,死者身分仍～。Despite all the investigations the identity of the dead remains unknown. /比赛结果尚～。The final score of the match has not come out.

不得法 bùdéfǎ not know the ropes; not know the right way to do sth.

不得劲 bù déjìn 〈口语〉❶ awkward; not handy:这枝笔使起来～。This pen is not handy. /这些书放在高层书架上拿起来～。These books on the higher shelves are not within easy reach. ❷ be indisposed; not feel well:我浑身～,像是感冒了。I'm not feeling my usual self; it seems I've caught a cold. ❸〈方言〉embarrassed:大家都这么看着他,弄得他怪～的。He looked very much embarrassed under the public gaze.

不得了 bùdéliǎo ❶ disastrous; terrible:～,出了大事啦! Something terrible has happened! /这事儿闹大了可～。It would be disastrous if the matter got out of control. /没什么～的事儿。There's nothing really serious. ❷ (often used after 得 to indicate degree or extent) extremely; exceedingly:高兴得～ be extremely happy; be wild with joy /急得～ be in a tearing hurry /后悔得～ look back with deep regret /坏得～ can't be worse; be wicked to the extreme/热得～ be awfully hot

不得其门而入 bùdé qí mén ér rù can't find the door and get in; not know the ropes

不得人心 bùdé-rénxīn not enjoy popular support; be unpopular:这样干问题倒是能解决,但是～,值得吗? We might solve the problem if we made this move, but that would be unpopular. Is it worth it? /她在左邻右舍很～。She is not getting along with her neighbours.

不得上诉 bùdé shàngsù 〈法律〉be denied the right to appeal to a higher court

不得烟儿抽 bùdé yānr chōu 〈方言〉unpopular; not in favour:他在我们这里一直～,所以他想换个单位。He has never been well liked here, so he is hunting a new job.

不得要领 bùdé-yàolǐng fail to grasp the main points; fail to get the nick of sth.; be not to the point; be at sea:说话～ fail to speak to the point /对文件的领会～ fail to grasp the essence of the document /他说了半天,我还是～。He talked at great length, but I just couldn't see what he was driving at.

不得已 bùdéyǐ act against one's will; have no alternative but to; have to:～的办法 last resort /不到万～,决不放弃原计划。Not until every means is exhausted would I give up my original plan. /没有请你来也是～。We would have invited you had we our own choice.

不得已而求其次 bùdéyǐ ér qiú qí cì have to be content with the

second best; settle for the second best: ～，采取了另一个办法。They had to give up their preference and content themselves with another choice.

不得已而为之 bùdéyǐ ér wéi zhī have no alternative but to do sth.; do sth. against one's will: 采取这样的措施，也是～。We will take this measure simply because we have no alternative.

不登大雅之堂 bù dēng dàyǎ zhī táng 〈书面〉 not appeal to refined tastes; be unpolished; be coarse and vulgar: 我这是随便画画而已，～。This painting of mine is not a serious effort, not presentable at all.

不等 bùděng vary; differ: 数量～ vary in amount /大小～ differ in size /尺码～的鞋子 shoes of different sizes /汽车装载量从两吨至十八吨～。The trucks vary in loading capacity from two to eighteen tons.

不等边三角形 bùděngbiān sānjiǎoxíng 〈数学〉 scalene triangle

不等额选举 bùděng'é xuǎnjǔ competitive election; multi-candidate election

不等号 bùděnghào 〈数学〉 sign of inequality

不等价交换 bùděngjià jiāohuàn 〈经济〉 exchange of unequal values

不等式 bùděngshì 〈数学〉 inequality; inequation

不抵抗主义 bùdǐkàngzhǔyì policy of non-resistance

不抵事 bù dǐshì *also* "不顶事" useless; in vain; good for nothing: 大家都嫌他～。Everybody regards him as useless. /这药～。The medicine is not effective.

不第 bùdì ❶ fail in the imperial civil service examination: 屡试～ fail in one civil service examination after another ❷ 〈书面〉 not only

不点儿 bùdiǎnr little bit; tiny bit: 小～ little one (meaning a small baby or kid) /～小事，值得大惊小怪么? It's a mere trifle. Do we have to kick up a fuss about it?

不迭 bùdié ❶ hastily; too late: 跑～ run away hastily; take to one's heels /忙～地要看一看 be in a hurry to take a look /后悔～ too late to regret; overtaken by repentance ❷ incessantly: 叫苦～ complain incessantly; pour out endless grievances

不丁点儿 bùdīngdiǎnr very little; very small in amount or size: 那年我才八岁，～高。I was eight that year, just a tiny kid.

不定 bùdìng ❶ not for certain: 他～来不来呢。It's not certain if he's coming at all. /结果还～会怎么样呢。It's hardly predictable how things will turn out. /她今天～哭过多少回了。She's cried God knows how many times today. ❷ indefinite; indeterminate: 主意～ be undecided /心神～ feel perturbed; be in a flutter /漂泊～ drift from place to place

不定变异 bùdìng biànyì 〈生物〉 indeterminate variation

不定方程 bùdìng fāngchéng 〈数学〉 indeterminate equation

不定根 bùdìnggēn 〈植物〉 adventitious root

不定冠词 bùdìng guàncí 〈语言〉 indefinite article

不定积分 bùdìng jīfēn 〈数学〉 indefinite integral

不定判 bùdìngpàn 〈法律〉 indeterminate sentence

不定期 bùdìngqī at irregular intervals; with no fixed date; indefinitely; *sine die*: ～休会 adjourn *sine die* /～航班 nonregular flight service /～存款 undated deposit /～航线 tramp steamer route /～刊物 publication issued at irregular intervals

不定式 bùdìngshì 〈语言〉 infinitive

不定芽 bùdìngyá 〈植物〉 adventitious bud

不动产 bùdòngchǎn real-estate; immovable property; immovables: ～保险 immovable insurance /～抵押 real estate mortgage /～抵押银行 hypothec bank /～遗赠 〈法律〉 devise

不动点 bùdòngdiǎn 〈数学〉 fixed point

不动声色 bùdòng-shēngsè *also* "不露声色" maintain one's composure; stay calm and collected: ～地问 ask calmly /～地看着他 look at him without batting an eyelid /这些话使小林脸上飞红，而老李却～。Xiao Lin blushed at these words, but Lao Li showed no change of expression (*or* countenance). /说的是关于边境军事冲突的话，可他却像谈家常琐事，丝毫～。Though he was talking about the military clashes at the borders, he did not betray any emotion as if he were chatting about everyday trivialities. /他俩～就把喜事给办了。They had their wedding very quietly without informing a lot of people.

不冻港 bùdònggǎng ice-free port; open port

不冻溶液 bùdòng róngyè non-freezing mixture or solution

不冻润滑油 bùdòng rùnhuáyóu non-freezable lubricating oil

不冻土 bùdòngtǔ never frozen soil

不独 bùdú not only: 今年水稻～种植面积比去年有所扩大，而且长势也比去年好。Not only has more land been sown to rice this year but the crop is growing better than last year.

不端 bùduān improper; dishonourable: 行为～ dishonourable behaviour; immoral conduct

不断 bùduàn unceasing; uninterrupted; continuous; constant: ～努力 sustained efforts /～前进 uninterrupted progress /～调整 continual readjustment /～完善 steady improvement /事故～ accidents occurring in succession /绵延～的群山 unbroken chain of mountains/经济～增长。The economy has grown continuously. /街上车辆～。There is a constant stream of motor vehicles in the street. /新鲜蔬菜四季～。Fresh vegetables are available all (the) year round. /他住院期间，～有人前来看望。While he was in hospital, people kept coming to see him.

不断革命论 bùduàn gémìnglùn theory of uninterrupted revolution

不对 bùduì ❶ incorrect; wrong: 你的想法～。It's wrong of you to think so. *or* It is your thinking that is wrong. /那样对待老朋友是～的。It's not right to treat old friends like that. ❷ No (as opposite to "Yes"): ～，我没有那么说。No, I didn't say that. ❸ amiss; abnormal; queer: 菜的味道～。This dish doesn't taste right. /机器声音～。The engine makes a queer noise. /她神色有点儿～。She doesn't look quite her usual self. /颜色不大对。There's something wrong with the colour. ❹ not in harmony; not on good terms: 他俩素来～。They've always been at loggerheads.

不对碴儿 bùduìchár *also* "不对茬儿" 〈口语〉 not proper; not fit for the occasion: 他刚开腔，觉得～，就停住了。Hardly had he started talking when he realized that his words might not suit the occasion, and he stopped short.

不对称 bùduìchèn asymmetrical; dissymmetrical; nonsymmetrical: ～性 asymmetry /～失真 asymmetrical distortion /～图案 dissymmetrical design (*or* pattern)

不对称矿脉 bùduìchèn kuàngmài 〈矿业〉 asymmetrical vein

不对劲 bùduìjìn 〈口语〉 ❶ not easy to use; not handy: 这把剪子太大，我用着～。The scissors are too big and feel clumsy in my hand. ❷ not in harmony: 我跟他～。We don't get along with each other. ❸ not feel well: 我有点儿发烧，一整天觉得混身～。I had a fever and felt out of sorts all day long.

不对头 bùduìtóu *see* "不对 ❶❸"

不…而… bù…ér… *used to indicate a result achieved without a direct cause or condition*: 不战而胜 win without fighting a battle; win hands down /不约而同 act simultaneously without prior agreement /不谋而合 agree without consulting each other beforehand /不药而愈 recover without taking medicine

不二法门 bù'èr-fǎmén one and only way; only proper course to take; inevitable resort

不二价 bù'èrjià uniform price

不二论 bù'èrlùn 〈佛教〉 *Advaita*

不贰过 bù'èrguò 〈书面〉 not repeat a previous mistake

不发达国家 bùfādá guójiā underdeveloped country: 最～ least developed country (LDC)

不发光体 bùfāguāngtǐ 〈天文〉 non-luminous body

不发火 bùfāhuǒ 〈机械〉 misfire or misfiring

不发言权 bùfāyánquán right to remain silent

不乏 bùfá 〈书面〉 no lack of; not rare: ～先例 such things are not without precedent (*or* not unprecedented) /～其事 such things are not rare

不乏其人 bùfá-qírén there is no lack of such people: 持这种见解的～。Many people hold such views. /以貌取人者～。There is no lack of people who judge by appearances.

不法 bùfǎ lawless; illegal; unlawful: ～之徒 lawless person /～活动 illegal activity /～收益 illegal earnings/～侵害 unlawful infringement /～行为 unlawful practice; illegal act /～行为国家 delinquent state /～行为者 delinquent /～行为责任 delinquent responsibility or liability

不凡 bùfán extraordinary; out of the common run; unconventional: 自命～ consider oneself out of the ordinary; have an unrealistic estimate of one's own ability /身手～ be extremely talented and capable /仪表～ look impressive /～的才能 unusual talent

不犯 bùfàn *also* "犯不着" fànbuzháo 〈方言〉 not worth doing: 咱们～跟他争论。It's not worth arguing with him.

不防 bùfáng not ready or prepared; taken by surprise; caught unawares: ～之事 sth. unexpected /乘其～ catch sb. unawares /把敌人打了个冷～ catch the enemy off guard

不防头 bùfángtóu (often used in the early vernacular) inattentively; carelessly: 刚一进门，～跟他撞了个满怀。On entering the door,

I bumped right into him.

不妨 bùfáng there is no harm in; might as well:～多打听打听。There is no harm in making further inquiries. /你～把事情经过统统跟她讲清楚。You might as well tell her the whole story.

不飞鸟 bùfēiniǎo 〈考古〉 Diatryma (a genus of large fossil birds of the earliest epoch of the Tertiary)

不菲 bùfěi considerable; great:待遇～ excellent pay /价值～ of great value; invaluable

不费吹灰之力 bù fèi chuī huī zhī lì as easy as blowing off dust — without the slightest effort; as easy as pie; like duck soup:那些湖边长大的孩子,下水捕几条鱼,自然～。To those kids growing up on the lake, diving into the water to catch fish is simple and easy.

不分彼此 bùfēn-bǐcǐ share everything (as between friends or among members of the same family); share everything one has with another

不分敌我 bùfēn-díwǒ fail to draw a line between the enemy and ourselves

不分高低 bùfēn-gāodī ❶ irrespective of social status, high or low ❷ be equally matched; be on a par:他俩的学习成绩～。They are equally good in their studies.

不分泾渭 bùfēn-jīngwèi *also* "泾渭不分" fail to distinguish between good and evil

不分巨细 bùfēn-jùxì regardless of the degree of importance:事～,他都揽到了身上。He takes charge of everything, big or small. *or* He monopolizes everything, big or small.

不分亲疏 bùfēn-qīnshū no matter whether sb. is close to one or not:用人～ appoint people on their merits rather than by favouritism /赏罚～。Everybody is equal when it comes to reward and punishment.

不分青红皂白 bùfēn qīnghóng-zàobái without distinguishing between right and wrong; indiscriminately:岂能～地乱批评一通! How can you just come and criticize without even finding out the truth of the matter!

不分轻重缓急 bùfēn qīngzhòng-huǎnjí fail to handle matters according to their relative importance or urgency; have no sense of priority

不分胜负 bùfēn-shèngfù draw; come out even:比赛～。The game ended in a draw (*or* tie). /两队～。The two teams tied (*or* came out even).

不分是非 bùfēn-shìfēi not distinguish between right and wrong; fail to tell right from wrong

不分轩轾 bùfēn-xuānzhì be even with; be equally matched

不分畛域 bùfēn-zhěnyù regardless of distinctions

不分昼夜 bùfēn-zhòuyè day and night; round the clock

不忿 bùfèn refuse to admit one's defeat, inferiority, etc.; feel indignant or resentful:～其事 feel indignant about sth. /意甚～ look resentful; be unwilling to admit defeat

不孚众望 bùfú-zhòngwàng not enjoy popularity; be unpopular

不服 bùfú ❶ refuse to obey or comply; plead not guilty; remain unconvinced by; not give in to:～裁判 refuse to accept the referee's ruling /～上诉〈法律〉 appeal a sentence (*or* arbitration) /～老 refuse to bow to old age /对批评表示～ disagree with the criticism /～管教 defy discipline /在事实面前,你～也得服。You will have to bow to the facts, whether you like them or not. /只能说服,压是压～的。One can only convince through persuasion, not by pressure. ❷ not used to; not accustomed to:这种香烟我抽～。I just can't get used to this brand of cigarettes. *or* These cigarettes don't agree with me.

不服软 bùfúruǎn 〈口语〉 not to go soft; refuse to bend

不服水土 bùfú-shuǐtǔ (of a stranger) not accustomed to the climate, food, etc. of a new place; not acclimatized

不服罪 bùfúzuì ❶〈法律〉 plead not guilty; plea of not guilty ❷ not recognize or admit one's crime; not accept one's punishment

不符 bùfú not agree or square with; not conform to; be inconsistent with:名实～ have an undeserved reputation /言行～ one's words do not tally with one's deeds /与事实～ be inconsistent with the facts /账目～ not square with the accounts

不复 bùfù no longer:～存在 no longer in existence

不干 bùgān have nothing to do with; be unrelated:你甭插嘴,～你的事。Shut up! It's none of your business.

不干不净 bùgān-bùjìng unclean; filthy:嘴里～ be foul-mouthed /～,吃了生病。Unclean food causes disease.

不干胶 bùgānjiāo adhesive; scotch tape

不干涉 bù gānshè noninterference; nonintervention:互～内政 noninterference in each other's internal affairs /～政策 policy of noninterference

不甘 bùgān be unreconciled to; not resign oneself to; be unwilling:～束手待毙 not willing to resign oneself to one's fate /～失败 not take one's defeat lying down

不甘雌伏 bùgān-cífú refuse to reconcile oneself to an undistinguished career; refuse to play second fiddle:～的大丈夫 man who is not resigned to remaining obscure

不甘后人 bùgān-hòurén not willing to lag behind:她是一个要强的人,凡事～。She is ambitious, and eager to excel in everything she does.

不甘寂寞 bùgān-jìmò be unwilling to live an obscure life; be eager for publicity; seek the limelight:他虽已退隐,却又～,暗中操纵朝政。Though he was retired, he was unwilling to live an obscure life, and tried to control the court from behind the scenes.

不甘落后 bùgān-luòhòu not ready to reconcile oneself to a state of backwardness; not content to lag behind

不甘示弱 bùgān-shìruò unwilling to be outdone:在全校运动会上,哪个班都～。At the sports meet of the college, no class was willing to be outshone.

不甘心 bù gānxīn not reconciled to; not resigned to:～失败 be unreconciled to one's defeat; not take one's defeat lying down

不尴不尬 bùgān-bùgà 〈方言〉 in a dilemma; in an awkward position; embarrassed:这件事搞得我～,不知如何是好。It put me in an awkward position, at a loss what to do. /一个大小伙子,似这般～地长住在叔父家,也不是事。As a full-blooded young man, how can he loaf around unabashedly in his uncle's home for long?

不敢 bùgǎn ❶ dare not; not dare:～说话 daren't air one's views /～说半个不字 not dare even to mutter disagreement /～正视事实 have no courage to face up squarely to the facts /我～惹他。I dare not offend him. *or* I am afraid to ruffle his feathers. ❷〈谦词〉 *see* "不敢当"

不敢当 bùgǎndāng 〈谦词〉(used in response to compliments) I am flattered; you flatter me; I wish I deserved your compliment:～,您过奖了。I am flattered. I wish I could deserve your compliments. *or* It's very kind of you to say so, but it is more than I deserve.

不敢告劳 bùgǎn-gàoláo ❶〈谦词〉 be willing to work hard without complaint ❷ work conscientiously and think nothing of the toil

不敢恭维 bùgǎn-gōngwei could not offer compliments:他的大作实在～。I wish I had compliments to offer about his writing.

不敢领教 bùgǎn-lǐngjiào beg to disagree:你的观点,我实在～。I wish I could go along with your arguments. *or* I could hardly accept your arguments.

不敢问津 bùgǎn-wènjīn not dare even to inquire (about the price of expensive commodities or into an abstruse subject)

不敢越雷池一步 bùgǎn yuè Léichí yī bù dare not overstep the limit:刘先生办事十分谨慎,从来～。Mr. Liu is very cautious. He never oversteps the mark.

不更事 bù gēngshì inexperienced in life:少～ young and inexperienced; too young to know the world

不公 bùgōng unjust; unfair:社会分配～ unfair social distribution /待人～ treat people unfairly

不攻自破 bùgōng-zìpò collapse by itself:谎言在事实面前～。Facts scotched the rumour.

不恭 bùgōng disrespectful; impolite; rude:言词～ use impolite language; speak rudely /却之～ it would be impolite to decline (a gift, an invitation, etc.) /倨傲～ arrogant and rude

不共戴天 bùgòng-dàitiān swear not to live under the same sky (with one's enemy) — be absolutely irreconcilable:～的敌人 sworn (*or* mortal) enemy /～之仇 inveterate hatred; deep-seated enmity

不苟 bùgǒu never deviating an inch from what is proper; conscientious; careful:工作一丝～ work most conscientiously; be meticulous in the discharge of one's duties /临危～ never stoop to anything even in the face of danger

不苟言笑 bùgǒu-yánxiào reserved; reticent; sober:老诚持重,～ be prudent and reserved /～的年轻人 reticent young man /他～,架子十足地走了进来。He was all business as he walked in imposingly.

不够 bùgòu not enough; insufficient; inadequate; lacking:魄力～ not decisive and resolute enough /准备～ be inadequately prepared /

人手～ be understaffed /～本 sell at a loss /～朋友 not much of a friend

不穀 bùgǔ ❶〈书面〉not competent; not worthy ❷〈谦词〉my unworthy self (used by feudal lords in ancient China to refer to themselves)

不顾 bùgù ❶ never think of; never care: 只顾自己, ～别人 think only of oneself and nobody else ❷ in spite of; regardless of: ～后果 regardless of the consequences /～一再警告 despite repeated warnings /～一切 at any cost; recklessly /～自身安危 have no thought of one's own safety/～个人劳累 have no regard for physical discomfort /～大局 ignore the overall interests /～情面 have no consideration for someone's sensibilities; not be afraid to hurt sb.'s feelings /～事实 disregard the facts /～死活 be willing to risk one's life

不关 bùguān not get involved; have nothing to do: ～你的事不用管。Don't poke your nose into matters that are not your concern.

不关宏旨 bùguān-hóngzhǐ *also*"无关宏旨" wúguān-hóngzhǐ have little to do with the theme; be irrelevant: ～的小事 trivial (*or* irrelevant) matter

不关紧要 bùguān-jǐnyào *also*"无关紧要" wúguān-jǐnyào unimportant; not essential: 此事～。This is not an important matter. /他在会上尽说些～的话。He often made irrelevant remarks at the meeting.

不关痛痒 bùguān-tòngyǎng ❶ irrelevant; insignificant; trivial; not to the point: 讲些～的话 make some irrelevant remarks /说两三句～的同情话 mouth a few meaningless (*or* superficial) words of sympathy ❷ have nothing to do with one's personal interest; show no concern: 这里倒是有两、三个人, 可都是些～的。There are two or three people here, but none of them is concerned about the matter.

不管 bùguǎn no matter (what, how, etc.); regardless of: ～怎样 in any case; anyway /～谁参加会都行。It doesn't matter who is to attend the meeting. /～困难多大, 都要完成任务。Whatever the difficulties, we'll have to fulfil the task. /～发生什么情况, 这件事都要坚持下去。Come what may, we will carry on the work.

不管不顾 bùguǎn-bùgù ❶ take no care of: 做父亲的, 对孩子哪能～? As a father, how can you leave your children to fend for themselves? ❷ impetuous; rash: 他发起火来, 什么也～。He forgets everything when he is in a rage.

不管部部长 bùguǎnbù bùzhǎng minister without portfolio

不管三七二十一 bùguǎn sān qī èrshíyī cast all caution to the winds; act recklessly: 他～地大发了一通脾气。He flew into a rage, casting all caution to the winds. /～, 先去了再说。We mustn't start worrying now. Let's get there first and then see what to do next.

不光 bùguāng ❶ not the only one; not the only thing: 不同意的～是他。He is not the only one to show disapproval. ❷ not only: ～是你, 其他人也都大吃一惊。It is not you alone but many other people who were taken by surprise.

不规则 bùguīzé irregular: ～变化〈语言〉irregular inflection /～动词 irregular verb /～曲线 irregular curve

不规则碎片形 bùguīzé suìpiànxíng 〈计算机〉fractal

不轨 bùguǐ act against the law or discipline: 图谋～ engage in conspiracy /～行为 lawless (*or* conspiratorial) act

不过 bùguò ❶ *used after an adjective to form the superlative degree*: 再好～ can't be better; superb /再坏～ couldn't be worse /最快～ fastest /聪明～ exceedingly bright ❷ only; merely; no more than: ～眨眼的工夫 in a mere split second /～二十人左右 some twenty people only ❸ but; however; yet: 法语他倒会说, ～发音不算很好。He can speak French all right, though his pronunciation isn't of the best. /实验失败了, ～他并不灰心。The experiment failed, but he didn't lose heart.

不过尔尔 bùguò-ěr'ěr 〈书面〉mediocre; just middling; nothing much; just so-so: 他的作品一度被吹得神乎其神, 其实也～。His works, which were once lauded to the skies, are merely mediocre.

不过如此 bùguò-rúcǐ just so-so; passable; barely acceptable: 他的成就～。His achievement is not at all remarkable.

不过意 bù guòyì sorry; apologetic; regretful: 给您添了许多麻烦, 真～。I am terribly sorry to have given you so much trouble.

不含糊 bù hánhu 〈口语〉❶ unambiguous; unequivocal; explicit: 毫～地作出回答 reply in clear-cut, unequivocal terms /他说话一点儿也～。There was no ambiguity in his words. ❷ not ordinary; excellent; really good: 这事办得～。The matter was well handled. /他待人真～。He is really good to people. /东西不错, 价码儿也～。The quality is high and so is the price. ❸ show no fear: ～你们。I am not afraid of you. /怎么办, 我听您一句话, 决～。Whatever you want me to do, just let me know. I'm completely at your disposal.

不寒而栗 bùhán'érlì shiver all over though not cold; tremble with fear; shudder: 使人～ make one's flesh creep; give one the creeps; make one's hair stand on end /瞻念前途, ～ shudder at the thought of the future /他眼里射出使人～的凶光。The cruel glitter in his eyes was enough to make your hair stand on end.

不好惹 bù hǎorě not to be trifled with; not to be made light of; not to be pushed around: 这种人～。Such people are not to be trifled with.

不好意思 bù hǎoyìsi ❶ embarrassed; shy; coy; bashful: 他被姑娘们笑得～了。He was embarassed by the laughing girls. ❷ find it embarrassing (to do sth.): ～再提什么问题 feel it embarrassing to raise any more questions /～推辞 find it difficult to decline

不合 bùhé ❶ not conform to; be out of keeping with: ～要求 fail to meet the requirements /～手续 not comply with the formalities /～心意 not to sb.'s liking; unsatisfactory /～情理 unreasonable /～标准 not up to the (required) standard(s); below the mark /～条件 fall short of the requirement /～传统习惯 be out of keeping with tradition /～乎事实 at variance with the facts /～口味 not to sb.'s taste; not appeal to sb. ❷〈书面〉should not; ought not: 此举殊属～。This act is indeed far from proper. ❸ on bad terms; at odds: 姑嫂～ The girl and her sister-in-law do not get along.

不合时宜 bùhé-shíyí be out of keeping with the times; be inopportune: ～的举动 inopportune (*or* inappropriate) action /他为人孤僻, ～。He is aloof and uncommunicative, and quite an anachronism. /我们这样做～。It would be against the present trend of things to act the way we did.

不合台 bùhétái 〈方言〉be on bad terms with; not get on well with: 这两个人一向～, 难以共事。They can hardly collaborate for they have never been on good terms.

不合作运动 bùhézuò yùndòng Non-Cooperation Movement, movement launched by M.K. Gandhi (1869-1948) from Sept. 1920 to Feb. 1922 for autonomy in India

不合作主义 bùhézuòzhǔyì doctrine of non-cooperation; satyagraha (doctrine advocated by M.K. Gandhi of India)

不和 bùhé ❶ not get along well; be on bad terms; be at odds: 父子～。Father and son are at loggerheads. ❷ discord: 制造～ sow discord

不哼不哈 bùhēng-bùhā remain quiet; refrain from expressing one's own view about sth.: 事关原则, 你怎么能～呢? This is a matter of principle. How can you remain silent?

不怀好意 bùhuái-hǎoyì harbour evil designs; cherish malicious intentions: ～的一笑 malicious smile /～地吹捧 flattering remarks motivated by evil intentions

不欢而散 bùhuān'érsàn part in a foul mood; break up in discord: 晚会闹得～。The evening party broke up on a sour note. /会议～。The meeting broke up on a note of discord.

不慌不忙 bùhuāng-bùmáng unhurriedly; leisurely: ～地回答 calmly answer questions /～地走上台去 go on the stage with great assurance /他～, 把事情仔细地调查了一番。He took his time to make a careful inquiry.

不遑 bùhuáng 〈书面〉there is not enough time (to do sth.): ～顾及 be too busy to attend to the matter /～宁处 too busy with work to lead a peaceful life

不灰木 bùhuīmù 〈旧语〉asbestos

不挥发性 bùhuīfāxìng 〈物理〉non-volatility

不会 bùhuì ❶ be unlikely; will not (act, happen, etc.): 她～不知道。It's unlikely that she is still in the dark. /他今天～来了。Most probably, he won't be here today. ❷ have not learnt to; be unable to: 他～骑自行车。He hasn't learned to ride a bike. /我～抽烟。I don't smoke. ❸ *used to show displeasure*: 你就～当心点儿吗? Can't you be a little more careful?

不会儿 bùhuìr in no time; in a little while

不讳 bùhuì 〈书面〉❶ without concealing anything: 供认～ candidly confess; make a clean breast of everything /直言～ tell the honest, naked truth; be frank and outspoken ❷〈婉词〉die

不惑 bùhuò 〈书面〉not to be perplexed; self-confident: 四十～。When one reaches forty, one is no longer perplexed by the complexities of the world. /～之年, 竟有如此丑行。Fancy a man of forty getting himself involved in such a scandal.

不羁 bùjī 〈书面〉uninhibited; unconventional: 落拓～ endowed with a romantic temperament /放荡～ unconventional and unrestrained; untrammelled /～之才 unconventional talent

不及 bùjí ❶ not as good as; inferior to: 我的考试成绩～他。My exam results are not as good as his. ❷ find it too late: 准备～ be unable to get things ready in time; be caught unprepared /躲避～ can hardly dodge /后悔～ repent too late ❸ fall short of: 力所～ beyond one's power (*or* reach) /有过之而无～ go even further /过犹～。Going too far is just as bad as not going far enough.

不及物动词 bùjíwù dòngcí 〈语言〉intransitive verb

不吉之兆 bùjízhīzhào *also* "不祥之兆" bad omen: 他的批评虽不重, 却是～。His criticism, though mild, was ominous. /此乃大病将至的～。This is a symptom of an impending attack of serious disease.

不即不离 bùjí-bùlí be neither too close nor too distant; keep at arm's length: 从那以后, 我跟他保持一种～的关系。I have since kept a relationship with him which is neither too close nor too distant. *or* I have since kept him at a respectful distance.

不急之务 bùjízhīwù matter of no great urgency: 他尽忙些～。He always busies himself with matters of no great urgency. /把办教育视为～是错误的。It is erroneous to think that educational undertakings require no immediate attention.

不计 bùjì disregard; not take into account; ignore: ～个人得失 take no account of personal gains or losses /～报酬 regardless of pay (*or* remuneration) /～成败 leave success or failure out of account /～名利 not mindful of fame and gain

不计其数 bùjì-qíshù countless; innumerable: ～的珍宝 countless treasures /死伤～。The casualties were innumerable. /山下来了大批兵马, ～! Large numbers of troops have reached the foot of the mountain. They are too many to count!

不记名 bùjìmíng unnamed; blank: ～背书 blank (*or* general) endorsement /～股票 blank stock; bearer stock /～提单 open bill of lading /～债券 unregistered bond /～证券 bearer security /～委托书 blank power of attorney /～支票 bearer check; blank check

不记名投票 bùjìmíng tóupiào secret ballot: 进行～ take a secret ballot; vote by secret ballot

不济 bùjì 〈口语〉no good; of no use: 时运～ bad luck /精力～ not as energetic as before /眼神儿～ one's sight is failing /你觉得他不行, 其实你比他还～! Don't you snap your fingers at him. In fact, you can hardly compare with him.

不济事 bù jìshì no good; (of) no use; of no avail: 事已至此, 发脾气是～的。Such being the case, it is no use getting into a temper.

不加可否 bùjiā-kěfǒu *also* "不置可否" refuse to comment; not commit oneself; be non-committal

不假辞色 bùjiǎ-císè not mince one's words; be stern and blunt: 父亲为人严厉, 常～地指出别人的过失。Father was strict and stern. He would point out other people's mistakes without mincing words.

不假思索 bùjiǎ-sīsuǒ *also* "不加思索" without hesitation; readily; without thinking: ～, 点头应允 nod assent without thinking /～, 援笔而就。He took up the brush and wrote on.

不检 bùjiǎn not cautious about what one says or does; indiscreet: 行为～ indiscreet in one's behaviour

不减当年 bùjiǎn-dāngnián by no means inferior to what one used to be: 勇气～ bold as ever

不简单 bù jiǎndān ❶ not simple; fairly complicated: 那件案子～。That case is rather complicated. /这个家伙看起来呆头呆脑, 内心可～。The chap looks like a simpleton but he is very shrewd. ❷ remarkable; marvellous: 他人小志大, 真～。It is remarkable for a boy of his age to cherish such lofty aspirations.

不见 bùjiàn ❶ not see; not meet: ～不散 not leave till we meet /非公～ see nobody except on business /多年～, 你还是那么年轻。Haven't seen you for ages but you look as young as ever. ❷ (followed by 了) disappear; be lost: 他走进人群就～了。He disappeared into the crowd.

不见得 bù jiànde not necessarily; not likely: 补药吃多了对身体～好。Taking too much tonic may not be conducive to health. /他今晚～能回来。He is not likely (*or* may not be able) to come back this evening.

不见棺材不落泪 bù jiàn guāncai bù luò lèi 〈比喻〉cry only when one sees the coffin — refuse to give up or remain unconvinced until faced with grim reality

不见经传 bùjiàn-jīngzhuàn not be found in the classical canon — not authoritative; unknown: ～的小人物 nonentity /～的事情 events that cannot be verified in the classics /此人名～。He is not a well-known figure. *or* He is a nobody.

不讲价钱 bù jiǎngjiàqian never bargain about the price; never haggle about assignments: 他接受任务从来～。He always accepts an assignment without any reservation.

不骄不躁 bùjiāo-bùzào free from conceit and impetuosity; neither arrogant nor rash

不教而诛 bùjiào'érzhū *also* "不教而杀" punish without prior admonition

不结果枝 bùjiēguǒzhī 〈植物〉sterile shoot

不结盟 bùjiéméng nonalignment: ～国家 nonaligned country /～政策 nonalignment policy /～运动 nonaligned movement /～国家和政府首脑会议 Conference of Heads of State and Government of Non-Aligned Countries

不解 bùjiě ❶ fail to comprehend; not understand: ～其意 fail to grasp sb.'s point (*or* meaning) /～之事 puzzle; enigma /大惑～ extremely puzzled; unable to make head or tail of sth.; wide at sea ❷ indissoluble: ～之仇 irreconcilable enmity

不解之谜 bùjiězhīmí unsolved riddle or puzzle; enigma: 这件事成了千古～。This has become an enigma of all time (*or* an insoluble mystery).

不解之缘 bùjiězhīyuán indissoluble bond: 他从此与艺术结下了～。He has since forged an indissoluble bond with art.

不介意 bù jièyì not mind; not care: 装出～的神气 put on a nonchalant look /我抽支烟您～吧? You don't mind my smoking, do you? /他对老李的严词厉语似乎毫～。He seemed unruffled at Lao Li's harsh remarks. *or* He didn't seem to mind Lao Li's harsh criticism.

不价 bùjie *also* "不家" 〈方言〉❶ *used to indicate negation*: ～, 那不是我的上衣。No. It isn't my jacket. ❷ *used to decline a request*: "今晚咱俩看电影去好吗?" "～, 我不去。" "Shall we go to the cinema tonight?" "No, I'm sorry I won't go."

不禁 bùjīn can't help (doing sth.); can't refrain from: ～要问 cannot but ask /～暗暗赞叹 cannot help admiring sb. secretly /～失声痛哭 burst out crying /～吓了一跳 be startled

不禁不由 bùjīn-bùyóu 〈口语〉involuntarily; unintentionally: 看孩子们跳舞, 他～地打起拍子来。Watching the children dance, he began to beat time without knowing it.

不矜不躁 bùjīn-bùzào be neither swollen-headed nor short-tempered

不仅 bùjǐn ❶ not the only one: 发言的～他一人。He was not the only one of those who took the floor. ❷ not only: ～如此 not only that; nor is this all; moreover /这～是你的事, 也是大家的事。Not only does this concern you, it's also a matter of concern to all of us.

不尽 bùjìn ❶ incomplete; not fully: ～合理 not fully rational; partly reasonable ❷ endless: 感恩～ be filled with boundless gratitude /说～的痛苦 untold suffering /～长江滚滚来。Ceaselessly flows the Yangtze.

不尽然 bù jìnrán not exactly (so); not necessarily (so)

不近人情 bùjìn-rénqíng be alien to human nature; not amenable to reason; unreasonable: 这事情办得太～! This is really too unreasonable!

不进则退 bùjìn-zétuì not to forge ahead is to slip backward; not to advance is to retreat: 治学如逆水行舟, ～。Learning is like rowing a boat against the stream. If you do not make progress (*or* move ahead) you fall behind.

不经 bùjīng absurd; groundless: 荒诞～ preposterous; fantastic

不经事 bùjīngshì ❶ useless: 我感到自己～了。I felt I was no longer useful. ❷ inexperienced: 几个少～的小青年 a few inexperienced young men; a few youngsters green to the ways of the world

不经一事, 不长一智 bù jīng yī shì, bù zhǎng yī zhì wisdom stems from experience; knowledge increases with practice

不经意 bùjīngyì carelessly; by accident; thoughtlessly: 他骑车～碰倒了一个小孩。While riding a bike he knocked down a child by accident. /这个人～走进一处禁区。The man thoughtlessly wandered into a restricted area.

不经之谈 bùjīngzhītán absurd statement; tall tale; nonsense; cock and bull story: 他常有些～, 并无人理会。No one ever paid any attention to his crazy talk. *or* He is apt to make absurd statements, but nobody ever pays attention to them.

不景气 bùjǐngqì ❶ 〈经济〉depression; recession; slump: ～之后便是经济危机。An economic crisis follows a depression. ❷ depressed state: 这个季节生意～。Business is slack in this season of the year.

B

不景气综合征 bùjǐngqì zōnghézhēng 〈经济〉 depression syndrome

不胫而走 bùjìng'érzǒu run apace; spread like wildfire: 坏消息～。Ill news runs apace. /这个传闻～。The news spread like wildfire.

不久 bùjiǔ soon; before long; not long after: ～以前 not long ago; recently /～的将来 in the near future; in the not too distant future /过后～ soon afterwards /大桥～就能完工。The bridge will be completed soon.

不久人事 bùjiǔ-rénshì one's days are numbered; won't be long for this world

不咎既往 bùjiù-jìwǎng not censure sb. for his past mistakes; let bygones be bygones: 只要你能痛改前非，我们是可以～的。So long as you are determined to mend your ways, we'll let bygones be bygones.

不拘 bùjū ❶ not stick to; not confine oneself to: 文章长短～ set no limit on the length of an article ❷ whatever; whoever; whenever: ～何人，他都能合得来。He can get along with anyone.

不拘礼节 bùjū-lǐjié not care about formalities (in social intercourse); not stand on ceremony; not bother about etiquette or protocol

不拘小节 bùjū-xiǎojié not bother about small matters; not be punctilious; disregard trifles or niceties; not be fettered by petty conventions: 他性格豪放，～。With an uninhibited character, he never cares about conventional decorum. *or* Bold and uninhibited in character, he never bothers about petty conventions.

不拘形迹 bùjū-xíngjì dispense with formalities: 他们原是～的密友。They were close friends who had no use for formalities between them.

不拘形式 bùjū-xíngshì not be particular about form; skip the formalities; not stand on ceremony: ～的座谈会 informal forum

不拘一格 bùjū-yīgé not stick to one pattern; not be confined to one form: 选用人才，～ discard uniformity of standards in selecting and employing people of talent

不具 bùjù 〈书面〉❶〈旧语〉not detailed here (used to wind up a letter): 知名～。(formula for winding up an anonymous letter) I'll omit my name as it is known to you. *or* Yours anonymously. ❷ incomplete: 旧籍散亡，典章～。As ancient documents are either fragmentary or missing, our knowledge of the legal and political systems of the antiquity is incomplete.

不倦 bùjuàn tireless; untiring; indefatigable: 诲人～ be tireless in teaching; teach with tireless zeal /读书～ read tirelessly

不绝如缕 bùjué-rúlǚ ❶ hanging by a thread; very precarious: 这门技艺后继乏人，目前已处于～的状态。This craftsmanship is on the verge of extinction for lack of successors. ❷ (of sound) linger in the ears: 那琴声余音袅袅，～。The notes came forth from the harp like a far-floating endless thread.

不均匀分布 bùjūnyún fēnbù nonuniform or uneven distribution

不均匀加热 bùjūnyún jiārè uneven heating

不均匀性 bùjūnyúnxìng 〈物理〉 nonuniformity; unevenness

不刊之论 bùkānzhīlùn idea or argument that admits of no modification or change; sacrosanct statement; absolute truth: 父亲总认为自己说过的话就是～，不允许我有一点不同意见。Father always considered what he said was absolute truth, and tolerated no slight contradiction from me.

不堪 bùkān ❶ cannot bear; cannot stand: ～受辱 cannot swallow the insult /～其苦 cannot stand the hardship /～奴隶主的压迫 cannot endure the oppression of the slaveowner ❷ (of sth. unpleasant or bad) unbearably; impossibly: ～入目 not fit to be seen; revolting; unbearably vulgar; most shameful and ugly /～收拾的局面 situation which is running out of control (*or* getting out of hand) ❸ utterly; extremely: 疲惫～ dog-tired; exhausted; overcome with fatigue /破烂～ very much tattered (*or* ragged); worn to shreds /狼狈～ in a very embarrassing situation /痛苦～ extremely miserable; in great agony /恶劣～ outrageously vile; extremely vicious; abominable /拥挤～的住房 cramped (living) quarters ❹ extremely bad: 这个人太～了。This chap is wicked to the extreme. /尤其～的是他那追求地位和金钱的欲望。Worst of all is his lust for position and wealth.

不堪回首 bùkān-huíshǒu cannot bear to recall or think of the past; find it unbearable to look back: ～话当年 cannot bear to recollect and speak about the past (events) /他历经宦海升沉，深感往事～。He had experienced so many ups and downs in politics that he could not recall the past without a deep sense of regret.

不堪入耳 bùkān-rù'ěr offensive to the ear; too sordid for decent ears; revolting: ～的辱骂 sordid (*or* filthy) abuse

不堪设想 bùkān-shèxiǎng too dreadful to contemplate: 后果～。The consequences would be too dreadful to contemplate. /事情已经到了～的地步。Things have come to a dreadful pass.

不堪一击 bùkān-yījī cannot withstand a single blow: 敌人已～。The enemy would collapse at our first blow. *or* The enemy could not withstand a single blow. /这个谬论～。This is an untenable fallacy.

不堪造就 bùkān-zàojiù unworthy of instruction; hopeless: ～的蠢货 hopeless fool /这个年青人并非是～。The young man is not unworthy of further education.

不看僧面看佛面 bù kàn sēngmiàn kàn fómiàn (do sth.) not for the monk's sake, but for the Buddha's — do sth. out of consideration for sb. else

不亢不卑 bùkàng-bùbēi *see* "不卑不亢"

不可 bùkě ❶ cannot; should not; must not: ～一概而论 should not make sweeping statements; must not indulge in generalizations /～剥夺的权利 inalienable right /～避免的冲突 unavoidable conflict; inevitable conflict /～辩驳的事实 irrefutable fact ❷ *used together with* 非 *to indicate what one is set to do*: 这部电影太精彩了，我非看～。The film is really great; I just cannot miss it. /看来这步棋非走～了。It seems that we simply have to make this move.

不可比因素 bùkěbǐ yīnsù incomparable factor; factor not subject to comparison

不可撤回的诉状 bùkě-chèhuíde sùzhuàng 〈法律〉 irrevocable indictment

不可撤消的判决 bùkě-chèxiāode pànjué 〈法律〉 irrevocable judgment

不可兑换的货币 bùkě-duìhuànde huòbì 〈经济〉 non-convertible currency

不可多得 bùkě-duōdé hard to come by; rare; exceptional: ～的人才 person of exceptional gift /～的机会 rare opportunity /～的佳作 unusual specimen of good writing (*or* painting)

不可分割 bùkě-fēngē indivisible; inseparable: ～的权利 undivided right /～的整体 organic whole /～的部分 inseparable part /统一而～的联邦 one and indivisible union

不可分解 bùkě-fēnjiě 〈化学〉 undecomposable

不可告人 bùkě-gàorén to be held in secrecy; covert: ～的目的 ulterior motives /～的勾当 sinister (*or* dirty) deal

不可估量 bùkě-gūliàng inestimable; incalculable; beyond measure: ～的损失 incalculable loss

不可或缺 bùkě-huòquē absolutely necessary; indispensable: ～的条件 indispensable condition; sine qua non

不可接触者 bùkě-jiēchùzhě *also* "贱民" jiànmín "untouchable" — member of lowest hereditary Hindu caste (use of the term and social restrictions accompanying it was declared illegal in India in 1949 and Pakistan in 1953)

不可接受 bùkě jiēshòu unacceptable; inadmissible: ～的解释 unacceptable explanation /～的证据 inadmissible evidence /～的人〈外交〉 person not acceptable

不可救药 bùkě-jiùyào ❶ incurable; beyond cure; without cure; past praying for: 病入膏肓，～。The disease which has attacked the vital organs is beyond cure. ❷ incorrigible; hopeless: 失足青年并非全是～的。Not all juvenile deliquents are hopeless.

不可开交 bùkě-kāijiāo (used after 得 as its complement) be locked in; be tied up: 打得～ be locked in a fierce fight /忙得～ be up to one's ears in work; be awfully busy /闹得～ make a hell of a fuss / 他们争得～。They argued heatedly among themselves.

不可抗拒 bùkě-kàngjù irresistible; inexorable: ～的自然规律 inexorable law of nature /～的历史潮流 irresistible trend of history

不可抗力 bùkěkànglì 〈法律〉 force majeure; act of God

不可理喻 bùkě-lǐyù cannot be persuaded by reasoned argument; refuse to obey the dictates of reason: 此人完全～。The guy is blind to reason.

不可弥补 bùkě-míbǔ irretrievable; irrecoverable; irremediable; irreparable: ～的错误 irreparable mistake; irremediable error /～的缺陷 irredeemable defect /～的损失 irretrievable loss

不可名状 bùkě-míngzhuàng *also* "不可言状" indescribable; beyond description: ～的喜悦 indescribable joy /山路险峭，～。The mountain path is rugged and steep beyond description. /她心中突然升起一种～的悲哀。A sudden feeling of sadness gripped her, a feeling that no words could describe.

不可磨灭 bùkě-mómiè indelible; inerasable; monumental: 留下～的印象 leave an indelible impression (on sb.) /～的功绩 ineffaceable merit; unforgettable deed /～的痕迹 inerasable mark
不可逆 bùkěnì non-reversible: ～反应〈化学〉non-reversible reaction /～式轧钢机〈冶金〉non-reversing rolling mill /～运算〈数学〉irreversible operation
不可逆转 bùkě-nìzhuǎn not to be turned back; irreversible: ～的历史潮流 irreversible trend of history /改革～。The reform is irreversible.
不可偏废 bùkě-piānfèi neither should be neglected: 学好功课与锻炼身体, 二者～。Neither study nor physical training should be overemphasized to the neglect of the other.
不可企及 bùkě-qǐjí beyond one's power of attainment: 钱教授的成就, 是我辈～的。Prof. Qian's attainments are beyond what you and I can ever hope to achieve.
不可侵犯权 bùkě-qīnfànquán〈外交〉inviolability
不可燃性 bùkěránxìng incombustibility
不可溶性 bùkěróngxìng insolubility
不可胜数 bùkě-shèngshǔ countless; innumerable; untold: 因海洋污染而死的海鸟～。The sea-birds that have died of pollution are beyond counting.
不可收拾 bùkě-shōushi irremediable; unmanageable; out of hand; hopeless: ～的局面 irremediable situation /事情到了～的地步。Things are getting out of hand. /出了大乱子就～了。If big trouble should start, the situation could hardly be taken in hand.
不可思议 bùkě-sīyì inconceivable; unimaginable: ～的举动 inconceivable behaviour /～的表情 mysterious look
不可调和 bùkě-tiáohé irreconcilable; incompatible: ～的矛盾 irreconcilable contradiction
不可同日而语 bùkě tóngrì ér yǔ cannot be mentioned in the same breath; cannot be put on a par: 这两件事～。These two things cannot be mentioned in the same breath. /他俩的社会地位～。They were poles apart in social status. /她现在的经济状况与几年前相比简直～了。There is no comparison between her financial situation today and that of a few years ago.
不可推卸 bùkě-tuīxiè unshirkable; inescapable: 对世界和平负有～的责任 have unshirkable responsibility for world peace
不可挽回 bùkě-wǎnhuí irremediable; irreparable; irretrievable; irrevocable: ～的损失 irretrievable losses /～的败局 certain defeat
不可为训 bùkě-wéixùn cannot be taken as a rule; cannot be taken as an example (for others to follow)
不可违背 bùkě-wéibèi infrangible; inviolable: ～的自然法则 infrangible law of nature
不可无一,不可有二 bùkě wú yī, bùkě yǒu èr unique; peerless: 如此异才, 求之天下, ～。You can't find another such extraordinary talent in this world.
不可限量 bùkě-xiànliàng limitless (opportunities); very promising
不可向迩 bùkě-xiàng'ěr cannot be approached: 烈火燎原, ～。The raging fire kept people from coming near.
不可行性 bùkěxíngxìng infeasibility
不可言宣 bùkě-yánxuān unable to describe in words; beyond description
不可延展性 bùkě-yánzhǎnxìng inextensibility
不可氧化性 bùkě-yǎnghuàxìng inoxidizability; non-oxidizability
不可一世 bùkě-yīshì flaunting one's superiority; extremely arrogant: 一副～的架势 air of extreme arrogance /这位大少爷在旧社会可是～。The young master used to bluster and swagger like a lord in the old society.
不可逾越 bùkě-yúyuè impassable; insurmountable; insuperable: ～的鸿沟 impassible chasm /～的障碍 insurmountable (*or* insuperable) barrier /～的长江天堑 impassable natural moat of the Yangtze River
不可约 bùkěyuē〈数学〉irreducible: ～方程 irreducible equation /～多项式 irreducible polynomial
不可争辩 bùkě-zhēngbiàn beyond dispute; irrefutable: 她用～的事实说服了每一个人。She convinced everyone by her powerful presentation of irrefutable facts.
不可知论 bùkězhīlùn〈哲学〉agnosticism: ～者 agnostic
不可终日 bùkě-zhōngrì have no peace of mind all day: 惶惶～ be very worried; be eaten up with anxiety
不可转让 bùkě-zhuǎnràng non-assignable; non-transferable; unalienable: ～的义务 non-assignable duty /～的债券 non-transferable bond
不可转移性 bùkě-zhuǎnyíxìng untransferability: 恶债的特点在于它的～。The characteristic of odious debts lies in their untransferability.
不可捉摸 bùkě-zhuōmō hard to size up; unpredictable; elusive: ～的性格 unpredictable character /～的形势 volatile situation /他行为古怪, ～。He is eccentric and unpredictable. /他的意图～。It was difficult to see what he had in mind.
不克 bùkè〈书面〉❶ be unable to; cannot: ～亲临 be unable to come in person /～当此重任 be unequal to this position of great responsibility ❷ fail to capture: 屡攻～ attack many times without success /攻无～ all-conquering; ever-victorious; invincible
不客气 bù kèqi ❶ impolite; rude: 说句～的话 to put it bluntly /说了几句～的话 make some rude remarks ❷〈套语〉(in reply to expressions of thanks) don't mention it; you are welcome; not at all ❸ *indicating polite refusal to accept an offer*: "抽支烟。" "～。" "Have a cigarette." "No, thanks." /"我能帮你忙吗?" "哦, ～, 我能行。" "Can I help you?" "Oh, that's very kind of you, but I can manage."
不空成就 Bùkōngchéngjiù〈宗教〉*Amoghasiddhi*
不快 bùkuài ❶ be unhappy; be displeased; be in low spirits: 心中～ feel unhappy about sth.; be in low spirits /令人～ annoying /深感～ feel very much displeased ❷ be indisposed; feel under the weather; be out of sorts: 身体偶感～。It happens that I feel a bit under the weather. ❸ slow; not fast: 增长速度～。The growth rate is low.
不愧 bùkuì be worthy of; deserve the title of: ～为人民英雄 be worthy of the title of People's Hero
不愧不怍 bùkuì-bùzuò have nothing to be ashamed of; have a clear conscience; be open and aboveboard
不扩散核武器条约 Bù Kuòsàn Héwǔqì Tiáoyuē Treaty on the Non-Proliferation of Nuclear Weapons (NPT)
不赖 bùlài〈方言〉not bad; good; fine: 手艺～ piece of fine craftsmanship /表演真～。The performance was superb. /画得～。The picture is well-drawn.
不郎不秀 bùláng-bùxiù neither fish nor fowl — good for nothing; ne'er-do-well; worthless: 她倒是个令人喜欢的孩子, 可是她～的哥哥真令人讨厌。She is a pleasant girl, but her brother is an unpleasant good-for-nothing.
不劳而获 bùláo'érhuò reap without sowing: 每个人都要自食其力, 不能～。Everybody must earn his own bread and nobody should live by sponging off others.
不老少 bùlǎoshǎo〈方言〉lots of; a great number of: 今儿晚儿观众可～。There're quite a lot of spectators tonight. *or* The house is quite full tonight.
不冷不热 bùlěng-bùrè ❶ moderately warm; lukewarm: 昆明四季如春, ～。It is pleasantly warm like spring all the year round in Kunming. /那里的气候～, 适合种水稻。The climate there is neither too hot nor too cold, and just right for growing rice. ❷ lukewarm in one's attitude: ～的关系 lukewarm relationship /他那种～的态度真叫人受不了。His lukewarm attitude is exasperating.
不离儿 bùlír〈方言〉❶ not bad; pretty good: 他画得还真～。He draws pretty well. ❷ pretty close: 酒饭吃个～, 老王把话转入正题。Dinner almost over, Lao Wang brought up the matter.
不理 bùlǐ refuse to acknowledge; pay no attention to; take no notice of; ignore: 这孩子不懂礼貌, 常见人～。The child often passes people by; he has no manners. /他故意～我。He cut me dead deliberately. /我对闲言碎语一概～。I turn a deaf ear to all gossip.
不力 bùlì not exert oneself; be ineffective; incompetent: 办事～ prove incompetent for one's job; lack efficiency /领导～ not exercise effective leadership; have weak leadership
不利 bùlì ❶ unfavourable; disadvantageous; harmful; detrimental: ～条件 unfavourable condition /～地形 disadvantageous terrain (*or* topographic features) /～天气 adverse weather /～时机 inopportune moment /于私于公皆～ detrimental both to oneself and to the public /处于～地位的国家 disadvantaged state /～于团结的言行 action and words harmful (*or* detrimental) to unity ❷ unsuccessful: 出师～ lose the first battle
不连续性 bùliánxùxìng〈物理〉discontinuity
不良 bùliáng bad; harmful; unhealthy: ～倾向 unhealthy trend /～影响 harmful (*or* adverse) effect /存心～ harbour ill intent /消化～ poor digestion; indigestion /～分子 bad elements /～作风 unde-

sirable work style /～嗜好 bad habit; addiction /～动机 evil motive / 营养～ under-nourishment /发育～ physically underdeveloped

不良导体 bùliáng dǎotǐ 〈物理〉poor conductor

不量力 bù liànglì fail to estimate one's own ability or strength correctly; not take a proper measure of oneself

不了 bùliǎo (often used after 个) without end:吃个～ keep eating/忙个～ be as busy as a bee /雨下个～。The rain kept pouring.

B

不了了之 bùliǎo-liǎozhī let things take their natural course; end up by letting the matter drop:事情一拖再拖,恐怕要～。The matter has been delayed time and again; it will probably be shelved in the end.

不料 bùliào unexpectedly; to one's surprise:～事与愿违。To my surprise, the event ran counter to my wishes. /偶然的一个疏忽,～竟成了大错。An accidental oversight has unexpectedly led to a gross error.

不列颠百科全书 Bùlièdiān Bǎikē Quánshū Encyclopaedia Britannica

不列颠博物馆 Bùlièdiān Bówùguǎn British Museum

不列颠哥伦比亚 Bùlièdiān Gēlúnbǐyà British Columbia, westernmost province of Canada

不列颠合金 Bùlièdiān héjīn britannia metal, alloy of tin and antimony, first made in England in 1770

不列颠群岛 Bùlièdiān Qúndǎo British Isles

不列颠人 Bùlièdiānrén Briton; Brit

不列颠战役 Bùlièdiān Zhànyì Battle of Britain, 1940-1941

不劣方头 bùliè-fāngtóu *also* "方头不劣" (often used in the early vernacular) obdurate; difficult of approach

不吝 bùlìn 〈套语〉(used in soliciting comments) not stint; not grudge; not spare:望～指教。I hope you will feel free to make suggestions.

不灵 bùlíng not work; be ineffective:你的办法～。Your method doesn't work. /我的表～了。My watch doesn't work properly. /老太太耳朵～了。The old lady is hard of hearing.

不留后路 bùliú-hòulù cut off all retreat; leave no leeway; cross the Rubicon

不留情面 bùliú-qíngmiàn not spare sb.'s sensibilities; not be afraid to hurt sb.'s feelings:他这个人办事铁面无私,从来～。Impartial and upright, he has never stretched a point to spare people's sensibilities.

不留意 bù liúyì careless:路那么滑,稍～就会跌倒。The road is so slippery that if you are off guard the least bit, you'll slip and fall.

不留余地 bùliú-yúdì leave no room; make no allowance:说话～往往会陷入被动。You'll land yourself in a difficult position if you make no allowances in your statement.

不露锋芒 bùlù-fēngmáng not display one's talents; try to cover up or hide one's abilities

不露圭角 bùlù-guījiǎo not be eager to show off; not display one's abilities

不露声色 bùlù-shēngsè not betray one's feelings, intentions, etc.:他虽已掌握情况,却丝毫～。Although he had been duly informed, he did not show it.

不伦不类 bùlún-bùlèi neither fish nor fowl; nondescript:～的比喻 far-fetched analogy; incongruous metaphor /一帮～的人 group of nondescripts /他的言论～。His remarks are neither here nor there.

不论 bùlùn ❶ no matter (what, who, how, etc.); whether... or...; regardless of:～性别、年龄,都可报名参赛。Anyone can sign up for the contest, regardless of sex and age. /～困难有多大,他们从未屈服。Whatever the difficulties, they never yielded. /～情况怎样,你都要跟我们保持联系。No matter what the situation is like, you must keep in touch with us. ❷〈书面〉not discuss; not debate:存而～ not be going to discuss sth.; leave the matter alone for the time being

不落窠臼 bùluò-kējiù 〈书面〉not follow the beaten track; not be restricted by convention; be original:这篇小说在写法上新颖别致,～。This novel is written in a graceful and original style departing from literary conventions.

不落俗套 bùluò-sútào depart from convention; be unconventional

不买账 bùmǎizhàng not buy it; not care:你摆架子,人们就不买你的账。If you put on airs, nobody would buy it. /我说破了嘴皮,他也～。However hard I tried to explain, he just wouldn't listen.

不满 bùmǎn resentful; discontented; dissatisfied:心怀～ nurse a grievance /散布～言论 raise complaints (usu. behind sb.'s back) /表示～ show displeasure

不蔓不枝 bùmàn-bùzhī not branching out; terse; succinct; to the point:一篇～的好文章 concise, well-organized article

不忙 bùmáng there's no hurry; take one's time:"别误了飞机。" "～,还早呢。" "Hurry up, or you'll miss the plane." "No hurry; it's early." /～,三点前完成就行了。Take your time. It will be fine if you can finish it by three o'clock.

不毛之地 bùmáozhīdì barren land:原先的～,如今变成了良田。The barren land has now become an expanse of fertile fields. /这里水土流失严重,几乎成了～。Serious soil erosion has turned the fields into barren land.

不免 bùmiǎn unavoidable:～感到失望 cannot help feeling disappointed /忙中～有错。We are prone to make mistakes when we do things in a hurry. /初次见面,～有些拘束。As we met for the first time, we were naturally a little stiff in our manners.

不妙 bùmiào not too encouraging; far from good; anything but reassuring:感到～ feel anything but reassured /情况～。Things are not encouraging.

不敏 bùmǐn 〈书面〉〈谦词〉not intelligent; slow-witted:敬谢～。I appreciate your kindness, but I'm afraid I have to decline the offer (*or* the present, etc.). /彭某～,愿聆指教。Slow-witted as I am, I'd like to hear your advice (彭某 being the speaker's modest way of referring to himself).

不名数 bùmíngshù 〈数学〉abstract number

不名一文 bùmíng-yīwén *also* "不名一钱" without a penny to one's name; penniless; broke:我～,如何能出国旅行呢? I haven't got a penny to my name. How can I afford to go on trips abroad? /他穷得～,无法维持家庭的生活了。He was so hard up that he could not support his family.

不名誉 bùmíngyù disreputable; disgraceful; infamous:你为何干出这种～的事? How could you have done such a disgraceful thing?

不明 bùmíng ❶ not clear; unknown:下落～ sb.'s whereabouts (is) unknown /情况～ the situation is murky /～国籍的飞机 plane of unidentified nationality; unidentified aircraft /身分～的人 person of unknown identity ❷ fail to understand; not know:～底蕴 not understand the true picture; not know the inside story /～真相 be unaware of the truth; be ignorant of the facts; be kept in the dark /～是非 confuse right and wrong; not know chalk from cheese /～事理 lack common sense; be unreasonable

不明不白 bùmíng-bùbái obscure; dubious; unclear:死得～ die a mysterious death /我不能～地辞职。I can't resign under a cloud.

不明飞行物 bùmíng fēixíngwù *also* "幽浮" yōufú; "飞碟" fēidié unidentified flying object (UFO); flying saucer

不明就里 bùmíng-jiùlǐ *also* "不知就里" not know the inside story; be in the dark:他的所作所为,总让～的人莫名其妙。His behaviour always puzzles the outsiders.

不摸头 bù mōtóu 〈口语〉not be acquainted with (the situation); have no inkling of:这个问题我一点儿也～。I haven't the haziest idea of the question.

不谋而合 bùmóu'érhé agree without prior consultation; happen to hold identical views:我们的见解～。Our views happened to coincide.

不睦 bùmù 〈书面〉unfriendly; not amicable; at odds (with):兄弟～ brothers at odds with each other

不能 bùnéng cannot; must not; should not:～置之不理 cannot stand idly by; cannot remain indifferent; cannot ignore /～盲从 cannot follow (sb. or sth.) blindly; must not have blind faith (in sb. or sth.) /你的这些要求我们～满足。We cannot meet your demands.

不能不 bùnéngbù cannot but; have to:～感到担忧 cannot help but feel worried /～表示反对 cannot but voice our opposition; feel impelled to object /～指出,这是不符合外交惯例的。It must be pointed out that this is not in keeping with international diplomatic practice.

不能繁殖 bùnéng fánzhí 〈生物〉sterility

不能通约 bùnéng tōngyuē 〈数学〉incommensurability

不能忘怀 bùnéng-wànghuái be unable to forget; often think of

不能赞一辞 bùnéng zàn yī cí unable to say a word (in criticism of an impeccable piece of writing):这篇文章好极了,我实在～。This essay is excellent, and I don't think I can offer a word of criticism.

不能自拔 bùnéng-zìbá unable to extricate oneself (from a difficult or embarrassing situation):陷于官僚主义泥潭而～ get inextricably bogged down in the quagmire of bureaucracy

不能自已 bùnéng-zìyǐ lose control over oneself; be unable to restrain oneself:泪如雨下,~。Tears streamed down one's cheeks involuntarily.

不念旧恶 bùniàn-jiù'è forget past grudges; let bygones be bygones; forget about old grievances:他~,重修前好。He did not allow the old grievances to stand in the path of renewing friendship.

不宁 bùning 〈书面〉❶ would rather...(than):与其尸位素餐,~告老还乡。I would rather plead old age and retire to my hometown than hold on to my official position doing nothing all day. ❷ not only; what is more; moreover

不宁唯是 bùningwéishì 〈书面〉not only... but also; moreover

不佞 bùning 〈书面〉〈谦词〉your dull-witted servant; I:此事足下讳莫如深,~颇为不解。You seem to be very guarded about the matter, and I must confess I am rather perplexed.

不怕 bùpà ❶ not be afraid of; not fear:~艰难困苦 fear no difficulties and hardships /为正义~牺牲 be ready to lay down one's life in a righteous cause ❷〈方言〉no matter how; even if; even:~雨再大,我也要去上班。No matter how hard it rains I will go to work.

不怕不识货,就怕货比货 bù pà bù shíhuò, jiù pà huò bǐ huò you needn't worry about not knowing the quality of the goods, you'll know which is better when you compare them; the worth of a thing is shown through comparison

不怕官,只怕管 bù pà guān, zhǐ pà guǎn it is not the official, but the clerk, that is to be feared; it is the person in direct control, however low his position, that has to be reckoned with; fear no officials, except those who officiate over you

不怕慢,只怕站 bù pà màn, zhǐ pà zhàn it's better to move ahead slowly than just to stand still; slow progress is better than none

不怕邪 bùpàxié be unafraid of sinister forces; not be daunted by anything sinister:我们~。We are not scared by evil forces. *or* We are not to be scared.

不配 bùpèi ❶ be unworthy of; not deserve; be unqualified for:她~当翻译。She is not a qualified interpreter. /他~得金牌。He didn't deserve the gold medal he got. ❷ not match:这一对儿真有点~。They are not a well-matched pair. /领带颜色与上装~。The colour of the tie doesn't match that of the jacket.

不偏不倚 bùpiān-bùyǐ even-handed; impartial; unbiased; without leaning to either side:~的态度 impartial attitude /在这种争论中,要保持~实在太难。To remain unbiased in a debate of this kind is really hard. *or* It is extremely difficult to maintain an even-handed attitude in such polemics.

不平 bùpíng ❶ uneven; not level; not smooth:凹凸~的地面 uneven ground /崎岖~的山路 rugged mountain path /表面~。The surface is not smooth. ❷ injustice; unfairness; wrong; grievance:~之事 injustice; wrong /路见~,拔刀相助 stand out boldly to redress a social injustice; come to the rescue of a wronged party one does not know ❸ indignant (about sth. unjust); resentful:愤愤~ boil with resentment (*or* indignation) /这并不能消除我心中的~。This does not in any way allay my deep-seated resentment.

不平等条约 bùpíngděng tiáoyuē unequal treaty

不平衡 bùpínghéng disequilibrium; imbalance:贸易~ trade imbalance /心里~ lose one's psychological equilibrium; feel unhappy /导致世界格局新的~ lead to a new disequilibrium in the global power structure

不平则鸣 bùpíngzémíng where there is injustice, there is complaint; people will give vent to their grievances; man will cry out against injustice

不破不立 bùpò-bùlì no construction without destruction; no making without breaking

不欺暗室 bùqī-ànshì do nothing one will be ashamed of even where no one knows what one is doing; be a hundred per cent honest even when nobody is around

不期而遇 bùqī'éryù meet by chance; have a chance encounter:日前散步,与他~。I ran into him the other day when I was taking a stroll.

不期然而然 bù qī rán ér rán *also* "不期而然" happen unexpectedly; turn out contrary to one's expectations

不起眼 bùqǐyǎn 〈方言〉negligible; unimportant:她是一位平凡而~儿的姑娘。She is an ordinary girl who attracts no one's attention. /他住在一条~儿的小胡同里。He lives in an inconspicuous small lane.

不巧 bùqiǎo unfortunately; as luck would have it:真~,他今天又不在家。Unfortunately, he is out again today. /~得很,路上碰到堵车把时间耽误了,没赶上火车。As luck would have it, I was caught in a traffic jam and missed the train.

不切实际 bùqiè-shíjì unrealistic; impractical; impracticable:~的想法 unrealistic notion /~的计划 impracticable plan /这种想法~。The idea flies in the face of reality.

不切题 bù qiètí irrelevant to the topic; off the mark; beside the point:发言~ speak (wide) off the mark; speak beside the point /你的高论太~。Your idea has little to do with the subject under discussion.

不亲和性 bùqīnhéxìng 〈植物〉incompatibility

不情之请 bùqíngzhīqǐng 〈套语〉my presumptuous request:~,敬希谅察。My request may be presumptuous, and I respectfully beg your pardon.

不求名利 bùqiú-mínglì not care for fame or wealth:我的座右铭是~。My motto is "seek neither fame nor fortune".

不求上进 bùqiú-shàngjìn have no desire for progress; be contented with one's lot:~无异自甘落后。Seeking no progress is tantamount to resigning oneself to lagging behind.

不求甚解 bùqiú-shènjiě not seek to understand things thoroughly; be content with a superficial understanding:好读书而~ love reading but have no desire to go too deeply into it /这是粗枝大叶,~的作风。This is a careless and superficial style of work.

不求仕进 bùqiú-shìjìn not embark on an official career; not seek public offices

不屈 bùqū unyielding; unbending:宁死~ would rather die than surrender /英勇~ valiant and unyielding /顽强~ obstinate and unbending

不屈不挠 bùqū-bùnáo unyielding; indomitable:~的意志 indomitable will /~的性格 unyielding character /~地去战胜困难 try to overcome the difficulties with great fortitude /~的反帝反殖斗争 the unrelenting struggle against imperialism and colonialism

不全骨折 bùquán gǔzhé 〈医学〉incomplete fracture

不全流产 bùquán liúchǎn 〈医学〉incomplete abortion

不然 bùrán ❶ not so:他表面谦虚,其实~。He is modest on the surface, but not so at heart. /这件事对你说很容易,对我就~了。This is easy for you, but not for me. ❷ (used at the beginning of a sentence to indicate disagreement) No:~,事情没那么简单。No, it's not as simple as that. ❸ or (else); otherwise; if not:请关上窗户,~病人要受凉的。Close the window please, or the patient may catch cold.

不燃物 bùránwù 〈化学〉incombustible; non-combustible

不燃性 bùránxìng 〈化学〉incombustibility

不人道 bù réndào inhuman:种族灭绝是~的。Genocide is inhuman.

不仁 bùrén ❶ not benevolent; heartless:~不义 show no benevolence; be heartless /为富~ one who shows no benevolence in the pursuit of riches; the heartless rich ❷ benumbed:麻木~ apathetic

不忍 bùrěn cannot bear:~卒读 cannot bear to read to the end /~离去 cannot tear oneself away /~坐视 have no heart to stand by /~之心 compassion

不妊症 bùrènzhèng (of a woman) infertility;sterility

不日 bùrì within the next few days; in a few days:~抵京 will soon arrive in Beijing /工程~即可完成。The project will be completed in a matter of days.

不容 bùróng not tolerate; not allow; not brook:~辩解 allow of no excuse /~干涉 tolerate (*or* brook) no interference /天理~ be tolerated nowhere under heaven /法理~ not to be permitted by law /~申辩 be immune to all pleas /~否认的事实 undeniable (*or* indisputable) fact /自尊心~侮辱 stomach no insult to one's sense of pride /~讨论 not negotiable

不容置辩 bùróng-zhìbiàn indisputable; incontestable; incontrovertible; beyond all question:~,他已卷入这场斗争。It is indisputable that he has got involved in the struggle.

不容置喙 bùróng-zhìhuì allow of no interference by any one; not allow others to butt in; brook no intervention:这是我俩之间的事,旁人~。This is a matter which involves only the two of us. We want no interference from others.

不容置疑 bùróng-zhìyí beyond doubt; undoubtedly:~,他对情况的分析是很正确的。Without doubt, his analysis of the situation is correct.

不如 bùrú not so good as; inferior to; would be better:今年收成~去年。The harvest this year is not as good as last year's. /我认为看电视~看书。I think I'd rather read books than watch TV. /既然看不

进书,~去散散步吧。Since you can't concentrate on reading, you might as well go for a walk.

不入虎穴,焉得虎子 bù rù hǔxué, yān dé hǔzǐ how can one catch tiger cubs without walking boldly into the tiger lair; nothing venture, nothing gain

不三不四 bùsān-bùsì ❶ dubious; shady:~的人 person of dubious (*or* shady) character; questionable character /~的勾当 disreputable (*or* shady) doings ❷ nondescript; neither one thing nor the other; neither fish nor fowl:说些~的话 make frivolous remarks

不塞不流,不止不行 bù sè bù liú, bù zhǐ bù xíng no flowing without damming and no motion without rest

不衫不履 bùshān-bùlǚ wear outlandish or weird clothes; be improperly dressed:他这个人~,我看见就讨厌。I hate the very sight of the chap, as he's always wearing weird clothes.

不善 bùshàn ❶ bad; ill; evil:处理~ not handle matters properly; mishandle matters /来者~。Those who came might not be motivated by friendship. *or* They did not come with the best of intentions. ❷ *also* "不善于" not good at:~经营 not good at business management /~交际 not a good mixer; not a good socializer /~言谈 not a good talker (*or* conversationalist); not be particularly articulate ❸ *also* "不善乎" 〈方言〉 quite impressive; to be reckoned with:别看他个头儿不高,打起球来可~。Short as he is, he is a player to be reckoned with in any ball match. /他那张嘴可~,能把白的说成黑的。He has such a glib tongue that he can talk black into white.

不善自谋 bùshàn-zìmóu not good at looking after oneself and one's family; not know how to fend for oneself

不上不下 bùshàng-bùxià be kept in suspense; dangle in mid-air; be in a pretty fix:~,惊喜不定 be kept in suspense, hovering between fear and joy

不舍昼夜 bùshě-zhòuyè no matter whether it is day or night; day and night; ceaselessly:逝者如斯夫,~。Thus things do flow away, day and night.

不设防城市 bùshèfáng chéngshì open city; undefended city; unfortified city

不甚了了 bùshèn-liǎoliǎo have only a hazy idea (about sth.); be not clear (about sth.)

不渗透层 bùshèntòucéng non-permeable stratum or layer

不渗透性 bùshèntòuxìng impermeability; tightness:~内衬 impervious lining /~石墨 impervious graphite

不声不响 bùshēng-bùxiǎng secretly; quietly:他~地继续工作。He went on quietly with his work.

不胜 bùshèng ❶ cannot bear or stand:~其烦 be bored beyond endurance /~其苦 undergo untold sufferings /弱~衣 so fragile that one seems unable to bear the weight of one's clothes; extremely weak ❷ *used between two identical verbs to indicate one's inability to do sth. or to complete sth.*:防~防 cannot avoid (danger, mistake, etc.) in all cases; cannot find a foolproof solution /数~数 countless; innumerable /这种漏洞堵~堵。Such leaks (*or* loopholes) are too numerous to plug (*or* stop). ❸ (used to indicate degree of emotion) very; extremely; tremendously; deeply:~感激 be very much obliged; be deeply grateful /未能及时奉告,~遗憾。I am very sorry for not having kept you informed in time. *or* Much to my regret, I failed to keep you informed in time. ❹ 〈方言〉 less than; worse than:老爷子的身体一年~一年。The old man got more frail with each passing year.

不胜枚举 bùshèng-méijǔ too numerous to be mentioned individually or one by one; far too numerous; so many as to defy enumeration:好人好事,~。Good people and good deeds are too numerous to be listed in detail. /诸如此类,~。Things like this are legion.

不胜庆幸 bùshèng-qìngxìng have great cause for rejoicing; be overjoyed

不失时机 bùshī-shíjī seize the opportune moment; lose no time; not let the opportunity slip (through one's fingers):~地提出新任务 seize the opportune moment to set forth new tasks /~地努力制止军备竞赛 lose no time in making efforts to stop the arms race

不失为 bùshīwéi can still serve as; may as well be accepted:这~解决问题的好办法。This may after all be a good solution. /这~一个应急办法。This can still serve as a contingency measure.

不识大体 bùshí-dàtǐ fail to take the overall interest into account; fail to recognize the larger issues:他如此~,真让我们失望。We are very disappointed at his total disregard of the overall interest of the public.

不识时务 bùshí-shíwù fail to appreciate the realities of the times; cannot read the trends of the times:众人笑他~。People ridicule him for not being sensible to the changing realities. *or* He is generally regarded as an old stick-in-the-mud.

不识抬举 bùshí-táijǔ not know which side one's bread is buttered; fail to appreciate favours from above:怎么开导也不行,看来他有点~。He has refused to take any advice. It seems he doesn't know what is good for him.

不识闲儿 bùshíxiánr 〈方言〉 be kept busy:她从早到晚,手脚~。She is on the trot all day long.

不识相 bù shíxiàng 〈方言〉 have no sense of propriety; not know what is the right thing to do:人们都讨厌他~。People dislike him for being such a bumpkin. /我们全都是为你好,你可不要~! Don't you bite the hand that feeds you. We're all trying to help.

不识之无 bùshí-zhīwú not know a single character:他从前是个~的文盲。He used to be an illiterate who did not know a single character.

不时 bùshí ❶ frequently; often; from time to time:~发生 occur from time to time; be a common occurrence /大厅里~爆发出热烈的掌声。The hall echoes with hearty rounds of applause. ❷ at any time; at an unexpected moment

不时之需 bùshízhīxū (for a) rainy day; time of want:以备~ provide for a rainy day

不食人间烟火 bù shí rénjiān yānhuǒ show little concern with material life; have no interest in mundane affairs; be other-worldly

不世之才 bùshìzhīcái unrivalled talent; rare talent

不是话 bùshìhuà 〈口语〉 unreasonable; absurd; amiss:她真~,到处无故大吵大闹。She is very unreasonable, making a scene everywhere without provocation. /~! 有你这样说话的吗? Nonsense! How can you say that?

不是玩儿的 bù shì wánrde 〈口语〉 it's no joking matter; it's no joke:你小小的年纪,落下个病根,可~! It's no joking matter if you cannot completely get rid of your disease at this tender age.

不是玩艺儿 bù shì wányìr 〈口语〉 be a person of despicable character; be a rotter:他到处无理取闹,真~。He is a rotter, kicking up a row everywhere.

不是味儿 bù shì wèir *also* "不是滋味儿" ❶ not have the right taste:这烤鸭做得~。The roast duck hasn't got the right taste. ❷ fishy; amiss:他的话我越听越~。The more he said, the more fishy he sounded. ❸ feel bad; be upset:事情虽已过去了,他心里仍觉得~。Though the matter is over and forgotten, it has left behind an unpleasant aftertaste with him. /我越想越觉得~。The more I thought about it, the less happy I became.

不是冤家不聚头 bù shì yuānjiā bù jù tóu 〈俗语〉 it's fate that lovers and enemies are thrown together; adversaries are bound to meet

不是 bùshi fault; blame:这是你的~,还是我的~? Is it your fault, or mine? /她好心劝他,到头来却落了个满身~。She offered him advice with the best of intentions only to get all the blame in the end. /我来给你赔~了。I've come to apologize to you.

不适 bùshì not well; out of sorts; under the weather:身上~ not feel very well; be out of sorts /他近来身体稍感~。He has not been in the pink of health lately.

不适时令 bùshì-shílìng unfit for the season; out of season

不受欢迎的人 bù shòu huānyíngde rén 〈外交〉 *persona non grata*:被驻在国政府宣布为~ be declared *persona non grata* by the receiving government

不受理 bù shòulǐ ❶〈法律〉 reject a complaint ❷〈外交〉 refuse to entertain (a proposal)

不受阻碍通过 bùshòu zǔ'ài tōngguò 〈法律〉 unimpeded passage

不爽 bùshuǎng ❶ not well; out of sorts; in a bad mood:心情~ in low spirits /身子~ feel out of sorts ❷ accurate; without discrepancy:~分毫 be correct in every detail /屡试~。It has proved a success again and again.

不顺手 bù shùnshǒu ❶ not easily available; not handy:剪子放在这儿,用起来~。It is not handy (*or* convenient) to put the scissors here. ❷ not as one wishes; not smooth; difficult:这件事办得可真~。The matter turned out to be so frustrating. /他想起那些~的事,心里就别扭。He felt unhappy at the recollection of those unfortunate experiences.

不送气 bù sòngqì 〈语言〉 *also* "不吐气" unaspirated:~音 unaspirated stop

不速之客 bùsùzhīkè uninvited guest; unexpected visitor; gatecrasher
不随意肌 bùsuíyìjī 〈生理〉involuntary muscle
不遂 bùsuì 〈书面〉not succeed; backfire:谋事～ fail to find a job /此计～。The plan backfired (*or* failed).
不碎玻璃 bùsuì bōli 〈化工〉nonshattering glass; laminated glass; safety or shatter-proof glass
不特 bùtè 〈书面〉not only:对此好人好事,～应表扬,亦应广加宣传。We must not only praise such good people and deeds but also give them wide publicity. /～无益,反而有害。It'll do one no good; it can only do one harm.
不祧之祖 bùtiāozhīzǔ *also*"不祧之宗"〈书面〉esteemed founding father
不停堆换料 bùtíngduī huànliào on-power refueling
不停炉清焦 bùtínglú qīngjiāo 〈冶金〉on-stream decoking
不通 bùtōng ❶ be blocked up; be obstructed; be impassable:此路～ not a through road; no thoroughfare /鼻子～ have a stuffy nose /电话～ cannot get through (on the phone) /邮路～ no postal service/～煤气 no gas supply /计划行～。The plan doesn't work. /谁都想～。Nobody is convinced. ❷ illogical; unreadable; ungrammatical:这篇文章文理～。This essay is illogical and unreadable. /这个句子～。This sentence is ungrammatical. ❸ not know; not understand:～情理 unreasonable /～文墨 not know how to read and write; be illiterate /～世故 know nothing about the ways of the world
不通透性 bùtōngtòuxìng imperviousness
不同 bùtóng different; distinct:国情～ different national realities (*or* conditions) /兴趣～ different in taste /性格～ not alike in character; temperamentally incompatible /背景～ dissimilar social backgrounds /有～癖好 have distinct likes and dislikes of their own /在～程度上 in varying degrees /他的结论和你的～。His conclusion differs from yours.
不同凡响 bùtóng-fánxiǎng outstanding; out of the ordinary; out of the common run:～的人物 person pre-eminent in his field /这篇作品～。This work is genuinely original.
不痛不痒 bùtòng-bùyǎng scratching the surface; superficial; perfunctory:～的批评 superficial criticism /他说了半天,都是些～的话。He held forth at great length, but what he said was perfunctory.
不透明色 bùtòumíngsè body colour
不透明体 bùtòumíngtǐ opaque body
不透明性 bùtòumíngxìng opacity
不透气 bù tòuqì airtight; hermetic:～性 impermeability to gas; air-tightness
不透水 bù tòushuǐ waterproof; watertight; impermeable:～层〈地质〉impermeable stratum; impervious bed
不图 bùtú ❶ not seek; not pursue:～名,～利,图的是祖国繁荣富强。We strive neither for fame nor for profit, but for the prosperity of our country. ❷〈书面〉unexpectedly; to one's surprise:～夭折 die young unexpectedly
不吐气 bù tǔqì 〈语言〉*see*"不送气"
不妥 bùtuǒ not proper; inappropriate:如此决定,似有～。It seems inappropriate to make such a decision. /此事办得～。The matter was not properly handled. /～之处,请予指正。Please feel free to point out the inadequacies.
不外 bùwài *also*"不外乎" not beyond the scope of; nothing more than; only:他俩谈论的～是工作问题。They are only talking shop (*or* business). /他打电话找我,～是有事相求。He called (*or* rang, *or* phoned) me up simply to ask a favour. /问题解决不了的原因～以下三点。Failure to solve the problem is merely due to the following three points. /老板～把我辞退了事。The boss can do no worse than sack me.
不完全 bùwánquán incomplete; imperfect:～承认 imperfect recognition /～的国际人格 imperfect international personality /～接受 imperfect (*or* partial) acceptance /～批准 incomplete ratification/ ～行为 imperfect act /～义务 imperfect obligation /～主权 imperfect sovereignty /～票据 incomplete bill /～竞争市场 imperfect market
不完全变态 bùwánquán biàntài 〈动物〉incomplete metamorphosis
不完全叶 bùwánquányè 〈植物〉incomplete leaf
不完全中立 bùwánquán zhōnglì 〈法律〉imperfect neutrality
不为所动 bùwéi-suǒdòng remain unmoved (esp. under pressure or temptation):他不为金钱所动,一心只想着回国效力。Money could not shake his determination to go back and serve his country.
不为已甚 bùwéi-yǐshèn 〈书面〉not go to extremes (esp. in apportioning blame or meting out punishment):他办事向来～。He has always shown moderation in handling affairs.
不违农时 bùwéi-nóngshí not miss the farming season; do farm work in the right season
不惟 bùwéi 〈书面〉not only:～如此,更有甚者。There are worse cases than this.
不韪 bùwěi 〈书面〉serious error; grievous fault:冒天下之大～ defy world opinion; risk universal condemnation /敌人必败,因为他们出兵犯境犯了五～。The enemy were simply courting defeat because they had committed five grievous errors in invading our border area.
不畏 bùwèi be unafraid of; defy:～强暴 defy brutal force /～艰险 brave hardship and danger
不谓 bùwèi 〈书面〉❶ (used in the negative) cannot be regarded as:负担～不重 the load is not really light; the burden is heavy /时间～不长 not a short time at all; quite a long time ❷ unexpectedly; to one's surprise:这事～竟然如此复杂。Never did I imagine that the problem was so complicated.
不闻不问 bùwén-bùwèn take no notice of; be indifferent to; show no interest in:她只关心自己,别人的事一概～。She cares about no one but herself, and what is happening to others never bothers her. /别人有困难,我们不能～。We shouldn't remain indifferent while other people are in trouble.
不稳 bùwěn ❶ unstable; unsteady:局势～ unstable situation /政局～ fluid political situation; political instability /桌子放在这儿～。The table does not stand steady here. /这几天蔬菜价格～。Vegetable prices have been fluctuating these days. ❷ erratic; precarious:这个人不太稳,我信不过他。I don't trust him because he is erratic. ❸ uncertain; hesitant:我在这儿总觉得～。I feel somewhat worried while I am here. /是否接受这个工作,我还拿～。I am not quite sure whether I will take on the job.
不稳定导热 bùwěndìng dǎorè 〈物理〉unsteady heat conduction
不稳定基因 bùwěndìng jīyīn 〈生物〉unstable gene
不稳定遗传 bùwěndìng yíchuán 〈生物〉unstable inheritance
不稳定因素 bùwěndìng yīnsù destabilizing factor
不稳平衡 bùwěn pínghéng 〈物理〉unstable equilibrium
不问 bùwèn ❶ pay no attention to; disregard; ignore:～事实真相 ignore the facts /～社会地位高低 irrespective of social status /～青红皂白,一律三十大板 order 30 flogs for each party, right or wrong ❷ let off; let (sb.) go unpunished:胁从～。Those who acted under duress shall go unpunished.
不无 bùwú not without:～可取之处 not without merit; not altogether unacceptable /～效果 not without effect
不无小补 bùwú-xiǎobǔ not without some benefit; of some help (if not much):这点钱虽不足以解决你的困难,但也～。Inadequate as it is for your needs, this sum of money will be of some help to you.
不务空名 bùwù-kōngmíng not seek undeserved fame, reputation, honour, etc.:他～,只干实事。He does solid work and never hankers after vain glory.
不务正业 bùwù-zhèngyè ❶ do no decent work; not engage in honest work:这人游手好闲,终日～。This chap does no decent work, loitering all day long. ❷ ignore one's proper occupation; not attend to one's proper duties:如果一个医生忙于小说写作,你是不是会说他～呢? If a physician is busy writing novels, would you say he is neglecting his own duties?
不惜 bùxī not spare; not stint; not scruple:～工本 spare neither labour nor money; spare no expenses /～任何代价 at all costs; at any cost /～忍受最大的牺牲 be willing and ready (*or* not hesitate) to bear the heaviest loss (*or* to make the maximum sacrifice) /～用最卑劣的言词诽谤人 not scruple to slander sb. in most vicious terms /为了帮助残疾人,他～付出宝贵的时间和精力。He unstintingly gave of his time and energy to help the handicapped.
不暇 bùxiá be too busy to (do sth.); have no time (for sth.):应接～ have too much work or too many things to cope with /～顾及 be too busy to attend to it /自顾～ too busy even to attend to one's own business
不下 bùxià ❶ *see*"不下于" ❷ *used after a verb to indicate incompletion or inefficacy*:放心～ cannot rest reassured; be worried /相持～ be at a standstill; be tied
不下于 bùxiàyú ❶ no less than; no fewer than:报考者～三千。There are no fewer than three thousand applicants. /成交额～五千万美元。The volume of business is worth as much as $50 million. ❷

not inferior to; as good as:这种吸尘器的质量～进口货。The quality of this kind of vacuum cleaner is as good as imported ones.

不显性感染 bùxiǎnxìng gǎnrǎn 〈医学〉not apparent infection; latent affection

不限 bùxiàn unrestricted; open; without limit: ～人数 without any restriction on the number of persons /申请者年龄、性别～ regardless of applicant's age and sex /毕业班的学生都可以报名,名额～。It is open to all the graduating students without restriction on the number of applicants.

不相称 bù xiāngchèn unsuited; unmatched; out of proportion:窗帘的颜色跟屋里的摆设～。The colour of the curtain doesn't match the furnishings in the room. /导言写得太长,似与文章其他部分～。The introductory remarks are so long as to seem out of proportion to the rest of the essay. /他的活动与外交官的身分极～。The activities he has been engaged in are quite incompatible with his status as a diplomat.

不相干 bù xiānggān be irrelevant; have nothing to do with:别尽说些～的话。Keep off such irrelevant remarks. *or* Don't speak off the point. /我的事自己决定,与你～。I'll decide my own affairs, and you mind your business. /你走你的,跟我才～呢! Quit if you like for all I care.

不相容 bù xiāngróng incompatible: 水火～ incompatible like fire and water; mutually antagonistic /二人性格～。The two of them are temperamentally uncongenial (*or* incompatible).

不相容性 bùxiāngróngxìng incompatibility; 〈物理〉incongruity

不相上下 bùxiāngshàngxià more or less equal (in strength, value, etc.); about the same:水平～ of about the same level /实力～ equal in strength /年龄～ about the same age /各有所长,～。As both have their own merits, they are nearly equal in ability.

不相往来 bùxiāngwǎnglái stay away from each other; not be on speaking terms:鸡犬之声相闻,而老死～。Though they could hear each other's cocks crow and dogs bark, the two villages had no contact with each other from cradle to grave. /我跟我的表弟大吵了一场后便～了。I have not been on speaking terms with my cousin after a bitter quarrel.

不详 bùxiáng 〈书面〉❶ not quite clear:下落～ sb.'s whereabouts are unknown /地址～ sb.'s address is unclear /家世～。Little is known about his family background. ❷ not in detail; unspecified:语焉～ be mentioned briefly; not go into detail /此事我当面陈,此处～。I will give you a full account when we meet instead of going into particulars here.

不祥 bùxiáng ominous; inauspicious:～之日 inauspicious day /～的预感 ominous presentiment /～的消息 ominous tidings; bad news

不祥之兆 bùxiángzhīzhào ill omen:老人的这些病象恐怕是～。I'm afraid, these symptoms of the old man are an ill omen.

不想 bùxiǎng not expect:～事情会闹到这个地步。I did not imagine (*or* expect) that things would come to such a pass.

不像话 bù xiànghuà ❶ unreasonable; absurd:他要你替他写论文,真太～了。It was ridiculous (*or* absurd) of him to ask you to write the thesis for him. /这本是我的错,让你来承担就～了。It was my fault; I wouldn't dream of asking you to take the blame. ❷ outrageous; shocking; scandalous:乱得～ (in a) shocking mess; total confusion /他们这样欺侮孤寡老人,真是太～了! It was atrocious of them to bully the helpless old people. /这个地方～的事情还真是不少。There is no lack of such scandals around here.

不像样 bù xiàngyàng ❶ unpresentable; not fit to be seen:这篇文章写得太～,无法刊登。This article is too unseemly for publication./这种～的话怎么说得出口! How can you allow yourself to be so foul-mouthed? ❷ *used as a complement after* 得 *to indicate extremity or unrecognizability*:破得～ shabby beyond recognition; worn to shreds /瘦得～ emaciated; be skin and bones /邋遢得～ extremely unkempt /有些房子简直糟得～。Some buildings have fallen into shockingly bad disrepair.

不消 bùxiāo 〈方言〉not require:～说 needless to say /原来你们都认识,我就～介绍了。As you all know each other, I'll forego my introduction. /～几日,必有回音。The reply will come in a few days.

不消化 bù xiāohuà 〈医学〉indigestion

不孝 bùxiào ❶ fail to practise filial piety; be unfilial:在中国,～是会受到社会谴责的。In China, lack of filial piety is condemned by public opinion. ❷ 〈旧语〉"I, the unfilial son," — a term referring to oneself in an obituary announcing the death of one's parents

不肖 bùxiào 〈书面〉unworthy:～之徒 undesirable elements /家门不幸,出了这样～子孙! It is very unfortunate of the family to have produced such unworthy descendants.

不屑 bùxiè ❶ disdain to do sth.; regard sth. as unworthy of notice:～置辩 not worth rebutting /～计较 consider it beneath one's dignity to fuss about (such trivial matters) /～为伍 be unworthy of one's company ❷ scorn; slight; despise: ～的语气 disdainful tone /～于逢迎上司 scorn to curry favour with one's boss /他皱一皱鼻子,以示～。He wrinkled his nose in contempt.

不屑一顾 bùxiè-yīgù be unworthy of serious consideration:此类电影～。Films of such type are not worth a glance.

不谢 bùxiè 〈套语〉don't mention it; not at all; you are welcome

不懈 bùxiè unremitting; untiring; indefatigable:坚持～ persevere unremittingly /在学术上～地追求 make persevering efforts in intellectual pursuit /作了～的努力 make a sustained effort

不信任案 bùxìnrèn'àn no-confidence motion:就～进行表决 vote on the no-confidence motion

不信任投票 bùxìnrèn tóupiào vote of no-confidence

不信邪 bùxìnxié *also* "不怕邪" not believe in fallacies; not dread evil forces:我们第一～,第二说话算数。First, we do not believe in fallacies; second, we mean what we say. /他是一个有原则的人,从～。He is a man of principle, who is never afraid of sinister forces.

不兴 bùxīng ❶ outmoded; out of fashion; outdated; obsolete:这种式样早就～了。This style of dress went out of fashion long ago. /那套老规矩现在～了。Those old regulations are out of date now. /现在～这种笨重的家具了。Such cumbersome furniture is completely outmoded nowadays. ❷ not allowed; impermissible:开会时谁也～抽烟。No one is allowed to smoke when the meeting is in session. /小孩子～这样称呼大人。Children shouldn't address adults in such a manner. /就兴你去,～别人去,这是哪来的规矩? What kind of rule is it that nobody but you can go? ❸ (used only in rhetorical questions) can't:你就～说简单点儿吗? Can't you cut your story short? *or* Can't you be brief?

不行 bùxíng ❶ be not permissible; be not allowed; be out of the question:～! 你们不能去。No, you can't go. /就让我看一眼还～啊? Wouldn't you let me to take a peek? /这根本～,你就别再提了。This is out of the question, and I suggest you drop the matter altogether. ❷ not work; not be equal to:这个办法～。This method won't work. /他干重活～。He is incapable of strenuous physical work. /～就是～,不要装行。If you are not equal to a job, say you are not and never pretend you are. ❸ dying:他看来～了。It seems he is on his last legs. /他直到最后～了才把秘密告诉他女儿。He kept the secret from his daughter until he was breathing his last. *or* Only when he was on his death-bed did he confide his secret to his daughter. ❹ be no good:产品包装～。The packing is no good. *or* The packing is not up to the standard. /电梯的质量～。The lift is not of good quality. ❺ *used after* 得 *to indicate degree, intensity, etc.*:困得～了 be terribly drowsy; can hardly keep one's eyes open /潮湿得～ be awfully damp /渴得实在是～了 be terribly thirsty; be parched /热闹得～ extremely busy; as busy as a beehive /我这几天忙得～。I am completely snowed under with work these days.

不省人事 bùxǐng-rénshì ❶ be unconscious; lose consciousness; go into a coma:烧得～了 so feverish as to fall unconscious /他倒在地上,～。He fell on the ground and lost consciousness. /她已经～,对她说又有什么用? What's the use of saying this to her when she is in a coma? /一阵眼黑,我便跌倒在地,～了。Everything went black, and I fell down in a faint. ❷ not know about the ways of the world:～之谈 statement which betrays an ignorance of worldly affairs /他涉世不深,～。He is still inexperienced and does not know about the ways of the world.

不幸 bùxìng ❶ unfortunate; ill-fated; sad: ～的人 unlucky person; person born under an unlucky star /～的事 disaster; misfortune /～的遭遇 mishap; sad experience /～的岁月 unfortunate years ❷ unfortunately:～而言中。The prediction has unfortunately come true. ❸ misfortune; bad luck; disaster; adversity:～降临到头上 misfortune befalls one /默默地忍受着～ bear an adversity with fortitude /他可能遭到了～。He may have met with a mishap.

不幸之幸 bùxìngzhīxìng stroke of good luck in misfortune:这算是不幸中之大幸。This is a most fortunate aspect of this unfortunate business. *or* This is indeed the silver lining of a black cloud.

不休 bùxiū (used as a complement) endlessly; ceaselessly; incessantly:争论～ argue endlessly; never cease arguing; engage in an endless argument /纠缠～ pester sb. incessantly

不修边幅 bùxiū-biānfú not care about one's appearance; be slovenly; be untidy:他是个大大咧咧，～的人。He is a casual sort of person, who cares not a fig about his appearance.

不朽 bùxiǔ immortal; perpetual; eternal:～的功绩 enduring achievements /～的艺术作品 imperishable work of art /西湖的美是～的。West Lake is an immortal image of beauty. /革命先烈永垂～! Eternal glory to the fallen heroes of the revolution.

不锈钢 bùxiùgāng stainless steel

不虚此行 bùxū-cǐxíng to take a journey like this is a rewarding experience; this is a worthwhile trip

不许 bùxǔ ❶ not allow; not permit; must not:～入内 out of bounds; no admittance /只许成功，～失败。You must succeed; you must not fail. ❷ (used in rhetorical questions) can't; couldn't:你就～干好点? Can't you do better? /你就～自己去? Can't (*or* couldn't) you go yourself?

不恤 bùxù 〈书面〉 not mind; not care; ignore:～人言 turn a deaf ear to gossip and criticism

不宣而战 bùxuān'érzhàn open hostilities without declaring war; start an undeclared war

不旋踵 bùxuánzhǒng 〈书面〉 in an instant:～而城陷。Before long, the city fell into enemy hands.

不学无术 bùxué-wúshù have neither learning nor ability:此人养尊处优，～。Enjoying a high position and a life of ease and comfort, he is an unmitigated ignoramus.

不逊 bùxùn 〈书面〉 rude; insolent; impertinent; discourteous:出言～ make impertinent remarks; speak rudely

不雅观 bù yǎguān offensive to the eye; unbecoming; unseemly; unsightly:举止殊～ have no manners at all /垃圾箱放在那里颇～。The dustbin over there is an eyesore.

不亚于 bùyàyú not inferior to; quite equal to:～任何人 second to none

不言不语 bùyán-bùyǔ not utter a single word; remain silent

不言而喻 bùyán'éryù it goes without saying; it is self-evident:运动可以强健身体，这是～的。It is self-evident that physical exercise builds up a person's health (*or* helps a person keep fit).

不厌 bùyàn ❶ not mind doing sth; not tire of:作为营业员，对顾客要百问～。As a salesman, you should not feel bored even when the customer asks you for the hundredth time. ❷ not exclude:兵～诈。All deception is fair in war.

不厌其烦 bùyàn-qífán not mind taking all the trouble; take great pains; be very patient

不厌其详 bùyàn-qíxiáng get down patiently to minute details; never tire of the smallest details; enumerate details with great patience

不扬 bùyáng (of one's appearance) homely; ugly:其貌～ have plain features; look ugly

不氧化铁 bùyǎnghuàtiě oxidation-free iron

不要 bùyào don't:～听信谣言。Give no credence to rumours. /～轻视他们在科研上所起的作用。Don't belittle their importance in scientific research. *or* Don't make light of the role they play in scientific research.

不要紧 bù yàojǐn ❶ be of no importance; not be serious; not matter:不懂～，但是不要不懂装懂。It doesn't matter if you don't know, but never pretend to know what you don't. /天黑～，我们备有手电。Never mind the gathering dusk, for we have brought electric torches with us. /有点伤风，～。Just a slight cold, nothing serious. ❷ it does not seem serious...but...:你开玩笑～，可把她吓坏了。Apparently, you were cracking a harmless joke, but she was terribly scared.

不要脸 bùyàoliǎn with no sense of shame; without a sense of shame; shameless; brazen:给脸～。I gave him (*or* her) the chance to save face but he (*or* she) wouldn't take it. /想不到他会做出这种～的事情。Never did I expect him to do something so shameless.

不一 bùyī vary; differ:型号～ vary in type /前后～ self-contradictory /长短～ with different sizes; differ in length (*or* size) /他心口～。He does not mean what he says. /说法～。Different people give different versions.

不一而足 bùyī'érzú not just once but on numerous occasions; by no means rare; legion:诸如此类，～。Similar cases are legion. /形形色色，～。They are of various types and descriptions. /字句和标点上的错误～。It teems with errors in wording and punctuation.

不一样 bù yīyàng of different kinds:诗人与诗人～。There are poets and poets.

不依 bùyī ❶ not comply; not obey; refuse:说什么也～ just won't listen, whatever you say; wouldn't comply or go along under any circumstances /孩子要什么，她没有～的。She never refuses the child anything it wants. ❷ not let off easily; not let sb. get away with it:～不饶 wouldn't let sb. off; be hard on sb. /你要不陪我去，我可～你。I will give you a hard time if you don't come along.

不宜 bùyí not suitable; inadvisable; inappropriate:儿童～ (of movies, books, etc.) not fit for children; X-class /饭后～做剧烈运动。Strenuous exercise immediately after a meal is harmful. /年高～远行。Old people should not go on distant journeys. /事关重大，～操之过急。The importance of the matter precludes any hasty action.

不遗传 bù yíchuán 〈生理〉 nonheritable:～变异 nonhereditary variation

不遗余力 bùyí-yúlì spare no effort; stint no effort; do sth. to the best of one's ability; do one's utmost:工作起来～ stint no effort in whatever one undertakes /经过医生～的抢救，病人转危为安。As a result of the doctor's painstaking rescue effort, the patient is out of danger.

不已 bùyǐ continually; continuously; incessantly; unremittingly:痛哭～ cry one's eyes out /赞叹～ no end of praise /后悔～ be overtaken by everlasting remorse; find it a matter of eternal regret /风雨如晦，鸡鸣～。With wind and rain going on, the day is as dark as night, and the cocks crow again and again.

不以为然 bùyǐwéirán object to; take exception to; not approve of; disagree:他听完议论，～地耸耸肩膀。After listening to these comments, he shrugged disapprovingly. /口里答应着，心里大～。He showed compliance in words but kept disagreement to himself.

不以为意 bùyǐwéiyì not take seriously; not feel upset about; not care:他已几经挫折，仍～。He has suffered several setbacks, but he doesn't seem to care.

不义之财 bùyìzhīcái ill-gotten or undeserved wealth; dishonest gains:我岂取～! How can I obtain wealth by dishonest means!

不亦乐乎 bùyìlèhū ❶ isn't it a great pleasure?:有朋自远方来，～? Is it not a great pleasure to have friends coming from afar? ❷ (often used as complement, after 得) extremely; awfully:累得～ be extremely tired from work /忙得～ awfully (*or* terribly) busy; as busy as a bee /笑得～ laugh heartily; burst into roars of laughter /一场大雨，把我们淋了个～。We were caught in a downpour and got soaked to the skin.

不易之论 bùyìzhīlùn unalterable truth; perfectly sound proposition:此说乃～。This is a watertight argument. /时间将证明其言乃～。Only time will show the truth of his statement.

不意 bùyì 〈书面〉 ❶ unexpectedly:～班机晚点，当日未能成行。Unexpectedly the plane was behind schedule, thus making it impossible for us to start off on the day. /～成绩如此之好。To our surprise, the results turned out to be so remarkable. ❷ unpreparedness:出其～，攻其不备 catch sb. unprepared; take sb. by surprise

不翼而飞 bùyì'érfēi ❶ disappear unexpectedly; vanish without a trace:架上好几本杂志～。Several magazines are missing from the shelves (*or* stacks). /保险柜里的文件～。The documents in the safe have vanished without a trace. ❷ spread fast; spread like wildfire:坏消息～。Ill news runs apace.

不阴不阳 bùyīn-bùyáng assume an ambiguous attitude

不应期 bùyìngqī 〈生理〉 refractory period or phase

不用 bùyòng need not; be unnecessary:～多说了。No need to say any more. /都是熟人，～客气。Since we are all friends, you don't have to stand on ceremony. /～说，这次你又输了。Evidently (*or* Needless to say), you lost again this time. /你～管。It's none of your business.

不由得 bùyóude ❶ as a necessary consequence:说得那么肯定，～你不信。This was said with such certainty that you were naturally led to believe it. ❷ can't help (doing sth.):听到这个喜讯，她～高兴得跳起来了。She could not help jumping with joy when she heard the exciting news.

不由分说 bùyóu-fēnshuō *also* "不容分说" allow no explanation; refuse to listen:父亲～地骂了我一顿。My father gave me a good scolding, refusing to listen to my explanation.

不由自主 bùyóu-zìzhǔ can't help; can hardly prevent:她的声音～直发颤。Her voice quivered involuntarily. /他双膝～地跪了下去。He almost instinctively went down on his knees. /船一失舵，就～地随波飘荡。A boat without its rudder will automatically float with the

waves.

不渝 bùyú 〈书面〉not change; remain faithful: 忠贞～ faithful to the end; unswervingly loyal

不虞 bùyú 〈书面〉❶ unexpected; unanticipated: ～走漏消息。Unexpectedly the secret leaked out. ❷ eventuality; contingency: 以备～ provide against any contingency (*or* eventualities) ❸ not worry about: ～匮乏 not dread the scarcity of supplies

B

不虞之誉，求全之毁 bùyú zhī yù, qiú quán zhī huǐ unexpected praise and excessive censure

不予 bùyǔ not grant; refuse; withhold: ～理会 take no notice of / ～批准 refuse to approve; reject approval / ～办理 refuse to attend to

不育 bùyù 〈植物〉sterile: ～花 sterile flower / ～种子 sterile seed

不育系 bùyùxì 〈农业〉sterile line: 雄性～ male sterile line

不育性 bùyùxìng 〈农业〉*also* "不孕性" bùyùnxìng sterility; infertility

不育症 bùyùzhèng 〈医学〉barrenness; sterility

不豫 bùyù 〈书面〉❶ displeased: 有～之色 look displeased ❷〈婉词〉unwell; out of sorts; ill

不远千里 bùyuǎn-qiānlǐ make light of travelling a thousand *li*; go to the trouble of travelling long distances: 门徒～而来。People come from afar to learn his skill as apprentice.

不约而同 bùyuē'értóng take identical action or share identical views without previous consultation: 几个人～地站起来表示反对。As if by prior arrangement, several people rose simultaneously to voice their objections. / 大家～地把目光转向他。Everyone spontaneously riveted their eyes on him.

不匀磨损 bùyún mósǔn uneven wear

不载人飞船 bùzàirén fēichuán 〈航天〉unmanned spaceship

不在 bùzài ❶ not be in; be out; be absent: 他～办公室，你过一会儿再来电话。He is not in the office. Please call back after a while. / 老张～，我只见了他的爱人。Lao Zhang was out, and I saw only his wife. ❷〈婉词〉(often used before 了) die; be dead: 我祖母两年前就～了。My grandma died (*or* passed away) two years ago.

不在乎 bùzàihu not mind; not care: 满～ not care a pin / 工作如此劳累，他丝毫也～。No matter how tiring the work is, he just doesn't mind. / ～他怎么说，要看他怎么做。It does not really matter what he says; what counts is what he does.

不在话下 bùzài-huàxià be not worth mentioning: 生活艰苦倒～，只是远离家人，可真受不了。Hardship is nothing; only it is terrible having to stay away from home. / 区区小事，～。That's a small matter I can easily manage. / 大李尚不是他的对手，小刘就更～了。Even Da Li is no match for him, to say nothing of Xiao Liu.

不在其位，不谋其政 bù zài qí wèi, bù móu qí zhèng one who holds no official position does not discuss official business or affairs

不在意 bù zàiyì ❶ pay no attention to; take no notice of; not mind: 这些小事，我毫～。I never bother about such trivial things. / 别人背后议论，他毫～。He doesn't care at all what people speak of him behind his back. ❷ neglect; ignore: 这病你别～。Don't take this ailment lightly.

不赞一词 bùzàn-yīcí 〈书面〉keep silent; make no comment: 他滔滔不绝，我～。He talked on and on but I just kept quiet.

不则声 bù zéshēng 〈方言〉keep silent; say nothing: 他躲在他们背后～。He hid himself behind them and kept silent.

不择手段 bùzé-shǒuduàn by fair means or foul; by hook or by crook; unscrupulously: ～地捞钱 make money by unscrupulous methods / 有人相信为了达到目的可以～。Some people believe that the end justifies the means.

不怎么 bù zěnme not very; not particularly: 巷子～长。The lane is not particularly long. / 天还～黑。It's not quite dark yet.

不怎么样 bù zěnmeyàng mediocre; indifferent; not as good as one or it should be: 这部电影～。This is an indifferent film. / 你要小心点儿，此人可～啊！You'd better be careful. He is not a decent chap. / 文章写得～。This essay is only mediocre.

不粘锅 bùzhānguō non-stick pan

不战不和 bùzhàn-bùhé no war, no peace: 两国处于～的状态。The two countries are locked in a stalemate of "no war, no peace".

不战而胜 bùzhàn'érshèng win without firing a single shot; conquer without a battle; defeat without a fight

不战而降 bùzhàn'érxiáng surrender without a fight

不着调 bùzháodiào 〈方言〉eccentric; abnormal: 他这个人～儿。He is an eccentric.

不折不扣 bùzhé-bùkòu hundred per cent; to the letter; out-and-out: ～的骗子 out-and-out swindler / 政策要～地贯彻执行。Policies should be implemented to the letter. / 只有～的白痴，才会对此感兴趣。Only a total idiot would be interested in it.

不振 bùzhèn dejected; in low spirits; listless: 精神～ languid; listless / 食欲～ lose one's appetite; have a jaded appetite / 士气～。Morale is low. / 国势～。The state is on the decline.

不争气 bù zhēngqì disappoint one's hopes; be disappointing: 他怨儿子～，终日闲荡，无所事事。He said he was bitterly disappointed that his son was loitering all day long. / 我这腿～，最后跑不动了。My legs failed me and I wasn't able to finish the race.

不正之风 bùzhèngzhīfēng unhealthy social trends; evil social practices: 制止～ check unhealthy social trends / 这里的大多数干部作风正派，～刮不起来。None of the evil social practices will prevail here, for the people in power in this district are mostly honest and upright.

不知不觉 bùzhī-bùjué unconsciously; without one's being aware of it: 钱～地就花光了。We had spent every penny before we knew it. / 两人说得投机，～天已昏黑。The two of them had been talking congenially when, to their surprise, it was already dark. / 她很坦率，有时～地伤害了别人。She was outspoken and sometimes hurt people unthinkingly.

不知凡几 bùzhī-fánjǐ innumerable; countless: 六合之中，珍禽怪兽，～。No one can tell how many rare birds and animals inhabit the earth.

不知分寸 bùzhī-fēncùn have no sense of propriety; be tactless

不知甘苦 bùzhī-gānkǔ can't tell the sweet from the bitter — know nothing of the difficulties of life

不知好歹 bùzhī-hǎodǎi not know what's good for one: 你这小子～！You idiot! Don't you know what's good for you? / 你又不是傻子，为何这样～？You are no fool. Don't you know which side your bread is buttered ?

不知进退 bùzhī-jìntuì lack tact; not know how to behave properly: 我这个人～，招人嫌。As I don't know how to act tactfully, I am liable to incur people's displeasure.

不知就里 bùzhī-jiùlǐ be unaware of the real reason, cause, etc.: 起初人家～，还愿意借钱给他。Unaware of the true situation at first, they agreed to lend him money.

不知轻重 bùzhī-qīngzhòng rash; brash; hasty and unthinking: 他年纪小，～，你不要和他一般见识。As he is young and brash, please forgive him (for his words or behaviour).

不知人间有羞耻事 bù zhī rénjiān yǒu xiūchǐ shì be past all sense of shame; be shameless beyond description: 那个卑鄙龌龊的小人，简直～！That despicable fellow doesn't know there is such a thing as human decency in this world! *or* That mean fellow has lost all sense of shame!

不知死活 bùzhī-sǐhuó act recklessly: 你这个人～，现在已招惹麻烦了。You've been acting so recklessly that you are already in for trouble. / 你这个～的东西，你给我闯下了大祸！You reckless fool! You've got me into big trouble now!

不知所措 bùzhī-suǒcuò be at a loss; be at one's wits' end; not know what to do: 惊恐得～ be scared out of one's wits / 这个意外的相逢，使他一时～。He was somewhat disconcerted by this unexpected encounter.

不知所以 bùzhī-suǒyǐ not know why: 他突然冲我发火，使我茫然～。I was stunned as I had no idea why he had suddenly flown into such a rage.

不知所云 bùzhī-suǒyún not know what sb. is talking about; be unintelligible: 他说话吞吞吐吐，～。As he hemmed and hawed, no one knew what he was driving at. / 这篇文章写得太乱，～。This piece of writing is too confused to be intelligible.

不知所终 bùzhī-suǒzhōng not know where sb. spent the last years of his life: 此人后来弃家修道，～。Later he left his family for good to be a Taoist and no one knows what became of him.

不知天高地厚 bù zhī tiān gāo dì hòu not know the immensity of the cosmos; have an exaggerated notion of one's abilities; be too arrogant: 想起幼年时那些～的话来，真觉惭愧。I feel deeply ashamed of myself whenever I recall boastful words as a child.

不知者不罪 bùzhīzhě bù zuì one should not be blamed for any wrong thing he does if he is not conscious of it

不值 bùzhí not worth: ～一提 not worth mentioning / 买得～ not worth the money / ～识者一笑 can only earn the contempt of the discerning; the clear-eyed will dismiss it with a contemptuous smile /

我看～那么多。I don't think it's worth that much.
不值一驳 bùzhí-yībó not worth refuting:这种言论～。These arguments are not worth refuting (*or* rebutting).
不值一钱 bùzhí-yīqián *also* "不值一文";"一钱不值" not worth a penny; utterly worthless; mere trash:这等粗俗作品,～。This kind of crude writing is mere trash. /他把对方贬得～。He derided his opponent as utterly worthless.
不止 bùzhǐ ❶ incessantly; without end:咳嗽～ cough incessantly/血流～ keep on bleeding /大笑～ cannot refrain from laughter; roar with laughter ❷ more than; not limited to:受到奖励的～他们俩。The two of them are not the only people who have been awarded. /这部电影我看了～两遍。I've seen the film more than twice. /他的贡献～在医学方面。His contribution is not limited to medicine.
不只 bùzhǐ not only; not merely:这～是我个人的意见,大家也都有这个要求。This is not my opinion alone, but the request of us all.
不至于 bùzhìyú cannot go so far; be unlikely:他要走,也～这样匆忙吧? He couldn't be in such a hurry even if he insisted on going. /要是好好想想,～答不上来。Think it over carefully and you'll be able to answer the question. /他～连这一点道理也不明白。He must have more sense than that.
不忮不求 bùzhì-bùqiú be neither jealous nor greedy; live a simple life and be free from worldly desires
不治之症 bùzhìzhīzhèng incurable disease:这些弊端是资本主义社会的～。These evils are symptoms of an incurable disease of capitalist society.
不致 bùzhì be unlikely to (cause inconvenience or trouble):如果你事先作好准备,也～那么被动。Had you cared to prepare in advance, you wouldn't have landed yourself in such a mess.
不置 bùzhì 〈书面〉 keep on; continue to do:赞叹～ praise profusely (*or* endlessly) /懊丧～ be given to moods of depression and remorse
不置褒贬 bùzhì-bāobiǎn pass no judgment on; neither praise nor censure:对于那幅画,他只是～地笑了笑。He gave a smile, making no comment on the painting.
不置可否 bùzhì-kěfǒu decline to comment; not express an opinion; be noncommittal; hedge:～地淡然一笑 dismiss it with a faint smile /他不愿意立即表态,只好～,拿别的话岔开。Since he didn't want to declare his position just then he had to remain noncommittal while trying to sidetrack the issue.
不中 bùzhōng 〈方言〉 be no good; be useless; will not do:这个办法～,还得另打主意。This method is no good. We've got to think up another one.
不中用 bù zhōngyòng no good; useless:看您说的,我就那么～? What are you talking about? Am I that useless? /人们全走了,无论怎么吆喝也～。People are all gone, and it is no use shouting after them.
不中意 bù zhòngyì not to one's liking:这些料子她都～。These dress materials are not to her liking. *or* None of these dress materials caught her fancy.
不周 bùzhōu inattentive; thoughtless:招待～ inadequate hospitality
不周延 bù zhōuyán 〈逻辑〉 undistributed
不抓辫子 bùzhuā biànzi without seizing sb.'s queue — without capitalizing on sb.'s mistakes or shortcomings
不准 bùzhǔn not allow; forbid; prohibit:～停车! No parking! /～入内。No admittance. /～动手! Hands Off! /～喧哗。Silence. /火车上～携带易燃易爆物品。Combustibles and explosives are not allowed onto the train.
不着边际 bùzhuó-biānjì not to the point; wide of the mark; neither here nor there; irrelevant:～的空谈 all irrelevant, empty talk /他越讲越～。As he talked, he strayed further and further from the subject.
不着痕迹 bùzhuó-hénjì without any trace; invisible
不着陆飞行 bùzhuólù fēixíng nonstop flight
不赀 bùzī 〈书面〉(of wealth, value or expenses) immeasurable; incalculable; valuable:工程浩大,所费～。The cost of this gigantic project is hard to calculate. /损失～。The loss in wealth is incalculable. /价值～。The price is fabulously high.
不赀之费 bùzīzhīfèi fabulous expenses
不自量 bùzìliàng not take a proper measure of oneself; overrate one's own abilities:蚍蜉撼大树,可笑～ ridiculously overrate oneself like a mayfly trying to topple a giant tree /他如此狂妄,太～。He is so arrogant that he doesn't have a realistic estimate of his own abilities.
不自量力 bùzìliànglì *also* "自不量力" overrate one's own abilities; put a quart into a pint pot:他敢承担这项任务的确有些～。The fact that he offered to do the job demonstrates his inability to give a realistic estimate of his own abilities.
不自由,毋宁死 bù zìyóu, wúnìng sǐ give me liberty, or give me death (Patrick Henry, 1736-1799)
不足 bùzú ❶ not enough; insufficient; inadequate:资源～ inadequate resources; insufficient mineral wealth /产量～ inadequate output /经验～ lack experience /先天～ be congenitally deficient; suffer from an inherent deficiency /给养～ be short of supplies /人手～ be shorthanded; be under-staffed /信心～ lack confidence /～之处 deficiency; inadequacy /～一千 less than a thousand ❷ not worth:～介意 need not take it to heart /～为据 cannot be cited as evidence ❸ cannot; should not:非团结～以图存 cannot survive without unity
不足道 bùzúdào insignificant; of no consequence:微～ not worth mentioning; insignificant; negligible /个人得失～。Personal gain or loss is of no consequence.
不足挂齿 bùzú-guàchǐ *also* "不足齿数" not worth mentioning; not worth taking seriously; nothing to speak of:些须小事,～。These trifling matters are not worth mentioning.
不足为虑 bùzú-wéilǜ cause no anxiety:癣疥之疾,～。It is only a bodily ailment which is no cause for alarm. *or* The trouble which is of no great dimensions needs not worry us.
不足为凭 bùzú-wéipíng cannot be taken as evidence:这些话～。These words cannot be quoted as evidence. /白条子没有公章～。A mere IOU note without an official seal on it is no proof (*or* is invalid).
不足为奇 bùzú-wéiqí *also* "不足为怪" nothing remarkable; not to be wondered at; not at all surprising:学生迟到、旷课的事,在这个学校经常发生,～。It's not unusual, let alone surprising, that students in this school are often late for class or cut classes.
不足为训 bùzú-wéixùn not to be taken as an example; not to be followed as an example; not to be taken as authoritative:用这种办法推销产品实在～。This kind of sales promotion cannot really serve as a model. /他的话～。His words are by no means authoritative.
不足为外人道 bù zú wèi wàirén dào not to be mentioned to outsiders; not wash one's dirty linen in public:此事敏感,～。The matter is sensitive, and you should not breathe a word about it to others.
不足与谋 bùzú-yǔmóu not worth consulting with:此人胆小怕事,～。He is so overcautious and timid that we had better not consult with him.
不做声 bù zuòshēng keep silent; not say a word:你明知他不对,为何～? You knew perfectly well he was wrong. Why didn't you speak up?

钚

bù 〈化学〉 plutonium (Pu)
钚弹 bùdàn 〈军事〉 plutonium bomb
钚反应堆 bùfǎnyìngduī plutonium reactor

布[1]

bù ❶ cloth:棉～ cotton cloth /麻～ linen /～鞋 cloth shoes /花～ cotton prints ❷ an ancient Chinese copper coin ❸ (Bù) a surname

布[2](佈)

bù ❶ declare; announce; publish; proclaim:发～ issue; release /公～ make public; announce; make known to the public ❷ spread; disseminate:阴云密～ covered with dark clouds; overcast /铁路、公路遍～全国。Railways and roads crisscross the country. /室内满～蛛网灰尘。The room is covered with dust and cobwebs. /他的名声远～海外。His fame has spread overseas. ❸ dispose; arrange; deploy:～下天罗地网 cast a gigantic escape-proof net (for catching a fugitive criminal, etc.) /～岗 deploy sentinels
布帛 bùbó cloth and silk; cotton and silk fabrics
布帛菽粟 bùbó-shūsù cloth, silk, beans and grain; food and clothing
布菜 bùcài serve dishes (to the guests); serve food
布达拉宫 Bùdálāgōng Potala Palace (in Lhasa, Tibet)
布达拉山 Bùdálāshān Potala Hill
布达佩斯 Bùdápèisī Budapest, capital of Hungary
布道 bùdào 〈宗教〉 preach; evangelize:～词 sermon /～坛 pulpit

布店 bùdiàn cloth store; draper's; piece-goods store
布丁 bùdīng (transliteration) pudding
布尔代数 Bù'ěr dàishù 〈数学〉 Boolean algebra
see also "逻辑代数" luójí dàishù
布尔计算机 Bù'ěr jìsuànjī 〈计算机〉 Boolean Computer
布尔乔亚 bù'ěrqiáoyà (transliteration) bourgeoisie
布尔人 Bù'ěrrén Boer (person of Dutch descent living in South Africa)
布尔什维克 Bù'ěrshíwéikè (transliteration) Bolshevik
布尔什维克革命 Bù'ěrshíwéikè Gémìng *also* "十月革命" Shíyuè Gémìng Bolshevik Revolution; October Revolution
布防 bùfáng deploy troops for defence; garrison a town or fort
布干达 Bùgāndá Buganda (a former powerful kingdom of East Africa, on the north shore of Lake Vidoria, now part of Uganda)
布告 bùgào ❶ notice; bulletin; proclamation:张贴～ put up a notice /～栏 notice board; bulletin board ❷ announce in a bulletin; make known; proclaim: ～天下 proclaim throughout the country; make known to the whole country
布告栏服务 bùgàolán fúwù 〈信息〉 Bulletin Board Service (BBS)
布谷 bùgǔ 〈动物〉 cuckoo
布鼓雷门 bùgǔ-léimén carry a cloth drum to a city gate well known for its colossal drum — display one's poor skill before a master; teach one's grandma to suck eggs
布褐 bùhè 〈书面〉 coarse cotton clothing
布基纳法索 Bùjīnàfǎsuǒ Burkina Faso (formerly known as Upper Volta)
布加勒斯特 Bùjiālèsītè Bucharest, capital of Romania
布景 bùjǐng ❶ setting; scenery: ～设计师 set designer ❷ composition (of a traditional Chinese painting)
布局 bùjú ❶ overall arrangement; layout; distribution:国民经济～ over-all arrangement of the national economy /博物馆的～ layout of the museum /工业的合理～ rational distribution of industry /调整作物～ readjust crop patterns ❷ composition (of an article, painting, etc.) ❸ opening moves (in a chess game): 下棋～极为重要。The opening strategic moves in chess are of the utmost importance.
布控 bùkòng have (sb.) under surveillance:对作案对象进行了严密～ have the suspects under strict surveillance
布拉柴维尔 Bùlācháiwéi'ěr Brazzaville, capital of the Republic of the Congo
布拉格 Bùlāgé Prague, capital of the Czech Republic
布拉吉 bùlājí *also* "连衣裙" liányīqún (transliteration from the Russian *platye*) woman's button-through dress
布拉耶盲字 Bùlāyē mángzì Braille system of reading for the blind; Braille
布朗 Bùlǎng John Brown (1800-1859), American abolitionist commemorated in the popular song "John Brown's Body".
布朗轨道 Bùlǎng guǐdào 〈数学〉 Brownian trajectory
布朗基主义 Bùlǎngjīzhǔyì Blanquism
布朗运动 Bùlǎng yùndòng 〈物理〉 Brownian movement
布朗族 Bùlǎngzú Blang nationality, a national minority inhabiting Yunnan Province
布雷 bùléi lay mines; mine: 在水道～ mine waterways /深水～ depth mining /在港口～ mine a harbour /～区 minefield
布雷兵 bùléibīng mine planter
布雷场 bùléichǎng minefield
布雷顿森林 Bùléidùn sēnlín (US) Bretton Woods: ～会议 Bretton Woods Conference (1944) /～制度 Bretton Woods system
布雷舰 bùléijiàn minelayer; mine vessel
布雷潜水艇 bùléi qiánshuǐtǐng 〈军事〉 submarine minelayer
布里纸 bùlǐzhǐ cloth-lined paper
布料 bùliào cotton dress material (including coating, shirting, etc.)
布列斯特和约 Bùlièsītè Héyuē Treaty of Brest-Litovsk (1918)
布隆迪 Bùlóngdí Burundi: ～人 Burundian
布鲁金斯学会 Bùlǔjīnsī Xuéhuì (US) Brookings Institution
布鲁塞尔 Bùlǔsài'ěr Brussels, capital of Belgium
布鲁士摇摆乐 bùlǔshì yáobǎiyuè rhythm and blues (popular music with a blue theme and a strong rhythm)
布鲁氏菌 bùlǔshìjūn brucella: ～病 brucellosis; undulant fever
布罗肯宝光环 Bùluókěn bǎoguānghuán *also* "峨嵋宝光" Éméi bǎoguāng Brocken bow; Brocken spectre
布面 bùmiàn cloth cover (of a book): ～精装本 clothbound de luxe edition
布匹 bùpǐ cloth; piece goods; yard goods
布票 bùpiào cloth coupon; clothing coupon
布琼布拉 Bùqióngbùlā Bujumbura, capital of Burundi
布设 bùshè lay; make arrangement: ～地雷 lay (land) mines /～圈套 set (*or* lay) a trap
布施 bùshī 〈书面〉〈宗教〉 alms giving; charities
布氏硬度 Bùshì yìngdù 〈机械〉 Brinell hardness: ～计 Brinell tester / ～试验 Brinell (hardness) test
布头 bùtóu ❶ leftover material (form a bolt of cloth) ❷ odd bits of cloth
布娃娃 bùwáwa doll made of cloth; cloth doll
布网船 bùwǎngchuán netlayer
布纹纸 bùwénzhǐ 〈摄影〉 wove paper
布线 bùxiàn wiring: ～图 wiring diagram
布鞋 bùxié cloth shoe
布须曼人种 Bùxūmàn rénzhǒng Bushman race, aboriginal race in S. Africa
布衣 bùyī ❶ cotton clothes: ～蔬食 wear cotton clothes and eat vegetables — live a simple and plain life; be thrifty ❷ 〈书面〉 person in coarse cotton clothes, not in silks; person of humble social status; commoner
布依族 Bùyīzú Buyei or Bouyei nationality, national minority living in Guizhou
布宜诺斯艾利斯 Bùyínuòsī'àilìsī Buenos Aires, capital of Argentina
布招 bùzhāo cloth streamer (outside a shop)
布政局 Bùzhèngjú (HK) Urban Council
布政司 Bùzhèngsī (HK before 1 July 1997) Chief Secretary: ～署 (HK) Government Secretariat
布置 bùzhì ❶ tidy up; arrange: ～会场 tidy up a meeting room /～展品 arrange exhibits ❷ assign; make arrangements for; give instructions about: ～作业 assign homework /～学术讲座 arrange academic lectures

怖

bù fear; be afraid of:景象可～。The scene was frightful. *or* It was a horrible sight. /山洪突发,众人大～。People were seized with fright when torrents of water rushed down the mountain.

步[1]

bù ❶ step; pace:脚～ footstep /跑～ double march /寸～难行 can hardly move a step; be unable to advance or act freely /大～流星 stride; walk in big strides /没几～远 only a few steps farther; at a stone's throw /一～好棋 an excellent move ❷ stage; step:作为第一～,你必须交一份申请书。As a first step, you'll have to send in an application. /我们必须考虑下一～该怎么办。We must consider the next step to be taken (*or* to take). /我们必须一～一～地执行训练计划。We must push ahead our training programme step by step. ❸ condition; situation; state:你怎么会落到这一～? How did you get into such a wretched state? *or* How did you manage to land yourself in such a plight? ❹ ancient unit for measurement of length, equivalent to five *chi* (*or* about two yards) ❺ walk; go on foot:散～ take a walk /～入会场 walk into the meeting room ❻〈书面〉 tread: ～其后尘 follow in sb.'s footsteps ❼〈方言〉 pace off: ～一～这段距离,看有没有二十米长。Pace off this distance to see if it is about 20 metres. ❽ (Bù) a surname

步[2]

bù *used in the same way as* 埠, *often in place names*: 盐～ Yanbu (*or* Salt Port) in Guangdong
步兵 bùbīng infantry; foot:第四～团 4th Regiment of Foot; No.4 Infantry Regiment /～、骑兵协同动作 foot and horse move in coordination /两名～ two foot soldiers (*or* infantrymen) /～班 rifle squad/～技术 infantry technique
步步进逼 bùbù-jìnbī press forward steadily
步步为营 bùbù-wéiyíng consolidate at every step; move with great care; be always on the alert:有人泣,为营步步嗟何及! A voice is heard wailing; His "bastion at every step" avails him nought!
步测 bùcè measure by pace (usu. with a double pace of 1.5 metres as the unit); pace off; pace out
步道 bùdào ❶〈口语〉 pavement; sidewalk ❷〈书面〉 path
步调 bùdiào pace; step:统一～ take concerted action; make concerted efforts; act in unison

步伐 bùfá step; pace: ～整齐 march in step /～不整 march out of step /加快～ quicken one's pace /放慢～ slow down (one's pace) /跟上时代的～ keep pace with the times; keep abreast of the times /士兵们迈着坚定的～前进。The soldiers strode ahead with firm steps.

步法 bùfǎ 〈体育〉〈舞蹈〉footwork

步幅 bùfú step; pace; stride

步弓 bùgōng *also* "弓" wooden measuring divider

步话机 bùhuàjī *also* "步谈机"; "对讲机" duìjiǎngjī; "步行机" walkie-talkie

步甲 bùjiǎ ground beetle (*Carabidae*)

步进电机 bùjìn diànjī *also* "步进电动机" 〈电工〉 step motor; stepper motor; stepping motor; repeating motor

步进式电位器 bùjìnshì diànwèiqì 〈电工〉step potentiometer

步进式炉 bùjìnshìlú 〈冶金〉walking beam furnace

步进制 bùjìnzhì *also* "步进系统" step-by-step system

步犁 bùlí walking plough

步履 bùlǚ 〈书面〉walk: ～蹒跚 hobble along; limp /～维艰 walk with difficulty; walk with unsteady steps

步辇 bùniǎn 〈古语〉sedan chair

步撵 bùniǎn 〈方言〉go on foot; walk: 赶不上车就只好～啦。If we miss the bus, we'll have to walk (*or* foot it).

步枪 bùqiāng rifle: 小口径～ small-bore rifle /半自动～ semi-automatic rifle /气～ air rifle /自选～ free rifle /～火力 rifle fire /～射程 rifle shot /～子弹 rifle bullet

步趋 bùqū 〈书面〉❶ walk (quickly) ❷ imitate; copy: ～原著,一成不变 follow the original (writing) mechanically /～古人,没多大出息。Those who copy the ancients will not accomplish much.

步人后尘 bùrénhòuchén follow in sb.'s footsteps; follow upon sb.'s heels; trail along

步哨 bùshào sentry; sentinel

步态 bùtài gait: ～轻盈 graceful walking gait; walk in a graceful manner /～蹒跚 walk in a difficult manner; totter along

步谈机 bùtánjī *see* "步话机"

步头 bùtou *also* "埠头" bùtou wharf; pier

步武 bùwǔ 〈书面〉❶ ancient unit of measurement, equivalent to two and a half *chi* (about a yard) — a short distance ❷ follow upon sb.'s heels — follow sb.'s example: ～前贤 follow the example of ancient men of virtue

步校 bùxiào infantry school; army academy

步行 bùxíng go on foot; walk: 他不是乘车而是～来的。He came here not by car but on foot.

步行虫 bùxíngchóng 〈动物〉ground beetle

步行机 bùxíngjī *see* "步话机"

步行街 bùxíngjiē pedestrian mall

步行桥 bùxíngqiáo pedestrian overpass

步行式挖掘机 bùxíngshì wājuéjī 〈建筑〉walker excavator; walking scoop dredge

步眼 bùyǎn 〈方言〉step: 稳健的～ steady steps

步韵 bùyùn use the same rhyme sequence (when writing a poem in reply to a friend)

步战车 bùzhànchē 〈军事〉infantry fighting vehicle

步骤 bùzhòu step; move; measure: 采取适当～,使过热的经济冷却下来。Take proper steps to cool down the overheated economy.

步子 bùzi step; pace: ～轻快有力 walk with springy vigorous steps /～迈得更大一些 take bigger strides (in doing sth.); take a bolder approach (to reform and opening-up) /队伍的～很整齐。The procession was parading in step.

步卒 bùzú 〈书面〉foot soldier; infantry man

B

C

C

cā

礤 cā see“礓礤儿”jiāngcār

擦 cā ❶ rub; scratch:～着双手乐滋滋的 rub one's hands with pleasure /～破了手 scratch one's hand /～火柴 strike a match ❷ towel; wipe with rags:～～脸 wipe your face (with a towel) /～桌子 wipe the desk clean /～地板 mop (*or* scrub) the floor /～黑板 clean the blackboard /～皮鞋 polish (*or* shine) shoes ❸ apply:～药水 apply medicinal lotion /～唇膏 apply lip stick /～粉 powder one's face /～胭脂 put on rouge ❹ approach; touch; brush past; shave:球～着桌边了。The ball touched the edge of the table. /滑翔机～着山坡飞过。The glider shaved the mountain slopes. ❺ shred (vegetables or melons):～萝卜丝 shred a turnip /～土豆丝 shred potatoes

擦棒球 cābàngqiú 〈体育〉foul tip (in baseball, etc.)

擦背 cābèi 〈方言〉scrub the back (with a towel, etc., usu. when one is taking a bath):用毛巾给孩子～ scrub the child's back with a towel

擦边 cābiān close to; near:老王才四十～,老张已六十出头了。Lao Wang is still on the right side of forty while Lao Zhang is over sixty already.

擦边球 cābiānqiú ❶〈体育〉edge ball; touch ball (in table tennis) ❷ something almost, but not quite, illegal; circumventing the law or regulation by doing something quasi-legal:这位律师最会钻空子,打～了。The lawyer is extremely good at finding loopholes and circumventing the law.

擦擦 cācā tsha-tsha, clay miniature figures (of Buddha, pagoda, etc.) used by Tibetan Buddhists for redeeming their vows to Buddha

擦菜板 cācàibǎn *also*“擦子”grater

擦除 cāchú scratch; erase

擦光机 cāguāngjī 〈机械〉scratch lathe

擦黑儿 cāhēir 〈方言〉about or towards dusk; dusk:天～我们才收工。We did not knock off till dark. /他是～回来的。He returned home at dusk.

擦痕 cāhén ❶ scratch ❷ ledge formed by rocks (carried by a glacier) rolling down a cliff

擦净 cājìng scour:把锈迹～ scour the rust off

擦亮 cāliàng shine:把铜像～ shine the bronze statue

擦亮儿 cāliàngr 〈方言〉at dawn; at daybreak

擦亮眼睛 cāliàng-yǎnjīng remove the scales from one's eyes; sharpen one's vigilance; alert oneself:我们要～,不为对手的花招所迷惑。We must sharpen our vigilance so as not to be confused by our adversary's tricks.

擦磨 cāmó 〈机械〉scouring

擦屁股 cā pìgu 〈比喻〉clean up the mess:他一走了事,倒要我来替他～。He's vanished for good, leaving me to clean up the mess for him.

擦破 cāpò 〈医学〉abrasion

擦拳摩掌 cāquán-mózhǎng *also*“摩拳擦掌”rub one's fists and palms — be ready to fight; be eager to have a go

擦伤 cāshāng scrape; abrasion; chafe

擦拭 cāshì wipe; cleanse; clean:～机床 clean the lathe /他把窗玻璃～得干干净净。He wiped the windowpanes spotlessly clean.

擦网球 cāwǎngqiú 〈体育〉net ball

擦洗 cāxǐ wipe clean; wash; clean:～手枪 clean one's pistol

擦洗器 cāxǐqì 〈矿业〉scrubber

擦眼抹泪 cāyǎn-mǒlèi wipe one's eyes; shed tears:听了这些伤感故事,她～,深受感动。These sad stories so moved her that they brought tears to her eyes. *or* These sentimental tales moved her to tears.

擦音 cāyīn 〈语言〉fricative

擦澡 cāzǎo rub oneself down with a wet towel; take a sponge bath:用温水～ rub oneself down with warm water /在家里～ have a sponge bath at home /擦一擦澡身上舒服多了 feel much more comfortable after rubbing oneself down with a wet towel

嚓 cā 〈象声〉scraping sound:～的一声,汽车停住了。The car stopped with a screech. /外面响起～～的脚步声。Heavy steps were heard from outside.
see also chā

拆 cā 〈方言〉discharge (faeces or urine); shit or piss
see also chāi

拆烂污 cā lànwū 〈方言〉do slovenly work; leave things in a mess; be irresponsible:他这个人总是～,没法让人相信。He's so irresponsible that you can never trust him.

cǎ

礤 cǎ 〈书面〉❶ coarse stone ❷ (same as 擦) rub; scrub; shred

礤床儿 cǎchuángr vegetable shredder

cāi

偲 cāi 〈书面〉with a wide range of knowledge; learned; erudite:其人美且～。He is a handsome, learned scholar.
see also sī

猜 cāi ❶ guess; conjecture; speculate:你～妈妈送我什么礼物? Guess what present Mother has given me? /让他～着了。He has guessed right. ❷ suspect; be doubtful:不要乱～疑。Don't entertain groundless suspicions. /我～他知道这事的内幕。I suspect he knows the inside story (*or* what is going on).

猜测 cāicè guess; conjecture; surmise:这不过是一种～而已。That is nothing but a conjecture. /与其凭空～,不如实地调查。On-the-spot investigation is preferable to pure surmise.

猜忖 cāicǔn guess; surmise

猜断 cāiduàn guess and assess

猜度 cāiduó surmise; conjecture; gather:这件事一点痕迹也没有,倒叫人难以～。This incident left no trace, making it difficult to get at the truth (*or* ascertain the cause).

猜忌 cāijì be suspicious and jealous of:相互～ be suspicious of each other /好～是他最大的毛病。His greatest weakness is that he often falls victim to groundless suspicion and jealousy.

猜奖 cāijiǎng guessing game with prizes for winners

猜料 cāiliào surmise; estimate:结果如何,还很难～。It is still hard to say what will eventually come of this. *or* It's still hard to anticipate the consequences.

猜枚 cāiméi play a guessing game (usu. at a drinking party):～助兴 play a guessing game to enliven the atmosphere

猜谜儿 cāimèir ❶ guess a riddle：晚会上的最后一个节目是～。The last item on the evening's programme was guessing riddles. ❷ guess：有话直说，别让我们～。Come straight to the point. Don't keep us guessing.

猜谜 cāimí 〈书面〉guess a riddle

猜摸 cāimo try to fathom; speculate：这个人的心思总是叫人～不透。It is hard to fathom the man's mind.

猜破 cāipò guess correctly：他这点心思我一猜就破。I can easily figure out what's on his mind.

猜拳 cāiquán *also* "划拳" huáquán finger-guessing game：一边～，一边饮酒，好不热闹。It is great fun playing a finger-guessing game while drinking.

猜思 cāisī 〈方言〉guess; reckon：我～她有点不高兴。I guess she is a little offended.

猜透 cāitòu make out (what's on sb.'s mind); figure out; see through：我真猜不透他的心事。I absolutely have no idea what is weighing on his mind.

猜嫌 cāixián harbour suspicions; be suspicious：他与同事们搞不好关系的原因就是爱～。The reason why he cannot get along with his colleagues is that he is too suspicious.

猜详 cāixiáng make guesses; conjecture

猜想 cāixiǎng suppose; suspect; guess：凭空～ make a wild guess / 反复～ keep guessing / 我～他正在阅览室读报。I suppose he is reading newspapers in the reading-room. / 我～他今天不会回来了。I guess he won't come back today.

猜哑谜 cāi yǎmí try to guess the real meaning or truth (behind sth.)

猜疑 cāiyí have suspicions (often groundless); have misgivings; distrust：互相～只能损害团结。Mutual distrust can only serve to undermine unity.

猜中 cāizhòng guess correctly; solve a riddle：这个谜语你没有～。Sorry, you haven't solved this riddle.

cái

裁 cái ❶ cut (paper, cloth, etc.) into parts：～纸 cut paper into sheets / 上衣～好了。The jacket is cut out. / 把塑料薄膜～开。Cut the plastic film open. ❷〈印刷〉size of paper cut：对～folio / 八～纸 octavo ❸ reduce; cut back：今年的经费～了二十万元。This year's budget was reduced by 200,000 *yuan*. / 这个工厂最近～了二十人。This factory recently laid off 20 workers. ❹ (often used in art and literature) mental planning; selection：别出心～ adopt an original approach; try to be different / 《唐诗别～》*Selected Tang Poems* ❺ type or form of writing：体～ style (of a literary work) ❻ judge; decide; determine：仲～ arbitrate / 总～ president (of a corporation) ❼ control; check; sanction：经济制～ economic sanction / 独～ arbitrary rule; dictatorship

裁兵 cáibīng 〈旧语〉reduce troops; cut down troop strength

裁并 cáibìng cut down and merge：这个工厂最近～了几个科室。Several sections in the factory have recently been either abolished or merged.

裁撤 cáichè dissolve; disband：～重叠的机构 trim overlapping organs / 学校的基建处去年被～了。The construction department of the school was dissolved last year.

裁处 cáichǔ deal with; handle：这几件事要及时～。We'll have to look into and settle these matters in good time.

裁答 cáidá 〈书面〉compose a letter of reply

裁定 cáidìng 〈法律〉❶ pass judgment; rule：主席～该发言人违反程序。The chairman ruled the speaker out of order. ❷ ruling：中级法院对这个案件的～是公允的。The intermediate court's ruling on the case was fair and just.

裁断 cáiduàn consider and decide：大胆～ decide on sth. boldly; make a bold decision / 慎作～ give careful consideration to something before making a decision; be circumspect in making decisions

裁夺 cáiduó consider and decide; decide：这件事如何处理，请厂长～。It is up to the factory manager to decide how the problem should be handled.

裁度 cáiduó 〈书面〉surmise; judge：时局不明，不好～。The situation being murky, it is difficult to predict how it will develop.

裁缝 cáiféng make (a dress); tailor：他～的衣服无不合体。All the clothes he made fitted his customers perfectly.

裁缝 cáifeng tailor; dressmaker：这套衣服是在～那里定制的。This suit is tailor-made.

裁复 cáifù 〈书面〉make a decision and reply：以上请示妥否，请～。(at the end of an official report) Your reply and decision on the feasibility of the above suggestions is hereby awaited.

裁革 cáigé cut out; abolish：～冗员 cut redundancy / ～陋规 abolish bad practices

裁画 cáihuà 〈书面〉decide on a plan：此事尚待阁下～。It remains for Your Excellency to decide on the plan.

裁减 cáijiǎn reduce; cut down; lay off：～军备 reduce armaments / ～非生产机构 cut down the number of non-productive units / ～支出 cut back on expenditure

裁剪 cáijiǎn cut out：～衣服 cut out a garment

裁决 cáijué ruling; adjudication：依法～ adjudicate according to law / 主席团将对这件事情作出～。The presidium is going to give its ruling on the matter.

裁决令 cáijuélìng 〈法律〉adjudication order; judicial order

裁决者 cáijuézhě 〈法律〉adjudicator

裁军 cáijūn disarmament：～谈判 disarmament negotiations / ～会议 disarmament conference / 单方面～ unilateral disarmament / 全面～ all-round (*or* comprehensive) disarmament / ～机构 disarmament mechanism (*or* machinery) / ～骗局 fraudulent disarmament proposal / ～审议委员会 Disarmament Commission (DC) / ～谈判委员会 Committee on Disarmament (CD) / 专门讨论～问题的联大特别会议 Special Session of the UN General Assembly devoted to disarmament / 欧洲～会议 Conference on Disarmament in Europe (CDE)

裁可 cáikě approve officially; judge and approve

裁判 cáipàn ❶〈法律〉judgment：两家公司的纠纷，将由法院作出～。The court will give its verdict on the dispute between the two firms. ❷〈体育〉referee (a match)：这场球赛～得不公平。The umpire for the match was not quite even-handed. ❸ referee; umpire; judge：这场足球赛，由你担任～。You'll act as referee for the football match.

裁判权 cáipànquán jurisdiction

裁判司法庭 Cáipàn Sīfǎtíng (HK) Magistrate's Court

裁判员 cáipànyuán judge; referee; umpire：国际～ international referee (*or* judge) / 一级～ first class referee (*or* judge)

裁判长 cáipànzhǎng head judge; chief judge; chief referee

裁片 cáipiàn 〈方言〉cut parts (of a garment)

裁汰 cáitài 〈书面〉reduce; trim; remove; lay off：～多余人员 trim overstaffing; lay off redundant employees

裁许 cáixǔ 〈方言〉*see* "裁可"

裁员 cáiyuán lay off; reduce：厂方为减少开支，决定大量～。In order to cut down expenditure, the factory management decided to lay off a large number of employees. / 因～酿起工潮。The laying off of employees has triggered a strike.

裁择 cáizé make a choice

裁纸刀 cáizhǐdāo paper cutter; paper knife

裁纸机 cáizhǐjī paper trimmer; cutter

裁制 cáizhì ❶ sanction; punish ❷ check; restrain：感情应该受到理智的～。One's emotions should be restrained by reason. ❸ cut and sew; make a dress; tailor

裁酌 cáizhuó weigh and decide; exercise judgment

才¹ cái ❶ ability; talent; gift：德～兼备 be both politically conscious and professionally competent; have both talent and political integrity / 人尽其～ give full play to everyone's talent ❷ capable person; talent：英～ man of outstanding talent / 天～ genius ❸ person of a certain type：庸～ mediocre person; mediocrity ❹ (Cái) a surname

才²(纔) cái 〈副词〉❶ *used to indicate that sth. has just happened*：会议～开始。The meeting has just begun. / 我～来他就走了。He left the moment I arrived. ❷ *used to indicate that sth. happens later than is expected*：感冒了一星期，他～到医院去。He did not go to hospital until he had been down with flu for a whole week. / 大风直刮到半夜～停。The gale did not stop until midnight. ❸ *used to indicate that sth. happens only on certain conditions*：只有齐心协力，～能完成任务。The task can only be completed when everybody works in close concert. ❹ *used to indicate sth. new has happened*：经他说明之后，我～知道真相。I learned the truth only after

C

he told me what had actually happened. ❺ *used to indicate that by comparison sth. is small in amount or low in frequency, or that sb. is weak in ability*：我们班～十个人。There are only ten people in our class. /这四本书～两块钱。These four books cost only two *yuan*. /这孩子～六岁，已经认得不少字了。The child is barely six years old, and he has learned quite a number of words. ❻ *used for emphatic assertion* (often followed by 呢 at the end of the sentence)：我～不去呢！I definitely won't go! /那演技～叫绝呢！The acrobatic performance was simply wonderful.

才调 cáidiào *see* "才情"

才分 cáifèn innate ability; inherent capability：～甚高 be endowed with rare talent; be highly gifted /～超群 of no ordinary talent

才赋 cáifù literary gift or talent

C

才干 cáigàn ability; competence：增长～ enhance one's abilities /～是锻炼出来的。Competence is acquired through training. *or* Competence comes with practice.

才刚 cáigāng 〈方言〉just now：他～还在这里。He was here a moment ago.

才高八斗 cáigāo-bādǒu outstanding literary talent

see also "八斗才" bādǒucái

才高识远 cáigāo-shíyuǎn of great talent and insight; talented and far-sighted

才华 cáihuá literary or artistic talent; talent：～出众 have brilliant talent /他是一个有～的作家。He is a gifted writer.

才华横溢 cáihuá-héngyì *see* "才气横溢"

才具 cáijù 〈书面〉ability; capability：此人～有限，不可大用。As a person of rather limited ability, he should not be placed in a responsible position.

才俊 cáijùn 〈书面〉❶ man of outstanding talent ❷ superb talent

才力 cáilì gift; ability：论文旁征博引，颇见作者～。You can visualize the author's gift and erudition from this well-documented paper.

才路 cáilù method of cultivating talented people; way of providing opportunities for the talented; ways to bring people's abilities into full play：广开～ provide ample opportunities for the talented to come to the fore

才略 cáilüè ability and sagacity (in political and military affairs)：～过人 be endowed with exceptional intelligence; be exceptionally sagacious /雄才大略 of great talent and bold vision /他具有军事家的～。He is endowed with the genius of a military strategist.

才貌 cáimào talent and looks：～出众 of remarkable talent and good looks

才貌双全 cáimào-shuāngquán both talented and good-looking; brilliant and handsome：他总想娶一个～的姑娘，因此拖到今天仍是单身。As he wants to marry a girl who is both beautiful and talented, he has remained single to this day.

才名 cáimíng reputation for talent and brilliance：颇有～ be reputed for one's talent

才能 cáinéng ability; talent; natural gift：工作～ practical ability /管理～ managerial ability /他没有施展自己～的地方。There is no scope for him to exercise his talent.

才女 cáinǚ talented woman; woman with a literary talent

才气 cáiqì literary talent：～超人 peerless literary talent

才气横溢 cáiqì-héngyì brim or overflow with talent; brilliant：她是～的作家。She is a writer of overflowing brilliance. /此人～，颇遭妒忌。The man aroused much jealousy for his rare gifts.

才器 cáiqì 〈书面〉talent and magnanimity

才情 cáiqíng literary talent; literary aptitude：卖弄～ show off (*or* vaunt) one's talent /我们都很钦佩他的～。We all admire him for his literary talent and skill.

才人 cáirén ❶ gifted scholar ❷〈古语〉woman scholar serving at court; woman official; imperial concubine of a lower rank

才识 cáishí talent and insight：～过人 be gifted with unusual talent and insight

才士 cáishì man of great ability or talent; gifted scholar

才疏学浅 cáishū-xuéqiǎn 〈谦词〉have little talent and learning：我～，不堪当此重任。Inadequate in talent and learning, I feel unequal to such an important post. /～，难成大事。Ambition cannot make mediocrities achieve greatness.

才思 cáisī (in writing) imaginative power; creativeness：～敏捷 have a facile imagination

才望 cáiwàng talent and prestige：他的～几乎没有人不景仰的。Few people remain unimpressed by his talent and the prestige he enjoys.

才绪 cáixù 〈书面〉literary talent; literary gift

才学 cáixué talent and learning; scholarship：～人品俱佳 be sound in scholarship and noble in character /王先生很有～。Mr. Wang is a man of great erudition.

才艺 cáiyì talent and skill

才藻 cáizǎo 〈书面〉literary talent

才智 cáizhì ability and wisdom：发挥聪明～ give full play to people's wisdom and creativeness

才子 cáizǐ gifted scholar：他是个～。He is a man of literary talent. /江南多～。Regions south of the Yangtze River boast a galaxy of talents.

才子佳人 cáizǐ-jiārén talented scholars and beautiful ladies (often heroes and heroines of traditional Chinese romances)

材

cái ❶ timber; raw materials：木～ timber /板～ steel sheet /钢～ steel products; rolled steel /药～ medicinal herb /树木已经成～。The trees have matured into timber. ❷ coffin：寿～ coffin ❸ material; matter：题～ subject-matter; theme; topic /教～ teaching material /素～ source materials (of art and literature) ❹ ability; talent; aptitude：人～ talents /将～ person with all the qualifications of a general /长大成～ grow into a useful (*or* talented) person

材积 cáijī volume (of timber)

材料 cáiliào ❶ material：建筑～ construction material /原～ raw material ❷ data; material：收集～ gather material; collect data /档案～ archival material /原始～ original data /学习～ material for study/掌握第一手～ have first-hand information /我写了一个调查～。I've prepared a report on my findings. ❸ makings; stuff：她既温和又活泼，是幼儿教师的～。Gentle and lively, she has the makings of a preschool teacher. /他是块搞科研的好～。He has good research potential.

材料工艺学 cáiliào gōngyìxué material technology

材料经济学 cáiliào jīngjìxué material economics

材料科学 cáiliào kēxué materials science

材料力学 cáiliào lìxué mechanics of materials

材料试验 cáiliào shìyàn 〈机械〉materials testing：～机 material testing machine

材树 cáishù timber tree

材质 cáizhì texture; quality of material：～要求特殊 special requirement for material quality /改进～和造型，提高产品质量 improve the quality of material and the shape of the product so as to upgrade the quality

财

cái wealth; money：理～ manage financial matters /爱～如命 love money more than one's life; have a craving for wealth

财办 cáibàn (short for 财务办公室) office of financial affairs

财宝 cáibǎo money and valuables：金银～ gold and silver pieces and other valuables

财帛 cáibó money and silk (often used as gifts); wealth：广施～，收揽人心 give money lavishly to people in order to win them over /他多有～，为富一方。Possessed of great wealth, he is recognized as the richest man in his district.

财产 cáichǎn property：保护人民的生命～ protect the life and property of the people /国家～ state property /集体～ collective property /私有～ private property /～处理权 *jus disponendi*; the right of disposing of property /～分类账 property ledger /～估价 property valuation /～关系 property relation /～目录 property inventory /～清理 property inspection /～索赔 property claims /～损失 property damage /～所有人 property owner /～债券 property bond

财产权 cáichǎnquán property right：拥有～ have a claim to the property; have a right to the property /移交～ transfer the property right /涉及～的民事诉讼 civil lawsuit involving property rights

财产税 cáichǎnshuì property tax

财大气粗 cáidà-qìcū he who rolls in money speaks loud; wealth breeds arrogance

财东 cáidōng ❶〈旧语〉shopowner; business man：拥有几家工厂的～ owner of several factories ❷ rich man; moneybags：乡下的小～ small rural moneybags /骡马成群的大～ rich farmer who owns many teams of farm animals

财蠹 cáidù 〈书面〉people who waste or squander huge financial resources; financial termites

财阀 cáifá financial magnate; plutocrat; tycoon：第二次世界大战

前,德国一小撮垄断～完全控制了国家的经济命脉。Before World War II, a handful of financial magnates in Germany had complete control over the lifelines of the national economy.

财富 cáifù wealth; riches:物质～ material wealth /精神～ intellectual wealth /社会～ social wealth /人类共同继承的～ common heritage of mankind /劳动创造～。Labour creates wealth. /人才是国家最宝贵的～。Able and educated people are the most precious wealth of a country.

财赋 cáifù 〈书面〉 finance and taxation

财货 cáihuò money and property; wealth

财经 cáijīng finance and economy:～纪律 financial and economic discipline /健全～体制 put the financial and economic system on a sound basis

财会 cáikuài book-keeping and accounting:～人员 book-keepers and accountants

财礼 cáilǐ betrothal gifts (from the bridegroom to the bride's family):下～ give betrothal gifts /收～的旧习俗 outdated custom of taking betrothal gifts

财力 cáilì financial power; financial resources:～充足 plentiful financial resources /由于～不足,许多事业无法兴办。Many undertakings have not been started for lack of financial resources.

财路 cáilù means to acquire wealth:广开～ open (*or* exploit) all possible avenues for wealth

财贸 cáimào finance and trade or commerce:～工作 work in finance and trade /～战线 on the finance and trade front /～部门 departments of finance and trade

财贸系统 cáimào xìtǒng departments of finance and trade and affiliated organizations; finance and trade sector:～职工 people working in the finance and trade sector

财迷 cáimí money-grubber; miser:远近有名的～ notorious miser

财迷心窍 cáimí-xīnqiào money-grubbing; crazy about making money

财气 cáiqi luck in money matters
see also "财运"

财权 cáiquán ❶ right of ownership; property right:继承～ inherit property rights /判定～的归属 determine who is to inherit the right of ownership ❷ financial control; control over financial matters:夺取～ seize financial control /～在握 be in control of financial matters /她在家里是掌～的。She holds the purse strings in the family.

财神 cáishén *also* "财神爷" God of Wealth; extremely rich person; person or institution in charge of financial affairs:过路～ God of Wealth through whose hands money passes /～奶奶〈戏谑〉 woman in charge of finance (*or* money matters); Goddess of Wealth /他掌管本单位的财权,因此常被称为～爷。Being in charge of the department's finance, he is often referred to as the God of Wealth.

财势 cáishì wealth and power:追求～ thirst (*or* lust) for wealth and power; seek wealth and position /他原是本镇最有～的人。He used to be the richest and most powerful person in the township.

财税 cáishuì finance and taxation:～秩序混乱 chaos in finance and taxation /～制度 financial and taxation system (*or* regime)

财团 cáituán financial group; consortium:摩根～ (US) Morgan financial group /大宇～ (ROK) Daewoo Group /现代～ (ROK) Hyundai Group /国际～ international consortium /金融～ financial consortium

财务 cáiwù financial affairs:～安排 financial arrangement /～报告 financial report /～报表 financial reporting; financial statement /～大检查 general financial audit /～代理人 financial agent /～工作 financial work /～顾问 financial adviser /～监督 financial supervision /～计划 financial plan /～结算 financial settlement /～人员 financial personnel /～条例 financial regulations /～往来 financial transaction /～行政管理 financial administration and management/～指标 financial target /～制度 financial system (*or* regime) /～主管人员 financial administrator; financial officer /～自主 financial autonomy

财务包干 cáiwù bāogān be responsible for one's own finances

财务杠杆 cáiwù gànggǎn gearing; leverage:～调整 gearing adjustment /运用～ use finance as leverage

财务科 cáiwùkē finance section

财务会计 cáiwù kuàijì financial accounting

财务审计 cáiwù shěnjì financial audit

财务总监 cáiwù zǒngjiān CFO (Chief Financial Officer)

财物 cáiwù property; belongings:个人～ personal effects; personal property /爱护公共～ take good care of public property

财喜 cáixǐ 〈旧语〉 income; earnings; money obtained:意外的～ unexpected fortune; windfall

财雄势大 cáixióng-shìdà wealthy and influential

财源 cáiyuán financial resources; source of revenue:～茂盛 abundant financial resources /～枯竭 drain (*or* exhaust) the sources of revenue /～充足 sufficient financial resources /广开～ open up broad ways of revenue

财运 cáiyùn luck in money matters or transactions:～亨通 (have a) run of good luck in money transactions /～不佳 be down on one's luck in money matters

财政 cáizhèng public finance:～收支平衡 balance of revenue and expenditure /～年鉴 financial yearbook /～拨款 budgetary appropriations /～界 financial community /～信用 financial credit /～纪律 financial discipline /～拮据 financial embarrassment /～稳健政策 financial prudence /～担保 financial guarantee /～实力 financial solvency /～巨头 financial magnate /～垄断 financial monopoly /～稳定 financial stability

财政包干制 cáizhèng bāogānzhì contract system in which each unit is responsible for its own surplus or deficit in fiscal matters; fiscal contract responsibility system

财政补贴 cáizhèng bǔtiē financial subsidy

财政部 cáizhèngbù Ministry of Finance; (UK) Exchequer; (US) (Department of the) Treasury:～长 Minister of Finance; (US) Secretary of the Treasury

财政赤字 cáizhèng chìzì financial deficits

财政大臣 Cáizhèng Dàchén (UK) Chancellor of the Exchequer

财政独立 cáizhèng dúlì financial autonomy; independent finances

财政放权 cáizhèng fàngquán decentralization of fiscal powers or authority

财政分级管理 cáizhèng fēnjí guǎnlǐ transference of financial management responsibility to the local levels

财政寡头 cáizhèng guǎtóu *also* "金融寡头" jīnróng guǎtóu financial oligarch:～统治 financial oligarchy

财政机关 cáizhèng jīguān financial institutions

财政监督 cáizhèng jiāndū financial control; financial supervision

财政年度 cáizhèng niándù fiscal year

财政审计 cáizhèng shěnjì financial audit

财政收入 cáizhèng shōurù revenue:～递增包干 contract system based on progressively increased revenue

财政司 Cáizhèngsī (HK before 1 July 1997) Financial Secretary

财政危机 cáizhèng wēijī financial crisis

财政政策 cáizhèng zhèngcè financial or fiscal policy

财政支出 cáizhèng zhīchū expenditure

财政驻厂员 cáizhèng zhùchǎngyuán resident supervisor of the financial department in an enterprise under the direct control of the central authorities

财政专项债券 cáizhèng zhuānxiàng zhàiquàn special treasury bonds

财政资本 cáizhèng zīběn *also* "金融资本" jīnróng zīběn financial capital

财主 cáizhu 〈旧语〉 rich man; moneybags

cǎi

采[1]**(採)** cǎi ❶ pick; pluck; gather:～莲 pick lotus seeds /～茶 pick tea /～药 cull medicinal herbs /～蘑菇 gather (*or* collect) mushrooms ❷ mine; extract:开～天然气 extract natural gas ❸ collect; gather:～标本 collect specimens /～矿样 gather mineral samples ❹ choose; adopt; select:～取措施 adopt measures /他的文章被一家杂志社～用了。His article was accepted by a magazine.

采[2] cǎi spirit; complexion:神～飞扬 be bubbling over with energy and enthusiasm; be in high spirits /丰～ graceful bearing (*or* appearance); elegant manner (*or* mien) /无精打～ be listless; be crestfallen

采[3] cǎi *see* "彩" cǎi
see also cài

采拔 cǎibá select (people); scout:～人才 scout for talent

采办 cǎibàn buy (a fairly large amount of goods); purchase:为

所乡村学校～生活用品 purchase articles of daily use for a village school

采编 cǎibiān gather and edit (news material)：新闻～ news coverage and editing /～人员 reporters and editors; staff writers

采捕 cǎibǔ dive to catch：～牡蛎 dive for oysters

采茶灯 cǎichádēng folk dance in which each dancer carries a basket for holding tea-leaves in the left hand and a fan in the right

采茶机 cǎichájī 〈农业〉tea-plucking machine; tea plucker; tea-leaf picker

采茶戏 cǎicháxì tea-plucking opera (local opera popular in provinces such as Jiangxi, Hubei, Anhui, etc.)

采场 cǎichǎng 〈矿业〉stope：露天～ open-cast stope /第四号～ stope No.4 /～管理制度 stope management rules

C

采出 cǎichū 〈石油〉extraction

采伐 cǎifá cut; fell：～树木 cut (*or* fell) trees

采伐迹地 cǎifá jìdì cutover

采伐量 cǎifáliàng amount of timber cut; cut

采访 cǎifǎng (of a reporter) gather material; cover：～新闻 gather news /～大会消息 cover the conference /～一位小学教师 interview a primary school teacher /王教授接受～。Professor Wang has agreed to give an interview.

采风 cǎifēng collect folk songs：深入内地～ go far into the interior to collect folk songs

采割 cǎigē collect (lacquer or latex) by cutting into barks

采购 cǎigòu ❶ make purchases for an institution; purchase：～图书 order books for a library /～农副产品 purchase farm and side-line products ❷ purchasing agent; payer

采购团 cǎigòutuán purchasing mission

采购员 cǎigòuyuán purchasing agent; payer

采购站 cǎigòuzhàn purchasing station

采光 cǎiguāng 〈建筑〉lighting; daylighting：～性能良好 excellent lighting function /～天井 light well

采集 cǎijí gather; collect：～标本 collect specimens /～小麦良种 seek out good strains of wheat

采精 cǎijīng 〈畜牧〉semen collection

采景 cǎijǐng locate outdoor scenes (for shooting a film)：北京电影制片厂的摄制组去南方～去了。The production unit of the Beijing Film Studio has gone to the south to photograph outdoor scenes.

采掘 cǎijué excavate：～矿石 excavate ores /～设备 equipment for excavation

采掘电铲 cǎijué diànchǎn 〈矿业〉mining shovel

采掘进尺 cǎijué jìnchǐ excavation footage

采空区 cǎikōngqū 〈矿业〉mined-out area; worked-out section; goaf：～充填 goaf-filling

采矿 cǎikuàng mining：露天～ opencut (*or* opencast) mining /地下～ underground mining /～工业 mining industry

采矿工程 cǎikuàng gōngchéng mining engineering

采矿机 cǎikuàngjī mining machine

采捞 cǎilāo dive for：～这种菜要潜入海底进行。One needs to dive to the bottom of the sea for this kind of seaweed.

采莲船 cǎiliánchuán "row-boat" dance (a form of traditional folk dancing)
see also "跑旱船" pǎo hànchuán

采录 cǎilù ❶ collect and record：～民歌 collect and record folk songs /～民间传说 gather folklore ❷ have a tape-recorded interview (with sb.); have a television interview (with sb.) ❸〈书面〉select and employ

采买 cǎimǎi ❶ purchase; buy：～日用品 buy articles of daily use /～办公用品 purchase articles for office use /～医疗设备 procure medical equipment ❷ purchasing agent; buyer

采煤 cǎiméi coal mining; coal extraction; coal cutting：露天～ opencast coal mining /人工～ manual coal mining /机械～ mechanized coal mining /～工人 coal miner

采煤工作面 cǎiméi gōngzuòmiàn coal face

采煤回收率 cǎiméi huíshōulǜ coal recovery rate

采煤机 cǎiméijī 〈矿业〉coal-mining machine; coal cutter

采棉机 cǎimiánjī cotton picker

采纳 cǎinà accept; adopt：～群众建议 accept recommendations made by the public /～合理化建议 adopt rationalization proposals /他的方案被领导～。The plan he proposed won the approval of the leadership.

采暖 cǎinuǎn heating：～设计 heating designing /～效果 heating effect

采气 cǎiqì gas production

采取 cǎiqǔ adopt; take：～有效措施 adopt (*or* take) effective measures /～主动 take the initiative /～具体行动 take concrete action /～克制态度 adopt a restrained attitude /～诡辩方法 resort to sophistry /～以攻为守的策略 employ the tactic of attacking for the sake of defence /～启发式的教学方法 use the elicitation (*or* heuristic) method of teaching

采沙场 cǎishāchǎng sand quarry

采石 cǎishí 〈建筑〉quarrying：～工 quarryman /～机 quarrying machine

采石场 cǎishíchǎng quarry; stone-pit

采食 cǎishí (of an animal) hunt for food

采收 cǎishōu pick (fruit); gather (berries or seeds)

采收率 cǎishōulǜ 〈石油〉recovery ratio

采挖 cǎiwā cull or dig out (Chinese medicinal herbs)

采撷 cǎixié 〈书面〉❶ pick; pluck：～芳草 pluck fragrant herbs /～奇花异草 collect exotic flowers and grass ❷ gather：～一尽 collect everything there is to collect

采写 cǎixiě interview sb. and write about his or her life and work

采血 cǎixiě 〈医学〉blood-taking; blood-collection：～作试验 take some blood for a test /医院明天派人来～，献血者请登记。The hospital will send its staff to collect blood tomorrow. Donors, please sign up.

采薪之忧 cǎixīnzhīyōu 〈书面〉be ill; be taken ill：家君有～。My father has been taken ill.

采样 cǎiyàng ❶〈矿业〉sampling ❷ sample; spot-check：食品～检查 food spot-check

采用 cǎiyòng adopt; use; employ：～先进技术 adopt advanced technology /～优良品种 use improved seed strains /～新式农具 employ new farm implements

采油 cǎiyóu 〈石油〉oil extraction; oil recovery：气举～ air-lift recovery /二次～ secondary recovery

采油队 cǎiyóuduì oil production crew

采育 cǎiyù fell trees and plant saplings：～兼顾将带来林业发展。Paying proper attention to both cutting down and planting trees helps to develop forestry.

采运 cǎiyùn cut down and transport：～木材 fell trees and transport timber

采择 cǎizé select and adopt：从各种方案中～最佳方案 select and adopt the best from various plans

采摘 cǎizhāi pick; pluck：～桑叶 pick mulberry leaves /～花朵 pluck flowers

采脂 cǎizhī 〈林业〉(resin) tapping

采摭 cǎizhí 〈书面〉select from various sources：～菁华 select the essence /～宏富 rich harvest of selections

采制 cǎizhì ❶ collect and process：～标本 collect and process specimens ❷ have a tape-recorded interview：～电视新闻 have an interview tape-recorded for TV news

采种 cǎizhǒng 〈农业〉seed collecting

采擢 cǎizhuó 〈书面〉select; choose：～优秀人材 select able and virtuous persons; choose the best and brightest

宷

cǎi 〈旧语〉official：～地 feudal estate /僚～ colleague

睬(倸)

cǎi pay attention to; take notice of：不理不～ ignore totally /小王太傲气，我不想理～他。Xiao Wang is so conceited that I intend to cut him dead.

踩(跴)

cǎi ❶ step on; trample：～了一脚泥 step into mud /～高跷 walk on stilts /不要～麦苗儿。Don't tread on the young wheat shoots. ❷〈比喻〉belittle; trample on：这种人既会捧人，也会～人。This sort of person knows well how to flatter and how to belittle others. ❸〈旧语〉track down bandits or robbers; investigate a criminal case：～缉 hunt down bandits (*or* robbers)

踩捕 cǎibǔ 〈旧语〉search for wanted criminals

踩蛋儿 cǎidànr (of birds) mating

踩道 cǎidào (of thieves and robbers) "tread out the path" — spy out the land before taking action

踩点 cǎidiǎn ❶ *see* "踩道" ❷ (in dancing) keep time; keep in

step:学跳舞先得学～。The first thing to do in learning ballroom dancing is to learn to keep time.
踩访 cǎifǎng *see* "踩捕"
踩咕 cǎigu 〈方言〉belittle; disparage; look down upon:为什么你总是～我? Why are you always picking on me?
踩藕 cǎi'ǒu (of cross talkers) move about aimlessly:～是相声表演的一大忌讳。In a comic dialogue, moving about aimlessly is a serious fault for the performing artists.
踩伞 cǎisǎn parachute jumping with one parachutist on top of another
踩墒 cǎishāng tread hard on a seed bed so as to preserve soil moisture
踩水 cǎishuǐ tread water
踩踏 cǎità step on; crush underfoot:小麦拔节后不要～。Don't tramp on wheat at its elongation stage.
踩线 cǎixiàn step on the line; foot-fault
踩秧草 cǎi yāngcǎo remove weeds in a paddy field by treading them:在田里～ tread weeds in the fields /瘦田要多～,多施灰肥。Poor soil needs more weeding and application of ash manure.
踩闸 cǎizhá step on the brake

彩(❷綵) cǎi ❶ colour:水～ water colour /五～ five colours (blue, yellow, red, white and black); multicoloured ❷ coloured silk:剪～ cut the ribbon (at opening ceremonies of exhibitions, etc.) /张灯结～ be decorated with lanterns and colourful festoons ❸ cheer; applaud:喝～ acclaim /他刚唱完,立刻～声四起。Applause arose in all directions the moment he finished singing. ❹ variety; splendour:精～ wonderful; splendid; superb /丰富多～ rich and colourful; rich and varied ❺ prize:中～ win a prize (in a lottery, etc.) /～金 prize money; award ❻ stage craft used in traditional opera to achieve a special effect; jugglery:火～ special effect symbolizing blood or fire ❼ blood from a wound:他在战斗中挂～了。He was wounded in the battle.
彩扮 cǎibàn *see* "彩唱 ❷"
彩蚌 cǎibàng 〈工美〉painted shell; painting on shell
彩笔 cǎibǐ coloured pencil (for drawing pictures); crayon
彩唱 cǎichàng ❶ dress performance in Chinese opera (as opposed to 清唱, singing opera without stage make-up or accompaniment) ❷ *also* "彩扮" Chinese folk art performance with actors or actresses somewhat dressed up for the roles
彩车 cǎichē float (in a parade); specially decorated cart or car:迎娶新娘的～ specially decorated wedding car /游行队伍中的～ floats in a parade
彩绸 cǎichóu coloured silk; silk with colourful patterns:～迎风飘舞 colourful silk ribbons fluttering in the wind /车上挂着一条～。A piece of coloured silk hung over the car.
彩带 cǎidài colourful ribbon; colourful streamer:金色的～ golden ribbon /七色～ rainbow-like ribbon /腰上系着一条～。A colourful sash is worn round the waist.
彩旦 cǎidàn 〈戏曲〉female clown role
彩蛋 cǎidàn ❶〈工美〉painted eggshells; painting on eggshells ❷〈方言〉preserved egg
彩灯 cǎidēng coloured light; coloured lantern:除夕街上挂满了～。Coloured lanterns are hung all over the streets on New Year's Eve.
彩电 cǎidiàn colour television; colour TV set
彩雕 cǎidiāo coloured carving; painted sculpture
彩调 cǎidiào local opera of the Guangxi Zhuang Autonomous Region
彩坊 cǎifāng *see* "彩牌楼"
彩凤随鸦 cǎifèng-suíyā a phoenix becomes the mate to a crow — a pretty girl married to a good-for-nothing
彩号儿 cǎihàor wounded soldier
彩虹 cǎihóng *also* "虹" rainbow
彩虹云 cǎihóngyún 〈气象〉iridescent cloud
彩画 cǎihuà *see* "彩绘"
彩绘 cǎihuì coloured drawing; coloured pattern:～瓷瓶 porcelain vase decorated with coloured drawings /这次出土的陶器都有美丽的～。The porcelain wares recently excavated all have beautiful coloured patterns. /古老的建筑～一新。Ancient buildings took on a new look after being repainted.
彩轿 cǎijiào bridal sedan chair:上～ mount a bridal sedan chair — (of a girl) get married
彩卷 cǎijuǎn colour film
彩口 cǎikǒu wound of a soldier
彩扩 cǎikuò (short for 彩色扩印) make enlargements from a colour film
彩礼 cǎilǐ betrothal gifts (from the bridegroom to the bride's family):男方送来的～ betrothal gifts from the bridegroom's family /改变旧习俗,婚嫁不送～ change the old custom of giving betrothal and wedding gifts
彩练 cǎiliàn coloured ribbon:一条七色～横贯长空。A beautiful rainbow streams across the sky. /赤橙黄绿青蓝紫,谁持～当空舞? Red, orange, yellow, green, blue, indigo, violet — Who is dancing, waving this coloured ribbon against the sky?
彩楼 cǎilóu *see* "彩门"
彩门 cǎimén decorated gateway (erected on festival occasions)
彩排 cǎipái dress rehearsal:本剧定于明晚～。The dress rehearsal of the play is fixed for tomorrow evening. /我观看了昨晚举行的奥运会开幕式～。I watched the dress rehearsal of the opening ceremony of the Olympiad last night.
彩牌 cǎipái ❶ colourful poster:～上公布了最新记录。The latest records are displayed on the colourful poster. ❷〈方言〉*see* "彩牌楼"
彩牌楼 cǎipáilou *also* "彩门";"彩坊" ornamental arch (erected on festive occasions)
彩佩 cǎipèi colourful ornament
彩棚 cǎipéng decorated or colourful tent (set up on festive occasions):公园门口搭起了一座～。A decorated tent was set up at the entrance of the park.
彩片 cǎipiàn colour film
彩票 cǎipiào lottery ticket:买～ buy lottery tickets /中了～头奖 get (*or* win) first lottery prize /发售～ sell lottery tickets
彩旗 cǎiqí coloured flag; bunting:～迎风招展 colourful buntings fluttering in the breeze
彩球 cǎiqiú ❶ colour balloon ❷ ball of coloured silk:抛～ ceremony at which a princess or the daughter of an aristocratic family throws an embroidered ball to a crowd of suitors to decide whom she is to marry
彩券 cǎiquàn lottery ticket
彩色 cǎisè multicolour; colour:～缤纷 a riot of colours
彩色玻璃 cǎisè bōli stained glass; end-of-day glass
彩色传真电报系统 cǎisè chuánzhēn diànbào xìtǒng 〈无线电〉colour facsimile telegraph system
彩色传真机 cǎisè chuánzhēnjī 〈无线电〉colour facsimile apparatus
彩色底片 cǎisè dǐpiàn colour negative; autochrome
彩色电视 cǎisè diànshì colour television:～机 colour television set; colour TV
彩色电影 cǎisè diànyǐng colour movie; colour motion picture; colour film
彩色对比度 cǎisè duìbǐdù colour contrast
彩色粉笔 cǎisè fěnbǐ pastel
彩色感光计 cǎisè gǎnguāngjì colour sensitometer
彩色合成 cǎisè héchéng 〈摄影〉colour composite
彩色胶片 cǎisè jiāopiàn colour film
彩色片儿 cǎisèpiānr 〈口语〉colour film
彩色片 cǎisèpiàn colour film
彩色铅笔 cǎisè qiānbǐ colour pencil; crayon
彩色强度调整 cǎisè qiángdù tiáozhěng colour intensity control
彩色摄影 cǎisè shèyǐng colour photography
彩色失真 cǎisè shīzhēn 〈无线电〉colour distortion
彩色石印术 cǎisè shíyìnshù 〈印刷〉chromolithography
彩色石英石 cǎisè shíyīngshí 〈矿业〉colour quartzite
彩色瓦 cǎisèwǎ 〈建筑〉encaustic tile
彩色显像管 cǎisè xiǎnxiàngguǎn colour trace tube; colour pick-up tube; colour picture tube; chromoscope
彩色显影液 cǎisè xiǎnyǐngyè colour developing solution
彩色音乐 cǎisè yīnyuè colourful music
彩色印片法 cǎisè yìnpiànfǎ technicolour
彩色印刷 cǎisè yìnshuā colour printing
彩色照相术 cǎisè zhàoxiàngshù *see* "彩色摄影"
彩色砖 cǎisèzhuān 〈建筑〉encaustic brick
彩砂 cǎishā coloured paint for spraying over the outer layer of a building
彩声 cǎishēng applause; cheers; acclaim:赢得一阵～ draw a burst

of applause
彩饰 cǎishì coloured ornament; coloured decoration
彩苏 cǎisū coloured tassels
彩塑 cǎisù colour modelling; painted sculpture:～泥人 coloured clay figurine /～花鸟 painted flower and bird sculptures
彩陶 cǎitáo ancient painted pottery
彩陶文化 cǎitáo wénhuà 〈考古〉painted-pottery culture
see also"仰韶文化" Yǎngsháo wénhuà
彩头 cǎitóu ❶〈旧语〉stage property and simple backdrop used in traditional Chinese opera ❷ good luck (in business, gambling, etc.):一出门就听见喜鹊叫,今天～不错。Good luck must be coming my way for I heard a magpie chirping the moment I stepped out of the room.
彩霞 cǎixiá rosy clouds; pink clouds:西边天幕上～朵朵。There are rosy clouds in the western sky.
彩印 cǎiyìn ❶(short for 彩色印刷) colour printing ❷ develop and print colour film
彩釉 cǎiyòu colour glaze:～砖 colour glazed tile
彩釉陶 cǎiyòutáo glazed colour pottery
彩云 cǎiyún rosy or pink clouds (that appear at dawn or dusk on a clear day)
彩照 cǎizhào 〈摄影〉colour picture; colour photo
彩纸 cǎizhǐ ❶ coloured paper ❷〈摄影〉colour photographic paper

cài

采(埰) cài

see also cǎi
采地 càidì *also*"采邑" fief; vassalage

菜 cài

❶ vegetable; greens:种～ grow vegetables /择～ trim vegetables (for cooking, etc.) /干～ dried vegetable /泡～ pickled vegetables; pickles /市场上细～很少。There is a scarcity of choice vegetables in the market. ❷ rape:～油 rapeseed oil; rape oil ❸ dish; course:荤～ meat dish /素～ vegetable dish /粤～ Guangdong cuisine /拿手～ the dish one cooks best /点～ order dishes; dine *à la carte* /饭桌上摆满了～。The table is covered with dishes. ❹ wild herb:糠～半年粮 live on chaff and wild herbs half the year
菜案 cài'àn job of preparing dishes (at a restaurant, etc.)
see also"红案" hóng'àn
菜板儿 càibǎnr chopping board
菜帮儿 càibāngr outer leaves (of a cabbage, etc.):把～切碎了喂鸡 chop outer leaves of a cabbage for chicken feed /腌～ pickled cabbage outer leaves
菜场 càichǎng *see*"菜市"
菜畜 càichù livestock (raised for meat)
菜单 càidān ❶ *also*"菜单子" menu; bill of fare ❷〈信息〉menu
菜单驱动界面 càidān qūdòng jièmiàn 〈信息〉menu-driven interface
菜刀 càidāo kitchen knife; chopper
菜地 càidì vegetable plot
菜点 càidiǎn dishes and cakes; cooked food and light refreshments
菜豆 càidòu kidney bean
菜墩子 càidūnzi chopping block (made of a tree stump)
菜饭 càifàn ❶ dishes and rice or other cereals ❷ rice, peas and vegetables all cooked together; rice cooked with vegetables
菜粉蝶 càifěndié cabbage butterfly
菜瓜 càiguā snake melon
菜馆 càiguǎn *also*"菜馆子"〈方言〉restaurant
菜花 càihuā ❶ cauliflower ❷ rape flower:一片金光灿灿的～ expanse of golden rape flowers
菜货 càihuò 〈方言〉〈粗话〉cowardly and incompetent person; good-for-nothing
菜窖 càijiào vegetable cellar; clamp
菜金 càijīn money earmarked for meats and vegetables
菜枯 càikū rapeseed cake (used as fertilizer)
菜篮子 càilánzi ❶ vegetable basket; shopping basket for food ❷ non-staple food supply:管好～ see to it that there is plentiful supply of non-staple food
菜篮子工程 càilánzi gōngchéng "vegetable basket" project — a project for establishing production bases and increasing non-staple food supply
菜码儿 càimǎr 〈方言〉shredded or sliced vegetables to go with noodles; vegetable trimmings
菜牛 càiniú beef cattle
菜农 càinóng vegetable grower
菜圃 càipǔ vegetable farm; vegetable plot
菜谱 càipǔ ❶ menu; bill of fare ❷ cookery-book; cookbook:《大众～》*Cookbook for Every Home*
菜畦 càiqí small section of a vegetable plot; vegetable bed
菜青 càiqīng dark grayish green:脸色～ dull greenish face
菜青虫 càiqīngchóng cabbage caterpillar
菜色 càisè be pallid due to hunger; look famished or emaciated:灾害连年,民有～。Suffering from natural disasters for years running, the people looked famished.
菜市 càishì food market
菜蔬 càishū ❶ vegetables; greens:瓜果～ fruits and vegetables ❷ dishes at a meal:明日过节,现在要赶紧备些～。We must get a few dishes ready in good time for tomorrow's festival.
菜薹 càitái tender petiole (of rape, mustard, etc.)
菜摊 càitān vegetable stall:摆个小～ run a small vegetable stall /马路两边有几十处～。There are scores of vegetable stalls on either side of the road.
菜系 càixì style of cooking; school of culinary art:我国有八大～。Chinese cuisine can be subdivided into eight major distinctive styles.
菜心儿 càixīnr heart (of a cabbage, etc.)
菜蚜 càiyá vegetable aphid
菜羊 càiyáng mutton sheep
菜肴 càiyáo cooked food (usu. meat dishes):各色～ various kinds of (*or* a variety of) cooked food /美味～ delicious cooked food
菜油 càiyóu *also*"菜子油" rapeseed oil; rape oil
菜园 càiyuán *also*"菜园子" vegetable garden
菜子 càizǐ ❶ vegetable seeds ❷ rapeseed
菜子饼 càizǐbǐng rapeseed cake
菜子油 càizǐyóu *see*"菜油"

蔡[1] Cài

❶〈历史〉principality of the Zhou Dynasty, lying southwest of present Shangcai County, Henan Province ❷ a surname

蔡[2] cài

〈书面〉big turtle or tortoise:蓍～ *shi* stalks and tortoise-shells used in divination; divination
蔡锷 Cài È Cai E (formerly translated as Ts'ai Ao, 1882-1916), Yunnan general and strategist who became famous as commander-in-chief of the National Salvation Armies (1915-1916) against Yuan Shikai (袁世凯)
蔡伦 Cài Lún Cai Lun (formerly translated as Ts'ai Lun, ? -121), known as inventor of paper making
蔡司 Càisī Carl Zeiss (1816-1888), German entrepreneur and manufacturer of precision optical instruments:～透镜 Zeiss lens
蔡特金 Càitèjīn Clara Zetkin (1857-1933), left-wing leader of the Second International and German Social Democratic Party as well as leader of women's movement in Germany
蔡襄 Cài Xiāng Cai Xiang (1012-1067), calligrapher of Northern Song Dynasty
蔡元培 Cài Yuánpéi Cai Yuanpei (formerly translated as Ts'ai Yuan-p'ei, 1868-1940), educationist

𦈢 cài

see"綷𦈢" cuìcài

cān

餐(飡、湌) cān

❶ eat:会～ dine together; have a dinner party /野～ have a picnic /就～ go (to a dining-hall or restaurant) for one's meal /饱～一顿 have a square meal; eat one's fill /少食多～ have more (than three) meals daily but eat less each time ❷ food; meal:中～ Chinese food /西～ Western food /快～ fast food; snack /晚～ dinner; supper /自助～ buffet /圣～ Holy Communion

❸〈量词〉*used for meals*：一日三～ three meals a day

餐车 cānchē restaurant car; dining car; diner

餐点 cāndiǎn refreshments; pastry

餐风宿露 cānfēng-sùlù *also* "风餐露宿" eat in the wind and sleep in the dew — endure the hardships of an arduous journey

餐馆 cānguǎn restaurant：～文化 restaurant culture

餐后酒 cānhòujiǔ after-dinner drinks

餐会 cānhuì dine together (usu. on festive occasions); have a dinner party

餐巾 cānjīn table napkin

餐巾纸 cānjīnzhǐ paper napkin; napkin paper

餐酒 cānjiǔ dinner wine

餐具 cānjù tableware; dinner service or set

餐盘 cānpán dinner plate

餐前酒 cānqiánjiǔ aperitif

餐券 cānquàn meal coupon;

餐室 cānshì dining-room

餐贴 cāntiē food allowance; food subsidy

餐厅 cāntīng dining room; dining hall; restaurant

餐位 cānwèi seats (for customers) in a restaurant

餐饮 cānyǐn food and drink：提供～ provide food and drinks

餐饮业 cānyǐnyè catering (trade)

餐桌 cānzhuō dining table

餐桌转盘 cānzhuō zhuànpán lazy Susan

鲹 cān

鲹鲦 cāntiáo 〈动物〉*Hemiculter leucisculus*

参[1]（參） cān

❶ join; take part in; participate：他去年～了军。He joined the army (*or* enlisted) last year. ❷ refer; consult：内～ reference news for restricted circulation

参[2]（參） cān

❶ call to pay one's respects; pay homage to ❷ impeach an official before the emperor：～他一本 bring a charge against him at imperial court / ～倒当朝宰相 impeach the chief minister and succeed in bringing about his removal from office

参[3]（參） cān

〈书面〉explore and grasp (the meaning, significance, etc.)

see also cēn; shēn

参拜 cānbài pay homage to; pay respects to：～中山陵 pay homage to the Mausoleum of Dr. Sun Yat-sen (1866-1925)

参半 cānbàn half; fifty-fifty：疑信～ half believing, half doubting / 毁誉～ get both praise and censure

参变量 cānbiànliàng 〈数学〉parameter

参禅 cānchán Buddhist's practice of meditation for penetration of truth：～悟道 try to reach into the realm of truth by meditation

参处 cānchǔ ❶ consider and solve (a problem) ❷ impeach and punish：自请～ ask for disciplinary action to be taken against oneself

参订 cāndìng participate in revising (a plan, treaty, book, etc.)

参定 cāndìng participate in the drawing up or mapping out (of a plan, programme, etc.)：～大计 jointly work out a policy of cardinal importance

参革 cāngé 〈书面〉impeach and remove from office

参股 cāngǔ buy shares; become a shareholder：企业之间可以互相～。Different enterprises may buy one another's shares.

参观 cānguān visit; look around：～历史博物馆 visit the Museum of History / 组织～ organize a visit (to a place) / ～团 visiting group / ～日程 programme of a visit; itinerary / 欢迎～。Visitors are welcome.

参合 cānhé 〈书面〉draw on：～其要 draw on the essence (of sth.) / ～各地经验，并在理论上作了些探索 explore and synthesize the experience of various localities from the theoretical point of view

参劾 cānhé 〈书面〉impeach

参会 cānhuì attend a meeting：～单位 organizations attending the meeting; participating organizations

参稽 cānjī 〈书面〉inspect and examine; investigate and check

参加 cānjiā ❶ join; take part in; be a member of：～作家协会 join the Writers' Union / ～工作 begin one's career / ～学术会议 participate in an academic meeting (*or* conference, *or* symposium) / ～考试 take an exam; sit for an exam / ～开学典礼 attend a school's opening ceremony / 积极～体育活动 actively go in for sports ❷ give advice, suggestion, etc.：工会工作如何开展，请你～意见。Hope you will give your opinion about how to do a good job of trade union work.

参加国 cānjiāguó 〈法律〉(of treaties and conventions) acceding state

参见 cānjiàn ❶ see also; cf.：～《中国近代史》第一章第一节。See also Section 1, Chapter 1 of *Modern History of China*. ❷ pay one's respects to (a superior, etc.)：群僧～主持。All the monks came to pay respects to the abbot.

参校 cānjiào ❶ revise; read and examine (the text of a book)：这部著作有三位著名学者～。The manuscript of the book was carefully read and checked by three eminent scholars. ❷ collate：本书以通行本为底本，另外～过其他七种版本。The book is based on the popular text as the master copy while seven other versions have been consulted.

参决 cānjué take part in decision-making：～政事 take part in making decisions for the government

参军 cānjūn join the army; join the services; enlist：他～后不久即开赴前线。He was sent to the front shortly after he joined the army.

参看 cānkàn ❶ consult：这个问题，你可～《北京年鉴》。As for this question, you may as well consult *the Annals of Beijing*. ❷ see also：～第三章第二节。See also Section II, Chapter III.

参考 cānkǎo ❶ read; consult; refer to：他写这本书～了几十种书刊。He read scores of books and journals before he started writing the book. / 必须～有关资料。It is necessary to consult relevant materials. / 不～原来的方案就很难提出妥善的建议。We cannot make appropriate recommendations without reference to the original plan. ❷ information; reference：有～价值 may serve as reference / 仅供～ for one's information (*or* reference) only ❸ *see* "参看 ❷"

参考点 cānkǎodiǎn 〈建筑〉reference point

参考群体 cānkǎo qúntǐ reference group

参考书 cānkǎoshū reference book：查阅～ consult reference books / 必读～ required reading (list)

参考书目 cānkǎo shūmù list of reference books; bibliography：列举有关的～ make a list of books consulted / 附有～。A bibliography is attached.

参考图书馆 cānkǎo túshūguǎn reference library

参考系 cānkǎoxì *also* "参照系" reference frame

参考资料 cānkǎo zīliào reference material：提供～ provide materials for reference

参量 cānliàng reference quantity; 〈数学〉parameter：～元件电子计算机 〈计算机〉parametric electronic computer

参量变化 cānliàng biànhuà parametric variation

参谋 cānmóu ❶ staff officer：作战～ combat (*or* operations) staff (officer) / 侦察～ reconnaissance staff (officer) / 通讯～ communications staff (officer) ❷ give advice; advise; serve as an adviser：这件事你给我～～。I would like to have your advice on this matter. / 老王真是你的好～。Lao Wang serves as a good adviser for you.

参谋部 cānmóubù general staff

参谋长 cānmóuzhǎng chief of staff

参谋长联席会议 Cānmóuzhǎng Liánxí Huìyì (US) Joint Chiefs of Staff (JCS)：～主席 (US) Chairman of the Joint Chiefs of Staff

参评 cānpíng be sent in for public appraisal or competitive selection：这次图书奖评比，他有两本著作～。He has two of his works nominated for appraisal and selection for the Book Awards.

参赛 cānsài take part in the competition：～的田径选手 athletes for track and field events

参事 cānshì counsellor; adviser：国务院～ consultant to the State Council / 当时国民政府驻巴黎使馆～ counsellor of the embassy of the then Nationalist Government (of China) in Paris

参事官 cānshìguān (Japan) counsellor：日本防卫厅～ Counsellor of the Defence Agency of Japan

参事室 cānshìshì office of consultants：国务院～ Office of Consultants to the State Council

参试 cānshì ❶ take part in an experiment：～的科研人员 scientific research personnel who take part in the experiment ❷ take or sit for an exam：报名～ sign up for the exam / ～者达万人。Around 10,000 people took the exam.

参数 cānshù 〈数学〉parameter

参数函数 cānshù hánshù parametric function

参孙 Cānsūn Samson, Israeli hero of vast strength in *The Book*

of Judges, Old Testament

参天 cāntiān reaching to the sky; towering into the clouds; very tall: ～大楼 high-rise building; skyscraper /～古木 tall ancient trees /松柏～。The pine and cypress trees soared into the skies.

参透 cāntòu have or gain a thorough understanding: 参不透 fail to understand /～禅理 have a deep understanding of Zen-Buddhist philosophy /～机关 see through the scheme

参悟 cānwù understand by meditation

参详 cānxiáng consider and examine; study in detail: ～许久 study (sth.) carefully for a long while /我把拟定的计划摆出来，请大家～。I am putting forward the draft plan for your consideration.

参选 cānxuǎn ❶ enter into an election contest; run in an election: ～的政界头面人物 prominent political figures running in the election ❷ enter a contest for public appraisal: ～作品 works entered for appraisal and selection (in a contest)

C

参演 cānyǎn put on a performance (at a party, gala, etc.)

参验 cānyàn examine and verify; compare and evaluate: 这些措施是否正确尚待～。Whether these measures are correct remains to be verified.

参谒 cānyè pay one's respects; pay homage: ～国画大师 pay one's respects to a master of Chinese painting /～烈士陵园 pay homage at the martyrs' mausoleum /～无名英雄纪念碑 pay one's respects at the monument to unknown heroes

参议 cānyì ❶〈书面〉take part in the planning or deliberation (of sth.): ～国事 take part in the deliberation of state affairs ❷ adviser; counsellor

参议员 cānyìyuán senator

参议院 cānyìyuàn senate; (Japan) House of Councillors

参映 cānyìng present a film in a film festival

参与 cānyù *also* "参预" participate in; have a hand in: ～其事 have a hand in the matter /～其间 have a finger in the pie /～工程设计 participate in the designing of the project /～决策 take part in decision-making /～政治阴谋 be involved in a political plot /～意识 sense of participation

参预 cānyù *see* "参与"

参院 cānyuàn (short for 参议院) senate: 参、众两院 (US) the Senate and the House

参阅 cānyuè see also; consult; refer to: 请～第23页第二段。Please see p.23, paragraph 2. /此材料启发思路，足资～。The material is thought-provoking and well worth reading.

参杂 cānzá mix; mingle: 河滩上乱石～。Rugged stones of all sizes intermingled on the beach. /她～在民工中间，直奔工地。She mingled among the labourers, heading straight for the worksite.

参赞 cānzàn ❶ counsellor: 政务～ political counsellor /商务～ commercial counsellor /文化～ cultural counsellor (*or* attaché) /教育～ educational counsellor /经济～ economic counsellor /科技～ counsellor for scientific and technological affairs /公使衔～ minister-counsellor ❷〈书面〉act as adviser on a matter of importance: ～军务 advise (sb.) on military affairs

参展 cānzhǎn supply exhibits for an exhibition; participate in an exhibition: ～作品 works on display (at an exhibition) /～厂家 factories and enterprises participating in the exhibition

参战 cānzhàn enter a war; go to war: ～部队 combat troops

参战国 cānzhànguó belligerent state

参照 cānzhào consult; refer to: 这个办法好，你可～实行。This method is fine, and you may as well try it. /～兄弟单位的经验，制订了本规定。These regulations were drawn up in the light of the experience of other organizations.

参照物 cānzhàowù object of reference

参照系 cānzhàoxì 〈物理〉reference frame

参证 cānzhèng corroborate; check: 那本书可作我们意见的～资料。That book can serve to corroborate our opinion.

参政 cānzhèng participate in managing the state: ～议政 participate in the deliberation and administration of state affairs

参政党 cānzhèngdǎng participating party (i. e. party participating in government and state affairs alongside the ruling party)

参酌 cānzhuó deliberate; consider sth. in the light of actual conditions: ～处理 handle (sth.) at one's discretion /上级部门再三～，才批准了这个项目。It was after much deliberation that the higher authorities approved this project.

骖(驂) cān

〈古语〉outside two (one on either side) of a team of horses

cán

惭(慚) cán

feel ashamed: 自～ feel ashamed of oneself; feel small /大言不～ be shamelessly boastful; brag brazenly

惭惶 cánhuáng feel ashamed and uneasy: 深感～ feel very much embarrassed and consider oneself unworthy of other people's regard

惭愧 cánkuì be ashamed: ～不安 feel ashamed and uneasy /工作没做好，我很～。I feel guilty for not having done my work properly.

惭恧 cánnǜ 〈书面〉be ashamed

惭色 cánsè 〈书面〉expression of shame; guilty countenance: 面带～ look ashamed

惭颜 cányán 〈书面〉ashamed look; guilty expression: 令人～ make one feel ashamed

惭怍 cánzuò 〈书面〉be ashamed; feel sorry: 自增～ feel increasingly ashamed (*or* sorry)

蚕(蠶) cán

silkworm: 家～ Chinese silkworm /野～ wild silkworm /柞～ tussah

蚕宝宝 cánbǎobǎo 〈方言〉silkworm

蚕匾 cánbiǎn 〈方言〉*see* "蚕箔"

蚕箔 cánbó bamboo tray for raising silkworms

蚕蔟 káncù small bundle of straw for silkworms to spin cocoons on

蚕豆 cándòu broad bean

蚕豆病 cándòubìng 〈医学〉favism

蚕豆象 cándòuxiàng bruchid weevil

蚕蛾 cán'é silk moth

蚕腐败病 cánfǔbàibìng gattine

蚕褐僵病 cánhèjiāngbìng bronen muscarine

蚕茧 cánjiǎn silkworm cocoon: ～大战 silkworm cocoon trade war

蚕眠 cánmián chrysalis state of the silkworm before it emerges (*or* sheds) its skin from the cocoon

蚕农 cánnóng silkworm raiser; sericulturist

蚕桑 cánsāng growing mulberry and raising silkworms; sericulture

蚕沙 cánshā silkworm excrement

蚕山 cánshān 〈方言〉small bundle of straw for silkworms to weave cocoons on

蚕食 cánshí nibble: ～邻国领土 nibble away a neighbour's territory /强国～弱国 case of a big country nibbling at a small country

蚕食鲸吞 cánshí-jīngtūn nibble away like a silkworm and swallow like a whale — seize another country's territory by piecemeal encroachment or wholesale annexation

蚕食政策 cánshí zhèngcè policy of piecemeal encroachment; nibbling policy

蚕事 cánshì all kinds of work involved in silkworm breeding

蚕室 cánshì ❶ room for raising silkworms ❷〈古语〉prison where people were castrated as a punishment

蚕丝 cánsī natural silk; silk

蚕蚁 cányǐ newly-hatched silkworm

蚕蛹 cányǒng silkworm chrysalis

蚕蛹油 cányǒngyóu oil extracted from silkworm chrysalis (for industrial use); silkworm chrysalis oil

蚕纸 cánzhǐ paper with silkworm eggs

蚕子 cánzǐ silkworm seed or egg

残(殘) cán

❶ incomplete; deficient; disabled: ～本 incomplete text /因公致～ become disabled on public account ❷ remnant; remaining: ～敌 remnants of the enemy forces /～冬 last days of winter /～夜 end of night /风卷～云 strong wind scattering wisps of clouds — making a clean sweep of sth. ❸ injure; damage: 摧～ beat cruelly; tread underfoot; ride roughshod over ❹ savage; barbarous; ferocious: 凶～ cruel; ruthless

残败 cánbài dilapidated; decrepit: ～不堪 totally defaced; be damaged beyond recognition /～破落 be in bad repair /村子里呈现出战后的～景象。The village was a scene of desolation after the battle (*or* war).

残暴 cánbào cruel and ferocious; ruthless; brutal; savage: ～的敌

人 cruel and ferocious enemy /～的统治 ruthless rule /极尽～之能事 reach the height of cruelty and savagery; brutal (*or* ruthless) to the extreme /匪徒烧杀抢掠,非常～。The savage bandits wouldn't stop burning, killing and looting.

残杯冷炙 cánbēi-lěngzhì *also*"残羹冷炙";"残桨冷炙";"残羹剩饭" leftovers of a meal:为人要有骨气,不能靠别人施舍的～生活。A man should have a sense of dignity; he should not live on others' handouts.

残本 cánběn incomplete ancient text

残编断简 cánbiān-duànjiǎn fragments of ancient texts *see also*"残篇断简"

残兵 cánbīng remnants of an army after defeat

残兵败将 cánbīng-bàijiàng remnants of a routed army:～,难以收拾。The troops were so badly battered in battle that they could not be regrouped. /～,士气不振。The routed troops were entirely demoralized.

残部 cánbù remnants of a routed army

残喘 cánchuǎn last gasps (as of a dying person):苟延～ be at one's last gasp; be on one's last legs

残次 cáncì defective or substandard:～品 defective product /用～零件拼装的计算机 computer assembled with substandard parts

残存 cáncún remnant; remaining; surviving:一场火灾过后,仅有这些东西～下来。These are the only things which survived the fire.

残灯末庙 cándēng-mòmiào the lights are going out and the fair is drawing to a close — a period of decline; on the verge of extinction:他只赶上了清朝的～。He happened to live in the last days of the Qing Dynasty.

残敌 cándí remnants of enemy troops

残毒 cándú ❶ savage:～掠夺 savage plunder ❷ residual poison:～积累 residual poison accumulation /蔬菜中的农药～ residual toxicant from farm pesticides in vegetables

残而不废 cán'érbùfèi disabled but still useful to the community

残匪 cánfěi remaining or residual bandits

残废 cánfèi ❶ maimed; disabled:他身体～了。He has been disabled for life. ❷ disabled or maimed person:车祸之后,他成了个～。He was disabled (*or* maimed) in the traffic accident.

残废军人 cánfèi jūnrén disabled serviceman:～证 disabled serviceman's certificate

残废证 cánfèizhèng ❶disabled serviceman's certificate ❷ certificate for the handicapped

残羹剩饭 cángēng-shèngfàn leftovers (of a meal) *see also*"残杯冷炙"

残骸 cánhái remains; wreckage:失事飞机～ wreckage of a crashed plane

残害 cánhài brutally injure or kill:～生命 kill wantonly; inflict serious (*or* mortal) injuries on human lives /～无辜 slaughter innocent people /～忠良 ruthlessly persecute the loyal and virtuous

残花败柳 cánhuā-bàiliǔ faded flowers and withered willows — faded beauty or fallen woman

残毁 cánhuǐ broken; dilapidated; wrecked; disabled:～的躯体 physical wreck /庙宇～ dilapidated temples

残货 cánhuò shopworn goods; damaged goods; substandard goods:退换～ return and exchange damaged goods /清仓处理～ clearance sales of substandard goods

残积 cánjī *also*"残积物"〈地质〉saprolite; eluvium:～相 eluvial facies

残迹 cánjì faint trace or sign; indistinct vestige:劫后～ vestiges of the scourge /～犹存。Faint traces are still visible.

残疾 cánji deformity; handicap:从小落下的～ deformity contracted in childhood /身体～ physical deformity

残疾人 cánjirén disabled person; the handicapped:～福利基金会 welfare fund for the handicapped /～保障法 law on the protection of the handicapped

残疾人奥运会 Cánjirén Àoyùnhuì (shortened as 残奥会) Paralympics

残烬 cánjìn cinders; ashes

残旧 cánjiù broken and shabby; dilapidated:房舍～不堪。The buildings are in a state of disrepair.

残局 cánjú ❶ final phase of a game of chess; endgame:～多变。A game of chess is often full of surprises in the final phase. ❷ situation resulting from a debacle or social unrest:收拾～ clear up the mess; pick up the pieces /～已无法挽回。The situation is beyond (*or* past) retrieval.

残苛 cánkē 〈书面〉cruel; ruthless; merciless:施政～ tyrannical rule; carry out a ruthless policy /蠲除～ be rid of (*or* be free from) cruelty

残刻 cánkè 〈书面〉❶ cruel and mean:～狠毒 cruel and vicious ❷ brutally injure:互相～ engage in mutual slaughter

残酷 cánkù cruel; brutal; ruthless:～的手段 ruthless method /～镇压 brutally suppress /～地折磨 cruelly torment /～地杀害 kill people in cold blood /～的战争环境锻炼了他。He was steeled in the harsh turmoil of war.

残联 Cánlián (short for 残疾人联合会) Association of Physically Challenged Persons

残留 cánliú remain; be left over:被烧的衣物只～一些碎片。Of the burnt clothes only bits and pieces remained.

残留电弧 cánliú diànhú 〈物理〉residual arc

残留量 cánliúliàng residual amount:～测定 determination of the residual amount

残留物 cánliúwù residue

残年 cánnián ❶ evening of one's life; declining years:人至七十,已届风烛～。At seventy, a person is like a candle in the wind. ❷ last days of the year:～腊月 last month of the year /天寒地冻,又近～。It was freezing cold towards the end of the year.

残孽 cánniè remnant evil-doers; evil elements from a previous regime; diehards of the *ancien régime*

残虐 cánnüè ❶ savage and ferocious; brutal:采取～的手段 by brutal means ❷ treat cruelly:～囚犯 ill-treat prisoners

残篇断简 cánpiān-duànjiǎn *also*"断编残简" fragments of ancient texts:出土的～ unearthed fragments of ancient texts /浩劫中幸存的～ fragments of ancient texts that survived the catastrophe

残品 cánpǐn damaged article; defective goods:仔细找出～和次品 carefully sift out the defective and substandard goods /～率逐月下降。The rate of defective products declined month by month.

残破 cánpò broken; dilapidated:～的水罐 broken water jar /几间～的房舍 several dilapidated houses

残棋 cánqí last phase of a chess or *weiqi* game; endgame:下～他最拿手。He is at his best in the last phase of a chess (*or weiqi* game). /～很有看头。Endgames are always interesting to watch.

残缺 cánquē incomplete; fragmentary:一套～的餐具 an incomplete dinner service /一方～的古砚 a broken ancient inkstone /这本书已～不全。This book has missing pages.

残忍 cánrěn cruel; ruthless:～成性 brutal by nature /这个杀人犯的手段十分～。The way in which the murderer perpetrated his crime was cruel beyond measure.

残杀 cánshā murder; massacre; slaughter:自相～ mutual slaughter

残山剩水 cánshān-shèngshuǐ *also*"剩水残山" desolate state of a broken country after disaster (e.g. national chaos or foreign invasion)

残生 cánshēng ❶ one's remaining years:了此～ conclude one's last years; put an end to one's remaining life /老先生孑然一身,在清贫中苦度～。The old gentleman was all alone and lived out his remaining years in poverty. ❷ surviving span of life:他在纳粹监狱里受尽折磨,幸保～。He suffered all forms of torture in a Nazi prison, and came out alive by sheer luck.

残剩 cánshèng remaining; remnant:～的茶饭 leftovers (of a meal) /雨停了,低空～着灰暗的云彩。The rain stopped, the dark-grey clouds still hanging low.

残数 cánshù 〈数学〉residue

残损 cánsǔn (of goods) broken; damaged:由于商品包装不好,在运输途中～较多。As a result of poor packaging, a considerable amount of goods was damaged in transit.

残效 cánxiào residual toxicity (of pesticides):～期 time of residual toxicity

残雪 cánxuě melting snow; thawing snow

残压 cányā 〈电学〉residual voltage

残阳 cányáng setting sun:～西下。The waning sun is setting in the west. /从头越,苍山如海,～如血。We are crossing its summit, The rolling hills sea-blue, The dying sun blood-red.

残佚 cányì (of books) damaged or lost; scattered and lost:所藏图书,战乱中～甚多。Many of his collected books were damaged or lost during the war.

残油 cányóu residual oil

残余 cányú remnants; remains; survivals; vestiges:封建～ vestiges of feudalism /～势力 remnant forces
残余奥氏体 cányú àoshìtǐ 〈冶金〉residual or retained austenite
残余电流 cányú diànliú aftercurrent
残余国会 Cányú Guóhuì Rump Parliament (that part of the Long Parliament which continued to sit after Pride's Purge in 1648 in England)
残余应力 cányú yìnglì 〈物理〉residual stress or strain
残垣断壁 cányuán-duànbì *also* "断壁残垣"; "颓垣断壁" tuíyuán-duànbì broken walls:一眼望去,尽是～。There was nothing but ruins as far as the eye could see.
残月 cányuè ❶ waning moon:～如钩。The waning moon became a crescent. ❷ setting moon:天幕上悬挂着淡淡的～。The setting moon hangs dim in the sky.
残渣 cánzhā residue; dregs
残渣余孽 cánzhā-yúniè evil elements from the old society; dregs of the old society:他被当作～开除了。He was labelled an evil element from the old society and sacked.
残照 cánzhào afterglow of the setting sun; evening glow:～中群山似乎抹上了一层神奇的色彩。The evening glow seemed to daub the hills with a fantastic colour.
残值 cánzhí 〈经济〉scrap value

cǎn

憯 cǎn 〈书面〉*see* "惨" cǎn
惨(慘) cǎn ❶ miserable; pitiful; tragic:～遭不幸 be killed in an accident; meet with a tragic death /～不忍闻 be too horrifying to hear /她早年的遭遇很～。She had a tragic early life. ❷ roundly; terribly; exceedingly:冻～了 suffer terribly from the cold / 这场球赛我们败～了。We were roundly defeated in the ball game. ❸ cruel; savage
惨案 cǎn'àn ❶ massacre:流血～ bloody massacre /制造一起空前残酷的～ engineer savage massacre never heard of before ❷ disastrous incident; disaster:列车相撞的～ disastrous trains collision
惨白 cǎnbái ❶ pale:～的月光 pale moonlight ❷ look deathly pale: 他说话时面容～。He looked deathly pale while he was speaking.
惨败 cǎnbài crushing or disastrous defeat:遭到～ suffer a crushing defeat /险遭～ all but suffer a devastating defeat; narrowly escape a disastrous defeat
惨变 cǎnbiàn ❶ disastrous turn of events:经此～,他显得衰老了。He looked aged after the disastrous turn of events. ❷ (of complexion) change greatly out of fear, sorrow, illness, etc.:他脸色～。His face turned frightfully pale.
惨不忍睹 cǎnbùrěndǔ too horrifying to look at; so appalling that one could not bear the sight:空难现场～。The scene of the air crash was just horrible.
惨惨 cǎncǎn ❶ depressed; worried:忧心～ heavy-hearted; be eaten up with anxiety ❷ gloomy; dark:阴风～。Gusts of chilly wind added to the settled gloom.
惨恻 cǎncè 〈书面〉wretched; miserable; tragic
惨怛 cǎndá 〈书面〉heartbroken; grieved; grief-stricken:家人离散,心中～。He was grief-stricken when he thought of his dispersed family.
惨淡 cǎndàn *also* "惨澹" ❶ gloomy; dull; bleak; dismal:天色～ gloomy sky (*or* weather) /～的灯光 dim lamp light /残阳～的余光 bleak rays of the setting sun ❷ dreary; desolate; depressed:秋风～ desolate autumnal wind /神情～ desolate (*or* sad) look /生意～ *also* "市面～" slack business; depressed trade ❸ painstaking; laborious
惨淡经营 cǎndàn-jīngyíng build up a business by laborious effort and persistence; keep an enterprise going by painstaking effort; take great pains to carry on one's work under difficult circumstances:老王～,商店才有现在的规模。The department store has grown to the present size thanks to Lao Wang's painstaking effort.
惨毒 cǎndú merciless; ruthless; cruel:心肠～ merciless heart /～的刑罚 cruel torture (*or* punishment)
惨祸 cǎnhuò horrible disaster; frightful calamity:飞机失事,造成了二百多人罹难的～。The plane crash took a toll of more than two hundred lives.
惨叫 cǎnjiào heart-rending cry; heart-breaking shriek; blood-curdling scream
惨景 cǎnjǐng tragic scene; miserable picture
惨境 cǎnjìng miserable condition; tragic circumstances; dire straits:这个小女孩七岁时父母双亡,陷入被人拐卖的～。The little girl lost both parents when she was barely seven, and fell into the clutches of kidnappers.
惨沮 cǎnjǔ 〈书面〉miserable; depressed; dejected
惨剧 cǎnjù tragedy; calamity:人间～ human tragedy /一个烟头引起大火,酿成了家毁人亡的～。An unextinguished cigarette butt caused a big fire which took a toll of human lives on top of the loss of homes.
惨绝人寰 cǎnjué-rénhuán tragic beyond compare in this human world; extremely tragic; exceedingly brutal or horrible:～的暴行 atrocities unprecedented in human history; most atrocious brutalities
惨刻 cǎnkè 〈书面〉vicious; venomous:狡诈～ crafty and venomous
惨苦 cǎnkǔ miserable; wretched:～的生活 miserable life /命运～ wretched fate /～的面容 woeful appearance
惨酷 cǎnkù very cruel; ruthless:～的遭遇 bitter experience; hard lot /～的浩劫 terrible calamity; hear-trending turmoil
惨况 cǎnkuàng tragic condition; pitiful sight
惨厉 cǎnlì sorrowful; hear-trending; mournful:～的哀乐声 sorrowful funeral strains /西北风～地叫着。A northwestern wind was shrieking mournfully.
惨烈 cǎnliè ❶ miserable; tragic:～的景象 miserable scene ❷ heroic:～牺牲 give one's life heroically; die a heroic death ❸ fierce; terrible:冰霜～ severe frost /～的寒风 cold wind cutting one to the quick /一场～的战斗在山下展开了。A fierce battle was unfolding at the foot of the mountain.
惨绿愁红 cǎnlǜ-chóuhóng withered leaves and flowers; worries of a young woman in love
惨然 cǎnrán saddened; grieved:心中～ heartbroken; heartsore /她～一笑,显露出内心有莫大的悲哀。She gave a sad smile as if to show that she was eating her heart out.
惨杀 cǎnshā murder; massacre; kill in cold blood:～无辜百姓 massacre innocent civilians /遭人～ be killed in cold blood
惨死 cǎnsǐ die a tragic death
惨痛 cǎntòng extremely grieved; painful; bitter:～的教训 bitter lesson /～的遭遇 tragic experience /～的话语 sad (*or* hear-trending) remarks
惨无人道 cǎnwúréndào very cruel and inhuman:～的血案 inhuman murder case
惨象 cǎnxiàng miserable situation; tragic scene
惨笑 cǎnxiào wan smile:无声的～ silent wan smile
惨遭不测 cǎnzāo-bùcè *also* "惨遭不幸" die an unexpected death; meet a tragic end:他在那次空难中～。He died a tragic death in the air crash.
惨重 cǎnzhòng heavy; grievous; disastrous:损失～ extremely heavy losses /伤亡～ suffer grievous casualties
惨壮 cǎnzhuàng tragic and heroic:～的厮杀 tragic and heroic fight at close quarters
惨状 cǎnzhuàng miserable condition; pitiful sight:～使人目不忍睹。It was (a sight) too dreadful to look at. /见此～,心中悲愤万分。The sight of the tragic scene filled me with boundless grief and indignation.
黪(黲) cǎn 〈书面〉❶ dark; darkly:～黩 dismally dark ❷ dim; dusky
篸(篸) cǎn 〈方言〉a kind of bin or pan
see also zān
穇(穇) cǎn
穇子 cǎnzi 〈植物〉billion-dollar grass

càn

灿(燦) càn bright; resplendent; dazzling:～若云锦

bright as brocade /黄～～的油菜花 bright-yellow rape flowers

灿烂 cànlàn magnificent; splendid; resplendent; bright: 灯光～ brightly lit /繁星～ brilliantly shining stars /辉煌～的时代 magnificent (*or* splendid) era /～的古老文明 glorious ancient civilization /经济改革取得了光辉～的成就。Magnificent achievements have been scored in economic reforms. /花园里的鲜花～夺目。The flowers in the garden are a dazzling sight of beauty. /前途无比～。The prospects are incomparably bright.

灿然 cànrán bright; beaming: 窗外阳光～。The sun shines brightly outside the window. /室内灯光～。The room is brilliant with the lights on. *or* The room is brightly lit.

粲

càn 〈书面〉❶ bright; beaming ❷ smile beamingly: 以博一～ for your entertainment

粲然 cànrán 〈书面〉❶ brilliant; bright: 文采～ brilliant style of writing ❷ remarkable; obvious; apparent: ～可见的成就 marked achievements ❸ broad smile; smilingly: ～一笑 give a beaming smile; grin with delight

璨

càn ❶ beautiful jade ❷ *see* "粲" càn

掺(摻)

càn a kind of ancient drum music

see also chān; shǎn

孱

càn

see also chán

孱头 càntou 〈方言〉〈粗话〉weakling; coward

cāng

仓(倉)

cāng ❶ warehouse; storeroom; storehouse: 粮～ barn; granary /颗粒归～ every grain to the granary ❷ (Cāng) a surname

仓廒 cāng'áo 〈书面〉granary

仓巴噶波 Cāngbā Gābō 〈佛教〉Tshangs-pa Dkar-po, one of eight guardians in Tibetan Buddhism

仓储 cāngchǔ keep grain, goods, etc. in a storehouse; put goods in storage: ～的粮食十分充足。We have a plentiful store of grain. /尽量避免商品在～过程中的损耗。It is necessary to reduce as far as possible the spoilage of goods during storage.

仓储式超市 cāngchǔshì chāoshì warehouse-type supermarket

仓储销售 cāngchǔ xiāoshòu cash and carry: ～商店 cash-and-carry store

仓促 cāngcù *also* "仓猝"; "仓卒" hurriedly; hastily; suddenly: 时间～ be pressed for time; be in a hurry /～应战 accept battle in haste; put up a flurry of resistance /～离去 leave all of a sudden; leave hastily /不要～下结论。Don't jump to conclusions.

仓猝 cāngcù *see* "仓促"

仓房 cāngfáng warehouse; storehouse

仓庚 cānggēng *also* "鸧鹒" cānggēng oriole

仓皇 cānghuáng *also* "仓黄"; "苍黄" cānghuáng in panic; in a flurry; flustered: ～逃遁 flee in panic; flee helter-skelter; flee in confusion /～退却 retreat in confusion; beat a hasty retreat

仓皇失措 cānghuáng-shīcuò be scared out of one's wits; be panic-stricken; get into a panic: 剧场失火时, 观众～。When the theatre caught fire, the audience was thrown into panic. /在危险情况下, 千万不可～。Don't panic when faced with danger — that's the most thing.

仓颉 Cāng Jié Cang Jie (formerly translated as Ts'ang Chieh), legendary creator of Chinese characters

仓库 cāngkù warehouse; storehouse; depository: 文物～ antique storeroom /～保管员 warehouseman /清理～ check warehouse stocks; make an inventory of warehouse stocks

仓廪 cānglǐn 〈书面〉granary: ～实而天下安。With the granaries full, people feel secure all over the country. /～实而知礼节。When the granaries are full, people learn rites and etiquette.

仓容 cāngróng storage capacity: ～有限 (due to) limited storage capacity

仓舍 cāngshè barn

仓鼠 cāngshǔ 〈动物〉hamster

仓务员 cāngwùyuán warehouseman

仓鸮 cāngxiāo barn owl

仓租 cāngzū warehouse storage charge

沧(滄)

cāng (of water) dark blue

沧海 cānghǎi the sea; the deep blue sea

沧海横流 cānghǎi-héngliú the deep, blue sea running high and wide — chaotic situation or social turmoil like turbulent tides from a vast ocean sweeping over the land; the political situation is chaotic and society unstable: ～, 方显出英雄本色。It's in a turbulent world that a hero shows his mettle.

沧海桑田 cānghǎi-sāngtián *also* "桑田沧海" seas change into mulberry fields — time brings great changes to the world

see also "沧桑"

沧海一粟 cānghǎi-yīsù one grain afloat on a vast ocean; a drop in the ocean: 在亿万群众之中, 个人不过是～罢了。An individual in the midst of hundreds of millions of people is but a drop in the ocean.

沧海遗珠 cānghǎi-yízhū a pearl left in the vast sea — neglected, undiscovered talent; neglected talented people

沧浪诗话 Cānglàng Shīhuà *Essays on Poetry*, written by Yan Yu (严羽) of the Southern Song Dynasty

沧桑 cāngsāng (short for 沧海桑田): 饱经～ have experienced many vicissitudes of life (*or* fortune) /天若有情天亦老, 人间正道是～。Were nature sentient, she too would pass from youth to age, But Man's world is mutable, seas become mulberry fields.

苍(蒼)

cāng ❶ green; blue: ～松翠柏 verdant pines and cypresses /～天 blue sky ❷ grey; ashy: ～髯 grey beard ❸ 〈书面〉heaven; sky: 上～ heaven above ❹ (Cāng) a surname

苍白 cāngbái ❶ pale; pallid; wan: ～无力 pale and weak /吓得面色～ turn pale with fear ❷ feeble; weak; insufficient: 论据～无力 feeble argument

苍苍 cāngcāng ❶ greyish white; ashen: 两鬓～ have greying temples /白发～ hoary-haired ❷ deep-blue: 天～ the sky is blue ❸ luxuriant; endless; boundless: 郁郁～ green woodland stretches far into the distance /山海～ great expanse of hills and sea /西山～。The western hills are distant and hazy.

苍葱 cāngcōng dark green; verdant: ～的松柏 green (*or* verdant) pine and cypress

苍翠 cāngcuì dark green; verdant: ～的竹林 verdant groves of bamboo /～的山峦 verdant hills; green mountains

苍耳 cāng'ěr 〈植物〉Siberian cocklebur (*Xanthium Sibiricum*); clotbur: ～子〈中药〉achene of Siberian cocklebur

苍古 cānggǔ austere and vigorous: 笔势～ austere and vigorous sweep (in brushwork or calligraphy)

苍黑 cānghēi ❶ (of trees and grass) dark green: 夕阳下山林显得格外～。The wooded mountains look especially dark in the setting sun. ❷ (of colour) dark: 皮肤～ dark complexion ❸ dusky

苍黄 cānghuáng ❶ greenish-yellow; greyish-yellow: 面色～ have a sallow complexion /～的天空 sombre skies ❷ 〈书面〉green and yellow — changeable: ～翻覆 undergo constant change; change irregularly ❸ in panic; in a flurry: 钟山风雨起～。Over Zhongshan (i. e. Nanjing) swept a storm, headlong.

苍劲 cāngjìng ❶ old and strong: ～青松 hardy, old, green pines ❷ (of calligraphy or painting) vigorous; bold: ～有力 vigorous and forceful /笔法～ bold, vigorous strokes of brushwork

苍空 cāngkōng sky; heaven: 阴沉的～ gloomy sky

苍老 cānglǎo ❶ (of appearance, voice) old; aged: 母亲显得～了。Mother looks old (*or* aged). /忧虑使他一夜之间变得～了。Anxiety aged him overnight. ❷ (of calligraphy or painting) firm and vigorous; forceful

苍凉 cāngliáng desolate; bleak: ～的山坡 desolate mountainside /月色～ melancholy moonlight /过去这一带满目～, 现在高楼大厦林立。Numerous high-rise buildings have sprung up in this once desolate area.

苍龙 cānglóng ❶ *also* "青龙" qīnglóng grey dragon, collective name for the eastern group (Nos. 1-7) of the twenty-eight constellations (二十八宿) ❷ mythical monster having a scaly reptilian body, wings, claws, and a long tail ❸ 〈比喻〉grey dragon, tyrannical power or evil influence: 今日长缨在手, 何时缚住～? Today we hold the long cord in our hands, When shall we bind fast the Grey Dragon?

C

苍鹭 cānglù 〈动物〉heron
苍绿 cānglǜ green; verdant: ～的树林 green woods
苍茫 cāngmáng ❶ vast; boundless: ～的大海 vast ocean; boundless seas /问～大地，谁主沉浮？I ask, on this boundless land, Who rules over man's destiny? ❷ indistinct: 海天～ vast expanse of sea and sky /暮色～。Dusk is gathering, stretching far into the distance.
苍莽 cāngmǎng 〈书面〉boundless; immeasurable, infinite: ～的林海 endless sea of forest
苍旻 cāngmín 〈书面〉blue sky; heavens
苍鸟 cāngniǎo 〈古语〉❶ a kind of eagle: ～群飞。Eagles fly in groups. ❷ goose
苍铅 cāngqiān bismuth
see also "铋" bì
苍穹 cāngqióng *also* "穹苍" 〈书面〉vault of heaven; the firmament: 高大的杉树直指～。The huge fir reaches up to the sky.
苍生 cāngshēng common people: 天下～ ordinary people across the land /～涂炭。The common people were plunged into an abyss of misery.
苍天 cāngtiān ❶ blue sky: 茫茫～ infinite blue sky ❷ *also* "上苍" shàngcāng Heaven: ～不容! Heaven forbid! /～保佑! May Heaven preserve us (*or* me)! /老人向～默默祷告。The old man silently prayed to Heaven.
苍头 cāngtóu 〈书面〉❶ servant ❷ soldier
苍哑 cāngyǎ (of voice) hoarse; husky; raucous (with age)
苍鹰 cāngyīng 〈动物〉goshawk
苍蝇 cāngying fly: ～见血 like a fly spotting blood — extremely greedy /老虎头上拍～ try to swat a fly on the tiger's head; bell the cat /～不叮无缝的蛋。〈俗语〉Flies go for cracked eggs — evil people (*or* influences) corrupt only those who have weaknesses.
苍蝇拍子 cāngying pāizi fly-swatter
苍郁 cāngyù 〈书面〉verdant and luxuriant: 草木～ verdant trees and grass
苍术 cāngzhú 〈中药〉rhizome of Chinese atractylodes (*Atractylodes chinensis*)

伧(傖)

cāng 〈书面〉rude; uncouth; boorish
see also chen
伧父 cāngfù *also* "伧夫" 〈书面〉boor; bumpkin
伧俗 cāngsú vulgar; uncouth; coarse: ～无知 vulgar and ignorant /～不堪 extremely vulgar (*or* coarse)

舱(艙)

cāng ❶ cabin; hold: 客～ (passenger) cabin /货～ hold /机～ engine room /燃油～ fuel tank /装～ stow the hold ❷ module: 指挥～ command module
舱壁 cāngbì bulkhead
舱单 cāngdān 〈运输〉manifest (list of goods carried on a ship)
舱口 cāngkǒu hatchway; hatch: ～盖 hatch door; hatch cover
舱门 cāngmén cabin door; hatch door
舱面 cāngmiàn deck: ～货 deck cargo
舱内货 cāngnèihuò 〈运输〉underdeck cargo
舱室 cāngshì cabin
舱外 cāngwài 〈航天〉outside the cabin of the vehicle in space; extra-vehicular: ～活动 extra-vehicular activities /～操纵设备 extravehicular maneuvering unit
舱外操作 cāngwài cāozuò 〈航天〉extravehicular operation
舱外航天服 cāngwài hángtiānfú 〈航天〉extravehicular suit
舱外环境 cāngwài huánjìng 〈航天〉extravehicular environment
舱外生命维持系统 cāngwài shēngmìng wéichí xìtǒng 〈航天〉extravehicular life support system (ELSS)
舱位 cāngwèi ❶ cabin seat or berth: 这架客机共有 260 个～。This passenger plane has 260 seats. ❷ shipping space

鸧(鶬)

cāng
鸧鹒 cānggēng *also* "黄鹂" huánglí oriole

cáng

藏

cáng ❶ hide; conceal: ～在门后 hide behind the door /把话～在心里 hide one's feelings /这人肚子里～不住话。This chap has got a big mouth. ❷ collect; store; lay by: 大量～书 large collection of books /～粮于民 store grain among the people
see also zàng
藏躲 cángduǒ *also* "躲藏" hide oneself; lie low: 四处～ hide hither and thither
藏锋 cángfēng ❶ 〈书面〉conceal one's brilliance; hold back one's vim; restrain one's overflowing talent: ～抑锐 refrain from displaying one's talent (*or* brilliance) /～守拙 conceal one's brilliance and behave humbly ❷ (in calligraphy) not make one's strokes forceful in a superficial manner; wield one's brush with contained vigour
藏富 cángfù conceal one's wealth: 别看这老头儿一副穷样，他这是～! Don't be misled by the old man's apparent poverty; he's just trying to conceal his wealth.
藏垢纳污 cánggòu-nàwū *also* "藏污纳垢" shelter evil people and uphold evil practices: 首善之区岂是～之地! As the best of all places, the capital should not be a cesspool of iniquity (*or* a sewer where all evil finds a home).
藏奸 cángjiān ❶ harbour evil intentions: 笑里～。Evil intentions are hidden in smiles. *or* Beneath that veneer of polite behaviour there lurks a cunning old fox. ❷ 〈方言〉unwilling to exert all one's strength or do one's best to help others: 他干活有点儿～。He wouldn't care to exert himself in work.
藏经阁 cángjīnggé depository of Buddhist scriptures
藏龙卧虎 cánglóng-wòhǔ hidden dragons and crouching tigers — talented or outstanding people who remain obscure to the undiscerning eye: ～之地 place full of talented (*or* outstanding) people unrecognized by careless observers; veritable den of unrecognized talent
藏猫儿 cángmāor 〈口语〉play hide-and-seek: 小孩～玩。Children play hide-and-seek. /甭给我～，总得把事情交代清楚。Stop playing hide-and-seek with me. You'll have to make a clean breast of things.
藏闷儿 cángmēnr 〈方言〉play hide-and-seek
藏匿 cángnì hide; go into hiding; conceal: 匪徒～在山洞里。The bandits hid out in a cave.
藏品 cángpǐn collected article: 博物馆～ museum collection; museum piece
藏身 cángshēn hide oneself; go into hiding: 无处～ have nowhere to hide /～之所 hiding place; hideout
藏书 cángshū ❶ collect books: 他爱好～。Book-collecting is his hobby. ❷ collection of books; library: 北京的国家图书馆～十分丰富。The National Library in Beijing boasts a rich collection of books.
藏书票 cángshūpiào book-collector's stamp (bearing date of collection, name of collector, etc.)
藏头露尾 cángtóu-lùwěi hide the head but show the tail — tell part of the truth but withhold the rest: 说话～的 tell only part of the story; speak evasively/你不要～，有什么说什么! No more of your evasive tricks. Out with the whole story, please!
藏头诗 cángtóushī verse in which the first character of each line, put together, form a sentence that expresses the intended idea
藏蓄 cángxù keep; cherish: ～在心中的理想 long-cherished ideal
藏掖 cángyē ❶ try to cover up: ～躲闪 dodge and hide ❷ covert malpractice: 光明正大，从来没有～ be open and aboveboard without hiding anything
藏运 cángyùn ship or transport contraband secretly: 非法～违禁品 secretly transport contraband in defiance of the law /～的香烟被查获。The contraband cigarettes were captured.
藏拙 cángzhuō hide one's incompetence by keeping quiet: 在诸位书法家面前，我只能～了。I dare not reveal my slight skill before such celebrated calligraphers.
藏踪 cángzōng leave no trace or track behind; hide: 闹市～ hide one's tracks in a busy town; vanish in a bustling area /他多年～于山野。For years he hid himself in the hills.

cāo

糙

cāo rough; coarse: ～纸 rough paper /这活儿干得太～。This is a very sloppy piece of work.
糙粮 cāoliáng 〈方言〉coarse food grain (e.g. maize, sorghum, millet, etc.)

糙米 cāomǐ brown rice; half-polished rice

糙皮病 cāopíbìng pellagra

操 cāo ❶ grasp; hold; wield: ～起扁担 grasp the carrying-pole /稳～胜券 find success within one's grasp; be sure to win /～生杀大权 wield power of life and death over people; have people completely at one's mercy ❷ do; act; operate: 重～旧业 resume one's old profession; take up one's old trade again ❸ speak (a language or dialect): ～本地口音 speak with a local accent /老外～着一口流利的中国话。The foreigner speaks fluent Chinese. ❹ drill; exercise: 早～ morning exercises /广播～ setting-up exercises to radio music /工间～ work-break exercises /课间～ class-break exercises /保健～ keep-fit exercises /徒手～ free-standing exercises /健美～ callisthenics /会～ gather together for military drill /战士们在上～。The soldiers are drilling. ❺ conduct; behaviour: 节～ one's moral principles; personal integrity /风～ graceful bearing and upright character ❻ (Cāo) a surname

see also cào

操办 cāobàn attend to; arrange; take care of; handle: ～丧事 attend to funeral arrangements /工地所需之粮,正在～。Food needed at the construction site is being taken care of.

操必胜之券 cāo bì shèng zhī quàn be assured of certain success; be confident of winning (victory)

操场 cāochǎng sports ground; playground; drill ground: 到～去打篮球。Go and play basketball on the playground.

操持 cāochí ❶ manage; handle: ～家务 manage household affairs /学校的日常事务由他～。He manages the daily routine of the school. /这件事由你～一下。I'll leave the matter to you. ❷ plan and prepare; make arrangements: 会议的准备工作由老王～。Lao Wang will make arrangements for the meeting.

操刀 cāodāo hold a knife, cleaver, scalpel, etc.; be in command: 由刘大夫～做手术。Doctor Liu will perform the operation. /～必割。Having got hold a knife, one must cut — Do not lose an opportunity when there is one.

操典 cāodiǎn drill regulations; drill manual; drill book: 步兵～ infantry drill manual /～要领 digest of the drill book

操舵 cāoduò 〈航海〉 con; steer: ～员 helmsman /～轮 steering wheel /～索 wheel rope; tiller rope /～系统 steering control system /我们正在接受～训练。We are being trained for steering.

操舵室 cāoduòshì wheelhouse; pilothouse; steering room

操舵台 cāoduòtái steering stand

操法 cāofǎ methods and rules for military drill or physical exercise

操课 cāokè 〈军事〉 ❶ military drill ❷ lecture as part of military training: ～时间 time for drill (*or* lecture)

操劳 cāoláo ❶ work hard: ～过度 overwork (*or* strain) oneself /他终年为国事～。He attends to state affairs with assiduity all the year round. ❷ take care; look after: 这事请你多～。Would you mind looking after this?

操练 cāoliàn drill; practise; train: 课堂～ class drill /～就业的本事 have vocational training; learn a trade /士兵们每天～刺杀。Soldiers have bayonet-charge drill every day. /一匹马从小驹喂养大,又～成这个样子,老饲养员不知费了多少心血。It took the old breeder God knows how much effort to raise and discipline the horse from a colt.

操坪 cāopíng 〈方言〉 playground; sports ground; drill ground

操切 cāoqiè hasty; rash; head-over-heels: 凡事不宜～ never rush into anything

操琴 cāoqín play *huqin* (a kind of two-stringed bowed musical instrument)

操神 cāoshén tax (one's mind); bother: ～受累 tax one's brain and strength /她为女儿的婚礼～。She took a lot of trouble over her daughter's wedding.

操守 cāoshǒu personal integrity: 李教授是个有～有学问的人。Professor Li is a man of great learning and moral integrity.

操心 cāoxīn worry about; trouble about; rack one's brains; take pains: 请别为我～。Please don't worry about me. / 为了把事情搞出个眉目,他可没有少～。He spared no effort to get things into shape.

操行 cāoxíng behaviour or conduct (usu. of a student): ～评语 comment (*or* remarks) on a student's behaviour

操演 cāoyǎn demonstration; exercise; drill (of military or physical training): ～用鱼雷 exercise torpedo /～动作之前要明了要领。Get the gist of the movements before drilling.

操之过急 cāozhī-guòjí act too hastily; make undue haste: ～,会把事情搞糟。Undue haste would spoil the show. *or* Haste makes waste.

操置 cāozhì ❶ buy; purchase: ～犁耙 buy ploughs and rakes ❷ attend to; take care of: ～公司产业 take care of a company's property

操舟 cāozhōu 〈书面〉 pilot a ship or boat

操纵 cāozòng ❶ operate; control: ～机器 operate machines /手动～ manual control; manual operation /无线电～ radio control /远距离～ remote control ❷ rig; manipulate: ～市场 rig the market /～公众舆论 manipulate public opinion /幕后～ manipulate from behind the scenes; pull the strings

操纵舱 cāozòngcāng control compartment

操纵程序 cāozòng chéngxù steering programme

操纵舵 cāozòngduò 〈航空〉 control vane

操纵杆 cāozònggǎn operating lever; control rod; control stick

操纵基因 cāozòng jīyīn 〈医学〉 operator gene; operator

操纵台 cāozòngtái control panel; control board

操纵装置 cāozòng zhuāngzhì control device

操纵子 cāozòngzǐ 〈医学〉 operon (the region of a chromosome which contains the operator gene and any structural genes involved in the production of messenger RNA for a given synthesis)

操作 cāozuò operate; manipulate: ～部分 working (*or* operation) part /～方法 method of operation /～说明书 operating manual /独立～ operate by oneself /手工～ manual operation

操作程序 cāozuò chéngxù operation sequence

操作程序图 cāozuò chéngxùtú flow diagram; flow chart

操作符 cāozuòfú 〈自控〉 operator

操作规程 cāozuò guīchéng operating rules; operating instructions; working order: 技术～ technical operating instructions /安全～ safety operating regulations

操作码 cāozuòmǎ 〈自控〉 operation code; command code

操作系统 cāozuò xìtǒng operating system (OS)

操作线 cāozuòxiàn 〈化工〉 operating line

操作性能 cāozuò xìngnéng 〈机械〉 serviceability

操作性条件反射 cāozuòxìng tiáojiàn fǎnshè 〈心理〉 operant conditioned reflex

操作指令 cāozuò zhǐlìng operational order

操作自如 cāozuò zìrú handle with skill

cáo

曹[1] cáo ❶ 〈书面〉 *used to indicate plural number*: 尔～ you gentlemen; all of you; you /吾～ all of us; we ❷ 〈古语〉 department of government under the monarch

曹[2] Cáo ❶ name of a principality of Zhou Dynasty located in the western part of present Shandong Province ❷ a surname

曹白鱼 cáobáiyú *also* "鳓" lè Chinese herring

曹操 Cáo Cāo Cao Cao (formerly translated as Ts'ao Ts'ao, 155-220), military strategist, statesman and writer during the Three Kingdoms

曹国舅 Cáo Guójiù Cao Guojiu (formerly translated as Ts'ao Kuo-chiu), one of the Eight Immortals in Taoist mythology

曹雪芹 Cáo Xuěqín Cao Xueqin (formerly translated as Ts'ao Hsueh-ch'in, c. 1715-1763 *or* 1764), author of *A Dream of Red Mansions* (also known as *The Story of the Stone*)

曹植 Cáo Zhí Cao Zhi (192-232), poet of the State of Wei during the Three Kingdoms and younger son of Cao Cao

漕 cáo water transport (esp. of grain)

漕船 cáochuán ship for carrying grain

漕渡 cáodù 〈军事〉 cross a river by boat or raft

漕河 cáohé waterway by which grain is transported: ～直达京畿。The waterway over which grain was transported reached the outskirts of the ancient capital.

漕粮 cáoliáng grain transported by water: 押解～ escort the grain transported by water

漕运 cáoyùn 〈旧语〉 transporting grain to the capital or for mili-

tary use by water：大运河在～中起了重要作用。The Grand Canal played an important role in transporting grain to the capital.

槽 cáo ❶ trough：水～ water trough／揉面～ dough trough；kneading trough／集气～〈化学〉pneumatic trough／马～ manger ❷ groove；slot：开～ cut a groove (*or* notch)；slot／键～ key groove／润滑油～ oil groove ❸〈方言〉〈量词〉(of doors，windows，etc.)：一～窗户 a window ❹〈方言〉time taken to raise a piglet until it is big enough for sale：明年我们计划养两～猪。We plan to raise two litters of piglets next year.

槽刨 cáobào 〈机械〉notching tool；grooving plane
槽车 cáochē tank car；tank truck
槽床 cáochuáng trough bed；groove or slot bed；trough stand；groove or slot stand
槽坊 cáofang traditional brewery or distillery：～酒气飘香。The distillery is permeated with the aroma of wine.
槽钢 cáogāng *also*"槽铁"〈冶金〉U-bar；U-steel；channel (steel)
槽糕 cáogāo *also*"槽子糕"〈方言〉cake made with moulds：各色风味的～ cakes of various flavours
槽谷 cáogǔ 〈地理〉trough valley
槽焊 cáohàn slot welding
槽距 cáojù 〈机械〉slot pitch
槽口 cáokǒu 〈机械〉notch
槽头 cáotóu trough (in a livestock shed)：～兴旺 stable full of sturdy livestock／两匹马在一个～吃食 feed two horses in one manger
槽铣刀 cáoxǐdāo 〈机械〉channeling cutter；slitting cutter；slot cutter；slot mill；milling cutter
槽形轨 cáoxíngguǐ grider or grooved rail
槽形框架 cáoxíng kuàngjià 〈机械〉channel frame
槽牙 cáoyá molar
槽子 cáozi trough：酒～ wine trough／马～ horse manger／在木头上挖个～ make a groove in a log
槽子糕 cáozigāo *see*"槽糕"
槽钻 cáozuàn 〈机械〉slotting drill

嘈 cáo noise；din

嘈杂 cáozá noisy：人声～ hubbub of voices／～的市场 bustling market／声音～聒耳。The noise grates on one's ears.

螬 cáo *see*"蛴螬" qícáo

艚 cáo

艚子 cáozi wooden cargo ship (with living quarters in the stern)

cǎo

草[1]（艸、❹騲） cǎo ❶ grass：青～ green grass／枯～ withered grass／野～ wild grass／杂～ weeds／疾风劲～ hardy grass in the storm ❷ straw：～绳 straw rope／稻～ paddy straw／稻～人 scarecrow ❸〈旧语〉the wild；the country：落～为寇 take to the greenwood and become a bandit ❹〈口语〉female (of certain domestic animals or fowls)：～马 mare

草[2]（艸） cǎo ❶ careless；hasty；sloppy：字写得很～。The handwriting is very sloppy. ❷ (of calligraphy) cursive hand；running style；handwritten forms (of romanized letters)：大～ (in) large handwritten form ❸ draft：起～文件 draft a document／起～委员会 drafting committee

草氨酸 cǎo'ānsuān 〈化学〉oxamic acid
草庵 cǎo'ān 〈方言〉*also*"草庵子" thatched hut
草案 cǎo'àn draft (of a plan，law，etc.)：决议～ draft resolution／宪法～ draft constitution／国会议案～ draft for a parliamentary bill／文本～ draft text／计划～ draft plan／建议～ draft proposal／条约～ draft treaty／协议～ draft agreement／议定书～ draft protocol／议程～ draft agenda／尚待核准的～ proposal *ad referendum*
草把 cǎobǎ *also*"草把子" bundle of straw or hay
草包 cǎobāo ❶ straw bag；straw sack：成车的～、木料、石块 truck-loads of straw sacks，timber and stones ❷ idiot；blockhead；good-for-nothing：难怪别人骂他是没用的～。No wonder people call him good-for-nothing!
草被 cǎobèi *see*"草本植被"
草本 cǎoběn ❶ herbaceous：～花与木本花 herbaceous and woody flowers／～水果 herbaceous fruit ❷ original draft (of a manuscript)
草本植被 cǎoběn zhíbèi herbosa
草本植物 cǎoběn zhíwù herb
草编 cǎobiān straw knitting；straw plaiting
草标儿 cǎobiāor wisp of straw marking sth. for sale：插～ mark sth. to be sold in the market
草草 cǎocǎo carelessly；hastily：～过目 read through carelessly；skim through
草草了事 cǎocǎo-liǎoshì rush through the work；get the work done any old way：这样的大案，怎么能～？How could you wind up such a major case so hastily? *or* Is it proper to rush through such a major case?
草草收场 cǎocǎo-shōuchǎng hastily wind up (the show)；come to a hasty end：这小说的结尾过于匆忙，给人以～的感觉。The ending of the novel is so hasty as to give the reader an impression of anticlimax.
草测 cǎocè preliminary survey：工程～业已完成。The preliminary survey of the project has been completed.
草叉 cǎochā pitch-fork
草场 cǎochǎng grazing land；pastureland；pasture
草虫 cǎochóng ❶ grass insects；grass hoppers ❷〈美术〉flower-grass-and-insect painting：工山水，善～ be versed in painting landscapes，flowers and insects
草除灵 cǎochúlíng benazolin
草创 cǎochuàng start (an enterprise，a troupe，etc.)；take the initial step in a process：～阶段 initial stage／～之时，我们一切从简。At the pioneering stage，we'll stick to the principle of economy and thrift.
草蝽 cǎochūn grassbug
草刺儿 cǎocìr tiny thing；sth. tiny：一根～他也休想拿去。Don't imagine that he can take away a tiny bit.
草苁蓉 cǎocōngróng *also*"列当" lièdāng〈植物〉broomrape (*Boschniakia rossica*)
草丛 cǎocóng thick growth of grass：～树底 in the thick grass under the trees／没入～ disappear into a thick growth of grass
草大青 cǎodàqīng 〈植物〉*Isatidis tintoria L.*，whose root is used as medicine for colds (板兰根)
草底儿 cǎodǐr 〈口语〉draft；manuscript：打个～ make a draft／按～抄一遍 make a clean copy of the manuscript
草地 cǎodì ❶ lawn：～网球 lawn tennis ❷ grassland；meadow：～改良 grassland improvement／～上牧放着成群的牛羊。Herds of cattle and sheep grazed on the grassland.
草地播种机 cǎodì bōzhǒngjī 〈畜牧〉grassland sod drill；grass reseeder
草地郎 cǎodìláng 〈方言〉country bumpkin；country folk
草地螟 cǎodìmíng 〈动物〉meadow webworm (*Loxostege sticticalis*)
草地农业 cǎodì nóngyè ley farming
草地生态学 cǎodì shēngtàixué grassland ecology
草甸鼠 cǎodiànshǔ 〈动物〉meadow mouse
草甸土 cǎodiàntǔ meadow soil；grassy marshland
草甸子 cǎodiànzi 〈方言〉grassy marshland：村外方圆十里全是～。Grassy marshland extends far and wide all around the village.
草垫子 cǎodiànzi straw mattress；pallet：几张～ several pallets／故乡的～干燥、暖和，更有一股清香。The straw mattresses made in my hometown are dry and warm. Besides，they have a pleasant smell.
草豆蔻 cǎodòukòu *also*"草蔻"〈植物〉*Alpinia katsumadai*，whose seeds are used as medicine
草垛 cǎoduò haystack；hayrick
草方 cǎofāng folk remedy；folk recipe
草房 cǎofáng thatched cottage
草稿 cǎogǎo rough draft；draft：打～ work out a draft／在～上修改 make corrections in the draft；revise the draft／～脱手了。The handwritten draft is finished.
草根 cǎogēn grass root：荒年吃树皮～ feed on tree barks and grass roots in a famine
草根阶层 cǎogēn jiēcéng people at the grass roots；people of lower classes
草菇 cǎogū straw mushroom
草果 cǎoguǒ 〈植物〉❶ *Amomum tsao-ko*，whose seeds are used

as medicine ❷〈方言〉strawberry ❸ round cardamom
草海桐 cǎohǎitóng 〈植物〉naupaka; native cabbage
草狐 cǎohú greyish-yellow fox
草花 cǎohuā ❶ herbaceous flower ❷ (playing-card) club:~老 K king of the clubs
草荒 cǎohuāng farmland running to weeds; farmland with more weeds than crops:这块地~严重。The plot is overgrown with weeds.
草灰 cǎohuī ❶ plant ash (used as fertilizer) ❷ greyish yellow:~色的大衣 greyish yellow overcoat /脸色~ have an ash-coloured face
草鸡 cǎojī 〈方言〉❶ hen ❷〈比喻〉cowardly; timid; chicken-hearted:临上阵,他有些~了。He got cold feet moments before the contest began.
草菅人命 cǎojiān-rénmìng treat human life as if it were not worth a straw:~的酷吏 cruel official who treats human life as if it were not worth a straw /他~,为所欲为。In total disregard of human lives, he did whatever he liked.
草碱 cǎojiǎn 〈化学〉potash; potassium carbonate
草荐 cǎojiàn pallet:清贫斗室,唯有~而已。Living in abject poverty, he had nothing but a pallet in his small room.
草浆 cǎojiāng straw pulp
草芥 cǎojiè trifle; mere nothing:视如~ regard as trash; treat like dirt
草决明 cǎojuémíng *also*“决明”cassia
草棵 cǎokē *also*“草棵子”thick growth of grass
草寇 cǎokòu 〈旧语〉robber in the greenwood; bandit
草库伦 cǎokùlún enclosed grazing land
草莱 cǎolái 〈书面〉❶ thick growth of weeds ❷ fields; wilderness
草兰 cǎolán cymbidium; orchid
草隶 cǎolì ❶ (of Chinese calligraphy) cursively executed characters in an ancient Han style, precursor to the cursive hand ❷ cursive script and official script:兼善~ be good at both cursive and official scripts
草笠 cǎolì bamboo hat
草帘 cǎolián straw curtain; straw mat
草寮 cǎoliáo thatched cottage
草料 cǎoliào forage; fodder
草蛉 cǎolíng lacewing
草驴 cǎolǘ female donkey; jenny ass
草履虫 cǎolǚchóng paramecium (*Paramecium caudatum*)
草绿 cǎolǜ grass green
草马 cǎomǎ mare
草码 cǎomǎ *also*“苏州码子”Sūzhōu mǎzi Suzhou numerals, traditionally used by shopkeepers to mark prices
草莽 cǎomǎng ❶ rank growth of grass ❷ uncultivated land; wilderness:出身~ rise from the common people; originate as a greenwood hero ❸ *see*“草野”
草莽英雄 cǎomǎng-yīngxióng hero of the bush; greenwood hero
草帽 cǎomào straw hat
草帽缏 cǎomàobiàn *also*“草帽辫”plaited straw (for making hats, baskets, etc.)
草莓 cǎoméi 〈农业〉strawberry:~冰淇淋 icecream with strawberry flavour /~黄边病 strawberry yellow edge (*Fragaria virus 1*)
草莓雀 cǎoméiquè *also*“红梅花雀”hóngméi huāquè strawberry finch
草煤 cǎoméi peat
草昧 cǎomèi 〈书面〉uncultivated; primitive; uncivilized:~状态 primitive state
草棉 cǎomián cotton; levant cotton
see also“棉花”miánhua
草灭平 cǎomièpíng chloramben
草民 cǎomín ❶ common people; commoner ❷〈旧语〉〈谦词〉I; me (as a commoner)
草茉莉 cǎomòli *also*“紫茉莉”zǐmòli four-o'clock (*Mirabilis jalapa*)
草木 cǎomù grass and trees; plants and trees
草木灰 cǎomùhuī plant ashes
草木皆兵 cǎomù-jiēbīng every bush and tree looks like an enemy soldier — the panicky state of a defeated army:风声鹤唳,~。The moan of the wind, the cry of the cranes and the rustle of the grass all sounded like an oncoming enemy army. /民兵沿途伏击,使侵略军大有~之感。The invaders were panic-stricken when they were ambushed by the militia all along the route.
草木犀 cǎomùxi 〈植物〉sweet clover
草拟 cǎonǐ draft; draw up:~一个计划 draft a plan /~和约 draw up a peace treaty
草棚 cǎopéng thatched shack; straw shed
草皮 cǎopí sod; turf
草坪 cǎopíng lawn:这~的草要割了。The lawn needs mowing.
草圃 cǎopǔ garden plot for growing grass
草器 cǎoqì article made of straw plaits; straw article
草签 cǎoqiān ❶ *see*“草标儿”❷ initial:~协定 initial an agreement /~文本 initialled text /~禁止在大气层进行核武器试验条约 initial a treaty banning nuclear tests in the atmosphere
草雀 cǎoquè grass finch
草裙舞 cǎoqúnwǔ hula (a Polynesian dance); hula-hula
草苫子 cǎoshānzi *also*“草帘”straw mat; straw curtain
草珊瑚 cǎoshānhú (popular term for 九节茶)〈植物〉*Sarcandra glabra*
草圣 cǎoshèng 〈古语〉master of the cursive hand
草石蚕 cǎoshícán *also*“甘露”gānlù;“宝塔菜”bǎotǎcài 〈植物〉Chinese artichoke (*Stachys sieboldii*)
草食 cǎoshí plant-eating
草食动物 cǎoshí dòngwù plant-eating animal; herbivore
草市 cǎoshì country fair
草书 cǎoshū (in Chinese calligraphy) characters executed swiftly and with strokes flowing together; cursive hand; running style
草鼠 cǎoshǔ grass mouse
草率 cǎoshuài careless; rash; perfunctory:失败的原因之一就是~。Carelessness was one of the causes of the defeat. /~下结论经常出错。Drawing hasty conclusions often leads to error.
草率从事 cǎoshuài-cóngshì act rashly or carelessly; do sth. rashly or carelessly; do a sloppy or perfunctory job:他领导这项工作,绝不会~。With him in charge of the work, there can be no sloppishness, you may be sure. /娶进这样一位大家闺秀,自然不能~。It was no simple affair, of course, to marry the daughter of such a distinguished family.
草酸 cǎosuān 〈化学〉oxalic acid
草酸铵 cǎosuān'ǎn 〈化学〉ammonium oxalate
草酸钙 cǎosuāngài calcium oxalate
草酸钠 cǎosuānnà sodium oxalate
草酸铁 cǎosuāntiě ferric oxalate
草酸盐 cǎosuānyán 〈化学〉oxalate
草索 cǎosuǒ straw rope
草台班子 cǎotái bānzi small travelling theatrical troupe (performing in small towns or villages)
草滩 cǎotān expanse of grassland near a river, lake or sea
草炭 cǎotàn *also*“泥炭”nítàn;“草煤” peat
草堂 cǎotáng (real or alleged) “thatched abode” — residence for ancient poets or hermits
草塘 cǎotáng pond covered with waterweeds
草体 cǎotǐ ❶ *see*“草书”❷ *also*“手写体”shǒuxiětǐ running hand of a phonetic alphabet
草田轮作法 cǎotián lúnzuòfǎ 〈农业〉grassland agriculture; grassland farming (rotating grass with other crops)
草头王 cǎotóuwáng chieftain of greenwood heroes; bandit chief
草图 cǎotú sketch (map); draft
草委 cǎowěi (short for 起草委员会) drafting committee
草乌 cǎowū *Aconiti agrestis*, a kind of medicinal herb
草屋 cǎowū thatched hut
草席 cǎoxí straw mat
草虾 cǎoxiā (small) shrimps
草鸮 cǎoxiāo grass owl
草鞋 cǎoxié straw sandals
草鞋没样,边打边像 cǎoxié méi yàng, biān dǎ biān xiàng straw sandals need no last; the shape comes with the weaving — work things out as you go along; play by ear
草写 cǎoxiě *see*“草体”
草雁 cǎoyàn grassgoose
草样 cǎoyàng draft design
草窑 cǎoyáo cave for housing livestock and storing firewood
草药 cǎoyào 〈中医〉medicinal herbs
草药医生 cǎoyào yīshēng 〈医学〉herbalist
草野 cǎoyě ❶ common people; ordinary people:~之人 untitled commoner; man in the street /退居~ (of an official) retire from

public life; retire from politics ❷〈书面〉uncouth; coarse; crude
草业 cǎoyè undertakings for cultivating or growing herbage
草医 cǎoyī 〈方言〉village doctor practising traditional herb medicine
草鱼 cǎoyú *also* "鲩" huàn grass carp
草原 cǎoyuán grassland; prairie: 辽阔的～ vast expanse of grassland /～带 steppe belt
草原化 cǎoyuánhuà steppification
草原狼 cǎoyuánláng coyote
草原气候 cǎoyuán qìhòu steppe climate; semiarid climate
草原退化 cǎoyuán tuìhuà grassland deterioration
草约 cǎoyuē draft treaty; draft agreement; protocol; *ad referendum* contract: 双方就～的未定事项再次磋商。The two sides are negotiating again the items which were not agreed on in the draft agreement.
草泽 cǎozé ❶ grassy marsh; swamp; morass: 深山～ remote mountains and grassy marshes /匿迹～ hide oneself in remote country ❷〈书面〉ordinary people: ～医生 folk doctor
草贼 cǎozéi outlaw in the greenwood; bandit; brigand
草长灭 cǎozhǎngmiè carbetamide
草纸 cǎozhǐ ❶ rough straw paper ❷ toilet paper
草质茎 cǎozhìjīng (of rice and wheat) herbaceous stalk
草猪 cǎozhū sow
草子 cǎozǐ 〈方言〉green manure crop (Chinese milk vetch, bur clover, etc.)
草籽 cǎozǐ grass seed
草籽收割机 cǎozǐ shōugējī seed stripper
草字 cǎozì ❶ (of Chinese calligraphy) grass character — character written in the cursive hand ❷ modest mention of one's own courtesy name

慅 cǎo

慅慅 cǎocǎo 〈书面〉be worried and ill at ease; disquieted: 终日～ be worried and depressed all day long

cào

操 cào 〈粗话〉(same as 肏) fuck

see also cāo
操蛋 càodàn 〈粗话〉be a damned nuisance; be a motherfucker: 这小子真～，借了钱不还，还打人! What a motherfucker! He actually hit me and refused to pay his debt!

肏 cào 〈粗话〉fuck

cè

测 cè ❶ survey; fathom; measure: ～气温 measure the temperature /～体温 take sb.'s temperature /目～山的高度 gauge the height of the mountain with one's eyes /水深不可～。The water is fathomless. ❷ conjecture; infer; predict: 变化莫～ change unpredictably /居心叵～ have ulterior motives /前途莫～。It's hard to tell what lies ahead. *or* We don't know what the future has in store for us. /人心难～。The public mood is difficult to judge.

测报 cèbào survey or measure and report: ～虫情 forecast the insect pest situation /完成水文～任务 accomplish the work of hydrologic survey and forecast /气象～是对工农业生产很重要的一项工作。Weather forecasting is very important for industrial and agricultural production.
测标 cèbiāo surveying mark
测波计 cèbōjì wave gauge
测产 cèchǎn calculate the approximate output; estimate the yield: 据初步～，今年这个地区皮棉总产量可达五百万担。According to preliminary estimation, the output of ginned cotton in this area will reach 250,000 tons this year.
测潮计 cècháojì tide gauge
测尘器 cèchénqì dust counter
测程仪 cèchéngyí 〈交通〉log; mileage meter
测锤 cèchuí 〈测绘〉plumb
测磁学 cècíxué magnetometry
测地卫星 cèdì wèixīng geodetic satellite
测地学 cèdìxué 〈测绘〉geodesy
测点 cèdiǎn landmark; measuring point
测电笔 cèdiànbǐ test pencil
测电阻仪 cèdiànzǔyí apparatus of resistance
测定 cèdìng determine (through measuring or testing): 示踪～ tracer determination /～年代 dating /经～，这台机器的性能符合要求。The test determines that the performance of the machine meets the specified requirements. /这种植物的含糖量已被～。The sugar content of the plant has been determined.
测度 cèdù 〈数学〉measure: ～空间 measure space /～代数 measure algebra /～函数 measure function
测度论 cèdùlùn measure theory
测度 cèduó estimate; infer: 根据风向～，今天要下雨。Judging by the direction of the wind, it will be raining today. /市场行情难以～。The quotations of the market are difficult to calculate.
测风经纬仪 cèfēng jīngwěiyí pilot balloon theodolite
测风气球 cèfēng qìqiú pilot balloon
测辐射计 cèfúshèjì pyranometer
测杆 cègān measuring staff; surveying rod
测高法 cègāofǎ altimetry; hypsometry
测高仪 cègāoyí 〈机械〉height finder
测光笔 cèguāngbǐ photometric pen
测规 cèguī gauge
测厚仪 cèhòuyí pachymeter
测候 cèhòu astronomical and meteorological observation: ～网〈气象〉reseau
测谎器 cèhuǎngqì lie detector; polygraph
测绘 cèhuì surveying and mapping; mapping; cartography: ～板 plotting board /～飞机 air-mapping plane /～员 surveyor; cartographer /～部队 mapping unit; topographic troops
测绘卫星 cèhuì wèixīng cartographic satellite
测交 cèjiāo 〈生物〉testcross
测焦距术 cèjiāojùshù focometry
测角 cèjiǎo goniometry: ～仪 goniometer
测井 cèjǐng 〈石油〉well logging: 电～ electric logging /放射性～ radioactivity logging
测径规 cèjìngguī 〈机械〉calliper gauge
测距 cèjù range finding: ～仪 range finder; diastimeter
测控 cèkòng observe and control: 卫星～中心 satellite observation and control centre
测力计 cèlìjì 〈物理〉dynamometer
测量 cèliáng survey; measure; gauge: ～地形 survey the topography /～高度 measure the height /～队 survey party /～仪器 surveying instrument /大地～ geodetic survey /航空～ aerial survey; air survey
测量标记 cèliáng biāojì survey mark
测量船 cèliángchuán surveying ship
测量学 cèliángxué surveying
测量员 cèliángyuán surveyor
测流计 cèliújì current meter
测漏 cèlòu tracking down a leak; leak hunting
测热计 cèrèjì calorimeter
测热学 cèrèxué calorimetry
测深锤 cèshēnchuí sounding bob; sounding lead
测深仪 cèshēnyí fathometer; depth-sounder; echo sounder
测湿法 cèshīfǎ hygrometry
测湿学 cèshīxué psychrometry
测试 cèshì test: ～机器 test a machine /～仪表 test an instrument; test a meter /～设备 testing equipment; checkout gear /～台 test-board; test desk /～图 resolution chart; test pattern /～数据 test data
测速计 cèsùjì velocimeter; speedometer
测算 cèsuàn measure or gauge and calculate; calculate: 用地震仪～地震震级 measure the magnitude of an earthquake by a seismograph /经过反复～，这项工程年内可以完成。Repeated calculation affirms that the project will be completed this year.
测探 cètàn ❶ find out; fathom; ferret out: ～心事 find out what is on sb.'s mind /～他的内心奥秘 ferret out the innermost secrets in his heart ❷ measure and survey; survey: ～矿藏 survey for mineral deposits

测体积学 cètǐjīxué stereometry
测听 cètīng audiometry
测图摄影机 cètú shèyǐngjī mapping camera
测温计 cèwēnjì temperature tester
测温学 cèwēnxué thermometry
测隙计 cèxìjì clearanceometer
测向计 cèxiàngjì goniometer
测斜仪 cèxiéyí inclinometer
测压计 cèyājì manometer
测验 cèyàn test:期中～ mid-term test /小～ quiz; quick test /～机械性能 test the performance of a machine
测验对象 cèyàn duìxiàng *also*“受试者”shòushìzhě testee
测音 cèyīn sound monitor; sound location
测远术 cèyuǎnshù telemetry
测云气球 cèyún qìqiú 〈气象〉ceiling balloon
测云器 cèyúnqì 〈气象〉nephoscope
测震学 cèzhènxué seismometry
测知 cèzhī learn after a survey or test
测字 cèzì fortune-telling by analyzing the component parts of a Chinese character; divine by means of characters; glyphomancy:算命～ tell sb.'s fortune by analyzing a Chinese character
测字先生 cèzì xiānsheng fortune-teller; glyphomancer
测醉器 cèzuìqì alcometer

恻 cè ❶ sorrowful; sad:凄～ sad; deeply grieved ❷〈书面〉sincere; earnest
恻恻 cècè 〈书面〉❶ grieved; sad ❷ earnest; sincere
恻楚 cèchǔ 〈书面〉saddened at heart; deeply grieved
恻然 cèrán sad; sorrowful:我心～。I was filled with sorrow.
恻隐 cèyǐn 〈书面〉compassion; pity:对受苦受难的人寄予～之情 show compassion for those suffering
恻隐之心 cèyǐnzhīxīn compassion; tenderheartedness:起了～ one's compassion is aroused; one's heart goes out (to sb. over sth.) /～,人皆有之。Compassion is human nature.

厕[1](**廁**) cè lavatory; toilet; washroom; restroom; WC:男～ men's; gents; men's room /女～ women's; ladies; women's room /公～ public toilet

厕[2](**廁**) cè 〈书面〉be mixed up in; be mingled with; be involved in:杂～ be mixed up
厕身 cèshēn 〈书面〉〈谦词〉work in a particular field or department:～社会 take one's place in society /～教育界 be a member of the teaching profession
厕所 cèsuǒ lavatory; toilet; WC
厕纸 cèzhǐ toilet paper
厕足 cèzú participate; set foot in:～其间 get involved in the matter

侧 cè ❶ side; lateral:左～ left side /鱼的～鳍 lateral fin of a fish /楼的两～各有一哨兵。On each side of the building stands a guard. ❷ lean; incline:她～过脸望着窗外的树木。She turned over to look at the trees outside the window.
see also zè; zhāi
侧柏 cèbǎi 〈植物〉arborvitae
侧扁 cèbiǎn laterally flat
侧步 cèbù pacing (in horse racing)
侧槽式溢洪道 cècáoshì yìhóngdào 〈水利〉side-channel spillway; lateral flow spillway
侧铲推土机 cèchǎn tuītǔjī 〈建筑〉side dozer; angledozer
侧吹 cèchuī 〈冶金〉side-blown
侧吹转炉 cèchuī zhuànlú side-blown converter
侧唇 cèchún lateral lip
侧捣淘矿机 cèdǎo táokuàngjī 〈矿业〉side-shake vanner
侧耳 cè'ěr ❶ incline one's ears:～而听 incline one's head to listen; prick up one's ears ❷ a kind of gill fungus
侧飞 cèfēi 〈航空〉fly laterally; crab
侧风 cèfēng sidewind; crosswind:～起飞 (make a) crosswind take-off
侧根 cègēn 〈植物〉lateral root
侧光 cèguāng 〈摄影〉sidelight
侧击 cèjī flank attack:正面佯攻,奇兵～ launch a surprise flank attack while feinting a frontal one
侧记 cèjì (usu. used in titles of news reports) sidelights:《北京艺术节～》*Sidelights on the Beijing Art Festival*
侧架犁 cèjiàlí 〈农业〉side-frame plow
侧角 cèjiǎo 〈动物〉lateral horn
侧近 cèjìn nearby:找～的人打听一下。Ask someone nearby. *or* Make inquiries in the neighbourhood.
侧颈龟 cèjǐngguī side-necked turtle
侧镜 cèjìng side mirror; telescope-axle mirror
侧力 cèlì side or lateral force
侧链 cèliàn 〈生物〉lateral chain
侧链理论 cèliàn lǐlùn 〈生物〉side-chain theory; lateral-chain theory
侧门 cèmén side door; side entrance
侧面 cèmiàn side aspect; flank:～攻击 flank attack /从～了解 find out from indirect sources /在大楼的～ on the side of the building /生活的一个～ one facet of life /这只是问题的一个～。This is only one side of the coin (*or* picture).
侧面进针 cèmiàn jìnzhēn 〈纺织〉raking
侧面图 cèmiàntú *see*“侧视图”
侧面像 cèmiànxiàng profile
侧目 cèmù sidelong glance:恶少横行,路人～。The passers-by looked askance at the hooligans running amuck.
侧目而视 cèmù'érshì look askance at sb. (with fear or indignation):重足而立,～ stand transfixed with fear and cast sidelong glances (*or* eye sb. askance)
侧倾 cèqīng (of a ship) heel; list
侧射 cèshè discharging a flank shot; flank fire:山顶正是一个～的火力点。The hill top happens to be a good flank firing point.
侧身 cèshēn ❶ on one's side; sideways:～匍匐前进 crawl on one's side /他～躲到树后。He turned over sideways and hid behind a tree. ❷ *also*“厕身”cèshēn 〈书面〉〈谦词〉work or move in a particular field or department
侧石 cèshí curbstone; curb
侧蚀力 cèshílì 〈地质〉side erosion
侧视 cèshì look askance at; shoot a sideglance at; give (sb. or sth.) a sidelong look
侧视图 cèshìtú *also*“侧面图”side view; lateral view; profile
侧室 cèshì 〈旧语〉❶ side room; side chamber ❷ concubine
侧手翻 cèshǒufān 〈体育〉cartwheel; turn a cartwheel
侧卫 cèwèi 〈军事〉flank guard
侧闻 cèwén learn from indirect sources; learn by hearsay:～高论 hear of sb.'s enlightening views; learn of sb.'s brilliant ideas
侧卧 cèwò lie on one's side
侧线 cèxiàn ❶〈铁路〉siding ❷〈动物〉lateral line:～系 lateral line system
侧向摆动 cèxiàng bǎidòng sideshake; lateral swing
侧向分力 cèxiàng fēnlì cross component force
侧向加速 cèxiàng jiāsù side acceleration; transverse acceleration
侧向搂草机 cèxiàng lōucǎojī 〈农业〉side (delivery) rake
侧卸 cèxiè (short for 侧向卸载) side discharge:～铲式装载机〈建筑〉side-discharge shovel
侧卸车 cèxièchē 〈建筑〉side discharging truck; side-tip truck; side-tipping dump truck
侧卸式货车 cèxièshì huòchē 〈建筑〉side-tip truck
侧旋 cèxuán 〈体育〉(in table tennis) sidespin
侧压力 cèyālì *also*“旁压力”pángyālì lateral pressure
侧芽 cèyá *also*“腋芽”yèyá 〈植物〉lateral bud; auxiliary bud
侧艳 cèyàn 〈书面〉(of language) flowery and frivolous:～之词 flowery and frivolous language
侧翼 cèyì 〈军事〉flank:从～包抄敌军 outflank the enemy; make a flank attack on the enemy
侧影 cèyǐng silhouette; profile:从景山西望,可以看到北海白塔的～。Looking westward from Jingshan Hill, you can see the profile of the white dagoba in Beihai Park. /通过小说《青春之歌》可以看到当时学生运动的一个～。The novel *The Song of Youth* gives a reflection of the student movement of the time.
侧泳 cèyǒng 〈体育〉sidestroke
侧枝 cèzhī 〈植物〉side shoot; offshoot
侧制动器 cèzhìdòngqì side brake
侧重 cèzhòng lay particular emphasis on; focus on; stress:他～风

C

景画。His emphasis is on landscape painting. /这篇文章～谈二次大战的历史根源。This essay focuses on the historical roots of World War II. /副经理～抓销售预测。The deputy manager devoted himself specially to sales forecast. /在讲话中,他～谈了通货膨胀问题。The keynote of his speech was inflation.

侧足 cèzú 〈书面〉❶ stand motionless with one's feet turned sideways as in fright ❷ *also* "厕足" cèzú participate; be involved (in sth.)

筴(筞) cè *see* "策" cè
see also jiā

策[1](筞) cè ❶ bamboo or wooden slips used in ancient China for writing on ❷ type of essay which candidates at imperial examination were required to write, mostly on political and economic issues; discourse on politics:《天人三～》*Three Discourses on Heaven and Man* ❸ plan; scheme; strategy:善～ sound strategy; wise decision /失～ wrong move or decision /万全之～ perfectly safe policy or plan; sure-fire measure ❹〈书面〉engineer; plan; arrange ❺ (Cè) a surname

策[2](筞) cè ❶ riding-crop; hunting-crop:执～ hold the crop ❷ use such a crop to urge a horse on:扬鞭～马 whip a horse on with a crop ❸〈书面〉crutches:扶～而行 walk on crutches

策动 cèdòng instigate; stir up:～叛乱 instigate a rebellion /～一场政变 plot (*or* engineer) a *coup d'état*

策反 cèfǎn instigate or incite defections within the enemy camp:敌后～ instigate defections in the enemy's rear /对卫队进行～ incite sb.'s guards to change sides (*or* mutiny)

策划 cèhuà plan; plot; scheme:～新的战役 plan a new campaign /～阴谋 hatch a plot /幕后～ plot behind the scenes /～于密室 scheme behind closed doors

策励 cèlì encourage; spur on:～我们更加努力 spur us on to greater efforts /你的话是对我们大家的一种～。What you have said is a great encouragement to us all.

策略 cèlüè ❶ tactics:斗争～ tactics of struggle /～上的失误 tactical error ❷ tactful:你这种作法不～。It was not tactful of you to act as you did. *or* It was tactless of you to behave like this. /下次跟他谈话时要更～一些。Be more tactful when talking to him next time.

策论 cèlùn discourse on politics (required essay at civil service examinations in imperial China):善作～ be good at writing political essays

策勉 cèmiǎn urge; encourage; spur on

策士 cèshì strategist:～谋臣 court counsellors and strategists

策试 cèshì examinations in politics, economics, and military affairs taken by candidates at the palace examinations presided over by the emperor

策问 cèwèn type of essay (often required at imperial examinations) giving answers to questions on Confucian canonical writings and state affairs

策应 cèyìng 〈军事〉support by taking coordinated action:遥相～ coordinate one's action with that of sb. else in a distant place /一营主攻,二营～。Battalion One will spearhead the attack while Battalion Two will lend it coordinated support.

策源地 cèyuándì source; place of origin:革命的～ cradle of revolution /战争～ hotbed of war

箣 cè

箣竹 cèzhú 〈植物〉*Bambusa stenostachya*, a kind of sturdy tall bamboo much used in building, and making furniture

册(冊) cè ❶ volume; book:首～ first volume; volume one /相～ album of photographs; photo album /画～ album of paintings /纪念～ autograph album /装钉成～ bind into book form /名～ official list of names; roll; register ❷〈书面〉confer a title:～为太子 make (sb.) the crown prince /～授勋位 bestow an order of merit ❸〈量词〉copy:这本书印了一万～。Ten thousand copies of this book have been printed. /这部小说分两～。This novel is in two volumes.

册封 cèfēng confer a title of nobility on:～诸侯 confer the title of duke on

册府元龟 Cèfǔ Yuánguī *Guide to Books*, a work on court life consisting of 1,000 volumes with 9.4 million words, compiled by Wang Qinruo (王钦若), Yang Yi (杨亿) and others (1005-1013)

册立 cèlì make a crown prince or empress:～皇后 make sb. empress; crown sb. queen (*or* empress)

册页 cèyè album of paintings or calligraphy:花卉～ album of flower paintings /展品中有二十幅《红楼梦》人物～。Among the exhibits was an album of 20 portraits of characters in *A Dream of Red Mansions*.

册子 cèzi book; volume:小～ pamphlet; booklet; brochure

cèi

䇲 cèi 〈口语〉break:瓶子～了。The bottle is broken.

cēn

参(參) cēn
see also cān; shēn

参差 cēncī ❶ irregular; uneven:～错落 uneven and irregular /屋檐～。The eaves are unevenly shaped. ❷〈书面〉well-nigh; almost:～是。Almost so. ❸〈书面〉go wrong; be delayed:佳期～。The wedding was delayed.

参差不齐 cēncī-bùqí not uniform; uneven; varying:程度～ uneven in level; to varying degrees /进度～ make uneven progress /人一多,认识就难免～。When you have a lot of people together, they are bound to vary in their understanding of things.

参错 cēncuò 〈书面〉❶ uneven and irregular:险岸岩石～。By the steep shore are rocks of irregular sizes and shapes. ❷ errors and omissions:文中颇多～。There are many errors and omissions in the essay.

cén

岑 cén ❶〈书面〉high hill:遥～ distant high hills /～楼 high tower ❷〈书面〉cliffy shore ❸ (Cén) a surname

岑岑 céncén 〈书面〉causing pain in the head:～作痛 have a splitting pain (*or* headache)

岑寂 cénjì 〈书面〉quiet; solitary; lonely:山中～,了无人声。All is quiet and still in the mountains, without a human voice.

涔 cén 〈书面〉❶ rain water in puddles ❷ excessive rain

涔涔 céncén 〈书面〉❶ dripping; streaming (of sweat, tears or rain):热汗～ dripping with sweat; sweating all over /泪～ tears streaming down ❷ gloomy; overcast (of weather):雪意～。It looks as if it's going to snow. *or* It threatens to snow. ❸ suffering from swelling pain; depressed; worried:心绪～ be laden with anxiety; emotionally upset; in a flutter

cēng

噌[1] cēng 〈象声〉麻雀～的一声飞上了屋顶。The sparrow flew across and landed on the roof.

噌[2] cēng 〈方言〉give a dressing down; scold:挨～ get a scolding (*or* dressing down)
see also chēng

céng

曾 céng 〈副词〉once:我～向他表示过我有出国留学的愿望。I once told him that I had the desire to study abroad. /他不～有过这种意图。He has never had such intentions. /她～到过伦敦。She's been to London.
see also zēng

曾几何时 céngjǐhéshí 〈书面〉before long; not long after:～,沙漠变为绿洲。In a short space of time, the desert had turned into green

land. /～他已成为一个享有盛名的学者。Before long he had become a scholar of repute.

曾经 céngjīng 〈副词〉once:他～是个京剧演员。He was once an actor of Beijing opera. /是的,我是～有过这个疑问。Yes, I did have this doubt.

曾经沧海 céngjīng-cānghǎi have sailed the seven seas; have experienced much:～难为水 to a sophisticated person there is nothing new under the sun /此人～,这些小花样骗不过他。A sophisticated person like him won't buy such apparent tricks.

曾用名 céngyòngmíng previous name

嶒 céng see "崚嶒" léngcéng

层(層) céng ❶ one on top of another; overlapping:看万山红遍,～林尽染。I see a thousand hills crimsoned through, By their serried woods deep-dyed... ❷ one of several overlapping layers or tiers:外～ outer layer /云～ tiers (*or* layers) of cloud ❸〈量词〉layer; tier; stratum:一～奶油 a layer of cream /两～油漆 two coats of paint /一～薄冰 a sheet of ice /地球的最里～ inner-most stratum of the earth /这块婚礼大蛋糕有三～。This wedding cake has three tiers. /双～玻璃的窗户 double-glazed window /这剧院有两～座位。The theatre has two tiers of seats. ❹〈量词〉storey; floor:三～楼 three-storey building /高～建筑 high building; high block; tower block; high-rise /他家在三～。He lives on the 3rd floor. ❺〈量词〉component part in a sequence:这话还有一～意思。This remark has another implication. /这个词有几～意思。This word has several shades of meaning.

层报 céngbào submit or report a matter to the higher authorities level by level:这个案子经过～,终于到了最高检察院。This case was finally brought before the Supreme Procuratorate after it had been submitted from one level to another.

层层 céngcéng at each level; layer upon layer; ring upon ring; tier upon tier:～动员 mobilize (the people) at all levels /～加码 the target (*or* quota) is raised at each level; increase at each level /～把关 check at each level /～包围 surround ring upon ring /～梯田 tier upon tier of terraced fields

层出不穷 céngchū-bùqióng emerge in an endless stream; come thick and fast:新款式～。New fashions are coming out fast one after another. /新事物、新思想～。New things and new ideas are emerging in quick succession.

层次 céngcì ❶ arrangement or sequence of ideas:这篇论文～不清。This essay lacks unity and coherence. /讲话要有～。One should organize one's ideas in a logical sequence when delivering a speech. ❷ level:知识～ levels of knowledge /管理～ administrative levels /高～的技术人员 technical personnel of high calibre /减少～,提高效率 simplify the administrative structure and improve work efficiency; cut down the overlapping levels and improve efficiency ❸ gradation:颜色的～ colour gradations /～不分明。The gradation is not clear. /这幅印象派的画真实地反映了光线的～。This impressionist painting shows the true colour components of light.

层叠 céngdié one on top of another; overlapping:冈峦～ range upon range of mountains; never-ending mountain ranges

层峰 céngfēng peaks rising one after another

层积木 céngjīmù laminated wood

层积云 céngjīyún 〈气象〉stratocumulus

层见叠出 céngjiàn-diéchū *also* "层出叠见" occur frequently; appear repeatedly:不知是怎么回事,这几年这类事～。I wonder why such things have occurred repeatedly in recent years.

层卷云 céngjuǎnyún 〈气象〉stratocirrus

层浪 cénglàng rolling waves:～迭起 roaring waves rush on one after another

层理 cénglǐ 〈地质〉bedding; stratification

层林 cénglín tier upon tier of woods; endless stretch of woods:深秋季节,山上～尽染,景色宜人。The mountain scenery in late autumn is delightful when all the trees are touched with gold.

层流 céngliú 〈物理〉laminar flow

层流层 céngliúcéng 〈气象〉laminar layer

层峦 céngluán range upon range of mountains or hills:～起伏 range upon range of undulating mountains /～叠翠 rolling hills with varying shades of greenery

层峦叠嶂 céngluán-diézhàng range upon range of mountains:～,山势奇伟。Meandering mountain ranges present a view of rare magnificence. /～,尽收眼底。Range upon range of mountains came into view.

层面 céngmiàn ❶〈地质〉bedding:～构造 bedding plane structure ❷ scope or aspect of sth. on a certain level or of a cross section:作品在语言～上有新的尝试。The author blazed a trail in the use of language in his writing.

层压 céngyā 〈化学〉lamination:～玻璃 laminated glass

层压压机 céngyā yājī 〈机械〉laminating press

层云 céngyún 〈气象〉stratus; many-layered clouds

层状矿脉 céngzhuàng kuàngmài 〈矿业〉stratified vein; bedded vein

层子 céngzǐ 〈物理〉straton:～模型 straton model

cèng

蹭 cèng ❶ rub; grind; scratch:把刀在石头上～两下 grind the knife on the stone /我～破了皮。I got a scratch. /她摔了一跤,把膝盖～破了。She fell and grazed her knee. /黑板上的字给～掉了。The words on the blackboard were erased. /他用袖子在桌上～。He is wiping the table with his sleeve. ❷ be smeared with:～了一脸的白灰 (one's) face smeared with whitewash /小心～油漆。Mind the fresh paint. ❸〈方言〉get sth. free (of charge); scrounge:坐～车 be given a free ride (*or* lift) /吃～饭 have a free meal /看～戏 go to the theatre (*or* an opera) free of charge ❹ dawdle; dillydally; loiter:一步步地往前～ inch one's way forward; drag along /快点,别～了。Hurry up! You are too slow! /她～了一个早上。She dawdled all morning.

蹭蹬 cèngdèng 〈书面〉meet with setbacks; be down on one's luck:他一生～,很不如意。He was unhappy all his life, overtaken by one misfortune after another.

蹭棱子 cènglèngzi 〈方言〉deliberately dawdle

蹭抹 cèngmǒ rub:用脚在地上～ rub one's feet against the floor /作案现场的痕迹被～一光。All the traces at the scene of the crime were scrubbed off.

chā

差 chā ❶ difference; discrepancy:时～ time difference; jet lag /温～ range of temperature; difference in temperature /一丝不～ perfectly correct; in total agreement /他们的性格～得很远。They are poles apart in temperament. *or* They have very different temperaments. /相～不大。There's not much difference between them. *or* There is very little to choose between them. ❷〈数学〉*also* "差数" mathematics difference:五与三的～是二。Five minus three equals two. ❸〈书面〉a little; somewhat; slightly:天气～暖。It's getting somewhat warmer.

see also chà; chāi; chài; cī

差巴 chābā 〈旧语〉one of the grades of serfs in Tibet

差别 chābié difference; disparity:年龄～ disparity of age /缩小城乡～ narrow the gap between the city and the countryside (*or* between town and country) /巨大的～ world of difference /我们的看法没什么～。There is little difference between our views.

差别关税 chābié guānshuì differential rates of duty; differential duties

差别汇率 chābié huìlǜ discriminatory cross-rates or exchange rates

差别心理学 chābié xīnlǐxué differential psychology

差别阈限 chābié yùxiàn 〈心理〉difference limen; difference threshold:差别感觉阈限 differential sensory threshold

差池 chāchí *also* "差迟" *see* "差错"

差错 chācuò ❶ error; mistake:计算上的～ calculating errors /她的工作从来没有出过～。She has never made mistakes in her work. /万一手术有个～,怎么办? What if the operation goes wrong? /技术上的～贻误了工作。A technical hitch delayed the work. ❷ mishap; trouble; accident:他怎么还没有回来? 准是出了～。Why isn't he back yet? Something untoward must have happened. /这汽车很安全,途中不会出什么～。This car is very reliable. It won't break down on the way.

差错文件 chācuò wénjiàn 〈计算机〉error file

差动 chādòng 〈机械〉〈电学〉differential:～变压器 differential

C

transformer
差动齿轮 chādòng chǐlún differential gear
差动滑轮 chādòng huálún differential pulley
差动轴 chādòngzhóu differential shaft
差讹 chā'é mistake; error
差额 chā'é difference; balance; margin:借方～ debit balance /贷方～ credit balance /进出口贸易～ imbalance (*or* gap) between imports and exports /～地租 differential rent /～表 balance sheet /补足～ make up the balance
差额选举 chā'é xuǎnjǔ competitive election; multi-candidate election
差分 chāfēn 〈数学〉difference:～方程 difference equation
差分电路 chāfēn diànlù 〈电学〉differential circuit

C

差价 chājià price difference:地区～ regional price differences /季节～ seasonal price differences /～关税 variable import levy /利润来自批发和零售之间的～。The profit comes from the price difference between wholesale and retail.
差距 chājù gap; disparity; difference:缩小～ reduce (*or* narrow) the gap /弥合～ bridge (*or* close) the gap /两个国家在经济上～很大。There is a big gap in the economies of the two countries. /你应该找找～。You should find out where you fall short. /跟人民的要求比起来,我的～还很大。I have a long way to go before I can live up to the expectations of the people.
差堪 chākān barely:～自慰的是事情总算有点眉目了。It is some solace that things are getting into shape.
差可 chākě more or less serve the purpose:成绩～ passable result; fair mark /～告慰 feel it a matter of some consolation
差频 chāpín 〈电学〉difference frequency; slip or beat frequency
差强人意 chāqiáng-rényì passable; barely satisfactory:去年的工作～。Last year's work was barely satisfactory. /拙作不日问世,但愿能～。My work will soon be published. I hope that it will be favourably received.
差热分析 chārè fēnxī 〈物理〉differential thermal analysis (DTA)
差三错四 chāsān-cuòsì in confusion; at sixes and sevens; topsy-turvy
差失 chāshī mistake; error:传送中要避免出～。Avoid any error or mishap in the transmission.
差数 chāshù mathematics difference
差忒 chātè 〈书面〉error; mistake:毫无～ no mistake whatsoever
差误 chāwù mistake; error; slip:他的工作出了～。Something went wrong with his work.
差异 chāyì difference; divergence; diversity:气候～ difference in climate /人们的思想有～。People vary in thinking. /他们的意见～很大。There is wide discrepancy between their views.
差异分析 chāyì fēnxī variance analysis
差之毫厘,谬以千里 chā zhī háolí, miù yǐ qiānlǐ *also* "差以毫厘,失之千里" an error the breadth of a single hair can lead you a thousand *li* astray; a small discrepancy often leads to an error of serious consequence; grave consequences may attend a small error committed at the start:统计工作要十分严格,～,因此一定要非常细心。Statistical work is highly exacting, as a minor mistake may lead to grave consequences. Therefore, meticulous care is required.
差值 chāzhí D-value; differential value
差值图 chāzhítú 〈气象〉differential chart
差转台 chāzhuǎntái differential transmission station; relay station

艖 chā 〈书面〉small boat; skiff

碴 chā *see* "胡子拉碴" húzilāchā
see also chá

喳 chā
see also zhā
喳喳 chāchā whispering sound:他俩喊喊～地说了许久。The two of them whispered to each other for quite some time.
喳喳 chācha whisper:他在～些什么? What is he whispering about?
喳喳舞 chāchāwǔ cha-cha; cha-cha-cha

馇 chā ❶ cook and stir (feed for pigs):～猪食 cook feed for pigs ❷〈方言〉cook porridge:～粥 cook porridge
see also zha

嚓 chā 〈象声〉*see* "喀嚓" kāchā; "啪嚓" pāchā
see also cā

臿 chā ❶〈书面〉spade; shovel ❷〈方言〉thresh:～米 thresh rice

插 chā ❶ insert; stick in:在书里～张书签 insert a bookmark between the pages of the book /～门 latch (*or* bolt) the door /把花～在花瓶里 put the flowers in a vase /山峰直～云端。The peak towers into the clouds. /他感到胸部剧痛,好像～了一把刀。He felt a sharp pain, as if a dagger had been stuck in his chest. ❷ interpose; insert:在报道中间～些评论 insert (*or* interpose) some comments in a report /～楔子 drive a wedge /我们说话时,她总想～上几句。When we talk, she always tries to chip in. /再版时要～入这张示意图。This sketch map will have to be included in the next edition.
插班 chābān join a class in the middle of the school year or a course:～生 mid-course student
插棒式继电器 chābàngshì jìdiànqì 〈电工〉plunger relay
插播 chābō insert (an item) in a radio or TV programme; broadcast or televise impromptu:在节目中～广告 insert commercials in a programme /现在～奥运会最新消息。Here's the latest news about the Olympic Games.
插车 chāchē (of individual farmers) pool horses to pull a cart
插齿机 chāchǐjī 〈机械〉gear shaper
插翅难飞 chāchì-nánfēi *also* "插翅难逃" unable to fly away even if given wings — impossible to escape
插床 chāchuáng 〈机械〉slotting machine; slotter:齿轮～ gear slotter
插袋 chādài *see* "插兜"
插戴 chādài ornament worn in the hair:男家下聘礼时,送来了几件崭新的～。A few brand-new hair ornaments were among the betrothal gifts from the bridegroom's family.
插刀 chādāo 〈机械〉slotting tool
插定 chādìng gift sent by the boy's family to the girl's to mark their betrothal; engagement gift:男方送了～,眼看这桩婚事就成了。It looks as though the wedding will soon take place since the fiancé has already sent over engagement gifts.
插兜 chādōu with one's hands in one's pants' pockets
插断 chāduàn interpose (a remark, etc.); chip in; interrupt:他讲话时几次被别人～,差点没讲完。He was almost unable to finish his speech because of several interruptions.
插队 chāduì ❶ cut in a line; jump the queue:请按顺序买票,不要～。Please buy your tickets in turn; don't jump the queue. ❷ (as in the 60's and 70's) go to live and work in a production team of a rural commune:下乡～ go to live and work in a production team in the countryside
插队落户 chāduì-luòhù go and settle as a member of a production team
插队知青 chāduì zhīqīng school graduate living and working as a member of a rural production team
插杠子 chā gàngzi poke one's nose into sb.'s business; meddle; butt in:别到处～! Don't poke your nose in everybody's business. /我没想到他会在我们中间～。Little did I imagine that he would try to drive a wedge between us.
插管 chāguǎn 〈医学〉intubate:～法 intubation
插关儿 chāguanr 〈方言〉small door-latch
插花 chāhuā ❶ mingle; intermingle:～地 land belonging to one production unit but enclosed in that of another /我们在玉米地里还～种着豆子。We grow soybeans in between the corn crops. ❷ flower arrangement; ikebana:日本妇女擅长～艺术。Japanese women are good at ikebana. ❸〈方言〉embroider
插话 chāhuà ❶ interpose; chip in:别～! 让他讲下去。Don't interrupt. Let him go on. /这时,母亲～说她不愿意去。At this point, mother chipped in saying that she didn't want to go. /大人谈事情,小孩子插什么话! Children mustn't butt in when adults are talking! ❷ interruption:她妹妹的～很值得思考。Her sister's remark in the middle of the conversation is worth pondering. ❸ digression; episode:文章中有这么一段～就更吸引人了。With this digression, the article becomes all the more interesting.

插画 chāhuà illustration:这本书的~很精美。This book has beautiful illustrations. /谁为这本书做的~? Who did the illustrating for the book?
插架 chājià ❶ shelve (books); put on shelf:~的地方志有五百部。There are 500 local chronicles on the shelves. ❷〈旧语〉hanging (book) shelf
插肩袖 chājiānxiù raglan sleeve
插件 chājiàn plug-in board, module, unit, etc.
插脚 chājiǎo ❶ gain a foothold; find a place to rest one's feet:屋里人太多,根本无法~。The room was so crowded that it was difficult for me to squeeze in. ❷ be engaged in; be involved in:事情太复杂,我们不宜~其间。The matter is so complicated that we'd better stay away from it. /这是他们家的内政,外人最好不要~。As this is their domestic affair, outsiders had better not intervene.
插接 chājiē 〈植物〉peg graft
插接板 chājiēbǎn 〈电工〉wiring board; pinboard
插接式程序设计 chājiēshì chéngxù shèjì pinboard programming
插进式铣削 chājìnshì xǐxiāo 〈机械〉plunge-cut milling
插犋 chājù (of individual farmers) pool farm implements and draft animals:两家合伙~,亲密如同一家。Pooling their farm implements and draft animals for joint farming, the two families became as close as though they were of the same household.
插科打诨 chākē-dǎhùn ❶ (of an actor) make impromptu comic gestures and remarks:这丑角的~令人绝倒。The clown's impromptu gestures and remarks are absolutely hilarious. ❷ jesting, buffoonery:老张就喜欢~。Lao Zhang is so fond of jesting (*or* making gags).
插孔 chākǒng socket; cutlet; jack; spigot
插孔板 chākǒngbǎn jack base; jack board; jack panel; female receptacle
插空 chākòng find time (out of a busy schedule):我~写了两封信。I managed to find time to write a couple of letters.
插口 chākǒu ❶ socket; jack; spigot:收音机~ socket for the radio /电器~ sockets for electric appliances ❷ interrupt; chip in; cut in:他妹妹~说道,她不喜欢那个人。His sister chipped in, saying that she did not particularly like that man.
插屏 chāpíng 〈工美〉table plaque; table screen
插瓶 chāpíng vase; big-bellied vase
插曲 chāqǔ ❶ songs in a film or play ❷〈音乐〉interlude ❸ episode; interlude:这是他生活中一个小小的~。This is an episode in his life.
插入 chārù ❶ insert:小说中~的这几个细节十分感人。Several of the episodes in the novel are very moving. ❷〈电工〉plug in:~部件 plug-in unit
插入卡 chārùkǎ plug-in card
插入器 chārùqì inserter
插入语 chārùyǔ parenthesis
插入杂交 chārù zájiāo cross-breeding
插身 chāshēn ❶ squeeze in; edge in:难以~ difficult to squeeze in ❷ take part in; get involved in:~某事 get involved in sth. /他不愿~派别斗争。He wants to steer clear of (*or* keep away from) factional strife.
插手 chāshǒu ❶ take part in; lend a hand:我是想帮忙,可是插不上手啊。I do want to help but do not know how to. ❷ have a hand in; meddle in:反对任何外来势力~ oppose interference by any outside force /超级大国的~ superpower interference (*or* intervention) /别人的事,不用你~! Don't poke your nose into other people's affairs! *or* Mind your own business! /每样事他都要~。He wants to have a finger in every pie.
插穗 chāsuì *see* "插条"
插条 chātiáo *also* "插枝"; "插穗"〈植物〉transplant a cutting
插头 chātóu *also* "插销"〈电工〉plug:三脚~ three-pin plug
插图 chātú illustration; plate:彩色~ colour illustration; colour plate /~本 illustrated edition (of a book)
插线程序计算机 chāxiàn chéngxù jìsuànjī 〈计算机〉wired-program computer
插销 chāxiāo ❶ bolt; latch (of a door or window):门上没安~。The door has no bolt. ❷ *see* "插头"
插销口 chāxiāokǒu pin clamp
插叙 chāxù flashback:这个故事中有几段精彩的~。The story contains several well-contrived flashbacks.
插言 chāyán *see* "插话"
插秧 chāyāng transplant rice seedlings or shoots:~季节 time for rice-transplanting; rice-transplanting period
插秧机 chāyāngjī rice transplanter; seedling planting machine
插页 chāyè inset; insert:这本导游书有好些~。The tourist guide book has quite a few insets.
插枝 chāzhī *see* "插条"
插足 chāzú ❶ gain a foothold; put one's foot in:这屋子里挤得没法儿~。The room is too crowded even to put one's foot in. *or* There is not even standing room here. ❷ get involved in:第三者~ involvement of a third party /他在这件事上~太深。He is too deeply involved in the matter.
插嘴 chāzuǐ interrupt; chip in:插不上嘴 can't get a word in edgeways /你别~,先听我说完。Don't interrupt. Let me finish first. /她一口气说下去,不让别人~。She spoke without a pause, leaving no chance for anyone to chip in.
插座 chāzuò 〈电工〉socket; outlet:弹簧~ cushion socket /三用~ three-way socket /多用~ multiple-purpose socket
插座转接器 chāzuò zhuǎnjiēqì socket adapter

锸 chā spade; shovel

叉 chā ❶ fork:刀~ knife and fork/木~ wooden fork /钢~ steel fork /鱼~ fish spear /干草~ hayfork ❷ work with a fork; fork:~稻草 fork hay /~鱼 spear fish ❸ (of a mark, "×", indicating a mistake or sth. to be erased) cross:打~号 put a cross on it; cross it out /这道题算错了,应打~。As the answer is wrong, a cross should be put over it.
see also chá; chǎ; chà
叉车 chāchē *also* "铲运车" chǎnyùnchē forklift
叉齿试验 chāchǐ shìyàn 〈林业〉prong test
叉规 chāguī fork gauge
叉角羚 chājiǎolíng 〈动物〉pronghorn (*Antilocapra americana*)
叉接 chājiē 〈机械〉forked joint
叉麻雀 chā máquè 〈方言〉play mah-jong
叉烧 chāshāo roasting of salted lean pork on a skewer:~肉 skewer-roasted pork
叉式起重机 chāshì qǐzhòngjī 〈机械〉fork-lift
叉式装载机 chāshì zhuāngzàijī 〈机械〉forklift loader
叉手 chāshǒu fold both hands (as in greeting):~直立 stand upright folding both hands in greeting
叉丝 chāsī *also* "十字丝" shízìsī cross hair; spider line
叉形接头 chāxíng jiētóu fork joint
叉形指针 chāxíng zhǐzhēn split pointer
叉腰 chāyāo akimbo:两手~ with arms akimbo
叉子 chāzi fork:用~吃饭 eat with a fork /发~ U-shaped hair pin /干草~ pitchfork; hayfork

杈 chā wooden fork; hayfork; pitchfork
see also chà

扠 chā work with a fork; fork

chá

茬 chá ❶ stubble:麦~儿 wheat stubble /豆~儿 bean stubble /须~ stubbly moustache ❷ crop:二~韭菜 second crop of Chinese chives /这块菜地一年能种四、五~。The vegetable plot can produce four or five crops a year. ❸ *variant for* "碴儿" chár
茬地 chádì stubble field:~放养 (of poultry, etc.) stubble feeding
茬口 chákou ❶ crops for rotation:他会安排~,所以年年丰收。He is able to select the right crops for rotation and so reaps a good harvest every year. ❷ soil on which a crop has been planted and harvested:油菜~ land on which rape seed has been grown and harvested /有些~壮,换茬儿时可以多种。As some crops enrich the soil, we can plant more after they are harvested. ❸〈方言〉opportune moment; juncture:在这个~上出了问题,真是糟透了。It is extremely unfortunate that things should go wrong at this juncture. /趁着这个~,我们辞职吧。Let's seize the present opportunity to hand in our resignations.
茬子 cházi stalks and roots of a harvested crop:~地 stubble land /

C

刨～ dig out the stubble

茶 chá ❶ tea; tea leaves:种～ grow tea /采～ pick tea leaves /绿～ green tea /红～ black tea /花～ jasmine tea /砖～ brick tea /龙井～ Dragon Well tea /清～ tea without refreshments /浓～ strong tea /冰～ ice-tea /沏～ make tea ❷〈旧语〉betrothal gift (formerly consisting of tea):下～ present betrothal gifts ❸ dark brown: *see* "～镜";"～色" ❹ certain kinds of drink or liquid food: 奶～ cream tea /草药～ herb-tea /油～ paste made of flour, beef fat and other ingredients /杏仁～ almond paste /菊花～ chrysanthemum tea ❺ tea-oil tree; oil-tea camellia ❻ camellia

茶杯 chábēi teacup

茶博士 chábóshì 〈旧语〉waiter in a teahouse

茶场 cháchǎng tea farm; tea plantation

茶匙儿 cháchír teaspoon

茶炊 cháchuī *also* "茶汤壶";"茶炊子";"烧心壶" shāoxīnhú tea-urn:龙头大～ dragon-head tea-urn /黄铜～ copper tea-urn /俄国～ samovar

茶道 chádào (Japan) tea ceremony

茶底儿 chádǐr tea dregs

茶点 chádiǎn tea and pastries; tea and cookies; refreshments:晚会备有～。Light refreshments will be provided at the evening party.

茶碟儿 chádiér saucer

茶饭 cháfàn food and drinks; meal;粗茶淡饭 simple meals /～不进 neither eat nor drink /他心情沉重,不思～。Deeply worried, he lost his appetite for meals.

茶房 cháfang 〈旧语〉waiter; steward

茶杆竹 chágǎnzhú *also* "篱竹" lízhú tonkin (cane), a kind of bamboo

茶缸子 chágāngzi (esp. enamel) mug

茶倌 cháguān 〈旧语〉waiter in a teahouse

茶馆 cháguǎn teahouse:开～儿 run (*or* own) a teahouse /坐～儿 drink tea in a teahouse

茶褐色 cháhèsè *also* "茶色" dark brown

茶壶 cháhú teapot; tea kettle

茶花 cháhuā camellia:院子里～盛开。The camellias in the yard are in full bloom. /她在手帕上绣了两朵～。She embroidered a couple of camellias on her handkerchief.

茶话会 cháhuàhuì informal meeting or get-together over tea and refreshments; tea reception; tea party:新年～ get-together to see in the New Year; New Year tea-party /开～ give (*or* organize) a tea party

茶会 cháhuì tea party:举行～招待文艺界的朋友。A tea party was given to entertain friends in art and literature as well as the performing arts.

茶几 chájī tea table; teapoy; side table; coffee table:玻璃～ glass tea table /不锈钢～ tea table made of stainless steel

茶鸡蛋 chájīdàn egg boiled in water blended with tea, spices, soy sauce, etc.

茶剂 chájì herbal mixture; herb tea

茶碱 chájiǎn 〈化学〉theophylline

茶巾 chájīn tea towel; tea cloth

茶经 Chájīng *The Classic of Tea* by Lu Yu (陆羽,733-804) of the Tang Dynasty

茶晶 chájīng citrine; yellow quartz

茶镜 chájìng glasses made of citrine or dark brown glass

茶居 chájū 〈方言〉teahouse

茶具 chájù tea set; tea service:一套精致的～ a beautiful tea set /这套～有十八件。This tea set has eighteen pieces.

茶客 chákè ❶ customer in a teahouse ❷〈旧语〉tea-dealer

茶枯 chákū *also* "茶子饼" tea dregs made into cakes

茶楼 chálóu teahouse (usu. of two storeys)

茶炉 chálú boiler (for drinking water); boiler house (for supplying boiling water)

茶卤儿 chálǔr strong tea (to be diluted before drinking)

茶毛虫 chámáochóng 〈动物〉*Euproctis pseudo conspersa*

茶末 chámò tea dust

茶农 chánóng tea grower; tea farmer

茶盘 chápán *also* "茶盘子" tea tray

茶钱 cháqian ❶ payment for tea:我已经付了～。I have paid for the tea. ❷ (another name for 小费) tip

茶青 cháqīng yellowish dark green

茶色 chásè dark brown:～玻璃 dark brown glass /～眼镜 dark brown sunglasses

茶色镜 chásèjìng dark brown sunglasses

茶社 cháshè teahouse

茶室 cháshì (Japan) *cha-shitsu*

茶食 cháshi cookies, cakes and sweetmeats

茶树 cháshù tea plant; tea tree; tea shrub

茶水 cháshuǐ tea or boiled water:～站 tea-stall /供应～ supply tea /迅速给旅客提供～。Tea was promptly brought to the passengers.

茶肆 chásì 〈书面〉teahouse

茶素 chásù *also* "咖啡碱" kāfēijiǎn caffeine

茶摊 chátān tea-stall

茶汤 chátāng ❶ (Beijing flavour) paste or custard made of millet or sorghum flour ❷〈书面〉tea or boiled water

茶汤壶 chátānghú 〈方言〉tea-urn

茶堂 chátáng 〈方言〉teahouse

茶亭 chátíng tea-booth; tea-stall; tea-kiosk

茶托 chátuō saucer

茶碗 cháwǎn tea cup; tea bowl

茶味儿 cháwèir tea flavour:品一品～ sip tea for the flavour /～不正。The tea doesn't have a good flavour. *or* The tea doesn't taste right.

茶文化 cháwénhuà tea culture; tea etiquette

茶锈 cháxiù tea stain

茶叶 cháyè tea; tea leaves:～加工 tea processing /～要泡一会儿,味道才能出来。Let the tea steep a little while, and the flavour will come out. /我带了点～,以备旅途中饮用。I've brought some tea with me so that I can enjoy a ready cup on the journey.

茶叶蛋 cháyèdàn 〈方言〉*see* "茶鸡蛋"

茶叶干燥机 cháyè gānzàojī 〈农业〉tea-leaf withering machine

茶叶罐 cháyèguàn tea canister

茶叶盒 cháyèhé tea box

茶叶花 cháyèhuā *also* "罗布麻" luóbùmá bluish dogbane (*Apocynum venetum*)

茶叶剪修机 cháyè jiǎnxiūjī tea plant pruning machine

茶叶碱 cháyèjiǎn 〈化学〉theocin

茶叶筛分机 cháyè shāifēnjī tea sifting and grading machine

茶叶收获机 cháyè shōuhuòjī 〈农业〉tea cropper

茶叶压实机 cháyè yāshíjī 〈农业〉tea-leaf rolling machine

茶艺 cháyì China's tea ceremony

茶役 cháyì 〈旧语〉waiter; steward

茶油 cháyóu *also* "清油" qīngyóu; "茶子油" tea-seed oil; tea oil

茶余饭后 cháyú-fànhòu *also* "茶余酒后" over a cup of tea or after a meal — at one's leisure:～,大家常在一起聊天。We often get together and chat in our spare time. /这种书只能供～消遣而已。You only read those books for entertainment at your leisure.

茶园 cháyuán ❶ tea farm; tea plantation ❷ tea house; tea garden

茶盅 cházhōng handleless teacup

茶砖 cházhuān *also* "砖茶" tea brick

茶资 cházī expense for tea served in a teahouse

茶座 cházuò ❶ teahouse (usu. outdoor); tea stall ❷ seat in a teahouse or at a tea stall

搽 chá put on or rub into the skin; apply:～粉 powder (one's face) /～雪花膏 put on vanishing cream /～油 put on lotion; apply ointment /～药水 apply liquid medicine

搽剂 chájì liniment

搽脂抹粉 cházhī-mǒfěn *also* "涂脂抹粉" túzhī-mǒfěn apply powder and paint; prettify; whitewash

槎[1] chá 〈书面〉raft:浮～ floating raft

槎[2] chá *see* "茬" chá

查 chá ❶ check; examine; inspect:～卫生 check sanitary conditions; make a sanitation check (*or* inspection) /～电表 read the electricity meter /～血 have a blood test /～尿 have a urine test ❷ look into; investigate:～谣言 chase down a rumour /～清事实的真相 find out the truth about sth. /没有～出 nothing comes of the investigation /～个水落石出 get to the bottom of a matter; investigate sth. thoroughly ❸ look up; consult:～词典 look up a word in the

dictionary; consult a dictionary /～数据 consult the data /～出处 find out the source (of a word, data, etc.); find out chapter and verse (for a quotation, etc.) /～资料 read the literature (on a special subject) /～书目 look in the catalogue /～电话簿 check a telephone directory /～档案 look into the archives /～地图 try to locate a place on the map

see also zhā

查办 chábàn investigate and deal with accordingly: 撤职～ dismiss a person from office and have him prosecuted /～一个案子 investigate a case

查抄 cháchāo make an inventory of a criminal's possessions and confiscate them: ～家产 check on and confiscate the property of a family /～充公 confiscate /奉旨～ be instructed by the emperor to confiscate sb.'s property

查处 cháchǔ investigate and deal with accordingly: 严肃～违反财经纪律的案件 severely deal with transgression of financial regulations

查档 chádàng look into the files; rummage through the archives

查道车 chádàochē track testing trolley; line inspection trolley or car

查点 chádiǎn check the number or amount of; make an inventory of: ～人数 check the number of people present /～库存 make an inventory of the goods in stock; take stock /～办公用品 make an inventory of office stationery

查定能力 chádìng nénglì 〈矿业〉 checked and adjusted capacity

查对 cháduì check; verify: ～材料 check the data /～账目 check the account /～原文 check the original text; check (a quotation or translation) against the original text /～数字 verify the figures /～无误 examined and found correct; verified

查尔平原 Chá'ěr Píngyuán Plaine des Jarres (in Laos)

查尔斯顿舞 chá'ěrsīdùnwǔ Charleston, a lively American dance of the 1920's with side-kicks from the knee

查尔斯王储 Chá'ěrsī Wángchǔ Charles, Prince of Wales (1948-), heir apparent to the British throne

查房 cháfáng make or go the rounds of the wards; (in some hostels) make a routine check of the rooms: 大夫每日上午～。Doctors make their rounds of the wards every morning.

查访 cháfǎng go around and make inquiries; investigate: ～被盗名画的下落 try to track down the stolen famous painting /经过警方多方～,终于找到了逃匿的罪犯。The police made extensive inquiries and eventually found the criminal in hiding.

查封 cháfēng seal up; close down: ～黄色书刊 seal up and ban pornographic publications /这家公司违法经营,已经～。The company has been closed down for conducting business activities forbidden by the law.

查岗 chágǎng go the rounds of guard posts; inspect the sentries

查戈尔斯群岛 Chágē'ěrsī Qúndǎo Chagos Archipelago, consisting of Diego Garcia and other islands in the Indian Ocean

查号台 cháhàotái 〈通信〉 directory inquiries; information: 北京的～是114。If you want to make directory inquiries in Beijing, dial 114.

查核 cháhé check; examine: ～账目 check (*or* examine) accounts /反复～,计算无误。We have verified the calculation by repeated checks.

查户口 chá hùkǒu check residence cards; check house occupants against household registration

查获 cháhuò hunt down and seize; ferret out; track down: ～一批走私品 seize some smuggled goods /～大量违禁录像带 ferret out a good number of contraband video-tapes /～逃犯 track (*or* hunt) down a fugitive criminal

查缉 chájī ❶ search for (contraband, tax evasion, etc.): ～走私物品 search for smuggled goods ❷ hunt down; track down; ferret about for: ～逃犯 track down an escaped convict

查检 chájiǎn ❶ consult; look up: 这部书分类得法,～方便。The book is well organized and convenient for the reader to consult. ❷ check: ～行李 luggage check

查禁 chájìn ban; prohibit: ～赌博 ban gambling

查究 chájiū investigate and ascertain (cause, responsibility, etc.): ～责任 find out who should be held responsible /这是个重大事故,一定要～。This is a serious accident which must be thoroughly investigated.

查勘 chákān survey; prospect: ～矿产资源 prospect for mineral deposits /～三峡地形 survey the Three Gorges of the Yangtze River

查看 chákàn look over; inspect; examine: ～水位 check the water (*or* flood) level /～身分证 check sb.'s identity card /～地图 look up (a place) on a map; look up a map

查考 chákǎo examine; do research on: ～这批古瓷的年代 try to ascertain the date of this lot of ancient porcelain /无处～。There is no source for verification.

查扣 chákòu find out and seize: ～违禁物品 track down and seize contraband goods

查理定律 Chálǐ dìnglǜ 〈化学〉 Charles' law

查明 chámíng prove through investigation; find out; ascertain: ～情况 ascertain the facts /～原因 find out the cause (of sth.) /～他有罪 find him guilty /现已～,他听到的都是毫无根据的谣言。It has been established that what he heard was sheer rumour.

查谟和克什米尔 Chámò hé Kèshímǐ'ěr Jammu and Kashmir (in South Asia) disputed by India and Pakistan

查票 chápiào examine or check tickets

查破 chápò solve a case; clear up a case; crack a criminal case; track down a criminal: 公安机关～各类案件三十余起。The police cleared up over 30 cases of various kinds.

查铺 chápù go the rounds of the beds at night; make a bed check: 连长每天夜里～。The company commander made a bed check in the barracks every night.

查讫 cháqì checked: 这笔账目现已～。The account has been checked.

查勤 cháqín check the rate of attendance; check attendance

查清 cháqīng make a thorough investigation of; check upon: ～他的来历 check up on him; find out his background /要～这个事故是怎么发生的。It is necessary to find out the cause of the accident.

查哨 cháshào *also* "查岗" go the rounds of guard posts; inspect the sentries: 排长每晚都到各哨所～。The platoon leader went the rounds of guard posts every night.

查实 cháshí check and verify: 案情已经～。The case has been unravelled.

查收 cháshōu (often used in letter writing) please find (sth.) enclosed: 寄上文稿,请～。Please find the manuscript enclosed herewith. *or* Enclosed herewith is the manuscript.

查税 cháshuì tax inspection: 本人一向守法,自然就不怕～。As a law-abiding businessman, I am of course not afraid of tax inspection.

查私 chásī seize smuggled goods; suppress smuggling

查文文化 Cháwén wénhuà Chavin culture (about 900-200 BC in today's Peru)

查问 cháwèn ❶ question; interrogate: ～证人 interrogate a witness /～口令 challenge (for a password) ❷ inquire: ～是否收到此信 check to see if the letter is received /此事请你代为～。It is hoped that you will make inquiries on our behalf.

查无实据 cháwúshíjù investigation reveals no evidence (against the suspect): 事出有因,～。The charge may not be without cause, but investigation furnishes no real (*or* solid) evidence.

查寻 cháxún search for; inquire about: 去邮局～邮包 inquire about a parcel at the post office /～失散多年的兄弟 look for a long-missing brother

查巡 cháxún (of police, etc.) make the rounds; go on the patrol: 这一地区夜间有武警～。The armed police patrol this neighbourhood at night.

查询 cháxún inquire about: ～电话号码 inquire about a telephone number /～某事 inquire into sth. /我不知道开车时间,得去～一下。As I don't know the exact time of the train's departure, I must go and inquire.

查询台 cháxúntái information desk

查亚峰 Cháyàfēng Mount Jaya, highest peak in New Guinea

查验 cháyàn check; examine: ～证件 check sb.'s papers /～护照 examine a passport /～行李 inspect the luggage

查夜 cháyè go the rounds at night; make a night patrol

查阅 cháyuè look up; consult: ～历史文献 consult historical documents /～会议记录 look up the minutes of the meeting /为了写这篇文章,他～了十几种参考书。He read up on a dozen of books to write this article.

查阅表 cháyuèbiǎo 〈计算机〉 look-up table

查账 cházhàng check accounts; audit accounts; examine accounts: ～报告 audit report

查找 cházhǎo look for: ～资料 gather data /～失主 look for the owner of a lost article

查找故障程序 cházhǎo gùzhàng chéngxù 〈自控〉 malfunction routine

查照 cházhào 〈旧语〉 please note：即希～ please note／希～办理。Please note and take action accordingly.

查证 cházhèng investigate and verify；check：～属实 be checked and found to be true；be verified／我说的话，句句可以～。Every word of mine can bear close scrutiny.／这件事我们要派人去～。We'll send somebody down to verify the matter.

楂 chá

楂子 cházi 〈方言〉 coarsely ground maize

楂 chá

❶ short，bristly hair or beard；stubble：胡子～ stubbly beard／脖子上还有点头发～。There is some hair on your neck. ❷ *see* "茬" chá

see also zhā

碴 chá

〈方言〉 be cut (by broken glass，chinaware，etc.)：这孩子的手让玻璃～破了。The little boy cut his fingers on the broken glass.

see also chā

碴口 chákǒu broken end；cut：警察正在检查输电线断的～。The police are examining the broken ends of the power line.

碴儿 chár ❶ broken piece；fragment：冰～ small pieces of ice／玻璃～ fragments of glass／骨头～ bits of bones；crushed bones ❷ sharp edge of broken glass，china，etc.：小心碗～，别扛了手！Don't cut yourself on the sharp edge of the broken bowl! ❸ cause of a quarrel；quarrel：没～找～ find fault with sb.；pick a quarrel with sb.／他俩有～，经常吵架。They bore a grudge against each other and often had rows. ❹ sth. just said or mentioned；cue：答～ follow up (on what sb. said)；speak in reply／接～ take the cue ❺ 〈方言〉 look of things：一看不是～，他跑了。Sensing that the odds were against him，he ran away.

猹 chá

badger-like animal

詧 chá

see "察" chá

察 chá

examine；look into；scrutinize：～其言，观其行 examine his words and watch his deeds；check what he says against what he does／体～民情 acquaint oneself with the condition of the people；watch the public mood

察察为明 cháchá-wéimíng be shrewd in small matters：他以～，甚是自得。He prides himself on the cleverness he shows in trifling matters.

察访 cháfǎng investigate through visit and observation：实地～ make an on-the-spot investigation／～江南 make an inspection tour in the area south of the Yangtze／到基层～ make an investigation at the grassroots level

察哈尔人 Cháhā'ěrrén Chahar (formerly translated as Chakhar)，eastern branch of China's Mongolian nationality active during the 15th and 16th centuries

察核 cháhé examine and verify；examine and approve

察觉 chájué be conscious of；become aware of；perceive：我们对他的犯罪活动已有所～。We are aware (*or* have some inkling) of his criminal activities.／我没有～到有什么危险。I didn't sense (*or* see) any danger.／一个人的感情变化不易～。It is difficult to perceive the change in a person's feeling.

察勘 chákān make a field survey：～水源 make an on-the-spot investigation of water resources

察看 chákàn watch；inspect；examine；observe：～灾情 inspect the aftermath of a disaster；ascertain the extent of damage caused by a disaster／～地形 survey the terrain／～现场 examine the site (*or* scene) of an accident (*or* a crime)／～风向 watch which way the wind is blowing／～动静 look around to see if anything is afoot

察探 chátàn investigate；detect；scout：～敌情 scout an area to obtain information about the enemy；gather intelligence about the enemy

察沃国家公园 Cháwò Guójiā Gōngyuán Tsavo National Park (biggest in Kenya)

察言观色 cháyán-guānsè try to read sb.'s thoughts from his words and facial expressions；weigh sb.'s words and watch the expression on his face：～，相机行事 watch sb.'s mood and act accordingly／为得主人欢心，她时刻～。She watches every mood of her master so as to curry favour with him.

察验 cháyàn examine；check；test：对产品质量进行～ check the quality of products／～项链的成色 examine the percentage of gold in a necklace

檫 chá

〈植物〉 sassafras

垞 chá

earthern mound

叉 chá

〈方言〉 block；jam：河里的冰块～住了。The ice blocked up the river.／车辆～住了路口。The vehicles jammed the road.

see also chā；chǎ；chà

chǎ

蹅 chǎ

trudge (in mud，snow，etc.)：～了两脚泥 step into a mud puddle and get both feet soiled／把鞋～湿了 get one's shoes wet while walking

镲 chǎ

〈乐器〉 cymbal：打～ strike a pair of cymbals

叉 chǎ

part so as to form a fork；fork：～开双腿 open one's legs／～着腿站着 stand with one's legs apart

see also chā；chá；chà

衩 chǎ

see "裤衩" kùchǎ

see also chà

chà

差 chà

❶ differ：意见之～ difference of opinion／相～甚远 be extremely different；differ greatly (from each other)／这哥儿俩的性格～得远。The two brothers are poles apart in character. ❷ wrong；mistaken：小～小错 minor mistakes；small errors；peccadilloes／判断之～ mistake in judgement／你这话说～了。What you said is wrong. *or* You are mistaken. ❸ be wanting；fall short of：～一道手续 have yet one more formality to go through／～十分两点 ten (minutes) to two／离目标还～得很远 be (*or* fall) far short of the goal／还～两天就开学了。There are two more days before the new term starts.／就～十块钱。We are ten *yuan* short. *or* The sum comes short by ten *yuan*.／我还～你五块钱。I still owe you five *yuan*.／还～一个人。There is one person short. *or* We are short of one person. ❹ not up to standard；poor；inferior：质量～ of low (*or* inferior) quality／设备～ poorly equipped／我的英语比她～。My English is not as good as hers.／这人太～，你别理他。You'd better keep away from him；he is such a mean guy.

see also chā；chāi；chài；cī

差不点儿 chàbudiǎnr nearly；on the verge of：小张心里难过得～要哭出来。Xiao Zhang was so upset that she was on the verge of tears.

差不多 chàbuduō ❶ almost；nearly：他～五十了。He is nearly fifty years old (or getting on towards fifty).／～六点了。It's almost six o'clock.／我～快干完了。I am winding up my work. *or* I'm almost done. ❷ about the same；similar：兄弟俩长得～。The two brothers look very much alike.／两国的自然情况～。The natural conditions of the two countries are similar. ❸ just about right or enough；not bad；not far off；just so-so："～"思想 mentality of "That's good enough"；complacency／我没有那么大的雄心，～就行了。I'm not that ambitious. I'm quite happy being average.

差不多的 chàbuduōde average person；ordinary people：这种常理，～都明白。This is understood by the man in the street.／这样的事，～都不会去做。People with common sense would not do things like that.

差不离儿 chàbulír *see* "差不多"

差等 chàděng (of students level) below the average：～生 poor student

see also cīděng

差点儿 chàdiǎnr *also*"差一点儿" ❶ not quite up to the mark; not good enough: 他的数学～。His math is not quite up to the mark. /这套西服的做工～。The tailoring of the suit is not good enough. /这点心味道～。The cake doesn't taste very nice. ❷ almost; nearly: ～就迟到了 be almost late /～没赶上飞机 very nearly miss the plane /～没哭出来 hold back one's tears with difficulty /～就完了 make a narrow escape; escape by the skin of one's teeth

差劲 chàjìn no good; disappointing: 两队打得都很～。Neither of the two teams played well. *or* Both teams were disappointing. /这幅画画得够～的了。This painting is no good at all. /这椅子可～啦,没用几天就坏了。This chair was shoddy stuff. It collapsed after a few days. /他办事拖拖拉拉,太～了。He is very disappointing with his dilatory style of work.

差生 chàshēng slow student; poor student: 帮助～补习功课 help a slow student with his lessons

差事 chàshì no good; of inferior quality: 这书的装订太～,全散了! The binding of the book is really poor. Look, it's all in loose pages!
see also chāishi

差样 chàyàng 〈方言〉 different kind; variety: 王大妈把他当成亲生儿子,吃口什么～的饭菜都给他留点儿。Aunt Wang treated him as a son of her own, always saving some food for him whenever they had something special for a change.

侘 chà

侘傺 chàchì 〈书面〉 feel low; look disconsolate

诧 chà

be surprised: ～为奇事 be surprised at sth. unusual; regard as a wonder

诧愕 chà'è 〈书面〉 be astounded; be astonished

诧怪 chàguài *see*"诧异"

诧然 chàrán be taken by surprise; be astonished: 此言一出,举座～。The remark astonished everybody present.

诧异 chàyì be surprised; be amazed; be astonished: 他反常的举动,使大家十分～。People were taken aback by his aberrant behaviour. /她用～的目光看着他。She gave him an astonished look. *or* She looked at him with bewilderment.

侘 chà

侘傺 chàchì 〈书面〉 feel low; look disconsolate

姹(奼) chà

〈书面〉 beautiful

姹紫嫣红 chàzǐ-yānhóng brilliant purples and reds; blaze of colours: 节日的广场,是一片～的花海。The square decked out with flowers during the festival was a blaze of colours.

刹 chà

Buddhist temple; Buddhist monastery: 古～ ancient temple /宝～ Buddhist dagoba; 〈敬词〉 your temple
see also shā

刹地利 Chàdìlì Kshatriya — caste of warriors in traditional India

刹那 chànà instant; split second: 一～ in an instant; in a flash /～间 in a split second; in the twinkling of an eye

岔 chà

❶ branch off: 从主干线上～开 branch off from the main line /从右边分～ branch off to the right /鹿角的～枝 branched horns of a male deer; stag's antler /这棵树在中部～开。This tree branches off in the middle. ❷ turn off; diverge: 自行车～上了左边的小道。The cyclist turned off into a trail on the left. /他讲着讲着就～到一边去了。He strayed from the main subject as he spoke. ❸ change the topic or subject of conversation: 打～ interrupt; butt in /他有意把话～开了。He changed the topic on purpose. ❹ stagger: 把两个会的时间～开 stagger the time of the two meetings /～开办公时间 stagger office hours /咱们～开时间去看他。Let us call on him separately. ❺ accident; mistake: 你放心吧,出不了～儿。Don't worry. Everything will be all right. *or* Don't worry. Nothing will go wrong. ❻ 〈方言〉 be hoarse; lose one's voice: 他高声大叫,嗓音都～了。He shouted himself hoarse.

岔道儿 chàdàor *see*"岔路"

岔管 chàguǎn branch pipe

岔换 chàhuàn 〈方言〉 ❶ swap by mistake or on purpose: 看好自己的行李,别被人家～了! Keep an eye on your luggage! Otherwise, it might be mistaken for that of somebody else. ❷ (of mood, taste, etc.) for a change; change: 我们晚上吃饺子,～一下口味。We are going to have dumplings for supper, just for a change.

岔口 chàkǒu fork (in a road): 你到了～就往东走。Turn east when you get to a fork in the road.

岔流 chàliú *also*"汊流" chàliú (of a river) tributary outlet into the sea; branch of a river: 这条河有四条～。This river has four tributary outlets into the sea.

岔路 chàlù *also*"岔道儿" branch road; byroad; side road: 三～ fork in the road; junction of three roads /过了石桥,有一条到刘庄的～。On the other side of the stone bridge, there is a side road leading to the Liu Village. /前面～很多,不要走错了。There are quite a few branch roads ahead. Don't get lost.

岔气 chàqì feel a pain in the chest when breathing: 没关系,是笑得太厉害,～了。Nothing serious. It's the kind of pain you often get in the chest when you are seized with spasms of laughter.

岔曲儿 chàqǔr lyrical prelude to single-stringed fiddle recital: 一段～唱过,听众慢慢静了下来。The audience gradually quieted down after the prelude.

岔头 chàtou 〈方言〉 accident; mistake; trouble
see also"岔子❷"

岔眼 chàyǎn (of draught animals) misjudge by sight and be alarmed: 这匹马一～,飞也似地跑起来。The horse had false vision and started galloping like mad.

岔子 chàzi ❶ *see*"岔路" ❷ accident; trouble; mistake: 他还没回来,该不是出了什么～吧? He is still not back. Has something gone wrong? /他开车很有经验,从来没出过～。He is a good driver, and has never had an accident. /是我自己出的～,不能怪别人。No one is to blame but myself for the mistake.

叉 chà

see"劈叉" pǐchà
see also chā; chá; chǎ

汊 chà

also"汊子" branch of a river; tributary: 湖～ arm of a lake /河～ river branch; river arm

汊港 chàgǎng tributary: 江南水乡,满布江河～。The region south of the Yangtze River is criss-crossed with rivers and their tributaries.

汊流 chàliú tributary outlet into the sea
see also"岔流" chàliú

汊子 chàzi branch of a river; tributary

衩 chà

slit or vent in the side of a garment: 旗袍在两边开～。The banner robe (*or* traditional Chinese long dress) has slits on both sides. /这条裙子的后～太长了。The rear slit of the skirt is much too long.
see also chǎ

杈 chà

branch (of a tree): 树～ tree branch /打～ trim; trim branches off a tree /打棉花～ trim cotton plants
see also chā

杈子 chàzi branch of a tree

chāi

差 chāi

❶ send on an errand; dispatch: ～人去请医生 send for a doctor /～他去联系业务。He was sent there on a business trip. ❷ 〈旧语〉 one sent on such an errand; errand-boy; hireling: 听～ errand-boy; servant /支～ on an errand /他过去在县衙里当过～。He used to serve as a runner (*or* be a runner) in the county government office (*or yamen*). ❸ job; official post: 兼～ hold more than one job concurrently /(因公)出～ be away on official business /交～ report back to the leadership after finishing a task /美～ cushy job; lucrative job
see also chā; chà; chài; cī

差拨 chāibō ❶ send on an errand or mission; dispatch ❷ 〈旧语〉 (often used in the early vernacular) *yamen* runner

差船 chāichuán 〈旧语〉 boat commandeered by the government

差馆 chāiguǎn 〈方言〉 police station

差佬 chāilǎo 〈方言〉 cop; policeman

差旅费 chāilǚfèi travel accommodation and other expenses paid

on official business; allowances for a business trip:报销～ have all the expense for one's business trip reimbursed

差妹 chāimèi 〈方言〉woman gatekeeper; woman janitor

差婆 chāipó 〈方言〉policewoman

差遣 chāiqiǎn send on an errand or mission; dispatch; assign:听候～ be at sb.'s disposal; be at sb.'s beck and call /经理～他到上海调查工厂产品的销路。The manager sent him to Shanghai to investigate the market conditions for the factory's products.

差缺 chāiquē 〈旧语〉vacant position; vacancy

差人 chāirén 〈旧语〉policeman

差使 chāishǐ send; assign; appoint:他是受人～才这样干的。He did this at somebody else's instigation. /我才不愿受人～呢! I don't want to be ordered about.

差使 chāishi 〈旧语〉official post; billet; commission:托人找～ ask sb. to recommend one for a job /他被派了一个好～。He was assigned to a good post.

差事 chāishi ❶ errand; assignment:你这次去天津的～是什么? What's the purpose of your Tianjin trip? /给你一件～去办。Here is a job for you. ❷ see "差使" chāishi

see also chàshì

差饷 chāixiǎng salary; pay

差役 chāiyì ❶ corvée:服～ do (*or* serve) one's corvée ❷〈旧语〉runner *or* bailiff in a *yamen*:衙门里的～ bailiff in a *yamen* /官府～ runner in a government office

拆 chāi ❶ (tear) open; take apart; undo:把包裹～开 (tear) open a parcel /～信 open a letter /～封 break the seal /～衣服 unstitch (*or* unpick) a garment /～毛衣 unravel a sweater /～机器 take a machine apart; disassemble a machine; strip a machine /把这个组～了 break up the group /～帐篷 break (*or* strike) a tent (*or* camp) ❷ pull down; demolish; dismantle:～房子 pull down (*or* demolish) a house /～桥 dismantle a bridge /～障碍物 remove the obstacles

see also cā

拆白 chāibái 〈方言〉swindle:到处～ swindle right and left

拆白党 chāibáidǎng gang of swindlers; swindler

拆包机 chāibāojī bale breaker

拆包钳 chāibāoqián bale hoop cutter

拆除 chāichú pull down; demolish; dismantle; remove:～违章建筑 pull down (*or* demolish) buildings put up in violation of municipal rules /～碉堡 demolish a pillbox /～危房 tear down crumbling houses /～军事基地 dismantle military bases /～铆钉 unrivet

拆穿 chāichuān expose; unmask; debunk:～骗局 expose a fraud /～伪装 strip off sb.'s mask; unmask /～谎言 nail a lie to the counter; give the lie to sth. /～阴谋 uncover a conspiracy /～西洋镜 expose a trick; give away the show

拆东墙,补西墙 chāi dōngqiáng, bǔ xīqiáng 〈俗语〉tear down the east wall to repair the west wall — resort to a make-shift solution; rob Peter to pay Paul:～,就这样对付着过日子。Rob Peter to pay Paul — that's how they manage to eke out a minimal living.

拆兑 chāiduì 〈方言〉borrow (money or sth.) for a short while (to tide over an unforeseen difficulty)

拆股 chāigǔ dissolve a partnership:～分息 dissolve the partnership and divide up the dividends /干脆～拉倒,省得大家合不来。Since the partners cannot get along, the simplest thing to do would be to break up the partnership altogether.

拆股发行 chāigǔ fāxíng 〈经济〉scrip issue

拆毁 chāihuǐ tear down; pull down; demolish:这一带的古建筑不幸被～了。The ancient buildings in this area have been torn down, to our regret.

拆伙 chāihuǒ dissolve a partnership; part company:那个戏班子已经～了。That opera troupe has been dissolved already.

拆建 chāijiàn demolish old buildings to make room for new ones:～工程进展顺利。The demolition of old houses to make land available for building new ones has made smooth progress.

拆借 chāijiè make a short-term loan (usu. at a daily interest):银行之间的相互～ interbank short-term loans /～一百万元 make a short-term loan of one million *yuan*

拆开 chāikāi open; take apart; separate; disassemble:把邮包～ open the parcel /这小孩把玩具～了自己装不上。The child has taken the toy apart but can't put the pieces back together. /任何力量也不能把这对夫妻～。Nothing on earth could separate this couple.

拆零 chāilíng sell piece by piece (instead of the whole lot):～销售 sell piece by piece; sell piecemeal /这家夫妻店卖针可以～。You can buy one or two needles at this Pop-and-Mom store (instead of a whole packet).

拆卖 chāimài dismantle and sell the parts:成套的家具怎么能～呢? How could a set of furniture be sold piece by piece?

拆模 chāimú 〈建筑〉form removal; form stripping

拆迁 chāiqiān pull down old houses and resettle the inhabitants:～工程 resettlement project /这座水坝估计要～一千户居民。This dam project is estimated to involve the resettlement of 1,000 households.

拆迁户 chāiqiānhù household to be resettled

拆墙脚 chāi qiángjiǎo undermine; pull the rug (out) from under sb.:你这样做,就是拆公司的墙脚。What you're doing is undermining the company.

拆散 chāisǎn break apart:这些瓷器是成套的,打包时不要～了。These pieces (of china) form one set, don't pack them separately.

拆散 chāisàn break up:～婚姻 break up a marriage /很多幸福的家庭在战争中给～了。Many happy families were broken up during the war.

拆梢 chāishāo 〈方言〉cheat; swindle:这是流氓～。That's a shameless swindle set up by hooligans.

拆台 chāitái cut the ground from under sb.'s feet; pull away a prop:互相～ counteract each other's efforts /你不能趁机拆大家的台。You mustn't cut the ground from under everybody's feet at this juncture.

拆息 chāixī daily interest (of banking):～如此之高,令人咋舌。The daily interest is astonishingly high.

拆息率 chāixīlǜ offer rate:银行～ interbank offer rate

拆洗 chāixǐ ❶ wash (padded coats, quilts, etc.) after removing the padding or lining; unpick and wash:～棉大衣 unpick and wash a cotton padded coat /～被褥 unpick and wash beddings ❷ (of a machine) strip and clean:这台机床的主要部件要～。The main parts of the machine need to be stripped for cleaning.

拆线 chāixiàn 〈医学〉unstitch; take out the stitches or sutures:伤口愈合,很快就要～。The stitches will soon be removed as the wound has healed.

拆线刀 chāixiàndāo 〈医学〉seam ripper

拆卸 chāixiè dismantle; disassemble; dismount:～引擎 dismantle an engine /～车床 disassemble a lathe

拆用 chāiyòng take sth. apart and use the parts thereof:这台旧机器还可以～。This old machine may be taken apart so as to use some of its parts. /～虽然麻烦,但可以省些钱。Though it is a lot of trouble dismantling the machine and using its parts, yet it could save some money.

拆账 chāizhàng ❶〈旧语〉(of opera troupes, or catering, hairdressing and other service trades) pay wages in proportion to earnings /明天～,给大家发工钱。The earnings will be distributed tomorrow, and all of you will get paid. ❷ divide (profit, income, etc.) on a percentage basis:三、七～ divide the profit on a 30 to 70 percent basis

拆装 chāizhuāng dismantle and reassemble:私自～ unauthorized dismantling and reassembling

拆字 chāizì fortune-telling by taking a character apart

see also "测字" cèzì

钗 chāi hairpin (formerly worn by women for adornment):荆～布裙 (of women) plainly dressed

chái

柴(❷瘵) chái ❶ firewood:上山砍～ gather (*or* collect) firewood in the mountains ❷〈方言〉bony; not fleshy:骨瘦如～ bony; be all skin and bone /这牛肉又～又硬。The beef is dry and tough. ❸〈方言〉poor; shoddy; inferior:棋下得特～ be extremely poor at chess /这车刚开了一个月就坏了,太～了。The car is of such poor quality that it broke down after only one month. ❹ (Chái) a surname

柴草 cháicǎo firewood; faggot:烧～做饭 cook food on a faggot fire; cook food by burning firewood /他推着一辆破车给大家分～。He was pushing a rickety cart to deliver firewood.

柴达木盆地 Cháidámù Péndì Qaidam Basin (in Qinghai Province)
柴刀 cháidāo firewood chopper
柴扉 cháifēi 〈书面〉door made of small sticks and broken pieces of wood: ～虚掩。The wicket door is left unbolted.
柴胡 cháihú 〈中药〉Chinese thorowax (*Bupleurum chinensis*)
柴火 cháihuo firewood; faggot: 一堆～ a heap of faggots / 下工的路上,他顺手拾些～。On his way home from work, he picked up some firewood.
柴鸡 cháijī small-bodied chicken
柴可夫斯基 Cháikěfūsījī Peter Ilich Tchaikovsky (1840-1893), Russian composer
柴门 cháimén door made of twigs; wicket door; poor family: 一扇～ door made of twigs; wicket door / 出身～ be born to a poor family / 农家院落～半开。The wicket gate to a rural cottage was left ajar.
柴米 cháimǐ firewood and rice — daily necessaries: 不当家不知～贵。You never know how much it takes to keep a family going, until you begin to manage its finances.
柴米夫妻 cháimǐ-fūqī impoverished couple who married for convenience
柴米油盐 chái-mǐ-yóu-yán fuel, rice, oil and salt — daily necessities: 一个家庭主妇得每日为～发愁。A housewife has to worry about the food on the table every day.
柴爿 cháipán 〈方言〉firewood; kindling
柴炭 cháitàn ❶ faggot ❷ charcoal
柴窑 Cháiyáo Chai kiln, said to be located near present Zhengzhou (郑州), whose porcelain was popular in the Song Dynasty
柴油 cháiyóu diesel oil: ～指数 diesel index
柴油泵 cháiyóubèng 〈机械〉diesel pump
柴油机 cháiyóujī *also* "狄赛尔机" dísài'ěrjī diesel engine: 船用～ marine diesel engine / 陆用～ stationary diesel engine / ～动力装置 diesel power plant / ～发电机组 diesel set; diesel-engine generator set / ～发电站 diesel generating station; diesel electric power station / ～直流发电机 diesel dynamo
柴油机车 cháiyóu jīchē 〈交通〉diesel locomotive; diesel-engine
柴油发电机 cháiyóu fādiànjī diesel generator
柴油发动机 cháiyóu fādòngjī diesel motor

豺 chái *also* "豺狗" jackal
豺狼 cháiláng jackals and wolves — cruel and evil people: 像～一般凶狠 as cruel and ferocious as jackals and wolves
豺狼成性 cháiláng-chéngxìng wolfish; rapacious and ruthless: 奴隶主～,令人发指。The ruthlessness and cruelty of the slaveowners make people bristle with anger.
豺狼当道 cháiláng-dāngdào jackals and wolves hold sway; evil people are in power: ～,安问狐狸? When the wolf is rampant, why pick on the fox? / ～,民不聊生。With evil people in power, the common folks were rendered destitute.

侪(儕) chái 〈书面〉peers; fellows; associates: 吾～ we; people like us
侪辈 cháibèi 〈书面〉people of the same generation or kind; peers
侪类 cháilèi *see* "侪辈"

chǎi

茝 chǎi a kind of fragrant plant referred to in ancient books

蹅 chǎi ground beans or maize: 豆～儿 ground beans / 把玉米磨成～儿 grind the maize into powder

chài

差 chài *see* "瘥" shài
see also chā; chà; chāi; cī

瘥 chài 〈书面〉recover (from illness): 久病初～ have just recovered from a long illness / 他偶感风寒,不治而～。He caught a cold and recovered without taking medicine.

see also cuó

虿(蠆) chài a kind of scorpion: 蜂～ wasps and scorpions

chān

搀¹(攙) chān help by the arm; support with one's hand: ～她一把 help her along / 他～奶奶进屋。He helped grandma into the room.

搀²(攙) chān mix; adulterate: 在玉米面里～点豆面 mix some bean powder into the corn meal / 粥太稠了,～点水。The porridge is too thick. Add some water to it. / 油和水～不到一块儿。Oil and water do not mix. / 牛奶里～了水了。This milk has been adulterated (*or* diluted) with water.
搀兑 chānduì mix: 啤酒里～点柠檬水 mix some lemonade into the beer
搀扶 chānfú support with one's hand: ～老人过马路 help elderly people across the street / 他行走不便,需要人～。He has difficulty walking and so needs help.
搀混 chānhùn mix: 两种药～在一起了。The two kinds of medicine got mixed.
搀和 chānhuo ❶ mix; mingle: 粗细粮～着吃 eat a mixed diet of fine and coarse grain / 用水把鸡饲料～一下。Mix the chicken feed with water. ❷ meddle; interfere; tamper: 不是你的事就别～。Don't meddle with what is not your business. / 人家正忙着,别在这里瞎～。We are very busy. Please stop messing things up here.
搀假 chānjiǎ adulterate: 搀了假的食物 adulterated food / 酒～了。The wine has been adulterated.
搀沙子 chān shāzi mix sand into cement — place other people into a monolithic group; appoint outsiders to posts in an otherwise monolithic organization
搀水 chānshuǐ dilute: 这酒准搀了水了。The liquor must have been diluted.
搀水股票 chānshuǐ gǔpiào watered stock
搀水文凭 chānshuǐ wénpíng diploma obtained with very poor marks
搀言 chānyán 〈书面〉interpose; interrupt
搀杂 chānzá mix; mingle: 真话假话～在一起 truth mingled with falsehood / 不能把质量不同的羊毛～在一起。Don't mix up wool of different qualities.

掺(摻) chān *see* "搀²" chān
see also càn; shǎn

觇 chān 〈书面〉observe; survey
觇标 chānbiāo 〈测绘〉surveyor's beacon

襜 chān 〈书面〉❶ short jacket ❷ carriage curtain
襜褕 chānyú 〈书面〉a kind of short casual jacket worn in ancient times

幨 chān 〈书面〉carriage curtain

chán

澶 chán
澶渊之盟 Chányuān Zhī Méng Treaty of Chanyuan (in present-day northeastern Henan) signed in 1005 between the Liao Dynasty and the Northern Song Dynasty on humiliating terms for the latter

廛 chán 〈古语〉house of a commoner's family: 市～ marketplace (usu. among commoners' houses)

躔 chán 〈书面〉❶ footprints of animals ❷ course of a celestial body: 日运为～。The sun revolves in its orbit.

缠(纏) chán ❶ twine; wind: ～铅丝 wind lead-wire

(onto a reel or round sth.) /把毛线~成一个团儿 wind the wool into a ball /用手绢~住受伤的手臂 tie a handkerchief round the wounded arm /一条藤~在树干上。A vine twines about (*or* round) the tree. /用铁丝把椅子腿~上。Twine the leg of the chair with wire. /她头上~着绷带。Her head was bandaged. /几股线~在一起了。These threads got tangled up. /钓鱼线和水草~在一起了。The fishing line got entangled in weeds. ❷ tangle; tie up; pester: ~着不放 fasten onto (sb. or sth.) like a leech /女儿老~着我要一起去逛商店。My daughter has always been pestering me to go window-shopping with her. /这件事他也被~进去了。He, too, got entangled in the affair. ❸〈方言〉deal with: 阎王好惹,小鬼难~。It's easier to deal with the King of Hell than with the imps — better speak to the master than the servant.

C

缠绑 chánbǎng bind; tie up: 受伤的左腿还~着纱布。His wounded left leg is still bandaged.

缠缚 chánfù tie up; bind up

缠夹 chánjiā 〈方言〉bind; entangle; harass: ~不清 too entangled to unravel

缠搅 chánjiǎo pester; bother; disturb

缠绵 chánmián ❶ (of illness, emotion, etc.) lingering; abiding; harassing: 病势~ have a lingering illness /情意~ abiding affection /~病榻 be bedridden with a lingering (*or* chronic) disease /忧思~ be a victim of melancholy; cannot shake off one's melancholia; be tormented by loneliness and depression /梅雨~ harassing never-ending drizzles ❷ touching; moving; sentimental: ~的故事 sentimental story /她是个有名的歌唱家,歌声柔和~。She is a well-known singer, whose voice is soft and sweet. /笛声~。The tune of the flute is melodious and sentimental.

缠绵悱恻 chánmián-fěicè sad and sentimental; mushy: 这封信写得~。The letter was written in a sentimental vein. /他终日~,完全忘记了自己的理想。Feeling mushy day in and day out, he completely lost sight of his goal in life.

缠磨 chánmo 〈口语〉bother; pester: 这男孩老拿没完没了的问题来~他爸爸。The boy keeps bothering his father with endless questions. /这孩子真~人,怎么老不肯睡觉! What a trying child! He just wouldn't fall asleep!

缠扰 chánrǎo *see* "缠绕❷"

缠绕 chánrào ❶ twine; wind: 竹篱上~着牵牛花 morning glories winding round the bamboo fence ❷ bother; pester; harass: 被日常琐事~ be bogged down in trivial everyday duties /她受不了这些男人的~。She can't stand these men's harassment. /我无法摆脱他的~。I cannot shake him off. He sticks to me like a burr.

缠绕接线法 chánrào jiēxiànfǎ 〈电工〉wrapping connection

缠绕茎 chánràojīng vine

缠绕植物 chánrào zhíwù 〈植物〉twiner; climbing plant

缠身 chánshēn twine round one; bog one down; be tied down: 重病~ be down with a serious disease /家务~ be bogged down in housework /债务~ be debt-ridden /疾病~ be pestered by illness; come down with illness /公务~ be tied up with official business

缠手 chánshǒu thorny; troublesome; hard to deal with: 这问题有些~。This is a rather thorny problem. /病情复杂,真有点儿~。The illness is very complicated and it's really hard to treat.

缠足 chánzú foot-binding: 在封建社会女孩子被迫~。Young girls were often forced to bind their feet in feudal China.

单(單) chán

see also dān; Shàn

单于 chányú king of the *Xiongnu* (匈奴) in ancient China

禅(禪) chán

〈佛教〉❶ prolonged and intense meditation (for cleansing the mind); *dhyana*; *Chan*: 坐~ sit in meditation (with crossed legs) /~定 lost in Buddhist meditation ❷ Buddhism; Buddhist

see also shàn

禅床 chánchuáng bed or divan for meditation

禅房 chánfáng Buddhist abode; Buddhist temple

禅画 chánhuà *Chan* school of brush painting

禅机 chánjī Buddhist allegorical word or gesture; subtleties

禅偈 chánjì *Gatha* or short verse containing a *Chan* (*or* Zen) message

禅经 chánjīng Buddhist scripture

禅客 chánkè one who practises Buddhist meditation

禅理 chánlǐ Buddhist doctrine; Buddhist tenets: 精通~ be well versed in Buddhist doctrine

禅林 chánlín Buddhist monasteries or temples

禅门 chánmén gate to Buddhism; Buddhism: ~澹泊 simple life devoted to Buddhism

禅那 chánnà *dhyana*

禅师 chánshī (complimentary term of address for a Buddhist monk) master

禅堂 chántáng Buddhist shrine hall; meditation hall

禅悟 chánwù 〈佛教〉awakening to truth; realization of truth

禅心 chánxīn 〈佛教〉mind totally at peace

禅学 chánxué doctrine of *Chan* or Zen Buddhism

禅院 chányuàn Buddhist temple or monastery

禅杖 chánzhàng Buddhist monk's staff

禅宗 Chánzōng ❶ *Chan* sect of Buddhism in China ❷ (Japan) Zen

蝉(蟬) chán

(popularly called 知了) cicada

蝉联 chánlián continue to hold a post or title: ~世界冠军 win a world championship for yet another time; retain a world championship

蝉蜕 chántuì ❶ cicada slough (used as traditional medicine) ❷〈书面〉free or extricate oneself from: ~世俗观念 free oneself from worldly considerations

蝉衣 chányī 〈中药〉cicada slough

蝉翼 chányì cicada's wing: 绸子薄如~ silk as thin as a cicada's wings

蝉翼纱 chányìshā 〈纺织〉organdie

婵(嬋) chán

婵娟 chánjuān 〈书面〉❶ (often used of women) lovely; graceful: ~之女 graceful maiden ❷ moon: 但愿人长久,千里共~。May we live a long life, And together share the beauty of the moonlight, Though thousands of miles apart.

婵媛 chányuán 〈书面〉❶ *see* "婵娟" ❷ be linked together; be joined: 垂条~。Drooping twigs are all intertwined.

蟾 chán

see "蟾蜍"

蟾蜍 chánchú ❶ *also* "癞蛤蟆" làiháma toad ❷ moon (as legend has it that there is a three-legged toad in the moon)

蟾蜍色胺 chánchúsè'àn 〈药学〉bufotenine

蟾蜍试验 chánchú shìyàn toad test

蟾毒素 chándúsù bufotoxin

蟾宫 Chángōng 〈书面〉moon: 传说嫦娥是~中的仙女。Legend has it that Chang'e is a goddess in the moon.

蟾宫折桂 Chángōng-zhéguì win laurels in the moon palace — be successful in the highest imperial examination

蟾光 chánguāng 〈书面〉moonlight: ~照人间。The moon shines on earth.

蟾皮病 chánpíbìng 〈医学〉toadskin

蟾酥 chánsū 〈中药〉dried venom of toads; toad-cake

蟾鱼 chányú toadfish (*Batrachoididae*)

铤 chán

short spear with an iron shaft

谗(讒) chán

accuse or slander (sb. behind his back); backbite: 信~ (of a superior) believe false accusations (against sb.) /进~ (of a subordinate) falsely accuse sb. (to his superior)

谗害 chánhài slander sb. in order to harm him; frame somebody; persecute: ~忠良 vilify and harm loyal courtiers /~无辜 persecute the innocent /受到别人的~ be the target of vicious slander; be calumniated

谗佞 chánnìng 〈书面〉slanderer-cum-toady: ~之辈 slanderers and toadies

谗言 chányán malicious, false accusation; calumniation: 屡进~ (of a court official) repeatedly bring false charges against another court official /误信~ (of a feudal ruler) take a false charge for truth

 chán 〈书面〉dangerously steep; precipitous

巉峻 chánjùn 〈书面〉(of mountains, cliffs, etc.) precipitous:悬崖～ steep cliff /峰峦叠起,群山～。Steep peaks and craggy mountains rise one after another.
巉崖 chányá steep cliff; precipice
巉岩 chányán 〈书面〉precipitous crag:～绝壁 precipitous cliff /～林立 forest of precipitous crags

馋(饞)

chán greedy; gluttonous:嘴～ gluttonous; interested in eating anything delicious /这人太～。He is too greedy. /他看见人家打乒乓球就～得慌。His hand itches when he sees others playing table-tennis.
馋鬼 chánguǐ greedy pig; greedy-guts; glutton:你这个小～,见着什么都想吃! You little glutton, eating whatever food you set eyes upon!
馋痨 chánláo very greedy for food; gluttonous:～鬼 glutton
馋猫 chánmāo greedy-guts
馋涎 chánxián saliva (secreted at the sight of food)
馋涎欲滴 chánxián-yùdī (make) one's mouth water:看见烤鸭就～ start drooling (*or* one's mouth water) at the sight of a roast duck
馋嘴 chánzuǐ ❶ gluttonous ❷ glutton

镵

chán ❶〈古语〉trowel; shovel ❷〈书面〉touch; prick:山高～天。The mountain towers into the sky.

孱

chán weak; frail
see also càn
孱儿 chán'ér〈医学〉thin and weak child; child suffering from malnutrition
孱羸 chánléi 〈书面〉frail; weak and feeble
孱弱 chánruò 〈书面〉❶ (of physique or health) weak; frail; feeble:身体～ have a weak constitution; have fragile health; be frail ❷ weak; impotent; powerless:国力～ poor in national strength /那时国家～,不能抵御强敌。The nation was then too weak to withstand powerful foes. ❸ thin; insubstantial
孱微 chánwēi 〈书面〉small; insignificant:～之人 man of no consequence /出身～ be from a humble family; be of humble origin

潺

chán 〈象声〉*used to indicate the sound of flowing water*
潺潺 chánchán 〈象声〉murmur; babble; gurgle:～流水 murmuring stream; babbling brook /水声～ murmuring water; gurgling water
潺湲 chányuán 〈书面〉(of water) flow slowly:涕泪～ tears stream down one's cheeks /山脚下溪水～。The stream flows gently in its course at the foot of the mountain.

僝

chán
僝僽 chánzhòu 〈书面〉❶ haggard; careworn; fretful:几处笙歌,几家～。Some halls resound with music and song while more families are unhappy and careworn. ❷ torment; harass:天气如此把人～。The weather is so oppressive. ❸ complain; blame:休要无端～他人。Do not put unwarranted blame upon others. ❹ divert oneself (from loneliness and boredom):他吟诗作画,～情怀。He diverted himself from a feeling of loneliness and boredom by reciting poems and painting.

chǎn

产(産)

chǎn ❶ give birth to; be delivered of; bear; breed:每胎～仔一、二只 bear one or two young at a birth /流～ miscarriage /生～ be in labour /难～ difficult delivery /顺～ easy (*or* normal) delivery /死～ still birth /早～ premature birth /人工流～ (artificial) abortion /先兆性流～ augural (*or* threatened) miscarriage /横～ cross birth /剖腹～ caesarean section; caesarean /预～期 expected date of childbirth /助～ midwifery /妇～科 gynecology and obstetrics department /这只狮子就要～小狮了。The lioness is expecting cubs. /有的动物关在笼子里就不～仔。Some animals will not breed when kept in captivity. ❷ produce; yield:高～ high yield /低～ low yield /亩～ per *mu* yield /国～ home made; made in one's own country /～煤区 coal-mining area /这个县盛～红枣。This county produces red dates in large quantities. ❸ product; produce:土～ local product /特～ special local product; speciality; specialty /水～ aquatic product /矿～ minerals; mineral resources; mineral products ❹ property; estate:公～ public property /私～ private property /家～ family property; family possession /房地～ real estate; real property
产程 chǎnchéng parturition; childbirth
产出 chǎnchū output:资本～率 output-capital ratio /～系数 output coefficient /～投入比率 output-input ratio /～劳动率 output-labour ratio /～潜力 output potential
产床 chǎnchuáng 〈医学〉obstetric table
产蛋鸡 chǎndànjī laying hen; layer
产道 chǎndào 〈生理〉birth canal; obstetric canal; parturient canal
产地 chǎndì place of production; place of origin:柑桔～ citrus growing area /熊猫～ native haunt of the panda /原料～ source of raw materials /景德镇是中国著名的陶瓷～。Jingdezhen is well known in China for its pottery and porcelain.
产地国 chǎndìguó country of origin
产地证明书 chǎndì zhèngmíngshū certificate of origin
产犊 chǎndú 〈畜牧〉calving:～季节 calving season
产额 chǎn'é yield; output
产儿 chǎn'ér ❶ newborn baby ❷ outcome; product:技术革命的～ product of the technological revolution
产房 chǎnfáng 〈医学〉delivery room; lying-in room:～护理 delivery room care
产妇 chǎnfù lying-in woman; puerpera; puerperant:待～ woman expecting confinement; expecting mother /初～ primipara
产妇死亡率 chǎnfù sǐwánglǜ maternal mortality rate
产羔 chǎngāo 〈畜牧〉lambing; kidding
产供销 chǎn-gòng-xiāo production, supply and marketing:～一条龙 integration of production, supply and market
产后 chǎnhòu following childbirth; postpartum; postnatal:～护理 postnatal care; puerperal care
产后出血 chǎnhòu chūxuè 〈医学〉postpartum haemorrhage
产后热 chǎnhòurè 〈医学〉puerperal fever
产后痛 chǎnhòutòng 〈医学〉after-pains
产后抑郁 chǎnhòu yìyù 〈医学〉puerperal or postnatal depression
产假 chǎnjià maternity leave:休～ take maternity leave
产经新闻 Chǎnjīng Xīnwén (Japan) *Sankei Shimbun*
产驹 chǎnjū 〈畜牧〉foaling
产科 chǎnkē obstetrical department; obstetrics; maternity department:～病房 maternity (*or* obstetrical) ward
产科学 chǎnkēxué obstetrics
产科医生 chǎnkē yīshēng obstetrician
产科医院 chǎnkē yīyuàn maternity or lying-in hospital
产量 chǎnliàng output; yield:钢～ steel output /粮食～ grain output /总～ total output; total yield /年～ annual output /单位面积～ yield per unit area /～和质量应当并重。Equal emphasis should be laid on both the quality and quantity of the output.
产卵 chǎnluǎn (of birds and poultry) lay eggs; (of fish, frogs, etc.) spawn; (of insects) oviposit:～洄游 spawning migration /～期 egg-laying (*or* spawning) season
产卵器 chǎnluǎnqì ovipositor
产门 chǎnmén 〈生理〉vaginal orifice
产品 chǎnpǐn product; produce:农～ farm produce /副～ sideline product /畜～ livestock product/工业～ industrial product /海～ marine product /民用～ civilian industry product /军需～ defence product /长线～ product in excessive supply /短线～ product in short supply /劳动密集型～ labour-intensive product /资本密集型～ capital-intensive product /技术密集型～ technology-intensive product /精神～ intellectual product /创汇～ product for export; product earning foreign currency /合格～ qualified product /不合格～ reject; substandard product /优质～ quality product /冒牌～ fake product /劣质～ shoddy product /没有销路的～ unsalable product /有竞争力的～ competitive product /过时～ obsolescent product /新～ pioneer product /名优～ superior product /～质量 quality of a product/～性能 properties of a product /～识别 product identification /～开发 product development /～系列 product line /～寿命周期 product life cycle /～专利 product patent /～成品 finished product
产品保证书 chǎnpǐn bǎozhèngshū product warranty
产品成本 chǎnpǐn chéngběn cost of product:～核算 product costing

C

产品分析 chǎnpǐn fēnxī product analysis
产品结构 chǎnpǐn jiégòu product mix：调整～ adjust the product mix
产品责任法 chǎnpǐn zérènfǎ PL law (law of product liability)
产品组合 chǎnpǐn zǔhé product mix
产婆 chǎnpó 〈旧语〉 midwife
产前 chǎnqián prenatal; antenatal：～检查 prenatal (*or* antenatal) examination /～应有适当的运动。Prenatal women should take a certain amount of physical exercise.
产前补饲 chǎnqián bǔsì 〈动物〉 steaming up
产前出血 chǎnqián chūxuè 〈医学〉 ante-partum haemorrhage
产前护理 chǎnqián hùlǐ 〈医学〉 antenatal or prenatal care
产钳 chǎnqián 〈医学〉 obstetric forceps：～分娩 forceps delivery
产权 chǎnquán property right; title：拥有～ have title to property /～要求 property claim /提出～要求 bring forward a claim to property /放弃～ renounce one's claim to property /获得～ acquire title to property /～转让 transference of title to property
产权管理 chǎnquán guǎnlǐ property rights administration
产权交易市场 chǎnquán jiāoyì shìchǎng property rights exchange; equity market
产权拍卖 chǎnquán pāimài equity auctioning
产褥感染 chǎnrù gǎnrǎn 〈医学〉 puerperal infection
产褥期 chǎnrùqī 〈医学〉 puerperium
产褥热 chǎnrùrè 〈医学〉 puerperal fever
产伤 chǎnshāng injury done to the newborn baby during the delivery; birth injury
产生 chǎnshēng ❶ produce; engender; cause：～热量 produce heat /～效力 be effective; take (*or* come into) effect /～影响 exert an influence; have impact /～深刻的印象 make a deep impression /～误解 cause (*or* give rise to) misunderstanding /～纠纷 cause (*or* lead to) disputes /～变化 bring about changes; undergo changes /～困难 create difficulties; difficulties have cropped up /～疑问 call into question; cast doubt; arouse suspicion /～信心 inspire confidence /～悲观情绪 be pessimistic /～副作用 have side-effects /～连锁反应 produce a chain-reaction /肮脏的环境容易～疾病。Filthy environment engenders disease. ❷ emerge; come into being; arise：一种新概念的～ emergence (*or* birth) of a new concept /一个新的政党～了。A new political party came into being. /由此～的一切后果，甲方应负全部责任。Party A must be held responsible for all the consequences arising therefrom. /在唐、宋两代，～了许多著名的诗人。The Tang and Song dynasties produced a good number of outstanding poets.
产痛 chǎntòng labour pain
产物 chǎnwù product; outcome; result：必然～ inevitable result (*or* outcome) /集体智慧的～ product of collective wisdom /互相妥协的～ outcome of mutual concession; result of compromise /十年辛勤劳动的～ fruit of ten years' hard work
产销 chǎn-xiāo production and marketing：～关系 relation between production and marketing /～对路 production based on marketing; market-oriented production /～平衡 balance between production and marketing; coordination of production and marketing /～挂钩 hook-up (*or* direct contact) between producing and marketing departments /～合一 integration of production and marketing operations /～结合 coordination between production and marketing /～两旺。Both production and marketing are thriving.
产需 chǎn-xū production and demand：～平衡 production-demand balance
产业 chǎnyè ❶ estate; property：家庭～ family property /国家～ state property /没收某人的～ confiscate sb.'s property /他继承了祖上的～。He inherited the property of his ancestors. /这宗～已传给了继承人。The property has fallen to the heir. ❷ industrial：～工会 industrial union /～界 industrial circles
产业分析 chǎnyè fēnxī industry analysis
产业革命 chǎnyè gémìng *also* "工业革命" gōngyè gémìng Industrial Revolution
产业工人 chǎnyè gōngrén industrial worker
产业后备军 chǎnyè hòubèijūn industrial reserve army; reserve army of labour
产业结构 chǎnyè jiégòu 〈经济〉 set-up of production; industrial structure
产业军 chǎnyèjūn industrial army
产业情报 chǎnyè qíngbào industrial intelligence or espionage
产业税 chǎnyèshuì 〈经济〉 industrial tax
产业心理学 chǎnyè xīnlǐxué industrial psychology
产业政策 chǎnyè zhèngcè industrial policy
产业资本 chǎnyè zīběn industrial capital
产油国 chǎnyóuguó oil producing country
产院 chǎnyuàn maternity hospital
产值 chǎnzhí value of output; output value：工业总～ total industrial output value /农业总～ total agricultural output value /商品～ value of product /国民经济总～ gross national product (GNP) /国内总～ gross domestic product (GDP)
产仔 chǎnzǐ give birth to young animals; farrow; calve; foal：～数 litter size

铲(鏟、剗) chǎn

❶ shovel：煤～ coal shovel /电～ electrical shovel /铁～ iron shovel /锅～ slice /煎饼～ pancake turner ❷ lift or move with a shovel; shovel：～土 shovel dirt /把地～平 scrape the ground even; level the ground with a shovel (*or* spade) /～草 remove weeds; weed
铲车 chǎnchē forklift truck
铲齿车床 chǎnchǐ chēchuáng 〈机械〉 relieving lathe; backing-off lathe
铲除 chǎnchú root out; uproot; eliminate; eradicate：～杂草 root out the weeds /～旧思想 do away with old-fashioned ideas /～异己 get rid of dissidents; exclude alien elements; exclude people not of one's own clique
铲床 chǎnchuáng 〈机械〉 gear milling lathe
铲斗 chǎndǒu 〈建筑〉 scoop; bucket; scraper bucket
铲斗挖掘机 chǎndǒu wājuéjī scoop shovel
铲斗装载机 chǎndǒu zhuāngzàijī scoop loader
铲路机 chǎnlùjī road planer
铲球 chǎnqiú 〈体育〉 sliding tackle
铲式刮土运输机 chǎnshì guātǔ yùnshūjī 〈机械〉 scraper chain conveyor
铲式装载机 chǎnshì zhuāngzàijī 〈建筑〉 shovel loader
铲蹚 chǎntāng 〈农业〉 weeding; loosening soil and hilling
铲土机 chǎntǔjī *also* "铲运机" earth remover; earth shovel; bulldozer
铲鱼 chǎnyú 〈动物〉 spadefish (*Ephippidae*)
铲运车 chǎnyùnchē scraper; carry-scraper
铲子 chǎnzi shovel

阐(闡) chǎn

explain; expatiate
阐发 chǎnfā elucidate：他详尽地～了改革的重要意义。He elucidated the significance of the reform in great detail.
阐明 chǎnmíng expound; clarify; make clear：～观点 clarify one's view /～立场 make clear one's position; clarify one's position /～案情真相 state the facts of a case /他没有～究竟为什么要取消这个计划。He didn't explain exactly why this plan should be cancelled. /这个观点需要进一步地～。This idea needs to be further expounded. *or* This idea calls for more elaboration.
阐释 chǎnshì explain; expound; interpret：她详细地～下一步的做法。She gave a detailed explanation of the steps to be taken afterwards. /主席的意图他无权～。He has no right to interpret the chairman's intention.
阐述 chǎnshù expound; elaborate：～观点 elaborate one's views /双方各自～了自己的立场。Each side set forth its position on the question. /这篇文章的理论～还不够。This article is inadequate in theoretical exposition.
阐扬 chǎnyáng expound and advocate：～爱国主义 expound and advocate patriotism

焯(燀) chǎn

〈书面〉 ❶ burn; be on fire ❷ send out sparks in all directions; sparkle ❸ intense heat

啴(嘽) chǎn

〈书面〉 lenient; relaxed：～缓 mild and lenient
see also tān

冁(囅、辴) chǎn

〈书面〉 the way one smiles：～然而笑 give a smile; break into a smile

谄 chǎn

flatter; fawn on

谄媚 chǎnmèi flatter; fawn on; toady: ～于人 fawn on sb. /～奉承是他惯用的伎俩。Flattery is his familiar trick.
谄佞 chǎnnìng ingratiate oneself servilely; fawn on; toady: 一副～相 ingratiating look
谄上欺下 chǎnshàng-qīxià be servile to one's superiors and tyrannical to one's subordinates; fawn on those above and bully those below
谄笑 chǎnxiào ingratiating smile: 胁肩～ cringe and smile obsequiously
谄谀 chǎnyú ingratiate oneself by obsequious flattery: ～邀宠 ingratiate oneself with sb. by obsequious flattery

刬(剗) chǎn remove with a shovel: ～除 eradicate; eliminate
see also chàn

蒇 chǎn 〈书面〉 finish; complete: ～事 finish the work; be through with the job

骣 chǎn ride an unsaddled horse: ～骑 ride a horse without a saddle

chàn

颤 chàn quiver; tremble; vibrate: 冻得浑身打～ tremble (*or* shiver) with cold /他激动得声音都发～了。His voice quivered with excitement. /一想到将要发生的事,他的心就发～。He shuddered at the thought of what was going to happen. /她笑得身体都～起来了。She was shaking with laughter.
see also zhàn
颤动 chàndòng quiver; vibrate: 手指～ trembling fingers /声带～ vibration of the vocal cords /树叶在风中～。The leaves of the tree quivered in the wind. /他脸上的肌肉～了一下。The muscles on his face gave a twitch.
颤抖 chàndǒu shake; tremble; shiver: 吓得两腿～ shake in one's shoes /她兴奋得双手都～起来。Her hands trembled with excitement.
颤忽 chànhu 〈方言〉 *see* "颤悠"
颤巍巍 chànwēiwēi in a tottering manner; unsteadily: 奶奶～地走到床边。Grandma tottered over to the bed. /老头儿～地朝门口走去。The old man hobbled towards the door.
颤巍 chànwei quiver; shake; tottering: 他的花白胡子不停地～着。His grey beard kept quivering all the time.
颤音 chànyīn 〈语言〉〈音乐〉 trill; shake: 逆～ inverted trill
颤音琴 chànyīnqín 〈音乐〉 vibraphone
颤悠 chànyou *also* "颤悠悠" shake; quiver; flicker: ～的烛光 flickering candle light /～的滑竿 swinging litter /他肩上的扁担随着脚步不停地～。The carrying-pole on his shoulder swayed to the rhythm of his footsteps.

忏(懺) chàn ❶ repent; be penitent: 他深感愧～。He felt deeply ashamed. ❷〈宗教〉 *ksama*, scripture read to atone for sb.'s sins: 拜～ (of a monk or nun) read scripture (to atone for sb.'s sins)
忏悔 chànhuǐ ❶ repent; be penitent: ～自己的罪过 deeply repent of one's sin /他～自己虚度了青春年华。He regretted that he had wasted his youth. ❷〈宗教〉 confess: 向神父～自己的罪过 confess one's sins to a priest /听取临终的～ hear deathbed confessions
忏悔节 Chànhuǐjié 〈宗教〉 Shrovetide; Shrove Tuesday: ～诙谐戏剧 Fastnachtsspiel
忏悔录 Chànhuǐlù ❶ *Confessions* by St. Augustine (354-430), bishop of Hippo (in present-day Algeria) ❷ *Les Confessions* by French Enlightenment scholar Jean-Jacques Rousseau (1712-1778), published after the author's death

刬(剗) chàn *see* "一刬" yīchàn
see also chǎn

韂 chàn *see* "鞍韂" ānchàn

羼 chàn mix; adulterate
羼杂 chànzá mix; mingle; adulterate: 米里～着沙子。The rice got mixed with grains of sand.

chāng

昌 chāng ❶ prosperous; flourishing: 万物得～。All things on earth flourish. *or* A scene of prosperity prevails on earth. ❷〈书面〉 proper; meet; fair ❸ (Chāng) a surname
昌巴尔河 Chāngbā'ěrhé Chambal River, in northern India
昌都 Chāngdū Changdu (formerly translated as Qamdo), third largest city in Tibet
昌化石 chānghuàshí 〈地质〉 a kind of stone available in quantity in Changhua County, Zhejiang Province, which is precious for making seals
昌隆 chānglóng prosperous; flourishing; thriving: 国运～。The country is flourishing.
昌明 chāngmíng ❶ flourishing; thriving; well-developed: 有了和平和稳定,科学方能～。Science flourishes only when there is peace and stability. ❷ make flourish; prosper; promote: ～文化 make culture flourish; promote culture
昌盛 chāngshèng prosperous; flourishing: 国家～ national prosperity /和平带来～。Peace brings prosperity. /把中国建设成一个富强、繁荣～的社会主义国家。We will turn China into a strong and prosperous socialist country.
昌言 chāngyán 〈书面〉 ❶ correct statement; appropriate remarks; worthy advice: 善纳～ follow good advice readily ❷ speak frankly; make a straightforward statement: ～无忌 state one's views unreservedly; not mince words

阊 chāng
阊阖 chānghé 〈书面〉 gate of the palace in heaven; heavenly gate; palatial entrance: 九天～ palatial entrance to the heaven of heavens

菖 chāng
菖兰 chānglán 〈植物〉 sweet flag
菖蒲 chāngpú 〈植物〉 calamus; sweet flag

倡 chāng ❶〈书面〉 professional entertainer in singing and dancing or playing musical instruments ❷ *see* "娼" chāng
see also chàng
倡狂 chāngkuáng *see* "猖狂" chāngkuáng
倡佯 chāngyáng *also* "徜徉" chángyáng roam leisurely
倡优 chāngyōu ❶〈古语〉 song-and-dance or comic entertainer ❷〈书面〉 prostitutes as well as actors and actresses

猖 chāng 〈书面〉 ferocious; fierce; savage
猖獗 chāngjué ❶ ferocious and rampant; wild and unrestrained: 这种病在世界一些地区仍很～。This disease is still rampant in some parts of the world. /这里走私活动曾～一时。Smuggling used to be quite prevalent here. /当年谣言～。Rumours were rife (*or* spread unchecked) in those days. ❷〈书面〉 collapse; decline: 智术浅短,遂用～。Intellectual inactivity led to the decline of the state.
猖狂 chāngkuáng fierce; outrageous; savage: ～进攻 ferocious attack /～挑衅 reckless provocation /～反扑 furious (*or* savage) counterattack /发出～的战争叫嚣 make wild war clamour /那伙歹徒～到了极点。The gangsters were wild and lawless to the extreme.

鲳 chāng butterfish; silvery pomfret
鲳鱼 chāngyú *also* "银鲳" yínchāng; "镜鱼" jìngyú; "平鱼" píngyú silvery pomfret; butterfish

娼 chāng prostitute: 逼良为～ drive a woman to prostitution /男盗女～ behave like thieves and whores /暗～ unlicensed prostitute; unregistered prostitute
娼妇 chāngfù (often used as a swearword) bitch; whore: 无耻～ shameless bitch /小～ little whore
娼妓 chāngjì prostitute; whore: 沦为～ become a prostitute /市长决心在这一地区清除～。The mayor decided to rid the area of prostitutes. *or* The mayor decided to stamp out prostitution in this area.
娼寮 chāngliáo *also* "娼窑" brothel

C

娼门 chāngmén brothel; whorehouse; house of ill repute: 沦落～ become a prostitute

伥(倀) chāng see "为虎作伥" wèihǔ-zuòchāng

伥鬼 chāngguǐ ghost of the man who devoured by a tiger helps the tiger to devour others

see also "为虎作伥" wèihǔ-zuòchāng

cháng

尝[1](嘗、嚐) cháng ❶ try (food); taste; have a taste of: ～～咸淡 try a bit to see if it tastes just right /这菜我～了～，味道很好。I have tried the dish. It tastes nice. ❷ experience; be aware of: ～到甜头 come to know the good of; have a foretaste of the joy /艰苦备～ experience all the hardships /他以前学习不努力，现在～到了苦头。He did not work hard enough at his studies and now he has to suffer for it.

尝[2](嘗) cháng ever; once: 我们未～晤面。We have never met before. /我何～想这样做，只是不得已罢了。I never meant to act the way I did; only I couldn't help it.

尝鼎一脔 chángdǐng-yīluán taste a piece of the meat in the pot and you know the whole lot — learn the whole by sampling a part; a straw shows which way the wind blows: 这仅是他创作的一个选本，但我们已可～了。This is only a selection of his works. Nevertheless, we can get a clear idea of the whole after reading the part.

尝试 chángshì attempt; try; venture; have a go at: 这是一次寻求解决争端的～。This is an attempt to seek a settlement of the dispute. /为什么不～～? Why not have a try? /他做过许多～，都失败了。He tried again and again, but failed each time.

尝受 chángshòu experience; go through (hardships, sufferings)

尝味 chángwèi ❶ have a taste of (food): 这种名菜早就没有了，不料今晚在这里又～到。I did not expect to taste this delicious dish here tonight, for it has not been seen for a long time. ❷ try; attempt; experience: 他对工作的各个方面都想～一下。He wanted to get the feel of the job in all its aspects.

尝鲜 chángxiān taste what is just in season; have delicious food

尝新 chángxīn have a taste of what is just in season: 主人捧出刚从果园摘下的苹果，请客人们～。The host brought for his guests apples right from the orchard.

偿(償) cháng ❶ repay; redeem; compensate: ～债 pay a debt; redeem a debt /补～损失 compensate for the loss /得不～失 the loss overweighs the gain; win a Pyrrhic victory ❷ meet the need of; fulfil; satisfy: 得～夙愿 have one's long-cherished wish realized /如愿以～。One's wish is fulfilled.

偿付 chángfù pay back; reimburse: 延期～〈法律〉moratorium; deferred payment

偿付能力 chángfù nénglì solvency: 有～ solvent /无～ insolvent

偿还 chánghuán repay; redeem; pay: 如期～债务 repay a debt as scheduled /分期～ pay in instalments /如数～ pay back the required amount /延期～ delayed repayment; moratorium /债务～比率 debt service ratio /债务～能力 debt servicing capacity /可以多种货币、货物或劳务～的债务 debt repayable in multiple currencies, goods or services

偿命 chángmìng pay with one's life (for a murder): 杀人～ a life for a life

偿清 chángqīng clear off; settle: ～债务 clear off one's debts

偿债 chángzhài debt service; debt redemption: ～义务 debt service obligation

偿债比率 chángzhài bǐlǜ debt service ratio

偿债基金 chángzhài jījīn sinking fund; debt service fund

偿债能力 chángzhài nénglì debt servicing ability; liquidity; solvency

裳 cháng skirt (in ancient China)

see also shang

常 cháng ❶ ordinary; common; normal: 反～ unusual; abnormal; weird: 一切照～ do everything as usual /习以为～ get used (*or* accustomed) to sth. /他有些失～。He is not quite himself. ❷ constant; invariable: 冬夏～青 remain green throughout the year; evergreen /这些东西市场～有。These goods are never in short supply. *or* These goods are always available in the market. ❸ often; frequently; usually: ～来～往 pay frequent calls on each other /她～觉得内疚。She often feels guilty about it. /他不～来。He seldom comes here. ❹〈书面〉morality; mores: 三纲五～ three cardinal guides and five constant virtues (in Confucian ethics) ❺ (Cháng) a surname

常备 chángbèi be always on hand or available; constantly stand by: ～药 household medicine; common medicine /～车辆 vehicles that are constantly in service (*or* standing by) /家里～着灭火器，以应不时之需。We have a fire-extinguisher in our house in case of a fire.

常备不懈 chángbèi-bùxiè always be on the alert; be ever prepared: 枕戈待旦，～ be on the alert all the time and never lower one's vigilance /军队要～。Troops should be ever prepared against any eventuality.

常备军 chángbèijūn standing army

常常 chángcháng often; frequently; usually; generally: 那时他周末～加班。In those years, he usually worked overtime on weekends. /他～独坐沉思。He often sat alone deep in thought.

常川 chángchuān frequently; constantly: 这两家商号在业务上～往来。The two firms have constant business contacts. /这个农场～向附近居民供应鲜菜。The farm supplies the local people with fresh vegetables all the year round.

常春藤 chángchūnténg 〈植物〉Chinese ivy

常春藤联合会 Chángchūnténg Liánhéhuì Ivy League, a group of long-established eastern US universities of high academic and social prestige, including Harvard, Yale, Princeton, and Columbia

常度 chángdù ❶ one's normal way of behaving: 不失～ be one's normal self /改变～ depart from one's norm; be not quite one's old self ❷〈书面〉fixed law; norm

常俸 chángfèng regular pay or salary

常服 chángfú daily wear; ordinary clothes: 外出着西装，居家穿～。He goes out dressed in a western suit, but changes into daily clothes when he returns home.

常规 chángguī ❶ convention; rule; routine; common practice: 打破～ break with conventions /礼仪～ conventional rule of etiquette /照～办事 follow the routine /这样做是～。This is the usual way of doing things. ❷〈医学〉routine: 血～ routine blood test /尿～ routine urine test /便～ routine stool test

常规裁军 chángguī cáijūn conventional disarmament

常规检查 chángguī jiǎnchá 〈医学〉routine physical check-up

常规疗法 chángguī liáofǎ routine treatment

常规能源 chángguī néngyuán conventional source of energy

常规武器 chángguī wǔqì conventional weapons or weaponry

常规战争 chángguī zhànzhēng conventional warfare

常轨 chángguǐ normal practice or course: 纳入～ follow normal procedure /这类事件，可以遵循～解决。These matters can be resolved (*or* settled) in conformity with normal practice.

常果植物 chángguǒ zhíwù ever-bearer; ever-bloomer

常衡 chánghéng avoirdupois (weight)

常会 chánghuì regular session or meeting: 每月有一次业务～。A regular business session is held every month.

常见 chángjiàn often seen; common; commonplace: 这些事情是～的。Such things are common occurrences.

常见病 chángjiànbìng common disease; common ailment

常见问题 chángjiàn wèntí 〈信息〉frequently asked question (FAQ)

常景 chángjǐng normal circumstances; common situation; usual scene

常客 chángkè frequent guest

常礼 chánglǐ regular or normal etiquette

常理 chánglǐ common sense; customary practice: 按～我应该去看望他。I should go and see him by social convention.

常例 chánglì common practice; normal procedure: 按照～，这个病人该出院了。According to customary practice, this patient should be discharged from hospital. /他们违背了在重大问题上双方互通情报的～。They departed from the normal practice of keeping each other informed on major issues.

常量 chángliàng *also* "恒量" héngliàng 〈物理〉constant: ～与变量 constants and variables

常流河 chángliúhé 〈水文〉perennial stream
常绿 chánglǜ evergreen:～灌木 evergreen shrub /～树 evergreen (tree)
常绿林 chánglǜlín evergreen forest
常绿植物 chánglǜ zhíwù evergreen plant
常年 chángnián ❶ all the year round; over a long period of time; year in and year out:他～坚持游泳。He swims regularly all the year round. ❷ average year:今年的降雨量不及～的一半。This year's rainfall is less than half of the average year's.
常平仓 chángpíngcāng official granary set up in ancient China to provide against famine (which purchased grain at a higher than normal price when the harvest was good and sold at a lower price in a lean year in order to stabilize food prices)
常青 chángqīng evergreen:～树 evergreen /松柏～ evergreen pine and cypress trees /～不老 remain fresh and vigorous
常情 chángqíng reason; common sense; human nature:不合～ contrary to reason; against common sense /他们对考试成绩不满意,也合乎～。It stands to reason that they should be displeased with their examination results. /希望生活一天天好起来,这也是人之～。It is only human nature that one hopes that life gets better and better.
常人 chángrén ordinary person; man in the street:～不懂得这种局面是多么微妙。The man in the street does not understand how delicate the situation is. /损失之大远非～所能想像。The scale of the damage is beyond the imagination of ordinary people.
常任 chángrèn permanent; standing:安理会～理事国 permanent member of the Security Council
常任代表 chángrèn dàibiǎo permanent representative
常任理事 chángrèn lǐshì standing member of a council
常任制 chángrènzhì permanent tenure of office
常山 chángshān 〈中药〉root of antipyretic dichroa (*Dichroa febrifuga*)
常设 chángshè permanent; standing:～委员会 permanent (*or* standing) committee /～秘书处 permanent secretariat /～调查委员会 permanent commission of enquiry /～部队 permanent force /～小组 permanent group /～国际机构 permanent international institution /～维持和平部队 permanent peacekeeping force
常设机构 chángshè jīgòu standing body; permanent organization
常设理事会 chángshè lǐshìhuì permanent council
常设仲裁委员会 chángshè zhòngcái wěiyuánhuì Permanent Court of Arbitration
常胜将军 chángshèng-jiāngjūn ever-victorious general:事实上的～是没有的。There is no such thing as an ever-victorious general in actual life.
常胜军 chángshèngjūn invincible army
常时 chángshí ❶ often; frequently:他～到农村去体验生活。He often goes to the countryside to see at first hand how the farmers live. ❷〈方言〉sometimes
常识 chángshí ❶ common knowledge; general or elementary knowledge; ABC:现代科学～ ABC of modern science /他连起码的文体学～都没有。He does not even have the rudimentary knowledge of stylistics. ❷ common sense:逃税犯法,这是～。It is common sense that tax evasion is an offence against the law.
常事 chángshì common occurrence; everyday experience:他看书至深夜是～。It is almost a matter of everyday experience with him to sit up reading far into the night.
常数 chángshù 〈数学〉constant:～项 constant term
常态 chángtài normalcy; normality; normal behaviour; normal state of affairs:一反～ contrary to one's normal behaviour /失去～ act oddly (*or* abnormally) /恢复～ come back to normal /保持～ maintain one's bearing
常态曲线 chángtài qūxiàn 〈统计〉normal curve
常谈 chángtán trite remark; commonplace; platitude:老生～ same old platitude; banal remarks; cliché
常套 chángtào convention; set routine; set formula:摆脱才子佳人小说的～ break away from the old convention of portraying gifted scholars and beautiful ladies in fiction
常微分方程 chángwēifēn fāngchéng 〈数学〉ordinary differential equation
常委 chángwěi ❶ *see* "常委会" ❷ (short for 常务委员) member of the standing committee:党委～ member of the Party standing committee
常委会 chángwěihuì (short for 常务委员会) standing committee:人大～ standing committee of the People's Congress /正开～。The standing committee is now in session.
常温 chángwēn ❶ normal atmospheric temperature (between 15°C and 25°C) ❷ homoiothermy
常温动物 chángwēn dòngwù *also* "温血动物" wēnxuè dòngwù homoiothermal animal; warm blood animal
常蚊 chángwén *also* "库蚊" kùwén 〈动物〉culex
常务 chángwù ❶ standing; permanent:～秘书 permanent secretary /～理事 executive council member /～副部长 executive vice-minister ❷ routine; day-to-day business:主持～ be in charge of day-to-day business; run routine work
常务次长 chángwù cìzhǎng (Japan) administrative vice-minister
常务董事 chángwù dǒngshì 〈商业〉managing director
常务委员 chángwù wěiyuán member of the standing committee
常务委员会 chángwù wěiyuánhuì standing committee
常锡文戏 Cháng-Xī wénxì *also* "锡剧" xījù Wuxi opera, local opera popular in southern Jiangsu and Shanghai
常项 chángxiàng 〈数学〉constant
常行军 chángxíngjūn (of an army) march at normal speed
常性 chángxìng ❶ perseverance; tenacity:他无论学什么都没～。He hardly perseveres with whatever he tries to learn. ❷〈书面〉habit; custom; nature
常压 chángyā ❶〈化学〉atmospheric pressure:蒸汽～灭菌器 Arnold sterilizer; steam sterilizer ❷〈物理〉ordinary pressure
常压沸点 chángyā fèidiǎn 〈化学〉atmospheric boiling point
常压塔 chángyātǎ 〈化学〉atmospheric tower
常压蒸馏 chángyā zhēngliú 〈化学〉atmospheric distillation
常言 chángyán saying; proverb:～道:众志成城。As the saying goes, unity is strength. /～说得好:有理走遍天下,无理寸步难行。It is well said that with justice on your side, you can go anywhere and without it, you can't take a step.
常业 chángyè regular profession:严惩以走私、投机倒把为～的人 mete out severe punishment to professional smugglers and speculators
常业犯 chángyèfàn 〈法律〉habitual offender; repeater
常用 chángyòng in common use; often used or quoted:～词语 everyday expression /～字 basic word; basic vocabulary /～典故 frequently quoted allusions /～药材 medicinal herbs most in use
常用对数 chángyòng duìshù *also* "十进制对数" shíjìnzhìduìshù 〈数学〉Brigg's logarithm; common logarithm
常志美 Cháng Zhìměi Chang Zhimei, Chinese Islamic scholar of the early Qing Dynasty
常住 chángzhù ❶ reside permanently; stay (at a place) frequently:～之地 permanent residence; place one has frequently visited; somewhere one has resided ❷〈宗教〉permanency; immutability ❸〈宗教〉Buddhist or Taoist temple and its assets
常住居民 chángzhù jūmín inhabitant; permanent resident:～证 permanent residence card
常住人口 chángzhù rénkǒu permanent population
常驻 chángzhù resident; permanent:～大使 resident ambassador /～观察员 permanent observer /～观察团 permanent observer mission /～外交使团 permanent diplomatic mission /～外交使节 permanent diplomatic envoy /～公使团 permanent legation /这位采购员～上海。This purchasing agent is stationed in Shanghai.
常驻代表 chángzhù dàibiǎo permanent representative:～团 permanent mission /常驻联合国代表 permanent representative to the United Nations /常驻副代表 deputy permanent representative
常驻记者 chángzhù jìzhě resident correspondent:路透社常驻北京记者 Reuters resident correspondent in Beijing

嫦 cháng

嫦娥 Cháng'é Goddess of the Moon (the lady in the legend who swallowed an elixir stolen from her husband and flew to the moon):～奔月 Chang'e flying to the moon /月里～ lady as beautiful as Chang'e, Goddess of the Moon

倘 cháng

see also tǎng
倘佯 chángyáng *see* "徜徉" chángyáng

徜 cháng

徜徉 chángyáng *also* "倘佯" chángyáng 〈书面〉stroll; saunter; amble:～于青山绿水之中 saunter over green hills and along crystal-clear streams / 在知识的海洋中～ sail in the vast ocean of knowledge

长(長) cháng ❶ long:～杆 long pole / 历史～ with a long history / 昼～夜短 long days and short nights / 中国有很～的海岸线。China has a long coastline. / 这衣服她穿着～。The dress is long on her. ❷ length:这个房间的～度和宽度设计得很相称。The length and width of the room are proportionately designed. ❸ strong point; forte:取人之～,补己之短 make up one's deficiencies by learning from others' strong points / 人各有～短。Everyone has his strong and weak points. ❹ be strong in; be good at:他～于演讲。He is an eloquent speaker. *or* He is good at making speeches. ❺ surplus; spare; extra
see also zhǎng

C

长安 Cháng'ān Chang'an, China's capital during the Han and Tang dynasties, situated roughly where Xi'an (西安), capital of Shaanxi Province now stands

长白山 Chángbáishān Changbai Mountain, in northeast China:～自然保护区 Changbai Mountain Reservation

长班 chángbān 〈旧语〉❶ attendant (of an official) ❷ errand boy (in a guild)

长鼻 chángbí 〈动物〉proboscis

长鼻猴 chángbíhóu proboscis monkey (*Nasalis larvatus*)

长鼻目 chángbímù 〈动物〉*Proboscidea*

长壁采矿法 chángbì cǎikuàngfǎ 〈矿业〉longwall working

长壁工作面 chángbì gōngzuòmiàn 〈矿业〉coal wall; long wall:～采煤机 longwall coal cutter

长臂挖掘机 chángbì wājuéjī 〈矿业〉high-front shovel

长臂虾 chángbìxiā 〈动物〉*Palaemon gravieri*

长臂猿 chángbìyuán 〈动物〉gibbon:～属 *Hylobates*

长编 chángbiān draft; draft edition:我披阅三载,辑此～。I had spent three years reading up on the topic before I edited this draft edition.

长别 chángbié ❶ long separation; long absence:倾诉～的心情 unbosom oneself of one's feelings (to sb.) after a long separation ❷ part forever; be parted by death

长兵 chángbīng 〈旧语〉❶ long-handled weapon like a spear ❷ weapons such as arrows, etc. which can be shot

长柄大镰刀 chángbǐng dàliándāo scythe

长柄锅 chángbǐngguō skillet

长波 chángbō long wave:～通讯 long-wave communication / ～发报机 long-wave transmitter

长波电热疗法 chángbō diànrè liáofǎ long-wave diathermy

长玻璃纤维 chángbōli xiānwéi long glass fibre

长策 chángcè good policy; sound plan; long-term strategy:治国～ sound plan for running a state / 自顾无～,空知返旧林。For myself I have no long-term strategy, Except returning to my native woods.

长长短短 chángcháng-duǎnduǎn of uneven length

长城 Chángchéng ❶ Great Wall:中国的～是世界奇观之一。China's Great Wall is one of the wonders of the world. / 不到～非好汉,屈指行程二万。If we fail to reach the Great Wall we are not men; We have already measured twenty thousand *li*. ❷ impregnable bulwark:军队是国家的钢铁～。The armed forces are the wall of bronze of a country.

长程 chángchéng long distance; long trip:～车票 long-distance ticket / ～旅行 long journey / 制定本公司的～发展规划 draw up a long-term plan of development of this company

长虫 chángchong 〈口语〉snake

长抽短吊 chángchōu-duǎndiào 〈体育〉(in table tennis) long drives coupled with drop shots

长处 chángchu strong point; merit; virtue; forte:要发挥每个人的～。It is necessary to bring everybody's strengths into full play. / 他的～之一是肯讲老实话。Honesty is one of his virtues. / 做工精细是王师傅的～。Master Wang is distinguished for his meticulous craftsmanship.

长川 chángchuān *also* "常川" chángchuān frequently; often

长传 chángchuán 〈体育〉throw a long pass

长春 Chángchūn Changchun, capital of Jilin Province:～电影制片厂 Changchun Film Studios

长春花碱 chángchūnhuājiǎn *also* "长春花素" vinblastine

长蝽 chángchūn 〈动物〉chinch bug:高粱～ sorghum chinch bug

长辞 chángcí leave forever — die; leave this world; pass away:与世～ depart from the world for ever; pass away

长此 chángcǐ continue this way:～下去 go on and on like this / 此处虽好,总不能～逗留。A nice place though it is, we cannot stay here for good.

长此以往 chángcǐyǐwǎng if things go on like this; if things continue this way; if things remain what they are:他总熬夜,～,健康状况会愈来愈糟。He often stays up late working, and his health will deteriorate if he goes on like this.

长存 chángcún live forever; be everlasting:他的业绩与世～。His achievements are immortal. *or* His achievements will be carved in history. / 艰苦奋斗的精神应永世～。The spirit of arduous struggle should be carried on from generation to generation.

长刀鱼 chángdāoyú knifefish

长岛 Chángdǎo (US) Long Island, an island of New York State:～海峡 Long Island Sound / ～战役 Battle of Long Island (27 August 1776)

长凳 chángdèng bench

长笛 chángdí flute

长笛鱼 chángdíyú 〈动物〉flutemouth

长度 chángdù length:～规 length scale / ～计 length gauge / ～测量 linear measurement / ～公差 length tolerance / 这张桌子的～为一米五十。The table is 1.5 metres long.

长短 chángduǎn ❶ length:这条裙子～正合适。This skirt is just the right length for you. / 这两根线～相当。These two lines are almost identical in length. *or* The two cords are about the same length. ❷ accident; mishap:老人家万一有个～,我们如何交代。How are we going to account for it if anything should happen to the old man? ❸ right and wrong; merits and demerits; good and bad:她好背后议论别人的～。She is fond of gossiping about people behind their backs. ❹〈方言〉anyway; whatsoever:跟他说了半天,他～不去。We tried to persuade him to go for quite a while, but he flatly refused. / 这件新衣服他～不喜欢。He does not like this new coat whatever you say.

长短句 chángduǎnjù ❶ another name for *ci* poem (词) ❷ a kind of classical poetry consisting chiefly of seven-character lines interspersed with shorter or longer ones
see also "古体诗" gǔtǐshī

长吨 chángdūn long ton (2,240 lb avoirdupois or 1,016.05 kg)

长法 chángfǎ overall solution; long-term solution:得有个～儿才行。A long-term solution has yet to be worked out. / 总这么将就,不是～儿。It won't get us anywhere if we go on putting up with all this for ever.

长方体 chángfāngtǐ cuboid; rectangular parallelepiped

长方形 chángfāngxíng *also* "矩形" jǔxíng rectangle; oblong

长俸 chángfèng (HK) pension:九折～ 90% pension / 每月～ monthly pension / 根据物价指数调整的～ index-linked pension

长歌当哭 chánggē-dàngkū sing in a loud voice to give vent to one's grief; compose poetry to express one's sorrow and indignation

长庚 Chánggēng 〈天文〉ancient Chinese name for Venus

长工 chánggōng farm labourer hired by the year; long-term hired hand:打～ be a farmhand; work as a farm labourer by the year / ～出身 used to be a farmhand

长弓 chánggōng long bow

长骨 chánggǔ 〈生理〉long bone

长鼓 chánggǔ 〈音乐〉long drum, narrowing towards the middle, used by the Korean and Yao ethnic groups as a musical instrument

长鼓舞 chánggǔwǔ drum dance of Yao or Korean nationality

长跪 chángguì kneel down with a straight back:～不起 fall on one's knees and refuse to get up (until one's request is granted, etc.)

长航 Chángháng ❶ (short for 长江航运) navigation along the Yangtze River ❷ (short for 长江航运管理局) Administration of Yangtze River Navigation

长号 chánghào *also* "拉管" lāguǎn 〈音乐〉trombone:～手 trombonist

长号筒 chánghàotǒng *dung-chen*, a brass instrument used in Buddhist monasteries in Tibet

长河 chánghé ❶ long river; large river:～落日圆。The disc of the evening sun is setting on the horizon of the river. ❷〈书面〉milky way ❸ endless flow:人类历史的～ long process of human history / 在真理的～中,认识是无止境的。In the endless flow of truth, cognition

is without limit.

长话 chánghuà long-distance telephone call: ～局 long-distance telephone exchange; toll centre

长话短说 chánghuà-duǎnshuō make a long story short

长活 chánghuó ❶ long-term job (of a hired farmhand): 扛～ be hired as a long-term farmhand ❷〈方言〉long-term hired hand

长技 chángjì expert skill: 别无～ have no other skill to speak of

长假 chángjià ❶ long leave; extended leave: 他因病请了～。He asked for long leave on account of illness. ❷〈旧语〉resignation from office or active military service

长江 Chángjiāng Changjiang River; Yangtze River: ～天堑。The Yangtze River is an impregnable natural barrier.

长江后浪推前浪 Chángjiāng hòulàng tuī qiánlàng in the Yangtze River the waves behind drive on those before — the new would always push on the old: ～，世上新人胜旧人。As in the Yangtze River the waves behind drive on those before, so the new generation excels the old.

长江三角洲 Chángjiāng Sānjiǎozhōu Yangtze River Delta

长江三峡 Chángjiāng Sānxiá Three Gorges of the Yangtze River: ～工程 Three Gorges project

长江中下游平原 Chángjiāng zhōng-xiàyóu píngyuán middle and lower Yangtze valley plains

长焦距 chángjiāojù long-focus: ～镜头 long-focus lens

长角羚 chángjiǎolíng〈动物〉gemsbok

长脚 chángjiǎo long-distance transport by cart

长颈鹿 chángjǐnglù giraffe

长颈烧瓶 chángjǐng shāopíng〈化工〉kjeldahl flask

长久 chángjiǔ prolonged; protracted; lasting: ～打算 long-term plans / ～以来 for a long time now; long since / 但愿人～。I wish we would all live long. / 这种搪瓷器皿外形美观，但用不～。This kind of enamelware, though outwardly beautiful, is not durable.

长久之计 chángjiǔzhījì long-term plan; permanent solution: 还是想个～为好。It would be best to work out a long-term plan. / 这不是～。This is not a permanent solution. *or* It's just a temporary arrangement.

长局 chángjú (often used in a negative sentence) permanent situation; lasting solution: 终究不是～。This is not a settled arrangement after all.

长距离 chángjùlí long distance: ～赛跑 long-distance race

长距离通信光纤 chángjùlí tōngxìn guāngxiān〈通信〉optic telecommunication cable (*or* fiber-optic telecommunication cable)

长距离通信激光器 chángjùlí tōngxìn jīguāngqì〈通信〉telecommunication laser

长卷 chángjuàn long scroll (of painting or calligraphy): 民俗～ long scroll depicting social customs and folkways

长靠武生 chángkào wǔshēng〈戏曲〉actor playing a martial role, wearing platform boots, wielding long-handled weapons, and good at acrobatics

长空 chángkōng sky: 飞机在～翱翔。The airplanes are soaring in the skies. / 寂寞嫦娥舒广袖，万里～且为忠魂舞。The lonely moon goddess spreads her ample sleeves To dance for these loyal souls in infinite space.

长裤 chángkù trousers; pants; slacks

长跨度 chángkuàdù long span: ～桥梁 long span bridge

长款 chángkuǎn〈会计〉more cash than can be accounted for

长廊 chángláng ❶ long covered corridor; gallery ❷ Long Corridor (of the Summer Palace in Beijing)

长里 chángli〈口语〉length

长龄 chánglíng〈书面〉advanced age; old age; long life: 克享～ live to a ripe old age

长龙 chánglóng long queue: 买火车票的人排成～。People stood in a long queue to buy train tickets.

长脉冲激光器 chángmàichōng jīguāngqì long-pulse laser

长脉冲雷达 chángmàichōng léidá〈无线电〉long-pulse radar

长毛 chángmáo ❶〈纺织〉long-wool ❷ (Chángmáo)〈旧语〉〈贬义〉long-haired Taiping rebels
see also zhǎngmáo

长毛绒 chángmáoróng〈纺织〉plush

长矛 chángmáo long spear; pike

长眠 chángmián〈婉词〉eternal sleep; death: ～地下 lie buried / 烈士们～在这座山冈上。The martyrs are buried on the slope of the hill.

长明灯 chángmíngdēng altar lamp which burns day and night

长命百岁 chángmìng-bǎisuì (used as a blessing) long life of 100 years: 祝你～! May you live to be a hundred! *or* I wish you a long, long life.

长命锁 chángmìngsuǒ "long-life lock", worn by a child as a mascot for longevity

长年 chángnián ❶ all the year round; from year to year; for a long time: ～冰雪覆盖 be clad with ice and snow all the year round / 他～在农村进行小麦品种试验。He stayed in the countryside over the years to experiment on wheat strains. ❷〈方言〉*see* "长工" ❸〈书面〉long life; longevity: 富贵～ wealth, position and a long life
see also zhǎngnián

长年累月 chángnián-lěiyuè year in year out; over the years; all the year round: ～的努力 long years of hard work; long-sustained efforts / 他～地积累材料。He worked hard for years to gather useful information and data.

长袍儿 chángpáor traditional Chinese long gown: 过去读书人多穿～。In the old days scholars used to wear long gowns.

长跑 chángpǎo long-distance running; distance race: ～运动员 long-distance runner

长篇 chángpiān ❶ of length; long: ～叙事诗 long narrative poem / ～论文 long treatise ❷ long fiction; novel: 他善于写～。He's good at writing long fiction. *or* He's a good novelist.

长篇大论 chángpiān-dàlùn lengthy speech or article: 他会上作的报告真可谓～。He made a long speech at the meeting. *or* He held forth at great length at the meeting. / 我不喜欢～的文章。I don't like lengthy articles.

长篇小说 chángpiān xiǎoshuō novel

长期 chángqī long-term; prolonged; protracted: ～以来 over a long period of time; since a long time ago / ～政策 long-term policy / ～合同 long-term contract / ～存在的问题 long-standing problem / ～天气预报 long-range weather forecast / ～奋斗 protracted struggle / ～贸易逆差 chronic trade deficit / ～亏损 be at a loss for years / ～占有 *longi temporis possessio*

长期贷款 chángqī dàikuǎn long-term loan

长期共存 chángqī gòngcún long-term coexistence: ～，互相监督，肝胆相照，荣辱与共 long-term coexistence and mutual supervision of the various parties, treating each other with all sincerity and sharing weal and woe

长期国会 Chángqī Guóhuì Long Parliament, summoned by Charles I in 1640, sitting through the English Civil War and finally voting its own dissolution in 1660

长期抗战 chángqī kàngzhàn long war of resistance against Japanese aggression (1937-1945);〈比喻〉prolonged efforts in doing sth.

长期失业 chángqī shīyè chronic unemployment: ～者 hardcore unemployed

长期信贷 chángqī xìndài long-term credit

长期行为 chángqī xíngwéi action taken for the long-term interest; far-sighted measure

长期性 chángqīxìng protracted nature: 斗争的艰苦性、～ how hard and how long a struggle will be

长期债权 chángqī zhàiquán long-term claim

长期债券 chángqī zhàiquàn long-term bond

长崎 Chángqí Nagasaki (Japanese city hit by the second atom bomb on 9 August, 1945)

长枪 chángqiāng ❶ spear ❷ long-barrelled gun; old-type rifle

长枪党 Chángqiāngdǎng Falange, Spanish Fascist movement founded in 1933, merged in 1937 with right-wing elements to form the ruling party, and formally abolished in 1977

长驱 chángqū (of an army) make a long drive; push deep: 他们～万里，直抵边塞。They drove over a distance of ten thousand *li* straight to the frontier.

长驱直入 chángqū-zhírù (of an army) drive straight in: ～，势如破竹 drive straight in and carry everything on the way

长拳 chángquán (a style of Chinese shadow-boxing) long punch boxing

长日照植物 chángrìzhào zhíwù〈植物〉long-day plant

长沙 Chángshā Changsha, provincial capital of Hunan

长衫 chángshān long gown: 身着～ be wearing a long gown

长舌 chángshé long-tongued — fond of gossip; gossipy: ～妇 gossipy woman

长蛇阵 chángshézhèn single-line battle array: 排成一字～ deploy

the troops in a long line / 店门前排起了～。There is a long queue of customers in front of the shop.

长蛇座 Chángshézuò 〈天文〉Hydra

长生 chángshēng long life; longevity: ～不老 perpetual rejuvenation

长生不老药 chángshēng-bùlǎoyào elixir of life

长生草 chángshēngcǎo 〈植物〉houseleek; live-forever (*Sempervivum*)

长生殿 Chángshēngdiàn title of a drama by Hong Sheng (洪升, 1645-1704) of the Qing Dynasty

长生果 chángshēngguǒ 〈方言〉peanut; groundnut
see also "落花生" luòhuāshēng

长生花 chángshēnghuā 〈植物〉hen-and-chicken

长绳系日 chángshéng-jìrì tie the sun with a long rope — be reluctant to let time go by

长石 chángshí 〈矿业〉feldspar

长时记忆 chángshí jìyì 〈心理〉long-term memory

长时优惠 chángshí yōuhuì 〈通信〉duration discount

长逝 chángshì pass away; be gone forever: 溘然～ pass away quite unexpectedly

长寿 chángshòu long life; longevity: ～老人 person who lives to a ripe old age / 祝你健康～。Wish you good health and a long life.

长寿菜 chángshòucài *also* "马齿苋" mǎchǐxiàn purslane

长寿灌顶 chángshòu guàndǐng *tshe-dbang*, annual ceremony to pray for long life in Tibetan Buddhism

长丝 chángsī 〈纺织〉filament

长随 chángsuí *also* "跟班" gēnbān 〈旧语〉attendant; retainer; follower: 带来了几个～ have a few escorts around

长榻 chángtà couch

长滩 Chángtān Long Beach, a resort city in California, US

长叹 chángtàn deep sigh: ～一声 heave a deep sigh

长天 chángtiān ❶ vast sky: 秋水共～一色。The autumn water merged into the azure sky in the distance. ❷ day; daytime

长条校样 chángtiáo jiàoyàng 〈印刷〉galley proof

长挑 chángtiao (of a person) tall and slender; lanky

长亭 chángtíng 〈古语〉wayside pavilion outside a city or town: 送别十里～ bid a friend farewell at a wayside pavilion 10 *li* from the town

长统皮靴 chángtǒng píxuē high boots

长统袜 chángtǒngwà stockings

长痛 chángtòng long, dull pain: ～不如短痛 be better to have short, sharp pains than long, dull pains; be better to have a quick, though painful, solution

长途 chángtú ❶ long-distance: ～旅行 long trip / ～飞行 long flight / ～运输 long-distance transport / ～奔袭敌后要塞 make a long-distance (*or* long-range) raid on a fortress in the enemy rear ❷ long-distance call or bus: 打～ make a trunk call / 坐～ take a long-distance bus

长途跋涉 chángtú-báshè make a long, difficult journey: 他经过～,终于重返故乡。After a long, difficult journey, he finally returned to his native town.

长途电话 chángtú diànhuà 〈通信〉long-distance or trunk call; toll call

长途电话局 chángtú diànhuàjú long-distance exchange; toll office; toll centre

长途电缆 chángtú diànlǎn 〈通信〉toll cable; long-distance cable

长途汽车 chángtú qìchē long-distance bus; coach

长途直拨电话 chángtú zhíbō diànhuà direct distance dialing (DDD)

长途自动电话网 chángtú zìdòng diànhuàwǎng automatic telephone trunk network

长网 chángwǎng (in papermaking) Fourdrinier wire: ～造纸机 Fourdrinier machine

长尾猴 chángwěihóu guenon (*Cercopithecus*)

长尾鲨 chángwěishā thresher shark (*Alopiidae*)

长尾鹟 chángwěiwēng 〈动物〉paradise fly-catcher

长物 chángwù surplus; anything that can be spared; valuables: 平生无～ own nothing but articles of everyday use all one's life / 他除了书籍之外,别无～。He possesses nothing of value except books.

长线 chángxiàn (as opposed to 短线) overproduction; oversupply: 缩短～,发展短线,把国民经济的比例关系协调好。Coordinate the national economy by reducing overproduced goods and increasing production of those in short supply.

长线产品 chángxiàn chǎnpǐn product in excessive supply

长项 chángxiàng sth. one is good at; one's strong point

长效 chángxiào enduring effect; lasting effect

长效避孕药 chángxiào bìyùnyào long-acting contraceptive

长效发酵饲料 chángxiào fājiào sìliào slow-acting fermentation feed

长效肥料 chángxiào féiliào depot fertilizer; long-lasting fertilizer; slow-release fertilizer

长效磺胺 chángxiào huáng'àn 〈药学〉sulphamethoxypyridazine (SMP)

长效胶囊 chángxiào jiāonáng 〈药学〉spansule

长效胰岛素 chángxiào yídǎosù 〈药学〉protamine zine insulin

长啸 chángxiào give a sustained loud cry; cry long and loud into the air

长行 chángxíng 〈书面〉go on a long journey

长性 chángxìng patience; constancy; perseverance; power of concentration: 这孩子没～。This child has little power of concentration.

长袖善舞 chángxiù-shànwǔ long sleeves lend grace to dancing; powerful backing ensures success; the wealthy know how to manoeuvre: ～,多财善贾。With long sleeves one will be good at dancing and with plentiful money one will be good at business.

长吁短叹 chángxū-duǎntàn moan and groan; whine: 她愁容满面,～。She looked very worried and sighed like a furnace.

长须鲸 chángxūjīng 〈动物〉finback

长阳人 Chángyángrén 〈考古〉Changyang Man (a type of primitive man of about 100,000 years ago whose fossil remains were found in Changyang, Hubei Province, in 1956 and 1957)

长夜 chángyè ❶ long night; eternal night: 漫漫～ endless night / 作～之饮 spend the whole night carousing ❷ period resembling dark night: ～难明。There seemed to be no end to the dark days. *or* One cannot see the light at the end of the tunnel. / ～难明赤县天。The night was long and dawn came slow to the Crimson Land.

长揖 chángyī make a long bow with clasped hands reaching to the knees

长缨 chángyīng 〈书面〉long rope (alluding to a young man in the Han Dynasty who volunteered to serve in the army, asking for a long rope with which to truss up the enemy chief): 今日～在手,何时缚住苍龙? Today we hold the long cord in our hands, When shall we bind fast the Grey Dragon?

长影 Chángyǐng (short for 长春电影制片厂) Changchun Film Studios

长于 chángyú be good at; specialize: ～文学 specialize in literature / ～骑术 be good at equestrian art / ～奉迎 be adept at flattery and touting

长余 chángyú surplus; more than what is due: ～的粮食 surplus grain

长元音 chángyuányīn 〈语言〉long vowel

长圆 chángyuán oval: ～脸 oval face / ～形 oval shape

长远 chángyuǎn long-term; long-range: ～打算 long-term plan / ～利益 long-term interest / ～目标 long-range objective / 这不是～的办法。This is only a stopgap measure. / 我们要把目光放～些,不要只看到鼻子底下的事儿。We must see farther than what is under our nose.

长斋 chángzhāi (Buddhists') permanent abstention from meat, fish, etc.; vegetarian diet: 吃～ be on a permanent vegetarian diet

长征 chángzhēng ❶ expedition; long march: 迈步在新～的大路上 advance on the road of a new long march / 万里～,始于足下。A long journey of ten thousand *li* begins with a single step. ❷ Long March (a major strategic movement of the Chinese Workers' and Peasants' Red Army which succeeded in reaching the revolutionary base area in northern Shaanxi after traversing eleven provinces and covering 25,000 *li*, or 12,500 kilometres, 1934-1935): ～干部 cadres who took part in the Long March; Long March veterans ❸ (Chángzhēng) Truong Chinh (1907-1988), Vietnamese leader, writer and poet

长征二E号大推力捆绑式火箭 Chángzhēng Èr-Yì Hào dàtuīlì kǔnbǎngshì huǒjiàn Long March-2E heavy thrust cluster carrier rocket

长征号运载火箭 Chángzhēnghào yùnzài huǒjiàn Long March launch vehicle

长支 chángzhī (formerly of a shop assistant, etc., paid by the year) advanced pay: 扣除～,他工钱所剩无几。With the advanced pay

deducted, little was left of his wages.
长至 chángzhì Summer Solstice
长治久安 chángzhì-jiǔ'ān long period of peace and stability; prolonged political stability:～之策 policy of long-term political stability / 国家～,人民永享太平。The people will forever enjoy peace and tranquillity in a country where there is prolonged political stability.
长昼 chángzhòu long day
长住 chángzhù live in a place for a long time; reside permanently; settle
长勺之战 Chángzhuó Zhī Zhàn *also* "齐鲁长勺之战" Qí-Lǔ Chángzhuó Zhī Zhàn Battle of Changzhuo of 684 BC, in which the Kingdom of Lu defeated the invading army of the Kingdom of Qi against heavy odds
长足 chángzú 〈书面〉by leaps and bounds:取得～的进步 make rapid progress; make great strides forward / 有了～的发展 score considerable achievements

苌(萇) cháng

苌楚 chángchǔ 〈古语〉a kind of kiwi fruit

场(場、塲) cháng

❶ level open space; threshing ground:看～ keep watch at the threshing ground (when harvested crops are stored there) / 晒～ sun the harvested crops on the threshing ground / 翻～ turn the harvested crops over on the threshing ground (for better sunning) / 打～ threshing ❷ 〈方言〉country fair; rural market:赶～ go to the country fair ❸ 〈量词〉*used to indicate a process*:一～大雪 a heavy snowfall / 一～战斗 a battle / 生了一～大病 have been very ill / 大干一～ go all out; exert one's utmost
see also chǎng; chang
场坪 chángpíng 〈方言〉level ground
场圃 chángpǔ garden plot
场屋 chángwū threshing-ground lodge (for the watchman to rest in, as well as for storing farm tools)
see also chǎngwū
场园 chángyuán threshing ground
场院 chángyuàn threshing ground; sunning ground:～里堆满了粮食。Grain mounds are everywhere on the threshing ground.

肠(腸) cháng

❶ *also* "肠管" intestines:大～ large intestine / 小～ small intestine ❷ sausage:鱼～ fish sausage
肠阿米巴病 cháng'āmǐbābìng 〈医学〉intestinal amebiasis
肠癌 cháng'ái 〈医学〉intestinal cancer
肠出血 chángchūxuè 〈医学〉enterorrhagia
肠穿孔 chángchuānkǒng 〈医学〉intestinal perforation
肠道病 chángdàobìng 〈医学〉enteropathy:～学 enterology; gastroenterology / ～学家 enterologist / ～毒 enterovirus / ～细菌 entric bacteria
肠淀粉酶 chángdiànfěnméi entero-amylase
肠断 chángduàn heart-broken; broken-hearted; grief-stricken:柔肠寸断 be grief-stricken / 那种惨景令人～。The horrible sight touched one to the heart.
肠肥脑满 chángféi-nǎomǎn *also* "脑满肠肥" (of sb. who eats well without working for it) heavy-jowled and pot-bellied
肠风 chángfēng *also* "肠风下血" 〈中医〉*Changfeng* or intestines attacked by wind, referring to haemorrhoid bleeding caused by internal injury, or dysentery discharging faeces with blood
肠缝合 chángfénghé 〈医学〉enterocleisis
肠梗阻 chánggěngzǔ 〈医学〉*also* "肠阻塞" intestinal obstruction
肠骨 chánggǔ *also* "髂骨" qiàgǔ 〈医学〉ilium
肠管 chángguǎn intestine
肠灌洗 chángguànxǐ 〈医学〉enteroclysis
肠环缝术 chánghuánféngshù 〈医学〉enterorrhaphy circularis; circular enterorrhaphy
肠激酶 chángjīméi 〈生化〉enterokinase
肠寄生虫 chángjìshēngchóng 〈医学〉enterozoon; intestinal parasite
肠绞痛 chángjiǎotòng intestinal colic
肠结核 chángjiéhé 〈医学〉abdominal phthisis; intestinal tuberculosis
肠痉挛 chángjìngluán 〈医学〉enterospasm
肠镜 chángjìng 〈医学〉enteroscope:～检查 enteroscopy
肠鸣 chángmíng borborygmus
肠黏膜 chángniánmó intestinal mucosa
肠扭转 chángniǔzhuǎn 〈医学〉volvulus
肠脓毒症 chángnóngdúzhèng 〈医学〉enterosepsis
肠切除术 chángqiēchúshù 〈医学〉enterectomy
肠切开术 chángqiēkāishù 〈医学〉enterotomy; Nelaton's operation
肠儿 chángr 〈口语〉sausage:泥～ frankfurter / 肉泥～ minced-meat sausage / 腊～ Chinese sausage / 香～ sausage
肠绒毛 chángróngmáo 〈生理〉intestinal villus
肠蠕动 chángrúdòng 〈医学〉enterocinesia
肠疝 chángshàn 〈医学〉enterocele
肠伤寒 chángshānghán *also* "伤寒" 〈医学〉typhoid fever; typhoid
肠肽酶 chángtàiméi 〈生化〉erepsin
肠套叠 chángtàodié 〈医学〉intussusception
肠外科 chángwàikē 〈医学〉enterochirurgia
肠胃 chángwèi intestines and stomach; stomach:～不好 suffer from indigestion / ～外饲法 parenteral feeding
肠胃炎 chángwèiyán 〈医学〉enterogastritis
肠息肉 chángxīròu intestinal polyp
肠系膜 chángxìmó 〈生理〉mesentery
肠线 chángxiàn catgut
肠炎 chángyán 〈医学〉enteritis
肠液 chángyè 〈生理〉intestinal juice
肠衣 chángyī casing for sausages
肠痈 chángyōng 〈中医〉appendicitis
肠粘连 chángzhānlián 〈医学〉ankylenteron; intestinal adhesion
肠子 chángzi intestines
肠阻塞 chángzǔsè *see* "肠梗阻"

chǎng

昶 chǎng

❶〈书面〉long day ❷〈书面〉relaxed and easy; unimpeded; unblocked:乐声和～ melodious and mellow music ❸ (Chǎng) a surname

场(場、塲) chǎng

❶ place where people gather for a specific purpose:会～ meeting-place / 战～ battlefield / 足球～ football field / 篮球～ basketball court / 运动～ sports ground (*or* field) / 广～ square / 剧～ theatre / 农～ farm / 赌～ gambling house / 入～ enter the stadium (*or* arena, etc.) / 退～ march out; walk out / 市～ market (place) ❷ stage:上～ enter stage (used in a script, scenario, libretto, etc.) / 下～ exit stage ❸ 〈戏剧〉scene:第三幕第二～ Act III, Scene II / 这出戏共分四幕十二～。The play consists of twelve scenes in four acts. ❹ spot; scene:出～ come on the scene; appear on the stage / 在～ be present / 当～ on the spot ❺ 〈量词〉:一～球赛 a ball game / 两～电影 two films / 一～恶梦 a nightmare / 一～演出 a performance (*or* show) ❻ 〈物理〉field:磁～ magnetic field
see also cháng; chang
场波 chǎngbō field wave
场畴 chǎngchóu field domain
场磁铁 chǎngcítiě 〈电学〉field magnet
场次 chǎngcì number of showings of a film, play, etc.:这个戏已演出一百多～。This play has had a run of over a hundred performances.
场地 chǎngdì space; place; site:比赛～ competition arena (*or* ground) / 活动～ playground; space for activities / 施工～ construction site / ～狭小 limited floor space / 群众性体育活动的～不足。There isn't enough space for mass sports activities.
场电路 chǎngdiànlù field circuit
场分布 chǎngfēnbù field distribution
场感应电流 chǎnggǎnyìng diànliú field-generated current
场馆 chǎngguǎn gymnasiums and stadiums; grounds:体育～ sports grounds and gymnasiums / 比赛～ gymnasiums and stadiums for holding competitions
场合 chǎnghé occasion; situation:正式～ formal occasions / 社交～ social occasion / 外交～ diplomatic occasion / 公开～ in public; openly / 热闹～ place bustling with activity / 说话要分～。Think of the social context whenever you speak. *or* One's speech must suit the occasion. / 他在人多的～说话常口吃。He often stammers when he speaks to a large audience.

场记 chǎngjì 〈影视〉❶ log ❷ *also* "场记员" log keeper; script holder; script girl
场界灯 chǎngjièdēng 〈航空〉boundary lights
场景 chǎngjǐng ❶〈戏剧〉〈影视〉scene: 富有特色的～ scene with special features of its own; scene with a distinctive flavour ❷ sight; scene; picture: 热火朝天的劳动～ picture of overflowing labour enthusiasm / 依依惜别的～ sentimental parting scene
场控晶体管 chǎngkòng jīngtǐguǎn field transistor; fieldistor
场理论 chǎnglǐlùn *also* "场论"〈物理〉field theory
场粒子 chǎnglìzǐ 〈物理〉field particle
场面 chǎngmiàn ❶〈戏剧〉〈影视〉〈文学〉scene: 精彩～ thrilling scene; superb scene / 这一～是全剧的高潮。This scene is the climax of the play. / 这部电视剧有不少感人的～。There are quite a number of moving scenes in this TV play. ❷〈戏曲〉musical accompaniment: 文～ orchestral accompaniment / 武～ percussional accompaniment ❸ spectacle; occasion; scene: ～壮观 grand spectacle (*or* occasion) / 热烈友好的～ manifestation of warm feeling and good friendship / 盛大的欢迎～ grand reception ❹ appearance; front; facade: 撑～ keep up appearances / 摆～ go in for ostentation and extravagance; go in for pomp; be ostentatious
场面话 chǎngmiànhuà polite platitude for the occasion; civil banalities; unctuous words
场面人 chǎngmiànrén ❶ man about town; very sociable person ❷ person of prestige; celebrity
场面上 chǎngmiànshang on social occasions; in social life: ～的人 socializer; man about town / 他在～吃得开。He knows his way about in social life. *or* He's a good socializer.
场内交易 chǎngnèi jiāoyì 〈经济〉transaction on exchange
场内经纪人 chǎngnèi jīngjìrén floor broker; board broker
场能 chǎngnéng 〈物理〉field energy
场频 chǎngpín 〈物理〉field frequency
场强 chǎngqiáng 〈物理〉intensity of field; field intensity
场所 chǎngsuǒ place (for an activity); venue: 公共～ public place / 娱乐～ place of entertainment / 幽静的～ quiet (*or* secluded) spot / 热闹～ place bustling with noise and activity / 蚊蝇孳生的～ breeding ground of flies and mosquitoes / 强盗出没的～ bandit-infested area
场外交易 chǎngwài jiāoyì 〈经济〉over the counter (OTC); over-the-counter dealing: ～市场 over-the-counter market / ～证券 over-the-counter securities / 外国股票的～ over-the-counter dealing of foreign stocks
场屋 chǎngwū 〈旧语〉hall for the imperial civil service examination
see also chángwū
场效应 chǎngxiàoyìng 〈物理〉field effect: ～变阻器 field-effect varistor
场效应晶体管 chǎngxiàoyìng jīngtǐguǎn 〈无线电〉field-effect transistor
场致发射 chǎngzhì fāshè 〈物理〉field emission
场子 chǎngzi place (for an activity): 大～ big place (*or* ring, *or* hall) / 空～ empty place (*or* ring)

厂(廠、厰)

chǎng ❶ factory; mill; plant; works: 服装～ clothing factory / 面粉～ flour mill / 钢铁～ iron and steel works / 汽车制造～ auto plant / 化工～ chemical works / 酿酒～ winery / 造船～ shipyard / 食品～ food products factory; bakery and confectionery / 电机～ electrical machinery plant / 电影制片～ studio; film studio / 糖～ sugar refinery ❷ yard; depot: 煤～ coal yard / 木材～ timber yard
厂标 chǎngbiāo emblem (of a factory): 设计～ design an emblem mark / 这个工厂的～分外醒目。The emblem of the factory is eye-catching.
厂房 chǎngfáng ❶ factory building: 宽敞明亮的～ bright and spacious premises of the factory ❷ workshop: 高大的～ huge workshop
厂风 chǎngfēng overall management and working style of a factory
厂规 chǎngguī factory regulations
厂籍 chǎngjí factory roll: 开除～ dismiss from a factory; strike off the factory roll
厂纪 chǎngjì factory discipline
厂家 chǎngjiā ❶ factory: 参展的有几百个～。Several hundred factories are represented at the exhibition. ❷〈方言〉factory owner; factory management
厂警 chǎngjǐng (security) guard of a factory
厂矿 chǎngkuàng factories and mines: ～企业 industrial enterprises; factories, mines and other enterprises / ～协作 cooperation between factories and mines / 深入～调查 conduct deep-going investigations in factories and mines
厂礼拜 chǎnglǐbài *also* "厂休日" day off for a factory (usu. on a weekday): 周三是我们的～。Wednesday is our day off.
厂龄 chǎnglíng length of service in a factory
厂内待业 chǎngnèi dàiyè be temporally without work, but still on factory payroll
厂区 chǎngqū production area of a factory
厂容 chǎngróng appearance or look of a factory; environmental features of a factory
厂商 chǎngshāng ❶ factory owner: 承包～ contractor / 营造～ manufacturer ❷ factories and shops: 许多～前来洽谈合资。Many factories and companies have sent representatives to negotiate the establishment of a joint venture.
厂史 chǎngshǐ history of a factory; story of an enterprise: 编写～ compile (*or* write) the history of a factory / ～展览 exhibition on the history of the factory / 向新来的工人讲～。The newly recruited workers were briefed on the story of the enterprise.
厂丝 chǎngsī 〈纺织〉filature silk
厂校挂钩 chǎng-xiào guàgōu establish contact between a school and a factory
厂卫 Chǎngwèi *also* "东厂" Dōngchǎng 〈历史〉Eastern Depot, the emperor's intelligence and prosecution department in the Ming Dynasty
厂休 chǎngxiū day of rest for staff as specified by the factory management
厂长 chǎngzhǎng factory director; factory manager
厂长负责制 chǎngzhǎng fùzézhì system of overall responsibility by the factory manager
厂长任期目标责任制 chǎngzhǎng rènqī mùbiāo zérènzhì system under which the factory director is held responsible for attaining given goals during his term of office
厂址 chǎngzhǐ site or location of a factory
厂主 chǎngzhǔ factory owner; millowner: ～易人 replace the factory owner
厂子 chǎngzi ❶〈口语〉factory; mill; workshop: 他和我在一个～干活。We both work at the same factory. ❷ yard; depot: 木～ timber-yard / 家具～ furniture depot

惝

chǎng
see also tǎng
惝恍 chǎnghuǎng *also* "惝怳"〈书面〉❶ depressed; upset; unhappy: 他徘徊～。He wandered about aimlessly, feeling upset. ❷ vague; hazy: 视听～ have poor sight and hearing; be weak in eyesight and hard of hearing

敞

chǎng ❶ (of houses, yards, etc.) spacious; roomy: 这院子太～了。The courtyard is very spacious indeed. ❷ open; uncovered: ～着门 leave the door open / 窗户～着。The windows were wide open. / 车篷～着 with the bonnet (*or* hood) open / ～胸露怀 with one's coat (*or* shirt) unbuttoned; bare one's chest
敞舱驳船 chǎngcāng bóchuán 〈交通〉scow; open barge
敞车 chǎngchē ❶ open wagon; open car ❷〈铁路〉flatcar
敞房 chǎngfáng salle; finishing house
敞怀 chǎnghuái ❶ with one's shirt unbuttoned; with one's chest bare ❷ unrestrainedly; open mindedly: ～大笑 laugh to one's heart's content
敞开 chǎngkāi ❶ open wide; open: 把门～ keep the door wide open / ～衬衫 unbutton one's shirt / ～胸怀 speak one's mind freely / ～思想 speak up; get things off one's chest ❷ put no limit on; de-regulate; decontrol: ～价格，随行就市 de-regulate the prices and let them fluctuate in the market / ～供应 supply without limit; ensure an open-ended supply / 你有什么想法，就～说吧。Say whatever's on your mind. *or* Get everything off your chest.
敞开儿 chǎngkāir 〈口语〉unlimited; unrestricted: ～吃 eat one's fill; do full justice to the food / ～喝 drink one's fill / ～说 get everything off one's chest; pour out (one's troubles, sorrows, grievances, complaints, etc.)
敞开式锻模 chǎngkāishì duànmó 〈机械〉open die

敞口儿 chǎngkǒur 〈方言〉unlimited：今年的白菜～供应。There will be ample supply of Chinese cabbage for this winter's storage.
敞口项目 chǎngkǒu xiàngmù open-ended project
敞快 chǎngkuai frank；straightforward；forthright：他是个～人，说做就做。He is a forthright chap who gets down to business the moment his mind is made up.
敞阔 chǎngkuò spacious；roomy；wide；open：～的洼地 open low-lying land／胸怀～ broad-minded；unprejudiced；unbiased
敞亮 chǎngliàng bright and spacious；clear-minded：～的房间 bright and spacious room／经你一讲，我心里～多了。I've got a clearer picture now that I have heard your explanation.
敞露 chǎnglù open；bare
敞喷 chǎngpēn 〈石油〉open flow
敞篷车 chǎngpéngchē open car
敞式车身 chǎngshì chēshēn open body（of a car）
敞着口儿 chǎngzhekǒur ❶ not healed；not settled：伤口还～呢。The cut hasn't healed up yet.／这个问题还～呢。This is still an open question. ❷〈方言〉unrestrained：我们不能～过日子。We should not live beyond our means.

氅 chǎng cloak：大～ cloak／毡～ felt coat／外～ overcoat

鋹（鋹） chǎng 〈书面〉sharp；keen-edged：盾坚矛～ strong shields and sharp spears

chàng

唱 chàng ❶ sing：～国歌 sing the National Anthem／～京戏 sing an aria from Beijing opera／渔舟～晚 sing folk songs in a fishing boat returning at dusk／二重～ duet／三重～ trio／四重～ quartet／五重～ quintet／表演～ item combining singing，dancing and acting／独～ solo／轮～ round／齐～ sing in unison／合～ chorus ❷ call；cry：～好 hail；applause；cheer loudly／雄鸡～晨 cock crowing at dawn ❸ song or singing part of a Chinese opera：小～ ditty；popular tune ❹（Chàng）a surname
唱白脸 chàng báiliǎn wear the white makeup of the stage villian；play the villian；pretend to be harsh and severe；play the bad cop：一个唱红脸，一个～。One coaxes，while the other bullies. *or* One plays the good cop while the other plays the bad cop.
唱本 chàngběn libretto or script of a ballad-singer：旧～儿 outdated（*or* old）libretto／他记性好，从来不用～。He always sings without looking at the words，for he has a good memory.
唱酬 chàngchóu 〈书面〉write and reply in regulated verse between friends，usu. using the same rhyme sequence
唱词 chàngcí libretto；words of a ballad
唱碟 chàngdié 〈方言〉record；gramophone record
唱独角戏 chàng dújiǎoxì play a monodrama；put on a one-man show；go it alone；work alone：要发动群众，不要～。Mobilize the masses instead of going it alone. *or* Try to rouse the public to action rather than take everything upon yourself.
唱段 chàngduàn aria：戏中的精彩～ wonderful aria from the opera
唱对台戏 chàng duìtáixì put on a rival show；enter into rivalry：他有意跟我～。He is deliberately putting on a rival show against me.
唱反调 chàng fǎndiào sing a different tune；sound or strike a discordant note：故意～ sing a different tune on purpose／他总～，很难合作。Holding contrary opinions on every occasion，he is hard to get along with.
唱付 chàngfù （of a salesman）shout the amount of money when giving the change to a customer
唱高调 chàng gāodiào make high-sounding statements；indulge in high-flown rhetoric：这纯粹是～。These are purely high-sounding words.／～无济于事。Fine-sounding words won't help matters. *or* Fair words butter no parsnips.
唱歌 chànggē sing：她爱～。She likes singing.
唱工 chànggōng 〈戏曲〉*also*"唱功" art of singing；singing：这位京剧女演员～好。This Beijing Opera actress is good at singing.
唱工戏 chànggōngxì Chinese opera featuring singing（rather than acting or acrobatics）
唱功 chànggōng *see*"唱工"
唱和 chànghè ❶ one sings a song and the others join in the chorus：彼此～ when one starts singing，another joins in；echo each other ❷ when one writes a poem，the other comes up with another in reply，usu. using the same rhyme sequence：饮酒～ write and respond to poems by each other over cups of wine
唱红脸 chàng hóngliǎn wear the red makeup of the stage hero；play the hero；appear generous and kind；play the good cop：大家当然喜欢他喽，他老是～。He is of course popular，for he is always playing the part of a warm-hearted and generous gentleman.
唱机 chàngjī gramophone；phonograph：电～ electric record player
唱经 chàngjīng 〈宗教〉cantillation
唱剧 chàngjù a kind of Korean folk opera
唱空城计 chàng kōngchéngjì ❶ play the empty-city stratagem（bluffing the enemy by opening the gates of a weakly defended city）；present a bold front to conceal a weak defence ❷ have all or most of the staff vacated：人都上街搞推销去了，只留下秘书一人～。With everybody else promoting sales in the streets，only the secretary is left behind.
唱老调 chàng lǎodiào sing the hackneyed tune；harp on the same old theme：走老路，～ traverse the same old route and sing the same old tune／文章要有新意，不要总是～。You must have fresh ideas when you write. Don't always harp on the same old theme.
唱名 chàngmíng ❶ roll call：～表决 vote by roll call ❷〈音乐〉sol-fa；solmization：七～ sol-fa syllables（i.e. do，re，mi，fa，sol，la，ti）
唱名法 chàngmíngfǎ 〈音乐〉tonic sol-fa；solmization：固定～ fixed-do system／首调～ movable-do system
唱盘 chàngpán turntable
唱片儿 chàngpiānr 〈口语〉record
唱片 chàngpiàn gramophone or phonograph record：放～ play a gramophone record／灌～ cut a disc；make a record／密纹～ long-playing record／～套 jacket（for a record）
唱票 chàngpiào call out the names of candidates while counting ballots：～人 teller
唱腔 chàngqiāng 〈戏曲〉melodies in a Chinese opera：～设计 melody designing／～凄婉动人 moving，sad melodies
唱曲 chàngqǔ sing a song or tune
唱喏 chàngrě 〈方言〉make a vocal response while bowing with folded hands held out before one；bow
唱诗 chàngshī ❶〈基督教〉sing hymns ❷〈书面〉recite poetry：～吟对 write and recite poetry in response to each other
唱诗班 chàngshībān （in a church）choir
唱收 chàngshōu （of a salesman）shout the amount of money when receiving money from a customer
唱衰 chàngshuāi 〈方言〉speak ill of；spread pessimistic views about；play down：企图～香港（try to）bad-mouth Hong Kong
唱双簧 chàng shuānghuáng ❶〈戏曲〉give a two-man comic show（with one gesticulating in front and the other speaking or singing behind him）：两个演员在台上～。The two actors are performing a comic show on the stage. ❷ collaborate with each other：你俩别～，还是老实说吧。Stop acting and come clean.
唱头 chàngtóu pick-up（of a gramophone，etc.）
唱戏 chàngxì 〈口语〉sing in an opera；put on a theatrical performance：爱～ be fond of acting in an opera／会～ be good at acting／请名角儿～ get famous actors or actresses to put on a theatrical performance
唱针 chàngzhēn gramophone needle；stylus
唱主角 chàng zhǔjué play the leading role：这个课题组由你来～。You'll play the leading role in this research team.
唱做念打 chàng-zuò-niàn-dǎ 〈戏曲〉singing，acting，recitation and acrobatics

倡 chàng ❶ initiate；advocate：首～ initiate；start ❷〈书面〉*see*"唱" chàng
see also chāng
倡办 chàngbàn initiate（an activity，etc.）；propose to start（an undertaking，etc.）：～文学社 propose to form a literary society／～疑难病治疗中心 launch a medical centre for treatment of difficult and complicated cases
倡导 chàngdǎo initiate；propose；promote：～实事求是的作风 promote a practical work style／～和平共处五项原则 initiate the Five Principles of Peaceful Coexistence
倡始 chàngshǐ initiate；originate；start：～人 initiator；founder
倡首 chàngshǒu initiate；take the lead in：为残疾人募捐的事，是工会

～的。The collection of donations for the handicapped was sponsored by the Trade Union.

倡言 chàngyán 〈书面〉propose; initiate; advocate:～共和 promote republicanism /～改革开放 advocate reform and open policy

倡议 chàngyì propose:～书 written proposal; proposal /～者 initiator /～权〈外交〉initiative /～组织一次讨论会 propose holding a seminar /～开展劳动竞赛 propose launching a labour emulation drive / 提出裁军新～ put forward a new proposal for disarmament /这一～得到了各方支持。The proposal won support from all quarters (*or* parties).

鬯[1] chàng 〈古语〉sacrificial wine

鬯[2] chàng 〈书面〉*see* "畅" chàng

韔(韔) chàng 〈书面〉❶ bow case ❷ put a bow in its case

怅(悵) chàng disappointed; sorry:深以为～ feel very much disappointed

怅怅 chàngchàng 〈书面〉disappointed; upset:～不乐 disappointed and unhappy /～离去 depart with regret /数十年一事无成,于心～。I feel dispirited when I think that I have accomplished nothing in several decades.

怅恨 chànghèn regretful:～不已 chew the bitter cud of regret /每念仓促离家,～交加。I cannot think of my hurried departure from home without a touch of regret.

怅然 chàngrán disappointed; upset:～不语 be speechless with sad disappointment /～离去 walk away dejectedly /～若失 feel depressed and perplexed; feel sad and distracted

怅惋 chàngwǎn sigh with regret; deeply regret:～不已 can hardly repress a feeling of deep regret

怅惘 chàngwǎng anxious and in low spirits; listless:无限～ be overcome with a feeling of infinite anxiety /～良久 be lost in depression and sadness /～之情形于眉梢 look anxious and sad /展诵来书,不胜～。I was full of solicitude for you after I read your letter.

怅望 chàngwàng look (at sth.) wistfully:凭栏～ lean on the railing looking wistfully into the distance

玚(瑒) chàng *also* "玚圭"〈古语〉a type of elongated pointed jade used for worship

see also yáng

畅(暢) chàng ❶ smooth; unimpeded:流～ easy and smooth; fluent /～通无阻 pass unimpeded; go unhindered /下水道排水不～。The sewer is partly blocked. /信息不～。The flow of information is impeded. /图书发行渠道不通～。The channels for distributing books are inadequate. ❷ free; uninhibited:～饮 drink one's fill ❸ (Chàng) a surname

畅达 chàngdá fluent; smooth:文辞～ read smoothly /本市交通～无阻。The city has a good transport and communications network.

畅怀 chànghuái to one's heart's content; as much as one likes:～痛饮 drink one's fill

畅快 chàngkuài free from inhibitions; carefree; happy:精神～ feel relaxed /心情～ have ease of mind; be in a happy mood /～地玩了一天 have a splendid time the whole day

畅茂 chàngmào 〈书面〉luxuriant; exuberant; flourishing:草木～。The grass and trees are lush and luxuriant.

畅适 chàngshì carefree and fit:安闲～ be at leisure and free from care; lead a life of ease and comfort; enjoy good health and a life of leisure

畅抒 chàngshū express freely:～已见 speak one's mind freely

畅顺 chàngshùn smooth; unhindered:他呼吸似乎不很～。It appears that he is breathing with difficulty.

畅所欲言 chàngsuǒyùyán speak without reservation; speak one's mind freely /大家都能～。Everybody said what was in his mind. *or* Everybody had his say.

畅谈 chàngtán chat or talk freely and cheerfully:每个人都～了自己的人生理想。Everyone of us talked frankly and eagerly about his or her ambition in life.

畅通 chàngtōng unblocked; unimpeded:河道～。The river is open to navigation. /公路～无阻。Road traffic is normal. /言路～。Public opinion has easy access to the government. *or* Opinion at the grass roots level finds easy access to the leadership. /输油管道～。The oil pipelines are functioning properly.

畅旺 chàngwàng prosperous; flourishing; thriving:生机～ full of energy and vitality

畅想 chàngxiǎng set no bounds to imagination or one's thoughts; give free rein to one's imagination; imagine freely what the future holds in store:～未来 call up in one's mind a delightful picture of the future /～发展远景 boldly visualize prospects for development

畅销 chàngxiāo be in great demand; sell well; have a ready market:工具书十分～。Dictionaries and other reference books are in great demand. /这种小型拖拉机～山区。Mini tractors of this type have a ready market in the mountain areas.

畅销书 chàngxiāoshū best-seller

畅行 chàngxíng pass unimpeded:一路～ pass unimpeded the whole way /车辆～无阻。The traffic proceeds without hindrance. /政令～无阻。The government decrees are carried out without obstruction.

畅叙 chàngxù chat cheerfully (usu. about old times):～友情 relive an old friendship /～离情别绪 chat about the sad feelings at parting

畅饮 chàngyǐn drink one's fill:让我们开怀～。Let's make merry and drink to our hearts' content.

畅游 chàngyóu ❶ enjoy a sightseeing tour:～泰山 make a delightful trip to Mount Tai ❷ have a good swim:～长江 have a good swim in the Yangtze River

chang

场 chang *see* "排场" páichang

see also cháng; chǎng

chāo

焯 chāo scald (as a way of cooking):～菠菜 scald spinach / 把胡萝卜～一下再炒。Scald the carrots a little before stir-frying them.

see also zhuō

绰[1] chāo grab:～起铁锹就干活 grab a shovel and start working (with it); grab a shovel and plunge right into the job

绰[2] chāo *see* "焯" chāo

see also chuò

抄[1] chāo ❶ copy; transcribe:～笔记 copy sb.'s notes /～乐谱 make a copy of a musical score; transcribe a musical score /照～原文 make a verbatim transcription of the original; copy out the original /这首诗我～了两份。I made two copies of the poem. /把黑板上的问题～下来。Copy the questions down from the blackboard. ❷ copy; plagiarize; lift:～别人的作业 copy from sb.'s homework /这一段是从一本小说里～来的。This paragraph is lifted straight from a novel. /你这个答案是～小王的。You copied the answer off Xiao Wang.

抄[2] chāo ❶ search and confiscate; make a raid upon; pinch:～赃物 search for and confiscate the booty /～出大量毒品 search (a place) and find a big quantity of drugs /警方～了那个赌场。The police made a raid on that gambling-den. /谁把桌子上的词典给～走了? Who made away with the dictionary on the desk? ❷ take a shortcut; outflank:～近道走 take a shortcut /～敌人侧翼 outflank the enemy ❸ fold (one's arms) in the sleeves:～着手站在一旁 stand by with arms folded in the sleeves

抄[3] chāo grab:～起扁担就打 grab a carrying-pole and hit sb. with it

抄靶子 chāo bǎzi 〈方言〉〈旧语〉(of a patrolling policeman) search a pedestrian; frisk sb.

抄本 chāoběn hand-copied book; transcript: 明代～ handwritten copy of the Ming Dynasty; Ming text
抄查 chāochá search for and confiscate (contraband goods): ～非法枪支 search for and confiscate illegal arms
抄撮 chāocuō 〈书面〉 make extracts and copy: ～古籍 make extracts from ancient writings
抄道 chāodào 〈口语〉 take a shortcut: ～追赶 pursue by taking a shortcut /～去县城要近好几里路。It will save us quite a few *li* if we take the shortcut to the county town.
抄掇 chāoduō collect and copy: ～稗史 collect and copy manuscripts of unofficial history
抄肥 chāoféi 〈方言〉 wangle extra income: ～自搂 wangle extra income for oneself /他这几天没上班,不定上哪儿～去了。He's been absent for the last few days. God knows where he is, raking in money for himself!
抄后路 chāo hòulù outflank and attack (the enemy) in the rear; turn the enemy's rear: ～拦住他 intercept him from behind /那样他就会让对方抄了后路。That would allow his adversary to outflank him.
抄获 chāohuò search and seize; search and confiscate; ferret out: ～毒品 ferret out drugs /～赃款 search for and confiscate illicit money
抄家 chāojiā search the home of a court official found guilty and confiscate his property; ransack sb.'s home: "文革"中他被～。His home was ransacked during the Cultural Revolution.
抄件 chāojiàn copy; duplicate (of a report, document, etc.): 兹将报告～四份发给你们。We are forwarding to you four copies of the report.
抄浆机 chāojiāngjī pulp machine (used in paper-making)
抄近路 chāo jìnlù take a shortcut: 我们穿过树林,～赶到他们前面。Let's cut through the woods and get ahead of them.
抄近儿 chāojìnr 〈口语〉 take a shortcut: ～能节省不少时间。We can save a lot of time by taking a shortcut.
抄录 chāolù make a copy of; quote: 这里,我～了一段达尔文的话。Here, I have quoted a paragraph from Darwin. /把前三段～下来。Copy out the first three paragraphs.
抄掠 chāolüè *also* "抄略" 〈书面〉 plunder; rob; pillage
抄没 chāomò ransack and confiscate: ～家产 search sb.'s house and confiscate his property; ransack sb.'s house
抄拿 chāoná illegally take away; make away with: ～公物 take away public property without permission
抄身 chāoshēn search sb.; frisk sb.: ～检查 body search /挨个儿～ search one by one /过去,工人进出厂门还要被～。In the old days, workers were subjected to body search when going into or coming out of the factory.
抄收 chāoshōu receive and record (radio signals)
抄手 chāoshǒu ❶ 〈方言〉 dumpling soup; wonton: 川味～,全国驰名。Dumpling soup with a Sichuan flavour is famous throughout the country. /街头有好几处卖～的摊点。There are stalls selling wonton soup on street corners. ❷ fold one's arms (in the sleeves): 人家有困难,你能～不管吗? Can you stand idly by with folded arms when somebody is in trouble?
抄送 chāosòng make a copy (usu. of a report or document) for; send a duplicate to: ～下列机关 C.C. (carbon copies) to the following departments /～有关单位 send copies to the relevant units; C. C. to the departments concerned
抄网 chāowǎng dip net
抄袭 chāoxí ❶ plagiarize; copy; lift: ～行为 (an act of) plagiarism /这首诗是从哪里～的? Where is this poem lifted from? /这小说的主要部分有～之嫌。It is suspected that the main part of the novel is mere plagiarism. ❷ borrow indiscriminately (from other's experience); copy: 不能生搬硬套地～别国的经验。Never copy foreign experience blindly (*or* mechanically). ❸ launch a surprise attack (on the enemy) by making a detour: ～敌人的后勤基地 make a detour into the enemy's rear and launch a surprise attack on its supply base /～敌军侧翼 outflank the enemy
抄写 chāoxiě copy; transcribe: 把文件～两份。Make two copies of this document.
抄写员 chāoxiěyuán copyist
抄胥 chāoxū 〈旧语〉 scribe; copyist; scrivener (in governmental offices)
抄用 chāoyòng apply mechanically; imitate; copy: 机械地～别人经验是愚蠢的。It's stupid to apply other people's experience mechanically.
抄造 chāozào make (pulp into) paper: 改进旧的～工艺 improve the outdated paper-making technology /引进先进的～流水线 import advanced paper-making production lines
抄斩 chāozhǎn (in feudal times) confiscate sb.'s property and have him executed: 满门～ confiscate the family property and have all family members executed

吵 chāo

see also chǎo
吵吵 chāochao 〈方言〉 be noisy; make a row: 安静点儿,不要瞎～。Be quiet. Stop making such a row.
吵吵巴火 chāochao-bāhuǒ 〈方言〉 make a racket; shout in confusion; rend the air: 什么人在大门外～呢? Who is making all that racket outside the gate?

钞[1] chāo

paper money; banknote: 现～ cash /外～ foreign currency /美～ US dollar /破～ incur an expense

钞[2] chāo

see "抄[1]❶" chāo
钞票 chāopiào banknote; paper money; bill: ～发行银行 note issuing bank /印刷～ print notes /大额～ notes of large denominations /流通中的～ banknotes in circulation /假～ counterfeit banknotes /百元面值的～ one-hundred-*yuan* bill /这张～是伪造的。This is a forged note.
钞票纸 chāopiàozhǐ banknote paper

怊 chāo

〈书面〉 grieved and indignant
怊怅 chāochàng 〈书面〉 grieved and disheartened: ～若失 look sad and distracted

超 chāo

❶ exceed; surpass; overtake: ～计划完成任务 overfulfil the plan (*or* target) /这个村子的户均年收入已经～万元。The annual income for the average household in this village exceeded (*or* topped) ten thousand *yuan*. ❷ ultra-; super-; extra-: ～高温 superhigh temperature /他的技术今天得到～水平的发挥。His performance did more than justice to his skill today. ❸ transcend; go beyond: ～现实 go beyond reality; be unrealistic /友谊是～国界的。Friendship transcends national boundaries. ❹ 〈书面〉 leap over; stride over: 挟泰山以～北海 carry Mount Tai over the North Sea — attempt to do the impossible
超拔 chāobá ❶ outstanding; transcendant; superb: 才情～ of outstanding talent /她演技～。Her acting is superb. ❷ be promoted: 他因行为不端而未被～。He was not promoted because of his loose behaviour. ❸ break away from; free from (an undesired environment or habit): 把他从罪恶的泥潭中～出来。Pull him out of the sink of iniquity.
超薄 chāobáo ultra-thin: ～磁带 ultra-thin magnetic tape /～镜片 ultra-thin glasses /～切片 ultra-thin section
超饱和 chāobǎohé over-saturation: ～的核力量 over-saturation nuclear capacity
超倍体 chāobèitǐ hyperploid
超倍显微镜 chāobèi xiǎnwēijìng ultramicroscope
超编 chāobiān exceed the personnel quota; be overstaffed: ～人员 excess personnel; redundant staff
超标 chāobiāo surpass the set standard; exceed a quota: 因～占用住房而受到批评 be criticized for moving into an apartment in excess of the set standard of floor space due to one /因～排放废水而被罚款 be fined for excessive discharge of waste water
超产 chāochǎn overfulfil a production target or quota: ～粮 grain output in excess of a production quota /～百分之十五 15% in excess of a production target /争取～ strive to overfulfil the production quota
超长期预报 chāochángqī yùbào extra long-range forecast
超长裙 chāochángqún maxi (skirt)
超常 chāocháng hypernormal; supernormal; extraordinary: ～儿童 supernormal child /～的努力 extraordinary effort /～的生理功能 supernormal physical ability /～发挥 give a supernormal performance; surpass (*or* outperform) oneself
超常记忆 chāocháng jìyì hypermnesia

C

超超短裙 chāochāoduǎnqún micromini (skirt)
超车 chāochē overtake other vehicles on the road:违章～ overtaking other vehicles in violation of the traffic regulations /不准～! No overtaking.
超尘拔俗 chāochén-bású *also* "超尘出俗";"超尘脱俗" transcend the petty and vulgar; be outstanding (*or* out of the common run) in moral character; stand head and shoulders above the vulgar crowd
超出 chāochū overstep; go beyond; exceed: ～规定 overstep the regulations /～定额 exceed the quota /～意料 exceed one's expectations; be quite unexpected /～职权范围 overstep one's authority /～限制 go beyond the limits (*or* bounds) /～法律权限 go beyond the law; overstep one's jurisdiction; be extralegal
超纯度 chāochúndù superpurity
超纯水 chāochúnshuǐ superpure water
C
超大规模集成电路 chāodàguīmó jíchéng diànlù very large-scale integrated circuit (VLSI)
超大型数据库 chāodàxíng shùjùkù very-large data base
超大型油船 chāodàxíng yóuchuán supertanker
超导 chāodǎo 〈物理〉superconduction: ～元件 superconducting component
超导材料 chāodǎo cáiliào superconducting material; superconductor
超导存储器 chāodǎo cúnchǔqì 〈自控〉superconducting memory
超导电机 chāodǎo diànjī superconducting motor
超导电缆 chāodǎo diànlǎn superconductive cable
超导电性 chāodǎodiànxìng 〈物理〉superconductivity
超导发电机 chāodǎo fādiànjī superconducting generator
超导计算机 chāodǎo jìsuànjī superconducting computer
超导技术 chāodǎo jìshù superconducting technology
超导输电 chāodǎo shūdiàn superconducting power transmission
超导体 chāodǎotǐ 〈物理〉superconductor
超导物理学 chāodǎo wùlǐxué 〈物理〉superconductor physics
超导元素 chāodǎo yuánsù superconducting element
超等 chāoděng of superior grade; extra fine: ～质量 of superior quality /成绩～ get excellent examination results; have an excellent academic record /才能～ of outstanding talent
超等离子体 chāoděnglízǐtǐ 〈物理〉epiplasmă
超低空飞行 chāodīkōng fēixíng minimum altitude flying; hedge-hopping
超低量喷雾器 chāodīliàng pēnwùqì ultra-low volume sprayer
超低频 chāodīpín 〈物理〉ultra-low frequency (ULF): ～放大器 ULF amplifier
超低温 chāodīwēn ultra-low temperature
超低噪声天线 chāodī zàoshēng tiānxiàn ultra-low noise antenna
超地平线雷达 chāodìpíngxiàn léidá over-the-horizon radar
超地球导弹 chāodìqiú dǎodàn extraterrestrial missile
超帝国主义论 chāodìguózhǔyìlùn theory of ultra-imperialism
超度 chāodù 〈宗教〉release souls from the purgatory; expiate the sins of the dead: ～众生 save the living souls from the sea of misery
超短波 chāoduǎnbō ultrashort wave
超短光脉冲 chāoduǎn guāngmàichōng 〈物理〉ultrashort light pulse
超短裙 chāoduǎnqún miniskirt
超额 chāo'é overfulfil or exceed the quota: ～征税 overtaxation /～完成任务 overfulfil the task
超额度融资 chāo'édù róngzī overfunding
超额奖金税 chāo'é jiǎngjīnshuì tax on above-norm bonuses
超额利润 chāo'é lìrùn superprofit; excess profit: 榨取～ extract superprofit /获取～ obtain excess profit /～税 windfall tax
超额认购 chāo'é rèngòu oversubscription
超凡 chāofán ❶ overcome the worldly desire and attain sainthood ❷ out of the common run; unusual; outstanding: 品格～ of noble character /技艺～ unusually skilful /林子里显得～的安静。The woods are extremely quiet and still.
超凡入圣 chāofán-rùshèng transcend worldliness and attain holiness; reach the pinnacle of literary fame; become a man of unrivalled wisdom
超分子 chāofēnzǐ supermolecule: ～复合体 supermolecular complex
超负荷 chāofùhè overload; excess load: 机器～运转。The machine is running with excess load. /别使电力系统～。Don't overload the electrical system. /他的工作太多,已经～了。He is overloaded with work as it is.
超感官知觉 chāogǎnguān zhījué *also* "超感觉力"〈心理〉extra-sensory perception (ESP)
超高 chāogāo freeboard (height)
超高倍显微镜 chāogāobèi xiǎnwēijìng ultramicroscope
超高空 chāogāokōng superaltitude: ～飞行 superaltitude flying
超高频 chāogāopín 〈电学〉ultrahigh or superhigh frequency: ～变压器 ultrahigh-frequency transformer
超高强度材料 chāogāoqiángdù cáiliào ultrastrength material
超高速 chāogāosù 〈物理〉ultrahigh-speed; hypervelocity
超高速弹道学 chāogāosù dàndàoxué hyperballistics
超高温 chāogāowēn 〈物理〉extraordinarily high temperature; ultrahigh-temperature
超高压 chāogāoyā ❶〈物理〉superhigh pressure ❷〈电学〉ultra-high voltage (UHV); extra-high tension: ～设备 extra-high-tension unit /～线路带电作业 working on live extra-high-tension power lines
超高压电网 chāogāoyā diànwǎng 〈电工〉supergrid
超高压输电系统 chāogāoyā shūdiàn xìtǒng 〈电工〉UHV or ultra-high-voltage transmission system
超工业时代 chāogōngyè shídài superindustrial age
超固态 chāogùtài state of ultrasolidity
超光电摄像管 chāoguāngdiàn shèxiàngguǎn super iconoscope; super emitron
超光速粒子 chāoguāngsù lìzǐ tachyon
超过 chāoguò overtake; outstrip; surpass; exceed: ～国外先进水平 surpass advanced world levels /质量～同类产品 have better quality than other products of the same category /在数量上～ outnumber /～原有最高记录 top all previous records /他的车已经～我们了。His car has overtaken ours. /北京在面积和人口上都～天津。Beijing exceeds Tianjin in both size and population. /在这方面谁也没有～他。No one has ever done better than he in this field.
超函数 chāohánshù hyper-function: 超几何函数 hypergeometric function
超基因 chāojīyīn supergene; hypergene
超级 chāojí super: ～炸弹 superbomb /～油轮 supertanker /～间谍 superspy /～明星 superstar /～豪华旅馆 super luxury hotel
超级大国 chāojí dàguó superpower
超级橄榄球赛 Chāojí Gǎnlǎnqiúsài 〈体育〉Super Bowl (championship games of the National Football League in the US, played annually in January from 1967 onwards)
超级公路 chāojí gōnglù 〈交通〉superhighway; supermotorway; freeway
超级航空母舰 chāojí hángkōng mǔjiàn 〈军事〉supercarrier
超级轰炸机 chāojí hōngzhàjī 〈军事〉superbomber
超级化学 chāojí huàxué *also* "原子结构化学" yuánzǐ jiégòu huàxué metachemistry
超级潜艇 chāojí qiántǐng 〈军事〉supersubmarine
超级燃料 chāojí ránliào 〈化工〉superfuel
超级市场 chāojí shìchǎng supermarket
超级细菌 chāojí xìjūn superbacteria (used to eliminate pollution, etc.)
超计划生育 chāojìhuà shēngyù have more children than what the plan allows; give unplanned births
超假 chāojià overstay one's leave: 按时返校,不要～。Return to the school on schedule. Don't overstay your home leave.
超阶级 chāojiējí transcending classes; supra-class
超经济剥削 chāojīngjì bōxuē 〈经济〉extraeconomic exploitation
超经济强制 chāojīngjì qiángzhì supra-economic coercion: ～手段 supra-economic means of coercion
超精度 chāojīngdù 〈机械〉ultraprecision
超精加工 chāojīngjiāgōng 〈机械〉superfinishing: ～机床 superfinisher
超巨星 chāojùxīng 〈天文〉supergiant star
超巨型计算机 chāojùxíng jìsuànjī 〈计算机〉super-super computer
超绝 chāojué superb; unique; unexcelled; extraordinary: 工艺～ extraordinary craftsmanship /～的技艺 superb skill (*or* performance)
超绝缘 chāojuéyuán superinsulation
超空间 chāokōngjiān 〈物理〉superspace; hyperspace
超冷中子 chāolěng zhōngzǐ 〈物理〉ultra-cold neutron
超离心机 chāolíxīnjī *also* "超速离心机"〈机械〉ultracentrifuge
超离子晶体 chāolízǐ jīngtǐ superionic crystal

超立体全息像 chāolìtǐ quánxīxiàng 〈物理〉 hyperstereoscopic holographic image
超临界反应堆 chāolínjiè fǎnyìngduī 〈核物理〉 supercritical reactor
超临界速度 chāolínjiè sùdù supercritical speed
超临界状态 chāolínjiè zhuàngtài supercriticality; supercritical state
超龄 chāolíng overage:～队员 overage member of a team /～团员 overage League member /按照兵役法,我已经～了。According to the draft law, I am overage for military service.
超流理论 chāoliú lǐlùn superfluidity theory
超流体 chāoliútǐ superfluid
超流性 chāoliúxìng 〈物理〉 superfluidity
超伦 chāolún far above the average; peerless; unequalled; unexcelled:才能～ unmatched talent
超迈 chāomài exceed; outstrip:～古今 have never been surpassed since ancient times; have enjoyed unrivalled fame through the ages /禀赋～ endowed with outstanding intelligence; extremely gifted
超媒体 chāoméitǐ 〈信息〉 hypermedia
超敏断路器 chāomǐn duànlùqì hypersensor
超敏反应 chāomǐn fǎnyìng hypersensitivity
超敏感化 chāomǐngǎnhuà hypersensitization
超耐热合金 chāonàirè héjīn 〈冶金〉 superalloy
超期 chāoqī exceeding or beyond the fixed term of service:这辆车的使用年限大大～了。The car has been running far beyond its guaranteed life.
超期服役 chāoqī fúyì extended service in the army; extended active duty:～的老队员 veteran member who continues to serve on the team beyond the usual age limit; overage team member
超迁 chāoqiān 〈书面〉 promote sb. by more than one grade at a time:他才干卓异,～任用。He has been promoted by several grades on account of his outstanding ability and talent.
超前 chāoqián ❶ transcending the present; ahead of the times; aiming at the future:～教育 future-oriented education /～意识 foresight; far-sight ❷ surpassing past generations:～绝后 unrivalled in the past and not likely to be matched in the future ❸ 〈电学〉 lead:～角 angle of lead
超前消费 chāoqián xiāofèi unduly high level of consumption; over consumption; excessive consumption; premature consumption
超前叙述 chāoqián xùshù 〈文学〉 flash-forward
超强度材料 chāoqiángdù cáiliào ultrastrength material
超轻合金 chāoqīng héjīn ultralight alloy
超轻坦克 chāoqīng tǎnkè superlight tank
超清晰度 chāoqīngxīdù superresolution
超群 chāoqún preeminent; head and shoulders above all others:技艺～ be unequalled in skill /才学～ be outstanding both in knowledge and talent
超群绝伦 chāoqún-juélún peerless; unrivalled; unmatched:棋艺～ be unrivalled (*or* unmatched) in playing chess
超然 chāorán aloof; detached:～自得 be detached and contented /～不群 stand aloof from the common crowd; be stand-offish /一副～的样子 with an air of detachment /他用～的眼光看了看四周。He looked around in a detached manner.
超然物外 chāorán-wùwài ❶ keep away from unpleasant social reality; be above worldly considerations:～,寄情山水 be free from worldly care and enjoy the beauty of nature /～,隐居山林 live as a recluse in the hills far away from the madding crowd ❷ stay away from trouble; keep aloof from the scene of worldly contention:要切实解决群众的实际问题,不能采取～、漠不关心的态度。We should take realistic steps to solve the practical problems of the ordinary people instead of adopting an attitude of apathy and indifference.
超热中子反应堆 chāorèzhōngzǐ fǎnyìngduī 〈核物理〉 epithermal reactor
超热中子钍反应堆 chāorèzhōngzǐ tǔfǎnyìngduī 〈核物理〉 epithermal thorium reactor
超人 chāorén ❶ out of the common run; superhuman:智力～ endowed with superior intelligence /～的毅力 superhuman fortitude (*or* perseverance) ❷ superman
超杀伤 chāoshāshāng overkill:拥有～的核力量 possess an overkill nuclear capacity
超深海动物 chāoshēnhǎi dòngwù ultra-abyssal fauna
超深井 chāoshēnjǐng 〈石油〉 extradeep well
超深渊海域 chāoshēnyuān hǎiyù hadal zone
超深钻 chāoshēnzuàn 〈地质〉 Mohole:～探 Mohole drilling
超升 chāoshēng ❶ 〈佛教〉 human soul going up to the paradise after death:佛教徒认为行善积德,乃～之道。Buddhists believe that doing good and practising virtue is the way to the paradise of great happiness. ❷ 〈书面〉 promote by more than one grade:破格～为教授 be promoted to full professorship as an exceptional case
超生 chāoshēng ❶ 〈宗教〉 reincarnation ❷ be lenient; spare sb.:笔下～ spare sb. when one gives the verdict; show tolerance in passing judgment; be lenient in one's critique (*or* comments) ❸ have more children than the family planning policy allows; give unplanned births:～子女 children born outside family planning /如今在农村,～现象减少了。There are fewer unplanned births in the rural areas today.
超声波 chāoshēngbō supersonic wave; ultrasonic wave:～疗法 ultrasonic therapy /～探伤仪 ultrasonic flaw detector
超声波干扰仪 chāoshēngbō gānrǎoyí ultrasonic interferometer
超声波加工 chāoshēngbō jiāgōng 〈机械〉 ultrasonic machining
超声波水下通信 chāoshēngbō shuǐxià tōngxìn 〈无线电〉 ultrasonic underwater communication
超声波洗浴 chāoshēngbō xǐyù supersonic wave bath
超声传感器 chāoshēng chuángǎnqì sonar
see also "声纳" shēngnà
超声电视 chāoshēng diànshì ultrasonovision
超声多普勒诊断仪 chāoshēng Duōpǔlè zhěnduànyí ultrasonic Doppler method diagnostic equipment
超声辐射 chāoshēng fúshè ultrasonic radiation
超声全息图 chāoshēng quánxītú ultrasonic hologram
超声全息照相 chāoshēng quánxī zhàoxiàng ultrasonic holography
超声速 chāoshēngsù *also* "超音速" supersonic speed:～飞行 supersonic flight
超声探伤仪 chāoshēng tànshāngyí supersonic (flaw) detector
超声图像记录仪 chāoshēng túxiàng jìlùyí 〈医学〉 ultrasonograph
超声物理学 chāoshēng wùlǐxué ultrasonic physics
超声心动图 chāoshēng xīndòngtú ultrasound cardiogram
超声学 chāoshēngxué ultrasonics
超视距雷达 chāoshìjù léidá 〈通信〉 over-the-horizon radar
超收 chāoshōu ❶ earn or receive more than planned for or stipulated:今年财政～。This year's financial revenues surpassed the original estimates. /学校不能～学杂费。No school or college is allowed to demand more tuition and other fees than stipulated. ❷ earnings or receipts in excess of what is stipulated
超手扣球 chāoshǒu kòuqiú 〈体育〉 spike over the block
超数染色体 chāoshù rǎnsètǐ 〈生物〉 supernumerary (chromosome)
超俗 chāosú be free from vulgarities; not be inhibited by conventions; be unconventional:风流潇洒,～绝世 graceful and unrestrained, incomparably free from all conventions
超速 chāosù ❶ exceed the speed limit:～行车 speeding ❷ hypervelocity:～粒子 hypervelocity particle
超塑性 chāosùxìng 〈物理〉 superplasticity
超缩微卡片 chāosuōwēi kǎpiàn ultrafiche
超脱 chāotuō ❶ free from convention; unconventional:举止～,不拘常规 uninhibited in spirit and free from all conventions /他的字体潇洒～,自成一家。His calligraphy has an unconventional grace of its own. ❷ be detached; keep or stand aloof; not get involved in; keep one's distance from:～日常事务 detach oneself from routine business /任何人不可能～现实。No one can possibly detach himself (*or* keep aloof) from reality.
超外差 chāowàichā 〈电子〉 superheterodyne; superhet:～式收音机 superheterodyne (radio set)
超微波 chāowēibō 〈物理〉 ultramicrowave
超微分析 chāowēi fēnxī 〈化学〉 ultramicroanalysis
超微技术 chāowēi jìshù 〈物理〉 ultramicrotechnique
超微粒 chāowēilì amicron
超微生物 chāowēishēngwù 〈生理〉 ultramicroorganism
超微天平 chāowēi tiānpíng 〈测绘〉 ultramicrobalance
超文本 chāowénběn 〈信息〉 hypertext
超文本传送协议 chāowénběn chuánsòng xiéyì 〈信息〉 hypertext transfer protocol (HTTP)
超文本语言 chāowénběn yǔyán 〈信息〉 hypertext make-up language (HTML)

超我 chāowǒ 〈心理〉superego
超细纤维 chāoxì xiānwéi superfine fibre
超弦理论 chāoxián lǐlùn 〈物理〉superchord theory, according to which the universe is 10-dimensional instead of 4-dimensional
超显微病毒 chāoxiǎnwēi bìngdú 〈医学〉ultravirus
超显性 chāoxiǎnxìng superdominance; overdominance
超现实主义 chāoxiànshízhǔyì surrealism
超限数 chāoxiànshù 〈数学〉transfinite number
超小型管 chāoxiǎoxíngguǎn 〈电子〉subminiature tube
超小型化 chāoxiǎoxínghuà 〈机械〉superminiaturization
超小型汽车 chāoxiǎoxíng qìchē subcompact (car)
超新星 chāoxīnxīng 〈天文〉supernova
超星体 chāoxīngtǐ *also* "超星"〈天文〉superstar
超星团 chāoxīngtuán 〈天文〉supercluster
超性杂交 chāoxìng zájiāo 〈生物〉supersexual hybridization
超验哲学 chāoyàn zhéxué *also* "超验主义" transcendentalism
超氧化物 chāoyǎnghuàwù 〈化学〉superoxide
超一流 chāoyīliú incomparably superior; super: ～棋手 super chess player; ultra-class chess player (as in go)
超逸 chāoyì unconventional and graceful; free and natural: 笔意～ write with rare grace and ease / 神采～ gracious demeanour
超音速 chāoyīnsù supersonic speed: ～喷气机 superjet / ～战斗机 supersonic fighter / ～地铁系统 supersonic subway system
超音速低空导弹 chāoyīnsù dīkōng dǎodàn supersonic low altitude missile (SLAM)
超音速风洞 chāoyīnsù fēngdòng supersonic wind tunnel
超铀元素 chāoyóu yuánsù transuranic or transuranium element
超宇宙 chāoyǔzhòu 〈天文〉superuniverse
超育 chāoyù have more children than the family planning policy stipulates; give unplanned birth
超员 chāoyuán exceed the designated number: ～百分之二十 (of a vehicle) carry 20% more passengers than stipulated; (of a unit) have 20% more staff than required / 这趟列车大大～。This train is overloaded with passengers.
超越 chāoyuè overstep; transcend; surpass: ～障碍 surmount an obstacle / ～常规 overstep the normal (*or* routine) procedure; break the convention / ～国力 go beyond the state's capability (*or* the national strength); outstrip the national capacity / ～前人 surpass one's predecessor(s) / ～工作范围 overstep one's responsibility (*or* duty) / ～职权范围 go beyond one's authority (*or* jurisdiction, *or* competence) / ～自我 outdo oneself; transcend self / ～历史阶段 bypass (*or* skip) a stage of history; overstep historical conditions; be historically premature
超越射击 chāoyuè shèjī 〈军事〉overhead fire
超载 chāozài 〈交通〉overload: ～能力 overload capacity / ～渡轮 overcrowded ferry / ～百分之十 carry 10% more freight (*or* passengers) than allowed
超增益天线 chāozēngyì tiānxiàn supergain antenna
超真空 chāozhēnkōng ultravacuum
超支 chāozhī overspend; overdraw; live beyond one's means: ～户 household (*or* family) living perpetually in debt; overdrawn account / 办公费不能～。We mustn't overspend the budget for administration expenses. / 我的户头～三百元。My account is overdrawn by 300 *yuan*. / 他这个人不会计划,月月～。He is such a bad planner that he lives beyond his income every month.
超质子 chāozhìzǐ 〈物理〉superproton
超智 chāozhì exceptionally intelligent: ～儿童 exceptionally intelligent child; child prodigy
超重 chāozhòng ❶ overweight: 行李～ overweight (*or* excess) luggage / 这封信～。This letter is overweight. ❷〈物理〉superheavy: ～核 superheavy nucleus / ～夸克 superheavy quark ❸ overload: 这辆卡车～。The truck is overloaded.
超重量级 chāozhòngliàngjí 〈体育〉super-heavyweight
超重氢 chāozhòngqīng tritium (T or $^3_1$H); superheavy hydrogen
超重元素 chāozhòng yuánsù 〈化学〉superheavy element
超轴 chāozhóu 〈铁路〉over haulage: ～牵引 train hauling above-normal tonnage
超卓 chāozhuó 〈书面〉superb; outstanding; splendid: 文辞～。The language is superb. *or* The style is elegant.
超擢 chāozhuó 〈书面〉promote by more than one grade: 他由讲师～为教授。He has been promoted to professor straight from lecturer.
超子 chāozǐ 〈物理〉hyperon
超紫外 chāozǐwài 〈物理〉extreme ultraviolet
超自然 chāozìrán supernatural: ～的力量 supernatural force(s) / ～主义 supernaturalism

弨 chāo 〈书面〉❶ loosened bow ❷ bow

剿(勦) chāo 〈书面〉plagiarize

see also jiǎo
剿说 chāoshuō 〈书面〉take ideas from sb. and use them as one's own; plagiarize: 毋～,毋雷同。Refrain from plagiarizing or parroting others' views.
剿袭 chāoxí copy; plagiarize; lift
see also "抄袭 ❶❷" chāoxí

cháo

朝 cháo ❶ court; government (as contrasted with the opposition): 在～ be in power / 在～党 ruling party; party in power / 争名于～ jockey for position at court / ～野意见不一。The ruling party and the opposition hold different views. ❷ dynasty: 明～ Ming Dynasty / 改～换代 dynastic changes / 封建王～ feudal dynasty ❸ emperor's reign: 乾隆～ reign of Qianlong; Qianlong period / 三～元老 senior minister who serves more than two reigns of a dynasty; elderly politician who survives more than two administrations / 一～天子一～臣。Each emperor has his own courtiers. *or* Courtiers change with the ruler. *or* Every leader chooses his own retinue. ❹ have an audience with (a king, emperor, etc.); make a pilgrimage to: ～见天子 seek an audience with the emperor / 他们是去麦加～圣的。They were pilgrims to Mecca. ❺ facing; towards: ～后退 go backward; retreat / 四脚～天 lie (*or* fall down) flat on one's back / 这屋坐北～南。This house has a southern exposure. *or* This house faces south. / 大门～东开。The gate opens towards the east. / 他～我招手。He waved at me. / 我们应该～这方面想。We must think along these lines. ❻ (Cháo) a surname

see also zhāo
朝拜 cháobài pay respects to (a sovereign); pay homage to; worship: 群臣～天子 ministers paying respects to the emperor / 焚香～ worship (Buddha) by burning incense
朝臣 cháochén courtier; government official: 身为～ being a courtier; as a court official
朝代 cháodài dynasty; reign: 百年兴衰,～更替。Prosperity is followed by decline, and one dynasty is replaced by another. / 皇权之争贯穿了整个～。The struggle for power among members of the royal family ran through the whole reign.
朝顶 cháodǐng (of a Buddhist) ascend a mountain to worship Buddha in a monastery
朝房 cháofáng 〈旧语〉chamber in the palace where courtiers meet before court is held
朝奉 cháofèng ❶ middle-ranking official title in the Song Dynasty ❷〈旧语〉〈方言〉rich man ❸〈旧语〉〈方言〉manager of a pawnshop; pawnbroker
朝服 cháofú court dress
朝纲 cháogāng court discipline: ～崩圮 collapse of court discipline / 整顿～ tighten up court discipline
朝贡 cháogòng pay tribute (to an imperial court); present tribute
朝贵 cháoguì senior official wielding great power in court; powerful courtier
朝贺 cháohè pay one's respects to (the sovereign): 新君登基,百官～。When the new emperor ascended the throne, all the courtiers came to pay their respects.
朝会 cháohuì (of courtiers) have an audience with a monarch
朝见 cháojiàn have an audience with; be received by (the emperor): 百官～天子。All the senior officials at court were granted an audience with the emperor.
朝觐 cháojìn ❶〈书面〉*see* "朝见" ❷ go on a pilgrimage: ～圣地 go on a pilgrimage to a sacred place
朝聘 cháopìn (of princes or feudal lords) have a regular audience with the monarch or overlord
朝山 cháoshān 〈佛教〉make a pilgrimage to a temple on a moun-

tain:～进香 make a pilgrimage to a mountain temple and burn incense before Buddha

朝圣 cháoshèng 〈宗教〉pilgrimage; hadj:到麦加去～ make a pilgrimage to Mecca /去耶路撒冷～ go as pilgrims to Jerusalem /去麦加的～者 pilgrims to Mecca

朝堂 cháotáng 〈旧语〉hall where the sovereign discusses state affairs with senior officials

朝廷 cháotíng ❶ royal or imperial court ❷ royal or imperial government

朝鲜 Cháoxiǎn Korea:～人 Korean /～语 Korean (language) /～南北两方 North and South of Korea/～停战协定 Korean Armistice Agreement (July 1953) /～自主和平统一 independent and peaceful reunification of Korea /～祖国解放战争 Fatherland Liberation War of Korea /～军事停战委员会 Korean Military Armistice Commission (MAC) /～南北协调委员会 Korean North-South Coordinating Committee

朝鲜半岛 Cháoxiǎn Bàndǎo Korean peninsula

朝鲜劳动党 Cháoxiǎn Láodòngdǎng Worker's Party of Korea (WPK)

朝鲜民主主义人民共和国 Cháoxiǎn Mínzhǔzhǔyì Rénmín Gònghéguó Democratic People's Republic of Korea (DPRK)

朝鲜圆 cháoxiǎnyuán Won

朝鲜战争 Cháoxiǎn Zhànzhēng Korean War (June 1950-July 1953)

朝鲜中央新闻社 Cháoxiǎn Zhōngyāng Xīnwénshè Korean Central News Agency

朝鲜族 Cháoxiǎnzú ❶ Korean nationality in China ❷ Korean people

朝香 cháoxiāng burn joss sticks at Buddhist temples

朝向 cháoxiàng ❶ face:向日葵总是～太阳。Sunflowers always face the sun. ❷ exposure:他认为这个房子的～不理想,不愿意搬进去。He would not move into the house because it has an unfavorable exposure. /两座大楼的～不同。The two buildings have different exposures. ❸〈伊斯兰〉*qiblah*, the direction of the Kaaba shrine in Mecca towards which all Muslims turn in ritual prayer

朝阳 cháoyáng illuminated by the sun; sunny:～的窗户 window which gets bright sunlight /这个山坡～。This is the sunny side of the hill. /葵花～开。Sunflowers open towards the sun.
see also zhāoyáng

朝阳花 cháoyánghuā sunflower

朝野 cháo-yě ❶ the court and the commonalty; government and populace; whole nation:～一致。The government and the people are of one mind. *or* The nation is united as one. /～上下,一片混乱。Chaos reigns both at court and among the populace. *or* The whole nation is in chaos. ❷ ruling party and opposition:面对民族危机,～必须团结起来。In the face of national crisis, the ruling party and the opposition must unite.

朝谒 cháoyè *see* "朝觐"

朝仪 cháoyí court ceremony; court etiquette (esp. during an audience)

朝真 cháozhēn (of a Taoist priest) sit in meditation

朝政 cháozhèng court affairs; affairs of state:议论～ discuss state affairs; talk politics /把持～〈贬义〉control the court; monopolize state power /处理～ handle state affairs /～混乱。Government affairs are in chaos. *or* Chaos reigns in the government.

朝中有人好做官 cháozhōng yǒu rén hǎo zuòguān *also* "朝里有人好做官"〈俗语〉You can easily embark on an official career, if you have friends at court. *or* You will have a bright official career if you have powerful backing in the government.

朝珠 cháozhū long string of beads (usu. made of coral or agate, and worn by senior officials of the Qing Dynasty)

潮[1]

cháo ❶ tide:浪～ tide /高～ high tide /小～ neap tide /心～ surge of emotion; surging thoughts /心血来～ be seized with a sudden impulse; have a sudden whim; have a brainwave; act on the spur of the moment /涨～了。The tide is coming in (*or* flowing). /退～了。The tide is ebbing (*or* receding). ❷ social upsurge; current; tide:工～ worker's strike; industrial unrest; workers' movement /学～ student movement; student unrest /新～ new current; new trend; new fashion ❸ damp; moist:这房间阴冷～湿。This room is cold and dank. /阴雨天东西容易返～。Things easily get damp in wet weather.

潮[2]

cháo 〈方言〉❶ of low or inferior quality:～银 inferior silver ingot /～金 impure gold ingot ❷ not skilled; not skilful:手艺～。The workmanship is quite poor.

潮[3]

Cháo (short for 潮州) Chaozhou, a city in Guangdong Province

潮白 cháobái a kind of sugar made from sugarcane (produced at Chaozhou 潮州)

潮差 cháochā tide range

潮虫 cháochóng 〈动物〉sow bug; wood louse

潮锋 cháofēng high tide; upsurge

潮幅 cháofú tidal amplitude

潮港 cháogǎng 〈水利〉tidal harbour

潮红 cháohóng (of face or skin) flush:两颊～ be flushed in both cheeks

潮呼呼 cháohūhū damp; dank; clammy; moist:～的手 clammy hands /被单～的。The sheet is pretty damp. /喷过一点水,草坪～的。The lawn has just been sprayed with water, and it is still moist. /别呆在那～的屋子里! Don't stay in that dank room!

潮解 cháojiě 〈化学〉deliquesce:～作用 deliquescence

潮剧 cháojù Chaozhou opera (popular in eastern Guangdong, southern Fujian and Taiwan Provinces)

潮流 cháoliú ❶ tide; tidal current:～汹涌 surging tide ❷ trend (of social change); current:时代～ current of the times /跟上时代的～ follow (*or* keep abreast of) the trend of the times /那些违背历史～的人总要失败。Those who go against the historical trend will come to grief (*or* are doomed to failure).

潮脑 cháonǎo *also* "樟脑" zhāngnǎo camphor

潮坪 cháopíng tidal flat

潮气 cháoqì moisture in the air; damp; humidity:仓库里～大,粮食就容易发霉。The grain is liable to mildew when the humidity in the barn is high. /地下室～太大,不能住人。The basement is too dank to serve as living quarters. /空气中的～使墙皮剥落了。The moisture in the air caused the walls to peel.

潮热 cháorè 〈中医〉hectic fever

潮润 cháorùn ❶ (of soil, air, etc.) wet; damp; humid:海风轻轻吹来,使人觉得～而有凉意。The gentle breeze drifting from the sea carries with it a touch of dewy coolness. ❷ teary; blurred (with tears):两眼～ eyes blurred (*or* moist) with tears

潮湿 cháoshī moist; damp:太～了,东西都发霉了。Things got mildewed from the damp. /海风吹来,有种～的感觉。Ocean wind feels moist. /连日阴雨,室内～。The room is damp as it has been raining for days. /她的眼睛～了。Her eyes were moist with tears.

潮水 cháoshuǐ tidewater; tidal water; flood water:～时涨时落。The tidal water surges and recedes. /孩子们像～一般涌进公园。Hordes of children streamed into the park.

潮位 cháowèi tide mark:～曲线 tide curve

潮汐 cháoxī morning and evening tides; ocean tide:～表 tide table /～测站 tide station /～预报 tide prediction

潮汐波 cháoxībō 〈水利〉tidal wave

潮汐发电站 cháoxī fādiànzhàn 〈水利〉tidal power station; tide-plant

潮汐发动机 cháoxī fādòngjī 〈水利〉tide-motor

潮汐能 cháoxīnéng tidal energy

潮信 cháoxìn ❶ flood tide; tidewater ❷〈书面〉〈婉辞〉menstruation

潮绣 cháoxiù Chaozhou embroidery (embroidery produced in Chaozhou, Guangdong Province)

潮汛 cháoxùn spring tide

潮音 cháoyīn ❶ sound of the waves ❷ chanting of Buddhist monks

潮涌 cháoyǒng surge forward like a tide:心事如～。All feelings welled up in one's heart like tidal waters. /人从四面八方～而来。The crowd surged in from all directions.

潮灾 cháozāi calamity caused by tidal waters

潮滋滋 cháozīzī wet; damp; soggy:～的泥土 soggy soil

嘲(謿)

cháo ridicule; deride; sneer:冷～热讽 withering irony and caustic satire; biting sarcasm /讥～ ridicule; sneer at; jeer at /解～ try to ward off a taunt with a lame excuse; try to sort

oneself out
see also zhāo
嘲讽 cháofěng sneer at; ridicule; deride: ～某人 cast (*or* throw) ridicule upon sb.; hold sb. in derision; sneer at sb. /受到～ be held up to ridicule; be sneered at; expose oneself to derision /～的笑 ironical (*or* sardonic) smile /他话里带着～。There is a sting in his remark.
嘲剧 cháojù *hat cheo* (a popular rural opera in Vietnam)
嘲骂 cháomà sneer and swear: 气势汹汹地～ sneer and swear at sb. viciously
嘲弄 cháonòng mock; poke fun at; ridicule: 成了别人～的对象 become a butt for ridicule /～某人 make fun of sb.; mock at sb.; hold sb. up to mockery /受到历史的～ be mocked by history
嘲诮 cháoqiào ridicule and criticize; taunt
嘲笑 cháoxiào laugh at; ridicule; jeer at; deride: 轻蔑的～ scornful derision /被人～ be a target for derision /～某人，使其窘态毕露 sneer sb. out of countenance /忍受别人的～ endure the taunt of others /他们～他胆小。They derided (*or* taunted) him for being cowardly. /演讲者在一阵～声中被轰下了台。The speaker was jeered off the stage. /这个提议在一片～声中被否定了。The proposal was sneered down.
嘲谑 cháoxuè banter: 互相～ exchange banter

晁（鼂） Cháo a surname

巢 cháo ❶ nest: 鸟～ bird's nest /蜂～ beehive /蚁～ ant hill /匪～ hideout of bandits; bandits' den (*or* lair) ❷ (Cháo) a surname
巢菜 cháocài 〈植物〉 common vetch
巢蛾 cháo'é ermine moth
巢居 cháojū dwell in trees
巢窟 cháokū lair; den; nest; hideout
巢鼠 cháoshǔ harvest mouse
巢穴 cháoxué lair; den; nest; hideout: 匪徒～ bandits' den /山中～ hideout in the hills /～之中 be in the lair

chǎo

炒 chǎo ❶ stir-fry; fry; *sauté*: ～一个菜 stir-fry a dish /～肉片 stir-fried sliced pork /～鸡丁 stir-fried chicken cubes /～瓜子 roasted melon seeds /～鱼片 *sautéed* fish slices /～鸡蛋 scrambled eggs ❷ speculate; promote: ～股票 speculate in stocks /～地皮 speculate in real estate /～得很热 promote sth. so that it becomes a hot item; be raised artificially high in price ❸ 〈方言〉 sack; fire
炒冰 chǎobīng rolled frozen confection
炒菜 chǎocài ❶ stir-fry: 她正在厨房～。She is cooking in the kitchen. ❷ stir-fried dish: 我要了两个～，一瓶啤酒。I ordered two stir-fried dishes and one bottle of beer.
炒饭 chǎofàn fried rice: 蛋～ fried rice with eggs
炒肝 chǎogān *chaogan*, stew made of pig liver, intestines, Chinese onion, bean plaster and starch
炒更 chǎogēng 〈方言〉 moonlighting: 他用～的钱买了台空调。He bought an air-conditioner with the money he earned by moonlighting.
炒锅 chǎoguō wok, Chinese pan for stir-frying
炒汇 chǎohuì trade illegally in foreign currency; speculate in foreign currency
炒货 chǎohuò roasted seeds and nuts
炒家 chǎojiā skilful broker or speculator
炒金热 chǎojīnrè stock market fever
炒冷饭 chǎo lěngfàn heat leftover rice — rehash; dish up the same old stuff; say or do the same old thing: 局长的讲话尽是～。The director's speech was nothing but a rehash of the same old platitudes. *or* There's nothing new in the director's speech.
炒买炒卖 chǎomǎi-chǎomài speculation: ～外汇 speculation in foreign currencies
炒米 chǎomǐ ❶ parched rice: ～花 puffed rice /～团 puffed rice ball ❷ millet stir-fried in butter (a staple of Mongolian food)
炒面 chǎomiàn ❶ chow mein; fried noodles: 肉丝～ fried noodles with shredded pork ❷ parched flour: 开水冲～ mix parched flour with boiling water
炒青 chǎoqīng process of curing tea-leaves
炒勺 chǎosháo round-bottomed frying pan with a handle
炒鱿鱼 chǎo yóuyú 〈方言〉 stir-fry squid — give sb. the sack; fire sb.; boot sb. out: 他被公司炒了鱿鱼。He was fired by the company.
炒友 chǎoyǒu 〈方言〉 broker; speculator

麨（麵） chǎo 〈书面〉 parched rice or wheat flour

吵 chǎo ❶ make a noise: 屋里太～，我们出去吧。It's too noisy in the room. Let's go out. /别把她～醒了！Don't wake her up! /别～他。Don't disturb him. /～得我没法儿睡。I can't go to sleep with so much noise around. *or* I can't get a wink in such noisy surroundings. /别～了！Stop that racket! *or* Be quiet! /～成一锅粥。There is a hell of a hullabaloo. ❷ quarrel; squabble; wrangle: 为一点小事就～ quarrel over a mere trifle /～红了眼 quarrel bitterly and fiercely; be beside oneself in the heat of a quarrel /你们在～什么？What are you quarreling about? /他们最后～翻了。They fell out at last. /前几天他同经理～得很凶。He had a terrible row with the manager the other day.
see also chāo
吵包子 chǎo bāozi 〈方言〉 quarrel; bicker
吵架 chǎojià quarrel; squabble; bicker: 我本来不想同他～的。I didn't mean to quarrel with him. /别人家里～，你介入是很不明智的。It is unwise to intervene in a family quarrel. /他们老是为了钱～。They are always bickering over money matters.
吵骂 chǎomà quarrel and shout abuse
吵闹 chǎonào ❶ wrangle; kick up a row: 我要不答应，她就要跟我大吵大闹。If I don't agree, she will kick up a row with me. /这夫妻俩常为孩子的事～。This couple are always wrangling over their children. ❷ disturb: 他在写文章，不要去～他。Don't disturb him; he's writing an article. ❸ din; hubbub: 人声～ din of confused voices /隔壁一片～声。A hubbub was heard from next door. /孩子们～不休，我精神无法集中。The children were making so much din that I could hardly concentrate.
吵嚷 chǎorǎng make a racket; clamour: 孩子们一个劲地～着要吃冰淇淋。The children clamoured for ice-cream. /别吵吵嚷嚷地跑来跑去！Don't dash around shouting! /大门外一片～声。There was confused shouting and screaming outside the gate.
吵扰 chǎorǎo ❶ disturb others by making a lot of noise: 请你不要～别人。Please don't disturb. /～你半天，很过意不去。Sorry for having given you so much bother. ❷ 〈方言〉 quarrel
吵人 chǎorén noisy; disturbing: 车声～ noisy traffic /吵死人了！The noise is getting on my nerves! *or* Oh, I can't stand the noise!
吵秧子 chǎo yāngzi 〈方言〉 quarrel; kick up a row: 大年初一，我不跟你～。It's New Year's Day, and I wouldn't quarrel with you today.
吵仗 chǎozhàng 〈方言〉 quarrel; wrangle; have a row
吵子 chǎozi 〈方言〉 cause of quarrel; bone of contention: 有什么～回家再说。If there's anything you're unhappy about, leave it until we get home.
吵嘴 chǎozuǐ quarrel; bicker: 他俩总是没完没了地～。They are forever bickering. /我跟他吵了嘴了。I had a quarrel with him.

chào

耖 chào ❶ harrow-like implement for pulverizing sods ❷ level land with such an implement: ～田 level land with a harrow

chē

车（車） chē ❶ vehicle: 汽～ motor vehicle; motor car; automobile /军用～ army (*or* military) vehicle /火～ train /电～ tram; street car /无轨电～ trolley bus /自行～ bicycle; bike /救护～ ambulance /消防～ fire engine /卡～ truck; lorry /大客～ coach /货～ freight truck; goods wagon /面包～ minibus; van; coaster /旅行～ station wagon /大～ horse cart /三轮～ pedicab; tricycle /手推～ hand cart /灵～ hearse /警～ police car /人力～ rickshaw /餐～ dining car /油～ tank truck /洒水～ water spray truck /骑～ ride a bike; cycle /开～ drive (a car) ❷ wheeled machine or instrument:

纺～ spinning wheel /水～ water wheel /滑～ pulley /吊～ crane; hoist ❸ machine:开～ start a machine; set the machine going /试～ trial run; test run (of the machine) /停～ stop the machine ❹ lathe; turn:～零件 lathe a machine part /～光 smooth (*or* polish) sth. on a lathe /～螺帽 lathe a screw nut ❺ lift water by waterwheel ❻〈方言〉carry in a vehicle:～垃圾 cart away the garbage; carry away the refuse in a truck ❼〈方言〉sew by machine:～衣 make garments on a sewing machine ❽〈方言〉turn (one's body or limb):～过头来 turn about /把身子往左边～一下。Turn a bit to the left. ❾ (Chē) a surname

see also jū

车把 chēbǎ handle bar; shaft

车把式 chēbǎshi *also* "车把势" cart-driver; carter:村里最棒的～ best cart-driver in the village

车班 chēbān ❶ train number:早上发了好几个～。Several trains departed in the morning. /～已经定好了。The train number has been decided on. ❷ motorcoach number (indicating order of departure)

车帮 chēbāng side or sideboard of a cart or truck

车厂 chēchǎng ❶ *also* "车厂子"〈旧语〉place where rickshaws or pedicabs are hired or rented; rickshaw or pedicab renter ❷ workshop that makes rickshaws or pedicabs; rickshaw or pedicab factory or workshop

车场 chēchǎng ❶ place where automobiles are parked, serviced and repaired; garage ❷〈铁路〉marshalling yard ❸ administrative unit in charge of road transport or urban public transit (usu. under a company); road transport or public transit pool

车臣 Chēchén Chechen; Chechenya:～人 Chechen /～语 Chechen language

车臣-印古什 Chēchén-Yìngǔshí Chechen-Ingush, an autonomous republic of the Russian Federation

车程 chēchéng distance covered by car in a certain amount of time:学校就在附近,几分钟～而已。The school is very close — only a few minute's ride.

车程计 chēchéngjì *also* "里程计" lǐchéngjì odometer

车床 chēchuáng *also* "旋床" xuànchuáng lathe; turning machine:～卡盘 lathe chuck /～拖板 lathe carriage /精密～ precision lathe /万能～ universal lathe /重型～ heavy duty lathe /普通机动～ engine lathe /程序控制～ programme-control lathe /多刀～ multicut lathe

车次 chēcì ❶ train number:你的～是多少? What is your train number? /北京开往东北方向的～很多。There are many trains bound for the northeast from Beijing. ❷ motorcoach number (indicating order of departure)

车带 chēdài〈口语〉tyre

车刀 chēdāo lathe tool; turning tool:木工～ wood turning tool /深割～ undercutting turning tool

车到山前必有路 chē dào shānqián bì yǒu lù〈谚语〉the cart will find its way round the hill when it gets there — things will eventually sort themselves out:～,不用担心。As things will always sort themselves out, there is no need to worry.

车道 chēdào traffic lane:快～ speed lane/慢～ normal lane /六～的高速公路 six-lane expressway

车道沟 chēdàogōu ❶ *also* "车辙沟" rut ❷ road that looks like a rut; rut-shaped road

车灯 chēdēng light or lamp on a vehicle:车前灯 head-lights /车后灯 rear-lights; taillights /自行车～ bicycle lamp

车队 chēduì ❶ convoy; motorcade ❷ transport pool (of an institution or company)

车尔尼雪夫斯基 Chē'ěrníxuěfūsījī Nikolai Gavrilovich Chernyshevsky (1828-1889), Russian philosopher and literary critic

车费 chēfèi fare

车份儿 chēfènr〈方言〉rent paid(by the rickshaw-puller, etc.) to the rickshaw-owner or pedicab-owner; rent paid (by the taxi-driver, etc.) to the taxi-company

车夫 chēfū〈旧语〉driver:人力～ rickshaw boy; rickshaw man /三轮～ pedicab driver

车工 chēgōng ❶ lathe work:～车间 turning shop ❷ turner; lathe operator

车公里 chēgōnglǐ (unit equivalent to) vehicle per kilometre; vehicle-kilometre

车沟 chēgōu rut

车钩 chēgōu〈铁路〉coupling

车轱辘 chēgūlu〈口语〉wheel (of a vehicle)

车轱辘话 chēgūluhuà〈方言〉repetitious, rambling talk; same old stuff:他说的尽是些～。He always speaks in a rambling, repetitious manner.

车轱辘会 chēgūluhuì regular dinner party with one member standing host in rotation

车号 chēhào licence number (of a vehicle)

车祸 chēhuò traffic accident; road accident:一起严重的～ serious traffic accident

车技 chējì〈杂技〉trick-cycling

车驾 chējià royal wagon; imperial carriage:～东巡。The emperor's carriage was heading east.

车架 chējià frame (of a bicycle, etc.); chassis

车间 chējiān workshop; shop:翻砂～ foundry /工具～ tool shop /锻工～ blacksmith tool shop /制模～ pattern shop /木工～ carpentry workshop /冷锻～ cold hammering shop /量具～ measuring gauge shop /装配～ assembly shop; fitting shop /～主任 workshop director

车捐 chējuān tax paid by vehicle owner

车口 chēkǒu〈方言〉parking lot for taxis (along a street)

车库 chēkù garage:大使馆的～里有辆大面包。In the embassy's garage there is a big van.

车筐 chēkuāng bicycle basket

车况 chēkuàng condition of a vehicle:～正常 (vehicle) in normal condition; running normally

车老板 chēlǎobǎn carter

车梁木 chēliángmù *also* "毛株" máolái〈方言〉long-petioled dogwood

车辆 chēliàng vehicle:～周转率 average turnaround rate of vehicles /前面施工,～绕行。Construction Ahead. Road Blocked. *or* Road Construction Ahead. Please make a detour.

车裂 chēliè tearing a person asunder by five carts (a cruel punishment in ancient China)

车铃 chēlíng bells on a bicycle or pedicab

车流 chēliú traffic flow

车绺子 chēliǔzi〈方言〉❶ car thief ❷ pickpocket on a bus or train

车轮 chēlún wheel (of a vehicle)

车轮驱动装置 chēlún qūdòng zhuāngzhì wheel drive:四轮～ four-wheel drive

车轮战 chēlúnzhàn tactic of several persons taking turns in fighting one opponent to tire him out — gruelling tactic:棋王雄风不减当年,～也奈何不了他。The king of chess is as skilful as he used to be, and even the gruelling tactics of a number of players challenging him in turn cannot wear him down.

车马费 chēmǎfèi travel allowance; transport allowance

车马坑 chēmǎkēng〈考古〉chariot pit

车马盈门 chēmǎ-yíngmén the gate is thronged with carriages and horses; the house is filled with rich and distinguished visitors

车幔 chēmàn *see* "车帷" chēwéi

车门 chēmén ❶ door of a vehicle ❷ special gate for a horse wagon to go through

车牌 chēpái licence plate; numberplate

车袢 chēpàn thick rope or strap tied to the handlebar of a pushcart (worn across the shoulders of the carter when the pushcart is in motion)

车棚 chēpéng shed for parking bicycles; bicycle (parking) shed

车篷 chēpéng awning for a vehicle

车皮 chēpí railway wagon or carriage; freight truck

车票 chēpiào ticket:火车～ train ticket /汽车～ bus ticket /请买～! Fares, please!

车骑 chēqí ❶ vehicles and horses ❷ military rank in the Han Dynasty:～将军 *cheqi* general

车前 chēqián *also* "车前草"〈中药〉Asiatic plantain (*Plantago asiatica*)

车钱 chēqián fare

车圈 chēquān rim (of a bicycle wheel, cart wheel, etc.)

车身 chēshēn ❶ body of a vehicle:～修理铺 body shop ❷〈方言〉(of a person) turn round:没等我说完,他～就走了。He turned away and left before I finished speaking. /她又车过身来看了看熟睡的孩子。She turned round and took another look at the sleeping child.

车身千斤顶 chēshēn qiānjīndǐng body jack

车手 chēshǒu (racing) motorist

车守 chēshǒu 〈旧语〉railway policeman：货车～ car caboose
车水 chēshuǐ lift water by waterwheel
车水马龙 chēshuǐ-mǎlóng endless stream of horses and carriages — heavy traffic：大街上～。The street looks very busy with a constant stream of cars and buses. /如今这个城市已是高楼耸立，～，一片繁荣景象。Now the whole city seemed like a forest of tall buildings with busy traffic and signs of prosperity everywhere.
车速 chēsù ❶ speed of a vehicle ❷ speed of a lathe
车胎 chētāi tyre
车条 chētiáo spoke (of a wheel)
车贴 chētiē commuter's allowance
车头 chētóu ❶ locomotive ❷ front part of a vehicle：～撞瘪了。The front of the car was smashed in.
车瓦 chēwǎ rim (of a wooden wheel)
车帷 chēwéi curtain in a carriage
车尾 chēwěi rear of a vehicle：保持车距，严防追～。Keep a distance from the car ahead. Don't smash into its rear.
车位 chēwèi parking place：这个停车场有五十个～。The parking lot has fifty parking places.
车厢 chēxiāng railway carriage; railway car
车箱 chēxiāng *see* "车厢"
车削 chēxiāo 〈机械〉metal-turning (with a lathe)
车辕 chēyuán shaft (of a cart, etc.)
车载 chēzài vehicle mounted：～天线 vehicle-mounted antenna / ～通信设备 vehicular communication equipment
车载斗量 chēzài-dǒuliáng be enough to fill carts and measured by the *dou* — common and numerous：这种水平的流行歌手这里～。Pop singers like this come by the bushel here.
车载式吊车 chēzàishì diàochē 〈林业〉cherry-picker
车闸 chēzhá brake (of a vehicle)：～失灵。The brake didn't work.
车站 chēzhàn station; stop; depot：～站长 station-master / ～候车室 station hall; waiting room
车长 chēzhǎng *also* "列车长" lièchēzhǎng head of a train crew; conductor
车照 chēzhào driving licence
车辙 chēzhé rut
车轴 chēzhóu axletree; axle
车轴草 chēzhóucǎo clover (*Trifolium*)
车主 chēzhǔ owner of a vehicle
车转 chēzhuǎn 〈方言〉turn round：他～身就走。He turned and left.
车资 chēzī fare
车子 chēzi ❶ vehicle (usu. small ones such as cars, pushcarts, etc.) ❷ 〈方言〉bike
车组 chēzǔ crew (of a bus, train, etc.)：全体～人员 the entire crew /二路公共汽车 583 号～ crew No. 583 of No. 2 Route Bus
车座 chēzuò seat
车座安全带 chēzuò ānquándài safety belt

砗 chē
砗磲 chēqú 〈动物〉giant clam; tridacna

唓 chē
唓嗻 chēzhē (often used in the early vernacular) terrific; much

俥 chē *see* "大车❷❸" dàchē

chě

扯(撦) chě ❶ pull; drag：小男孩～住妈妈的大衣。The boy pulled (at) his mother's coat. *or* The boy pulled his mother by the coat. /他俩打起来了，快～开！Pull them apart. They are coming to blows! /把裤腿儿～平了再晾。Pull the (trouser) legs straight before you air the trousers. /再去～两个人来打桥牌。Go and grab two more people to make up a bridge party. /他硬是要把两件事～在一起。He insisted on lumping the two things together. ❷ tear：外衣～了个口子 tear a hole in one's jacket / ～下假面具 tear off the mask /他大衣上的一颗钮扣～掉了。He had a button torn off his coat. /他急忙把信封～开。He tore the envelope open with impatience. /把墙上那张画～下来。Pull that picture off the wall. ❸ chat; gossip：～闲话 gossip / ～家常 chit-chat; chat about everyday family affairs / 咱俩好好扯一扯。Let's have a good chat. /你瞎～些什么？What are you chattering about? /他们说着说着又～回去了。They drifted back to the old topic. /别把话～远了。Don't digress (from the topic).
扯把子 chěbǎzi 〈方言〉chit-chat; chin-wag
扯巴 chěba 〈方言〉❶ tear; tear up：他把旧床单～了，做了个拖把。He tore up the old sheets and made a mop out of it. ❷ chat：客人们等着吃饭，就～开了。The guests chatted while they were waiting for dinner to be served.
扯白 chěbái 〈方言〉lie; tell a lie：～蒙人 cheat by lying / ～坑人 tell lies to lead people astray
扯常 chěcháng 〈方言〉often; frequently：他～来。He comes here very often.
扯淡 chědàn 〈方言〉talk nonsense：别～了，说点正经事吧！Let's stop talking idly and get down to business!
扯后腿 chě hòutuǐ hold back from action; be a drag on; be a hindrance to：去吧，我不会扯你的后腿的。Go ahead as you wish. I will not hold you back. /农业上不去，就会扯现代化的后腿。A backward agriculture would be a drag on China's modernization.
扯后衣襟 chě hòuyījīn 〈方言〉*see* "扯后腿"
扯谎 chěhuǎng tell a lie; lie：谁也不能～！Nobody should tell lies!
扯伙 chěhuǒ 〈方言〉gang up; band together：那些人～闹事。Those people banded together to make trouble.
扯筋 chějīn 〈方言〉❶ chat; gossip; talk nonsense ❷ quarrel; bicker
扯诓 chěkuáng 〈方言〉tell a lie; lie
扯拉 chěla ❶ grip; seize hold of：他～着树棵子向山上爬去。He climbed up the mountain by seizing hold of one clump after another. ❷ involve; implicate; drag in：这件事你不要再～上别人。Don't get others involved in this matter. ❸ chat; chit-chat：休息的时候，咱们再到一块～～。Let's have another chat during the break.
扯裂 chěliè 〈医学〉divulsion; tear
扯铃 chělíng diabolo
扯皮 chěpí dispute over trifles; argue back and forth; wrangle：没完没了的～ keep wrangling without getting anywhere /双方互相～，推卸责任。They argued back and forth, each trying to shift the blame onto the other. /我说这件事一次解决了好，免得今后～。I want a final settlement of the matter so as to avoid future disputes.
扯平 chěpíng break even; even up：～汇率 break even exchange rate / ～价格 average price /你再给我一百元，咱俩就～了。Give me another hundred *yuan*, and we're quits.
扯臊 chěsào 〈方言〉talk nonsense; shoot off one's mouth：别在这儿瞎～，就欠你老子揍你了！Don't you go shooting off your mouth; you seem to want a good beating!
扯手 chěshou 〈方言〉bridle (for a horse, etc.)
扯顺风旗 chě shùnfēngqí trim one's sail; swim with the current：有些人不敢说真话，而是随大溜，～。Some people dare not tell the truth, but always swim with the tide (*or* current).
扯谈 chětán chat：他们一边吃，一边～赶集的事。They were chatting about the fair over their meal.
扯腿 chětuǐ ❶ *see* "扯后腿" ❷ 〈方言〉lift the foot (and begin to run, chase, etc.)：话没说完，他～就走。He took to his heels before he finished talking.
扯闲篇 chě xiánpiān *also* "扯闲天儿" chat; chit-chat：别在那儿～浪费时间了。Don't waste your time chit-chatting.

尺 chě 〈音乐〉note of the scale in *gongchepu* (工尺谱), corresponding to 2 (*re*) in numbered musical notation
see also chǐ

chè

澈 chè (of water) clear; limpid：澄～ clear /清～见底 crystal clear; crystaline
澈底 chèdǐ *also* "彻底" chèdǐ thorough; thoroughgoing

撤 chè ❶ remove; take away：职务被～了 be stripped of one's post; be dismissed from office / ～火 (of cooking) put out the fire; stop heating / ～一道菜 take a dish away /把碗盘～下去 clear away the dishes / ～桌子 remove the table /把她的名字从名单上～下去。Take her name off the list. *or* Strike her name off the list. ❷

withdraw; retreat:立即后～ retreat immediately /～下一个排 withdraw one platoon /～伤员 evacuate the wounded /岗哨都～了。All the sentries have been removed. /居民已～出危险地带。The inhabitants have been withdrawn (*or* evacuated) from the danger area. ❸〈方言〉(of smell, weight, etc.) reduce; take off:～味儿 reduce the smell /～分量 take some weight off

撤编 chèbiān disestablish; deactivate; inactivate:～两个师 disestablish two divisions

撤兵 chèbīng withdraw troops:从前沿～ withdraw troops from the forward positions /双方～ mutual withdrawal (*or* pullout) of troops /停火～ cease hostilities and pull back troops

撤差 chèchāi 〈旧语〉be removed from office

撤除 chèchú remove; dismantle:～障碍 remove obstacles; remove barriers /～军事设施 dismantle military installations /～他的职务 dismiss him from office

撤佃 chèdiàn forcibly terminate tenancy:东家这一～,日子没法过了。Life became very difficult for me after the landlord evicted me from the land I had rented from him.

撤防 chèfáng withdraw a garrison; withdraw from a defended position:部队～ withdraw troops from fortified positions /颁布～命令 issue an order for evacuation

撤岗 chègǎng withdraw the guard or sentry

撤换 chèhuàn dismiss and replace; replace; recall:～人选 recall candidates /～三个人 replace three people /这些旧机器应全部～。These old machines must all be replaced.

撤回 chèhuí ❶ recall; withdraw:～使馆人员 recall embassy personnel /～军队 withdraw troops /～岗哨 withdraw the sentry /登山队员～大本营。The mountaineers returned to the base area. ❷ retract; revoke; withdraw:～提案 retract a proposal /～声明 retract a statement /～起诉 withdraw a charge; revoke a court action /～任命 withdraw an appointment

撤军 chèjūn withdraw troops:限期～ withdraw troops within a stated period; set a deadline for withdrawal of troops

撤离 chèlí withdraw from; evacuate; leave:～回国 be withdrawn (*or* evacuated) to one's own country /～战场 evacuate the battlefield /部队已经～。The forces have been withdrawn.

撤诉 chèsù (of the plaintiff) drop the lawsuit; withdraw a charge

撤退 chètuì evacuate; withdraw; retreat:～非战斗人员 evacuate non-combatants (from...) /部分～ partial withdrawal /全面～ full pullout; total withdrawal /主动～ withdraw on one's own initiative /～方向 line of withdrawal /向后方～ retreat to the rear /士兵～的地区 area vacated by the soldiers /敌人已有～的迹象。There are signs of the enemy retreating.

撤围 chèwéi lift a seige

撤席 chèxí clear the table (after a feast)

撤消 chèxiāo *see* "撤销"

撤销 chèxiāo *also* "撤消" cancel; revoke; rescind:～命令 cancel (*or* countermand) an order /～任命 revoke an appointment /～机构 dismantle (*or* dissolve) an organization /～定货单 recall an order /～合同 abandon a contract /～一切职务 dismiss a person from all his posts /～处分 rescind (*or* annul) a penalty /～禁令 lift a ban /～决议 annul a decision /～原判 revoke; (*or* disaffirm) the court decision /～邀请 withdraw an invitation /～法令 repeal a decree /他～了自己的意见。He withdrew his opinion.

撤职 chèzhí remove from office; dismiss or discharge from post:～查办 discharge sb. from his post and prosecute him /～反省 dismiss sb. from his post and order him to do (*or* conduct) self-criticism

撤走 chèzǒu withdraw:～驻军 withdraw the garrison troops

彻(徹) chè

thorough; penetrating; complete:透～的理解 thorough understanding /响～云霄 resounding across the skies

彻查 chèchá investigate thoroughly:～积年旧案 thoroughly investigate cases that have been pending over the years

彻底 chèdǐ thorough; thoroughgoing:～治疗 thorough treatment /～改正错误 correct a mistake thoroughly /～调查 full investigation /～否定 totally reject (*or* negate); reject categorically /～修理 overhaul /做事～ do things in a thoroughgoing way /～胜利 utter victory /～改变 radical change /～完蛋 be finished for good /～解决问题 solve a problem once and for all; find a radical solution

彻骨 chègǔ to the bone:寒风～。The cold wind chills one to the bone. /寒气～。The cold cuts one to the marrow.

彻亮 chèliàng very bright; shiny:桌子擦得～。The table was wiped bright and clean.

彻头彻尾 chètóu-chèwěi out and out; through and through; sheer; downright:～的骗局 downright fraud; sheer fraud; deception from beginning to end /～的谎言 sheer lie /一个～的种族主义者 an out-and-out racist; every inch a racist

彻悟 chèwù ❶ be fully conscious of; come to fully realize ❷ complete awakening

彻夜 chèyè all night; all through the night:～不眠 lie awake all night /～工作 work all night; burn the midnight oil /灯火～通明。The lights were ablaze all through the night.

坼 chè

〈书面〉split open; crack:天旱地～。During the drought, the land was so dry that it cracked. /天寒地～。The earth cracked in the severe cold.

坼裂 chèliè 〈书面〉split open; crack:土地～。The dry land cracked.

掣 chè

❶ pull; tug; drag:～后腿 hold sb. back ❷ draw:～签 draw lots /～回手去 draw back one's hand /从后～其笔 pull sb.'s pen away from behind his shoulders ❸ flash past:风驰电～ swift as the wind and quick as lightning; go at lightning speed

掣电 chèdiàn 〈书面〉(of lightning) flash

掣肘 chèzhǒu hold sb. back by the elbow; impede:由于有人～,事情办得不顺利。Owing to obstruction by some people, the matter didn't proceed very smoothly. /他大权在握,别人无从～。As he wielded absolute power, nobody could restrain him. /搞工作切不可互相～。In collective work we should never deliberately create difficulties for others.

chēn

琛 chēn

〈书面〉treasure

綝 chēn

〈书面〉❶ stop; cease ❷ good; kind

see also lín

嗔 chēn

〈书面〉❶ angry; displeased:含～ look displeased or angry /娇～ pout with displeasure /～诟 vilify; berate angrily /似～非～ look as if angry /转～为喜 one's anger turning into pleasure ❷ be annoyed (with sb.); blame:他～我多嘴。He was annoyed with me for butting in.

嗔斥 chēnchì reprimand; rebuke; reproach

嗔怪 chēnguài blame; rebuke; upbraid:他自己作错了事,却～别人。He shifted the blame on to other people for what he did wrong.

嗔睨 chēnnì glare at angrily:～不语 glare at sb. angrily without saying anything; stare at sb. in silent anger

嗔怒 chēnnù become angry; get angry:～而言 speak angrily /休要～! Refrain from anger! *or* Control your temper!

嗔色 chēnsè angry expression; sullen look:面带～ look displeased; look angry

嗔怨 chēnyuàn complain; grumble

嗔责 chēnzé blame; scold

嗔着 chēnzhe 〈口语〉be angry; be displeased; blame:你别～我多嘴,我说这些是为了你好。Don't take my words to heart; I said all this for your own good.

瞋 chēn

〈书面〉stare angrily; glare

瞋目 chēnmù stare angrily; glare:～而视 stare (*or* glare) at sb. angrily /～叱之 stare at sb. angrily and denounce him (*or* her)

膜 chēn

〈书面〉swollen

抻(捵) chēn

pull out; stretch:～长了 stretch too long /～着脖子看 crane to see /衣服～～就合适了。Give the clothes a stretch and they'll be all right.

抻面 chēnmiàn ❶ make noodles by drawing out the dough by hand ❷ hand-pulled noodles

chén

沉(沈) chén ❶ sink:～底儿 sink to the bottom /船迅速下～。The boat is sinking fast. /木头在水里不～。Wood doesn't sink in water. /月落星～。The moon is down and the stars have set. ❷ subside:地基下～ subsidence of foundations ❸ (usu. of abstract matters) keep down; lower; sink:～下脸来 put on a stern expression; pull a long face /～下心来 settle down (to one's work); concentrate (on one's work, study, etc.) /～不住气 unable to hold back one's excitement or anger /听到这个消息,我的心都～下去了。My heart sank at the news. /她不由得心里一～。A sinking feeling came over her. ❹ (of degree) deep; profound:睡得很～ be in a deep sleep; be fast asleep /阴～的天 gloomy sky; overcast sky ❺ heavy:这口袋真～。The sack is rather heavy. /他感到肩上担子很～。He felt that he was shouldering a heavy responsibility. ❻ feel heavy or uncomfortable:头～,身上也痛 feel dizzy and be aching all over /我的两腿发～。My legs feel heavy.

沉沉 chénchén ❶ heavy:麦穗儿～的 ears of wheat hanging heavy on the stalks ❷ deep; heavy; to a great extent:～入睡 sink into a deep sleep /～的乌云 heavy(*or* overcast) with dark clouds /心事～ have a heavy heart; be deeply troubled /暮气～ lifeless; lethargic; apathetic /寒夜～。The cold night is long.

沉甸甸 chéndiāndiān heavy:～的钱包 heavy wallet /迈着～的步子 walk with heavy steps; trudge /心情～的 with a heavy heart /这事儿在我心里～的。This matter weighs heavily on my mind.

沉淀 chéndiàn ❶ settle; precipitate:等咖啡渣～下来 wait for the coffee grounds to settle /瓶里积有厚厚的一层～。There is a thick layer of sediment in the bottle. /水～一下就清了。Let the water settle for a while and it'll become clear. /把两种药水混在一起,就会出现～。The mixture of these two solutions will precipitate. ❷ accumulation; accretion:几千年的文化～ accretion of culture over thousands of years /情感需要～,才能写出好诗。Good poetry requires the accumulation of emotions.

沉淀池 chéndiànchí 〈环保〉precipitating or sedimentation tank

沉淀剂 chéndiànjì 〈化学〉precipitating agent

沉淀物 chéndiànwù sediment; precipitate

沉浮 chénfú ❶ sink and swim; drift:一只小船在海上随波～。A little boat is drifting about in the sea. ❷ vicissitude:与世～ swim with the tide; drift along /问苍茫大地,谁主～? I ask, on this boundless land Who rules over man's destiny?

沉痼 chéngù 〈书面〉❶ serious chronic illness:～在身 suffer from a lingering grave disease ❷ stubborn habit; inveterate habit:因循守旧的～ attitude of tenaciously clinging to one's old ideas; stubborn habit of a stick-in-the-mud /说谎是他的～了。He is an inveterate liar.

沉管 chénguǎn immersed tube

沉酣 chénhān indulge; be lost (in sth.):歌舞～ indulge in dance and song /～经史 be absorbed in the study of Confucian classics /香梦～ indulge in daydreaming; live in a fool's paradise

沉厚 chénhòu ❶ (of colour) thick and heavy:这幅画墨色～。This picture is drawn with heavy ink shading. ❷ (of demeanour, expression, etc.) sedate; staid:表情～ look staid

沉缓 chénhuǎn ❶ deep; steady and slow:～的声音 deep voice /他～地点点头。He languidly nodded his head. ❷ (in traditional Chinese medicine) slow and weak (pulse)

沉积 chénjī ❶ deposit; sediment:陆相～ continental deposit /海相～ marine deposit /～旋回 cycle of sedimentation /～作用 deposition; sedimentation /河水夹带的泥沙～下来,使河床逐年增高。The silt that is deposited in the riverbed raises it each year. ❷ sedimentation; settlement:浑浊的池水经过几天的～,变得清澈了。The muddy water in the pool became clear again after a few days of sedimentation. ❸ (often used of abstract matters) accumulation; accretion:文化～ cultural sediment /历史～ accretion of history

沉积构造 chénjī gòuzào 〈地质〉sedimentary structure

沉积盆地 chénjī péndì 〈地质〉sedimentation basin

沉积物 chénjīwù 〈地质〉deposit; sediment

沉积相 chénjīxiàng sedimentary facies

沉积岩 chénjīyán *also* "水成岩" shuǐchéngyán sedimentary rock

沉寂 chénjì ❶ quiet; still:山村的夜晚～得没有一点声息。All was quiet and still at the mountain village during the night. /枪声划破了深夜的～。The crack of gunfire broke the silence of the night. /会场突然～下来,谁也不说话。The meeting hall suddenly quieted down (*or* fell silent). No one spoke a word. ❷ no news:音讯～。There has been no news whatsoever. /战况～。Nothing is reported about the war.

沉降 chénjiàng subside:地面～ earth subsidence

沉降缝 chénjiàngfèng 〈建筑〉settlement joint

沉浸 chénjìn be immersed in; be steeped in; be permeated with:～在甜蜜的梦幻中 be immersed in visionary pleasure /～在深思中 be deep in thought /～在胜利的欢乐中 be intoxicated with the joy of victory /～在极大的悲痛之中 be plunged into deep grief /山峦～在金色的霞光里。The mountains are bathed in bright sunshine. /会场～在一片友谊的气氛之中。The conference hall is permeated with an atmosphere of friendship.

沉井 chénjǐng 〈建筑〉open caisson

沉静 chénjìng ❶ quiet; calm:人们经过激烈的争吵后,～下来。People finally calmed down after the heated debate. /四周一片～。All was quiet around. ❷ calm; serene; placid:神色显得很～ look calm and composed /～的心情 in a placid mood /性情～ quiet by temperament /她～地叙述这次事故的经过。She spoke calmly about the accident.

沉疴 chénkē grave and lingering illness; serious chronic illness:～绵绵 be gravely ill; be terminally ill /～不起 be unable to recover from a lingering illness

沉雷 chénléi muffled thunder:外面下大雨,～响个不停。It was raining heavily outside, with incessant muffled roars of thunder. /火炮～般地响着。The artillery fire sounded like rumbling thunder.

沉沦 chénlún sink into (sin, vice, degradation, etc.):～于罪恶的深渊里 sink deep into the iniquity of sin /不甘～ refuse to submit to degradation /饮酒和赌博使他彻底～了。Drinking and gambling made him a reprobate beyond redemption.

沉落 chénluò sink; drop; fall:心绪～ depressed; gloomy /月亮从树林的黑影里～下去。The moon sank into the dark shadows of the trees.

沉埋 chénmái ❶ lie buried deep ❷ immersed in; submerged by:山村～在云雾里。The mountain village lies hidden in the misty clouds. /他～在愉快的回忆里。He is engrossed in pleasant memories of the past.

沉脉 chénmài 〈中医〉deep pulse (which can be felt only by pressing hard)

沉闷 chénmèn ❶ (of weather, atmosphere, etc.) dull; oppressive; depressing:～的空气 oppressive atmosphere /～的局面 depressing situation /～的生活 dull life /～的故事 dull (*or* insipid) story ❷ (of a person) in low spirits; in a mood; (of character) withdrawn; retiring:心情～ feel depressed /性格～ have a retiring nature /这个人很～。He is rather withdrawn.

沉迷 chénmí indulge; wallow:～于奢侈的生活 wallow in luxury and extravagance /～在幻想之中 indulge in illusions /～酒色 be excessively fond of wine and woman; be addicted to drinking and womanizing /～赌博 take to gambling

沉眠 chénmián fast asleep:～不醒 fall into a heavy slumber

沉绵 chénmián 〈书面〉be afflicted with a lingering illness:积劳成疾,～不起 fall ill from overwork and become bedridden

沉湎 chénmiǎn 〈书面〉indulge; be given to:～于儿女之情 indulge in romantic sentiments /～于杯中之物 take to heavy drinking

沉没 chénmò sink:打捞～已久的商船 salvage a long-sunken merchant ship /载着数百名旅客的海轮～在大洋里。The ship went to the bottom of the ocean with hundreds of passengers on board.

沉默 chénmò ❶ taciturn; reticent; quiet:～寡言 taciturn; reticent; of few words /他变得更～了。He's become more reticent than before. ❷ silent; speechless:保持～ keep quiet; remain silent; remain speechless /他的～并不是没有原因的。His silence is not unaccountable.

沉溺 chénnì indulge; wallow; be given to:～于醉生梦死的生活里 indulge in dissipation /～声色 wallow in sensual pleasures /～在幻想里 luxuriate in fanciful imagination

沉潜 chénqián ❶ lie hidden under water:这种鱼常～于水底。This kind of fish always lie hidden at the bottom of the water. ❷〈书面〉reserved; unruffled; composed:他～坚忍,处逆境而不馁。A man of equanimity and fortitude, he never feels disheartened in adversity. ❸ act with great concentration:他～在研究工作中,废寝忘食。He was

cult to shake off bad habits.
陈朝 Chéncháo Tran Dynasty (1225-1400) of Vietnam
陈淳 Chén Chún Chen Chun (formerly translated as Ch'en Ch'un, 1483-1544), Chinese brush painter of the Ming Dynasty
陈词 chéncí ❶ state one's views, reasons, etc.:慷慨～ speak vehemently; make a vehement statement ❷ cliché; hackneyed expression
陈词滥调 chéncí-làndiào cliché; stereotyped phrase; hackneyed expression; platitude:这个评论通篇～。This commentary is cliché-ridden./他每章结尾时少说点～就好了。One could only wish that he had found a less trite and commonplace way of ending his chapters.
陈醋 chéncù mature vinegar
陈独秀 Chén Dúxiù Chen Duxiu (formerly translated as Ch'en Tu-hsiu, 1879-1942), one of the founding members and first General Secretary (1921-1927) of the Communist Party of China, expelled from the CPC in 1929
陈放 chénfàng put on display; lay out:摇曳的烛光照着～在桌上的糕点,干果等供品。The flickering candlelight fell on the offerings — the pastry and candied fruit that were laid out on the table.
陈废率 chénfèilǜ 〈经济〉rate of obsolescence
陈旉农书 Chén Fū Nóngshū *Agricultural Treatise of Chen Fu*, published in 1149
陈腐 chénfǔ stale; old and decayed; outworn; obsolete:～之言 platitudinous remark/内容～ stale in content/～习俗 outworn custom
陈古 chéngǔ 〈方言〉old and outmoded; ancient:～的图画 ancient picture/不要把～几十年的事都翻出来。Don't bring up stuff that is ancient history.
陈谷子烂芝麻 chén gǔzi làn zhīma old millet and stale sesame — dull and uninteresting things of the past; old garbage:这些～的,她抖落它有啥用? Why does she have to pull out all this ancient garbage? *or* There is no point in her digging up the past.
陈规 chénguī outmoded convention:打破～ break with outmoded conventions/死守～ stick to old customs and habits
陈规陋习 chénguī-lòuxí outmoded conventions and practices:革除～ do away with outmoded conventions and practices
陈果夫 Chén Guǒfū Ch'en Kuo-fu (1892-1951), a politician of the KMT
陈洪绶 Chén Hóngshòu Chen Hongshou (formerly translated as Ch'en Hung-shou, 1598-1652), Chinese brush painter of the late Ming and early Qing dynasties
陈化 chénhuà ageing; maturing; seasoning
陈货 chénhuò old stock; shopworn goods:减价出售～ sale of old stock
陈迹 chénjì thing of the past; old traces:历史的～ historical record; historical site/向之所新,俯仰之间,已为～。What was once regarded as new has shortly become a thing of the past.
陈见 chénjiàn outmoded idea; old-fashioned concept
陈酒 chénjiǔ old wine; mellow wine:百年～ century-old wine/～味醇。The old wine has a mellow flavour.
陈旧 chénjiù old; shabby; outmoded; old-fashioned:～的照片 old photos/衣著～ shabbily dressed/观点～ outmoded notion/～的服装 old-fashioned clothes/设备～outdated equipment; obsolete equipment/语言～ obsolete language/～的思想方法 antiquated way of thinking
陈粮 chénliáng surplus grains of the preceding year(s)
陈列 chénliè display; exhibit:～品 exhibit/～柜 show case/～室 exhibition room; show room/～馆 exhibition hall/他的画被送到美术馆～。His paintings are on display in the art gallery.
陈米 chénmǐ *also*"老米" lǎomǐ rice of the preceding year(s)
陈纳德 Chénnàdé Claire Lee Chennault (1890-1958), US Brigadier General who organized the American Volunteer Group — the Flying Tigers — to assist the Chinese people's War of Resistance Against Japanese Aggression
陈年 chénnián of many years' standing:～老酒 old wine
陈年老账 chénnián-lǎozhàng ❶ long-standing debt; old score ❷ sth. that happened a long time ago
陈酿 chénniàng old wine; mellow wine
陈皮 chénpí 〈中药〉dried tangerine or orange peel
陈皮梅 chénpíméi preserved prunes; preserved plums
陈桥兵变 Chénqiáo Bīngbiàn Chenqiao Mutiny engineered by Zhao Kuangyin (赵匡胤, 927-976) in 960, who thereby became the first emperor of the Song Dynasty
陈情 chénqíng state one's case; explain oneself; make a plea:恳切～ make an earnest plea
陈请 chénqǐng submit a request to a higher or relevant organization for consideration:～上级审定 report to the higher authorities for approval
陈容 Chén Róng Chen Rong (formerly translated as Ch'en Jung), Chinese brush painter during the Southern Song Dynasty
陈绍 chénshào Shaoxing rice wine of many years' standing
陈绍禹 Chén Shàoyǔ Chen Shaoyu, better known as 王明 (Wang Ming, 1904-1974), chief representative of the third "Left" opportunist line in the history of the Chinese Communist Party
陈设 chénshè ❶ exhibit; display; set out:客厅里～着几色古玩。A few antiques are displayed in the sitting room. ❷ furnishings:豪华的～ luxurious furnishings/客厅里的～优雅古朴。The furniture in the drawing room has a taste of simplicity and elegance. *or* The drawing room is furnished in simple and elegant taste./居室的一切～都保持着他生前的原状。Everything in the room is kept exactly as it was before his death.
陈设饼 chénshèbǐng 〈宗教〉shewbread
陈胜吴广起义 Chén Shèng Wú Guǎng Qǐyì *also*"大泽乡起义" Dàzéxiāng Qǐyì Chen Sheng-Wu Guang Uprising (209 BC), the first large-scale peasant uprising in China's history
陈氏定理 Chénshì dìnglǐ Chen Jingrun's (陈景润) theorem
陈世美 Chén Shìměi Chen Shimei, a notorious character in traditional Chinese opera, now a derisive title for a person who abandons his wife and seeks new romance with the elevation of his position
陈饰 chénshì decoration; ornament; embellishment
陈寿 Chén Shòu Chen Shou (223-297), a historian of the Western Jin Dynasty, who compiled *History of the Three Kingdoms* (三国志)
陈述 chénshù state; explain:～理由 state one's reasons/～事情的经过 explain (*or* recount) what happened/～自己的看法 set out one's views
陈述句 chénshùjù 〈语言〉declarative sentence
陈说 chénshuō state; explain:～道理 enumerate the reasons/～利害关系 explain the advantages and disadvantages
陈诉 chénsù state; recite; make a plea:～冤屈 state one's grievances/～苦恼 recite one's vexations/～不幸遭遇 recount one's sufferings (*or* ordeal)/你得找一个律师替你～。You must get a lawyer to plead your case.
陈套 chéntào outmoded style:这幅画构思新颖,不落～。This painting is fresh in design and free from conventional techniques.
陈香梅 Chén Xiāngméi Ch'en Hsiang-mei (1925-), wife of C. L. Chennault (陈纳德)
陈谢作用 chénxiè zuòyòng 〈生物〉catabolism
陈言 chényán ❶ state one's views; make remarks:率直～ state one's view in a straightforward manner ❷ hackneyed expression; cliché:务去～ delete the clichés by all means
陈玉成 Chén Yùchéng Chen Yucheng (formerly translated as Ch'en Yu-cheng, 1837-1862), one of the leaders of the later Taiping Heavenly Kingdom (1851-1864)
陈账 chénzhàng old score; long-standing debt
陈芝麻烂谷子 chén zhīma làn gǔzi *see*"陈谷子烂芝麻"

chěn

碜[1](**磣、硶**) chěn (food) mixed with pieces of grit or grains of sand

碜[2](**磣、頳**) chěn ugly; unsightly; hideous:这件外套真～。This jacket is ugly.

墋(**墋**) chěn ❶ *see*"碜[1]" chěn ❷〈书面〉unclear; turbid; muddy:～黩 not clear; turbid

踸 chěn
踸踔 chěnchuō *see*"踔踔" chěnchuō

踸 chěn

踸踔 chěnchuō 〈书面〉 leap; bound

chèn

疢 chèn 〈书面〉 ill; sick:～疾 disease

榇(櫬) chèn 〈书面〉 coffin

儭(儭、嚫) chèn alms given to Buddhist or Taoists monks

C

儭钱 chènqian *also* "衬钱" chènqian money given to Buddhist or Taoist priests; religious donation; alms

衬(襯) chèn ❶ line; place sth. underneath:～上一层布 put a piece of cloth underneath /里面～着一件羊毛衫 wear a woollen sweater underneath ❷ sth. worn underneath ❸ cloth lining; liner: 帽～儿 cap lining /袖～儿 cuff lining ❹ serve as a foil to; set off:绿叶把红花～得更好看。The green leaves set off the red flowers beautifully.

衬布 chènbù lining cloth

衬层 chèncéng 〈机械〉lining:炉壁～ furnace lining

衬垫 chèndiàn 〈机械〉liner:接合～ joint liner

衬垫板 chèndiànbǎn 〈建筑〉sarking

衬褂 chènguà 〈方言〉shirt

衬架裙 chènjiàqún crinoline

衬裤 chènkù underpants; pants

衬里 chènlǐ ❶ lining:大衣～ coat lining /水泥～ cement lining ❷ *see* "衬料"

衬料 chènliào stuffing (between the outside and lining of a garment); dunnage

衬领 chènlǐng detachable collar lining (of a coat)

衬砌 chènqì lining for roadside or riverbank or inner wall of a tunnel:用水泥～渠道 line an irrigation canal with cement

衬钱 chènqian *also* "儭钱" chènqian alms; religious donation

衬圈 chènquān 〈机械〉bush ring; gasket; burr

衬裙 chènqún underskirt; petticoat

衬衫 chènshān shirt; blouse:花～ bright-coloured blouse

衬套 chèntào 〈机械〉bush; bushing:隔离～ dividing bushing /减震～ shock absorbing bushing

衬托 chèntuō set off; serve as a foil to:金色的镜框将油画～得很美。The gold frame sets off the painting very well. /小说中叛徒的可耻行径～出爱国志士的崇高品质。The shameless acts of the traitor serve as a foil to the noble qualities of the patriots in the novel.

衬胸 chènxiōng stomacher

衬页 chènyè endpaper; endleaf

衬衣 chènyī underclothes; underwear; shirt; blouse

衬映 chènyìng set off:朱墙碧瓦互相～。The vermilion walls and the green tiles set off each other.

衬纸 chènzhǐ slip sheet; interleaving paper

衬字 chènzì word inserted in a line of verse for balance or euphony

谶 chèn 〈书面〉augury (in the form of predictions or omens)

谶记 chènjì written prophecies believed to have been fulfilled

谶纬 chènwěi divination by augury and mystical interpretation of Confucianist texts (prevalent during the Eastern Han Dynasty):～之学 esoteric study of auguries and Confucianist texts (for prophecies)

谶语 chènyǔ prophecy believed to have been fulfilled:昔日戏谑之言竟成～。The words I said in a playful mood turned out to be a fulfilled augury.

趁(趂) chèn ❶ take advantage of; avail oneself of:我们～此机会向东道主表示诚挚的感谢。We wish to take this opportunity to extend our hearty thanks to the hosts. /他～别人不注意的时候偷偷溜走了。He sneaked away while nobody took any notice of him. ❷〈方言〉own; possess:～几头牲口 own (*or* have) a few draught animals ❸〈书面〉chase; pursue:山蜂～人。Mountain bees chase after people.

趁便 chènbiàn when it is no extra trouble; when it is convenient:我出差去上海时要～看望几位老朋友。When I am on a business trip to Shanghai, I will call on some old friends there.

趁火打劫 chènhuǒ-dǎjié plunder a burning house; take advantage of sb.'s misfortune to make trouble; fish in troubled waters:别人有难,他不但不肯帮助,而且还～。He not only refused to help out when people were in trouble, but unashamedly cashed in on their difficulties.

趁机 chènjī *also* "趁机会" seize the chance (to do sth.):～调整计划 seize the chance to readjust the plan /～捣乱 make use of the opportunity to start trouble

趁空 chènkòng when one has time to spare; in one's leisure or spare time:～学习英语 study English in one's spare time /～到底下转一转。Go and see people at the grass roots when you've time to spare.

趁亮儿 chènliàngr before dusk falls:～开始吧。Let's start before dark.

趁坡 chènpō 〈口语〉take advantage of a favourable situation; seize the opportunity:～下驴 seize the opportunity to back down

趁钱 chènqián 〈方言〉have lots of money; be rich:他的老板很～。His boss is rolling in money. /你趁几个臭钱有什么了不起的! What is there to be proud of, even if you have some stinking money!

趁热打铁 chènrè-dǎtiě strike while the iron is hot; make hay while the sun shines:这件事要～,抓紧进行。You must take advantage of the opportunity to speed up the matter.

趁墒 chènshāng when there is sufficient moisture (in the soil):～下种 go ahead with the sowing when there is sufficient moisture in the soil

趁势 chènshì make the best of the opportunity when it arises:他见经理有兴致,就～把自己的主意全盘说了出来。He promptly brought forward his entire plan when he found the manager was interested.

趁手 chènshǒu 〈方言〉when it is no extra trouble:你离开时请～把灯关上。Please turn off the lights before you leave.

趁水和泥 chènshuǐ-huóní get down to business when conditions are favourable; make hay while the sun shines

趁心 chènxīn to one's heart's content; satisfactory:找一个～郎君 find a husband after one's heart

趁圩 chènxū 〈方言〉go to a rural fair

趁愿 chènyuàn have one's wish fulfilled:这次没有～,他自是很不甘心。He was naturally quite unhappy about the frustration of his plans.

趁早 chènzǎo as soon as possible; at an early date; better sooner than later:这事得～儿打个主意。We'd better make a prompt decision about the matter. /你气色不太好,～去看看大夫。You look a bit off colour. You'd better go and see a doctor right away.

龀 chèn 〈书面〉(of a child) grow permanent teeth:始～ begin to grow permanent teeth

称(稱) chèn fit; match; suit:相～ be well-matched /匀～ symmetrical; well-proportioned /这顶帽子和你的上衣不相～。The hat doesn't match your jacket. 他的行为同一个外交官的身分是不相～的。His behaviour is incompatible with the status of a diplomat. *see also* chēng

称对 chènduì (of man and woman) match; suit:这两个年轻人很～。The young couple are a perfect match.

称钱 chènqián *also* "趁钱" chènqián have lots of money; be rich

称身 chènshēn fit:你穿这套西服很～。This suit fits you well. *or* This suit is a beautiful fit (for you).

称体裁衣 chèntǐ-cáiyī *also* "量体裁衣" liàngtǐ-cáiyī cut the cloth according to one's measurements; act in conformity with the circumstances

称心 chènxīn find sth. gratifying; give complete satisfaction:日子过得很～ live contentedly /买一对～的花瓶 get a pair of vases one fancies

称心如意 chènxīn-rúyì *also* "称心遂意" after one's own heart; to one's heart's content:他很想找一个美丽的、～的配偶。He hoped to find a pretty girl after his own heart. /问题解决得好,大家都～。The problem was settled to the satisfaction of all parties concerned.

称意 chènyì gratifying; satisfactory:不～ unsatisfactory /快心～

after one's own heart

称愿 chènyuàn feel gratified (esp. at the misfortune of a much-hated person)：他被免了职，大家都～。People were gratified at his dismissal from office.

称职 chènzhí qualified; competent：～的教师 qualified (*or* competent) teacher / 作为学者他是有成就的，但是作为教师他是不～的。He is a success as a scholar, but a failure as a teacher.

chen

伧(傖) chen *see* "寒伧" hánchen

see also cāng

chēng

琤 chēng

琤琤 chēngchēng 〈书面〉〈象声〉 jangling; twanging; gurgling：涧流～ gurgling creek / ～的吉他声 twang of a guitar

琤瑽 chēngcōng 〈书面〉〈象声〉 clink (of jade pieces); gurgling (of flowing water)：玉佩～ clink of jade ornaments knocking together / ～的小溪 gurgling of a stream

赪(赬) chēng 〈书面〉 red; vermillion

瞠 chēng 〈书面〉 *see* "撑" chēng

see also chèng

撑(撐) chēng ❶ prop up; support：～起身子 prop oneself up / 两手～着下巴沉思 be deep in thought, with one's chin held in both hands / 护士～着病人的头，让他喝些水。The nurse propped up the patient's head to give him a drink of water. ❷ move (a boat) with a long pole pushed against the bottom of the river：～船 pole a boat; punt ❸ maintain; keep up：这几根柱子～不住这破房子。These props can't keep up (or sustain) the tottering house. / 他病得实在～不住了。He is so ill that he can't hold out any longer. / 听了她的话，老张～不住笑了。On hearing her words, Lao Zhang couldn't help laughing. ❹ open; unfurl：～开雨伞 open an umbrella ❺ fill to the point of bursting：吃～了 be full up; be bursting at the seams / 上衣太瘦，～破了。The jacket has burst; it is such a tight fit. ❻ 〈机械〉 brace; stay：角～ corner brace

撑臂 chēngbì 〈机械〉 brace; supporting arm

撑场面 chēng chǎngmiàn *also* "撑门面" keep up appearances：为了～，他常常不能量入为出。He often lives beyond his means just to keep up appearances. / 一个饭店总要有一两个像样的厨师～。A restaurant has to have a couple of master chefs to give it a boost.

撑持 chēngchí prop up; shore up; sustain：～摇摇欲坠的政权 shore up a tottering regime / 没有资金，这个店如何～？How can we keep the store going without funds? / 这个家～不了多久了。The family can't hold on much longer.

撑得慌 chēngdehuang have eaten so much as to feel uncomfortable：我吃得太多，～。I have eaten so much that I'm bursting at the seams. / 他就爱管闲事，吃多了～。He always pokes his nose into others' business; maybe he has too much extra energy.

撑杆 chēnggān ❶ flexible long pole：～跳 pole vault ❷ 〈机械〉 stay bar; stay-pole

撑竿跳高 chēnggān tiàogāo *also* "撑竿跳" 〈体育〉 pole jump; pole vault：～运动员 pole-vaulter

撑篙 chēnggāo long wood or bamboo pole for punting a boat; punt pole

撑门面 chēng ménmian *see* "撑场面"

撑木 chēngmù 〈矿业〉 gallows timber; stull

撑死 chēngsǐ 〈方言〉 at the outside limit; at most：这堆西红柿～也就一公斤。These tomatoes will weigh one kilo at the outside limit. / 这件上衣～不过一百元。The jacket is worth 100 *yuan* at most.

撑台 chēngtái 〈方言〉 support; back up; bolster; buttress：要是没人～，她一天也混不下去。She couldn't last for a single day if she had no backing.

撑条 chēngtiáo 〈机械〉 stay：斜～ diagonal stay / 横～ cross stay

撑腰 chēngyāo support; back up; bolster：～打气 bolster and pep up / 大胆去干吧，大家给你～。Go ahead! We are all behind you.

撑柱 chēngzhù 〈矿业〉 jack post

瞠 chēng 〈书面〉 stare

瞠乎其后 chēnghū-qíhòu stare helplessly without being able to catch up：他在前面飞速奔跑，我们几个人～。He raced ahead while the rest of us lagged helplessly behind.

瞠目 chēngmù stare (as in fear or embarrassment)：～以对 stared blankly in reply / ～不知所答 stare tongue-tied

瞠目结舌 chēngmù-jiéshé stare tongue-tied; be amazed and speechless：她被问得～。The questions put her on the spot. / 他的一番高论，弄得大家～。Amazed by his glibness, we were all at a loss for words. / 眼前的情景使他脸色苍白，～地靠在墙上。He turned pale at the sight and leant against the wall tongue-tied.

瞠然 chēngrán dumbfounded; dazed：～木立 stare blankly transfixed to the ground; stand frozen with wide-open eyes / ～若失 feel dumbfounded; be at a loss

瞠视 chēngshì stare in fear or surprise; stare with astonishment：他惊得两眼～，不知所措。He stared with astonishment, at a loss what to do.

铛(鐺) chēng pan：饼～ pan

see also dāng

称[1](稱) chēng ❶ call; style：自～ call (*or* style) oneself / 人们～他为"胖子"。People call him "Fatty". / 他～得上是个英雄。He deserves the title of hero. ❷ name：俗～ popular name / 湖南省简～湘。"Xiang" is the abbreviation for Hunan Province. / 四川素～"天府之国"。Sichuan has long been known as the "Kingdom of the Heaven". ❸ say; state：满口～是 say "yes" again and again / 据消息灵通人士～ according to well-informed sources ❹ 〈书面〉 praise; commend：～叹不已 praise profusely / ～贤举能 commend the virtuous and promote the capable / 这座城市以风景优美著～。The city is noted for its beautiful scenery.

称[2](稱) chēng weigh：用秤～一～ weigh sth. in the balance / 把盐～出来零售 weigh out the salt for retail / 给我～一公斤橙子。One kilo of oranges, please. / ～～西瓜有多重。See how much the watermelon weighs.

称[3](稱) chēng 〈书面〉 raise：～觞祝寿 raise one's drinking vessel to toast sb.'s health; drink a toast to sb.'s health

see also chèn

称霸 chēngbà play the bully; seek or maintain hegemony; dominate：～世界 dominate the world / 永不～ never seek hegemony / ～一方 wield influence and exercise control over a region / ～地方的恶棍 local bully

称便 chēngbiàn find sth. to be a great convenience：游客无不～。Tourists all consider it a great convenience. / 宾馆服务周到，旅客～。The hotel provides excellent service to the satisfaction of all guests.

称兵 chēngbīng 〈书面〉 launch a military attack：～邻国 launch a military expedition against a neighbouring state

称病 chēngbìng plead illness：长期～ have long been absent on the excuse of illness / ～不出 claim to be ill and stay at home / 他～不肯会客。Pleading illness, he declined to see visitors.

称臣 chēngchén swear fealty (to a feudal ruler)

称大 chēngdà vaunt one's seniority; put on airs：他喜欢在年轻人面前～。He simply loves to vaunt his seniority before youngsters.

称贷 chēngdài borrow money from others：～度日 live by borrowing from others

称道 chēngdào speak approvingly of; commend; praise：值得～ be praiseworthy / 无足～ be not worthy of praise; be of little consequence / 他办事公道，人人～。He is praised for being fair in handling matters.

称得起 chēngdeqǐ deserve to be called; be worthy of (the name)：她～我公司的秀才。She is worthy of the name of the firm's best writer.

称帝 chēngdì proclaim oneself emperor

称孤道寡 chēnggū-dàoguǎ look upon oneself as the supreme leader; assume the airs of a leader：他这样的人居然也～起来了。It's ridiculous, isn't it, that a man like him should be strutting about

and assuming the airs of a leader.

称号 chēnghào title; name; designation: 她获得了优秀教师的光荣～。She won the glorious title of best (*or* model) teacher. /先进工作者的～对我来说实在受之有愧。I'm truly unworthy of the title of advanced worker.

称贺 chēnghè congratulate: 登门～ call on sb. to offer one's congratulations

称呼 chēnghu ❶ call; address: 我们应该怎么～他? What should we call him? *or* How should we address him? /论年龄,我得～您"叔叔"。So far as age is concerned, I should call you uncle. ❷ form of address; way in which one is addressed: "老兄"是熟人之间常用的一种～。"Buddy" is a form of address often used among acquaintances.

称斤掂两 chēngjīn-diānliǎng *also* "称斤约两" calculate carefully; weigh the pros and cons

称快 chēngkuài express one's satisfaction: 拍手～ clap one's hands with satisfaction /主犯落网,人人～。People were wild with joy at the news that the archcriminal had been captured.

称量 chēngliáng measure an object's weight: 他试举的杠铃经过～,正好是151.5公斤。The weight of the barbell he used for a trial lift has been checked; it is exactly 151.5 kgs.

称量体重 chēngliáng tǐzhòng 〈体育〉 weighing-in

称美 chēngměi 〈书面〉 enumerate sb.'s merits: ～颂德 extol sb. for his virtues /交相～ exchange praise

称奇 chēngqí speak admiringly of; regard as amazing: 啧啧～ praise sb. profusely (for his superb ability, skill or performance)

称庆 chēngqìng congratulate: 额手～ raise one's hands in jubilation; be wild with joy

称赏 chēngshǎng commend; praise; speak highly of: 他的学位论文颇得导师～。His graduation thesis was highly rated (*or* commended) by his supervisor. /他办事认真,领导颇为～。The leadership praised him for his conscientious work.

称述 chēngshù narrate; mention; describe: 这种花品种繁多,难以一一～。There are so many varieties of the flower that it would take too much time to describe them one by one. /我的那点事不足～。What little I have done is not worth mentioning.

称说 chēngshuō name; describe: 人们用种种美好的字眼来～各种不同的菊花。People have beautiful names for various kinds of chrysanthemums.

称颂 chēngsòng praise; extol; eulogize; pay tribute to: 大加～ heap praises upon sb.; extol (*or* commend) sb. profusely /人们～他的业绩。Everybody pays tribute to his outstanding achievements. /他没有因为人们的～而陶醉。He didn't indulge in illusions about himself because of popular eulogy.

称叹 chēngtàn praise; admire: 连声～ praise again and again /他对杂技演员的精湛技艺啧啧～。He was full of admiration for the superb skill of the acrobatic performers.

称王 chēngwáng proclaim oneself king

称王称霸 chēngwáng-chēngbà act like an overlord; lord it over; domineer: 我们决不能关起门来自吹自擂,～。We should not brag about ourselves behind closed doors and try to lord it over other people.

称为 chēngwéi be called or named: 食盐在化学上～氯化钠。Salt is called sodium chloride in chemistry.

称谓 chēngwèi appellation; form of address; title: 时代不同,～常发生一些变化。Forms of address often change with the times.

称羡 chēngxiàn admire; envy: ～不已 admire boundlessly /他的博学令人～。His erudition commands admiration.

称谢 chēngxiè thank: 点头～ nod one's thanks

称兄道弟 chēngxiōng-dàodì call each other brothers; be on very good terms: 二人～,吃喝不分。The two are on intimate terms, sharing food and drink with each other.

称雄 chēngxióng exercise control over a region by sheer force; be dominant: ～一时 hold a dominant position for a period of time /割据～ break away from the central authorities and exercise exclusive control over a locality /二十年来,这位画家一直～于艺坛。For twenty years this painter has been the leading light in the art circles.

称许 chēngxǔ praise; commendation: 他的近作受到同行们的～。His latest work received the praise of his colleagues.

称扬 chēngyáng extol; admire: 极口～ speak in lavish praise of

称引 chēngyǐn 〈书面〉 quote: ～史实以论证观点 quote historical facts to back up one's argument

称誉 chēngyù sing the praises of; praise; acclaim: 人们～他是"人民诗人"。He was acclaimed as a "people's poet".

称赞 chēngzàn praise; acclaim; commend: 外国专家～葡萄长得好。The foreign expert spoke in glowing terms of the excellent condition in which the grapes were growing. /在一片～声中,他保持了冷静的头脑。He kept cool amidst cheers from all round.

偁 chēng

〈书面〉 *see* "称[1]" chēng

柽(檉) chēng

柽柳 chēngliǔ *also* "三春柳" sānchūnliǔ; "红柳" hóngliǔ 〈植物〉 Chinese tamarisk

蛏(蟶) chēng

〈动物〉 razor clam: 竹～ razor shell

蛏干 chēnggān dried razor clam

蛏田 chēngtián razor clam bed; razor clam farm

蛏子 chēngzi razor clam

噌 chēng

see also cēng

噌吰 chēnghóng 〈书面〉 (of bells and drums) booming: ～之声,不绝于耳。The continual booming of the bells lingered in one's ears.

chéng

枨(棖) chéng

〈书面〉 touch

枨触 chéngchù 〈书面〉 ❶ touch: 以手～之 touch it with one's hand ❷ move; impress: ～甚深 be deeply impressed

成[1] chéng

❶ accomplish; succeed: 完～ achieve; accomplish /此事必～。This is bound to succeed. /功到自然～。Constant effort yields sure success. ❷ help sth. to materialize; help sb. to achieve sth.: 玉～其事 help bring a matter to success ❸ become; turn into: 切～两半 cut sth. in half (*or* into halves) /纸烧～灰。The paper was burned to ashes. /他～了街头谈论的中心。He has become the talk of the town. /～什么话? What will people say? ❹ achievement; result: 坚持下去,事必有～。Perseverance means success. ❺ fully developed; fully grown: 长大～人 have grown up; become an adult /树大～材。The trees have grown into useful timber. ❻ established; ready-made: 既～事实 established facts; *fait accompli* /墨守～规 stick to conventions; stay in a rut ❼ in considerable numbers or amounts: ～千上万栋楼房 tens of thousands of buildings /～捆的报纸 bundles of newspapers /～天～夜地抢修铁路 race against time in repairing the railway; work round the clock to rush-repair the railway ❽ OK; all right: ～不～? Is that all right? *or* Will that do? /什么时候都～。Any time will do. /～了,我答应了。OK, I promise. /你不去可不～。No. You must go. ❾ able; capable: 你真～,竟然把他说通了。It was really smart of you to bring him around. ❿ (Chéng) a surname

成[2] chéng

one tenth; ten per cent: 九～九的金子 99% gold /七～新 seventy per cent new /增产一～ ten percent increase in output; the output has increased by ten per cent

成案 chéng'àn ❶ precedent: 无～可循。There's no precedent to fellow. ❷ legal precedent; judicial precedent

成败 chéngbài success or failure: ～在此一举。Success or failure hinges on this final effort. /不以～论英雄。Do not judge a person by his success or failure in the world. *or* Let no worldly success or failure be the criterion of a person's ability. /这项工作的～关系全局,务必重视。Great attention must be paid to this task whose success or failure has a direct bearing on the over-all situation.

成败利钝 chéngbài-lìdùn success or failure, plain sailing or rough going: ～,在所不计。We will not ask (*or* do not care) whether this will lead to success or end up in failure.

成报 Chéngbào (HK) *Sing Pao Daily News*

成本 chéngběn cost: 降低～ reduce (*or* cut) the cost /不计～ regardless of the cost /生产～ production cost /固定～ fixed cost /可变～ variable cost /直接～ direct cost /总～ aggregate cost /单位产品～ cost per unit product /劳务～ cost of labour /可控～ controllable cost /混合～ mixed cost /边际～ marginal cost /～因素 cost factor /～、保险和运费 cost, insurance and freight (CIF) /投产两年,收回全部～。

The cost was fully recovered (*or* recouped) in two years after the article went into production.
成本参数 chéngběn cānshù cost parameter
成本分析 chéngběn fēnxī cost analysis
成本工程师 chéngběn gōngchéngshī cost engineer
成本管理 chéngběn guǎnlǐ cost control or management:《~条例》Regulations on Cost Management
成本核算 chéngběn hésuàn cost accounting or calculation
成本核算单位 chéngběn hésuàn dānwèi cost accounting unit
成本价格 chéngběn jiàgé cost price
成本结构 chéngběn jiégòu cost structure
成本会计 chéngběn kuàijì cost accounting:~师 cost accountant
成本推动型通货膨胀 chéngběn tuīdòngxíng tōnghuò péngzhàng cost-push inflation:~论 theory of cost-push inflation
成本效率 chéngběn xiàolǜ cost effectiveness or efficiency
成本效益 chéngběn xiàoyì cost benefit:~分析 cost-benefit analysis
成本意识 chéngběn yìshi cost-consciousness
成本账 chéngběnzhàng cost account
成本折耗 chéngběn zhéhào cost depletion
成本指数 chéngběn zhǐshù cost index
成才 chéngcái become an accomplished or talented person:自学~ become an accomplished person through self-study; be self-taught / 父母希望他早日~。His parents hope that he will soon become a useful citizen.
成材 chéngcái ❶ grow into useful timber; grow to full size:这种树数年之后即可~。This kind of trees can grow into useful timber in a few years. ❷ become a useful person:老师总是希望每个学生都能~。Every teacher hopes that his pupils will eventually become useful members of society.
成材林 chéngcáilín standing or mature timber
成虫 chéngchóng 〈动物〉imago; adult
成仇 chéngchóu become enemies; turn hostile (to each other):反目~ fall out and become enemies
成丁 chéngdīng (of men) come of age; become an adult:古代十六为~。In ancient China a young man came of age at sixteen.
成洞 chéngdòng *also* "成腔"〈医学〉cavitation
成都 Chéngdū Chengdu, capital of Sichuan Province
成堆 chéngduī form a pile; be in heaps:~的白菜 heaps of cabbage / ~的砖瓦 piles of bricks and tiles / 问题~。Problems are piling up. *or* We have a whole heap of trouble.
成对 chéngduì be in pairs:成双~ pairs of men and women / ~核子 paired nuclei / ~联想法 method of paired association
成法 chéngfǎ ❶ established laws and decrees ❷ conventional method; recipe
成方 chéngfāng 〈中医〉set prescription; ready recipe
成分 chéngfen *also* "成份" ❶ composition; component part; element; ingredient:土壤~ composition of the soil / 化学~ chemical composition / 这个结论含有主观~。There is an element of subjectivism in the conclusion. / 香烟都含有尼古丁~。All cigarettes contain a certain amount of nicotine. ❷ one's class status, original or current; one's profession:~不好 of bad class status / 他的~是教师。His status is that of a teacher. / 过去,人们往往错误地强调个人~和家庭出身。In the past people often made the mistake of stressing a person's social origin and family background.
成风 chéngfēng become a common practice; become the order of the day:助人为乐蔚然~。It has become a common practice to render help readily. / 如今集邮~。Stamp-collecting is all the rage today. / 这里一度赌博~。Gambling was once prevalent here.
成佛 chéngfó become a Buddha; attain Buddhahood:立地~ attain Buddhahood instantly
成服 chéngfú ❶〈旧语〉〈书面〉mourning dress worn by the relatives of the deceased:遵礼~。Mourning dresses were worn in observance of funeral rituals. ❷ ready-made clothes; off-the-peg or off-the-rack clothes:~一般要便宜些。Off-the-rack clothes are usually cheaper.
成皋之战 Chénggāo Zhī Zhàn *also* "楚汉成皋之战" Chǔ-Hàn Chénggāo Zhī Zhàn first major battle between Xiang Yu (项羽) and Liu Bang (刘邦), fought at Chenggao and Xingyang (荥阳) in present Henan from 205-203 BC, won by Liu Bang against great odds
成个儿 chénggèr ❶ grow to a good size:苹果~了。The apples have grown to a good size. ❷ be in the right shape; be well formed or shaped:我余的丸子不~。The meat balls I prepared do not seem to be in the right shape. / 他的字写得不~。The characters he writes are shapeless. *or* His handwriting is a scribble.
成功 chénggōng success:演出~ successful performance / 取得初步~ score initial success / 试制~一种新产品。A new product has been successfully trial-produced. / 良好的开端,是~的一半。A good beginning is half the battle. *or* Well begun is half done. / 祝你~。Wish you success.
成骨细胞 chénggǔ xìbāo 〈医学〉osteoblast
成规 chéngguī established practice; set rule; groove; rut:突破~ break set rules / 墨守~ stick to conventions; get into a rut / 他的操作符合~。His operation conforms to established practice.
成果 chéngguǒ achievement; fruit; gain; positive result:劳动~ fruit of one's labour / ~累累 an abundance of achievements (*or* results) / 谈判取得了~。The negotiations have achieved positive results.
成裹 chéngguo 〈方言〉make; complete:这几块破板子一~起来就是件有用的家具。These old boards can be made into a very useful piece of furniture.
成红细胞 chénghóngxìbāo 〈医学〉erythroblast:~瘤 erythroblastoma
成化 Chénghuà Chenghua, title of the reign (1465-1487) of Zhu Jianshen (朱见深), 9th emperor of the Ming Dynasty, called reverently Ming Xianzong (明宪宗) after death
成婚 chénghūn get married:他们是前年~的。They got married the year before last.
成活 chénghuó survive:充足的水分是树苗~的关键。Abundant water is essential to the survival of saplings.
成活率 chénghuólǜ survival rate
成绩 chéngjì result; achievement; success:公布考试~ publish examination results / 评定学生的学业~ evaluate the achievements of the students / 我们工作中的~是主要的。What we have achieved in our work merits primary consideration. / 有了~不能骄傲。We should not get conceited over what we have accomplished. / 不能满足已有的~。One must not rest on one's laurels.
成绩单 chéngjìdān *also* "成绩册" school report; report card
成吉思汗 Chéngjísīhán Genghis Khan (1162-1227), born Temujin (铁木真), founder of the vast Mongol empire of the Middle Ages
成家 chéngjiā ❶ (of a man) get married:他~了吗? Is he married? ❷ become a recognized authority *see also* "成名成家"
成家立业 chéngjiā-lìyè get married and start one's career:孩子们如今都已长大成人,~了。Now the children are all grown up with families and careers of their own.
成见 chéngjiàn preconceived idea; bias; prejudice:消除~ remove prejudices / 固守~ be prejudiced (*or* biased, *or* opinionated) / 不要有~。You should rid yourself of any bigotry. / 他俩~极深。The two of them have deep-rooted prejudices against each other.
成交 chéngjiāo strike a bargain; conclude a transaction; clinch a deal:拍板~ strike a bargain / 一宗成衣出口的大买卖即将~。A deal on the export of large quantities of garments is to be clinched.
成交额 chéngjiāo'é volume of business
成交欺诈 chéngjiāo qīzhà gazump, or demand a higher price after the original price has been accepted
成就 chéngjiù ❶ achievement; accomplishment; attainment; success:卓有~的科学家 scientist of great attainments / 艺术~ artistic merits / 在数学方面取得了突出~ score outstanding successes in mathematics ❷ achieve; accomplish:~革命大业 accomplish a great revolutionary task / 他用毕生精力~了这部不朽著作。He devoted his whole life to writing this immortal work.
成句 chéngjù ❶ ready sentence (from previous writing):古人的~ ready quotation (*or* sentence) from ancient writings ❷ form a complete sentence:英语说不~ speak broken English
成矿 chéngkuàng 〈矿业〉mineralize:~作用 mineralization; metallogenesis / ~带 metallogenic belt / ~理论 metallogenic theory / ~时期 mineralization (*or* metallogenic) period
成矿构造 chéngkuàng gòuzào 〈矿业〉ore-forming structure
成矿区 chéngkuàngqū 〈矿业〉metallogenic province or region
成了 chéngle ❶ be all right or OK; do:屋子粉刷成这个样子也就~。It's all right to have the room whitewashed like this. ❷ sufficient; enough:有这么多原料~,多了浪费。That's enough; too much material would be a waste. ❸ succeed; be done:试验终于~。The

C

experiment succeeded at last. /事情~。The thing's done.

成礼 chénglǐ ❶ go through a ceremony:草草~ bring the ceremony to a hasty end; hurry through a ceremony ❷ have one's wedding;hold one's wedding ceremony; get married:匆匆~ marry in haste

成立 chénglì ❶ establish; found; set up:宣告中华人民共和国~ proclaim the founding of the People's Republic of China /书法研究会~起来了。A calligraphy society has been set up. /昨天出版社开~大会。The publishing house held its inaugural meeting yesterday. ❷ be tenable; hold water:这个新说法可以~。The new thesis is tenable. /你的结论根据不足,~不了。Your conclusion cannot stand for lack of evidence. /这个估计能不能~,还要看一看。We'll have to wait and see if the estimate will hold water.

成例 chénglì precedent; existing model:援引~ cite a precedent; quote an authoritative example /请查一查此事有无~可援。Please check up and see if there are any precedents to follow in this case.

成粒器 chénglìqì 〈机械〉granulator

成殓 chéngliàn encoffin:死者~事毕。The deceased has been encoffined.

成林 chénglín (of trees) grow into a wood:几年功夫,这一片小树已长大~。In a few years the young trees have grown into woods.

成龙配套 chénglóng-pèitào also "配套成龙" combine the different parts into a whole; complete a system or chain:使灌溉工程~ complete an irrigation system /这里农用机械不少,可惜没有~。There is a lot of farming machinery around here, but unfortunately it doesn't form a complete set.

成寐 chéngmèi 〈书面〉fall asleep; go to sleep:浮想联翩,夜不~。Thoughts thronged my mind and I could not sleep.

成眠 chéngmián fall asleep; go to sleep:思念往事,不能~。Reflecting on the past, I could hardly fall asleep. /他心事重重,终夜不能~。Weighed down with worries, he lay awake through the night.

成名 chéngmíng establish one's reputation; make a name for oneself:~作 work that establishes one's reputation; work that brings the author instant fame /他以小说~。He became famous for his novels. or He established his reputation as a novelist. /时无英雄,使竖子~。The absence of outstanding figures brought that bloke to the fore. or A mediocrity like him comes to the fore for lack of talented people.

成名成家 chéngmíng-chéngjiā establish one's reputation as an authority; establish oneself as a recognized authority:一心想~ have a burning desire for fame and (academic) recognition /这位教授三十年前就已~了。This professor made a name for himself and became a recognized authority as early as thirty years ago.

成命 chéngmìng order already issued; decision already announced:收回~ countermand (or retract) an order; revoke a command /此事按~处理。The matter is to be handled in accordance with the issued instructions.

成年 chéngnián ❶ grow up; come of age:未~ be under age /在中国,年满十八岁为~。In China, a person comes of age at eighteen. ❷ adult; grown-up:~教育 adult (or continuing) education /~树 grown tree ❸〈口语〉year in and year out; year after year; all the year round:他们~劳累,仅得温饱。Toiling all the year round, they barely managed to keep body and soul together.

成年累月 chéngnián-lěiyuè year in year out; for years and years:勘探队员们~在荒山野岭工作。Year in and year out, the surveyors worked in remote mountainous areas.

成年人 chéngniánrén adult

成批 chéngpī group by group; in batches:~的学生 groups of students /~的新产品 batches of new products /~生产 mass production; serial production /新产品已~投放市场。New products are on the market in large quantities.

成品 chéngpǐn end or finished product:~质量 quality of the end product /半~ semifinished products /从原料到~ from raw material to finished product

成品合格证 chéngpǐn hégézhèng certificate of quality of finished product

成品检验 chéngpǐn jiǎnyàn finished product testing

成品粮 chéngpǐnliáng processed grain (like rice, flour, etc.)

成气候 chéng qìhòu be hopeful; be promising (often used in the negative):不~ will get nowhere /连这么点小事也犹犹豫豫的,真成不了气候。You won't get anywhere if you hesitate over such trifles.

成器 chéngqì grow up to be a useful person:但愿这些青年将来能~。I wish these youth would prove really useful in the future. /玉不琢,不~。A piece of jade cannot be made into anything valuable unless it is carved. or The finest diamond must be cut.

成千成万 chéngqiān-chéngwàn also "成千上万" tens of thousands; thousands upon thousands; myriad:~的人群拥向街头。Thousands of people spilled into the streets.

成亲 chéngqīn 〈口语〉get married:他还未~。He is not yet married. /他俩什么时候成的亲? When did they get married?

成寝 chéngqǐn fall asleep:夜不~ fail to get a wink of sleep at night; spend a sleepless night

成趣 chéngqù be of interest:这位老人画画,涉笔~。Whatever the old man paints, it forms a picture of some interest. /湖光塔影,相映~。The reflection of the pagoda in the shimmering lake presents a scene of exquisite beauty.

成全 chéngquán help sb. (achieve his aim):~好事 help bring about a happy event /尽一切力量来~她 do everything possible to help her succeed /你得~~我! You must help me out.

成群 chéngqún in large numbers; in crowds:~的孩子 hordes of children /~的游客 swarms of tourists /~的人拥入广场。Crowds of people swarmed into the square. /二人结伴,三人~。Two's company, three's a crowd.

成群结队 chéngqún-jiéduì in crowds:来参观这个小型展览的人~。Crowds of visitors swarmed to the small exhibition.

成人 chéngrén ❶ grow up; become full-grown:长大~ be grown to manhood /抚养~ bring sb. up ❷ adult; grown-up:~男装 men's clothes

成人高考 chéngrén gāokǎo exams for adults to gain degrees or certificates (usu. at the bachelor's or associate's level) through self-study:~教材 textbooks for adult education

成人教育 chéngrén jiàoyù adult or continuing education:~部 department of continuing education

成人之美 chéngrénzhīměi help sb. to fulfil his wish; help sb. in doing a good deed or achieving sth. desirable:君子~。A gentleman is always ready to help others fulfil their wishes.

成仁 chéngrén 〈书面〉die for a righteous cause:杀身~ die a martyr's death /不成功,便~ fulfil one's mission or die a martyr's death; succeed or die

成日 chéngrì 〈方言〉all day long; all the time; the whole day:~成夜 day and night /他为何~蹲在家里? Why does he stay at home all day long?

成三破二 chéngsān-pò'èr 〈旧语〉3 percent from buyer, 2 percent from seller (in real estate transactions, the commission for a broker was 5 per cent of the total amount, the buyer paying 3 per cent and the seller 2 per cent)

成色 chéngsè ❶ percentage of gold or silver (in a coin, etc.); relative purity of gold or silver:这个金项链的~高。This gold necklace contains a high percentage of gold. ❷ quality:这块料子的~很好。This material is of good quality.

成纱车间 chéngshā chējiān 〈纺织〉bundling and baling room

成式 chéngshì formula

成事 chéngshì ❶ succeed; accomplish sth.:~之后,定当重谢。When this is accomplished, I shall express my thanks by a big reward. /谋事在人,~在天。The planning lies with man, the outcome with Heaven. or Man proposes, God disposes. ❷〈书面〉sth. that is finished or past; bygones:~不说。Let bygones be bygones.

成事不足,败事有余 chéng shì bùzú, bài shì yǒuyú accomplish nothing oneself but can very well serve as a mischief-maker; not able to accomplish anything but quite capable of ruining it; never make but always break:这个人~,这种大事不能交给他。The guy can never make but always break; he must not be entrusted with such an important task.

成实 chéngshi 〈方言〉(of seeds) full; plump:稻穗沉甸甸的,个个子粒~。The ears of rice are hanging heavy, all with plump kernels.

成手 chéngshǒu 〈方言〉old hand; past master:他赶车可是把~。He is a skilled cart driver.

成书 chéngshū ❶ finish (writing a book); appear in book form:《本草纲目》~于明代。The *Compendium of Materia Medica* was written in the Ming Dynasty. /这些零散的史料,已有人搜辑~。These scattered historical data have been collected and compiled into a book. ❷ book already in circulation

成熟 chéngshú ripe; mature:不~的水果 unripe fruit /智力~ intellectually mature /秋天是谷物~季节。Autumn is the season of ripen-

ing crops. /时机～。The time is ripe. /条件～。The conditions are ripe. /意见很不～。This may not be a well-considered opinion.
成熟产业 chéngshú chǎnyè mature industry
成熟分裂 chéngshú fēnliè maturation division
成熟林 chéngshúlín mature forest
成熟期 chéngshúqī 〈农业〉mature period
成数 chéngshù ❶ round number:五、十、二百、三千等都是～。Five, ten, two hundred and three thousand are all round numbers. ❷ ratio; percentage:这种酒含酒精的～小。This liquor contains a small percentage of alcohol.
成双 chéngshuāng form a pair:鸳鸯～地嬉水。The mandarin ducks and drakes swam about in pairs.
成说 chéngshuō accepted theory or formulation:科学家要勇于创新,不可囿于～。It is important for scientists to break new ground and refuse to be fettered by accepted theories.
成讼 chéngsòng go to court (to settle a dispute):双方因版权争执而～。They went to court over a copyright dispute.
成诵 chéngsòng be able to recite by rote; be able to repeat from memory; have a retentive memory:过目～ able to repeat from memory what one has just read
成俗 chéngsú become social custom or convention
成算 chéngsuàn preconceived idea or plan:已有～ have already worked out a plan (about how to go about sth.)
成套 chéngtào form a complete set:～课本 complete set of textbooks /～唱腔 complete score for voices (in an opera) /引进～项目 introduce whole plants /这些仪器都是～的。These instruments form a complete set.
成套转让 chéngtào zhuǎnràng package transfer
成体 chéngtǐ 〈动物〉adult
成天 chéngtiān 〈口语〉all day long; all the time:楼上人家～放音乐,闹得四邻不安。The family upstairs plays music all the time and the neighbours cannot have a moment's quiet.
成土母质 chéngtǔ mǔzhì *also* "母质";"亚土" yàtǔ 〈地质〉parent material; matrix; mother material
成为 chéngwéi become; turn into:～学者 become a scholar /把我国建设～现代化强国 turn our country into a powerful modern state /他由一个农民～一个企业家。He used to be a farmer, but has since become an entrepreneur.
成文 chéngwén ❶ existing writings:抄袭～ copy ideas or sections from a book or article ❷ written:年度计划已有～。The annual plan is in written form.
成文法 chéngwénfǎ 〈法律〉written law; statute law; statutory law:～典 code of written law; written code /～律 codified law
成问题 chéng wèntí be a problem; be open to question or doubt:技术水平～。The technical level is a problem. /产品销路不～。Marketing of the product presents no problem. /旅馆的服务态度真～。The hotel service is really a headache.
成细胞作用 chéngxìbāo zuòyòng 〈生物〉cellulation
成仙 chéngxiān become an immortal
成想 chéngxiǎng (often used in the negative) expect
see also "承想" chéngxiǎng
成像 chéngxiàng formation of image; imagery
成像系统 chéngxiàng xìtǒng imaging system:立刻～ instant imaging system
成效 chéngxiào effect; result:卓有～ highly effective /～显著 produce a marked effect; achieve remarkable success /坚持就会有～。Perseverance yields results.
成心 chéngxīn intentionally; on purpose; deliberately:～捣蛋 make trouble on purpose /他～跟你过不去。He was deliberately making things difficult for you. /你～拆我的台。You intentionally pulled the rug from under my feet. /你可别～气我! You'd better not provoke me.
成行 chéngxíng go on a trip:友好访日团将于年底～。The goodwill mission will visit Japan by the end of the year.
成形 chéngxíng ❶ develop a definite form (either by natural growth or by processing); take shape:浇铸～ pour molten steel into a mould /新建中的公寓大楼已经～。The new apartment house has begun to take shape. /文章初稿已经～。The first draft is completed. ❷〈医学〉repair damaged tissues or organs:骨～术 osteoplasty ❸〈医学〉have a normal shape:大便～。The stool is normal in shape.
成形刀具 chéngxíng dāojù 〈机械〉forming tool or cutter
成形机 chéngxíngjī 〈机械〉shaper; shaping machine
成形切削 chéngxíng qiēxiāo form-cutting
成形外科 chéngxíng wàikē plastic surgery
成形压力机 chéngxíng yālìjī forming press
成型 chéngxíng shaping; forming:爆炸～ explosive forming /冷滚～ cold roll forming /经多道工序产品才～。The product has to go through a series of processes to be shaped.
成型轧制 chéngxíng zházhì formation rolling
成型铸件 chéngxíng zhùjiàn mould casting
成性 chéngxìng by nature; become second nature:侵略～ aggressive by nature /这班人虚伪～了。It is second nature for these people to speak and act hypocritically.
成宿 chéngxiǔ 〈口语〉all night:～的不睡觉,那怎么行。It won't do to stay up all night.
成岩作用 chéngyán zuòyòng 〈地质〉diagenesis
成样儿 chéngyàngr 〈口语〉❶ take shape or form:再有几天,这座大型雕塑就快～了。A few more days of work, and the giant sculpture will take shape. ❷ (often used in the negative) seemly; presentable:她闹得太不～了! What an unseemly scene she has made!
成药 chéngyào medicine ready-made by a pharmacy; patent medicine:中～ ready-made traditional Chinese medicine
成也萧何,败也萧何 chéng yě Xiāo Hé, bài yě Xiāo Hé the same person can contribute to both your success and downfall; success and failure (of sb. or sth.) are both due to the same person or factor
成夜 chéngyè 〈口语〉all night:～不睡 stay up all night
成衣 chéngyī ❶ tailoring ❷ ready-made clothes
成衣匠 chéngyījiàng tailor; dress maker
成衣铺 chéngyīpù tailor's shop; tailor's
成议 chéngyì agreement already reached:这个问题双方已有～。The two sides have already reached an agreement on this issue.
成因 chéngyīn cause (of formation); contributing factor:海洋的～ causes of the formation of the ocean /这次通货膨胀的～很复杂。The contributing factors of the current inflation are rather complicated. *or* The current inflation has been brought about by a series of complex factors.
成阴 chéngyīn *also* "成荫" (of trees) give shade:路边杨树都已～。The poplars on either side of the road are already tall enough to give shade.
成鱼 chéngyú adult fish
成语 chéngyǔ set phrase; idiom:汉语的～很丰富。The Chinese language is rich in idiomatic expressions. /要恰当地使用～。Idioms must be used properly.
成员 chéngyuán member:家庭～ family member /科研小组～ members of a scientific research group
成员国 chéngyuánguó member state:有几个～没有参加投票。Several member states did not participate in the voting.
成约 chéngyuē existing agreement:两国边界问题应按～解决。The boundary question between the two countries should be settled in accordance with the existing agreements.
成灾 chéngzāi cause disaster:暴雨～ disaster brought by torrential rain /会议～ deluge of meetings
成则为王,败则为寇 chéng zé wéi wáng, bài zé wéi kòu *also* "成者为王,败者为寇" the winner is the king, the loser a bandit; losers are always in the wrong; nothing succeeds like success
成章 chéngzhāng ❶ constitute a good piece of writing:下笔～。One's words flow as if from the pen of a master. ❷ logical; systematic:这是顺理～的事。It is the logical conclusion of the matter. *or* This follows as a matter of course.
成长 chéngzhǎng ❶ grow up; grow to maturity:健康～ healthy growth; sound growth /前年栽的果树还没有～好。The fruit trees planted the year before last have not grown to maturity yet. /他已～为出色的工程师。He has grown into a fine engineer. ❷〈方言〉development; growth:～率 growth rate /经济～加速 accelerating growth of the economy
成长股 chéngzhǎnggǔ growth stock
成竹在胸 chéngzhú-zàixiōng have well-thought-out ideas
see also "胸有成竹" xiōngyǒu-chéngzhú
成总儿 chéngzǒngr 〈口语〉❶ in lump sum:～付钱 pay in a lump sum ❷ in quantities; in bulk:～买 buy in quantities

宬 chéng archives:皇史～ Imperial Archives

C

C

诚 chéng ❶ sincere; honest:开~相见 treat each other sincerely /以~待人 treat people with sincerity ❷〈书面〉actually; really:~非易事 be by no means an easy task /此~危急存亡之秋也。This is indeed a time of grave national crisis.

诚笃 chéngdǔ extremely sincere:情意~ exceedingly sincere feelings; feeling of implicit faith and sincerity

诚服 chéngfú comply in earnest; have genuine admiration:心悦~ be genuinely convinced of sb.'s superiority (*or* righteousness)

诚惶诚恐 chénghuáng-chéngkǒng (formerly used as a set formula in an official's memorial to the emperor) in fear and trepidation:他们都~,小心翼翼地行事,生怕出什么差错。Awe-stricken, they all acted with the utmost caution, lest something might go wrong. /如此重要的工作竟然落到了我身上,真让我~。It fills me with awe that I have been entrusted with such an important task.

诚恳 chéngkěn sincere; earnest:待人~ treat people earnestly and sincerely /~地接受批评 accept criticism in all sincerity /表示~的感谢和敬意 extend to sb. one's heart-felt thanks and respect

诚朴 chéngpǔ simple and honest:~的农民 simple and honest farmer

诚悫 chéngquè〈书面〉honest; sincere

诚然 chéngrán ❶ indeed; truly; really:这里河网纵横,~是个鱼米之乡。Crisscrossed by streams and lakes, the area is indeed a land of plenty. ❷ to be sure; admittedly:问题~不少,但总有办法解决。True, there are quite a lot of problems, but we can always find solutions. /~,他是很聪明的,但有时却过了头。To be sure, he is clever, but he sometimes overreaches himself.

诚实 chéngshí honest:~可靠 honest and dependable /说话~ speak candidly (*or* honestly) /没有~的狐狸,没有不吃人的老虎。There are no guileless foxes any more than there are friendly tigers.

诚心 chéngxīn ❶ sincere desire; wholeheartedness:一片~ in all sincerity /他的帮助完全出于~。He offered his help out of complete sincerity. ❷ sincerely; earnestly:~劝告 sincerely advise /~悔过 repent earnestly

诚心诚意 chéngxīn-chéngyì earnestly and sincerely; in all sincerity

诚信 chéngxìn faith; honesty:以~为本 take honesty as one's cardinal principle /刘先生素重~。Mr. Liu always honours his word.

诚意 chéngyì good faith; sincerity; bona fides:以实际行动来表示自己的~ show one's sincerity (*or* good faith) by actual deeds /他的一番~,感动了老人。The old man was moved by his sincerity. /双方都没有~,谈判怎能成功? How could the negotiations succeed in the absence of good faith on both sides?

诚挚 chéngzhì sincere; cordial:~的祝愿 sincere wishes /怀着~的感情 cherish sincere feelings /~的友谊 genuine friendship /~的谢意 heartfelt gratitude /会谈在~友好的气氛中进行。The talks proceeded in a cordial and friendly atmosphere.

城 chéng ❶ city wall; wall:长~ Great Wall /~外 outside the city; outside the city wall /金~汤池 impregnable fortified city ❷ city:东~ eastern part of the city ❸ (as opposed to 乡) town:县~ county town / 省~ provincial capital /山~ mountain city

城邦 chéngbāng city-state

城堡 chéngbǎo castle; citadel

城标 chéngbiāo symbol of a city

城池 chéngchí〈书面〉city wall and moat; city:一座古老而坚固的~ ancient and solidly-built city

城雕 chéngdiāo sculptures placed in a city's public places

城堞 chéngdié *also*“城垛”battlements

城垛 chéngduǒ *also*“城垛口”;“城垛子”❶ parapet; rampart ❷ battlements

城防 chéngfáng city defence:巩固~ strengthen the defence of a city /~工事 defence works of a city /~部队 city garrison

城府 chéngfǔ〈书面〉subtlety or astuteness of mind; sophistication; native shrewdness:~很深 astute; sophisticated /胸无~ unsophisticated /颇具~的政治家 astute (*or* shrewd) politician

城根 chénggēn sections of a city close to the city wall:皇~ sections close to the wall of the imperial palace

城关 chéngguān area just outside a city gate

城郭 chéngguō inner and outer city walls; city walls:~巍峨 imposing city walls

城壕 chéngháo moat

城狐社鼠 chénghú-shèshǔ *also*“社鼠城狐”fox in the city wall and rat in the village temple — evildoers with strong backing

城隍 chénghuáng ❶〈书面〉moat ❷ town god; city god:~庙 town god's temple

城建 chéngjiàn urban construction:~规划 city planning; urban planning

城郊 chéngjiāo outskirts of a town:~有所农业大学。There is an agricultural university on the outskirts of the town.

城里 chénglǐ inside the city; in town:~人 townspeople; city dweller /~生活 city life; urban life /到~去买东西 go shopping in town

城楼 chénglóu gate tower:天安门~上宫灯高悬。Palace lanterns hang on Tian An Men gate tower.

城门 chéngmén city gate

城门失火,殃及池鱼 chéngmén shīhuǒ, yāng jí chí yú when the city gate is on fire, the fish in the moat will suffer — innocent people often fall victim to what others do; be a scapegoat for sb. else's wrongdoing

城濮之战 Chéngpú Zhī Zhàn *also*“晋楚城濮之战”Jìn-Chǔ Chéngpú Zhī Zhàn Battle of Chengpu, in which the State of Jin defeated the State of Chu in 633 BC and its king became the hegemon of all the feudal states

城墙 chéngqiáng city wall

城区 chéngqū city proper:~高楼林立。There is a forest of tall buildings in the city proper. /~空气不新鲜。The air in the city area is polluted.

城圈 chéngquān area of a town:那是一座边关古城,~并不大。As an ancient border town, it is naturally not large in area.

城阙 chéngquè〈书面〉❶ watch tower on either side of a city gate ❷ palace:~金碧辉煌。The palace is resplendent and magnificent.

城市 chéngshì town; city:工业~ industrial city /消费~ consumer city /~居民 city dwellers; urban population /~规划 urban planning; town planning /~建设 urban construction /~环境 urban environment /~住宅区 urban residential area; uptown (area) /~美容师〈婉词〉(environmental) sanitation worker

城市化 chéngshìhuà urbanization

城市经济学 chéngshì jīngjìxué urban economics

城市科学 chéngshì kēxué urban science

城市贫民 chéngshì pínmín urban poor; city poor; pauper

城市生态学 chéngshì shēngtàixué urban ecology

城市学 chéngshìxué urbanology:~家 urbanologist

城台 chéngtái raised platform on top of a city wall built for defence purposes; city wall platform

城头 chéngtóu ❶ top of a city wall:站在~可以望见远处蜿蜒的河流。If you stand on the city wall, you can see the winding course of the river in the distance. ❷ gate tower; tower over a city gate

城下之盟 chéngxiàzhīméng treaty concluded with the enemy outside the city wall; terms accepted under duress:结~ sign a treaty with the enemy when they are at the city gate; accept harsh terms under duress (*or* pressure)

城乡 chéng-xiāng urban and rural areas; town and country; city and countryside:~并重 laying equal stress on urban and rural areas /~差别 difference between town and country /~结合 integration of town and country /~结合部 area joining town and country /~人民的收入成倍增长 multiple increase of the income of the urban and rural population

城乡交流 chéng-xiāng jiāoliú exchange (of goods, etc.) between the city and the countryside; interflow between town and country

城厢 chéngxiāng city proper and area outside its gates:~一带变化很大。Great changes have taken place in and around the city. /地近~,该地区人口稠密。Close to the urban area, this district is densely populated.

城邑 chéngyì〈书面〉town; city

城垣 chéngyuán〈书面〉city wall

城运会 chéngyùnhuì (short for 城市运动会) city sports meet

城镇 chéngzhèn cities and towns:~商业区 downtown area of a city or town /~失业人口 urban unemployed /~户口 urban residence registration

城址 chéngzhǐ townsite

盛 chéng ❶ fill; ladle:~稀饭 ladle out porridge /给我~一碗饭。Give me a bowl of rice. ❷ hold; contain:车厢能~一百五十人。

The compartment can hold 150 people. /缸里～着水。The jar is filled with water. /箱子～了许多旧瓷器。The box contains a lot of old china.
see also shèng
盛殓 chéngliàn encoffin
盛器 chéngqì vessel; container:给我找个装废品的～来。Get me a container for the junk.

呈

chéng ❶ assume (form, colour, etc.); manifest:液体～黄色。The liquid is yellow in colour. /他面～不豫之色。His face took on a vexed expression. ❷ submit; present:谨～ respectfully submit ❸ petition; memorial:这个农民只好找个秀才替他写了个～儿。This peasant had to ask a local scholar to write a petition for him.
呈报 chéngbào report to (one's superior, etc.) in writing:计划已～上级审查。The plan has been submitted to the higher level for examination. /立即向上～。Report to the higher authorities at once.
呈递 chéngdì present; submit:～国书 present one's credentials (*or* letter of credence) /～报告 submit a report /～公文 present an official document /～申请书 submit (*or* file) an application
呈览 chénglǎn submit (sth. to a higher authority) for perusal
呈露 chénglù show; present; exhibit:～出雄伟庄严的气概 present a spectacle of grandeur and magnificence /丰收景象～眼前。Before us is a picture of a bumper harvest. /到处～出一片荒凉。A scene of desolation meets the eye everywhere.
呈请 chéngqǐng apply (to higher authorities for consideration or approval):～辞职 request to resign /办学事项须～上级批准。We must secure the approval of higher authorities for the setting up of new schools.
呈送 chéngsòng submit:此项目应～主管方面审批。The project must be submitted to the relevant authorities for approval.
呈文 chéngwén official document submitted to a superior; memorial; petition:递～ submit a petition
呈现 chéngxiàn present (a certain appearance); appear; emerge:当年与家人离别的情景又～在他眼前。The scene of parting with his family reappeared before his eyes. /海港～出一片紧张繁忙景象。The harbour bustled with activity. /雨后,田野～出一片碧绿。After the rain, the fields look like a carpet of bright green.
呈献 chéngxiàn respectfully present:～礼物 present a gift
呈祥 chéngxiáng 〈旧语〉bring good luck or felicity:龙凤～。The dragon and phoenix harbinger prosperity.
呈阅 chéngyuè submit for perusal (and approval):文件尚在～过程中。The documents are being circulated (among the leaders) for perusal and approval.
呈正 chéngzhèng *also* "呈政"〈敬词〉submit a piece of writing (to a friend) for criticism:特～于先生。Your criticisms (on my essay) are hereby requested.
呈子 chéngzi petition; appeal:递～ submit a petition

裎

chéng naked; with nothing on
see also chěng

埕[1]

chéng razor clam bed; razor clam farm

埕[2]

chéng 〈方言〉wine jar

酲

chéng 〈书面〉unconscious due to inebriation; drunken:解～ counteract the effect of alcohol /愁～ be weighed down by worry

程

chéng ❶ rule; regulation:章～ rules; constitution /操作规～ operation rules ❷ order; procedure:议～ agenda/进～ process ❸ journey; leg of a journey:登～ set out on a journey /全～ entire journey /送他一～ accompany sb. on the first leg of his journey (*or* part of the way) ❹ distance:远～ long-range; long-distance /中～ intermediate range; medium range /射～ range of fire /路～ distance travelled; journey /行～万里 travel a distance of 10,000 *li* /计～他今日可到广州。Judging by the distance, he ought to be in Guangzhou today. ❺〈书面〉measure; estimate:计日～功 measure achievements by the day ❻ (Chéng) a surname
程度 chéngdù ❶ level; degree:文化～ level of education; degree of literacy /觉悟～ level of political consciousness /达到大专毕业～ reach the level of junior college education /他对情况的熟悉～,令人吃惊。His familiarity with the situation is simply amazing. ❷ extent; degree:在一定～上 to a certain extent (*or* degree) /在不同～上 in varying degrees /破坏～很小。The extent of damage is very limited.
程颢 Chéng Hào Cheng Hao (1032-1085), Confucian philosopher and educator of the Northern Song Dynasty
程控 chéngkòng (short for 程序控制) program control:～设备 stored program control equipment /～机床 program-controlled machine tool
程控电话 chéngkòng diànhuà program-controlled telephone:～交换机 program-controlled exchange
程门立雪 Chéngmén-lìxuě (of a student) stand in snow at the gate of one's teacher's house; wait upon one's teacher with humble reverence
程式 chéngshì form; pattern; formula:公文～ forms and formulas of official documents /～动作 stylized movements (as in Beijing opera)
程式化 chéngshìhuà stylization; formulism:～表演形式 stylized forms of artistic performance /这几部小说有～倾向。These novels reveal a certain trend towards formulism.
程途 chéngtú distance of a journey
程限 chéngxiàn 〈书面〉❶ ready formula and limits:创作是没有一定的～的。There is no ready formula governing literary creation. ❷ prescribed progress; assignment:宽其～ relax the assignment /读书日有～。There is a daily reading assignment.
程序 chéngxù ❶ order; procedure; course; sequence:工作～ working procedure /会议～ procedure of a meeting /生产～ production procedure /医疗～ course of treatment /法律～ legal procedure /～问题 point of order /～性动议 procedural motion /机器按照规定的～进行操作。The machine operates according to a set programme. ❷〈计算机〉program:～分配 program allocation /～分析 program analysis /～区 program area /～卡 program card /～校验 program check; program checkout /～计数器 program counter /～文件 program file /～流程图 program flow diagram /～方式 program mode/～包 program (*or* routine) package /～参数 program parameter /～系统 program system /～设计技术 programming technique /～编制器 program compiler /～存储器 program memory (*or* storage) /～寄存器 program register /～库 program (*or* routine) library /修改～ program modification
程序处理机 chéngxù chǔlǐjī program processor
程序法 chéngxùfǎ 〈法律〉procedural law; adjective law
程序复制 chéngxù fùzhì program copy
程序管理 chéngxù guǎnlǐ program management
程序机 chéngxùjī 〈计算机〉scheduler
程序兼容 chéngxù jiānróng program compatibility
程序教学 chéngxù jiàoxué programmed instruction; programmed learning
程序可控只读存储器 chéngxù kěkòng zhǐdú cúnchǔqì Programmable Read Only Memory (PROM)
程序控制 chéngxù kòngzhì program control:～控制器 program controller
程序控制计算机 chéngxù kòngzhì jìsuànjī 〈计算机〉program-controlled computer; sequence-controlled computer
程序设计 chéngxù shèjì 〈计算机〉program(m)ing:～语言 program(m)ing language
程序时钟 chéngxù shízhōng program clock
程序谈判 chéngxù tánpàn formula bargaining
程序信息块 chéngxù xìnxīkuài program information block
程序语法 chéngxù yǔfǎ program syntax
程序语言 chéngxù yǔyán program language
程序员 chéngxùyuán *also* "程序设计员"〈计算机〉programmer
程序指令 chéngxù zhǐlìng program instruction
程序转换 chéngxù zhuǎnhuàn program conversion
程仪 chéngyí 〈书面〉gift from a relative or friend meant to cover one's travel expenses; gift for a departing friend
程颐 Chéng Yí Cheng Yi (1033-1107), Confucian philosopher, educator and younger brother of Cheng Hao, considered to be one of the founders of the *Li* school of Confucianism (理学)
程子 chéngzi 〈方言〉period of time:呆一～ stay for a while /老张那～精神特别好。Lao Zhang was in a very good mood at the time. /这～他很忙。At present, he is pretty busy.

乘[1] chéng ❶ ride:～车 ride in a car /～马 ride a horse /～船 go by boat /～公共汽车到火车站 go to the railway station by bus /旅游团～飞机去杭州。The tourist group is going to Hangzhou by plane. ❷ (often replaced in colloquial speech by 趁) avail oneself of; take advantage of:～胜前进 advance on the crest of a victory; push on in the flush of victory /～人不备 take sb. by surprise /～夜出击 attack under cover of night ❸〈佛教〉main division of Buddhism:大～ *Mahayana*, the "greater vehicle" /小～ *Hinayana*, the "lesser vehicle" ❹ (Chéng) a surname

乘[2] chéng multiply:长～宽 length by width /二～四等于八。Two times four is eight.
see also shèng

C

乘便 chéngbiàn when there is a chance; when it means no extra trouble; at one's convenience:请你～给我捎封信。Please take a message for me at your convenience. /路过北京,～逛逛王府井百货大楼。You may as well go window-shopping in the Wangfujing Department Store when you stop over in Beijing.

乘除 chéngchú ❶ multiplication and division; calculations:他肚里另有～。He has his own calculations. ❷〈书面〉vicissitudes

乘法 chéngfǎ 〈数学〉multiplication

乘法表 chéngfǎbiǎo multiplication table

乘法器 chéngfǎqì 〈计算机〉multiplier; multiplying unit

乘方 chéngfāng 〈数学〉❶ involution ❷ *also* "乘幂" power:N 的五次～ fifth power of N; N(raised) to the power of 5 (*or* N^5)

乘风凉 chéng fēngliáng 〈方言〉enjoy the cool

乘风破浪 chéngfēng-pòlàng ride the wind and cleave the waves; brave the wind and waves:那船～,很快就消失在远方。Braving the wind and waves, the ship is fast disappearing in the distance. /我们的事业正～,迅猛向前。We are riding on the crest of a wave and making rapid headway in our undertaking.

乘号 chénghào 〈数学〉multiplication sign

乘火打劫 chénghuǒ-dǎjié loot a burning house; take advantage of a state of emergency for selfish ends; fish in troubled waters

乘机 chéngjī seize the opportunity:～行事 act according to the circumstances; act when an opportunity offers itself /～反驳 seize the opportunity to give a retort

乘积 chéngjī *also* "积"〈数学〉product

乘积累加器 chéngjī lěijiāqì 〈计算机〉product accumulator

乘坚策肥 chéngjiān-cèféi drive a solidly-built carriage or ride a sturdy horse — live in clover or extravagance

乘间 chéngjiàn make use of one's spare time; seize an opportunity:～窃发 seize an opportunity to secretly launch (an attack, etc.)

乘间伺隙 chéngjiàn-sìxì exploit a loophole or watch for an opening (to do evils)

乘警 chéngjǐng train police

乘客 chéngkè passenger:车厢里～十分拥挤。The compartment is crowded with passengers.

乘凉 chéngliáng enjoy the cool; relax in a cool place:在花园里～ enjoy the cool in a garden /夏天晚上,乡亲们常在大树下～。The villagers often relax in the shade of a big tree on summer evenings.

乘龙 chénglóng (of a woman) ride a dragon — be happily married to a brilliant young man:～快婿 son-in-law with a bright future

乘幂 chéngmì 〈数学〉power
see also "乘方 ❷"

乘骑 chéngqí ❶ sit on horseback:把马让给病员～ give one's horse to an invalid to ride ❷ horse ❸ rider

乘人之危 chéngrénzhīwēi take advantage of sb.'s precarious position:他是惯于～的卑劣小人。He's a mean fellow ready to pounce upon anybody in trouble.

乘时 chéngshí make use of an opportunity

乘势 chéngshì avail oneself of a favourable situation:～前进 press on at an opportune moment; advance when the situation is favourable

乘数 chéngshù 〈数学〉multiplier

乘务 chéngwù service on airliners, trains, buses, etc.:～组 crew (of a train or plane)

乘务员 chéngwùyuán attendant on a train; steward or stewardess; conductor or conductress

乘隙 chéngxì get hold of a loophole; seize the opportunity:～而入 sneak in when people are off guard

乘兴 chéngxìng while one is in high spirits:～一直爬到山顶 climb all the way to the top of the hill in a happy mood /～而来,兴尽而归 one arrives in ebullient good spirits and does not depart till one has thoroughly enjoyed oneself /～而来,败兴而归 set out cheerfully and return disappointed

乘虚 chéngxū take advantage of a weak point or an opening in an opponent's defence; act when sb. is off guard:～直闯篮下投中得分 dash under the basket and score a goal when there is an opening in the opponent's defence

乘虚而入 chéngxū'érrù break through at a weak point:你身体虚弱,疾病就～。Disease will attack you as soon as you become weak physically.

乘员 chéngyuán crew (member); passenger

乘员舱 chéngyuáncāng 〈航天〉crew module; manned module

乘晕宁 chéngyùnníng 〈药学〉dramamine

乘子 chéngzǐ 〈数学〉multiplicator; multiplier

乘坐 chéngzuò take (a plane or boat); ride (in a train or vehicle):～飞机 take a plane; travel by plane /～轮船 take a ship; travel by ship /～公共汽车 take a bus; ride in a bus; travel by bus

椉 chéng 〈书面〉*see* "乘" chéng
see also shèng

塍(堘) chéng 〈方言〉path between fields

惩(懲) chéng ❶ punish; penalize:严～贪污犯 severely punish embezzlers ❷〈书面〉guard against; warn:～忿窒欲 suppress one's anger and check one's desire

惩办 chéngbàn punish; penalize:严加～ mete out severe (*or* rigorous) punishment /～杀人凶手 severely punish the murderer /实行～少数改造多数的原则 carry out the principle of punishing the few and reforming the many

惩处 chéngchǔ punish; penalize:依法～罪犯 punish a criminal in accordance with the law /贪污受贿者,一律依法～。All embezzlers and bribe-takers will be dealt with according to law.

惩创 chéngchuàng 〈书面〉penalize; punish

惩恶劝善 chéng'è-quànshàn punish evildoers and encourage people to do good

惩罚 chéngfá punish; penalize:因犯罪受到～ be punished for an offence /免于～ exempt from punishment /违背科学是会受到～的。Those who act against science will come to grief.

惩罚权 chéngfáquán power of punishment; punitive power

惩羹吹齑 chénggēng-chuījī burnt child dreads the fire; once bitten, twice shy; overcautious

惩教署 Chéngjiàoshǔ (HK) Commission of Correctional Services:～署长 Commissioner of Correctional Services

惩戒 chéngjiè punish as a warning (either to the delinquent himself or to others); discipline as a warning:工厂给他记过一次,是对他的及时～。The factory management put his error on record as a timely warning to him.

惩前毖后 chéngqián-bìhòu learn from past mistakes to avoid future ones:批评的目的是为了～,治病救人。The purpose of criticism is to help people learn from past mistakes and avoid future ones, and to cure the sickness to save the patient.

惩劝 chéngquàn *also* "惩恶劝善" punish evildoers and encourage people to do good:～不明则风俗污浊。Indiscriminate punishment and encouragement will contaminate the moral atmosphere.

惩一警百 chéngyī-jǐngbǎi *also* "惩一儆百" punish one to warn a hundred; make an example of sb.:狠狠打击首犯,以收～之功效。Severe punishment of the chief culprit is aimed at warning others.

惩艾 chéngyì 〈书面〉punish; penalize

惩膺 chéngyīng 〈书面〉go on a punitive expedition or send a punitive force against a recalcitrant vassal state

惩治 chéngzhì punish; mete out punishment to:～腐败官吏 punish corrupt officials

澄(澂) chéng ❶ (of water, etc.) clear; transparent; limpid:～江似练。A limpid river resembles a scarf of white gauze. ❷ clear up; clarify:～心 purify the heart

see also dèng
澄碧 chéngbì clear and blue: 海天～。The sky and sea are azure and clear. /湖水～。The lake is crystal-clear and blue.
澄彻 chéngchè *see* "澄澈"
澄澈 chéngchè *also* "澄彻" transparently clear; limpid: ～的月光 bright moonlight /潭水～。The pond is transparently clear.
澄净 chéngjìng fresh and clear: 空气～。The air is fresh and clear.
澄静 chéngjìng clear and calm: 一泓～的潭水 a pool of clear, serene water
澄空 chéngkōng cloudless sky: ～无际。The cloudless sky stretches to infinity.
澄明 chéngmíng clear and bright: 河水～。The river is bright and crystal-clear.
澄清 chéngqīng ❶ clear; bright: ～的溪水 transparent brook/湖水～。The lake is crystal clear. ❷ purify; put an end to: ～混乱局面 put an end to a chaotic situation /～吏治 stamp out political corruption ❸ clear up; clarify: ～事实 clarify facts /～误会 clear up misunderstanding
see also dèngqīng
澄莹 chéngyíng 〈书面〉 crystal-clear; limpid: 溪水～。The brook is clear and bright.
澄湛 chéngzhàn 〈书面〉 clear and transparent: 月色～如水。The moonlight is as transparent as water.

橙 chéng ❶ orange: ～树 orange tree /甜～ sweet orange /酸～ sour (*or* bitter) orange ❷ orange (colour)
橙红 chénghóng orange red
橙黄 chénghuáng orange: 桌子的颜色是～的。The desk is orange in colour.
橙皮苷 chéngpígān *also* "橘皮苷" júpígān 〈生化〉 hesperidin
橙子 chéngzi orange (fruit)

承 chéng ❶ hold; bear; carry: 这几根柱子～住了房顶的巨大压力。The columns bear the heavy weight of the roof. ❷ undertake; contract (to do a job): ～做家具 undertake to make furniture /～印名片 contract to print visiting cards; undertake the printing of visiting cards ❸ 〈套语〉 be indebted (to sb. for a kindness); be granted a favour: 多～照顾 be indebted to sb. for his kindness /～您过奖。You flatter me. /昨～热情招待，不胜感激。I am deeply grateful for the cordial hospitality you showered on me yesterday. ❹ continue; carry on: 继～ inherit; carry on /子～父业。The son carries on his father's business. / 汉～秦制。The Han Dynasty inherited the institutions of the Qin Dynasty. ❺ accept (orders, instructions, advice, etc.): 敢不～命〈套语〉 dare not refuse to comply with your instructions; cannot but do as you say ❻ (Chéng) a surname
承办 chéngbàn undertake: ～汽车维修业务 undertake automobile maintenance service /～宴席 undertake catering /～单位是市卫生局。The responsible organization is the Municipal Bureau of Public Health.
承包 chéngbāo contract: ～单位 contracting unit /～工程 undertake contracted projects /～基数 base quota of a contract /～十亩稻田 contract to farm 10 *mu* of rice paddy /各种形式的～经营 various kinds of contractual operations /把工程～给一家建筑公司 contract a project out to a building company /把房屋维修工作～给房屋维修工 contract with the house maintenance workers for the repairs
承包合同 chéngbāo hétong contract
承包商 chéngbāoshāng contractor
承包田 chéngbāotián land contracted by a farmer for cultivation
承包责任制 chéngbāo zérènzhì system of contracted responsibility; contract system
承包制 chéngbāozhì contracting system: 家庭联产～ contracted responsibility system based on the household with remuneration linked to output
承保 chéngbǎo undertake or accept insurance: ～火险 undertake fire insurance /～人 insurer /～范围 insurance coverage /～通知书 (insurance) cover note
承保单 chéngbǎodān 〈商业〉 open cover
承尘 chéngchén ❶〈古语〉 canopy over a chair ❷〈方言〉 ceiling
承担 chéngdān undertake; bear; assume: ～风险 undertake (*or* run) risks /～一项重要使命 assume an important mission /～最大的牺牲 bear the greatest sacrifice /～起建设祖国的重任 shoulder the heavy task of building up one's motherland /对一切后果～全部责任 accept (*or* bear) full responsibility for all the consequences /～不首先使用核武器的义务 commit oneself (*or* undertake) not to be the first to use nuclear weapons
承当 chéngdāng ❶ take up; take on; bear: ～责任 bear the responsibility /他们希望经理一职由你来～。They all hope that you will take up the post of manager. ❷〈方言〉 promise; agree: 当时你对这件事曾一口～。You didn't hesitate to take charge at the time.
承德 Chéngdé city and summer resort in Hebei Province: ～避暑山庄 Qing Emperor's Summer Mountain Resort in Chengde
承佃 chéngdiàn 〈旧语〉 contract tenancy; rent land to farm: ～数亩薄田 rent a few *mu* of infertile land
承兑 chéngduì 〈经济〉 honour (a check, etc.); accept: ～汇票 accepting a draft; acceptance /～票据 accepting a bill; acceptance /此处～旅行支票。Traveller's cheques (are) cashed here.
承兑行 chéngduìháng accepting house
承兑人 chéngduìrén accepter
承兑信用证 chéngduì xìnyòngzhèng acceptance letter of credit; acceptance credit
承恩 chéng'ēn 〈旧语〉 be a grateful recipient of royal favours: ～邀宠 bask in the emperor's favour
承乏 chéngfá 〈书面〉〈谦词〉 take up a post (for lack of a better candidate): 副会长一职暂由我～。I'll have to take up the post of vice-president of the society for the time being.
承奉 chéngfèng accept and carry out (instructions, orders, etc.)
承付 chéngfù undertake to pay (a loan, etc.): 加工厂～全部贷款。The processing factory undertakes to pay the entire loan.
承购 chénggòu undertake to purchase: ～公债 undertake to buy government bonds; underwrite treasury bonds /产品由数家公司～包销。Its products are under contract with a few firms to sell exclusively.
承管 chéngguǎn take charge of; be responsible for: 此事当由有关部门～。This matter should be left in the charge of a relevant department.
承欢 chénghuān do everything possible to please (especially one's parents or sovereign): ～膝下 attend on one's parents at home
承继 chéngjì ❶ be adopted as heir to one's uncle: 他自小～给伯父。He was adopted by his uncle when a child. ❷ adopt one's brother's son (as one's heir): 他把弟弟的小儿子～了过来。He adopted his brother's youngest son as his heir. ❸ inherit: ～祖业 inherit ancestral property
承建 chéngjiàn (of a project) contract to construct: 宾馆由建筑公司～。A construction company has contracted to build the guesthouse.
承教 chéngjiào 〈书面〉 have the benefit of sb.'s instruction: 奉命～ have received instructions to seek your wise counsel
承接 chéngjiē ❶ hold out a vessel for liquid to be poured into it: 用脸盆～屋漏 hold (*or* place) a bowl to receive dripping water from the leak in the roof ❷ continue; carry on: ～上文 continued from the preceding paragraph /～对方的语气说 carry on talking in the same tone of the other party; take over the floor in the same tone of one's counterpart ❸ support; back up; prop up: 用臂膀～病人的后背 prop up the patient's back with one's own shoulder ❹ undertake; take in; accept: ～来料加工 undertake to process materials supplied /～文物修复业务 accept to restore artifacts to their original shapes
承揽 chénglǎn undertake or contract to do a job: ～合同 contract of work; contractor's agreement /建筑队～土建工程。The construction team contracts to build civil engineering projects.
承梁 chéngliáng 〈机械〉 bolster: 防松～ check bolster
承梁垫石 chéngliáng diànshí padstone
承领 chénglǐng accept an allotment: ～荒山办林场 receive an allotment of bare hills to run a forestry farm
承溜 chéngliù 〈书面〉 gutter (on a roof)
承蒙 chéngméng 〈书面〉 be granted a favour; be indebted (to sb. for a kindness): ～惠顾 be grateful to sb. for his patronage /～关照 be thankful to sb. for his kind attention /～鼎力相助，不胜感激。I'm deeply appreciative of your generous assistance.
承诺 chéngnuò promise; commit oneself (to do sth.); undertake to do: 已经～的任务，不能反悔。Since we have accepted the task, we cannot go back on our word.
承诺费 chéngnuòfèi commitment fee
承诺计谋 chéngnuò jìmóu 〈经济〉 (in negotiations) commitment

C

ploy
承诺人 chéngnuòrén accepter
承诺书 chéngnuòshū letter of undertaking (L/U); letter of commitment
承盘 chéngpán tray; plate:高脚～ high-based plate
承平 chéngpíng 〈书面〉 peaceful; tranquil:～岁月 piping times of peace /天下～,万民乐业。Peace reigns in the country with the people happily engaged in their own pursuits.
承前启后 chéngqián-qǐhòu see "承先启后"
承情 chéngqíng 〈套语〉 be much obliged; owe a debt of gratitude: 您给我的许多帮助,～不尽。I'll always remain indebted to you for your kind assistance in various ways.
承认 chéngrèn ❶ admit; recognize; acknowledge; concede:～现状 recognize the status quo /～失败 concede defeat /～他的工作能力 acknowledge sb.'s ability (*or* capability); do justice to his ability / ～党的章程 accept the Constitution of the Party /他～自己有缺点。He admitted he had shortcomings. /在证据面前,他不得不～自己的罪行。Faced with irrefutable evidence, he had to plead guilty. ❷ give diplomatic recognition; recognize:世界上许多国家都～了那个国家。Many countries in the world have recognized that state.
承上启下 chéngshàng-qǐxià *also* "承上起下" form a connecting link between the preceding and the following (as in a piece of writing, etc.):这段文字起～的作用。These lines serve as a link between what goes before and what comes after.
承审员 chéngshěnyuán trial judge (of a case)
承受 chéngshòu ❶ bear; endure; appreciate:～考验 endure every kind of trial /你的心意我～了,但东西我不能收。I fully appreciate your kindness, but I cannot accept the present. /这么大的压力,她～得住吗? Can she withstand such tremendous pressure? ❷ inherit (a legacy, etc.):她～了伯父的全部遗产。She inherited all her uncle's property.
承受能力 chéngshòu nénglì bearing capacity; affordability; tolerance; ability to sustain or forebear:超过人们的～ beyond the people's capacity to bear
承顺 chéngshùn be obedient to; submit to; obey:他是个很听话的小孩,事事～母亲。He is such a docile child that he is all obedience to his mother.
承索即寄 chéngsuǒ jíjì will be mailed (free) on request
承题 chéngtí second sequence (of three or four sentences) of an "eight-legged" essay; exposition of the theme
see also "八股" bāgǔ
承祧 chéngtiāo become heir (to one's uncle who has no son)
承头 chéngtóu 〈方言〉 take the lead:大家就盼望有你这么个人出来～呢。We have been expecting a person of your calibre to take the lead.
承托 chéngtuō bear the weight of; support; hold up:这个岩层下面有一层页岩～着。This rock stratum is supported by a layer of shale beneath. *or* A layer of shale lies beneath this rock stratum.
承望 chéngwàng (often used in the negative) expect:谁都认为这场足球准输,不～却赢了。They won the football match although everybody had predicted that they would lose.
承袭 chéngxí ❶ adopt; follow (a tradition, etc.):～前人的见解 adopt ideas of one's predecessors /～旧制 follow the old system (*or* convention)/社会发展有不断变化的一面,也有世代～的一面。Social development consists of both constant changes and the retention of traditions. ❷ inherit (a peerage, etc.):他～了父亲的地位和权力。He inherited the position and power of his father. /一个小孩子～了皇位。A young child succeeded to the throne.
承袭海 chéngxíhǎi 〈法律〉 patrimonial sea
承先启后 chéngxiān-qǐhòu *also* "承前启后" inherit the past and usher in the future; serve as a link between past and future:这位大师在语言研究上占有～的地位。The great master occupies a unique position in linguistic research, in which he combines traditional heritage and contemporary contributions.
承想 chéngxiǎng *also* "成想" chéngxiǎng (often used in the negative) expect:不～ contrary to one's expectations /没～会得到这样的结果。I didn't expect things would end up that way. /谁～今天又刮大风呢? Who would have thought it would be terribly windy again today?
承销 chéngxiāo 〈商业〉 consignment-in; consignment inward; underwriting:～货物 goods on consignment-in /～品 consigned goods; goods on consignment-in
承销费用 chéngxiāo fèiyòng underwriting expenses
承销人 chéngxiāorén sales agent; underwriter; consignee:～协议 agreement among underwriters /～预付款 advances from the consignees
承修 chéngxiū undertake to repair (machines, electric applicances, etc.):本店～各种电视机。We undertake to repair all kinds of TV sets.
承续 chéngxù inherit; carry on:～家产 inherit family property /～友好关系 carry on friendly relations
承颜 chéngyán 〈书面〉 ❶ win the favour of one's superiors (by observing their facial expression and acting accordingly):顺心～ win favour with one's superiors by conforming to their wishes; never contradict one's superiors ❷ 〈敬词〉 feel honoured to meet sb.:～接辞。I regard it as a great honour to meet you.
承印 chéngyìn undertake the printing of:～书刊 undertake the printing of books and periodicals
承印物 chéngyìnwù 〈印刷〉 stock
承迎 chéngyíng 〈书面〉 ❶ greet:笑面～ greet sb. with a smiling face ❷ cater to; pander to:～低级趣味 pander to vulgar tastes /～上级 suit one's words or action to one's superior
承应 chéngyìng agree to do; accept; promise:满口～ readily agree / 慨然～此项任务 readily accept the assignment
承允 chéngyǔn consent to; promise
承运 chéngyùn ❶ (of transport department) undertake transport services:行李～处 baggage check-in counter; baggage-handling counter ❷ 〈书面〉 (of a ruler) be ordained by Heaven:奉天～ be ordained by Heaven to rule
承运人 chéngyùnrén carrier
承载 chéngzài bear the weight of:～能力 bearing capacity; load-bearing capacity; carrying capacity
承造 chéngzào undertake to manufacture, build or construct for others:向航空公司交付～的四架客机 hand over to the airline the four passenger planes built for it /～商 contractor
承制 chéngzhì undertake to manufacture:将设计方案提交～单位鉴定。Submit the draft design to the manufacturing department for assessment.
承重 chéngzhòng bearing; load-bearing
承重墙 chéngzhòngqiáng 〈建筑〉 bearing or load-bearing wall
承重孙 chéngzhòngsūn eldest grand son (of the eldest branch) serving as chief mourner during grandparent's funeral when his father is already dead (thus acting in "doubly heavy" responsibility)
承重柱 chéngzhòngzhù 〈建筑〉 bearing column
承转 chéngzhuǎn forward (a document to the next level above or below):这个县给国务院的报告,省办公厅已及时～。The general office of the provincial government has promptly forwarded the county's report to the State Council.
承租 chéngzū contract to lease (shop, enterprise, etc.):～合同 contract for leasing; lease /～招标 invite biddings for lease
承租人 chéngzūrén lessee; tenant
承做 chéngzuò undertake to make garments, etc.:～各式男女服装 accept orders for men's and women's wear

丞 chéng 〈旧语〉 assistant; assistant officer:县～ county magistrate's assistant/府～ petty official in prefectural magistrate's office
丞相 chéngxiàng 〈书面〉 chief minister (in ancient China)

chěng

逞 chěng ❶ show off; flaunt:～威风 show off one's strength or power; swagger about /～英雄 pose as a hero /～本事 flaunt one's abilities ❷ carry out (an evil design); succeed (in a scheme):阴谋得～ succeed in a plot /以求一～ in a bid for success in the conspiracy ❸ indulge; give free rein to:～性妄为 be reckless in doing evil
逞脸 chěngliǎn 〈方言〉 ❶ be wilful and arrogant because one is in sb.'s good graces:你别～,这里不用你多嘴。Stop acting like a spoilt child and save your breath. ❷ spoil; pamper:我没有答应她的要求,怕逞了她的脸。I did not comply with her request so as not to spoil her.
逞能 chěngnéng show off one's skill or ability; parade one's ability:没有那个本事就别～! If you are not up to it, you'd better not try

to display your ability. *or* If you are not the stuff, you'd better be quiet! /这人爱～。This fellow is fond of showing off.
逞强 chěngqiáng flaunt one's superiority; exhibit one's power: ～蛮干 parade one's ability and act recklessly /～好胜 parade one's superiority and strive to outshine others
逞性 chěngxìng *also* "逞性子" act wilfully; be wayward; act on impulse: 希望你遇事冷静,再也不要～。We hope that you'll keep cool in all circumstances and not act on impulse.
逞凶 chěngxiōng act violently; go berserk: 在光天化日之下～行抢 commit robbery in broad daylight
逞臆 chěngyì 〈书面〉 be a mere conjecture: 此说～,不可凭信。This theory is not to be credited, for it is based entirely on conjecture.
逞嘴 chěngzuǐ 〈方言〉 boast; brag: 别～,做不好自己出丑。Stop boasting, or you'll be making a fool of yourself.

裎 chěng 〈古语〉 Chinese-style jacket with buttons down the front
see also chéng

骋 chěng 〈书面〉 ❶ gallop: 驰～ gallop about ❷ give free rein: ～望 look as far as one's eyes can see
骋怀 chěnghuái 〈书面〉 enjoy oneself to one's heart's content
骋目 chěngmù 〈书面〉 look into the distance: ～远望 scan distant horizons
骋足疾驰 chěngzú-jíchí run quickly; gallop

chèng

牚 chèng ❶ buttress: 给危房打～ buttress the crumbling houses with piles ❷ rung between two legs of a desk, table or chair
see also chēng

秤(称) chèng balance; steelyard: 用～称一称 weigh sth. in a balance (*or* on the scales) /杆～ steelyard; lever scales /地～ platform balance; platform scales /弹簧～ spring scales /案～ counter scales /重力～ gravity balance /市～ Chinese scale of weights /过～ weigh /开～ begin business /折～ (of goods) lose weight (in transit, storage, etc.) /压～ relatively heavy per unit volume
秤锤 chèngchuí *also* "秤砣" sliding weight of a steelyard
秤杆 chènggǎn arm or beam of a steelyard
秤钩 chènggōu steelyard hook
秤毫 chèngháo lighting cord of a steelyard
秤花 chènghuā 〈方言〉 *see* "秤星"
秤纽 chèngniǔ *see* "秤毫"
秤盘子 chèngpánzi pan of a steelyard
秤砣 chèngtuó 〈口语〉 sliding weight of a steelyard
秤星 chèngxīng gradations marked on the beam of a steelyard

chī

痴(癡) chī ❶ silly; idiotic; stupid; foolish: 白～ idiot; moron /他说这些糊涂话真有点发～。It was stupid of him to say such rubbish. ❷ be infatuated; be crazy: 书～ bookworm /情～ person who is head over heels in love ❸ 〈方言〉 deranged; insane; crazy: 由于这场悲剧,他已经变～了。The tragedy has unhinged his mind.
痴骇 chī'ái stupid; slow-witted: ～的表情 dull expression; blank look /～的样子 look stupid (*or* wooden-headed)
痴爱 chī'ài dote on: ～孙子 dote on one's grandson
痴呆 chīdāi ❶ silly; idiotic; stupid: 一副～相 look like an idiot /～的眼睛 glassy eyes ❷ deranged; crazy: ～儿童 mentally retarded children ❸ *see* "痴呆症"
痴呆症 chīdāizhèng dementia: 老年性～ senile dementia /早老性～ Alzheimer's disease /先天性～ congenital dementia
痴钝 chīdùn stupid; idiotic; dull-witted
痴肥 chīféi abnormally fat; obese: ～臃肿 corpulent and ugly
痴话 chīhuà silly words; nonsense: ～连篇 whole spiel of silly words /姑娘,你尽说～,那是不可能的事。You're talking nonsense, miss. What you suggested is just impossible.
痴狂 chīkuáng infatuation; obsession: 爱到了～的程度 love (sb. or sth.) to infatuation /如痴如狂 crazy with infatuation
痴愣 chīlèng be dazed; stare blankly; be in a trance: 他～地看着她,一句话也说不出来。He stared at her blankly, tongue-tied.
痴梦 chīmèng daydream; illusion; hallucination: 哪有那种好事,你是在做～吧! You must be daydreaming about pie in the sky!
痴迷 chīmí infatuated; obsessed; crazy: ～不悟 be so infatuated (*or* obsessed) as to be unable to shake free /～于声色 wallow in sensual pleasure /他陷入单相思,已经变得～了。Unrequited love has made him almost crazy.
痴男怨女 chīnán-yuànnǚ pining lovers (usu. those who for some reason cannot get married)
痴念 chīniàn foolishly sentimental attachment; wishful thinking; illusion
痴情 chīqíng ❶ deep passionate love; sentimental attachment; sentimental longing: 他是一片～。He is all passionate devotion. ❷ be sentimentally attached; infatuated: ～女子 foolishly (*or* mawkishly) sentimental girl; infatuated girl: 他对艺术太～了。He is obsessed with art.
痴人 chīrén idiot; fool: ～自有～福。Even idiots have their own blessings. *or* Fortune favours fools.
痴人说梦 chīrén-shuōmèng tale told by an idiot; idiot's daydream; idiotic nonsense: 时间将证明,他的话不过是～而已。Time will prove that his words are no more and no less than a tale told by an idiot.
痴傻 chīshǎ feeble-minded; stupid
痴头痴脑 chītóu-chīnǎo silly head and brain — idiotic and crazy
痴想 chīxiǎng ❶ be lost in thought or reverie: 他呆呆地～着,身上淋湿了也不觉得。He was so lost in thought that he didn't even feel the rain drenching him. ❷ wishful thinking; daydreaming; illusion: 指望他马上改变主意乃是一种～。It is daydreaming to expect him to change his mind right away.
痴笑 chīxiào give an idiotic laugh; giggle
痴心 chīxīn infatuation; obsession; adoring love: ～女子负心汉 innocent girl in deep love with a heartless man — favourite theme of traditional romances /不要辜负了她的一片～。Don't disappoint her adoring love for you. /真是一片～。It is a case of pure infatuation.
痴心妄想 chīxīn-wàngxiǎng illusion; wishful thinking; daydreaming: 如果你以为一切都会一帆风顺,那简直是～。It is sheer illusion if you believe that everything will be plain sailing. /不肯努力而想成名,岂不是～? To achieve fame without hard work — isn't it the fond dream of a fool?
痴愚 chīyú imbecility; idiocy: ～行为 imbecile act
痴长 chīzhǎng 〈谦词〉 be older; be sb.'s senior: 我虽比你～两三岁,但阅历却不如你丰富。I am two or three years your senior, but I don't have your rich experience.
痴滞 chīzhì (of one's expression) dull
痴子 chīzi 〈方言〉 ❶ idiot; fool; dupe ❷ mad person; lunatic
痴醉 chīzuì infatuated; fascinated; spellbound: 他的演唱,曾使不少少男少女～。His acting and singing held a lot of youngsters spellbound.

摛 chī 〈书面〉 spread; sprawl
摛藻 chīzǎo write in an ornate style; indulge in rhetoric: ～如春华 diction as colourful as spring flowers

螭 chī ❶ hornless dragon (a decorative motif) ❷ *see* "魑" chī

魑 chī 〈书面〉 (of ancient folklore) evil spirits dwelling in mountains
魑魅 chīmèi 〈书面〉 man-eating spirits in mountains
魑魅魍魉 chīmèi-wǎngliǎng demons and monsters; evil people of every description: 社会黑暗,～横行。As the society was dark, evil people ran amuck.

眵 chī gum (of the eye); gum-like excretion of the eyes: 眼～ gum of the eye
眵泪 chīlèi 〈中医〉 eye secretion and tears
眵目糊 chīmuhū 〈方言〉 gum of the eye

哧 chī 〈象声〉: ～的一声撕下一块布 rip off a piece of cloth

with a splitting sound /她只是～～地笑。She was tittering. *or* She had a fit of giggling.

哧溜 chīliū 〈象声〉sound of slipping or sliding:他踩在香蕉皮上，～一下滑倒了。He slipped on a banana peel and fell with a thump.

吃[1]**(喫)** chī ❶ eat; take:～早饭 eat (*or* have, *or* take) breakfast /～茶 drink tea /～饼干 have (*or* take) biscuits /～零食 take snacks between meals /～奶 (of a baby) take milk from its mother; suck at its mother's breast /～药 take medicine /请～help yourself, please /～饱 eat one's fill; be full ❷ have one's meals; eat (at a restaurant or by a certain standard); dine:～食堂 dine in a canteen /～馆子 eat at a restaurant; eat out; dine out /～中灶 eat in a special mess for middle-ranking cadres in years of war and revolution /～在广东。It's in Guangdong that you get the best food. *or* Guangdong is the home of the gourmet (*or* an epicureans' paradise). ❸ live off; live on; scrounge off:～利息 live on interest /～父母 live off one's parents /坐山～山 live off the mountains where your home is /干一行，～一行。One's profession is one's livelihood. ❹ absorb; soak up:宣纸～墨。Rice paper absorbs ink. ❺ take in (sth.): *see* "～刀"; "～水" ❻ annihilate; wipe out; take (in a chess game):拿车～他的马。Take his horse with your chariot. /～掉敌人一个团的兵力。Wipe out a regiment of the enemy force. ❼ grasp; understand:他打算干什么，我可～不准。I'm not sure (*or* don't understand) what he's up to. ❽ endure; withstand; take:我才不～他那一套呢! I'm not going to put up with that! ❾ suffer; incur:脑门上～了一拳 get a blow on the head /～败仗 suffer a defeat; be defeated in battle ❿ exhaust; consume:这活儿～劲。This job is energy-consuming. ⓫ by (as used in the passive voice in the early vernacular):～他笑话 be laughed at by him

吃[2] chī stammer; stutter
see also "口吃" kǒuchī

吃白饭 chī báifàn ❶ eat rice alone (without anything to go with it) ❷ have meals at others' expense; have free meals:要生活好就得好好干，没处～去! You have to work hard if you want to improve your life. There's no free lunch! ❸ sponge on sb.:～的 parasite; good-for-nothing

吃白食 chī báishí 〈方言〉eat at others' expense; have free meals; live off others

吃白眼 chī báiyǎn 〈方言〉be looked on with contempt; be looked down upon:他破产之后，到处～。After he went bankrupt, people gave him the cold shoulder everywhere.

吃饱了撑的 chībǎole chēngde 〈方言〉be restless from overeating — do sth. senseless:下这么大雨要出去骑车兜风，这不是～吗! It is absolutely silly to cycle in such heavy rain.

吃闭门羹 chī bìméngēng find the door closed on one — be denied a reception; find the door locked — fail to see sb. when one calls on him:我昨天去拜访他，不成想吃了闭门羹。I went to visit him yesterday, only to find him out and the door locked.

吃瘪 chībiē 〈方言〉❶ be humiliated; eat humble pie:当众～ be humiliated in public ❷ be forced to admit or concede defeat

吃瘪子 chī biězi 〈方言〉stand to lose; get the worst of it; be embarrassed:你如果与他争论，定会～。If you get involved in a dispute with him, you'll get the worst of it.

吃不饱 chībubǎo ❶ have not enough to eat ❷ (of enterprises, factories, etc.) operate under capacity

吃不得 chībudé ❶ cannot eat; be not edible:葡萄太酸，～。The grapes are too sour to eat. ❷ cannot bear; cannot stand:～苦 cannot endure hardships

吃不服 chībufú not be used to certain food:西餐我～。I have yet to get used to Western food. /我～辣味菜。Hot dishes do not agree with me.

吃不开 chībukāi be unpopular; won't work:过去的那一套～了。The old practices are no longer popular. *or* The old way of doing things just doesn't work any more. /这种作风哪儿都～。Such a work style is frowned on everywhere. /没背景的人在这儿～。If you don't have a certain background, you don't have a place here. *or* You don't get ahead here without patronage.

吃不来 chībulái not be fond of (certain food):我～辣的。I don't care for hot food. /油腻的东西我～。I have an aversion to rich food.

吃不了，兜着走 chībuliǎo, dōuzhezǒu 〈方言〉get more than one has bargained for; land oneself in serious trouble; be left holding the bag:把他做的这些事情抖搂出来，教这小子～! Tell everyone what he has been doing, and give him his deserts, the beast!

吃不上 chībushàng have nothing to eat; cannot afford to eat; cannot get (sth. to eat):一天～一顿饱饭 cannot afford (to eat) one square meal a day /没有煤气，连热饭都～。Without gas you cannot even get a hot meal. /太晚了，我们～午饭了。We are too late for lunch now.

吃不下 chībuxià can eat no more; have no appetite for:我饱了，实在～了。I'm full. Really, I can't eat any more. /他病了，一点东西都～。He is ill and doesn't feel like eating. /～就算了，不要勉强。You needn't eat up everything if you don't want to.

吃不消 chībuxiāo cannot bear; cannot endure or stand:天气热得～。It is unbearably hot. /长途旅行，叫人～。We can hardly stand the fatigue of a long journey. /这工作太累了，我～了。This job is too much for me. I can't take it any more.

吃不住 chībuzhù not be strong enough to sustain heavy weight:书太多，这个书架～。The bookshelf is not strong enough to accommodate so many books. /工作难度太大，我怕～。I am afraid I'm not equal to this difficult task.

吃不准 chībuzhǔn not quite understand; not be sure:这个词儿的意思我～。I'm not sure of the exact meaning of the word.

吃长斋 chī chángzhāi (of a Buddhist, etc.) be on a vegetarian diet all the year round

吃吃 chīchī titter; chuckle:姑娘们在～地笑。The girls are tittering.

吃吃喝喝 chīchi-hēhē eat and drink and be merry; wine and dine:他不应该整天跟这些人～混日子。He shouldn't idle away his time hobnobbing with these people.

吃穿 chī-chuān food and clothing:讲究～ be particular about one's food and dress /不愁～ not have to worry about food and clothing /够吃够穿 have enough to eat and wear

吃醋 chīcù be jealous:争风～ be bitterly and openly jealous of one's rival in love affairs (especially in a love triangle)

吃大锅饭 chī dàguōfàn eat from the same big pot — get the same pay whether one works hard or does not work at all:大家～，吃亏的是国家。If everybody eats from the same big pot, the state is the only loser (*or* the state alone stands to lose).

吃大户 chī dàhù ❶ (formerly of starving peasants in times of famine) eat free meals or seize grain in landlords' homes ❷ dine on the rich guy; get the rich guy to pay up:今天你得奖，我们可要～啊! Now that you've won a prize, we'll all dine on you. /都什么时候了，还到赢利企业来～! Times have changed. You can't use the funds of a profitable enterprise any more!

吃刀 chīdāo 〈机械〉cutting tool's penetration

吃得开 chīdekāi be popular; be much sought after:新农具在农村很～。New farm tools are in great demand in the villages. /这个人头脑灵，在单位～。Clever and resourceful, he is getting on very well in his work unit.

吃得苦中苦，方为人上人 chīde kǔ zhōng kǔ, fāng wéi rén shàng rén 〈俗语〉only by enduring the hardest lot can a person aspire to rise above all others

吃得来 chīdelái not mind eating:海参我～。I don't mind eating sea-cucumber. /牛肉我还～，羊肉就不行了。Beef is all right, but mutton doesn't agree with me.

吃得上 chīdeshàng ❶ be available on the market:现在冬天也～西红柿。Nowadays tomatoes are available even in winter. ❷ can afford to eat:农民现在～大米和白面了。Farmers can afford rice and wheat flour now. ❸ be in time for a meal:马上去，还～午饭。If you go right now, you will be in time for lunch.

吃得下 chīdexià have an appetite for:再多他也～。He's got such an enormous appetite that he can't have too much. *or* The more the merrier, for he has got such an enormous appetite. /她好点儿了，已经～东西了。She is better and has got an appetite now.

吃得消 chīdexiāo can endure or stand (hardship, arduous work, etc.):熬个通宵，我也～。I can stand working throughout the night. /这个工作你～吗? Are you sure this job is not too much for you?

吃得住 chīdezhù be strong enough to sustain (heavy weight):货物再多一点儿，船也～。The vessel is good for still more cargo. /这座木桥过大卡车也能～。This wooden bridge can bear the weight of a heavy-duty lorry.

吃等食 chī děngshí 〈方言〉eat food prepared by others; lead an

idle life; be a loafer or sponger

吃地面儿 chī dìmiànr 〈旧语〉 live by exacting payments from the local people

吃豆腐 chī dòufu 〈方言〉 ❶ dally (with a woman); flirt: 别想吃我的豆腐! Don't you try to flirt with me! ❷ crack a joke; tease: 他性情活泼，总爱～。He is good fun and makes jokes all the time. ❸ *also* "吃豆腐饭" 〈旧语〉 express one's condolences to the bereaved and share in the beancurd meal

吃独食 chī dúshí have things all to oneself; refuse to share with others: 她从小娇生惯养，养成了～的习惯。As a spoiled child, she has developed the habit of not sharing nice things with others. /有好处大家共享，不要少数人～。An advantage should be shared rather than monopolized. *or* Good things should be shared by all and not monopolized by a few.

吃耳光 chī ěrguāng get a slap on the face; get a box on the ears: 让他～ slap him across the face

吃饭 chīfàn ❶ eat a meal: ～了! Dinner is ready! *or* Meal time! /你在哪儿～? Where do you have your meals? /～了吗? Have you eaten? (phatic language) /～防噎，行路防跌。Beware of choking when you eat, and stumbling when you walk. *or* You can't be too cautious in whatever you do. ❷ live; make a living: 靠教书～ make a living by teaching /靠天～ live at the mercy of nature /吃社会主义公有制的饭 live off socialist public ownership /一要～，二要建设。First, feed the people, and second, build the country. /不要靠老资格～。Don't live on your seniority.

吃饭财政 chīfàn cáizhèng payroll budgeting

吃粉笔灰 chī fěnbǐhuī 〈戏谑〉 live off chalk dust — live by teaching: 我吃了几十年粉笔灰。I've lived off chalk dust for decades now.

吃干醋 chī gāncù be jealous without reason: 你何必为不相干的事～。Why are you so jealous about something that you have nothing to do with?

吃功夫 chī gōngfu require great effort; be strenuous: 这出戏要演四个多小时，是一出相当～的重头戏。It requires considerable effort to put on the play that lasts over four hours.

吃挂络 chī guàlao *also* "吃挂落" 〈方言〉 be involved or implicated in trouble caused by sb. else: 这小伙子招灾惹祸的，害得他一家人都跟着～。The boy is always the source of trouble, getting the whole family involved.

吃官粮 chī guānliáng receive a salary from the government: 他是～的。He is a government official (*or* employee).

吃官司 chī guānsi be prosecuted or sued; be punished by law; be imprisoned: 在旧社会，他因还不起债而吃了官司。In the old days he was put in jail for failing to pay his debt. /这件事搞不好要～的。We'd better be careful, or else we'll get ourselves involved in a lawsuit.

吃馆子 chī guǎnzi 〈口语〉 eat in a restaurant; dine out

吃喝不分 chīhē-bùfēn share food and drink — be cronies

吃喝风 chīhēfēng unhealthy practice of feasting on public money

吃喝嫖赌 chīhē-piáodǔ go dining, wining, whoring and gambling — lead a life of dissipation

吃喝儿 chīhēr 〈口语〉 food and drink: 除了有时添置几件衣服，他把钱都花在～上了。He spends all his money on food and drink except for occasional purchase of clothing.

吃喝玩乐 chīhē-wánlè eat, drink and be merry; seek pleasure: 我们难道没有比～更高的人生目的吗? Can we have no higher aim in life than mere pleasure-seeking?

吃黑枣儿 chī hēizǎor 〈方言〉 get a bullet — be shot to death; be executed

吃红牌 chī hóngpái 〈体育〉 get a red card; be sent off (as in a football match)

吃后悔药 chī hòuhuǐyào cry over spilt milk; repent only too late

吃花酒 chī huājiǔ 〈旧语〉 carouse in the company of prostitutes

吃皇粮 chī huángliáng receive salaries, subsidies, or other support from the government: 靠"～"过日子的企业 enterprise supported (entirely) by government subsidies; state-subsidized enterprise

吃黄牌 chī huángpái 〈体育〉 get a yellow card; be booked: 因手球～ be booked for handball /吃了两张黄牌 pick up two bookings; get two yellow cards

吃回扣 chī huíkòu accept a commission: 吃百分之三的回扣 take a three per cent commission

吃荤 chīhūn eat meat: 爱～ be fond of meat; prefer meat /和尚不应～。Buddhist monks are supposed to refrain from eating meat.

吃货 chīhuò 〈粗话〉 good-for-nothing

吃讲茶 chī jiǎngchá 〈方言〉 meet at a tea-house to settle a dispute; drink mediation tea

吃教 chījiào 〈旧语〉 be converted to and live off christianity

吃角子老虎 chījiǎozi lǎohǔ slot machine

吃紧 chījǐn ❶ tense; critical: 形势～。The situation is tense. /战局～。The war is in a critical moment. /市场货源～。Goods are in short supply in the market. /任务～。The task is urgent. /银根～。The money market is tight. ❷ important; essential: 先把那些～的地方整修一下，过几年再大修吧。Let's first fix those parts which require immediate attention and put off the overhaul for a few years.

吃劲 chījìn requiring much effort; strenuous: 他年轻，多干点活儿不～。As a young man, he can take on a heavy load without feeling the strain. /每周上十五小时课够～的。It is a lot of strain teaching fifteen hours per week.

吃惊 chījīng be surprised; be amazed or shocked; be taken aback: 这个消息使我大吃一惊。This news came to me as a big surprise (*or* shock). /他的记忆力令人～。His memory is amazing. /他忽然变卦，令大家～。We were all taken aback by his sudden change of mind. /他睁大双眼，～地看着我。He stared at me, dumfounded.

吃开口饭 chī kāikǒufàn 〈旧语〉 make a living as an entertainer

吃空额 chī kòng'é *also* "吃空饷" put imaginary names on the payroll and draw pay: 军阀部队由于军官～而总是人员不足。The warlord armies were always under strength, as the commanding officers pocketed the pay for non-existing troops.

吃口 chīkǒu ❶ dependent: 他家里～多，生活比较困难。He is a bit hard up for he has many mouths to feed in the family. ❷ taste: 这种梨水分多，～略差。This kind of pear is juicy, but doesn't taste as good as it should. ❸ (of livestock) intake of feed: 这头牛～好，不挑食。This ox has a good appetite and is not choosy about the feed.

吃苦 chīkǔ bear hardships; suffer: ～在前，享受在后 be the first to bear hardships and the last to enjoy comforts /她太娇了，一点也不能～。She is much too spoiled to get used to even a little hardship.

吃苦耐劳 chīkǔ-nàiláo bear hardship and hard work; be used or inured to hardship and toil: ～的传统 tradition of hard work and self-denial /中国农民～。Chinese farmers are inured (*or* used) to hardship and hard work.

吃苦头 chī kǔtou suffer; get into trouble: 他流浪异乡，吃过很多苦头。He led a vagrant's life and suffered many hardships. /蛮干准～。You will pay for your recklessness. /无知和愚昧是要～的。One is bound to come to grief for one's stupidity and ignorance.

吃亏 chīkuī ❶ suffer losses: 吃眼前亏 immediately get the worst of it /不让顾客～ give the customers a fair deal /那些一心想占小便宜的人准会吃大亏。Those who hanker after petty gains are bound to suffer big losses. /他吃了自私的亏。He suffered from his own selfishness. *or* He was a victim of his own selfishness. ❷ at a disadvantage; in an unfavourable position: 他口吃，学语言吃了亏。As a language learner, he was at a disadvantage for his bad stammer. /这次打了败仗，～在对敌方军力估计不足。The defeat was due to our underestimation of the enemy.

吃劳保 chī láobǎo 〈口语〉 live off the labour insurance (on account of disablement or prolonged illness)

吃老本 chī lǎoběn live off one's past gains or achievements: 不能靠～过日子。One should not rest on one's laurels. /谁要～，谁就会落伍。Whoever constantly looks back on his or her past achievements will fall behind.

吃累 chīlèi ❶ requiring great effort; strenuous; fatiguing: 干这种活不觉得太～。This job does not seem strenuous to me. ❷ 〈方言〉 burden: 老王家里～多，生活困难。Lao Wang is badly off, as he has a heavy family burden.

吃里爬外 chīlǐ-páwài *also* "吃里扒外" eat sb.'s food and cater to his enemy; live on one person while secretly serving another; secretly work for the opponent of one's benefactor: 我们不能肯定在我们队伍里就没有～的人。We can't say with absolute certainty that there are no double-dealers within our ranks who serve our enemy.

吃力 chīlì requiring effort; laborious; strenuous: 这篇文章他写得相当～。It took him much effort to write the article. /他的文章写得毫不～。He writes with grace and ease. *or* He writes in an effortless style. /我干这项工作并不觉得～。I was not conscious of any strain while doing the job.

吃力不讨好 chīlì bù tǎohǎo do a thankless job; work hard (for

sb.) but get little thanks; spare no pains but get no gains

吃粮 chīliáng 〈旧语〉be on the pay-roll of the army; be a soldier: 他叔叔在军阀时期当过兵,吃过粮。His uncle once served in the army in the warlord period.

吃零嘴 chī língzuǐ *also* "吃零食" take snacks between meals; eat between meals: 小孩子爱~。Children like to nibble between meals.

吃码头 chī mǎtou earn a living by working on the docks

吃闷亏 chī mènkuī 〈方言〉swallow a bitter pill in silence; have to keep one's grievances to oneself: 这人胆小怕事,凡事宁肯~,也不愿意惹是非。He is so chicken-hearted that he would rather swallow the bitter pill in silence than air his grievances for fear of getting into trouble.

吃奶 chīnǎi (of a baby) suck at its mother's breast: ~的婴儿 sucking baby /使出~的力气 use all one's strength; strain every nerve; make every effort

C

吃排头 chī páitou 〈方言〉be blamed; be scolded: 快走吧,迟了又要害得我~。Hurry up! I'll be blamed if you are late.

吃派饭 chī pàifàn (of officials who go to inspect work in the country) board with different peasant families in rotation

吃碰 chīpèng 〈方言〉meet with a rebuff; be rebuffed: 他正在生气,你去找他准得~。You are bound to meet with a rebuff if you try to talk to him now, as he is in a fit of anger.

吃偏饭 chī piānfàn *also* "吃偏食" eat better-than-average meals in the mess; enjoy special privilege: 这孩子是个长跑的好苗子,教练何不给他吃点偏饭? The child has great potential for long-distance running. Why doesn't the coach give him some special training?

吃气 chīqì 〈方言〉be bullied; be insulted; be wronged; suffer wrong

吃枪药 chī qiāngyào be in a bad temper and not amenable to reason; be irritable: 怎么,你今天~了! Why! You are so irritable today.

吃枪子儿 chī qiāngzǐr 〈粗话〉be hit by a bullet; be shot dead

吃青 chīqīng get in a crop for food before it is ripe

吃请 chīqǐng accept an invitation to dinner (often extended for a favour): ~受礼是腐败的一种表现。Accepting gifts and invitations to dinner is a sign of corruption.

吃屈 chīqū 〈方言〉be wronged; suffer wrong: 那人可不是~让人的。He is not the kind of person to take an insult lying down.

吃儿 chīr 〈口语〉food; feed; things to eat: 今天午饭有什么好~? What do we have for lunch today? /猪在圈里嗡嗡着要~。The pig is snorting for feed in the pigsty.

吃人不吐骨头 chīrén bù tǔ gǔtou 〈俗语〉devour a man without spitting out the bones — treat people ruthlessly; show no mercy at all

吃软不吃硬 chīruǎn bù chīyìng susceptible to persuasion rather than coercion: 他是那种~的人: 如果你一硬起来,他就会大叫大嚷的。He is the sort of person who yields to soft rather than hard tactics. If you get tough, he'll give you hell.

吃烧饼 chī shāobǐng (in shooting) lay an egg — shoot wide of the mark

吃生活 chī shēnghuó 〈方言〉get a beating

吃十方 chī shífāng (as of a monk) live off donations from all quarters

吃食 chīshí (of bird or animal) eat; feed: 母鸡生病,不~儿了。The hen is bad and doesn't feed. /这鱼~水草。The fish feeds on water-weeds.

吃食 chīshi 〈口语〉food: 餐桌上摆满了~。The dinner table is covered with all kinds of food.

吃水 chīshuǐ ❶〈方言〉drinking water: 这里的~来自地下。Here drinking water comes from underground. ❷ absorb water; be absorbent: 这种吸墨纸可~了! This type of blotting paper is very absorbent. ❸〈船舶〉draught; draft: 满载~ load draught /空载~ light draught /这艘江轮~两米。This steamer has a draught of two metres.

吃水线 chīshuǐxiàn 〈船舶〉waterline

吃私 chīsī 〈方言〉embezzle; take bribes: ~舞弊 engage in fraudulent practices; be guilty of graft and corruption

吃素 chīsù ❶ be a vegetarian; be on a vegetarian diet: 基本~ be basically a vegetarian /吃一个月素 be on a vegetarian diet for a month /长年~ be a regular vegetarian ❷ (usu. used in the negative) not killing; not effective (as a weapon, etc.): 小心点,他的拳头可不是~的。Be careful. His fists are not for decorative purposes.

吃太平饭 chī tàipíngfàn live a peaceful life

吃通 chītōng ❶ (in gambling) win all through ❷ be popular; find favour in everybody's eyes

吃透 chītòu understand thoroughly; have a thorough grasp of sth.: 吃得透 be able to understand correctly (*or* thoroughly) /吃不透 fail to understand correctly; cannot quite see; be not sure /~两头 have a thorough understanding of the Party's policies and the people's views (*or* actual circumstances)/重在~文件精神,而不能拘泥于字面的理解。It is more important to grasp the essence of the document than to define the phraseology. *or* It is more important to grasp the spirit than the letter of the document.

吃瓦片儿 chī wǎpiànr live on tiles — make one's living on rent; live on rent

吃席 chīxí attend a feast

吃闲饭 chī xiánfàn be a loafer; lead an idle life: 他不愿在家~,就找了个工作。He didn't want to stay idle at home, so he got himself a job.

吃闲话 chī xiánhuà be an object of gossip; cause a good deal of talk

吃现成饭 chī xiànchéngfàn eat meals prepared by sb. else; benefit from other people's labour: 如今他老伴退休了,教授下课后吃上了现成饭。Now that his wife is retired, the professor goes back home to enjoy ready meals after class. /村里的老人们也干点力所能及的活儿,不愿在家~。Unwilling to sit back and be taken care of at home, elderly people in the village tried to do what they could.

吃香 chīxiāng 〈口语〉be in great demand; be much sought-after; be popular: 夏天啤酒到处~。Beer is popular everywhere in summer. /大学毕业生在我们公司里很~。College graduates are most sought-after in our company.

吃香的喝辣的 chī xiāngde hē làde enjoy tasty food and drinks; live in clover

吃相 chīxiàng table manners: 没个~ have no table manners at all /吃要有~。When you eat, pay attention to your table manners.

吃小亏占大便宜 chī xiǎokuī zhàn dàpiányi take small losses for the sake of big gains; the best gain is to lose first

吃小灶 chī xiǎozào eat at a small mess where better food is prepared and served for a restricted number of diners (formerly, high-ranking cadres in years of war and revolution) — enjoy some privilege: 给困难学生~ give problem students special tutorials

吃心 chīxīn 〈方言〉❶ be suspicious; be oversensitive: 她这个人容易~,你跟她说话时注意点。Be careful how you speak to her; she tends to be oversensitive. /为这点事不必那么~。Don't let this little accident upset you. ❷ absorbed; engrossed: 他~地阅读那本书。He was absorbed in the book.

吃鸭蛋 chī yādàn fail an exam; win no score at a competition; lay an egg

吃哑巴亏 chī yǎbakuī swallow a bitter pill in silence; have to keep one's grievances to oneself

吃洋荤 chī yánghūn *also* "开洋荤" kāi yánghūn 〈方言〉eat sth. for the first time; have a new experience

吃夜草 chī yècǎo eat midnight fodder — moonlight

吃一堑,长一智 chī yī qiàn, zhǎng yī zhì a fall into the pit, a gain in your wit

吃硬不吃软 chīyìng bù chīruǎn be prone to hard tactics, but not soft tactics; be open to coercion rather than persuasion: 这小子的为人,~。He's a bully who understands force only.

吃赃 chīzāng share stolen goods: 直接参与这个案件的盗窃、~人员达二十余人。As many as over twenty people are directly involved in the case, including the housebreakers and receivers of the stolen goods.

吃斋 chīzhāi ❶ practise abstinence from meat and fish for religious reasons; abstain from meat and fish; be a vegetarian: ~念佛 abstain from meat and fish and chant Buddhist scriptures ❷ (of Buddhist priests) eat meals: 和尚们正在~。The Buddhist priests were having their meal. ❸ (of lay people) eat vegetarian food at a Buddhist temple

吃着碗里看着锅里 chīzhe wǎnli kànzhe guōli keep looking at the pot while eating from one's bowl — be covetous of what one does not yet have; be insatiably greedy: 这人贪心不足,~。He's so greedy that he's never contented with what he has but always covets more.

吃重 chīzhòng ❶ heavy (responsibility); arduous (task): 他担任校

长以后，工作很～。The post of university president placed heavy responsibilities on his shoulders. ❷ strenuous; laborious; hard: 编字典可是件很～的事啊。It is strenuous work compiling a dictionary. ❸ (loading) capacity: 这辆车～五吨。This truck has a loading capacity of five tons.

吃主 chīzhǔ ❶ patron of a restaurant; customer in a food market ❷ *see* "吃货" ❸ gourmet

吃准 chīzhǔn 〈方言〉 affirm; be sure: 这筐苹果有多少个，我吃不准。I am not sure how many apples there are in the basket.

吃租 chīzū live on rent; live as a renter

吃嘴 chīzuǐ 〈方言〉 ❶ *see* "吃零嘴" ❷ fond of eating; greedy

吃罪 chīzuì take the blame: ～不起 cannot afford to take the blame

瓻 chī wine (pottery) pot

絺 chī fine linen (cloth)

笞 chī 〈书面〉 beat with a whip, cane, split bamboo, etc.: ～责 censure; severe criticism / 鞭～ whip; flog

笞刑 chīxíng flogging with a split bamboo or stick (as a punishment): 有些国家至今仍保留着～。Some countries still retain flogging as a punishment for offenders.

胵 chī *see* "膍胵" píchī

鸱 chī 〈动物〉 owl

鸱尾 chīwěi ceramic decoration shaped somewhat like an owl's tail, fixed at both ends of the ridge of the roof of an old-fashioned Chinese house

鸱吻 chīwěn *see* "鸱尾"

鸱鸮 chīxiāo *also* "鸱枭" 〈动物〉 birds of the owl family

鸱鸺 chīxiū 〈动物〉 owl

鸱张 chīzhāng 〈书面〉 rampant; violent: 群凶～。A gang of violent elements went on the rampage.

蚩 chī 〈书面〉 ignorant; idiotic

蚩骇 chī'ái *also* "痴骇" chī'ái stupid; slow-witted

蚩尤 Chīyóu legendary leader of the Jiuli (九黎) tribes living in the eastern part of what is now the North China Plain, who fought Huangdi (黄帝) at Zhuolu (涿鹿) in present Hebei Province, and was defeated and killed by the latter

蚩拙 chīzhuō 〈书面〉 crude and clumsy

嗤 chī sneer

嗤鄙 chībǐ 〈书面〉 sneer at; scorn; hold in contempt

嗤嗤 chīchī hiss; fizzle; giggle; sizzle: 两人交头接耳，～地笑着。The two of them are whispering and giggling.

嗤诋 chīdǐ 〈书面〉 mock; deride; laugh scornfully

嗤溜 chīliū *also* "哧溜" chīliū 〈象声〉 sound of slipping or sliding

嗤笑 chīxiào jeer at; laugh at: 为人～ be made a laughing-stock

嗤之以鼻 chīzhīyǐbí look down one's nose at; give a snort of contempt; despise: 如此自吹自擂，人们都～。By blowing his own trumpet, he incurred nothing but ridicule and contempt.

媸 chī 〈书面〉 ugly; unsightly: 妍～不分 fail to distinguish between beauty and ugliness; fail to see what is beautiful and what is ugly

chí

漦 chí 〈书面〉 saliva

坻 chí 〈书面〉 sand bar

墀 chí 〈书面〉 landing (on top of a flight of steps); steps: 丹～ vermillion steps (leading to the imperial palace)

迟(遲) chí ❶ slow; tardy: 事不宜～。The matter brooks no delay. *or* Procrastination is the thief of time. / ～于作复，歉甚。I wish to apologize for my tardy reply. ❷ late; delayed; belated: 姗姗来～ be slow in coming; be late / 来～了的贺年卡 belated new year card / 我来～一步，没有见到她。I arrived too late to meet her. *or* I didn't arrive in time to meet her. ❸ (Chí) a surname

迟笨 chíbèn clumsy: 动作～ move clumsily

迟迟 chíchí slow; tardy: ～不来 slow in coming / ～不表态 be reluctant (*or* hesitate) to commit oneself / ～定不下来 fail to come to a decision even after so much delay / 春日～。Spring days pass slowly.

迟到 chídào late (to come or arrive): 抱歉，～了。I'm sorry I am late. *or* I wish to apologize for my late arrival. / 上课不得～。Coming late for class is not permitted. / ～者共五人。Altogether five persons arrived late. / 她～了几分钟。She was a few minutes late.

迟钝 chídùn slow; slow-witted; obtuse: 反应～ be slow in reaction; react slowly / 头脑～ slow-witted; obtuse; unintelligent / 他今天特别～。He is particularly obtuse today.

迟缓 chíhuǎn slow; tardy; sluggish: 行动～ act (*or* move) slowly / 迈着～的步子 walk with a heavy step / 这项工程进展～。This project isn't making good progress. *or* The pace of the project is painfully slow.

迟留 chíliú delay; stay on; stop over: ～数日 stay for a few more days

迟脉 chímài 〈中医〉 retarded pulse (less than 60 beats per minute)

迟慢 chímàn slow; sluggish: 步履～ walk slowly; be slow in movement

迟明 chímíng 〈书面〉 break of day; dawn

迟暮 chímù ❶ dusk; evening: 天色已近～。Dusk is gathering. ❷ old age; twilight of life: 年近～ approach old age; become advanced in years / ～之感 feel one's age

迟误 chíwù hinder by delay; procrastinate: 抓紧办理，不得～。Get down to brass tacks without delay.

迟效肥料 chíxiào féiliào slow-acting or slow-release fertilizer

迟延 chíyán delay; procrastinate; retard: ～方 party in delay / 为了不使火势蔓延，消防队必须立即出动，不能～。To check the spread of the fire, the fire brigade must set out without delay. *or* To bring the conflagration under control, fire engines must be rushed to the spot right away.

迟延税 chíyánshuì deferred tax

迟疑 chíyí be indecisive; hesitate: 毫不～ act resolutely (*or* without the least hesitation) / ～未决 remain undecided; hesitate irresolutely / 行动～ act indecisively / ～的神情 hesitant (*or* irresolute) look / ～坐困 land in a predicament as a result of procrastination / 不可～。Don't lose any time.

迟早 chízǎo sooner or later: 他～会明白的。He will understand sooner or later. / 骄傲的人～要失败。A conceited person is bound to come a cropper. / 谎言～会被揭穿。No lie can long escape exposure.

迟滞 chízhì ❶ sluggish; stagnant: 河道淤塞，水流～。The river is silted up and the water flows sluggishly. ❷ dull; slow: 眼光～ dull expression; glazed eyes / 精神～ be listless ❸ slow down; hold up: ～敌人的行动 slow down the enemy's operation

迟重 chízhòng slow and heavy: 他走起路来脚步有些～。He walks with somewhat slow and heavy steps.

持 chí ❶ hold; grasp: ～笔 hold a pen (in hand); wield a pen / ～相同意见 hold identical views / ～反对意见 hold dissenting views / ～敌对态度 take (*or* adopt) a hostile attitude / ～币抢购 rush to buy with cash in hand ❷ support; maintain: 支～ support / 坚～ persist; insist / 维～秩序 keep (*or* maintain) order ❸ manage; run; handle: 操～家务 manage household affairs / 大家都同意这件事由你主～。It is agreed that you'll take charge of the matter. ❹ control; hold under duress: 劫～ abduct; kidnap; hijack / 挟～ hold under duress ❺ oppose; confront: 相～不下 come to a deadlock; be locked in stalemate

持不同政见者 chí bùtóng zhèngjiàn zhě dissident

持法 chífǎ enforce the law: ～严谨 be strict and meticulous in the enforcement of law

持服 chífú 〈旧语〉 in mourning

持股公司 chígǔ gōngsī 〈经济〉 holding company

持恒电流 chíhéng diànliú 〈电学〉 constant current

持己 chíjǐ behave: ～端方 behave with equity and dignity

持家 chíjiā run one's home; manage household affairs; keep house: 勤俭～ be industrious and thrifty in running one's home; manage domestic affairs with diligence and thrift / 这位主妇很会～。

She is a very good housewife.
持节 chíjié hold the imperial insignia (as credentials) — serve as a diplomatic envoy
持戒 chíjiè (of a Buddhist monk) observe monastic rules
持久 chíjiǔ lasting; enduring; protracted:～和平 lasting peace /～目标 long-term objective /他对数学的兴趣不会～。His interest in mathematics will only be transient. /但愿这种热情能够～。We wish this kind of enthusiasm would last.
持久力 chíjiǔlì staying power; endurance; stamina
持久战 chíjiǔzhàn protracted warfare
持论 chílùn present an argument; express an opinion:～有据 put forward a well-grounded argument /～新颖 be original in approach /～公允 set forth a sound argument; be fair in judgement or criticism

C

持票人 chípiàorén bearer (of a cheque, etc.)
持平 chípíng ❶ unbiased; fair; impartial:～之论 unbiased view ❷ even; balanced; equal:这家商场的销售额与去年～。The sales of the shop this year equal those of last year.
持枪 chíqiāng ❶ hold a gun:～歹徒 armed bandit; armed robber /～抢劫 armed robbery ❷〈军事〉port arms
持球 chíqiú 〈体育〉(as in volleyball) holding
持身 chíshēn conduct oneself:～严正 be self-disciplined and upright
持续 chíxù continuous; sustained; steady:产量～上升 steady growth of production /～努力 sustained effort /战斗～了一昼夜。The battle lasted for 24 hours. /暴雨从下午三点～到午夜十二点。The storm raged from 3:00 p.m. till midnight.
持续电流 chíxù diànliú 〈电学〉sustained current
持续性抽搐状态 chíxùxìng chōuchù zhuàngtài 〈医学〉status epilepticus; status convulsivus
持续性肌阵挛 chíxùxìng jīzhènluán 〈医学〉myoclonic status
持续增长 chíxù zēngzhǎng 〈经济〉sustained growth:产值～steady increase in output values /经济可～ sustainable economic growth
持续罪 chíxùzuì 〈法律〉continuing offence
持议 chíyì view; argument:～公允。One's views are fair and reasonable.
持有 chíyǒu hold:～债券 hold bonds /股票～者 stockholder /～护照 hold a passport /对流行音乐～偏见 have a prejudice against pop music
持斋 chízhāi abstain from meat and fish or abide by other restrictions on food for religious reasons:～素食 confine oneself to a vegetarian diet on religious grounds
持照人 chízhàorén passport holder; passport bearer:中华人民共和国外交部请各国军政机关对～予以通行的便利和必要的协助。The Ministry of Foreign Affairs of the People's Republic of China requests all civil and military authorities of foreign countries to allow the bearer of this passport to pass freely and afford assistance in case of need.
持针钳 chízhēnqián 〈医学〉needle holder; needle forceps
持正 chízhèng 〈书面〉❶ uphold justice; be just:～不阿 be just and uncompromising ❷ be impartial; be even-handed:平心～ be equitable and even-handed
持证人 chízhèngrén holder (of certificate)
持之以恒 chízhīyǐhéng pursue a matter with determination; make consistent efforts; persevere; persist:做学问要～。Perseverance is essential for intellectual pursuit.
持之有故 chízhīyǒugù be well-grounded in one's views; hold well-supported or valid arguments:写文章应～。You must present well-grounded arguments in your essay. *or* You must have something valid to say and say it cogently in your writing.
持重 chízhòng prudent; cautious; circumspect; discreet:老成～ steady (*or* experienced) and prudent /老吴为人极为～。Lao Wu is the soul of discretion. /他仍然～、自信、含蓄、谦逊。He is still prudent, self-confident, reserved and modest.

匙

chí spoon:汤～ soup spoon /茶～ teaspoon
see also shi
匙骨 chígǔ 〈生理〉cleithrum
匙子 chízi spoon

踟

chí

踟蹰 chíchú *also* "踟躇"〈书面〉hesitate; waver:～不前 hesitate to move forward; stand still irresolutely /搔首～ scratch one's head in hesitation /前程似锦，切莫～。The future is bright, and you should forge ahead without hesitation.

篪(箎、竾)

chí ancient bamboo flute with eight holes

池

chí ❶ pond; pool:游泳～ swimming pool /水～ pool /荷花～ lotus pond /鱼～ fish pond /盐～ salt lake ❷ place that resembles a pool:浴～ bath (esp. in a bathhouse) /舞～ dance floor /乐～ orchestra pit ❸〈旧语〉stalls (in a theatre) ❹〈书面〉moat:城～ city ❺ (Chí) a surname
池杉 chíshān *also* "池柏"〈植物〉pond cypress; pond bald cypress
池汤 chítāng pool in a bathhouse; bath:洗～ take a bath in a pool (as distinct from bathing in a bathtub)
池塘 chítáng ❶ pond:～生春草。Grass grows around the pond in spring. ❷ *see* "池汤"
池田勇人 Chítiányǒngrén Ikeda Hayato (1899-1965), Japanese Prime Minister from 1960 to 1964
池盐 chíyán lake salt
池鱼笼鸟 chíyú-lóngniǎo fish in a pond and birds in a cage — people without freedom
池鱼之殃 chíyúzhīyāng disaster that one is unfortunately involved in
see also "城门失火，殃及池鱼" chéngmén shīhuǒ, yāng jí chí yú
池浴 chíyù take a bath in a common bathing pool
池沼 chízhǎo large pool or pond
池中物 chízhōngwù (often used in the negative) fish in a pond — person without any ambition:此人终非～。He is no mediocre, unambitions person. *or* He will certainly go far.
池子 chízi ❶ pond; pool:把水灌进～。Fill the pool with water. ❷ pool in a bathhouse ❸ dance floor ❹〈旧语〉stalls (in a theatre)
池座 chízuò front seat in a theatre; front stall

弛

chí 〈书面〉loosen; relax; slacken:文武之道，一张一～。The cardinal principle of governance is to alternate tension with relaxation.
弛废 chífèi 〈书面〉be lax and even abandoned:纲纪～。Discipline and order are lax or practically non-existent.
弛缓 chíhuǎn ease; relax:～双方的紧张关系 ease tension in the bilateral relationship; relax the strained relations between the two sides /紧张的空气渐渐地～下来。The tension eased gradually.
弛禁 chíjìn 〈书面〉rescind a prohibition; lift a ban
弛懈 chíxiè relax; slack; slacken:刻苦攻读，不可一日～。You must work hard at your studies without relaxing for a single day.
弛张理论 chízhāng lǐlùn 〈物理〉relaxation theory
弛张热 chízhāngrè 〈医学〉remittent fever
弛张振荡 chízhāng zhèndàng 〈物理〉relaxation oscillation

驰

chí ❶ race; gallop; speed:一辆汽车飞～而过。A car sped past. ❷ promulgate; spread ❸〈书面〉desire; aspire; crave:心～神往 (make) one's thoughts go to (sb. or sth.)
驰骋 chíchěng 〈书面〉gallop:～在辽阔的草原上 gallop across the boundless grassland /～疆场 gallop about on the battlefield; fight bravely in war /～文坛 play a dominant role in the literary world
驰道 chídào 〈旧语〉road for royal carriages; royal road
驰电 chídiàn send a cable in haste; telegraph hurriedly:～召之 hurriedly send a cable to recall sb.
驰马 chímǎ gallop (on a horse)
驰名 chímíng *also* "驰誉" well known; famous:国内～的特产 local product well known throughout the country /～中外 renowned at home and abroad /他在学术界久已～。He has long been an eminent figure in the academic world.
驰目 chímù 〈书面〉look as far as the eye can see:～远眺 look far into the distance
驰念 chíniàn 〈书面〉think about people far away; concern oneself with distant events:时切～。My thoughts often go back to you and the old days.
驰驱 chíqū ❶ gallop:千里～ gallop a thousand *li* ❷ do one's utmost in sb.'s service:某虽不才，敢效～。Unworthy as I am, I ven-

ture to offer my service.
驰书 chíshū 〈书面〉send an urgent message; send a letter in haste:～告急 send sb. an urgent message about the dangerous (*or* critical) situation
驰思 chísī 〈书面〉*see* "驰念"
驰突 chítū 〈书面〉dash; rush:往来～,如入无人之境 charge about as if no one were in the way; dash back and forth unchallenged
驰骛 chíwù 〈书面〉❶ (of a horse) gallop ❷ run after (fame, power, money, etc.)
驰行 chíxíng (of a vehicle) drive at a high speed; speed:火车向北～。The train sped northward. /我们一行人分乘四辆大卡车,～在公路上。We sped down the highway in four trucks.
驰誉 chíyù *see* "驰名"
驰援 chíyuán rush to the rescue:火速～ rush to sb.'s rescue posthaste /千里～ come to sb.'s rescue from over a long distance
驰骤 chízhòu 〈书面〉gallop; race:纵横～ ride back and forth; charge about gallantly
驰逐 chízhú ❶ ride on horseback; chase on horseback:地多沼泽,不利～。The land, full of marshes, is not fit for horse-riding. ❷ horse-race

chǐ

耻(恥) chǐ ❶ shame:知～ have a sense of shame /恬不知～ have no sense of shame /～于人后 be ashamed to lag behind /不～下问 not regard it as beneath one's dignity to consult people below ❷ humiliation; ignominy; infamy:引以为～ regard as a disgrace /雪～ avenge an insult
耻骨 chǐgǔ 〈生理〉pubic bones; pubics:～切开术 pubiotomy
耻骂 chǐmà abuse; insult; hurl insults:这件事惹得很多人讥笑～。The affair has been a target of ridicule and abuse among many people.
耻辱 chǐrǔ shame; disgrace; humiliation:蒙受极大的～ suffer dreadful humiliation; suffer a gross insult /洗刷～ revenge an insult
耻笑 chǐxiào hold sb. to ridicule; sneer at; mock; ridicule:不要～失败者。Never sneer at the loser. /他在讲话中～这位"专家"的狂妄与无知。In his speech, he ridiculed the self-styled expert for his arrogance and ignorance. /人们～他卖弄本领的拙劣企图。People laugh at him for his awkward attempt to show off.

豉 chǐ *see* "豆豉" dòuchǐ
豉虫 chǐchóng *also* "豉甲"〈动物〉whirligig beetle

齿(齒) chǐ ❶ tooth:牙～ tooth /恒～ permanent tooth /乳～milk tooth /臼～ mortar /门～ front tooth; incisor /犬～ canine tooth /义～ false tooth /智～ wisdom tooth /蛀～ decayed tooth /龋～ dental caries; decayed tooth /儿～ (of some old people) new teeth after the falling off of the original ones ❷ tooth-like part of an object; tooth:锯～儿 teeth of a saw /梳～儿 teeth of a comb /轮～ teeth of a cogwheel ❸ toothed:～轮 toothed wheel; gear ❹〈书面〉stand side by side; regard as of one's own:不～于人类 not be regarded as one of humanity; be not worthy of the name of a human ❺〈书面〉age:稚～ very young /～德俱尊 command respect on account of both one's age and one's moral integrity /马～徒增 grow older but no wiser ❻〈书面〉mention; speak of:何足挂～ not worth mentioning /这些人是我们所不～的。They are such people as we scorn to mention.
齿唇音 chǐchúnyīn *also* "唇齿音" labio-dental sound
齿及 chǐjí 〈书面〉speak of; mention:此事尚未～。This matter has not been brought up yet.
齿间留香 chǐjiān-liúxiāng leave an unforgettable taste in one's mouth after a meal
齿鲸 chǐjīng toothed whale
齿科学 chǐkēxué 〈医学〉odontology
齿冷 chǐlěng 〈书面〉arouse one's infinite scorn:这班人的作风如此恶劣,实在令人～。By acting so atrociously, these people have laid themselves open to infinite scorn.
齿录 chǐlù 〈书面〉hire; employ
齿绿松石 chǐlǜsōngshí odontolite
齿轮 chǐlún gear; toothed or cog wheel:正～ spur gear /斜～ helical gear /伞～ bevel gear /～传动 gear drive /～间隙 gear clearance /～箱 gear box /～组 gear cluster
齿轮泵 chǐlúnbèng 〈机械〉gear pump
齿轮珩床 chǐlún héngchuáng 〈机械〉gear honing machine
齿轮精削机床 chǐlún jīngxiāo jīchuáng 〈机械〉gear cutting and finishing machine
齿腔 chǐqiāng 〈生理〉dental cavity
齿舌 chǐshé 〈生理〉radula
齿舌音 chǐshéyīn 〈语言〉dentilingual
齿数 chǐshǔ mention; speak of:不足～ not worth mentioning
齿髓 chǐsuǐ 〈生理〉tooth pulp
齿条 chǐtiáo 〈机械〉rack
齿舞群岛 Chǐwǔ Qúndǎo Habomai Islands (formerly Japanese, under Russian jurisdiction after World War II)
齿音 chǐyīn 〈语言〉dental; dental sound
齿龈 chǐyín 〈生理〉(tooth) gum
齿质 chǐzhì dentine; dentinum

哆 chǐ 〈书面〉open (one's mouth):～口 open one's mouth; talk
see also duō

侈 chǐ 〈书面〉❶ wasteful; extravagant:穷奢极～ live in extreme extravagance ❷ exaggerate:～言 exaggerated terms; exaggeration
侈论 chǐlùn exaggerated talk; hyperbole
侈靡 chǐmí 〈书面〉extravagant; wasteful:过着荒淫～的生活 lead a life of dissipation and debauchery /民俗～ popular craze for luxury and extravagance
侈谈 chǐtán 〈书面〉❶ talk glibly about; prate about; prattle about:～大道理 talk glibly about what one regards as major principles ❷ high-sounding words:这种～一文不值。Such idle talk is worth nothing.

褫 chǐ 〈书面〉❶ take off; doff:解佩而～绅 take off one's jade ornaments as well as one's broad belt ❷ dismiss; divest; deprive:～职 be dismissed from office
褫夺 chǐduó deprive; divest; dispossess:～政治权利 be deprived of political rights; deprive (sb.) of his political rights
褫革 chǐgé 〈书面〉dismiss (sb.) from office; relieve (sb.) of his post

尺 chǐ ❶ *chi*, unit of length equalling one third of a metre ❷ rule; ruler:鲁班～〈旧语〉carpenter's square /直角～ square /卡～ sliding callipers /三棱～ three-square rule; triangular scale /米突～ metre scale /折～ folding ruler /卷～ tape measure; band tape /钢～ steel rule /皮～ tape measure; tape /标～〈测绘〉surveyor's rod /量油～ oil dip rod; dipstick ❸ tool for drawing:放大～ pantograph /丁字～ T-square ❹ instrument in the shape of a ruler:计算～ slide ruler /镇纸～ horizontal bronze paperweight /戒～ ruler used by a teacher in old days to hit the palm of a pupil as a punishment ❺〈中医〉one of the three points where the pulse is felt
see also chě
尺八 chǐbā shakuhachi, Japanese bamboo flute
尺寸 chǐcùn ❶ a jot; an iota:无～之功 without the least contribution ❷ small; narrow:～之兵 small or short weapons /无～之地 not have an inch of land; not have enough room to swing a cat
尺寸 chǐcun ❶ measurement; dimension; size:衣服的～ measurement of a garment /量～ take sb.'s measurements ❷〈口语〉propriety; suitability:办事有～ have a sense of propriety in handling matters /说话很注意～ speak properly on social occasions
尺动脉 chǐdòngmài 〈生理〉ulnar artery
尺牍 chǐdú 〈旧语〉correspondence; letters; epistolary writing
尺度 chǐdù standard; yardstick; criterion; measure:货币是价值的～。Money is the measure of value. /不可放宽～。The standard cannot be lowered.
尺短寸长 chǐduǎn-cùncháng (short for 尺有所短,寸有所长) sometimes a *chi* (foot) may prove short while a *cun* (inch) may prove long — everyone has his strong and weak points
尺幅千里 chǐfú-qiānlǐ panorama of a thousand *li* on a one-foot scroll — rich content within a small compass; a good artist can

paint mountains and rivers on a foot of paper
尺骨 chǐgǔ 〈生理〉ulna
尺蠖 chǐhuò 〈动物〉looper; inchworm; geometer
尺蠖蛾 chǐhuò'é 〈动物〉geometrid moth
尺码 chǐmǎ ❶ (of shoes, hats, etc.) size:各种～的鞋帽一应俱全。We supply shoes and hats of all sizes. /你穿多大～的鞋子? What size shoes do you wear? ❷ standard; yardstick:问题在于用什么～来衡量。It depends on what yardstick you will apply.
尺脉 chǐmài 〈中医〉*chi* pulse; proximal position of radial pulse
尺素 chǐsù ❶ one-foot-long piece of white silk; small hanging scroll:这幅画～之间烟波云海,幽谷峻崖,气象万千。This picture drawn on a one-foot-long piece of white silk presents a magnificent view of impenetrable mists and clouds, and of secluded valleys and craggy mountains. ❷〈书面〉epistle; letter
尺头儿 chǐtóur 〈方言〉❶ measurement; size:这双鞋～大。This pair of shoes is of large size. ❷ odd bits of cloth:这个摊位专卖～。This counter is reserved exclusively for sales of odd bits of cloth.
尺头 chǐtou 〈方言〉cloth; textile:拿走了一匹～ take away a bolt of cloth
尺腕骨 chǐwàngǔ 〈生理〉ulnare
尺页 chǐyè painting or calligraphy on a sheet one *chi* in diameter; book of such paintings or calligraphy
尺有所短,寸有所长 chǐ yǒusuǒ duǎn, cùn yǒusuǒ cháng *see* "尺短寸长"
尺泽 chǐzé 〈中医〉*Chize*, an acupuncture point
尺中 chǐzhōng *see* "尺❺"
尺子 chǐzi rule; ruler

呎

chǐ *also* yīngchǐ 〈旧语〉foot (as a measurement of length)

chì

啻

chì 〈书面〉only; merely:不～于此。It is so not only in this respect.

炽(熾)

chì burning; flaming; ablaze:～炭 burning charcoal /～焰 raging flames
炽烈 chìliè flaming; white-hot:～的感情 ardent affection /～的爱情 passionate love /～的气氛 fervent atmosphere /炉火～。The stove is burning vigorously.
炽情 chìqíng passion; ardent emotion
炽热 chìrè white-hot; blazing; fervent:～的岩浆 white-hot magma /～的情感 consuming passion /对祖国～的爱 fervent love for one's motherland /言词～ impassioned words
炽盛 chìshèng flaming; blazing; flourishing:火势～。The fire is blazing. /他有着～的求知欲。He has a burning desire for knowledge.
炽燥 chìzào hot and dry:天气～。The weather is hot and dry.
炽灼 chìzhuó ❶ blazing (fire) ❷ enormous (power):威权～ enormous power ❸ burn; scorch; singe

瘛

chì
瘛疭 chìzòng 〈中医〉spasm

瘈

chì
see also zhì
瘈疭 chìzòng *see* "瘛疭" chìzòng

赤

chì ❶ a kind of red slightly lighter than vermillion ❷ red:～日 red sun; scorching sun /面红耳～ get red in the face; be flushed /近朱者～ what's near cinnabar goes red — one becomes good in good company ❸ revolutionary; Communist:～色政权 Red power; nevolutionary government ❹ loyal; devoted; faithful:～心 devotion ❺ bare:～着脚 barefoot ❻ empty ❼ pure (gold):金无足～。There is no such thing as a hundred percent pure gold.
赤白痢 chìbáilì 〈中医〉dysentery with purulent and bloody stools
赤背 chìbèi naked to the waist; barebacked
赤崩 chìbēng 〈中医〉vaginal discharge of blood and leucorrhea
赤壁之战 Chìbì Zhī Zhàn Battle of Chibi (208 AD), which resulted in the prolonged balance of power among the Three Kingdoms
赤膊 chìbó be naked to the waist:打～ be stripped to the waist; barebacked / 烈日下,不可～干活。One should not work naked to the waist under a scorching sun.
赤膊上阵 chìbó-shàngzhèn ❶ (of a warrior in ancient times) go into battle stripped to the waist; challenge one's enemy or accept a challenge to single combat with no armour on ❷ take personal charge and go it alone despite opposition ❸〈贬义〉throw away all disguise and tactics; come out into the open as a result of desperation or of foolhardiness
赤潮 chìcháo *also* "红潮" hóngcháo red tide
赤忱 chìchén 〈书面〉❶ absolute sincerity:～相待 be absolutely sincere ❷ sincere wish; ardent expectations:你不可辜负他的一片～。You should prove yourself worthy of his ardent expectations.
赤诚 chìchéng absolute sincerity:～待人 treat people with all sincerity
赤带 chìdài 〈中医〉red leucorrhea; leucorrhea with blood discharge
赤胆忠心 chìdǎn-zhōngxīn absolute loyalty; utter devotion; complete dedication:～为人民服务 serve the people heart and soul /对人民事业～ be absolutely loyal (*or* completely dedicated) to the cause of the people
赤道 chìdào ❶ equator:～气候 equatorial climate /～无风带 doldrums ❷〈天文〉celestial equator:～面 equatorial plane
赤道非洲 Chìdào Fēizhōu Equatorial Africa
赤道几内亚 Chìdào Jǐnèiyà Equatorial Guinea:～人 Equatorial Guinean
赤道洋流 chìdào yángliú equatorial current
赤道仪 chìdàoyí equatorial telescope
赤地 chìdì 〈书面〉barren land:此国大旱,～三载。Stricken by a severe drought, the country got in no crops for three years running.
赤地千里 chìdì-qiānlǐ vast expanse of barren land; scene of utter desolation:大旱三年,～。Three successive years of dire drought left a vast expanse of barren land.
赤豆 chìdòu red bean; adzuki bean
赤褐色 chìhèsè russet
赤红 chìhóng crimson; flushed:～脸儿 flushed cheeks /这孩子发热,脸色～。The child was feverish and looked flushed. *or* The child flushed with fever.
赤狐 chìhú 〈动物〉red fox
赤脚 chìjiǎo bare-footed; barefoot:～趟水 wade across a stream barefoot /～穿草鞋 wear straw sandals without socks on /～大仙 the Barefoot Immortal; (jocularly) barefoot guy
赤脚医生 chìjiǎo yīshēng barefoot doctor (term created in the late 1960's to refer to part-time paramedical workers who serve rural people)
赤金 chìjīn pure gold; solid gold
赤经 chìjīng 〈天文〉right ascension
赤嵌之战 Chìkàn Zhī Zhàn Battle of Chikan (1661), in which Zheng Chenggong (郑成功) defeated the Dutch occupation army and recovered Taiwan
赤口白舌 chìkǒu-báishé ❶〈方言〉talk nonsense:年轻人不要～。Young people should not babble such nonsense. ❷ (usu. used in the early vernacular) misunderstanding or dispute caused by words
赤口毒舌 chìkǒu-dúshé venomous tongue; vile language
赤佬 chìlǎo *also* "赤老"〈方言〉〈粗话〉devil; bastard
赤栎 chìlì 〈植物〉red oak
赤痢 chìlì 〈中医〉dysentery characterized by blood in the stool
赤练蛇 chìliànshé a kind of poisonous snake (*Dinodon rufozonatum*)
赤磷 chìlín red phosphorus
赤露 chìlù bare:～着脊背 be stripped to the waist; with one's naked back exposed
赤裸 chìluǒ ❶ naked:全身～ stark-naked /～着上身 stripped to the waist; topless /他～着脚走路。He walked barefoot. ❷ totally unsheltered:～的原野 open country; open fields
赤裸裸 chìluǒluǒ ❶ (stark) naked:婴儿～地躺在摇篮里。The baby lay naked in the cradle. ❷〈贬义〉undisguised; naked; open:～的侵略行为 naked aggression /～的强盗逻辑 out-and-out gangster logic /～地进行抢劫 commit robbery in the open; rob in broad daylight
赤眉起义 Chìméi Qǐyì Chimei Uprising (peasant uprising led by Fan Chong 范崇 from 18 to 25 AD, which helped to overthrow Wang Mang's 王莽 reign, but was eventually defeated by Liu Xiu

刘秀, founder of the Eastern Han Dynasty. The rebels dyed their eyebrows red, hence the name Chimei or Red Eyebrows Uprising.)
赤霉病 chìméibìng wheat scab
赤霉素 chìméisù 〈生化〉gibberellin
赤贫 chìpín extreme or dire poverty; destitution: ～如洗 be poverty-stricken; be destitute; be as poor as a church mouse
赤热 chìrè red-hot; white-hot
see also "炽热" chìrè
赤日 chìrì scorching sun
赤芍 chìsháo 〈中药〉unpeeled root of herbaceous peony (*Paeonia lactiflora*)
赤身 chìshēn ❶ naked; without a stitch of clothing: ～露体 stark-naked ❷ destitute; penniless: 他上无片瓦,下无立锥之地,真是十足的～汉。He had neither a roof over his head, nor an inch of land under his feet. He was every inch a pauper.
赤绳系足 chìshéng-xìzú *also* "红绳系足" hóngshéng-xìzú bind the feet with a red rope — be united in wedlock
赤石脂 chìshízhī 〈中药〉red halloysite
赤手 chìshǒu bare-hand; unarmed: ～搏斗 fight bare-handed; fist fight
赤手空拳 chìshǒu-kōngquán barehanded; unarmed; with bare fists: ～同歹徒搏斗 fight gangsters barehanded
赤手起家 chìshǒu-qǐjiā start from scratch
赤松 chìsōng 〈植物〉Japanese red pine
赤塔 Chìtǎ Chita, Russian town near China's northeastern border with a railway line to China
赤陶 chìtáo terracotta
赤条条 chìtiáotiáo have not a stitch on; be stark-naked: 两个婴儿～地在床上玩耍。Two naked babies are playing in bed.
赤铁矿 chìtiěkuàng red iron ore; hematite
赤铜矿 chìtóngkuàng red copper ore; cuprite
赤纬 chìwěi 〈天文〉declination
赤卫队 chìwèiduì Red Guards (local armed units in the revolutionary base areas in the Second Revolutionary Civil War from 1927 to 1937)
赤县 Chìxiàn 〈书面〉China: ～神州 Sacred Earth of China
赤小豆 chìxiǎodòu red bean; adzuki bean
赤心 chìxīn utter devotion; complete loyalty: ～报国 utter dedication to one's country / 彼此～相待 be absolutely sincere and loyal to each other
赤血盐 chìxuèyán 〈化学〉potassium ferricyanide; red prussiate of potash
赤眼蜂 chìyǎnfēng 〈动物〉trichogramma
赤子 chìzǐ 〈书面〉new-born baby: ～之心 (with) complete innocence; (with) an unquestioning trust / 海外～ overseas compatriot
赤字 chìzì deficit; red ink: 财政～ financial deficit / 外贸～ foreign trade deficit / ～预算 deficit budget / ～余额 red balance / ～财政 deficit financing / ～开支 deficit spending/ ～公债 deficit-covering bond / 有～ be in the red / 弥补～ make up (*or* meet, *or* cover) a deficit
赤足 chìzú barefoot; barefooted: ～而行 walk in one's bare feet

敕(勅、勑)

chì imperial edict: 宣～ promulgate an imperial edict; announce or read out an imperial edict / ～命 decree by imperial edict
敕封 chìfēng appoint (sb.) to a post or confer a title (on sb.) by imperial order
敕建 chìjiàn build by imperial edict: 这座寺庙是～的。The temple was built by imperial order.
敕令 chìlìng ❶ (of an emperor) issue an edict ❷ imperial edict
敕书 chìshū imperial edict to court officials
敕造 chìzào build by imperial edict

鹈

chì *see* "鸂鹈" xīchì

翅(翄)

chì ❶ wing: 展～飞翔 (of a bird) move its wings to fly in the sky ❷ samara's wings ❸ shark's fin ❹ wing-like part of an object
翅膀 chìbǎng ❶ wing ❷ part of an object which looks or functions like a wing: 飞机～ airplane's wing(s) / 风筝～ wings of a kite
翅果 chìguǒ 〈植物〉samara
翅脉 chìmài 〈动物〉vein of the wing of an insect
翅鞘 chìqiào *also* "鞘翅" 〈动物〉elytrum
翅席 chìxí banquet that includes shark's fin
翅翼 chìyì *also* "翅膀" elytrum
翅子 chìzi ❶ shark's fin ❷ 〈方言〉wing

扶

chì 〈书面〉flog; whip; cane

眙

chì 〈书面〉❶ stare; gaze ❷ stare in surprise

叱

chì 〈书面〉denounce or rebuke loudly; roundly rebuke; shout at: 怒～其无状 roundly rebuke him for his insolence / 痛～朝奸 vehemently denounce treacherous courtiers
叱呵 chìhē shout at; bawl at: 大声～ bawl at; shout abuse at
叱喝 chìhè shout; yell; bellow: 我听见老板在～人。I heard the boss yelling at somebody.
叱呼 chìhū shout; cry out
叱令 chìlìng shout at and order; order loudly: ～退出 shout at sb. to get out / ～凶手放下武器 order the murderer loudly to lay down his weapon
叱骂 chìmà scold; abuse: 挨父母～ be scolded by one's parents; get a dressing-down from one's parents
叱问 chìwèn interrogate angrily; question loudly
叱责 chìzé scold; upbraid; rebuke: 受到上级的～ be severely censured by higher-ups
叱咤 chìzhà 〈书面〉shout angrily: ～左右 shout (*or* yell) at one's subordinates
叱咤风云 chìzhà-fēngyún commanding wind and storm; shaking heaven and earth; thundering; enormously powerful: ～的英雄人物 all-conquering hero / ～的英雄气概 earth-shaking heroism / 那些～的政治家们 those thundering statesmen

憏

chì *see* "侘憏" chàchì

傺

chì *see* "侘傺" chàchì

斥[1]

chì ❶ scold; upbraid; reprimand; denounce: 训～ take to task / 痛～ severely reprimand / ～为邪说 denounce as heresy ❷ repel; exclude; dismiss: ～退左右 dismiss one's entourage / 排～异己 weed out members of all rival factions; exclude people not of one's own clique / 同电相～。Two like electric charges repel each other. ❸ 〈书面〉pay; spend ❹ expand; open up

斥[2]

chì 〈书面〉scout; reconnoitre: ～骑 mounted scout

斥[3]

chì 〈书面〉saline soil
斥地 chìdì 〈书面〉expand one's territory: ～千里 expand one's territory by one thousand *li*
斥革 chìgé 〈书面〉dismiss: ～功名 strip sb. of his titles and positions
斥候 chìhòu 〈旧语〉reconnoitre; scout
斥力 chìlì 〈物理〉repulsion
斥卤 chìlǔ 〈书面〉(of soil) saline; alkaline
斥骂 chìmà scold; rebuke; berate: 高声～ scold loudly / 经理厉声～秘书。The manager gave his secretary a severe reprimand (*or* a good dressing-down).
斥卖 chìmài 〈书面〉sell: ～房产 sell off one's real estate
斥退 chìtuì ❶ 〈旧语〉dismiss; expel: 以小过而被朝廷～。He was banished from court for a petty offence. / 他因考试不及格而被学校～。He was expelled from school for failing his examinations. ❷ shout at sb. to go away: ～左右的仆人 dismiss the servants from one's presence
斥责 chìzé reprimand; rebuke; denounce: ～不讲公德的行为 denounce unethical conduct / 作者在文中愤怒地～了官僚主义者。The author makes a scathing criticism of the bureaucrats in his book.
斥逐 chìzhú 〈书面〉expel; dismiss; banish from court: ～入侵之敌 expel invaders / 皇帝愚昧,竟然～贤臣。The emperor was so foolish as to send his good ministers into exile.
斥资 chìzī 〈书面〉pay the expenses: ～创建学校 donate money to

found a school

彳 chì

彳亍 chìchù 〈书面〉 walk slowly; saunter; stroll: ～在乡间小路上 saunter along a country path

饬 chì

〈书面〉 ❶ put in order; readjust; rectify: 整～纪律 strengthen (*or* straighten out) discipline ❷ order: ～其照办无误 order sb. to act in conformity with the demand ❸ prudent: 谨～ prudent and conscientious

饬厉 chìlì *also* "饬励" 〈书面〉 encourage the rank and file to work still harder: ～将士 boost the morale of officers and men

饬令 chìlìng order: 朝廷～他火速进击。The imperial court ordered him to mount an immediate attack.

C

chōng

充 chōng

❶ sufficient; full: 粮～食足 have plenty of food / 供应～分 have ample supply / 内容～实 substantial in content ❷ fill; stuff: ～气 pump air (into sth.) / 按时纳税，以～国库。Pay taxes in time to fill the national treasury. ❸ serve as; act as: 我为两队比赛～裁判。I acted as referee for the two contesting teams. ❹ pretend to be; pose as: ～行家 pretend to be an expert / 以次～好 pass inferior stuff off as quality goods / 打肿脸～胖子 slap one's face until it's swollen in an effort to look imposing — puff oneself up at one's own cost / 他不过是在老板面前～能干。He is only trying to show off in front of his boss. ❺ (Chōng) a surname

充畅 chōngchàng 〈书面〉 ❶ (of supply of goods) plentiful and constant: 货源～ plentiful and constant supply of goods / 国内市场上物资丰富，产品～。There is ample supply and smooth transit of goods in the home market. ❷ (of style of writing) fluent and smooth: 文句～ smooth and fluent writing

充斥 chōngchì flood; congest; be full of: 不能让不健康的书刊～图书市场。We mustn't allow books of unhealthy tendencies to flood our book market. / 奸商～全城。There are profiteers everywhere in town.

充磁 chōngcí magnetize

充当 chōngdāng serve as; act as; play the part of: ～炮灰 serve as cannon fodder / ～工具 act as a cat's paw; be a pawn / ～主角 play the leading part (*or* role) / 这个代表团由他来～领队。He will lead the delegation.

充电 chōngdiàn charge (a battery, etc.): ～发电机 charging generator / ～机组 charging set / ～站 charging station / ～电池 rechargeable battery

充电器 chōngdiànqì battery charger

充耳不闻 chōng'ěr-bùwén refuse to hear; turn a deaf ear to: 对别人的意见他～。He always turns a deaf ear to others' views and advice.

充分 chōngfèn ❶ full; ample; abundant; sufficient: 证据～ have ample evidence / 理由～ have well-grounded (*or* well justified) reasons / 思想准备很～ be well prepared mentally / 人民享有～的自由。The people enjoy full freedom. ❷ to the best of one's ability; as far as possible: ～发挥水平 give full play to one's ability / ～利用时间 make good use of one's time

充分就业 chōngfèn jiùyè 〈经济〉 full employment: ～政策 policy of full employment / ～经济 full employment economy

充公 chōnggōng confiscate: 海关把走私的货物～了。The Customs confiscated the contraband.

充饥 chōngjī allay or appease one's hunger: 以野菜～ eat wild herbs to stave off hunger; survive on herbs / 带着干粮，准备在路上～。Take with you some dry food in case you are hungry on the way.

充军 chōngjūn be deported to a distant place for penal servitude; be banished

充满 chōngmǎn ❶ fill: 欢呼声～了会场。The conference hall resounded (*or* was filled) with applause. ❷ be full of; be imbued with; be brimming with; be permeated with: 内心～喜悦 be overjoyed / ～青春的活力 be full of youthful vigour / ～矛盾 teem with contradictions / 这首诗～着乐观主义的精神。The poem is imbued with the spirit of optimism. / 她心里～了激情。Her heart overflowed with enthusiasm. / 我们～必胜的信心。We are absolutely confident of success.

充沛 chōngpèi plentiful; abundant; full: 雨水～ ample rainfall / 精力～ be energetic; be full of vim and vigour / ～的爱国热情 boundless patriotic enthusiasm

充其量 chōngqíliàng at most; at best: 一个月～挣三百元 make 300 *yuan* a month at most / 书法比赛他～能得个第三名。He can at best win a third prize in the calligraphy contest. / 这次出差～一周时间就够了。This business trip will take no more than one week.

充气 chōngqì 〈机械〉 air charging; air inflation: ～机 inflator / ～轮胎 inflated tyre / ～压力 inflation pressure

充气灯泡 chōngqì dēngpào 〈电工〉 gas-filled lamp bulb

充气电缆 chōngqì diànlǎn 〈电工〉 gas-filled cable; GF cable; pressure cable

充气光电池 chōngqì guāngdiànchí 〈电工〉 gas cell

充气式结构 chōngqìshì jiégòu inflatable structure

充气艇 chōngqìtǐng inflatable boat

充气压力 chōngqì yālì inflation pressure

充任 chōngrèn fill the post of; hold the position of: ～部长助理 serve as assistant minister / ～银行经理 hold the position of bank manager

充塞 chōngsè fill up; cram: 进口货～市场。Imported goods flooded the market. / 吵闹声～整个大厅。The din filled the whole hall. *or* The hall buzzed with noises.

充实 chōngshí ❶ substantial; rich: 设备～。The equipment is adequate. / 这个系的教学力量～。The department is well-staffed. / 文字流畅，内容～。The language is fluent, and the content substantial. ❷ substantiate; enrich; replenish: ～基层 strengthen organizations at the grassroots level / ～各级领导 strengthen the leadership at all levels / ～论据 substantiate one's argument / ～师资队伍 augment the teaching staff

充数 chōngshù make up the number; serve as a stopgap; pass muster: 有些人参加表演不过是～而已。Some people who took part in the performance were there simply to make up the number. / 不能以次品～。We must not make up the amount with products of poor quality. / 他不能胜任这项工作，暂时～是可以的。He is not equal to the job, but he is all right as a stopgap. / 如果你找不到更好的人，我或许可以～。If you have no better choice, I can perhaps pass muster.

充填 chōngtián fill up (a space); stuff: ～了氢气的气球，能漂浮在空中。Balloons filled with hydrogen can float in the air.

充填材料 chōngtián cáiliào 〈矿业〉 filler; mine-fill; filling material

充血 chōngxuè 〈医学〉 hyperaemia; congestion of blood: 他双目～。His eyes were bloodshot.

充压 chōngyā pressurize

充氧 chōngyǎng oxygen charging

充溢 chōngyì be full to the brim; overflow; be permeated: 会议～着团结友爱的精神。The meeting is permeated with the spirit of friendship and unity. / 大厅～着欢乐的气氛。The atmosphere of the hall overflows with joy and merriment. / 他脸上～着幸福的笑容。His face lit up with a happy smile.

充盈 chōngyíng ❶ plentiful; full: 仓廪～。The granaries are full. / 眼眶里～着泪水。Eyes brimmed with tears. ❷ 〈书面〉 full and round; well-developed; full-grown: ～的肌体 well-developed body

充裕 chōngyù plentiful; abundant; ample; sufficient: 物资～ abundant supply of materials / 时间～ have plenty of time; have ample time / 粮食～ ample supply of grain

充足 chōngzú adequate; sufficient; abundant; ample: 光线～ well-lit / 经费～ have sufficient (*or* ample) funds / 商品～。Commodities are in abundant supply.

充足理由律 chōngzú-lǐyóulǜ 〈逻辑〉 law of sufficient reason

茺 chōng

茺蔚 chōngwèi 〈植物〉 motherwort

舂 chōng

pound; pestle: ～米 husk rice with mortar and pestle / ～药 pound medicinal herbs in a mortar

惷 chōng

〈书面〉 stupid; foolish

冲[1]（沖、衝） chōng

❶ thoroughfare; important place: 要～ hub (of transport, etc.); strategically important place ❷

charge; rush; dash: ~出重围 break loose from heavy enemy encirclement /向山下~去 rush down the mountain /~向敌人阵地 charge towards the enemy lines /~啊! Charge! ❸ clash; collide: ~撞 offend; contradict /缓~ buffer; cushion ❹ *see* "冲喜" ❺〈书面〉young: ~年 childhood; infancy ❻〈天文〉opposition: 大~ favourable opposition

冲[2]**(冲、衝)** chōng ❶ pour boiling water on: ~奶粉 pour boiling water in powdered milk /~茶 make tea /~咖啡 make (instant) coffee ❷ rinse; wash away; flush: 手绢洗过后,用清水~一~。After washing the handkerchief, rinse it out. /小屋被洪水~垮了。The hut was washed away by the flood. /星期三的讨论让运动会给~了。The Wednesday discussion clashed with the sports meet and was cancelled. ❸〈摄影〉develop: ~胶卷 develop a film ❹ offset; cancel out: 将这笔账~了罢。Write off the item when you balance the accounts.

冲[3]**(冲)** chōng 〈方言〉stretch of flatland in a hilly area: 小村座落在山~之中。The small village nestles on a piece of level land among the hills.
see also chòng

冲程 chōngchéng 〈机械〉stroke

冲冲 chōngchōng in a state of excitement: 喜~ be jubilant /气~ be fuming with anger /急~ be in a great hurry /兴~ be in high spirits; burst with enthusiasm

冲刺 chōngcì 〈体育〉spurt; sprint: 做最后的~ make a final spurt /向终点~ make a dash (*or* spurt) towards the tape /~速度 spurting speed; top speed

冲淡 chōngdàn ❶ dilute: 用凉开水~橘子汁 dilute orange juice with cold boiled water ❷ water down; weaken; play down; downgrade: 改编~了原著的悲剧气氛。The adaptation watered down the tragic tone of the original. /岁月的流逝没有~他对故乡的思念。The passage of time did not reduce his longing for his hometown.

冲荡 chōngdàng (of water current) pour; lash: 大树被洪水~得东倒西歪。Lashed by the flood, the big trees were either tottering or lying athwart in water.

冲抵 chōngdǐ *see* "冲销"

冲动 chōngdòng ❶ impulse: 凭一时~ act on impulse; act on the spur of the moment; act on a brain wave ❷ get excited; be impetuous: 不要~。Don't get excited. /如果你遇事~,你会后悔的。If you act rashly, you will regret it.

冲断层 chōngduàncéng 〈地质〉thrust fault

冲犯 chōngfàn hurt; offend: 他的话~了上司。His words offended his boss. /谁也没有~你,你为什么这样发火? Why are you flaring up since nobody has said anything to offend you?

冲锋 chōngfēng charge; assault: 向敌人发起~ launch an assault against the enemy; charge at the enemy

冲锋队员 chōngfēng duìyuán storm trooper

冲锋号 chōngfēnghào bugle call to charge

冲锋枪 chōngfēngqiāng assault rifle; submachine gun; tommy gun

冲锋陷阵 chōngfēng-xiànzhèn ❶ charge against the enemy line; charge ahead in battle; fight bravely: 他在战场上~,立下了许多战功。He won distinction on the battlefield for his extraordinary valour. ❷ fight valiantly for a just cause: 他是文化战线上~的民族英雄。His image is that of a national hero charging ahead bravely on the literary front.

冲服 chōngfú take (medicine) after mixing it with water, wine, etc.

冲沟 chōnggōu gully; ravine; washout

冲昏头脑 chōnghūn-tóunǎo turn sb.'s head; be or get carried away: 被胜利~ be dizzy with success; be carried away by success /他怕她让预想不到的胜利冲昏了头脑。He was afraid that her head would be turned by the unexpected victory.

冲击 chōngjī ❶ lash; beat against; break on: 狂涛~着堤岸。Furious waves lashed the dyke. ❷ charge; assault: 向敌人阵地迅猛~ launch a swift and fierce attack on the enemy position /向顶峰~ make an assault on the highest peak ❸ challenge; affect: 在外国商品~下,有些工厂停产了。Some factories went out of production under the impact of foreign merchandise. /人们的思想受到科学发现的~。Man's thinking is affected by the discoveries of science. /传统观念受到新思想的~。Traditional concepts have been challenged by new ideas. ❹ subject to attack or criticism: 在"十年动乱"中没有受到~的人很少。Few people were immune from attack during the ten years of chaos. ❺〈物理〉impact; shock;〈医学〉ictus: ~器〈机械〉impacter /~扳手 impact wrench /~测量 shock measurement /~钻〈机械〉percussion driller

冲击摆 chōngjībǎi 〈物理〉ballistic pendulum

冲击波 chōngjībō blast wave; shock wave

冲击电流 chōngjī diànliú impulse or impact current

冲击机 chōngjījī 〈军事〉(old name for 战斗机) fighter plane

冲击力 chōngjīlì force of impact

冲击伤 chōngjīshāng blast injuries

冲击式截煤机 chōngjīshì jiéméijī 〈矿业〉coal puncher

冲击式破碎机 chōngjīshì pòsuìjī 〈机械〉impact crusher

冲击式水轮机 chōngjīshì shuǐlúnjī 〈机械〉impulse or action turbine

冲击试验 chōngjī shìyàn impulse test; shock or percussion test; blow test; falling-weight test

冲积 chōngjī 〈地理〉alluviation

冲积层 chōngjīcéng alluvium

冲积平原 chōngjī píngyuán alluvial plain

冲积扇 chōngjīshàn alluvial fan

冲积土 chōngjītǔ alluvial soil

冲积锥 chōngjīzhuī alluvial cone

冲激 chōngjī lash; beat against; break on: 海浪~着礁石。Sea waves lashed (against) the reefs.

冲剂 chōngjì 〈中药〉instant herbal mixture

冲减 chōngjiǎn deduct: ~财政收入 deduct from treasury revenues

冲决 chōngjué burst; smash: ~罗网 smash the trammels /~堤坝 burst the dykes

冲口而出 chōngkǒu'érchū say sth. without thinking; blurt out: 那是他~的气话,请别在意。Those are remarks he blurted out when he was angry. Don't take them to heart.

冲垮 chōngkuǎ break down; burst; shatter: 洪水~了河堤。The floods burst the river embankment. /新思想~了封建迷信。New ideas have broken down feudalistic superstitions.

冲扩 chōngkuò 〈摄影〉develop and enlarge: ~彩卷 develop and enlarge a roll of colour film

冲浪板 chōnglàngbǎn surfboard

冲浪运动 chōnglàng yùndòng surfing

冲力 chōnglì impulsive force; thrust; momentum

冲凉 chōngliáng 〈方言〉take a cold shower: 广州几乎每户人家都有个~的地方。There is a cold shower in almost every household in Guangzhou.

冲量 chōngliàng 〈物理〉impulse

冲龄 chōnglíng (at a) tender age; very young: ~即位 be enthroned at a tender age

冲破 chōngpò break through; breach: ~防线 breach the defences /~封锁 break through a blockade /~河堤 burst a dyke /~禁区 break into a forbidden zone; do sth. regarded as out of bounds /火光~漆黑的夜空。The blaze pierced the darkness of the night skies.

冲散 chōngsàn break up; scatter; disperse: 队伍被人流~。The procession was scattered by the onrush of crowds.

冲杀 chōngshā charge; rush ahead; fight: 拼死~ risk one's life in battle; fight desperately /战场上一片~声。The battleground resounded with battle cries.

冲沙闸 chōngshāzhá 〈水利〉scouring sluice

冲晒 chōngshài 〈摄影〉develop and print

冲绳 Chōngshéng Okinawa, in the southern Ryuku islands of Japan

冲刷 chōngshuā ❶ wash down; wash off: 把汽车~干净 wash down the car /墙上的字已被雨水~掉了。The words on the wall have been washed off by the rain. ❷ erode; scour: 岩石上有被洪水~过的痕迹。The rocks still bear the marks of scouring floods.

冲刷作用 chōngshuā zuòyòng 〈水利〉scouring

冲塌 chōngtā (of floodwater, etc.) cause to collapse; burst: ~桥梁 (of a flood) collapse bridges /~房屋 (of a flood) tear down houses

冲腾 chōngténg (of gases) rise up; rush out: 热气从排气管~而出。Steam rushed out from the exhaust pipe.

冲天 chōngtiān towering; soaring: 怒气~ in a towering rage /干劲~ with boundless enthusiasm /不飞则已,一飞~。If the bird ever

flies, it soars right into the sky. — (of one who appears common and mediocre) show one's mettle and accomplish an astonishing feat
冲天炉 chōngtiānlú 〈冶金〉cupola (furnace)
冲田 chōngtián paddy fields in lowland of hilly country
冲突 chōngtū conflict; clash; contradict: 言语～ verbal conflict / 武装～ armed conflict / 边境～ border clashes / 意见～ opinions in conflict with each other; conflicting opinions / 贸易～ trade conflict / 职权～ conflict of competence / 管辖权～ conflict of jurisdictions / 法律的～ conflict of laws / 解决两国的～ resolve the conflict between two countries / ～研究所 Institute for the Study of Conflict (ISC) / ～国 conflicting power / 内容前后～。The content is self-contradictory. / 新旧思想～。The old ideas collide with the new. / 我们之间没有利害～。There is no conflict of interests between us.
冲洗 chōngxǐ ❶ wash away; rinse: ～伤口 wash a wound / 把这些瓶子～一下。Rinse the bottles. ❷〈摄影〉develop: ～照片 have a film developed and printed; develop prints / ～放大 develop and enlarge (a film)
冲洗机 chōngxǐjī scouring machine
冲洗液 chōngxǐyè flushing liquid
冲喜 chōngxǐ 〈旧语〉wedding arranged in the hope that the joyous occasion would ward off the evils and bring the bridegroom back to health
冲销 chōngxiāo write off; abate: ～坏账 write off a bad debt / ～记录 reverse an entry
冲霄 chōngxiāo tower or soar into the skies: ～的高楼 buildings towering into the clouds
冲泻 chōngxiè (of water) rush down from a height: 雨水从山坡上～而下。Rain water rushed down the slope.
冲压空气涡轮 chōngyā kōngqì wōlún 〈航空〉ram-air turbine
冲压式喷气发动机 chòngyāshì pēnqì fādòngjī 〈航空〉ramjet engine; athodyd (aero-thermo-dynamicduct)
冲压式压气机 chòngyāshì yāqìjī 〈机械〉ram compressor
冲要 chōngyào ❶ strategically important: 地处～ be a place of strategic importance ❷〈书面〉key position or post: 他久居～。He has been in that key position for a long time.
冲澡 chōngzǎo take a shower
冲账 chōngzhàng 〈会计〉balance an account; reverse an entry
冲撞 chōngzhuàng ❶ hit; bump; strike; ram: 小轿车被卡车～翻倒。The car was hit and overturned by a truck. ❷ offend; give offence to: 我后悔不该失言～他。I regret I had a slip of the tongue and offended him.

忡(㤝) chōng 〈书面〉restless with anxiety
忡忡 chōngchōng in an unhappy mood; laden with anxiety: 忧心～ heavyhearted; careworn; unhappy / 他终日～，不知有何心事。I don't know what is on his mind. He looks so worried all day long.

翀 chōng 〈书面〉(of birds) soar

憧 chōng
憧憧 chōngchōng flickering; moving: 烛影～ flickering shadows of candlelight / 人影～ shadows of people moving about
憧憬 chōngjǐng long for; look forward to: ～着幸福生活 long for a happy life / ～未来，他信心百倍。He looked forward to the future with redoubled confidence.

罿 chōng 〈书面〉bird-net

艟 chōng *see* "艨艟" méngchōng

涌 chōng 〈方言〉branch (of a river)
see also yǒng
涌滘 chōngjiào 〈方言〉branch or fork of a river

chóng

虫(蟲) chóng ❶ insect; worm: 益～ beneficial insect / 害～ harmful insect / 蝗～ locust / 萤火～ firefly; glowworm / 甲～ beetle / 昆～ insect / 毛毛～ caterpillar / 寄生～ parasite / 鱼～ water flea (used as fish feed) ❷〈贬义〉certain sort of people: 懒～〈口语〉lazybones; idler / 可怜～ pitiful creature / 糊涂～ muddle-head; blockhead / 应声～ yes-man
虫草 chóngcǎo 〈中药〉Chinese caterpillar fungus (*Cordyceps sinensis*)
虫吃牙 chóngchīyá *see* "虫牙"
虫果 chóngguǒ wormed fruit
虫害 chónghài insect pest
虫积 chóngjī 〈中医〉parasitic disease (usually in the stomach or intestines)
虫胶 chóngjiāo shellac: ～清漆 shellac (varnish)
虫口 chóngkǒu number of insects in a particular area: ～密度 insect density
虫媒传粉 chóngméi chuánfěn 〈植物〉insect pollination
虫媒花 chóngméihuā 〈植物〉entomophilous flower
虫漆 chóngqī 〈化工〉lacca
虫情 chóngqíng insect pest situation: ～测报站 pest forecasting station / 今年～严重。The insect pest is serious this year.
虫蚀 chóngshí (of clothes, books or other articles) be moth-eaten: 你要防止衣服被～。Make sure that your clothes are not moth-eaten.
虫牙 chóngyá (popular term for 龋齿) carious or decayed tooth
虫眼 chóngyǎn wormhole
虫蚁 chóngyǐ ❶ insects and ants; all kinds of insects: 老人心地善良，走路连～都不愿踩死。The old man is so kind-hearted that he does not even want to trample an insect while walking. ❷〈方言〉bird
虫瘿 chóngyǐng gall (on plants)
虫灾 chóngzāi plague of insects
虫豸 chóngzhì 〈书面〉insects
虫子 chóngzi insect; worm

种 Chóng a surname
see also zhǒng; zhòng

崇 chóng ❶ high; lofty; sublime: ～山 high mountain ❷ esteem; worship; respect: 推～ hold sb. in esteem; praise sb. highly / ～实 practical; pragmatic; realistic; down-to-earth ❸ (Chóng) a surname
崇拜 chóngbài worship; adore; admire: ～偶像 worship of idols; idolatry / 英雄～ hero worship / 个人～ personality cult / 盲目～ blind worship / 他们对教师有一种非常～的心理。They had an admiration that bordered on worship for teachers.
崇奉 chóngfèng believe in (a religion, philosophy, etc.): ～道教 believe in Taoism / ～佛教 believe in Buddhism; worship Buddha
崇高 chónggāo lofty; sublime; high; noble: ～的理想 lofty ideal / ～的事业 noble cause / ～的品德 virtuous character; nobility of character / ～的气节 moral integrity / ～的形象 sublime image / 享有～的威望 enjoy high prestige / 顺致最～的敬意。I avail myself of this opportunity to express (*or* renew) to you (*or* Your Excellency) the assurances of my highest consideration.
崇敬 chóngjìng esteem; respect; revere: 怀着无比～的心情 hold sb. in great reverence; cherish a feeling of great reverence for sb. / 他受到广大青年的～。He is held in great respect by young people.
崇论闳议 chónglùn-hóngyì *also* "崇论宏议" brilliant comments or ideas: 书中关于教育的～征服了许多读者。The brilliant ideas on education expounded in the book have won the hearts of a great many readers.
崇山峻岭 chóngshān-jùnlǐng high mountains and lofty ridges: 此地～，在在险阻。This is an area of high mountains and towering ridges, making it difficult and dangerous for people to get through.
崇尚 chóngshàng uphold; advocate: ～正义 uphold justice / ～助人为乐的道德观念 advocate an altruistic moral standard / ～艰苦朴素的作风 foster a life style of hard work and simple living
崇信 chóngxìn believe in (a religion); trust (a person): ～奸邪 trust evil people; take evil people into confidence
崇洋 chóngyáng worship things foreign: 盲目～ have blind faith in things foreign
崇洋媚外 chóngyáng-mèiwài worship things foreign and fawn on foreigners or foreign powers
崇洋迷外 chóngyáng-míwài worship and have blind faith in things foreign
崇洋哲学 chóngyáng zhéxué philosophy of worshiping things

foreign
崇仰 chóngyǎng advocate; hold in esteem:～真理 advocate truth
崇祯 Chóngzhēn Chongzhen, title of the reign (1628-1644) of Zhu Youjian (朱由检, 1611-1644), 17th and last emperor of the Ming Dynasty, called reverently Ming Sizong (明思宗) after death

重 chóng ❶ repeat; duplicate:外衣买～了 duplicate the purchase of a jacket by mistake ❷ again; once more:～写 rewrite /～读一遍 read all over again (*or* read once more)/～修黄鹤楼 give the Yellow Crane Pavilion a facelift /～访英伦 revisiting Britain; Britain revisited /这封信写得太乱, 我得～抄一遍。The letter is too messy, and I have to make a clear copy of it. ❸ layer:突破一～又一～的包围 break through layer after layer of encirclement /多～关卡 numerous checkpoints /双～领导 dual leadership /这句话有双～意义。This remark has a double meaning. ❹〈方言〉pile up; stack up:把这些席子～在一起。Pile these mats up.
see also zhòng
重版 chóngbǎn reprint; republish:～书 reprint (of a book) /此书已多次～。This book has been reprinted several times.
重瓣花 chóngbànhuā 〈植物〉double flower; multiple flower:～冠 multiple corolla
重瓣胃 chóngbànwèi *also* "瓣胃"〈动物〉manyplies; omasum; psalterium
重播 chóngbō ❶ (of radio or TV programme) rebroadcast; retransmit:～新闻联播节目 retransmit the network news programme ❷ resow; seed the fields for a second time:这块地被水淹过, 需～。This plot has been flooded. We must sow seeds again.
重操旧业 chóngcāo-jiùyè resume one's old trade; work at one's old job:这位厂长退休后, ～, 又当上了小学教师。The retired factory director resumed his old job as a schoolteacher.
重茬 chóngchá 〈农业〉continuous cropping
重唱 chóngchàng 〈音乐〉ensemble of two or more singers, each singing one part:二～ duet /三～ trio /四～ quartet
重重 chóngchóng layer upon layer; ring upon ring:陷入～包围 be encircled ring upon ring /受到～剥削 be fleeced right and left /忧虑～ deeply worried; careworn /顾虑～ full of misgivings /受到～阻力 faced with multiple obstructions /抵住外来的～压力 withstand outside pressure in countless forms /心事～ fall into a pensive mood /消失在～迷雾中 disappear into the heavy fog
重出 chóngchū reappear; recur:这种症状万一～, 就可能导致死亡。Recurrence of such symptoms could be fatal.
重床叠屋 chóngchuáng-diéwū *also* "叠床架屋" diéchuáng-jiàwū needless duplication; redundancy
重打锣鼓另开张 chóng dǎ luógǔ lìng kāizhāng 〈俗语〉reopen a business to the beating of gongs and drums — make a fresh start
重蹈覆辙 chóngdǎo-fùzhé take the road where carts have been wrecked; follow the same old disastrous road; meet with the same fate:必须谨慎从事, 避免～。Be cautious and steer clear of the same old disastrous course.
重叠 chóngdié one on top of another; overlapping:山峦～ range upon range of mountains /～影像 superimposed image /精简～的机构 streamline overlapping organizations /最后两段意思～。The ideas expressed in the last two paragraphs overlap.
重读 chóngdú ❶ read again:我最近～了这本书, 获益匪浅。I reread the book recently, to my great benefit. ❷ repeat one's studies:～生 repeater
see also zhòngdú
重发球 chóngfāqiú 〈体育〉let service; let
重返 chóngfǎn return; go back:难民获准～家园。The displaced persons were allowed to return to their homeland. /他伤愈后～前线。He went back to the front after his wound had healed.
重返大气层运载工具 chóngfǎn dàqìcéng yùnzài gōngjù re-entry vehicle (as rockets, spaceships, etc.)
重犯 chóngfàn repeat (an error or an offence):避免～错误 avoid repeating the same mistake /～老毛病 relapse into one's old bad habits; have a relapse
重放 chóngfàng replay:把这一段～一下。Please replay this part (of a record or video-tape).
重逢 chóngféng meet again; have a reunion:久别～ meet again after a long separation
重复 chóngfù ❶ reappear; repeat:这篇文章～冗赘。This article is repetitive and tedious. ❷ repeat; duplicate:～保险 overlapping insurance; double insurance /～课税 double taxation /～劳动 duplication of labour /机器人自动～全部操作过程。The robot automatically repeats the whole operation. /她又～一遍要大家赶快干, 因为时间快到了。She reiterated that we had to hurry up for time was running out.
重复感染 chóngfù gǎnrǎn 〈医学〉superinfection
重复耕作 chóngfù gēngzuò 〈农业〉repeated tillage
重复建设 chóngfù jiànshè building redundant projects; duplication of similar projects
重复课税协议 chóngfù kèshuì xiéyì double-taxation agreement
重复利用 chóngfù lìyòng recycle
重复模拟计算机 chóngfù mónǐ jìsuànjī 〈计算机〉repetitive analogue computer
重复染色体 chóngfù rǎnsètǐ duplicated chromosome
重复引进 chóngfù yǐnjìn importation of redundant technical facilities; duplicate importation of similar plants or technologies
重根 chónggēn 〈数学〉repeated root
重光 chóngguāng ❶ see light again:大地～。There was light again over the earth. ❷ recover:～河山 recover lost territory
重光葵 Chóngguāngkuí Mamoru Shiemitsu (1887-1957), Japanese war criminal in WW II, who signed the surrender papers as Foreign Minister and became Foreign Minister again (1954-1956)
重归于好 chóngguīyúhǎo be reconciled; be reunited:双方在法庭调解下～。The two parties became reconciled through the mediation of the court. *or* Husband and wife were reunited through the good offices of the court.
重合 chónghé 〈数学〉coincide
重婚 chónghūn 〈法律〉bigamy
重婚罪 chónghūnzuì 〈法律〉offence of bigamy; bigamy
重积分 chóngjīfēn 〈数学〉multiple integral
重茧 chóngjiǎn ❶〈书面〉thick silkwaste padded clothes ❷ *see* "重趼"
重趼 chóngjiǎn 〈书面〉thick callus
重见天日 chóngjiàn-tiānrì *also* "重睹天日" see the light of day again; be delivered from oppression or persecution:他们推翻了殖民统治, 使人民得以～。They overthrew the colonial rule so that the people saw the light of day again.
重建 chóngjiàn rebuild; reconstruct; reestablish:～家园 rebuild one's homeland
重九 Chóngjiǔ *see* "重阳"
重聚 chóngjù meet again; reunite:王先生和他妻子分别多年后, 现在～了。After years of separation, Mr. Wang and his wife were reunited.
重考 chóngkǎo resit an exam
重录 chónglù re-record
重峦叠嶂 chóngluán-diézhàng *also* "重岩叠嶂" range upon range of mountains
重落 chóngluo 〈方言〉become worse after an initial improvement:他的病又～了。His illness became worse.
重名儿 chóngmíngr of the same name:他和我～。He is my namesake.
重起炉灶 chóngqǐ-lúzào set up a new stove or kitchen — start afresh; begin all over again:我们只得放弃原计划, ～。We had to scrap our original plan and make a fresh start.
重庆谈判 Chóngqìng Tánpàn Chongqing Negotiations (August-October 1945), peace talks held between the representatives of the Chinese Communist Party led by Mao Zedong and those of the Kuomintang under Chiang Kai-shek
重熔 chóngróng 〈冶金〉refusion
重申 chóngshēn reaffirm; reiterate:～我国政府的一贯立场 reaffirm (*or* reiterate) the consistent stand of our government
重审 chóngshěn try again after the original court verdict has been nullified by the higher court; retrial
重生 chóngshēng ❶ be revived or resurrected; be resuscitated:基督徒都相信耶稣的～。All Christians believe in the resurrection of Jesus Christ. ❷ (of a tissue or organ after sustaining an injury or loss) regrow:蜥蜴的尾巴掉了, 还会～。The lizard can regrow its tail after losing it.
重生父母 chóngshēng-fùmǔ *also* "再生父母" zàishēng-fùmǔ person who has rescued one from danger or misery; benefactor whose kindness is comparable to that of a parent
重施故伎 chóngshī-gùjì play the same old trick; repeat a stock

trick：这些人是造谣专家，现在又～了。These people are rumour-mongers and now they are playing the same old trick again.

重适 chóngshì 〈书面〉(of women) remarry

重孙 chóngsūn great-grandson

重孙女 chóngsūnnǚ great-granddaughter

重沓 chóngtà 〈书面〉redundant; wordy; repetitive：句子～ redundant sentences／避免语言～ avoid wordiness

重弹老调 chóngtán-lǎodiào *also*"老调重弹" harp on the same string; sing the same old tune：对那些～的人，我们有些不耐烦了。We are fed up with those who are striking up the same tune again.

重提 chóngtí bring up again：这是往事，何必～？This is a thing of the past. Why bring it up again? *or* It is no use harking back to what is past.／我也许是老话～。What I am going to say may be nothing but a platitude.

C

重贴现 chóngtiēxiàn *also*"再贴现" zàitiēxiàn 〈金融〉rediscount

重围 chóngwéi tight encirclement：敌军陷入～。The enemy found themselves trapped in a tight encirclement.

重温 chóngwēn review; relive：～往事，宛如一梦。They relived the past and felt as if it had been a dream.／今天～鲁迅的著作，我们更感到他政治上的敏锐。When we review Lu Xun's works in the present-day context, we feel all the more impressed by his political acumen.

重温旧梦 chóngwēn-jiùmèng revive an old dream; relive an old experience：他们默默地坐在湖边，～。They sat silently by the lake, reliving their past experience.

重文 chóngwén 〈书面〉variant (of a character)

重午 Chóngwǔ *also*"重五"(old name for 端午) Dragon Boat Festival (the 5th day of the 5th lunar month)

重现 chóngxiàn reappear：这种歪风在"文化大革命"后曾一度～。This evil trend reappeared in the wake of the Cultural Revolution.／童年生活又～在她的眼前。The life of her childhood years flashed across her mind.

重像 chóngxiàng 〈电子〉double or ghost image

重霄 chóngxiāo *also*"九重霄" jiǔchóngxiāo 〈书面〉zenith of the sky; seventh heaven; heaven of heavens

重新 chóngxīn ❶ again; once more：～上台 regain power／从那以后，中国农村～走上健康发展的道路。Since then, the Chinese countryside has been put back on the road of sound development. ❷ start afresh：～编排 reprogramme; rearrange／我们将～考虑他的要求。We will reconsider his request.／内阁要～调整。There will be a cabinet reshuffle.

重新定位 chóngxīn dìngwèi repositioning

重新做人 chóngxīn-zuòrén begin a new life; turn over a new leaf：他决心痛改前非，～。He made up his mind to mend his ways and start a new life.

重行 chóngxíng start afresh; begin again：～起草宪法 draft a constitution anew

重修 chóngxiū ❶ reconstruct; renovate (a building, etc.)：～古寺 renovate an ancient temple ❷ revise; recompile：～县志 recompile the county annals

重修旧好 chóngxiū-jiùhǎo renew cordial relations; become reconciled; bury the hatchet：经过多年战争之后，两国～。After years of war, the two countries decided to bury the hatchet.／这两国～，对该地区的局势起了稳定作用。A rapprochement between the two states will exercise a stabilizing influence on the region.

重言 chóngyán *also*"叠字" diézì 〈修辞〉reduplicated word; reduplication

重檐 chóngyán 〈建筑〉double-eaved roof

重眼皮 chóngyǎnpí *also*"双眼皮" shuāngyǎnpí double-fold eyelids

重演 chóngyǎn ❶ restage; put on an old play：《茶馆》下月将～。The *Teahouse* will be restaged next month. ❷ recur; reenact; repeat：历史的悲剧不容～。The historical tragedy should never be repeated.

重阳 Chóngyáng Double Ninth Festival (9th day of the 9th lunar month)

重阳木 chóngyángmù 〈植物〉*Biscofia polycarpa*

重洋 chóngyáng seas and oceans：远涉～ travel across the oceans／远隔～ be separated by the seas and oceans

重样 chóngyàng of the same style or form：她买了五张纪念邮票，没有一张～的。She bought five commemorative stamps, each of a different design.

重译 chóngyì ❶ translate a number of times ❷ retranslate from a translation ❸ translate again; retranslate

重印 chóngyìn reprint：～本 reprint

重影 chóngyǐng double image; ghost image

重映 chóngyìng (of an old film) be shown again

重圆 chóngyuán reunion：在战乱中离散之后，他们夫妻～了。The husband and wife were reunited after the turmoil of war.／破镜～。The man and wife eventually pieced together the wreckage of their married life.

重孕 chóngyùn 〈生理〉superfetation

重张 chóngzhāng restart a business

重振军威 chóngzhèn-jūnwēi reestablish one's prestige in military prowess; make an army's might felt once again

重整旗鼓 chóngzhěng-qígǔ *also*"重振旗鼓" rally one's forces after a defeat：他们现在有～的机会了。Now they have gained an opportunity to regroup their forces after the debacle.

重置成本 chóngzhì chéngběn replacement cost

重置需求 chóngzhì xūqiú replacement demand

重铸 chóngzhù 〈机械〉remould

重奏 chóngzòu 〈音乐〉ensemble of two or more instrumentalists, each playing one part：二～ duet／三～ trio

重足而立 chóngzú'érlì stand transfixed with terror; be extremely terrified：～，钳口而不言 stand transfixed and keep one's mouth shut in fear

重组 chóngzǔ ❶ reorganize; reshuffle：～内阁 reshuffle of the cabinet ❷〈信息〉re-engineering

chǒng

宠(寵) chǒng dote on; bestow favour on; indulge：得～ be in sb.'s favour／这孩子给～坏了。The child is spoiled.

宠爱 chǒng'ài make a pet of; dote on：老奶奶特别～小孙子。Grandma dotes on her grandson.

宠儿 chǒng'ér pet; favourite; darling：时代的～ darling of the times／上司的～ darling of the boss

宠妃 chǒngfēi favourite imperial concubine

宠惯 chǒngguàn pamper or spoil (a child); indulge

宠姬 chǒngjī 〈书面〉favourite concubine

宠任 chǒngrèn favour and trust：他得到司长的～。He has won the favour and confidence of the director of the department.

宠容 chǒngróng *see*"宠惯"

宠辱不惊 chǒngrǔ-bùjīng keep one's head cool whether bestowed with favour or subjected to humiliation, or whether one achieves success or suffers defeat; be neither carried away by success nor upset by failure

宠物 chǒngwù pet：～商店 pet shop／～食品 pet food／电子～ electronic pet

宠信 chǒngxìn 〈贬义〉cherish excessive fondness for and place undue trust in：受到皇帝～的奸臣 evil court officials in the emperor's favour

宠幸 chǒngxìng bestowing favour on a person of inferior rank; favour bestowed by a person of superior rank：那恶奴深得主子的～。That vicious flunkey was very much in his master's good graces.

宠用 chǒngyòng assign to a post out of favouritism

chòng

眈 chòng 〈方言〉short sleep; nap：瞌～ doze off／～一～ take a nap

铳 chòng blunderbuss; shotgun：火～ shotgun／鸟～ fowling piece

铳子 chòngzi *also*"冲子" chòngzi punching pin

冲[1](衝) chòng ❶ vigorously; with plenty of dash; bluntly：他干活很～。He works with vim and vigour.／这司机开车真～。This chauffeur drives with plenty of dash. *or* He is a reckless driver.／这小伙子说话太～。This young fellow speaks too bluntly.／干事太～了会惹麻烦的。If you act impulsively (*or* impetuously), you will get into trouble. ❷ (of smell) strong：这酒很～。This liquor is

for an exhibition /～演讲比赛会 plan to hold a speech contest

筹备 chóubèi prepare; arrange:～贷款 arrange for a loan /～运动会 make plans for a sports meet /～修建体育馆 prepare for the building of a gymnasium /～工作 preparatory work; preparations /～会议 preparatory (*or* preliminary) meeting /正式上马之前还得做不少～工作。We have to do a lot of spade work before we get down to business.

筹备委员会 chóubèi wěiyuánhuì preparatory committee

筹备组 chóubèizǔ planning group; preparatory team

筹策 chóucè ❶ a kind of calculation instrument in ancient times, made of wood or bamboo ❷〈书面〉stratagem; plan; tactics

筹措 chóucuò raise (money):为农村小学～经费 raise funds for a village school /他得～自己的旅费。He had to scrape up enough money for his travelling expenses.

筹划 chóuhuà plan and prepare:～生计 scrape a living /～建造核电站 plan the building of a nuclear power station /～有方 be good at planning

筹集 chóují raise (money):～基金 raise funds

筹建 chóujiàn prepare to construct or establish:这条公路正在～。Preparations are being made for the construction of this highway.

筹借 chóujiè make arrangements for a loan:～款项 try to arrange a loan

筹虑 chóulǜ see "筹思"

筹略 chóulüè tactics; strategy

筹码 chóumǎ *also* "筹马" ❶ chip; counter:政治交易的～ bargaining counters in political deals /有人常用钢镚儿作～。Coins are often used as chips in gambling. ❷〈旧语〉currency or substitute for currency

筹谋 chóumóu rack one's brains to find a way out:那些日子,他整日为生计～。In those days he had to try hard to make both ends meet.

筹募 chóumù collect (funds):为灾区～捐款 collect donations for the disaster area

筹拍 chóupāi plan to shoot a film:他们正在～一部有关清朝末代皇帝的故事片。They are planning to shoot (*or* produce) a feature film on the last emperor of the Qing Dynasty.

筹商 chóushāng discuss; consult:～对策 discuss countermeasures /～如何解决职工住房问题 exchange views on how to solve the housing problem of the employees

筹思 chóusī deliberate over (a matter):他～再三,仍犹豫不决。He is still hesitating after thinking the matter over and over again.

筹算 chóusuàn calculate:此人颇善～,大概是块理财的料儿。He has a good head for figures, and probably has the makings of a financier.

筹委会 chóuwěihuì (short for 筹备委员会) preparatory committee

筹议 chóuyì hold consultations about; discuss:～对策 discuss future moves to cope with the situation; consider counter-measures

筹资 chóuzī fund raising:～办学 raise funds for schools

筹组 chóuzǔ prepare and form:～学术团体 make arrangements for setting up an academic society

俦(儔)

chóu〈书面〉❶ companion:良～ good companion ❷ likes; peers

俦类 chóulèi *also* "畴类" chóulèi〈书面〉persons of the same generation; people of similar tastes or inclinations

俦侣 chóulǚ *also* "俦伴" companion; partner

酬(酧、醻)

chóu ❶〈书面〉propose a toast; toast ❷ repay a kindness:无以为～ can offer nothing in return (for sb.'s kindness) ❸ pay; payment; remuneration:男女同工同～。Men and women have equal pay for equal work. ❹ social intercourse:这一向我的应～特别多。I have had many social engagements lately. ❺ fulfil; realize:壮志未～身先死。He died without fulfilling his noble aspirations.

酬报 chóubào reward; recompense; remuneration:他热心帮助别人,但谢绝任何～。He is always ready to extend assistance to others but accepts no recompense in any form.

酬宾 chóubīn bargain sales; sales at preferential rates:～活动 bargain sales /～月 bargain sales month /春节大～ special season sale during Spring Festival holidays /开业头三天,以九五折～。All sales at the shop will be at five per cent discount during the first three days after it opens.

酬唱 chóuchàng reciprocate (each other) by writing poems (often using the same rhyme sequence and expressing kindred feelings):二人以诗～。The two of them often reciprocated each other by writing poems.

酬答 chóudá ❶ reward sb. for his kindness:以厚礼～ reward sb. with expensive gifts ❷ respond with a poem or speech:这是一首～友人的小诗。This is a short poem written in response to a friend's poem.

酬对 chóuduì respond; reply; retort:在宾客面前,他从容～。He talked with ease and grace before the guests.

酬和 chóuhè respond to a poem with another:主人即席赋诗,客人也以诗～。The host improvised a poem, to which his guests responded with theirs.

酬金 chóujīn payment for one's service; monetary reward; remuneration:付～ pay for sb.'s service

酬劳 chóuláo ❶ reward (sb.) for his service:应该～那些超时工作的人。Those who worked overtime should be properly rewarded. ❷ recompense; reward:应该送点什么～给他。We should send him something as a token of our appreciation.

酬谢 chóuxiè reward sb. for his kindness:应该重重地～他为我们出这么多力。We should richly reward him for the trouble he has taken on our behalf. /以此薄礼聊表～。We are sending you this humble gift as a token of gratitude.

酬应 chóuyìng ❶ socializing:不善～ socially inept /此人善于～。He is good at socializing. *or* He is a good mixer. ❷〈书面〉respond; reply; retort:～如流 quick at response

酬庸 chóuyōng〈书面〉remuneration for service or help

酬载 chóuzài *also* "有效载重" yǒuxiào zàizhòng payload:航天飞机的军用～由五角大楼控制。The military payload of the space shuttle is under Pentagon control.

酬酢 chóuzuò〈书面〉❶ exchange of toasts ❷ friendly intercourse; socializing:终日～ spend all one's time socializing

愁

chóu ❶ be worried; be anxious:我不～找不到工作。I'm not worried if I can find a job. /注意别～坏了身体。Take care not to let anxiety wear you down. /她～得直哭。She is so worried that she cannot refrain from tears. ❷ melancholy; sadness; sorrow:离～ sorrow at parting /乡～ homesickness

愁惨 chóucǎn distressing; sad:面容～ sad expression; forlorn (*or* miserable) look

愁肠 chóucháng pent-up feelings of sadness:～寸断 be eaten up with deep sorrow /～百结 with anxiety gnawing at one's heart; weighed down with anxiety /～九转 be haunted by a pent-up feeling of sadness

愁城 chóuchéng〈书面〉grief; misery:陷入～ be eaten up with anxiety; be overcome with grief; be plunged into deep misery /坐困～ be inactivated by cares and worries

愁楚 chóuchǔ anxiety and sorrow:满腹～ be deeply worried and grieved

愁烦 chóufán worried and vexed:他～得坐立不安。He was so worried that he looked as if he were sitting on pins and needles.

愁怀 chóuhuái mood of anxiety and gloom:一腔～ be full of anxiety and gloom

愁苦 chóukǔ anxiety; distress:世上多有令人～之事。The world teems with afflictions and anxieties.

愁虑 chóulǜ worry; be worried:收入多了,他再也不为生活～了。He is no longer worried about his livelihood as his income has increased.

愁帽 chóumào worry; depression; anxiety:戴～ feel worried; fall into a mood; be depressed

愁眉 chóuméi knitted brows; worried look:～不展 look downcast; knit one's brows /～解锁 become cheerful gradually; one's furrowed brows gradually clear

愁眉苦脸 chóuméi-kǔliǎn have a worried look; look miserable; wear a distressed expression:一副～的样子 look gloomy and depressed /他整天～,遇事就大发脾气。He wore a distressed expression all day long and would explode into uncontrollable rages whenever something came up.

愁眉锁眼 chóuméi-suǒyǎn with knitted brows and lowered eyes — be laden with sorrow; look sad

愁闷 chóumèn feel gloomy; be in low spirits:升学考试落榜,他异常～。He was very much discouraged by his failure at the entrance examinations.

C

愁戚 chóuqī be worry-ridden：他满脸～。There were signs of worry and anxiety all over his face.
愁容 chóuróng worried look：～满面 look deeply worried；with sorrow written all over one's face／她脸上没有丝毫～。She has not the faintest trace of sadness on her face.
愁思 chóusī gloomy thoughts；melancholy reveries：～如麻 be distressed by a skein of gloomy thoughts
愁绪 chóuxù 〈书面〉gloomy mood：～全消 have a load taken off one's mind；one's gloom has totally disappeared
愁郁 chóuyù dejected；grieved：她听了这个消息，满布～的脸上露出一丝笑容。A smile flitted across her troubled face when she heard the news. *or* Her sad face was lit up with a fleeting smile at the news.
愁云 chóuyún worried expression；melancholy look：喜讯传来，人们脸上的～消失了。When the good news came，the look of anxiety disappeared from everyone's face.
愁云惨雾 chóuyún-cǎnwù gloomy clouds and dismal mists — depressing atmosphere；desolate scene

C

雠[1]（讎、讐） chóu compare texts；collate：校～ textual criticism；collation (of texts)

雠[2]（讎、讐） chóu *see*"仇"chóu
雠校 chóujiào textual criticism；text collation
雠问 chóuwèn 〈书面〉seek answers to difficult questions

仇（讎、讐） chóu ❶ enemy；foe：亲痛～快 sadden one's friends and gladden one's enemies／反目成～ (usu. of a married couple) fall out with each other and become enemies；enmity ensues from a bitter quarrel ❷ hatred；enmity；grudge：记～ nurse a grievance／旧～ old score／有恩报恩，有～报～ return good for good and evil for evil／我跟他有～。I have a grudge against him.
see also Qiú
仇雠 chóuchóu 〈书面〉foe；enemy
仇敌 chóudí foe；enemy：不共戴天之～ sworn foe／最凶恶的～ most ferocious foe／我不想使他成为我的～。I don't want to make an enemy of him.
仇恨 chóuhèn hatred；enmity；hostility：～敌人 hate one's enemy／怀有强烈的～ nurse (*or* harbour) bitter (*or* intense) hatred／满腔～ be burning with hatred／招来～ incur sb.'s enmity／挑起种族～ stir up ethnic hatred (*or* enmity)／他用～的眼光望了我一下。He gave me a hostile look.
仇家 chóujiā enemy；foe
仇口 chóukǒu 〈方言〉❶ grievance；grudge；feud：两家种下了～。A feud has developed between the two families. ❷ foe；enemy
仇气 chóuqì enmity；rancour；resentment
仇人 chóurén personal enemy；enemy：他们俩是不共戴天的～。They are sworn enemies.／～相见，分外眼红。When enemies face each other，their eyes blaze with hatred.
仇杀 chóushā murder committed in revenge：这人死于～。This man was killed in a feud (*or* vendetta). *or* The man was murdered in revenge.
仇深似海 chóushēn-sìhǎi entertain a hatred as great as the ocean：我和他们～。My hatred for them is as great as the ocean.
仇视 chóushì look upon with hostility；be hostile to；regard as an enemy：他们对入侵者极端～。They were extremely hostile to the invaders.
仇外 chóuwài cherish hostile feelings towards foreign countries：～心理 anti-foreign sentiment；xenophobia
仇隙 chóuxì 〈书面〉hatred；enmity；feud：两国久有～。There has been a long-standing feud between the two countries. *or* The two countries have had a bitter quarrel over a long period of time.
仇冤 chóuyuān enmity；rancour；hatred：结～ earn sb.'s hatred／报～ revenge oneself；avenge a wrong
仇怨 chóuyuàn grudge；grievance；hatred：两人深结～。The two of them cherish inveterate hatred for each other.

惆 chóu 〈书面〉disappointed；aggrieved
惆怅 chóuchàng melancholy；disconsolate；sad：辞别老友，他骤然产生一种～失落之感。After bidding farewell to his old friends，he was suddenly seized with a feeling of ennui and melancholy.

裯 chóu ❶ single-layered quilt ❷ bed curtains；mosquito-net

稠 chóu ❶ thick：～粥 thick porridge／墨还不够～。The ink (on the inkslab) is not thick enough. ❷ dense：人～物穰 thriving in population and rich in natural resources
稠糊 chóuhu 〈方言〉thick and sticky：早饭我要吃～粥，外加一碟泡菜。I'll have thick porridge for breakfast and a dish of pickles to go with it.
稠化 chóuhuà 〈化工〉thicken
稠胶 chóujiāo 〈化工〉thick glue
稠密 chóumì dense；thick：森林～ thick (*or* dense) forest／人口～ dense population／炮声～ intense artillery／树叶～ thick foliage／这块地里的棉花长得太～。The cotton plants on this plot are too close together.
稠人广众 chóurén-guǎngzhòng *also*"稠人广坐" big crowd；big gathering；large audience：他在～的地方闹了个大笑话。He made a big fool of himself before a large audience.
稠油 chóuyóu 〈石油〉thick oil

绸（紬） chóu silk fabric；silk：～布 silk fabric／一块～料 a piece of silk／～巾 silk scarf
绸缎 chóuduàn silks and satins
绸缪 chóumóu 〈书面〉❶ sentimentally attached：情意～ be deeply in love ❷ *see*"未雨绸缪"wèiyǔ-chóumóu
绸纹纸 chóuwénzhǐ 〈摄影〉matte (paper) — standard paper for photography：这照片您要～还是光纸？Do you want this matte or glossy?
绸子 chóuzi silk fabric

chǒu

瞅（矁） chǒu 〈方言〉look at：我瞪着眼睛～他。I gave him a stare.／让我～一～。Let me have a look.
瞅见 chǒujiàn 〈方言〉see；have or catch a glimpse (of sth. or sb.)：远远～一片树林。A wood came into view at a distance.／我什么也没有～。I didn't see anything.
瞅空儿 chǒukòngr 〈方言〉seek an opportunity；find time：这件事你～和他谈谈。Talk the matter over with him when you have time. *or* Bring up the matter with him when you are free，will you?
瞅冷子 chǒu lěngzi 〈方言〉*also*"抽冷子"chōu lěngzi do sth. when people are off guard

丑[1] chǒu ❶ second of the twelve Earthly Branches ❷ (Chǒu) a surname

丑[2]（醜） chǒu ❶ ugly；unsightly；hideous：其状甚～ look ugly；have hideous features／人家说她愈变愈～了。People said she was getting more homely all the time. ❷ disgraceful；scandalous；unpleasant ❸ 〈方言〉bad：脾气～ bad-tempered

丑[3] chǒu 〈戏曲〉clown；comedian：武～ clown specialized in acrobatics／文～ comedian in civil plays
丑八怪 chǒubāguài 〈口语〉very ugly person；hideous looking person；monster：这人长得～似的。The fellow has all the hideous features of a monster.
丑表功 chǒubiǎogōng brag shamelessly about one's deeds；claim an undeserved merit：他～，恰恰把自己搞得很臭。He is only making himself despicable when he tries to laud his own merits to the skies.
丑旦 chǒudàn 〈戏曲〉female clown
丑诋 chǒudǐ slander；vilify；calumniate；defame：～别人，也会玷污自己。If you throw mud at others，you will soil your own fingers.
丑恶 chǒu'è ugly；repulsive；hideous：～灵魂 ugly soul／～行径 wicked act／～面目 repulsive features／～行为 disgusting behaviour
丑怪 chǒuguài ugly；unsightly
丑化 chǒuhuà discredit；smear；vilify：～现实生活 paint a distorted picture of everyday life／～英雄形象 deliberately damage the image

of a hero
丑话 chǒuhuà ❶ vulgar or coarse language：这种～，真是不堪入耳。This sort of filthy language is absolutely revolting. ❷ blunt words：咱们～说在前头，以后要再发生这种事，别来找我。Let me not mince words. Don't come to me for advice if such things happen again.
丑剧 chǒujù farce：演了一出～ put on a farce
丑角 chǒujué ❶ clown；buffoon：马戏～ circus clown ❷ ignoble role：此人在未遂政变中扮演了～。The man played a very ignoble part in the aborted coup.
丑类 chǒulèi the wicked；rascals；scoundrels：～恶物 evildoers
丑劣 chǒuliè ugly；inferior；repulsive：～不堪 utterly disgusting；extremely ugly
丑陋 chǒulòu ugly；hideous：相貌～，心地善良 ugly in appearance but kind at heart／最美丽的猴子与人相比也是～的。The most handsome ape becomes ugly beside a human being.
丑婆子 chǒupózi 〈戏曲〉 female clown playing the part of a middle-aged or old woman
丑时 chǒushí 〈旧语〉 period of the day from 1 a.m. to 3 a.m.
丑史 chǒushǐ story of a sinful life；scandalous past
丑事 chǒushì disgraceful affair；scandal：揭露某人的～ expose sb.'s disgraceful affairs
丑态 chǒutài ugly or ludicrous performance；buffoonery：他的～实在令人作呕。His scandalous behaviour is simply disgusting.
丑态百出 chǒutài-bǎichū cut a despicable figure；put on an abominable show
丑态毕露 chǒutài-bìlù reveal all one's hideous features；be utterly nauseating
丑闻 chǒuwén scandal：水门～ Watergate scandal (in 1972)／官场～ scandals among the officialdom／他家的那些～，成了人们街谈巷议的话题。Scandals about his family have become the talk of the town.
丑媳妇也得见公婆 chǒuxífu yě děi jiàn gōngpó 〈俗语〉 an ugly bride will sooner or later have to come face to face with her parents-in-law；whatever the faults or shortcomings of sth., it has to be shown to those concerned
丑相 chǒuxiàng ugly features
丑行 chǒuxíng scandalous conduct；misconduct；misdemeanour：极力掩盖自己的～ try to cover up one's misconduct by all means

chòu

臭 chòu ❶ smelly；foul；stinking：～鸡蛋 rotten egg／～不可当 give off an unbearable stink／除～剂 deodorant／鱼～了。The fish has gone bad.／你的脚好～！Your feet smell awful. ❷ disgusting；disgraceful：摆～架子 put on disgusting airs／名声～ have a bad reputation／这个人在我们学校可～了。He is such a notorious figure in our school. ❸ inferior；poor；bad：这一着真～！What a bad move！*or* That was a poor trick！❹ harsh；severe；relentless：～呲儿了一顿 give sb. a good dressing-down ❺〈方言〉(of a bullet) dud
see also xiù
臭鼻症 chòubízhèng 〈医学〉 ozena
臭吃臭喝 chòuchī-chòuhē 〈方言〉〈贬义〉 eat and drink lavishly or greedily：家里这点钱全让他～了。He spent all the money left in the family eating and drinking lavishly.
臭虫 chòuchóng bedbug
臭椿 chòuchūn 〈植物〉 tree of heaven (*Ailanthus altissima*)
臭葱石 chòucōngshí 〈矿物〉 scorodite
臭大姐 chòudàjiě popular name for a kind of stinkbug
臭弹 chòudàn ❶ stink bomb；stinkball ❷ bomb, shell, or bullet that fails to go off；dud
臭豆腐 chòudòufu strong-smelling fermented bean curd：～闻起来臭，吃起来香。The fermented bean curd smells bad but tastes good. *or* Something may be quite enjoyable though it looks bad. *or* A person may prove very useful though he is despised for one reason or another.
臭瓜 chòuguā 〈植物〉 calabazilla (*Cucurbita foetidissima*)
臭烘烘 chòuhōnghōng foul；odorous；stinking：这水沟～的味儿很难闻。The ditch gives off a terribly foul smell.
臭乎乎 chòuhūhū somewhat foul-smelling：这块肉～的，是不是坏了？How come the meat smells a bit foul? Is it rotten?
臭火 chòuhuǒ 〈方言〉 ❶ (of a bullet, etc.) fail to go off；misfire ❷ inactivated bullet；dud
臭老九 chòulǎojiǔ 〈贬义〉 stinking people ninth category (i.e. after the eight usual categories of bad people such as landlords, counter-revolutionaries, traitors, etc. — a term labelled on intellectuals in the Cultural Revolution)；damned intellectual
臭骂 chòumà curse roundly；scold angrily：被人～了一顿 be cursed roundly；get a dressing-down
臭美 chòuměi show off one's smartness；feel immensely pleased with oneself：别～，谁不知道你那两下子。Don't show off, for everybody knows how much you are worth.
臭名 chòumíng bad reputation；notoriety
臭名远扬 chòumíng-yuǎnyáng be notorious far and wide：这是些～的人物，没有什么评论的价值。These people are too notorious to deserve comments on.
臭名昭著 chòumíng-zhāozhù *also*"臭名昭彰" of ill repute；notorious：这种理论早已～。Such a theory has long been thoroughly discredited.
臭皮囊 chòupínáng 〈佛教〉 vile skin-bag — the human body；mortal flesh
臭棋 chòuqí bad move (in chess)；inferior skill in playing chess：走了几步～ make a few ill-calculated moves／下一手～ be a lousy chess player
臭气 chòuqì bad smell；offensive odour；stink：～冲天 stink to the sky／～熏人 be horribly stinking
臭钱 chòuqián stinking or filthy money：有几个～ have a few rotten coins；have some stinking money
臭球 chòuqiú 〈口语〉 lousy pass, stroke, or shot in a ball game；rotten game or match：这场～！看得我真腻味。What a rotten game! I was totally disgusted.
臭水沟 chòushuǐgōu sewage ditch；stinking open ditch
臭死 chòusǐ 〈口语〉 terribly；to death：吓了个～ be scared to death／累得～ be terribly tired；be dog-tired／骂了个～ give sb. a sound telling-off
臭味相投 chòuwèi-xiāngtóu be birds of a feather；be two of a kind：这二人～，勾得很紧。The two of them are birds of a feather and work hand in glove with each other.
臭腺 chòuxiàn 〈动物〉 foetid gland
臭熏熏 chòuxūnxūn stinking；smelly
臭氧 chòuyǎng 〈化学〉 ozone：～设备 ozone equipment／～中毒 ozone poisoning
臭氧层 chòuyǎngcéng ozone layer；ozonosphere
臭氧发生器 chòuyǎng fāshēngqì ozonizer；ozonator
臭氧计 chòuyǎngjì 〈化学〉 ozonometer
臭氧降解 chòuyǎng jiàngjiě 〈化学〉 ozone degradation
臭油 chòuyóu tar (oil)
臭鼬 chòuyòu 〈动物〉 skunk
殠 chòu 〈书面〉 *see*"臭" chòu

chū

初 chū ❶ at the beginning of；in the early part of：年～ at the beginning of the year／～入世途 embark on one's career in life ❷ first (in order)：～十 tenth day (of a lunar month)／最～几天 first few days ❸ for the first time；only just begun：～次见面 first meeting／～见成效 begin to take effect／大病～愈 have just recovered from a serious illness ❹ elementary；rudimentary：～步知识 rudimentary knowledge ❺ original：当～的计划 original plan／并非～衷 not one's original intention／和好如～ be reconciled ❻ (Chū) a surname
初版 chūbǎn ❶ be published for the first time：本书～于 1960 年。The book was first published in 1960. ❷ first edition：～很快告罄。The first edition soon ran out (*or* was soon sold out).
初冰 chūbīng first freeze in winter
初步 chūbù tentative；initial；preliminary：～设想 tentative idea／～方案 tentative programme／～分析 preliminary analysis／～概算 initial estimate (of costs, etc.)／～繁荣昌盛的社会主义国家 socialist country with the beginnings of prosperity／这些问题已得到～解决。Initial solution of the problems has been achieved.
初产 chūchǎn primiparity：～妇 primipara
初潮 chūcháo 〈生理〉 menophania

初出茅庐 chūchū-máolú (said of Zhuge Liang who came out of his thatched cottage to embark on a brilliant career as Liu Bei's military strategist during the period of the Three Kingdoms) at the beginning of one's career; fledgling: ~的指挥官 fledgling commander / 他~，毫无经验。He has no experience whatever, as he is as green as grass.
初创 chūchuàng newly established; initial: ~阶段 initial stage / ~的企业 newly established enterprise
初春 chūchūn ❶ first month of spring, namely, first month of the lunar year ❷ early spring
初次 chūcì first time: ~露面 make a first public appearance / ~上阵 (of soldiers) go into battle for the first time
初等 chūděng ❶ elementary: ~数学 elementary mathematics / ~函数 elementary functions / ~代数 elementary algebra ❷ primary: ~学校 primary school

C

初等教育 chūděng jiàoyù primary or elementary education
初等小学 chūděng xiǎoxué 〈旧语〉lower primary school
初冬 chūdōng ❶ first winter month, namely, tenth month of the lunar year ❷ early winter
初读 chūdú (of a bill in Parliament) first reading
初度 chūdù 〈书面〉birthday: 四十~ fortieth anniversary of one's birthday; one's fortieth birthday
初犯 chūfàn ❶ first offender ❷ first offence
初伏 chūfú *also* "头伏" tóufú ❶ first day of the first period of the hot season (falling usu. in mid-July) ❷ first of the three ten-day periods of the hot season
初稿 chūgǎo first draft: 完成文章~ finish the first draft of an essay / 修改剧本~ revise the first draft of a play
初花 chūhuā ❶ come into flower for the first time in a year ❷ early flowers of a plant
初会 chūhuì first meeting or encounter: 他们是~，彼此都有点拘束。They were both a bit restrained as it was the first time they had ever met.
初婚 chūhūn ❶ first marriage ❷ newly married; newly wed: 这对夫妇~便不和。The couple fell out soon after marriage.
初吉 chūjí 〈旧语〉first day of each month of the lunar year; period from the first to the eighth
初级 chūjí primary; elementary; junior: ~市场 primary market / ~抵押市场 primary mortgage market / ~证券市场 primary securities market / ~销售 primary marketing / ~律师 (UK) solicitor / ~班 junior class; elementary course
初级产品 chūjí chǎnpǐn primary product: ~生产国 primary producing country / ~出口国 primary exporting country
初级产业 chūjí chǎnyè primary industry
初级读本 chūjí dúběn primer
初级阶段 chūjí jiēduàn primary or preliminary stage: 社会主义的~ primary or initial stage of socialism
初级农业生产合作社 chūjí nóngyè shēngchǎn hézuòshè elementary agricultural producers' cooperative (in which collective income was distributed according to the amount of work each member did as well as the amount of land and other assets he contributed)
初级人民法院 chūjí rénmín fǎyuàn *also* "基层人民法院" jīcéng rénmín fǎyuàn primary people's court
初级社 chūjíshè (short for 初级农业生产合作社) elementary agricultural producers' cooperative
初级线圈 chūjí xiànquān 〈电工〉primary coil
初级小学 chūjí xiǎoxué primary grades of elementary school; lower primary school
初级中学 chūjí zhōngxué junior high school; junior secondary school
初加工 chūjiāgōng 〈机械〉preliminary working
初见 chūjiàn first meeting; first encounter
初交 chūjiāo newly acquainted: 我们仅仅是~，对他不大了解。I don't really know much about him, as we are merely new acquaintances.
初校 chūjiào first check; first proof-reading
初晶 chūjīng primary crystal
初几儿 chūjǐr (used usu. in questions) one of the first ten days of a lunar month; date: 今天~啦? What date is it today?
初亏 chūkuī 〈天文〉first contact (of an eclipse); beginning of a solar or lunar eclipse
初来乍到 chūlái-zhàdào newly arrived; new (to a job or place): 我是~，请各位诸事多关照。As I am new to the job, I hope, you'll all help me whenever you can.
初恋 chūliàn ❶ first love: ~的甜蜜 happiness of one's first love ❷ just fall in love: 他们还在~阶段。They have just fallen in love with each other.
初馏塔 chūliútǎ 〈石油〉primary tower
初龙 Chūlóng 〈考古〉Archosaurus
初露端倪 chūlù-duānní surfacing of the incipient symptoms of sth.: 两派倾轧已~。Initial symptoms of the strife between the two factions have surfaced.
初露锋芒 chūlù-fēngmáng display one's talent for the first time: 他在外交界~。He began to distinguish himself in the diplomatic world.
初露头角 chūlù-tóujiǎo begin to show one's ability and talent: 这次展出的作品，作者大都是~的青年画家。The paintings on show this time are mostly works by young fledgling artists.
初民 chūmín people of remote antiquity; ancients
初磨 chūmó 〈机械〉preliminary grinding; preparatory grinding
初年 chūnián early part of a historical period: 清朝~ in the early years of the Qing Dynasty
初捻纱 chūniǎnshā 〈纺织〉single
初评 chūpíng preliminary appraisal; first round of evaluation: 进行~ make preliminary appraisal
初期 chūqī initial stage; early days: 战争~ in the early phase of the war / 19世纪~ early in the nineteenth century; in the early nineteenth century; in the early 1800's
初切 chūqiē 〈天文〉ingress
初秋 chūqiū first month of autumn, namely, seventh month of the lunar year; early autumn
初日 chūrì rising sun
初赛 chūsài 〈体育〉preliminary trial; preliminary contest
初丧 chūsāng died not long ago; died recently: 其母~，诸事急需料理。His mother died recently, and he has many things to take care of.
初审 chūshěn ❶ preliminary check or examination; preliminary evaluation: ~合格 pass the preliminary check (*or* examination) ❷ preliminary interrogation; initial questioning: 何时对涉嫌人进行~? When will the suspect be interrogated preliminarily? ❸〈法律〉trial of first instance; first trial: ~案件 case of first instance / ~裁决 ruling of first instance / ~法官 judge of first instance / ~法院 trial court; court of original jurisdiction; court of first instance
初生态 chūshēngtài 〈化学〉nascent state
初生之犊 chūshēngzhīdú newborn calf: ~不畏虎〈谚语〉newborn calves are not afraid of tigers — young people dare do anything and fear nothing
初时 chūshí at first; at the beginning; originally: 来任教的事，他~不肯，过后才答应。At first, he did not agree to take the teaching position. It was some time before he accepted.
初始 chūshǐ initial; inaugural: ~速度 initial velocity
初试 chūshì ❶ first try ❷ preliminary examination: 他通过了~，但复试时太紧张，没考好。He got through the preliminary examination, but felt very nervous at the final and didn't do very well.
初霜 chūshuāng first frost
初速度 chūsùdù 〈物理〉initial velocity
初酸洗 chūsuānxǐ 〈纺织〉lime sour; gray sour
初岁 chūsuì 〈书面〉initial period of a year
初探 chūtàn (often used in titles of articles or books) initial exploration; studies: 《写作心理学~》*Studies in Writers' Psychology*
初头 chūtóu 〈方言〉early in the year or month: 1995年~ beginning of 1995; in early 1995
初夏 chūxià first month of summer, namely, fourth month of the lunar year; early summer
初小 chūxiǎo (short for 初级小学) lower primary school; primary grades of elementary school
初心 chūxīn 〈书面〉original intention or aspiration: 事虽如此，~不改。My original intention remains unchanged for all that has happened.
初选 chūxuǎn primary election: ~获胜 win a primary election / 在~中投票 vote in a primary election
初学 chūxué begin to learn; be a beginner: ~打字 begin to learn typing / ~英语 beginner in English / ~者通用符号指令代码〈计算机〉BASIC (Beginner's All-Purpose Symbolic Instruction Code)

初雪 chūxuě first snow
初旬 chūxún first ten days of a month: 十月～ first ten days of October
初叶 chūyè early years (of a century): 20 世纪～ early in the twentieth century; in the early twentieth century; in the early 1900's
初夜 chūyè ❶ not long after dark; early at night ❷ first night after a marriage ceremony; wedding night
初夜权 chūyèquán *jus primae noctis* — feudal lord's privilege to sleep with a vassal's bride on her wedding night; *droit du seigneur*
初愿 chūyuàn original wish; original desire: 鲁迅的～是当医生,后来弃医从文。Initially, Lu Xun intended to be a doctor, but he gave up medicine later on and became a writer.
初月 chūyuè crescent moon
初轧 chūzhá 〈冶金〉 blooming; breakdown: ～方坯 cogged bloom / ～轧辊 bloom roll
初轧机 chūzhájī blooming mill; cogging mill; roughing mill; bloomer
初战 chūzhàn *also* "序战" xùzhàn first battle; prelude to major battle: ～获胜。We won the first battle.
初绽 chūzhàn (of flowers) be opening: 梅花～。The plum blossoms are opening.
初诊 chūzhěn (of a patient) first visit (to a doctor or hospital)
初值 chūzhí 〈数学〉 initial value
初志 chūzhì original ambition: ～未遂 fail to fulfil one's original ambition
初中 chūzhōng (short for 初级中学) junior secondary school
初衷 chūzhōng original intention: 未改～ original intentions remain unchanged

樗

chū *also* "臭椿" chòuchūn 〈植物〉 tree of heaven (*Ailanthus altissima*)
樗蚕 chūcán *also* "椿蚕" chūncán castor silkworm
樗蒲 chūpú a kind of ancient game like dice-throwing

摴

chū
摴蒱 chūpú *see* "樗蒲" chūpú

出[1]

chū ❶ go or come out: ～壳 break the (egg) shell / ～城 go out of town / ～狱 be released from prison / 火车～站了。The train has left the station. ❷ come; arrive: ～席 be present; attend ❸ exceed; go beyond: 这孩子刚～满月。The baby is a little over one month old. / 篮球～了端线。The basketball is out of bounds. ❹ issue; put up; offer; give: ～证明 issue a certificate / ～布告 post an announcement; put up a notice / ～钱 offer money / ～主意 offer advice; make suggestions / ～节目 give a performance / ～考题 set the examination questions; set the (examination) paper / 今晚比赛,你们～谁? Whom are you going to field in tonight's match? ❺ produce; yield; turn out: ～煤 produce coal / ～油 yield oil / ～成果 yield results / 这种茶～在杭州。This kind of tea is produced in Hangzhou. / 实践～真知。Genuine knowledge comes from practice. ❻ arise; emerge; happen; occur: ～问题 go wrong; go amiss / 防止～同样事故 prevent the recurrence of similar accidents / 近年来我国～过不少杰出的科学家。Quite a few outstanding scientists have emerged in our country in recent years. / 故事～在两千年前。The story happened (*or* took place) two thousand years ago. ❼ publish: ～了不少好书 publish many good books ❽ put forth; vent: ～疹子 have measles / ～天花 have smallpox; contract smallpox / ～了一身大汗 sweat all over / 拿某人～气 vent one's spleen on sb.; take it out on sb. ❾ be quoted from: 语～《论语》。The saying is quoted from *The Analects of Confucius*. *or* It's a quotation from *The Analects of Confucius*. ❿ emerge; appear; show: 水落石～ when the water subsides the rocks emerge — the whole thing comes to light / 人才辈～ people of talent are coming to the fore in large numbers ⓫ (of rice, etc.) rise well (with cooking) ⓬ pay out; spend; expend: 入不敷～ one earns less than one spends; be unable to make (both) ends meet; one's earnings are insufficient for one's needs / 量入为～ keep one's expenditure within the limits of one's income; live within one's means; cut one's coat according to one's cloth ⓭ 〈方言〉 *used after* 往 *to indicate direction of movement*: 散场了,人们往～走。The opera being over, people began to come out.

出[2](齣)

chū dramatic piece; chapter in a romance: 一～戏 a play; an opera

出

chu ❶ *used after a verb to indicate direction or completion of an action*: 拿～证件 produce one's papers / 走～办公室 come out of the office / 发～命令 issue an order / 找～毛病 detect the flaw; find out what goes wrong / 看～问题 see where the problem lies; realize that something is wrong ❷ *used after an adjective to indicate a higher degree*: 多～了六个人。We have six more people (than needed, expected, etc.).

出埃及记 Chū Āijí Jì *Exodus* (a book of the *Old Testament* relating the departure of the Israelites under Moses from Egypt)
出版 chūbǎn come off the press; publish; come out: ～合同 contract for publication / ～自由 freedom of the press
出版界 chūbǎnjiè publishing; the press
出版权 chūbǎnquán right of publication
出版社 chūbǎnshè publishing house
出版物 chūbǎnwù publication
出版者 chūbǎnzhě publisher
出榜 chūbǎng ❶ publish a list of successful candidates or examinees: 考完试三天就～。A list of successful examinees will be published three days after the examination. ❷ 〈旧语〉 put up a notice: ～安民 put up a notice to set the people's minds at ease; put out a bulletin to reassure the public / ～招贤 put up a notice to recruit able and virtuous people; advertise for qualified persons
出包儿 chūbāor 〈方言〉 pickpocket
出奔 chūbēn run away; leave: ～他乡 flee (from) one's native place / 在易卜生的《玩偶之家》里,娜拉离家～,但是以后她会怎样呢? In Ibsen's *A Doll's House* Nora runs away from home, but what will happen to her?
出殡 chūbìn carry a coffin to the cemetery; hold a funeral procession
出兵 chūbīng dispatch troops: ～御敌 dispatch troops to resist enemy invasion
出彩 chūcǎi ❶ 〈戏曲〉 use red liquid to indicate bleeding ❷ make a fool of oneself: 当场～ make a fool of oneself then and there; cut a sorry figure right on the spot
出操 chūcāo drill or do exercises: 士兵一早就～。The soldiers have drill first thing in the morning.
出岔子 chū chàzi go wrong; amiss: 莫非～了? Has something gone wrong? *or* Is there something amiss?
出差 chūchāi ❶ be away on official business; be on a business trip: ～费 allowance for a business trip / 他～去上海了。He has gone to Shanghai on business. ❷ do short-term tasks in transport, construction, etc.
出产 chūchǎn ❶ produce; manufacture: 云南～大理石。Yunnan Province produces marble. / 江西景德镇～的精美瓷器遐迩闻名。The fine porcelain produced in Jingdezhen, Jiangxi Province, is known far and near. ❷ produce; products: 四川的农业～很丰富。Sichuan Province is rich in agricultural produce.
出厂 chūchǎng (of products) leave the factory: 产品检验合格方能～。Products cannot leave the factory until they are examined and granted certificates of quality.
出厂价 chūchǎngjià producer price; ex-factory price
出厂日期 chūchǎng rìqī date of production or manufacture
出场 chūchǎng ❶ come on the stage; appear on the scene: 今晚～的都是名演员。The actors and actresses appearing tonight are all celebrities. ❷ (used in a libretto) enter ❸ enter the arena or sports ground: ～的运动员名单 list of players for the match / 体操运动员们马上要～了。The gymnasts will soon enter the arena.
出超 chūchāo favourable balance of trade: 国际贸易～几亿美元 have a favourable international trade balance of several hundred million US dollars / 这个国家对外贸易每年都～。The country has a balance of exports over imports every year.
出车 chūchē ❶ dispatch a vehicle: 班车每天上午七点～。The shuttle bus service starts at 7 a.m. every day. ❷ be out driving a vehicle: 所有的司机都～了。All the drivers are out at work.
出尘 chūchén ❶ (of painting, calligraphy, poetry, etc.) have extraordinary grace and beauty: 他的书画潇洒～,名噪一时。His roman-

tic and exceedingly graceful paintings and calligraphy won him instant fame in his time. ❷〈佛教〉be above worldly considerations

出乘 chūchéng (of attendants on a train or a ship) be on one's job or on duty

出丑 chūchǒu make a fool of oneself; cut a poor or sorry figure; bring shame on oneself: 当众~ make an exhibition of oneself / 有意叫人~ deliberately make a fool of sb. / 我若和他分辩,就要让他~了。If I argue with him, it will only be washing his dirty linen in public.

出处 chūchǔ 〈书面〉taking up an official post and retirement from public life

出处 chūchù source (of a quotation or allusion): 查清典故的~ locate the source of the allusion / 注明~ indicate the source; give references; give chapter and verse / ~同上 ibid.; ib.; ibidem

C

出错 chūcuò make mistakes; go wrong: 他打字很少~。He seldom makes a mistake in typing. / 难保不会~。It is hardly possible to prevent any error from cropping up. / 此事重大,不可~。This is an extremely important matter; we must make sure nothing will go wrong. *or* This is too important a matter to go wrong.

出倒 chūdǎo *also* "出盘" (of an owner) sell one's establishment when it is difficult to keep it any longer

出道 chūdào (formerly of an apprentice) start working as a journeyman after serving one's apprenticeship; make one's début in society; embark on one's career; become known: 论业务,他比才~的年轻人强不了多少。As far as his professional ability is concerned, he is not much better than the fledglings. / ~前她也拍过电视剧。She played some parts in TV plays before she became known (as a film star, etc.).

出典 chūdiǎn ❶ *see* "出处" chūchù ❷ mortgage: ~厂房 mortgage one's plant

出点子 chū diǎnzi offer advice; make suggestions: 他常帮人~。He is always ready with advice for others. / 咱们怎么干,大家来~。What's to be done? Let's put our heads together. / 有人在背后出坏点子。Someone is manipulating the show from behind the scenes.

出店 chūdiàn 〈方言〉〈旧语〉errand-boy for a shop

出顶 chūdǐng 〈方言〉sublet; re-lease (a building, house, etc.)

出动 chūdòng ❶ set out; start off: 部队待命~。The troops are awaiting orders to move. / 小分队提前~了。The detachment set off ahead of schedule. ❷ send out; dispatch; call out: ~军舰 dispatch warships / ~飞机一百架次 fly 100 sorties / ~伞兵,协同作战 call out paratroops to join the battle ❸ turn out; go into action: 全城~欢迎这位宇航员。The whole town turned out to welcome the astronaut.

出动机场 chūdòng jīchǎng departure airfield

出尔反尔 chū'ěr-fǎn'ěr go back on one's word; contradict oneself: 诺言应该遵守,不可~。You are supposed to keep a promise and not to break it. / 他不是那种~的人。He is not the sort of man to go back on his word.

出发 chūfā ❶ set off; set out; start (off); leave: 准备~ get ready to start off / 香山离这里相当远,我们明天要早点~。We'll have to set out early tomorrow as the Fragrant Hill is quite a distance from here. / 他们将~去罗马。They are leaving for Rome. ❷ start from; proceed from: 从国家的大局~ from the overall interests of the state / 从睦邻的愿望~ out of the desire for good neighbourliness / 他是从全球战略观点~来分析亚洲问题的。He analyses Asian problems from the viewpoint of global strategy.

出发点 chūfādiǎn ❶ starting point of a journey: 上海是我们这次旅行的~。We started from Shanghai on this journey. ❷ intention; aim; purpose; point of departure: 为人民服务是我们的~。Our aim (*or* point of departure) is to serve the people. / 他的~是好的,但考虑问题不全面。He is well-intentioned but lacks an overall approach to the problem. / 我们的~一致,但在具体问题上有不同的看法。We share the same basic position, but hold different views on specific matters. / 我们在这个问题上观点相同,但~不一样。We hold similar views on this issue, but out of different considerations.

出发港 chūfāgǎng port of departure

出饭 chūfàn (of rice, etc.) rise well (in cooking): 糙米~。Brown rice rises well when it's cooked.

出访 chūfǎng go abroad on an official visit; visit (foreign countries): 五年来,我国领导人~了很多国家。Our government leaders have visited many countries in the last five years. / 这次~进一步加强了我国与非洲国家的友好关系。This tour has further strengthened the friendly relations between China and African countries.

出份子 chū fènzi club together (to buy a gift for sb., etc.)

出风头 chū fēngtou seek the limelight; be in the limelight; get a lot of publicity: 喜欢~ seek the limelight; be fond of the limelight; be fond of publicity / 不爱~ be publicity-shy / 你不知道我们的老板就讨厌女人们~! Don't you know that our boss really hates women pushing themselves forward. / 他在上海可~呢! He was quite the man in Shanghai!

出佚 chūfū send people for corvée

出伏 chūfú ending of the dog days or hot season

出钢 chūgāng 〈冶金〉tapping (of molten steel)

出港 chūgǎng clear a port; leave port: ~呈报表 bill of clearance / ~证 clearance (papers)

出阁 chūgé 〈旧语〉(of a woman) leave her boudoir; get married; marry: 尚未~ be still unmarried

出格 chūgé ❶ out of the ordinary; outstanding: 这位诗人写诗不拘常法,每有~之佳作。The poet did not follow conventional patterns, and often produced unusually exquisite pieces. ❷ exceed what is proper: 这样做可有些~。That's going a bit too far.

出工 chūgōng go to work; show up for work: 天不亮就~下地 go to work in the fields before dawn / ~的时候到了。It's time to go to work.

出恭 chūgōng go to the lavatory (for bowel movement)

出乖露丑 chūguāi-lòuchǒu *also* "出乖弄丑" make an exhibition of oneself; cut a sorry figure

出轨 chūguǐ ❶ be derailed; go off the rails: 一列火车~。A train was derailed. ❷ overstep the bounds: 我们不能容忍任何~行为。We will not tolerate any behaviour which oversteps the bounds of decency (*or* goes against the sense of propriety).

出国 chūguó go abroad: ~留学 go and study abroad; pursue one's studies abroad / ~讲学 go abroad on a lecture tour / ~访问 go on a visit to foreign countries

出海 chūhǎi put (out) to sea: ~捕鱼 go fishing on the sea / 全村渔民都~了。All the fishermen in the village have put to sea. / 我们的舰队从大连~。Our fleet sailed from Dalian.

出海通道 chūhǎi tōngdào access to the sea

出汗 chūhàn sweat; perspire: 出一身汗 break into a sweat; sweat all over / 天气太热,我们~不止。It was very hot, and we were covered in sweat.

出航 chūháng ❶ set out on a voyage; sail: ~日期 date for sailing / 邮船明天~。The mail steamer sails tomorrow. ❷ (of a plane) take off; set out on a flight: ~航线 outbound course / 飞机早上七点~。The plane takes off at 7 a.m.

出号 chūhào ❶〈旧语〉(of a shop assistant) quit one's job ❷ outsize; extra-large (size): ~夹克衫 outsize jacket / 他身高两米,要买~的衣服。He is two metres tall. Buy him extra-large clothes.

出乎意料 chūhū-yìliào unexpected; unforeseen; exceeding one's expectations; contrary to one's expectations: ~的慷慨 unexpected generosity / 工作完成得~的快。The work was finished much sooner than expected. / 事情会到这种地步,真~。I had not expected that things would come to such a pass.

出花儿 chūhuār be infected with smallpox; come down with smallpox

出活 chūhuó yield good results in work; be efficient: 这样干,很~。This is an efficient way to work. / 这姑娘心灵手巧,~快。The girl is clever and deft, and works quickly. / 这种机器既轻巧,又~。This kind of machine is efficient as well as easy to handle.

出货 chūhuò delivery of goods: ~单 delivery order (D/O)

出击 chūjī ❶〈军事〉launch an attack; make a sally: 主动~ take the initiative to launch an attack ❷ hit out; attack: 不要四面~。Don't strike out in all directions.

出籍 chūjí 〈法律〉expatriation

出继 chūjì be legally adopted as heir: 他从小~给伯父。He was adopted by his uncle when he was little.

出家 chūjiā go to a monastery or a nunnery; become a monk or nun: 他年轻时~当了和尚。He became a Buddhist priest when he was a young man.

出家人 chūjiārén Buddhist or Taoist priest; monk; nun: ~慈悲为本。Monks and nuns are guided by the principle of mercy.

出价 chūjià offer a price; bid: ~最高的投标人 highest bidder / ~太低了 offer too little for it

出嫁 chūjià (of a woman) get married; marry: 传说这个美女不肯~,除非她父亲答应她三个条件。Legend has it that the beautiful girl

refused to marry unless her father granted her three conditions.

出尖 chūjiān ❶ tiptop; outstanding:～露众 stand head and shoulders above the common run; be outstanding ❷〈方言〉overfill a container:给客人盛饭，别～。Don't overfill a guest's rice bowl.

出将入相 chūjiàng-rùxiàng 〈旧语〉person of talent in both political and military fields who could be entrusted with the command of the armies or with the direction of the government — be qualified to be either a general or a chief minister

出脚 chūjiǎo 〈方言〉❶ take a step; step forward; move about:他刚～，就摔倒了。He fell down the moment he took a step. ❷ a little over:你怕是二十～了吧? You look a little over twenty.

出街 chūjiē 〈方言〉go into town; go to town

出结 chūjié sign an undertaking or statement:～保释受嫌人 sign a bail bond for a suspect; stand bail for a suspect /～领回失物 sign a receipt for one's lost property

出界 chūjiè 〈体育〉outside; out-of-bounds; out

出借 chūjiè lend; loan:图书馆～录像带。The library lends out videotapes.

出惊 chūjīng 〈方言〉be alarmed

出境 chūjìng ❶ leave the country:经由深圳～ leave the country via Shenzhen /递解～ send out of the country under escort /办理～手续 go through exit formalities /～登记 departure registration /～回执 exit receipt /～签证 exit visa /～许可证 exit permit /～证书 exit certificate /驱逐～ deport ❷ leave a certain district (county, province, etc.)

出九 chūjiǔ after the nine periods (of nine days each) following the winter solstice; out of the coldest days of the year:虽说还没有～，天气却暖和多了。Though the nine periods are scarcely over, the weather has become much warmer than before.

出局 chūjú bowl out; (in baseball or soft ball) be out

出具 chūjù write; issue:～证明 issue a certificate /～介绍信 write a reference (*or* letter of introduction)

出圈 chūjuàn remove manure from a pigsty, sheepfold, etc.

出科 chūkē 〈旧语〉graduate from old-type traditional opera school

出客 chūkè 〈方言〉go visiting; be entertained:～时穿的西装 western-style suit for social occasions /～时多少总得带点礼品吧。It is necessary to carry some gift when you go visiting.

出口 chūkǒu ❶ speak; utter:～伤人 speak bitingly /～粗野 swear like a trooper; be foul-mouthed /他的话还未～，她就知道他要说什么了。She knew what he was going to say before he opened his mouth. ❷ leave the port:货轮已经～。The freightship has left the port. ❸ export:～刺激 export incentives /无外汇～ export without foreign exchange ❹ exit; way out:会场的～ exit of a conference hall /影院～ exits from a cinema

出口保险 chūkǒu bǎoxiǎn export insurance

出口补贴 chūkǒu bǔtiē export subsidy

出口产品退税 chūkǒu chǎnpǐn tuìshuì tax refund or rebate on exports

出口成章 chūkǒu-chéngzhāng words flow from one's mouth as from the pen of a master:他才思敏捷，～。He is so quick-witted that words flow from his mouth as from the pen of a master.

出口代办行 chūkǒu dàibànháng export commission house

出口代理商 chūkǒu dàilǐshāng export agent

出口贷款 chūkǒu dàikuǎn export loan

出口单据 chūkǒu dānjù export document

出口港 chūkǒugǎng port of export

出口管制 chūkǒu guǎnzhì export control

出口行 chūkǒuháng export house

出口加工区 chūkǒu jiāgōngqū export processing zone

出口检疫 chūkǒu jiǎnyì export quarantine

出口结关 chūkǒu jiéguān customs clearance for exports

出口禁令 chūkǒu jìnlìng export ban

出口净值 chūkǒu jìngzhí net export value

出口贸易 chūkǒu màoyì export trade

出口免税区 chūkǒu miǎnshuìqū tax-free export zone

出口配额 chūkǒu pèi'é export quota:～管理 export quota administration /～公开招标制 public bidding system for export quotas

出口融资 chūkǒu róngzī export finance

出口商 chūkǒushāng exporter; export merchant; export trader

出口商品 chūkǒu shāngpǐn export commodities or goods:～结构 export commodity mix

出口申报单 chūkǒu shēnbàodān export declaration

出口市场 chūkǒu shìchǎng export market

出口税 chūkǒushuì export duty

出口提单 chūkǒu tídān export bill of lading

出口限制 chūkǒu xiànzhì export restriction

出口信贷 chūkǒu xìndài export credit:～担保 export credit guarantee /～保险 export credit insurance

出口信用证 chūkǒu xìnyòngzhèng export letter of credit

出口型工业 chūkǒuxíng gōngyè export-oriented industry

出口许可证 chūkǒu xǔkězhèng export licence

出口银行 chūkǒu yínháng export bank

出口转内销 chūkǒu zhuǎn nèixiāo ❶ commodities intended for export but sold on the domestic market (usu. because of substandard quality) ❷〈比喻〉domestic news learned from foreign broadcasts and publications

出来 chūlai ❶ come out; go out:太阳～了。The sun has come out. ❷ appear; emerge:化验结果～了。The laboratory test report is ready.

出来 chulai ❶ *used after certain verbs to indicate the direction of motion from inside*:从抽屉里跳～一只耗子。A mouse jumped out of the drawer. /你拿～个办法嘛! Think of a way of doing it, please! ❷ *used after a verb to indicate the completion or realization of an action*:计划已订～了。The plan has been worked out. /她把嗓子练～了。Her voice has become resonant and mellow through continual practice. ❸ *used after a verb to indicate the change from a hidden or ambiguous state to certainty*:我一眼就认出他来了。I recognized him the moment I saw him. /她禁不住哭～了。She could not help crying out. /你能不能从别人那儿打听～点儿消息? Could you try to find some information about it from other sources?

出栏 chūlán ❶ (of pigs or sheep) be taken to the slaughterhouse ❷〈方言〉*see*"出圈"

出栏率 chūlánlǜ number of heads of livestock delivered to the slaughterhouse; number of heads of livestock for sale

出蓝 chūlán 〈书面〉(of pupils) surpass one's masters; (of new generation) surpass the older generation:有～之誉 be reputed for surpassing one's teachers /青出于蓝而胜于蓝。Blue is extracted from the indigo plant, but is bluer than the plant it comes from — the pupil learns from the teacher but surpasses him.

出类拔萃 chūlèi-bácuì stand out from one's fellows; be out of the ordinary run:～的人物 outstanding figure; the best and the brightest /她是年轻女知识分子中～的。She is one of the best and the brightest among young women intellectuals.

出力 chūlì ❶ put forth one's strength; exert oneself; make great efforts:为农业现代化～ do sth. for the modernization of agriculture /每人多出把力，提前完成任务。Let's put in an extra effort to get the job done ahead of time. /他从不肯～帮助别人。He never cares to lift a finger to help anybody. ❷ output power:～试验 service test /～效率 power efficiency

出列 chūliè 〈军事〉come out of the ranks:～! Fall out!

出猎 chūliè go hunting

出溜 chūliu 〈方言〉slide; slip:我脚底一～，摔了一跤。I slipped and fell.

出笼 chūlóng ❶ just off the steamer:热乎乎的馒头刚～。The hot buns are just off the steamer. ❷〈贬义〉(sth. bad) come out into the open; come forth; appear:这谬论一～，立即受到舆论界的抨击。As soon as the fallacies came out, they met with withering criticism from the press. ❸ sell in large quantities; dump; inflate (the paper currency)

出漏子 chū lòuzi *also*"出娄子" get into trouble; be in trouble; go wrong:我想他也许出了大漏子。I think he has probably got into serious trouble.

出炉 chūlú come out of the oven or furnace:这火烧刚～。The pie is just out of the oven. /高炉准点～。Molten steel came out of the furnace on time.

出路 chūlù ❶ way out:生活～ opportunity to earn a living; means of livelihood /自谋～ try to find a way out by oneself /山谷只有这一条～。This is the only way out of the valley. /发展中国家的根本～是自力更生。The fundamental way out for a developing country is through self-reliance. ❷ outlet:他们必须为自己的产品寻找新～。They have to find new outlets for their products.

出露 chūlù emerge; show:潜艇的上部～水面。The top of the submarine emerged above water. /这个地质结构有油气～。This geological formation has shown signs of oil and gas.

出乱子 chū luànzi go wrong; get into trouble: 除非我们牢牢控制局势, 否则就会出大乱子。Something disastrous would happen unless we take the situation well in hand.

出落 chūluo grow (prettier, etc.): 这几年姑娘~得更漂亮了。The girl has grown even prettier in recent years.

出马 chūmǎ go into action; take: 这件事我恐怕要亲自~。I'm afraid I'll have to take care of (*or* attend to) the matter personally.

出卖 chūmài ❶ offer for sale; sell: 这家商店正在减价~服装。There is a sale for suits in this store. *or* This store is selling suits at reduced prices. ❷ sell out; betray; barter away: ~灵魂 sell one's soul / ~朋友 betray one's friend / ~民族利益 sell out national interests / ~原则 barter away principles

出满月 chū mǎnyuè ❶ (of a woman) one month after giving birth to a baby ❷ (of a baby) one month old

C

出毛病 chū máobing be or go out of order; go wrong; break down: 汽车中途出了毛病。The car broke down on the way. / 检查一下, 看毛病出在哪里。Please check and see what's wrong with it. / 仪表~了。The meter doesn't work properly.

出梅 chūméi *also* "断梅" duànméi the rainy season is over

出门 chūmén ❶ go out: 我拜访经理, 他恰巧~了。The manager happened to be out when I called. / 他刚~, 我估计一会就会回来。He's just left. I think he'll be back in a minute. ❷ be away from home; go on a journey: ~后, 常接到家里来信。I have often heard from home since I left. / 他明天就要~办事。He is going away on business tomorrow. ❸〈方言〉(of a woman) get married; marry: 姐姐十八岁那年~。My sister got married at the age of 18.

出门子 chū ménzi 〈方言〉(of a woman) get married; marry

出面 chūmiàn act in one's own capacity or on behalf of an organization; appear personally: 自己不~ keep oneself in the background / 以个人名义~ act in his own name / 他以部长身分~调解纠纷。He tried to mediate the dispute in his capacity as minister.

出苗 chūmiáo 〈农业〉(of seedlings) germinate; sprout; come out: ~率 rate of emergence; rate of germination

出名 chūmíng ❶ famous; well-known; celebrated: ~的电影明星 well-known film star / 以英勇善战~ be noted for one's bravery in war / 以好客~的城市 city famous for its hospitality ❷ use the name of; lend one's name (to an occasion or enterprise): 下周由红梅公司~儿举办义卖。A charity bazaar will be held next week under the auspices of The Hong Mei Company.

出没 chūmò appear and disappear; haunt: 这一带有老虎~。This region is the haunt of tigers.

出没无常 chūmò-wúcháng appear and disappear suddenly and unpredictably: 土匪~ infested by bandits / 在这原始森林里, 野兽~。The virgin forest is haunted by wild beasts.

出谋划策 chūmóu-huàcè give (evil) counsel; make (evil) designs: 毫无疑问, 有人躲在后面~, 散布谣言。No doubt there are people hiding behind the scenes, spreading rumours and hatching plots. / 这件事是由他~的。He's the brain behind this.

出牧 chūmù graze sheep and cattle at a distant pasture

出纳 chūnà ❶ receive and pay out money or bills ❷ cashier; teller ❸ receive and lend books, etc.

出纳台 chūnàtái (library) circulation desk; (bank) cashier's or teller's desk

出纳员 chūnàyuán cashier; teller

出盘 chūpán 〈方言〉 *see* "出倒"

出票 chūpiào draw a bill: ~人 drawer / ~日 date of draft; date of issue

出品 chūpǐn ❶ produce; manufacture; make: 本厂~新式家具。Our factory manufactures stylish furniture. ❷ product: 新~ new product / 本地的~ local product

出聘 chūpìn ❶ (of a girl) marry: ~女儿 marry off a daughter / 妹妹于去年~。My sister married last year. ❷〈书面〉be sent on an official mission abroad; go abroad as an envoy

出圃 chūpǔ remove young plants from a nursery for transplantation

出妻 chūqī 〈旧语〉❶ divorce a wife ❷ divorced wife

出其不备 chūqíbùbèi catch sb. unprepared: 进攻敌人, 要~。Attack when the enemy are not on the alert.

出其不意 chūqíbùyì take sb. by surprise; catch sb. unawares; catch sb. on the hop: 这个问题提得~, 他真不知如何回答是好。The question caught him off guard and he was at a loss what to say. / 攻其不备, ~。Attack where the enemy is unprepared and act where they do not expect it.

出奇 chūqí unusually; extraordinarily: 考题难得~。The paper is unusually stiff. / 这东西没有什么~的地方。There's nothing extraordinary about it. / 这个老汉沉默得~, 动作也慢得~。This old fellow was incredibly taciturn and slow.

出奇制胜 chūqí-zhìshèng win by making a surprise move: 敌众我寡, 我们唯有~。As we are outnumbered, the only chance to win is to make a surprise attack.

出气 chūqì vent one's spleen; take it out on sb.; give vent to one's anger: 拿别人~是很不对的。It is very wrong to vent your spleen on others. / 他发誓迟早要出这口气。He vows to avenge himself sooner or later. / 为什么老拿我~? Why do you always pick on me? / 你一定有什么不如意, 借我~。Something must be troubling you, and you just let off some steam on me.

出气口 chūqìkǒu vent hole; gas outlet

出气筒 chūqìtǒng 〈方言〉person on whom to vent one's anger; punching bag: 他常常把老婆当~。He often vented his anger on his wife. / 我可不是你的~。I am in no way a punching bag of yours.

出勤 chūqín ❶ turn out for work: 按时~ turn out for work on time / 全体~ full attendance ❷ be out on duty; make a business trip: 每年他总有几次到上海南京一带~。He would go on several business trips to Shanghai and Nanjing every year.

出勤率 chūqínlǜ (rate of) attendance

出去 chūqu go out; get out: ~散散步 go for a walk / ~透口气 go out for a breath of air

出去 chuqu *used after a verb to indicate outward movement*: 从屋里溜~ sneak out of the room / 把入侵者赶~ drive the invaders out / 今天运~二十袋粮食。Twenty bags of grain were carried away today.

出圈儿 chūquānr go too far; overstep the bounds of normal social behaviour: 这样做就~了。This is going too far indeed.

出缺 chūquē (of a high post) fall vacant: 一位部长最近去世, 职位~了。The post was left vacant by the recent death of a minister.

出让 chūràng sell articles of one's own (usu. not for profit): ~摩托车 sell one's motorcycle

出人命 chū rénmìng involve the loss of human life: 这件事处理不当, 可能~。The matter, if mishandled, might take a toll of human lives.

出人头地 chūréntóudì rise head and shoulders above others; stand out among one's fellows; become outstanding: 他希望有一天能~。He hopes he will find himself famous some day. *or* He hopes he will be well ahead of others.

出人意料 chūrényìliào *also* "出人意表"; "出人意外" exceeding all expectations; beyond all expectations; coming as a surprise: 他们竟招待得如此殷勤, 真是~。Little did we expect that they would go out of their way to treat us so generously. / 演出效果之佳~。The performance turned out unexpectedly to be a great success.

出任 chūrèn 〈书面〉take up the post of: ~外交部长 be appointed foreign minister

出入 chūrù ❶ come in and go out: ~请随手关门。Please close the door behind you when you come in or go out. / 骑自行车~请下车。Cyclists please dismount at the gate. ❷ discrepancy; divergence; difference: 这两个声明有~。There is some discrepancy between the two statements. / 现金与账面有~。Cash on hand does not tally with the figure in the accounts.

出入证 chūrùzhèng pass (identifying a staff member, etc.)

出塞 chūsài go beyond the Great Wall: 昭君~。Wang Qiang (王嫱), a beauty of the Han Dynasty, went to the frontier areas (to marry the chieftain of a northern tribe).

出赛 chūsài 〈体育〉take part in a sports competition

出丧 chūsāng *see* "出殡"

出色 chūsè outstanding; remarkable; splendid: ~的科学家 outstanding scientist / ~的文章 remarkable piece of writing / 干得很~ do a splendid job; be doing splendidly / 她没有什么特别~的地方。There was nothing particularly striking about her.

出山 chūshān ❶ leave a hilly region ❷〈比喻〉enter politics as a government official; take up a post or task: 为了备战全运会, 非请他~担任我队教练不可。In order to be well prepared for the National Games, it is essential to ask him to be coach to our team.

出射 chūshè 〈物理〉outgoing; emergent: ~波 outgoing wave / ~中子 outgoing neutron

出身 chūshēn ❶ family background; class origin: 工人~ have a

working-class background /～知识分子家庭 be born and brought up in an intellectual's family /～卑贱 be of a humble origin /～寒微 come from an impoverished family ❷ one's previous experience or occupation：此人科班～。This man has a record of professional training. ❸〈旧语〉first appointment in the ladder of official promotion：翰林～ be first appointed as a member of the Imperial Academy

出神 chūshén be spellbound; be lost in thought：看得～ watch spellbound /听得～ listen with rapt attention /坐在那儿～ sit there, lost in thought /他～地望着远方。He gazed into the distance, as if in a trance. /她一个人独自坐在房里，两眼望着窗户～。She sat alone in her room, her eyes staring blankly at the window.

出神入化 chūshén-rùhuà reach the height or acme of perfection：～的表演 spellbinding performance /画笔～ superb brushwork

出生 chūshēng be born：～于战乱之中 be born in the turmoil of war /～登记 registration of birth /～日期 date of birth

出生地 chūshēngdì birthplace

出生地法 chūshēngdìfǎ law of the place of one's birth; *jus soli*

出生率 chūshēnglǜ birthrate

出生入死 chūshēng-rùsǐ go through fire and water; brave untold dangers：他在战场上～地战斗。He fought bravely on the battle ground, forgetting all about his own safety.

出生证 chūshēngzhèng birth certificate

出声 chūshēng utter a sound：大家别～，先仔细听听。Don't make any noise and listen carefully.

出师 chūshī ❶ finish one's apprenticeship ❷〈书面〉launch a campaign：～不利 meet with initial setbacks; get off to a bad start /～未捷身先死，长使英雄泪满襟！Before seeing victory, he died in the camp ground; It oft makes later heroes weep with sighs profound!

出使 chūshǐ serve as an envoy abroad; be sent on a diplomatic mission：～日本 serve as ambassador to Japan; be accredited to Japan

出示 chūshì ❶ show; produce：～身分证 produce one's identity card /搭乘出境飞机前必须～护照。You must show your passport before you board a plane. ❷〈书面〉put up a notice：～安民 put up a notice to reassure the public

出世 chūshì ❶ come into the world; be born：一个婴儿～了。A new baby was born. ❷ come into being or existence; be born：旧制度要灭亡，新制度要～了。A new system will come into being in place of the crumbling old system. ❸ renounce human society; stand aloof from the mortal world：～思想 other-worldly thoughts /产生了～的念头 think of renouncing human society and becoming a monk ❹ soar into the skies：横空～ (of mountains) tower majestically into the heavens

出世作 chūshìzuò〈旧语〉virgin work; maiden work; first effort (as a writer, etc.)

出仕 chūshì〈旧语〉serve as an official; take up an official career：隐居山野，终身不再～ retire to the mountains and never serve as an official again

出市壁垒 chūshì bìlěi〈外贸〉barrier of exit

出事 chūshì meet with a mishap; have an accident：飞机～ air-crash; air disaster /～地点 site of an accident /没有出什么事。Nothing is wrong. *or* Nothing has gone wrong.

出手 chūshǒu ❶ get (hoarded goods, etc.) off one's hands; dispose of; sell：这批货要尽快～。We should try to dispose of these goods as soon as possible. ❷ produce; offer：他一～就是几百元钱。He would flash money around several hundred *yuan* at a time. /这点钱实在拿不～。I really couldn't offer such a trifling sum without blushing. ❸ length of sleeve：衣袖的～正好。The sleeves are just the right length. ❹ skill displayed in making opening moves：～不凡 make skilful (*or* masterly) opening moves (in martial arts, chess, etc.) ❺ come to blows *see also* "打出手" dǎ chūshǒu

出首 chūshǒu ❶ inform against (an offender)：到派出所～歹徒 go to the local police station to inform against the gangster; report the gangster to the local police station ❷ (often used in the early vernacular) give oneself up; surrender (to the police, etc.)

出售 chūshòu offer for sale; sell：高价～ sell sth. at a good price /减价～ sell sth. at a reduced price /这房子～吗？Is the house for sale?

出书 chūshū publish books：～计划 publication plan /该出版社每年～数百种。The press publishes hundreds of titles a year.

出数儿 chūshùr〈口语〉(of rice) rise well with cooking

出水 chūshuǐ ❶ surface from water：～才看两腿泥 only when a man comes out of the water can the mud on his legs be seen — only the end can tell ❷ (water) surface from underground：这口井挖了六米，还未～。Six metres have been dug for the well, and there is still no water in sight. ❸〈旧语〉(of a prostitute) leave the brothel for good

出水芙蓉 chūshuǐ-fúróng lotus flower just emerging from water; beautiful woman; beautiful verse or graceful calligraphy

出死入生 chūsǐ-rùshēng *see* "出生入死"

出台 chūtái ❶ appear on the stage; enter：～亮相 strike a pose on the stage /名角儿还没～。The famous stars have not appeared yet. ❷ come out from behind the scenes; come into the open：～干涉 come out into the open to interfere ❸ make sth. public; publicize：工资改革方案即将～。A plan for reforming the wage system will be made known (*or* publicized) soon.

出摊 chūtān set up a stall (in the open)：～卖盒饭 set up a stall selling lunch boxes /老王今天没有～。Old Wang did not set up his stall today.

出逃 chūtáo run away (from one's home or country); flee

出题 chūtí ❶ set examination paper ❷ set a topic

出粜 chūtiào sell (grain)

出挑 chūtiao ❶ *see* "出落" ❷ grow into：不满十年，这位少女就～为一名出色的芭蕾舞演员。In less than ten years, the young girl had grown into a superb ballet dancer.

出铁 chūtiě〈冶金〉tap a blast furnace：出一炉铁 tap a heat of molten iron /～口 taphole; iron notch

出庭 chūtíng appear in court; enter an appearance：～作证 appear in court as a witness; serve as a witness at court /～受审 appear in court as a defendant /～辩护 defend a case in court /～通知 memorandum of appearance; notice of appearance

出头 chūtóu ❶ extricate oneself from miserable circumstances：第三帝国灭亡之后，欧洲的犹太人才有了～之日。Not until after the fall of the Third Reich did the Jews in Europe come out of the abyss of misery. ❷ (of sth.) show its tip; jut out; stand out：堆放杉篙，不能～太多。When you pile up fir poles, make sure not too many of them jut out. ❸ appear personally; act on behalf of; take the lead：亲自～调解纠纷 come in person to mediate a dispute /他～组织了一次高校校际演说比赛。He initiated the organization of an intercollegiate oratorical contest. /枪打～鸟。The leading bird gets shot first. — One who takes the lead usually bears the brunt of attack. ❹ a little over; odd：一百～ one hundred odd /这人四十～的年纪。The man is just a little over forty.

出头的椽子先烂 chūtóude chuánzi xiān làn rafter that juts out rots first; those who come to the fore are most liable to attack

出头露面 chūtóu-lòumiàn make a public appearance; be in the limelight：他不爱～。He does not like the limelight. *or* He is publicity shy. /我们注意到他近来不大～。We notice that he hasn't made many public appearances lately.

出徒 chūtú complete one's apprenticeship

出土 chūtǔ ❶ be unearthed; be excavated：一批汉代古物在西安～。A number of archaeological relics of the Han Dynasty were unearthed in Xi'an. ❷ come up out of the ground：小苗刚～。The sprouts have just come up.

出土文物 chūtǔ wénwù unearthened relic; excavated artifact

出脱 chūtuō ❶ manage to sell; dispose of：靠降低价格咱们这批货才得～。It's the low price which sold our goods. ❷ *see* "出落" ❸ acquit; absolve：～罪名 acquit sb. of a charge /自我～ self-absolution

出外 chūwài leave home; be away：～度假 be away on holiday; be vacationing somewhere /～公干 be away on official business /～经商 leave home to do business /～一里，不如屋里 better to stay at home than even roam one *li*; east and west, home is best

出亡 chūwáng flee; live in exile：为了躲避迫害，他～海外达十年之久。To escape persecution, he fled the country and lived in exile for as long as ten years.

出污泥而不染 chū wūní ér bù rǎn emerge unsullied from the filth — remain undefiled in spite of general corruption

出席 chūxí attend; be present：～会议 attend a meeting /～开幕式 be present at the opening ceremony /以观察员身分～大会 attend the conference as an observer /～人数 number of persons present; attendance

出息 chūxi ❶ promise; prospects; future：有～的青年 promising youth /他志坚如玉，一定会有～的。He is tenacious of purpose and bound to go far. /所有全心全意为人民而工作的人都是有～的。All

those who work singleheartedly for the people have a bright future. / 这个人真没～。This chap is a good-for-nothing. ❷〈方言〉progress:这孩子比去年～多了。The boy has improved greatly since last year. ❸〈方言〉temper; cultivate; train:艰苦的条件往往更～人。Arduous circumstances tend to temper people. ❹〈方言〉benefit:种棉花～大。Growing cotton brings great benefit.

出险 chūxiǎn ❶ (of people) be out of danger:战斗开始时,妇女儿童已全部～。Women and children had all got out of danger when the fighting began. ❷ (of a dyke or similar structure) be in danger; be threatened:河水上涨,堤坝～。The river has risen, and the dyke is threatened.

出现 chūxiàn appear; arise; emerge:一只巡洋舰突然～在地平线上。A cruiser suddenly appeared on the horizon. /当机会～的时候,不要让它溜走了。Don't let slip an opportunity when it arises. /讨论中～了新见解。Fresh ideas emerged from the discussion.

C

出线 chūxiàn (of athletes) become qualified for the next round of competition in a sports meet

出项 chūxiàng item of expenditure; spending; outlay:这几年科学研究的～大大增加。The outlay on scientific research has increased greatly in recent years.

出血 chūxiě 〈方言〉pay up; cough up:老爷子平时非常节俭,这回娶儿媳妇可出了不少血。Thrifty as he usually was, the old man coughed up quite a bit of money for his son's wedding.

出心 chūxīn motive; intention; purpose:～要正。One must be soundly motivated.

出行 chūxíng go on a trip to other places:会议日内在京召开,何时～,盼告。The conference will be held in Beijing in a few days. Will you kindly let us know the date of your departure?

出雄 chūxióng *also* "抽雄" chōuxióng (of plants) put forth staminal ears

出秀 chūxiù 〈方言〉*see* "出落"

出虚恭 chū xūgōng 〈婉词〉break wind; fart

出血 chūxuè 〈医学〉haemorrhage; bleeding:大～ massive haemorrhage /胃～ gastric haemorrhage /内～ internal haemorrhage /皮下～ subcutaneous haemorrhage /～胆囊炎 haemocholecystitis /～性麻疹 haemorrhagic measles; black measles /～性胸膜炎 haemorrhagic pleuritis /伤口大量～。The wound bled freely.

出巡 chūxún royal progress; tour of inspection:总统正～各地。The president is on a tour of inspection around the country.

出芽 chūyá ❶ sprout; germinate ❷〈植物〉prolification

出言 chūyán speak; remark:～有章 speak in a methodical manner

出言不逊 chūyán-bùxùn make impertinent or rude remarks

出言无状 chūyán-wúzhuàng make flippant comments or remarks

出演 chūyǎn perform; play the role of; act as

出殃 chūyāng 〈迷信〉(of a dead person's soul) return home (to say farewell)

出洋 chūyáng 〈旧语〉go abroad:～考察 go on a study mission (*or* tour) abroad /～留学 pursue one's studies abroad; study abroad

出洋相 chū yángxiàng cut a sorry figure; make an exhibition of oneself:他在宴会上喝醉了酒,大～。He got drunk at the dinner party and made an exhibition of himself. /他想来点俏皮话,可是又讲得那么拙劣,真是出尽洋相。He cut a very sorry figure by trying, rather awkwardly, to be witty and humorous. /我就是爱看那些人～。I enjoyed watching those people make fools of themselves.

出以公心 chūyǐgōngxīn keep the public interest in mind; act without any selfish consideration:办事要～。Whatever one does, one should have the public interest at heart. *or* One should be fair in handling all matters.

出迎 chūyíng go or come out to meet sb.:列队～ line up to welcome sb. /～贵宾 turn out to greet a distinguished guest

出油井 chūyóujǐng 〈石油〉producing well

出游 chūyóu go on a (sightseeing) tour or trip:我们常于假日～郊区。We often go on sightseeing trips to suburban districts on holidays.

出于 chūyú stem from; be motivated or dictated by; proceed from:～自愿 of one's own free will /～无奈 have no alternative (but to do sth.) / 狂妄往往～愚昧无知。Arrogance often stems from ignorance and stupidity. /我们的批评完全～加强团结的真诚愿望。Our criticism proceeds from a genuine desire for unity. /他的这番讲话是～理智,而不是闹个人意气。His speech was dictated by reason rather than by personal feeling.

出渔 chūyú go fishing on the sea

出语 chūyǔ speak; utter remarks:～惊人 utter remarks that astonish people; leave a vivid impression on everybody with one's words; one's words make people sit up

出狱 chūyù come out of prison; be released from prison

出院 chūyuàn leave hospital:～证明 hospital discharge certificate /～处 discharge office /他已病愈～。He has been discharged from hospital (after recovery).

出月 chūyuè next month:这篇文章～才能脱稿。This article will not be finished until next month.

出月子 chū yuèzi (of a woman) one month after giving birth to a baby

出渣 chūzhā 〈冶金〉tap; slag tap

出渣口 chūzhākǒu 〈冶金〉slag notch; cinder notch

出展 chūzhǎn hold an exhibition abroad or in a place other than one's own; be exhibited:这种新产品计划年内～美国。It is planned that the new product will be exhibited in the US this year. /岭南画家代表作品～北京,获得好评。The exhibition of Guangdong painters' representative works in Beijing received a good press.

出战 chūzhàn go into battle:～失利 have lost the battle /今晚由北京队～天津队。Tonight, the Beijing team will lock horns with the Tianjin team.

出账 chūzhàng ❶ enter an item of expenditure in the accounts ❷〈方言〉(item of) expenditure

出蛰 chūzhé 〈生物〉(of some animals) end of winter sleep; end of hibernation

出针 chūzhēn *also* "引针" yǐnzhēn; "排针" páizhēn pull the acupuncture needle out

出诊 chūzhěn (of a doctor) visit a patient at home; pay a home visit; make a house call:～费 house visit charges; charges for a house visit

出阵 chūzhèn ❶ go into battle ❷ take part (in a kind of activity):今晚的演讲比赛,班上许多同学都要～。Many students of my class will take part in this evening's oratorial contest.

出征 chūzhēng go on an expedition; be sent to the front:这首唐诗描写一位少妇怀念～的丈夫。This Tang poem depicts a young woman pining for her husband who has gone to fight in a distant land.

出证 chūzhèng give evidence; bear witness; testify:不肯～ refuse to testify

出众 chūzhòng be out of the common run; be out of the ordinary; be outstanding:人才～ of outstanding ability /智力～ unusually gifted; of exceptional intelligence /容貌～ (of a girl) exceedingly attractive

出资 chūzī provide funds; put in capital:～办厂 provide capital for setting up a factory /～作主 pay the piper and call the tune /～而不参与经营的合伙人 dormant partner

出自 chūzì come from; proceed from; stem from:～肺腑 from the bottom of one's heart /这个典故～何处? Where does this literary allusion come from?

出走 chūzǒu leave; run away; flee:贾宝玉离家～,那情景催人泪下。The scene when Jia Baoyu flees home is truly pathetic. /他自知大祸临头,仓卒～。He knew he was in for dreadful trouble and ran away in a hurry.

出租 chūzū let; rent out; hire out:～房屋。House to let. /～自行车。Bicycles on hire. /游船～按小时计费。Rowboats for hire by the hour.

出租柜台 chūzū guìtái rent or hire out counters (in a store, shop, etc.)

出租汽车 chūzū qìchē taxi; cab; taxicab

出租人 chūzūrén leasor; lessor

chú

厨(廚、㕑) chú ❶ kitchen:下～ work in the kitchen; serve as a cook ❷ cook; chef:名～ famous chef /大～ head cook; chef

厨房 chúfáng kitchen:～用具 kitchen (*or* cooking) utensils /～有人好进餐,朝里有人好做官。If you have a pal in the kitchen, you can always enjoy a good meal; if you have a friend in the government, you can always hold on to a good job.

厨行 chúháng cooking trade; culinary skills

厨具 chújù kitchen utensils

厨娘 chúniáng 〈旧语〉woman cook
厨师 chúshī cook; chef:名～ master cook /广东～ Guangdong chef
厨司 chúsī 〈方言〉cook; chef
厨子 chúzi 〈旧语〉cook:～太多倒把汤烧糟了。Too many cooks spoil the broth.

橱(櫥) chú cabinet; closet:衣～ wardrobe /五斗～ chest of drawers /书～ bookcase /碗～ cupboard /壁～ built-in cabinet
橱窗 chúchuāng ❶ show window; display window; shop window; showcase:～设计 shop-window design ❷ glass-fronted billboard
橱柜 chúguì ❶ cupboard ❷ low cupboard that also serves as a table; sideboard

蹰(躕) chú see "踟蹰" chíchú

躇 chú see "踌躇" chóuchú

蜍 chú see "蟾蜍" chánchú

除[1] chú ❶ get rid of; eliminate; abolish; remove:为民～害 rid the people of a scourge ❷ except; except for; in addition to:～此而外,别无他图 have no other plan in mind except this /他的动向如何,～你之外谁也不清楚。Everyone is in the dark about his future moves excepting (*or* except) you. /～汉族外,中国还有五十五个民族。There are fifty-five ethnic groups in China besides the Han. ❸ divide:六～以三得二。Six divided by three is two. /三～九得三。Three goes into nine three times. /任何奇数都不能被二～尽。Any odd number is indivisible by two. ❹〈书面〉offer or confer(official positions)

除[2] chú 〈书面〉steps to a house; doorsteps:黎明即起,洒扫庭～ rise at dawn and sweep the courtyard
除暴安良 chúbào-ānliáng get rid of bullies and bring peace to the people; eliminate local tyrants to reassure the public
除弊 chúbì abolish what is harmful; eradicate abuses:兴利～ promote what is beneficial and abolish what is harmful
除冰 chúbīng de-icing:～器 de-icer
除草 chúcǎo weeding:～机 weeder
除草定 chúcǎodìng Bromacil, a brand of chemical herbicide
除草剂 chúcǎojì weed killer; herbicide; weedicide
除颤 chúchàn eliminate quivers in atrium or ventricle by mechanical means
除尘 chúchén remove dust:～设备 dust removing plant; dust-cleaning apparatus
除尘器 chúchénqì dust remover; vacuum cleaner
除虫菊 chúchóngjú 〈植物〉*Dalmatian chrysanthemum*
除虫菊酯 chúchóngjúzhǐ 〈化学〉pyrethrins
除臭 chúchòu 〈化工〉deodorizae
除臭剂 chúchòujì 〈化学〉deodorant; deodoriferant; deodoriser
除恶务尽 chú'è-wùjìn *also* "除恶务本" one must be thorough in exterminating evil; evil must be eradicated or rooted out
除法 chúfǎ 〈数学〉division:～题 division problem
除非 chúfēi ❶ (indicating a premise, followed by 否则,不然) only when; only if; unless:～接到命令,他决不撤退。He would not retreat unless he received orders to do so. /若要人不知,～己莫为。If you don't want people to know, you'd better not do it. ❷ except:～他,我谁都不信任。I trust no one except him. /～雨天,我天天晚饭后散步。I take a walk after supper every day except when there is rain.
除服 chúfú 〈旧语〉take off mourning clothes; go out of mourning
除干扰天线 chúgānrǎo tiānxiàn balancing antenna
除根 chúgēn dig up the roots; root out; be cured once and for all; get a permanent cure:斩草～。Dig up the roots when you weed. *or* If you spare the roots of an evil, you spare the evil itself. /这种病很麻烦,不易～。This kind of disease is troublesome and very difficult to shake off for good.
除号 chúhào 〈数学〉division sign
除籍 chújí 〈书面〉remove sb.'s name from the rolls; expunge sb.'s name from a list; expel; dismiss
除旧布新 chújiù-bùxīn *also* "除旧更新" do away with the old, usher in the new; ring out the old, ring in the new
除开 chúkāi *see* "除了"
除了 chúle ❶ except; except for:这道题～他全班谁都不会做。Nobody can resolve this problem in our class except him. /那对孪生兄弟～高矮略有差别外,长相看上去完全一样。The twin brothers looked exactly alike except for some slight difference in height. /～沙沙的树叶声,小树林别无动静。The wood was silent and still except for the rustling of the leaves. ❷ besides; in addition to; apart from:这个设计～费用低,还有许多其他优点。This design has many other advantages besides lower cost. /我～教书,有时还做点翻译。Apart from teaching, I do some translation. ❸ (used in coordination with 就是) either... or:这些日子～刮风,就是下雨。It has been either windy or rainy these days.
除名 chúmíng expel; dismiss:被学校～ be expelled from school; be sent down
除沫剂 chúmòjì anti-foaming agent
除气 chúqì 〈冶金〉degassing; degasifying:～钢 degasifying steel /～剂 degasifier; degasifying agent
除却 chúquè ❶ except; besides:小丘上～一座宝塔外,什么都没有。There is nothing on the hill except a pagoda. ❷ exclude; get rid of
除日 chúrì 〈书面〉last day of the twelfth month of the lunar year
除丧 chúsāng *see* "除服"
除湿 chúshī dehumidify:～作用 dehumidification
除授 chúshòu 〈书面〉confer an official post or position
除数 chúshù 〈数学〉divisor
除霜 chúshuāng defrosting:快速～ fast defrosting /自动～ auto-defrosting /手动～ manual defrosting /～器 defroster; frost remover
除四害 chú sìhài eliminate the four pests (i.e. rats, bedbugs, flies and mosquitoes)
除岁 chúsuì *see* "除夕"
除外 chúwài except; not counting; not including:图书馆每天都开放,节日～。The library is open every day except on holidays. /公共汽车上有四十个人,司机～。There were forty people in the bus, not counting the driver.
除夕 chúxī New Year's Eve:～之夜他们联欢睡得很晚。They had a get-together on New Year's Eve and stayed up very late.
除息 chúxī 〈金融〉ex-div
除锈 chúxiù remove the rust; get the rust off:～器 rust removal /～剂 rust inhibitor; rust remover
除夜 chúyè *see* "除夕"
除莠剂 chúyǒujì herbicide; weed-killer
除渣 chúzhā 〈冶金〉slag removal; slagging

篨 chú see "籧篨" qúchú

钼 chú see "锄" chú
see also jǔ

锄(耡) chú ❶ hoe:鹤嘴～ mattock ❷ work with a hoe; hoe:～庄稼地 hoe up weeds in the cropland /～草 hoe up weeds; weed with a hoe ❸ uproot; eliminate; wipe out
锄地 chúdì weed or loosen the soil with a hoe
锄奸 chújiān ferret out traitors and spies:～工作 anti-espionage activities
锄强扶弱 chúqiáng-fúruò eliminate the bullies and help the downtrodden
锄式开沟器 chúshì kāigōuqì hoe coulter
锄头雨 chútóuyǔ 〈方言〉rain that comes just before hoeing
锄头 chútou ❶〈方言〉hoe ❷ pickaxe (used in southern China)

刍(芻) chú 〈书面〉❶ hay; fodder:反～ ruminate; chew the cud ❷ cut grass; weed ❸〈谦词〉my:～见 my (humble) opinion
刍狗 chúgǒu 〈书面〉straw dog (used in ancient times as a sacrificial offering, to be discarded when the ritual was over); worthless stuff:天地不仁,以万物为～。The universe is ruthless, and treats all living things as worthless stuff to be discarded.
刍豢 chúhuàn 〈书面〉domestic animals
刍粮 chúliáng 〈书面〉fodder and food
刍灵 chúlíng 〈古语〉straw men and horses buried with the dead
刍秣 chúmò 〈书面〉fodder
刍荛 chúráo 〈书面〉❶ cut grass and firewood:～有禁。There are

C

limits on cutting grass and firewood. ❷ woodcutter：询于～ inquire of a woodcutter ❸〈谦词〉this rustic, untutored person；I：～之言 my superficial remarks

刍言 chúyán 〈书面〉〈谦词〉my insignificant words；my humble opinion

刍议 chúyì 〈书面〉〈谦词〉my humble opinion：以上～，请诸位指正。Please feel free to criticize what I have just said.

雏(雛) chú young (bird)：～鸭 duckling /～莺乳燕 young orioles and swallows

雏凤 chúfèng young phoenix — promising young man or woman

雏凤声清 chúfèng-shēngqīng *also*“雏凤清于老凤声”children are more talented than their parents

C

雏鸡 chújī chick

雏妓 chújì child prostitute

雏鸟 chúniǎo nestling；fledgling

雏儿 chúr 〈口语〉❶ young bird ❷ young inexperienced person；fledgling：他缺少经验，还是个～。Lacking in experience, he is no more than a young bird just learning to fly.

雏形 chúxíng ❶ embryonic form；embryo：汉字在商朝前就有了～。Chinese characters appeared in an embryonic form as early as the pre-Shang period. ❷ model；miniature：在桌上你可以看到本城即将修建的大剧院的～。On the table you can see a model of the new theatre to be built in this town.

鸰(鶵) chú 〈书面〉*see*“雏”chú

chǔ

褚 Chǔ a surname
see also zhǔ

楮 chǔ ❶〈植物〉paper mulberry ❷〈书面〉paper

楮币 chǔbì *also*“楮券”paper currency made from paper mulberry bark (and in use from the Northern Song Dynasty)

楮墨 chǔmò 〈书面〉❶ paper and ink-stick：堪付～ may be sent to the press；be fit for publication ❷ poetry, painting or calligraphy：寄心～ dedicate oneself entirely to painting, calligraphy and poetry

楮实 chǔshí 〈中药〉paper mulberry fruit

储(儲) chǔ ❶ store up；keep in reserve：～款 savings /～粮备荒 store up grain against natural disasters /冬～白菜 cabbages stored for the winter ❷ heir to the throne：立～ appoint the crown prince ❸ (Chǔ) a surname

储备 chǔbèi ❶ store for use；lay in；lay up：～粮食 store up grain；build up supplies of grain /～过冬饲料 lay up fodder for the winter ❷ reserve：黄金～ gold reserve /外汇～ foreign exchange reserve /银行～金 bank's reserves /军需～品 war reserves /战略～ strategic reserves /现金～ cash reserves /国际货币基金组织中的～地位 reserve position in the IMF

储备货币 chǔbèi huòbì reserve currency

储备基金 chǔbèi jījīn reserve fund

储备粮 chǔbèiliáng reserve grain；grain reserve

储备银行 chǔbèi yínháng reserve bank

储采比 chǔcǎibǐ 〈矿业〉reserve and production ratio

储藏 chǔcáng ❶ save and preserve；store；keep：鲜果～ preservation of fresh fruit /冷冻～ cold storage /把货物～起来 place the goods in storage ❷ deposit：天然气～丰富 abound in natural gas deposits；be rich in natural gas deposits

储藏量 chǔcángliàng 〈矿业〉reserves；deposit

储藏室 chǔcángshì storeroom；room for storage

储存 chǔcún lay in；lay up；store；stockpile：～战略物资 stockpile strategic materials /～商品 store up goods /～以备匮乏 provide against a rainy day

储贰 chǔ'èr 〈书面〉crown prince

储放 chǔfàng store；deposit：～行李 deposit one's luggage

储宫 chǔgōng 〈书面〉crown prince's palace；crown prince

储罐 chǔguàn storage tank

储户 chǔhù depositor：这些～大部分是附近工厂的工人。The majority of the depositors are workers from the nearby factories.

储积 chǔjī ❶ store up；accumulate：～余粮，以便急需。Store up surplus grains to provide for urgent needs. ❷ accumulated wealth；savings：素无～ have never had any savings

储集 chǔjí collect and store up：～油气 stock up on oil and gas

储集层 chǔjícéng 〈石油〉reservoir stratum or bed

储君 chǔjūn crown prince

储量 chǔliàng 〈矿业〉reserves：探明～ proved (*or* verified) reserves /可采～ recoverable reserves；workable reserves /远景～ prospective reserves /～等级 ore reserve classification

储频装置 chǔpín zhuāngzhì frequency memory

储气 chǔqì gas storage：～构造 gas-bearing structure /～罐 gas tank

储气筒 chǔqìtǒng steam reservoir

储青 chǔqīng store up green fodder

储蓄 chǔxù deposit；savings：个人～ individual (*or* personal) savings /私人～ private savings /自愿～ voluntary savings /强制～ compulsory savings /实际～ effective savings /国民～ national savings /定期～ fixed deposit /活期～ current deposit /～会 savings society /把富余的钱～起来 put one's spare money in the bank /～存款不断增长。Savings deposits have shown a steady increase.

储蓄存折 chǔxù cúnzhé savings account book

储蓄代办所 chǔxù dàibànsuǒ savings agency

储蓄贷款协会 chǔxù dàikuǎn xiéhuì saving and loan association (S & L)

储蓄额 chǔxù'é total savings deposits

储蓄所 chǔxùsuǒ savings bank

储蓄银行 chǔxù yínháng savings bank

储氧筒 chǔyǎngtǒng oxygen cylinder

储油 chǔyóu 〈石油〉oil storage

储油构造 chǔyóu gòuzào oil-bearing structure

储油罐 chǔyóuguàn 〈石油〉oil storage tank；oil tank：浮顶～ floating roof tank /球形～ spherical tank

储运 chǔyùn store up and transport：～网 storage and transport network /～站 storage and transport depot

楚¹ chǔ ❶〈书面〉pang；suffering：苦～ distress；suffering ❷ clear；neat：清～ be clear /一清二～ perfectly clear

楚² Chǔ ❶ name of a state under the Zhou Dynasty and later one of the seven hegemonic states of the period of the Warring States (c. 11th century BC-223 BC) ❷ name for the region covering Hunan and Hubei, esp. Hubei ❸ a surname

楚帛书 Chǔ bóshū silk book of the State of Chu

楚材晋用 chǔcái-jìnyòng people of talent brought up in the State of Chu finding employment in the State of Jin — a case of brain drain

楚楚 chǔchǔ ❶ clear；tidy；neat：衣冠～ immaculately dressed ❷ graceful；delicate：～动人 delicate and attractive；lovely /门前垂柳，～可人。Outside the door are drooping willows, graceful and enchanting.

楚楚可怜 chǔchǔ-kělián delicate and charming；attractive

楚辞 Chǔcí *Chu Ci* or *The Poetry of Chu* (anthology of poetry of the State of Chu, mainly of Qu Yuan 屈原, compiled by Liu Xiang 刘向 of the Western Han Dynasty)

楚弓楚得 chǔgōng-chǔdé one man in the State of Chu loses his bow, but another man of Chu finds it — there is no loss as far as the country or organization is concerned；there is no real loss

楚馆秦楼 chǔguǎn-qínlóu *also*“秦楼楚馆”quarters of courtesans；public houses of pleasure

楚汉战争 Chǔ-Hàn Zhànzhēng The War Between Chu and Han (206-203 BC), in which Liu Bang (刘邦) defeated Xiang Yu (项羽) and founded the Han Dynasty

楚河汉界 chǔhé-hànjiè borderline on the Chinese chessboard；border of two contesting powers

楚剧 chǔjù Chu opera (popular in Hubei and part of Jiangxi)

楚囚 chǔqiú native of the State of Chu captured and taken to the State of Jin；a man caught in a predicament：～对泣 unhappy souls weep together lamenting a common misfortune

楚天 chǔtiān 〈书面〉skies above the middle and lower reaches of the Yangtse River：暮霭沉沉～阔。Dusk is gathering over the vast Chu skies.

楚瓦什人 Chǔwǎshírén Chuvash, a minor ethnic community in Russia:～语言 Chuvash language
楚腰 chǔyāo (of a woman) slender waist; slim figure

齼 chǔ 〈书面〉toothache

础(礎) chǔ plinth:～润而雨 a damp plinth predicts rain — sign that sth. serious is going to happen; portent of what is going to happen
础石 chǔshí ❶ stone base of a column or statue; plinth ❷ base; foundation; pillar:这种人才是社会的～。It is they who are pillars of the society. *or* They are salt of the earth.

杵 chǔ ❶ pestle:木～ wooden pestle /～臼 mortar and pestle /～药 pestle medicinal herbs ❷ wooden club used to pound clothes in washing ❸ poke (with sth. long and slender):把纸～个窟窿 poke a hole in the paper /你的铅笔差一点～着我的眼。You nearly jabbed my eye with your pencil.
杵臼关节 chǔjiù guānjié 〈生理〉enarthrosis:～炎〈医学〉enarthritis
杵臼时代 chǔjiù shídài mortar-and-pestle age; age of the hand-pestle
杵乐 chǔyuè *also* "杵舞" pestle dance (a kind of folk song-and-dance performance popular among the Gaoshan nationality in Taiwan Province)
杵杖 chǔzhàng ❶ staff for a sedan to rest upon ❷ walking stick
杵状指 chǔzhuàngzhǐ 〈医学〉clubbed finger

处(處、處、処) chǔ ❶〈书面〉dwell; live; inhabit:五方杂～ people from different parts of the country living together in one community /穴居野～ live in the wild and dwell in caves ❷ get along (with sb.):他脾气好,容易～。He is good-natured and easy to get along with. /你跟他～得来吗? Do you hit it off well with him? /两国人民和睦相～。The people of the two countries live in peace and amity. ❸ be situated in; be in a certain condition:地～东海之滨 be situated on the coast of the East China Sea /～在困难的环境之中 be in a difficult situation /我们正～在一个伟大的历史时代。We are living in a historic era. ❹ manage; handle; deal with:善自～之 deal with the matter properly by oneself ❺ punish; sentence:～以重刑 inflict a harsh sentence /～以无期徒刑 sentence sb. to life imprisonment
see also chù
处变不惊 chǔbiàn-bùjīng keep presence of mind or be calm in the face of disaster
处罚 chǔfá punish; penalize:经济～ impose a monetary penalty on sb.; fine sb. /减轻～ mitigate a punishment /免除～ absolve sb. from punishment; remit a penalty /受到应有的～ meet with well-deserved punishment /超速行驶要受到～。Speeding shall be penalized.
处方 chǔfāng ❶ write out a prescription; prescribe:大夫必先对病人确诊,然后才能～。A doctor must diagnose the illness of his patient before he can prescribe correctly. ❷ prescription; recipe:开～ write out a prescription /照大夫的～抓药 compound (*or* make up) a prescription
处方药 chǔfāngyào prescription drug; prescription medicine
处分 chǔfèn ❶ take disciplinary action against; punish:行政～ administrative disciplinary measure /党内～ disciplinary action within the Party /罚款～ punish by a fine; fine /予以警告～ give sb. disciplinary warning /免于～ exempt sb. from punishment /怎么～他,由领导决定。It's up to the leadership to decide what disciplinary action to take against him. ❷〈书面〉handle; deal with; settle:诸事均已～停当。All the affairs have been attended to.
处境 chǔjìng unfavourable situation; plight:～尴尬 be in a predicament /～危险 be in a dangerous (*or* precarious) situation; be in peril /他必须顶住两边的压力,～十分困难。He found himself in a sad plight as he had to resist pressure from both sides.
处决 chǔjué ❶ put to death; execute:依法～ put to death in accordance with the law ❷ deal with and settle:～此事并不那么容易。It will not be easy to pass judgment on the matter and deal with it accordingly.
处理 chǔlǐ ❶ handle; deal with; dispose of; settle:～污水 dispose of sewage /～纠纷 settle disputes /～家务 run the household /～国家大事 conduct state affairs /～日常工作 handle day-to-day work; deal with routine matters /学术问题不能用简单的行政方法去～。Academic problems should not be settled by simple administrative measures. ❷ punish; penalize:依法～ punish according to law:这些不法之徒应从严～。These lawless people should be dealt with sternly. /对人的～要十分慎重。We have to be very cautious in rendering disciplinary punishment to people who make mistakes. ❸ sell at reduced prices:降价～ sell at a discount /～价格 bargain price /生意人善于利用季节变换～积压商品。Businessmen know how to make use of the change of seasons to dispose of old stock. ❹ treat by a special process:～器 treater /热～ heat treatment /用硫酸～ treat with sulphuric acid
处理机 chǔlǐjī processor:文字～ word processor /数据～ data processor /中央～ central processor
处理品 chǔlǐpǐn shop-worn or substandard goods that are ready to be sold at reduced prices
处女 chǔnǚ ❶ virgin; maiden:老～ old maid; spinster ❷〈比喻〉first effort; first experience
处女地 chǔnǚdì virgin land; virgin soil
处女峰 chǔnǚfēng virgin mount or peak
处女航 chǔnǚháng maiden voyage or flight
处女膜 chǔnǚmó 〈生理〉hymen
处女作 chǔnǚzuò maiden work; first effort
处身 chǔshēn behave in society; face a certain situation:～涉世 conduct oneself in society /战士们～在一个异常艰难的环境中。The troops found themselves in an exceedingly difficult and dangerous situation.
处士 chǔshì 〈古语〉man of virtue and wisdom in ancient times leading the life of a hermit; scholar who never held a public office; recluse
处世 chǔshì conduct oneself in society:深知～之道 experienced in the ways of the world; worldly-wise /"不要惹事生非"是他的～哲学。"Letting sleeping dogs lie" is his philosophy of life. /他为人～,无瑕可击。He is flawless in the way he behaves in society.
处事 chǔshì manage one's affairs:～精明 be sharp and shrewd in handling matters /～谨慎 act cautiously /他～严肃,态度却十分和蔼。He treats everything seriously, but he manages to be very affable.
处暑 Chǔshǔ ❶ Limit of Heat, 14th seasonal division point, marking the sun's position at 150° on the ecliptic ❷ day marking such a seasonal division point, usu. falling on the 23rd or 24th of August ❸ period lasting from such a seasonal division point till the next one (White Dew 白露)
see also "节气" jiéqì;"二十四节气" èrshísì jiéqì
处死 chǔsǐ 〈法律〉put to death; execute
处窝子 chǔwōzi 〈方言〉timid or shy guy
处心积虑 chǔxīn-jīlǜ rack one's brains (to achieve evil ends); incessantly scheme; bend every effort (to achieve one's purpose):～地要搞垮对方公司 bend every effort to wreck the rival company
处刑 chǔxíng 〈法律〉condemn; sentence:免于～ exempt sb. from punishment
处以 chǔyǐ inflict (sth. on sb.):～死刑 inflict or pass the death sentence /他被判有罪并～一年缓刑。He was convicted and sentenced to probation for one year.
处于 chǔyú be (in a certain condition):～有利地位 find oneself in an advantageous position /～水深火热之中 be plunged in the depths of misery /～逆境 be in adverse circumstances /～同等地位 be on an equal footing /当时革命～高潮。At that time the revolution was at high tide. /同其他的竞争对手相比,他明显地～优势地位。He has a conspicuous advantage over the rest of the contestants.
处之泰然 chǔzhī-tàirán *also* "泰然处之" take things calmly; remain unruffled:对紧张局势～ take a tense situation calmly; remain unruffled in a tense situation /他听到这个坏消息时仍然～。He retained his composure when he heard the bad news.
处治 chǔzhì punish:惩治腐败,首先必须～贪污犯。To combat corruption, one should first of all punish grafters. /对违法乱纪者,应及时～。Violators of law and discipline should be dealt with promptly.
处置 chǔzhì ❶ handle; deal with; dispose of:～失当 handle matters inappropriately; mishandle matters /必须谨慎小心地～这个很微妙的问题。One must handle this highly delicate problem with care and caution. /他把事情～得很妥贴。He has dealt with the problem in a very proper manner. ❷ punish:一定要依法从严～这些骗子。These swindlers must be punished severely according to law.
处子 chǔzǐ 〈书面〉virgin; maiden

chù

畜 chù domestic animal; livestock: 六～ six domestic animals (pig, ox, goat, horse, fowl and dog) /～群 herd of livestock / 耕～ farm animal /家～ livestock /役～ draught animal /幼～ young animal /母～ female animal
see also xù

畜肥 chùféi animal manure
畜圈 chùjuàn *also* "畜舍" animal pen, sty or shed
畜类 chùlei domestic animals; livestock
畜力 chùlì animal power: ～车 animal-drawn cart /～农具 animal-drawn farm implements /～牵引 animal traction; animal hauling
畜生 chùsheng ❶ domestic animal ❷〈粗话〉beast; swine
畜疫 chùyì epidemic disease of domestic animals

滀 chù 〈书面〉(of water) gather

搐 chù twitch; 〈医学〉tic
搐动 chùdòng slight, involuntary movement (of a muscle); quick, jerky movement (of some part of the body); twitch: 他的脸有点～。His face twitched.
搐搦 chùnuò *also* "抽搐" chōuchù twitch
搐缩 chùsuō contract; twitch: 这孩子嘴角～,像是要哭。The child's mouth twitched as if she were about to cry.

怵(怵) chù 〈书面〉fear; fright: 她头一次登台,心里直犯～。She was quite afraid to go on the stage, as it was her first experience.
怵场 chùchǎng *also* "憷场" chùchǎng feel nervous before a large audience; have stage fright
怵惧 chùjù 〈书面〉dread; fear: 局面险恶,令人～。The situation was pregnant with danger and filled people with fear.
怵目惊心 chùmù-jīngxīn be extremely nervous, afraid, or shocked at the sight of sth.: 我不愿看这些令人～的恐怖镜头。I don't want to watch these shocking scenes of horror.
怵然 chùrán be startled; be scared but watchful: 心中～ seized with fear
怵惕 chùtì 〈书面〉feel apprehensive but watchful
怵头 chùtóu *also* "憷头" chùtóu 〈方言〉shrink from difficulties; be timid, be somewhat reluctant

憷 chù fear; flinch: 发～ feel uneasy; feel nervous /这孩子～见生人。The child is shy of strangers.
憷场 chùchǎng 〈方言〉feel nervous before a large audience; have stage fright
憷头 chùtóu 〈方言〉shrink from difficulties; be timid; be somewhat reluctant (to do sth.): 这姑娘遇事就～。The girl always shrinks from difficulties. /这种事从没办过,还真有点～。As I've never dealt with such matters, I do find it somewhat hard to set about them.

亍 chù *see* "彳亍" chìchù

矗 chù 〈书面〉stand tall and upright
矗立 chùlì stand tall and upright; tower (over sth.): 广场四周,大厦～。High buildings tower all around the square.
矗入 chùrù tower aloft; soar into: ～云霄 tower aloft into the clouds.

柷 chù ancient musical instrument made of wood and shaped like a square grain measure

諔 chù
諔诡 chùguǐ 〈书面〉❶ bizarre; queer; strange ❷ facetious; comic

俶 chù 〈书面〉❶ begin; start; commence ❷ tidy up; put in order: ～装 pack (for a trip)
see also tì

俶尔 chù'ěr 〈书面〉abruptly; suddenly: 鱼游水中,～远逝。A fish swimming in water disappeared into the distance all of a sudden.
俶扰 chùrǎo 〈书面〉harass; disturb; upset: 兵戈～ scourge of war

处(處、處、処) chù ❶ place: 住～ accommodation; lodging; living quarters /别～ in another place; elsewhere /某～ in a certain place; somewhere /近～ in a nearby place; in the neighbourhood /远～ in a faraway place; in the distance /问讯～ inquiry office (*or* desk) /登记～ registration office /售票～ booking office /停车～ parking place (*or* lot); car park ❷ part; point: 长～ strong point; forte /短～ weak point; weakness /心灵深～ deep down in one's heart; in the inmost recesses of one's mind /两者有相同之～。There is some resemblance between the two. *or* One has something in common with the other. ❸ division; office; department: 人事～ personnel division /总务～ general affairs division /联络～ liaison office ❹〈量词〉: 两～印刷错误 two misprints /此地有几～古迹。There are several historical relics here.
see also chǔ

处处 chùchù everywhere; in all respects: ～掣肘 hinder (sb.) at every step; make difficulties (for sb.) at every turn /～碰壁 meet with rebuffs everywhere /～严格要求自己 set strict demands on oneself in all respects /他们～受到热烈欢迎。They were warmly welcomed wherever they went.
处所 chùsuǒ place; location: 这里是可以提供很好休养条件的～。This is a place with excellent conditions for rest.
处长 chùzhǎng head of a department or office; division or section chief

黜 chù 〈书面〉remove or dismiss sb. from office; reject: 因贪污被～ be dismissed from office because of corruption /罢～百家,尊崇儒术 establish Confucianism as the sole authority by rejecting all other schools of thought
黜斥 chùchì 〈旧语〉dismiss from office; expel (a student) from school or college
黜免 chùmiǎn 〈书面〉dismiss (a government official): 他被～官职。He was removed (*or* dismissed) from office.
黜退 chùtuì relieve sb. of a post
黜陟 chùzhì 〈书面〉dismissal and promotion
黜逐 chùzhú 〈书面〉dismiss from office and send into exile: ～能臣 dismiss and banish able courtiers

绌 chù 〈书面〉❶ inadequate; insufficient: 左支右～ be unable to meet the needs of all sides; have no adequate means to cover the expenses /相形见～ appear weaker when compared with another; pale by comparison; be outshone by another ❷ *see* "黜" chù

触(觸) chù ❶ touch; contact; hit: ～雷 hit a mine; run into a mine /雪花一～到脸上就化了。Snowflakes melted as soon as they fell on one's face. ❷ move sb.; stir up sb.'s feelings: ～到痛处 touch a sore spot; touch sb. to the quick; hit (*or* touch) a nerve /～起前情 stir up an old sentiment
触变性 chùbiànxìng 〈物理〉thixotropy
触处 chùchù 〈书面〉everywhere: 杨花～飞。Catkins are floating here and there.
触电 chùdiàn get an electric shock: ～身亡 die of electric shock /小心～! Danger! Electricity! *or* Danger! Live wire!
触电保护器 chùdiàn bǎohùqì electric shock protector
触动 chùdòng ❶ touch sth., moving it slightly; touch: 我无意中～电门,电灯全亮了。I unknowingly touched the switch and all the lights were turned on. ❷ collide (against sth.); offend; affect: ～现行体制 collide against the current regimen /这次检查无疑地会～某些人的既得利益。This investigation will undoubtedly affect some people's vested interests. ❸ move; touch; stir up: 同事们对他的尖锐而又诚恳的批评使他有所～。He was somewhat moved by the sharp but sincere criticism of his colleagues. /近来发生的几件事对她～很大。Some recent events gave her quite a shake-up. /他的话～了我的心弦。What he said touched me to the heart.
触发 chùfā detonate by contact; touch off; spark off; trigger: ～热核聚变 trigger thermonuclear fusion /～乡思 touch off a train of home thoughts; cause nostalgia /这件事～了一场大战。The incident sparked (off) a major war.

触发地雷 chùfā dìléi contact mine; trap mine
触发电路 chùfā diànlù trigger circuit
触发器 chùfāqì trigger; flip-flop
触犯 chùfàn offend; violate; infringe: ～校规 violate school regulations / ～法律 break (*or* violate) the law / ～某人的尊严 hurt sb.'s pride / ～人民利益 encroach on the interests of the people / 最好不要去～他。You'd better not offend him. *or* You'd better leave him alone.
触感 chùgǎn tactile impression; (sense of) touch
触击 chùjī ❶〈体育〉(in baseball or softball) bunt ❷ ram; dash against: 他跑着，衣袋里有银圆～的声音。As he ran, there was a clattering of silver coins in his pocket.
触机 chùjī have a brainwave; have an inspiration: 不假思索，～即发。When you have an inspiration, all ideas naturally come into your mind, and you don't have to stop to think.
触及 chùjí touch: ～敏感问题 touch on a sensitive issue / ～事物的本质 get to the essence of a matter
触礁 chùjiāo ❶ run (up) on rocks; strike a reef or rock: ～沉没 (of a ship) sink after striking a reef ❷ run into difficulty; be snarled: 谈判～。The negotiations ran into difficulties. / 婚事～。One's marriage is snarled.
触角 chùjiǎo *also* "触须"〈动物〉antenna; feeler; tentacle
触景生情 chùjǐng-shēngqíng the sight strikes a chord in one's heart; the scene brings back past memories: 他节日里～，不禁有思乡之叹。He sighed, moved by the festive occasion to thoughts of home.
触觉 chùjué〈生理〉tactile or tactual sensation; sense of touch; 〈动物〉touch reception: ～器官 tactile organ
触觉传感器 chùjué chuángǎnqì tactile sensor
触类旁通 chùlèi-pángtōng grasp a typical example and you will master the whole category; comprehend by analogy
触媒 chùméi〈化学〉catalyst; catalytic agent
触霉头 chù méitóu *also* "触楣头"〈方言〉have a stroke of bad luck; be unfortunate; come to grief
触摸 chùmō stroke: 我轻轻地～那小猫。I gently stroked the kitten. / 请勿～展品。Please don't touch the exhibits.
触目 chùmù ❶ meet the eye: ～皆是 can be seen everywhere / ～伤心 feel sad at the sight ❷ conspicuous; attracting attention: 墙上写着"危险"二字，十分～。The word "danger" on the wall is very conspicuous.
触目惊心 chùmù-jīngxīn startling; shocking: ～的景象 shocking scene / 看到反映农奴制度下西藏人民生活的那些展品，真是～。It was soul-stirring to see the exhibits of Tibetan life under serfdom.
触怒 chùnù make angry; infuriate; enrage: 这句话～了他。This remark infuriated him.
触碰 chùpèng touch: 他用肩～了我一下。He nudged me with his shoulder.
触气 chùqì〈方言〉annoying; disgusting: 真～，又停电了。It's really annoying that there is a power cut again.
触杀 chùshā ❶ kill by contact ❷〈体育〉(in baseball or softball) tag out
触杀剂 chùshājì〈农业〉contact insecticide
触身式橄榄球 chùshēnshì gǎnlǎnqiú〈体育〉touch football
触手 chùshǒu〈动物〉tentacle
触痛 chùtòng ❶ touch a tender or sore spot: 这句话深深地～了他。The remark touched him to the quick. ❷〈医学〉tenderness
触网 chùwǎng〈体育〉touch net
触线水雷 chùxiàn shuǐléi antenna mine
触须 chùxū *also* "触毛"〈动物〉cirrus; vibrissa: 鱼类～ barbel / 无脊椎动物～ palp
触靴 chùxuē〈电工〉contact shoe
触眼 chùyǎn〈方言〉eye-catching; conspicuous: 她的穿着这么鲜艳，走在路上有些～。She was so loudly dressed that she attracted quite a bit of notice in the street.
触诊 chùzhěn〈医学〉palpation
触珠蛋白 chùzhū dànbái〈生化〉haptoglobin

歜 chù〈书面〉❶ wild with anger; in a rage ❷ overbearing; haughty

chuā

欻(欻) chuā〈象声〉: 仪仗队迈着坚定有力的步伐，～～地走过来。Tramp, tramp, the guard of honour marched past with firm, vigorous steps. / 他～的一声，把信撕开了。He ripped the letter open with a crisp sound.
see also xū
欻拉 chuālā〈象声〉: ～一声，肉片倒进了滚油锅里。The pork slices dropped onto the frying pan with a sizzle.

chuāi

揣 chuāi ❶ hide or carry in one's clothes; tuck: ～在怀里 hide sth. in the bosom / ～着明白装糊涂 pretend to know nothing while knowing all about it ❷〈方言〉(of animals) be pregnant: 骒马～上驹了。The mare is in (*or* with) foal.
see also chuǎi; chuài
揣手儿 chuāishǒur tuck each hand in the opposite sleeve

搋 chuāi ❶ rub; knead: ～面 knead dough / ～衣服 give the clothes a rub ❷ clear a drain with a suction pump
搋子 chuāizi suction pump

chuái

膗 chuái〈方言〉fat and flabby; overweight: 看他那～样。How fat and flabby he looks.

chuǎi

揣 chuǎi ❶〈书面〉estimate; conjecture; surmise: ～知其意 have an idea of what sb. has in mind / 不～浅陋〈谦词〉shallow as I am; despite my shallowness ❷ (Chuǎi) a surname
see also chuāi; chuài
揣测 chuǎicè guess; suppose; conjecture: 纯属～ mere conjecture; anybody's guess / 我～这件事难办。I have a feeling that the problem is hard to tackle. *or* I guess it is not easy.
揣度 chuǎiduó〈书面〉make a rough estimate of; appraise; estimate; calculate: 妄加～ make wild conjectures / 股票行情一时不好～。It is hard to form an accurate estimation of the stock market for the moment. / 他最能～妻子的心思。He could always read his wife's mind.
揣摩 chuǎimó *also* "揣摸" try to fathom; try to figure out; elicit by careful study: ～他的意思 try to fathom his meaning / ～不透他的用意 cannot figure out his intention / 仔细～写作方法 carefully study writing techniques
揣情度理 chuǎiqíng-duólǐ weigh the pros and cons; judge by reason and by the normal conduct of human affairs
揣想 chuǎixiǎng guess; conjecture: 他心里～着究竟发生了什么问题。He was trying to figure out what had actually happened.

chuài

揣 chuài *see* "囊揣" nāngchuài; "挣揣" zhèngchuài
see also chuāi; chuǎi

踹 chuài ❶ kick (forward with sole and heel): 把门～开 kick the door open / 他一脚把暴徒～倒。He knocked the gangster down with a kick. ❷ trample; tread; step in: 一脚～在水坑里 step in a puddle / 用脚把它～入泥里。Trample it into the mud.
踹腿儿 chuàituǐr〈方言〉kick the bucket; die

膪 chuài *see* "囊膪" nāngchuài

闧 chuài *see* "闸闧" zhèngchuài

嘬 chuài 〈书面〉bite; eat: 这个孩子怎么～也胖不了。No matter how much you feed the child, he does not put on weight.
see also zuō

chuān

穿 chuān ❶ pierce through; penetrate: 一箭～透靶心 penetrate the bull's eye with one arrow /把墙～个洞 make a hole in the wall ❷ *used after certain verbs to indicate thoroughness or completeness*: 磨～ wear through (shoes, etc.); grind through /戳～阴谋 show up (*or* expose) a plot /我看～了他。I have seen through him. /说～了,他不过是江湖骗子。To put it bluntly, he is nothing but a charlatan. ❸ go through; pass through; cross: 横～公路 cross the highway /乱～马路 jaywalk /从小胡同～过去 pass through the lane /从人群中～过去 thread one's way through the crowd /把线～过针眼 pass a thread through the eye of a needle /阳光～过树叶的缝隙射进来。The sunlight was shining in through the foliage. ❹ thread: 用珠子～成项链 thread the beads to make a necklace ❺ wear; put on; be dressed in; have... on: ～轻便鞋 wear walking shoes /～得很朴素 be simply dressed /～上最好的衣服 put on one's best clothes /～红衣服的女士是大使夫人。The lady in red is the ambassador's wife. /～得这么少,不冷吗? Aren't you feeling cold with so little on?

穿煲 chuānbāo 〈方言〉let the cat out of the bag; give the game or show away: 这样岂不～了? You'll give the game away this way.

穿贝海绵 chuānbèi hǎimián 〈动物〉clionidue

穿鼻草约 Chuānbí Cǎoyuē Draft Agreement of Chuanbi or Chuenpi (1841), imposed by the British but rejected by the Qing court

穿插 chuānchā ❶ alternate; arrange by turns; do or perform by turns: 音乐和相声节目～进行。Music alternated with comic dialogues. ❷ insert; weave in; interweave: 这部电影～了一些有趣的细节。The film is spiced with interesting episodes. ❸ thrust deep into the enemy forces: ～营〈军事〉deep-thrust battalion /～分割敌人 penetrate and cut up the enemy forces

穿刺 chuāncì 〈医学〉puncture: 肝～ liver puncture /腰椎～ lumbar puncture /～放液 tapping

穿刺术 chuāncìshù 〈医学〉centesis; paracentesis

穿戴 chuāndài dress; apparel: 讲究～ be particular about one's dress /～整齐 be neatly dressed; dress neatly

穿耳 chuān'ěr punch a hole in the earlobe for wearing an ear-ring

穿过 chuānguò walk from one side to the other; cross (over): 行人～马路,要注意来往车辆。Pedestrians should watch out for passing vehicles while crossing the street.

穿甲弹 chuānjiǎdàn 〈军事〉armour-piercing projectile; armour piercing shell or bullet; armour piercer

穿甲燃烧弹 chuānjiǎ ránshāodàn 〈军事〉armour-piercing incendiary (API)

穿甲炸弹 chuānjiǎ zhàdàn 〈军事〉armour-piercing bomb

穿孔 chuānkǒng ❶〈医学〉perforation: 溃疡～ perforated ulcer /胃～ gastric perforation /阑尾～ appendicular perforation ❷ bore a hole; punch a hole; perforate: ～纸带 punched tape; chadded tape

穿孔带读器 chuānkǒng dàidúqì perforated tape reader

穿孔腐蚀 chuānkǒng fǔshí 〈化学〉pitting corrosion

穿孔机 chuānkǒngjī punch; perforator

穿孔金属板 chuānkǒng jīnshǔbǎn perforated metal

穿孔卡 chuānkǒngkǎ punched card: ～输入机〈计算机〉punched card reader /～转录器〈计算机〉punch card transcriber

穿廊 chuānláng covered corridor on either side of the second gate in an old-style Chinese compound

穿连裆裤 chuān liándāngkù 〈方言〉work cheek by jowl; act in collusion with each other; shield each other

穿颅术 chuānlúshù 〈医学〉craniotomy

穿墙套管 chuānqiáng tàoguǎn 〈电学〉wall bushing

穿山甲 chuānshānjiǎ ❶ *also* "鲮鲤" línglǐ 〈动物〉pangolin ❷〈中药〉pangolin scales

穿梭 chuānsuō shuttle back and forth: 往来～ shuttle to and fro /～飞行 shuttle flight /～外交 shuttle diplomacy /日月如～ the sun and the moon shuttle back and forth — time flies

穿梭机 chuānsuōjī *also* "太空穿梭机" tàikōng chuānsuōjī space shuttle

穿堂风 chuāntángfēng draught

穿堂门 chuāntángmén passageway

穿堂儿 chuāntángr hallway (connecting two courtyards in an old-style Chinese compound)

穿透 chuāntòu pass through; penetrate: 阳光～树林照到地上。The sunlight penetrated the woods and reached the ground.

穿透粒子 chuāntòu lìzǐ 〈物理〉penetrating particle

穿透性溃疡 chuāntòuxìng kuìyáng 〈医学〉penetrating ulcer

穿臀瘘 chuāntúnlòu 〈中医〉multiple anal fistula

穿线 chuānxiàn serve as go-between or liaison: 他俩靠我从中～。They two depended on me as their go-between.

穿小鞋 chuān xiǎoxié give sb. tight shoes to wear — (of a bureaucrat) make things difficult for one's subordinate out of revenge; deliberately put sb. to trouble: 他怕他的上司给他～。He is afraid that his superior might deliberately make things hot for him.

穿孝 chuānxiào be in mourning; wear mourning

穿心莲 chuānxīnlián 〈中药〉creat (*Andrographis paniculata*)

穿新鞋,走老路 chuān xīnxié, zǒu lǎolù tread the same old path in new shoes — do sth. old in a new form; old wine in a new bottle: 这家工厂的改革有～之嫌。The reform of this factory looks like going through the motions.

穿行 chuānxíng pass through; cut through: 火车在隧道中～。The train was passing through a tunnel.

穿靴戴帽 chuānxuē-dàimào *also* "穿鞋戴帽" use stereotypes devoid of content in one's writing or speech, esp. at the beginning and end of it: 你这篇文章提出的新想法很好,可是～太多了! There are a few excellent ideas in your article, but why use so much padding?

穿一条裤子 chuān yītiáo kùzi wear the same pair of pants — gang up; collude

穿衣镜 chuānyījìng full-length mirror

穿窬 chuānyú 〈书面〉cut through a wall or climb over it (in order to rob the house): ～之盗 burglar /口谈道德,而志在～ contemplate burglary while mouthing morality; prate about virtue but think of vice

穿越 chuānyuè pass through; cut across: 公路～崇山峻岭。The highway runs across high mountains.

穿云裂石 chuānyún-lièshí pierce the clouds and split the rocks — (of instrumental or vocal music) penetrating; resounding

穿凿 chuānzáo give a farfetched or strained interpretation; read too much meaning into sth.

穿凿附会 chuānzáo-fùhuì give strained interpretations and draw farfetched analogies — distort (the evidence, the original, etc.): 这篇文章多处～。This essay gives wrong interpretations in many places.

穿章儿 chuānzhangr 〈方言〉dress; apparel

穿针 chuānzhēn thread a needle

穿针器 chuānzhēnqì needle threader

穿针引线 chuānzhēn-yǐnxiàn act as a go-between; try to make a match: 为促进双方的合作～ serve as a go-between for the two sides to promote their cooperation /他忙着为这桩婚事～。He was busy trying to arrange this match.

穿着 chuānzhuó dress; apparel: ～入时 be dressed à la mode /～整洁 be neatly dressed /～高雅 dress elegantly

川 chuān ❶ river: 高山大～ high mountains and big rivers /冰～ glacier ❷ plain: 一马平～ vast expanse of flat land; great stretch of land ❸ (Chuān) (short for 四川) Sichuan Province

川贝 chuānbèi *also* "川贝母" 〈中药〉tendril-leaved fritillary bulb

川菜 chuāncài dishes of Sichuan flavour; Sichuan cuisine: ～馆 Sichuan restaurant /～师傅 chef specializing in Sichuan cuisine

川地 chuāndì low-lying flat land along a river or between hills

川费 chuānfèi *see* "川资"

川红 chuānhóng 〈农业〉black tea grown in Sichuan

川剧 chuānjù 〈戏剧〉Sichuan opera

川军 chuānjūn *also* "大黄" dàihuáng 〈中药〉Chinese rhubarb

川流不息 chuānliú-bùxī flow past in an endless stream: 立交桥上下,车辆～。Vehicles on and under the flyover come and go in an endless stream. *or* There is a lot of traffic on and under the flyover.

川马 chuānmǎ 〈动物〉Sichuan horse

川木香 chuānmùxiāng 〈中药〉root of *Vladimiria souliei*

川崎 Chuānqí Kawasaki, industrial city on Honshu (本州),

Japan：～制铁公司 Kawasaki Steel Corpration, Japanese transnational established in 1950／～重工工业公司 Kawasaki Heavy Industries Ltd., one of Japan's major manufacturers of transport machinery
川芎 chuānxiōng *also*“芎䓖” xiōngqióng 〈中药〉*Ligusticum wallichii*
川续断 chuānxùduàn 〈植物〉teasel
川资 chuānzī travelling expenses：～短缺 short of travelling expenses

氚 chuān *also*“超重氢” chāozhòngqīng〈化学〉tritium（T or $^3_1$H）
氚核 chuānhé 〈物理〉triton：～反应 triton reaction
氚水 chuānshuǐ HTO

chuán

传（傳） chuán ❶ pass；convey；hand down：～口信 convey（*or* pass on）an oral message／祖～秘方 secret recipe handed down from an early ancestor of the family／世代相～ hand sth. down from generation to generation ❷ pass on（knowledge, skill, etc.）；impart；teach：～手艺 teach the skill／～经验 pass on the experience ❸ spread：～谣信谣 spread rumours and give them credence／恶事～千里。Ill news runs apace.／谣言很快在村里～开了。The rumour quickly spread in the village.／一股幸福的暖流顿时～遍全身。A warm current began to course through my whole being. ❹ transmit；conduct：～电 conduct electricity／～热 transmit heat／水～音。Water transmits sound.／卫星把数据～到地面。Data collected by the satellite were transmitted to the ground station. ❺ convey；express：其中奥妙，不可言～。What's behind it beggars description（*or* defies all description）. ❻ summon：～审 summon sb. to court／～证人 summon a witness ❼ infect；be contagious：～上流感 have come down with the flu／她怕把病～给孩子。She was afraid of giving the disease to her child.
see also zhuàn
传帮带 chuán-bāng-dài （of experienced people）pass on experience, help and guide new hands（in their work）
传本 chuánběn circulating edition；extant book：此书世有～。There are still extant copies of the book.
传病昆虫 chuánbìng kūnchóng 〈动物〉insect vector
传播 chuánbō ❶ spread widely；publicize；disseminate：～基督教教义 spread the Christian faith／制止病菌～ check the spread of germs／蜜蜂～花粉。Bees spread pollen.／电视和广播是～新闻的有力工具。Television and radio are powerful news media. ❷〈物理〉propagation：直线～ rectilinear propagation／散射～ scatter propagation／～损耗 propagation loss
传播媒介 chuánbō méijiè mass media；the media
传播效果 chuánbō xiàoguǒ media or propagation effect
传播学 chuánbōxué media studies
传布 chuánbù circulate；spread：优秀文学作品常常～较广。Good literary works often gain wide circulation.
传唱 chuánchàng circulate and sing：广为～ be widely circulated and sung
传抄 chuánchāo make hand-written copies（of a manuscript, document, etc. for secret circulation）
传承 chuánchéng pass on and inherit：历代～的手艺 handicraft skills that were passed on from generation to generation
传出神经 chuánchū shénjīng *also*“运动神经” yùndòng shénjīng 〈生理〉efferent nerve：～元 efferent neuron
传达 chuándá ❶ convey；transmit；relay：～命令 convey（*or* transmit）an order／～上级指示 communicate the instructions of the higher level ❷ reception and registration of callers at a public establishment ❸ janitor
传达报告 chuándá bàogào ❶ relay a report：昨天校长传达了上级的报告。Yesterday the president relayed to us a report from the higher leading body. ❷ relayed report：昨天听了～。We heard a relayed report yesterday.
传达室 chuándáshì reception or receptionist's office；janitor's room
传代 chuándài go down to posterity；go down to future generations
传单 chuándān leaflet；handbill；propaganda sheet
传导 chuándǎo conduction；transmission：热的～ conduction of heat／～场 conduction field／刺激向大脑的～ conduction of impulses to the brain
传导电流 chuándǎo diànliú conducting current
传导放电 chuándǎo fàngdiàn conductive discharge
传导率 chuándǎolǜ conductivity；conduction
传道 chuándào ❶〈宗教〉preach；deliver a sermon ❷〈旧语〉propagate the doctrines of ancient sages：师者，所以～、授业、解惑也。It is a teacher's job to propagate cardinal principles, impart professional knowledge, and resolve doubts.
传灯 chuándēng 〈佛教〉teach the Buddhist doctrine：～弟子 initiated disciple
传递 chuándì transmit；deliver；transfer：～信息 transmit messages／～信件 deliver mail／～接力棒 pass on the relay baton
传递系统 chuándì xìtǒng transmission system
传递效率 chuándì xiàolǜ transmission efficiency
传动 chuándòng 〈机械〉transmission；drive：变速～ change drive／齿轮～ gear drive／液压～ hydraulic drive
传动比 chuándòngbǐ drive ratio；transmission ratio
传动齿轮 chuándòng chǐlún transmission or drive gear
传动带 chuándòngdài transmission belt
传动箱 chuándòngxiāng transmission case
传动轴 chuándòngzhóu transmission shaft
传动装置 chuándòng zhuāngzhì gearing；transmission
传粉 chuánfěn 〈植物〉pollination：～媒介 pollination medium
传粉昆虫 chuánfěn kūnchóng 〈动物〉insect pollinator
传感 chuángǎn sense
传感电路 chuángǎn diànlù sensing circuit
传感器 chuángǎnqì 〈电学〉sensor；transducer：激光～ laser sensor
传感器计算机 chuángǎnqì jìsuànjī sensor-based computer
传告 chuángào pass on（a message）；relay：奔走～ go about spreading the news
传观 chuánguān pass round for others to see：他拿出纪念册让我们～。He took out his autograph album and passed it round among us.
传号 chuánhào 〈通信〉mark：～空号比 mark-space ratio／～脉冲 marker pulse；marking pulse／～电路 order-wire circuit
传呼 chuánhū ❶ notify sb. of a phone call；pass on a message left by phone ❷ issue an order to summon sb.
传呼电话 chuánhū diànhuà neighbourhood telephone service
传呼员 chuánhūyuán 〈法律〉crier
传话 chuánhuà pass on a message：～给别人 send word to sb.
传唤 chuánhuàn 〈法律〉summon to court；subpoena：～当事人 summon the litigant／被～作证 be summoned as a witness
传家 chuánjiā pass on from generation to generation in a family：忠厚～久。Honesty and kindness bring lasting prosperity to a family.
传家宝 chuánjiābǎo family heirloom；hereditary treasure；cherished heritage：这剑是他家的～。This sword is his family treasure.／勤俭是我们的～。Industry and frugality are our precious heritage.
传见 chuánjiàn summon（a subordinate）
传教 chuánjiào 〈宗教〉do missionary work
传教士 chuánjiàoshì missionary
传戒 chuánjiè 〈佛教〉initiate sb. into monkhood or nunhood
传经 chuánjīng ❶ teach Confucian canon ❷ pass on one's valuable experience
传经送宝 chuánjīng-sòngbǎo pass on one's valuable experience：来～ come and pass on one's valuable experience
传看 chuánkàn pass（sth.）round for a look
传令 chuánlìng transmit orders；dispatch orders：～嘉奖 cite sb. in a dispatch／～兵 messenger
传流 chuánliú spread；circulate；hand down
传媒 chuánméi ❶（short for 传播媒介）mass media；the media ❷ medium；vehicle：疾病的～ medium for transmitting a disease
传名 chuánmíng spread one's or sb.'s reputation：替人～ spread sb.'s name；make sb. known／～后世 carve a name in history；be remembered by progeny；go down in history
传票 chuánpiào ❶〈法律〉summons；subpoena：下～ issue a summons ❷〈会计〉voucher：清理～ check the vouchers
传奇 chuánqí ❶ short stories of the Tang and Song dynasties ❷ long, serial dramas of the Ming and Qing dynasties ❸ legend；romance：～式的人物 legendary figure；legend／～文学中的人物 charac-

ter in a romance /这个故事带有~色彩。The tale has the character of a romance.

传情 chuánqíng convey one's amorous feelings: 眉目~ flash amorous glances; make sheep's eyes (at sb.)

传球 chuánqiú 〈体育〉pass: 低手~ underhand pass /反手~ reverse pass /反弹~ bounce pass /横~ parallel pass /间接~ indirect pass /肩上~ shoulder pass /凌空~ volley pass /手腕~ snap pass /头上~ overhead pass /斜~ diagonal pass /直接~ direct pass

传染 chuánrǎn infect; be contagious: 接触~ contagion /空气~ infection through air /水~ waterborne infection /~媒介 vehicle of disease; vector /夫妻之间容易~疾病。Husband and wife often transmit diseases to each other. /他的热情~给了和他一起工作的每一个人。His enthusiasm infected everyone who worked with him.

C

传染病 chuánrǎnbìng infectious disease; contagious disease: ~医院 hospital for infectious diseases; infectious hospital /~报告 infectious disease notification /~房 infectious ward /~管理 communicable disease control

传染性 chuánrǎnxìng infectious; infective: ~肝炎 infectious (*or* infective) hepatitis

传染源 chuánrǎnyuán source of infection; infectious agent

传热 chuánrè 〈物理〉heat-transfer: ~系数 heat-transfer coefficient /金属~快。Metal transfers heat quickly.

传人 chuánrén ❶〈书面〉disciple; offspring: 龙的~ offspring of the dragon /梅派~ foremost exponent of the Mei Langfang school (of Beijing opera) ❷ pass on (skill) to sb.: 他这技术不会轻易~。He would think twice about passing his skill to anyone. ❸ transmit (a disease): 流感容易~。Flu is highly infectious. ❹ summon sb.: ~问话 summon sb. for questioning

传入神经 chuánrù shénjīng 〈生理〉*also* "感觉神经" gǎnjué shénjīng afferent nerve

传舌头 chuán shétou 〈方言〉pass on a misrepresented message: 这人就是好~，惹是非。This chap is fond of gossip and often stirs up trouble.

传神 chuánshén vivid; lifelike: ~之笔 vivid touch (in writing or painting) /他画的奔马非常~。The galloping horses he drew are very life-like.

传审 chuánshěn subpoena

传声 chuánshēng sound or acoustic transmission: ~系数 sound (*or* acoustic) transmission coefficient; acoustic transmissivity

传声器 chuánshēngqì microphone

传声清晰度 chuánshēng qīngxīdù 〈无线电〉articulation

传声筒 chuánshēngtǒng ❶ megaphone; loud hailer ❷ one who parrots another; sb.'s mouthpiece: 当敌人的~ act as the mouthpiece of the enemy /她是她丈夫的~。She parrots every word of her husband.

传声性 chuánshēngxìng 〈物理〉acoustic conductivity

传世 chuánshì be handed down from ancient times: ~之作 work that will be handed down to posterity; enduring work /~珍宝 treasure handed down from ancient times /他早年去世，有诗文集~。He died young, leaving behind a collection of poems and writings.

传授 chuánshòu pass on; teach; impart: ~知识 impart knowledge; teach /~成功的秘诀 pass on the recipe for success; teach (sb.) the secret of success /他把祖传医术~给徒弟。He imparted to his apprentice the knowledge of traditional medicine which he had inherited from his ancestors.

传输 chuánshū 〈电工〉transmission: ~损耗 transmission loss

传输层 chuánshūcéng 〈信息〉transport layer

传输电路 chuánshū diànlù transmission circuit or channel

传输方式 chuánshū fāngshì transmission mode

传输功率 chuánshū gōnglǜ transmission power

传输控制协议 chuánshū kòngzhì xiéyì 〈信息〉transmission control protocol

传输线 chuánshūxiàn transmission line

传述 chuánshù *see* "传说❶"

传说 chuánshuō ❶ pass from mouth to mouth; circulate; it is said; they say: ~他已辞职了。It is said he has resigned. /~如此。So the story goes. /这只不过是~而已。That's only hearsay. /这故事在城里~开了。The story circulated throughout the town. ❷ legend; tradition: 中世纪~ medieval legend /民间~ folklore; popular legend

传送 chuánsòng convey; transmit; deliver: ~电报 transmit a telegram /~消息 pass on information

传送带 chuánsòngdài conveyor belt

传诵 chuánsòng be on everybody's lips; be widely read: 为世人所~ be read with admiration by people /至今还~着他的英雄事迹。His heroic deeds are still on the lips of the people.

传颂 chuánsòng be eulogized everywhere; be on everybody's lips

传统 chuántǒng tradition: ~观念 traditional ideas /~友谊 traditional (ties of) friendship /~艺术 traditional art /~剧目 traditional theatrical repertoire /~的民族形式 traditional national style /革命~ revolutionary tradition /优良~ fine tradition /~习惯边界线 traditional customary line of the border

传为话柄 chuánwéi-huàbǐng *also* "传为笑柄" become a subject for ridicule; become a laughing-stock

传为佳话 chuánwéi-jiāhuà become a favourite topic; be handed down as a popular tale: 牛郎织女的故事历代~。The story of the Cowherd and the Weaving Maid was passed on from generation to generation as a popular tale.

传为美谈 chuánwéi-měitán pass from mouth to mouth with approbation: 他急人之难的事早就在这里~。His readiness to help people has long been a household word around here.

传闻 chuánwén ❶ it is said; they say: ~他病倒了。It is said he has fallen ill. /~不如亲见。To see it is better than to hear about it. *or* Seeing is believing. ❷ hearsay; rumour; talk: ~失实。The rumour proved unfounded. /早有~。It has been in the air for quite some time.

传闻异辞 chuánwén-yìcí the same story has different versions after being passed on from one person to another

传习 chuánxí teach and learn: ~武术 teach and learn *wushu* or martial art

传习录 Chuánxílù *Records of the Teachings of the Master*, a book by philosopher Wang Shouren (王守仁, 1472-1528) of the Ming Dynasty

传檄 chuánxí 〈书面〉promulgate and circulate an official call to arms; promulgate an official denunciation: ~声讨复辟阴谋 issue an official circular denouncing the attempt to restore the monarchy

传销 chuánxiāo 〈商业〉pyramid selling

传写 chuánxiě 〈书面〉make private copies (of a manuscript, document, etc. which is being circulated): 几经~，讹误颇多。It has been copied and recopied so many times that the present version contains quite a lot of errors.

传心 chuánxīn communicate one's thoughts; exchange ideas and feelings

传心术 chuánxīnshù 〈迷信〉telepathy

传薪 chuánxīn 〈书面〉(of a teacher) impart knowledge to students

传信 chuánxìn ❶〈书面〉pass on to others what one believes in ❷ pass on a message

传讯 chuánxùn 〈法律〉summon for interrogation or trial; subpoena; cite

传言 chuányán ❶ hearsay; rumour: ~不可轻信。Do not readily believe rumours. ❷ pass on a message: 互相~送语 send messages to each other ❸〈书面〉make a speech

传扬 chuányáng spread (from mouth to mouth): 美名~天下。One's good name spread far and wide.

传艺 chuányì teach a skill or trade: 收徒~ take apprentices for passing on one's skills

传译 chuányì translate one language into another: 同声~ simultaneous interpretation

传语 chuányǔ take a message

传谕 chuányù 〈旧语〉relay instructions from a superior or an elder

传阅 chuányuè pass around for perusal; circulate for perusal: 这份文件请委员们~。Please pass the document around among the committee members.

传召大法会 Chuánzhào Dàfǎhuì *Monlam* or Grand Summons Ceremony, a tradition in Tibetan Buddhism

传真 chuánzhēn ❶ portraiture ❷〈通信〉facsimile; fax: 无线电~ radio fascimile; radiophotography /~邮件 fax-mail /收到~ receive a fax /给某人发~ send sb. a fax

传真电报 chuánzhēn diànbào phototelegraph: ~机 telectrograph

传真机 chuánzhēnjī fax machine; fax

传真照片 chuánzhēn zhàopiàn radiophoto; telephoto

传真照相机 chuánzhēn zhàoxiàngjī telephoto camera

传知 chuánzhī transmit and notify

传旨 chuánzhǐ pronounce an imperial edict

传种 chuánzhǒng propagate; reproduce: 择优~ select a good

strain for propagation
传宗接代 chuánzōng-jiēdài have a son to carry on one's family name

舡 chuán 〈书面〉see "船" chuán

船(舩) chuán ship; boat: 木～ wooden boat / 轮～ steamer / 帆～ sailing-ship / 商～ merchant ship / 靶～ target ship / 破冰～ icebreaker / 驳～ barge; lighter / 冷藏～ refrigerator ship / 气垫～ hovercraft / 水翼～ hydrofoil / 货～ freighter; cargo ship / 客货～ passenger-freighter / 龙～ dragon boat / 挖泥～ dredger / 水泥～ concrete boat; plastered boat / 缉私～ anti-smuggling patrol boat / 双体～ catamaran / 拖～ tug-boat; tow boat / 拖网～ trawler / 游～ pleasure boat / 飞～ airship; dirigible / 机耕～ boat tractor / 乘～ take ship; go on board a ship; go by boat / 去划～ go boating
船板 chuánbǎn deck of a boat
船帮 chuánbāng ❶ side of a ship; shipboard ❷ merchant fleet
船边交货 chuánbiān jiāohuò free alongside ship; free from alongside
船边提货 chuánbiān tíhuò alongside delivery; shipside delivery
船舶 chuánbó ships; shipping: ～证书 ship's papers / ～登记证书 certificate of registry / ～大修 overhaul (of ships) / ～设计师 marine architect / ～经纪人 ship-broker
船埠 chuánbù wharf; quay
船舱 chuáncāng ❶ ship's hold ❷ cabin
船厂 chuánchǎng shipyard; dockyard
船次 chuáncì ❶ number indicating the order of a ship's departure; (ship's) voyage number ❷ (number of) voyages made by a ship or ships
船到江心补漏迟 chuán dào jiāngxīn bǔ lòu chí 〈俗语〉it's too late to plug up the leak when the boat is in midstream; it will be too late to mend a boat when it has reached the middle of the river
船底 chuándǐ bottom: ～破漏 bilging
船底星座 Chuándǐ Xīngzuò 〈天文〉Carina
船东 chuándōng 〈旧语〉ship owner
船队 chuánduì fleet; flotilla
船帆星座 Chuánfān Xīngzuò 〈天文〉Vela
船方 chuánfāng 〈商业〉the ship: ～不负担装货费用 free in (FI) / ～不负担卸货费用 free out (FO) / ～不负担装、卸、理舱费用 free in and out and stowed (FIOS)
船夫 chuánfū 〈旧语〉boatman: ～曲 boatman's song
船工 chuángōng ❶ boatman; junkman; sailor ❷ maker of wooden boats
船棺葬 chuánguānzàng 〈考古〉boat-coffin burial
船户 chuánhù ❶ one who owns a boat and makes a living as a boatman; boatman ❷ 〈方言〉boat dweller
船货 chuánhuò freight; cargo: ～清单 manifest
船级 chuánjí ship's classification; ship's class: ～证书 classification certificate
船级社 chuánjíshè classification society: 劳氏～ Lloyd's Register of Shipping
船籍 chuánjí registry; nationality of a ship; flag under which a ship sails
船籍港 chuánjígǎng port of registry; home port
船家 chuánjiā 〈旧语〉see "船户❶"
船脚 chuánjiǎo ❶ boatman ❷ cost of water transport
船壳 chuánké hull
船老大 chuánlǎodà 〈方言〉❶ chief crewman of a wooden boat ❷ boatman
船龄 chuánlíng length of service of a ship
船民 chuánmín ❶ people engaged in transport by boat; boat people ❷ refugees who flee by boat: 越南～ Vietnamese boat people
船模 chuánmó ship model
船篷 chuánpéng ❶ mat or wooden roofing of a boat: ～里坐满了人。People crowded together under the roofing of the boat. ❷ sail: ～高扬 ship in full sail
船票 chuánpiào steamer ticket; boat or ship ticket: 我三日前预定了去上海的～。I booked my passage to Shanghai three days ago.
船破又遇顶头风 chuán pò yòu yù dǐngtóufēng meet a head wind when the boat is broken — double misfortune
船期 chuánqī sailing date: ～表 sailing schedule
船旗国 chuánqíguó flag state
船钱 chuánqian ship fare; boat fare
船桥 chuánqiáo (ship's) bridge
船蛆 chuánqū 〈动物〉shipworm
船上交货 chuánshàng jiāohuò 〈贸易〉free on board (FOB)
船艄 chuánshāo stern
船身 chuánshēn hull: ～倾斜 listing hull; listing ship
船手 chuánshǒu boatman; junkman
船首 chuánshǒu stem; bow; prow: ～楼 forecastle
船台 chuántái (building) berth; shipway; slipway; slip: 干式～ dry shipway / ～周期 berth period
船体 chuántǐ body of a ship; hull
船桅 chuánwéi mast
船尾 chuánwěi stern: ～部 quarter / ～楼 poop / ～轴 stern shaft
船位 chuánwèi ❶ ship's position: 测定～ fix a ship's position (at sea); position finding / ～推算法 dead reckoning ❷ accommodation (on a ship): 订～ book one's passage (on a ship)
船坞 chuánwù dock; shipyard: 浮～ floating dock / 干～ dry dock; graving dock / ～费 dockage / 这座～能承造十万吨巨轮。Ocean-going vessels of 100,000 tons can be built at this dock.
船舷 chuánxián side (of a ship or boat); gunwale: 游客们靠着～，谈笑风生。The tourists leaned against the ship's rail, talking and laughing cheerfully.
船小好调头 chuán xiǎo hǎo diàotóu 〈俗语〉it is easier for a small boat to turn round — it is easier for a small enterprise to change its line of products or a small company to change its business orientation
船形帽 chuánxíngmào garrison cap; field cap
船用柴油机 chuányòng cháiyóujī marine diesel
船用海水淡化设备 chuányòng hǎishuǐ dànhuà shèbèi marine desalination equipment
船用雷达 chuányòng léidá ship or marine radar
船用罗盘 chuányòng luópán mariner's compass
船用油 chuányòngyóu bunker oil
船员 chuányuán (ship's) crew; seaman; sailor
船运 chuányùn ship; transport by water
船闸 chuánzhá (ship) lock
船长 chuánzhǎng captain; skipper
船只 chuánzhī vessels; shipping
船主 chuánzhǔ ❶ captain (of a ship); skipper ❷ shipowner

遄 chuán 〈书面〉❶ fast; quickly: ～返南京 return quickly to Nanjing ❷ make frequent trips to and fro

篅(圌) chuán 〈方言〉a kind of grain bin made of bamboo strips, wicker, paddy straw, or mat

椽 chuán rafter
椽笔 chuánbǐ 〈敬词〉writing brush as big as a rafter — your magnificent writing
椽条 chuántiáo rafter
椽子 chuánzi also "椽条" rafter

chuǎn

喘 chuǎn ❶ breathe heavily; gasp for breath; pant: ～粗气 puff and blow / ～不过气来 gasp for breath; be out of breath / 跑到公共汽车站后，他～得相当厉害。He was almost breathless after running to the bus stop. ❷ 〈医学〉asthma: 他有～病。He is a victim of asthma.
喘咳 chuǎnké cough and breathe with difficulty; pant and cough: 她按住胸口～着。She kept her hand on her chest, panting for breath in a coughing fit.
喘气 chuǎnqì ❶ breathe (deeply); pant; gasp: 他费力地喘着气。He was breathing hard. ❷ take a breather: ～的功夫 breathing-space / 喘喘气儿再干。Let's take a breather before we go on.
喘息 chuǎnxī ❶ pant; gasp for breath: ～未定 before regaining one's breath; before one has a chance to catch one's breath ❷ breather; breathing spell; respite: 乘胜追击，不让敌人有～的机会 follow up the victory with hot pursuit so as not to allow the enemy a breathing spell

喘哮 chuǎnxiào *also* "哮喘" asthma
喘吁 chuǎnxū *also* "喘嘘" be short of breath
喘吁吁 chuǎnxūxū *also* "喘嘘嘘" puff and blow; pant：他跳上公共汽车时～的。He was panting when he jumped on to the bus.

舛 chuǎn 〈书面〉❶ error ❷ run counter to：～驰 run in the opposite direction ❸ mishap：命途多～ suffer many a setback during one's life
舛驳 chuǎnbó 〈书面〉jumbly; disorderly; messy
舛错 chuǎncuò ❶ error：音韵～ error in rhyming ❷ accident; mishap：万一有个～，懊悔也来不及了。If anything untoward should happen, it would be too late for regret. ❸ uneven; not uniform：互相～ jigsaw; intertwine
舛讹 chuǎn'é 〈书面〉run counter to; contradict
舛误 chuǎnwù 〈书面〉error; mishap：判断的～ error of judgment

荈 chuǎn 〈书面〉late-picked tea leaves

chuàn

串 chuàn ❶ string together：贯～ run through; penetrate; permeate / 把钥匙～起来 string the keys together ❷〈量词〉string; bunch; cluster：一～珠子 a string of beads / 一～钥匙 a bunch of keys / 一～葡萄 a cluster of grapes ❸ conspire; gang up：～骗 gang up to swindle (sb.) ❹ get things mixed up：收音机～台 get two or more (radio) stations at once / 电话～线 get the (telephone) lines crossed ❺ go from place to place; go about; rove：～亲访友 go visiting one's relatives and friends / 走村～寨 go from village to village / 到处乱～ scurry in all directions ❻ play a part (in a play); act：反～play a role one is not trained for / 客～ be a guest performer ❼〈信息〉string
see also guàn
串并联 chuàn-bìnglián 〈电工〉series-parallel connection
串灯 chuàndēng string of lanterns：楼前的～大放光彩。The strings of lanterns in front of the building sent out a brilliant lustre.
串地 chuàndì loosen up topsoil with a plough (without attaching the mouldboard)
串岗 chuàngǎng leave one's own post without permission; wander away from one's post：凡～者扣发奖金。Anyone who leaves his post without permission will have his bonus deducted.
串供 chuàngòng act in collusion to make each other's confessions tally (so as to cover up sth.)
串行 chuànháng ❶ (in reading or typing) skip a line; confuse two lines：字印得太小，很容易看～。The print is so small that you can easily miss (*or* skip) a line. ❷〈计算机〉series：～计算机 series machine / ～成批处理系统 serial batch system / ～处理系统 serial processing system / ～累加器 serial accumulator
串行线接口协议 chuànhángxiàn jiēkǒu xiéyì 〈信息〉serial line interface protocol (SLIP)
串花 chuànhuā (of plants) cross; hybridize：这两种菜不能种得太近，以免～。It is important to grow these two vegetables far apart so as to avoid crossing them.
串话 chuànhuà *also* "串扰"；"串话干扰"〈通信〉cross talk; babble：～补偿 cross talk compensation / ～测试器 crosstalk meter
串换 chuànhuàn exchange; change; swap：～坐位 change seats
串激 chuànjī *also* "串励"〈电工〉series excitation：～电动机 series motor / ～发电机 series generator; series dynamo
串讲 chuànjiǎng ❶ (of a teacher) explain a text sentence by sentence：～一段文章 explicate a passage ❷ give a summing-up of a text after going over it paragraph by paragraph
串联 chuànlián *also* "串连" ❶ establish ties; contact：他～了几位工会领导人，组织了一次罢工。He contacted several trade union leaders and organized a strike. ❷〈电学〉series connection：～绕组 series winding / ～谐振 series resonance / ～电路 series circuit / ～电池组 series battery / ～电阻 series resistance
串列 chuànliè 〈机械〉tandem; line：～道岔 tandem turnout/ ～结构 in-line configuration / ～式薄板轧机〈冶金〉tandem sheet-mill / ～式拉拔机〈冶金〉tandem drawing-machine / ～式冷轧机〈冶金〉tandem cold-mill
串铃 chuànlíng ❶ hollow metal ring with small metal balls in it, used in old times by pedlers, fortune-tellers and itinerant doctors to draw customers ❷ string of bells hung round the neck of a horse, mule, etc.
串门子 chuàn ménzi 〈口语〉*also* "串门儿" call on sb.; drop in：有空来～。Drop in when you are free.
串皮 chuànpí effect of medicine or alcohol being diffused to the skin of the human body
串骗 chuànpiàn act in cahoots to swindle (sb.); conspire in a fraud
串气 chuànqì gang up; collude with：暗中～ be in secret collusion
串亲戚 chuàn qīnqi go visiting one's relatives：春节期间人们相互～。Relatives pay calls on each other (*or* exchange visits) during the Spring Festival.
串儿红 chuànrhóng scarlet sage (*Salvia splendens*)
串通 chuàntōng ❶ gang up; collaborate; collude：法官与证人暗中～。The judge acted in collusion with the witness. ❷ establish contact with; get in touch with：几个青年教员～好了要建立一个现代文学研究组。A few young teachers made contact with each other to set up a research team on modern literature.
串通一气 chuàntōng-yīqì work hand in glove; act in close collaboration：两人～，互相包庇。Acting in collaboration, the two of them shielded each other.
串痛 chuàntòng pain (in one's body) moving from place to place
串味 chuànwèi (of food or drinks) absorb the smell of sth. with a peculiar odour; be tainted in flavour：茶叶与化妆品不应该放在一起，以免～。Tea should not be put beside cosmetics, or it might get a peculiar odour.
串戏 chuànxì (of amateurs) perform with a professional troupe; act in a play or opera
串线 chuànxiàn get the lines crossed：电话～了，重打一下吧。The lines have got crossed; please dial again.
串乡 chuànxiāng go to the rural area; go from village to village (to sell or purchase goods or to give road performances, etc.)
串烟 chuànyān ❶ (of food) smell of smoke ❷ wisp of smoke when incense is burnt
串演 chuànyǎn play the role of; act the role of：他在电影《西游记》中～孙悟空。He plays the role of the Monkey King in the film *Pilgrimage to the West*.
串秧儿 chuànyāngr crossbreed; hybridize
串音 chuànyīn 〈通信〉cross talk; babble：～测试器 cross talk meter
串游 chuànyou roam; wander; loaf：到处瞎～ go loafing about
串珠 chuànzhū string of beads
串子 chuànzi string; chain：钱～ chain of coins

钏 chuàn bracelet
钏子 chuànzi bracelet：玉～ jade bracelet

chuāng

窗（窓、窻、牎） chuāng window：纱～ screen window / 屋顶～ skylight; dormer window / 双层～ double window / 落地长～ French window / 气～ transom / 凸～ bay window / 圆花～ rose window / 花格～ lattice window / 百叶～ shutters / 框格～ sash window
窗玻璃 chuāngbōli windowpane
窗洞 chuāngdòng opening in a wall (to let in light and air)
窗扉 chuāngfēi casement (of a window)
窗格子 chuānggézi window lattice
窗钩 chuānggōu window catch
窗户 chuānghu window; casement
窗花 chuānghuā paper-cut for window decoration：剪～ make paper-cuts
窗花格 chuānghuāgé 〈建筑〉tracery
窗槛 chuāngkǎn windowsill
窗口 chuāngkǒu ❶ window：站在～ stand by the window / 往～外望去 look out of the window ❷ wicket; window：大门上有一个小～。The big door has a wicket in it. / 在这个～挂号。Register (at a hospital, etc.) at this wicket. / 去北京的火车票在那个～卖。Train tickets to Beijing are sold at that window. ❸ window on people's life — serving the people directly：～单位 institution bearing directly on people's life ❹ channel; medium：在引进先进技术上发挥～作用 serve as a medium for introducing advanced technology from abroad ❺

reflection; showcase:眼睛是心灵的～。Eyes are the window of the soul. /王府井是北京商业的～。The Wangfujing area is a showcase of commerce in Beijing.
窗口行业 chuāngkǒu hángyè various service trades (e. g. commerce, catering, public transport, etc.)
窗框 chuāngkuàng window frame
窗框式天线 chuāngkuàngshì tiānxiàn window frame aerial
窗帘 chuānglián curtain; drape
窗棂 chuānglíng *also* "窗棂子"〈方言〉window lattice
窗幔 chuāngmàn large window curtain
窗门 chuāngmén 〈方言〉window
窗明几净 chuāngmíng-jījìng with bright windows and clean tables; bright and clean
窗纱 chuāngshā gauze for screening windows; window screening; window gauze
窗扇 chuāngshàn casement (of a window)
窗台 chuāngtái windowsill
窗台板 chuāngtáibǎn window board
窗屉子 chuāngtìzi 〈方言〉wooden frame for fixing screen or gauze on a window
窗挺 chuāngtǐng 〈建筑〉stile (of a window)
窗帷 chuāngwéi *also* "窗帏"; "窗幔" large window curtain
窗沿 chuāngyán *see* "窗台"
窗友 chuāngyǒu 〈旧语〉fellow pupil; schoolmate
窗牖 chuāngyǒu 〈书面〉window
窗纸 chuāngzhǐ window paper (for lattice windows)
窗子 chuāngzi window

牕(牕) chuāng *see* "窗" chuāng

疮(瘡) chuāng

❶ sore; skin ulcer:褥～ bed sore /恶～ malignant sore /冻～ chilblain /头上长～，脚底流脓 with the head growing boils and feet running with pus — rotten from head to foot; rotten to the core ❷ wound:刀～ sword wound /金～ metal-inflicted wound; incised wound
疮疤 chuāngbā ❶ scar:腿上留有～ scar on the leg /好了～忘了疼 forget the pain after the wound is healed; forget the bitter past when one is relieved of one's suffering ❷ sore spot; tender spot:揭人～ pull the scab right off sb.'s sore; touch sb.'s sore spot
疮痕 chuānghén scar
疮痂 chuāngjiā 〈医学〉scab
疮口 chuāngkǒu open part of a sore
疮痏 chuāngwěi 〈书面〉scar:生～于玉肌 scar on the fair skin
疮痍 chuāngyí *also* "创痍" chuāngyí 〈书面〉wound; devastation:战争的～ wounds of war /～未瘳。The wounds of war are far from healed.
疮痍满目 chuāngyí-mǎnmù *also* "满目疮痍" a scene of devastation meets the eye everywhere; one sees suffering and destruction everywhere

创(創) chuāng

wound; trauma:予以重～ inflict heavy casualties (on the enemy)
see also chuàng
创痕 chuānghén scar
创巨痛深 chuāngjù-tòngshēn badly injured and in great pain; in deep distress from severe wounds or trauma
创口 chuāngkǒu wound; cut
创面 chuāngmiàn surface of a wound
创伤 chuāngshāng wound; trauma:精神上的～ emotional trauma /战争～ wounds of war; war scar /没有受过～的人才会嘲笑别人的伤疤。Only those who have never received any injuries will laugh at other people's scars. *or* He who has suffered no emotional trauma has no sympathy for its victims.
创痛 chuāngtòng pain from an injury
创痍 chuāngyí *also* "疮痍" chuāngyí wound; devastation

摐(摐) chuāng 〈书面〉hit; strike; beat (sth.)

chuáng

噇 chuáng

〈方言〉eat or drink without restraint; guzzle:～得烂醉 be roaring drunk

幢 chuáng

❶〈古语〉pennant or streamer ❷ stone pillar inscribed with Buddha's name or Buddhist incantation
see also zhuàng
幢幢 chuángchuáng 〈书面〉flickering (shadows); dancing (reflections):人影～ shadows of people moving about

床(牀) chuáng

❶ bed:单人～ single bed /双人～ double bed /双层～ double-deck bed; bunk bed /帆布～ camp bed; cot /行军～ camp bed /折叠～ folding bed /小孩～ child's cot /铺～ make the bed ❷ implement or appliance shaped like a bed:车～ lathe /机～ machine tool ❸ ground shaped like a bed:河～ riverbed /苗～ seedbed ❹〈量词〉*used of sth. that covers a bed*:一～被子 one quilt (*or* duvet) /一～被套 one tick /两～铺盖 two sets of bedding
床板 chuángbǎn wooden boards (of a bed)
床播 chuángbō 〈农业〉sowing in bed
床次 chuángcì 〈书面〉bed:呻吟～ moaning in bed /卧病～ take to one's bed; be laid up in bed
床单 chuángdān *also* "床单子" (bed) sheet
床单布 chuángdānbù sheeting
床垫 chuángdiàn mattress:弹簧～ spring mattress /斜纹布包面的泡沫～ foam mattress with drill tick
床架 chuángjià bedstead
床框架 chuángkuàngjià bed frame
床铺 chuángpù bed; bunk
床蓐 chuángrù straw bedding; bedding:卧病～ be laid up in bed; be bedridden
床上用品 chuángshàng yòngpǐn bedclothes
床上戏 chuángshàngxì 〈影视〉sex scene; plot on bed
床身 chuángshēn 〈机械〉lathe bed
床虱 chuángshī bed bug
床榻 chuángtà bed
床头 chuángtóu head of a bed; bedside:～灯 bedside lamp
床头板 chuángtóubǎn headboard
床头柜 chuángtóuguì ❶ bedside cabinet ❷〈戏谑〉henpecked husband
床头箱 chuángtóuxiāng 〈机械〉headstock; spindle head
床帏 chuángwéi curtain over bed; sexual relations or affairs:此书多涉～秘事。The book relates many intimate affairs.
床位 chuángwèi bed; bunk; berth:这所医院总共有五百个～。The hospital has a total of 500 beds.
床沿 chuángyán edge of a bed; bedside
床罩 chuángzhào bedspread; counterpane:～布 sheetings
床笫 chuángzǐ 〈书面〉bed clothes, especially referring to boudoir intimacies as between husband and wife
床笫之言 chuángzǐzhīyán *also* "床笫之私" intimate words exchanged as between husband and wife when in bed
床子 chuángzi ❶〈机械〉lathe ❷〈方言〉bed-shaped shelf for goods:菜～ vegetable shelf

chuǎng

闯 chuǎng

❶ rush; dash; charge:～进来 rush in; break in; force one's way in /横冲直～ charge about furiously; run amuck ❷ temper oneself (by battling through difficulties and dangers):～出一条新路来 break a new path; blaze a trail /这孩子已经～出来了。The lad has hewed out his path in life. ❸ go around (in order to accomplish certain goals); be busy running about:走南～北 journey north and south; travel widely ❹ get into or bring on (sth. undesirable):～乱子 get into trouble; bring on a disaster
闯荡 chuǎngdàng venture out into the world; try to make a living away from home
闯关 chuǎngguān fight one's way through a fortress; break through barriers:～夺隘 fight one's way through fortresses /该队连闯五关，夺得决赛权。The team overcame five rivals in succession before it entered the finals.
闯关东 chuǎng Guāndōng 〈旧语〉brave a risky journey to the Northeast to earn a living; go and settle down in northeast China
闯红灯 chuǎng hóngdēng ❶ go against a red light; jump a red

C

light ❷ violate law and discipline; break down a barrier or limit

闯祸 chuǎnghuò get into trouble; bring disaster:你净给我～! You are always getting me into trouble. /这是谁闯的祸? Who's done it? /你开车要小心,千万别～。Drive carefully and steer clear of trouble.

闯江湖 chuǎng jiānghu 〈旧语〉make a living wandering from place to place (as a fortune-teller, acrobat, quack doctor, etc.)

闯将 chuǎngjiàng daring general; pathbreaker:技术革新的～ pathbreaker in technological innovations

闯劲 chuǎngjìn spirit of a pathbreaker; pioneering spirit:稳重有余,～不足 care too much about striking sure blows, but lack the pioneering spirit /这人有一股～。This man has the fearless spirit of a pathbreaker.

C

闯练 chuǎngliàn go out into society to temper oneself; get tempered in the world:到实际工作中去～ temper oneself in practical work

闯路 chuǎnglù break a new path; blaze a trail

闯牌子 chuǎng páizi work hard to establish a name for oneself:想办法闯出牌子来 try every means to establish a name for oneself /我们公司正处在～的时期。Our company is still in its initial stage.

闯世界 chuǎng shìjiè venture out into the world; try to make a living away from home:现在有许多青年农民进城～。Nowadays many young farmers swarm into cities to seek a better life.

闯王 Chuǎngwáng Chuang Wang or Daring King, a title for Gao Yingxiang (高迎祥) and then Li Zicheng (李自成), leaders of a peasant uprising in the late Ming Dynasty

chuàng

沧(滄) chuàng 〈书面〉frigid; cold

怆(愴) chuàng 〈书面〉sorrowful:内心～～ feel sad

怆恻 chuàngcè 〈书面〉sorrowful; sad:心情～ feel very sad; be overcome with sorrow

怆恍 chuànghuǎng *also* "怆怳"〈书面〉feel frustrated; be disheartened

怆恼 chuàngnǎo be annoyed; be upset:～的情绪 frustrated mood

怆然 chuàngrán 〈书面〉look sad; seem sorrowful:～泪下 shed sad tears

怆痛 chuàngtòng grieved; sad:万分～ be extremely grieved

创(創、刱、剏) chuàng start (doing sth.); achieve (sth. for the first time); create:～高产 achieve a high yield /～奇迹 create miracles; work wonders; achieve prodigious feats /～新说 found a new theory /粮食产量～历史最高水平。The grain output recorded an all-time high. /实行改革后,该厂年～利税一亿多元。The profits made and taxes paid by the factory totalled over one hundred million *yuan* a year after the reforms had been instituted.
see also chuāng

创办 chuàngbàn establish; set up:～工厂 set up a factory /这所医院～于1956年。The hospital was established in 1956.

创编 chuàngbiān write; create:他正忙于～一个历史剧。He is busy writing a historical play.

创汇 chuànghuì earn net foreign exchange profit from exports:～五千万美元 earn (a net profit of) 50 million US dollars

创汇产品 chuànghuì chǎnpǐn foreign-exchange-earning (export) products

创汇工业 chuànghuì gōngyè export-oriented industry

创获 chuànghuò gain (for the first time); discover:有不少～ make many new gains and discoveries

创纪录 chuàng jìlù break a record; register a new record

创价学会 Chuāngjià Xuéhuì *Sokagakkai*, a Buddhist association in Japan associated with the Komeito Party (公明党)

创见 chuàngjiàn original idea; creative thinking:这篇文章有～。This essay contains original ideas.

创建 chuàngjiàn found; establish:～一座新城市 build a new city /～工业基地 establish an industrial base /～新的学派 found a new school of thought

创举 chuàngjǔ pioneering work or undertaking:伟大的～ great undertaking

创刊 chuàngkān start publication:《人民日报》于1948年6月15日～。The *People's Daily* started publication on June 15, 1948.

创刊号 chuàngkānhào first issue or number

创立 chuànglì found; originate:～一所综合性大学 found a comprehensive university /这个理论是爱因斯坦～的。The theory was originated by Einstein.

创利 chuànglì make or earn a profit

创牌子 chuàng páizi (of enterprises) produce and establish a brand name

创设 chuàngshè ❶ found; create; set up:～疗养院 set up a sanatorium /～新的研究所 establish a new research institute ❷ create (conditions, etc.):为业余教育～有利的条件 create favourable conditions for sparetime education

创始 chuàngshǐ originate; initiate:马克思和恩格斯是科学社会主义的～人。Marx and Engels were the founders of the theory of scientific socialism. /中国是联合国的～国之一。China is a founding member of the United Nations.

创世记 Chuàngshìjì 〈基督教〉*Genesis*, the first book of the *Old Testament*

创世外记 Chuàngshì Wàijì 〈基督教〉*Genesis Apocrypha*

创世主 Chuàngshìzhǔ 〈宗教〉Creator

创收 chuàngshōu increase income (by providing paid services, etc.)

创树 chuàngshù create; set up:～新的艺术风格 create a new artistic style

创税 chuàngshuì pay taxes:～大户 big taxpayer /每年～上千万元 pay taxes of more than ten million *yuan* a year

创新 chuàngxīn bring forth new ideas; blaze new trails:大胆～ be bold in blazing new trails /在科学技术上不断～ constantly bring forth new ideas in science and technology

创新立异 chuàngxīn-lìyì break new paths; be innovative

创新霉素 chuàngxīnméisù 〈药学〉creatmycin

创演 chuàngyǎn put on (a performance) for the first time; première:这出戏几年前由上海京剧团～。The drama was first performed (*or* premièred) by the Shanghai Beijing Opera Troupe several years ago.

创业 chuàngyè start an undertaking; do pioneering work:～难,守业更难。It is difficult to start an enterprise but even more difficult to keep it going.

创业精神 chuàngyè jīngshén pioneering spirit; enterprising spirit

创议 chuàngyì ❶ propose; initiate:～开展劳动竞赛 propose to start a labour emulation drive ❷ proposal:这一～得到大家的响应。The proposal gained general support.

创意 chuàngyì create a new concept of art; break fresh ground in imaginative art:颇有～ rather original in concept

创意部 Chuàngyìbù (as in ad business) creative department

创优 chuàngyōu ❶ achieve success ❷ make brand-name or high quality products

创造 chuàngzào create; produce; bring about:～世界新记录 set a new world record /～奇迹 work wonders; create miracles; perform daring exploits /在小说中～了许多有趣的人物 create many wonderful characters in the novel /人民,只有人民,才是～世界历史的动力。The people, and the people alone, are the motive force in the making of world history.

创造力 chuàngzàolì creative power or ability

创造性 chuàngzàoxìng creativeness; creativity:～思维 creative thinking /调动每个人的积极性和～ give free rein to everyone's initiative and creativity

创造性进化论 chuàngzàoxìng jìnhuàlùn 〈哲学〉creative evolution

创制 chuàngzhì formulate; institute; create:～拼音文字 formulate an alphabetic system of writing

创作 chuàngzuò ❶ write; produce; create:～美术作品 produce works of art /～技巧 artistic technique; craftsmanship /～思想 ideas guiding artistic (*or* literary) creation /他正在～一个电影剧本。He is writing a scenario. /这本书是集体～的。This book is the work of many hands. ❷ creative work; creation:文艺～ literary and artistic creation /划时代的～ epoch-making creative work

创作方法 chuàngzuò fāngfǎ mode of writing:现实主义～ realistic mode of writing /浪漫主义～ romantic mode of writing /自然主义～ naturalist mode of writing

chuī

炊 chuī cook a meal:晨~ morning cooking; cooking breakfast /家贫难~ be of an impoverished family and eke out a bare subsistence /无米之~ cook a meal without rice; make bricks without straw

炊饼 chuībǐng steamed round flat cake

炊爨 chuīcuàn cook; prepare food:~的家什 cooking utensils

炊火 chuīhuǒ 〈方言〉❶ light a fire; build a fire in the stove:在灶下~ attend to the fire in the kitchen ❷ kitchen fire

炊具 chuījù cooking utensils

炊沙作饭 chuīshā-zuòfàn cook sand for rice; work hard but to no avail; work fruitlessly; make futile efforts

炊事 chuīshì cooking; kitchen work:~员 cook (*or* kitchen) staff; cook /~班 cookhouse (*or* mess, *or* kitchen) squad /~用具 cooking utensils

炊烟 chuīyān smoke from kitchen chimneys:~袅袅 smoke spiraling from kitchens /~弥漫的山村 mountain village enveloped in cooking smoke

炊艺 chuīyì art of cuisine

炊帚 chuīzhou brush for cleaning pots and pans; pot-scouring brush

吹 chuī ❶ blow; puff:把火~旺 blow a fire into flames /将食物~凉 blow on one's food to cool it (down) /~一口气 give a puff ❷ play (wind instruments):~箫 play the vertical flute /~口琴 play the mouth organ /~口哨 whistle /~军号 blow the bugle ❸ (of wind) blow:雨打风~ be weather-beaten /风一阵阵地~。The wind blows in gusts. /门~开了。The door blew open. /什么风把你给~来了? What wind blows you here? /~皱一池春水,干卿底事? If the wind troubles the surface of the water, what has it to do with you, dear? ❹〈口语〉boast; brag:自~自擂 blow one's own trumpet /~得天花乱坠 boast in most fantastic terms /此人就爱自~。He is boastful. *or* He is fond of bragging. ❺ flatter; compliment:又~又拍 do one's utmost to flatter ❻〈口语〉break off; break up; fall through:他们俩~了。The couple have broken up. /这项工程最终告~了。Eventually the project fell through.

吹玻璃 chuī bōli 〈化工〉glass blowing:~机 glass blower

吹除 chuīchú 〈化工〉blowdown

吹吹打打 chuīchui-dǎdǎ beating drums and blowing trumpets; piping and drumming; making an ostentatious (*or* exaggerated) show

吹吹拍拍 chuīchui-pāipāi flattery and toadying:~,拉拉扯扯 resort to flattery and touting

吹唇 chuīchún 〈方言〉whistle

吹打 chuīdǎ ❶ play wind and percussion instruments ❷ be hit (by a rainstorm):经受暴风雨的~ withstand the onslaught of storms

吹打 chuīda ❶ blow off (dust, etc.) ❷〈方言〉hurt sb. by offensive remarks:说话~人 speak sarcastically; use offensive language ❸〈方言〉blow one's horn; brag:别~,谁不知道你那点儿能耐! Stop bragging! Everybody knows the few tricks you are capable of.

吹打乐 chuīdǎyuè 〈音乐〉ensemble of Chinese wind and percussion instruments

吹大气 chuī dàqì 〈方言〉boast; blow one's horn

吹荡 chuīdàng stir (by wind):春风~着明净的湖水。The spring breeze ruffles the crystal-clear water of the lake.

吹灯 chuīdēng ❶ blow out a lamp:~睡觉 blow out the lamp and go to sleep ❷〈方言〉die; go west; kick the bucket:去年一场病,差点儿~。I very nearly kicked the bucket when I fell ill last year. ❸〈方言〉fail; collapse:前几回都没搞成,这回又~了。We have failed several times before, and things are fizzling out again.

吹灯拔蜡 chuīdēng-bálà 〈方言〉kick the bucket; fall from power:这些坏人眼看就要~了。The days of the evildoers are numbered.

吹动 chuīdòng (of wind) blow; sway:凉风~着他斑白的头发。The cool wind blew about his grey hair.

吹法螺 chuī fǎluó *also* "大吹法螺" dàchuī-fǎluó blow one's horn or trumpet; brag; boast

吹风 chuīfēng ❶ be in a draught; catch a chill:小心~受凉。Be careful not to get in a draught and catch cold. ❷ dry (hair, etc.) with a blower ❸ let sb. in on sth. in advance; give a cue; brief:这件事要向他吹吹风。Brief him on what this is all about. /她~儿要大伙儿一起给她做寿。She hinted that we should pool to throw a birthday party for her.

吹风会 chuīfēnghuì (background) briefing

吹风机 chuīfēngjī blower (for drying hair); hair drier

吹拂 chuīfú ❶ sway; stir:晨风~着垂柳。The morning breeze is swaying the weeping willows. /微风~她的头发。The wind caressed her hair. ❷〈书面〉commend; speak favourably of:他在经理面前对我多有~。He commended me several times before the manager.

吹歌 chuīgē instrumental music popular in China's rural areas with mainly *sheng*, the trumpet and other pipe instruments:~会 performance of traditional wind instruments

吹鼓手 chuīgǔshǒu ❶ trumpeter; bugler ❷ eulogist:封建礼教的~ eulogist of feudal ethics

吹管 chuīguǎn 〈机械〉blowpipe:氢氧~ oxyhydrogen blowpipe /氧乙炔~ oxyacetylene blowpipe

吹胡子瞪眼 chuīhúzi-dèngyǎn froth at the mouth and glare with rage; foam with rage; snort and stare in anger:他对手下的人总是~。He was always fuming with rage at those working under him.

吹呼 chuīhu *also* "吹唬"〈方言〉❶ brag; boast:他又在那里瞎~。He is blowing his own trumpet again. ❷ reprimand; dress down:老王狠狠地把他~了一顿。Lao Wang gave him a good dressing-down.

吹画 chuīhuà breath painting (created by blowing ink on paper)

吹灰之力 chuīhuīzhīlì (used in the negative) effort needed to blow away a speck of dust; just a small effort:不费~ as easy as blowing away dust; without the least effort

吹火筒 chuīhuǒtǒng bamboo pipe used for blowing a stream of air into a stove to make the fire burn more quickly

吹糠见米 chuīkāng-jiànmǐ rice appears when the chaff is blown off; produce speedy results:这个新办法产生了~的效果。This new measure has achieved instant success (*or* has yielded quick results).

吹口 chuīkǒu 〈音乐〉mouthpiece

吹拉弹唱 chuī-lā-tán-chàng blow, pull, pluck and sing — perform various kinds of instrumental as well as vocal music:她可是多才多艺,~,无所不能。She is quite a versatile artist, good at all kinds of instrumental as well as vocal music. /这次晚会,~样样都有。There will be all kinds of performances in the evening party.

吹喇叭 chuī lǎba given to unctuous praise:~,抬轿子 sheer unctuous praise (*or* downright flattery) of sb.

吹擂 chuīléi boast:自我~ make loud boasts

吹冷风 chuī lěngfēng blow a cold wind over; throw cold water on:不要对人家参加体育活动的热情~。Don't pour cold water on other's enthusiasm for sports.

吹炼 chuīliàn 〈冶金〉blowing

吹毛求疵 chuīmáo-qiúcī find fault; pick holes; nitpick; cavil at:她对女佣人常常~。She often finds fault with her maid. /对别人~的人往往看不到自己的缺点。He who cavils at others often fails to see his own faults.

吹模法 chuīmúfǎ blow moulding

吹牛 chuīniú *also* "吹牛皮" boast; brag; talk big:~拍马 boast and flatter /~大王 boaster; braggart /他~说下象棋没有碰到过真正的对手。He bragged that he had met no real match in chess.

吹拍 chuīpāi flatter; toady upon:这个人惯于~,人们都讨厌他。People dislike him for his proneness to flatter.

吹捧 chuīpěng flatter; laud to the skies; lavish praise on; extol:互相~ flatter each other; blow each other's trumpet /将某人~得上了天 extol sb. to the skies /大凡~别人的人总有自己的目的。He who flatters always has an axe to grind.

吹腔 chuīqiāng one of the main tunes of Anhui opera with flute accompaniment

吹求 chuīqiú find fault with; pick holes in:对青年同志不要过于~。Don't be nitpicking with young people.

吹蚀 chuīshí 〈地理〉deflation; wind erosion

吹手 chuīshǒu wind instrumentalist; player of a wind instrument

吹塑 chuīsù blowing; blow moulding:~机 blow moulding machine

吹台 chuītái fall through; fizzle out:他们的新计划也~了。Their new plan flopped too. /他俩的事儿肯定要~。The two of them are bound to part company.

吹弹 chuītán play musical instruments:~之声,不绝于耳。The sound of the musical instruments lingers in one's ears.

C

吹腾 chuīteng 〈方言〉brag:别那样～自己! Don't speak of yourself in such inflated terms!

吹筒 chuītǒng ❶ bamboo pipe for blowing air into a kitchen stove ❷ instrument used by hunters to lure animals by imitating their cries

吹袭 chuīxí (of wind) blast; sweep:寒风～着卖火柴的小姑娘。A chilly wind was lashing the little match girl.

吹嘘 chuīxū lavish praise on (sb.); boast:自我～ self-praise /～领导 lavish praise on one's superiors; flatter one's boss /～自己打桥牌的本事 boast about one's skill at bridge

吹氧 chuīyǎng 〈冶金〉oxygen blast

吹氧炼钢 chuīyǎng liàngāng 〈冶金〉oxygen furnace steel /～转炉 oxygen-blown converter

吹氧转炉 chuīyǎng zhuànlú oxygen-blown converter

吹制玻璃 chuīzhì bōli blow-moulded glass

吹制机 chuīzhìjī 〈化工〉blow-and-blow machine

吹奏 chuīzòu play (wind instruments):他用笛子～一首新曲子。He played a new tune on his flute.

吹奏乐 chuīzòuyuè wind music

吹奏乐队 chuīzòu yuèduì wind band; band

chuí

椎 chuí ❶ tool with a heavy head and handle, used for breaking or beating:铁～ hammer /木～ mallet ❷ beat; thump; pound:～鼓 beat drums /～杀 kill with a hammer

see also zhuī

椎心泣血 chuíxīn-qìxuè beat one's chest and burst into tears in deep sorrow; cry one's eyes out:想起父母惨死在敌寇的屠刀下,他每每～。His heart bleeds whenever he recalls his parents' tragic death under enemy's bayonets.

槌 chuí mallet; beetle:棒～ wooden club (used to beat clothes in washing) /鼓～儿 drumstick

槌球 chuíqiú 〈体育〉croquet

垂 chuí ❶ hang down; droop:柳条～在水面上。Willow branches drooped down to the water. /屋檐下～着几根冰柱。Icicles are hanging from the roof. ❷〈书面〉〈敬词〉*used of kind action of other people (usu. one's seniors) towards one*:～问 condescend to inquire /～念 show kind concern for ❸〈书面〉spread; hand down; go down in history; bequeath to posterity:功～竹帛 be recorded in history in letters of gold /名～千古 one's reputation will resound throughout the ages; one's good name will be recorded in history /～示后世 set a shining example for posterity ❹〈书面〉approach; near; be close to; verge on

垂爱 chuí'ài 〈书面〉〈敬词〉(often used in correspondence) kindness that a person of senior status has shown to one; your gracious concern for me

垂成 chuíchéng 〈书面〉on the verge of success:功败～ suffer defeat when success is in sight

垂垂 chuíchuí 〈书面〉gradually:～老矣 approaching old age

垂钓 chuídiào fish with a hook and line; go angling:湖边～ sit fishing by a lake; angle by a lake

垂范 chuífàn pass on to posterity as a shining example:～后世 set an example for posterity

垂拱 chuígǒng 〈书面〉let things take their own course; laissez-faire:～而治 rule by laissez-faire

垂挂 chuíguà hang down:卧室里～着绿色的窗帘。Green curtains hang over the windows of the bedroom.

垂花饰 chuíhuāshì swag

垂花门 chuíhuamén (in a traditional compound house) ornamental inner gate having a decorative roof with short carved posts hanging down from the four corners

垂绝 chuíjué 〈书面〉❶ dying; moribund ❷ almost extinct:此种～之技艺,如今又获新生。This type of craftsmanship which was on the verge of extinction has acquired a new lease of life.

垂老 chuílǎo approach old age; get on in years

垂泪 chuílèi shed tears; weep:～不止 cannot refrain from tears

垂怜 chuílián show sympathy (as for one's subordinates who have met with misfortune):上天～,你我还有见面之日。With heaven's blessing, you and I will be reunited some day.

垂帘听政 chuílián-tīngzhèng (of an empress or mother queen) attend to court affairs from behind a screen

垂柳 chuíliǔ *also* "垂杨柳" weeping willow

垂纶 chuílún 〈书面〉fish with a hook and line; retire from politics; live as a recluse

垂落 chuíluò droop; fall:眼泪簌簌地从脸上～。Tears rolled down his face.

垂暮 chuímù 〈书面〉❶ just before sundown; near sunset:～之时,炊烟四起。Towards dusk smoke is seen curling up from village chimneys. ❷ old age:～之年 in old age; in the evening of one's life /不觉渐入～之年。I am suddenly aware that old age is creeping up on me.

垂念 chuíniàn 〈书面〉〈敬词〉kind attention that one receives from a person:承蒙～,不胜感奋。I am indeed grateful to you for the kind attention you have paid to me.

垂盼 chuípàn 〈书面〉〈敬词〉solicitude from a senior person

垂盆草 chuípéncǎo 〈中药〉stringy stonecrop (*Sedum sarmentosum*)

垂泣 chuíqì shed tears; weep

垂青 chuíqīng 〈书面〉look upon sb. with favour:他得到这位老专家的～,真有点受宠若惊。He was overwhelmed by the favour that the distinguished expert had bestowed upon him.

垂手 chuíshǒu ❶ with hands down; easily:～而得 obtain sth. without lifting a finger ❷ with the hands at one's side; respectfully:～侍立 stand beside sb. with great reverence

垂手可得 chuíshǒu-kědé *also* "垂手而得" (can) obtain sth. without lifting a finger; be extremely easy to obtain:此城～。It will be extremely easy to capture the city. *or* The city is easy game.

垂首 chuíshǒu bow one's head:她～拭泪。She bowed her head and wiped the tears from her eyes.

垂首帖耳 chuíshǒu-tiē'ěr extremely docile and obedient

see also "俯首帖耳" fǔshǒu-tiē'ěr

垂死 chuísǐ dying; moribund:～挣扎 put up a last-ditch (*or* desperate) struggle; be in one's death throes

垂体 chuítǐ *also* "脑下垂体" nǎoxià chuítǐ 〈生理〉hypophysis; pituitary body or gland:～性矮小症〈医学〉pituitary dwarfism /～制剂 pituitary extract

垂体后叶素 chuítǐ hòuyèsù 〈药学〉pituitrin

垂体机能减退 chuítǐ jīnéng jiǎntuì 〈医学〉hypopituitarism; panhypopituitarism

垂体机能亢进 chuítǐ jīnéng kàngjìn 〈医学〉hyperpituitarism

垂体瘤 chuítǐliú 〈医学〉hypophysoma

垂体炎 chuítǐyán 〈医学〉hypophysitis

垂髫 chuítiáo 〈书面〉early childhood:黄发～,并怡然自乐。People, old and young, are happy and pleased with themselves.

垂头 chuítóu bend one's head:他垂着头往前走。He walked ahead, head bent.

垂头丧气 chuítóu-sàngqì crestfallen; dejected; downcast:打得敌人～ inflict a demoralizing defeat upon the enemy /他们～而去。They left crestfallen.

垂危 chuíwēi ❶ critically ill; at one's last gasp:病势～ gravely ill; mortally ill /生命～ dying; at one's last gasp /～的病人 patient in a critical condition ❷ (of a nation) be in grave danger:他们要挽救～的祖国。They tried to deliver the nation from the jaws of danger.

垂问 chuíwèn *also* "垂询"〈书面〉〈敬词〉condescend to inquire:小儿患病,承蒙～,不胜感激。I am very grateful for your kind inquiry after my child's illness.

垂涎 chuíxián drool; salivate; slaver; covet:他看见那么多好吃的,不禁～。He could not help salivating at the sight of so much nice food. /这是他们～的一块土地。This is the land they covet.

垂涎三尺 chuíxián-sānchǐ have one's saliva or spittle three feet long — drool with envy

垂涎欲滴 chuíxián-yùdī ❶ one's mouth waters; one's mouth drools with greed ❷ be greedy

垂线 chuíxiàn 〈数学〉*also* "垂直线" perpendicular line; vertical line:直线的两条～是平行的。Two vertical lines from the same straight line are always parallel.

垂心 chuíxīn 〈数学〉orthocentre

垂悬 chuíxuán hang down; droop:一条彩带从屋顶～下来。A coloured streamer hangs down from the roof.

垂询 chuíxún 〈书面〉*see* "垂问"

垂杨柳 chuíyángliǔ weeping willow

垂直 chuízhí perpendicular; vertical: ～俯冲 steep dive; nose dive / ～天线 vertical antenna / ～贸易 vertical trade / ～流动 vertical mobility / 两线～相交。The two lines meet at right angles.

垂直度 chuízhídù verticality; perpendicularity

垂直舵 chuízhíduò vertical rudder

垂直发射 chuízhí fāshè vertical firing; vertical launching (of a missile); vertical take off (VTO)

垂直面 chuízhímiàn perpendicular or vertical plane

垂直平分线 chuízhí píngfēnxiàn vertical bisector

垂直起落 chuízhí qǐluò vertical take-off and landing (VTOL)

垂直起落飞机 chuízhí qǐluò fēijī vertical take off and landing aircraft; VTOL aircraft: 垂直短距起落飞机 VSTOL / 垂直或短距起落飞机 V/STOL

垂直升降机 chuízhí shēngjiàngjī vertical conveyor or lift

垂直线 chuízhíxiàn vertical line

垂直型一体化 chuízhíxíng yītǐhuà vertical integration

垂直中心线 chuízhí zhōngxīnxiàn Vertical Center Line (VCL)

垂直轴 chuízhízhóu (of a ship or aircraft) vertical axis

垂注 chuízhù 〈书面〉❶ look downwards: 他的目光～在地上。He gazed at the ground. ❷ be recorded: ～史册 be recorded in history

棰

chuí 〈书面〉❶ short wooden club; cudgel ❷ beat with a cudgel: ～楚 caning (as a form of punishment in the past) ❸ *see* "箠" chuí ❹ *see* "槌" chuí

捶(搥)

chuí beat (with a stick or fist); thump; pound: 怒冲冲地～着桌子 pound the table with rage / ～衣裳 beat clothes (when washing them) / ～背 pound sb.'s back (as in massage) / ～鼓 beat a drum / 把某人好好～一顿 give sb. a good thrashing

捶打 chuídǎ strike; beat; thump: 用榔头～铁板 strike an iron-plate with a hammer

捶打 chuída ❶ beat with light blows; tap: 我腿痛, 你给～～。Please beat on my aching leg. ❷ temper; toughen: 他在艰苦生活中～出来了。He was tempered in a life of hardship.

捶拓 chuítà make rubbings (from inscriptions, pictures, etc. on stone tablets): 未经批准, 不得～石碑。It is forbidden to make rubbings on stone tablets without permission.

捶胸顿足 chuíxiōng-dùnzú thump one's chest and stamp one's feet; beat one's breast and stamp about with sorrow: 他～, 放声大哭。He beat his bosom and stamped in agony, crying bitterly.

箠

chuí 〈书面〉❶ whip ❷ flog with a whip; whip

锤(鎚)

chuí ❶ metal ball with a chain or long handle (used as a weapon in ancient times); hammer: 铜～ copper hammer ❷ sth. shaped like a hammer: 秤～ steelyard weight / 纺～ spindle ❸ hammer: 铁～ iron hammer / 钉～ nail hammer; claw hammer / 汽～ steam hammer ❹ hammer into shape; knock with a hammer: 千～百炼 thoroughly tempered (*or* steeled)

锤锻 chuíduàn 〈机械〉hammer forging

锤骨 chuígǔ 〈生理〉malleus

锤光 chuíguāng 〈机械〉planish

锤击夯 chuíjīhāng 〈机械〉hammer blow tamper or ram

锤击选矿 chuíjī xuǎnkuàng 〈矿业〉cobbing

锤磨机 chuímójī 〈机械〉hammermill

锤炼 chuíliàn ❶ temper: 在艰苦的环境里～自己的意志 temper one's willpower under hard conditions / 经过炮火的～ go through the baptism of war ❷ polish; refine: ～语言 refine one's diction / ～文笔 polish one's style of writing / 这戏经过反复～, 比较成熟了。The play has been polished several times and is relatively mature.

锤头 chuítou 〈方言〉hammer

锤子 chuízi hammer

陲

chuí 〈书面〉frontier; border: 边～ frontier or border area

chūn

春

chūn ❶ spring: 初～ early spring / ～景 scenery of springtime / 开～ when spring comes round again; in the Lunar New Year season / ～去秋来 with the change of seasons; with the passage of time / ～天的温暖 warmth of spring days / ～暖花开。Spring has come and the flowers are in bloom. ❷ a year's time; year: 退隐南山二十～ have retired into the Southern Mountain for twenty years ❸ love; lust: 有女怀～ girl longing for love; girl in love / 猫叫～ cat's caterwauling courtship ❹ vital energy; life: 着手成～ bring the dying back to life ❺ (Chūn) a surname

春冰 chūnbīng 〈书面〉thin ice on the water in spring; things that easily vanish; precarious situation

春饼 chūnbǐng spring pancake (usu. eaten on Beginning of Spring day)

春播 chūnbō spring sowing: ～作物 spring-sown crops / ～时间 time for spring sowing / 大部分农作物是～的。Most crops are sown in spring.

春不老 chūnbùlǎo 〈方言〉〈植物〉potherb mustard

春茶 chūnchá ❶ tea leaves picked in spring ❷ tea made with leaves picked in spring: 沏一杯～ make a cup of spring tea

春潮 chūncháo springtide; vigorous sweep of the waves: 人群～般地拥向天安门广场。People surged towards Tian'anmen Square like a rising tide.

春城 chūnchéng city of spring (referring to Kunming, provincial capital of Yunnan)

春绸 chūnchóu silk fabric with a geometric design (for spring wear)

春川 Chūnchuān Ch'unch'on (in the Republic of Korea)

春大麦 chūndàmài 〈农业〉spring barley

春凳 chūndèng old-fashioned rectangular stool

春地 chūndì cultivated land

春肥 chūnféi 〈农业〉spring top-dressing

春分 Chūnfēn ❶ Vernal Equinox, 4th seasonal division point, marking the sun's position at 0° on the ecliptic ❷ day marking such a seasonal division point, usu. falling on the 20th or 21st of March ❸ period lasting from such a seasonal division point till the next one (Pure Brightness 清明)

see also "节气" jiéqì; "二十四节气" èrshísì jiéqì

春分点 chūnfēndiǎn vernal equinox point

春风 chūnfēng ❶ spring breeze: ～送暖。The spring breeze brings warmth into the air. / 朵朵野花在～中摇摆。Wild flowers dance gaily here and there in the spring breeze. ❷ 〈书面〉favour; kindness ❸ kind and pleasant countenance

春风得意 chūnfēng-déyì be flushed with success; ride on the crest of success

春风化雨 chūnfēng-huàyǔ life-giving spring breeze and rain — salutary influence of education or teachers

春风满面 chūnfēng-mǎnmiàn *also* "满面春风" beaming with satisfaction; radiant with happiness: 他近来很顺利, ～。He beams with pleasure, for he has been quite successful these days.

春耕 chūngēng spring ploughing

春宫 chūngōng ❶ official residence of a crown prince ❷ *also* "春画" pornographic picture

春菇 chūngū spring mushroom

春灌 chūnguàn 〈农业〉spring irrigation

春光 chūnguāng sights and sounds of spring; spring scenery: ～明媚 enchanting scene of spring / ～如海 boundless spring scenery / ～融融。Spring fills the air with warmth.

春寒 chūnhán cold spell in spring: 倒～ unexpected cold spell in spring (usu. following a relatively warm winter) / ～料峭。There is a nip in the cold air in spring.

春旱 chūnhàn dryness or aridity in spring; spring drought

春洪 chūnhóng mountain torrents in spring resulting from the melting snow

春花作物 chūnhuā zuòwù crop that flowers in spring; vernal flowering crop

春华秋实 chūnhuá-qiūshí blossom in spring and fruit in autumn — change of seasons; hard work and its fruit; literary talent and moral integrity

春化 chūnhuà 〈农业〉*also* "催青" cuīqīng vernalization: ～处理 vernalization

春画 chūnhuà pornographic picture

春荒 chūnhuāng temporary food shortage in spring: 度～ tide over the food shortage in spring

春晖 chūnhuī 〈书面〉beams of spring; parental love: 祖国山河满～。

The mountains and rivers of our country are bathed in the warm light of springtime.

春季 chūnjì spring; springtime; spring season: ～作物 spring crops / ～运动会 spring sports meet

春交会 Chūnjiāohuì (short for 中国出口商品春季交易会) Spring Fair for Chinese Export Commodities (held annually in Guangzhou from April 14 to 24)

春假 chūnjià spring vacation; spring holidays: 利用～组织郊游 organize an outing during the spring holidays

春节 Chūnjié Spring Festival; Chinese New Year's Day

春景 chūnjǐng spring scenery; sights and sounds in springtime: ～如画。The scenery in spring is picturesque.

春景天 chūnjingtiān 〈方言〉 spring

C

春酒 chūnjiǔ ❶ wine distilled or mellowed in spring ❷ feast celebrating the Spring Festival

春卷 chūnjuǎn spring roll (a thin sheet of dough, rolled, stuffed and fried)

春困 chūnkùn feeling of lethargy that comes over many people in spring: 患～ overcome with drowsiness on spring days

春兰 chūnlán *also* "兰花" lánhuā orchid; cymbidium

春兰秋菊 chūnlán-qiūjú spring orchids and autumn chrysanthemums — each has its own peculiar charms; everybody has his strong points

春雷 chūnléi spring thunder

春雷霉素 chūnléiméisù 〈药学〉 kasugarnycin

春联 chūnlián Spring Festival couplets (pasted on gateposts or door panels); New Year scrolls: 写～儿 write Spring Festival couplets / 贴～儿 stick on New Year couplets

春令 chūnlìng ❶ spring: 时交～ in spring ❷ spring weather: 冬行～。The winter is mild like spring.

春麦 chūnmài *see* "春小麦"

春梦 chūnmèng spring dream; pipe dream: 一场～ nothing but a spring dream; pleasant dream on a spring night / ～无痕 vanish without a trace like a pipe dream

春明 chūnmíng 〈书面〉 Gate of Spring Brightness (the middle one of the three eastern gates of Chang'an City, capital of the Tang Dynasty); capital city

春牛 chūnniú clay ox (used in old days as a symbol to greet spring at the Beginning of Spring)

春情 chūnqíng stirring of love or desire

春秋 chūnqiū ❶ spring and autumn; year: ～四季 throughout the year; all the year round / 几度～ several years have passed / 苦度～ eke out a living year in and year out / 他在这个工厂度过了五十个～。He has worked in the factory for fifty years. ❷ age: ～正富 in the prime of life / ～已高 be advanced in years

春秋 Chūnqiū ❶ annal; chronicle; history ❷ the Spring and Autumn Period (formerly 722-481 BC as covered by *The Spring and Autumn Annals* attributed to Confucius, now generally considered to last 770-476 BC): ～无义战。There was no just war during the Spring and Autumn Period.

春秋笔法 chūnqiū bǐfǎ euphemistically critical approach in historical narrative or other writings, said to have been adopted by Confucius in compiling *The Annals*

春秋鼎盛 chūnqiū-dǐngshèng in the prime of life; be in the full vigour of manhood

春秋衫 chūnqiūshān jacket suitable for spring or autumn wear

春日 chūnrì ❶ spring ❷ 〈书面〉 spring sun

春色 chūnsè ❶ spring scenery: ～满神州。Spring reigns in all its gorgeous beauty in this Sacred Land. ❷ flushed look under the influence of alcohol; joyful look: 满面～ be flushed with joy; one's face is radiant with happiness

春色满园 chūnsè-mǎnyuán signs of spring are visible everywhere in the garden

春山 chūnshān 〈书面〉 dark-green mountains in spring; women's eyebrows (as in former times, women used a black pigment to paint their eyebrows)

春上 chūnshang in spring: 我们今年～去过南京。We visited Nanjing last spring.

春试 chūnshì 〈旧语〉 spring examination (for the imperial service)

春事 chūnshì 〈书面〉 spring farming; spring ploughing

春树暮云 chūnshù-mùyún *also* "暮云春树" spring trees and sunset clouds — yearning for a friend who is far away

春笋 chūnsǔn spring bamboo shoots: ～怒发。Bamboo shoots are springing up and growing vigorously.

春天 chūntiān spring; springtime: 燕子和～一起来了。Swallows come in company with spring.

春条 chūntiáo 〈方言〉 strips of red paper containing auspicious words pasted on the walls in the Spring Festival; Spring Festival scrolls

春帖 chūntiě ❶ *see* "春条" ❷ *see* "春联"

春头 chūntóu 〈方言〉 in early spring; at the beginning of spring: 时值冰雪融化的～ when ice and snow start to thaw at the beginning of spring

春蛙秋蝉 chūnwā-qiūchán croaks of frogs in spring and chirps of cicadas in autumn — loud but empty talk

春闱 chūnwéi 〈书面〉 *see* "春试"

春瘟 chūnwēn 〈中医〉 pestilence in spring; spring fever

春宵 chūnxiāo spring night; 〈比喻〉 night of sexual bliss: ～苦短。Spring nights are lamentably short. *or* Night for lovers are always too short.

春小麦 chūnxiǎomài *also* "春麦" spring wheat

春心 chūnxīn ardent desire for love; ardent love; lust

春汛 chūnxùn ❶ 〈水利〉 spring flood; spring freshet ❷ spring (fishing) season

春阳 chūnyáng warm sunshine in spring

春药 chūnyào aphrodisiac

春意 chūnyì ❶ breath of spring; hint of spring: ～盎然。Spring is very much in the air. / ～阑珊。Spring is on the wane. / 这里正是阴雨初晴，～葱茂，一派清新的农村景色。The sky has just cleared after rain. Spring has arrived and covered the countryside with fresh verdure. ❷ *see* "春心"

春蚓秋蛇 chūnyǐn-qiūshé 〈比喻〉 cacography; scrawling hand

春游 chūnyóu spring outing

春雨 chūnyǔ spring shower; spring rain: ～贵如油。Rain during springtime is as precious as oil.

春运 chūnyùn (passenger) transport during the Spring Festival period

春种 chūnzhòng spring sowing: ～秋收 spring sowing and autumn harvest

春装 chūnzhuāng spring clothing; spring dress

堾 chūn 〈方言〉 stone wall along the edge of fields against dust storms, etc.

椿 chūn ❶ 〈植物〉 Chinese toon ❷ tree of heaven ❸ (Chūn) a surname

椿白皮 chūnbáipí 〈中药〉 bark of the root or trunk of the tree of heaven

椿庭 chūntíng 〈旧语〉〈敬词〉 your father

椿象 chūnxiàng *also* "蝽" chūn 〈动物〉 stinkbug; shieldbug

椿萱 chūnxuān 〈书面〉 parents; father and mother: ～并茂。Both parents are living and healthy.

蝽 chūn 〈动物〉 stinkbug; shieldbug

鰆 chūn *also* "鰆鱼"; "马鲛" mǎjiāo 〈动物〉 chorinemus

輴 chūn ❶ 〈书面〉 hearse ❷ ancient vehicle for muddy roads

chún

淳 chún 〈书面〉 pure; honest: ～白 pure; clear

淳风 chúnfēng 〈书面〉 unsophisticated way of life

淳古 chúngǔ (of custom) simple and honest

淳和 chúnhé 〈书面〉 honest and kind

淳厚 chúnhòu *also* "醇厚" chúnhòu simple and honest; simple and plain; unsophisticated: 民风～ unsophisticated folk customs / 风格～ simple and plain style / 为人～ simple and honest by nature

淳良 chúnliáng simple and kind

淳美 chúnměi pure and sweet: 这位歌剧演员的音色很～。The opera singer's voice has a mellow timbre.

淳朴 chúnpǔ *also* "纯朴" chúnpǔ pure and simple: 风俗～ simple

and pristine custom /语言～ simple and unadorned language
淳于 Chúnyú a surname

醇 chún ❶〈书面〉strong alcoholic drink; liquor: ～酿 liquor; spirits ❷〈书面〉pure; unadulterated; mellow: ～粹 pure and unadulterated /北京～ mellow Beijing liquor ❸〈化学〉alcohol: 乙～ ethanol; alcohol
醇胺 chún'àn 〈化学〉hydramine; alcohol amine
醇和 chúnhé pure and mild: 酒味～。The wine is (*or* tastes) mellow.
醇厚 chúnhòu ❶ (of taste, smell, etc.) pleasantly strong: 花香～。The scent of the flowers is pleasantly strong. /这蜂蜜的滋味～。The honey has a pure and unadulterated taste. ❷ *also* "淳厚" chúnhòu pure and honest; simple and kind; unsophisticated: ～的乡下人 honest (*or* unsophisticated) countrymen
醇化 chúnhuà ❶ refine; purify; perfect: ～技艺 perfect one's skill (*or* technique) /表演日臻～。The performance is approaching perfection with each passing day. ❷〈化学〉alcoholization: ～物 alcoholate
醇解 chúnjiě 〈化学〉alcoholysis
醇酒 chúnjiǔ mellow and pure wine
醇酒妇人 chúnjiǔ-fùrén wine and women — life of dissipation
醇醪 chúnláo mellow wine
醇美 chúnměi pure and sweet: ～的嗓音 beautiful voice
醇酿 chúnnóng ❶ (of flavour) pure and strong: ～的奶茶 pure and strong cream tea ❷〈书面〉pure and simple: 她的演唱韵味～。Her singing has a mellow flavour.
醇朴 chúnpǔ *also* "淳朴" chúnpǔ pure and simple
醇醛 chúnquán 〈化学〉alcohol aldehyde
醇溶谷蛋白 chúnróng gǔdànbái 〈化学〉prolamin
醇溶清漆 chúnróng qīngqī 〈化学〉spirit varnish
醇酸 chúnsuān 〈化学〉alcohol acid; alcoholic acid: ～树脂 alkyd resin
醇烯橡胶 chúnxī xiàngjiāo 〈化学〉alfin rubber
醇香 chúnxiāng (of smell, taste, etc.) pure and fragrant
醇正 chúnzhèng strong but mellow: 酒味～。The wine tastes mellow. /这种香水香味～。The perfume smells pure and pleasant.
醇中毒 chúnzhòngdú alcoholism; alcoholic poisoning

鹑 chún quail
鹑衣 chúnyī 〈书面〉ragged clothes: ～百结 in rags; tattered

漘 chún 〈书面〉water's edge; waterside

唇(脣) chún *also* "嘴唇" zuǐchún lip: 上～ upper lip / 下～ lower lip
唇齿 chúnchǐ lips and teeth: 互为～ be like lips and teeth to each other /两国为～之邦。The two countries are as close as lips and teeth. *or* The two countries are mutually dependent as close neighbours.
唇齿相依 chúnchǐ-xiāngyī be as interdependent as lips and teeth
唇齿音 chúnchǐyīn 〈语言〉labiodental (sound); dentilabial
唇读 chúndú understand by reading sb.'s lips
唇缝术 chúnféngshù 〈医学〉labiorrhaphy
唇膏 chúngāo lipstick
唇红齿白 chúnhóng-chǐbái (usu. of children and youngsters) red lips and white teeth — have handsome features: 这姑娘出落得～, 眼秀眉清。The girl has handsome features, with delicate eyes, beautiful brows, red lips and shining white teeth.
唇环 chúnhuán lip ring
唇焦舌敝 chúnjiāo-shébì talk till one's tongue and lips are parched; expostulate at great length
唇裂 chúnliè *also* "兔唇" tùchún; "豁嘴" huōzuǐ 〈医学〉harelip; cleft lip
唇枪舌剑 chúnqiāng-shéjiàn cross verbal swords; engage in a battle of words; have a heated verbal exchange: 双方～, 各不相让。The two sides were engaged in a battle of words, each refusing to yield.
唇舌 chúnshé words; argument; talking round; persuasion: 颇费～ take a lot of persuading /白费～ waste of breath /你不知道我为了说服他费了多少～。You don't know how hard I have tried to talk him round.
唇亡齿寒 chúnwáng-chǐhán if the lips are gone, the teeth will be exposed to the cold; share a common lot: 两国利害攸关, ～。The two countries share weal and woe. If one of them falls, the other is in danger.
唇纹 chúnwén wrinkles of the lip
唇吻 chúnwěn 〈书面〉lips; words; eloquence
唇炎 chúnyán 〈医学〉cheilitis
唇音 chúnyīn 〈语言〉labial (sound)
唇印 chúnyìn lip print
唇脂 chúnzhī lipstick

纯 chún ❶ pure; unmixed: ～棉 pure cotton /～羊毛 pure wool ❷ simple; pure and simple: ～黑 all black /～白 pure white /成分不～ (of an organization, etc.) composed of people of diverse political hues (*or* of different class backgrounds) /～属污蔑 sheer slander /动机不～ actuated by an impure motive ❸ skilful; practised; well versed; fluent: 技艺不～ not skilful enough
纯粹 chúncuì ❶ pure; unadulterated: ～的人 man of gold /～的北京话 pure (*or* standard) Beijing dialect ❷ (usu. followed by 是) solely; purely; only: ～是虚构 sheer fabrication /～是浪费时间 just a waste of time /～是骗人的鬼话 downright lies /～是一派胡言 utter nonsense /～是故意捣乱 make trouble entirely on purpose /这不～是给我出难题吗? Is this not simply creating difficulties for me? *or* Isn't it simply an attempt to put me on the spot?
纯粹地租 chúncuì dìzū pure rent
纯粹数学 chúncuì shùxué pure mathematics
纯粹主义 chúncuìzhǔyì 〈美术〉purism
纯导弹防空 chúndǎodàn fángkōng 〈军事〉all-missile air defence
纯度 chúndù purity; pureness
纯钢 chúngāng 〈冶金〉clean steel
纯厚 chúnhòu *also* "淳厚" chúnhòu pure and honest; unsophisticated
纯化 chúnhuà purification
纯碱 chúnjiǎn 〈化学〉soda ash; sodium carbonate
纯洁 chúnjié ❶ pure and honest; with a spotless reputation: 思想～ unsophisticated /心地～ pure of heart /～性 purity /她～善良。She is pure and kindhearted. ❷ purify: ～组织 purify an organization
纯洁冰 chúnjiébīng blue ice
纯金 chúnjīn pure gold; fine gold
纯金属 chúnjīnshǔ 〈物理〉fine metal
纯谨 chúnjǐn 〈书面〉honest and prudent
纯净 chúnjìng ❶ pure; clean: 溪水～。The water of the brook is crystal clear. ❷ purify
纯亏损 chúnkuīsǔn net loss; net deficiency
纯利 chúnlì net profit
纯良 chúnliáng honest and sincere: 心地～ pure of heart
纯林 chúnlín *also* "单纯林" dānchúnlín woods or forest with a single species of trees growing; pure forest
纯律 chúnlǜ 〈音乐〉just intonation
纯美 chúnměi innocent and charming; simple and pure: 风俗～ simple and fine customs /～的少女 innocent and charming maiden
纯朴 chúnpǔ honest and simple; unsophisticated: ～可爱 honest and lovable /忠厚～ good-natured and sincere
纯情 chúnqíng pure love (of a girl, etc.); innocent love: 一片～ full of innocent love /～少女 girl of innocent love; *ingénue*
纯然 chúnrán purely; merely: 这段描写～是为了主题的需要而臆造出来的。This descriptive passage is created out of pure imagination to suit the demands of the theme.
纯收入 chúnshōurù net income
纯熟 chúnshú skilful; practised; well versed: ～的艺术技巧 dexterous artistic technique; accomplished craftsmanship /小提琴拉得～ play the violin with superb skill
纯水 chúnshuǐ pure water
纯态 chúntài 〈化学〉pure state
纯文学 chúnwénxué serious literature; belles-lettres: ～主义 belletrism
纯系 chúnxì 〈农业〉pure line: ～育种 pure-line breeding
纯小数 chúnxiǎoshù pure decimal
纯一 chúnyī single; simple: 目标～ singleness of purpose; single-mindedness

纯艺术 chúnyìshù pure art
纯音 chúnyīn 〈物理〉pure tone; simple tone
纯育 chúnyù 〈农业〉pure breeding
纯贞 chúnzhēn pure and devoted:～的爱情 love of undivided loyalty
纯真 chúnzhēn pure; true; sincere:～的爱情 true love /一颗金子般～的心 a heart of gold /这位妹妹真是～。She is really a pure and innocent girl.
纯正 chúnzhèng ❶ pure; perfect:发音～ flawless pronunciation /他讲～的英语。He speaks standard English. ❷ pure and upright:学习目的～ proper motivation in study /思想～ pure and sound in mind; ideologically sound
纯挚 chúnzhì true and sincere:～的感情 sincere and true sentiment
纯稚 chúnzhì innocent; naive:孩子们～的心灵 children's pure and innocent minds
纯种 chúnzhǒng 〈生物〉purebred:～家畜 purebred livestock /～繁育 pure breeding

C

莼(蓴) chún

莼菜 chúncài 〈植物〉water shield
莼羹鲈脍 chúngēng-lúkuài *also*"莼鲈之思" be homesick and decide to give up one's official post

chǔn

蠢[1] chǔn 〈书面〉wriggle; squirm

蠢[2](惷) chǔn ❶ stupid; foolish; dull:这人太～了。What a fool (he is)! /他从不做那种～事。He is above such folly. /这是最～最坏的做法。This is the silliest and worst possible thing to do. ❷ clumsy; awkward:一头又憨又～的狗熊 a silly and clumsy bear

蠢笨 chǔnbèn ❶ awkward; stupid:～无知 stupid and ignorant /～如牛 as silly as an ass ❷ unwieldy; clumsy:～的牛车 unwieldy oxcart /动作～ clumsy in one's movement
蠢材 chǔncái idiot; fool; dumbbell; blockhead:你什么也不会,真是个～! You are good for nothing, you idiot! /你这个～! You bloody fool!
蠢蠢 chǔnchǔn 〈书面〉❶ the way an insect or worm moves:一条毛虫～而动。A caterpillar is wriggling. ❷ turbulent; restless; in a turmoil:征战不已,天下～。Torn asunder by warfare, the land is in a turmoil.
蠢蠢欲动 chǔnchǔn-yùdòng ready to start wriggling; ready to make trouble; be restless and about to create disturbances:据点里的敌人又～。The enemy in the stronghold seemed ready to start something again.
蠢动 chǔndòng ❶ wriggle; squirm:惊蛰一过,百虫～。After the third solar term all worms and insects begin to turn about and move. ❷ create disturbances; carry on disruptive activities; stir up trouble:警察擒获了几名正在～的歹徒。The police arrested several evildoers red-handed.
蠢话 chǔnhuà stupid remark; foolish words
蠢货 chǔnhuò 〈粗话〉blockhead; dunce; idiot
蠢驴 chǔnlǘ 〈粗话〉idiot; silly ass
蠢然 chǔnrán ❶ in a wriggling manner:～思动 be wriggling for motion; be making a stupid effort to create disturbances ❷ idiotic:～的笑脸 idiotic smile
蠢人 chǔnrén fool; blockhead:～办蠢事。It's a case of a fool acting foolishly.
蠢事 chǔnshì stupid thing:我们再也不干那种亲者痛、仇者快的～了。We must by all means refrain from such stupidities as would only grieve our friends and gladden our enemies.
蠢俗 chǔnsú stupid and vulgar:～不堪 unbearably stupid and vulgar
蠢头蠢脑 chǔntóu-chǔnnǎo looking like an idiot; stupid-looking
蠢猪 chǔnzhū 〈粗话〉idiot; stupid swine; ass
蠢拙 chǔnzhuō stupid and clumsy:～的伎俩 stupid and clumsy tricks

chuō

逴 chuō 〈书面〉❶ distant; far ❷ transcend; surpass

踔 chuō 〈书面〉❶ leap; bound ❷ transcend; surmount

踔厉 chuōlì 〈书面〉in high spirits; full of élan:～风发 full of enthusiasm; full of vim and vigour

戳 chuō ❶ jab; poke; stab:向他头上～了一指头 poke him in the head with a finger /小心毛衣针～了我眼睛。Be careful not to jab my eyes with your knitting needle. ❷〈方言〉get sprained; blunted:手腕子～了 sprain one's wrist /钢笔尖儿～了。The nib is blunted. ❸〈方言〉stand sth. on end; stand erect:把粮食口袋～起来。Stand the bag of grain on end. /有话进来说,别在门口～着。Come on in, if you want to speak. Don't stand at the door. ❹ stamp; seal:邮～ postmark /盖～ stamp (sth.)

戳壁脚 chuō bìjiǎo 〈方言〉speak ill of sb.:背后～ gossip behind sb.'s back
戳不住 chuōbuzhù unable to stand the test
戳穿 chuōchuān ❶ pierce; puncture:这小孩用棍儿把气球～了。The child pierced his balloon with a stick. ❷ lay bare; expose; explode:～阴谋 lay bare a plot /～鬼花招 expose a dirty trick /～西洋景 strip off the camouflage; give away the show
戳搭 chuōda knock the end of sth. (in the form of a strip) against an object:他掏出一支烟,在烟盒上～着。He took out a cigarette and tapped it against the case.
戳得住 chuōdezhù be firm and able to stand the test:要在危难面前～。It is necessary to stand your ground in face of great difficulty (*or* danger).
戳份儿 chuōfènr 〈方言〉show off; flaunt one's superiority:你算老几,敢在这儿～! Who are you to flaunt your seniority here?
戳个儿 chuōger 〈方言〉figure; stature:她那～跟她姐姐差不多。Her figure is much the same as her sister's. *or* She very much resembles her sister in stature.
戳咕 chuōgu 〈方言〉egg sb. on from behind the scenes; instigate:这事都是他～的。He was the one that pulled the strings.
戳祸 chuōhuò get into serious trouble:咱们差点儿戳了祸。We were nearly in for dreadful trouble.
戳脊梁骨 chuō jǐlianggǔ criticize sb. behind his back:办事要公正,别让人家～。You must be fair and reasonable in handling matters so that no one could criticize you behind your back.
戳记 chuōjì stamp; seal:这是我厂的独家产品,凡未盖我厂～者均系假货。This product is exclusively from our factory and is marked with our seal. All others are fakes.
戳破 chuōpò puncture; expose; unmask
戳儿 chuōr *also*"戳子"〈口语〉stamp; seal:刻一个～ engrave a seal /用邮～盖销邮票 cancel a stamp with a postmark /没盖上～的收据 receipt without a stamp on it
戳伤 chuōshāng stab wound
戳子 chuōzi 〈口语〉stamp; seal:盖～ affix one's seal

chuò

龊 chuò *see*"龌龊" wòchuò

娖 chuò 〈书面〉❶ prudent; cautious ❷ regroup (troops, etc.); reorganize

辵 chuò 〈书面〉keep stopping and starting again

惙 chuò 〈书面〉❶ anxiety; worry ❷ fatigue ❸ feeble; weak (breath):气息～然 breathe feebly

歠 chuò 〈书面〉❶ suck; drink ❷ liquid food; soup; porridge

辍 chuò stop; cease:时作时～ work by fits and starts /工作日夜不～ work day and night (*or* round the clock) /岂能中～? How can we stop halfway?

辍笔 chuòbǐ stop in the middle of writing or painting
辍学 chuòxué discontinue one's studies; leave off school:因病～ drop out from school because of illness
辍演 chuòyǎn suspend or discontinue a performance

辍止 chuòzhǐ cease; stop; discontinue: 母亲渐渐～哭声。Gradually, mother ceased sobbing.

啜 chuò 〈书面〉❶ sip; suck: ～茗 sip tea /～粥 have porridge /～菽饮水 live on coarse grain and drink plain water — live a simple life ❷ sob

啜泣 chuòqì sob: 低声～ subdue one's sobbing /～着睡着了 sob oneself to sleep /她边～边诉说自己的不幸。She sobbed out her grievances. /孩子的～声渐渐消逝。The child's sobs gradually died down.

婼 chuò 〈书面〉with difficulty

婥 chuò

婥约 chuòyuē also "绰约" chuòyuē 〈书面〉(of a girl) graceful

绰 chuò 〈书面〉ample; spacious: 宽～的房间 spacious room

see also chāo

绰绰有余 chuòchuò-yǒuyú enough and to spare; more than sufficient; more than enough: 这些钱买一台洗衣机～。The money is more than enough for a washing-machine.

绰号 chuòhào nickname: 那个男孩的～叫胖子。That boy's nickname is Fatty. /人们给他起了一个～叫机灵鬼儿。People nicknamed him Smartie.

绰有余裕 chuòyǒuyúyù ❶ enough and to spare; have more than needed; abundant: 这些钱做路费～。The money more than covers the fare. /他收入供养一家老小，～。His income is more than sufficient to support the whole family. ❷ composed; calm and collected: 他处理任何难局，都是～、恢宏大度。When he came upon any difficulty, he would always handle it with composure and magnanimity.

绰约 chuòyuē 〈书面〉(of a girl) graceful

绰约多姿 chuòyuē-duōzī graceful and lovely

cī

粢 cī

粢饭 cīfàn 〈方言〉steamed rice made from glutinous and round rice

see also zī

差 cī ❶〈书面〉grade; class; grading ❷ see "参差" cēncī

see also chā; chà; chāi; chài

差等 cīděng 〈书面〉grade; class

see also chàděng

刺 cī 〈象声〉: ～～地直冒火星 keep spattering sparks /～的一声，他滑倒了。Wham! He slipped and fell.

see also cì

刺打 cīda also "呲打" cīda 〈方言〉scold; haul over the coals

刺啦 cīlā 〈象声〉splitting sound: ～一声，我的上衣撕了个口子。With a splitting sound, something tore a hole in my jacket.

刺棱 cīlēng 〈象声〉sound of quick movement: 猫～一下跑了。Whew! The cat scampered away.

刺溜 cīliū 〈象声〉sound of slipping or sliding: 那子弹～一声从他身边擦过去。The bullet whistled past his ears. /自行车～一下从身边驶过。A bike whooshed past. /～一下，他栽倒在冰冻的路上。He slipped on the icy road with a thump.

疵 cī flaw; defect; blemish; fault: 瑕～ flaw; blemish /～毛 defective wool /吹毛求～ fault finding; nitpicking

疵病 cībìng defect; shortcoming; flaw

疵点 cīdiǎn flaw; blemish; defect

疵品 cīpǐn defective product; substandard product

疵瑕 cīxiá flaw; blemish

呲 cī give a talking-to, a tongue-lashing or dressing-down; scold: 他一～上人就没完没了。Once he gives somebody a lecture, he goes on and on. /他妈妈狠～了他一顿。He was severely scolded by his mother.

跐 cī slip; slide: 我登～了，差点摔下来。I missed my footing and nearly fell off.

see also cǐ

跐溜 cīliū ❶ slip; trip: 他～一滑，摔了个脸朝天。He slipped and fell on his back. ❷ very quick; swift: 小猫～就逃出了屋子。The kitten all of a sudden scampered out of the room.

骴 cī 〈书面〉skeleton retaining some of flesh

cí

茨 cí ❶ thatch (a roof) ❷〈植物〉puncture vine

茨冈人 Cígāngrén (Russian name for 吉普赛人) Gypsy

茨菰 cígu also "慈姑" cígu 〈植物〉arrowhead

茨莨 cíliáng 〈植物〉dye yam (*Dioscorea cirrhosa*)

茨藻 cízǎo 〈植物〉*Najas marina*

薋 cí 〈书面〉heap of weeds and grass

瓷(甆) cí porcelain; china: 细～ fine china /青花～ blue and white porcelain /青～ celadon /洋～〈口语〉enamel

瓷雕 cídiāo also "瓷刻"〈工美〉porcelain carving

瓷饭碗 cífànwǎn (in contrast with 铁饭碗) porcelain ricebowl — insecure position or job

瓷公鸡 cígōngjī china cock; skinflint; miser: 这个人是个～，一毛不拔。He is a miser who would not part with a farthing.

瓷婚 cíhūn china wedding; 20th wedding anniversary

瓷瓶 cípíng ❶ porcelain vase; porcelain bottle ❷ (popular term for 绝缘子)〈电工〉insulator

瓷漆 cíqī enamel paint; enamel

瓷器 cíqì porcelain; chinaware: 薄胎～ eggshell china

瓷实 císhi 〈方言〉solid; firm; substantial: 地上的雪冻得很～。The snow on the ground is frozen solid. /他睡得多～！How soundly he is sleeping! /他腿上的肌肉很～。He has got strong legs.

瓷头 cítóu 〈方言〉stupid; foolish: ～老公 foolish husband

瓷土 cítǔ porcelain clay; china clay

瓷碗 cíwǎn china bowl; porcelain bowl

瓷窑 cíyáo porcelain kiln

瓷釉 cíyòu porcelain glaze

瓷砖 cízhuān ceramic tile; glazed tile

兹 cí see "龟兹" Qiūcí

see also zī

糍 cí

糍粑 cíbā cooked glutinous rice pounded into paste; glutinous rice cake

慈 cí ❶ kind; loving: 心～手软 kindhearted and merciful ❷〈书面〉(usu. of a senior person) love; affection; kindness: 敬老～幼 respect the old and care for the young ❸ mother: 家～ my mother /～亲 mother ❹ (Cí) a surname

慈蔼 cí'ǎi affectionate; kind: ～的笑容 kindly smile

慈爱 cí'ài love; affection; kindness: 老师的声音里充满了～。The teacher spoke in an affectionate tone.

慈悲 cíbēi mercy; benevolence; pity: ～心肠 merciful heart /大发～ show great compassion (for sb.) /佛门弟子～为怀。The Buddhists always have mercy at heart.

慈姑 cígu 〈植物〉also "茨菰" cígu arrowhead

慈航 cíháng 〈佛教〉journey of salvation

慈和 cíhé kind and gentle: 老人待人～。The old man always behaves with gentle courtesy.

慈惠 cíhuì ❶ affectionate; kindly: 老太太脸上露出～的微笑。A kindly smile appeared on the old lady's face. ❷ benevolent; kind

慈江道 Cíjiāngdào Chagang-do, prefecture in DPRK bordering China

慈怜 cílián kind and sympathetic: ～的眼神 kind eyes

慈眉善目 címéi-shànmù wearing a kindly look; kind-faced: 走出来一位～的老人。Out came a kind-faced elderly gentleman.

C

慈命 címìng mother's wish or instruction
慈母 címǔ loving mother; tender mother; mother:～手中线,游子身上衣。The sewing at the mother's hands has become the coat on the wandering son's back. /他～般地关心我们。He cared for us like a loving mother.
慈亲 cíqīn kind parents, especially kind mother
慈善 císhàn charitable; benevolent; philanthropic:～心肠 tender heart /～行为 act of benevolence; charity
慈善机关 císhàn jīguān charitable institution or organization; philanthropic institution
慈善家 císhànjiā philanthropist
慈善事业 císhàn shìyè charities
慈善学校 císhàn xuéxiào charity school
慈石 císhí *also* "磁石" císhí 〈书面〉magnet
慈禧 Cíxǐ Empress Dowager Cixi (1835-1908)
慈祥 cíxiáng kindly:～可亲 be kindly and affable /～的笑容 benign smile /他～地抚摸着孩子的头。He fondly stroked the child's head.
慈心 cíxīn ❶ benevolent heart:大发～ actuated by extraordinary benevolence ❷ kind-hearted:～的邻居 kind-hearted neighbour
慈颜 cíyán benevolent face (of a parent or anybody of parent's generation)
慈竹 cízhú 〈植物〉*Sinocalamus affinis*

磁[1] cí magnetism:电～ electromagnetism /防～ antimagnetic

磁[2] cí porcelain; china

磁安 cí'ān 〈电学〉abampere, equal to 10 ampere
磁板存储器 cíbǎn cúnchǔqì magnetic-plate storage
磁棒 cíbàng bar magnet:圆型～ round bar magnet /扁型～ flat bar magnet
磁饱和 cíbǎohé magnetic saturation
磁暴 cíbào 〈物理〉magnetic storm:～效应 magnetic storm effect
磁北 cíběi magnetic north:～记录器 magnetograph
磁测 cícè 〈物理〉magnetic survey
磁层 cícéng 〈天文〉magnetosphere
磁场 cíchǎng 〈物理〉magnetic field
磁场强度 cíchǎng qiángdù magnetic field intensity or strength:～矢量 magnetic intensity vector /～计 oersted meter
磁赤道 cíchìdào 〈物理〉magnetic equator (an imaginary line on the earth's surface near the equator, where a magnetic needle has no dip)
磁畴 cíchóu 〈物理〉magnetic domain
磁存储器 cícúnchǔqì 〈计算机〉magnetic memory
磁带 cídài (magnetic) tape:～录音 tape recording /录像～ video tape
磁带盒 cídàihé cassette; cartridge
磁带库 cídàikù tap library
磁带录音机 cídài lùyīnjī tape recorder
磁带录像机 cídài lùxiàngjī VTR (video tape recorder)
磁带驱动器 cídài qūdòngqì 〈信息〉tape drive
磁带失真度 cídài shīzhēndù tap distortion
磁带涂层 cídài túcéng tape coating
磁带文件 cídài wénjiàn magnetic tape file
磁导率 cídǎolǜ *also* "磁导系数"; "导磁率" 〈物理〉magnetoconductivity; magnetic conductivity; magnetic permitivity; permeability
磁等离子体 cíděnglízǐtǐ 〈物理〉magnetoplasma:～发电机 magnetoplasma dynamic generator
磁电机 cídiànjī 〈电工〉magnetor
磁电学 cídiànxué 〈物理〉magnetoelectricity
磁碟 cídié magnetic disk; floppy disk; disk
磁方位 cífāngwèi magnetic bearing:～角 magnetic azimuth
磁放大器 cífàngdàqì 〈无线电〉magnetrol
磁粉 cífěn magnetic particle or powder:～探伤 magnetic-particle inspection
磁感应 cígǎnyìng 〈物理〉magnetic induction:～强度 magnetic induction intensity
磁钢 cígāng magnet steel
磁共振 cígòngzhèn 〈物理〉magnetic resonance:～加速器 magnetic resonance accelerator
磁鼓 cígǔ 〈计算机〉drum:～记录 drum memory /～存储计算机 drum computer /～式信息收发器 drum information assembler and dispatcher /～信息转储 drum dump
磁光激光器 cíguāng jīguāngqì magneto-optical laser
磁光学 cíguāngxué 〈物理〉magneto-optics
磁合金 cíhéjīn magnet alloy
磁化 cíhuà 〈物理〉magnetization:～功率 magnetizing power /～半导体 magnetic semi-conductor
磁化率 cíhuàlǜ magnetic susceptibility
磁化器 cíhuàqì magnetizer
磁化水 cíhuàshuǐ magnetized water
磁化学 cíhuàxué 〈化学〉magnetochemistry
磁极 cíjí 〈物理〉magnetic pole:～强度 magnetic pole intensity (*or* strength)
磁检波器 cíjiǎnbōqì magnetodetector
磁镜 cíjìng 〈物理〉magnetic mirror
磁卡 cíkǎ magnetic card:～电话 magnetic card phone; card telephone
磁开关 cíkāiguān 〈电工〉magnetic switch
磁空气动力学 cíkōngqì dònglìxué magneto-aerodynamics
磁控管 cíkòngguǎn 〈电工〉magnetron
磁力 cílì 〈物理〉magnetic force:～测定 magnetometry /～勘探 magnetic prospecting /～选矿 magnetic dressing
磁力除尘 cílì chúchén magnetic dust removal:～器 magnetic dust collector
磁力探矿仪 cílì tànkuàngyí magnetic detector (for ore deposits)
磁力探伤器 cílì tànshāngqì magnetic flaw detector
磁力线 cílìxiàn magnetic line of force
磁力学 cílìxué 〈物理〉magnetomechanics
磁力仪 cílìyí magnetometer
磁疗 cíliáo magnetotherapy
磁流体 cíliútǐ 〈物理〉magnetic fluid:～力学 magnetofluiddynamics /～发电 magnetohydrodynamic generation
磁流体动力学 cíliútǐ dònglìxué magnetohydrodynamics (MHD); hydromagnetics
磁流体力学 cíliútǐ lìxué magnetofluidmechanics
磁漏 cílòu 〈物理〉magnetic-flux-leakage; magnetic leakage
磁路 cílù 〈物理〉magnetic circuit
磁能 cínéng 〈物理〉magnetic energy
磁盘 cípán 〈计算机〉magnetic disk:～存储器〈计算机〉magnetic disk store
磁盘操作系统 cípán cāozuò xìtǒng 〈信息〉disk operating system (DOS)
磁盘驱动器 cípán qūdòngqì 〈计算机〉disk drive
磁偏角 cípiānjiǎo 〈物理〉magnetic declination
磁偏转 cípiānzhuǎn 〈电子〉magnetic deflection; magnetic deviation
磁屏蔽 cípíngbì 〈物理〉magnetic shielding
磁漆 cíqī 〈化工〉lacquer enamel
磁强计 cíqiángjì magnetometer
磁强记录图 cíqiáng jìlùtú magnetogram
磁倾角 cíqīngjiǎo 〈物理〉magnetic dip inclination
磁热效应 círèxiàoyìng magnetothermal effect
磁石 císhí ❶〈矿业〉magnetite ❷〈电工〉magnet:～发电机 magneto /～录音机 magnetophone /～检波器 magnetodetector
磁体 cítǐ 〈物理〉magnet
磁铁 cítiě *also* "磁石"; "吸铁石" xītiěshí 〈物理〉magnet:电～ electromagnet /永久～ permanent magnet /条形～ bar magnet /马蹄形～ horseshoe magnet
磁铁矿 cítiěkuàng magnetite
磁通量 cítōngliàng 〈物理〉magnetic flux
磁头 cítóu 〈物理〉magnetic head
磁向 cíxiàng magnetic heading
磁效应 cíxiàoyìng magnetic effect:电流～ magnetic effect of electric current
磁心 cíxīn 〈计算机〉(magnetic) core:～储存器 (magnetic) core memory
磁性 cíxìng 〈物理〉magnetism; magnetic:顺～ paramagnetism /抗～ diamagnetism /铁～ ferromagnetism /～水雷 magnetic mine /～炸弹 magnetic bomb /～瓷 magnetic porcelain
磁性开关 cíxìng kāiguān magnetic switch
磁性全息照相 cíxìng quánxī zhàoxiàng magneto hologram

磁悬法 cíxuánfǎ magnetic suspension
磁悬浮 cíxuánfú magnetically levitated: ～列车 magnetically levitated train; magnetic suspension train
磁选 cíxuǎn 〈矿业〉magnetic separation: 湿法～ wet magnetic separation /～厂 magnetic ore dressing plant
磁学 cíxué magnetics
磁异常 cíyìcháng magnetic anomaly
磁针 cízhēn magnetic needle
磁振子 cízhènzǐ magnon
磁州窑 Cízhōuyáo Cizhou kiln (in today's Hebei Province, producing black and white porcelain in the Song Dynasty)
磁轴 cízhóu also "磁轴线" magnetic axis
磁砖 cízhuān 〈建筑〉ceramic tile
磁子 cízǐ 〈物理〉magneton
磁阻 cízǔ 〈物理〉magnetoresistance

鹚(鷀) cí see "鸬鹚" lúcí

雌 cí female: ～兔 female rabbit /～鹿 female deer
雌儿 cí'ér 〈旧语〉〈贬义〉female
雌蜂 cífēng female bee; queen bee or worker bee
雌伏 cífú 〈书面〉❶ be placed in a position unworthy of one's ability; come under sb.'s control: 大丈夫当雄飞,安能～! A real man must aim high and should never be content with his lowly position. ❷ lie low: 在此国难当头之时,你我岂能～草野! When our nation is in crisis, how can we remain on the sidelines, doing nothing?
雌花 cíhuā female flower; pistillate flower
雌黄 cíhuáng ❶〈矿业〉orpiment ❷ tamper with (a text); argue falsely over (an issue): 信口～ make irresponsible remarks
雌激素 cíjīsù 〈生物〉estrin; estrogen: ～过多 hyperestrogenism
雌老虎 cílǎohǔ tigress — shrew; virago; termagant
雌麻 címá 〈植物〉pistillate hemp
雌配子 cípèizǐ 〈生物〉oogamete; megagamete
雌蕊 círuǐ 〈植物〉pistil
雌酮 cítóng 〈生物〉oestrone; estrone
雌性 cíxìng female
雌雄 cí-xióng ❶ male and female ❷ victory and defeat: 他们两人要一决～。The two of them are determined to fight it out.
雌雄单性生殖 cí-xióng dānxìng shēngzhí 〈生物〉amphitoky
雌雄同体 cí-xióng tóngtǐ 〈动物〉hermaphrodite; monoecism
雌雄同株 cí-xióng tóngzhū 〈植物〉hermaphrodite
雌雄异体 cí-xióng yìtǐ 〈动物〉gonochorism; dioecism
雌雄异型遗传 cí-xióng yìxíng yíchuán 〈生物〉anisogeny
雌雄异株 cí-xióng yìzhū 〈植物〉dioecious plant

辞[1](辭、辤) cí ❶ diction; phraseology: 措～ wording; diction /修～ rhetoric ❷ genre of classical Chinese literature: see "～赋" ❸ form of classical Chinese poetry: 《木兰～》*The Ballad of Mulan*

辞[2](辭、辤) cí ❶ take leave: 告～ take one's leave; say good-bye /不～而别 leave without saying goodbye /～世 pass away ❷ resign; hand in one's resignation: ～官 resign one's government post /～去兼职 resign one's concurrent job ❸ dismiss; discharge: 他被店主～了。He was dismissed by the shopkeeper. ❹ shirk; evade; dodge; decline: 坚～不受 firmly decline /万死不～ willing to risk one's life (for a cause); ready to lay down one's life (for sb.)
辞别 cíbié bid farewell; take one's leave; say good-bye: ～家乡 leave one's hometown /～亲人 bid farewell to one's relatives /～好友 take leave of one's close friends
辞呈 cíchéng resignation; letter of resignation: 递交～ hand in (*or* submit) one's resignation /他的～已被批准。His resignation is accepted.
辞典 cídiǎn dictionary; lexicon
辞费 cífèi wordy; verbose: 文字要简练,不可～。Conciseness is preferred to verbosity.
辞赋 cífù also "词赋" cífù genre of classical Chinese poetry (as represented by *The Poetry of Chu* 《楚辞》); special form of rhapsodic poem, chiefly in parallel constructions; descriptive poetic prose
辞格 cígé figure of speech
辞工 cígōng ❶ (of an employer) dismiss a worker: 东家辞了他的工。The shopowner discharged him. ❷ (of a worker) ask for a discharge; resign: 他～回家了。He resigned and went back home.
辞活 cíhuó see "辞工"
辞旧迎新 cíjiù-yíngxīn bid farewell to the old and usher in the new; ring out the old year and ring in the new
辞诀 cíjué also "辞决" 〈书面〉bid farewell; part: ～而行 bid farewell and depart
辞灵 cílíng bow to a coffin before it is interred
辞令 cílìng also "词令" cílìng language appropriate to the occasion: 娴于～ gifted with a silver tongue /不擅～ not good at speech /外交～ diplomatic language
辞年 cínián see the old year out
辞聘 cípìn decline a job offer; refuse to accept an appointment
辞却 cíquè decline: 婉言～ decline politely
辞让 círàng politely decline: 老先生再三～,不肯到主席台就坐。The old gentleman repeatedly decline to take a seat on the rostrum.
辞色 císè 〈书面〉one's speech and facial expression: 假以～ look at sb. encouragingly /他这个人喜怒形于～。You can easily detect from his speech and countenance whether he is pleased or displeased. *or* He never cares to hide his joy or anger.
辞世 císhì pass away; die
辞书 císhū dictionary and other reference books: 充分利用～ make full use of reference books
辞讼 císòng also "词讼" císòng legal case; legal action
辞岁 císuì bid farewell to the outgoing year; celebrate the lunar New Year's Eve: ～迎新 see the old year out and the new year in; see off the old year and usher in the new; ring out the old year and ring in the new
辞退 cítuì ❶ dismiss; discharge: ～几名职工 lay off several employees ❷ decline: ～礼物 decline a gift
辞歇 cíxiē 〈方言〉dismiss; discharge
辞谢 cíxiè politely decline; decline with thanks: 送来的礼物,他一概～。He politely declined to accept any gift.
辞行 cíxíng say good-bye (to one's friends) before setting out on a journey: 不及～ have no time for farewell calls
辞严义正 cíyán-yìzhèng also "义正辞严" speak sternly from a sense of justice
辞藻 cízǎo diction; rhetoric: 浮华的～ grandiloquent language; pure rhetoric /～华丽 flowery language; ornate diction /玩弄～ juggle with words
辞灶 cízào bid farewell to the kitchen God who is going back to heaven (on the 23rd or 24th day of the twelfth month of the lunar year, as one of the rites held in preparation for lunar New Year celebrations)
辞章 cízhāng also "词章" cízhāng ❶ poetry and prose: 酷爱～ be passionately fond of prose and poetry ❷ art of writing: 讲究～ be particular about one's writing
辞职 cízhí resign; hand in one's resignation: ～书 letter of resignation /申请～ hand in one's resignation; ask to be relieved of one's duties
辞旨 cízhǐ 〈书面〉language and intent: ～甚切 earnest in language and intent
辞致 cízhì also "词致" cízhì 〈书面〉appeal or charm of one's diction: ～高雅 refined language
辞宗 cízōng also "词宗" cízōng one who is respected for his literary achievement: 一代～ literary master of a period

词 cí ❶ wording; words; language: 歌～ words of a song /演讲～ speech /祝酒～ toast /用～准确 use words accurately; be accurate in the choice of words ❷ *ci*, poetry written to certain tunes with strict tonal patterns and rhyme schemes and in fixed numbers of lines and words, originating in the Tang Dynasty and fully developed in the Song Dynasty: 填～ compose a *ci* poem ❸ word; character: 名～ noun /同音～ homonym; homophone /创造新～ coin words /这五个～构成一个句子。The sentence consists of five words.
词不达意 cíbùdáyì the words fail to convey the idea; the language does not express the meaning
词臣 cíchén official in charge of imperial edicts and mandates, etc.
词典 cídiǎn also "辞典" cídiǎn dictionary; lexicon: 《现代汉语～》

A Dictionary of Modern Chinese Language /古汉语～ lexicon of classical Chinese /发音～ pronouncing dictionary /综合～ comprehensive dictionary /分类插图～ classified and illustrated dictionary /双语～ bilingual dictionary /成语～ dictionary of idioms /活～ walking dictionary /查～ consult a dictionary; look up a word in a dictionary

词典学 cídiǎnxué lexicography:～家 lexicographer

词调 cídiào tonal patterns and rhyme schemes of *ci* poetry

词法 cífǎ 〈语言〉morphology

词锋 cífēng eloquent or forceful writing:～犀利 incisive in writing

词赋 cífù *see* "辞赋" cífù

词干 cígàn 〈语言〉stem

词根 cígēn 〈语言〉root; radical

词根语 cígēnyǔ *also* "孤立语" gūlìyǔ 〈语言〉radical language

词华 cíhuá ornate diction in poetry and prose

词话 cíhuà ❶ notes and commentaries on *ci* poetry ❷ storytelling interspersed with songs and ballads, originating in the Song Dynasty ❸ novel with parts in verse, popular during the Ming Dynasty

词汇 cíhuì 〈语言〉vocabulary; words and phrases:～丰富 abundant vocabulary; rich in vocabulary /～贫乏 meagre vocabulary; poor in vocabulary /基本～ basic vocabulary; basic word-stock /一般～ common words /科技～ technical terms

词汇表 cíhuìbiǎo word list; glossary; vocabulary

词汇学 cíhuìxué lexicology

词句 cíjù 〈语言〉words and phrases; expressions:推敲～ weigh one's words /～畅达。The language is fluent. /要注意～的准确性。It is important to use the right words and expressions.

词库 cíkù lexicon; dictionary

词类 cílèi 〈语言〉parts of speech

词令 cílìng *also* "辞令" cílìng language appropriate to the occasion

词律 cílǜ prosody of *ci* poetry

词牌 cípái ❶ names of tunes to which *ci* poems are composed ❷ names of songs to be a sung at dinner

词谱 cípǔ collection of tunes of *ci* poems

词曲 cíqǔ ❶ general term for *ci* (词) and *qu* (曲) ❷ words and music (of a song):这首歌的～都是他写的。He composed both the words and the music of the song.

词人 círén writer of *ci* poetry; *ci* writer

词讼 císòng *also* "辞讼" císòng legal case; legal action:包揽～ (of a shyster lawyer, etc.) monopolize all legal actions (for profit) /认真处理每一件～ be serious in handling every legal case

词素 císù 〈语言〉morpheme:～在语言学中指最小的意义单位。A morpheme is the smallest unit of meaning in linguistic studies.

词坛 cítán circles of *ci* writers:～故事 anecdotes of *ci* writers

词条 cítiáo entry (in a dictionary):本词典收进了十万多～。This dictionary consists of over 100,000 entries.

词头 cítóu 〈语言〉prefix

词尾 cíwěi 〈语言〉suffix

词形 cíxíng 〈语言〉morphology:～变化 morphological changes; inflections

词性 cíxìng 〈语言〉syntactical functions and morphological features that help determine a part of speech

词序 cíxù 〈语言〉word order:复合句中的～ word order in compound sentences

词严义正 cíyán-yìzhèng *also* "辞严义正" cíyán-yìzhèng speak sternly from a sense of justice

词义 cíyì 〈语言〉meaning or sense of a word

词余 cíyú alternative term for *qu* (曲)

词语 cíyǔ words and expressions; terms:生僻～ rarely used terms; rare words /废弃的～ obsolete words /这篇文章的～丰富。The essay is rich in expressions.

词源 cíyuán 〈语言〉origin of a word; etymology:～学 etymology

词韵 cíyùn ❶ rhymes of *ci* poetry ❷ rhyming dictionary (of *ci* poetry)

see also "词❷"

词藻 cízǎo flowery language; rhetoric; ornate diction

词章 cízhāng *also* "辞章" cízhāng poetry and prose; art of writing

词致 cízhì *also* "辞致" cízhì appeal or charm of one's diction

词缀 cízhuì 〈语言〉affix

词宗 cízōng *also* "辞宗" cízōng one respected for his literary achievement

词组 cízǔ 〈语言〉word group; phrase

祠 cí ancestral temple; memorial temple:宗～ clan hall /生～ memorial temple to a living person /烈士～ memorial temple to martyrs

祠庙 címiào *also* "祠宇" ancestral temple; memorial temple

祠墓 címù ancestral temple and tomb

祠堂 cítáng ❶ ancestral hall; ancestral temple ❷ memorial hall:成都有诸葛亮的～。There is a memorial hall to Zhuge Liang in Chengdu.

cǐ

此 cǐ ❶ this:～次 this time /～人 this person /～种 this kind /顾～失彼 attend to one thing to the neglect of the other ❷ now; then; here:从～ from then on; from now on /由～往西 go west from here /故事就～结束。The story ends here.

此岸 cǐ'àn 〈宗教〉this shore; temporality

此岸性 cǐ'ànxìng 〈哲学〉this-sideness:知识的～ this-sidedness of knowledge

此辈 cǐbèi people of this type or ilk; such people:～都不是好人。These are by no means honest people.

此地 cǐdì this place; here:～盛产水果。This place abounds in fruits.

此地无银三百两 cǐdì wú yín sānbǎi liǎng the 300 taels of silver is not buried here (the sign put up by the man in the folk tale over the place where he had hidden the money) — a guilty person gives himself away by conspicuously protesting his innocence; protest one's innocence too much:他的解释是～。His explanation gave himself away.

此伏彼起 cǐfú-bǐqǐ *see* "此起彼伏"

此后 cǐhòu after this; hereafter; henceforth:五年前他到过我家,～我再也未曾见到过他。He dropped in five years ago. I have never seen him since then.

此呼彼应 cǐhū-bǐyìng as one calls, another echoes:口号声如海涛回旋,～。Shouts of slogans followed one after another like roaring waves.

此际 cǐjì 〈书面〉this moment

此间 cǐjiān around here; here:～消息灵通人士 well-informed sources here /～天气渐暖。It's getting warm around here.

此举 cǐjǔ this action; this step; this measure:人们对他的～甚感突然。People were surprised at this action of his.

此刻 cǐkè this moment; now; at present:此时～她正在想什么呢? What is she thinking of at the very moment? /～就动身,你还能赶上火车。Start off right now, and you won't miss the train.

此路不通 cǐlù-bùtōng dead end; blind alley:～! Not a Through Road. *or* No Thoroughfare! /～,另想他法。It's a blind alley, and you have to go another way. *or* This method doesn't work; you'll have to find another way.

此起彼伏 cǐqǐ-bǐfú *also* "此伏彼起" as one falls, another rises; rise one after another; rise here and subside there:歌声～ undulating sound of singing

此前 cǐqián before:～我对这事一无所知。I did not know anything about it before.

此山望着那山高 cǐ shān wàngzhe nà shān gāo 〈俗语〉the mountain beyond this one always seems higher; the grass is always greener on the other side of the hill or fence

此生 cǐshēng this life

此时 cǐshí this moment; right now:～此地 here and now /～此刻 at this very moment /～无声胜有声。At this moment silence is better than speech. /～不走,更待何时? Go while the going is good.

此外 cǐwài besides; in addition; moreover:他喜欢下棋,～再没有其他爱好。Apart from playing chess, he has no other hobbies. /他会说北京话和上海话,～还懂点广州话。Besides speaking Beijing and Shanghai dialects, he understands a little Cantonese.

此一时,彼一时 cǐ yīshí, bǐ yīshí this is one situation and that was another; circumstances have changed with the passage of time; things are now different from what they were; times have changed:～,过去短发时兴,现在长发时髦。Things are now different from what

they were. Long hair is in fashion while bobbed hair is out.
此致 cǐzhì (often used at the end of a letter) here I wish to convey:～敬礼 my best regards
此中 cǐzhōng in this; herein:～奥妙外人不得而知。The secret behind all this is not known to outsiders.
泚 cǐ 〈书面〉❶ bright; limpid ❷ perspire; sweat ❸ dip one's brush in ink:～笔作画 dip one's brush in ink and start to paint
跐 cǐ ❶ step on:～着门槛儿 step on the threshold／脚～两只船 straddle two boats; have a foot in both camps; sit on the fence ❷ walk on tiptoe:～着脚往里瞧 stand on tiptoe and look in
see also cī
鮆 cǐ a kind of marine fish living in coastal waters

cì

次 cì ❶ order; sequence:名～ position in a name list; place in a competition／车～ train number／班～ order of classes at school; number of runs／席～ seating arrangement／顺～入内 enter in due order; come in one at a time ❷ second; next:～女 second daughter／主～ primary and secondary; priorities ❸ shoddy; second-rate; inferior:～布 shoddy cloth／这种照相机很～。This kind of camera is of poor quality.／她的书法并不～于他。Her handwriting is not inferior to his. ❹〈化学〉hypo-:～氯酸 hypochlorous ❺〈量词〉time; occasion:四～ four times／首～ first; first time／无数～胜利 countless victories／十三～列车 No. 13 train／举行几～会议 hold several meetings／一～～地解释 explain time and again ❻〈书面〉stopping place on a journey; stopover:舟～ during a voyage／旅～ at a stopover; at a hotel ❼〈书面〉middle:言～ during one's talk; in between one's words ❽ (Cì) a surname
次表面层 cìbiǎomiàncéng 〈地质〉subcrust
次波 cìbō 〈物理〉secondary wave
次存储器 cìcúnchǔqì 〈计算机〉secondary storage
次大陆 cìdàlù subcontinent:南亚～ South Asia subcontinent
次等 cìděng second class; second-rate; inferior:～品 inferior product／～货 shoddy goods (*or* stuff)
次第 cìdì ❶ order; sequence:按年代～排列历史事件 place the historical events in chronological sequence／优胜者按得分多少排～。The winners are listed in order of their scores. ❷ one after another:～入场 enter one after another
次货 cìhuò inferior goods; substandard goods; shoddy stuff
次级 cìjí secondary:～规则 secondary rules／～义务 secondary obligation
次级产品 cìjí chǎnpǐn secondary product
次级线圈 cìjí xiànquān 〈电工〉secondary coil
次经 cìjīng 〈宗教〉deuterocanonical book
次口径火箭弹 cìkǒujìng huǒjiàndàn 〈军事〉subcalibre rocket
次磷酸 cìlínsuān 〈化学〉hypophosphorous acid:～钾 potassium hypophosphite／～钠 sodium hypophosphite
次硫酸 cìliúsuān 〈化学〉sulphoxylic acid:～盐 sulphoxylate
次氯酸 cìlǜsuān 〈化学〉hypochlorous acid:～钙 calcium hypochlorite／～钠 sodium hypochlorite
次女高音 cìnǚgāoyīn mezzo-soprano
次贫 cìpín relatively poor
次品 cìpǐn substandard product; defective goods:提高质量,减少～ raise quality to reduce the number of substandard products
次轻量级 cìqīngliàngjí 〈体育〉featherweight
次日 cìrì next day:他们～起程。They set out the next day.
次生 cìshēng secondary:～休眠 secondary dormancy／～扩大 secondary enlargement／～生长 secondary growth／～射线 secondary ray／～周皮 secondary periderm／～污染物 secondary pollutant／～根 secondary root／～孢子 secondary spore／～构造 secondary structure／～加厚 secondary thickening／～壁 secondary wall
次生矿物 cìshēng kuàngwù 〈矿业〉secondary mineral
次生林 cìshēnglín (of forest) second growth; secondary forest
次声 cìshēng 〈物理〉infrasonic sound; infrasound
次声波 cìshēngbō infrasonic sound wave
次声学 cìshēngxué infrasonics; subsonics
次数 cìshù number of times; frequency:数不清的～ innumerable times; for the umpteenth time／我去那儿～不多。I have seldom been there.
次帅 cìshuài 〈军事〉vice marshal
次序 cìxù order; sequence:～颠倒 in reversed order／～井然 in good (*or* apple-pie) order／按姓氏笔划多少排列～ arrange the list according to the number of strokes of the surnames
次要 cìyào less important; secondary; subordinate; minor:～特征 less important characteristic／～方面 secondary aspect／～成分 secondary element／～角色 secondary role／～养分 minor nutrient／退居～地位 retreat (*or* be relegated) to a less important position／这个理由是～的。This reason is of minor importance.
次要矛盾 cìyào máodùn secondary contradiction
次耀斑 cìyàobān 〈天文〉subflare (of the sun)
次优 cìyōu second best:～方案 second best solution／～方法 second best measure
次有限战争 cìyǒuxiàn zhànzhēng 〈军事〉sub-limited war
次于 cìyú second to:他认为自己的爱国心不～任何人。He thinks he is second to none in patriotism.／这幅画在技巧上远～那幅。This painting is far inferior to that one in technique.
次宇宙线 cìyǔzhòuxiàn secondary cosmic radiation
次韵 cìyùn *also* "步韵" bùyùn write a poem with the same tonal pattern and rhyme words in response to a previous poem
次长 cìzhǎng vice-minister; under-secretary
次之 cìzhī take second place:当地土特产中,黄豆产量第一,玉米～。Among the local specialities, the yield of soybeans comes first, and that of corn comes second.／母鸡孵蛋最好,孵蛋器～。In hatching eggs, hens are better than incubators.
次殖民地 cìzhímíndì semi-colony
次中音大号 cìzhōngyīn dàhào 〈音乐〉euphonium
次中音鼓 cìzhōngyīngǔ 〈音乐〉tenor drum
次中音号 cìzhōngyīnhào 〈音乐〉tenor horn
次重量级 cìzhòngliàngjí 〈体育〉middle heavy weight
次篆 cìzhuàn person's second or courtesy name
次最轻量级 cìzuìqīngliàngjí 〈体育〉flyweight
佽 cì 〈书面〉help; assist:～助 help
刺 cì ❶ prick; pierce; stab:针～ acupuncture／胸部被～伤 be stabbed in the chest／用注射针～入手臂 jab the needle into one's arm／我的手指让针～了一下。I had my finger pricked by a needle.／他的话像利箭一样～伤了她的心。His words pierced her heart like a sharp arrow. ❷ irritate; stimulate:辣味～鼻。The pungent smell irritates the nose (*or* assails the nostrils).／说话别～人。Don't speak of others with such sarcasm. ❸ assassinate:遇～ be attacked by an assassin; be assassinated ❹ spy; pry; make roundabout or secret inquiries ❺ criticize:讥～ satirize／辛辣的讽～ biting satire ❻ sting; thorn; splinter:鱼～ fishbone／他说话带～儿。There is a sting in his remark.／玫瑰花好看,但有～。Roses are lovely but prickly. *or* It's difficult to win the love of a beautiful girl.／她话里有～。Her words were barbed. ❼〈书面〉visiting card; calling card:名～ visiting (*or* calling) card
see also cī
刺柏 cìbǎi Chinese juniper; Taiwan juniper
刺柴 cìchái wild thorny shrubs which can be gathered as firewood
刺刺不休 cìcì-bùxiū rattle on; babble on
刺丛 cìcóng thorny bushes
刺促 cìcù 〈书面〉busy and hard pressed for time
刺刀 cìdāo bayonet:上～ fix bayonets／拼～ bayonet-fighting／用～刺 stab with a bayonet
刺耳 cì'ěr grating on the ear; jarring; ear-piercing; harsh:～之言 harsh words (*or* remarks)／～的尖叫声 discordant scream／每句话都十分～。Every word grates on the ear.
刺骨 cìgǔ piercing to the bones; piercing; biting:寒风～。The cold wind pierced one to the marrow.
刺槐 cìhuái 〈植物〉locust (tree)
刺黄瓜 cìhuángguā 〈植物〉bur cucumber
刺激 cìjī ❶〈生理〉excite; stimulate; irritate:～神经的药物 drugs that stimulate the nerves／～疗法 irritation (*or* stimulation) therapy／～作用 excitation; irritation; stimulation／机械性～ mechanical irritation／阳光～眼睛。The glare of the sun dazzles the

C

eyes. /噪音～耳朵。Noise is harsh to the ear. ❷ stimulate; give play or incentive to:～生产力 stimulate productive forces /～人们的积极性 bring people's initiative into play /物质～ material incentive ❸ provoke; irritate; upset:这话对他～很厉害。He felt terribly upset at this remark. *or* This remark stung him to the quick. /她的精神受到了强烈～。She had a terrible traumatic experience.

刺激素 cìjīsù 〈药学〉stimulant

刺激物 cìjīwù stimulus; stimulant

刺激性皮炎 cìjīxìng píyán irritant dermatitis

刺客 cìkè assassin

刺鳗 cìmán spiny eel

刺目 cìmù dazzling:～的光线 dazzling light

刺挠 cìnao 〈口语〉itchy:背上很～ have an itch on one's back /蚊子咬的地方仍～。The mosquito bites are still itching.

刺配 cìpèi tattoo the face of a convict and banish him to a remote, barren place (a punishment in imperial China)

刺取 cìqǔ 〈书面〉❶ dig into:～故书 dig into ancient classics ❷ pry into; gather information by making secret enquiries:～情报 collect secret information; gather intelligence

刺儿菜 cìrcài 〈植物〉field thistle (*Cephalanoplos segetun*)

刺儿话 cìrhuà sarcastic and ironical remarks

刺儿头 cìrtóu 〈方言〉troublesome or difficult person:他是个惹不得的～。He is such a troublesome person that it's best to steer clear of him.

刺杀 cìshā ❶ assassinate:被人～ be assassinated ❷ bayonet charge:练～ practise bayonet charge

刺伤 cìshāng 〈医学〉puncture wound; stab wound

刺参 cìshēn *also* "沙噀" shāxùn a kind of sea cucumber (*Stichopus japonicus*)

刺史 cìshǐ 〈古语〉provincial or prefectural governor

刺丝 cìsī ❶〈动物〉ecthoraeum; nema ❷ barbed wire

刺探 cìtàn spy; make roundabout or secret inquiries:～军事设施 spy on a military installation

刺体动物门 cìtǐ dòngwùmén *Phylum Acantho cephala*

刺铁丝 cìtiěsī *also* "刺丝" barbed wire

刺桐 cìtóng Indian coral tree

刺网 cìwǎng gill net

刺猬 cìwei *also* "猬" wèi hedgehog

刺细胞 cìxìbāo 〈动物〉cnidoblast

刺绣 cìxiù ❶ embroider:在衬衣上～红花 embroider red flowers on a shirt /她正在～被面。She is embroidering a quilt cover. ❷ embroidery:华丽的～ gorgeous embroidery /真丝～ pure silk embroidery

刺绣机 cìxiùjī embroidery machine

刺绣品 cìxiùpǐn embroidery

刺眼 cìyǎn ❶ dazzling:探照灯发出～的白光。The searchlight shot out dazzling beams. ❷ offensive to the eye:她那个打扮呀,别提多～啦! You can hardly imagine how loudly she is dressed!

刺痒 cìyang 〈口语〉itchy; itch

刺鱼 cìyú stickleback

刺针 cìzhēn ❶〈中医〉felting needle; lance ❷〈植物〉〈动物〉aculeus

刺字 cìzì ❶ tattoo, especially on the face of a convict in ancient China ❷〈书面〉card, visiting card; calling card

赐 cì

❶ (of a senior person) confer; bestow:此乃校长所～。This was bestowed by the president. ❷〈敬词〉(of the person addressed) grant; favour:敬希～复。I am looking forward to a reply from you. ❸〈敬词〉gift; favour:受～良多,实不敢当。I feel unworthy of the many favours and gifts you have granted me.

赐光 cìguāng do honour to one by making one's appearance:请～ request the pleasure of your gracious presence

赐婚 cìhūn 〈古语〉imperial order sanctioning a marriage

赐教 cìjiào 〈敬词〉care to enlighten me with your instructions:不吝～。Hope you'll favour me with your enlightening remarks. *or* Hope you'll be so kind as to give me timely advice.

赐死 cìsǐ 〈古语〉ancient form of death penalty (for members of royal family or court officials who were ordered to commit suicide for their alleged crimes)

赐予 cìyǔ *also* "赐与" grant; bestow:～尚方宝剑 bestow the imperial sword (a symbol of high authority, investing the bearer with discretionary powers) on sb.; give sb. a carte blanche

伺 cì

see also sì

伺候 cìhou wait upon; serve:～病人 attend a patient /难～ hard to please /不能把服务行业的工作与～人等同起来。We must not equate working in the service trade with waiting on people in the conventional sense.

cōng

囱 cōng

see "烟囱" yāncōng

熜 cōng

〈书面〉❶ low fire ❷ hot air

璁 cōng

〈书面〉stone that looks like jade

璁珑 cōnglóng 〈书面〉bright and clean

骢 cōng

〈书面〉piebald horse

聪(聰) cōng

❶〈书面〉faculty of hearing:两耳失～ become deaf in both ears; become stone deaf ❷ acute hearing:耳～目明 see and hear clearly ❸ bright; clever; intelligent

聪慧 cōnghuì bright; intelligent:～能干 bright and capable /给人～的印象 impress people as an intelligent person

聪加人 Cōngjiārén Tsonga, indigenous people in the southeastern part of Africa

聪敏 cōngmǐn bright; keen; sharp-witted:～过人 unusually bright

聪明 cōngming clever; bright; intelligent:～才智 intelligence and ability /～伶俐 bright and clever /自作～ think oneself clever (in making suggestions, etc.) /耍小～ resort to clever tricks /过去的教训使人～起来。People become wiser for their past lessons. *or* Experience is a severe teacher.

聪明反被聪明误 cōngming fǎn bèi cōngming wù clever people may be their own victims; cleverness may overreach itself:他考试舞弊被学校除名,这岂不是～! He was expelled from school for cheating in the exam. Isn't he the victim of his own "cleverness"?

聪明一世,糊涂一时 cōngming yīshì, hútu yīshí smart all one's life but foolish for once; a wise man is not free from momentary stupidities:这种暴利也是图得的? 你可真是～! For all your cleverness, you must have taken leave of your senses to grab such huge profits.

聪睿 cōngruì 〈书面〉intelligent; bright

聪颖 cōngyǐng 〈书面〉intelligent; clever; bright:他自幼～过人。He was exceedingly bright from childhood.

匆(悤、怱) cōng

hastily; hurriedly

匆匆 cōngcōng hurriedly; in a rush; in haste:来去～ come and go in haste; make a hurried trip from one place to another and back again /行色～ be in a rush getting ready for a journey /不要～忙忙作出结论。Don't be hasty in drawing conclusions. *or* Don't jump to conclusions. /他～道了别,就走了。He hurried away after saying good-bye.

匆促 cōngcù hastily; in a hurry:～启程 set out hastily /部队～应战,损失很大。The troops gave battle in a hurry and suffered a heavy loss.

匆猝 cōngcù *also* "匆卒" *see* "匆促"

匆遽 cōngjù 〈书面〉in a hurry; in haste:～而定 decide in haste; make a hasty decision

匆忙 cōngmáng hastily; in a hurry; in haste:～赶来 rush to a place /走得～ leave in a hurry /～作出反应 make a hasty response /不必如此～! There is no tearing hurry!

葱 cōng

❶ onion; scallion:小～ spring onion; shallot /大～ scallion; green Chinese onion /洋～ onion ❷ green:青～ green

葱白 cōngbái very light blue

葱白儿 cōngbáir scallion stalk

葱葱 cōngcōng verdant:松柏～ verdant pines and cypresses

葱翠 cōngcuì fresh green; luxuriantly green:～的松林 lush green pine forest

葱花 cōnghuā chopped green onion:面里放点～儿 add some chopped green onion to the noodles /～饼 green onion pancake

葱黄　cōnghuáng　light yellow; yellowish:～的雏鸡 yellowish chick
葱茏　cōnglóng　verdant; luxuriantly green:草木～ luxuriant vegetation /～的山坡 green mountain slope /田野披上了～的春装。Spring clothed the fields in green. /一山飞峙大江边,跃上～四百旋。Perching as after flight, the mountain towers over the Yangtze; I have overleapt four hundred twists to its green crest.
葱绿　cōnglǜ　❶ *also* "葱心儿绿" pale yellowish green; light green:～的上衣 light green jacket ❷ lush green; verdant:河两岸是一片～的灌木和竹林。Both banks of the river are overgrown with green bushes and bamboo groves.
葱茂　cōngmào　verdant and luxuriant:林木～ verdant and luxuriant trees
葱头　cōngtóu　onion
葱头形穹顶　cōngtóuxíng qióngdǐng　〈建筑〉pointed dome
葱头形圆顶　cōngtóuxíng yuándǐng　〈建筑〉imperial dome
葱头猪排　cōngtóu zhūpái　fried pork chops with onion
葱油鸡　cōngyóujī　steamed chicken with scallion oil
葱郁　cōngyù　verdant; luxuriantly green:～茂密的大森林 verdant and luxuriant forest

玐(瑽)　cōng
玐瑢　cōngróng　〈书面〉〈象声〉jingling of jade ornaments

苁(蓯)　cōng
苁蓉　cōngróng　〈中药〉desert cistanche (*Cistanche deserticola*)

枞　cōng　〈植物〉fir

锹(鏦)　cōng　short spear
锹锹　cōngcōng　〈书面〉〈象声〉clang (of metal)

cóng

淙　cóng
淙淙　cóngcóng　〈象声〉murmuring; gurgling; babbling:溪水～ babbling brook

悰　cóng　〈书面〉mood:欢～ happy mood /离～ feelings at parting

琮　cóng　long hollow piece of jade with rectangular sides
琮琤　cóngzhēng　〈象声〉jingle (of jade and stone); gurgle (of water flowing over stones):泉水～ gurgling spring /玉佩～ jingling of jade pendants

藂　cóng　〈书面〉gather together; assemble

从[1](從)　cóng
❶ follow:愿～其后 will follow sb. in his footsteps /～俗 follow the general custom ❷ comply with; conform with; follow; obey:盲～ follow blindly /～其计 take sb.'s advice /愿天～人愿。May Heaven grant us our wishes! ❸ join; be engaged in:～政 go into politics ❹ act in a certain manner or according to a certain principle:～缓 be in no hurry; put sth. off till a later time /～宽处理 treat sb. with leniency /～轻发落 let sb. off lightly ❺ follower; attendant:仆～ footman; flunky ❻ secondary; accessary:分别主～ distinguish between the principal and the secondary; distinguish between the chief culprit and the accessary; sort out the priorities ❼ relationship between cousins, etc. of the same paternal grandfather, great-grandfather or a yet earlier common ancestor; of the same clan:～兄弟 cousin of the same clan; cousin ❽ (Cóng) a surname

从[2](從)　cóng
❶ from:～今以后 from now on; in the future /～天津到北京 from Tianjin to Beijing /～本质上看问题 look at the problem from its essential aspect /～实际出发 proceed from the actual situation /～工作上考虑 out of consideration for the actual work /～脚步声就能听出是谁 recognize sb.'s footsteps ❷ through; by:～大路 by the main road /～空中 by air /列车～隧道里穿过。The train passed through the tunnel. ❸ (used before a negative) ever:～未见过她 have never seen her /～不骄傲 never get conceited /～没有到过江南 have never been to the region south of the Yangtse River

从便　cóngbiàn　whenever convenient:请～给他捎个信。Please give him a message when it's convenient.
从长计议　cóngcháng-jìyì　consider the matter carefully before making a decision; need further consideration; take more time to consider:这个问题很复杂,应该～。Since the matter is complicated, we should give it further thought. /这件事我们改天再～。We'll discuss the matter at full length some other time.
从此　cóngcǐ　from now on; from then on; henceforth; thereupon:误解～消除。Misunderstanding was thereupon dispelled. /他搬家后,我们～失去了联系。We have lost contact since he moved away.
从打　cóngdǎ　〈方言〉since (that day, etc.):～入夏以来,就没下过一场雨。It has never rained since summer set in.
从…到…　cóng…dào…　from... to...:从古到今 from ancient times to the present /从南到北 from the south to the north /从生到死 from the cradle to the grave /从简到繁 from the simple to the complex /从猿到人 from ape to man /从不了解到比较了解 from knowing very little to knowing fairly well
从动　cóngdòng　〈机械〉driven:～齿轮 driven gear; follower gear
从而　cóng'ér　〈连词〉thus; thereby:工厂盖起了公寓,～解决了职工住房问题。The factory has built new apartment houses, thus solving the housing problem for the staff and workers.
从犯　cóngfàn　〈法律〉accessary criminal; accessary
从父　cóngfù　〈书面〉paternal uncle
从价税　cóngjiàshuì　〈经济〉*ad valorem* duties
从简　cóngjiǎn　act according to the principle of simplicity:接待～ give a simple reception /一切～ dispense with all unnecessary formalities /婚事～。The wedding is to be celebrated in a modest way. /一切手续～。All formalities will be simplified.
从谏如流　cóngjiàn-rúliú　(of a sovereign) listen to court officials' exhortations or advice readily
从教　cóngjiào　be engaged in the teaching profession; be a teacher:给～三十年的教工颁奖。Awards are conferred on those who have been engaged in educational work for thirty years.
从井救人　cóngjǐng-jiùrén　jump into a well to rescue sb. from drowning — risk one's life or harm one's own interest without doing anybody any good; rescue another at the risk of one's own life or at a tremendous risk
从句　cóngjù　〈语言〉subordinate clause
从军　cóngjūn　join the army; join the services; enlist:他～二十年,屡建战功。He has rendered outstanding service many times during his twenty years of active service in the army.
从来　cónglái　always; at all times; all along:他对工作～认真负责。He has always been very conscientious in his work. /这个问题～没有搞清楚过。This problem has never been thrashed out.
从良　cóngliáng　〈旧语〉(of a prostitute) reform and marry a decent man
从量税　cóngliàngshuì　〈经济〉specific duties
从轮　cónglún　〈机械〉driven wheel
从略　cónglüè　be omitted:其余～。The other details are omitted.
从命　cóngmìng　comply with sb.'s request; do sb.'s bidding:欣然～ comply with sb.'s request gladly
从母　cóngmǔ　〈书面〉mother's sister; maternal aunt
从女　cóngnǚ　〈书面〉brother's daughter; niece
从前　cóngqián　before; formerly; in the past:我～是工人。I used to be a worker. /他～去过那里。He has been there before.
从权　cóngquán　as a matter of expediency:～处理 do what is expedient; act from expediency
从戎　cóngróng　〈书面〉enlist:投笔～ put aside the writing brush and follow the career of a soldier; renounce the pen for the sword
从容　cóngróng　(formerly pronounced cōngróng) ❶ calm; unhurried; leisurely:举止～ carry oneself with ease /那女人应酬很～,说话也得体。The woman behaved with great self-possession and spoke in appropriate terms. ❷ ample (time or money):手头～ be in easy circumstances; have plenty of cash /生活～ be well-off /时间～。There is plenty of time yet.
从容不迫　cóngróng-bùpò　calm and unhurried; composed and steady:他～地申述了理由。He calmly stated his reasons.
从容就义　cóngróng-jiùyì　go to one's death unflinchingly; meet one's death like a martyr or hero

从容自若 cóngróng-zìruò remain composed; have the presence of mind:错了板眼,他也能～地往下唱。Though he was out of tune, he still went on singing as if nothing had happened.

从善如登 cóngshàn-rúdēng to follow what is right is like climbing up a hill — it's not easy to be virtuous:～,从恶如崩。It's difficult to follow the path of virtue but easy to succumb to vice.

从善如流 cóngshàn-rúliú follow good advice as naturally as a river follows its course; readily accept good advice:年轻的经理和蔼可亲,～。Friendly and amiable, the young manager readily accepts all good advice.

从师 cóngshī serve one's apprenticeship with sb.:～习艺 be apprenticed to a master worker

从实 cóngshí according to the facts; truthfully:～回答 answer according to the facts /你要～招来。You have to confess truthfully.

C

从事 cóngshì ❶ go in for; be engaged in:～革命 dedicate oneself to the cause of revolution /～技术革新 go in for technical innovations /～科学研究 be engaged in scientific research /～社会活动 take part in communal activities ❷ deal with:不可鲁莽～ must not act rashly; refrain from any rash action /军法～ deal with according to military law; court-martial

从属 cóngshǔ subordinate:～地位 subordinate status /上层建筑～于经济基础。The superstructure is subordinate to the economic base. /这是一家大公司的～机构。It is a branch organization affiliated with a large company.

从俗 cóngsú ❶ according to custom; in conformity with convention:～就简 follow the custom and dispense with all unnecessary formalities ❷ swim with the tide; follow the fashion:难免～ cannot but swim with the tide

从速 cóngsù as soon as possible; without delay:～处理 deal with the matter as soon as possible

从天而降 cóngtiān'érjiàng descend from heaven — be quite unexpected

从头 cóngtóu ❶ from the beginning:～念 read from the very beginning ❷ anew; afresh; once again; all over again:这套动作,你得～儿再练。You have to practise this set of movements all over again.

从违 cóngwéi compliance or refusal; approval or disapproval:比较各种译本以定～。We can compare the different versions of the text to decide what to follow and what to exclude.

从先 cóngxiān 〈方言〉before:这里的居民比～多多了。There is a much bigger population here than before.

从小 cóngxiǎo from childhood; as a child:他～儿就爱运动。He has loved sports ever since he was a child.

从心所欲 cóngxīnsuǒyù do as one pleases; have one's own way; follow one's inclinations:不法商贩们～地抬高物价。Lawless pedlars charge excessive prices as they please.

从新 cóngxīn again; anew; afresh:～生活 turn over a new leaf /这事得～做。It'll have to be done all over again.

从刑 cóngxíng *also* "附加刑" fùjiāxíng 〈法律〉accessary punishment

从性遗传 cóngxìng yíchuán 〈生物〉sex-influenced inheritance

从严 cóngyán be strict; maintain a high demand on:～治党 be strict in Party discipline /～惩处 punish severely

从业 cóngyè be engaged in; obtain employment; get a job:～机会 job opportunities /～人员 employees

从业员 cóngyèyuán those employed in commerce and the service trades

从一而终 cóngyī'érzhōng 〈旧语〉not remarry after one's husband dies; be faithful to one's husband to the very end

从艺 cóngyì be engaged in performing arts:这位老演员～近六十年。The old actor has been engaged in the performing arts for almost sixty years.

从影 cóngyǐng be engaged in film-making; be a movie actor:她～仅十年,演了几十部影片。During her ten years in the film world, she acted in dozens of movies.

从优 cóngyōu give preferential treatment to:价格～ offer preferential prices /条件～ provide favourable conditions /工资和福利待遇～。Preferential treatment will be given with regard to salary and welfare.

从葬 cóngzàng be buried together with:～陶俑 terra cotta figurines buried together with the deceased

从者 cóngzhě follower; attendant:～如云 have a large following

从征 cóngzhēng go on a military expedition:他以记者身分～。He went on a military expedition as a journalist.

从政 cóngzhèng enter politics; embark on a political career

从中 cóngzhōng out of; from among; therefrom:～渔利 profit from; cash in on /～斡旋 mediate between two sides /～作梗 hinder sb. from carrying out a plan; place obstacles in the way; put a spoke in sb.'s wheel

从众 cóngzhòng follow the populace; follow public opinion:～行事 act in conformity with the majority (*or* most of the people)

从兹 cóngzī 〈书面〉from now on

从子 cóngzǐ 〈书面〉brother's son; nephew

从坐 cóngzuò 〈书面〉be punished for being related to an offender

丛(叢、藂)

cóng ❶ crowd together; cluster:草木～生 be overgrown with bushes and trees ❷ clump; thicket; grove:灌木～ bushes and shrubs ❸ crowd; collection:人～ crowd of people /译～ collection of translations; choice translations ❹ (Cóng) a surname

丛残 cóngcán 〈书面〉multifarious anecdotes:掇拾～ collect anecdotes

丛簇 cóngcù 〈书面〉crowd together; (of plants) grow thickly together:花木～ thick growth of trees and flowers

丛脞 cóngcuǒ 〈书面〉loaded down with trivial details

丛集 cóngjí ❶ crowd together:债务～ debts piling up /诸事～。A multitude of things crop up. /百感～。All sorts of feelings well up. ❷ collection:青年文学～ collection of youth literature

丛聚 cóngjù gather; get together; (of plants) grow together

丛刊 cóngkān series of books; collection

丛刻 cóngkè collection of block-printed books

丛林 cónglín ❶ jungle; forest:～热 jungle fever /～战 jungle warfare ❷ Buddhist or Taoist monastery

丛莽 cóngmǎng stretch of dense luxuriant grass:密林～ dense forest with luxuriant grass

丛密 cóngmì dense; thick:林木～ dense wood

丛山 cóngshān ranges of mountains:～峻岭 ranges of mountains with steep ridges

丛生 cóngshēng ❶ (of plants) grow thickly:荆棘～ overgrown with thorny bushes /～的野草 overgrowth of weeds ❷ (of diseases, evils, etc.) break out in profusion:险象～ be riddled with danger /百病～ all kinds of diseases and ailments breaking out

丛书 cóngshū series of books; collection; set of books issued in the same format by a publisher:百科～ encyclopaedia /知识青年自学～ school-leavers' self-study series

丛谈 cóngtán (usu. used in titles of articles or books) series of talks or articles:《美学～》*Talks on Aesthetics* /《科学知识～》*Talks on Popular Science*

丛杂 cóngzá motley:建校伊始,诸事～。Numerous things call for attention as the school has just been set up.

丛葬 cóngzàng group burial

丛冢 cóngzhǒng 〈书面〉group of usually unkept graves:荒岭～ groups of graves on wild hills /这片果园过去是穷人的～。This orchard used to be the site of graves for poor people.

丛子 cóngzi 〈方言〉bush:灌木～ thick growth of bushes; a clump of bushes

còu

凑(湊)

còu ❶ gather together; pool; collect:～钱办个刊物 pool money to start a magazine /～了一整套古籍 collect a complete set of ancient texts /把这些事～在一起 piece together all these facts /我们～在一起研究一下要采取的步骤。We got together to discuss the steps to be taken. ❷ take advantage of:～空儿看望老朋友 try to find time to see one's old friends /我要～机会去一趟上海。I'll make a trip to Shanghai if such an opportunity offers itself. ❸ move close to; press near:往前～～ move on (in a queue); move forward /～着烛光看书 read by candlelight

凑巴 còuba 〈口语〉scrape up:他有点积蓄,～～就可以买台彩电。As he has a little savings, he will be able to scrape up enough to buy a coloured TV set.

凑搭 còuda 〈方言〉piece together; club together

凑胆子 còu dǎnzi 〈方言〉round up a few friends to help boost one's courage

凑份子 còu fènzi ❶ club together (to buy a present for sb.); pool:小张结婚,大家～送些礼物。Let's club together to buy Xiao Zhang a wedding gift. ❷〈方言〉add to the trouble, esp. by poking one's nose into others' business:这儿又没有你什么事,你说三道四地凑什么份子呀! You have no business to be here; why should you add to the confusion by wagging your tongue!

凑合 còuhe ❶ assemble; collect; gather together:昨天大家～在一起练歌。We assembled here yesterday to practise singing. ❷ improvise:这篇文章是临时～的,组织得不好。This article was written hurriedly on the spur of the moment; it is not well-organized. ❸ make do:这个自行车棚还可以～着用。We can still make do with this bicycle shed. /这台旧打字机先～着使吧。Just make this old typewriter do for the time-being. ❹ so-so; passable

凑合事儿 còuheshìr do sth. half-heartedly; go through the motions:做事要认真负责,～可不行呀! You must do everything conscientiously instead of just going through the motions.

凑乎 còuhu ❶ knock together:我临时～了一篇讲稿。I worked out an impromptu draft for my speech. ❷ make do with:我这点钱能～过一个月。I can make this much money do for a month.

凑集 còují gather together; collect:我们～了一点儿钱给他作路费。We raised some money for his travel expenses. /把大家～在一块儿说个事儿。Round up everybody for a brief discussion.

凑近 còujìn come near to; draw close to:他～王先生,叽里咕噜地说了一阵。Drawing close to Mr. Wang, he whispered something to him.

凑拢 còulǒng move closer:大家～点儿,商量一下明天的工作。Let's come closer and discuss tomorrow's work.

凑钱 còuqián pool money; raise a fund:大家～买了些图书资料。They clubbed together to buy books and other reference materials.

凑巧 còuqiǎo luckily; fortunately; as luck would have it:真不～,我手头正好没有钱。Unfortunately, I happen to be running out of money. /说也～,机会就在眼前。As luck would have it, a chance has just presented itself. /我正想去找他,～他来了。I was about to look for him when he turned up.

凑趣儿 còuqùr ❶ join in (a game, etc.) just to please others:他故意开个玩笑～。He cracked a joke just to make everybody laugh. ❷ make a joke about; poke fun at:他是拿我～呢。He was making fun of me.

凑热闹 còu rènao ❶ join in the fun:见大家说得很高兴,他也走过来～。Seeing that we were chattering cheerfully, he came over to join in the fun. /想好了再决定,别跟着～。Think carefully before you decide, and don't just follow others for the fun of it. ❷ add trouble to:我们够忙的了,别再来～。We're busy enough as it is, don't give us more trouble.

凑手 còushǒu at hand; on hand; within easy reach:我一时钱不～,到外地旅游也只好作罢。As I haven't got enough money on hand, I have to shelve my plan of going out for travel.

凑数 còushù ❶ make up the number or amount:凑个整数 make up a round number /我们得凑足数以组成旅游团。We have to make up the required number of people to form a tourist group. ❷ serve as a stopgap; pass muster:也许我还能凑个数。Maybe I can barely pass muster.

凑整儿 còuzhěngr make sth. a round number:我有九十八元,你给我两元,凑个整吧。I have 98 *yuan*. Give me 2 *yuan* to make it a round number.

辏

còu 〈书面〉centre on sth. (as spokes of a wheel on the hub):～集 centre on sth.

辏力 còulì 〈物理〉central force:～场 central force field

腠

còu

腠理 còulǐ 〈中医〉space between skin and muscle

cū

粗(觕、麤、麁)

cū ❶ wide (in diameter); thick:～棍子 thick stick /桌面上有一条很～的划痕。A thick cut can be seen on the table. ❷ not close in breadth; broad; thick:～眉 thick (*or* heavy) brows /～轮廓 in broad (*or* rough) outline ❸ coarse; crude; rough:～沙 coarse sand; grit /手又～又黑 have rough, work-soiled hands /～瓷碗雕不出细花儿来。It's impossible to carve delicate flowers on a coarse porcelain bowl. *or* You can't make a silk purse out of a sow's ear. ❹ gruff; husky:～声～气 deep, gruff voice ❺ rough; unrefined:～呢子 woolen suiting /去～存精 discard the dross and choose the essential /活干得～。The job was hastily done. ❻ careless; negligent:他这人～,你得要多提醒他。He is often careless. You have to keep reminding him. ❼ rude; unpolished; vulgar:说话很～ speak rudely; use offensive language ❽ slightly; roughly:～通日语 have a smattering of Japanese

粗暴 cūbào rude; harsh; uncouth; crude:～态度 rude attitude /作风～ crude style of work /行为～ uncouth behaviour /～的批评 harsh criticism /～践踏别国主权 wantonly trample on the sovereignty of another country /～违反国际关系准则 grossly violate the norms of international relations

粗笨 cūbèn ❶ clumsy; ungainly:他身高体大,但动作并不～。Though tall and of powerful build, he is not clumsy in movement. ❷ unwieldy; cumbersome:～的家具 unwieldy piece of furniture

粗鄙 cūbǐ vulgar; coarse; sordid; mean:言语～ coarse language /行为～可憎 vulgar and abominable behaviour

粗脖子 cūbózi bull-necked

粗布 cūbù ❶ coarse cloth ❷ handwoven cloth; homespun cloth

粗菜 cūcài vegetable for popular consumption; common vegetable

粗糙 cūcāo ❶ rough; coarse; unrefined:皮肤～ rough skin ❷ crudely made; of poor workmanship:工艺～ crude craftsmanship /～的雕像 rough-hewn statue /文章写得～。The article is crudely written. /他的用心是好的,但做法上有些～。Although he meant well, he was not tactful enough.

粗糙度 cūcāodù 〈机械〉roughness:～测定仪 roughmeter

粗茶淡饭 cūchá-dànfàn plain tea and simple food; homely meal:吃点儿～,招待不周。Take potluck with us if you don't mind.

粗柴油 cūcháiyóu gas oil

粗齿锯 cūchǐjù rip saw; ripper

粗粗咧咧 cūcu-liēliē (of a person) careless; slapdash; casual:这个人～,有点马大哈。He's a rather slapdash sort of person, something of a scatterbrain if you like.

粗大 cūdà ❶ thick; bulky:胳膊～有力 have strong and powerful arms /～的树干 thick tree trunk ❷ (of voice) loud:声音～ loud voice /鼾声～ thunderous snoring

粗蛋白 cūdànbái crude protein

粗锻 cūduàn 〈机械〉rough forging; blocking

粗墩墩 cūdūndūn (of a person) stocky; thickset

粗恶 cū'è ❶ (of a person) savage and fierce ❷ coarse:～的食物 coarse food

粗帆布 cūfānbù canvas duck

粗纺 cūfǎng slubbing; roving:～工序 roving process /～车间 roving shop

粗放 cūfàng ❶〈农业〉extensive:～耕作 extensive cultivation /～型经济增长 extensive economic growth /由～型经营过渡到集约型经营 change over from extensive to intensive management ❷ crude; careless; sloppy:生产～ crude (*or* sloppy) production ❸ unconstrained and bold:～的笔触 bold strokes; whirlwind energy of one's brush; free and bold style of writing

粗浮 cūfú (of a person) rude and impetuous:气质～ rude and impetuous by temperament

粗钢 cūgāng 〈冶金〉crude steel

粗工 cūgōng ❶ crude work; rough work; unskilled labour ❷ unskilled labourer

粗估 cūgū rough estimate:～这块玉值五千元。This jade may be worth 5000 *yuan* by my rough estimate.

粗光纤 cūguāngxiān macrofibre

粗犷 cūguǎng ❶ rough; rude; boorish:一身～的习气 be rustic and boorish in behaviour /一个剽悍而～的汉子 uncouth and intrepid man /～的说笑声 ribald talk and laughter ❷ straightforward and uninhibited:～的性格 be straightforward and unconventional in character /～洒脱的气质 bold and romantic in temperament /～的山歌 rustic folk song /他为人～豪爽。He is frank, bold and scornful of convention.

粗顸 cūhān 〈方言〉thick and hard:～的手指 thick hard fingers

粗豪 cūháo ❶ straightforward; outspoken:～坦率 be forthright and candid ❷ loud and clear; raucous; strident:汽笛发出～的声音。The sirens whistled loud and long.

粗忽 cūhū careless; neglectful; negligent:他干工作向来～,常常出

错。He often makes mistakes of one kind or another as he is habitually careless in work.
粗花呢 cūhuāní 〈纺织〉tweed
粗话 cūhuà vulgar language:满嘴～ be foulmouthed
粗活 cūhuó heavy manual labour; unskilled work
粗货 cūhuò shoddy goods
粗加工 cūjiāgōng 〈机械〉rough machining; roughing
粗具规模 cūjù guīmó be roughly in order; be roughly in shape
粗糠 cūkāng chaff
粗犷 cūkuáng crude and bold; rough and uninhibited:人类祖先的作品体现了一种～、原始的美。Artifacts of the earliest humans reveal a kind of crude primeval beauty.
粗拉 cūla 〈口语〉crude; careless:新买的家具太～。The new furniture is of crude workmanship. /这个～人干细致活哪儿行啊! How on earth can a careless person like him do a job which requires minute care?
粗厉 cūlì ❶ (of voice) gruff and stern; harsh ❷ peremptory and stern:～地下令 issue stern orders; give peremptory instructions
粗粝 cūlì ❶〈书面〉unpolished rice ❷ coarse; rough:～的饭食 coarse food
粗粒盐 cūlìyán bay salt
粗粮 cūliáng coarse food grain (e.g. maize, sorghum, millet, etc. as distinct from wheat and rice):搭配着吃点～ eat some coarse grain for a change
粗料 cūliào coarse fodder
粗劣 cūliè of poor quality; cheap; shoddy:质量～ be of poor (*or* inferior) quality /～的赝品 crude imitation /插图～ shoddy illustrations
粗陋 cūlòu ❶ coarse; crude:房舍～ crudely built house /字迹～ poor clumsy handwriting /食物～ coarse and poor food ❷ coarse and ugly:面貌～ coarse and ugly features ❸ crude and shallow:文章～ crude and shallow writing
粗鲁 cūlu *also* "粗卤" rude; coarse; boorish:言语～ coarse language /说话～ be rough in speech /～的彪形大汉 boorish husky fellow /看他这样～,倒还有点儿聪明呢。He looks like an oaf but he does have some brains.
粗铝 cūlǚ crude aluminum
粗略 cūlüè sketchy; rough:～的估计 rough estimate /～地阅读一遍 read through quickly; leaf through /～地一看 take a cursory look /～地介绍一下经过 give a sketchy account of what has happened /我对俄语有一些～的知识。I have a smattering of Russian.
粗麻布 cūmábù burlap; gunny; sacking
粗莽 cūmǎng rough and rude:～汉子 rough character
粗毛 cūmáo coarse wool
粗毛羊 cūmáoyáng coarse-wooled sheep; coarse wool
粗眉大眼 cūméi-dàyǎn brushy eyebrows and big eyes; heavy features
粗磨 cūmó 〈机械〉coarse grinding; rough grinding
粗朴 cūpǔ (of a person) simple and plain
粗鳍鱼 cūqíyú dealfish (*Trachipterus*)
粗浅 cūqiǎn shallow; superficial; simple:～的认识 superficial understanding /～看法 shallow view /～的想法 not well-thought-out idea
粗人 cūrén ❶ blunt man; rash person ❷ (often used in self-depreciation) uneducated or unlettered man:我是个～,说得不对请包涵。I'm a bit of a boor, so I hope you'll forgive me for my bluntness.
粗绒大衣呢 cūróng dàyīní 〈纺织〉fearnaught
粗鞣革 cūróugé rough-tanned leather; crust leather
粗嗓子 cūsǎngzi husky voice
粗涩 cūsè ❶ coarse; rough; unsmooth:～的土布 coarse homespun cloth ❷ (of voice) raucous
粗纱 cūshā 〈纺织〉roving
粗纱机 cūshājī fly frame; roving frame
粗砂 cūshā 〈冶金〉open sand; coarse sand grit
粗砂轮 cūshālún 〈机械〉coarse wheel
粗砂岩 cūshāyán gritstone
粗生 cūshēng (of a plant) thrive even under unfavourable conditions
粗食 cūshí coarse food; low diet
粗使 cūshǐ (of maids or servants) do unskilled manual labour:～丫头 maid who works as a cleaner in a house; maid of all work
粗实 cūshi strong and sturdy:～的腰身 strong and sturdy body /这桌子腿很～。The table has solid legs.
粗手笨脚 cūshǒu-bènjiǎo clumsy; ham-fisted:别看他～的,心眼可鬼呢。He is full of tricks though he looks a bit clumsy.
粗梳 cūshū 〈纺织〉carding:～机 carding machine /～条子 card sliver
粗梳毛纺 cūshū máofǎng 〈纺织〉woollen spinning
粗梳棉纱 cūshū miánshā 〈纺织〉carded yarn
粗疏 cūshū ❶ careless; neglectful; inattentive:办事～ careless in work /她因为～而出了不少错误。She made quite a few mistakes on account of her carelessness. ❷ (of wool, hair, etc.) coarse and thin; crude and sparse
粗率 cūshuài rough and careless; thoughtless; ill-considered:～的决定 ill-considered decision /～的处理 casual treatment /这个计划订得比较～。This plan was cursorily drawn up.
粗饲料 cūsìliào coarse fodder; roughage
粗俗 cūsú vulgar; obscene; indecent:举止～ vulgar in behaviour /说话～ use coarse language /～的轶闻 scandalous anecdotes; scandals
粗算 cūsuàn rough estimate or calculation
粗糖 cūtáng unrefined sugar
粗陶 cūtáo coarse pottery
粗体 cūtǐ 〈印刷〉bold face:～字 bold faced word /用～印 print in bold type
粗通 cūtōng know a little about; have a smattering of; be slightly acquainted with:～文墨 only have a rudimentary knowledge of letters; be partially literate
粗腿病 cūtuǐbìng *also* "丝虫病" sīchóngbìng filariasis
粗纹 cūwén coarse texture
粗纹唱片 cūwén chàngpiàn coarse groove record
粗细 cūxì ❶ (degree of) thickness:手指～的钢筋 steel rods as thick as a finger /同样～的木料需要一百根。We need a hundred planks of the same size. ❷ crudeness or fineness; degree of finish; quality of work:工艺的～决定产品的质量。The degree of finish determines the quality of the product.
粗纤维 cūxiānwéi 〈植物〉coarse fibre
粗线条 cūxiàntiáo ❶ thick lines; rough outline:～的勾画 rough sketch ❷ rough-and-ready; slapdash:他干什么都是那样～的。He is slapdash with whatever he undertakes. ❸ outline; sketch:情节的～已有了,但还需要充实丰富。The outline of the story has been worked out, but it has yet to be fleshed out.
粗斜棉布 cūxiémiánbù 〈纺织〉denim
粗心 cūxīn careless; thoughtless:～气浮 careless and hasty /考试失败的原因就在于～。His failure in the examinations stemmed from his carelessness.
粗心大意 cūxīn-dàyì careless; negligent:一时～铸成大错。Momentary carelessness led to a grave mistake.
粗锌 cūxīn spelter
粗选 cūxuǎn 〈矿业〉roughing
粗哑 cūyǎ (of voice) hoarse and husky; raucous
粗野 cūyě rough; boorish; uncouth:比赛中他们动作～。They played rough in the match.
粗硬 cūyìng ❶ (hair) thick and stiff:～的头发 thick stiff hair ❷ (of voice) loud and harsh:～的语言 uncouth language
粗窳 cūyǔ 〈书面〉shoddy; of poor quality:陶器～ crude earthenware
粗轧 cūzhá 〈冶金〉roughing (down):～机 roughing mill
粗支纱 cūzhīshā 〈纺织〉coarse yarn
粗枝大叶 cūzhī-dàyè ❶ crude and careless; sloppy; slapdash:做事～,容易出错。Carelessness leads to error. ❷ rough sketch; brief outline:细说起来三天三夜也说不完,还是～地告诉你吧。It would take too long to give you the detailed story; Let me just sketch out the main points for you.
粗直 cūzhí (of a person) blunt and straightforward:为人～ be outspoken and straightforward
粗纸板 cūzhǐbǎn chipboard
粗制滥造 cūzhì-lànzào produce in a rough and slipshod way; turn out rough and slipshod work:～的翻译 shoddy translation /～的产品 slipshod product
粗制品 cūzhìpǐn semifinished product
粗中有细 cūzhōng-yǒuxì there's subtlety in what seems to be crudeness:他这人～,这一次倒看出了问题。Careless though he might be usually, he was careful enough for once to detect the problem.
粗重 cūzhòng ❶ (of voice, etc.) rough and loud:～的嗓音 gruff

voice /～的喘气声 heavy panting ❷ big and strong:～的手 big and strong hand ❸ heavy and clumsy; bulky:那机器特别～。That machine is exceptionally bulky. ❹ thick and heavy:浓黑～的双眉 black, heavy brows /～的笔道 (of calligraphy) heavy strokes ❺ (of work) heavy; strenuous:再～的活儿他也愿意干。He's ready to take on any strenuous work.

粗壮 cūzhuàng ❶ sturdy; thickset; brawny:那人结实～。That man is strong and sturdy. ❷ thick and strong:～的树干 thick tree trunk /庄稼长得～。The crops are growing sturdy. ❸ (of voice) deep and resonant:声音～ have a deep resonant voice

粗拙 cūzhuō ❶ crudely made; of inferior workmanship ❷ (of a person) rough and clumsy:这个人貌似～,但善于思考。He looks clumsy, but he is capable of deep thinking.

cú

殂

cú 〈书面〉death; demise

殂谢 cúxiè 〈书面〉pass away; die

徂

cú 〈书面〉❶ go; get:由西～东 go east; from west to east ❷ pass; elapse:岁月其～。How time passes (*or* flies). ❸ begin; start:六月～暑。Summer begins in June. ❹ *see* "殂" cú

cù

憱

cù 〈书面〉feeling uneasy

蹴(蹵)

cù 〈书面〉❶ kick:～鞠 kick the ball ❷ tread:一～而就 reach the goal in one step; accomplish one's aim in one move

see also jiu

蹴踏 cùtà 〈书面〉tread; stamp:马蹄～着石阶,发出嗒嗒的响声。The sound of the hoofs became audible as the horse rumbled up the stone steps.

卒

cù *see* "猝" cù

see also zú

卒卒 cùcù 〈书面〉in a hurry

卒中 cùzhòng *also* "中风" zhòngfēng 〈中医〉suffer from a stroke of apoplexy; have a stroke

猝

cù 〈书面〉sudden; abrupt; unexpected:～毙 die suddenly; drop dead /～变 sudden change /心脏病～发 have a sudden heart attack

猝不及防 cùbùjífáng be taken by surprise:对敌人施行～的袭击 launch a surprise assault on the enemy; make a surprise raid on the enemy /敌人～,慌了手脚。Taken by surprise, the enemy were thrown into disarray.

猝倒 cùdǎo 〈医学〉cataplexy

猝倒病 cùdǎobìng 〈农业〉damping off:松苗～ damping off of pine seedlings

猝尔 cù'ěr 〈书面〉sudden; unexpected:～夭逝 pass away all of a sudden when still young

猝灭 cùmiè 〈冶金〉quenching

猝然 cùrán abruptly; unexpectedly; suddenly:～变色 suddenly change countenance

猝死 cùsǐ sudden death

蔟

cù bundle of straw, etc. for silkworms to spin cocoons on:上～ (of silkworms) start spinning cocoons (on a bundle of straw)

簇

cù ❶ form a cluster; pile up:蜂～野花。Bees are swarming over wild flowers. ❷ cluster; pile:花团锦～ like bouquets of flowers (*or* piles of brocade) — rich colourful decorations ❸ 〈量词〉cluster; bunch:一～桃花 a bunch of peach blossoms

簇虫 cùchóng gregarine

簇居 cùjū live in clusters:他的祖辈～山区多年。His forefathers lived close together in the hilly region for many years.

簇聚 cùjù gather in clusters; cluster:花丛中蝴蝶～。The butterflies clustered round the flower bushes.

簇射 cùshè 〈物理〉shower:宇宙线～ cosmic ray shower /高能～ energetic shower

簇生 cùshēng (of a plant) grow in clusters; cluster

簇新 cùxīn brand new:一套～的衣服 a brand new suit

簇拥 cùyōng cluster round:人们～着演讲人提问题。People gathered round the speaker, asking questions. /他一下飞机,迎接的人们便～上来。The moment he alighted from the plane, those waiting to meet him thronged forward.

瘄

cù

瘄子 cùzi *also* "麻疹" mázhěn 〈方言〉measles

醋

cù ❶ vinegar:陈～ mature vinegar ❷ jealousy (particularly in love affairs):争风吃～ feel bitterly jealous and fight for (sb.'s) attention (*or* love)

醋大 cùdà *also* "措大" cuòdà impoverished scholar

醋罐子 cùguànzi *also* "醋坛子" person eaten up with jealousy; jealous woman or man; jealousy:打翻了～ be overwhelmed by jealousy

醋海生波 cùhǎi-shēngbō storm raised by a jealous woman or man

醋化 cùhuà acetify:～器 acetifier; acetator

醋劲儿 cùjìnr jealousy:～十足 consumed with jealousy; green with jealousy /～大发 make a big scene out of jealousy; be seized with a fit of jealousy

醋精 cùjīng vinegar concentrate

醋栗 cùlì 〈植物〉gooseberry

醋酸 cùsuān 〈化学〉*also* "乙酸" yǐsuān acetic acid

醋酸酐 cùsuāngān acetic oxide

醋酸铅 cùsuānqiān lead acetate

醋酸纤维 cùsuān xiānwéi acetate fibre

醋酸盐 cùsuānyán acetate

醋酰苯胺 cùxiānběn'àn 〈药学〉acetanilide

醋心 cùxīn 〈口语〉belching of acid from the stomach

醋意 cùyì feeling of jealousy; jealousy (usu. in a love triangle)

醋渍 cùzì vinegar cure; marinate:～食物 marinated food

酢

cù *see* "醋" cù

see also zuò

酢浆草 cùjiāngcǎo 〈植物〉creeping oxalis (*Oxalis corniculata*)

顣

cù 〈书面〉knit (one's brows)

蹙

cù 〈书面〉❶ pressed; cramped:穷～ in dire straits ❷ knit (one's brows):～眉 knit one's brows

蹙额 cù'é knit one's brows; frown:疾首～ knit one's brows and shake one's head (in disapproval, etc.)

蹙金 cùjīn embroider with golden thread

蹙缩 cùsuō ❶ shrink; shrivel; contract:她的脸～得像一只干苹果。Her face was shrivelled like a dried apple. ❷ recoil; flinch; wince:畏难～ flinch from difficulty

蹙皱 cùzhòu shrink; wrinkle

踧¹

cù 〈书面〉in panic and fear

踧²

cù 〈书面〉*see* "蹙" cù

促

cù ❶ (of time) short; urgent; hurried:短～的一生 short lifetime /急～的脚步声 hurried steps ❷ urge; promote; hurry:催～他早日归来 urge him to return home as soon as possible /～其实现 bring about (*or* facilitate) realization (of a plan, policy, etc.) /把生产～上去 promote production ❸ 〈书面〉close to; near

促成 cùchéng help to bring about; facilitate:大力～ make a great effort to bring the matter to success /好事要积极～。We must actively help bring all good things to fruition.

促红细胞生成素 cùhóngxìbāo shēngchéngsù 〈生化〉erythropoietin

促进 cùjìn promote; advance; accelerate:～友谊 promote friendship /～工作 give impetus to work; push work forward /～团结 strengthen unity /起～作用 serve to spur the progress of events;

help quicken the pace of progress /～祖国统一大业 advance (*or* further) the cause of the reunification of the country /～两国关系的正常化 speed up the normalization of relations between the two countries

促进剂 cùjìnjì 〈化学〉promoter

促进派 cùjìnpài promoter of progress

促卵泡激素 cùluǎnpāo jīsù follicle-stimulating hormone (FSH)

促脉 cùmài 〈中医〉quick pulsation

促凝剂 cùníngjì coagulant

促迫 cùpò ❶ urgent; pressing; in a hurry:时间～ be in a tearing hurry; be hard pressed for time; time is running out ❷ urge; impel; spur:他的良心～他承担责任。His conscience drove him to accept the responsibility.

C

促请 cùqǐng urge and request:我们应～上级早作决定。We should request the higher authorities to make a prompt decision.

促染剂 cùrǎnjì 〈纺织〉accelerant

促肾上腺皮质激素 cùshènshàngxiàn pízhì jīsù adrenocorticotrophic hormone (ACTH):～试验 ACTH test

促生长素 cùshēngzhǎngsù 〈植物〉auxin

促声 cùshēng 〈语言〉entering tone (one of the four tones in classical Chinese pronunciation, still retained in certain dialects)

促使 cùshǐ impel; urge; spur:～双方达成协议 urge the two sides to reach agreement /祖国的需要,～他下决心学科学。The needs of the country inspired him to go in for science. /学校要开展各种活动,～学生全面发展。The school should organize various activities to help the students develop in an all-round manner. /你去跟她谈谈,一定要～她悬崖勒马。Go and have a chat with her and try to make her rein in at the edge of the precipice.

促退 cùtuì retard progress; promote retrogression:对工作,不能～,要促进。One should help and not retard the progress of work.

促退派 cùtuìpài supporter of retrogression

促胃液素 cùwèiyèsù *also*“促胃酸激素”gastrin

促膝 cùxī sit knee to knee; sit close together:～谈心 sit knee to knee in a cosy tête-à-tête; sit close together for a heart-to-heart talk; have a heart-to-heart talk

促狭 cùxiá 〈方言〉mischievous:～鬼 mischievous person; mischief /这是谁这么～,吓了我一大跳! Who was so mischievous as to give me such a start!

促销 cùxiāo promote the sale of goods; sales promotion

促销预算 cùxiāo yùsuàn promotional budget

促织 cùzhī 〈动物〉cricket

促装 cùzhuāng make haste to pack up:～就道 make haste to pack up and set out on a journey

cuān

撺(攛) cuān 〈方言〉❶ throw; fling:他把瓶子～到窗外。He threw the bottle out of the window. ❷ jump in; throw oneself in:～入水中 jump into the water ❸ do in a hurry:临时现～ improvise; make a hasty last-minute effort ❹ be infuriated; fly into a rage; get into a temper:你先别～儿,等他把话说完。Don't flare up. Let him finish what he has to say.

撺掇 cuānduo urge; egg on; instigate:我本不愿提,是有人～的。I wouldn't have mentioned this without somebody pushing me. /他不想去,也～我不要去。As he didn't want to go, he urged me to stay behind too.

撺弄 cuānnong *see*“撺掇”

撺怂 cuānsǒng *see*“撺掇”

蹿(躥) cuān ❶ leap up or forward:他身子一～就上了房顶。He got on to the roof in one leap. /鹿突然～上岩石,消失在林中。The deer suddenly leapt up on the rock and disappeared in the woods. ❷〈方言〉spurt; gush:他鼻子直往外～血。Blood gushed from his nose.

蹿蹦 cuānbèng leap; jump; bounce:一群猴子在假山上～。A troop of monkeys were leaping and bouncing on the rockery.

蹿房越脊 cuānfáng-yuèjǐ leap over housetops and roofs

蹿个儿 cuāngèr (of a child or adolescent) grow rapidly within a relatively short time:这孩子真～,一年不见,比我都高了。How the boy has grown since I saw him a year ago. He is taller than I now.

蹿火 cuānhuǒ 〈方言〉get angry; burn or boil with anger:听了他的话,她心里更～。His words made her all the more angry.

蹿货 cuānhuò 〈方言〉goods in great demand

蹿腾 cuānteng 〈方言〉jump around; bounce about:那马～开了。The horse broke into a trot.

蹿跳 cuāntiào leap; bounce

蹿稀 cuānxī 〈口语〉have loose bowels; get the trots; have running stool

镩(鑹) cuān ❶ ice pick; ice chisel ❷ cut or break (ice) with an ice pick or chisel:～冰 break ice with an ice chisel

镩子 cuānzi ice pick or chisel

汆 cuān ❶ quick-boil (a way of preparing food):～丸子 quick-boiled meat balls with soup ❷〈方言〉boil water in a small cylindrical iron pot thrust into a fire

汆子 cuānzi small cylindrical pot that can be thrust into a fire to boil water quickly

cuán

攒(欑) cuán gather together; collect; assemble:～钱 acquire money; amass wealth /他给弟弟～了台电视机,作为生日礼物。He assembled a TV set and gave it to his brother as a birthday present. /四支箭都～在靶心。The four arrows all hit the bull's eye.

see also zǎn

攒簇 cuáncù gather together:瓦屋～的村庄 village with a cluster of brick houses

攒动 cuándòng crowd together and move back and forth:灯会上人头～。There was a sea of bobbing heads at the Lantern Festival.

攒盒 cuánhé box with several layers or compartments for various kinds of food

攒集 cuánjí gather closely together

攒聚 cuánjù gather closely together:一伙人～在路旁。A crowd of people gathered at the roadside.

攒眉 cuánméi knit one's brows; frown:～苦思 rack one's brains with knitted brows

攒三聚五 cuánsān-jùwǔ (of people) gather in threes and fours:人们～,争论不休。Little knots of people had formed, arguing among themselves.

攒射 cuánshè (of arrows or guns) shoot at the same target; concentrate fire on:机枪、步枪、冲锋枪向着目标～。Machine guns, rifles and sub-machine guns all shot at the target.

cuàn

窜(竄) cuàn ❶ (of bandits, enemies, animals, etc.) flee; scurry; skedaddle:东奔西～ flee in all directions /鼠～ scurry like rats /狼狈逃～ flee in panic; flee helter-skelter /屋子里～出一条恶狗来。A fierce cur darted out of the house. ❷〈书面〉banish; exile; expel:～逐 send sb. into exile ❸ change (the wording in a text, manuscript, etc.); alter:点～ make alterations (in wording)

窜定 cuàndìng revise (a text); finalize (a draft)

窜犯 cuànfàn raid; make inroads into:～边境 raid (*or* invade) the border area

窜改 cuàngǎi alter; tamper with; falsify:～文件 tamper with a document /～原文 alter the original text /～账目 falsify the accounts /～得面目全非 be distorted beyond recognition

窜踞 cuànjù flee to and occupy (a place):敌人～了这个岛屿。The enemy fled to and occupied the island.

窜扰 cuànrǎo harass:～领海 intrude into the territorial waters /警惕敌人～ guard against enemy harassment

窜逃 cuàntáo flee in disorder; scurry off:狼狈～ flee in utter confusion /全歼～之敌 completely wipe out the fleeing enemy troops

篡 cuàn usurp; seize illegally

篡党 cuàndǎng usurp supreme power in a party:～夺权 usurp party and state powers

篡夺 cuànduó usurp; seize illegally:～领导权 usurp leadership

篡改 cuàngǎi tamper with; falsify:～历史 falsify history /～事实

distort facts /～上级指示 tamper with instructions from one's superior /～记录 alter the minutes
篡国 cuànguó usurp state power
篡窃 cuànqiè usurp (position, power, etc.); seize; grab
篡权 cuànquán usurp power (usually political power):窃国～ usurp supreme power in a country
篡位 cuànwèi usurp the throne

爨 cuàn ❶〈书面〉cook:分居异～(usu. of brothers) divide up family property and set up their separate kitchens ❷〈书面〉earthen cooking stove:执～ be in charge of the kitchen ❸ (Cuàn) a surname

cuī

衰 cuī ❶ *see* "等衰" děngcuī ❷ *see* "缞" cuī
see also shuāi

榱 cuī 〈书面〉rafter

缞 cuī 〈旧语〉funeral garment (formerly made of coarse linen); mourning outfit

崔 cuī ❶ *see* "崔巍" ❷ (Cuī) a surname
崔圭夏 Cuīguīxià Choi Kyu Hah (1919-), President of the Republic of Korea from 1979 to 1980
崔可夫 Cuīkěfū Vasily Ivanovich Chuikov (1900-1982), marshal of the former Soviet Union
崔巍 cuīwēi 〈书面〉lofty; towering:～的山岭 lofty craggy mountains
崔嵬 cuīwéi 〈书面〉❶ earthen hill with rocks ❷ high; towering: ～的宫墙 high palace walls /巨雕～。The massive sculpture stands high and imposing.
崔庸健 Cuīyōngjiàn Choi Yong Kun (1900-1976), Korean revolutionary leader and statesman, elected Vice President of DPRK in 1972

摧 cuī break; destroy:～锋陷阵 annihilate enemy forces and overrun their positions /无坚不～ be capable of destroying any stronghold; can carry all before one
摧残 cuīcán wreck; destroy; devastate:～身体 ruin (*or* wreck) one's health /～意志 wreck (*or* blunt) one's will power /～文化 cause the culture to wither /～民主 trample on democracy /～致死 persecute to death; torture to death
摧挫 cuīcuò 〈书面〉setback; frustration
摧毁 cuīhuǐ destroy; smash; wreck:～敌人的抵抗 break all enemy resistance /阵地为大炮所～。The positions were destroyed by gunfire.
摧枯拉朽 cuīkū-lāxiǔ (as easy as) crushing dry weeds and smashing rotten wood; destroy with overwhelming force:击溃匪军,犹如～ rout the bandits as easily as smashing rotten trees
摧眉折腰 cuīméi-zhéyāo bow and scrape; fawn on:安能～事权贵,使我不得开心颜。Why should I — with lowered eyes, on bent knees — serve the high and mighty? Such things can never gladden my heart!
摧陷 cuīxiàn break through and capture
摧陷廓清 cuīxiàn-kuòqīng wipe out (old ideas, etc.) completely: 这些人在五四时代有～、标新立异之功。They did a great service at the time of the May Fourth Movement (1919) by helping to wipe out wornout antiquated ideas and introduce what was new and different.
摧心剖肝 cuīxīn-pōugān tearing one's guts out; terribly traumatic:噩耗传来,～。The sad news almost tore his guts out. /每思亡妻,～。Whenever I think of my deceased wife, I am overwhelmed by grief.
摧折 cuīzhé 〈书面〉❶ break; snap:暴风雨～了路边的许多大树。The storm brought down a lot of tall trees along the road. ❷ setback:试验受到～。The experiment met with setbacks.

催 cuī ❶ urge; hurry; press:～稿子 urge sb. to send in his manuscript; press sb. for a promised article /～孩子们睡觉 hurry the children to bed ❷ hasten; expedite; speed up:春风～绿。The spring wind speeds the greening of the plants. /这块地还得用化肥～～。The crop on this plot needs to be stimulated with more fertilizer.
催巴儿 cuībar 〈方言〉flunkey; errand-boy:喂,我简直成了你的～。Why, I'm almost your errand-boy now. /他这个人很骄傲,从不给人当～。He is too proud to be at anybody's beck and call.
催办 cuībàn press sb. to do sth.:发函～ send an official letter to press the completion of sth. /派人～ send sb. to expedite some business on the spot
催逼 cuībī press for:～欠款 press sb. for payment of debt
催产 cuīchǎn *also* "催生" expedite (child) delivery; hasten parturition
催产素 cuīchǎnsù 〈药学〉alpha-hypophamine; oxytocin
催促 cuīcù urge; hasten; press:我多次打电话,～他来京参加会议。I called him many times, urging him to come to Beijing to attend the conference.
催动 cuīdòng ❶ press for action; spur on:～坐骑 spur on one's horse ❷ hasten; expedite:春风～着花事。The spring wind hastens the budding of flowers.
催肥 cuīféi fatten
催肥期 cuīféiqī 〈畜牧〉finishing period
催复 cuīfù press sb. for an answer
催函 cuīhán reminder letter
催化 cuīhuà 〈化工〉catalysis
催化反应 cuīhuà fǎnyìng catalytic reaction
催化剂 cuīhuàjì catalyst; catalytic agent
催化加氢精制 cuīhuà jiāqīng jīngzhì 〈化工〉catalytic hydrofinishing
催化裂化器 cuīhuà lièhuàqì catalytic cracker
催化转化器 cuīhuà zhuǎnhuàqì catalytic converter
催化作用 cuīhuà zuòyòng 〈化学〉catalysis; acceleration
催款单 cuīkuǎndān 〈金融〉prompt; prompt-note
催泪弹 cuīlèidàn tear bomb; tear-gas grenade
催泪气 cuīlèiqì *also* "催泪瓦斯" 〈军事〉tear gas; lacrimator gas
催眠 cuīmián hypnotize; mesmerize; lull sb. (to sleep)
催眠暗示 cuīmián ànshì 〈心理〉hypnotic suggestion
催眠疗法 cuīmián liáofǎ 〈心理〉hypnotherapy
催眠曲 cuīmiánqǔ lullaby; cradlesong
催眠术 cuīmiánshù hypnotism; mesmerism
催眠药 cuīmiányào hypnotic; somniferous potion; soporific; sleeping pill
催命 cuīmìng ❶ hasten sb. on his or her way to death:～小鬼〈迷信〉devil who comes to fetch sb. to hell when he or she is dying ❷〈比喻〉persistently urge; continually press:我就来,别～。I'll be right over; don't press me like mad.
催命鬼 cuīmìngguǐ person who keeps pressing another for sth.
催奶 cuīnǎi stimulate the secretion of milk; promote lactation:炖猪蹄能～。Stewed pig's trotter stimulates lactation.
催奶激素 cuīnǎi jīsù *also* "催乳激素"〈药学〉prolaction
催奶剂 cuīnǎijì galactagogue
催迫 cuīpò *see* "催逼"
催青 cuīqīng ❶ *see* "催情" ❷〈农业〉hasten the hatching of silkworms (by adjusting temperature and humidity) ❸〈旧语〉〈农业〉vernalization
催情 cuīqíng stimulate the oestrus of a female animal by artificial means
催生 cuīshēng hasten child delivery
催收 cuīshōu *see* "催讨"
催熟 cuīshú 〈农业〉accelerate the ripening (of fruit, etc.)
催熟栽培 cuīshú zāipéi 〈农业〉accelerating culture
催讨 cuītǎo press for repayment (of debt, etc.):～货款 press for payment for the purchase of goods
催吐剂 cuītùjì 〈药学〉emetic
催醒剂 cuīxǐngjì 〈药学〉analeptic
催芽 cuīyá hasten the budding (of soybeans, etc.)
催欲剂 cuīyùjì *also* "春药" chūnyào aphrodisiac
催债 cuīzhài press for payment of debt
催租 cuīzū press for payment of rent

獕 cuī *see* "猥獕" wěicuī

C

cuǐ

漼 cuǐ 〈书面〉❶ deep (water) ❷ streaming with tears and snivel

璀 cuǐ

璀璨 cuǐcàn 〈书面〉lustrous; bright; resplendent:～的明珠 dazzling pearls /～的诗篇 splendid poem /大楼里灯光～。The building was brilliantly lit up.

皠 cuǐ 〈书面〉pure white; white and clean

cuì

淬(焠) cuì temper by dipping (hot metal) in water, oil, chemicals, etc.; quench

淬火 cuìhuǒ (generally called 蘸火) quench:～液 quench bath /～油 quenching oil

淬火钢 cuìhuǒgāng chilled steel

淬火剂 cuìhuǒjì quenching agent; hardening liquid

淬火炉 cuìhuǒlú glowing or hardening furnace

淬透性 cuìtòuxìng 〈冶金〉quenching degree; hardenability

淬砺 cuìlì 〈书面〉temper oneself through severe trials:～意志 harden one's will

淬硬 cuìyìng 〈冶金〉harden; quench:～钢 quenched steel /～钢板 hardened plate

淬针 cuìzhēn 〈医学〉heat needling; ignipuncture

瘁 cuì 〈书面〉overworked; exhausted:毕生精力尽～于斯 devote the energy of a lifetime to the work /鞠躬尽～ bend oneself to a task and exert oneself to the utmost; devote all one has to a cause /心力交～ be physically and mentally worn out from overwork

悴 cuì see "憔悴" qiáocuì

粹 cuì 〈书面〉❶ pure:～而不杂 pure and unadulterated ❷ essence; the best:精～ essence; quintessence; cream of the crop /国～ quintessence of a nation's culture; cultural treasure of a nation

粹白 cuìbái 〈书面〉❶ pure; unadulterated ❷ pure white:～之裘 pure-white fur (coat)

粹美 cuìměi 〈书面〉perfect:品学～ have sound scholarship and moral integrity

萃 cuì 〈书面〉❶ come together; assemble:人才荟～ galaxy of talent ❷ gathering of people or collection of things:出类拔～之人 outstanding people; the best and the brightest ❸ (Cuì) a surname

萃萃蝇 cuìcuìyíng 〈动物〉tsetse or tzetze fly (an African fly that causes sleeping sickness)

萃集 cuìjí gather together:艺术节各国民歌手～,演出十分精彩。Folk singers from all over the world gathered at the Festival and gave brilliant performances.

萃聚 cuìjù (of distinguished people or exquisite objects) assemble; gather together:为庆祝伟大诗人诞辰五百周年,各界代表～一堂。Representatives of all circles gathered to celebrate the 500th birthday of the great poet.

萃取 cuìqǔ 〈化学〉extraction:～塔 extraction tower /～溶剂 extracting solvent; extractant /～分离设备 extraction and stripping apparatus /～蒸馏 extractive distillation

膵(脺) cuì

膵脏 cuìzàng 〈旧语〉〈生理〉pancreas

顇 cuì see "顦顇" qiáocuì

啐 cuì ❶ spit; expectorate:他拿出手帕,～了一口。He took out a handkerchief and spat into it. /她急了,～了那人一口。She got furious and spat at the man. ❷ 〈叹词〉*make a sound of disapproval, reprimand or insult*:呀～! 休得胡来! Tut-tut! Don't you dare run wild!

翠 cuì ❶ emerald green; green:～竹 green bamboos /青松～柏 green pines and cypresses /苍～ dark green; verdant ❷ kingfisher:点～ handicraft using kingfisher's feather for ornament ❸ jadeite:～花 jadeite flower /珠～ pearls and jade; jewellery

翠碧 cuìbì dark green

翠菊 cuìjú 〈植物〉China aster (*Callistephus chinensis*)

翠蓝 cuìlán bright blue colour; azure

翠鸡 cuìlì 〈动物〉motmot:～科 motmotidae

翠绿 cuìlǜ emerald green; jade green; vivid green:雨后竹林格外～。The bamboo thicket looked especially fresh and green after the rain. /他欣赏着窗外花园里～的龙柏。Through the window he was enjoying the emerald-green cypresses in the garden.

翠鸟 cuìniǎo kingfisher

翠绕珠围 cuìrào-zhūwéi (of ancient women) in beautiful clothes and jewels; (of ancient wealthy families) be attended upon by throngs of maids

翠生生 cuìshēngshēng fresh and green; verdant:～的柳枝在阳光下显得分外妖娆。Weeping willows, radiant and green, looked particularly graceful in the sunshine.

翠微 cuìwēi green mountain scenery; green hill

翠玉 cuìyù green jade; jadeite

毳 cuì 〈书面〉fine hair on birds or animals; down

毳毛 cuìmáo 〈医学〉fine fair on the human body (other than the hair on the head and armpit, or public hair)

脆(脃) cuì ❶ fragile; brittle:这种玻璃杯很好看,但太～。This kind of glass looks nice but is too fragile. /碳素钢性硬而～。Carbon steel is hard and brittle. ❷ crisp; crunchy:～炸土豆片 potato chips /豆角炒得又绿又～。The fried beans are fresh and crisp. /我就喜欢吃生菜那个～劲儿。I adore lettuce for its crunchiness. ❸ (of voice, sound, etc.) clear; crisp:清～的嗓子 clear, ringing voice /清～的枪声 clear and sharp sound of gunfire ❹ 〈方言〉neat; tidy; crisp:干～利落的回答 crisp reply /说话干～ speak in a straightforward, clear-cut style /这事干得真～。The job was neatly done.

脆绷 cuìbeng 〈口语〉❶ (of food) crisp ❷ (of voice) clear and melodious

脆变 cuìbiàn 〈冶金〉embrittlement

脆骨 cuìgǔ gristle (as food)

脆骨症 cuìgǔzhèng 〈医学〉fragilitas ossium

脆化 cuìhuà embrittlement

脆甲症 cuìjiǎzhèng 〈医学〉onychorrhexis

脆快 cuìkuài 〈方言〉straightforward; direct; neat:说～的,你到底签名不签名? To put it bluntly, are you going to sign up or not? /老张办事～。Lao Zhang is a no-nonsense man and gets things done.

脆沥青 cuìlìqīng 〈化工〉grahamite

脆亮 cuìliàng (of voice) clear and crisp:山里很静谧,笛声更显得～。In the tranquillity of the mountains, the flute sounded especially clear and crisp.

脆裂 cuìliè brittle rupture:～强度 bursting strength

脆美 cuìměi ❶ (of food) crisp and delicious:～的天津大麻花 crisp and tasteful Tianjin frid ❷ (of voice) clear and sweet:歌声～情意长。The singing was clear, sweet and full of emotion.

脆嫩 cuìnèn crisp and tender:这黄瓜真～。The cucumbers are really crisp and tender.

脆弱 cuìruò fragile; frail; weak:感情～ be emotionally fragile; be sentimental /意志～ be weak-willed /～的经济 fragile economy

脆弱性骨硬化 cuìruòxìng gǔyìnghuà 〈医学〉osteopecilia; osteopoikilosis

脆蛇 cuìshé *also* "蛇蜥" shéxī 〈动物〉glass snake

脆生生 cuìshēngshēng see "脆生"

脆生 cuìsheng 〈口语〉❶ crisp:这萝卜真～。The turnip is crisp and refreshing. ❷ (of sound) clear and sharp:她有六十了,可嗓音还挺～。At the age of sixty, she still has a resonant voice.

脆爽 cuìshuǎng ❶ (of food) crisp and refreshing:～可口 crisp and palatable ❷ (of voice) crisp and clear:～的回答 clear and definite reply

脆响 cuìxiǎng clear and loud:巴掌拍得～。There was a clear and

loud clapping of hands.
脆性 cuìxìng brittleness; fragileness:～断裂应力 brittle stress fracture
脆性材料 cuìxìng cáiliào fragile material; hard brittle material
脆性试验 cuìxìng shìyàn brittleness test
脆银矿 cuìyínkuàng 〈矿业〉stephanite; black silver; brittle silver ore
脆云母 cuìyúnmǔ 〈矿业〉brittle mica
脆枣 cuìzǎo 〈方言〉*also*"焦枣" jiāozǎo crisp dates
脆真真 cuìzhēnzhēn 〈方言〉crisp; crunchy

cūn

村(❶邨) cūn ❶ village; hamlet:渔～ fishing village /城市和乡～ town and country; cities and countryside ❷ populated place or area:工人新～ housing area for workers ❸rustic; boorish:～风乡俗 customs of a rustic community /她这身打扮太～。She was too rustically dressed.
村办企业 cūnbàn qǐyè village enterprise; rural enterprise
村坊 cūnfāng 〈方言〉village
村夫 cūnfū villager; country bumpkin; uncouth rustic
村夫俗子 cūnfū-súzǐ boorish philistine; vulgar, uncouth person; common herd:此等高论,是我们这些～所不能理解的。Such high-sounding arguments are indeed beyond the ken of men in the street like us.
村姑 cūngū young country woman
村话 cūnhuà coarse language
村口 cūnkǒu village entrance; end of a village
村醪 cūnláo 〈书面〉home-made wine of the village
村落 cūnluò village; hamlet
村民 cūnmín villager:～委员会 villagers' committee /《中华人民共和国～委员会组织法》*The Organic Law of Villagers' Committees of the People's Republic of China*
村气 cūnqì rustic; uncouth
村山富市 Cūnshānfùshì Tomiichi Murayama (1924-), leader of Japanese Social Democratic Party, and Prime Minister of Japan (1994-1995)
村舍 cūnshè cottage
村史 cūnshǐ village history
村市 cūnshì village fair
村塾 cūnshú 〈旧语〉old-style private school in a village
村俗 cūnsú ❶ coarse; crude:谈吐～ speak with a vulgar taste ❷ unrefined; gaudy; vulgar:这裙子显得太～。This seems to be a rather loud skirt.
村头 cūntóu village entrance; end of a village
村坞 cūnwù 〈书面〉village
村圩 cūnxū 〈方言〉village fair; village
村学 cūnxué old-style private school in a village; private primary school in a village
村野 cūnyě ❶ village with its fields; country ❷ rustic; boorish: ～之人 rustic
村妪 cūnyù old country woman
村寨 cūnzhài village; stockaded village
村长 cūnzhǎng village head
村镇 cūnzhèn villages and small towns
村庄 cūnzhuāng village; hamlet
村子 cūnzi village; hamlet

踆 cūn 〈书面〉❶ kick ❷ retreat; stop
踆乌 cūnwū legendary three-legged bird on the sun; sun

皴 cūn ❶ (of skin) chapped (from the cold); cracked:冬天手容易～。Hands easily get chapped from winter cold. /手、脸～了,用这种油最好。This ointment is very good for chapped hands and cheeks. ❷〈方言〉dirt accumulated on the skin ❸〈美术〉method of showing the shades and texture of rocks and mountains by light ink strokes in traditional Chinese landscape painting
皴法 cūnfǎ 〈美术〉light-ink stroke; method of showing the shades and texture of rocks and mountains in traditional Chinese landscape painting
皴裂 cūnliè (of skin) chapped (from the cold):孩子的手脚都～了。The child's hands and feet are chapped from the cold.

cún

存 cún ❶ exist; live; survive:生～ exist; subsist /共～ coexistence /苟～ survive in humiliation /与世长～ live as long as the universe; be eternal ❷ store; keep; preserve:～粮于民 store up grain among the people /地窖里～有大白菜。Cabbages are kept in the cellar. /香蕉～不了几天。Bananas don't keep very long. ❸ accumulate; gather; collect:～点钱买冰箱。Save (*or* scrape) up money for a refrigerator. /下水道坏了,一下雨路上就会～水。With the drain-pipe blocked, there would be puddles of water on the road if it rained. ❹ deposit:他在银行～了不少钱。He has deposited a large sum in the bank. *or* He has a considerable amount of savings in his bank account. ❺ leave (for safekeeping); check:～自行车 leave one's bicycle in a bicycle park /～行李 check one's luggage /小件行李寄～处 checkroom /能把书～在你这儿吗? Could I leave my books with you? ❻ reserve; retain:去伪～真 discard the sham and retain the true /求同～异 seek common ground while shelving the differences /他这个人有话就是～不住。He has got a big mouth. ❼ remain on balance; be in stock:商品库～ commodity stock /净～七百元 net surplus of 700 *yuan* ❽ cherish; harbour:～有很大希望 cherish high hopes /心～疑虑 have misgivings; worry /心～不良 harbour evil intentions /～有侥幸心理 trust things to chance; bank on chance
存案 cún'àn register with the proper authorities
存本付息储蓄 cúnběn fùxī chǔxù time deposit with the interest payable at fixed intervals before maturity
存仓 cúncāng keep in store:～费 storage expenses
存查 cúnchá file for reference:此件交有关部门～。Let the department concerned keep the document on file for future reference.
存车处 cúnchēchù bicycle park; bicycle shed; bicycle parking lot
存储 cúnchǔ ❶〈电子〉memory; storage:～二极管 storage diode /～元件 memory element /～管 memory tube ❷ storage:～成本 carrying cost /～地点 location of storage /～费 storage charges
存储程序计算机 cúnchǔ chéngxù jìsuànjī 〈计算机〉storage-program computer
存储读出 cúnchǔ dúchū 〈计算机〉memory read
存储键 cúnchǔjiàn 〈计算机〉storage or memory key
存储器 cúnchǔqì *also*"存贮器"〈计算机〉memory (storage)
存储容量 cúnchǔ róngliàng 〈计算机〉storage capacity; memory capacity
存储设备 cúnchǔ shèbèi 〈自控〉storage device
存储转发 cúnchǔ zhuǎnfā 〈信息〉store and forward
存单 cúndān deposit receipt:定期～ time certificate /活期～ demand certificate
存档 cúndàng file; place on file; keep in the archives:这批资料要～。These documents should be filed.
存底 cúndǐ keep the original draft; keep a file copy
存而不论 cún'érbùlùn leave the question open:一时弄不清,不如～。As it takes time to clear up the matter, we'd better leave it open.
存放 cúnfàng leave with; leave in sb.'s care:～行李 leave one's luggage with sb. /这家电影院里衣物无处～。There's no cloakroom in the cinema.
存抚 cúnfǔ 〈书面〉provide care; placate; appease:～孤弱 provide care for the orphaned and the handicapped
存根 cúngēn counterfoil; stub:发票～ receipt stub /支票～ cheque stub
存候 cúnhòu 〈书面〉bring comfort to:～父老 offer greetings and comfort to the elders
存户 cúnhù depositor
存活 cúnhuó survive; exist:三名垂危病人,经抢救全部～。The three patients, who were critically ill, all survived after emergency treatment.
存活率 cúnhuólǜ *also*"存活比" survival ratio or rate
存货 cúnhuò ❶ store up goods ❷ goods in stock; existing stock; inventory:～核算 inventory accounting /～价值 inventory value /～成本和控制 inventory costs and control /～周期 inventory cycle (*or* turnover) /～损益 inventory holding gain or loss /～指数 inventory index /～模式 inventory model /～政策 inventory policy /～销售比率 inventory-sales ratio /～不多,欲购从速。As there isn't much in stock, customers are advised to buy early.

C

存货簿 cúnhuòbù stock book
存货分类账 cúnhuò fēnlèizhàng stock ledger
存据 cúnjù written receipt or pledge to be kept for future reference
存款 cúnkuǎn ❶ deposit money in the bank：～日期 depositing date /办理～手续 go through the depositing formalities ❷ deposit; bank savings：提取～ draw money from a bank; withdraw a bank deposit /个人～ personal savings account /活期～ current (*or* demand) account (*or* deposit) /定期～ time (*or* fixed) account (*or* deposit)
存款单 cúnkuǎndān certificate of deposit
存款利率 cúnkuǎn lìlǜ deposit rate
存款利息 cúnkuǎn lìxī interest on deposit：～所得税 income tax on interest
存款人 cúnkuǎnrén depositor
存栏 cúnlán 〈畜牧〉livestock on hand：牲畜～数比去年增加15%。The amount of livestock is 15% more than last year.
存粮 cúnliáng ❶ store up grain ❷ stockpiled grain; stored grain
存留 cúnliú preserve; keep：他的著作～下来的不多。Not many of his works are still extant. *or* Many of his works have been lost.
存念 cúnniàn keep as a memento or souvenir：刘先生～。(of a photo, etc.) For Mr. Liu.
存取 cúnqǔ 〈计算机〉access
存取方式 cúnqǔ fāngshì 〈计算机〉access mode
存取控制 cúnqǔ kòngzhì 〈计算机〉access control
存取器 cúnqǔqì 〈计算机〉memory access
存取顺序 cúnqǔ shùnxù 〈计算机〉access sequence
存取周期 cúnqǔ zhōuqī storage cycle; access cycle
存入 cúnrù deposit：把一笔款项～银行 deposit a sum of money in a bank
存身 cúnshēn take shelter; make one's home：无处～ have no place one can call one's home; have no roof over one's head
存食 cúnshí suffer from indigestion
存世 cúnshì survive; be extant：这位画家的作品～不多。Only a few of the painter's works are extant.
存亡 cún-wáng live or die; survive or perish：生死～的斗争 life-and-death struggle /～未卜 sb.'s fate remains unknown /与阵地共～ defend the position to death
存亡绝续 cúnwáng-juéxù life or death, survival or extinction — a most critical juncture：～之际 at a moment when the fate of the state hangs by a thread
存问 cúnwèn 〈书面〉express sympathy and solicitude for; extend one's regards to; convey greetings to：～长老 extend one's regards to the elders
存息 cúnxī interest on deposit
存项 cúnxiàng credit balance; balance：手里留点儿～以备不时之需 always have some extra money on hand against emergencies
存心 cúnxīn ❶ cherish certain intentions：～不良 cherish evil designs (*or* intentions) /～欺骗 attempt to cheat /他说这番话不知～是何? What was his motive behind such words? ❷ intentionally; on purpose：他这样做是～跟我过不去。He did this deliberately to irritate me. /我不是～这么做的。I didn't do it on purpose. *or* I didn't mean to do it.
存休 cúnxiū *also* "存假" accumulate days-off for later need
存恤 cúnxù 〈书面〉express sympathy for and give relief to a bereaved family：～孤寡 give sympathy and relief to widows and orphans
存蓄 cúnxù ❶ store; preserve：雨季～饮用水 preserve (*or* store) drinking water in rainy season ❷ goods or money kept in stock; savings：这些年来你难道毫无～? Haven't you got any savings all these years?
存衣处 cúnyīchù cloakroom; checkroom
存疑 cúnyí leave a question open; leave a matter for future consideration：问题一时搞不清，则可～。If we cannot clarify the matter for the time being, we'd better leave it open.
存油 cúnyóu trapped oil (in a tank, etc.)
存余 cúnyú surplus; leftover; remainder：略有～ have a little surplus
存约国政府 cúnyuēguó zhèngfǔ 〈外交〉depository government
存在 cúnzài ❶ exist; be：矛盾普遍～。Contradictions exist everywhere. /只要～人剥削人的现象，就～事实上的不平等。So long as there is exploitation of man by man, there is *de facto* inequality. /矛盾～于一切事物发展的过程中。Contradiction is present in the process of development of all things. ❷ 〈哲学〉being; substance; objective world; reality：客观～ objective reality /～决定意识。Man's social being determines his consciousness.
存在主义 cúnzàizhǔyì 〈哲学〉existentialism：～者 existentialist
存照 cúnzhào ❶ keep a document for future reference; file a document：口说无凭，立此～。As verbal statements are no guarantee, a written agreement is hereby made. ❷ document on file：立有～ have a contract (*or* document) on file
存折 cúnzhé deposit book; account book; bankbook; passbook
存执 cúnzhí counterfoil; stub：汇款～ remittance stub
存贮 cúnzhù store up; deposit
存贮器 cúnzhùqì 〈计算机〉memory; storage

蹲 cún 〈方言〉hurt (one's legs or feet) while jumping：他跳下来时～了腿。He hurt his legs when he jumped down.
see also dūn

cǔn

忖 cǔn turn over in one's mind; ponder; mull over：自～ think to oneself; turn over in one's mind /思～〈书面〉ponder; mull over /暗暗自～ ponder in solitude
忖度 cǔnduó speculate; conjecture; surmise; fathom：～对方心理 try to fathom the other party's intention /你不要任意～人。Don't go imagining things about people like that.
忖量 cǔnliàng ❶ conjecture; gauge：～这事的后果 take stock of its possible consequences /我一边说话，一边～着他的真正来意。As I was speaking, I kept wondering what he had come for. ❷ think over; consider：这事我几经～仍犹豫不决。I thought hard about this matter for quite some time but still could not come to a decision.
忖摸 cǔnmo estimate; figure out：你可要～着自己的伤，量力而行啊! You have to think about the injury you have sustained and act accordingly.

刌 cǔn 〈书面〉cut; amputate

cùn

寸 cùn ❶ *cun*, a unit of length (1/30 metre) ❷ very little; very short; very small：仍图～进 attempt to make even the smallest progress (in one's studies or career) /～土尺地 tiny bit of land /手无～铁 bare-handed; unarmed; defenceless ❸ 〈方言〉just right (timing, exertion, way of doing, etc. for sth. good or bad); coincidental; as luck would have it：你来得可真～。You've come just at the right time (for sth.). ❹ *also* "寸口" the three places at the wrist where the pulse is taken ❺ (Cùn) a surname
寸白虫 cùnbáichóng tapeworm (*Tauchurng*)
寸步 cùnbù tiny step; single step
寸步不离 cùnbù-bùlí follow sb. closely; keep close to sb.; follow sb. like his own shadow; be always at sb.'s elbow：小两口如鱼似水，～。The young couple are glued together with love. /他和皇上～。The emperor never went a step without him.
寸步不让 cùnbù-bùràng refuse to yield a single inch; not budge an inch：你这个人做生意怎么～? How can you do business if you never yield an inch?
寸步难行 cùnbù-nánxíng *also* "寸步难移" be unable to move even a single step; be in an extremely difficult situation：他两脚俱肿，～。His feet were too swollen to move a single step. /有理走遍天下，无理～。With justice, one can go everywhere; without it, one can't take even a simple step.
寸草 cùncǎo small grass; blade of grass
寸草不留 cùncǎo-bùliú not leave even a blade of grass — total destruction：敌军过处，～。Wherever the enemy troops passed, they looted and killed all, leaving nothing behind.
寸草不生 cùncǎo-bùshēng not even a blade of grass grows：～的荒山 (totally) bare hill /这地方～。This place does not even grow a blade of grass.
寸草春晖 cùncǎo-chūnhuī the grass cannot repay the spring sun-

shine for its warmth; one can never repay one's parents' kindness enough

寸长 cùncháng 〈书面〉merit of no great significance; small merit: 奖掖后进,不遗～。One leaves no merit unnoticed however insignificant, when one wants to encourage (*or* award) the younger generation.

寸楮 cùnchǔ 〈书面〉❶ visiting card; calling card ❷ letter

寸断 cùnduàn (as of string, rope, etc.) break into short pieces:肝肠～ be heartbroken; be deeply grieved

寸功 cùngōng small contribution; meagre achievement:身无～ can claim no merit (*or* credit) for oneself; have rendered no meritorious service whatever

寸关尺 cùn-guān-chǐ 〈中医〉*cun*, *guan* and *chi*, three places at the wrist where the pulse is usually taken

寸晷 cùnguǐ 〈书面〉very short duration of time

寸金难买寸光阴 cùn jīn nán mǎi cùn guāngyīn 〈谚语〉money can't buy time; time is more precious than gold

寸进 cùnjìn a little progress:蹉跎岁月,未有～。He idled away his time and failed to make the slightest progress.

寸进尺退 cùnjìn-chǐtuì advance by inches and retreat by feet; retrogress is faster than progress; one step forward, two steps backward

寸劲儿 cùnjìnr 〈方言〉❶ knack of using one's strength cleverly or appropriately:干这活儿全靠～,不能使蛮劲。You got to know the knack (*or* trick) of doing this; brute force wouldn't do. ❷ (by) chance; coincidence:这部书已经绝版,赶上～,能买到旧的。This book is out of print. Perhaps you can get a second-hand one by chance.

寸楷 cùnkǎi (in Chinese calligraphy) one-square-inch block character

寸刻 cùnkè very short time:～不离 not stay away (from sb. or sth.) for a single moment

寸口 cùnkǒu 〈中医〉❶ *also* "寸口脉" one of the three places at the wrist (i. e. *cun*, *guan* and *chi*) where the pulse is taken ❷ (specifically) *cun*, the position nearest the wrist

寸丝不挂 cùnsī-bùguà without a stitch of clothing on; totally nude; stark naked

寸铁 cùntiě (usu. used in the negative) short weapon; small firearm:手无～ unarmed

寸头 cùntóu crew cut:留～ wear a crew cut /理个～ have one's hair crew-cut

寸土 cùntǔ single inch of land:～尺地 single inch of land /～不让 not yield a single inch of land

寸土必争 cùntǔ-bìzhēng fight for every inch of land; contest every inch of land

寸隙 cùnxì 〈书面〉temporary leisure:勤奋攻读,略无～ very diligent in study and have no leisure

寸心 cùnxīn ❶ (inner) heart:～如割 be cut up in one's innermost heart; be in acute agony /～不忘 never forget (sth.); always bear in one's mind /得失～知。I know full well the strong and weak points of my own writing. ❷ feelings:聊表～ as a small token of friendship (*or* good will); just to show my appreciation

寸阴 cùnyīn 〈书面〉time indicated by a shadow moving an inch — very short time:～尺璧。An inch of time is equal to a foot of jade. *or* Time is more precious than priceless jade.

寸有所长,尺有所短 cùn yǒu suǒ cháng, chǐ yǒu suǒ duǎn an inch has its length and a foot sometimes falls short — everybody has his or her strengths and weaknesses

寸衷 cùnzhōng 〈书面〉feelings:聊表～ as a small token of my appreciation

吋

cùn *also* yīngcùn 〈旧语〉inch

cuō

磋

cuō ❶ grind ivory, or other bones or horns, into utensils, implements, wares, etc. ❷ consult; deliberate

磋磨 cuōmó 〈书面〉learn from each other by exchanging views

磋切 cuōqiē 〈书面〉*see* "磋磨"

磋商 cuōshāng consult; exchange views:政治～ political consultation /与某人～某事 consult with sb. about sth. /双方经反复～,终于取得一致。After repeated exchanges of views they finally reached agreement.

搓

cuō ❶ rub with the hands:～耳取暖 rub one's ears to keep warm /～背 scrub sb.'s back /～衣服 give the clothes a scrubbing /～肥皂 apply soap /急得直～手 wring one's hands in anxiety ❷ twist with both hands:～麻绳 make cords by twisting hemp fibres between the palms /～线 twist threads /～纸捻 roll paper spills ❸〈体育〉chop:这球应该～,不该扣。That should be a chop, not a smash.

搓板 cuōbǎn washboard

搓磨 cuōmó rub; scrab

搓弄 cuōnong rub or twist idly:她手里～着手绢,一句话也不说。She played with a handkerchief in her hands, not saying a word.

搓球 cuōqiú 〈体育〉chop:～过网 return the shot with a chop

搓揉 cuōróu rub; knead; twist:洗脚时多～几下,促进血液流通。When you wash your feet, give them a good massage to help the blood circulation. /他把信～成一团,扔进废纸篓。He crumpled the letter into a ball and threw it into the waste paper basket.

搓绳机 cuōshéngjī cording machine

搓手顿脚 cuōshǒu-dùnjiǎo wring one's hands and stamp one's feet — get anxious and impatient:你得想个办法,光～有什么用。You got to work out a solution. There's no use wringing your hands and stamping your feet.

搓洗 cuōxǐ scrub (clothes, etc.)

搓澡 cuōzǎo give sb. a rubdown with a damp towel; rub oneself down (with a towel)

蹉

cuō

蹉跌 cuōdiē 〈书面〉slip and fall; make a mistake

蹉跎 cuōtuó waste time:一再～ miss one's chances repeatedly /莫见长安行乐处,空令岁月易～。Linger not in Chang'an's pleasure quarters; There months and years are turned to empty waste.

蹉跎岁月 cuōtuó-suìyuè idle away one's time; let time slip by without achieving anything:不甘～ be unwilling to idle away one's time /～,误尽时机 let time and opportunity pass one by

撮

cuō ❶〈书面〉gather; bring together:～其部卒三万之众 gather 30,000 troops under his command ❷ scoop up (with a dustpan or shovel):～垃圾 scoop up refuse /～煤 shovel coal ❸〈方言〉pick up (powdery stuff) with fingers:～点儿胡椒面儿 take a pinch of powdered pepper ❹ extract; summarize:～全书之要 make a précis of the book /～其旨意 outline the essentials of sb.'s instructions ❺〈方言〉have a meal; eat:等我得了钱,请你们大伙～一顿。When I get the money, I'll invite you all to a meal. ❻ unit of capacity (= millilitre) ❼〈量词〉(a)〈方言〉*used of sth. powdery one can pick up with one's fingers*:一～儿芝麻 a pinch of sesame seeds /一～白发 a tuff of white hair (b)〈贬义〉*used to indicate a tiny number*:一小～坏人 a handful of evil-doers

see also zuǒ

撮合 cuōhe make a match; act as a match-maker or go-between:经双方的一个朋友～,他俩才相互认识,建立了美满的家庭。With a mutual friend acting as a go-between, they got acquainted and happily married.

撮合山 cuōheshān 〈旧语〉go-between; match-maker

撮箕 cuōjī 〈方言〉dustpan

撮口呼 cuōkǒuhū 〈语言〉class of syllables with ü as the final (韵母) or a final beginning with ü

see also "四呼" sìhū

撮弄 cuōnòng ❶ make fun of; play a trick on; tease:他一有机会就爱～人。He would like tease others at every opportunity. ❷ abet; instigate; incite:谁～这些人来大吵大闹的? Who incited these people to kick up a row here?

撮要 cuōyào ❶ make an abstract; outline essential points:将文件～上报 submit an outline of the document to the higher organization ❷ abstract; synopsis; extracts:论文～ abstract of a thesis

撮药 cuōyào make up or fill a prescription of Chinese herbal medicine; have a prescription of Chinese herbal medicine made up or filled

cuó

cuó 〈书面〉illness

C

see also chài

鹾（鹺） cuó 〈书面〉❶ salt ❷ salty

嵯 cuó

嵯峨 cuó'é 〈书面〉(of mountains, etc.) high and steep：大楼高耸，～入云。Skyscrapers tower into the clouds.

痤 cuó

痤疮 cuóchuāng 〈医学〉acne

痤疮炎 cuóchuāngyán 〈医学〉acnitis

矬 cuó ❶〈方言〉short：这小孩长得有点儿～。The child is a bit short for his age. ❷ lower one's body; crouch：你越拉他，孩子越往下～。The more you try to pull him up, the more the child crouches. ❸ cut; dock：～他十块钱奖金。Dock ten *yuan* from his bonus.

矬子 cuózi 〈方言〉short person; dwarf：他的绰号是"小～"。His nickname is "shorty".

cuǒ

脞 cuǒ 〈书面〉minute and numerous; trivial：～语 trivial remarks or words /～谈 trivial conversation; gossip /丛～ trifling; trivial

cuò

厝 cuò ❶〈书面〉lay; place ❷〈书面〉place a coffin in a temporary shelter pending burial ❸〈方言〉house

厝火积薪 cuòhuǒ-jīxīn *also* "积薪厝火" put or place a fire under a pile of faggots — be blind to a grave danger

措 cuò ❶ arrange; manage; conduct; handle：无所～手足 be embarrassed; find oneself in an awkward situation /惊慌失～ panic-striken; scared out of one's wits /不知所～ be at a loss what to do; be at one's wits' end ❷ make plans：筹～款项 raise funds

措办 cuòbàn map out a plan for an undertaking：～粮草 prepare army provisions /～善后事宜 plan to tackle the problems in the aftermath of an event

措辞 cuòcí *also* "措词" wording; diction：～尖锐 couched in harsh terms /～不当 inappropriate wording /～强硬 sharply worded /在～上多下些功夫 pay more attention to the choice of words

措大 cuòdà *also* "穷措大" qióngcuòdà; "醋大" cùdà penniless scholar：在旧社会，人们把他看作～。In the old society, he was regarded as an impoverished, indifferent scholar.

措举 cuòjǔ measure; action; step：～不当 inappropriate measure /采取这些～实出无奈。We have no alternative but to take such actions.

措施 cuòshī measure; step：具体～ concrete (*or* specific) measure /应急～ emergency measure /补救～ remedial steps; remedies /预防～ preventive measure /反通货膨胀～ anti-inflation measure /紧缩～ austerity measure /强制性～ compulsory (*or* coercive) measure /折衷的～ middle-of-the-road measure; half measure /高压～ high-handed measure /临时～ makeshift (*or* temporary, *or* interim) measure /报复～ retaliatory measure /保安～ security measure /战时～ wartime measure /立即采取～ take immediate measures

措手 cuòshǒu set one's hand to; set about：难以～ difficult to handle (*or* deal with) /何以～ not know how to go about it

措手不及 cuòshǒu-bùjí be caught unprepared; be caught unawares：被弄得～ be caught unprepared; be taken by surprise /打他个～ spring a surprise attack on sb. /有备无患，以防临时～。Preparedness ensures freedom from danger, for it puts one on the alert for eventualities.

措意 cuòyì 〈书面〉pay attention to; keep one's eyes open：对此我已不复～。I have scarcely paid any attention to it.

措置 cuòzhì handle; manage; arrange：～得当 handle a matter properly /～失当 mishandle a problem; not deal with a question properly

措置裕如 cuòzhì-yùrú handle matters with competence and ease

剒（斮） cuò 〈书面〉cut; reap

错[1] cuò ❶ interlocked and jagged; intermeshed; intricate：纵横交～ criss-cross /犬牙交～ jigsaw-like; interlocking ❷ grind; rub：～牙 grind one's teeth (as in one's sleep) ❸ cross; miss：劳驾把车往外～一点。Please move your car a bit outward. ❹ alternate; stagger：把上下班时间～一下 stagger office hours ❺ wrong; mistaken; erroneous：你～了。You are mistaken. /我弄～了。I've got it wrong. /你认～人了。You've got the wrong person. *or* You've taken me for somebody else. ❻ mistake; error; fault; demerit：挑～儿 find fault with /认～ admit one's fault /有～就改。Correct the mistake once you have made it. /全是我的～，不能怪别人。I have nobody to blame but myself. ❼ (used in the negative) bad, poor：画得不～ well-drawn /生意不～。Business is not half bad. /他们的私交相当不～。They are on very good terms. ❽〈方言〉except; but for：～了你，谁会饶了他！Nobody except you would have let him off.

错[2] cuò 〈书面〉inlay or plate with gold, silver, etc.：～金匾额 horizontal gold-inscribed board

错[3] cuò 〈书面〉❶ grindstone for polishing jade：他山之石，可以为～。Stones from other hills may serve to polish the jade of this one; advice (*or* experience) from others may help one overcome one's shortcomings ❷ polish jade：攻～ polish jade; hone

错爱 cuò'ài 〈谦词〉undeserved kindness：承蒙～，今后一定倍加努力。I feel honoured by your favour, which I don't really deserve, and I pledge to make redoubled efforts in the future.

错案 cuò'àn 〈法律〉misjudged case

错别字 cuòbiézì wrongly written or mispronounced character

错彩镂金 cuòcǎi-lòujīn (of carvings and coloured drawings) extremely exquisite; (of writings) flowery language; ornate diction：这篇文章语言～，但多华而不实。This piece of writing is full of ornate expressions but without much substance.

错车 cuòchē (of a vehicle) give another vehicle the right of way：～岔道 layby

错处 cuòchu fault; mistake; error

错待 cuòdài treat unfairly; treat shabbily：放心吧，我们不会～她的。You can rest assured that she will be treated well here.

错动 cuòdòng 〈地质〉move; dislocate：发生了～。A dislocation occurs. /这两个断层～了十厘米。The two faults were dislocated (*or* moved) for ten centimetres.

错讹 cuò'é (of record) error; mistake：校对不严，～甚多。There are quite a few errors due to careless proofreading.

错愕 cuò'è stunned; dumbfounded

错非 cuòfēi 〈方言〉except; not... but：～他爸，谁也管不了他。Nobody but his father can take him in hand.

错缝儿 cuòfèngr 〈方言〉fault; mistake：他总是找我的～。He is always finding fault with me.

错格 cuògé 〈语言〉anacoluthon

错构瘤 cuògòuliú 〈医学〉hamartoma

错怪 cuòguài blame wrongly：你～人了。You've blamed the wrong person.

错过 cuòguò ❶ miss; let slip：～机会 miss an opportunity /～农时 miss the farming season ❷ mistake; fault：她从未在我面前说过你的半点～。She has never said a word against you in my presence.

错话 cuòhuà mistaken remarks; wrong words：说了～，办了错事 say and do wrong things /请不要计较我说的那些～。Please forgive my mistaken remarks.

错踝 cuòhuái wrenched or sprained anklebone

错会 cuòhuì misunderstand; get wrong：避免出现～ avoid misunderstanding /他～了你的意思。He got you wrong.

错简 cuòjiǎn error in the order of bamboo slips (used for writing on in ancient times) — textual error

错角 cuòjiǎo 〈数学〉alternate angle

错金 cuòjīn inlay gold：～器皿 gold-inlaid ware; metal-inlaid ware

错觉 cuòjué wrong impression; misconception; illusion：产生～ have a misconception (*or* wrong impression) /造成～ give a false impression

错开 cuòkāi stagger：～上课时间 stagger the class hours /我们～日

子值班。We work on shifts, each on alternate days.
错漏 cuòlòu mistakes and omissions:严重的～ serious commissions and omissions
错乱 cuòluàn in disorder; in confusion; deranged:精神～ mental disorder; derangement; insanity /颠倒～ topsy-turvy /思绪～ confused in thought (*or* mind)
错落 cuòluò scattered here and there; strewn at random:苍松翠柏,高低～。Green pines and cypresses stood here and there, varying in height.
错落不齐 cuòluò-bùqí disorderly and uneven
错落有致 cuòluò-yǒuzhì apparently scattered about but properly spaced; in graceful disorder
错码 cuòmǎ error code
错谬 cuòmiù error; mistake
错判 cuòpàn 〈体育〉misjudge
错失 cuòshī mistake; slip; fault:他工作认真负责,没有发生过～。He is very conscientious and has never committed a mistake in his work.
错时 cuòshí stagger working hours:我们已要求各工厂～上下班,以避免交通堵塞。We have asked factories to stagger their work hours in order to avoid the traffic jam.
错听 cuòtīng 〈医学〉otosis
错位 cuòwèi ❶ misplacement; dislocation:～煤层〈矿业〉dislocated seam ❷〈医学〉malposition:～咬合 malocclusion
错误 cuòwù ❶ wrong; mistaken; erroneous; incorrect:～言论 erroneous statement /～的结论 incorrect conclusion /在～的时间,～的地点,打了一场～的战争 fight a wrong war at a wrong time and in a wrong place ❷ mistake; error; blunder; incorrect behaviour or conduct:犯～ make a mistake; commit an error
错误百出 cuòwù-bǎichū full of mistakes; error-ridden
错误分析 cuòwù fēnxī error analysis
错误检测 cuòwù jiǎncè error detection
错误检索 cuòwù jiǎnsuǒ false retrieval
错误校正功能 cuòwù jiàozhèng gōngnéng error correction function
错误输人 cuòwù shūrù misinput
错误数据 cuòwù shùjù misdata
错盐 cuòyán *also*"络盐" luòyán complex salt
错银 cuòyín handicraft with inlaid silver filigree
错语症 cuòyǔzhèng 〈医学〉paraphasia
错杂 cuòzá mixed; heterogeneous; jumbled; of mixed content:各类书刊～地放在一起。Books and journals of different kinds are jumbled together.
错账 cuòzhàng account error
错诊 cuòzhěn 〈医学〉erroneous diagnosis
错字 cuòzì wrongly written character; misprint:～连篇 full of misprints or wrongly written characters
错综 cuòzōng criss-cross; intricate:～的公路 criss-crossing highways /～的喧嚷 confused din
错综复杂 cuòzōng-fùzá intricate; complex:～的情节 intricate plot /情况～。The situation is most complicated.
错子 cuòzi 〈方言〉mistake; error; slip:出了～怎么办? What if something goes wrong?

莝

cuò 〈书面〉❶ chop (grass or hay) ❷ chopped grass or hay

挫

cuò ❶ defeat; frustrate:连连受～ suffer one setback after another ❷ subdue; lower; deflate:～敌人的锐气 deflate the enemy's arrogance
挫败 cuòbài ❶ frustration; setback; defeat:屡遭～ suffer repeated frustrations (*or* setbacks) ❷ defeat; frustrate:～敌人的阴谋 thwart the enemy's conspiracy /～反动势力的进攻 frustrate (*or* foil) the offensive of the reactionary forces
挫磨 cuòmo 〈方言〉maltreat; torment
挫伤 cuòshāng ❶〈医学〉contusion; bruise:他腿部～,疼痛不已。He got injured in the leg, which hurts badly. ❷ deflate; dampen; discourage:～上进心 discourage (*or* thwart) sb.'s desire for progress /～感情 hurt sb.'s feelings /～生产积极性 dampen enthusiasm in production
挫失 cuòshī lose heart because of the setbacks one has suffered:～锐气 lose heart; be frustrated
挫损 cuòsǔn weaken or lose because of setbacks:～斗志 lose one's fighting spirit /～信心 lose confidence
挫折 cuòzhé ❶ inhibit; suppress; check; frustrate ❷ setback; reverse:重大～ major setback /遭到～ suffer a defeat /一受～就灰心丧气 be easily discouraged by setbacks; be easily upset

剉

cuò ❶〈书面〉fracture ❷ *see*"锉" cuò

锉

cuò ❶ file:钢～ file /木～ (wood) rasp /圆～ round file /细～ smooth file ❷ make smooth with a file:～光 file sth. smooth /～平 file away rough edges
锉程 cuòchéng file stroke
锉床 cuòchuáng 〈机械〉rasper
锉刀 cuòdāo 〈机械〉file:～车床 filing lathe /～切削机床 file cutting machine
锉蛇 cuòshé 〈动物〉file snake
锉削 cuòxiāo 〈机械〉filing away; file finishing; file cutting; filing
锉屑 cuòxiè filing
锉座 cuòzuò filing block

C

D

dā

褡 dā

褡包 dābao *also*“褡膊”;“褡布” long, broad girdle or sash (usu. made of silk or cloth and worn outside one's garment):摔跤手腰上系着一条蓝色的～。The wrestler wore a broad blue girdle around his waist.

褡膊 dābo *also*“搭膊” dābo *see*“褡包”

褡布 dābù *also*“搭布” dābù *see*“褡包”

褡裢 dālian ❶ long, rectangular bag sewn up at both ends with an opening in the middle (usu. worn round the waist or across the shoulder); waist-bag; shoulder-bag:旅客肩上的～鼓鼓囊囊,装满了零七八碎的东西。The passenger carried a big shoulder-bag bulging with odds and ends. ❷ wrestler's jacket made of several layers of cloth:他穿着白色的～。He wore a white wrestler's jacket.

褡子 dāzi *see*“褡裢❶”

搭 dā ❶ put up; build:～草棚 put up a straw hut /～帐篷 pitch a tent /～瓜架子 set up a trellis ❷ hang over; lay or put over:肩上～了条毛巾 with a towel (hanging) over one's shoulder/往电线上～衣服是危险的。It is dangerous to hang washing on electric wires. /我感到有只手轻轻地～在我的肩上。I felt a hand put lightly on my shoulder. ❸ join together; lap over:前言不～后语 speak disconnectedly; give a disjointed account of sth./两根竹竿～上了。The two bamboo poles lapped over (*or* touched) each other. ❹ throw in more (people, money, etc.); add:今天我们将再～上一个排的兵力。We will throw in another platoon today./为了修改这个报告,我已经～进五个钟头。It took me five hours to revise the report. *or* I put in five hours revising the report. ❺ mixed together; in combination: 大小苹果～着卖 sell big and small apples mixed together/白薯、玉米最好和细粮～着吃。It is best to supplement fine grains with sweet potatoes and maize in one's diet. ❻ lift sth. together:这铜桌子要八个人才能～起来。It takes eight people to lift (up) the copper table./这箱子太沉,请帮我～上一把。The trunk is too heavy. Give me a hand, please. ❼ take (a ship, bus, plane, etc.); travel or go by (plane, train, etc.):～汽车进城 go to town by bus; take a bus to town/没有～上火车 fail to catch the train; miss the train

搭白 dābái 〈方言〉answer; reply; respond

搭班 dābān ❶ join a theatrical troupe or company on a short-term basis:当年我在一个剧团～。In those years, I performed in a theatrical troupe on a short-term basis. ❷ join a work team temporarily; enter into a temporary partnership: 出车时,老张总是找老工人～,装卸车时助他们一臂之力。When he drives out on an assignment, Lao Zhang always teams up with older workers and lends them a helping hand when loading and unloading lorries.

搭班子 dā bānzi set up a (work) team or group:把领导班子搭起来 form a leading group; get a leading group set up/先搭好一个精干的班子,再商量其他事情。We must have an efficient set-up before getting down to business.

搭伴 dābàn join sb. on a trip; travel together: ～旅游 travel in company (with sb.)/她也去上海,你们正好～儿。As she's also going to Shanghai, you two will be travelling companions.

搭帮 dābāng 〈方言〉❶ (of a number of people) form a group:我们～走。We are going in a group. /谁也不愿跟他～走。No one would like to travel in a group with him. ❷ owe... to...:～你,我们的计划才能搞成。We owe it to you that we have made a success of our plan.

搭帮 dābang 〈方言〉help:大家相互～着点,困难就解决了。Let's help each other and the difficulty will soon be resolved.

搭背 dābèi 〈方言〉*see*“搭腰”

搭便 dābiàn 〈方言〉conveniently; in passing:他是出差来这里的,～看看大家。He is here on official business and would like to take the opportunity to see you.

搭膊 dābo *also*“褡包” dābao long, broad girdle or sash

搭补 dābǔ 〈方言〉subsidize; give financial assistance: ～家用 eke out household expenses; help support one's family/这笔钱很快就～完了。This sum of money will drain off easily if doled out as regular allowance.

搭布 dābù *also*“褡包” dābao long, broad girdle or sash

搭茬儿 dāchár *also*“答茬儿” dāchár join in a conversation; chip in

搭车 dāchē ❶ go by bus, car, etc.; hitchhike:搭火车去北京 go to Beijing by train/让人～ give sb. a lift/搭别人的便车 get a lift in sb.'s car/我是一路～来的。I hitchhiked my way here. ❷〈比喻〉take the opportunity:不准～涨价。Ban unauthorized, chain reaction price rise.

搭乘 dāchéng travel by (plane, train, ship, etc.): ～客轮去上海 go to Shanghai by ship

搭档 dādàng *also*“搭当” ❶ cooperate; work together:我跟他～一起干。I'll team up with him to do the job. ❷ partner:桥牌桌上他们是～。They are partners at the bridge table./咱俩是老～了。We are old workmates (*or* colleagues).

搭调 dādiào ❶ in tune (with):他嗓子没有正规练过,唱起来总是不～。He hasn't got a trained voice and keeps going out of tune when he sings. ❷ stand to reason; be reasonable:你这话说得可不～。You sound unreasonable the way you talk. ❸ match; coordinate:有的词和曲与整个影片不～。Some words and melodies are out of harmony with the film as a whole.

搭盖 dāgài build or put up (make-shift houses, etc.): ～几间茅屋临时住住 put up a few thatched cottages as makeshift dwellings

搭钩 dāgōu strike up a relationship with; make connection with; establish contact with: 这家工厂跟一个研究所搭上钩了。This factory has established a sort of hook-up with a research institute.

搭咕 dāgu 〈方言〉❶ strike up a relationship with; establish contact with:你这个人也真怪,怎么一下子就和他～起来了呢。It is surprising, isn't it, that you struck up a relationship with him in such a short time. ❷ consult; discuss; talk over

搭挂 dāguà ❶ hang over; put over:一棵已经伐倒的榆树～在一棵槐树上。A felled elm is hanging over a locust tree. ❷〈方言〉respond; answer:我干我的活儿,没～他。I went on with my work and ignored him.

搭焊 dāhàn 〈机械〉lap welding

搭焊机 dāhànjī 〈机械〉lap (seam) welder

搭话 dāhuà ❶ talk to each other; join in the conversation:大家抢着跟他～。Everyone was anxious for a chance to talk to him. ❷〈方言〉convey a verbal message: 他娘～来了,说过了年要到北京来看他。His mother sent word that she would come to Beijing to see him after the New Year Festival.

搭伙 dāhuǒ ❶ join as partners:他们明天去郊游,我们也想～一道去。They will go on an outing tomorrow and we are thinking of joining them. ❷ have a meal-arrangement with (a restaurant, canteen, etc.):我们要在那里住宿并～。We'll board and lodge there.

搭架子 dā jiàzi ❶ build a framework; get (an undertaking, composition, etc.) roughly into shape:关于技术革新小组,已经搭了个架

子。We have got the group for technical innovation into shape./我写文章总是先～。I usually work out an outline before I start writing an article. ❷〈方言〉put on airs:你凭什么～? What gives you such airs?

搭肩 dājiān ❶ help lift heavy weights onto the shoulders of porters:你～,我扛包。Help shove the sack onto my shoulder, will you? ❷ reach a high place by standing on sb.'s shoulders:战士们～爬上墙头。The men scaled the wall by climbing on each other's shoulders.

搭建 dājiàn ❶ put up; rig up; build; construct: ～工棚 put up a work shed ❷ set up (an organization, institution, etc.): 各级领导班子刚刚开始～。Leading bodies at various levels are being set up. *or* Work has just started to set up leading groups at various levels.

搭箭 dājiàn get ready to shoot an arrow

搭脚儿 dājiǎor 〈方言〉get a lift (in sb.'s car); get a free ride (on a bus, boat, etc.); hitchhike:这两个县城之间没有班车,我只好想法～了。I had to hitchhike as there was no regular bus service between the two counties. /您这车是进城吧,让我搭个脚儿吧。Are you going to town? Be so good as to give me a lift.

搭接 dājiē ❶ connect; link up; join:注意抓好劳动组合和工序～。Pay close attention to the organization of the labour force and the link-up in work procedures. ❷〈机械〉lap joint:～焊 lap weld /～点焊 lap spot weld/～铆 lap riveting /～铆钉 lap-rivet

搭街坊 dā jiēfang 〈方言〉live as neighbours:两家～已有多年了。They have been next-door neighbours for years.

搭界 dājiè ❶ border on; be adjacent to:这里是两国～的地方。This is where the two countries border on each other. ❷〈方言〉(usu. in a negative sense) strike up a relationship with; establish contact with; have to do with:这两家从不～。The two families would never meet socially (*or* would never have any social contact). /这件事跟他毫不～。This has nothing whatsoever to do with him. /咱们还是少跟这种人～为好。We'd better stay away from such people.

搭救 dājiù rescue; go or come to the rescue of; save: ～措施 rescue measures/他们去前线～伤员。They rushed to the front to rescue the wounded. /我们从虎口里把他～出来。We saved him from the jaws of death.

搭犋 dājù *also* "插犋" chājù 〈方言〉pool livestock, ploughs, etc. and farm cooperatively

搭客 dākè 〈方言〉❶ (of boat, car, etc.) take (on) passengers:小面包一路搭了五位客。The minibus picked up five passengers on the way. ❷ passengers

搭扣 dākòu 〈方言〉hasp; bolt

搭拉 dāla *also* "耷拉" dāla droop; hang down

搭理 dāli *also* "答理" dāli (usu. used in the negative) respond; answer; acknowledge

搭链 dāliàn door chain

搭凉棚 dā liángpéng ❶ set up a mat shelter:在西瓜地里搭个凉棚 set up a mat shelter in the watermelon plot ❷ shade one's eyes with one's hand

搭卖 dāmài package sale: ～条款 tied-in clause /硬性～滞销商品 package sale tied to inclusion of some goods in least demand

搭脉 dāmài 〈方言〉feel the pulse: 医生正给病人～。The doctor is feeling the patient's pulse.

搭赔 dāpéi incur additional loss; shoulder responsibilities or defray expenses for sb. else:这件事他非但没得任何好处,还差点儿把老命都～进去了。Not only did he gain nothing from the adventure; it very nearly cost him his life. /这一大笔钱,我可～不起。I can't afford to pay such a big sum for anybody.

搭配 dāpèi ❶ arrange according to given requirements; organise in pairs or groups:分组时男女要～开。There should be a proper proportion of boys and girls when they are divided into groups. /咱俩～参加男子双打比赛吧。Let's pair up for the men's doubles./食物里这两种成份要合理～。The two ingredients of the food should be mixed in due proportions. ❷〈语言〉collocation:英语～词典 dictionary of English collocations/这两个词～不当。These two words don't go together (*or* do not collocate). ❸ co-operate; work together:哥俩一唱一和,～得好极了。The two brothers worked so well together that they fitted each other like a glove. ❹ match; fit:这两种颜色太不～了。The two colours don't match at all.

搭配销售 dāpèi xiāoshòu bundling

搭腔 dāqiāng *also* "答腔" dāqiāng ❶ answer; respond:问谁谁都不～。The question drew no response, whoever it was asked. ❷〈方言〉talk to each other:她们俩很少～。The two of them seldom spoke to each other.

搭桥 dāqiáo ❶ build a bridge:逢山开路,遇水～ (of an army) hew a path if there is a mountain, and put a bridge across if there is a river ❷〈比喻〉act as a go-between; introduce; establish links; form liaison:为两地贸易穿针引线,铺路～ help establish and facilitate direct trade relations between the two localities/我们给未婚青年～,举办各种联谊活动。We organize all kinds of social gatherings for unmarried youths to meet each other. ❸〈医学〉bypass:做心脏～手术 perform a heart bypass surgery

搭桥牵线 dāqiáo-qiānxiàn *also* "牵线搭桥" act as a go-between; bring (people, etc.) into contact:换房站积极为居民换房～。The house-exchange office acts as a go-between for people who wish to exchange houses.

搭儿 dār 〈方言〉place:他不知道小王藏在哪～,找了半天没找着。As he had no idea where Xiao Wang was hiding, he spent a long time vainly looking for him.

搭撒 dāsa droop; hang down: ～着眼皮儿 with drooped eyelids /他～着脸。He pulled a long face.

搭讪 dāshan *also* "搭赸";"答讪" dāshan try to make conversation; say sth. to smooth over an awkward situation:和漂亮姑娘～ try to strike up a conversation with a pretty girl; accost a pretty girl /他见人们不理他,就点了一支烟,不再～了。Realizing that people were paying no attention to him, he lit up a cigarette and made no further effort to mix.

搭设 dāshè put up; rig up (shed, tent, scaffolding, etc.):～脚手架 rig up scaffolding

搭手 dāshǒu give sb. a hand:搭把手 lend a hand; give a hand/我想帮你一把,苦于搭不上手。I would like very much to help you, only I have no idea how to do it.

搭售 dāshòu (short for 搭配销售) package sale tied to unsalable commodities; bundling:必须刹住商品～的歪风。It is necessary to ban the wrong practice of making undesirable or substandard goods part and parcel of a sale package.

搭套 dātào 〈方言〉draught animals and farm tools shared by two or more farm families

搭头 dātou ❶ sth. thrown in (to go with the mainstay); subsidiary goods: 这些黄瓜只是个～。These cucumbers were thrown in to go with other goods. ❷ lap:～焊 end lap weld

搭线 dāxiàn ❶ make contact: 他们是在一家旅馆舞厅搭上线的。They made contact with each other in a hotel ballroom. ❷ act as a match-maker or go-between: 他俩结婚是我搭的线。It was I who played Cupid for them.

搭言 dāyán *also* "答言" dāyán respond

搭腰 dāyao *also* "搭背" pad for harness (on the back of a draught animal)

搭载 dāzài (of boat or truck) take on additional passengers or goods:上水船大多是些货船,～客人的很少。Most of the boats sailing upstream are freighters, few of which take on passengers.

搭制 dāzhì make and put up:～布景 make and put up settings /园内的亭台楼阁、假山水榭～得非常巧妙。The pavilions, towers, rockeries and fish-ponds in the garden are laid out with good taste.

搭置 dāzhì 〈方言〉❶ prepare; arrange: 饭菜已经～停当。Dinner is ready. ❷ make up; dress up; deck out: 小伙子～一下挺英俊。The young man looks very handsome when well-groomed.

搭住 dāzhù take up temporary quarters (with a friend or in a hotel); put up:他在一个亲戚家里～了几天。He stayed for a few days with a relative of his.

搭嘴 dāzuǐ *also* "答嘴" dāzuǐ answer; reply; respond

搭坐 dāzuò travel by:我是～汽车来的。I came here by car.

嗒

dā 〈象声〉:马蹄～～ hoofbeats of a horse; clatter of horses' hoofs/挂钟的～～声 ticktocks of a wall clock/机枪～～地响着。The machine gun rattled away.

see also tà

铬

dā "铁铬" *see* "铁搭" tiědā

答(荅)

dā *used in the following phrases*

see also dá

答白 dābái *also* "搭白" dābái 〈方言〉answer; respond; reply:从容地～ answer unhurriedly (*or* with assurance) /任你怎讲,他总是不

D

～。Whatever you said to him, he just refused to talk.

答茬儿 dāchár *also*"搭茬儿"dāchár 〈方言〉follow up on what has just been said; pick up the thread and join in the conversation; chip in:他的话叫人不摸头脑，没法～。Unable to make out what he meant, I said nothing in response. /我跟他认真说话，你少～！He and I are in serious conversation, so would you be good enough not to interrupt us?

答理 dāli *also*"搭理"dāli (usu. used in the negative) acknowledge (sb.'s greeting, etc.); respond; answer:不爱～人 be standoffish; be distant in manner/我连写三封信，他毫不～。I wrote three letters in succession, but he answered none. /他俩路上见了熟人也不～。When they met acquaintances on the way, the two of them did not even seem to know them.

答聘 dāpìn 〈旧语〉formally pay a return visit to a friendly country

答腔 dāqiāng *also*"搭腔"dāqiāng answer; respond

答讪 dāshan *also*"搭讪"dāshan try to make conversation (with sb.); say sth. to smooth over an awkward situation

答声 dāshēng answer aloud:我叫了好半天，没听见有人～儿。I called out for God knows how long, but heard no answer.

答言 dāyán *also*"搭言"dāyán respond:老师一连问了几遍，都没有人～。The teacher repeated the question several times but there was no response.

D

答应 dāying ❶ answer; reply; respond:老人敲了好几次门，也不见有人～。The old man knocked repeatedly, but nobody answered the door. ❷ agree; promise; comply with:～给予帮助 promise to help/我很难～你的要求。I find it difficult to comply with your request. /你胃口太大，不能～。You are asking too much, I can't buy it.

答允 dāyǔn consent to sb.'s request; promise:满口～ agree (*or* consent) readily

答嘴 dāzuǐ *also*"搭嘴"dāzuǐ answer; reply; respond:问得他直发愣，答不上嘴来。He was so dazed by a barrage of questions that he was at a loss for words. *or* Confronted by a barrage of questions, he stood dumbfounded.

耷 dā ❶〈书面〉big-eared ❷ droop; hang down:她～下脸来，很不高兴。Disappointed, she put on a long face. *or* Her face darkened with displeasure.

耷拉 dāla *also*"搭拉"dāla droop; hang down:～着脑袋 hang one's head /黄狗～着尾巴跑了。The yellow dog limped off, with its tail between its legs. /她把眼皮一～，假装没看见。She let her eyelids droop and pretended to see nothing. /灰溜溜的，两眼无光，脸儿～着，好像老了20岁。With his face drawn and his eyes glazed, he looked as if he were twenty years older than his age.

聹 dā *see*"肥聹聹"féidādā

吖 dā 〈象声〉gee up; giddyap (sound made by a driver to spur a draught animal on)

哒(噠) dā ❶〈象声〉*used in the same way as* 嗒 dā ❷ (used to urge on a draught animal) gee; giddyap

哒嗪 dāqín 〈化学〉pyridazine; diazine ($C_4H_4N_2$)

dá

瘩 dá

瘩背 dábèi 〈中医〉carbuncle on the back

阘 dá 〈方言〉window of upstairs room; upstairs room window

see also tà

达(達) dá ❶ go through to; extend:这地方虽小，但铁路却四通八～。Railway lines extend in all directions from the place, small as it is. /从北京可乘火车直～广州。There is a through train from Beijing to Guangzhou. ❷ reach; arrive at; achieve; amount to:目的已～。Our aim has been achieved. /费用高～三千元以上。The cost amounted to upward of 3,000 *yuan*. /会议长～四小时。The session lasted four hours. ❸ understand thoroughly; be understanding:～于事理 be understanding (of the ways of the world) and amenable to reason/通情～理 be understanding and reasonable; be sensible; show common sense /通权～变 adopt flexible measures in the face of a rapidly changing situation ❹ express; convey; communicate:转～口信 pass on a (verbal) message /传～上级指示 relay directives from higher authorities ❺ eminent; prominent; distinguished:仕途显～ become a prominent figure in the political world ❻ (Dá) a surname

达标 dábiāo attain the required standards; qualify:未能～ fail to reach (*or* attain) the required standards; fail to qualify/花样滑冰～赛 qualifying match in figure skating

达成 dáchéng reach (agreement):～谅解 reach an understanding /～交易 strike a bargain; close a deal /～一致 achieve unanimity/双方就会议议程～协议。The two parties reached agreement on the agenda of the meeting.

达达尼尔海峡 Dádání'ěr Hǎixiá Dardanelles, a narrow strait between European and Asiatic Turkey

达达主义 Dádázhǔyì Dadaism (early 20th-century international movement in art, literature, music and film repudiating conventions)

达旦 dádàn until dawn:工作通宵～ work all through the night

达到 dádào achieve; attain; reach:～目的 achieve (*or* attain) the goal /～标准 be up to standard /～要求 meet the requirements /～高潮 reach a high tide; reach the climax /～预期效果 attain the anticipated results/～先进水平 come up to (*or* reach) advanced levels /他身高～2.15米。He is 2.15 metres tall. *or* His height comes to 2.15 metres.

达尔文 Dá'ěrwén Charles Robert Darwin (1809-1882), English natural historian who propounded the theory of evolution by natural selection

达尔文主义 Dá'ěrwénzhǔyì Darwinism; Darwin's theory

达·芬奇 Dá Fēnqí Leonardo da Vinci (1452-1519), Italian painter and designer whose works include the portrait *Mona Lisa* (c.1504-1505)

达观 dáguān take a philosophical view; take things philosophically:～安命 be philosophical and take things as they are/处事～ take things philosophically in society /他生性～，素不知忧愁为何物。He always takes a philosophical view of things and is carefree.

达官 dáguān high official:～贵人 high officials; ranking officials /～显宦 political dignitaries

达哈 dáhǎ (Mongolian) fur coat with the hair on the outside

达荷美 Dáhéměi Dahomey, former name (until 1975) of Benin

达吉斯坦 Dájísītǎn Dagestan, autonomous republic of Russia on the western shore of the Caspian Sea

达金氏溶液 Dájīnshì róngyè 〈化学〉Dakin's solution

达喀尔 Dákā'ěr Dakar, capital of Senegal

达卡 Dákǎ Dacca or Dhaka, capital of Bangladesh

达赖喇嘛丹增嘉措 Dálài Lǎma Dānzēngjiācuò Dalai Lama Tenzin Gyatso (1935-), 14th Dalai Lama

达朗伯 Dálǎngbó *also*"达兰伯"Jean Le Rond d'Alembert (1717-1783), French philosopher and mathematician:～原理 d'Alembert's principle/～算符〈数学〉d'Alembertian

达累斯萨拉姆 Dálèisīsàlāmǔ Dar es Salaam, former capital and chief port of Tanzania

达令草地 Dálìng Cǎodì Darling Downs, northeastern Australia

达令河 Dálìnghé Darling River, southeastern Australia

达摩 Dámó *also*"达磨"〈佛教〉Bodhidharma, a Mahayana (大乘) Buddhist who came to China in the 6th century and developed a Chinese Buddhist school (*Chan* or Zen Buddhism)

达姆弹 dámǔdàn 〈军事〉dumdum (bullet)

达人 dárén 〈书面〉❶ sensible person ❷ optimist

达人知命 dárén-zhīmìng a wise man understands the will of Heaven

达斡尔族 Dáwò'ěrzú Daur or Tahur nationality, distributed over Heilongjiang Province and the Xinjiang Uygur Autonomous Region

达意 dáyì express or convey one's ideas:词不～。One's words do not convey one's ideas.

达因 dáyīn 〈物理〉dyne:～计 dynemeter

莶(薘) dá *see*"莙莶菜"jūndácài

鞑(韃) dá

鞑靼 Dádá Tartar (used by the Hans in ancient times to refer to

all the nomadic peoples in the north, and specifically in the Ming Dynasty to mean eastern Mongolian tribes living in present Inner Mongolia and eastern part of the Republic of Mongolia, or used to refer to a nationality in the former Soviet Union)：～人 Tartar /～语 Tartar language

鞑靼海峡 Dádá Hǎixiá Tartar Strait

打 dá 〈量词〉dozen：半～ half a dozen /一～毛巾 a dozen face towels /两～圆珠笔 two dozen ball-pens
see also dǎ

怛 dá 〈书面〉❶ sad; in deep sorrow; miserable：～伤 saddened; in deep sorrow ❷ fear; be afraid

靼 dá *see* "鞑靼" Dádá

笪 dá ❶〈方言〉bamboo mat (usu. used for airing grains) ❷〈书面〉tow rope; tow line (for boats) ❸ (Dá) a surname

妲 dá given name：～己 Daji, notorious favourite concubine of King Zhou, last ruler of the Shang Dynasty

舷(韃) dá *see* "舭舷" bǐdá

答(荅) dá ❶ answer; reply; respond：～记者问 press interview /本书以问～形式写成。The book is written in question-and-answer form. ❷ return (a visit, etc.); reciprocate; repay：报～ repay a favour
see also dā

答案 dá'àn answer; solution; key：练习的～ key to an exercise /问题的～ solution to a problem /～不容易找到。The answer is hard to come by.

答拜 dábài *also* "回拜" huíbài return a courtesy call; pay a return visit

答报 dábào repay; requite：～他的盛情 repay him for his gracious kindness

答辩 dábiàn reply (to a charge, query or an argument)：允许被告～ allow the defendant to reply to the charges/论文～ oral defence of one's thesis

答词 dácí thank-you speech; answering speech; reply：致～ give a speech of thanks

答对 dáduì (usu. used in the negative) answer; reply：无言～ can say nothing in reply; feel tongue-tied

答访 dáfǎng pay a return visit

答非所问 dáfēisuǒwèn give an irrelevant answer; sidestep a question：把题目理解准确，避免～。Try to grasp the questions accurately and avoid giving irrelevant answers.

答复 dáfu answer; reply：不予～ make no reply /这个问题无法～。The question is unanswerable. /须及时～他的询问。It is necessary to reply to his inquiry in good time (*or* without delay). /～稽迟，至为歉疚。I'm sorry for my belated reply.

答话 dáhuà answer; reply：我们问她许多问题，她都不～。We asked her many questions, but she didn't reply. /他～彬彬有礼。He was very polite when he spoke in reply.

答卷 dájuàn ❶ answer examination or test papers：认真地～ answer the examination paper carefully /答完卷的同学请出场。Will those students who have finished their papers please leave the room? ❷ examination paper finished by an examinee：标准～ key to the examination questions

答礼 dálǐ *also* "还礼" huánlǐ reciprocate sb.'s courtesy; return a salute

答数 dáshù 〈数学〉answer

答问 dáwèn ❶ answer sb.'s questions; reply to sb.'s queries ❷ book or essay written in question-answer form：《英语语法～》*Questions and Answers in English Grammar*

答谢 dáxiè express appreciation (for sb.'s kindness or hospitality); acknowledge：写信～ write a letter of thanks /～宴会 return banquet /真不知道怎样～你才好。I do not know how to repay your favour.

答谢词 dáxiècí speech of thanks; thank-you speech

答疑 dáyí answer sb.'s questions

沓 dá 〈量词〉pile (of paper, etc.); pad：一～报纸 a pile of newspaper /一～信纸 a writing pad /一～钞票 a wad of banknotes
see also tà

沓子 dázi 〈量词〉pile of (paper, etc.); pad：一～拾元钞票 a wad of ten-*yuan* notes /一～贺年片 a pile of New Year cards

dǎ

打[1] dǎ ❶ strike; hit; knock：～锣 beat (*or* strike) a gong /～铃 ring a bell/～钟 toll (*or* ring) a bell /～稻子 thresh rice /有人～门。Somebody is knocking at the door. ❷ break; smash：杯子～了。The cup is broken. ❸ fight; attack; batter：～败仗 be defeated; suffer a defeat/～碉堡 attack a stronghold/～老婆 batter one's wife /～了就跑的战术 hit-and-run tactics ❹ come into contact with; deal with：*see* "～交道" ❺ construct; build：～土坯 make adobe bricks /～地基 lay the foundation ❻ make (as in a smithy); forge：～耳环 make ear-rings /～一把刀 forge a knife /～家具 make furniture ❼ mix; stir; beat：～浆糊 mix paste/～鸡蛋 beat eggs ❽ tie up; pack：～行李 pack one's luggage; pack up /～捆儿 bundle up / ❾ knit; weave：～草鞋 weave straw sandals /～草绳 spin straw ropes/～毛衣 knit a sweater ❿ apply (sth. to sth. else); draw; paint; mark：～邮戳 stamp a letter /～鞋油 polish shoes /～手印 put one's fingerprint on (a document)/给家具～油漆 varnish furniture/给果树～药 spray insecticide on fruit trees ⓫ open; dig：～井 dig (*or* sink) a well /～(炮)眼 drill a (blasting) hole ⓬ raise; hold up; hoist：～帘子 raise the curtains /～旗帜 hold up a flag; raise a banner/～伞 hold an umbrella; put up an umbrella /～起精神 cheer up; pluck up courage ⓭ project; send; dispatch：～电话 make a phone call /～手电 flash a torch/～信号 signal; give a signal ⓮ issue or receive (a certificate, etc.)：～病假条 get a doctor's certificate for sick leave /～收条 write out a receipt /～介绍信 get a letter of introduction /～借条 write an IOU (*or* loan receipt) ⓯ remove; get rid of：～蛔虫 take worm medicine /～树杈 trim a tree ⓰ ladle; draw：～一碗粥 ladle out a bowl of porridge /～井水 draw water from a well/～开水 fetch boiled water ⓱ buy：～酒 buy some liquor /～票 buy a ticket ⓲ hire (a taxi)：～车 hire (*or* get) a taxi /他刚刚～了辆小面包走了。He just left by a mini-taxi. ⓳ catch; hunt：～鱼 go fishing; catch fish ⓴ gather in; collect; reap：～柴 gather firewood/每亩地～一千斤稻子。We can get in 1,000 *jin* of rice from each *mu* of land. ㉑ draw up; work out; calculate; reckon：～底稿 make a first draft /旅费～低了 underestimate the travel expenses /损耗已经～进去 wastage is counted in (*or* included) ㉒ do; engage in：～零工 take odd jobs; be (*or* work as) an odd jobber /～夜班 be on night shift ㉓ play：～桥牌 play bridge /～乒乓球 play table tennis /～秋千 play on the swing; get a swing ㉔ *indicating certain body movements*：～踉跄 stagger (along) /～手势 make gestures; gesticulate /～旗语 signal with a flag; use semaphore ㉕ adopt; use：～比方 draw an analogy ㉖ (as of a riddle) be about; concern：这个谜语～一物。The riddle is about a thing. ㉗ label; charge：被～成反革命 be labelled a counterrevolutionary

打[2] dǎ 〈介词〉from; since：～心眼里 from the bottom of one's heart/～那以后 since then/我～明儿起戒烟。I'll give up smoking right from tomorrow.
see also dá

打熬 dǎ'áo ❶ endure (hardship); sustain; hold out：他在旧社会～了二十多年。He endured all kinds of hardships in the old society for over twenty years. /她困得实在～不住，趴在桌子上睡着了。She was so tired that she fell asleep reclining on her desk. ❷ hardship; suffering; tribulation：不论什么样的～，他都经得住。He can put up with whatever hardship he may come up against. ❸ build up one's strength through physical exercise; toughen; temper; steel：～筋骨 toughen the body; build up one's physique

打把势 dǎ bǎshi *also* "打把式" ❶ practise martial arts or *wushu*：公园里有许多人在～。People are practising *wushu* in the park. ❷ dance for joy：这孩子在地上～时跌倒了。Dancing for joy, the boy slipped on the floor.

打靶 dǎbǎ target or shooting practice：/～归来 back from shooting practice /～比赛 shooting contest

D

打靶场 dǎbǎchǎng target range; shooting range
打白条 dǎ báitiáo write an IOU (instead of paying cash):收购粮食不准～。It is prohibited to write IOUs instead of paying the farmers when purchasing their grain.
打摆子 dǎ bǎizi 〈方言〉suffer from malaria; run a malarial fever
打败 dǎbài ❶ defeat (in war); vanquish; trounce; rout:～侵略者 defeat an aggressor /他们决心在这场比赛中～对手。They are determined to beat their opponents in the match. ❷ suffer a defeat (in war or competition); be defeated:主队～了。The host team lost the game.
打板子 dǎ bǎnzi ❶ beat on the palm with a ruler; flog; cane:爷爷小时候,不会背书老师就～。When my grandpa was a school boy, he was beaten on the palm with a ruler by the teacher if he couldn't recite the text. ❷〈比喻〉(often used humorously) scold; criticize; take to task:小心老婆～,你这个窝囊废。Take care, you idiot! Your wife'll bite your head off. /谁完不成定额,就打谁的板子。Whoever fails to fill his or her quota will be taken to task.
打扮 dǎban ❶ make up; deck out:～得花枝招展 be gorgeously dressed /～得干干净净 be well groomed/她得～一下才会出门。She will have to make herself up before she is ready to go out. /节日的北京～得格外壮丽。Beijing was magnificently decked out for the festive occasion. /他～成一个乡下佬。He disguised himself as a country cousin.❷ the way one is dressed:这些姑娘几乎都是一样～。These girls were dressed almost in the same way./看她的～,像是上海人。Judging by the style of her dress, she is from Shanghai.

D

打包 dǎbāo ❶ bale; pack:～费 packing charges/～钢丝 baling wire/～铁皮 baling hoop; steel baling hoop; steel baling strap/这些东西容易碎,必须妥善～装车。These things are fragile and must be properly packed and loaded. ❷ unpack:～检验 unpack for check ❸ put the leftovers in a doggie bag after eating in a restaurant:这两个菜～吗? Shall I put these two dishes in a doggie bag for you?
打包机 dǎbāojī 〈机械〉baler; baling machine; bale press; bagging machine; packaging machine
打包票 dǎ bāopiào vouch for; guarantee:这件事成不成,谁也不敢～。Nobody can guarantee whether the matter will turn out to be a success. /你可不能给他～。You mustn't vouch for him./我敢～,这项投资不会有风险。I can assure you that there is no element of risk in the investment.
打苞 dǎbāo (of wheat, sorghum, maize, etc.) form ears; ear up
打保 dǎbǎo 〈方言〉guarantee; vouch for:我敢用脑袋给你～。I can vouch for it upon my honour.
打饱嗝儿 dǎ bǎogér belch after a solid meal
打抱不平 dǎ bàobùpíng intervene on behalf of the injured party; defend sb. against an injustice:老张为人正直,好～。Old Zhang is honest and upright, and never hesitates to take up the cudgels for (*or* is always ready to defend) the injured party.
打奔儿 dǎbēnr 〈方言〉❶ stammer; get stuck:他讲话一动感情就～。He stammers whenever he gets excited. ❷ stagger; stumble:老太太病后走路有点～。The old lady tended to hobble after her illness.
打本 dǎběn rubbings of inscriptions on stone tablets
打蹦儿 dǎbèngr 〈方言〉jump; hop:听到这个好消息,他乐得直～。He jumped for joy when he heard the good news.
打比 dǎbǐ ❶ give or take examples; use an analogy:讲抽象道理最好拿具体事物来～。You'd better give concrete examples when you explain an abstract idea. ❷〈方言〉compare:老了,不能跟小伙子们～了。As an old man, I can no longer hold a candle to youngsters.
打笔墨官司 dǎ bǐmò guānsi engage in written polemics;carry on an academic feud; fight a battle of words:两位老先生在学术问题上打了几十年的笔墨官司。The two elderly scholars have crossed academic swords with each other for decades.
打边鼓 dǎ biāngǔ *also*"敲边鼓" qiāo biāngǔ say sth. from the sidelines:这件事由你去跟领导说,我～。You take this matter up with the leadership and I'll put in a word or two for you from the sidelines.
打摽 dǎbiào 〈方言〉be too weak to stand or walk because of fear, injury or illness:他心里明白腿～。He knew what it was all about but his knees were wobbly.
打冰出溜 dǎbīngchūliu glide across the ice by relying on momentum
打并 dǎbìng ❶ put in order; tidy up; get things ready; pack:～行李,等候出发 get packed and ready to start off ❷ (mostly used in the early vernacular) gather together:～得五十两银子 scrape together 50 *taels* of silver
打并伙 dǎ bìnghuǒ *see*"打平伙"
打补钉 dǎ bǔding patch up; mend:～的衣服 patched-up clothes/文章七拼八凑,到处～。The article was just a piece of patchwork.
打不平 dǎ bùpíng *see*"打抱不平"
打不住 dǎbuzhù ❶ more than (a certain amount):这件大衣一千元～。This overcoat must cost over one thousand *yuan*. ❷ not enough:我们出国前有许多准备工作要做,一个月的时间是～的。One month is too short for the various preparations we'll have to make before going abroad. ❸ miss the target; try in vain to hit:～黄鼬惹一股子臊 try to catch the weasel only to get oneself sick from its foul smell; go for wool and come back shorn
打草 dǎcǎo ❶ cut grass; mow:用镰刀～ mow with a sickle ❷〈方言〉work out a draft:说话不～ speak without a draft; speak extempore
打草稿 dǎ cǎogǎo make (out) a written draft; prepare a rough sketch
打草惊蛇 dǎcǎo-jīngshé stir the grass and alarm the snake — act rashly and alert the enemy; wake a sleeping wolf or dog:侦破过程中要不动声色,以免～。One should stay calm and collected in the process of investigation so as not to alert the criminal.
打喳喳 dǎchācha 〈方言〉whisper:开会的时候,她俩一直在～。The two of them whispered all the time at the meeting.
打茶围 dǎ cháwéi 〈旧语〉have a merry-making party in a brothel
打杈 dǎchà prune:果树要～了。The fruit trees need pruning.
打岔 dǎchà interrupt; cut in; chip in:别人谈话,你别～。Don't chip in when people are talking privately. *or* Don't interrupt anybody in a private conversation.
打禅 dǎchán 〈佛教〉sit in meditation
打长工 dǎ chánggōng work as a long-term hired farmhand
打场 dǎcháng thresh grain (on a threshing ground):～的工具都准备好了。All the tools for threshing grain are now ready.
打场子 dǎ chǎngzi (of street performers) beat drums and gongs to attract a crowd for one's performance:～卖艺 make a living as a street performer
打吵子 dǎ chǎozi 〈方言〉quarrel; have a row
打沉儿 dǎchénr 〈方言〉make a short pause:他听到外面的脚步声一～,又继续说下去。Hearing footfalls outside, he paused for a moment and then went on talking.
打趁语 dǎ chènyǔ 〈方言〉interrupt; interpose; chip in:人家在谈话,你就别总跟着～。Don't keep chipping in while we are talking. *or* Don't butt in on our conversation.
打成一片 dǎchéng yīpiàn become one with; identify oneself with; merge with; mix with:领导应该和群众～。Leaders should identify themselves with the masses. /军民～。The army should become one with the people.
打迟 dǎchí 〈方言〉hesitate for a moment in one's speech; pause:他见我打了迟,就接过话头自己讲开了。When he found me hesitating, he took over the conversation and started speaking himself.
打赤膊 dǎ chìbó 〈方言〉be naked to the waist:天气太热,小伙子都～下地。The weather was sultry, and all the young men went to work in the fields naked to the waist.
打赤脚 dǎ chìjiǎo 〈方言〉go barefooted:他～穿过泥塘。He walked through a mire barefooted.
打冲锋 dǎ chōngfēng ❶ (of attacking forces) charge (enemy positions, etc.):他带领全排～。He led the platoon in charging the enemy position. ❷ dash ahead of others in action; take the lead:青年人在各项工作中都应该～。Young people should be in the van in all spheres of work. /这个人做事磨洋工,吃饭～。A dawdler at work, the fellow is always in a headlong rush during mealtime.
打虫药 dǎchóngyào parasiticide
打虫子 dǎ chóngzi get rid of intestinal parasites or worms by taking medicine
打抽丰 dǎ chōufēng *see*"打秋风"
打出 dǎchū ❶ raise; hoist; unfurl:～某人的旗号 hoist the ensign of sb. (famous or influential) ❷ display; give play to:～水平,～风格 (in a tournament, etc.) give full play to one's skill and sportsmanship
打出手 dǎ chūshǒu ❶〈戏曲〉perform *wushu* in a fighting scene ❷〈方言〉come to blows
打憷 dǎchù be afraid; flinch; recoil:他在困难面前从不～。He never flinched from difficulty.

打春 dǎchūn ❶ *also* "立春" Lìchūn Beginning of Spring ❷〈旧语〉(as of amateur performers, usu. from the local riffraff) go from door to door singing and begging money during the Spring Festival

打从 dǎcóng ❶ since:~春上起，就没有下过透雨。There has been no soaker since spring. ❷〈介词〉(used before words or phrases of place) pass; go through; go by:他每天上班都~公园门口经过。He passed by the entrance to the park every day on his way to work.

打粗 dǎcū 〈方言〉do heavy manual labour; do unskilled work:她经常~打杂，上山下地，什么都干。She was always ready for any type of work, light or heavy, up in the hill or down in the fields.

打错算盘 dǎcuò suànpan miscalculate; make a wrong decision:如果他以为自己可以为所欲为，那是~了。He is miscalculating if he thinks he can do whatever he likes.

打蛋机 dǎdànjī egg-beater; egg-whisk; whisk

打倒 dǎdǎo ❶ attack and bring down on the ground; fell:我一拳头把他~了。I knocked him down with just one blow. ❷ topple; overthrow:~反动统治 overthrow reactionary rule/~帝国主义! Down with imperialism!

打道 dǎdào 〈旧语〉clear the road of pedestrians (for imperial officials to pass through):~回府〈戏谑〉go back home

打嘚嘚 dǎ dēde one's teeth chatter with fear or cold:冻得他直~。His teeth chattered with cold.

打得火热 dǎde huǒrè be on intimate terms; be cheek by jowl (with sb.); be as thick as thieves:他们似乎~。They seem to be on very intimate terms with each other. *or* It seems they have hit it off very well.

打灯谜 dǎ dēngmí *also* "打灯虎" guess or read lantern riddles

打提溜 dǎ dīliu *also* "打滴溜" dangle; swing; sway or hang in the air:这风筝一放起来就~。The kite keeps swinging when flying. /孩子们喜欢抓着大人的胳膊~。Children enjoy swinging around by holding on to the arms of grown-ups. /蚕豆豇豆挂满架，茄子黄瓜~。Broad and string beans hang heavy from the trellis, while eggplants and cucumbers dangle here and there.

打的 dǎdí 〈方言〉take a taxi:我~去了学校。I went to school by taxi./等了半天也没打上的。I waited for quite a while but couldn't get a taxi.

打底 dǎdǐ ❶ *also* "垫底" diàndǐ eat sth. before taking a drink:你不能空腹喝酒，一定要先吃点东西~。Don't drink on an empty stomach; make sure you eat something before you start drinking. ❷ free from anxiety; having peace of mind:从那次出车祸以后，他心里总有些不~。The traffic accident has upset his peace of mind. ❸ *see* "打底子" ❹〈纺织〉bottoming:~机 padding machine

打底子 dǎ dǐzi ❶ sketch (a plan, picture, etc.); draft:你画国画前也~吗? Do you have to make a sketch if you do a Chinese painting in the classical style? ❷ put at the bottom; apply as grounding:路基用细沙土~。Use fine sand and earth as the grounding for the roadbed. ❸ lay a foundation:前两年~，后两年提高。Lay a foundation in the first two years and build on it in the next two.

打地铺 dǎ dìpù sleep on the floor; have a shakedown on the floor or on the ground:我可以打个地铺。I can have a shakedown on the floor.

打地摊 dǎ dìtān sit or lie on the floor or ground:几个年岁大的坐在凳子上,其余的人全都~。Some elderly people were sitting on stools while everybody else was sitting on the floor.

打点滴 dǎ diǎndī (in nursing) put on a drip:手术后他一直在~。He has been on a drip since the surgery (*or* operation).

打点 dǎdian ❶ get (luggage, etc.) ready:~行装 pack up for a trip; get ready for a journey ❷ bribe:他企图上下~，求得开脱。He attempted to get himself acquitted by bribing everyone concerned in the case.

打电 dǎdiàn 〈方言〉make a telephone call:快去~要辆出租车。Please hurry and ring for a taxi (*or* call a taxi by telephone).

打掉 dǎdiào destroy; knock out; wipe out:~一颗门牙 have a front tooth knocked out/~敌人两个团 wipe out two enemy regiments/~一项提案 kill a motion /~他的狂妄气焰 deflate his arrogance

打叠 dǎdié arrange in order; get ready:~行李 pack (one's luggage)/~精神 cheer up; pluck up /把炊具~好。Get the cooking utensils ready.

打顶 dǎdǐng *see* "打尖❷"

打动 dǎdòng move; touch:这番话深深地~了我的心。I was deeply moved (*or* touched) by these words. /我编了一首歌去~他。I composed a song to prompt him into action.

打洞机 dǎdòngjī *also* "打眼机" perforator

打抖 dǎdǒu 〈方言〉shiver; shake; tremble:他冻得直~。He shivered all over with cold. /老爷子气得全身直~。The old man was so angry that he trembled all over. *or* The old man trembled with anger.

打斗 dǎdòu fight; fistfight; wrestle:拳打脚踢地~ engage in a fistfight/他们过去经常~，现在成了好朋友。They used to bicker with each other but have become pals now.

打斗片 dǎdòupiàn kung fu film; action movie

打逗 dǎdòu 〈方言〉make fun of; tease; banter:说笑~ crack jokes; exchange banter

打嘟噜 dǎ dūlu speak with a lisp; talk inarticulately:听不清他说些什么，光听到他嘴里~。I could only see he was murmuring to himself, but could not make out what he was saying.

打赌 dǎdǔ bet; wager:我敢~，这场球我们输定了。I bet we'll lose the game.

打肚皮官司 dǎ dùpí guānsi keep mulling over sth. but refuse to speak plainly:你我多年的老朋友，有话当面说，不兴~。We have known each other for years, so tell me what's on your mind and don't keep it to yourself (*or* don't hold anything back).

打短工 dǎ duǎngōng work as a casual labourer:农闲季节~ work as a casual labourer during the slack season

打短儿 dǎduǎnr 〈口语〉❶ *also* "打短工" work as a casual labourer ❷ be dressed in a (Chinese-style) jacket and trousers (instead of the traditional long gown):她爱~，看起来倒也精神。She likes to wear a jacket and trousers, and looks really smart in them.

打断 dǎduàn ❶ break:一颗流弹把他的腿~了。He was hit by a stray bullet and had his leg broken. ❷ interrupt; cut short:敲门声~了我的思路。A knock on the door interrupted my train of thought. /我在他的肩上拍了一下，~了他的沉思。Patting him on the shoulder, I woke him from his reveries. /他的讲话不时为愤怒的叫骂声所~。His speech was punctuated by bursts of angry shouting.

打堆 dǎduī 〈方言〉gather together; combine; associate; unite:少跟那种人~。Don't mix with such people. /他没有架子，能和群众~。He is modest and unassuming, and easily accessible.

打对面 dǎ duìmiàn ❶ opposite:我的座位和他的座位~。My seat is opposite his. ❷ come face to face with:天很黑，俩人打了对面才互相认出来。It was so dark that only when they came face to face did they recognize each other.

打兑 dǎduì 〈方言〉arrange; look after:她忙完了饭菜，~大伙吃饭。After getting the dishes ready, she served food to everybody.

打盹儿 dǎdǔnr doze off; take a nap:中午打了个盹，下午精神好。If you take a nap after lunch, you will feel fine the whole afternoon. /他听报告时~了。He dozed off while listening to the lecture.

打趸儿 dǎdǔnr ❶ buy or sell in batches:~买西瓜，便宜多了。It's much cheaper to buy watermelons by batches. ❷ altogether; in a lump:他回来后把一年的工资~领去了。He got his pay for the whole year after his return.

打顿 dǎdùn pause:他背书的时候，稍稍打个顿就得挨呲儿。He would be scolded for even the slightest pause he made when reciting a lesson from memory.

打哆嗦 dǎ duōsuo shiver; tremble:气得直~ tremble with rage /吓得~ tremble with fear; shudder /冷得~ shiver with cold

打呃 dǎ'è *see* "打嗝儿"

打耳光 dǎ ěrguāng box sb.'s ears; give a box on the ear:气得她打了他一个耳光。In a moment of uncontrollable rage, she slapped him across his face. /你这样粗心真该~。You really deserve a slap on the face for your carelessness.

打发 dǎfa ❶ send; dispatch:她~大女儿上街买点东西。She sent her eldest daughter to do some shopping. ❷ dismiss; send away:她连说带哄才把孩子们~走了。Partly by persuasion and partly by kidding, she managed to send the children away. /他好不容易才把闹事者~走了。It was with some difficulty that he finally got rid of the trouble-makers. ❸ while or wile away (one's time); kill time:我想在火车上读一本侦探小说~时间。I'm thinking of reading a detective novel on the train to kill time. ❹ (often used in the early vernacular) arrange; look after:~众人住下 see that everybody is settled down

打幡 dǎfān 〈旧语〉(of son of the deceased) hold a white streamer of mourning walking before the bier in the funeral procession

打翻 dǎfān overturn; capsize:小船让风浪给~了。The skiff cap-

D

sized (*or* was overturned) in the storm. /小孩把碗～了。The child knocked the bowl over.

打翻身 dǎ fānshēn toss about in bed:他老是心神不安,到夜里,不停地在床上～。He was so worried that he kept tossing and turning in bed at night.

打翻身仗 dǎ fānshēnzhàng work hard to bring about a fundamental change:大打农业翻身仗 work hard (*or* strive) to bring about an upswing in agriculture /工人们大～,一年时间扭转了企业亏损的局面。The workers went all out to make up for business losses and in a year's time succeeded in bringing the enterprise back on its feet.

打榧子 dǎ fěizi snap the fingers

打分 dǎfēn give grades; mark (students') papers:请给参赛者～。Please give the contestants grades (*or* marks).

打伏击 dǎ fújī ambush:这可是个～的好地方。This is favourable terrain for laying (*or* making) an ambush.

打杠子 dǎ gàngzi ❶ *see* "打闷棍" ❷ stop sb. (from doing); obstruct; bar the way:人家跟你毫无关系,你为什么～? Why get in the way of those who have nothing to do with you? ❸ fleece; diddle; bleed one white:他漫天要价,简直是想打我的杠子。He asked such an exorbitant price that it was obviously meant to bleed me white.

D

打稿 dǎgǎo *also* "打稿子" draft; make a draft: 打腹稿 make a draft in one's head; make mental notes (for an article or speech)

打嗝儿 dǎgér 〈口语〉❶ hiccup ❷ belch; burp

打跟头 dǎ gēntou turn a somersault; loop the loop

打更 dǎgēng ❶ sound the night watches ❷〈方言〉go on night patrol

打埂 dǎgěng 〈农业〉ridging

打哽 dǎgěng 〈方言〉choke with sobs:他讲到这里,不禁打起哽来。He broke down choking with sobs as he said this.

打工 dǎgōng hire out for work; do manual work (for sb. or temporarily); work part-time:给老板～ work for a boss/～糊口 make a living by manual labour /他在国外靠～上学。While abroad, he had to work part-time to support himself at college.

打工妹 dǎgōngmèi employed female worker (usu. referring to a rural girl working in a city)

打工仔 dǎgōngzǎi employed labourer (usu. referring to a rural young man working in a city)

打躬 dǎgōng *also* "打恭" make a deep bow: 频频向来宾～ greet the guests by bowing respectfully again and again; bow to the visitors respectfully again and again

打躬作揖 dǎgōng-zuòyī bow and scrape: ～赔不是 make deep bows and offer humble apologies

打拱 dǎgǒng salute with hands folded in front

打狗看主面 dǎgǒu kàn zhǔmiàn before you beat a dog, find out who's its master; love me, love my dog

打箍机 dǎgūjī 〈机械〉hoop-driving machine

打谷场 dǎgǔcháng threshing ground; threshing floor

打鼓 dǎgǔ ❶ beat a drum:敲锣～ beat gongs and drums ❷ feel nervous:领导叫我去接管总工程师的工作,我心里直～。When I was asked by the leadership to take over as chief engineer, I was very nervous.

打瓜 dǎguā a kind of watermelon grown mainly for its edible seeds

打卦 dǎguà 〈迷信〉cast lots by way of fortune-telling

打关节 dǎ guānjié 〈旧语〉bribe officials for favours

打官腔 dǎ guānqiāng *also* "打官话" mouth officialese; stall with bureaucratic jargon; assume bureaucratic airs:动不动就～训斥人 be ready to put on the airs of a bureaucrat and give people a severe reprimand; be prone to lecture people in a stream of jargon/你说得合乎情理,他不好再～。Your remarks struck home and he couldn't very well go on stalling with bureaucratic jargon.

打官司 dǎ guānsi go to court or law; engage in a lawsuit:打场官司 engage in a lawsuit/他们如果继续散布我的谣言,我就要同他们～。I'll take them to court if they keep spreading rumours about me.

打光 dǎguāng 〈机械〉polish

打光棍儿 dǎ guānggùnr remain a bachelor; stay single:旧社会他没钱娶媳妇儿,打了一辈子光棍。He could not afford to have a wife in the old society and stayed single all his life.

打鬼 dǎguǐ ❶ *also* "跳布扎" tiào bùzhá (as of Tibetan lamas) dance to exorcise ghosts and evil spirits ❷ chase away or annihilate ghosts and evil spirits

打滚 dǎgǔn ❶ roll about; toss about:痛得直～ writhe with pain; toss about in agony/有人在路上～。他一定是疯了,或是醉了。Somebody is tossing and turning on the road. He must be either mad or drunk. ❷〈比喻〉live under certain circumstances for a long time:从小在农村～长大 live and grow up in the country since childhood/在钱堆里～ roll in money

打棍子 dǎ gùnzi come down with the big stick (upon sb.); bludgeon; attack people vehemently and politically; accuse sb. of a crime without producing evidence:不～,不扣帽子。There will be no unfounded accusation and no political labelling. /让大家畅所欲言,不抓辫子,不～。Let everyone speak his mind without either picking on his mistakes or coming down upon him with the big stick.

打哈哈 dǎ hāha tease; make fun; crack a joke: 别跟他～,他情绪很坏。Don't tease him, he is in a foul mood. /要坏事,别～了。Don't joke about it, for there's going to be trouble.

打哈欠 dǎ hāqian yawn

打哈失 dǎ hāshi *also* "打呵欠"〈方言〉yawn

打鼾 dǎhān snore:他真能睡,一躺下就～。How easily he goes to sleep! He starts snoring the moment he lies down.

打寒噤 dǎ hánjìn *also* "打寒战";"打冷噤" tremble or shudder with cold or fear:一股冷气袭来,不禁浑身～。A blast of cold air sent him shivering all over.

打夯 dǎhāng ramming; tamping: ～机 ramming machine; rammer; tamper

打夯号子 dǎhāng hàozi rammer's rythmic chant

打号子 dǎ hàozi sing a work song to synchronize movements, with one person leading; sing a work chant

打呵欠 dǎ hēqian *see* "打哈失"

打黑枪 dǎ hēiqiāng shoot at from a hiding-place; shoot at from behind;〈比喻〉stab in the back

打哼哼 dǎ hēngheng moan; groan:她～惯了,其实没有什么了不起的病。She is habitually moaning like that; there's nothing seriously wrong with her.

打横 dǎhéng sit in the inferior seat at a square table:请老人坐上首,年轻人～。Let the elders take the seats of honour and the youngsters inferior ones.

打横炮 dǎ héngpào 〈比喻〉raise obstacles; deliberately complicate the issue or cause trouble

打呼噜 dǎ hūlu *also* "打呼" snore:小伙子好睡,头一贴枕头就～。It seems this young fellow can never have enough of sleep; the minute his head touches the pillow he starts snoring.

打忽闪 dǎ hūshǎn 〈方言〉*see* "打闪❸"

打花胡哨 dǎ huāhúshào 〈方言〉❶ speak perfunctorily; sweet-talk:他打了个花胡哨,一扭身就走了。After making a few perfunctory remarks, he turned and left./别尽跟我～,你到底答应不答应? Don't you try to sweet-talk me. Do you agree or not? ❷ joke; jest:年轻人喜欢在一起打个花胡哨。Young people enjoy cracking jokes among themselves (*or* in their own company).

打滑 dǎhuá ❶ (of vehicle wheels) turn without moving forward; spin:车轮在泥里～。The wheels spun in the mud. ❷ slip; slide:脚底下一～,险些摔倒了。I slipped and almost fell./汽车一～,冲上了便道。The car slid onto the pavement.

打滑点 dǎhuádiǎn point of slippage

打话 dǎhuà 〈方言〉talk:他们边走边打着话。They talked with each other while walking.

打谎 dǎhuǎng 〈方言〉lie:爱～ be fond of lying; be an easy liar/出家人不～。Monks are not supposed to lie.

打晃儿 dǎhuàngr stagger; hobble:他喝醉了,走起路来～。He was stumbling as he had got drunk.

打回票 dǎ huípiào 〈方言〉❶ return; go back:天不早了,我们该～了。It's getting late and time for us to go back. ❷〈比喻〉reject; send back: 送去的货几次～。The shipment was rejected several times.

打回头 dǎhuítóu *also* "打回转" turn back:他们听见前面有枪声,就赶紧～。Hearing gunshots ahead, they turned back immediately.

打诨 dǎhùn (as of a clown in a traditional opera) make a joke

打活 dǎhuó 〈方言〉work as a farm labourer:为了养活老母亲,他十来岁就开始～。In order to support his aged mother, he began to work as a farmhand when he was a teenager.

打火 dǎhuǒ strike sparks from a flint; strike a light

打火机 dǎhuǒjī cigarette lighter

打火枪 dǎhuǒqiāng device for lighting a gas flame, etc.; ignitor; lighter

打火石 dǎhuǒshí flint
打伙儿 dǎhuǒr join as partners：几个人～贩卖西瓜。Several people peddled watermelons in partnership.
打击 dǎjī ❶〈音乐〉percussion ❷ attack；strike；upset：～报复 retaliate；take revenge /～歪风邪气 combat unhealthy social trends/～投机倒把活动 crack down on speculation and profiteering/情绪上受的～很大 be terribly upset /这对他的尊严是沉重的～。It was a heavy blow to his pride. /不要～群众的积极性。Don't dampen public enthusiasm.
打击面 dǎjīmiàn scope of attack
打击乐器 dǎjī yuèqì percussion instrument：～四重奏 percussion quartet
打饥荒 dǎ jīhuang 〈方言〉be in debt；be in financial difficulty：村里～，人们穿不上，吃不上。People hadn't enough to eat and wear as the whole village was in a bad shape. /他到我家来～。He came to live with my family to tide over difficult days.
打挤 dǎjǐ 〈方言〉cram；pack；crowd：趁现时活还不～，抓紧给棉田浇遍水。Seize the time to water the cotton fields when there are not many other jobs to do yet.
打家劫舍 dǎjiā-jiéshè loot；plunder：这伙土匪经常～，搅得人心惶惶。The bandits often loot the neighbourhood, throwing the people into panic.
打假 dǎjiǎ crack down on counterfeit goods
打价 dǎjià 〈口语〉(usu. used in the negative) bargain；haggle：大百货公司不兴～。You cannot haggle in big stores.
打架 dǎjià come to blows；fistfight；scuffle：～斗殴 fistfights and scuffles/两个喝醉酒的年轻人吵得很凶，打起架来了。Two drunken young men had a bitter quarrel and came to blows.
打尖 dǎjiān ❶ stop for refreshment while travelling；have a snack (at a rest stop)：日近中午，到前边村里打个尖。It's almost midday, let's have a snack in the village ahead. ❷〈农业〉topping；pinching a crop for fuller production
打歼灭战 dǎ jiānmièzhàn fight a war of annihilation — pool all resources to get sth. done completely
打江山 dǎ jiāngshān seize state power through armed struggle：～不易，保江山更难。It is difficult to win state power and even more so to maintain it.
打浆 dǎjiāng pulp beating：～机 beating engine；beater
打讲 dǎjiǎng 〈方言〉talk；chat：两个老人一面抽烟，一面～。The two old men chatted while smoking. /两兄妹直打了一晚的讲。Brother and sister talked far into the night.
打桨 dǎjiǎng pull on the oars
打交道 dǎ jiāodao make or come into contact with；have dealings with：他常和外商～。He has frequent dealings (*or* contacts) with foreign businessmen. /此人不好～。This man is hard to deal with.
打脚 dǎjiǎo 〈方言〉(of tight shoes) pinch：这双鞋穿起来～。These shoes pinch.
打搅 dǎjiǎo ❶ disturb；trouble：他正在看书，别～。Don't disturb him；he is reading. /对不起，～您了。Sorry to have bothered you. /～您一下行吗？May I trouble you a minute? ❷〈婉词〉give trouble to (sb. for his entertainment or hospitality)：实在～您了，明儿见。Thank you for your hospitality. See you tomorrow.
打醮 dǎjiào 〈道教〉perform Taoist rites
打劫 dǎjié rob；plunder；loot：～财物 rob sb. of money or valuables /趁火～ loot (*or* plunder) a burning house
打结 dǎjié ❶ tie a knot；make a knot：打个结 make a knot /两撇眉毛都～了。His brows were knitted. ❷ be tongue-tied：他一时舌头～，半晌说不出话来。He felt tongue-tied and remained speechless for quite a while.
打结器 dǎjiéqì 〈纺织〉knotter
打结强度 dǎjié qiángdù knot strength
打筋斗 dǎ jīndǒu 〈方言〉turn a somersault；tumble
打紧 dǎjǐn 〈方言〉(usu. used in the negative) of consequence：这(件事)不～。This is (a matter) of no consequence.
打近乎 dǎ jìnhu cotton up to；try to establish a relationship with sb.：他千方百计和上司～。He is trying hard to ingratiate himself with the boss.
打噤 dǎjìn tremble；shiver；shudder
打京腔 dǎ jīngqiāng speak mandarin；speak the Beijing dialect
打救 dǎjiù succour；rescue：～难友 succour fellow sufferers /～掉在河里的孩子 rescue a boy who has fallen into a river；rescue a drowning child
打卡 dǎkǎ punch card：～机 punch-card machine；punched-card machine/这种～上夜班的生活他习惯了。He got used to working on night shift and punching in regularly.
打开 dǎkāi ❶ open；unfold：～箱子 open a trunk /～盖子 take off a lid /～包袱 untie a bundle ❷ turn on；switch on：～电视机 switch (*or* turn) on the TV ❸ open up；widen：～局面 open up a new prospect /～眼界 widen one's mental horizons /～销路 develop new markets for a product /～僵局 break a deadlock；bring a deadlock to an end；break an impasse/～缺口 make a breach /～方便之门 provide an outlet；make things easy (for sb. or sth.)
打开话匣子 dǎkāi huàxiázi 〈口语〉plunge into one's spiel；turn on the gas：这个女人只要一～，就说个没完。Once you let her plunge into her spiel, she will never stop.
打开天窗说亮话 dǎkāi tiānchuāng shuō liànghuà *also* "打开窗子说亮话" not beat about the bush；speak frankly；talk in explicit terms：我们～，不要再相互捉迷藏。Let's put our cards on the table and not indulge in a game of hide-and-seek.
打磕绊儿 dǎ kēbanr 〈方言〉pause：他背得很熟，一点也没有～。As he knew every word by heart, he got through without a pause.
打瞌眈 dǎ kēchòng 〈方言〉doze off；nod：他坐在那里一个劲儿～。He sat there nodding away.
打瞌睡 dǎ kēshuì doze off；nod off：看书～ doze over one's book /打起瞌睡来 fall (*or* drop off) into a doze /他在会上～。He dozed away at the meeting.
打搭 dǎké 〈方言〉pause；falter：他说话好～。He speaks in a halting voice. *or* He often falters in his speech. /他打了一个搭儿，接着说下去。He paused a while and then went on.
打孔 dǎkǒng drill a hole；punch a hole；perforate
打孔机 dǎkǒngjī pinhole plotter；punching machine；puncher
打垮 dǎkuǎ smash；rout；destroy：～封建势力 smash the forces of feudalism /～敌人的精锐师团 rout a crack enemy division
打诳 dǎkuáng 〈方言〉lie；tell a lie：他说的是真话，没有～。He was telling the truth, he was not lying. *or* He spoke nothing but the truth.
打捆机 dǎkǔnjī bander；tying machine；baler；baling machine
打蜡 dǎlà wax；polish：往地板上～ wax a wooden floor /给汽车～ give a car a polish
打来回 dǎ láihuí make a round or return trip：不用十分钟就可以打一个来回。It won't take ten minutes to make a round trip.
打赖 dǎlài 〈方言〉deny；disavow；act shamelessly；be perverse：说过的话不许～。Don't deny what you said. / 你装什么糊涂，还想～不成。Are you trying to get away with it by playing the fool?
打兰 dǎlán dram；drachm (equivalent to 60 grains or one eighth of an ounce)
打捞 dǎlāo ❶ get out of the water；salvage：～沉船 salvage a sunken ship /～落水的箱子 retrieve a box from the water ❷〈石油〉fishing：～工具 fishing tool /～装置 fishing gear/～浮筒 caisson
打捞船 dǎlāochuán 〈船舶〉rescue vessel；salvage ship；wrecker
打唠 dǎlào 〈方言〉chat；engage in chitchat
打雷 dǎléi thunder：光～，不下雨。There is all thunder but no rain. /打了一声响雷。Thunder crashed. *or* There was a loud crash of thunder.
打擂 dǎlèi onstage contest in feats of prowess；competition；emulation：车间各小组决心参加～。All the groups in the workshop decided to take part in the emulation campaign.
打擂台 dǎ lèitái contest in boxing or martial arts on stage；join in an open contest：那年有三家厂子来～，但哪一家都没获得全胜。That year, three factories joined in a contest, but none of them came off with flying colours.
打冷噤 dǎ lěngjìn shudder；shiver：令人～ send shivers down one's spine
打冷枪 dǎ lěngqiāng snipe；stab in the back：在丛林地带作战，小心敌人～。Beware of snipes when combatting the enemy in the jungle. /有话当面说，别在背后～。Speak up openly and don't snipe on the sly.
打冷战 dǎ lěngzhan *also* "打冷颤" tremble with cold or fear：冻得我直～。I am shivering with cold.
打愣儿 dǎlèngr 〈方言〉be in a daze；be in a trance：我跟他讲话时，他直～。He seemed to be in a trance while I was speaking to him.
打里 dǎlǐ take care of household chores：他们家有～的，有打外的，日子过得挺好。They are making a go of life, with some taking care

of household matters and others taking on work outside the house.

打理 dǎlǐ 〈方言〉❶ take care of; arrange; put in order: ~家务 take care of domestic affairs /~铺盖 make the bed; tidy up the bedclothes ❷ reply; respond: 人家问他的话，他也不~，只是吧唧他的旱烟袋。He would not say a word even when spoken to but sat there puffing at his long-stemmed Chinese pipe.

打连连 dǎ liánlian *also* "打联联" ❶ associate with; make friends with; cotton up to: 往后少跟那些不三不四的人~。Don't associate (*or* get mixed up) with those dubious characters any more. ❷ 〈方言〉 stay; stop: 快些动身吧，别在这里~了。Hurry up! Don't dawdle any longer. ❸ 〈方言〉 be reluctant to leave; cannot tear oneself away; hate to leave: 心里有点儿~ can hardly tear oneself away

打连厢 dǎ liánxiāng *also* "霸王鞭" bàwángbiān rattle stick used in folk dancing; rattle stick dance

打量 dǎliang ❶ measure with the eye; look up and down; size up: 那人从头到脚把她~了一番。The man looked at her from head to toe. /他迅速~了她一下，她精心的打扮也遮掩不住留华已逝的痕迹。As he ran his eyes quickly over her, he saw that despite her careful make-up she could not conceal the fact that her charms were fading. ❷ think; suppose; reckon: 我~他今天不会来。I suppose he won't show up today. /我~你不知道呢。I figured you were in the dark.

打猎 dǎliè go hunting: 喜欢~ be fond of hunting /以~为生 make a living by hunting

打零 dǎlíng 〈方言〉❶ do odd jobs; work as an odd jobber: 我目前无固定职业，在一个工地~。I don't have a regular position yet, but work as an odd jobber on a construction site. ❷ be all alone; be the odd man out

打零杂 dǎ língzá do odd jobs; do miscellaneous work: 打了半天零杂，该歇歇了。Let's have a break. We've been tinkering about for quite a while.

打卤面 dǎlǔmiàn noodles served with thick gravy as sauce

打乱 dǎluàn upset; disrupt; throw into confusion: ~计划 disrupt a plan; upset the apple cart/~顺序 disrupt a sequence /~座次 upset the seating arrangement/~阵脚 throw (the enemy, etc.) into confusion; cut the ground from under sb.'s feet; take the wind out of sb.'s sails

打骡子惊马 dǎ luózi jīng mǎ beat the mule to scare the horse — punish one person and the others will be scared; punish a person as a warning to others

打落水狗 dǎ luòshuǐgǒu beat a drowning dog — not let up one's attack but go on to crush a beaten enemy; hit a person when he is down

打麻 dǎmá 〈纺织〉❶ scutch: ~机 scutcher; scutching machine ❷ (short for 打麻将牌) play mahjong

打麻烦 dǎ máfan kick up a row; make trouble; make a fuss: 你不要~，你有事，就先回去。Don't make such a fuss. If you have something to attend to, you may go back first.

打马虎眼 dǎ mǎhuyǎn 〈方言〉 try to fool sb. by acting dumb; feign ignorance in order to swindle sb.: 他想~混过去。He was trying to muddle through by acting dumb.

打骂 dǎmà beat and scold; maltreat: 农奴经常遭到主人的~。The serfs often got beatings and scoldings from their owners.

打埋伏 dǎ máifu ❶ lie in ambush: 留下一个排~。A platoon stayed behind in ambush. ❷ hold sth. back for one's own use: 打了埋伏的预算 blown-up budget/你的问题已经暴露，不要再~。Your involvement has been revealed and it's no use trying to hold anything back now.

打卯 dǎmǎo 〈方言〉 make a formal appearance: 他去办公室打了个卯就走了。He left his office immediately after he put in an appearance.

打闷棍 dǎ mèngùn *also* "打杠子" ❶ rob a victim after beating him unconscious with a club; mug ❷ 〈比喻〉 deal sb. a heavy blow by surprise

打闷雷 dǎ mènléi 〈方言〉 leave sb. in suspense; puzzle or perplex sb.: 干脆点儿，省得让我~。Be succinct and to the point so as to save me from guessing.

打鸣儿 dǎmíngr (of a rooster) crow: 天将破晓，公鸡已经~。It's almost dawn, for the cock has crowed.

打抹 dǎmǒ clean with a duster or wiper; wipe clean; dust: 家具~得干干净净。The furniture has been wiped spotlessly clean.

打磨磨 dǎ mòmo *also* "打磨旋" 〈方言〉 walk round nervously: 他急得直~。He was so worried that he walked impatiently all over the room.

打磨 dǎmo polish; burnish; shine: 铜壶~得很光亮。The brass kettle was well shined. *or* The brass kettle was polished till it shone.

打闹 dǎnào ❶ act boisterously; be rowdy; quarrel and fight: 大家都在学习，你们别在这里~。Everybody is busy studying. Don't be so rowdy here. /这些孩子打打闹闹，把房间弄得不成样子。The kids have made a mess of the room, laughing, cursing, fighting, and running all over the place. /他俩常为芝麻大的事~。They two often fall out over trifles. ❷ 〈方言〉 try to get: 他到街上~点吃食来。He went out looking for something to eat.

打闹剧 dǎnàojù 〈戏剧〉 slapstick

打蔫儿 dǎniānr ❶ (of plants) wither; shrivel up: 高粱都旱得~了。The sorghum leaves are all shrivelling up in this spell of drought. ❷ 〈方言〉 droopy; listless; run down: 他今天下午有点~，一直耷拉着脑袋，不说话。He is listless and crestfallen this afternoon, saying not a word.

打拍子 dǎ pāizi beat time

打牌 dǎpái ❶ play cards or mahjong: 打了通宵的牌 play mahjong (*or* cards) all night long ❷ (in international or domestic politics) exploit for one's own end: 打"民意"牌 exploit "public opinion" for one's own end; play the "public opinion" card/中国不打别国牌，也不允许别人打中国牌。China does not play any other country as a card and will not allow other people to play the China card.

打派仗 dǎ pàizhàng engage in factional strife; fight for the interests of a particular faction

打盘 dǎpán ❶ *also* "打盘旋" circle round; spin ❷ 〈方言〉 rest: 牧羊人把羊群赶到阴凉地方~。The shepherd drove his flock to a shady place to rest. ❸ pile up earth round the root of a plant: 他冒雨给树培土、~，生怕雨水白白流掉。Braving the rain, he tried to pile up an earth bed round the foot of the tree to keep the rainwater from running away.

打泡 dǎpào blister; get a blister (on one's foot, hand, etc.): 鞋太紧，脚上就会~。If your shoes are too tight, you may get blisters on your feet.

打炮 dǎpào ❶ open fire with artillery; shell; bombard: 敌军又向我阵地~了。The enemy troops shelled our position again. ❷ 〈旧语〉 (of actors and actresses arriving at a new venue) perform one's best items; put on one's best show: ~戏 one's best item (*or* show)

打喷嚏 dǎ pēntì sneeze

打坯 dǎpī make adobe: ~筑墙 build a wall with adobe

打屁股 dǎ pìgu 〈戏谑〉 slap sb. on the buttocks; spank; severely criticize: 谁不听指挥，就打谁的屁股。Whoever disobeys orders shall be severely criticized. /主意是我出的，要~，打我的。The idea is mine, and if anyone is to get a spanking I offer myself.

打平伙 dǎ pínghuǒ *also* "打并伙" 〈方言〉 have a Dutch treat; go Dutch

打平手 dǎ píngshǒu (in contest) draw; tie: 甲乙两队打了个平手。The A and B teams had a draw (*or* were tied).

打破 dǎpò break; smash: ~垄断 break a monopoly/~僵局 break a deadlock; break the ice; find a way out of a stalemate/~洋框框 break with foreign conventions /~常规 break free from conventions /~界线 break down barriers/~平衡 overturn the balance /~情面 not spare people's sensibilities

打破饭碗 dǎpò fànwǎn break one's rice bowl — lose one's job; be fired: 打破铁饭碗 break the iron rice-bowl — get rid of lifelong employment; abolish the system of lifelong employment

打破脑袋 dǎpò nǎodai break sb.'s head; 〈比喻〉 act savagely: 商业上的竞争激烈，简直要~。There is cutthroat competition in business.

打破沙锅问到底 dǎpò shāguō wèn dàodǐ get to the bottom of things; acquaint oneself with every detail of the matter: 他学习钻研，什么问题都爱~。Having an inquiring mind, he would never stop until he got to the bottom of every question in his studies. /这件事还不能就此了结，我要~。I can't let the matter rest at that; I'll see it through to the end.

打破碗花花 dǎpòwǎnhuāhuā 〈植物〉 Hubei anemone (*Anemone hupehensis*)

打铺盖 dǎ pūgai tie up one's bedrolls; pack up: ~走人 pack up (*or* pull up stakes) and leave

打谱 dǎpǔ ❶ study a chess problem according to a chess manual ❷ make general plans: 你得先打好谱，然后跟人家谈合同。You have to know pretty well what you want before you negotiate the contract. ❸ calculate; figure out: 心里正在~ calculate in one's mind

打气 dǎqì ❶ inflate; pump up: 给轮胎～ pump up the tyre /～筒 bicycle pump; inflator ❷ boost the morale; encourage; cheer up: 给他们撑腰～ back them up and boost their morale

打千 dǎqiān salute by going down on the left knee while the right arm droops forward

打钎 dǎqiān drill a blasting hole in rock with a hammer and a drill rod

打前失 dǎ qiánshi (of a horse, etc.) trip; stumble: 马～, 把我摔了下来。I was thrown off the horse when it stumbled.

打前站 dǎ qiánzhàn act as an advance party: ～小组 advance party/派人为总理的访问～ send an advance party for the premier's visit /他明天出发给旅游团～。He'll set out tomorrow to make advance arrangements for the tourist group.

打钱 dǎqián (of a street-performer) collect money from the spectators

打枪 dǎqiāng ❶ open fire; fire ❷ *also* "枪替" qiāngtì sit for an exam in place of another person

打抢 dǎqiǎng 〈方言〉 rob: 白日～ rob people in broad daylight

打怯 dǎqiè fear; be scared: 心里有点～ get a little scared

打青 dǎqīng collect tender young twigs and weeds: ～积肥 collect twigs and weeds to be stored as compost

打情骂俏 dǎqíng-màqiào tease one's lover by pretending to be displeased; flirt with a member of the opposite sex

打秋风 dǎ qiūfēng *also* "打抽丰" collect or extort money under various pretences: 县官借着给他家老太爷做寿大～。The county magistrate extorted a lot of money under the pretense of celebrating his father's birthday.

打趣 dǎqù tease; banter; make fun of: 拿小孩子～是不对的。It is not right to make fun of the little child. /姑娘们没事也要找个借口跟他～。The girls always made up one excuse or another to crack jokes with him.

打圈子 dǎ quānzi *also* "打圈圈" ❶ circle round; whirl about: 老鹰在空中～。The eagle circled in the sky. ❷ beat about the bush: 他说话～, 我很不耐烦。I'm fed up with him beating about the bush. /不要在小事上～。Don't keep going back to minor issues.

打拳 dǎquán do Chinese shadowboxing: 学～ learn Chinese shadowboxing

打群架 dǎ qúnjià engage in a gang or dog fight; scuffle

打扰 dǎrǎo *see* "打搅"

打入冷宫 dǎrù lěnggōng banish a disfavoured queen or imperial concubines to a "cold" palace; consign to limbo; shelve

打入十八层地狱 dǎrù shíbā céng dìyù banish to the lowest depths of hell; condemn to eternal damnation

打软 dǎruǎn 〈方言〉 become limp; be weak from fatigue or poor health: 他劳累了一天, 上楼时腿直～。After a day's hard work, he felt weak in the legs when climbing the stairs.

打扫 dǎsǎo sweep; clean: ～卫生 have a general cleaning /～街道 clean the street/～院子 sweep the courtyard clean /～战场 clean up the battlefield

打杀 dǎshā kill; beat to death: ～害虫 exterminate the pests

打山 dǎshān 〈方言〉 hunt in mountains: 他从小就跟爷爷～, 谁不知道他的枪法好! He has been hunting in the mountains with his grandpa since childhood, and is known far and wide as a good (*or* crack) shot.

打闪 dǎshǎn ❶ lightning: 又打雷又～ there are flashes of lightning and crashes of thunder ❷ (of ideas, etc.) flash through the mind: "是敌人发现了我, 还是开我个玩笑。" 他的脑子里连打了两个闪。Two questions flashed through his mind: "Has the enemy spotted me, or is it just someone playing me a trick?" ❸ 〈方言〉 trip and fall; stumble and fall: 他光着脚走在倾斜而光滑的石板上, 稳稳实实, 从不～。He walked barefooted on the slippery, sloping flagstone with firm steps, not tripping even once.

打扇 dǎshàn use a fan; fan (sb.): 小女孩夏天经常给爷爷～。The little girl often kept fanning her grandpa in summer.

打伤耗 dǎ shānghao allow for damage or loss: 托运这筐梨要打10%的伤耗。We must allow for 10% damage or loss to this basket of pears in transit.

打赏 dǎshǎng 〈方言〉 bestow a reward; give tips: 主人～下人, 这是头一回。This is the first time the master has given his servants a reward. /这是给招待员的～。These are tips for the waiters.

打失 dǎshī 〈方言〉 lose: 她～了一个金戒指。She lost a gold ring.

打食 dǎshí ❶ (of birds and beasts) forage for food: 狼经常结群～。Wolves often go in packs in search of food. ❷ take medicine to relieve indigestion

打手 dǎshou hired roughneck or thug; hatchet man: 充当～ serve as a hatchet man/他们看起来就像下流社会的～。They looked exactly like thugs from the underworld.

打舒展 dǎ shūzhǎn stretch oneself: 他伸起胳膊, 打了个舒展。He raised his arms and stretched himself.

打水漂儿 dǎ shuǐpiāor play ducks and drakes; 〈比喻〉 squander: 一群小孩在江边～。A group of children were playing ducks and drakes by the river. /不要拿着钱～。Don't play loose with your money.

打水围 dǎ shuǐwéi hunt over water

打死老虎 dǎ sǐlǎohǔ flog a dead tiger — attack or criticize those who are no longer in power: 他专会～。He is adept at flogging a dead tiger.

打算盘 dǎ suànpan ❶ work or use an abacus ❷ calculate: 打小算盘 be calculating; be petty and scheming/打如意算盘 indulge in wishful thinking/打错算盘 miscalculate/要注意工作方法, 不能光在加班加点上～。One should improve one's working methods rather than prolong working hours.

打算 dǎsuan ❶ intend; plan; think of: 你～怎么办? What are you planning to do? /我～尽快开始。I intend to begin as soon as I can. /他一直～学一门技术。He's been thinking of learning a trade. /你真会～。You have a head for turning everything to good account. ❷ consideration; calculation: 长远～ long-term plan(s)/作最坏的～ be prepared for the worst /没有个人～ have no personal motives; have no selfish considerations; have no axe to grind

打胎 dǎtāi have an (induced) abortion: ～药 abortive (medicine)

打太极拳 dǎ tàijíquán ❶ practise *taijiquan* (a kind of traditional Chinese shadowboxing) ❷ dodge and shirk: 直说吧, 不要和我～了。Out with it. Don't beat about the bush any more. *or* Stop this shadowboxing.

打滩 dǎtān (of river boats) sail full steam past dangerous shoals

打谈 dǎtán 〈方言〉 talk: 我很想和他们～～。I would like very much to have a talk with them.

打探 dǎtàn try to find out secretly; fish for: 他四处～消息。He fished for information everywhere.

打嚏喷 dǎ tìpen *also* "打嚏" sneeze

打天秤 dǎ tiānchèng (of rickshaws, large handcarts, etc.) have the front tipped up because of imbalance

打天下 dǎ tiānxià ❶ seize state power by armed force ❷ start, establish or set up an enterprise: 他十五岁那年跟着父亲到天津开店～。At the age of fifteen, he went to Tianjin with his father to open a shop and start a career in the business world.

打铁 dǎtiě forge iron; work as a blacksmith: ～的 blacksmith /趁热～。Strike while the iron is hot.

打挺 dǎtǐng stretch oneself and bend backwards: 小孩不吃药, 在护士怀里直～。The kid refused to take the medicine. He stretched himself and bent backwards in the nurse's arms.

打听 dǎting ask about; inquire about: ～情况 ask for information about sth. /～消息 inquire about sth. or sb. /～老同学的下落 try to find out the whereabouts of one's old classmates

打通 dǎtōng get through; open up: 打不通电话 be unable to get through (on the telephone) /把墙～ make an opening in the wall /～思想 talk sb. round; persuade

打通关 dǎ tōngguān have a drinking game with each of those seated at one's table: 他自恃酒量大, 在席上～。Having a great capacity for liquor, he challenged each of the party to a drinking game.

打通宵 dǎ tōngxiāo work all night long: 那时的工作经常～。We often worked round the clock then. /玩牌又打了个通宵。We played cards till dawn again.

打头 dǎtóu ❶ take the lead: 跑道上～的是个黑人。Leading in the race is a Black athlete. ❷ 〈方言〉 from the beginning: 请～儿再说一遍。Please say it again from the beginning. ❸ take a cut of the money won in gambling

打头风 dǎtóufēng head wind; contrary wind: 船迟又遇～ the boat that set out late happened to have to sail against the wind — misfortunes never come singly

打头炮 dǎ tóupào fire the first shot; be the first to speak or act: 她在会上总爱～。She is always the first to speak at meetings.

打头阵 dǎ tóuzhèn fight in the van; spearhead the attack; take the lead: 由他～, 抗旱一定胜利。With him in the lead, the battle

D

against the drought is bound to be a success. /在这个研究所里，～的是一群中青年知识分子。Spearheading research work at this institute is a group of young and middle-aged intellectuals.

打退堂鼓 dǎ tuìtánggǔ beat a retreat; back out:在这节骨眼上你可不能～。You mustn't give up at this critical moment. /她为什么忽然～呢? Why is she backing out so suddenly? *or* Why is she beating a sudden retreat?

打哇哇 dǎ wāwā ❶ (in children's games) call for a pause or halt; ask for time-out ❷〈比喻〉suspend all of a sudden; change plans at the last minute:这个行动计划是集体研究决定的，谁也不许随便～。This plan of operation is a collective decision taken after careful consultation. Nobody can change it as he pleases.

打外 dǎwài do work outside the house:打里～全靠妈妈一个人。Mother had to take care of things both inside and outside the house.

打弯 dǎwān ❶ (of limbs) bend; flex: 他那条受过伤的腿不能～。He can't bend that knee owing to the wound. ❷ change (ideas or behaviour); change course:困难再大也不能～。We cannot change course no matter how great the difficulties may be. ❸ talk in a roundabout way; beat about the bush:他讲话一向直来直去，不～。He always says what he means and never beats about the bush.

D

打碗花 dǎwǎnhuā 〈中药〉ivy glorybind (*Calystegia hederacea*)

打网 dǎwǎng ❶ weave or make a net ❷〈方言〉cast a fishing net ❸〈比喻〉(often used in the early vernacular) lay a trap

打望 dǎwàng 〈方言〉look (in order to find out sth.): 四处～ look right and left /他凝神～着对面的山坡。He gazed intently at the opposite hillside.

打围 dǎwéi encircle and hunt down (animals); go hunting

打问 dǎwèn ❶〈方言〉inquire: 你去～一下航班。Will you please inquire about the flight number? ❷〈书面〉interrogate with torture; torture into confession:严刑～ put sb. to cruel torture to obtain a confession

打问号 dǎ wènhào put a question mark (to sth.); cherish doubt (about sth.):这事成不成，还得打个问号呢。It is doubtful whether this will be a success.

打问讯 dǎ wènxùn (of a Buddhist monk, etc.) salute by raising both palms and putting them together:那和尚未曾开言先打个问讯。The monk gave a Buddhist salute before speaking.

打硪 dǎwò operate or work a rammer; ram: 轮番～ operate the rammer by turns /～号子震天响。The sky reverberated with the work song sung by those working the rammer.

打下 dǎxià ❶ storm; capture: ～一座县城 capture a county town ❷ lay (a foundation): ～坚实基础 lay a solid foundation /为…～基础 lay the basis for

打下手 dǎ xiàshǒu act as assistant to: 行! 我给您～。OK, I'll be your assistant.

打先锋 dǎ xiānfēng ❶ (in battle or march) fight in the van; be the vanguard; be the advance party:这次战斗由一连～。The First Company will spearhead the attack. ❷〈比喻〉lead the way:要为社会主义建设～。We should take the lead in undertakings of socialist construction. *or* We should stride ahead in the van of socialist construction.

打闲 dǎxián 〈方言〉❶ be unemployed:不管做什么都比～儿强。Any employment would be better than no employment. ❷ be idle; loaf: 她从不～偷懒。She never loafs on the job.

打乡谈 dǎ xiāngtán 〈方言〉talk in Hakka dialect:你同他说话时最好～。You'd better speak Hakka dialect when talking to him.

打响 dǎxiǎng ❶ start shooting; open fire; begin to exchange fire:战斗～了。The battle began. /先头部队～了。The advance detachment has engaged the enemy. ❷ win initial success:第一炮就～了。The first attempt succeeded. /～秋收第一炮。The autumn harvest got off to a good start.

打响鼻 dǎ xiǎngbí (of a horse, mule, etc.) snort

打消 dǎxiāo give up (an idea, etc.); dispel (a doubt, etc.): ～顾虑 dispel misgivings /～念头 dismiss (*or* drop, *or* give up) an idea /～原计划 cancel (*or* drop) the original plan

打小报告 dǎ xiǎobàogào inform secretly on sb.; squeal:给人～ squeal on sb./他是个专爱～的人。He is a squealer (*or* ratfink).

打歇 dǎxiē 〈方言〉rest:赶集的人都在这里～。People going to the fair often take a rest (*or* break) here. /～的时候，大家谈起增产的问题。During the break, they talked about how to increase production.

打斜 dǎxié ❶ slant:太阳已经～了。The sun is setting. ❷ (of a boat or car) yield right of way by moving sideways:对面来了一辆载重汽车，手推车马上～，站住了。As a truck came up in the opposite direction, the pushcart quickly made way and stopped. ❸ (of a junior or a host) sit on the side to show respect:几个儿子～坐在两旁。His sons sat respectfully on either side.

打旋 dǎxuán turn round and round; spin:狂风吹得沙土直～。A gust of wind sent the dust swirling. /侦察机在空中打着旋。The reconnaissance plane was circling overhead.

打雪仗 dǎ xuězhàng have a snowball fight; throw snowballs

打鸭子上架 dǎ yāzi shàng jià *also* "赶鸭子上架" gǎn yāzi shàng jià drive a duck onto a perch — make sb. do sth. entirely beyond him:你们让我唱歌，这不是～吗。You are forcing a donkey to dance if you ask me to sing.

打牙 dǎyá ❶ one's teeth chatter with cold:一阵冷风扑过来，他冻得直～。A gust of cold wind arose and his teeth began to chatter. ❷〈方言〉come into the mouth:一连两天我们连粒米也没～哪! We haven't even taken a mouthful of food for two days running! ❸ joke at sb.'s expense; make fun of sb.:说正经事吧，别拿他～玩儿啦! Let's get down to business, and stop making fun of him.

打牙祭 dǎ yájì 〈方言〉have sth. special to eat; give oneself a special treat:每逢假日，大家凑几个钱～。On holidays, we used to pool our money for a good meal.

打哑谜 dǎ yǎmí speak in riddles; talk in code

打哑语 dǎ yǎyǔ talk in sign language

打掩护 dǎ yǎnhù ❶ provide cover for:为友军～ provide cover for friendly forces ❷ shield; cover up:给坏人～ shield evildoers/你不该为他的错误～。You shouldn't cover up his mistakes.

打眼 dǎyǎn ❶ punch or bore a hole; drill:在墙上打几个眼 drill a few holes in the wall ❷〈方言〉fail to detect the flaws in the goods one buys:买上衣打了眼，买了件次品。I didn't notice the flaws in the jacket when I bought it. So I got a substandard one. ❸〈方言〉catch the eye; attract attention:他那身打扮儿挺～。The way he was dressed was eye-catching.

打眼器 dǎyǎnqì puncher

打眼遮 dǎ yǎnzhē *also* "打眼篷";"打遮手";"打遮阳"〈方言〉shade the eyes with one's hand:他打着眼遮望着一个骑自行车飞跑的人。Shading his eyes with his hand, he watched a man cycling at top speed.

打佯儿 dǎyángr 〈方言〉pretend to be ignorant:我问他，他跟我～。He feigned ignorance when I asked him about it.

打烊 dǎyàng 〈方言〉(of shops, stores, etc.) close:今日～。Closed for the day./这时候各商店都该～了。It was closing time for the shop.

打样 dǎyàng ❶ draw a design ❷〈印刷〉make a proof; proof press

打腰 dǎyāo ❶ bend forward:～弯躬 bow and scrape ❷ *also* "打幺" be popular:她在班上很～。She's quite popular in her class.

打要子 dǎ yàozi weave straw, etc. into cords; make straw cords:割麦子时要有个人专门～、捆麦子。When we reap wheat, someone will make straw cords and tie the wheat up.

打药 dǎyào ❶ laxative ❷〈方言〉ointment for wounds and injuries sold by quacks ❸〈方言〉go and buy Chinese medicine

打噎 dǎyē ❶ hiccup; belch ❷ choke:吃点东西就～ choke on every bite

打野 dǎyě 〈方言〉❶ run around; dash about: 她不做家务，一天到晚在外面～。Instead of doing household chores, she is dashing about everywhere all day long. ❷ stay overnight in the open air:不要紧，没店咱～。It doesn't matter that there is no inn around. We might as well camp in the open air.

打野话 dǎ yěhuà 〈方言〉use obscene language; use coarse expressions:咱可不兴～。We should abstain from obscenities.

打野鸡 dǎ yějī 〈旧语〉shoot wild chickens;〈比喻〉visit low-class prostitutes

打野外 dǎ yěwài (of an army, etc.) carry out field exercises or manoeuvres

打野眼 dǎ yěyǎn 〈方言〉look around; fail to fix one's eyes on the target:看着字念，不要～。Keep your eyes on the text you're reading. Don't look elsewhere.

打夜作 dǎ yèzuò *also* "打夜工" work at night; be on night shift: 他接连打了两个夜作。He worked on night shift twice in succession.

打印 dǎyìn ❶ put a seal on; stamp:别忘了在文书上打个印。Don't

forget to have the document stamped. ❷ cut a stencil and mimeograph; mimeograph: 请将这篇文章～一下。Please have it mimeographed. ❸〈计算机〉print out
打印格式 dǎyìn géshì print format
打印机 dǎyìnjī printer: 点(阵)式～ dot printer/激光～ laser printer/喷墨～ inkjet printer/～接口 printer interface
打印机终端 dǎyìnjī zhōngduān typewriter terminal
打印计算器 dǎyìn jìsuànqì printing calculator
打印件 dǎyìnjiàn mimeographed copy: 计算机～ print-out
打印速度 dǎyìn sùdù print speed
打印台 dǎyìntái ink or stamp pad
打印子 dǎ yìnzi 〈旧语〉borrow from a usurer
打油 dǎyóu ❶ ladle oil; buy (cooking, lamp) oil at a retail shop: 妈妈叫我去打一瓶花生油。Mother told me to get a bottle of peanut oil. ❷〈方言〉extract oil: 棉籽可以～。Oil can be extracted from cotton seeds.
打油诗 dǎyóushī doggerel; ragged verse: 五行～ limerick/他写了几句～，便自诩为诗人。He claims to be a poet simply because he has written a few lines of doggerel.
打游击 dǎ yóujī ❶ wage guerrilla warfare; fight as a guerrilla: 在敌占区～ wage guerrilla warfare in enemy-occupied areas ❷〈口语〉(eat, sleep, etc.) at no fixed place: 他当时不名一文，也没个固定工作，天天在朋友们那里～。He was then literally broke and had no fixed job. He had to sponge off his friends here and there day after day.
打预防针 dǎ yùfángzhēn have a preventive injection — take precautions against sth.; caution against: 我说的这些话，就算是给你～吧。Let these words of mine serve as a warning to you.
打冤家 dǎ yuānjia fight blood feuds; engage in tribal vendettas
打圆场 dǎ yuánchǎng mediate a dispute; smooth things over: ～，赔不是 smooth out a dispute by offering apologies /后来还是他出面～。Finally, he stepped forward to smooth things over.
打援 dǎyuán attack enemy reinforcements; ambush enemy reinforcements: 围点～ besiege an enemy stronghold in order to strike at the reinforcements
打砸抢 dǎ-zá-qiǎng beating, smashing and looting: ～者 smash-and-grabber/严禁～。Acts of beating, smashing and grabbing are strictly forbidden.
打杂儿 dǎzár do odds and ends; do odd jobs: 外出～ go out charring /我在店里～。I worked in a shop as an odd-jobber.
打早 dǎzǎo ❶ long ago: 我们～想来，就是腾不出身儿。We intended to come long ago but couldn't find the time. ❷ before it is too late; at the first opportunity; as early as possible: 天气很热，得～动身。We must set off as early as possible in this hot weather.
打造 dǎzào forging; smithing: ～农具 make farm tools (by forging)
打斋 dǎzhāi *also* "化斋" huàzhāi (of a Buddhist or Taoist monk or nun) beg a vegetarian meal
打战 dǎzhàn *also* "打颤" shiver; shudder; tremble: 冻得浑身～ shiver all over with cold
打掌子 dǎ zhǎngzi 〈方言〉mend the sole of a shoe; resole a shoe
打仗 dǎzhàng go into battle; fight; go to war: 打恶仗 fight a fierce battle /打硬仗 fight a hard battle; fight the enemy head-on/在提高质量上争取打个胜仗 strive for success in quality improvement
打招呼 dǎ zhāohu ❶ greet; say hello: 看见熟人～是一种礼貌。It is a common courtesy to greet people you know. /见到老王，请替我打个招呼。Please say hello to Lao Wang for me when you meet him. ❷ notify; let sb. know: 想要我帮忙，尽管～。Please do not hesitate to let me know if you want any help. /事先已跟他们打过招呼了。I've warned them before. /万一出了岔子，我会设法给你～的。I'll try to tip you off if anything goes wrong.
打照面儿 dǎ zhàomiànr ❶ meet face to face; encounter: 他呀，我就是打个照面儿，也认不出来了。Even if I meet him face to face, I would hardly recognize him. ❷ show up; make an appearance: 他刚才在会上打了个照面儿就走了。He put in a brief appearance at the conference and left shortly afterwards.
打折扣 dǎ zhékòu ❶ sell at a discount; give a discount: 电视机现在～出售。TV sets now sell at a discount. ❷ fall short of a requirement, standard or promise: 说到做到，不～ carry out one's pledge to the letter /大学的报考条件必须坚持，不能～。The college admission requirements have to be met in their entirety.
打着灯笼没处找 dǎzhe dēnglong méi chù zhǎo not to be found even if one holds a lantern in one's search; hard to come by; rare: 这样的好人，你～。Such a good person is rarely seen.
打针 dǎzhēn give or have an injection: 打静脉针 inject into the veins; give or have an intravenous injection /打皮下针 inject under the skin; give or have a hyperdermic or subcutaneous injection
打整 dǎzheng 〈方言〉pack up; get ready: ～行装 pack for one's trip
打止 dǎzhǐ end; close: 咱们今天就谈到这里～。Let's call it a day.
打制 dǎzhì make (implements); forge: ～镰刀 make sickles by hand/～刀剑 forge swords
打制石器 dǎzhì shíqì 〈考古〉chipped stone implement
打中歇 dǎ zhōngxiē 〈方言〉break during work
打肿脸充胖子 dǎzhǒng liǎn chōng pàngzi try to look fat by slapping one's face till it's swollen — do sth. beyond one's means in order to look impressive: 有什么困难就如实说，不要～。Let me know if you have any difficulty, and don't just try to keep up appearances.
打中 dǎzhòng hit (the mark or target): ～敌机 hit an enemy plane /没有～目标 miss the target /～要害 hit the nail on the head; hit the vital spot
打皱 dǎzhòu 〈方言〉crease; crumple: 脸～ one's face creases/尼龙床单会～吗? Do nylon sheets crumple?
打主意 dǎ zhǔyi think of a plan; evolve an idea; try to obtain: 打错主意 miscalculate/光在钱上～ have one's eyes on money alone/今后的路怎样走，要及时早～。We'd better make up our minds as soon as possible about what course to take in the future. /大家正在～让老张做东。We are planning to make Lao Zhang play the host.
打住 dǎzhù ❶ bring or come to a halt (in speech or writing); stop: 他说到这儿突然～了。He stopped abruptly at this point. ❷〈方言〉put up; stay temporarily: ～几天 stay for a few days
打转 dǎzhuǎn *also* "打转身"〈方言〉turn round; turn back: 不要送了，你～吧! Don't bother to come any further, please stop here.
打转 dǎzhuàn *also* "打转转" spin; rotate; revolve: 急得乱～ be so anxious as to run round in circles/车轮在烂泥里～。The car's wheels kept spinning in the mud. /他的话老在我脑海里～。His words kept ringing in my mind.
打桩 dǎzhuāng pile driving; piling: ～机 pile driver
打坠 dǎzhuì swing; sway or hang in the air (by holding onto sb.'s arms, etc.)
打自 dǎzì since; from... on: ～入伏以后，天气还没怎么热过。The weather hasn't turned really hot since the dog days began.
打字 dǎzì typewrite; type: 隔行～ type every other line; type double space
打字带 dǎzìdài typewriter ribbon
打字稿 dǎzìgǎo typescript
打字机 dǎzìjī typewriter
打字员 dǎzìyuán typist
打字纸 dǎzìzhǐ typing-paper
打总儿 dǎzǒngr 〈口语〉in sum total; in a lump; altogether: ～算账 settle the whole business/～买 buy all on the list; buy altogether
打嘴 dǎzuǐ ❶ slap sb.'s face; box sb.'s ear(s): 说脏话，该～。You deserve a box on the ears for mouthing such dirty words. ❷〈方言〉slap one's own face (by making a poor show after boasting): ～现眼 make a fool of oneself in public immediately after boasting
打嘴仗 dǎ zuǐzhàng quarrel: 她们整天唧唧喳喳地～。They kept bickering all day long. /～我可不是你的对手。I'm not your equal in a slanging match.
打坐 dǎzuò (as of a Buddhist or Taoist monk) sit in meditation

dà

大[1] dà ❶ big; large; great: ～建筑 big or large building /～救星 great liberator; saviour/～片 big-budget film/房间～ spacious room/功～于过 one's achievements outweigh one's errors/～有～的难处。Big as something is, there are disadvantages to sheer size. /团结起来力量～。Unity is strength. ❷ heavy; strong: 雪～。It snows heavily. /这酒劲儿～。This liquor is very strong. /外面风～。It's blowing hard outside. ❸ main; major; important; general: ～路 main road /～手术 major operation /～问题 major issue; big problem /～进攻 general offensive /～作家 major (*or* important) writer/～案要案 major and severe cases in violation of law ❹ loud; high: ～声点说话 speak louder /把喇叭开～点 turn up the loudspeaker /痛痛快快地～哭一场 have a good cry ❺ size: 一立方～的冰块 block of ice one

cubic metre in size/这个瓶子有那两个～。This bottle is twice as big as that one. /他的身材和你的差不多～。He is about your size. /你穿多～号的? What size do you wear? ❻ (of) age:你女儿多～了? How old is your daughter? /他～我一岁。He is one year older than I. *or* He is my senior by a year. ❼ to a great extent or degree; greatly; fully:～为改观 change greatly (*or* considerably) /病已～好 be fully recovered; be up and about / ～出风头 be very much in the limelight /～醉如泥 dead or blind drunk/～力发展养猪事业 raise pigs on a large scale /～搞旅游业 make all-out efforts to develop tourism ❽ *used after* 不 *to indicate low degree or frequency*:不～好 not so good /不～容易 not very easy/听不～清楚 can't hear very clearly /不～爱说话 tend to speak little /不～出门 seldom go out ❾ eldest:老～ eldest among brothers and sisters/～儿子 eldest son ❿ adult; major; elder:一家～小 whole family (including both adults and children)/没～没小 not know how to treat elders and juniors in different ways; show no respect for elders ⓫ *used before a phrase of time for emphasis*:～冬天 cold winter day /～晴天 bright sunny day /～热天 exceedingly hot day /～过节的还加班哪! Why, you're working even on a festival! ⓬ *further back or on in time*:～～后天〈口语〉four days from now ⓭〈敬词〉your: *see* "～作";"～札" ⓮ (Dà) a surname

大[2] dà 〈方言〉❶ father:俺～ my dad; my father ❷ uncle:张～～ Uncle Zhang
see also dài

大阿尔伯图斯 Dà'ā'ěrbótúsī Saint Albertus Magnus (c. 1200-1280), Dominican theologian, philosopher and scientist

大安的列斯群岛 Dà'āndìlièsī Qúndǎo Greater Antilles, comprising Cuba, Jamaica, Hispaniola and Puerto Rico

大岸滩 Dà'àntān Grand Banks, continental shelf of North America in the Atlantic to the east of Canada

大螯虾 dà'áoxiā lobster

大巴 dàbā 〈方言〉bus; van

大巴哈马 Dàbāhāmǎ Grand Bahama, principal island and administrative centre of the Bahamas

大把 dàbǎ ❶〈方言〉(polite form of address for) cart driver ❷ many; much; a lot of:～～地进钱 money pours in in large amounts; earn big sums of money; be rolling in money

大白 dàbái ❶〈方言〉whiting:～浆〈建筑〉whitewash ❷ come out; become known; be fully exposed:真相～于天下。The truth has been brought to light.

大白菜 dàbáicài Chinese cabbage:冬储～ Chinese cabbage stored in winter

大白话 dàbáihuà vernacular; colloquial speech:快板的语言最好用～,越通俗越好。Clapper talk should be written in the vernacular, and the simpler the better.

大白天 dàbáitiān in broad daylight:～关着门干什么? Why shut yourself up behind closed doors in broad daylight?

大白天说梦话 dàbáitiān shuō mènghuà 〈比喻〉daydream; put forward impractical and groundless arguments:你说要亩产万斤粮食,这是～。You're only daydreaming when you say you can harvest 10,000 *jin* of grain for each *mu* of land.

大百科词典 Dàbǎikē Cídiǎn (Japan) *Dai Hyakka Jiten*, first published in Tokyo between 1931 and 1935

大百科全书 Dàbǎikē Quánshū (France) *Grand Encyclopédie*, first published in Paris between 1971-1978

大伯子 dàbǎizi 〈口语〉husband's elder brother; brother-in-law:～和她不和。She is not getting on with her husband's elder brother. *or* She is not on good terms with her husband's elder brother.

大败 dàbài ❶ defeat completely; trounce; put to rout:～对手 thoroughly trounce the opponent /A 队以五比零～B 队。Team A beat Team B by 5 to zero. ❷ suffer a crushing defeat:自由党在竞选中～。The Liberal Party was totally defeated in the election.

大班 dàbān ❶ top class in a kindergarten, usu. composed of children ranging from 5 to 6 years old ❷〈方言〉manager of a foreign firm in old China; taipan ❸〈旧语〉sedanchair-carrier

大阪 Dàbǎn Osaka (of Japan)

大板车 dàbǎnchē large handcart

大办 dàbàn go all out; do in a big way:～农业 go all out in agriculture /～水利 build irrigation works in a big way (*or* on a large scale)/反对～婚事 oppose extravagance in weddings /不要～宴席。Do not give lavish feasts.

大半 dàbàn ❶ more than half; greater part; majority:～年 over half a year; better part of a year /～天 more than half a day; most of the day /～辈子 most of one's life-time /～议员坚决反对这个议案。The majority of the congressmen were strongly against the bill. ❷ very likely; most probably:听口音,他～是上海人。Judging by his accent, he is most likely from Shanghai. /老先生～是给忘了。Most probably the old man has forgotten all about it.

大棒 dàbàng big stick — means of intimidation:～加胡萝卜政策 stick-and-carrot policy /挥舞～ wield a big stick

大棒政策 dàbàng zhèngcè big stick policy

大包大揽 dàbāo-dàlǎn take all responsibilities and power upon oneself; take on the whole thing (without considering whether one is capable of undertaking it):不管什么事,他都～。He is ready to take on the whole lot whatever he does.

大包干 dàbāogān all-round contract:我们这里实行了～。We have put into effect the all-round contract system here.

大宝 dàbǎo ❶ great treasure ❷ throne; imperial throne:新登～ newly crowned; recently enthroned ❸ Buddhist dharma; Buddhist doctrine; power of Buddha ❹ shoe-shaped 50-tael silver ingot

大鸨 dàbǎo *also* "地鹔" dìbǔ 〈动物〉great bustard

大堡礁 Dàbǎojiāo Great Barrier Reef (off northeastern Australia)

大报 dàbào major newspaper; newspaper (in contrast to tabloid)

大暴雨 dàbàoyǔ downpour with a 24 hour precipitation of 100-200 millimetres

大爆炸宇宙论 dàbàozhà yǔzhòulùn big-bang cosmology; big-bang theory:～者 big banger

大本营 dàběnyíng ❶〈军事〉general headquarters; supreme headquarters ❷ base camp:登山～ base camp of a mountaineering expedition ❸ centre; heart:反动势力的～ stronghold of political reaction

大本钟 Dàběnzhōng Big Ben (huge bell in the clock tower of the Parliament building in London or the clock itself)

大比 dàbǐ 〈旧语〉(used after the Sui and Tang dynasties) imperial civil service examinations; (used during the Ming and Qing dynasties) provincial civil service examinations:～之年 year of the imperial civil service examinations

大比武 dàbǐwǔ full-scale competition in military skills and tactics:全军～ PLA-wide competitions in military skills and tactics (conducted by the People's Liberation Army in 1963)

大笔 dàbǐ ❶ pen; writing brush:～如椽 writing brush as big as a rafter — forceful writing /他感觉似乎只要他～一挥,一切问题都可以解决了。He feels as if he could solve every problem with a stroke of the pen. ❷〈敬词〉your writing; your handwriting:这是您的～吧? Isn't this your handwriting? ❸ large amount of (capital, money, legacy, etc.):一～钱 a large sum of money /继承～遗产 inherit a large legacy

大便 dàbiàn ❶ defecate; have a bowel movement; shit:去～ go to stool; move the bowels; relieve oneself /～不通 (suffer from) constipation / ～不正常 irregular bowel movement/～失禁 incontinence of faeces (*or* feces) /一天～两次 have two movements a day ❷ stool; human excrement; shit; faeces:化验～ have one's stool examined

大辩论 dàbiànlùn great debate; mass debate

大别 dàbié make rough distinction; roughly classify:柿子可以～为甘柿、涩柿两大类。Persimmons fall roughly into two major types, the sweet and the puckery.

大冰期 Dàbīngqī 〈地质〉Great Ice Age

大兵 dàbīng ❶〈贬义〉serviceman; soldier ❷ great force; powerful army:～压境 threatened by an approaching army; confronted with a great force

大兵团 dàbīngtuán large troop formation:～作战 large formation warfare; movement of huge numbers of people (for the building of a dam, etc.)

大饼 dàbǐng ❶ a kind of large flatbread; pancake ❷〈方言〉*also* "烧饼" shāobing baked pancake with sesame seeds on it

大拨轰 dàbōhōng make all people do the same thing regardless of circumstances:那年头是～干活、大食堂吃饭。In those years, people had to work like a mass of ants and eat together in huge public canteens.

大般若波罗密多经 Dàbōrěbōluómìduōjīng 〈佛教〉*Prajñāpāramitā*

大伯 dàbó ❶ father's elder brother; uncle ❷ (polite form of ad-

dress for an elderly man) uncle
大脖子病 dàbózibìng 〈医学〉goitre
大不敬 dàbùjìng ❶〈古语〉high treason in showing contempt of the monarch ❷ great disrespect to or for one's superior or senior:你的话就是对长辈的~。Your words are a mark of disrespect for your elders.
大不列颠 Dàbùlièdiān Great Britain (comprising England, Wales and Scotland):~及北爱尔兰联合王国 the United Kingdom of Great Britain and Northern Ireland
大不了 dàbuliǎo ❶ at (the) worst; if the worst comes to the worst:~我们把会议取消就是了。If worst comes to worst, we'll cancel the meeting. /~在村子里过夜。At the worst, we'll stay at the village for the night. ❷ (mostly used in the negative) alarming; serious:没什么~的事,不必担心。There is nothing serious. Don't worry. /这不是什么~的成就。This is not a particularly remarkable success.
大布 dàbù 〈方言〉coarse cloth
大步流星 dàbù-liúxīng with vigorous strides; at a stride:~地向前走去 walk on with vigorous strides/他~地穿过草坪,走向篝火。He strode across the lawn towards the bonfire.
大部 dàbù greater part; mostly:~产品质量合格。The products are mostly up to standard. /他的著作~是散文。Most of his works are in prose.
大部头 dàbùtóu voluminous work:~的小说 novel in several volumes; long novel
大才 dàcái ❶ great talent; outstanding ability:此人有~。The man is very talented. ❷ talented person:他可是个~,文章写得漂亮极了。He is a man of talent, and writes beautiful prose.
大材小用 dàcái-xiǎoyòng put fine timber to petty use; waste one's talent on a petty job; assign trivial tasks to talented people:~,是人才的一种浪费。It is a sheer waste of talent to assign petty jobs to people of great ability.
大裁 dàcái 〈印刷〉foolscap
大菜 dàcài ❶ major course (usu. served in a large bowl or platter, and later on in a Chinese feast) ❷ Western food; European food:法国~ French food
大餐 dàcān ❶ sumptuous meal ❷ Western-style meal
大操大办 dàcāo-dàbàn go in for ostentation and extravagance:刹住婚事~的风气。The practice of arranging extravagant weddings should be stopped.
大草 dàcǎo (of Chinese calligraphy) cursive hand with characters and strokes flowing together
大肠 dàcháng 〈生理〉large intestines:~型细菌 coliform bacteria
大肠杆菌 dàcháng gǎnjūn colon bacillus:~群 coli group
大肠杆菌尿 dàcháng gǎnjūnniào 〈医学〉coliuria
大肠杆菌噬菌体 dàcháng gǎnjūn shìjūntǐ 〈医学〉coliphage
大氅 dàchǎng overcoat; cloak; cape
大钞 dàchāo large-denomination banknote:佰元~ hundred-*yuan* note/~换零 break a large-denomination banknote
大巢菜 dàcháocài *also* "巢菜" cháocài common vetch
大潮 dàcháo ❶ syzygial tide; flood tide ❷〈比喻〉current; surging tide:改革开放的~ surging tide of reform and opening up
大吵大闹 dàchǎo-dànào make a big scene:她稍不顺心就~。She would kick up a row (*or* make a big scene) whenever she felt annoyed.
大车 dàchē ❶ horse-drawn cart:赶~ drive a cart /胶轮~ rubber tyre cart/~店 inn for carters /用~运走垃圾 cart garbage away ❷ *also* "大伡" chief engineer (of a ship) ❸ *also* "大伡" engine driver (of a train)
大臣 dàchén (in a monarchy) minister; secretary:总理~ Prime Minister/外交~ (UK) Foreign Secretary /财政~ (UK) Chancellor of the Exchequer
大臣官房长 Dàchén Guānfángzhǎng (Japan) Chief of the Secretariat (of the Ministry of Foreign Affairs)
大成 dàchéng ❶ comprehensive collection or combination:这一工程集本领域各种先进技术之~。The project entails a combination of all advanced technologies in its field. ❷ accomplish great things:此人日后必有~。The man promises to become great in the future.
大成殿 dàchéngdiàn main hall of a Confucian temple
大城府 Dàchéngfǔ Phra Nakhon Si Ayutthaya, historic city in central Thailand
大乘 dàchéng 〈佛教〉Mahayana; Great Vehicle
大吃八喝 dàchī-bāhē *also* "大吃大喝" indulge in wining and dining; be given to lavish feasting:滥用公款~ squander public money wining and dining
大吃一惊 dàchī-yījīng be greatly surprised; be quite taken aback:问题竟如此严重,使我~。I was greatly surprised to find the problem was so serious.
大冲 dàchōng 〈天文〉favourable opposition
大虫 dàchóng 〈方言〉tiger
大出血 dàchūxuè ❶〈医学〉massive hemorrhage ❷〈比喻〉bargain sale; big spending:~价 bargain price/这回我就~,为乡亲们修条路。I'll dig deep into my pocket to pay for the construction of a road for the village.
大楚 Dà Chǔ Great Chu, regime set up by Chen Sheng (陈胜), leader of a major peasant uprising towards the end of the Qin Dynasty about 209 BC
大处落墨 dàchù-luòmò concentrate on the key points; keep the general goal in mind; have the overall interest in view:处理眼前的事情也要~,不能只从小处着想。You must have the long-range interest in mind and not confine yourself to petty considerations while you tackle immediate problems.
大处着眼,小处着手 dàchù zhuóyǎn, xiǎochù zhuóshǒu never lose sight of the general goal, but begin by tackling practical problems at hand
大串联 dàchuànlián establish nationwide ties (as during the Cultural Revolution, when Red Guards went all over the country to incite people to struggle against "capitalist roaders")
大疮 dàchuāng 〈口语〉ulcer on the body caused by venereal diseases
大吹大擂 dàchuī-dàléi make a big fanfare; trumpet loudly (about sth.); boast excessively:为了推销积压产品,他们在报上~地做广告。They advertised with a fanfare in the newspapers to sell their overstocked products. /不要有了点成绩就~。Don't brag when you have scored some modest achievement.
大吹法螺 dàchuī-fǎluó trumpet loudly; brag unashamedly; blow one's own horn or trumpet:这位先生~,我们干吗要听下去呢? Why should we stay and listen to the gentleman blowing his own trumpet?
大锤 dàchuí sledgehammer
大春 dàchūn 〈方言〉❶ spring; springtime ❷ *see* "大春作物"
大春作物 dàchūn zuòwù spring-sown crop
大醇小疵 dàchún-xiǎocī sound on the whole, though faulty in minor details:这篇论文总起来说是~。This thesis is well written on the whole except for a few minor defects.
大词 dàcí 〈逻辑〉major term
大慈大悲 dàcí-dàbēi 〈佛教〉be infinitely merciful; be infinitely compassionate; have immense mercy and compassion:~的观音菩萨 infinitely compassionate and merciful *Guanyin*
大葱 dàcōng large green Chinese onion
大错特错 dàcuò-tècuò completely mistaken; absolutely wrong:质言之,他们的战略就是~的。To put it bluntly, their strategy went badly wrong.
大打出手 dàdǎ-chūshǒu attack brutally; come to blows; get into a fistfight:你们怎么能对那个陌生人~? How could you attack the stranger so brutally? /为了一点小事,他们竟~。They came to blows over a trifle.
大…大… dà…dà… *used before a noun, a verb or an adjective to indicate scale or magnitude*:大鱼大肉 plenty of meat and fish; rich food /大红大绿 in glaring red and green; gaudy; loudly dressed/大吵大闹 kick up a row; make a scene; set up or raise a terrific racket /大摇大摆 walk with a swagger /大进大出 great inflow and outflow /大彻大悟 (of Buddhist philosophy) great awakening to eternal truth /大起大落 great ups and downs; violent fluctuations
大大 dàdà greatly; enormously; tremendously:~增强企业活力 add tremendous vitality to an enterprise/生产效率~提高。Productivity has risen sharply. /今年的出口~超过进口。This year's exports far exceeded the imports. /煤产量~增加。There has been a substantial increase in coal production. /~出乎意料,她考试竟然失利了。Quite contrary to our expectations, she failed the exams.
大大 dàda 〈方言〉❶ dad; pop; father ❷ father's elder brother; uncle ❸ (term of polite address for a man of father's generation) uncle:刘~ Uncle Liu ❹ grandpa; grandad; grandfather
大大咧咧 dàda-liēliē 〈方言〉(of a person) careless; casual;

D

happy-go-lucky：别看他～的，什么事都心里有数。He may seem somewhat careless, but nothing escapes his attention.

大大落落 dàda-luōluō 〈方言〉natural and poised：举止～的 behave with graceful poise/姑娘～地走了进来。The girl walked in with ease and grace.

大袋鼠 dàdàishǔ kangaroo

大胆 dàdǎn bold; daring; audacious：～的举措 bold measure/～的行动 daring act /正视困难，～向前 go ahead bravely while taking full account of the difficulty /～表示反对 venture (*or* dare) to disagree /～! How dare you!

大刀 dàdāo broadsword; glaive

大刀阔斧 dàdāo-kuòfǔ bold and resolute; drastic：采取～的措施 take drastic measures /～地裁减人员 resolutely cut down personnel/～进行改革 carry out radical reforms/此人办事一向～，气魄不凡。He is known for his drive and ability to make bold and resolute decisions.

大道 dàdào ❶ main road; broadway：林荫～ boulevard/院墙外是村边的～。Outside the wall of the courtyard is the wide road on the outskirts of the village. ❷ road of justice; way to a bright future：人要走光明～，不要搞歪门邪道。One should follow the road that leads to a bright future, and not take to evil ways. ❸〈书面〉correct principle; common sense; right thing to do：合乎～ in conformity with the correct principle ❹〈古语〉Great Way or *Tao* — highest political ideal; way of virtue and justice：～之行也，天下为公。When the way of virtue and justice prevails, the whole world is one community.

大道理 dàdàoli major principle; general principle; great truth：光讲～ talk in generalities only; talk nothing but platitudes/这些～人人都懂，但真正做到可不容易。These general principles are known to all, but it isn't easy to live up to them. /小道理要服从～。Minor principles should be subordinated to major ones.

大纛 dàdào 〈旧语〉(used by ancient armies or guards of honour) big banner; streamer

大灯 dàdēng 〈汽车〉headlight (of a car)

大堤 dàdī dike; levee; embankment

大迪克桑斯水坝 Dàdíkèsāngsī Shuǐbà (Switzerland) Grande Dixence Dam

大敌 dàdí ❶ formidable enemy; archenemy：～当前 confronted by a formidable foe ❷ major obstacle; main difficulty：惰性是成功的～。Laziness is the enemy of success.

大抵 dàdǐ generally speaking; approximately; more or less; on the whole：～相同 more or less the same/情况～如此。That is about all it is.

大地 dàdì ❶ earth; land; world：～母亲 Mother Earth/走遍祖国～ travel all over the country /春回～。Spring returns to the earth. /阳光普照～。The sun shines all over the world. /春天，～一片新绿。Spring has brought tender green to the land. ❷ of the earth; ground; terrestrial：～望远镜 terrestrial telescope/～折射 terrestrial refraction/～噪声 ground noise

大地测量学 dàdì cèliángxué geodesy

大地电流 dàdì diànliú earth or ground current

大地电阻 dàdì diànzǔ earth resistance

大地构造学 dàdì gòuzàoxué geotectology; tectonics

大地经线 dàdì jīngxiàn geographic longitude

大地水准面 dàdì shuǐzhǔnmiàn geoid

大地天文学 dàdì tiānwénxué gedetic astronomy

大地纬度 dàdì wěidù geographic latitude

大典 dàdiǎn ❶ grand ceremony：开国～ founding ceremony (of a state) /登基～ coronation ❷ body of classical writings; canon：《永乐～》*Yongle Canon*

大殿 dàdiàn ❶ audience hall; main hall (of a palace or temple) ❷ main hall of a Buddhist temple

大调 dàdiào 〈音乐〉major：C～奏鸣曲 sonata in C major

大东亚共荣圈 Dàdōngyà Gòngróngquān Greater East Asia Co-prosperity Sphere, aggressive and expansionist slogan advocated by Japanese militarists before and during World War II as a pretext under which to conquer Asia and the Pacific

大动干戈 dàdòng-gāngē go to war; go all out; raise a ballyhoo：为这么点小事而～，简直可笑。It is ridiculous to raise a ballyhoo over such a trifling matter.

大动肝火 dàdòng-gānhuǒ be furious; fly into a rage

大动脉 dàdòngmài main artery; aorta：交通～ main artery of communication

大斗兽场 dàdòushòuchǎng 〈历史〉Colosseum

大都 dàdōu for the most part; mostly; largely; mainly：来访者～是学生。The visitors were mainly students. /对他的支持～来自校外。His support came largely from outside the school.

大豆 dàdòu soybean; soya bean：～胶 soya butter (for industrial use)/～油 soybean oil

大豆根瘤菌 dàdòu gēnliújūn soybean nodule bacteria

大都 Dàdū Dadu or Khanbaliq, capital of China's Yuan Dynasty：元～ capital of the Yuan Dynasty

大都会歌剧院协会 Dàdūhuì Gējùyuàn Xiéhuì Metropolitan Opera Association, New York

大都会艺术博物馆 Dàdūhuì Yìshù Bówùguǎn Metropolitan Museum of Art, New York

大都市 dàdūshì large city; metropolis

大肚子 dàdùzi 〈口语〉❶ pregnant; pregnant woman ❷〈戏谑〉big eater ❸ paunch; potbelly

大肚子痞 dàdùzipǐ 〈中医〉swollen belly with ascites

大度 dàdù 〈书面〉magnanimous：～包容 magnanimous and tolerant /豁达～ open-minded and magnanimous

大端 dàduān 〈书面〉main aspects or features; salient points：举其～ point out the main features

大队 dàduì ❶ military unit corresponding to the battalion or regiment ❷ (in the air force) group：美国空军一个～由两个以上的中队组成。A group consists of two or more squadrons in the US Air Force. ❸ brigade (of a rural commune, etc.)：生产～ production brigade/消防～ fire brigade ❹ large body of：～人马 large contingent of troops; large body of marchers, paraders, etc.

大多 dàduō for the most part; mostly; mainly; largely：响尾蛇～在晚间出来觅食。The rattlesnake comes out for food mostly at night. /她的论点～以事实为根据。Most of her arguments are founded on facts.

大多数 dàduōshù great majority; vast majority; bulk：提案没有得到～人的赞同。The proposal did not get majority support. /在～情况下，这类谈判都无积极结果。In most cases these negotiations produce no positive results.

大额优惠 dà'é yōuhuì volume discount

大而化之 dà'érhuàzhī careless; casual; slapdash：他平时～，经常丢三落四。Usually, he is so careless that he is forgetting or mislaying things all the time.

大而全 dà'érquán big and self-contained or all-inclusive：追求～的方针 policy of setting up only big and comprehensive enterprises

大而无当 dà'érwúdàng large but impractical; big but unwieldy：～的计划 grandiose but impractical plan

大发雷霆 dàfā-léitíng be furious; fly into a rage; bawl angrily：他～，跺着脚骂她。He lost his temper completely, stamping his feet and swearing at her. /老板～，炒了他的鱿鱼。The boss flew into a rage and gave him the boot.

大发 dàfa 〈方言〉excessively; exceedingly; terribly：你我都错了，错～了! Both you and I are wrong, terribly wrong./事情闹～了。The thing has blown into a storm.

大法 dàfǎ ❶ fundamental law; constitution：宪法是国家～。The constitution is the basic law of a nation. ❷〈书面〉important law; major statute

大法官 dàfǎguān grand justice; chief justice; Lord Chancellor or Lord High Chancellor (the highest judicial official of the United Kingdom who is also keeper of the Great Seal and Speaker of the House of Lords)

大法会 Dàfǎhuì Great Prayer Festival, most important religious ceremony of the year in Tibet

大凡 dàfán generally; in most cases：～坚持锻炼的人，身体抵抗力都比较强。Generally speaking, those who exercise regularly have higher resistance to disease.

大方 dàfāng ❶〈书面〉experts; scholars; the initiated：～之家 learned man; expert/贻笑～ incur the ridicule of experts ❷ a kind of green tea produced in certain areas of Anhui and Zhejiang

大方 dàfang ❶ generous; liberal; open-handed：花钱～ be open-handed; be generous with money ❷ natural and poised; easy; unaffected：举止～ have an easy manner; carry oneself with ease and confidence /谈吐～ talk with easy grace; talk naturally /她看上去端庄～。She looks serene and unaffected. ❸ in good taste; tasteful：这件衣服款式很～。The style of the dress is in good taste.

大方广佛华严经 Dàfāngguǎngfóhuáyánjīng *also* "华严经" *Avatamsaka-sūtra*

大方脉 dàfāngmài 〈中医〉internal medicine (for adults):大小方脉 general practice in Chinese medicine (for both adults and children)

大方向 dàfāngxiàng general orientation or direction:～正确 have a correct orientation /要坚持为和平与人类进步而斗争的～。We must persist in the general direction of the struggle for peace and human progress.

大房 dàfáng ❶ eldest branch of a family ❷ primary or official wife (in polygamy)

大放厥词 dàfàng-juécí talk a lot of nonsense; spout a stream of empty rhetoric; deliver a harangue; be full of sound and fury:我不许你再～。I want no more of your nonsense. /他在会上～。He spouted a lot of rubbish at the meeting.

大放异彩 dàfàng-yìcǎi shine with dazzling splendour:唐代诗歌～。The Tang period was a scene of dazzling exuberance for classical poetry.

大费唇舌 dàfèi-chúnshé take a lot of persuading:让他把烟戒掉可～了。It took me a lot of persuading to make him give up smoking.

大分子 dàfēnzǐ 〈化学〉macromolecule:～超导体 macromolecular superconductor

大粪 dàfèn human excrement; night soil:掏～ collect night soil

大风 dàfēng ❶〈气象〉force 8 wind; fresh gale ❷ gale; strong wind:～警报 gale warning/海上刮起了～。A strong wind is blowing over the sea.

大风大浪 dàfēng-dàlàng ❶ wind and waves; great storms:这条船很坚固,经得住～。The ship is strong enough to ride out heavy storms. ❷〈比喻〉great social upheaval; social turbulence:经历了～,遇上这点小事就不算什么了。Compared with the great social upheavals we have gone through, this is nothing.

大风子 dàfēngzǐ 〈植物〉chaulmoogra (*Hydnocarpus anthelmintica*):～油 chaulmoogra oil

大夫 dàfū 〈古语〉senior official
see also dàifu

大幅度 dàfúdù substantially; drastically; by a big margin:～地裁减核武器 drastic reduction of nuclear weapons /工农业生产～增长 substantial growth in the industrial and agricultural output /粮食持续～增产 large continuous increase of grain output /～提高 increase by a big margin

大父 dàfù 〈书面〉❶ grandfather:先～ my late grandfather ❷ maternal grandfather

大副 dàfù (on a ship) first or chief mate; mate; chief officer

大腹贾 dàfùgǔ 〈贬义〉potbellied merchant; rich merchant

大腹皮 dàfùpí 〈中药〉shell of areca nut

大腹便便 dàfù-piánpián 〈贬义〉potbellied; paunchy:～的官僚 potbellied bureaucrats /那些大亨们个个～,盛气凌人。Those paunchy magnates all had an air of arrogance.

大盖帽 dàgàimào *also* "大檐帽" peaked cap; law enforcement or other officer who wears such a cap

大概 dàgài ❶ general idea; broad outline:关于这件事,我只知道个～。I have only a general idea of the matter. ❷ general; rough; approximate:～的估计 rough estimate /～的轮廓 broad outline; general picture /～的数字 approximate figure /～的印象 general impression ❸ probably; most likely; presumably:他到北京～有三十多天了。He has been in Beijing for thirty days or so. /会议～要延期。The meeting will probably be postponed. /他～不会来了。He is not likely to come.

大概其 dàgàiqí *also* "大概齐"〈方言〉roughly; generally:这本书我～地翻了一遍。I only leafed through that book. /他的话我只听了个～。I only got a rough idea of what he said.

大干 dàgàn work energetically; go all out; make all-out efforts:～四化 work energetically for the four modernizations/～快上 get going and go all out/我们得～一场,才能按时完成工作任务。We'll have to make an all-out effort to complete the work on time.

大纲 dàgāng outline:世界史～ outline of world history /教学～ teaching programme; syllabus

大哥 dàgē ❶ eldest brother ❷〈口语〉(polite form of address for a man about one's own age) elder brother

大哥大 dàgēdà 〈口语〉❶ mobile telephone; cellular phone ❷ boss; influential person

大革命 dàgémìng ❶ great revolution:法国～ French Revolution ❷ Great Revolution in China — the First Revolutionary Civil War (1924-1927):他父亲在～时期参加了中国共产党。His father joined the Chinese Communist Party during the Great Revolution.

大公 dàgōng *also* "大公爵" grand duke:～夫人 grand duchess /～领地 grand duchy

大公报 Dàgōngbào *Dagong Bao* (formerly translated as *L'impartial*), first published in 1902 in Tianjin, and now in Hong Kong known as *Tak Kung Pao*

大公国 dàgōngguó grand duchy:卢森堡～ the Grand Duchy of Luxembourg

大公无私 dàgōng-wúsī ❶ selfless; unselfish:我钦佩他～的精神。I admire him for his selfless spirit. ❷ just and fair; perfectly impartial:～的法官 impartial judge /他们对这件事的处理确实～。They are quite fair in handling the matter.

大功 dàgōng great merit; extraordinary service:立了～ have performed exceptionally meritorious services /他在部队立过～。He was awarded a special merit citation in the army. /她对本地教育事业的发展有～。She has made great contributions to the cause of education in this locality.

大功告成 dàgōng-gàochéng be crowned with success; come off with flying colours; be brought to a successful conclusion:桥梁施工已～。The construction of the bridge is at last completed.

大功率 dàgōnglǜ 〈电学〉high-power:～电缆 high-power cable/～显微镜 high-power microscope/～整流器 heavy-duty rectifier

大恭 dàgōng 〈书面〉excrement; stool:出～ have a bowel movement; defecate

大估摸 dàgūmo 〈方言〉approximately; roughly; about:枣子～得多少钱一斤? Approximately how much does one *jin* of dates cost? /你就说个～吧。Just give us a rough idea of it.

大姑子 dàgūzi 〈口语〉husband's elder sister; sister-in-law

大古力水坝 Dàgǔlì Shuǐbà (US) Grand Coulee Dam

大骨节病 dàgǔjiébìng Kaschin-Beck disease

大鼓 dàgǔ ❶ big drum;〈乐器〉bass drum ❷〈戏曲〉*dagu*, versified story sung to the accompaniment of a small drum and other instruments:京韵～ Beijing musical storytelling

大故 dàgù 〈书面〉❶ major disaster or incider:国有～。A major disaster fell on the country. ❷ death of a parent

大褂 dàguà unlined long Chinese-style gown; robe:蓝布～ blue cotton gown

大关 dàguān ❶ strategic pass; important junction ❷ (used after big numbers or amounts) mark; limit:小麦亩产突破了五百斤～。The per-*mu* yield of wheat exceeded (*or* topped) the 500 *jin* mark. /这个镇的人口已接近十万～。The population of this township has come close to the hundred thousand figure (*or* has grown to nearly one hundred thousand). ❸ (ancient instrument of torture) rack for the legs

大关节目 dàguān-jiémù 〈方言〉major parts; important details:你放心,这件事的～,我都查清楚了。Don't worry. I have found out all the major points about the matter.

大观 dàguān grand sight; magnificent spectacle:蔚为～ present a magnificent view /洋洋～ grand view

大观园 Dàguānyuán Grand View Garden, family garden of the Jias in classical novel *A Dream of Red Mansions* (红楼梦)

大管 dàguǎn 〈乐器〉bassoon

大归 dàguī 〈书面〉❶ return of a divorced woman to her own mother's home for good ❷ one's final resting place—death

大规模 dàguīmó large-scale; full-scale; extensive; massive:～生产 large-scale production /～毁灭性武器 weapon of mass destruction/举行～罢工 stage a massive strike /～报复 massive retaliation

大规模集成电路 dàguīmó jíchéng diànlù 〈电子〉large-scale integrated circuit; LSI circuit

大锅饭 dàguōfàn cooked rice in a big pot — indiscriminate egalitarianism:吃～ eat from the big rice-pot the same as everyone else; get an equal share of income without doing the same amount of work /改革"吃～"的体制 change the practice of eating from the same big rice-pot

大国 dàguó big country; big power; great power:工业～ big industrial power /军事～ military power/超级～ superpower/人口～,资源小国 big power in terms of its population but poor in its resources

大国沙文主义 dàguó shāwénzhǔyì *also* "大国主义" great-nation chauvinism

大国一致原则 dàguó yīzhì yuánzé principle of unanimity of the Five Powers (i. e. the five permanent members of the Security

Council of the United Nations)
大过 dàguò major demerit; serious offence; big mistake:记～一次 record a serious mistake
大海捞针 dàhǎi-lāozhēn fish for a needle in the ocean; look for a needle in a haystack; be next to impossible:谁知道他在哪儿躲着，要找到他好比～。Who knows where he is holed up? It's easier to look for a needle in a haystack than to find him.
大海鲢 dàhǎilián tarpon (*Elopidae*)
大海雀 dàhǎiquè great auk; garefowl (*Pinguinus impennis*)
大寒 Dàhán ❶ Great Cold, 24th seasonal division point, marking the sun's position at 300° on the ecliptic ❷ day marking such a seasonal division point, usu. falling on the 20th or 21st of January ❸ period lasting from such a seasonal division point till the next one (Beginning of Spring 立春)
see also "节气" jiéqi; "二十四节气" èrshísì jiéqì
大韩贸易振兴公司 Dàhán Màoyì Zhènxīng Gōngsī (ROK) Korea Trade Promotion Corporation
大韩民国 Dàhán Mínguó Republic of Korea (ROK)
大喊大叫 dàhǎn-dàjiào ❶ shout at the top of one's voice:一群孩子在窗外～。A group of children are making a great noise outside the window. ❷ conduct vigorous propaganda:为新生事物～ vigorously advertize newly emerging things
D
大汉 dàhàn big or burly fellow:彪形～ hefty fellow; man of strong build
大汉族主义 dàhànzúzhǔyì Han chauvinism
大旱逢甘霖 dàhàn féng gānlín auspicious rain during a serious drought; timely relief from distress
大旱望云霓 dàhàn wàng yúnní long for a rain cloud during a drought; look forward to relief from distress:灾区人民盼望医疗队有如～。People of the afflicted areas eagerly look forward to the arrival of medical teams.
大好 dàhǎo ❶ very good; excellent; superb; wonderful:～形势 excellent situation /～风光 superb view; wonderful sight /～河山 beautiful rivers and mountains of a country; one's beloved motherland /～时机 opportune moment; golden opportunity; finest hour/他是个～人。He has indeed a heart of gold. ❷ fully recover:他的病已～了。He is fully recovered from his illness.
大号 dàhào ❶〈敬词〉your (given) name ❷ large size:～的男衬衣 large-size shirt /特～ extra-large ❸〈乐器〉tuba; bass horn:圆型～ helicon /苏萨～ sousaphone
大合唱 dàhéchàng cantata;choral work or piece; chorus:《黄河～》*The Yellow River Cantata* /今天晚会第一个节目是～。The first item at tonight's party is a choral work.
大河 dàhé ❶ great river:～有水小河满，～无水小河干。The small streams rise when the main stream is high; when the main stream is low, the small streams run dry—individual well-being depends on collective prosperity. ❷ Yellow River:～上下，顿失滔滔。The Yellow River's swift current Is stilled from end to end.
大和绘 dàhéhuì *Yamato-e*, Japanese style of painting
大和魂 Dàhéhún (Japan) *Yamato-damashii*:在第二次世界大战中，"～"成了日本军国主义精神的代名词。During World War II, *Yamato-damashii* became a synonym for the spirit of Japanese militarism.
大和民族 Dàhé Mínzú Japanese nation; *Yamato*
大亨 dàhēng big shot; tycoon; magnate:上海滩上的～ big shot on the Shanghai Bund/石油～ oil tycoon /钢铁～ steel magnate
大轰大嗡 dàhōng-dàwēng engage in ostentatious mass action with little substance; raise a big fanfare; make a terrific bustle:搞建设要有计划，不可～。We should build the country in a planned way, and not rush headlong into ostentatious mass action.
大红 dàhóng bright red; scarlet:～大紫 bright red and purple; scarlet and violent;〈比喻〉(of people) at the height of influence or popularity; all the rage
大红人 dàhóngrén (figuratively referring to one who has won the trust of his superiors) favourite; trusted follower; golden boy or girl:那小子是咱们厂长的～。That fellow is the factory director's golden boy.
大后方 dàhòufāng ❶ vast rear area ❷ areas under KMT rule (in northwestern and southwestern China) during China's War of Resistance Against Japanese Aggression (1937-1945)
大后年 dàhòunián three years from now
大后天 dàhòutiān three days from now
大呼拉尔 Dàhūlā'ěr Great Hural, legislative body of Mongolia
大呼隆 dàhūlong much fanfare but few practical results; hustle and bustle:这个工地管理混乱，工人干活儿～，浪费现象严重。This construction site is poorly managed. There is much hustle and bustle but little work is done, and the waste is staggering.
大狐猴 dàhúhóu indri (*Indriidae*)
大户 dàhù ❶〈旧语〉rich and powerful family; well-to-do family:～人家 wealthy and influential family; rich family with ancient lineage/吃～ (of the rebellious poor in a famine) go and feed upon the rich ❷ large family; large clan:李、王二姓是本村的～。The Lis and Wangs are the largest clans in the village. ❸ unit or individual that produces the most or occupies a prominent place in a given field:种粮～ major grain producer/用电～ large consumer of power/本行业的创汇～ big foreign-exchange earner in the industry
大花脸 dàhuāliǎn ❶〈戏曲〉character with painted facial make-up in traditional Chinese opera, specializing in singing ❷ dirty funny face; besmirched face
大话 dàhuà big talk; boast; bragging:说～ talk big; brag /少说～。Stop swanking.
大患 dàhuàn great damage; major danger:他认为这班野心家日后终成～。He thought that those careerists would cause tremendous damage later on.
大荒 dàhuāng ❶ severe famine:～之年 year of severe famine ❷ vast wilderness; wasteland:北～ Great Northern Wilderness (in northeast China)
大荒儿 dàhuāngr 〈方言〉approximately; roughly:他～地看了看园子里的花木。He threw a cursory glance at the flowers and trees in the garden.
大黄 dàhuáng 〈植物〉rhubarb (*Rheum officinale*)
大黄蜂 dàhuángfēng hornet
大黄根酸 dàhuánggēnsuān chrysophanic acid
大黄鱼 dàhuángyú large yellow croaker
大回环 dàhuíhuán 〈体育〉giant circle; giant:单臂～ single-arm circle
大茴香 dàhuíxiāng 〈植物〉anise; star anise
大会 dàhuì ❶ plenary session; general (membership) meeting; conference; congress:联合国～ United Nations General Assembly / 全国科学～ National Science Conference /全国人民代表～ National People's Congress ❷ mass meeting; mass rally:举行群众～ hold a mass rally /纪念～ commemoration meeting /建校五十周年庆祝～ jubilee celebration of the founding of the university
大会战 dàhuìzhàn decisive battle into which both armies throw in most of their forces; big pitched battle — pooling all resources to complete a certain major project
大伙儿 dàhuǒr 〈口语〉*also* "大家伙儿" we all; you all; everybody:～一起干。Let all of us join in the work. /～都关心她。Everybody shows solicitude for her.
大祸 dàhuò dreadful trouble; great misfortune; calamity; disaster:闯下～ get into terrible trouble/ ～临头。A great misfortune has befallen us. *or* We are in for dreadful trouble.
大惑不解 dàhuò-bùjiě be extremely puzzled; be baffled or bewildered; be unable to make head or tail of sth.; be all at sea:令人～ extremely baffling/对他的所作所为，我感到～。I'm quite puzzled about what he did.
大吉 dàjí ❶ extremely lucky; very auspicious:开市～ (of a shop, etc.) open with everything auspicious; get off to a flying start/万事～ all's well; everything is just fine; everything goes off without a hitch ❷ *used after a verb to add a touch of humour*:溜之～ sneak away; slink off /关门～ close down; shut down for good /完事～ it's over, thank god; this is the end of the story
大吉大利 dàjí-dàlì extremely auspicious; very lucky:祝你新年～。Wish you every luck in the New Year.
大集体 dàjítǐ ❶ collective ownership on a large scale; enterprise founded on such ownership ❷ big family; big collective:生活在这个～里，他感到很舒心。He felt quite comfortable living in such a big collective.
大几 dàjǐ more than (twenty or thirty years of age):三十～的人，还没结婚呢! Though he's on the wrong side of thirty, he's still single.
大戟 dàjǐ 〈中药〉root of Beijing euphorbia (*Euphorbia pekinensis*)
大计 dàjì major issue; programme of lasting importance; matter

of fundamental importance：百年～ matter of fundamental importance for generations to come；major issue that will affect future generations /共商～ come together to discuss matters of vital importance
大祭司 dàjìsī pontifex，member of the principal college of priests in ancient Rome；archpriest
大蓟 dàjì 〈植物〉setose thistle
大家 dàjiā ❶ great master；authority：书法～ great master of calligraphy；master calligrapher /汉学～ leading expert on sinology/～手笔 work of a master；master-stroke ❷ well-known ancient family；distinguished family of long standing：～闺秀 daughter from a family of good social standing /～风范 manners of good breeding ❸ all；everybody；everyone：～来出主意。Let's put our heads together. *or* Let's have a brainstorming session together. /在这个小机构里，～都互相认识。In this small unit，everybody knows everybody else. /你不要辜负～的希望。You must never let us down. *or* You must never disappoint our hopes. /报告～一个好消息。I have a piece of good news for you all.
大家伙儿 dàjiāhuǒr 〈口语〉*see*“大家❸”
大家庭 dàjiātíng extended family；big family；community：四代同堂的～ big family with four generations living under the same roof/民族～ community of ethnic groups
大驾 dàjià ❶〈敬词〉you：恭候～ wait respectfully for your gracious presence/有劳～ have to rely on your efforts；have to ask you to take the trouble ❷〈古语〉carriage of a sovereign or emperor；sovereign or emperor
大件 dàjiàn ❶ bulky good or piece：～行李要托运。Bulky luggage has to be checked in. ❷ major possession (such as refrigerators，videos，recorders，TV sets，etc.)；prestigious item：自行车、手表、缝纫机是传统的“三～”。The bicycle，watch and sewing machine used to be the traditional “three major possessions” (of the average Chinese).
大间歇泉 Dàjiànxiēquán (Iceland) Great Geyser
大建 dàjiàn *also*“大尽” lunar month of 30 days
大江 dàjiāng ❶ great river ❷ Yangtze River：～南北 to the north and south of the Yangtze River
大奖 dàjiǎng grand prize；top prize；big award or prize：以～招揽顾客 attract customers with big prizes/这项发明获得～。The invention was awarded the grand prize.
大奖赛 dàjiǎngsài Grand Prix；prize-giving competition
大将 dàjiàng ❶〈军事〉senior general ❷ general (officer)：～之才 makings of a general ❸ person of special importance or outstanding ability：他是我们篮球队的一员～。He is a star player in our basketball team.
大将风度 dàjiàng-fēngdù poise of a great general；qualities of a great commander：他这个人有～。He has all the qualities befitting a great general. *or* He is a man of magnanimity and vision.
大蕉 dàjiāo 〈植物〉plantain
大角 dàjiǎo 〈天文〉Arcturus
大角斑羚 dàjiǎo bānlíng eland (*Taurotragus*)
大角羊 dàjiǎoyáng bighorn；mountain sheep
大脚 dàjiǎo 〈旧语〉(of women) unbound feet (in contrast to bound feet which were considered beautiful)：他家儿媳妇是～。Their daughter-in-law did not bind her feet.
大脚疯 dàjiǎofēng *also*“丝虫病” sīchóngbìng 〈方言〉filariasis
大轿车 dàjiàochē *see*“大客车”
大教堂 dàjiàotáng cathedral
大街 dàjiē main street；street；avenue：～小巷 streets and lanes /逛～ go window-shopping；go for a walk in a street
大节 dàjié ❶ matter of critical importance to a nation；major issue ❷ political integrity；strength of character /～凛然 awe-inspiring integrity /～不辱 maintain (*or* preserve) one's dignity/在～问题上，他丝毫不苟且，不迁就。On matters of political integrity，he never stoops or yields to temptation. ❸〈书面〉outline；cardinal principle
大劫 dàjié great calamity；cataclysm
大捷 dàjié resounding victory (of a major battle)
大姐 dàjiě ❶ eldest sister ❷ (polite form of address for a woman about one's own age) elder sister：刘～ Sister Liu
大姐大 dàjiědà 〈口语〉woman with power
大解 dàjiě have a bowel movement；defecate
大襟 dàjīn front of a Chinese garment with buttons on the right
大尽 dàjìn *see*“大建”
大进化 dàjìnhuà *also*“种外进化” zhǒngwài jìnhuà 〈生物〉macroevolution
大惊失色 dàjīng-shīsè turn pale with fright：人家告诉她这一事故时，她～。She turned pale when she was told about the accident.
大惊小怪 dàjīng-xiǎoguài be alarmed at sth. apparently normal；have a storm in a teacup；make a fuss about nothing：为什么这样～？Why make such a fuss about nothing? /真是～。This is really a tempest in a teapot. /这点儿小事，也值得～！Why get so excited over such a trifle!
大净 dàjìng 〈伊斯兰〉Ghusl
大竞技场 Dàjìngjìchǎng 〈历史〉Circus Maximus
大静脉 dàjìngmài 〈生理〉large vein；vena cava
大舅子 dàjiùzi 〈口语〉wife's elder brother；brother-in-law
大局 dàjú overall situation；general situation；overall public interest：顾全～ take the whole situation into account；take the interests of the whole into account /事关～ issues that concern (*or* have a vital bearing on) the overall situation /一切从～出发 proceed in all cases from the overall public interest /你们之间的分歧应服从于国家利益的～。You should subordinate your differences to the overall national interest. /～已定。The outcome is irreversible. *or* The dust has settled. *or* The die is cast.
大举 dàjǔ ❶ carry out (a military operation) on a large scale：～进攻 mount a large-scale offensive；attack in force /～反攻 launch an all-out counteroffensive ❷〈书面〉major action；important move：共图～ plan the decisive move together；pool efforts to bring about a major action
大剧院 Dàjùyuàn Bolshoi Theatre (in Moscow)
大锯 dàjù cross-cut saw；log saw
大军 dàjūn ❶ main forces；huge army：百万～ army a million strong /我们是先头部队，～随后就到。We are the advance detachment. The main force will be here soon. ❷ large contingent：筑路～ large contingent of road builders /文艺～ ranks of writers and artists
大卡 dàkǎ 〈物理〉kilocalorie；large calorie (Cal)
大开方便之门 dà kāi fāngbiàn zhī mén try to make it easy (for sb. to do sth.)；provide all the facilities；open the floodgates wide：他利用职权，为某些人的走私活动～。He has，by dint of his power and position，done everything possible to facilitate the smuggling activities of certain people.
大开眼界 dàkāi-yǎnjiè open one's eyes；broaden one's horizon；be an eye-opener：这次欧洲之行使我～。The European trip helped widen my mental horizon. *or* It was an eye-opener for me.
大楷 dàkǎi ❶ regular script in big characters，as used in Chinese calligraphy exercises ❷ (of Chinese phonetic alphabet) block letter；blockwriting
大砍刀 dàkǎndāo machete
大考 dàkǎo end-of-term examination；final exam：～总复习 general review for the finals
大可不必 dàkěbùbì not at all worth it；not necessary in the least；totally unnecessary：你～生这么大的气。You don't have to get so angry about it.
大课 dàkè lecture given to a large number of students；enlarged class；big-class lecture：上～ attend or give a big-class lecture
大客车 dàkèchē *also*“大轿车” bus；coach
大口径机枪 dàkǒujìng jīqiāng big-calibre large-bore machine gun
大口径输油管 dàkǒujìng shūyóuguǎn 〈石油〉big inch pipe
大跨径桥 dàkuàjìngqiáo long-span bridge
大快人心 dàkuài-rénxīn affording general satisfaction；most gratifying to the people；to the immense satisfaction of the people：～的事 thing that brings universal joy and happiness /～的消息 news that makes everybody happy；gratifying news；glad tidings
大块头 dàkuàitóu 〈方言〉tall and bulky fellow
大块文章 dàkuài-wénzhāng long article
大款 dàkuǎn moneybag；upstart；nouveau riche：傍～ find a sugar daddy
大魁 dàkuí 〈书面〉❶ (title conferred on the candidate who came out first in the highest imperial examination) *Zhuangyuan* (状元) or Number One Scholar ❷ chieftain；ringleader；head of a bandit gang
大括弧 dàkuòhú brace
大拉鲁斯百科词典 Dàlālǔsī Bǎikē Cídiǎn *Le Grand Larousse Encyclopédique*，first published between 1960-1964 in Paris
大剌剌 dàlālā 〈方言〉swaggering；ostentatious；pompous：～的派

D

头 throw one's weight about; behave ostentatiously; walk with a swagger

大牢 dàláo 〈口语〉 prison; jail: 关进～ cast into prison; put behind bars/坐～ be imprisoned; serve a sentence

大老 dàlǎo revered elder

大老粗 dàlǎocū uncouth fellow; uneducated person; rough and ready fellow: 他过去是个～，斗大的字识不了几筐。He used to be an uneducated person who knew just a few characters. /我是个～，文化浅，说错话您别见怪。I'm an uncouth and uneducated man. I hope you won't feel offended if I say anything out of place.

大老婆 dàlǎopo *also* "大婆儿" primary or official wife (as contrasted with concubines in polygamy)

大老爷儿们 dàlǎoyérmen 〈口语〉 man; guy

大老远 dàlǎoyuǎn far away: 你～来啦，多住几天吧。Do stay a bit longer since you've come all the way from far.

大礼 dàlǐ most solemn of ceremonies or greetings: 行～ greet in the most solemn manner

大礼拜 dàlǐbài ❶ alternate Sunday on which one has a day off; fortnightly holiday: 休～ have every other Sunday off ❷ two-day weekend (in contrast with one day off)

D

大礼服 dàlǐfú man's formal or ceremonial dress

大礼堂 dàlǐtáng big assembly hall; auditorium

大理石 dàlǐshí marble: ～雕像 marble statue/～粉 marble dust (*or* powder)/～木 marblewood

大理院 dàlǐyuàn 〈古语〉 supreme court

大力 dàlì energetically; vigorously: 出～ make an energetic effort/～支持农业 give energetic support to agriculture /～发展教育事业 devote major efforts to developing education /～协助 spare no efforts to help /谢谢您的～支持。Thank you for your generous support.

大力神 dàlìshén Hercules: ～导弹 (US) Titan (LGM-25)

大力士 dàlìshì man of extraordinary strength

大吏 dàlì important provincial administrator: 封疆～ governors and commanders of border provinces

大丽花 dàlìhuā 〈植物〉 dahlia

大联唱 dàliánchàng serial singing; hook-on singing: 民歌～ hook-on singing of folk songs

大殓 dàliàn encoffining ceremony

大梁 dàliáng ❶〈建筑〉 girder; roof beam; ridgepole: 这些木料可用来做～。These logs can be made into ridge beams. ❷〈比喻〉 most important part of work: 能挑～ be able to play a central role in the work; be qualified for the most important functions; be the main prop

大量 dàliàng ❶ large number; great quantity: ～人才 large numbers of talented people/～军火 large quantities of munitions /～财富 enormous wealth; large fortune /～引证 quote extensively or copiously/～库存 huge stocks /～时间 plenty of time /～事实 host of facts /收集～科学数据 collect a vast amount of scientific data /为国家积累～资金 accumulate large funds for the state ❷ generous; magnanimous: 宽宏～ magnanimous; liberal-minded; broad-minded

大料 dàliào 〈方言〉 *also* "八角" bājiǎo aniseed

大咧咧 dàliēliē *see* "大大咧咧"

大灵猫 dàlíngmāo zibet

大羚羊 dàlíngyáng oryx; eland

大龄青年 dàlíng qīngnián unmarried men or women of the age group between 28 and 35

大溜 dàliù main current; main trend; greater number (of persons); majority (of the people): 随～ follow the crowd; conform to the majority; follow the trend

大楼 dàlóu multi-storeyed building; tall building: 居民～ apartment house; block of flats /教学～ classroom building /办公～ office building /摩天～ sky-scraper /百货～ department store

大陆 dàlù ❶ continent; mainland: ～隆起 continental rise /～漂移说 theory of continental drift /～封锁 continental blockade /～台地 continental platform /～水域 continental waters /～地块 continental land mass /欧亚～ continent of Europe and Asia; Eurasia ❷ *also* "中国大陆" China's mainland; mainland of China: ～热 desire of Chinese compatriots in Taiwan or elsewhere to come to the mainland to visit or invest/每年都有大量台胞回～探亲访友。Large numbers of Taiwan compatriots return to the mainland to visit their relatives and friends every year.

大陆报 Dàlùbào *China Press*, English-language newspaper published in Shanghai before 1949

大陆岛 dàlùdǎo continental island

大陆法系 Dàlù Fǎxì Civil Law System: ～国家 Civil Law countries

大陆法学派 Dàlùfǎ Xuépài continental jurists

大陆国家 dàlù guójiā continental state or country

大陆海 dàlùhǎi continental sea

大陆会议 Dàlù Huìyì (US) Continental Congress (1774-1789)

大陆架 dàlùjià *also* "大陆棚" continental shelf: ～地区 continental shelf area /～公约 convention on the continental shelf /～边缘 continental shelf edge /～外缘 outer continental shelf

大陆块 dàlùkuài 〈地质〉 continental block

大陆坡 dàlùpō continental slope

大陆事务委员会 Dàlù Shìwù Wěiyuánhuì (Taiwan, China) Council of Mainland Affairs

大陆形成作用 dàlù xíngchéng zuòyòng 〈地质〉 continent formation

大陆性高压 dàlùxìng gāoyā 〈气象〉 continental anticyclone; continental high

大陆性气候 dàlùxìng qìhòu continental climate

大陆增长作用 dàlù zēngzhǎng zuòyòng 〈地质〉 continental growth

大辂椎轮 dàlù-chuílún spokeless cart-wheel; 〈比喻〉 initial crude stage of things

大路 dàlù ❶ high road; main street: 走～ take the high road/顺着～往前走 follow the high road/条条～通罗马。All roads lead to Rome. ❷ cheap and in great demand: ～产品 inexpensive goods catering to the majority of the public

大路菜 dàlùcài basic, common vegetables: 黄瓜是夏季的～。Cucumbers are a mainstay vegetable in summer.

大路活 dàlùhuó low-skill job; inferior, crude product

大路货 dàlùhuò run-of-the-mill goods; low-priced, popular goods: 附近小店只卖些～。The shop nearby only sells articles for popular use.

大略 dàlüè ❶ general idea; broad outline: 了解书的～ get a general idea of a book ❷ generally; roughly: ～相同 roughly the same /时间不多了，我就～地说说吧。As there isn't much time left, I'll just speak briefly. ❸ great vision and talent: 他是一个有着雄才～的政治家。He is a statesman with rare talents and great vision.

大仑丁 dàlúndīng 〈药学〉 dilantin; Dilantin Sodium

大伦敦市百科全书 Dàlúndūnshì Bǎikē Quánshū *Encyclopaedia Metropolitana*, first published between 1817-1845 in Great Britain

大妈 dàmā ❶ wife of father's elder brother; aunt: 她在她～家住了几天。She stayed with her aunt for a few days. ❷ (affectionate or respectful form of address for an elderly woman) aunt: 朱～ Aunt Zhu

大麻 dàmá ❶ *also* "线麻" xiànmá hemp: ～籽 hempseed ❷ marijuana; hashish; cannabis

大麻醇 dàmáchún canabinol

大麻风 dàmáfēng 〈医学〉 leprosy

大麻哈鱼 dàmáhǎyú *also* "大马哈鱼" chum salmon; dog salmon

大麻子 dàmázǐ ❶ hempseed ❷ castor-oil plant ❸ castor bean

大麻子油 dàmázǐyóu hempseed oil

大马金刀儿 dàmǎ-jīndāor 〈方言〉❶ striking a pose; with fuss; with fanfare: 他便～地干了起来，把别人都惊动了。He startled everybody by getting down to the job with much fanfare. ❷ with an air of importance; with a swagger; haughtily: ～地坐在贵宾席上 sit haughtily in the seat reserved for the guest of honour

大马趴 dàmǎpā flat on one's face: 摔了个～ fall flat on one's face

大马士革 Dàmǎshìgé Damascus, capital of Syria: ～大清真寺 Great Mosque of Damascus

大麦 dàmài barley: ～茶 barley water

大麦除芒器 dàmài chúmángqì barley awner

大麦粉碎机 dàmài fěnsuìjī barley breaker

大麦去壳机 dàmài qùkéjī barley sheller

大麦哲伦星云 Dàmàizhélún xīngyún 〈天文〉 Large Magellanic Cloud

大忙 dàmáng very busy: ～季节 busy season

大忙人 dàmángrén very busy person; person with many responsibilities

大猫熊 dàmāoxióng *also* "大熊猫" giant panda

大毛 dàmáo long-haired pelt

大帽子 dàmàozi exaggerated epithet used to categorize a person; unwarranted charge; political label: ～压人 try to intimidate people

by pinning political labels on them / ～底下开小差 intend to escape punishment (*or* criticism) by insincere, vague self-criticism

大媒 dàméi matchmaker

大门 dàmén street door; front door; gate: 看～的 door-keeper

大梦初醒 dàmèng-chūxǐng wake up from a dream; wake up to reality: 在经历了如许艰难之后，他才如～。It was not until he had gone through so much that he began to wake up to reality.

大米 dàmǐ (husked) rice: ～粥 rice porridge / 南方人爱吃～。Southerners prefer rice.

大面积 dàmiànjī large tracts of land; large area: ～丰收 bumper harvest over large areas; high yields over large areas / ～烧伤 large-area burns

大面儿 dàmiànr 〈方言〉❶ general appearance; surface: 这家具～上挺光亮，其实做工较粗。The furniture looks smooth and shiny, but is rather crude in workmanship. / 他只是～上表现得客气。His politeness is only on the surface. / ～还过得去。That passes muster all right. ❷ face: 顾全～ spare people's sensibilities; keep up appearances

大民主 dàmínzhǔ great democracy — open-ended democracy

大民族主义 dàmínzúzhǔyì big-nationality chauvinism

大名 dàmíng ❶ formal personal name; official name ❷〈敬词〉your (given) name: 请问尊姓～? May I know your name, please? ❸ great name; famous name: 久闻～。I've long known your famous name by reputation.

大名鼎鼎 dàmíng-dǐngdǐng famous; well-known; celebrated: ～的学者 famous scholar / 他已经是一个～的人物了。He has become a celebrity (*or* a well-known public figure).

大明大摆 dàmíng-dàbǎi in the open; openly: 这是机密文件，怎么～地放在桌子上? This is a confidential (*or* classified) document. How can it be left on the desk as if it were for everybody to read? / 这些要求要～地跟他提出来。These demands must be put forth to him in explicit terms.

大鸣大放 dàmíng-dàfàng have a free airing of views; speak out and air views in a big way

大螟 dàmíng 〈动物〉pink rice borer (*Sesamia inferens*)

大谬不然 dàmiù-bùrán entirely wrong; grossly mistaken: 此说～，不值一驳。This is a grossly mistaken idea unworthy of rebuttal.

大莫卧尔 Dàmòwò'ěr *also* "莫卧尔大帝" Great Mogul, title for emperor of Delhi in the 16th-19th centuries

大漠 dàmò great desert

大模大样 dàmú-dàyàng in an ostentatious manner; with a swagger; grandly: ～地走上讲台 mount the platform with a swagger / 经理～地走进了市长办公室。The manager strutted into the mayor's office. / 他总是像主人似的～推门而入。He would swagger in as if he owned the place.

大母 dàmǔ 〈书面〉❶ grandmother ❷ wife of father's elder brother; aunt

大拇哥 dàmugē 〈方言〉thumb: 大家伙儿谁不伸～说你好。Every one gives you a thumbs-up as a good guy.

大拇指 dàmuzhǐ thumb: 竖起～叫好 hold one's thumbs up in approval; give the thumbs-up

大拿 dàná 〈口语〉❶ person with power; boss: 我们这里厂长说了算，他是～。The director has the final say here. He is the boss. ❷ expert; authority: 在力学方面，他是我们这里的～。In mechanics, he is the expert (*or* an authority) here.

大男大女 dànán-dànǚ ❶ *see* "大龄青年" ❷ sons and daughters over 15 or 16 years of age who live with their parents

大男子主义 dànánzǐzhǔyì male chauvinism: ～者 male chauvinist

大难 dànàn catastrophe; disaster; calamity: ～临头 be faced with imminent disaster; be in immediate danger / ～不死，必有后福。He who survives a disaster is destined to good fortune in the future.

大脑 dànǎo 〈生理〉cerebrum: ～半球 cerebral hemisphere

大脑发育不全 dànǎo fāyù bùquán cerebral agenesia

大脑脚 dànǎojiǎo 〈生理〉cerebral peduncle

大脑局部缺血 dànǎo júbù quēxuè cerebral ischaemia

大脑皮层 dànǎo pícéng 〈生理〉cerebral cortex; pallium

大脑扫描 dànǎo sǎomiáo 〈医学〉brain scanning

大脑生理学 dànǎo shēnglǐxué cerebrophysiology

大脑死亡 dànǎo sǐwáng 〈医学〉cerebral death; brain death

大脑性巨人症 dànǎoxìng jùrénzhèng 〈医学〉cerebral gigantism

大脑性麻痹 dànǎoxìng mábì 〈医学〉cerebral palsy or paralysis

大脑性双瘫 dànǎoxìng shuāngtān 〈医学〉cerebral diplegia

大脑炎 dànǎoyán cerebritis; encephalitis

大脑溢血 dànǎo yìxuè 〈医学〉cerebral hemorrhage

大内 dànèi 〈旧语〉the Great Within; imperial palace

大鲵 dàní (popularly known as 娃娃鱼)〈动物〉giant salamander

大逆不道 dànì-bùdào high treason; treason and heresy; greatest outrage: 视为～ brand as traitors and heretics / 谁反对皇上，谁就是～。He who opposed the throne was considered guilty of high treason. / 对权威理论提出挑战，只能推动学术进步，绝不是什么～的事。Challenging the canon can only promote academic progress, and should never be regarded as heresy or outrage.

大年 dànián ❶ good year; year of bumper harvest; (of fruit trees) on-year: 今年是苹果～。We've had a bumper crop of apples this year. *or* This is an on-year for the apple crop. ❷ lunar year in which the last month has 30 days ❸ lunar New Year's Day; Spring Festival: 过～ celebrate the (lunar) New Year's Day / ～初三 third day of a lunar new year

大年初一 dànián chūyī 〈口语〉first day of the lunar year; lunar New Year's Day

大年夜 dàniányè 〈方言〉lunar New Year's Eve: ～，合家欢聚，吃团圆饭。All families have feasts at family reunions on lunar New Year's Eve.

大娘 dàniáng 〈口语〉❶ wife of father's elder brother; aunt ❷ (respectful form of address for elderly women) aunt

大农业 dànóngyè mega-agriculture

大奴湖 Dànúhú Great Slave Lake (in Canada)

大排行 dàpáiháng seniority among cousins in an extended family on the paternal side

大泡 dàpào 〈医学〉bulla

大泡性肺气肿 dàpàoxìng fèiqìzhǒng 〈医学〉bullous emphysema

大炮 dàpào ❶ artillery; big gun; cannon ❷〈口语〉one who speaks boastfully or forcefully; blunt man: 他是一个～，喜欢在会上提出些令人难堪的问题。He is a blunt man who likes to raise embarrassing questions at the meeting.

大陪审团 dàpéishěntuán grand jury

大配子 dàpèizǐ 〈生物〉macrogamete

大配子体 dàpèizǐtǐ macrogametocyte

大鹏 dàpéng Roc; Rokh (fabulous bird of prey in Arabian and Persian legend)

大篷车 dàpéngchē ❶ (covered) wagon ❷ covered truck or lorry (for carrying goods); caravan: 组织～送货下乡 send goods into the country in caravans

大批 dàpī large quantities; large numbers; large amounts: ～定货 large order / ～现钞 piles of cash / ～消费物资 huge quantities of consumer goods / ～出口棉花 export cotton in large quantities / ～生产 large batch production; large-scale manufacturing; mass production / 公司新近招进了～年轻人。The company has recently employed a large number of young people. / ～移民离开欧洲到美国定居。Floods of emigrants left Europe for America.

大批判 dàpīpàn mass criticism; mass criticism and repudiation (a practice prevalent in the turbulent years of the Cultural Revolution)

大披肩 dàpījiān (in ancient Greece or Rome) pallium

大辟 dàpì 〈旧语〉capital punishment; decapitation
see also "五刑" wǔxíng

大薸 dàpiáo 〈植物〉water lettuce; water cabbage

大票 dàpiào large-denomination banknote: 商场里设有～兑换处。There is a special booth for breaking large-denomination banknotes in the shopping-mall.

大屏幕 dàpíngmù 〈通信〉large screen: ～电视 large-screen television

大平正芳 Dàpíngzhèngfāng Ohira Masayoshi (1910-1980), Japanese Prime Minister between 1978 and 1980

大坡面 dàpōmiàn macrodome (of a crystal)

大破大立 dàpò-dàlì destroy and build in an extensive way; resolutely do away with old habits and ideas and establish the new (slogan often quoted in the Cultural Revolution)

大谱表 dàpǔbiǎo 〈音乐〉great stave

大谱儿 dàpǔr ❶ broad outline; general idea: 心里没个～ have nothing definite in mind / 究竟怎么做，心里应该先有个～。Before you start, you ought to have a general idea of what you're going to do. ❷ roughly; approximately: ～算一下 make a rough calculation

大瀑布 dàpùbù cataract

大漆 dàqī raw lacquer

大起大落 dàqǐ-dàluò great ups and downs; sharp rise and fall: 国

D

民经济的～ great ups and downs in the national economy /情绪～ experience abrupt swings in one's mood /股票价格～ sharp fluctuations in the price of shares

大气 dàqì ❶ atmosphere; air: ～干扰 atmospheric interference / ～污染 air pollution; atmospheric pollution /～电 atmospheric electricity /～辐射 atmospheric radiation/～腐蚀 atmospheric corrosion /～折射 atmospheric refraction; astronomical refraction /～密度 atmospheric density/～极限 limit of the atmosphere; atmospheric limit /～潮 atmospheric tides /～华 atmospheric corona /～湍流 atmospheric turbulence ❷ heavy breathing: 吓得连～也不敢出 catch one's breath from fear; hold one's breath in fear /跑得直喘～ breathe heavily from running; pant from running

大气波导 dàqì bōdǎo atmospheric duct

大气采样 dàqì cǎiyàng atmospheric sampling

大气层 dàqìcéng atmospheric layer; atmosphere: ～空间 atmospheric space /～试验 atmospheric test

大气尘粒 dàqìchénlì 〈气象〉 lithometeor

大气成分 dàqì chéngfèn air composition; atmospheric composition

大气阀 dàqìfá atmos-valve

D

大气光学 dàqì guāngxué atmospheric optics

大气候 dàqìhòu ❶〈气象〉 macroclimate ❷ overall situation in the world; general political climate

大气环流 dàqì huánliú atmospheric circulation; general circulation of atmosphere

大气监测 dàqì jiāncè atmospheric monitoring

大气科学 dàqì kēxué atmospheric science

大气磅礴 dàqì-pángbó of great momentum or power; of immense sweep: 这幅画可谓尺幅千里，～。Presenting a panoramic scene in limited space, this painting is impressive for its powerful sweep.

大气谱线 dàqì pǔxiàn 〈天文〉 telluric lines

大气声学 dàqì shēngxué atmospheric acoustics

大气数据系统 dàqì shùjù xìtǒng 〈航空〉 air data system; ADS

大气衰减 dàqì shuāijiǎn atmospheric attenuation

大气温度 dàqì wēndù free air temperature

大气雾霾 dàqì wùmái 〈摄影〉 atmospheric haze

大气压 dàqìyā 〈气象〉 ❶ atmospheric pressure; barometric pressure ❷ atmosphere: 两个～ two atmospheres

大气遥感 dàqì yáogǎn 〈气象〉 remote sensing of atmosphere

大气杂质 dàqì zázhì atmospheric impurities

大气蒸发 dàqì zhēngfā 〈水文〉 atmospheric evaporation

大器 dàqì ❶ treasure ❷〈比喻〉 great talent: 必成～ will become a prominent figure in the future; be promising /～小用 use a talented man in a menial job

大器晚成 dàqì-wǎnchéng great vessels take years to build; great minds mature slowly: 先生高才久屈，必是～。As a man of talent, you should have been better known. Perhaps all great minds prove their mettle later rather than sooner.

大千世界 dàqiān-shìjiè ❶〈佛教〉 universe of a billion worlds; boundless universe ❷ vast world: ～，无奇不有。Everything is possible under the sun.

大前年 dàqiánnián three years ago

大前提 dàqiántí 〈逻辑〉 major premise

大前天 dàqiántiān *also* "大前儿" three days ago

大钱 dàqián ❶ (old Chinese coin of low denomination) large copper coin: 值不了几个～ not worth much ❷ a lot of money; large amount of money: 赚～ make a lot of money; make piles of money/小钱不肯挣，～挣不来 contemptuous of working for a little money, yet unable to earn big money

大枪 dàqiāng rifle

大巧若拙 dàqiǎo-ruòzhuō a truly wise man often appears slow-witted

大清白日 dàqīng-báirì 〈口语〉 broad daylight: ～的，开着灯干什么? What's the point in having all the lights on in broad daylight?

大清洗 Dàqīngxǐ Great Purge (between 1934 and 1938 in the former Soviet Union)

大清早 dàqīngzǎo very early in the morning: 他～就走了。He left early in the morning.

大晴天 dàqíngtiān sunny day: 趁～，把衣服拿出来晒晒。Air the clothes while it is bright and sunny.

大庆 dàqìng ❶ grand celebration of an important event; great occasion: 建国五十年～ grand celebrations of the 50th anniversary of the founding of a state ❷〈敬词〉(usu. of every fifth or tenth) birthday (of an elderly person): 八十～ grand occasion of one's eightieth birthday ❸ (Dàqìng) Daqing Oilfield (in Heilongjiang Province)

大邱 Dàqiū Taegu, one of the major cities in the Republic of Korea

大秋 dàqiū ❶ harvest season in autumn ❷ crop harvested in autumn; autumn harvest: 今年的～获得丰收。We have brought in a good autumn harvest this year.

大秋作物 dàqiū zuòwù crop sown in spring and reaped in autumn; autumn-harvested crop: ～长势良好。The autumn-harvested crops are growing fine.

大球 dàqiú general term for football, basketball, volleyball, etc.

大曲 dàqū ❶ yeast for making hard liquor ❷ hard liquor made with such yeast

大趋势 dàqūshì megatrend; major trend: 时代～ dominent trend of the times

大去 dàqù 〈书面〉 ❶ leave a place not to return: ～其国 leave the country for good ❷〈婉词〉 die; pass away: ～之期 date of sb.'s death

大权 dàquán power over major issues; authority: ～在握 hold power in one's hands /掌握家庭财政～ hold the purse strings of the family/他掌握人事～。He has the final say in personnel matters.

大权独揽 dàquán-dúlǎn centralize power in one man's hands (to deal with major issues); arrogate all authority to oneself: ～，小权分散 monopolise absolute power on major issues while devolving authority on others concerning minor matters/他在农场里～，为所欲为。On the farm, he arrogated all power to himself, doing whatever he liked.

大权旁落 dàquán-pángluò power has fallen into the hands of others: 外戚逐渐得势，皇室～。With the influence of the queen's relatives mounting gradually, the authority of the royal family was slipping away.

大全 dàquán complete works; complete collection; complete volume: 美国俚语～ dictionary of American slang

大犬座 Dàquǎnzuò 〈天文〉 Canis Major (CMa); Greater Dog

大人 dàrén 〈敬词〉 *often used in letters as a respectful form of address for a person of an elder generation*: 母亲～ (used at the beginning of a letter) Dear Mother

大人 dàren ❶ adult; grown-up: ～说话，小孩别插嘴。Children are not supposed to chip in when adults are talking. ❷〈旧语〉 Your Excellency; His Excellency: 总督～ His Excellency the Governor

大人不记小人过 dàrén bù jì xiǎorén guò a great man does not bear grievance for faults committed by a petty person; an elder should not mind the faults of juniors

大人物 dàrénwù important person; dignitary; big shot; VIP: 他自以为是个～。He thinks he is really somebody.

大日本百科词典 Dàrìběn Bǎikē Cídiǎn *Dai Nihon Hyakka Jiten*, published between 1972 and 1976 in Tokyo

大容量 dàróngliàng high capacity; large volume: ～喷雾器 large-volume sprayer

大容量磁心存储器 dàróngliàng cíxīn cúnchǔqì 〈自控〉 large core memory

大容量存储器 dàróngliàng cúnchǔqì 〈自控〉 large scale memory; large(-capacity) storage; mass storage; bulk memory or storage; high-capacity memory

大容量光存储器 dàróngliàng guāngcúnchǔqì mass optical memory

大肉 dàròu pork

大儒 dàrú 〈旧语〉 scholar well known for his erudition; renowned scholar

大赛 dàsài important tournament; major contest: 网球～ major tennis tournament/全国青年歌手～ national contest for young singers/首届漫画～ first cartoon competition

大扫除 dàsǎochú general cleaning; thorough cleaning: 节前～ general cleaning on the eve of a holiday

大嫂 dàsǎo ❶ eldest brother's wife; sister-in-law ❷ (polite form of address for a married woman about one's own age) elder sister

大杀风景 dàshā-fēngjǐng spoil the fun; sink the spirits; mar the pleasure: 一场足球赛正在紧张进行时，忽然下起大雨，真是～。The downpour which came in the middle of an exciting football match marred the pleasure of all spectators.

大沙沙漠 Dàshā Shāmò (Australia) Great Sandy Desert

大厦 dàshà large building; mansion:高楼～ tall buildings and large mansions /上海～ Shanghai Mansion /～千间，夜眠七尺。〈谚语〉Despite the possession of a mansion with a thousand rooms, one sleeps in a bed seven feet long at night.

大厦将倾 dàshà-jiāngqīng the great building is about to collapse — the whole situation is beyond remedy

大衫 dàshān unlined long gown

大少爷 dàshàoye ❶ eldest son (of a rich family); young master ❷ spoilt son of a rich family; spendthrift: ～作风 wasteful habits typical of a spoiled son of a rich family; lavish spending

大舌头 dàshétou 〈口语〉thick-tongued person; one who lisps; lisper

大社会学 dàshèhuìxué macrosociology

大赦 dàshè amnesty; general pardon: ～一批犯人 grant amnesty to a group of prisoners / ～令 bill of oblivion; order of general amnesty /～条款 amnesty clause

大赦国际 Dàshè Guójì Amnesty International

大神农架 Dàshénnóngjià Mount Dashennongjia (in Hubei Province)

大婶儿 dàshěnr 〈口语〉❶ wife of father's younger brother; aunt ❷ (polite form of address for a married woman about one's mother's age) aunt

大声疾呼 dàshēng-jíhū raise a cry of warning; raise a hue and cry: 向全世界～保护野生动植物 make a passionate worldwide appeal for wildlife conservation /由于一些人大代表的～，人们越来越认识到计划生育的重要性。Thanks to the vociferous and passionate appeal of some people's deputies, there has been an increasing awareness among the people of the importance of family planning.

大牲畜 dàshēngchù draught animal

大牲口 dàshēngkou draught animal

大圣 dàshèng ❶ saint; man of impeccable moral integrity ❷〈佛教〉great saint, referring to Buddha, etc. ❸ spirit; immortal: 齐天～ Saint in Heaven (self-adopted title of the Monkey King in the classical novel *Pilgrimage to the West*《西游记》)

大失所望 dàshī-suǒwàng greatly disappointed; to one's great disappointment: 他高考落榜，使他的父母～。His failure in the university entrance exams was a bitter disappointment to his parents.

大师 dàshī ❶ great master; master: 国画～ master of traditional Chinese painting /文学～ literary giant/艺术～ leading artist ❷〈佛教〉Great Master, courtesy title for Buddhist monk

大师傅 dàshīfu Great Master, courtesy title used to address a Buddhist monk

大师傅 dàshifu cook; chef

大使 dàshǐ ambassador: 特命全权～ ambassador extraordinary and plenipotentiary /驻联合国～ ambassador to the United Nations /无任所～ ambassador at large /巡回～ roving ambassador/内定～ ambassador designate /～衔 ambassadorial rank /互派～ exchange ambassadors /～级会谈 talks at ambassadorial level /～级外交关系 diplomatic relations at ambassadorial level/～特权 ambassadorial privileges

大使馆 dàshǐguǎn embassy: 两国互设～。Each of the two countries is to open an embassy in the other.

大士 dàshì ❶〈旧语〉man of virtue ❷〈佛教〉Buddha; bodhisattva: 观音～ the Bodhisattva *Guanyin*

大事 dàshì ❶ great or major event; important matter; major issue: 头等～ matter of vital (*or* prime, *or* paramount) importance /国家～ state affair /天下～ world affairs /人生～ most important event in one's life (usually referring to one's marriage) /文化生活中的～ major cultural event/～不糊涂 be sober-minded on major issues/～做不来，小事又不做 be incapable of great undertakings, yet disdain minor tasks; disdain minor assignments though incompetent for major tasks/出～了! Something terrible has happened. /若得此三人，～必成。If we can get those three men to help, our great project is a sure thing. ❷ overall situation: ～不好。A disaster is imminent. /他见～不妙，赶紧溜走了。He slipped away as he saw the situation was turning against him. ❸ in a big way: ～宣传 play up; raise a ballyhoo /～渲染 exaggerate grossly; play up /～铺张 present with a great fanfare

大事化小，小事化了 dàshì huà xiǎo, xiǎoshì huà liǎo turn big problems into small problems and small problems into no problems at all; reduce a big trouble into a small one and a small one into nothing: 赔礼道歉讲好话，这是个～的好办法。Say "sorry" and follow it up with a stream of honeyed words — this is the way to reduce a big trouble into a small one and a small one into nothing (*or* the way to patch things up).

大事记 dàshìjì record of major events; chronicle of major developments

大势 dàshì general trend of events; main course of development: ～所趋，人心所向 trend of the times and will of the people; general trend and popular feeling /～已去。The game is up. *or* The game is as good as lost. /天下～，分久必合，合久必分。This is the way the world develops: prolonged division leads to unity; prolonged unity leads to division.

大是大非 dàshì-dàfēi major issue of principle; cardinal question of right and wrong: 区分～ distinguish between right and wrong on cardinal issues /在～的问题上，含糊不得! One should not be ambiguous on major issues of principle. *or* There's no room for ambiguity on fundamental questions of right and wrong.

大手笔 dàshǒubǐ ❶ work or writing of a great author or calligrapher ❷ famous writer 这篇文章显然出于～。This essay evidently comes from the pen of a great master.

大手大脚 dàshǒu-dàjiǎo be lavish or extravagant (with money); be wasteful (with things): 花钱～ spend lavishly /～的人 extravagant person; spendthrift /过日子不能～。One must be thrifty in everyday life. /他花钱～惯了，从不攒钱。He had a habit of throwing money around and had never saved any.

大寿 dàshòu 〈敬词〉birthday (usu. of an old man or woman in every fifth or tenth year): 六十～ 60th birthday

大书 dàshū storytelling; professional storytelling in a local dialect

大书特书 dàshū-tèshū record in letters of gold; write volumes about; write repeatedly and elaborately: 这种英雄行为值得～。Such an act of exemplary heroism deserves to be recorded in letters of gold.

大叔 dàshū 〈口语〉❶ younger brother of one's father; uncle ❷ (polite form of address for a man somewhat younger than one's father age) uncle: 约瑟夫～ Uncle Joseph/山姆～ Uncle Sam

大暑 Dàshǔ ❶ Great Heat, 12th seasonal division point, marking the sun's position at 120° on the ecliptic ❷ day marking such a seasonal division point, usu. falling on the 23rd or 24th of July ❸ period lasting from such a seasonal division point till the next one (Beginning of Autumn 立秋)

see also "节气" jiéqì; "二十四节气" èrshísì jiéqì

大树底下好乘凉 dàshù dǐxia hǎo chéngliáng 〈谚语〉a big tree affords good shade; an influential friend, relative or mentor provides protection and help

大数 dàshù 〈书面〉❶ predestined years to live; fate; destiny: 他～已尽。His days are numbered. ❷ matter of vital importance; major programme of lasting importance ❸ outline; summary: 用兵之～ general principles of the art of war ❹〈数学〉large number; googol ($=10^{100}$): ～定律 law of large numbers

大帅 dàshuài 〈旧语〉(form of respectful address for the chief officer in an army) commander-in-chief

大率 dàshuài 〈书面〉generally; roughly: ～如此。It is generally the case.

大水 dàshuǐ flood; inundation; spate: 那一带在发～。That area is flooded. /～冲了龙王庙。〈谚语〉The flood inundates the temple of the Dragon King — people on the same side fight each other by mistake.

大水漫灌 dàshuǐ mànguàn 〈农业〉flood or flooding irrigation

大司祭 dàsījì 〈宗教〉archpriest

大肆 dàsì without restraint; wantonly; viciously: ～污蔑 slander viciously; launch a slander campaign against /～攻击 wantonly attack; launch an unbridled (*or* all-out) attack against /～叫嚣 allege vociferously; clamour /～吹嘘 feverishly advertise; preach and trumpet; boast wildly /～宣扬 vigorously propagate; give unlimited publicity to /～挥霍 spend without restraint; squander /～歪曲事实 distort the facts wilfully

大溲 dàsōu 〈书面〉have a bowel movement; defecate

大苏打 dàsūdá 〈化学〉sodium thiosulfate; sodium hyposulfite; hypo

大蒜 dàsuàn garlic: 一头～ a head of garlic/～油 garlic oil

大踏步 dàtàbù in big strides; by leaps and bounds: ～前进 stride ahead; stride forward

大唐西域记 Dàtáng Xīyù Jì *Records on the Western Regions of*

the Great Tang Empire
大堂 dàtáng ❶〈旧语〉magistrate's courtroom ❷ lobby (of a hotel):～经理 manager on duty
大…特… dà…tè… *used each before the same verb, expressing magnitude and depth*:大干特干 work vigorously and energetically / 大讲特讲 talk at length and most emphatically/大吃特吃 eat and drink to one's heart's content
大提琴 dàtíqín violoncello; cello
大题小做 dàtí-xiǎozuò treat an important issue lightly; play sth. down:这件事不是一时能解决的,所以他采取了～的办法。As the problem cannot be solved right away, he is deliberately playing it down.
大体 dàtǐ ❶ cardinal principle; general interest:不识～ fail to keep the general interest in mind; ignore the major issues (and concentrate on one's petty concerns); be petty-minded /识～,顾大局 have the cardinal principles in mind and take the overall situation into account ❷ generally; more or less; in the main; by and large: ～上正确 correct in the main /～相同 more or less the same /收支～平衡。Income roughly balances expenditure. /～说来,结果是令人满意的。Generally speaking, the results are satisfactory. /生活～过得去。We can get by. *or* We can manage.
大天白日 dàtiān-báirì 〈口语〉in broad daylight:～的,他们就拦路抢劫。They waylay people even in broad daylight.
大田 dàtián land for growing field crops
大田作物 dàtián zuòwù field crop
大厅 dàtīng hall; lobby
大庭广众 dàtíng-guǎngzhòng (before a) big crowd; (on a) public occasion:她害怕在～之中丢丑。She is afraid to cut a sorry figure in the public eye. /他一定是疯了,在～之中做出那种丢人的事。He must be mad to have behaved so shamelessly in public.
大通曼哈顿银行 Dàtōng Mànhādùn Yínháng (US) Chase Manhattan Bank
大同 dàtóng ❶ Great Harmony; ideal or perfect society:～世界 ideal world /实现世界～ bring about universal harmony in the world ❷ identical view; consensus on major issues:求～,存小异 seek consensus on major issues and reserve differences on minor ones
大同江 Dàtóngjiāng (DPRK) Taedong River
大同书 Dàtóngshū *The Great Commonwealth*, written by Kang Youwei (康有为) and published in full in 1935
大同乡 dàtóngxiāng person from the same province (as one):我们三个是～。The three of us are from the same province.
大同小异 dàtóng-xiǎoyì largely identical despite minor differences; alike except for slight differences; almost the same; very much the same:两人的见解～。Their viewpoints are very much the same.
大统 dàtǒng 〈书面〉❶ great cause of national reunification or unity:以成～ to accomplish national reunification ❷ imperial throne:继承～ succeed to the throne
大头 dàtóu ❶ mask in the shape of a big head:～娃娃舞 Chinese folk dance, with each dancer made up as a child wearing a mask in the shape of a big head ❷ *also* "袁大头" Yuán dàtóu silver dollar with a bust of Yuan Shikai (then President of the Republic of China) ❸ larger or thicker end of sth.; major part:棍子的～ thicker end of a stick /搞工作要善于抓～儿。One should grasp major problems in work. ❹ *also* "冤大头" yuāndàtóu one who spends a big sum of money for nothing or achieves nothing despite great efforts; sucker:拿～ treat as a sucker; make a sucker of
大头菜 dàtóucài 〈植物〉rutabaga
大头钉 dàtóudīng tack; hobnail
大头龟 dàtóuguī 〈动物〉big-headed turtle (*Platysternon megacephalum*)
大头鱼 dàtóuyú cod (*Gadus morhua*)
大头针 dàtóuzhēn pin
大屠杀 dàtúshā massacre; holocaust
大团结 dàtuánjié 〈口语〉❶ 10-*yuan* banknote (with a design showing the great unity of the various nationalities of China):五张～ five ten-*yuan* notes ❷ *renminbi* (人民币)
大团圆 dàtuányuán ❶ happy family reunion ❷ happy ending:中国古代才子佳人小说一般是以～结局的。The classical Chinese fiction of the wit and beauty type has in most cases a happy ending.
大腿 dàtuǐ thigh
大碗茶 dàwǎnchá tea served in big bowls and sold in stalls
大腕 dàwàn top-notch artist; star; heavyweight:这个电视连续剧集中了五位～。There are five stars in the TV serial.
大王 dàwáng ❶ king; magnate; tycoon:钢铁～ iron and steel magnate /汽车～ automobile magnate ❷ person of a certain outstanding talent; master:爆破～ master at blasting/足球～ ace footballer
see also dàiwang
大王宫 Dàwánggōng (Thailand) Great Palace
大为 dàwéi to a high degree; on a large scale:～发展 develop greatly /～提高 improve significantly; be greatly raised /～改观 change markedly; see a marked change /～高兴 very much pleased; very glad
大位 dàwèi 〈书面〉❶ throne:初登～ have just ascended the throne ❷ office of great importance
大尉 dàwèi 〈军事〉senior captain
大慰平生 dàwèi-píngshēng great comfort or pleasure in one's life:我们又能见面,真是～。What a pleasure we're able to meet again!
大卫之星 Dàwèi Zhī Xīng *also* "大卫之盾" Star of David, insignia of the Jewish people; Magen or Mogen David
大蜗牛 dàwōniú 〈动物〉helix
大我 dàwǒ the collective (as contrasted with the individual):小我的利益要服从～。Individual interests are subordinate to collective interests. *or* Put collective interests before individual interests.
大屋顶 dàwūdǐng traditional curly-tiled Chinese roof; curly top
大无畏 dàwúwèi dauntless; utterly fearless; indomitable:～精神 intrepid spirit /～的英雄气概 dauntless heroism
大五金 dàwǔjīn large metallic materials (such as steel pipes and plates)
大西北 Dàxīběi Great Northwest (which covers Xinjiang, Qinghai, Gansu, Ningxia, Shaanxi and part of Inner Mongolia)
大西洋 Dàxīyáng Atlantic (Ocean):～公约 Atlantic Pact /～宪章 Atlantic Charter /～主义 Atlanticism /～盟军司令部 Allied Command Atlantic (ACLANT)
大西洋区 dàxīyángqū 〈地质〉Atlantic Provinces (in Canada)
大西洋银行 Dàxīyáng Yínháng BNU (*Banco Nacional Ultramarino*), bank of issue of (Macao) *pataca*
大席 dàxí sumptuous feast:大厅里摆了二十桌～。Twenty tables were laid out in the big hall for the feast.
大喜 dàxǐ ❶〈口语〉great rejoicing; great happiness:～若狂 wild with joy/您～啦! Congratulations! ❷ marriage:哪天是你们～的日子? What day will be your wedding day?
大喜过望 dàxǐ-guòwàng be delighted that things are better than one expected; be overjoyed:这真是件～的事。This is much better than expected. /爸爸带来的好消息使我～。I was overjoyed at the news papa brought us.
大戏 dàxì ❶ full-length traditional opera or drama ❷〈方言〉Beijing Opera
大虾 dàxiā prawn
大峡谷 Dàxiágǔ (US) Grand Canyon:～国家保护区 Grand Canyon National Monument
大显身手 dàxiǎn-shēnshǒu display one's prowess fully; give full play to one's abilities; distinguish oneself; cut a dashing figure:比赛场上～ give full play to one's skills at a tournament; distinguish oneself in competition
大显神通 dàxiǎn-shéntōng display one's remarkable skill or prowess; give full play to one's brilliant abilities:神枪手们在场上～。The sharp-shooters displayed their impressive marksmanship at the shooting range.
大限 dàxiàn 〈迷信〉fated end of one's life; predestined hour of one's death:～已到。The hour of death is approaching.
大相径庭 dàxiāngjìngtíng widely divergent; totally different:他们意见～。They hold diametrically opposite views. *or* Their views were poles apart.
大萧条 Dàxiāotiáo Great Depression (1929-1930's)
大小 dàxiǎo ❶ size:这双鞋我穿～正合适。These shoes are just my size. /它们一般～。They are of the same size. ❷ degree of seniority:说话没个～ speak without due respect for elderly people ❸ adults and children:全家～五口。There are five people in the family altogether. ❹ big or small; more or less:～是笔生意。That was a transaction all right, however small it was./国家不论～,应该一律平等。All countries, big or small, should be equal. ❺ big as well as small; all together:～要搭配公平 have an equal mix of the big and the small/～水库十座 ten reservoirs of varying sizes

大小姐 dàxiǎojie ❶〈旧语〉sb.'s daughter ❷〈敬词〉eldest daughter ❸ pampered girl (usu. of a rich family)
大小年 dàxiǎonián 〈农业〉biennial fruiting
大校 dàxiào 〈军事〉senior colonel
大协作 dàxiézuò large-scale or all-round cooperation; major pooling of efforts:县与县之间的～ large-scale cooperation between counties; major pooling of efforts of counties
大写 dàxiě ❶ capital form of Chinese numeral:～金额 amount in words ❷ capitalization:～字母 capital letters /这个字母要～。Please capitalize this letter.
大兴 dàxīng go in for in a big way:～水利 go in for water conservancy projects in a big way/～调查研究之风 energetically encourage the practice of conducting investigations and studies /～协作之风 greatly promote the spirit of cooperation /～问罪之师 point an accusing finger at sb.; condemn scathingly
大兴土木 dàxīng-tǔmù go in for large-scale construction; get busy building
大猩猩 dàxīngxing gorilla
大刑 dàxíng cruel torture:动～ apply ruthless torture
大行 dàxíng ❶ prevalent; popular; in vogue:南北朝时期佛教～。Buddhism spread widely in the Northern and Southern dynasties. ❷〈书面〉recent demise of an emperor:～皇帝 late emperor
大行星 dàxíngxīng 〈天文〉major planet — one of the nine planets of the solar system
大行政区 dàxíngzhèngqū greater administrative region (six in all China between 1949 and 1954)
大型 dàxíng large-scale; large; full-length; grand:～企业 large enterprise/～铸件 large or heavy casting /～歌剧 full-length opera/～彩色记录片 full-length colour documentary film /～运输机 giant transport or cargo aircraft; air freighter /～客机 jumbo /～轧钢厂 heavy steel rolling plant /～管弦乐队 grand orchestra /～电影招待会 grand film reception
大型浮游生物 dàxíng fúyóu shēngwù 〈生物〉macroplankton
大型机 dàxíngjī 〈计算机〉mainframe (computer)
大型汽轮发电机 dàxíng qìlún fādiànjī 〈电工〉large steam turbine-generator
大型人工神经网络 dàxíng réngōng shénjīng wǎngluò 〈自控〉large artificial nerve network
大型生物区系 dàxíng shēngwù qūxì macrobiota
大型油轮 dàxíng yóulún mammoth tanker; super-tanker
大型正负电子对撞机 dàxíng zhèngfù diànzǐ duìzhuàngjī 〈电子〉large electron-positron collider
大型植物 dàxíng zhíwù 〈生物〉macrophyte
大幸 dàxìng ❶ great blessing; capital luck; fortune:落水得救是不幸中的～。To be rescued from drowning is a piece of luck snatched out of misfortune. ❷〈书面〉love dearly; dote on
大姓 dàxìng ❶ distinguished family; large clan ❷ popular surname:张、王、刘、李是我国的～。Zhang, Wang, Liu, and Li are popular surnames in our country.
大雄 Dàxióng 〈佛教〉(respectful form of address used by Buddhists for Sakyamuni, the founder of Buddhism) Mahavira; Buddha:～宝殿 Hall of Sakyamuni, main hall of a Buddhist temple
大熊湖 Dàxiónghú (Canada) Great Bear Lake
大熊猫 dàxióngmāo *also* "大猫熊" giant panda
大熊座 Dàxióngzuò 〈天文〉Ursa Major; Great Bear
大休 dàxiū 〈口语〉take a day off every two weeks
大修 dàxiū 〈机械〉overhaul; major or general repair:这辆汽车要进厂～。The car needs an overhaul in the workshop.
大选 dàxuǎn general election:美国每四年举行一次总统～。The presidential election is held in the US every four years.
大学 dàxué ❶ university; college:综合性～ comprehensive university /理工科～ institute of science and engineering/广播电视～ radio broadcasting and television university /师范～ normal university; teachers' college /文科～ college of liberal arts /业余工业～ part-time engineering college /职工业余～ spare-time college for staff and workers /～入学注册 matriculation /～预科 preparatory course for college/具有～水平 have had a college education; be at college level ❷ *The Great Learning*, one of the Four Confucian Classics *see also* "四书" Sìshū
大学生 dàxuéshēng university student; college student:一年级～ freshman /二年级～ sophomore /三年级～ junior /四年级～ senior/低年级～ lower division student; lower grade student/高年级～ upper division student; upper grade student /男～ man (*or* boy) student/女～ woman (*or* girl) student/应届毕业～ graduating student; this year's graduate/住宿～ resident student; boarder /走读～ day student, non-resident student
大学生 dàxuésheng ❶ big schoolboy or schoolgirl ❷〈方言〉big boy; boy
大学士 dàxuéshì 〈旧语〉Secretary of the Grand Council, highest rank in China's imperial official hierarchy
大学学院 dàxué xuéyuàn university college:哈佛～ Harvard College
大雪 Dàxuě ❶ (dàxuě) heavy snow (with a 24-hour precipitation of 5 millimetres or more):～纷飞。It's snowing thick and fast. /～封山。The mountain is sealed off by heavy snow. ❷ Great Snow, 21st seasonal division point, marking the sun's position at 255° on the ecliptic ❸ day marking such a seasonal division point, usu. falling on the 7th or 8th of December ❹ period lasting from such a seasonal division point till the next one (Winter Solstice 冬至) *see also* "节气" jiéqi; "二十四节气" èrshísì jiéqì
大血藤 dàxuèténg *also* "红藤" hóngténg 〈植物〉*Sargentodoxa cuneata*
大勋位菊花章 Dàxūnwèi Júhuāzhāng Order of the Chrysanthemum, highest order in Japan
大循环 dàxúnhuán 〈生理〉systemic circulation
大牙 dàyá ❶ molar ❷ front tooth:你这样会叫人笑掉～。That would only make people split their sides with laughter. *or* You would only make a laughing stock of yourself.
大雅 dàyǎ 〈书面〉elegance; refinement; good taste:不登～之堂 not appeal to refined taste; not be in good taste /开个小玩笑，无伤～。Such a small joke would offend nobody's sensibilities.
大烟 dàyān opium
大烟鬼 dàyānguǐ 〈贬义〉❶ opium addict ❷ heavy smoker
大言不惭 dàyán-bùcán brag unblushingly; boast unashamedly:他～地称自己是艺术家。He claimed to be an artist without batting an eyelid.
大盐 dàyán crude salt
大盐湖 Dàyánhú (US) Great Salt Lake
大雁 dàyàn wild goose
大扬琴 dàyángqín dulcimer
大洋 dàyáng ❶ ocean:～彼岸 on the other side of the ocean; beyond the ocean/～隆起 oceanic rise ❷ silver dollar:现～ cash in the form of silver dollars; silver dollar
大洋带 dàyángdài oceanic zone
大洋岛 dàyángdǎo oceanic island
大洋断裂系 dàyáng duànlièxì 〈地质〉oceanic rift system
大洋鲈 dàyánglú ocean perch (*Scorpaenidae*)
大洋岩 dàyángyán oceanite
大洋中脊 dàyáng zhōngjǐ 〈地质〉mid-ocean ridge; oceanic ridge
大洋洲 Dàyángzhōu Oceania; Oceanica
大样 dàyàng ❶〈印刷〉(as of a newspaper) full-page proof ❷〈建筑〉detail drawing:足尺～ drawing to the last detail; detail drawing
大摇大摆 dàyáo-dàbǎi strutting; swaggering:他们～地在街上走着。They swaggered down the street. /小李～地闯进总经理办公室。Xiao Li swept into the General Manager's office as bold as brass. /她上个月不辞而别，现在却～地回来了。She went away without taking leave last month, and now she comes swaggering back.
大要 dàyào main points; gist:举其～ give the gist (of sth.) /知己知彼，兵家～。It is important above all else for military strategists to know their own strength and that of their enemy.
大爷 dàyé arrogant and self-willed man who does not do a stroke of work:～作风 arrogant manners /～脾气 rude, wilful temperament
大爷 dàye 〈口语〉❶ father's elder brother; uncle ❷ (respectful address for men around one's father's age or older) uncle:张～在家吗? Is Uncle Zhang at home?
大业 dàyè great cause; great undertaking:开创～ pioneer a great undertaking /国家统一～ great cause of national reunification
大叶性肺炎 dàyèxìng fèiyán 〈医学〉lobar pneumonia
大叶杨 dàyèyáng Chinese white poplar
大一统 dàyītǒng great national unity:～思想 concept of great national unity
大衣 dàyī overcoat; topcoat; greatcoat:风雪～ anorak; parka /夹～ light overcoat /军～ army greatcoat /棉～ cotton-padded

overcoat/皮～ fur coat
大衣呢 dàyīní heavy wool for making overcoat
大姨 dàyí mother's eldest sister; aunt
大姨子 dàyízi 〈口语〉wife's elder sister; sister-in-law
大义 dàyì cardinal principles of righteousness; righteous cause:深明～ be deeply conscious of what is righteous/微言～ subtle language with profound implications
大义凛然 dàyì-lǐnrán fearless with justice on one's side; firm and stern in upholding justice:刘胡兰～，视死如归。Liu Hulan faced death unflinchingly with a moral courage that commanded respect.
大义灭亲 dàyì-mièqīn sacrifice one's own flesh and blood on the altar of justice; place righteousness above family loyalty; uphold justice and righteousness at the sacrifice of blood relations:他～，检举了父亲的罪行。Placing righteousness above family loyalty, he reported his father's crime to the authorities./在国法面前是应该～的。Before the law, justice should come before ties of blood.
大异其趣 dàyì-qíqù have entirely different interests; be poles apart (in tastes and interests)
大意 dàyì general idea; main points; gist; tenor:文章～ gist of an article/歌词～ main content of a song /了解～ get a general idea /口授～由秘书起稿 dictate the main points for one's secretary to draw up a draft
大意 dàyi careless; negligent; inattentive:～出了错 make a mistake out of carelessness (*or* negligence)/他太～了，连这样明显的错误也没看出来。It was very careless (*or* thoughtless) of him to overlook such an obvious mistake.
大意失荆州 dàyi shī Jīngzhōu suffer a major setback as a result of negligence
大音阶 dàyīnjiē 〈音乐〉major scale
大印 dàyìn great seal; seal of power; official seal:盖～ affix an official seal /掌～ hold great power
大英百科全书 Dàyīng Bǎikē Quánshū *also*“不列颠百科全书” Bùlièdiān Bǎikē Quánshū Encyclopaedia Britannica
大英博物馆 Dàyīng Bówùguǎn British Museum (in London)
大勇若怯 dàyǒng-ruòqiè paramount courage appears like cowardice; a man of great courage often looks like a coward
大油 dàyóu 〈口语〉lard
大有 dàyǒu ❶ plenty; a great deal; of a great amount:～讲究 there is a great deal that calls for careful study/～裨益 be of great benefit (*or* advantage) / ～可看 be well worth reading (*or* seeing) ❷〈书面〉bumper harvest:～之年 year of abundance (*or* bumper harvest)
大有好处 dàyǒu-hǎochù be of great benefit; be of much good
大有可为 dàyǒu-kěwéi be well worth doing; have bright prospects:科学种田～。There are bright prospects for scientific farming.
大有区别 dàyǒu-qūbié poles apart; entirely different:你出席不出席，～。Whether you are present or not will make a world of difference.
大有人在 dàyǒurénzài there are plenty of such people; such people are by no means rare:打算火上加油的也～。Such people as want to add fuel to the fire are by no means rare.
大有文章 dàyǒu-wénzhāng there is something behind all this; there is more to it than meets the eye:其中～。There is something intricate (*or* hidden) behind all this apparent simplicity. *or* There's more in it than meets the eye.
大有作为 dàyǒu-zuòwéi there is plenty of scope for one's talents; be able to develop one's ability to the full:～的青年人 promising young man /年轻人在这里是～的。There are plenty of opportunities for young people here.
大鱼 dàyú big fish; major target; arch offender:放长线、钓～ cast a long line in order to catch a big fish; adopt a long-term plan to achieve sth. big /在反腐败斗争中抓到几条～ net some big fish in the drive against corruption
大鱼吃小鱼 dàyú chī xiǎoyú big fish swallowing little fish; the strong bullying the weak
大鱼大肉 dàyú-dàròu abundant fish and meat; rich food:吃腻了～ be cloyed with rich food
大宇财团 Dàyǔ Cáituán (ROK) Daewoo Group
大雨 dàyǔ heavy rain:～倾盆。It rains cats and dogs. *or* The rain is really bucketing down. /～如注。The heavy rain pours down in torrents. *or* The rain comes down in sheets.

大禹 Dà Yǔ respectful term of address for Yu (禹), founder of the Xia Dynasty:～治水 Da Yu leading the people in curbing floods /～陵 legendary mausoleum of Da Yu, located outside Shaoxing (绍兴), Zhejiang Province
大元帅 dàyuánshuài generalissimo
大员 dàyuán 〈旧语〉high-ranking official:接收～ official appointed to take over sth. (such as enemy property)/封疆～ governors of border provinces /听说那桩丑闻牵涉到该国政府的几位～。It was said that the scandal involved some high-ranking officials of the government of that country.
大圆 dàyuán great circle
大圆航向 dàyuán hángxiàng 〈航空〉great-circle course
大远 dàyuǎn very far; far distant:～的路 long way off; of long distance /～来的客人 guest from afar
大院 dàyuàn courtyard; compound:居民～ residential compound/机关～ compound of an institution (usu. including offices and residences)
大约 dàyuē ❶ approximately; about:怀里抱着一个～两周岁的孩子 with a child about two years old in one's arms /从这里到李庄～有三十里地。It is approximately 30 *li* from here to the Li Village. /出席会议的～有二十人。Some 20 people attended the meeting. ❷ probably:条件～尚未谈妥。Probably they have not agreed on the conditions.
大约摸 dàyuēmo 〈方言〉*see*“大约”
大月 dàyuè ❶ solar month of 31 days ❷ lunar month of 30 days
大跃进 dàyuèjìn great leap forward:～的年代 in the years of the Great Leap Forward (1958-1959)
大运河 Dàyùnhé Grand Canal (first dug in the 5th century BC)
大杂烩 dàzáhuì hodgepodge; hotchpotch:这篇文章是一个东抄西拼的～。This article is a hodgepodge of disconnected, pirated ideas.
大杂院儿 dàzáyuànr residential compound occupied by many households:故事发生在北京西城区的一个～里。The story took place in a residential compound in the Western District of Beijing.
大藏经 dàzàngjīng term for all the Buddhist scriptures in Chinese
大藏省 Dàzàngshěng (Japan) Ministry of Finance
大藏相 Dàzàngxiàng (Japan) Minister of Finance
大早 dàzǎo early morning:起了个～儿 get up very early in the morning /第二天一～，他就赶集去了。He set out for the fair early the next morning.
大灶 dàzào ❶ large fixed kitchen range or cooking stove (usu. built of brick and earth) ❷ (in contrast with 小灶 and 中灶) ordinary mess:吃～ have meals in the ordinary mess
大泽乡起义 Dàzéxiāng Qǐyì *also*“陈胜吴广起义” Chén Shèng Wú Guǎng Qǐyì large-scale peasant uprising led by Chen Sheng and Wu Guang which started in Dazexiang (in present Su County 宿县 of Anhui) in 209 BC
大札 dàzhá 〈敬词〉your letter:～拜读。I have read your letter (with much attention).
大斋节 Dàzhāijié 〈基督教〉Lent (period of fasting and penitence during the 40 days between Ash Wednesday and Holy Saturday before Easter)
大斋首日 dàzhāi shǒurì 〈基督教〉Ash Wednesday
大展宏图 dàzhǎn-hóngtú realize one's ambitious dream; one's ambitious plan will be crowned with success:到新岗位后定能～。After arriving at the new post you will be certainly able to fully realize your noble ambition.
大战 dàzhàn ❶ great war; great battle:世界～ world war /棉花～ fierce competition for cotton; battle for cotton ❷ wage large-scale warfare or fierce battle:～中原 fight fiercely on the Central Plains
大张旗鼓 dàzhāng-qígǔ on a grand scale; in a big way; with a great fanfare:～地开展反腐败斗争 launch a great campaign against corruption /～地宣传计划生育的意义 give wide publicity to the significance of family planning
大张挞伐 dàzhāng-tàfá launch a large-scale punitive expedition against; launch a big campaign against; criticize severely and openly:对于浪费现象就是要～。It is imperative to launch a massive campaign against waste.
大丈夫 dàzhàngfu true man; real man; man:～决不食言。A true man will never break his promise. /～敢作敢当。A real man has the courage to accept responsibility for what he does./～能屈能伸。A great man knows when to yield and when not. *or* A real man does not mind petty setbacks and humiliations. /真乃～! Truly a man of

noble generosity!

大昭寺 Dàzhāosì Jokhang Monastery (in Lhasa, Tibet)

大折刀 dàzhédāo jack-knife

大政 dàzhèng important government affairs or policies：总揽～ assume overall responsibility of state affairs; have overall authority /～方针 guiding principles (*or* policies) of fundamental importance; major policies

大枝 dàzhī 〈植物〉bough

大旨 dàzhǐ main points; important aspects; gist：他讲话的～是要大家团结对敌。The gist of his speech is that we should unite to fight the common enemy. /惩恶扬善是这篇小说的～。The moral the novel tries to drive home is to denounce vice and extol virtue.

大指 dàzhǐ ❶ *also* "大拇指" thumb ❷ *see* "大旨"

大志 dàzhì high or lofty aim; exalted ambition; high aspirations：胸怀～ cherish lofty aspirations; aim high /他是个有～的人。He is a man of noble ambition.

大治 dàzhì great order：从大乱到～ from utter chaos to great order/天下～ universal peace and prosperity in the country

大致 dàzhì ❶ in the main; on the whole; by and large：～相似 similar on the whole; largely alike /答案～是正确的。The answer is correct by and large. ❷ roughly; approximately; more or less：～相同 roughly the same /这项工程～两年可以完工。This project will take two years or so to complete.

大智若愚 dàzhì-ruòyú man of great wisdom often appears slow-witted：～，大巧若拙。A man of great wisdom appears like a fool; a man of great skill looks like a clumsy oaf.

大中型 dà-zhōngxíng large and medium-sized：建立了一批～骨干企业。A group of large and medium-sized key projects were established.

大众 dàzhòng common people; the public; broad masses of people：～食谱 recipes for daily cooking; people's cookbook /～歌曲 popular songs /～科学 popular science /～文艺 arts and literature for the masses; popular literature /为～说话 speak for the masses

大众化 dàzhònghuà popularize; do or make in a popular style：～的饭菜 popular low-priced dishes /～商品 run-of-mill, low-priced commodities /京剧只有走～的道路，才能赢得观众。Beijing Opera must cater to the taste and interest of the common people to win back viewers.

大众汽车公司 Dàzhòng Qìchē Gōngsī (Germany) Volkswagen Automobile Plant; Volkswagenwerk AG

大仲马 Dàzhòngmǎ Alexandre Dumas (Davy de La Pailleterie) or Dumas père (1802-1870), French novelist and dramatist

大洲 dàzhōu continent

大轴子 dàzhòuzi *also* "大轴" last (usu. the best) item on the programme：《凤还巢》是今儿晚上的～。*The Phoenix Returns to its Nest* is the last item on the theatrical programme tonight.

大主教 dàzhǔjiào 〈基督教〉archbishop：坎特伯雷～ Archbishop of Canterbury

大助祭 dàzhùjì 〈基督教〉archdeacon

大著 dàzhù 〈敬词〉your celebrated book, essay, work, etc.

大专 dàzhuān ❶ universities and polytechnics ❷ junior college (as distinct from 中专 technical school)：～生 junior college student/～水平 of junior college level; having received a junior college education

大专院校 dà-zhuān yuàn-xiào universities and polytechnics; institutions of higher education or learning

大篆 dàzhuàn ancient style of calligraphy, current in the Zhou Dynasty (c. 11th century-256 BC)

大庄稼 dàzhuāngjia 〈方言〉crop sown in spring and reaped in autumn; autumn-harvested crop

大资产阶级 dàzīchǎnjiējí big bourgeoisie

大子儿 dàzǐr 〈口语〉big coin (= 20 coppers)：～不称 penniless; clean broke

大字 dàzì ❶ (in Chinese calligraphy) large-sized character written with the brush：写一篇～ write a page of big characters ❷ (usu. used in the negative) character; word：～不识 not know a single character; be illiterate

大字报 dàzìbào *dazibao* — big-character poster (prevalent during the Cultural Revolution, 1966-1976)

大字本 dàzìběn ❶ copybook for practising big-character calligraphy ❷ 〈印刷〉large-character edition; large-type edition

大字标题 dàzì biāotí banner headline; bannerline streamer

大自流盆地 Dàzìliú Péndì (Australia) Great Artesian Basin

大自然 dàzìrán nature; Mother Nature：改造～ transform nature /人类不断地与～进行抗争。Man is engaged in a constant struggle with nature.

大宗 dàzōng ❶ large amount or quantity：～款项 large amount of money; large sum /～购买 purchase on a large scale /～交易 block trading ❷ staple：本地产品以茶叶为～。Tea is the staple produce here.

大总统 dàzǒngtǒng president

大足石窟 Dàzú Shíkū Dazu Grottoes (in Sichuan Province)

大族 dàzú large clan; big family

大作 dàzuò ❶ 〈敬词〉your celebrated work, book, article, etc. ❷ erupt; upheave：狂风～。There suddenly arose a strong wind. /枪声～。Dense gunfire broke out.

大作文章 dàzuò-wénzhāng *also* "大做文章" make a fuss; make a big issue：他抓住对手的失误～。He made a big issue of his rival's blunder.

汏 dà 〈方言〉wash; rinse：～手 wash one's hands /～面 wash one's face

da

嗒 da *see* "屹嗒" gēda

垯(墶) da *see* "圪垯" gēda

跶(躂) da *see* "蹬跶" dēngda; "跳跶" tiàoda

纮(繨) da *see* "纥纮" gēda

dāi

呆(獃) dāi ❶ slow-witted; dull; dumb：一脸～相 dull-looking; looking dumb /读书读～了 become dumb with useless book-learning ❷ blank; wooden; dumbstruck：～～地看 stare (*or* look) blankly (at sth. *or* sb.)/吓～了 be dumbfounded /～想 think absent-mindedly; be absorbed in thought /～～出神 be in a brown study/他听到消息后～住了。He froze at the news. ❸ *also* "待" dāi stay：～着别动 stay put; stand still /我在英国～了三年。I stayed in England for three years. *or* I spent three years in England.

呆板 dāibǎn stiff; rigid; inflexible; stereotyped：思想～ rigid in thinking /方法～ inflexible in method /举止～ stiff in manners /形式～ stereotyped in form /文章～。The essay is dull.

呆笨 dāibèn dull; dumb; slow; clumsy：～的眼光 dull eyes /他手脚灵活，一点儿也不～。He is not at all clumsy. In fact, he is quite nimble (*or* agile).

呆痴 dāichī stupid; dumb; muddle-headed：～的神气 glazed expression

呆登登 dāidēngdēng with a blank or wooden expression; in a daze; in a trance：他～地望着窗外。He stared blankly out of the window.

呆钝 dāidùn dull and slow：举止～ slow in movement /神情～ look stupified

呆磕磕 dāikēkē with a stupid or dazed expression：～地发怔 stare blankly as if in a trance

呆愣 dāilèng be in a trance; be in a daze：他低下头，～了一阵子。Hanging his head, he fell into a trance. /他～地站在那里，动也不动。He stood bewildered and transfixed to the spot.

呆料 dāiliào unused material long in stock; overstocked goods

呆气 dāiqi silly; quixotic：这个人有点～。There is something quixotic about the chap. *or* The chap looks a bit silly.

呆然 dāirán as if in a daze; as if in a trance：～而立 stand as if in a trance

呆若木鸡 dāiruòmùjī dumb as a wooden chicken or as a post; dumbstruck; transfixed (with fear or amazement)：吓得～ be transfixed with horror/他得知这个噩耗之后，～。On learning the sad news, he was struck dumb as a wooden chicken.

呆涩 dāisè dull; monotonous; clumsy：她勉强睁开了～的眼。With

an effort she opened her lacklustre eyes.

呆傻 dāishǎ dull-minded; slow-witted; muddle-headed: 又呆又傻 dumb and stupid /他一点儿也不～，内心明白得很。He is no idiot; he knows what is what.

呆傻儿 dāishǎ'ér moronic child or baby

呆头呆脑 dāitóu-dāinǎo dull and stupid; stupid-looking: 那些人好像都是～的。Those people are all like blockheads.

呆小症 dāixiǎozhèng *also* "克汀病"〈医学〉kètīngbìng cretinism: ～患者 cretin

呆性物质 dāixìng wùzhì 〈化学〉inert-material

呆月子 dāiyuèzi 〈方言〉confinement in childbirth; lying-in

呆账 dāizhàng bad debt

呆怔 dāizhèng 〈方言〉be in a daze; be in a trance; stare blankly: 他～了好一会儿才清醒过来。He stared vacantly for quite a while before he came to himself.

呆滞 dāizhì ❶ dull; inert; lifeless: 表情～ vacant expression /目光～ with a dull look in one's eyes ❷ sluggish; stagnant; slack; idle: 贸易～ sluggish trade /生意～ slack business /～的资金 idle capital; tied-up capital/～的资产 bad asset/市场～ dull (*or* stagnant) market /销路～ slow in sale

D

呆滞贷款 dāizhì dàikuǎn dead loan; bad loan

呆滞库存 dāizhì kùcún inert inventory; inactive stock

呆滞商品 dāizhì shāngpǐn unsalable commodity; drug on the market

呆子 dāizi idiot; simpleton; blockhead

呔(咑) dāi 〈叹词〉*usu. used in the early vernacular to draw attention*: ～，住口！你这势利的狗！Hey, shut up! You snobbish cur!
see also tǎi

待 dāi *also* "呆" dāi stay: ～在户外 stay out /～在屋里 stay indoors /他一会儿就来。It won't be long before he comes. *or* He'll be here soon.
see also dài

dǎi

歹 dǎi bad; evil; vicious: 好～不分 cannot tell the good from the bad; cannot distinguish between friend and foe/为非作～ do evil /不识好～ have no sense of propriety; not appreciate a favour; not know which side one's bread is buttered

歹毒 dǎidú vicious; malicious: 为人～ malicious by nature/心肠～ ill-hearted /他好～，居然如此待我。It was very nasty of him to let me down like this.

歹话 dǎihuà 〈方言〉unpalatable words; unpleasant truth: 咱们是～说在头里。Let's get all this straightened out at the very start, however unpleasant it may be.

歹人 dǎirén evil person; thief; burglar; robber

歹徒 dǎitú scoundrel; ruffian; robber; thug

歹心 dǎixīn evil or malicious intent; malice; malicious or evil design: 横起～ conceive an evil design; harbour evil intent

歹意 dǎiyì malice; malicious or evil intent: 心怀～ harbour malice; have malicious intent /可别把人家的好心当了～。Don't mistake goodwill for ill intent.

傣 Dǎi *see* "傣族"

傣剧 dǎijù Dai Opera (popular among the Dai people)

傣历 Dǎilì Dai or Tai calendar (a kind of lunisolar calendar with its first month falling in September): ～新年 Dai (*or* Tai) New Year's Day

傣族 Dǎizú Dai or Tai nationality, living in Yunnan Province

逮 dǎi capture; catch: ～扒手 catch a pickpocket/猫～老鼠 cats catch mice
see also dài

dài

戴 dài ❶ put on; wear; don: ～上帽子 put on one's hat /～假发 wear a wig/穿红～绿 be dressed in red and green — be gaily dressed/～有色眼镜看人 see people through coloured spectacles; view people with biases (*or* a jaundiced eye) ❷ respect; esteem; support: 受群众的爱～ enjoy the love and esteem of the public; enjoy popular support; enjoy great popularity /大家推～他为化学学会会长。He was chosen president of the Chemistry Society. ❸ (Dài) a surname

戴高乐 Dàigāolè de Gaulle (Charles André Marie Joseph de Gaulle, 1890-1970), leader of Free France in World War II, provisional president of France 1945-1946, and President of the Fifth Republic from 1959 to 1969

戴高帽子 dài gāomàozi ❶ wear a dunce's cap: ～游街 wear a dunce's cap and be paraded through the streets ❷ *also* "戴高帽儿"〈比喻〉praise unctuously; flatter; laud sb. to the sky: 人家给他～，他总信以为真，变得忘乎所以。He always looks upon unctuous praise as undeniable truth and thus becomes puffed up with insufferable pride.

戴进 Dài Jìn Dai Jin (formerly translated as Tai Chin, 1386-1462), Chinese brush painter of the Ming Dynasty

戴绿帽 dài lǜmào *also* "戴绿头巾" be a cuckold; be cuckolded; have an unfaithful wife

戴帽小学 dàimào xiǎoxué primary school with first-year middle school classes attached

戴帽子 dài màozi be branded as; bear the label of: 文革时，许多学者被戴上反动学术权威的帽子。Many scholars were denounced as reactionary academic authorities in the Cultural Revolution.

戴姆勒-奔驰有限公司 Dàimǔlè-Bēnchí Yǒuxiàn Gōngsī Daimler-Benz AG, German motor vehicle manufacturer

戴盆望天 dàipén-wàngtiān look at the sky while carrying a tray on the head — pursue one's goal in a self-defeating manner; attempt the impossible

戴胜 dàishèng *also* "呼哱哱" hūbōbō; "山和尚" shānhéshang 〈动物〉hoopoe

戴维灯 dàiwéidēng 〈矿业〉Davy lamp

戴维斯循环理论 Dàiwéisī xúnhuán lǐlùn Davis's cycle theory

戴维营 Dàiwéiyíng (US) Camp David: ～协议 Camp David Accord /埃、以、美～会谈 Camp David Summit Meeting of Egypt, Israel and the United States

戴孝 dàixiào wear mourning for a parent, relative, etc.; be in mourning: 他臂上戴着黑纱，可能是为他的亡母～。He wore a black armband. Probably he was in mourning for his deceased mother.

戴月披星 dàiyuè-pīxīng *also* "披星戴月" go out before dawn and come back after dark; travel day and night; work arduously

戴震 Dài Zhèn Dai Zhen (1723-1777), thinker and scholar of the Qing Dynasty

戴罪立功 dàizuì-lìgōng atone for one's offence by rendering good service; redeem oneself by doing good deeds: 司令命上尉～。The commander told the captain to atone for his error by war exploits.

襶 dài *see* "褦襶" nàidài

带[1](帶) dài ❶ belt; band; ribbon; tape: 皮～ leather belt /腰～ waist band; sash /丝～ silk ribbon /录像～ video tape /鞋～ shoestrings; shoelaces /背～ braces; suspenders /传送～ conveyor belt ❷ tyre: 汽车外～ car tyre ❸ zone; area; belt: 寒～ frigid zone/热～ torrid zone/温～ temperate zone/玉米～ Corn Belt (in the US) /无人地～ no man's land /这一～盛产西瓜。This area produces watermelons in abundance. ❹ leucorrhoea; whites

带[2](帶) dài ❶ take; bring; carry: 聪明点儿还是～雨伞去。It's sensible to take your umbrella along. /让她把有关文件都～来。Tell her to bring along all the relevant papers. /他们～来了好作风。They have brought with them a very good work style. /我没有～笔记本来。I haven't got my notebook with me. /我给你们～来好消息。I have good news for you. ❷ do in passing or by the way; do incidentally: 随手把门～上 close the door after one; pull the door to when one goes out (*or* comes in)/你上街时给我～一包烟。Get me a packet of cigarettes when you go out. /你写信给家里时，给我～上一笔。Give my best regards to your family when you write home. ❸ bear; reveal; show: ～有阶级的印记 bear the imprint of (one's) class /面～笑容 have a smile on one's face; wear a smile /她脸上～着

不屑一顾的神情。Her face showed a sign of infinite disdain. *or* She looked bored and scornful. ❹ contain; hold:~点盐味 have a touch of salt/他话里~着深刻的讽刺意味。There were overtones of biting sarcasm in his words. ❺ with; including; having sth. attached:树叶~着露珠 leaves with dew drops /连说~笑地走进来 enter laughing and talking /做饭~看孩子 be a baby-sitter as well as a cook /这茶叶~盒一共五元。The tea costs 5 *yuan*, including the canister. ❻ lead; head; supervise:~研究生 be a supervisor for graduate students /~客人参观故宫 show the visitors around the Palace Museum /~朋友来玩玩儿。Bring along some friends and we can have a good time. ❼ look after; bring up; raise:~孩子 look after children /早年丧失双亲后，他是叔叔~大的。He lost both parents when (he was) a child, and was brought up by his uncle./这两个孩子真不好~。Those two children are difficult to handle. ❽ drive; promote; give impetus to:以点~面 use the experience of pilot units to promote progress in an entire area /他的模范行为把一大批人都~起来了。His exemplary action kindled the enthusiasm of a large contingent of people.

带班 dàibān head or lead a group of people (on patrol duty, on a shift, or on an assignment of work):今夜排长~。The platoon leader will lead the patrol tonight./老厂长明天将亲自出马，~示范。The old factory director will personally lead a team of workers tomorrow for the demonstration.

带便 dàibiàn 〈方言〉avail oneself of the opportunity; do in passing:他是来北京出差的，~看望老同学。He has come to Beijing on business and will take the opportunity to call on some of his old schoolmates.

带兵 dàibīng lead troops; be in command of troops:~平乱 lead the troops in suppressing a rebellion;command one's men to quell a rebellion /他带过兵，打过仗。He was once a commander and fought in war.

带病 dàibìng in spite of illness:~参加比赛 take part in a competition (*or* game) despite one's illness

带材 dàicái 〈冶金〉strip:~轧机 strip mill

带彩 dàicǎi be wounded in battle or action:他在战争中带过彩。He was wounded in action.

带操 dàicāo 〈体育〉gymnastics with ribbons

带刺儿 dàicìr 〈比喻〉with a touch of sarcasm:说话~ speak with a touch of sarcasm; speak sarcastically/他话里~。There is a sting in his remark.

带刺植物 dàicì zhíwù muricated or thorny plant

带答不理 dàidā-bùlǐ *also* "待答不理" dàidā-bùlǐ be cold and indifferent; stand aloof

带道 dàidào lead the way; act as guide:老吴熟悉地形，就让他~吧。Let Lao Wu lead the way since he knows the terrain well.

带电 dàidiàn electrified; charged; live:~导线 live wire

带电粒子 dàidiàn lìzǐ charged particle

带电体 dàidiàntǐ charged or electrified body

带电作业 dàidiàn zuòyè live wire work

带动 dàidòng ❶ drive; operate:柴油机~的汽艇 boat driven by a diesel engine/用两部机车~货车 use two locomotives to pull a goods van /应该用水电~更多的机器。Hydro-electric power should be utilized on a more extensive scale to operate machines. ❷ bring along; give impetus to; promote:抓好典型~全局 take firm hold of typical examples to promote work as a whole /改革开放~了经济发展。The policy of reform and opening to the outside world has given impetus to the development of the economy.

带犊 dàidú *also* "带犊子" (of a widow) remarry and bring into the new family her son by her previous marriage

带队 dàiduì ❶ lead a group of people ❷ leader of a group

带分数 dàifēnshù 〈数学〉mixed fraction; mixed number

带钢 dàigāng 〈冶金〉strip steel; sheet strip; banding steel:~轧机 strip mill

带好儿 dàihǎor convey sb.'s regards:母亲让我替她给你~。Mother asks me to give you her regards. *or* Mother sends you her regards./你回校时给王老师~。Remember me to our teacher Mr. Wang when you go back to school (*or* on your return to school).

带花 dàihuā be wounded in battle:战斗中他~致残了。He was wounded in action and became disabled.

带话 dàihuà take a message; give a message:替人~ take a message for sb./请你带个话儿给他。Please give him my message.

带胶邮票 dàijiāo yóupiào adhesive stamp

带劲 dàijìn ❶ energetic; forceful:他工作起来真~。He works like a horse. /越表扬，他们干得越~。The more praise they received, the more vigorously they worked. ❷ interesting; wonderful; exciting:这部小说读起来真~。This novel is simply wonderful. *or* It's a gripping novel./昨天的足球赛可~了。Yesterday's football match was just terrific. /他下起棋来可~了。He plays chess with evident relish.

带锯 dàijù 〈机械〉band saw

带菌 dàijūn carry pathogenic bacteria:~体 bacteria-carrier/~率 bacteria-bearing rate

带菌者 dàijūnzhě 〈医学〉bacteria-carrier

带宽 dàikuān 〈通信〉bandwidth:按需分配~ bandwidth-on-demand

带累 dàilěi implicate; involve:我一人做事一人当，绝不~任何人。I am solely responsible for what I did, and will get nobody involved. /他~你们全家遭殃。He brought disaster upon your whole family. /是我~了你。It is I who have got you into this trouble.

带领 dàilǐng ❶ take to a place; guide:一位老工人~学生参观了工厂。An old worker showed the students around the factory. ❷ lead; direct:总工程师~工人搞技术革新。The chief engineer directs the workers in technical innovation. /经理~全店开展冬季销售活动。Led by the manager, the shop launched a winter sales drive.

带路 dàilù show or lead the way; serve as a guide:为人~ show sb. the way; lead the way for sb. /一位老猎户给我们~上山。We had an old hunter as our guide when we climbed the mountain.

带路人 dàilùrén guide; leader:他们需要一个好~，领导他们走出经济困境。They need a good leader who can guide them through the labyrinth of economic ills.

带卵鱼 dàiluǎnyú hard-roed fish

带挈 dàiqiè lead:那年春天,祖父~全家老小逃荒,离开了家乡。That spring, the grandfather led the whole family to flee from their famine-stricken hometown.

带身子 dài shēnzi be pregnant; be in the family way

带声 dàishēng *see* "带音"

带式分级机 dàishì fēnjíjī 〈机械〉belt grader

带式输送机 dàishì shūsòngjī 〈机械〉belt or band conveyer

带式装载机 dàishì zhuāngzàijī 〈机械〉belt truck loader

带手儿 dàishǒur 〈方言〉at sb.'s convenience; without extra trouble:你放心,这点儿事我~就做了。Don't worry, I'll take this bit of work in stride.

带田 dàitián 〈农业〉belt-like land for cross cropping

带头 dàitóu take the lead; take the initiative; be the first; set an example:~完成任务 take the lead in fulfilling one's task/~冲锋 lead the charge /起~作用 play a leading role /~发言 be the first to speak; break the ice

带头人 dàitóurén leader; forerunner

带头学科 dàitóu xuékē leading discipline (of learning)

带头羊 dàitóuyáng bellwether

带徒弟 dài túdi train or take on an apprentice:别看他年轻,可已经~了。Young as he is, he has taken on apprentices.

带土栽植 dàitǔ zāizhí 〈农业〉ball-planting

带土植物 dàitǔ zhíwù 〈农业〉ball-plant

带下 dàixià 〈中医〉morbid leucorrhoea

带小数 dàixiǎoshù whole number with a decimal

带孝 dàixiào *also* "戴孝" dàixiào wear mourning for a parent, relative, etc.; be in mourning:上个月他父亲去世了，他还在~。He's still in mourning for his father who died last month.

带信儿 dàixìnr take or bring an oral message

带形天线 dàixíng tiānxiàn ribbon antenna

带音 dàiyīn 〈语言〉voiced:~辅音 voiced consonant

带引 dàiyǐn lead the way; guide:猎人在前面~着我穿过森林。The hunter walked ahead and led me through the forest.

带鱼 dàiyú cutlass fish; hairtail

带职 dàizhí retain one's post during absence from duty:~学习 go on a study course without being formally relieved of one's post; go on a training course as a mid-career student/~培训 in-service training

带状矿脉 dàizhuàng kuàngmài 〈矿业〉banded lode

带状疱疹 dàizhuàng pàozhěn 〈医学〉herpes zoster; zoster

带子 dàizi ❶ belt; band; sash; ribbon ❷ 〈口语〉videotape; cassette tape; tape

带座 dàizuò (of waiters, usherers, etc.) show customers to their seats:巡堂~ walk around taking (*or* ushering) customers to their

seats

大 dài *used in the following phrases*
see also dà

大夫 dàifu doctor; physician: 外科～ surgeon/小儿科～ paediatrician
see also dàfū

大黄 dàihuáng *also* "川军" chuānjūn 〈植物〉 Chinese rhubarb

大王 dàiwang (used in traditional operas or old-time novels) ❶ king ❷ bandit chieftain: 山～ chieftain of mountain bandits
see also dàwáng

甙 dài *also* "葡糖苷" pútánggān; "糖苷" tánggān 〈化学〉 glucoside

代[1] dài ❶ take the place of; be a substitute for: 我～老王值夜班。I am on night shift in place of Lao Wang. /请～我向他问好。Please give him my regards. *or* Please remember me to him. ❷ acting: ～总理 acting premier ❸ (Dài) a surname

代[2] dài ❶ historical period or era: 古～ ancient times /现～诗歌 contemporary poetry ❷ dynasty: 唐～ Tang Dynasty/改朝换～ one dynasty to be replaced by another ❸ generation: 新一～ new generation /两国世世～～友好下去 maintain a friendly relationship between our two countries from generation to generation ❹ 〈地质〉 era: 古生～ Palaeozoic Era/中生～可分为三叠纪、侏罗纪和白垩纪。The Mesozoic Era is divided into the Triassic, Jurassic, and Cretaceous periods.

代办 dàibàn ❶ do sth. for sb.; act on sb's behalf: 这件事请你～吧。Could I leave the matter with you? *or* Could you act on my behalf? /～托运。We undertake commissions for shipments. ❷ 〈外交〉 chargé d'affaires: 临时～ *chargé d'affaires ad interim* /代理～ *chargé d'affaires en piea* /本任～ *chargé d'affaires en titre* /～处 Office of the Chargé d'Affaires /～级外交关系 diplomatic relations at the level of chargé d'affaires

代办行 dàibànháng 〈商业〉 commission house

代办所 dàibànsuǒ agency: 储蓄～ savings agency /邮政～ postal agency

代笔 dàibǐ write on sb.'s behalf: ～写申请 write an application on sb.'s behalf /父亲病重，女儿～给他的朋友们写信。The father, who was seriously ill, had his daughter write to his friends in his name.

代笔遗嘱 dàibǐ yízhǔ 〈法律〉 dictated testament; dictated will

代币 dàibì token money; token

代表 dàibiǎo ❶ deputy; delegate; representative; envoy: 党代会～ delegate to the Party Congress /区人大～ deputy to a district people's congress /作战双方～ representatives of the belligerant parties /常驻～ permanent representative; permanent delegate /全权～ envoy plenipotentiary/作为中国人类学家的～参加国际会议 participate in an international conference as a representative of Chinese anthropologists ❷ represent; stand for: ～自己国家的利益 represent the interests of one's country /批判现实主义的～作 representative work of critical realism /～新的方向 represent new orientation /～时代精神 embody the spirit of the times /这本书货真价实地～民族虚无主义。This book stands for nothing but national nihilism. ❸ on behalf of; in the name of: ～全院师生向你们表示衷心的感谢 extend heartfelt thanks to you on behalf of the faculty and students of the college /～全体同学讲话 speak in the name of all the students

代表大会 dàibiǎo dàhuì congress; representative assembly or conference: 全国人民～ National People's Congress /教工～ representative assembly of the teachers and staff members (*or* of the faculty and staff)

代表董事 dàibiǎo dǒngshì representative director

代表队 dàibiǎoduì team formed for the purpose of participating in a contest: 高校体育～ athletic team of the colleges and universities/各省、市都有～参加这次比赛。Each province or municipality has sent its team to the contest.

代表权 dàibiǎoquán representation

代表人物 dàibiǎo rénwù representative figure; leading exponent

代表团 dàibiǎotuán delegation; mission; deputation: 政府～ government delegation /经济～ economic mission /工会～ trade union's deputation

代表性 dàibiǎoxìng representativeness: 具有广泛～的爱国人士 patriot who represents broad sections of the people/他的这篇杂文～不强。This essay is not a typical example of his work.

代表资格 dàibiǎo zīgé qualifications of a representative: ～审查委员会 (delegate) credentials committee

代表作 dàibiǎozuò representative work

代步 dàibù 〈书面〉 ride instead of walk: 以车～ ride in a car instead of walking; go by car

代拆代行 dàichāi-dàixíng 〈旧语〉 be authorized to open letters and act for sb. who is absent; be deputed to take charge: 县长请病假，诸事由副县长～。As the magistrate is on sick leave, the deputy magistrate will be in charge.

代偿 dàicháng 〈医学〉 compensation

代偿服 dàichángfú 〈航天〉 pressure compensating suit

代偿功能 dàicháng gōngnéng 〈医学〉 compensation

代偿机能不全 dàicháng jīnéng bùquán 〈医学〉 broken compensation

代偿失调 dàicháng shītiáo 〈医学〉 decompensation

代偿性肺气肿 dàichángxìng fèiqìzhǒng 〈医学〉 compensatory emphysema

代偿性心脏肥大 dàichángxìng xīnzàng féidà compensatory cardiac hypertrophy; hypercardia compensatoria

代称 dàichēng *also* "代名" another name; nickname: 梨枣是木刻的～。Pear and jujube is another name for wood carving.

代词 dàicí 〈语言〉 pronoun: 人称～ personal pronoun/指示～ demonstrative pronoun/关系～ relative pronoun/ 疑问～ interrogative pronoun

代代红 dàidàihóng ❶ be of working-class or poor-peasant origin for generations (a term frequently used in the 1960's and 1970's) ❷ 〈贬义〉 one who is in favour from one reign to another; survivor

代代花 dàidàihuā *also* "玳玳花" dàidàihuā *Citrus aurantinum* var. *amara*

代电 dàidiàn (short for 快邮代电) 〈旧语〉 brief official message sent as express mail

代父 dàifù *also* "教父" jiàofù godfather

代耕 dàigēng ❶ 〈旧语〉 make a living by engaging in work other than farming: 以笔～ make a living as a writer ❷ do farm work for the family of an armyman or a revolutionary martyr (before the period of agricultural cooperation) ❸ (as of a tractor station) plough with machines for sb.

代沟 dàigōu generation gap: 两代人之间的～ gap between two generations/目前青年一代与老一代的～问题是一个热门话题。The generation gap between the old and the young is now a topic that often provokes lively discussion.

代购 dàigòu buy on sb.'s behalf; act as a purchasing agent: ～代销点 purchasing and marketing agency /我们办理～业务。We undertake commissions for purchases.

代号 dàihào code name

代价 dàijià price; cost: 以生命为～ at the cost of one's life/不惜任何～ prepared to pay any price; at any cost; at all costs /我们为胜利付出了昂贵的～。We have to pay dearly for our success.

代金 dàijīn money paid (to sb.) in place of goods or services; cash equivalent

代课 dàikè take over a class for an absent teacher; stand in for an absent teacher; be a substitute (teacher): ～教师 substitute teacher

代劳 dàiláo ❶ ask sb. to do sth. for oneself; request sb. to act on one's behalf: 我今天身体不适，这件事只好由你～了。I'm not very well today. I'll have to leave this to your care. ❷ do sth. for sb.; take trouble on sb.'s behalf: 不要紧，这件事由我～吧。No worry. I'll take care of it for you.

代理 dàilǐ ❶ act for a person in a responsible position: ～部长 acting minister/院长外出开会，院务由副院长～。As the president is away attending a conference, the vice-president will act for him. ❷ engage in certain activities on behalf of one's client; serve as an agent: 受当事人的委托，我将～他签订合同。At the request of the client, I'll sign the contract on his behalf.

代理行 dàilǐháng correspondent bank

代理理论 dàilǐ lǐlùn agency theory

代理领事 dàilǐ lǐngshì acting consul

代理权 dàilǐquán power of attorney; attorneyship; procuration

代理人 dàilǐrén ❶ 〈法律〉 procurator; attorney: 我已请一位律师做我的诉讼～。I've asked a lawyer to act as my procurator. ❷ agent;

deputy; proxy: 外国财团利益的～ agent for foreign financial interests/～战争 proxy war
代理融通 dàilǐ róngtōng 〈金融〉factoring
代理商 dàilǐshāng commercial agent; factor
代理制 dàilǐzhì agency system
代码 dàimǎ 〈自控〉code (language): ～读出器 code-reader
代脉 dàimài 〈中医〉slow, intermittent pulse
代面 dàimiàn 〈书面〉❶ mask ❷ compare notes by writing instead of talking face to face
代名 dàimíng *see* "代称"
代名词 dàimíngcí ❶ another name; synonym: 西施历来是美女的～。Xi Shi has always been a synonym for feminine beauty. ❷ *also* "代词"〈语言〉pronoun
代母 dàimǔ godmother
代庖 dàipáo 〈书面〉do what is sb. else's job; replace sb. else gratuitously: 这是他的工作，我不能越俎～。This is his business, and I must not overstep my jurisdiction.
代培 dàipéi train students for an organization: 我校为这个公司～了几十名专业人才。Our school has trained scores of specialists for this company.
代培生 dàipéishēng student recruited or trained for an organization
代人受过 dàirén-shòuguò suffer for the faults of another; bear the blame for sb.; be a whipping boy for sb. 他为人宽厚，就是～也从不抱怨。Kind-hearted and broad-minded, he never complains about the blame he gets for no fault of his own.
代乳粉 dàirǔfěn milk powder substitute
代售 dàishòu sell for sb. else; be commissioned to sell: ～月票 be commissioned to sell monthly tickets/～邮票 sell stamps on the sideline
代书 dàishū ❶ write for others: 请人～ ask sb. to write on one's behalf ❷ one who writes legal documents or letters for others
代数 dàishù algebra: ～和 algebraic sum; algebraic addition/～数 algebraic number/～数论 algebraic theory of numbers
代数簇 dàishùcù algebraic variety
代数方程 dàishù fāngchéng algebraic equation
代数函数 dàishù hánshù algebraic function
代数几何 dàishù jǐhé algebraic geometry
代数理论 dàishù lǐlùn algebraic theories
代数曲面 dàishù qūmiàn algebraic surface
代数式 dàishùshì algebraic expression
代数学 dàishùxué algebra
代替 dàitì replace; substitute for; take the place of: 内燃机车已经被电力机车所～。The internal combustion engine has been replaced by the electric locomotive. /在许多情况下，可以用硬塑料～钢材。Hard plastics can be a substitute for steel products in many cases. /这两个词可以互相～。The two words are interchangeable.
代为 dàiwéi for (sb.): ～保管 take care of... for sb. (*or* on sb.'s behalf)/～说项 put in a good word for sb.
代位 dàiwèi 〈法律〉subrogation: ～权 right of subrogation
代销 dàixiāo sell (for sb. or the state) on a commission basis; be commissioned to sell sth. (usu. as a sideline); act as a commission agent: ～商 commission agent/～店 shop commissioned to sell certain goods/～农产品 be commissioned to sell farm products /这些试制品全由我店～。We are the sole agent for these trial-products.
代谢 dàixiè ❶ supersession: 新旧事物的～ supersession of the old by the new/四时～ change of the seasons/人事～ vicissitudes of life ❷〈生物〉metabolism: 新陈～ metabolism/～分解 catabolism /～组成 anabolism/～过程 metabolic process
代谢病 dàixièbìng 〈医学〉metabolic disorder
代谢亢进 dàixiè kàngjìn 〈医学〉hypermetabolism
代谢期 dàixièqī metabolic stage
代谢物 dàixièwù metabolite
代谢性皮肤病 dàixièxìng pífūbìng dermotosis of metabolism disturbance
代谢作用 dàixiè zuòyòng metabolism
代行 dàixíng act on sb.'s behalf: ～职权 function in an acting capacity /～部长职务 act for the minister
代序 dàixù article used in lieu of a preface; article written by way of an introduction
代言人 dàiyánrén spokesman; mouthpiece: 那位专栏作家实际上是执政党的～。That columnist is none other than a spokesman for the ruling party.
代议制 dàiyìzhì *also* "议会制" yìhuìzhì representative system: ～政府 representative government/～机构 representative institution
代用 dàiyòng substitute: ～材料 substitute (*or* ersatz) material
代用品 dàiyòngpǐn substitute; ersatz
代远年湮 dàiyuǎn-niányān too long ago to be ascertained: 这件事～，详情无从查考了。The event has long since passed into oblivion and its details cannot be ascertained.
代职 dàizhí function in an acting capacity
代字号 dàizìhào swung dash (～)

袋

dài ❶ bag; sack; pocket; pouch: 旅行～ travelling bag /邮～ mailbag /工具～ tool kit /衣～ pocket /烟～ tobacco pouch/～装奶粉 milk powder in bags ❷〈量词〉sack; bag; packet: 一～玉米面 a sack of maizemeal /一～瓜子 a bag of melon seeds /一～白糖 a bag (*or* packet) of sugar ❸〈量词〉*used of tobacco*: 抽一～烟 smoke a pipe/一～烟功夫 time needed to smoke a pipe
袋茶 dàichá ❶ tea bag ❷ tea in bags
袋猴 dàihóu cuscus
袋獾 dàihuān Tasmanian devil (*Sarcophilus harrisii*)
袋狼 dàiláng Tasmanian wolf (*Thylacinus cynocephalus*)
袋狸 dàilí bandicoot
袋狸鼠 dàilíshǔ bandicoot rat (*Bandicota indica*)
袋猫 dàimāo marsupial cat
袋鼠 dàishǔ kangaroo
袋蛙 dàiwā marsupial frog
袋鼯 dàiwú glider; flying possum; flying phalanger
袋鼹鼠 dàiyǎnshǔ *also* "袋鼹" marsupial mole
袋鼬 dàiyòu marsupial mouse
袋子 dàizi bag; sack: 面～ flour sack/钱～ purse

玳(瑇) dài

玳玳花 dàidàihuā *also* "代代花" dàidàihuā *Citrus aurantinum* var. *amara*
玳瑁 dàimào 〈动物〉hawksbill turtle

黛

dài black pigment used by women in ancient times to paint their eyebrows
黛蓝 dàilán dark blue: ～的山峰 dark blue peaks
黛绿 dàilǜ 〈书面〉dark green: 傍晚，附近的树林都成了～色。Towards evening, the nearby woods were a vast expanse of dark green.
黛紫 dàizǐ purple: 雾霭蒙蒙，远山～。The distant mountains are purple in the mists.

贷

dài ❶ loan; credit: 信～ credit/农～ agricultural loan; credit for agricultural production ❷ borrow or lend: 向银行～款 borrow money from a bank; get a bank loan /银行给这家工厂～了几笔款。The bank granted several loans to the factory. ❸ shift (responsibility); shirk: 责无旁～ be one's unshirkable responsibility; be duty-bound ❹ pardon; mercy: 严惩不～ punish without mercy
贷方 dàifāng ❶〈会计〉credit; credit side: ～记录 credit entry /～金额 amount of credit side /～余额 credit balance /～票据 credit note; C/N ❷ creditor; lender: 这笔款～催得很紧。The creditor is pressing hard for the repayment of the loan.
贷款 dàikuǎn ❶ provide or grant a loan; extend credit; get or obtain a loan: 从银行～ arrange a loan from a bank; ask for a bank loan/中国银行～给几家公司进口先进设备。The Bank of China extended credit to a number of companies for the importation of advanced equipment. ❷ loan; credit: 取得一笔～ obtain a loan /无息～ interest-free loan /长期低息～ long-term low-interest loan/未偿～ outstanding loan/出口～ export loan (*or* credit) /软～ soft loan /抵押～ loan against collateral; loan on mortgage /专用～ loan for exclusive use/政策性～ policy-based (*or* -related) lending/票据抵押～ loan on bill (*or* note)/一日～ overnight loan /未确定数额的～ open-end loan /～与存款比率 loan-deposit ratio
贷款本金 dàikuǎn běnjīn principal of a loan
贷款财团 dàikuǎn cáituán loan consortium; loan syndicate
贷款规模 dàikuǎn guīmó volume of credit; size of a loan
贷款结构 dàikuǎn jiégòu loan mix
贷款利率 dàikuǎn lìlǜ loan interest rate

贷款人 dàikuǎnrén ❶ borrower (of a loan) ❷ lender; creditor
贷款协定 dàikuǎn xiédìng loan agreement
贷款业务 dàikuǎn yèwù loan transaction
贷学金 dàixuéjīn student loan; loan offered to student by future employer
贷主 dàizhǔ creditor; lender

岱 Dài another name for Mount Tai (泰山)
岱人 Dàirén Tays, one of the ethnic minorities in Vietnam
岱宗 Dàizōng *also* "岱岳" another name for Mount Tai

待[1] dài ❶ treat; deal with: 优~ give special (*or* preferential) treatment to / 以礼相~ treat with courtesy / 宽~俘虏 treat prisoners of war leniently / 宽以~人, 严以律己 be strict with oneself but lenient with others ❷ entertain: 在家~客 be at home to entertain guests; entertain guests at home

待[2] dài ❶ wait for; await: ~机行事 wait for an opportunity to act / 有~改进 have yet to be improved; need improvement / 尚~解决 have yet to be solved; be outstanding / 停工~料 work is being held up for lack of raw material ❷ need: 自不~言 this goes without saying; be taken for granted ❸ going to; about to: 我正~离家, 电话铃响了。I was about to leave when the telephone rang.
see also dāi
待承 dàicheng treat; entertain: 用丰盛的饭菜~客人 treat guests to a sumptuous dinner
待答不理 dàidā-bùlǐ *also* "带搭不理" dàidā-bùlǐ be stand-offish or distant; give the cold shoulder: 他~地嗯了一声。"H'm," he said half-heartedly.
待到 dàidào by the time; when: ~山花烂漫时, 她在丛中笑。When the mountain flowers are in full bloom, She will smile mingling in their midst.
待发 dàifā ready to leave; ready to be shipped: 整装~ be packed and ready to go
待机 dàijī bide one's time: ~行事 bide one's time until the opportunity comes up
待价而沽 dàijià'érgū wait for a good price; wait for the highest bid: 投机商人囤积居奇, ~。Profiteers store up commodities in short supply, and only sell them at high prices. / 他是个~的政客。He is a politician ready to sell himself to the highest bidder.
待建 dàijiàn to be constructed: 城里有许多~项目。There are many construction projects to be started in this city.
待见 dàijian 〈方言〉 like; be fond of: 这孩子真乖, 我可~他。The child is such a dear that I am really fond of him. / 他就不~小里小气的。He can't tolerate meanness.
待决 dàijué awaiting a decision: ~案件 〈法律〉 pending case
待决犯 dàijuéfàn prisoner sentenced to death and awaiting execution; death row prisoner
待考 dàikǎo remain to be verified; need checking: 这些出土文物的年代~。The age of these archeological finds remains to be determined.
待理不理 dàilǐ-bùlǐ look aloof and distant; be standoffish: 你跟他说话, 他总是~的。He always assumes an air of indifference when you speak to him.
待令 dàilìng await orders or instructions: ~出发 await orders to set out
待命 dàimìng await orders: 原地~ stand by to await orders
待聘 dàipìn ❶ waiting for an appointment: ~技术员 technician who has not signed a contract with any firm; unemployed technician ❷ *see* "待字"
待人 dàirén treat people; conduct oneself towards others: ~处世 the way one gets along with others and conducts oneself in society / 诚心实意~ treat people with sincerity; be sincere and true to others
待人接物 dàirén-jiēwù the way one gets along with people: ~, 谦逊有礼 modest and unassuming in one's behaviour towards people / 他们~, 和蔼可亲。They are kindly and affable in social intercourse.
待审 dàishěn 〈法律〉 pending trial
待时 dàishí 〈书面〉 bide one's time; await the opportune moment: 还兵~ recall one's troops to await a better opportunity (for attacking the enemy)
待时而动 dàishí'érdòng wait for the right time to act: 韬光养晦, ~ hide one's capabilities and await the opportune time for action
待售 dàishòu ready for sale: ~货 commodities for sale; offerings / ~商品目录 catalogue of goods for sale
待宵草 dàixiāocǎo *also* "山芝麻" shānzhīma; "月见草" yuèjiàncǎo *Oenothera odorata*
待续 dàixù to be continued: 未完~ (usu. used at the end of an instalment of a long article, etc.) to be continued
待业 dàiyè wait for employment; be unemployed: ~青年 (usu. of youngsters, fresh from school) youth waiting for employment / ~人员 people waiting for jobs; unemployed people / 去年下岗以后, 她一直在家~。Since laid off last year, she has stayed at home, looking for another job.
待业保险 dàiyè bǎoxiǎn unemployment insurance
待遇 dàiyù ❶ treat (people): 不能似一个陌生人~他。You should not treat him as a stranger. ❷ treatment: 最惠国~ most-favourednation treatment / 平等~ equal treatment / 国民~ national treatment / 政治~ political seniority (*or* status); political treatment / 这种冷淡的~使他感到很不高兴。He was highly displeased with the cold reception. ❸ remuneration; pay; wages or salary and benefits: 优厚的~ attractive salary / 生活~ material benefits / 罢工职员要求提高~。The striking staff demanded higher pay.
待字 dàizì 〈书面〉 (of a maiden) have yet to be betrothed: ~闺中 still a maiden (in her boudoir) not yet engaged to anybody

迨 dài 〈书面〉 ❶ till; until; by the time: ~后再议 discuss it later (*or* another time) / ~夜, 涛声不绝于耳。The waves kept roaring when night came. ❷ before sth. happens; while sth. lasts: ~天未雨而往 go there before it rains / ~其不备而击之 launch an attack while the enemy is off guard

怠 dài ❶ idle; lax; slack; negligent: 懈~ lax and sluggish ❷ slighting; disrespectful
怠惰 dàiduò idle; lazy; indolent: ~成性 be incorrigibly lazy / ~使他一事无成。He failed to accomplish anything in his life on account of indolence.
怠工 dàigōng go slow; slow down; work-to-rule: 消极~, 以示抗议 go slow as a protest
怠忽 dàihū be remiss; neglect: 他工作勤恳, 从无~。He works conscientiously and never neglects his duties.
怠倦 dàijuàn lax and tired; tired of work; idle and languid: 坚守岗位, 不敢~ stand fast at one's post and never slack off for a single moment
怠慢 dàimàn ❶ slight; cold-shoulder; neglect: 他从来不~人。He never cold-shoulders anybody. / 不要~了来宾。See that none of the guests are neglected. / 就是你不喜欢他, 你也不应该~他。You shouldn't slight him even if you don't like him. ❷ 〈套语〉 (used by a host to show his modesty) fail to give proper attention to one's guests: 真对不起, 太~了。I am sorry to have been a poor host.

殆 dài 〈书面〉 ❶ danger: 危~ great danger / 百战不~ fight a hundred battles without danger of defeat ❷ almost; nearly: 他的钱财挥霍~尽。His money and property have almost been squandered.
殆周期 dàizhōuqī 〈数学〉 almost periodic: ~函数 almost periodic function / ~解 almost periodic solution

骀 dài
see also tái
骀荡 táidàng 〈书面〉 ❶ invigorating; exhilarating: 春风~。The vernal wind is exhilarating. ❷ lax; bohemian; dissipated

绐 dài 〈书面〉 swindle; coax; dupe

逮[1] dài 〈书面〉 reach: 力所不~ beyond one's reach (*or* power) / 天阴沉沉的, ~晚方晴。The sky was overcast, and it didn't clear up till dusk.

逮[2] dài *see* "逮捕"
see also dǎi
逮捕 dàibǔ arrest; apprehend; take into custody: ~法办 arrest and deal with according to law; bring to justice / ~归案 bring to book (*or* justice) / 当场被~ be captured red-handed / ~证 arrest warrant

逮(𨔵) dài see "叆逮" àidài

埭 dài 〈方言〉(usu. used in place names) dam:石～ Shidai, place in Anhui Province

dān

单(單) dān ❶ one; single:～位数 single figure/～扇门 single-leaf door /～排纽扣的 single-breasted /～职工家庭 single breadwinner (*or* income) family ❷ odd:～只手套 odd glove /～周 odd-number week ❸ singly; alone:～门独户 house (*or* apartment) for one family/把农药～放在一个地方 put pesticides in a separate place /～方面撕毁合同 unilaterally tear up agreements ❹ only; alone:别的不说,～说这点。Let's take up this point alone. /不能～看表面现象。We cannot judge things by their appearances only. ❺ simple: 简～ simple; plain ❻ thin; weak: 势～力薄 weak and without much support ❼ unlined or unpadded (clothes) ❽ sheet:床～ bed sheet ❾ list; bill:名～ name list/价目～ price list/提货～ bill of lading/菜～ menu; bill of fare /节目～ programme /传～ leaflet /发货～ invoice

see also chán; Shàn

单摆 dānbǎi 〈物理〉simple pendulum

单板 dānbǎn ❶〈林业〉veneer:～干燥 veneer-drying/～切削机 veneer-slicer ❷〈计算机〉one board; single board:～存储器 one-board memory/～微型机 single board microcomputer

单帮 dānbāng 〈旧语〉travelling trader working on his own:跑～ travel around trading on one's own

单倍体 dānbèitǐ *also* "单元体"; "单倍体生物"〈生物〉monoploid; haploid:～育种 haploid breeding

单倍体植株 dānbèitǐ zhízhū *also* "单倍体植物" haplobiont

单本剧 dānběnjù *also* "单剧"〈影视〉single-episode TV play

单本位制 dānběnwèizhì 〈经济〉monometalic standard; monometallism:～货币 monometallic currency /单本位金属货币制 monometallic monetary system

单本栽插 dānběn zāichā individual plant transplanting

单崩儿 dānbēngr *also* "单崩个"〈方言〉singly; alone:这个人很不合群儿,干什么事情都是～。This chap is a loner, going about everything on his own. *or* This fellow is not gregarious and likes doing things all by himself. /一双筷子剩～的了。There's only one left of the pair of chopsticks.

单比 dānbǐ 〈数学〉simple proportion

单比例 dānbǐlì 〈数学〉simple ratio

单边 dānbiān 〈经济〉unilateral:～进口 unilateral import

单边贸易 dānbiān màoyì one-way trade; unilateral trade

单边限额 dānbiān xiàn'é unilateral quota restriction

单兵 dānbīng ❶ single soldier; ～负荷 equipment carried by a single soldier ❷〈书面〉troops cut off from the main body of the army; lone force

单兵导弹 dānbīng dǎodàn one-man missile

单兵教练 dānbīng jiàoliàn 〈军事〉individual drilling; drilling on a one-by-one basis

单兵装备 dānbīng zhuāngbèi 〈军事〉individual equipment

单薄 dānbó ❶ (of clothing) thin: 你穿得太～了。You should put on warmer clothes. ❷ delicate; frail: 身体～ in delicate health; frail /女孩子往往比男孩子身体～些。Girls are normally of lighter build than boys. ❸ insubstantial; flimsy; thin: 证据～ flimsy evidence /论据～ feeble argument /内容～ thin in content /我们国家的底子比较～。Our country has a relatively weak foundation to start with.

单步指令 dānbù zhǐlìng 〈计算机〉single-step instruction

单参数 dāncānshù 〈数学〉one parameter; single parameter:～法 single (*or* one) parameter method

单层 dāncéng single layer; monolayer:～焊 single layer welding

单层全息图 dāncéng quánxītú single layer hologram

单层丝包线 dāncéng sībāoxiàn single silk-covered wire

单产 dānchǎn (short for 单位面积产量) per unit area yield; unit yield:提高～,扩大种植面积 raise the per unit area yield and increase the acreage sown

单车 dānchē ❶ single vehicle; individual vehicle:～日收入 daily revenue per vehicle ❷〈方言〉bicycle

单程 dānchéng one way:～机票 one way (*or* single) air ticket/～出境签证 one way exit visa /这车只走～。This is a one-way bus.

单程清棉机 dānchéng qīngmiánjī 〈纺织〉single process scutcher

单处理机 dānchǔlǐjī uni-processor

单传 dānchuán ❶ (of a family) have only one son for several generations:他家几辈～,就这一根独苗儿。He was the only son of a family with a sole male heir for several generations. ❷ learn or derive (one's skill, etc.) from one master or school alone:梅派～ be of the pure Mei Lanfang school

单纯 dānchún ❶ simple; pure:思想～ unsophisticated /这工作很～。The work is simple and well-defined. ❷ alone; purely; merely: ～追求物质享受 seek purely material comfort /～计件工资制 straight piece-work pay system/这不是～的方法问题。This is not simply a question of methodology.

单纯词 dānchúncí 〈语言〉single-morpheme word

单纯骨折 dānchún gǔzhé 〈医学〉closed or simple fracture

单纯林 dānchúnlín *also* "纯林" pure forest

单纯疱疹 dānchún pàozhěn 〈医学〉herpes simplex

单纯性肥胖 dānchúnxìng féipàng 〈医学〉simple obesity

单纯性甲状腺肿 dānchúnxìng jiǎzhuàngxiànzhǒng 〈医学〉simple goiter

单纯性紫癜 dānchúnxìng zǐdiàn 〈医学〉purpura simplex

单词 dāncí ❶ single-morpheme word ❷ individual word; word: 记～ learn words by rote; memorize words

单打 dāndǎ 〈体育〉singles:女子～ women's singles/少年男子～ boy's singles/他在～中失利。He was beaten in the singles.

单打一 dāndǎyī ❶ concentrate on one thing alone:学外语不能～,光靠课堂是不行的。One cannot rely solely on classroom instruction in learning a foreign language. /发展农业不能～,光种粮食。In developing agriculture, we must not focus on grain production alone. ❷ have a one-track mind: 这个人～的头脑,遇事不知变通。He has a one-track mind and does not know that sometimes he has to be flexible in handling matters.

单单 dāndān only; alone:大家都喜欢吃米饭,～她爱吃面条。She alone cares for noodles while the rest of us prefer rice.

单刀 dāndāo ❶ short-hilted broadsword ❷ single-broadsword event (in *wushu*) ❸〈机械〉single-tool:～架 single tool holder

单刀直入 dāndāo-zhírù come straight to the point; speak out without mincing one's words:他为人直率,谈问题总是～。Frank and straightforward, he never minces matters in presenting his views. /我～地向他提出了这个问题。I put the question point-blank to him. /老人说话～,一点也不拐弯抹角。The old man drove his point home without beating about the bush.

单道焊 dāndàohàn 〈机械〉single-pass weld

单调 dāndiào monotonous; dull; drab: ～的生活 dull everyday life/色彩～ dull colouring/衣着～ drab clothing/饭菜～ monotonous food or diet /故事情节～。The plot (of the story) is insipid.

单丁 dāndīng 〈旧语〉only male adult among the offspring

单独 dāndú on one's own; by oneself; independent:～核算 independent accounting/～使用 for one's exclusive use /外商～投资 sole foreign investment /我要～去南京一趟。I'll make a trip to Nanjing by myself. /他总是～一个人,不合群。He is a bad mixer and likes to keep to himself.

单独关税区 dāndú guānshuìqū separate customs territory

单耳听觉 dān'ěr tīngjué monaural hearing

单发 dānfā 〈军事〉single shot:～射击 single shot

单发动机 dānfādòngjī monomotor; single engine:～飞机 single-engine airplane

单方 dānfāng *also* "丹方" dānfāng folk prescription; home remedy

单方面 dānfāngmiàn one-sided; unilateral:～裁军 unilateral disarmament /～义务 unilateral obligation /～承担义务的协定 unilateral agreement /～废除 unilateral denunciation /～规定的配额 unilateral quota /～转让 unilateral transfer /你怎么可以～做出这样的决定呢? How could you make such a decision without consulting others?

单放机 dānfàngjī ❶ cassette player ❷ *also* "放像机" fàngxiàngjī videotape player

单飞 dānfēi 〈航空〉solo flight:放～ make a solo flight; fly alone

单分子 dānfēnzǐ 〈化学〉monomolecular; of a single molecule:～反应 monomolecular reaction /～膜 monomolecular film

单峰驼 dānfēngtuó 〈动物〉one-humped camel; dromedary; Ara-

D

bian camel
单幅 dānfú 〈纺织〉single width:～布 single width cloth
单干 dāngàn ❶ work on one's own; go it alone; work by oneself; do sth. single-handed:她生性孤独,总愿意～。She is a lone wolf and likes to do things on her own. /有些工作必须合作,有些工作需要～。Some types of work presuppose cooperation in a collective effort whereas some other types require individuals to work by themselves. ❷ individual farming:农业生产过去不允许～。Individual farming was not allowed in the past.
单干风 dāngànfēng tendency to return to individual farming after collectivization
单干户 dāngànhù peasant family farming on its own after agricultural collectivization; self-employed businessman or farmer
单杠 dāngàng 〈体育〉❶ horizontal bar ❷ horizontal bar gymnastics
单睾畸形 dāngāo jīxíng 〈医学〉monorchism:～患者 monorchid
单个儿 dāngèr ❶ individually; alone:教授要你们集体去,而不是～行动。The professor expects you to go in a group, not individually. ❷ odd one:别的同学都搭对跳舞,只剩他～了。All the other students have paired off for a dance; he is the odd man out./这套家具不～卖。This set of furniture is not to be sold piecemeal.
单根独苗 dāngēn-dúmiáo only child
单挂号 dānguàhào registered mail which does not require the post office to deliver the recipient's acknowledgment of receipt to the sender
单管锅炉 dānguǎn guōlú 〈机械〉monotube boiler
单管炮 dānguǎnpào single-barrel gun
单轨 dānguǐ ❶ *also* "单线" single track:改～为双轨 double-track a single-track railway ❷ monorail:～起重机 monorail crane; monorail hoist /～运输机 monorail conveyer / ～火车 monorail train
单轨铁路 dānguǐ tiělù monorail:高架～ elevated monorail
单果 dānguǒ *also* "单花果" monothalmic fruit
单过 dānguò live alone; live by oneself; live on one's own:儿子结了婚,已经分居～了。The son has got married and now lives apart from his parents.
单寒 dānhán ❶ thinly clad in cold weather:时值严冬,衣着～。He was thinly clad even in inclement winter. ❷〈旧语〉of poor and low origin:家世～ come of an impoverished family
单号 dānhào odd number (of a ticket, seat, etc.)
单核 dānhé 〈生物〉monokaryon
单核细胞 dānhé xìbāo 〈生物〉monocyte
单核细胞瘤 dānhé xìbāoliú 〈生物〉monocytoma
单鹄寡凫 dānhú-guǎfú *also* "寡鹄单凫"〈比喻〉widow or widower
单花果 dānhuāguǒ *see* "单果"
单铧犁 dānhuálí single-furrow plough
单簧管 dānhuángguǎn *also* "黑管" hēiguǎn clarinet
单簧口琴 dānhuáng kǒuqín Jew's harp; Jews' harp
单机 dānjī single engine, generator or machine; single plane:～功率 single-machine (*or* single generator) capacity
单机组电站 dānjīzǔ diànzhàn 〈电工〉one-unit plant
单级火箭 dānjí huǒjiàn single-stage rocket
单级人轨飞行器 dānjí rùguǐ fēixíngqì 〈航天〉single stage to orbit vehicle
单计算机 dānjìsuànjī unicomputer
单季稻 dānjìdào single-crop rice:种～ planting single-crop rice; single cropping of rice
单价 dānjià ❶〈经济〉unit price ❷〈化学〉〈生物〉univalent:～抗体 univalent antibody
单间儿 dānjiānr ❶ one-room house:～公寓 one-room flat/～铺面 one-room shop front ❷ single room (as in a hotel); separate room (as in a restaurant):南屋是～,你住着合适。The room with a southern exposure is a single room, which suits you fine. /我为今天的宴会预订了一个～。I booked a separate room for the dinner today.
单件生产 dānjiàn shēngchǎn individual piece production
单件生产时间 dānjiàn shēngchǎn shíjiān piece rate
单件小批生产 dānjiàn xiǎopī shēngchǎn jobbing work
单键 dānjiàn 〈化学〉single bond
单交 dānjiāo 〈农业〉single cross:～种 single-cross stock
单脚跳 dānjiǎotiào 〈体育〉hop
单晶 dānjīng 〈物理〉monocrystalline; single crystal; unit crystal /～炉 single crystal growing furnace /～纤维 monocrystalline fibre
单晶硅 dānjīngguī 〈电子〉monocrystalline silicon
单晶体 dānjīngtǐ 〈物理〉monocrystal
单精受精 dānjīng shòujīng monospermy:～卵 monospermic egg
单镜头相机 dānjìngtóu xiàngjī single-lens camera
单静 dānjing *also* "单净" with few family members:他们夫妻俩过日子,上无父母,下无儿女,别提有多么～。The couple live in quiet conjugal bliss, unworried and undisturbed, with neither parents nor children to look after.
单居 dānjū live alone by oneself; live on one's own
单句 dānjù 〈语言〉simple sentence
单剧 dānjù *see* "单本剧"
单据 dānjù documents attesting to the giving or receiving of money or goods; receipts; bills; vouchers:～不符 discrepancy in the documents/货运～ shipping documents /凭～报销 be reimbursed by receipts
单卡 dānkǎ single cassette deck:～录放机 single-cassette recorder
单孔目 dānkǒngmù 〈动物〉*Monotremata*:～动物 monotreme
单口 dānkǒu 〈戏曲〉solo performance; one-man show:～快板 solo clapper talk
单口相声 dānkǒu xiàngsheng one-man comic talk
单跨 dānkuà 〈建筑〉single span:～桥 single-span bridge/～梁 single beam
单利 dānlì 〈经济〉simple interest
单恋 dānliàn unrequited love
单料 dānliào ❶ unfortified raw material ❷〈比喻〉(of people or things) pure; simple; unsophisticated:世界上哪儿有～的诗人哪? Where on earth can we find an unsophisticated poet?
单列 dānliè separately listed:计划～城市 cities specifically designated in the state plan (i. e. apart from the provinces they belong to administratively)
单列轴承 dānliè zhóuchéng single-row bearing
单另 dānlìng separately; alone and apart from the rest:～保存 keep sth. separate /我再～给他做吃的。I shall cook something specially for him.
单路载波 dānlù zàibō 〈通信〉single-channel carrier
单卵孪生 dānluǎn luánshēng chorioangiopagus
单卵双生 dānluǎn shuāngshēng monozygotic twins; identical twins
单轮脚踏车 dānlún jiǎotàchē unicycle; monocycle
单轮射箭 dānlún shèjiàn 〈体育〉single round archery:女子 30 米～ women's 30-metre single-round archery event
单面 dānmiàn single face or side:～焊接 single-side welding
单面山 dānmiànshān 〈地理〉cuesta
单名 dānmíng single-character given name
单模光纤 dānmó guāngxiān single mode (optical) fibre
单模激光器 dānmó jīguāngqì unimodal laser
单宁酸 dānníngsuān 〈化学〉tannic acid
单偶婚 dān'ǒuhūn monogamy
单皮 dānpí small drumlike percussion instrument for coordinating the other musical instruments in Chinese operas
单皮鼓 dānpígǔ *danpi* drum
单篇 dānpiān ❶ separate and unrelated (articles, papers, etc.):～论文集 collection of essays ❷ separately printed article or essay
单片存储器 dānpiàn cúnchǔqì 〈自控〉monolithic memory or storage
单片混合电路 dānpiàn hùnhé diànlù 〈电子〉monobrid circuit
单片机 dānpiànjī single or one chip computer
单片式集成电路 dānpiànshì jíchéng diànlù 〈电子〉monolithic integrated circuit
单片微型处理机 dānpiàn wēixíng chǔlǐjī 〈计算机〉single- or one-chip microprocessor
单片微型计算机 dānpiàn wēixíng jìsuànjī 〈计算机〉one-chip microcomputer
单片眼镜 dānpiàn yǎnjìng monocle
单枪彩色显像管 dānqiāng cǎisè xiǎnxiàngguǎn Uniray
单枪匹马 dānqiāng-pǐmǎ *also* "匹马单枪" single-handed; all by oneself; alone:～地解决难题 resolve a difficult problem single-handed /他～地突出重围。He broke through the heavy encirclement all alone.
单亲 dānqīn single parent
单亲家庭 dānqīn jiātíng single- or lone-parent family
单亲生殖 dānqīn shēngzhí 〈生物〉monogenic reproduction; monogeny

单人床 dānrénchuáng single bed
单人独马 dānrén-dúmǎ *also* "单身匹马" single-handed; all by oneself:他~活捉了一个俘虏。He captured an enemy soldier single-handed.
单人房 dānrénfáng single room
单人划艇 dānrén huátǐng 〈体育〉Canadian single
单人拦网 dānrén lánwǎng 〈体育〉single block
单人皮艇 dānrén pítǐng 〈体育〉one-man kayak; single kayak; K-1
单人艇 dānréntǐng one-man boat or shell
单人舞 dānrénwǔ solo dance:跳~ dance a solo /舞剧《天鹅湖》中的~很精彩。The solo dance in the ballet *Swan Lake* is wonderful.
单人纸牌戏 dānrén zhǐpáixì solitaire
单日 dānrì odd-number days (of the month)
单弱 dānruò delicate; frail; fragile:身体~ fragile constitution /他看起来很~。He looked very delicate.
单色 dānsè monochromatic: ~电视 monochromatic television; black-and-white TV
单色光 dānsèguāng 〈物理〉monochromatic light
单色光谱 dānsè guāngpǔ 〈物理〉monochromatic spectrum
单色画 dānsèhuà monochrome
单色胶印机 dānsè jiāoyìnjī single colour offset press
单色滤光片 dānsè lǜguāngpiàn 〈摄影〉monochromic filter
单色性 dānsèxìng monochromaticity
单色照片 dānsè zhàopiàn monochrome
单衫 dānshān Chinese-style unlined gown
单身 dānshēn ❶ unmarried; single:他已步入中年,还是~。He is still unmarried though he is nearing middle-age. ❷ not be with one's family; live alone:他~到海外谋生。He was away from home, making a living for himself abroad.
单身汉 dānshēnhàn bachelor:参加联谊晚会的大部分为~。Those who went to the party were mostly bachelors.
单身宿舍 dānshēn sùshè bachelor quarters; single dorm
单生花 dānshēnghuā 〈植物〉solitary flower
单声系统 dānshēng xìtǒng monophonic sound system
单声道 dānshēngdào 〈物理〉single track: ~录音机 single track recorder; monophonic recorder
单式 dānshì 〈会计〉single entry
单式编制 dānshì biānzhì monolevel grouping in teaching — putting students of the same level in the same class
单式预算 dānshì yùsuàn single budget system
单手进针法 dānshǒu jìnzhēnfǎ 〈中医〉single-hand needle insertion
单瘦 dānshòu weak and thin; emaciated: ~的身体 weak and thin /迎面走来一个短小~的中年人。Coming towards us was a short middle-aged man of thin build.
单数 dānshù ❶ odd number ❷ 〈语言〉singular number
单丝 dānsī 〈纺织〉monofilament
单丝不成线,独木不成林 dānsī bù chéng xiàn, dúmù bù chéng lín one strand of silk doesn't make a thread; one tree doesn't make a forest
单瘫 dāntān 〈医学〉monoplegia
单糖 dāntáng 〈化学〉monose; monosaccharide
单体 dāntǐ 〈化学〉monomer
单体计算机 dāntǐ jìsuànjī all-in-one computer
单体生物 dāntǐ shēngwù monosomic
单体物质 dāntǐ wùzhì monomeric substance
单条 dāntiáo single vertically-hung scroll of painting or calligraphy; individual wall scroll
单筒望远镜 dāntǒng wàngyuǎnjìng monocular (telescope)
单位 dānwèi ❶ unit (as a standard of measurement): ~重量 unit of weight/长度~ unit of length /货币~ monetary unit /~产值能耗 energy consumption per unit of output value /以公顷为~计算 measure in terms of the hectare; measure by the hectare ❷ unit (as an organization, department, division, section, etc.):直属~ unit under the direct jurisdiction of a higher authority /附属~ affiliated unit /行政~ administrative unit /生产~ production unit /基层~ basic (*or* grass-roots) unit /企业~ enterprise /事业~ institution
单位成本 dānwèi chéngběn unit cost:~技术 unit cost technique
单位价值指数 dānwèi jiàzhí zhǐshù unit value index
单位面积产量 dānwèi miànjī chǎnliàng yield per unit area
单位圆 dānwèiyuán 〈数学〉unit circle
单位增益 dānwèi zēngyì unit gain
单位制 dānwèizhì system of units
单位装机容量 dānwèi zhuāngjī róngliàng 〈电工〉unit installed capacity
单胃 dānwèi simple stomach
单细 dānxì 〈方言〉small and frail: ~的身子 of small and slight build /这根扁担太~,挑不了这么重的分量。This shoulder pole is too thin for carrying such a heavy weight.
单细胞 dānxìbāo single cell; monocell: ~动物 unicellular animal
单细胞生物 dānxìbāo shēngwù monad
单弦儿 dānxiánr 〈戏曲〉story-telling and singing to musical accompaniment, popular in north and northeast China
单线 dānxiàn ❶ single line or wire: ~天线 single-wire antenna /~缝纫机 single-thread sewing machine ❷ one-way (contact); single-line (link):这个特工与一位当地商人~联系。The spy had single-line contact with a local merchant. ❸ 〈交通〉single track: ~铁路 single-track railway; single-track line /~船闸 single lane lock
单相思 dānxiāngsī unrequited love; unreturned love: ~把他害苦了。He suffered the bitter pangs of unrequited love.
单向 dānxiàng one-way; unidirectional: ~电路 one-way circuit /~交通 one-way traffic /~磁化 unidirectional magnetization
单向阀 dānxiàngfá one-way or non-return valve
单向通道 dānxiàng tōngdào half-duplex or simple channel
单向元件 dānxiàng yuánjiàn unidirectional element
单向转动 dānxiàng zhuàndòng unidirectional rotation
单相 dānxiàng 〈电工〉〈冶金〉single-phase; one phase: ~电动机 single-phase motor /~电机 single-phase machine /~电流 single-phase current /~交流发电机 single-phase alternator /~合金 single-phase alloy /~电弧炉 single-phase (*or* one-phase) electric-arc furnace
单项 dānxiàng 〈体育〉individual event: ~比赛 individual competition
单项式 dānxiàngshì 〈数学〉monomial
单斜 dānxié 〈地质〉monocline: ~断层 monoclinal fault
单斜层 dānxiécéng 〈地质〉monoclinal stratum
单斜面 dānxiémiàn single bevel: ~T形接合 single-bevel T-joint
单行 dānxíng ❶ specific (to a particular situation or place); separate; special ❷ come singly:祸不~ misfortunes never come singly; it never rains but it pours ❸ print singly ❹ one-way; unidirectional
单行本 dānxíngběn ❶ separate edition ❷ collection (of newspaper articles, etc.); offprint
单行道 dānxíngdào *also* "单行线" one-way traffic; one-way road:上海有许多街道都是~。Many of the streets in Shanghai are one-way roads. /国际合作不是~。International cooperation is not one-way traffic.
单行法规 dānxíng fǎguī special or separate laws and regulations
单行条例 dānxíng tiáolì regulations to be implemented separately; specific regulations
单行线 dānxíngxiàn *see* "单行道"
单性花 dānxìnghuā 〈植物〉unisexual flower
单性生殖 dānxìng shēngzhí 〈生物〉parthenogenesis; parthenogenetic propagation or reproduction
单性现象 dānxìng xiànxiàng 〈生物〉unisexuality
单姓 dānxìng single-character Chinese surname such as Zhang, Wang, Liu, Li, etc.
单循环过程 dānxúnhuán guòchéng 〈机械〉one-cycle process
单眼 dānyǎn 〈动物〉simple eye
单眼皮 dānyǎnpí single-layer eyelids
单叶 dānyè 〈植物〉simple leaf
单一 dānyī single; unitary: ~政策 unitary policy; single policy /~的生产资料全民所有制 unitary system of the ownership of the means of production by the whole people /~文本的条约 single-instrument treaty /~整体方案 single integrated proposal /需求的~弹性 unitary elasticity of demand /~种植 monoculture; one-crop farming /样式~ stereotyped style; monotonous in style /过分~的所有制结构 structure of ownership in which undue emphasis is placed on a single form of ownership
单一的分配制度 dānyīde fēnpèi zhìdù single-mode system of wealth distribution
单一的公有制结构 dānyīde gōngyǒuzhì jiégòu single-sector system of public ownership
单一汇率 dānyī huìlǜ unitary rate; single exchange rate
单一婚制 dānyī hūnzhì monogamy

单一货币 dānyī huòbì single currency
单一价格 dānyī jiàgé single price; uniform price
单一经济 dānyī jīngjì single-product economy
单一税 dānyīshuì single tax; single tariff
单一税制 dānyī shuìzhì unitary tax system; single tariff system
单一预算制 dānyī yùsuànzhì unitary budgetary system
单一作物经济 dānyī zuòwù jīngjì single-crop economy
单衣 dānyī unlined garment
单翼机 dānyìjī 〈航空〉monoplane
单音词 dānyīncí 〈语言〉monosyllabic word; monosyllable
单元 dānyuán unit: 运算～ arithmetic unit /三号楼丙～四号 Flat 4, Entrance C, Building 3
单元化运输 dānyuánhuà yùnshū unit-load handling
单元楼 dānyuánlóu apartment building; block of flats
单元体 dānyuántǐ *see* "单倍体"
单元音 dānyuányīn 〈语言〉monophthong
单原子分子 dānyuánzǐ fēnzǐ monoatomic molecule
单原子金属 dānyuánzǐ jīnshǔ monoatomic metal
单原子气体 dānyuánzǐ qìtǐ monoatomic gas
单渣操作 dānzhā cāozuò 〈冶金〉single-slag practice

D

单只 dānzhǐ only; alone: ～借款的利息就超过百万美元。The interest on the borrowings alone amounts to over one million dollars.
单质 dānzhì 〈化学〉simple substance
单轴 dānzhóu 〈机械〉monospindle: ～镗床 monospindle boring machine /～自动机 single-spindle automatic /～挂车 monotrailer
单子 dānzǐ 〈哲学〉monad
单子 dānzi ❶ list; bill; form: 列出个～ work out a list /菜～ bill of fare; menu /填～ fill in a form ❷ cloth sheet: 床～ sheet (on a bed)
单子叶植物 dānzǐyè zhíwù monocotyledon
单字 dānzì ❶ individual Chinese character ❷ word (of a foreign language)
单作 dānzuò 〈农业〉single-crop farming
单座飞机 dānzuò fēijī single-seater (aeroplane)

瘅(癉) dān

see also dàn
瘅疟 dānnüè 〈中医〉a kind of malaria marked by a high fever but no shivers

禅(襌) dān 〈书面〉unlined garment

殚(殫) dān 〈书面〉devote; exhaust: ～心 devote oneself heart and soul to; be dedicated to /～力 spare no effort; stint no effort

殚见洽闻 dānjiàn-qiàwén 〈书面〉have vast learning and experience: 此人～，非我辈所能及也。He has both vast knowledge and extensive experience, and we cannot aspire to be his peer.
殚竭 dānjié 〈书面〉exhaust (human and material resources); use up: 国用～。The state treasury is drained. /储备～。All the reserve has been used up.
殚精竭力 dānjīng-jiélì tax one's energy to the limit; devote every effort: 他～，终于打败了世界乒坛名将。He put in his best effort and eventually succeeded in beating the world-famous table-tennis player.
殚精竭虑 dānjīng-jiélǜ rack one's brains; devote all one's knowledge and experience; dedicate oneself completely: 他在教学工作上～，是我们学习的榜样。His unqualified dedication to teaching is always an example to us all.

箪(簞) dān round food container made of bamboo used in ancient China

箪食壶浆 dānsì-hújiāng welcome (an army) with food and drink: 市民们～，迎接凯旋的将士们。Citizens welcomed back the victorious soldiers with abundant food and drink.
箪食瓢饮 dānsì-piáoyǐn live on a basket of rice and a gourd dipper of drinking water — lead a simple life; live frugally

郸(鄲) dān *see* "邯郸" Hándān

耽[1](躭) dān delay

耽[2] dān 〈书面〉abandon oneself to; indulge in: ～于游乐 indulge in merry-making /～酒 be a heavy drinker; indulge in (*or* be addicted to) drinking

耽爱 dān'ài be very fond of; have ardent or intense love for: ～书画 have a passion for painting and calligraphy
耽待 dāndài *also* "担待" dāndài ❶ forgive; excuse ❷ accept responsibility for sth.
耽搁 dānge *also* "担搁" dānge ❶ stop over; stay: 他去埃及途中，在迪拜～了三天。He stopped over at Dubai for three days on his way to Egypt. ❷ delay; procrastinate: 不得～ admit of no delay (*or* procrastination) /立即办理毫不～。Act without (the least) delay. ❸ hold up; spoil through delay: 庸医误诊，把病人给～了。His illness got worse through the wrong diagnosis of an incompetent doctor. /一忙就把事情～了。I have been busy and forgotten the whole thing.
耽乐 dānlè 〈书面〉❶ indulge in pleasure: 从早到晚，～在花厅里 indulge in merry-making in the garden parlour from morning till night ❷ be excessively fond of; be crazy about: ～田猎 be excessively fond of hunting
耽迷 dānmí indulge in; be intoxicated with: ～酒色 abandon oneself to wine and women; indulge in sensual pursuits
耽湎 dānmiǎn 〈书面〉be addicted to (drinking, etc.): 终日～声色犬马 indulge in sensual pleasures all day long
耽溺 dānnì be immersed in; indulge in (evil ways): ～于幻想之中 indulge in dreams and fantasies /～于腐化的生活 immerse oneself in a life of dissipation; sink into a quagmire of debauchery
耽误 dānwu delay; hold up; spoil through delay: ～了整个节目的演出 hold up the whole programme /把～的时间夺回来 make up for lost time /这本书的出版～得太久了。The publication of the book has long been delayed.
耽心 dānxīn *also* "担心" dānxīn worry; fear; feel anxious
耽延 dānyán delay; hold up: ～时日 cause delay; lose time /工作就这么～着，他心里很着急。He was deeply worried about the work being held up like that.
耽忧 dānyōu *also* "担忧" dānyōu worry; be anxious

眈 dān

眈眈 dāndān gaze at; stare at; fix one's eyes on: ～相向 stare at each other /虎视～ glare like a tiger (at its prey); eye covetously or fiercely

担(擔) dān ❶ carry on a shoulder pole: ～两筐土 carry two baskets of earth (with a shoulder pole) ❷ take on; undertake; shoulder: 把工作承～起来 take on a job /～风险 run risks /～责任 shoulder responsibility; take the blame /您这样称呼我，我可～不起。I'm afraid I do not deserve the honour of being so addressed. *or* I feel very much embarrassed by the way you address me.

see also dàn
担保 dānbǎo assure; guarantee; vouch for: 财政～ financial guarantee /出口信贷～ export credit guarantee /他肯定没有去过，我敢～。I can assure you he has never been there. /她来不来谁敢～。Nobody is sure whether she will come or not.
担保金 dānbǎojīn bail; bond
担保期 dānbǎoqī period of guarantee
担保企业 dānbǎo qǐyè guarantor enterprise
担保人 dānbǎorén guarantor; guarantee
担保信贷 dānbǎo xìndài secured credit
担不是 dān bùshi take the blame: 万一出了问题，也不能让他一个人～。In case something goes wrong, we won't pin all the blame on him. /本来为大家好，现在倒担了不是。I did it for everybody's sake, but now I have to take the entire blame.
担沉重 dān chénzhòng 〈方言〉accept responsibility; be held responsible for: 你到底是个闺女家，不～的。After all, you are a young girl and will not be held responsible for it. /要是他在家，得替你担多大沉重啊。If he were at home, what heavy responsibility he would have to bear for your sake.
担承 dānchéng undertake; bear; shoulder: 这个光荣任务，我们要～起来。We must shoulder this glorious task. /这笔债由我～。I undertake to pay this debt.
担待 dāndài ❶ forgive; excuse: 他不懂事，您多～着点儿。Forgive him for his thoughtlessness, please. ❷ accept responsibility for

sth.:没关系，一切由我～。Don't worry. I accept responsibility for everything.
担戴 dāndài take the responsibility; be responsible:只要您～，就没有问题了。Everything will be all right if you will take the responsibility.
担当 dāndāng take on; assume; undertake:～重任 take on heavy responsibilities /她决心～风险。She is determined to run the risks. /这项工作应由一位年轻人～。This job should be undertaken by a younger man.
担负 dānfù bear; shoulder; take on; be charged with: ～责任 shoulder responsibility /～损失 bear losses incurred /～领导工作 hold a leading post; be put in a position of leadership /～繁重的任务 be entrusted with heavy responsibility /～出访莫斯科的使命 be sent on a mission to Moscow
担纲 dāngāng play the leading role;star;be the mainstay: 这部戏由她来～演出。The play will star her. *or* She will star (*or* have a starring role) in the play.
担搁 dānge *also* "耽搁" dānge ❶ stop over; stay ❷ delay; procrastinate ❸ hold up; spoil through delay
担架 dānjià stretcher; litter: ～队 stretcher team /～队员 stretcher-bearer/人们用～把他抬到医院。He was carried to hospital on a stretcher (*or* litter).
担肩胛 dān jiānjiǎ 〈方言〉〈比喻〉shoulder responsibility:豆子减了产你～! You will be answerable for any reduced output of beans.
担惊 dānjīng be startled; be shocked; be worried:她替你担过多少惊啊。How she has worried about you!
担惊受怕 dānjīng-shòupà feel alarmed; get scared; be fidgety:在战争的岁月里，人们总是～。People were filled with anxiety and fear in war years.
担名 dānmíng bear the name of:他只担个虚名。He is in charge nominally (*or* only in name). /光担个空名的差事，我可不干。I don't want a nominal post(*or* sinecure). /这件事并没牵涉到他，不应该担这个罪名。He is not involved in the matter and so should not take the blame for it.
担任 dānrèn assume the office of; hold the post of: ～当地工会主席 be chairman of a local trade union /～联合国秘书长 hold the post of Secretary-General of the United Nations /～会议主席 chair a meeting /他～委员会的顾问。He acts as adviser to the committee.
担受 dānshòu undergo; experience; withstand; stand: ～不起 cannot withstand it /～风险 run risks
担险 dānxiǎn face danger; run risks: ～的事他不干。He never takes risks.
担心 dānxīn worry; feel anxious; fear: ～他的安全 be concerned about his safety /～他考试不及格 fear that he might fail (in) the examination /你能适应那里的环境吗? 我真～。I am deeply worried if you can adapt (yourself) to the circumstances there.
担忧 dānyōu worry; be anxious:地球上的环境污染日益严重，有识之士无不为之～。People of insight are all worried about the environmental pollution of the earth, which is getting worse every day. /还有一种令人～的猜测，就是他本人或许也听到了什么内幕消息。Another disquieting possibility is that he may also have got some inside information.

丹

dān ❶ red: ～凤 red phoenix ❷〈中药〉pellet; powder: 灵～妙药 panacea ❸ cinnabar ❹ (Dān) a surname
丹忱 dānchén *also* "丹诚" staunch loyalty
丹墀 dānchí *also* "丹陛"〈旧语〉stone terrace painted red in front of the great hall of the imperial palace
丹顶鹤 dāndǐnghè red-crowned crane
丹毒 dāndú *also* "流火" liúhuǒ 〈医学〉erysipelas
丹方 dānfāng ❶ *also* "单方" dānfāng folk prescription; home remedy: 祖传～ recipe handed down from one's ancestors ❷〈书面〉art or skill of making magical pellets
丹枫 dānfēng maple after the autumn frost
丹凤眼 dānfèngyǎn slanting eyes: 一双～，两道柳叶眉 with slanting eyes and arched brows
丹桂 dānguì 〈植物〉orange osmanthus
丹黄 dānhuáng ❶ red and yellow: ～的花卉 red and yellow flowers and plants ❷〈旧语〉cinnabar and ochre used in punctuating texts; collation: 藏书万卷，～皆遍 have a collection of ten thousand volumes full of his own marginal notes (in cinnabar and ochre)
丹雘 dānhuò ❶ red paint ❷ cinnabar-red and black colours
丹江 Dānjiāng Danjiang River, longest tributary of the Hanjiang River (汉江): ～口水利枢纽工程 Danjiang River Mouth Key Water Control Project (in Hubei Province, 1973)
丹剧 dānjù local opera popular in Danyang County, Jiangsu Province
丹荔 dānlì 〈植物〉litchi; lychee
丹麦 Dānmài Denmark: ～人 Dane /～语 Danish (language)
丹麦海峡 Dānmài Hǎixiá Denmark Strait
丹麦通讯社 Dānmài Tōngxùnshè Ritzaus Bureau
丹宁 dānníng *also* "鞣酸" róusuān (transliteration) tannin: ～酸 tannic acid
丹皮 dānpí 〈中药〉root bark of the tree peony
丹魄 dānpò 〈书面〉❶ loyalty ❷ amber
丹铅 dānqiān cinnabar and lead powder which were used in old times in punctuating old texts; 〈比喻〉collation of texts; textual criticism
丹青 dānqīng 〈书面〉❶ red and black colours; 〈比喻〉painting: ～手 painter /～妙笔 touch of a great master ❷ historical record; history: 留名～ carve a name in history
丹砂 dānshā cinnabar
丹参 dānshēn 〈中药〉root of red-rooted salvia (*Salvia miltiorrhiza*)
丹田 dāntián pubic region: ～之气 deep breath controlled by the diaphragm /气沉～ inhale a deep breath
丹心 dānxīn loyal heart; loyalty: 留取～照汗青 in the hope that my loyalty may remain a fine example in the annals of history

甔

dān 〈书面〉bottle; vase; flask

dǎn

掸(撢、撣、担)

dǎn brush lightly; whisk: ～掉身上的灰尘 brush the dust off one's clothes /～得干干净净 be dusted clean
see also Shàn
掸瓶 dǎnpíng duster holder (like a vase with a narrow neck but a big belly)
掸甩子 dǎnshuǎizi duster (made of strips of cloth or leather)
掸帚 dǎnzhou 〈方言〉duster
掸子 dǎnzi duster (usu. made of chicken feathers or strips of cloth): 鸡毛～ feather duster /用～拂去家具上的尘土 use a duster to clean furniture

黕

dǎn 〈书面〉❶ filth; stain ❷ pitch-black; jet-black

亶

dǎn 〈书面〉indeed; truly: ～其然乎? Is it indeed true?

疸

dǎn *see* "黄疸" huángdǎn

胆(膽)

dǎn ❶ gallbladder ❷ courage; guts; bravery: 壮～ pluck up one's courage; boost sb's courage /浑身是～ every inch a courageous man ❸ bladder-like inner container: 热水瓶～ glass liner of a vacuum flask /球～ rubber bladder of a ball
胆胺 dǎn'àn 〈生化〉cholamine
胆憷 dǎnchù *also* "胆怵" afraid; timid
胆大 dǎndà bold; audacious: 这小子没人不说他～的。Everybody says that he is an audacious guy.
胆大包天 dǎndà-bāotiān audacious in the extreme
胆大妄为 dǎndà-wàngwéi bold and reckless; devil-may-care: ～之徒 dare-devil fellow /他说这些人～，竟敢攻击朝廷命官。He said that these people were audacious enough to attack senior court officials.
胆大心细 dǎndà-xīnxì bold but cautious; courageous and wise
胆道 dǎndào *also* "胆管"〈生理〉biliary duct or passage: ～镜 choledochoscope
胆道蛔虫病 dǎndào huíchóngbìng biliary ascariasis
胆矾 dǎnfán *also* "蓝矾" lánfán 〈化学〉chalcanthite; blue vitriol
胆敢 dǎngǎn dare; have the audacity to: 你～骂我，我就揍你。I'll hit you if you dare to call me names.
胆固醇 dǎngùchún 〈生化〉cholesterol: 高密度～ high density cholesterol /医生说我的～太高。The doctor says that my cholesterol

level is too high.

胆管 dǎnguǎn *see* "胆道"

胆管癌 dǎnguǎn'ái cholangiocarcinoma

胆管瘤 dǎnguǎnliú cholangioma

胆管炎 dǎnguǎnyán cholangitis

胆管造影 dǎnguǎn zàoyǐng 〈医学〉cholangiography

胆寒 dǎnhán terrified; struck with terror; awestricken: 他的威名令敌人～。His name strikes the enemy's heart with terror (*or* strikes terror into the enemy). /看看那悬崖，真叫她～。The sight of the precipice sent a chill down her spine.

胆褐素 dǎnhèsù 〈生化〉bilifuscin

胆红素 dǎnhóngsù 〈生化〉bilirubin

胆黄素 dǎnhuángsù 〈生化〉biliflavin

胆碱 dǎnjiǎn 〈生化〉choline

胆绞痛 dǎnjiǎotòng 〈医学〉biliary colica

胆酒 dǎnjiǔ medicinal liquor and tonic containing the bile of animals

胆力 dǎnlì courage; boldness; bravery: 办事有～ be courageous in tackling things

胆量 dǎnliàng courage; guts; pluck; spunk: 有～ have plenty of guts /我真佩服你的～。I admire you for your courage.

D

胆绿素 dǎnlǜsù 〈化学〉biliverdin

胆略 dǎnlüè courage and resourcefulness; bold vision: ～过人 have unusual courage and resourcefulness /他以政治家的～开始了改革。He initiated the reforms with the bold vision of a statesman.

胆囊 dǎnnáng 〈生理〉gallbladder

胆囊结石 dǎnnáng jiéshí 〈医学〉cholecystolithiasis

胆囊切除术 dǎnnáng qiēchúshù cholecystectomy

胆囊切开术 dǎnnáng qiēkāishù cholecystomy

胆囊碎石术 dǎnnáng suìshíshù cholecystolithotripsy

胆囊炎 dǎnnángyán cholecystitis

胆瓶 dǎnpíng vase with a slender neck and a bulging belly

胆破心惊 dǎnpò-xīnjīng terror-stricken; frightened to death: 那爆炸声让人～。The explosion was soul-shattering.

胆魄 dǎnpò courage; guts; daring

胆气 dǎnqì boldness; courage; bravery: 他办事犹豫不定，缺乏～。He is always shilly-shallying because he has no guts.

胆怯 dǎnqiè timid; cowardly: 在困难面前，从不～ never flinch in face of difficulty /听了这番话，他感到心虚～。Hearing these words, he began to feel deflated and his courage was receding.

胆色素 dǎnsèsù 〈生化〉cholochrome; bile pigment

胆石 dǎnshí 〈医学〉cholelith; gallstone

胆石病 dǎnshíbìng cholelithiasis

胆石切除术 dǎnshí qiēchúshù 〈医学〉cholelithotomy

胆识 dǎnshí courage and insight; boldness and vision: 超人的～ with superhuman courage and vision

胆酸 dǎnsuān 〈生化〉cholic acid: ～盐 chleolate

胆突突 dǎntūtū afraid; scared: 他吓得～的，躲在角落里。Scared out of his wits, he hid himself in the corner.

胆小 dǎnxiǎo timid; cowardly: ～怕事 timid and overcautious

胆小鬼 dǎnxiǎoguǐ coward

胆小如鼠 dǎnxiǎo-rúshǔ as timid as a mouse; chicken-hearted

胆虚 dǎnxū afraid; timid: 我真有点～呢。I am a bit scared.

胆血症 dǎnxuèzhèng 〈医学〉cholemia

胆盐 dǎnyán 〈化学〉cholate

胆战心惊 dǎnzhàn-xīnjīng tremble with fear; be scared out of one's wits; be terror-stricken: 成天～地过日子 live in perpetual fear /唬得那老头子～。The old man was scared out of his wits. /望下去是万丈深渊，令人～。We shuddered at the sight of the bottomless pit down below. /我刚踏上独木桥时～。I had my heart in my mouth when I trod on the one-plank bridge.

胆汁 dǎnzhī 〈生理〉bile: ～病 biliousness /～疗法 bilitherapy

胆汁返流 dǎnzhī fǎnliú biliary regurgitation

胆汁分泌 dǎnzhī fēnmì bilifaction; choleresis

胆壮 dǎnzhuàng bold; audacious: 他见到有人支持他，就更～了。Seeing support for him, he became all the bolder.

胆子 dǎnzi boldness; courage; nerve: 放开～ pluck up one's courage /好大的～! What a nerve!

胆总管 dǎnzǒngguǎn choledochus; ductus communis: ～截除术 choledochectomy

赕 dǎn (transliteration from Dai or Tai language) offer; donate

赕佛 dǎnfó donate money, etc. to a Buddhist temple for the blessing of Buddha

dàn

澹 dàn 〈书面〉quietude; tranquillity

see also tán

澹泊 dànbó not hanker after fame and fortune

see also "淡泊" dànbó

澹澹 dàndàn ripple; undulate: ～的海波 rippling waves of the sea

澹然 dànrán indifferent; cool

see also "淡然" dànrán

瘅(癉) dàn 〈书面〉❶ illness resulting from physical exhaustion or overwork ❷ hate; detest; denounce: 彰善～恶 praise the good and denounce the evil; uphold virtue and condemn vice

see also dān

惮(憚) dàn 〈书面〉fear; dread: 不～烦 not mind the trouble /过则勿～改。Hesitate not to correct an error when it is found.

弹(彈) dàn ❶ ball; pellet ❷ bullet; shell; bomb: 穿甲～ armour-piercing bullet /烟幕～ smoke shell /燃烧～ incendiary bomb /手榴～ grenade /凝固汽油～ napalm bomb /～尽粮绝 run out of ammunition and provisions /～无虚发。Every shot hits the target.

see also tán

弹袋 dàndài *also* "弹带" cartridge belt

弹道 dàndào trajectory; ballistic path: ～弧线 ballistic curve

弹道导弹 dàndào dǎodàn ballistic missile: ～运载工具 ballistic missile carrier/～预警系统 ballistic-missile early warning system / 卫星发射的～ SLBM (satellite-launched ballistic missile)

弹道火箭 dàndào huǒjiàn ballistic rocket

弹道学 dàndàoxué ballistics: 内～ interior ballistics /外～ exterior ballistics

弹弓 dàngōng catapult; slingshot

弹痕 dànhén bullet or shell hole: ～累累。There are shell holes all over the place.

弹夹 dànjiā (cartridge) clip; charger: 机枪～ cartridge magazine of a machine-gun

弹壳 dànké ❶ cartridge case ❷ shell case

弹坑 dànkēng (shell) crater: 遍地～。The ground is full of craters.

弹流 dànliú bullets or shells fired in quick succession; barrage: 密集的～倾泻过来。A volley of bullets came pouring (*or* raining) down.

弹幕 dànmù barrage

弹盘 dànpán cartridge drum; magazine

弹片 dànpiàn shell fragment or splinter; shrapnel

弹伤 dànshāng bullet wound

弹膛 dàntáng chamber (of a gun)

弹体尾部 dàntǐ wěibù 〈航天〉afterbody

弹头 dàntóu bullet; projectile nose; warhead: 核～ nuclear warhead

弹丸 dànwán ❶ ball; pellet: ～射中了树上的小鸟。The bird on the tree was hit by the pellet shot. ❷ bullet; shot ❸ 〈书面〉(of land) tiny; small and narrow: ～之地 small bit of land; tiny plot

弹匣 dànxiá 〈军事〉magazine

弹药 dànyào ammunition: ～库 ammunition depot (*or* storehouse) /～手 ammunition man (*or* bearer) /～所 ammunition supply point /～箱 ammunition chest; cartridge box

弹雨 dànyǔ hail of bullets: 枪林～ hail of bullets; heavy fire /他冒着～抢救伤员。He gave first aid to wounded soldiers under heavy fire.

弹着 dànzhuó 〈军事〉impact: ～观察 spotting /～观察兵 spotter

弹着点 dànzhuódiǎn point of impact; hitting point

弹着角 dànzhuójiǎo angle of impact

弹着区 dànzhuóqū impact area; target area

弹子 dànzi ❶ pellet shot from a catapult ❷ marble:～游戏 game of marbles ❸〈方言〉billiards:打～ play billiards
弹子房 dànzifáng 〈方言〉billiard room
弹子锁 dànzisuǒ 〈方言〉spring lock

淡

dàn ❶ thin; light:天高云～。The sky is clear and the clouds are thin. ❷ tasteless; weak:～酒 weak wine /这菜太～。The food needs a little more salt. *or* It lacks a pinch of salt. ❸ (of colour) light:～绿 light green /～红 pink ❹ indifferent; cool; with little enthusiasm:～于名利 be indifferent to fame and wealth; care little about fame and fortune /争胜好强的心已经～了。The desire to outshine others has all but disappeared. ❺ dull; slack:生意清～。Business is slack. ❻ meaningless; unimportant; trivial:扯～ talk rubbish
淡巴菰 dànbāgū (transliteration of the Spanish word *tabaco*) tobacco
淡泊 dànbó *also*“澹泊”dànbó 〈书面〉not hanker after fame and fortune:～寡欲 not hanker after fame and fortune, and lead an ascetic life /他生性～。He is indifferent to worldly concerns.
淡泊明志 dànbó-míngzhì indifference to fame and fortune characterizes a high aim in life; simple living demonstrates lofty aspirations
淡薄 dànbó ❶ thin; light:朝雾渐渐地～了。The morning mist thinned gradually. ❷ weak; mild:酒味～。The wine is weak. /烟味～。The cigarette is mild. ❸ (of emotion, interest, etc.) become weak or cool; flag:他们感情～。They maintain a distant relationship. /兴趣～。One's interest has flagged. /人情～。Human ties are weak. ❹ faint; dim; hazy:时间久了,印象也就～了。With the passage of time, these impressions have become blurred.
淡菜 dàncài *also*“贻贝”yíbèi mussel
淡出 dànchū *also*“渐隐”jiànyǐn 〈影视〉fade out
淡淡 dàndàn ❶ thin; (of colour) light or pale; (of smell, flavour, etc.) mild or weak:～的浮云 pale, floating clouds /～的远山 hazy mountains looming in the distance; distant mountains shrouded in mist /随着和风飘来一股～的泥土味。The gentle breeze brought with it a faint aroma of moist earth. *or* A faint smell of moist earth came wafting on a gentle breeze. ❷ cool; indifferent; slight:她只是～地笑了一笑。She gave a faint smile. *or* She smiled drily. ❸〈书面〉(of waves) rippling; undulating
淡而无味 dàn'érwúwèi tasteless; flat; insipid; bland
淡饭 dànfàn simple and plain food:粗茶～ plain tea and simple food; homely meal; simple fare /粗衣～ plain clothing and simple food; simple life
淡化 dànhuà ❶ become faint, slight or unimportant; fade; weaken:家族观念～ weakening of clannish concepts ❷ give less prominence to; put less emphasis on:不能～思想教育。It is not right to relegate ideological education to a secondary place. ❸ desalination:海水～ desalination of sea water
淡话 dànhuà 〈方言〉meaningless talk; irrelevant remark:他只说了几句～,实质问题避而不谈。He made only a few irrelevant remarks while keeping silent on matters of substance.
淡积云 dànjīyún 〈气象〉cumulus humilis
淡季 dànjì slack or dull season; off season:旅游～ slack season for tourism /争取做到蔬菜～不淡,旺季不烂。Strive for an ample supply of vegetables in the off seasons and avoid waste in the peak periods.
淡漠 dànmò ❶ indifferent; unconcerned; apathetic:表情～ look indifferent; appear apathetic /他似乎对什么事都很～。He seems indifferent to everything. ❷ dim; faint; hazy:我们的印象已经～了。We have only a hazy impression now. /这件事我已～了。I have but a faint memory of the matter.
淡墨 dànmò light ink
淡青 dànqīng light greenish blue
淡然 dànrán *also*“澹然”dànrán 〈书面〉unconcerned; casual; indifferent:～处之 treat sth. with (an air of) complete indifference
淡入 dànrù *also*“渐显”jiànxiǎn 〈影视〉fade in
淡弱 dànruò ❶ (of light) weak; dim; faint:～的灯光 dim lamplight ❷ (of interest or emotion) weak; slight:法纪观念十分～ have hardly any sense of law and discipline /丧子的悲痛随着时间的流逝而逐渐～了。His grief over the loss of his son lessened with the passage of time (*or* was assuaged by time).
淡食 dànshí food or diet without salt:吃～ go on a diet of saltless food /由于敌人的封锁,乡亲们～已经一个多月了。As a result of the enemy blockade, the villagers had been cooking without salt for over a month.
淡事 dànshì 〈方言〉meaningless or trifling matter:我忙得不可开交,哪有工夫管这些～。With my hands so full, I simply have no time for such trifling matters.
淡水 dànshuǐ ❶ fresh water; sweet water:～养鱼 freshwater fish farming /船上的～快用光了。The fresh water on the ship is fast running out. ❷ (Dànshuǐ) Danshui or Tamshui, port city in Taiwan Province
淡水湖 dànshuǐhú freshwater lake
淡水螺 dànshuǐluó freshwater snail
淡水水母 dànshuǐ shuǐmǔ freshwater jelly fish
淡水养殖 dànshuǐ yǎngzhí freshwater aquaculture
淡水鱼 dànshuǐyú freshwater fish
淡素 dànsù (of colour) plain; quiet; simple:装束～ plainly dressed
淡退 dàntuì (of colour) fade (away):她脸上的红晕开始～。Her rosy cheeks began to fade.
淡忘 dànwàng fade from one's memory:这件事我早已～。I've clean forgotten about this matter.
淡雅 dànyǎ simple and elegant; quietly elegant:窗帘色调～。The curtain is quietly elegant. /室内陈设～。The room is simple but elegantly furnished.
淡幽幽 dànyōuyōu (of light) dim; faint:蜡烛快要着完了,屋子里～的。With the candle almost burnt out, the room was only dimly lit.
淡悠悠 dànyōuyōu casual; nonchalant:临走时,她～地同主人告了别。Before leaving, she said good-bye to the host in a casual manner.
淡远 dànyuǎn (of scenery or artistic conception of poetry or painting) simple but profound; chaste but full of meaning:墙上挂着一幅～的山水画。On the wall hangs a landscape painted in a simple but meaningful style.
淡月 dànyuè slack month
淡竹 dànzhú 〈植物〉henon bamboo (*Phyllostachys nigra* var. *henonis*)
淡妆 dànzhuāng in light make-up; dressed up in a quiet, good taste:二十多岁的女子以～为宜。Young women in their 20's look best in light make-up.
淡妆浓抹 dànzhuāng-nóngmǒ (in reference to two different styles of make-up and dress) simple and elegant or rich and gaudy:欲把西湖比西子,～总相宜。For varied charms, the West Lake I may well compare to Xizi, who, adorned or not, alike was fair.

啖¹(啗、噉)

dàn 〈书面〉❶ eat; feed:～荔枝 eat lychee /以肉～虎 feed a tiger with meat ❷ entice or lure with profit:～以重利 lure sb. with handsome rewards

啖²

Dàn a surname

氮

dàn 〈化学〉nitrogen (N):～当量 nitrogen equivalent
氮肥 dànféi nitrogenous fertilizer
氮化 dànhuà 〈化学〉nitrogenation; nitriding:～处理 liquid nitrogen quenching /～钢 nitriding steel; nitro-alloy /～铝 aluminium nitride
氮化硅陶瓷 dànhuàguī táocí silicon nitride ceramics
氮化镓 dànhuàjiā gallium-nitrogen (Ga-N)
氮化物 dànhuàwù 〈化学〉nitride:～耐火材料 nitride refractory material
氮激光器 dànjīguāngqì nitrogen laser
氮尿 dànniào azoturia
氮气 dànqì nitrogen; nitrogen gas:～灯 nitrogen lamp
氮稳定剂 dànwěndìngjì N-Serve
氮族 dànzú 〈化学〉nitrogenous family (comprising nitrogen, phosphorus, arsenic, antimony and bismuth)

饯

dàn 〈书面〉❶ *see*“啖¹”dàn ❷ pancake

诞¹

dàn ❶ birth ❷ birthday:五十华～ fiftieth birthday; fiftieth anniversary

诞²

dàn absurd; fantastic:荒～ fantastic; incredibly absurd

诞辰 dànchén birthday
诞谩 dànmàn 〈书面〉❶ absurd; fantastic; incredible: ～无实 absurd and groundless (*or* impractical); fantastic and without a shred of truth ❷ indulgent; self-indulgent; undisciplined
诞日 dànrì birthday
诞生 dànshēng be born; come into existence; emerge: 孔子～于公元前551年。Confucius was born in 551 BC.
诞生地 dànshēngdì place of birth
诞生石 dànshēngshí birthstone

髧 dàn 〈书面〉with hair drooping: ～彼两髦 that youngster with the drooping tresses

萏 dàn *see* "菡萏" hàndàn

禫 dàn 〈旧语〉ritual held to mark the end of the period of mourning

赕 dàn 〈书面〉❶ pay a deposit for sth. ❷ top of a scroll or back of a thread-bound book, usu. pasted with silk cloth

D

石 dàn *dan*, a unit of dry measure of grain (＝1 hectolitre): 十斗为～。Ten *dou* make a *dan*.
see also shí

旦[1] dàn ❶〈书面〉dawn; daybreak: 坐以待～ sit waiting for the dawn /通宵达～ all through the night ❷ day: 元～ New Year's Day

旦[2] dàn 〈戏曲〉female character type in Beijing opera, etc.

旦[3] dàn *also* "紞" dài 〈纺织〉denier, a unit of weight measuring the fineness of thread or yarn
旦角儿 dànjuér 〈戏曲〉female character type in Chinese opera
旦暮 dànmù 〈书面〉dawn and dusk; of short duration; transient; brief
旦日 dànrì 〈书面〉❶ tomorrow ❷ day; daytime
旦夕 dànxī 〈书面〉this morning or evening — in a short while: 危在～ in imminent danger; in instant peril /不能指望局面～之间就能转变。You can't expect the situation to change overnight.
旦夕祸福 dànxī-huòfú anyone may be lucky one moment and unlucky the next; fortune is fickle: 人有～。Men are subject to sudden changes of fortune. *or* Misfortunes always befall a person suddenly.

担(擔) dàn ❶ carrying pole and the loads on it; load; burden: 货郎～ loads of goods carried on a shoulder pole by an itinerant pedlar /为国家勇挑重～ ready to shoulder heavy tasks for the state ❷ *dan*, a unit of weight (＝50 kilograms) ❸〈量词〉*used of things carried on a shoulder pole*: 一～水 two buckets of water (carried on a shoulder pole) /两～柴 four bundles of firewood
see also dān
担担面 dàndanmiàn Sichuan noodles with peppery sauce
担杖 dànzhàng 〈方言〉carrying pole; shoulder pole
担子 dànzi ❶ carrying pole and the loads on it: 一副～ a carrying pole and the loads on it ❷ load; burden: 捡重～挑 choose to take on (*or* tackle) difficult jobs

但 dàn ❶ merely; only; just: ～说无妨。Just speak out what is on your mind. *or* It is all right to speak up. /不求有功，～求无过。I aspire after no merit but merely wish to be free from error. /在辽阔的原野上，～见麦浪随风起伏。On the vast fields, you find nothing but wheat billowing in the wind. ❷ but; yet; still; nevertheless: 他饱学多识，～总是那么谦虚。He is a learned scholar, yet he is so modest. /虽然遇到挫折，～他从不气馁。He never felt discouraged despite setbacks. ❸ (Dàn) a surname
但凡 dànfán as long as; in every case; without exception: ～有点办法，也不去求他。I won't go and ask for his help as long as I can manage myself. /～认识他的，都对他交口赞誉。Whoever knows him is full of praise for him.
但分 dànfen 〈方言〉so long as; provided: ～有一线希望，也要努力争取。So long as there is a gleam of hope, we'll do our best.
但丁 Dàndīng Dante Alighieri (1265-1321), Italian poet and author of *Divine Comedy*
但是 dànshì but; still; yet; nevertheless: 他虽然年过七十，～精力仍很健旺。Though over 70, he's still full of vitality. /我尽管很想去，～实在太忙，去不了啦。Much as I want to, I'm nevertheless too busy to go with you.
但书 dànshū 〈法律〉proviso
但以理书 Dànyǐlǐshū *The Book of Daniel* (a book of the *Old Testament* bearing the name of Daniel, a Hebrew prophet)
但愿 dànyuàn if only; I wish: ～如此。If only it were so. *or* I wish it were so. *or* I hope so. /～他健康长寿。I wish him good health and a long life.

黕 dàn *also* dǎn 〈书面〉black; dark: ～然 dark /～暗 dim; dusky

疍(蜑) dàn
疍民 dànmín boat dwellers; people living on boats

蛋 dàn ❶ egg: 鸟～ bird egg /下～ lay eggs /孵～ hatch (*or* sit on) eggs ❷ egg-shaped thing; ball: 泥～儿 mud ball
蛋白 dànbái ❶ *also* "蛋清" egg white; albumen ❷ protein: 动物～ animal protein /植物～ vegetable protein /高～ high protein
蛋白胨 dànbáidòng 〈化学〉peptone
蛋白合成 dànbái héchéng protein synthesis
蛋白激素 dànbái jīsù 〈生化〉proteohormone
蛋白酶 dànbáiméi 〈化学〉protease; proteinase
蛋白尿 dànbáiniào 〈医学〉albuminuria; proteinuria
蛋白石 dànbáishí 〈地质〉opal
蛋白水解 dànbái shuǐjiě 〈生化〉proteolysis: ～酶 proteolytic enzyme /～素 proteolysin
蛋白酥皮 dànbái sūpí meringue
蛋白相纸 dànbái xiàngzhǐ albumen paper
蛋白杏仁饼 dànbái xìngrénbǐng macaroon
蛋白银 dànbáiyín silver protein
蛋白脂 dànbáizhǐ 〈生化〉soap albumin; proteolipin
蛋白质 dànbáizhì *also* "朊" ruǎn protein: ～结构 protein structure /～塑料 protein plastics
蛋白质纤维 dànbáizhì xiānwéi protein fibre
蛋彩画 dàncǎihuà tempera painting
蛋雕 dàndiāo egg carving
蛋粉 dànfěn powdered eggs; egg powder
蛋糕 dàngāo cake: 奶油～ cream cake /巧克力～ chocolate cake /生日～ birthday cake
蛋羹 dàngēng egg custard
蛋花汤 dànhuātāng soup with egg flakes
蛋黄 dànhuáng *also* "卵黄" luǎnhuáng yolk
蛋黄酱 dànhuángjiàng mayonnaise
蛋鸡 dànjī layer; laying hen
蛋卷 dànjuǎn egg roll
蛋卷冰淇淋 dànjuǎn bīngqílín ice-cream cone
蛋壳 dànké eggshell
蛋奶糕 dànnǎigāo *also* "蛋奶沙司" custard
蛋奶酥 dànnǎisū *also* "苏发莱" sūfālái soufflé
蛋品 dànpǐn egg product
蛋青 dànqīng pale blue
蛋清 dànqīng *also* "蛋白" egg white
蛋松 dànsōng dried egg floss
蛋用鸡 dànyòngjī layer
蛋制品 dànzhìpǐn egg product
蛋子 dànzi egg-shaped thing

dāng

当[1]**(當)** dāng ❶ equal; match: 旗鼓相～ nearly equal in strength; equally matched in strength /门～户对 be of equal social status /得失相～。The gain equals (*or* matches) the loss. ❷ ought to; should; must: ～办不办 refuse to deal with a matter which re-

quires immediate attention /责任～由他负。He is to take the responsibility. ❸ facing; confronting; to sb.'s face; in sb.'s presence:～着他谈 talk about sth. in sb.'s presence /～胸一拳 punch sb. in the chest /首～其冲 be the first to bear the brunt ❹ just at (a time or place):～我回来时，她正在做饭。She was cooking when I came back. /～黄昏来临的时候，天忽然下起雨来。It suddenly started to rain towards evening.

当[2]（當） dāng ❶ serve or act as; work as; be:～官做老爷 act like an overlord /选他～班长 elect him monitor / 五年前他～会计。He was an accountant five years ago. ❷ deserve; bear; accept:敢做敢～ act boldly and never shirk responsibility /～此重任 be equal to this position of responsibility /一人做事一人～。One should accept the responsibility for what one does. *or* A person should hold himself responsible for whatever he does. ❸ manage; be in charge of; direct:我想你～不了家。I don't think you can run the household. *or* I don't think you wear the trousers in the house. ❹〈书面〉stop; prevent; obstruct:螳臂焉能～车? How can a mantis stop a chariot?

当[3]（當） dāng 〈书面〉tip; top:瓦～ eaves tile

当[4]（當、噹） dāng 〈象声〉*sound made by striking metals*:～～的钟声 tolling of a bell /铃声～～响了。The bell goes ding-dong.
see also dàng

当班 dāngbān be on duty; be on a shift:他下午～到七点。He is on duty in the afternoon till seven. /全班工人齐心协力，使～产量比定额提高百分之十。Thanks to the joint efforts of the shift workers, their output went up ten percent above the quota.

当兵 dāngbīng get into uniform; serve in the army (navy, air force, etc.); enlist

当差 dāngchāi 〈旧语〉❶ work as a petty official or runner in *yamen* ❷ be a servant

当场 dāngchǎng on the spot; then and there:～拍板 decide on the spot /～成交 clinch a deal then and there /有一个人被汽车撞倒，～就死了。Somebody was knocked down by a car and killed instantly. /罪犯被～抓住。The criminal was caught red-handed (*or* in the act). /他没有～表态。He did not commit himself under the circumstances.

当场出彩 dāngchǎng-chūcǎi make a spectacle of oneself then and there; give the whole show away on the spot:他冒充专家，不料～。He posed as an expert only to make a spectacle of himself then and there.

当朝 dāngcháo ❶〈书面〉current dynasty; present reign ❷ present emperor or prime minister ❸ be in power:小人～，排挤忠良。When evil men are in power, they exclude the loyal and virtuous (ministers).

当承 dāngchéng bear responsibility for; be responsible for:自己做的事自己～。One should be responsible for what one does.

当初 dāngchū at the beginning; originally; initially:～他打算参军，但后来改变了主意。He originally planned to join the army, but changed his mind later. /你～怎么想的? What did you have in mind then? /～你就不该那么盲目自信嘛! You should not have been so cocksure in the first place. /早知今日，何必～? If I had known that things would come to this, I would not have acted the way I did.

当代 dāngdài present age; contemporary era:～文豪 literary giant of our time /～意识 consciousness of the present age; willingness (*or* readiness) to keep up with the times /和平与发展是～的两大主题。Peace and development are the two major themes of the contemporary era.

当道 dāngdào ❶ in the middle of the road:别在这儿～站着! Don't stand in the way! ❷〈贬义〉be in power; hold sway:坏人～，好人遭殃。When scoundrels are in power, good people suffer. /豺狼～，安问狐狸? When jackals and wolves hold sway, why pick on foxes? ❸〈旧语〉influential officials; powers that be:取悦于～ curry favour with the powers that be

当地 dāngdì in the locality; local:～居民 local inhabitants /～时间下午七时 19 hours local time /～政府负有责任保护那里出土的文物。The government of a locality is responsible for the protection of its unearthed cultural relics.

当顶 dāngdǐng (of the sun, moon, etc.) right overhead:一直到太阳～才收工。They kept working until the sun was right overhead.

当东 dāngdōng play the host:今天由我～。It's my treat today.

当断不断 dāngduàn-bùduàn fail to make a decision when one should; be hesitant and indecisive:～，反受其乱。You are bound to suffer if you fail to decide when a decision is called for.

当关 dāngguān ❶ guard a strategic pass or checkpoint:一夫～，万夫莫开。Though only one man is guarding the pass, not even ten thousand can get through. ❷〈书面〉doorkeeper; guard

当归 dāngguī 〈中药〉Chinese angelica

当锅 dāngguō 〈方言〉❶ do the cooking; cook:母亲～，我放牛。Mother did the cooking and I herded the cattle. ❷ cook

当国 dāngguó hold the reins of government; rule the country

当行 dāngháng ❶ expert; adept:所作诗篇，语语～。Each word of his poems is well chosen. *or* Every line of his poetry demonstrates a mastery of poetic art. ❷〈旧语〉service by a craftsman to the government

当行出色 dāngháng-chūsè distinguish oneself in one's own trade or profession

当红 dānghóng be in favour; be in vogue:～歌星 popular singer; pop star

当机立断 dāngjī-lìduàn make a prompt decision:在关键时刻，我们要～。We must act promptly at critical junctures. /～，执法如山，使他出了名。It was his prompt decisions and strict enforcement of the law that brought him fame.

当即 dāngjí right away; at once; immediately:～点头同意 nod approval without hesitation /～向公安局报告 report to the police station immediately /部队接到命令，～出发。The troops set out at once upon receiving the order. /合同一签字，～生效。The contract became effective the moment it was signed.

当家 dāngjiā run a household; manage household affairs; rule the roost:她很会～。She is a very good housewife (*or* homemaker). /～才知柴米价，养子方晓爹娘恩。One has to keep house to know the price of rice and firewood, and raise children to appreciate parental affection. *or* No one appreciates the difficulty of running a household unless he is the head of a family, nor does he fully understand parental love until he becomes a parent himself. /这么多人瞎吵吵什么，到底谁～? Why are you all cackling like so many hens? Who is in charge any way?

当家菜 dāngjiācài basic, common vegetables essential for daily consumption

当家的 dāngjiāde ❶ master or mistress of a household; head of a family:他家大女儿是～。His eldest daughter is running the household. *or* His eldest daughter is mistress of the household. ❷ abbot (of a temple) ❸〈方言〉husband:我的～是工人。My husband is a factory worker.

当家肥 dāngjiāféi 〈方言〉fertilizer applied at a crucial stage of the growth of crops, for example, when cotton-plants are in flower and bolls are forming

当家作主 dāngjiā-zuòzhǔ be master in one's own house; be master of one's own affairs:人民～。The people are the masters of their own country.

当间儿 dāngjiànr 〈方言〉in the middle:客厅～摆着几张沙发。There are several sofas in the middle of the sitting room.

当街 dāngjiē ❶ near a street; facing a street:我的房子正～，整天不得安宁。My house is near a street, and there is no peace and quiet all day. /～是一溜商店。Facing the street is a row of shops. ❷〈方言〉in the street:出了车祸，～都是人。There is a car accident and the street is crowded with onlookers.

当今 dāngjīn ❶ now; at present; nowadays:～的世界格局 power structure of the present-day world /～国际形势，缓和之中有紧张。The situation of the world today is characterized by relaxation punctuated with tension. ❷ reference to the reigning monarch in feudal China

当紧 dāngjǐn 〈方言〉urgent; important:我们要把精力用在最～的事情上。We should concentrate on matters of cardinal importance.

当局 dāngjú authorities:政府～ authorities (*or* government) /学校～ school authorities /地方～ local authorities

当局者迷，旁观者清 dāngjúzhě mí, pángguānzhě qīng the spectators see the chess game better than the players; an outsider sees things more clearly than one involved; what is hidden from those concerned is plain to the bystanders; the spectator sees most of the

game

当空 dāngkōng high above in the sky:明月~。A bright moon hangs in the sky.

当口儿 dāngkour at this very moment:就在流氓捣乱的~,警察来了。The riffraff were stirring up trouble when police showed up.

当啷 dānglāng 〈象声〉clank; clang: ~一声,牢门关上了。The prison gate clanked shut.

当量 dāngliàng 〈化学〉equivalent (weight):电化~ electro-chemical equivalent /克~ gram equivalent /~比例定律 law of equivalent proportions /核装置的梯恩梯~ TNT equivalent of a nuclear device /高~核装置 high-yield nuclear device

当量浓度 dāngliàng nóngdù equivalent concentration

当令 dānglìng in season:伏天西瓜~。Watermelons are in season during the dog days. /~的果子趁鲜卖。Sell the fruit when it is still fresh. /她吃穿都是应时~的。She eats what is in season and wears what is in style.

当垆 dānglú *also* "当卢"; "当炉" sell alcoholic drinks (in a wineshop)

当路 dānglù ❶ be in the middle of the road; block the road:他站在~望了一会儿。Standing on the road, he glanced around for a while. ❷〈书面〉be in power; hold the reins of government: 奸臣~。Treacherous court officials held sway.

D

当门 dāngmén ❶ against the door or gate; blocking the door or gate:他~一站,挡住那人的去路。He stood against the door, blocking the man's way. ❷ in front of the door or gate:~搭着彩牌楼,显得花团锦簇,富丽堂皇。A decorated archway was put up in front of the gate, looking magnificent with all its gorgeous bouquets of flowers and piles of silks.

当面 dāngmiàn to sb.'s face; in sb.'s presence: ~直言 speak to sb.'s face /~取笑 laugh in sb.'s face /~对质 confront sb. (with facts, questions, etc.); challenge sb. face to face /~撒谎 tell a barefaced lie /~一套,背后一套 behave one way to sb.'s face and another way behind his back; double-deal /我们要~弄清楚这些事实。We must straighten out these facts face to face.

当面锣,对面鼓 dāngmiàn luó, duìmiàn gǔ negotiate directly and argue face to face:有什么事咱们~,说清楚。Let's thrash things out face to face.

当年 dāngnián ❶ in those years or days: ~,我靠助学金读完大学。In those years I worked through college on state scholarships. /想~,这里连一所高等学校都没有! Well, in those days, there was not even a single college around here! /老人的精力不减~。The old man is as energetic as ever. ❷ in the prime of life:他正~。He is in his prime.
see also dàngnián

当前 dāngqián ❶ before one; facing one:大敌~,我们必须团结得像一个人一样。Confronted by a formidable foe, we must be united as one. ❷ present; current: ~的中心任务是经济建设。The central task at present is economic development. /~国际形势的主要趋势是缓和。Détente is the main trend of the current international situation. /我们既要考虑长远利益,也要考虑~利益。We must take into account the immediate interests as well as the long-term interests.

当前用户 dāngqián yònghù 〈信息〉active user

当枪使 dāngqiāngshǐ 〈比喻〉be used by sb. as a tool for attacking another; serve as sb.'s hatchet man or cat's paw:不要给人~。Don't let yourself be used as somebody's cat's paw.

当权 dāngquán hold or wield power; be in power: ~派 person in power; people in authority; powers that be

当儿 dāngr ❶ this or that very moment:正在犯愁的~,他来帮忙了。Just when I was worrying myself to death, he offered his help. ❷ gap; break:两行玉米中间留一尺宽的~。Please leave a one-foot space between the two rows of maize.

当然 dāngrán ❶ it is only natural; it goes without saying: ~应该如此。That is just as it should be. /尊师爱生理所~。It goes without saying that students should respect teachers and teachers cherish students. ❷ certainly; of course; to be sure; without doubt:国家有难,我们~不能坐视不顾。When the state is in difficulty, we certainly cannot stand idly by. ❸ natural; *ex officio*: ~盟友 natural ally /~成员 *ex officio* (*or ipso facto*) member

当然官守议员 dāngrán guānshǒu yìyuán 〈旧语〉(HK) *ex officio* member:立法局~ *ex officio* member of the Legislative Council (before July 1997)

当然继承 dāngrán jìchéng 〈法律〉natural succession

当然继承人 dāngrán jìchéngrén heir apparent; natural heir

当仁不让 dāngrén-bùràng not pass on to others what one is called upon to do; feel duty-bound to shoulder a responsibility; the buck stops here:你有这个能力,就要~,承当重任。You should assume the heavy responsibility as your due, since you have the ability.

当日 dāngrì then; at that time; on the same day
see also dàngrì

当时 dāngshí then; at that time: ~我没有认识到这个问题的严重性。At that time, I did not realize the gravity of the matter. *or* I was not aware of the seriousness of the problem then.
see also dàngshí

当世 dāngshì ❶ present age; present time: ~之事 contemporary events; current affairs ❷〈书面〉influential official; bigwig:不交~ never seek the acquaintance of bigwigs; never curry favour with high officials ❸〈书面〉run the country; hold the reins of government

当事 dāngshì ❶ be in charge; take charge:坏人~,好人倒霉。When bad people are in charge, good people will suffer. ❷ concerned; related: ~各方 parties concerned; interested parties ❸〈书面〉when something is happening to one; when one is confronted with a situation: ~不乱 keep one's presence of mind when something happens; remain composed (*or* cool) in a crisis ❹ authorities; party or parties concerned; interested parties
see also dàngshì

当事国 dāngshìguó state directly involved; country concerned:争端~ party to a dispute

当事人 dāngshìrén ❶〈法律〉party (to a lawsuit); litigant: 法院传唤~。The litigants are summoned to court. ❷ person or party concerned; interested party:具体情况要向~了解。You have to go to the persons concerned for more detailed information.

当堂 dāngtáng 〈旧语〉in the magistrate's court; before the tribunal: ~作证 testify in court; bear witness in a lawcourt

当天 dāngtiān *also* "当空" high above in the sky
see also dàngtiān

当庭 dāngtíng in a lawcourt; in court:检察官~就认为这不能作为犯罪的证据。The prosecutor said right in court that this could not be accepted as evidence of guilt.

当头 dāngtóu ❶ right overhead; right on the head; head-on: 烈日~。The scorching sun is right overhead. ❷ facing or confronting one; imminent: 国难~ when disaster threatens a nation; when a nation is confronted with a crisis ❸ put in the first place; give priority to:他这个人怕字~,干什么都是畏首畏尾。The fear of getting into trouble has made a coward of him in whatever he does.
see also dàngtou

当头棒喝 dāngtóu-bànghè (as when monks of *Chan* Buddhism receive a learner) give a stunning blow or a stern warning to enlighten sb.:考试失败,给他一个~。His failure in the examinations gave him a serious warning.

当头炮 dāngtóupào (in Chinese chess) cannon directed at (the other side's) king;〈比喻〉direct attack; direct criticism

当头一棒 dāngtóu-yībàng ❶ *see* "当头棒喝" ❷ *also* "当头棒" head-on blow — surprise attack:他听到这个消息,就像是挨了~,半天说不出话来。The news came to him as a terrible blow, leaving him speechless for a long while.

当途 dāngtú *also* "当涂"〈书面〉be in power; hold sway: ~之人 people in power

当午 dāngwǔ noon; noontide; midday:锄禾日~,汗滴禾下土。He hoes the grain under a midday sun, Sweat dripping down on the soil beneath the grain.

当务之急 dāngwùzhījí burning issue or pressing matter of the moment:眼前搜集资料是~。The top priority task at present is collecting data.

当下 dāngxià instantly; immediately; at once: 听了这个消息,他~就吓得魂不附体。No sooner had he heard the news than he was scared stiff. /我一听这话,~就愣住了。I was immediately taken aback by what he said.

当下手 dāng xiàshǒu work as sb.'s subordinate or assistant; serve under sb.:他这个人很自负,不愿给人家~。As he is arrogant and opinionated, he does not want to take orders from anybody.

当先 dāngxiān ❶ in the van; in the front ranks; at the head:奋勇~ fight bravely in the van /作为一名军官,他一马~,立即参加抢救工作。As an officer, he took the lead in the rescue work. ❷〈方言〉at

the beginning; originally; initially

当心 dāngxīn ❶ be careful; beware; watch out: ～小偷。Beware of pickpockets. /～路滑。Watch your step. The road is slippery. /你要～，别说漏了嘴。Be careful not to blurt out our secret. /～别踩草地。Keep off the grass. ❷〈方言〉middle of the chest; middle or centre of sth.: 给他～一拳 hit him in the chest /请把桌子摆在屋子～。Please place the table in the centre of the room.

当墟 dāngxū 〈方言〉be a market day: 今天～ Today is a market day.

当选 dāngxuǎn be elected; win an election: 以多数票～ be elected by a majority vote /他～为学会秘书长。He was elected Secretary-General of the Society.

当选总统 dāngxuǎn zǒngtǒng president-elect

当眼 dāngyǎn conspicuous; showy: 她把新衣服挂在～的地方。She hung the new dress in a conspicuous place.

当央 dāngyāng 〈方言〉in the middle; in the centre: 屋～放了张八仙桌。Right in the centre of the hall is an old-fashioned square table for eight people.

当腰 dāngyāo middle (of an article of some length): 这根棍子两头粗，～细。The stick has a small waist. *or* The stick is thick at the ends and thin in the middle.

当一天和尚撞一天钟 dāng yī tiān héshang zhuàng yī tiān zhōng *also* "做一天和尚撞一天钟" go on tolling the bell as long as one is a monk — do the least that is expected of one; take a passive attitude towards one's work

当意 dāngyì satisfied; to one's liking: 她至今还没有～的人。She has yet to find a man of her heart.

当院儿 dāngyuànr 〈方言〉in the courtyard: 吃完晚饭后，全家都在～乘凉。After supper the whole family were enjoying the cool in the courtyard.

当政 dāngzhèng be in power; be in office: 该国如今是社会民主党～。The social democratic party is now in power in that country.

当之无愧 dāngzhī-wúkuì fully deserve (a title, an honour, etc.); be worthy of: "铁人"的称号，他～。He was worthy of the name "the iron man".

当之有愧 dāngzhī-yǒukuì not deserve (a title, an honour, etc.); not be worthy of: 如此荣誉，我实在～呀。I am afraid I am not really worthy of the honour accorded me. *or* I feel truly humbled by the honour.

当直 dāngzhí ❶ (often used in the early vernacular) domestic servant ❷ *see* "当值"

当值 dāngzhí 〈旧语〉be on duty

当中 dāngzhōng ❶ in the middle; in the centre: 广场～是个大花坛。In the centre of the square (there) is a large flower bed. /河～的水流最急。The current is the swiftest in the middle of the river. ❷ among; in the midst of: 他们是从大批有才华的知识分子～选拔出来的。They were selected from among the most brilliant intellectuals. /我校毕业生～许多人现在担任了重要职务。Many graduates of our school are now in positions of responsibility.

当中间儿 dāngzhōngjiànr 〈口语〉in the middle; in the centre

当众 dāngzhòng in the presence of all; in public: ～宣布 declare (*or* announce) in public

当众表态 dāngzhòng biǎotài take a public stance

当众出丑 dāngzhòng-chūchǒu make an exhibition of oneself; be disgraced in public

当轴处中 dāngzhóu-chǔzhōng hold a key post; be a leader of the government

当子 dāngzi 〈方言〉space; gap: 不要留这么大的～。Don't leave so much space in between.
see also dàngzi

裆(襠) dāng

❶ crotch (of trousers); rise: 立～ rise /开～裤 babies' pants with a vent in the seat; open-seat pants (for children) /～要长一点。I want a longer rise. /横～最好大一些。I'd prefer the cut to be a little loose in the hips. ❷〈生理〉crotch

珰(璫) dāng

〈书面〉❶ earring ❷ eunuch

珰珰 dāngdāng *see* "铛铛" dāngdāng

蟷(蟷) dāng

see "螳蟷" diédāng

筜(簹) dāng

see "筼筜" yúndāng

铛(鐺) dāng

〈象声〉clank; clang
see also chēng

铛铛 dāngdāng *also* "珰珰" dāngdāng clank; clang: 铜锣敲得～响。Brass gongs clanged.

dǎng

挡(擋、攩) dǎng

❶ keep off; ward off; get in the way of: 一件单衫可～不了夜里的寒气。An unlined garment cannot ward off the cold at night. /他～住我们的去路。He stood in our way. ❷ shelter or shield (one) against or from sth.; keep out; block: ～～风 keep out the wind; shelter one from the wind /遮风～雨 shelter one from wind and rain /前面一座高楼～住了我们的视线。A tall building in front blocked our view. /山高～不住太阳。Even the highest mountain cannot shut out the sun. ❸ fender; blind: 炉～儿 (fire) fender; fire screen /窗～子 window blind (*or* shade) ❹ gear: 前进～ forward gear /倒～ reverse gear /高速～ top gear /低速～ bottom gear ❺ (of some apparatuses and measuring instruments) indentation; grading
see also dàng

挡车 dǎngchē 〈纺织〉operate a number of looms: ～工 loom tender; spinner

挡尘板 dǎngchénbǎn dust board

挡风玻璃 dǎngfēng bōli 〈汽车〉windshield; wind screen

挡风墙 dǎngfēngqiáng windbreak: 拿他当～ use him as a shield (*or* protector)

挡寒 dǎnghán keep off the cold; shield from the cold: 穿上皮袄～ put on a fur-lined jacket to keep off the cold

挡横儿 dǎnghèngr intervene; interfere and make difficulties; get in the way: 要不是有人～，这事早就成了。If nobody had created difficulties, it would have been done long ago.

挡火墙 dǎnghuǒqiáng fire wall; fire stop

挡饥 dǎngjī stave off hunger; satisfy hunger: 孩子饿了，先给他两块点心挡挡饥。The child is famished. Give him a couple of cookies to stave off hunger.

挡驾 dǎngjià 〈婉词〉put off a visitor with some excuse; decline to see a guest: 走到大门口，他便被挡了驾。When he walked up to the entrance, he was denied admittance.

挡箭牌 dǎngjiànpái shield; excuse; pretext: 他想把小李当作～。He wanted to use Xiao Li as a shield and hide behind him. /他拿病作～，不参加会议。He refused to attend the meeting on the pretext that he was ill.

挡泥板 dǎngníbǎn 〈汽车〉mudguard; fender

挡热板 dǎngrèbǎn 〈航天〉heat shield (part of the external surface of a spacecraft designed to protect the interior from aerodynamic heating)

挡水板 dǎngshuǐbǎn 〈船舶〉dasher; dash plate

挡水檐 dǎngshuǐyán hoodmould

挡头阵 dǎng tóuzhèn fight as vanguard; take on the enemy in the front line

挡头 dǎngtou sth. that obstructs, checks, stops or impedes; obstruction; obstacle
see also dàngtou

挡土墙 dǎngtǔqiáng 〈建筑〉retaining wall

挡子 dǎngzi blind; shade; screen; fender: 窗～ window blind (*or* shade)

党(黨) dǎng

❶ political party; party: 执政～ ruling party /反对～ opposition (party) /参政～ party participating in the government /～内民主 inner-party democracy; democracy inside a party ❷ the Party (i.e. the Communist Party of China): 入～ join the Party /～的基本路线 the Party's basic line ❸ clique; faction; gang: 死～ sworn followers ❹〈书面〉be partial to; take sides with ❺〈书面〉kinsfolk; relatives: 父～ father's kinsfolk ❻ (Dǎng) a surname

党八股 dǎngbāgǔ stereotyped Party writing; Party jargon

党办 dǎngbàn (short for 党委办公室) office of the Party committee

党报 dǎngbào party newspaper or organ: 《人民日报》是中国共产党

～。The *People's Daily* is the organ of the Communist Party of China.

党部 dǎngbù party headquarters

党代表 dǎngdàibiǎo Party representative (political worker of the Chinese Communist Party assigned a leading role in the army during the First and Second Revolutionary Civil Wars, 1924-1937)

党阀 dǎngfá party boss; party tyrant

党法 dǎngfǎ rules and regulations of a political party：维护党规～ uphold the constitution and rules of a party

党费 dǎngfèi party membership dues

党风 dǎngfēng conduct of Party members; work style of a political party：～问题是关系执政党生死存亡的问题。The style of a political party in power determines its very survival.

党纲 dǎnggāng party programme

党锢 dǎnggù 〈旧语〉 restrictions placed on certain cliques or groups, forbidding their members to hold official posts or take part in political activities (esp. in the Han Dynasty)：～之禁 decree for excluding people of a certain group or clique from the country's political life / ～之祸 disaster brought on those concerned by such a decree prohibition or exclusion

D

党规 dǎngguī rules of a political party

党棍 dǎnggùn dirty politician who uses his party membership as a means to an ignoble end

党国 dǎngguó (used by the KMT) the party and the state：～要员 party and state bigwigs

党籍 dǎngjí party membership：开除～ expel from the party / 保留～ keep in the party

党纪 dǎngjì party discipline：～国法 party discipline and state laws

党建 dǎngjiàn (short for 党的建设) party building

党禁 dǎngjìn ❶〈旧语〉 ban on certain cliques or groups in feudal China, forbidding their members to take up official posts and participate in political activities ❷ ban on political parties and their activities：开放～ lift the ban on political parties

党刊 dǎngkān (in reference to a periodical) organ of a political party; party organ

党课 dǎngkè party lesson; party lecture：听～ attend a party lecture

党魁 dǎngkuí 〈贬义〉 party boss, chieftain, or chief

党龄 dǎnglíng party standing：此人既有学问，又有多年～和工作经验，在工作中当然可以起很好的作用。He is well-educated and has a long party standing and work experience. Naturally he can play a useful role in our undertaking.

党派 dǎngpài political parties and groups; party groupings：民主～ democratic parties / 左翼～ left-wing parties / ～关系 party affiliation

党票 dǎngpiào 〈贬义〉 party membership：捞～ grab Party membership (in order to use it for personal gains)

党旗 dǎngqí party flag

党人 dǎngrén ❶ partisan; member of a political party：联邦～ (US) Federalist / 保守～ (UK) conservative; tory ❷〈书面〉 member of a clique formed to pursue political interests

党日 dǎngrì day set off for activities by party organizations

党参 dǎngshēn 〈中药〉 *dangshen* (*Codonopsis pilosola*)

党史 dǎngshǐ history of a political party：中共～ history of the Communist Party of China / ～学习班 study course on the history of the Party

党同伐异 dǎngtóng-fáyì gang up with those who are of the same faction and attack those who are not; be narrowly partisan

党徒 dǎngtú 〈贬义〉 member of a clique or a political party; henchman

党团 dǎngtuán ❶ political parties and other organizations ❷ Chinese Communist Party and Chinese Communist Youth League：～员 Party and League members ❸ (as in some parliaments) caucus; group：议会～ parliamentary group of a political party; caucus

党外人士 dǎngwài rénshì non-Party personage; public figure outside the Party

党委 dǎngwěi Party committee：～制 Party committee system (for ensuring collective leadership in the Party)

党卫军 Dǎngwèijūn *Schutzstaffel* (SS), established in Germany by the Nazis in 1925

党务 dǎngwù party work; party affairs

党项 Dǎngxiàng 〈古语〉 branch of the Qiang (羌) nationality who set up the state of Xi Xia (西夏) covering the present Ningxia and parts of Gansu, Shaanxi and Inner Mongolia

党小组 dǎngxiǎozǔ Party group (smallest unit within the Party's organizational setup)

党校 dǎngxiào Party school

党性 dǎngxìng Party spirit; Party character：～强 have a solid Party character; be a staunch Party member / ～不纯的表现 sign of impurity in Party spirit

党羽 dǎngyǔ 〈贬义〉 members of a clique; adherents; henchmen：这个特务组织的头头及其～全部落网。The leader of the spy ring and its members have all been captured.

党员 dǎngyuán party member：～大会 general membership meeting of a party organization; meeting of all party members

党员登记 dǎngyuán dēngjì party member re-registration

党章 dǎngzhāng party constitution

党争 dǎngzhēng factional strife; partisan war

党证 dǎngzhèng party membership card

党政不分 dǎng-zhèng bùfēn failure to distinguish between the Party and government functions

党政分工 dǎng-zhèng fēngōng division of labour between Party and government; separation of Party work from government work

党政工团 dǎng-zhèng-gōng-tuán Party branches, government departments, trade unions and Youth League branches

党政机关 dǎng-zhèng jīguān Party and government organizations

党支部 dǎngzhībù Party branch：～书记 Party branch secretary

党中央 Dǎngzhōngyāng Central Committee of the Party; central leading body of the Party; Party Centre

党总支 dǎngzǒngzhī general Party branch

党组 dǎngzǔ leading Party group (in a government department or people's organization)

谠(讜) dǎng

〈书面〉 (of advice or comment) honest; unbiased

谠辞 dǎngcí 〈书面〉 sincere words

谠论 dǎnglùn 〈书面〉 unbiased comments

谠言 dǎngyán 〈书面〉 honest remarks

谠议 dǎngyì 〈书面〉 outspoken sincere comments

榄(欓) dǎng

see "簕榄" lèdǎng

dàng

宕 dàng

〈书面〉 ❶ delay：他一再延～，把最后的机会都丢了。He procrastinated until the last opportunity was lost. ❷ abandon; freedom from restraint：跌～ unrestrained; unbridled; varied

宕账 dàngzhàng outstanding loan; bad debt; arrears

砀 dàng

see "莨砀" làngdàng

当[1](當) dàng

❶ proper; right; appropriate：处理得～ handle properly / 用词不～ inappropriate wording / 比喻失～。The analogy is inept. ❷ be equal to; match：一个钱～两个钱花 make one cent do the job of two — be frugal (*or* economical) / 他一个人可以～两个人用。He can do the job of two persons. ❸ treat as; regard as; take for：把朋友～敌人 take a friend for an enemy / 死马～活马医 make every possible effort to save an apparently hopeless situation / 别把我～客人看待。Don't treat me as a guest. ❹ think：我～你走了。I thought you had left. / 我～是谁呢，原来是你。Oh, it's you. I thought it was somebody else. 你真的～我不知道? Do you really think I don't know? ❺ that very (day, year, etc.)：～天 that very day / 他～晚赶回来了。He hurried back that very evening.

当[2](當、儅) dàng

❶ pawn：～手饰 pawn one's jewelry; put one's jewelry in pawn / 把～出去的一副项链赎回 redeem a pawned necklace ❷ sth. pawned; pawn; pledge：赎～ take sth. out of pledge; redeem sth. pawned

see also dāng

当成 dàngchéng treat as; regard as; look upon as：不要把马克思主义～教条看待。We should not treat Marxism as dogma.

当当 dàngdàng pawn things

当户 dànghù 〈旧语〉 pawner or pawnor

当家子 dàngjiāzi 〈方言〉 member of the same clan
当卖 dàngmài pawn and sell: 以~度日 eke out an existence by pawning and selling articles one owns
当年 dàngnián same year; that very year: ~设计, ~施工, ~投产。It was designed, constructed and put into operation all in the same year. /这个水库一修成, ~受益。We began to benefit from the reservoir the very year it was completed.
see also dāngnián
当票 dàngpiào pawn ticket
当铺 dàngpu pawnshop: ~老板 pawnbroker /青年时代的鲁迅经常出入于~药店之间。As a young man, Lu Xun was a frequent customer of pawnshops and drugstores.
当日 dàngrì same day; that very day: ~有效 good for the day stipulated /~往返 one-day round trip
see also dāngrì
当时 dàngshí right away; at once; immediately: 见他不高兴, 我~便起身告辞。As he was not in a good mood, I immediately rose and took my leave. /一听到这消息, 她~就晕过去了。She fainted the moment she heard the news. *or* She fainted on hearing the news.
see also dāngshí
当事 dàngshì ❶ regard as serious business; take seriously: 他根本不拿这个工作当回事儿。He does not at all take this job seriously. ❷ serve the purpose; carry weight; count: 小孩子的话不~。What a child says doesn't count.
see also dāngshì
当是 dàngshi think: 我~小张来了, 原来是你。I thought Xiao Zhang was here, but it's you!
当天 dàngtiān same day; that very day: 办完事~就走了。He left the very day he was through with his business. /~的事, ~做完。Never leave today's work till tomorrow.
see also dāngtiān
当头 dàngtou ❶〈口语〉 sth. pawned; pawn; pledge: 拿皮袄当~ leave one's furcoat as a pledge ❷ *also* "挡头" dàngtou sth. that obstructs or stops; obstacle; barrier
see also dāngtóu
当晚 dàngwǎn that evening; on the evening of the same day: 他真是飞毛腿, ~就赶回来了。What a fleetfooted walker! He made his way back the same evening.
当押 dàngyā pawn; mortgage: ~衣物 pawn clothes and other articles
当夜 dàngyè that night; at night the same day: 他上午九时才住进医院, ~就去世了。He was hospitalized at 9 o'clock in the morning but passed away that very night.
当月 dàngyuè same month; that very month: 生产任务没完成好, 小马被扣发了~奖金。Xiao Ma's bonus for the month was withheld for his failure to meet the production quota. /月票~有效。The monthly pass is good only for the month stipulated.
当真 dàngzhēn ❶ take seriously: 开玩笑的事儿, 你别~。Don't take it seriously; I was joking. /你要是~, 可就上了他的当了。You will be playing into his hands if you take it to heart. ❷ really; really true: 此话~? Is it really true? /他说会参加会议, 他~来了。He said he would attend the meeting. Sure enough, he did.
当子 dàngzi *also* "档子" dàngzi 〈量词〉 *used before an event or incident*: 这~事儿我看现在该了结了。I think we should settle the matter here and now.
see also dāngzi
当做 dàngzuò treat as; regard as; look on as: 不把它~一回事 regard it as a matter of no consequence; treat it lightly /不要把别人的劝告~耳边风。Don't turn a deaf ear to advice. /他往往把来自下级的批评~对自己尊严的挑战。He often looks upon criticism from below as a challenge to his dignity.

垱(壋) dàng

〈方言〉 embankment built for irrigation: 筑~挖塘 build embankments and dig ponds for irrigation

档(檔) dàng

❶ shelves (for files); pigeonholes: 把文件归~ file a document; place a document on file ❷ files; archives: 查~ consult the files /存~备查 be kept on file for reference ❸ crosspiece (of a table, bed, etc.) ❹ grade: 高~商品 high-grade goods /分~出售 divide goods into different grades for sale ❺〈方言〉 open-air booth or stall: 鱼~ fish stall /大排~ cheap stall; cheap restaurant

档案 dàng'àn files; archives; record; dossier: ~管理员 archivist /机密~ secret archives; confidential (*or* classified) files /人事~ personnel dossier /故宫内保存着明清两代的~资料。In the Palace Museum there are archives of the Ming and Qing dynasties. /该公司保存着每一雇员的~。The firm keeps a dossier on every employee.
档案馆 dàng'ànguǎn archives (institution or building administering or housing records)
档案柜 dàng'ànguì filing cabinet
档次 dàngcì grading; grade: 这个工厂生产的提包规格多, ~全。This factory produces handbags of all grades and many different specifications. /奖金的~越拉越大。The gap between different grades of bonus payment is widening. /存本取息的定期储蓄分一年、三年、五年三个~。Time deposits whose interest is drawn at fixed dates are of three different durations: one year, three years and five years.
档级 dàngjí (of commodities, products, etc.) grade: 这批录音机~不高, 销路不畅。This batch of recorders, which aren't of a high grade, do not sell well.
档子 dàngzi 〈方言〉〈量词〉 ❶ *also* "档儿" *used before an event or issue*: 这~事我来管吧。Leave the matter to me. ❷ integrated group of performances: 刚过去两~龙灯, 又来了一~秧歌。Two groups of dragon lanterns had just passed when a group of *yangge* dancers appeared.

挡(擋) dàng

see also dǎng
挡头 dàngtou 〈方言〉 ends of a rectangular object: 被~ ends of a quilt /床~ head and foot of a bed /他俩坐在长方桌的~。They two sat at the ends of a rectangular table.
see also dǎngtou

荡[1](蕩、盪) dàng

❶ swing; sway; wave: ~秋千 play on a swing /~桨 pull on the oars /柳絮在空中飘~。Willow catkins were wafting in the air. ❷ loaf: 游~ loaf about /闲~ lounge around ❸ rinse: 冲~ rinse out; wash away /涤~ wash away; cleanse ❹ clear away; sweep off: 扫~ mopping up; mopping-up operation /倾家~产 lose the entire family fortune; be broke ❺ vast; broad and level: 浩~ vast and mighty /坦~ broad and level; magnanimous

荡[2](蕩) dàng

of loose morals; debauched; licentious: 放~ dissolute; dissipated /放~不羁 unconventional and romantic /淫~ lustful; lascivious; lewd

荡[3](蕩) dàng

❶ shallow lake; marsh: 芦苇~ reed marsh ❷ *also* "凼" dàng pond; pit; pool
荡除 dàngchú clear away; get rid of: ~积习 do away with old habits and customs
荡船 dàngchuán ❶ row a boat: ~湖上 go boating on a lake ❷ swingboat
荡荡 dàngdàng ❶ (of water, wind, etc.) wave; sweep; drift: 水波~ undulating waves /春风~ wafting spring breeze ❷ vast; broad: 黄沙~, 一望无际。A vast expanse of yellow sand stretches far into the distance. ❸ level; even; smooth: ~大道被山洪冲得坑坑洼洼。Mountain torrents left bumps and hollows in the smooth road.
荡荡悠悠 dàngdang-yōuyōu swing (back and forth); float about
荡涤 dàngdí 〈书面〉 cleanse; clean up; wash away: 暴风雨~了大城市污浊的空气。The storm purified the polluted air of the metropolis. /海风把空中的烟尘~一尽。The sea breeze blew away all the dust floating in the air. /要~旧社会遗留下来的污泥浊水。We must clean up the filth and mire left over from the old society. /必须把人们心灵上的污秽~干净。It is imperative to cleanse the human mind of all its spiritual filth.
荡妇 dàngfù 〈书面〉 ❶ dissolute woman; woman of loose morals ❷ prostitute
荡检逾闲 dàngjiǎn-yúxián abandon restraint and overstep propriety; be licentious; be dissolute
荡平 dàngpíng mop up and quell; suppress and wipe out: ~天下 quell all disturbances throughout the land /残匪被一举~。The remnants of the bandits were wiped out in one swoop.
荡气回肠 dàngqì-huícháng *also* "回肠荡气" (of music, poetry, etc.) stirring; thrilling; inspiring

荡然 dàngrán 〈书面〉all gone：资财～ with all one's property gone; clean broke

荡然无存 dàngrán-wúcún 〈书面〉all gone; with nothing left：山上的古庙已～。The old temple on the hill has vanished without a trace.

荡田 dàngtián land reclaimed from a lake; shoaly land

荡析 dàngxī 〈书面〉(of family, friends, etc.) scattered or separated (as in troubled times)：资财衣物，～一空。One's belongings — money, clothing and other articles — were all lost.

荡析离居 dàngxī-líjū 〈书面〉become separated and live apart：饥荒使成千上万的人～。The famine forced thousands of people to wander about homeless.

荡漾 dàngyàng ripple; undulate：湖上碧波～。The lake rippled gently. /歌声～。The song rose and fell like waves. /幸福的暖流在心中～。My mind overflowed, as it were, with warm feelings of happiness.

荡子 dàngzi 〈方言〉shallow lake

砀(碭) dàng

砀山 Dàngshān Dangshan, place in Anhui Province：～梨 *Dangshan* pear, famous pear produced at or round Dangshan

凼(氹) dàng 〈方言〉pool; pit; pond：粪～ cesspool /水～ pond

凼肥 dàngféi wet compost

dāo

氘 dāo 〈化学〉*also* "重氢" zhòngqīng deuterium (^2_1H or D)

氘氚反应堆 dāochuān fǎnyìngduī deuterium-tritium reactor

氘灯 dāodēng deuterium lamp

氘核 dāohé deuteron：～反应 deuteron reaction /～感生裂变 deuteron-induced fission

氘化 dāohuà 〈化学〉deuterate; deuterize：～(合)物 deuteride

氘束缚中子 dāoshùfù zhōngzǐ deuterium-bound neutron

氘水合物 dāoshuǐhéwù 〈化学〉deuterate

氘原子 dāoyuánzǐ D-atom

刀 dāo ❶ knife; sword; any kind of cutting tool：菜～ kitchen knife; kitchen chopper /铣～ milling cutter /车～ lathe tool /铡～ fodder chopper /指甲～ nail-clippers /剪～ scissors; shears /镰～ sickle /开～ have an operation; be operated on /～下留人! Hold the execution! ❷ sth. shaped like a knife：冰～ ice skates ❸〈量词〉*used with sheets of paper*：一～纸 one hundred sheets (of paper) ❹ (Dāo) a surname

刀把儿 dāobàr *also* "刀把子" ❶ handle (of a knife); hilt (of a sword) ❷ military power; power：～攥在手里 in control of military power ❸〈方言〉opportunity, reason or excuse for doing sth. harmful to one; handle：他把～递给自己的对手，真是笨透了。It was idiotic of him to provide his opponents with ammunition.

刀耙 dāobà blade harrow

刀背 dāobèi back of a knife blade

刀笔 dāobǐ 〈旧语〉knife and brush — writing of indictments and appeals; pettifoggery：～老手 old hand in drawing up indictments; seasoned pettifogger

刀笔吏 dāobǐlì petty official who draws up indictments, etc.; official pettifogger

刀币 dāobì *also* "刀布" knife-shaped coin of ancient China

刀兵 dāobīng weapons; arms; 〈比喻〉fighting; war：～相见 meet in battle; fight each other /动～ resort to arms; resort to force /千秋事业息～。It is our historical task to put an end to war for good and all.

刀兵之灾 dāobīngzhīzāi calamity of war; war

刀柄 dāobǐng knife handle; hilt

刀叉 dāo-chā knife and fork

刀齿 dāochǐ 〈机械〉cutter tooth

刀锉 dāocuò 〈机械〉knife file

刀豆 dāodòu 〈植物〉sword bean (*Canavalia gladiata*)

刀法 dāofǎ skill in the use of a knife in cookery or engraving, or of a sword in martial arts：～娴熟 skilful in using a carver (*or* graver, *or* kitchen knife); adept in swordsmanship

刀锋 dāofēng ❶ cutting edge of a knife：～锐利，当心不要伤了自己。Take care not to hurt yourself, for the edge of the knife is pretty sharp. ❷〈机械〉cutter point; tool point

刀斧手 dāofǔshǒu 〈旧语〉executioner

刀耕火种 dāogēng-huǒzhòng slash-and-burn farming or cultivation：世界一些原始地区仍处于～阶段。The slash-and-burn method of farming is still being practised in some primitive areas of the world.

刀功 dāogōng skill in the use of a kitchen knife (in preparing food)

刀光剑影 dāoguāng-jiànyǐng glint and flash of cold steel — fierce fighting：沙场上～，双方损失惨重。There was fierce fighting on the battleground, and both sides suffered heavy losses.

刀痕 dāohén mark or scar left by a knife-cut

刀架 dāojià 〈机械〉tool carrier; tool post

刀架导槽 dāojià dǎocáo 〈机械〉carriage guide; tool guide

刀尖 dāojiān ❶ point of a knife; point of a sword ❷〈机械〉nose of a tool

刀具 dāojù *also* "刃具" rènjù ❶ cutlery ❷〈机械〉cutting tool; cutter; knife tool; tool bit

刀具柄 dāojùbǐng shank of tool

刀具车床 dāojù chēchuáng lathe tool

刀具导轨 dāojù dǎoguǐ cutter guide

刀具工 dāojùgōng toolman

刀具规格 dāojù guīgé tool specification

刀锯 dāojù ❶〈机械〉knife saw ❷〈旧语〉knife and saw — instruments of torture; punishment

刀口 dāokǒu ❶ edge of a knife：好刀看～。Judge a knife by its edge. *or* A knife is good if its edge is sharp. ❷ where a thing can be put to best use; crucial point; right spot：把劲儿使在～上。Focus your effort on the right problem. /钱要花在～上。Use your money where it is most needed. *or* Your money should be spent on what is most essential. ❸ cut; incision：～尚未痊愈。The cut hasn't healed yet.

刀螂 dāolang 〈方言〉mantis：这人瘦得跟～似的。He is as thin as a mantis. *or* He is such a spindle!

刀马旦 dāomǎdàn 〈戏曲〉actress with skill in acrobatic fighting

刀片 dāopiàn ❶〈机械〉cutter blade; fly-bar ❷ razor blade：不锈钢～ stainless steel blade

刀枪 dāoqiāng sword and spear; weapons：～入库，马放南山 put the weapons back in the arsenal and graze the war horses on the hillside — war is over and there is peace throughout the land; enjoy peace and worry no longer about war

刀枪不入 dāoqiāng-bùrù ❶ (of a human body) no weapon can harm; be invincible ❷〈比喻〉(of a person) proof against criticism or admonition：他这个人～，说他也没用。It's no use trying to talk him round; he's simply proof against different ideas.

刀鞘 dāoqiào sheath; scabbard：这～真精致。This is a truly fine sheath.

刀儿 dāor small knife; pocket knife：小～ small knife /铅笔～ pencil sharpener; pen-knife

刀刃 dāorèn ❶ blade; knife-edge; cutting edge ❷ where a thing can be put to best use; crucial point：好钢用在～上 use the best steel to make the best blade — use resources where they are needed most

刀山火海 dāoshān-huǒhǎi *also* "火海刀山" mountain of swords and sea of flames — immense dangers and difficulties; most severe trials：这是一位在战争年代闯过～的老人。He is a veteran who underwent the most severe trials during the war years.

刀山剑林 dāoshān-jiànlín *also* "刀山剑树" mountain of daggers and forest of bayonets — most dangerous places or extremely severe trials：就是～，我也要去。I am determined to go whatever danger might lie ahead.

刀伤 dāoshāng knife wound; gash; stab

刀削面 dāoxiāomiàn *also* "削面" noodles cooked by whittling off the dough into the boiling pot, popular in Shanxi Province

刀形开关 dāoxíng kāiguān chopper switch; knife-blade switch

刀鱼 dāoyú *also* "带鱼" dàiyú 〈方言〉hairtail; cutlass fish

刀子 dāozi 〈口语〉small knife; pocketknife：软～杀人 harm a person imperceptibly

刀子嘴 dāozizuǐ ❶ sharp tongue; bitter tongue：你这张～，真能挖苦人。What a sharp tongue you have, speaking with such biting sar-

casm. ❷ person with a sharp or bitter tongue：她真是个～，把人都得罪尽了。She has such a sharp tongue that she has offended everyone around.
刀子嘴，豆腐心 dāozizuǐ，dòufuxīn (have) a sharp tongue but a soft heart
刀俎 dāozǔ 〈书面〉butcher's knife and chopping block：人为～，我为鱼肉。We are at other people's mercy (like fish or meat on a chopping board).

忉 dāo
忉忉 dāodāo 〈书面〉sorrowful；anxious：忧国意～ be deeply anxious about the fate of the country

叨 dāo
see also dáo；tāo
叨扯 dāoche 〈方言〉chat；engage in chitchat；chatter away：他俩一边抽着烟，一边～起来。While smoking，the two of them chattered away.
叨叨 dāodao talk on and on；chatter away：瞎～ talk nonsense /她总是～，烦死人了！She is a regular chatterbox！She is getting on my nerves.
叨登 dāodeng 〈方言〉❶ turn over and over；rummage：他～了所有的抽屉，才找到了那封信。He rummaged through all the drawers before he found the letter. /把衣服～出来晒晒。Take the clothes out to air. ❷ bring up an old case；harp an old score：事情已经过去了，还～什么！There is no point in raking up something that is long past.
叨唠 dāolao *also* "叨叨" chatter away；babble：我不知道这个老妇人在～些什么。I don't know what the old woman is babbling on about.
叨念 dāoniàn *also* "念叨" be always talking about：儿子不在家，母亲时时～。The mother often talked about her son while he was away.

dáo

捯 dáo 〈方言〉❶ pull (yarn, thread or string) hand over hand；wind round and round：我撑着，你帮我把这点毛线～上。I'll hold up my hands，will you help wind the wool round them？❷ step along (with alternating feet)：大人走得快，孩子小腿儿紧～都跟不上。As the adults were walking fast，the child could not keep up even though he did his best with his short legs. ❸ look into；find out；investigate：～老账 rake up (*or* look into) an old score /这件案子已经～出点眉目来了。We have found a clue to the mystery.
捯饬 dáochi 〈方言〉dress up；make up；decorate：这小姑娘挺爱～。The little girl loves to dress up.
捯根儿 dáogēnr 〈方言〉find out the source or origin；get to the bottom (of sth.)：这个谣言一定要～。We must track down the rumour.
捯链 dáoliàn 〈机械〉chain pulley
捯气儿 dáoqìr 〈方言〉❶ gasp for breath on one's death-bed ❷ short of breath；out of breath；panting：他说得那么快，都捯不过气儿来了。He talked so fast that he could hardly catch his breath.

叨 dáo
see also dāo；tāo
叨咕 dáogu 〈方言〉murmur away：不满地低声～ grumbled in a low voice /他嘴里不知在～什么。He is murmuring about god knows what.

dǎo

祷(禱) dǎo ❶ pray：为出征的儿子祈～ pray for one's son who is fighting at the front ❷〈旧语〉(used in correspondence) long for；hope for：盼～ earnestly hope (that...) /是所至～。That is what I am most eagerly looking forward to.
祷告 dǎogào pray；say one's prayers：～上苍 pray to heaven
祷念 dǎoniàn pray：心中默默～ pray silently；pray in one's heart
祷求 dǎoqiú pray for；beg for；ask for earnestly：～保佑 pray for blessings
祷文 dǎowén prayer
祷祝 dǎozhù pray and wish：她～亲人旅途平安。She prayed that her kinfolk might have a safe journey.

蹈 dǎo ❶〈书面〉tread；step：循规～矩 not step out of bounds；toe the line；observe rules and conventions /重～覆辙 follow the same old road to ruin；repeat the same mistake /赴汤～火 go through fire and water — defy all difficulties and dangers ❷ move up and down；skip；trip：手舞足～ move one's limbs up and down；dance for joy
蹈常袭故 dǎocháng-xígù go on in the same old way；get into a rut；follow a set routine；be conventional
蹈海 dǎohǎi 〈书面〉commit suicide by drowning oneself in the sea：～而死 drown oneself in the sea
蹈袭 dǎoxí follow slavishly；copy：～陈言 slavishly follow outmoded sayings；parrot clichés /～前人 mechanically follow one's predecessors

倒[1] dǎo ❶ fall；topple；tumble down：～在地上 fall on the ground /卧～ lie down /一边～〈比喻〉lean to one side /她脚下一滑，摔～了。She slipped and fell down. /墙～了。The wall collapsed. /大风把我们院子里一棵树刮～了。The strong wind felled (*or* uprooted) a tree in our yard. /我～在床上就睡着了。I fell asleep as soon as I got into bed. ❷ collapse；fail；go bankrupt；go out of business：这家银行～了。The bank went bankrupt. /公司～了。The firm has gone out of business. /内阁～了。The cabinet fell. ❸ overthrow；overturn；bring down：～袁运动 movement to overthrow Yuan Shikai (袁世凯) ❹ (of voice) become hoarse；(of a singer) lose one's voice：他的嗓子～了。He has lost his voice. ❺ spoil (appetite)：*see* "～胃口"

倒[2] dǎo ❶ change；exchange：在济南～火车 change trains at Jinan /我们工作三班～。We work on three shifts. /请二位把座位～一～。Can I ask you two gentlemen to swop (*or* change) seats？/让我～～肩。Let me shift the load from one shoulder to the other. ❷ move around：地方太小，～不开身。There is no room to move around. *or* We haven't enough room to swing a cat. /屋子太小，家具～不开。The room is too small for me to move the furniture around. ❸ sell out (a business，etc.)：铺子～出去了。The shop has been sold out. ❹ speculate；profiteer：～粮食 speculate in grain /～国库券 deal illegally in T-bonds /官～ speculation by bureaucrats or official institutions；official or bureaucratic profiteering ❺ *see* "倒爷"
see also dào
倒把 dǎobǎ profiteering；speculation：投机～ engage in speculation and profiteering
倒班 dǎobān change shifts；work in shifts；work by turns：昼夜～ work in shifts round the clock /我们每周倒一次班。We change shifts every week.
倒板 dǎobǎn *also* "导板" dǎobǎn 〈戏曲〉stylised tune in traditional Chinese opera，usu. preceding an integrated singing part
倒闭 dǎobì close down；go bankrupt；go into liquidation：企业～ bankruptcy of an enterprise /大批工厂～。Many factories closed down.
倒毙 dǎobì fall dead；drop dead：～街头 drop dead in the street
倒仓 dǎocāng ❶ take all the grain out of a granary to air ❷ transfer grain from one granary to another ❸〈戏曲〉change of voice (in puberty) of a young singer
倒槽 dǎocáo (of cattle，horses，etc.) the entire herd dies of epidemic disease or for want of proper care
倒茬 dǎochá *also* "轮作" lúnzuò 〈农业〉rotation of crops
倒车 dǎochē change buses；change trains：中途要倒两次车 have to change trains twice on the way
see also dàochē
倒动 dǎodòng *also* "捣动" dǎodòng ❶ move；shift：民兵冒着炮火，抢着抄起弹药箱往山上～。Braving enemy fire，the militia men and women lost no time in picking up the ammunition chests and moving them to the top of the hill. /小毛驴不安地打起响鼻，轮换着～四只蹄子。The donkey snorted uneasily and shifted its hoofs. ❷〈方言〉buy and sell；peddle；trade：～粮食 trade in food grain
倒伏 dǎofú (of crops) lodging：新稻种抗～。The new strain of rice is resistant to lodging.
倒戈 dǎogē change sides in a war；turn one's coat；transfer one's

allegiance:临阵～ change sides on the battlefield /～投敌 be a turncoat; become a renegade

倒阁 dǎogé bring down a cabinet; force a government to resign

倒钩 dǎogōu (of football) make a scissor kick

倒海翻江 dǎohǎi-fānjiāng *also* "翻江倒海" turbulent river and crashing sea — overwhelming; tremendous: 山, ～卷巨澜。Mountains! Like great waves surging in a crashing sea!

倒换 dǎohuàn ❶ rotate; take turns: ～着值班 be on duty by turns /他们～着放哨。They took turns keeping watch. /几种作物～着种 rotate crops in a field ❷ rearrange (sequence, order, etc.); replace; exchange: 上下午的课要～一下。The morning and afternoon classes will be swapped round. /卡片弄乱了,请按编号～一下。The cards are not in proper order. Please rearrange them according to their serial numbers.

倒汇 dǎohuì deal illegally in foreign currency; speculate in foreign exchange

倒嚼 dǎojiào *also* "倒嚥" (popular term for 反刍) ruminate; chew the cud

倒睫 dǎojié 〈医学〉 trichiasis

倒姐 dǎojiě 〈口语〉 girl engaged in profiteering

倒圈 dǎojuàn (of pigs, sheep, etc.) the entire litter dies of epidemic disease or for want of proper care

倒买倒卖 dǎomǎi-dǎomài speculative buying and selling

倒卖 dǎomài resell at a (usu. high) profit; speculate: ～汽车 resell cars at a huge profit /～违禁品 secretly sell contraband goods /～紧俏商品 speculative reselling of goods in short supply

倒霉 dǎoméi *also* "倒楣" have bad luck; be out of luck; be down on one's luck; be unlucky: ～透了! What bad luck! /真～,买东西时把钱包丢了。What lousy luck! I lost my wallet while shopping. /别看我现在～,将来总有出头之日。It's true I'm down on my luck right now, but I will make the grade one day. /这家公司倒了霉,不如从前了。This firm has fallen upon evil days and is not what it was.

倒弄 dǎonong ❶ move: 他把犁杖扫帚都～到厢房里。He moved all the ploughs and brooms into the wing-room. ❷ buy and sell; deal in: ～粮食 be engaged in buying and selling food grain ❸ manipulate; make a fool of

倒牌子 dǎo páizi ruin one's established trade name; lose or spoil one's good reputation: 这家工厂由于粗制滥造倒了牌子,已濒临破产。The factory ruined its own reputation through shoddy production and was on the verge of bankruptcy.

倒儿爷 dǎoryé *see* "倒爷"

倒嗓 dǎosǎng (of opera singers) lose one's voice; have a hoarse voice

倒手 dǎoshǒu ❶ shift or move from one hand to the other: 他没～,一口气把箱子提上了六楼。He carried the suitcase all the way to the 5th floor without ever shifting it from one hand to the other. ❷ (of merchandise, etc.) change hands: 这房子今年已～三次了。This house has changed hands three times this year.

倒塌 dǎotā collapse; topple over; tumble down: 小屋在暴风雨中～。The hut tumbled down in the storm. /一楼房～,造成5人死亡。Five people were killed when a building collapsed.

倒台 dǎotái fall from power; fall down; collapse: 内阁～后,国家一片混乱。The collapse of the cabinet left the country in chaos. /这个独裁者的残暴统治导致了他的～。The dictator's brutal rule led to his downfall.

倒坍 dǎotān fall down; topple down; collapse: 这座塔眼看就要～了。The pagoda is about to collapse.

倒腾 dǎoteng *also* "捣腾" dǎoteng 〈口语〉 ❶ rummage; move; shift: 把化肥～到地里去 carry the fertilizer to the fields /那小孩最喜欢的事是～他妈妈的手提包。Nothing delighted the child more than to turn out his mother's handbag. ❷ replace; exchange; rearrange: 人手少,事情多,～不开。It is hard to cope, with so few hands and so much to do. ❸ buy in and sell out; deal in; trade in: 他～旧家具。He deals (*or* trades) in second-hand furniture. /这一阵子,他在～邮票。Lately, he has been buying and selling stamps.

倒替 dǎotì take turns; work in turn: 我们～着开车,所以旅途上不觉得太累。Since we took turns driving, we did not find the trip very tiring.

倒头 dǎotóu ❶ touch the pillow; lie down: ～就睡 fall asleep the moment one touches the pillow; hit the sack instantly; tumble into bed ❷ 〈方言〉 (often used in cursing) die

倒胃口 dǎo wèikou ❶ spoil one's appetite; upset one's stomach: 什么东西吃多了都会～。A surfeit of any food will spoil one's appetite. ❷ kill one's interest; dampen one's spirits; be boring: 他翻来覆去就那几句话,真是～。His talk with its repeated platitudes is infinitely boring.

倒卧 dǎowò lie down: ～在地 lie down on the ground

倒卧 dǎowo 〈方言〉 person who drops dead in the street out of hunger and cold

倒向 dǎoxiàng 〈林业〉 felling direction

倒邪霉 dǎo xiéméi *also* "倒血霉" fall on evil days; have rough luck; hit a bad patch: 娶这么个老婆,他算是倒了八辈子邪霉了。He struck a bad patch marrying such a woman. *or* It was his lousy luck to have married this woman.

倒休 dǎoxiū (of workers and staff) exchange working days and holidays; stagger holidays

倒牙 dǎoyá 〈方言〉 set or put one's teeth on edge: 酸杏吃得人～。The sour apricots set my teeth on edge.

倒爷 dǎoyé 〈口语〉 speculator; profiteer: 小～ petty speculator or profiteer /这是些出手很大的～。These people are big profiteers buying and selling in large amounts.

倒运 dǎoyùn ❶ 〈方言〉 have a run of bad luck; be unlucky: 我这一阵子真～。I've had a run of bad luck lately. ❷ buy cheap in one place and sell dear in another place; profiteer: ～粮食 profiteer on grain ❸ ship from one place to another; transship

倒灶 dǎozào 〈方言〉 ❶ decline; collapse: 家业～ decline of the family fortune ❷ be down on one's luck; be out of luck: 今年～,碰到一个又一个的挫折。I've been most unlucky this year, meeting with one setback after another.

倒账 dǎozhàng ❶ evade or repudiate a debt: ～卷逃 evade debts by absconding with money and valuables ❷ debt that can not be recovered; bad debt: 店里今年出了三笔～。The store is faced with three bad debts this year. /就算是吃了几笔～! Just mark it off as a couple of bad debts!

岛(島) dǎo

island: 孤～ lone island /小～ islet /群～ archipelago /半～ peninsula /安全～ 〈交通〉 safety island; pedestrian island

岛港 dǎogǎng island harbour

岛国 dǎoguó country consisting of one or more islands; island country

岛弧 dǎohú island arc

岛架 dǎojià ocean shelf of an island

岛链 dǎoliàn archipelago

岛山 dǎoshān 〈地质〉 inselbeng

岛屿 dǎoyǔ islands and islets; islands

岛屿坡 dǎoyǔpō insular slope

岛宇宙 dǎoyǔzhòu 〈天文〉 island universe

岛状冰山 dǎozhuàng bīngshān ice island; iceberg

岛子 dǎozi 〈方言〉 island; islet

捣(搗、擣) dǎo

❶ pound with a pestle, etc.; beat; smash: ～米 husk rice with a pestle and mortar /～药 pound medicine in a mortar /～蒜 pound garlic into pulp /用胳膊肘～了他一下 nudge sb.; give sb. a nudge /直～匪巢 drive straight on to the bandits' den ❷ beat; strike: ～衣 beat clothes (in washing) ❸ *see* "捣乱"

捣棒 dǎobàng 〈机械〉 ramming or tamping bar

捣锤 dǎochuí ❶ pestle ❷ 〈机械〉 stamp hammer

捣蛋 dǎodàn make trouble: 调皮～ be mischievous /告诉那些小鬼头别在这儿～。Tell those naughty boys to stop acting up. /你要不答应他的要求,他就跟你～。He'll start giving you a hard time if you don't allow him to do what he wants.

捣动 dǎodòng ❶ pound and turn: 用铁杈子～粪堆 pound and turn a heap of animal fertilizer with an iron pitchfork ❷ 〈方言〉 instigate; incite; stir up; whip up: 背后～是非 stir up trouble or sow discord behind the scenes (*or* behind people's backs) ❸ *see* "倒动" dǎodòng

捣固 dǎogù make firm by ramming or tamping: ～机 tamping tool

捣鼓 dǎogu 〈方言〉 ❶ fiddle with; meddle with: 他在～我的自来水笔。He is fiddling with my fountain pen. /不要～我的打字机。Don't meddle with my typewriter. ❷ buy and sell; deal or trade in: ～股票 deal in stocks /～点儿小买卖 buy and sell on a small scale

捣鬼 dǎoguǐ play tricks; do mischief: 此事有人在背后～。Some-

body must have played dirty tricks behind my back. / 贪污分子常常在账面上～。An embezzler often juggles with his accounts. / 你们在这儿捣什么鬼? What are you up to here?
捣毁 dǎohuǐ smash up; demolish; destroy: ～抢劫团伙的巢穴 destroy the lair of a robbers' band
捣臼 dǎojiù ❶ mortar ❷〈机械〉stamp box
捣矿机 dǎokuàngjī 〈矿业〉stamping mill; crushing mill
捣烂 dǎolàn pound sth. into pulp
捣乱 dǎoluàn ❶ make trouble; create a disturbance: ～会场 create a disturbance at the meeting / 有人故意～。Someone is deliberately making trouble. ❷ make trouble for; disturb: 他在忙, 你不要去～。He is busy. Don't disturb him. / 孩子老～, 叫妈妈不得安心。The child is always making mischief and will not give his mother a moment's rest.
捣乱电话 dǎoluàn diànhuà *also* "骚扰电话" sāorǎo diànhuà crank call: 打～的人 nuisance caller
捣乱分子 dǎoluànfènzǐ troublemaker
捣麻烦 dǎo máfan 〈口语〉create trouble; make things hard for: 这事还是经过法院公了为好, 免得日后有人～。It will be better to get the matter settled in court to prevent any future trouble.
捣弄 dǎonong ❶ toy with; fiddle with: ～纸牌 toy with cards / 他放下饭碗就～那些齿轮、轴承, 一会儿也闲不住。He gets down to cogwheels and bearings the moment he finishes his meal, without even a moment's break. ❷ *see* "倒弄❶❷" dǎonong
捣碎 dǎosuì pound to pieces: 把玉米～ pound corn to pieces
捣腾 dǎoteng *see* "倒腾" dǎoteng

导(導) dǎo

❶ lead; guide; channel: 向～ guide / 领～ leader / ～河入海 channel a river into the sea / ～向正路 guide on to the right path; set on the right course ❷ transmit; conduct: ～电 conduct electricity / ～热 transmit heat ❸ instruct; give guidance to: 教～ teach; instruct / 指～ guide; instruct / 诱～ induce; lead / 劝～ persuade; advise ❹ direct (a performance, etc.): ～一出戏 direct the production of a play
导板 dǎobǎn *see* "倒板" dǎobǎn
导标 dǎobiāo 〈交通〉beacon
导播 dǎobō direct and broadcast a programme on radio or TV
导槽 dǎocáo conduit ferrule; guide slot
导出单位 dǎochū dānwèi derived unit *see also* "国际单位制" guójì dānwèizhì
导词 dǎocí 〈语言〉introductory word
导磁率 dǎocílǜ *also* "磁导率" magnetic inductivity
导弹 dǎodàn guided missile: 地对地～ surface-to-surface missile / 地对空～ ground-to-air missile; surface-to-air missile (SAM) / 空对地～ air-to-ground missile / 空对空～ air-to-air missile / 空对水下～ air-to-underwater missile / 寻的制导～ homing guided missile / 红外线寻的制导～ infrared seeker / 反导弹～ antimissile missile; contra-missile / 截击～ interceptor missile / 防空～ antiaircraft missile; interceptor missile / 机载～ guided aircraft missile; guided air rocket / 雷达制导～ radar homing missile; radar guided missile / 潜艇发射的～ submarine-launched missile / 洲际弹道～ intercontinental ballistic missile (ICBM) / ～弹头 missile warhead / 远程～ long-range missile / 中程～ intermediate (*or* medium) range missile / 中远程～ long and intermediate-range missile; longer range intermediate missile / 短程～ short-range missile / 中短程～ short- and intermediate-range missile; shorter-range intermediate missile / 巡航～ cruise missile / 潘兴 II～ Pershing II missile / "毒刺"防空～ "Stinger" anti-aircraft missile / 民兵～ Minuteman missile / 北极星～ Polaris missile / 海神～ Poseidon missile / 响尾蛇～ Sidewinder missile / 麻雀～ Sparrow missile / 大力神～ Titan missile / 陶式～ Tow missile / SS-20～ SS-20 missile / 飞鱼～ Exocet / ～防御警报系统 MIDAS (Missile Defence Alarm System) / ～防御警报卫星 missile defence alarm satellite
导弹部队 dǎodàn bùduì missile force; missilemen
导弹电子搜索系统 dǎodàn diànzǐ sōusuǒ xìtǒng electronic missile acquisition system
导弹发射场 dǎodàn fāshèchǎng (missile) launching site
导弹发射井 dǎodàn fāshèjǐng launching silo
导弹发射器 dǎodàn fāshèqì missile launcher
导弹发射台 dǎodàn fāshètái (missile) launching pad
导弹跟踪船 dǎodàn gēnzōngchuán missile-tracking vessel
导弹核潜艇 dǎodàn héqiántǐng nuclear submarine armed with guided missiles
导弹基地 dǎodàn jīdì missile base
导弹库 dǎodànkù missile hangar
导弹驱逐舰 dǎodàn qūzhújiàn guided missile destroyer
导弹系统 dǎodàn xìtǒng guided missile system
导弹巡洋舰 dǎodàn xúnyángjiàn guided missile cruiser
导弹专家 dǎodàn zhuānjiā missileer; missileman
导电 dǎodiàn electric conduction: ～板 current-carrying plate / ～玻璃 conductive glass / ～状态 conduction state / ～银糊 conductive silver paste
导电率 dǎodiànlǜ conductivity; electroconductivity
导电塑料 dǎodiàn sùliào conductive plastic
导电体 dǎodiàntǐ electric conductor
导电橡胶 dǎodiàn xiàngjiāo conductive rubber
导电性 dǎodiànxìng electric conductivity; conductance; condutibility
导洞 dǎodòng pilot tunnel
导读 dǎodú guide to reading: 《世界名著～》 *Guide to World Classics*
导发 dǎofā lead to; induce; cause: ～事故 cause an accident / ～疾病 be conducive to disease
导风板 dǎofēngbǎn 〈航空〉baffle
导杆 dǎogǎn ❶〈机械〉pilot; guide bar or rod ❷〈印刷〉drop bar
导购 dǎogòu provide guidance for purchase: ～小姐 sales girl; shopping guide
导管 dǎoguǎn ❶〈机械〉conduit; pipe; duct: 冷冻～ cooling duct / 金属～ metal conduit ❷〈生物〉vessel; duct: ～分子 vessel element; vessel segment ❸〈医学〉catheter: 插入～ catheterize ❹〈植物〉vessel; trachea: ～植物 tracheophyta
导光体 dǎoguāngtǐ light conductor
导轨 dǎoguǐ 〈机械〉slideway; guide; guide rail; guide way: ～面 guide pass; track surface / ～罩 way-cover / ～磨床 slideway grinder
导辊 dǎogǔn guide roll; deflector roll
导函数 dǎohánshù 〈数学〉derived function; differential coefficient
导航 dǎoháng navigation: 为船舶～ navigate (*or* pilot) a ship / 雷达～ radar navigation / 天文～ celestial navigation / ～台 navigation (*or* guidance) station; nondirection radio beacon (NDB) / ～灯 range lights / ～卫星 navigational satellite / ～仪 avigraph; navigator / ～传感器 navigation sensor / ～数据库 navigational route database / ～计算机 navigation computer / ～设备 navigational aid
导航罗盘 dǎoháng luópán navigation or course-setting compass
导航卫星 dǎoháng wèixīng Navsat (navigation satellite)
导航员 dǎohángyuán navigator; pilot
导火索 dǎohuǒsuǒ 〈军事〉*see* "导火线❶"
导火线 dǎohuǒxiàn ❶ *also* "导火索" (blasting) fuse: 定时～ time fuse ❷ apparently insignificant incident leading to a big conflict: 奥国王储裴迪南大公遇刺是第一次世界大战的～。The assassination of the Austrian crown prince Archduke Francis Ferdinand touched off the First World War.
导坑 dǎokēng *also* "导孔" feed hole; guide pit; guide hole
导流 dǎoliú 〈水利〉diversion: ～隧道 diversion tunnel
导流工程 dǎoliú gōngchéng 〈水利〉training works
导轮 dǎolún 〈机械〉guide pulley; pilot wheel
导论 dǎolùn introduction; introductory remarks: ～课 introductory course / 《当代英国文学～》 *An Introduction to Contemporary British Literature*
导螺杆 dǎoluógǎn 〈机械〉driving screw; lead screw: ～驱动 lead-screw drive
导眠能 dǎomiánnéng 〈药学〉glutethimide
导纳 dǎonà 〈电工〉admittance
导尿 dǎoniào 〈医学〉catheterization
导尿管 dǎoniàoguǎn catheter
导盘 dǎopán 〈纺织〉guide disc; godet
导热 dǎorè 〈物理〉heat conduction: ～体 heat carrier / ～计 conductometer of heat / ～系数 thermal conductivity / ～能力 capacity of heat transmission
导伞 dǎosǎn 〈航空〉pilot chute
导纱杆 dǎoshāgǎn 〈纺织〉lever jack; locker jack
导纱针 dǎoshāzhēn 〈纺织〉sley point
导生制 dǎoshēngzhì monitorial system, a teaching method which requires good students to help poor ones
导师 dǎoshī ❶ tutor; adviser; supervisor: 博士生～ supervisor of

D

Ph.D candidates ❷ guide of a great cause; teacher; mentor:革命～prophet (*or* mentor) of a revolution
导师制 dǎoshīzhì tutorial system
导数 dǎoshù 〈数学〉derivative
导体 dǎotǐ 〈物理〉conductor:非～ nonconductor /半～ semiconductor /超～ super-conductor
导线 dǎoxiàn 〈电工〉lead; (conducting) wire:玻璃纤维～ fiberglass wire /～管 conduit /～荷载 conductor load
导向 dǎoxiàng ❶ head towards; make for; lead to:这次会谈～两国关系的正常化。The talks led to the normalization of relations between the two countries. ❷ lead; guide:这种火箭的～性能良好。This type of rocket has an excellent guidance system (*or* excellent directivity). /气垫火车也同火车一样,是靠路轨～的。Like ordinary trains, air-cushion trains are also guided by rails. ❸ orientation; direction:以市场为～ market-oriented /社会思潮的～ direction (*or* guidance) of social trends /舆论～ orientation of media; media guidance of public opinion
导向架 dǎoxiàngjià 〈机械〉leading truck
导向轮 dǎoxiànglún 〈交通〉directive wheel; steerable wheel
导泻 dǎoxiè 〈医学〉catharsis; purgation; laxation
导言 dǎoyán *also* "绪论" xùlùn preamble; foreword; introduction; introductory remarks
导演 dǎoyǎn ❶ direct (a film, play, etc.):他～了许多莎士比亚的戏剧。He directed many Shakespearean plays. ❷ director:她丈夫是电影～。Her husband is a film director.
导扬 dǎoyáng 〈书面〉advocate; propagate
导引 dǎoyǐn ❶ guide; lead; direct:我们由交通员～,安全到达目的地。With the liaison man as our guide, we reached our destination safely. ❷ direct or control the course of sth. with an instrument; navigate ❸ Chinese traditional body-building exercise which combines breathing control, body and limb movements, concentration of mind, local massage, etc.
导游 dǎoyóu ❶ conduct a sightseeing tour; guide a tour:这位小姐将为大家～。This young lady will guide us in the tour. ❷ tour guide
导游图 dǎoyóutú tourist map
导语 dǎoyǔ synopsis (of a long article, etc.)
导源 dǎoyuán ❶ (of a river) have its source in:黄河～于青海。The Yellow River rises in Qinghai Province. ❷ originate; derive:认识～于实践。Knowledge derives from practice.
导致 dǎozhì lead to; bring about; result in; cause:忽视安全措施～了这次事故。The negligence of safety measures resulted in this accident. /这个问题如不及时妥善解决将会～一场灾难。This problem, if not properly solved in time, will cause a disaster. /过分劳累会～心脏病的突发。Over exhaustion will bring on heart attacks. /骄傲～失败。Pride goes before a fall.

dào

盗 dào ❶ steal; rob; burgle; burglarize:监守自～ steal what is entrusted to one's care /采取防～措施 take precautions against theft, robbery or burglary /欺世～名 gain fame by deceiving the public; win undeserved fame by cheap means / 这家银行昨晚被～。The bank was robbed last night. ❷ thief; robber; burglar:强～ robber; burglar /海～ pirate; sea-rover /开门揖～ open one's door to invite the robbers in /窃国大～ arch usurper of state power
盗案 dào'àn case of robbery or burglary; case of larceny or theft
盗版 dàobǎn illegal copy; pirate copy; piracy:～小说 illegally copied novel; pirate copy of a novel /～影碟 illegally copied video disc; pirated video disc /～现象 phenomenon of illegal copying; illegal copying; (copy) piracy
盗伐 dàofá fell trees without official permission:～林木 illicit logging
盗犯 dàofàn thief; criminal who has committed larceny
盗匪 dàofěi bandit; robber:～窝儿 bandits' nest; bandits' lair /缉拿～ capture bandits; bring bandits to justice
盗汗 dàohàn 〈医学〉night sweat:出～ perspire during sleep
盗劫 dàojié rob; ransack:结伙～ group robbery; gang robbery
盗掘 dàojué dig or excavate illicitly:～坟墓 tomb robbery
盗寇 dàokòu bandit; robber
盗魁 dàokuí chieftain of a gang of bandits or robbers; ringleader
盗录 dàolù copy illegally (sound or video tape, etc.):～行为 piracy /这影带还未正式发行就被～了。Pirated copies of the video tape came out before its formal distribution.
盗卖 dàomài steal sth. and offer it for sale:～公物 steal and sell public property
盗名欺世 dàomíng-qīshì *also* "欺世盗名" steal fame by hoodwinking the public
盗墓 dàomù rob a grave or a tomb; commit grave robbery:～人 grave robber
盗骗 dàopiàn steal and cheat:～他人财物 appropriate sb.'s property by dishonourable or illegal means
盗窃 dàoqiè steal; burgle:～国家机密 steal state secrets /～案 theft; burglary /～犯 thief; burglar /～惯犯 hardened (*or* habitual) thief /～集团 gang of thieves
盗窃癖 dàoqièpǐ kleptomania:～患者 kleptomaniac
盗窃罪 dàoqièzuì 〈法律〉robbery; theft; larceny
盗取 dàoqǔ steal:～机密文件 steal confidential (*or* classified) documents
盗薮 dàosǒu 〈书面〉thieves' lair; den of robbers
盗听 dàotīng *also* "窃听" qiètīng ❶ eavesdrop ❷ wiretap; bug (sb.'s phone, etc.)
盗亦有道 dàoyìyǒudào even thieves or robbers have their own code of conduct or honour
盗印 dàoyìn copy illegally; pirate copies (of books, tapes, etc.):～者 pirate /～录像带是违法的。It is illegal to pirate videotapes.
盗用 dàoyòng embezzle; usurp:～公款 embezzle public funds /～他人名义 usurp sb.'s name
盗运 dàoyùn ship illicitly; steal and ship off:～珍贵文物 steal and ship off valuable historical relics
盗贼 dàozéi thieves; robbers; bandits:～蜂起。Robbers (*or* Bandits) rose like swarms of wasps.

悼 dào mourn; grieve:哀～死者 mourn for the deceased; grieve over sb.'s death /追～会 memorial meeting
悼词 dàocí *also* "悼辞" memorial speech:致～ deliver a memorial speech (*or* a funeral oration)
悼念 dàoniàn mourn; grieve over:～死者 mourn over sb.'s death; grieve for the deceased; express one's condolences upon sb.'s death /～文章 essay written in commemoration of the deceased /沉痛～这位艺术家的逝世 mourn with deep grief the death of the great artist /参加～的有各界人士五百多人。Over five hundred people from all circles took part in the funeral.
悼念日 dàoniànrì (US) Memorial Day, last Monday in May, on which those who died in active military service are remembered
悼亡 dàowáng 〈书面〉❶ mourn over one's deceased wife:～诗 poem written in memory of one's wife ❷ have lost one's wife
悼惜 dàoxī mourn; grieve over:对他的逝世,我们深为～。We were deeply grieved over his death (*or* passing away).
悼唁 dàoyàn mourn for the dead and express condolences to the bereaved:致电～ telegraph or cable a message of condolences

道[1] dào ❶ way; road; path:街～ street; road /岔～ side-road; side track; siding /便～ sidewalk; pavement /弯～ crooked road; turn /山间小～ mountain path /人行横～ zebra-crossing; pedestrian crossing /快车～ motorway; fast (traffic) lane; speedway /慢车～ slow (traffic) lane; lane for non-motor vehicles /自行车～ bicycle lane or track /机动车～ motorway /非机动车～ traffic lane for non-motor vehicles /跑～〈体育〉track; path; cinder path /轨～ orbit; railway track /铁～ railway /隧～ tunnel /通～ passage /康庄大～ broad way leading to prosperity /走正～ follow the correct path /走歪～ go astray /坏人当～ bad people hold sway ❷ course; channel:河～ course of a river /航～ (navigation) channel /下水～ sewer /煤气管～ gaspipe /收音机频～ radio channel ❸ orientation; way; justice:志同～合 share the same orientation and aspirations; have a common goal /养生之～ way to keep fit /为人之～ way to get along with people /以其人之～还治其人之身 deal with a man as he deals with you; pay sb. back in his own coin /王～ kingly way; rule by benevolence /霸～ way of a tyrant; rule by force /他讲得头头是～。It seems that his argument is well reasoned. /得～多助,失～寡助。He who has justice on his side enjoys abundant support, while he who has not finds little. *or* A just cause enjoys great support while an unjust one finds little. ❹ morality; virtue:仁～ kindness;

benevolence /惨无人～ savage; ruthless /替天行～ do justice in the name of God /他是个有～长者。He is a man of virtue. ❺ technique; skill; art: 医～ medical skill; art of healing /茶～ art of serving tea; tea ceremony ❻ (academic, religious, or ideolological) doctrine; principle: 孔孟之～ doctrines of Confucius and Mencius /传～ preach; give a sermon; work as a missionary /尊师重～ respect teachers and revere the established doctrines /～不同, 不相为谋。There is little common ground for understanding between people of different principles. ❼ Taoism; Taoist: 老～ Taoist priest /～服 robe worn by a Taoist priest /～观 Taoist temple ❽ superstitious sect: 会～门 superstitious sects and secret societies ❾ line: 画～儿 draw a line /斜～ slanting line /细～ thin line ❿〈量词〉(a) *of rivers and certain long and narrow things*: 一～沟 a gully /万～霞光 myriads of sun rays /一～闪电 a flash of lightning /一～痕迹 a mark /一～伤疤 a scar (b) *of a door, wall, etc.*: 设两～岗 post double lines of sentries /过三～门 pass through three entrances one after another /上两～锁 double lock /一～防风林 a line of windbreak-trees (c) *of an order, question, etc.*: 一～命令 an order /一～手谕 a hand-written instruction /十～数学题 ten mathematical problems (d) *indicating times*: 上三～漆 have it painted three times /上最后一～菜 serve the last course of a meal /还有一～手续 have one more formality to go through ⓫ (popular term for 忽米) centimillimetre ($\frac{1}{100,000}$ of a metre)

道² dào ❶ prefecture, an administrative area in the Tang Dynasty (when it was equivalent to the present province 省), the Qing Dynasty and early years of the Republic of China (when it was under the province) ❷ (DPRK) province: ～人民会议 Provincial People's Assembly /平安南～ South Pyongan /平安北～ North Pyongan /慈江～ Jagang /黄海南～ South Hwanghai /黄海北～ North Hwanghai /江原～ Kangwan /咸镜南～ South Hamgyong /咸镜北～ North Hamgyong /两江～ Yanggang ❸ (ROK) province: 京畿～ Kyongqi-Do /江原～ Kangwon-Do /忠清北～ Chungchongbuk-Do /忠清南～ Chungchongnam-Do /庆尚南～ Kyongsangnam-Do /全罗北～ Chollabuk-Do /全罗南～ Chollanam-Do /济州～ Cheju-Do ❹ (Japan) prefecture: 北海～ Hokkaido

道³ dào ❶ say; talk; speak: ～出实情 tell the truth /能说会～ have the gift of gab; have a glib tongue /常言～ as the saying goes /说三～四 gossip; make comments on sth. without real understanding; make unwarranted (*or* carping) remarks /说东～西 engage in small talk; make rambling conversation /说古～今 talk about things past and present ❷ express; extend: *see* "～喜" ❸ (usu. used in the early vernacular) say: 老翁～: "后会有期。" The old man said: "Till we meet again." ❹ suppose; think: 我～是纯棉的呢, 原来是化纤的。So it's polyester! I thought it was pure cotton.

道白 dàobái *also* "念白" niànbái 〈戏曲〉 spoken parts in an opera

道班 dàobān 〈交通〉 railway or highway maintenance squad: ～工人 railway (*or* highway) maintenance worker /～房 maintenance workers' dormitory

道别 dàobié ❶ say good-bye; bid farewell: 握手～ shake hands and say good-bye /过了十字路口, 两人才～。Only after they had passed the crossroads did they bid each other farewell. ❷ take leave of; say good-bye (to) before setting out on a journey: 一清早他到王大妈家～。Early in the morning he went to Aunt Wang's home to say good-bye.

道…不… dào…bù… 〈方言〉 *usu. followed by two monosyllabic adjectives opposite in meaning, indicating "neither... nor..."*: 道高不矮 neither tall nor short /道长不短 neither long nor short /道大不小 neither big nor small /道多不少 neither too many nor too few

道不拾遗 dàobùshíyí *also* "路不拾遗" lùbùshíyí no one pockets anything found on the road — honesty prevails everywhere

道不是 dào bùshi apologize: 他们一个劲地给他赔小心、～。They kept apologizing to him. /去, 给爷爷道个不是。Go and say "sorry" to grandpa.

道岔 dàochà ❶ branch road; feeder road ❷〈铁路〉 switch; points: 扳～ pull railway switches; switch a train onto another track /～区 switch area; switch section

道场 dàochǎng ❶ Taoist or Buddhist rites (performed to save the souls of the dead): 她为母亲做了一次～。She had Taoist rites performed for her deceased mother. *or* She sponsored services to lay her mother to rest. ❷ place where such rites are performed

道成肉身 dàochéng ròushēn 〈基督教〉 Incarnation (embodiment of God the Father in Jesus Christ as human flesh)

道床 dàochuáng 〈铁路〉 roadbed; track bed: 整体～ monolithic roadbed

道道儿 dàodaor ❶ line: 电视屏幕上怎么有这么多黑白～? Why are there so many black and white lines on the TV screen? ❷ way; method; idea: 他的～多, 问他去。Go and ask him as he is a resourceful man. /我们一定要想出新～来提高产品质量。We must try to find out a new way to improve the quality of the product. ❸ way to do or understand sth.; what's what; knack: 小伙子听了半天也没听出～来。Though he listened for a long time, the young man still could not make head or tail of it. /这里面大有～, 可不是一眼能看懂的。There's much more to it than meets the eye. /你得说出个～来呀! You've got to give a convincing explanation.

道德 dàodé morality; morals; ethics: 遵守公共～ observe public morality /～标准 moral standards /不～ immoral; unethical; without morals /～败坏 morally degenerate /体育～ sportsmanship /职业～ professional ethics; work ethic /商业～ business ethics

道德法庭 dàodé fǎtíng court of conscience

道德规范 dàodé guīfàn moral standards or criteria; code of ethics: 合乎～ conform to moral standards

道德教育 dàodé jiàoyù education in ethics; moral education

道德经 Dàodéjīng *also* "老子" Lǎozǐ *Daode Jing* (formerly translated as *Tao Te Ching*), or *Classic of the Way and Virtue* (main classic of Taoism, attributed to Laodan 老聃, or Laozi 老子 of the late Spring and Autumn Period)

道德品质 dàodé pǐnzhì moral character; moral qualities: ～高尚 of high (*or* lofty) moral character

道地 dàodì ❶ produced in its famous place of origin; authentic: ～药材 authentic medicinal herbs ❷ genuine; real; pure: 一口～的北京话 standard (*or* pure) Beijing speech

道钉 dàodīng ❶〈铁路〉 spike ❷ *also* "猫眼道钉" māoyǎn dàodīng 〈交通〉 highway reflector; cat's eye

道恩电解池 Dào'ēn diànjiěchí 〈化工〉 Down's cell

道恩法 dào'ēnfǎ 〈化工〉 Down's process

道尔贝降噪系统 Dào'ěrbèi jiàngzào xìtǒng 〈电子〉 Dolby system *see also* "杜比降噪系统" Dùbǐ jiàngzào xìtǒng

道尔顿 Dào'ěrdùn John Dalton (1766-1844), English chemist and physicist: ～定律 Dalton's law

道乏 dàofá extend thanks for taking the trouble: 他要亲自来给你～。He would like to call in person and thank you for the trouble you have taken on his behalf.

道法 dàofǎ ❶ Buddhist or Taoist magic art: ～高强 excel in magic art ❷〈书面〉 laws and institutions; reason and law

道高一尺, 魔高一丈 dào gāo yī chǐ, mó gāo yī zhàng as virtue rises one foot, vice rises ten; while the priest climbs a foot, the devil climbs ten; the more illumination, the more temptation

道格拉斯 Dàogélāsī Donald Douglas (1892-1981), American aircraft designer and founder of Douglas Aircraft Company (now MacDonald-Douglas)

道姑 dàogū Taoist nun

道冠 dàoguān hair-fastener of a Taoist

道观 dàoguàn Taoist temple

道光 Dàoguāng Daoguang, title of the reign (1821-1850) of Aisin Gioro Minning (爱新觉罗·旻宁, 1783-1850), 6th emperor of the Qing Dynasty, called reverently Qing Xuanzong (清宣宗) after death

道号 dàohào name of a Taoist

道贺 dàohè congratulate: 见到她时代为～。Please pass on my congratulations when you meet her.

道行 dàoheng supernatural skill possessed by a Buddhist or Taoist priest; skill or workmanship: ～深 great (supernatural) skill

道家 Dàojiā Taoist school (school of thought originating in the Spring and Autumn and Warring States Periods); Taoists

道教 Dàojiào 〈宗教〉 ❶ Taoism, indigenous Chinese religion founded by Zhang Daoling (张道陵) of the Eastern Han Dynasty ❷ (Japan) Dokyo

道经 dàojīng Taoist scriptures

道具 dàojù stage property; prop

道口儿 dàokǒur ❶ road junction: 到前面～向左拐 turn left at the

next junction ❷ level crossing:～堵了。The crossing is blocked.
道劳 dàoláo see "道乏"
道里 dàolǐ 〈书面〉❶ distance travelled; journey:～悠长 long journey ❷ usual length:相去不可以～计。The two are poles apart.
道力 dàolì inner strength one gains from practising Taoism:～不凡 have acquired super strength by practising Taoism
道理 dàoli ❶ truth; principle; hows and whys:针灸的～ principles (*or* theories) of acupuncture /他短短的几句话里有着深刻的～。There is profound truth in the brief remarks he made. /光讲～不讲实际是无用的。It's no use dwelling on abstract ideas without reference to reality. ❷ reason; argument:他的话听起来满有～。He sounds reasonable (*or* plausible). /这个～站不住脚。The argument is untenable. *or* The argument doesn't hold water. /你讲不出～,我们就不改变主意。We won't change our minds unless you can make your point convincingly. /与这种丧心病狂的人无～好讲。It's impossible to reason with such frenzied and heartless people. /请你别吵,有～好好讲嘛。I wish you would calm down and reason things out. ❸ way to do sth.; intention; plan:请放心,怎么办我自有～。Please set your mind at ease; I know how to go about this. /先把情况了解清楚再作～。It is essential to find out about everything before making any decision.
道林纸 dàolínzhǐ Dowling paper; glazed printing paper
道流 dàoliú Taoist school or sect:崇奉～ believe in a school of Taoism
道路 dàolù ❶ road; way; path:宽阔、平坦的～ broad, level road /给救护车让开～ make way for the ambulance /为两国关系正常化铺平～ pave the way for normalizing the relations between the two countries /为经济改革扫清～ clear the path (*or* way) for economic reform /为航天工业开辟一条新的～ blaze a trail (*or* path) for the space industry /前途是光明的,～是曲折的。The way ahead is full of twists and turns, but the prospects are bright. *or* The road is tortuous, but the future is bright. ❷ passage (between two places)
道路以目 dàolùyǐmù 〈书面〉friends can only exchange glances when they pass each other on the road (for fear of arousing suspicion and getting into trouble under despotic rule); be frightened into complete silence
道貌岸然 dàomào-ànrán be sanctimonious; appear as if one were a person of high morals:装出一副～的样子 pose as a person of high morals /他～,其实是一个彻头彻尾的伪君子。He is an out-and-out sanctimonious hypocrite.
道门 dàomén ❶ Taoism ❷ superstitious sects and secret societies
道木 dàomù *also* "枕木" zhěnmù 〈铁路〉sleeper; railway tie
道恼 dàonǎo (usu. used in the early vernacular) express condolences to the bereaved family; condole with
道袍 dàopáo Taoist robe
道破 dàopò point out frankly; reveal; lay bare:一语～其中的奥妙 unveil the mystery with one remark
道歉 dàoqiàn make an apology; apologize:他已～,这事就算完了吧。You may let the matter rest at that since he has apologized to you. /不要认为～会丢面子。Don't imagine that offering an apology is losing face.
道情 dàoqíng *daoqing*, chanting folk tales to the accompaniment of percussion instruments
道-琼斯股票指数 Dào-Qióngsī gǔpiào zhǐshù (US) Dow Jones index
道-琼斯平均指数 Dào-Qióngsī píngjūn zhǐshù (US) Dow Jones average
道-琼斯收盘平均指数 Dào-Qióngsī shōupán píngjūn zhǐshù (US) Dow Jones Closing Average
道扰 dàorǎo thank sb. for his hospitality or kind reception
道人 dàoren ❶〈旧语〉(respectful form of address for a Taoist priest) holy man ❷〈旧语〉Buddhist disciple ❸〈方言〉person who does the cleaning and other odd jobs in a Buddhist temple
道山 dàoshān ❶〈书面〉place where men of letters meet; cultural centre ❷ celestial place where the immortals live:久归～ died long ago
道氏理论 Dàoshì lǐlùn 〈经济〉Dow theory
道是 dàoshì be said:有～人逢喜事精神爽。As is said, one's spirits rise when there is good news. /故垒西边,人～,三国周郎赤壁。West of the old fortress, So people say, Is Lord Zhou's red cliff in the time of the Three Kingdoms. /～无情却有情。There is affection in spite of apparent indifference.
道士 dàoshi Taoist priest
道听途说 dàotīng-túshuō hearsay; rumour; gossip:世上最可笑的是那些"知识里手",有了～的一知半解,便自封为"天下第一"。The most ridiculous person in the world is the "know-all" who picks up a smattering of hearsay knowledge and proclaims himself "the world's number one authority".
道统 dàotǒng Confucian orthodoxy
道徒 dàotú Taoist; follower or adherent of Taoism
道喜 dàoxǐ congratulate:他儿子结婚,邻居们都去～。Neighbours called at his house to congratulate him on his son's marriage.
道谢 dàoxiè express thanks; extend gratitude; thank:改日登门～。I'll call to extend my appreciation some other day.
道叙 dàoxù talk; recount; relate:人们～着当年红军经过这里的事。People are talking about how the Red Army passed through here many years ago.
道学 dàoxué ❶ *also* "理学" lǐxué Confucian School of philosophy of the Song Dynasty; Neo-Confucianism ❷ of pedantic learning:～先生 Confucian moralist; pedantic scholar /假～ canting hypocrite
道牙 dàoyá *also* "道牙子" curb; curbstone
道眼 dàoyǎn 〈方言〉❶ way; idea:～多,会办事 be resourceful and adept in handling matters /他一眨眼就想出一个～来。In the twinkling of an eye he came up with a new idea. ❷ reason; argument; sense; truth:这封信里的～,比书里写的还高明。There is more sense in this letter than you can find in a whole book. ❸ implied meaning:妹妹听出姐姐话里有～,便会意地点点头。Sensing the implication of her elder sister's remarks, she nodded knowingly. ❹ footpath in the wilderness
道义 dàoyì morality and justice:～上的支持 moral support /这在～上说不过去。This cannot be justified on moral grounds.
道引 dàoyǐn see "导引❶❸" dǎoyǐn
道院 dàoyuàn ❶ Taoist hermitage or temple:山腰里有一座～。There is a Taoist temple half way up the mountain. ❷ monastery or convent
道藏 dàozàng collected Taoist scriptures
道砟 dàozhǎ 〈铁路〉ballast
道子 dàozi line; cut:划了个～ cut a line; get a scratch

焘(燾) dào see "帱" dào

帱(幬) dào 〈书面〉cover

see also chóu

纛 dào big army banner used in ancient times

到 dào ❶ arrive; reach:他今晚～。He is arriving tonight. /快～新年了。New Year's Day is drawing near. /～了! Here we are. /～! (in a roll call) Here! /人还没有～齐。Not everyone is here yet. /时间～了,停止吧。Time is up. Let's stop. /～这个地步,什么药也不管用了。No medicine would be of any use at this stage. ❷ up until; up to; by:从一～十 from one to ten /～目前为止我们还没有收到有关这次会议的消息。So far (*or* Up to now) we haven't received any information about the conference. /～今年六月他就满二十岁了。He'll be twenty in June. /一～秋季枫叶就变红了。Maple leaves turn red when (*or* by the time) autumn comes. /～年底我就能写完这本书。I'll have finished the book by the end of the year. ❸ leave for; go to:我要～上海去。I'm leaving for Shanghai. /她～过英格兰。She has been to England. ❹ *as the complement of a verb indicating the result of an action*:说～做～ do what one says; be as good as one's word /你在那儿看～他了吗? Did you see him there? /想不～今天下雪了。I didn't expect it would be snowing today. /真没想～在这儿遇见你。Fancy meeting you here. ❺ considerate; thoughtful; thorough:不～之处请原谅。I hope you will forgive me if I have not been thoughtful enough. /该说的我都说～了,还是不顶用。I've said all I could, but it still didn't work. ❻ (Dào) a surname
到岸价格 dào'àn jiàgé cost, insurance and freight (CIF)
到案 dào'àn 〈法律〉(those involved in a case) appear in court
到差 dàochāi 〈旧语〉arrive at one's post; assume office
到场 dàochǎng turn up; show up; be present:～作证 attend as a witness /会议快结束,他才～。He didn't turn up until the meeting

was about to end. /市长亲自～指挥救火。The mayor rushed to the spot in person to direct the firefighting.

到处 dàochù everywhere; at all places:～受欢迎 be welcomed wherever one goes; be popular everywhere /屋里的报刊～乱扔。The room is littered with newspapers and periodicals. /那本书我～都找过了,还是没找到。I looked high and low for the book but still couldn't find it. /瓶子破了,水流得～都是。The bottle is broken with water flowing all over the place. /这件事不要～乱传。Don't bandy it about.

到达 dàodá reach; arrive; get to:～目的地 arrive at one's destination /～终点站 get to the terminal /～顶峰 reach the summit; attain the height of one's ambition /火车应于晚上十点～。The train is due at 10 p.m.

到达港 dàodágǎng port of arrival

到达站 dàodázhàn destination

到底 dàodǐ ❶ to the end:坚持～ stick (*or* persevere) to the end /拼～ fight to the bitter end; fight to the last man /说～,哪都不如家里好。In the final analysis, east or west, home is best. ❷ finally; at last; in the end:几经邀请,他～还是没来。He never came despite repeated invitations. /沉默了许久,他～开口了。After a long silence, he finally spoke out. ❸〈副词〉*used in an interrogative sentence for emphasis*:你～想干什么? What on earth are you up to? /这男孩～为什么从家里跑出来? Why the devil did the boy run away from home? /～是什么使你这样想的? What exactly makes you think so? ❹ after all; when all is said and done:～还是这主意行。It's this idea that works after all.

到点 dàodiǎn time is up:就要～了,快点走吧。Time is running out. Let's hurry up.

到顶 dàodǐng reach the top or limit; leave no room for improvement:增产～ reach the ceiling (*or* outside limit) in increasing production /这技术我学了一辈子也没～。I've spent my whole life learning the technique but I think there is still room for improvement.

到会 dàohuì be present at a meeting; attend a meeting:～人数不多。Not many people showed up at the meeting. *or* There was a small attendance. /～人数不少。There was a good turn-out at the meeting.

到货 dàohuò arrival of goods; shipment:～通知 arrival notice /～验收 inspection of goods received

到货港 dàohuògǎng port of delivery

到家 dàojiā ❶ arrive home:他已平安～。He has arrived home safe and sound. ❷ be perfect; be excellent; reach a very high level:功夫练得还不～。Your skill is still far from perfect. /他这笔字儿写得真～了。You could say he reached perfection in writing these characters. *or* As a calligrapher, he is superb.

到来 dàolái arrival; advent:雨季的～ arrival of the monsoon (season) /我们在这里欢迎朋友的～。We are here to welcome our friends.

到了儿 dàoliǎor 〈方言〉in the end; finally:紧叮嘱他注意身体,～还是病了。I advised him most earnestly to take good care of himself, but for all that he came down with illness in the end.

到临 dàolín arrival; advent; approach:我们要加紧工作,迎接最后胜利的～。We must step up our efforts to usher in the final victory.

到期 dàoqī become due; expire; mature:～利息 interest due /～本金 matured principal /～付款 payable at maturity /～未付单据 overdue bill /～收益率 yield to maturity /这本借阅的杂志已～。This magazine is due for return. /合同何时～? When does the contract expire? /存款月底～。The deposit matures at the end of the month. /他的休假早～了。He has long overstayed his vacation.

到期日 dàoqīrì date due; expiring date; maturity date

到任 dàorèn assume a post; take office:新市长～后,市里的工作就有了起色。Since the new mayor came to office there has been some notable improvement in municipal work.

到什么山唱什么歌 dào shénme shān chàng shénme gē sing different songs on different mountains — adapt oneself to a new situation; be adaptable or flexible

到手 dàoshǒu have in one's possession; take possession of; get hold of:这些善本书终于搞～了。We have succeeded in getting these valuable books. /权力一～,他就原形毕露。No sooner was he in power than he showed his true features. /眼看就要～的冠军,可别让人家夺走了。We have the championship in our pocket and must make sure that it does not slip away.

到庭 dàotíng appear in court:～作证 appear in court as witness

到头 dàotóu at an end; to the end:走～向右拐。Turn right at the end of the street. /一年～总是忙 be busy all the year round /他认为自己在事业上算是～了,用不着再向前拼了。He believes he has reached the peak of his career and doesn't have to race on.

到头来 dàotóulái in the end; finally:违法者～总要受到法律制裁。Offenders will be punished by the law in the end. *or* The law is bound to catch up with all offenders in the end. /她机关算尽,陷害别人,～反害了自己。She tried in every way to harm other people, only to trip herself up in the end.

到位 dàowèi reach the designated place; be in place or position:突击排按时～。The shock platoon reached the designated position in time. /由于传球不～,北京队失去了一次进球的机会。Because the ball was badly placed, the Beijing team missed the opportunity to score a goal. /这个体操运动员的左手放得不～。This gymnast's left hand is not in the right position. /工程开始前,百分之五十的资金必须～。Fifty per cent of the promised capital must be in place before the project starts.

到职 dàozhí assume office; take up one's post

倒[1]

dào ❶ inverted; upside down; inverse:挂～了 hang sth. upside down /这几本书次序放～了。These books are placed in the wrong order. ❷ reverse; obverse; converse:帮～忙 make things even worse; be more of a hindrance than a help ❸ move backward; turn upside down; reverse; invert:～抽一口冷气 draw a cold breath; give a gasp of astonishment /把这张照片～过来。Turn the picture back. /灭火器不用时千万不要～过去。A fire-extinguisher must not be turned upside down unless you want to use it. ❹ tip; pour; dump:～垃圾 dump (*or* tip) rubbish; empty garbage /请把牛奶～到锅里。Pour milk into the pot, please. /他把背包里的东西都～在桌上。He emptied the contents of the rucksack onto the table.

倒[2]

dào 〈副词〉❶ *contrary to what is expected or thought*:你太客气,～显得见外了。You are so polite that you make me feel like a stranger. /原想省点钱,不料～花多了。I meant to be frugal but spent more than I had expected. /我本想调解一下他们之间的紧张关系,不料～把事情弄得更僵了。Instead of straightening out their relations, I made them even more strained than before. /屋子不算宽敞,收拾得～也干净。The room isn't large but it is kept clean and tidy. /说起这事来,我～认为是你错了。Speaking of the matter, I'm inclined to think that you are in the wrong. /她～不是这个意思。Actually, this is not really what she meant. ❷ *used to indicate contrast*:说说～容易,做起来可不那么简单。It's easier said than done. ❸ *used to indicate concession*:东西是贵,～还值得买。It is expensive but still worth the money. /他人～不错,就是脾气有些急。He is a nice man alright, only a bit short-tempered. ❹ *used to urge sb. to respond quickly, indicating impatience*:你～快点呀,我们要晚了。Hurry up or we'll be late. /发生了什么事,你～是说呀! What happened? Out with it!.

see also dǎo

倒背如流 dàobèi-rúliú can recite sth. backwards fluently — know sth. thoroughly by heart:他对一些生产上的数字熟悉得～。He is so familiar with the production figures that he can reel them off without a hitch.

倒背手 dàobèishǒu with one's hands clasped behind one; with hands on the back:他倒背着手在院子里走来走去。With his hands behind his back, he paced up and down in the courtyard.

倒憋气 dàobiēqì choke with anger:小王这句呛人的话把李主任噎了个～。Xiao Wang's sarcastic remarks rendered Director Li speechless with fury. *or* Director Li choked with anger at Xiao Wang's sarcastic remarks.

倒彩 dàocǎi booing; hooting; catcall:那个演员忘了台词,观众喝～。The audience made catcalls when the actor forgot his lines.

倒插门 dàochāmén 〈口语〉(of a man) live with wife's family:他女儿招了个～女婿。His daughter married a man who came to live with her family.

倒产 dàochǎn 〈医学〉footling presentation

倒车 dàochē ❶ back a car; back up:倒一倒车 back one's car a little /开历史～ turn back the wheel of history; put the clock back ❷〈机械〉back running;〈航海〉astern running

see also dǎochē

倒持太阿 dàochí-Tài'ē *also* "太阿倒持" hold the sword by the blade — surrender one's sword to another at one's own peril; hand over one's power unwisely and suffer as a consequence

倒垂 dàochuí hang upside down:～的柳丝,随风摆动。The twigs of the weeping willows are swaying gently in the breeze.

倒春寒 dàochūnhán unusually cold spell in an otherwise warm early spring

倒刺 dàocì ❶ hangnail; agnail ❷ barb (as on a fish hook)

倒打一耙 dàodǎ-yīpá make unfounded countercharges; put the blame on one's victim; recriminate:他不仅不承认自己的错误,反而～。Instead of admitting his own mistake he blamed his critics. /没想到他～,把事故的责任推到我身上。I did not expect that he would shift the blame on to me, holding me responsible for the accident.

倒带 dàodài rewind a cassette or a tape; reverse:自动～ auto-reverse; automatically rewind a cassette

倒带键 dàodàijiàn rewind button

倒挡 dàodǎng reverse gear

倒读数 dàodúshù countdown:卫星发射进入～。The countdown to the launching of the satellite began.

倒反 dàofǎn *also* "反倒"〈方言〉on the contrary:他平日很大方,这次～显得小气了。He is usually liberal with his money, but seemed rather stingy this time.

倒飞 dàofēi 〈航空〉inverted or upside-down flight

倒粪 dàofèn turn over a heap of manure or a compost heap

倒风 dàofēng wind blowing in through a chimney choked with smoke

倒挂 dàoguà ❶ hang upside down:他的左肩～着崭新的冲锋枪。A brand-new tommy gun was slung upside down across his left shoulder. /崖壁上古松～。Old pine trees hang downwards from the precipice. ❷ be contrary to the natural order of things; be in an inverted order:脑体～ distortion of the ratio in pay between mental and physical labour (i. e. manual labourers earn more than mental workers) /购销价格～ inverted purchasing and selling prices

倒挂金钟 dàoguà jīnzhōng *also* "吊钟花" diàozhōnghuā fuchsia

倒灌 dàoguàn (of river and sea water) flow from a lower to a higher level (as on morning and evening tides or as a result of a typhoon); flow backward:水管堵塞,污水～入室。Clogged pipes caused drain water to back up into the house.

倒果为因 dàoguǒ-wéiyīn take effect for cause; put the cart before the horse

倒过儿 dàoguòr 〈方言〉in the reverse order:这两个名字写～了。These two names have been reversed in their order. *or* They are written in the wrong order. /把这两个数字～就对了。To correct the mistake, you only have to change the order of these two numbers.

倒好儿 dàohǎor catcall; boo; hoot:喊～ make catcalls; boo and hoot

倒虹吸管 dàohóngxīguǎn *also* "倒虹管" inverted siphon

倒剪 dàojiǎn with one's hands clasped or tied behind one's back:～着双手在屋里兜圈子 walk about in the room with hands (clasped) behind one's back /把他～了胳膊,五花大绑牵了进来。He was led in trussed up, his hands tightly tied behind his back.

倒接 dàojiē 〈植物〉reverse graft

倒金字塔 dàojīnzìtǎ inverted pyramid

倒经 dàojīng *also* "逆经" nìjīng 〈医学〉menometastasis

倒卷 dàojuǎn 〈摄影〉rewind a film:自动～ automatic rewinding

倒苦水 dào kǔshuǐ vent or air one's grievances; pour out one's woes

倒立 dàolì ❶ stand upside down:纪念碑的影子～在水中。The monument is reflected upside down in the water. ❷ *also* "拿大顶" nádàdǐng 〈体育〉handstand:～行走 walk on one's hands /你会单手～吗? Can you do a handstand with one hand?

倒流 dàoliú flow backwards:河水～ flowing backwards of the water in a river /出口商品～ flow of exported goods back to their place of origin /人口～ backward flow of population (e.g. from sparsely populated to densely populated areas); reverse migration

倒卵形 dàoluǎnxíng (of leaves) in the shape of an egg placed upside down; obovate:～叶 obovate leaf

倒轮闸 dàolúnzhá brake at the back axle of a bicycle, applied by pedalling backwards; coaster brake; backpedalling brake

倒脉冲 dàomàichōng inverted impulse

倒赔 dàopéi lose (money) instead of making a profit; earn less than the cost:在这种情况下,不～就算是好的了。Under the circumstances, it would be good enough if you don't incur a loss. /他没有赚一分钱,却～了两万元。He lost 20,000 *yuan*, instead of making any profit.

倒片 dàopiàn rewind (a film):～机 rewinder

倒欠 dàoqiàn go into the deficit instead of gaining anything:他不但没有赚钱,反而～三千元。Instead of making a profit, he has run a debt of 3,000 *yuan*.

倒摄遗忘 dàoshè yíwàng 〈心理〉retroactive or retrograde amnesia

倒是 dàoshì 〈副词〉❶ *used to indicate contrast with what is usually true*:妹妹～比姐姐高。The younger sister is actually the taller of the two. ❷ *used to indicate, with a touch of criticism, what is contrary to fact*:他想得～容易,事情哪儿有那么好办! How can it be as easy as he thinks? ❸ *used for sth. unexpected*:有这样的事? 我～要听听。Is that true? Please tell me about it. ❹ *used to indicate concession*:住这儿交通～很方便,就是周围太嘈杂。There are handy transport facilities around, only it is too noisy. ❺ *used to indicate a turn in meaning*:这小说的内容一般,语言～很生动。The novel is just so-so in terms of content, but its language is quite vivid. ❻ *used to modify or tone down a preceding statement*:咱们能一起去,那～挺好。It would be nice if we could go together. / 你说他不肯去,这～不见得。You said he wouldn't go. Well, that may not necessarily be true. ❼ *used to press or question sb.*:你～说句话呀! Say something, will you! /你～去不去呀? Are you going or not?

倒收付息 dàoshōu fùxī 〈经济〉negative interest

倒数 dàoshǔ count in reverse order:～第一名 last one on a list; the worst /第五十八页～第二行 second line from the bottom on page fifty-eight /坐在～第二排 sit in the last row but one

倒数计时 dàoshǔ jìshí *see* "倒读数"

倒数 dàoshù 〈数学〉reciprocal:～比 reciprocal proportion /～式 reciprocal expression

倒算 dàosuàn *also* "反攻倒算" fǎngōng-dàosuàn 〈贬义〉counterattack (as by reactionaries) to settle old scores

倒锁 dàosuǒ lock sb. in from the outside; lock sb. out from the inside:孩子睡了,妈妈～上门,上街去买菜。The mother locked the sleeping child in and went shopping at the greengrocer's. /她怕他再来,就把门～上。She locked herself in for fear that he might come again.

倒踏门 dàotàmén *see* "倒插门"

倒提壶 dàotíhú *also* "狗舌草" gǒushécǎo hound's-tongue (*Cynoglossum*)

倒贴 dàotiē ❶ post upside down ❷ lose money (instead of making a profit); pay (instead of receiving):在竞争剧烈的市场里,我不得不削价贱卖,～五百元。In the competitive market, I had to cut the price of my goods and lose 500 *yuan* as a consequence. /这东西～些钱都没人要。Nobody would want this even with an accompanying gift of money. ❸ 〈俗语〉(of a woman) pay her paramour; keep a gigolo

倒退 dàotuì go backwards; fall back; retrogress:他～一步,再往前跳。He fell one step back before springing forward. /～是没有出路的。Retrogression leads only to a dead end. *or* Retrogression is no way out.

倒相 dàoxiàng 〈电子〉phase inversion:～放大器 inverting amplifier /～器 phase inverter

倒像 dàoxiàng 〈物理〉inverted image

倒行逆施 dàoxíng-nìshī try to put the clock back; go against the historical trend; push a reactionary policy; act perversely:法西斯的～从反面教育了人民。The perverse acts of the Fascists taught the people by negative example.

倒许 dàoxǔ perhaps on the contrary; but perhaps:别看他理科功课不好,学文科～合适。He is weak in science, but he may do fairly well in the humanities.

倒序词典 dàoxù cídiǎn reverse dictionary

倒叙 dàoxù 〈修辞〉flashback

倒悬 dàoxuán 〈书面〉hang by the feet — be in sore straits:解庶民于～ retrieve the ordinary people from their dire predicament

倒烟 dàoyān smoke blowing in through the chimney

倒仰儿 dàoyǎngr 〈方言〉fall backwards

倒阴 dàoyīn 〈方言〉(of wet weather) clear up and turn cloudy again

倒因为果 dàoyīn-wéiguǒ take cause for effect; reverse cause and effect; put the cart before the horse

倒影 dàoyǐng inverted image; inverted reflection in water:宝塔的～ reflection of a pagoda

倒映 dàoyìng inverted image of one object reflected on another;

reflect:晚霞～在江面上,像一片飘浮的红色薄雾。The sunset clouds as reflected in the river look like a whirling mass of coral mists. /西斜的太阳把人们～在地上的影子拉得挺长。The setting sun lengthened people's shadows across the ground.
倒栽葱 dàozāicōng fall headlong; fall head over heels:一个～,扎进水里 jump headlong into the water /他脚一滑,跌了个～。He slipped and fell full length.
倒找 dàozhǎo pay instead of receiving:这双鞋如有质量问题,我们不仅包换,还要～你双倍的钱。If there's anything wrong with the quality of the shoes, we guarantee to pay you twice the original price, as well as exchange them.
倒置 dàozhì place upside down; invert:本末～ place the superficial above the essential /轻重～ place the unimportant before the important /请勿～。Please don't place it upside down. *or* This end up.
倒置发动机 dàozhì fādòngjī 〈机械〉inverted engine
倒转 dàozhuǎn ❶ turn the other way round; reverse:～来说,如果我是你,我也会同意的。Well, if I were you, I'd agree too. ❷〈方言〉contrary to reason or one's expectation:你把时间搞错了,～来怪我。You have got the time wrong and now you put the blame on me.
倒转 dàozhuàn turn backwards; go backwards:历史的车轮不会～。You can never put the clock of history back.
倒装 dàozhuāng 〈语言〉inversion; inverted order
倒装词序 dàozhuāng cíxù 〈语言〉inverted word order
倒装句 dàozhuāngjù 〈语言〉inverted sentence
倒座儿 dàozuòr 〈方言〉❶ room opposite the principal rooms (usu. facing south) in a quadrangle courtyard ❷ (of a bus or ship) seat facing the rear

稻 dào rice; paddy:种～ grow rice; cultivate rice /割～ reap rice /早～ early rice /水～ paddy /旱～ upland rice /单季～ single harvest rice /双季～ double harvest rice /三季～ triple harvest rice /～鱼兼作 rice-fish cultivation
稻白叶枯病 dàobáiyèkūbìng bacterial blight of rice
稻苞虫 dàobāochóng rice plant skipper
稻草 dàocǎo rice straw:一捆～ a bundle of rice straw
稻草人 dàocǎorén scarecrow
稻恶苗病 dào'èmiáobìng Bakanae disease of rice
稻飞虱 dàofēishī planthopper
稻谷 dàogǔ paddy:～满仓。The granary is full of paddy.
稻黑粒病 dàohēilìbìng black kernel
稻糠 dàokāng rice chaff
稻壳 dàoké rice husk or hull
稻烂秧 dàolànyāng seedling blight of rice
稻粒 dàolì rice grain
稻螟虫 dàomíngchóng rice borer
稻曲病 dàoqūbìng false smut; green smut
稻鼠 dàoshǔ rice rat (*Oryzomys*)
稻树 dàoshù 〈植物〉fontanesia
see also "雪柳❶" xuěliǔ
稻穗 dàosuì rice ear
稻田 dàotián paddy-field; rice-field:～养鱼 fish culture in paddy-fields; rice-field fish cultivation /～皮炎〈医学〉paddy-field dermatitis
稻瘟病 dàowēnbìng *also* "稻热病" rice blast
稻纹枯病 dàowénkūbìng sheath and culm blight of rice
稻秧 dàoyāng rice shoots; rice seedlings
稻种 dàozhǒng rice seeds
稻子 dàozi rice; paddy
稻纵卷叶螟 dàozòngjuǎnyèmíng rice leaf roller
稻作 dàozuò cultivation of paddy

dē

嘚 dē 〈象声〉clatter of a horse's hoofs:骑警们骑着马在石板地上～～跑过。The horses of the mounted police clattered over the flagged street.
see also dēi
嘚啵 dēbo 〈方言〉garrulous; long-winded:我可没功夫听他瞎～。I've no time for his long-winded chitchat.
嘚嘚 dēde 〈方言〉talk on and on; chatter away:一点小事,别再～了。Don't keep chattering over such a trifle.

dé

锝 dé technetium (Tc), a kind of radioactive element

得[1] dé ❶ get; obtain; gain; win:获～硕士学位 obtain an MA degree /取～成功 gain success /多劳多～ the more you do, the more you get; more pay for more work /语文考试～了5分 get an A for the examination in Chinese /～了感冒 have caught cold; have a cold; have a touch of flu /不～要领 miss the point; fail to grasp the essentials /这荣誉～来不易。The honour was hard won. ❷ (of a calculation) result in; make; equal:三加六～九。Three plus six equals nine. /二四～八。Twice four is eight. *or* Two multiplied by four is eight. ❸ fit; proper:这种鞋跑步很～穿。This sort of shoes is suitable for jogging. ❹〈书面〉satisfied; complacent:扬扬自～ be self-satisfied; show smug complacency ❺ be finished; be done; be ready:饭～了吗? Is dinner ready? /这牛排～了,关火吧。The steak is done. Turn off the gas. ❻〈口语〉*used in ending a statement to indicate agreement or prohibition*:～,就照你说的办。All right! We'll do as you say. /～,就这么办。OK! Just go ahead. /～了,别再绕圈子了。That's enough. Don't beat about the bush any more. ❼ *used in a bad situation indicating helplessness*:～,我又把饭烧糊了。Look! I've burnt the rice again. /～,我又忘带钥匙了。Oh, shoot! I forgot the key again.

得[2] dé ❶ (*usu. in documents and stipulations*) *used before other verbs, indicating permission*:未经许可,不～入内。No admittance without permission. /本学期末考试不及格者～在下学期开学时补考一次。Those who failed (in) the final examination of this term may resit for it at the commencement of next term. ❷〈方言〉*used before other verbs, usually in the negative, indicating probability*:谈判没有一星期不～完。The negotiation will last for over a week. /这本书刚动手写,一年也不～完。I've just started writing the book. It'll take at least one year and more to complete.
see also de; děi
得便 débiàn when it's convenient:～请来我处一叙。Drop in for a chat when you're free. /这本书请你～捎给他。Please give this book to him at your convenience.
得标 débiāo *also* "中标" zhòngbiāo (in open tender) win the contract; be awarded the contract
得病 débìng fall ill; contract a disease:他～刚好。He has just recovered from his illness. /五岁以下儿童易得这种病。Children under five are liable to this disease.
得不偿失 débùchángshī the loss outweighs the gain; pay too dear for one's whistle; get more kicks than halfpence; the game is not worth the candle:我们不做～的买卖。We won't make a deal in which we lose more than we gain. /好高骛远,往往～。If you aim too high, the gain will not make up for the loss. /为了面子连命都搭上了,这才叫～呢! So you are going to risk your life just for the sake of face? The game is not really worth the candle!
得步进步 débù-jìnbù *see* "得寸进尺"
得采 décǎi 〈旧语〉win a (lottery) prize
得逞 déchěng 〈贬义〉succeed; have one's way; prevail:一旦他们推翻政府的阴谋～,国家就会大乱。Should their plot to overthrow the government succeed the country would be plunged into chaos. /我们要尽一切可能使劫机者不能～。We must do everything possible to defeat (*or* foil) the hijackers.
得宠 déchǒng 〈贬义〉be in sb.'s good graces; find favour with sb.:他那张巧嘴利舌使他在上司那儿很～。His glib tongue has found him favour with his boss. /家里孩子中数她最～。Of all the children she is her parents' favourite. /～思辱。Think of possible future humiliations while you bask in somebody's favour. *or* Prepare for a rainy day while the sun shines.
得出 déchū find (an answer); reach (a conclusion); obtain or yield (a result):无法～正确的答案 unable to find a correct answer (to a problem)/这项实验～了令人满意的结果。The experiment has yielded a gratifying result. /经过调查我们～了他是蒙受冤枉的结论。After the investigation we came to the conclusion that he had been wrongly accused.
得寸进尺 décùn-jìnchǐ reach out for a yard after taking an inch;

D

give him an inch and he'll take a mile; be insatiable: 你一味妥协,他就会~。Your endless concessions will only serve to whet his appetite for more gain. /他~,提出一连串不合理的要求。Driven by an insatiable desire he made unreasonable demands one after another. /我们必须慎重考虑才能同意他们的要求,以免他们以后~。We must think twice before we accede to their request; we may find that is the thin end of the wedge.

得当 dédàng proper; appropriate; suitable: 处理~ deal with a problem properly /措词~ properly (*or* aptly) worded /组织~ well-organized /文章详略~。The essay is appropriate in length.

得到 dédào get; obtain; receive; gain: ~一次学习机会 get an opportunity for study /~迅速答复 receive a prompt reply /~奖状 be awarded a certificate of merit /她~精心的照料,不久恢复了健康。She was well taken care of and soon nursed back to health. /杀人犯被处决了,~了他应有的下场。The murderer got what was coming to him, the death penalty. /植物得不到阳光就会死亡。Plants would die without sunshine.

得道 dédào ❶ uphold justice; have justice on one's side: ~者多助。He who upholds justice shall not be alone. ❷ (in Buddhism or Taoism) attain the highest state of spiritual enlightenment
see also "一人得道,鸡犬升天" yī rén dédào, jī-quǎn shēng tiān

得道多助,失道寡助 dédào duō zhù, shīdào guǎ zhù a just cause enjoys abundant support while an unjust cause finds little support

得法 défǎ work in the proper way; get the knack: 公司经营不~就可能破产。A company may go bankrupt if it isn't properly managed. /学习~,掌握所学的知识就快。You'll learn fast if you have the right approach.

得分 défēn score (in a game, exam, etc.): 连得三分 win three points in a row /一分未得 fail to score /主队~多于客队。The host team gained more points than the visiting team. /能把我考试的~告诉我吗? May I know my exam results?

得过且过 déguò-qiěguò muddle along or on; drift along: ~的人将一事无成。One who drifts along will accomplish nothing. /你不能总是这样敷衍了事,~。You should stop muddling along and working half-heartedly.

得计 déjì succeed in one's scheme: 他自以为~,其实别人早识破了他的鬼把戏。He thought he was clever but his trick had long been seen through.

得济 déjì reap a reward for one's efforts (as from one's children or relatives): 早生儿子早~是一种陈腐观念。It is an outmoded idea that a man has an early blessing if he has sons in early life.

得间 déjiàn 〈书面〉❶ have an opportunity; gain a breathing spell ❷ spot loopholes; find out flaws: 读书~ read critically (*or* with a critical mind)

得奖 déjiǎng win an award; be awarded a prize: ~者 prize-winner /~论文 prize-winning essay /哪幅画得了一等奖? Which painting won first prize?

得劲 déjìn ❶ feel well: 我浑身不~。I'm feeling weak all over. /这几天心里不~。I'm feeling not quite myself lately. ❷ fit for use; just right; handy: 我用这把螺丝刀~。This screw-driver is just right for me. /这钢笔用起来很~。The pen writes smoothly.

得救 déjiù be rescued; be saved: 几十个落水的人~了。Scores of people who had fallen into the water were brought to safety. *or* Scores of people were rescued from drowning. /大火被扑灭了,这批珍贵的文物~了。With the fire put out, the invaluable relics were preserved.

得克萨斯 Dékèsàsī Texas, a state in the southern United States, bordering on the Gulf of Mexico: ~共和国 Republic of Texas (1836-1845)

得克萨斯石油公司 Dékèsàsī Shíyóu Gōngsī *also* "德士古石油公司" Déshìgǔ Shíyóu Gōngsī (US) Texaco Incorporated

得空 dékòng be free; have leisure: ~去香山玩 make a trip to the Fragrant Hills when free /我说过要到上海去看望他,可总不~。I said I would go and see him in Shanghai, but I just couldn't find time.

得了 déle ❶ *also* "得啦" (usu. indicating prohibition, dismissal, or agreement) well, well; it's enough; come off it: ~,你懂什么赛马? Oh, come off it! What do you know about horse racing? /你~吧,谁信你的! Well! Well! Who do you think will believe you? /别啰嗦了,我去就~呗。Will you stop nagging? Isn't it enough that I go? ❷〈助词〉*used in a declarative sentence to indicate affirmation*: 你走~,不用惦记我。Please go and don't worry about me.
see also déliǎo

得力 délì ❶ benefit from; be effective: 我吃这药很~。The medicine is very effective for me. /他的身体健壮是~于多年锻炼。He is in robust health, as a result of years of physical exercises. ❷ get help from; be assisted by: 别忘了你得他的力不小。Remember you benefited a lot from his assistance. ❸ competent; capable: ~助手 competent assistant; righthand man ❹ strong; efficient: 办事~ do things efficiently /领导~ exercise strong leadership /措施~ effective measure

得利 délì benefit from; profit from: 鹬蚌相争,渔翁~。When the snipe and the clam grapple, it's the fisherman who stands to benefit. *or* It's the third party that benefits from a tussle.

得脸 déliǎn 〈口语〉❶ gain favour; be in favour: 在兄弟几个中间,他是~的一个。Among the boys in the family, he was the favourite of his parents. ❷ gain face; gain honour or praise: 这回她可~了。She certainly made a wonderful showing of herself this time! /上级夸你两句,你就觉得~了? So one or two words of praise from your boss have sent you to the skies, eh?

得了 déliǎo 〈叹词〉*often used in the negative or a rhetorical question to express astonishment or shock*: 这怎么~啊? Oh, my God! How will all this end? /不~! 房子着火了。Good Heavens! The house is on fire! /他吃错药了,这可不~。How disastrous! He took the wrong medicine.
see also déle

得陇望蜀 délǒng-wàngshǔ covet Sichuan after capturing Gansu — have insatiable desires; give him an inch and he'll ask for a mile; avarice knows no bound: ~,欺人太甚。These avaricious people are driving me mad.

得名 démíng ❶ name; be named: 镜湖以水清如镜而~。The Mirror Lake is so named because it is crystal clear like a mirror. ❷ gain fame; be famous; be known: 她以高深的文学造诣~。She is well known for her literary accomplishments.

得墨忒耳 Démòtè'ěr Demeter, goddess of agriculture and marriage in Greek mythology

得其所哉 déqísuǒzāi find one's proper place; feel at home: 把这老龟放回太湖,可谓~。Why don't we put the old turtle back in the Taihu Lake? He'll certainly feel at home there.

得气 déqì 〈中医〉bring about the desired sensation (in acupuncture treatment)

得人 dérén 〈书面〉use people properly: 让他理财,堪称~。Putting him in charge of financial matters is an example of employing people according to their talents.

得人儿 dérénr 〈方言〉*see* "得人心"

得人心 dé rénxīn enjoy public support: ~者得天下,失人心者失天下。Those who command popular support will gain state power; those who forfeit popular confidence will lose it. /厂长几项措施大~。The measures adopted by the factory manager are very popular among the staff and workers.

得色 désè complacent or smug look: 面有~ look satisfied; have an air of complacency

得神 déshén ❶〈中医〉generally good condition of a patient (indicating that his illness is easy to cure) ❷〈方言〉happy; cheerful: 这几日~,去了一趟香山。I have been in a good mood these days; so I made a trip to the Fragrant Hills.

得胜 déshèng triumph; win a victory: 旗开~ win victory in the first battle /~归来 return home in triumph; make a triumphal return

得胜回朝 déshèng-huícháo return to the imperial court with flying colours; make a triumphal return

得失 dé-shī ❶ gain and loss; success and failure: 权衡~ weigh gains and losses /~参半 gains balance losses; break even /斤斤计较个人~ care too much about personal gains and losses; be obsessed with personal interest ❷ advantages and disadvantages; merits and demerits: 两种路子各有~。Each of the two approaches has its advantages and disadvantages.

得时 déshí be in luck; ride the crest of fortune: 万物~。Everything is flourishing.

得势 déshì 〈贬义〉be in power; get the upper hand; be in the ascendant: 坏人~,好人遭殃。Good people suffer when bad people hold sway. /这个势利鬼,谁~就巴结谁。What a snob he is, cottoning up to whoever is in power.

得手 déshǒu ❶ go smoothly; succeed; come or bring off: 侥幸~ bring sth. off by sheer luck /进攻~。The attack was successful. /五

号队员扣球频频～。Player No. 5 made several successful smashes in a row. ❷ come in handy; be convenient and easy to use:这把镰刀很～,使起来又轻又快。The sickle is very handy; it is both light and sharp. /怎么～就怎么干。Do whatever is convenient for you.

得数 déshù 〈数学〉solution (of a mathematical problem):对～(as among students) compare the solutions; check the solutions with the key

得泰尔线路 Détài'ěr xiànlù 〈电子〉Datel circuit

得体 détǐ (of language or behaviour) appropriate to the occasion; befitting one's position or dignity:穿着～ be dressed appropriately /应对～ give the right answers /说得很不～ speak in a most improper manner

得天独厚 détiān-dúhòu enjoy special favours of nature; abound in gifts of nature; be richly endowed by nature:这里的水利资源～。This area enjoys the special favour of nature in water resources. /这孩子有着～的聪慧。The child was endowed with superior intelligence.

得悉 déxī learn about; hear of:～病体康复,不胜欣慰。Learning of your recovery, I felt very much relieved.

得闲 déxián *see* "得空"

得心应手 déxīn-yìngshǒu ❶ with high proficiency; with facility; in one's element:他的生活底子厚,写起小说来～。As he has a wide range of experience, he is really in his element when he writes a novel. ❷ handy; serviceable:这架打字机已经旧了,用起来却很～。The typewriter is old but quite serviceable (*or* handy).

得行 déxíng 〈方言〉be good at (sth.); be competent:下棋～ be good at chess /他很～,你就放心让他干吧。He is fully competent. You can entrust him with the job.

得幸 déxìng be in favour; (usu.) enjoy the favour of the king or emperor

得样儿 déyàngr 〈方言〉(of clothes) nice; fine:她这身打扮很～。This dress looks very becoming on her.

得宜 déyí proper; suitable; appropriate:剪裁～ properly cut /处置～ duly handle

得以 déyǐ so that; so as to; as a result:～生存的条件 conditions essential to survival /由于大家共同努力,我们的计划才～实现。Thanks to (*or* As a result of) our common effort, the plan was finally brought to fruition. /必须为科研人员创造条件,使科研工作～顺利进行。It is essential to create conditions for scientists to carry on their researches smoothly.

得益 déyì benefit from; profit from:读者的意见使他～不小。He benefited considerably from the readers' comments. /落实农业政策,使农民～。The implementation of the agricultural policy will benefit the farmers.

得意 déyì pleased with oneself; proud of oneself; complacent; conceited:～的微笑 complacent smile /自鸣～ be very much pleased with what one has done; preen oneself (on sth.) /刚有了点小成就,他就～起来了。He became conceited with some initial successes.

得意门生 déyì ménshēng favourite pupil or protégé

得意忘形 déyì-wàngxíng be intoxicated by one's success; get dizzy with success:胜利使他～。He got dizzy with success. *or* Success turned his head. /一个人～的时候常常会遭霉运。More often than not, bad luck approaches a person quietly when he is beside himself with elation. /她获奖之后颇有些～。She has been walking on air since she won the prize.

得意扬扬 déyì-yángyáng *also* "得意洋洋" look triumphant; be immensely proud

得意之作 déyìzhīzuò (author's) favourite work:作家自己的～往往与最出名的作品不一致。An author's favourite works are not necessarily his or her most popular ones.

得用 déyòng ❶ handy; fit for use:这把剪刀很～。This pair of scissors is quite handy. ❷ competent; able; capable:他们都是很～的助手。They are all able assistants.

得鱼忘筌 déyú-wàngquán forget the trap as soon as the fish is caught; forget the means by which the end is attained; forget the things or conditions which bring one success:丢掉了艰苦奋斗的精神就等于～。To throw away the spirit of arduous struggle is to forget how we have achieved success.

得知 dézhī learn; get to know; become acquainted with:从天气预报～,今天傍晚有阵雨。We have learnt from the weather forecast that there will be passing showers towards evening.

得志 dézhì achieve one's ambition; have a successful career:郁郁不～ depressed over one's lack of success; unhappy not to have achieved one's ambition /少年～ achieve success in the first flush of youth; make a name for oneself when young /小人～,无所不为。When a mean-minded fellow is in power, he is capable of anything.

得中 dézhōng moderate; appropriate; suitable:长短～ of moderate length

得中 dézhòng ❶ (as in imperial examinations) be a successful candidate ❷ draw a prize-winning ticket (in a lottery); get the winning number:～头奖 win first prize

得主 dézhǔ winner:诺贝尔奖～ winner of the Nobel Prize; Nobel Laureate

得罪 dézuì offend; displease; give offence to:这种人～不起。We cannot afford to offend such people. /有些尖锐的话他不说了,怕～人。He kept back some sharp criticism for fear of giving offence.

德(悳)

dé ❶ morality; virtue; moral character:公～ social morality; civic virtue; social responsibility /品～ moral character; moral integrity /～、智、体全面发展 all-round development of moral, intellectual, and physical education /缺～少才 lacking in virtue and ability ❷ mind; heart:离心离～ dissension and discord; disharmony and disunity /同心同～ of one heart and one mind ❸ kindness; favour:恩～ favour; kindness /感恩戴～ be deeply grateful; feel deeply indebted /以怨报～ return evil for good; repay kindness with ingratitude ❹ (Dé) (short for 德国 or 德意志) Germany:～方 German side ❺ (Dé) a surname

德昂族 Dé'ángzú De'ang nationality, living in Yunnan Province

德奥班德学院 Dé'àobāndé Xuéyuàn Deoband School, Islamic school established in India in 1867

德奥合并 Dé-Ào hébìng Anschluss, annexation of Austria by Germany in 1938

德拜 débài ❶ 〈物理〉debye ❷ (Débài) P. J. W. Debye (1884-1966), American physicist and chemist, Nobel Laureate for chemistry (1936):～效应 Debye effect /～定律 Debye's law

德班 Débān Durban, major seaport and resort of South Africa on the coast of Natal Province, formerly known as Port Natal

德比瓷器 Débǐ cíqì Derby ware, porcelain made in Derby, England, between 1750 and 1848

德比尔斯联合矿业公司 Débǐ'ěrsī Liánhé Kuàngyè Gōngsī De Beers Consolidated Mines, world's biggest producer of diamonds in South Africa

德才兼备 décái-jiānbèi combine ability with political integrity; have both moral integrity and professional competence; be a person of ability and virtue:～、年富力强的中青年干部 energetic, young and middle-aged cadres who possess both political integrity and ability

德操 décāo moral integrity; moral conduct and personal integrity; virtuous behaviour:优美的～ sterling moral integrity

德川幕府 Déchuān Mùfǔ *also* "江户幕府" Jiānghù Mùfǔ (Japan) Tokugawa Shogunate (1603-1867)

德川时代 Déchuān Shídài (Japan) Tokugawa Period (1603-1867)

德尔塔航空公司 Dé'ěrtǎ Hángkōng Gōngsī (US) Delta Airlines Inc.

德福雷斯特 Défúléisītè Lee De Forest (1873-1961), American physicist and electrical engineer, one of the pioneers of radio broadcasting

德干高原 Dégān Gāoyuán (India) Deccan Plateau

德高望重 dégāo-wàngzhòng (of old people) enjoy moral eminence and high esteem; be of good moral standing and undisputed reputation

德国 Déguó Germany; Deutschland:～人 German /～的统一 unification of Germany /～马克 German mark; *Deutschmark* /～国会 *Reichstag* /～国家银行 *Reichsbank*

德国百科全书 Déguó Bǎikē Quánshū *Konversationslexikon*

德国国防军 Déguó guófángjūn 〈旧语〉*Reichswehr* (1919-1935)

德黑兰 Déhēilán Tehran or Teheran, capital of Iran:～会议 Tehran Conference of 1943 /～宣言 Proclamation of Tehran (1943)

德化 déhuà 〈旧语〉inculcate virtue by one's example; educate the public by inculcating virtue

德化瓷 Déhuàcí Dehua porcelain, white china made in Dehua, Fujian Province

德拉古法典 Délāgǔ Fǎdiǎn Draconian code (600 BC), laws codified by Draco in Athens, notorious for their severity

德莱塞 Déláisài Theodore Dreiser (1871-1945), American novel-

D

ist whose works include *Sister Carrie* (1900), *An American Tragedy* (1925), etc.

德兰士瓦省 Délánshìwǎshěng Transvaal, northernmost province of South Africa rich in mineral resources

德勒克吕泽 Délèkèlǚzé Louis-Charles Delescluze (1809-1871), French revolutionary and one of the leaders of the Paris Commune

德雷克海峡 Déléikè Hǎixiá Drake Passage, channel seperating South America from the Antarctic and named after Sir Francis Drake

德里 Délǐ Delhi, capital of India：新～ New Delhi

德鲁兹教派 Délǔzī Jiàopài Druzes, political and religious sect of Muslim origin

德谟克拉西 démókèlāxī (transliteration) democracy

德色 désè airs of a benefactor：面有～ put on airs of a benefactor

德苏互不侵犯条约 Dé-Sū Hùbùqīnfàn Tiáoyuē German-Soviet Nonaggression Pact, also known as the Ribbentrop-Molotov Pact (1939)

德王 Déwáng De Wang (formerly translated as Teh Wang) or Prince Demchukdongrub (1902-1966), head of the puppet regime propped up by Japan in Inner Mongolia during China's War of Resistance Against Japanese Aggression (1937-1945)

D

德望 déwàng virtue and prestige：他素有～，堪当大任。A man of virtue held in high esteem by the public, he is capable of shouldering great responsibility.

德文 Déwén ❶ German (language) ❷ Devon, county in southwestern England：～郡 Devonshire

德行 déxíng moral conduct; moral integrity：他很注意～修养。He is punctilious about the cultivation of his moral conduct.

德行 déxing (of manner, behaviour, etc.) disgusting; revolting; repulsive; repellent：瞧他那～。Look, how repulsive the chap is!

德性 déxìng ❶ moral character：她眉宇间充满怜悯慈爱，是一个～高尚的老妇人。Her eyes beaming with compassion and benevolent love, she is an old lady of lofty virtue. ❷ *see* "德行" déxing

德意志 Déyìzhì Germany; Deutschland：～人 German; *Deutschen* /～帝国 *Deutsches Reich*

德意志联邦共和国 Déyìzhì Liánbāng Gònghéguó Federal Republic of Germany

德意志民主共和国 Déyìzhì Mínzhǔ Gònghéguó German Democratic Republic (1949-1990)

德意志通讯社 Déyìzhì Tōngxùnshè *Allgemeiner Deutscher Nachrichtendienst* (ADN) (of the former German Democratic Republic)

德意志新闻社 Déyìzhì Xīnwénshè *Deutsche Presse-Agentur* (DPA)

德语 Déyǔ German (language)

德育 déyù moral education：既要注重智育也要重视～。Pay attention to both intellectual training and moral education.

德泽 dézé 〈书面〉favour; grace; bounty

德政 dézhèng political measure beneficial to the well-being of the people; popular political measure：解决本市饮用水净化问题，是前任市长的一大～。Purification of drinking water for the citizens was one of the most popular measures taken by the former mayor.

德治 dézhì (as advocated by Confucians) rule of virtue; benevolent rule; government by virtue

de

底 de *see* "的[1]❶(b)" de
see also dǐ

地 de 〈助词〉*used after an adjective or a phrase to form an adverbial adjunct before the verb*：雪花轻轻～落在树叶上。Snow flakes fell gently on the leaves. /他一阵风～跑了出去。He rushed out like a gust of wind. /天渐渐～变暖。It is getting warm.
see also dì

的[1] de 〈助词〉❶ *used after an attribute* (a) *when the attribute modifies the noun in the usual way*：圆圆～脸 oval face /古老～文明 ancient civilization /铁～纪律 iron discipline /担心～事情 worrisome problem /要考虑～问题 problem that requires consideration /破碎～玻璃片 pieces of broken glass /我们所追求～目标 goal we are after /我读过～一部小说 novel I have read (b) *when the attribute indicates possession*：他～父母 his parents /我～一位同事 a colleague of mine (c) *when the attribute is a personal pronoun or a name, and the modified noun indicates role or position*：你怎样认识你丈夫的？谁～介绍人？How did you meet your husband? Who played Cupid for you? /今天是我～东。It's my treat today. /这出戏是刘洪～主角，王山～配角。Liu Hong is the leading man in the play while Wang Shan plays a supporting role. (d) *when the attribute is a personal pronoun or a noun standing for a person, and the modified noun indicates the action received by the former*：开新郎～玩笑 crack a joke on the bridegroom /别尽看我～笑话，帮帮我。Don't just stand by and laugh at me. Give me a hand. ❷ *used at the end of a nominal structure* (*equivalent to a noun phrase*) (a) *to substitute for sth. or sb. already mentioned*：这张票是我～，那张票是你～。This ticket is mine while that one is yours. /我买了一斤红枣，有好～，也有坏～。I've bought one *jin* of dates, some good, some not so good. (b) *to indicate a class or category of people or things*：理发～ barber; hair-dresser /送信～ postman; messenger /值班～ person on duty /受伤～要马上转移。The wounded will have to be evacuated immediately. /去参观展览～在门口集合。Those who are visiting the exhibition will meet at the gate. /吃～、穿～、用～都不缺。We have no shortage of food, clothing or any other daily necessities. (c) *to emphasize what precedes it*：大星期天～，怎么不出去玩玩儿？Why don't you go out and have a good time, today being Sunday? /这里用不着你，你只管干你～去。You have no business to be here. Go and get down to your own work. ❸ *used between identical verbs, adjectives, etc. to constitute a sequence of contrasts*：说～说，笑～笑。Some talk while others laugh. /大～大，小～小。The big ones are too big while the small ones are too small. ❹ *used between a verb* (*of past time*) *and its object for emphasis*：是老马发～言，我可没吭气儿。It was Lao Ma who spoke at the meeting. I didn't say anything. /她是上个月结～婚。It was last month that she got married. /我们是严格按规定作～处理。We handled the matter strictly according to the regulations. ❺ *used at the end of a statement to indicate certainty*：这件事我是知道～。True, I know about this matter. /熊猫一般是不吃肉～。As a rule, pandas don't eat meat. *or* Pandas are usually not carnivorous. /你真够精明～！You are really smart! ❻ *used after words or phrases belonging to the same part of speech to imply further enumeration*：破铜烂铁～，他捡来一大筐。He picked up a basketful of scrap iron and stuff. /钢笔、本子～都放在书包里。Put into your satchel pens, exercise-books and the like. /她一天尽道张家长李家短～。She is forever gossiping about this neighbour or that. ❼ *used between two numerals* (a) *to indicate multiplication*：两米～四米，是八平米。Two metres by four is eight square metres. (b) 〈方言〉*to indicate addition*：两元～五元，共七元。Two *yuan* plus five *yuan* is seven *yuan*.

的[2] de *see* "得❷❸" de
see also dí；dì

的话 dehuà 〈助词〉*used at the end of a conditional clause*：要是你认为有必要～，我一定设法去办。If you think it's necessary, I'll do my best to get it done. /明天有空～，我就去。I'll go if I have time tomorrow. /你同意当然好，不然～，就得另找人。It would be nice if you agree. Otherwise I would have to get somebody else.

得 de 〈助词〉❶ *used after certain verbs to indicate possibility*：这种蘑菇吃～。Mushrooms of this kind are edible. /这东西晒～晒不～？Can we dry it in the sun or not? /篮子里有鸡蛋，压不～。There are eggs in the basket. Don't press it. ❷ *used between a verb and its complement to indicate possibility*：买～起 can afford sth. /办～到 can do sth. /过～去 passable; so-so /你到底拿～动还是拿不动？Can you carry this or not? ❸ *used after a verb or an adjective to introduce a complement of result or degree*：辣～狠 be terribly hot /甜～不厉害 not very sweet /玩～痛快 enjoy oneself to one's heart's content; have a wonderful time /疼～打哆嗦 shiver with pain /风刮～很大。The wind is blowing hard. /这男孩子写字写～很好。The boy writes an excellent hand. ❹ (usu. used in the early vernacular) *after a verb to indicate the completion of an action*：出～门来 have come out of the house
see also dé；děi

脦 de *also* te *see* "肋脦" lēde

dēi

嘚 dēi sound to urge on a donkey or mule
see also dē

děi

得 děi ❶ need; require; take:骑车来回～一个半小时。It will take an hour and a half to make a return journey by bicycle. /这事～你来做。You will have to handle the matter yourself. /买个新的,至少～五十元。It will cost at least 50 *yuan* to buy a new one. ❷ must; have to:要取得好成绩,就～努力学习。One must study hard to achieve good results. /你一个人在外,遇事就～自己拿主意,不用写信回来问我了。Since you'll be away by yourself, you'll have to make your own decision when any problem arises, instead of writing home to consult me. ❸ will; be sure to:他准～来。He is sure to come. /这么晚才回来,妈又～说你了。You came back so late. I'm sure mother will take you to task again. /要不快走,我们就～误火车了。Hurry up or we'll miss the train. ❹〈方言〉comfortable; cozy; contented:这床睡着真～。How cozy it is to sleep on this bed!
see also dé; de

得亏 děikuī 〈方言〉fortunately; luckily:～他及时赶来,不然局势就控制不住了。Fortunately, he came in time. Otherwise, things would have gone out of hand.

dèn

扽(撜) dèn ❶ pull (at both ends, or at one end with the other fixed); tug; yank:使劲儿～ pull hard /把绳子～直 pull a rope straight (*or* taut) /把衣服～平 pull out wrinkles on clothes /感到袖子被人～了一把 feel a tug at one's sleeve /从床上把他～起来 drag him out of bed /大衣扣子给～掉了。The button was yanked off the coat. ❷〈方言〉grasp tightly; pull hard; tug hard:你～住了,不要松手。Pull it hard and don't let go.

dēng

灯(燈) dēng ❶ lamp; light; lantern:煤油～ kerosene lamp; oil lamp /电～ electric lamp or light /日光～ fluorescent lamp /彩～ coloured lamp /宫～ palace lantern /马～ barn lantern /探照～ searchlight /霓虹～ neon light /台～ desk lamp /床头～ bedside lamp /落地～ floor lamp; standard lamp /壁～ wall light; bracket light /吊～ pendant light /枝形吊～ chandelier /顶～ ceiling lamp /路～ street lamp; road lamp /指示～ pilot light; indicator lamp /车～ (car) light /尾～ tail light (or lamp) /矿～ miner's lamp /闪光～ flash-light; flash /无影～ shadowless lamp /航标～ navigation light /红绿～ traffic lights /华～ colourfully decorated lantern /冰～ ice lantern /水晶～ crystal lamp /幻～ magic lamp show; slide show /～下夜读 read by lamplight /不是省油的～〈俗语〉lamp that consumes too much oil — difficult person ❷ burner:酒精～ alcohol burner; spirit lamp /本生～ Bunsen burner ❸〈俗语〉valve; tube:五～收音机 five-valve radio set

灯标 dēngbiāo ❶ beacon light ❷ (electrically) lighted decorations or sign

灯彩 dēngcǎi ❶ coloured lantern making:宫灯是北京著名的～。Beijing is well-known for its palace lantern making. ❷ coloured lanterns (formerly used on the stage):满台～。The stage is decorated with many coloured lanterns. ❸ decorative coloured lanterns and lights:国庆节用的～ coloured lanterns and lights for National Day Celebrations

灯草 dēngcǎo rush (used as lampwick)

灯船 dēngchuán lightship; light vessel

灯蛾 dēng'é moth that flits around a lamp

灯蛾扑火 dēng'é-pūhuǒ moth flying into the flame only to get itself burnt to death; be fatally attracted to one's destruction; bring destruction upon oneself

灯管儿 dēngguǎnr 〈口语〉fluorescent lamp:这个日光灯坏了,换个～吧。This daylight lamp is broken. Let's have a new one.

灯光 dēngguāng ❶ lamplight:柔和的～ soft light /～刺眼。The light is dazzling. ❷ (stage) lighting:～布景 lighting and scenery /舞台～ stage lights; lighting /～师 juicer /～渐暗 lights fade to dark; lights slowly dim /～太强。The light is too strong.

灯光捕鱼 dēngguāng bǔyú torch fishing

灯光球场 dēngguāng qiúchǎng floodlit or illuminated court, field, etc.

灯光诱杀 dēngguāng yòushā 〈农业〉light trap; light trapping

灯红酒绿 dēnghóng-jiǔlǜ red lanterns and green wine — scene of feasting and revelry; scene of debauchery; night scene of colour and bustle:过着～的生活 lead a life of luxury or debauchery

灯虎 dēnghǔ *see* "灯谜"

灯花 dēnghuā snuff (of a candlewick):～报喜。A lucky snuff is an omen of happiness.

灯会 dēnghuì *also* "灯展" lantern show; lantern festival

灯火 dēnghuǒ lights:万家～ myriad of twinkling lights (e.g. in a city) /不见一星～。Not a single light is visible anywhere.

灯火管制 dēnghuǒ guǎnzhì blackout

灯火辉煌 dēnghuǒ huīhuáng brilliantly lit or illuminated; ablaze with lights

灯架 dēngjià lamp bracket; lamp holder

灯节 Dēngjié Lantern Festival (15th of the first lunar month)

灯具 dēngjù lamps and lanterns

灯口 dēngkǒu ❶ socket ❷ bulb holder

灯亮儿 dēngliàngr lights; illumination of lights:漆黑的夜晚,连个～也没有。It was a pitch-dark night when not even a beam of lamplight was discernible. /把窗台上的～挪到桌子上。Please move the lamp on the windowsill onto the table.

灯笼 dēnglong lantern:这种丈夫打着～也难找啊。Such a husband is one in a million.

灯笼椒 dēnglongjiāo 〈方言〉*also* "柿子椒" shìzijiāo bell pepper; sweet pepper

灯笼裤 dēnglongkù sweat pants; knee-length or ankle-length loose sports trousers:穿着～的武术队员 martial artists in sweat pants

灯笼鱼 dēnglongyú lantern fish (*Myctophidae*)

灯谜 dēngmí riddles written on lanterns; lantern riddles:猜～ guess a lantern riddle

灯苗 dēngmiáo tongue of a flame (of a kerosene lamp)

灯明 dēngmíng illumination of lights; lamplight:远处见有～,急忙走去一看,只是个小作坊。There was a spot of light in the distance, and when they hurried on they found it was merely a small workshop.

灯捻 dēngniǎn *also* "灯捻子" wick; lampwick

灯泡 dēngpào *also* "灯泡子" light bulb; (electric) bulb:螺口～ screw socket bulb /卡口～ bayonet bulb /乳白～ opal bulb /25 瓦的～ 25 watt bulb

灯檠 dēngqíng lampstand; lamp holder; lamp bracket

灯伞 dēngsǎn umbrella lampshade

灯市 dēngshì lantern fair:逛～ have a look around the lantern fair

灯丝 dēngsī filament (in a light bulb or valve):这个灯泡的～断了。The filament in this bulb is broken.

灯丝功率 dēngsī gōnglǜ filament wattage; heater power

灯塔 dēngtǎ lighthouse; beacon

灯台 dēngtái lampstand

灯台树 dēngtáishù *also* "梾木" láimù large-leaved dogwood (*Cornus macrophylla*)

灯头 dēngtóu ❶ lamp holder; electric light socket:螺丝口的～ screw socket ❷ number of lamps:客厅里有三个～。There are three lamps in the sitting room. ❸ kerosene lamp holder for the wick and chimney

灯夕 dēngxī *also* "灯宵" night of the 15th of the first lunar month; Lantern Festival Night

灯心 dēngxīn *also* "灯芯" lampwick; wick

灯心草 dēngxīncǎo 〈植物〉rush

灯心虹吸输送 dēngxīn hóngxī shūsòng wick feeding

灯心绒 dēngxīnróng *also* "条绒" tiáoróng 〈纺织〉corduroy

灯芯 dēngxīn *see* "灯心"

灯影 dēngyǐng ❶ lamplight:暗淡的～ dim lamplight ❷ shadow

D

cast by an object blocking the light:～里突然钻出了一个小姑娘。A little girl bounced out of the shadows of the lamplight.

灯油 dēngyóu lamp-oil; kerosene; paraffin oil

灯语 dēngyǔ lamp signal

灯盏 dēngzhǎn oil lamps (minus their chimneys)

灯展 dēngzhǎn *see* "灯会"

灯罩 dēngzhào *also* "灯罩子" lampshade; chimney (of a kerosene lamp, etc.):这油灯的～打碎了。The lamp-chimney is broken.

灯烛 dēngzhú lights:～通明 brilliantly illuminated

灯炷 dēngzhù lampwick; candlewick; wick

灯柱 dēngzhù lampost

灯座 dēngzuò lamp or lantern stand

登[1] dēng ❶ climb; ascend; mount; scale (a height):～楼 climb stairs; go upstairs /～上讲台 mount the platform; become a teacher /～上顶峰 reach the summit (*or* the pinnacle of success) /一步～天 ascend to the heaven with a single step — attain the zenith of power in one jump ❷ publish; record; enter:～上光荣榜 be entered (*or* placed) in the roll of honour /～广告 advertise (in a newspaper) /本期杂志～有他的文章。The current issue of the magazine carries an article by him. /他的事迹昨天～了《人民日报》了。His good deeds were reported in yesterday's *People's Daily*. ❸ (of grain) ripen (so that it may be harvested and taken to the threshing ground):五谷丰～ bumper harvest of all the cereals

登[2] dēng ❶ tread; step; stand:～在椅子上擦灯罩 stand on a chair cleaning the lampshade ❷ put on; wear (shoes or trousers):脚～长统靴 wear a pair of high boots /他～上鞋就跑。He hurriedly put on his shoes and rushed out. ❸ press down with the foot; pedal:～三轮车 pedal a tricycle /～油门 press (down) the accelerator (of a car)/～自行车 ride a bicycle /～缝纫机 work on a sewing machine

登岸 dēng'àn land; disembark; go ashore:弃舟～ leave a ship and disembark

登报 dēngbào publish in the newspaper; appear in the newspaper:～声明 make a statement in the newspaper /这场火灾～了。The newspapers reported the fire.

登场 dēngcháng (of grain) be gathered and taken to the threshing ground:收拾好场院,准备小麦～ clean up the threshing ground for the wheat crops

登场 dēngchǎng come or go on stage; enter:粉墨～ make oneself up and go on stage; appear on the stage in full make-up /小丑～。Enter the clown. /这个戏的～人物多达五、六十人。The play has a cast of up to fifty or sixty persons. /她第一次～就引起了行家的注意。Her début on the stage drew the immediate attention of the professional critics.

登场人物 dēngchǎng rénwù characters in a play; dramatis personae

登程 dēngchéng set off; set out; start off on a journey:收拾行装,准备～。Pack up and get ready for the journey.

登第 dēngdì 〈旧语〉 pass imperial civil examinations, esp. the palace examination

登峰造极 dēngfēng-zàojí (of skill, learning, etc.) reach the acme of perfection; reach the pinnacle of fame; reach the limit:石桥建造之精巧,真是～了。The elegant structure of the stone bridge is a supreme embodiment of human ingenuity. /其阴险毒辣,可谓～。He is sinister and ruthless in the extreme. *or* He is a past master in treachery and ruthlessness.

登高 dēnggāo ❶ ascend a height; climb up:～望远 ascend a height to enjoy a distant view /～必跌重 the higher the climb the harder the fall ❷ climb a mountain on the Double Ninth Festival (9th day of the 9th lunar month)

登革热 dēnggérè *also* "骨痛病" gǔtòngbìng 〈医学〉 dengue fever

登机 dēngjī board an airplane

登机牌 dēngjīpái boarding-card;boarding-pass

登机入口 dēngjī rùkǒu boarding gate

登基 dēngjī mount the throne; be enthroned:～大典 ceremony at which a king or queen ascends the throne; coronation

登极 dēngjí *see* "登基"

登记 dēngjì register; enter one's name; check in:～财产 register one's property /户口～ residence registration /结婚～ marriage registration /～入册 register; make an entry in a register /～住宿 check in (at a hotel) /～借书 check out a book from the library /～图书 keep a record of the books in a library /请到大会秘书处～。Please check in at the secretariat of the conference. *or* Please register with the secretariat of the conference.

登记簿 dēngjìbù register; registry

登记处 dēngjìchù registration; registry

登记吨 dēngjìdūn 〈交通〉 registered tonnage

登科 dēngkē pass imperial civil examinations

登临 dēnglín climb (a hill, tall building, etc. which commands a broad view); visit (famous mountains, places of interest, etc.):素喜～,经日不归。He often went on trips to scenic spots for days on end.

登龙 dēnglóng 〈比喻〉 rise to a position of power and influence:文坛～ appear in the limelight in literary circles

登龙门 dēng lóngmén legend has it that silver carps swimming upstream in the Yellow River in springtime usually could not reach Longmen, or Dragon Gate(between present-day Shanxi and Shaanxi) and the few that did were transformed into dragons — enter on a successful career with the help of an influential patron; pass imperial examinations successfully

登龙术 dēnglóngshù secret of success; skill in securing a powerful person's support to advance one's political career

登陆 dēnglù land; disembark (from a ship):台风～ typhoon hitting land /～作战 landing operations /诺曼底～ Normandy Landing (on D-Day, 6 June 1944)

登陆部队 dēnglù bùduì landing force; landing troops

登陆场 dēnglùchǎng beachhead

登陆点 dēnglùdiǎn landing point; debarkation point

登陆母舰 dēnglù mǔjiàn landing-craft carrier

登陆艇 dēnglùtǐng landing craft

登录 dēnglù ❶ register:～在案 be recorded; be put on record ❷ 〈信息〉telnet

登门 dēngmén call at sb.'s house:～拜访 pay sb. a visit /～道谢 call at sb.'s place to express one's gratitude /～求教 call on sb. for advice

登攀 dēngpān *also* "攀登" climb; scale:向科学的顶峰～ scale the heights of science /世上无难事,只要肯～。There is nothing too difficult to overcome in this world as long as one is fortified with determination (*or* is willing to make the effort).

登山 dēngshān 〈体育〉 mountain climbing; mountaineering:～队 mountaineering expedition (*or* party)

登山服 dēngshānfú ❶ mountaineering apparel ❷ anorak; parka:薄～ cagoule

登山鞋 dēngshānxié climbing or mountaineering boots

登山运动 dēngshān yùndòng mountaineering:～员 mountaineer

登时 dēngshí (used in narration of past events) at once; immediately; then and there:听了这话,她～脸色就变了。She changed countenance instantly upon hearing these words. /消防队员～赶赴现场。The fire brigade rushed to the spot at once.

登市 dēngshì (of seasonal commodities) be in season:下月初,鲜桃即可～。Peaches will be in season early next month.

登仕 dēngshì 〈书面〉embark upon an official career

登台 dēngtái ❶ mount the platform; go on the stage:我初次～讲话心里有点紧张。I felt a bit nervous when I mounted the rostrum to address the audience for the first time. /他十三岁就～表演。He began to perform on the stage at thirteen. ❷〈比喻〉enter the political arena:这届内阁刚～,便面临垮台的危险。No sooner had the new cabinet come to power than it faced the danger of imminent collapse.

登台拜将 dēngtái-bàijiàng *also* "登坛拜将" formally appoint a general or some such key official; receive such formal appointment

登堂入室 dēngtáng-rùshì *also* "升堂入室" shēngtáng-rùshì pass through the hall into the inner chamber — be well initiated in one's studies; become highly proficient in one's profession:他是师门～的弟子。He is an outstanding pupil of his master.

登徒子 dēngtúzǐ rake; lecher; debauchee

登位 dēngwèi be enthroned; succeed to the throne

登样 dēngyàng 〈方言〉 fashionable; in vogue:这是今年夏天最～的连衣裙了。This dress is the latest fashion in the summer.

登月 dēngyuè 〈航天〉land on the moon:～宇航员 lunanaut; astronaut / ～人 moonwalker

登月舱 dēngyuècāng lunar module (LM)

登月车 dēngyuèchē lunar rover

登月飞船 dēngyuè fēichuán lunar excursion vehicle
登载 dēngzǎi publish (in newspapers or magazines); carry: 今天许多报纸都～了这篇报道。The report is carried in many newspapers today. /各报在显著的位置～了这条新闻。All the newspapers gave prominent coverage to the news.

噔 dēng 〈象声〉 thump; thud: 他～～～地走上楼梯来。He came thumping up the stairs. /什么东西～的一声摔在地上。Something fell thudding on the floor.

蹬 dēng see "登²" dēng
see also dèng
蹬跶 dēngda 〈方言〉 also "蹬打" ❶ stamp (one's feet); stomp: 他爬山累得直喘气，可是两条腿还是紧往前～。Although he was panting for breath climbing the mountain, he kept pressing onward in vigorous strides. ❷ struggle in pain; kick one's feet in mid-air: 那只快死的小山羊，躺在墙根旁边，有时还～～下蹄子。The young goat lay dying at the foot of the wall, kicking its feet from time to time. ❸ get or set things going: ～不开 unable to get things under way /没有她的帮助，我这一摊工作休想～得开。Without her help, I simply won't be able to get things going here.
蹬技 dēngjì 〈杂技〉 juggling with the feet
蹬腿 dēngtuǐ ❶ stretch one's legs: 他一～坐起身。With a stretch of his legs, he sat up. ❷ 〈口语〉 (with a touch of humour) kick the bucket; die

镫 dēng ❶ 〈古语〉 vessel for meat food ❷ 〈书面〉 oil lamp
see also dèng

簦 dēng ❶ 〈古语〉 bamboo or straw hat with a conical crown, broad rim and handle ❷ 〈方言〉 bamboo or straw hat with a conical crown and broad rim

děng

戥 děng weigh with a small steelyard: 把这包药～一～。Please weigh this package of medicine.
戥子 děngzi also "等子" děngzi small steelyard for weighing precious metal, medicine, etc.

等¹ děng ❶ class; grade; rank: 优～ excellent (or superior); first-rate /劣～ inferior /中～ fair; middling /一～奖 first prize /二～功 second-class merit /上～货 top quality goods; topnotch goods /头～舱 first-class cabin /中～城市 medium-sized city /中～教育 secondary school education /高～学府 institute of higher learning; universities and colleges ❷ kind; sort: 这～事 things like this /此～人 such people /他是何～人? What kind of person is he? ❸ equal: 高矮相～ equal in height /大小不～ different in size; of different sizes /平～ equal; equality ❹ see "戥" děng

等² děng ❶ wait; await: ～人 wait for sb. /～车 wait for the bus, train, etc. /～着轮到自己 wait one's turn /～一～再说。There is no hurry. or Let's wait and see. /请稍～片刻。Please wait a while. or I won't be a minute. /让您久～了。Sorry to have kept you waiting. /这事要～上级批准。We are awaiting approval on the matter by the higher authorities. /时间不～人。Time and tide wait for no man. ❷ by the time; when; till: ～你回来，事早就完了。It will be all over by the time you return. /～雨停了再走。Wait till the rain stops. /他不～天亮就起床了。He got up before daybreak.

等³ děng 〈助词〉 ❶ 〈书面〉 *used after a personal pronoun or a noun referring to people to indicate plural number*: 你～ all of you; you /我～三人 the three of us /闲杂人～ people who have no business ❷ and so on; and so forth; etc.: 加点葱、姜、蒜～ add some scallion, ginger, garlic and so on /去北京、上海、广州～地出差 go on business trips to Beijing, Shanghai, Guangzhou and other places /小张～四人 four of them including Xiao Zhang; Xiao Zhang and three others ❸ *used to end an enumeration*: 小提琴、钢琴、单簧管～乐器 musical instruments such as violin, piano and clarinet /亚洲、欧洲、非洲、北美洲、南美洲、大洋洲、南极洲～七大洲 seven continents, namely, Asia, Europe, Africa, North America, South America, Oceania and Antarctica
等倍数 děngbèishù 〈数学〉 equimultiple
等比级数 děngbǐ jíshù also "几何级数" jǐhé jíshù 〈数学〉 geometrical progression
等臂染色体 děngbì rǎnsètǐ 〈生物〉 isochromosome
等边三角形 děngbiān sānjiǎoxíng equilateral triangle
等差 děngchā ❶ 〈书面〉 gradations of difference: 按功劳大小，受奖各有～。Rewards are given according to one's deserts. ❷ 〈数学〉 arithmetic: ～中项 arithmetic mean
等差级数 děngchā jíshù also "算术级数" suànshù jíshù 〈数学〉 arithmetical progression
等长收缩 děngcháng shōusuō isometric contraction
等潮时 děngcháoshí co-tidal hour
等潮图 děngcháotú co-tidal map; co-tidal chart
等潮线 děngcháoxiàn co-tidal line
等成本曲线 děngchéngběn qūxiàn 〈经济〉 equal cost contour; equal cost curve; isocost curve
等持 děngchí 〈佛教〉 *samadhi* (a state of concentration induced by meditation)
等次 děngcì grade; rank; place in a series: 按茶叶质量划分～。The tea is graded according to quality.
等衰 děngcuī 〈书面〉 place in a series; rank; grade: 在封建宗法社会里，人的～是按血缘远近区分的。In feudal patriarchal society people were graded according to blood relationship.
等待 děngdài wait; await; expect: ～时机 bide one's time; wait for a favourable opportunity /～消息 await information /～形势转变 wait for the turning of the tide
等到 děngdào by the time; when; till: ～钱攒齐了，那东西也卖完了。By the time enough money was raised, it all had been sold out. /～学业有成，我才考虑成家。I won't think of getting married until I have achieved success in my studies. /～饭后再谈工作。Business can wait until after dinner.
等等 děngděng 〈助词〉 and so on; and so forth; etc.: 桌上摆的是花生、核桃、红枣、糖～。On the table are peanuts, walnuts, dates, sweets and so on and so forth.
等等 děngdeng wait a minute: 请～我。Please wait for me. /～，我还有一点意见要提。Wait a minute. I've another suggestion to make.
等第 děngdì 〈书面〉 rank; grade (of people): 论功行赏，各有～ award people according to their merits
等电势加速器 děngdiànshì jiāsùqì 〈物理〉 constant potential accelerator
等电子化合物 děngdiànzǐ huàhéwù 〈物理〉 isoelectronic compound
等额分期付款 děng'é fēnqī fùkuǎn equal amount instalment payment
等额选举 děng'é xuǎnjǔ nominating one candidate for election of each post; single-candidate election
等而下之 děng'érxiàzhī from that grade down; lower down: 最好的尚且如此，～的就不必说了。Even the best of the bunch is not worth much, to say nothing of those lower down.
等分 děngfēn divide in the middle; halve
等分线 děngfēnxiàn bisector; bisectrix
等份 děngfèn equal portion: 一块蛋糕分成五～。A cake is equally divided into five portions.
等风速线 děngfēngsùxiàn 〈气象〉 isotach
等辐 děngfú constant amplitude
等辐波 děngfúbō continuous wave (CW): ～干扰 continuous wave interference (or jamming)
等概率 děnggàilǜ 〈数学〉 equiprobability
等高线 děnggāoxiàn 〈地理〉 contour (line): ～地图 contour map
等高种植 děnggāo zhòngzhí contour farming or cropping
等号 děnghào 〈数学〉 equal-sign; equality sign: 划～ draw an equal-sign
等候 děnghòu wait; await; expect: ～命令 await orders; wait for instructions /～客人 be expecting guests /人们在车上～出发。People are sitting on the coach ready for departure. /你瞧，朋友们在月台上～我们呢。Look, our friends have come to meet us on the platform.
等级 děngjí ❶ grade; rank: 商品按～定价。Prices of goods are set according to their grades. /旅馆的房间是分～的。Rooms in a hotel are graded. ❷ order and degree; social stratum; social estate: ～观

念 concept of (social) status /～制度 hierarchy; social estate system /第三～ (as in 18th-century France) third estate /～森严的社会 rigidly stratified society /～差别 difference in (social) status
等级工资制 děngjí gōngzīzhì graded wage scale
等级赛 děngjísài 〈体育〉contest or competition held according to categories; classification competition
等级运动员 děngjí yùndòngyuán graded sportsman, athlete, player, etc.
等加速度 děngjiāsùdù 〈物理〉uniform acceleration:～运动 motion with uniform acceleration
等价 děngjià equal in value; of equal value; equivalent:～变数 equivalent variable
等价交换 děngjià jiāohuàn exchange of equal values; exchange at equal value
等价物 děngjiàwù 〈经济〉equivalent
等价物交换 děngjiàwù jiāohuàn exchange of equivalents
等价原理 děngjià yuánlǐ equivalence principle
等减速运动 děngjiǎnsù yùndòng uniformly decreasing motion
等焦透镜 děngjiāo tòujìng 〈物理〉equivalent lens
等角 děngjiǎo isogonism; equal angle:～形 isogon /～多边形 equiangular polygon /～投影 isometrical projection; equal-angle projection
等距离 děngjùlí equidistance:～外交 equidistant diplomacy /～原则 principle of equidistance; equidistance /～边界 equidistance boundary /～区域 equidistance area
等离子 děnglízǐ 〈物理〉plasma:～弧 plasma arc /～流 plasma jet /～切割 plasma cutting /～焊 plasma welding /～武器 plasma weapon
等离子层 děnglízǐcéng 〈天文〉plasmasphere (lower level of the magnetosphere from about 350 km altitude to the plasmapause):～顶 plasmapause
等离子态 děnglízǐtài 〈物理〉plasma state
等离子体 děnglízǐtǐ 〈物理〉plasma:～激光器 plasma laser /～加速器 plasmatron /～物理学 plasma physics
等量劳动 děngliàng láodòng equal amount of labour:～相交换规律 law of exchange of equal amounts of labour /～领取等量产品 rewarding (*or* compensating) equal labour with equal products; exchange of an equal amount of labour for an equal amount of products
等量齐观 děngliàng-qíguān equate one with the other; put on a par; mention in the same breath:今日中国的农村地区与昔日大不一样了,不可～。The village areas in old China couldn't be mentioned in the same breath with those of today.
等米下锅 děngmǐ-xiàguō have yet to get rice for the cooking pot — live from hand to mouth; stop production for lack of raw materials
等内 děngnèi (of quality) up to standard; of acceptable quality:～木材 timber of acceptable quality
等强度 děngqiángdù equal strength
等日 děngrì 〈方言〉some time later; in a few days:～我加倍奉还。One day, I'll repay your kindness twice as much.
等日照线 děngrìzhàoxiàn 〈气象〉isohel
等熵 děngshāng isentropy:～流 isentropic stream (*or* flow) /～变化 isentropic change
等熵面 děngshāngmiàn 〈气象〉isentropic surface
等熵图 děngshāngtú 〈气象〉isentropic chart
等熵线 děngshāngxiàn isentrope; constant entropy line
等身 děngshēn be equal to oneself in height or weight; be of a great number or amount:～雕像 full length statue /～金 (possess) enormous wealth /著作～ have published a great number of books; have many works to one's credit
等深线 děngshēnxiàn 〈地理〉isobath; bathymetric contour
等深线图 děngshēnxiàntú bathymetric map
等式 děngshì 〈数学〉equality
等速运动 děngsù yùndòng *also* "匀速运动" yúnsù yùndòng 〈物理〉uniform motion
等同 děngtóng be equal to; equate; put on a par (with):不能把主观愿望与客观现实～起来。You cannot regard your wishful thinking as an accomplished fact. /书面语来源于口语,但又不～于口语。Although written language originates from spoken language, it is by no means the same.
等同语 děngtóngyǔ equivalent word; equivalent
等外 děngwài substandard:～品 product not up to standard; substandard product
等位基因 děngwèi jīyīn 〈生物〉allelic gene; allele:～间互补 interallelic complementation
等温 děngwēn 〈冶金〉isothermic:～淬火 austemper(ing) /～退火 isothermal annealing
等温线 děngwēnxiàn 〈气象〉isotherm
等闲 děngxián 〈书面〉❶ ordinary; unimportant:～视之 treat lightly (*or* casually); regard as unimportant /不是～之辈 not a person to be trifled with ❷ easily; lightly; casually:莫～,白了少年头,空悲切。Should youthful heads in vain turn grey, We would regret for aye. /莫～错过良机。Do not let the golden opportunity slip through your fingers. ❸ for no reason; for nothing:～平地起风雷。A storm broke out over the calm sea — an undesirable event occurred unexpectedly.
等效 děngxiào equivalent:～电抗 equivalent reactance /～电路 equivalent circuit/～电源 equivalent source /～发动机 equivalent generator /～负载 equivalent load /～刚度 equivalent stiffness /～噪声 equivalent noise
等歇 děngxiē 〈方言〉in a moment:～我就走。I'm leaving in a jiffy.
等形 děngxíng equiform
等雪线 děngxuěxiàn 〈气象〉isochion
等压 děngyā 〈物理〉equipressure:～锅炉 equipressure boiler /～循环 equipressure cycle
等压面 děngyāmiàn 〈气象〉isobaric surface; constant pressure surface
等压线 děngyāxiàn 〈气象〉isobaric line; isobar
等腰三角形 děngyāo sānjiǎoxíng 〈数学〉isosceles triangle
等因奉此 děngyīn-fèngcǐ ❶〈旧语〉(used in official documents) in view of the above, we therefore...; whereas... therefore... ❷ officialese
等音 děngyīn 〈音乐〉enharmonic
等于 děngyú ❶ be equal to; be equivalent to:一米～三市尺。One metre is equal to three *chi*. /一加二～三。One plus two is three. /今年的收入～去年的三倍。This year's total income is three times that of last year. ❷ be the same as; amount to; be tantamount to:我错了并不～他就正确。I was wrong, but that does not mean (that) he was right. /你不说话就～默认。Your silence will be taken for tacit consent. /不珍惜时光～浪费生命。Whiling away one's time is wasting one's life.
等于零 děngyúlíng amount to nothing; be of no use:说了不办,还不是～。Words not backed up by deeds amount to nothing.
等雨量线 děngyǔliàngxiàn 〈气象〉isohyet
等着瞧 děngzheqiáo wait and see:～的政策 wait-and-see policy /究竟谁对谁错,咱们～。Let's wait and see who is right after all.
等震线 děngzhènxiàn 〈地质〉isoseismal line
等值 děngzhí equivalence:～系数 co-efficient of equivalence
等值线 děngzhíxiàn 〈气象〉isopleth:～图 isogram; isoline
等周问题 děngzhōu wèntí 〈数学〉isoperimetric problem
等轴晶 děngzhóujīng equiax crystal:～结构 equiax grain structure /～系 isometric system
等子 děngzi *see* "戥子" děngzi

dèng

澄 dèng ❶ (of liquid) become clear; settle:这水里有杂质,要～一～才能用。There are impure substances in the water. Let them settle before you use it. ❷〈方言〉strain; decant:把汤～出来。Decant the soup (without the substance in it).
see also chéng
澄浆泥 dèngjiāngní filtered fine clay (esp. for making delicate porcelain)
澄清 dèngqīng (of liquid) become clear; settle; clarify:把咖啡搅一搅,～了再喝。Stir the coffee to settle the grounds before you drink.
see also chéngqīng
澄沙 dèngshā sweetened bean paste
澄水池 dèngshuǐchí setting basin

磴 dèng ❶〈书面〉stone steps:拾～而上 climb up the stone steps ❷〈量词〉*used of steps and stairs*:那楼梯有十一～。There are eleven steps on that flight of stairs. /他一～一～慢慢往上走。He

went up slowly step by step.

磴道 dèngdào mountain path with stone steps

瞪 dèng ❶ open one's eyes wide:眼睛～得大大的 with one's eyes wide open ❷ glare; stare:生气地～了他一眼 give him an angry stare /～着眼睛发呆 stare blankly /你～着我作什么? Why are you glaring at me?

瞪视 dèngshì stare; glare:卫兵目不转睛地～着前方的动静。The guard was watching with close attention for any movement ahead.

瞪眼 dèngyǎn ❶ open one's eyes wide; stare; glare:干～ look on helplessly /孩子们好奇地～看着魔术师。The children are watching the magician with wide open eyes. /别瞪着眼让贼给跑了。Don't let the thief run away from right under your nose. ❷ get angry with sb.; glare and glower at:气得吹胡子～ snort and stare in anger; glare with rage /他就爱跟别人～。He is always glaring and glowering.

蹬 dèng *see* "蹭蹬" cèngdèng
see also dēng

嶝 dèng 〈书面〉 path up a hill:此山虽险,但可沿～而上。The mountain is steep, but there is a little path that will take you up to the top.

镫 dèng stirrup:马～ stirrup
see also dēng

镫骨 dènggǔ 〈生理〉 stapes; stirrup bone

镫里藏身 dènglǐ-cángshēn hide one's body behind one side of the horse (in order to stay clear of arrows, or not to be seen by the enemy)

镫子 dèngzi stirrup:他跳上战马,～一磕,飞奔而去。He jumped on his horse and galloped away with a click of the stirrups.

凳(櫈) dèng stool; bench:小板～ stool /长(板)～ bench /石～ stone bench /竹～ bamboo stool /琴～ music stool /方～ square stool /踏脚～ foot-stool

凳子 dèngzi stool; bench

邓(鄧) Dèng a surname

邓洛普 Dèngluòpǔ John Boyd Dunlop (1840-1921), Scottish veterinary surgeon and the first person to devise a successful pneumatic tyre (1888) which was manufactured by the company named after him

邓洛普-皮雷利联合公司 Dèngluòpǔ-Píléilì Liánhé Gōngsī Dunlop-Pirelli Union

邓小平 Dèng Xiǎopíng Deng Xiaoping (1904-1997), leader of the Communist Party and People's Republic of China, and architect of China's modernization programme:《～论教育》*Deng Xiaoping on Education*

邓小平理论 Dèng Xiǎopíng Lǐlùn Deng Xiaoping Theory:高举～伟大旗帜 hold high the great banner of Deng Xiaoping Theory

邓小平文选 Dèng Xiǎopíng Wénxuǎn (shortened as 邓选) *Selected Works of Deng Xiaoping* (in three volumes, published in 1989, 1983 and 1993 respectively)

dī

滴 dī ❶ drip:～水的龙头 dripping tap /农民锄地,汗往泥土上直～。Sweat dripped onto the soil while the farmer was hoeing the fields. /伞还在～水。The umbrella is still dripping water. ❷ let drop; drip:给鼻子～药 put drops of medicine in one's nose ❸ drop; bead:水～ drop of water/汗～ bead of sweat ❹〈量词〉 *used with dripping liquid*:两～墨水 two drops of ink /他为祖国流尽最后一～血。He shed his last drop of blood for his country.

滴鼻剂 dībíjì nose drops; collunarium

滴虫 dīchóng 〈医学〉 trichomonas; trichomonad:～病 trichomoniasis /～感染 trichomonas infection /～性阴道炎 trichomonas vaginitis

滴翠 dīcuì emerald green; jade green; green in the extreme:千山～,遍野葱绿。The mountains are emerald green, and the fields a carpet of verdure.

滴答 dīdā *also* "嘀嗒" dīdā 〈象声〉 tick; ticktack; ticktock:夜深人静,客厅壁钟～作响。It was quiet and still in the dead of night, and the wall clock was ticking away in the parlour. /雨滴滴答答地整夜不停。The rain kept pattering the whole night.

滴答 dīda *also* "嘀嗒" dīda drip:融化的雪水从房顶上～下来。Melted snow is dripping down from the roof.

滴滴涕 dīdītì DDT (dichloro-diphenyl-trichol-roethane):～中毒 DDT poisoning

滴定 dīdìng 〈化学〉 titration:～法 titration /比浊～ heterometric titration /～仪 titration apparatus; titrator

滴定度 dīdìngdù titre

滴定管 dīdìngguǎn buret; burette

滴定计 dīdìngjì titrimeter

滴定剂 dīdìngjì titrant

滴管 dīguǎn dropper; eye-dropper

滴灌 dīguàn 〈农业〉 drip irrigation; trickle irrigation

滴剂 dījì drops:白内障～ cataract drops

滴里耷拉 dīlidālā *also* "滴里搭拉" droop in disorder; hang down loosely:农舍的墙上～地挂着成串的玉米、大蒜和辣椒。All over the walls of the farmer's cottage hung strings of corn, garlic and hot pepper.

滴里嘟噜 dīlidūlū ❶ (of a whole series of things put loosely together) appear cumbersome or clumsy:他身上挂着～的一长串钥匙。A big bunch of keys hung clumsily on him. ❷ speak quickly and indistinctly:他～讲了老半天,可是谁都没有听懂。He rattled on for a long while, but nobody understood what he was talking about.

滴沥 dīlì 〈象声〉 dripping of rain or water:泉水～ dripping spring /雨水～～下了一整天。The rain pattered on the whole day.

滴溜溜 dīliūliū motion of rolling or flowing:～地转 turn round and round; spin round /一阵震耳欲聋的爆炸声后,大小石头～地向下滚。After the deafening explosion, rocks and stones started rolling down the hillside.

滴溜儿 dīliūr ❶ perfectly (round):～滚圆的珠子 perfectly round beads /他的两只眼睛瞪得～圆。He glared with wide open eyes. ❷ turn or flow round quickly; be on the go:眼珠～乱转 with one's eyes rolling round and round /忙得～转 be as busy as a bee

滴溜 dīliu 〈方言〉 drip; trickle; dribble:一阵雨过去了,屋檐上的水还不断地～。The rain had stopped, but water continued to drip down from the eaves.

滴漏 dīlòu water clock; clepsydra; hourglass

滴滤池 dīlǜchí 〈环保〉 trickling filter

滴尿症 dīniàozhèng 〈医学〉 dripping urination

滴瓶 dīpíng 〈化学〉 dropping bottle; drop bottle

滴水不进 dīshuǐ-bùjìn not take a single drop of water; not eat or drink at all

滴水不漏 dīshuǐ-bùlòu *also* "滴水不透" ❶ (speak) in a watertight or leakproof manner; leaving nothing for people to pick on; making one's argument flawless:她能言善辩,说出话来～。She has the gift of the gab, and leaves nothing for people to pick on when she speaks. ❷ very crowded; closely surrounded:乡亲们围了个～,争着看那人变戏法。The conjuror was tightly surrounded by a large crowd of villagers who were eager to see his performance.

滴水成冰 dīshuǐ-chéngbīng water freezes as soon as it drops; freezing cold:～的天气 freezing weather /这里严冬季节经常是～,呵气成霜。In the dead of winter here, dripping water freezes and one's breath frosts.

滴水穿石 dīshuǐ-chuānshí *also* "水滴石穿" dripping water wears holes in stone; little strokes fell great oaks:办成这事,须有～的功夫。You need tremendous patience and perseverance to bring the work to fruition.

滴水石 dīshuǐshí dripstone

滴水瓦 dīshuǐwǎ drip-tile (placed at either end of an eaves)

滴水檐 dīshuǐyán 〈建筑〉 dripping eaves

滴眼剂 dīyǎnjì eye drops

嘀 dī
see also dí

嘀嗒 dīdā *see* "滴答" dīdā

嘀嗒 dīda *see* "滴答" dīda

嘀里嘟噜 dīlidūlū *see* "滴里嘟噜" dīlidūlū

镝 dī 〈化学〉 dysprosium (Dy)

see also dí

堤(隄) dī dyke; embankment:河～ embankment along a river /修～拦洪 build a dyke to hold back flood water

堤岸 dī'àn embankment:～码头 bulkhead wharf /～工程 bund project

堤岸权 dī'ànquán 〈法律〉riparian right

堤坝 dībà dykes and dams

堤防 dīfáng dyke; embankment:加固～ strengthen a dyke /～工程 dyke building; embankment project

堤埂 dīgěng also "堤埂子" dyke; embankment:他们沿着一条～走了三里多地。They walked more than three *li* along a dyke.

堤埝 dīniàn dyke; embankment:村子周围筑有约两米高的环形～。Around the village is a two-metre tall circular embankment.

堤坡 dīpō dyke slope; dyke batter

堤墙 dīqiáng embankment wall

堤情 dīqíng state of the dyke or embankment:普测～ general survey of dykes

堤围 dīwéi dyke; embankment

D

堤堰 dīyàn embankment; dyke; levee:整修～ mend and reinforce an embankment

堤垸 dīyuàn flood or high-water structure similar to a dyke or embankment

提 dī same as "提❶" tí

see also tí

提防 dīfang be on guard against; beware of; be on the alert:～那些专门说恭维话的人。Beware of flatterers. /～隔墙有耳。Be careful: walls have ears. /为～火灾,我们采取了一系列措施。We have taken precautionary measures against fire.

提拉 dīla 〈方言〉carry in one's hand with the arm down; lift; raise:他～着水桶往外跑。He rushed out carrying a bucket.

提溜 dīliu 〈方言〉hold in hand; bring along:～着心 have one's heart in one's mouth; be very worried or anxious / 他手里～的是什么? What's that he is holding? /队长走在前边,手里～着灯笼。The captain walked in front, lamp in hand.

氐 dī ❶ one of the 28 constellations ❷ (Dī) ethnic group living in northwestern China around 400 AD

see also dǐ

羝 dī ram; billy goat

羝羊触藩 dīyáng-chùfān like a ram having its antlers caught in a hedge while trying to jump over — on the horns of a dilemma

低 dī ❶ at a small distance from the ground; low:水位降～了。The water level dropped. /燕子～飞。The swallow is flying low. /飞机绕机场～飞一周。The airplane flew round the airfield at low altitude. ❷ below the average; low:文化水平～ low in educational level /眼高手～ have high ambitions but little ability; have grandiose aims but puny abilities; be fastidious but incompetent /声音太～。The voice is too low. ❸ low in grade or rank:社会地位～ low in social status /～年级学生 students of the junior years; lower-division students /这种大米等级～。This is low-grade rice. ❹ hang down; droop:～头 hang one's head /杨柳～悬。The willows are drooping lazily.

低矮 dī'ǎi low:～的茅屋 low thatched cottage /～的酸枣树 short wild jujube tree

低昂 dī'áng rise and fall; fluctuate in height; swing up and down:他让两个小外孙分别骑在自己的左右腿上,～起来,使他们觉得像是在骑马。With his two little grandsons each sitting on one of his knees, he gently moved them up and down, making them feel as if they were on horseback.

低卑 dībēi petty and low; lowly:地位～ low in status or position / 不为出身～而感到羞耻 not ashamed of one's lowly origins

低倍 dībèi low power:～镜 low power lens

低倍显微镜 dībèi xiǎnwēijìng 〈物理〉low-power(ed) microscope

低标号 dībiāohào low-grade:～水泥〈建筑〉low-grade cement

低层 dīcéng ❶ of or on a lower level, floor, layer, etc.:他住高层,我住～。He lives on a higher floor than I do. ❷ low-ranking; lowly; low:～职员 junior clerk; petty functionary

低层大气 dīcéng dàqì lower atmosphere layer

低产 dīchǎn low yield:～田 low-yield plot (*or* land) /～作物 low-yielding crop /～油井〈石油〉stripper well; stripped well

低潮 dīcháo ❶ low tide; low ebb:～高地 low tide elevation /～海退现象 regression of the low watermark /今天的高潮时间是早晨六时,～是正午。Today, high tide was at 6 a.m. and low tide at midday. ❷ lowest point; nadir:两国关系目前正处于～。Relations between the two countries have reached their nadir.

低潮标 dīcháobiāo low-tide mark

低潮线 dīcháoxiàn low-water line; low-water mark

低沉 dīchén ❶ overcast; gloomy:天空笼罩着～的阴云。The sky is overcast (*or* covered) with low-lying dark clouds. /天色～得可怕。The weather is frightfully gloomy. ❷ (of voice) low and deep:语调～ speak in a low and deep tone /～的哀乐声 mournful funeral music ❸ low-spirited; downcast:情绪～ be in low spirits /他没有因为失败而～下去。Failure did not dishearten him.

低垂 dīchuí hang low:天色阴暗,乌云～。The sky is overcast and dark clouds hang low. /帘幕～。The window curtains are drawn. /夜幕～。Night has fallen. /那孩子羞愧地～着头。The child hung his head in shame. /湖边柳枝～水面。The branches of the willow bend low over the lake.

低搭 dīda 〈方言〉low; lowly; humble:这人以为唯有自己高贵,别人都～。The guy sets too much store by himself and regards everyone else as lowly.

低蛋白 dīdànbái low protein:～饮食 low protein diet /～血〈医学〉hypoproteinemia

低档 dīdàng low-grade; inferior in quality:这类～商品根本进不了超级市场。These low-grade (*or* poor-quality) goods can have no access to the supermarket.

低档产品市场 dīdàng chǎnpǐn shìchǎng down market

低等 dīděng lower; lower-class:～哺乳动物 lower mammal

低等动物 dīděng dòngwù lower animal

低等植物 dīděng zhíwù lower plant

低地 dīdì lowland; low-lying land:～人 lowlander /～农庄 lowland farm

低电离层 dīdiànlícéng lower ionosphere

低电压 dīdiànyā 〈电学〉low voltage

低调 dīdiào low-key; low-pitched:他在内阁只作了一个～的讲话。He made a low-key speech at the cabinet.

低度 dīdù (of wine, etc.) of low proof; weak:～酒 low-proof alcohol or wine

低分辨力 dīfēnbiànlì 〈物理〉low resolution:～遥感 low-resolution remote sensing

低峰 dīfēng low ebb; nadir

低功率 dīgōnglǜ 〈物理〉low power:～逻辑电路〈电子〉low power logic

低估 dīgū underestimate; underrate:这件事的影响不能～。You must not underrate the impact of the event. /～敌人的实力是很危险的。It is dangerous to underestimate the strength of one's enemy.

低谷 dīgǔ deep valley — all-time low; bottom:跌入～(of prices, goods, markets, etc.) bottom out /走出～ climb off the bottom; get out of the doldrums /职工情绪跌入～。The morale of the staff and workers is at an all-time low.

低轨道 dīguǐdào also "低地球轨道"〈航天〉low orbit:～卫星 low earth orbit (LEO)

低合金 dīhéjīn 〈冶金〉low alloy:～钢 low-alloy steel /～高强度结构钢 low-alloy high-strength structural steel

低缓 dīhuǎn ❶ (of sound and voice) low and slow:他语调～,但口气很坚决。He spoke in a low but firm voice. ❷ (in topography) low-lying and flat:地势～ lowland with a gentle slope; gently-sloping land

低回 dīhuí also "低徊"〈书面〉❶ pace up and down:～于林间 pace to and fro in the woods /在湖畔～ stroll leisurely by the side of a lake ❷ be reluctant to leave; linger; yearn:万里长城使你对千年往事～不已。The Great Wall makes you ponder over the history of a millennium. /～过去,不如憧憬未来。It is better to visualize the future than long for the past. ❸ full of twists and turns; tangled; sentimental:思绪～ lost in a tangle of thoughts /～婉转的乐曲 sentimental music

低徊 dīhuí see "低回"

低级 dījí ❶ elementary; rudimentary; low; junior:～阶段 lower stage /～哺乳动物 lower mammal /～生物 low form of life /～原生动

物 low protozoan ❷ vulgar; coarse; low:此人～庸俗,为人不齿。He was held in contempt because of his coarse and philistine tastes.

低级汽油 dījí qìyóu 〈石油〉 low-test gasoline

低级趣味 dījí qùwèi bad taste; vulgar interest:文艺表演不能迎合某些观众的～。Artistic performance should not cater to the vulgar tastes of some members of the audience.

低级燃料 dījí ránliào 〈化工〉 low-grade fuel

低级神经活动 dījí shénjīng huódòng activities of the lower nerves (under the cerebral cortex)

低钾血 dījiǎxuè 〈医学〉 hypokalemia

低价 dījià low price; reduced price; low cost:～货 low-priced goods /最～ lowest possible price /～住房 low cost housing /～购入,高价卖出 buy cheap and sell dear /这些货物将～出售。These goods will be sold at reduced prices.

低贱 dījiàn ❶ low and degrading; lowly; humble; mean:在往日,人们认为他出身～而不大理睬他。In the old days people considered him a man of humble birth unworthy of notice. ❷ cheap; low in price:谷价～ low grain prices; cheap grain

低精确度 dījīngquèdù 〈机械〉 low accuracy

低空 dīkōng low altitude; low level:～侦察 low-altitude reconnaissance /～飞行 low-altitude (*or* low-level) flying /～爆炸 low-level explosion /～轰炸 low-level bombing /～扫射 low-level strafing; ground strafing

低空导弹 dīkōng dǎodàn 〈军事〉 low-level missile; low-altitude missile

低栏 dīlán 〈体育〉 low hurdles:她在 400 米～中获第一名。She came first in the 400-metre low hurdles.

低利 dīlì low interest; small profit:～贷款 low interest loans /～政策 low interest policy

低廉 dīlián cheap; low-priced; low in price:价格～。Prices are low. /旅游业成本～,效益可观。Tourism requires small investment, but can reap considerable profit.

低劣 dīliè inferior; sub-standard; low-grade:～材料 shoddy (*or* inferior) material /如今市场上不时出现～的冒牌商品。Inferior, fake goods are often found in the market nowadays.

低烈度 dīlièdù low intensity:～战争战略 strategy of low-intensity warfare

低硫煤 dīliúméi low sulphur coal

低氯化物 dīlǜhuàwù subchloride

低落 dīluò low; depressed; downcast:情绪～ be crestfallen; be in low spirits /使～的士气重新振作起来 pep up the sagging morale /任何事情都不能使她摆脱～的心绪。Nothing could pull her out of her depression. *or* Nothing could help shake off her depression. /部分耐用商品物价已趋～。The prices of some durable goods have gone down.

低眉 dīméi look downward; be submissive or humble; be merciful and benevolent:～默想 look downward in meditation /～折腰 bow and scrape /拱手～ make a show of respect or submission by lowering one's head and folding one's hands

低眉顺眼 dīméi-shùnyǎn be submissive and servile

低迷 dīmí ❶ 〈书面〉 vague; indistinct; blurred; hazy:云雾～ hazy clouds /～思寝 feel (dully) drowsy ❷ (of prices, etc.) low; (of economy, etc.) stagnant:经济持续～。The economy remains in the doldrums. /这种产品的需求趋于～。The demand for such products tends to go down.

低能 dīnéng ❶ mental deficiency; feeble-mindedness:～儿童 retarded children /只有～的人才会走这步棋。Only an imbecile could make such a move. /他工作搞得一塌糊涂,不是由于～,而是由于不负责。He has made a mess of his work not because he is incompetent but because he is irresponsible. ❷ 〈物理〉 low-energy:～放射性元素 low-energy radioactive element /～物理 low-energy physics

低能儿 dīnéng'ér (mentally) retarded child; imbecile; simpleton

低黏度 dīniándù 〈化工〉 low viscosity:～润滑油 low-viscosity oil

低泡沫洗涤剂 dīpàomò xǐdíjì low-foaming detergent

低膨胀合金 dīpéngzhàng héjīn low-expansion alloy

低频 dīpín 〈物理〉 low frequency:～输出 low-frequency output /～音波 low-frequency sound waves

低频变压器 dīpín biànyāqì low-frequency transformer

低频段 dīpínduàn low-frequency range

低频放大器 dīpín fàngdàqì low-frequency amplifier

低频接收机 dīpín jiēshōujī low-frequency radio receiver

低频扬声器 dīpín yángshēngqì woofer

低品位 dīpǐnwèi low-grade:～矿石 low-grade ore /～耐火黏土〈化工〉 low-heat-duty clay

低平 dīpíng low-lying and flat:地势～。The terrain is low and flat. /村庄前面的山谷是一片开阔～的草地。In front of the village the valley opens into a broad, low-lying, flat meadow.

低气 dīqì (of status, position, etc.) humble; lowly; degrading:他过去嫌当营业员～,老想改行,现在让他改也不改了。He used to think that his job as a shop assistant was degrading and always wanted to change his occupation. But now he wouldn't do so even if you asked him to.

低气压 dīqìyā 〈气象〉 low pressure; depression:～槽 low-pressure trough

低气压病 dīqìyābìng hypobaropathy

低气压区 dīqìyāqū low pressure area

低强度 dīqiángdù low intensity:～辐射 low-intensity radiation

低热 dīrè *also* "低烧" low fever; low temperature

低热量 dīrèliàng low calorie:～饮食 low calorie diet

低热值 dīrèzhí 〈物理〉 low heat value

低人一等 dīrényīděng of inferior status; inferior to others:在我们的社会里,没有～的工作。No job is inferior to another in our society. /他很自卑,总觉得自己～。He has an inferiority complex and always feels as if he was actually inferior to others.

低熔点 dīróngdiǎn 〈物理〉 low melting point:～合金〈冶金〉 low-thermo metal; low-melting alloy

低柔 dīróu (of sound, voice, etc.) low and soft:～的乐曲 light melody /～的声音 soft voice

低弱 dīruò ❶ (of sound, voice, etc.) small and weak; low; indistinct:～的呼喊 feeble cry /远处的枪炮声～了。The gunfire in the distance calmed down (*or* subsided). ❷ inferior and weak; fragile; feeble:体质～ fragile in health; physically weak /智力～ feeble-minded; be of low intelligence

低三下四 dīsān-xiàsì abject; subservient; servile; obsequious:～地求饶 beg abjectly for mercy/可鄙的～的家伙 despicable, spineless person /他如此～,就连他的朋友都因此而瞧不起他。He is so subservient that even his friends despise him for it.

低烧 dīshāo *also* "低热" 〈医学〉 low fever; slight fever:发～ run a low fever; run a slight temperature

低声 dīshēng in a low voice; under one's breath:～谈话 talk in whispers; talk in a low voice /～点。Keep down your voice. /大夫～嘀咕了几句,就离开了。The doctor said something under his breath and then left.

低声波 dīshēngbō *also* "次声波" cìshēngbō 〈物理〉 infrasonic wave

低声下气 dīshēng-xiàqì speak humbly and submissively; be humble and meek:～地要求从宽处理 plead piteously for mercy/他跟上级说话的时候总露出～的样子。He sounded almost servile when he spoke to his superiors. /有求于人,有时就难免～。When you have a favour to ask of somebody, you may sometimes have to be humble and meek.

低湿 dīshī low and damp:～地带 marshy land /窄小～的房间 narrow, low and damp room

低手 dīshǒu poor player or performer; fumbler

低首下心 dīshǒu-xiàxīn obsequiously submissive; obedient and docile:他不习惯于～地同领导说话。He was not used to talking to his superiors in humble terms.

低水头 dīshuǐtóu 〈水利〉 low-head:～离心泵 low-head centrifugal pump /～水电厂 low-head hydroelectric power station

低水位 dīshuǐwèi 〈水利〉 low water:～阀 low-water valve /～警报器 low water alarm

低俗 dīsú in bad taste; vulgar; coarse:言语～ vulgar (*or* coarse) language /一些格调～的出版物已经从书市上清理出去了。Some publications which catered to low and vulgar tastes have been cleared from the book market.

低速 dīsù low speed:～轴 low-speed shaft (*or* axle) /～行驶 drive at low speed; drive slowly

低速传动 dīsù chuándòng low gear

低速电机 dīsù diànjī low-speed electric machine

低速电子扫描 dīsù diànzǐ sǎomiáo low-velocity scanning

低速发动机 dīsù fādòngjī low-speed engine

低速开关 dīsù kāiguān low-speed switching

低速空气动力学 dīsù kōngqì dònglìxué low-speed aerodynamics

低损耗 dīsǔnhào 〈电学〉 low loss:～光学波导 low-loss optical waveguide

低碳钢 dītàngāng 〈冶金〉low-carbon steel
低糖 dītáng low sugar:～食品 low sugar food
低头 dītóu ❶ hang or bow one's head:～不语 hang one's head in silence /～默哀 bow one's head in silent mourning /～认罪 hang one's head and admit one's guilt; plead guilty ❷ yield; submit:决不向困难～ never yield or bow to difficulties
低洼 dīwā low-lying:～地 low-lying land
低微 dīwēi ❶ (of voice or sound) low; faint:～的呻吟 faint groans ❷ low; little; meagre:待遇～ low pay /收入～ meagre (*or* low) income ❸ lowly; humble:这位总经理是二十年前从一桩～的工作起家的。The general manager began his career from a very humble position twenty years ago.
低纬度 dīwěidù low latitude:～地区 area of low latitudes
低位 dīwèi 〈数学〉low order:～数 low order digit
低温 dīwēn of low temperature; cryogenic; 〈气象〉microthermal; 〈医学〉hypothermic:～操作 low temperature operation /～箱 cryogenic box; low temperature cabinet /～手术 cryogenic operation /～气候 microthermal climate /～麻醉 hypothermic anesthesia /～疗法 cryotherapy
低温泵 dīwēnbèng cryopump
低温材料 dīwēn cáiliào cryogenic material
低温超导 dīwēn chāodǎo 〈物理〉cryogenic superconductivity:～体 cryogenic superconductor
低温储藏 dīwēn chǔcáng cryo-preservation
低温发生器 dīwēn fāshēngqì cryogenerator
低温固化 dīwēn gùhuà low-temperature setting
低温管 dīwēnguǎn cryotron
低温恒温器 dīwēn héngwēnqì cryostat
低温化学 dīwēn huàxué cryochemistry
低温计 dīwēnjì cryometer
低温技术 dīwēn jìshù cryonetics
低温生化学 dīwēn shēnghuàxué cryobiochemistry
低温生物学 dīwēn shēngwùxué cryobiology
低温外科 dīwēn wàikē cryosurgery
低温物理学 dīwēn wùlǐxué cryophysics
低温吸着 dīwēn xīzhuó cryosorption
低温学 dīwēnxué cryogenics
低温植物 dīwēn zhíwù microtherm
低温装置 dīwēn zhuāngzhì cryogenic device
低雾 dīwù 〈气象〉ground fog
低息 dīxī low interest:～贷款 low-interest loan; low-interest credit
低下 dīxià ❶ (as of status or living standard) below average; low; inferior:社会地位～ low in social status /生活水平～ low standards of living ❷ (as of taste, etc.) lowly; vulgar; cheap:情调～ in vulgar taste
低陷 dīxiàn sink; be sunken:地基已～。The foundations have sunk (*or* subsided). /在群山围绕中有一片～的盆地种着许多果树。There was a low-lying basin among the hills, planted with fruit trees. /他瘦得两颊都～下去了。He was so thin that his cheeks became sunken.
低消耗 dīxiāohào low consumption (of raw materials, fuel, etc.):高产～ high production, low consumption
低血糖 dīxuètáng 〈医学〉hypoglycemia
低血压 dīxuèyā 〈医学〉hypotension
低血脂 dīxuèzhī 〈医学〉hypolipemia
低压 dīyā ❶〈物理〉low pressure:～计 low-pressure gauge /～泵〈机械〉low-lift pump /～铸造〈机械〉low-pressure casting /～鼓风机〈冶金〉low-blast furnace ❷〈电学〉low tension; low voltage:～线 low-voltage line /～变压器 low-voltage transformer /～电源 low-voltage power supply /～开关 low-tension switch /～配电网 low-voltage network ❸〈气象〉low pressure; depression:～气流 low-pressure air current ❹〈医学〉minimum pressure
低压舱 dīyācāng hypobaric chamber
低压槽 dīyācáo trough
低压带 dīyādài low-pressure belt
低压炉 dīyālú low-pressure burner
低压输送 dīyā shūsòng 〈电学〉low-voltage transmission
低哑 dīyǎ low and hoarse; husky:他连日劳累,说话的声音都～了。He had been so busy the last few days that his voice became hoarse. /侦察机的声音～细长。The reconnaissance plane droned low and harshly.
低亚 dīyà 〈书面〉hang low; droop:树枝～。The branches of the tree hang low.
低氧 dīyǎng 〈医学〉hypoxia:～血症 hypoxemia
低音 dīyīn 〈音乐〉bass:～谱号 bass clef /女～ alto /男～ bass
低音管 dīyīnguǎn bass horn
低音吉他 dīyīn jítā bass guitar
低音喇叭 dīyīn lǎba 〈电工〉woofer; bass loudspeaker
低音提琴 dīyīn tíqín double bass; contrabass:～手 bassist; bassman
低吟 dīyín recite or chant in a low voice:～浅唱 recite a poem in a gentle voice; hum a song
低语 dīyǔ speak softly; speak under one's breath; whisper:～密谈 talk in whispers /他在我耳边～了几句。He whispered a few words in my ear.
低云 dīyún 〈气象〉low cloud (less than 2 km. above ground)
低噪声 dīzàoshēng 〈物理〉low noise
低噪声轴承 dīzàoshēng zhóuchéng noise-free or low-noise bearing
低智 dīzhì mentally deficient; retarded:～儿童 retarded child; imbecile
低姿态 dīzītài low profile:保持～ maintain a low profile

dí

涤(滌) dí 〈书面〉wash; cleanse:洗～ wash; wash up
涤除 díchú wash away; do away with; eliminate:～旧习 do away with outdated customs /～社会弊端 root out social malpractices
涤荡 dídàng *also* "荡涤" wash away; clean up:～人类社会上一切污泥浊水 clean up all the filth of human society /丑恶的东西都应该从地球上～干净。The earth should be cleansed of all that is evil and ugly.
涤卡 díkǎ 〈纺织〉dacron drill; dacron khaki
涤纶 dílún 〈纺织〉polyester fibre; dacron; terylene:棉～ polycotton /毛～ wool and polyester blend
涤纶长丝 dílún chángsī polyester filament
涤纶短纤维 dílún duǎnxiānwéi polyester staple fibre
涤纶絮棉 dílún xùmián polyester cotton
涤棉布 dímiánbù (popularly known as 棉的确良) mixed polyester-cotton fabric; polycotton
涤瑕荡秽 díxiá-dànghuì wash away stains and cleanse off dirt; do away with pernicious habits and bad practices
涤罪所 dízuìsuǒ 〈宗教〉purgatory

嘀(啾) dí
see also dī
嘀咕 dígu ❶ whisper; talk in whispers; gossip (in a low voice):两人在走廊里～了一阵后走开了。They left after talking in whispers for a while in the corridor. /她就爱嘀嘀咕咕。She is fond of gossip. /他嘴里～着走出房间。He left the room murmuring to himself. ❷ have misgivings; have sth. on one's mind:我心里一直～这件事。I have had some misgivings about the matter. *or* It has been on my mind all the while. /走了几个钟头也没找到那村子,心里有点～这地图是不是有问题。After walking for hours without finding the village, we began to suspect that there was something wrong with our map.

蹢 dí 〈书面〉trotter; hoof

镝 dí 〈书面〉arrowhead; arrow:锋～ blade and arrowhead — weaponry; war /正西风落叶下长安,飞鸣～。The west wind scatters leaves over Chang'an, And the arrows are flying, twanging.
see also dī

嫡 dí ❶ of or by the wife (as distinguished from a concubine under the feudal-patriarchal system):～长子 eldest son by wife ❷ of lineal descent; closely related ❸ orthodox; authentic
嫡出 díchū 〈旧语〉born of the wife (as distinguished from one born of a concubine under the feudal-patriarchal system)
嫡传 díchuán handed down in a direct line from the master; authentic:她是那位京剧大师的～弟子。She was an artist of Beijing opera, who had the benefit of the personal instruction and guidance of the master.

嫡母 dímǔ mother of the direct line (as used by children by a concubine in reference to their father's official wife in feudal times)

嫡派 dípài ❶ *see* "嫡系" ❷ disciples personally instructed by the master: ～真传 personal instruction by the master

嫡亲 díqīn closest by blood; by the same father; by the same paternal grandfather: ～兄弟 blood brothers; own brother; brother-german /～兄妹 brother and sister by the same father /～姑姑 daughter of one's paternal grandfather; own aunt /～侄子 son of one's own brother

嫡堂 dítáng once removed from the direct paternal line: ～兄弟姐妹 cousins having the same paternal grandfather; first cousins; cousins-german /～叔伯 first cousins of one's father; uncles

嫡系 díxì ❶ direct line of descent: ～后裔 progeny of direct line of descent (from sb.) ❷ under the direct control of a faction: ～部队 troops under the direct control of a faction

嫡子 dízǐ son or oldest son born of the wife (as distinguished from 庶子, son born of a concubine)

敌(敵) dí

❶ of diametrically opposed interests; of the enemy camp: ～军 enemy troops /～机 enemy plane ❷ enemy; foe: 劲～ formidable adversary; worthy opponent /死～ sworn enemy /残～ remnant enemy troops /分清～我 make a distinction between the enemy and ourselves /～强我弱 with the enemy stronger than we are; facing the enemy's stronger forces /如临大～ as if confronted by a formidable foe ❸ oppose; resist; stand up to: 寡不～众 be too few to resist (*or* stand up to) the numerous enemy; be hopelessly outnumbered /以寡～众 fight against heavy odds /所向无～ invincible; ever victorious ❹ equal in strength; match; rival: 匹～ be one's match /势均力～ evenly matched in strength /工力悉～ be one's peer in scholarship, attainment or mastery of a technique /富可～国 one's fortune rivals the wealth of a state

敌百虫 díbǎichóng 〈农业〉 dipterex

敌稗 díbài 〈农业〉 propanil; Stam F-34 (dichloropropionanilide)

敌草净 dícǎojìng 〈农业〉 desmetryn

敌草隆 dícǎolóng 〈农业〉 diuron

敌产 díchǎn enemy property

敌敌畏 dídíwèi 〈药学〉 DDVP (dimethyl-dichloro-vinyl-phosphate); dichlorvos

敌对 díduì hostile; antagonistic; belligerent: ～势力 hostile forces /～态度 hostile (*or* antagonistic) attitude /～情绪 antagonistic feelings; feelings of hostility; enmity /～双方 opposing (*or* warring) sides; belligerent parties /～阵营 rival camps

敌方 dífāng enemy: 俘虏～特工人员数名 capture several enemy agents /～占领地 enemy-occupied territory

敌国 díguó enemy state: ～国民 enemy national /～国籍 enemy nationality /～领土 enemy territory /～条款 enemy state clause

敌害 díhài animal which harms other living beings; enemy: 刺猬遇到～时,便把身子蜷作一团。A hedgehog curls itself up when it encounters an enemy.

敌后 díhòu enemy's rear: 挺进～ push (*or* drive) into the enemy's rear area /建立～根据地 establish base areas behind enemy lines /～武工队 (during the War of Resistance Against Japanese Aggression, 1937-1945) armed work team operating in the enemy's rear

敌货 díhuò enemy goods

敌机 díjī enemy plane; enemy aircraft

敌基督 Díjīdū 〈基督教〉 Antichrist, archenemy of Christ

敌舰 díjiàn enemy warship; enemy man-of-war: ～被击中沉没。The enemy ship was sunk by a direct hit.

敌境 díjìng enemy-controlled territory; enemy's territory: 深入～ penetrate deep into the enemy's territory

敌军 díjūn enemy troops; enemy: 歼灭～一个营 wipe out a battalion of enemy troops /部队拔营去迎战～。The army struck camp and advanced to meet the enemy.

敌菌灵 díjūnlíng 〈农业〉 anilazine

敌忾 díkài 〈书面〉 hatred towards the enemy

敌忾同仇 díkài-tóngchóu *also* "同仇敌忾" cherish a common feeling of hatred for the enemy

敌咳 díké 〈药学〉 dicough

敌寇 díkòu enemy bandits (a curse word for foreign invaders); aggressors; enemy

敌楼 dílóu watch tower; look-out tower: 从～上可以清楚地看到敌军的调动。The watch tower commands a good view of the enemy troops' movements.

敌旗 díqí enemy flag

敌侨 díqiáo enemy alien; enemy national

敌情 díqíng enemy's situation; enemy activities: 侦察～ reconnoitre the enemy situation; gather information about the enemy /仔细分析～ make a careful analysis of the enemy's situation /～有了变化。There have been changes on the part of the enemy. /～严重。Enemy activities pose a grave threat.

敌情观念 díqíng guānniàn awareness of the enemy's presence; alertness to or vigilance against the enemy: 缺乏～ not feel keenly the enemy's presence; lack of vigilance against the enemy

敌酋 díqiú enemy chieftain; enemy commander

敌区 díqū enemy-controlled area

敌人 dírén enemy; foe: 无形的～ invisible enemy /公开的～ open enemy /隐藏的～ enemy in disguise; hidden foe /来自内部的～ enemy from within /虚假的朋友比公开的～更可怕。A false friend is worse than an open foe.

敌视 díshì be hostile or antagonistic to; take a hostile attitude towards: 有些人对改革总是持～态度。Some people are always hostile to reforms. /我猜想他们一直～我们。I have a hunch that they have been antagonistic to us all along.

敌手 díshǒu ❶ match; opponent; adversary: 不是他的～ not his match (*or* rival) /竞选人指责他的～回避基本问题。The candidate charged his opponent with evasion of the basic issue. ❷ enemy hands: 落入～ fall into enemy hands

敌台 dítái ❶ enemy broadcasting or TV station ❷ watch tower or defence works built on a city wall or strategic spot

敌探 dítàn enemy spy

敌特 dítè enemy spy; enemy agent

敌顽 díwán (during the War of Resistance Against Japanese Aggression, 1937-1945) enemy and the diehards — Japanese aggressor troops, and KMT forces who persisted in fighting the Communist troops instead of the Japanese: 狠狠打击～ hit hard at the Japanese aggressors and the diehards

敌伪 díwěi enemy and the puppet regime (during the War of Resistance Against Japanese Aggression, 1937-1945): ～人员 enemy and puppet personnel

敌我矛盾 dí-wǒ máodùn contradiction between ourselves and the enemy

敌穴 díxué den of the enemy: 捣毁～ destroy the enemy's den; smash the enemy's hideout /这里是个～。The place is a lair of the enemy.

敌焰 díyàn enemy's arrogance: ～嚣张。The enemy's arrogance is rampant.

敌意 díyì hostility; enmity; animosity; antagonism: 他没有表露出明显的～。There is no obvious antagonism on his part. /充满～的人群把演讲者轰下了台。The speaker was hooted down by the hostile crowd.

敌营 díyíng enemy camp

敌占区 dízhànqū enemy-occupied area; enemy-occupied territory

敌阵 dízhèn enemy position: 冲入～ charge into the enemy position

髢 dí

髢髢 dídi 〈方言〉 wig

觌(覿) dí

〈书面〉 see; meet

觌面 dímiàn 〈书面〉 meet: 未能～ unable to meet

迪(廸) dí

〈书面〉 enlighten; guide: 启～ enlightenment; inspiration

迪拜 Díbài Dubai, one of the seven member states of the United Arab Emirates

迪戈加西亚岛 Dígējiāxīyàdǎo Diego Garcia, largest island of the Chagos Archipelago in the Indian Ocean

迪斯科 dísīkē (transliteration) disco (dancing): ～舞 disco /～舞曲 disco music /～舞厅 discotheque /跳～ dance at a discotheque; disco

迪斯尼乐园 Dísīní Lèyuán Disneyland

笛 dí

❶ *also* "横笛" héngdí bamboo flute; flute: 长～ flute

/短～ piccolo ❷ whistle：汽～ steam whistle /警～ police whistle

笛福 Dífú Daniel Defoe (1660-1731), English novelist and journalist, author of *Robinson Crusoe* (1719)

笛卡尔 Díkǎ'ěr René Descartes (1596-1650), French philosopher, mathematician, and man of science：～儿何 Cartesian geometry

笛卡尔坐标 Díkǎ'ěr zuòbiāo 〈数学〉Cartesian coordinate

笛膜 dímó bamboo membrane (for holes in a Chinese flute)

笛式存储器 díshì cúnchǔqì 〈自控〉flute storage

笛子 dízi *dizi*, Chinese bamboo flute; eight-holed bamboo flute：～独奏 flute solo /他十岁开始学～。He began to learn to play the flute at the age of 10.

的

dí 〈书面〉true; really：～是高手 truly a master

see also de; dì

的当 dídàng 〈书面〉proper; appropriate; suitable：用词～ use words properly /这个评语十分～。This is an appropriate comment.

的的喀喀湖 Dídíkākāhú Lake Titicaca (in the Andes between Peru and Bolivia, the highest large lake in the world)

的款 díkuǎn reliable sum of money

的黎波里 Dílíbōlǐ Tripoli, capital and chief port of Libya

D

的情 díqíng 〈书面〉actual fact; truth：所报俱系～，并无虚夸。The report is based entirely on facts, and there is not the least exaggeration.

的确 díquè indeed; really：我～没有什么不满意的。I have nothing to complain of really. /她的那些小故事～引人入胜。Her little stories are indeed very fascinating.

的确良 díquèliáng 〈纺织〉dacron; terylene：棉～ polycotton

的士 díshì 〈方言〉(transliteration) taxi; cab

的真 dízhēn true to life; lifelike：这个角色她演得～。The part she acted in the play was true to life. *or* Her performance in the play was wonderfully realistic.

的证 dízhèng reliable evidence; irrefutable proof：有～表明他是无罪的。Indisputable evidence proved that he was not guilty.

狄

Dí ❶ ancient name for ethnic groups in north China ❷ a surname

狄慈根 Dícígēn Joseph Dietzgen (1828-1888), German writer and philosopher

狄德罗 Dídéluó Denis Diderot (1713-1784), French philosopher and man of letters, compiler of the *Encyclopédie*

狄盖特 Dígàitè Pierré de Geyter (1848-1932), French worker, composer of *The Internationale*

狄更斯 Dígēngsī Charles Dickens (1812-1870), English novelist

狄克推多 díkètuīduō (transliteration, now replaced by 独裁者) dictator

狄拉克 Dílākè Paul A. M. Dirac (1902-), British physicist, founder of quantum physics, and Nobel laureate for 1933：～粒子 Dirac particle

狄赛尔 Dísài'ěr Rudolf Diesel (1858-1913), German engineer who invented the diesel engine

狄赛尔机 dísài'ěrjī diesel engine

鬏

dí

鬏髻 díjì 〈书面〉bun (of false hair worn at the back or on top of the head)

荻

dí a kind of reed

荻芦竹 dílúzhú giant reed

籴(糴)

dí buy in (grain)

翟

dí ❶〈古语〉long-tailed pheasant ❷〈古语〉pheasant feather (used for dancing) ❸ (Dí) a surname

see also Zhái

dǐ

氐

dǐ 〈书面〉foundation; base

see also dī

底[1]

dǐ ❶ bottom; base：井～ bottom of a well /海～ seabed /战斗到～ fight to the end /这条船～朝天，漂在水上。The boat was found floating bottom upwards. ❷ origin or bottom of sth.; heart of the matter; ins and outs：心里没～ feel uncertain of sth. /摸摸他的～ try to sound him out /刨根问～ get to the bottom of sth. /交～ give someone the bottom line; put all the cards on the table /亮～ show one's hand ❸ rough draft; draft text：留个～儿 keep a copy on file; duplicate and file (a document, letter, etc.) /我先打个～。I'll make a draft first. ❹ end of a year or month：年～ end of a year /月～ end of a month ❺ background; foundation：蓝～白花 white flowers on a blue background ❻ (short for 底数❶) base number ❼〈书面〉end up with; end up in; come to：终～于成 end in victory; succeed in the end /伊于胡～？Where will all this end? ❽ (Dǐ) a surname

底[2]

dǐ 〈书面〉what：～事 what matter; what

底[3]

dǐ 〈书面〉❶ here; this：～是藏春处。Here is where spring resides. ❷ so; such：长歌～有情。The song is so sentimental.

see also de

底板 dǐbǎn *also* "下盘" xiàpán 〈矿业〉baseboard; backboard; base plate

底版 dǐbǎn negative; photographic plate

底包 dǐbāo *also* "班底" bāndǐ 〈旧语〉ordinary members of a theatrical troupe

底本 dǐběn ❶ original copy for the record or for duplication; master copy：原稿作为～存档。The original copy will be put on file as master copy. ❷ text used in proof reading or against which other texts are checked

底部 dǐbù bottom; bottom side

底财 dǐcái real estate; immovables (such as land, houses etc.)

底舱 dǐcāng ship's bottom compartment; bilge

底册 dǐcè bound copy of documents kept on file; file copy

底层 dǐcéng ❶〈建筑〉ground floor; first floor：大楼的～是商店。The ground (*or* first) floor of the building houses shops. ❷ bottom; lowest rung; rock bottom：处在社会的～ at the bottom of society/他工作从～干起，惨淡经营，终底于成。He started his career at the lowest rung and worked his way up to success.

底层浮游生物 dǐcéng fúyóu shēngwù bottom plankton

底层鱼类 dǐcéng yúlèi demersal fish

底衬 dǐchèn ❶〈印刷〉under blanket ❷ bottom liner; bottom lining

底垫 dǐdiàn 〈方言〉capital; fund：生产～ production fund /拿出一部分现款作～。A part of the cash was set aside as capital.

底定 dǐdìng 〈书面〉restore peace in a region after an insurgence is put down; have rebellion suppressed and law and order restored：畿辅～。Peace and order were restored in the areas around the capital.

底肥 dǐféi *also* "基肥" jīféi 〈农业〉base fertilizer

底粪 dǐfèn base manure

底稿 dǐgǎo draft; manuscript：他的新诗～ manuscript of his new poem

底工 dǐgōng *also* "底功" grounding in basic skills：这位京剧演员的～扎实。The Beijing opera actor has a good grounding in basic skills.

底火 dǐhuǒ ❶ fire in a stove before fuel is added：注意不要让～熄灭了。Make sure that the fire (in the stove) does not go out. ❷〈军事〉primer; ignition cartridge

底极 dǐjí 〈书面〉end; ultimate point; extremity

底价 dǐjià *also* "底码" base price; bottom price; floor

底架 dǐjià 〈机械〉chassis

底角 dǐjiǎo 〈数学〉base angle

底孔 dǐkǒng 〈水利〉bottom outlet

底里 dǐlǐ exact details; ins and outs：～不明 not know the inside story of the matter

底码 dǐmǎ ❶ (of price, loan interest, etc.) floor：规定～ fix the floor /提高～ raise the floor /这批棉花～是每公斤五元。The cotton will be sold at the floor price of 5 *yuan* per kilo. ❷ basic factors; fixed plan or figure; bottom line：摸清～，才好开展工作。We must find out the basic factors before we proceed with the work.

底牌 dǐpái cards in one's hand; bottom line：亮～ show one's

hand /摸清对方~ find out the other party's bottom line /不到万不得已,别打这张~。Don't play this final card until and unless it's absolutely necessary.

底盘 dǐpán ❶ chassis (of an automobile):~车架 chassis frame /~高度 chassis height ❷ board or plate on which most components or parts are fixed in an electronic apparatus ❸〈方言〉base or foundation of sth.

底片 dǐpiàn negative; photographic plate:~处理 film processing /~盒 cartridge /~对比率 film contrast

底栖生物 dǐqī shēngwù benthon:~群落 benthonic community

底漆 dǐqī priming paint; primer:先涂~。Lay priming paint first.

底气 dǐqì ❶ (in speech and singing) resonance; breath:~不足 be lacking in resonance or breath /他~足,唱起来嗓音洪亮。As he has good resonance he sings in a deep and loud voice. ❷ energy; drive; vigour; force:教师们看到自己的工作受到领导的支持,做好工作的~更足了。The leadership's support has provided the teachers with a fresh spurt of energy in a bid to improve their work.

底情 dǐqíng inside story; true state of affairs; actual condition of things:我不摸~,无法表示意见。I am not in a position to express an opinion since I don't know how matters actually stand.

底裙 dǐqún *also* "衬裙" chènqún underskirt; slip

底燃火炉 dǐrán huǒlú baseburner

底色 dǐsè ❶〈纺织〉bottom ❷ underpainting

底墒 dǐshāng 〈农业〉soil moisture (before sowing or planting):今冬雪少,~不好。As there wasn't enough snowfall this winter, the soil is too dry (for spring sowing).

底视图 dǐshìtú 〈机械〉bottom view

底数 dǐshù ❶〈数学〉base number ❷ truth or root of a matter:告诉你个~。I'll give you a tip. /此项工作如何进行,我已有了~。I have some idea how the matter should be carried out.

底水 dǐshuǐ water used to irrigate the fields before the sowing season:要保丰收,最好先浇灌~。It is advisable to irrigate the fields before sowing in order to guarantee a good harvest.

底特律 Dǐtèlǜ Detroit, major industrial city in southeastern Michigan and centre of the US automobile industry nicknamed Motown (short for motor town)

底图 dǐtú 〈地理〉base map

底土 dǐtǔ subsoil:~层〈地质〉substratum

底细 dǐxi ins and outs; inside story:你去了解一下这事的~。Go and find out the ins and outs of the matter. /镇上来了一个货郎,没人知道他的~。Nobody knows anything about the street vendor who has recently come to the village.

底下 dǐxia ❶ under; below; beneath:桌子~ under the table /楼~有一个小花园。Below the building there was a small garden. /我们觉得脚~的土很松。The earth felt soft under (*or* beneath) our feet. /大树~好乘凉。One can enjoy the cool in the shade of a big tree. *or* A man's career is assured as long as he has influential friends. /请大家~交换意见。You can exchange views when the session is over. ❷ next; later; afterwards:~该干什么了? What shall we do next? /爆炸之后我昏倒了,~的事就不知道了。Everything went black after the explosion, and I did not know what happened later.

底下人 dǐxiarén ❶ servant ❷ subordinate; underling:老板不表态,我们~不好说话。How can we say anything when the boss hasn't made his position clear?

底限 dǐxiàn minimum; least possible amount; lowest limit:厂主付给工人的工资仍旧低于~。The mill owners still pay the workers less than the minimum wage.

底线 dǐxiàn ❶ (of tennis court, etc.) baseline ❷ planted agent; stooge; stoolpigeon:要是没有~,他们是不会得逞的。They could not have succeeded without their stooges (*or* stoolpigeons).

底薪 dǐxīn basic salary; base pay

底蕴 dǐyùn 〈书面〉details; inside story; ins and outs:不知其中~ not know the details

底账 dǐzhàng original accounts; original account book; first copy of the account book

底止 dǐzhǐ 〈书面〉end; limit:永无~ limitless; endless

底子 dǐzi ❶ bottom; base:鞋~ sole of a shoe ❷ ins and outs; bottom line; basic position:摸清了他们的~ get to know their basic position ❸ foundation; base; grounding:我国~薄。We have a weak economic foundation. /她的英文~好。She has a good grounding in English. ❹ copy kept as a record; rough draft or sketch:每个文件都要留个~。Make sure that a copy of each document is kept on file. /画画儿先用铅笔打个~。When drawing a picture make a rough sketch in pencil first. ❺ remnant:货~ remnants of stock ❻ background; ground:她穿着一件白~小花的短衫。She is wearing a white shirt with coloured flowers.

底座 dǐzuò base; pedestal; foundation; support:塑像的~ pedestal (*or* base) of a statue /圆柱的~ base of a column /台灯的~ stand of a reading lamp /~螺丝 base screw

诋

dǐ 〈书面〉speak ill of; slander; defame:丑~ call names; defame

诋斥 dǐchì condemn; denounce:~军阀 denounce the warlords

诋毁 dǐhuǐ slander; vilify; calumniate; defame:~别人声誉 vilify sb.'s reputation /你如此~他,他可以控告你犯了诽谤罪。If you slander him like this, he may sue you for libel.

诋辱 dǐrǔ 〈书面〉slander and insult:肆为~ slander and insult at will

柢

dǐ root (of a tree):根深~固 deep-rooted; ingrained

砥

dǐ (formerly also pronounced zhǐ)〈书面〉whetstone

砥砺 dǐlì 〈书面〉❶ whetstone ❷ whet; temper:好剑也常需~。Even a good sword needs constant whetting. /处逆境可以~意志。One may temper one's will in adverse circumstances. ❸ encourage; spur on:我们应该互相~,互相帮助。We should encourage and help one another.

砥石 dǐshí whet-slate; whetstone; grindstone

砥柱 dǐzhù *see* "砥柱中流"

砥柱中流 dǐzhù-zhōngliú *also* "中流砥柱";"砥柱" stand rockfirm in the middle of the turbulent Yellow River like Dizhu Hill (in Sanmen Gorge) — be a mainstay

抵[1]

dǐ ❶ support; prop; hold; sustain:旧墙由几根大柱~着。The old wall is shored up by several poles. /他用手~住下巴,陷入沉思。He propped his chin in both hands, deep in thought. /这椅子不结实,~不住他的分量。This chair is not solid enough to hold him. ❷ resist; withstand:这个排~住了敌人的几次反攻。The platoon withstood several counterattacks by the enemy. /有些人犯罪是因为~不住物质的诱惑。Some people commit crimes because they cannot resist material temptations. ❸ compensate for; make good; make up for:怎么赔也~不了她的损失。Nothing can compensate for her loss. /怎么报答也~不了他对我的恩情。There is nothing I can do to repay his kindness. ❹ mortgage:用银行的存款作~ mortgage bank deposits /他把房子~了一万元。He mortgaged his house for 10,000 *yuan*. ❺ balance; set off:收支正好相~。Income and expenditure are exactly equal. *or* We manage to strike a balance between revenue and expenditure. ❻ be equal to; match:一个鸡蛋的蛋白质~得上半磅牛肉。An egg is equal to half a pound of steak in protein value. /他的体力~得上你,但脑瓜子不行。He can compare with you physically but not mentally. / 忠言~万金。A word of advice is worth 10,000 taels of gold. *or* Advice is more valuable than gold.

抵[2]

dǐ 〈书面〉arrive at; reach:我已安~上海。I have arrived in Shanghai safe and sound. /代表团将于日内~京。The delegation is arriving in Beijing in a day or two.

抵补 dǐbǔ make up for; compensate (for):这些金钱就能~她蒙受的屈辱么? Can the money compensate for the humiliations she has suffered?

抵偿 dǐcháng compensate (for); make up for; make good:~损耗 make up the depreciation (*or* loss) /实物~ compensation in kind /他蒙受的损失终于得到了~。The loss he sustained was finally made good.

抵充 dǐchōng pay with money or materials originally earmarked for other uses; use sth. as a substitute:实验费一时不够用,组员们先拿出自己的生活费来~。Members of the team offered their living allowances to cover the temporary shortfall in the expenses of the experiment.

抵触 dǐchù *also* "牴触" dǐchù conflict; contravene; clash; oppose:利益~ conflicting interests /有~情绪 be resentful /两个考察组的结论发生~。The findings of the two study missions contradict each other. /朋友的婚礼与我的上海之行有~,所以参加不成了。The wedding of a friend clashes with my trip to Shanghai, so I have to

excuse myself. /这是与法律相～的。This contravenes (*or* goes against) the law.

抵达 dǐdá arrive; reach:～目的地 reach one's destination /正点～东京 arrive at Tokyo on time /红军经过两万五千里长征终于在1935年～陕北。The Red Army finally got to northern Shaanxi in 1935 after a long march of 25,000 *li*.

抵挡 dǐdǎng withstand; keep out; ward off:这种临时的木棚～不住风寒。This makeshift shed cannot keep out the wind and the cold. /这些沙袋也许能暂时～住上涨的洪水。These sandbags will perhaps withstand the rising flood-waters for a moment. /部队～敌人的进攻达48小时之后撤至安全地带。The troops resisted the enemy onslaught for 48 hours before they withdrew to a safe place.

抵当 dǐdàng offer as collateral; give as equivalent:～权〈法律〉right of the creditor to receive payment on priority basis upon the selling of the property which has been offered as security by the debtor

抵法 dǐfǎ 〈书面〉(of convicts) be executed

抵还 dǐhuán compensate with goods of equal value:作价～ compensate at the price fixed

抵换 dǐhuàn exchange; substitute for; take the place of:他用一台彩电～我的冰箱。He exchanged (*or* traded) a coloured TV set for my refrigerator. /我们不用现金支付,而用实物～。We will pay not in cash but in kind.

抵交 dǐjiāo hand in sth. as a substitute for sth. else:股份资金可以用实物～。Share capital can be paid in kind instead of cash.

抵近 dǐjìn come close to:～射击 shooting at close range; point-blank firing

抵拒 dǐjù resist; keep off:无法～ irresistible

抵抗 dǐkàng resist; fight against; stand up to:增强对疾病的～力 build up one's resistance to disease /顽强～ put up a stubborn resistance /人民奋起～侵略者。The people rose in resistance against the invaders.

抵赖 dǐlài deny; disavow; disclaim:不容～ brook no denial /他对自己说过的话矢口～。He disavowed having ever made such remarks. /～是无用的,还是老实交待为好。It's no use denying facts. Better own up.

抵临 dǐlín arrive (at a place)

抵命 dǐmìng give a life for a life; pay with one's life (for a murder, etc.):杀人～,欠债还钱。He who kills has to give his life; he who borrows has to pay his debt.

抵塞 dǐsè ❶ stall sb. off:他怕挨说,就编造了一些理由来～一下。He invented some excuses to stave off reproach. ❷ contradict; talk back to:他不但不接受意见,反而冷冷地～人家。He not only rejected all criticism, but gave his critics a stinging retort.

抵事 dǐshì 〈方言〉be useful; serve the purpose; work:虽然这不是最佳方案,但能～。The plan may not be the best one, but it will serve the purpose. /这孩子太小,还不～。The boy is still too young to be of any help. /药量太小不～。The dosage is too small to be effective.

抵数 dǐshù make up the number; serve as a stopgap; balance an account:他的技术也许不够熟练,但还能～。He may not be very skilful, but he can probably pass muster.

抵死 dǐsǐ risk one's life; fight desperately:～不从 obstinately refuse to comply

抵牾 dǐwǔ *also*"牴牾" dǐwǔ contradiction; conflict:文章中的提法多有～。We find contradictory arguments in this essay.

抵瑕蹈隙 dǐxiá-dǎoxì pick holes; find fault

抵消 dǐxiāo offset; counteract; cancel out; neutralize; countervail:～影响 offset an influence /～药物的副作用 counteract side-effects of a medicine /两种力量互相～。The two forces cancel out one another. /保险公司的赔偿一定程度上～了火灾带来的损失。Compensation made by the insurance company mitigated to some extent the losses caused by the fire.

抵消关税 dǐxiāo guānshuì countervailing duty

抵押 dǐyā mortgage; pledge:～资产 mortgage asset /受～者 mortgagee; pledgee /以家产作～ raise a mortgage on one's family estate /把钻石戒指～给他 leave a diamond ring with him as a pledge

抵押贷款 dǐyā dàikuǎn mortgage financing; mortgage loan

抵押法 dǐyāfǎ law of mortgages

抵押合同 dǐyā hétong mortgage contract

抵押经纪人 dǐyā jīngjìrén mortgage middleman

抵押品 dǐyāpǐn security; pledge

抵押人 dǐyārén mortgager; mortgagor; pledger

抵押市场 dǐyā shìchǎng mortgage market

抵押销售 dǐyā xiāoshòu mortgage sale

抵押信贷 dǐyā xìndài mortgage credit

抵押银行 dǐyā yínháng mortgage bank

抵押债券 dǐyā zhàiquàn mortgage bond

抵用 dǐyòng be of use or help; serve the purpose:她吓得心里发毛,腿也不～了。She was frightened out of her wits and could not even move her legs. *or* She was so scared that her legs simply refused to move.

抵御 dǐyù resist; withstand; ward off:～外敌的侵略 resist foreign aggression /用防风林来～风沙的袭击 use windbreaks to withstand the onslaught of duststorms; build a shelter belt against sandstorms /入睡前她们烧起了几堆火以～寒气。Before going to sleep, they started several camp fires to ward off the cold.

抵债 dǐzhài pay a debt in kind or by labour:干活～ pay a debt with one's work /解放前有些穷人被迫卖儿卖女以～。Before liberation, poverty-stricken families were often compelled to sell their children to pay off their debts.

抵账 dǐzhàng *see*"抵债"

抵制 dǐzhì boycott; resist; combat; reject:～腐朽思想的侵蚀 resist the corrosive influence of decadent ideas /～歪风邪气 combat evil social trends /那次会议遭到众人的～。People boycotted the meeting.

抵罪 dǐzuì be punished for a crime; be punishable by law:伤人致残,即使是无意的,也要～。Action resulting in people's disability, even unpremeditated, is punishable by law.

骶 dǐ

骶骨 dǐgǔ *also*"骶椎";"荐骨" jiàngǔ;"荐椎" jiànzhuī 〈生理〉sacrum:～融合 sacralization /～痛 sacralgia

骶骨麻醉 dǐgǔ mázuì 〈医学〉sacral block

骶神经 dǐshénjīng 〈生理〉sacral nerve

骶椎 dǐzhuī 〈生理〉sacrum; sacral vertebra

牴(觝) dǐ

牴触 dǐchù *see*"抵触" dǐchù

牴牾 dǐwǔ *see*"抵牾" dǐwǔ

邸 dǐ

❶ residence of a high official ❷ (Dǐ) a surname

邸报 dǐbào *also*"邸抄"〈旧语〉official gazette

邸第 dǐdì 〈旧语〉residences of nobility and senior officials

邸舍 dǐshè ❶〈旧语〉residences of nobility and senior officials ❷〈书面〉hotel; inn; tavern

邸宅 dǐzhái mansion; mansion house

dì

帝 dì

❶ Supreme Being; the Divine:玉皇大～ Jade Emperor (supreme ruler of heaven according to Taoism) /上～ God /天～ supreme ruler of heaven ❷ emperor; monarch:称～ proclaim oneself emperor /三皇五～ three rulers (天皇 the ruler of heaven, 地皇 the ruler of the earth, and 人皇 the ruler of humanity) and five emperors (黄帝 Huangdi, 颛顼 Zhuanxu, 帝喾 Di Ku, 唐尧 Tang Yao, and 虞舜 Yu Shun) ❸ (short for 帝国主义) imperialism:反～斗争 struggle against imperialism; anti-imperialist struggle

帝都 dìdū *also*"帝京" imperial capital

帝俄 Dì-É *also*"沙俄" Shā-É Tsarist Russia; Tzarist Russia; Czarist Russia

帝国 dìguó ❶ empire:殖民～ colonial empire /东罗马～ Eastern Roman Empire /西罗马～ Western Roman Empire /第一～ *also*"神圣罗马～" First Reich (the Holy Roman Empire, 962-1806) /第二(德意志)～ Second Reich (1871-1918) /第三(德意志)～ Third Reich (1933-1945) /拿破仑～ Napoleonic Empire (first French Empire under Napoleon, 1804-1815) ❷〈比喻〉huge monopolistic corporation; empire:石油～ oil empire

帝国大厦 Dìguó Dàshà Empire State Building (in New York City)

帝国化学工业公司 Dìguó Huàxué Gōngyè Gōngsī Imperial Chemical Industries Limited (ICI)

帝国主义 dìguózhǔyì imperialism:～分子 imperialist /～者 imperi-

alist /～侵略 imperialist aggression /～时代 era of imperialism
帝号 dìhào name of the reign of an emperor
帝虎 dìhǔ clerical or typographical errors made through confusing Chinese characters of similar form; wrongly written character similar to the intended word in form
see also "鲁鱼帝虎" lǔyú-dìhǔ
帝君 dìjūn title for higher deities, usu. in the Buddhist or Taoist hierarchy:关～ Guan Yu (god of military prowess, loyalty, etc.) / 文昌～ Wen Chang (god of literature and learning)
帝王 dìwáng emperor; monarch:～将相 kings and princes, generals and ministers /～思想 mentality of a feudal emperor; autocratic mentality
帝王谷 Dìwánggǔ (Egypt) Valley of the Tombs of the Kings
帝汶 Dìwèn Timor, largest of the Lesser Sunda Islands in the southern Malay Archipelago
帝业 dìyè great undertaking of an emperor
帝制 dìzhì autocratic monarchy; monarchy:建立～ establish a monarchy /恢复～ restore the monarchy /改～为民国 abolish the monarchy and proclaim the establishment of a republic
帝雉 dìzhì 〈动物〉mikado pheasant
帝子 dìzǐ princes and princesses; children of a monarch

谛

dì 〈书面〉❶ attentively; carefully ❷ meaning; significance:妙～ ingenious remark; wisdom /寻求革命的真～ seek revolutionary truth
谛视 dìshì examine closely; scrutinize:凝神～ scrutinize with rapt attention
谛思 dìsī 〈书面〉ponder deeply; consider carefully:凝神～ be buried in thought
谛听 dìtīng 〈书面〉listen attentively:屏息～ listen attentively with bated breath

蒂(蔕)

dì base of a fruit:并～莲 twin lotus flowers of the same root

碲

dì 〈化学〉tellurium (Te)
碲化物 dìhuàwù 〈化学〉telluride
碲金矿 dìjīnkuàng 〈矿业〉calaverite
碲酸 dìsuān 〈化学〉telluric acid; hydrogen tellurate
碲铜矿 dìtóngkuàng 〈矿业〉rickardite

缔

dì form; establish; conclude
缔合 dìhé 〈化学〉association:～热 heat of association /～液体 associated liquid
缔交 dìjiāo ❶〈书面〉establish friendship:他们～三十年,始终如一。The friendship (that) they forged over 30 years ago has remained unchanged. ❷ establish diplomatic relations:两国～以来,我们的传统友谊有了进一步发展。Since the establishment of diplomatic relations between our two countries, we have further developed our traditional friendship.
缔结 dìjié conclude; establish:～条约 conclude a treaty (*or* an agreement) /～邦交 establish diplomatic relations
缔盟 dìméng form an alliance
缔姻 dìyīn be united in wedlock
缔约 dìyuē conclude or sign a treaty or an agreement:～各方 each of the contracting parties; all contracting parties /～双方重申严守协定条款。Both contracting parties reaffirm their commitment to the provisions of the treaty.
缔约方 dìyuēfāng 〈法律〉contracting party
缔约国 dìyuēguó signatory (state) to a treaty; party to a treaty; (high) contracting party
缔造 dìzào found; create; establish:共和国的～者 founders of the republic /～大业 create and complete a grand cause

弟

dì ❶ younger brother:二～ second younger brother /小～ kid brother ❷ younger brother-in-law or (male) cousin ❸〈谦词〉I (usu. in letter writing):～近日身体不适。I don't feel quite well these days. ❹ (Dì) a surname
弟弟 dìdi ❶ younger brother; brother ❷ younger male cousin:叔伯～ first cousin
弟妇 dìfù younger brother's wife; sister-in-law
弟妹 dìmèi ❶ younger brother and sister:～均已长大成人。My younger brother and sister have both grown up. ❷ younger brother's wife; sister-in-law:我～比弟弟办法多。My younger brother's wife is more resourceful than my brother.
弟兄 dìxiong brothers:他～二人 he and his brother; the two brothers /支援农民～ give aid to peasant brothers /他没有～,只有一个姐姐。He has an elder sister but no brothers.
弟子 dìzǐ disciple; pupil; follower:据说孔子有三千～。It is said that Confucius had three thousand disciples.

第[1]

dì ❶ *indicating ordinal numbers*:～一 first /宪法～三条 Article 3 of the Constitution /我住在～十四层。My flat is on the 14th floor. ❷〈书面〉grades in which successful candidates in the imperial examinations were placed:及～ pass the imperial examinations /落～ fail the imperial examinations

第[2]

dì 〈旧语〉residence of a high official:宅～ residence; house /府～ mansion; mansion house /门～ family status

第[3]

dì 〈书面〉❶ but; however ❷ only; alone
第比利斯 Dìbǐlìsī Tbilisi or Tiflis, capital of the Republic of Georgia
第二把手 dì'èrbǎshǒu second in command; number two man:这个厂的～是从工人中选举产生的。The second in command of the factory was elected from among the workers.
第二产业 dì-èr chǎnyè secondary industry
第二次打击能力 dì-èr cì dǎjī nénglì 〈军事〉second-strike capability
第二次国内革命战争 Dì-èr Cì Guónèi Gémìng Zhànzhēng *also* "土地革命战争" Tǔdì Gémìng Zhànzhēng Second Revolutionary Civil War or Agrarian Revolutionary War (1927-1937), waged by the Chinese people under the leadership of the Chinese Communist Party against KMT rule
第二次世界大战 Dì-èr Cì Shìjiè Dàzhàn Second World War (1939-1945); World War II
第二次限制战略武器会谈 dì-èr cì xiànzhì zhànlüè wǔqì huìtán Strategic Arms Limitation Talks II (SALT II)
第二次鸦片战争 Dì-èr Cì Yāpiàn Zhànzhēng Second Opium War (known in the West as the Arrow War, 1856-1860)
第二国际 Dì-èr Guójì Second International (1889-1914)
第二人称 dì-èr rénchēng 〈语言〉second person:～复数 second person plural
第二审 dì'èrshěn 〈法律〉second instance:～法院 court of second instance; court of second hearing
第二声 dì'èrshēng 〈语言〉rising tone, second of the four tones in modern standard Chinese pronunciation
第二十二条军规 dì-èrshí'èr-tiáo-jūnguī Catch-22, a dilemma in which one is trapped by contradictory regulations or conditions
第二世界 dì-èr shìjiè Second World (composed of developed countries other than the superpowers)
第二现场 dì-èr xiànchǎng 〈法律〉secondary scene
第二信号系统 dì-èr xìnhào xìtǒng 〈生理〉second signal system
第二性 dì'èrxìng 〈哲学〉secondary
第二宇宙速度 dì-èr yǔzhòu sùdù second cosmic velocity (11.2 km per second); earth escape velocity
第二职业 dì-èr zhíyè second job; sparetime job; moonlighting:～者 moonlighter
第二主犯 dì-èr zhǔfàn 〈法律〉principal in the second degree
第六感觉 dì-liù gǎnjué sixth sense
第聂伯河 Dìnièbóhé Dnieper River (flowing some 2,200 km through Russia, Belorussia and Ukraine to the Black Sea)
第三产业 dì-sān chǎnyè tertiary industry; service sector
第三次国内革命战争 Dì-sān Cì Guónèi Gémìng Zhànzhēng *also* "解放战争" Jiěfàng Zhànzhēng Third Revolutionary Civil War or War of Liberation (1945-1949), which saw the final overthrow of KMT rule and the founding of the People's Republic of China
第三当事人 dì-sān dāngshìrén 〈法律〉third party
第三等级 dì-sān děngjí third estate; third class
第三国际 Dì-sān Guójì Third International (1919-1943)
第三纪 Dìsānjì 〈地质〉Tertiary Period
第三人 dìsānrén third party (in a law case)

D

第三人称 dì-sān rénchēng 〈语言〉third person:~单数 third person singular
第三声 dìsānshēng 〈语言〉falling-rising tone, third of the four tones in modern standard Chinese pronunciation
第三世界 dì-sān shìjiè Third World (composed of the developing countries in Asia, Africa, Latin America, etc.)
第三系 Dìsānxì 〈地质〉Tertiary System
第三宇宙速度 dì-sān yǔzhòu sùdù third cosmic velocity (16.7 km per second); solar escape velocity
第三债务人 dì-sān zhàiwùrén 〈法律〉garnishee
第三者 dìsānzhě ❶ third party (to a dispute):这件事的是非曲折,可向~了解。Ask a third party for the rights and wrongs of the case. ❷ person having an affair with either the husband or the wife; third party:他的悲剧是由~的插足造成的。His tragedy was caused by the involvement of a third party in his family life.
第四国际 Dì-sì Guójì Fourth International (set up by Trotsky in 1937)
第四纪 Dìsìjì 〈地质〉Quaternary Period
第四声 dìsìshēng 〈语言〉falling tone, fourth of the four tones in modern standard Chinese pronunciation
D
第五纵队 dì-wǔ zòngduì fifth column, group of enemy agents working in a country at war:~队员 fifth columnist
第一 dì-yī ❶ first:~副总理 first deputy prime minister; first vice premier /~号种子选手 No.1 seeded player; No.1 seed /考了~ come first in an exam; get a first in an exam /~卷 first volume; volume one /~小提琴手 first violin /~版 first edition /~抵押权 first mortgage /(影片)~轮放映 first run /~次参观故宫 one's first visit to the Palace Museum /下午讨论会上你~个发言。You'll be the first to speak in the afternoon's session. /什么事情都有~次。There is a first for everything. ❷ most important; primary; foremost:把劳动看作是生活的~需要 regard labour as life's prime want /产品质量~,服务态度~。We give (*or* attach) primary importance to the quality of commodities and the service attitude of shop assistants. /安全~。Safety first.
第一把交椅 dì-yī bǎ jiāoyǐ top post; number one position; most important post (in a government organ, a factory, etc.)
第一把手 dìyībǎshǒu first in command; number one man; person holding primary responsibility:这位就是我们农场新当选的~。This is the top man recently elected by the staff of the farm.
第一被告 dì-yī bèigào 〈法律〉first-mentioned defendant
第一产业 dì-yī chǎnyè primary industry
第一次打击能力 dì-yī cì dǎjī nénglì 〈军事〉first-strike capability
第一次国内革命战争 Dì-yī Cì Guónèi Gémìng Zhànzhēng First Revolutionary Civil War (1924-1927), waged against the imperialists and the Northern warlords
第一次世界大战 Dì-yī Cì Shìjiè Dàzhàn First World War (1914-1918); World War I
第一次鸦片战争 Dì-yī Cì Yāpiàn Zhànzhēng First Opium War (1840-1842)
第一夫人 dì-yī fūren First Lady (wife of head of state)
第一副本 dì-yī fùběn first authentic copy
第一国际 Dì-yī Guójì First International (1864-1876)
第一家庭 dì-yī jiātíng First Family (family of head of state)
第一流 dìyīliú first rate; first class:~作家 first-class writer /~产品 top-grade (*or* top-notch) products
第一劝业银行 Dì-yī Quànyè Yínháng (Japan) Dai-Ichi Kangyo Bank
第一人称 dì-yī rénchēng 〈语言〉first person
第一审 dìyīshěn 〈法律〉first instance:~法院 court of first instance
第一声 dìyīshēng 〈语言〉high and level tone, first of the four tones in modern standard Chinese pronunciation
第一世界 dì-yī shìjiè First World (composed of the superpower or superpowers)
第一手 dìyīshǒu firsthand:~材料 firsthand information (*or* material)
第一线 dìyīxiàn ❶ front line; front:敌军将大部分兵力投入~,造成后方空虚。With the greater part of his troops concentrated at the front, the enemy has left his rear weakly defended. *or* The enemy's concentration of troops at the front has made his rear vulnerable. ❷ forefront; first line:奋斗在社会主义建设的~ struggle in the forefront of socialist construction /教学~ classroom lecturing /农业生产~ field work in farming /~人员 people in the front line of production /老干部退出~ veterans stepping down from active government service /领导干部要深入~。Leaders should get to know intimately about the situation at the grass-roots level.
第一现场 dì-yī xiànchǎng 〈法律〉primary scene
第一信号系统 dì-yī xìnhào xìtǒng 〈生理〉first signal system
第一性 dìyīxìng 〈哲学〉primary:物质是~的,意识是第二性的。Matter is primary while consciousness is secondary.
第一宇宙速度 dì-yī yǔzhòu sùdù first cosmic velocity (7.9 km. per second); circular or orbital velocity
第一主犯 dì-yī zhǔfàn 〈法律〉principal in the first degree
第宅 dìzhái 〈旧语〉mansions of princes, lords, and senior court officials

递(遞)

dì ❶ hand over; pass; deliver:~口信 deliver an oral message /向会议主席~条子 pass a note to the chairman of the meeting /把盐~给我。Pass me the salt, please. /他~给我一支烟。He offered me a cigarette. ❷ successively; in the proper order:~进 move forward in order of sequence; progress
递变 dìbiàn change progressively or successively
递补 dìbǔ fill vacancies in the proper order:正式委员出现缺额,由后补委员~。Any vacancies in full membership shall be filled by alternate members in the proper order.
递归 dìguī 〈数学〉recursion:~算术 recursive arithmetic /~过程 〈自控〉recursive procedure
递加 dìjiā increase progressively or successively; increase by degrees:财政赤字逐年~。The budget deficit has increased progressively every year.
递价 dìjià bid price
递减 dìjiǎn decrease progressively or successively; decrease by degrees:收益~〈经济〉diminishing returns /外贸逆差逐月~。There has been a progressive decrease in the foreign trade deficit for months.
递降 dìjiàng decrease or reduce gradually; fall gradually
递交 dìjiāo hand over; present; submit; table:~国书 present one's credentials (*or* letter of credence) /~申请书 submit an application /~抗议书 lodge a protest /~声明 deliver a statement /~照会 send in a note /把这封信~给他本人。Have the letter hand delivered to him.
递解 dìjiè escort (usu. a prisoner) from one place to another:~回籍 send back (a convict, etc.) to his native place under escort
递解出境 dìjiè chūjìng deportation:被~ be deported from a country
递嬗 dìshàn 〈书面〉develop gradually; alternate successively:盛衰~。Prosperity and decline alternate. /春秋时代是新旧势力~的时代。The Spring and Autumn Period was an age when the new forces gradually replaced the old.
递升 dìshēng rise or increase progressively; promote to the next grade or rank
递送 dìsòng send; deliver:他的职责是~文件。His duty is delivering documents. /按快件~这份公函。Send this official letter by express mail.
递条子 dì tiáozi send a note asking for favour:有人~要求学校给这名考生以照顾。Somebody has sent a note asking the school to give preference to this candidate.
递推 dìtuī *see* "递归"
递嘻和儿 dì xīher 〈方言〉put on a smiling face to show one is ready to conciliate or apologize:吵了几句嘴没什么关系,谁先递个嘻和儿就算了。It doesn't matter much if you had a few words. Why doesn't either of you give a big smile? All will be well again.
递眼色 dì yǎnsè wink at; give a wink:她向我递了个眼色。She gave me a knowing look. /他一面说,一面~给大妈。While he was so saying, he winked at auntie.
递增 dìzēng increase progressively; increase by degrees:粮食产量逐年~。There has been a progressive increase in the grain output each year. /上缴利润每年~5%。The profit handed over to the state increases at an annual rate of 5 per cent.

睇

dì ❶〈书面〉look askance; cast a sidelong glance:~视 look askance; cast a sidelong glance (at sb.) /回眸凝~ turn around and cast a sidelong glance in her direction ❷〈方言〉look; glance

娣

dì ❶〈古语〉wife of husband's younger brother; sister-in-

law:~姒 sisters-in-law ❷〈古语〉(used by a woman) younger sister

地 dì ❶ the earth:天与~之间 between heaven and earth /上天无路,入~无门。There is absolutely no way out. /天~不仁。The universe is pitiless. ❷ land; soil:山~ hilly land /高~ highland /低~ low-lying land; lowland ❸ fields; land:棉花~ cotton field/盐碱~ saline and alkaline land /锄~ hoe the land/在~里干活 work in the fields /劳力不够,~都荒了。The land is running to weeds for shortage of labour. ❹ surface; ground; floor:砖~ brick floor/用大理石铺~ pave the ground with marble ❺ place; locality; area:各~ various localities; all localities/内~ hinterland; interior (of a country)/墓~ burial place; cemetery /目的~ destination /~处闹市 be located in the downtown area /罪犯的滋生~ hotbed of crimes ❻ position; situation; room:立于不败之~ be in an invincible position /留有余~ leave some margin; allow some leeway /设二人易~,其结果必迥异。If the two people changed places, they would end up differently. ❼ background; ground:白~青花大瓷盘 white porcelain platter with a pattern of blue flowers on it /白~红字,非常醒目。The red characters on a white background are very eye-catching. ❽ distance:二十里~ distance of twenty *li* /两站~ a couple of bus stops away

see also de

地巴唑 dìbāzuò 〈药学〉dibazol

地板 dìbǎn ❶ floor; floorboard:硬木~ hardwood floor /瓷砖~ tile floor /水磨石~ terrazzo floor /~上铺着一块土耳其地毯。The floor is covered with a Turkish carpet. ❷〈方言〉cultivated field

地板革 dìbǎngé plastic floor covering; plastic flooring

地板蜡 dìbǎnlà floor wax

地磅 dìbàng *see* "地秤"

地保 dìbǎo (during the Qing Dynasty and early republican days) neighbourhood chief in charge of local law and order

地堡 dìbǎo 〈军事〉bunker; blockhouse; pillbox

地标 dìbiāo 〈航海〉land mark

地表 dìbiǎo the earth's surface:~温度 surface temperature

地表径流 dìbiǎo jìngliú surface runoff

地表水 dìbiǎoshuǐ 〈地理〉surface water

地鳖 dìbiē (usu. called 土鳖 tǔbiē) ground beetle (*Eupolyphage sinensis*)

地波 dìbō *also* "表面波" biǎomiànbō 〈无线电〉surface wave

地鹔 dìbǔ 〈动物〉bustard

地步 dìbù ❶ (usu. bad) condition or situation; plight; predicament:你怎么混到这样的~? How did you get into such a frightful plight? *or* How did you come to such a pass? /局面已闹到不可收拾的~。The situation has got out of control (*or* hand). /事情还没有坏到这种~。Things are not as bad as that. /他的生意已到了山穷水尽的~。He has come to a dead end in his business. ❷ extent; degree:发展到公开对抗的~ develop into an open clash /到了欲罢不能的~ go too far to retreat (*or* back down) /她的病已到了危险的~。She is critically ill. ❸ room for action; leeway; elbowroom:留有回旋的~ leave room for manoeuvre; have some leeway; give oneself elbowroom

地财 dìcái 〈方言〉valuables hidden in the ground (to avoid discovery)

地蚕 dìcán 〈方言〉cutworm

地槽 dìcáo 〈地质〉geosyncline:~学说 theory of geosyncline

地层 dìcéng 〈地质〉stratum; layer

地层表 dìcéngbiǎo table of strata

地层沉裂 dìcéng chénliè subsidence break

地层图 dìcéngtú stratigraphic map

地层序 dìcéngxù stratigraphic succession or sequence

地层学 dìcéngxué stratigraphic geology; stratigraphy:~家 stratigrapher

地层油田 dìcéng yóutián stratigraphic oilfields

地产 dìchǎn landed property; real estate:~公司 estate company /房~税 real estate tax

地颤 dìchàn earth tremor; earthquake

地场 dìcháng 〈方言〉open space used as threshing ground

地场 dìchang 〈方言〉open ground for carrying out various activities:村边大槐树下是歇凉的好~。The big locust tree on the edge of the village provides an ideal place for enjoying the cool.

地秤 dìchèng *also* "地磅" weighbridge; bathroom scale

地出 dìchū 〈航天〉earthrise

地处 dìchu 〈方言〉space; place; room:这一带的山坡上,已经有不少~垒了梯田。Quite a few terraced fields have been built on the mountain slopes in this area.

地磁 dìcí 〈物理〉terrestrial magnetism; geomagnetism:~暴 geomagnetic storm /~变化 geomagnetic variation /~测量 magnetic survey /~记录仪 magnetograph /~仪 magnetometer

地磁场 dìcíchǎng geomagnetic field; terrestrial magnetic field

地磁赤道 dìcí chìdào aclinic line; geomagnetic equator; magnetic equator

地磁极 dìcíjí geomagnetic pole

地磁制导系统 dìcí zhìdǎo xìtǒng Terrestrial Magnetic Guidance System (TMGS)

地大物博 dìdà-wùbó vast in territory and rich in natural resources; big country abounding in natural resources

地带 dìdài region; area; zone; belt:沙漠~ desert region /森林~ forest area /绿化~ green belt (of a city) /火山~ belt of volcanoes /危险~ danger zone /无人~ no man's land

地蛋 dìdàn 〈方言〉potato

地道 dìdào tunnel:挖~ dig a tunnel /~战 tunnel warfare /~口 entrance to a tunnel; subway entrance

地道 dìdao ❶ from a place well known for the product; genuine:~货 genuine product of the locality /~的新疆哈密瓜 genuine Hami melon (from Xinjiang) ❷ pure; typical:~的英国口音 pure British accent /地地道道的教条主义 unadulterated (*or* out-and-out) dogmatism /这是一座~的中式四合院。This is a typical Chinese quadrangle. ❸ up to standard; of high quality; excellent:~的木工活 excellent carpentry /(服装)做工~ excellent (*or* exquisite) tailoring

地点 dìdiǎn place; site; location; venue:犯罪~ scene of a crime /考古~ archaeological site /~适中 conveniently located /开会~在大礼堂。The meeting will be held in the assembly hall. /他们还没有就下一次会议~达成协议。They haven't agreed on the venue for the forthcoming conference.

地电 dìdiàn terrestrial electricity

地丁 dìdīng ❶〈植物〉Chinese violet (*Violo philippica*) ❷〈旧语〉land tax plus poll tax

地东 dìdōng 〈旧语〉landlord; rich-peasant

地动 dìdòng 〈口语〉quake; earthquake

地动仪 dìdòngyí mobile celestial globe invented by the Chinese scientist Zhang Heng (张衡) in AD 132 for observation of earthquakes

地洞 dìdòng hole in the ground; burrow:鼹鼠钻入~逃之夭夭。The mole quickly burrowed out of sight.

地段 dìduàn sector or section of an area:重点开发~ key section for development /~医院 neighbourhood hospital (*or* clinic) /全市最热闹的商业~ downtown shopping area of a city /这一~实行宵禁。Curfew has been enforced in the area.

地对地导弹 dìduìdì dǎodàn ground-to-ground (guided) missile; surface-to-surface missile:东风4型远程~ Dongfeng IV long-range ground-to-ground missile

地对空导弹 dìduìkōng dǎodàn ground-to-air (guided) missile; surface-to-air missile; anti-aircraft missile:毒刺~ Stinger anti-aircraft missile

地方 dìfāng ❶ locality (as distinct from the central administration):~武装 local armed forces /~财政 local finance /~财政收入 budgetary revenues of the locality /~报刊 local newspapers /~人民政府 people's government at the local level/~法院 (US) district court/~性的民间关系 non-governmental relations at the local level/充分发挥中央和~两个积极性 give full play to the initiative of both central and local authorities ❷ this locality (as distinct from other localities); local government and people (as distinct from the army garrisoned there):~产品 product of the locality; local product/~特产 local speciality /军队与~的关系 relations between the army and the local government and people

地方 dìfang ❶ place; space; room:不管他到什么~,他总是那么谦虚而无架子。Wherever he is, he is always modest and unassuming. /沈教授是什么~人? Where is Prof. Shen from? /什么~都找不到她。She is nowhere to be found (*or* nowhere in sight). /汽车里没~了。There is no room in the car. /我这个~有点疼。I've got a pain here. ❷ part:他的建议有些~我同意。I agree in part with his proposal.

地方病 dìfāngbìng endemic (disease)

地方裁判所 dìfāng cáipànsuǒ (Japan) district court

地方法院 dìfāng fǎyuàn local court

地方干部 dìfāng gànbù local cadre; local official

地方观念 dìfāng guānniàn localism; localistic prejudice
地方国营 dìfāng guóyíng state-owned but locally-administered: ~企业 locally administered state enterprise / ~农场 state farm under local administration
地方军 dìfāngjūn local force; regional troops
地方民族主义 dìfāng mínzúzhǔyì local nationalism; local-nationality chauvinism
地方气候 dìfāng qìhòu local climate
地方区域联网 dìfāng qūyù liánwǎng local area network (LAN)
地方时 dìfāngshí local time
地方税 dìfāngshuì local tax
地方外办 dìfāng wàibàn local foreign affairs office
地方戏 dìfāngxì local opera; local drama
地方性 dìfāngxìng endemic: ~流感 endemic influenza / ~甲状腺肿 endemic goiter / ~传染 endemic infection
地方性流行病 dìfāngxìng liúxíngbìng 〈医学〉 endemic (disease)
地方性植物 dìfāngxìng zhíwù endemic plant
地方志 dìfāngzhì *also* "方志" local chronicles; annals of local history; local records
地方主义 dìfāngzhǔyì localism: ~的做法 localistic practice
地方自治 dìfāng zìzhì local self-government; autonomy: 民族~区域 national autonomous area or region
地肤 dìfū 〈植物〉 summer cypress (*Kochia scoparia*)
地肤子 dìfūzǐ 〈中药〉 fruit of summer cypress
地府 dìfǔ lower or nether world: 阴曹~ home of the dead; Hades
地富反坏右 dì-fù-fǎn-huài-yòu landlords, rich-peasants, counter-revolutionaries, bad elements and rightists (a term often used in 1950's-1970's)
地覆天翻 dìfù-tiānfān *also* "天翻地覆" earthshaking
地高辛 dìgāoxīn 〈药学〉 digoxin
地阁 dìgé *also* "地格" chin; lower jaw: ~方圆 double chin
地根儿 dìgēnr 〈方言〉 (usu. used in the negative) ever; at all: ~不行。It will never do. *or* No can do. / 我~不认识他。I don't know him at all.
地梗 dìgěng low bank of earth between fields; ridge
地宫 dìgōng ❶ underground palace — coffin chamber of an emperor's tomb ❷ terrestrial palace — underground shrine housing Buddhist relics
地沟 dìgōu ❶ sewer; drain-pipe: ~堵了。The drain-pipe is blocked. ❷ 〈地理〉 trench
地骨皮 dìgǔpí 〈药学〉 root bark of Chinese wolfberry (*Lycium Chinese*)
地瓜 dìguā 〈方言〉 ❶ sweet potato: ~干 dried sweet potato chips ❷ yam bean
地光 dìguāng flashes of light preceding an earthquake
地广人稀 dìguǎng-rénxī wide but sparsely populated area
地滚球 dìgǔnqiú ❶ *also* "保龄球" bǎolíngqiú bowling: 打~去 go bowling ❷ (in a baseball game) groundball; grounder
地棍 dìgùn local bully; local scoundrel or ruffian
地核 dìhé 〈地质〉 earth's core
地黄 dìhuáng 〈中药〉 glutinous rehmannia (*Rehmannia glutinosa*)
地黄牛 dìhuángniú bamboo top: 打~ play bamboo tops
地积 dìjī measure of land; acreage; area
地基 dìjī ❶ foundation; ground; subgrade: 盖房首先要打好~。In house building, what is of primary importance is the laying of the foundation. ❷ *see* "地皮"
地极 dìjí 〈地理〉 terrestrial pole
地级市 dìjíshì prefecture-level city
地甲病 dìjiǎbìng (short for 地方性甲状腺肿病) endemic goitre
地价 dìjià price of land
地角 dìjiǎo ❶ remote and far-away place; end of the world ❷ cape; promontory ❸ chin
地角天涯 dìjiǎo-tiānyá *also* "天涯地角" ends of the earth; remotest corners of the world
地脚 dìjiǎo lower margin (of a page); 〈印刷〉 tail: 天头~ upper and lower margins / 留出四公分~ leave a lower margin of 4 cm. 〈方言〉 foundation: 打~ lay the foundation (for a building)
地脚 dìjiao *also* "地基"
地脚螺丝 dìjiǎo luósī *also* "地脚螺栓" 〈机械〉 foundation bolt; anchor bolt; anchor rod
地窖 dìjiào cellar: 冬天储菜的~ cellar for storing vegetables in winter / ~通道 cellarway
地界 dìjiè ❶ demarcation of land; boundary: ~纠纷 disputes over land demarcations / 去掉田垅~,增加耕地面积。The boundaries and earth banks between fields were removed to bring more land under cultivation. ❷ space; area; jurisdiction: 这里是四乡农民赶集的~。This is where the peasants from the villages nearby have fairs. / 出了北京市,就是河北省的~。As soon as you go outside the municipality of Beijing, you are in Hebei Province.
地锦 dìjǐn 〈植物〉 humid euphorbia (*Euphorbia humifusa*)
地久天长 dìjiǔ-tiāncháng *also* "天长地久" as long and enduring as heaven and earth; everlasting
地炕 dìkàng traditional heating range in north China, built into a rectangular pit in the ground of the veranda and connected to the various rooms with heating flues
地空通信 dì-kōng tōngxìn ground-air communication
地窟 dìkū cellar; underground vault
地块 dìkuài plot (of land); 〈地质〉 massif: 地温高的壤土~宜于种棉花。Loamy land with a high ground temperature is most suitable for growing cotton.
地矿部 Dìkuàngbù Ministry of Geology and Mineral Resources
地拉那 Dìlānà Tirana or Tirane, capital of Albania
地蜡 dìlà 〈矿业〉 earth wax; mineral wax; ozocerite: 纯~ ceresin wax
地缆 dìlǎn underground cable
地牢 dìláo dungeon; underground prison
地老虎 dìlǎohǔ *also* "地蚕"; "土蚕" tǔcán cutworm
地老天荒 dìlǎo-tiānhuāng *also* "天荒地老" till the aging of earth and heaven; ages and ages; all eternity
地雷 dìléi (land) mine: 杀伤~ antipersonnel mine / 触发~ contact mine / 防坦克~ antitank mine / ~战 (land) mine warfare / 埋~ plant (*or* lay) mines / 探~ detect mines / 扫~ sweep mines
地雷搜索器 dìléi sōusuǒqì 〈军事〉 mine-detector
地垒 dìlěi 〈地质〉 horst
地梨 dìlí ❶ a kind of wild water chestnut (*Eleocharis tuberosa*) ❷ *also* "荸荠" bíqi 〈方言〉 water chestnut
地里 dìlǐ 〈书面〉 ❶ mileage; distance travelled ❷ *see* "地理"
地理 dìlǐ ❶ geographical features of a place: ~条件 geographical conditions / ~环境 geographical surroundings / ~上接近 geographical proximity / ~上接壤 geographical propinquity / ~上毗连 geographical contiguity / ~上统一 geographical unity / ~一体化 geographical integration / ~区域 geographical area / ~特点 geographical features / ~位置 geographical position / ~坐标 geographical coordinates / 上知天文,下知~ know everything under the sun; possess a wide knowledge of the world / 熟悉~民情 be familiar with the place and its people ❷ geography: 自然~ physical geography / 经济~ economic geography / 世界~ world (*or* global) geography / 商业~ applied geography ❸ 〈方言〉 geomancy; *feng shui*
地理景观 dìlǐ jǐngguān *also* "景观" landscape
地理先生 dìlǐ xiānsheng 〈旧语〉 geomancer; *feng shui* expert
地理学 dìlǐxué geography: ~家 geographer: 历史~ historical geography / 人文~ human geography / 自然~ physical geography / 政治~ political geography
地力 dìlì soil fertility: ~不足 of poor fertility; infertile
地利 dìlì ❶ favourable geographical position; topographical advantages: 天时~ favourable climate and geographical advantages/ ~人和 favourable terrain and friendly people ❷ soil condition; land productivity: 充分发挥~ give full play to (*or* make full use of) land productivity
地沥青 dìlìqīng asphalt; bitumen
地栗 dìlì 〈方言〉 water chestnut
地裂 dìliè (of ground, land, etc.) rift; crack: 山崩~。The mountains are collapsing and the earth is cracking up.
地邻 dìlín neighbours who have plots of land adjacent to each other: 他们两家是~。The two families are neighbours whose land lies adjacent.
地灵人杰 dìlíng-rénjié *also* "人杰地灵" a remarkable place produces outstanding talents; famous people add lustre to a beautiful place
地瘤 dìliú 〈地质〉 geotumor
地龙 dìlóng earthworm (used as medicine)
地龙墙 dìlóngqiáng 〈建筑〉 sleeper wall
地垄 dìlǒng rows of low earth banks in the fields

地漏 dìlòu 〈建筑〉floor drain
地炉 dìlú underground heater
地脉 dìmài 〈迷信〉veins of the earth (according to geomancy); geomantic features of a place
地幔 dìmàn 〈地质〉earth's mantle; mantle
地貌 dìmào general configuration of the earth's surface; geomorphology
地貌结构 dìmào jiégòu geomorphological structure
地貌图 dìmàotú geomorphic map
地貌学 dìmàoxué geomorphology: ～学家 geomorphologist
地面 dìmiàn ❶ earth's surface; ground: ～高低不平 rugged ground; rough and uneven ground /高于～ above ground /～压力 geostatic pressure; ground pressure/～能见度〈航空〉control-tower visibility; ground visibility ❷〈建筑〉ground; floor: 水磨石～ terrazzo floor /～砖 floor tiles ❸ region; area; territory: 这里已是河北～。We're now in Hebei Province. ❹ locality: 他在～儿上很有威信。He enjoys a good deal of prestige among the local people. *or* He is held in high esteem by the public here.
地面部队 dìmiàn bùduì land forces; ground forces
地面沉降 dìmiàn chénjiàng surface subsidence
地面储罐 dìmiàn chǔguàn above-ground storagetank
地面导航 dìmiàn dǎoháng 〈航空〉area navigation: ～设备 ground-based navigation aid
地面电阻 dìmiàn diànzǔ earth resistance
地面风 dìmiànfēng surface wind
地面分辨率 dìmiàn fēnbiànlǜ ground resolution
地面辐射 dìmiàn fúshè 〈气象〉terrestrial radiation; surface radiation; earth radiation
地面灌溉 dìmiàn guàngài surface irrigation
地面核爆炸 dìmiàn hébàozhà surface nuclear explosion
地面核试验 dìmiàn héshìyàn surface nuclear test
地面距离 dìmiàn jùlí ground distance
地面控制中心 dìmiàn kòngzhì zhōngxīn ground control (centre)
地面气压 dìmiàn qìyā surface pressure
地面数据 dìmiàn shùjù ground data
地面数据处理系统 dìmiàn shùjù chǔlǐ xìtǒng ground data handling system
地面卫星站 dìmiàn wèixīngzhàn ground satellite station
地面位置 dìmiàn wèizhì 〈航空〉ground position
地面遥测装置 dìmiàn yáocè zhuāngzhì ground telemetering equipment
地面站 dìmiànzhàn ground station
地面子午线 dìmiàn zǐwǔxiàn terrestrial meridian
地名 dìmíng place name: ～辞典 dictionary of place names; gazetteer
地名学 dìmíngxué toponymy: ～家 toponymist
地膜 dìmó plastic film for covering young plants; mulch film: ～式覆盖栽培 plastic film mulching
地亩 dìmǔ land; fields: 丈量～ measure land
地脑 dìnǎo 〈方言〉ends of a field: 地头～ ends of a field /连地边～都要种上作物。Even the edges and ends of a field were to be sown with crops.
地牛 dìniú 〈方言〉large handcart
地排车 dìpǎichē large handcart
地盘 dìpán territory under one's control; turf; domain; sphere: 争夺～ fight for turf; compete for spheres of influence /把集体企业作为个人的～ regard a collective enterprise as one's personal domain
地陪 dìpéi local guide; local escort
地皮 dìpí ❶ ground: 昨晚下了雨后，～现在还湿着。The ground is still wet from last night's rain. /雨太小了，刚湿了点～。It was only a light rain, which has scarcely moistened the ground. ❷ land for building; plot: 买～盖住宅楼 buy land freehold for a housing project /～处置费 land clearance fee; expense for the disposal of land /互惠无偿提供～ provide land gratis on a reciprocal basis /这块～已经有主了。This plot of land has a new owner.
地皮风 dìpífēng 〈方言〉sensational rumour: 扯～ spread sensational rumours
地痞 dìpǐ local ruffian; local riffraff
地平俯角 dìpíng fǔjiǎo 〈测绘〉dip of the horizon
地平经度 dìpíng jīngdù 〈天文〉azimuth
地平经纬仪 dìpíng jīngwěiyí 〈天文〉altazimuth
地平纬度 dìpíng wěidù 〈天文〉altitude
地平线 dìpíngxiàn horizon: 远远的～上有一处村落。There is a village on the distant horizon. /太阳已从～上消失。The sun has sunk below (*or* beyond) the horizon.
地平坐标 dìpíng zuòbiāo 〈天文〉horizontal coordinates
地坪 dìpíng 〈方言〉flat ground around a house
地铺 dìpù shakedown; makeshift bed on the floor: 睡～ sleep on a makeshift bed on the floor; make a bed on the floor
地祇 dìqí 〈旧语〉god of the land
地气 dìqì ❶ vapour: 不要趴在地上，怕～太大着了凉。You'll catch cold from the rising vapour if you lie prone on the ground. ❷ ground temperature; weather; climate: ～凉了，苗出了土会怕冻。It is already cold, and the seedlings just out of the soil won't be able to stand it. /这新品种的棉花倒适合上海的～。This new strain of cotton is suited to the climate of Shanghai.
地契 dìqì title deed for land: 办理～过户手续 go through formalities for the transfer of ownership of a title deed
地堑 dìqiàn 〈地理〉graben: ～盆地 graben basin
地壳 dìqiào 〈地质〉earth's crust
地壳板块 dìqiào bǎnkuài 〈地质〉crustal plate; tectonic plate
地壳构造物理学 dìqiào gòuzào wùlǐxué tectonophysics
地壳均衡 dìqiào jūnhéng 〈地质〉isostasy
地壳运动 dìqiào yùndòng crustal movement; diastrophism
地勤 dìqín 〈航空〉ground service: ～人员 ground crew; ground personnel /在机场搞～ work as an airport ground serviceman
地球 dìqiú earth; globe: ～保护日 Earth Day /～反照〈天文〉earthshine /～时 earth time /～站〈无线电〉earth station /～年 earth year /～引力 gravitational attraction /～自转〈天文〉earth rotation
地球村 dìqiúcūn global community; globe (seen as a village)
地球化学 dìqiú huàxué geochemistry
地球静止气象卫星 dìqiú jìngzhǐ qìxiàng wèixīng 〈气象〉geostationary meteorological satellite (GMS)
地球科学 dìqiú kēxué earth science; geoscience
地球人 dìqiúrén Terran; earthling
地球日 dìqiúrì Earth Day (a day in April set aside to stress pollution control)
地球同步卫星 dìqiú tóngbù wèixīng 〈航天〉geostationary satellite; synchronous satellite
地球同步转移轨道 dìqiú tóngbù zhuǎnyí guǐdào geosynchronous transfer orbit: 将质量为5000公斤的有效负荷送入～ carry a five-ton payload into a geosynchronous transfer orbit
地球外生物学 dìqiúwài shēngwùxué exobiology
地球外天文学 dìqiúwài tiānwénxué extraterrestrial astronomy
地球外智能生物 dìqiúwài zhìnéng shēngwù extraterrestrial intelligence
地球卫星 dìqiú wèixīng earth satellite
地球物理学 dìqiú wùlǐxué geophysics
地球演化 dìqiú yǎnhuà earth evolution
地球仪 dìqiúyí terrestrial globe
地球与轨道间往返飞行器 dìqiú yǔ guǐdàojiān wǎngfǎn fēixíngqì 〈航天〉earth orbiting shuttle vehicle
地球资源观测卫星 dìqiú zīyuán guāncè wèixīng earth resources observation satellite (EROS)
地球资源技术卫星 dìqiú zīyuán jìshù wèixīng 〈航天〉landsat; earth resources technology satellite (ERTS)
地区 dìqū ❶ area; district; region: 京津～ Beijing-Tianjin area /华北～ (area over) northern China /亚太～ Asia and Pacific region /撒哈拉以南～ sub-Saharan region /邻近～ adjacent regions; neighbouring districts /边境～ border region /潮湿～ humid region /半沙漠～ half-desert region /多山～ mountainous region /干旱～ arid region /城市～ urban district (*or* area) /农村～ rural district (*or* area) /～集团 regional group/～司 regional department /～特惠税 regional preferential duties /～性销售 regional distribution /～专业化 regional specialization ❷ prefecture (administrative division below the province and above the county): 该省共有10个～，102个县。There are ten prefectures under the province, governing 102 counties. ❸ region of the world as distinguished from an independent state; territory: 亚洲国家和～ Asian countries and regions
地区霸权 dìqū bàquán regional hegemony: ～主义 regional hegemonism
地区差别 dìqū chābié regional disparities or differences
地区差价 dìqū chājià regional price differences
地区冲突 dìqū chōngtū regional conflict

D

地区封锁 dìqū fēngsuǒ barriers between regions
地区经济 dìqū jīngjì regional economies
地圈 dìquān geosphere (the solid and liquid portion of the earth; the lithosphere plus the hydrosphere)
地权 dìquán land ownership: 平均～ equalization of land ownership
地券 dìquàn title deed for land
地儿 dìr place; space; room: 腾个～ make room /哟,这里没～了。Oh, there is no room for us here. /旅馆已满了,到别处找～吧。This hotel is full (*or* booked up), please contact another one.
地热 dìrè 〈地质〉 geotherm; terrestrial heat: ～资源 geothermal resources /～发电 geothermal power generation /～能源 geothermal energy
地热电站 dìrè diànzhàn geothermal power plant; geothermic electropower station
地热田 dìrètián geothermal land
地热学 dìrèxué geothermics
地煞 dìshà ❶ (in astrology) evil star; star determining killings on earth ❷ monster; thug; gangster: 本地的一伙～ gang of local thugs
地上茎 dìshàngjīng 〈植物〉 aerial stem
地上 dìshang on the ground: 穿着旱冰鞋,刚迈步就摔在了～。He fell flat on the ground the moment he tried to move on roller-skates.
地生物学 dìshēngwùxué geobiology
地声 dìshēng earthquake sound
地史学 dìshǐxué historical geology
地势 dìshì physical features of a place; terrain; topography: ～险要。The terrain is of strategic importance and difficult of access.
地刷 dìshuā *also* "地刷子" scrubber; long-handled scrubbing brush
地税 dìshuì land tax
地台 dìtái 〈地质〉 platform
地摊 dìtān roadside stall: 摆～ set up a stall on the street
地毯 dìtǎn carpet; rug: 提花～ jacquard carpet /铺～ cover with a carpet (*or* rug) /铺红～欢迎贵宾 roll out the red carpet for distinguished guests /全部铺上～ cover with wall-to-wall carpet
地毯式轰炸 dìtǎnshì hōngzhà carpet or blanket bombing
地铁 dìtiě ❶ subway; tube; Metro; underground railway: ～站 subway station; Metro station ❷ underground train: ～来了。Here comes the underground train. *or* The subway train is arriving.
地头 dìtóu ❶ edge or end of a field: 在～休息 have a break at the edge of the field ❷ 〈方言〉 destination: 快到～了。We'll be there in no time. ❸ 〈方言〉 place; locality: 你～熟,联系起来方便。You know the place well, so you can make easy contacts there. ❹ foot margin (of a page); lower margin: 他在书的～上写了些批语。He made some comments on the lower margins of the book.
地头蛇 dìtóushé snake in its old haunt — local villain or bully: 强龙难压～。Even a dragon (from the outside) finds it hard to control a snake in its old haunt. *or* Powerful outsiders can hardly afford to neglect local bullies. /此人作恶多端,人称～。As he had done evil of all kinds, he was called the "local snake".
地图 dìtú map: 绘制～ draw a map /查看～ consult a map /～投影 map projection /世界～ world map /军用～ military map /～册 atlas
地图集 dìtújí atlas: 世界～ world atlas
地图学 dìtúxué cartography
地土 dìtǔ fields; farmland; cropland: ～贫瘠 barren land /房产～ houses and land; real estate /这里牲口羊群一年比一年多,～也一年比一年肥。Here the number of draught animals and cattle grows larger and the farmland more fertile from year to year.
地推子 dìtuīzi wheeled push broom; sweeper
地外文明 dìwài wénmíng extraterrestrial civilization
地望 dìwàng 〈书面〉 position and prestige
地委 dìwěi prefectural Party committee
地位 dìwèi ❶ position; standing; place; status: 政治～ political position (*or* standing) /经济～ economic status /社会～ social position (*or* status) /国际～ international standing (*or* prestige) /学术～ academic standing /～平等 equal in status; on an equal footing /公民～ citizenship; one's status as a citizen /侨民～ status of a resident foreign national ❷ place (as occupied by a person or a thing): 处于偏僻的～ be located in an out-of-the-way place
地温 dìwēn 〈气象〉 ground or earth temperature: ～表 ground (*or* earth) thermometer; geothermometer /～梯度 geothermal gradient
地文学 dìwénxué physical geography; physiography
地窝子 dìwōzi *also* "地窝铺" pit dwelling or house, a kind of simple and crude dwelling place
地物 dìwù surface features (usu. man-made features of a region)
地峡 dìxiá isthmus: 巴拿马～ Isthmus of Panama /苏伊士～ Isthmus of Suez
地下 dìxià ❶ underground; subterranean: ～宫殿 underground palace /～核试验 underground nuclear test/在～铺设输电线路 lay power lines underground ❷ secret (activity); underground: 转入～ go underground /～报纸 underground newspaper /～印刷厂 underground press /～工作 underground work
地下 dìxia on the ground: 掉到～ fall to the ground /从～拣起 pick up from the ground /把席子铺在～ spread a straw mat on the ground
地下党 dìxiàdǎng underground party; underground party organization: 他于1929年加入～。He joined an underground (Communist) Party organization in 1929.
地下发射井 dìxià fāshèjǐng underground launching silo
地下工厂 dìxià gōngchǎng underground factory; unlicensed factory
地下管道 dìxià guǎndào underground piping
地下河流 dìxià héliú subterranean river or stream
地下火 dìxiàhuǒ underground fire
地下茎 dìxiàjīng 〈植物〉 subterranean stem
地下渗流 dìxià shènliú underground percolation
地下室 dìxiàshì basement; cellar
地下水 dìxiàshuǐ groundwater: ～的过分开采使水荒问题日益严重。A water crisis is imminent due to indiscriminate exploitation of groundwater resources.
地下水位 dìxià shuǐwèi groundwater level; water table
地下铁道 dìxià tiědào underground railway; subway; tube
地下铁路公司 Dìxià Tiělù Gōngsī (HK) Mass Transit Railway Corp (MTR)
地下通道 dìxià tōngdào underground passage
地下油管 dìxià yóuguǎn 〈石油〉 buried oil pipeline
地线 dìxiàn 〈电工〉 ground or earth wire: 使用洗衣机时别忘了接好～。Don't forget to connect the earth wire before using the washing machine.
地陷 dìxiàn (of land) subsidence or caving in: 山崩～。The mountains collapse and the land caves in.
地心 dìxīn 〈地质〉 earth's core; core: ～圈 barysphere; centrosphere /～坐标 geocentric coordinates
地心说 dìxīnshuō geocentrism; geocentricity
地心引力 dìxīn yǐnlì terrestrial gravity; gravity
地形 dìxíng topography; terrain: ～复杂 varied topography /～测量 topographic survey /～侦察 terrain reconnaissance /～优越 enjoy topographical advantages /战斗前参谋们仔细研究了～。The staff officers made a careful study of the terrain before the battle.
地形分析 dìxíng fēnxī terrain analysis
地形模型 dìxíng móxíng relief model
地形图 dìxíngtú topographic map; relief map
地形学 dìxíngxué topography
地形雨 dìxíngyǔ 〈气象〉 orographic rain
地形云 dìxíngyún 〈气象〉 orographic cloud
地学 dìxué earth science
地衣 dìyī 〈植物〉 lichen
地役权 dìyìquán 〈法律〉 easement (on a piece of land)
地音探听器 dìyīn tàntīngqì *see* "地震检波器"
地窨子 dìyìnzi ❶ basement ❷ cellar
地应力 dìyìnglì 〈地质〉 crustal stress: ～场 (crustal) stress field
地榆 dìyú 〈植物〉 garden burnet
地舆图 dìyútú 〈旧语〉 atlas
地狱 dìyù ❶ hell; inferno: 但丁的《～篇》*The Inferno* by Dante /打入～ be condemned (*or* consigned) to hell; cast to outer space ❷ place of torment like hell; hell on earth: 解放前,她的日子苦得就跟在～里似的。She suffered like hell before liberation.
地域 dìyù ❶ vast area; region: ～辽阔 vast in territory /美洲～ American continent /特定～ in a particular region ❷ locality: ～观念 regionalism
地缘经济学 dìyuán jīngjìxué geoeconomics
地缘政治 dìyuán zhèngzhì *also* "地理政治" geopolitics: ～学 geopolitics /～学家 geopolitician /～上的考虑 geopolitical considerations

地照 dìzhào title deed for land; land certificate

地震 dìzhèn earthquake; seism; tremor:国家～局 State Bureau of Seismology /里氏7.1级～ tremor measuring 7.1 on the Richter scale /～台 seismograph (*or* seismic) station /～工作者 seismologist /～预报 seismic forecast /～海啸 seismic sea wave; tsunami

地震波 dìzhènbō seismic wave

地震带 dìzhèndài seismic belt

地震观测 dìzhèn guāncè seismological observation

地震活动 dìzhèn huódòng seismic activity:～性 seismicity

地震计 dìzhènjì seismometer

地震检波器 dìzhèn jiǎnbōqì geophone

地震检测法 dìzhèn jiǎncèfǎ seismography

地震勘探 dìzhèn kāntàn seismic prospecting

地震烈度 dìzhèn lièdù earthquake intensity

地震烈度表 dìzhèn lièdùbiǎo scale of seismic intensity

地震区 dìzhènqū seismic area or region

地震物理学 dìzhèn wùlǐxué seismophysics

地震学 dìzhènxué seismology

地震仪 dìzhènyí seismograph

地震源 dìzhènyuán seismic origin or focus

地震震级 dìzhèn zhènjí (earthquake) magnitude

地政 dìzhèng land administration:～问题涉及面广,必须谨慎对待。Land administration must proceed with great care as it covers a wide range of problems.

地支 dìzhī *also*"十二支" shí'èrzhī twelve Earthly Branches (used in combination with the Heavenly Stems to designate years, months, days and hours)

地址 dìzhǐ address:通信～ mailing address /家庭～ family (*or* home) address; residence address /回信～ return address /永久～ permanent address /临时～ temporary address

地址解析协议 dìzhǐ jiěxī xiéyì 〈信息〉address resolution protocol (ARP)

地志 dìzhì topography

地志学 dìzhìxué 〈地理〉topology

地质 dìzhì geology:～博物馆 geological museum /～调查 geological survey /～图 geologic map

地质储量 dìzhì chǔliàng geological reserve or deposit

地质构造 dìzhì gòuzào geological structure

地质勘探 dìzhì kāntàn geological prospecting

地质力学 dìzhì lìxué geomechanics

地质年代 dìzhì niándài *also*"地质时期" geological time; geological eras

地质年代学 dìzhì niándàixué geochronology

地质时期 dìzhì shíqī 〈地质〉geologic age

地质学 dìzhìxué geology:～家 geologist

地中海 Dìzhōnghǎi the Mediterranean (Sea):～舰队 Mediterranean fleet /～沿岸国家 Mediterranean country

地中海果蝇 Dìzhōnghǎi guǒyíng Mediterranean fruit fly; Med fly

地轴 dìzhóu earth's axis

地主 dìzhǔ ❶ landlord:恶霸～ despotic landlord ❷ host:尽～之谊 extend the courtesies of the host; play the host

地主阶级 dìzhǔjiējí landlord class

地啄木 dìzhuómù 〈动物〉wryneck

地子 dìzi (of patterns, figures, calligraphy, etc.) background:白～ white background

地租 dìzū land rent; ground rent; rent:～剥削 exploitation through land rent /货币～ money rent /级差～ differential rent /绝对～ absolute rent /劳役～ labour rent /合同～ contract rent /追收～ back rent /实物～ natural rent; rent in kind /准～ quasi-rent /收取～者 rent-taker

杕

dì 〈书面〉(of a tree) grow in isolation; stand alone:有～之杜。A birchleaf pear tree stands all by itself.

棣[1]

dì ❶〈植物〉kerria ❷ *see*"棠棣" tángdì

棣[2]

dì 〈书面〉younger brother:贤～ my worthy brother /仁～ my kind brother

棣棠 dìtáng 〈植物〉kerria

蝃(蝃、蝃) dì

蝃蝀 dìdōng 〈书面〉rainbow

踶

dì 〈书面〉kick; tramp:两马相～。Two horses were kicking at each other.

玓

dì

玓瓅 dìlì 〈书面〉gleam or shine of jewels

的

dì bull's-eye; target:无～放矢 shoot an arrow without a target — aimless and fruitless /众矢之～ target of public criticism (*or* censure)

see also de; dí

菂

dì 〈书面〉lotus seed

diǎ

嗲

diǎ 〈方言〉❶ act or speak like a pampered child; speak or act in an arch, or coquettish manner:发～ act the pampered child; act the coquet /～声～气 in an affectedly childish voice; in a coquettish manner ❷ nice; good; pretty:这件衣裳～哦? Isn't this dress pretty (*or* nice)?

diān

掂(敁)

diān weigh in the hand:用手～一下金戒指的分量 weigh a gold ring in one's hand

掂对 diāndui 〈方言〉❶ think over; consider; weigh (up):～得失 weigh the pros and cons /让他～～,看怎么办吧。Let him think it over and decide what is to be done. ❷ exchange; swap:用玉米～点儿麦子 swap maize for wheat

掂掇 diānduo ❶ weigh (up); think over; consider:你～着办吧。You may act at your own discretion. ❷ estimate; reckon; appraise:我～这辆自行车能值三百元。I figure the bike is worth 300 *yuan*.

掂斤播两 diānjīn-bōliǎng *also*"掂斤簸两" weigh up every *jin* and *liang*; haggle over every little gain or loss; be calculating:他是个心胸狭窄、～的人。He is a narrow-minded, calculating chap.

掂量 diānliang ❶ weigh in the hand:卖瓜人～了一下大西瓜,说有十五斤重。Weighing the big water-melon in his hand, the pedlar said it was about 15 *jin*. ❷ think over; weigh up:咱们～着办得了。We may as well act as we see fit.

掂算 diānsuàn estimate; calculate; figure:～一下路途费用,最少得花八百元。The travel expenses are estimated to be around 800 *yuan* at least. /我～着有二十个人能来出席会议。I figure there will be twenty people at the meeting. /你要～好了再干。You should think it over before you start doing anything.

滇

Diān another name for Yunnan (Province):～藏公路 Yunnan-Tibet highway/～池 Lake Dian (in Kunming, Yunnan)

滇红 diānhóng Yunnan black tea

滇剧 diānjù Yunnan opera (traditional opera popular in Yunnan and parts of Guizhou and Sichuan)

傎

diān 〈书面〉confused; disordered

颠[1]

diān ❶ crown (of the head):华～ grey-crowned ❷ top; peak; summit:山～ mountain top /塔～ top of a pagoda /越过山～ cross over the peak of a mountain

颠[2]

diān ❶ jolt; bump:公共汽车在山路行驶～得厉害。Buses jolt (*or* bump) violently on the mountain road. ❷ fall; topple down; turn over: *see*"～覆" ❸〈方言〉jump up and run; run; make off:整天跑跑～～ be running about all day long; be on the go from morning till night /他早就～儿了。He has already gone away (*or* left).

颠[3]

diān *also*"癫" diān mentally deranged; insane

颠簸 diānbǒ jolt; bump; toss:卡车在崎岖的道路上～着前进。The

D

truck bumped along on the rugged road. /小船在波涛汹涌的海上～不定。The boat was tossed about on the rough sea.

颠达 diānda *also* "颠搭"; "颠嗒" ❶ (of the body) jerk or jolt upwards and downwards: 这人走路～～的。This man walks jerkily. /他在车上～了一路，觉得胃里有点不舒服。As the car jolted along all the way, he felt somewhat uncomfortable in his stomach. ❷〈方言〉be busy running about; bustle: 他终日在野地里～。He was busy working in the open fields all day long.

颠荡 diāndàng jolt; bump; toss: 车身～，摇得人也颤颤巍巍的。As the car bumped along, the passengers kept shaking all the time.

颠倒 diāndǎo ❶ put or turn upside down; invert; transpose; reverse: ～乾坤 reverse heaven and earth; create total chaos /～主次 reverse the order of importance; confuse the priorities /～事实 turn the truth upside down; stand the facts on their heads /～敌友关系 take enemies for friends and friends for enemies /墙上的画挂～了。The picture on the wall is hung upside down. /把这两个部分～过来句子就通顺了。Transpose these two parts and the sentence will read well. /你完全弄～了，是我欠他的钱呀。You've got hold of the wrong end of the stick. It's I who owe him money. ❷ confused; disordered: 神魂～ suffer from a disordered mind; be distraught; be infatuated

D

颠倒黑白 diāndǎo-hēibái confound black and white; stand the facts on their heads: ～，混淆视听 turn black into white in an attempt to mislead the public

颠倒是非 diāndǎo-shìfēi confound right and wrong; confuse or reverse truth and falsehood; turn the truth upside down: ～是他的惯用伎俩。Confounding right and wrong was his favourite trick.

颠覆 diānfù overturn; subvert; topple: ～活动 subversive activities /汽车～在沟里。The car fell into a ditch and was overturned. /～新政府的阴谋以失败而告终。The plot to subvert the new government ended in fiasco.

颠来倒去 diānlái-dǎoqù over and over; again and again; over and again: 如果你～就这几句陈词滥调，那没有人会听你的。No one will care to listen if you keep harping on just a few shopworn clichés.

颠连 diānlián 〈书面〉❶ hardship; trouble; difficulty: ～无告 have nowhere to air one's grievances ❷ continuous; unending: 群山起伏～ undulating range of mountains

颠末 diānmò 〈书面〉beginning and end of a story; whole story: 题诗纪～ write a poem in memory of the event /属笔于予，俾记～。I was asked to write an essay recounting the experience.

颠沛流离 diānpèi-liúlí drift from place to place; have nowhere to live and little to eat; wander about homeless and penniless: 当年他～，形同乞丐。In those years he led a vagrant life and looked like a beggar. /那个地区战乱不已，人民～。In that war-torn area, people drifted away from home, destitute and miserable.

颠仆 diānpū fall down; fall over: ～在地 fall on the ground

颠扑不破 diānpū-bùpò indestructible; irrefutable; indisputable: ～的真理 irrefutable truth /论点精确，～。The argument is sound and indisputable.

颠茄 diānqié 〈药学〉belladonna

颠三倒四 diānsān-dǎosì disorderly; confused; disconnected; incoherent: 说话～ talk incoherently (*or* disconnectedly) /把事情搞得～ mess things up; make a mess of sth.

颠危 diānwēi 〈书面〉❶ (of a regime or situation) on the verge of collapse or disintegration; in jeopardy; tottering: 国势～。The nation is facing imminent danger. *or* The fate of the nation is hanging in the balance. ❷ topple; subvert: ～社稷 topple a state or regime

颠张醉素 Diānzhāng-Zuìsù Crazy Zhang and Drunken Su, referring to Zhang Xu (张旭, ?-c.759) and Huai Su (怀素, 725-785), calligraphers excelling in the cursive hand during the Tang Dynasty

颠踬 diānzhì ❶ stagger along; totter or dodder along; tumble: 马在崎岖的山路上～着。The horse staggered along the rugged mountain path. /中弹的老虎～了一下，倒下去了。Hit by the bullets, the tiger tottered a minute before it fell. ❷〈比喻〉in danger; in peril

癫

diān mentally deranged; insane: 疯～ insane; mad /～和尚 mentally deranged monk; mad monk

癫狂 diānkuáng ❶ insanity; schizophrenia ❷ (of behaviour) frivolous and arrogant

癫痫 diānxián (usu. known as 羊角风 or 羊痫风)〈医学〉epilepsy

癫子 diānzi 〈方言〉madman; lunatic

攧

diān (usu. used in the early vernacular) fall; drop: ～下来 fall down

巅

diān mountain top; peak; summit: 登山队终于登上了珠峰之～。The mountaineers finally reached the summit of Mount Qomolangma.

巅峰 diānfēng mountain peak; summit

蹎

diān 〈书面〉fall down: ～仆 fall over

diǎn

踮(跕)

diǎn *also* "点" diǎn stand on tiptoe: ～着脚轻轻地走出房间 walk out of the room on tiptoe; tiptoe out of the room

踮脚 diǎnjiǎo 〈方言〉walk on a lame leg: 他昨天滑了一跤，走路还有点～。He is walking on a lame leg for he slipped and got a sprain yesterday.

点[1](點)

diǎn ❶ drop (of liquid): 雨～儿 raindrops /外边掉～儿了。It's spotting with rain. ❷ stain; spot; speck: 斑～儿 stain; spot; speckle /霉～儿 speck of mould /墨～儿 ink spot ❸ dot stroke (in Chinese characters): 汉字可由不同笔画组成，～是其中之一。A Chinese character may be made up of several basic strokes, one of which is the dot stroke. ❹〈数学〉point: 两线的交～ point of intersection of two lines /基准～ datum point (*or* mark) /接触～ point of contact ❺ decimal point; point: 七～儿一 seven point one (7.1) ❻〈量词〉a little; a bit; some: 大一～儿 a little bigger /差一～儿 slightly inferior /一～儿小事 a mere trifle /吃～儿东西 have sth. to eat; have a bite /懂～儿法语 know a little French; know French after a fashion /不能有一(*or* 半)～儿差错 not allow the smallest error /你觉得好～儿了吗? Are you feeling (somewhat) better? ❼〈量词〉*used in counting items*: 两～不成熟的意见 two tentative proposals (*or* comments) /鉴于以上几～理由 in view of the above-mentioned reasons /文章内容大致有四～。The article contains roughly four points. /在这一～上他是正确的。He is right on this point (*or* in this respect). ❽ mark (of a given degree or level); point (bearing a given characteristic); place (distinguished by a certain trait): (水位的)顶～ high-water mark /起～ starting point /沸～ boiling point /终～ destination /居民～ residential area /制高～ commanding height ❾ aspect (of the whole); point; feature: 疑～ dubious point /要～ main points; the gist; essentials /优～ strong point; merit; virtue; advantage /重～ point for emphasis; focal point /特～ characteristic; feature ❿ put a dot: ～句 punctuate sentences in an ancient Chinese text /～三个点表示省略 put three dots to indicate an omission ⓫ touch on briefly; mention in passing; skim: 船夫用篙轻轻一～，船就离岸了。The boatman pushed the boat off with only a shove of the pole. /他在讲话结束前～了这件事。He touched on the matter before he concluded his speech. ⓬ *also* "踮" diǎn on tiptoe ⓭ incline one's head or hand briefly: *see* "～头" ⓮ drip: ～眼药 put drops in the eyes /把润滑油～到车轴里 drip lubricating oil into the axle ⓯ plant in holes; dibble: 往地里～花生 dibble groundnuts in the soil ⓰ check or count one by one: ～钱 check (*or* count) the money /～货 check over goods; take stock ⓱ select; choose: *see* "～菜"; "～戏" ⓲ make clear directly or indirectly; hint; point out: ～到了要害 hit the nail on the head; hit (*or* drive) home /聪明人一～就明白。Bright people take a hint quickly. *or* A word to the wise. ⓳ light; kindle; ignite: ～烟 light a cigarette /～炮 detonate (*or* ignite) a charge; cause a blowup /～炉子 make a fire in the stove /湿柴不易～着。Wet wood doesn't light easily. /火爆性子，一～就着。He's got a fiery temper and flares up at the slightest provocation. ⓴ embellish; ornament; adorn: 装～庭园 embellish the courtyard and the flower garden ㉑〈书面〉stain; tarnish

点[2](點)

diǎn ❶ iron bell or clapper used to announce the hour or rally the people: 敲～ strike an iron clapper or bell to announce the hour ❷〈旧语〉unit of time during the night ($\frac{1}{5}$ of 更, or about 24 minutes) ❸ o'clock: 清晨六～ six o'clock in the morning /三～半 half past three; three thirty /十一～见。See you at eleven. ❹ appointed time: 准～ on time; on the dot /误～ behind

time; delayed; late /正～到达 arrive on schedule (*or* time) /快到～了。It's almost time.

点[3]**(點)** diǎn refreshments; snack; cake: 糕～ cake; pastry /茶～ tea; tea and cake /早～ breakfast

点[4]**(點)** diǎn 〈印刷〉point, a unit of measurement (about 3.5 millimetres) for type and matrix

点兵 diǎnbīng 〈旧语〉muster troops; gather men for a roll call or a review: 沙场秋～。On the desert front, the troops were parading in autumn.

点波束 diǎnbōshù spot beam; point beam

点播 diǎnbō ❶ *also* "点种" dibble seeding; dibbling: ～玉米 dibble corn seeds /～器 dibbler ❷ request an item or programme for broadcasting (*or* televising): 听众～音乐节目 music item requested by the radio or TV audience; music programme by request

点拨 diǎnbo teach; instruct; show how (to do sth.): 他学艺时受过名师～。He was personally instructed by a master while he was learning his trade.

点补 diǎnbu have a snack to stave off hunger; have a bite: 还不到吃晚饭时间,先～一点儿。Let's have a bite first as dinner is not ready yet.

点菜 diǎncài choose dishes from a menu; order food (in a restaurant): 你～好吗? Would you like to order? /我吃份饭,不～了。I'll have the *table d'hôte* rather than *à la carte*.

点唱 diǎnchàng (of an audience) request a performing artist to sing a certain song or aria

点穿 diǎnchuān bring sth. out into the open; lay bare; point out bluntly

点窜 diǎncuàn change (wording, etc.); alter; revise: 经他一～,这篇文章就好多了。The essay reads much better now that he has touched it up.

点打印 diǎndǎyìn 〈计算机〉dot printing

点滴 diǎndī ❶ a bit; a little; a small amount: ～经验 limited experience /～成就 small achievement /点点滴滴积累 accumulate (*or* collect) little by little /从～小事做起 start in life from humble jobs /要注意～节约。It is necessary to practise economy in every conceivable way. ❷ scattered things; random notes; bits of information: 大奖赛～ random notes on the Grand Prix ❸〈医学〉intravenous drip: 打～ place sb. on a drip /葡萄糖～ intravenous glucose drip /静脉～ intravenous drip

点定 diǎndìng 〈书面〉(in editing) decide on correct morphology among variant forms; make corrections or revisions: 操笔而成,无所～。The article was done at one stroke and needed no polishing.

点厾 diǎndū 〈美术〉free stroking (by a painter)

点对点协议 diǎnduìdiǎn xiéyì 〈信息〉point-to-point protocol (PPP)

点发 diǎnfā *see* "点射"

点分十进制记法 diǎnfēn shíjìnzhì jìfǎ dotted decimal notation

点焊 diǎnhàn spot or point welding

点化 diǎnhuà ❶ transform by magic; (of Taoist or Buddhist priests) awaken people to the truth by enlightening words; convert (to religious truth) ❷ enlighten; guide; teach

点画 diǎnhuà ❶ (of Chinese characters) stroke (such as dots, vertical & horizontal strokes and left or right-falling strokes) ❷ *also* "点划" point (with fingers) and gesture: 他～着小李说:"你一个人留在这里实在不方便。" Pointing at Xiao Li, he said: "It would cause some inconvenience to leave you here all by yourself." ❸ decorate; set off: 满天的红云把天空～得绚丽多彩。Set off by rosy clouds, the sky looked bright-coloured and beautiful.

点火 diǎnhuǒ ❶ light a fire; ignite; fire: 点把火 make a fire /自动～ automatic ignition /火箭～ firing of a rocket /二次～〈航天〉second burn ❷ stir up trouble: 煽风～ fan the flames; inflame popular feeling; stir up trouble

点火脉冲 diǎnhuǒ màichōng firing pulse

点火喷嘴 diǎnhuǒ pēnzuǐ ignition burner

点火试验 diǎnhuǒ shìyàn firing run or experiment

点火装置 diǎnhuǒ zhuāngzhì ignition device; ignitor; squib

点饥 diǎnjī have a snack to stave off hunger; have a bite: 备点饼干～。Let's take some biscuits with us in case we get hungry. /先吃点儿东西点点饥。Let's have a bite to take the edge off our hunger.

点将 diǎnjiàng ❶〈旧语〉muster one's officers and assign them tasks ❷ assign sb. a particular job; name sb. for a given task: 厂长～让他担任推销部主任。The factory manager appointed him head of the sales department. /你可是总经理亲自点的将啊。You were named for the job (*or* task) on the personal recommendation of the general manager, you know.

点交 diǎnjiāo hand over item by item

点金成铁 diǎnjīn-chéngtiě turn gold into iron by touching it — spoil a piece of writing by ill-advised changes or corrections

点金石 diǎnjīnshí philosopher's stone

点睛 diǎnjīng (short for 画龙点睛) bring a picture of a dragon to life by putting in the pupils of its eyes: ～之笔 the touch that brings a work of art to life; the finishing touch

点卯 diǎnmǎo call the roll in the morning; check in at one's job (before one leaves again): 他每天到办公室点个卯就走。He leaves quickly after he puts in an appearance at the office every day.

点面结合 diǎn-miàn jiéhé combine work at selected spots with that of the whole area

点名 diǎnmíng ❶ call the roll: 早～ morning roll call /～册 roll book; roll ❷ mention sb. by name; name sb. explicitly: ～批评 criticize (explicitly) by name /经理～要我当采购员。The manager wanted me to be a purchasing agent. /校长在会上讲了这件事,但没有～。The president talked about the matter at the meeting, but he didn't mention anybody's name.

点明 diǎnmíng point out; pinpoint; put one's finger on: ～问题所在 point out (*or* pinpoint) the cause of the trouble; show where the shoe pinches /～这次调查的重要意义 point out the significance of the investigation

点派 diǎnpài appoint; name; designate: 上级～他到外单位取经。He was sent to another work unit on a study tour.

点破 diǎnpò bring to light; lay bare; point out bluntly: 事情既已～,我也就不在乎了。Now that the matter has been brought to light, I won't have to beat about the bush any more. /我知道他的来意,却不～。I kept my mouth shut although I knew what he was after. /她直截了当地～他为何故弄玄虚。She went straight to the point and called his bluff.

点球 diǎnqiú 〈体育〉penalty kick

点燃 diǎnrán light; kindle; ignite: ～蜡烛 light a candle /～一支烟 light a cigarette /～人民仇恨的火焰 ignite the hatred of the people

点染 diǎnrǎn add details and apply colours to a painting; touch up or polish: 这幅画最后还得～一番。We still have to add a few more details to the painting. *or* We are to give finishing touches to the painting. /他请人将稿子略加～。He has asked somebody to polish the essay.

点射 diǎnshè 〈军事〉firing in bursts: 他用自动步枪打了三个～,发发打中靶心。He fired three bursts with his automatic rifle, and hit the bull's eye each time.

点施 diǎnshī *also* "穴施" xuéshī apply fertilizer by dibbling

点石成金 diǎnshí-chéngjīn turn stone into gold with a touch; turn sth. worthless into sth. valuable; turn a crude essay into a literary gem: 真是～,只改了二十个字,就通篇改观了。With the change of some twenty words, the essay is entirely different. Isn't it a magic touch?

点收 diǎnshōu check and accept: 按清单～ check the goods against a list before acknowledging delivery

点手 diǎnshǒu 〈方言〉beckon; wave: ～呼唤 beckon to sb. and call him

点首 diǎnshǒu nod

点数 diǎnshù check the number or amount; count: 这是五百块钱,请～。Here is five hundred *yuan*. Please count it.

点题 diǎntí bring out the theme: 本文～的方法很高明。The way the writer brings out the theme of his essay is masterly.

点铁成金 diǎntiě-chéngjīn *see* "点石成金"

点头 diǎntóu nod one's head; nod: ～同意 nod assent (*or* approval) /～之交 nodding (*or* bowing) acquaintance /他还没～。He hasn't given the go-ahead (*or* approval) yet.

点头哈腰 diǎntóu-hāyāo bow servilely or unctuously; bow and scrape: 他进办公室来,逢人便～。When he came into the office, he nodded and bowed to everyone he saw.

点污 diǎnwū 〈书面〉stain; tarnish; sully

点戏 diǎnxì select a play from a repertoire offered

点心 diǎnxīn 〈方言〉*see* "点饥"

点心 diǎnxin refreshments; pastry; dim sum: ～铺 bakery; snack

D

bar

点醒 diǎnxǐng 〈方言〉drop a hint; remind:经小王一～,她立即领会这话的意思了。After Xiao Wang dropped her a hint, she immediately grasped the meaning of the remark.

点穴 diǎnxué (said of a master of the martial arts) hit sb. at selected points with one's finger and cause temporary paralysis or internal bleeding; hit a vital point:他打架时让人点了穴。He got hit at a vital point in a scuffle.

点验 diǎnyàn examine item by item:成品正在～中。The products are being examined one by one.

点阅 diǎnyuè ❶ check or inspect one by one ❷ mark off sentences by dots and make circles alongside words for emphasis while reading:～古籍 punctuate ancient texts and make circles alongside important words or sentences

点阵 diǎnzhèn 〈物理〉(space) lattice; dot matrix:～理论 lattice theory /～能 lattice energy /～字符 dot character

点阵式打印机 diǎnzhènshì dǎyìnjī dot matrix printer

点阵无序 diǎnzhèn wúxù lattice disorder

点种 diǎnzhǒng dibble in the seeds

点种 diǎnzhòng *see* "点播❶"

点缀 diǎnzhui ❶ embellish; adorn; decorate:彩旗和鲜花～校园 campus decorated with bunting and flowers /～着野花的陵园 cemetery dotted with wild flowers / 梅花把雪后的园林～得格外美丽。With the plum trees silhouetted against the snowy background, the garden was refreshingly beautiful. *or* With the snowy background setting off the plum trees, the garden was a scene of enchanting beauty. ❷ use merely for show:他在书柜里摆了几本大书,不过是为了～而已。He has several big volumes placed in the bookcase, for show only.

点字 diǎnzì *also* "盲字" mángzì braille

点子 diǎnzi ❶ drop (of liquid):雨～ raindrop ❷ spot; dot; speck:泥～ speck of dirt or mud /油～ grease stain ❸ beat (of percussion instruments):鼓～ drumbeat ❹〈方言〉〈量词〉a little; a bit; a tiny amount:抓～药 get some medicine ❺ key point; crux:劲儿要使在～上。Put on a spurt at the right moment. /工作要抓到～上来。Get down to key problems in your work. /他的话说到～上了。His remark hit the nail on the head. ❻ idea; pointer:鬼～多 be full of clever ideas; be resourceful /出～ offer advice; make suggestions

典[1] diǎn ❶ standard; canon; law:赏功而不罚罪,非国～也。Giving rewards for good service without punishment for offence is against the canon of the state. ❷ standard work of scholarship; definitive work; code:词～ dictionary /佛教经～ Buddhist scripture / 刑法～ code of criminal law; criminal code /经～著作 classics ❸ allusion; literary quotation:用～ use allusions ❹ ceremony:开国盛～ grand founding ceremony of a state /庆～ celebrations ❺〈书面〉be in charge of:～试 act as chief examiner ❻ (Diǎn) a surname

典[2] diǎn pawn; lease; mortgage:～衣 pawn clothes /～妻 (former custom in backward areas) lease one's wife to another man (for a period of time) /他穷得只好出～他的房子。He was so poor that he had to mortgage his house.

典当 diǎndàng ❶ *also* "典押" mortgage; pawn:～一套西服 pawn a suit of clothes /他把家产～了两万元。He mortgaged his family property for 20,000 *yuan*. ❷〈方言〉pawnshop

典范 diǎnfàn model; example; paragon:勤俭的～ model of industry and thrift /自称美德的～ claim to be a paragon of virtue /他是我们学习的光辉～。He is a shining example for us to learn from.

典故 diǎngù allusion; literary quotation:他的诗用了许多～。His poems teem with literary allusions.

典籍 diǎnjí ancient codes and records; ancient books and records:保存完好的～ well-preserved ancient codes and records /我国保存下来的～极其丰富。There is a rich collection of extant ancient texts in China.

典借 diǎnjiè mortgage; pawn

典礼 diǎnlǐ ceremony; celebration:毕业～ graduation ceremony; commencement (ceremony) /就职～ inauguration ceremony /开幕～ opening ceremony /结婚～ wedding (ceremony) /加冕～ coronation (ceremony) /奠基～ cornerstone laying ceremony /远洋轮的下水～ launching ceremony of a new ocean liner /独立～ independence ceremony /国庆～ national day celebrations

典丽 diǎnlì refined and elegant:文词～ refined writing

典卖 diǎnmài 〈旧语〉mortgage; pawn

典铺 diǎnpù 〈方言〉pawnshop

典契 diǎnqì 〈旧语〉mortgage contract

典守 diǎnshǒu 〈书面〉be in charge; be custodian of:～者 person in charge; custodian

典刑 diǎnxíng 〈书面〉penalties according to law:明正～ carry out capital punishment in accordance with law

典型 diǎnxíng ❶ typical case or example; model; type:德才兼备的～ model of both ability and integrity /抓～ grasp typical cases /这个企业是艰苦创业的～。This is an example of building an enterprise through arduous work. ❷ typical; representative:～代表 typical representative /～事件 typical instance (*or* case)/～的北京四合院 typical quadrangle courtyard of the Beijing type /他举的例子都很～,能够说明问题。The examples he has cited are typical enough to explain how things stand. ❸ (used in art and literature) typicalness; representativeness:塑造～ portray the typical /小说的主人公是当代青年农民的～形象。The hero of the novel is a typical young farmer in the contemporary era.

典押 diǎnyā *see* "典当"

典雅 diǎnyǎ refined; elegant; in good taste:客厅布置得很～。The parlour is elegantly furnished. /这篇作品用词～。The language of the essay is refined.

典要 diǎnyào 〈书面〉❶ refined and succinct ❷ norm; standard; model:不可据为～。This must not be taken as a model. *or* This is not to be regarded as a criterion.

典狱 diǎnyù prison warden

典狱长 diǎnyùzhǎng prison warden

典则 diǎnzé rule; law

典章 diǎnzhāng institutions; decrees and regulations:文物～ historical records, decrees and regulations /～制度 historical institutions

典质 diǎnzhì mortgage; pawn

典制 diǎnzhì laws and institutions (of a society)

典重 diǎnzhòng refined and solemn

典租 diǎnzū land rent paid to the mortgagee by the mortgagor who retains use of the mortgaged land; rent for use of land mortgaged to sb. else; mortgaged land rent

碘 diǎn 〈化学〉iodine:～试验 iodine test /～中毒 iodism /～值 iodine number (*or* value)

碘处理 diǎnchǔlǐ iodine treatment

碘蛋白 diǎndànbái iodoprotein

碘酊 diǎndīng 〈药学〉tincture of iodine

碘仿 diǎnfǎng 〈化学〉iodoform

碘酚酞 diǎnfēntài 〈化学〉iodophthalein

碘化法 diǎnhuàfǎ 〈冶金〉iodide process

碘化物 diǎnhuàwù iodide

碘化盐 diǎnhuàyán iodized salt

碘化银 diǎnhuàyín 〈化学〉silver iodine

碘化油 diǎnhuàyóu iodized oil

碘酒 diǎnjiǔ 〈药学〉tincture of iodine

碘木 diǎnmù iodine bush

碘片 diǎnpiàn iodine tablet

碘缺乏 diǎnquēfá iodine deficiency

碘酸 diǎnsuān 〈化学〉iodic acid:～盐 iodate

碘钨灯 diǎnwūdēng iodine-tungsten lamp; iodine tungsten filament lamp:～放影机 tungsten-iodine lamp film projector

diàn

淀[1](澱) diàn form sediment; settle; precipitate:沉～物 sediment

淀[2] diàn (often used in place names) shallow lake:白洋～ Baiyang Lake (in Hebei Province)

淀粉 diànfěn starch; amylum

淀粉酶 diànfěnméi 〈生化〉amylose

淀粉水解 diànfěn shuǐjiě amylolysis:～酶 amylolytic enzyme

淀积 diànjī 〈地质〉illuviation:～层 illuvium /～土壤 illuvial soil /

～作用 illuviation

靛 diàn ❶ indigo ❷ indigo-blue

靛红 diànhóng 〈纺织〉isatin

靛颏儿 diànkér 〈口语〉general term for both *Luscinia calliope* and *Luscinia svecica svecica*

靛蓝 diànlán indigo：～色 indigo-blue

靛青 diànqīng ❶ indigo-blue ❷〈方言〉indigo

奠[1] diàn establish; settle: *see* "～基"

奠[2] diàn make offerings to the spirits of the dead：祭～ hold a ceremony for Heaven or one's ancestors

奠边府战役 Diànbiānfǔ Zhànyì Battle of Dien Bien Phu (1954) in Vietnam

奠定 diàndìng establish; settle：～基础 lay a foundation /这部著作～了他在史学界的地位。This work established his reputation among historians.

奠都 diàndū establish or found a capital：～北京。Beijing was made the capital.

奠基 diànjī lay a foundation：那座摩天大楼是两年前的今天～的。The foundation of the skyscraper was laid today two years ago.

奠基礼 diànjīlǐ foundation (stone) laying ceremony

奠基人 diànjīrén founder

奠基石 diànjīshí foundation stone; cornerstone

奠祭 diànjì (perform) libation; (hold) a memorial ceremony (for)

奠敬 diànjìng *see* "奠仪"

奠酒 diànjiǔ libation：～者 libationer

奠仪 diànyí *also* "奠敬" gift of money given by a relative or friend on the occasion of a funeral

垫(墊) diàn ❶ put sth. under sth. else to raise it; spread sth. over sth. else; make level by filling up; pad：～路 repair a road by filling the holes /把茶几～平 put sth. under the leg of a tea table to make it level /在床板上～个褥子。Put a cotton-padded mattress on the bed. ❷ fill in gap; insert：在几个歌手的独唱之间，～上些小节目。Some small items were inserted in between the solos of the well-known singers. ❸ pay for sb. and expect to be paid back later：我带的钱不够，你先替我～上吧。I haven't enough money on me. Will you please pay for me now (so that I can repay you later)? ❹ pad; cushion; mattress; mat：靠～ cushion /草～ straw mat /鞋～ inner sole; insole /床～ mattress /沙发～ sofa cushion

垫板 diànbǎn 〈印刷〉make-ready

垫办 diànban ❶ *see* "垫用" ❷ take care (of sth.) on behalf of sb.; do for sb.：我出差期间，这些事就由你～了。Please take care of these matters for me while I am away on business.

垫背 diànbèi 〈方言〉take the blame for sb.; be a scapegoat：出了事儿他不拿你～才怪呢。You can be sure he'll put the blame on you if something goes wrong. /甭想让我给你当～的。Don't you try to use me as a scapegoat (*or* shift all the blame on to me).

垫补 diànbu 〈方言〉❶ use money earmarked for other purposes; borrow money as a stopgap：这点存款先～着花。Let's use these savings for the time being. ❷ have a bite before a meal：先吃块蛋糕～～。Have a piece of cake before the meal is ready.

垫场 diànchǎng put on a substitute performance (when a scheduled item is not ready)

垫喘儿 diànchuǎnr 〈方言〉vent one's anger; use as outlet for one's anger：他心里不痛快，倒拿我们～。He was in a bad mood and vented his spleen on us.

垫底儿 diàndǐr ❶ put on the bottom：金鱼缸里是用细沙～的。There is a layer of fine sand on the bottom of the goldfish bowl. /报考时，最好选一个一般学校～。When you apply for universities and colleges, it would be best to choose a middling one as your last resort. ❷ take a bite to stave off hunger：你先吃点东西垫垫底儿，我们还得等几位客人。You can take a bite first, for we have to wait for some guests yet. ❸ lay the foundation; serve as a basis：有了你以前的工作～，今后我们的工作就好开展了。On the basis of what you have accomplished, we will be better able to get on with the work.

垫付 diànfù pay for sb. and expect to be repaid later：你本月的房租已由老孙～了。Lao Sun has paid the month's rent for you.

垫话 diànhuà prologue of a comic dialogue or crosstalk

垫肩 diànjiān ❶ shoulder pad (for a carrying pole) ❷ shoulder padding; padded shoulder

垫脚石 diànjiǎoshí stepping-stone：有些人跟你交朋友只不过把你当作获取名利的～。Some people make friends with you simply because they want to use you as a stepping-stone to fame and profit.

垫脚 diànjiao earth, grass, etc. spread in a pigsty, cowshed, etc.

垫圈 diànjuàn *see* "垫脚"
see also diànquān

垫款 diànkuǎn money paid or advanced for sb. to be paid back later：索回～ get back the advanced money /还清～ pay back the advanced money

垫密片 diànmìpiàn 〈机械〉gasket：气缸～ cylinder gasket

垫片 diànpiàn 〈机械〉❶ spacer：绝缘～ insulation spacer ❷ shim：轴承～ bearing shim

垫圈 diànquān 〈机械〉washer; cushion ring; grommet：毡～ felt washer /锁紧～ locking washer /开口～ snap washer
see also diànjuàn

垫上运动 diànshàng yùndòng 〈体育〉mat tumbling; mat work

垫戏 diànxì fill-in performance

垫用 diànyòng spend or use money earmarked for other purposes on a temporary basis：那笔钱我拿去～一下，年底归还。I'll have to use that money for some other purpose, but I'll return it by the end of the year.

垫支 diànzhī *see* "垫付"

垫子 diànzi mat; mattress; pad; cushion：椅～ chair cushion /体操～ gym mat /茶杯～ teacup mat (*or* coaster) /弹簧～ spring mattress

店 diàn ❶ inn：开～ keep an inn /住～ put up at an inn /客～ inn /骡马～ roadside inn with sheds for carts and animals ❷ shop; store：开～ open (up) shop /关～ close up (shop) /酒～ wine shop; bar /布～ drapery store /零售～ retail shop; retail store /古玩～ antique shop /小吃～ snack bar /副食～ grocery; grocer's /熟食～ delicatessen (shop) /理发～ barber's or hairdresser's (shop) /百货商～ department store

店东 diàndōng 〈旧语〉shopkeeper; storekeeper; innkeeper

店倌 diànguān 〈方言〉shop assistant; salesclerk; salesman or saleswoman

店伙 diànhuǒ 〈旧语〉shop employee; clerk; salesclerk

店家 diànjiā ❶〈旧语〉shopkeeper; innkeeper; shopowner; shop manager ❷〈方言〉shop

店面 diànmiàn shop front (where sales are conducted)：～房 shop building /装饰～ decorate the shop front

店铺 diànpù shop; store

店钱 diànqián inn or hotel bill

店容 diànróng look of a store or shop：～整洁。The shop looks clean and tidy.

店肆 diànsì 〈书面〉shop; store

店堂 diàntáng main room or hall (of a shop or restaurant) where business is conducted

店小二 diànxiǎo'èr (usu. used in the early vernacular) waiter; attendant; shop assistant

店员 diànyuán shop assistant; salesclerk; clerk; salesman or saleswoman

店主 diànzhǔ proprietor (of a shop or store); shopowner; shopkeeper

店子 diànzi 〈方言〉shop; store

惦 diàn be concerned about; keep thinking about：～着某人 keep thinking of sb. /他虽患重病，心里仍～着工作。He is still concerned about his work though seriously ill.

惦挂 diànguà remember with concern; be concerned about; keep thinking about：她总～着孩子们。She is always concerned about her children.

惦记 diànji cannot take one's mind off; keep thinking about; worry about：你不用～我，我很好。Don't worry about me. I am fine. /他～着那篇没写完的文章。He cannot take his mind off the unfinished article.

惦念 diànniàn keep thinking about; be concerned about; worry about：分别多年，他一直～着我。He has always thought about me although it is many years since we parted. /我一切均好，请勿～。You need not worry, for everything is fine with me. /她～着远方的亲人。

D

She is concerned about her family who live so far away.

玷 diàn ❶ flaw in a piece of jade:白玉之～ flaw in a white jade ❷ tarnish; disgrace:有～令誉 be a blemish to one's good reputation

玷辱 diànrǔ bring disgrace or shame on; be a disgrace to:他这样做一定会～祖宗,遗臭万年。By so doing, he would bring shame upon his forebears and be pilloried throughout the ages.

玷污 diànwū ❶ stain; sully; tarnish:他的行为～了自己的名誉。By his behaviour he smeared (*or* tarnished) his own good name. ❷ ravage; rape; seduce

坫 diàn ❶〈古语〉indoor earthen platform (for food and wine vessels) ❷〈书面〉protective screen or barrier

阽 diàn *also* yán 〈书面〉on the verge of (danger):～于死亡 on the verge of death

阽危 diànwēi 〈书面〉(of situation, plight, etc.) in grave or imminent danger:国势～。The nation is in peril./天下～。The world situation is pregnant (*or* fraught) with danger.

D

电(電) diàn ❶ electricity; electric power:发～ generate electricity (*or* power)/充～ charge (a battery)/放～ discharge/正～ positive electricity/负～ negative electricity/停～ cutting off power supply; power cut; blackout ❷ give or get an electric shock:～了我一下。I got a shock. ❸ telegram; cable:急～ urgent telegram/贺～ message of congratulations; congratulatory telegram/唁～ telegram of condolence; message of condolence/复～ cable reply/致敬～ message of greetings/复～费已付 reply prepaid ❹ send a cable; cable; send a telegram; telegraph:即～上级请示 telegraph (*or* cable) the higher authorities immediately for instructions

电按摩法 diàn'ànmófǎ 〈医学〉electromassage

电霸 diànbà (of those who control power supply and use their position despotically, usu. to further their own interests) overlord or despot in the electricity business

电棒 diànbàng 〈方言〉(electric) torch; flashlight

电报 diànbào ❶ telegraphy; telegraph:一般认为是莫尔斯发明了～。Samuel Morse is generally thought to be the inventor of the telegraph. ❷ telegram; cable:无线～ wireless telegraph; radiotelegram/有线～ wire telegram/海底～ cablegram/国内～ inland telegram/国外～ foreign cable/国际～ international telegram/明码～ plain code telegram/密码～ cipher telegram/新闻～ press cable/用户～ telex/传真～ photo telegram; fax/无线电传真～ photoradiogram/～费 telegram charge/特急～ most urgent telegram/加急～ urgent (*or* express) telegram/公事～ official telegram/书信～ letter telegram/～通知 cable advice/～信用证 cable order/译～ decode a telegram/～报盘 cable an offer/～确认 cable confirmation/我把父亲病故的消息打～告诉亲友。I telegraph (*or* cable) the news of father's death to our relatives and friends.

电报等级 diànbào děngjí telegram message precedence

电报挂号 diànbào guàhào cable address; telegraphic address

电报机 diànbàojī telegraph

电报局 diànbàojú telegraph office

电报纸 diànbàozhǐ telegram form; telegram blank:填写～ fill in the telegraph form; fill in the telegram form

电笔 diànbǐ 〈电工〉test pencil; electroprobe

电表 diànbiǎo ❶ electricity measuring meter; ammeter; voltmeter ❷ kilowatt-hour meter; watt-hour meter; electric meter:我家的～坏了。The electric meter in my house is out of order.

电冰柜 diànbīngguì freezer

电冰箱 diànbīngxiāng (electric) refrigerator; fridge:单门～ single-door refrigerator/双门～ double-door refrigerator

电波 diànbō electric wave:～的发射 emission of radio waves/～的反射 reflection of radio waves

电波折射 diànbō zhéshè radio wave refraction

电铲 diànchǎn electric shovel

电厂 diànchǎng (electric) power plant

电场 diànchǎng electric field:～强度 electric field intensity

电唱机 diànchàngjī electric gramophone; phonograph; record player:～插孔 socket for pick-up

电唱头 diànchàngtóu pick-up

电唱针 diànchàngzhēn (gramophone) stylus; needle

电车 diànchē tram; tramcar; streetcar:～钢轨 tram rail/有轨～ tram; tramcar; streetcar/无轨～ trolleybus; trolley/～售票员 conductor; conductress

电掣风驰 diànchè-fēngchí *also* "风驰电掣" swift as wind and quick as lightning

电陈 diànchén state or declare by telegraph:他向上级领导～自己的不同意见。He telegraphed to the higher level stating differing views.

电池 diànchí cell; battery:～组 battery/干～ dry cell/太阳能～ solar cell

电传 diànchuán ❶ facsimile; fax:将复函用～发过去。Send the reply by fax. ❷ (short for 电传打字电报) telex

电传打印机 diànchuán dǎyìnjī teleprinter:汉字～ Chinese teleprinter

电传打字电报 diànchuán dǎzì diànbào telex:～机 teletypewriter; teletype

电传打字机 diànchuán dǎzìjī teletype

电传机 diànchuánjī fax machine

电瓷 diàncí electroceramics; electric ceramics

电磁 diàncí electromagnetism:～成形 electromagnetic forming

电磁波 diàncíbō electromagnetic wave

电磁场 diàncíchǎng electromagnetic field

电磁干扰 diàncí gānrǎo electromagnetic interference (EMI)

电磁感应 diàncí gǎnyìng electromagnetic induction:～圈 electromagnetic coil

电磁兼容性 diàncí jiānróngxìng 〈物理〉electromagnetic compatibility

电磁炉 diàncílú electromagnetic cooker or oven

电磁脉冲 diàncí màichōng radioflash

电磁扫雷器 diàncí sǎoléiqì electromagnetic minesweeping gear

电磁示波器 diàncí shìbōqì electromagnetic oscillograph

电磁铁 diàncítiě electromagnet

电磁选矿机 diàncí xuǎnkuàngjī 〈矿业〉electromagnetic ore separator

电磁学 diàncíxué electromagnetics

电磁引信 diàncí yǐnxìn electromagnetic fuse

电磁振荡器 diàncí zhèndàngqì herz oscillator

电刺激 diàncìjī electrostimulation

电催化 diàncuīhuà 〈化学〉electrocatalysis

电大 diàndà *see* "电视大学"

电导 diàndǎo conductance; conductivity:～仪 conductivity gauge

电灯 diàndēng electric lamp; electric light

电灯泡 diàndēngpào electric (light) bulb

电动 diàndòng power-driven; electrically-operated; electric:～玩具 electric toy/～泵 electric pump/～车 electrically operated motor car/～发电机 motor generator/～割草机 power-operated mower/～旗杆 electric mast

电动打字机 diàndòng dǎzìjī electric typewriter

电动机 diàndòngjī 〈电工〉motor:～驱动 motor drive/～转子 motor rotor/～增益 motor gain/～组 motor unit

电动记分牌 diàndòng jìfēnpái electric scoreboard

电动力学 diàndòng lìxué electrodynamics

电动人行道 diàndòng rénxíngdào speedwalk

电动势 diàndòngshì electro-motive force (EMF)

电动剃须刀 diàndòng tìxūdāo electric shaver

电度表 diàndùbiǎo kilowatt-hour meter; watt-hour meter; electric meter

电镀 diàndù electroplate:无氰～ electroplating without using cyanide

电锻 diànduàn 〈机械〉electro-forge

电法勘探 diànfǎ kāntàn 〈矿业〉electrical prospecting

电饭煲 diànfànbāo *also* "电饭锅" electric cooker

电费 diànfèi power rate; power bill:交～ pay one's power bill/～不贵 reasonable power rate

电风扇 diànfēngshàn electric fan

电腐蚀 diànfǔshí 〈机械〉electro-etching; electro-corrosion

电复 diànfù answer or reply by cable:请立即～。Please cable reply at once.

电杆 diàngān wire pole

电感 diàngǎn inductance:～电桥 inductance bridge

电感光材料 diàngǎnguāng cáiliào electrophoretic material

电镐 diàngǎo electric pick
电稿 diàngǎo draft of a cable message
电告 diàngào cable to inform (sb.); inform (sb.) by telegraph: 把谈判结果立即～外交部。Telegraph negotiation results to the Foreign Ministry instantly.
电工 diàngōng ❶ electrical engineering: ～技术 electrotechnics / ～器材厂 electrical appliances factory ❷ electrician
电工学 diàngōngxué electrical engineering; electrotechnics
电功率 diàngōnglǜ electric power
电购 diàngòu purchase by telephone, telegraph or fax
电挂 diànguà (short for 电报挂号) cable address; telegraphic address
电灌 diànguàn electric pumping: ～站 electric pumping station (*or* house)
电光 diànguāng light produced by electricity; lightning
电光工艺 diànguāng gōngyì 〈纺织〉 schreinering
电光石火 diànguāng-shíhuǒ lightning and sparkle — anything that vanishes in a flash
电滚子 diàngǔnzi 〈方言〉 ❶ generator; dynamo ❷ motor
电焊 diànhàn electric welding: ～工 electric welder / ～机 electric welding machine; electric welder / ～条 welding electrode; welding rod
电贺 diànhè telegraph one's congratulations; cable a message of congratulations: 国务院～大坝合龙成功。The State Council telegraphed congratulations on the successful closure of the huge dam.
电荷 diànhè electric charge; charge: 正～ positive charge / 负～ negative charge / ～密度 charge density
电弧 diànhú electric arc: ～炉 arc furnace / ～切割机 arc cutting machine
电弧焊接 diànhú hànjiē arc welding
电化当量 diànhuà dāngliàng electrochemical equivalent
电化教学 diànhuà jiàoxué (shortened as 电教) instruction or teaching with electrical audio-visual aids: ～设备 (electrical) audio-visual aids / ～试验室 audio-visual (instruction) laboratory / ～大楼 audio-visual instruction building
电化教育 diànhuà jiàoyù education with electrical audio-visual aids; audio-visual education
电化学 diànhuàxué electrochemistry: ～加工〈机械〉electrochemical machining; electrochemical processing
电话 diànhuà ❶ telephone; phone; (telephone) line: 无线～ radio (*or* wireless) telephone/电视～ picture telephone; video telephone / 自动～ automatic (*or* dial) telephone / 程控～ program-controlled telephone / 热线～ hot line / 专线～ special line / 当地～ local call / 郊区～ suburban telephone / 长途～ trunk (*or* long distance) call / 直拨长途～ direct distance dialing call / 国际～ international call / 传呼～ message call / 叫人～ person to person call; personal call / 预约(*or* 定时)～ sequency (*or* fixed time) call / 受话人付费～ *also* "对方付费～" collect call; reverse charge call / 加急～ urgent call / 普通～ ordinary call / 政务～ government telephone / ～用户 telephone subscriber / ～接线员 telephone operator; switchboard operator / 安装～ install a telephone / 切断～ ring off the telephone; hang up / ～坏了。The phone is out of order. / 别把～挂了。Hold the line a minute. *or* Hold on a minute. ❷ phone call: 打～ make a phone call; phone sb.; call sb. up; ring sb. up; give sb. a ring / 打个对方付费～ call collect / 接～ answer the phone / ～留言 leave a telephone message / 打～通知 inform by telephone / ～打不通 can't get through / 接通～ put a call through / 窃听～ tap a telephone / ～占线。Number engaged. *or* The line is busy. / ～听不清。The connection is poor. / ～一点声音也听不到。The line is dead. / ～断了。The phone is disconnected. / 有你的～。You're wanted on the phone. *or* There's a phone call for you. / 有人在打～。There is somebody at the telephone. / 李先生正在接～。Mr. Li is on the telephone just now. / 我没有接到他的～。I didn't receive his call.
电话传真 diànhuà chuánzhēn telefacsimile; telefax
电话分机 diànhuà fēnjī extension (telephone)
电话号码 diànhuà hàomǎ telephone number: 您拨错了～。Sorry, wrong number.
电话会议 diànhuà huìyì telephone conference; audio conferencing: 有关部门召开～，布置今年的防汛工作。The relevant departments held a telephone conference to make arrangements for this year's flood prevention.
电话机 diànhuàjī telephone
电话交换台 diànhuà jiāohuàntái *also* "总机" zǒngjī telephone exchange; switchboard
电话局 diànhuàjú telephone office; exchange: 长途～ trunk exchange; long distance office
电话卡 diànhuàkǎ phone card; calling card
电话录音机 diànhuà lùyīnjī 〈通信〉 answering machine
电话亭 diànhuàtíng telephone box, booth, or kiosk
电话增音机 diànhuà zēngyīnjī telephone repeater
电话中继线 diànhuà zhōngjìxiàn main line: ～号码 general number
电汇 diànhuì telegraphic money order; remittance by telegram; telegraphic transfer: ～汇率 rate for telegraphic transfer / 请立将购书款～我处。Prompt telegraphic remittance to my office for book subscription is kindly requested.
电火花 diànhuǒhuā electric spark: ～加工 electric spark machining / ～加工机床 electric spark machine tool
电击 diànjī electrical shock
电机 diànjī electric machinery; electric engineering: ～厂 electrical machinery plant / ～系 electric engineering department (EE) / ～工程 electrical engineering
电机车 diànjīchē *see* "电气机车"
电积 diànjī (short for 电解淀积) 〈冶金〉 electrodeposition
电吉他 diànjítā electric guitar
电极 diànjí electrode: 阳～ anode; positive electrode / 阴～ cathode; negative electrode
电加工 diànjiāgōng electric processing: ～机床 electric processing lathe
电价 diànjià ❶ *see* "电费" ❷ 〈化学〉 electrovalence: ～键 electrovalent bond
电剪 diànjiǎn electric scissors; electric shears: ～羊毛 electric shearing of wool
电键 diànjiàn telegraph key; key; button
电教 diànjiào (short for 电化教育) education with electrical audio-visual aids; audio-visual education
电教馆 diànjiàoguǎn audio-visual education centre or building
电解 diànjiě electrolysis: ～分离 electrolytic dissociation / ～炉 electrolytic furnace / ～铜 electrolytic copper/ ～槽 electrolyzing cell; electrolysis bath; electrolytic tank / ～加工 electrochemical machining; electromachining
电解液 diànjiěyè 〈化学〉 electrolyte
电解质 diànjiězhì electrolyte: ～导体 electrolytic conductor
电介基 diànjièjī dielectrophore
电介质 diànjièzhì dielectric
电警棍 diànjǐnggùn electric baton
电锯 diànjù electric saw
电抗 diànkàng reactance: ～器 reactor
电烤箱 diànkǎoxiāng electric oven; electric roaster
电缆 diànlǎn 〈电工〉 electric cable: ～管道 cable channel / ～盘 hank of cable / ～箱 cable box / 同轴～ coaxial cable
电老虎 diànlǎohǔ ❶ *see* "电霸" ❷ big power or electricity consumer
电烙术 diànlàoshù 〈医学〉 electrocautery; electric cautery
电烙铁 diànlàotie ❶ electric iron ❷ electric soldering iron
电离 diànlí ionization: ～室 ion chamber / ～化 ionize
电离层 diànlícéng 〈气象〉 ionosphere
电力 diànlì electric power; power: ～工程 electric power project / ～供应 supply of electricity; power supply/ ～拖动 electric traction / ～机械 electrical power equipment / ～消耗 power consumption / ～系统 power system / ～系统自动化 automation of electric-power system
电力捕鱼 diànlì bǔyú electrofishing
电力工业 diànlì gōngyè power industry
电力机车 diànlì jīchē electric locomotive
电力网 diànlìwǎng power network; power grid
电力线 diànlìxiàn ❶ electric flux line; electric line of force ❷ power line; power main
电量 diànliàng electric quantity; quantity of electricity
电疗 diànliáo 〈医学〉 electrotherapy: 短波～ short-wave therapy / 超短波～ ultrashort-wave therapy
电疗机 diànliáojī 〈医学〉 electrizer
电疗学 diànliáoxué electrology
电料 diànliào electrical materials and appliances

D

电铃 diànlíng electric bell
电令 diànlìng ❶ transmit an order by telegram; cable an order:～驻军火速开拔 cable the troops to set out at top speed ❷ order transmitted by telegram
电流 diànliú electric current:负载～ load current /载波～ carrier current /定额～ nominal current /反向～ reverse current /接通～ turn on electricity
电流表 diànliúbiǎo *also* "安培计" ānpéijì ammeter; amperemeter
电流计 diànliújì galvanometer
电流强度 diànliú qiángdù current intensity
电溜子 diànliùzi 〈矿业〉chain conveyor; face conveyor
电漏 diànlòu 〈电工〉leakance
电炉 diànlú electric stove; electric furnace:家用～ electric stove; hot plate /工业～ electric furnace /电阻～ resistance electric furnace /感应～ induction electric furnace /～钢 electric steel /～炼钢法 electric furnace process /速熔～ rapid electromelt furnace /交流～ alternating current furnace /佛尔顿～ Fulton furnace /阿贾斯-瓦特～ Ajax-Watt furnace /无(铁)心高频感应～ Ajax-Northrup furnace
电路 diànlù 〈电工〉circuit
电路图 diànlùtú circuit diagram
电驴子 diànlǘzi 〈方言〉motorcycle; motor bicycle; motorbike
电麻醉 diànmázuì 〈医学〉electro-anesthesia
电码 diànmǎ ❶ (telegraphic) code:莫尔斯～ Morse code /～本 code book ❷ (telegraphic) code representation of Chinese characters (each consisting of four Arabic numbers)
电鳗 diànmán 〈动物〉electric eel
电门 diànmén 〈电工〉switch:～在进门左手的墙壁上。The switch is on the left-hand side of the wall at the entrance.
电母 diànmǔ goddess of lightning:雷公～ god of thunder and goddess of lightning
电木 diànmù 〈化学〉bakelite:～粉 phenolic moulding powder /～插座 bakelite receptacle; bakelite socket
电纳 diànnà 〈物理〉susceptance
电脑 diànnǎo electronic brain; computer:微～ micro-computer /个人用～ personal computer (PC) /第五代～ fifth-generation computer /带～的彩电 colour television set with a built-in computer/～洗印〈摄影〉computer-controlled developing and printing /～电视终端 minitel /这部机器由～控制。The machine is computer controlled.
电脑病毒 diànnǎo bìngdú computer virus:清除～ remove computer virus
电脑记事簿 diànnǎo jìshìbù personal digital assistant
电脑空间 diànnǎo kōngjiān 〈信息〉cyberspace
电能 diànnéng electric energy
电鲇 diànnián 〈动物〉electric catfish (*Malapterurus electricus*)
电钮 diànniǔ push button; button:按～ press (*or* push) a button /转动～ turn a button /扳动～ pull a button
电耙 diànpá 〈矿业〉scraper
电抛光 diànpāoguāng 〈机械〉electropolishing; electrolytic polishing; electrolytic brightening
电平 diànpíng electrical level
电瓶 diànpíng storage battery; accumulator:～船 boat operated by storage battery; battery-operated boat
电瓶车 diànpíngchē storage battery car; electromobile
电气 diànqì electric:～工程 electrical engineering /～设备 electrical equipment /～开关 electric switch
电气动 diànqìdòng electro-pneumatic:～控制 electro-pneumatic control
电气孵卵器 diànqì fūluǎnqì 〈农业〉electric incubator
电气化 diànqìhuà electrification:农业～ electrification of agriculture /～铁路 electric railway
电气机车 diànqì jīchē electric locomotive
电气石 diànqìshí 〈矿业〉tourmaline
电气栽培 diànqì zāipéi 〈农业〉electroculture
电气自动化 diànqì zìdònghuà electric automatization
电器 diànqì ❶ electric device; electrical equipment ❷ (household) electrical appliance:家用～ household (*or* home) electrical appliances
电桥 diànqiáo 〈电工〉bridge:～电路 bridge circuit
电切除术 diànqiēchúshù 〈医学〉electroresection
电热 diànrè electric heat; electrothermal:～丝 (electric) heating wire /～处理 electrothermal treatment
电热杯 diànrèbēi electric heating mug
电热厂 diànrèchǎng heat and power plant
电热疗法 diànrè liáofǎ 〈医学〉electrothermotherapy
电热器 diànrèqì electric heater
电热毯 diànrètǎn electric blanket;〈医学〉electrothermal pad
电热针灸 diànrè zhēnjiǔ electrothermal acupuncture
电容 diànróng ❶ electric capacity; capacitance:～率 permittivity ❷ *see* "电容器"
电容器 diànróngqì *also* "容电器" condenser; capacitor:单联～ single capacitor; single-connection /可变～ variable (*or* adjustable) capacitor /双联～ double-connection; double capacitor
电熔炼 diànróngliàn 〈冶金〉electric smelting
电扫描 diànsǎomiáo electronic scanning
电扇 diànshàn electric fan:台式～ table electric fan /立式～ standing electric fan /吊式～ ceiling electric fan
电烧灼 diànshāozhuó 〈医学〉galvanocautery
电渗析 diànshènxī 〈化学〉electrodialysis
电生理学 diànshēnglǐxué electrophysiology
电声系统 diànshēng xìtǒng electro-acoustic system
电声学 diànshēngxué electro-acoustics
电石 diànshí 〈化学〉calcium carbide:～灯 acetylene lamp
电石气 diànshíqì 〈化学〉acetylene
电蚀加工 diànshí jiāgōng 〈机械〉electro-erosion machining:～法 electro-erosion process
电示 diànshì notify or instruct by telegram:以上建议妥否,盼～。Please instruct by cable whether the above proposal is appropriate.
电视 diànshì ❶ television; TV:彩色～ colour television /黑白～ black-and-white television /立体～ stereoscopic television /高清晰度～ high-definition television /闭路～ closed-circuit television (CCTV) /全频道彩色～ all-channel colour TV set /～电影 telecine /～天线 television antenna /～频道 television channel /～网 television network /～屏幕 television screen /～摄像转播车 television pickup station ❷ television programme:～转播 television relay /～实况转播 live television coverage; live telecast /发表～讲话 deliver a televised speech /看～ watch TV /上～ be publicized on TV/昨晚的～很好。Yesterday's TV programme was excellent.
电视病 diànshìbìng television syndrome
电视大学 diànshì dàxué (shortened as 电大) telecast higher education programme; TV university
电视电话 diànshì diànhuà video telephone; video-phone; vision phone; picture telephone
电视发射机 diànshì fāshèjī television transmitter
电视发射塔 diànshì fāshètǎ *see* "电视塔"
电视购物 diànshì gòuwù teleshopping
电视广播 diànshì guǎngbō television broadcasting; telecasting; videocast
电视机 diànshìjī *also* "电视接收机" television receiver; television set:投影式～ projection television receiver
电视讲座 diànshì jiǎngzuò telecourse
电视接收机 diànshì jiēshōujī *see* "电视机"
电视剧 diànshìjù TV play or drama
电视雷达导航仪 diànshì léidá dǎohángyí teleran
电视连续剧 diànshì liánxùjù TV serial play or drama
电视录像 diànshì lùxiàng telerecording
电视片 diànshìpiàn television film; telefilm
电视扫描 diànshì sǎomiáo television scanning
电视摄影机 diànshì shèyǐngjī television camera; telecamera
电视摄影记者 diànshì shèyǐng jìzhě television cameraman
电视塔 diànshìtǎ television tower
电视台 diànshìtái television station
电视文化 diànshì wénhuà television culture
电视系列片 diànshì xìlièpiàn TV series
电视新闻 diànshì xīnwén television news
电视诊断 diànshì zhěnduàn videognosis
电视制式 diànshì zhìshì television system:～转换器 television system converter
电视转播 diànshì zhuǎnbō telecast; televise; relay or transmit (a TV programme):～车 mobile television unit; remote pickup unit (*or* van) /～卫星 television transmission satellite
电势 diànshì *see* "电位"
电枢 diànshū armature:～线圈 armature coil /～绕组 armature winding

电刷 diànshuā 〈机械〉brush:～触点 brush contact
电台 diàntái ❶ transmitter-receiver; transceiver ❷ broadcasting or radio station
电烫 diàntàng permanent wave effected by electric hair rollers; electric perm
电梯 diàntī lift; elevator:～司机 lift operator; elevator runner /乘～上去 go up by lift /乘～到十一层 take the lift to the 11th floor
电梯井 diàntījǐng elevator shaft
电筒 diàntǒng torch; pocket torch; flashlight
电头 diàntóu dateline
电涂 diàntú 〈化工〉electropainting; electrocoating; electrophoretic coating
电推拿法 diàntuīnáfǎ 〈医学〉electromassage
电网 diànwǎng ❶ electrified wire netting; live wire entanglement ❷ electric network (including generators and transmitting systems); power grid:并入～ enter into electricity grid
电位 diànwèi *also* "电势"〈电学〉potential:～分布 potential distribution /～稳定器 potential stabilizer
电位差 diànwèichā *also* "电势差" potential difference
电位计 diànwèijì potentiometer
电文 diànwén text (of a telegram):草拟～ draw up the text of a telegram; draft a cable
电匣子 diànxiázi 〈方言〉radio set
电线 diànxiàn wire:～杆 (wire) pole
电信 diànxìn telecommunications:～业务 telecommunications service /～事业 telecommunications undertaking /～局 telecommunications bureau / ～零售业 retail telecoms /他在～部门工作多年。He has been in telecommunications for many years.
电信办公 diànxìn bàngōng teleworking
电刑 diànxíng ❶ torture by electric instrument ❷ electrocute
电休克 diànxiūkè electric shock:～疗法〈医学〉electroplexy
电须刀 diànxūdāo electric razor
电学 diànxué electricity (as a science)
电讯 diànxùn ❶ (telephone, telegraph, or radio) dispatch:各地记者发来的～ dispatches from reporters stationed in various places /把这条重要的～放在本报头版。Set the important dispatch on the first page of the newspaper. ❷ telecommunications:～协定 agreement on telecommunications matters /国际～公约 International Telecommunications Convention (1973) /国际～联盟 International Telecommunications Union (ITU)/～联系中断。Telecommunications connection is cut off.
电讯稿 diànxùngǎo news dispatch; news release:新华社～ Xinhua News Release
电压 diànyā voltage:～不足 undervoltage; undertension /～调整 voltage control
电压表 diànyābiǎo voltmeter
电压分压器 diànyā fēnyāqì voltage divider
电压计 diànyājì voltmeter
电压调压器 diànyā tiáoyāqì voltage regulator
电压稳定器 diànyā wěndìngqì voltage stabilizer
电眼 diànyǎn tuning eye; electric eye; magic eye
电唁 diànyàn send a telegram or message of condolence:这位科学家病逝时,国内外朋友纷纷～。When the scientist died, messages of condolence poured in from his friends, both Chinese and foreign.
电邀 diànyāo invite by telegram:～来京 invite sb. by cable to come to the capital
电冶金 diànyějīn electrometallurgy
电椅 diànyǐ electric chair
电影 diànyǐng film; movie; motion picture:有声～ sound film /无声～ silent film /彩色～ colour film /黑白～ black and white film /立体～ three-dimensional film; stereoscopic film /宽银幕～ wide-screen film /全景式宽银幕～ Cinerama /遮幅式宽银幕～ superscope /～观众 movie-goer; cinema-goer/～发行公司 film distribution company /～放映队 film projection team (*or* unit) /～剪辑机 film editing machine /～胶片 cinefilm; motion-picture film /～字幕 film caption; film subtitles /～制片人 film producer /～摄影师 cinematographer; cameraman /～说明书 film synopsis
电影导演 diànyǐng dǎoyǎn film director
电影放映机 diànyǐng fàngyìngjī (film) projector
电影节 diànyǐngjié film festival
电影剧本 diànyǐng jùběn scenario
电影明星 diànyǐng míngxīng film or movie star
电影片子 diànyǐng piānzi *also* "电影片" film; movie; motion picture
电影摄影机 diànyǐng shèyǐngjī cinecamera
电影演员 diànyǐng yǎnyuán film actor or actress
电影译制厂 diànyǐng yìzhìchǎng film dubbing studio
电影院 diànyǐngyuàn cinema; movie (house)
电影招待会 diànyǐng zhāodàihuì film reception
电影制片厂 diànyǐng zhìpiànchǎng (film) studio
电影周 diànyǐngzhōu film week
电泳 diànyǒng 〈物理〉electrophoresis
电玉粉 diànyùfěn 〈化学〉urea-formaldehyde moulding powder
电谕 diànyù issue an order by telegram; instruct by telegram
电源 diànyuán power supply; power source; mains:接上～ connect with the mains /切断～ cut off the electricity supply /～变压器 power transformer; mains transformer /～开关 power switch
电晕 diànyùn 〈物理〉corona:～放电 corona discharge /～管 corona tube
电熨斗 diànyùndǒu electric iron
电灶 diànzào electric cooking stove or range
电渣 diànzhā electroslag:～重熔〈冶金〉electroslag refining; electroslag remelting
电渣焊 diànzhāhàn electroslag welding
电渣炉 diànzhālú 〈冶金〉electroslag furnace
电闸 diànzhá electric brake; main switch; master switch
电站 diànzhàn power station
电针疗法 diànzhēn liáofǎ 〈中医〉acupuncture with electric stimulation; galvano-acupuncture
电针麻醉 diànzhēn mázuì 〈中医〉galvano-acupunctural anesthesia
电诊断法 diànzhěnduànfǎ 〈医学〉electro-diagnosis
电震疗法 diànzhèn liáofǎ electroshock therapy
电钟 diànzhōng electric clock; electroclock
电珠 diànzhū small bulb:手电的～坏了。The bulb of the flashlight doesn't work.
电铸 diànzhù 〈机械〉electric forming; electroforming
电铸版 diànzhùbǎn 〈印刷〉electrotype
电转儿 diànzhuànr 〈方言〉electric gramophone or phonograph; record player:他的收音机带～。There is an electric gramophone to go with his radio.
电子 diànzǐ electron:热～ thermal electron /正～ positive electron; positron /负～ negative electron; negatron /～电荷 electron charge /～程序控制 electron program control /～刻版机 electronic engraving machine /～器件 electronic device /～分色机 electronic colour scanner /～监视 electronic surveillance /～壳层 electron shell /～人工喉 artificial electronic larynx /～稳压器 electronic voltage regulator /～照相术 electro-photography /～印相机 electronic printer
电子表 diànzǐbiǎo quartz watch; accutron
电子表格 diànzǐ biǎogé 〈信息〉spreadsheet
电子秤 diànzǐchèng electronic scale; electronic-weighing system
电子对 diànzǐduì 〈物理〉duplet; electron pair
电子对抗 diànzǐ duìkàng 〈通信〉electronic countermeasures; electron warfare:～接收机 electronic-countermeasures receiver /～搜索仪〈军事〉electronic fence /～导弹 countermeasures missile; ECM-carrying missile /～卫星 electronic countermeasure satellite (*or* countermeasures satellite)
电子反对抗 diànzǐ fǎnduìkàng 〈军事〉(electronic) counter-countermeasures
电子伏特 diànzǐ fútè electron-volt
电子干扰 diànzǐ gānrǎo 〈军事〉electronic jamming or countermeasure
电子工业 diànzǐ gōngyè electronics industry
电子管 diànzǐguǎn electron tube; valve:～收音机 valve radio set
电子光学 diànzǐ guāngxué electron optics
电子函件 diànzǐ hánjiàn *also* "电子邮件" E-mail; electronic mail
电子回旋加速器 diànzǐ huíxuán jiāsùqì betatron
电子货币 diànzǐ huòbì cybermoney
电子货币系统 diànzǐ huòbì xìtǒng electronic monetary system (EMS)
电子计算机 diànzǐ jìsuànjī electronic computer:微型～ microcomputer
电子加速器 diànzǐ jiāsùqì electron accelerator
电子经济 diànzǐ jīngjì cybereconomy

电子流 diànzǐliú electron current
电子炉 diànzǐlú electronic oven
电子排版 diànzǐ páibǎn electronic composition
电子枪 diànzǐqiāng electron gun
电子窃听 diànzǐ qiètīng electronic eavesdropping or bugging
电子琴 diànzǐqín electronic organ; electronic keyboard
电子扫描 diànzǐ sǎomiáo electronic scanning: ～雷达〈军事〉electronically steerable array radar
电子闪光灯 diànzǐ shǎnguāngdēng electronic flash
电子商务 diànzǐ shāngwù E-commerce; electronic commerce
电子石英钟 diànzǐ shíyīngzhōng electronic quartz clock
电子束 diànzǐshù electron beam
电子数据处理机 diànzǐ shùjù chǔlǐjī 〈电子〉electronic data processing machine; electronic data processor
电子数据交换 diànzǐ shùjù jiāohuàn electronic data interchange (EDI)
电子陶瓷 diànzǐ táocí 〈无线电〉electronic porcelain; electronic ceramics
电子望远镜 diànzǐ wàngyuǎnjìng electronic telescope
电子物理学 diànzǐ wùlǐxué electron physics
电子显微镜 diànzǐ xiǎnwēijìng electron microscope: 八十万倍～ electron microscope with a magnification of 800,000 times
电子学 diànzǐxué electronics: 无线电～ radio-electronics
电子业务 diànzǐ yèwù 〈信息〉E-business (including commerce, customer support, employee work, etc. on the Internet)
电子音乐 diànzǐ yīnyuè electronic music
电子邮件 diànzǐ yóujiàn *see* "电子函件"
电子游戏 diànzǐ yóuxì video game; TV game: ～机 video game player; TV game player
电子乐器 diànzǐ yuèqì electrophone; electronic instrument
电子云 diànzǐyún electron cloud
电子战 diànzǐzhàn 〈军事〉electronic warfare
电子钟 diànzǐzhōng electronic clock
电阻 diànzǔ resistance: ～器 resistor /～炉〈冶金〉resistance furnace /～率 resistivity; specific resistance /～表 ohmmeter /～对焊〈机械〉upset butt welding
电钻 diànzuàn electric drill
电嘴 diànzuǐ 〈方言〉sparking plug; spark plug; ignition plug

钿 diàn flower-patterned ornament made of gold foil; shell-inlaid flower pattern on wooden or lacquer ware: 金～ woman's hair ornament of gold flowers /螺～ shell-inlaid flower pattern; mother-of-pearl inlay /翠～ woman's hair decoration studded with kingfisher feathers
see also tián

佃 diàn rent land (from a landlord)
see also tián
佃东 diàndōng 〈旧语〉(used by tenants) landlord
佃户 diànhù tenant (farmer): 解放前他父亲给地主当～。Before liberation, his father worked as a tenant for a landlord.
佃客 diànkè ❶〈旧语〉liege tenant ❷ tenant (farmer)
佃农 diànnóng tenant-peasant; tenant farmer: 这位老人当过～。The old man used to be a tenant farmer.
佃契 diànqì tenancy contract
佃权 diànquán right to tenancy
佃租 diànzū land rent

甸 diàn ❶〈旧语〉open country outside a town ❷ *used in place names*: 桦～ Huadian (in Jilin Province) /宽～ Kuandian (in Liaoning Province)
甸子 diànzi 〈方言〉pastureland

簟 diàn 〈方言〉bamboo mat

殿[1] diàn hall; palace: 佛～ Buddhist hall; hall for worshipping Buddha /宫～ palace /太和～ Hall of Supreme Harmony

殿[2] diàn at the rear; in the rear: ～其卒而退 bring up the rear in retreat
殿版 diànbǎn *see* "殿本"
殿本 diànběn palace edition (imperial block-printed edition of the Qing Dynasty)
殿后 diànhòu bring up the rear; follow in the rear; close the rear: 你打头阵，我～。You go in front while I'll bring up the rear.
殿军 diànjūn ❶ rearguard: 行军时，警卫团总是部队的～。When the troops were on march, the guards regiment were the rearguard. ❷ person who comes last in a contest or last among the winners; last of the successful candidates: 他是这次羽毛球友好邀请赛的～。He is the last-placed winner of the Badminton Friendship Invitational Tournament.
殿试 diànshì final imperial examination (presided over by the emperor); palace examination
殿堂 diàntáng ❶ palace; temple ❷ hall in a palace or temple: 寺院内～焕然一新。The halls in the temple have put on an entirely new look.
殿下 diànxià His, Her, or Your Highness (for addressing princes or princesses); His, Her, or Your Royal Highness (for crown prince or princess); His, Her, or Your Imperial Highness (for imperial crown prince or princess): 太子～ His Royal Highness the Crown Prince /亲王～ His Royal Highness the Prince
殿宇 diànyǔ palace; temple: 宏伟的～ magnificent palace (*or* temple)

癜 diàn purplish or white patches on the skin: 紫～ purpura /白～疯 vitiligo

diāo

貂(鼦) diāo marten; ermine: 紫～ mink /黑～ sable
貂皮 diāopí (fur or pelt of) marten; mink; ermine
貂裘 diāoqiú marten coat; mink coat
貂熊 diāoxióng *also* "狼獾" lánghuān 〈动物〉glutton (*Gulo gulo*)

凋(彫) diāo wither: 岁寒然后知松柏之后～。Only when winter comes do you realize that the pine and cypress will not wither.
凋败 diāobài wither and decay; wither: 草木～ with all vegetation withered and decayed
凋敝 diāobì ❶ (of life) in straitened circumstances; hard; destitute: 民生～。The people lived in destitution. ❷ (of business) languishing; depressed: 百业～。All business languished.
凋残 diāocán ❶ ruined; ramshackle; dilapidated; tumble-down: ～的古庙 dilapidated (*or* ramshackle) ancient temple ❷ withered; fallen and scattered about: 百花～。All flowers have withered and fallen. ❸〈书面〉*see* "凋敝"
凋枯 diāokū *see* "凋萎"
凋零 diāolíng ❶ withered; fallen and scattered about: 花草～。Flowers and grasses have withered. /万物～。All things have fallen into decay. ❷ decline; go downhill; be on the wane or decline: 家道～。His family is on the decline. ❸ pass away; die: 亲友～。Many of my relatives and friends have passed away. /老辈～。Many of the old generation have departed this life.
凋落 diāoluò wither and fall: 秋风起处，树叶～。Chilly gusts of the autumn wind denuded the trees of their leaves. /亲朋故旧，～殆尽。Few relatives, friends and acquaintances have survived.
凋丧 diāosàng 〈书面〉❶ disheartened; discouraged; downhearted; depressed ❷ pass away; die: 老友～殆尽。Nearly all my old friends are gone.
凋萎 diāowěi withered and fallen: 枝叶～。The twigs and leaves were withered and fallen.
凋谢 diāoxiè ❶ wither and fall: 庭院中的花都～了。Flowers in the courtyard have withered away. ❷ die of old age: 老成～ passing away of worthy old people

碉 diāo pillbox; blockhouse: 明～暗堡 blockhouses and bunkers
碉堡 diāobǎo pillbox; blockhouse; bulwark
碉楼 diāolóu watchtower

雕[1]**(彫、琱)** diāo ❶ carve; engrave; sculpt: 在铜器

上～花样 engrave designs on copper /椅子靠背上～着花纹。The back of the chair was carved with floral patterns. ❷ carving; sculpture: 玉～ jade carving /骨～ bone sculpture (*or* carving) /泥～ clay sculpture /牙～ ivory sculpture /瓷～ carved porcelain; porcelain carving /浮～ relief /半浮～ bas-relief; low relief /根～ root carving /石～佛像 stone statue of Buddha /木～像 wood figure; wooden statue /黄杨木～ boxwood carving /竹板平～ bamboo board with shallow carving ❸ decorated with coloured drawings: 峻宇～墙 tall buildings with walls decorated with coloured drawings

雕[2]（鵰）

diāo 〈动物〉eagle; vulture

雕鞍 diāo'ān saddle decorated with carvings

雕版 diāobǎn block printing; engraving: ～印刷品 engraving(s)

雕虫小技 diāochóng-xiǎojì insignificant skill; trifling skill of a scribe; literary skill of small order: 有人把写作技巧统统视为～，这显然是不对的。It is obviously wrong to consider all techniques of writing insignificant skills.

雕红漆 diāohóngqī *also* "剔红" tīhóng carved (red) lacquerware

雕花 diāohuā ❶ carving: ～艺术 carving art /～匠 carver /～家具 furniture with carved patterns /～烟盒 engraved cigarette case ❷ carve patterns or designs on woodwork: 正屋的两扇门上有～，十分好看。Designs on the two doors of the principal room are beautifully carved.

雕花玻璃 diāohuā bōli cut glass

雕画 diāohuà carve and paint: 柱头上～得很华丽。The top of the column is magnificently carved and painted.

雕绘 diāohuì *see* "雕画"

雕镌 diāojuān 〈书面〉carve; engrave

雕刻 diāokè carve; engrave; sculpt: ～品 carvings; carved works /象牙～ ivory carving /～玻璃 engraved glass /玉石～ jade carving /铜板～ copperplate engraving /用玉～一个人像 sculpt a statue out of jade /在石头上～图案 engrave a stone with designs /大理石很难～。It's difficult to engrave in marble.

雕刻刀 diāokèdāo carving tool; burin

雕刻工艺 diāokè gōngyì artistic carving

雕刻师 diāokèshī carver; engraver

雕空绣 diāokōngxiù cutwork

雕栏玉砌 diāolán-yùqì carved balustrades and marble stairs — beautifully ornamented palace buildings: ～应犹在，只是朱颜改。The carved balustrades and marble steps must still be there, But rosy faces cannot be as fair.

雕梁画栋 diāoliáng-huàdòng richly ornamented building: 园中有两座亭子，～，金碧辉煌。Two pavilions decorated with coloured drawings stand in the garden, splendid and magnificent.

雕镂 diāolòu 〈书面〉*see* "雕刻"

雕漆 diāoqī *also* "漆雕" 〈工美〉carved lacquerware: ～花瓶 carved lacquer vase /～盘 carved lacquer tray

雕砌 diāoqì write in a laboured and ornate style: 通篇～，毫无新意。The essay is full of ornate words and devoid of literary originality.

雕青 diāoqīng 〈书面〉tattoo

雕饰 diāoshì ❶ carve and decorate: 精心～ carve and decorate with loving care /柱子上的盘龙～得很生动。The column is decorated with a graphically carved coiling dragon. ❷ carved designs and patterns; carving: 门扇上的～已经残破了。The carvings on the doors are already worn down and broken. ❸ over-decorate; overdo; overact: 她表演适度，不加～，显得很自然。Her performance struck the right note of balance, effortless and perfectly natural.

雕塑 diāosù sculpture: ～品 sculpture /精于～ be skilled in sculpture /～技巧 technique of sculpture

雕塑家 diāosùjiā sculptor or sculptress

雕像 diāoxiàng statue; carved figure: 青铜～ bronze statue /半身～ bust /小～ statuette

雕展 diāozhǎn sculpture exhibition

雕琢 diāozhuó ❶ cut and polish (jade, etc.); carve: 这尊佛像是用玉石～的。The statue of Buddha is carved out of jade. ❷ write in an ornate style: 这篇文章过于～了。The style of the essay is too elaborate.

鲷

diāo 〈动物〉porgy: 真～ genuine porgy; red porgy

刁

diāo ❶ sly; wily; cunning; tricky: 逞～ act like a cunning fox /～风不可长。We should do nothing to encourage wily practices. /他这人很～。He is very (*or* singularly) sly. ❷ create difficulties; make things difficult: 不～卡用户 not deliberately create difficulties for consumers ❸ 〈方言〉take (things from others) by force: ～别人的钱财 seize other people's money ❹ 〈方言〉be picky about food: 嘴～ be too picky (*or* choosy) about food ❺ (Diāo) a surname

刁斗 diāodǒu 〈古语〉brass rice pot with a handle, used in the army as a gong during night watch

刁恶 diāo'è wicked; cunning and vicious: ～之徒 wicked fellow

刁妇 diāofù unruly woman; virago

刁怪 diāoguài sly and capricious; perverse; cranky: 性情～ be of a cranky temperament

刁棍 diāogùn ruffian; scoundrel; bully

刁悍 diāohàn cunning and fierce: 为人～ cunning and ferocious

刁横 diāohèng cunning and peremptory

刁滑 diāohuá cunning; crafty; artful: 生性～ cunning by nature

刁赖 diāolài sly and unreasonable: 别看他外表很有礼貌，为人～得很。He is cunning and unamenable to reason despite his veneer of politeness.

刁利 diāolì cunning and fierce

刁蛮 diāomán 〈方言〉crafty and savage

刁民 diāomín 〈旧语〉(as used by officials to refer to common people under their jurisdiction) unruly people; ungovernable people: 大胆～! You brazen rowdies!

刁难 diāonàn create difficulties; make things difficult: 故意～ deliberately make things difficult (for sb.) /百般～ create obstructions of every description; raise all manner of difficulties

刁巧 diāoqiǎo tricky and self-serving

刁顽 diāowán cunning and stubborn; cunning and obstinate: 此人一生～不化。He remained cunning and incorrigibly obstinate throughout his life.

刁羊 diāoyáng *also* "叼羊" diāoyáng traditional sport of Kazakh, Uygur, Tajik and Kirgiz nationalities, held on festival days with riders competing for a headless goat, the winner being the one capturing and carrying it to the designated spot

刁钻 diāozuān cunning; wily; artful; tricky: 发球～ tricky service /此人很～。This man is very cunning and unreliable.

刁钻古怪 diāozuān-gǔguài sly and capricious: 这个主意够～的! What a sly idea!

叼

diāo hold in the mouth: ～着烟卷儿 with a cigarette dangling from one's lips /老鹰～走了一只小鸡。A hawk swooped down on a chick and carried it off.

叼口 diāokǒu 〈印刷〉gripper edge: ～边 pitch edge

叼羊 diāoyáng *see* "刁羊" diāoyáng

貂

diāo 〈古语〉*also* "蝉" chán cicada

diǎo

鸟（鳥）

diǎo *also* "屌" diǎo 〈粗话〉(used in old-style novels) fucking; damned: 作甚～事? What fucking business are you up to?

see also niǎo

屌

diǎo 〈粗话〉penis

diào

调[1]

diào ❶ transfer; shift; move: 对～ (of officials, etc.) exchange posts; be swapped /南水北～ divert water from the south to the north /～部队 bring in (*or* move) troops /我刚～到北京来。I've just been transferred to Beijing. ❷ investigate: 函～ investigate by letter /内查外～ investigate both inside and outside (a unit)

调[2]

diào ❶ accent; tone: 他说话的～儿有点儿怪。He speaks with a queer accent. ❷ argument; view; tone (of one's words): 唱高～ utter high-sounding words /老～重弹 strike up an old tune;

harp on one's string ❸〈音乐〉key: B~ key of B /D大~ D major / D小~ D minor ❹ air; tune; melody: 定~ call the tune; set the keynote /这个~儿很好听。This tune sounds pleasant to the ear. ❺〈语言〉tone; tune: 升~ rising tone (*or* tune) /降~ falling tone (*or* tune)
see also tiáo
调包 diàobāo *see* "掉包" diàobāo
调兵遣将 diàobīng-qiǎnjiàng ❶ move troops; deploy forces; dispatch armies: 敌军频繁~, 企图反攻。The enemy are busy moving troops in an attempt to launch a counteroffensive. ❷ mobilize and organize manpower: 总指挥正在~, 力保工程如期完成。The general director is mustering manpower to make sure that the project will be completed on schedule.
调拨 diàobō ❶ transfer and allocate (goods or funds); allot: ~款项购置设备 allocate funds for purchase of equipment /~价格 transfer pricing ❷ *see* "调遣"
see also tiáobō
调茬 diàochá *also* "轮作" lúnzuò crop rotation
调查 diàochá investigate; inquire into; look into; survey: 现场~ on-the-spot investigation /刑事~ criminal investigation /农村~ rural survey /~事故原因 investigate the cause of an accident /~报告 report on the findings of an investigation /~机关 investigatory apparatus /~人 investigator; inquirer /~提纲 questionnaire; outline for investigation /~委员会 board of inquiry /案件尚在~中。The case is under investigation. /这件事必须彻底~。We must get to the bottom of the matter.
调查会 diàocháhuì fact-finding meeting
调查团 diàochátuán fact-finding mission
调车场 diàochēchǎng 〈铁路〉switchyard
调挡 diàodǎng shift gears
调档 diàodàng ask for the transfer of sb.'s file of records
调调 diàodiao ❶ *see* "调²❹" ❷ view; argument; tone (of one's words): 她说话的~儿不对头。Her remarks sound fishy to me. /他的话你听出点~儿来没有? Did you smell a rat in what he said?
调动 diàodòng ❶ transfer; shift; move (troops); manoeuvre: ~工作 transfer sb. to another post /边境部队~频繁。There have been numerous troop movements on the border. ❷ bring into play; arouse; muster; mobilize: ~群众积极性 arouse (*or* mobilize) the enthusiasm of the masses /当务之急是为这次总攻~五万军队, 一千辆坦克。The task of top priority now is to muster fifty thousand troops and a thousand tanks for the general offensive.
调度 diàodù ❶ manage; control; dispatch (trains, buses, etc.): ~车辆 dispatch cars (*or* buses) / 这里的生产~搞得很好。Production management is good here. ❷ dispatcher: 汽车公司的~ dispatcher at the bus company
调度室 diàodùshì dispatcher's office; control room
调度员 diàodùyuán dispatcher; controller
调防 diàofáng 〈军事〉relieve a garrison; (of a garrison) be relieved or transferred: 他回来时, 正好部队~。He came back just when the army was being transferred.
调赴 diàofù be transferred or dispatched to (a place): ~前线 be dispatched (*or* sent) to the front
调干 diàogàn cadre temporarily relieved of his or her work and waiting for new assignment (usu. to study at an institution of formal education)
调干学员 diàogàn xuéyuán mid-career student; cadre student
调函 diàohán (official) letter of transfer: 他的~今天已经发出。The official letter for his transfer was sent today.
调号 diàohào ❶〈语言〉tone mark ❷〈音乐〉key signature
调猴儿 diàohóur *also* "吊猴儿" diàohóur 〈方言〉naughty; mischievous; unruly
调虎离山 diàohǔ-líshān lure the tiger out of his mountain or lair; entice the enemy away from his entrenchment; tempt sb. into leaving vantage ground: 中了敌人的~之计 be fooled by the enemy's trick of "luring the tiger from his mountain"; be tempted by the enemy into leaving one's vantage ground
调换 diàohuàn *also* "掉换" diàohuàn exchange; change; swap: 他要~工作。He wants to change to another job. /咱俩~一下坐位, 好吗? May I exchange my seat with yours?
调回 diàohuí order to return; recall: 把军队~北京 recall the troops to Beijing
调集 diàojí assemble; muster: ~军队 assemble forces /~防汛器材 mobilize (*or* muster) flood prevention equipment
调卷 diàojuàn *also* "吊卷" diàojuàn send for sb.'s file or examination papers; ask for the transfer of sb.'s file or examination papers
调侃儿 diàokǎnr *also* "调坎儿" 〈方言〉speak jargon or cant
调看 diàokàn ask for sth. for examination: ~档案 send for sb.'s files for examination
调类 diàolèi 〈语言〉tone category
调离 diàolí be transferred from one place or job (to another): 他已~该厂。He has been transferred from this factory (to another place).
调令 diàolìng transfer order: 下~ issue a transfer order
调门儿 diàoménr ❶ pitch (of one's voice): ~定得太低 pitch a tune too low /这歌儿~定高了, 我唱不上去。The song is pitched too high for my voice. ❷ view; argument; tone (of one's words): 跟他的那篇文章相比, 这篇文章的~就不那么高了。This article of his has a rather moderate tone as compared with his earlier one.
调派 diàopài send; assign; allocate: ~干部下基层 send cadres to the grass-roots units /合理~人员很重要。Rational allocation of personnel is an important job.
调配 diàopèi allocate; deploy: ~农具 allocate farm implements / 合理~劳动力 deploy manpower rationally
see also tiáopèi
调遣 diàoqiǎn dispatch; assign: ~军队 dispatch troops /听从~ (be ready to) accept an assignment; be at sb.'s disposal; be at sb.'s command /不服从~ disobey (*or* reject) an assignment
调取案卷令状 diàoqǔ ànjuàn lìngzhuàng 〈法律〉*certiorari*
调任 diàorèn be transferred (to another post): ~别的工作 transfer sb. (*or* be transferred) to another job /他已~办公室主任。He has been transferred to take charge of the office.
调式 diàoshì 〈音乐〉mode
调头 diàotóu ❶ *also* "掉头" diàotóu turn round: 汽车怎么~了? Why has the bus changed its direction? ❷ argument; view; tone (of one's words): 空洞的~ empty rhetoric
调头 diàotou 〈方言〉❶ tune; melody ❷ manner of speaking
调歪 diàowāi *see* "掉歪" diàowāi
调性 diàoxìng 〈音乐〉tonality
调训 diàoxùn assemble and train: ~干部 assemble cadres for further training
see also tiáoxùn
调研 diàoyán (short for 调查研究) investigate and study
调研员 diàoyányuán researcher
调演 diàoyǎn joint performance (by chosen theatrical troupes of different localities); invitational theatrical festival: 全省戏剧~ provincial invitational theatrical festival /中青年京剧演员观摩~将在北京举行。Middle-aged and young Beijing Opera artists will assemble in Beijing by invitation to give performances and exchange experiences.
调用 diàoyòng transfer (under a unified plan): ~干部 transfer cadres (to a specific job) /~物资 appropriate materials
调阅 diàoyuè send for (related papers or data) for inspection, verification or reference
调运 diàoyùn allocate and transport: ~救灾物资 allocate and transport relief materials /蔬菜从农场~到市内各菜场。Vegetables are transported from the farms to various grocery stores in the city.
调值 diàozhí 〈语言〉tone pitch
调职 diàozhí be transferred to another post; be appointed to a new post: 我近日将去上海商量~问题。I am going to Shanghai one of these days to arrange for a transfer from my job.
调转 diàozhuǎn ❶ be transferred (to a new job); change jobs: 他的~手续已经办好了。He has completed (*or* gone through) the formalities for his transfer. ❷ *see* "掉转" diàozhuǎn
调子 diàozi ❶〈音乐〉mode ❷ tune; melody: 定~ call the tune; set the tone (*or* keynote) /这个~挺熟。The tune sounds quite familiar. /钢琴与小提琴用的不是一个~。The piano and the violin are not in tune. ❸ tune; tone; vein: 改变~ change one's tune; sing another (*or* a different) tune / 把批评的~降低点儿。Tone down the criticism. /这篇文章带有争论的~。The article has a polemical tone. /他以悲观的~谈了他的看法。He spoke of the matter in a pessimistic vein. ❹ view; argument; tone (of one's words): 他今天发言的~值得深思。The tone of his speech today is worth pondering.

掉[1] diào ❶ fall; drop; shed; come off: ~眼泪 shed tears /~头发 one's hair is thinning /屋顶~土。Dust fell from the roof. /扣子~了。The button has come off. /这里水很深,小心别~进去。The water is deep here; take care not to fall in. ❷ fall behind; lag behind: 走得太慢,~在大伙后面 walk so slowly as to fall behind all the others /他的数学考试成绩由前十名~到第二十名。He dropped from among the first ten to the twentieth place in the math examination. ❸ lose; be missing: 我把钢笔给~了。I've lost my fountain pen. /这本书~了四页。Four pages are missing from the book. ❹ reduce; cut down; drop; lower: 一年之内他体重~了五公斤。He lost 5 kg within the year.

掉[2] diào ❶ wag; wave; shake: 尾大不~ the tail is too big to wag — the tail wags the dog; the organization is too cumbersome to be efficient ❷ turn; turn round; turn back: ~过头来 turn one's head round /~过脸去 avert one's face; turn one's face away ❸ change; exchange; swap: ~座位 change seats; exchange seats; swap places with sb. ❹ show off; vaunt: *see* "~文"

掉[3] diào *used after some verbs, indicating the result of an action*: 改~坏习气 correct bad habits; rectify undesirable practices /割~肿瘤 have a tumour removed /脱~鞋袜 pull off one's shoes and stockings /刷~靴子上的泥 brush the mud off one's boots /洗~衣服上的油渍 wash out the greasy stains from the clothes /把没用的东西扔~ throw away the junk /蠹虫几乎把整本书都给吃~了。The moths have eaten up almost the whole book.

掉包 diàobāo stealthily replace sth. genuine or valuable with sth. fake or worthless: 这批衣料跟样品不一样,肯定被人~了。The dress materials must have been stealthily changed, for they are different from the samples.

掉膘 diàobiāo (of livestock) become thin; lose weight

掉秤 diàochèng 〈方言〉(of perishable or wholesale goods) lose weight when reweighed or retailed: 这只鸡我买回几小时就~了。The chicken lost weight only a few hours after I bought it.

掉点儿 diàodiǎnr start to rain: ~了,赶快回去吧! It's starting to rain. Let's hurry back.

掉队 diàoduì drop out or off; fall or lag behind: 在急行军中,没有一个~的。No one dropped out on the forced march. /你再不抓紧学习就要~了。You'll lag behind if you don't study hard.

掉过儿 diàoguòr exchange or swap places: 这两张桌子~放才合适。It would be better to swap these two desks around.

掉换 diàohuàn *also* "调换" diàohuàn ❶ exchange; swap: 我想同住在西城的人~房子。I would like to swap apartments with someone living in the western part of the city. /我们~一下座位好吗? Could I exchange seats with you? ❷ change; replace: ~工作 change to a new job; be transferred to another post /货物售出,概不~。(sign in shop) No exchanges. /这件衬衫不合适,请~一下。This shirt is not of the right size. Could I change it for another?

掉魂 diàohún be frightened out of one's wits; be numb with fear

掉价 diàojià ❶ (of price) go down; fall or drop in price: 菠菜~了。The price of spinach has gone down. ❷ lower one's social status; lose face: 你认为大学生参加体力劳动就~了吗? Do you really think it beneath the dignity of a college student to do some physical labour?

掉脑袋 diào nǎodai lose one's head; be beheaded; get killed

掉枪花 diào qiānghuā 〈方言〉play tricks; double-cross: 有啥讲啥,不要~。Own up and play no tricks.

掉色 diàoshǎi lose colour; fade: 这块布不~。This piece of cloth won't fade. *or* This piece of cloth is colour fast.

掉舌 diàoshé 〈书面〉go about drumming up support for an idea; go canvassing

掉书袋 diào shūdài show off one's erudition by making literary quotations or historical allusions; lard one's speech or writing with quotations and allusions: 他这人特爱~,说话总是文绉绉的。He's excessively fond of using literary quotations and allusions, and never speaks plainly.

掉头 diàotóu ❶ turn; turn round; turn about: 掉过头去 turn one's head away /小偷见了警察,~就跑。At the sight of a policeman, the thief turned round and took to his heels. ❷ *also* "调头" diàotóu (of vehicles, vessels, etc.) turn round or about; make a U-turn: 车辆~处 turnaround /船到下一个港口就~返回。The ship will turn back after calling at the next port. ❸ 〈书面〉shake one's head: ~叹息 shake one's head and utter a sigh

掉歪 diàowāi *also* "调歪" diàowāi; "吊歪" diàowāi 〈方言〉deliberately make things difficult for sb.; be mischievous: 这小子~,又出难题了。This guy is creating difficulties again.

掉文 diàowén show off one's literary talent; lard one's speech or writing with literary allusions: 你甭~了,有话直说吧。Drop your flowery rhetoric and come straight to the point.

掉向 diàoxiàng 〈方言〉lose one's bearings; get lost; lose one's way

掉腰子 diào yāozi *see* "吊腰子" diào yāozi

掉以轻心 diàoyǐqīngxīn lower one's guard; treat lightly: 对伪装的敌人~ be off one's guard against disguised enemies /这件事我们决不可~。Under no circumstances can we treat the matter lightly.

掉转 diàozhuǎn *also* "调转" diàozhuǎn turn round: ~船头 turn a boat round /叛变的士兵~枪口,朝司令部开火了。The mutineers turned their guns on the headquarters.

吊[1]**(弔)** diào ❶ hang; suspend; dangle: 房檐下~着成串的红辣椒。Strings of red peppers hang from the eaves. /把篮子~起来。Hang up the basket. ❷ lift up or let down with a rope, etc.; haul: 起重机正把预制板~上顶层。The crane is hauling prefabricated parts to the top floor. ❸ 〈体育〉drop (the ball or shuttle) where one's rival or rivals find it hard to retrieve: 近网轻~ drop the ball (*or* shuttle) just over the net ❹ put in a fur lining; line: ~皮袄 line a coat with fur; fix a cover on a fur coat ❺ revoke; withdraw: *see* "~销" ❻ crane: 塔~ tower crane

D

吊[2]**(弔)** diào (monetary unit in ancient China) a string of 1,000 cash

吊[3]**(弔)** diào condole; mourn

吊膀子 diào bàngzi *also* "吊膀" 〈方言〉flirt; fool around (with a girl): 我知道他和那个姓李的女人~。I know he is carrying on with that woman named Li.

吊钹 diàobó 〈乐器〉suspension cymbal

吊车 diàochē *also* "起重机" qǐzhòngjī crane; hoist: 桥式~ overhead crane /~轨道 crane runway /~梁 crane beam /~工 craneman /~起重能力 lifting capacity of a crane; hoisting power

吊窗 diàochuāng window hinged on top

吊床 diàochuáng hammock

吊打 diàodǎ hang up and beat: ~勒索 torture a victim by hanging him up and extort money

吊带 diàodài *also* "吊袜带" (stocking) suspenders; (US) garters; braces

吊蛋 diàodàn purposely make trouble; be naughty and unruly: 这个人真~。This chap is really troublesome and unruly. /牲口~,他依旧耐着性子驯服。The beast was wild and vicious, but he managed to bring it under control with great patience.

吊灯 diàodēng pendent lamp: 枝形~ chandelier

吊灯花 diàodēnghuā 〈植物〉rosary vine (*Hibiscus schizopetalus*)

吊兜 diàodōu loosely hanging pocket (without the bottom end stitched to jacket or trousers)

吊斗 diàodǒu cableway bucket

吊儿郎当 diào'erlángdāng fool around; be careless and casual: 学习上~是学不扎实的。You cannot make solid progress in your studies if you are careless and casual. /他整天~,不正经干事。He fools around all day doing nothing.

吊放式声纳 diàofàngshì shēngnà dipping sonar

吊杆 diàogān 〈机械〉boom; jib: (船用)起重~ derrick /起重机~ crane boom /~托架 boom crutch

吊杠 diàogàng 〈体育〉trapeze

吊钩 diàogōu 〈机械〉(lift) hook; hanger

吊古 diàogǔ reminisce about the past on visiting a historical site

吊挂 diàoguà ❶ hang; suspend; dangle: 屋角~着蛛网。There are cobwebs dangling from the corners of the ceiling. ❷ 〈方言〉*also* "吊钱儿" paper cut with auspicious signs and words, pasted over the door

吊罐 diàoguàn *also* "罐笼" guànlóng 〈矿业〉cage

吊诡 diàoguǐ 〈书面〉eccentric; singular; bizarre; odd: ~矜奇 ex-

ceedingly eccentric
吊猴儿 diàohóur *see*“调猴儿”diàohóur
吊环 diàohuán 〈体育〉rings：摆荡～ swinging rings /静止～ still rings
吊货网 diàohuòwǎng cargo net
吊机 diàojī ❶ crane; hoist ❷ a kind of loom suspended from a beam
吊祭 diàojì hold a funeral ceremony; attend a funeral ceremony
吊架 diàojià 〈机械〉hanger：平衡～ balance hanger
吊脚楼 diàojiǎolóu 〈方言〉*see*“吊楼❶”
吊颈 diàojǐng 〈方言〉hang oneself
吊景 diàojǐng 〈戏剧〉drop scenery
吊具 diàojù hoisting device
吊卷 diàojuàn *see*“调卷”diàojuàn
吊卡 diàokǎ 〈石油〉elevator：油管～ tubing elevator
吊坎儿 diàokǎnr *see*“调侃儿”diàokǎnr
吊客 diàokè one who pays a condolence call; one who visits the bereaved to offer condolences; mourner
吊扣 diàokòu (of certificates, etc. that have been issued) recall and suspend：违者～驾驶执照。Those who violate the regulations shall have their driving licences suspended.
吊裤带 diàokùdài shoulder straps; braces; suspenders
吊兰 diàolán *also*“挂兰”guàlán *Chlorophytum comosum*：蛛状～ spider plant
吊雷 diàoléi 〈军事〉hanging mine
吊链 diàoliàn chain sling; sling chain
吊楼 diàolóu ❶ *also*“吊脚楼” house whose rear part is supported on piles over water ❷ (in certain hilly regions) house made of timber or bamboo and supported by wooden stakes over ground
吊毛 diàomáo 〈戏曲〉throw oneself headlong, turn a backward somersault, and fall on one's back (to indicate a sudden fall on stage)
吊眉 diàoméi *also*“吊梢眉” thick eyebrows sticking out at the end
吊民伐罪 diàomín-fázuì punish the tyrant and comfort the people; strike the oppressors to succour the people：农民军～，一路受到百姓的欢迎。Punishing the tyrant to reassure the public, the peasant army won the hearts of the people.
吊盘 diàopán moveable platform in building a vertical shaft; hanging scaffold
吊铺 diàopù hanging bed or bunk
吊钱儿 diàoqianr 〈方言〉*see*“吊挂❷”
吊桥 diàoqiáo ❶ drawbridge ❷ suspension bridge
吊丧 diàosāng call on the bereaved to offer one's condolences; pay a condolence call：～问疾 offer condolences to the bereaved and comfort to the ill; show concern for all who suffer
吊嗓子 diào sǎngzi (of singers, etc.) train one's voice; exercise one's voice
吊扇 diàoshàn ceiling fan
吊梢眉 diàoshāoméi *see*“吊眉”
吊死鬼 diàosǐguǐ 〈迷信〉ghost of a person who hanged himself or herself
吊索 diàosuǒ sling：钢丝～ steel wire sling /绳～ rope sling
吊塔 diàotǎ tower crane
吊梯 diàotī rope ladder
吊艇柱 diàotǐngzhù 〈航海〉davit
吊桶 diàotǒng well-bucket; bucket：～落在井里 like a bucket fallen on the bottom of a well, one is unable to extricate oneself; be on a tight spot /十五个～打水，七上八下 like fifteen buckets going up and down a well, one's mind is in a turmoil; one's heart pounds incessantly; be extremely nervous
吊袜带 diàowàdài *see*“吊带”
吊歪 diàowāi *see*“掉歪”diàowāi
吊胃口 diào wèikǒu whet sb.'s appetite; hold in suspense; tantalize：别～了，到底是什么事？Out with it, and stop holding us in suspense. /小孩子拿着一块肉，吊笼里的虎崽的胃口。The child tantalized the tiger cub in the cage by dangling a piece of meat beyond its reach.
吊慰 diàowèi *see*“吊问”
吊问 diàowèn *also*“吊慰” visit the bereaved to offer one's condolences：表示深切的～ express (*or* extend) one's sincere condolences
吊线 diàoxiàn plumb line
吊线板 diàoxiànbǎn 〈电学〉ceiling plate
吊线缆 diàoxiànlǎn 〈电学〉messenger cable
吊销 diàoxiāo revoke; withdraw：～营业执照 revoke a business licence /～汽车执照 suspend a motor licence /～护照 withdraw a passport
吊孝 diàoxiào *see*“吊丧”
吊唁 diàoyàn pay homage to the deceased and offer condolences to the bereaved; condole：～函电 messages of condolence /总理亲自前往～。The premier went to offer his condolences in person.
吊腰子 diào yāozi *also*“掉腰子” diào yāozi 〈方言〉cause mischief; play tricks：从那以后，他改邪归正，再没吊过腰子。Since then, he has mended his ways and never made trouble again.
吊影 diàoyǐng 〈书面〉the body has only its shadow for company — be all alone; be lonely
吊运 diàoyùn hoist up and carry (to a place)：～物品 hoist things up and carry them to another place
吊钟花 diàozhōnghuā *also*“倒挂金钟”dàoguà jīnzhōng 〈植物〉fuchsia
吊装 diàozhuāng 〈建筑〉hoisting
吊子 diàozi *also*“铫子”diàozi metal or clay pot or kettle for boiling water or herbal medicine; pot; kettle：铜～ brass kettle; 药～ pot for boiling herbal medicine

铞 diào *see*“钌铞儿”liàodiàor

铫 diào
see also yáo
铫子 diàozi *also*“吊子”diàozi metal or clay pot or kettle for boiling water or herbal medicine; pot; kettle

钓 diào ❶ fish with a hook and line; angle：～鱼 angle; go fishing ❷ fish or angle for; hunt for; seek：沽名～誉 fish (*or* angle) for fame and compliments; hanker after fame ❸ fishhook：操竿下～ hold the pole and throw the fishhook in
钓场 diàochǎng fishing ground (kept for anglers)
钓饵 diào'ěr bait：～虽好，可连一条鱼也没钓上。Though I had the best possible bait, no fish ever took it. /他以金钱美女为～。He used money and pretty women as bait.
钓竿 diàogān fishing rod or pole
钓钩 diàogōu fishhook
钓技 diàojì fishing skills; angling：～颇高 be an expert angler
钓具 diàojù fishing tackle
钓手 diàoshǒu angler
钓丝 diàosī fish line
钓友 diàoyǒu fellow angler
钓鱼岛 Diàoyúdǎo Diaoyu Islands, Chinese islands about 180 km northeast of Taiwan Province (referred to as Senkaku Islands 尖阁群岛 by Japan)：～等岛屿 Diaoyu and adjacent islands
钓鱼郎 diàoyúláng *also*“翠鸟”cuìniǎo 〈动物〉kingfisher
钓鱼台 diàoyútái place where emperors and high officials used to go fishing; fishing terrace：～国宾馆 Diaoyutai State Guesthouse
钓针 diàozhēn hook

窎 diào remote; distant
窎远 diàoyuǎn (of distance) far; remote

diē

跕 diē 〈书面〉fall; tumble; land; descend

跌 diē ❶ fall; tumble：～入水池 tumble into a pond /头朝下地～下楼梯 fall headlong down a flight of stairs /吓得他们～～跄跄，连连倒退 send them all scurrying and stumbling backward in terror ❷ drop; fall：物价骤～。Prices drop steeply (*or* have plummeted).
跌膘 diēbiāo (of livestock) lose flesh; lose weight
跌打损伤 diē-dǎ sǔnshāng injuries from falls, fractures, concussions and strains：这种药膏专治～。This plaster is a special cure for injuries from falls, fractures, concussions and strains.
跌宕 diēdàng *also*“跌荡”〈书面〉❶ free and easy; bold and unconstrained：～不羁 free and unrestrained /他简傲～，即使在达官贵人

面前，也不拘常礼。Proud and unconventional, he didn't even show normal courtesies to the dignitaries and high officials. ❷ undulating; varied：节奏～ undulating rhythm /～起伏的乐曲 well-modulated tune /这篇文章～有致，出自名家手笔。The essay is rich and varied in style; it must be the work of a master.

跌倒 diēdǎo fall or tumble down：他直挺挺地～在地上。He fell full length on the ground.

跌跌撞撞 diēdie-zhuàngzhuàng stagger along; dodder along; totter：他酒喝多了，～地走了过来。He came staggering along as he had a drop too much.

跌份 diēfèn 〈方言〉do discredit; lose face; humiliate：虚心请教并不～。It is not humiliating to be modest and ask for advice. *or* You don't lose face by asking for advice with an open mind. /他这种行为可真给北京人～。His deplorable behaviour dishonoured all Beijingers. *or* He did discredit to all Beijingers by acting like that.

跌风 diēfēng downward trend (of prices)

跌幅 diēfú volume or amount of decrease or fall：这种股票的～不小。This stock fell by a large margin.

跌跟头 diē gēntou ❶ tumble; trip and fall ❷ suffer a setback; come a cropper：他在情场上跌了跟头。He was unlucky in love.

跌价 diējià go down in price; devalue; decline in value：日用品～了。The prices of articles of daily use have dropped. /世界市场上黄金～了。Gold is devalued in the world market.

跌跤 diējiāo *also* "跌跤子" ❶ trip and fall; stumble and fall; fall：路滑，当心～。The road is slippery. Be careful not to stumble. ❷ make a mistake; meet with a setback：他这一跤跌得很重。He has made a grievous mistake (*or* suffered a serious setback).

跌落 diēluò ❶ fall; drop：风起处，树叶纷纷～。Leaves came whirling down when the wind rose. ❷ (of prices, output, etc.) go down; decrease; fall：粮价～。Grain prices have come down.

跌爬滚打 diē-pá-gǔn-dǎ 〈比喻〉go through all kinds of hardships; be full of sufferings

跌水 diēshuǐ ❶ abruptly dropping stream; waterfall; cascade ❷ 〈水利〉drop：河流至此～十公尺。The river has a drop of ten metres here.

跌水式溢洪道 diēshuǐshì yìhóngdào drop spillway

跌销 diēxiāo sales fall off; sales are down：这种牌子的计算机上个月～二百万元。This brand of computer went down in sales by two million *yuan* last month.

跌眼镜 diē yǎnjìng 〈方言〉go contrary to expectations; come as a surprise：球场上风云突变，令球迷们大～。The sudden changes of fortune in the field came as a total surprise to the fans.

跌足 diēzú 〈书面〉stamp one's foot (in bitter remorse, sorrow or despair)

爹

diē 〈口语〉father; dad; pa：～娘 parents; father and mother; mum and dad; ma and pa

爹爹 diēdie 〈方言〉❶ father; dad; pa ❷ grandfather; grandpa

dié

谍

dié ❶ espionage ❷ intelligence agent; spy：防～工作 anti-spy work; anti-espionage work

谍报 diébào information obtained through espionage; intelligence：干～工作 be in the intelligence service /收到一份重要～ receive an important intelligence report

谍报部门 diébào bùmén secret service

谍报网 diébàowǎng spy ring; intelligence network

谍报员 diébàoyuán intelligence agent; spy

谍报组 diébàozǔ espionage team

惵

dié 〈书面〉fear; terror：～息 hold one's breath in fear; be struck dumb with terror

堞

dié battlements：城～ battlements

堞墙 diéqiáng battlements

碟

dié (small) dish; saucer：一副杯～ a cup and saucer /一～油炸花生米 a dish of fried peanuts /飞～ flying saucer

碟形环形山 diéxíng huánxíngshān 〈天文〉saucer crater

碟形天线 diéxíng tiānxiàn disc antenna

碟子 diézi small dish; saucer

揲

dié 〈书面〉fold up

喋

dié

see also zhá

喋喋不休 diédié-bùxiū chatter away; rattle on; talk endlessly：我希望你不要～地谈你不了解的事。I wish you'd stop prating about things you do not quite understand.

喋血 diéxuè *also* "啑血" diéxuè; "蹀血" diéxuè 〈书面〉extensive bloodshed; bloodbath：边城～ bloodbath in a border town

蝶(蜨)

dié butterfly

蝶耳狗 dié'ěrgǒu 〈动物〉papillon

蝶骨 diégǔ 〈生理〉sphenoid bone

蝶兰 diélán 〈植物〉butterfly orchid (*Platanthera* or *Habenaria*)

蝶形花 diéxínghuā papilionaceous flower

蝶泳 diéyǒng butterfly stroke

蹀

dié 〈书面〉tread; step; stamp one's foot

蹀躞 diéxiè 〈书面〉❶ walk in small steps：～而前 walk with mincing steps ❷ pace up and down：～林中 walk to and fro in the wood

蹀血 diéxuè *see* "喋血" diéxuè

牒

dié ❶ official document; certificate：公～ official (*or* business) document /度～ letter of credence for a travelling Buddhist priest /最后通～ ultimatum ❷ record; book：谱～ book of family lineage /史～ history (book)

艓

dié 〈书面〉small boat; skiff

鲽

dié 〈动物〉right-eyed flounder; flatfish

啑

dié *see* "喋" dié

see also shà

啑血 diéxuè *see* "喋血" diéxuè

垤

dié 〈书面〉mound：丘～ small hill /蚁～ ant hill

耋

dié 〈书面〉age of seventy or eighty; old age：耄～之年 in one's seventies or eighties; advanced in age

螲

dié

see also zhì

螲蟷 diédāng *also* "戴氏拉土蛛" dàishìlātǔzhū 〈动物〉ctenizid (*Latouchia davidi*)

绖

dié linen belt on ancient mourning apparel

嵽(嵽)

dié

嵽嵲 diéniè 〈书面〉(of mountains) towering; lofty; high

迭

dié ❶ alternate; replace; change：人事更～ personnel change /他二人～为组长。They acted as group leader alternately. ❷ repeatedly; time and again：～挫来犯之敌 inflict repeated reverses on the invaders /最近盗窃案件～有发现。Quite a few burglaries and thefts have been reported lately. ❸ in time：她忙不～给我倒了杯热茶。She hurriedly poured me a hot cup of tea.

迭出 diéchū crop up one after another; happen again and again：花样～ present one pattern after another; produce a whole series of tricks /差错～ make repeated mistakes or errors /名家～。Famous masters emerged one after another.

迭次 diécì repeatedly; time and again：～磋商后达成协议 reach agreement after repeated consultations /～造访 call on sb. on many occasions

迭句 diéjù 〈语言〉refrain, a recurring phrase or number of lines, esp. at the end of each stanza

迭连 diélián on end; in a row; in succession：这几天他～受到批评。He was criticized several times these days.

迭忙 diémáng promptly; at once: 他听到敲门声，就～去开门。He went to open the door the moment he heard someone knocking.

迭起 diéqǐ occur repeatedly; happen frequently: 两国边界争端～。Frontier disputes between the two countries occurred frequently. /掌声～。There was one round of applause after another. /高潮～。One climax followed another.

昳 dié 〈书面〉(of the sun) incline to the west: 日～。The sun has inclined to the west.
see also yì

瓞 dié 〈书面〉small melon: 绵绵瓜～。May your family grow and prosper like spreading melon-vines.

氎 dié 〈书面〉cotton cloth

叠(疊、曡) dié ❶ pile up; repeat: 把书～放在桌上 pile up books on a desk /层见～出 (of events) appear repeatedly /这本书中的错误～见。Errors crop up everywhere in this book. /贺函～至。Letters of congratulation kept pouring in. *or* Congratulatory messages came in thick and fast. ❷ fold: 折～椅 folding chairs /把信～好，装在信封内。Fold up the letter and put it in an envelope.

叠层石 diécéngshí 〈地质〉stromatolite

叠床架屋 diéchuáng-jiàwū pile one bed upon another or build one house on top of another — senseless piling up (of phrases, etc.); needless duplication (of institutions, etc.): 建立新机构一定要防止～。It is essential to avoid needless duplication in establishing new institutions. /这样～，文章就太啰嗦了。Repetition and superfluity make the essay practically unreadable.

叠翠 diécuì layers of green: 层林～ row upon row of green woods; serried green woods

叠氮酸 diédànsuān hydrazoic acid

叠焊 diéhàn 〈电工〉stitch welding

叠句 diéjù 〈语言〉reiterative sentence

叠罗汉 diéluóhàn 〈体育〉pyramid

叠涩 diésè 〈建筑〉corbelling

叠印 diéyìn 〈印刷〉overprint; super imposition

叠影 diéyǐng *also* "重像" chóngxiàng 〈影视〉ghosting

叠韵 diéyùn 〈语言〉two or more characters with the same vowel formation (e.g. 阑干 lángān); vowel rhyme

叠嶂 diézhàng range after range of mountains: ～重峦 peak after peak rising ever higher and stretching far into the distance; mountains upon mountains

叠锥构造 diézhuī gòuzào 〈地质〉cone-in-cone structure

叠字 diézì 〈语言〉reiterative locution (e.g. 天天 or 跌跌撞撞); reduplication

dīng

丁[1] dīng ❶ male adult; man: 抓～ press-gang able-bodied men into service /成～ reach manhood /家有三～。There are three male adults in the family. ❷ members of a family; population: 添～ have another baby born into the family /人～兴旺 have a growing family; have a flourishing population ❸ person engaged in certain types of labour: 园～ gardener /家～ domestic servant /庖～ cook; chef ❹ (Dīng) a surname

丁[2] dīng ❶ fourth of the ten Heavenly Stems: *see also* "干支" gānzhī ❷ fourth: ～级 fourth grade; grade D /～种维生素 Vitamin D

丁[3] dīng small cube (of meat or vegetable): 肉～ meat cubes /萝卜～ diced turnip

丁[4] dīng 〈书面〉meet; encounter: ～母忧 be in mourning for one's mother
see also zhēng

丁胺 dīng'àn butyl amine

丁坝 dīngbà 〈水利〉groyne spur dike; groyne

丁苯 dīngběn 〈化学〉butylbenzene

丁苯橡胶 dīngběn xiàngjiāo butadiene styrene rubber

丁部 dīngbù *also* "集部" jíbù one of the four traditional categories for classification of written works, consisting mainly of poetry and works related to poetry
see also "四部" sìbù

丁册 dīngcè 〈旧语〉household registration book

丁醇 dīngchún 〈化学〉butyl alcohol

丁村人 Dīngcūnrén Dingcun Man, primitive man of about 100,000 years ago whose fossil remains were found at Dingcun, Shanxi Province, in 1954

丁当 dīngdāng *also* "叮当" dīngdāng; "玎珰" dīngdāng 〈象声〉(of metal, jade or china) ding-dong; jingle; clatter: 驼铃～ jingling of camel bells /穷得～响 as poor as a church mouse; penniless

丁点儿 dīngdiǎnr 〈方言〉〈量词〉tiny bit; wee bit; jot: 布袋里只有一～面粉了。There is only a handful of flour left in the bag. /～问题也没有了。There is no problem at all. /你的答案～不错。You have got all the answers correct.

丁丁 dīngdīng 〈书面〉〈象声〉tinkle; drip: ～～，水从漏壶中徐徐滴下。Tink, tink, the water keeps dripping from the clepsydra.
see also zhēngzhēng

丁东 dīngdōng *also* "丁冬" 〈象声〉(of metal, jade or stone) tinkle: 玉佩～ one's jade pendants tinkle (as one moves)

丁冬 dīngdōng *see* "丁东"

丁对 dīngdui 〈方言〉proper; appropriate; just right: 你来了，他也来了，真～。It is really great that both of you have come.

丁二酸 dīng'èrsuān 〈化学〉succinic acid

丁方 dīngfāng 〈方言〉square: 房间很小，～不到五平米。The room is very small, no more than 5 square metres.

丁赋 dīngfù *also* "人头税" réntóushuì 〈书面〉poll tax; capitation tax

丁基 dīngjī 〈化学〉butyl group: ～氯 butyl chloride /～醚 butyl ether /～橡胶〈化工〉butyl rubber

丁艰 dīngjiān 〈书面〉*see* "丁忧"

丁腈 dīngjīng 〈化学〉butyronitrile; butanenitrile; propyl cyanice: ～橡胶〈化工〉nitrile rubber (*or* nitrile-butadiene rubber); acrylonitrile rubber (*or* acrylonitrile-butadiene rubber)

丁克夫妇 dīngkè fūfù DINK (Double Income, No Kid); childless couple

丁口册 dīngkǒucè *see* "丁册"

丁零 dīnglíng 〈象声〉(of bell or small metal ware) tinkle; jingle: 闹钟的～声将他从睡梦中惊醒。The tinkling of the alarm clock awoke him.

丁零当啷 dīngling-dānglāng 〈象声〉jinglejangle; ding-dong: 钟～地乱响。The bell jinglejangled wildly.

丁醚 dīngmí 〈化学〉butyl ether

丁男 dīngnán 〈书面〉able-bodied man (subject to conscription); male adult

丁尼生 Dīngníshēng Alfred Tennyson (1809-1892), English poet

丁宁 dīngníng *also* "叮咛" dīngníng urge again and again; warn; exhort: 她再三～学生要防止骄傲自满。She exhorted her students over and over again to guard against pride and conceit. /他时刻牢记老师的～。He always keeps his teacher's admonitions at heart.

丁宁周至 dīngníng-zhōuzhì give thoughtful advice; give repeated admonitions

丁钱 dīngqián 〈书面〉poll tax

丁醛 dīngquán 〈化学〉butyraldehyde; butaldehyde

丁是丁，卯是卯 dīng shì dīng, mǎo shì mǎo *also* "钉是钉，铆是铆" dīng shì dīng, mǎo shì mǎo keep *ding* (a Heavenly Stem) distinct from *mao* (an Earthly Branch) — be meticulous; be precise; be unaccommodating: 他办起事来～，从不含糊。He is very exacting in his work.

丁税 dīngshuì 〈书面〉poll tax

丁酸 dīngsuān 〈化学〉butyric acid; butanoic acid: ～发酵 butyric fermentation /～甲酯 methyl butyrate /～盐 butyrate

丁酮 dīngtóng 〈化学〉butanone: ～二酸 butanone diacid

丁烷 dīngwán 〈化学〉butane

丁烷气 dīngwánqì butagas

丁屋地段 dīngwū dìduàn (HK) small house plot

丁烯 dīngxī 〈化学〉butene

丁香 dīngxiāng 〈植物〉❶ lilac: ～紫 lilacky, lilac ❷ clove: ～种植

园 clove plantation
丁香结 dīngxiāngjié clove hitch
丁香油 dīngxiāngyóu clove oil
丁徭 dīngyáo corvée imposed on families that have male adults
丁一卯二 dīngyī-mǎo'èr ❶ *also* "丁一确二" true; definite: 我的话～。What I said is absolutely true. ❷ reliable; dependable: 他办事～。One could always rely on him to handle things well.
丁役 dīngyì *see* "丁徭"
丁忧 dīngyōu 〈书面〉 be afflicted with the misfortune that one's parents have passed away; meet with the misfortune of parental bereavement
丁肇中 Dīng Zhàozhōng Samuel Chao Chung Ting (1936-), Chinese-American physicist
丁壮 dīngzhuàng 〈书面〉 ❶ strong; robust; powerful ❷ male adult; able-bodied man
丁字 dīngzì T-shaped: ～形 T-shaped /～把手 T-handle
丁字布 dīngzìbù T-shaped signal at an airport, made of two pieces of white cloth
丁字尺 dīngzìchǐ T-square
丁字钢 dīngzìgāng T-steel
丁字街 dīngzìjiē T-shaped road junction

疔

dīng 〈中医〉 malignant boil or furuncle
疔疮 dīngchuāng malignant boil or furuncle
疔毒 dīngdú 〈中医〉 serious furunculosis
疔疽 dīngjū miliary vesicle under the nose or on either side of the mandible

玎

dīng
玎珰 dīngdāng *see* "丁当" dīngdāng
玎玲 dīnglíng 〈象声〉 (often of jade or stone) clink; jingle; tinkle

耵

dīng
耵聍 dīngníng cerumen; earwax

靪

dīng repair or mend sole of a shoe: ～后掌 repair the heel of a shoe

酊

dīng tincture: 碘～ tincture of iodine
see also dǐng
酊剂 dīngjì 〈药学〉 tincture

叮

dīng ❶ sting; bite: 这是蚂蚁～的包。This is an ant bite. ❷ urge again and again; exhort; admonish: *see* "～嘱" ❸ say or ask again to make sure: 再～他一句，免得忘了。Remind him again just in case.
叮当 dīngdāng *see* "丁当" dīngdāng
叮咛 dīngníng *see* "丁宁" dīngníng
叮问 dīngwèn 〈方言〉 question or inquire closely: 我不断～，他只是支吾。He only hummed and hawed despite my repeated queries.
叮咬 dīngyǎo sting or bite: 蚊虫的～ mosquito bites
叮嘱 dīngzhǔ urge again and again; admonish; exhort: 父亲～我要好好学习。Father exhorted me to work hard at school.

盯

dīng *also* "钉" dīng fix one's eyes on; gaze at; stare at: 他两眼～着地板，陷入了沉思。He fixed his eyes on the floor, lost in reverie. /～着人看很不礼貌。It is bad manners to stare at people. /～住这个坏蛋。Keep a close watch on the scoundrel.
盯梢 dīngshāo *also* "钉梢" dīngshāo shadow; tail: 他被警察～。He was tailed by the police.
盯视 dīngshì look fixedly at; gaze at; fix one's eyes on: 母亲愉快地～着女儿的笑脸。The mother gazed with delight at the smiling face of her daughter.

钉[1]

dīng nail; tack: 钢～ steel nail /平头～ hobnail /图～ drawing pin; thumb tack /木～ peg /把～子钉进木板 drive nails into a wooden board

钉[2]

dīng ❶ follow closely; shadow; tail: 便衣～着一个形迹可疑的人。The plainclothesman is tailing a suspicious character. /一名后卫队员紧～着对方的中锋。A full back followed closely the centre forward of the other team. ❷ urge; press; keep asking or reminding: 你要～着点，让他们把危房快点修好。You should keep pressing them to get the crumbling house repaired as soon as possible. ❸ *see* "盯" dīng
see also dìng
钉齿耙 dīngchǐbà spike-tooth harrow
钉锤 dīngchuí nail hammer; claw hammer
钉螺 dīngluó 〈动物〉 oncomelania; snail: ～是血吸虫寄生的媒介。The freshwater snail is the intermediate host of the blood fluke.
钉帽 dīngmào head of a nail
钉耙 dīngpá (spike-toothed) rake
钉胼 dīngpián *also* "鸡眼" jīyǎn 〈医学〉 clavus; corn
钉人 dīngrén 〈体育〉 watch or mark an opponent in a game
钉人防守 dīngrén fángshǒu man-for-man defence; man-to-man defence
钉梢 dīngshāo *see* "盯梢" dīngshāo
钉是钉，铆是铆 dīng shì dīng, mǎo shì mǎo *see* "丁是丁，卯是卯" dīng shì dīng, mǎo shì mǎo
钉问 dīngwèn 〈方言〉 inquire in great detail about; question closely
钉鞋 dīngxié ❶ old fashioned rainproof shoes made of oiled cloth uppers and hobnailed soles ❷ spiked shoes; spikes
钉住汇率 dīngzhù huìlǜ 〈金融〉 pegged exchange rate
钉住价格 dīngzhù jiàgé price pegging
钉子 dīngzi ❶ nail; tack; pin ❷ snag: 拔～ remove a snag (*or* obstacle) /碰～ hit (*or* strike) a snag; meet with a rebuff (*or* stout opposition) ❸ stinger: 他话里有～。His remarks carried a stinger. ❹ planted agent, stool, or saboteur: 他是敌人在我们内部安插的～。He is an agent planted in our ranks by the enemy.
钉子户 dīngzihù person or household who refuses to move and bargains for unreasonably high compensation when the land is requisitioned for a construction project
钉子精神 dīngzi jīngshén spirit of the nail — make the best use of one's time and work persistently to achieve one's purpose

仃

dīng *see* "伶仃" língdīng

dǐng

酊

dǐng *see* "酩酊" mǐngdǐng
see also dīng

顶

dǐng ❶ top; peak; crown (of the head): 平～ flat-topped /山～ mountain peak; hilltop /屋～ roof /到～ reach the peak (*or* limit) /秃～ be bald ❷ hold or carry on the head: 头～着水罐 carry a pitcher of water on one's head ❸ push from below or behind; push up: 用千斤顶把汽车～起 jack up a car /嫩芽把土～了起来。The sprouts have pushed through the earth. ❹ gore; butt: 这牛常～人。The bull often gores people. ❺ prop up: 把门闩好，～上。Bolt the door and prop it up. ❻ go against: 他们～着暴风雨前进。They marched ahead in the teeth of the storm. ❼ answer back; retort; rebuff: 我～了他几句。I said a few words in retort. /他的抗议给我～了回去。I rejected his protest. ❽ undertake; cope with; stand up to: 工作虽重，他们俩还是～下来了。Arduous as the work was, they two managed to get it done (*or* cope with it). ❾ equal; be equivalent to: 他一个人能～两个人用。He can do the job of two persons by himself. ❿ take the place of; substitute; replace: 以次～好 substitute shoddy stuff for quality goods /我得找人～他的缺儿。I must get somebody to replace him. /一个士兵在缺口处倒下去，另一个马上～了上来。When one soldier fell in the breach, another pushed ahead from behind. ⓫ transfer business licence, or lease of real estate; sublease: ～进一套公寓 sublease an apartment ⓬ 〈方言〉 at a specified time: ～下午两点你再来吧。You can come at, say, two o'clock in the afternoon. ⓭ 〈量词〉 *used of sth. that has a top*: 一～帽子 a cap; a hat /一～帐子 a mosquito net ⓮ most; very; extremely: ～有用 most useful /～大 biggest; largest; oldest /～漂亮 very beautiful /他～喜欢运动。He is very keen on sports.
顶班 dǐngbān ❶ work as a temporary substitute; take over sb.'s shift: 有人去外地度假了，由我这个科长～。As section chief I had to

work as a substitute when someone was away on holiday. ❷ work on regular shifts; work full time:厂长上午在车间～劳动。The factory director worked on the morning shift today.

顶板 dǐngbǎn ❶〈矿业〉roof (of a shaft, etc.):直线～ immediate roof /～陷落 roof caving ❷ ceiling ❸〈方言〉clash; be at loggerheads:他和妻子常为一些鸡毛蒜皮的事～。He often quarrelled with his wife over trivial matters.

顶承 dǐngchéng ❶ bear responsibility; be held responsible; answer for:出了什么乱子,由他去～。He will be held responsible in case anything goes wrong. ❷ inherit (a legacy, etc.):那笔遗产全部由他～了去。He inherited the entire legacy.

顶吹 dǐngchuī 〈冶金〉top blown:～转炉 top-blown converter

顶戴 dǐngdài ❶〈书面〉salute; give a salute ❷ official hat accessories showing various ranks in the Qing Dynasty

顶挡 dǐngdǎng ❶ ward off; withstand; stand up to:这里虽然只有一个排的兵力,也能～一阵子。Although there is only one platoon here, it can withstand the onslaught for quite a while. ❷ bear responsibility; be held responsible; answer for:天大事由我来～。Come what may, I'll answer for the consequences.

顶灯 dǐngdēng 〈汽车〉overhead light; toplight; dome light

顶颠 dǐngdiān peak; summit; pinnacle:他好不容易才爬到了～。With much effort, he reached the peak.

顶点 dǐngdiǎn ❶〈数学〉vertex; apex ❷ apex; zenith; acme; pinnacle:他在文学方面的声望已达到～。He has reached the pinnacle of literary fame.

顶丁 dǐngdīng 〈旧语〉pay for the corvée due; buy oneself out (as a conscript)

顶端 dǐngduān ❶ top; peak; apex:他们上了塔的～。They climbed to the top of the tower. ❷ end:桥的～ end of a bridge

顶端淬火法 dǐngduān cuìhuǒfǎ end hardening

顶端饰 dǐngduānshì 〈建筑〉finial

顶端压条法 dǐngduān yātiáofǎ tiplayering

顶多 dǐngduō at (the) most; at best:他～是个二流政客。He is at best a second-class politician. /她～也不过十八岁。She is at most eighteen.

顶风 dǐngfēng ❶ against the wind:～骑车 cycle against the wind /～逆水 go against the wind and current; go upstream against the wind /～冒雪 brave wind and snow /～作案〈比喻〉commit a crime in defiance of a law-enforcement campaign ❷ head wind:回家正好是～。We faced a head wind on the way home.

顶封 dǐngfēng top seal

顶峰 dǐngfēng peak; summit; pinnacle:泰山～ top of Mount Tai / 前十年是他事业的～时期。He was at the zenith of his career in the past ten years.

顶腐病 dǐngfǔbìng 〈农业〉top rot

顶缸 dǐnggāng 〈口语〉bear responsibility for others; be a scapegoat:拿人～ use sb. as a scapegoat /我的事,我负责,不要你～。I'm responsible for what I do, and don't want you to take the blame for it.

顶岗 dǐnggǎng 〈方言〉*see*"顶班"

顶杠 dǐnggàng ❶ argue for argument's sake; be quarrelsome:他脾气坏,爱跟人～。He is bad-tempered and quarrelsome. ❷ be a scapegoat:儿子犯法,总不能拿老子～吧。You cannot punish the father for a crime committed by the son, can you?

顶格 dǐnggé (of typing, typesetting, etc.) flush:请～打,不用缩进。Please type it flush, without any indentation.

顶骨 dǐnggǔ 〈生理〉parietal bone

顶刮刮 dǐngguāguā *also*"顶呱呱" tip-top; first-rate; excellent:他的业务是～的。His professional skill is first-rate.

顶冠 dǐngguān 〈生理〉apical cap

顶光 dǐngguāng 〈摄影〉top light

顶好 dǐnghǎo ❶ best; very good; excellent ❷ had better; it would be best:你～快点儿回来。You'd better come back soon.

顶花坛 dǐng huātán 〈杂技〉balancing a jar (on the head)

顶换 dǐnghuàn substitute; replace:这位厂长不称职,必须找人～他。The factory director is not competent for his job and must be replaced.

顶火 dǐnghuǒ *see*"顶门火"

顶家 dǐngjiā 〈方言〉run the household; keep house:～过日子 take charge of household affairs

顶价 dǐngjià ❶ top price; ceiling price:这个商店竟把次西红柿以～出售。That grocery went so far as to sell low-grade tomatoes at top price. ❷〈方言〉rent deposit

顶尖 dǐngjiān ❶ top; tip:宝塔的～ tip of a tower /桅杆的～ masthead /打掉棉花的～ top cotton plants /大厦的～高耸入云。The top of the skyscraper towers into the clouds. ❷ best; first-rate:～大学 first-rate university /球队里的～队员 best player on the team /～的象棋高手 topmost master of chess ❸〈机械〉centre:死～ dead centre /～距 distance between centres

顶交 dǐngjiāo 〈农业〉topcross

顶角 dǐngjiǎo 〈数学〉vertex angle

顶枯病 dǐngkūbìng 〈农业〉withertip

顶礼 dǐnglǐ 〈宗教〉lay oneself down in the dust and press one's head against sb.'s feet (Buddhist salute of the highest respect)

顶礼膜拜 dǐnglǐ-móbài 〈贬义〉prostrate oneself in worship; make a fetish of; pay homage to

顶梁柱 dǐngliángzhù pillar; backbone:社会的～ pillar of society; salt of the earth /他是家里的～。He is the pillar of the family.

顶凌 dǐnglíng (till the land) when the topsoil begins to thaw on the surface:～耙地 harrow the fields when the topsoil begins to thaw

顶楼 dǐnglóu 〈建筑〉attic

顶马 dǐngmǎ ❶〈旧语〉men riding as outriders or heralds in front of the carriage of a high official ❷ horses of such an advance party

顶门杠 dǐngméngàng thick stick propped against the door from behind when closed

顶门火 dǐngménhuǒ *also*"顶火" bullet inside a loaded gun:掏出上好～的左轮手枪 take out a loaded revolver

顶门立户 dǐngmén-lìhù be the mainstay of the family; keep the family going; bolster up the respectability of the family

顶门儿 dǐngménr front top of the head:他～上的头发已经脱光了。He has a large bald patch on the front top of his head.

顶门子 dǐngménzi 〈方言〉*see*"顶门火"

顶名 dǐngmíng ❶ go under sb. else's name:～假冒 go under a fake identity ❷ exist in name only:～是个公司,其实没有任何资产。Despite the facade of a commercial firm, they actually had no assets.

顶命 dǐngmìng pay with one's life (for a murder, etc.); give a life for a life:杀人要～。A life for a life. *or* Life must be paid in kind.

顶牛 dǐngniú be at loggerheads with sb.:他们俩说不上两句话就又～了。They had only exchanged a few words before they got locked in a wrangle again.

顶盘 dǐngpán buy a bankrupt or poorly-managed shop or factory and keep it going; take over a business

顶棚 dǐngpéng ceiling

顶碰 dǐngpèng ❶ lash; dash against; pound:洪峰～。Flood crests dash against each other. ❷ clash; quarrel; contradict:老张在会上和他～,弄得他很不痛快。Lao Zhang clashed with him at the meeting, making him feel very bad.

顶球 dǐngqiú 〈体育〉head (a ball)

顶少 dǐngshǎo ❶ least:与其他车相比,这种车耗油～。Compared with other models, this type consumes least gasoline. ❷〈方言〉at least:～也有五百来人参加竞赛。At least over five hundred people took part in the competition.

顶生 dǐngshēng 〈植物〉acrogenous; terminal:～花 terminal flower /～芽 terminal bud /～叶 acrophyll

顶生植物 dǐngshēng zhíwù acrogen

顶视图 dǐngshìtú *also*"俯视图" fǔshìtú vertical view

顶事 dǐngshì be useful; serve the purpose:这辆自行车很～。This bicycle is quite serviceable. /这药～不? Is the medicine effective? / 他在我们这里可～啦! He is a great asset to us here.

顶饰 dǐngshì 〈建筑〉cresting

顶首 dǐngshǒu ❶〈方言〉rent deposit ❷〈旧语〉buy sb.'s practice or property

顶数 dǐngshù ❶ swell the total; make up the number; be a nonentity:拿次品～ make up the number (*or* total) with substandard products /他只是～的,什么事也干不了。He does no more than making up the number. ❷ (usu. used in the negative) have effect or influence; count:他说的顶不得数。What he says doesn't count.

顶水 dǐngshuǐ ❶ carry water (in a pitcher) on one's head ❷ against the current:～上溯 sail against the current

顶死病 dǐngsǐbìng 〈植物〉dieback

顶趟儿 dǐngtàngr be equal to others; can keep up with others:他五十来岁了,干活不～了。As a man of over 50, he can no longer keep

up with young people in physical labour.

顶替 dǐngtì ❶ take sb.'s place; replace; substitute:冒名～ assume sb.'s name and act under false pretences /我想不出有谁能～他。I can think of nobody to replace him. ❷ (usu. of manual work) get a job at one's parent's place when the latter retires

顶替工 dǐngtìgōng replacer; substitute; one who takes a job in place of one's retired parent

顶天 dǐngtiān tower into the sky; be extremely high; reach the outside limit:～岭 towering mountain ranges /这块地打二百公斤粮食就～了。You can get 200 kilos of grain from this plot at the very most.

顶天立地 dǐngtiān-lìdì of titanic, noble stature; of the highest order; of dauntless spirit:～的英雄 hero of gigantic stature /～的汉子 dauntless man; real man; he-man /～的事业 earth-shaking undertaking

顶头 dǐngtóu ❶ coming directly towards one:～风 head wind /他俩在胡同里正好走了个～。They bumped into each other in the alley. ❷ top; end:房子～有个小书柜。There is a small bookcase at the end of the room.

顶头上司 dǐngtóu shàngsi one's immediate superior or boss; institution of immediately higher level

顶推力 dǐngtuīlì jacking force

顶托 dǐngtuō (of high tide, etc.) block the downcoming water of a river

顶拖 dǐngtuō refuse to do; deliberately delay:人民迫切需要办的事,不能～不办。We cannot refuse to do what is urgently needed by the public.

顶碗 dǐngwǎn 〈杂技〉 balancing a stack of bowls on the head; pagoda of bowls:表演～ balance a stack of bowls on the head; do a pagoda of bowls on the head

顶箱 dǐngxiāng box on top of a wardrobe; top-box

顶心 dǐngxīn *also* "顶尖" tip (of a cotton plant, etc.)

顶凶 dǐngxiōng 〈旧语〉 be hired to bear the punishment due to a homicide, etc.

顶芽 dǐngyá 〈植物〉 terminal bud

顶叶 dǐngyè 〈植物〉 terminal leaf

顶用 dǐngyòng be of use or help; be effective or serviceable:这玩艺儿不～。This is no use. /这机器真～,能干二十个人的活。The machine is very efficient; it can do the job of twenty workers.

顶载天线 dǐngzài tiānxiàn top-loaded antenna

顶账 dǐngzhàng pay a debt with sth. equal in value:替人家看小孩～ pay off a debt by serving as a baby-sitter

顶真 dǐngzhēn ❶ 〈方言〉 conscientious; earnest; meticulous; scrupulous:他办事～。He is conscientious in whatever he does. ❷ *also* "顶针" 〈修辞〉 a kind of rhetorical device calling for a sentence to begin with the final word or phrase of the previous sentence

顶针 dǐngzhen thimble

顶证 dǐngzhèng 〈方言〉 bear witness; give evidence:她答应替你～。She agreed to bear witness for you.

顶珠 dǐngzhū *also* "顶子" jewel or bead on a Qing official's hat that indicates his rank; top jewel or bead

顶住 dǐngzhù withstand; stand up to; hold out against:～外来的巨大压力 withstand tremendous outside pressure /～一切诱惑 resist all temptation

顶撞 dǐngzhuàng contradict (one's elder or superior); answer or talk back; retort:～父母 answer (or talk) back to one's parents /他和他的顶头上司～了几句。He had a few words with his immediate superior. /他俩因为一点小事儿互相～起来。They quarrelled over a trifling matter.

顶子 dǐngzi ❶ decorative top (of a pavilion, pagoda, etc.) ❷ *also* "顶珠" jewel or bead on a Qing official's hat ❸ roof (of a house):挑～ thorough repair of the roof

顶租 dǐngzū ❶ pay the rent in kind or by labour ❷ 〈方言〉 rent deposit

顶嘴 dǐngzuǐ 〈口语〉 reply defiantly; answer back; talk back:爸爸不喜欢儿女们跟他～。Father didn't like his children to talk back.

顶罪 dǐngzuì ❶ answer for the crime of another; bear blame for sb. else; be a scapegoat ❷ (of punishment, etc.) be equal to the crime; be appropriate:罚不～。The punishment falls short of the crime.

鼎[1] dǐng ❶ *ding* — ancient cooking vessel with two loop handles and three (sometimes four) legs:三足～ tripod /四足～ quadripod ❷ 〈书面〉 the throne; state power:问～ vie for the throne; compete for state power /定～ establish oneself as emperor ❸ 〈书面〉 great; grand: *see* "～鼎";"～力" ❹ 〈方言〉 pot; pan

鼎[2] dǐng 〈书面〉 just when; at the very time

鼎鼎 dǐngdǐng grand; magnificent:大名～ well-known; renowned; celebrated /新春～来。Spring comes in all its magnificence.

鼎沸 dǐngfèi 〈书面〉 like a boiling cauldron; clamorous; noisy and confused:人声～ hubbub or babel of voices; seething mass of people; bawling crowd /群情～。Public feeling runs high.

鼎革 dǐnggé 〈书面〉 do away with the old; change dynasty or regime:天地～,万物维新。As the new succeeds the old, all nature is rejuvenated.

鼎罐 dǐngguàn coarse pottery pot or jar

鼎锅 dǐngguō cylindrical iron cauldron

鼎甲 dǐngjiǎ ❶ (of feudal society) the most prestigious family in a patriarchal clan ❷ top three successful candidates in the palace examination

鼎力 dǐnglì 〈书面〉〈敬词〉 your kind effort; your great help:～相助 make unstinting effort to help sb. (esp. in an undertaking) /务请～玉成。Please render your help to accomplish this.

鼎立 dǐnglì stand like the three legs of a tripod; (of three parties) confront one another on an equal footing:呈～之势 be (*or* confront one another) in a tripartite balance

鼎盛 dǐngshèng in a time of great prosperity; at the height of power and glory:春秋～ in the prime of manhood /国力～ in the heyday of a nation

鼎式甲根固定 dǐngshì jiǎgēn gùdìng 〈中医〉 tripod-shaped splint fixation

鼎新 dǐngxīn 〈书面〉 reform:革故～ introduce reforms; restructure

鼎言 dǐngyán 〈书面〉 weighty words; valuable opinion or advice

鼎彝 dǐngyí 〈书面〉 ancient sacrificial utensil (often carved with words extolling people of merit):功铭～ have one's merits mentioned in carved inscriptions on a sacrificial utensil; have achieved eternal fame; go down in history

鼎峙 dǐngzhì 〈书面〉 tripartite confrontation

鼎助 dǐngzhù 〈书面〉〈敬词〉 your generous help:多承～,不胜感激。My gratitude for your generous help knows no bounds. *or* I'm deeply grateful to you for your kind help.

鼎足 dǐngzú three legs of a tripod — three rival powers:～之势 (situation of) tripartite confrontation; triple power balance; triangular balance of power

dìng

定 dìng ❶ calm; still; stable:立～ stand still /心神不～ be restless; be distracted; be on tenterhooks /人心思～。Everyone looks forward to a stable situation. ❷ fix; set: *see* "～影" ❸ decide; fix; make certain:以销～产 fix output on the basis of orders and sales; suit output to sales /～计划 make a plan /出发时间～在明天上午九点。The departure time is set for 9:00 tomorrow morning. /候选人还没～下来。It has not yet been decided which candidates will be nominated. /他今天是否来还说不～。It's still uncertain whether he will come today. ❹ determined; settled; established: *see* "～局" ❺ stipulated; provided; fixed: *see* "～量" ❻ subscribe to (a newspaper, magazine, etc.); book (seats, tickets, etc.); order (merchandise, etc.):～《人民日报》subscribe to the *People's Daily* /～去日本的机票 book a plane ticket to Japan /～一千辆拖拉机 order 1,000 tractors ❼ 〈书面〉 surely; certainly; definitely:～可取胜 be sure to win /～能胜任 be certainly competent for the job /～可办成 be sure of success ❽ (Dìng) a surname

定案 dìng'àn ❶ decide on or pass a verdict; reach a conclusion on a case; make the final decision:难以～ difficult to reach a verdict or conclusion /这类大事必须厂长亲自拍板～。It is up to the factory manager himself to make final decisions on such important matters. ❷ verdict; final decision:推翻～ overturn a verdict /此次事件已有～。A conclusion has been drawn about the incident.

定板 dìngbǎn have the final say; make the final decision:这事就等着第一、二把手～了。It's up to the first or second in command to

make the decision.
定本 dìngběn definitive edition
定比定律 dìngbǐ dìnglǜ 〈化学〉 law of definite or constant proportions
定臂起重机 dìngbì qǐzhòngjī fixed boom crane
定编 dìngbiān fix the number of staff; set personnel quota or complement
定标 dìngbiāo ❶ set goals ❷ decide on the awarding of a contract or bid
定产 dìngchǎn (system of) fixed quotas for (grain) production
定常流 dìngchángliú 〈物理〉 steady flow; steady motion of a fluid
定场白 dìngchǎngbái soliloquy introducing the character's background (in traditional Chinese opera)
定场诗 dìngchǎngshī verse (usu. four lines) recited by a character in traditional Chinese opera when he strikes a pose on stage at the beginning of a play
定单 dìngdān order (for goods); order form
定当 dìngdàng 〈方言〉 ready; settled; finished: 一切已安排～。Everything is in order. /我们已商量～。We have talked the matter over and reached agreement.

D

定点 dìngdiǎn chosen location; designated place; selected point: 组织～生产 organize production at designated factories (*or* places)
定点厂 dìngdiǎnchǎng factory designated (by the state, etc.) to make a particular product; designated factory
定点供应 dìngdiǎn gōngyìng rationed supply at designated locations
定调子 dìng diàozi set the tone or keynote
定鼎 dìngdǐng 〈书面〉 establish a capital; establish a dynasty
定定心心 dìngdìng-xīnxīn 〈方言〉 feel carefree; feel at ease: ～读书 get down to one's studies free from worry
定都 dìngdū choose a site for the capital; establish a capital: ～北京 make Beijing the capital; decide on Beijing as the capital
定夺 dìngduó make a final decision; decide: 这项工作如何进行由领导～。It is for the leaders to decide how to go about the work. /等会后再行～。We won't make a decision till after the meeting.
定额 dìng'é ❶ stipulate an amount or number; fix or set a quota: ～计酬 payment on the basis of fixed quotas ❷ quota; norm: 生产～ production quota /～奖 bonus payment based on the fulfilment of quotas
定额补贴 dìng'é bǔtiē set quota subsidy
定额分期付款 dìng'é fēnqī fùkuǎn fixed installment
定额工资制 dìng'é gōngzīzhì wage scale based on work quota; remuneration according to quota
定额管理 dìng'é guǎnlǐ quota management
定额流动资金 dìng'é liúdòng zījīn turnover of state-allocated working capital
定额投资基金 dìng'é tóuzī jījīn fixed-amount investment fund; closed end investment fund
定额温度 dìng'é wēndù rated temperature
定额制 dìng'ézhì quota system (for production)
定岗 dìnggǎng fix number of posts with well-defined tasks and responsibilities; define job requirements
定高气球 dìnggāo qìqiú 〈航空〉 constant-level balloon
定稿 dìnggǎo ❶ finalize a manuscript, text, etc.: 课本要到四月份才能～。The manuscript of the textbook will not be finalized until April. ❷ final version or text: ～将于年底付印。The final text will go to press towards the end of the year.
定格 dìnggé ❶ 〈影视〉 freeze frame ❷ fixed pattern or norm; stereotype: 写小说哪有～? How can there be any fixed pattern or norm for writing fiction?
定更 dìnggēng 〈旧语〉 beat or sound the first watch at 8 p.m. indicating the beginning of the five two-hour periods into which the night was divided
定工定产 dìnggōng dìngchǎn (contract for) production based on fixed work and output quotas
定购 dìnggòu *see* "订购" dìnggòu
定购粮 dìnggòuliáng quota grain to be sold by peasants to the state at fixed price
定冠词 dìngguàncí 〈语言〉 definite article
定规 dìngguī ❶ established rule or practice; set pattern: 无～可循。There's no hard and fast rule to follow. /新生入学教育已成～。It is now established practice for new students to attend an orientation course at the beginning of the first semester. /这种药的炮制方法已有～。There's a set formula for this herbal medicine to be concocted. ❷ 〈方言〉 be bent on; be determined: 他～要去。He insists on going. ❸ 〈方言〉 decide; settle: 大会议程已经～好了。The agenda of the meeting has been worked out.
定户 dìnghù *see* "订户" dìnghù
定滑轮 dìnghuálún fixed pulley
定婚 dìnghūn *also* "订婚" dìnghūn be engaged (to be married); be betrothed: ～仪式 engagement ceremony /他们已经～了。They are already engaged.
定货 dìnghuò *see* "订货" dìnghuò
定级 dìngjí fix one's grade in official or professional hierarchy
定计 dìngjì devise a stratagem; work out a scheme
定价 dìngjià ❶ fix a price: 给商品～ fix the prices of goods ❷ fixed price; list price: 明码～ marked prices /这些商品都有～。All of these commodities have been priced.
定见 dìngjiàn definite opinion; set or settled view: 对这个问题我没有～。I have no settled view on this matter.
定界 dìngjiè determine a border alignment; delimit a boundary
定金 dìngjīn *also* "定钱" earnest money; down payment
定睛 dìngjīng fix one's eyes upon: ～细看 gaze fixedly at
定居 dìngjū settle (down) in; reside in; live in: 他们祖祖辈辈在这里～。They have lived here for generations. *or* Their ancestors came here to settle down.
定居点 dìngjūdiǎn settlement: 牧民～ herdsmen's settlement
定居证书 dìngjū zhèngshū certificate of resettlement
定局 dìngjú ❶ final settlement: 等调查有了～再说。Let's wait till we have received the findings of the investigation. ❷ foregone conclusion; inevitable outcome: 这个计划失败已成～。It's a foregone conclusion that the plan will fall through.
定礼 dìnglǐ betrothal gifts (from the bridegroom to the bride's family); bride-price
定理 dìnglǐ theorem: 基本～ fundamental theorem
定例 dìnglì usual practice; set pattern; routine: 周末舞会已成～。It is regular practice that we have a dance on every weekend.
定量 dìngliàng ❶ determine the amounts of the components of a substance ❷ fix the amount or quantity: ～供应 fixed quantity supply; rationing /饮食～有助于身体健康。It is good for one's health to have a regular diet. ❸ fixed quantity; ration: 超出～ exceed the fixed quantity (*or* ration)
定量分析 dìngliàng fēnxī 〈化学〉 quantitative analysis
定陵 Dìnglíng Ding Ling, tomb of Emperor Zhu Yijun (reign: 1573-1620) of the Ming Dynasty which was excavated in 1956 and has been open to the public since 1959: ～博物馆 Dingling Museum /～的地下宫殿 underground palace of Dingling
定律 dìnglǜ law: 万有引力～ law of universal gravitation
定论 dìnglùn accepted opinion; final conclusion: 不作～ leave a matter open /如何评价这本书，目前尚无～。There is no consensus of opinion about this book.
定苗 dìngmiáo 〈农业〉 final singling or thinning (of seedlings)
定名 dìngmíng name; denominate: 这家公司～为"蓝星"。The firm is named Blue Star.
定牧 dìngmù (of nomads) settle down: 在适当的条件下，可使游牧逐渐变为～。Nomads may gradually settle down given appropriate conditions.
定牌生产 dìngpái shēngchǎn 〈外贸〉 manufacture of goods for export with trade mark either given or designated by the client
定盘星 dìngpánxīng ❶ first or lowest marking on the beam of a steelyard or portable balance ❷ 〈比喻〉 definite idea, view, opinion, etc.: 他做事没有～。He has never had any definite ideas of his own. /别看姑娘年轻，她可是家里的～。Young as she is, the girl is the brainy one (*or* decision-maker) in the family.
定评 dìngpíng accepted opinion; universally accepted appraisal: 这部作品早有～。There has been a generally accepted opinion about the book.
定期 dìngqī ❶ fix or set a date: 会议尚未～。The date for the meeting has not been decided. ❷ regular; fixed; at regular intervals; periodical: ～体格检查 regular physical check-ups /～轮换 rotate at regular intervals /～汇报工作 regularly report back on one's work /～刊物 periodical publication; periodical /不～刊物 non-periodical publication/～租船 time charter (of a ship) /不～磋商 irregular consultations /～逐级加薪 periodic step wage increase

定期存款 dìngqī cúnkuǎn fixed deposit; time deposit
定期贷款 dìngqī dàikuǎn term loan; time loan; fixed loan
定期抵押 dìngqī dǐyā term mortgage:～贷款 time mortgage loan
定期付款 dìngqī fùkuǎn scheduled payment
定期合同 dìngqī hétong fixed term contract
定期汇票 dìngqī huìpiào date draft; time bill; fixed bill
定期交货 dìngqī jiāohuò time delivery; delivery on term
定期信用证 dìngqī xìnyòngzhèng time letter of credit
定期债券 dìngqī zhàiquàn fixed-maturity bonds; term bond
定钱 dìngqian deposit; earnest (money):～已付。Earnest money is paid. /租房子要先付～。One has to pay a deposit when renting a house.
定亲 dìngqīn engagement (usu. arranged by parents); betrothal: ～日 date of engagement
定情 dìngqíng ❶ (of lovers) pledge enduring affection (usually by exchanging gifts):～诗 poem written on the occasion of taking a vow of eternal love ❷ get married:～之夕 on the night of marriage
定然 dìngrán certainly; definitely:事情～如此。This is how events will develop.
定日镜 dìngrìjìng 〈天文〉 heliostat
定神 dìngshén ❶ concentrate one's attention:他一动不动,～沉思。He was motionless, lost in thought. / 我～细看,这鼻烟壶上雕刻着几朵梅花。Looking hard, I found that on the snuff-box were carved plum blossoms. ❷ collect oneself; compose oneself; pull oneself together:我定下神来仔细琢磨事情的来龙去脉。I pulled myself together to ponder over the matter from beginning to end. /先定定神再往下讲。Calm down before you go on with your story.
定时 dìngshí ❶ at fixed time; at regular intervals:～起床 rise at a fixed time every day /～吃饭 take regular meals /～吃药 take medicine at regular intervals ❷ fix the time; time:～引爆 time an ignition or explosion
定时脉冲 dìngshí màichōng timing pulse:～发生器 timing pulse generator
定时器 dìngshíqì timer; timing controller
定时锁 dìngshísuǒ time lock
定时炸弹 dìngshí zhàdàn ❶ time bomb; delayed action bomb ❷ hidden danger; latent crisis:威胁两国关系的～ time bomb that endangers the relations between the two countries
定时装置 dìngshí zhuāngzhì clockwork; timer
定式 dìngshì *also* "定势" fixed pattern; stereotype; set:思维～ fixed pattern of thinking; set frame of mind /心理～ psychological set
定数 dìngshù ❶ destiny; fate:在迷信的人看来,什么事都有一个～。To superstitious people, everything is predestined (*or* determined by fate). ❷ fixed amount; fixed number; quota:这台机车的牵引～,由原来拉一千五百吨提高到两千吨。The pulling force fixed for this locomotive has increased from 1,500 to 2,000 tons. /今天的任务已经分下去了,每个人都定了数。Work for today has been assigned, each person given a set quota.
定说 dìngshuō ❶ say with certainty; assert categorically:他～这些碗碟是孩子们打碎的。He insisted that these bowls and plates were broken by the children. ❷ accepted view; conclusion:推翻～ give lie to accepted theories. /这种病的起因尚无～。The cause of the disease is still an open question.
定天镜 dìngtiānjìng 〈天文〉 coelostat
定位 dìngwèi ❶ orientate; position: 为船舶～ determine a ship's position /～式谈判〈经济〉 positional bargaining ❷ fixed position; location; orientation ❸ put... in proper perspective and evaluate:一定要给自己正确～,才能心理平衡。It is essential to put oneself in a proper place if one wants to feel psychologically balanced.
定位测定 dìngwèi cèdìng position-finding
定位键 dìngwèijiàn positioning key
定位器 dìngwèiqì 〈矿业〉 positioner
定息 dìngxī fixed interest (usu. in reference to the rate of interest paid annually by the state for a number of years to capitalists whose assets were transformed into joint state-private ventures in 1956)
定弦 dìngxián ❶ tune a stringed instrument ❷〈方言〉 have a fixed idea; make up one's mind:我夏天去不去西藏旅行还未～儿呢。I have not made up my mind whether I'll make a trip to Tibet this summer.
定限 dìngxiàn ❶ fixed number or amount; limit: 饮酒有～。There's a limit to one's capacity for liquor. ❷ fixed date; deadline: 上缴公粮,例有～。There is a deadline for paying the agricultural tax in grain. *or* There is a fixed date set for sending in tax grain.
定向 dìngxiàng ❶ find or determine the direction of; fix the orientation of; orient:无线电～ radio range orientation /～台 direction finder ❷ directional; orientational:～广播 directional broadcasting / ～钻井 directional drilling; directed drilling
定向爆破 dìngxiàng bàopò directional or directed blasting
定向地雷 dìngxiàng dìléi oriented mine; fougasse
定向分配 dìngxiàng fēnpèi fixed direction assignment; predetermined assignment of job (for a student, etc.)
定向航行 dìngxiàng hángxíng constant-bearing navigation
定向进化 dìngxiàng jìnhuà 〈生物〉 directed evolution
定向聚合 dìngxiàng jùhé stereospecific or stereoregular polymerization
定向培训 dìngxiàng péixùn training for specific post; job-oriented training
定向培养 dìngxiàng péiyǎng training for a certain region or work unit; target training
定向培育 dìngxiàng péiyù 〈农业〉 directive breeding
定向天线 dìngxiàng tiānxiàn directional antenna
定向仪 dìngxiàngyí 〈气象〉 direction finder
定向招生 dìngxiàng zhāoshēng enrol students who are preassigned to specific posts or areas
定销 dìngxiāo (system of) fixed quotas for marketing
定心 dìngxīn ❶ feel relieved; feel at ease:定一定心 collect one's wits; pull oneself together; calm oneself down /他近来情绪不好,工作不～。He could not concentrate on his work as he had been rather depressed lately. ❷〈机械〉 centring:～装置 centring device
定心骨 dìngxīngǔ *also* "主心骨" zhǔxīngǔ ❶ backbone; mainstay; pillar ❷ definite view; one's own judgment
定心丸 dìngxīnwán sth. capable of setting sb.'s mind at ease; reassurance:他的一席话使我吃了～。What he said reassured me.
定星镜 dìngxīngjìng 〈天文〉 siderostat
定刑 dìngxíng (of a judge, etc.) fix the punishment; decide on the sentence:～过轻 decide on too light a sentence (for a crime)
定形 dìngxíng ❶ setting; boarding:热～ heat setting /〈纺织〉～机 boarding machine ❷ take form; take shape:计划尚未～。The plan has not taken shape yet.
定形轰炸 dìngxíng hōngzhà 〈军事〉 pattern bombing
定型 dìngxíng finalize the design; fall into a pattern; take shape or form:这种牌子的汽车正在试制,尚未～。This make of cars is being trial-produced, for the design has not been finalized. /青少年正处在成长阶段,思想、性格还未～。As teenagers are in their formative years, they are not fixed (*or* are still malleable) either in outlook or in character.
定型反应 dìngxíng fǎnyìng 〈生物〉 stereotyped response
定省 dìngxǐng 〈书面〉 fulfil filial duties by inquiring after one's parents:晨昏～ inquire after one's parents both in the morning when they get up and in the evening when they retire
定性 dìngxìng ❶ determine the nature (of an offence or a case): 他的错误已经～。The nature of his error is determined (*or* clarified). ❷ determine the chemical composition of a substance:～试验 qualitative test
定性分析 dìngxìng fēnxī 〈化学〉 qualitative analysis
定性预测 dìngxìng yùcè qualitative forecasting
定序器 dìngxùqì 〈航天〉 sequencer (equipment which generates appropriately timed signals to command a series of operations by a spacecraft)
定谳 dìngyàn 〈书面〉〈法律〉 pass a verdict
定洋 dìngyáng *see* "定钱"
定窑 Dìngyáo Dingzhou kiln, famous for producing porcelain in the Song Dynasty
定义 dìngyì definition:下～ give a definition; define
定音鼓 dìngyīngǔ kettledrums; timpani
定银 dìngyín earnest money; down payment
定影 dìngyǐng 〈摄影〉 fixing:～罐 fixing tank /～剂 fixer /～液 fixing bath; fixing solution
定于一尊 dìngyúyīzūn look up to one man as the supreme authority (as in learning or moral excellence)
定语 dìngyǔ 〈语言〉 attribute:～从句 attributive clause
定员 dìngyuán fixed number of staff, army unit, or passengers:这节车厢～一百二十人。This carriage has a seating capacity of 120 peo-

ple./我们部门的职工已经超过～。Our department is already overstaffed.
定约 dìngyuē *see*“订约”dìngyuē
定约桥牌 dìngyuē qiáopái contract bridge
定阅 dìngyuè *see*“订阅”dìngyuè
定则 dìngzé 〈物理〉rule:左手～ left-hand rule /右手～ right-hand rule
定章 dìngzhāng established regulations
定值美元 dìngzhí měiyuán constant dollar
定职定编 dìngzhí dìngbiān fix the number of posts and staff
定植 dìngzhí 〈植物〉field planting or setting (of seedlings)
定址 dìngzhǐ ❶ set the location of a project:总装厂～重庆。The assembly factory was set at Chongqing. ❷ permanent address:他成年东跑西颠,没有个～。He has no permanent address, travelling from one place to another (*or* from place to place) all the year round.
定制 dìngzhì ❶ established rule or practice ❷ *see*“订制”dìngzhì
定置网 dìngzhìwǎng set or fixed net
定准 dìngzhǔn ❶ set principle; fixed standard:作人行事要有个～。A person should live in conformity with certain principles of conduct. ❷ certainly; definitely:这场电影你～满意。I'm sure you will like the film.
定子 dìngzǐ 〈电学〉stator:～绕组 stator winding /～转子组 stator-rotor unit
定阻抗电路 dìngzǔkàng diànlù constant impedance circuit
定罪 dìngzuì declare guilty; convict (of a crime):要量刑～。Penalty should be given in accordance with guilt.
定做 dìngzuò *see*“订做”dìngzuò

碇(矴、椗) dìng heavy stone used as an anchor; killick:拔锚起～ weigh anchor
碇泊 dìngbó anchor; berth:～在岸边的渔船有五、六十艘。More than 50 fishing boats lay at anchor near the bank.
碇泊费 dìngbófèi *also*“碇泊税”anchorage dues; anchorage
碇手 dìngshǒu 〈方言〉weigh heavy in the hand:这块怀表很～。This pocket watch weighs heavy in the hand.

啶 dìng *see*“吡啶”bǐdìng

锭 dìng ❶〈纺织〉spindle:一座五十万～纱厂 a half-million-spindled textile mill /开工～数 spindles in operation ❷ (of medicine, Chinese ink, etc.) ingot-shaped tablet:～墨 ink stick /～铁 ingot iron /～钳 ingot dogs (*or* tongues) ❸〈量词〉*used of sth. like an ingot*:一～银子 a silver ingot
锭剂 dìngjì 〈药学〉lozenge; pastille; troche
锭模 dìngmú 〈冶金〉ingot mould
锭速 dìngsù rotational speed of a spindle
锭子 dìngzi 〈纺织〉spindle
锭子油 dìngziyóu spindle oil

腚 dìng 〈方言〉buttocks

订 dìng ❶ conclude; draw up; agree on:～条约 conclude a treaty /～合同 enter into (*or* make) a contract /～计划 formulate (*or* draw up, *or* work out) a plan /～日期 fix (*or* agree on) a date /～生产指标 set a production target ❷ subscribe to (a newspaper, etc.); book (a seat, ticket, etc.); order (merchandise, etc.):增～ make additional bookings or subscriptions; place a new order /续～ renew one's subscription /～三桌酒席 reserve three tables for a feast (at a restaurant) ❸ make corrections; revise:修～ revise /校～ check against a reliable text; collate ❹ staple together:把散页～起来 staple the loose sheets together
订舱 dìngcāng book cargo space; charter space:～单 booking memo; booking note
订单 dìngdān *also*“定单”dìngdān order (for goods); order form
订费 dìngfèi subscription rate
订购 dìnggòu *also*“定购”dìnggòu order goods; place an order (for sth.)
订户 dìnghù *also*“定户”dìnghù subscriber (to a newspaper or periodical); person or household with a standing order (for milk, etc.)
订婚 dìnghūn *also*“定婚”dìnghūn be engaged (to be married); be betrothed:～戒指 engagement ring /～启事 engagement announcement
订货 dìnghuò *also*“定货”dìnghuò order goods; place an order for goods:～确认书 confirmation of order /向厂家～ place orders with a factory
订货代理人 dìnghuò dàilǐrén indent agent
订货单 dìnghuòdān order list
订货付款 dìnghuò fùkuǎn cash with order (CWO)
订货会 dìnghuòhuì meeting for the placement of orders; order-placing meeting
订货量 dìnghuòliàng quantity or size of order
订交 dìngjiāo make friends (with sb.); forge ties of friendship (with sb.)
订金 dìngjīn *also*“定金”dìngjīn down payment; earnest money
订立 dìnglì conclude (a treaty, agreement, etc.); make (a contract, etc.):～贸易协定 conclude a trade agreement /～攻守同盟 forge an offensive and defensive alliance; pledge (*or* vow) to shield each other
订书机 dìngshūjī ❶ stapling machine; stapler ❷ bookbinding machine
订约 dìngyuē *also*“定约”dìngyuē conclude a treaty; make or sign a contract:～方 party to treaty; contracting party
订约人 dìngyuērén contractor
订约书 dìngyuēshū document of contract
订阅 dìngyuè *also*“定阅”dìngyuè subscribe to (a newspaper, periodical, etc.):我们许多人都～了《中国日报》。Many of us have subscribed to *China Daily*.
订造 dìngzào have sth. made to order
订正 dìngzhèng make corrections; emend:要对书中的错误一一加以～。All errors should be removed from the book, one by one, after examination.
订制 dìngzhì *also*“定制”dìngzhì have sth. made to order; have sth. custom-made:～特大号鞋 have extra-size shoes made to order /欢迎选购和～服装。Orders for ready-made or custom-made costumes are welcome.
订做 dìngzuò *also*“定做”dìngzuò have sth. made to order or measure:～的套服 tailor-made suit; suit made to measure

钉 dìng ❶ nail:～鞋掌 nail on a sole; sole a shoe /～钉子 drive in a nail /把地图～在墙上 nail up a map on the wall ❷ sew on:～扣子 sew a button on
see also dīng

饤 dìng *see*“饾饤”dòudìng

铤 dìng 〈书面〉pig iron or crude copper
see also tǐng

diū

丢(丟) diū ❶ lose; mislay:我～了本杂志。I lost a magazine./图书馆～了几本书。Several books are missing from the library./你把我的笔～哪儿了? Where did you leave my pen? ❷ throw; cast; toss:把果皮～在垃圾箱里。Throw the fruit peels into the dustbin./不要随地～烟头。Don't litter by dropping the cigarette ends around./艰苦奋斗的传统不能～。We cannot dispense with the tradition of arduous struggle. ❸ put or lay aside; shelve:～不开 cannot put (sth. or sb.) out of one's mind; keep worrying about (sth. or sb.) /他早已把这事～在脑后。He has clean forgotten all about the matter./我的德语～了好几年,都忘得差不多了。My German has become rusty as I have not used it for years./问题已弄清楚,我～了一个沉重的包袱。I have had a heavy burden removed now that I am cleared.
丢丑 diūchǒu be disgraced; make a fool of oneself:当众～ make a fool of oneself in public; make an exhibition of oneself /他这样做太～了。It was disgraceful of him to act like that.
丢掉 diūdiào ❶ lose:我把钱包～了。I lost my wallet. ❷ throw away; cast away; discard:他们把不要的东西都～了。They have

thrown away everything they did not want. /～幻想，面对现实。Cast away illusions and face the reality. /为人民服务的原则决不能～。The principle of serving the people should by no means be discarded. /必须～官气。One must shed one's bureaucratic airs.

丢番图　Diūfāntú　Diophantus (c. 246-330), Greek mathematician of Alexandria, the first to attempt an algebraical notation: ～方程 Diophantine equation

丢份儿　diūfènr　〈方言〉disgraceful; shameful: 这么抠抠搜搜的，真～! How shameful it is behaving like a miser!

丢荒　diūhuāng　(of fields) be left uncultivated: 由于水源断绝，这一片地～了。This plot of land is left uncultivated because the water source has run dry.

丢魂落魄　diūhún-luòpò　*also* "失魂落魄" shīhún-luòpò　be panic-stricken; be scared out of one's wits

丢盔卸甲　diūkuī-xièjiǎ　*also* "丢盔弃甲" throw away one's shield and armour; be badly defeated: 敌人被打得～，落荒而逃。Badly battered, the enemy fled in disorder.

丢勒　Diūlè　Albrecht Dürer (1471-1528), German painter and engraver

丢脸　diūliǎn　lose face; be disgraced: 这件事给大家丢了脸。This brought disgrace upon all of us. /他今天的表现出人意料地糟，真～。His performance today ran counter to all expectations; it was a humiliating fiasco.

丢面子　diū miànzi　lose face; feel humiliated: 怕～ be afraid of losing face /当着众人被训斥，太～了。Being reprimanded in public is just too humiliating.

丢弃　diūqì　abandon; discard; get rid of: ～无用的东西 discard all the junk /～一切坏作风 get rid of all evil practices /那种遗憾的心情至今不能～。To this day I still cannot put that feeling of regret out of my mind.

丢却　diūquè　❶ *see* "丢弃" ❷ lose: 那本书让我不慎～了。I was so careless as to lose that book.

丢人　diūrén　*see* "丢脸"

丢人现眼　diūrén-xiànyǎn　make a fool of oneself; be disgraced: 有你～的时候。You are sure to make a spectacle of yourself one day.

丢三落四　diūsān-làsì　be always forgetting things; be careless and sloppy

丢失　diūshī　lose; let slip; miss: 我连着～了三本书。I lost three books in a row.

丢手　diūshǒu　wash one's hands of; give up: 这件事他～不管了。He washed his hands of the business.

丢眼色　diū yǎnsè　wink; signal with a wink: 他几次向他妻子～，但他妻子没有理会。He winked at his wife several times; but she didn't take his cue.

丢置　diūzhì　leave unused; lay aside: 这些钢管长期～不用，已经锈了。These steel tubes have gone rusty as they have not been used for so long.

丢卒保车　diūzú-bǎojū　(as in playing chess) give up a pawn to save a castle — sacrifice minor things to save major ones

铥　diū　〈化学〉thulium (Tm)

dōng

东(東)　dōng　❶ east: 城～三十公里 thirty kilometres east of the city /～城 eastern part of the city /～郊 eastern suburbs /长江～去入海流。The Yangtze River flows east into the sea. ❷ master; owner: 房～ landlord /股～ stockholder ❸ host: 今天上餐馆，我做～。Let's dine out today. I will be the host (*or* stand host). ❹ (Dōng) a surname

东半球　dōngbànqiú　Eastern Hemisphere

东宝影片公司　Dōngbǎo Yǐngpiàn Gōngsī　Toho Motion Picture Company, a major film studio in Japan

东北　dōngběi　❶ northeast; northeasterly: 风向～ (with a) northeasterly wind ❷ (Dōngběi) northeast China (formerly known as Manchuria); the Northeast

东北大鼓　Dōngběi dàgǔ　*also* "辽宁大鼓" Liáoníng dàgǔ　〈戏曲〉a kind of *dagu* popular in the Northeast (a versified story sung to the accompaniment of a small drum, usu. a solo, but sometimes a duet or a chorus to the accompaniment of a three- or four-stringed fiddle)

东北虎　dōngběihǔ　〈动物〉Manchurian tiger

东北抗日联军　Dōngběi Kàng-Rì Liánjūn　Anti-Japanese Amalgamated Army of the Northeast (organized and led by the Communist Party of China after Japanese seizure of the region through the September 18th Incident of 1931)

东北民主联军　Dōngběi Mínzhǔ Liánjūn　Northeast Democratic Allied Army (reorganized from all Communist-led forces in the region on 14 Jan. 1946, and renamed the Fourth Field Army of the People's Liberation Army in October, 1948)

东北平原　Dōngběi Píngyuán　Northeast Plain, largest in China, covering an area of 350,000 sq. km.

东奔西窜　dōngbēn-xīcuàn　run from place to place; flee in all directions

东奔西跑　dōngbēn-xīpǎo　run here and there; bustle about; rush about; rush around: 他终日～，并无怨言。He was rushed off his feet all day, but never complained. /我没有时间为你～! I've no time to go on (*or* run) errands for you!

东边　dōngbian　east; east side: 城市～有条河。There is a river to the east of the city.

东柏林　Dōng Bólín　East Berlin, Soviet occupation zone of the city 1945-1949, and capital of the German Democratic Republic from 1949 till reunification of Germany in 1990

东不拉　dōngbùlā　*also* "冬不拉" dōngbùlā　plucked string instrument, used by the Kazak nationality

东部裕固语　Dōngbù Yùgùyǔ　Eastern Yugur language, used by China's Yugur nationality

东厕　dōngcè　〈方言〉lavatory; WC

东昌纸　dōngchāngzhǐ　*also* "毛头纸" máotóuzhǐ　a kind of coarse soft white paper, used for papering windows or for wrapping

东厂　Dōngchǎng　Eastern Depot, emperor's secret service set up in 1420 during the Ming Dynasty

东窗事发　dōngchuāng-shìfā　the plot hatched in secret is exposed (the eastern window refers to the place where Qinhui 秦桧 had plotted with his cronies against Yuefei 岳飞, the most loyal and brave general of the Southern Song Dynasty); the conspiracy is unmasked; murder is out

东床　dōngchuáng　son-in-law: 招为～ choose (sb.) as one's son-in-law

东大阪　Dōng Dàbǎn　(Japan) Higashi-Osaka, satellite town of Osaka

东大寺　Dōngdàsì　Todai-ji, temple completed in 752 in Nara (奈良), Japan

东丹　dōngdān　(popular term for 铅丹) red lead; minium

东倒西歪　dōngdǎo-xīwāi　❶ stumble; stagger; totter: 老头醉得厉害，～地跌进大门，砰地一声关了门。The old man drunkenly stumbled through the gate and slammed it behind him. ❷ lying in disorder or aslant; tumbledown; rickety: ～的家具 rickety furniture /～的屋子 tumbledown houses

东道　dōngdào　❶ one who treats sb. to a meal; host: 尽～之谊 fulfil the obligations of a host; extend the courtesies of the host ❷ role of the host: 做～ play host; be the host

东道国　dōngdàoguó　host country: ～委员会 (UN) Committee on Host Country /～协定 host agreement

东道主　dōngdàozhǔ　*see* "东道❶"

东德　Dōng Dé　(popular brief term for 德意志民主共和国) East Germany: 东西德的统一 reunification of the two Germanies (1990)

东帝汶　Dōng Dìwèn　East Timor, eastern part of the largest and easternmost island of the Lesier Sundas, (a Portuguese colony until 1975, when it was taken by Indonesia, and declared independent by referendum in 1999)

东佃　dōng-diàn　landlord and tenant

东丁　dōngdīng　〈象声〉tinkle; clink; jingle: 玉佩～ jingle of jade ornaments

东躲西藏　dōngduǒ-xīcáng　hide here and there; flee hither and thither

东方　dōngfāng　❶ east: 日出～。The sun rises in the east. /～不亮西方亮，黑了南方有北方。When it is dark in the east, it is bright in the west; when it is murky in the south, there is still light in the north. — There is always plenty of room for manoeuvring. ❷ (Dōngfāng) the East; the Orient ❸ (Dōngfāng) a surname

东方航空公司　Dōngfāng Hángkōng Gōngsī　❶ China Eastern Airlines ❷ (US) Eastern Air Lines Inc.

东方号 Dōngfānghào 〈航天〉Vostok (Soviet spacecraft that launched the first man into the earth's orbit on 12 April 1961):～火箭 Vostok rocket
东方汇理银行 Dōngfāng Huìlǐ Yínháng (France) *Banque de l'Indo-Chine*
东方快车 Dōngfāng Kuàichē Orient Express, name of a train which, from 1883 to 1961, ran between Paris and Istanbul
东方学 dōngfāngxué orientalism
东非 Dōng Fēi East Africa:～大裂谷 East African Rift Valley
东风 dōngfēng ❶ east wind; spring wind:～化雨。The east wind brings rain. ❷〈比喻〉driving force of revolution; propitious or favourable circumstance:～压倒西风。The east wind prevails over the west wind. /万事具备,只欠～。Everything is ready except one key element. /这件事还要借你的～哟。I'll have to count on your help in this.
东风吹马耳 dōngfēng chuī mǎ'ěr like the east wind blowing at the ear of a horse — go in one ear and out the other:我劝他多少次,可就如～,毫无效果。I talked to him time and again, but it was just so much wasted breath.
东风带 dōngfēngdài 〈气象〉easterlies
东干人 Dōnggānrén Dungans, Russian name for the Hui nationality and its descendants in the former republics of the Soviet Union
东宫 dōnggōng ❶〈旧语〉Eastern Palace — place where the crown prince lived ❷ crown prince
东郭 Dōngguō a surname
东郭先生 Dōngguō xiānsheng Master Dongguo, the foolish, soft-hearted scholar who narrowly escaped being eaten by a wolf which he had helped to hide from a hunter; naive person who gets into trouble through being soft-hearted to evil people
东海 Dōnghǎi East China Sea
东海银行 Dōnghǎi Yínháng (Japan) Tokai Bank Ltd.
东汉 Dōng Hàn Eastern Han Dynasty (25-220)
东汉铜奔马 Dōng Hàn tóngbēnmǎ bronze galloping horse of the Eastern Han Dynasty, excavated in 1969 in Wuwei County, Gansu Province
东胡 Dōnghú Eastern Hu, ancient ethnic group inhabiting what is now southeastern Inner Mongolia
东伙 dōnghuǒ shop owner and shop assistant; employer and those employed; boss and employee:他们是～关系。Theirs is a relationship between employer and employee.
东加里曼丹 Dōng Jiālǐmàndān Kalimantan Timur, Indonesian province on the island of Borneo
东家长,西家短 dōngjiā cháng, xījiā duǎn *also*"张家长,李家短" Zhāngjiā cháng, Lǐjiā duǎn gossip about people:她们一天吃饱饭,闲的没事做,当然只有～。They've nothing to do but stuff themselves all day. Naturally, they're full of gossip.
东家 dōngjia master; boss:少～ young master
东晋 Dōng Jìn Eastern Jin Dynasty (317-420)
东京 Dōngjīng ❶ former name for Kaifeng (开封), Henan Province ❷ Tokyo:～–横滨都市区 (Japan) Tokyo-Yokohama Metropolitan Area /～警视厅 (Japan) Tokyo Metropolitan Police Board
东京都 Dōngjīngdū (Japan) Tokyo-to; Greater Tokyo
东京广播公司 Dōngjīng Guǎngbō Gōngsī Tokyo Broadcasting System (TBS)
东京时报 Dōngjīng Shíbào Tokyo Times
东京湾 Dōngjīngwān Gulf of Tonkin, also known as Beibu Gulf (北部湾)
东京银行 Dōngjīng Yínháng (Japan) Bank of Tokyo
东京芝浦电气公司 Dōngjīng Zhīpǔ Diànqì Gōngsī (Japan) Tokyo Shibaura Electric
东经 dōngjīng 〈地理〉east longitude:位于～50度 at 50° east longitude
东净 dōgjìng (usu. used in the early vernacular) lavatory; WC
东拉西扯 dōnglā-xīchě drag in all sorts of irrelevant matters; talk at random; ramble:别～的,有话请直说。Don't beat about the bush. Come to the point, please. /两个人～,有时谈到过去的熟人。They talked in a wandering way, sometimes about their past acquaintances.
东林党 Dōnglíndǎng Donglin Clique, political organization composed of scholars and court officials in the late Ming Dynasty
东鳞西爪 dōnglín-xīzhǎo odds and ends; bits and pieces; fragments:这首长诗他只能～地背得几句。He can only recite a few lines here and there from the long poem.
东罗马帝国 Dōng Luómǎ Dìguó Eastern Roman Empire or Byzantine Empire (330-1453)
东盟 Dōngméng (short for 东南亚联盟) Association of Southeast Asian Nations (ASEAN)
东面 dōngmiàn ❶ face east:～而坐 sit facing the east ❷ eastern side; east
东南 dōngnán ❶ southeast; southeasterly:～风 southeasterly wind ❷ (Dōngnán) southeast China; the Southeast
东南亚 Dōngnán Yà Southeast Asia:～条约组织 Southeast Asia Treaty Organization (SEATO) (formed on 8 September 1954 and dismantled on 20 February 1976)
东挪西借 dōngnuó-xījiè borrow from everybody; solicit loans from all quarters
东欧 Dōng Ōu Eastern Europe:～国家 East European countries
东派教会 Dōngpài Jiàohuì 〈宗教〉Eastern Church
东跑西颠 dōngpǎo-xīdiān dash here and there; run busily around; bustle about
东拼西凑 dōngpīn-xīcòu scrape together; knock together:～借了一笔钱 have to borrow from different quarters to make up the sum /那篇文章没有什么新意,全是～的。There is nothing new in that essay. It is a scissors-and-paste job.
东萨摩亚 Dōng Sàmóyà Eastern Samoa
东三省 Dōngsānshěng Three Northeast Provinces (Heilongjiang, Jilin, and Liaoning)
东沙群岛 Dōngshā Qúndǎo Dongsha Islands or Eastern Sand Islands, northernmost of the four major groups of Chinese islands in the South China Sea
东山再起 dōngshān-zàiqǐ stage a comeback:策划～ plot a comeback /多年默默无闻后,他在政界又～了。After lying low for years, he staged a comeback in the political arena.
东施效颦 Dōngshī-xiàopín Dong Shi, an ugly woman, knitting her brows in imitation of the famous beauty Xi Shi, only to make herself all the uglier — blind imitation with ludicrous effect:对别人的经验要消化吸收,～地机械模仿是毫无用处的。Though we should assimilate and absorb other people's experience, blind imitation would lead nowhere.
东条英机 Dōngtiáoyīngjī Hideki Tojo (1884-1948), Japanese general and Prime Minister from 1941 to 1944, hanged on 23 December 1948 for war crimes
东魏 Dōng Wèi Eastern Wei Dynasty (534-550), one of the Northern Dynasties
东西 dōng-xī ❶ east and west:房子的～两边都有树。There are trees on both east and west sides of the house. ❷ from east to west:这个镇子不大,～约千米,南北才五百米。This is not a big town, about 1,000 metres from east to west and 500 metres only from north to south.
东…西… dōng…xī… ...here...there:东一榔头,西一棒子 hammer here and batter there; act or speak haphazardly; act in a hit-or-miss fashion /东一个,西一个 (of things) be scattered here and there /东一句,西一句 say one sentence here and another there; drag in irrelevant matters; talk incoherently /东诓西骗 cheat everybody and everywhere possible /东涂西抹 scribble here and daub there; smear all over
东西 dōngxi ❶ stuff; thing:屋子里～摆得太多了。The room is cluttered with stuff. /收拾好～再走。Put your things in order before you leave. /写～要看对象。One should know for whom one writes. /他买～去了。He is out shopping. ❷ (used to express affection or hatred for person or animal) thing; creature:这小～别提有多乖。What a clever little creature! /蠢～! What a fool! /真不是～! What a mean creature!
东西方效应 dōngxīfāng xiàoyìng 〈航天〉east-west effect
东西方中心 Dōng-Xīfāng Zhōngxīn (short for 东西方文化技术交流中心) East-West Center; Center for Cultural and Technical Interchange Between East and West (located in Honolulu, Hawaii)
东乡族 Dōngxiāngzú Dongxiang or Tunghsiang nationality, living in Gansu Province
东亚 Dōng Yà East Asia
东洋 Dōngyáng 〈旧语〉Japan:～人 Japanese /～货 Japanese goods
东洋车 dōngyángchē 〈旧语〉rickshaw
东洋工业公司 Dōngyáng Gōngyè Gōngsī (Japan) Toyo Kogyo

Ltd., manufacturer of Mazda cars
东印度公司 Dōng Yìndù Gōngsī East India Company:英属～ British East India Company (1600-1858) /荷属～ Dutch East India Company (1602-1798)
东印度群岛 Dōng Yìndù Qúndǎo East Indies, off the SE coast of Asia
东瀛 Dōngyíng 〈书面〉❶ East China Sea ❷ Japan:留学～ study in Japan
东映影片公司 Dōngyìng Yǐngpiàn Gōngsī (Japan) Toei Motion Picture Company
东隅 dōngyú east; sunrise; morning:失之～,收之桑榆 lose at sunrise and gain at sunset—what you lose on the swings, you gain on the roundabouts
东吁王朝 Dōngyù Wángcháo (Burma) Toungoo Dynasty (c. 15th-18th centuries)
东岳 Dōngyuè Eastern Sacred Mountain (another name for Mount Tai 泰山)
see also "五岳" Wǔyuè
东张西望 dōngzhāng-xīwàng gaze or peer around; glance around; look about in all directions:他站在那儿～。He stood there glancing around.
东正教 Dōngzhèngjiào Eastern Orthodox Church
东芝公司 Dōngzhī Gōngsī (Japan) Toshiba Corporation
东周 Dōng Zhōu Eastern Zhou Dynasty (770-256 BC)
东周铜矿遗址 Dōng Zhōu Tóngkuàng Yízhǐ site of Eastern Zhou copper mine, discovered in 1973 in Daye (大冶), Hubei Province

蛴(蝀) dōng *see* "蝃蛴" dìdōng

鸫(鶇) dōng 〈动物〉thrush

冬[1] dōng ❶ winter:隆～ deep winter; in the depths of winter /在北京住了两～ spend two winters in Beijing /今～雪不多。There hasn't been much snow this winter. ❷ (Dōng) a surname

冬[2](鼕) dōng 〈象声〉(used to indicate sound of beating a drum, knocking on a door, etc.) dub-a-dub; rat-tat:战鼓～～ booming (*or* dub-a-dub) of war drums /～～地敲门 drum at (*or* thump on) the door
冬不拉 dōngbùlā 〈乐器〉*also* "东不拉" dōngbùlā plucked stringed instrument, used by the Kazak nationality
冬菜 dōngcài ❶ preserved, dried Chinese cabbage or mustard greens ❷ vegetables (to be) stored for winter use
冬虫夏草 dōngchóng-xiàcǎo (shortened as 虫草)〈中药〉Chinese caterpillar fungus (*Cordyceps sinesis*)
冬储 dōngchǔ store sth. in winter or for winter use:他～了一千公斤白菜。He has stored 1,000 kgs of Chinese cabbage for the winter.
冬耕 dōnggēng winter ploughing
冬宫 Dōnggōng Winter Palace, former Russian imperial residence in St. Petersburg and now used as a museum and art gallery
冬菇 dōnggū (dried) mushrooms picked in winter
冬瓜 dōngguā wax gourd; white gourd
冬瓜条 dōngguātiáo slices of wax gourd preserved in sugar
冬灌 dōngguàn winter irrigation
冬寒 dōnghán winter cold:松柏耐～。Pines and cypresses can stand cold weather in winter.
冬烘 dōnghōng shallow and old-fashioned; pedantic:～先生 old-fashioned man full of superficial, half-baked ideas; pedant
冬候鸟 dōnghòuniǎo winter bird
冬花 dōnghuā *also* "款冬" kuǎndōng 〈植物〉coltsfoot
冬季 dōngjì winter:～施工 winter construction /～体育运动 winter sports /～作物 winter crop /～饲养 winter feeding
冬季奥林匹克运动会 Dōngjì Àolínpǐkè Yùndònghuì Olympic Winter Games
冬节 Dōngjié *see* "冬至"
冬景天 dōngjingtiān 〈方言〉winter
冬葵 dōngkuí 〈植物〉cluster mallow (*Malva verticillata*)
冬令 dōnglìng ❶ winter ❷ winter weather:春行～。The weather in spring was as cold as that in winter.
冬麦 dōngmài winter wheat
冬眠 dōngmián 〈生物〉winter sleep; hibernation
冬眠疗法 dōngmián liáofǎ hibernation therapy
冬眠灵 dōngmiánlíng 〈药学〉wintermin; chlorphomazine
冬青 dōngqīng 〈植物〉Chinese ilex
冬青油 dōngqīngyóu 〈化学〉wintergreen
冬日 dōngrì ❶ winter:即使是～,他也是天刚亮就起床。He gets up at dawn even in winter. ❷〈书面〉sun in winter:～融融。The sun in winter fills the air with warmth. *or* The sun feels pleasantly warm in winter.
冬笋 dōngsǔn winter bamboo shoots
冬天 dōngtiān winter
冬瘟 dōngwēn 〈中医〉winter febrile disease
冬闲 dōngxián slack farming season in winter:利用～做好室内选种工作 make use of the slack winter season to select seeds indoors
冬小麦 dōngxiǎomài *also* "冬麦" winter wheat
冬性植物 dōngxìng zhíwù 〈植物〉winter plant
冬学 dōngxué winter school for farmers
冬训 dōngxùn winter training
冬汛 dōngxùn winter fishing season
冬衣 dōngyī winter clothes
冬泳 dōngyǒng swim in freezing water in winter; winter swimming
冬月 dōngyuè 11th month of the lunar calendar
冬运 dōngyùn (short for 冬季运输) winter transport
冬运会 dōngyùnhuì (short for 冬季运动会) winter sports meet
冬蛰 dōngzhé 〈生物〉winter sleep; hibernation
冬至 Dōngzhì *also* "冬节" ❶ Winter Solstice, 22nd seasonal division point, marking the sun's position at 270° on the ecliptic ❷ day marking such a seasonal division point, usu. falling on the 22nd or 23rd of December ❸ period lasting from such a seasonal division point to the next one (Slight Cold 小寒)
see also "节气" jiéqi; "二十四节气" èrshísì jiéqì
冬至点 dōngzhìdiǎn southernmost point of the ecliptic, through which the sun is supposed to pass at Winter Solstice
冬至线 dōngzhìxiàn Tropic of Carpricon
see also "回归线" huíguīxiàn
冬装 dōngzhuāng winter dress; winter clothing

咚 dōng *see* "冬[2]"

氡 dōng 〈化学〉radon (Rn)

dǒng

董 dǒng ❶〈书面〉direct; superintend; supervise:～其成 supervise a project until its completion /～理 manage ❷ director; trustee:校～ school trustee ❸ (Dǒng) a surname
董必武 Dǒng Bìwǔ Dong Biwu (1885-1975), founding member and leader of the Chinese Communist Party, Vice-premier, President of the Supreme People's Court and Vice-President of the People's Republic of China successively
董鸡 Dǒngjī water cock (*Gallicrex cinerea*)
董建华 Dǒng Jiànhuá Tung Chee-hwa (1937-), first Chief Executive of Hong Kong Special Administrative Region (1 July 1997-)
董酒 dǒngjiǔ *Dongjiu*, strong liquor produced in Zunyi, Guizhou Province
董其昌 Dǒng Qíchāng Dong Qichang (formerly translated as Tung Ch'i-ch'ang, 1555-1636), Chinese calligrapher and brush painter of the Ming Dynasty
董事 dǒngshì director; trustee:常务～ executive director
董事会 dǒngshìhuì board of directors; (of schools, etc.) board of trustees
董事长 dǒngshìzhǎng chairman of the board of directors
董源 Dǒng Yuán Dong Yuan (?-c.962), painter of the Later Tang of the Five Dynasties
董仲舒 Dǒng Zhòngshū Dong Zhongshu (formerly translated as Tung Chung-shu, 179-104 BC), Chinese philosopher of the Western Han Dynasty

懂 dǒng understand; know:～日语 know Japanese /～规矩

know the rules; be well-behaved /～礼貌 have good manners /～人情世故 be experienced in the ways of society; be worldly-wise

懂得 dǒngde understand; know; grasp:没有人～他在笑什么。No one knew what he was laughing at. /你～他话中的含义吗? Do you see the point of his remarks? /要使群众更清楚地～交通法规的重要性。It is necessary to make the public understand more clearly the importance of traffic rules.

懂行 dǒngháng know the business; know the ropes; know the tricks:搞银行他很～。He knows banking thoroughly.

懂局 dǒngjú know the business; know the ropes; be in the know:他这句话说在点子上了,是个～的。He spoke directly to the point, so he really knows the business.

懂门儿 dǒngménr 〈方言〉know much about sth.; be well versed:他对兽医不～。He knows nothing about veterinary science.

懂事 dǒngshì sensible; intelligent:～明理 sensible and understanding /这孩子很～。The child is well-behaved. /你怎么这样不～? How can you be so silly?

懂眼 dǒngyǎn 〈方言〉have considerable knowledge of; be experienced in sth.; be in the know; be proficient in:买计算机,你得向～的请教。You must consult an expert if you want to buy a computer.

D

dòng

动(動) dòng ❶ move; stir:～如脱兔 move like a hare /四个人把他按在地上,～也不能～。Held down by four men, he couldn't move a bit. /谁也没有～过你的收音机。Nobody has touched (*or* tampered with) your radio set. ❷ act; get moving:轻举妄～ act rashly /只要大家都～起来,就没有解决不了的困难。No difficulty is insurmountable when all of us get moving. ❸ change; alter:～几个字 change a few words /作一些改～ make some alterations /这种设计要作一些变～,使它更科学一点。The design has to be modified to make it more scientific. ❹ use; wield:～脑筋 use one's head /～嘴皮子 pay lip service /～心眼 think up a trick /～了多年的存款 draw the savings one has had for years ❺ touch (one's heart); arouse:不为所～ remain untouched (*or* unaffected); not be swayed (by sb.'s words, etc.) /～感情 be carried away by emotion; get worked up ❻ moving; touching:漠然不～ remain indifferent /晓之以理,～之以情 appeal to reason as well as human compassion /这个故事很～人。The story is very touching. ❼ 〈方言〉(mostly used in the negative) eat; drink:不～荤腥 never eat meat or fish; be a vegetarian /他从不～酒。He never touches alcohol. ❽ easily; often:～辄骂人 be given to swearing; be foul-mouthed

动笔 dòngbǐ take up the pen or brush; start writing or painting:～作画 take up one's brush and start painting /想清楚了再～。Think everything through before setting pen to paper.

动宾 dòng-bīn 〈语言〉verb and object:～短语 verb-object phrase /～结构 verb-object structure

动兵 dòngbīng resort to force; appeal to arms

动不动 dòngbudòng easily; frequently; at every turn:～就发火 flare up at the slightest provocation; flare up easily /～就请假 frequently ask for leave of absence /～哭鼻子 be apt to cry; often break down and weep

动产 dòngchǎn personal property; movable property; movables:～和不～ movable and immovable property; personal and real estate /～税 movable property tax

动词 dòngcí 〈语言〉verb:～短语 phrasal verb; verbal phrase

动粗 dòngcū 〈方言〉resort to violence; hit sb.

动荡 dòngdàng ❶ undulating; rolling:湖水～ undulating surface of the lake ❷ turbulence; upheaval; unrest:～年代 age of turmoil; turbulent years /该国局势依然紧张～。The situation remains tense and volatile in that country.

动荡不安 dòngdàng-bù'ān turbulent; intranquil:国家局势～。The country is in turmoil.

动电学 dòngdiànxué electrokinetics

动肝火 dòng gānhuǒ flare up; get angry:大～ fly into a towering rage /有话慢慢说,不要～。It's no good flying into a temper, as we can always talk things over at our leisure.

动感 dònggǎn dynamic; graphic:这塑像极富～。It is a very dynamic statue.

动工 dònggōng ❶ begin construction; start building:公路尚未～。The construction of the highway hasn't started yet. ❷ under construction:前方正在～,车辆禁止通行。The road is closed to traffic, for construction is under way. *or* Construction under way; closed to traffic.

动关节 dòngguānjié 〈生理〉diarthrosis

动滑轮 dònghuálún movable pulley

动画片儿 dònghuàpiānr *see* "动画片"

动画片 dònghuàpiàn animated cartoon; cartoon

动换 dònghuan move; stir:坐了一整天,也该起身～～。You should get up and stretch yourself, as you've been working at the desk the whole day.

动火 dònghuǒ get angry; flare up:你不必为这些区区小事～。You don't have to flare up over such trifles.

动机 dòngjī motive; intention:～不纯 have impure (*or* mixed) motives /你的～很好,但效果欠佳。You failed to achieve good results though you meant well. /他这样做的～是什么? Why did he do so? *or* What's behind his action?

动劲儿 dòngjìnr 〈方言〉make efforts; try to do sth.:光说不～ never put one's words into practice; pay lip service only

动静脉分流术 dòng-jìngmài fēnliúshù 〈医学〉surgical arteriovenous shunt

动静脉瘤 dòng-jìngmàiliú 〈医学〉arteriovenous aneurism

动静脉吻合术 dòng-jìngmài wěnhéshù 〈医学〉arteriovenostomy

动静 dòngjing ❶ sound of sth. astir:他一听到～便惊醒。He is apt to wake up at the slightest sound. /周围没有一点～。It was dead quiet all around. ❷ movement; activity:监视敌人的～ keep a close eye (*or* watch) on the enemy's movements /打听～ try to find out how things stand /一有～就来报告。Report at once if anything happens. /他们早就答应办理,可至今还不见～。They have long pledged to attend to the matter, but so far nothing concrete is in sight.

动觉 dòngjué 〈心理〉kinaesthesia

动口 dòngkǒu use one's tongue; reason things out:君子～不动手。A gentleman uses his tongue but not his fists. *or* A gentleman argues but does not fight with his fists.

动力 dònglì ❶ motive power; power:～设备 power plant ❷ motive or driving force; impetus:社会发展的～ motive force of social development /他学习的～很大。He is strongly motivated in his studies.

动力传送 dònglì chuánsòng power transmission

动力反应堆 dònglì fǎnyìngduī power reactor

动力干线 dònglì gànxiàn power main

动力机 dònglìjī *also* "发动机" fādòngjī motor; engine

动力时 dònglìshí 〈天文〉dynamic time

动力头 dònglìtóu 〈机械〉unit head:～车床 unit head turning machine /～拉床 unit head broaching machine /～铣床 unit head milling machine

动力系统 dònglì xìtǒng dynamic or power system

动力心理治疗 dònglì xīnlǐ zhìliáo dynamic psychotherapy

动力学 dònglìxué dynamics; kinetics

动力增殖反应堆 dònglì zēngzhí fǎnyìngduī power breeder

动力装置 dònglì zhuāngzhì power set

动量 dòngliàng 〈物理〉momentum:广义～ generalized momentum /～矩 moment of momentum /～守恒定律 law of conservation of momentum

动令 dònglìng 〈军事〉command of execution

动乱 dòngluàn turmoil; disturbance; upheaval; turbulence:～时期 time of turmoil /社会～ social unrest /～年代 years of upheaval /制止～ curb the disturbance /国家当时正处在～之中。The nation was in a state of turmoil.

动轮 dònglún 〈机械〉driving wheel:从～ driven wheel /反～ reaction wheel /回～ reverse wheel /主～ driver wheel; running wheel

动脉 dòngmài 〈生理〉artery:～血 arterial blood /～脉搏 arterial pulse /～血压 arterial pressure

动脉穿刺 dòngmài chuāncì 〈医学〉arteriopuncture

动脉导管 dòngmài dǎoguǎn arterial duct

动脉弓 dòngmàigōng arch of aorta

动脉痉挛 dòngmài jìngluán 〈医学〉arteriospasm

动脉瘤 dòngmàiliú 〈医学〉aneurysm; arterial tumour:～切除术 aneurysmectomy

动脉炎 dòngmàiyán 〈医学〉arteritis

动脉硬化 dòngmài yìnghuà 〈医学〉arteriosclerosis

动脉粥样硬化 dòngmài zhōuyàng yìnghuà atherosclerosis

动名词 dòngmíngcí 〈语言〉gerund
动摩擦 dòngmócā 〈物理〉dynamical friction
动目 dòngmù attract attention; catch the eye: 艳丽～ gorgeous and eye-catching
动能 dòngnéng 〈物理〉kinetic energy
动念 dòngniàn ❶ be attracted; have one's desire, interest or enthusiasm aroused: 钱财堆如山,他也不～。No amount of wealth can move him. ❷ idea; thought: 他脑子里突然出现一个奇怪的～。A strange idea suddenly dawned upon him. /听了他这番话,她便有了～。His story went to her heart.
动怒 dòngnù lose one's temper; flare up; get worked up: 何必～? Why get worked up? /不必那样～。No need to fly into a temper.
动拍镜头 dòngpāi jìngtóu travel shot; truck shot
动平衡 dòngpínghéng 〈物理〉dynamic balance; running balance: ～机〈机械〉dynamic balancer
动气 dòngqì take offence; get angry; lose one's temper: 我从未见他～过。I have never seen him lose his temper.
动迁 dòngqiān relocate; resettle; remove: 此项工程需～三家工厂和一千多户居民。The project involves the relocation of three factories and over 1,000 residential households.
动迁户 dòngqiānhù family or household to be relocated (so that the land can be used for other purpose)
动情 dòngqíng ❶ be moved or touched; get worked up; become excited: 他的演奏令我十分～。His performance touched me deeply. /不要～,那只能坏事。Don't get excited. It would only make matters worse. ❷ become enamoured: 看来他为她～了。It seems he has fallen for her.
动情期 dòngqíngqī estrus; oestrus
动人 dòngrén moving; touching: ～的场面 moving scene /～的事迹 stirring deeds /楚楚～ (of women) beautiful; attractive
动人心弦 dòngrénxīnxián *also* "动人心魄" strike or touch a deep chord in one's heart; tug at one's heartstrings; touch one's heart: 这是一幅多么～的画面! What a moving scene!
动容 dòngróng 〈书面〉change countenance; be visibly moved: 其情哀婉,听者为之～。The audience was visibly moved by the sad story.
动身 dòngshēn go or set out on a journey; leave (for a distant place): 明天一早我们就～。We leave early tomorrow morning. /趁着天还没黑,我们得赶快～。We have to set off before it gets dark.
动势 dòngshì kinetic potential
动手 dòngshǒu ❶ start work; get to work; do: ～搞卫生 start cleaning /亲自～ do it oneself /越早～越好。The sooner we get moving, the better. /人人～。Let everyone join in. ❷ touch; handle: 爱护展品,请勿～。Please don't touch the exhibits. ❸ raise a hand to strike or hit; hit out: ～打人 raise one's hand to hit sb. /是他先动的手。He struck the first blow. /卫士们该没有～吧? The guards didn't join the fray, did they?
动手动脚 dòngshǒu-dòngjiǎo ❶ strike sb. with hands and feet; kick and cuff ❷ molest a woman; take liberties with a woman; be or get fresh with sb. of the opposite sex: "你怎么～!"尼姑满脸通红地说,一面赶快走。"Who are you pawing?" demanded the nun, blushing crimson as she began to hurry away.
动手术 dòng shǒushù ❶ perform an operation; operate (on sb.): 给病人脑部～ operate on a patient's brain ❷ have an operation; be operated on: 他的眼睛～了。He had an operation on the eyes. ❸〈比喻〉effect a big change: 这个厂的管理太差,非动大手术不可。The factory is poorly managed; it has to have a major overhaul.
动态 dòngtài ❶ trends; developments: 科技新～ recent developments in science and technology /了解敌人的～ find out about enemy movements /舆论～ trend of public opinion ❷ motion and expression; behaviour: 画中人物,～各异,栩栩如生。Differing each from the other in expression and behaviour, the figures in the picture are vivid and life-like. ❸ dynamic state: ～电流 dynamic current /～变量 dynamic variable /～社会 dynamic society /～文化 mobile culture
动态电阻 dòngtài diànzǔ dynamic resistance
动态度 dòng tàidu be rudely impatient; lose one's temper; get angry: 我昨天对你有点～,实在对不起。I am sorry I was a bit short with you yesterday.
动态分析 dòngtài fēnxī dynamic analysis
动态光学 dòngtài guāngxué 〈物理〉active optics
动态经济 dòngtài jīngjì dynamic economy
动态经济学 dòngtài jīngjìxué dynamic economics
动态平衡 dòngtài pínghéng dynamic equilibrium or balance
动态随机存取存储器 dòngtài suíjī cúnqǔ cúnchǔqì dynamic random access memory (DRAM)
动态特性 dòngtài tèxìng 〈电学〉dynamic characteristic
动态学 dòngtàixué dynamics
动态艺术 dòngtài yìshù kinetic art
动态噪声 dòngtài zàoshēng dynamic noise
动弹 dòngtan move; stir: 他被绑住手脚,～不得。He was bound hand and foot and could not move. /他的嘴唇～了一下,但什么话也没说出来。His lips twitched, but not a single word came out of his mouth.
动天地,泣鬼神 dòng tiāndì, qì guǐshén earth-shaking and soul-stirring
动听 dòngtīng interesting or pleasant to listen to: 娓娓～ pleasant to the ear /别为他～的言辞所迷惑。Don't let his fine-sounding words affect your judgment.
动土 dòngtǔ break ground; start construction
动问 dòngwèn 〈套语〉Excuse me, (but): 不敢～,您是上海人吗? Excuse me, (but) are you from Shanghai?
动窝儿 dòngwōr 〈方言〉start moving; make a move: 他坐错了位置,可就是不肯～。He is sitting in the wrong seat but refuses to budge.
动武 dòngwǔ use or resort to force; start a fight; come to blows: 通过谈判解决争端而不要～ settle a dispute through negotiations without resorting to force /他们俩好像要～了。They seem to be coming to blows.
动物 dòngwù animal: ～界 animal kingdom
动物病毒 dòngwù bìngdú 〈医学〉animal virus
动物崇拜 dòngwù chóngbài 〈宗教〉animal cult
动物地理学 dòngwù dìlǐxué zoogeography
动物淀粉 dòngwù diànfěn animal starch
动物化学 dòngwù huàxué zoochemistry
动物胶 dòngwùjiāo 〈化学〉animal sizing or glue
动物恐怖 dòngwù kǒngbù zoophobia
动物区系 dòngwù qūxì *also* "动物志" fauna
动物圈 dòngwùquān zoosphere
动物群落 dòngwù qúnluò animal community
动物生态学 dòngwù shēngtàixué ecology; zooecology
动物纤维 dòngwù xiānwéi 〈纺织〉animal fiber
动物心理学 dòngwù xīnlǐxué animal psychology
动物型植物 dòngwùxíng zhíwù zoophyte
动物性蛋白 dòngwùxìng dànbái animal protein
动物学 dòngwùxué zoology
动物油 dòngwùyóu animal oil
动物园 dòngwùyuán zoological garden; zoo: 北京～ Beijing Zoo
动物志 dòngwùzhì fauna
动响 dòngxiǎng sound of sth. or sb. moving: 他没有听到什么～。He heard nothing.
动向 dòngxiàng trend; tendency: 新～ new trend /这个人行踪诡秘,没人摸得清他的～。He is very secretive; nobody knows what he is up to.
动心 dòngxīn have one's enthusiasm or interest aroused; be attracted or lured: 见财～ attracted (*or* lured) by wealth /这么多好的展品,不由得你不～。There is such an array of exhibits that your interest is naturally aroused. /她被那番甜言蜜语说～了。She was carried away by those honeyed words.
动刑 dòngxíng subject to torture; torture
动凶 dòngxiōng resort to violence; use brute force
动眼神经 dòngyǎn shénjīng 〈生理〉oculomotor nerve
动摇 dòngyáo ❶ vacillate; waver: 在不同意见之间～不定 vacillate between different opinions /信仰～ waver in one's conviction /～分子 wavering element; vacillating element ❷ shake; undermine: ～军心 undermine the morale /这点小挫折不可能～他的信心。This minor setback cannot shake his confidence.
动议 dòngyì motion: 紧急～ urgent motion /提出一项～ put forward a motion /通过～ adopt (*or* carry) a motion /拒绝一项～ reject a motion /搁置～ shelve a motion /撤消～ withdraw a motion /修改～ amend a motion; submit an amendment to a motion /对～进行表决 vote on a motion; put a motion to vote /提出休会～ move for recess (*or* adjournment) of the meeting.
动用 dòngyòng use; employ; draw on: ～武力 use force /～后备力量 employ the reserve /～库存 draw on the stock
动员 dòngyuán ❶ national or general mobilization: ～令 mobiliza-

D

tion order /全国总～ national mobilization ❷ arouse; mobilize: 作～报告 give a mobilization speech (*or* pep talk) /～大会 mobilization rally /～大家参加冬季锻炼 mobilize people to go in for winter training

动辄 dòngzhé 〈书面〉easily; frequently; at every turn: ～训人 start to lecture people at every opportunity /～发怒 fly into a rage on the slightest provocation

动辄得咎 dòngzhé-déjiù be often taken to task; be frequently blamed for what one does

动真格的 dòng zhēngéde do sth. for real; work in earnest; take sth. seriously: 这回他们可要动～了。This time they will be serious about it. /纠正不正之风，就要～。We must take action to correct malpractices in real earnest.

动支 dòngzhī pay out; expend; draw on: ～公款 expend public money (*or* funds)

动植物 dòng-zhíwù animals and plants: ～检疫 quarantine of animals and plants

动转 dòngzhuǎn move; turn; move about: 只要能～一天，就要干一天的活。I shall keep on working as long as I can move about.

动嘴 dòngzuǐ wag one's tongue; speak; talk: 光～，不动手 pay lip-service only /光坐在旁边～不行，要干点活儿。Don't sit on the sidelines babbling. Get down to some serious work.

动作 dòngzuò ❶ movement; motion; action: ～敏捷 quick in motion (*or* movement) /优美的体操～ graceful gymnastic movements /在双边关系中搞小～ make petty moves in the bilateral relations /他的滑稽～引得观众哄堂大笑。His funny performance set the spectators roaring with laughter. ❷ act; move; use: 弹钢琴要十个手指都～。You have to employ (*or* use) all your fingers in playing the piano. /分析一下他下一步如何～。Let's examine what his next move may be.

冻(凍) dòng

❶ freeze: 不～港 ice-free port /盆里的水～了。The water in the basin has frozen. /这些土豆～坏了。These potatoes were damaged by frost. /把肉～上。Put the meat in the freezer. ❷ jelly: 肉～儿 jellied meat /果子～儿 fruit jelly ❸ feel very cold; freeze; be frost-bitten: ～手～脚 freezing (*or* ice) cold /防～ keep from frost /小心别～着。Take care so you won't catch cold. /她手脚都～了。Both her hands and feet were frost-bitten.

冻冰 dòngbīng freeze: 湖面～了。The lake is frozen on the surface. /马路上～了。There was ice on the road.

冻藏 dòngcáng keep in the freezer; keep in cold storage: ～间 freezer

冻疮 dòngchuāng frostbite; chilblain: 生～ have chilblains

冻豆腐 dòngdòufu frozen beancurd

冻害 dònghài 〈农业〉frost; freeze injury

冻僵 dòngjiāng frozen stiff; numb with cold: 我简直快～了。I'm freezing. /我手～了。My hands are numb with cold.

冻结 dòngjié ❶ freeze; congeal: 水～成冰。Water has frozen into ice. ❷ (of wages, prices, etc.) freeze: ～存款 freeze an account or deposit /～的资产 frozen assets /工资～ wage freeze /资金～ freeze of funds /人员～ personnel freeze /核～ nuclear freeze ❸ suspend: ～协议 suspend an agreement /～双方关系 suspend bilateral relations

冻结编制 dòngjié biānzhì freeze the number of posts and staff of a department

冻结核 dòngjiéhé 〈气象〉freezing nucleus

冻结账户 dòngjié zhànghù escrow account

冻凌 dònglíng 〈方言〉ice

冻馁 dòngněi cold and hunger: 百姓有～之忧。The common people suffered from cold and hunger.

冻凝 dòngníng congeal: ～点 congealing point

冻肉 dòngròu frozen meat

冻伤 dòngshāng frostbite: 他的手上有～。His hands are frostbitten.

冻死 dòngsǐ freeze to death; freeze and perish; die of cold

冻土 dòngtǔ frozen earth, ground, or soil: ～学 cryopedology /～带 area of frozen soil

冻雨 dòngyǔ 〈气象〉sleet

冻原 dòngyuán *also* "苔原" táiyuán tundra

冻瘃 dòngzhú 〈方言〉frostbite; chilblain

栋(棟) dòng

❶〈书面〉ridgepole: 雕梁画～ (of buildings) with rich interior decorations ❷〈量词〉*used of housing*: 一～楼房 a building

栋号 dònghào 〈建筑〉serial number (of a building)

栋梁 dòngliáng ridgepole and beam; pillar: 社会～ pillar of the society; salt of the earth

栋宇 dòngyǔ 〈书面〉building; mansion

胨(腖) dòng

(short for 蛋白胨)〈生化〉peptone

洞 dòng

❶ hole; cavity: 窑～ (mountain) cave /地～ dugout; tunnel /无底～ bottomless pit /漏～ loophole /城门～儿 archway of a city gate/桥～ bridge opening /小～不补，大～吃苦。A stitch in time saves nine. ❷〈书面〉penetrate; pierce: 弹～其腹。A bullet pierced his belly. ❸ *used in speaking to stand for the number* "0": 1503 yāo wǔ dòng sān ❹ penetratingly; thoroughly

洞察 dòngchá see clearly; have an insight into: ～是非 see clearly the rights and wrongs of a case; distinguish unequivocally between right and wrong /～一切 see everything clearly; take in all with one's observant eyes; be omniscient /～秋毫 have eyes sharp enough to perceive an animal's autumn hair — be perceptive of the minutest detail; have discerning eyes /～下情 be well-acquainted with the situation at the grass-roots level

洞察力 dòngchálì insight; discernment; acumen

洞彻 dòngchè understand thoroughly; see clearly: ～事理 be sensible and wise

洞穿 dòngchuān ❶ pierce (through); penetrate (through): 子弹～他胸部。The bullet pierced (through) his chest. ❷ have a thorough understanding; see clearly: ～万恶的根源 see clearly the root of all evils

洞达 dòngdá understand thoroughly: ～人情世故 understand the ways of the world thoroughly; be world-wise /他思虑～。He is a man of keen insight.

洞房 dòngfáng bridal or nuptial chamber: 闹～ (of guests, etc.) celebrate a wedding by making noisy fun of the couple in the bridal chamber

洞房花烛 dòngfáng-huāzhú wedding festivities; wedding: ～夜，金榜挂名时 your nuptial chamber is softened in candle light and your name is on the list of the successful candidates — happiest moments in life

洞府 dòngfǔ (in Chinese mythology) mountain retreat where the immortals live: 神仙～ immortals' cave dwellings

洞贯 dòngguàn ❶ pierce (through); penetrate (through): ～坚甲 pierce (through) heavy armour ❷ have a thorough understanding of; be proficient in: 方书医理，无不～ be versed in the theory and practice of traditional medicine

洞黑 dònghēi dark; dim; gloomy: ～的峡谷 gloomy canyon

洞见 dòngjiàn see clearly: ～症结 see clearly where the disease is — have a clear understanding of what is wrong; understand clearly the crux of the matter

洞见肺腑 dòngjiàn-fèifǔ wear one's heart on one's sleeve; be open and honest

洞鉴 dòngjiàn 〈书面〉see clearly; have an insight into; have a thorough understanding of: ～积弊 know the age-old malpractices inside out /～衷曲 fully understand how sb. feels in the inmost recesses of his heart

洞究 dòngjiū 〈书面〉make a thorough study: ～历法 make a thorough study of the calendrical principles

洞开 dòngkāi wide open: 门户～。The door is wide open.

洞窟 dòngkū cave; cavern: 幽深的～ deep dark cave

洞库 dòngkù man-made cave used as a warehouse: 弹药～ man-made cave for storing ammunition

洞里萨湖 Dònglǐsàhú Tonle Sap, lake in central Cambodia linked to the Mekong River by the Tonle Sap River

洞明 dòngmíng see clearly; see through: ～世故 be worldly-wise

洞启 dòngqǐ *see* "洞开"

洞然 dòngrán 〈书面〉❶ thorough; clear: 事之本末，～可知。The whole story is well known to all. *or* You can grasp the whole story from beginning to end. ❷ bright: 阳光射入，殿中～。The hall of the temple is bright with sunshine. ❸ empty; hollow: ～无物 empty all around ❹ sound of water: 投以小石，～有声。Throw a pebble in and you'll hear the sound of water.

洞若观火 dòngruòguānhuǒ see sth. as clearly as a blazing fire: 他对当前局势～。He has a complete understanding of the current situa-

tion.

洞识 dòngshí know clearly; have a clear knowledge of:～其奸 see through sb.'s plot or trick

洞视 dòngshì see clearly; have a good view of

洞室 dòngshì cave-room; grotto

洞天 dòngtiān ❶〈道教〉dwelling of immortals ❷ place of unique beauty; scenery of exceptional charm:别有～。It's an enchanting place of unique beauty.

洞天福地 dòngtiān-fúdì ❶〈道教〉dwelling of immortals ❷ (in reference to scenic mountain or other resort) blessed spot; fairyland; scenery of exceptional charm

洞庭湖 Dòngtínghú Dongting Lake, second largest freshwater lake of China in the north of Hunan Province

洞悉 dòngxī know clearly; understand thoroughly:～内情 know the inside story; be in the know /作家要～生活。Writers should know life at first hand.

洞箫 dòngxiāo vertical bamboo flute; Chinese flageolet

洞晓 dòngxiǎo have a clear knowledge of:～其中利弊 have a clear understanding of both the advantages and the disadvantages involved /琴棋书画,无不～ be conversant with musical instruments, chess, calligraphy and painting; be versatile

洞熊 dòngxióng cave bear

洞穴 dòngxué cave; cavern:～鱼 cave fish /～墓 catacomb /～学 speleology

洞眼 dòngyǎn small hole:口袋上有个小～。The pocket has a small hole in it.

洞幽烛微 dòngyōu-zhúwēi have a penetrating insight into matters

洞烛 dòngzhú see through; see clearly:～敌人的阴谋 see through the enemy's plot

洞烛其奸 dòngzhú-qíjiān see through sb.'s treachery, tricks, or schemes

洞子 dòngzi ❶〈方言〉greenhouse:花儿～ greenhouse for flowers ❷ cave

洞子货 dòngzihuò 〈方言〉greenhouse products — flowers or vegetables grown in a greenhouse

恫

dòng 〈书面〉fear; fright; terror

see also tōng

恫吓 dònghè threaten; intimidate:武力～ threaten with force /虚声～ bluff; bluster /～是无济于事的。It is useless trying to intimidate anybody.

垌

dòng 〈方言〉(usu. used in names of places) field:儒～ Rudong (in Guangdong Province)

垌田 dòngtián 〈方言〉level fields along a river

硐

dòng cave; pit; cavern

硐子 dòngzi cave; cavern; pit

峒

dòng (mostly used in names of places) cave; cavern:五里～ Five Li Cave

see also tóng

峒室 dòngshì chamber in a mine or pit (for storing tools, equipment, etc.)

侗

Dòng Dong or Tung nationality

see also tóng

侗族 Dòngzú Dong or Tung nationality, distributed over Guizhou, Hunan, and Guangxi

胴

dòng ❶ trunk; body ❷〈书面〉large intestine

胴体 dòngtǐ ❶ trunk (of a slaughtered animal); carcass ❷ (human) body

dōu

都

dōu 〈副词〉❶ all; both; every:我们大家～认为他是合格的技术员。We are all agreed that he is a qualified technician. /夫妻俩～病了。Both husband and wife were taken ill. /每道题孩子～答对了。The child answered every one of the questions correctly. /无论干什么工作,他～非常认真。He is very conscientious in whatever he does. /怎么办～可以。Do as you please. /横竖～一样。It's as broad as it is long. *or* It makes no difference one way or the other. ❷ *used together with* 是 *to indicate cause*:～是你一句话把他惹翻了。He was provoked just by one remark of yours. /～是这场暴雨,害得我们耽误了一天工。It was all because of the storm that we had to stop work for one day. ❸ even:他悄悄地走了,一声～不吭。He left quietly, without a word. /连他老婆～不知道是怎么回事。Nobody, not even his wife, knew anything about it. /连个人影儿～看不见。Not (even) a soul was in sight. ❹ already:～十二点了,还不睡觉! Why don't you go to bed? It's already twelve o'clock.

see also dū

兜[1]

dōu ❶ pocket; bag:裤～儿 trouser pocket /网～儿 string bag ❷ wrap up or hold as if in a bag:用手巾～着 wrap sth. up in a towel /小姑娘的衣襟里～着几个苹果。The little girl held some apples in the front of her dress. ❸ move round; go in a circle; make a detour:晚饭后我们乘车在市区～了一圈。We went round the city after supper. /许多感想～上心头。A multitude of feelings welled up in my heart. ❹ canvass; solicit:～生意 canvass business; solicit customers ❺ take upon oneself; assume responsibility for:一切后果我～着。I am answerable for all the consequences. ❻ disclose all the details of the matter:他把内情全～出去了。He has brought to light the whole inside story. ❼ confronting; facing: *see* "～头" ❽ *see* "篼" dōu

兜[2]

dōu *see* "蔸" dōu

兜捕 dōubǔ surround and seize; encircle and catch; round up:～流氓 round up street ruffians /警察四面～,很快就把逃犯逮住了。The police started a search all over the place and captured the escaped convict in no time.

兜抄 dōuchāo close in from the rear and flanks; encircle and attack; round up:～残敌 round up remnant enemy troops

兜搭 dōuda ❶ engage in small talk; chat; chitchat:他们一边喝茶,一边～着。They sat chatting over a cup of tea. ❷ pay attention to; show interest in:他见没人～他,就讪讪地走了。Seeing that nobody paid him any attention, he walked away looking embarrassed. ❸ seduce; lure; entice ❹〈方言〉gang up with:他们又～上了。They have ganged up again. ❺ (usu. used in the early vernacular) complication; implicity; trouble:倘有些～,恐不方便。We'll find ourselves in a predicament in case there is some trouble. *or* It will be a nuisance if anything untoward should happen.

兜挡 dōudǎng 〈方言〉shoulder responsibility for; cope with; deal with:万一有个啥,我可～不了呀! I'm afraid the responsibility would be too great for me in case anything should go wrong.

兜的 dōude suddenly:他刚一出门,～想起一件事来。Scarcely had he left home when he suddenly remembered something.

兜底 dōudǐ disclose all the details (of sth. disreputable or sb.'s disreputable past); reveal sth. disreputable for what it is; show up sb. for the wretch he is:兜一个人的老底 drag up the seamy side of sb.'s life; disclose the whole inside story of sb.'s past /他进行诈骗的事儿全给人兜了底。His swindle was thoroughly exposed.

兜兜 dōudou *see* "兜肚"

兜兜裤儿 dōudoukùr sunsuit (for a child)

兜兜嘴儿 dōudouzuǐr *see* "兜肚"

兜肚 dōudu *also* "兜兜"; "兜兜嘴儿" diamond-shaped cloth worn (usu. by a child) over the chest and abdomen and attached by a loop round the neck and strings fastened behind the back; bib

兜翻 dōufan 〈方言〉❶ turn over (things one holds precious); rummage through (old things):天天～他那几箱破书。He is rummaging through the few boxes of musty old books of his every day. ❷ bring up again; rake up:过去的那些事别～了。Don't rake up past things. *or* Let bygones be bygones. ❸ expose; lay bare; reveal; show up:他说要当众把那桩丑事～出来。He threatened to make the scandal public.

兜风 dōufēng ❶ catch the wind; shield against the wind:破帆兜不住风。Broken sails won't catch the wind. ❷ go for a (joy) ride or sail; go for a spin:咱们乘车去兜兜风。Let's go for a ride (*or* spin).

兜剿 dōujiǎo surround and put down; encircle and suppress:～残匪 surround the remnants of the bandits and wipe them out

兜揽 dōulǎn ❶ canvass; solicit; tout:～生意 tout for business ❷ take upon oneself (sb. else's work); take up the cudgels for others;

这些麻烦事都是他～来的。These troubles are all of his own making.

兜脸 dōuliǎn right in the face：一根大棒～打来。A huge club was swung at his face.

兜拢 dōulǒng become reconciled：谈了好几次，好容易～了，两个人和好如初。They have finally made it up after several contacts and now they are on good terms again.

兜鍪 dōumóu helmet (worn in ancient battles)

兜圈子 dōu quānzi ❶ go round in circles；circle：飞机降落前围着机场～。The airplane circled over the airport before it landed. ❷ beat about the bush：你直说吧，没有时间～。Speak straight to the point；there is no time for beating about the bush.

兜售 dōushòu peddle；hawk：～假冒伪劣商品 peddle fake or shoddy goods／各国对他极力～的方案反应冷淡。Many countries responded coldly to the plan he was hawking round.

兜水母 dōushuǐmǔ 〈动物〉lobed comb jelly

兜头 dōutóu head-on；straight on the head：～一棒 head-on blow／～泼了一桶冷水 pour a pail of cold water over sb.'s head — cool sb.'s passion or dampen sb.'s enthusiasm

兜头盖脸 dōutóu-gàiliǎn *also* "兜头盖脑" straight on the head；right in the face：他拿起擀面杖，对孩子～一顿打。He seized a rolling pin and beat the child up.

兜网球 dōuwǎngqiú 〈体育〉lacrosse

兜销 dōuxiāo peddle；hawk

兜子 dōuzi ❶ pocket；bag：衣～ coat pocket ❷ *see* "篼子" dōuzi

兜嘴 dōuzuǐ 〈方言〉❶ bib ❷ muzzle

蔸(橷)

dōu 〈方言〉❶ root and lower stem of some plants：禾～ roots of rice ❷〈量词〉piece；clump：一～白菜 a head of Chinese cabbage／两～禾 two clumps of paddy

蔸距 dōujù 〈方言〉spacing between clumps

蔸子 dōuzi 〈方言〉root and lower stem of certain plants

篼

dōu bamboo, cane, or wicker basket：背～ basket carried on the back

篼子 dōuzi *also* "兜子" dōuzi bamboo chair tied to two bamboo poles serving as a sedan chair；bamboo sedan chair

dǒu

斗

dǒu ❶ *dou*, unit of dry measure for grain (now about a decalitre) ❷ *dou* measure, square or drum-like, made of wood or bamboo ❸ sth. shaped like a *dou* measure；object shaped like a cup or a dipper：漏～ funnel／风～ vent／车～ sidecar (body)；tipping body／烟～ pipe／拖～ trailer ❹ whorl (of a fingerprint) ❺ ancient wine vessel ❻ (usu. called 南斗) eighth of the 28 constellations into which the celestial space was divided in ancient Chinese astronomy ❼ (short for 北斗星) Big Dipper ❽ *see* "陡" dǒu

see also dòu

斗笔 dǒubǐ giant writing brush with a container for its head shaped like a *dou* measure

斗柄 dǒubǐng handle of the Dipper

斗车 dǒuchē (in a mine or at a construction site) trolley；tram；tub：翻～ end-tipper；end-tip lorry；end-dump truck；rear-dump truck

斗胆 dǒudǎn 〈谦词〉make bold；venture：恕我～进言。I venture to offer a suggestion.

斗店 dǒudiàn 〈旧语〉grain shop

斗方 dǒufāng ❶ square paper for writing and drawing ❷ calligraphy or painting done on a square sheet of paper one or two *chi* in diameter

斗方名士 dǒufāng-míngshì literary hack who regards himself as a man of highbrow tastes

斗拱 dǒugǒng *also* "枓拱" dǒugǒng；"枓栱" dǒugǒng 〈建筑〉system of tiers of brackets inserted between the top of a pillar and a crossbeam (each bracket being formed of a bow-shaped arc, called *gong*, and cushioned with a block of wood, called *dou*)

斗行 dǒuháng 〈旧语〉wholesale grain shop

斗箕 dǒuji *also* "斗记" fingerprint

斗筐 dǒukuāng a kind of bamboo basket, about one metre in diameter, with a handle on either end

斗笠 dǒulì wide-rimmed bamboo hat

斗轮 dǒulún 〈机械〉bucket wheel；scoop wheel：～挖掘机 scoop wheel excavator；bucket wheel excavator

斗门 dǒumén 〈农业〉sluice valve；sluice gate

斗篷 dǒupeng ❶ sleeveless cloak；cape ❷〈方言〉bamboo hat

斗篷草 dǒupengcǎo 〈植物〉lady's mantle (*Alchemilla*)

斗渠 dǒuqú 〈水利〉lateral canal

斗筲 dǒushāo 〈书面〉narrow-mindedness；poor ability；shallow understanding：～之人 narrow-minded person／～之辈 petty-minded people；minnows／～之材 man of shallow understanding；indifferent scholar

斗式水泵 dǒushì shuǐbèng 〈机械〉bucket-pump

斗式提升机 dǒushì tíshēngjī 〈机械〉bucket elevator

斗式挖泥机 dǒushì wāníjī 〈机械〉scoop dredger

斗式挖土机 dǒushì wātǔjī 〈机械〉bucket excavator

斗室 dǒushì 〈书面〉tiny room：身居～，心怀天下。A scholar has the whole world in mind, though he may live in a tiny room.

斗烟丝 dǒuyānsī pipe tobacco

斗转参横 dǒuzhuǎn-shēnhéng the Dipper handle turns and the Constellation Orion lies horizontal；day breaks

斗转星移 dǒuzhuǎn-xīngyí turning of the Dipper and rotating of the stars — change of season；passage of time：～又一秋。Another year passed by.

斗子 dǒuzi ❶ coal bucket ❷ bucket：料～〈建筑〉mortar bucket；mortar trough

枓

dǒu

枓拱 dǒugǒng *also* "枓栱" *see* "斗拱" dǒugǒng

抖

dǒu ❶ tremble；shiver；quiver：浑身直～ tremble all over／气得发～ quiver with rage ❷ shake；jerk；flick：～掉衣服上的土 shake the dirt off one's clothes／～缰绳 jerk the reins／～开床单 flick open a sheet；spread the sheet with a flick／～空竹 play with a diabolo／把这条毯子好好～一～。Give the blanket a good shake. ❸ disclose the inside story；expose：这些事弄不好咱们就～出来。We will disclose the whole story if something unexpected happens. ❹ rouse；muster up；stir up：～起精神 pluck up one's spirits；cheer up ❺〈讽刺〉throw one's weight about；preen oneself：张小三～起来了。Zhang Xiaosan is having his day.

抖颤 dǒuchàn shake；tremble；shiver：浑身～ be trembling all over

抖袋机 dǒudàijī bag cleaner

抖动 dǒudòng ❶ shake；tremble；quiver：他激动得嘴唇都在～。His lips trembled with excitement. ❷ shake；jerk；flick：她把布料～了一下，问我喜欢不喜欢。She flicked the material and asked if I liked it.

抖动式滑槽 dǒudòngshì huácáo vibrating chute

抖翻 dǒufān turn inside out；disclose the whole inside story：你那老底儿都叫人家～出来了。They have dragged the skeleton out of your cupboard.

抖劲 dǒujìn 〈贬义〉be immensely proud；feel proud：他穿上礼服，觉得挺～。Putting on his formal dress, he was proud as a peacock.

抖搂 dǒulou 〈方言〉❶ shake off；shake out of sth.：把帽子上的雪～干净 shake the snow off one's hat／把上衣好好～～。Give the jacket a good shake. ❷ shake out (a container, etc.)；make a clean breast of (a secret)；expose；bring to light：～箱子底儿 shake out a suitcase／他们干的那些事全被～出来了。Everything they did has been brought to light. ❸ waste；squander：别把钱～光了！Don't spend every penny you have.

抖露 dǒulou *see* "抖搂 ❶❷"

抖落 dǒuluo *see* "抖搂"

抖瑟 dǒuse tremble；shiver；quiver

抖神 dǒushén 〈方言〉take or steal the limelight；be the focus of public attention；strut about self-importantly：这一下咱们可～了，得了一等奖。We are in the limelight now that we have won first prize.／买辆摩托车有什么了不起，抖的什么神！What if you've bought a motorbike? You needn't strut about for that!

抖手 dǒushǒu swing one's hand：他怒气冲冲，一～就走了。With a swing of his hand, he hurried away indignantly.

抖擞 dǒusǒu enliven；rouse；invigorate：精神～ full of energy；full of beans／我劝天公重～，不拘一格降人才。O Heaven! Bestir yourself, I beseech you, And send down men of all the talents.

抖擞精神 dǒusǒu jīngshen brace or cheer up；pull oneself together；pep oneself up；summon up one's spirits：他抖擞着精神，堆起满脸

的笑容。He bolstered his sagging spirit, with a broad smile plastered on his face.

抖索 dǒusuo shiver; tremble; quiver：她冻得浑身直～。She was shivering all over with cold. /他～着嘴唇,激动得一句话也说不出。He was too excited to say a word, his lips quivering with emotion.

抖威风 dǒu wēifēng throw one's weight around; swagger about：在大庭广众中～是非常可笑的。It is ridiculous to swagger about in public.

抖战 dǒuzhàn shake; tremble; shiver：两手不住地～ with hands shaking continuously

蚪 dǒu see“蝌蚪”kēdǒu

陡 dǒu ❶ steep; precipitous：这个山坡太～。The mountain slope is very steep. ❷ suddenly; abruptly：see“～变”

陡隘 dǒu'ài precipitous and narrow：～的山路 steep and narrow mountain path

陡壁 dǒubì cliff; precipice：～悬崖 precipices and cliffs; sheer precipices and overhanging rocks

陡变 dǒubiàn change suddenly or abruptly：天气～。There was a sudden change in the weather. *or* The weather changed suddenly. /他面色～。His countenance changed abruptly.

陡地 dǒudì *also*“陡的”suddenly; abruptly：精神～振作起来 brace up at once; feel instantly invigorated /他～打了个寒噤。Suddenly a chill shot through him (*or* ran down his spine).

陡度 dǒudù 〈物理〉gradient; grade：压力～ pressure gradient

陡绝 dǒujué precipitous; dangerously steep：山势～。The mountain is dangerously steep.

陡峻 dǒujùn precipitous and perilous：～的山崖 sheer cliff

陡棱棱 dǒulēnglēng very steep：～的山坡 very steep mountain slope

陡立 dǒulì rise steeply：险峰～。Perilous peaks rise steeply.

陡坡 dǒupō steep slope or declivity

陡起 dǒuqǐ occur suddenly; spring up abruptly：～恶意。An evil idea occurs to one suddenly. /他怒火～。He exploded into a rage.

陡峭 dǒuqiào precipitous; sheer：山峰～ precipitous mountain peak /～的深谷 sheer ravine

陡然 dǒurán suddenly; unexpectedly; abruptly：脸色～苍白 suddenly turn pale /～响起一阵鞭炮。All of a sudden there came a burst of firecrackers. /山势～下降。The mountain terrain descends abruptly.

陡险 dǒuxiǎn dangerously precipitous：山峰异常～。The mountain peak is extremely precipitous.

陡斜 dǒuxié sloping precipitously; steep

陡削 dǒuxuē perpendicular from top to bottom as if cut by a sword：～的山崖 perpendicular or sheer cliff

陡崖 dǒuyá precipitous cliff：～峭壁 precipice

陡直 dǒuzhí very steep; precipitous; sheer

dòu

斗(鬥、鬭、鬬) dòu ❶ fight; tussle：群～ communal fighting; gang fighting /拳～ fist fight; fisticuffs ❷ struggle against; denounce; fight：战天～地 fight against nature; brave the elements ❸ make animals fight (as a game)：～蛐蛐儿 cricket fight; cricket duel ❹ compete with; contend with; contest：～智～勇 contest of wits and courage /狐狸再狡猾也～不过好猎手。No matter how crafty the fox is, it cannot outwit a seasoned hunter. ❺ come together; fit together; put together：那条桌子腿还没有～榫。The leg tenons of the table haven't been fitted into their mortises. /大家把意见～一～。Let's put our heads together to size up the situation. /把我们收集的情报～起来,看情况究竟如何。Let's piece together the information we have gathered and see how matters stand.
see also dǒu

斗法 dòufǎ ❶ fight (each other) with magic powers; contest in magic arts ❷ contend by artifice or trickery; carry on a covert struggle by underhand means：为了争夺议会席位,各党派正在那里～。The political parties are covertly fighting for seats in parliament.

斗份子 dòu fènzi 〈方言〉club together to present a gift to sb. or for some joint undertaking

斗富 dòufù compete or contest in wealth

斗拱 dòugǒng see“斗栱”dǒugǒng

斗鸡 dòujī ❶ gamecock ❷ cockfight ❸ game in which all players hop round on one leg and each tries to strike the other with the (other) leg held in both hands

斗鸡脚 dòujījiǎo see“斗脚”

斗鸡眼 dòujīyǎn cross-eye：长着～的男人 cross-eyed man

斗鸡走狗 dòujī-zǒugǒu *also*“斗鸡走马”go in for cockfighting and dog-racing; idle about and keep away from honest work

斗架 dòujià 〈方言〉fight; scuffle; come to blows

斗脚 dòujiǎo *also*“斗鸡脚”splay feet with heels turning outwards

斗劲 dòujìn have a contest of strength; match strength (with or against sb.)

斗经纪 dòu jīngji 〈方言〉provoke：他既然认输了,你何必跟他再～。Now that he has conceded defeat, why provoke him further?

斗口 dòukǒu quarrel; bicker：老头看他们～,便连忙走过来排解。The old man hastened to intervene when he saw them start quarrelling.

斗口齿 dòu kǒuchǐ 〈方言〉see“斗嘴”

斗闷子 dòu mènzi *also*“逗闷子”dòu mènzi 〈方言〉make or crack a joke; kid：就他爱～。He loves to crack a joke from time to time. *or* He is such a joker.

斗牛 dòuniú bullfighting; bullfight

斗牛场 dòuniúchǎng bullring

斗牛狗 dòuniúgǒu bulldog

斗牛士 dòuniúshì matador; bullfighter：～导弹〈军事〉matador

斗弄 dòunong tease：人家都快哭了,你还去～她。Why do you tease her? She's almost in tears.

斗殴 dòu'ōu fight with fists; have a fisticuff：相互～ locked in a fist fight /寻衅～ pick a quarrel and start a fist fight

斗牌 dòupái have a game of mah-jong, cards or dominoes

斗批改 dòu-pī-gǎi struggle-criticism-transformation (slogan of the Cultural Revolution, 1966-1976)

斗气 dòuqì take things personally and nurse a grudge (against sb.); act perversely out of resentment or anger：两个老头下棋斗起气来了。The two old men started quarrelling over a game of chess. /两口子～就不管孩子了,这可让别人笑话。You'll only make a joke of yourselves if you two neglect the child just because you're angry with each other.

斗巧 dòuqiǎo ❶ by coincidence; as luck would have it：你来的不～,他刚出门。What bad luck! He has just gone out. ❷ contend in ingenuity：争奇～ contend (*or* vie) with each other in ingenuity

斗趣儿 dòuqùr *also*“逗趣儿”dòuqùr set people laughing (by telling jokes or acting facetiously)

斗拳狗 dòuquángǒu 〈动物〉boxer

斗杀 dòushā kill in a brawl

斗伤 dòushāng wound in an affray

斗士 dòushì fighter (for a cause); champion; proponent：反封建的～ champion against feudalism

斗私批修 dòusī-pīxiū fight selfishness, repudiate revisionism (slogan of the Cultural Revolution, 1966-1976)

斗心眼儿 dòu xīnyǎnr contend in petty scheming; try to outwit (usu. over trifling matters)：你们怎么彼此斗起心眼儿来了? How come you are trying to outwit each other? /～我斗不过他。I'm no match for him in petty scheming.

斗妍 dòuyán see“斗艳”

斗眼 dòuyǎn *also*“斗鸡眼”cross-eye

斗艳 dòuyàn contend in beauty; vie in splendour; compete in gorgeousness or magnificence：群芳～。The flowers vie with each other for beauty.

斗阵 dòuzhèn 〈方言〉quarrel; wrangle; have a row

斗争 dòuzhēng ❶ struggle; fight; combat：～性 fighting spirit; militancy /阶级～ class struggle /思想～ ideological struggle /内心～ mental struggle; soul-searching /与落后的现象～ struggle against (*or* combat) backward trends /新与旧的～ conflict between the new and the old /有史以来,人类就同自然不断地～。Since the beginning of recorded history, mankind has battled incessantly against nature. ❷ expose; denounce; accuse：～贪污犯 denounce embezzlers ❸ strive; fight; work energetically：为真理而～ fight for truth /他为祖国解放事业～了一生。He dedicated his whole life to the liberation of his country.

斗争会 dòuzhēnghuì public accusation or denunciation meeting

斗志 dòuzhì will to fight; fighting will; morale：～昂扬 have high

D

morale; be militant / 丧失~ have no will to fight; be demoralized / 鼓舞人民的~ inspire the people's will to fight; boost the fighting spirit of the people / ~不减当年 one's militant fervour has not diminished with the years; be as militant as ever before

斗智 dòuzhì have a battle or duel of wits; pit one's intelligence against sb.'s: 解决争端要靠~。We should rely on reasoning to settle (*or* resolve) a dispute. / 和敌人既要斗勇,也要~。We will contend with the adversary not merely in strength but in resourcefulness as well.

斗嘴 dòuzuǐ ❶ quarrel; have an angry exchange: ~呕气 fall out with sb. and get heated about it / 你们俩天天~,岂不叫人笑话。People will laugh at you if you two bicker with each other all the time. ❷ exchange banter; joke with each other; make fun of each other: 取笑~ pull each other's leg; poke fun at and play practical jokes on each other

窦(竇)

dòu ❶ hole; opening; aperture: 狗~ dog hole / 疑~ suspicious point ❷〈生理〉sinus; antrum: 鼻~ paranasal / 鼻旁~ paranasal sinus / 额~ frontal sinus / 横~ lateral sinus ❸ (Dòu) a surname

窦传刺术 dòuchuáncìshù 〈医学〉sinusopuncture

窦娥冤 Dòu'é Yuān *also* "六月雪" Liùyuèxuě *Snow in Midsummer*, play by Guan Hanqing (关汉卿) of the Yuan Dynasty

窦房 dòufáng 〈生理〉antrum

窦房结 dòufángjié 〈生理〉❶ sinoatrial node ❷ sinus

窦建德 Dòu Jiàndé Dou Jiande (formerly translated as Tou Chienteh, 573-621), leader of a peasant uprising which contributed to the downfall of the Sui Dynasty in 618

窦切除术 dòuqiēchúshù 〈医学〉antrectomy

窦性心动过速 dòuxìng xīndòng guòsù 〈医学〉nodal tachycardia

窦性心率失常 dòuxìng xīnlǜ shīcháng 〈医学〉sinus arrhythmia

窦炎 dòuyán 〈医学〉sinusitis

读(讀)

dòu short pause in reading a Chinese sentence

see also dú

豆[1]

dòu ❶ ancient stemmed cup or bowl: 一~之羹 a cup of soup — very little food or a light meal ❷ (Dòu) a surname

豆[2](❶荳)

dòu ❶ legumes; pulses; beans; peas: 黄~ soya beans; soybeans / 蚕~ broad beans / 豌~ peas / 扁~ hyacinth beans ❷ sth. like a bean; bean-like thing: 花生~儿 peanut / 土~儿 potato / 玉米~儿 kernel of corn; grain of corn

豆瓣 dòubàn ❶ two segments of a bean or pea ❷ cotyledon of a bean or pea

豆瓣儿酱 dòubànrjiàng thick broad-bean sauce

豆包 dòubāo steamed bun with sweetened bean paste filling

豆饼 dòubǐng soya-bean cake; bean cake

豆䜴儿 dòuchǎir 〈方言〉*also* "豆䜴子" crushed beans: ~粥 crushed bean porridge

豆豉 dòuchǐ fermented soya beans, salted or otherwise

豆腐 dòufu tofu; bean curd: ~房 bean-curd mill

豆腐饭 dòufufàn 〈方言〉dinner (usu. vegetarian) for friends and relatives attending a funeral

豆腐干 dòufugān dried bean curd

豆腐老虎 dòufu-lǎohǔ bean curd tiger — outwardly fierce but inwardly weak

豆腐脑儿 dòufunǎor jellied bean curd

豆腐皮 dòufupí ❶ skin of soya-bean milk ❷〈方言〉thin sheet of dried bean curd

豆腐乳 dòufurǔ *also* "腐乳" fǔrǔ; "酱豆腐" jiàngdòufu fermented bean curd

豆腐衣 dòufuyī 〈方言〉*see* "豆腐皮 ❶"

豆腐渣 dòufuzhā *also* "豆渣" residue from beans after making soya-bean milk; bean dregs: "~"工程 construction project with building materials like bean dregs; project built with skimped materials

豆花儿 dòuhuār 〈方言〉condensed bean curd jelly

豆荚 dòujiá pod

豆浆 dòujiāng *also* "豆腐浆"; "豆乳" soya-bean milk

豆角儿 dòujiǎor fresh beans in pod

豆秸 dòujiē beanstalk after threshing

豆科 dòukē 〈植物〉pulse family; bean or pea family: ~植物 legume; leguminous plant

豆棵 dòukē bean plant

豆蔻 dòukòu *also* "草果" cǎoguǒ; "草豆蔻" cǎodòukòu 〈植物〉round cardamom (*Amomum cadarmomum*): 肉~ nutmeg

豆蔻年华 dòukòu-niánhuá (of a girl) thirteen or fourteen years of age; early teens; adolescence: ~的少女 girl in her early teens

豆蔻山脉 Dòukòu Shānmài (Cambodia) Kravanh Mountains

豆绿 dòulǜ *also* "豆青" pea green

豆面 dòumiàn bean flour; beanmeal

豆娘 dòuniáng 〈动物〉damselfly

豆皮 dòupí 〈方言〉❶ dried sheets of bean curd ❷ a kind of fried pancake made of glutinous rice, minced meat, cubes of bamboo shoots, etc., wrapped in sheets of rice and mung bean flour mixed with eggs

豆剖瓜分 dòupōu-guāfēn *also* "瓜剖豆分" divide up (just as one separates pea-pods or cuts melons into slices)

豆萁 dòuqí 〈方言〉beanstalk

豆青 dòuqīng *see* "豆绿"

豆蓉 dòuróng ❶ fine bean mash, used as stuffing in cakes: ~月饼 moon cake with mashed bean filling ❷〈方言〉pigeonpea; *Cajanus cajan*

豆乳 dòurǔ ❶ soya-bean milk ❷〈方言〉fermented bean curd

豆沙 dòushā sweetened bean paste: ~月饼 moon cake with sweetened bean paste filling

豆石 dòushí 〈地质〉pisolite

豆薯 dòushǔ *also* "凉薯" liángshǔ; "地瓜" dìguā jicama; yam bean

豆象 dòuxiàng 〈动物〉seed beetle; bean weevil

豆蟹 dòuxiè 〈动物〉pea crab

豆芽儿 dòuyár *also* "豆芽菜" bean sprouts

豆雁 dòuyàn 〈动物〉bean goose

豆油 dòuyóu soya-bean oil

豆渣 dòuzhā *see* "豆腐渣"

豆汁 dòuzhī ❶ fermented drink made from water used in grinding green beans ❷〈方言〉soya-bean milk

豆纸 dòuzhǐ coarse toilet paper

豆制品 dòuzhìpǐn bean product

豆猪 dòuzhū pig with parasitic cysticercosis; pig suffering from cysticercosis

豆子 dòuzi ❶ legumes; pulses; beans; peas ❷ seeds of legumes, pulses, beans or peas ❸ sth. like a bean; bean-like thing: 糖~ candies / 花生~ peanuts

豆嘴儿 dòuzuǐr soaked soya beans; soya beans with sprouts (cooked as vegetable)

痘

dòu ❶ smallpox; variola ❷ vaccine (lymph): 种~ vaccinate; be vaccinated / 种~者 vaccinee ❸ smallpox pustule

痘病毒 dòubìngdú poxvirus

痘疮 dòuchuāng variola; smallpox

痘痂 dòujiā variola scab

痘浆 dòujiāng smallpox liquid containing filterable virus

痘苗 dòumiáo *also* "牛痘苗" niúdòumiáo (bovine) vaccine

痘疱 dòupào 〈医学〉pock pustule

逗[1](鬥、閗、鬭)

dòu ❶ tease; tantalize; play with: 别上当,他在~你呢! He's pulling your leg; don't be taken in. / 她拿一束花~小孩儿玩。She is tantalizing a child with a bunch of flowers. / 动物园里不准~猴子。It is forbidden to bait the monkeys in the zoo. ❷ entice; attract: 这孩子的一双大眼睛~人喜欢。The child has a pair of big lovely eyes. ❸〈方言〉amusing; funny: 爱说爱~的小伙子 lad who is fond of chatting and joking; rollicking young fellow / 他讲的那个故事真~。What a funny story he told!

逗[2]

dòu ❶ stay; stop; sojourn ❷ *also* "读" dòu short pause in reading a Chinese sentence

逗点 dòudiǎn comma (,)

逗动 dòudòng arouse; stir up: ~小孩的好奇心 arouse the curiosity of children

逗哏 dòugén 〈戏曲〉provoke laughter with funny remarks (esp.

in a comic dialogue)

逗哈哈 dòu hāha 〈方言〉make jokes; make funny remarks; provoke laughter:你这个人,真会～。You are a regular joker.

逗号 dòuhào *also* "逗点" comma (,)

逗乐儿 dòulèr 〈方言〉provoke laughter; amuse:熊猫的一举一动都非常～。The movements of the panda amused all onlookers.

逗留 dòuliú stay; stop:去年,我在故乡～了一段时间。I stayed in my hometown for some time last year. /蝴蝶在花间盘旋～。The butterflies fluttered from flower to flower. /父亲看着文稿,笑意～在嘴角边。Father wore a smile on his lips while reading the manuscript.

逗遛 dòuliú *see* "逗留"

逗闷子 dòu mènzi *also* "斗闷子" dòu mènzi 〈方言〉crack a joke; joke; make fun of:您吃饱了饭没事儿,可别拿我们～。If you have nothing else to do, it is your business, but don't crack jokes at our expense.

逗闹 dòunào have fun; play a joke:一群小青年在那儿～。A group of young lads are having fun there.

逗弄 dòunong ❶ play with; have fun by inducing sb. to do sth.:我们～狗熊作个揖。We had a lot of fun by making a bear bow to us with both forelegs folded. ❷ tease; kid; make fun of:再～下去这孩子就要哭了。If you go on teasing him the boy will start crying.

逗情 dòuqíng make amorous advances

逗趣儿 dòuqùr 〈方言〉set people laughing (by making jokes): amuse:他真会～。He is very good at cracking jokes.

逗人 dòurén arouse interest; amuse:～发笑 make people laugh; provoke laughter /～喜爱的孩子 lovable (*or* lovely) child /憨态～amusingly naive

逗笑儿 dòuxiàor 〈方言〉amusing:这人可滑稽了,说出话来老那么～。He is a regular comedian. He never opens his mouth without making funny remarks.

逗引 dòuyǐn play with; tease:～小孩儿玩 play with a child

逗嘴 dòuzuǐ joke; kid; make jokes; tell jokes:他们经常～。They often tease each other.

脰

dòu 〈书面〉neck:绝～而死 commit suicide by cutting one's own throat

饾

dòu

饾版 dòubǎn 〈旧语〉wood block printing

饾饤 dòudìng 〈书面〉❶ food for display ❷ load one's writing with fancy phrases:文中所用典故,信手拈来,不露～堆砌之痕迹。The allusions which appear in the essay are perfectly natural, leaving no trace of rhetorical flourish.

酘

dòu 〈书面〉wine or liquor from second brew

dū

阇

dū 〈书面〉platform above a city gate

see also shé

都

dū ❶ capital:建～ establish a capital ❷ big city; metropolis:钢～ steel city /通～大邑 big city; metropolis ❸ 〈旧语〉local government between the county and township levels ❹ 〈书面〉beautiful; lovely: *see* "～丽" ❺ (Dū) a surname

see also dōu

都柏林 dūbólín Dublin, capital of Ireland

都城 dūchéng capital

都督 dūdu ❶ 〈古语〉commander-in-chief ❷ (in the early years of the Republic of China) provincial military governor who was also in charge of civil administration

都凡 dūfán 〈书面〉in all; altogether:每册～四百幅图画。There are altogether 400 pictures in each book. *or* Each book contains 400 pictures in all.

都会 dūhuì city; metropolis

都江堰 Dūjiāngyàn Dujiang Weirs in Sichuan (ancient irrigation network built in 3rd century BC and in use to this day)

都丽 dūlì 〈书面〉beautiful; gorgeous; handsome:服饰～ in gorgeous dress

都灵 Dūlíng Turin or Torino, city in NW Italy and capital of unified Italy 1861-1864

都门 dūmén gate of the capital city; capital:凯旋～ return to the capital in triumph

都市 dūshì city; metropolis:～生活 city (*or* urban) life; life in a metropolis

都市化 dūshìhuà urbanization:人口的～ urbanization of population

都统 dūtǒng chief of each of the "Eight Banners"

see also "八旗" bāqí

都雅 dūyǎ 〈书面〉elegant; refined; cultured:仪貌～ elegant in manner; refined in behaviour

嘟[1]

dū 〈象声〉toot; honk:汽车喇叭～～地响。The cars tooted.

嘟[2]

dū 〈方言〉pout:她气得～着嘴。She pouted peevishly.

嘟噜 dūlu 〈口语〉❶ 〈量词〉bunch; cluster:一～钥匙 a bunch of keys /一～葡萄 a cluster (*or* bunch) of grapes ❷ hang down in a bunch; dangle; sag:他胖得下巴都～下来了。He is so fat that his chin sags. ❸ trill:打～儿 pronounce with a trill; trill

嘟囔 dūnang *also* "嘟哝" mutter to oneself; mumble:别瞎～啦! Stop that foolish mumbling. /他边走边～。He muttered to himself as he walked.

嘟念 dūniàn 〈方言〉talk to oneself; mutter to oneself:她坐在地上～着。She sat on the ground, mumbling to herself.

嘟哝 dūnong *see* "嘟囔"

嘟嚷 dūrǎng talk loudly to oneself; clamour indistinctly:你在那里～些什么呀? What on earth are you clamouring about there?

督

dū superintend and direct:监～ supervise /～工 supervisor; overseer

督办 dūbàn ❶ superintend; supervise; oversee:～粮秣 superintend the supply of army provisions ❷ superintendent; supervisor

督察 dūchá ❶ superintend; supervise ❷ superintendent; supervisor

督促 dūcù supervise and urge:～学生专心学习 urge the students to apply themselves to their studies /县长下乡检查～秋收工作。The county magistrate went down to the countryside to inspect and supervise the autumn harvest.

督导 dūdǎo 〈书面〉supervise and direct; superintend:～员 superintendent; supervisor /～司 department of supervision /敬请莅临～。Your presence and guidance is requested.

督抚 dū-fǔ governor-general and inspector-general (highest local officials during the Ming and Qing dynasties):～大员 highest provincial officials

督教 dūjiào supervise and give guidance

督军 dūjūn military governor (in the early years of the Republic of China)

督理 dūlǐ 〈书面〉superintend and handle; supervise and manage:～军务 superintend and handle military affairs; be in charge of military affairs

督励 dūlì 〈书面〉urge and encourage:～将士 urge and encourage officers and men

督迫 dūpò 〈书面〉urge in categorical terms; compel:～就道 strongly urge sb. to set out on his journey

督师 dūshī supervise military operations:亲赴前线～ go in person to the front to take charge of military operations; assume personal command of the troops at the front

督率 dūshuài *also* "督帅" command; lead:～将士 command one's officers and men /～民工抢修堤坝 lead the labourers in rush-repairing the dike

督学 dūxué inspector of schools; educational inspector

督造 dūzào superintend the manufacture of:～兵器 superintend the manufacture of ordnance

督责 dūzé 〈书面〉❶ inspect and mete out punishment to:～大臣 go on an inspection tour and punish erring ministers ❷ supervise and urge sb. to measure up to a certain standard; admonish:良友不时～,进步较快。With the frequent admonition of my close associates, I am making good progress. ❸ give instructions and see that they are carried out:～诸军克日进兵 order all troops to advance on a fixed date

督战 dūzhàn supervise military operations:亲临～ personally supervise military operations

督阵 dūzhèn supervise a battle at the front

丑(㲘) dū strike or tap slightly with a finger or a stick:～一个点儿 make a dot by tapping lightly (with one's finger or a stick) /点～ wield one's brush lightly (in traditional painting)

豖(启) dū

豖子 dūzi 〈方言〉❶ buttocks; bottom; behind; bum ❷ tail end of a bee or a scorpion

dú

毒 dú ❶ poison; toxin:蛇～ snake poison /蜂～ bee poison /病～ virus /食物中～ food poisoning ❷ anything pernicious to the mind:洗刷旧社会的污～ wash away all the corrupt and pernicious leftovers from the old society ❸ narcotics; drugs:吸～ take drugs /贩～ traffic in drugs; engage in drug-trafficking /缉～ suppress drug-trafficking ❹ poisonous; noxious; poisoned; toxic: *see* "～液"; "～箭" ❺ kill with poison; poison:～耗子药 rat poison; ratsbane /用药～老鼠 poison rats ❻ vicious; cruel; fierce:心～ heartless; cruel; full of venom /说话刻～ have a wicked tongue /太阳很～。The sun was blazing.

毒八角 dúbājiǎo *also* "莽草" mǎngcǎo 〈植物〉poisonous anis

毒扁豆 dúbiǎndòu 〈植物〉calabar bean:～碱〈药学〉physostigmine; eserine

毒草 dúcǎo poisonous weeds;〈比喻〉harmful speech or writings (from an ideological point of view):分辨香花与～ distinguish between (*or* tell apart) fragrant flowers and poisonous weeds

毒刺 dúcì poisonous sting

毒打 dúdǎ beat up; beat relentlessly:遭到～ get a vicious beating /挨了一顿～ be beaten black and blue

毒蛋白 dúdànbái 〈生物〉toxalbumin

毒蛾 dú'é tussock moth

毒饵 dú'ěr poisoned bait

毒番石榴 dúfānshíliu 〈植物〉manchineel; poison guava (*Hippomane mancinella*)

毒谷 dúgǔ 〈农业〉poisoned grain (made from half-boiled rice, soybeans or maize mingled with insecticide and planted with seeds to kill harmful insects)

毒害 dúhài ❶ defile; poison (sb.'s mind); harm (sb.'s health) with narcotics:色情文学～青少年。Pornographic literature defiles the minds of young people. /吸烟对人～很大。Smoking is very harmful to health. /当年鸦片的大量输入,严重地～和摧残了中国人民的身心健康。The large quantities of opium smuggled into China in those years played havoc with the health of the Chinese people, both physically and mentally. ❷ pernicious influence; poisonous stuff:清除一切～ get rid of anything pernicious

毒狠 dúhěn vicious; venomous:用心～ with vicious intent

毒化 dúhuà poison (sb.'s mind); spoil:～人们的思想 poison (*or* defile) people's thinking /散布谣言～两国的关系 spread rumours in an attempt to poison the relations between the two countries

毒计 dújì venomous scheme; deadly trap:设下一条借刀杀人的～ set the deadly trap of killing one's adversary with a borrowed knife (*or* by sb. else's hand)

毒剂 dújì toxic; toxicant

毒箭 dújiàn poisoned arrow

毒辣 dúlà sinister; diabolic; malignant:手段～ ruthless means /阴险～ sinister and ruthless

毒理学 dúlǐxué 〈医学〉toxicology

毒烈 dúliè (of the sun) scorching; burning; fierce:夏天的骄阳～无比。The blazing summer sun was beating down on us most relentlessly.

毒瘤 dúliú malignant tumour; cancer

毒骂 dúmà curse roundly; scold savagely

毒麦 dúmài 〈植物〉darnel

毒酶 dúméi 〈生化〉toxenzyme

毒谋 dúmóu sinister and treacherous scheme; deadly trap:设下～ set a deadly trap (for sb.)

毒品 dúpǐn narcotic drugs; narcotics:～走私 drug traffic /～贩子 drug trafficker; drug pusher

毒气 dúqì ❶ (as used in war) poisonous gas; toxic gas; gaseous poison:～室 gas chamber /～弹 gas shell; gas bomb /芥子～ mustard gas /神经～ nerve gas ❷ harmful or poisonous gas in general:一氧化碳是一种～。Carbon monoxide is a poisonous gas.

毒芹 dúqín 〈植物〉water hemlock; cowbane

毒区 dúqū contaminated area (in chemical warfare); gassed area

毒热 dúrè (of the sun) scorching; burning; fierce:冒着～的太阳赶路 press ahead on one's journey under the scorching sun

毒杀 dúshā kill with poison:～田鼠 poison voles

毒杀芬 dúshāfēn 〈农业〉toxaphene; octachlorocamphene

毒砂 dúshā *also* "砷黄铁矿" shēnhuángtiěkuàng 〈矿业〉arsenopyrite; mispickel

毒舌 dúshé venomous tongue; poisonous words; abusive language:摇动～ wag one's venomous tongue

毒蛇 dúshé poisonous or venomous snake; viper

毒手 dúshǒu violent treachery; murderous scheme; wicked trap:下～ resort to violent treachery; lay murderous hands (on sb.) /险遭～ nearly fall victim to a murderous scheme

毒素 dúsù ❶ toxin; poison:抗～ antitoxin /中和～ neutralize a toxin or poison ❷ pernicious influence:封建～ pernicious feudal influence; feudal poison /灌输军国主义～ instil (into people) pernicious ideas of militarism

毒瓦斯 dúwǎsī poisonous gas; poison gas

毒物 dúwù poisonous substance; poisonous matter; poison

毒物学 dúwùxué 〈生化〉toxicology

毒腺 dúxiàn 〈动物〉poison gland

毒刑 dúxíng cruel corporal punishment; torture:受尽～ be subjected to all kinds of tortures

毒性 dúxìng toxicity; poisonousness:～发作 a toxin or poison makes itself felt

毒血症 dúxuèzhèng 〈医学〉toxemia; toxicohemia

毒蕈 dúxùn poisonous fungus; toadstool

毒牙 dúyá poison fang; venom fang

毒焰 dúyàn ❶ raging fire; raging flames; roaring blaze:村舍被～吞没。The village huts were engulfed in a raging fire. ❷ arrogance of evil force:～嚣张 give arrogant play to one's evil power; display blatantly the arrogance of one's evil force

毒药 dúyào poison; toxicant

毒液 dúyè liquid poison; venom

毒瘾 dúyǐn drug addiction:有～者 drug addict /他的～发作了。He has a craving for the drug. *or* He's craving the drug.

毒皂角苷 dúzàojiǎogān sapotoxin

毒瘴 dúzhàng toxic miasma

毒汁 dúzhī liquid poison; venom

毒资 dúzī money for buying drugs or narcotics; money from sale of drugs

渎[1](凟、瀆) dú 〈书面〉show disrespect or contempt:亵～ blaspheme; profane /烦～ put sb. to trouble; trouble sb.; bother sb. /有～清神 (used as a formula of courtesy in correspondence) have subjected you to so much inconvenience; have given you tremendous bother

渎[2](瀆) dú 〈书面〉ditch; drain:沟～ ditch

渎犯 dúfàn offend; affront

渎神 dúshén blasphemy (as against God)

渎圣 dúshèng 〈书面〉sacrilege

渎职 dúzhí malfeasance; dereliction of duty:贪污～ jobbery /他因～而受到惩罚。He was punished for dereliction of duty.

渎职行为 dúzhí xíngwéi malfeasance; malpractice; dereliction of duty

渎职者 dúzhízhě 〈法律〉malfeasant

渎职罪 dúzhízuì 〈法律〉crime of misconduct in office; offence of dereliction of duty

读(讀) dú ❶ read out; read aloud:宣～ read aloud; proclaim /朗～课文 read a text aloud ❷ read:默～ read /本文值得一～。The present article (*or* essay) is worth reading. ❸ attend (school):～中学 attend secondary school /～完师范 finish normal school ❹ pronounce:这两个字形状相同,～法不同。These two characters are identical in shape but different in pronunciation.

see also dòu

读本 dúběn reader; textbook:古汉语～ reader in classical Chinese

读出 dúchū 〈自控〉readout:～管 readout-tube /～器 reader /～装置 readout unit; reading station

读后感 dúhòugǎn notes on a book or an essay; comments after reading a book or an essay; impressions of a book or an essay

读经 dújīng ❶ study Confucian classics ❷〈宗教〉read scriptures

读经台 dújīngtái 〈基督教〉lectern; ambo

读卡机 dúkǎjī card reader

读卖新闻 Dúmài Xīnwén *Yomiuri Shimbun*, one of the popular daily newspapers in Japan

读破 dúpò variant pronunciation (of a Chinese character)

see also "破读"

读破句 dú pòjù pause at wrong places when reading aloud (esp. traditional unpunctuated writing); make wrong stops in reading

读入 dúrù 〈计算机〉read-in:～程序 read-in program

读史方舆纪要 Dúshǐ Fāngyú Jìyào *An Outline of Historical Geography*, compiled before 1692 by Gu Zuyu (顾祖禹) of the Qing Dynasty

读书 dúshū ❶ read a book; read:～声 sound of reading aloud /利用业余时间好好读点书。Make use of your spare time to do some serious reading. /～破万卷,下笔如有神。After poring over ten thousand volumes, You can write like one inspired. ❷ study:他～很用功。He studies very hard. *or* He is very diligent in his studies. ❸ go to school; attend school:我还在～时她就已结婚了。She got married when I was still at school.

读书班 dúshūbān study course (usu. for a particular purpose):部级干部～ study course for officials at ministerial level

读书笔记 dúshū bǐjì reading notes

读书人 dúshūrén ❶ scholar; intellectual ❷〈方言〉student; pupil

读数 dúshù reading:自动～ automatic reading /温度计～ thermometer reading /标度～ scale reading /～误差 reading (*or* indication) error /里氏震级～为 7.8 级的大地震 earthquake of 7.8 magnitude on the Richter scale

读数器 dúshùqì 〈自控〉reader

读帖 dútiè imitate calligraphy models mentally by scrutinizing them; learn calligraphy by mental imitation of models

读头 dútóu 〈计算机〉reading head

读图 dútú interpret blueprints; interpret drawings

读物 dúwù reading matter or material:儿童～ reading matter for children; children's books /青年～ books for the consumption of youth; reading matter for youth /通俗～ popular literature

读写磁头 dú-xiě cítóu 〈计算机〉read-write head

读音 dúyīn pronunciation

读者 dúzhě reader:～来信 letters from readers; letters to the editor; letters page /～园地 readers' forum

读者文摘 Dúzhě Wénzhāi *Reader's Digest*, popular American magazine

讟(讟)

dú 〈书面〉complaint:民无谤～。There is no complaint from the people.

椟(櫝、匵)

dú 〈书面〉casket; case; box:买～还珠 buy the (glittering) casket but decline the (valuable) pearls—show lack of judgment and make wrong choices

黩(黷)

dú 〈书面〉❶ sully; defile:先贞而后～ be pure and virtuous only to end up being defiled; remain unsullied till later in life ❷ act rashly:敬而不～ show reverence and never let slip any flippant remarks

黩武 dúwǔ militaristic; warlike; bellicose:穷兵～ engage in unjust military ventures; indulge in incessant wars of conquest; use all one's military might in a war of conquest /～主义 militarism; jingoism

犊(犢)

dú calf:初生之～不畏虎。Newborn calves are not afraid of tigers. *or* Young people are fearless.

犊子 dúzi calf:护～ protect calves; protect one's young

牍(牘)

dú ❶ wooden tablets or slips for writing (in ancient times) ❷ documents; archives; correspondence:文～ official documents and correspondence /尺～ correspondence; models of epistolary writing

顿

dú *see* "莫顿" Mòdú

see also dùn

髑

dú

髑髅 dúlóu 〈书面〉skull (of a dead person):此人骨瘦如柴,形同～。He is a bag of bones, practically a walking skeleton.

髑髅地 Dúlóudì 〈基督教〉Calvary, place near Jerusalem where Jesus was crucified

独(獨)

dú ❶ one; single:无～有偶 not come singly but in pairs (generally used in reference to evil-doers or evil deeds); curious coincidence ❷ alone; by oneself; on one's own; in solitude:～居 live in solitude /他这个人～来～往,很少跟人在一起。He is a loner and is seldom seen in company. ❸ old people without offspring; the old and childless:鳏寡孤～ widowers, widows, orphans and the old and childless ❹ only; alone:～有她持不同意见。She alone holds a different view. /大家都同意,惟～他反对。Everybody agreed except him. ❺ selfish; egoistic and not tolerant:他这个人太～。He is too self-centred. *or* He is too much of a loner.

独霸 dúbà dominate exclusively; monopolize:～市场 corner the market /～一方 lord it over a district; be a local despot /企图～天下 seek world domination

独白 dúbái soliloquy; monologue:这幕戏的主角用～表露自己的内心世界。In this scene, the hero is revealing his inner mind through soliloquy.

独步 dúbù be unequalled; be unmatched:～天下 be unmatched (*or* unrivalled) in the world /～文坛 be unsurpassed in the literary world; be a titan in the world of letters

独步一时 dúbù-yīshí be unequalled in one's time; be unmatched in one's generation

独裁 dúcái dictatorship; autocratic rule:～政治 autocracy /～政权 dictatorship /～统治 autocratic rule /～专断 autocratic; dictatorial

独裁者 dúcáizhě autocrat; dictator:《大～》*The Great Dictator* (film starring Charlie Chaplain)

独唱 dúchàng solo:～歌曲 solo song /～音乐会 recital (of a vocalist)

独出心裁 dúchū-xīncái show originality; be original; attempt to be different from others:～的设计 original (*or* novel) design /我相信这篇小说有～的地方。I am inclined to believe that there is something original in this novel.

独处 dúchǔ live on one's own; live alone:长期～ live in solitude for a long time /小姑～ young girl staying single; single girl

独创 dúchuàng speciality; original creation:～精神 creative spirit /这种产品是我厂～的。This product is a speciality of our factory. /艺术家必须～一格。An artist should create a distinctive style of his own.

独创性 dúchuàngxìng originality:好的艺术要有～。Originality is a hallmark of good art.

独词句 dúcíjù 〈语言〉one-member or one-word sentence

独胆 dúdǎn fearless against heavy odds:发扬～作战的精神。Carry forward the spirit of daring to pit oneself against heavy odds.

独当一面 dúdāng-yīmiàn cope with one sector or field on one's own; assume sole responsibility in one's job; take charge of a whole department or locality:他在公司里能～。He can cope with his job in the company all on his own.

独到 dúdào original:学术上有～的见解 show originality in one's academic research

独到之处 dúdàozhīchù distinctive feature; unique style:他的演出有～。His performance has a distinctive style of its own.

独断 dúduàn arbitrary; dictatorial:为人～ arbitrary and despotic

独断专行 dúduàn-zhuānxíng *also* "独断独行" make arbitrary decisions and take peremptory actions; act wilfully on one's own; act arbitrarily or despotically:他向来～,遇事不同别人商量。He always acts on his own without consulting others.

独夫 dúfū cruel and wicked ruler spurned and hated by the people; tyrant; autocrat:～民贼 autocrat and enemy of the people; tyrant spurned by the people

独个 dúgè alone; by oneself:他～住在乡间,潜心著述。He lives

alone in the country, devoting himself to writing.

独根 dúgēn *also* "独根苗";"独苗" only son of a family; only male offspring of a clan

独孤 Dúgū a surname

独活 dúhuó general name for several kinds of plants:浙～ *also* "毛当归" *Angelica pubescens* (whose roots are used as herbal medicine) /牛尾～ *Heracleum hemsleyanum* /九眼～ *Arolia cordata*

独家 dújiā exclusive:～新闻 exclusive report; exclusive / ～分销 exclusive distribution /～经营 be the sole agent of (a product, etc.)

独家代理 dújiā dàilǐ sole agency; exclusive agent

独角鲸 dújiǎojīng 〈动物〉narwhal (*Monodon monoceros*)

独角兽 dújiǎoshòu unicorn

独角戏 dújiǎoxì *also* "独脚戏" ❶ monodrama; one-man show:唱～ put on a one-man show; go it alone ❷ comic talk (usu. by one performer)

独角仙 dújiǎoxiān 〈动物〉rhinoceros beetle

独脚金 dújiǎojīn 〈植物〉witchweed

独居石 dújūshí 〈矿业〉monazite

独具匠心 dújù-jiàngxīn show unusual ingenuity; have originality:情节构思～。The plot is ingenious in structure. *or* The plot is a model of structural ingenuity.

独具只眼 dújù-zhīyǎn see what others fail to see; show unusual insight and judgment:他那番见解～。His judgment is insightful and enlightening.

独来独往 dúlái-dúwǎng come and go all alone; keep (oneself) to oneself; be a loner

独揽 dúlǎn arrogate to oneself; monopolize:大权～ arrogate all power to oneself

独力 dúlì by one's own efforts; on one's own:～经营 manage affairs by oneself; go into business on one's own

独立 dúlì ❶ stand alone:～旷野的大树 huge tree standing alone in the wilderness /～寒秋。Alone I stand in the autumn cold. ❷ independence:宣布～ proclaim independence /～运动 independence movement /～庆典 independence ceremony /～战争 war of independence /给予殖民地国家和人民～的宣言 Declaration on the Granting of Independence to Colonial Countries and Peoples (UN resolution No.1514, 1960) ❸〈军事〉independent:～营 independent battalion ❹ become independent or separate:这个系已～出去,成为一个学院了。The department has now become an independent institute. ❺ independently; on one's own:～生活的能力 ability to provide for (*or* look after) oneself /～思考 think for oneself /他在经济上已经～了。He is no longer dependent on his family for support.

独立成分 dúlì chéngfen *also* "独立结构"〈语言〉independent element:主格～ nominative independent; nominative absolute

独立董事 dúlì dǒngshì independent director

独立法人 dúlì fǎrén independent legal person

独立国 dúlìguó independent country; sovereign state

独立函数 dúlì hánshù 〈数学〉independent function

独立核算 dúlì hésuàn keep separate accounts; practise independent accounting

独立核算单位 dúlì hésuàn dānwèi independent accounting unit

独立权 dúlìquán right to independence

独立王国 dúlì wángguó 〈比喻〉independent kingdom — a realm, department or an area under one's absolute control and free from any higher authority or outside scrutiny:搞～ refuse to obey the leadership /把自己的部门变成～ turn the department under one's jurisdiction into an organization independent of central authority / 针插不入、水泼不进的～ independent kingdom where nothing could penetrate and nobody from the outside could gain a toehold

独立性 dúlìxìng independent character; independence:闹～ assert one's "independence" — disregard established discipline and refuse to obey the leadership

独立宣言 Dúlì Xuānyán (US) Declaration of Independence (4 July 1776)

独立制冷系统 dúlì zhìlěng xìtǒng self-contained refrigerating system

独立自主 dúlì-zìzhǔ maintain independence and keep the initiative in one's own hands; act independently and rely on oneself:～的和平外交政策 independent foreign policy of peace /她姐姐是有志气的,能够～。Her sister is a girl of resolute character and always relies on herself.

独联体 Dúliántǐ (short for 独立国家联合体) Commonwealth of Independent States (CIS)

独龙族 Dúlóngzú Derung nationality, living in Yunnan

独轮车 dúlúnchē wheelbarrow

独门 dúmén ❶ (of a family, etc.) having one's own entrance or gate:～独户 single house or apartment with its own entrance /～独院 compound with houses around a courtyard occupied by a single family; one-household quadrangle ❷ (of a skill, recipe, etc.) possessed by one individual or family only:～儿绝活 special skill possessed solely by an individual or family

独苗 dúmiáo *see* "独根"

独木不成林 dúmù bù chéng lín one tree does not make a woods — one person without support cannot achieve anything of significance

独木难支 dúmù-nánzhī a single log cannot support a big house — one person alone cannot accomplish a major undertaking:要完成这样艰巨的任务,一个人的力量再大也是～。No matter how capable a person is, he cannot fulfil such an arduous task single-handed. /主队败局已定,换上一名顶尖队员恐怕也是～了。The host team has as good as lost the game, and fielding an ace player will probably not save the situation.

独木桥 dúmùqiáo single-plank or single-log bridge; 〈比喻〉difficult path:你走你的阳关道,我过我的～。Take what you think is the open road, and leave me to travel along my rugged path. *or* You go your way, and I'll go mine.

独木舟 dúmùzhōu dugout canoe

独幕剧 dúmùjù one-act play

独女 dúnǚ *see* "独生女"

独辟蹊径 dúpì-xījìng blaze a new trail or open up a new road for oneself; create a new style or method of one's own:一个伟大的艺术家必须能够摆脱前人的窠臼,～。A great artist should not allow himself to be fettered by convention and should strike out on his own.

独善其身 dúshàn-qíshēn seek one's personal edification alone; be self-centred:他只是～,从不关心他人。He is interested only in self-improvement, and never shows any concern for other people.

独擅 dúshàn be the only one to possess (some skill, etc.); be exceptionally good at:～此技 possess a unique skill /～其利 be the sole beneficiary of sth.

独擅胜场 dúshàn-shèngchǎng collect all the laurels (in a contest, etc.); be exceptionally good:他少年酷爱书画,中年后～。He loved painting and calligraphy as a young man and became exceptionally good at them in later life.

独身 dúshēn ❶ live alone; live away from home and family:早年,他～一人,流落异国他乡。In his early years, he drifted homeless into an alien land. ❷ unmarried; single:～女子 single woman; spinster /他决心过一辈子～生活。He is determined to remain single all his life.

独身主义 dúshēnzhǔyì remaining unmarried or single (as a principle); celibacy:～者 celibatarian; celibate

独生 dúshēng ❶ only child born into the family ❷ live one's life alone; survive by oneself:誓共存亡,义不～ vow to live or die together, never seeking personal survival

独生女 dúshēngnǚ only daughter

独生子 dúshēngzǐ only son

独生子女 dúshēng zǐnǚ only child:～家庭 one-child family or couple /～证 certificate of a single-child family

独树一帜 dúshù-yīzhì fly one's own colours; blaze one's own path; be unique:中国绘画在世界绘画中～,自成体系。Chinese painting constitutes a unique school in the world of art, apart from any other artistic tradition.

独特 dútè unique; distinctive; peculiar:～风光 sight of no ordinary attraction; unusual tourist attraction /～的民族音乐 exotic national music /～的表现手法 novel way of expression /文章的构思新颖～。The plot of the writing is original and has a distinctive mark of its own.

独体 dútǐ 〈语言〉(of a Chinese character) single-element; one-unit:汉字按结构可分为～和合体。Chinese characters fall structurally into two categories — the single-element and the combined.

独体字 dútǐzì 〈语言〉single-element character

独头 dútóu ❶ one; only (one); single:～蒜 one-clove bulb of garlic ❷〈方言〉lonely person

独吞 dútūn keep all to oneself; take exclusive possession of; hog:～巨款 appropriate (*or* pocket) a huge sum of money /～胜利果实 hog the fruits of victory

独舞 dúwǔ *also* "单人舞" dānrénwǔ solo dance
独弦琴 dúxiánqín 〈音乐〉monochord
独行 dúxíng ❶ walk alone: 踽踽～ walk in solitude and silence ❷ go one's own way; stick to one's own way of doing things: 独断～ make one's own decisions and go one's own way; be arbitrary in everything one does /～其是 go it alone; take a different course from others; paddle one's own canoe ❸〈书面〉unique character; distinctive behaviour
独眼龙 dúyǎnlóng person blind in one eye; one-eyed person
独一 dúyī only: ～的女儿 only daughter
独一无二 dúyī-wú'èr unique; unrivalled; unmatched: 有什么理由能说太阳系的构成在宇宙中是～的呢? How can we be sure that the formation of the solar system is unique in the universe?
独异 dúyì peculiar; exceptional; out of the ordinary: 性情～ have a peculiar disposition
独营 dúyíng independent management; independent operation
独有权 dúyǒuquán sole ownership
独院儿 dúyuànr one-household compound
独占 dúzhàn have all to oneself; monopolize
独占鳌头 dúzhàn-áotóu come out first; head the list of successful candidates; be the champion: 这次围棋赛, 他一路斩关夺寨, ～。In this *weiqi* (*or* go) tournament, he eliminated all his rivals and came out first.
独占资本 dúzhàn zīběn 〈经济〉monopoly capital
独资 dúzī single proprietorship
独资经营 dúzī jīngyíng exclusive ownership and management: 外商～企业 enterprise with exclusive foreign capital and management
独资企业 dúzī qǐyè enterprise of exclusive ownership (usu. referring to foreign-owned enterprise); foreign-owned enterprise
独子 dúzǐ *also* "独生子" only son
独自 dúzì alone; by oneself: ～盘算 think over the matter by oneself /～谋生 earn one's (daily) bread /他～在树林里转悠着。He is strolling in the woods alone.
独奏 dúzòu (of instrumental music) solo: 钢琴～ piano solo
独奏会 dúzòuhuì (of instrumental music) recital

dǔ

堵 dǔ ❶ stop up; block; plug up: 把窟窿～上 plug up a leak /水沟～住了。The ditch is blocked. /路口～着很多汽车。There is a traffic jam at the cross-roads. /别～着路! Don't stand in the way. ❷ stifled; suffocated; oppressed: 胸口～得慌 feel suffocated; feel a constriction of the chest /心里～得难受 have a load on one's mind ❸〈书面〉wall: 观者如～。There was a big crowd of spectators. *or* There was a big crowd watching. ❹〈量词〉*used of walls*: 一～墙 a wall ❺ (Dǔ) a surname
堵车 dǔchē traffic jam; traffic congestion: 绕道避免～ take a detour to avoid traffic jams /这条大街上～现象严重。The avenue is often congested with traffic.
堵挡 dǔdǎng block; stop up; stem; plug: ～敌人 intercept the enemy /水流太急, ～不住。The current is too swift to be stemmed.
堵击 dǔjī intercept and attack: 分兵～ divide the forces for interception and attack /～逃敌 intercept the fleeing enemy; cut off the enemy's retreat route
堵截 dǔjié intercept: 围追～ encircle, pursue and intercept /～敌机 intercept enemy planes
堵口 dǔkǒu gag sb.; silence sb.: 你别用恐吓来～。Don't try to gag people by intimidation.
堵搡 dǔsang *also* "堵丧" try to prevent sb. from speaking up by blunt or rude remarks; choke off: 别拿这话来～我! Don't you ever try to choke me off by such words!
堵塞 dǔsè stop up; block up: 交通～ traffic hold-up; traffic jam; traffic congestion /～工作中的漏洞 stop up loopholes in work /垃圾和污泥又～了下水道。Garbage and mud have blocked (*or* choked) the sewer again.
堵心 dǔxīn depressing; frustrating: 这东西真不顺眼, 瞧着怪～的。This is absolutely an eyesore. It looks so depressing.
堵噎 dǔyē choke off; try to stop sb. from going on by blunt or rude remarks: 你去～他几句, 杀杀他的威风。Go and speak sternly to him to deflate his arrogance (*or* to take him down a peg or two).
堵嘴 dǔzuǐ gag sb.; silence sb.: 请客送礼往往是要堵住人家的嘴。Banqueting or giving gifts is often a means of gagging criticism.

睹(覩) dǔ see: 目～ see with one's own eyes; be an eyewitness to /先～为快 consider it a pleasure to be among the first to read (a poem, article, etc.) or see (a play, film, etc.)
睹物思人 dǔwù-sīrén think of the person at the sight of the thing; the souvenir reminds one of the person who gave it: 他～, 悲不自胜。His sorrow knew no bounds when he saw the articles once used by the deceased.

赌 dǔ ❶ gamble: 禁～ ban gambling /聚～ set up a gambling party /他已～得倾家荡产。He has gambled away his family fortune. ❷ bet: 打～ make a bet; bet /～赛马 bet on horse racing
赌本 dǔběn money to gamble with; gambling money
赌博 dǔbó gambling: ～成瘾 be given to gambling /政治～ political gamble /严禁～。Gambling is strictly prohibited.
赌场 dǔchǎng gambling house; gambling den: 私设～ set up an illegal gambling house
赌东道 dǔ dōngdào *also* "赌东儿" bet a treat (on sth.): 我敢跟你～他不会来了。I'll bet a treat with you on his not coming.
赌风 dǔfēng vice of gambling: 这里文化活动少, ～甚盛。There are few cultural events in this area, and gambling is widespread.
赌鬼 dǔguǐ gambler
赌棍 dǔgùn professional gambler; hardened gambler
赌局 dǔjú ❶ gambling party ❷ gambling house
赌具 dǔjù gambling paraphernalia; gambling device: 没收～ confiscate gambling devices
赌窟 dǔkū gambling den; gambling joint
赌气 dǔqì be discontented and act rashly; act wilfully or in a pique: 他～走了。He went off in a fit of pique. /她撅着嘴, ～不吃饭。She pouted her lips refusing to eat. /我偏要跟他赌这口气。I'm bent on having (*or* determined to have) it out with him.
赌钱 dǔqián gamble
赌誓 dǔshì swear; vow; pledge: 对天～ pledge to heaven
赌徒 dǔtú gambler
赌窝 dǔwō gambling den
赌咒 dǔzhòu take an oath; swear: 他～发誓要痛改前非。He swore to mend his ways.
赌注 dǔzhù stake: 下～ put down a stake
赌资 dǔzī money to gamble with; gambling money

笃 dǔ ❶ faithful; earnest; sincere: 情爱甚～ be deeply in love with each other /～行而不倦 go in for sth. tirelessly and in all sincerity ❷ be seriously ill; be in a critical condition: 危～ be mortally ill; be terminally ill
笃爱 dǔ'ài love deeply; be devoted to: ～自身的职业 be devoted to one's profession
笃诚 dǔchéng sincere and faithful: ～之士 sincere and faithful man
笃定 dǔdìng 〈方言〉❶ be sure of; be certain of: ～办好 be sure of success; be bound to succeed ❷ be completely at ease; be composed: 妻子到家里, 他才感到～了。He did not feel completely at ease until his wife got back home.
笃厚 dǔhòu honest and kind-hearted: 乡村里的人往往很～。People from rural areas are often honest and kind-hearted.
笃论 dǔlùn 〈书面〉appropriate remark; fitting commentary
笃情 dǔqíng deep affection; sincere feeling
笃实 dǔshí ❶ honest and loyal: 为人～敦厚 be loyal and sincere ❷ solid; sound: 学问～ sound scholarship
笃守 dǔshǒu abide by faithfully; faithfully follow the teachings of: ～遗教 faithfully abide by the instructions of the deceased /～诺言 keep one's word meticulously
笃信 dǔxìn faithfully believe in; be an ardent believer in: ～佛教 be a devout believer in Buddhism
笃性 dǔxìng genuine affection; feeling of sincerity
笃学 dǔxué be diligent in study; be devoted to study; be studious: 他少年～, 现在已成为一代宗师。As he was extremely diligent when a young man, he has become a great scholar of the present generation.
笃志 dǔzhì 〈书面〉devote oneself to; concentrate on: ～学习, 孜孜不倦 devote oneself, heart and soul, to one's studies
笃挚 dǔzhì 〈书面〉sincere and earnest: 友情～ sincere and deep

friendship

肚

dǔ tripe:牛～ beef tripe
see also dù

肚子 dǔzi tripe:猪～ pork tripe
see also dùzi

dù

度

dù ❶ linear measure: *see* "～量衡" ❷ degree of a given quality:烈～ (degree of) intensity /热～ (degree of) heat /硬～ hardness /湿～ humidity /浓～ density; concentration ❸ degree as a unit of measure (a) *for arcs and angles*:一～弧 a one-degree arc /四十五～角 an angle of 45 degrees /钝角大于九十～。An obtuse angle is larger than 90 degrees. (b) *for latitude or longitude*:北纬三十二～ latitude 32°N. (c) *for kilowatt-hours*:两～电 2 kilowatt-hours (d) *for temperature, percentage (of alcohol), etc.*:水的沸点是摄氏一百～。The boiling point of water is 100 degrees centigrade. /这种酒是三十八～。This liquor contains 38 per cent alcohol. /你的眼镜有多少～? What's the strength of the lenses of your glasses? ❹ extent; degree:透明～ transparency; openness /灵敏～ sensitivity /难～极高 extremely difficult /高～的爱国热情 strong sense of patriotism ❺ limit; bound; extent:长短适～ be of the right length /兴奋过～ be overexcited /将铁棍加热,以能弯曲为～。Heat the iron bar to the point that it can bend. ❻ rule; standard; criterion:法～ law /制～ institution; system; regulation ❼〈哲学〉cross-over point (between quantitative and qualitative change) ❽ tolerance; magnanimity:气～ tolerance /豁达大～ open-minded and magnanimous ❾ temperament; bearing; mien; attitude:风～不凡 of graceful bearing /态～谦和 modest, genial attitude ❿ space or time of a given extent:国～ country /年～计划 annual (*or* yearly) plan ⓫ calculation; consideration:把个人安危置之～外 give no thought to personal safety; with no thought for one's own safety ⓬〈量词〉occasion; time:一年一～ once a year; annually /两～公演 give public performances on two occasions /再～声明 state once again; reaffirm; reiterate ⓭ spend; pass:虚～光阴 fritter away one's time /欢～春节 joyously celebrate the Spring Festival /～过一生 live out one's days /只有～过了严冬,才能找到暖人春光里的欢欣。Only after weathering a harsh winter can one find joy in the warming rays of spring sunlight. ⓮ (of Buddhists or Taoists) (try to) convert:剃～ tonsure /普～众生 deliver all living creatures from suffering ⓯ (Dù) a surname
see also duó

度牒 dùdié〈旧语〉*also* "戒牒" jièdié certificate of ordination; letter of credence issued by the government to a Buddhist monk or nun

度荒 dùhuāng tide over a famine:贮粮准备～ store up grain to provide against a lean year

度假 dùjià spend one's holidays; go vacationing:～者 holiday maker; vacationer /～胜地 holiday resort; vacationland

度假村 dùjiàcūn holiday village

度冷丁 dùlěngdīng〈药学〉dolantin

度量 dùliàng *also* "肚量" dùliàng tolerance; magnanimity:～大 broad-minded; magnanimous /～小 narrow-minded /很有～ be large-minded

度量衡 dùliànghéng length, capacity and weight; weights and measures:～学 metrology

度命 dùmìng barely keep oneself alive; make a meagre living; live at subsistence level; subsist:乞讨～ keep oneself alive by begging /一家人靠父亲微薄的收入～。My family managed to make a bare living on father's small income. *or* We could hardly keep body and soul together by relying on father's meagre income.

度盘 dùpán dial; disk:～指示器 dial indicator /～指针 dial pointer

度盘式变阻器 dùpánshì biànzǔqì dial-type resistor

度曲 dùqǔ〈书面〉❶ set to music; compose (music):工于～ be a skilled composer ❷ sing to a tune

度人经 Dùrénjīng (short for《太上洞玄灵宝无量度人上品妙经》) *Scripture of Divine Deliverence*, classic works of Taoism in 61 volumes

度日 dùrì eke out a living or an existence:艰难～ drag out a miserable existence /她靠卖唱～。She made a living by singing.

度日如年 dùrì-rúnián one day seems like a year; days wear on like years; every hour seems an eternity; time hangs heavy:～的岁月 days that drag on like years /我整天如坐针毡,～。All day long I would feel as though I were sitting on a bed of thorns, and each day seemed like a year.

度数 dùshu number of degrees; reading:用电～ consumption of electricity (*or* power) /那个表上的～是多少? What does the meter read?

度宿 dùsù *also* "度夜" spend the night; stay overnight:天色已晚,只得在那里～了。It was getting late, so I had to stay there for the night.

度越 dùyuè ❶〈书面〉surpass; exceed; excel:～前人 surpass one's predecessors ❷ *see* "渡越" dùyuè

渡

dù ❶ go across; cross:～河 cross a river /飞～大洋 fly (across) the great ocean /强～天险 force one's way across a natural barrier ❷ tide over; pull through:～过难关 tide over a difficulty; pull through /过～时期 transitional period ❸ ferry (people, goods, etc.) across:老船夫～我们过河。An old boatman ferried us across the river. ❹ (usu. used in place names) ferry crossing:风陵～ Fengling Ferry Crossing

渡槽 dùcáo aqueduct

渡场 dùchǎng ferry crossing; ferry:过了山口就到了～。The ferry crossing is beyond the pass. /～有一只小船。There is a small boat at the ferry.

渡船 dùchuán ferryboat; ferry:乘～过江 cross a river by ferry; ferry across

渡渡鸟 dùdùniǎo〈动物〉dodo (*Raphus cucullatus*)

渡河点 dùhédiǎn point of crossing

渡江战役 Dùjiāng Zhànyì Crossing Yangtze Campaign (about one million PLA men crossed the Yangtze River on 21 April 1949 to overthrow the KMT government)

渡口 dùkǒu ferry crossing; ferry

渡轮 dùlún ferryboat; ferry

渡桥 dùqiáo temporary or makeshift bridge:架设～ build a temporary bridge across the river; build a floating (*or* pontoon) bridge

渡头 dùtóu ferry crossing

渡鸦 dùyā〈动物〉raven

渡越 dùyuè cross; surmount; negotiate:～天险 cross a natural barrier

镀

dù plating:电～ electroplating; galvanizing

镀铂 dùbó platinum plating

镀槽 dùcáo coating bath

镀层 dùcéng coating:～钢板 coated steel /～金属 coated metal

镀铬 dùgè chromium-plating; alphatizing:～钢 chrome-plated steel

镀合金 dùhéjīn alloy plating

镀金 dùjīn ❶ gold-plating; gilding:～器皿 gilded household utensils ❷〈讽刺〉become gilded (said of people attending school or studying abroad with the express purpose of raising their reputation and social status); acquire a gilded reputation

镀金属塑料 dùjīnshǔ sùliào metallized plastics

镀铑 dùlǎo rhodanizing

镀铝 dùlǚ aluminize:～钢 aluminium-plated steel /～膜 aluminizer

镀膜 dùmó coating film:～镜头 coated lens

镀镍 dùniè nickel plating:～铁丝 nickel-coated iron wire

镀铅 dùqiān lead plating:～薄钢板 lead-coated sheet; mat iron

镀青铜 dùqīngtóng bronzing; bronze plating

镀铜 dùtóng brassing; copper plating

镀锡 dùxī tin-plating; tinning:～铁皮 tinplate; tinned sheet iron

镀锡铁 dùxītiě *also* "马口铁" mǎkǒutiě tinplate

镀锌 dùxīn zinc-plating; galvanizing:～层 zinc coat /～钢丝 zinc-coated wire /～设备 galvanizing equipment

镀锌铁 dùxīntiě galvanized iron

镀银 dùyín silver-plating; silvering

芏

dù *see* "茳芏" jiāngdù

杜[1]

dù ❶ *also* "杜树" *see* "杜梨" ❷ (Dù) a surname

杜[2]（**敷**） dù block; stop; forestall：以～流言 so as to forestall gossip
杜阿拉 Dù'ālā Douala, chief port and largest city of Cameroon
杜邦财团 Dùbāng Cáituán (US) Du Pont Interest Group
杜比系统 Dùbǐ xìtǒng *also* "杜比降噪系统"；"道尔贝降噪系统" Dào'ěrbèi jiàngzào xìtǒng 〈电子〉Dolby System; Dolby：装备～的音响 Dolbyized hi-fi
杜波伊斯 Dùbōyīsī William Edward Burghard Du Bois (1868-1963), sociologist and leader of the Afro-Americans
杜甫 Dù Fǔ Du Fu (formerly translated as Tu Fu, 712-770), poet of the Tang Dynasty
杜父鱼 dùfùyú sculpin; bullhead; sea scorpion
杜衡 dùhéng *also* "杜蘅"〈植物〉wild ginger
杜蘅 dùhéng *see* "杜衡"
杜渐防微 dùjiàn-fángwēi *also* "防微杜渐" stamp out sth. evil before it rears its ugly head; nip in the bud
杜鹃 dùjuān ❶ *also* "杜宇"；"布谷" bùgǔ；"子规" zǐguī 〈动物〉cuckoo ❷ *also* "映山红" yìngshānhóng 〈植物〉azalea
杜绝 dùjué ❶ stop; put an end to; uproot：～贪污浪费 put an end to corruption and waste /～漏洞 plug a loophole /～走后门儿 stop the "back door" practice /～后患 destroy the root of future trouble /～弊端 uproot all evil practices; eradicate all corruption ❷〈旧语〉waive all right to buy back real estate one sells
杜康 dùkāng legendary figure who first distilled liquor;〈比喻〉wine or liquor：何以解忧？惟有～。There is nothing but wine to assuage my sorrow.
杜口裹足 dùkǒu-guǒzú speechless and motionless with fear; too scared to speak and move
杜兰线 Dùlánxiàn Durand Line (border line drawn in 1893 between Afghanistan and British India)
杜勒斯 Dùlèsī John Foster Dulles (1888-1959), American international lawyer and secretary of state (1953-1959)
杜梨 dùlí *also* "棠梨" tánglí birchleaf pear (*Pyrus betulaefolia*)
杜林 Dùlín Karl Eugen Duhring (1833-1921), German philosopher：《反～论》*Anti-Duhring* (1878, by Engels)
杜鲁门 Dùlǔmén Harry S. Truman (1884-1972), 33rd President of the US (1945-1953)
杜鲁门主义 Dùlǔménzhǔyì Truman Doctrine (policy statement by US President Truman in 1947 against the alleged threat of Soviet expansion)
杜马 Dùmǎ Duma, Russian Council of State or Lower House
杜梅 Dù Méi Do Muoi (1917-), Chairman of the Council of Ministers (1988-1991) and General Secretary of the Central Committee of the Communist Party of Vietnam (1991-1997)
杜门 dùmén 〈书面〉close one's door; shut oneself up：～谢客 close one's door to visitors; shut oneself up and refuse to see visitors /～思过 shut oneself up to meditate upon one's errors and faults
杜灭芬 dùmièfēn 〈药学〉domiphen
杜牧 Dù Mù Du Mu (803-c.852), poet and writer of the Tang Dynasty
杜塞 dùsāi stop up; plug; block up：～漏洞 plug a leak /～言路 stifle (*or* gag) criticism
杜松 dùsōng 〈植物〉❶ *also* "崩松" bēngsōng needle juniper ❷ Chinese fir
杜松子酒 dùsōngzǐjiǔ gin; geneva; jacky
杜瓦瓶 dùwǎpíng 〈物理〉Dewar flask
杜威 Dùwēi ❶ John Dewey (1859-1952), American philosopher, psychologist, and educator：～主义 Deweyism ❷ Melvil Dewey (1851-1931), American librarian：～十进分类法 Dewey decimal (classification) system
杜宇 dùyǔ 〈动物〉cuckoo
杜仲 dùzhòng ❶〈植物〉eucommia (*Eucommia ulmoides*) ❷〈中药〉bark of eucommia ❸ gutta-percha tree
杜仲胶 dùzhòngjiāo gutta-percha
杜撰 dùzhuàn fabricate; make up; coin：全部情节纯系～。The whole story was a pure fabrication. /通讯报道的事实，决不能～。A news report is based upon facts and must not be the figment of one's imagination. /这个词是你～的。This word is your own coinage.

肚 dù belly; abdomen; stomach：挺胸凸～ stick out one's chest and belly (as a posture of self-confidence)
see also dǔ
肚才 dùcái 〈方言〉hidden talent; inward wisdom：这人有～。He is quite talented, though he doesn't look it.
肚肠 dùcháng ❶ stomach and intestines; stomach：暖～ warm up one's stomach (*or* inside) /饿～ suffer from hunger; go hungry ❷ heart; intention：热心热～ enthusiastic and warm-hearted
肚带 dùdài bellyband; girth; cummerbund
肚量 dùliàng ❶ *see* "度量" dùliàng ❷ appetite; capacity or need for food：小伙子～大。Young men have good appetites. *or* Young men eat a great deal.
肚囊 dùnáng 〈方言〉❶ tolerance; magnanimity：～宽 broad-minded ❷ *also* "肚囊子" belly
肚皮 dùpí 〈方言〉belly：填饱～ fill the stomach /笑破～ laugh till one's sides split; hold one's sides with laughter
肚脐 dùqí *also* "肚脐眼儿" navel; belly button
肚子 dùzi ❶ belly; abdomen; stomach：～痛 have a stomach-ache; suffer from abdominal pain /生一～气 be overcome with anger; be full of pent-up grievances /她～大了。She is pregnant. *or* She is in a family way. ❷ bulging and round part (of sth.); sth. like the belly：腿～ calf (of one's leg) /这瓶子是口小～大。The bottle is narrow at the neck and big in the body.
see also dǔzi

蠹（**蠧**、**螙**、**蠹**） dù ❶ insect that eats into books, clothing, etc.; moth：衣～ moth (for clothes) /书～ bookworm ❷ (of moths or worms) eat：流水不腐，户枢不～。Running water is never stale and a door-hinge never gets worm-eaten.
蠹弊 dùbì 〈书面〉malady; evil; malpractice
蠹虫 dùchóng ❶ moth; worm; vermin ❷〈比喻〉vermin; harmful person：他们是国家的～。They are vermin to the state.
蠹害 dùhài harm (like vermin); endanger：～人民 do harm to the people; jeopardize the interests of the people
蠹鱼 dùyú *also* "衣鱼" yīyú fish moth; silverfish; bookworm
蠹蛀 dùzhù get moth-eaten：竹简已遭～，字迹漫漶。As the bamboo slips are moth-eaten, the writing on them has become illegible.

斁 dù 〈书面〉ruin; corrupt; undermine
see also yì

妒（**妬**） dù be jealous of; be envious of; envy
妒害 dùhài be jealous of and do harm to
妒恨 dùhèn hate out of jealousy; be jealous of
妒火 dùhuǒ agony of jealousy：～中烧 burn with jealousy; be consumed with envy; be green with jealousy
妒嫉 dùjí *see* "妒忌"
妒忌 dùjì be jealous of; be envious of：～心 jealousy /人家受表扬，你干吗～呢？Why should you feel jealous when somebody is praised?
妒贤嫉能 dùxián-jínéng *also* "嫉贤妒能" be jealous of capable and virtuous people
妒羡 dùxiàn envy and admire：令人～ inspire envy and admiration; be enviable
妒意 dùyì feeling of jealousy; jealousy：满脸～ very image (*or* picture) of jealousy

duān

端[1] duān ❶ tip; end; extremity：笔～ tip of a pen /两～ both ends /县城西～ western end of a town ❷ beginning; start; source：开～ beginning /发～ make a start /祸～ source of disaster ❸ reason; cause; occasion：无～ without rhyme or reason; groundless; unwarranted; unprovoked /借～ use sth. as a pretext ❹ aspect; point; item：仅举数～ just to mention a few points /举其大～ take for example the important aspects of the matter

端[2] duān ❶ upright; proper：～坐 sit bolt upright /品行不～ of loose morals; of improper behaviour ❷ hold sth. level with both hands; carry：～两碗饭 carry two bowls of rice /～饭上菜 serve a meal /有什么意见都～出来。Whatever you have in your mind, out with it. ❸ (Duān) a surname

端底 duāndǐ ❶ exactly; after all:～像啥呢? What exactly does it look like? ❷ ins and outs; heart of the matter:此事～不详。The cause of the matter is not clear. /要知事情～,需从头说起。I have to tell the story from the very beginning if you want to know the ins and outs of the matter.
端的 duāndì (often used in the early vernacular) ❶ really; indeed; sure enough:在下～不知。Your humble servant surely does not know. ❷ after all; in the end:这人～是谁? Who is he after all? ❸ what actually happened; whole story; ins and outs:不知～ not know the whole story; not know what actually happened
端点 duāndiǎn 〈数学〉end point
端方 duānfāng 〈书面〉proper; upright; correct:品格～ proper and upright; of integrity
端公 duāngōng ❶〈方言〉wizard; sorcerer ❷〈旧语〉runner or bailiff in a feudal *yamen*
端架子 duān jiàzi 〈方言〉put on airs:康老二在一般群众面前是很会～的。Kang Lao'er was apt to put on airs before ordinary people.
端节 Duānjié *see*“端午”
端静 duānjìng dignified and serene:她有一副～自重的外表。She appears dignified and serene.
端楷 duānkǎi (in Chinese calligraphy) regular script
端口 duānkǒu 〈信息〉port
端丽 duānlì neat and beautiful; graceful:字体～ write (in) a fair hand /姿容～ have graceful delicate features
端梁 duānliáng end beam; end girder
端量 duānliang look up and down; size up:他把我浑身上下～了一番。He looked me up and down.
端面 duānmiàn surface (of a cylinder); face:～车削〈机械〉facing /～铣削〈机械〉face milling
端木 Duānmù a surname
端脑 duānnǎo 〈生理〉telencephalon
端倪 duānní ❶ clue; indication; inkling:毫无～ have no clue whatever /略有～ have an inkling of the matter /问题解决已见～。There are indications of a solution of the problem. *or* The solution of the problem is in the offing. ❷ conjecture; predict:事态复杂,不可～。Prediction is not possible as things are too complicated.
端凝 duānníng dignified; sedate; grave; solemn:风度～ with a dignified bearing
端平 duānpíng ❶ just; fair; impartial; unbiased ❷ make fair and just; put things right:～法度 make the system of law a model of justice; make the law fair and just ❸ hold level:把一碗水～ hold a bowl of water level — treat people and matters even-handedly; be even-handed
端然 duānrán upright; proper:～正坐 sit up straight; sit bolt upright
端日 duānrì 〈书面〉first day of the first lunar month; New Year's Day (of the lunar calendar)
端梢 duānshāo tip; end:树木的～ tip of a tree; treetop /村镇的～有个水塘。There is a pool at one end of the village.
端射定向天线 duānshè dìngxiàng tiānxiàn end-on directional antenna
端视 duānshì look attentively; gaze:～良久 gaze fixedly (at sb. *or* sth.) for a long while
端视图 duānshìtú end-view
端午 Duānwǔ *also*“端五”;“端阳”;“端五节” Dragon Boat Festival (5th day of the 5th lunar month)
端铣削 duānxǐxiāo 〈机械〉end milling
端线 duānxiàn 〈体育〉end line
端详 duānxiáng ❶ details:细说～ give a full account of the story; give full particulars; speak in detail ❷ dignified and serene:举止～ dignified and serene in manner
端详 duānxiang look up and down; size up; look searchingly about:他并不坐下,站在屋子当中四面仔细地～起来。Instead of sitting down, he stood in the middle of the room looking around searchingly.
端相 duānxiang (now usu. replaced by 端详) look at closely; look up and down:对着镜子仔细～ look at oneself closely in the mirror
端秀 duānxiù delicate:容貌～ delicate features /她～的脸庞被炉火映得格外美丽。Her delicate face became all the more beautiful before a glowing stove.
端绪 duānxù thread of thought; inkling; clue:会议开了好几天,仍然毫无～。The meeting lasted for quite a few days without getting anywhere. /他心乱如麻,无论如何也理不出个～。He was so agitated that he could in no way sort the matters out.
端雅 duānyǎ dignified and elegant; serene and graceful:字体～ neat fair hand /风度～ elegant manners
端严 duānyán dignified and serene:容止～ carry oneself with dignity; with a serene deportment
端砚 duānyàn high-quality ink-slab made from stone produced in Duanxi (端溪), Guangdong Province
端阳 Duānyáng *see*“端午”
端由 duānyóu cause; reason:说说事情的～ relate (*or* recount) the cause of an incident
端月 duānyuè *also*“正月” zhēngyuè 〈书面〉first lunar month
端整 duānzhěng ❶ neat; regular:容貌～ have regular features ❷ smooth; tidy:床上收拾得很～。The bed was tidily made. ❸ tidy up; arrange; get ready:他回到家,妻子已为他～下很好的饭菜。When he got home, his wife had prepared a nice meal for him.
端正 duānzhèng ❶ balanced and symmetrical; regular; upright:五官～ have regular features /坐得～ sit bolt upright /字写得～ write a fair (*or* neat) hand /衣服穿得端端正正的 be neatly dressed ❷ proper; upright; correct:人品～ be upright; behave with moral rectitude; be a person of integrity ❸ rectify; correct:～工作作风 rectify the style of work /～动机 straighten out one's intentions /把错误的态度～过来 change one's wrong attitude
端直 duānzhí ❶ honest; upright:品行～ upright in behaviour ❷ straight on:这条街～走去,通向天安门。Go straight down the street and you will find Tian An Men.
端重 duānzhòng dignified:举止～ behave with dignity
端庄 duānzhuāng stately; dignified and sedate:神情～ look calm and sedate; look dignified /举止～大方 have a graceful and dignified manner
端子 duānzǐ 〈电工〉terminal:～电压 terminal voltage
端坐 duānzuò sit bolt upright in one's seat:～读书 sit straight in one's seat reading

duǎn

短 duǎn ❶ short; brief:～棍 short stick /～身材 short in stature /他的报告很～。His talk was brief. /这条裤子不～也不长。This pair of trousers is just the right length. ❷ lack; owe:理～ not fair and reasonable; not on just grounds; in the wrong /一年～两天 two days short of a year /我～他一百元钱。I owe him 100 *yuan*. /那次会人人都来了,就～他一个。Everybody attended the meeting except him. ❸ shortcoming; deficiency; fault:互相学习,取长补～ learn from each other and make up each other's deficiencies /不应该护～。It is wrong to shield a fault. /背后不应该说长道～。We should not make irresponsible remarks about anyone behind his back. /他就是爱揭别人的～儿。He likes to rub people on the raw.
短壁 duǎnbì 〈矿业〉shortwall:～采煤法 shortwall coal mining method /～工作面 shortwall /～截煤机 shortwall coal cutter
短臂染色体 duǎnbì rǎnsètǐ 〈生物〉cephalobrachial chromosome
短兵相接 duǎnbīng-xiāngjiē fight at close quarters; engage in hand-to-hand fight; come to grips with each other; cut and thrust:一场～的外交斗争 a fight at close range on the diplomatic front; a cut-and-thrust diplomatic battle
短波 duǎnbō 〈通信〉shortwave:～段 shortwave band /～传播 shortwave propagation /～疗法〈医学〉shortwave therapy /～可以收到。You can get it on shortwave.
短不了 duǎnbuliǎo ❶ cannot do without; find indispensable:搞建设～科学技术。Construction can make no headway without the help of science and technology. /生命～水。Water is indispensable to life. ❷ cannot avoid; have to:搞技术革新,～要找老师傅商量。To go in for technical innovation, we will have to consult veteran workers.
短长 duǎncháng ❶ strong points and weak points; merits and shortcomings:识其～而量才使用。Acquaint yourself with both the merits and shortcomings of a person and put him on a job commensurate with his ability. ❷ right and wrong; good and bad:议论别人的～ gossip about other people /胜负不在一时之～。Victory or defeat does not hinge on temporary advantages. ❸ accident (threatening sb.'s life); mishap:如果孩子有个～,我可如何是好? What shall I do if anything should happen to the baby?
短程 duǎnchéng short distance; short range:～航行 short-distance

navigation /～导弹 short-range missile /～飞机 short-haul airplane
短秤 duǎnchèng give short measure or weight
短翅水鸡 duǎnchì shuǐjī takahe; notornis (*Notornis mantelli*)
短绌 duǎnchù inadequate; insufficient: 资金～ suffer from inadequate funds /劳力～ be short of hands; be short-handed
短处 duǎnchu shortcoming; failing; fault; weakness: 我们都有～,谁也不能说是完人。None of us can claim to be perfect, for we all have our failings. /国家不论大小,各有长处和～。Countries, (whether) big or small, have their weaknesses as well as their strengths.
短传 duǎnchuán 〈体育〉short pass
短粗 duǎncū ❶ short and thick; stocky: ～的棒子 short and thick stick /～的身材 short and thickset ❷ short and heavy; quick and heavy: ～的呼吸 quick and heavy breathing
短促 duǎncù very short; very brief: ～的一生 short (*or* brief) life /～突击 short, swift thrusts; quick and sudden assaults /呼吸～ be short of breath; gasp; pant /时间～,要干的事情又那么多。There is so much to do and so little time to do it. /期限十分～。The time allowed is very short. *or* The notice is very short.
短打 duǎndǎ ❶〈戏曲〉hand-to-hand fight in tights: ～戏 hand-to-hand fight scene ❷ *see* "短装"
短打扮儿 duǎndǎbànr 〈口语〉*see* "短装"
短打武生 duǎndǎ wǔshēng 〈戏曲〉(in Chinese opera) actor usu. dressed in jacket and trousers, and playing a martial role; actor in tights fighting at close range with short weapons
短大衣 duǎndàyī short overcoat; carcoat
短刀 duǎndāo dagger; short sword
短导 duǎndǎo (short for 短程导弹)〈军事〉short-range missile
短笛 duǎndí piccolo
短吊 duǎndiào 〈体育〉drop shot (as in table tennis or badminton)
短吨 duǎndūn *also* "美吨" měidūn short ton
短发 duǎnfà bob; shingle: ～姑娘 girl with bobbed hair
短工 duǎngōng casual labourer; seasonal labourer: 打～ work as a casual labourer
短骨 duǎngǔ 〈生理〉short bone
短号 duǎnhào 〈乐器〉cornet
短简 duǎnjiǎn *also* "短柬" brief note: 他写了一封～。He wrote a brief note.
短见 duǎnjiàn ❶ short-sighted view: 这是一种只顾眼前利益的～。It is short-sighted only to take the immediate interests into consideration. ❷ suicide: 寻～ attempt suicide; commit suicide
短焦距镜头 duǎnjiāojù jìngtóu short-focus lens
短角牛 duǎnjiǎoniú 〈动物〉shorthorn
短角球 duǎnjiǎoqiú 〈体育〉(in hockey) short corner
短斤缺两 duǎnjīn-quēliǎng *also* "缺斤短两" give short weight or measure
短距离 duǎnjùlí short distance: ～赛跑 short-distance run; dash; sprint /～运输 short-distance transport /～起落飞机 short take-off and landing airplane; STOL
短撅撅 duǎnjuējuē 〈口语〉very short: ～的小袄儿 very short padded jacket
短裤 duǎnkù short pants; shorts
短款 duǎnkuǎn the amount of cash on hand being less than that registered in the accounts
短路 duǎnlù ❶〈电工〉short circuit; short: ～快速切断 short-out rapid cut-off /～事故 short-out accident /发生～ short; short-circuit ❷〈方言〉waylay; mug
短路保护装置 duǎnlù bǎohù zhuāngzhì short-circuit protection device
短路触点 duǎnlù chùdiǎn short-circuit contact
短路电压 duǎnlù diànyā short-circuit voltage
短脉冲激光器 duǎnmàichōng jīguāngqì short-pulse laser
短命 duǎnmìng die young; be short-lived: ～鬼 the short-lived /～的政权 short-lived regime /好人～。Those whom the gods love die young.
短跑 duǎnpǎo dash; sprint: ～运动员 dash man; sprinter
短跑道速度滑冰 duǎnpǎodào sùdù huábīng short track speed skating
短篇小说 duǎnpiān xiǎoshuō short story: ～集 collection of short stories /～选 selected short stories /中、～ novelette
短片 duǎnpiàn 〈影视〉short film; short
短平快 duǎn-píng-kuài ❶〈体育〉short, quick smash (as in volleyball) ❷ (enterprise or project) of little investment, short duration but quick returns: ～项目 project with relatively little investment but yielding quick returns
短评 duǎnpíng short commentary; brief comments: 时事～ brief comments on current events; brief news commentary
短期 duǎnqī of short duration; short-term: ～合作 short-term cooperation /～打算 short-term plans /～外出 leave for a short duration /～休假 go on a short leave /～训练班 short-term training-course /～轮训 short-term in-service training /～分析 short-run analysis /在～内完成 accomplish (a task) in the near future
短期保险 duǎnqī bǎoxiǎn short-term insurance
短期贷款 duǎnqī dàikuǎn short-term loan
短期国会 Duǎnqī Guóhuì Short Parliament (first of two Parliaments summoned by Charles I in 1640 in England which lasted only three weeks)
短期国库券 duǎnqī guókùquàn short-term treasury bond; short-term government bond
短期经济预测 duǎnqī jīngjì yùcè short-term economic forecast
短期票据 duǎnqī piàojù short bill
短期行为 duǎnqī xíngwéi action or behaviour aimed at achieving short-term results only; short-sighted action
短期债权 duǎnqī zhàiquán short-term claim
短期债券 duǎnqī zhàiquàn shorts
短期证券 duǎnqī zhèngquàn short-dated securities
短期资本流动 duǎnqī zīběn liúdòng short-term capital movement
短期资产 duǎnqī zīchǎn short-lived assets; short-term assets
短期资金市场 duǎnqī zījīn shìchǎng short-term fund market
短气 duǎnqì lacking in confidence; be depressed: 振作起来,不要说这种～的话。Cheer up and drop such depressing talk.
短浅 duǎnqiǎn narrow (in vision) and shallow (in understanding); superficial: 目光～〈比喻〉be short-sighted /见识～ be superficial in one's view; be inexperienced
短欠 duǎnqiàn owe; be in arrears; lack: 我厂～银行一笔借款。Our factory still has to pay off a loan to the bank. /一切准备都做好了,现在只～人力。We have got everything ready except manpower. *or* Everything is ready except for the shortage of manpower.
短枪 duǎnqiāng side arm; small arm; handgun; pistol
短球 duǎnqiú 〈体育〉short ball; drop shot: 发～ serve a short ball /吊～ drop the ball near the net
短拳 duǎnquán 〈体育〉(in *wushu*) short-jab boxing
短缺 duǎnquē short; deficient; scarce; lacking: 资金～ be short of funds; funds are scarce /这种商品货源～。These commodities are in short supply. /目前劳动力～,但还不会成为严重问题。The present scarcity (*or* lack, *or* shortage) of labour does not yet constitute a serious problem.
短缺商品 duǎnquē shāngpǐn scarce item or commodity; goods in short supply
短裙 duǎnqún short skirt: 超～ mini skirt /苏格兰～ kilt
短日照植物 duǎnrìzhào zhíwù short-day plant
短衫 duǎnshān (traditional) Chinese jacket
短少 duǎnshǎo deficient; short; missing: ～一页。One page is missing. /你们需要的钢材我们保证供应,一吨也不～。We guarantee full supply of the required steel products.
短时负载 duǎnshí fùzài short-time load
短时过载试验 duǎnshí guòzài shìyàn short-time overload test
短时记忆 duǎnshí jìyì 〈心理〉short-term memory
短视 duǎnshì ❶ near-sightedness; myopia ❷ lack foresight; be short-sighted: 这种见解,未免～。This is a short-sighted view of the matter.
短寿 duǎnshòu of short life; short-lived
短统靴 duǎntǒngxuē ankle boots
短途 duǎntú short distance: ～运输 short-distance transport; short haul
短袜 duǎnwà *also* "短统袜" socks; anklets; half-hose stockings
短尾矮袋鼠 duǎnwěi ǎidàishǔ 〈动物〉quokka
短尾雕 duǎnwěidiāo *also* "短尾鹫"〈动物〉bateleur (*Terathopius ecaudatus*)
短尾猴 duǎnwěihóu 〈动物〉stump-tailed monkey; macaque
短纤维 duǎnxiānwéi ❶ short-staple: ～棉花 short-staple cotton ❷〈纺织〉staple: ～切断器 staple cutter
短线 duǎnxiàn in short supply; in great demand: 增加～钢材的生产 increase the output of steel products that are in short supply

D

短线产品 duǎnxiàn chǎnpǐn goods in short supply; goods in great demand; undersupplied product

短线专业 duǎnxiàn zhuānyè (of graduates) specialities which are much sought after in the labour market:减少长线专业招生,增加～名额 reduce the number of students enrolled for specialities for which there is little demand, and expand enrollment of students for specialities for which there is great demand

短小 duǎnxiǎo short and small:篇幅～ limited in length /～的曲子 short song; short musical piece /身材～ of small stature

短小精悍 duǎnxiǎo-jīnghàn ❶ (of a person) short but strong and tough ❷ (of writing) short and pithy; terse and forceful:报上应多登些～的文章。The press should carry more articles which are short, terse and pithy.

短讯 duǎnxùn news in brief

短训 duǎnxùn short-term training; short training

短训班 duǎnxùnbān short-term training course

短语 duǎnyǔ 〈语言〉 phrase:～动词 phrasal verb

短元音 duǎnyuányīn 〈语言〉 short vowel

短暂 duǎnzàn of short duration; transient; brief:生命是～的,艺术是永久的。Art is long, while life is short. /我们在贵国访问的时间虽然～,但结下的情谊是深长的。Our visit to your country has been brief, but the friendship we have forged is lasting.

短装 duǎnzhuāng be dressed in a Chinese jacket and trousers (instead of wearing a long gown)

duàn

断[1]**(斷)** duàn ❶ cut (sth. long) in two or more sections; break; snap:～砖 broken brick /一刀两～ sever at one cut—make a clean break /绳子绷得太紧,忽然～了。The rope was stretched so taut that it suddenly snapped. /琴弦～了。The string broke with a snap. ❷ break off; cut off; stop:～电 cut off the supply of electrical power; cut power /～了联系 break off relationships (*or* ties); be out of touch (*or* contact) /电话中～ be temporarily disconnected /他～了给前妻的赡养费。He stopped his ex-wife's alimony. ❸ intercept:他把球～了下来,传给前锋。He intercepted the ball and passed it to the forward. ❹ quit; give up; abstain from:～烟 give up (*or* quit) smoking /～酒 keep off alcohol /～荤 go on a vegetarian diet

断[2]**(斷)** duàn ❶ judge; decide:诊～ diagnosis /当机立～ decide promptly; make a prompt decision /我～他不敢这样做。I just don't think he has the nerve to take such a course. ❷〈书面〉(often used in the negative) absolutely; utterly; decidedly:～不能信 absolutely incredible; beyond belief /～无可能 absolutely impossible; decidedly untrue /～不可轻信这类谣言。You must never give credence to such rumours.

断垵 duàn'ǎn cut up a ridge planted with millet etc., to thin out the plants and form clusters of earth round the remaining plants

断案 duàn'àn ❶ try or hear a case; settle a lawsuit:秉公～ settle a lawsuit with impartiality ❷ *also* "结论" jiélùn 〈逻辑〉 conclusion (of a syllogism)

断壁 duànbì ❶ broken walls:残垣～ dilapidated walls ❷ cliff; precipice:～绝崖 sheer cliff; bluff

断臂再植 duànbì zàizhí rejoin a severed arm or limb

断编残简 duànbiān-cánjiǎn *also* "断简残编";"断简残篇";"残篇断简" cánpiān-duànjiǎn broken (bamboo or wooden) slips inscribed with characters; stray fragments of texts

断层 duàncéng ❶〈地质〉fault:～带 fault zone; distributed fault /～面 fault-plane /～线 fault-line /～作用 faulting /盆地～ fault basin /倾向～ dip fault /走向～ strike fault ❷ break; gap: 文化～ break in cultural continuity /文化大革命的后果之一是出现了一个十年的人才～。One consequence of the Cultural Revolution was a 10-year break in China's intellectual lineage.

断层地震 duàncéng dìzhèn *also* "构造地震" gòuzào dìzhèn fault earthquake

断层湖 duàncénghú fault lake

断层矿脉 duàncéng kuàngmài 〈矿业〉fault vein

断层落差 duàncéng luòchā fault throw; fault drop

断层山 duàncéngshān fault mountain

断层崖 duàncéngyá fault cliff

断层岩 duàncéngyán fault rock

断层移位 duàncéng yíwèi 〈地质〉 fault displacement

断层褶皱 duàncéng zhězhòu fault fold

断肠 duàncháng be heartbroken; be overwhelmed with grief:～人在天涯 heart-broken man roaming the corners of the earth /未老莫还乡,还乡须～! Till he grows old, from Southland he won't part. To leave this land for home would break his heart.

断炊 duànchuī run out of rice and firewood; can't keep the pot boiling; go hungry:他告贷无门,已～数日。Since he had no one to turn to, he was forced to go hungry for several days.

断代 duàndài ❶ *see* "断后 ❶" ❷ (of a profession or undertaking) have no successors to carry on; be interrupted ❸ division of history into periods; periodization:研究～文学史 study the history of literature in separate periods

断代史 duàndàishǐ dynastic history; periodic history

断档 duàndàng out of stock; sold out:这些小百货早就～。These small articles of daily use have long been out of stock.

断道 duàndào 〈方言〉❶ waylay; commit highway robbery ❷ block; obstruct:这条路常在雨季塌方～。This road is often blocked by landslides during the rainy season.

断电 duàndiàn power failure; power cut; blackout: 经常～ frequent blackouts /部分～ brownout

断定 duàndìng form a judgment; conclude; determine:我敢～,他会后悔的。I am certain that he will repent. /有没有这回事,谁也不能～。Nobody is sure if this sort of thing ever occurred.

断断 duànduàn (often used in the negative) absolutely; utterly; ever:～信不得 absolutely incredible; utterly beyond belief /～骄傲不得。One should never get conceited. /～不可灰心丧气。Never on any account should you lose heart.

断断续续 duànduàn-xùxù on and off; intermittently:～的枪声 intermittent gunshots; sporadic gunfire /雨～地下着。It has been raining intermittently. /他～地学了三年法语。He studied French off and on for three years. /她～地说出了这番话。She forced the words out brokenly.

断顿 duàndùn can't afford the next meal; go hungry:过去家里穷得三天两头～。The family was so poor that they often had to go hungry.

断发文身 duànfà-wénshēn cut one's hair short and tattoo one's body (regarded as a primitive custom in traditional Chinese culture)

断根 duàngēn ❶ have no offspring; die without issue; be childless:～绝种 have no male offspring in one's family lineage ❷ be completely cured; effect a permanent cure:他的气管炎～了。He is completely cured of his bronchitis.

断喝 duànhè give a loud shout; bawl suddenly:他一声～,狗不再叫了。He gave a loud shout and the dog stopped barking.

断鹤续凫 duànhè-xùfú shorten the legs of a crane and use them to lengthen those of a wild duck — go against nature:不要做～的蠢事。Don't indulge in obvious stupidities, which are impossible of fulfilment.

断黑 duànhēi dusk:从天亮忙到～ be busy working from dawn till nightfall /天色已经～了。Dusk has fallen.

断后 duànhòu ❶have no progeny or offspring ❷ cover a retreat; bring up the rear

断乎 duànhū (often used in the negative) absolutely; decidedly:～不可 absolutely impermissible /这件大事,少数人～干不了。This being a major task, a handful of people cannot possibly cope with it.

断魂 duànhún be overwhelmed with sorrow or grief; feel transported:清明时节雨纷纷,路上行人欲～。As the rain falls thick and fast on Clear Purity day, The men and women sadly move along the way.

断简残编 duànjiǎn-cánbiān *see* "断编残简"

断交 duànjiāo break off a relationship; sever ties; sever diplomatic relations:他们～已有多年。It is many years since they severed all ties with each other. /两国已经～。The two countries have broken off diplomatic relations.

断经 duànjīng 〈纺织〉 cracked ends

断井颓垣 duànjǐng-tuíyuán broken wells and tumble-down walls — a dilapidated scene

断句 duànjù make pauses in reading unpunctuated ancient writings; punctuate:给一篇古文～ punctuate an ancient text

断绝 duànjué break off; cut off; sever: ～邦交 break off (*or*

sever) diplomatic relations /～交通 cut off transport; stop all traffic /～经济来源 cut off all financial support /～后患 remove causes of future trouble
断口 duànkǒu 〈矿业〉fracture:结晶形～ crystalline fracture
断口金相学 duànkǒu jīnxiàngxué 〈冶金〉fractography
断块 duànkuài 〈地质〉fault-block:～盆地 block basin
断粮 duànliáng run out of grain or food:～绝草 run out of grain and forage; be out of provisions
断裂 duànliè ❶ split; break; be rent asunder:船身～。The body of the ship has broken (*or* cracked). ❷ crack; fracture
断裂带 duànlièdài fault zone; fracture zone; rift zone
断裂力学 duànliè lìxué fracture mechanics
断裂油层 duànliè yóucéng 〈石油〉faulted deposit
断裂载荷 duànliè zàihè breaking or crushing load
断流 duànliú ❶ water has ceased to flow in the riverbed; run dry:长期干旱,小河都～了。The streams have run dry due to the long dry spell. ❷〈电学〉cut off; cut out:～熔丝 cut-out fuse /～器〈电工〉cutout; safety cutout
断垄 duànlǒng patches of a drill-sown ridge devoid of plants:缺苗～(fields) with seedlings missing and ridges blanked here and there
断路 duànlù ❶ block the road in order to rob; waylay:～劫财 commit highway robbery ❷〈电工〉open circuit; broken circuit:～器 circuit breaker
断梅 duànméi *also* "出梅" chūméi end of the rainy season
断面 duànmiàn section:横～ cross-section
see also "剖面" pōumiàn
断面图 duànmiàntú cross-section drawing
断命 duànmìng forfeit one's life; drive sb. to his death; kill:还不起～的阎王账 unable to pay off the shark's loan, which is driving one to one's death
断奶 duànnǎi wean:给婴儿～ wean a baby /～羊羔 weaner
断念 duànniàn give up the idea; give up all hope:一切都～了 give up all hope; surrender to despair /他叹口气～地说:"看来这是命中注定的呀!" He sighed and said in resignation, "Well, this seems to be my fate."
断片 duànpiàn extract; fragment; passage; part:这是一部长篇小说的几个～。These are a few passages of the novel.
see also "片段" piànduàn
断七 duànqī 〈迷信〉49th day after sb.'s death, when Buddhist monks or nuns are called in to perform religious rites for the dead
断气 duànqì ❶ breathe one's last; die:这家伙～了。The fellow has snuffed it now. ❷ cut off or stop the gas (supply)
断球 duànqiú *also* "截球" jiéqiú 〈体育〉intercept the ball:～三次 make (*or* have) three intercepts
断然 duànrán ❶ resolute; drastic:采取～措施 take drastic measures /～拒绝 flatly refuse /～反对 resolutely oppose ❷ absolutely; categorically:～没有这个道理 absolutely unreasonable /强加于人的种种罪名,我们～不能承认。We categorically reject all the charges against us.
断乳 duànrǔ *see* "断奶"
断送 duànsòng forfeit or lose (one's life, future, etc.); ruin:～性命 lose one's life /～前程 ruin one's career /他饮酒过度,～了自己的健康。He forfeited his health by excessive drinking.
断头 duàntóu ❶〈纺织〉broken end:～率 end breakage rate ❷ cut off sb.'s head; behead:宁可～也不屈服 would rather lose one's life than submit
断头将军 duàntóu-jiāngjūn general who would rather die than surrender
断头台 duàntóutái guillotine; block (on which one's head is placed to receive the axe)
断尾 duànwěi 〈畜牧〉docking
断纬 duànwěi 〈纺织〉broken picks
断弦 duànxián snap the lute string — lose one's wife:～之痛 grief over the death of one's wife /～未续 not yet remarry after one's wife's death
断线 duànxiàn ❶ (of string or thread) break:放的风筝断了线啦。The flying kite has broken away from its string. ❷ discontinue; be interrupted; be cut off:面临～危险 face the danger of being discontinued (*or* cut off from sth.)
断线风筝 duànxiàn-fēngzheng kite with a broken string; person or thing gone beyond recall
断想 duànxiǎng brief comments; notes:新春～ random thoughts on New Year's Day /看完电影我写了一篇～的小文。I wrote a brief commentary on the film after the show.
断行 duànxíng resolutely execute or carry out:～有效办法 resolutely take effective measures
断续 duànxù 〈书面〉intermittently; on and off; off and on:远处的歌声～可闻。The singing could be heard intermittently from afar. /病人嘴里发出～的呻吟。The patient groaned now and then with pain.
断续光源 duànxù guāngyuán intermittent light source
断续器 duànxùqì 〈电学〉interrupter; chopper
断续振荡 duànxù zhèndàng interrupted oscillation; intermittent oscillation; discontinuous oscillation
断崖 duànyá cliff:～绝壁 sheer crag; bluff
断言 duànyán say or state with certainty; assert or affirm categorically:当前的困难虽然很多,但可以～,我们的前途是光明的。We can say with certainty that despite numerous difficulties our future is bright.
断语 duànyǔ conclusion; judgment:妄下～ make (*or* draw) unwarranted conclusions /事情尚未调查清楚,不可轻下～。As the matter is still under investigation, we must not jump to conclusions.
断狱 duànyù hear or try a case; give a verdict:～如神 give a verdict with miraculous accuracy /老吏～ experienced and skilful (as a veteran magistrate trying a case)
断垣残壁 duànyuán-cánbì *also* "断壁残垣" (desolate scene of) dilapidated walls; ruins; debris:可惜这处古迹只剩下～了! It is a pity that this historic site is only a heap of broken walls.
断缘 duànyuán cut off all relations with; give up:他决心和文学～,专攻医学。He decided to give up literature to devote himself to medicine.
断章取义 duànzhāng-qǔyì quote out of context; garble a statement, etc.:这篇评论颇有～之嫌。This commentary gives one the impression that it quotes remarks out of context.
断折 duànzhé break; break off:路轨～。The rail was broken.
断肢 duànzhī severed limb:重接～ rejoin (*or* reattach, *or* replant) a severed limb
断肢再植 duànzhī zàizhí 〈医学〉replantation of a severed limb
断制 duànzhì 〈书面〉consider and decide; judge:～谨严 be meticulous in judgment
断种 duànzhǒng have no progeny; die without issue
断子绝孙 duànzǐ-juésūn 〈粗话〉may you die without issue; may you be the last of your line
断奏 duànzòu 〈音乐〉staccato

簖(籪) duàn

bamboo weir (for catching fish, etc.):鱼～ bamboo fish weir

段 duàn

❶〈量词〉(a) *used of a section or segment of sth. long*:一～衣料 a length of suiting /一～弧 a sector of a circle /边界中～ middle sector of the boundary /受到感染的一～肠子 affected segment of the bowel /锯下一～木头 saw off a part from the log /把绳子剪成两～ cut the rope into two (with scissors) /这～路崎岖不平。This part of the road is very rugged. (b) *used to indicate time or distance*:步行了一大～路 cover a long distance on foot /一～时间 a period of time /我过～时间再来看你。I'll come and see you again some time later. (c) *used to indicate part of a whole*:一～话 a passage of a speech /一～文章 a paragraph of an article ❷ rank (in *weiqi*):九～国手 rank as level 9 *weiqi* master (the highest in go); ninth-dan go master /业余五～ fifth-dan amateur ❸ section (as an administrative level in a mine or factory):工～ work section; (work) shop ❹ (Duàn) a surname
段落 duànluò ❶ paragraph:～大意 main idea of a paragraph /文章～分明。This article is well paragraphed. ❷ phase; stage:告一～ come to the end of a stage
段位 duànwèi 〈体育〉level; dan:一般地说,～越高,棋艺的水平越高。Generally speaking, the higher the level (*or* dan), the more skilful the player is.
段子 duànzi 〈戏曲〉aria; piece:新～ new arias /传统～ traditional arias /这个相声～挺带劲儿。This comic dialogue is very amusing. /这个评书～不怎么样。This piece of story-telling is not particularly interesting.

煅 duàn

❶ calcine ❷ *see* "锻" duàn

D

煅烧 duànshāo calcination; incineration:～粉末 calcined powder / ～车间 calcination plant /～矿 calcined ore
煅烧炉 duànshāolú calcar; calcinator; calcining furnace
煅烧窑 duànshāoyáo 〈化工〉 calcining kiln; calciner
煅石膏 duànshígāo calcined gypsum; plaster of Paris; plaster
煅石灰 duànshíhuī *also* "石灰" lime

塅 duàn 〈方言〉(used mostly in place names) vast plain area:他们在～上栽稻子。They are planting rice seedlings in the plain fields.

椴 duàn 〈植物〉(Chinese) linden
椴木 duànmù (Chinese) linden

碫 duàn 〈书面〉whetstone; grindstone

锻 duàn forge:～铁 forge iron
锻锤 duànchuí forging hammer
锻打 duàndǎ ❶ beat with a forging hammer; forge; smith:～牙轮 forge a gear wheel ❷ temper; steel; toughen:人也像钢铁一样,～得越多,就越坚硬。Like steel, the more tempered a man is, the stronger he is.
锻工 duàngōng ❶ forging:～车间 forging shop; forge /～钳 band jaw tongs ❷ forger; blacksmith
锻焊 duànhàn 〈机械〉forge welding; fire welding; hammer welding
锻件 duànjiàn forging(s)
锻接 duànjiē forge welding
锻炼 duànliàn ❶ forge; smelt ❷ do exercises; have physical training:注意～身体 pay attention to physical training /我通过体育～保持健康。I have managed to keep fit through physical exercise. ❸ temper; steel; toughen; build up:～坚强的意志 build up a strong will /～在大庭广众前讲话的本领 improve one's ability to speak in public /青年人要不怕苦,才能得到～。Young people should fear no hardship so that they may get tempered.
锻炉 duànlú forge
锻模 duànmú forging die
锻坯 duànpī 〈机械〉forging stock
锻铁 duàntiě *also* "熟铁" shútiě wrought iron
锻铁炉 duàntiělú forge
锻压 duànyā forging and pressing
锻压机 duànyājī forging press
锻冶 duànyě ❶ smelt and forge:～厂 smelting and forging plant / ～车间 hammering shop ❷ temper; steel:投身到实践中去,把自己～得更成熟些。Temper yourself in practice so as to become even more mature.
锻造 duànzào 〈机械〉forging; smithing:压力～ press forging /～合金 wrought alloy /～毛坯 forging blank /～起重机 forging crane / ～水压机 forging pump press /～生产线 forging line
锻轧机 duànzhájī 〈冶金〉forging roll

缎 duàn satin:软～ soft silk fabric in satin weave /绸～ silks and satins
缎花 duànhuā 〈植物〉honesty
缎木 duànmù satinwood (*Chloroxylon swietenia*)
缎纹 duànwén 〈纺织〉satin weave
缎子 duànzi satin

duī

堆 duī ❶ pile (up); heap (up); stack (up):～木料 pile logs (*or* timber) /黄灿灿的玉米在场上～成了山。Ears of golden maize were heaped in a mound on the threshing ground. /他的案头～满了文件。His desk is piled with documents. *or* Documents are piled up on his desk. /把砖头靠墙～起。Stack the bricks up against the wall. ❷ heap; pile; stack:瓦砾～ (pile of) debris /柴火～ pile (*or* stack) of firewood /草～ haystack /雪～ heap of snow /粪～ manure (*or* dung) heap; dunghill /沙～ sand mound ❸〈量词〉heap; pack; pile; crowd:一～灰烬 a heap of ashes /一大～谎话 a pack of lies /一大～困难 numerous difficulties /论～卖 sell by the heap /给某人加上一大～罪名 bring a number of charges against sb.; accuse sb. of numerous offences /一大～看热闹的人 a huge crowd watching the fun ❹ (often used in place names) hillock; mound:马王～ Mawangdui (place in Hunan Province, where a Han tomb of high archaeological value was excavated)
堆场 duīchǎng freight yard; stacking ground:矿石～ ground for stacking ore /废汽车～ car dump
堆存 duīcún store up; keep in store:猪饲料～在仓库里。The pig feed is kept in the storehouse.
堆叠 duīdié pile one upon another; pile up; stack:书架上～着许多新书。A great many new books are neatly stacked on the shelves. /礁石四周浪花～。One after another, the waves crashed upon the rocks.
堆垛 duīduò ❶ pile up; heap up; stack:场上～着麦秸和豆秸。Wheat-stalks and bean-stems are piled up on the threshing ground. ❷ stack; heap:村子前后到处是干草～。Heaps of hay can be seen everywhere in front of and behind the village.
堆垛机 duīduòjī (hay) stacker
堆放 duīfàng pile up; stack:刚收割的麦子都～在场院里。Newly reaped wheat was piled up on the threshing ground. /不许在此～建筑材料。It's not allowed to leave building materials about here. *or* No stacking building materials here.
堆房 duīfang storeroom; storehouse
堆肥 duīféi 〈农业〉compost
堆焊 duīhàn 〈机械〉built-up welding
堆红 duīhóng 〈工美〉plaster patterns painted red on lacquer ware
堆积 duījī ❶ pile up; heap up:～如山 (of things) heap in a mound; (of work, etc.) pile up like a mountain /院子里～着木料。The yard is piled high with timber. /事情要及时处理,以免～。Matters should be promptly dealt with so that they may not accumulate. ❷〈地理〉accumulation:～相 accumulative facies /泥沙～ accumulation of sand (*or* silt)
堆集 duījí pile up; heap up:他案头～着画轴。Scrolls of painting are piled up on his desk.
堆金积玉 duījīn-jīyù store up gold and jade articles — accumulate wealth; amass a fortune; possess huge wealth
堆聚 duījù gather; collect; pile up:～成山 be piled up mountain-high
堆绢 duījuàn 〈工美〉flowers and figures of coloured silk sewn on a screen
堆垒 duīlěi pile one upon another
堆垒数论 duīlěi shùlùn 〈数学〉additive theory of numbers
堆摞 duīluò pile one upon another:床上～着被卧。Quilts are piled up one upon another on the bed.
堆码 duīmǎ pile up neatly; pile one upon another:货架上的商品～得整整齐齐。Commodities are neatly arranged on the shelves.
堆漆 duīqī 〈工美〉embossed lacquer
堆砌 duīqì ❶ pile up (hewn rocks, cobbles, etc. to build sth.):墙是乱石和泥～而成的。The wall is built with cobbles, rocks and clay. ❷ pile up fancy vocabulary in one's writing; write in an ornate and redundant style:他的文章～了许多华丽的形容词。His essay is heavily loaded with fancy adjectives.
堆石坝 duīshíbà rock-filled dam
堆笑 duīxiào put on a smile; wear a grin from ear to ear:满脸～ be all smiles; one's face is wreathed in smiles
堆心菊 duīxīnjú 〈植物〉sneezeweed; sneezewort (*Helenium*)
堆芯 duīxìn 〈核物理〉reactor core:～紧急冷却系统 emergency core cooling system /～喷淋系统 core spray system /～栅板 reactor diagrid
堆绣 duīxiù 〈工美〉padded flowers made of satin of different colours
堆栈 duīzhàn storehouse; warehouse
堆子 duīzi heap; pile; stack:柴火～ pile (*or* stack) of firewood / 草～ haystack

锻 duī 〈古语〉steamed pie

duì

敦 duì 〈古语〉ancient grain container
see also dūn

憝 duì 〈书面〉❶ resentment; grudge ❷ evil; wicked: 大～ arch-criminal; man of iniquity

兑[1] duì ❶ exchange (old for new); convert: 把人民币～成美元 convert RMB into US dollars / 她到金匠那里把耳环～了一只金戒指。She exchanged her earrings for a gold ring with the goldsmith. ❷ honour (a bill, etc.); cash (a money order, cheque, etc.): 汇～ remittance ❸ pour from one container into another; mix; mingle: 往锅里～点水 pour some water into the pot / 往水泥中～水 mix the cement with water / 牛奶里～了水。The milk is adulterated with water.

兑[2] duì one of the Eight Trigrams, standing for marsh

兑付 duìfù cash (a cheque, etc.): 不知怎么搞的, 银行不肯～这张支票。I'm wondering why the bank refused to honour this cheque.

兑换 duìhuàn exchange; convert: 把外币～成人民币 convert foreign currency into RMB; change foreign currency for RMB / ～价格 conversion price; exchange rate / ～制度 convertibility system / ～危机 convertibility crisis / 平价～ conversion at par / 可～货币 convertible currency / 可～债券 convertible bond; convertible loan stock / 可～证券 convertible security

兑换率 duìhuànlǜ rate of exchange; exchange rate

兑换券 duìhuànquàn (short for 外汇兑换券) Foreign Exchange Certificate (FEC) — *Renminbi* equivalent of hard currencies, no longer in use

兑奖 duìjiǎng claim a prize; cash in a lottery ticket (that has won a prize)

兑现 duìxiàn ❶ cash (a cheque, IOU, etc.); pay a dividend, bonus or balance in cash (when the accounts are made up): ～白条 pay off an IOU in cash / 那年生产队年终～时, 他家才分了 10 元钱。That year, his family got a mere ten *yuan* at the year-end distribution of the production team's cash income. ❷ honour (a commitment, etc.); fulfil; make good: 说了话不～ not live up to one's word; fail to make good one's promise / 签订的合同应该～。Any signed contract should be honoured.

碓 duì treadle-operated tilt hammer for hulling rice; stone mortar

碓房 duìfáng *also* "碓屋" hulling house

对(對) duì ❶ reply; answer: 踌躇未～ hesitate to reply / 无言以～ have nothing to say in reply / 无以为～ not know how to answer ❷ treat; cope with; confront: 面～强敌 be confronted (*or* faced) with a formidable enemy / 中国队～美国队 the Chinese team versus the American team / 刀～刀、枪～枪 sword against sword, spear against spear; tit for tat; an eye for an eye / 你怎么可以这样～她? How could you treat her like that? / 我们～事不～人。We are concerned with facts rather than individuals. ❸ be trained on; be directed at: 枪口～外 train one's guns on the invaders / ～着镜子梳头 comb one's hair looking into the mirror / 这篇文章不是～着你的。This article is not directed at you. ❹ facing each other; face to face: 面～面 face to face; vis-à-vis ❺ opposite; opposing: 偏和我作～ be set specifically against me ❻ bring into coordination or contact; fit; match: 把门～上 fit the two leaves of a door together; close a door / ～暗号 exchange code words / 这幅对联～不上。The two parts of the antithetical couplet do not quite match. ❼ suit; agree; fit: 文不～题 content of an essay at variance with its title; be irrelevant / 驴唇不～马嘴 a donkey's lips don't match a horse's jaws — be beside the point ❽ compare; check; identify: ～地址 check the address / ～笔迹 identify the handwriting / 校～ proofread / 翻译查～原文 check the translation against the original ❾ set; adjust: ～表 set one's watch; synchronize watches / ～焦距 adjust the focus of (a telescope, camera, etc.) / ～琴弦 tune up a fiddle ❿ right; correct; normal: 你弄～了。You've got it (right). / 数目不～。The number is not correct. / ～, 他当然不会来了。No, he certainly won't be here. / 她今天神色不大～。She doesn't quite look herself today. ⓫ add; mix; adulterate: 酒里～了水。The wine has been adulterated with water. / 咖啡里～一点牛奶。Pour a little milk in the coffee. ⓬ divide into halves: ～股分成 go halves in profits ⓭ (antithetical) couplet: 五言～儿 five-character couplet / 喜～ wedding couplet ⓮ 〈量词〉pair; couple: 一～石狮子 a pair of stone lions / 一～青年夫妇 a young married couple ⓯ 〈介词〉concerning; regarding: 绝不～压力屈服 never submit to pressure / ～老人表示尊重 show respect for the elderly / ～案件进行调查 investigate (into) a case / ～实验的结果有信心 have confidence in the outcome of an experiment / ～我的健康很关心 be very concerned about my health / 这便是我～这个问题的看法。This is how I look at the problem.

对氨水杨酸 duì'ān shuǐyángsuān *also* "对氨基小杨酸" 〈药学〉para-aminosalicylic acid

对氨水杨酸钠 duì'ān shuǐyángsuānnà *also* "对氨基小杨酸钠" 〈药学〉sodium para-aminosalicylate (PASNa)

对岸 duì'àn opposite bank; other side of the river, lake, etc.: 从河～向这边打枪 fire from across the river

对案 duì'àn 〈外交〉counterproposal

对白 duìbái 〈戏剧〉dialogue: 这段～足以表现两个角色的不同心情。This dialogue suffices to show the different moods of the two characters.

对半 duìbàn ❶ half-and-half; fifty-fifty: 切成～ cut sth. in half / 我可以同你～分。I can go halves with you. *or* Let's split the profits between the two of us. ❷ double: 如果再等两个月, 我们就可以得到～儿利。If we can wait for a couple of months longer, we will get a double profit.

对保 duìbǎo 〈旧语〉confirm or verify a guaranty (with the guarantor)

对杯 duìbēi (of two persons) drink together: ～痛饮 raise and clink glasses, drinking to heart's content

对本 duìběn profit or interest equivalent to capital: ～利 one hundred percent interest or profit

对比 duìbǐ ❶ compare; contrast; balance: 新旧～ compare (*or* contrast) the new with the old / ～灵敏度 contrast sensitivity / 形成鲜明～ make a striking (*or* sharp) contrast / 对双方力量作一～ make a comparison of the relative strength of the two sides / ～之下, 黯然失色 pale by comparison / 如果我们将他的错误和他的成就作一～, 他仍不失为一位伟人。If we balance his errors against his achievements, he will remain a great man. ❷ ratio: 师生人数～是一对十。The teacher-student ratio is one to ten.

对比度 duìbǐdù contrast: ～失真 contrast distortion / ～调节 contrast control

对比分析 duìbǐ fēnxī comparative analysis

对比剂 duìbǐjì 〈医学〉contrast medium

对比色 duìbǐsè contrast colour

对簿 duìbù 〈书面〉be interrogated; be tried (in court): ～公堂 be cross-examined in court; be interrogated in court; go to court (over sth.)

对不起 duìbuqǐ *also* "对不住" ❶ 〈套语〉I am sorry; excuse me; pardon me; I beg your pardon: ～, 叫你久等了。Sorry to have kept you waiting so long. / ～, 我得走了。Excuse me, I must be going now. / ～, 我没听懂你的意思。I beg your pardon. I didn't quite catch what you said. *or* Beg your pardon? ❷ let down; be unworthy of; do a disservice to; be unfair to; disappoint: ～列祖列宗 be unworthy heirs of one's ancestors / 我没有说过任何～你的话。I've said nothing about you that I should be sorry for (*or* I need to regret). / 我决不做任何～你们的事情。I shall never do any disservice to you.

对策 duìcè ❶ 〈古语〉policies to be employed in running a state (as required in the imperial examination) ❷ way to cope with a situation; solution; countermeasure; countermove: 解决失业问题的～ solution for unemployment / 对目前形势, 我们要有新的～。We must find ways and means to cope with the present situation. / 上有政策, 下有～。Whatever policy the higher-ups may adopt, people down below know how to circumvent it.

对策论 duìcèlùn 〈数学〉game theory

对茬儿 duìchár 〈方言〉tally with (reality); conform to (rules); correspond to (fact); agree with (each other): 他所谈的和我所听到的对上茬了。His account tallied with what I heard. / 这事听起来不～, 我们应调查一下。The matter doesn't sound right, and we'll have to look into it.

对唱 duìchàng musical dialogue in antiphonal style; antiphonal singing (between two singers or two groups of singers): 他们俩的～优美动听。Their musical dialogue is beautiful and enthralling.

对称 duìchèn symmetry: ～变换 symmetry transformation / ～平面 symmetry plane / 这座城市的建筑是～的。The city is symmetrical in its layout.

对称轴 duìchènzhóu axis of symmetry
对冲基金 duìchōng jījīn hedge fund
对词 duìcí (of actors) practise lines together:演员在一起～。The actors are practising their lines together.
对答 duìdá answer; reply:他不知如何～才是。He didn't know how to reply.
对答如流 duìdá-rúliú respond fluently; reply readily without any difficulty
对待 duìdài ❶ be relative to:高山与平地～,不见高山,哪见平地。Plains are relative to mountains, without which they would not be plains. ❷ take or adopt a certain attitude towards; treat; approach; handle:我们应该认真地～排练中所出现的问题。We should adopt a serious attitude towards the problems that crop up in the rehearsals. / 以客观的态度～一切事物。Take all things objectively. /用辩证的观点～历史人物。Treat historical figures from a dialectical point of view.
对得起 duìdeqǐ *also* "对得住" treat fairly; do justice to:你这样做也就～他了。By so doing, you have done him full justice. / 我没有做过错事,～自己的良心。As I have done nothing wrong, I have got a clear conscience.
D
对等 duìděng reciprocal; equal in rank or status:在～的基础上 on a reciprocal basis /双方代表的地位是～的。The delegates of both sides are equal in status. /～原则是外交事务中一项重要的原则。Reciprocity is an important principle in diplomacy.
对等待遇 duìděng dàiyù reciprocal treatment
对等贸易 duìděng màoyì counter-trade
对敌 duìdí ❶ deal with the enemy; oppose the enemy:团结起来,共同～。Close our ranks to oppose the enemy. /～狠、对己和。Be ruthless to your enemies, but kind to your comrades. ❷ hostile; antagonistic:双方～,相持不下。The two opposing sides are locked in a stalemate.
对调 duìdiào exchange; swop:～住房 exchange housing (with each other) /～工作 exchange jobs /～座位 swop seats
对顶角 duìdǐngjiǎo 〈数学〉vertically opposite angles
对方 duìfāng other side; opposite side; other party:中了～的计 play into the hands of the other party (*or* one's rival, enemy, etc.) /我们还未接到～的答复。We've not received a reply from the other side yet. /李教授快要结婚了,～是他原来的学生。Professor Li is getting married, his fiancée is a former student of his.
对方付款电话 duìfāng fùkuǎn diànhuà *also* "对方付费电话" collect call:(给家里)打～ call (one's family) collect
对付 duìfu ❶ deal with; cope with; handle; tackle:他知道如何～蛮不讲理的人。He knows how to handle those who are stubborn and unreasonable. /此人不易～。This chap is a hard nut to crack. /我能～。I can manage. /必须采取有力措施～目前的干旱。It is necessary to take effective measures to relieve the severe drought. /他学英语还不到一年,只能～最简单的会话。He has studied English for less than a year and can barely carry on a very simple conversation in that language. ❷ make do:这台旧打字机我们暂时～着用吧。We have to make do with this old typewriter for the time being. ❸〈方言〉get along (with sb.); be on agreeable terms:这两人好像有些不～。The two of them don't seem to get along.
对歌 duìgē (esp. of folk singers of ethnic minorities in China) sing in antiphonal style:夫妻～ antiphonal singing between husband and wife
对工 duìgōng ❶〈戏曲〉part or role appropriate for an actor or actress:他演这出戏～。He is the right person to play this part in the opera. ❷〈方言〉suitable; appropriate; proper:你说得～。What you've said is quite right.
对光 duìguāng set a camera; focus a camera, telescope, microscope, etc.:自动～ automatic focusing (of a camera)
对过 duìguò opposite; across:他从街～向我打招呼。He greeted me from across the road. /～的房间就是他的办公室。His office is just opposite mine. /他家～有一家副食店。Opposite his house there is a grocery.
对焊 duìhàn 〈冶金〉butt welding:～机 butt welding machine /～钢管 butt-welded tube
对焊接头 duìhàn jiētou butt joint
对号 duìhào ❶ check the number:这场演出不～。Sit wherever you like for the performance. ❷ fit; tally; match:统计里几个数字对不上号。There are a few figures in the statistics that don't tally. /我听说过这人,但一直没有和他本人对上号。I know of the man but haven't been able to identify him. ❸ mark used to show that an answer is correct (usu. "O" or "√")
对号入座 duìhào-rùzuò check the number before taking one's seat; sit in the right seat; see where one fits into sth., or how sth. or sb. relates to one:本书人物全属虚构,请勿～。All characters in the novel are fictious; please do not relate any of them to yourself in any manner.
对话 duìhuà dialogue; conversation:父子～ dialogue between father and son /南北～ North-South dialogue /～可以导致政治问题的合理解决。Dialogue may lead to a reasonable settlement of political issues.
对话处理 duìhuà chǔlǐ 〈自控〉conversational processing
对话统计学 duìhuà tǒngjìxué conversational statistics
对话终端 duìhuà zhōngduān conversational terminal; interactive terminal
对换 duìhuàn exchange; swop:我跟你～一下,你坐这个位置。Let's swop our seats; you sit here, will you?
对火 duìhuǒ light one's cigarette from another:他们利用～的一瞬间交换了一下眼色。They winked at each other the moment one lit his cigarette from the other's. /对不起,对个火儿。Give me a light, please.
对击式镦锻机 duìjīshì dūnduànjī double swage hammer
对家 duìjiā ❶ party sitting opposite oneself (in mah-jong, etc.):打～ sit opposite one in a game /该～出牌了。Now, it's the turn of the party sitting opposite me to lead. ❷ other party in a proposed marriage; intended husband or wife:妹妹现在正考虑结婚,～是个会计。Sister is thinking of getting married, the man being an accountant.
对讲电话 duìjiǎng diànhuà intercommunicating telephone set
对讲机 duìjiǎngjī intercom
对角 duìjiǎo 〈数学〉opposite angle
对角式通风 duìjiǎoshì tōngfēng diagonal ventilation
对角线 duìjiǎoxiàn 〈数学〉diagonal line
对接 duìjiē ❶〈航天〉dock; connect; link up:空间～ connect in space; dock in space; perform a link-up (*or* mooring) operation /～舱 docking module; docking unit / 宇宙飞行器成功地完成～。The spacecraft successfully completed the docking. ❷〈机械〉butt joint; abutting joint
对接触点 duìjiē chùdiǎn 〈电学〉butt contact
对接滚焊 duìjiē gǔnhàn 〈机械〉butt seam welding
对接结合器 duìjiē jiéhéqì 〈航天〉docking adapter
对襟 duìjīn Chinese-style jacket with buttons down the front:～小袄 front-buttoned padded jacket
对劲 duìjìn ❶ be to one's liking; suit one:这钢笔不贵,但写起字来～。This pen is cheap but it writes well. ❷ normal; right:我今天觉得不～儿。I am not feeling very well today. /这事儿看起来不大～儿。There seems to be something fishy about it. ❸ get along (well); be on good terms with:他俩一向不～儿。The two of them have never been on good terms.
对进突击 duìjìn tūjī 〈军事〉two-pronged assault from opposite directions; pincer movement
对酒当歌 duìjiǔ-dānggē cup to cup calls for song; one should sing merrily over one's wine:～,人生几何? Cup to cup calls for song. Man's life — how long? *or* Let's drink and be merry, for life is all too short.
对局 duìjú play a game of chess, etc.:他们的～非常精彩。They played a fascinating game of chess.
对句 duìjù couplet
对开 duìkāi ❶ (of trains, buses or ships) run from opposite directions:天津和北京间每天～十列客车。There are ten trains running between Tianjin and Beijing daily. ❷〈印刷〉folio ❸ divide into two halves; go fifty-fifty:我们～支付这次宴会开支。We'll equally share the expenses for the dinner party.
对抗 duìkàng ❶ antagonism; confrontation:阶级～ class antagonism /电子～ electronic warfare /超级大国之间的～已成为过去。Confrontation between the two superpowers has become a thing of the past. /议会辩论引起党派～。The parliamentary debate gave rise to factional rivalry. ❷ resist; oppose:武力～ resist by force /～上级指示 disobey (*or* defy) the instructions of the higher organization /有～情绪 be defiant; appear antagonistic; show signs of disobedience
对抗疗法 duìkàng liáofǎ 〈医学〉allopathy
对抗赛 duìkàngsài 〈体育〉dual meet
对抗生物 duìkàng shēngwù antibiont

对抗声纳 duìkàng shēngnà countermeasure sonar
对抗效应 duìkàng xiàoyìng antagonistic effect
对抗性 duìkàngxìng antagonism:矛盾的～ antagonistic nature of a contradiction
对抗性矛盾 duìkàngxìng máodùn antagonistic contradiction
对课 duìkè 〈旧语〉exercise in matching antithetical couplets
对空监视哨 duìkōng jiānshìshào antiaircraft lookout or scout; aircraft spotter; ground observer
对空射击 duìkōng shèjī 〈军事〉antiaircraft firing
对空台 duìkōngtái 〈航空〉ground radar navigation station
对口 duìkǒu ❶〈中医〉deep-rooted ulcer in the back of the head (above the nape):～疮 boil at the top of the nape ❷ (of two performers) speak or sing alternately:～山歌 mountain song sung by two singers by turns ❸ (of two parties, etc.) correspond in nature or field of work; (of training, etc.) fit in with one's job or speciality:～协作 cooperation between similar departments of different institutions /～训练 training specially designed for a job's requirements /～专业 the kind of work one is trained for ❹ to one's taste; palatable; agreeable:做了几个～的菜 cook some palatable dishes (*or* dishes one likes)
对口词 duìkǒucí 〈戏曲〉rhymed dialogue
对口会谈 duìkǒu huìtán talks between representatives of corresponding organizations of two countries or parties; negotiations between counterparts
对口快板儿 duìkǒu kuàibǎnr 〈戏曲〉rhymed clapper talk
对口味 duì kǒuwèi *also* "对胃口" suit one's taste
对口相声 duìkǒu xiàngsheng comic dialogue; cross talk (by two performers)
对垒 duìlěi confront each other in battle or contest; be pitted against each other (in chess, tennis, basketball, etc.); fight each other:两军～ two armies confronting each other on the battlefield; two armies pitted against each other /机缘偶然,这两支最强的队将在四分之一决赛中～。As luck would have it, the two strongest teams will meet in the quarter-finals.
对立 duìlì contradict; oppose; be antagonistic to:～物 opposite; antithesis /～情绪 antagonistic mood; antagonism /两套～的政策 two sets of sharply contrasting policies; two sets of diametrically opposed policies /自由与纪律并不～。Freedom and discipline are not contradictory to each other. /不要把这两种意见完全～起来,它们实际上是可以互为补充的。Don't think that these two views are mutually exclusive; in fact, they complement each other.
对立面 duìlìmiàn opposite; antithesis:矛盾的～ opposites in a contradiction /谁是你的～? Who is your rival (*or* opponent)? /他为自己树立了～。He created an adversary for himself.
对立统一规律 duìlì tǒngyī guīlǜ 〈哲学〉law of the unity of opposites
对联 duìlián antithetical couplet (often written on a scroll or carved on a pillar)
对脸 duìliǎn face to face; directly opposite:～坐着一个工人。A worker sat directly opposite him. /他和老张走了个～儿。He met Lao Zhang face to face.
对流 duìliú convection; convection current:～传热 convective heat transfer /～冷却 convection cooling /～式断路器 convection circuit breaker /～云 convective cloud
对流层 duìliúcéng *also* "变温层" biànwēncéng 〈气象〉troposphere
对流气流 duìliú qìliú 〈气象〉convection current; convective current
对流热交换 duìliú rèjiāohuàn convective heat exchange
对流雨 duìliúyǔ 〈气象〉convective rain
对硫磷 duìliúlín 〈农业〉parathion
对路 duìlù ❶ meet the requirement; satisfy the need; be just right:～商品 marketable goods; goods that sell well /这种鞋子销到山区正～。These shoes can readily find a market in the mountainous regions. ❷ be to one's liking; suit one:这些改革都是～的。These are welcome reforms. /这把菜刀用起来有点不～。This is not a handy chopper.
对马岛 Duìmǎdǎo Tsushima, a group of Japanese islands in the Korea Strait
对马海峡之战 Duìmǎ Hǎixiá Zhī Zhàn Battle of Tsushima, a sea battle between Japan and Russia in 1905
对骂 duìmà trade abuse; call each other names
对门 duìmén ❶ (of two houses) face each other:我们是～儿户。We live in houses which face each other across the street. ❷ the building or room opposite:住在～ live in the house opposite; live right across the way /医院～是一所邮电局。There is a post office opposite the hospital.
对面 duìmiàn ❶ opposite; across:街～有一家戏院。There is a theatre on the opposite side of the road (*or* from across the street). ❷ right ahead:～走过来一群小学生。A group of school kids came towards us. ❸ face to face; vis-à-vis:这事你最好同他本人～谈。You'd better take up the matter with him personally.
对命 duìmìng 〈方言〉❶ quarrel bitterly with; fight like mad:你这是和谁～呀? Who are you quarrelling with so bitterly? ❷ give a life for a life; pay with one's life (for a murder)
对内 duìnèi internal; domestic; home:～政策 domestic (*or* home) policy /～销售 sell at home (*or* in the home market) /～搞活 invigorate (*or* enliven) the domestic economy
对年 duìnián 〈方言〉anniversary; whole year
对牛弹琴 duìniú-tánqín play the lute to a cow—address the wrong audience; cast pearls before swine; talk over sb.'s head:你跟他们谈相对论,等于～。If you talk to them about the theory of relativity, you will be barking up the wrong tree.
对偶 duì'ǒu ❶〈语言〉antithesis *see also* "律诗" lǜshī ❷〈数学〉dual:～运算 dual operations /～空间 dual space /～图 dual graph
对偶函数 duì'ǒu hánshù 〈数学〉dual function
对偶婚 duì'ǒuhūn (transition from group marriage to monogamous marriage in primitive society) pairing marriage, with the man marrying into and living with the wife's family, and their children belonging to the mother
对偶晶体管 duì'ǒu jīngtǐguǎn matched pair transistor
对偶粒子 duì'ǒu lìzǐ dual particle
对偶原理 duì'ǒu yuánlǐ 〈数学〉principle of duality
对偶坐标 duì'ǒu zuòbiāo 〈数学〉dual coordinates
对脾味 duì píwèi *also* "对脾气" find each other congenial; be temperamentally compatible; hit it off
对撇子 duì piězi 〈方言〉find each other congenial:他们夫妻俩平时挺～。The couple get on very well.
对瓶 duìpíng 〈工美〉twin vases
对亲 duìqīn 〈方言〉❶ become engaged or betrothed ❷ meeting between man and woman to be engaged, or between their parents
对日照 duìrìzhào 〈天文〉counterglow
对生 duìshēng 〈植物〉opposite:～叶 opposite leaf
对式 duìshì 〈方言〉❶ proper; suitable; fitting:我需要一名秘书,有～儿的人,你给我介绍一个。I need a secretary. Perhaps you can recommend one in case you have somebody in mind. ❷ get on well; be on friendly terms:他俩可～儿啦,在许多重大问题上看法都很一致。The two of them get along so well that they always see eye to eye on many important issues.
对手 duìshǒu ❶ opponent; adversary; rival:击倒～ (in boxing, etc.) fell (*or* flatten) one's opponent /生意竞争～ business rival (*or* competitor) /谈判～ one's counterpart in negotiation ❷ match; equal:棋逢～ find one's match /下棋你不是他的～。You are no match for him in chess games.
对数 duìshù 〈数学〉logarithm:～表 logarithmic table /～函数 logarithmic function
对台戏 duìtáixì rival show:演～ stage a rival show /他现在何必和咱们唱～呢? Why should he be having a shouting-match with us now? *or* Why should he challenge us at present?
对谈 duìtán talk to each other; talk face to face:他们花前月下,娓娓～。They talked intimately among the moonlit flowers.
对头 duìtóu ❶ right and proper; correct; on the right track:这种想法很不～。This way of thinking is absolutely erroneous. /你这样看问题就～了。Now you are thinking along the right line. ❷ (often used in the negative) normal; right:你的脸色不～。You are not looking well. /他的情绪不～。He is in a bad mood. ❸ (often used in the negative) get on well; hit it off:他俩过去不大～,现在却十分合得来。The two of them didn't get along very well before but they are now hitting it off with each other.
·对头 duìtou ❶ enemy; foe:死～ sworn enemy /冤家～ inveterate enemy ❷ opponent; adversary; rival:他们俩在学术观点上是～。They hold conflicting academic views.
对外 duìwài external; foreign:～代表权 external representation /～扩张 external expansion /～事务 external (*or* foreign) affairs /～

关系 foreign (*or* external) relations /～清偿能力 external liquidity /～经济合作 economic cooperation with foreign countries /～文化交流 cultural exchange with foreign countries /～经济贸易管理体制 system of administering foreign trade and other foreign economic relations /新华社～部 Home News for Overseas Service Department of Xinhua News Agency

对外关系委员会 Duìwài Guānxì Wěiyuánhuì (US) Council on Foreign Relations

对外函件 duìwài hánjiàn correspondence in foreign affairs

对外经济贸易部 Duìwài Jīngjì Màoyìbù Ministry of Foreign Economic Relations and Trade (Mofert)

对外开放 duìwài kāifàng opening to the outside world; open policy: ～, 对内搞活 opening to the outside world and invigorating the domestic economy

对外开放口岸 duìwài kāifàng kǒu'àn open port

对外贸易 duìwài màoyì foreign trade: ～逆差 foreign trade deficit; unfavourable balance of trade /～顺差 foreign trade surplus; favourable balance of trade /～管制 foreign trade control /～仲裁 foreign trade arbitration /～指数 foreign trade index number /～体制 foreign trade regime /～商品结构 foreign trade commodity structure /～区 foreign trade zone /～商 foreign trader

D

对外贸易仲裁委员会 Duìwài Màoyì Zhòngcái Wěiyuánhuì (China) Foreign Trade Arbitration Commission (FTAC)

对外友协 Duìwài Yǒuxié (short for 中国人民对外友好协会) Chinese People's Association for Friendship with Foreign Countries

对外政策 duìwài zhèngcè foreign policy: ～分析研究所 (US) Institute for Foreign Policy Analysis

对味儿 duìwèir ❶ suit one's palate; be tasty; be nice: 这个菜很～。This dish is very nice. *or* The dish suits my palate. ❷ (often used in the negative) sound right; seem all right: 你这番话似乎不太～。What you said doesn't sound quite right. /他说的话总不对我的味儿。Whatever he says does not particularly appeal to me.

对胃口 duì wèikou ❶ suit one's taste; be to one's taste: 他做的菜很对我的胃口。The dishes he cooked suit my taste perfectly. /辣菜不对他的胃口。Hot dishes don't agree with him. ❷ be interesting or pleasant: 昨天的晚会开得真～。We enjoyed every minute of the party yesterday evening.

对舞 duìwǔ contredanse; contradance

对物权 duìwùquán 〈法律〉 *jus ad rem*; right to possess a thing

对席 duìxí opposite seat: 他坐在～。He took the opposite seat.

对虾 duìxiā *also* "明虾" míngxiā prawn

对象 duìxiàng ❶ target; object: 攻击～ target of attack /调查～ object for investigation /团的发展～ sb. for the Youth League to recruit; prospective League member /讲话要看～。One should bear the audience in mind while delivering a speech. /讲话的～主要是知识分子。The speech was mainly addressed to intellectuals. /这些文化古迹是重点保护～。These cultural relics are designated for special protection. /本书的～是青年教师。This book is intended for young teachers. ❷ prospective partner in marriage; boy or girl friend: 找～ look for a partner in marriage /她找～的条件很高。She is very demanding in choosing a boy friend.

对象连接与嵌入 duìxiàng liánjiē yǔ qiànrù object linking and embedding (OLE)

对象数据库 duìxiàng shùjùkù object database

对象语言 duìxiàng yǔyán object language; target language

对消 duìxiāo offset; cancel each other out: 买书你替我付了十块钱, 今天中午吃午饭我为你也付了十块钱。咱们～, 谁也不欠谁。You paid 10 *yuan* for my book while I paid the same amount for your share of the lunch. Now we're quits.

对销贸易 duìxiāo màoyì counter-trade

对心 duìxīn *also* "对心眼儿" find each other's company congenial: 外表上这一对很相称, 但是他们不～。To all appearances the couple are well matched, but they are temperamentally incompatible.

对眼 duìyǎn 〈口语〉 ❶ to one's liking: 这块布料～。I rather like this cloth material. ❷ cross-eye: 这孩子怎么有点～儿? The child seems a little cross-eyed, doesn't he?

对弈 duìyì 〈书面〉 play chess; have a game of chess

对应 duìyìng ❶ homologous; corresponding: ～物 homologue /～原理〈物理〉 correspondence principle /～资金 counterpart fund ❷ relevant; suitable; corresponding: ～措施 corresponding (*or* reciprocal) measure; countermeasure

对应词 duìyìngcí 〈语言〉 equivalent

对应点 duìyìngdiǎn 〈数学〉 corresponding point

对应染色体 duìyìng rǎnsètǐ 〈生理〉 homologue

对于 duìyú about; concerning; with regard to: ～这种人, 我们要严格些。We must be strict with this kind of people. /教育～社会进步是至关重要的。Education is vital to social progress. /～这种事情, 他向来是不介入的。He never intervenes in such matters.

对仗 duìzhàng (in poetry, etc.) antithesis formed by lines or sentences matched in sound and sense

对照 duìzhào ❶ check (a piece of writing) against another; place side by side: 英汉～读物 bilingual English-Chinese reader /～原文再核对一遍译文 check the translation once more against the original ❷ contrast; compare: 形成鲜明的～ make a striking contrast; contrast sharply /新旧～ draw a comparison between the old and the new

对折 duìzhé ❶ 50% discount: 所有残损商品将以～出售。All damaged goods are to be sold at fifty percent discount (*or* at half price). ❷ fold (a piece of paper, cloth, etc.) in half

对辙儿 duìzhér 〈方言〉 *see* "对心"

对着干 duìzhegàn ❶ adopt a confrontational approach; set oneself against ❷ compete with sb. in work

对阵 duìzhèn ❶ stand facing each other, ready for battle; be pitted against each other: 两军～ two armies pitted against each other ❷ engage in a contest: 两国排球队五次～, 主队三胜二负。The volleyball teams of the two countries played five games, and the host team won three of them (*or* three to two).

对证 duìzhèng give testimony at court; establish evidence through personal confrontation or signed statements, etc.; verify; check: 上法庭～ give witness (*or* testimony) in a law court / 我们必须～事实然后作出判断。We must verify the facts before passing judgement. /死无～。Dead men bear no witness (*or* tell no tales).

对症 duìzhèng give a correct diagnosis; be the right cure (for sth.): ～良药 highly effective medicine; right remedy

对症下药 duìzhèng-xiàyào administer the medicine that cures the malady; give the right prescription for an illness; take proper steps: 必须对社会弊端作出正确分析, 然后～。We must make a correct diagnosis of social ills and take appropriate measures.

对直 duìzhí 〈方言〉 ❶ directly: 你可以～去找他。You can go and see him directly. ❷ straight; directly: 他～朝着小屋走去。He made straight for the small hut.

对蹠点 duìzhídiǎn *also* "对踵点" antipodes

对质 duìzhì confrontation in a law court between two parties: 让被告与原告～。Make the plaintiff and the defendant confront each other in court. /如果他不承认, 我敢当面～。If he denies the accusation, I'm ready to face him in court.

对质权 duìzhìquán 〈法律〉 right of confrontation

对峙 duìzhì stand facing each other, neither side willing to give in; confront each other: 武装～ military confrontation /两军～。The two armies are locked in a face-off. /两岸奇峰～。Grotesque mountains stand facing each other on both sides of the river.

对盅 duìzhōng 〈方言〉 *see* "对杯"

对撞机 duìzhuàngjī 〈物理〉 collider; colliding beam machine

对准 duìzhǔn ❶ aim at; point at: ～靶子 aim at the target ❷ 〈机械〉 alignment: 轴～ shaft alignment

对酌 duìzhuó (of two persons) have a drink together

对字 duìzì *see* "对课"

对子 duìzi ❶ pair of antithetical phrases, sentences, etc.: 对～ write a pair of antithetical sentences; provide the second of a pair of antithetical sentences ❷ *see* "对联" ❸ pair of persons or things: 他们俩结成～, 常在一起练习英语口语。They often paired off, practising spoken English together.

怼(懟)

duì 〈书面〉 rancour; resentment: 怨～ bitterly resentful

队(隊)

duì ❶ row of people; line; queue: 站～ line up; queue up; stand in line /请跟上～。Keep up in the line, please. /～里给我留个位置。我就来。Save a place for me in the queue. I'll be right back. ❷ team; group; band: 排球～ volleyball team /军乐～ military band /消防～ fire brigade /石油钻井～ oil drilling crew /敢死～ dare-to-die corps /拉拉～ cheering squad /舰～ fleet /合唱～ chorus /登山～ mountaineering expedition /商～ trade caravan /梯～ echelon formation /卫～ armed escort /仪仗～ guard(s) of honour ❸ Chinese Young Pioneers: ～歌 Young Pioneers' song ❹ 〈量词〉: 一～

士兵 a column of soldiers
队部 duìbù office or headquarters of a team, organization, etc.:消防队～ headquarters of the fire brigade
队礼 duìlǐ Young Pioneer's salute
队列 duìliè formation:～整齐 in neat formation /～训练〈军事〉drill; formation drill
队旗 duìqí 〈体育〉team pennant:互换～ exchange team pennants
队日 duìrì Young Pioneers' activity day
队商 duìshāng company or band of travelling merchants
队伍 duìwu ❶ armed force; troops:～扩充了。The troops have been augmented (*or* expanded). ❷ contingent; force:知识分子～contingent of intellectuals ❸ ranks; formations:革命～ revolutionary ranks /游行～ procession; parade
队形 duìxíng formation:成战斗～ in battle formation /以密集～前进 advance in close order /以散开～包围敌人 surround the enemy in open order
队友 duìyǒu fellow player; fellow member of a group or team
队员 duìyuán team member
队长 duìzhǎng ❶〈体育〉captain:足球队～ captain of a football team ❷ team leader:工作队～ work team leader /拉拉队～ cheerleader

dūn

惇 dūn 〈书面〉honest and sincere:为人～谨 be honest and prudent

敦 dūn ❶ sincere; honest ❷ (Dūn) a surname
see also duì
敦促 dūncù urge; press:～赴会 urge sb. to attend a meeting /～对方早日答复 request the other side to make an early reply; ask the other side to reply at their earliest convenience /～双方采取克制态度,以免事态扩大 urge both sides to exercise restraint to avoid further complications
敦厚 dūnhòu honest and sincere:温柔～ gentle and honest /质朴～simple and sincere
敦煌石窟 Dūnhuáng Shíkū Dunhuang Grottoes, Gansu Province, dating from 366 AD, containing Buddhist statues, frescoes, and scriptures
敦煌学 Dūnhuángxué Dunhuang Studies
敦刻尔克 Dūnkè'ěrkè Dunkirk; Dunkerque (in northern France):～大撤退 Dunkirk retreat (27 May-4 June 1940) /～条约 Treaty of Dunkirk (4 March 1947)
敦伦 dūnlún 〈书面〉❶ bring about good interpersonal relationships ❷ make love
敦睦 dūnmù 〈书面〉promote good relations:～邻好 promote good-neighbourly relations
敦聘 dūnpìn 〈书面〉offer to engage; cordially invite (sb. to serve in a position):～您为本会顾问。We wish to offer you a position as adviser to the association. *or* You are cordially invited to serve as adviser to the association.
敦朴 dūnpǔ 〈书面〉honest and sincere; simple and honest
敦请 dūnqǐng sincerely request; cordially invite:～阁下本星期五莅临历史博物馆参观指导。We cordially invite your Excellency to visit the Historical Museum on Friday and offer us your kind advice.
敦劝 dūnquàn earnestly advise or admonish
敦实 dūnshi 〈方言〉stocky; thickset; squat:～的坛子 squat jar /他长得很～。He is of stocky build.

墩 dūn ❶ mound:垒土为～ heap earth into a mound ❷ block of stone or wood; foundation made of brick or cement:石～ stone block /树～ stump /桥～ pier of a bridge ❸ squat stool or cushion:锦～ silk-covered cushion /坐～儿 stool ❹ mop (the ground, etc.):先扫干净了再～。Sweep the floor clean before mopping it. ❺〈量词〉cluster:一～稻秧 a cluster of rice seedlings /一～一～的野蔷薇 clusters of briers or roses
墩布 dūnbù mop; swab (for use on a ship)
墩墩个儿 dūndūngèr (of one's build) pudgy; dumpy; stumpy
墩头 dūntou 〈方言〉round, thick mat woven with cattail or wheat straw used as a seat; cattail hassock; rush cushion
墩子 dūnzi block of wood or stone:菜～ chopping block

礅 dūn large stone:石～ stone block

撴 dūn 〈方言〉catch hold of; seize:伸手把他～住 catch hold of him

蹾(擎) dūn 〈方言〉lay down heavily; put down with force; dump:请别～。Please lay it down softly.

镦 dūn 〈机械〉❶ stamping; punching:冷～ cold punching /热～ hot punching ❷ castrate
镦粗 dūncū 〈机械〉upset:冷～ cold upsetting /～机 upsetter (machine); upsetting machine
镦锻 dūnduàn 〈机械〉upset:～机 upsetter; upsetter machine /～压力机 upset forging press
镦焊 dūnhàn 〈机械〉upset butt welding; upset welding

驐 dūn 〈方言〉castrate:～牛 castrate a bull

吨(噸) dūn ❶ ton (t):公～ metric ton; tonne /长～ long ton /短～ short ton ❷ register ton ❸ (in shipping) tonnage
吨公里 dūn-gōnglǐ ton kilometre
吨海里 dūn-hǎilǐ ton sea mile; ton nautical mile
吨时 dūnshí ton hour
吨位 dūnwèi ❶ tonnage ❷ register ton

蹲 dūn ❶ squat on the heels:他们～在树下乘凉呢。They are squatting under a tree, enjoying the cool. /门口～着一对石狮子。There are a pair of stone lions squatting by the gate. ❷ be idle; stay:她整天～在图书馆。She stayed all day in the library. /不能老～在家里。It won't do to idle away one's time at home. /他不知犯了什么罪,～监牢了。He committed I don't know what offence and was thrown into jail.
see also cún
蹲班 dūnbān (of pupils, etc.) fail to advance to the next grade or year; stay down; repeat the year's work:他去年蹲了一班。He stayed down (*or* failed to pass) last year.
蹲班房 dūn bānfáng 〈口语〉be in jail; be imprisoned
蹲膘 dūnbiāo (of cattle, pigs, etc.) fatten in the shed:这猪该～了。The pig needs to be kept in and fattened up./你这五尺高的汉子在家～,也不找个活计干干。Look at you, a big strong man staying at home all day long doing nothing but getting fattened!
蹲点 dūndiǎn (of leaders, etc.) work for a period of time at a chosen grass-roots unit to get firsthand experience:～跑面 gain firsthand experience at a chosen grass-roots unit and then apply it in the whole area /我想到一个国营农场～去。I am thinking of working for some time on a state farm to gain firsthand experience.
蹲伏 dūnfú crouch:他～在草丛里窥视敌人的动静。He crouched in the thick growth of grass, keeping close watch on the movements of the enemy.
蹲踞 dūnjù crouch; squat or sit on the heels:～式起跑 crouch start; crouch /～在田埂上 squat on a ridge between fields
蹲坑 dūnkēng ❶ squat over a latrine pit to relieve oneself ❷〈方言〉dig holes in the fields (for planting vegetables)
蹲苗 dūnmiáo 〈农业〉restrain the growth of seedlings for the roots to develop better
蹲腿 dūntuǐ ❶ crouch:先～后出拳。Crouch before you hit out with your fists. ❷ pull a muscle in one's leg or sprain one's ankle when jumping
蹲窝 dūnwō ❶ (of birds or animals) lie in the nest or lair ❷ stay indoors; shut oneself up in one's house

dǔn

不 dǔn
不子 dǔnzi 〈方言〉❶ *see* "墩子" dūnzi ❷ bricks of clay used to make porcelain

趸(躉) dǔn ❶ wholesale:～买～卖 buy and sell whole-

sale ❷ buy wholesale (for retail trading):～货 buy goods wholesale
趸船 dǔnchuán landing stage; pontoon
趸卖 dǔnmài sell wholesale
趸批 dǔnpī wholesale:～买进 buy wholesale
趸售 dǔnshòu *see* "趸卖"

盹 dǔn doze; take a nap:午饭后打个～儿 have a nap after lunch /他听报告时经常打～。He often dozes off when listening to a lecture.
盹睡 dǔnshuì doze off; have a nap

dùn

沌 dùn *see* "混沌" hùndùn

炖(燉) dùn ❶ stew:～牛肉 stewed beef /清～鸡 water-boiled chicken without salt or soy sauce ❷ warm sth. by putting it in a container in boiling water:～药 warm (herbal) medicine in a container /～酒 warm wine

砘 dùn ram loose soil with a stone-roller after sowing
砘子 dùnzi roller

顿[1] dùn ❶ pause:说到这里他～了一下。He paused briefly when he came to this in his account. ❷ (in Chinese calligraphy) pause in writing in order to reinforce the beginning or ending of a stroke:一横的两头都要～一～。Reinforce both the beginning and the ending when you write a horizontal stroke. ❸ kowtow; stamp: *see* "～首"; "～足捶胸" ❹ arrange; handle:整～ consolidate; straighten out /安～ settle in ❺ suddenly; immediately:～止 suddenly stop ❻ 〈量词〉 *used to indicate frequency*:一日三～饭 three meals a day ❼ (Dùn) a surname

顿[2] dùn tired:困～ dog-tired; fatigued
see also dú
顿巴敦橡树园会议 Dùnbādūn Xiàngshùyuán Huìyì Dumbarton Oaks Conference (21 August-7 October 1944)
顿挫 dùncuò pause and transition (in rhythm or tone):抑扬～ lowering, raising, pausing and transition — all the variations of one's tone; modulation in tone
顿宕 dùndàng up and down; twist and turn:故事情节曲折～。The story is complicated and full of twists and turns.
顿号 dùnhào slight-pause mark (、), usu. used to set off items in a series
顿河 Dùnhé Don (River in European Russia)
顿即 dùnjí at once; immediately; promptly:剧场里～鸦雀无声。A silence fell on the theatre.
顿开茅塞 dùnkāi-máosè *also* "茅塞顿开" become suddenly enlightened; open one's eyes; make one see the light:聆听指教,～。I was instantly enlightened by your instructions.
顿刻 dùnkè ❶ immediately; at once; forthwith ❷ for the moment
顿然 dùnrán suddenly; immediately:一阵风吹过,～雨住天晴。When the wind blew over, the rain stopped all at once and the sun came out again. /登上顶峰,～觉得周围山头矮了一截。Reaching the peak, I suddenly felt as if all the hills around were visibly lower.
顿时 dùnshí at once; instantly:消息一传来,村子里～就沸腾起来。The village was boiling with excitement at the news.
顿首 dùnshǒu (usu. used after the signature in formal or conventional letters) yours humbly
顿悟 dùnwù suddenly come to realize (the truth); be suddenly enlightened; realize in a flash
顿歇 dùnxiē stop temporarily or for the time being; come to a halt; pause
顿足不前 dùnzú-bùqián come to a standstill
顿足捶胸 dùnzú-chuíxiōng stamp one's feet and beat one's chest:听说儿子因车祸死去,她～,号啕大哭。When she learned that her son had been killed in a traffic accident, she burst out crying bitterly, hammering her chest and stamping her feet.
顿钻钻井 dùnzuàn zuànjǐng churn drilling; percussion drilling; cable tool drilling

囤 dùn grain bin:大～满,小～流。All bins, big or small, were bursting with grain (from a bumper harvest).
see also tún

钝 dùn ❶ blunt; dull:这刀太～,不好使。This knife is too blunt, not at all handy. ❷ stupid; dull-witted:迟～ slow; dull-witted /言辞讷～ slow and halting in speech /他脑子～。He has a slow mind. *or* He is slow-witted.
钝化 dùnhuà passivation; inactivation:～晶体管 passivation transistor /～剂 passivator /～金属 passive metal /～-活化电池 passive-active cell
钝化酸 dùnhuàsuān 〈石油〉 retarded acid
钝角 dùnjiǎo 〈数学〉 obtuse angle:～三角形 obtuse triangle
钝器伤 dùnqìshāng blunt force injury; injury from blunt utensil
钝涩 dùnsè dull:～的眼睛 lacklustre (*or* glazed) eyes
钝痛 dùntòng dull pain
钝吻鳄 dùnwěn'è *also* "短嘴鳄" duǎnzuǐ'è alligator
钝响 dùnxiǎng thud; clang:远处传来除夕鞭炮的～,打破了夜空的寂静。The explosion of firecrackers in the distance thudded through the silent night of the new year eve.
钝性物质 dùnxìng wùzhì 〈化学〉 inactive substance
钝滞 dùnzhì ❶ slow and dull-witted:～的眼光 glassy (*or* glazed) look; dull eyes ❷ not sharp; dull:变～为锋利 sharpen sth.
钝重 dùnzhòng booming noise:～的炮声 boom of the guns
钝拙 dùnzhuō clumsy; awkward; stupid:言语～ be clumsy of speech

盾[1] dùn ❶ shield; buckler:他带剑拥～闯入军帐。He strode into the commander's tent with sword and buckler. ❷ shield-shaped:～背椅 shieldback

盾[2] dùn money unit of Holland (*guilder*), Vietnam (*dong*), Indonesia (*rupiah*), etc.
盾牌 dùnpái ❶ shield; buckler ❷ pretext; excuse:他以此为～,想逃避应负的责任。He used this as an excuse to evade his responsibility.
盾牌星座 Dùnpái Xīngzuò 〈天文〉 Scutum; Shield
盾形纹章 dùnxíng wénzhāng coat of arms

遁(遯) dùn ❶ escape; flee; run away:仓皇～去 scamper off in panic /远～他乡 flee far away from home /报道敌军宵～。Word comes the enemy has fled into the night. ❷ hide; lie low; disappear:隐～ lie low; go into hiding
遁北 dùnběi 〈书面〉 be routed and flee in disorder
遁藏 dùncáng 〈书面〉 run away and go into hiding:～草中 run away and hide oneself in the grass
遁词 dùncí subterfuge; quibble:这不过是避开正题的～。This is only a subterfuge to sidetrack the main issue.
遁迹 dùnjì 〈书面〉 live in seclusion; withdraw from society and live in solitude:～山林 lead a reclusive life in the woods
遁甲 dùnjiǎ *also* "奇门" qímén magic of invisibility
遁入空门 dùnrù kōngmén withdraw from secular life and become a Buddhist monk or nun
遁世 dùnshì 〈书面〉 withdraw from the world; live in seclusion:～绝俗 withdraw from the world and renounce all secular life
遁逃 dùntáo flee; escape; run away:仓皇～ flee in panic; flee in confusion; flee helter-skelter /～山中 escape to the mountains
遁形 dùnxíng lie low; hide one's identity

楯 dùn 〈书面〉 *see* "盾" dùn
see also shǔn

duō

多[1] duō ❶ many; much; more; a lot of:朋友～ many friends /时间～ much (*or* a lot of) time / ～品牌战略 multi-brand strategy /～愁～病 be laden with sorrow and illness; be prone to

anxiety and illness /～听少说 give every man thine ear, but few thy voice /要学的知识还很～。There is a lot more to learn. /请～～指教。I hope you will feel free to make your suggestions. /冬季～风干旱，夏季～雨湿润。It is windy and dry in winter and rainy and damp in summer. ❷ exceed the original, correct or required number or amount; be or have too many or too much：恰恰～了一个人。There is one person too many. /他～喝了一点儿。He had a drop too much. ❸ excessive; over: *see* "～疑" ❹ (used after a numeral) more; over; odd：二百～人 more than (*or* over) two hundred people /全书有两千～页。The book runs to 2,000-odd pages. /现在五点～钟。It's a little past five. /功效提高了一倍～。The efficiency has more than doubled. ❺ much more; much less; far more; far less：前景好～了。The prospects are much brighter. /她现在比以前身体差～了。Her health is not at all as good as before. ❻ (Duō) a surname

多² duō 〈副词〉❶ *used in questions to indicate degree or extent*：这孩子～大了？How old is the boy? ❷ *used in exclamations to indicate a high degree or great extent*：～好的年轻人啊！What a fine young man! /瞧这姑娘的手有～巧！Look, how dexterous the girl is! /他是～么傲慢！How arrogant he is! ❸ *used to indicate a certain degree or extent*：无论路～难走，他总是走在前面。He was always in the lead no matter how hard the journey was. /～复杂的算术题他也能做出来。He could work out even the most difficult math problem. /需要我呆～久，我就干～久。I'll stay for as long as I'm needed.

多胺 duō'àn polymine

多半 duōbàn ❶ greater part; majority; most：考生～是南方人。Most of the examinees are from the south. /他的节假日也～用在科研上了。He spent most of his holidays on scientific research. ❷ probably; most likely：他好久没有来信。～已出国了。I haven't heard from him for a long time. Most likely he has gone abroad. /台风～发生在夏季。Typhoons usually occur in summer.

多瓣抓斗 duōbàn zhuādǒu 〈机械〉Orange-peel bucket

多宝槅 duōbǎogé *also* "多宝架" curio stand with many sections; curio shelves; knick-knack shelf

多倍体 duōbèitǐ *also* "多元体"〈生物〉polyploid：～育种 polyploid breeding

多倍体植物 duōbèitǐ zhíwù polyploid plant

多臂机 duōbìjī 〈纺织〉dobby

多边 duōbiān multilateral：～会谈 multilateral talks or negotiations /～清算 multilateral clearing /～机构 multilateral agency /～援助 multilateral assistance /～渠道 multilateral channel /～承诺 multilateral commitment /～核力量 multilateral nuclear forces /～一体化 multilateral integration /～最惠国条款 multilateral most favoured nation clause /～保证 multilateral guarantee /支付～化 multilateralization of payment

多边公约 duōbiān gōngyuē multilateral pact or convention

多边贸易 duōbiān màoyì multilateral trade：～谈判 multilateral trade negotiations

多边条约 duōbiān tiáoyuē multilateral treaty

多边外交 duōbiān wàijiāo multilateral diplomacy

多边形 duōbiānxíng 〈数学〉polygon

多边主义 duōbiānzhǔyì multilateralism

多变 duōbiàn changeable; fickle; varied：色彩～ varied colours /天气～ changeable (*or* fickle) weather /形势～ volatile situation /性情～ mercurial temperament

多兵种合成部队 duōbīngzhǒng héchéng bùduì combined force of different arms (*or* military services)

多波段 duōbōduàn 〈无线电〉multiple-band：～遥感 multiband scanner /～接收机 multiple-band receiver

多波束 duōbōshù 〈无线电〉multi-beam：～天线 multi-beam antenna /～卫星 multi-beam satellite

多不饱和酸 duōbùbǎohésuān 〈化学〉polyunsaturated acid

多不饱和脂肪 duōbùbǎohé zhīfáng 〈化学〉polyunsaturated fat

多部门 duōbùmén multisectional：～情报网 multisectional information network (MSIN)

多才多艺 duōcái-duōyì versatile：他是个～的人。He is a versatile man. *or* He's a man of many talents (*or* a man of parts).

多财善贾 duōcái-shàngǔ with plenty of money one will be good at business; given the means success is easy

see also "长袖善舞" chángxiù-shànwǔ

多层安全玻璃 duōcéng ānquán bōli multiplex safety glass

多层板 duōcéngbǎn multiply wood

多层波束雷达 duōcéng bōshù léidá stacked-beam radar

多层薄膜电路 duōcéng bómó diànlù multilayer film circuit

多层次 duōcéngcì multiple echelons; multilevel; multilayer：～教育 multilevel education

多层镀膜 duōcéng dùmó multicoating

多层建筑 duōcéng jiànzhù multi-storied building; highrise

多层屏蔽 duōcéng píngbì multilayer screen

多层天线 duōcéng tiānxiàn stacked antenna

多层元件 duōcéng yuánjiàn sandwich type element

多产 duōchǎn ❶ prolific：～作家 prolific writer ❷ multiparity：～妇女 multiparous woman

多车道 duōchēdào multilane：～公路 multilane highway

多吃多占 duōchī-duōzhàn take more than is due to one; get more (from the state, etc.) than is proper; grab more than one's share：～的干部大大降低了他们在人民中的威望。Officials who take more from the state than is due them lower themselves considerably in the estimate of the people.

多重公民资格 duōchóng gōngmín zīgé multiple citizenship

多重国籍 duōchóng guójí plural nationality; multiple nationality

多重开关 duōchóng kāiguān multi-break switch or circuit-breaker

多重人格 duōchóng réngé 〈医学〉multiple personality

多重调制 duōchóng tiáozhì compound or double modulation

多重图像 duōchóng túxiàng 〈摄影〉multi-image (set of images taken of the same location at different times, at different wavelengths, with different sensors, or with different polarizations)

多重信息处理机 duōchóng xìnxī chǔlǐjī polyprocessor

多愁善感 duōchóu-shàngǎn excessively sentimental; mawkish：她生性～。She is sentimental (*or* mawkish) by nature.

多处理机 duōchǔlǐjī 〈计算机〉multiprocessor：～交叉 multiprocessor interleaving

多此一举 duōcǐyījǔ be superfluous; carry coals to Newcastle; make an unnecessary move：何苦～？Why go to all this bother? /如果他改变了原先的想法，我们就不必～了。If he changed his mind, we would not have to make the move.

多次 duōcì many times; repeatedly; on many occasions：～提出忠告 offer repeated advice /～崭露头角 distinguish oneself on many occasions /～入境签证 multiple entry visa

多弹头 duōdàntóu multiple warhead：～分导重返大气层运载工具 multiple independently-targeted reentry vehicle (MIRV)

多党合作和协商制 duōdǎng hézuò hé xiéshāngzhì system of multi-party cooperation and consultation

多党制 duōdǎngzhì multi-party system

多刀车床 duōdāo chēchuáng 〈机械〉multiple-tool lathe

多刀切削 duōdāo qiēxiāo 〈机械〉multiple cut; multicut

多道程序处理机 duōdào chéngxù chǔlǐjī 〈计算机〉multi-list processor

多斗挖土机 duōdǒu wātǔjī 〈建筑〉multi-bucket excavator; digging ladder

多端 duōduān ❶ varied; in various ways：变化～ most changeable; highly volatile /诡计～ have a whole bag of tricks; be very crafty ❷〈计算机〉multi-port; multi-terminal：～网络 multi-port or multi-terminal network /～输入 multi-input

多多马 Duōduōmǎ Dodoma, capital of Tanzania since 1990

多多益善 duōduō-yìshàn the more, the better; the more, the merrier; plenty is no plague：韩信用兵～。When Han Xin, the military strategist, directed a battle, his principle was "the more troops, the better". *or* The more, the better, as Han Xin said of his ability to command troops in battle.

多发 duōfā occur frequently：事故～地段 accident-prone area or section (of a road, etc.)

多发病 duōfābìng frequently occurring disease; disease of frequent occurrence

多发性 duōfāxìng 〈医学〉multiple：～肿瘤 multiple tumour /～骨髓瘤 multiple myeloma; Kahler's disease

多发性淋巴肉瘤 duōfāxìng línbā ròuliú 〈医学〉lymphosarcoma malignum multiplex

多发性息肉 duōfāxìng xīròu 〈医学〉polyposis

多发性脂肪瘤 duōfāxìng zhīfángliú 〈医学〉lipomatosis

多方 duōfāng in many ways; in every way：～阻挠 hinder in many ways; place many obstacles (in sb.'s way, etc.) /～譬喻 explain by

all sorts of analogies /～设法挽救局面 try in many ways to save the situation /医院经过～抢救,病人才转危为安。The dying patient eventually pulled through after all available emergency treatments at the hospital.

多方面 duōfāngmiàn many-sided; multiple; in many ways:他失败的原因是～的。His defeat was caused by a number of factors. /蒙他们～给以帮助,我们才得以及时完成任务。Thanks to their help in every possible way, we fulfilled our task in time.

多哥 Duōgē Togo:～人 Togolese

多功能 duōgōngnéng multifunction; multi-purpose:～传感装置 multifunction sensor

多功能厅 duōgōngnéngtīng multi-purpose hall

多寡 duōguǎ number; amount:不知～ not know the exact amount (*or* number) /～不等 vary in number or amount /报酬不计～ not mind how much one will be paid for the job

多管 duōguǎn 〈军事〉multibarrel:～炮 multibarreled gun /～高射机关炮 pompom /～火箭炮 multibarrel (rocket) launcher

多光点扫描 duōguāngdiǎn sǎomiáo 〈通信〉multiple-spot scanning

多光子 duōguāngzǐ 〈物理〉multiphoton

多轨录音 duōguǐ lùyīn multitrack recording

多滚立式延压机 duōgǔn lìshì yányājī vertical multi-roller

多国 duōguó multinational:～维持和平部队 multinational peace-keeping force /～经济组织 multinational economic organization /～河流 multinational river /～委派 multiple accreditation /～货币调整 multinational currency realignment

多国公司 duōguó gōngsī multinational corporation

多国银行 duōguó yínháng multinational bank

多辊轧机 duōgǔn zhájī 〈冶金〉cluster mill; rolling mill

多哈 Duōhā Doha, capital of Qatar

多汗症 duōhànzhèng 〈医学〉hyperhidrosis

多行播种机 duōháng bōzhǒngjī 〈农业〉multiple-row seeder

多行中耕机 duōháng zhōnggēngjī 〈农业〉multiple-row cultivator

多核白细胞 duōhé báixìbāo 〈生物〉multinuclear leucocyle

多核苷酸 duōhégānsuān 〈生化〉nucleotide

多核细胞 duōhé xìbāo 〈生物〉polykaryocyte

多铧犁 duōhuálí multishare plough; multifurrow plough

多会儿 duōhuìr 〈口语〉❶ when; what time:那笔贷款～到期? When will that loan be due? ❷ ever; at any time:～我休假,就来看您。I'll come and see you when I am on holiday.

多基地雷达 duōjīdì léidá 〈军事〉multistatic radar

多基因 duōjīyīn 〈生物〉polygenes

多级泵 duōjíbèng 〈机械〉multi-stage pump

多级抽样 duōjí chōuyàng multi-stage sampling (technique for acquiring statistics by studying various selected samples of a population with the most detailed studies being done on very small samples)

多级火箭 duōjí huǒjiàn multi-stage rocket

多极 duōjí 〈电学〉multipolar:～发电机 multipolar generator

多极化 duōjíhuà multi-polarization:当今世界正在向～方向发展。The world is moving towards multipolarity.

多极世界 duōjí shìjiè multipolar world

多价染色体 duōjià rǎnsètǐ multivalent chromosome

多价元素 duōjià yuánsù polyad

多键 duōjiàn multikey

多晶硅 duōjīngguī 〈电子〉polycrystalline silicon

多晶激光器 duōjīng jīguāngqì polycrystalline laser

多晶体 duōjīngtǐ 〈物理〉polycrystal

多精受精 duōjīng shòujīng polyspermy:～卵 polyspermic egg

多镜 duōjìng multi-mirror:～望远镜 multi-mirror telescope; multiple mirror telescope

多镜头 duōjìngtóu multi-lens:～摄影机 multi-lens camera

多聚糖 duōjùtáng *also* "多糖"〈化学〉polysaccharide; polysaccharose

多菌灵 duōjūnlíng 〈农业〉carbendazim; carbendazol

多孔 duōkǒng porous:～不锈钢〈冶金〉porous stainless steel /～(反应)堆〈核物理〉porous reactor /～金属〈冶金〉porous metal /～玻璃〈化工〉cellular glass; foamed glass

多孔板 duōkǒngbǎn multi-orifice; perforated plate

多孔动物 duōkǒng dòngwù porifera

多孔混凝土 duōkǒng hùnníngtǔ 〈建筑〉cellular concrete

多孔砖 duōkǒngzhuān porous brick; perforated brick

多口词 duōkǒucí 〈戏曲〉rhymed dialogue performed by more than two persons

多口相声 duōkǒu xiàngsheng cross talk or comic dialogue performed by more than two persons

多跨结构 duōkuà jiégòu 〈建筑〉multispan structure

多跨桥 duōkuàqiáo 〈建筑〉multispan bridge

多快好省 duō-kuài-hǎo-shěng achieve greater, faster, better and more economical results

多亏 duōkuī thanks to; luckily:～你的支持。We owe everything to your support. /～有你在场。Luckily you were on the scene.

多劳多得 duōláo-duōdé more work, more pay:贯彻～的方针 implement the policy of more work, more pay

多类寄生虫感染 duōlèi jìshēngchóng gǎnrǎn 〈医学〉polyparasitism

多棱镜 duōléngjìng *also* "棱镜"(optical) prism; triangular prism

多列士 Duōlièshì Maurice Thorez (1900-1964), General Secretary of the French Communist Party (1930-1964)

多路 duōlù 〈自控〉multichannel; multipath:～联机 multiple on-line /～通信〈通信〉multichannel communication

多路传输 duōlù chuánshū 〈无线电〉multiplex transmission

多路传真 duōlù chuánzhēn multichannel facsimile:～机 multichannel fax machine

多路载波通路 duōlù zàibō tōnglù multichannel carrier path

多虑 duōlǜ be over-anxious; be full of misgivings:请勿～。There is no cause for anxiety. /我没有那个意思,您～了。I didn't mean that. You are oversensitive.

多伦多 Duōlúnduō Toronto, largest city in Canada

多轮汽车 duōlún qìchē multiwheeler

多毛症 duōmáozhèng 〈生理〉hirsutism; pilosis

多么 duōme 〈副词〉❶ (used in questions, often without 么 in spoken language) to what extent; how:西安离这里有～远? How far is Xi'an from here? /泰山有～高? What is the height of Mount Tai? ❷ (used in an exclamatory sentence to indicate high degree) what; how:～讨厌! What a nuisance! /～好玩! What fun! /～滑稽! How funny! ❸ to a great extent:不管～忙,他总是挤出时间来读书。However busy he was, he always managed to find spare time for reading.

多媒体 duōméitǐ multimedia:宽带～ broadband multimedia /～光盘 multimedia CD /～效应 multimedia effect

多酶 duōméi multienzyme:～复合物 multienzyme complex

多米尼加 Duōmǐníjiā Dominica, island in the Caribbean:～共和国 Dominican Republic /～人 Dominicans

多米诺骨牌 duōmǐnuò gǔpái dominoes:～理论 domino theory /经济危机一来,许多企业就成了～,一个接着一个地倒闭。Hit by economic depression, enterprises went bankrupt one after another like dominoes.

多面角 duōmiànjiǎo *also* "立体角" lìtǐjiǎo 〈数学〉solid angle

多面手 duōmiànshǒu many-sided person; versatile person; all-rounder; person of many parts:他是个～。He is an all-rounder.

多面体 duōmiàntǐ 〈数学〉polyhedron

多民族国家 duōmínzú guójiā multinational country; country with many ethnic groups

多明戈 Duōmínggē Placido Domingo (1941-), Spanish tenor

多明我会 Duōmíngwǒhuì 〈宗教〉Dominican Order

多模光纤 duōmó guāngxiān multimode optical fibre; multimode fibre

多谋善断 duōmóu-shànduàn resourceful and decisive; sagacious and resolute:那次战役,充分表现了将军的～。The general's resourcefulness was fully demonstrated in that battle.

多幕剧 duōmùjù play of many acts; full-length drama

多那太罗 Duōnàtàiluó Donato di Niccolo Donatello (1386-1466), Italian sculptor in early Renaissance

多难兴邦 duōnàn-xīngbāng trials and tribulations regenerate a nation; foreign aggression or internal distress helps invigorate a nation

多囊肾 duōnángshèn 〈医学〉polycystic kidney

多瑙河 Duōnǎohé Danube (River):～文化 Danubian culture /"蓝色的～" *Blue Danube* (by Johann Strauss Jr.)

多年 duōnián many years; for years:为之奋斗～ fight for a cause for many years /他～没有音信。I haven't heard from him for ages.

多年生 duōniánshēng 〈植物〉perennial:～植物 perennial plant

多黏菌素 duōniánjūnsù polymyxin

多尿症 duōniàozhèng 〈医学〉polyuria

多胚生殖 duōpēi shēngzhí polyembryony
多配偶制 duōpèi'ǒuzhì polygamy
多频 duōpín 〈无线电〉multifrequency：～接收机 multifrequency receiver /～遥控系统 multifrequency remote control system
多频道 duōpíndào multichannel：～电视 multichannel television
多频发电机 duōpín fādiànjī 〈电工〉multifrequency generator
多普勒 Duōpǔlè Christian Doppler (1803-1853), Austrian physicist：～导航〈航空〉Doppler navigation /～雷达〈通信〉Doppler radar
多普勒位移 Duōpǔlè wèiyí 〈物理〉Doppler shift (change in the apparent frequency of sound or electromagnetic waves caused by the motion of the source towards or away from the observer)
多普勒效应 Duōpǔlè xiàoyìng 〈物理〉Doppler effect
多普线照相 duōpǔxiàn zhàoxiàng multispectral photography
多谱段 duōpǔduàn 〈物理〉multi-spectrum：～扫描 multispectral scanning /～航天摄影 multispectral space photography /～系统 multispectral system /～图像 multispectral image /～测量 multi-band survey
多谱段扫描仪 duōpǔduàn sǎomiáoyí multiple spectrum scanner
多羟基 duōqiǎngjī 〈化学〉polyhydroxy
多情 duōqíng tender and affectionate (to a person of the opposite sex)：她～地看着他。She looked at him affectionately (*or* fondly). /～自古伤离别。Lovers always suffer the sorrows of parting.
多儿 duōr 〈方言〉❶ how much; how many：他无论有～钱都不够花。He never has enough money to spend, no matter how much he has. ❷ what time; when：您～来的？When did you come?
多染色性 duōrǎnsèxìng 〈医学〉polychromasia; polychromatophilia
多刃刀具 duōrèn dāojù 〈机械〉multiple cutting-edge tool; multi-point tool
多任务卫星 duōrènwù wèixīng multi-mission satellite
多日 duōrì many days; long time：～不见。Haven't seen you for a long time. /我们已等候～。We have been waiting for many days.
多如牛毛 duōrúniúmáo too numerous to enumerate; countless; innumerable：苛捐杂税，～。There were as many taxes and levies as there are hairs on an ox. /这种平庸的作品市上～。Such mediocre works are innumerable on the book market.
多色 duōsè polychrome：～染料 polygenetic dye /～印刷 polychrome printing
多少 duōshǎo ❶ number; amount：～不等 vary in amount or number /衣服不在～，而在质量。The quality of one's clothes carries more weight than the number. ❷ somewhat; more or less; to some extent：～有点沾沾自喜 feel somewhat conceited /不要多，给我一点儿就行。I don't need much. Just something will do. /对这件事，你多多少少总有些耳闻吧。You must have got an inkling of what has happened. ❸ a little; slightly：初秋的天气，～有点凉意了。One begins to feel a slight chill in the air when autumn comes.
多少 duōshao ❶ how many; how much：医学知识他究竟懂～？How much medical knowledge does he have? /这苹果～钱一公斤？How much are those apples per kilo? ❷ *indicating an uncertain quantity*：我不知道他在上海要呆～天。I don't know how long he will stay in Shanghai.
多神教 duōshénjiào polytheism
多神论 duōshénlùn 〈宗教〉polytheism：～者 polytheist
多时 duōshí long time：等候～ wait a long time /～不见。Haven't seen you for a long time (*or* for ages).
多事 duōshì ❶ do what is unnecessary or superfluous：这些问题自有他处理，你何必～！It is up to him to handle these matters. Why should you bother? ❷ stick one's nose in; be meddlesome：～的人 busybody; Nosey Parker /不必～。Don't poke your nose into the matter. *or* Let sleeping dogs lie. *or* Mind your own business. ❸ troubled; eventful：国家～，百姓不安。The people shall have no peace when the country is in trouble.
多事之秋 duōshìzhīqiū eventful period of time; troubled times
多数 duōshù majority; most：绝大～ overwhelming majority /简单～ simple majority /特定～ qualified majority /绝对～ absolute majority /相对～ relative majority; plurality /三分之二～ two-thirds majority /～通过的决议 majority decision /～票 majority vote /在～情况下，利多弊少。In most cases, advantages outweigh disadvantages. /大～人过着小康的生活。Most people are moderately well off. /决议以微弱～通过。The resolution was carried by a small (*or* narrow) majority. /团结～，孤立少数。Unite the many and isolate the few.
多速电动机 duōsù diàndòngjī multispeed motor
多胎妊娠 duōtāi rènshēn 〈医学〉polycyesis
多肽 duōtài 〈生化〉polypeptide：～酶 polypeptidase
多糖 duōtáng 〈化学〉polysaccharide; polysaccharose：～酶 polysaccharase; polyase
多特蒙德-埃姆斯运河 Duōtèméngdé-Āimǔsī Yùnhé Dortmund-Ems Canal in Germany
多通道放大器 duōtōngdào fàngdàqì 〈计算机〉multichannel amplifier
多头 duōtóu ❶ (on the stock exchange) bull; long：做～ take a long position; be long (*or* on the long side) /～市场 bull market ❷ many chiefs or leaders; more than one channel：领导～ control by many leaders (*or* bosses)
多头对外 duōtóu duìwài 〈外贸〉multichannel management in foreign trade
多头条虫 duōtóu tiáochóng 〈医学〉multiceps
多头条虫蚴 duōtóu tiáochóngyòu 〈医学〉coenurus：～病 coenurosis
多头政治 duōtóu zhèngzhì polyarchy
多退少补 duōtuì-shǎobǔ 〈商业〉refund for any overpayment or supplementary payment for any deficiency (after a round sum is paid in advance for a batch of goods)
多维 duōwéi 〈数学〉multidimensional：～积分 multidimensional calculus
多维空间 duōwéi kōngjiān hyperspace; multidimensional space
多维球面 duōwéi qiúmiàn hypersphere
多维曲面 duōwéi qūmiàn hypersurface
多闻 duōwén well-informed; knowledgeable：博学～ learned and well-informed; have extensive knowledge and experience
多系杂交 duōxì zájiāo multiple crossing
多细胞生物 duōxìbāo shēngwù multicellular organism
多纤光缆 duōxiān guānglǎn multiple fibre-optic cable
多线铁路 duōxiàn tiělù multiple-line railway
多嫌 duōxian 〈方言〉regard (sb.) as superfluous; cold-shoulder：你别担心，决不会～你一个。Don't worry. You are not one too many.
多相 duōxiàng ❶〈电工〉〈物理〉multiphase; polyphase：～电动机 multiphase (*or* polyphase) motor /～电流 polyphase current /～发电机 multiphase generator; multiphaser /～流 multiphase flow ❷〈化学〉heterogeneous：～催化 heterogeneous catalysis /～合金 heterogeneous alloy /～聚合 heterogeneous polymerization
多项式 duōxiàngshì 〈数学〉polynomial; multinomial：～表示 polynomial representation /～函数 polynomial function
多谢 duōxiè 〈套语〉many thanks; thanks a lot：～～。Thank you ever so much. /～款待。Thanks for your hospitality. /～关照。Thank you for your kindness.
多心 duōxīn oversensitive; suspicious：他无恶意，你别～。He meant no harm. Please don't take it to heart. /她太～了，我根本不是这个意思。She is just hopelessly oversensitive and got me completely wrong. *or* She is paranoid about what I said.
多芯电缆 duōxìn diànlǎn multicore cable
多芯光缆 duōxìn guānglǎn multifilament cable; multifibre cable
多行不义必自毙 duō xíng bùyì bì zì bì he who perpetrates many injustices is doomed to destruction; he who keeps on doing evil is only digging his own grave; an evil-doer is his own grave-digger; those who commit unrighteous acts bring ruin on themselves
多学科 duōxuékē multidisciplinary; interdisciplinary
多氧菌素 duōyǎngjūnsù polyoxin
多样 duōyàng diverse; varied：款式～ many diverse styles /形式～ diversified (*or* varied) in form
多样化 duōyànghuà diversify; vary：～经营 diversification /生产结构～ diversification of the production structure /投资的～规划 diversified programme of investment /作品的艺术风格应～。The work should be varied in artistic style.
多耶 duōyē folk dance of the Dong (*or* Tung) nationality
多一半 duōyībàn more than half; good half：这个厂的产品～有质量问题。More than half of the products turned out by this factory are defective in quality.
多一事不如少一事 duō yī shì bùrú shǎo yī shì avoid trouble wherever possible; the less trouble, the better; let sleeping dogs lie
多一位菩萨多一炉香 duō yī wèi púsà duō yī lú xiāng more Buddhas, more incense burning; get another Buddha and you will have to burn more incense; if you get more people in leading positions,

D

you will increase red tape rather than efficiency

多疑 duōyí oversensitive; oversuspicious; given to suspicion; prone to suspicion: 不该～。One must not be suspicious without cause.

多义 duōyì 〈语言〉polysemy

多义词 duōyìcí 〈语言〉polysemous word; polysemant

多音节词 duōyīnjiécí 〈语言〉polysyllabic or multisyllabic word

多用插座 duōyòng chāzuò multitap

多余 duōyú ❶ surplus: ～农产品 surplus farm produce / 这是～的讲稿。Here are extra copies of the speech. ❷ unnecessary; superfluous; uncalled for; redundant: 删除～的词语 delete redundant words and expressions / 你的猜疑是～的。Your suspicion is uncalled for. / 也许这些话是～的。Perhaps, these words are superfluous.

多元 duōyuán multifactor; multielement; multivariate; multiple: ～计划 multifactor scheme / ～地震计 multielement seismoscope / ～分析 multivariate analysis / ～联接 multiple access / ～主义 pluralism

多元大学 duōyuán dàxué multiversity; polyversity

多元激光雷达 duōyuán jīguāng léidá 〈军事〉multilasered optical radar

多元论 duōyuánlùn 〈哲学〉pluralism: 政治～ political pluralism / ～历史观 pluralistic concept of history / ～者 pluralist

多元社会 duōyuán shèhuì pluralistic society

多元酸 duōyuánsuān 〈化学〉polybasic acid

多元体 duōyuántǐ *see* "多倍体"

多元文化 duōyuán wénhuà multicultural: ～社会 multicultural society / ～主义 multiculturalism

多云 duōyún 〈气象〉cloudy: ～转阴, 有时有阵雨 (turning) from cloudy to overcast, with occasional showers

多灾多难 duōzāi-duōnàn be dogged by bad luck; be plagued by frequent disasters: 他的病刚好, 儿子又出了车祸, 真是～。No sooner had he recovered from illness than his son had a car accident. What bad luck!

多栽花少栽刺 duō zāi huā shǎo zāi cì plant more flowers and fewer thorns — adopt a placatory attitude and avoid offending people

多咱 duōzan 〈方言〉what time; when: 你记得这是～的事? Can you remember when it happened? / ～动身, 你告诉我一声。Let me know when you wish to leave.

多早晚 duōzaowǎn *see* "多咱"

多趾畸形 duōzhǐ jīxíng 〈生理〉polydactylia: ～的男孩 polydactyl boy

多中心 duōzhōngxīn polycentric: ～主义 polycentrism

多种 duōzhǒng diversified; varied; manifold: ～形式的合作 multiform cooperation / ～语言的通知 multilingual notice / ～工业联合企业 conglomerate / ～汇价 multiple rates / ～货币贷款 multicurrency loan / ～用途 multipurpose

多种多样 duōzhǒng-duōyàng varied; manifold: ～的促销形式 various forms of sales promotion / 生产更多的东西满足消费者～的需要。Produce more to meet the manifold needs of consumers.

多种钙 duōzhǒnggài polycalcium

多种经营 duōzhǒng jīngyíng diversified economy; diversification: ～的趋向 tendency towards diversification / ～, 全面发展。Develop a diversified economy and ensure all-round development.

多种所有制经济 duōzhǒng suǒyǒuzhì jīngjì economy with different modes of ownership

多种纤维协定 Duōzhǒng Xiānwéi Xiédìng Multifibre Arrangement (MFA)

多轴 duōzhóu 〈机械〉multiple-spindle; multi-axle: ～车床 multiple-spindle lathe / ～拉床 multiple-spindle broaching machine / ～钻床 multiple-spindle drill

多助 duōzhù abundant support: 得道～, 失道寡助。A just cause enjoys abundant support while an unjust cause finds little support.

多柱式 duōzhùshì 〈建筑〉polystyle

多姿 duōzī very charming: ～多彩 very charming and colourful / 婀娜～ graceful and enchanting

多子多福 duōzǐ-duōfú 〈旧语〉to have many sons is to have many blessings

多子叶 duōzǐyè 〈植物〉polycotyledony: ～植物 polycotyledon

多足动物 duōzú dòngwù myriopod

多嘴 duōzuǐ shoot off one's mouth; have a big mouth: 因为他～, 咱们弄得这么被动! His big mouth has been an embarrassment to us. / 初来乍到, 别～! Being a stranger here, you'd better keep your mouth shut!

多嘴多舌 duōzuǐ-duōshé gossipy and meddlesome; long-tongued: 不要～! Don't interrupt! / 她立刻瞪了他一眼, 怪他～。She tossed him a quick glance to indicate that he had said too much.

哆 duō

see also chǐ

哆嗦 duōsuo tremble; shiver: 气得直～ tremble with rage / 冷得直打～ shiver with cold / 她脸色苍白, 嘴唇不住地～。She turned pale, her lips trembling.

裰 duō ❶ mend; patch: 补～ mend (*or* patch) clothes ❷ *also* "直裰" zhíduō loose robe worn by a Buddhist monk or Taoist priest

掇(敠) duō ❶ pick up: ～而置于室中 pick up sth. and keep it in the house / 她把房间拾～得整整齐齐。She tidied up the room. ❷ 〈方言〉hold with both hands (a chair, stool, etc.); carry: 把凳子～开。Take the stool away. *or* Put the stool aside.

掇弄 duōnòng 〈方言〉❶ repair; fix: 我的电视机坏了, 找个人给～一下。My TV set has broken down. Please get somebody to repair it for me. / 闹钟经他一～就好了。The alarm clock worked again after he fixed it up. ❷ incite; manipulate; stir up: 谁都知道是他在她后面～。Everybody knows that she is manipulated by him. / 不要受人～。Don't let yourself be twisted (*or* turned) round somebody's (little) finger.

掇拾 duōshí 〈书面〉❶ tidy up; put in order ❷ collect; gather

剟 duō 〈书面〉❶ stab; attack ❷ cut down on; delete ❸ cut down and take

咄 duō 〈书面〉❶〈叹词〉*used to show amazement or to berate*: ～! 休得无理! Tut! None of your cheek! ❷ berate; be shocked: 酒肉朋友, 终必相～。Fair-weather friends are bound to fall out in the end.

咄咄 duōduō tut-tut: ～称奇 cannot help wondering loudly / ～奈老何! Tut-tut, I'm an old man now!

咄咄逼人 duōduō-bīrén arrogant; overbearing; aggressive: 他那～的态度, 大家都厌烦。His overweening manner annoyed every one of us.

咄咄怪事 duōduō-guàishì height of absurdity: 岂非～? Isn't this monstrous absurdity?

咄嗟 duōjiē 〈书面〉shout (an order); cry out; call

咄嗟立办 duōjiē-lìbàn carry out (an order) immediately: 这项规定虽然重要, 但还不能～。This is a policy of great importance. However, it cannot be put into practice immediately.

咄呐 duōnè 〈方言〉be garrulous; nag: 老伴整天在他身边～, 搞得他心烦意乱。His wife's constant nagging made him nervous and flustered. *or* He was upset by his wife's endless nagging.

咄念 duōniàn 〈方言〉babble; be garrulous; be long-winded: 她整天穷～, 搞得大家都心烦。She is babbling all day and getting on everybody's nerves.

duó

度 duó 〈书面〉surmise; estimate: 审时～势 judge the timing and size up (*or* estimate) the situation

see also dù

度德量力 duódé-liànglì take a proper measure of one's own strength or ability; make correct appraisal of one's own position: 我倒是愿意干的, 但～, 确实难以胜任。I'd very much like to take on the job, but judging by my ability, I do not think I am equal to it.

踱 duó pace; stroll: ～来～去 pace to and fro (*or* up and down) / 他独自一人在草坪上～着方步。He strolled across the lawn with measured steps (*or* walked in a leisurely manner).

夺[1](奪) duó ❶ take by force; seize; wrest: 巧取豪～ take away by force or fraud / 强词～理 resort to sophistry ❷ contend for; compete for; strive for: ～高产 strive for high yields / ～走金牌

carry off the gold medal ❸ overwhelm; defeat; surpass: 巧～天工 ingenuity surpassing nature /眼泪～眶而出 tears trickle (*or* spill, *or* gush) from one's eyes; be unable to hold back the tears ❹ deprive: 剥～权利 deprive sb. of a right ❺〈书面〉lose: 勿～农时。Don't miss the farming season.

夺²(奪) duó 〈书面〉decide: 定～ make a final decision /裁～ give a verdict

夺³(奪) duó 〈书面〉omission (in a text): 讹～ errors and omissions

夺杯 duóbēi win the (first) prize (in a contest); win the championship: 在这次乒乓球团体赛中,我男女队双双～。Both China's men's team and women's team carried off the first prizes in the table tennis championships team events.

夺标 duóbiāo ❶ win the trophy; win a championship: ～呼声最高 be favoured for the championship ❷ have one's tender accepted; win bid: 这项工程被北京的一家建筑公司～。The bid for the project was won by a Beijing construction company.

夺佃 duódiàn eviction of peasants from land leased to them by landlords

夺冠 duóguàn win the championship; come first; take first place: 该队在大赛中接连～。The team won one championship after another at major events.

夺回 duóhuí recapture; retake; seize back; wrest back: ～一局 win a game (after losing one or more) /～失去的时间 make up for lost time

夺获 duóhuò capture; seize; wrest: ～了大批战利品 capture large quantities of spoils

夺魁 duókuí come first; win the first prize; win the championship: 这个厂的电视机在全国评比中～。TV sets produced by this factory won first prize in the nationwide evaluation. /在这次篮球锦标赛中,我队再次～。Our team once again came out first in the basketball championship.

夺门而出 duómén'érchū make for the door and rush out

夺门而入 duómén'érrù force one's way into a room or house

夺目 duómù dazzle the eyes: 灿烂～ dazzling; brilliant /光彩～的项链 shining necklace

夺氢反应 duóqīng fǎnyìng 〈化学〉hydrogen abstraction reaction

夺取 duóqǔ ❶ capture; seize; wrest; take by force: ～敌人的阵地 capture an enemy position /～主动权 seize the initiative ❷ strive for: ～更大的胜利 strive for even greater victories

夺权 duóquán seize power; take over power by force

夺神 duóshén daze; dazzle; amaze: 彩色缤纷,眩目～ be dazzled by a riot of colours

夺胎换骨 duótāi-huàngǔ (originally a Taoist expression) seize sb.'s body and be reincarnated as an immortal; 〈比喻〉follow sb.'s example creatively in writing

夺占 duózhàn capture; seize; carry: 敌人乘虚～了我们一个据点。Taking advantage of the weak links in our defence, the enemy captured one of our strongholds.

夺志 duózhì 〈书面〉force sb. to give in: 匹夫不可～。Man's will cannot be conquered.

泽(澤) duó *see* "凌泽" língduó

铎(鐸) duó big bell used in ancient China in times of war or when a proclamation was issued: 木～ wooden bell /振～ strike a bell; issue a clarion call

duǒ

朵(朶) duǒ ❶〈量词〉*used of flowers, clouds, etc.*: 一～花 a flower /一～白云 a whitish cloud ❷ (Duǒ) a surname

朵儿 duǒr ❶ flower; blossom ❷〈量词〉: 一～梅花 a Chinese plum flower

朵颐 duǒyí 〈书面〉munch; chew: 大快～ eat with great relish; enjoy hugely

垛(垜) duǒ ❶ crenel; battlements ❷〈量词〉*used of a window, wall, etc.*: 砌一～砖墙 build a brick wall

see also duò

垛堞 duǒdié battlement; crenel: 有～的城堡 crenellated castle

垛口 duǒkǒu battlement; crenel

see also duòkǒu

垛子 duǒzi battlement; crenel: 城～ battlements on a city wall

see also duòzi

哚 duǒ *see* "吲哚" yǐnduǒ

躲(躱) duǒ ❶ go into hiding; hide (oneself): ～在角落里 hide in a corner ❷ avoid; dodge: ～雨 take shelter from the rain /她讨厌他,总设法～他。She hated him and always tried to steer clear of him.

躲避 duǒbì ❶ hide (oneself) ❷ avoid; elude; dodge: ～困难 shy away from difficulties

躲藏 duǒcáng hide or conceal oneself; go into hiding: 躲躲藏藏终非良策。Hiding is after all not the best solution.

躲躲闪闪 duǒduo-shǎnshǎn dodge; evade: 他的话说得～的,内中必有缘故。There must be something behind his evasive statement.

躲风 duǒfēng go into hiding or lie low until sth. blows over: 为了～,老板把一些伪劣商品都撤下去了。In order not to be caught red-handed, the boss unshelved all the conterfeit and shoddy goods.

躲懒 duǒlǎn shy away from work: 也有人～,上班不好好干。There are also lazy ones who shirk work.

躲了初一躲不过十五 duǒle chūyī duǒbuguò shíwǔ one may get off today, but not necessarily tomorrow — you have to face it sooner or later

躲难 duǒnàn take refuge; seek asylum: 到乡下～ lie low in the countryside

躲年 duǒnián stay away from home at the end of the lunar year to avoid creditors (formerly it was the custom to have all debts settled before the lunar New Year's; once into the New Year, the debtor got a reprieve)

躲穷 duǒqióng 〈方言〉〈旧语〉live with a relative to tide over difficult days

躲让 duǒràng dodge; evade; make way: 一辆救火车飞驰而来,人们纷纷往两边～。A fire-engine came speeding over, and people quickly stepped aside to dodge it.

躲闪 duǒshǎn dodge; evade: 老太太～不及,被汽车撞倒了。It was too late for the old woman to get out of the way and she was knocked down by the car. /别找理由～,你应对此事负全部责任。Don't hedge, you are entirely responsible for all this.

躲债 duǒzhài avoid a creditor

亸(嚲、軃) duǒ 〈书面〉hang down; droop: 城边柳～地 at the edge of the city where the willows droop

埵 duǒ 〈书面〉hard soil

duò

舵(柁) duò rudder; helm: 方向～ rudder /升降～ elevator /掌～ be at the helm

舵柄 duòbǐng tiller

舵杆 duògǎn 〈船舶〉rudder stock

舵工 duògōng *also* "舵公" quartermaster; helmsman; wheelsman

舵令 duòlìng word of command to turn the rudder

舵轮 duòlún steering wheel; helm

舵盘 duòpán *also* "舵轮" steering wheel; helm

舵师 duòshī quartermaster; helmsman; wheelsman

舵手 duòshǒu steersman; helmsman: 大海航行靠～。Sailing the seas we rely on our helmsman.

舵索 duòsuǒ rudder-line

舵位 duòwèi quartermaster's grating; helmsman's post

惰 duò lazy; idle; indolent: 懒～ lazy; slothful

惰轮 duòlún 〈机械〉idle roll; idle gear; idle pulley; idle wheel

惰态光学 duòtài guāngxué 〈物理〉passive optics

惰态金属 duòtài jīnshǔ 〈物理〉passive metal

惰性 duòxìng ❶〈化学〉inertia; inertness: ~金属 inert metal ❷ passive attitude (towards life and work); passivity
惰性化 duòxìnghuà 〈冶金〉deactivation
惰性气体 duòxìng qìtǐ 〈化学〉inert gas; noble gas: ~保护电弧焊〈机械〉inert gas-shielded arc welding; Heliarc welding /~保护切割〈机械〉inert-gas cutting
惰性气体激光 duòxìng qìtǐ jīguāng noble gas laser
惰性元素 duòxìng yuánsù inert element
惰转 duòzhuàn 〈机械〉idling

堕(墮)

duò fall; sink: ~地 fall on the ground
堕落 duòluò ❶ degenerate; sink low: ~成为罪犯 degenerate into a criminal /自甘~ resign oneself to degeneration; give oneself up to a life of degeneration /腐化~ corruption and degeneration /这儿便种下了他~的种子。Here lies the seed of his downfall. ❷ (often used in the early vernacular) fall low; come down in the world
堕落风尘 duòluò-fēngchén stoop to street-walking; be driven to prostitution
堕马 duòmǎ 〈书面〉fall from horseback; fall off a horse
堕入 duòrù sink into; lapse into; land oneself in: ~陷阱 fall into a trap /~情网 fall in love; be hit by Cupid's arrow /~五里雾中 be puzzled (*or* perplexed); be wide at sea
堕胎 duòtāi have an (induced) abortion

D

驮

duò
see also tuó
驮架 duòjià pannier
驮子 duòzi ❶ load carried by a pack-animal; pack: 卸下~ put down the load; unload the animal ❷〈量词〉*used of caravan goods*: 有三~货。There are three loads of goods.

柮

duò *see* "榾柮" gǔduò

柂(杝)

duò 〈书面〉❶ *see* "舵" duò ❷ communicate; connect; link: ~以漕渠 connect by canals
see also yí

垛(垜、稖)

duò ❶ pile up neatly: 把干草打好捆~起来。Bale the hay and pile it up. ❷ pile; stack: 柴禾~ pile of firewood
see also duǒ
垛叠 duòdié stack; heap up
垛口 duòkǒu 〈戏曲〉sing rhymed lines in neat succession
see also duǒkuǒ
垛子 duòzi pile; stack: 麦秸~ wheat (stem) pile
see also duǒzi

剁(剁)

duò chop; cut: ~去头尾 chop off the head and tail (of a fish, etc.) /~肉馅 chop up (*or* mince) meat /~为肉泥 hack to pieces
剁斧石 duòfǔshí *also* "剁假石" artificial stone made of stone powder and bits with cement, whose texture is made by hacking with an axe during solidification

跺(跥、跢)

duò stamp (one's foot)
跺跶 duòda step heavily on the ground: 他~着皮靴走路。He stomped along in his thumping boots.
跺脚 duòjiǎo stamp one's foot: 气得直~ stamp one's foot with fury (*or* in irritation)

E

ē

阿[1] ē ❶ play up to; pander to; cater to:～其所好 pander to sb.'s whims /刚正不～ standing on principles and not yielding to pressure; upright and above flattery ❷〈书面〉big hill; large mound:崇～ lofty hill ❸〈书面〉twist or turn in terrain:山～ turn of a mountain range

阿[2] Ē (short for 东阿) Dong E, place in Shandong
see also ā; à

阿堵物 ēdǔwù 〈书面〉cash; money
阿附 ēfù 〈书面〉fawn on and echo; toady to and chime in with:～权贵 cotton to the powerful; attach oneself to powerful and influential officials
阿胶 ējiāo *also* "驴皮胶" lǘpíjiāo 〈中药〉donkey-hide gelatin
阿弥陀佛 Ēmítuófó 〈宗教〉❶ (Sanskrit) *Amitabha*; *Amitayus* ❷ (in prayers) may Buddha preserve us; merciful Buddha:南无～。*Namo Amitabha*. *or* Blessed be (*or* Glory to) *Amitabha*!
阿弥陀经 Ēmítuójīng 〈宗教〉*Amitabhasutra*
阿弥陀宗 Ēmítuózōng 〈宗教〉Amidism (a form of Mahayana Buddhism which places faith above works)
阿房宫 Ēpánggōng grand palace built by the first Emperor of Qin Dynasty at Epang (in Shaanxi), started in 212 BC and burnt down, when still uncompleted, in 206 BC
阿魏 ēwèi ❶〈植物〉*Ferula asafoetida* ❷ Chinese herbal medicine extracted from the root of *Ferula asafoetida*.
阿谀 ēyú fawn on; flatter:～曲从 go against one's conscience to flatter sb. /～取容 flatter and toady to; fawn upon /～之词 words of flattery; soft soap
阿谀逢迎 ēyú-féngyíng *also* "阿谀奉承" curry favour with; lick sb.'s boots

痾 ē 〈书面〉disease; illness

屙 ē 〈方言〉discharge (excrement or urine):～屎 discharge excrement; shit /～尿 discharge urine; piss

婴 ē *see* "媕婴" ān'ē

婀 ē
婀娜 ēnuó (usu. of a woman's bearing or figure) lithe and graceful; supple and charming:体态～ be of lithe and graceful figure; have supple and charming bearing
婀娜多姿 ēnuó-duōzī very pretty and charming:杨柳～,可谓妩媚极了。Those lithe, pretty willows are extremely charming.

妸 ē
妸娜 ēnuó 〈书面〉*see* "婀娜" ēnuó

é

额[1] é ❶ forehead:蹙～ knit one's brows; frown ❷ horizontal tablet:碑～ top of a tablet /匾～ horizontal inscribed board

额[2] é specified number, sum, volume, or amount:营业～ turnover; volume of business /贸易～ volume of trade /全～ full amount of money /巨～ huge sum /差～ balance (in bookkeeping); difference /定～ quota /超～ above quota

额定 édìng specified (number or amount); rated:～人数 maximum number of persons allowed; stipulated number of personnel /～功率 rated power /～马力 rated horsepower /～吨位 specified tonnage
额定输出功率 édìng shūchū gōnglǜ rated output power
额定值 édìngzhí ❶〈电工〉nominal value ❷〈机械〉rating
额度 édù quota; specified amount
额尔德尼 É'ěrdéní Erdeni, scholar of the Manchu nationality of the 16th century who created the Manchu script
额尔古纳河 É'ěrgǔnàhé Ergun River, in Heilongjiang Province
额枋 éfāng 〈建筑〉architrave
额驸 éfù 〈旧语〉(of the Man nationality) emperor's son-in-law
额骨 égǔ 〈生理〉frontal bone
额角 éjiǎo frontal eminence
额颅 élú 〈方言〉forehead
额鲁特 Élǔtè 〈旧语〉general term used in the Qing Dynasty for China's western Mongolian tribes, called Wala (瓦剌) in the Ming Dynasty
额门 émén forehead:宽阔的～ broad forehead /突出的～ prominent forehead /他急得～冒汗。He was so worried that beads of sweat stood out on his forehead.
额面 émiàn denomination:～一百元的人民币 *Renminbi* note of 100 *yuan* denomination; 100 *yuan* banknote
额脑 énǎo 〈方言〉forehead
额手称庆 éshǒu-chēngqìng lay one's hand on one's forehead in jubilation; be overjoyed:消息传来,村民无不～。The villagers were beside themselves with joy at the good tidings.
额数 éshù specified amount; quota
额头 étou forehead
额外 éwài extra; additional; added:～开支 extra expenses /～报酬 extra pay /～损失 extraneous loss /～收入 additional income /～负担 added burden /～补贴 perk; perquisite

莪 é
莪蒿 éhāo species of artemisia; sagebrush
莪术 ézhú aromatic turmeric (*Curcuma aromatica*) of the ginger family

哦 é 〈书面〉softly chant (poetry):吟～ recite (poetry) with a cadence; chant
see also ó; ò

蛾 é moth:蚕～ silk moth /螟～ snout moth
see also yǐ
蛾兰 élán moth orchid (*Phalaenopsis*)
蛾螺 éluó whelk (*Buccinidae*)
蛾眉 éméi *see* "娥眉" éméi
蛾子 ézi moth

峨(峩) é 〈书面〉high; lofty; towering:嵯～ high and steep /巍～ towering; lofty
峨峨 é'é ❶ high and craggy; towering and precipitous:南岭～

E

southern craggy peaks ❷ solemn; awe-inspiring
峨冠博带 éguān-bódài high hat and wide waistbelt (worn by officials and scholars in ancient China)
峨嵋山 Éméishān Mount Emei, Sichuan Province

睋
é 〈书面〉❶ look; watch ❷ suddenly; soon

锇
é 〈化学〉osmium (Os)
锇笔尖合金 ébǐjiān héjīn osmium pen alloy
锇处理 échǔlǐ 〈化学〉osmification
锇黑 éhēi osmium black
锇丝灯 ésīdēng osmium lamp
锇酸 ésuān 〈化学〉osmic acid /～盐 osmate

俄[1]
é 〈书面〉shortly; presently; suddenly

俄[2]
É (short for 俄罗斯) ❶ Russian Empire (1721-1917) ❷ Russian Soviet Federated Socialist Republic (as a member of the Union of Soviet Socialist Republics, 1922-1990) ❸ (formerly used in the West as another name for) Union of the Soviet Socialist Republics ❹ Russian Federation (1990-);
俄巴底亚书 Ébādǐyàshū *Book of Obadiah*, shortest book of the *Old Testament*
俄而 é'ér *also* "俄尔" before long; not long after: ～日出。Presently the sun rose. /～雨过天晴。The rain soon stopped and the sky cleared up (*or* the sun came out).
俄国 Éguó Russia:沙皇～ Tsarist (*or* Czarist) Russia /苏维埃～ Soviet Russia /～社会民主工党 Russian Socialist Democratic Workers' Party /～1917年革命 Russian Revolution of 1917
俄亥俄 Éhài'é (US) Ohio:～河 Ohio River
俄里 élǐ verst (＝1.067 km.)
俄罗斯 Éluósī Russia:～人 Russian /～语 Russian language /～正教会 Russian Orthodox Church /～公教会 Russian Catholic Church
俄罗斯帝国 Éluósī Dìguó Russian Empire (1721-1917)
俄罗斯联邦 Éluósī Liánbāng Russian Federation
俄罗斯族 Éluósīzú ❶ Eluosi or Russian nationality, distributed over the Xinjiang Uygur Autonomous Region and Heilongjiang Province ❷ the Russians, majority people in the Russian Federation
俄顷 éqǐng 〈书面〉in a moment; presently: ～雨止。Presently the rain stopped.
俄然 érán suddenly; in a flash: ～消失 disappear suddenly (*or* in a flash); vanish like soap bubbles
俄文 Éwén Russian (language)
俄延 éyán delay; stall:他～了一会儿,只好失望地走了。He lingered for a while and left in disappointment.
俄语 Éyǔ Russian (language)

鹅(鵞、䳘)
é goose: 一群～ a flock of geese /企～ penguin /天～ swan
鹅蛋脸 édànliǎn egg-shaped face; oval face
鹅耳枥 é'ěrlì 〈植物〉*Carpinus turczaninowii*
鹅观草 éguāncǎo *Roegneria kamoji*, fine fodder for cattle and geese
鹅黄 éhuáng light yellow:他穿一件～色的上衣。He is wearing a light yellow jacket.
鹅颈管 éjǐngguǎn 〈机械〉gooseneck
鹅颈起重机 éjǐng qǐzhòngjī gooseneck crane
鹅颈式压铸机 éjǐngshì yāzhùjī gooseneck die-casting machine
鹅口疮 ékǒuchuāng 〈医学〉thrush
鹅涟 élian 〈方言〉stain; spot:衣服上沾了油漆,起了一片～。The clothes are stained with paint.
鹅卵石 éluǎnshí cobblestone; cobble
鹅毛 émáo goose feather: ～扇子 goose feathers fan /千里送～,礼轻情意重。The gift itself may be as light as a goose feather, but sent from afar, it conveys deep feeling.
鹅毛雪 émáoxuě snow flakes as big as goose feathers — heavy snow:下了一场～。There was a heavy snowfall.
鹅绒 éróng goose down
鹅喜 éxǐ 〈方言〉fertilised goose egg which has not hatched out: ～大量上市。There is an ample supply of fertilised goose eggs on the market.
鹅行鸭步 éxíng-yābù waddle along like a duck or goose
鹅掌柴 ézhǎngchái 〈植物〉*Schefflera octophylla*
鹅掌风 ézhǎngfēng 〈中医〉fungal infection of the hand; tinea manuum
鹅掌楸 ézhǎngqiū 〈植物〉Chinese tulip tree (*Liriodendron chinense*)

娥
é pretty young woman:宫～ palace maid; maid of honour/嫦～〈书面〉goddess of the moon
娥眉 éméi *also* "蛾眉" éméi ❶ delicate eyebrows ❷ beautiful woman
娥眉皓齿 éméi-hàochǐ fine eyebrows and white teeth — (a woman's) beauty; beautiful woman
娥眉月 éméiyuè new moon; crescent; crescent moon:天上一轮～。A crescent moon is hanging in the sky.

讹(❶譌)
é ❶ erroneous; wrong; mistaken: ～字 wrong words (in a text) /以～传～ circulate erroneous reports; spread a wrong message (*or* falsehood) /～言～语 erroneous and irresponsible comments ❷ blackmail; extort; bluff: ～人 blackmail sb.; bluff sb. /～钱 extort money by blackmail
讹传 échuán false or unfounded rumour:前一阵子～老张病了。There was a rumour days ago that Lao Zhang was ill.
讹舛 échuǎn 〈书面〉error (in a text):此书颇多～。There are quite a lot of errors in the book. *or* The book is full of mistakes.
讹夺 éduó 〈书面〉error and omission (in a text)
讹赖 élài 〈方言〉blackmail and act like a rascal:不要耍～! Don't you ever try to blackmail us like a rascal!
讹谬 émiù error; mistake
讹索 ésuǒ blackmail; extort under false pretences
讹头 étóu 〈方言〉pretext; excuse:找～生事 pick a quarrel (with sb.); find fault (with sb. or sth.) /想出～来讹人 find some excuse with which to blackmail sb.
讹脱 étuō error and omission (in a text): 补正～ correct errors and supply omissions
讹误 éwù error (in a text):绝无～ free from errors
讹言 éyán ❶〈书面〉rumour; hearsay: ～惑众 spread rumours to mislead people /此必～。This must be an unfounded rumour. ❷ (often used in the early vernacular) nonsense; rubbish:口出～ talk nonsense
讹诈 ézhà ❶ extort under false pretences: ～钱财 extort money under false pretences ❷ blackmail; bluff:核～ nuclear blackmail

吪
é 〈书面〉❶ move; act ❷ change; teach

囮
é
囮子 ézi *also* "圝子" yóuzi decoy

ě

恶(惡、噁)
ě
see also è; wū; wù
恶心 ěxin ❶ feel nauseated; feel like vomiting; feel queasy; feel sick:有的人见了血就～。Some people feel nauseated (*or* sick) at the sight of blood. ❷ disgusting; repugnant:那人做的事真叫人～。His conduct is disgusting. *or* His behaviour is repugnant. ❸〈方言〉lousy; terrible; rotten:你这车开得真～。What a lousy driver you are! ❹〈方言〉show up; embarrass; humiliate:这种人太假模假式了,得找个机会～～他。This guy is just too smug and hypocritical for words; we must find an opportunity to show him up.

è

颏
è 〈书面〉bridge of the nose

阏
è 〈书面〉❶ block; stop; close up: ～其势 stop sb.'s momentum; block sb.'s advance ❷ sluice-gate
see also yān

恶(惡) è ❶ evil; guilt; wickedness:罪～ crime; evil; guilt /无～不作 stop at nothing in doing evil /十～不赦 guilty of unpardonable evil; unpardonably wicked /疾～如仇 hate evil as much as one hates an enemy; hate injustice like poison ❷ fierce; vicious; ferocious:～狼 ferocious wolf /穷凶极～ extremely cruel and vicious ❸ bad; evil; wicked:～衣菲食 poor clothing and meagre food *see also* ě; wū; wù

恶霸 èbà local tyrant or despot; local bully:～地主 despotic landlord

恶报 èbào retribution for evildoing; judgment:恶有～。Evil is rewarded with evil. /恶人早晚会得～。Retribution for evil will come sooner or later. *or* Evildoers will come to no good end.

恶变 èbiàn 〈医学〉become cancerous; cancerate

恶病质 èbìngzhì 〈医学〉cachexia

恶叉白赖 èchā-báilài (often used in the early vernacular) savage and rascally

恶臭 èchòu ❶ foul smell; stench:沟里一股～扑上来。A foul smell is coming up from the ditch. ❷ foul; stinking:～的烂鱼 stinking fish /名声～ foul reputation /屠宰场充满了～味。The slaughter house was filled with a foul odour.

恶道 èdào ❶ evil ways; vice:堕入～ fall into evil ways; get into a bad habit; go astray ❷〈佛教〉home of evil people after death; hell

恶德 èdé vile conduct; abominable behaviour

恶斗 èdòu fierce fight; ferocious fist fight:在一场～中,他被打得鼻青脸肿。He was beaten black and blue in a fist fight.

恶毒 èdú vicious; malicious; venomous:～的诽谤 venomous slander /用心～的流言蜚语 malicious gossip /手段～ vicious means /想不到他会说出这样～的话来。That he should use such malicious (*or* vile) language is quite unexpected.

恶恶实实 è'e-shīshī 〈方言〉merciless; ruthless; relentless:～地坑了他一笔 mercilessly cheat him of a big sum (of money)

恶感 ègǎn ill or hard feeling; ill will:造成～ cause ill feeling /对某人有～ bear ill will against sb.; have a grudge against sb. /我们俩人之间向无～。There have never been any hard feelings between us.

恶贯满盈 èguàn-mǎnyíng be guilty of too many crimes to escape punishment; face retribution for one's sum of iniquity:严厉惩处了那个～的贩毒头子。The drug baron whose sum of iniquity is made up will be severely punished.

恶鬼 èguǐ ❶ evil spirit; demon ❷ wicked person:你这个～,老天爷是不会放过你的! You devil, Heaven will not let you off lightly.

恶棍 ègùn ruffian; scoundrel; bully

恶果 èguǒ evil consequence; bad result:招致～ entail dreadful consequences /自食～ suffer the consequences of one's evildoings; sow the wind and reap the whirlwind /这些就是管理不善所造成的～。These are the deplorable results of mismanagement.

恶耗 èhào *see* "噩耗" èhào

恶狠 èhěn vicious; cruel; merciless:用心～ vicious intention (*or* design) /～的打手 merciless hatchet man

恶狠狠 èhěnhěn venomous; fierce; ferocious:他～地瞪着我。He stared fiercely at me. /"活该!"她～地说。"It serves him right!" she said venomously.

恶化 èhuà worsen; deteriorate; take a turn for the worse:迅速～的经济形势 rapidly worsening economy /病人病情～了。The patient's condition is deteriorating. /相互指责～了两国关系。Mutual recriminations worsened the relations between the two countries. /战斗情况突然～。The battle took a sudden turn for the worse.

恶疾 èjí foul or nasty disease

恶迹 èjì evildoing; evil deed:～昭昭 notorious evil deed

恶口 èkǒu vicious abuse; foul verbal attack; vile language:～伤人 attack sb. with virulent words; use vile language to attack sb.; vilify sb.

恶辣 èlà fierce and brutal; savage and cruel:手段～ by savage and cruel means; by venomous means

恶浪 èlàng ❶ surging waves; swashing waves:狂风～ wild wind and roaring waves; howling wind and surging waves; stormy (*or* tempestuous) sea ❷〈比喻〉evil forces

恶劣 èliè bad; vile; odious:心情～ in a bad mood /天气～ inclement (*or* foul) weather /影响～ exert a baneful influence /品质～ be morally corrupt /～行径 odious conduct (*or* behaviour) /～环境 adverse circumstances /劫机是一种任何政府都不能容忍的～罪行。Hijacking is a vile crime tolerated by no government.

恶露 èlù 〈中医〉lochia

恶骂 èmà shout vicious abuse

恶眉恶眼 èméi-èyǎn fierce look; ferocious look

恶梦 èmèng *also* "噩梦" èmèng bad dream; nightmare

恶苗病 èmiáobìng *also* "白秆" báigǎn bakanae disease

恶名 èmíng bad reputation; infamy:～昭彰 infamous; notorious /背～ be subjected to vilification

恶名昭著 èmíng-zhāozhù *also* "臭名昭著" chòumíng-zhāozhù notorious:～的骗子 notorious swindler

恶魔 èmó ❶ demon; devil; evil spirit ❷ monster; vicious thug:杀人～ bloodthirsty monster

恶念 èniàn evil design; wicked intention:萌生～。An evil idea occurs to one.

恶癖 èpǐ bad habit:沾染～ be addicted to bad habits

恶气 èqì ❶ foul smell; bad odour:他打开盖子,一股～直冲而来。He opened the lid and was instantly greeted by a foul smell. ❷ insult; humiliation:你就这么默默地忍受他的～? But are you going to swallow his insults? ❸ grudge; resentment; hatred:法官的公平裁决替我们出了一口～。The judge's fair verdict helps to redress our grievances. ❹ anger; rage:他满脸～地吼叫道:"我要砸了你的店!" "I'll smash your shop!" he stormed angrily.

恶趣 èqù ❶ low, cheap, or vulgar taste:此等描述,流于～,可厌之至。This sort of description which all but caters to the lowest tastes is indeed very disgusting. ❷〈佛教〉misery for evildoers in the nether world

恶人 èrén evil person; vile creature; villain:～当道。Evil people were in power. /～自有～磨。A wicked person will be harassed by another of like ilk.

恶人先告状 èrén xiān gàozhuàng he who offends is always the first to complain; the guilty party files the suit first; the villain sues his victim before he himself is prosecuted

恶煞 èshà ❶ fierce-looking god in charge of punishment ❷ fierce and savage person

恶少 èshào wicked young man from a wealthy or influential family; young ruffian:洋场～ rich young bully in a metropolis infested with foreign adventurers; young ruffian in a cosmopolitan city

恶声 èshēng ❶ angry tone:～对骂 trade angry insults; call each other names angrily ❷〈书面〉music of low taste ❸〈书面〉bad reputation; infamy:此人在官场颇有～。He was quite infamous in official circles.

恶声恶气 èshēng-èqì angry voices and rude remarks:老李瞪了他一眼,～地说:"你这个笨蛋,你在这儿干什么?" Lao Li gave him a stare and roared: "You damned fool, what are you up to here?"

恶事传千里 èshì chuán qiānlǐ scandal travels fast; scandal has wings; ill news runs apace:好事不出门,～。Good deeds are never heard of outside the door, but bad deeds are proclaimed for three hundred miles. *or* Good travels at a snail's pace, but evil has wings.

恶势力 èshìlì evil force; pernicious pressure group

恶水 èshuǐ ❶ unruly river:穷山～ barren mountains and unruly rivers; harsh natural conditions ❷〈方言〉dirty water:倒～ pour away dirty water

恶俗 èsú ❶ evil practices or customs ❷ philistine; vulgar:～趣味 philistine taste /这样摆设才显高雅而不～。The furnishings are arranged in an elegant style without a trace of bad taste.

恶岁 èsuì 〈书面〉famine year

恶徒 ètú scoundrel; villain

恶习 èxí bad or pernicious habit:染上～ contract a bad habit; fall into evil ways

恶相 èxiàng sinister look:他一脸～。He has a fierce look on his face.

恶行 èxíng abominable behaviour; evil conduct

恶性 èxìng malignant; pernicious; vicious:～刑事事件 case of vicious crime /～通货膨胀 galloping (*or* runaway) inflation /～交通事故 grave traffic accident

恶性高血压 èxìng gāoxuèyā accelerated or malignant hypertension

恶性淋巴瘤 èxìng línbāliú 〈医学〉lymphadenoma; lymphoma

恶性疟疾 èxìng nüèji subtertian malaria; falciparum malaria

恶性贫血 èxìng pínxuè pernicious anaemia

恶性葡萄胎 èxìng pútaotāi 〈医学〉invasive mole; malignant mole; metastasizing mole

E

恶性水肿 exìng shuǐzhǒng malignant edema
恶性循环 èxìng xúnhuán vicious circle
恶性肿瘤 èxìng zhǒngliú malignant tumour; cancer
恶凶凶 èxiōngxiōng fierce; ferocious:他临走时还~地对大家发了一阵子脾气。He bawled furiously at us even when he was on the point of leaving.
恶谑 èxuè taunt; gibe
恶言 èyán coarse language; abuse:口出~ shout abuse; be foul-mouthed /~相报 let loose a stream of invective in return; reply with a curse
恶衣恶食 èyī-èshí poor clothing and coarse food — simple life
恶意 èyì evil or ill intention; ill will; malice:~攻击 spiteful attack /~中伤 slander /有人在~地散布有关他的谣言。Some people are maliciously spreading rumours about him.
恶因 èyīn cause of disaster
恶语 èyǔ vicious slander; foul language:他不该~伤友。He shouldn't have said such nasty things about his friends.
恶语伤人 èyǔ-shāngrén hurt sb. by hurling wicked slanders at him or her:~六月寒。Wicked slanders make one shudder even in the hottest weather.
恶语中伤 èyǔ-zhòngshāng viciously slander; calumniate
恶运 èyùn bad luck:交了~ have a run of bad luck; be down on one's luck
恶债 èzhài odious debts:~不予继承。Odious debts are not the responsibility of heirs. *or* Odious debts are not hereditary.
恶战 èzhàn fierce battle; savage fighting:两个对手在最后一个回合的比赛中展开了一场~。The two opponents were locked in a furious battle in the last round of the tournament. /两队旗鼓相当,必有一场~。As the two teams are well-matched, their battle will be a fierce one.
恶仗 èzhàng *see* "恶战"
恶兆 èzhào ill or bad omen; writing on the wall:一些人认为黑猫从眼前走过是一种~。Some people believe that a black cat's crossing one's path is a bad omen.
恶浊 èzhuó foul; filthy:室内空气~。The air in the room is foul.
恶阻 èzǔ 〈中医〉vomiting during early pregnancy; morning sickness
恶作剧 èzuòjù mischief; prank; practical joke:闹~be up to mischief; play a practical joke

垩(堊) è ❶ chalk:用白~擦绳子画线 rub a cord with chalk to mark a line ❷〈书面〉whiten with chalk; chalk:~墙 whitewash the wall /~了一下弹子棒梢 chalk a billiard cue ❸〈方言〉apply (fertilizer)

噩 è shocking; frightening
噩耗 èhào sad news (as of the death of sb. one loves, respects, or values):飞机失事的~把大家都惊呆了。Every one was stunned by the sad news of the plane crash.
噩梦 èmèng nightmare; frightening or horrible dream:他从~中醒来,吓得直打冷战。He woke cold and shaking from a nightmare. /那些日子的生活真是一场~。Life in those days was a real nightmare.
噩运 èyùn *see* "恶运" èyùn
噩兆 èzhào *see* "恶兆" èzhào

厄(戹、[1]阨) è 〈书面〉❶ strategic point:险~ strategic pass; strategic point ❷ disaster; adversity; hardship:困~ dire straits; difficult situation /遭~ meet with disaster or adversity ❸ be in distress; be stranded:登山队~于风暴,未能如期登上顶峰。The mountaineers were stranded (*or* caught) in a storm and failed to reach the peak on schedule.
厄尔尼诺现象 è'ěrnínuò xiànxiàng 〈气象〉*El Niño* phenomenon
厄瓜多尔 Èguāduō'ěr Ecuador:~人 Ecuadorian
厄境 èjìng miserable plight; predicament:迭遭~ land oneself in one predicament after another; have a run of bad luck
厄立特里亚 Èlìtèlǐyà Eritrea, African country with Asmara as the capital
厄难 ènàn suffering; trials and tribulations
厄运 èyùn adversity; misfortune:他感到自己难逃这一~。He felt it was difficult for him to escape this misfortune.

苊 è 〈化学〉acenaphthene

扼 è ❶ clutch; grip:~其手腕 clutch at his wrist ❷ guard; control:~据峻岭 be entrenched on a steep mountain
扼吭 èháng choke; suffocate:~之地 strategic position
扼吭拊背 èháng-fǔbèi clutch at sb.'s throat and hit his spine — hold the best strategic position and have the enemy at one's mercy
扼流圈 èliúquān 〈电学〉choke (coil):~变压器 choke-transformer
扼杀 èshā strangle; smother; throttle:~新生事物 smother new emerging things /企图把新思想~在萌芽状态中 try to nip new ideas in the bud /想把新生的共和国~在摇篮里 attempt to strangle the new republic in the cradle
扼守 èshǒu hold (a strategic point); guard:~山海关 guard the Shanhai Pass /~阵地 hold a position
扼死 èsǐ strangle (to death); throttle
扼腕 èwàn 〈书面〉wring one's hands in sorrow or despair:为之~ be sorry for sth. or sb.
扼要 èyào concise; to the point:简明~ brief and precise; concise; succinct /~传达指示精神 relay the key points of the instructions /~地介绍情况 give a briefing; brief sb. on sth.
扼制 èzhì control; restrain:~心中的怒火 restrain (*or* control, *or* contain) one's anger /~通往内河的航道 control the access to all routes of inland navigation

轭 è yoke

呃 è 〈叹词〉*used to express an exclamation, a reminder, etc.*:~,你还在这里啊! Why, so you're still here. /~,别忘了带钥匙。Well, don't forget to bring your key.
see also e
呃逆 ènì 〈医学〉hiccups

呝 è 〈书面〉❶ *see* "呃" è ❷ cry or chirp (of a bird)

遏 è check; restrain; prohibit:沮~〈书面〉stop; prevent /怒不可~ cannot restrain one's anger; be in a towering rage; boil with indignation
遏抑 èyì keep down; suppress; contain:他~不住内心的愤怒。He could no longer contain his anger.
遏止 èzhǐ check; hold back; restrain:~侵略 check aggression /不可~的洪流 irresistible tide
遏制 èzhì restrain; curb; contain; keep within limits:~内心的恐惧 try to keep one's fear under control /~革命 contain a revolution /~恶性通货膨胀 curb the runaway inflation
遏制政策 èzhì zhèngcè policy of containment

愕 è astounded; stunned; dazed:惊~ be stunned; be shocked
愕然 èrán stunned; astounded:她~地瞪大了眼睛。She was stunned, her eyes wide open. /听到这个消息,他~失色。He was taken aback by the news and turned pale.
愕视 èshì look in astonishment; stare wide-eyed
愕异 èyì 〈书面〉astonished; astounded; stunned:~不置 greatly astonished

谔 è
谔谔 è'è 〈书面〉speak bluntly; call a spade a spade:千人之诺诺,不如一士之~。It is better to have one person speaking the blunt truth than a thousand yes-men nodding agreement.

萼 è 〈植物〉calyx
萼片 èpiàn 〈植物〉sepal

遻 è 〈书面〉come across; meet

崿 è 〈书面〉cliff:危岩峭~ dangerous crags and sheer cliffs

颚 è ❶ mandible (of an arthropod); jaw:上~ upper jaw ❷ palate
颚骨 ègǔ jawbone
颚式破碎机 èshì pòsuìjī 〈机械〉jaw crusher; jawbreaker

E

锷 è 〈书面〉blade of a sword; edge of a knife

鹗 è (generally called 鱼鹰) osprey; fish hawk; sea eagle

腭 è (generally called 上膛)〈生理〉palate: 硬～ hard palate / 软～ soft palate

腭窦 èdòu sinus palatinus

腭化 èhuà 〈语言〉palatalization

腭裂 èliè 〈医学〉cleft palate

腭修补术 èxiūbǔshù 〈医学〉palatorrhaphy

腭炎 èyán 〈医学〉palatitis

腭音 èyīn 〈语言〉palatal

腭针鱼 èzhēnyú needlefish (*Belonidae*)

鳄(鱷) è crocodile; alligator

鳄梨 èlí avocado

鳄式碎矿机 èshì suìkuàngjī 〈矿业〉alligator

鳄式压轧机 èshì yāzhájī 〈冶金〉alligator squeezer

鳄蜥 èxī crocodile lizard

鳄牙剪 èyájiǎn 〈机械〉alligator shears

鳄鱼 èyú crocodile; alligator

鳄鱼眼泪 èyú-yǎnlèi crocodile tears: 不要相信他那鳄鱼的眼泪。Don't believe him. He is shedding crocodile tears.

鄂 È ❶ another name for Hubei ❷ a surname

鄂毕河 Èbìhé Ob River, one of the major rivers in northern Asia flowing into the Arctic

鄂博 èbó *also* "敖包" áobāo Mongolian cairn or obo for boundary marking

鄂尔多斯高原 È'ěrduōsī Gāoyuán Ordos Plateau (in the Inner Mongolia Autonomous Region)

鄂伦春族 Èlúnchūnzú Oroqen nationality, one of China's minority nationalities, living in Inner Mongolia and Heilongjiang

鄂温克族 Èwēnkèzú Ewenki nationality, one of China's minority nationalities, living in Inner Mongolia and Heilongjiang

饿 è ❶ hungry: 挨～ go hungry; starve / 我～极了。I'm famished. / ～了甜如蜜。Any food is tasty when one is hungry. *or* Hunger is the best sauce. ❷ starve: 敌人妄图～死村民。The enemy tried in vain to starve the villagers to death.

饿饭 èfàn 〈方言〉go hungry; go without food

饿鬼 èguǐ *also* "饿死鬼" ❶〈迷信〉ghost of one who died of starvation ❷〈戏谑〉ravenous eater

饿虎扑食 èhǔ-pūshí like a hungry tiger pouncing on its prey: 那人～般的扭住了我。He pounced on me like a hungry tiger.

饿狼 èláng hungry wolf — greedy person

饿殍 èpiǎo 〈书面〉bodies of those who died of hunger: ～遍野。The bodies of the starved could be seen everywhere. *or* Famine stalks the country.

e

呃 e 〈助词〉*placed at the end of a sentence to express admiration, surprise, etc.*: 红霞多美～! How beautiful the rosy clouds are!
see also è

ē

欸(誒) ē *also* ēi〈叹词〉*used to call attention*: ～, 快来看。Hey! Come and have a look.

é

欸(誒) é *also* éi〈叹词〉*used to express surprise*: ～, 怎么人都走了! Why, everybody has left.

ě

欸(誒) ě *also* ěi〈叹词〉*used to express disapproval or disagreement*: ～, 你这么说可不对呀! Now, you shouldn't say that.

è

欸(誒) è *also* èi〈叹词〉*used to express approval or consent*: ～, 我看可以。Yes, I think it will do. / ～, 我这就来。All right, I'm coming.
see also āi; ǎi

ēn

恩 ēn ❶ kindness; favour; grace: 报～ repay a kindness (*or* favour) / 施～ bestow favours / 开～ show mercy; grant special favour / 忘～ be ungrateful; be devoid of gratitude / 谢～ thank sb. (esp. the emperor or a high official) for his favour (*or* kindness) / ～礼有加 shower sb. with kindness and courtesy ❷ (Ēn) a surname

恩爱 ēn'ài conjugal love: 小两口恩恩爱爱, 从未拌过嘴。They are an affectionate couple and have never fallen out with each other.

恩宠 ēnchǒng 〈书面〉(usu. bestowed by the monarch) prerogatives and royal favours: ～有加 (of a subject) receive many royal favours and promotions; (of a monarch) bestow many prerogatives and favours (upon sb.)

恩仇 ēnchóu kindness and hatred: ～分明 distinguish between what is motivated by kindness and what is prompted by hatred; know one's friend from one's enemy / 相逢一笑泯～。Grudges vanish when you greet your opponent with a smile.

恩赐 ēncì bestow (favours, charity, etc.); patronize: 大自然的～ bounty of nature / 摆出一副～的态度 adopt a patronizing attitude / 我们不接受别人～。We do not want to accept handouts. / 援助是相互的, 不是什么～。Aid is mutual; it is not bestowed as a favour.

恩德 ēndé kindness; favour; grace: ～无量 infinite kindness; numerous favours / 我们将永远记住你的～。We'll always remember the kindness that you have shown us.

恩典 ēndiǎn ❶ favour; grace; benevolence: 皇上的～ royal favour ❷ bestow a favour or kindness on sb.; be clement to sb.: 恳请大人～。I beg for the clemency (*or* kindness) of Your Honour.

恩断义绝 ēnduàn-yìjué all love and kindly feeling are dead; a marriage or friendship breaks down completely: ～, 各奔东西。With the marriage (*or* relationship) broken down completely, the two each went his or her own way.

恩格斯 Ēngésī Friedrich Engels (1820-1895), one of the founders of scientific socialism or Marxism

恩公 ēngōng 〈旧语〉polite form of address for one's benefactor

恩惠 ēnhuì favour; kindness; grace; bounty: 小恩小惠 petty favours

恩贾梅纳 Ēnjiǎméinà N'Djamena, capital of Chad

恩将仇报 ēnjiāngchóubào return evil for good; requite kindness with enmity; bite the hand that feeds one: 他～, 出卖他的救命恩人。He returned evil for good and sold out the man who had saved his life.

恩眷 ēnjuàn 〈书面〉kindly bestow favours on sb.

恩科 ēnkē imperial examination held on a special occasion such as a coronation and other royal celebration (as distinguished from regular imperial examinations); special imperial examination

恩克彗星 Ēnkè huìxīng 〈天文〉Encke's comet

恩克鲁玛 Ēnkèlǔmǎ Kwame Nkrumah (1909-1972), first Prime Minister of Ghana

恩情 ēnqíng loving kindness; favour: 老一辈人对我们的～很深。We are deeply indebted to the older generation.

恩人 ēn'rén benefactor: 以～自居 assume the airs of a benefactor; play the benefactor

恩荣 ēnróng grace and glory: 旷世～ unprecedented grace and glory

恩赦 ēnshè special pardon granted to an offender by the emperor

恩深义重 ēnshēn-yìzhòng deep and great debt of gratitude：他对我～。I owe him a great debt of gratitude.

恩师 ēnshī (usu. used as a form of address for one's teacher to whom one owes a debt of deep gratitude and for whom one has great respect) esteemed teacher; honourable master; kind benefactor

恩同再造 ēntóngzàizào extraordinary kindness tantamount to giving one a new lease on life：您对我～，我将永世不忘。I will be for ever indebted to you for your profound kindness.

恩威并用 ēnwēi-bìngyòng *also* "恩威并行"；"恩威并重" resort to both benevolence and severity; combine justice and mercy; use both the carrot and the stick：他历来赏善罚恶，～。He always meted out rewards to the good and punishments to the wicked, and combined mercy with justice.

恩物 ēnwù favorite toy or gadget：动画片是孩子们的～。cartoons are children's special favorites.

恩义 ēnyì ❶ love and friendship：他们之间～已绝。They have severed ties of love and friendship for good. ❷ kindness：我永远不会忘记他对我的～。I will never forget the kindness he has showered on me.

恩遇 ēnyù 〈书面〉treat with unusual kindness, generosity or courtesy：～甚厚 shower generosity (*or* hospitality, *or* kindness) on sb.

恩怨 ēnyuàn gratitude and resentment; resentment; grievance：～分明 know whom one should love or hate／不计较个人～ not allow oneself to be swayed by personal ill-will／我和他并无～。He and I have no personal grudges against each other.

恩泽 ēnzé bounties bestowed by a monarch or an official

恩重如山 ēnzhòng-rúshān kindness as heavy as a mountain; great favour：～，刻骨铭心。He has showered great favours on me, and my gratitude to him knows no bounds.

恩准 ēnzhǔn 〈敬词〉gracious approval of the monarch

蒽 ēn 〈化学〉anthracene：～酸 anthroic acid

蒽醌 ēnkūn 〈化学〉anthraquinone：～染料 anthraquinone dye

蒽油 ēnyóu 〈化学〉anthracene oil

èn

摁 èn press (with the hand or finger)：～电钮 press (*or* push) a button／～电铃 ring an electric bell／～手印 register one's fingerprint／～住不放 press sth. (*or* sb.) down and not let go

摁钉儿 èndīngr drawing pin; thumbtack

摁扣儿 ènkòur snap fastener

ēng

鞥 ēng 〈书面〉reins (for a horse); halter

ér

而 ér 〈连词〉❶ *used to express coordination* (a) *by joining two parallel adjectives or other elements*：朴素～大方 simple but with good taste／美丽～富饶的土地 beautiful and richly-endowed land; land of plenty and charm (b) *by joining two elements that form a sequence in meaning*：战～胜之 fight and defeat sb.; defeat sb.／生～有之的本能 instinct one is born with; innate instinct／通过实践～发现真理 find truth through practice (c) *by joining an affirmative and a negative element that complement each other*：忙～不乱 busy but not disorderly／艳～不俗 colourful and in good taste (d) *by joining two elements opposite in meaning that show a contrast*：大～不甜 big but not sweet／华～不实 flashy without substance／有其名～无其实 in name but not in reality／不在数量多～在质量好。It is not quantity but quality that counts.／应该怪我～不应该怪你。I am to blame, not you. (e) *by connecting cause and effect or aim and means*：由于成功～骄傲 become conceited because of one's success; be dizzy with success／因病～辞职 resign on health grounds／为找工作～奔忙 busy hunting for a job ❷ *used to indicate change from one state to another*：由上～下 from top to bottom／由远～近 approach from afar／一～再，再～三 again and again; time and again ❸ *used to connect an adverbial phrase of time or manner with a verb*：日出～作 start working at sunrise／顺流～下 go downstream／不战～胜 win a battle without a fight／不欢～散 part in discord ❹ *inserted between subject and predicate to indicate a condition*：科学研究～无进取精神，是不会有所成就的。Scientific research would never get anywhere without the pioneering spirit.

而后 érhòu (used only after another element) after that; then：我们先去颐和园，～再去故宫。We shall go to the Summer Palace first, and then the Forbidden City.／三思～行。Think twice before you act. *or* Look before you leap.／学～知不足。One discovers one's ignorance only through learning.

而今 érjīn now; at the present time：过去这里是荒滩，～成了米粮仓。It used to be wasteland here, but now it has become a breadbasket.

而今而后 érjīn-érhòu from now on：～我俩永不分离。From now on, we shall never part.

而况 érkuàng 〈连词〉(not to be used in connection with 更 or 又) much less; let alone：这种房子我租都租不起，～把它买下来。I couldn't afford even to rent a house like that, let alone buy it.

而立 érlì 〈书面〉thirty years of age (from *The Analects*《论语》)：三十～ at thirty one should be well established in one's life／年近～ approaching thirty

而立之年 érlìzhīnián thirty years old：他在～便事业有成了。He was well advanced in his career at the age of 30.

而且 érqiě 〈连词〉(often used after an element introduced by 不但 or 不仅) and; and also; but also; moreover：这房子很宽敞，～光线充足。The room is spacious and bright.／他不但是一位历史学家，～还是个诗人。He is not only a historian, but also a poet.／骑自行车不仅能锻炼身体，～还不污染空气。Cycling provides good physical exercise; moreover, it does not pollute the air.

而外 érwài ❶ besides：除了英语～，他还自学日语和德语。Besides English, he taught himself Japanese and German. ❷ except：我除了报上看到的～，别的什么也不知道。I know nothing of it except what I've read in the paper.

而已 éryǐ 〈助词〉nothing more; nothing but; only：这不过是个烟幕弹～。This is nothing but a smoke-screen.／如此～，岂有他哉！That's all there is to it.／说说～，别当真。Don't take it too seriously; it was only a casual remark.

洏 ér *see* "涟洏" lián'ér

轜(輀) ér 〈书面〉hearse：灵～ hearse

栭 ér 〈书面〉❶ *also* "斗拱" dǒugǒng set of brackets on top of a column supporting the beam within and roof eaves without ❷ fungus that grows on rotten wood

栭栎 érlì 〈植物〉white oak

鸸 ér

鸸鹋 érmiáo 〈动物〉emu

胹 ér 〈书面〉boil; boil sth. until it becomes mushy or soft

鲕 ér 〈书面〉(fish) roe

鲕石 érshí oolite; oolith

鲕状体 érzhuàngtǐ oolitic ore

儿¹(兒) ér ❶ child; baby：小～ little child／产～ new-born baby／早产～ premature baby／婴～ baby; infant ❷ youngster; youth; young man：英雄～女 young heroes and heroines／体育健～ athlete ❸ son：生～育女 raise children／～不嫌母丑。A mother never looks ugly to her son.／小～不懂事，多有冒犯。My son is too young to behave properly; he may have given you offence, I'm afraid. ❹ male：*see* "～马"

儿²(兒) ér (used as a suffix and transcribed as r in Pinyin) ❶ *used as a noun suffix*：(a) *added to a noun to indicate smallness*：帽～ hat; cap／零碎～ odds and ends／小车～ small cart (b) *added to a verb or an adjective to turn it into a noun*：吃～ eat-

ables; food /亮～ light /热闹～ fun (c) *added to a concrete noun to turn it into an abstract noun*：摸到了办这件事的门～ get the knack of doing the work /这生意油水～不大。You cannot make much profit from this business. (d) *added to a noun to change its original meaning*：白面～ heroin (with 白面 meaning wheat flour) ❷ *used as suffix of a limited number of verbs*：我不玩～了。I don't want to play any more. /他火～了。He blew up.

see also "儿化"

儿茶 érchá 〈植物〉〈中药〉catechu (*Acacia catechu*)：～单宁〈化学〉catechotannin

儿夫 érfū 〈旧语〉(used by a young woman in the early vernacular) my husband

儿妇 érfù daughter-in-law

儿歌 érgē children's song; nursery rhymes

儿化 érhuà 〈语言〉suffixation of a nonsyllabic r to nouns and sometimes verbs or adjectives, causing a retroflexion of the preceding vowel, typical of the pronunciation of standard Chinese and of some dialects

儿皇帝 érhuángdì puppet emperor

儿科 érkē (department of) paediatrics：～医生 paediatrician

儿郎 érláng 〈书面〉❶ young man; man ❷ son ❸ troops; men：三千～ three thousand troops

儿麻 érmá (short for 小儿麻痹) polio; poliomyelitis; infantile paralysis

儿马 érmǎ 〈口语〉male horse; stallion

儿男 érnán ❶ man ❷ boy

儿女 érnǚ ❶ sons and daughters; children：～都已成家立业了。The children have all married and started their careers. /他们都是中华民族的优秀～。They are all fine sons and daughters of the Chinese nation. ❷ young man and woman (in love)：～之情 love between a man and a woman

儿女情长 érnǚ-qíngcháng (of a man and a woman) cherish deep affection for each other; be sentimentally attached to each other：英雄气短，～。(said of a man who sacrificed his career for the sake of love) While the aspiration of a hero is short, the love between a man and a woman is long. *or* The aspirations of a hero are overwhelmed by the love between man and woman.

儿时 érshí childhood：～故乡的景物至今记忆犹新。The scenes of my hometown where I spent my childhood are still fresh in my memory.

儿孙 érsūn children and grandchildren; descendants; posterity：～满堂 many children and grandchildren in the family

儿孙自有儿孙福 érsūn zì yǒu érsūn fú 〈俗语〉the children will have their own happiness and fortunes; the children can take care of themselves when they grow up：～，莫为儿孙作马牛。As your children will seek their own happiness and fortunes when they grow up, don't work and worry for them all your life.

儿童 értóng children：～读物 children's book /～广播剧 radio play for children /～节目 children's programme /～医院 children's hospital /～保育事业 child care /～福利 child welfare /～期疾病 childhood disease /～权利宣言 Declaration of the Rights of the Child (20 November 1959)

儿童发育障碍 értóng fāyù zhàng'ài 〈医学〉child development disorder

儿童节 Értóngjié *also* "六一儿童节" Liù-Yī Értóngjié (International) Children's Day (1 June)

儿童攀爬具 értóng pānpájù jungle gym

儿童失语症 értóng shīyǔzhèng 〈心理〉childhood aphasia

儿童受虐综合征 értóng shòunüè zōnghézhēng 〈心理〉battered child syndrome

儿童团 Értóngtuán Children's Corps (set up and led by the Chinese Communist Party in the revolutionary base areas before 1949)；战争期间，～放哨、送信，起了很大作用。In the war years, the Children's Corps played an important role, standing sentry and taking messages from one place to another.

儿童文学 értóng wénxué children's literature; juvenile literature

儿童心理学 értóng xīnlǐxué child psychology

儿童学 értóngxué pedology

儿嬉 érxī ❶ child's play ❷ trifling matter：此非～。It's no joking matter.

儿媳妇儿 érxífur daughter-in-law

儿戏 érxì trifling matter：这可不是～。It's no trifling matter. /不要把这样重要的工作视同～。You should not treat such an important task as a matter of no consequence.

儿影 Éryǐng (short for 儿童电影制片厂) Children's Film Studio

儿韵 éryùn 〈语言〉r-ending retroflexion

儿子 érzi son

ěr

耳[1] ěr ❶ ear：内～ inner ear /中～ middle ear /外～ external ear; outer ear /逆～ unpleasant to the ear; unpalatable /悦～ pleasing to the ear; melodious; sweet-sounding /顺风～ legendary person who can hear voices a long way off; well-informed person ❷ any ear-like appendage; ear of a utensil：银～ tremella /木～ edible fungus; a kind of mushroom /鼎～ ears (*or* loop-handles) of a tripod ❸ on both sides; flanking; side：*see* "～房"

耳[2] ěr 〈书面〉〈助词〉only; just：距此不过二里～。It is only two *li* from here. /此戏言～。I am only joking.

耳巴 ěrbā 〈方言〉❶ *also* "耳巴子" box on the ear ❷ earflaps of a hat

耳报神 ěrbàoshén 〈方言〉one who reports on sb.'s activities; informer：你们就是有～，不然，怎么知道得这么快。You certainly have your own intelligence people. Otherwise, how could you have learnt about this in such a short time?

耳背 ěrbèi hard of hearing; deaf

耳鼻喉科 ěr-bí-hóukē ❶ ENT (ear-nose-throat) department; otolaryngological department ❷ otolaryngology：～医生 ENT specialist; otolaryngologist

耳边风 ěrbiānfēng *also* "耳旁风" breeze flitting by one's ears; unheeded advice; sth. that goes in one ear and out the other：他把朋友的劝告当作～。He turned a deaf ear to his friends' advice.

耳鬓厮磨 ěrbìn-sīmó 〈书面〉(of a boy and girl) play together ear to ear and temple to temple; often play together during childhood：青梅竹马，～ be childhood playmates, sharing the joys of innocent intimacy. /当年我和他～，两小无猜。In those years, we were both naive and innocent children and were always together.

耳病 ěrbìng ear diseases;〈医学〉otopathy：此人有～，听力不好。He is suffering from ear disease and is hard of hearing.

耳病性眩晕 ěrbìngxìng xuànyùn 〈医学〉aural vertigo

耳沉 ěrchén 〈方言〉*also* "耳朵沉" hard of hearing

耳垂 ěrchuí 〈生理〉earlobe

耳唇 ěrchún 〈方言〉auricle

耳聪目明 ěrcōng-mùmíng ❶ have good ears and eyes; have good eyesight and hearing; can hear and see well：老爷子年近八旬，依然～。My father is approaching 80, but can still hear and see quite well. ❷ clear-headed and clear-sighted; have a good grasp of the situation

耳珰 ěrdāng ear pendant

耳底 ěrdǐ 〈生理〉eardrum; tympanum

耳朵 ěrduo ear：～尖 have sharp ears

耳朵底子 ěrduo dǐzi 〈方言〉otitis media; tympanitis

耳朵软 ěrduoruǎn credulous; easily influenced; susceptible to flattery：他～，别人说啥他信啥。He is credulous of hearsay.

耳朵眼儿 ěrduoyǎnr ❶ (common name for 外耳门) external auditory canal ❷ aperture pierced in the earlobe (for wearing earrings)

耳房 ěrfáng smaller rooms on both sides of the main room or of the wings (usu. in a courtyard)

耳粪 ěrfèn 〈方言〉earwax

耳风 ěrfeng 〈方言〉hearsay; rumour：你不能听到一点～就急于下结论。You can't jump to conclusions by hearsay evidence.

耳福 ěrfú good fortune of listening to wonderful music, opera, etc.：大饱～ have the good fortune to fully enjoy wonderful music (*or* opera); fully satisfy one's acoustic sense /今天的音乐会使我一饱～。I enjoyed every minute of today's concert.

耳根 ěrgēn ❶ root of the ear ❷ ear ❸〈佛教〉ear regarded as a source of sin

耳根清净 ěrgēn qīngjìng have peace for one's ears (free from nagging, quarrel, etc.); have a quiet and peaceful environment：图个～ hope to live in peace and tranquillity far from the madding crowd

耳垢 ěrgòu earwax; cerumen
耳骨 ěrgǔ ear bone
耳鼓 ěrgǔ *also* "鼓膜" gǔmó eardrum; tympanic membrane
耳刮子 ěrguāzi *see* "耳光"
耳掴子 ěrguāizi 〈方言〉 *see* "耳光"
耳管 ěrguǎn 〈生理〉 external auditory canal
耳光 ěrguāng slap on the face; box on the ear: 打～ slap sb.'s face; box sb.'s ear / 事实给了那些散播谣言的人一记响亮的～。The truth was a resounding slap on the face of the rumour-mongers.
耳郭 ěrguō 〈生理〉 auricle; pinna
耳锅 ěrguō pot with loop-handles on both sides
耳乎 ěrhu 〈方言〉 ❶ pay attention to; notice; catch: 他说什么我没～。I didn't catch what he was saying. ❷ vaguely: 这事我～听说过。I have heard something about it, but only in vague terms.
耳化浓 ěrhuànóng 〈医学〉 otopyosis; otohelcosis
耳环 ěrhuán earring
耳机 ěrjī *also* "耳机子"; "听筒" tīngtǒng ❶ earphone; ear cup; earpiece ❷ (usu. telephone, etc.) receiver
耳际 ěrjì in one's ears: 他的话还在我～萦绕。His words are still ringing in my ears. *or* His words still linger in my ears.
耳尖 ěrjiān sharp of hearing: 还是这姑娘～, 听到了极轻的敲门声。The girl was really sharp of hearing; she heard the almost inaudible knocking.
耳镜 ěrjìng 〈医学〉 auriscope; ear mirror; ear speculum; otoscope: ～检查 otoscopy
耳科学 ěrkēxué 〈医学〉 auristics; otology
耳科医师 ěrkē yīshī 〈医学〉 aurist; otologist
耳孔 ěrkǒng earhole
耳溃疡 ěrkuìyáng 〈医学〉 otohelcosis
耳廓 ěrkuò 〈生理〉 *see* "耳郭"
耳力 ěrlì power of hearing; hearing: ～不好 have poor hearing; be hard of hearing
耳瘤 ěrliú 〈医学〉 otoncus
耳聋 ěrlóng deaf: ～眼睛 deaf and blind / ～眼花 hard of hearing and bleary-eyed
耳漏 ěrlòu 〈医学〉 otorrhoea
耳轮 ěrlún 〈生理〉 helix
耳毛 ěrmáo tragus (hair of external auditory meatus)
耳帽 ěrmào ear-warmer; earmuff
耳门 ěrmén smaller door on either side of the gate, or beside the main entrance
耳鸣 ěrmíng 〈医学〉 tinnitus; ringing in the ear
耳膜 ěrmó *also* "鼓膜" gǔmó eardrum; tympanum
耳目 ěrmù ❶ ears and eyes: 掩人～ deceive sb. by confusing his ears and eyes; prevent sb. from seeing or hearing of sth. ❷ what one sees and hears; information; knowledge: ～闭塞 ill-informed / ～所及 from what one sees and hears; from what one knows / 我一到此处, ～顿新。Everything I see and hear here is new to me. ❸ one who spies for sb. else; informer: 广有～ have many people around watching or listening; have many agents around / 他是皇帝的亲信和～。He was a trusted aide to the emperor and served as his informer.
耳目一新 ěrmù-yīxīn find everything fresh and new: 我们一到这个小山村, 顿时觉得～。We found everything fresh and new the moment we entered the small mountain village.
耳旁风 ěrpángfēng *see* "耳边风"
耳屏 ěrpíng 〈生理〉 tragus (prominence in front of external auditory meatus)
耳切开术 ěrqiēkāishù 〈医学〉 ototomy
耳热 ěrrè one's ears burn: 酒酣～。One's ears begin to burn after one has drunk much. *or* One has drunk so much that one is having burning ears. / 她脸红～, 心扑通扑通直跳。She blushed, her heart throbbing with excitement.
耳濡目染 ěrrú-mùrǎn be imperceptibly influenced by what one constantly sees and hears: 人们在旧社会～, 往往把腐化现象看作理所当然的事。People whose minds were defiled by the foul atmosphere in the old society often took corruption for granted. / 他父母都是歌唱家, 平日～, 所以他也爱好音乐。His parents are both singers and, under their daily influence, he is passionately fond of music.
耳软 ěrruǎn susceptible to flattery and spiteful gossip; easily influenced; gullible: 老张就是～, 容易受人拉拢。Lao Zhang is gullible enough to be taken in by intriguers.
耳软心活 ěrruǎn-xīnhuó credulous and pliable: 此人～, 不可大用。This chap is not worthy of trust, as he is too trustful and changes his position easily.
耳塞 ěrsāi ❶ mini-earphone ❷ earplug
耳塞 ěrsai *see* "耳垢"
耳沙 ěrshā *also* "耳石" otolith
耳扇 ěrshàn ❶ earflap; earlap ❷ 〈生理〉 auricle; pinna
耳勺子 ěrsháozi box on the ear; slap on the face
耳神经痛 ěrshénjīngtòng 〈医学〉 otoneuralgia
耳神经学 ěrshénjīngxué 〈医学〉 otoneurology
耳生 ěrshēng be unfamiliar to the ear; sound rather strange: 这个人的话音听起来～。This man's voice sounds unfamiliar to me.
耳石 ěrshí 〈生理〉 otolith: ～病 otolithiasis
耳食 ěrshí 〈书面〉 readily believe what one is told; be credulous: ～不化 readily believe what one hears without really understanding it / ～之谈 hearsay
耳屎 ěrshǐ 〈口语〉 earwax
耳饰 ěrshì earring; ear ornament
耳熟 ěrshú familiar to the ear: 这名字听起来很～, 他好像来过。The name sounds quite familiar. It seems he's been here before.
耳熟能详 ěrshú-néngxiáng one can always repeat what is frequently heard; one will get to know pretty well what one hears many times
耳顺 ěrshùn 〈书面〉 ❶ sixty years of age (from *The Analects*《论语》): 年近～ near sixty / 六十而～。At sixty, one's ears are an obedient organ for the reception of Truth. *or* One could hear the biddings of Heaven with docile ears. ❷ pleasing to the ear: 这种戏我听起来倒～。This kind of local opera sounds pleasant to me.
耳堂 ěrtáng 〈建筑〉 transept
耳提面命 ěrtí-miànmìng pour advice and exhortations into sb.'s ears; constantly give sb. one's advice and instructions: 多承～, 殊深感荷。I am deeply grateful to you for your frequent kind exhortations.
耳听八方 ěrtīngbāfāng have keen ears; be very alert: 领导者应该～, 眼观六路。A leader should be very alert to what is going on in the world.
耳痛 ěrtòng 〈医学〉 ear pain; otalgia; otodynia: ～药 otalgic
耳挖勺儿 ěrwāsháor 〈方言〉 *see* "耳挖子"
耳挖子 ěrwāzi earpick
耳闻 ěrwén hear of or about: 此事早有～。I heard about it long ago. / ～为虚, 眼见为实。What one hears may not be true, but what one sees is. *or* Seeing is believing.
耳闻不如目见 ěrwén bùrú mùjiàn seeing is believing
耳闻目睹 ěrwén-mùdǔ *also* "耳闻目击"; "耳闻目见" what one sees and hears: 其间他～了不少新鲜事儿。During the time he saw and heard many things which were new to him. / 他叙述的是他～的事实。This is his eyewitness account.
耳闻证人 ěrwén zhèngrén 〈法律〉 earwitness
耳蜗 ěrwō 〈生理〉 cochlea; acoustic labyrinth
耳蜗炎 ěrwōyán 〈医学〉 cochlitis
耳息肉 ěrxīròu 〈医学〉 otopolypus
耳下腺 ěrxiàxiàn *also* "腮腺" sāixiàn 〈生理〉 parotid gland
耳性青光眼 ěrxìng qīngguāngyǎn 〈医学〉 auricular glaucoma
耳性 ěrxing (often used with children in the negative) ability to remember exhortations or warning one hears; memory: ～不好 have a poor memory (for exhortations and warnings)
耳穴 ěrxué ear acupuncture point
耳熏目染 ěrxūn-mùrǎn *see* "耳濡目染"
耳丫子 ěryāzi 〈方言〉 ear
耳咽管 ěryānguǎn 〈生理〉 Eustachian tube; auditory tube
耳炎 ěryán 〈医学〉 otitis: 内～ otitis interna / 外～ otitis externa / 中～ otitis media
耳音 ěryīn hearing: 瞧你这～, 连我的声音也听不出来! How poor your hearing is! You can't even recognize my voice!
耳硬化症 ěryìnghuàzhèng 〈医学〉 otosclerosis
耳语 ěryǔ whisper in sb.'s ear; whisper: 几个妇女在大树下低声～。Several women are whispering under a tall tree.
耳针 ěrzhēn ear acupuncture: ～麻醉 ear acupuncture anesthesia
耳针疗法 ěrzhēn liáofǎ 〈中医〉 auriculotherapy; ear-acupuncture therapy
耳坠 ěrzhuì *also* "耳坠子" earring; eardrop
耳子 ěrzi ear of utensil or container

洱 ěr

洱海 Ěrhǎi Erhai Lake, fresh-water lake in Yunnan Province

珥 ěr 〈书面〉earring made of jade or pearl

铒 ěr 〈化学〉erbium (Er)

铒激光器 ěrjīguāngqì erbium laser

饵 ěr ❶ cakes; pastry: 果～ candies and cakes; confectionery / 饼～ cakes; pastry ❷ bait: 鱼～ fishing bait ❸〈书面〉entice; tempt: ～以重利 entice sb. with the prospect of wealth; tempt sb. by offering pots of money

饵敌 ěrdí lay a trap for the enemy

饵雷 ěrléi booby trap

饵料 ěrliào ❶ fishing bait ❷ insect killer; insecticide

饵子 ěrzi fishing bait

駬 ěr see "騄駬" lù'ěr

尔(爾) ěr 〈书面〉❶ you; your: ～等 you; all of you / ～父 your father ❷ so; like that: 果～ if so / ～许 so many / 何其相似乃～。What a striking similarity! ❸ that; this: ～时 at that time / ～夜月朗。The moon was bright that night. ❹〈助词〉only; just; merely: 无他，但手熟～。It is just that I am familiar with this. ❺ *used after an adjective*: 率～ hastily; rashly / 卓～不群 be preeminent

尔曹 ěrcáo 〈书面〉you people; you and your kind: ～身与名俱灭，不废江河万古流。Your names will perish along with your bodies, but the river will flow on for ever—the names of mediocre writers will be forgotten, but those of the great masters will live.

尔代节 Ěrdàijié *also* "开斋节" Kāizhāijié 〈伊斯兰〉Lesser Bairam; Fast-breaking Festival

尔耳 ěr'ěr *also* "尔尔" 〈书面〉nothing out of the ordinary; just so-so: 不过～。It's nothing out of the ordinary. / 聊复～。This is just a brief note in reply.

尔格 ěrgé 〈物理〉erg: ～子 ergon

尔后 ěrhòu 〈书面〉thereafter; subsequently: ～的事情我不清楚了。I have no idea what happened afterwards.

尔刻 ěrkè 〈方言〉now; for the moment: ～他学习比较努力了。He studies (*or* works) much harder now.

尔来 ěrlái 〈书面〉since then; lately: ～四十余载。It has been over 40 years since then.

尔许 ěrxǔ 〈书面〉so; such; so very: ～多 so many or much / ～闲暇 so much leisure

尔雅 ěryǎ ❶〈书面〉cultured; refined; elegant: 温文～ gentle and elegant / 雍容～ cultured and dignified. ❷ (Ěryǎ) *Er Ya* or *Near to Correctness*, earliest Chinese dictionary compiled between 221 BC-220 AD

尔虞我诈 ěryú-wǒzhà *also* "尔诈我虞" mutual deception; each trying to cheat or outwit the other: 派系之间～。These factions were trying to cheat and deceive each other.

迩(邇) ěr 〈书面〉near: 遐～驰名 known far and wide / 年关在～。It is approaching the year's end (when all debts must be paid and extra expenses incurred). *or* The year is drawing to a close.

迩来 ěrlái 〈书面〉recently; lately: ～天气变幻无常。The weather has been very changeable lately.

迩言 ěryán 〈书面〉simple words; simple and plain language

èr

二 èr ❶ two: ～十 twenty / ～楼 (UK) first floor; (US) second floor / 他们村离我们村只有～里地。Their village is only two *li* (*or* one kilometre) away from ours. / 这事我略知一～。I know a little about it. / ～者必居其一，其它的道路是没有的。Either one or the other, there is no other choice. / ～者不可兼得。You can't eat your cake and have it too. ❷ different: 不～价 fixed price; no bargaining / 不～法门 same old trick / 三心～意 of two minds; shilly-shally

二八 èrbā 〈书面〉sixteen: 小女年方～。My daughter is sixteen.

二八佳人 èrbā jiārén maiden of sixteen; nubile girl of sweet sixteen

二把刀 èrbǎdāo 〈方言〉❶ have a smattering of a subject; have half-baked knowledge or skill: 我的英语可是～呀! I only know a smattering of English. *or* My English is only half-baked. ❷ dabbler; smatterer: 他在书法方面只算是个～。He is no more than a dabbler in calligraphy.

二把手 èrbǎshǒu number two person; second-in-command; first or executive deputy (to the head of a unit): 他是我们厂里的～。He is the second-in-command of our factory.

二百二 èrbǎi'èr *also* "二百二十" (common name for 汞溴红) mercurochrome

二百五 èrbǎiwǔ ❶〈口语〉one who is not all there; stupid person: 你别～了! Don't play the fool! ❷〈方言〉dabbler; smatterer; dilettante

二倍体 èrbèitǐ 〈生物〉diploid

二苯胺 èrběn'àn 〈化学〉diphenylamine

二遍苦，二茬罪 èr biàn kǔ, èr chá zuì be subjected to oppression and exploitation all over again: 谁都不愿再吃二遍苦，受二茬罪。Nobody is willing to suffer oppression and exploitation for a second time.

二部制 èrbùzhì two-shift system; two part-time shifts: ～学校 school with two part-time shifts; double-shift school

二长岩 èrchángyán 〈矿业〉monzonite

二冲程 èrchōngchéng 〈机械〉two stroke: ～循环 two-stroke cycle / ～发动机 two-stroke engine

二重唱 èrchóngchàng 〈音乐〉(vocal) duet

二重处理 èrchóng chǔlǐ dual processing

二重胶片 èrchóng jiāopiàn 〈摄影〉bipack

二重透视 èrchóng tòushì double perspective

二重性 èrchóngxìng dual character or nature; duality

二重奏 èrchóngzòu 〈音乐〉(instrumental) duet

二传手 èrchuánshǒu (in volleyball) setter; tosser

二次方程 èrcì fāngchéng 〈数学〉quadratic equation

二次函数 èrcì hánshù 〈数学〉quadratic function

二次互反率 èrcì hùfǎnlǜ 〈数学〉quadratic reciprocity law

二次加工能力 èrcì jiāgōng nénglì capacity to reprocess

二次能源 èrcì néngyuán secondary energy source (such as electricity, etc.); second energy

二次曲面 èrcì qūmiàn 〈数学〉conicoid; quadratic surface

二次曲线 èrcì qūxiàn 〈数学〉conic section; curve of the second degree; quadratic curve

二道贩子 èrdào fànzi 〈贬义〉private businessman or trader who makes exorbitant profits by buying cheap and selling dear

二等 èrděng second-class; second-rate

二等兵 èrděngbīng (US and UK Army, US Marine Corps, etc.) private; (UK Marine Corps) marine second class; (US Navy) seaman second class; (UK Navy) able seaman; (US Air Force) airman second class; (UK Air Force) leading aircraftsman

二等残废军人 èrděng cánfèi jūnrén disabled soldier, second class

二等舱 èrděngcāng second-class cabin

二等分 èrděngfēn 〈数学〉bisect: ～线 bisector

二等公民 èrděng gōngmín second-class citizen

二等功 èrděnggōng merit citation class II; second-class merit

二等奖 èrděngjiǎng second prize

二等秘书 èrděng mìshū (shortened as 二秘)〈外交〉second secretary

二等品 èrděngpǐn second-class goods; seconds

二地主 èrdìzhǔ sub-landlord

二叠纪 Èrdiéjì 〈地质〉Permian Period; the Permian

二叠系 Èrdiéxì 〈地质〉Permian system

二段式 èrduànshì 〈音乐〉binary form

二恶英 èr'èyīng 〈化学〉dioxin, a cancer-causing chemical: 不含～ dioxin-free / 受到～污染的食物 food contaminated by dioxin; dioxin-contaminated food

二·二八起义 Èr-Èrbā Qǐyì Uprising of February 28, 1947 (popular revolt against the Kuomintang in Taiwan Province)

二二丝丝 èr'èr-sīsī 〈方言〉hesitant; indecisive: 她～地拿不定主意去不去。She was hesitant about the trip. / 他就是这么一个～的人。He is such a typically indecisive character.

二房 èrfáng ❶ second male branch of an extended family; branch

E

headed by the second son; cadet branch ❷ concubine
二房东 èrfángdōng sublessor (of a room or house); sub-landlord
二分点 èrfēndiǎn 〈天文〉the equinoxes:~风暴 equinoctial storm
二分法 èrfēnfǎ 〈逻辑〉dichotomy; 〈哲学〉theory that everything divides into two
二分裂 èrfēnliè 〈生物〉binary fission
二分音符 èrfēn yīnfú 〈音乐〉minim; half note
二伏 èrfú *also* "中伏" zhōngfú ❶ second of the three ten-day periods of the hot season ❷ first day of the second period of the hot season
二副 èrfù 〈航海〉second mate; second officer
二杆子 èrgǎnzi 〈方言〉❶ impetuous; rude; fiery: ~脾气 fiery temper (*or* temperament) ❷ impetuous person
二鬼子 èrguǐzi (used to refer to those who collaborated with the enemy during the Anti-Japanese War) traitor; collaborator; quisling
二辊式轧机 èrgǔnshì zhájī two-high rolling mill
二锅饭 èrguōfàn rice from different pots; 〈比喻〉different minds; different approaches:一家人不吃~ members of one family eat from the same pot — family members are of one mind (*or* heart)
二锅头 èrguōtóu strong spirit usu. made from sorghum, popular in northern China
二合土 èrhétǔ 〈农业〉loam
二合元音 èrhé yuányīn 〈语言〉diphthong
二胡 èrhú *erhu* fiddle; two-stringed Chinese fiddle
二虎 èrhǔ 〈方言〉rash; reckless; impetuous: ~劲儿 impetuous way of doing things; rash behaviour /说~话 talk impetuously
二虎相斗,必有一伤 èr hǔ xiāng dòu, bì yǒu yī shāng 〈俗语〉when two tigers fight one is bound to be the loser
二乎 èrhu *also* "二忽"〈方言〉❶ shrink back in fear; flinch:他在困难面前向来不~。He never flinches from difficulties. ❷ feel uncertain and hesitant; be puzzled:你越说越把我弄~了。The more you talk about it, the more puzzled I am. ❸ unpromising; of little hope:我看这件事~了。It seems that the thing is fizzling out.
二花脸 èrhuāliǎn *also* "架子花" jiàzihuā 〈戏曲〉a kind of *hualian*, or multicoloured face, so named because the actor's face is painted in multiple colours
二化螟 èrhuàmíng striped rice borer (*Chilo suppressalis*)
二话 èrhuà (often used in the negative) demur; objection; complaint:~没说,他们就干起来了。They started working right away without more ado. /你尽管吩咐吧,我决没有~。If you have any instructions, please let me know and I will not hesitate to carry them out.
二荒地 èrhuāngdì land once cultivated but later gone to waste
二黄 èrhuáng *also* "二簧"〈戏曲〉*erhuang* melodies (one of the chief types of music in traditional Chinese operas)
二婚 èrhūn (usu. of women) remarry
二婚头 èrhūntóu *also* "二婚儿"〈贬义〉woman or man who has married twice
二混子 èrhùnzi 〈方言〉good-for-nothing; loafer; loiterer:他放着工作不做,甘愿当一个~。He chose to stay away from his job and just dillydally.
二级风 èrjífēng 〈气象〉force 2 wind; light breeze
二级公路 èrjí gōnglù second-class highway
二级火箭 èrjí huǒjiàn booster-missile combination; two-stage rocket
二级市场 èrjí shìchǎng secondary market
二级准尉 èrjí zhǔnwèi (UK) warrant officer (Class II); (US Army and Air Force) warrant officer, junior grade; (US Navy and Marine Corps) warrant officer
二极管 èrjíguǎn 〈电子〉diode:~整流器〈电子〉diode rectifier
二甲苯 èrjiǎběn 〈化学〉xylene
二价 èrjià 〈化学〉bivalence:~酸 dibasic acid /~染色体〈生物〉bivalent chromosome /~元素 dyad
二尖瓣 èrjiānbàn 〈生理〉mitral valve:~狭窄 mitral stenosis /~闭锁不全 mitral insufficiency
二尖瓣切开术 èrjiānbàn qiēkāishù 〈医学〉cardiovalvulotomy
二进宫 èrjìngōng ❶ traditional play in Beijing opera ❷ detained or sentenced for a second time; in and out of prison twice ❸ do sth. for a second time:他这次~,又来本院学英文了。This is his second stint at the college to learn English.
二进位 èrjìnwèi 〈计算机〉binary bit:~编码 binary coding /~编码信息 binary coded information /~计数器 binary counter
二进制 èrjìnzhì 〈计算机〉〈数学〉binary system; binary mode:~编码器 binary coder /~乘法器 binary multiplier /~计算机 binary computer /~加法器 binary adder (*or* adding device)/~标度 binary scale /~数 binary number /~数字 binary digit
二聚物 èrjùwù 〈化学〉bipolymer
二赖子 èrlàizi loafer; idler
二郎神 Èrlángshén Erlangshen, popular god in Chinese legend who has a third and vertical eye in his forehead enabling him to see through all monsters and demons, and so is good at fighting them
二郎腿 èrlángtuǐ cross-legged:跷起~ sit cross-legged
二老 èrlǎo father and mother:~身体还好。My parents are in good health.
二愣子 èrlèngzi rash fellow
二愣 èrleng 〈方言〉❶ shrink back in fear; flinch:既然我已下了决心,再难也决不~。Now that I've made up my mind, I will not shy away from any difficulties, no matter how great they are. ❷ hesitate; shilly-shally
二里头文化 Èrlǐtóu wénhuà 〈考古〉Erlitou Culture, early bronze culture (about 21st-17th centuries BC) usu. associated with Xia Dynasty, excavated at Erlitou in Yanshi (偃师) County, Henan Province
二连浩特 Èrliánhàotè Erenhot, border town in the Inner Mongolia Autonomous Region
二流 èrliú second-class; second-rate: ~作家 second-rate writer
二流子 èrliúzi loafer; idler; bum
二硫化物 èrliúhuàwù 〈化学〉bisulphide
二氯化物 èrlǜhuàwù 〈化学〉bichloride
二路儿 èrlùr *see* "二流"
二轮摩托 èrlún mótuō two-wheeled motorcycle; two wheeler
二毛 èrmáo 〈书面〉❶ grey or grizzled hair ❷ old people with grey hair or greying temples
二门 èrmén (of spacious courtyard) second gate leading to the main court; inner gate:大门不出,~不迈 (of girls in feudal times) never step beyond the inner gate, much less the outer one; never expose oneself to the world outside
二米饭 èrmǐfàn boiled rice mixed with millet or corn
二面角 èrmiànjiǎo 〈数学〉dihedral angle
二名法 èrmíngfǎ 〈生物〉binomial nomenclature
二拇指 èrmuzhǐ index finger; forefinger
二能极激光器 èrnéngjí jīguāngqì two-level laser
二年生 èrniánshēng 〈植物〉biennial:~植物 biennial plant
二炮 Èrpào (short for 中国人民解放军第二炮兵) Second Artillery Force (of the People's Liberation Army of China); Rocket Force
二七大罢工 Èr-Qī Dà Bàgōng Great Strike of February 7, 1923 (anti-imperialist, anti-warlord strike of the Beijing-Hankou Railway workers led by the Chinese Communist Party)
二汽 Èrqì (short for 中国第二汽车制造厂) No. 2 Motor Vehicle Plant (at Xiangfan 襄樊, Hubei Province)
二全音符 èrquán yīnfú 〈音乐〉breve
二人台 èrréntái ❶ popular Inner-Mongolian song-and-dance duet ❷ local opera based on such song-and-dance duets
二人同心,其利断金 èr rén tóngxīn, qí lì duàn jīn 〈谚语〉if two people unite as one, their strength is powerful enough to cut metal — unity is strength
二人转 èrrénzhuàn ❶ song-and-dance duet popular in northeast China ❷ local opera based upon such duets
二三其德 èrsān-qídé 〈书面〉be of two minds; shilly-shally
二色镜 èrsèjìng dichroic mirror
二审 èrshěn *also* "第二审" dì'èrshěn second appeal; second instance; second trial:~法院 court of second instance
二十八星瓢虫 èrshíbāxīng piáochóng 〈动物〉*also* "花大姐" huādàjiě potato ladybird or ladybug
二十八宿 èrshíbāxiù 〈天文〉lunar mansions; twenty-eight constellations, into which ancient Chinese astronomers divided all the visible stars in the sky: the constellations further formed four major groups, each taking up one of the four quadrants of the sky, with the eastern group called Dragon (苍龙), comprising the constellations of *jiao* (角), *kang* (亢), *di* (氐), *fang* (房), *xin* (心), *wei* (尾) and *ji* (箕); the northern group called Black Warrior (玄武), comprising *dou* (斗), *niu* (牛), *nü* (女), *xu* (虚), *wei* (危), *shi* (室) and *bi* (壁); the western group called White Tiger (白虎),

comprising *kui* (奎), *lou* (娄), *wei* (胃), *mao* (昴), *bi* (毕), *zi* (觜), *shen* (参); and the southern group called Vermillion Bird (朱雀), comprising *jing* (井), *gui* (鬼), *liu* (柳), *xing* (星), *zhang* (张), *yi* (翼) and *zhen* (轸)

二十世纪福克斯影片公司 Èrshí Shìjì Fúkèsī Yǐngpiàn Gōngsī (US) 20th Century-Fox Film Corporation

二十四节气 èrshísì jiéqì twenty-four seasonal division points by which the solar year is divided under the traditional Chinese calendar according to the sun's apparent movement along the ecliptic (黄经), with Vernal Equinox (春分) marking 0° on this imaginary line and each of the twenty-four points spaced by 15° from the next, but with the Beginning of Spring (立春) at 315° as the first point starting the solar year. The twenty-four seasonal division points are Beginning of Spring (立春), with the sun at 315°, falling on 4 or 5 Feb.; Rain Water (雨水), at 330°, 19 or 20 Feb.; Waking of Insects (惊蛰), at 345°, 5 or 6 March; Vernal Equinox (春分), at 0°, 20 or 21 March; Pure Brightness (清明), at 15°, 5 or 6 April; Grain Rain (谷雨), at 30°, 20 or 21 April; Beginning of Summer (立夏), at 45°, 5 or 6 May; Grain Budding (小满), at 60°, 21 or 22 May; Grain in Ear (芒种), at 75°, 6 or 7 June; Summer Solstice (夏至), at 90°, 21 or 22 June; Slight Heat (小暑), at 105°, 7 or 8 July; Great Heat (大暑), at 120°, 23 or 24 July; Beginning of Autumn (立秋), at 135°, 7 or 8 August; Limit of Heat (处暑), at 150°, 23 or 24 August; White Dew (白露), at 165°, 7 or 8 Sept.; Autumnal Eqinox (秋分), at 180°, 23 or 24 Sept.; Cold Dew (寒露), at 195°, 8 or 9 Oct.; Frost's Descent (霜降), at 210°, 23 or 24 Oct.; Beginning of Winter (立冬), 225°, 7 or 8 Nov.; Slight Snow (小雪), at 240°, 22 or 23 Nov.; Great Snow (大雪), at 255°, 7 or 8 Dec.; Winter Solstice (冬至), at 270°, 22 or 23 Dec.; Slight Cold (小寒), at 285°, 5 or 6 Jan.; Great Cold (大寒), at 300°, 20 or 21 Jan.

二十四开 èrshísìkāi ❶ 24-carat gold; pure gold ❷ (of paper size) 24mo

二十四史 èrshísìshǐ ❶ Twenty-Four Histories (dynastic histories from remote antiquity till the Ming Dynasty), i.e. *Historical Records* (史记), *History of Han* (汉书), *History of Eastern Han* (后汉书), *History of the Three Kingdoms* (三国志), with the above comprising the "four early Histories" (前四史), *History of Jin* (晋书), *History of Song* (first of the Southern Dynasties, 宋书), *History of Southern Qi* (second of the Southern Dynasties, 南齐书), *History of Liang* (third of the Southern Dynasties, 梁书), *History of Chen* (fourth and last of the Southern Dynasties, 陈书), *History of Weis* (three Weis of the Northern Dynasties, called Northern Wei, Eastern Wei, and Western Wei respectively, 魏书), *History of Northern Qi* (one of the Northern Dynasties, 北齐书), *History of Zhou* (last of the Northern Dynasties, 周书) *History of Sui* (隋书), *History of the Southern Dynasties* (南史), *History of the Northern Dynasties* (北史), *Old History of Tang* (旧唐书), *New History of Tang* (新唐书), *Old History of the Five Dynasties* (旧五代史), *New History of the Five Dynasties* (新五代史), *History of the Song Dynasty* (宋史), *History of Liao* (辽史), *History of Jin* (金史), *History of Yuan* (元史), and *History of Ming* (明史) ❷ long intricate story: 一部～，不知从何说起。It's such a long story that I hardly know where to start. *or* It is a long and involved story.

二十五史 èrshíwǔshǐ ❶ Twenty-Four Histories plus the *New History of Yuan* ❷ Twenty-Four Histories plus the *Draft History of Qing*

二十一点 èrshíyīdiǎn blackjack: 玩～ play blackjack

二十一世纪委员会 èrshíyī shìjì wěiyuánhuì Twenty-first Century Committee: 中日友好～ 21st Century Committee for China-Japan Friendship

二十一条 Èrshíyītiáo Twenty-one Demands (forced on Chinese warlord government by Japan in 1915)

二手 èrshǒu ❶ helper; assistant: ～活儿 play a supporting role / 我给你当～。I'll act as your assistant. ❷ second-hand: ～货 second-hand goods / ～资料 second-hand information / ～设备 second-hand equipment

二竖为虐 èrshù-wéinüè 〈书面〉 fall victim to a disease hard to cure: ～，他竟一病不起。He got an incurable disease and could not leave his bed again.

二四滴 èrsìdī 〈农业〉 2,4-D; 2,4-dichlorophenoxyacetic acid

二糖 èrtáng 〈生化〉 disaccharide: ～酶 disaccharidase

二踢脚 èrtījiǎo double-bang firecracker

二天 èrtiān 〈方言〉 some other time; some other day: 我～再来。I'll come some other time.

二烃基 èrtīngjī 〈化学〉 dialkyl

二头肌 èrtóujī 〈生理〉 bicephalous muscle; biceps

二万五千里长征 Èrwàn Wǔqiānlǐ Chángzhēng Long March of 25,000 *li* (made by the Chinese Workers' and Peasants' Red Army, 1934-1935)
see also "长征"

二维 èrwéi 〈物理〉 two-dimension: ～流 two-dimensional current / ～基本形 two-dimensional fundamental form

二维存储 èrwéi cúnchǔ two-dimensional storage

二维电路 èrwéi diànlù two-dimensional circuit

二维矢量 èrwéi shǐliàng two-dimensional vector

二五眼 èrwuyǎn 〈方言〉 ❶ of inferior ability or quality: 那些业务上～的，出工不出力的，全要裁下去。All those who are unqualified or loaf on the job will be given the sack. ❷ incompetent person

二弦 èrxián ❶ silk string of medium thickness for musical instruments ❷ a kind of bowed instrument

二线 èrxiàn ❶ second line of defence ❷ semi-retirement for veteran cadres: ～工作者 second liner (a person who is due to retire but still does some less strenuous or less responsible work) / 许多老干部退居～以后，仍关心单位的工作。Many veteran cadres still care a lot about the work of their departments after stepping down from active service.

二项式 èrxiàngshì 〈数学〉 binomial (expression)

二象性 èrxiàngxìng 〈物理〉 dual property; duality: 物质的～ dualistic nature of matter / 波粒～ wave-particle duality

二硝基本酚 èrxiāojīběnfēn 〈化学〉 dinitrophenol

二心 èrxīn *also* "贰心" èrxīn ❶ disloyalty; unfaithfulness: 她怀疑丈夫对自己有～。She suspects that her husband is unfaithful. *or* She suspects her husband of disloyalty. ❷ half-heartedness; two minds

二形人 èrxíngrén *also* "二体人" *see* "二性子"

二性霉素 èrxìngméisù 〈药学〉 amphotericin B

二性土 èrxìngtǔ 〈农业〉 loam

二性子 èrxìngzi bisexual person; hermaphrodite

二溴化物 èrxiùhuàwù 〈化学〉 dibromide

二氧化硅 èryǎnghuàguī 〈化学〉 silicon dioxide; silica

二氧化硫 èryǎnghuàliú 〈化学〉 sulphur dioxide

二氧化碳 èryǎnghuàtàn 〈化学〉 carbon dioxide: ～保护焊 carbon-dioxide arc welding / ～激光器 carbon-dioxide laser / ～灭火器 carbon-dioxide bottle; carbon-dioxide cylinder; carbon-dioxide fire extinguisher

二氧化物 èryǎnghuàwù 〈化学〉 dioxide

二一添作五 èr yī tiānzuò wǔ share on a fifty-fifty basis; go halves: 来，这点东西咱们～，对半平分。Hey, let's share it on a fifty-fifty basis.

二乙基 èryǐjī 〈化学〉 diethyl

二尾子 èryǐzi 〈方言〉 bisexual person; hermaphrodite

二意 èryì ❶ disloyalty; unfaithfulness: 终无～ remain loyal; work with utter devotion ❷ half-heartedness; two minds 三心～ be of two minds; be half-hearted

二意 èryi 〈口语〉 shilly-shally; hesitant: ～忽忽 be irresolute

二元 èryuán duality; binary: ～式〈化学〉dualistic formula / ～推进剂〈航天〉bipropellant / ～布尔运算 dyadic Boolean operation

二元方程式 èryuán fāngchéngshì binary equation: 二元二次方程式 binary quadratic equation

二元化合物 èryuán huàhéwù binary compound

二元化学武器 èryuán huàxué wǔqì binary chemical weapon

二元经济 èryuán jīngjì dual economy

二元论 èryuánlùn 〈哲学〉 dualism

二元燃料 èryuán ránliào 〈化学〉 bipropellant

二元溶液 èryuán róngyè binary solution

二元酸 èryuánsuān 〈化学〉 binary acid; diacid

二元体 èryuántǐ *see* "二倍体"

二月 èryuè ❶ February ❷ second month of the lunar year; second moon

二月革命 Èryuè Gémìng February Revolution (1917) in Russia

二战 Èrzhàn (short for 第二次世界大战) WWII; World War Two: ～史 History of World War Two

二者必居其一 èrzhě bì jū qí yī either one or the other; one way or the other

E

二指 èrzhǐ index finger
二至点 èrzhìdiǎn 〈天文〉solstice
二致 èrzhì (often used in the negative) different; not the same：他俩的看法实质上并无～。Their views do not differ in essence.
二足动物 èrzú dòngwù biped

弍 èr *see* "二" èr

贰 èr ❶ two (used for the numeral 二 to avoid mistakes or alterations) ❷ transfer one's allegiance; turn one's coat
贰臣 èrchén court official who transferred his allegiance to a new ruler; turncoat official
贰心 èrxīn *see* "二心" èrxīn

刵 èr cutting off of the ear as punishment in ancient times

咡 èr 〈书面〉cheek

F

fā

发(發) fā ❶ issue; send (out); give out; distribute: 颁～ issue; promulgate /签～ sign and issue (a document, certificate, etc.)/印～ print and distribute; issue /～传真 send a fax /～考卷 give out exam papers /～奖金 distribute bonuses /～信号 give a signal /～驾驶执照 issue a driving licence /～解雇通知 hand out a dismissal notice /给优胜者～奖品 award prizes to winners /我们上星期五～了那批货。We dispatched the goods last Friday. ❷ discharge; shoot; fire; launch: 单～ *also* "点～" (fire a) single shot /连～ fire in bursts /～炮 fire a cannon /～导弹 launch a missile /百～百中 every shot hits the target; shoot with unfailing accuracy /引而不～ draw the bow without shooting the arrow ❸ generate; produce; bring or come into existence: 萌～ germinate; sprout /旧病复～ have a recurrence of an old illness /有一分热,～一分光 give as much light as the heat can produce; do one's utmost ❹ speak; utter; express: 大～议论 speak at great length /她坐在角落里一言不～。She sat in a corner without uttering a word. ❺ develop; expand: 局部开～ develop partially ❻ become rich; make a fortune: ～横财 get a windfall; make money illegally /暴～户 nouveau riche; overnight millionaire; upstart /这几年,他～起来了。He made a fortune the last few years. ❼ (of foodstuffs) rise or expand when fermented or soaked: ～海带 soak dried kelp in water /～木耳 raise edible fungus /盆里的面～了。The dough has risen in the bowl. ❽ disperse; diffuse: 挥～ volatilize /蒸～ evaporate /散～热气 give forth steam (*or* heat) ❾ open up; discover; expose: 当众揭～ expose in public /向警方告～某人罪行 denounce sb.'s crime to the police /东窗事～。The crime has come to light. *or* Murder is out. ❿ get into a certain state; become; turn: ～硬 become stiff (*or* rigid) /枫叶开始～红。Maple leaves were beginning to turn red. /小草～绿。The slender grass was greening. /这块料子看上去～旧。The material looks used. ⓫ show (one's feeling); elicit: ～慈悲 show mercy (*or* pity) /～善心 show charity; be kind /引～诗兴 draw poetic inspiration (from sth.) ⓬ feel (usu. sth. unpleasant): ～冷 feel cold; feel chilly /～麻 feel numb; tingle /～黏 feel sticky; be sticky to the touch /嗓子～哑 sound husky (*or* hoarse) /他身上～烫。He was burning with fever. ⓭ start on a journey; set out; depart: 整装待～ be fully equipped for a journey; be ready to start; pack up and get ready to start /朝～夕至 set off in the morning and arrive in the evening ⓮ begin(an action); start: 先～制人 gain the initiative by striking first /引～一连串爆炸 set off a chain of explosions ⓯ 〈量词〉 *used for ammunition*: 两～炮弹 two shells / 五十～子弹 50 rounds of ammunition; 50 cartridges (*or* bullets)
see also fà

发案 fā'àn (of a case) occur; take place: ～率 incidence (of criminal cases) /～时间 time of the occurrence of a case /到～地点进行调查 investigate a case on the scene (of its occurrence)

发榜 fābǎng publish a list of successful candidates or applicants: 新生录取名单已经～。The list of students to be admitted has been published.

发包 fābāo put out to contract; contract out: ～工程 contract project /把工程～给一家建筑公司 contract a project out to a building company

发报 fābào transmit a message by radio, telegraphy, etc.: ～速度 transmitting speed; transmission speed /到了上海立即～给我。Be sure to send me a telegram when you arrive in Shanghai.

发报机 fābàojī transmitter

发报台 fābàotái transmitting station

发背 fābèi ❶〈中医〉carbuncle on the back ❷ become hard of hearing: 父亲的耳朵有点儿～。My father became somewhat hard of hearing.

发变 fābiàn 〈方言〉(of a teenager) grow up

发标 fābiāo ❶〈方言〉make a show of one's power or authority; throw one's weight about; throw a tantrum ❷ issue bidding documents

发表 fābiǎo ❶ state; announce; issue; deliver: ～任命 announce an appointment /～联合公报 issue (*or* make) a joint communique /即席～演说 deliver (*or* make) an impromptu speech /～个人意见 voice one's opinion; state (*or* air) one's view /向全国人民～讲话 address the nation ❷ publish; (of newspapers, journals, etc.) carry: 学报～了他的几篇学术论文。The university (*or* college) journal carried a few academic papers of his. /社论～在头版头条。The editorial was published at the top of the front page.

发兵 fābīng send troops; dispatch troops: 已经～前去救援。Troops were sent to the rescue.

发病 fābìng (of a disease) come on; (of a person) fall ill; be taken ill: 突然～ be suddenly taken ill (with diarrhea, etc.) /艾滋病的～原因尚不清楚。The cause (*or* pathogeny) of Aids is still unknown. /在母亲的精心照料下,父亲一整年都没有再～。Father has not had another attack for the last year as a result of mother's good care.

发病机理 fābìng jīlǐ pathogeny; pathogenesis

发病率 fābìnglǜ incidence (of a disease): 减少并发症～ reduce the incidence of complications /在成年男子中,心脏病的～较高。There is a higher incidence of heart diseases among male adults.

发布 fābù issue; promulgate; release: ～命令 give an order; promulgate a decree /～通缉令 issue a wanted circular /～嘉奖令 issue an order of commendation /～新闻 release news /～消息 give out information /新闻～会 press briefing; news conference; press conference

发财 fācái ❶ get rich; make a fortune; make a pile: ～致富 become rich; make a fortune /恭喜～。〈套语〉Wish you a happy and prosperous year. /他们在这笔交易中发了大财。They made a pile out of the deal. ❷〈套语〉seek a fortune — get a job: 您这阵子在哪儿～? Where have you been working these days?

发颤 fāchàn quiver; tremble; vibrate: 他激动得声音都～了。His voice quivered with emotion.
see also fāzhàn

发潮 fācháo become damp; feel damp: 衣服有点～。The clothes feel a bit damp. /不要睡在～的被单上。Don't sleep on a damp sheet.

发车 fāchē ❶ dispatch or send off a car (bus, truck, etc.) ❷ depart; leave: ～时间 time of departure; departure time /～信号 outbound (*or* departure) signal /早七点半～。The train (*or* bus) departs (*or* leaves) at 7:30 a.m.

发车场 fāchēchǎng 〈铁路〉departure track or yard

发痴 fāchī 〈方言〉❶ look blank; be in a daze; be in a trance: 他坐在那里～。He sat there as if in a trance. ❷ go mad; go crazy; become insane; be out of one's mind: 他悲伤得几乎要～。He was nearly driven mad by grief.

发愁 fāchóu worry; be anxious; become sad: 你大可不必为这事～。You don't have to worry about this at all. /他为找不到工作而十分～。He was filled with anxiety over his failure to find work. /由于为钱～,他显得老了。Money worries (*or* troubles) made him look old.

发出 fāchū ❶ produce (sound, etc.); generate; send forth: ～刺

F

耳的声音 produce a piercing (*or* grating) sound /～爽朗的笑声 laugh a hearty laugh /～热能 generate thermal energy /树叶在微风中～沙沙声响。The leaves rustled gently in the breeze. ❷ issue (orders, etc.); send out; promulgate:～逮捕证 issue an arrest warrant /～警报 sound (*or* send out) a warning /～指示 give (*or* issue) a directive /～紧急呼吁 send out an urgent appeal /～行政命令 promulgate an executive order (*or* decree) ❸ send (letters, messages, etc.); dispatch:～传票 send out (*or* issue) a summons /～新闻稿 file a news dispatch /文件已全部～。The documents have all been dispatched.

发憷 fāchù 〈方言〉 feel timid and uneasy; become nervous; be keyed up; grow apprehensive:要她讲英语,她就～。She feels uneasy when she has to speak English.

发喘 fāchuǎn be short of breath; gasp for breath; pant:累得直～ pant from exertion /爬三层楼就～ be short of breath after climbing three flights of stairs

发达 fādá ❶ developed; flourishing:～市场经济 developed market economy /大脑～ have powerful brains /生意～ do a booming (*or* flourishing) business /市场越来越兴旺～。The market is growing more and more prosperous. ❷ promote; develop; expand:～经济 develop (*or* promote) the economy

发达国家 fādá guójiā developed country:欠～ under-developed country; less-developed country

发呆 fādāi look blank; be in a trance; be in a daze; be stupefied:他话也不说,眼直直地,坐在那儿～。Without a word, he sat there staring blankly. /这个消息使他们惊得～。The news left them dazed (*or* stupefied).

发单 fādān *also* "发票" invoice; bill

发嗲 fādiǎ 〈方言〉 ❶ speak or act like a spoiled child ❷ (of a woman) speak or behave coquettishly

发电 fādiàn ❶ generate electricity or power:水力～ hydro-power; water power /火力～ thermal power /地热～ geothermal power /原子能～ atomic power; nuclear power /海洋热能～ generate electricity with oceanic thermal energy /～能力 generating capacity /～成本 generating cost /～设备 generating equipment; generating plant; generation set ❷ send a telegram:向死者家属～吊唁 send a message of condolences to the bereaved family

发电厂 fādiànchǎng power plant; generating plant:～容量 power plant (*or* station) capacity /～设备 power plant (*or* station) equipment

发电机 fādiànjī generator; dynamo:永磁～ magneto generator /双水内冷汽轮～ turbogenerator with inner water-cooled stator and rotor /～容量 generator capacity /～组 generating set; generating unit; power set /～磁场 generator field /～输出功率 generator (*or* dynamo) output /～控制台 generator control desk

发电量 fādiànliàng generated energy; electric power production

发电站 fādiànzhàn power station:核能～ nuclear power station

发动 fādòng ❶ start; launch:～引擎 start an engine; set an engine going; get an engine started /～进攻 launch an attack /～政变 stage a *coup d'état* /～战争 unleash (*or* start) a war ❷ call into action; arouse; mobilize:放手～群众 boldly arouse (*or* mobilize) the masses /植树造林需要～各行各业来搞。Afforestation requires mobilization of people of all walks of life.

发动机 fādòngjī *also* "动力机" dònglìjī engine; motor:柴油～ diesel engine /内燃～ inner-combustion engine /涡轮喷气～ turbojet engine /～动力学 engine dynamics /～试车 engine test /～传动 engine drive /～功率 engine power /～汽缸 (engine) cylinder /～汽缸排气量 engine cylinder displacement/～输出功率 engine output /～性能 engine performance /～罩 (engine) hood (*or* cover) /～房 engine room

发抖 fādǒu shiver; quiver; shake; tremble:冻得～ shiver with cold /气得浑身～ shake all over with anger /他紧张得声音有些～。He was so worked up that his voice quivered.

发堵 fādǔ feel oppressed; feel suffocated; be depressed:胸口～ feel a tightness in the chest /心里～ have a load on one's mind; feel depressed

发端 fāduān make a start; begin; originate:故事的～ the beginning (*or* origin) of the story /这件事～于三年前。It all started three years ago.

发凡 fāfán 〈书面〉 introduction (to a subject or a book):～起例 introduction and guide (to a book) /《汉语修辞～》 *An Introduction to Chinese Rhetoric*

发烦 fāfán be vexed; be impatient; be fidgety; be agitated:故事太长会使小孩～。A long tale gives a child fidgets. /听到消息她心里～。She was agitated at the news.

发放 fāfàng ❶ provide; grant; extend; distribute:～贷款 grant (*or* extend) credits /～救济 distribute (*or* deal out) relief /～宣传资料 hand out (*or* distribute) publicity material ❷ send out; send up:～信号弹 send up a signal flare ❸ deal with (an offender):被告对查清案情有立功表现,将从轻～。The accused will be given a lighter sentence as he has shown repentance by contributing to the clearing up of the case.

发粉 fāfěn baking powder; ferment

发奋 fāfèn ❶ work energetically; exert oneself:～有为 energetic and promising /～读书 work hard at one's studies; study assiduously ❷ *see* "发愤"

发愤 fāfèn *also* "发奋" make a firm resolution; make a determined effort:～学习 put all one's energy into one's study; be assiduous in one's study

发愤图强 fāfèn-túqiáng *also* "发奋图强" work with a firm will to make the country strong; make determined efforts to better oneself

发愤忘食 fāfèn-wàngshí be so absorbed in one's work or study as to forget one's meals; work or study so hard as to forget to eat

发疯 fāfēng go mad or crazy; become insane; be out of one's mind; lose one's senses:被逼得～ be driven to madness; be driven mad /～似地工作 work like crazy (*or* mad) /爱得～ be madly in love (with sb.) /正逢暴风雪,你还要出去,真是～了。It is crazy of you to rush out into such a snow storm.

发福 fāfú (usu. said of older people as an euphemism or in a jocular manner) put on weight; grow stout:近来他愈见～。He has gained much weight recently. /哟,您～了。Why, you are rounding out. *or* Well, you've put on weight.

发付 fāfù (often used in the early vernacular) send on an errand; dispatch

发绀 fāgàn *also* "青紫" qīngzǐ 〈医学〉 cyanosis

发糕 fāgāo steamed sponge cake (usu. sweetened):江米～ glutinous rice cake

发稿 fāgǎo ❶ distribute news dispatches:～截止时间 deadline for submitting (*or* filing) news reports /截至～时 at press time ❷ send manuscripts to the press:～付印 send a manuscript for printing

发给 fāgěi issue; distribute; grant:～毕业证书 issue a diploma /～签证 grant (*or* issue) a visa /～营业执照 issue a business license /把报纸～订户 distribute newspapers to subscribers

发功 fāgōng (used in *qigong* or kung fu) release or deliver energy

发光 fāguāng ❶ emit light; shine; be luminous or glow:～的天体 luminous heavenly body /她兴奋得两眼～。Her eyes shone with excitement. /星星在夜空中闪闪～。The stars twinkled in the night sky. /露珠在早晨的阳光下闪闪～。Dewdrops sparkled in the morning sun. ❷ shiny; luminous; luminescent:乌黑～的头发 shiny black hair /～标志 luminous sign /～动物 luminous animal /～材料 luminescent material

发光度 fāguāngdù luminosity; luminance; radiance

发光二级管 fāguāng èrjíguǎn light-emitting diode (LED)

发光浮标 fāguāng fúbiāo lighted buoy

发光管 fāguāngguǎn luminotron

发光菌 fāguāngjūn photogen

发光漆 fāguāngqī luminous paint or glazing

发光器 fāguāngqì illuminator

发光强度 fāguāng qiángdù luminous intensity

发光体 fāguāngtǐ luminous body; 〈物理〉 luminaire; luminophor

发函清单 fāhán qīngdān mailing list

发汗 fāhàn (induce) perspiration; sweat; diaphoresis:姜汤可以～。Ginger tea can induce perspiration. /医生给病人～。The doctor sweated his patient. /～可以治感冒。A good sweat will cure a cold.

发汗药 fāhànyào sudorific; diaphoretic

发行 fāháng sell wholesale
see also fāxíng

发号施令 fāhào-shīlìng issue orders; order people about:领导切忌坐在办公室里～。Leaders should not just sit in their offices issuing orders. /你有什么资格向别人～? What right have you to order people about?

发黑 fāhēi ❶ turn black or dark; look black or dark:天色～。It was getting dark. ❷ (of one's vision, etc.) blackout:眼前突然～

have a sudden blackout

发狠 fāhěn ❶ make a determined effort:～戒烟 make a determined effort to give up smoking; be dead set to quit smoking /她～要赶上其他同学。She made up her mind to catch up with the other students. ❷ be furious:你发什么狠? What is there to be angry about? /她一～,把手表也摔了。Flying into a rage, she flung away her watch.

发恨 fāhèn feel resentful; be piqued; take umbrage:因受到粗鲁对待而～ resent (*or* take umbrage at) being treated rudely /一看到儿子不争气,他不由得心中～。He felt resentment surging up when he saw his son had let the family down.

发横 fāhèng act in an unreasonable or headstrong way; go berserk:这小子脾气一上来就～。The guy will go berserk when he flares up.

发花 fāhuā (of the eyes) grow dim; see things in a blur:他的头发白了,眼睛也开始～了。His hair turned grey and eyes grew dim. /灯光太亮,使我两眼～。The strong light dazzled me.

发话 fāhuà ❶ give a verbal order; say or speak the word:只要你～,我们一定全都使劲儿。Whenever you speak the word, we'll all pitch in. ❷ speak angrily:冲妻子～ speak angrily at his wife

发话器 fāhuàqì *also* "话筒" huàtǒng telephone transmitter or mouthpiece

发坏 fāhuài 〈方言〉do mischief; play a dirty trick:要不是他～,这件事就办成了。It would have been successful but for his sabotage.

发还 fāhuán return (usu. to a subordinate or the original owner); give or send back:～失物 return lost properties (to their owners) /把计划～给起草人作修改 send a plan back to its drafter for revision /我的作文,老师为何迟迟未～? Why is the teacher taking so long to return my composition?

发慌 fāhuāng feel nervous; get flustered; get flurried:心里～ feel nervous /饿得～ feel faint with hunger; be famished /演说者并没有因为听众喝倒彩而～。The speaker was not flustered by the jeers of the crowd.

发皇 fāhuáng 〈书面〉❶ magnificent; grand ❷ broaden (one's mind, etc.); enlighten:～耳目 broaden one's vision; make one see things in a clear light; bring about one's enlightenment

发挥 fāhuī ❶ bring into play; give play or scope to; give rein to:～骨干作用 play a key role /～学生的积极性 bring the initiative of the students into full play; give full scope to the initiative of the students /～想像力 give free rein to one's imagination /～投资效益 make full use of the investment /～优势 exploit one's advantages to the full; put something to the best use /～优越性 give play to one's superiority /充分～潜力 maximize the potential; tap the potential to the full /～得不理想 (as in a match, test, etc.) not be in good form; not do well ❷ develop (an idea, theme, etc.); elaborate; expand:～主题思想 develop a theme /根据笔记～ expand on one's notes /借题～ make use of a topic under discussion to put across one's own ideas (which are not related to it); seize upon a pretext to give vent to one's own views or feelings /文章的最后一个问题～得不够。The last point in the article needs further elaboration.

发昏 fāhūn ❶ feel giddy; feel dizzy:我的头有点～。I feel a bit giddy. *or* I feel somewhat light in my head. /他的头撞在书架上,他感到一阵～。Banging his head on the bookcase he was dazed for a moment. ❷ lose one's head; become confused; be out of one's mind:你这样干简直是～了。You are simply out of your mind in so doing.

发昏章第十一 fāhūnzhāng dì-shíyī extremely; heavily:打了个～ be badly (*or* soundly) beaten

发火 fāhuǒ ❶ catch fire; fire; ignite:～机制 firing device; ignition /～速度 firing speed ❷ detonate; go off:幸好,枪没有～。Fortunately, the gun didn't go off. ❸〈方言〉(of a stove) draw well:这种型号的炉子～好。This type of stove draws well. ❹〈方言〉(of a fire) break out; be on fire:他家～时,他正好不在。When the fire occurred in his house, he was not in. ❺ get angry; flare up; lose temper:发大火 hit the ceiling; go through the roof /不～ keep one's shirt on; keep one's hair on /你干吗发这么大的火儿? Why are you in such a temper?

发火点 fāhuǒdiǎn ignition point; firing point

发货 fāhuò send out or dispatch goods; deliver goods:～通知单 consignment note /～单位 forwarding unit /～港 port of dispatch /一定要按期～。Be sure to dispatch (*or* deliver) the goods on schedule.

发货单 fāhuòdān dispatch list; (consignment) invoice; delivery order

发货人 fāhuòrén consignor; shipper

发急 fājí become impatient; get excited; chafe; fret:等得～ become impatient at waiting; wait impatiently /不要为这种小事～。Don't fret over such trifles. /本地队输了一个球,许多球迷就～了。Many fans got excited (*or* began to chafe) when the local team lost a goal.

发迹 fājì (of sb. poor and obscure) gain fame and fortune; rise to power and position; make the grade:他的～纯属偶然。His rise to power was a sheer accident. /他到中年开始～。He began to rise in the world at middle age. /穷孩子～了。The poor boy has made good.

发悸 fājì 〈方言〉be scared; be seized with terror:心里～ be seized with terror

发家 fājiā build up a family fortune:勤劳～ (of a family) become rich through honest labour

发家致富 fājiā-zhìfù build up a family fortune; get rich

发奸擿伏 fājiān-tīfú 〈书面〉expose evildoing without reserve; uncover hidden iniquities; bring hidden treason and crime to light:～,其事甚难。It is extremely difficult to bring hidden iniquities to light.

发贱 fājiàn act cheap; make oneself cheap:我干吗要多此一举,这不是～吗? Why should I take the trouble and make myself so cheap? *or* Why should I stoop to doing such a thing?

发奖 fājiǎng award prizes; present prizes:给优胜者～ award prizes to the winners /～大会 prize-giving meeting

发酵 fājiào *also* "酦酵" fājiào ferment; leaven:未经～的面团 unleavened dough

发酵粉 fājiàofěn yeast powder; baking powder

发酵计 fājiàojì zymometer

发酵剂 fājiàojì leavening agent

发酵酒 fājiàojiǔ *also* "酿造酒" niàngzàojiǔ liquor made through fermentation

发酵饲料 fājiào sìliào fermented feed

发酵学 fājiàoxué fermentology

发酵作用 fājiào zuòyòng fermentation

发解 fājiè (of local authorities) send candidates to the captial for the imperial examinations during the Tang and Song dynasties; succeed in the provincial examinations during the Ming and Qing dynasties

发紧 fājǐn ❶ feel choked or uncomfortable (in the chest, etc.):胸口～ feel uncomfortable (*or* choked) in one's chest /嗓子～ feel a lump in one's throat ❷ feel nervous; be keyed up:他当众讲话心里直～。He was nervous when he spoke in public.

发窘 fājiǒng feel embarrassed; be ill at ease:令人～的场合 embarrassing occasion (*or* situation)

发酒疯 fā jiǔfēng be in a drunken fit or brawl; be roaring drunk:他三杯下肚就大～。He would get into a drunken fit after three glasses. *or* He would get quite belligerant after three drinks.

发觉 fājué find; discover; detect; realize:我～她话里有话。I realized that there was more to it than what she said. /贪污受贿案件一经～,必须追查到底。Cases of corruption and bribery must be thoroughly investigated.

发掘 fājué excavate; unearth; explore:～古代遗址 excavate ancient ruins /～宝贵文物 unearth valuable relics /～人才 seek out gifted (*or* talented) people; hunt for talent /～潜力 tap potentials /兵马俑的～震动了全世界。The excavation of terra cotta warriors and horses shook the whole world.

发刊词 fākāncí foreword or introduction to a periodical:《共产党人～》*Introducing the Communist* /校长为校刊撰写了～。The president wrote a foreword for the school journal.

发棵 fākē 〈方言〉❶ *also* "分蘖" fēnniè tiller ❷ (of plant) grow gradually

发狂 fākuáng go mad or crazy; go berserk:这种噪音简直要使我～。This noise is driving me mad (*or* crazy). /一曲新歌,使成千上万的歌迷～。Tens of thousands of pop fans were crazed about the new song.

发聩振聋 fākuì-zhènlóng *see* "发聋振聩"

发困 fākùn 〈口语〉feel sleepy; feel drowsy:火生得暖融融的,我不觉有些～。The warmth of the fire made me sleepy.

发赖 fālài 〈方言〉behave like a spoiled child:这孩子见到妈妈就～。The child behaves like a cheeky brat before his mother.

发蓝 fālán 〈冶金〉blueing:～加热 blue heating; blue working /～

退火 blue annealing

发懒 fālǎn feel lazy; feel languid or sluggish: 思想上～ mentally lazy /他因为～而不想做这事。Only laziness prevented him from doing it. /天气热得让人浑身～。The hot weather makes one feel torpid.

发冷 fālěng feel cold; feel chilly: 浑身～ feel cold all over

发愣 fālèng 〈口语〉stare blankly; be in a daze; be in a trance; be stunned: 别站在那里～! 帮我一把。Don't just stand there staring! Lend me a hand. /这消息使他～。The news left him dazed.

发利市 fā lìshì 〈方言〉❶ make the first transaction after opening shop — be a propitious omen; make a good beginning in business: 大～ do brisk (*or* good) business ❷ profit (in general terms)

发亮 fāliàng shine; glow: 把钢精壶擦得～ polish an aluminium kettle till it shines; put a good shine on an aluminium kettle /天开始～。Day begins to break.

发令 fālìng ❶ give or issue an order: ～开火 give an order to fire / 团长～紧急集合。The regimental commander ordered an emergency muster. ❷ give a password

发令枪 fālìngqiāng 〈体育〉starting gun or pistol

发聋振聩 fālóng-zhènkuì *also* "发聩振聋" rouse the deaf and awaken the unhearing; enlighten the ignorant and the benighted: 您这番议论, 对我真有～的作用。Your arguments were indeed most enlightening to me.

发露 fālù become visible; manifest oneself; appear

发落 fāluò deal with (an offender): 从轻～ deal with sb. leniently /听候法院的～ wait for the court's decision /你们如何～此案? What is your verdict on the case?

发卖 fāmài put out for sale; sell: 该杂志不公开～。The magazine is not for general sale.

发毛 fāmáo ❶〈口语〉get gooseflesh; be scared; be frightened: 别说那个, 听了心里直～。Don't say that; it gives me gooseflesh (*or* it scares me). ❷〈方言〉lose one's temper

发霉 fāméi go mouldy; become mildewed: ～的乳酪 mouldy cheese /～的味道 mouldy smell /梅雨季节东西容易～。Things easily get mildewed in the rainy season.

发闷 fāmēn ❶ stuffy; close: 今天天气～。It's stuffy today. ❷ muffled: ～的声音 muffled sound (*or* voice)

发闷 fāmèn be sulky; be depressed; be in low spirits: 他碰了钉子, 正在楼上～。He was having a bit of a sulk upstairs over the rebuff.

发蒙 fāmēng 〈口语〉get confused; become bewildered; be at a loss: 你越讲我越～。The more you talk, the more confused I get. /一进考场, 他脑子就～。He felt all muddled up as soon as he entered the examination room.

发蒙 fāméng 〈旧语〉teach a child to read and write; teach a child his ABC: ～读物 children's primer /～启滞 enlighten the young and open the minds of the dull

发蒙振落 fāméng-zhènluò as easy as ABC; easily accomplished; effortless

发面 fāmiàn ❶ leaven dough: 发过面了吗? Has the dough been leavened? ❷ leavened dough: ～饼 leavened pancake

发明 fāmíng ❶ invent: ～家 inventor /～构思 inventive concept / ～专利 patent for an invention /古代四大～ four major inventions of the ancient world /玻璃是在史前～的。Glass was invented in prehistoric times. /需要乃～之母。Necessity is the mother of invention. ❷〈书面〉expound: 在《论语》的诠解上颇多～ do much to expound *The Analects*

发明权 fāmíngquán patent rights of an inventor

发墨 fāmò (of inkstones) good for grinding an inkstick: 这种砚石细腻如玉, ～快。Smooth as jade, this inkstone is good for grinding an inkstick.

发木 fāmù feel numb: 我的手冻得～。My hands are numb with cold.

发奶 fānǎi (of food or medicine) stimulate the secretion of milk; promote lactation: 吃炖猪蹄可以～。Stewed pig's trotters are good for promoting lactation.

发难 fānàn ❶ rise in revolt; start a rebellion; launch an attack: 公开～ rise in open revolt; launch an open attack /率先～ take the initiative in starting a rebellion; be the first to rise in revolt (*or* launch an attack) ❷ raise a difficult question for discussion; start discussion on a doubtful or difficult point: 向他的观点～ raise questions about his view

发恼 fānǎo 〈方言〉get angry; flare up; fly into a rage

发腻 fānì be sick (of sb. or sth.); be fed up; be disgusted: 闲得～ be sick of being idle /～的小旅店 disgusting (*or* nasty) inn /他的故事我们已听得～了。We are fed up with his story, which we've heard so many times. *or* We're sick of listening to his story again and again.

发蔫 fāniān ❶ wither; shrivel up; droop: 剪下的花很快就～。Cut flowers soon wither (*or* shrivel up). ❷ listless; lethargic; spiritless; droopy: 他最近有点～, 怕是病了。He looks a bit listless recently. I'm afraid he is not well.

发茶 fānié *see* "发蔫❷"

发怒 fānù get angry; flare up; fly into a rage: 无端～ flare up for no reason at all /只要有人拿老王的肥胖开玩笑, 他就～。Whenever anyone teased Lao Wang about his weight, he would flare up.

发排 fāpái send a manuscript to the compositor: 您的大作已经～了。Your manuscript (*or* work) has already been sent to the compositor (*or* printer).

发胖 fāpàng put on or gain weight; get fat: 她～了, 过去的连衣裙已穿不了啦。She gained so much weight that she could not put on the dresses she used to wear.

发泡 fāpào foam: ～黏合剂 foam glue /～纤维 foamed fibre /～物质 foaming substance /～饮料 fizz

发泡剂 fāpàojì foaming or blowing agent; inflating agent

发泡塑料 fāpào sùliào *also* "泡沫塑料" pàomò sùliào foam plastic; expanded plastic

发配 fāpèi transport to a distant place for penal servitude; banish; exile: ～边疆十年 be exiled (*or* banished) to a border area for ten years

发脾气 fā píqi lose one's temper; fly into a rage; throw a tantrum: 他不常～, 但这回是真火了。He did not often lose his temper, but this time he saw red. /有话好说, 何必～。Speak calmly. There is no need to throw a tantrum. /别冲我～! Don't vent your spleen on me! *or* Don't take out your anger on me!

发飘 fāpiāo not have firm control of sth; feel weak: 我大病初愈, 脚底下～。I've just recuperated from a major illness and am still a bit shaky. /这菜刀太轻, 使着～。This chopper is too light and doesn't feel right.

发票 fāpiào bill; receipt; invoice: 开～ make out a bill; write a receipt (*or* an invoice) /～存根 invoice stub /～本 invoice book /～副联 duplicate invoice /凭～报销 reimburse one's expenses with the receipts

发泼 fāpō 〈方言〉be unreasonable and make a scene; act the termagant: 你那嘴干净点, 这不是你～的地方。Don't be that foul-mouthed. This is not the place for you to make a scene.

发起 fāqǐ ❶ initiate; sponsor: ～反腐败运动 initiate an anti-corruption compaign /这个学术团体是由沈教授～组织的。The learned society was organized under the sponsorship of Professor Shen. ❷ start; launch: ～进攻 launch an attack /～宣传攻势 start a press campaign

发起国 fāqǐguó sponsor nation

发起人 fāqǐrén initiator; sponsor; promoter: ～股〈经济〉promoter's stock; founder's stock

发气 fāqì 〈方言〉❶ lose one's temper; get angry: 你在发谁的气? Who are you angry with? /他从来没有像这样～过。He has never been so furious before. ❷ give vent to one's anger; vent one's spleen or anger: 向周围的人～ vent one's spleen (*or* anger) on everybody around one ❸ (used in *qigong* or kung fu) release or give out one's inner energy

发遣 fāqiǎn 〈书面〉❶ send back; repatriate: ～回籍 send (sb.) back to his or her native place /～回国 repatriate ❷ banish; send into exile

发情 fāqíng 〈动物〉oestrus or oestrum; heat; rut: 同步～ sychronization of oestrus /大象～时, 是极危险的动物。The elephant is a most dangerous animal when it is in heat.

发情期 fāqíngqī heat (period); oestrus

发情周期 fāqíng zhōuqī oestrous cycle

发球 fāqiú 〈体育〉serve a ball: 换～ change service /～抢攻 smash after service /～擦网 net ball /～得分 (in volleyball or tennis) ace / ～失误 miss a service /发怪球 make a tricky service (*or* serve) /接～得分 kill a service /由你～。It's your service.

发球区 fāqiúqū service area

发热 fārè ❶ have or run a fever; have or run a temperature: 他因～而卧床休息。He is in bed with a fever. ❷ generate heat; give out heat: 恒星本身发光～。Fixed stars send out light and heat themsel-

ves. ❸ be hotheaded:盲从和头脑～使他们陷入目前的困境。Blind faith and impetuosity have landed them in their present plight.

发热剂 fārèjì exothermic compound or agent

发热量 fārèliàng 〈化学〉calorific capacity

发人深思 fārénshēnsī set people thinking; call for or provoke deep thought; provide food for thought:这个问题～。What a thought-provoking question! /电影的结尾不落俗套,～。The unconventional ending of the film gave the viewers much to think about.

发人深省 fārénshēnxǐng *also*"发人深醒" make one wake up to reality or the truth; make one wide awake; stir up one's soul:～的肺腑之言 soul-stirring words from the bottom of one's heart /这场大火教训很多,～。The disastrous fire taught us many lessons and made us wide awake.

发轫 fārèn 〈书面〉commence or launch an undertaking; set sth. afoot:这个小小的实验室,也许就是我们今后伟大事业的～。This modest laboratory may be the starting place for our great undertaking.

发荣 fāróng flourish; prosper; boom:～滋长 flourish and develop

发散 fāsàn ❶ (of rays, etc.) diverge; diffuse:～光 divergent light /气体～ diffusion of gases /蛇毒渐渐～到他的全身。The snake poison gradually diffused through his body. ❷〈中医〉disperse the internal heat (with sudorifics); let out the internal heat:吃点发汗药～一下。Take a sudorific to sweat out the cold.

发散波 fāsànbō 〈物理〉divergent wave; diverging wave

发散度 fāsàndù *also*"发散量"〈物理〉divergence

发散镜 fāsànjìng *also*"凸面镜" tūmiànjìng 〈物理〉convex mirror

发散透镜 fāsàn tòujìng *also*"凹透镜" āotòujìng 〈物理〉concave lens; divergent lens; diverging lens

发丧 fāsāng ❶ announce a death; send out an obituary:秘不～ (as in dynastic days) not announce sb.'s death; make a secret of sb.'s death /向亲友～ send out an obituary to relatives /登报～ put an obituary in the newspaper ❷ hold a funeral (procession); carry a coffin to the graveyard:～的队伍缓缓地穿过肃静的街道。The funeral procession made its way slowly through the silent streets.

发色团 fāsètuán 〈纺织〉chromophore

发痧 fāshā 〈方言〉have a heatstroke or sunstroke:没关系,她只是～。It's nothing serious; she's only having a heatstroke.

发傻 fāshǎ ❶ be dumbstruck; be stupefied:惊得～ be dumbfounded with amazement /这消息使他一下子～了。He was stupefied at the news. ❷ be foolish:他这个人平时挺精明,可遇事就～。He appears smart but gets muddled up when things happen.

发烧 fāshāo ❶ *also*"发热" have or run a fever; have or run a temperature:～病倒了 be down with fever /发高烧,说胡话 run a high fever and talk deliriously ❷ give oneself to; be infatuated:他这两年对集邮有点～。Over the past two years he has been obsessed with stamp-collecting.

发烧友 fāshāoyǒu 〈方言〉enthusiastic fan; fancier; zealot:只要她一演出,就会有一批～为她捧场。A crowd of fans would be there to cheer her whenever she gave a performance.

发射 fāshè ❶ launch; project; discharge; fire:～航天飞机 launch a space shuttle /～导弹 launch (*or* fire) a guided missile /～炮弹 discharge (*or* fire) shells /～点 *also*"火力点" firing point /～角 angle of departure; launching angle /～塔 launch(ing) tower ❷〈物理〉transmit; emit:～电波 transmit radio waves /～强度 emission power /～功率 transmitting power /～脉冲 transmitted pulse /～天线 transmitting antenna

发射场 fāshèchǎng launching site; launch site

发射光谱 fāshè guāngpǔ 〈物理〉emission spectrum (ES):～测定法 emission spectrometric method /～分析 emission spectrographic analysis

发射机 fāshèjī transmitter; sender; launcher:～不稳定性 transmitter instability /～冷却系统 cooling system of a transmitter

发射极 fāshèjí 〈电子〉emitter:～电流 emitter current /～脉冲 emitter pulse /～接地 grounded emitter

发射架 fāshèjià launcher:火箭～ rocket launcher

发射井 fāshèjǐng launching silo

发射坪 fāshèpíng 〈军事〉pad; flight pad; firing pad; launch(ing) pad:浮坞～ floating drydock launch pad /(导弹)平放式～ horizontal pad /移动式综合～ integrate (transfer) launch pad

发射台 fāshètái launching pad; launching stand

发射药 fāshèyào propellant powder; gun propellant

发射装置 fāshè zhuāngzhì launcher:垂直～ launch(ing) tower /火箭～ rocket launcher (*or* projector); firing vehicle /导弹～ missile launcher /卫星～ satellite launcher

发身 fāshēn puberty:～期 age of puberty; pubescence

发神经 fā shénjīng go mad; go crazy; go out of one's mind; go bonkers:有时他酒后大～。He sometimes went raving mad after drinking. /做这种事纯粹是～。It would be sheer madness to do such a thing.

发瘆 fāshèn have the creeps; be scared:夜深了,路上没有一个行人,他心里一阵阵发紧,头皮～。As he walked all alone in the deserted streets late at night, he could not help but shiver from the tips of his hair to the marrow of his bones.

发生 fāshēng ❶ happen; occur; arise; take place:～兴趣 become interested (in sth.); take an interest (in sth.) /～冲突 come to a clash; have a conflict /～关系 establish a relationship; have sth. to do (with sb.); have sexual intercourse; have an affair /什么情况都可能～。Anything may happen. /他们之间偶尔也～争论。Disputes occasionally occurred between them. /～了新的问题。New problems cropped up. /双方～误会。Misunderstanding arose between the two parties. /汽车～故障。The car broke down. ❷ development of an embryo (from a fertilized egg); genesis:～学 embryology /～生物学 developmental biology /～心理学 genetic psychology /～遗传学 development genetics /～认识论 genetic epistemology /～定义〈逻辑〉genetic definition

发生器 fāshēngqì 〈化学〉generator; producer:煤气～ gas generator /蒸气～ steam generator

发声 fāshēng emit or produce sounds; vocalize:～术 vocalism /～器官 vocal organ /练习～ practise vocalization; exercise one's voice

发市 fāshì 〈旧语〉make the first transaction of a day's business:开门半天,尚未～。There was no business long after the shop had opened its door.

发事 fāshì have an accident; meet with a mishap:～地点 site (*or* scene) of an accident

发誓 fāshì take an oath; vow; pledge; swear:～为死去的兄弟报仇 vow to avenge one's dead brother /～保守秘密 be pledged to secrecy /～不再抽烟 swear off smoking /我对神明～我不是这个意思。I swear before God I didn't mean it.

发实 fāshi 〈方言〉sturdy; stout; brawny:个子不高但很～ short but sturdy /两条～的绳子 two stout ropes

发售 fāshòu sell; put on sale:通过代理商～ sell through an agent /按成本～ sell at cost price /这种新型彩电在本市各大商场均有～。This new-model colour TV is on sale in all major department stores in the city.

发抒 fāshū express; voice:～己见 voice one's own view /～思乡之情 express one's nostalgia for home

发水 fāshuǐ flood:这条河夏天～,冬天枯竭。The river floods in the summer but runs dry in the winter.

发思古之幽情 fā sī gǔ zhī yōuqíng muse over persons or things of the remote past; reminisce about people or things of the ancient times

发送 fāsòng ❶ transmit (by radio):～电报 transmit a telegram (*or* cable message) ❷ dispatch (letters, etc.); send:～消息 send a news dispatch /～货物 dispatch (*or* forward, *or* deliver) goods

发送 fāsong carry a coffin to the cemetery; hold a funeral procession:新媳妇自杀后第二天就被草草～了。The young bride was hastily buried the day after her suicide.

发送机 fāsòngjī (radio) transmitter

发酸 fāsuān ❶ turn sour; taste sour:牛奶在热天会很快～。Milk turns sour quickly in hot weather. /碱放少了,馒头有些～。The steamed buns taste a bit sour, as too little soda was used in mixing the dough. ❷ (of one's nose, eyes, etc.) tingle with sorrow, grief or compassion (before breaking down and weeping):鼻子～ feel a tingle in one's nose /提起往事,她不由得两眼～,泪水不停地流了下来。Recalling her past sufferings, she felt a tingle in her eyes and tears began to roll down her cheeks. ❸ feel weak and sore; ache:浑身～ feel sore all over /腰有点～ have a slight backache /走了一天路,大家都两腿～。We all felt weak and sore in the legs after walking the whole day.

发态度 fā tàidu put on a show of bad temper; throw a tantrum

发条 fātiáo 〈机械〉spiral power spring; clockwork spring:闹钟的～ spring of an alarm clock /给表上～ wind up a watch

发旺 fāwàng ❶ vigorous; exuberant:禾苗长势缓慢,不～。The seedlings are growing too slowly; they are not vigorous. ❷〈方言〉put on weight; round out:生病期间体重减轻不少,现在又开始～了。I

lost much weight during my illness, but I am beginning to round out again.

发威 fāwēi make a show of authority; assume an air of haughtiness; throw one's weight about:在众人面前～ assume an air of importance in public

发文 fāwén ❶ issue; dispatch (a document, etc.):中央三部委联合～。The three major departments of the Party's Central Committee jointly issued a document. ❷ outgoing message or document, or correspondence; dispatch:～簿 register of outgoing documents, letters, etc.

发问 fāwèn ask or put, or pose a question:～技巧 questioning techniques /根据所学课文～ ask questions on the text learnt /向某人～ put a question to sb.; ask sb. a question

发物 fāwu 〈中医〉 food which stimulates or aggravates certain clinical conditions:上火时不要吃鱼、虾、羊肉等～。When one has too much internal heat, one should not eat any stimulating food such as fish, shrimp, or mutton.

发现 fāxiàn ❶ find; discover:～漏洞 find a loophole /～线索 find clues /～错误 spot a mistake; detect an error /考古～ archaeological finds /鲁迅的一份手稿被～。A manuscript of Lu Xun's was brought to light. /雷达～了一个不明飞行物。A UFO was picked up (*or* detected) by our radar. /他的科研导致一次重大～。His scientific research resulted in a discovery of major importance. ❷ detect; notice; become aware of:～自己陷入进退两难的困境 find oneself in a dilemma /她～丈夫有心事。She noticed that there was something on her husband's mind. /我没有～她生气。I wasn't aware that she was angry.

发祥 fāxiáng 〈书面〉 ❶ occurrence of a propitious event ❷ originate; begin:仰韶文化～于黄河流域中游。Yangshao culture originated in the middle reaches of the Yellow River.

发祥地 fāxiángdì place of origin; birthplace:中国古代文化的～ birthplace of China's ancient culture

发饷 fāxiǎng 〈旧语〉 issue pay (usu. to soldiers or police):明天～。Pay will be issued tomorrow. *or* Tomorrow is pay day.

发笑 fāxiào burst out laughing; laugh:不由得～ cannot help laughing; burst out laughing /引人～ make one laugh; provoke laughter; be ridiculous

发泄 fāxiè give vent to; let off:～不满 air one's grievances; give vent to one's discontent /将心中的郁愤一股脑儿～出来 deliver oneself of all the pent-up hatred

发心 fāxīn set one's mind (on sth.); make up one's mind:只要～去学,定会学成的。If you make up your mind to learn something, you are sure to learn it well.

发薪 fāxīn pay wages or salaries:～日 pay day

发信 fāxìn post or mail a letter; send a letter:～人 addresser; sender /我今天～去上海,什么时候可以收到? If I post (*or* send) a letter to Shanghai today, when will it be received?

发行 fāxíng (of currency, bonds, books, etc.) issue; publish; release; distribute:～者 publisher /～量 amount issued; circulation /～日期 date of issuance (*or* publication) /～年限 maturity period /～金融债券 float bond issues/～国库券 issue treasury bonds /～纪念邮票 issue commemorative stamps /～新书 publish a new book /～影片 release a film /～渠道 channel for distribution /～费用 issuer's cost; cost of distribution /本书将由新华书店～。The book will be distributed by Xinhua Bookstore.
see also fāháng

发行审计局 fāxíng shěnjìjú audit bureau of circulation (ABC)

发行银行 fāxíng yínháng bank of issue:中国银行是港币的～之一。The Bank of China is one of the issuing banks for the Hong Kong dollar.

发虚 fāxū ❶ lack in self-confidence; be diffident:准备不足,心中～ be diffident from lack of preparation ❷ feel feeble and weak:他最近生了一场病,身体仍很～。He is still weak from his last illness.

发噱 fāxué 〈方言〉 amusing; funny

发芽 fāyá germinate; sprout:～试验 germination test /～力 germinating ability (*or* capacity) /把种子浸在温水中～ sprout the seeds in warm water /柳树发出了新芽。The willows put forth (*or* shot out) new buds. *or* The willows burgeoned forth.

发芽率 fāyálǜ germination or sprouting percentage

发芽势 fāyáshì germination percentage during the initial period of seeding; vigour of germination

发言 fāyán speak; make a statement; deliver a speech; take the floor:～稿 text of a statement or speech /一般性～ general statement /举手～ raise (*or* put up) one's hand to ask for the floor; ask to be heard /报名～ enter one's name on the list of speakers /即席～ speak impromptu (*or* extempore) /～很踊跃。People took the floor one after another. /下面该轮到我～了。It's now my turn to speak.

发言权 fāyánquán right to speak:保留～ reserve the right to speak /没有调查,就没有～。No investigations, no right to speak. /在这个问题上你没有～。You have no say in the matter.

发言人 fāyánrén spokesman; spokesperson:女～ spokeswoman /官方～ official spokesperson /新闻～ press spokesperson /外交部～ spokesperson of the foreign ministry /～名单 list of speakers

发炎 fāyán inflammation:伤口～了。The wound became inflamed. /引起急性～ set up acute inflammation

发扬 fāyáng ❶ develop; carry on or forward; promote; foster:～独特风格 develop one's unique style /～优良传统 carry on (*or* forward) a fine tradition /～民主 promote democracy /～合作精神 foster the spirit of cooperation /～成绩 add to one's achievements /～艰苦朴素的作风 keep up the practice of hard work and plain living /～优点,改正缺点 carry on with one's strong points and overcome one's shortcomings ❷ make the most of; make full use of; bring (latent power, etc.) into full play:～舰艇火力 make full use of the ships' firepower /～大无畏英雄气概 bring one's dauntless heroism into full play / ～我军善于夜战的优势,一举击溃敌人。Rout the enemy at one go by pressing home our superiority in night fighting.

发扬踔厉 fāyáng-chuōlì *also* "发扬蹈厉" vigorous and full of spirit

发扬光大 fāyáng-guāngdà carry forward; build on; further develop; enhance:～先辈的事业 carry forward the cause of the older generation

发洋财 fā yángcái make a big fortune; get a windfall; strike it rich

发痒 fāyǎng ❶ itch; tickle:浑身～ itch all over /喉咙～ one's throat tickles /穿这件衬衫身上就～。This shirt itches. ❷ have an itch for sth.:他歇工一天,就觉得手～。Whenever he has a day off, his hands start itching for work.

发疟子 fā yàozi have an attack of malaria; suffer from malarial fever

发音 fāyīn pronounce; articulate; enunciate; vocalize:～方法〈语言〉 manner of articulation /～清晰 enunciate or articulate one's words clearly /这个字母如何～? How do you pronounce this letter? /这个字母在这里不～。The letter is silent (*or* not pronounced) here. /他的～很准确。His pronunciation is quite accurate.

发音部位 fāyīn bùwèi point of articulation

发音困难 fāyīn kùnnan 〈医学〉 dysphonia

发音器官 fāyīn qìguān vocal organs; speech organs

发音学 fāyīnxué 〈语言〉 phonetics

发引 fāyǐn carry out the coffin at a burial; carry the bier

发语词 fāyǔcí *also* "发端词" function words such as 夫 fú, 盖 gài, etc., in classical Chinese writings

发育 fāyù growth; development:～期 period of growth; (of people) adolescence /～健康 healthy growth (*or* development) /充分～ reach full growth /秧苗～情况良好。The young saplings are coming on well.

发育不全 fāyù bùquán 〈医学〉 underdevelopment; hypoplasia

发育心理学 fāyù xīnlǐxué developmental psychology

发育异常 fāyù yìcháng 〈医学〉 maldevelopment; dysplasia

发源 fāyuán rise; originate:黄河、长江均～于青海。Both the Yellow and the Yangtze rivers rise in Qinghai Province.

发源地 fāyuándì place of origin; source; birthplace:亚洲是人类文明的～之一。Asia is one of the birthplaces (*or* cradles) of human civilization.

发愿 fāyuàn express one's wish or desire; make a pledge or promise:发了愿可是要还的啊。When you make a pledge, you should be prepared to redeem it.

发晕 fāyūn feel dizzy or giddy:头～ one's head swims /她一阵阵～。She was having a dizzy spell.

发运 fāyùn send by freight; ship (goods):～人 shipper /～单 shipping order /～代理 forwarding agent /货物已于上周～。The goods were shipped last week.

发躁 fāzào be irritable; be fidgety; be impatient:被孩子的哭声弄得心里～ be irritated by the cries of the baby /炎热的天气使人～。Sultry weather gives people the fidgets.

发乍 fāzhà have one's hair stand on end and flesh creep; have the

creeps; have gooseflesh：凄厉的叫声听来叫人毛孔～。The agonized, shrill cries made one's hair stand on end. *or* The agonized, shrill cries gave one the creeps.

发展 fāzhǎn ❶ develop; expand; grow; promote：～规划 development plan /～势头 trend of development; momentum of growth /～性失语症〈心理〉developmental aphasia /～组织 expand an organization (*or* membership) /日益～ grow with each passing day /～各项民间往来 promote people-to-people exchanges in various fields /～生产，繁荣经济 develop production and bring about economic prosperity /～进步势力，争取中间势力，孤立顽固势力 develop the progressive forces, win over the middle-of-the-roaders and isolate the die-hard forces /～体育运动，增强人民体质 promote physical culture and build up people's health /～安定团结的政治局面 enhance (*or* promote) political unity and stability /～同各国人民的友谊 foster the friendship with the people of all countries /～壮大 go from strength to strength /有～前途 have good prospects /～到一个新的阶段 reach a new stage /用～的眼光看人 look at a person by taking into account his possible changes in future ❷ recruit; admit：～新会员 recruit (*or* admit) new members /～会员国 admit as a member state; add new member states

发展基金 fāzhǎn jījīn development fund

发展经济学 fāzhǎn jīngjìxué development economics

发展模式 fāzhǎn móshì mode of development

发展权 fāzhǎnquán right of development

发展中国家 fāzhǎnzhōng guójiā developing country; developing world

发颤 fāzhàn *also* "发战" shake; tremble; quiver; shiver：气得～ quiver (*or* shake) with anger /他激动得浑身～。He was so overcome with emotion that he shook (*or* trembled) all over.

see also fāchàn

发胀 fāzhàng ❶ swell：头脑～ have or suffer from a swelled head /肚子～ feel bloated ❷〈中医〉feel distended

发疹 fāzhěn 〈医学〉exanthema; eruption; rash

发证银行 fāzhèng yínháng opening bank; issuing bank

发怔 fāzhèng stare blankly; be in a daze or trance; be stupefied：她默默地坐在那里，望着远山～。She sat there quietly, staring blankly at the distant mountains.

发肿 fāzhǒng swell; become swollen：他的两腿～。His legs are swelling out (*or* swollen).

发冢 fāzhǒng 〈书面〉dig up a grave; excavate a tomb

发咒 fāzhòu vow; swear; take an oath：发个死咒 take a terrible oath

发紫 fāzǐ ❶ turn purple; turn blue：她的嘴唇冻得～。Her lips were blue from the cold. ❷ be at the height of one's popularity or influence：红得～ be at the height of one's power and influence; enjoy great popularity

发纵指示 fāzòng-zhǐshì *also* "发踪指示" hound a dog at quarry; set a dog on quarry; command and dispatch; pull the strings

发作 fāzuò ❶ break out; show effect：胃病～ have a stomachache /药性开始～。The medicine began to take effect. /他的关节炎又开始～了。His arthritis began to act up again. ❷ have a fit of anger; flare up：他恼羞成怒，突然～起来。His shame turned into anger, and he suddenly flared up. /你在众人面前～，有失身分。It's unbefitting of you to fly into a rage in public.

酦(醱) fā ferment

see also pō

酦酵 fājiào *also* "发酵" fājiào ferment

fá

罚(罸) fá punish; penalize; fine; forfeit：受～ be punished /～站 make (a pupil, etc.) stand as punishment /赏～分明 be fair in meting out rewards and punishments; be fair in passing critical judgment /～一百元 fine sb. 100 *yuan* /～饮一杯 (make sb.) drink a cup of wine as a forfeit /～俸一年〈旧语〉suspend sb.'s salary for a year as punishment; forfeit one's salary for a year /～而不教，不足正人。Discipline without education will not put anyone on the right course.

罚不当罪 fábùdāngzuì the punishment is not commensurate with the crime or misdemeanor; be unduly (often too severely) punished; suffer inappropriate punishment：这位法官处理案子，～的极少。Very seldom has the punishment been incommensurate with the crime in the cases tried by this judge. /他被判了三年，似乎有些～。He was sentenced to three years' imprisonment, which seems somewhat too severe.

罚出场 fá chūchǎng 〈体育〉be ordered or sent off the field for foul play; foul out：那位足球队员因不服从裁判被～。The footballer was sent off the field for disobeying the referee. /篮球运动员侵人犯规五次即被～。A basketball player is allowed five personal fouls before fouling out.

罚锾 fáhuán 〈书面〉fine; forfeit：因扰乱秩序被处～五十元 be fined 50 *yuan* for disturbing public order

罚金 fájīn fine; forfeit：处以～ impose a fine on sb.; fine sb. /交纳～ pay a fine /～二千元 fine sb. 2,000 *yuan*

罚酒 fájiǔ make sb. drink wine or be made to drink wine as a forfeit：～三杯 (make sb.) have three drinks as a forfeit

罚款 fákuǎn ❶ impose a fine or forfeit; fine：店主因逃税被～一万元。The shopowner was fined ten thousand *yuan* for tax evasion. ❷ fine; forfeit; penalty：超速行车～ fine for speeding /违章停车～ parking fine /逾期～ fine for being overdue (with a loan, etc.); fine for delay /违约～ fine for breaching a contract (*or* agreement) /免除～ remit a fine /禁止乱扔废物，违者～十元。No littering; penalty 10 *yuan*.

罚款条款 fákuǎn tiáokuǎn penalty clause

罚没 fámò fine and confiscate; forfeit：这是一笔～的赌款。This is a sum of confiscated gambling money.

罚球 fáqiú (in soccer) penalty kick; (in basketball) penalty shot; foul shot; free throw：罚点球 take a spot kick /罚角球 take a corner kick /罚任意球 take a free kick /～得分 score a penalty shot; convert a free throw

罚球区 fáqiúqū penalty area (in basketball)

罚球线 fáqiúxiàn penalty line (in basketball)

乏 fá ❶ lack; be short of：～力 lacking in strength; weak /贫～ impoverished; destitute /不～其人。There is no lack of such people. *or* Such people are not rare. ❷ tired; weary：浑身～得很 feel weary all over /人困马～ both the men and horses are exhausted; everybody is tired out ❸〈方言〉exhausted; worn-out; useless：～话 ineffective talk; useless words /～茶叶 tea dregs /贴～了的橡皮膏 worn-out (adhesive) plaster /炭烧～了。The charcoal fire is going out. *or* The charcoal fire is burning low.

乏地 fádì 〈方言〉exhausted soil; poor land

乏顿 fádùn 〈书面〉weary; fatigued：连日行军，人马～。The entire force (*or* contingent) was fatigued after marching for days on end.

乏货 fáhuò 〈方言〉good-for-nothing; ne'er-do-well：没想到你也是个不中用的～。I did not know you were also a good-for-nothing.

乏倦 fájuàn fatigued; tired：登上山顶，大家都～了。We all felt very tired when we reached the top of the mountain.

乏困 fákùn tired; weary; fatigued：旅途～ fatigued by a journey; travel-worn

乏累 fálèi tired; run-down：让他休息一会儿，他太～了。Let him have a rest; he is overworked.

乏力 fálì ❶ weary; worn-out：浑身～ feel dog-tired ❷ short of strength; incapable (of doing sth.)：回天～ not able to turn the tide (*or* save a desperate situation)

乏煤 fáméi used (but not thoroughly burned) coal

乏汽 fáqì dead steam; steam exhaust

乏人 fárén useless person; good-for-nothing; ne'er-do-well

乏术 fáshù lack means; have no effective measures：进攻～ have no means of launching an offensive

乏嗣 fásì without (male) offspring

乏味 fáwèi dull; insipid; tasteless; uninteresting：～的谈话 insipid conversation /单调～的建筑 drab building /枯燥～的工作 dull and tedious work /他感到生活～。Life seems flat to him.

乏戏 fáxì dull or boring play or opera

伐[1] fá ❶ fell; cut down：采～ fell (trees); log (an area) /～竹编筏 cut bamboo to make rafts /房前的杨树被～了。The poplar in front of the house was cut down. ❷ send an expedition against; attack; strike：征～ send a punitive expedition (against sb.) /北～ Northern Expedition (1926-1927) /口诛笔～ condemn both in

F

speech and in writing; denounce both by the spoken word and by writing /武王～纣。King Wu led an expedition against King Zhou (of the Shang Dynasty).

伐[2] fá 〈书面〉sing one's own praises; boast about oneself: 不矜不～ neither conceited nor boastful; modest and unassuming

伐倒 fádǎo 〈林业〉fell: ～木 felled timber

伐柯 fákē 〈书面〉be a matchmaker; act as a go-between (in arranging a marriage): ～人 matchmaker; go-between

伐毛洗髓 fámáo-xǐsuǐ cut the hair and wash the marrow of the bones — cast off one's old self; remold oneself thoroughly

伐木 fámù lumbering; logging; felling: ～工人 lumberman; lumberjack /～场 lumber-mill /～许可证 felling licence /～为舟 fell timber to make a boat /在树林中～ log in the woods

伐木业 fámùyè lumbering

伐区 fáqū 〈林业〉cutting or felling area

伐善 fáshàn 〈书面〉sing one's own praises: 他为人谦虚，从不～。He is a modest man and never boasts about his own accomplishments.

伐性之斧 fáxìngzhīfǔ sexual indulgence that vitiates one's vitality; sth. that endangers one's life

伐罪 fázuì 〈书面〉send or launch a punitive expedition against an oppressive ruler: 吊民～ (slogan often used in launching a revolt) relieve the people of their sufferings and punish the oppressive ruler

阀[1] fá powerful person or family: 军～ warlord /财～ financial magnate; plutocrat /学～ scholar-tyrant /门～ family of power and influence

阀[2] fá *also* "凡尔" fán'ěr (transliteration) valve: 汽～ steam valve /油～ oil valve /水～ water valve /安全～ safety valve /止回～ check valve /提升～ poppet valve /回转～ rotary valve /～套 valve bush; valve pocket

阀簧 fáhuáng 〈机械〉valve spring: ～减振器 valve spring damper

阀门 fámén 〈机械〉valve: ～帽 *also* "阀帽" bonnet /关闭～ turn off the valve

阀阅 fáyuè 〈书面〉❶ meritorious service; exploit ❷ distinguished, meritorious family

阀座 fázuò 〈机械〉valve seat; valve base: ～磨光机 valve seat refacer

垡[1] fá 〈方言〉❶ turn up soil: 耕～ turn up soil; plough a field ❷ upturned soil: 深耕晒～ plough deep to sun the upturned soil

垡[2] fá *used in place names only*: 榆～ Yufa (in Beijing) /落～ Luofa (in Tianjin)

垡子 fázi 〈方言〉❶ *also* "垡头" upturned soil ❷ fairly long period of time: 这一～ these days

筏(栰) fá raft: 竹～ bamboo raft /木～ wooden raft /橡皮～ rubber raft /乘～游江 tour a river on a raft

筏道 fádào log chute; logway

筏夫 fáfū rafter: 有经验的～ experienced rafter

筏子 fázi raft: 羊皮～ raft made of sheepskin; sheepskin raft

fǎ

法[1] fǎ ❶ law; statute: 守～ observe the law; be law-abiding /执～ enforce the law /立～ make laws; legislate /犯～ break (*or* violate) the law; go against the law /刑～ criminal law /刑事诉讼～ law of criminal procedure/民～ civil law /成文～ written law; statute law; statute /不成文～ unwritten law /公～ public law (*or* statute) /私～ private law (*or* statute) /宪～ constitution /选举～ electoral law /组织～ organic law /婚姻～ marriage law /国籍～ nationality law /普通～ common law /习惯～ customary law /衡平～ (rules of) equity /无～无天 defy laws human and divine /绳之以～ punish sb. according to law; bring sb. to justice /～不徇情。The law does not yield to personal considerations. *or* The law is impartial. /～不阿贵。The law does not bend before the powerful. ❷ method; way; mode: 教学～ teaching method; pedagogical methodology /表达～ mode of expression /操作～ method of operation /做～ way of doing (sth.) /设～ try in one way or another /得～ in the right way /用～ usage /兵～ art of war; military strategy and tactics ❸ standard; criterion; model: 不足为～ be not fit to serve as a standard (*or* model); cannot be taken as a model (*or* an example) /取～乎上 set a high standard (*or* criterion); aim high ❹ follow; emulate; pattern or model after: 效～ take as a model; follow (suit) /～先王 (political slogan for looking into the past for model government) follow the ancient kings (such as Yao 尧 and Shun 舜) /～其遗志 carry out sb.'s unfulfilled wish ❺ 〈佛教〉dharma; the Law; the Way: *see* "～轮" ❻ magic; trick; magic arts: 戏～ conjuring trick; sleight of hand; magic /作～ resort to magic; exercise magic ❼ (Fǎ) (short for 法家) Legalists; Legalist school: 儒～之争 struggle between the Confucian and Legalist schools ❽ (Fǎ) (short for 法兰西 or 法国) France; French: 英～ Britain and France /～属圭亚那 French Guyana /～式大菜 French cuisine /普～战争 Franco-Prussian War (1870-1871) ❾ (Fǎ) a surname

法[2] fǎ (short for 法拉)〈物理〉farad (F)

法案 fǎ'àn proposed law; bill: 提出～ propose a bill; introduce a bill /通过一项～ pass a bill (*or* proposed law); adopt a bill /将～提交大会审议 submit (*or* present) a bill to a congress for deliberation

法办 fǎbàn deal with according to law; punish by law; bring to justice: 对犯罪分子必须～。Criminals must be punished by law. *or* Criminals must be brought to justice.

法半夏 fǎbànxià *also* "法夏" fǎxià 〈中药〉Rhizoma pinellinae praeparata — traditional Chinese medicine made from the tuber of pinellia

法宝 fǎbǎo ❶〈佛教〉Sutras; monk's mantle, almsbowl, staff, and other paraphernalia ❷〈道教〉something of magic power that can subdue or kill monsters and demons ❸ magic weapon or formula; talisman: 克敌制胜的～ magic weapon with which to defeat the enemy /勤奋是他成功的～。Diligence is his key to success.

法币 fǎbì ❶ paper currency issued by the KMT government from 1935 to 1948 ❷ legal tender; legal currency (of a country)

法场 fǎchǎng ❶ place where Buddhist or Taoist rites are performed ❷ execution ground: 将犯人押赴～ take a convict to the execution ground under escort /劫～ (as in traditional novels) raid an execution ground to rescue the condemned

法典 fǎdiǎn code; statute book: 民～ civil (law) code /刑～ penal (law) code; criminal code /《拿破仑～》*Napoleonic Code*; *Code Napoléon* (1804)

法定 fǎdìng legal; lawful; statutory; official: ～权利 lawful right; legal right /～手续 legal formalities; legal procedure /～资格 *also* "～身分" legal capacity /～标准 statutory standard /～多数 statutory majority; required majority /～贴现率 official discount rate /～价格 official price; officially fixed price /～资本 authorized capital; declared capital /～单位 legal entity /～资产 legal asset /～所有者 legal owner /～团体 statutory body /～最高限额 statutory ceiling

法定代理人 fǎdìng dàilǐrén legal representative; statutory agent

法定股本 fǎdìng gǔběn authorized share capital

法定汇率 fǎdìng huìlǜ official rate of exchange; pegged rate of exchange; pegged exchange parity

法定货币 fǎdìng huòbì legal tender

法定继承人 fǎdìng jìchéngrén legal heir; heir at law

法定价格 fǎdìng jiàgé legal price

法定监护人 fǎdìng jiānhùrén legal guardian

法定年龄 fǎdìng niánlíng lawful age; legal age: 法定结婚年龄 legal or lawful age for marriage

法定期限 fǎdìng qīxiàn *also* "时效" shíxiào; "法定时效"〈法律〉legal time limit; statutory limitation; prescription

法定人数 fǎdìng rénshù (legal) quorum: 达到～ reach a quorum /已到～。We have a quorum now. *or* There is a quorum now.

法定休假日 fǎdìng xiūjiàrì *also* "法定假日" legal holiday; official holiday

法定证据 fǎdìng zhèngjù 〈法律〉legal evidence

法定准备 fǎdìng zhǔnbèi *also* "法定储备"〈金融〉legal reserve; statutory reserve: ～基金 legal reserve fund

法度 fǎdù ❶ law: ～不行，何以服众? If the laws are not enforced, how can we win the trust of the people? ❷ moral standard; established norm: 做工作总得有个～。There must be a norm or standard for the conduct of our work.

法服 fǎfú *also* "法衣" monastic habit
法古 fǎgǔ follow the example of ancient sages or figures:他的书法~而又不泥古。His calligraphy does not merely copy but draws on the styles of ancient masters.
法官 fǎguān judge; justice:大~ chief justice / ~裁定那些供述不能作为证据。The judge ruled that the testimony could not be allowed as evidence.
法规 fǎguī laws and regulations; statutes:国家~ state laws and regulations / 经济~ economic statutes; economic laws and regulations / 教会~ canon law / 颁布~ promulgate laws and statutes / ~汇编 statute book
法国 Fǎguó France:~人 French; Frenchman / ~化 Frenchify / ~菜 French cooking; French cuisine / ~式屋顶〈建筑〉French roof / ~电视广播公司 Organization Radio Television de France
法国白兰地 Fǎguó báilándì cognac
法国大革命 Fǎguó Dàgémìng French Revolution (1789-1799), overthrowing the Bourbon monarchy in France
法国航空公司 Fǎguó Hángkōng Gōngsī Air France
法国号 fǎguóhào 〈音乐〉French horn
法国梧桐 Fǎguó wútóng plane tree:街道两旁是高大的~。Standing on either side of the street are rows of tall plane trees.
法号 fǎhào *also* "法名" Buddhist monastic name; clerical name
法华经 Fǎhuájīng (short for 妙法莲华经) *Saddharma-pundarika Sutra*; *Lotus Sutra*
法会 fǎhuì Buddhist service
法纪 fǎjì law and discipline:目无~ act in total disregard of law and discipline; flout (*or* defy) law and discipline / 遵守~ observe law and discipline / 加强~观念 enhance one's awareness of law and discipline
法家 Fǎjiā Legalists; Legalist school (a school of thought in the Spring and Autumn and Warring States Periods, 770-221 BC)
法界 fǎjiè 〈佛教〉*dharmahātu*; dharma-realm
法警 fǎjǐng bailiff
法拉 fǎlā 〈物理〉farad (F):微~ microfarad / ~计 farad meter
法拉第 Fǎlādì Michael Faraday (1791-1867), English chemist and physicist:~常数 Faraday constant / ~效应 Faraday effect / ~旋转器 Faraday rotator
法拉第定律 Fǎlādì dìnglǜ 〈物理〉Faraday's law
法兰 fǎlán 〈机械〉(transliteration) flange:~保护 flange protection / ~密封 flange seal
法兰克福 Fǎlánkèfú Frankfurt or Frankfurt am Main, a port and commercial city on the River Main in Germany
法兰盘 fǎlánpán flange plate
法兰绒 fǎlánróng flannel:~裤 flannels
法兰西 Fǎlánxī (transliteration) France:~人 French / ~第一帝国 First French Empire (1804-1815) / ~第一共和国 First Republic of France (1789-1804) / ~联邦 *Union Française* (renamed as French Community in 1958) / ~共同体 French Community / ~石油公司 *Compagnie Française des Pétroles*
法兰西银行 Fǎlánxī Yínháng *Banque de France*
法郎 fǎláng franc:比利时~ Belgian Franc / 法国~ French Franc / 瑞士~ Swiss Franc / ~区 French Franc Area
法老 fǎlǎo Pharaoh, title of the king of ancient Egypt
法理 fǎlǐ ❶ legal principle; theory of law:此项规定缺乏~依据。This rule wants legal basis. *or* There is no legal basis for this rule. ❷〈书面〉rules; law:事物发展变化之~ laws governing the evolution of things ❸ Buddhist doctrine:妙解~ ingenious interpretation of the Buddhist tenets
法理学 fǎlǐxué jurisprudence
法力 fǎlì ❶〈佛教〉dharma power; power of the Buddhist doctrine:~无边。The dharma is all-powerful. *or* There is infinite power to the dharma. ❷ supernatural power; magic power:施展~ bring one's supernatural power into play; exercise one's magic power
法例 fǎlì legal provision; legal clause:此事有无~可据? Is there any legal provision to go by on this question?
法令 fǎlìng laws and decrees; decree; order; ordinance:政府~ government ordinance / 行政~ (US) executive order / 颁布~ promulgate a statute or decree
法律 fǎlǜ law; statute:制定~ enact a law / 执行~ enforce a law / 解释~ interpret a law / ~根据 legal basis / ~规定 legal provisions / ~程序 legal procedure (*or* process) / ~地位 legal status / ~实体 legal entity / ~用语 legal language / ~保护 legal protection / ~漏洞 legal loophole / ~咨询 legal advice; legal consultancy service / ~手段 legal means / ~诉讼 legal proceedings; action at law / ~人格 legal personality / ~权利 legal right / ~义务 legal duty (*or* obligation) / ~主权 legal sovereignty / ~意识 awareness of law; legal consciousness / ~补救 legal redress / ~体制 legal framework / ~界 legal circles / ~范围 scope of law / 以~形式规定下来 be institutionalized in the form of law; be enacted into law / ~面前,人人平等。All are equal before the law.
法律博士 fǎlǜ bóshì (US) Juris Doctor; JD — basic degree for practising law in US
法律承认 fǎlǜ chéngrèn *de jure* recognition
法律冲突 fǎlǜ chōngtū conflict of laws
法律顾问 fǎlǜ gùwèn legal adviser; legal counsel
法律化学 fǎlǜ huàxué legal chemistry
法律事务所 fǎlǜ shìwùsuǒ law office; law firm
法律效力 fǎlǜ xiàolì legal validity; legal effect:法律域外效力 extraterritorial effect of law
法律责任 fǎlǜ zérèn legal liability, legal responsibility:追究~ investigate and affix sb.'s legal responsibility
法律制裁 fǎlǜ zhìcái legal sanction:受到~ be punished according to law
法律咨询 fǎlǜ zīxún legal advice; legal consultancy
法轮 fǎlún 〈佛教〉*dharmacakra*; Wheel of the Law; dharma; doctrine:~常转。The power of dharma (*or* Buddhist doctrine) is constant and infinite.
法罗群岛 Fǎluó Qúndǎo Faeroe Islands, a group of islands in the North Atlantic between Iceland and the Shetlands
法螺 fǎluó ❶〈动物〉triton; triton shell ❷ conch shell used as trumpet (as in Buddhist and Taoist services or by fishermen):自吹~ blow one's own trumpet
法盲 fǎmáng person ignorant of the law; person with little legal knowledge
法门 fǎmén ❶〈佛教〉*dharmaparāya*; dharma door; gateway to the Law; way to become initiated in Buddhist doctrine:不二~ only approach (to a subject); only method (to do sth.) ❷ access; approach; method:挽救这家企业你有何~? What key measures are you going to take to salvage this enterprise?
法名 fǎmíng 〈宗教〉*see* "法号"
法器 fǎqì 〈宗教〉ritual implement, including musical instrument (used in Buddhist or Taoist services)
法权 fǎquán right; privilege:治外~ extraterritorial rights; extraterritoriality / 资产阶级~ bourgeois right
法人 fǎrén 〈法律〉legal or juridical person; artificial person; *legalis homo*; corporation:集体~ corporation aggregate / 独任~ corporation sole / ~代表 legal representative / ~股 shares held by legal persons; corporate shares / ~税 corporation tax
法人团体 fǎrén tuántǐ body corporate; corporate body; corporation
法身 fǎshēn 〈佛教〉❶ *dharmakāya*; embodiment of Truth and the Law; body of Buddha ❷ body of a holy monk
法绳 fǎshéng ropes used by bailiffs or police to truss up criminals
法师 fǎshī (title of respect for a Buddhist or Taoist priest) *dharmācarya*; master (of the Law)
法式 fǎshì rule; method; model:《营造~》*Rules of Architecture* (written around 1100)
法事 fǎshì Buddhist or Taoist service or ceremony
法书 fǎshū ❶ model calligraphy ❷〈敬词〉your calligraphy; your writing
法术 fǎshù ❶ (in legalist thought) law and methods of governing — law for guiding and keeping in line both the officials and the common people and methods for guiding the ruler in wielding power and controlling the men under him ❷ magic arts; witchcraft:施~ exercise magic arts / 戳穿骗人的~ lay bare sb.'s deceitful tricks
法塔赫 Fǎtǎhè Al Fatah (guerrilla organization associated with the Palestine National Liberation Movement)
法坛 fǎtán *also* "斋坛" zhāitán locus for holding a Buddhist or Taoist service; tabernacle
法堂 fǎtáng ❶〈旧语〉hall where a magistrate hears cases; law court:上~ go to court ❷ hall for preaching Buddhist doctrines
法帖 fǎtiè copy of, or rubbings from, model calligraphy:临摹~ imitate model calligraphy

法庭 fǎtíng court; tribunal: 军事～ military tribunal; court-martial / 刑事～ criminal court / 民事～ civil court / 仲裁～ arbitration tribunal; court of arbitration / 警务～ police court / 海事～ maritime court / 国际～ international court / 道德～ forum of conscience / 对簿～ take a matter to court; go to court
法庭保释 fǎtíng bǎoshì court bail
法庭执达员 fǎtíng zhídáyuán 〈法律〉 catchpole
法统 fǎtǒng legally constituted authority
法王 fǎwáng ❶ *Dharma-raja*; King of the Law, respectful term of address used by Buddhists for Sakyamuni ❷ title conferred on the head of Lamaism in the Yuan and Ming dynasties
法网 fǎwǎng net of justice; arm of the law: ～难逃 can not escape the meshes of law; will eventually be brought to justice / 落入～ be caught in the net of justice; be brought to justice / ～恢恢，疏而不漏。Large though its meshes may be, the wide net of justice lets no criminal through.
法无我 fǎwúwǒ 〈佛教〉 nonself of things
法务部 Fǎwùbù (ROK) Ministry of Justice: ～长官 (ROK) Minister of Justice
法务大臣 Fǎwù Dàchén (Japan) Minister of Justice
法务省 Fǎwùshěng (Japan) Ministry of Justice
法物 fǎwù musical instruments, etc., used in ancestral temples; instruments used by the guard of honour of an emperor
法西斯 fǎxīsī fascist: ～化 fascistization / ～党 Fascist Party (1922-1943) / ～组织 fascist organization / ～统治 fascist rule / ～分子 fascist
法西斯蒂 fǎxīsīdì (transliteration from Italian) Fascisti: 意大利～ Italian Fascista (1922-1943) / ～分子 Fascist
法西斯主义 fǎxīsīzhǔyì fascism: 新～ neo-fascism / ～者 fascist
法系 fǎxì genealogy of law; system of law: 罗马～ system of Roman law
法夏 fǎxià *see* "法半夏"
法显 Fǎxiǎn Faxian (formerly translated as Fa-hsien, c. 337-422), Chinese monk and translator of Buddhist literature of the Eastern Jin Dynasty
法线 fǎxiàn 〈数学〉 normal (line)
法相 fǎxiàng 〈佛教〉 ❶ *dharmalakasana*; aspects of an object in the universe: 众生～ myriad aspects (*or* images) of life ❷ image of Buddha: ～庄严 solemn image (*or* figure) of Buddha
法像 fǎxiàng figure or image of Buddha
法新社 Fǎxīnshè *Agence France-Presse* (AFP)
法学 fǎxué science of law; jurisprudence: 研究～ study law; study jurisprudence / ～士 bachelor of laws; *legum baccalaureus* (LLB) / ～硕士 master of laws; *legum magister* (LLM) / ～博士 doctor of laws; *legum doctor* (LLD)
法学会 fǎxuéhuì 〈法律〉 jurisprudence society; law society
法学家 fǎxuéjiā jurist; jurisprudent
法眼 fǎyǎn ❶ 〈佛教〉 Buddhas' Dharma-eye (which perceives both past and future) ❷ discernment; insight; acumen: 我不具～，看不出其中的奥妙。Not a man of acumen, I fail to see the subtlety.
法衣 fǎyī monastic habit; garment worn by a Buddhist or Taoist priest at a religious ceremony
法医 fǎyī legal medical expert: ～病理学家 forensic pathologist
法医化学 fǎyī huàxué 〈法律〉 forensic chemistry
法医鉴定 fǎyī jiàndìng 〈法律〉 medicolegal expertise
法医死因学 fǎyī sǐyīnxué 〈法律〉 forensic thanatology
法医学 fǎyīxué medical jurisprudence; forensic medicine
法语 Fǎyǔ French (language): ～国家 French-speaking countries; Francophone countries / ～区 Francophone area; French-speaking area
法院 fǎyuàn court of justice; law court; court: 最高人民～ Supreme People's Court / 高级人民～ higher people's court / 中级人民～ intermediate people's court / 初级人民～ primary people's court / 地方～ local court / 初审～ trial court; court of first instance / 上诉～ court of appeal; appellate court / 终审～ court of last instance; court of final appeal (CFA) / 国际～ International Court of Justice / 巡回～ circuit court / 高等～ (UK) High Court of Justice / 行政～ (US) Court of Claims / ～判决 court sentence / ～裁决 court decision / ～院长 president of the court / ～开庭日 court day / ～规则 rules of the court / ～正在开庭。The court is now sitting.
法则 fǎzé ❶ law; rule: 自然～ law of nature / 客观～ objective law ❷ 〈书面〉 laws and regulations: 遵守～ abide by the laws and regulations ❸ 〈书面〉 model; fine example: 足以为天下之～ suffice as a model for all to emulate
法政 fǎzhèng 〈旧语〉 law and politics: ～系 department of law and political science
法旨 fǎzhǐ 〈旧语〉 god's wish; will of Buddha
法治 fǎzhì ❶ Legalist thought prior to the Qin Dynasty ❷ rule of law; government by law: ～管理 administration of law / ～国家 country under the rule of law
法制 fǎzhì legal system; legal institutions; legality: 完善～ 建设 build and perfect the legal system / ～教育 education or instruction in the law / 提高人民的～观念 enhance the people's awareness of law / ～观念薄弱 have a weak sense of legality; have a poor understanding of law; know little about legal institutions / 加强社会主义～ strengthen the socialist legal system
法子 fǎzi way; method: 想～ think of some way; find a way / 用这个～可以解决问题。The problem can be solved this way. / 我有～了! I have an idea.

砝 fǎ

砝码 fǎmǎ weight (used on a balance): ～盘 scale-pan

fà

珐(琺) fà

珐琅 fàláng enamel: ～制品 enamelware
珐琅质 fàlángzhì 〈生理〉 enamel (of teeth)

发(髮) fà

hair: 白～ grey hair; white hair / 直～ straight hair / 卷～ curly hair / 金～ blonde hair; golden hair; fair hair / 银～ silver hair / 做头～ do one's hair / 烫～ have a permanent wave; have a perm / 染～ have one's hair dyed / 理～ have one's hair cut; have a haircut / 留长～ wear one's hair long / 留短～ wear one's hair short (*or* bobbed) / 蓬头散～ dishevelled hair
see also fā

发辫 fàbiàn plait; braid; pigtail: 留～ wear one's hair in plaits (*or* braids); wear one's hair in a pigtail
发鬓 fàbìn *also* "鬓发" hair on the temples
发菜 fàcài *also* "头发菜" tóufacài; "羊栖菜" yángqīcài 〈植物〉 hair weeds; flagelliform nostoc (*Nostoc commune*)
发带 fàdài (hair) ribbon; hairband: 系了一根色彩鲜艳的～ wear a colourful ribbon (in one's hair)
发雕 fàdiāo hair sculpture
发短心长 fàduǎn-xīncháng though one's hair is sparse from age, one's wisdom is great from experience; be short in the hair but long in wisdom
发膏 fàgāo pomade; hair cream
发箍 fàgū hair slide; headband
发际 fàjì hairline: 前～ hairline on the forehead / 后～ hairline on the nape
发髻 fàjì bun; chignon: 梳成～ (of a woman) wear one's hair in a bun
发夹 fàjiā hairclip; hairpin; bobby pin; barrette: 卷～ hair-curler
发胶 fàjiāo hair jelly; gel-mousse
发蜡 fàlà pomade: 抹～ apply pomade to one's hair; rub one's hair with pomade
发廊 fàláng 〈方言〉 *see* "发屋"
发妻 fàqī 〈旧语〉 first wife
发卡 fàqiǎ hairpin; bobby pin; hairclip; barrette: 小～ hairpin; bobby pin; hairgrip / 用～把头发夹住 pin up one's hair; pin one's hair with a barrette (*or* hairclip)
发乳 fàrǔ hair cream
发式 fàshì hair style; hairdo; coiffure
发刷 fàshuā hairbrush
发网 fàwǎng hairnet
发屋 fàwū *also* "发廊" 〈方言〉 ❶ barber's; hairdresser's ❷ beauty salon
发型 fàxíng hairstyle; hairdo; coiffure; hair fashion: 最新～ latest hairstyle (*or* hair fashion) / ～设计师 hairtician
发绣 fàxiù 〈工美〉 hair embroidery (done with processed human hair)

F

发癣 fàxuǎn 〈医学〉 ringworm of the scalp; scurfy ringworm; tinea capitis

发油 fàyóu hair oil; hair tonic; brilliantine

发指 fàzhǐ bristle or boil with anger; be filled with indignation:罪犯凶残的杀人行径令人～。The cold-blooded murder committed by the criminal got one's hackles up.

发指眦裂 fàzhǐ-zìliè with one's hair bristling and the corners of one's eyes splitting — become so angry that one's hair stands on end and one's eye sockets burst; boil with anger

fɑ

哦 fɑ 〈方言〉〈助词〉 *used at the end of a sentence to form a question*:同意～? Do you agree?

fān

帆 fān ❶ sail:扬～ unfurl a sail; set sail /降～ lower a sail /白～点点 dotted with white sails /鼓足风～ in full sail /一～风顺 plain or smooth sailing /孤～远影碧空尽。The only sail in sight disappears into the distant blue sky. *or* Your sail, a single shadow, becomes one with the blue sky. ❷〈书面〉 sailing boat; sailboat:千～竞发。Thousands of sails shoot ahead.

帆板 fānbǎn 〈体育〉 sailboard; windsurfer

帆板运动 fānbǎn yùndòng sailboarding; windsurfing:～员 windsurfer

帆布 fānbù canvas; sailcloth:～船 canvas boat /～篷 canvas roof; (canvas) awning /～输送带 canvas conveyor /～衣裤 ducks

帆布包 fānbùbāo canvas bag; kit bag

帆布床 fānbùchuáng cot; campbed

帆布带 fānbùdài 〈机械〉 canvas belt:～传送装置 canvas belting /～升降机 canvas sling elevator

帆布鞋 fānbùxié canvas shoes; plimsolls; sneakers; deck shoes

帆船 fānchuán sailing boat or ship; sailing vessel; sailboat; junk:～比赛 regatta; yacht race /～俱乐部 yacht club

帆船运动 fānchuán yùndòng 〈体育〉 sailing; yachting:～员 sailor; yachtsman

帆桁 fānhéng yard:～索 yard rope

帆具 fānjù rigging (of a sailboat); tackle

帆篷 fānpéng sail; canvas

帆樯 fānqiáng mast:～林立 forest of masts

飒 fān 〈书面〉 *see* "帆" fān

番[1] fān foreign; barbarian; aboriginal:～人〈旧语〉 foreigner; alien; barbarian /生～〈旧语〉 aboriginal savage

番[2] fān 〈量词〉 ❶ (used with the numeral 一 only) kind; sort:出自一～好意 out of good will (*or* good intentions) /呈现一～新气象 put on a new look /另有一～娇媚 charming in a totally different way /别具一～风味 have an altogether different flavour; have a distinctive style of one's own /进入水帘洞中,又是一～天地。Entering the cave behind the waterfall, one seemed to have stepped into a fairyland (*or* a land of unique beauty). ❷ *used often with the numeral* 一, *but sometimes with* 几, *or* 三 *in given collocations, in reference to a process or action that takes time and effort*:作出一～努力 make an effort /认真考虑一～ give careful consideration (to sth.) /一～感人肺腑的话语 a heart-warming talk /费一～口舌 take a lot of talking or persuasion /下一～功夫 put in a lot of time and effort /三～五次 *also* "几次三～" time and again /几～较量 repeated trials of strength /老板把他好一～训斥。The boss berated him for a good while. /经过了几～周折,会议终于达成了一致。The conference had gone through quite a few twists and turns before it finally reached consensus. ❸ (used after the verb 翻) time; -fold:翻一～ increase twofold; double /翻两～ increase four-fold; quadruple
see also pān

番邦 fānbāng 〈旧语〉 foreign country; barbarian land; alien people or nation

番菜 fāncài 〈旧语〉 Western-style food; foreign food

番瓜 fānguā 〈方言〉 pumpkin

番号 fānhào designation (of a military unit):这个团的～是 8361。The regiment's designation is 8361. *or* The regiment is designated as 8361.

番椒 fānjiāo 〈中医〉 chilli; pepper; *Capsicum*

番客 fānkè 〈旧语〉 foreigner; alien

番荔枝 fānlìzhī sweetsop (*Annona squamosa*)

番木鳖 fānmùbiē 〈植物〉 vomiting nut (*Nux vomica*)

番木鳖硷 fānmùbiējiǎn 〈药物〉 strychnine

番木瓜 fānmùguā 〈植物〉 papaya (*Carica payaya*); pawpaw (*Asimina triloba*)

番茄 fānqié *also* "西红柿" xīhóngshì tomato:～酱 tomato sauce; (tomato)ketchup (*or* catsup) /～汁 tomato juice

番石榴 fānshíliu 〈植物〉 guava (*Psidium guajava*)

番薯 fānshǔ 〈方言〉 sweet potato:烤～ baked sweet potato

番泻 fānxiè 〈植物〉 *Cassia angustifolia*

番杏 fānxìng *also* "白番杏" báifānxìng; "滨莴苣" bīnwōju 〈植物〉 aizoaceae (*Tetragonia expansa*)

蕃 fān *see* "番[1]" fān
see also fán

藩 fān ❶ fence; hedge ❷〈书面〉 (protective) screen; barrier; defence ❸ vassal state; feudatory:外～ outlying vassal state /三～之乱 (1673-1681, at the beginning of the Qing Dynasty) Rebellion of the Three Feudatories

藩国 fānguó vassal state

藩篱 fānlí fence; hedge; (protective) barrier:围有～的庭院 fenced-in courtyard /不可或缺的～ essential protective barrier (for a country etc.); indispensable defence

藩属 fānshǔ feudatory; vassal state

藩镇 fānzhèn (of the Tang Dynasty) military governorship (at first only in command of the army in a prefecture, later taking over all power in the prefecture, and finally wresting control of outlying prefectures as well):～割据 (from the late Tang till the establishment of the Song Dynasty) separatist rule by military governors

幡(旛) fān long narrow flag; streamer

幡儿 fānr *also* "引魂幡" yǐnhúnfān long narrow white flag carried in a funeral procession; funeral streamer

幡然 fānrán (change) quickly and completely
see also "翻然" fānrán

幡子 fānzi 〈方言〉 long narrow white flag carried in a funeral procession; funeral streamer

翻 fān ❶ turn (over, up, upside down, inside out, etc.):～唱片 turn over a phonograph record /～口袋 turn a pocket or sack inside out /～衣领 turn the collar up /犁地～土 plough a field and turn up the soil /碰～了酒杯 knock over a wine cup /人仰马～ both men and horses are thrown off their feet — be utterly routed /巨浪把小船打～。A big wave turned the boat over. *or* A big wave capsized the boat. /清风不识字,何必乱～书。Knowing not how to read, O Breeze, why dost thou turn the pages? ❷ rummage; search; look through:～箱子 rummage about a suitcase /～某人的行李 search sb.'s luggage /～文件 look through the documents /～资料 look for data or information /抽屉都～遍了,也没找到笔记本。I rummaged through all the drawers, but still could not find the notebook. ❸ reverse; overturn:～口供 withdraw a confession; retract a testimony ❹ cross; get over:～过山头 cross a mountain /～墙越脊 climb over walls and roofs /～越障碍物 get over a barrier ❺ multiply; double:粮食产量～了几番。The grain output has doubled and redoubled. /国民生产总值～了两番。The GNP has quadrupled. ❻ translate; interpret:把小说～成英文 translate or turn a novel into English /这本书是从法文～过来的。This book was translated from the French. ❼〈口语〉 fall out; quarrel; break up:一家人闹～了。The family fell out with each other. /别把我惹～了! Don't get my back up!

翻案 fān'àn reverse or overturn a verdict:为受冤枉的好人～ overturn or reverse the wrong verdict passed on an innocent person /为历史人物～ completely change the traditional evaluation of a historical figure /铁证如山,他翻不了案。He cannot get his case reversed as

the evidence is irrefutable.

翻案风 fān'ànfēng trend towards reversing verdicts

翻案文章 fān'àn wénzhāng article or work presenting a radically different view on a historical incident or figure:这件事的~恐怕不好做。It is not easy to change the original evaluation of this event.

翻把 fānbǎ 〈方言〉❶ take the upper hand again:不能让对手~。Don't give your rival a chance to take the upper hand again. ❷ deny what one has said or done:刚说过的话怎么就想~? How can you go back upon your word so quickly?

翻白眼 fān báiyǎn show the whites of one's eyes (as from dissatisfaction, despair, resentment, or illness):他朝我翻了翻白眼,但仍然一声没吭。He glared at me but kept his silence.

翻版 fānbǎn reprint; reproduction; refurbished version; copy:拙劣的~ inferior reproduction (of sth.); bad copy (*or* duplicate) /艺术形象不应是现实生活的机械~。Artistic images should not be mechanical duplicates from real life.

翻本 fānběn win back (money lost in gambling, etc.); make up or recoup one's losses:他原指望~,结果输了个精光。Trying to win back what he had lost, he gambled away all his money.

翻茬 fānchá 〈农业〉plough under the stubble after a harvest:这块地已翻过茬。The stubble has been ploughed under in the field.

翻场 fāncháng turn over the grain on the threshing ground:你需要几个人晒场、~? How many people do you need to sun the grain and turn it over?

翻场 fānchǎng 〈戏曲〉show up fellow actors' or actresses' faults on the stage

翻车 fānchē ❶ (of a vehicle) overturn:这是一起~交通事故。It was a traffic accident in which a car turned over. ❷ suffer a setback midway through one's work:干得好好的,不料想中间翻了车。We had started well but unexpectedly things went wrong half way through. ❸〈方言〉change the original decision or plan; fail to keep one's promise:既应了人家就别~。Since you have made the promise, don't break it. ❹〈方言〉quarrel; fall out:今天我跟他~了。I had a row with him today. ❺〈方言〉waterwheel

翻车机 fānchējī 〈矿业〉tipper; dumper; tipple

翻车鱼 fānchēyú ocean sunfish; headfish

翻船 fānchuán ❶ (of a boat) capsize:在大海里翻了船。The ship capsized on the sea. ❷ suffer a setback or an upset; be defeated:阴沟里~ capsize in a ditch; suffer an upset with all odds on one's side /女排在比赛中险些~。The women's volleyball team almost lost the game. /不要笑话人家的失败,谁也保不齐日后不~。Don't laugh at others when they have a failure. Nobody can be a sure winner forever.

翻地 fāndì turn up the soil:播种前先~ turn up the soil before seeding /~筑垄 ridge the land

翻动 fāndòng shift (sth. from its original place); move:屋里东西被人~过了,椅子也挪了地方。Someone has moved things in the room; the chairs are not where they were.

翻斗 fāndǒu tipping bucket; skip bucket:~提升机 skip hoist or elevator /~坏了,卸不了货。As the skip bucket broke down, it was impossible to unload the goods.

翻斗车 fāndǒuchē tipcart; skip car; end tipper

翻斗卡车 fāndǒu kǎchē tipping lorry; tip lorry; tip truck; tipper truck; tipper

翻番 fānfān double; be twice as much or many as:这个县的工农业总产值三年~。The total agricultural and industrial output value of the county doubled in three years.

翻飞 fānfēi ❶ (of birds, butterflies, etc.) fly about; fly up and down; flit to and fro:蜻蜓在湖面上~。Dragonflies were flitting to and fro over the lake. ❷ flap; flutter:迎风~的红飘带 red ribbon flapping in the wind

翻覆 fānfù ❶ overturn; turn upside down:火车脱轨~。The train was derailed and overturned. ❷ great and thorough change:天地~ earth-shaking change; world-shaking change ❸ toss and turn; toss from side to side:夜间~不能入眠 toss and turn sleepless at night ❹〈书面〉vacillate; chop and change; back out (of a commitment, promise, etc.):此公为人常有~,不可信赖。Chopping and changing all the time, this man is totally unreliable.

翻改 fāngǎi turn (old clothes); remake:~大衣 have an overcoat turned or remade /她把她的旧连衣裙~成了一条百褶裙。She turned her old dress into a pleated skirt.

翻盖 fāngài rebuild; renovate (a house):这所旧房子需要~了。The old house needs renovation.

翻杠子 fān gàngzi 〈体育〉do gymnastics on a horizontal bar or parallel bars

翻个儿 fāngèr 〈口语〉turn over:场上晒的麦子该~了。It is time to turn over the wheat on the threshing ground. /把饼翻个个儿再烙一会儿。Turn the cake over and bake it some more.

翻跟头 fān gēntou *also* "翻斤头";"翻筋斗" ❶ turn a somersault; loop the loop:在地毯上~ turn somersaults on the carpet /飞机在半空中连翻三个跟头。The plane looped the loop three times in the sky. ❷suffer a setback:如何搞教改,起初我们也没经验,翻过跟头。As we hadn't had any experience in educational reform, we, too, suffered a few setbacks at the beginning. ❸ (of prices, etc.) double:这种外衣批发价才六十元,到零销商手里就起码要翻个跟斗。The wholesaler's price for this jacket is only 60 *yuan*, but the retailers will at least double the price.

翻耕 fāngēng plough; turn over (soil)

翻工 fāngōng 〈方言〉do (poorly-done work) over again:这项工程必须全部~。Work on the project will have to be done all over again.

翻供 fāngòng withdraw or revoke a confession; retract one's testimony:在大量事实面前,罪犯无法~。The criminal had no way to revoke his confession when confronted with so much evidence.

翻古 fāngǔ 〈方言〉speak or talk about the past; bring up old stories:听老人~ listen to old people talk about the past

翻滚 fāngǔn ❶ (of waves, water, etc.) seethe; churn; roll:麦浪~ rolling sea of wheat /思绪~ disquieting thoughts seething (*or* surging) in one's mind /牛肉汤在大锅中~。The beef soup was roiling (*or* boiling) in the cauldron. ❷ toss and turn; tumble about:几只小猫在草地上~嬉戏。Several kittens tumbled about on the lawn. /病人痛苦地在床上辗转~。The sick man tossed and turned painfully in his bed.

翻过儿 fānguòr ❶ turn upside down; turn over:谁知道他在找什么,把房里的箱子、柜子都翻了个过儿。Who knows what he is looking for; he has rummaged through all the boxes, chests and drawers in the room. ❷ turn about (in one's view, etc.); change one's mind:他~一想,她说的话是有道理的。On second thoughts, he realized that there was something in what she said.

翻黄 fānhuáng *also* "翻簧" handicraft ware made from bamboo with its green covering removed

翻悔 fānhuǐ back out (of a commitment, promise, etc.); renege:你我一言为定,不许~。It is agreed, and nobody should renege. /一旦签了合约,就无可~。Once you sign the contract, there is no turning back.

翻检 fānjiǎn turn over and check; look through:~书信文件 look through sb.'s books and papers

翻建 fānjiàn rebuild:~危房 rebuild dilapidated or rundown housing /这个餐厅停业~。The restaurant is closed for renovation.

翻江倒海 fānjiāng-dǎohǎi *also* "倒海翻江" overturning rivers and seas — overwhelming; earth-shaking; stupendous; tremendous:~之势 overwhelming momentum; momentum of an avalanche /~之力 prowess to perform astounding feats of valour; tremendous power

翻浆 fānjiāng (of road surface) burst and become muddy (when a spring thaw sets in):~作用 congeliturbation /春天开冻,道路~。Road surfaces became sodden and muddy in spring when the thaw set in.

翻搅 fānjiǎo stir; ruffle:拿棍子~灰浆 stir plaster with a stick /湖水被大风~得波涛汹涌。Driven by high wind, the waves churned furiously in the lake.

翻旧账 fān jiùzhàng bring up old scores again; rake up old grievances
see also "翻老账"

翻卷 fānjuǎn whirl round; wheel about; roll:树叶在风中~。The leaves whirled about in the wind. /雪花在空中~。Snowflakes were dancing in the air. /汽车飞驰而过,~起一股尘土。A car sped past, raising a cloud of dust in its wake.

翻刻 fānkè (in blockprinting) cut the blocks based on a printed book or article (for the purpose of reprinting):~重印 reprint a book by cutting the blocks again /~本 book reprinted in this way

翻来覆去 fānlái-fùqù ❶ toss and turn; toss from side to side:他~,直到临晨才入睡。He tossed and turned in bed, unable to sleep till near daybreak. ❷ again and again; repeatedly:她~地说了很多遍,大家才听明白。She repeated herself over and over again before everybody understood her. /他独自坐在屋里,~地想着这件事。Sitting

alone in his room, he mulled over the matter.

翻老账 fān lǎozhàng *also* "翻旧账" bring up old scores again; rake up old grievances：你就是爱～。哼，这有什么用？You do love raking up old grievances, don't you? What's the use, huh? /不要再去翻那些陈年老账了。Don't bring up those old scores again.

翻脸 fānliǎn suddenly turn hostile; fall out; turn (against sb.)：他们终于翻了脸。They finally fell out.

翻脸不认人 fānliǎn bù rèn rén turn against a friend; turn one's back on an old associate; cut sb. dead：他会～，对你下毒手。He could turn hostile any time and do you in.

翻脸无情 fānliǎn-wúqíng be treacherous and ruthless; turn against a friend without mercy：此人～惯了，我们不能不提高警惕。He is such a treacherous man that we have to keep a watchful eye on him.

翻两番 fān liǎngfān quadruple; increase by four times：到 20 世纪末使 1980 年的工农业年总产值～ quadruple the gross annual value of industrial and agricultural output of 1980 by the end of the 20th century

翻领 fānlǐng turndown collar：～衬衣 shirt with a turndown-collar /大～上衣 jacket with a wide lapel

翻录 fānlù duplicate (tapes)：版权所有，～必究。All rights reserved; duplicators (of the tape) will be prosecuted.

翻毛 fānmáo ❶ fur：～大衣 fur coat ❷ suede：～皮鞋 suede shoes

翻木机 fānmùjī 〈林业〉cant hook; peavey; peavy

翻弄 fānnòng turn (back and forth)：他心不在焉地～着报纸。He was turning the pages of the newspaper absent-mindedly. /我漫不经心地将书～了一遍。I casually leafed through the book.

翻拍 fānpāi reproduce (a photo, etc.)：～一张老相片 reproduce an old photo

翻皮 fānpí suede：～靴子 suede boots /～手套 suede gloves

翻然 fānrán *also* "幡然" fānrán (change) quickly and completely：～改进 make quick, marked improvements or progress

翻然改图 fānrán-gǎitú quickly change one's plans or ways：你如能～，前途仍然光明。You still have a bright future if you mend your ways without delay.

翻然悔悟 fānrán-huǐwù wake up to one's error; make a clear break with one's past：他这次出的问题可不小，但愿能～。He made a serious mistake this time and we hope that he would realize it as soon as possible.

翻砂 fānshā 〈机械〉founding; moulding; casting：～铸铁 sand-cast pig iron

翻砂车间 fānshā chējiān foundry shop; moulding floor

翻砂工 fānshāgōng foundry worker; caster

翻晒 fānshài turn over in the sun (to dry)：～被褥 turn over quilts in the sun /～粮食 turn over grain on the threshing ground; turn over grain in the sun

翻山涉水 fānshān-shèshuǐ cross (over) rivers and hills

翻山越岭 fānshān-yuèlǐng cross over mountain after mountain; tramp over hill and dale; go uphill and down dale：地质队员们～，终于找到了这种矿石。After crossing over mountain after mountain the geological prospectors finally found the ore.

翻梢 fānshāo 〈方言〉❶ win back (what is lost in gambling); recoup or make up one's losses ❷ pull oneself together and extricate oneself from an unfavourable situation

翻身 fānshēn ❶ turn over：～落马 (turn and) fall from one's horse /～从床上爬起来 roll off the bed /他翻了个身又睡着了。He turned over in bed and fell asleep again. ❷ free oneself; stand up; stand on one's own feet：～农奴 emancipated serfs /～做主人 stand up and be master(s) of one's own fate ❸ change (from poverty) to favourable conditions; improve dramatically：帮助贫穷地区～ help the poor areas stand on their own feet /办了奶牛场以后，咱们村可是～了。Our village has prospered since the dairy farm was set up. ❹ 〈方言〉turn round：他脸一沉～就走了。His face fell, and he turned round and left.

翻身仗 fānshēnzhàng battle to improve one's lot fundamentally; effort to bring about a decisive change for the better：大打农业～ make a determined effort (*or* go all out) to bring about a steady upswing in agriculture

翻绳儿 fānshéngr (children's game) cat's cradle

翻手为云，覆手为雨 fān shǒu wéi yún, fù shǒu wéi yǔ produce clouds with one turn of the hand and rain with another — wield one's power capriciously; be shifty and capricious; be tricky and deceitful

see also "翻云覆雨"

翻腾 fānténg 〈体育〉tuck dive：向前～三周半 forward tuck dive with three-and-a-half somersaults /向内～两周半 backward tuck dive with two-and-a-half somersaults

翻腾 fānteng ❶ seethe; churn; surge：瀑布下，水浪～。Water churned under the falls. /各种思想在她脑海里～。Her mind was seething with conflicting ideas. ❷ turn sth. over and over：他把书柜～遍了，也没找到那本书。He rummaged through all the bookcases but still could not find the book. /我的胃一个劲儿地～想吐。I felt sick and my stomach was turning over and over. /那些事儿，不去～为好。It is better not to rake up those things again.

翻天 fāntiān ❶ make a violent noise or row; roughhouse：闹～ make (*or* raise) a rumpus; roughhouse /吵～ start a violient quarrel; kick up a terrific row ❷ rebel against (the establishment, etc.); overthrow：不许敌人～。We shall never allow the enemy to run berserk. /凭他们几个人想～，岂不笑话。It is nothing less than a farce for a handful of them to try to rock the boat (*or* upset the applecart).

翻天覆地 fāntiān-fùdì ❶ earth-shaking; world-shaking：～的时代 world-shaking era; era of turbulence and upheaval ❷ quarrel furiously：两口子不和，家里常常闹得～。Not getting along with each other, the couple often kicked up a terrible row.

翻蔓儿 fānwànr turn the vines (of sweet potato, etc.)

翻胃 fānwèi *also* "反胃" fǎnwèi suffer or cause nausea due to gastric disorder; regurgitate; feel nauseated; feel sick：屠宰场的冲天恶臭使我直想～。The stink from the slaughterhouse turned my stomach.

翻箱倒柜 fānxiāng-dǎoguì *also* "翻箱倒箧" rummage through chests and cupboards (in a thorough search); ransack boxes and chests：他一进家就～地找他的皮夹子。As soon as he got home, he rummaged through chests and cupboards in search of his wallet.

翻新 fānxīn renovate; revamp; recondition; make over：工厂～ renovate a factory /旧车～ revamp an old car /旧大衣～ make over an old overcoat /车胎～ retread a tyre /花样～ present (the same old thing) in a new guise; ring changes (on an old subject)

翻修 fānxiū rebuild; restore to good condition; renovate：～老房子 renovate an old house /～地板 relay the floor /～店面 give the shop a face-lift

翻扬 fānyáng (of prices) soar; skyrocket：纸价～。The price of paper is skyrocketing.

翻译 fānyì ❶ translate; interpret：笔头～ written translation /口头～ oral interpretation /逐字～ word-for-word (*or* literal) translation /～电码 decode (*or* decipher) a telegram /中国～工作者协会 China Translators' Association /外交部～室 Department of Translation and Interpretation of the Ministry of Foreign Affairs /～司 (UN) Translation Division /～会议司 (European Union) Joint Service Interpretation Conferences /她的～忠实于原文。Her translation is faithful to the original. ❷ translator; interpreter：高级～ senior translator or interpreter; high-level interpreter or translator /～职称 professional titles for translators /他在联合国做同声～。He works as a simultaneous interpreter for the United Nations.

翻译本 fānyìběn translation

翻译机 fānyìjī electronic translator; translation machine

翻译片 fānyìpiàn dubbed film

翻印 fānyìn (usu. of sb. other than the original author or publisher) reprint; reproduce：把这篇文章～几份。Make some copies of this article. /这幅画从未被～过。The painting has never been reproduced. /版权所有，～必究。All rights reserved; those responsible for unauthorized reproduction will be prosecuted.

翻涌 fānyǒng seethe; rise; surge：极目望去，处处波涛～。As far as the eye could reach, billows were rolling in all directions. /许多问题在我脑海中～。My mind was seething with questions.

翻阅 fānyuè leaf through; look over; glance over：～图书目录 leaf through a catalogue (of books) /～报刊杂志 look over newspapers and magazines /我只是随手～一下。I was just turning over the pages.

翻越 fānyuè climb over; get over; surmount：～障碍物 get over (*or* surmount) an obstacle /～荒山野岭 climb over barren mountains and hills

翻云覆雨 fānyún-fùyǔ (short for 翻手为云，覆手为雨) produce clouds with one turn of the hand and rain with another — wield

one's power capriciously; be tricky and deceitful; be shifty and capricious:此人历来～,老是让人琢磨不透。Shifty and capricious, the man is most unpredictable. /你这样～的,究竟为了什么? What are you playing fast and loose like this for?

翻造 fānzào rebuild; renovate

翻嘴 fānzuǐ 〈方言〉❶ retract or modify one's previous remark; renege:他原先是那么说的,现在又～了。That's what he said at first, but he has gone back on his word. ❷ quarrel; bicker:他脾气温和,从不见他和谁翻过嘴。He has a mild temper and never has been known to quarrel with anyone.

缂

fān see "翻❻" fān

see also fán

缂译 fānyì see "翻译" fānyì

fán

烦

fán ❶ vexed; upset; irritated; annoyed:心～意乱 be terribly upset; be vexed and at a loss /～死人了! How annoying! ❷ fed up; tired:厌～ be fed up /不耐～ be impatient /这些陈词滥调我都听～了。I have had enough of such platitudes. ❸ superfluous and confusing:要言不～ give the essentials in a few words; be terse and to the point /不胜其～ be too much bother ❹ trouble:～您帮我寄封信好吗? May I trouble you to post a letter for me? *or* Could you post a letter for me? /～交王先生。Please forward this to Mr. Wang.

烦愁 fánchóu worried and depressed

烦劳 fánláo ❶〈敬词〉trouble:能～您给李小姐捎几本书吗? May I trouble you to take a few books to Miss Li? *or* Would you mind taking a few books to Miss Li for me? ❷ numerous and tiresome:这里的日常工作颇为～。The routine here is quite numerous and tiresome. ❸ be depressed; feel low

烦乱 fánluàn ❶ depressed and perturbed:心神～,坐立不安 feel upset and fidgety /外面的嚷嚷声使他心情～。The noise outside got on his nerves. ❷ see "繁乱" fánluàn

烦忙 fánmáng also "繁忙" fánmáng busy

烦闷 fánmèn unhappy; heavyhearted; moody; depressed:丈夫的责备使她～不安。Her husband's criticism depressed and disquieted her. /连日阴雨,真叫人～。The unbroken spell of wet weather is really vexing.

烦难 fánnán troublesome; knotty

see also "繁难" fánnán

烦恼 fánnǎo vexed; upset; worried:～已极 be extremely upset (*or* vexed) /你何必自寻～! Why should you bring all this vexation upon yourself? /～使她久久不能入睡。Worry kept her wide awake for a long time. /他终日为家里拮据的经济状况而～。He never stopped fretting over the family's financial straits.

烦腻 fánnì bored; fed up:那出戏令人～。The play was a bore. /饭菜天天老一套,我都～了。I'm tired of having the same kind of food every day.

烦气 fánqì 〈口语〉be annoyed; be vexed; be fed up:他一见还是老套子,心里就～。He was annoyed to see the same old stuff again.

烦请 fánqǐng 〈敬词〉request; ask:～光临。May I request the honour of your presence.

烦扰 fánrǎo ❶ bother; disturb:刚才～您了,非常抱歉。I'm sorry to have disturbed you just now. /正要睡觉,不想一只蚊子却来～我。A mosquito kept bothering me just when I was going to sleep. ❷ feel disturbed:他被白天发生的事情所～。He was disturbed by what had happened during the day.

烦人 fánrén vexing; annoying:～的毛毛雨 vexing prolonged drizzle /天天洗衣服真～。Doing laundry every day is a terrible bother.

烦冗 fánrǒng also "繁冗" fánrǒng ❶ (of one's affairs) diverse and complicated:每日忙于～的事务,无暇他顾。I'm busy with daily chores of all sorts and have no time for other matters. ❷ (of speech or writing) long and tedious; wordy and insipid; prolix:他的讲话极其～乏味。His speech was awfully long and tedious.

烦神 fánshén take pains; take trouble:这些小事您就无需～了。You need not trouble yourself over such trifles. /对不起,让您～了。I'm sorry to trouble you.

烦碎 fánsuì also "繁碎" fánsuì trivial; trifling; petty:这些～的事何不让秘书去管? Why don't you leave these trivial matters to your secretary?

烦琐 fánsuǒ、also "繁琐" fánsuǒ loaded down with trivial details; overelaborate; petty and tedious:这些手续真～。These formalities (*or* procedures) are overelaborate. /写文章切忌平庸～。In writing one must shun commonplaces and tedious details.

烦琐哲学 fánsuǒ zhéxué ❶ scholasticism ❷ overelaboration; hairsplitting:别搞你的～了,挑重要的说吧。Forget your hairsplitting details; give us the main points.

烦文缛节 fánwén-rùjié red tape

see also "繁文缛节" fánwén-rùjié

烦恶 fánwù 〈方言〉detest; abhor:老厂长最～溜须拍马的事。The old manager detested shameless flatteries.

烦嚣 fánxiāo 〈书面〉noisy and annoying:往来车辆行人的～声 hubbub of traffic; traffic din /大厅里人声～。The hall was filled with the racket of conversation.

烦心 fánxīn ❶ annoying; wearying; vexatious; worrisome:～的事 trouble; worry; vex /如此久等真叫人～。It is annoying having to wait so long. ❷〈方言〉take a lot of trouble:这孩子淘气,让奶奶～。He is such a mischievous child that grandma must have taken a lot of trouble caring for him.

烦絮 fánxù miscellaneous and disorderly:他整天忙些个零七八碎的事儿,也不嫌～。He busied himself with trivial matters all day long and did not seem to mind at all.

烦言 fányán 〈书面〉❶ complaint; grievance:口无～ have no complaints whatever; never grumble /啧有～ be full of complaints; grumble time and again ❷ also "繁言" fányán tedious words or remarks

烦言碎辞 fányán-suìcí also "烦言碎语" overlaborate and tedious remarks; tiresome loquacities:～,不必细叨 cut out the irrelevant details

烦厌 fányàn tired of; fed up with:要做好工作,就不能～小事。If you want to do your work well, you should not tire of details.

烦忧 fányōu worried and depressed

烦郁 fányù unhappy and gloomy; depressed

烦杂 fánzá miscellaneous

see also "繁杂" fánzá

烦躁 fánzào irritable and restless; fretful; agitated or fidgety:～地来回走动 walk to and fro in a terrible fidget /天热人容易～。People easily get fretful (*or* irritable and restless) in hot weather. /她讲话时～之情露于言表。As she spoke, she was obviously in a fret. /他迟迟不出来,其他人～不安地在车上等着。He stayed inside the house for a long time, while others waited impatiently in the car.

樊

fán ❶〈书面〉fence ❷ (Fán) a surname

樊篱 fánlí ❶ fence; hedge:修补～ fix a fence ❷ barriers; trammels; restriction:冲破旧礼教的～ shake off the shackles of the old (*or* conventional) ethical code

樊笼 fánlóng bird cage — place or condition of confinement:她被锁裹在旧传统的～里。She is imprisoned (*or* trapped) by outdated traditions.

燔

fán 〈书面〉❶ burn; set on fire:～柴取暖 burn firewood to keep warm ❷ bake; roast

燔针 fánzhēn 〈中医〉one of the needling techniques, puncturing with a hot needle

璠

fán 〈书面〉beautiful jade

墦

fán 〈书面〉tomb; grave

蕃

fán ❶ (of grass, trees, etc.) luxuriant; growing in abundance; lush ❷ reproduce rapidly; multiply; proliferate

see also fān

蕃昌 fánchāng luxuriant and flourishing

蕃茂 fánmào luxuriant; lush

蕃息 fánxī multiply quickly; proliferate

蕃衍 fányǎn also "繁衍" fányǎn multiply; increase gradually in number or quantity

蹯

fán 〈书面〉paw:熊～ bear's paw

鷭 fán 〈动物〉coot

膰 fán 〈古语〉sacrificial meat

墦 fán

see also fān

繙帑 fányuān 〈书面〉❶ flutter ❷ grab

繁(緐) fán ❶ in great numbers; numerous; manifold; complicated:多似～星 like a multitude of (*or* a galaxy of) stars /事务纷～ have too many things to attend to /删～就简 simplify by weeding out superfluities; reduce to bare essentials /～霜夜降 heavy frost at night ❷ propagate; procreate; multiply:农民自～自养的牲畜 livestock propagated and raised by farmers themselves

繁本 fánběn unabridged book or version

繁博 fánbó (of citation or quotation) numerous and wide-ranging:论据～ broadly based (*or* well-grounded) argument

繁多 fánduō various; numerous:花样～ of all shapes and colours /品种～ various in kind; of great variety /名目～,不胜枚举。The names of items are too many to enumerate. /学校图书馆拥有种类～的图书。The college library has a wide collection of books.

繁分数 fánfēnshù 〈数学〉complex fraction

繁复 fánfù heavy and complicated:～的组织工作 complex organizational work /电脑把统计人员从～的运算中解脱出来。A computer can free statisticians from complicated calculations.

繁富 fánfù ❶ great many; numerous:他一生著述～。He was a prolific author. ❷ thriving and prosperous:都市～。The city (*or* metropolis) is flourishing.

繁花 fánhuā full-blown flowers; variety of flowers:～满树。The tree was in full blossom. /公园里万紫千红,～怒放。Flowers of all sorts are blooming in a riot of colour in the park.

繁花似锦 fánhuā-sìjǐn flowers blooming like a piece of brocade; a multitude of blossoming flowers; flourishing scene of prosperity

繁华 fánhuá flourishing; thriving; prosperous; bustling; busy:～的商业区 busy downtown area (*or* quarter) /整个城市非常～热闹。The whole city is a scene of bustling activity.

繁剧 fánjù 〈书面〉strenuous; onerous:任务～。The tasks are arduous.

繁丽 fánlì (of language, diction, etc.) rich and flowery:～的文辞 ornate language /词藻～的散文 luxuriant prose; ornate prose /他的诗写得～。He writes poems in a flowery style.

繁乱 fánluàn *also* "烦乱" fánluàn many and diverse; miscellaneous

繁忙 fánmáng *also* "烦忙" fánmáng busy; bustling:公务～ be busy with official duties /世界上最～的海港之一 one of the busiest seaports in the world /工地上一片～景象。The work site bustled with activity. /人来人往,市井～。The marketplace was full of people coming and going. /圣诞节前商店里十分～。The shops are doing a brisk business before Christmas.

繁茂 fánmào lush; luxuriant:热带森林中草木～。Vegetation luxuriates in tropical forests. /杉树枝叶～,高耸入云。The towering cedar tree was thickly covered with foliage.

繁密 fánmì dense; thick:林木～的植物园 densely wooded botanical garden /～交错的电缆 thicket of cables /炮声依旧～。The gunfire was still intense.

繁难 fánnán *also* "烦难" fánnán hard to tackle; troublesome; knotty:～的问题 knotty problem /～的数学题 complicated mathematical problem /～的任务 arduous task

繁闹 fánnào prosperous and lively:～的城市 prosperous and bustling city

繁荣 fánróng ❶ flourishing; thriving; prosperous; booming:经济～ thriving economy /市场～ flourishing market /商业～ brisk business /～兴旺的景象 scene of prosperity /维护国家的稳定和～ maintain the stability and prosperity of the country /工业发展的～时期 period of industrial boom ❷ make prosper; promote:～市场,活跃经济 stimulate the market and reinvigorate the economy /～文艺创作 boost literary and artistic creation /～祖国文化 promote the cultural prosperity of one's country

繁荣昌盛 fánróng-chāngshèng thriving and prosperous:祝贵国～,人民幸福。May your country enjoy prosperity and her people happiness. *or* We wish your country prosperity and her people wellbeing. /国家日益～。Our country is thriving and prospering day by day. /我们正在建设一个～的现代化强国。We are building a prosperous and powerful modern country.

繁荣富强 fánróng-fùqiáng rich, powerful and prosperous:祝愿我们的祖国更加～。May our motherland become even more prosperous and powerful.

繁荣通货膨胀 fánróng tōnghuò péngzhàng 〈经济〉boomflation

繁冗 fánrǒng *also* "烦冗" fánrǒng ❶ (of one's affairs) diverse and complicated ❷ (of speech or writing) lengthy and tedious; prolix

繁缛 fánrù overelaborate:礼仪～ overelaborate rituals /～的手续 redundant procedures

繁盛 fánshèng ❶ thriving; flourishing; prosperous:这座城市日渐～。The city is thriving day by day. /文艺创作的～时期已经到来。We are witnessing a flourishing period of creative work in art and literature. *or* A period of literary and artistic efflorescence has set in. ❷ luxuriant; exuberant:花草～ exuberant growth of flowers and grass

繁庶 fánshù in abundance:土产～ abundant variety of local products

繁碎 fánsuì many and in bits:～的脚步声 sound of light and hurried footsteps

繁琐 fánsuǒ *also* "烦琐" fánsuǒ loaded down with trivial details

繁体 fántǐ ❶ (of Chinese characters) in the original complex form:一般报刊不使用～的汉字。In general, newspapers and magazines do not use the original complex Chinese characters. ❷ *see* "繁体字"

繁体字 fántǐzì original complex form of the simplified Chinese characters; full-form characters:"東"是"东"的～。東 is the original complex form of 东.

繁蔚 fánwèi 〈书面〉various; luxuriant; flourishing:花木～。Flowers are in full bloom and trees with luxuriant foliage.

繁文缛节 fánwén-rùjié *also* "繁文缛礼" overelaborate formalities; red tape:改革的目的就是为了革掉～,提高工作效率。The purpose of reform is to improve work efficiency by cutting out red tape.

繁芜 fánwú burdened with unnecessary words; wordy; prolix; verbose:文笔～ prolix style of writing /删除～ cross (*or* cut) out unnecessary words

繁细 fánxì overloaded with details; excessively detailed:分类过于～。The classification is too minute (*or* fine-drawn).

繁弦急管 fánxián-jíguǎn *also* "急管繁弦" fast beat or quick rhythm in music

繁嚣 fánxiāo *also* "烦嚣" fánxiāo noisy and annoying:～的集市 noisy market

繁兴 fánxīng crop up frequently; appear constantly:灾祸～ one calamity after another /谣言～。Rumours came thick and fast.

繁星 fánxīng array of stars:月黑之夜,～满天。The sky was studded with stars in the moonless night.

繁喧 fánxuān noisy; bustling:～的车马声 noise of heavy traffic

繁言 fányán *also* "烦言" fányán tedious talk

繁衍 fányǎn *also* "蕃衍" fányǎn 〈书面〉multiply; proliferate; procreate:自古以来,我们的祖先就在这块土地上～生息。From time immemorial our forefathers have lived and procreated on this land. /树木靠种子～。Trees propagate themselves by seeds.

繁育 fányù breed; raise:～纯种马 raise thoroughbred (*or* purebred) horses /～水稻新品种 breed a new strain of rice /～良种蚕 cultivate fine breeds of silkworms

繁杂 fánzá *also* "烦杂" fánzá many and diverse; various; miscellaneous:～的家务活 miscellaneous household chores /从～的事务中解脱出来 relieve sb. from all sorts of daily chores

繁征博引 fánzhēng-bóyǐn quote from many sources; quote extensively

繁殖 fánzhí 〈生物〉breed; reproduce; procreate; propagate:～鱼苗 breed fry /自我～ self-reproduction; autosynthesis /近亲～ close breeding; inbreeding /同种～ breed in and in /异种～ breed out and out /那些热带花卉只适合在暖和的气温中生长～。Those tropical plants will grow and propagate only in warm temperature.

繁殖场 fánzhíchǎng breeding ground

繁殖力 fánzhílì reproductive capacity; fecundity; fertility

繁殖率 fánzhílǜ rate of reproduction; breeding rate; breeding potential

繁重 fánzhòng heavy; strenuous; toilsome; onerous:～的体力劳动

strenuous manual labour; toilsome labour /～的负担 onerous burden /～的工作 heavy work

蘩 fán 〈书面〉〈植物〉wormwood; artemisia

凡[1]**(凢)** fán ❶ commonplace; ordinary: 自命不～ consider oneself out of the ordinary /成就非～ achieve extraordinary successes; make remarkable achievements /超～绝俗 rise above the general run of people /～家子弟 children of a humble family ❷ this mortal world; the earth: 思～ (of an immortal) long for this mortal world

凡[2]**(凢)** fán ❶ all; every; any: ～我国公民，均有受教育的权利和义务。In our country, every citizen has the right and duty to receive an education. /～违章建筑，一律限期拆除。All houses built in violation of the regulations shall be pulled down (*or* demolished) within the specified time. ❷〈书面〉altogether; in all; all inclusive: 全书～十二章，五十万字。The work has twelve chapters, 500,000 words in all. ❸〈书面〉outline; gist: 大～ generally; in most cases /发～ introduction (to a subject or a book)

凡[3]**(凢)** fán 〈音乐〉note of the scale in *gongchepu* (工尺谱), corresponding to 4 in numbered musical notation

凡百 fánbǎi 〈方言〉all; every; everything: 我和他很知己，～事情都向他说。I take him as my bosom friend and confide everything to him.

凡尘 fánchén this world; this mortal life: 脱离～ stay away from wordly affairs; become an immortal

凡尔 fán'ěr valve

凡尔丁 fán'ěrdīng 〈纺织〉(transliteration) valetin

凡尔赛 Fán'ěrsài Versailles: ～和平会议 Versailles Peace Conference (1919) /～和约 Treaty of Versailles (1919) /～宫 Palace of Versailles; Chateau de Versailles /～体系 Versailles System

凡夫 fánfū ordinary person: 我等～，不堪当此重任。We are only ordinary people, incapable of shouldering such heavy responsibilities.

凡夫俗子 fánfū-súzǐ ❶〈佛教〉layman ❷ ordinary people; common run of people: 内中的奥妙，不是我这个～能搞明白的。An ordinary person like me can't expect to see what's behind the facade.

凡·高 Fán Gāo Vincent van Gogh (1853-1890), Dutch post-impressionist painter

凡间 fánjiān mortal world

凡近 fánjìn 〈书面〉wanting in ability and shallow in knowledge

凡立丁呢 fánlìdīngní *also* "凡尔丁"〈纺织〉valetin

凡立水 fánlìshuǐ *also* "清漆" qīngqī 〈方言〉varnish

凡例 fánlì notes on or guide to the use of a reference book, etc.: 使用工具书之前最好先看看该书的～。Before consulting a reference book, one should read the guide to its use first.

凡木有本，是水有源 fán mù yǒu běn, shì shuǐ yǒu yuán 〈俗语〉every tree has its roots, and every river has its source

凡人 fánrén ❶〈书面〉ordinary person; common people: ～小事 ordinary people and trifling matters ❷ mortal (man)

凡士林 fánshìlín *also* "矿脂" kuàngzhī vaseline; petrolatum

凡世 fánshì mortal world

凡事 fánshì everything: ～小心不为过。There is nothing wrong in being careful in whatever you do. *or* It always pays to be prudent. /～有因。Every event has its cause. /～有兆。Coming events cast their shadows before. /～当留余地。In what one does, one must always leave some leeway.

凡事开头难 fánshì kāitóu nán 〈俗语〉beginning is always difficult; it's the first step that costs

凡事预则立，不预则废 fánshì yù zé lì, bù yù zé fèi preparedness ensures success, and unpreparedness spells failure

凡是 fánshì ❶ every; any; all: ～愿意参加的人都将受到邀请。Everyone who wishes to attend will be invited. /～违反本规定者将予以罚款。Whoever breaks this regulation is subject to a fine. /～错误的思想都应该受到批评。All erroneous ideas must be criticized. ❷〈政治〉whatever (has been said and done by Mao Zedong is right): 两个"～" two whatever's (i.e. what has been said by Mao Zedong is right, and whatever has been stipulated by him must not be changed) /～派 whateverists (those who insist on the "two whatever's")

凡俗 fánsú ordinary; common: 不同～ out of the ordinary; out of the common run

凡响 fánxiǎng common or ordinary music: 非同～ quite extraordinary

凡心 fánxīn mortal desires; worldly desires: 他虽已出家，却依然为～所困。Though he has become a monk, he is still tormented by desires of the flesh.

凡庸 fányōng (of a person) ordinary; commonplace: ～之才 person of mediocre abilities; common herd

矾(礬) fán 〈化学〉vitriol: 明～ alum /胆～ blue vitriol; chalcanthite /绿～ green vitriol; copperas

矾石 fánshí 〈矿业〉aluminite

矾土 fántǔ 〈矿业〉alumina

矾土肺 fántǔfèi *also* "矾沉着病" atuminosis

矾土水泥 fántǔ shuǐní alumina cement

钒 fán 〈化学〉vanadium (V): ～钢 vanadium steel /～铁 ferro-vanadium /～土 vanadine

钒铝合金 fánlǚ héjīn 〈冶金〉vanalium

钒酸 fánsuān 〈化学〉vanadic acid: ～盐 vanadate (e.g. 钒酸铁 ferric vanadate)

钒中毒 fánzhòngdú vanadiumism

fǎn

反 fǎn ❶ in an opposite direction; reverse; inverse; inside out: 袜子穿～了 wear one's socks inside out; wear one's socks the wrong side out /正～两穿的羽绒服 reversible down jacket /相～相成 (of two things) be both opposite and complementary to each other /适得其～。The result is just the opposite. ❷ turn over; turn; reverse: 易如～掌 as easy as turning one's palm over; easy as pie /～守为攻 turn from the defensive to the offensive; turn the tables on the attackers /一～常态 depart from one's normal behaviour; not be one's usual self /～其道而行之 act in a diametrically opposite way; do exactly the opposite /物极必～。Things turn into their opposites when they reach the extreme. ❸ return; counter: *see* "～问"; "～光" ❹ oppose; combat; be against: ～倒退 oppose retrogression /～侵略 resist aggression /～腐化 combat corruption /～法西斯 fight against fascism /～窃听 debug /～人民 antipopular /～政变 counter-coup ❺ revolt; rebel: 造～ rise in rebellion; rebel /策～ incite defection /谋～ conspire against the state; plot a rebellion /官逼民～。Oppressive government drives the people to revolt. ❻ counterrevolutionaries; reactionaries: 肃～ elimination of counterrevolutionaries ❼ analogize; reason by analogy: 举一～三 draw inferences about other cases from one instance ❽ on the contrary; instead: 听他一说，大伙～倒大笑起来。At his words, everybody burst into a fit of laughter instead. /他吃了半年补品，身体～不如从前。He has taken tonic for half a year, only to find himself in worse health. ❾ *see* "反切" fǎnqiē

反把 fǎnbǎ *also* "翻把" fānbǎ 〈方言〉(of one's defeated opponent, etc.) gain the upper hand again

反霸 fǎnbà ❶ oppose hegemonism (of any superpower): ～斗争 struggle against hegemonism ❷ struggle against local despots (during the land reform)

反败为胜 fǎnbài-wéishèng turn defeat into victory; turn the tables (on sb.); turn the tide: 客队在终场前一分钟内连进两球，～。The visiting team turned the tables towards the end of the game by scoring two goals successively.

反绑 fǎnbǎng with one's hands tied behind one's back: 将土匪～ tie the bandit's hands behind his back

反比 fǎnbǐ ❶ inverse relation ❷〈数学〉inverse ratio or proportion: 成～ be in inverse proportion; be inversely proportional

反比例 fǎnbǐlì 〈数学〉inverse proportion or ratio

反病毒软件 fǎnbìngdú ruǎnjiàn 〈计算机〉anti-virus (software)

反驳 fǎnbó refute; retort; rebut: ～无理的攻击 rebut an unjustified accusation /被～得体无完肤 be refuted down to the last point; be thoroughly repudiated; be torn to shreds /在辩论会上，她机智有力的～赢得了阵阵掌声。During the debate, she won repeated applause for her witty and sharp retorts.

F

反补贴税 fǎnbǔtiēshuì countervailing duty; anti-subsidy duty

反哺 fǎnbǔ feed the mother bird in return when fully grown — repay one's parents for their upbringing when they get old: ～之情 loving kindness to one's parents; filial piety

反侧 fǎncè 〈书面〉❶ toss and turn; toss from side to side: 辗转～ toss about in bed; toss and turn ❷ be disobedient; be insubordinate: ～之民 rebellious people ❸ changeable; capricious: 天命～。The will of God is capricious.

反差 fǎnchā contrast: ～度〈摄影〉contrast grade / 强烈～ striking contrast / 对于这件事是否能办成，她的看法正好与丈夫的悲观情绪形成明显～。In contrast to (*or* with) her husband's pessimism, she believed they would succeed in the undertaking.

反常 fǎncháng unusual; abnormal; perverse; strange: ～的行为 abnormal behaviour / 今年冬天冷得～。It is unusually cold this winter. / 最近他的态度有点～。His attitude is a bit strange these days.

反超子 fǎnchāozǐ 〈物理〉antihyperon

反潮流 fǎncháoliú go against the tide; swim against the stream: ～而动 act against the prevailing mood (*or* current)

反衬 fǎnchèn set off by contrast; serve as a foil to: 画面上寥寥几笔黑色鲜明地～了白茫茫的雪原。On the picture the few strokes of black set off pretty well the white dim expanse of snow. / 绿色的丝绒～出红宝石的光泽。Green velvet foiled the ruby's brilliance.

反冲 fǎnchōng 〈物理〉recoil; kick

反冲电子 fǎnchōng diànzǐ recoil electrons

反冲核 fǎnchōnghé recoil nucleus

反冲力 fǎnchōnglì *also* "坐力" zuòlì; "后坐力" hòuzuòlì recoil

反冲效应 fǎnchōng xiàoyìng recoil effect

反刍 fǎnchú ❶ *also* "倒嚼" dǎojiào ruminate; chew the cud ❷ mull over (past events): 他～着上月的那段经历。He is mulling over what he experienced last month.

反刍动物 fǎnchú dòngwù ruminant

反刍胃 fǎnchúwèi ruminant stomach

反串 fǎnchuàn (of Chinese opera actors or actresses) not play one's customary role; act a role other than one's own; play a reversed role: 这位花旦在戏中～老生。The *huadan* (a female role of the coquettish type) singer acted *laosheng* (the part of an older man) in the opera.

反唇相讥 fǎnchún-xiāngjī *also* "反唇相稽" answer back sarcastically; reply with a sarcastic rebuttal: 他对别人善意的批评置若罔闻，甚至～。He not only turned a deaf ear to well-intentioned criticism but answered back with withering sarcasm.

反磁性 fǎncíxìng 〈物理〉diamagnetism: ～材料 anti-magnetic material

反担保 fǎndānbǎo 〈经济〉counter guarantee; counter letter of undertaking

反弹道导弹 fǎndàndào dǎodàn anti-ballistic missile (ABM): ～发射器 ABM launcher

反党 fǎndǎng anti-Party; opposed to the Chinese Communist Party: ～分子 elements opposed to the Party / ～集团 anti-Party clique (*or* group)

反氘 fǎndāo antideuterium: ～核 antideuteron

反倒 fǎndào on the contrary; quite the reverse; instead: 困难没有使我们泄气，～增强了我们的决心。Instead of dampening our spirits, difficulties only strengthen our resolve to go ahead. / 虽然好心，事情～弄糟了。For all our goodwill, the whole thing has fallen through.

反帝 fǎndì (short for 反对帝国主义) be anti-imperialist; oppose imperialism: ～反封建的资产阶级民主革命 bourgeois democratic revolution against imperialism and feudalism

反颠覆 fǎn diānfù counter-subversion: 颠覆与～的斗争 struggle between subversion and counter-subversion / ～斗争 struggle against subversion; anti-subversion struggle

反电子 fǎndiànzǐ 〈物理〉anti-electron

反调 fǎndiào different tune; different view: 唱～ sing a different tune; express opposite views

反动 fǎndòng ❶ reactionary: ～统治 reactionary rule / ～势力 forces of reaction; reactionary forces / ～卖国政府 reactionary traitorous government / ～透顶 reactionary to the extreme; ultra-reactionary ❷ reaction: 从历史来看，党八股是对五四运动的一种～。In historical perspective, stereotyped Party writing was a reaction to the May 4th Movement. / 他弃家出走，是对社会和家庭压力的～。He left home in order to counteract the pressure of the society and his family.

反动分子 fǎndòngfènzǐ reactionary element; reactionary

反动会道门 fǎndòng huìdàomén reactionary secret societies

反动派 fǎndòngpài reactionaries; reactionary group or clique

反对 fǎnduì oppose; be against; fight; combat: ～大国霸权主义 oppose big-power hegemonism / ～官僚主义 combat bureaucratism / ～不正之风 battle against unhealthy trends or practices / ～种族歧视 fight racial discrimination / 持～意见 hold opposite opinions / 有没有～意见? Are there any objections? / 我～你这样做。I object to your doing that. / 我们坚决～任何形式的国际恐怖主义。We are firmly against international terrorism of any kind.

反对党 fǎnduìdǎng opposition party; the opposition: ～领袖 leader of the opposition / 我国的民主党派不是～，而是参政党。Our country's democratic parties are not the opposition; rather, they are parties participating in the administration of state affairs.

反对派 fǎnduìpài opposition faction

反对票 fǎnduìpiào dissenting vote; negative vote: 结果是投～的获胜。The nays won when the vote was taken.

反而 fǎn'ér on the contrary; instead: 遭到挫折之后，他并没有失去信心，～工作更努力了。He didn't lose heart after the setbacks. On the contrary, he worked even harder than before. / 失败～使我们的斗争决心更坚定了。The failure only strengthened our determination to carry on the struggle.

反方 fǎnfāng (as of a debate) con side: 辩论中～占了上风。In the debate the con side got the upper hand.

反封建 fǎn fēngjiàn oppose feudalism; be anti-feudal: 反帝、～的运动 anti-imperialist, anti-feudal movement

反腐 fǎnfǔ combat corruption: ～倡廉 combat corruption and build a clean government

反复 fǎnfù ❶ repeatedly; again and again; over and over again: ～强调 stress over and over again / ～较量 repeated trials of strength / ～琢磨 turn sth. over in one's mind again and again; ponder on; mull over / ～辩论 argue back and forth / 他一再～说他很忙。He repeated several times that he was busy. ❷ chop and change; back out; go back on one's word: 我讲话是算数的，决不～。I mean what I say and shall never retract my words. ❸ reversal; setback; relapse: 有很多～和曲折 full of setbacks and twists and turns / 病情又有～。The patient has suffered another relapse. / 形势出现～。There has been a reversal in the situation.

反复记号 fǎnfù jìhào 〈音乐〉repeat

反复无常 fǎnfù-wúcháng be changeable; be fickle; be capricious; play fast and loose: 天气～ fickle weather / ～的人 capricious person; inconsistant sort of fellow / ～的情绪 in a mercurial mood

反感 fǎngǎn be disgusted with; be averse to; loathe; dislike: 我对他的话很～。I'm disgusted with his remarks. / 我对阿谀奉承极为～。Flattery is repugnant to me. / 她对吸烟颇为～。She has an aversion to smoking.

反戈 fǎngē turn one's weapon around: 阵前～ turn against one's ownside in battle

反戈一击 fǎngē-yījī turn one's weapon around and strike — turn against one's own side; change sides and turn back to hit: 你必须～，立功赎罪。You must hit hard at your own camp and do good deeds to atone for your crimes.

反革命 fǎngémìng ❶ counterrevolutionary: ～政变 counterrevolutionary *coup d'état* / ～组织 counterrevolutionary organization ❷ counterrevolutionaries: 镇压～ crack down on counterrevolutionaries

反攻 fǎngōng counteroffensive; counterattack: 发动～ launch a counterattack / 大举～ mount a large-scale counteroffensive / 我们没料到敌人这么快就～过来。We didn't expect the enemy to strike back so quickly.

反攻倒算 fǎngōng-dàosuàn (as of members of an overthrown class) counterattack to settle old scores; stage a vengeful or vindictive counterattack; retaliate: 决不允许敌人～ never allow the enemy to stage a comeback and retaliate

反躬自问 fǎngōng-zìwèn *also* "抚躬自问" fǔgōng-zìwèn examine oneself; examine one's conscience: 我不禁～，自己到底错在哪儿。I couldn't help searching my heart (*or* soul), trying to find out where I had been wrong.

反骨 fǎngǔ (of a person) with a treacherous nature: ～毕露 reveal one's renegade character / 长一身～ person who is traitorous by nature

反顾 fǎngù 〈书面〉look back: 义无～ be duty-bound not to turn back; go ahead without hesitation

反卦 fǎnguà *also* "变卦" biànguà 〈方言〉 change one's mind; go back on one's word; break an agreement: 你自己说的话, 怎么就～了? How could you go back on your word?

反光 fǎnguāng ❶ reflect light: 镜子在阳光下～, 耀人眼目。The mirror reflects the dazzling light in the sunshine. ❷ reflection of light: ～把我弄得头昏眼花。The reflection of light made me feel dizzy.

反光灯 fǎnguāngdēng reflector lamp

反光镜 fǎnguāngjìng reflector

反过来 fǎnguolai ❶ conversely; the other way round: 我～再数一遍。I'll count it again in reverse order. /这话可不能～说。The converse of this statement may not hold water. ❷ in reverse order; vice versa: 理论来源于实践, ～又指导实践。Theory comes from practice and in turn guides practice. /男青年可以和女青年约会, ～女青年也可以和男青年约会。Boys can date girls, and vice versa.

反氦 fǎnhài antihelium

反函数 fǎnhánshù 〈数学〉 inverse function: $X=\sqrt[3]{Y}$是 $Y=X^3$的～。$X=\sqrt[3]{Y}$ is the inverse function of $Y=X^3$.

反汗 fǎnhàn 〈书面〉 go back on one's word or promise

反和平演变 fǎn hépíng yǎnbiàn counter-"peaceful evolution" (the struggle against external attempts to subvert socialism by peaceful means): "和平演变"与～的斗争是长期的。The struggle between "peaceful evolution" and counter-"peaceful evolution" will last a long time.

反核子 fǎnhézǐ 〈物理〉 anti-nucleon

反华 fǎn-Huá ❶ persecute overseas Chinese; anti-Chinese ❷ oppose the People's Republic of China in the international arena; anti-China

反话 fǎnhuà irony: 他没有发觉她是在说～。He did not realize that she was speaking ironically.

反悔 fǎnhuǐ go back on one's word; go back on one's promise: 我说过的话, 决不～。I will never go back on my word. /他本来答应帮忙, 后来又～了。He did promise to help but then backed out.

反火箭导弹 fǎnhuǒjiàn dǎodàn 〈军事〉 antirocket missile

反击 fǎnjī strike or hit back; beat back; counterattack: 进行自卫～ launch a counterattack in self-defence /对敌人的挑衅给予有力的～ deal a vigorous counterblow at the enemy's provocation

反季节 fǎnjìjié 〈农业〉 out of season: ～蔬菜 vegetables grown out of season; out-of-season vegetables

反剪 fǎnjiǎn ❶ hold one's hands behind one's back: 他～着双手, 大模大样走了进来。He swaggered in, holding his hands behind his back. ❷ have one's hands tied behind one's back: 罪犯被～双手, 带走了。The convict was taken away with his hands tied behind his back.

反间 fǎnjiàn sow distrust or dissension among one's enemies; sow discord within the enemy camp: 他们略施小计, 成功地～了敌人。They succeeded in setting the enemies at odds by a little trick. *or* With a minor ruse, they set the enemies at each other.

反间谍 fǎn jiàndié *also* "反情报" counterespionage; counter-intelligence; antiespionage: ～机构 antiespionage agency; counter-espionage institution

反间计 fǎnjiànjì stratagem of sowing distrust or discord among one's enemies: 要提防敌人的～。We must guard against the enemy plot of driving a wedge between us.

反建议 fǎnjiànyì counterproposal: 他们提出了一个～。They put forward a counterproposal.

反骄破满 fǎnjiāo-pòmǎn oppose arrogance and shatter complacency; combat haughtiness and conceit

反接 fǎnjiē 〈书面〉 have one's hands tied behind one's back

反诘 fǎnjié ask in retort; counter with a question

反经行权 fǎnjīng-xíngquán adopt a flexible approach without following old rules; accommodate oneself to circumstances: 在这种非常情况下, 我们不能不～了。We have to adapt ourselves to such special circumstances.

反抗 fǎnkàng revolt; rebel; resist: ～侵略 resist invasion or aggression /～专制统治 revolt against tyranny (*or* despotic rule) /～精神 spirit of revolt; rebellious spirit /消极～ passive resistance /如果敌人继续～, 就把他们消灭干净。If the enemy should continue to hold out against us, we'll wipe them out completely.

反科学 fǎnkēxué anti-science; opposition to science, scientific research or the scientific method: 坚决反对任何～的行为。Any anti-scientific approach should be vigorously opposed.

反客为主 fǎnkèwéizhǔ turn from a guest to a host — gain the initiative (from a passive position); turn the tables (on an early comer or established person); take the initiative into one's own hands

反空降 fǎn kōngjiàng 〈军事〉 anti-airborne defence: ～部队 anti-airborne defence troops

反恐怖主义 fǎn kǒngbùzhǔyì anti-terrorism: ～活动 anti-terrorist activities

反控 fǎnkòng 〈法律〉 countercharge; recriminate

反口 fǎnkǒu go back on one's word or promise; back out: 话已说出, 不能～。Since you have already given your word, you can't go back on it.

反口相诘 fǎnkǒu-xiāngjié ask in retort; counter with a question

反夸克 fǎnkuākè 〈核物理〉 antiquark

反馈 fǎnkuì feedback: 正～ 〈电子〉〈医学〉 positive feedback /负～ negative feedback /我们欢迎来自读者的信息～。We welcome feedback from our readers.

反馈编码 fǎnkuì biānmǎ 〈电子〉 feedback encoding

反馈电路 fǎnkuì diànlù 〈电子〉 feedback circuit

反馈控制 fǎnkuì kòngzhì 〈电子〉 feedback control

反馈抑制 fǎnkuì yìzhì 〈电子〉 feedback inhibition

反雷达导弹 fǎnléidá dǎodàn 〈军事〉 antiradar missile; anti-radiation missile: 高速～ High-Speed Anti-Radiation Missile (HARM)

反雷达涂层 fǎnléidá túcéng 〈军事〉 antiradar coating

反离子 fǎnlízǐ 〈物理〉 contra-ion

反例 fǎnlì counterexample

反粒子 fǎnlìzǐ 〈物理〉 antiparticle: ～束 antiparticle beam

反乱 fǎnluàn social turmoil; turbulence; upheaval; disturbance

反面 fǎnmiàn ❶ reverse side; wrong side; back: 布料的～ wrong side of the cloth /硬币的正～ obverse and reverse sides of a coin; head and tail /在本页的～你将找到答案。On the reverse of this page, you will find the answer. ❷ opposite; contrary; negative side: 走向～ change (*or* turn) into one's opposite /吸取～教训 learn a lesson from negative (*or* bitter) experience; gain wisdom from hard knocks /～意见 adverse (*or* antithetical) opinion /起～作用 set a negative example ❸ other or reverse side of a state of affairs, a problem, etc.: 既看到事物的正面, 也看到事物的～。We must see the reverse as well as the obverse side of things.

反面教材 fǎnmiàn jiàocái negative example which may serve as a lesson; unpleasant experience which may serve as a warning.

反面教员 fǎnmiàn jiàoyuán teacher by negative example

反面人物 fǎnmiàn rénwù negative character; negative role; villain

反目 fǎnmù fall out (esp. between husband and wife): 夫妻～, 孩子遭罪。When husband and wife fall out, the children suffer.

反目成仇 fǎnmù-chéngchóu quarrel with each other (esp. among man and wife) and become enemies

反扒 fǎnpá crack down on pickpockets: ～能手 good hand at catching pickpockets

反派 fǎnpài villain (in drama, etc.); negative character: 扮演～人物 act the part of the villain /善演～ be good at playing a negative role

反叛 fǎnpàn betray; revolt; rebel; defect: ～投敌 defect to the enemy side /～朝廷 rebel against the imperial court

反叛 fǎnpan 〈口语〉 traitor; renegade; turncoat

反批评 fǎnpīpíng counter-criticism

反聘 fǎnpìn be employed or reposted after one's retirement

反扑 fǎnpū (of a beast of prey) pounce on sb. again after being beaten off; (of enemy forces) launch a counteroffensive (to retrieve lost ground): 老虎又一次向他～过来。The tiger came pouncing upon him once again. /敌人向我前沿阵地疯狂～。The enemy launched a fierce attack on our forward position.

反璞归真 fǎnpú-guīzhēn *see* "返璞归真" fǎnpú-guīzhēn

反其道而行之 fǎn qí dào ér xíng zhī do exactly the opposite of what the other side does; act in a diametrically opposite way

反气旋 fǎnqìxuán 〈气象〉 anticyclone

反潜 fǎnqián 〈军事〉 antisubmarine: ～防御 antisubmarine defence /～武器 antisubmarine weapon

反潜机 fǎnqiánjī antisubmarine plane; sub-hunter

反潜舰艇 fǎnqián jiàntǐng antisubmarine vessel

反潜战 fǎnqiánzhàn antisubmarine warfare (ASW)

反潜直升机 fǎnqián zhíshēngjī antisubmarine helicopter; antisub chopper

反切 fǎnqiē 〈语言〉traditional method of indicating the pronunciation of a Chinese character by using two other characters, the first having the same consonant as the given character and the second having the same vowel and tone (e.g. the pronunciation of 同 tóng is indicated as 徒红切, meaning a combination of the consonant t from 徒 tú and the compound vowel ong from 红 hóng)
反侵略 fǎn qīnlüè counter aggression; resist aggression:中国人民的抗日战争是一场正义的～战争。The anti-Japanese war waged by the Chinese people in 1937-1945 was a just war against aggression.
反氢 fǎnqīng 〈物理〉antihydrogen
反倾销 fǎn qīngxiāo anti-dumping:～税 anti-dumping duties /～法 anti-dumping law /～法案 anti-dumping code /～补贴 countervailing subsidy /～调查 anti-dumping investigation
反情报 fǎn qíngbào *see* "反间谍"
反求诸己 fǎnqiúzhūjǐ seek the cause in oneself (instead of in sb. else):出了问题应该～,不要推卸责任,委过于人。When trouble occurs, one should seek the cause in oneself rather than shirk responsibility and shift the blame onto others.
反三角函数 fǎnsānjiǎo hánshù 〈数学〉inverse trigonometric function
反射 fǎnshè ❶〈物理〉reflection:光～ reflection of light /声音～ reflection of sound /热～ reverberation of heat /镜子能～光线。Mirrors reflect light. ❷〈生理〉reflex:条件～ conditioned reflex /非条件～ unconditioned reflex /膝腱～ knee-jerk (reflex)
反射比 fǎnshèbǐ 〈物理〉reflectance
反射波 fǎnshèbō 〈物理〉back wave; reflected wave
反射测云器 fǎnshè cèyúnqì reflecting nephoscope
反射弧 fǎnshèhú 〈生理〉reflex arc
反射计 fǎnshèjì reflectometer
反射角 fǎnshèjiǎo 〈物理〉angle of reflection
反射镜 fǎnshèjìng reflector; mirror
反射炉 fǎnshèlú 〈冶金〉reverberatory furnace
反射率 fǎnshèlǜ *also* "反照率"〈物理〉albedo
反射望远镜 fǎnshè wàngyuǎnjìng reflecting telescope
反射线 fǎnshèxiàn 〈物理〉reflected ray
反身 fǎnshēn (of a person) turn round; face about:她～要走,小王急忙拦住。She turned round and was about to leave when Xiao Wang hurriedly stopped her.
反身代词 fǎnshēn dàicí 〈语言〉reflexive pronoun
反身动词 fǎnshēn dòngcí 〈语言〉reflexive verb
反诗 fǎnshī poem or verse with rebellious contents
反市场原理 fǎn shìchǎng yuánlǐ 〈经济〉anti-market principle
反是 fǎnshì on the contrary; quite the reverse; just the opposite
反噬 fǎnshì 〈书面〉trump up a countercharge against one's accuser; make a fake countercharge:他疯狂地～检举者。He frenziedly made a false countercharge against the accuser.
反手 fǎnshǒu ❶〈体育〉backhand:～抽球 backhand drive /～握拍 backhand grip ❷ turn one's hand over; have one's hand(s) behind one's back:～把门关上 pull the door to behind one ❸ be as easy as turning one's palm over; get sth. done easily:～可得 can be got easily
反衰退 fǎn shuāituì 〈经济〉anti-recession:～计划 anti-recession programme
反水 fǎnshuǐ 〈方言〉❶ turn one's coat; defect:他～后向敌人提供情报。He provided information to the enemy after his defection. ❷ go back on one's word; break a promise:你已经同意了,不兴～。You've already agreed and should not change your mind.
反水不收 fǎnshuǐ-bùshōu *also* "覆水难收" fùshuǐ-nánshōu spilt water can't be gathered up — what is done can't be undone; it's no use crying over spilt milk
反思 fǎnsī reflect; introspect:～过去 reflect upon one's past /这件事值得我们好好～。It gives us much food for thought (*or* reflection).
反诉 fǎnsù 〈法律〉countercharge; counterclaim:同本案有直接关系的～ counter-lawsuit filed by the defendant directly concerning the case /～案件 counter case /他对警方的指控提出～。He made a countercharge against the police's accusation.
反酸 fǎnsuān 〈医学〉sour regurgitation; acidic reflux
反锁 fǎnsuǒ be locked in or be locked out:门被人从外边～了。The door was locked from outside.
反弹 fǎntán rebound:球从墙壁上～回来。The ball rebounded from the wall. /股市猛烈～。The stock market saw a sharp rebound in price.
反坦克 fǎntǎnkè 〈军事〉antitank:～炮兵 antitank artillery
反坦克地雷 fǎntǎnkè dìléi antitank mine
反坦克火箭 fǎntǎnkè huǒjiàn antitank rocket
反坦克炮 fǎntǎnkèpào antitank gun
反特 fǎntè counterespionage:～影片 spy film; anti-espionage film
反提案 fǎntí'àn counter-proposal
反题 fǎntí 〈哲学〉antithesis
反铁电 fǎntiědiàn 〈物理〉antiferroelectric:～现象 antiferroelectricity
反通货膨胀 fǎn tōnghuò péngzhàng disinflation; anti-inflation:～措施 anti-inflation measures /～计划 anti-inflation programme /～刺激 counter inflationary impact
反推力 fǎntuīlì 〈物理〉reverse thrust
反托拉斯 fǎntuōlāsī anti-trust:～法 anti-trust legislation; anti-trust law
反危机 fǎn wēijī anti-crisis:～措施 anti-crisis measures
反围盘 fǎnwéipán 〈机械〉reverse repeater (used in steel rolling)
反卫星 fǎnwèixīng antisatellite
反卫星导弹 fǎnwèixīng dǎodàn antisatellite missile
反卫星武器 fǎnwèixīng wǔqì satellite active nullifier
反胃 fǎnwèi *also* "翻胃" fānwèi 〈医学〉regurgitation; gastric disorder causing nausea; feeling nauseated or queasy
反文化 fǎnwénhuà counter-culture; anticulture
反问 fǎnwèn ❶ ask (a question) in reply; ask in retort:她惊愕地望着我,～道:"是谁告诉你这些的?" She looked at me in great surprise and asked: "Who told you all this?" ❷〈语言〉rhetorical question
反污染 fǎn wūrǎn anti-pollution:～措施 anti-pollution measure
反诬 fǎnwū deny the charge and make a countercharge; countercharge:提防对方～ be on guard against the countercharge by the other side
反物质 fǎnwùzhì 〈物理〉anti-matter
反响 fǎnxiǎng repercussion; echo; reverberation:观众～热烈 hearty response from the audience /引起不同～ evoke conflicting responses /这件看来微不足道的事件却在很多人心中产生了巨大的～。This seemingly insignificant event had unexpectedly found an echo in the hearts of many people.
反向 fǎnxiàng opposite direction; reverse
反向铲 fǎnxiàngchǎn backhoe
反向电流 fǎnxiàng diànliú reverse current
反向器 fǎnxiàngqì 〈航空〉thrust reverser; reverser:引擎～故障 engine thrust reverser trouble /～失灵。The thrust reverser was inoperative.
反向卫星 fǎnxiàng wèixīng retrograde satellite
反效应 fǎnxiàoyìng countereffect
反效用 fǎnxiàoyòng 〈经济〉disutility
反斜面 fǎnxiémiàn 〈军事〉reverse slope; rear slope
反信风 fǎnxìnfēng 〈气象〉antitrades; countertrades
反星系 fǎnxīngxì 〈天文〉anti-galaxy
反省 fǎnxǐng introspection; retrospection; self-questioning; self-examination:～自己的言行 examine one's own words and deeds /停职～ be suspended from one's duties for self-examination /闭门～ shut oneself up and make an introspection /表示深刻的～之意 express one's deep remorse for sth.
反修 fǎnxiū oppose revisionism; be anti-revisionist
反宣传 fǎnxuānchuán ❶ counterpropaganda ❷ slander campaign
反压力 fǎnyālì 〈物理〉anti-vacuum; counterpressure; opposite pressure; reverse pressure
反咬 fǎnyǎo trump up a countercharge (against one's accuser, ect.):你还想～我? Are you trying to shift the blame onto me?
反咬一口 fǎnyǎo-yīkǒu retort with a countercharge; make a false countercharge:他自己错了不承认,还反咬我一口。Instead of admitting his own mistake, he turned on me with some slanderous accusation.
反义词 fǎnyìcí 〈语言〉antonym
反应 fǎnyìng react; respond:～迟钝 slow to react; slow in response /碱性～ alkaline reaction /酸性～ acid reaction /化学～ chemical reaction /阴性～ negative reaction /阳性～ positive reaction /过敏～〈医学〉allergic reaction /热核～ thermo-nuclear reaction /链式～ chain reaction /聚合～ fusion reaction /吸热～ endothermic reaction /发言引起代表们的不同～。The speech drew a mixed response from the delegates. /～不一。Reactions vary. /群众对我们所作的努力

F

～良好。People responded favourably to our efforts. /他对这个药物的～很强烈。He had a strong reaction to the drug. /我怀孕时什么～也没有。I didn't experience any morning sickness in my pregnancy.
反应本领 fǎnyìng běnlǐng 〈物理〉reaction capacity
反应堆 fǎnyìngduī 〈物理〉reactor: 核～ nuclear reactor /高温～ high-temperature reactor /增殖～ breeder reactor /轻水慢化～ light-water-moderated reactor /热中子～ thermal neutron reactor /石墨减速～ graphite-moderated reactor /浓缩铀～ enriched uranium reactor /重水～ heavy-water reactor /沸水～ boiling water reactor
反应塔 fǎnyìngtǎ reaction tower
反应物 fǎnyìngwù reactant
反应性能 fǎnyìng xìngnéng 〈物理〉reactive worth
反应学 fǎnyìngxué reactology
反映 fǎnyìng ❶ reflect; mirror; manifest; show: 时代的～ mirror the times /～人民的愿望 give expression to the wishes of the people /民族感情的真实～ genuine manifestation of the feelings of the nation /展览会～了我们在发展旅游业方面所取得的巨大成就。The exhibition shows the tremendous achievements in the development of tourism. /犯罪率高是社会不稳定的～。A high crime rate is a reflection of an unstable society. /这个决定～了广大市民的愿望。This decision conveys the wishes of the city residents. ❷ report; make known: 向上级～情况 report to the higher authorities /向政府有关部门～群众的意见 transmit the opinions at the grassroots to the government departments concerned /报纸向读者～世界最新动态。Newspapers inform their readers of the latest developments in the world. /我会如实向你～。I will let you know the truth. ❸〈生理〉reflect: 人脑能以感觉、知觉和思维等～现实。Human brains can reflect reality through sensation, perception and thinking.
反映论 fǎnyìnglùn 〈哲学〉theory of reflection: 唯物论的～ materialist theory of reflection
反犹太分子 fǎnyóutàifènzǐ anti-Semite
反犹太主义 fǎnyóutàizhǔyì anti-Semitism
反右派斗争 fǎn yòupài dòuzhēng Anti-Rightist Campaign (1957-1958)
反余切 fǎnyúqiē 〈数学〉anticotangent
反余弦 fǎnyúxián 〈数学〉anticosine
反宇宙 fǎnyǔzhòu 〈物理〉anti-universe
反语 fǎnyǔ 〈语言〉irony
反原子 fǎnyuánzǐ 〈物理〉anti-atom (an atom of antimatter)
反战 fǎnzhàn anti-war: ～运动 anti-war movement /～力量 forces against war
反战术弹道导弹 fǎnzhànshù dàndào dǎodàn 〈军事〉anti-tactical ballistic missile (ATBM)
反掌 fǎnzhǎng turn over one's palm: ～一击 turn over one's palm and hit (at sb.) /易如～ as easy as turning one's palm over
反照 fǎnzhào *also* "返照" fǎnzhào reflection of light; glow: 夕阳～ evening glow; sunset glow /～着满天星斗的湖面 lake which reflects a starry sky /在数千只彩灯的～下，整幢大楼光彩夺目，十分壮观。Under the glow of thousands of coloured electric lamps the building makes a brilliant and spectacular picture.
反照镜 fǎnzhàojìng rearview mirror
反照率 fǎnzhàolǜ *see* "反射率"
反侦察 fǎn zhēnchá 〈军事〉anti-reconnaissance: 雷达～ radar anti-reconnaissance /通信～ communication anti-reconnaissance
反正 fǎnzhèng ❶ restore things to order; put things on the right track: 拨乱～ bring order out of chaos ❷ come over from the enemy's side; stage an uprising
反正 fǎnzheng 〈副词〉❶ *used to indicate the same result despite different circumstances*: 不管怎么样，～我不准备干。In any case I am not going (*or* prepared) to do it. /明天可能下雨，但不管怎样，～我们要回家。It may rain tomorrow, but we are going home anyway. /去不去～都一样。It makes no difference whether you go or not. ❷ *used to convey certainty or resolution*: 你别着急，～不是什么要紧的事。There is no need to worry, as it is nothing important. /～我不信。I don't believe it anyhow. /～你已经知道，我也没有必要再瞒着。Since you know it already, I won't hide anything from you.
反正切 fǎnzhèngqiē 〈数学〉antitangent
反正弦 fǎnzhèngxián 〈数学〉arcsine; anti-cine
反证 fǎnzhèng disproof; counterevidence: 辩护律师为被告提出了有力的～。The defence counsel produced convincing counterevidence for the defendant.
反证法 fǎnzhèngfǎ reduction to absurdity; *reductio ad absurdum*
反之 fǎnzhī conversely; on the other hand; otherwise; whereas: ～亦然 vice versa /只有坚持改革开放，才能实现四化。～，四化就难以实现。Only by persisting in the policy of reform and opening-up can we succeed in our modernization drive, otherwise we'll fail.
反殖 fǎnzhí (short for 反对殖民主义) oppose colonialism; be anti-colonialist
反治 fǎnzhì 〈中医〉treat a patient by reverse process, e.g. administering medicine of a hot nature to cure a pseudofebrile disease
反质子 fǎnzhìzǐ 〈物理〉antiproton
反中子 fǎnzhōngzǐ 〈物理〉anti-neutron
反种族主义 fǎnzhǒngzúzhǔyì antiracism; antiracist
反周期行动 fǎnzhōuqī xíngdòng 〈经济〉countercyclical action
反周期政策 fǎnzhōuqī zhèngcè 〈经济〉anti-cyclical policy
反转 fǎnzhuǎn reverse turn; reverse
反转来 fǎnzhuǎnlái ❶ conversely; the other way round ❷ in reverse order; vice versa
反转片 fǎnzhuǎnpiàn 〈摄影〉reversal film
反嘴 fǎnzuǐ 〈方言〉❶ answer or talk back; retort ❷ go back on one's word or promise: 说话算数，不许～。You must keep your promise and never go back on it.
反坐 fǎnzuò 〈旧语〉sentence an accuser to the punishment facing the person he falsely accused
反作用 fǎnzuòyòng counteraction; reaction: 上层建筑与经济基础的作用与～ action and reaction between the superstructure and the economic base /不要起～。Don't set a bad example. /如果由你去替他说话，只能起～。It would be counterproductive if you go and speak on his behalf.
反作用力 fǎnzuòyònglì 〈物理〉reacting force

返

fǎn return; come or go back: 重～ return /遣～ repatriate /往～ journey to and fro /流连忘～ linger on with no thought of leaving /迷途知～ realize one's errors and mend one's ways /～其本真 return to one's original nature
返场 fǎnchǎng (of a performer) give an encore: 他应听众的要求在～时演奏了肖邦的一支小夜曲。He played a Chopin nocturne for his encore at the request of his audience.
返潮 fǎncháo get damp; get moist: 连日下雨，屋里～。A continuous rain for days on end made the house damp.
返程 fǎnchéng return journey; on one's way back
返防 fǎnfáng 〈军事〉return to station: 演习结束后，部队立即～。The troops immediately returned to their barracks when the military exercises were over.
返工 fǎngōng do poorly done work over again; redo one's job: 这件上衣需要～。This jacket needs to be remade. /这段公路正在～。This section of the road is being built all over again.
返归 fǎnguī go back; return: 艺术市场出现向高雅艺术～的势头。The art market has shown a tendency to return to highbrow art.
返航 fǎnháng return to base or port; be on the homeward journey: 飞机在～途中。The plane is on the homebound flight. /远洋船队顺利～。The oceangoing fleet returned to port safely.
返还 fǎnhuán return; give or send back; restore: ～公物 return public property /～定金 give back down payment
返回 fǎnhuí return; come or go back: ～家园 return to one's homeland /人造卫星～地面 return of a satellite to the earth's surface /他下周将结束假期～学校。He will go back to school from his vacation next week.
返回式卫星 fǎnhuíshì wèixīng retrievable or recoverable satellite
返魂 fǎnhún revive after being pronounced dead; (of the soul) return to the body; return from the grave
返碱 fǎnjiǎn 〈农业〉accumulation of salt in the surface soil
返老还童 fǎnlǎo-huántóng regain one's youthful vigour; feel rejuvenated in one's old age
返里 fǎnlǐ 〈书面〉return to one's hometown or birthplace
返料 fǎnliào 〈冶金〉revert; return (product): ～皮带 return conveyer
返聘 fǎnpìn *also* "反聘" fǎnpìn be employed or reposted after one's retirement
返璞归真 fǎnpú-guīzhēn *also* "归真返璞" recover one's original purity and simplicity; go back to nature
返青 fǎnqīng 〈农业〉(of winter crops or transplanted seedlings) turn green: 冬小麦～了。The winter wheat has turned green.

返任 fǎnrèn return to one's post：大使回国述职后～。The ambassador has returned to his post after going home for consultations.
返润 fǎnrùn (of soil) become moist or damp
返俗 fǎnsú (of Buddhist monks and nuns or Taoist priests) return to secular life
返销 fǎnxiāo resell to the place of production：吃～粮 live on "resold grain" (state-purchased grain sold back to a grain-producing area in case of natural disaster, etc.)/国家每年将一部分征购的粮食～给欠收的农民。Every year the state sells part of its purchased grain back to the farmers suffering from a shortfall in grain output. /制成品大量～发展中国家。Manufactured goods are sold back to developing countries in great quantities.
返校 fǎnxiào (of students) return to school：今天是暑假的最后一天，明天就～了。Today is the last day of summer vacation, and tomorrow we will all go back to school.
返修 fǎnxiū refix or repair again (at the previous repair shop) sth. poorly fixed：这几台机器需要～。These machines need to be repaired again.
返盐 fǎnyán *see* "返碱"
返照 fǎnzhào *also* "反照" fǎnzhào reflection of light; glow
返祖现象 fǎnzǔ xiànxiàng 〈生理〉atavism; reversion：全身长毛是一种典型的～。A person with hairy skin all over is a typical case of atavism.

fàn

泛(汎、⑤氾) fàn ❶〈书面〉float：～萍浮梗 floating duckweed and plant stems ❷ emerge; turn; spread out; send forth：东方地平线上开始～白。Dawn is beginning to break over the eastern horizon. /树叶～黄了。The leaves are turning yellow. /小姑娘的脸蛋儿白里～红。The little girl has a fair and glowing face. /兰花～出淡淡的香味儿。The orchild sends forth delicate fragrance. /晨光下，湖面～着粼粼波光。The ripples of the lake danced and glistened in the dawn light. ❸ extensive; general; nonspecific：双方就共同关心的问题进行了广～的交谈。Both sides (*or* The two parties) had wide-ranging talks on matters of common concern. ❹ superficial; shallow：浮～ superficial and full of generalities ❺ flood; inundate：黄～区 areas formerly flooded by the Yellow River ❻ pan-：阿扎尼亚～非主义者大会 Pan-Africanist Congress of Azania (PAC)
泛常 fàncháng general; ordinary; not deepgoing：视为～ regard as ordinary
泛称 fànchēng general term：动物是一切有感觉、能行动、并以有机物为食粮之生物的～。Animal is a general term for any living thing that feels, moves and has organic substance as its food.
泛代数 fàndàishù 〈数学〉universal algebra：～曲线 pan-algebraic curve
泛德意志 Fàn-Déyìzhì Pan-German：～主义 Pan-Germanism
泛读 fàndú extensive reading：～课文 texts for extensive reading
泛恶 fàn'ě 〈中医〉nausea
泛泛 fànfàn ❶ general; not deepgoing：他～地敷衍了几句。He made a few casual remarks. ❷ common; ordinary：～之辈 mediocre person; mediocrity
泛泛而谈 fànfàn'értán speak in vague terms; talk in generalities; merely touch on a subject
泛泛之交 fànfànzhījiāo nodding acquaintance; casual acquaintance：我和他只是～。I am merely on speaking terms with him.
泛灌 fànguàn 〈农业〉broad irrigation
泛光灯 fànguāngdēng floodlight
泛函分析 fànhán fēnxi 〈数学〉functional analysis
泛碱 fànjiǎn *also* "返碱" fǎnjiǎn 〈农业〉accumulation of salt in the surface soil
泛览 fànlǎn read extensively; browse：～群书 be well-read /～史书 read a lot of history books
泛滥 fànlàn ❶ be in flood; overflow; overspill; inundate：尼罗河一年一次的～ annual overflow of the Nile ❷ spread unchecked：不能让黄色作品任意～。We must not allow pornography to spread unchecked. /外国货在该国～。There is an overflow of foreign goods in the country. *or* The country was flooded with foreign goods.
泛滥成灾 fànlàn-chéngzāi disaster caused by flooding waters; deluge; run rampant; run wild：洪水～ be seriously inundated with flood /每至年底，各类报表～。At the end of each year we are plagued with a flood of reports and statistical forms.
泛论 fànlùn have a general discussion (on sth.)：～哲理 talk generally on philosophy
泛逻辑主义 fànluójìzhǔyì 〈哲学〉panlogism
泛美 Fàn-Měi Pan-American; inter-American：～会议 Pan-American conference /～世界航空公司 Pan-American World Airways, Inc. (Pan Am) /～运动会 Pan-American Games /～联盟成立纪念日 Pan-American Day (April 14)
泛美主义 Fàn-Měizhǔyì Pan-Americanism
泛神论 fànshénlùn 〈哲学〉pantheism：～者 pantheist
泛生论 fànshēnglùn 〈生物〉pan-genesis
泛水 fànshuǐ 〈建筑〉flashing
泛斯拉夫主义 Fàn-Sīlāfūzhǔyì Pan-Slavism
泛酸 fànsuān 〈化学〉pantothenic acid
泛心论 fànxīnlùn 〈哲学〉panpsychism
泛漾 fànyàng 〈书面〉❶ float; drift：小船随波～。The boat was drifting with the tide. ❷ appear; unfold before one's eye; emerge：一种天真活泼的神情～在她脸上。A lively and innocent look appeared on her face.
泛溢 fànyì ❶ overflow; flood：江水～。The river was in flood. ❷ send forth; diffuse：花儿～着芳香。The flowers send forth fragrance. ❸ brim with; be permeated with：～着少女的欢乐 be filled to the brim with girlish glee
泛音 fànyīn *also* "陪音" péiyīn 〈音乐〉overtone; harmonic
泛音列 fànyīnliè 〈音乐〉harmonic series
泛指 fànzhǐ make a general reference; be used in a general sense：他的发言只是～一般情况，不针对某一具体事件。His remarks refer to things in general, not to any particular event.
泛舟 fànzhōu 〈书面〉go boating; float about on a boat：月夜湖上～ go boating upon the lake on a moonlit night

范[1](範) fàn ❶〈书面〉pattern; mould; matrix：铜～ copper matrix /钱～ coin mould ❷ model; criterion; example：典～ example; model to be followed /示～ demonstrate; set an example /规～ standard; norm /模～ model; fine example ❸ limits; range：就～ submit; give in ❹〈书面〉restriction：防～ be on guard; remain vigilant

范[2] Fàn a surname
范本 fànběn model for calligraphy or painting：习字～ model for calligraphy /把他的书法作为～ take his handwriting as a model /临摹～ copy a model of calligraphy or painting
范畴 fànchóu ❶ category：基本～ basic (*or* primary) category /派生～ derivative category /语言学的～ linguistic category ❷ domain; realm; scope; range：不在我研究的～里。The subject is outside my range.
范宽 Fàn Kuān Fan Kuan, originally called Fan Zhongli (范中立), painter of the Northern Song Dynasty, and founder of one of the three major northern schools of Chinese brush painting of scenery
范例 fànlì example; model：典型～ typical example /他的写作是文字清晰的～。His writing is a model of lucidity.
范围 fànwéi ❶ scope; limits; range; extent：活动～ range of activities /知识～ extent of knowledge /实际控制～ extent of actual control /目视～ range of vision /职责～ one's scope of responsibility /在可能的～内 within the realm of possibilities /扩大势力～ enlarge one's sphere of influence /全省～ within the whole province /在协议规定的～内 within the framework of the agreement /职权～ terms of reference /城市的发展已超出了原来的～。The city has outgrown its original limits. ❷〈书面〉set limits to; limit the scope of：纵横四溢，不可～ overflow all the limits
范文 fànwén model essay：他的作文被作为～发给全班。His composition was distributed to the whole class as a model.
范文同 Fànwéntóng Pham Van Dong (1906-2000), Chairman of the Council of Ministers of the Socialist Republic of Viet Nam in 1981-1987.
范性 fànxìng *also* "塑性" sùxìng 〈物理〉plasticity：物质的～ plasticity of substance
范晔 Fàn Yè Fan Ye (398-445), historian of Song (420-479) of the Southern Dynasties and author of the *History of Eastern Han*
范缜 Fàn Zhěn Fan Zhen (formerly translated as Fan Chen,

F

c. 450-515), materialist philosopher and atheist of the Southern Dynasties

范仲淹 Fàn Zhòngyān Fan Zhongyan (formerly translated as Fan Chung-yen, 989-1052), politician and scholar of the Song Dynasty

梵 fàn ❶ of ancient India: see "～语" ❷ Buddhist ❸ (in Hinduism) Brahman; Supreme Being

梵呗 fànbài *Pathaka*; eulogy to the Buddha

梵刹 fànchà Buddhist temple

梵蒂冈 Fàndìgāng Vatican: ～城 Vatican City /～教皇宫 Vatican Palace

梵宫 fàngōng Buddhist temple

梵花 fànhuā Buddhist nun

梵经 fànjīng 〈宗教〉*Brahmasūtra*

梵衲 fànnà Buddhist monk

梵师 fànshī 〈敬词〉Buddhist monk

梵王 fànwáng 〈佛教〉King of Heaven

梵文 Fànwén Sanskrit

梵哑铃 fànyǎlíng (transliteration) violin

梵宇 fànyǔ Buddhist temple

梵语 Fànyǔ see "梵文"

梵钟 fànzhōng Buddhist temple bell

畈 fàn 〈方言〉❶ (often used in place names) land; field: 周党～ Zhoudangfan (in Henan Province) /葛～ Gefan (in Zhejiang Province) ❷〈量词〉*used for large tracts of land*

畈田 fàntián big tract of farmland

贩 fàn ❶ buy to resell: ～粮食 buy grain for resale /～鸦片 traffic in opium ❷ trader; monger; pedlar; vendor: 小～ vendor; hawker /摊～ street pedlar; vendor /商～ small retailer; pedlar /报～ newspaper seller in the street

贩毒 fàndú traffic in narcotics; drug trafficking: ～者 drug trafficker

贩夫 fànfū 〈旧语〉vendor; pedlar; peddler; hawker: ～走卒 small tradesmen and porters; people of lowly occupations

贩卖 fànmài peddle; sell; trade: ～旧货 peddle secondhand goods /～奴隶 engage in slave trade /～牲口 deal in draught animals /～人口 traffic in human beings (especially women); white slavery

贩私 fànsī traffic in smuggled goods; sale of illegal goods; illegal vending

贩运 fànyùn transport goods for sale; traffic: 长途～ long-distance transport of goods for sale /～私货 smuggle (goods) /～国家保护动物是犯法的。Traffic in animals protected by the state is illegal.

贩子 fànzi 〈贬义〉trader; monger: 鱼～ fishmonger /牲口～ cattle trader /皮货～ fur dealer /毒品～ drug trafficker /战争～ warmonger

饭 fàn ❶ cooked rice or other cereals: 干～ cooked rice /稀～ congee; porridge /炒～ fried rice /蒸～ steamed rice /夹生～ half-cooked rice /小米～ cooked millet /八宝～ eight-treasure rice pudding ❷ meal: 一天三顿～ three meals a day /～后服用 to be taken after meals /早～ breakfast /中～ lunch /晚～ supper /客～ meal specially prepared for visitors at a canteen; set meal /便～ simple meal /～后百步走，活到九十九。Walk 100 paces after meals and you will live to ninety-nine. ❸ means of livelihood or living; job: 混～吃 just to make a living /这口～不好吃。It is not an easy job.

饭菜 fàncài ❶ meal; repast; food: ～可口 tasty (*or* delicious) food /这里的～吃得惯吗? Are you used to the food here? /～全好了。Lunch (*or* dinner) is ready. ❷ dishes to go with staple food like rice, steamed buns, etc.: 中午有什么～? What dishes do you serve for lunch? /～摆了一桌。The table was loaded with all kinds of food.

饭单 fàndān ❶ table napkin ❷〈方言〉menu; bill of fare ❸〈方言〉apron ❹〈方言〉bib

饭店 fàndiàn ❶ hotel: 五星级～ five-star hotel; first class hotel /豪华～ luxury hotel /下榻锦江～ stay at the Jinjiang Hotel ❷〈方言〉restaurant; eatery: 中午就近在一家～就餐。We had lunch at a nearby restaurant.

饭豆 fàndòu ❶〈植物〉snailflower ❷ beans of snailflower (often cooked with rice in some areas); rice beans

饭馆 fànguǎn restaurant; eatery: 这条街上有好几家～。There are several restaurants in the street.

饭锅 fànguō ❶ pot for cooking rice; rice cooker ❷ job; means of livelihood: 砸～ lose one's job

饭盒 fànhé lunch-box; mess tin; dinner pail: 带～上学 take a lunch-box to school

饭局 fànjú banquet; feast; dinner party: 天天有～ attend dinner parties every day

饭口 fànkǒu 〈方言〉meal time; dinner time; time to eat: 一到～时间，饭店顾客络绎不绝。At meal time, the restaurant is busy with a stream of customers.

饭来张口，衣来伸手 fàn lái zhāngkǒu, yī lái shēnshǒu have only to open one's mouth to be fed and hold out one's arms to be dressed — lead an easy life, with everything provided; live the life of a parasite

饭粒 fànlì grain of cooked rice: 你嘴边粘着～。There is a grain of rice on the corner of your mouth.

饭量 fànliang appetite: ～不大 have a poor appetite; be a light eater /他～比我大，身体也结实得多。He eats more than I do and also looks much stronger.

饭门 fànmén means of livelihood; job; profession: 另找～ find another job

饭囊 fànnáng ❶ rice bag ❷ fathead; good-for-nothing

饭票 fànpiào meal ticket; mess card

饭铺 fànpù (small) restaurant; eating house: 街道拐角上有个小～。There is an eatery at the street corner.

饭糗茹草 fànqiǔ-rúcǎo eat dry rice and wild herbs — live a simple life

饭时 fànshí 〈方言〉meal time; time for breakfast, lunch, or dinner

饭食 fànshi food (esp. with regard to its quality): ～挺不错，花样多。The food is pretty good, with a great variety.

饭摊 fàntān food stall or stand; fast-food stall

饭堂 fàntáng 〈方言〉dining hall; dining room; mess hall; canteen

饭厅 fàntīng dining hall; dining room; mess hall: 在～就餐 eat at the dining room /能同时容纳三百人就餐的大～ large dining hall with a seating capacity of 300 people

饭桶 fàntǒng ❶ rice bucket ❷ big eater; gourmand: 他真能吃，简直是个～! He is really a big eater! ❸ fathead; good-for-nothing: 你真是个～，这点小事儿都办不了。You're such a dunderhead; you can't even do such a simple thing.

饭碗 fànwǎn ❶ rice bowl ❷ job; means of livelihood: 找～ look for a job /丢～ lose one's job; be out of work /铁～ iron rice bowl — a secure lifelong job /他自己把～给砸了。He was fired through his own fault.

饭辙 fànzhé 〈方言〉means of livelihood; job: 找个～。Find a job (to support oneself).

饭庄 fànzhuāng also "饭庄子" (big) restaurant: 今晚去东来顺～吃涮羊肉。Let's go and have instant-boiled mutton at Donglaishun Restaurant tonight.

饭桌 fànzhuō dining table

饭座儿 fànzuòr customers at a restaurant

犯 fàn ❶ violate; encroach on; go against; offend (against the law, etc.): ～忌讳 offend a person's sensitivity; touch a person's sore spot; break taboos /～校规 violate school regulations /明知故～ deliberately do sth. wrong; deliberately break a rule /秋毫无～ (of highly disciplined troops) not encroach on the interests of the people to the slightest degree /众怒难～。One cannot afford to incur public wrath. ❷ attack; assail; invade: 井水不～河水。Well water does not intrude into river water — everybody minds their own business. /人不～我，我不～人；人若～我，我必～人。We will not attack unless we are attacked, if we are attacked, we will certainly counterattack. ❸ criminal; offender; culprit: 战～ war criminal /惯～ habitual offender; hardened criminal /初～ first offender; first offence /主～ principal offender; principal culprit /从～ accomplice /盗窃～ thief; robber /贪污～ embezzler /杀人～ murderer /嫌疑～ suspect /少年～ juvenile offender; juvenile delinquent /囚～ prisoner /诈骗～ swindler /现行～ offender caught red-handed /刑事～ criminal offender; criminal /教唆～ abettor; abetter /纵火～ arsonist; incendiary /未决～ prisoner awaiting trial ❹ have a recurrence of (an old illness); revert to (a bad habit): ～老毛病 revert to

one's bad habit/又～心脏病了 get another heart attack /～脾气 flare up; fly off the handle; be in a bad mood /～糊涂 become confused; get mixed up /～胃病 have a stomach-ache ❺ commit (a mistake, crime, etc.):～死罪 commit a capital crime; incur the death penalty /～主观主义 succumb to subjectivism

犯案 fàn'àn (of an offender) be found out and brought to justice:听说他又～了。I have heard he was caught again for law-breaking.

犯病 fànbìng have an attack of one's old illness; have a relapse; fall ill again:冬天一到,他就常～。He gets sick quite often after winter sets in. /他的老毛病又犯了。He is having a relapse.

犯不上 fànbushàng 〈口语〉 *see* "犯不着"

犯不着 fànbuzháo *also* "犯不上"〈口语〉 not worthwhile; not worth doing:～为这点小事生气 not worth getting angry at such trifles /～在枝节问题上计较。It is not worthwhile to argue over minor problems (*or* side issues).

犯冲 fànchòng contradictory; inharmonious:～的色彩 incongruous colours

犯愁 fànchóu worry; feel uneasy; be anxious:现在不再为汽油短缺～了。There are no more worries now over gasoline shortage. /孩子没考上大学,真让人～。I'm so troubled by my son's failure in the college entrance exam. /他们小两口最～的是住房问题。Housing is the young couple's biggest headache.

犯憷 fànchù 〈方言〉 feel timid; be nervous; grow apprehensive:初次登台,她心里直～。She felt quite nervous as it was her first experience to perform on stage.

犯刺儿 fàncìr find fault; pick holes; pick a quarrel; set oneself against

犯得上 fàndeshàng *see* "犯得着"

犯得着 fàndezháo *also* "犯得上" (often used in rhetorical questions) is it worthwhile:为这点小事～再去麻烦他吗? Is it worthwhile bothering him again with such trifles?

犯嘀咕 fàn dígu have misgivings about sth.; have sth. on one's mind; have doubts about sth.:听到这个消息,我心里直～。I feel rather uneasy at hearing the news.

犯而不校 fàn'érbùjiào not take to heart the offences committed against oneself:～是儒家所提倡的恕道。To put up with offences or insults against oneself is the spirit of forbearance advocated by Confucian scholars.

犯法 fànfǎ violate or break the law:～的人 law-breaker; offender /执法～ violate the law while enforcing it /这是～行为。It is an illegal act. *or* It is an offence against the law.

犯风 fànfēng emission of smoke out of the air inlet of a cooking range (instead of through the chimney)

犯规 fànguī ❶ break the rules or regulations:～的职工都受到公司的处罚。All the staff members who had violated the regulations were penalized by the company. ❷〈体育〉 foul:侵人～ personal foul /技术～ technical foul /双方～ double foul /发球～ foul service /出球～ foul stroke /～者 offender /因～而罚出场 be sent off for fouling; foul out

犯讳 fànhuì ❶〈旧语〉 mention the names of one's elders or superiors — a practice regarded as irreverent ❷ break or violate taboos:小孩子莫乱说,～要倒霉的。You children watch what you say. It would bring bad luck if you break taboos.

犯浑 fànhún be perversely tactless in one's behaviour or speech; act unreasonably:我一时～,说话冲撞了您,请别生气。I'm sorry to have offended you by the improper remarks I made offhand. /他犯起浑来,谁的话都不听。When he runs wild, he would not listen to anybody's admonition.

犯急 fànjí become impatient; get restless:等得人心里直～ become impatient after waiting so long

犯忌 fànjì violate a taboo:对多数人来说,节育已不再是～的话题。For most people, birth control is no longer a taboo.

犯贱 fànjiàn conduct oneself below one's dignity; behave badly:当叔叔的别在小辈面前～。You're their uncle and should not be frivolous when they are around.

犯犟 fànjiàng ❶ stubborn; obstinate; bullheaded:他总爱～,谁劝都不听。He is often too opinionated to take others' advice. ❷ run into a snag:这把锁跟我犯上犟了,怎么也开不开,该上点油了。This lock is rather stubborn; it needs some oiling to get it opened.

犯节气 fàn jiéqi suffer from a seasonal illness:一到春天我的关节炎就～。Every spring, I would have an attack of arthritis.

犯戒 fànjiè violate religious discipline or commandment; break one's vow of abstinence:我昨天～抽了一支烟。I broke my abstinence yesterday and smoked a cigarette.

犯禁 fànjìn violate a ban or prohibition:戒严期间,他因晚上外出而～。During the martial law period, he violated the ban by going out at night.

犯境 fànjìng invade the territory of another country; make inroads into another country:敌军屡次～。The enemy troops repeatedly invaded our frontiers.

犯科 fànkē 〈书面〉 violate laws and decrees:作奸～ commit crimes in violation of the law; commit offences against the law

犯困 fànkùn feel sleepy or drowsy

犯赖 fànlài ❶ be mischievous or perverse; act shamelessly:这孩子一有人来就～。The child tends to be naughty in company. ❷ be listless; feel languid; be in low spirits:夏日炎炎,使人～。The sweltering summer makes one feel languid.

犯难 fànnán feel embarrassed; feel uneasy; get perplexed:～的事 awkward matter /心里直～ have sth. on one's mind; have misgivings about sth. /为找到一个合适的选题而～ be at a loss for a suitable topic /我们一点也不想使他～。We are not trying to embarrass him in any way.

犯人 fànrén prisoner; convict

犯傻 fànshǎ 〈方言〉 ❶ pretend not to know; feign ignorance; pretend to be naive or stupid:这事你很清楚,别～了。You know it full well. Don't pretend ignorance. ❷ act foolishly:我真～,费力不讨好。It was stupid of me to take up this thankless job. ❸ stare blankly; be in a daze:他坐在那儿～。He sat there staring blankly.

犯上 fànshàng rebel against the king or emperor; defy one's superiors, elders, etc.

犯上作乱 fànshàng-zuòluàn go against one's superiors and make trouble; rebel against authority

犯舌 fànshé 〈方言〉 speak out of turn; shoot off one's mouth; wag one's tongue

犯神经 fàn shénjīng 〈方言〉 go mad; go crazy; be out of one's mind

犯事 fànshì commit a crime or an offence:这个家伙又～了。This guy has committed a crime again.

犯死凿儿 fàn sǐzáor obstinate; stubborn; bullheaded

犯嫌疑 fàn xiányí raise or arouse suspicion; come under suspicion

犯相 fànxiàng ❶〈迷信〉(of a man and woman) contradict each other in their symbolic animals (and be unsuitable for marriage); have contradictory horoscopes ❷ incompatible in temperament; unable to get along (well)

犯心 fànxīn 〈方言〉 be cross with sb.; be at odds with sb.:她这会儿又在～怄气。She is in one of her sulks. *or* She is having a fit of the sulks.

犯性 fànxìng lose one's temper; fly off the handle:他又～了,怎么说也不成。He lost his temper again and couldn't be talked to reason.

犯颜 fànyán 〈书面〉 offend the dignity of the monarch or one's elders:～直谏 voice one's outspoken criticisms before the monarch without considering the consequences

犯夜 fànyè break or violate curfew

犯疑 fànyí *also* "犯疑心" be suspicious:对某人的行为～ become suspicious of sb.'s conduct

犯意 fànyì 〈法律〉 criminal intent; malice aforethought; malice prepense

犯由 fànyóu cause of an offence or a crime

犯嘴 fànzuǐ 〈方言〉 argue; quarrel; have a row

犯罪 fànzuì commit a crime or an offence:～行为 criminal offence; criminal act /～分子 offender; criminal /～的中止 desistance from offence /共同～ joint offence /故意～ intentional offence /过失～ offence through negligence; involuntary crime

犯罪成因 fànzuì chéngyīn aetiology or cause of a crime

犯罪工具 fànzuì gōngjù tools or devices used to commit a crime (e.g. burglary tools)

犯罪环境 fànzuì huánjìng physical setting of a crime

犯罪集团 fànzuì jítuán criminal gang

犯罪客体 fànzuì kètǐ criminal object; object of a crime

犯罪率 fànzuìlǜ crime rate

犯罪社会学 fànzuì shèhuìxué criminal sociology

犯罪未遂 fànzuì wèisuì attempted crime; criminal attempt

犯罪现场 fànzuì xiànchǎng scene of a crime

犯罪心理学 fànzuì xīnlǐxué criminal psychology

犯罪学 fànzuìxué criminology
犯罪主体 fànzuì zhǔtǐ subject of a crime

嬔 fàn 〈方言〉(of fowls) lay an egg:鸡～蛋。Hens lay eggs.

fāng

方[1] fāng ❶ square:～凳 square stool /长～ rectangle /正～ square ❷〈数学〉involution; power:平～ square /立～ cube /X的五次～ fifth power of X /三的三次～是二十七。The cube of 3 is 27. ❸〈量词〉*used for square things*:一～桌布 a tablecloth /一～砚台 an ink-stone /三～图章 three seals /五～石碑 five stone tablets ❹〈量词〉(short for 平方 or 立方) square metre; cubic metre:一～地板 a square metre of floor /土～ cubic metres of earth; earthwork /卧室的面积是十～。The bedroom has a floor space of 10 square metres. ❺ morally square; upright; honest:品行端～ have an upright character /外圆内～ outwardly gentle but inwardly strict ❻ (Fāng) a surname

方[2] fāng ❶ direction:北～ north /东南～ southeast /四面八～ in all directions ❷ side; party:己～ our side /敌～ enemy side /双～ both sides (*or* parties) /对～ other party /有关各～ (all) the parties concerned /甲～和乙～ party A and party B /多～协作 coordinated efforts by all quarters /官～人士 official quarters; official sources ❸ place; region; locality:远～ faraway (*or* remote) place /后～ the rear (area) /一～水土,一～人情。Conditions and customs vary from place to place.

方[3] fāng ❶ method; means; way:想～设法 try in all possible ways (*or* by every means); leave no stone unturned; do one's utmost /领导有～ exercise competent leadership /教子有～ good at educating one's own children ❷ prescription:处～ make out a prescription /秘～ secret recipe /偏～〈中医〉folk prescription /成～〈中医〉set prescription

方[4] fāng 〈书面〉〈副词〉❶ then; just at the time; just then:血气～刚 full of vitality /来日～长 there will be plenty of time; there will be time for that ❷ only; just; just now:年～二八 sweet sixteen; in one's teens; young /如梦～醒 just like awakening from a dream

方案 fāng'àn ❶ work plan; work programme:制订～ draw up a programme /切实可行的～ practical or feasible plan /提出新～ put forward a new proposal /批准施工～ approve the construction project /提出解决危机的～ offer solutions to a crisis ❷ formula; scheme:汉语拼音～ formula or scheme for the Chinese phonetic alphabet

方便 fāngbiàn ❶ convenient; handy:为了～起见 for convenience' sake /～顾客 make things convenient for the customers /交通～ have a good transport service /～群众生活 make life easy for the people /给乘客提供～ offer conveniences to passengers /前面一个街区就有商店,十分～。The store in the next block is quite handy. ❷ appropriate; proper; suitable:周末到那里去,恐怕不太～。The weekend will not be the right time to go there. /如果～的话,我将于周二和你会面。If it suits you, I will meet you Tuesday. /欢迎您在～的时候访问中国。You are always welcome to visit China at your convenience. ❸〈婉词〉have money to spare or lend:你如果手头～就借给我点儿钱。If you have money to spare, pleace lend me some. ❹〈婉词〉go to the lavatory:我得找地方～一下。I'll have to find a restroom. /现在休息,大家可以～～。Let's have a break and you may go and wash your hands if you want to.

方便米 fāngbiànmǐ instant rice
方便面 fāngbiànmiàn instant noodles:牛肉～ instant noodle with beef flavour
方便食品 fāngbiàn shípǐn instant food; convenience food; ready-to-serve food
方便之门 fāngbiànzhīmén convenience:大开～ make things easy (*or* convenient) for others
方波 fāngbō 〈物理〉square wave
方步 fāngbù measured steps:踱～ walk with a measured tread; walk with measured steps

方才 fāngcái ❶ just now; just:～这里发生的事,你不要对别人说。Don't tell anybody else what happened here just now. /我～看见他了。I saw him just a moment ago. /～我上图书馆了。I've just been to the library. ❷ not until:直到天黑他～回来。He didn't come back until it was dark. /我举了许多例子,他～明白过来。Only after I had given many examples did he come to understand it.
方材 fāngcái *also* "方子"〈林业〉square or rectangular timber
方册 fāngcè 〈书面〉ancient books and records; classic works
方策 fāngcè 〈书面〉❶ general plan; strategy ❷ ancient books and records
方程 fāngchéng *also* "方程式"〈数学〉equation:二次～ quadratic equation /三次～ cubic equation /高次～ equation of higher degree /微分～ differential equation /线性～ linear equation /不等～ inequation /化学～ chemical equation/解～ solve an equation /～组 group of equations /～根 root of equation
方尺 fāngchǐ square *chi* (= $\frac{1}{9}$ square metre)
方寸 fāngcùn ❶ square *cun* (= $\frac{1}{9}$ square decimeter) ❷〈书面〉mind; heart:～未定 be undecided what to do
方寸已乱 fāngcùn-yǐluàn with one's heart troubled and confused; with one's mind in a turmoil; greatly upset
方寸之地 fāngcùnzhīdì (human) heart
方单 fāngdān 〈方言〉❶ title deed for land ❷ folk prescription
方鲷 fāngdiāo boarfish (*Caproidae*)
方队 fāngduì phalanx; square array
方法 fāngfǎ method; way; approach; means:～灵活 adopt a flexible approach /改变教学～ change one's teaching method /用最简便的～运算 employ the simplest way of calculation /用尽一切～ explore every possible avenue; leave no stone unturned
方法论 fāngfǎlùn 〈哲学〉methodology:辩证唯物主义的～ methodology of dialectical materialism
方法论者 fāngfǎlùnzhě methodologist
方方面面 fāngfāng-miànmiàn all sides:干工作要处理好～的关系。If you want to do a job well, you'll have to maintain good working relations with all concerned.
方钢 fānggāng 〈冶金〉square steel:～锭 square ingot /～坯 square billet
方格 fānggé check; pattern of squares:～床单 check or checked bedcover /～纸 squared paper; graph paper; checked paper /～画法 graticulation
方格布 fānggébù 〈纺织〉gingham
方格木栅 fānggé mùzhà trellis
方根 fānggēn 〈数学〉root:二次～ square root /均～ root-mean-square
方钴矿 fānggǔkuàng skutterudite
方黄铜矿 fānghuángtóngkuàng cubanite
方技 fāngjì 〈旧语〉general term for certain professions, esp. for medicine, necromancy, clairvoyance, astrology and physiognomy, etc.
方剂 fāngjì *also* "方药"〈中医〉prescription; recipe
方济各会 Fāngjìgèhuì 〈基督教〉Franciscan Order
方家 fāngjiā expert; scholar; great master:国画～ great master of traditional Chinese brush painting /书法～ great master of calligraphy; noted calligrapher
方尖碑 fāngjiānbēi 〈建筑〉obelisk
方将 fāngjiāng 〈书面〉about to do sth.:～离开之际 on the point of leaving or departing
方结 fāngjié square knot
方解石 fāngjiěshí 〈矿业〉calcite
方巾 fāngjīn kerchief worn by scholars of the Ming Dynasty
方巾气 fāngjīnqì (of one's thoughts, remarks or behaviour) pedantic:～十足 sheer pedantry
方今 fāngjīn nowadays; at present:～盛世 in this age of prosperity; in the present golden age
方近 fāngjìn 〈方言〉nearby; in the neighbourhood:～不远 just nearby; not far off; in the vicinity /住在学校～ live close to a school
方孔 fāngkǒng square hole:～筛 square-hole screen
方块 fāngkuài square; diamond (in cards)
方块舞 fāngkuàiwǔ square dance
方块字 fāngkuàizì square-shaped characters — Chinese characters
方框 fāngkuàng square-shaped frame; square frame; square case
方框图 fāngkuàngtú *also* "框图";"方块图" block diagram; skele-

F

ton diagram
方括号 fāngkuòhào square brackets ([ ])
方腊起义 Fāng Là Qǐyì Fang La Uprising (a peasant uprising led by Fang La, ? -1124, during the last years of the Northern Song Dynasty)
方里 fānglǐ square *li* (¼ square kilometre)
方略 fānglüè general plan; overall strategy: 作战～ battle plan; line of action /建国～ grand design or programme for national reconstruction /胸中自有～ have a general plan in one's mind
方螺纹 fāngluówén 〈机械〉square thread: ～车刀 square thread tool
方镁石 fāngměishí 〈矿业〉periclase
方面 fāngmiàn respect; aspect; side; field: 矛盾的主要～ principal aspect of a contradiction /在这一～ in this respect or connection /经济～取得的巨大成就 great achievements in the economic sphere (*or* field) /从各～学到很多东西 learn a lot from all sides /征求各～的意见 solicit opinions from different quarters /在人民生活～ in regard to the people's life /他在数学～有重大贡献。He has made great achievements in mathematics.
方面军 fāngmiànjūn front army: 中国工农红军有三个～。The Chinese Workers' and Peasants' Red Army consisted of three front armies.
方命 fāngmìng 〈书面〉defy orders; disobey: ～之处, 尚希见谅。I hope you will excuse me for disobeying.
方钠石 fāngnàshí 〈矿业〉sodalite
方铅矿 fāngqiānkuàng 〈矿业〉galena
方钳 fāngqián 〈机械〉square tongs
方枘圆凿 fāngruì-yuánzáo *also* "圆凿方枘" square tenon for a round mortice; square peg in a round hole; at odds with one another: 两种办法～, 不能同时使用。The two methods are at variance with each other (*or* are incompatible) and can't be used at the same time. /他俩可谓～, 很难配合。Since the two of them never agree with each other, they can hardly act in concert.
方石英 fāngshíyīng 〈矿业〉cristobalite
方始 fāngshǐ not until: 直到见了她本人, 他～相信是真的。Only when he saw her in person did he believe it to be true.
方士 fāngshì ❶ alchemist ❷ necromancer
方式 fāngshì way; mode; pattern; fashion: 生活～ way or mode of life; lifestyle /生产～ mode of production /注意～方法 pay attention to method and style /管理～ style of management /他以佛教徒的～双手合十, 微微鞠躬。He joined his hands together in the Buddhist fashion and gave a little bow. /以无记名投票的～选出了五名代表。Five representatives were elected by secret ballot.
方书 fāngshū ❶ books on traditional Chinese medicine ❷ books on alchemy
方术 fāngshù *see* "方技"
方俗 fāngsú local custom
方糖 fāngtáng sugar cube; lump sugar
方铁 fāngtiě 〈冶金〉square iron: ～条 square bar; square bar iron
方头不劣 fāngtóu-bùliè *also* "不劣方头" (often used in the early vernacular) be obstinate; be disagreeable: 见一个～后生欺侮一个年老的。I saw a headstrong young man bullying an elderly person.
方外 fāngwài ❶ beyond this world; beyond this mortal life: ～之人 Buddhist monk; Taoist priest ❷ foreign country or land
方位 fāngwèi ❶ point of the compass: 东、南、西、北为四个基本～。East, west, north and south are the four cardinal points of the compass. ❷ direction and position; bearing: 目标～ target bearing /敌军的～ location of the enemy troops /测定船在海上的～ fix or locate a ship's position at sea
方位词 fāngwèicí 〈语言〉noun of direction or locality
方位角 fāngwèijiǎo 〈天文〉azimuth
方位罗盘 fāngwèi luópán 〈测绘〉azimuth compass
方位天文学 fāngwèi tiānwénxué positional astronomy
方位物 fāngwèiwù 〈军事〉topographic marker; landmarker
方物 fāngwù 〈书面〉local or native produce: 献～ present local products
方响 fāngxiǎng ancient percussion instrument consisting of 16 iron pieces of the same size but of different thicknesses
方向 fāngxiàng ❶ geographical direction: ～朝南 face south /善于辨别～ have a good sense of direction /向相反～走去 go in an opposite direction /请问火车站在哪个～? Can you tell me where the railway station is? ❷ orientation: 大～ general orientation /确定～ find one's bearings /坚持为人民服务的～ adhere to the orientation of serving the people /指明了前进的～ point out the way forward /如果情况继续向坏的～发展 if things continue to get worse /决定历史发展的～ determine the course of history /改变政府经济政策的～ change the thrust of the government's economic policy
方向 fāngxiang 〈方言〉situation; circumstances: 看～做事 act according to the circumstances; steer according to the wind; go with the flow
方向舵 fāngxiàngduò rudder
方向盘 fāngxiàngpán steering wheel: 他是个握～的。He is a driver. /他熟练的转动～, 船沿着航道稳稳前进。He skilfully turned the wheel, and the ship steered a steady course.
方兴未艾 fāngxīng-wèi'ài be just unfolding; be in the ascendant: 旅游业的发展～。The tourist industry is on the upswing.
方形 fāngxíng square-shaped: ～大脸 broad and square face
方言 fāngyán ❶ 〈语言〉dialect; local dialect; patois: ～土话 dialects of various regions /广东～ Guangdong dialect ❷ (Fāngyán) *Fangyan*, or *Dialects*, first Chinese lexicon on dialects, written by Yang Xiong (扬雄, 53BC-18AD) of the Han Dynasty
方言学 fāngyánxué dialectology
方药 fāngyào *also* "方剂" 〈中医〉prescription; recipe
方以智 Fāng Yǐzhì Fang Yizhi (formerly translated as Fang I-chih, 1611-1671), thinker and scientist of the late Ming and early Qing dynasties
方音 fāngyīn ❶ phonetic aspect of dialects ❷ dialectal accent: 他讲英语带很重的～。He speaks English with a strong accent.
方舆图 fāngyútú mercator projection map
方圆 fāngyuán ❶ squares and circles: 不以规矩, 不能成～。You cannot draw squares and circles without the compass and square — nothing can be accomplished without norms or standards. ❷ neighbourhood; surrounding area: ～左近, 大名鼎鼎 well-known in the neighbourhood /～数百里的平原上不见人烟。There was no trace of human habitation on the plains for hundreds of miles around. ❸ circumference: 这个湖～三百里。The lake has a circumference of 300 *li*.
方丈 fāngzhàng square *zhang* (= 11 1/9 square metres)
方丈 fāngzhang ❶ abbot's room in a Buddhist temple ❷ abbot
方照 fāngzhào 〈天文〉quadrature
方针 fāngzhēn policy; guiding principle: 基本～ fundamental policy /总～ general guiding principle /制定～政策 formulate general and specific policies /坚持自主～ adhere to the principle of independence /战略～ strategy /事业的成功将充分证明我们的～是正确的。The success of our cause will be eloquent proof of the correctness of our policies.
方阵 fāngzhèn ❶ 〈军事〉phalanx; square array ❷ 〈计算机〉square matrix
方正 fāngzhèng ❶ foursquare and upright: 一张～的脸膛 square face; broad face /他的字写得很～。He writes square and upright characters. ❷ straightforward; upright; righteous: 为人～ upright person; person of integrity /～不阿 upright and never stooping to flattery; frank and honest
方趾圆颅 fāngzhǐ-yuánlú creature with rectangular feet and a round head — human being
方志 fāngzhì *also* "地方志" dìfāngzhì local records; local annals; local gazetteer (the records or a general description of the history, geography, etc. of a town, county, or township): 《绍兴～》*Shaoxing Gazetteer*
方舟 fāngzhōu ❶ 〈书面〉two boats chained together and sailing abreast ❷ ark: 挪亚～ Noah's Ark
方轴 fāngzhóu 〈机械〉square shaft
方柱 fāngzhù square column
方柱石 fāngzhùshí 〈矿业〉scapolite
方桌 fāngzhuō square table
方字 fāngzì square cards with characters for children to learn
方子 fāngzi ❶ prescription: 照～抓药 make up a doctor's prescription of Chinese herbal medicine ❷ formula for chemicals ❸ squared timber
方钻杆 fāngzuàngǎn 〈石油〉kelly (bar)

芳 fāng ❶ sweet-smelling; aromatic; fragrant: 芬～馥郁 very fragrant ❷ flowers and plants: 孤～自赏 a solitary flower admiring its own beauty — self-admiration; narcissism ❸ good (name

F

or reputation); virtuous:万古流～ be remembered throughout the ages; one's name will go down in history and shine forever ❹〈书面〉〈敬词〉your:～札 your letter ❺ (Fāng) a surname

芳草 fāngcǎo fragrant grass; fragrant plant:天涯何处无～ the sweet green grass grows everywhere — there is no lack of virtuous and talented people

芳草如茵 fāngcǎo-rúyīn carpet of green grass

芳醇 fāngchún fragrant and mellow:茶味～ rich and fragrant tea

芳菲 fāngfēi 〈书面〉❶ (of flowers and grass) fragrant:青草～。The fragrant grass grows lush and green. ❷ flowers and plants:十亩～ ten *mu* of flowers and grasses

芳馥 fāngfù (of flowers) rich in fragrance:～的花朵 sweet-smelling flowers

芳华 fānghuá youth; youthfulness:～虚度 idle away one's youthful years

芳基 fāngjī 〈化学〉aryl:～化 arylation /～化物 arylate; arylide

芳槿 fāngjǐn 〈植物〉hibiscus

芳烈 fāngliè ❶ strong fragrance ❷〈书面〉wonderful achievements; meritorious service

芳邻 fānglín 〈书面〉❶ good neighbour ❷〈敬词〉your neighbour

芳龄 fānglíng age of a girl

芳名 fāngmíng ❶ name of a girl ❷ good name or reputation:～远扬 be known far and wide /～永垂。One's name will remain immortal. *or* One's name will be remembered forever.

芳年 fāngnián one's prime; best time of one's life

芳炔 fāngquē 〈化学〉aryne

芳容 fāngróng good looks (of a woman):未睹～ have never seen (*or* met) her /病后～略见清瘦。You look rather thin after your illness.

芳烃 fāngtīng 〈化学〉aromatic hydrocarbon

芳酮 fāngtóng 〈化学〉arone

芳香 fāngxiāng (of flowers, etc.) fragrant; aromatic:～植物 aromatic plant /～馥郁 rich in fragrance /～扑鼻 sense or smell a sweet aroma; fragrance assails one's nostrils /～四溢。Sweet perfumes are diffused all around.

芳香胺 fāngxiāng'àn aromatic amine

芳香醇 fāngxiāngchún aromatic alcohol

芳香剂 fāngxiāngjì aromatic

芳香油 fāngxiāngyóu perfume oil

芳香浴 fāngxiāngyù bathe in water prepared with fragrant plants and herbs (said to have curative effect)

芳香族化合物 fāngxiāngzú huàhéwù 〈化学〉aromatic compound; aromatic

芳心 fāngxīn heart of a young lady:～已许 love a man in her heart /～无主 (of a young woman) not yet betrothed /～已碎。Her heart is broken. /～既许,永矢不变。Once a girl has given her heart to a man, she will remain faithful to him forever.

芳馨 fāngxīn fragrant; aromatic:桂花盛开,～浓郁。The sweet osmanthus is in full bloom, diffusing rich fragrance.

芳泽 fāngzé ❶ scented hair tonic (used by women in old days) ❷ fragrance:～扑鼻。The fragrance strikes the nostrils. ❸ (of a woman) good looks; good manners:我曾在一次招待会上有幸一睹这位大明星的～。I was lucky to see the famous movie star in person at a reception.

芳姿 fāngzī beautiful carriage; graceful posture

芳族 fāngzú 〈化学〉aromatics

芳族化合物 fāngzú huàhéwù aromatic compound; aromatic

芳族酸 fāngzúsuān 〈化学〉aromatic acid

坊 fāng ❶ lane (usu. as part of a street or lane name); alley:白纸～ White Paper Lane (in Beijing) /街～ neighbourhood ❷ memorial archway or gateway

see also fáng

坊本 fāngběn 〈旧语〉block-printed edition prepared by a bookshop

坊间 fāngjiān in the streets (often referring to bookshops in old times):这是从～觅来的孤本。The only extant copy of the book was found in a bookshop.

坊巷 fāngxiàng lane; alley; street

枋[1] fāng 〈古语〉tree whose timber is good for making vehicles

枋[2] fāng ❶ square-shaped lumber; squared timber ❷〈书面〉square timber placed horizontally between two pillars; crossbeam

枋子 fāngzi ❶ square-shaped lumber; square timber ❷〈方言〉coffin

蚄 fāng *see* "虸蚄" zǐfāng

钫[1] fāng 〈化学〉francium (Fr)

钫[2] fāng ❶〈考古〉bronze round-bellied wine vessel with a square mouth ❷〈书面〉cooking utensil; pot

fáng

房[1] fáng ❶ house; building:平～ single-storey house /楼～ building of two or more storeys; storeyed building /厂～ factory building /瓦～ tile-roofed house /民～ private house /草～ thatched cottage ❷ room; chamber:卧～ bedroom /客～ guest room /病～ sickroom; ward /闺～ young lady's chamber /新～ bridal chamber /厢～ wing of a house /牢～ prison cell /书～ study /伙～ kitchen (in a school, factory, etc.) /上～ main room /下～ servants' quarters ❸ house-like structure:蜂～ beehive /莲～ lotus pod ❹ branch of an extended family:长～ eldest branch, i.e. eldest son and his family /正～ legal wife /偏～ concubine /填～〈旧语〉woman married to a man whose first wife is dead ❺〈量词〉*used for branches of an extended family*:有两～儿媳妇 have two daughters-in-law ❻ shop; store:药～ drug store; pharmacy; chemist's shop /面包～ bakery /票～ box office; booking office ❼ one of 28 constellations in ancient Chinese astronomy ❽ (Fáng) a surname

房[2] fáng *see* "坊" fáng

房舱 fángcāng passenger cabin in a ship:只有一间～空着。Only one cabin is available.

房产 fángchǎn house (property); real estate:继承～ inherit a house

房产税 fángchǎnshuì house (property) tax

房产主 fángchǎnzhǔ owner of a house; landlord or landlady

房地产 fángdìchǎn real estate; real property:～公司 company doing real estate business; real estate agency /～经纪人 real estate agent; house agent; realtor /～市场 real estate market

房顶 fángdǐng roof (of a house); housetop

房东 fángdōng owner and lessor of a house or room; landlord or landlady

房改 fánggǎi (short for 住房改革) housing reform

房管局 fángguǎnjú housing administration

房荒 fánghuāng housing shortage

房基 fángjī foundations (of a building)

房脊 fángjǐ ridge (of a roof)

房间 fángjiān room:租一套～ rent a suite or an apartment /这套住房有四个～。The apartment has four rooms.

房客 fángkè tenant (of a flat, room, house, etc.); lodger:收～ take in tenants /～是位大学生。The lodger is a college student.

房契 fángqì title deed (for a house)

房纤 fángqiàn 〈方言〉middleman or broker in housing business:他在过去做过拉～的事。He used to work as a housing broker.

房钱 fángqian house or flat rent; room rent; rent

房山 fángshān ❶ *also* "山墙" shānqiáng gable ❷ walls of a house:前～ front wall of a house

房舍 fángshè house; building

房师 fángshī 〈旧语〉(respectful form of address by successful candidates) assistant examiner who recommended one in the imperial examinations

房事 fángshì (of a married couple) sexual intercourse

房室 fángshì room

房贴 fángtiē subsidy of house rent; rent subsidy

房帖 fángtiě house-for-rent notice; house-to-let ad:张贴～ put up a house-to-let notice

房头 fángtóu 〈旧语〉branch of a family
房柁 fángtuó 〈建筑〉girder
房屋 fángwū house; building:房前屋后 both the front and the rear of a house — all around the house /危旧~ dilapidated and unsafe housing /许多~被飓风摧毁。Many buildings were demolished by the hurricane.
房下 fángxià 〈旧语〉wife and concubine(s)
房牙 fángyá 〈旧语〉middleman in housing business; housing agent or broker
房檐 fángyán eaves
房院 fángyuàn house with a courtyard:一座大~ big house with a large courtyard
房照 fángzhào house property certificate or licence
房主 fángzhǔ house-owner
房柱 fángzhù pillars of a house
房子 fángzi house; building:修缮~ renovate a house /三卧室的~ three-bedroom house /两户合住的~ duplex house /不与他屋相连的~ detached house /到处在建造新~。New buildings are going up everywhere.
房租 fángzū rent (for a house, flat, etc.):这套房子每月~是多少? What's the monthly rent for this flat?

坊 fáng workshop; mill; shop:作~ workshop /染~ dyehouse; dye-works /油~ oil mill /酱~ shop making and selling sauce, pickles, etc. /碾~ grain mill /茶~ teahouse
see also fāng

肪 fáng *see* "脂肪" zhīfáng

鲂 fáng 〈动物〉triangular bream (*Megalobrama terminalis*)
鲂鮄 fángfú 〈动物〉gurnard

防 fáng ❶ prevent; guard against; provide against:提~ guard against (sth. or sb.); be on the alert for (sth. or sb.) /严~ take strict precautions /~病治病 prevention and cure of diseases /以~万一 be prepared for all contingencies; be ready for any eventuality /猝不及~ be caught off guard; be taken by surprise /谨~扒手。Beware of pickpockets. ❷ defend; protect:海~ coast defence /边~ frontier or border defence /设~ set up defence /布~ place troops on garrison duty; organize a defence /驻~ be on garrison duty /调~ relieve a garrison ❸ dyke; embankment:加固堤~ strengthen the dykes ❹ (Fáng) a surname
防暴 fángbào anti-riot:~器具 anti-riot equipment /~任务 riot duty
防暴催泪瓦斯 fángbào cuīlèi wǎsī riot gas; tear gas
防暴盾 fángbàodùn riot shield
防暴警察 fángbào jǐngchá riot police; riot squad
防暴枪 fángbàoqiāng riot gun
防爆震系统 fángbàozhèn xìtǒng 〈汽车〉detonation suppressor system
防备 fángbèi be on the alert for; guard against; take precautions against:~天灾 be prepared against (*or* for) natural disasters /缺乏~ not prepared; without adequate preparation /他这个人不诚实，我得~着点。As he is quite dishonest, I should keep a watchful eye on him.
防变 fángbiàn be prepared for an unfavourable turn of events; get ready for any emergency
防波堤 fángbōdī breakwater; mole
防不胜防 fángbùshèngfáng impossible to defend effectively; very hard to guard against:~，还是要防。Though it's difficult to reckon with all eventualities, we must still try our best to prevent anything untoward from happening.
防潮 fángcháo ❶ dampproof; moistureproof ❷ protection against the tide:~堰堤 tidal barrage /~闸门 tidal gate
防潮层 fángcháocéng 〈建筑〉dampproof course; damp course
防潮火药 fángcháo huǒyào moistureproof powder; nonhygroscopic powder
防潮剂 fángcháojì drying agent
防潮密封 fángcháo mìfēng moisture seal
防潮纸 fángcháozhǐ moistureproof or tarred paper
防潮砖 fángcháozhuān moistureproof brick
防尘 fángchén dustproof
防尘密封 fángchén mìfēng dust seal
防尘圈 fángchénquān 〈机械〉dust ring
防尘罩 fángchénzhào dust cover
防臭剂 fángchòujì deodorant
防除 fángchú prevent and kill off:~白蚁 prevent and wipe out termites
防磁 fángcí 〈物理〉antimagnetic:~手表 antimagnetic watch; nonmagnetic watch
防弹 fángdàn bulletproof; shellproof:~车 bulletproof car; bubbletop car /~背心 bulletproof vest /~玻璃 bulletproof glass
防盗 fángdào guard against theft; take precautions against burglars:采取~措施 take precautions against theft and burglary
防盗警报器 fángdào jǐngbàoqì burglar alarm
防盗门 fángdàomén burglar-proof door; anti-theft door
防盗锁 fángdàosuǒ burglar-proof lock
防地 fángdì 〈军事〉defence sector; station (of a unit)
防冻 fángdòng ❶ frostbite prevention:~药品 frostbite preventive ❷ freeze-proof; antifreeze:~剂 antifreeze; antifreezing agent /~液 anti-icing fluid /~阀 frost valve
防毒 fángdú protect (men or animals) against toxins; protect against poison gas:~器材 gas protection equipment
防毒面具 fángdú miànjù gas mask
防毒手套 fángdú shǒutào (toxin) protective gloves
防毒衣 fángdúyī (toxin) protective clothing
防范 fángfàn be on guard; keep a lookout:~敌人的破坏 guard against the enemy's sabotage /严密~森林火灾 keep a close lookout for any possible outbreak of forest fire
防风 fángfēng ❶〈中药〉root of *fangfeng* (*Saposhnikovia divaricata*) ❷ protect against the wind; provide shelter from the wind:~防沙 check the wind and fix the shifting sand
防风带 fángfēngdài windbreak belt
防风灯 fángfēngdēng hurricane lamp
防风林 fángfēnglín windbreak (forest):~带 shelterbelt
防风衣 fángfēngyī windcheater
防风障 fángfēngzhàng windbreak
防风罩 fángfēngzhào windshield
防辐射 fángfúshè radiation protection:~材料 radiation-proof materials
防腐 fángfǔ antiseptic; antirot:~处理 antiseptic treatment /~材料 antirot material; antiseptics
防腐剂 fángfǔjì antiseptic; preservative
防腐蚀 fángfǔshí ❶ anticorrosion:~绝缘层 anti-corrosion insulation /~电器设备 corrosion-proof electric equipment /~水泥 corrosion-resistant cement ❷ guard against corruption:~，永不沾 fight corrosive influence and always remain honest
防寒 fánghán protect against cold weather:采取~措施 take precautions against the cold weather
防寒服 fánghánfú winter outerwear; eiderdown outerwear
防旱 fánghàn prevent or control drought
防洪 fánghóng prevent or control flood:~工程 flood control works /修筑~大堤 build a flood dyke /~设施 flood-control facilities /数万军民沿江~。Along the river tens of thousands of soldiers and civilians are fighting the flood.
防护 fánghù protect; shelter:人体~〈军事〉physical protection /~涂层 protective coating
防护堤 fánghùdī (protection) embankment; levee
防护林 fánghùlín shelter-forest:~带 shelterbelt /三北~体系 the shelter-forests in northern, northwestern and northeastern China
防滑 fánghuá antiskid:~公路 antiskid highway /~路面 antiskid surface
防滑链 fánghuáliàn 〈汽车〉skid chain; tyre chain
防滑轮胎 fánghuá lúntāi nonskid tyre
防化学兵 fánghuàxuébīng *also* "防化兵" antichemical warfare corps
防患未然 fánghuàn-wèirán take preventive measures; provide against possible trouble:与其补救于已然，不如防患于未然。To forestall is better than to amend. *or* Prevention is better than cure. /我们最好公开发表声明，~，以免引起误会。We'd better take precautionary action by making a public statement to avoid any possible misunderstanding.

防荒 fánghuāng prepare against famine: 积谷～ store up grain against (*or* for) a lean year
防火 fánghuǒ ❶ prevent fires: ～瞭望台 fire watch tower /节假日要特别注意～防盗。Special care must be taken to guard against fire and theft during public holidays. ❷ fireproof: ～设备 fireproof installations
防火层 fánghuǒcéng fireproof layer
防火隔板 fánghuǒ gébǎn (used in airplane or automobile engine) fire wall
防火隔离线 fánghuǒ gélíxiàn 〈林业〉 fire lane
防火漆 fánghuǒqī fire resistant paint
防火墙 fánghuǒqiáng fire wall (also used on the Internet to mean a security screen separating and protecting a sub-net)
防己 fángjǐ 〈中药〉 root of *fangji* (*Stephania tetrandra*)
防空 fángkōng air defence; antiaircraft defence: ～炮 air defence artillery
防空部队 fángkōng bùduì air defence force
防空导弹 fángkōng dǎodàn air defence missile; antiaircraft missile
防空洞 fángkōngdòng ❶ air-raid shelter ❷ hideout for evildoers; cover for wrong thoughts: 这里成了走私分子的～。It became a hideout for smugglers.
防空壕 fángkōngháo air-raid dugout
防空警报 fángkōng jǐngbào air-raid warning; air alert
防空识别区 fángkōng shíbiéqū air defence identification zone
防空掩体 fángkōng yǎntǐ air-raid shelter
防空演习 fángkōng yǎnxí air defence exercise or practice; air-raid drill
防老 fánglǎo provide for one's old age: 这笔储蓄用于～。He keeps the savings against old age.
防老剂 fánglǎojì antideteriorant
防涝 fánglào prevent waterlogging
防凌 fánglíng reduce the menace of ice run
防漏电 fánglòudiàn 〈电工〉 anticreep: ～开关 anticreeping switch / ～设备 anticreeper
防民之口，甚于防川 fáng mín zhī kǒu, shènyú fáng chuān It is more dangerous to stop the mouths of the people than to block the course of a river; to gag or suppress criticism is to court disaster
防区 fángqū defence area; garrison area
防染剂 fángrǎnjì 〈纺织〉 resist
防沙堤 fángshādī sand-control dyke
防沙林 fángshālín sand-break forest; sand-break; barrier forest; forest belt for protection against the advance of sand dunes
防身 fángshēn act in self-defence; protect oneself: ～招数 self-protection techniques / ～术 art or skill of self-defence
防渗 fángshèn seepage control: ～层 impervious layer / ～墙 cut-off wall
防守 fángshǒu defend; guard: ～阵地 defend or hold one's position (in battle) / ～军火库 guard an arsenal / ～边境 keep guard on the frontier; guard the frontier / ～要塞 garrison a fort /人盯人～〈体育〉 man-to-man defence
防暑 fángshǔ heatstroke or sunstroke prevention: ～降温 lower the temperature to prevent heatstroke / ～药 heatstroke preventive / 多喝大麦茶能～。To drink plenty of barley tea will stave off sunstroke.
防霜林 fángshuānglín forest belt for crop protection against frost; anti-frost forest belt
防水 fángshuǐ waterproof: ～水泥 waterproof cement
防水表 fángshuǐbiǎo waterproof watch
防水布 fángshuǐbù waterproof cloth
防水层 fángshuǐcéng 〈建筑〉 waterproof layer
防缩 fángsuō 〈纺织〉 shrinkproof; shrink-resistant: ～布料 shrinkproof materials / ～整理 shrinkproof finish; shrinkage control finish
防坦克 fángtǎnkè antitank defence: ～阵地 antitank position / ～壕 tank or antitank ditch
防坦克地雷 fángtǎnkè dìléi antitank mine
防坦克炮 fángtǎnkèpào antitank gun
防特 fángtè guard against enemy agents or spies
防头 fángtóu (often used in the negative) be careful; take care: 不～摔了一跤 have a fall by accident
防微杜渐 fángwēi-dùjiàn nip (an evil) in the bud; check (erroneous ideas) at the outset: 对不良倾向要～。We must nip harmful tendencies in the bud.
防卫 fángwèi defend; guard: ～能力 defence capabilities / ～行为 act of defence /我们足球队的～线很强。Our football team has a good defence.
防卫厅 Fángwèitīng (Japan) Defence Agency: ～长官 Director General of the Defence Agency / ～防卫局 Defence Bureau of the Defence Agency
防污 fángwū antifouling: ～剂 antifouling composition; antifoulant / ～漆 antifouling coating
防务 fángwù defence matters; defence: ～会议 conference (*or* meeting) on defence /讨论～问题 discuss defence affairs (*or* matters)
防雾 fángwù antifog: ～剂 antifoggant / ～林 fog-damage control forest
防闲 fángxián 〈书面〉 guard and restrict
防线 fángxiàn line of defence: 建立一道～ set up a defence line /突破敌人的～ break through the enemy's defence line
防修 fángxiū prevent revisionism
防锈 fángxiù rustproof; rust-resistant: ～材料 rust-resistant materials
防锈层 fángxiùcéng antirust coating
防锈剂 fángxiùjì rust inhibitor; antirusting agent
防锈漆 fángxiùqī antirust; anticorrosive paint
防锈脂 fángxiùzhī rust grease; antirust grease
防汛 fángxùn flood prevention or control: ～人员 flood-fighters / ～办公室 office for flood control; flood-control office / ～器材 flood-relief equipment / ～设施 flood-control facilities
防氧化 fángyǎnghuà 〈化学〉 oxidation protection
防疫 fángyì epidemic prevention or control: ～措施 epidemic control measures / ～员 health worker for the prevention of epidemics
防疫站 fángyìzhàn epidemic prevention station
防疫针 fángyìzhēn (prophylactic) inoculation
防意如城 fángyì-rúchéng guard against one's inordinate desire as if guarding a city against an enemy: 守口如瓶，～ bite one's tongue and curb one's desire
防鱼雷装置 fángyúléi zhuāngzhì antitorpedo device
防雨布 fángyǔbù waterproof cloth; tarpaulin
防御 fángyù defend; guard: 纵深～ defence in depth /由～转入进攻 go over from the defensive to the offensive / ～外来侵略 guard against external aggression /处于～地位 be on the defensive / ～手段 means of defence /共同～条约 mutual security treaty /进攻是最好的～。The best defence is to attack.
防御部队 fángyù bùduì defending force or troops; defence unit
防御部署 fángyù bùshǔ defensive disposition
防御地带 fángyù dìdài zone of defence
防御工事 fángyù gōngshì defences; fortifications; defence works
防御力量 fángyù lìliàng defence capabilities
防御性军备 fángyùxìng jūnbèi defensive armament
防御战 fángyùzhàn defensive warfare
防御阵地 fángyù zhèndì defensive position
防御正面 fángyù zhèngmiàn 〈军事〉 frontage in defence; front of defence
防灾 fángzāi take precautions against natural calamities: ～抗灾 prevent and fight natural adversities / ～救灾 prevent natural disasters and relieve people in the stricken areas
防震 fángzhèn ❶ shockproof; quakeproof; antiseismic: ～建筑 antiseismic building / ～表 shockproof watch; watch with shock absorber ❷ take precautions against earthquakes: ～措施 precautionary measures against earthquakes; antiquake measures
防震棚 fángzhènpéng temporary shelter for earthquake victims
防止 fángzhǐ prevent; deter; guard against; avoid: ～海洋污染 prevent marine pollution / ～传染 keep off the infection of a disease / ～吸毒 avoid drug addiction / ～故步自封 guard against conservatism /制定这些规则意在～事故。These rules are intended to forestall accidents.
防治 fángzhì prevention and cure; prophylaxis and treatment: ～病虫害 prevention and control of plant diseases and elimination of pests / ～传染病 prevention and cure of infectious or contagious diseases /地方病的～工作取得了可喜的进展。We have made encouraging progress in the prevention and cure of some endemic diseases.

妨 fáng hinder; hamper; impair; harm：不～事 no harm done; no hindrance /～功害能 suppress people of achievement or talent /试试又何～？What harm is there to have a try? /不～先跟他商量商量。We might as well talk it over with him first.

妨碍 fáng'ài hinder; hamper; impede; obstruct：～别人的自由 hamper others' freedom /～进步 impede progress /～视线 obstruct the view /～和平进程 hinder the peace process /～经济的发展 hamper the growth of the economy /～安定团结 harm or undermine stability and unity /这不应～正常的国家关系。This should not be an obstacle to the normal relations between states. /请不要～我。Please don't stand in my way. *or* Please keep out of my way. /我们在这里谈话，会不会～你？Would we disturb you if we speak here?

妨害 fánghài impair; jeopardize; harm; damage：～公共卫生 cause damage to public hygiene /～治安 threaten public security or law and order /这对你并无～。It will not do you any harm.

fǎng

访 fǎng ❶ pay a visit; visit; call on：拜～ pay a visit; pay a call /互～ exchange visits /回～ pay a return visit /过～ drop in /家～ (of a teacher, etc.) visit to the parents of schoolchildren; family visit /出～ visit a foreign country; make a trip overseas /顺～ make a stop-over visit /～亲问友 call on one's relatives and friends ❷ seek by inquiry or search; try to get or gather：采～ (of a reporter) gather material; have an interview with sb. /明察暗～ observe publicly and investigate privately; conduct a thorough investigation

访查 fǎngchá go about making inquiries; inquire; investigate：～民情 go about making inquiries about the conditions of the people /～亲人的下落 inquire about or trace a relative's whereabouts

访古 fǎnggǔ search for ancient relics; look for places of historic interest：河套～ in quest of antiquities in the Hetao area (at the top of the Great Bend of the Yellow River)

访旧 fǎngjiù visit one's old friends or native land：寻根～ visit one's ancestral land to search for one's own roots

访客 fǎngkè visitor; caller; guest

访拿 fǎngná search for and seize; track down (criminals, etc.)

访贫问苦 fǎngpín-wènkǔ visit impoverished people

访求 fǎngqiú search for; seek; look for：～善本古籍 make a search for original copies of ancient books /～贤能 look for men of virtue and ability; scout talent

访视 fǎngshì (of a doctor, etc.) pay a house call：～病人 make a house call to see a patient

访听 fǎngtīng 〈方言〉ask about; inquire about：～当地的情形 inquire about the local situation

访问 fǎngwèn visit; call on; interview：非正式～ unofficial (*or* informal) visit /友好～ friendly visit; goodwill visit /国事～ state visit /私人～ private visit /突然～ surprise visit /～团 visiting mission (*or* group) /记者～了几位专家教授。The reporter interviewed a number of experts and professors. /这次～促进了两国间的友谊和合作。The visit has promoted the friendship and cooperation between the two countries.

访问学者 fǎngwèn xuézhě visiting scholar

访销 fǎngxiāo sales promotion through visits or house calls

访寻 fǎngxún ask about and look for; inquire about：～失散亲人 look for a relative whom one has lost touch with /～草药 search for a medicinal herb

访员 fǎngyuán 〈旧语〉field reporter

髣 fǎng

髣髴 fǎngfú *see* "仿佛" fǎngfú

昉 fǎng 〈书面〉❶ bright ❷ begin; start

仿(倣) fǎng ❶ imitate; model on; copy：效～ imitate; follow the example /模～ model on; pattern after or upon; imitate /～唐制品 imitations or replicas of Tang Dynasty articles ❷ resemble; be like：他俩模样儿相～。The two of them look very much alike. ❸ characters written after a calligraphy model：写了一张～ have written a page of Chinese characters after a calligraphy model

仿办 fǎngbàn follow the example of; imitate; model on：依例～ follow a precedent /这个办法很好，各地可～。This is a good method which may be applied in other localities.

仿单 fǎngdān instructions on the use of a commodity sold; instruction manual：请看～后再使用本产品。Please read the instructions in the manual before use (*or* using the product).

仿佛 fǎngfú *also* "彷佛" fǎngfú；"髣髴" fǎngfú ❶ seemingly; as if：他张开嘴，～要说什么。He opened his mouth as if to say something. /我～听到有人在叫喊。I seem to hear someone calling. /他对工作满腔热情，～从不疲倦似的。He works with such enthusiasm as if he is never tired. ❷ be more or less the same; be similar：他看起来～和十年前一样。He looks almost the same as he did ten years ago.

仿古 fǎnggǔ modelled after an antique; in the style of the ancients：～瓷器 imitation of ancient porcelain; chinaware of an ancient design /～建筑 pseudo-classic architecture

仿建 fǎngjiàn copy the style of another building

仿冒 fǎngmào counterfeit; forge：～名牌 counterfeit of a well-known brand /他～名家的字画发了一笔财。He made a fortune with the forgery of renowned calligraphy and paintings.

仿若 fǎngruò as if; as though：～隔世 feel as if in another life; seem to belong to another world /登上此山，～进入仙境。On top of this mountain one feels as if one were in a fairyland.

仿生学 fǎngshēngxué bionics：～家 bionicist

仿书 fǎngshū brush hand-writing on checked paper

仿宋 fǎngsòng *also* "仿宋体"〈印刷〉imitation Song-Dynasty-style typeface; write in such a style：写得一手～ write a good imitation-Song hand

仿宋本 fǎngsòngběn publications with Song-Dynasty-style typeface

仿宋街 Fǎngsòngjiē Song-Dynasty-Style Street, in Kaifeng, Henan Province

仿效 fǎngxiào imitate; follow the example of; pattern after; model on：不要总是盲目～别人，要走自己的路。One must always try to blaze a new path and never blindly follow others. /他的行为值得我们每一个人～。His conduct is a good example to each and every one of us.

仿效榜样 fǎngxiào bǎngyàng example to follow; role model

仿行 fǎngxíng follow suit; pattern on：这种做法很难在大城市～。This practice can hardly be followed in metropolitan cities.

仿形 fǎngxíng 〈机械〉profile modelling：～车床 copying lathe; repetition lathe /～机械 profiling mechanism

仿影 fǎngyǐng Chinese calligraphy model placed beneath thin checked paper for children to see and imitate

仿造 fǎngzào copy; model on：这台机器是根据国外产品～的。This machine is modelled on (*or* a copy of) a foreign product. /他～的工艺品可以乱真。His imitations of handicraft articles look just like the original.

仿造珍珠 fǎngzào zhēnzhū imitation pearl; olivet

仿照 fǎngzhào pattern on or after; imitate; follow：～办理 follow the example; do (*or* act) accordingly /这些别墅是～德国式样建造的。These villas were built after German architectural style. /这座公园是～《红楼梦》里的大观园设计的。This park is patterned after the Garden of Grand View in the novel of *A Dream of Red Mansions*.

仿真 fǎngzhēn 〈计算机〉simulate; emulate：～技术 simulation technology /～程序 emulation programme /～器 emulator /～终端 terminal emulator

仿真喉 fǎngzhēnhóu artificial throat

仿纸 fǎngzhǐ checked lettering sheet for children to practise Chinese calligraphy; thin checked paper

仿制 fǎngzhì copy; imitate; model on：～的古董 imitation curio; replica of an antique /依照原样～ made to imitate the original pattern

仿制品 fǎngzhìpǐn imitation; replica; copy

彷 fǎng

see also páng

彷佛 fǎngfú *see* "仿佛" fǎngfú

舫 fǎng boat：游～ pleasure-boat /画～ gaily-painted pleasure-boat /石～ Marble Boat (in the Summer Palace)

F

纺 fǎng ❶ spin：～纱织布 spin yarn and weave cloth；spinning and weaving /手～ spin by hand /粗～ rove /混～ blend；blending /毛～ wool spinning /棉～ cotton spinning /绢～ silk spinning ❷ thin silk fabric：杭～ soft plain-weave silk fabric made in Hangzhou /小～ thin，soft plain-weave silk fabric

纺车 fǎngchē spinning wheel

纺绸 fǎngchóu soft plain-weave silk fabric

纺锤 fǎngchuí spindle

纺锭 fǎngdìng spindle

纺纱 fǎngshā spinning：～工人 spinner /～机 spinning machine /～厂 cotton spinning mill /～车间 spinning workshop

纺丝 fǎngsī spinning：～泵 spinning pump /～罐 spinning box /～机 spinning machine /～浴 spinning bath /～头 spinning nozzle；spinneret

纺液染色 fǎngyè rǎnsè dope dyeing：～纤维 dope-dyed fibre

纺织 fǎngzhī spinning and weaving；textile：～厂 textile mill /～工人 textile worker /国家～工业局 State Bureau of Textile Industry /～废水 textile waste /～印花 textile printing

纺织娘 fǎngzhīniáng 〈动物〉katydid；long-horned grass-hopper

纺织品 fǎngzhīpǐn textile；fabric

fàng

放 fàng ❶ let go；set free；free；release：释～ set free；release /解～思想 free oneself from old ideas；emancipate one's thinking /把人质～了 release the hostage /把鸟儿从笼子里～出来。Let the birds out of the cage. ❷ stop (work，etc.)；knock off；have a holiday：*see* "～学"；"～工"；"～假" ❸ let oneself go；act with abandon；give way to：大～厥词 talk a lot of nonsense /为人豪～ bold and unconstrained /热情奔～ bubbling with enthusiasm ❹ put out to pasture：～牛 put cattle out to pasture；pasture or graze cattle /～马 herd horses /～鸭 tend ducks；put ducks out to feed ❺ show；play；turn on：～电视 turn on the TV /～电影 show a film /～录像 play a video tape /～录音 play a recording ❻ send away；banish；exile：流～ send into exile ❼ set or let off；give out：～焰火 set off fireworks /～爆竹 light firecrackers；let off firecrackers /～风筝 fly a kite /～箭 shoot an arrow /～气球 let go a balloon /茉莉花～出芳香。The jessamine sends out a sweet perfume. ❽ light；kindle；ignite：坏人～了一把火烧了仓库。The evildoer set fire to the storehouse. ❾ lend (money) at interest；loan：*see* "～债"；"～高利贷" ❿ let out；expand；make larger：把上肩～宽一些 let the jacket out a little bit across the shoulders /把裤腿～长半寸 let down (*or* lower) half a *cun* the hemline of the trousers /把照片～一～ make enlargements of a photograph；have a photograph enlarged ⓫ (of flowers) blossom；bloom；open：红梅～蕊。The plums are in red blossom. /牡丹初～。Peonies are beginning to bloom. ⓬ leave alone；lay aside；put aside；keep：我们最好存～点钱将来用。We'd better put some money aside for future use. /这问题咱们暂～一～。Let's shelve the question for the time being. /屋子太热，鱼～不住。This room is too hot，and the fish won't keep. ⓭ fell；cause to fall to the ground：～树 fell trees；cut down trees /一拳把他～倒 knock him down to the ground with one blow ⓮ put；place：把衣服～在箱子里 put the clothes into the chest /把国家利益～在首位 place national interests above everything else；give first priority to national interets /阅后～回原处。Put the book (*or* magazine，etc.) back where it was after reading. ⓯ put in；add：咖啡里再～勺糖。Add one more spoonful of sugar in the coffee. /汤里～点味精。Put in some gourmet powder in the soup. ⓰ readjust or moderate (one's attitude，behaviour，etc.)：～尊重些。Behave yourself. /说话～和气点儿。You should speak politely. /～仔细点儿。Be more careful. /～冷静点。Calm yourself down. *or* Cool off a bit. ⓱ (followed by 着… 不…) allow sth. to remain (undone，etc.)：～着正路不走，走邪路 refuse to do the right thing，but stick to the evil way /～着这么大的事不管，后果不堪设想。The consequences will be disastrous when such important matters are not attended to.

放暗箭 fàng ànjiàn shoot an arrow from behind — stab sb. in the back；injure people by treacherous means

放榜 fàngbǎng publish a list of successful candidates or applicants

放包袱 fàng bāofu remove a load on one's mind：放下包袱，轻装前进 remove the load on one's mind and advance without hindrance

放步 fàngbù walk in stride：～前进 stride forward

放长线，钓大鱼 fàng chángxiàn，diào dàyú throw a long line to catch a big fish — adopt a long-term plan to secure sth. big；fly at higher game：他们是～，先给点甜头，引我们上钩。They are carrying out a long-term plan，trying to lure us into their trap by allowing us to gain some benefits first.

放出 fàngchū give out；let out；emit：～能量 release energy /～蒸气 let off steam /～一股清香 send forth a refreshing fragrance /烟囱里～浓浓的黑烟。Clouds of black smoke were belching from the chimney. /他刚从监狱里～来。He has just been discharged from prison.

放黜 fàngchù 〈书面〉send into exile；banish；dismiss sb. from his post

放存 fàngcún deposit；leave in sb.'s care；put under sb.'s care：先把行李～在这儿。Let's deposit our luggage here first.

放达 fàngdá 〈书面〉(of one's words and deeds) unconventional and uninhibited：言行～ be unconventional in one's speech and behaviour

放大 fàngdà enlarge；magnify；blow up；amplify：～点声 speak a bit louder；turn up the volume a little /～照片 enlarged photograph；enlargement；blowup /～一张八寸的照片 make an eight-inch enlargement of the photograph /把物像～五十倍 magnify an object by 50 times

放大倍数 fàngdà bèishù magnifying power

放大尺 fàngdàchǐ pantograph

放大机 fàngdàjī 〈摄影〉enlarger

放大镜 fàngdàjìng magnifying glass；magnifier

放大率 fàngdàlǜ magnifying power；amplification

放大炮 fàng dàpào ❶ talk big；boast；brag；blow one's own horn：别信他～，要看他的行动。Don't be taken in by his big talk. We'll see what he does. ❷ shoot off one's mouth：你为啥不和主任商量，在会上～呢？Why didn't you discuss it with the director before you shot your mouth off at the meeting?

放大器 fàngdàqì ❶〈电子〉amplifier：功率～ power amplifier /视频～ video amplifier /音频～ audio-frequency amplifier ❷ *see* "放大尺"

放大纸 fàngdàzhǐ 〈摄影〉enlarging paper；bromide paper

放贷 fàngdài grant or extend credits

放胆 fàngdǎn act boldly and with confidence：～去干吧 go ahead boldly with your work

放诞 fàngdàn wild in speech and behaviour

放诞不经 fàngdàn-bùjīng absurd (talk，behaviour，etc.)：做事～ sink into absurdity in what one does；act wildly

放荡 fàngdàng ❶ dissolute；debauched；dissipated：过着～的生活 lead a dissolute or dissipated life；sow one's wild oats /～的女人 loose woman；woman of easy virtue /行为～ licentious conduct ❷ unconventional

放荡不羁 fàngdàng-bùjī unconventional and unrestrained；Bohemian

放电 fàngdiàn 〈物理〉❶ (electric) discharge：火花～ spark discharge /尖端～ point discharge ❷ (of a battery，etc.) produce electricity：电池不～了。The battery is dead.

放电灯 fàngdiàndēng 〈电工〉discharge lamp

放刁 fàngdiāo make difficulties for sb.；create troubles deliberately；act in a rascally manner：～撒赖 act in a rascally and unreasonable manner /别在我面前～。Don't try to play dirty tricks on me.

放定 fàngdìng 〈旧语〉betrothal gifts (from the bridegroom to the bride's family)，usu. of gold or silver ornaments on the occasion of engagement

放毒 fàngdú ❶ put poison in food，water，etc.；poison；harm with poison ❷ make vicious remarks；poison minds with evil ideas：向青少年～ corrupt the youth with evil propaganda /农村里又有人～，宣传封建迷信。Some people tried to poison (*or* pervert) the minds of the rural people again by disseminating feudal and superstitious ideas.

放对 fàngduì ❶〈方言〉rivals posturing before a martial arts contest ❷〈方言〉set oneself against；oppose：他总是和我～。He always sets himself against me. ❸ (of animals) mate

放飞 fàngfēi ❶ (of airplanes) allow to take off ❷ let go of (birds)；release：这批信鸽从济南市～，赛程约五百公里。This batch of carrier pigeons were released from Jinan City for a flying contest of about 500 kilometres.

F

放风 fàngfēng ❶ let in fresh air; ventilate: 打开窗户～ open the window to let in some fresh air; give the room an airing; ventilate the room ❷ let prisoners out for exercise or to relieve themselves: 犯人们每天有一次～。Prisoners were let out for exercise and air once every day. ❸ divulge information; circulate news or rumours: 有人～说他将辞去内阁职务。It is rumoured that he is going to resign from the cabinet. ❹〈方言〉be on the lookout; act as a lookout: 我们进去后你在外面～。You keep a lookout outside while we are inside.

放高利贷 fàng gāolìdài lend money at an exorbitant rate of interest; practise usury: ～的人 usurer

放告 fànggào 〈旧语〉periodic announcements by a county magistrate to receive indictments

放歌 fànggē sing heartily and loudly; sing to one's heart's content: ～一曲 sing a song heartily

放工 fànggōng (of workers) knock off; get off work: 我们每天下午五点～。We get off (work) at 5 p.m. every day.

放过 fàngguò let off; let slip by: 不～一个罪犯 not let a single criminal go unpunished / 切莫～这个好机会。Don't let this good opportunity slip through your fingers.

放虎归山 fànghǔguīshān *also* "纵虎归山" zònghǔguīshān set free a tiger and let it return to the mountains — breed calamity for the future: 那不是～, 又给咱多添麻烦吗? That is like letting the tiger go back to its den and would make more troubles for us later.

放怀 fànghuái to one's heart's content; as much as one wants: ～畅饮 drink to one's heart's content / ～大笑 sidesplitting laughter; laughing heartily

放还 fànghuán ❶ release; return; let go: ～原主 return (a draught animal) to its owner / 交保～ release on bail ❷ put back (to its original place); place back: 看完后把书～原处。Place the book back where it was when you finish reading.

放荒 fànghuāng burn the bush on waste land: ～开地 burn the bush on waste land and bring it under cultivation

放活 fànghuó loosen control and enliven; invigorate: ～小企业和小商品 adopt flexible measures with regard to small enterprises and minor commodities / "宏观指导, 微观～"的政策 policy of "macro guidance and micro flexibility"

放火 fànghuǒ ❶ set fire to; commit arson: ～烧荒 burn grass on waste land / 杀人～ commit murder and arson ❷ create disturbances: 此人到处煽风～, 造谣滋事。That fellow has stirred up a lot of trouble by rumourmongering everywhere he goes.

放火犯 fànghuǒfàn arsonist

放假 fàngjià have a holiday or vacation; have a day off: 放暑假 be on summer vacation / ～期间, 他将去欧洲旅行。He will go on a trip to Europe during his holidays.

放开 fàngkāi relax or loosen control; give a free hand to; let go: ～肚皮吃饭 eat as much as one can; eat to one's heart's content / ～手脚让年轻人干 give the young people a free hand to do their work / ～他 let go of him / ～价格 relax control over prices / ～视野 widen one's vision / ～经营 allow more freedom over management

放开搞活 fàngkāi-gǎohuó open up and invigorate; adopt a flexible policy to enliven the economy

放课 fàngkè after class; after school

放空 fàngkōng (of truck, bus, etc.) make an empty run; go unloaded or without passengers: 这辆卡车返程～。The truck returned unloaded.

放空炮 fàng kōngpào talk big; spout hot air; indulge in idle boasting; pay lip service: 他尽～。He is all talk. *or* He is a windbag. / 这件事我们无能为力, 只能放放空炮。We can only voice some verbal support on the matter, as we are unable to render any concrete help.

放空气 fàng kōngqì drop a hint; spread word; create an impression: 放出种族关系日趋紧张的空气 try to create an impression of mounting racial tensions / 不知是谁～, 说电视机要涨价。It was rumoured that the price for TV sets would go up.

放宽 fàngkuān relax (restrictions); liberalize (control): ～尺度 relax the requirements / ～期限 extend or prolong the time limit / ～政策 introduce more flexible policies / ～利率 liberalize interest rates / ～入学年龄限制 lower the age limit for school admission / ～非关税壁垒 liberalize (*or* relax) non-tariff barriers

放款 fàngkuǎn make loans; lend; extend credit: 短期～ short-term credit / 中期～ medium-term credit / 长期～ long-term credit / ～政策 lending policy / ～财团 loan syndicate / ～风险担保计划 lending risk guarantee programme / ～及贴现 loans and discounts (L&D) / ～利率 lending rate / ～人 moneylender; lender / ～市场 loan market

放旷 fàngkuàng 〈书面〉unconventional; unconstrained

放赖 fànglài 〈方言〉act shamelessly; play the rascal: 你别～讹人。Stop playing the rascal and blackmailing people.

放浪 fànglàng 〈书面〉❶ dissolute; debauched; Bohemian: 他年轻时生活够～的, 但现在改邪归正了。He sowed his wild oats when he was young, but now he has reformed. ❷ unrestrained: ～于山水之间 enjoy oneself freely among the mountains and rivers; enjoy beautiful scenery to the full

放浪形骸 fànglàng-xínghái fly in the face of convention; be unconventional and unrestrained

放冷风 fàng lěngfēng spread slanderous rumours: 谁要批评了她, 她就对谁～。She will slander anyone who ventures to criticize her.

放冷箭 fàng lěngjiàn *also* "放暗箭" injure with an arrow shot from behind; stab in the back; snipe: 小心有人～ guard against people who try to stab you in the back; beware of snipers

放亮 fàngliàng 〈方言〉begin to shine; give out light: 天刚～, 我们就动身了。We set out when the day was just dawning (*or* breaking). / 东方已经～。The first gleam of dawn has shimmered in the east.

放量 fàngliàng to the limit of one's capacity (in eating or drinking): ～痛饮 drink to one's heart's content / ～地吃 eat as much as one likes; eat one's fill

放疗 fàngliáo (short for 放射疗法) radiotherapy: 两次～ two sessions of radiotherapy

放流 fàngliú release (fry, etc.) into river, lake or sea: ～鱼苗 release the fry into the river / ～鱼尾数 number of fish released

放马后炮 fàng mǎhòupào fire belated shots; flog a dead horse; comment on sth. when it is already over: 你这个建议虽好, 但却是～了。Your proposal, though very good, is too late to be useful.

放牧 fàngmù put out to pasture; pasture; graze; herd: ～牛羊 herd or graze sheep and cattle / ～作物 grazing crops

放牧地 fàngmùdì grazing land

放牧期 fàngmùqī grazing season; grazing period

放牛娃 fàngniúwá child cowherd

放排 fàngpái *also* "放簰"〈林业〉rafting

放盘 fàngpán (of a shop) sell at reduced prices or buy in at higher prices

放炮 fàngpào ❶ fire a gun: 向敌人阵地～ fire cannons on the enemy position ❷ set off firecrackers ❸ blasting; shotfire: ～工 shot firer / ～开山 blast through a mountain / 危险, 正在～! Danger! Blasting in progress! / 就要～开隧道了, 请大家撤到安全地带。We are going to blast a tunnel. Please move to the safe area. ❹ blowout (of a tyre, etc.): 车胎～了。The tyre has had a blowout. ❺ shoot off one's mouth: 他在会上放了一通炮。He shot his mouth off at the meeting.

放屁 fàngpì ❶ break wind; fart ❷〈粗话〉talk nonsense: ～! What crap! / ～胡说 flatulence and foolish talk; rubbish / 他说话等于～。His words were all rot.

放泼 fàngpō 〈方言〉rude and unreasonable; shrewish

放弃 fàngqì abandon; give up; forfeit; renounce: ～机会 give up an opportunity / ～原来的意见 abandon one's original view / ～发言权 forfeit the right to speak / ～表决权 abstain from voting / ～优厚的待遇 give up a well-paid job / ～使用武力 renounce the use of force / ～国籍 renounce one's nationality; divest oneself of one's nationality / ～索赔 abandonment of claim / ～特权 waive a privilege / ～王位 abdicate one's throne

放钱 fàngqián 〈方言〉lend money for interest

放青 fàngqīng put (cattle, etc.) out to pasture; graze

放青苗 fàng qīngmiáo 〈旧语〉(of landlords or merchants) purchase standing crops at very low prices from poor peasants before the harvest; buy standing crops dirt cheap

放情 fàngqíng to one's heart's content; as much as one likes: ～歌唱 sing to one's heart's content; sing heartily / ～山水 enjoy mountains and rivers; enjoy oneself in the embrace of nature

放晴 fàngqíng (of sky) clear up: 天马上会～。It is going to clear up soon. / 天一～我们就去旅行。We will begin our trip on the first fine day.

放权 fàngquán delegate powers to lower levels: 简政～ simplify or streamline the administration and delegate more decision-making powers to lower levels

F

放热 fàngrè 〈化学〉emitting; exothermic; exothermal: ～现象 emission of heat
放热反应 fàngrè fǎnyìng 〈化学〉exothermic reaction
放热率 fàngrèlǜ heat release rate; exothermic rate
放任 fàngrèn not interfere; let alone; indulge; laissez-faire: 对孩子～不管 leave one's children to themselves / 采取～态度 take an indulgent attitude / ～不羁 unconventional and unrestrained / 决不能～这种行为。Such behaviour should not be tolerated.
放任政策 fàngrèn zhèngcè policy of laissez-faire
放任主义 fàngrènzhǔyì laissez-faireism; laissez-faire (doctrine)
放任自流 fàngrèn-zìliú let things drift or slide; let people do as they like
放散 fàngsàn (of smoke, scent, etc.) diffuse; disperse: 光的～ diffusion of light
放山 fàngshān 〈方言〉go hunting
放哨 fàngshào stand sentry or sentinel; be on sentry or on patrol: 站岗～ be on sentry duty / 在门口～ be posted as a sentry at the front gate
放射 fàngshè radiate; emit: 太阳～出耀眼的光芒。The sun is radiating dazzling light.
放射病 fàngshèbìng radiation sickness
放射虫 fàngshèchóng radiolarian
放射镜 fàngshèjìng radioscope
放射疗法 fàngshè liáofǎ radiotherapy
放射路 fàngshèlù system of roads radiating from the centre in all directions; radiating roads
放射区域 fàngshè qūyù radioactive area
放射生态学 fàngshè shēngtàixué radioecology
放射生物学 fàngshè shēngwùxué radiobiology
放射现象 fàngshè xiànxiàng 〈物理〉radioactivity
放射线 fàngshèxiàn radioactive rays
放射形 fàngshèxíng pattern of radiation; radiation
放射性 fàngshèxìng ❶〈物理〉radioactivity; activity ❷〈医学〉(of pain, etc.) radiating (from a central point): ～疼痛 spreading pain; pain that radiates around
放射性示踪物 fàngshèxìng shìzōngwù radioactive tracer
放射性碳素断代法 fàngshèxìng tànsù duàndàifǎ 〈考古〉radiocarbon dating
放射性同位素 fàngshèxìng tóngwèisù radio isotope: 人造～ induced radio isotope
放射性微尘 fàngshèxìng wēichén radioactive dust; fallout
放射性污染 fàngshèxìng wūrǎn radioactive pollution
放射性元素 fàngshèxìng yuánsù radioactive element; radioelement
放射性沾染 fàngshèxìng zhānrǎn radioactive contamination
放射性战剂 fàngshèxìng zhànjì radioactive agent
放射学 fàngshèxué radiology: ～家 radiologist
放生 fàngshēng (of Buddhists) free captive or bought animals
放声 fàngshēng at the top of one's voice: ～大喊 shout at the top of one's voice / ～大笑 scream with laughter / ～痛哭 burst into loud weeping; cry loudly / ～歌唱 sing heartily
放手 fàngshǒu ❶ let go; let go one's hold: 小女孩把玩具紧紧地抓住, 不肯～。The little girl took a firm hold of the toy and would not let go. ❷ give a free hand; go all out: ～发动群众 go all out to mobilize the masses; fully arouse the masses / 让他～干下去。Give him a free hand in the matter. ❸ remove one's control: 一切事情都抓在自己手里, 从不～。He keeps everything in his own hands without letting anyone else have a say.
放水 fàngshuǐ ❶ turn on the water ❷ (of a reservoir) draw off water
放肆 fàngsì unbridled; wanton; rude; impudent: 说话～ talk wantonly; speak rudely / ～之至 throw all restraint to the winds / 胆敢如此～! How dare you take such liberties! *or* What impudence! / 小伙子, 休得在我面前～! Don't get wise with me, young man!
放松 fàngsōng relax; slacken; lower; loosen: ～警惕 lower one's vigilance; let down one's guard / 别紧张, ～点。Loosen up! Don't be nervous. / ～学习 slacken one's efforts in studies / 把螺丝钉～ loosen the screw / ～缰绳 slacken the reins / 我出去～一下。I will go and relax a little bit outside.
放送 fàngsòng broadcast; send out (over a loudspeaker, etc.): ～电视节目 broadcast a TV programme / 实况～新年联欢会 broadcast live the New Year's party
放卫星 fàng wèixīng ❶ launch a satellite into orbit ❷ report extraordinary, often exaggerated, achievements during the "Great Leap Forward" in China
放下屠刀, 立地成佛 fàngxià túdāo, lìdì chéng fó drop one's cleaver and become a Buddha — achieve salvation the moment one gives up evil
放下 fàngxia lay down; put down; let go; release: ～武器! Lay down your arms! / ～思想包袱 cast off one's mental burdens / 把百叶窗～ pull down the blinds / 手头的工作一时还放不下。I can't put aside the work on hand for the time being. / 我认为你应该～架子向他道歉。I think you should pocket your pride and apologize to him.
放线菌 fàngxiànjūn 〈微生物〉actinomyces
放像 fàngxiàng video reproduction; video playback: ～室 video (show) room
放像机 fàngxiàngjī videocassette player; video player
放血 fàngxiě ❶〈医学〉blood-letting; phlebotomy ❷〈口语〉inflict grievous wound on sb.; bleed sb. even to death: 那伙坏蛋要他交出钱包, 否则就要放他的血。The hooligans threatened to take his life if he did not hand over his wallet.
放心 fàngxīn set one's mind at rest; rest assured; have confidence; trust: ～不下 be kept in suspense; feel anxious / 请～, 我决不会让你失望的。You can rest assured that I'll never let you down. / 威胁不消除, 我们能～吗? How can we feel easy if this threat is not removed? / 他做这事大家都很～。Everyone trusts him to do the job. / 他对大夫的医术一百个～。He has full confidence in the doctor's skill. / 此人总不让人～。The man is not reliable at all.
放行 fàngxíng let (sb. or sth.) pass; get clearance: 申请～ request clearance / 海关免税～这批外交车辆。The customs office has granted duty-free clearance for these diplomatic cars. / 凡过哨卡没有证件的一律不予～。Don't let anyone without an identity card pass through the sentry post.
放行单 fàngxíngdān release permit; clearance paper
放学 fàngxué ❶ classes are over; dismiss class: 孩子们中午～就玩开了。The children start to play happily as soon as the morning classes are over. / 每天～以后, 我都要练习小提琴。Every day I practise the violin after school. ❷ school holidays: 七月十五号开始～。The summer vacation starts on July 15.
放烟幕 fàng yānmù throw up a smokescreen
放眼 fàngyǎn take a broad view; scan widely: 他们站在山顶～眺望美丽的景色。They stood at the top of the hill and viewed the beautiful landscape in the distance.
放眼世界 fàngyǎn-shìjiè have the whole world in view: 胸怀祖国, ～ have one's country at heart (*or* in mind) and the entire world in view
放羊 fàngyáng ❶ graze sheep; pasture sheep; look after sheep: ～娃 shepherd boy ❷〈贬义〉be reinless; throw (the) reins off; drift along: 昨天老师病了, 学生可就～了。As the teacher fell ill yesterday, pupils were free to do what they pleased.
放洋 fàngyáng ❶〈旧语〉serve as an envoy abroad; be sent on a diplomatic mission or to study abroad ❷〈书面〉(of a ship) go to sea; set out on a voyage: 商船明日～。The merchant ship will set out tomorrow.
放养 fàngyǎng breed (fish, silkworm, etc.) in a suitable environment; culture: ～各种淡水鱼 breed various kinds of freshwater fish / ～海带 culture kelp
放样 fàngyàng moulding; laying off; setting out; 〈船舶〉lofting
放音 fàngyīn sound reproduction; audio playback; playback: ～扩大器 playback amplifier
放音机 fàngyīnjī cassette player; tape player
放印子 fàng yìnzi 〈旧语〉practise usury
see also "印子钱" yìnziqián
放鹰 fàngyīng ❶ go hawking; hunt with falcons ❷〈旧语〉use women to trap people for money ❸ lose everything; lose completely: 他的钱全都放了鹰了。He lost all his money. *or* He went clean broke.
放映 fàngyìng show; project: ～电影 show a film; have a film show / ～幻灯 have a slide show
放映队 fàngyìngduì film projection team
放映机 fàngyìngjī (film) projector
放映室 fàngyìngshì projection room
放映员 fàngyìngyuán projectionist
放淤 fàngyū 〈农业〉warp: ～造田 land reclamation by warping

放债 fàngzhài *also* "放账" lend money for interest; lend money at (a certain rate of) interest: ～人 money-lender
放账 fàngzhàng *see* "放债"
放赈 fàngzhèn 〈书面〉provide disaster relief; distribute relief to people in stricken areas
放之四海而皆准 fàng zhī sìhǎi ér jiē zhǔn universally applicable; valid everywhere: ～的真理 universally applicable truth
放置 fàngzhì lay up; lay aside; place; put: ～不用 lay up (machinery, equipment, etc.); lie idle /把仪器～好。Put the instruments in their proper place. /墓前～着花圈。Wreaths were laid at the tomb.
放逐 fàngzhú 〈旧语〉send into exile; exile; banish
放恣 fàngzì 〈书面〉arrogant and imperious; domineering and wilful
放纵 fàngzòng ❶ let sb. have his own way; connive at; indulge: ～孩子 indulge one's child; be indulgent towards one's child ❷ unrestrained; undisciplined; uncultured; boorish: 骄奢～ given to boastful luxury and debauchery /行为～ unbridled behaviour / 性～社会 permissive society

fēi

非[1] fēi ❶ wrong; wrongdoing; error; evil: 是～曲直 rights and wrongs; truth and flasehood /混淆是～ confuse right and wrong /习～成是 accept what is wrong as right as one grows accustomed to it /文过饰～ cover up one's errors (*or* mistakes) ❷ not conform to; go against; run counter to: *see* "～法"; "～礼"; "～分" ❸ censure; oppose; find fault with: 未可厚～ not altogether inexcusable /口是心～ say yes and mean no; say one thing and mean another /是古～今 praise everything ancient and condemn everything present ❹ not; non-; un-; in-: 答～所问 give an irrelevant answer /似懂～懂 have only a hazy notion; not quite understand /～人生活 inhuman life/～政府机构 non-governmental organization /～言语所能表达 no words can adequately express; be beyond words /此～我本意。It is not my wish (*or* intention). ❺ have got to; simply must: 长跑～得有耐力不可。One has got to have staying power in long distance running. ❻ *used to indicate wilfulness or determination*: 不让他去,他～要去。We didn't want him to go, but he insisted. /为什么～要他来? Why must he come? ❼〈书面〉deteriorate; degenerate: 世道日～。The moral standards of the society are degenerating day by day.

非[2] Fēi (short for 非洲) Africa: 泛～ pan-African /～统首脑会议 Summit of the Organization of African Unity
非暴力 fēibàolì nonviolence: ～主义者 exponent of nonviolence /～抗议 nonviolent protest /～反抗 civil disobedience
非本质 fēiběnzhì nonessential; inessential
非比寻常 fēibǐxúncháng out of the ordinary; unusual; extraordinary: ～的外交行动 unusual diplomatic move /此事～,应密切关注。The matter is rather out of the ordinary and deserves close attention.
非必需品 fēibìxūpǐn nonessential goods; nonessentials
非标准 fēibiāozhǔn nonstandard: ～分析〈数学〉nonstandard analysis
非病原菌 fēibìngyuánjūn nonpathogenic bacterium
非…不… fēi…bù… ❶ simply must; have to: 我今天非见到他不可。I simply must see him today. /这事你今天非做完不行。You've got to finish it today. /难道非要我一个人去不成? Must I really go alone? ❷ be sure to; be bound to: 你车开得这么快,非出事不可。You'll surely end up in an accident if you go on speeding like that. /非经批准不能动用这笔资金。You can not use the fund without formal approval.
非常 fēicháng ❶ extraordinary; unusual; uncommon; special: ～的举动 unusual behaviour /～情况 special circumstances /～时期要采取～措施。Extraordinary times call for extraordinary measures. ❷ very; extremely; exceedingly; highly: ～有意思 highly interesting /～感谢 very grateful /～激动 extremely excited /～好 wonderful; marvellous /～健康 as fit as a fiddle /～愚蠢 height of stupidity; stupidity incarnate /集市上人来人往,热闹～。With people streaming in and out, the country fair was bustling with noise and activity.
非常规 fēichángguī non-conventional: ～能源 non-conventional energy /～战争 non-conventional warfare
非常任 fēichángrèn nonpermanent: ～代表 nonpermanent representative
非常任理事国 fēichángrèn lǐshìguó nonpermanent member (of the UN Security Council)
非常设机构 fēichángshè jīgòu ad hoc organization
非常时期 fēicháng shíqī time of emergency
非常征用权 fēicháng zhēngyòngquán 〈法律〉angary (the right of a belligerent state, subject to compensation for loss, to seize or destroy neutral property under military necessity)
非成本 fēichéngběn noncost: ～项目 noncost item
非成员国 fēichéngyuánguó non-member country
非承重墙 fēichéngzhòngqiáng 〈建筑〉non-load-bearing wall
非池中物 fēichízhōngwù be not confined to a small pond — one who has a great future: 这位经理认为他的副经理乃是～,总想及早把他排挤掉。Believing that his deputy is a person of no small ambition, the manager has always wanted to get rid of him.
非处方药 fēichǔfāngyào OTC (over-the-counter) medicine or drug
非创始国 fēichuàngshǐguó non-original member state
非此即彼 fēicǐ-jíbǐ either this or that; one or the other
非但 fēidàn not only: 那姑娘～长得俊,手还特别巧。The girl is not only beautiful but also very clever with her hands. /他～不感谢我的好意,反而记恨在心。Far from appreciating my kindness, he bore me grudges.
非当事方 fēidāngshìfāng non-party; not a party
非当事国 fēidāngshìguó non-party state; non-participant
非党人士 fēidǎng rénshì non-Party personage
非导体 fēidǎotǐ *also* "绝缘体" juéyuántǐ non-conductor
非得 fēiděi (usu. followed by 不 or 才) have to; have got to; must: 练字～下几年苦功夫才成。You've got to keep on practising for years before you can get somewhere in calligraphy. /～经过批准,才能动用这笔资金。You must get approval for using the fund.
非敌性 fēidíxìng 〈法律〉non-hostile: ～目的地 non-hostile destination /～交往 non-hostile intercourse /～关系 non-hostile relations
非缔约方 fēidìyuēfāng 〈法律〉non-contracting party
非缔约国 fēidìyuēguó 〈法律〉non-contracting power; non-contracting state
非电解质 fēidiànjiězhì 〈化工〉anelectrolyte; non-electrolyte
非定额 fēidìng'é non-quota: ～移民 non-quota immigrant /～签证 non-quota visa
非定期 fēidìngqī non-scheduled: ～飞行 non-scheduled flight /～国际航空服务 non-scheduled international air service
非独 fēidú 〈书面〉not merely: 吃这种药～没治好病,反而产生了不良反应。This medicine is not only inefficacious, but has harmful side effects.
非对称 fēiduìchèn asymmetric(al): ～辐射 asymmetric radiation /～性 asymmetry
非对称型数字用户线路 fēiduìchènxíng shùzì yònghù xiànlù 〈信息〉asynchronous digital subscriber loop (ADSL)
非对抗性 fēiduìkàngxìng nonantagonism
非对抗性矛盾 fēiduìkàngxìng máodùn nonantagonistic contradiction
非法 fēifǎ illegal; unlawful; illegitimate; illicit: ～合同 illegal contract /～手段 illegal means /～集会 unlawful assembly /～行为 illegitimate action /～监禁 illegal detention /～移民 illegal immigration /～收入 illicit income; illegal income /～同居 illicit cohabitation /～解雇 wrongful dismissal /～翻印 pirate /～侵入〈法律〉trespass /～政府 outlaw government /被宣布为～ be outlawed; be declared illegal; be illegalized
非法结社 fēifǎ jiéshè 〈法律〉illegal association
非凡 fēifán outstanding; extraordinary; uncommon: ～的学术成就 outstanding scholarship/～的见解 unusually perceptive views /才能～ exceptional ability; remarkable talent /仪表～ have an imposing appearance; cut a fine figure /抱负～ cherish extraordinary aspirations
非防火材料 fēifánghuǒ cáiliào 〈建筑〉non-fireproof material
非…非… fēi…fēi… neither... nor...: 非敌非友 neither friend nor foe
非分 fēifèn ❶ overstepping one's bounds; assuming; presumptuous: ～的企求 presumptuous desires ❷ not belonging to oneself; not one's due: ～的钱他一文都不贪。He accepts nothing, not even a penny, that is not honestly earned.
非分之想 fēifènzhīxiǎng inordinate ambition or desire: 他心存～,

F

干了许多非法活动。Driven by inordinate desires, he has engaged in many illegal activities.
非封锁港 fēifēngsuǒgǎng 〈法律〉nonblockaded port
非刚性塑料 fēigāngxìng sùliào non-rigid plastics
非高峰期 fēigāofēngqī 〈通信〉off-peak period
非公莫入 fēigōng-mòrù no admittance except on business: 仓库重地，～。Warehouse. No admittance except on business.
非固体 fēigùtǐ non-solid
非关税壁垒 fēiguānshuì bìlěi non-tariff barrier
非官方 fēiguānfāng unofficial: ～消息 news from unofficial sources /～机构 unofficial or nongovernmental institution
非国际性 fēiguójìxìng non-international: ～武装冲突 non-international armed conflict
非国家实体 fēiguójiā shítǐ 〈法律〉non-state entity
非国民 fēiguómín non-national: ～的引渡 extradition of non-nationals
非国有化 fēiguóyǒuhuà denationalization
非核化 fēihéhuà denuclearization: ～体系 denuclearization regime
非和平 fēihépíng non-peaceable; non-amicable: ～方法〈法律〉non-amicable means
非互惠 fēihùhuì nonreciprocal: ～优惠 nonreciprocal preference /～贸易 nonreciprocal trade /～待遇 nonreciprocal treatment /～概念 (concept of) nonreciprocity
非会员 fēihuìyuán nonmember: ～国 nonmember country /～国政府 nonmember government /～银行 nonmember bank
非婚生子女 fēihūnshēng zǐnǚ children born out of wedlock; illegitimate children
非货币 fēihuòbì nonmonetary: ～账目 nonmonetary account /～经济 nonmonetary economy /～收入 nonmonetary income /～黄金 nonmonetary gold
非机械化 fēijīxièhuà nonmechanized
非…即… fēi … jí … either... or...: 非醉即疯 either drunk or mad /非涝即旱 (suffer from) either flood or drought
非集团原则 fēijítuán yuánzé non-bloc principle
非价格 fēijiàgé 〈经济〉nonprice: ～竞争 nonprice competition /～刺激 nonprice stimuli
非建交国 fēijiànjiāoguó 〈外交〉country that has no diplomatic relations with China; countries that have no diplomatic relations (with each other)
非交战国 fēijiāozhànguó nonbelligerent
非交战状态 fēijiāozhàn zhuàngtài nonbelligerency
非金属 fēijīnshǔ nonmetal: ～材料 nonmetallic material /～元素 nonmetallic element
非晶体 fēijīngtǐ amorphous body; noncrystal
非晶质 fēijīngzhì 〈化学〉noncrystalline; amorphous
非竞争性 fēijìngzhēngxìng noncompetitive
非静态 fēijìngtài nonstatic: ～经济 nonstatic economy
非居民 fēijūmín nonresident: ～外国人 nonresident alien /～机构 nonresident organization /～账户 nonresidential account
非军事 fēijūnshì non-military: ～目标 non-military objective /～用途 non-military use /～国家 non-military state
非军事化 fēijūnshìhuà demilitarize
非军事区 fēijūnshìqū demilitarized zone
非军事人员 fēijūnshì rényuán civilian personnel
非开放港 fēikāifànggǎng closed port
非矿物燃料 fēikuàngwù ránliào nonfossil fuel
非劳动收入 fēiláodòng shōurù *also* "非劳动所得" income which does not come from one's own labour; unearned income
非累计 fēilěijì 〈金融〉noncumulative: ～信用证 noncumulative credit /～股息 noncumulative dividend /～优先股 noncumulative preferred stock
非礼 fēilǐ ❶ rude; impolite; improper: ～之举 indecorous conduct; improper behaviour /来而不往，～也。It is impolite not to reciprocate. *or* One should return as good as one receives. ❷ assault (a woman) sexually; violate; rape: 欲行～ attempt to assault a woman
非理性主义 fēilǐxìngzhǔyì 〈哲学〉irrationalism
非零和 fēilínghé non-zero sum (where the gains of one side do not mean the losses of the other): ～解决方案 non-zero-sum solution; win-win solution
非流动性 fēiliúdòngxìng nonliquid: ～资产 nonliquid asset
非垄断 fēilǒngduàn nonmonopoly
非驴非马 fēilú-fēimǎ neither ass nor horse; neither fish nor fowl; neither fish, flesh, nor good red herring: 这种似通非通、～的文字叫人无法卒读。One could hardly finish reading an article full of such incongruous words and expressions.
非轮回亲本 fēilúnhuí qīnběn 〈农业〉nonrecurrent parent
非卖品 fēimàipǐn article not for sale
非贸易 fēimàoyì noncommercial; nontrade: ～账户 noncommercial account /～合同 noncommercial contract /～开支 noncommercial payment /～收入 nontrade receipt
非贸易外汇收入 fēimàoyì wàihuì shōurù foreign exchange earned from sources other than trade; nontrade foreign exchange earnings
非美活动委员会 Fēi-Měi Huódòng Wěiyuánhuì (US) House Un-American Activities Committee (HUAC, 1938-1975)
非美元 fēiměiyuán nondollar: ～国家 nondollar country
非盟国 fēiméngguó non-allied country: ～的友好国家 non-allied friendly country
非命 fēimìng ❶ unnatural death; violent death: 死于～ die a violent death ❷〈哲学〉refute fatalism
非那更 fēinàgēng 〈药学〉phenergan
非耐用品 fēinàiyòngpǐn nondurable: 非耐用消费品 nondurable consumer goods
非难 fēinàn (often used in the negative) blame; condemn; censure; reproach: 无可～ above criticism; blameless; irreproachable /遭到无理～ receive unfair censure (*or* blame) /他这样做没有什么可以～的。He has done nothing reproachable.
非农产业 fēinóng chǎnyè non-agricultural industry
非农业人口 fēinóngyè rénkǒu non-agricultural population
非欧几何 fēi'ōu jǐhé 〈数学〉noneuclidean geometry
非配额产品 fēipèi'é chǎnpǐn quota-free product
非毗连国 fēipíliánguó 〈法律〉non-contiguous state
非破坏性 fēipòhuàixìng nondestructive
非歧视性 fēiqíshìxìng nondiscriminatory: ～措施 nondiscriminatory measures /～政府采购 nondiscriminatory government procurement
非契约 fēiqìyuē noncontractual: ～索赔 noncontractual claim /～收益 noncontractual income /～性责任 noncontractual liability
非签字国 fēiqiānzìguó non-signatory state
非强制性 fēiqiángzhìxìng nonmandatory: ～国际范本 nonmandatory international model
非强迫行为 fēiqiǎngpò xíngwéi 〈法律〉non-coercive act
非亲非故 fēiqīn-fēigù neither relative nor friend; neither kith nor kin; not in any way related
非请莫入 fēiqǐng-mòrù no admittance except on invitation
非权益股票 fēiquányì gǔpiào 〈金融〉non-equity share
非燃料 fēiránliào nonfuel: ～商品贸易 nonfuel merchandise trade /～初级产品 nonfuel primary product
非人 fēirén ❶〈书面〉not the right person: 所嫁～ marry the wrong man ❷ inhuman: 受到～的待遇 receive inhuman treatment
非人道 fēiréndào inhuman: ～行为 inhuman act /～待遇 inhuman treatment
非商品 fēishāngpǐn nonmerchandise: ～贸易 nonmerchandise trade
非商业 fēishāngyè noncommercial: ～性能源 noncommercial energy /～储备 noncommercial reserve
非上市证券交易市场 fēishàngshì zhèngquàn jiāoyì shìchǎng 〈金融〉unlisted securities market (USM)
非生产部门 fēishēngchǎn bùmén nonproductive department
非生产劳动 fēishēngchǎn láodòng nonproductive labour
非生产性 fēishēngchǎnxìng unproductive; nonproductive: ～工程 nonproductive construction /～开支 nonproductive expenditure /～人员 nonproductive personnel
非市场 fēishìchǎng nonmarket: ～经济 nonmarket economy /～因素 nonmarket factor
非受益者 fēishòuyìzhě nonbeneficiary
非水 fēishuǐ 〈化学〉nonaqueous: ～溶剂 nonaqueous solvent
非税收 fēishuìshōu nontax: ～收入 nontax receipt (*or* revenue) /～支出 nontax payment
非司法 fēisīfǎ non-judicial: ～解释 non-judicial interpretation /～方法 non-judicial means /～机关 non-judicial organ
非斯大林化 fēi-Sīdàlínhuà de-Stalinization, systematic moves by leaders of the former Communist Party of the Soviet Union to discredit Joseph Stalin and dissociate themselves from him
非诉讼管辖 fēisùsòng guǎnxiá 〈法律〉non-contentious jurisdic-

tion

非特 fēitè 〈书面〉not only:此文~简练,而且寓意深刻。The essay is not only succinct in style but profound in meaning.

非条件刺激 fēitiáojiàn cìjī unconditioned stimulus

非条件反射 fēitiáojiàn fǎnshè unconditioned reflex

非通货膨胀 fēitōnghuò péngzhàng noninflationary:~性经济增长 noninflationary economic growth

非同儿戏 fēitóng'érxì no child's play; sth. very important:婚姻大事,~。Marriage is an important matter, not child's play.

非同小可 fēitóngxiǎokě no small or trivial matter:人命关天,~。This is no joking matter, for a person's life is at stake.

非统组织 Fēitǒng Zǔzhī *see*"非洲统一组织"

非投票股权 fēitóupiào gǔquán non-voting share

非徒 fēitú not merely; not only:揠苗助长,~无益,而且有害。It is not merely useless, but harmful to try to help the shoots grow by pulling them upwards.

非外交 fēiwàijiāo non-diplomatic:~代表 non-diplomatic representative (*or* agent) /~使团 non-diplomatic mission /~人员 non-diplomatic person

非违禁品 fēiwéijìnpǐn noncontraband

非我莫属 fēiwǒmòshǔ I, and I alone, deserve it; it is definitely mine:我自以为这次全国象棋赛冠军~。I thought that this time I would definitely be the champion of the National Chess Competition.

非我族类 fēiwǒzúlèi persons or things alien to oneself:他们把不同社会制度的国家视为~,总想除之而后快。They always try to subvert countries with different social systems, which they regard as beyond the pale.

非物质 fēiwùzhì nonmaterial:~货物 nonmaterial goods /~需要 nonmaterial need /~性劳务 nonmaterial service

非系统论 fēixìtǒnglùn non-systematology

非现金 fēixiànjīn noncash:~投入 noncash input /~支出 noncash outlay

非线性 fēixiànxìng 〈经济〉nonlinear:~规划 nonlinear programming /~经济学 nonlinear economics /~相关 nonlinear (*or* nonrectilinear) correlation /~回归 nonlinear regression

非限制性 fēixiànzhìxìng nonrestrictive:~定语从句 nonrestrictive attributive clause

非项目 fēixiàngmù nonprogrammed:~援助 nonprogrammed aid /~贷款 nonprogrammed lending

非消耗性 fēixiāohàoxìng nonexpendable:~设备 nonexpendable equipment /~部件 nonexpendable part /~基金 nonexpendable fund

非笑 fēixiào ridicule; jeer at; sneer at; deride:他那本著作,颇遭同行~。The book he wrote was held up to ridicule among his fellow writers.

非刑 fēixíng (unlawful) brutal torture; cruel and illegal punishment

非刑拷打 fēixíng kǎodǎ torture sb. brutally; subject sb. to brutal torture

非沿海 fēiyánhǎi non-coastal; non-maritime:~国 non-coastal state

非要素 fēiyàosù nonfactor:~劳务 nonfactor service

非移民 fēiyímín non-immigrant:~签证 non-immigrant visa

非议 fēiyì reproach; blame; condemn; censure:无可~ beyond (*or* above) reproach; irreproachable/不希望我们的学生在德才上受人~。We do not want our students to get reproached for lack of integrity or professional competence.

非银行 fēiyínháng nonbank:~筹资项目 nonbank financing project /~背书 nonbank endorsement

非饮用水 fēiyǐnyòngshuǐ 〈环保〉non-potable water

非盈利 fēiyínglì nonprofit; nonprofitable:~事业 nonprofit business /~营销 non-profit marketing /~公司 nonprofit company /~性社团 nonprofit-making association

非营业性 fēiyíngyèxìng nonoperating; nonoperative:~公司 nonoperating company /~收入 nonoperating income (*or* earnings) /~停泊时间 nonoperative lay-time /~支出 nonoperating outlay (*or* expense)

非优惠性 fēiyōuhuìxìng nonconcessional; nonpreferential:~官方贷款 nonconcessional official lending /~条件 nonconcessional terms /~循环办法 nonconcessional recycling mechanism /~关税 nonpreferential duty

非优先 fēiyōuxiān nonpriority:~目标 nonpriority objective /~项目 nonpriority project

非约定继承 fēiyuēdìng jìchéng 〈法律〉non-conventional succession

非约束性条款 fēiyuēshùxìng tiáokuǎn permissive provision

非再生 fēizàishēng non-renewable:~资源 non-renewable resources

非战斗人员 fēizhàndòu rényuán non-combatant

非战公约 fēizhàn gōngyuē anti-war pact

非正规军 fēizhèngguījūn irregular troops; irregulars

非正式 fēizhèngshì unofficial; informal:~声明 unofficial statement /~译文 unofficial (*or* tentative) translation /~会议 informal meeting

非正统 fēizhèngtǒng unorthodox:~意见 unorthodox view

非正义战争 fēizhèngyì zhànzhēng unjust war

非政府 fēizhèngfǔ nongovernment; nongovernmental; nonestablishment:~实体 nongovernmental entity /~组织 nongovernmental organization (NGO)/~专业协会 nongovernmental professional association /~交往 nongovernmental exchanges

非政治 fēizhèngzhì non-political:~行为 non-political act /~协定 non-political agreement /~犯 non-political criminal /~性国际组织 non-political organization of states /~性军事法院 non-political military court

非执行董事 fēizhíxíng dǒngshì non-executive director

非殖民化 fēizhímínhuà decolonization:~委员会 Committee on Decolonization

非制造业 fēizhìzàoyè nonmanufacturing industry

非周期性 fēizhōuqīxìng nonperiodicity

非洲 Fēizhōu Africa:西南~人民组织 South West Africa People's Organization (SWAPO) /~发展基金 African Development Fund /~前线国家 African frontline states /~人国民大会 African National Congress (ANC) /~铁路联盟 African Union of Railways /~邮政联盟 African Postal Union

非洲艾虎 Fēizhōu àihǔ zoril; zorille

非洲刺毛鼠 Fēizhōu cìmáoshǔ spiny mouse

非洲大羚羊 Fēizhōu dàlíngyáng gemsbok

非洲妇女日 Fēizhōu Fùnǚrì African Women's Day (July 31)

非洲河燕 Fēizhōu héyàn river martin

非洲昏睡病 Fēizhōu hūnshuìbìng 〈医学〉lethargus

非洲鲫鱼 Fēizhōu jìyú *also*"罗非鱼" luófēiyú African crucian; tilapia

非洲解放日 Fēizhōu Jiěfàngrì African Liberation Day (May 25)

非洲经济共同体 Fēizhōu Jīngjì Gòngtóngtǐ African Economic Community

非洲开发银行 Fēizhōu Kāifā Yínháng African Development Bank

非洲南猿 Fēizhōu nányuán *Australopithecus africanus*

非洲树蛇 Fēizhōu shùshé boomslang (*Dispholidus typus*)

非洲水羚 Fēizhōu shuǐlíng waterbuck

非洲司 Fēizhōusī Department of African Affairs (of the Ministry of Foreign Affairs)

非洲蹄兔 Fēizhōu títù hyrax

非洲统一组织 Fēizhōu Tǒngyī Zǔzhī (shortened as 非统) Organization of African Unity (OAU):~首脑会议 Summit of the Organization of African Unity /~国家和政府首脑会议 Assembly of Heads of State and Government of the Organization of African Unity

非洲议会联盟 Fēizhōu Yìhuì Liánméng African Parliamentary Union

非洲运动会 Fēizhōu Yùndònghuì African Games; Pan-African Games; All-African Games

非洲之角 Fēizhōu Zhī Jiǎo Horn of Africa

非洲自由日 Fēizhōu Zìyóurì African Freedom Day (April 15)

非主权 fēizhǔquán non-sovereign:~行为 non-sovereign act

非主要矛盾 fēizhǔyào máodùn nonprincipal contradiction

非专利技术 fēizhuānlì jìshù nonproprietary technology

非专属经济区 fēizhuānshǔ jīngjìqū 〈法律〉non-exclusive economic zone

非专业 fēizhuānyè non-professional:~领事〈外交〉non-professional consul

非自治 fēizìzhì nonselfgoverning; not autonomous:~领土 nonselfgoverning territory

非组织活动 fēizǔzhī huódòng non-organizational activity; factional activity

F

上～。The gulls were wheeling over the sea.
飞檐 fēiyán 〈建筑〉upturned eaves
飞檐走壁 fēiyán-zǒubì (of swordsmen, etc., in old Chinese novels) leap onto roofs and vault over walls:～的功夫 roof-climbing and wall-scaling skills
飞眼 fēiyǎn make eyes; ogle:他对她的～假装没有看见。He pretended not to notice when she made eyes at him.
飞扬 fēiyáng *also* "飞飏" ❶ fly upward; rise; float:汽车过后,尘土～。Clouds of dust rose behind the car. /歌声～。The sound of singing is floating in the air. ❷ in high spirits; elated:神采～ glowing with pride and happiness
飞扬跋扈 fēiyáng-báhù arrogant and domineering; unruly and haughty; throw one's weight around:这位部长夫人把儿子娇惯得～。The minister's wife has spoiled her son so much that he is unruly and arrogant in the extreme.
飞蝇症 fēiyíngzhèng *see* "飞蚊症"
飞鱼 fēiyú flying fish
飞鱼导弹 fēiyú dǎodàn Exocet (missile)
飞语 fēiyǔ *also* "蜚语" fēiyǔ rumour; hearsay; gossip
飞跃 fēiyuè ❶〈哲学〉leap:认识的～ leap in the process of cognition ❷ leap:～前进 leap forward /纺织业在～发展。Textile industry is developing by leaps and bounds. ❸ (of birds) leap or fly swiftly upward
飞越 fēiyuè ❶ overfly:～大西洋 fly over (*or* across) the Atlantic ❷〈书面〉in high spirits; elated; uplifted:他独自凭栏,神思～。Alone, he leaned on a railing, engrossed in elevated thoughts.
飞灾 fēizāi sudden disaster; unexpected calamity
飞仔 fēizǎi 〈方言〉hooligan
飞贼 fēizéi ❶ burglar who makes his way into a house over walls and roofs; cat burglar ❷ intruding enemy airman; air marauder or pirate
飞涨 fēizhǎng (of prices, etc.) soar; shoot up; skyrocket:物价～ soaring prices /医疗费用～。Medical costs have skyrocketed.
飞针走线 fēizhēn-zǒuxiàn ply one's needle nimbly; be skilful in needlework:～绣荷花 embroider lotus flowers quickly and skilfully
飞舟 fēizhōu swift boat:曾记否,到中流击水,浪遏～? But don't you remember How, venturing midstream, we struck the waters And waves stayed the speeding boats?
飞转 fēizhuàn (of wheels, etc.) turn or revolve swiftly:车轮～。The wheels (of the cart) turned swiftly.

F

妃 fēi ❶ imperial concubine:贵～ highest ranking imperial concubine ❷ wife of a prince, etc.:王～ princess consort
妃红 fēihóng light pink
妃嫔 fēipín imperial concubine
妃色 fēisè light pink
妃子 fēizi imperial concubine

féi

腓[1] féi calf (of the leg)

腓[2] féi 〈书面〉become diseased; wilt; wither:百卉俱～。All the plants have wilted.
腓肠肌 féichángjī 〈生理〉gastrocnemius
腓肠神经 féicháng shénjīng 〈生理〉sural nerve
腓骨 féigǔ 〈生理〉fibula
腓骨肌 féigǔjī 〈生理〉peroneal muscle (*musculus peroneus*)
腓尼基 Féiníjī 〈历史〉Phoenicia (in present-day coastal Syria and Lebanon):～人 Phoenician /～语 Phoenician (language)

肥 féi ❶ fat:～猪 fat pig ❷ fertile; rich: *see* "～美"; "～田❷" ❸ make fertile; fertilize: *see* "～田❶" ❹ fertilizer; manure; compost:农家～ farmyard manure /绿～ green manure /氮～ nitrogenous fertilizer /磷～ phosphorous fertilizer /钾～ potash fertilizer /积～ manure accumulation; stock up manure; store compost /沤～ make compost /施～ spread manure; apply fertilizer /施底～ apply base manure to the subsoil /追～ apply additional fertilizer; apply topdressing ❺ yielding good profits; lucrative; profitable:他专挑～活儿干。He always picks lucrative jobs for himself. ❻ feather one's nest; line one's pocket or purse:以公～私 fatten oneself on public funds /那警察接受贿赂以～私囊。The policeman lined his pockets by taking bribes. ❼ benefit; profit:分～ divide up the spoils ❽ loose-fitting; loose:这件大衣腰身～。The coat is large in girth. /鞋子太～不跟脚。These shoes are too loose to fit my feet.
肥差 féichāi lucrative post; fat job:这是一桩～。This is a fat job.
肥肠 féicháng pig's large intestines (used as food)
肥吃海喝 féichī-hǎihē 〈方言〉eat and drink extravagantly
肥膪膪 féidādā fatty; plumpy; corpulent:一个大小伙子养得～的,多难看! What an ugly-looking obese young chap!
肥大 féidà ❶ loose; large:他穿了件～的外套。He is wearing a loose coat. ❷ fat; plump; corpulent:～的白熊 fat polar bear /果实～甘美。The fruit is plump and sweet. ❸〈医学〉hypertrophy:心脏～ hypertrophy of the heart /～性肝硬变 hypertrophic cirrhosis; Hanot's cirrhosis; Todd's cirrhosis
肥大细胞 féidà xìbāo mast cell; mastocyte
肥嘟嘟 féidūdū 〈方言〉fatty; plump:～的脸蛋儿 plump cheeks
肥鹅肝 féi'égān foie gras
肥分 féifèn 〈农业〉(the percentage of) nutriment in a fertilizer
肥甘 féigān 〈书面〉delicious food; choice food:嗜食～ dote on delicious food; be a gourmet
肥羔 féigāo 〈畜牧〉fat lamb
肥厚 féihòu ❶ plump; fleshy:～的手掌 plump palm /果肉～。The pulp is full and fleshy. ❷ (of human organs) hypertrophic ❸ (of soil, etc.) fertile and deep:土层～ fertile and deep top soil ❹〈书面〉(of food) rich and delicious
肥厚性鼻炎 féihòuxìng bíyán 〈医学〉hypertrophic rhinitis
肥厚性胃炎 féihòuxìng wèiyán 〈医学〉hypertrophic gastritis
肥力 féilì 〈农业〉fertility (of soil)
肥料 féiliào fertilizer; manure:化学～ chemical fertilizer /有机～ organic fertilizer /无机～ inorganic fertilizer /细菌～ bacterial fertilizer /腐殖酸～ humic acid fertilizer /颗粒～ granulated fertilizer; pellet fertilizer /抗生素～ antibiotic fertilizer /～有效成分 effective fertilizer composition
肥溜溜 féiliūliū ❶ (of animals) stout and sleek; fat and smooth or shiny:～的黄牛 nice fat bullock ❷〈方言〉well-to-do; affluent; prosperous:～的日子 comfortable life
肥马轻裘 féimǎ-qīngqiú ride stout horses and wear light fur coats — live an extravagant or luxurious life:～,仆从如云 live in clover and be waited on by throngs of servants
肥煤 féiméi bituminous coal (used in coking)
肥美 féiměi ❶ fertile; fecund; rich:～的黑土地 rich black soil ❷ luxuriant; plump; fat; fleshy:～的牧场 rich pasture ❸ fleshy and delicious
肥胖 féipàng fat; corpulent; obese:他日渐～。He's getting fat. *or* He's putting on weight. /他年纪大了,逐渐～起来。He became stout as he grew older.
肥胖症 féipàngzhèng *also* "肥胖病"〈医学〉obesity; adiposis
肥缺 féiquē lucrative job or post:那是个～。That's a real bit of fat. /他新得到的那份差事可是个～。This new job he's got is a real plum (*or* a plum job).
肥肉 féiròu fat meat; fat:他不甘心到口的～让人抢了去。He is loath to let others snatch away the profits already within his reach.
肥腮鼓腹 féisāi-gǔfù fat cheeks and a big belly
肥实 féishi ❶ fat; stout:这汉子长得倒很～。He is a stout man. ❷ rich in fat:这块肉真够～的。This piece of meat is very fat indeed. ❸ rich; affluent:日子过得挺～ lead an affluent life; live in affluence
肥瘦儿 féishòur ❶ girth of a garment, etc.:这件外衣的～挺合适。The coat fits very well. *or* It's neither too loose nor too tight. ❷ proportion of fat and lean:给我来一块～肉。I'd like to take a chunk of meat, half fat half lean.
肥水 féishuǐ water rich in nutrients; liquid fertilizer:～不流外人田。〈俗语〉No rich water should be let out of one's own fields. *or* One should always keep all benefits for one's own people.
肥水外流 féishuǐ-wàiliú benefits meant for oneself accrue to others:这种商品,我们自己生产也很容易,何必进口,让～? Why should we import this kind of commodity, which we ourselves can very well produce, and thus let others reap the benefits?
肥硕 féishuò ❶ (of fruit) big and fleshy:～的大鸭梨 big and fleshy pear ❷ (of limbs and body) large and firm-fleshed
肥田 féitián ❶ fertilize or enrich the soil:～要多用有机肥。Better use more organic fertilizer to enrich the soil. ❷ fertile land; rich

soil
肥田草 féitiáncǎo fabaceous herbs (such as clover); herbal fertilizer
肥田粉 féitiánfěn 〈口语〉"soil-fertilizer" — ammonium sulphate
肥头大耳 féitóu-dà'ěr (of a man) big and fat; (of a child) plump; chubby:他家大儿子长得～。His eldest son is fat and bulky.
肥土 féitǔ rich soil; fertile land
肥尾鼠狐猴 féiwěi shǔhúhóu 〈动物〉fat-tailed lemur
肥沃 féiwò fertile; rich:～的黏土 rich clay /土地～。The land is fertile.
肥效 féixiào 〈农业〉fertilizer efficiency or effect; manurial effect
肥腴 féiyú ❶ fertile; rich:～的土壤 rich soil ❷ round and full; fat; plump:～的面颊 fat cheeks
肥育 féiyù 〈畜牧〉fattening
肥育地 féiyùdì feedlot
肥育期 féiyùqī stage of fattening
肥育猪 féiyùzhū fattening pig
肥源 féiyuán 〈农业〉source of manure or fertilizer
肥皂 féizào *also* "胰子" yízi soap:洗脸～ toilet soap /～泡 soap bubble /一块～ a cake of soap /一条～ a bar of soap /～盒 soap box /这种～起泡多。This soap lathers nicely.
肥皂粉 féizàofěn soap powder
肥皂剧 féizàojù 〈戏剧〉soap opera
肥皂片 féizàopiàn soap flakes
肥皂润滑 féizào rùnhuá suds lubrication
肥皂水 féizàoshuǐ soapsuds:～灌肠 soapsuds enema
肥壮 féizhuàng stout and strong:牲口～ thriving herds of cattle /禾苗～ healthy and strong seedlings (of cereal crops)

淝 Féi (short for 淝河) Feihe River (in Anhui Province)
淝水 Féishuǐ *also* "淝河" Feihe River (in Anhui Province):～之战 Battle of the Feihe River (383 AD), in which the Eastern Jin (东晋) army crushed the far more numerous army of the Former Qin (前秦)

fěi

斐 fěi 〈书面〉rich with literary grace; of striking literary talent
斐济 Fěijì Fiji:～人 Fijian /～语 Fijian (language)
斐林溶液 Fěilín róngyè Fehling's solution (used in the detection and estimation of certain sugars)
斐然 fěirán 〈书面〉❶ of striking literary talent:文采～ of great literary talent ❷ brilliant; splendid:功绩～ outstanding exploits; illustrious accomplishment; brilliant achievements
斐然成章 fěirán-chéngzhāng show striking literary merit or talent:平凡之文,往往经他修饰,便可～。His polishing can often turn a mediocre essay into a piece of beautiful prose.

悱 fěi 〈书面〉be at a loss for words; not know what to say
悱恻 fěicè 〈书面〉laden with sorrow; sad at heart; melancholy:缠绵～ exceedingly sentimental; extremely sad

诽 fěi slander; calumniate:腹～〈书面〉unspoken criticism
诽谤 fěibàng slander; calumniate; defame; libel:散布～之词 spread slanders /造谣～ cook up a story to vilify sb. /～名誉 character assassination; character defamation /～诉讼 libel action
诽谤案 fěibàng'àn case of libel
诽谤罪 fěibàngzuì crime of defamation; offence of libel; libel

菲 fěi ❶〈古语〉radish or red turnip ❷〈书面〉〈谦词〉humble; poor; unworthy:～礼 my humble gift /～材 my humble (*or* unworthy) talent
see also fēi
菲薄 fěibó ❶ humble; poor:～的物质生活 living plain /待遇～ poorly paid ❷ belittle; look down on; despise:妄自～ unduly belittle oneself; be excessively humble
菲敬 fěijìng 〈谦词〉small gift:聊备～,务望笑纳。Please kindly accept this small gift of mine.
菲食薄衣 fěishí-bóyī simple food and coarse clothing — lead a simple life
菲仪 fěiyí 〈谦词〉my small or humble, or unworthy gift
菲酌 fěizhuó 〈谦词〉simple meal:敬备～,恭候光临。We request the pleasure of your company at a simple dinner.

棐 fěi 〈书面〉assist; support

匪[1] fěi bandit; robber; brigand; gangster:土～ bandit; brigand; outlaw /盗～ bandit; robber /惯～ hardened bandit; professional brigand /绑～ kidnapper

匪[2] fěi 〈书面〉not; no:获益～浅 reap no little benefit; profit immensely /夙夜～懈 never slacken one's efforts; work day and night
匪帮 fěibāng bandit gang:～出没之处 place infested with bandits
匪巢 fěicháo bandits' lair or den
匪盗 fěidào bandit; robber; brigand
匪患 fěihuàn scourge of banditry; banditry
匪祸 fěihuò *see* "匪患"
匪军 fěijūn bandit troops; 〈贬义〉bandit army:蒋～ Chiang's bandit army (i. e. the Kuomintang army headed by Chiang Kai-shek)
匪窟 fěikū bandits' lair or hideout
匪酋 fěiqiú bandit chief or chieftain
匪首 fěishǒu bandit chieftain
匪徒 fěitú robber; brigand; gangster; bandit:一帮～ gang (*or* band) of bandits /抢银行的～ bank robber
匪穴 fěixué *see* "匪巢"
匪夷所思 fěiyísuǒsī 〈书面〉(of ideas, events, etc.) out of the ordinary; unimaginably queer; fantastic; bizarre:其设计之奇巧,～。The design is unimaginably ingenious.

榧 fěi 〈植物〉Chinese torreya
榧螺 fěiluó olive shell
榧子 fěizi 〈植物〉❶ Chinese torreya ❷ Chinese torreya-nut

篚 fěi 〈书面〉round bamboo basket

蜚 fěi 〈古语〉insects like locusts
see also fēi
蜚蠊 fěilián *also* "蟑螂" zhāngláng cockroach; roach

翡 fěi 〈古语〉〈动物〉halcyon
翡翠 fěicuì ❶〈动物〉halcyon (a kind of kingfisher) ❷ *also* "硬玉" yìngyù jadeite:～绿 jade green
翡翠羹 fěicuìgēng green vegetable soup
翡翠婚 fěicuìhūn emerald wedding anniversary, 55th wedding anniversary

朏 fěi 〈书面〉(of the crescent moon) begin to shine

fèi

吠 fèi bark; yap; yelp:狂～ bark furiously; howl /鸡鸣犬～。Cocks crow and dogs bark.
吠叫 fèijiào bark:夜里传来狗的阵阵～声。There were intermittent barks of dogs in the night.
吠犬不咬人 fèiquǎn bù yǎo rén barking dogs seldom bite; great barkers are no biters
吠舍 Fèishè Vaisya (third of the four Hindu castes in India, comprising merchants and farmers)
吠形吠声 fèixíng-fèishēng *also* "吠影吠声" when one dog barks at a shadow all the others join in — slavishly echo others:这群鼓噪的人中,有见解者少,～者多。Among those who are now raising a hubbub, few have any original ideas, and most of them are merely echoing others.

痱(疿) fèi prickly heat
痱子 fèizi 〈医学〉prickly heat:白～ sudamen; sudamina

F

痱子粉 fèizifěn prickly-heat powder

剕(踑) fèi amputating the feet (a cruel punishment in ancient China)

see also "五刑" wǔxíng

废(廢) fèi ❶ give up; abandon; reject; abolish: 半途而～ give up halfway / 国家兴～ rise and fall of a nation / 因噎～食 give up eating for fear of choking — refrain from doing what is right for fear of running a risk / 不以人～言。Do not reject an opinion because of the speaker. ❷ lie waste; decline: ～园 garden lying waste ❸ waste; useless; disused: ～弹壳 spent case / 修旧利～ repair old equipment and make use of waste materials / 作～ invalidate; declare invalid / 百～待举。A thousand things remain to be undertaken. ❹ disabled; maimed: ～疾 disability; cripplehood ❺〈书面〉depose; dethrone: ～太子 depose a crown prince / 皇帝被权臣所～。The emperor was dethroned by his powerful ministers.

废弛 fèichí (of a law, custom, etc.) cease to be binding; (of discipline, etc.) become lax: 纲纪～。Discipline has become lax and morale low.

废除 fèichú abolish; abrogate; annul; repeal: ～农奴制 abolish serfdom / ～一切不平等条约 abrogate all unequal treaties / ～陈规旧俗 annul outmoded customs and habits / ～过时的法律 repeal an obsolete law / ～不合理的规章制度 do away with unreasonable rules and regulations / ～债务 cancel a debt

废除令 fèichúlìng 〈法律〉abatement order

废黜 fèichù ❶〈书面〉banish; dismiss from office ❷ dethrone; depose: ～国王 dethrone the king

废船 fèichuán disabled ship; hulk; scrap boat

废帝 fèidì ❶ dethroned emperor ❷ depose or dethrone an emperor

废钢 fèigāng scrap steel

废耕 fèigēng (of land) be left uncultivated; lie waste

废话 fèihuà ❶ superfluous words; nonsense; rubbish: ～少说。No more rubbish! / 少说～，多干实事。No more idle words, but more solid work. / ～! 谁还不知道这么办不行? You're wasting your breath! Who doesn't know this won't work? ❷ talk nonsense: 别再～了! Don't talk nonsense!

废话连篇 fèihuà-liánpiān reams of rubbish; pages and pages of nonsense; load of garbage: 他的报告～。His speech was nothing but verbiage.

废金属 fèijīnshǔ metal scrap

废井 fèijǐng disused well

废旧 fèijiù old and useless (things): ～物资 waste materials; scrap / ～货市场 junk market / ～资产处理费用 cost of scrap disposition

废矿 fèikuàng abandoned mine

废料 fèiliào waste material; waste; scrap; junk: ～场 junk yard / ～堆 scrap heap; waste heap; junk / ～仓 reject bin / ～槽 reject chute / ～报告单 report on scrap materials / ～处理 waste disposal; scrap handling; waste treatment

废料艺术 fèiliào-yìshù junk art: ～家 junk artist

废棉 fèimián cotton waste

废木料 fèimùliào wood waste

废奴运动 Fèinú Yùndòng 〈历史〉Abolition Movement (1783-1888)

废圮 fèipǐ 〈书面〉be in ruins and deserted: 这座古刹久已～。The ancient temple has long fallen into ruin.

废票 fèipiào ❶ invalidated ticket ❷ invalidated ballot; spoilt vote

废品 fèipǐn ❶ waste product; reject: ～率 reject rate ❷ scrap; waste; junk: 收～的 scrap collector; rags-and-bone man

废品处理 fèipǐn chǔlǐ salvaging

废品袋 fèipǐndài litterbag

废品回收 fèipǐn huíshōu waste recovery; salvage of waste material

废品收购站 fèipǐn shōugòuzhàn salvage station (where waste materials may be turned in for payment)

废气 fèiqì waste gas or steam; exhaust steam; exhaust: ～处理 waste gas treatment / ～综合利用 multipurpose use of waste gas / 汽车～ car exhaust

废气阀 fèiqìfá exhaust gas valve

废弃 fèiqì discard; abandon; cast aside; fall into disuse: 久已～的旧货场 long discarded old freight yard / ～财产 abandoned property / ～费用 abandonment charge; obsolescence charge / ～一项协定 denounce an agreement / 旧机器已～不用。The old machinery has been dumped.

废寝忘食 fèiqǐn-wàngshí (so absorbed or occupied as to) forget all about food and sleep; (work day and night) without eating or sleeping: ～地工作 devote oneself whole-heartedly to work / 一工作，他就～。Once he gets down to work, all thoughts of sleep or food vanish from his mind.

废然 fèirán 〈书面〉dispirited and disappointed: ～而返 come back disappointed

废燃料 fèiránliào 〈环保〉waste fuel

废热 fèirè 〈环保〉waste heat: ～供暖 waste heating / ～锅炉 waste heat boiler; gastube boiler; exhaust boiler / ～回收 waste heat recovery / ～蒸汽机 waste heat engine / ～发电 cogeneration

废人 fèirén ❶ disabled person ❷ simpleton; good-for-nothing: 你这点活也干不好，真是个～! What a dunce! You can't even do such a simple job.

废水 fèishuǐ waste water; liquid waste: ～渗透 waste water infiltration

废水处理场 fèishuǐ chǔlǐchǎng waste water processing station

废水处理池 fèishuǐ chǔlǐchí purification tank for liquid waste

废水分流系统 fèishuǐ fēnliú xìtǒng effluent segregation system

废水氧化池 fèishuǐ yǎnghuàchí waste oxidation basin

废丝 fèisī 〈纺织〉waste silk

废铁 fèitiě scrap iron: ～压块机 scrap baling press

废铜烂铁 fèitóng-làntiě metal scrap

废物 fèiwù waste material; junk; trash: ～利用 make use of waste material; convert waste into useful material; recycling of wastes / ～处理 waste treatment; waste disposal / ～综合处理 integrated treatment of waste

废物 fèiwu 〈粗话〉dimwit; good-for-nothing: 老～ old vegetable / ～点心〈方言〉good-for-nothing; worthless person

废物处理场 fèiwù chǔlǐchǎng wasteyard

废物袋 fèiwùdài litterbag

废物商 fèiwùshāng junk dealer

废墟 fèixū ruins; debris: 地震使这座城市成了～。The earthquake reduced the city to ruins.

废学 fèixué discontinue one's studies; drop out of school

废液 fèiyè waste or used water; liquid waste: ～处理 waste liquor treatment

废油 fèiyóu waste oil; used oil; refuse oil: ～处理设施 waste oil disposal facility

废渣 fèizhā waste residue; slag; dross: ～堆 slagheap

废蒸汽 fèizhēngqì exhaust steam; waste steam

废止 fèizhǐ abolish; annul; nullify; put to an end: ～协议 nullify an agreement / ～婚约 annul a marriage contract / ～应试教学 put an end to learning merely for the sake of exams / ～流通 demonetization / ～契约 defeasance

废址 fèizhǐ abandoned site

废纸 fèizhǐ waste paper: ～篓 wastebasket; scrap basket / 请勿乱扔～。Please don't litter the place with waste paper. / 和平条约连一张～都不如。The peace treaty was not worth a scrap of paper (*or* not worth the paper it was written on).

废置 fèizhì put aside as useless: 那台旧发电机久已～。The old generator has long been out of use.

篚(籭) fèi 〈书面〉bamboo mat

芾 fèi *see* "蔽芾" bìfèi

see also fú

肺 fèi lung

肺癌 fèi'ái carcinoma of the lung; cancer in the lung; lung cancer

肺病 fèibìng pulmonary tuberculosis (TB); lung disease

肺不张 fèibùzhāng 〈医学〉atelectasis (of a newborn baby)

肺肠炎 fèichángyán pneumoenteritis

肺尘病 fèichénbìng pneumoconiosis; pneumokoniosis

肺充血 fèichōngxuè pneumonemia

肺出血 fèichūxuè pneumorrhagia

肺动脉 fèidòngmài pulmonary artery: ～瓣 pulmonary valve / ～瓣狭窄 pulmonary stenosis

肺动脉高血压 fèidòngmài gāoxuèyā pulmonary hypertension
肺腑 fèifǔ bottom of one's heart：发自～ from the depths of one's heart／感人～ move one deeply；touch one to the depths of one's soul
肺腑之交 fèifǔzhījiāo bosom friend；deep and sincere friendship：平生只有二三～。I have had only a couple of bosom friends in all my life.
肺腑之言 fèifǔzhīyán words from the bottom of one's heart：他这番～你不可不听。You must heed these words that come from the bottom of his heart.
肺活量 fèihuóliàng （of lungs）vital capacity：～计 spirometer／～测定法 spirometry
肺结核 fèijiéhé *also* "肺病" pulmonary tuberculosis（TB）
肺静脉 fèijìngmài pulmonary vein
肺镜 fèijìng 〈医学〉pneumoscope
肺痨 fèiláo 〈中医〉consumption；tuberculosis
肺螺 fèiluó 〈动物〉pulmonate
肺囊肿 fèinángzhǒng pulmonary cyst
肺脓肿 fèinóngzhǒng pulmonary or lung abscess
肺泡 fèipào 〈生理〉pulmonary alveolus（*alveolus pulmonum*）：～炎 pulmonary alveolitis／～音 vesicular sound／～蛋白沉积症 pulmonary alveolar proteinosis／～小结石病 pulmonary alveolar microlithiasis
肺气 fèiqì 〈中医〉lung *qi* or vital energy：～不宣 lung *qi* obstruction／～上逆 lung *qi* upward reversal／～虚 lung *qi* deficiency
肺气肿 fèiqìzhǒng pulmonary emphysema（*emphysema pulmonum*）；pneumonectasis：～病（of a horse）broken wind
肺切除术 fèiqiēchúshù pneumonectomy
肺肾虚 fèishènxū 〈中医〉lung-kidney deficiency
肺栓塞 fèishuānsè pulmonary embolism
肺水肿 fèishuǐzhǒng pulmonary edema；pneumonedema
肺外科 fèiwàikē pneumochirurgia；pneumosurgery
肺吸虫 fèixīchóng *also* "肺蛭" lung fluke
肺吸虫病 fèixīchóngbìng paragonimiasis
肺细胞 fèixìbāo pneumonocyte
肺线虫 fèixiànchóng thread lungworm：～病 lungworm disease
肺心病 fèixīnbìng *also* "肺原性心脏病" pulmonary heart disease
肺胸膜炎 fèixiōngmóyán pneumopleuritis
肺循环 fèixúnhuán *also* "小循环" xiǎoxúnhuán 〈生理〉pulmonary circulation
肺压计 fèiyājì pneumatometer
肺炎 fèiyán pneumonia：大叶～ lobar pneumonia／小叶～ lobular pneumonia／双～ double pneumonia／～球菌 pneumococcus／～杆菌 pneumobacillus
肺叶 fèiyè 〈生理〉lobe of the lung
肺硬变 fèiyìngbiàn 〈医学〉cirrhosis of lung；pulmonary cirrhosis
肺鱼 fèiyú lungfish；sirenoid；dipnoan
肺原性心脏病 fèiyuánxìng xīnzàngbìng （shortened as 肺心病）pulmonary heart disease
肺脏 fèizàng lungs
肺蛭 fèizhì *also* "肺吸虫" lung fluke

沸

fèi boil；bubble：～水 boiling water／街上人声鼎～ great commotion in the street／扬汤止～ try to stop water from boiling by scooping it out and pouring it back（without removing the fire underneath）— apply a palliative
沸点 fèidiǎn 〈物理〉boiling point：～温度 boiling temperature／～升高测定法〈化学〉ebullioscopy
沸点测定计 fèidiǎn cèdìngjì ebulliometer
沸点测高计 fèidiǎn cègāojì hypsometer
沸反盈天 fèifǎn-yíngtiān raise a hullabaloo；kick up a rumpus；be in an uproar：刚到门口，就听见里面哭得～。When I was about to step in, I heard a pandemonium of weeping and wailing in the room.
沸沸扬扬 fèifèi-yángyáng bubbling and gurgling；in a hubbub：这件事在居民院儿里～地议论起来。A hubbub arose over the matter in the compound.／这消息～，不胫而走。The news spread like wildfire.
沸滚 fèigǔn boiling：～的油锅 cauldron containing boiling oil
沸绿岩 fèilǜyán teschenite
沸泉 fèiquán 〈地质〉near-boiling spring（a spring with a temperature of over 80°C）
沸热 fèirè boiling hot；steaming hot：气温～ very hot weather／此人心肠～。He is extremely warm-hearted.
沸石 fèishí *also* "泡沸石" pàofèishí zeolite：～催化 zeolite catalysis／～酯 zeolite ester
沸水 fèishuǐ boiling water
沸水反应堆 fèishuǐ fǎnyìngduī boiling water reactor：～核电厂 boiling water reactor power plant
沸汤 fèitāng 〈方言〉boiling water
沸腾 fèiténg ❶ boil；bubble；reach ebullition：～的熔岩 bubbling lava／～的钢水 boiling steel；rimmed steel／～反应 boiling reaction ❷ seethe with excitement；boil over：热血～ one's blood boils／沿途所见，使我们感受到处处有～的生活。We felt from what we saw during our trip that life was seething with excitement everywhere. ❸ noisy and confused：人声～ hubbub of voices
沸腾炉 fèiténglú fluosolid furnace
沸扬 fèiyáng seethe with excitement；bubble over：～的感情 bubbling over with excitement；very excited／心情～ ebullient；in a state of ebullience／街上人声、爆竹声一阵阵～起来。The street was in pandemonium with the sounds of people and firecrackers.
沸涌 fèiyǒng boil over；surge：波涛～ seething（*or* surging）waves／心潮～ feel an upsurge of emotion

费

fèi ❶ fee；charge；expenses；fare：经～ expenses；expenditure／学～ tuition（*or* schooling）fee；tuition／注册～ registration fee／生活～ living expenses／办公～ administrative expenses／水电～ charges for water and electricity／修理～ repair charge／会～ membership dues（*or* fee）／医药～ medical costs／报～ subscription for a newspaper／房～ rent／车～ fare／车马～ travel allowance／养路～ road toll／免～ free of charge；gratis／工本～ production cost ❷ cost；spend；expend：买这房子～了我们不少钱。This house cost us a lot of money.／修这部车～了我好多时间。It took me quite some time to fix the car.／让你破～了。Sorry to have made you go to some expense. ❸ be wasteful；consume too much；expend too quickly：枉～口舌 waste one's breath／～时间的工作 time-consuming job／～燃料的锅炉 energy-consuming boiler／白～力 labour in vain／这种冰箱～电。This kind of fridge consumes too much electricity.／这种车～油。The car is a gas guzzler.／孩子很～鞋。Children wear out shoes quickly. ❹（Fèi）a surname
费边社 Fèibiānshè Fabian Society, a socialist organization aiming at the gradual change of society（founded in 1883-1884 in London）
费边主义 Fèibiānzhǔyì *also* "费边社会主义" Fabianism
费城 Fèichéng （short for 费拉德尔菲亚）Philadelphia（in Pennsylvania）, fourth largest city in the United States
费唇舌 fèi chúnshé take a lot of talking or explaining：事已至此，我就不必多～了。Such being the case, I might as well save my breath.／我费尽唇舌，才算把他说通了。I finally convinced him after nearly talking myself dry.
费尔斯通轮胎和橡胶公司 Fèi'ěrsītōng Lúntāi Hé Xiàngjiāo Gōngsī Firestone Tire and Rubber Company, major American tire producer, founded in 1900
费工 fèigōng take a lot of work；require a lot of labour：加工这种零件太～。It takes too much work to manufacture this kind of spare parts.
费工夫 fèi gōngfu *also* "费功夫" take time and energy；be time-consuming：不怕～ not stint one's time；spare no pains or efforts／做景泰蓝很～。Making cloisonné is very time-consuming（work）.／试制这种产品，可～了。It took a lot of time and energy to trial-produce this product.
费话 fèihuà take a lot of arguing or explaining：费了我不少话才使他回心转意。It took me a lot of persuading to bring him round.
费解 fèijiě hard to understand；obscure；puzzling；unintelligible：他这句话着实令人～。What he said is almost inscrutable.／你的观点有点儿令人～。Your views are a bit obscure（*or* vague）.
费尽心机 fèijìn-xīnjī rack one's brains（in scheming）：敌人～在人民中间散播各种疑虑，但这一切都是枉然的。The enemies were at pains to sow seeds of doubt among the people, but all to no avail.
费劲 fèijìn exert much effort；go to great pains；be strenuous：一点不～ without any difficulty；quite easy／他费了好大的劲儿去说明这一点。He went to great pains to drive the point home.／改这篇稿子很～。It's no easy task revising this article.
费力 fèilì require or need great effort；be strenuous：我没怎么～就完成了这件工作。It took me little effort to accomplish the work.／他费了九牛二虎之力才找到那首诗的手稿。With a Herculean effort he finally located the original manuscript of the poem.

费力不讨好 fèilì bù tǎohǎo do a hard but thankless job; work hard but to no avail; be arduous but useless or fruitless: ～的工作 tough but thankless work; demanding but unrewarding job

费率 fèilǜ 〈通信〉 tariff: ～再平衡 tariff rebalancing

费率分割 fèilǜ fēngē 〈通信〉 accounting separation

费米 fèimǐ ❶ (Fèimǐ) Enrico Fermi (1901-1954), Italian-born American atomic physicist: ～－狄拉克统计 Fermi-Dirac statistics ❷ 〈核物理〉 fermi (1 fermi = 10^{-13} cm)

费米子 fèimǐzǐ 〈核物理〉 fermion

费难 fèinán 〈方言〉 find sth. difficult to do; give sb. trouble; be hard put to it: 要她当众发言,她可费了难了。She was hard put to it to speak in public.

费钱 fèiqián cost a lot; be costly: 白～ waste of money /房子装修～。Fitting up a house costs a lot of money.

费神 fèishén ❶ 〈套语〉 may I trouble you (to do sth.); would you mind (doing sth.): 请您～给照看一下。Would you be so kind as to take care of it? /～之处,容后面谢。I'll thank you in person for the trouble you've taken on my behalf. ❷ tax one's energy; be exhausting: 在家里我不愿理财,太～。It's too much of a tax on the brain to run the family budget, so I shun the job.

费时 fèishí take time; be time-consuming: 编写词典～费力。Compiling a dictionary drains both time and energy.

费事 fèishì give or take a lot of trouble; be troublesome: "别～了,随便吃点就可以了。" "一点也不～。" "Don't bother to cook. Anything ready will do with me." "Oh, it's no trouble at all." /他费了不少事才把这件事办成。He went to a lot of trouble to get it done.

费手脚 fèi shǒujiǎo need or require much effort: 这件事请你费点手脚去张罗一下。Would you mind sparing some effort to attend to this matter?

费唾沫 fèi tuòmo take a lot of explaining or arguing: 谈了半天,白～,没有什么结果。I wasted a lot of time and breath in the talk I had with him.

费心 fèixīn ❶ give great care; take much trouble: 她为编那本书可费了不少心。She devoted a lot of care to editing the book. /非常感谢您为我儿子的事～。Thank you ever so much for the trouble you've taken for my son. ❷ 〈套语〉 may I trouble you (to do sth.); would you mind (doing sth.): 下次您见到他时,～把这本书交给他。Would you kindly give him the book when you see him next time?

费眼神 fèi yǎnshén strain the eye(s): 这字太小,～。The print is too small. It strains the eyes. *or* The small print taxes the eye.

费用 fèiyong cost; expenses: 生产～ production cost /～概算 cost estimate /生活～ cost of living; living expenses /他的医疗～尚无着落。We still don't know how to pay his medical expenses. /我付不起请一个家庭教师的～。I cannot pay for the luxury of a private tutor.

费正清 Fèizhèngqīng John King Fairbank (1907-1991), US historian and sinologist

费嘴皮子 fèi zuǐpízi waste one's breath; talk nonsense: 事情已经这样定了,不必再～了。It's decided. Don't waste your breath any more.

镄

fèi 〈化学〉 fermium (Fm)

狒

fèi

狒狒 fèifèi 〈动物〉 baboon

fēn

分

fēn ❶ divide; separate; split; part: 全书～为若干章节 divide a book into several chapters /～组座谈 hold talks in groups /河流在此～为三条支流。The river splits into three tributaries at this point. /从地形地貌上美国可以～成三个主要地区。Physiographically and topographically the United States may be divided into three major regions. /这副中药～两天服用。This Chinese medicine is to be taken in two days. /他们道别时感到难舍难～。They found it difficult (*or* couldn't bear) to part from each other. /本地区的植物大致～为三类。The plants in this region fall roughly into three categories. ❷ distribute; assign; allot: 我来～电影票。Let me distribute the film tickets. /每人都～到一项具体任务。Each person was assigned a specific task. /厂方给每个雇员～了一套住房。The factory allotted a flat to each employee. ❸ tell; distinguish; differentiate: 五谷不～ unable to distinguish one food crop from another /不～青红皂白 make no distinction between black and white (*or* right and wrong) /不～伯仲 be equally matched ❹ branch (of an organization): ～公司 branch company /～局 branch office; sub-bureau /第三～册 Book III; third volume (of a work) /新华社香港～社 Hong Kong Branch of the Xinhua News Agency ❺ fraction: 约～ reduce a fraction /通～ reduce fractions to a common denominator ❻ *used in fractions and percentages*: 五～之二 two fifths /七～之一 one seventh /百～之三 three per cent ❼ one-tenth: 七～成绩,三～错误 70 per cent achievements, 30 per cent mistakes /有十～把握 be hundred per cent sure /有一～热,发一～光 give as much light as the heat can produce; exert every bit of one's energy /酒劲儿上来,他的话不免多了几～。He became talkative under the influence of the alcohol. ❽ *fen*, a unit of length (= $\frac{1}{3}$ centimetre): 一尺二寸三～ one *chi* and two *cun* and three *fen* ❾ *fen*, a unit of area (one tenth of a *mu*, = 66.666 square metres): 一亩三～地 1.3 *mu* of land ❿ *fen*, a unit of weight (one tenth of a *qian*, = $\frac{1}{2}$ gram): 这条金项链重一两二钱五～。This gold necklace weighs one *liang* and two and a half *qian*. ⓫ *fen*, a fractional unit of money in China (= $\frac{1}{100}$ of a *yuan* or $\frac{1}{10}$ of a *jiao*): 十元五角三～ ten *yuan* and fifty-three *fen* ⓬ minute (= $\frac{1}{60}$ of an hour): 剧场下午七点十五～开演。The opera began at a quarter past seven p.m. /我每晚十一点三十～睡觉。I went to bed at half past eleven p.m. every night. ⓭ minute (= $\frac{1}{60}$ of a degree): 北纬 70 度 23～ 70 degrees and 23 minutes (70°23′) north latitude ⓮ *of interest rate*: 月利二～ a monthly interest of 2% /年利一～二厘 12% annual interest ⓯ point; mark: 上半场结束时我队领先五～。Our team led by five points in the first half. /这次算术考试他得 95～。He got 95 marks out of 100 in the arithmetic exam. ⓰ 〈方言〉 banknote; ten-*yuan* note: 捞～ make money

see also fèn

分包合同 fēnbāo hétong subcontract

分包人 fēnbāorén *also* "分包商" subcontractor

分保 fēnbǎo reinsurance

分保合同 fēnbǎo hétong reinsurance treaty

分贝 fēnbèi 〈物理〉 decibel (db): 高出正常标准几～ several decibels above the norm

分贝计 fēnbèijì decibel or db meter

分崩离析 fēnbēng-líxī disintegrate; fall to pieces; come or fall apart; crumble: 傀儡政权～,处境极为狼狈。The puppet regime began to fall apart and was in dire straits.

分辨 fēnbiàn ❶ distinguish; differentiate: ～美丑 distinguish the beautiful from the ugly /～是非 distinguish between right and wrong; tell right from wrong /～字迹 identify sb.'s handwriting /这种年月,好人坏人难以～。In times like this, it's difficult to separate the sheep from the goats. ❷ 〈物理〉 resolution; resolve: ～度 resolution /～力 resolution (capacity); resolving power /～系数 resolution ratio /～误差 resolution error

分辩 fēnbiàn defend oneself (against a charge); offer an explanation: 不容～ allow no explanation

分别 fēnbié ❶ part; say goodbye to each other: ～前咱们合个影吧。Let's have a picture taken before we say good-bye to each other. /他们～有年。They have been parted for years. ❷ distinguish; differentiate: ～好坏 distinguish good from bad /对工作要～轻重缓急,合理安排。We must differentiate the important and urgent from the less important and less urgent in our work. *or* We must arrange our work in order of importance and urgency (*or* priority). ❸ distinction; difference: 两者在颜色上没有什么～。There is no difference between the two in colour. /两种意见没有什么～。There is no distinction between the two views. /这两件事性质不同,应该～对待。They are problems of different character and should be treated differently. ❹ respectively; separately: ～进行调整 be adjusted each on its own /两支巡逻队到达目的地后～执行任务。The two patrol teams went about their respective missions immediately after arriving at their destination. /两案～处理。The two cases will be dealt with separately.

分兵 fēnbīng divide forces: ～把守要隘 divide forces to defend strategic passes

分拨 fēnbō ❶ allocate and transfer (goods or funds); allot: 货物已～各销售网点。The merchandise has been transferred to the various stores for sale. ❷ assign; dispatch: ～部分劳力去植树 dispatch some workers to plant trees ❸ divide into groups or batches: 我们分三拨儿参观电站。We are going to visit the power station in three groups.

分布 fēnbù be distributed (over an area); be spread over; be dispersed; be scattered:人口～ population distribution /这些少数民族主要～在云贵境内。These ethnic (*or* national minority) groups are mainly distributed over Yunnan and Guizhou provinces. /我国森林～地区很广。Forests are widely dispersed over our country. /电话亭～全市。Telephone booths are scattered all over the city.

分布函数 fēnbù hánshù 〈数学〉distribution function

分布区 fēnbùqū distribution (range); range:大熊猫～ range of the giant panda

分布式计算机 fēnbùshì jìsuànjī 〈计算机〉distributed computer

分布式人工智能 fēnbùshì réngōng zhìnéng 〈信息〉distributed AI (artificial intelligence)

分布式网络 fēnbùshì wǎngluò distributed network

分布式运算 fēnbùshì yùnsuàn 〈信息〉distributed computing

分部 fēnbù subsection; branch (department)

分餐 fēncān *also* "分食" meal served individually; (a dinner or banquet at which) each has his own portion of food (instead of sharing food from common plates on the table)

分册 fēncè separately published part of a book; fascicle:第三～ Book Three

分叉管接 fēnchā guǎnjiē Y-joint

分汊 fēnchà (of rivers) diverge; fork out:这条河在这里～。The river forks out here. /这条小河是淮河的～。This stream is a tributary of the Huaihe River.

分杈 fēnchà ❶ branch; fork; diverge:树干长到这儿～。The trunk forks here. /棉花～时节快到了。It's almost branching time for cotton. ❷ branch; ramification:打掉～ trim off the branches

分拆 fēnchāi 〈数学〉partition:～函数 partition function

分成 fēnchéng divide into tenths; share:～收入 shared revenue /～税 shared tax /四六～ divide into two shares of four and six tenths (with one party getting 40% and the other 60%)

分词 fēncí 〈语言〉participle:现在～ present participle /过去～ past participle /～短语 participial phrase

分爨 fēncuàn 〈书面〉(of brothers) cook separately — live apart:兄弟～。The brothers are living apart now.

分寸 fēncun proper limits for speech or action; sense of propriety or proportion:有失～ have gone too far; overstep the limits /这个年轻人做事不知～。The young man has no sense of propriety in doing things. /他的措词很有～。He chose his words appropriately. /在公共场合讲话,有时不易掌握～。On public occasions, it is sometimes difficult to know what is proper to say and what is not.

分担 fēndān share; contribute:责任～和危机处理 shared responsibility and crisis management /～风险和亏损 share risks and losses /平均～ share and share alike /～利益及～价值 contributing interests and value /我们共同～这笔费用。Let's split up the cost. /他们夫妇～家务。The couple share household chores.

分导式多弹头再入飞行器 fēndǎoshì duōdàntóu zàirù fēixíngqì multiple independently-targeted reentry vehicle (MIRV):～导弹 MIRV missile

分道 fēndào 〈体育〉lane:第二～ second lane

分道扬镳 fēndào-yángbiāo *also* "分路扬镳" separate and go different ways; part company; each going his own way:你既然坚持己见,我恐怕只好和你～了。I am afraid I must part company with you, as you are so opinionated.

分得 fēndé get one's share:最近他～了父亲的部分遗产。He got his share of his father's legacy recently.

分等 fēnděng grade; classify:皮棉按质～ grade (*or* price) ginned cotton according to quality /客房～论价 fix rates of hotel rooms according to their grades /～销售 selling by grades

分店 fēndiàn branch (of a shop):～独立会计制 decentralized branch accounting /～间送货运费 freight on inter-branch transfers

分度 fēndù graduation (of a measuring instrument)

分段 fēnduàn in sections; section by section; sector by sector:～解决(边界问题) sector-by-sector solution (of the border question)

分队 fēnduì troop unit corresponding to the platoon or squad; detachment; element:侦察小～ scout squad

分而治之 fēn'érzhìzhī divide and rule; *divide et impera*:采取"～"的策略 adopt the tactics of "divide and rule"

分发 fēnfā ❶ distribute; hand out; issue:～试卷 hand out examination papers /向灾民～救济食品 distribute relief food to disaster victims /～证书 issue certificates individually ❷ assign (to a post); appoint (to a job):这项工作～谁干好? Who shall we assign the job?

分肥 fēnféi share out ill-gotten gains; divide booty; divide up the spoils

分肥制 fēnféizhì spoils system (in US politics)

分封 fēnfēng enfeoff:～诸侯 award hereditary titles and invest the nobles with fiefs

分封制 fēnfēngzhì system of enfeoffment (as of the Western Zhou Dynasty, investing nobles with hereditary titles, territories and slaves)

分赴 fēnfù leave for different destinations:～各个战场 leave for the various war fronts /毕业生已～不同的工作岗位。The graduates have gone to take up different posts.

分付 fēnfu tell; order; instruct
see also "吩咐" fēnfu

分割 fēngē cut apart; carve up; separate; break up:～销售 split sale /连体婴～手术 operation to separate Siamese twins /～围歼敌人 break up the enemy forces into many pockets and wipe them out one by one; carve up and wipe out the enemy /台湾是中国领土不可～的一部分。Taiwan is an inalienable (*or* inseparable) part of Chinese territory.

分割铸造法 fēngē zhùzàofǎ 〈冶金〉separated casting

分隔 fēngé isolate; separate; partition:一间房～为前店后厂。The house was partitioned into two, the one at the front serving as a store and the other at the back as a workshop. /一家人被～在军事分界线的两边。The family was separated by the military demarcation line. /与其说海洋把世界～开,倒不如说它们将世界连成一体。Oceans don't so much divide the world as unite it.

分隔板 fēngébǎn demarcation strip

分隔变压器 fēngé biànyāqì isolating transformer

分隔信息系统 fēngé xìnxī xìtǒng isolation information system

分工 fēngōng division of labour:专业～ division of labour based on specialization /国际～ international division of labour /职员各有～。Each staff member has his or her own responsibility. /有～也有协作。There is division of work as well as coordination of effort.

分工合作 fēngōng-hézuò share out the work and help one another; have division of labour as well as cooperation

分管 fēnguǎn assume personal responsibility for; be in charge of:他是～技术革新的副厂长。He is the deputy director in charge of technological innovations. /我受命～这个部门。I am authorized to take charge of the department.

分光吃光 fēnguāng-chīguāng divide and eat up everything; consume all one's income and resources

分光辐射计 fēnguāng fúshèjì 〈物理〉spectroradiometer

分光光度学 fēnguāng guāngdùxué 〈物理〉spectrophotometry

分光计 fēnguāngjì 〈物理〉spectrometer

分光镜 fēnguāngjìng 〈物理〉spectroscope:～分析 spectroscopic analysis

分规 fēnguī *see* "分线规"

分行 fēnháng branch (of a bank):国内～ home (*or* domestic) branch /国外～ overseas branch /～间往来 inter-branch exchanges

分毫 fēnháo fraction; iota:与原设计～不差 precisely the same as the original design; without an iota of difference from the original blueprint

分号 fēnhào ❶ semicolon(;) ❷ branch (of a firm, etc.):小店在本市有三家～。Our shop has three branches in the city. /只此一家,别无～。Our shop is the only one bearing the name; there are no branches. *or* Ours is the only authentic kind.

分红 fēnhóng share out bonus; draw dividends or profits:～制度 bonus system; premium system /～人寿保险 life insurance with dividend /按股～ dividends on shares; dividends to the shareholders

分洪 fēnhóng flood diversion:～工程 flood-diversion project

分洪区 fēnhóngqū flood-diversion area

分洪闸 fēnhóngzhá flood-diversion sluice

分户账 fēnhùzhàng ledger

分化 fēnhuà ❶ become divided; split up; break up:贫富两极～ polarization of rich and poor /执政党已经～为三大派。The ruling party has split up into three major factions. /顽固派正在～。The diehards are disintegrating (*or* falling apart). ❷ divide:可从对方营垒中把她～出来。We can win her over from the rival camp. ❸〈生物〉(of cells, etc.) differentiate:～变异 dissociation /～期 idiophase /～素 differone /～转移 transdifferentiation

分化瓦解 fēnhuà-wǎjiě divide and demoralize; disintegrate; split:～敌人 disintegrate the enemy (forces)

F

分会 fēnhuì branch (of a society, committee, association, etc.); sub-committee; chapter
分机 fēnjī (telephone) extension:～号码 extension number
分级 fēnjí grade; gradate; classify:本店商品均～销售。All commodities in the shop are sold in grades.
分级淬火 fēnjí cuìhuǒ 〈冶金〉graded hardening
分级存货管理 fēnjí cúnhuò guǎnlǐ ABC control; selective inventory control
分级护理 fēnjí hùlǐ classified system of nursing
分级机 fēnjíjī 〈农业〉grader; sorter:水果～ fruit grader /马铃薯～ potato sorter
分级数据模型 fēnjí shùjù móxíng hierarchical data model
分家 fēnjiā ❶ (of family members, usu. grown and married children) divide up family property and live apart:父母过世后,兄弟俩便分了家。After the death of their parents, the two brothers shared out the family property and lived apart. ❷ split up; break up:我们分工不～。We divide the work but still coordinate our efforts.
分拣 fēnjiǎn sort (letters):～机 sorter
分阶段 fēn jiēduàn phased; in phases; phase by phase:～安排工业投资 phasing of industrial investment /～撤军 phased withdrawal of troops; phase out troops; phaseout
分节歌 fēnjiégē 〈音乐〉stanzaic song, folk or popular song with several paragraphs of lyrics set to the same notes of music
分解 fēnjiě ❶ separate into parts; break up; break down; dismantle:做体操～动作 do gymnastic exercises by the numbers /～武器 take a weapon apart (*or* to pieces); disassemble a weapon /力的～〈物理〉resolution of force /因式～〈数学〉resolve into factors ❷〈化学〉decompose; resolve:水可以～为氢和氧。Water can be resolved (*or* decomposed) into hydrogen and oxygen. /该混合物可～为两种物质。The mixture will resolve into two simple substances. ❸ mediate; make peace:让他替你们～～。Let's ask him to help you sort things out. ❹ disintegrate:从内部～ disintegrate from within ❺ (used in traditional Chinese novels) recount; disclose:欲知后事如何,且听下回～。What happened thereafter will be disclosed in the ensuing chapter.
分解代谢 fēnjiě dàixiè 〈生物〉catabolism:～产物 catabolite /～基因活化蛋白 catabolite gene activation protein
分解反应 fēnjiě fǎnyìng 〈化学〉decomposition reaction
分解热 fēnjiěrè 〈化学〉decomposition heat
分界 fēnjiè ❶ have as the boundary; be demarcated:两国以河～。The two countries have the river as their common boundary. ❷ dividing line; line of demarcation:正确与错误的～ dividing line between right and wrong /竖立石碑作为两国的～ erect a stone tablet to mark the line of demarcation between the two countries
分界线 fēnjièxiàn line of demarcation; boundary:军事～ military demarcation line /划定～ delimitation of boundary
分斤掰两 fēnjīn-bāiliǎng ❶ count pennies — be stingy; pinch pennies; pinch and scrape; pinch and save:～的小气鬼 penny pincher /她为人吝啬,钱财往来上一向～。A stingy woman, she always pinches and scrapes to save money. ❷ niggle over personal gains
分进合击 fēnjìn-héjī 〈军事〉make a concerted attack by converging columns
分镜头 fēnjìngtóu 〈影视〉story-board:～剧本 continuity
分居 fēnjū ❶ (of a married couple) live separately; separate:法定～ judicial separation /～赡养费 separate maintenance /他们婚后不到半年就～了。They separated less than six months after marriage. ❷ (of family members) live apart:一家人～全国各地。Members of the family live in different parts of the country.
分局 fēnjú 〈通信〉out-station; minor office
分句 fēnjù 〈语言〉clause
分开 fēnkāi ❶ be away from each other; part:这对同居的男女早已～。The two cohabitors have long parted from each other. ❷ (cause to) separate or part:把头发从中间～ part one's hair in the middle /把两个打架的孩子～。Separate the two kids locked in a fight. /请你把中文书和英文书～。Please sort out the Chinese books from the English ones. /两件事要～解决。The two matters should be solved separately.
分克 fēnkè decigram (dg)
分类 fēnlèi classify:～整理 collect and classify /按题材～ classify according to subjects /国民经济部门～ classification of the branches of national economy /会计科目～ classification of account
分类测度学 fēnlèi cèdùxué taximetrics
分类单元 fēnlèi dānyuán 〈生物〉taxon
分类法 fēnlèifǎ classification
分类广告 fēnlèi guǎnggào classified advertisement
分类机 fēnlèijī sorting machine; sorter
分类数字 fēnlèi shùzì breakdown figures
分类索引 fēnlèi suǒyǐn classified index
分类学 fēnlèixué taxology; taxonomy; systematics:植物～ plant taxonomy; systematic botany /动物～ animal taxonomy; systematic zoology
分类账 fēnlèizhàng ledger
分厘 fēnlí very small amount; tiny bit:船在险滩上,顺流直下,稍差～,便会撞得粉身碎骨。Rushing downstream over the dangerous reefs, the boat would be smashed to pieces at the slightest error.
分厘卡 fēnlíkǎ micrometer; milscale
分离 fēnlí ❶ separate; sever:从空气中～稀有气体 separate rare gases from air /理论不可与实践～。Theory must not be divorced from practice. /战争使国家一分为二,也使得他骨肉～。War tore the country in two and severed him from his own flesh and blood (*or* kith and kin). ❷ part; leave:～半辈子的好友终于在耄耋之年在首都北京见面了。The two friends met in their old age at Beijing after decades of separation.
分离度 fēnlídù separating degree
分离段 fēnlíduàn 〈航天〉fallaway section
分离器 fēnlíqì splitter; separator
分理处 fēnlǐchù 〈经济〉subbranch (of a bank); suboffice
分力 fēnlì 〈物理〉component (of force)
分列式 fēnlièshì 〈军事〉march-past; pass in review; ceremonial march
分裂 fēnliè ❶〈生物〉division;〈物理〉fission:细胞～〈生物〉cell division /核～〈物理〉nuclear fission /减数～〈生物〉meiosis; reduction division /有丝～〈生物〉mitosis ❷ split; divide; break up:制造～ create dissensions /国家处于～状态。The country is divided. /他们企图～我们的政党。They try to split our Party. /他们从联合阵线中～出去了。They broke away from the united front.
分裂腔 fēnlièqiāng *also* "囊胚腔" nángpēiqiāng 〈医学〉blastocele; segmentation cavity
分裂生殖 fēnliè shēngzhí 〈生物〉fission
分裂主义 fēnlièzhǔyì splittism:～分子 splittist /～路线 splittist line; divisive line
分流 fēnliú ❶ distributary; split-flow:～河道 distributary channel ❷ split-flow of human resources:我国青少年从中学阶段开始～,初中毕业生一部分升入高中,一部分进入职业学校。The split-flow of the youth in our country starts in secondary school years. Of the junior secondary school leavers, some go to senior secondary schools, some to vocational schools. ❸ (of communications and transport) split-flow; diversion:铁路客运～业务 railway passenger split-flow operation /开辟客运～线路 open up a passenger diversion line ❹ (in economic restructuring) repositioning of redundant personnel
分流电路 fēnliú diànlù divided circuit
分流电阻 fēnliú diànzǔ shunt resistance
分流河口坝 fēnliú hékǒubà distributary mouth bar
分流器 fēnliúqì shunt; splitter; (current) divider
分流术 fēnliúshù 〈医学〉shunt; bypass
分馏 fēnliú 〈化学〉fractional distillation; fractionation
分馏塔 fēnliútǎ fractionating tower; fractional column
分路 fēnlù ❶ along separate routes; from several directions:你我在此～,各奔前程。You and I must part company here, each going his own way. ❷〈电学〉shunt:～电流 branch current /～电阻 shunt resistance /～电容 shunt capacitance
分脉 fēnmài 〈矿业〉dropper
分袂 fēnmèi 〈书面〉bid farewell to each other; part:自南京与君～,倏已兼旬。It has been 20 days since we took leave of each other in Nanjing.
分门别类 fēnmén-biélèi put into different categories; classify
分米 fēnmǐ decimetre (dm)
分米波 fēnmǐbō decimetric wave
分泌 fēnmì ❶〈生理〉secrete; excrete:～胃液 secrete gastric juice /内～ endocrine; internal secretion /外～ exocrine; external secretion ❷ (of cracks in rocks, etc.) fill up (with fluid minerals)
分泌基因 fēnmì jīyīn secretory gene
分泌素 fēnmìsù secretin
分泌物 fēnmìwù secretion; secreta

分泌细胞 fēnmì xìbāo secretory cell
分泌腺 fēnmìxiàn secreting gland
分泌组织 fēnmì zǔzhī secretory tissue
分蜜 fēnmì purging; extraction of sugar from dross
分蜜机 fēnmìjī honey or sugar extractor; honey or sugar centrifuge
分娩 fēnmiǎn ❶ childbirth; delivery; labour; parturition: ～顺利 smooth delivery /～机理 mechanism of labour ❷ (of animals) give birth to the young
分娩合并症 fēnmiǎn hébìngzhèng 〈医学〉 labour complication
分娩急速 fēnmiǎn jísù 〈医学〉 oxytocia
分娩室 fēnmiǎnshì *also* "产房" chǎnfáng delivery room
分娩延缓 fēnmiǎn yánhuǎn 〈医学〉 bradytocia
分秒 fēnmiǎo minute and second; instant: 时间不饶人，～赛黄金。Time flies! (*or* Time waits for nobody.) Every minute or second is as precious as gold.
分秒必争 fēnmiǎo-bìzhēng seize every minute and second; every second counts; not a second is to be lost; make the best use of one's time
分明 fēnmíng ❶ clear; obvious; distinct; unmistakable: 这件事情是非～，无可争辩。The rights and wrongs of the case are perfectly clear and admit of no dispute. /赏罚要～。We must be strict and fair in meting out rewards and punishments. ❷ clearly; plainly; evidently: 有些人～是打着人权的旗号搞强权政治。Obviously some people are playing power politics under the signboard of human rights. /他～在说谎。It's as plain as the nose on your face that he is lying.
分母 fēnmǔ 〈数学〉 denominator
分蘖 fēnniè 〈农业〉 tiller: 有效～ effective tillering /小麦正在～。The wheat is tillering.
分蘖节 fēnnièjié tillering node
分蘖期 fēnnièqī tillering stage
分蘖造林 fēnniè zàolín planting by suckers
分派 fēnpài ❶ assign (a task, etc.): 队长～工作任务。The team leader assigned tasks to his members. ❷ apportion (money); share (the expenses): 按人头～ share out the expenses on a per capita basis
分配 fēnpèi ❶ distribute; allot; allocate: ～产品 distribute products /～资金 give out monetary rewards /～住房 allot housing /～投资贷款 allocate investment credits /按劳～ to each according to his work ❷ assign: 给大学毕业生～工作 assign jobs to college graduates /大学毕业生工作～制度 job placement system for university graduates /服从～ accept the job assigned to one /合理～劳力 rational disposition of manpower ❸ 〈经济〉 distribution; allocation: ～理论 theory of distribution /～制度 distribution system /～基础 distribution basis /～率 distribution rates /按比例～ proportional allocation
分配律 fēnpèilǜ 〈数学〉 distributive law
分批 fēnpī ❶ in batches; in groups: ～出发 set out in batches /～参加培训 go to a training course group by group ❷ 〈经济〉 job; lot; instalment: ～订货 job order /～购买 instalment buying /～交货 partial shipment /～生产 batch production; job production /～成本计算 job costing; job-order costing /～装船 instalment shipment
分片包干 fēnpiàn-bāogān divide up the work and assign a part to each (individual or group)
分频 fēnpín 〈通信〉 frequency demultiplication; frequency division: ～器 frequency divider; frequency demultiplier /～制 frequency division system
分期 fēnqī by stages: ～实施 implement by stages /～分批交货 instalment deliveries
分期偿还借款 fēnqī chánghuán jièkuǎn instalment loan
分期偿还债务 fēnqī chánghuán zhàiwù amortization of debt
分期定额折旧法 fēnqī dìng'é zhéjiùfǎ depreciation-fixed-instalment method
分期付款 fēnqī fùkuǎn payment by instalments; (UK) hire purchase; (US) instalment plan: ～信贷 instalment credit /～债务 instalment debt /全额～ instalment in full /～销售 instalment sale
分歧 fēnqí dispute; difference; divergence: 观点～ divergence of views; conflicting opinions /政治上的～ differences of a political nature /加深～ sharpen a dispute; deepen discord /讨论时大家的～很大。There was a deep chasm in opinion during the discussion.
分清 fēnqīng distinguish; tell from or between; draw a clear distinction between; draw a clear line of demarcation between: ～敌友 know (*or* distinguish) a friend from an enemy /～善恶 draw a distinction between good and evil /～是非 distinguish between right and wrong /他分不清真假。He could not tell truth from falsehood.
分权 fēnquán divide up power; decentralize: ～制 decentralization of power /～管理 decentralized management /中央和地方适当～。The central authorities should give the local governments adequate power. *or* There should be a proper division of power between the central and local governments.
分群 fēnqún (of bees) hive off; swarm to form a subcolony
分润 fēnrùn share in the profit or benefit
分散 fēnsàn ❶ disperse; scatter; diffuse; decentralize: ～精力 diffuse one's energies (*or* strength) /～兵力 dispersion of forces /～指挥 decentralized command; separate command /居住～ live far apart from one another /～注意力 distract sb.'s attention; divert one's attention; take sb.'s mind off sth. /～活动 carry out individual (*or* small group) operations; act on one's own /～的商品市场 decentralized commodity market /～资金 proliferation of funds /工业布局太～。The industries were spread too thin. ❷ distribute; hand out: 在会场上～传单 distribute leaflets at a meeting
分散复制 fēnsàn fùzhì dispersive replication
分散剂 fēnsànjì 〈化学〉 dispersing agent
分散胶体 fēnsàn jiāotǐ dispersion colloid
分散染料 fēnsàn rǎnliào disperse dye
分散数据处理 fēnsàn shùjù chǔlǐ decentralized data processing
分散胎盘 fēnsàn tāipán diffuse placenta
分散主义 fēnsànzhǔyì decentralism
分色机 fēnsèjī 〈印刷〉 colour scanner
分色镜 fēnsèjìng colour selective mirror
分色镜头 fēnsè jìngtóu process lens
分色棱镜 fēnsè léngjìng colour splitting prism
分设 fēnshè set up or establish as a branch: 公司下面～五个部门。The firm has five departments under it.
分身 fēnshēn (often used in the negative) spare time (from one's main work to attend to sth. else); find time: ～无术 cannot replicate oneself; cannot attend to many things at the same time /这两天太忙了，实在分不开身来看你。I've been busy these days and really can't find the time to call on you.
分身术 fēnshēnshù magic of replicating oneself: 孙悟空会～，可以变出许多个小孙悟空来。Monkey King could replicate himself at will, creating numerous little Monkey Kings.
分神 fēnshén ❶ 〈套语〉 give some attention to: 这件事务请～办一办。I earnestly request you to take some time off your crowded schedule to attend to this matter. ❷ divert sb.'s attention; be distracted: ～的事太多 too many distractions /开车时万万不可～。Don't get distracted while driving.
分升 fēnshēng decilitre (dl)
分生孢子 fēnshēng bāozǐ 〈生物〉 conidium
分时 fēnshí 〈信息〉 time sharing
分式 fēnshì 〈数学〉 fraction
分式方程 fēnshì fāngchéng 〈数学〉 fractional equation
分手 fēnshǒu part company; part; say good-bye: 我们是在巴黎～的。We parted at Paris. /火车要开了，我们就此～吧。The train is leaving. We'll have to say good-bye now.
分数 fēnshù ❶ mark; grade; score; point: 好～ good mark /高～ high mark /～不及格 failing mark ❷ 〈数学〉 fraction; fractional number: 带～ mixed number /繁～ complex fraction /假～ improper fraction /真～ proper fraction
分数式 fēnshùshì 〈数学〉 fractional expression
分数线 fēnshùxiàn bottom or floor mark (as for enrolment eligibility)
分水岭 fēnshuǐlǐng ❶ *also* "分水线" 〈地理〉 watershed; divide: 北美大陆～ Continental Divide; Great Divide (i.e. the Rockies) ❷ line of demarcation; dividing line; watershed: 善与恶的～ watershed (*or* divide) between good and evil
分水岭工业 fēnshuǐlǐng gōngyè watershed industry
分水线 fēnshuǐxiàn dividing line
分水闸门 fēnshuǐ zhámén 〈水利〉 bifurcation gate
分税制 fēnshuìzhì system of tax distribution: 实行中央和地方～ introduce a system of sharing tax revenue between the central and local authorities
分说 fēnshuō (usu. used in the negative) defend oneself (against a charge); explain matters: 不容～ allow no explanation
分送 fēnsòng send; distribute: 把教材～到各位老师手中。Distribute

F

the teaching materials to every teacher.
分诉 fēnsù see "分说"
分速度 fēnsùdù component velocity
分摊 fēntān share; apportion; contribute:合理~ rational (*or* reasonable) apportionment /责任~ responsibility sharing /费用由签约诸方~。The expenses are to be shared out among the contracting parties.
分摊保险 fēntān bǎoxiǎn contributory insurance
分摊税 fēntānshuì apportioned tax
分庭抗礼 fēntíng-kànglǐ stand up to sb. as an equal; make rival claims as an equal; act independently and defiantly:有些地方居然想跟中央平起平坐,~。Some local authorities went so far as to try to sit as equals at the same table with the central authorities.
分头 fēntóu ❶ separately; severally:明天开会,咱们~通知。As the meeting will be held tomorrow, let's notify the people concerned severally (*or* separately). ❷ parted hair:留~ have parted hair (*or* a hair parting, *or* a part in one's hair)
分文 fēnwén (usu. used in the negative) single cent or penny:~不值 not worth a farthing; not worth a straw; worthless /身无~ penniless; broke; stony broke
分文不取 fēnwén-bùqǔ not take or charge a single cent; free of charge; gratis:非分之财,~ not take a single dishonest penny /他常在节假日下乡为农民看病,~。He often goes to the country on holidays and festive ocassions to give treatment to peasants free of charge.
分析 fēnxī analyse:~问题的能力 ability to analyse problems (*or* reason things out) /~当前形势 analyse (*or* size up) the present situation /深入的~ in-depth analysis /市场动态~ market trend analysis /综合~ analysis by synthesis /~员 analyst
分析化学 fēnxī huàxué analytical chemistry
分析会计 fēnxī kuàijì analytical accounting
分析器 fēnxīqì 〈化工〉 analysor; analyzer
分析天平 fēnxī tiānpíng 〈化学〉 analytical balance
分析心理学 fēnxī xīnlǐxué analytic(al) psychology
分析语 fēnxīyǔ 〈语言〉 analytical language
分析哲学 fēnxī zhéxué analytic philosophy
分线规 fēnxiànguī dividers
分享 fēnxiǎng share (joy, rights, etc.); partake of:~好处 share the benefits
分享经济 fēnxiǎng jīngjì *also* "分成经济" share economy
分相 fēnxiàng 〈电学〉 split phase
分相电动机 fēnxiàng diàndòngjī split-phase motor
分相放大器 fēnxiàng fàngdàqì paraphase amplifier
分相器 fēnxiàngqì phase splitter
分销 fēnxiāo 〈商业〉 distribution:~渠道 distributional channel
分销店 fēnxiāodiàn retail shop or store
分晓 fēnxiǎo ❶ (often used after 见) outcome; result; solution:此事还未见~。The outcome of the affair is still uncertain. ❷ see or understand clearly:问个~ try to find out the whys and wherefores of sth.; inquire about and get to the bottom of sth. /且看下图,便知~。Read the diagram below and you'll undertand the whole thing clearly. ❸ (usu. used in the negative) reason:这话多没~。The remark is most unreasonable.
分校 fēnxiào branch school; branch campus
分心 fēnxīn ❶ divert or distract sb.'s attention:实验正在关键时刻,不要让他~。Don't distract his attention; his experiment is at a crucial stage. /外面的噪嚷,使我~。I can hardly concentrate for the noise outside. ❷ 〈套语〉 may I trouble you:这件事您多~吧。May I trouble you to attend to the matter? *or* Would you be kind enough to take care of the matter?
分选 fēnxuǎn ❶ sizing; size classification ❷ 〈矿业〉 separation:~机 separator /~炉〈冶金〉 selector
分压 fēnyā differential pressure; partial pressure
分压电路 fēnyā diànlù bleeder circuit
分压力 fēnyālì partial pressure:~传感器 partial pressure sensor
分压器 fēnyāqì 〈电工〉 voltage divider:~电流 voltage-divider current
分秧 fēnyāng 〈农业〉 separate seedlings for planting
分野 fēnyě dividing line; line of demarcation:两种学派的~ dividing line between the two schools of thought
分页 fēnyè 〈信息〉 paging
分一杯羹 fēnyībēigēng take or have a share of the spoils or profits
分益 fēnyì shared profits (in business)
分阴 fēnyīn short moment; instant:惜~ treasure every second; make the best use of one's precious time
分忧 fēnyōu share sb.'s worries; help solve difficult problems:为妈妈~ share mother's worries and burdens /为国~ contribute one's share in solving difficult problems for the country; do one's bit for the country in times of trouble or crisis
分赃 fēnzāng ❶ divide the spoils; share the booty or loot:坐地~ (of a fence, schemer, etc.) take a share of the spoils without participating in the robbery ❷ 〈比喻〉 share ill-gotten gains or power
分灶吃饭 fēnzào-chīfàn each having his meal cooked from a separate stove — each administrative level having its own source of revenue and expenditure
分张 fēnzhāng 〈书面〉 part company; take leave; bid farewell
分账 fēnzhàng divide money in a ratio:三七~ divide the money in the ratio 3:7 (*or* the ratio of 3 to 7)
分针 fēnzhēn minute hand (of a watch or clock)
分争 fēnzhēng argue; quarrel; defend oneself (against a charge):和人~起来 begin arguing with sb.; pick a row with sb. /不容~ allowing no explanation
分支 fēnzhī branch (of an organization, etc.); affiliate:~机构 branch; affiliate; affiliated agency /~机构网 branch network /~电缆 branch cable /~代理 subagent /~学科 subdiscipline
分支光缆 fēnzhī guānglǎn branch optical cable
分支酶 fēnzhīméi 〈生化〉 branching enzyme
分值 fēnzhí cash value of a workpoint, etc. (as in the production team)
分至点 fēnzhìdiǎn general term for the four division points of the Vernal Equinox, Autumnal Equinox, Summer Solstice and Winter Solstice
分钟 fēnzhōng minute
分子 fēnzǐ ❶ 〈数学〉 numerator (in a fraction) ❷ 〈化学〉 molecule:克~ gram molecule /高~ high molecule
see also fènzǐ
分子病 fēnzǐbìng molecular disease
分子病理学 fēnzǐ bìnglǐxué molecular pathology
分子电子学 fēnzǐ diànzǐxué 〈电子〉 molecular electronics; mole-electronics; molectronics
分子动力学 fēnzǐ dònglìxué molecular dynamics
分子仿生学 fēnzǐ fǎngshēngxué molecular bionics
分子激光器 fēnzǐ jīguāngqì molecular laser
分子结构 fēnzǐ jiégòu molecular structure
分子力 fēnzǐlì molecular force
分子量 fēnzǐliàng molecular weight; molecular mass
分子论 fēnzǐlùn molecular theory
分子溶液 fēnzǐ róngyè molecular solution
分子筛 fēnzǐshāi molecular sieve
分子生物学 fēnzǐ shēngwùxué molecular biology
分子式 fēnzǐshì molecular formula
分子天文学 fēnzǐ tiānwénxué molecular astronomy
分子遗传学 fēnzǐ yíchuánxué molecular genetics
分租 fēnzū sublet; sublease:把包租来的房间~出去 sublet a rented room to sb.
分组 fēnzǔ ❶ divide into groups:~学习 study in groups; group study /~抽样 group sampling /~编码 block encoding /按年龄大小~ be grouped according to age /她对~情况不满意。She's not satisfied with the grouping. ❷ 〈信息〉 packet
分组分析 fēnzǔ fēnxī 〈经济〉〈商业〉 cluster analysis
分组交换 fēnzǔ jiāohuàn 〈信息〉 packet-switching

雰

fēn 〈书面〉 mist; air; atmosphere
雰雰 fēnfēn 〈书面〉 (of snow, frost, etc.) heavy:雨雪~。It is snowing heavily.
雰围 fēnwéi *see* "氛围" fēnwéi

玢

fēn *see* "赛璐玢" sàilùfēn
see also bīn

芬

fēn sweet smell; fragrance:清~ delicate fragrance; faint scent

F

芬芳 fēnfāng sweet-smelling; fragrant:～的野花 sweet-smelling wild flowers /～郁馥 rich in fragrance /清风徐来,遍野～。A cool breeze blows gently and the sweet smell fills the open country.
芬兰 Fēnlán Finland:～人 Finn; Finlander /～语 Finnish (language)
芬香 fēnxiāng fragrance; sweet smell:泥土的～ sweet smell of the soil /丁香花散发着～。The lilacs send forth their fragrance.

棻

fēn 〈书面〉fragrant wood

酚

fēn 〈化学〉phenol
酚醇 fēnchún phenolic alcohol
酚磺酞 fēnhuángtài 〈药学〉phenolsulphonphthalein (PSP)
酚解 fēnjiě 〈化学〉phenolysis
酚酶 fēnméi 〈生化〉phenolase
酚醛 fēnquán 〈化学〉phenolic aldehyde
酚醛层板 fēnquán céngbǎn phenolic laminate
酚醛树脂 fēnquán shùzhī phenolic resin:～清漆 phenolic resin varnish
酚醛塑料 fēnquán sùliào phenolic plastics; phenolics; phenoplast; bakelite
酚酞 fēntài 〈化学〉phenolphthalein
酚酞试纸 fēntài shìzhǐ phenolphthalein test paper
酚纤维 fēnxiānwéi 〈化工〉phenol fibre
酚盐 fēnyán 〈化学〉phenolate; phenoxide
酚衍生物 fēnyǎnshēngwù 〈化学〉amphyl

吩

fēn
吩咐 fēnfu *also* "分付" fēnfu tell; instruct; bid; order:她～女儿不要出门。She told her daughter not to go outdoors. /您有什么事儿,尽管～。In case you need anything, please don't hesitate to let me know. /我的车子和司机听凭阁下～。I shall gladly put my car with chauffeur at your disposal. /恭候～。I am humbly at your service. *or* I am awaiting your instructions.

氛

fēn atmosphere:亲切友好的气～ cordial and friendly atmosphere
氛围 fēnwéi *also* "雰围" fēnwéi atmosphere; ethos:文化～ cultural ethos /她觉得自己的情绪与眼前欢乐的～不协调。She felt that her mood was out of harmony with the joyful atmosphere around her.

纷

fēn ❶ many and various; diverse; numerous; profuse:五彩缤～ colourful; blazing with colour; riotous with colour /雪片～飞。Snow flakes flutter about. ❷ confused; tangled; chaotic; disorderly:乱～～ disorderly; confused; chaotic /纠～ dispute; quarrel /排难解～ solve problems and mediate disputes; pour oil on troubled waters
纷呈 fēnchéng present oneself one after another or all at once:色彩～ be a riot of colour /流派～的戏曲艺术 opera art of a variety of schools
纷繁 fēnfán numerous and complicated:手续～ numerous and complicated procedures (*or* formalities) /从～的工作头绪中抓住主要矛盾 grasp the principal contradictions out of the complexities of work /春天,～的桃花染红了小山坡。In spring, a profusion of peach blossoms turns the hillside red.
纷飞 fēnfēi swirl in the air; fly about disorderly:战火～的年代 war-ridden years /大雪～。The snow is falling in thick flakes. *or* It is snowing heavily.
纷纷 fēnfēn ❶ numerous and confused; profuse:落叶～。Leaves fall in profusion. /大家对这事议论～。This has become the subject of much discussion. ❷ one after another; in succession; all at once:人们～退出该组织。People withdrew from the organization one after another. /他们～要求发言。They all clamoured to take the floor.
纷纷扬扬 fēnfēn-yángyáng (of snowflakes, flowers, leaves, etc.) flying or fluttering in confusion:柳絮～,漫天飞舞。Willow catkins are swirling in the air. /午饭刚过,竟～地下起雪来。Shortly after lunch, snowflakes began to flutter like feathers in the air.
纷华 fēnhuá 〈书面〉❶ flourishing and splendid:～富丽的王府井大街 prosperous and magnificent Wangfujing Street ❷ glorious:有功者显荣,无功者虽富无所～。A meritorious deed brings glory, while wealth does not if its owner has no merit.
纷乱 fēnluàn numerous and disorderly; helter-skelter; chaotic:～的说话声 hullabaloo /心绪～ unsettling mood /～的事情 swirl of events /一头～的长发 a head of dishevelled hair /天下～,群雄逐鹿。The ambitious and powerful vied for supreme power in times of national turmoil.
纷纶 fēnlún 〈书面〉profuse and confused; numerous and disorderly
纷忙 fēnmáng in a rush and a muddle; extremely busy:事务～ busily engaged /终日～ busy all day long (*or* all the time); always busy
纷拏 fēnná 〈书面〉confused; chaotic; in tangled fighting:两军相～。The two armies were locked in a tangled fight.
纷披 fēnpī 〈书面〉spreading disorderly:枝叶～。The tree branches and leaves spread out in all directions.
纷扰 fēnrǎo confusion; tumult; chaos; turmoil:内心的～使她无法保持镇静。She felt so perturbed that she could hardly keep her composure.
纷冗 fēnrǒng ❶ many and diverse; redundant:删除～ cut what is redundant; trim ❷ in bustling disorder; busy and confusing:连日～,未能顾及此事。I've been too busy for days on end to take care of this.
纷纭 fēnyún diverse and confused:众说～,莫衷一是。Opinions differ widely, and there is no consensus at all.
纷杂 fēnzá diverse and confused; numerous and disorderly:头绪～ have too many things to attend to /～的思绪 confused state of mind; confused train of thought
纷争 fēnzhēng dispute; quarrel; wrangle:国际～ international dispute /～不已 endless wrangle
纷至沓来 fēnzhì-tàlái come in a continuous stream; come thick and fast; come as thick as hail; keep pouring in:内忧外患,～。Domestic troubles and foreign invasions come in quick succession. /慕名求医者～。People keep pouring in to see the doctor out of admiration.

赠(𠶛)

fēn 〈方言〉have not:～来过 have never been here

fén

坟(墳)

fén grave; tomb:祖～ ancestral grave /上～ visit a grave (to honour the memory of the dead) /扫～ to sweep the graves of the dead (at the festival of Pure Brightness 清明节)
坟包 fénbāo grave mound
坟场 fénchǎng graveyard; cemetery
坟地 féndì *see* "坟场"
坟堆 fénduī *see* "坟包"
坟墓 fénmù grave; tomb:自掘～ dig one's own grave; be one's own grave digger; be one's own undoing
坟起 fénqǐ swell; bulge
坟丘 fénqiū *also* "坟丘子" grave mound; grave; tomb
坟山 fénshān 〈方言〉❶ graveyard; cemetery ❷ big grave mound ❸ *also* "坟山子" protective mound behind the grave
坟头 féntóu grave mound
坟茔 fényíng ❶ grave; tomb ❷ graveyard; cemetery
坟冢 fénzhǒng grave; tomb

渍

fén 〈书面〉water margin; waterside

豮

fén 〈方言〉male domestic animal:～猪 boar

焚

fén burn:自～ burn oneself /玉石俱～ jade and stone burned together — destruction of good and bad alike /忧心如～。Anxiety gnaws at one's heart.
焚风 fénfēng 〈气象〉foehn; fohn
焚膏继晷 féngāo-jìguǐ burn a candle to prolong the day — burn the midnight oil:这位先生发愤读书,～,昼夜不倦。This gentleman devoted himself tirelessly to his studies day and night.
焚化 fénhuà incinerate; cremate:～尸体 cremate a dead body
焚化炉 fénhuàlú incinerator; crematorium; cremator

焚毁 fénhuǐ destroy by fire; burn down: 整座城市在战火中～。The entire city was burned down in the war.
焚掠 fénlüè burn and loot: 入侵者四处～。The invaders burned and looted everywhere they went.
焚琴煮鹤 fénqín-zhǔhè *also* "煮鹤焚琴" burn a lute for fuel and cook a crane for food — offend against good taste; act like a philistine or barbarian; spoil the fun
焚烧 fénshāo burn; set on fire; consume with flames: 侵略者一把火～了圆明园。The foreign invaders burned down the old Summer Palace (Yuan Ming Yuan).
焚尸炉 fénshīlú crematory; crematorium
焚尸灭迹 fénshī-mièjì burn the corpse to cover up the crime or destroy the evidence
焚尸扬灰 fénshī-yánghuī burn the corpse and scatter the ashes (regarded as the severest treatment of the dead in feudal times)
焚书坑儒 fénshū-kēngrú burn books and bury Confucian scholars alive (by the first emperor of the Qin Dynasty)
焚香 fénxiāng ❶ burn joss sticks (before an idol): ～拜佛 burn joss sticks and prostrate oneself before Buddha ❷ burn incense: ～静坐 burn incense and sit in quietitude / ～操琴 play *guqin* (a stringed musical instrument) with incense burning

黂 fén ❶〈古语〉seeds of hemp ❷〈书面〉coarse hemp or linen

汾 Fén name of a river in Shanxi Province: ～河 Fen River
汾酒 fénjiǔ a kind of spirit distilled in Fenyang (汾阳), Shanxi Province

棼 fén 〈书面〉confused; ravelled; tangled: 治丝益～ try to sort out silk threads only to tangle them further — try to do sth. only to make it worse; make confusion worse

鼢 fén
鼢鼠 fénshǔ *also* "盲鼠" mángshǔ zokor (a kind of mole)

fěn

粉 fěn ❶ powder: 奶～ powdered milk; milk powder / 面～ (wheat) flour / 藕～ lotus root starch / 花～ pollen / 漂白～ bleaching powder / 爽身～ talcum powder / 磨成～ grind into powder; pulverize ❷ powdered cosmetics: 香～ face powder / 脂～ rouge and face powder; cosmetics / 涂脂抹～ apply powder and paint; prettify ❸ noodles or vermicelli made from flour, bean, sweet potato starch, etc.: 凉～ bean jelly / 炒米～ fried rice-flour noodles / 菠菜炒～ bean noodles stir-fried with spinach / 通心～ macaroni ❹〈方言〉turn to powder: 生石灰放得太久，已经～了。The quick lime has turned to powder over time. ❺〈方言〉whitewash: 房间刚～过。The room has just been whitewashed. ❻ white (with white powder): ～墙绿瓦 white walls and green tiles ❼ pink: 他家的窗帘是～的。His house has pink window curtains.
粉白 fěnbái powder-like white
粉白黛绿 fěnbái-dàilǜ *also* "粉白黛黑" (of a woman) with face powdered and eyebrows darkened: ～者，列屋而闲居。The fair ladies lived an idle, dependent life.
粉孢子 fěnbāozǐ 〈植物〉oidium
粉本 fěnběn rough sketch or draft of a painting
粉笔 fěnbǐ chalk: 两枝彩色～ two coloured chalks / 用～勾出草图 chalk out a sketch
粉笔槽 fěnbǐcáo blackboard chalk ledge
粉笔画 fěnbǐhuà chalk drawing; crayon
粉彩 fěncǎi 〈工美〉mixed glaze; *famille rose*: ～画 pastel drawing
粉肠 fěncháng sausage stuffed mainly with bean starch paste; starch sausage
粉尘 fěnchén (industrial) dust: 去除～ dusting / 爆炸性～ explosive dust
粉尘爆炸 fěnchén bàozhà dust explosion
粉尘病 fěnchénbìng koniosis; coniosis
粉尘处理 fěnchén chǔlǐ dust-management; ash-handling
粉尘监测器 fěnchén jiāncèqì dust monitor
粉尘浓度 fěnchén nóngdù dust concentration
粉刺 fěncì *also* "痤疮" cuóchuāng 〈医学〉acne; comedo
粉翠 fěncuì 〈工美〉Beijing jade
粉黛 fěndài 〈书面〉❶ face powder and eyebrow pigment ❷ beautiful ladies in the palace or of a rich family: 回眸一笑百媚生，六宫～无颜色。Her smiling glance unleashed a hundred charms That turned to pallor all the paint and colour of the women's quarters.
粉箪竹 fěndānzhú *also* "箪竹" a kind of bamboo with a tall stem and powder on it between sections
粉底霜 fěndǐshuāng foundation cream
粉蝶 fěndié 〈动物〉white butterfly; pierid: 菜～ cabbage butterfly
粉蠹 fěndù powder-post beetle
粉坊 fěnfáng workshop where starch noodles, sheet jelly, etc., are produced
粉盒 fěnhé powder box; compact
粉红 fěnhóng pink; rosy: ～的脸 rosy cheeks; pinkish complexion
粉化 fěnhuà pulverization; powdering; chalking; dusting
粉剂 fěnjì ❶〈医药〉powder ❷〈农业〉dust
粉蚧 fěnjiè mealy bug
粉连纸 fěnliánzhǐ a kind of thin, transparent paper used to copy patterns underneath
粉蛉 fěnlíng 〈动物〉dusky wing
粉瘤 fěnliú 〈医学〉sebaceous cyst; atheroma
粉煤 fěnméi powdered coal; pulverized coal
粉煤灰 fěnméihuī flyash: ～水泥 flyash cement / ～砖 flyash brick
粉螟 fěnmíng 〈动物〉flour moth
粉末 fěnmò powder: ～金属 powdered metal
粉末电弧法 fěnmò diànhúfǎ powder arc method
粉末镀锌 fěnmò dùxīn sherardizing
粉末喷涂 fěnmò pēntú powder spraying
粉末热锻 fěnmò rèduàn powder hotforging
粉末衍射 fěnmò yǎnshè powder diffraction
粉末冶金 fěnmò yějīn powder metallurgy
粉墨登场 fěnmò-dēngchǎng 〈贬义〉make oneself up and go on stage — embark upon a political venture: 在侵略军的扶植下，傀儡们匆匆忙忙地～了。The puppets (*or* quislings) hurriedly assumed office with the backing of the aggressor forces.
粉嫩 fěnnèn fair and delicate; soft and fair: 姑娘～的小脸 girl's fair and tender little face
粉牌 fěnpái white memo plate or board
粉皮 fěnpí sheet jelly (made from bean or sweet potato starch)
粉扑儿 fěnpūr powder puff
粉芡 fěnqiàn pasty mixture of water and starch (for cooking)
粉墙 fěnqiáng ❶ whitewash a wall ❷ plaster wall
粉砂 fěnshā silt: ～黏土 silt soil
粉砂岩 fěnshāyán siltstone; aleuvite
粉身碎骨 fěnshēn-suìgǔ have one's body smashed to pieces and one's bones be crushed to (a) pulp; be ground to powder: ～在所不辞 do not flinch (*or* shrink) even if one is threatened with destruction / 被历史的车轮碾得～ be ground to dust by the wheels of history
粉虱 fěnshī whitefly
粉饰 fěnshì gloss over; prettify; whitewash: ～自己 try to whitewash oneself / 一堆～之词 load of whitewash / ～现实 prettify reality / ～门面 window dressing
粉饰太平 fěnshì-tàipíng present a fake picture of peace and prosperity: 借大办庆典以～ maintain a facade of peace and stability by holding a grand celebration
粉刷 fěnshuā ❶ whitewash: ～一下厨房 whitewash a kitchen / ～一新 look brand new after being whitewashed ❷〈方言〉plaster ❸〈方言〉layer of protective plaster ❹〈信息〉rendering
粉丝 fěnsī vermicelli made from bean starch, etc.
粉碎 fěnsuì ❶ broken into or to pieces: 锅被砸得～。The pot was smashed to smithereens. / 他把信撕得～。He tore the letter to pieces. ❷ smash; shatter; crush: ～思想桎梏 smash ideological shackles / ～一切达成妥协的希望 shatter all hopes of reaching a compromise / ～敌人的阴谋 crush the enemy conspiracy
粉碎机 fěnsuìjī pulverizer; grinder; kibbler: 饲料～ fodder grinder / 球磨～ ball mill pulverizer
粉碎性骨折 fěnsuìxìng gǔzhé 〈医学〉comminuted fracture
粉条 fěntiáo starch noodles (made from bean or sweet potato starch)
粉头 fěntóu 〈旧语〉prostitute

粉纹夜蛾 fěnwén yè'é cabbage looper
粉戏 fěnxì pornographic opera
粉线 fěnxiàn tailor's chalk line
粉蒸肉 fěnzhēngròu pork steamed with ground rice flour
粉装玉琢 fěnzhuāng-yùzhuó (of human skin) fair and delicate; (of a snow scene) silvery white: ～的可人儿 fair and delicate young lady /眼前一片～的世界，好像人间仙境。I found myself in a world of silvery white, a veritable fairy land on earth.
粉状橡胶 fěnzhuàng xiàngjiāo powder rubber

fèn

粪(糞) fèn ❶ excrement; faeces; dung; droppings: 大～ human excrement; night soil /马～ horse dung /鸟～ birds' droppings; guano ❷〈书面〉apply manure: ～地 manure the fields ❸〈书面〉have a cleaning; clear away; *see* "～除"
粪便 fènbiàn excrement and urine; night soil: ～检查 stool examination /～处理 faecal treatment /～微生物 faecal microorganism /～污水 faecal sewage /～无害处理 decontamination of faeces /～清除设备 manure and slurry cleaning equipment
粪便学 fènbiànxué coprology
粪车 fènchē dung-cart; night-soil cart
粪池 fènchí manure pit; cesspool; stercorary
粪臭素 fènchòusù skatole; scatole
粪除 fènchú 〈书面〉thoroughly clean (a place); wipe out
粪袋 fèndài 〈医学〉colostomy bag
粪胆素 fèndǎnsù stercobilin
粪道 fèndào (of birds, reptiles, etc.) coprodaeum; coprodeum
粪毒 fèndú 〈中医〉ground-itch; dermatitis uncinariasis
粪堆 fènduī dunghill; manure pile or heap
粪肥 fènféi muck; manure; dung
粪夫 fènfū 〈旧语〉night-soil collector
粪化石 fènhuàshí coprolite
粪积 fènjī 〈医学〉coprostasis; scatoma
粪箕子 fènjīzi *also* "粪箕" manure basket
粪坑 fènkēng *also* "粪坑子" ❶ manure pit ❷ latrine
粪筐 fènkuāng ❶ manure collector's bin ❷ manure basket
粪瘘 fènlòu faecal or stercoral fistula
粪门 fènmén 〈方言〉anus
粪生动物 fènshēng dòngwù coprozoon
粪石 fènshí coprolith; bezoar; faecalith
粪桶 fèntǒng night-soil bucket; manure bucket
粪土 fèntǔ dung and dirt; muck: 视名利如～ look upon fame and fortune as dirt /～当年万户侯。We counted the mighty no more than muck.
粪蝇 fènyíng dung fly

瀵 fèn 〈书面〉(of underground water) gush out and overflow
瀵泉 fènquán geyser

愤 fèn anger; fury; indignation; resentment: 悲～ grief and indignation /激～ wrathful; infuriated /气～ furious; resentful /义～ righteous indignation; moral indignation /民～ popular fury; the people's wrath /公～ public resentment; popular anger
愤愤 fènfèn *also* "忿忿" fènfèn angry; indignant; furious: 提起这件事，他便～然。He becomes very angry whenever the matter is mentioned. /这话使她～不已。She was exasperated by (*or* at) these words.
愤愤不平 fènfèn-bùpíng be indignant; feel aggrieved; be resentful: 他因没有得到提拔而感到～。He is fuming with anger because he has failed to win promotion.
愤恨 fènhèn indignantly resent; furiously detest: 激起天下人的～ arouse popular resentment
愤火 fènhuǒ fury; flames of fury: 一腔～ be filled with fury
愤激 fènjī excited and indignant; furious: ～若狂 be wild with fury /他怀着～的心情离开了会场。He walked out of the conference room, fuming (*or* seething) with anger.
愤慨 fènkǎi (righteous) indignation: 对杀害无辜人民表示～ express (*or* voice) one's indignation at the killing of innocent people /激起了群众的极大～ arouse the great resentment of the masses; stir up (*or* excite) immense popular resentment
愤懑 fènmèn 〈书面〉disgruntled; resentful: ～之情 resentment; disgruntled expression
愤怒 fènnù indignation; fury; anger; wrath: ～到了极点 be overwhelmed with indignation /他两眼燃烧着～的火焰。Both of his eyes were flazing with wrath. /～声讨 angrily denounce
愤然 fènrán angry; indignant: ～作色 flush with anger /～离去 leave in anger; walk off in a huff; shake the dust off one's feet
愤世嫉俗 fènshì-jísú detest human injustices; loathe the ways of the world; be cynical: ～之作 work that is highly critical of the world and its ways /他变得越来越～。He is getting more cynical about life.
愤愠 fènyùn anger; wrath; resentment: 她想借此把胸中的郁闷、～驱散。In this way she was trying to drive away her vexation and pent-up anger.

偾 fèn 〈书面〉destroy; spoil; ruin
偾事 fènshì 〈书面〉spoil an affair: 一言～。One word can spoil the whole thing. /鲁莽只能～。Impetuosity will only bring failure.

鲼 fèn 〈动物〉eagle ray

奋(奮) fèn ❶ brace up; exert oneself; act vigorously: 兴～ feel excited; be in high spirits /发～ work energetically; exert oneself; make a determined effort /振～ rouse oneself; brace oneself up; feel inspired /勤～ diligent; industrious ❷ take up; raise; lift: ～笔疾书 take up a pen and write swiftly; wield one's (writing) brush energetically /～臂高呼 raise one's arms and hail
奋不顾身 fènbùgùshēn (charge forward) regardless of personal safety: ～的战斗精神 fighting spirit that defies personal danger; dauntless militant spirit /他～地冲进大火中救人。Disregarding his own safety, he rushed to rescue the people trapped in the big fire.
奋斗 fèndòu fight; struggle; work hard; strive: 艰苦～ work arduously /～到底 struggle to the very end /～目标 objective of a struggle /为农业现代化而～ strive for the modernization of agriculture /为人民幸福而～终身 work all one's life for the wellbeing of the people; dedicate one's life to the people's welfare
奋发 fènfā rouse oneself; exert oneself; brace oneself up: 作品给人一种～向上的力量。This book spurs people on to something higher and better. *or* The book has an uplifting quality.
奋发图强 fènfā-túqiáng go all out to achieve success; work hard for the prosperity of the country; work with stamina and diligence: 我们这一代青年要学好本领，～。The youth of our generation should acquire knowledge and skills and strive for the prosperity of our country.
奋发有为 fènfā-yǒuwéi energetic and promising: ～的青年 diligent and promising young man
奋飞 fènfēi (of birds) spread the wings and soar; take off at flying speed — undergo rapid development: 工业的～ rapid industrial advance; swift industrial take-off /海燕在暴风雨中展翅～。The storm petrels were flying with a vengeance in the teeth of the storm.
奋击 fènjī strike out with great force; rise up and fight; attack bravely: 对敌～ make a spirited attack on the enemy /歌颂先驱者的～精神 extol the pioneers' trail-blazing spirit
奋激 fènjī be elated; be roused to enthusiasm: ～的心情 feel excited and elated /群情～。Popular feelings were running high.
奋进 fènjìn advance bravely; forge ahead courageously: 在艰难中～ boldly forge ahead amid difficulties
奋亢 fènkàng *also* "亢奋" extremely excited
奋力 fènlì do all one can; exert oneself to the utmost; spare no effort: ～反抗 do all one can to resist /～挣扎 struggle with all one's might /～抢救 exert every ounce of energy to rescue (sb.) /他为人民～工作了四十年。He has worked for the people to the best of his ability for forty years.
奋励 fènlì be spirited; exert oneself: 精神～ be high-spirited
奋袂 fènmèi 〈书面〉roll up one's sleeves for action
奋袂而起 fènmèi'érqǐ 〈书面〉flick one's sleeves and stand up; rise up and be ready for action: 一部屈辱的近代史，使多少人～，投入振兴祖国的事业。A modern history of humiliation has made large numbers of people rise up and dedicate themselves to the cause of national re-

F

juvenation.
奋勉 fènmiǎn make a determined effort
奋乃静 fènnǎijìng 〈药学〉 perphenazine
奋起 fènqǐ ❶ rise with force and spirit; brace up; rise:～行动 brace oneself for action /～自卫 rise in self-defence /～反抗殖民统治 rise up against colonial rule ❷ raise or lift with force:金猴～千钧棒,玉宇澄清万里埃。The Golden Monkey wrathfully swung his massive cudgel And the jade-like firmament was cleared of dust.
奋起直追 fènqǐ-zhízhuī do one's utmost or exert all one's strength to catch up:不甘落后的人要～。Those who do not wish to be left behind must make every possible effort to forge ahead.
奋然 fènrán animated; energetic; high-spirited
奋迅 fènxùn enthusiastic and swift
奋勇 fènyǒng summon up all one's courage and energy; be dauntless:～前进 advance valiantly; forge ahead boldly /～当先 charge at the forefront of the struggle /自告～ volunteer (to do sth. difficult or dangerous)
奋战 fènzhàn fight bravely:浴血～ engage in bloody battle /～到底 struggle to the bitter end /为保卫国土而英勇～ fight bravely to defend the country /他们～七个月,建成这座大型立交桥。After seven months of strenuous work, they finished building the huge flyover.
奋争 fènzhēng struggle with might and main
奋志 fènzhì make a determined effort (to achieve sth.):～读书 be bent on learning /～从军 be determined to join the army /～从事教育工作 resolve to dedicate one's life (*or* oneself) to education

分[1] fèn ❶ component; element:水～ moisture content /养～ nutrient ❷ what is within one's right or obligation:过～ excessive; too much; going too far; over-done /恰如其～ appropriate; just right /这是我的本～。This is my duty. /这人很不安～。He is an ambitious person. ❸ friendly feeling; affection:情～ (mutual) affection /看在老关系的～ for old times' sake ❹ *see* "份" fèn

分[2] fèn 〈书面〉 expect; think; know:自～难以肩此重任 know very well that one is not up to the arduous task; be well aware of one's inability to shoulder such a heavy responsibility
see also fēn
分地 fèndì piece of land worked by a serf who paid rent in corvee
分际 fènjì 〈书面〉 ❶ proper limits for speech or action; sense of propriety:不知～ have no sense of propriety ❷ condition; plight; extent:闹到了不可收拾的～ have come to such a sorry pass; have made a hopeless mess /我真想不到他竟糊涂到这个～。I just can't imagine that he can be so muddled up.
分量 fènliang weight:给足～ give full measure /～给得不足 give short measure / 有～的国家 countries of no small consequence; countries with considerable clout; countries that carry weight /这个手提包很有～。The handbag is quite heavy. /文中的这几个词儿加大了全文的～。These words added to the weight of the whole article. /要把这几件事在全局中的～摆恰当。We must do justice to the importance of these matters in the scheme of things.
分内 fènnèi (within) one's job or duty:这是我～的事,不必感谢。No trouble at all. This is what I should do.
分外 fènwài ❶ particularly; especially:～寒冷 particularly cold /～激动 very excited /～妖娆 enchantingly beautiful /天空～晴朗。The sky was extraordinarily clear. /月到中秋～明。The moon at the Mid-autumn Festival is especially bright. ❷ beyond one's duty or job; beyond one's due:～之想 inordinate wish (*or* ambition) /他干工作从来不分分内～。He always does whatever he thinks is right, no matter whether it's his job or not.
分子 fènzǐ member; element:骨干～ core member; key member /积极～ active member; activist /先进～ advanced element /知识～ intellectual /中坚～ pillar /后进～ laggard /死硬～ diehard /动摇～ vacillating element; waverer
see also fēnzǐ

忿[1] fèn *see* "愤" fèn

忿[2] fèn *see* "不忿" bùfèn;"气不忿儿" qìbùfènr
忿忿 fènfèn *see* "愤愤" fènfèn
忿詈 fènlì 〈书面〉 scold out of anger

份 fèn ❶ share; portion; part:股～ stock; share /双～ double portion /全～ complete set /等～ equal share /付自己的一～钱 pay one's share /为建设家乡出一～力 do one's bit in building one's hometown ❷ 〈量词〉 (a) set:一～儿咖啡 a coffee /一～儿饮料 a drink /两～儿快餐 two sets of fast food /三～儿冰淇淋 three ice-creams (b) copy:一～报纸 a copy of newspaper /一～电报 a telegram (*or* cable)/合同一式两～。The contract was done in duplicate. (c) *used for certain abstract things*:瞧他那～儿神气! Look what airs he puts on. ❸ *used after* 年,月,省,县 *to form a unit*:县～ county /省～ province /月～ month /年～ year
份额 fèn'é share; portion:～提款 tranche drawings (in the IMF) /～制度 quotient system
份礼 fènlǐ gift in the form of cash
份儿 fènr ❶ portion; share:这一～是你的。This is your share. ❷ status; position:他的～可不小。He is quite somebody. /这个团体里没有我的～。I'm a person of no weight (*or* consequence) in this organization. ❸ 〈方言〉 face; self-respect:丢～ lose face /他的～上怕不好看。I'm afraid this won't do his reputation much good. ❹ extent; degree:都闹到这～上了! 我还有啥好说的? As things have come to such a sorry pass, what can I say about it? ❺ 〈方言〉 good; excellent:演得～ excellent performance /你瞧,她多～! Look! She is simply marvellous!
份儿菜 fènrcài set-portion dish
份儿饭 fènrfàn table d'hôte; set meal:今天午餐吃～。We had a set meal for lunch.
份子 fènzi ❶ one's share of expenses for a joint undertaking (as in buying a gift for a mutual friend):凑～ club together to present a gift to sb. /出～ give one's share of expenses (for a joint undertaking) ❷ gift in the form of cash

fēng

丰[1]（豐） fēng ❶ rich; plentiful; abundant:人寿年～ the land yields good harvests and the people live to a great age /羽毛未～ not yet full-fledged; immature; young and inexperienced /收入颇～ earn a large income; be well-paid /从～ give generously ❷ great: *see* "～碑" ❸ (Fēng) a surname

丰[2] fēng good (looks); fine (appearance); graceful (carriage)
丰碑 fēngbēi monument; monumental work:他在地质学上的伟大成就,为我国的科技事业树立了一块～。His great achievements in geology are a monument to China's science and technology. /《红楼梦》是中国文学史上的～。*A Dream of Red Mansions* is a monumental work in the history of Chinese literature.
丰采 fēngcǎi *also* "风采" fēngcǎi elegant demeanour; graceful bearing
丰产 fēngchǎn high yield; bumper crop; plenteous harvest:三亩～田 three *mu* of high-yield cropland /～不丰收 raise a good crop but fail to get it in /这一块地今年～。This plot of land yielded fine crops this year.
丰登 fēngdēng bumper harvest:五谷～ abundant harvest of all crops; bumper grain harvest /愿乡亲们年年～,岁岁平安。May all the villagers be safe and sound and get in bumper harvests year after year.
丰度 fēngdù ❶ graceful bearing or carriage ❷ 〈物理〉 abundance:～比 abundance ratio
丰富 fēngfù ❶ rich; wealthy; plentiful; abundant:物产～ large variety of products /自然资源～ rich in natural resources /营养～ nutritious; nourishing /种类～ profusion of varieties /词汇～ abundant (*or* large, *or* copious) vocabulary /感情～ emotional; sentimental /在工作中积累了～的经验 accumulate a wealth of experience in work /她做生意经验～。She has wide (*or* rich) experience in business. ❷ enrich:～学生的娱乐活动 lend (*or* add) variety to students' recreational activities /读书可以～我们的知识。Reading can enrich our knowledge.
丰富多彩 fēngfù-duōcǎi rich and varied; luxuriant and colourful:～的生活 interesting and full life /体育活动～ varied and colourful sports activities /～的手工艺品 fine and diverse handicrafts /～的汉

F

语方言 great variety of Chinese dialects /暑假生活~。We had an interesting and colourful summer vacation.

丰富文本格式 fēngfù wénběn géshì 〈信息〉 rich text format (RTF)

丰功伟绩 fēnggōng-wěijì *also* "丰功伟业" signal or monumental contributions; magnificent exploits and great feats:他们为人民建立了~。They have made great contributions to the people.

丰厚 fēnghòu ❶ rich and thick:海狸皮绒毛~ rich and thick beaver (fur) /植被~ rich vegetation ❷ rich and generous:待遇~ excellent pay and perks /奖品~ generous prizes /收入~ handsome income

丰满 fēngmǎn ❶ full; plentiful:~的麦穗 full ears of wheat /嗓音圆润~ rich and mellow voice ❷ full and round; well-developed; full-grown:~的胸脯 full and round breasts; ample bosom /~的身材 well-rounded (*or* plump) figure /面颊~ chubby (*or* plump) face /羽毛~ be full-fledged /这姑娘发育得健壮~。The girl is physically well-developed. /她这两年~多了。Her figure has filled out a good deal in the past couple of years.

丰茂 fēngmào luxuriant; lush; profuse:~的草木 luxuriant vegetation /须眉~ have thick eyebrows and dense beard /湖区芦苇~。The reeds in the lake are thriving.

丰美 fēngměi lush:水草~的牧场 lush pasture

丰年 fēngnián bumper harvest year; good year; year of abundance:~要当歉年过 spend a year of plenty the way you spend a year of want; practise frugality in plenty /瑞雪兆~。A timely snow foretells a bumper harvest. *or* A snow year is a good year.

丰年虫 fēngniánchóng 〈动物〉fairy shrimp

丰沛 fēngpèi (of rain) plentiful; abundant:水源~ abundant water resources /今年雨水~。There has been plenty of rain this year.

丰取刻与 fēngqǔ-kèyǔ take much and give little; cruelly plunder (the people)

丰饶 fēngráo rich and fertile: ~的长江流域 rich and fertile Yangtze River valley

丰稔 fēngrěn 〈书面〉bumper harvest

丰润 fēngrùn plump and smooth-skinned: ~的双臂 plump and smooth-skinned arms

丰赡 fēngshàn 〈书面〉rich; abundant; plentiful:谷米~ have plenty of grain

丰神 fēngshén *also* "风神" fēngshén elegant bearing or demeanour

丰盛 fēngshèng rich; abundant; lavish; sumptuous: ~的宴席 sumptuous banquet; lavish feast /摆了一大桌~的瓜果 set an abundant table of fruits and melons /食堂每天的晚饭很~。The canteen serves a good square meal every evening. /菜肴不很~,但味道鲜美。The dishes had small portions but were very delicious.

丰收 fēngshōu bumper harvest; big harvest: ~补歉 make up for a crop failure with a bumper harvest /连续三年小麦~ reap bumper wheat harvests for three years running /今年水稻~在望。There is every prospect of a good rice harvest this year. *or* This year promises a good rice harvest. /可望教学科研双~。Great achievements are expected in both education and scientific research.

丰硕 fēngshuò plentiful and enormous; abundant;rich:成果~ rich reward; great successes /树上满挂着~的柿子。The persimmon trees are thickly hung with fruit. /这位作家作品~。This is a prolific writer.

丰田汽车公司 Fēngtián Qìchē Gōngsī (Japan) Toyota Motor Company Ltd.

丰沃 fēngwò fertile; rich:~土地 fertile land

丰衣足食 fēngyī-zúshí have ample food and clothing; be well-fed and well-clad:这个村家家~。Every family in the village leads a fairly comfortable life.

丰仪 fēngyí *also* "风仪" fēngyí charm; graceful bearing

丰盈 fēngyíng ❶ (of one's figure) full; well-rounded:体态~ have a full (*or* well-rounded) figure ❷ rich; plentiful:衣食~ have ample food and clothing; have enough and to spare

丰腴 fēngyú ❶ (of one's figure) plump; well-rounded:女方长得~白净。The girl has a plump figure and fair complexion. ❷ fertile; rich; abundant; plentiful:~的酒席 sumptuous feast /~的大平原 fertile plain /在~的草甸上放牧 graze on rich (*or* lush) pasture

丰裕 fēngyù in plenty; well provided for:粮草~ be well-stocked with grain and fodder /牧民的生活一年比一年~。The herdsmen are getting better off year by year.

丰韵 fēngyùn graceful bearing
see also "风韵" fēngyùn

丰姿 fēngzī charisma
see also "风姿" fēngzī

丰足 fēngzú plentiful; abundant:这里风调雨顺,百姓~。The weather is favourable here and the people are living in plenty.

酆

Fēng a surname

酆都城 Fēngdūchéng 〈迷信〉nether world

封[1]

fēng ❶ confer (a title, territory, etc.) upon:分~ grant titles and fiefs to the nobles /敕~ confer a title on sb. by imperial edict /加~ confer a title upon sb. ❷〈旧语〉boundary; scope; limit: *see* "~疆❶" ❸ (short for 封建主义) feudalism:反帝反~ struggle against imperialism and feudalism ❹ (Fēng) a surname

封[2]

fēng ❶ seal; close:密~ seal up; seal airtight (*or* hermetically) /查~ seal up; close down /尘~ be covered with dust; be dust laden /铅~ lead sealing /~住井口 seal up the mouth of the well /~信 seal (up) a letter /拆~ break the seal /他企图用金钱~住我的嘴。He tried to seal my lips with money. /气温骤降,江河冰~。A sudden fall in temperature caused the rivers to freeze over. /别忘了~炉子。Don't forget to bank up the fire. ❷ envelope; wrapper:信~ envelope /护~ book jacket /启~ unseal; open an envelope or wrapper /原~不动 be left intact /赏~〈旧语〉gratuity or small gift wrapped in red paper ❸〈量词〉:一~信 a letter /一~电报 a telegram / 一~请帖 an invitation

封闭 fēngbì ❶ seal; cap:把门窗~起来 seal up the doors and windows /用蜡~瓶口 seal a bottle with wax /~油井 cap an oil well /全~式学校 immersion school /进行~式训练 conduct closed-door training; conduct training in total immersion /不能自我~,与世隔绝。One shouldn't cut oneself off from the outside world. ❷ seal off; close: ~机场 close an airport /~新闻 shut out the media /这家参与走私的公司被~了。The company that had a hand in smuggling was closed down.

封闭层 fēngbìcéng 〈石油〉confining bed

封闭剂 fēngbìjì sealer

封闭结构 fēngbì jiégòu 〈建筑〉enclosed construction

封闭抗体 fēngbì kàngtǐ 〈医学〉blocking antibody

封闭疗法 fēngbì liáofǎ 〈医学〉block therapy

封闭式公司 fēngbìshì gōngsī closed or close corporation

封闭式核爆炸 fēngbìshì hébàozhà contained nuclear explosion

封闭式基金 fēngbìshì jījīn 〈经济〉closed-end fund

封闭系统 fēngbì xìtǒng closed system

封闭性社会 fēngbìxìng shèhuì closed society (in contrast with an open society)

封闭液 fēngbìyè 〈化工〉confining liquid

封舱 fēngcāng 〈船舶〉hatch sealing

封存 fēngcún seal up for safekeeping:~历史档案 seal up historical archives for safekeeping /~备查 be sealed up for later examination /~基金 sterilized fund /~资金 blocked fund /~账户 blocked account

封底 fēngdǐ *also* "封四"〈印刷〉(of bookbinding) back cover

封地 fēngdì fief; manor; feudal estate

封顶 fēngdǐng ❶ (of the terminal bud) stop growing ❷ put a ceiling on; set the maximum rate; cap:奖金不~ put no ceiling on bonuses; set no maximum for bonuses /税率~ rate-capping

封冻 fēngdòng ❶ (of river, etc.) freeze over:湖一~,我们就可以滑冰了。We can go skating as soon as the lake is frozen over. ❷ (of soil) be frozen over; be frozen hard:地全~了。The earth is frozen solid.

封冻期 fēngdòngqī period of freezing weather; freeze

封二 fēng'èr 〈印刷〉inside front cover

封港 fēnggǎng close a port

封官许愿 fēngguān-xǔyuàn 〈贬义〉hand out official posts and make lavish promises; promise high posts and other favours;利用~来收买人 buy sb. off by offering him a high post or other favours

封罐机 fēngguànjī tin seamer; can seamer

封焊 fēnghàn solder and seal

封行 fēngháng 〈农业〉closing of furrow by crop foliage

封河 fēnghé (of a river) be frozen over

F

封火 fēnghuǒ bank a fire:炉子还没有～。The fire hasn't been banked up yet.
封建 fēngjiàn ❶ system of enfeoffment *see also* "分封制" fēnfēngzhì ❷ feudalism:反～ anti-feudal /～剥削 feudal exploitation ❸ pertaining to feudalism; feudal:头脑～ feudal-minded /～毒素 feudal poison /～习俗 feudal customs (*or* conventions) /～余孽 spawn of feudalism
封建把头 fēngjiàn bǎtou feudal gangmaster
封建割据 fēngjiàn gējù feudal separationist rule
封建社会 fēngjiàn shèhuì feudal society
封建王朝 fēngjiàn wángcháo feudal monarchy or dynasty
封建主 fēngjiànzhǔ feudal lord
封建主义 fēngjiànzhǔyì feudalism
封建专制主义 fēngjiàn zhuānzhìzhǔyì feudal despotism
封疆 fēngjiāng ❶ boundary; frontier ❷〈旧语〉governors or commanders of border provinces:～大吏 governor (*or* commander) of a border province
封接 fēngjiē〈电工〉seal in
封禁 fēngjìn ❶ seal up; seal off; close:～府库 seal up the government repository ❷ prohibit; ban; forbid:这本书遭到～。The book was banned.
封镜 fēngjìng finish making a film:这部影片已经～。They have finished making the film.
封局 fēngjú *also* "封盘";"封棋" (chess game) go into recess; adjourn:下到中午～时,双方仅走了三十五手棋。By noon when the chess game adjourned, the two players had only made 35 moves.
封君 fēngjūn〈旧语〉❶ noble who held his fief from the sovereign ❷ person granted a posthumous title thanks to his descendants' successes in their official careers
封口 fēngkǒu ❶ seal; close; heal:～机 sealer /他带来一封没有～的信。He brought an unsealed letter. / 脖子上的疮还没有～。The sore on the neck has not healed yet. ❷ shut up; speak with a tone of finality:他都～了,再谈也没有用。He spoke with such finality that there is no use to talk to him anymore.
封蜡 fēnglà sealing wax
封里 fēnglǐ (of books or magazines) inside front cover; inside back cover
封垄 fēnglǒng〈农业〉*see* "封行"
封炉 fēnglú〈冶金〉bank; bank up the furnace
封门 fēngmén ❶ seal up a door (so that people are forbidden to enter the room or house):他破产了,被人家封了门。As he went bankrupt, his house was sealed up. ❷ speak with a tone of finality; shut up:他不想交代罪行,一开口就～。As he had no intention to confess his crimes, he flatly denied the charge against him. ❸〈方言〉〈旧语〉(of a bereaved family when an elder of the family passed away) cover the couplets or picture of the door-god pasted on the gate with white paper
封面 fēngmiàn ❶ title page of a thread-bound book ❷ front and back cover of a book ❸ *also* "封一" front cover
封泥 fēngní ❶ *also* "泥封" sealing clay used in the Qin and Han dynasties ❷〈冶金〉lute
封皮 fēngpí ❶ *see* "封面❷" ❷ envelope ❸ wrapper; paper wrapping ❹〈方言〉strip of paper used for sealing
封妻荫子 fēngqī-yìnzǐ〈旧语〉win a title for one's wife and hereditary official positions for one's descendants (by one's meritorious service to the sovereign)
封三 fēngsān〈印刷〉inside back cover
封杀 fēngshā strangle; smother:这股歪风一冒头即遭～。That unhealthy trend was nipped in the bud.
封山 fēngshān seal or close a mountain pass:～期 period when hillsides are closed /大雪～。Heavy snow has sealed the mountain passes.
封山育林 fēngshān-yùlín close hillsides (to livestock grazing and fuel gathering) to facilitate afforestation
封禅 fēngshàn〈旧语〉(of an emperor) offer sacrifices to heaven and earth on Mount Tai
封豕长蛇 fēngshǐ-chángshé like a large boar and a long serpent — rapacious and ruthless:这群贪暴的侵略者有如～。These cruel aggressors were as rapacious and ferocious as boars and serpents.
封四 fēngsì〈印刷〉back cover
封锁 fēngsuǒ ❶ blockade:经济～ economic blockade /信息～ information blackout /实行～ enforce a blockade /解除～ lift (*or* raise) a blockade /突破～ break a blockade/～边境 close (*or* seal off) the border /～交通要道 block vital communication lines ❷〈信息〉lock
封锁线 fēngsuǒxiàn blockade line; blockade:偷越～ run a blockade /突破～ break through a blockade line (*or* blockade)
封套 fēngtào big envelope (for holding documents, books, etc.)
封条 fēngtiáo strip of paper bearing an official seal and the date for the sealing of doors, drawers, etc.; paper strip seal
封土 fēngtǔ ❶ grave mound; tumulus ❷〈书面〉fief; feudal estate; manor
封网 fēngwǎng〈体育〉(in volleyball) block
封箱戏 fēngxiāngxì〈旧语〉last opera performances put on before the Spring Festival
封檐板 fēngyánbǎn〈建筑〉eaves board
封一 fēngyī〈印刷〉front cover
封邑 fēngyì〈旧语〉manor, estate or district granted by a monarch; fief
封印 fēngyìn seal (on mail)
封邮 fēngyóu seal the mail; seal an envelope
封斋 fēngzhāi *also* "封斋节"〈伊斯兰〉Ramadan
封装 fēngzhuāng seal up and pack:塑料～ plastic packing /邮寄瓶装酒,应单独～。Bottles of wine should be sealed up and packed separately when they are sent by post.
封子 fēngzi *also* "红封子" hóngfēngzi money or gift (to children, servants, employees, etc.) wrapped up in red paper; red package
封嘴 fēngzuǐ ❶ speak with a tone of finality ❷ seal sb.'s lips

烽 fēng beacon

烽火 fēnghuǒ ❶ beacon-fire (for giving border alarm in ancient China); beacon:～狼烟 beacon-fire and the smoke of wolves' dung burnt to signal alarm; times of war /燃起～,传递消息 send a message by lighting signal fires ❷ flames of war:该国又起～。War broke out again in the country. /～连三月,家书抵万金。With turmoil of battle three months on end, A letter from home is worth a fortune in gold.
烽火连天 fēnghuǒ-liántiān flames of war raging all over the land:他出生在～的岁月。He was born at a time when flames of battle were raging everywhere.
烽火台 fēnghuǒtái beacon tower
烽燧 fēngsuì〈书面〉〈旧语〉beacon fire lit at night (烽) and smoke of wolves' dung burnt in the daytime (燧) to raise alarms at border posts; alarm signal
烽烟 fēngyān beacon fire; beacon; flames of war:～四起 flames of war raging all over the country

蜂(蠭) fēng ❶ wasp:马～ hornet; wasp /黄～ wasp; yellow jacket /泥～ mud dauber ❷ bee:工～ working bee; worker bee /雄～ drone /蜜～ honeybee /养～ keep bees /养～业 bee-keeping; apiculture /养～场 apiary; bee yard /养～人 bee-keeper; apiarist; apiculturist ❸ in swarms; flocking:*see* "～拥"

蜂虿有毒 fēngchài-yǒudú the wasp and the scorpion are venomous — little things may do one harm:他刚要发作,又怕～,惹出祸来,只好咽下这口气。He was on the point of flaring up when he checked himself, fearing his loss of temper might cause greater trouble.
蜂巢 fēngcháo honeycomb; beehive
蜂巢胃 fēngcháowèi〈动物〉honeycomb stomach; reticulum
蜂刺 fēngcì sting of a bee or wasp
蜂毒 fēngdú bee venom
蜂房 fēngfáng beehive; honeycomb
蜂糕 fēnggāo steamed sponge cake (made of wheat or rice flour)
蜂虎 fēnghǔ〈动物〉bee eater
蜂皇精 fēnghuángjīng royal jelly
蜂集 fēngjí gather in swarms; swarm together:几千人～在广场上。Thousands of people gathered in the square.
蜂聚 fēngjù gather in swarms; swarm together
蜂蜡 fēnglà *also* "黄蜡" huánglà beeswax
蜂螨 fēngmǎn bee mite
蜂蜜 fēngmì *also* "蜜" honey
蜂蜜酒 fēngmìjiǔ mead
蜂鸣器 fēngmíngqì buzzer

F

蜂鸟 fēngniǎo hummingbird
蜂农 fēngnóng bee-keeper; apiarist
蜂起 fēngqǐ rise in swarms:战乱时代盗匪～。Bandits ran rampant in those war-ridden years. /注家～。Scholars swarmed to annotate the book.
蜂群 fēngqún (bee) colony
蜂乳 fēngrǔ royal jelly
蜂王 fēngwáng queen bee; queen wasp
蜂王精 fēngwángjīng *see* "蜂皇精"
蜂窝 fēngwō ❶ honeycomb; beehive ❷ honeycomb-like thing:～胃〈动物〉honeycomb stomach; reticulum /混凝土结构中的～现象 gas hole in concrete
蜂窝炉 fēngwōlú honeycomb briquet stove
蜂窝煤 fēngwōméi honeycomb briquet
蜂窝式电话 fēngwōshì diànhuà cellular phone
蜂窝织炎 fēngwōzhīyán 〈医学〉phlegmon; cellulitis
蜂窝组织 fēngwō zǔzhī 〈医学〉areolar tissue; cellular tissue
蜂舞 fēngwǔ bees' dance — signal to each other as to what to do
蜂箱 fēngxiāng beehive; hive
蜂响器 fēngxiǎngqì *see* "蜂鸣器"
蜂腰鹤膝 fēngyāo-hèxī defects or shortcomings in the rhythm of words in poems
蜂音 fēngyīn hum; buzz
蜂拥 fēngyōng swarm; flock:～而入 swarm into; come swarming; come pouring in /农民～入城。The peasants came to town in swarms.
蜂拥而至 fēngyōng'érzhì come swarming:展览会刚刚开幕,参观者～。Visitors flocked to the exhibition as soon as it was opened.
蜂子 fēngzi 〈方言〉bee; wasp

峰(峯)

fēng ❶ peak; summit:山～ mountain peak /顶～ peak; summit; pinnacle /险～ perilous peak /主～ highest peak in a mountain range /群～ mountains; mountain range /冰～ iceberg /攀登科学高～ scale the heights of science ❷ peak-like thing; hump:驼～ camel's hump /单～驼 one-humped camel; dromedary; Arabian camel /洪～ flood peak /浪～ crest of a wave ❸ 〈量词〉*used of camels*:一～骆驼 a camel
峰巅 fēngdiān summit; peak:登上了珠穆朗玛峰的～ reach the summit of Mount Qomolangma
峰回路转 fēnghuí-lùzhuǎn (of mountain paths) be full of twists and turns; be circuitous; (of writing) make an abrupt transition
峰会 fēnghuì summit (meeting):五国～昨已开幕。The summit meeting of the five countries began yesterday.
峰立 fēnglì tower up like mountain peaks:剑眉～ straight eyebrows slanting upwards
峰峦 fēngluán ridges and peaks:～重叠 ridges and peaks rise one after another /～起伏 mountain ranges rise and fall /～连绵 rolling hills
峰年 fēngnián peak year:那年是地震活动的～。Earthquake activity reached its peak that year.
峰态 fēngtài 〈数学〉kurtosis
峰值 fēngzhí 〈电学〉peak or crest value:～计 peak meter /～点 peak point

锋

fēng ❶ sharp point or cutting edge of a sword, knife, etc.:刀～ cutting edge of a knife /笔～ tip of a writing brush; firm stroke; vigour of style in writing /话～ thread of discourse; topic of conversation /词～ incisive style of writing; pungent language /交～ cross swords; engage in a battle or contest /针～相对 tit for tat ❷ (as of an army, etc.) van; forefront; leading edge:前～ vanguard; forward /边～ wing; wing forward /先～ vanguard ❸ 〈气象〉front:冷～ cold front
锋镝 fēngdí 〈书面〉❶ cutting edge of a knife (锋) and arrowhead (镝) ❷ weaponry; weapons; arms:销～ destruction of weapons ❸ war:～余生 survive a war
锋钢 fēnggāng high speed steel; rapid steel
锋快 fēngkuài ❶ sharp:他把菜刀磨得～。He sharpened the knife. ❷ incisive; sharp; pungent; stinging:～的反驳 scathing retort
锋棱 fēngléng ❶ edge; pointedness:久经风雨的汉唐雕刻,失去了往日的～和光泽。The weather-beaten carvings of the Han and Tang dynasties have lost their former bold relief and lustre. ❷ dashing spirit; outward show of talent; drive:岁月流逝,～磨尽。The passage of years gradually took the edge off his spirit. *or* With the passage of time, he has gradually drawn in his horns.
锋利 fēnglì ❶ sharp; keen:～的匕首 keen dagger /猫有～的爪子。The cat has sharp claws. ❷ incisive; biting; piercing; sharp:言辞～ biting remarks /文笔简洁～ concise and incisive style of writing /～的目光 piercing look /两片嘴皮子比刀子都～ have a tongue sharper than a knife
锋芒 fēngmáng *also* "锋铓" ❶ cutting edge; spearhead:斗争的～ spearhead of struggle /会上他把批评的～转向了我。He directed (*or* levelled) pointed criticisms against me at the meeting. /对方一再避开他的～,不肯应战。The other side kept avoiding his challenge. ❷ outward show of one's talent:小试～ make a modest display of one's talent and ability
锋芒逼人 fēngmáng-bīrén display one's talent in an aggressive manner; be sharp:他批评我的缺点时～。He made trenchant (*or* caustic) comments about my shortcomings.
锋芒毕露 fēngmáng-bìlù make a full display of one's talent; show off one's ability:太～会招至忌恨。Too much glare of your talent will court jealousy and hate. /他已经不像刚上任时那样～了。He is no longer as assertive as when he first took office.
锋芒所向 fēngmáng-suǒxiàng target of attack:大军南下,势不可挡,～,无不披靡。Our troops swept southward irresistibly, carrying everything before them.
锋铓 fēngmáng *see* "锋芒"
锋面 fēngmiàn 〈气象〉frontal surface:暖～ anaphalanx /～低压 frontal low
锋刃 fēngrèn sharp point or cutting edge of a knife, sword, etc.
锋锐 fēngruì ❶ (of knives, swords, etc.) sharp; keen ❷ sharp; keen; incisive; poignant:目光～ have sharp eyes; be keen-eyed ❸ dashing spirit; drive:挫败敌人的～ take the edge off the enemy's spirit
锋头 fēngtou ❶ public attention; limelight:大出～ cut a dashing figure; catch a lot of attention ❷ edge; incisiveness:译文未能保存原文的～。The biting (*or* incisive) edge of the original work is lost in the translation.

风(風)

fēng ❶ wind; breeze; gale:大～ strong wind; high wind /强～ fierce wind; vehement wind; gale /和～ gentle wind or breeze /贸易～ trade wind /春～ spring breeze /季～ monsoon /台～ typhoon /飓～ hurricane /旋～ whirlwind; cyclone /龙卷～ tornado; twister /暴～雨 storm; tempest /阵～ gust /一级～ light air /二级～ light breeze /三级～ gentle breeze /四级～ moderate breeze /五级～ fresh breeze /六级～ strong breeze /七级～ moderate (*or* near) gale /八级～ fresh gale /九级～ strong gale /十级～ whole gale /十一级～ storm /十二级～ hurricane /顺～ fair (*or* tail, *or* favourable) wind /顺～而行 go before the wind (*or* with the wind, *or* off the wind) /逆～ head wind /逆～行船 sail in the teeth of the wind (*or* against the wind, *or* into the wind) /顶～冒雨 brave wind and rain /一股～ a gust of wind /起～了。The wind is rising (*or* springing up). /轻～拂面。The breeze was softly stroking one's face. /海上吹过一阵凉～。A cool wind blew off the sea. /～刮得正紧。The wind is blowing hard. /～停了。The wind has lulled (*or* subsided). *or* The wind died away. /～小了。The wind is abating. /什么～把你给吹来了? What wind blows you here? *or* What good wind brings you here? ❷ put out to dry; winnow:晒干～净 sun-dried and well winnowed ❸ air-dried:～肉 air-dried meat ❹ as swift as wind; speedily:雷厉～行 with the power of a thunderbolt and the speed of lightning ❺ practice; custom; atmosphere:世～ general trend (*or* common practice) of a society /校～ school spirit /移～易俗 change established (*or* prevailing) habits and customs; transform social traditions /蔚然成～ become prevalent; become the order of the day /歪～邪气 unhealthy tendencies ❻ scene; view:*see* "～光"; "～景" ❼ attitude; style:文～ style of writing /作～ style of work /八面威～ be awe-inspiring in every respect ❽ news; information:通～报信 give sb. secret information; tip sb. off /闻～丧胆 become panic-stricken (*or* terrified) at the news ❾ hearsay; rumour:捕～捉影 catch at (*or* chase) shadows /听见～就是雨 speak or act on hearsay; react impetuously; hastily overreact ❿ section in *The Book of Songs* (诗经) consisting of ballads:采～ collect ballads; collect folk songs ⓫ 〈中医〉*used in names of certain diseases*:抽～ convulsion /伤～ cold /破伤～ tetanus /中～ apoplexy; stroke /痛～ gout /喉～ sore throat /羊痫～ epilepsy /鹅掌～ fungal

F

infection of the hand; tinea manuum /白癜～ vitiligo /麻～ leprosy / 祛～ relieve rheumatic pains, colds, etc. ⓬ (Fēng) a surname

风暴 fēngbào windstorm; storm; tempest:看天气正孕育着一场～。A storm is brewing (*or* gathering). /大～肆虐了数小时。The tempest raged for hours. /革命～席卷全国。A revolutionary storm swept across the country. /美元～再起。The upheaval over the greenback starts all over again.

风泵 fēngbèng *also* "气泵" qìbèng ❶ air pump ❷ air compressor

风痹 fēngbì 〈中医〉 wandering arthritis

风标 fēngbiāo weathercock; weather vane

风波 fēngbō disturbance; rumpus; trouble:挑起一场～ make (*or* kick up) a rumpus /闹出～ touch off a tumult /平息～ put down (*or* quell) a disturbance /平地～ a storm out of the blue

风伯 Fēngbó God of Wind in Chinese mythology

风采 fēngcǎi 〈书面〉 ❶ *also* "丰采" fēngcǎi graceful bearing; elegant demeanour; charisma:这女人聪明漂亮，～不凡。The woman is bright and beautiful and has uncommon grace. /她决定去参加晚会，让他们一睹她的～。She decided to go and grace the soiree by her presence. /此人有学者的～。The man has the charm of a scholar. ❷ literary grace or talent:其文章别具一格，极有～。His writings have an elegant style of their own. ❸ 〈旧语〉 uprightness and integrity (of an official):天下士人皆仰慕其～。His upright personality is admired by all.

风餐露宿 fēngcān-lùsù *also* "露宿风餐" eat in the wind and sleep in the dew — go through the rigours of an arduous journey or fieldwork:长期的勘探生涯，使他习惯于～。A seasoned prospector, he was used to the hardships of living in the open.

风操 fēngcāo 〈书面〉 graceful demeanour and personal integrity:少好学，有～。Eager to learn as a child, he was well-mannered when grown-up.

风铲 fēngchǎn 〈矿业〉 pneumatic or air shovel; pneumatic or air chipper

风潮 fēngcháo agitation; unrest; disturbance:政治～ political unrest /闹～ agitate (for reform, etc.) /一场抢购德国马克的～ panic purchases of the Deutschmark /银行挤兑～ run on the bank

风车 fēngchē ❶ windmill ❷ winnower ❸ pinwheel (a toy)

风尘 fēngchén ❶ travel fatigue:满面～ travel-stained /一路～ endure the hardships of a long journey ❷ hardships or uncertainties of an unstable society or a wandering life:～侠士 chivalrous man in times of social unrest /沦落～ (of a woman) be driven to prostitution ❸ 〈书面〉 war and unrest:～之警 threat of war; alarm of war

风尘女子 fēngchén nǚzǐ prostitute; street walker

风尘仆仆 fēngchén-púpú worn out by a long journey; travel-stained; travel-worn and weary:他一路跋涉，～地走进了家门。After a long and difficult journey, he got home, travel-stained and exhausted. /～的脸上挂着一丝苦笑。On his weather-beaten face a wry smile appeared.

风成 fēngchéng aeolian; windblown; windborne:～地貌 aeolian landform /～沙丘 aeolian sand dune; windborne sand dune /～岩 aeolian rock; aeolith

风驰电掣 fēngchí-diànchè swift as the wind and quick as lightning:那马～般地向西奔去。The horse dashed westward. /一列火车～般地驶过大桥。A train whizzed across the bridge at full speed.

风传 fēngchuán hearsay; rumour:这不过是～，不可轻信。This is mere hearsay. You should not give it any credence. /～他已经逃跑了。He is rumoured to have escaped.

风吹草动 fēngchuī-cǎodòng rustle of grass in the wind — a sign of disturbance or trouble; sign of anything untoward brewing:有什么～要及时通报。Inform us immediately if there is anything untoward brewing. /我必须立即动身，万一今晚有个什么～，就走不了啦。I must set out at once. I won't be able to get away if there should be any sign of trouble tonight.

风吹浪打 fēngchuī-làngdǎ being beaten by wind and waves; being battered by a storm; storm and stress of struggle:不管～，胜似闲庭信步。Let the wind blow and waves beat, Better far than idly strolling in a courtyard.

风吹雨打 fēngchuī-yǔdǎ ❶ the wind blows and the rain beats; be buffeted by wind and rain:小茅屋经不起～。A thatched cottage can't stand wind and rain (*or* rough weather). ❷ rough conditions; upheaval; storm and stress:小农经济的弱点之一，是经不起～。One of the weaknesses of small-scale peasant economy is its vulnerability to natural calamities (*or* storm and stress).

风锤 fēngchuí pneumatic hammer

风挡 fēngdǎng 〈汽车〉 windscreen; windshield

风刀霜剑 fēngdāo-shuāngjiàn ❶ the wind cuts like a knife and the frost bites like a sword; severely cold weather; frosty weather:塞外的冬天，～，异常寒冷。It is terribly cold in winter beyond the Great Wall, with piercing wind and biting frost. ❷ adverse circumstances:封建家庭～般的桎梏摧毁了她的一生。Her life was ruined by the ruthless shackles of her feudal family.

风灯 fēngdēng ❶ *also* "风雨灯" storm lamp or lantern; hurricane lamp or lantern ❷ 〈方言〉 decorative family lantern

风笛 fēngdí 〈音乐〉 bagpipe

风动 fēngdòng 〈机械〉 pneumatic; wind-driven:～工具 pneumatic tool

风洞 fēngdòng 〈航空〉 wind tunnel:～试验 wind tunnel test

风斗 fēngdǒu wind scoop

风度 fēngdù demeanour; manner; bearing:～潇洒 have a graceful and easy manner; have a free and easy style /军人～ military (*or* soldierly) bearing /大将～ bearing of a general /有男子汉～ be manly; be man enough /他有学者～。He bears himself as a scholar (*or* in a scholarly manner). /此人颇有～。The man has poise. /他很快就带着长者的那种宽容的～，表示理解。He readily assumed the tolerant air of an elder, saying that he understood.

风度翩翩 fēngdù-piānpiān elegant demeanour; graceful manner or bearing:～一少年 elegant young man

风铎 fēngduó *see* "风铃"

风发 fēngfā ❶ swift as the wind; speedily:～相赴 lose no time in getting there ❷ energetic:意气～ daring and energetic

风帆 fēngfān ❶ sail:扬起～ hoist the sails; set sail ❷ sailing boat; sail; junk:海面上点点～在阳光下闪闪发光。The sea is dotted with sails glittering in the sun.

风范 fēngfàn demeanour; bearing; manner:颇有大家～ have the air of a great master; have refined manners; bear oneself in a way that shows one's fine upbringing

风风火火 fēngfēng-huǒhuǒ ❶ in a hurry; hastily and rashly; hustling and bustling:有个人～地闯进会议室。A man rushed into the meeting room. /做事稳重些，不要～的。Act calmly, not rashly. ❷ active; dynamic:～的战争年代 hectic war years

风风雨雨 fēngfēng-yǔyǔ ❶ repeated difficulties and hardships:六十年来的～，一起涌上他的心头。He recalled the countless hardships of the last sixty years. ❷ groundless talk; gossip:她过门没几天，满村就～起来，说什么的都有。All kinds of gossip about her went round the village a few days after she got married. ❸ 〈方言〉 changing mood; mercurial temper:干活要有耐性，～突击一阵子可不成。You've got to have patience in your work. You can't accomplish anything in erratic spurts.

风干 fēnggān air-dried; air-dry:～木材 seasoned timber /～腊肉 air-dried bacon

风镐 fēnggǎo 〈矿业〉 pneumatic pick; air pick

风格 fēnggé ❶ character; integrity:见义勇为的高尚～ noble character as shown by one's readiness to take up the cudgels for a just cause /运动员们赛出了水平，赛出了～。The athletes gave a good account of themselves and displayed fine sportsmanship. ❷ style; spirit:一位具有独特～的艺术家 artist with a unique style

风格学 fēnggéxué stylistics

风骨 fēnggǔ ❶ strength of character:～峭峻 be upright and never stoop to flattery /～高洁 be of noble and stainless character ❷ vigour of style:文笔～雄健 forceful and vigourous style of writing

风光 fēngguāng scene; view; sight:～旖旎 beautiful (*or* wonderful) view /～迷人 scenery of enchanting beauty /田园～ idyllic scene /领略祖国的大好～ appreciate the wonderful (*or* splendid) sights of our motherland /北京的～名胜 scenic spots in Beijing

风光 fēngguang 〈方言〉 ostentatious and extravagant; in style:他想把母亲的丧事办得～一些。He wants to hold his mother's funeral in style. /他一辈子辛劳，现在也该～～了。Having slaved all his life, he deserves a little extravagance now.

风光不再 fēngguāng-bùzài lose one's past glory, splendour, etc.; be no longer beautiful, attractive, etc.

风光片 fēngguāngpiàn 〈影视〉 scenic

风害 fēnghài damage caused by a windstorm; windburn

风寒 fēnghán cold; chill:偶染～ catch a chill (*or* cold) by chance /除去～ take the chill off /他衣衫单薄，难挡～。His clothes are too thin to keep out the cold.

风耗 fēnghào erosion by wind:这些措施减少了煤炭的~。These measures reduced the coal erosion by wind.

风和日丽 fēnghé-rìlì gentle breeze and bright sunshine; sunny and genial weather (in spring):~艳阳天 bright and balmy spring day

风庐 fēnghù wind-powered or wind-driven waterwheel

风花雪月 fēnghuā-xuěyuè ❶〈文学〉wind, flowers, snow and moon (used to refer originally to the subject matter in certain classical literary works and later to effete and sentimental writings in general) ❷ love affair ❸ lead a dissipated life; visit prostitutes

风华 fēnghuá 〈书面〉charisma and talent

风华正茂 fēnghuá-zhèngmào in the flower of youth; in one's prime; at life's full flowering:恰同学少年,~;书生意气,挥斥方遒。Young we were, schoolmates, At life's full flowering; Filled with student enthusiasm Boldly we cast all restraints aside.

风化 fēnghuà ❶ morals; decency:有碍~ offence against decency ❷〈地质〉weathering:~石 weathered rock /岩石~成土。The rock has weathered away into soil. ❸〈化学〉efflorescence

风化壳 fēnghuàqiào 〈地质〉crust of weathering

风怀 fēnghuái ❶〈旧语〉love (between man and woman):~诗 romantic poetry ❷ refined feeling

风火墙 fēnghuǒqiáng fire wall

风火事儿 fēnghuǒshìr 〈方言〉urgent or pressing matter:这是件~,可得紧着办。The matter is pressing and must be tackled without delay.

风机 fēngjī air-blower; blower

风鸡 fēngjī air-dried chicken

风级 fēngjí 〈气象〉wind scale:~表 wind scale; Beaufort scale *see also* "风❶"

风纪 fēngjì conduct and discipline; discipline:~严明 have strict discipline /军人应注意~。A soldier should observe discipline and pay attention to his appearance and bearing.

风纪扣 fēngjìkòu hook and eye on the collar of a uniform:系上~ button up the collar (of one's uniform)

风教 fēngjiào 〈书面〉customs and education; moral edification

风节 fēngjié 〈书面〉strength of character; moral integrity; morals:~日颓 moral decline; decay of morals

风井 fēngjǐng 〈矿业〉ventilating shaft; air shaft

风景 fēngjǐng scenery; landscape:游览西湖~ enjoy the scenery of the West Lake /大杀~ take all the fun out of it; spoil the fun /桂林~如画。Guilin is as beautiful as a painting. /三峡以~壮丽著称。The Three Gorges are famous for their scenic splendours. /蓬莱偎山抱海,~别致。Situated at the foot of a mountain and overlooking the sea, Penglai presents a unique sight. /踏遍青山人未老,~这边独好。Crossing these blue hills adds nothing to one's years, The landscape here is beyond compare.

风景画 fēngjǐnghuà landscape painting

风景林 fēngjǐnglín scenic forest

风景区 fēngjǐngqū scenic spot

风景树 fēngjǐngshù scenic tree

风镜 fēngjìng goggles

风卷残云 fēngjuǎncányún a strong wind scatters wisps of clouds — make a clean sweep of sth.:众人如~,吃了个干净。Everybody ate ravenously and the food was swallowed up like clouds dispelled by a strong wind.

风口 fēngkǒu ❶ place where there is a draught:她站在~上着了凉。She caught cold by standing in the draught. ❷〈地质〉wind gap ❸〈冶金〉(blast) tuyere:渣~ slag tuyere

风口浪尖 fēngkǒu-làngjiān where the wind and waves are highest; in the teeth of the storm; at the centre of storm and stress:青年人应该到~上去摔打摔打。Young people should temper themselves in the storm and stress of struggle.

风快 fēngkuài very fast; as swift as the wind:他跑得~。He ran very fast. /消息~地传遍全城。The news quickly spread all over (*or* got round) the city.

风籁 fēnglài 〈书面〉whistle of the wind

风浪 fēnglàng ❶ stormy waves; storm:海上~很大。The sea is rough. /船在海上遇到~。The ship was caught in a heavy gale on the sea. ❷ stormy experience; hardship:他准备迎战任何~。He is ready to brave any storm.

风雷 fēngléi wind and thunder; tempest:~激荡。The storm is raging. /一从大地起~,便有精生白骨堆。A thunderstorm burst over the earth, So a devil rose from a heap of white bones.

风力 fēnglì force or power of wind:~减弱。The wind has dropped (*or* subsided).

风力发电 fēnglì fādiàn wind power (generation):~机 wind-driven generator; windmill generator /~站 wind power station

风力输送机 fēnglì shūsòngjī pneumatic conveyor

风力提水机 fēnglì tíshuǐjī wind-driven water pump; wind pump

风里来,雨里去 fēngli lái, yǔli qù come in the wind and go in the rain — be busy running about with one's work despite hardship:他终年~地奔波在山区邮路上。He delivers mail in this mountainous area all the year round, rain or shine.

风凉 fēngliáng cool:在~处休息 rest in the cool

风凉话 fēngliánghuà irresponsible and sarcastic remarks:站在一旁说~ make derisive comments from the sidelines

风量 fēngliàng 〈机械〉input air; wind rate

风裂 fēngliè (of timber) wind crack

风铃 fēnglíng aeolian bell (hung on the eaves of pagodas or temple buildings); wind chime

风流 fēngliú ❶ distinguished and accomplished; outstanding: *see* "~人物" ❷ talented in letters and unconventional in life style:~儒雅 learned and graceful /~倜傥 easy and elegant bearing /~才子 free-mannered gifted scholar ❸ romantic; dissolute; loose:~韵事 romantic (*or* love) affair /~艳史 romance /~寡妇 widow on the loose /此人过于~。The man is too licentious.

风流人物 fēngliú rénwù truly great man; hero:每个时代都有它的~。There are great men in each era. *or* Each generation has its heroes.

风流云散 fēngliú-yúnsàn *also* "云散风流" dispersed by the wind and scattered like the clouds — separated and scattered:毕业以后,同窗好友们都天各一方,~了。After graduation, my schoolmates separated and lived far apart from one another.

风流蕴藉 fēngliú-yùnjiè graceful but not showy; natural and unaffected; urbanely charming

风炉 fēnglú ❶〈方言〉stove ❷〈旧语〉bronze or iron tea brewer with two loop handles and three or four legs

风轮机 fēnglúnjī 〈机械〉wind turbine

风马牛不相及 fēng mǎ niú bù xiāng jí have nothing at all to do with each other; be totally irrelevant:我说的和你说的是两码事,~。The remarks I made are entirely different from what you said. /法官告诉证人他的话与案子~。The judge told the witness that his remarks were beside the point.

风帽 fēngmào ❶ cowl-like hat worn in winter ❷ hood

风貌 fēngmào ❶ characteristic style and features; ethos:时代~ style and features of the time; ethos /当代中国青年的精神~ mental outlook of contemporary Chinese youth ❷ appearance and manner; looks and bearing:~娉婷 (of a woman) have elegant looks and bearing ❸ view; scene; appearance:恢复这座小城的古老~ restore the small town to its ancient appearance

风玫瑰图 fēngméiguītú *also* "风向图"〈气象〉wind rose

风媒传粉 fēngméi chuánfěn 〈农业〉wind pollination

风媒花 fēngméihuā 〈植物〉anemophilous flower

风门 fēngmén ❶〈矿业〉air door; ventilation door ❷ storm door

风门子 fēngménzi *also* "风门" storm door

风靡 fēngmǐ fashionable; in vogue:一时间呼拉圈~京城。For a while the hula hoop was all the rage (*or* vogue) throughout Beijing.

风靡一时 fēngmǐ-yīshí become fashionable for a time:这种时尚在全国曾~。The fad once swept the country.

风魔 fēngmó *see* "疯魔" fēngmó

风磨 fēngmò windmill

风能 fēngnéng *also* "风力" wind power

风鸟 fēngniǎo *also* "极乐鸟" jílèniǎo 〈动物〉bird of paradise

风派 fēngpài weathercock; fence-sitter; time-server; opportunist:~人物 opportunist; chameleon

风平浪静 fēngpíng-làngjìng the wind has abated and the waves have calmed down; calm and tranquil:今晚海上~。The sea is calm tonight. /任何社会改革都不会是~的。No social reform is plain sailing.

风起云涌 fēngqǐ-yúnyǒng ❶ rising wind and rolling clouds:~,雷电交加。The wind rose and clouds scudded; the thunder roared and lightning flashed. ❷ surging and fast-changing; rolling on with full force:~的群众斗争 surging mass struggles

风气 fēngqì general mood; common practice; atmosphere:败坏社会～ corrupt public (*or* social) morals /树立良好的社会～ foster a healthy social atmosphere/眼下有一种结婚讲排场的～。It has become a common practice now to have extravagant weddings. /这里学习～很浓。There is a good learning climate here.

风切变 fēngqiēbiàn 〈气象〉wind shear

风茄儿 fēngqiér 〈植物〉datura

风琴 fēngqín organ:管～ pipe organ; organ /簧～ reed organ; harmonium /手～ accordion /弹～ play the organ

风情 fēngqíng ❶(information about) wind-force and wind direction ❷〈书面〉bearing; demeanour:～都雅 have graceful bearing; be refined in manner ❸〈书面〉thoughts and feelings:这首诗寄托了他的～。This poem embodies his thoughts and feelings. ❹ flirtatious expression; amorous feeling:卖弄～ play the coquette; coquet temptingly; be coquettish; flirt ❺ lifestyle; local conditions and customs:塞外～ lifestyle north of the Great Wall /民族～ cultures and customs of the ethnic minorities /这条大街的店铺门面还保留着昔日～。The shop front in this street is still kept in its former style.

风趣 fēngqù humour; wit:～话 witty remarks; wisecrack /这位老人很有～。He is an old man of charm and wit. /这篇文章缺乏～。The article is rather dull (*or* lacks humour).

风圈 fēngquān solar or lunar halo

风人 fēngrén 〈书面〉poet

风骚 fēngsāo ❶〈书面〉literature in general ❷〈书面〉literary excellence:独领～ claim top excellence; enjoy the highest reputation ❸ coquettish; flirtatious:卖弄～ play the coquette /～女人 flirtatious woman; coquette

风色 fēngsè ❶ how the wind blows:～突然变了,由西往东刮,而且风势越来越大。The wind suddenly veered round to the east, and it was blowing harder and harder. ❷ how things stand; trend of events; circumstances; situation:善观～ be good at seeing which way the wind blows; be expert in sizing up the situation

风沙 fēngshā sand blown by the wind; dust storm:北国多～。It's very windy and dusty in the north.

风扇 fēngshàn ❶ electric fan ❷〈机械〉fan:散热～ radiator fan /通风～ draught fan; ventilation fan

风尚 fēngshàng prevailing custom or practice:树立良好的社会道德～ build up good social ethics /年轻人中流行的～ fad among young people /文明礼貌已成为一种社会～。It has become a common practice to stress decorum and manners.

风神 fēngshén *also* "丰神" fēngshén elegant demeanour and romantic charm

风声 fēngshēng ❶ sighing or soughing of the wind ❷ news; word; rumour:探听～ fish for information /走漏～ leak information /听到～ get wind of sth. /放出～ let out certain information on purpose; put out feelers /～越来越紧。The situation is getting tense.

风声鹤唳 fēngshēng-hèlì moaning of the wind and cry of cranes — fleeing army's suspicion of danger at the slightest sound:～,草木皆兵 afraid of the wail of the wind and the cry of the cranes, and fearing ambush from every tree and tuft of grass — the retreating force fled in panic and confusion

风师 Fēngshī God of Wind in Chinese mythology

风湿 fēngshī 〈医学〉rheumatism:类～ rheumatoid arthritis

风湿病 fēngshībìng rheumatism; rheumatic disease

风湿热 fēngshīrè rheumatic fever

风湿性关节炎 fēngshīxìng guānjiéyán rheumathritis

风湿性心脏病 fēngshīxìng xīnzàngbìng rheumatism of heart

风蚀 fēngshí 〈地质〉wind erosion

风势 fēngshì ❶ wind-force:～越来越大。The wind blew harder and harder. /夜间～减弱了。The wind fell during the night. ❷ how the wind blows; how things stand:探探～ try to find out how things stand (*or* which way the wind blows) /他一看～不对,拔腿就溜。He slipped off when he saw trouble was brewing.

风霜 fēngshuāng wind and frost — hardships experienced in life or on a journey:久经～ weather-beaten /几十年的～染白了她的头发。Decades of hardships whitened her hair.

风水 fēngshuǐ 〈中医〉acute essential edema; rheumatismal edema

风水 fēngshui *feng shui*, traditional Chinese practice of determining the location of a house, tomb, etc., supposed to have a vital bearing on the fortune of a family, owner, user, etc.; geomancy; geomantic omen:～宝地 place of good geomantic omen /看～ practise *feng shui* (*or* geomancy)

风水轮流转 fēngshui lúnliú zhuàn 〈俗语〉even luck rotates; your mileage may vary

风水先生 fēngshui xiānsheng *feng shui* practitioner; geomancer

风说 fēngshuō *see* "风传"

风丝 fēngsī breath of air:天热得很,连一点儿～儿也没有。It's very hot. There isn't a breath of air.

风俗 fēngsú social custom:～习惯 customs and habits /过春节是我国古老的～。It is an old Chinese custom to celebrate the Spring Festival. /各地～大不相同。Customs vary greatly from place to place.

风俗画 fēngsúhuà 〈美术〉genre painting; genre

风速 fēngsù wind speed; wind velocity:～表 anemometer ～计 anemograph /～器 wind gauge

风瘫 fēngtān *also* "疯瘫" fēngtān paralysis

风涛 fēngtāo stormy waves; storm

风调雨顺 fēngtiáo-yǔshùn propitious winds and rains; favourable weather (for the crops):今年～,五谷丰登。We reaped a bumper harvest this year as the weather was quite favourable.

风头 fēngtóu way the wind blows:密切观察～和水势 keep a close watch on the wind and water

风头 fēngtou ❶trend of things; developments (esp. those affecting one's interests); straw or straws in the wind:看～行事 act according to circumstances /避避～ lie low until the dust has settled /我看～不对。I smell a rat. *or* I think there is something fishy about it. ❷ publicity one receives; public attention; the limelight:喜欢出～ like to be in the limelight; seek the limelight; seek publicity /她在舞会上大出～。She cut quite a figure at the dance (*or* ball).

风土 fēngtǔ natural conditions and social customs (of a place)

风土人情 fēngtǔ-rénqíng local conditions and customs:你跟我说说这里的～。Please tell me about the conditions and customs here.

风土性植物 fēngtǔxìng zhíwù *also* "地方性植物" dìfāngxìng zhíwù endemic plant

风土驯化 fēngtǔ xùnhuà 〈农业〉acclimatization

风味 fēngwèi distinctive flavour; local colour:地方～ local flavour /这道菜很有些法国菜的～。The dish has a rich taste of French cuisine. /这种东北民间小调别具一番～。This kind of northeastern folk ditty has a special flavour.

风味菜 fēngwèicài typical local dish; local delicacy

风味小吃 fēngwèi xiǎochī typical local snack; local delicacy

风闻 fēngwén learn through hearsay; hear; get wind of:此事我已有～。It has reached my ears. /～他要高升了。I got wind of his oncoming promotion. /早就～他在背后说我的坏话。I heard long ago that he had maligned me behind my back.

风物 fēngwù scenery (typical of a place):～宜人 delightful scenery /牢骚太盛防肠断,～长宜放眼量。Beware of heartbreak with grievance overfull, Range far your eye over long vistas.

风习 fēngxí custom and habit:～人情 local conditions and customs /多年的～ long-established custom; time-honoured custom

风匣 fēngxiá 〈方言〉*see* "风箱"

风险 fēngxiǎn risk; hazard; danger:冒～ run (*or* take) a risk /招致～ invite (*or* incur, *or* court) a risk /承担～ assume (*or* undertake) a risk /避免～ avoid a risk /减少～ reduce (*or* decrease, *or* minimize) a risk /～太大的保险户 poor risk for insurance /～转移 passing of risks /～分担 allocation (*or* sharing) of risks /股票投资是要承担很大～的。Investment in stocks is highly risky. *or* It is highly risky to invest in stocks.

风险报酬 fēngxiǎn bàochou risk premium

风险分析 fēngxiǎn fēnxī risk analysis

风险公司 fēngxiǎn gōngsī risk investment company

风险工资 fēngxiǎn gōngzī subsidy for taking risks (in doing a job)

风险管理 fēngxiǎn guǎnlǐ crisis management

风险合同 fēngxiǎn hétong risk contract

风险赔偿 fēngxiǎn péicháng indemnity for risk

风险资本 fēngxiǎn zīběn risk capital; venture capital

风箱 fēngxiāng bellows; wind chest:拉～ pump (*or* work) a bellows

风向 fēngxiàng ❶ wind direction; how the wind blows:辨别～ try to tell the direction of the wind; try to find out which way the wind blows ❷ situation; circumstances:看～行事 trim one's sails; act according to circumstances /善辨～ be like a weathercock in the wind

风向标 fēngxiàngbiāo weathervane; wind vane; weathercock

风向袋 fēngxiàngdài wind sleeve; wind sock
风向计 fēngxiàngjì registering weather vane
风向图 fēngxiàngtú 〈气象〉wind rose
风向仪 fēngxiàngyí anemoscope
风心病 fēngxīnbìng 〈医学〉rheumatism of heart
风信 fēngxìn ❶ news; information; rumour:他一听到～就赶去了。He hurried there as soon as he heard the news. ❷〈书面〉monsoon
风信鸡 fēngxìnjī weathercock
风信子 fēngxìnzǐ 〈植物〉hyacinth
风信子石 fēngxìnzǐshí 〈矿业〉zircon
风行 fēngxíng ❶ be in fashion or vogue; become prevalent; be popular:～全国 be popular throughout the country /不过是一时～ nothing but a passing fad /通俗音乐目前十分～。Pop is all the rage now. ❷ fast; rapidly; vigorously:雷厉～ do sth. vigorously and speedily
风行一时 fēngxíng-yīshí be in great vogue for a while; be all the rage for a time:这种发式曾在青年中～。This hair style was once all the vogue (*or* rage) among young people.
风选 fēngxuǎn 〈农业〉selection by winnowing or wind
风选机 fēngxuǎnjī winnowing machine; winnower
风雪 fēngxuě wind and snow; snowstorm:～交加 blinding (*or* smothering) snowstorm /《～夜归人》*Return in a Snowstorm*
风压 fēngyā 〈气象〉wind pressure
风雅 fēngyǎ 〈书面〉❶ literary pursuits:附庸～ mingle with men of letters and pose as lovers of art and culture ❷ polite; elegant; refined:举止～ have refined manners; be elegant in manner
风雅颂 fēng-yǎ-sòng three parts that make up *The Book of Songs* (诗经)
see also "诗经" Shījīng
风烟 fēngyān smoke blown about by the wind:～滚滚 rolling smoke
风言风语 fēngyán-fēngyǔ slanderous gossip; groundless talk; canard:文艺圈内的～ backbiting in the literary and art circles /她的古怪行为引起了不少～。Her strange behaviour gave rise to a lot of gossip.
风谣 fēngyáo 〈旧语〉folk rhyme; ballad
风衣 fēngyī windcheater; windbreaker
风仪 fēngyí *also* "丰仪" fēngyí graceful bearing; charm
风义 fēngyì *also* "风谊" ties of friendship; morality
风油精 fēngyóujīng 〈药学〉essential balm
风雨 fēngyǔ ❶ wind and rain; the weather:在亭子里避一避～ take shelter from the wind and rain in a pavilion ❷ stress and storm; trials and hardships:经～,见世面 face the world and brave the storm
风雨不透 fēngyǔ-bùtòu watertight and airtight; completely surrounded (by a lot of people):里三层外三层地围了个～ be surrounded by ring upon ring of people /消息封锁得～。There is a watertight block of information.
风雨灯 fēngyǔdēng *see* "风灯❶"
风雨交加 fēngyǔ-jiāojiā the wind howls and the rain pours down; it's raining and blowing hard; be wet and windy:～的夜晚 stormy night
风雨飘摇 fēngyǔ-piāoyáo swaying in the midst of a raging storm; shaky; precarious; tottering:那个政权正处于内忧外患、～之中。Beset with domestic troubles and foreign invasion, the regime was tottering. /他的公司负债累累,已经处于～的境地。Burdened with a heavy debt, his company is already on the verge of bankruptcy.
风雨如晦 fēngyǔ-rúhuì wind and rain sweeping across a gloomy sky — a grim and grave situation
风雨如磐 fēngyǔ-rúpán ❶ continuous rain; succession of storms; gloomy skies:～,三日不霁。The grey and rainy weather lasted three days without clearing up. ❷ dark society; straitened circumstances:在～的旧社会 in the dark old society
风雨同舟 fēngyǔ-tóngzhōu in the same storm-tossed boat — stand together through adversity; tide over difficulties together:～的朋友 friend in adversity /现在你我双方是～,合作则两利,争斗则两亡。We are now in the same boat. If we cooperate, we'll both benefit; if we fight, we'll both perish.
风雨无阻 fēngyǔ-wúzǔ stopped by neither wind nor rain — regardless of the weather; rain or shine:比赛将准时举行,～。The game will start promptly as scheduled, rain or shine.
风雨衣 fēngyǔyī weathercoat; stormcoat; mackintosh
风浴 fēngyù wind bath
风源 fēngyuán ❶ source of wind ❷ root of some prevailing practice or popular trend:要纠正这股不正之风,就要找到它的～。To rectify the unhealthy tendency we have to find out its root cause.
风月 fēngyuè ❶ wind and moon — scenery:～清幽。The landscape is quiet and beautiful. /～无边。The wonders of natural beauty are boundless. ❷〈旧语〉sexual love:渐知～ gradually become aware of sexual urges
风云 fēngyún wind and cloud — stormy or unstable situation:战争～ winds of war /叱咤～ earth-shaking; all-powerful /天有不测～,人有旦夕祸福。In nature there are unexpected storms and in life unpredictable vicissitudes. *or* Storms gather without warning, and bad luck befalls men overnight.
风云变幻 fēngyún-biànhuàn changeable or fast-changing situation:～的世界 fast changing world /国际形势～。The international situation is highly volatile.
风云人物 fēngyún rénwù man of the hour:时代的～ hero of the time /他是本地的一位众所周知的～。He is a well-known influential figure here.
风云突变 fēngyún-tūbiàn abrupt change of the weather; sudden change in the situation:下半场～,我队最终落了个败局。Things took a sudden turn in the second half, and in the end our team lost the game. /～,军阀重开战。Sudden veer of wind and rain, The warlords are clashing anew.
风韵 fēngyùn *also* "丰韵" fēngyùn graceful bearing; charm:她已年过半百,但～犹存。She is over fifty, but her charm still remains.
风灾 fēngzāi disaster caused by a windstorm:此地屡遭～。The place was frequently hit by windstorms.
风凿 fēngzáo 〈矿业〉pneumatic chipping hammer; pneumatic chisel
风闸 fēngzhá 〈机械〉pneumatic brake
风障 fēngzhàng 〈农业〉windbreak; windscreen
风疹 fēngzhěn 〈医学〉nettle rash; urticaria
风疹块 fēngzhěnkuài wheal
风筝 fēngzheng kite:放～ fly a kite /～比赛 kiteflying competition
风致 fēngzhì 〈书面〉❶ good looks; graceful bearing; charm ❷ special flavour; humour; wit:别有～ have a flavour (*or* charm) of one's own /他的诗充满田园～。His poems are imbued with idyllic charm.
风中之烛 fēngzhōngzhīzhú candle guttering in the wind — (of a person or thing) may die or perish at any time
风烛残年 fēngzhú-cánnián old and ailing like a candle guttering in the wind; have one foot in the grave:老太太已是～了。The old lady looks as though her days are numbered.
风姿 fēngzī *also* "丰姿" fēngzī graceful bearing; charm; charisma:～绰约 (of a woman) carry oneself in a graceful manner; have graceful bearing
风钻 fēngzuàn pneumatic drill; rock drill

沨 fēng 〈书面〉〈象声〉sound of flowing water; gurgle

疯 fēng ❶ mad; deranged; insane; crazy:发～ go mad; become insane; be out of one's mind; go off one's head; go nuts /装～ feign madness /撒酒～ be roaring drunk ❷ without restraint:～玩 enjoy oneself with abandon /～嚷～闹 shout and fool around like mad ❸ (of a grain crop, plant, etc.) spindle:这些棉花～了。The cotton spindled.
疯杈 fēngchà *see* "疯枝"
疯癫 fēngdiān insane; mad; demented; moon-struck
疯疯颠颠 fēngfeng-diāndiān be mentally deranged; act like a lunatic; be dotty; be flighty:这姑娘成天～的。The girl is flighty all the time.
疯狗 fēnggǒu mad dog; rabid dog
疯话 fēnghuà incoherent utterance; rot; nonsense:别说～! Don't talk nonsense!
疯狂 fēngkuáng wild; crazy; frenzied; unbridled:～的大屠杀 unbridled mass slaughter /～的报复 frenzied revenge /～反扑 desperate counterattack /乐队～地奏着一支支乐曲。The band struck up one tune after another in a frenzy. /他们～地唱呀,跳呀。They were singing and dancing like mad.
疯魔 fēngmó *also* "风魔" fēngmó ❶ mad; insane ❷ be fascinated; be infatuated:看足球赛时,他简直～了。He watched the football match spellbound. /这孩子终于从电子游戏机的～中解脱出来了。The

kid at last recovered from his infatuation with computer games. ❸ fascinate; enchant; hold spellbound：足球比赛～了成千上万的球迷。Football matches have thrilled hundreds of thousands of football fans.
疯牛病 fēngniúbìng mad cow disease; bovine spongiform encephalopathy (BSE)
疯抢 fēngqiǎng panic buying：汽油储备不足，造成～。Petrol is in short supply, which has led to panic buying.
疯人 fēngrén deranged person; lunatic; madman; nut
疯人院 fēngrényuàn lunatic asylum; madhouse; mental hospital
疯瘫 fēngtān *also*"风瘫" fēngtān paralysis
疯长 fēngzhǎng 〈农业〉❶ overgrow; spindle：防止作物～ prevent the spindling of a crop ❷ (of plants) grow over but not bloom：阳光过足，水仙～。Too much sunshine made the narcissus overgrow without any flowers.
疯枝 fēngzhī *also*"疯杈"〈农业〉spindling stem (of cotton, etc.)
疯子 fēngzi lunatic; madman; nut; loony

枫 fēng 〈植物〉❶ Chinese sweet gum ❷ maple
枫丹白露 Fēngdānbáilù Fontainebleau, a town about 65 kilometres southeast of Paris known for the magnificent palace built by King Francis I
枫树 fēngshù ❶ Chinese sweet gum ❷ maple
枫香树 fēngxiāngshù Chinese sweet gum (*Liquidambar taiwaniana*)
枫杨 fēngyáng 〈植物〉beech (*Pterocarya stenoptera*)
枫叶 fēngyè leaves of Chinese sweet gum, maple, etc.

砜 fēng 〈化学〉sulphone

féng

F

冯 Féng a surname
see also píng
冯梦龙 Féng Mènglóng Feng Menglong (formerly translated as Feng Meng-lung, 1574-1646), writer of the Ming Dynasty
冯雪峰 Féng Xuěfēng Feng Xuefeng (1905-1976), modern Chinese writer and literary critic
冯友兰 Féng Yǒulán Feng Youlan (1895-1990), Confucian scholar and philosopher
冯玉祥 Féng Yùxiáng Feng Yuxiang (1882-1948), renowned Chinese general and patriot
冯云山 Féng Yúnshān Feng Yunshan (formerly translated as Feng Yun-shan, 1822-1852), one of the leaders of the Taiping Heavenly Kingdom (1851-1864)

逢 féng ❶ meet; encounter; come across：久别重～ meet again after a long separation / 萍水相～ (of strangers) meet by chance like patches of drifting duckweed / 棋～对手 meet one's match in a game of chess; meet one's peer / 千载难～ occurring only once in a thousand years; once in a blue moon / 游泳馆每～一、三、五开放。This swimming pool opens on Mondays, Wednesdays, and Fridays. *or* It opens every Monday, Wednesday and Friday. / 独在异乡为异客，每～佳节倍思亲。All alone in a foreign land, I am twice as homesick on this festive day. ❷ (Féng) a surname
逢场作戏 féngchǎng-zuòxì join in the fun on occasion; have fun in keeping with the occasion：朋友聚会，他也喝上两杯，但不过是～，并无酒瘾。When he was together with friends he would drink a cup or two to join in the fun, but was not addicted to alcohol. / 此人很会～，并不认真。He isn't serious. He is only playing games.
逢集 féngjí on market day：小镇～便热闹起来。The small town bustled with activity on market days.
逢年过节 féngnián-guòjié on New Year's Day or other festivals：～时队长总是自己值班，让别人回家团聚。On New Year's Day or other festivals, the team leader would always send others home and stay on duty himself.
逢人但说三分话 féng rén dàn shuō sānfēn huà *also*"逢人只说三分话" talk always with reserve：～，未可全抛一片心。〈俗语〉Think twice before you speak, and talk always with reserve. *or* Talk always with reserve and never speak your mind totally.
逢人说项 féngrén-shuōxiàng praise sb. or sth. everywhere：为了办成这件事，他便～。To get this done, he spared no effort and sang its praises everywhere he went.
逢山开路，遇水搭桥 féng shān kāilù, yù shuǐ dāqiáo cut paths through mountains and build bridges over rivers; remove obstacles and make things easy (for sb. or sth.)
逢凶化吉 féngxiōng-huàjí turn ill luck into good; turn misfortune into fortune：～，遇难呈祥 turn calamities into blessings and ill luck into good
逢迎 féngyíng ingratiate oneself with; make up to; fawn on; curry favour with：阿谀～ flatter and toady / ～上司，笼络部下 curry favour with one's superiors and rope in one's subordinates
逢遇 féngyù meet; come across：～节日，周围几十里的人都赶来集会欢庆。On a festival, people from miles away gathered here for celebrations.

缝 féng stitch; sew：～衣服 sew clothes / ～扣子 sew on a button / ～被子 stitch a cover on a quilt; stitch a quilt cover on / ～刀口 (in a surgery) stitch up an incision / 伤口～了三针 sew up a wound with three stitches
see also fèng
缝包机 féng bāojī sack closer
缝边 féngbiān stitch-hem; hem
缝边器 féngbiānqì hem-stitcher; hemmer
缝补 féngbǔ sew and mend：～外衣 mend a jacket
缝缝连连 féngfeng-liánlián do sewing and mending：她下班后有时也做点～的活儿。She sometimes does some sewing and mending after work.
缝合 fénghé suture; sew up：～手臂上的伤口 suture (*or* sew up) a cut on sb.'s arm
缝合线 fénghéxiàn ❶ suture ❷〈地质〉stylolite; suture line
缝连 féngliàn sew and mend：拆洗～ wash and sew
缝穷 féngqióng 〈旧语〉sew and mend clothes for a pittance：～过日 make a living by sewing and mending
缝纫 féngrèn sewing; tailoring：～车间 tailoring workshop
缝纫工 féngrèngōng stitcher; sewer
缝纫机 féngrènjī sewing-machine：手摇～ hand-operated sewing machine / 脚踩～ pedal sewing-machine / 电动～ electric sewing-machine / ～针 sewing-machine needle / ～油 sewing-machine oil
缝线 féngxiàn 〈医学〉suture：吸收性～ absorbable suture / 羊肠～ catgut suture
缝叶莺 féngyèyīng 〈动物〉tailorbird
缝制 féngzhì sew：～军衣 sew (*or* make) army uniforms / 她买了一块布料学着～衣服。She bought a piece of cloth to learn how to make clothes.
缝缀 féngzhuì stitch; sew：～破外套 stitch up a torn coat / ～领章帽徽 sew up collar badges and cap insignias

fěng

讽 fěng ❶ allude or admonish euphemistically; satirize; mock：～示 hint (at sth.); allude euphemistically (to sth.) / 讥～ ridicule; satirize / ～一劝百 satirize one person in order to teach a lesson to others / 冷嘲热～ burning satire and freezing irony ❷〈书面〉chant; intone：*see*"～诵"
讽嘲 fěngcháo satirize; mock; sneer：～的口吻 sarcastic tone / ～的笔调 satiric style / 恶意～ mock maliciously
讽刺 fěngcì satirize; ridicule; mock：～小说 satirical novel / 辛辣的～ bitter irony; biting sarcasm / 乘机～他几句 seize an opportunity to mock at (*or* ridicule) sb.
讽刺画 fěngcìhuà satirical cartoon; caricature
讽刺诗 fěngcìshī satirical poem
讽刺文学 fěngcì wénxué satirical or ironical literature; satire
讽刺小品 fěngcì xiǎopǐn satirical essay; satirical skit
讽谏 fěngjiàn 〈书面〉remonstrate with the sovereign by euphemism：以谈笑～ make implicit remonstrances amid talking and laughter
讽诵 fěngsòng 〈书面〉read with intonation and expression; chant：～古诗 chant classic poems
讽喻 fěngyù parable; allegory：～时政 allude to current politics in parables / 文章使用了～手法。The essay can be read as an allegory

(*or* parable). *or* The essay is written in an allegorical style.
讽喻诗 fěngyùshī parabolical or allegorical poem

覂 fěng 〈书面〉(of a cart, etc.) overturn

唪 fěng chant in a loud voice
唪经 fěngjīng (of Buddhists or Taoists) recite or chant scripture aloud

fèng

奉 fèng ❶ give or present with respect; submit; offer: ～上报告一份 submit a report /～上一片爱心 offer one's love or affection ❷ receive (orders, etc.): 昨～来书。Your letter was received yesterday. /～上级紧急指示，机场暂时关闭。The airport is temporarily closed on emergency orders from above. ❸ regard with respect; esteem; revere: ～为楷模 hold up (*or* look upon) as a model /～为经典 regard as a classic ❹ believe in; espouse (a religion): ～佛 believe in Buddhism ❺ wait upon; attend to: 侍～父母 take care of one's parents; look after one's parents ❻〈敬词〉*used to refer to sth. one does for the other party*: *see* "～告"; "～陪"; "～托" ❼ (Fèng) a surname
奉安 fèng'ān 〈旧语〉removal of the remains of an emperor or empress or a leader of a political party or government to the mausoleum; official burial of such remains after removal
奉承 fèngcheng bow and scrape; flatter; fawn upon; toady: 当面～ flatter sb. to his (*or* her) face /向他～讨好的人可不少。Quite a few people try to curry favour with him.
奉承话 fèngchenghuà flatteries: 爱听～ fall for (*or* dote on) flatteries
奉辞伐罪 fèngcí-fázuì send an expedition to punish a guilty party: 这个国家好像是～，其实另有算盘。That country seems to have taken punitive action on righteous grounds, but in fact, it has other axes to grind.
奉达 fèngdá 〈敬词〉inform; express: 特此～ (usu. used in a letter) that is what this letter is for; sincerely yours
奉复 fèngfù 〈敬词〉reply (to a letter, etc.): 谨此～。(at the beginning of one's letter) May I now reply to your letter; (at the end of one's letter) The above is my reply to your letter.
奉告 fènggào 〈敬词〉inform you; let you know: 现将有关决定～如下。Allow me to inform you of the relevant decisions as follows. /详情容当面～。I'll give you the details when I see you. /特此～，请参酌。The above information is for your consideration. /无可～。No comment. *or* I have no comment to make.
奉公 fènggōng act for public interests: 克己～ be selfless and work devotedly for public interests
奉公守法 fènggōng-shǒufǎ law-abiding: 本人一向～，连擦边球都不打。I have always abided by the law and never tried to stretch it the least bit.
奉还 fènghuán 〈敬词〉return with thanks: 如期～ give (sth.) back on schedule; return on time /如数～ repay (a sum of money, etc.) in full /这本书借我一用，五日内定当～。Please lend me the book and I promise to return it within five days.
奉敬 fèngjìng offer as a gift; offer or present with respect: 奉茶敬烟 serve tea and offer cigarettes (to a guest) /向皇上～方物 present the emperor with local specialities
奉令 fènglìng *see* "奉命"
奉命 fèngmìng *also* "奉令" receive orders; act under orders: ～出击 be ordered to attack; attack on orders /发言人～声明。The spokesman was authorized (*or* instructed) to make a statement. /奉总经理命前来通知你们停产。By order of the general manager, I am here to tell you to stop production. *or* I've been instructed by the general manager to come here and tell you to stop production.
奉命唯谨 fèngmìng-wéijǐn obey orders scrupulously; be punctilious: 在处理公务上他向来～。He always obeys orders to the letter in performing his official duties. *or* He is always punctilious about his official duties.
奉陪 fèngpéi 〈敬词〉keep sb. company: 有些公务需要处理，恕不～了。As I've some business to take care of, I'm afraid I won't be able to keep you company.
奉陪到底 fèngpéi-dàodǐ keep sb. company till the very end: 既然您有如此雅兴，我当然要～了。Since you're so interested (in the party, game, etc.), I'll certainly stay till the end. /他们一定要打，我们就～。If they insist on attacking us, we will take them on and fight to a finish.
奉劝 fèngquàn 〈敬词〉offer a piece of advice: ～你把这些问题好好考虑一下。I suggest that you think over all this carefully. /～你不要鲁莽从事。You would be well advised not to act rashly.
奉若神明 fèngruòshénmíng *also* "敬若神明" jìngruòshénmíng make a fetish of; worship: 他们为什么要把这样一个人物～? Why do they worship someone like this?
奉使 fèngshǐ be instructed or ordered to serve as an envoy abroad: ～西欧 be sent to Western Europe on a diplomatic mission
奉侍 fèngshì *also* "奉事" wait upon; attend to; look after: ～老人 look after the old people; take care of one's aged parents
奉祀 fèngsì 〈书面〉offer sacrifices to (gods or ancestors)
奉送 fèngsòng give away free; offer as a gift: 凡参加本项活动者～纪念章一枚。Everyone participating in the activity will be given a badge as a souvenir.
奉天承运 fèngtiān-chéngyùn by the Grace of God
奉天大鼓 Fèngtiān dàgǔ (old term for 东北大鼓, as Fengtian was the former name for Shenyang, major metropolis and political centre of Northeast China) versified story-singing to the accompaniment of a small hand-drum and other instruments
奉托 fèngtuō 〈敬词〉request sb. to do sth.: 这件事就～您了。I'd like to ask you to take care of this matter.
奉为圭臬 fèngwéi-guīniè look up to as the standard; regard as a model: 现在世界上有不少人把《孙子兵法》～。Many people in the world regard *The Art of War* by Sun-tzu as a model of enlightenment.
奉为楷模 fèngwéi-kǎimó look up to as a model: 把这位好干部奉为自己的楷模 take this honest public servant (*or* cadre) as one's model
奉献 fèngxiàn present with respect; offer as a tribute; devote; dedicate: ～洁白的哈达 present a white *hada* (to sb.) /把青春～给儿童 devote one's youth to children /把新作～给曾经一同出生入死的战友 dedicate the new book to one's comrades-in-arms who fought and defied death together /为祖国做～ make contributions to one's motherland /为听众～一首我最新创作的歌曲。Now I'll sing for you a song I've just written.
奉行 fèngxíng pursue (a policy, etc.): ～独立自主的外交政策 pursue an independent foreign policy
奉行故事 fèngxíng-gùshì 〈书面〉follow tradition; act in accordance with established practice: 请你办这些手续不过是～。You are asked to go through these procedures as a formality.
奉养 fèngyǎng support and wait upon: ～父母 support and look after one's parents
奉谒 fèngyè 〈敬词〉call reverently on (sb. holding a high office or sb. senior in clan hierarchy)
奉迎 fèngyíng ❶ flatter; fawn on; curry favour with: 他不会～上级。He doesn't know how to curry favour with his superiors. ❷〈书面〉〈敬词〉greet; meet: 经理特命我前来～。The manager sent me to meet you.
奉赠 fèngzèng 〈敬词〉give as a present; present as a gift: 临别～小诗一首。Allow me to present you with a poem of mine as something to remember me by.
奉召 fèngzhào receive a summons: ～进京 be summoned to (go to) Beijing /大使～回国述职。The ambassador has been recalled (*or* summoned home) to report on his work.
奉赵 fèngzhào 〈书面〉return sth. intact to its owner; return sth. with thanks
see also "完璧归赵" wánbì-guīzhào
奉旨 fèngzhǐ by decree of the emperor; by imperial edict: ～查办 investigate and try a case by imperial edict (*or* decree)

俸 fèng salary; stipend; pay: 薪～ salary (usu. of an official); stipend
俸给 fèngjǐ salary (usu. of an official); stipend
俸金 fèngjīn *also* "俸钱" sum of official's salary; stipend
俸禄 fènglù 〈旧语〉official's salary or stipend
俸钱 fèngqián *see* "俸金"

赗 fèng 〈书面〉❶ help with a funeral by presenting gifts or money to the bereaved family: 赙～ present a funeral gift to a be-

F

reaved family ❷ gift for a funeral

覅 fèng 〈方言〉no need; not necessary

凤(鳳) fèng ❶ phoenix:龙～ dragon and phoenix (traditional symbols of the monarch, dragon for the emperor or king and phoenix for the empress or queen) /～求凰 (of a young man seeking a girl's love) like a male phoenix seeking its mate ❷ (Fèng) a surname

凤雏 fèngchú 〈书面〉fledgeling phoenix; handsome and spirited youth:龙驹～ young dragon or fledgeling phoenix — promising youth; intelligent and promising young people

凤蝶 fèngdié 〈动物〉swallowtail (butterfly); *Papilio*:黑色玉带～ *Papilio polytes*

凤肝龙心 fènggān-lóngxīn liver of a phoenix and heart of a dragon — rare delicacy

凤阁龙楼 fènggé-lónglóu pavilions and halls sculpted or ornamented with phoenix and dragon patterns — imperial palace; beautiful mansion:～连霄汉。Gorgeous palaces and pavilions reach up to heaven.

凤冠 fèngguān phoenix coronet (worn by an empress or imperial concubine and formerly also as a bride's headdress):～霞帔 phoenix coronet and embroidered tasselled cape (worn formerly by a woman of high rank)

凤凰 fènghuáng phoenix (with 凤 being the male and 凰 being the female):～来仪 phoenix being seen to salute people — an auspicious omen

凤凰木 fènghuángmù royal poinciana; flamboyant tree; flame tree; *Delonix regia*

凤凰衣 fènghuángyī 〈中医〉chorion ovi; chorion of a hatched egg

凤凰于飞 fènghuáng-yúfēi pair of phoenixes flying side by side — (compliment for) conjugal harmony and happiness

凤凰竹 fènghuángzhú *also* "观音竹" guānyīnzhú ledge bamboo (*Bambusa multiplex*)

凤凰座 Fènghuángzuò 〈天文〉Phoenix

凤梨 fènglí *also* "菠萝" bōluó pineapple

凤螺 fèngluó conch

凤毛麟角 fèngmáo-línjiǎo phoenix feathers and unicorn horns — rarity of rarities:如今这样好的小说竟是～了。Nowadays such a good novel is very rare indeed.

凤体 fèngtǐ 〈敬词〉(mostly used in traditional operas and novels) health of the empress or high-ranking imperial concubine:皇后娘娘～欠安。Her majesty the empress is indisposed.

凤头鹦鹉 fèngtóu yīngwǔ *also* "葵花鹦鹉" kuíhuā yīngwǔ cockatoo

凤尾草 fèngwěicǎo *also* "凤尾蕨" 〈植物〉(used as herbal medicine) phoenix-tail fern (*Pteris multifida*)

凤尾鱼 fèngwěiyú (general term for 鲚 jì) anchovy

凤尾竹 fèngwěizhú fernleaf hedge bamboo (*Bambusa multiplex* var. *nana*)

凤仙花 fèngxiānhuā 〈植物〉garden balsam; touch-me-not

凤眼 fèngyǎn (usu. of a woman) eyes of a phoenix; upwardly slanting eyes:～柳眉 (usu. of a beautiful woman) eyes of a phoenix and brows like willow-leaves; delicate, beautiful eyes and brows

凤眼莲 fèngyǎnlián *also* "凤眼蓝"; "水葫芦" shuǐhúlu water hyacinth (*Eichhornia crassipes*)

缝 fèng ❶ seam:骑～ junction of edges of two sheets (of paper) /焊～ welding seam; weld line /无～钢管 seamless steel tubing ❷ chink; crack; crevice:门～ crack between a door and its frame /见～插针 stick in a pin wherever there's room — make use of every bit of time or space /衣柜裂了许多～儿。There are a lot of cracks in the cupboard.

see also féng

缝隙 fèngxì chink; rift; fissure; a crack; crevice:～腐蚀 crevice corosion /桌面上有一道～。There's crack in the table. /一棵青松耸立在悬崖～间。A green pine towers aloft in the crevice of the cliff.

缝隙分析 fèngxì fēnxī 〈经济〉〈商业〉gap analysis

缝子 fèngzi 〈口语〉crack; chink; crevice:泥土屋顶裂了好些～。The mud roof has cracked in many places.

fó

佛 fó ❶ Buddha:～骨 relic (*or* remains) of Buddha /活～ living Buddha /放下屠刀,立地成～ a butcher becomes a Buddha the moment he drops his cleaver — a wrongdoer achieves salvation as soon as he gives up evil ❷ Buddhism:信～ believe in (*or* espouse) Buddhism ❸ image or statue of Buddha:大～ giant statue of Buddha /石～ stone statue of Buddha /拜～ worship Buddha; pay respects to Buddha /神龛里供着一尊～。There is a Buddha in the shrine. ❹ name of Buddha (*Amitabha*); Buddhist scripture or sutra; Buddhist sacred literature:念～ pray to Buddha

see also fú

佛得角 Fódéjiǎo Cape Verde:～人 Cape Verdean

佛得角半岛 Fódéjiǎo Bàndǎo Cape Verde Peninsula, the most westernly cape of Africa

佛灯 fódēng oil lamp burning in front of the statue of Buddha

佛典 fódiǎn Buddhist scripture or sacred literature

佛肚竹 fódùzhú a kind of bamboo with short bulging cane lengths between joints

佛法 fófǎ ❶ *Buddhadharma*; Buddha's teachings; Buddhist doctrine:弘扬～ spread Buddha's teachings; spread the dharma ❷ power of Buddha:～无边。The power of Buddha is infinite. *or* There is no limit to Buddha's power.

佛法僧 fófǎsēng 〈佛教〉Buddha, dharma and sangha (Buddhist religious community)

佛光 fóguāng ❶ Buddha's halo ❷ brocken bow; brocken spectre; anticorona

佛光山 Fóguāngshān Mount of Buddhist Glory, in Gaoxiong (高雄), Taiwan Province

佛光寺 Fóguāngsì Foguang Temple or Temple of Buddhist Glory, in Wutai (五台) County, Shanxi Province

佛国记 Fóguójì *also* "高僧法显传" Gāosēng Fǎxiǎnzhuàn; "历游天竺记" Lìyóu Tiānzhújì *Record of Buddhist Kingdoms* or *Faxian's Pilgrimage to India*, by Buddhist monk Fa Xian (c. 337-c. 422) of the Eastern Jin Dynasty

佛号 fóhào name of Buddha (Amitabha):口诵～ chant the name of Buddha

佛家 Fójiā ❶ Buddhist religion; Buddhism:道家与～ Taoism and Buddhism ❷ Buddhist:～不打妄语。Buddhists are forbidden to lie.

佛教 Fójiào Buddhism:～徒 Buddhist

佛经 fójīng Buddhist scripture; Buddhist sutra

佛龛 fókān niche for a statue of Buddha

佛口蛇心 fókǒu-shéxīn *also* "佛面蛇心" have a Buddha's tongue or face but a viper's heart; be honeyed-lipped but evil at heart; be a malicious hypocrite

佛兰德 Fólándé Flanders, a medieval principality in the southwest part of the Low Countries, now divided between Belgium, France and the Netherlands

佛兰芒人 Fólánmángrén *also* "佛兰德人" Flemish

佛兰芒语 Fólánmángyǔ Flemish (language)

佛老 Fó-Lǎo Buddha and Lao-tzu; Buddhism and Taoism

佛罗里达 Fóluólǐdá Florida, a state in the southeasten United States

佛门 fómén Buddhism:～弟子 follower of Buddha; Buddhist /皈依～ be converted to Buddhism

佛青 fóqīng ultramarine

佛身 fóshēn 〈宗教〉*Buddhakāya*; body of Buddha

佛事 fóshì Buddhist ceremony; Buddhist service:做～ hold a Buddhist service

佛手 fóshǒu *also* "佛手柑" 〈植物〉fingered citron; Buddha's-hand; *Citrus medica* var. *sarcodactylis*

佛手瓜 fóshǒuguā 〈植物〉chayote (*Sechium edule*)

佛寺 fósì Buddhist temple

佛塔 fótǎ Buddhist pagoda; dagoba

佛堂 fótáng (family) hall for worshipping Buddha

佛头着粪 fótóu-zhuófèn smear Buddha's head with dung; put a black spot in a piece of fine writing; desecrate; spoil

佛陀 Fótuó Buddha (title for Sakyamuni given by Buddhists)

佛像 fóxiàng image or statue of Buddha

佛协 Fóxié (short for 佛教协会) Buddhist Association

佛性 fóxìng *Buddhata*; nature of Buddha (believed to be present in every living creature)
佛学 fóxué Buddhist learning; Buddhist philosophy
佛牙 fóyá Buddha's tooth; tooth relic of Buddha
佛眼相看 fóyǎn-xiāngkàn regard with (Buddha's) mercy; treat sb. with kindness
佛要金装，人要衣装 fó yào jīn zhuāng, rén yào yī zhuāng 〈俗语〉 as Buddha needs a gilt statue, man needs fine clothes; fine feathers make fine birds; fine clothes make the man
佛爷 Fóye Buddha
佛音 Fóyīn *Buddhaghosa*
佛争一炷香，人争一口气 fó zhēng yīzhù xiāng, rén zhēng yīkǒu qì *also* "佛靠一炷香，人靠一口气"〈谚语〉 as Buddha needs incense, so man needs self-respect
佛珠 fózhū beads; rosary: 她闭目静坐，捻着一串～。Sitting quietly with closed eyes, she was twirling a string of beads.
佛子 fózǐ ❶ *Bodhisattva*; Buddha ❷ follower of Buddha; Buddhist monk ❸ all human creatures
佛祖 Fózǔ Buddha; founder of a Buddhist sect

fǒu

否 fǒu ❶ negate; deny: 他的方案被上级～了。His proposal was turned down by the superiors. ❷〈书面〉 no; nay: 你们同意他的意见吗？～。Do you agree with him? No. ❸〈书面〉 *used at the end of a question*: 知～? Do you know? /此物可得一见～? May we look at it? ❹ *used after* 是，能，可，*etc. to indicate a choice or question*: 此事可～见告? Can you tell me about it? /明日能～出发，尚待最后决定。Whether or not we will start off tomorrow is yet to be decided. *see also* pǐ
否定 fǒudìng ❶ negate; deny: ～之～〈哲学〉 negation of negation /对自己过去信仰的～ negation of one's former belief /工作的成绩不能～。What has been accomplished can not be denied. ❷ negative: ～判断 judgement in the negative /持～态度 hold a negative attitude /结论是～的。The conclusion is a negative one.
否决 fǒujué vote down; reject; veto; overrule: 总统的～ presidential veto /投～票 cast a veto /这个提案被大会～。The motion was voted down at the assembly. /法官～了辩护律师的抗议。The judge overruled the objection of the defense counsel.
否决权 fǒujuéquán veto power; veto: 行使～ exercise the veto /拥有～ have a veto (on sth.)
否认 fǒurèn ❶ deny; disavow; repudiate: 这些事实谁也～不了。No one can deny these facts. /刚刚说过的话，他却矢口～。He flatly disavowed what he had just said. ❷〈信息〉 negative acknowledgment
否则 fǒuzé 〈连词〉 otherwise; if not; or else: 我今天下午一定得去，～就没有机会了。I'll have to go this afternoon; otherwise I won't have another chance. /穿上你的大衣，～你会受凉的。Wear your overcoat or (else) you'll catch cold.

缶 fǒu ❶〈书面〉 long-necked earthern jar; amphora-like jar ❷〈考古〉 clay percussion instrument

fū

夫 fū ❶ husband: 丈～ husband /前～ ex-husband /妹～ younger sister's husband; brother-in-law /姑～ husband of father's sister; uncle /～仁则妻贤。A good husband makes a good wife. ❷ man: 匹～ ordinary man /武～ man of prowess; warrior; soldier /懦～ coward /万～不当之勇 of such prowess that even 10,000 men are not his match ❸ person engaged in manual labour: 更～ night watchman /农～ farmer /车～ carter /渔～ fisherman ❹〈旧语〉 conscripted labourer; corvée labourer: 拉～ pressgang /民～ coolie for an army *see also* fú
夫唱妇随 fūchàng-fùsuí *also* "夫倡妇随" the husband sings and the wife follows — (traditional concept of) domestic harmony; wife being her husband's echo: 他们俩～，变着法儿宰顾客。In close collaboration the couple fleeced their customers by hook or by crook.
夫妇 fūfù husband and wife; married couple: 新婚～ newly-married couple; newlyweds /老年～ elderly couple
夫君 fūjūn 〈书面〉 ❶ (form of address for one's husband) my husband ❷ (form of address for a friend) my friend
夫妻 fūqī husband or man and wife: ～和美 harmony between husband and wife; conjugal felicity /～恩爱 conjugal affection; connubial love /～感情破裂 alienation of mutual affection (between husband and wife) /～同居权 conjugal rights /～共有财产 property held in common by husband and wife; 〈法律〉 estates by the entirety /一日～百日恩。The affection of those who are husband and wife for one day will last a hundred days thereafter. *or* No affection endures like conjugal love. /～本是同林鸟，大限到来各自飞。Husband and wife are like birds sharing the same grove, who each fly away at the time of death (*or* a catastrophe).
夫妻店 fūqīdiàn small shop run by husband and wife; mom-and-pop store
夫妻关系 fūqī guānxi 〈法律〉 conjugal relations
夫妻无隔夜之仇 fūqī wú géyè zhī chóu enmity between husband and wife doesn't last the night; nothing can come between husband and wife
夫权 fūquán authority of the husband; 〈法律〉 manus: ～社会 male-dominated society
夫人 fūren 〈敬词〉 lady; madame: 第一～ First Lady /居里～ Madame Curie /王～ Mrs. Wang /驻华外交官和他们的～ foreign diplomats in China and their wives /大使～ wife of an ambassador
夫婿 fūxù 〈书面〉 husband
夫役 fūyì 〈旧语〉 hired hand; conscripted labourer; coolie
夫子 fūzǐ ❶〈旧语〉 term of address for a scholar: 孟～ Master Meng; Mencius ❷〈旧语〉 form of address for a teacher (usu. used in letters): ～教诲，敢不从命。I will abide by your instructions without fail. ❸〈旧语〉 my husband ❹〈讽刺〉 pedant: 老～ old pedant /～气 pedantic attitude; pedantry
夫子庙 fūzǐmiào Confucian temple: 南京～ Confucian temple in Nanjing /～前卖文章 peddle one's articles in front of the Confucian temple — carry coals to Newcastle; teach fish to swim
夫子自道 fūzǐ-zìdào the master exposes himself (while criticizing others); one's criticism boomerangs: 他说别人不谦虚，其实是～。He criticized others for bragging, which was just what he did.

玞 fū *see* "珷玞" wǔfū

麸(麩) fū (wheat) bran
麸皮 fūpí (wheat) bran: ～糊 bran mash
麸皮面包 fūpí miànbāo whole-wheat bread; brown bread
麸子 fūzi *also* "麸皮" (wheat) bran

砆 fū *see* "碔砆" wǔfū

呋 fū
呋喃 fūnán 〈化学〉 (transliteration) furfuran; furan: ～糖 furanose /～唑酮 *also* "痢特灵"〈药学〉 furazolidone /～甲醛 *also* "糠醛" furfural
呋喃树脂 fūnán shùzhī 〈化学〉 furane resins
呋喃妥英 fūnántuǒyīng 〈药学〉 nitrofurantoin
呋喃西林 fūnánxīlín 〈药学〉 nitrofuranzone; furancilin

趺 fū ❶ instep ❷ pedestal of a stone tablet: 石～ stone pedestal
趺坐 fūzuò 〈书面〉 sit cross-legged (as Buddhists do)

𫓧 fū 〈书面〉 fodder chopper; hand hay cutter

伕 fū 〈旧语〉 conscripted labourer; corvée labourer; coolie
伕子 fūzi 〈方言〉 conscripted labourer; corvée labourer; coolie

肤(膚) fū ❶ skin: 肌～(human) skin /皮～ skin /体无完～ have cuts and bruises all over the body; be a mass of bruises ❷ superficial: *see* "～泛"; "～浅" ❸〈书面〉 big; great: *see* "～功"
肤泛 fūfàn skin-deep; shallow; superficial: 内容～ shallow content /这种看法失之～。This view is rather superficial.
肤功 fūgōng 〈书面〉 outstanding service; great achievement: 克奏～ achieve great success
肤觉 fūjué 〈生理〉 dermal sensation; cutaneous sensation

F

肤廓 fūkuò 〈书面〉(of content) empty; shallow; unrealistic:～之论 shallow and impractical idea (*or* view)
肤皮潦草 fūpí-liáocǎo *also* "浮皮潦草" fúpí-liáocǎo cursory; casual; perfunctory; barely skimming the surface:作业完成得～。His homework was done hastily.
肤浅 fūqiǎn superficial; shallow; skin-deep:～的认识 superficial knowledge (*or* understanding) /这篇文章的论点既～又乏味。The arguments of this essay are both shallow and tedious. /我来说一点～的意见,算是抛砖引玉吧。Let me offer a few cursory ideas to set the ball rolling.
肤轻松 fūqīngsōng 〈药学〉fluocinolone acctonide
肤色 fūsè colour of skin:不论民族、信仰、性别或～ without regard to ethnicity, creed, gender, or (skin) colour
肤癣病 fūxuǎnbìng dermatophytosis

痡

fū 〈书面〉fall ill; be fatigued

敷

fū ❶ apply (powder, ointment, etc.):～药 apply ointment /热～ hot compress /只可外～ for external application only /在脸上～粉 powder one's face ❷ spread; lay out: *see* "～设" ❸ sufficient; enough:粮草不～。There were not sufficient provisions. *or* Provisions fell short. /收入刚刚～用。Income barely covers expenditure. *or* One can just make both ends meet.
敷陈 fūchén 〈书面〉relate in great detail; elaborate:～其事 relate sth. in detail; elaborate sth.; set forth sth. /他把历史上的一个小故事～为数万言的小说。He expanded (*or* wrote up) a historical incident into a novel of tens of thousands of words.
敷料 fūliào 〈医学〉dressing:～钳 dressing forceps
敷设 fūshè ❶ lay out; lay; install:～铁轨 lay a railway track ❷ place; lay (mines, etc.):～地雷 place (*or* lay) land mines
敷贴 fūtiē apply (plaster, ointment, etc. to a particular part of the human body)
敷叙 fūxù 〈书面〉narrate in great detail; elaborate:～观感 relate one's impressions in great detail
敷衍 fūyǎn *also* "敷演"〈书面〉elaborate; expound; develop:～教义 elaborate (*or* expound) a tenet /～成篇 develop (an anecdote, idea, etc.) into a story /这部小说根据历史故事～而成。The novel was written on the basis of a historical event.
敷衍 fūyan ❶ be perfunctory; go through the motions; muddle through:采取～态度 take a perfunctory attitude; act in a perfunctory manner; go through the motions /～几句 dismiss (sb. *or* sth.) with a few perfunctory remarks; make a few casual remarks; say sth. just for the occasion /这是件生死攸关的大事,你怎能用假话～过去? This is a matter of life and death. How can you muddle through by lying? /他这么说只不过是～那个女孩子,其实并不打算和她结婚。He said that just to humour the girl for the time being; actually, he did not intend to marry her. ❷ just manage; barely get by:对他来说,一天三顿能～过去,也就不错了。Three meals a day was good enough for him. /这笔钱,也只够全家～几天而已。The money is just enough for the family to get by a few days. *or* The money can last the family only a few days.
敷衍了事 fūyan-liǎoshì do sth. perfunctorily; muddle through sth.; skimp a job:如此重大的考试,你怎么可以～! How could you expect to muddle through such an important examination? /她做事认真,从不～。She is very conscientious and never skimps her work. /他们想跟我～。They tried to stall me off.
敷衍塞责 fūyan-sèzé perform one's duty in a perfunctory manner; make a show of doing one's duty; muddle through one's work:这人办事总是～。He always performs his duty in a casual manner. /这完全是一个～的答复。It's a sheer perfunctory reply.
敷衍搪塞 fūyan-tángsè go through the motions; do (sth.) perfunctorily; stall (sb.) off; explain away:对顾客的投诉,绝不可～。It is impermissable to stall off customers who make complaints. /出了这样大的事故,你还想～吗? How could you try to explain away such a serious accident?
敷余 fūyu 〈方言〉have more than needed; have enough and to spare; have a surplus:没有～的钱 have no money to spare /他们那里劳动力有～。They have surplus labour there. *or* They have more than enough workers there. /该的账都还了,手里还能～点儿钱。After paying off the debts we still had some money left.

稃

fū husk; chaff; bran:内～ bran /外～ husk; chaff

孵

fū hatch; brood; incubate:～出一窝小鸭 hatch a brood of ducklings
孵化 fūhuà hatch; incubate:人工～ artificial incubation /～率 rate of hatchability /～期 incubation period
孵化场 fūhuàchǎng hatchery (for poultry, etc.)
孵化池 fūhuàchí hatchery (for fish, etc.)
孵化器 fūhuàqì hatcher; incubator
孵卵 fūluǎn hatch; brood; incubate:～鸡 brooding hen; sitter
孵卵期 fūluǎnqī incubation period
孵卵器 fūluǎnqì incubator
孵育 fūyù hatch; incubate:刚～出来的小鸡 newly-hatched chicks

柎

fū 〈书面〉❶〈植物〉calyx ❷ leg of the stand for a bell or drum; foot of a bell or drum rack

跗

fū 〈生理〉instep
跗骨 fūgǔ 〈生理〉tarsal bones; tarsus:～炎 tarsitis
跗骨切开术 fūgǔ qiēkāishù tarsotomy
跗关节 fūguānjié tarsal joint; hock
跗面 fūmiàn 〈生理〉instep
跗痛 fūtòng tarsalgia
跗蹠 fūzhí *also* "跗跖骨" tarsometarsus (of a bird)

fú

夫

fú 〈书面〉❶ this; that:～人不言,言必有中。This man never speaks but to the point. ❷ he:～非而仇乎? Is he not your enemy? ❸〈助词〉*used at the beginning of a sentence*:～青年者,国家之精华也。The youth are the cream of a nation. ❹〈助词〉*used at the end of a sentence or of a pause in a sentence to express an exclamation*:悲～! How tragic! /逝者如斯～! 不舍昼夜。Thus do things flow away, day in and day out!
see also fū

芙

fú
芙蕖 fúqú 〈书面〉lotus
芙蓉 fúróng 〈植物〉❶ cottonrose hibiscus ❷ lotus ❸〈比喻〉fresh and original poem; beautiful woman
芙蓉出水 fúróng-chūshuǐ *also* "出水芙蓉" lotus flower appearing just above the water:其诗如～。His poems were fresh and original. /娇艳如出水芙蓉。She was delicate and charming like a fresh lotus flower.
芙蓉国 Fúróngguó land of hibiscus (in poetical reference to Hunan Province):我欲因之梦廖廓,～里尽朝晖。And I am lost in dreams, untrammelled dreams Of the land of hibiscus glowing in the morning sun.
芙蓉鸡片 fúróngjīpiàn stir-fried chicken slices with egg white

扶

fú ❶ place a hand on sb. or sth. for support; support with the hand:～杖而行 walk with (the support of) a stick /～着椅子站起来 get on one's feet by leaning on a chair /～病人上车 help an invalid into a car (by giving him or her a hand) /小家伙现在不用～就可走路了。The toddler can now walk without support. ❷ hold up; straighten up:把小树苗～起来 straighten up a young sapling /～他起来吃药。Prop him up to take the medicine. ❸ lend a hand; help; assist: *see* "～弱抑强" ❹ (Fú) a surname
扶壁 fúbì 〈建筑〉buttress; counterfort:～墩 buttress pier
扶病 fúbìng (do sth.) in spite of illness:他一直～工作。In spite of illness, he worked all along.
扶不起的阿斗 fúbuqǐde Ā Dǒu weakling whom nobody can help to succeed
扶持 fúchí ❶ help sb. to stand and walk; support:摔伤以后,他坐卧都要人～。Hurt by the fall, he needed help whenever he wanted to sit up or lie down. ❷ give aid to; help sustain; foster:～乡镇企业 help (*or* give aid to) township enterprises /～正气 help sustain a healthy atmosphere; encourage healthy trends (in a society, etc.) /红花虽好,也要绿叶～。Beautiful as a red flower is, it needs green leaves to sustain it. *or* For all its beauty, the red flower needs green leaves to set it off. *or* However capable one is, one needs the

support of others.

扶乩 fújī see "扶箕"

扶箕 fújī also "扶乩"; "扶鸾"〈迷信〉planchette writing: ～请仙 consult deities (*or* spirits) through planchette writing

扶柩 fújiù also "扶灵" escort a coffin (as in a funeral procession); serve as a pallbearer: ～返乡 escort a coffin to the native place of the deceased

扶老携幼 fúlǎo-xiéyòu help the aged along and lead the young by the hand; bring along both the old and the young: ～, 四处逃荒 flee from the famine, taking along both the old and the young; entire families flee from the famine

扶犁 fúlí put one's hand to the plough; follow the plough

扶鸾 fúluán see "扶箕"

扶轮国际 Fúlún Guójì Rotary International, a worldwide society for business and professional men

扶轮社 Fúlúnshè Rotary Club: ～成员 Rotarian

扶苗 fúmiáo straighten up the seedlings (after they have been lodged by wind or rain)

扶贫 fúpín help the poor; aid a poverty-stricken area; alleviate poverty: 技术～ help the poor (*or* poverty-stricken area) with technology / 教育～ aid a poverty-stricken area by promoting education there / ～计划 aid-the-poor programme (government programme to provide aid to poverty-stricken areas) / 这几年, 农村～工作大有成效。In recent years, the work of helping the poor has made much headway in the countryside.

扶弱抑强 fúruò-yìqiáng also "抑强扶弱" help the weak and restrain the powerful; help the weak against the strong

扶桑 fúsāng ❶ also "榑桑" fúsāng (in ancient mythology) huge mulberry tree beyond the seas, where the sun rises ❷ (Fúsāng) also "榑桑" Fúsāng legendary name of an ancient country beyond the East China Sea, used later to refer to Japan ❸〈植物〉*Hibiscus rosa-sinensis*

扶上马,送一程 fú shàng mǎ, sòng yī chéng help sb. get on the horse and escort him for a distance; (of a retired veteran) help a new appointee to get familiar with his or her post by serving as advisor for a while

扶手 fúshou ❶ handrail; rail; banister: ～绳 manrope ❷ armrest

扶手椅 fúshouyǐ armchair; fauteuil

扶疏 fúshū〈书面〉luxuriant and well-spaced: 花园里花木～。The flowers and trees in the garden are luxuriant but well spaced.

扶梯 fútī ❶ staircase with banisters ❷〈方言〉ladder

扶危济困 fúwēi-jìkùn also "扶危救困"; "扶危济急" help those in distress and aid those in peril; help those in danger and relieve those in need; rescue the endangered and succour the poor

扶阳退阴 fúyáng-tuìyīn〈中医〉reinforce healthy factors *yang* to eliminate pathogenic factors *yin* (in the human body)

扶养 fúyǎng provide for; foster; bring up: ～老人 provide for the elderly; support one's parents

扶养费 fúyǎngfèi support payment; alimony

扶摇 fúyáo〈书面〉cyclone spiralling up steeply: 鲲鹏展翅, 九万里, 翻动～羊角。The roc wings fanwise, Soaring ninety thousand *li* And rousing a raging cyclone

扶摇直上 fúyáo-zhíshàng soar as if on the wings of a cyclone; be promoted quickly in official career; rise steeply; skyrocket: 物价～ prices rise steeply; prices skyrocket / 步步高升, ～ rise higher and higher (usu. in one's official career) as if soaring on the wings of a cyclone; make a meteoric rise

扶掖 fúyè〈书面〉support; assist; help: ～后进 help one's juniors (*or* subordinates) / 不遗余力地鼓励和～青年演员 do one's utmost to encourage and assist young actors and actresses

扶正 fúzhèng ❶〈旧语〉make a concubine one's official wife ❷ set upright or straight: 把树苗～ set a sapling upright ❸〈中医〉foster or build up resistance to disease / ～祛邪 foster resistance to disease and dispel pathogenic influences

扶植 fúzhí foster; cultivate; promote; prop up: ～新生力量 foster new emerging forces / ～傀儡政权 prop up a puppet (*or* quisling) regime / ～亲信 cultivate one's sworn followers / 热心～业余作家 help amateur writers enthusiastically

扶助 fúzhù help; assist; support: ～穷人 assist the poor / ～贫困地区 help the poverty-stricken areas

蚨

fú see "青蚨" qīngfú

榑

fú

榑桑 fúsāng see "扶桑❶❷" fúsāng

福

fú ❶ good fortune; luck; blessing; happiness: ～、禄、寿 happiness, high rank and longevity (considered the three major blessings of life) / 为民造～ work for the wellbeing of the people / 有～同享, 有难同当 share weal and woe alike / 一饱眼～ feast one's eyes / ～兮祸之所伏。In good fortune lurks bad luck. ❷〈旧语〉(of a woman) make a curtsy: ～了一～ make a curtsy / 道万～ (of a woman) make a greeting while curtsying ❸ (short for 福建) Fujian Province: see "～橘" ❹ (Fú) a surname

福地 fúdì ❶ (of Taoism) place where immortals live: 洞天～ cave inhabited by immortals; beautiful scenic place ❷ place of happiness: 身在～不知福。Growing up in happiness, one fails to appreciate it.

福尔马林 fú'ěrmǎlín〈化学〉(transliteration) formalin

福尔摩斯 Fú'ěrmósī Sherlock Holmes, the central figure of Arthur Conan Doyle's detective stories

福分 fúfen〈口语〉happy lot; good fortune: 能到这里一游, ～不浅啊! We are fortunate enough to be able to visit this place. *or* It is our good fortune to visit this place.

福冈 Fúgāng Fukuoka, a commercial and industrial city and port in Kyushu (九州), Japan

福建 Fújiàn Fujian (Province)

福建柏 fújiànbǎi〈植物〉*Fokienia hodginsii*

福将 fújiàng fortune's favourite: 这事儿他去准成, 他是我们的～。He is sure to succeed in the task, for he always has fortune on his side.

福晋 fújìn wife of a Manchu prince; (Manchu) princely consort

福橘 fújú tangerine produced in Fujian Province

福克兰群岛 Fúkèlán Qúndǎo Falkland Islands; Falklands; or Malvinas Islands as called by Argentina

福利 fúlì ❶ material benefits; well-being; welfare: 公众～ public welfare / 儿童～ child welfare / 附加～ fringe benefits / 为当地群众谋～ work for the wellbeing of the local people / ～社会 welfare society ❷〈书面〉bring material benefits to: 发展生产, ～人民 promote production to benefit the people; improve the people's livelihood through developing production

福利国家 fúlì guójiā welfare state

福利基金 fúlì jījīn welfare fund

福利经济学 fúlì jīngjìxué welfare economics

福利设施 fúlì shèshī welfare facilities

福利事业 fúlì shìyè welfare projects or services

福利主义 fúlìzhǔyì doctrine of working solely for material benefits; exclusive emphasis on welfare; welfarism

福气 fúqi happy lot; good fortune: 这么贵重的礼品, 我可没～消受。I'm afraid I don't have the happy lot to enjoy such expensive gifts. / 老太太有～, 儿子媳妇们都这么孝顺。The old lady has the good fortune to be cared for by her loving sons and their wives.

福人 fúrén person of good fortune; person born under a lucky star

福如东海,寿比南山 fú rú dōnghǎi, shòu bǐ nánshān〈套语〉happiness as boundless as the sea and longevity comparable to that of the hills; may you live a long and happy life: 祝您老人家福如东海长流水, 寿比南山不老松。I wish you happiness and a long life.

福特 Fútè ❶ Henry Ford (1863-1947), engineer and founder of the Ford Motor Company ❷ Gerald Rudolph Ford (1913-), 38th President of the United States (1974-1977)

福特基金会 Fútè Jījīnhuì Ford Foundation (established in 1936)

福特汽车公司 Fútè Qìchē Gōngsī Ford Motor Company, first established in 1903 in the United States

福田赳夫 Fútiánjiūfū Fukuda Tadeo (1905-1995), Japanese Prime Minister (1976-1978)

福无双至,祸不单行 fú wú shuāng zhì, huò bù dān xíng〈谚语〉blessings do not come in pairs and calamities never come singly; luck comes but once but trouble comes in droves

福物 fúwù〈旧语〉sacrificial offerings (such as wine, meat, etc.)

福相 fúxiàng features or countenance of good fortune: 长得一副～ have features suggestive of good fortune; look as if born under a lucky star

福星 fúxīng lucky star; mascot: ～高照 the lucky star shines high above; have one's star in the ascendant; ride the high tide of luck; be under the smiles of fortune

福音 fúyīn ❶〈基督教〉Gospel:《马太～》*The Gospel according to Matthew* /～传道士 evangelist /～音乐 gospel music ❷ happy news; glad tidings:这一决定给我们厂带来了～。The decision brought glad tidings to our factory.
福音派教义 fúyīnpài jiàoyì〈基督教〉evangelicalism
福音书 Fúyīnshū 〈基督教〉Gospels (of the Bible)
福音堂 fúyīntáng church; chapel
福荫 fúyìn 〈旧语〉benefits derived from the good fortune of one's elders or ancestors; protection of one's elders or ancestors
福佑 fúyòu bless and protect:～子孙 give blessings and protection to posterity /～一方 bless and protect people of an area (where one is magistrate, etc.)
福祉 fúzhǐ 〈书面〉happiness; well-being
福至心灵 fúzhì-xīnlíng when good luck comes, one's mind works like magic; luck brings wisdom:～,祸来神昧。Luck makes one wise while misfortune dulls one's wit.
福州 Fúzhōu Fuzhou, capital of Fujian Province
福州戏 fúzhōuxì *also* "闽剧" mǐnjù a kind of local opera popular in northeastern Fujian Province

辐

fú spoke:轮～ spoke of a wheel
辐辏 fúcòu *also* "辐凑"〈书面〉converge:四方～ converge from all around
辐合 fúhé 〈气象〉convergence:～降水 convergent precipitation /～场 convergence field
辐散 fúsàn 〈气象〉divergence:～场 divergence field
辐射 fúshè ❶ radiate:太阳向行星～光芒。The sun radiates light to its planets. /该国的铁路以首都为中心,向四方～。Railways radiate in all directions from the capital of the country. ❷〈物理〉radiation:核子～ nuclear radiation /电磁～ electromagnetic radiation /受激～ stimulated radiation /自发～ spontaneous radiation
辐射保鲜 fúshè bǎoxiān *also* "辐射保藏" radiation preservation
辐射病 fúshèbìng radiation disease
辐射波 fúshèbō radiation or radiated wave
辐射测量 fúshè cèliáng radiometry;〈天文〉actinometry
辐射场 fúshèchǎng radiation or radioactive field
辐射带 fúshèdài 〈天文〉radiation zone; radiation belt
辐射防护剂 fúshè fánghùjì radioprotector
辐射功率 fúshè gōnglǜ radiation or radiant power
辐射计 fúshèjì radiometer
辐射剂量 fúshè jìliàng radiation dosage
辐射灭菌 fúshè mièjūn radiosterilize
辐射能 fúshènéng 〈物理〉radiation energy
辐射频率 fúshè pínlǜ radiation frequency
辐射强度 fúshè qiángdù radiation intensity; radiance
辐射热 fúshèrè radial or radiated heat
辐射容限 fúshè róngxiàn radiotolerance
辐射衰变 fúshè shuāibiàn radioactive decay
辐射体 fúshètǐ radiating body; radioactive object
辐射危险 fúshè wēixiǎn radiation hazard; radiation danger
辐射线 fúshèxiàn radiation ray
辐射性损伤 fúshèxìng sǔnshāng radiation injury
辐射学 fúshèxué radiology
辐射遗传学 fúshè yíchuánxué radiogenetics; radiation genetics
辐射育种 fúshè yùzhǒng 〈农业〉radioactive breeding
辐射源 fúshèyuán radiation source; radiant
辐条 fútiáo 〈口语〉spoke
辐照 fúzhào 〈物理〉irradiation
辐照度 fúzhàodù irradiance

幅

fú ❶ width (of cloth, etc.):单～ single width /双～ double width /宽～白布 white cloth of broad width; extra-wide white cloth ❷ breadth (in general); size:振～ amplitude of vibration;〈电学〉amplitude /巨～画像 portrait of gigantic size ❸〈量词〉*used for cloth, pictures, scrolls, etc.*:两～布 two pieces of cloth /一～国画 a traditional Chinese painting /一～地毯 a carpet /一～标语 a slogan
幅度 fúdù range; margin; scope; extent:变动～不大 fluctuate within a narrow range /大～上升 increase or rise by a big margin / 近来,他的学习进步～挺大。Recently, he has made considerable progress in his studies.
幅面 fúmiàn width of cloth:宽～的床单 bed sheet of extra-width
幅员 fúyuán area (of a country's territory); size (of a country):～辽阔 vast territory /这个国家～不大,但油藏丰富。In spite of its small size, the country is rich in oil deposits.

蝠

fú 〈动物〉bat
蝠鲼 fúfèn devil ray; manta ray; *Mobula japonica*

匐

fú *see* "匍匐" púfú

市

fú *see* "黻" fú

芾

fú 〈书面〉❶ lush; luxuriant ❷ *see* "黻" fú
see also fèi

芣

fú
芣苢 fúyǐ 〈古语〉〈植物〉Asiatic plantain (*Plantago asiatica*)

罘

fú
罘罳 fúsī *also* "罦罳" fúsī ❶ screen or latticed partition placed outside the door in ancient China ❷ metal network under eaves to ward off birds

袚

fú ❶〈旧语〉offer sacrifices to gods for giving blessings and averting disasters; exorcistic ceremony ❷〈书面〉general cleaning or cleansing
袚除 fúchú ❶〈旧语〉eliminate diseases and avert disasters by ritual cleansing or offering sacrifices to gods ❷〈书面〉have a general cleaning; cleanse; clear away

韨(韍)

fú ❶ ceremonial gown in ancient China ❷ silk ribbon tying the imperial seal

黻

fú ❶ half-blue, half-black pattern embroidered on a ceremonial gown in ancient China ❷ *see* "韨" fú

绂

fú ❶ silk ribbon used to tie a seal in ancient China ❷〈书面〉*see* "黻" fú

襆

fú ❶〈书面〉(bed) sheet ❷〈书面〉wrap ❸ *see* "袱" fú
襆被 fúbèi 〈书面〉wrap up clothes and bedding; pack:～前往 pack up and go

幞

fú ❶ a kind of scarf worn by men in ancient China ❷ *also* "袱" fú cloth-wrapper; cloth covering
幞头 fútóu a kind of scarf worn by men in ancient China

孚

fú inspire confidence (in sb.):以信～人 win trust with good faith

浮

fú ❶ float; emerge:鸡汤上～着油花 drops of oil floating on the chicken soup /干部～在上层 cadres (*or* officials) confining themselves only to the leading institutions (instead of going down to the grassroots) /泛泛扬舟,载沉载～。It floats about, the willow boat, now going down, now rising again. /潜艇～出水面。The submarine emerged from the water. /老人的脸上～着微笑。A faint smile was playing on the old man's face. ❷〈方言〉swim:他好不容易才～了二百米。He had a hard time swimming 200 metres. ❸ on the surface; superficial:～灰 surface dust ❹ movable; portable:这台机器是～放着的,还没有安装。The machine is not fixed, as it has not been installed yet. ❺ temporary; provisional; transient:～借～支 borrow and expend on a temporary basis; provisional accounts of borrowings and expenditures ❻ flighty; frivolous; shallow; superficial:轻～的行为 frivolous conduct /工作很～ superficial (*or* shallow) work/ 这孩子心～,总是坐不下来看书。The child was too flighty to sit down to read a book. ❼ hollow; empty; inflated:虚～ hollow and inflated ❽ exceed; be surplus or redundant:人～于事 (there are) more people than required (by the work); be overstaffed; be redundant
浮报 fúbào report more than the actual number, amount, or achievement; give inflated figures in a report:～开支 report more expenditure than actually defrayed
浮标 fúbiāo buoy:灯～ light buoy /航向～ marker buoy

浮冰 fúbīng floating ice; (ice) floe: ～冰碛 floe till /河里漂着～。Ice floated about in the river.
浮薄 fúbó shallow and superficial; insincere and flippant: 世情～ superficial and insincere ways of the world /～少年 frivolous youth
浮财 fúcái movable property; portable property: 拿出些～来赈灾 distribute some of one's movable property to relieve people in the stricken area
浮尘 fúchén floating dust; surface dust: 空中满是～。The air was filled with floating dust. /桌上有一层～。There's a sheet of dust on the table.
浮尘子 fúchénzǐ 〈动物〉leafhopper
浮沉 fúchén now sink, now emerge; go up and down; drift along: 与世～ follow the trend (*or* current) /宦海～ vicissitudes in the world of officialdom; ups and downs of an official career /远处，一群海豚在海浪里～追逐。In the distance, a shoal of dolphins were chasing and drifting over the waves.
浮船坞 fúchuánwù floating (dry) dock
浮词 fúcí *also* "浮言" empty words; groundless remarks; verbiage: 此文～连篇。The article is full of verbiage.
浮厝 fúcuò place a coffin in a temporary place and cover it with bricks or stones pending burial
浮袋 fúdài water wings (used as a support while learning to swim)
浮荡 fúdàng ❶ float in the air; float about: 几缕炊烟在村子上空～。Wisps of smoke from kitchen chimneys floated over the village. /落叶在湖面～。Fallen leaves floated about on the lake. /小舢板在江面上随波～。The small sampan was drifting on the river. ❷ dissolute; loose in morals: ～女子 woman of easy virtue
浮点 fúdiǎn 〈计算机〉floating point: ～表示法 floating-point representation /～程序 floating-point procedure /～记数法 floating-point notation /～计算机 floating-point computer /～运算 floating-point arithmetic (*or* calculation) /～软件包 floating-point package
浮雕 fúdiāo 〈美术〉relief: ～木刻 wood carvings in relief /～群像 relief sculpture of a group of figures /深～ high relief /浅～ low relief; bas relief /空心～ conclave relief
浮雕压印 fúdiāo yāyìn embossing
浮吊 fúdiào 〈机械〉floating crane
浮动 fúdòng ❶ float; drift: 黑夜里点点渔火在江面上～。In the dark night, lights on the fishing boats floated here and there on the river. /一些模糊的思想在我的脑海里～。Some confused ideas drifted across my mind. ❷ rise and fall; fluctuate; be unsteady: 价格～ price fluctuation /人心～ widespread feeling of insecurity ❸ 〈经济〉float: 货币共同～ joint currency float /～供给 floating supply
浮动摆轮 fúdòng bǎilún floating balance (as in a clock)
浮动程序 fúdòng chéngxù 〈计算机〉relocatable programme; relocatable routine: ～库 relocatable programme library
浮动工资 fúdòng gōngzī floating or fluctuating wages: ～制 floating wage system
浮动汇率 fúdòng huìlǜ floating (exchange) rate: ～体制 floating exchange rate system
浮动价格 fúdòng jiàgé floating price
浮动利率 fúdòng lìlǜ floating interest rate: 浮动基本利率 floating prime rate (of interest) /～期票 floating-rate note
浮动平台 fúdòng píngtái 〈建筑〉floating platform
浮动水雷 fúdòng shuǐléi 〈军事〉floating mine
浮动轴 fúdòngzhóu 〈机械〉floating axle
浮法 fúfǎ float glass process: ～玻璃 float glass
浮泛 fúfàn ❶ 〈书面〉float about: 小舟～于平湖之上。A small skiff floated about on the calm lake. ❷ reveal; show; display: 她脸上～出喜悦和兴奋。Her face beamed with happiness and excitement. /小女孩的脸蛋上～着天真的表情。Innocence showed on the little girl's face. ❸ superficial; too generalized: 见解～ superficial view /内容～ superficial and full of generalities
浮根 fúgēn 〈植物〉floating root
浮光掠影 fúguāng-lüèyǐng skimming over the surface; hasty and casual; superficial; cursory: ～的印象 hasty and casual impressions /～地看了几个地方 visit a few places in a hasty and superficial manner
浮华 fúhuá vain; showy; ostentatious; flashy: 风气～ customs of vanity /生活～ life of vanity; showy and luxurious life style /他这篇文章尽是些～无用之言。His article is full of flashy but useless remarks.
浮滑 fúhuá slick and frivolous: 习性～ given to slick and frivolous ways
浮记 fújì keep a tally of a transaction before entering it in the regular accounts; tally sth. for the time being
浮家泛宅 fújiā-fànzhái dwell on a boat; live a wandering life on the water; lead the life of a recluse
浮夸 fúkuā be boastful; exaggerate: 工作作风～ work style characterized by boasting and exaggeration; proneness to boasting and hyperbole /～之词 boastful words; pompous remarks /这个汇报很实事求是，绝无～。The report is truthful and realistic, free from any exaggeration.
浮夸风 fúkuāfēng trend or tendency to boast and exaggerate (one's achievements, etc.)
浮浪 fúlàng frivolous and dissipated: ～子弟 frivolous and dissipated young man
浮雷 fúléi 〈军事〉floating mine
浮礼儿 fúlǐr 〈方言〉insincere politeness; empty courtesy
浮力 fúlì 〈物理〉buoyancy: ～参数 buoyancy parameter /这种木料～很大。This kind of timber has great buoyancy. /海水比淡水更有～。Sea water is more buoyant than fresh water.
浮露 fúlù ❶ show; reveal: 脸上～出满意的神情 look pleased; reveal an expression of satisfaction ❷ direct but unsubtle; explicit but not profound: 辞气～ written in straightforward language
浮码头 fúmǎtou floating pier
浮脉 fúmài 〈中医〉surface pulse (which can be felt when touched lightly)
浮锚 fúmáo 〈船舶〉drogue; drag anchor; sea anchor; floating anchor
浮面 fúmiàn surface: ～上有一层保护膜。There's a sheet of protective film on the surface. /他～上还装出没事的样子。He looked as if nothing had happened.
浮名 fúmíng empty name; vain glory; bubble reputation: 何苦追逐～? Why bother to pursue a bubble reputation?
浮木 fúmù 〈林业〉flood wood
浮沤 fú'ōu ❶ bubble on water: 曲涧漾～。The winding ravine rippled and bubbled. ❷ transient life; fickle ways of the world
浮皮 fúpí ❶ outer skin; cuticle; epidermis ❷ surface
浮皮蹭痒 fúpí-cèngyǎng scratching the surface; skin-deep; superficial: ～磨洋工 work in a slapdash and dawdling manner /我只不过～地说了一句，倒像捅了马蜂窝似的! Although my criticism merely scratched the surface of the matter, it seemed as if I had brought down a hornets' nest!
浮皮潦草 fúpí-liáocǎo *also* "肤皮潦草" fūpí-liáocǎo superficial and careless; cursory; casual; perfunctory: ～地翻一下 look over (*or* through) casually; glance through perfunctorily /这篇作文写得太～了! What a cursory composition this is!
浮漂 fúpiāo (of a person or his work) flighty; careless; superficial: 工作～ superficial work
浮萍 fúpíng 〈植物〉duckweed
浮签 fúqiān note pasted on the margin of a page
浮浅 fúqiǎn superficial; shallow: 认识～ shallow understanding /学识～ superficial learning
浮桥 fúqiáo pontoon or floating bridge
浮生 fúshēng ❶ brief and illusory life; fleeting life: 《～六记》*Six Chapters of a Floating Life* /～若寄。Life is transient. *or* Life passes in a flash. ❷ grow on water: 浮萍～在池塘中。The duckweed grows and floats on the surface of the pond.
浮生若梦 fúshēng-ruòmèng life passes or is like a dream
浮尸 fúshī dead body floating on river; floating corpse
浮石 fúshí pumice (stone)
浮士德 Fúshìdé Faust, a wandering astronomer and necromancer who lived in Germany c. 1488-1541 and was reputed to have sold his soul to the Devil
浮水 fúshuǐ swim: 他很小就会～了。He learnt to swim as a child.
浮说 fúshuō groundless remarks; unfounded statement
浮筒 fútǒng float; pontoon; buoy: ～导杆 float guide /～飞机 *also* 水上飞机 float plane /～起落架 float landing gear
浮头 fútóu (of fish) breathe with its mouth sticking out of the water (as a result of lack of oxygen in the fish pond)
浮头儿 fútóur 〈方言〉surface: 一筐苹果，～一层是大的，底下全是小的。In the basket there were some big apples on top, and all those below were small ones.
浮屠 fútú *also* "浮图" 〈佛教〉❶ Buddha ❷ 〈旧语〉Buddhist monk

F

❸ pagoda; stupa:救人一命,胜造七级～。(Buddhist saying) Saving one life is more meritorious than building a seven-storey pagoda.

浮土 fútǔ ❶ loose surface soil ❷ dust collected on furniture, etc.; surface dust:掸去衣服上的～ whisk the dust off the clothes

浮文 fúwén verbiage; padding (in writing):～妨要。Verbiage hampers the expression of important subject-matter.

浮息票据 fúxī piàojù floating-rate note (FRN)

浮现 fúxiàn ❶ appear before one's eyes:眼前不断地～母亲的面影。Mother's image appeared repeatedly before my eyes. ❷ reveal; show:她脸上～出绝望的神色。An expression of despair showed on her face.

浮想 fúxiǎng ❶ thoughts or ideas flashing across one's mind:他沉浸在～之中。He was lost in rambling thoughts. ❷ recollect; recall:拿起这张旧照,我不禁～起逝世的表哥来。Picking up the old photo, I couldn't help recalling my deceased cousin.

浮想联翩 fúxiǎng-liánpiān thoughts thronging one's mind:～,夜不能寐。As thoughts thronged my mind, I could not sleep.

浮嚣 fúxiāo 〈书面〉 frivolous and licentious

浮小麦 fúxiǎomài 〈中医〉 shrivelled wheat that can float on the water (used as a sedative to stop abnormal sweating)

浮性 fúxìng buoyant capacity

浮选 fúxuǎn 〈矿业〉 flotation:～法 flotation (process) /～厂 flotation mill

浮选剂 fúxuǎnjì flotation agent; flotating chemical

浮言 fúyán see "浮词"

浮岩 fúyán 〈地质〉 pumicite; pumice

浮艳 fúyàn ❶ flashy; gaudy; gorgeous:衣饰～ gorgeously dressed ❷ (of writing, etc.) showy and unsubstantial

浮漾 fúyàng ❶ reveal; display:脸上～着欣慰的微笑。One's face beams with gratification. ❷ float and ripple; float about; drift along:一叶扁舟在水面上～。A small boat floated about on the water. /田野中～着稀薄的雾气。Thin vapour drifted over the fields.

F

浮一大白 fúyīdàbái drink a large glass of wine when in high spirits

浮游 fúyóu ❶ swim:鲸鱼在海上～觅食。Whales swim and seek food in the sea. ❷〈书面〉 roam about; go on a pleasure trip:～于天地之间 roam between heaven and earth

浮游动物 fúyóu dòngwù zooplankton

浮游生物 fúyóu shēngwù plankton

浮游植物 fúyóu zhíwù phytoplankton

浮游资金 fúyóu zījīn floating fund

浮语虚辞 fúyǔ-xūcí empty bragging; hollow words; verbiage

浮员 fúyuán redundant personnel:裁减～ cut down the redundant personnel

浮云 fúyún floating cloud:～朝露 floating clouds and morning dew — sth. transient /～富贵 look upon wealth and power as transient and immaterial; despise money and status

浮云蔽日 fúyún-bìrì like a floating cloud obscuring the sun — in reference to treacherous court officials deluding the monarch

浮躁 fúzào impetuous; impulsive:性情～ impetuous temperament /办事～ act on impulse

浮渣 fúzhā 〈冶金〉 dross

浮肿 fúzhǒng 〈医学〉 dropsy; oedema; edema

浮舟 fúzhōu pontoon

浮子 fúzi ❶(of fishery) float ❷〈汽车〉 carburettor float

莩

fú 〈书面〉 thin membrane inside a rush stalk

see also piǎo

桴[1]

fú ❶〈书面〉 little raft:乘～浮于海 sail the sea on a raft ❷〈方言〉 small beam on the main beam; tie:～子 tie (on the main beam)

桴[2](枹)

fú 〈书面〉 drum stick

桴鼓相应 fúgǔ-xiāngyìng the drum responds to the drumsticks — cooperate in perfect harmony; work in perfect coordination:筹建亚洲文学研究会的事,幸蒙各地同仁～,才有今日这个成立大会。Thanks to the concerted efforts of our colleagues all over the country, we are now able to hold this inaugural meeting of the Institute of Asian Literature.

桴子 fúzi ❶〈方言〉 small raft ❷ small beam on the main beam

蜉

fú

蜉蝣 fúyóu 〈动物〉 mayfly

罦

fú 〈书面〉 bird net; bird trap

罦罳 fúsī *also* "罘罳" fúsī ❶〈旧语〉 screen or latticed partition that one could see through ❷ wire netting

俘

fú ❶ capture; seize; take prisoner:生～ capture alive; take a prisoner alive /上尉离开军营后被～。The captain was taken prisoner after leaving the camp. ❷ prisoner of war; captive:战～ prisoner of war (POW) /伤～ wounded prisoner /遣～ repatriate prisoners of war

俘获 fúhuò ❶ capture:～敌机十余架 seize over a dozen enemy planes /～甚众 capture many enemy soldiers; take many prisoners ❷〈物理〉 capture:中子～ neutron capture /裂变～ fission capture

俘虏 fúlǔ ❶capture; take prisoner:～敌将官三名 capture three enemy generals ❷ captive; captured personnel; prisoner of war (POW):抓～ take prisoners of war /优待～ treat prisoners of war leniently /～营 prisoner camp; POW camp

俘囚 fúqiú imprisoned captive:释放全部～ release all imprisoned captives

郛

fú outer wall of a city:～郭 outer wall of a city

伏[1]

fú ❶ lean or bend over; lie prostrate:～几假寐 bend over one's desk having a nap /～在床上 lie prostrate on the bed /～地请罪 throw oneself on the ground to apologize or ask for punishment (for one's faults) ❷ fall; subside; go down:起～ rise and fall ❸ hide:潜～ hide; lie low /埋～ lie in wait; ambush /危机四～ beset with crisis; crisis-ridden /昼～夜行 hide by day and come out at night ❹ any of the three nine-day periods constituting the hottest season of the year; dog days:入～ begin (*or* enter into) the hottest season /三～天 three nine-day periods constituting the hottest season of the year; dog days ❺ yield; admit (defeat, guilt, etc.): *see* "～罪" ❻ subdue; overcome; vanquish:降龙～虎 subdue the dragon and tame the tiger — overcome powerful adversaries ❼ (Fú) a surname

伏[2]

fú (short for 伏特) 〈电学〉 volt

伏安 fú'ān (short for 伏特安培) 〈电学〉 volt-ampere (va):～小时 volt-ampere hour /～特性 volt-ampere (va) characteristic; current-voltage characteristics /～计 *also* "～表" voltammeter

伏安法 fú'ānfǎ 〈化学〉 voltammetry

伏案 fú'àn bend over one's desk:～写作 bend over one's desk writing /～入睡 fall asleep leaning over a table (*or* desk) /～工作 (do) sedentary work

伏笔 fúbǐ hint foreshadowing later developments in a story, essay, etc.; foreshadowing:为后文设下～ foreshadow later developments

伏辩 fúbiàn *also* "服辩" fúbiàn 〈旧语〉 written document of repentance; written confession (of one's guilt, etc.)

伏兵 fúbīng (troops in) ambush:设～ lay an ambush /～四起。Troops in ambush came out from all around.

伏藏 fúcáng 〈书面〉 hide; remain under cover; go into hiding:无处～ have nowhere to conceal oneself /罪犯～于荒山之中。The criminals were hiding in the uninhabited mountains.

伏打 fúdǎ 〈电学〉 voltaic:～电池 voltaic cell; volta cell /～电流 voltaic current /～定律 Volta's law /～表 voltameter

伏地 fúdì 〈方言〉 locally-produced:～面 locally-produced wheat flour /～小米儿 local millet

伏都教 Fúdūjiào Voodoo; voodooism:～徒 voodooist

伏尔加河 Fú'ěrjiāhé Volga River (major river in western Russia)

伏尔泰 Fú'ěrtài Voltaire (1694-1778), French Enlightenment scholar and philosopher, whose real name is Francois Marie Arouet:～主义 Voltairianism /～的信徒 Voltairian

伏法 fúfǎ be executed:杀人犯昨已～。The murderer was executed yesterday.

伏旱 fúhàn drought in summer:战胜～,夺取丰收。Combat the summer drought and strive for a good harvest.

伏击 fújī ambush; ambuscade:遭到～ fall into an ambush /打了敌人一个～ ambush the enemy

伏击圈 fújīquān ambush ring
伏剑 fújiàn kill oneself with a sword:～而亡 fall victim to a sword; be killed by a sword
伏流 fúliú 〈地质〉subterranean drainage; underground stream
伏热 fúrè 〈中医〉latent heat:～在里 accumulated latent heat inside the body
伏侍 fúshi *also* "服侍" fúshi wait upon; attend to
伏输 fúshū *also* "服输" fúshū admit or acknowledge defeat:他有一种永不～的劲头。He would never concede victory to his adversary.
伏暑 fúshǔ hot season; height of summer:～难挨。The dog days are too hot to bear.
伏特 fútè 〈电学〉volt:～安培 voltampere /～分贝 decibel volt (dbv) /～数 voltage
伏特计 fútèjì *also* "电压表" diànyābiǎo; "电压计" diànyājì 〈电学〉voltmeter
伏特加 fútèjiā vodka
伏天 fútiān hot summer days; dog days
伏帖 fútiē ❶ comfortable; at ease:心里很～ feel at ease ❷ docile; obedient; submissive
伏贴 fútiē ❶ fit perfectly:这件连衣裙穿着很～。This dress fits perfectly. ❷ *see* "伏帖❶"
伏惟尚飨 fúwéi-shàngxiǎng 〈书面〉〈套语〉(used at the end of an elegiac address to the deceased) may you taste of the offerings
伏卧 fúwò lie on one's stomach; lie prone; drop to the ground:照明弹一亮,侦察兵就～在地上。The scouts lay still on the ground at the lighting of a flare.
伏羲 Fúxī *also* "庖牺" Páoxī; "包牺" Bāoxī Fuxi (formerly translated as Fu-hsi), a legendary Chinese ruler who taught people how to fish, hunt, and raise livestock
伏线 fúxiàn hint foreshadowing later developments (in a story, essay, etc.); foreshadowing; clue
伏汛 fúxùn summer flood:～期 period of summer flooding
伏诛 fúzhū 〈书面〉be executed
伏罪 fúzuì plead guilty:证据确凿,犯人低头～。Before the ironclad evidence, the prisoner lowered his head and admitted his guilt.

洑 fú ❶ (of water) spin round; turn round ❷ whirlpool; eddy; vortex:湍～ swift vortex
see also fù

袱 fú cloth-wrapper; covering cloth
袱子 fúzi 〈方言〉❶ piece of cloth for wrapping up things; cloth-wrapper ❷ scarf; kerchief ❸ handkerchief

茯 fú
茯苓 fúlíng 〈中药〉*fuling* (*Poris cocos*), edible fungus often used as medicine; tuckahoe
茯苓饼 fúlíngbǐng *fuling* cake

栿 fú 〈书面〉beam

苻 fú ❶ membrane inside a rush stalk ❷ (Fú) a surname

符 fú ❶ tally issued by a ruler to a general or envoy as credentials in ancient China:兵～ tally issued to a general as imperial authorization for troop movement in ancient China ❷ symbol; mark; sign:声～ phonetic sign (of a pictophonetic character) /音～ musical note ❸ match; tally with; accord with:数目不～ the figures do not tally /与事实相～ accord (*or* tally) with the facts /言行相～ one's deeds match one's words ❹ magic figure or sign drawn by a Taoist priest to invoke or expel spirits and bring good or ill forture:画一张～ draw a magic sign /护身～ amulet; protective talisman ❺ (Fú) a surname
符号 fúhào ❶ symbol; mark; sign:标点～ punctuation mark /注音～ phonetic symbol /代数～ algebraic symbol ❷ insignia
符号编码 fúhào biānmǎ symbolic coding or programming
符号处理 fúhào chǔlǐ symbol manipulation or processing
符号处理假定 fúhào chǔlǐ jiǎdìng 〈信息〉symbol-processing hypothesis
符号读出 fúhào dúchū mark sensing; character reading
符号函数 fúhào hánshù sign function; symbolic function
符号论 fúhàolùn symbol theory; 〈哲学〉semiotics
符号逻辑 fúhào luójí symbolic logic; algebraic logic
符号数位 fúhào shùwèi 〈计算机〉sign digit
符号学 fúhàoxué 〈语言〉semiology:～家 semiologist
符合 fúhé ❶ accord with; tally with; be in line with:～大家的心愿 accord with everyone's wish /～人民的利益 be in keeping with the people's interests /～客观实际 conform to objective reality /～标准 meet a criterion; be up to the standard /不～条件 not qualified /～要求 meet one's requirement; fill the bill /他的理论与实际观测相～。His theory tallies with actual observations. ❷ 〈物理〉coincidence:～校正 coincidence correction
符合摆 fúhébǎi coincidence pendulum
符合传感器 fúhé chuángǎnqì coincidence sensor
符节 fújié tally issued by a ruler to a general, or an envoy, as credentials in ancient China
符拉迪沃斯托克 Fúlādíwòsītuōkè Vladivostok (also known as 海参崴 Haishenwai), Russia's principal seaport on the Pacific east coast
符箓 fúlù Taoist talisman, magic figure or sign drawn by Taoist priests to invoke or expel spirits and bring good or ill fortune
符咒 fúzhòu Taoist magic figures and incantations

凫(鳬) fú ❶ wild duck:～趋雀跃 in high spirits; jubilant; elated /～燕难明 hard to distinguish between high-flying wild ducks and swallows — things easily confused ❷ swim:～水 swim
凫翁 fúwēng 〈动物〉water cock

服 fú ❶ clothes; garments; dress; attire:西～ western-style clothes /便～ everyday (*or* informal) clothes; mufti /礼～ full dress; formal attire /制～ uniform ❷ mourning (apparel):有～在身 be in mourning ❸ wear (clothes):～孝 wear mourning clothes (*or* be in mourning) for one's parent (*or* husband) ❹ take (medicine):内～ to be taken orally ❺ serve:～兵役 serve in the army /～三年徒刑 serve a three-year sentence ❻ obey; submit (oneself to); be convinced:不～裁判 refuse to obey the referee /心～口～ be convinced completely /不～管理 not submit oneself to sb.'s management /李师傅说的我都～。I believe every word Master Li says. ❼ convince:以理～人 convince people by reason /何以～天下人? How could you convince the people? ❽ be accustomed to; be used to; be acclimatized to:不～水土 not acclimatized to the local environment /这东西我吃不～。I'm not used to eating such food. *or* This does not agree with me. ❾ (Fú) a surname
see also fù
服辩 fúbiàn *see* "伏辩" fúbiàn
服从 fúcóng obey; submit (oneself) to; be subordinated to:～法律 obey the law /～真理 submit to the truth /～命令 follow orders /～纪律 observe discipline /～大多数人的意见 bow to the opinion of the majority /～全局利益 subordinate one's own interests to the overall interests /～分配 accept one's assigned job
服毒 fúdú take poison
服法 fúfǎ obey or abide by the law:认罪～ admit one's guilt and submit oneself to the law
服法 fúfa directions on how to take a medicine:这种药丸,怎么个～? How does one take these pills?
服劲 fújìn 〈方言〉be convinced
服老 fúlǎo (mostly used in the negative) admit that one is old and not as energetic as before; be reconciled to one's age and failing health:不～ would not admit that one is old; refuse to give in to age; not be reconciled to one's age and failing health
服满 fúmǎn be out of mourning; leave off mourning
服气 fúqì be convinced; be won over:你撅什么嘴,还不～吗? Why such a pout? Aren't you convinced yet? /选他当劳动模范,大家都～。Everyone gave his or her hearty consent when he was elected a model worker.
服勤 fúqín serve in a civilian capacity (with an army, etc.):随军～人员 civilians who serve with an army
服劝 fúquàn accept advice; be amenable to advice; be persuaded:他既是不～,你何苦操这份儿心呢? Since he won't accept your advice, why bother any more?
服阕 fúquè 〈书面〉be out of mourning; leave off mourning
服软 fúruǎn ❶ admit or acknowledge defeat; acknowledge or admit a mistake; give in:不在困难面前～ not be cowed by difficulties /

他知道是自己错了,可嘴上还不～。He knew that he was in the wrong, but wouldn't admit it. ❷ be amenable to persuasion:～不服硬 be amenable to persuasion but would not submit to coercion

服丧 fúsāng be in mourning (for the death of a kinsman, etc.)

服色 fúsè style and colour of clothes:民族～ national costume (with all its unique styles and colours); styles and colours of ethnic garments

服式 fúshì dress style; fashion:新潮～ trendy dress; latest fashion

服饰 fúshì dress and personal adornment; dress; attire:～俗气 be gaudily attired (*or* dressed) /本店专营妇女～。This shop specializes in women's garments and accessories.

服侍 fúshi *also* "服事";"伏侍" fúshi wait upon; attend to; nurse:～病人 nurse the sick /～老人 wait upon (*or* care for) the old

服输 fúshū *also* "伏输" fúshū admit or acknowledge defeat:从不～ never take defeat hands down; never acknowledge (*or* admit) defeat /在事实面前,他不得不～,承认对方的办法更为有效。Confronted with the facts, he could not but acknowledge that he was wrong, and that his rival's method was more effective than his.

服帖 fútiē ❶ *also* "伏帖" fútiē docile; compliant; obedient; submissive:像绵羊一样～ as docile as a lamb /他对上级服服帖帖,唯唯诺诺。He was a yes-man and was always obedient towards his superiors. ❷ fitting; neat; well-arranged:她做事有条不紊,一切事情都办得服服帖帖。She is so methodical that everything she does is in apple-pie order.

服务 fúwù serve; give or render service to; be in the service of:开展"微笑～" render smiling service; serve one's customers with a smiling face /～不周 unsatisfactory service /在驻外使领馆～ work in the foreign service /她们的～质量大大提高了。They have vastly improved their service. /对不起,我们没有这个～项目。Sorry, we don't offer such service here.

服务行业 fúwù hángyè service trades or sector

服务经济 fúwù jīngjì service economy

服务器 fúwùqì 〈计算机〉server

服务台 fúwùtái (as on a hotel floor) service desk or counter; (as in a hotel lounge) information and reception desk

服务态度 fúwù tàidu attitude in serving one's customers; quality of service; service:改进～ improve one's service /～耐心、和蔼 be patient and amiable in serving customers /什么～! What abominable service!

服务员 fúwùyuán attendant; assistant:列车～ train attendant; guard /商店～ shop assistant /饭店～ hotel attendant; bell boy; bell hop /餐厅～ waiter; waitress

服务站 fúwùzhàn *also* "服务中心" (neighbourhood) service centre

服务质量 fúwù zhìliàng quality of service

服刑 fúxíng serve a sentence (in prison); serve time:在劳改农场～ serve a sentence on a reform-through-labour farm /～期满 complete a term of imprisonment

服药 fúyào take medicine:按时～ take medicine on time

服役 fúyì ❶ *also* "服现役" be on active service; enlist or serve in the army:在炮兵部队～ serve in the artillery /～期间有立功表现 do deeds of merit during one's term of military service (*or* during the period of enlistment) /～期满 complete one's term of service /服后备役 be on reserve duty; be in reserve service /超期～ be on an extended term of service ❷〈旧语〉do corvée labour

服膺 fúyīng 〈书面〉bear in mind; be deeply convinced:终身～ bear in mind all one's life /拳拳～ believe sincerely; be deeply convinced

服用 fúyòng ❶〈书面〉wear (clothes) and use (utensils); live:～甚俭 be frugal in one's life; live frugally ❷ take (medicine):～补药 take tonics /这个运动员由于～了兴奋剂被取消资格。The athlete was disqualified for taking stimulants.

服装 fúzhuāng clothing; dress; garment; costume:儿童～ children's clothing /中式～ Chinese-style clothing /西式～ Western-style clothes /中老年～ clothes for middle-aged and old people /特体～ clothes for people of a special type of build /流行～ fashionable clothing /民族～ national costume /～设计 dress designing /～设计师 apparel stylist; fashion designer /～剪裁 dress tailoring /～款式 dress style (*or* fashion) /～厂 clothing factory /～商店 clothes (*or* clothing) store

服装表演 fúzhuāng biǎoyǎn fashion show

服装工业 fúzhuāng gōngyè garment industry; apparel industry

服装模特儿 fúzhuāng mótèr fashion model; mannequin

服罪 fúzuì *also* "伏罪" fúzuì plead guilty; admit one's guilt:认罪～ admit one's guilt and be determined to atone for it

菔

fú *see* "莱菔" láifú

箙

fú 〈书面〉quiver

弗

fú 〈书面〉not:～如 not as good as; not equal to /自愧～如 feel ashamed of one's inferiority; feel one's inferiority keenly; acknowledge one's inferiority

弗拉芒语 Fúlāmángyǔ *also* "佛兰芒语" Fólánmángyǔ Flemish (language)

怫

fú 〈书面〉❶ gloomy; depressed; worried ❷ indignant; angry; glowering

怫然 fúrán 〈书面〉look angry or offended; glower:～作色 flush with anger; glower /～不悦 wear an offended expression; look angry

怫郁 fúyù 〈书面〉gloomy and indignant; depressed and angry; depressed:壮志未酬常～ feel depressed and discontented because one's lofty aspirations have not been realized

髴

fú *see* "髣髴" fǎngfú

茀

fú 〈书面〉❶ be overgrown with weeds; weedy ❷ good luck; fortune

砩

fú

砩石 fúshí *see* "氟石" fúshí

拂

fú ❶ stroke; caress; touch:春风～过湖面。A spring breeze swept over the lake. ❷ whisk; flick:～去身上的尘土 whisk the dust off one's clothes ❸〈书面〉run counter to; go against (sb.'s wishes):不忍～其意 not have the heart to go against sb.'s wishes; not wish to refuse sb. /忠言～于耳。Good advice jars on the ear.

拂尘 fúchén horsetail whisk

拂荡 fúdàng sway; swing; wave; flutter:低垂的柳枝随风～。The drooping willows swayed in the breeze.

拂动 fúdòng sway gently; flap; brush slightly against; stroke:他站在窗前,晚风～着他那稀疏的白发。He stood by the window, with the evening breeze brushing gently against his thin grey hair. /绸带随着轻盈优美的舞姿上下～。Long silk ribbons flapped up and down with the lithe and graceful movements of the dancers.

拂拂 fúfú (of winds) blow gently

拂菻 Fúlǐn Fulin, ancient Chinese name for the Eastern Roman Empire

拂逆 fúnì ❶ go against; run counter to:他不敢～老人家的意旨。He dared not go against the old man's wish. ❷ contrary; adverse; full of setbacks:坎坷一生,～多舛 life of frustrations and setbacks; frustrating and adverse life

拂拭 fúshì wipe off; whisk off:用手帕轻轻～书上的尘土 wipe the dust off the book gently with a handkerchief

拂晓 fúxiǎo before dawn:～出发 set off before dawn /～前结束战斗 end the battle before daybreak

拂袖 fúxiù 〈书面〉give a flick of one's sleeve in anger:～而起 rise to one's feet in anger

拂袖而去 fúxiù'érqù leave with a flick of one's sleeve; leave in a huff; storm out:一言不合,～ go off in a huff at the slightest disagreement

拂煦 fúxù 〈书面〉(of wind) bring warmth:春风～。The spring breeze is warm and pleasant.

拂意 fúyì be contrary to one's wish; not suit sb.; not appeal to sb.:稍有～,他就大发雷霆。He would fly into a rage if anything was not quite to his liking.

刜

fú 〈书面〉cut with a knife; hit

氟

fú 〈化学〉fluorine (F):～缺乏症 fluorine deficiency

氟斑 fúbān (as in teeth) fluoride spot

氟化 fúhuà fluoridize; fluorinate; fluridize:～铵 ammonium fluo-

ride
氟化低价物 fúhuà dījiàwù subfluoride
氟化法 fúhuàfǎ fluoration or fluorination process
氟化反应 fúhuà fǎnyìng fluoration or fluorination reaction
氟化合物 fúhuàhéwù fluorine compound
氟化剂 fúhuàjì fluridizer; fluorinating agent
氟化氢 fúhuàqīng hydrogen fluoride (HF)
氟化物 fúhuàwù fluoride:～中毒 fluoride poisoning /～浓度 fluoride concentration
氟利昂 fúlì'áng *also*"氟氯烷"〈化学〉freon; CFC (chlorofluorocarbons, chemicals used in air conditioning and refrigeration and believed to be depleting stratospheric ozone)
氟氯烷 fúlǜwán *see*"氟利昂"
氟氢可的松 fúqīng kědìsōng 〈药学〉fludrocortison
氟石 fúshí *also*"萤石" yíngshí fluorite; fluorspar
氟树脂 fúshùzhī 〈化工〉fluororesin
氟橡胶 fúxiàngjiāo fluorubber; fluoroelastomer; viton
氟乙烯 fúyǐxī 〈化工〉fluorothene
氟乙酰胺 fúyǐxiān'àn *also*"敌蚜胺" díyá'àn 〈化工〉fluoroacetamide
氟中毒 fúzhòngdú fluorosis

佛 fú 〈书面〉*see*"拂❸"
see also fó
佛戾 fúlì 〈书面〉violate; go against; run counter to

彿 fú *see*"彷彿" fǎngfú

艴 fú *see*"魴艴" fángfú

艴 fú 〈书面〉look angry; look offended:～然 be angry; be offended

绋 fú 〈书面〉big (hemp) rope; cord tying the coffin or leading the hearse:执～ serve as a pallbearer (at a funeral ceremony or procession)

fǔ

府 fǔ ❶ seat of government; government office:官～ government (esp. in reference to the local government); the authorities /首～ capital (of a province) ❷〈旧语〉archive or treasury of (local) government ❸ official residence; mansion:王～ residence (*or* palace) of a prince /总督～ official residence of the governor /总统～ presidential palace ❹〈敬词〉your home; your house:尊～ your home; your house ❺ (from the Tang to the Qing dynasties) prefecture (above the county):绍兴～ prefecture of Shaoxing /知～ prefect ❻ (Fǔ) a surname
府城 fǔchéng seat of a prefecture; prefectural city
府绸 fǔchóu 〈纺织〉poplin:～绉 crepe poplin /山东～ Shandong pongee; shantung
府邸 fǔdǐ *also*"府第" mansion; mansion house; residence
府第 fǔdì mansion; mansion house; residence:宰相～ mansion house of the prime minister /亲王～ residence (*or* mansion) of a prince
府库 fǔkù 〈旧语〉government repository (for archives, valuables, etc.)
府上 fǔshang 〈敬词〉❶ your home; your house:改日到～拜访。I'll call at your home some other day. /～还有什么人? Who else is there in your family? ❷ your native place:～在哪里? Where are you from?
府试 fǔshì (in the Qing Dynasty) imperial examination at the prefectural level
府尹 fǔyǐn 〈旧语〉chief magistrate of a prefecture; prefect
府治 fǔzhì seat of a prefectural government; prefectural seat

腐 fǔ ❶ rotten; putrid; corroded; stale:～鱼 rotten (*or* putrid) fish /～米 rotten rice /陈～ stale; outworn /防～剂 preservative; antiseptic /流水不～。Running water is never stale. ❷ beancurd
腐败 fǔbài ❶ putrid; foul; rotten; decayed:～变质的食品 putrid (*or* rotten) food /防止菜、肉～ prevent vegetables and meats from rotting (*or* decaying) ❷ (of ideas) decadent; musty; (of behaviour) degenerate; corrupt:～分子 corrupt (*or* decadent) elements; degenerates /生活～ lead a decadent (*or* dissolute) life /思想～ musty (*or* decadent) ideology ❸ (of a system, organization, measure, etc.) chaotic; dark; corrupt:～的社会 decadent (*or* degenerate) society /政治～ corrupt (*or* decadent) politics /～无能的政府 corrupt and inept government
腐臭 fǔchòu smelly; stinking; putrid:沤肥坑里冒出～的气味。The compost pit sends forth (*or* emits) a putrid smell. *or* The compost pit stinks.
腐恶 fǔ'è corrupt and evil:六月天兵征～,万丈长缨要把鲲鹏缚。In June Heaven's armies chastise the corrupt and evil, Seeking to bind roc and whale with a league-long cord.
腐化 fǔhuà ❶ degenerate; corrupt; dissolute; depraved:贪污～ practise graft and live a dissolute life; be corrupt and depraved /生活～ lead a dissipated life ❷ corrupt; corrode:那些有毒的思想～了他的灵魂。Those poisonous thoughts corroded his soul. ❸ rot; decompose; go putrid:尸体已经～,奇臭无比。The corpse was decomposed and smelled terribly.
腐化堕落 fǔhuà-duòluò become corrupt and degenerate:追求～的生活方式 be after a dissolute lifestyle
腐化分子 fǔhuàfènzǐ corrupt elements; depraved persons; degenerates
腐旧 fǔjiù old and decayed; corrupt and outmoded; stale:思想～ outworn ideas; stale thoughts
腐烂 fǔlàn ❶ rot; decompose; go putrid:仓库里的食品开始～。The food in the warehouse began to rot. /路边堆着～的果皮蔬菜。Rotting (*or* putrescent) peels and vegetables were piled by the roadside. ❷ *see*"腐败❷" ❸ *see*"腐败❸"
腐泥 fǔní *also*"腐植泥" sapropel; humic soil
腐泥煤 fǔníméi sapropelic coal
腐气 fǔqì odour of the old and decayed; stale smell
腐儒 fǔrú pedantic scholar; pedant
腐乳 fǔrǔ fermented beancurd or tofu
腐生 fǔshēng 〈生理〉saprophytic:～细胞 saprophytic cell /～植物 saprophyte /～微生物 saprophytic microbe /～链 saprophyte chain
腐蚀 fǔshí ❶ corrode; etch:～船体 corrode a hull /～性物质 corrosive material /～性很强 very corrosive /～速度 corrosion rate /～酸 corrosive acid ❷ corrupt; deprave:黄色书刊～人们的心灵。Pornography depraves (*or* corrupts) people's souls.
腐蚀版 fǔshíbǎn 〈印刷〉etched plate
腐蚀机 fǔshíjī 〈印刷〉etching machine
腐蚀剂 fǔshíjì 〈化学〉corrosive; corrodent
腐熟 fǔshú 〈农业〉(of compost, etc.) become thoroughly decomposed:～的人粪尿是很好的有机肥料。Thoroughly decomposed night-soil is an excellent organic fertilizer.
腐心 fǔxīn 〈书面〉❶ hate bitterly; utterly detest:～切齿 gnash one's teeth in bitter hatred ❷ be extremely worried or anxious:～焦虑 be gnawed by anxiety
腐刑 fǔxíng *also*"宫刑" gōngxíng 〈历史〉castration as a punishment
腐朽 fǔxiǔ ❶ rot; decay:房顶的木结构已经～。The wooden structure of the roof has rotted (*or* decayed). ❷ decadent; depraved; dissolute; degenerate; rotten:～本质 decadent nature /～生活 dissolute (*or* depraved) life /～的文化 decadent culture /～的生活方式 degenerate way of life /～的观念 rotten ideas; decadent concept /～庸俗的思想作风 decadent, philistine way of thinking /化～为神奇 turn the rotten into the miraculous; change sth. degenerate (*or* stale) into sth. vigorous; blow the breath of vigour into the dying
腐殖煤 fǔzhíméi humic coal
腐殖酸 fǔzhísuān humic acid:～肥料 humic acid fertilizer /～分解细菌 humic acid decomposing bacteria /～盐 humate
腐殖土 fǔzhítǔ 〈农业〉humus soil
腐殖质 fǔzhízhì 〈地质〉humus
腐竹 fǔzhú rolls of dried bean-milk cream

俯 fǔ ❶ bow (one's head); bend forward or down:～而纳履 bend down to put on one's shoes ❷〈敬词〉〈旧语〉(often used in official documents or letters) deign to; condescend to
俯察 fǔchá 〈书面〉❶ look down:仰观～ look up and down /～两边山谷的地形 look down to examine the terrain of the valleys on

both sides ❷〈敬词〉deign to examine; kindly understand:～下情 deign to examine what is going on at the lower levels; kindly understand the situation at the lower levels
俯冲 fǔchōng 〈航空〉dive:～扫射 dive-strafe; strafe
俯冲角 fǔchōngjiǎo dive angle
俯伏 fǔfú lie prostrate:～在草丛中 lie prostrate in the grass
俯角 fǔjiǎo 〈测绘〉angle of depression
俯就 fǔjiù ❶〈敬词〉condescend to take or accept (a post, etc.): 秘书一职,务请～。Please be kind enough to take the post of secretary. ❷ yield to; make do with:看得出,他有点巴结～对方。Obviously, he is accommodating himself to curry favour with the other guy.
俯瞰 fǔkàn look down at; overlook:～大地 look down over the land /～全城 overlook the whole town
俯瞰摄影 fǔkàn shèyǐng crane shot; boom shot
俯临 fǔlín overhang; overlook:岩洞～着波光闪烁的河流。The cave overlooks (*or* looks out on) a sparkling river.
俯念 fǔniàn 〈敬词〉kindly bear in mind; be kind enough to consider:～群情 give sympathetic consideration to public sentiments
俯拍 fǔpāi *also* "俯摄"〈摄影〉take a crane or boom shot; shoot downwards
俯射 fǔshè shoot at sth. below; plunge-fire
俯摄 fǔshè (short for 俯瞰摄影) shoot downwards; take a crane shot; take a boom shot:这张全景是从大厦顶上～的。This panorama is a boom shot taken from the top of the tall building.
俯身 fǔshēn bend down; stoop:她～看了看孩子的腿。She bent down to take a look at the child's leg.
俯拾即是 fǔshí-jíshì can be found everywhere; be easily available; be extremely common:这类贝壳在海边～。Such shells can be found anywhere by the sea. /这篇文章中的错字～。This article is full of wrongly written characters.
俯视 fǔshì look down at; overlook:从山上～蜿蜒的公路 look down at a meandering road from a hilltop
俯视图 fǔshìtú *also* "预视图" yùshìtú 〈机械〉vertical view
俯首 fǔshǒu ❶ bow one's head; stoop:～作画 stoop to paint a picture ❷ obey submissively:～听命 obey submissively; be at sb.'s beck and call /～就范 submit meekly; give in without a struggle /～就缚 bow one's head and allow oneself to be bound; surrender without a struggle /～称臣 bow one's head to acknowledge one's allegiance; acknowledge one's inferiority; admit defeat
俯首甘为孺子牛 fǔshǒu gān wéi rúzǐniú humbly serve the people with one's heart and soul
俯首帖耳 fǔshǒu-tiē'ěr be docile and obedient; be servile; take lying down:他凡事颇有主见,对领导也从不～。He knew his own mind and never obeyed his superiors blindly. /在主人面前,他只是个～的奴隶。Before his master, he was nothing but a yesman.
俯首听命 fǔshǒu-tīngmìng bow down and obey submissively; be at sb.'s beck and call; be all obedience
俯顺 fǔshùn 〈旧语〉〈敬词〉kindly comply with; be kind enough to accommodate:～民情 kindly comply with the sentiments of the people
俯卧 fǔwò lie on one's stomach; lie prostrate
俯卧撑 fǔwòchēng 〈体育〉press-up; push-up
俯仰 fǔyǎng 〈书面〉bend or lift one's head; act; move:～随人 act as sb. orders; be at sb.'s beck and call /～自得 feel contented and happy whatever one does /我在这井畔～徘徊,不忍离去。I paced up and down by the well, reluctant to leave.
俯仰机翼 fǔyǎng jīyì 〈航空〉pitching wing
俯仰角 fǔyǎngjiǎo 〈航空〉angle of pitch
俯仰角偏差 fǔyǎngjiǎo piānchā 〈航空〉pitch angle deviation
俯仰陀螺仪 fǔyǎng tuóluóyí 〈航空〉pitch gyroscope
俯仰无愧 fǔyǎng-wúkuì not feel ashamed of one's behaviour; have nothing on one's conscience:做一个～的男子汉 be a man with a clear conscience
俯仰由人 fǔyǎng-yóurén be at sb.'s beck and call:摆脱～的地位 be rid of one's dependent and subservient position /～的日子是不好过的。Life is hard when you have to be at the beck and call of others.
俯仰运动 fǔyǎng yùndòng 〈航空〉pitching movement
俯仰之间 fǔyǎngzhījiān in the twinkling of an eye; in an instant:～,快艇已驶出了港口。In a flash, the motor boat had sailed out of the harbour.
俯泳 fǔyǒng 〈体育〉breaststroke:男子一百米～决赛 men's one-hundred-metre breaststroke finals
俯允 fǔyǔn 〈敬词〉condescend to grant; deign to approve:承蒙～所请,不胜感激。My gratitude knows no bounds, as you have so kindly granted my request.

腑 fǔ *see* "脏腑" zàngfǔ

拊 fǔ 〈书面〉clap
拊手 fǔshǒu 〈书面〉clap hands:～称快 clap one's hands with joy; clap and cheer /～欢笑 clap and laugh heartily
拊膺 fǔyīng 〈书面〉slap one's chest to express grief:～长叹 slap one's chest and heave a deep sigh
拊掌 fǔzhǎng *also* "抚掌" fǔzhǎng 〈书面〉clap hands:～大笑 clap hands and laugh out loud

甫[1] fǔ ❶ man's courtesy name:台～ your name ❷ (Fǔ) a surname

甫[2] fǔ 〈书面〉just; only; only just:惊魂～定 not quite recovered from a fright; still badly shaken /一言～毕 have just finished one's words /年～十八 only just turned eighteen

辅 fǔ ❶ assist; complement; supplement:相～而行 go along by assisting one another /相～相成 complement each other /抑制通货膨胀,以经济、法律手段为主,行政手段为～。To bring inflation under control, we should rely mainly on economic and legal measures supplemented by administrative means. ❷〈书面〉areas round a national capital:畿～ environs of a national capital
辅币 fǔbì (short for 辅助货币) fractional currency or money
辅弼 fǔbì 〈书面〉assist a sovereign in ruling a country; serve as prime minister:～之臣 official who assisted a ruler in governing a country
辅车相依 fǔchē-xiāngyī the jowls and the jaws are mutually dependent — be closely linked up with each other in fate or fortune; be interdependent
辅导 fǔdǎo give guidance in study or training; guide; tutor; coach:课外～ after-school tutoring /课外阅读～ after-class reading guide /～材料 guidance material /～讲座 guidance lecture /～学生打篮球 coach the students in playing basketball /个别～ individual coaching or tutorial /他由王教授～。He was tutored by Prof. Wang.
辅导员 fǔdǎoyuán counsellor; assistant; instructor:校外～ after-school activities counsellor; outside instructors invited to give guidance to students /理论～ instructor in political theory /少先队～ Young Pioneers counsellor
辅课 fǔkè subsidiary course
辅料 fǔliào supplementary materials; subsidiary materials:许多工厂需用的原料和～得靠农业供应。Many factories depend on agriculture for raw and supplementary materials.
辅酶 fǔméi 〈生化〉coenzyme
辅仁大学 Fǔrén Dàxué Catholic University (originally established in Beijing by the Vatican in 1925 and merged into Beijing Normal University in 1952)
辅食 fǔshí supplementary food (for a baby):对婴儿定时加～ give supplementary food to a baby at regular intervals
辅药 fǔyào 〈医学〉adjuvant
辅翼 fǔyì 〈书面〉assist (a ruler in governing a country); give assistance
辅音 fǔyīn 〈语言〉consonant
辅助 fǔzhù ❶ assist; aid:多加～ offer plenty of assistance /～他完成任务 help him to finish the job ❷ supplementary; supplemental; auxiliary; subsidiary:～材料 supplementary material /～读物 supplementary reading material /～作用 auxiliary function
辅助车间 fǔzhù chējiān auxiliary shop
辅助单位 fǔzhù dānwèi auxiliary unit
辅助货币 fǔzhù huòbì *see* "辅币"
辅助机构 fǔzhù jīgòu auxiliary body or organization
辅助舰船 fǔzhù jiànchuán auxiliary vessels
辅助劳动 fǔzhù láodòng auxiliary labour
辅助人员 fǔzhù rényuán auxiliary personnel; auxiliary staff member
辅助授粉 fǔzhù shòufěn 〈农业〉supplementary pollination

辅助仪器 fǔzhù yíqì supplemental instrument
辅助因子 fǔzhù yīnzǐ 〈生化〉cofactor
辅佐 fǔzuǒ assist (a ruler in governing a country)

黼 fǔ patterns of black and white embroidered on ancient official robes

簠 fǔ 〈考古〉square utensil containing grain for sacrifice

脯 fǔ ❶ dried meat:肉～ dried meat /兔～ dried hare meat ❷ preserved fruit:各色果～ sundry candied fruit /杏～ preserved apricot
see also pú
脯氨酸 fǔ'ānsuān 〈生化〉proline

抚(撫) fǔ ❶ comfort; console:安～ aid and comfort /优～ give special care to disabled servicemen and to family members of revolutionary martyrs and servicemen /招～ offer amnesty and enlistment to rebels ❷ protect; nurture; foster:～孤 bring up the orphaned ❸ press lightly; stroke:*see* "～摩" ❹ *see* "拊" fǔ
抚爱 fǔ'ài caress; fondle; take care of:～儿女 cherish one's children
抚躬自问 fǔgōng-zìwèn *also* "反躬自问" fǎngōng-zìwèn examine one's own conscience; hold communion with oneself
抚古思今 fǔgǔ-sījīn recall the remote past and compare it with the present
抚辑 fǔjí 〈书面〉comfort and help settle down:～流亡 console exiles and help them settle down
抚今追昔 fǔjīn-zhuīxī contemplate the present and recall the past; reflect on the past in the light of the present:～,感慨系之。I cannot but sigh with deep emotion when reflecting on the past in the light of the present. /～,物是人非。Comparing the present with the past one finds that while things remain the same, people are not what they used to be.
抚摸 fǔmō stroke; caress:妈妈～着女儿的头发。Mother was stroking her daughter's hair.
抚摩 fǔmó stroke; caress:风吹窗帘拂面,仿佛有一只柔软的手在脸颊上～着。The wind blew the curtain over the face, as if a soft hand were stroking the cheeks.
抚弄 fǔnòng caress; stroke, fondle:她～着儿子的手。She fondled her son's hand. /孩子们～着那只小猫。The children stroked the kitten.
抚琴 fǔqín 〈书面〉play the zither:焚香～ burn incense and play the zither
抚绥 fǔsuí 〈书面〉aid and comfort; reassure; appease:～万方 reassure and pacify all quarters
抚慰 fǔwèi comfort; console; soothe:好言～ comfort with kind words /～受灾群众 console the people in the stricken area /她那受到创伤的心灵亟待～。Her traumatized soul needs most special comfort.
抚恤 fǔxù comfort and compensate a bereaved family
抚恤金 fǔxùjīn pension for the disabled or for the family of the deceased
抚循 fǔxún 〈书面〉aid and console; reassure and pacify:～百姓 placate the common people
抚养 fǔyǎng foster; raise; bring up:～成人 bring up a child /父母对子女有～教育的义务,不得虐待或遗弃。Parents have the obligation to rear and educate their children and must not maltreat or abandon them.
抚养费 fǔyǎngfèi child support payment (after divorce)
抚育 fǔyù ❶ foster; nurture:～孤儿 foster (*or* bring up) orphans ❷ tend; look after:～森林 tend the forest
抚掌 fǔzhǎng *also* "拊掌" fǔzhǎng clap one's hands

父 fǔ 〈书面〉❶ respectful term for an elderly man:渔～ old fisherman /田～ old farmer ❷ *used as part of a courtesy name in ancient times*
see also fù

斧 fǔ ❶ axe; hatchet:板～ broad axe /大刀阔～ bold and resolute; drastic ❷ battleaxe, a kind of weapon in ancient China
斧柄 fǔbǐng *see* "斧柯❶"
斧蛤 fǔgé 〈动物〉coquina clam (*Donax variobilis*)
斧斤 fǔjīn 〈书面〉axe; hatchet
斧柯 fǔkē 〈书面〉❶ shaft of an axe or hatchet ❷ political power; power; authority
斧石 fǔshí axinite
斧头 fǔtou axe; hatchet
斧头鱼 fǔtouyú hatchetfish
斧削 fǔxuē 〈书面〉〈敬词〉chop with an axe — make corrections:这稿子还得请你～。Please kindly make corrections in this article.
斧钺 fǔyuè axe and battle-axe — ancient weapons used for execution; capital punishment:甘冒～以陈 state one's opinions at the risk of one's life
斧凿 fǔzáo 〈书面〉❶ axe and chisel ❷ (of literary works, etc.) affected; artificial
斧凿痕 fǔzáohén 〈书面〉marks of hatchet and chisel — traces of man-made embellishment:这部电影片的有些情节存在着～。The plot of this film is rather artificial in some places.
斧藻 fǔzǎo 〈书面〉carve and decorate; adorn; embellish
斧正 fǔzhèng *also* "斧政"〈书面〉〈敬词〉(please) make corrections
斧锧 fǔzhì executioner's block and axe (used in ancient China)
斧子 fǔzi axe; hatchet
斧足类 fǔzúlèi 〈动物〉pelecypodia (comprising oysters, clams, scallops, etc.)

釜 fǔ a kind of cauldron used in ancient China:破～沉舟 break the cauldrons and sink the boats (after crossing the river) — cut off all means of retreat; burn one's boats (*or* bridges)
釜底抽薪 fǔdǐ-chōuxīn take away the firewood from under a cauldron; take drastic measures to deal with a critical situation; cut the ground from under sb.'s feet:禁止吸毒,要采取～的办法,断绝毒品入境。To prohibit the use of narcotics, we must take drastic measures to bar the drugs from entering the country.
釜底游鱼 fǔdǐ-yóuyú *also* "釜中之鱼" fish swimming in the bottom of a cauldron — person whose fate is sealed:他们已是～,或降或死,别无他途。Like fish swimming in a cauldron, they had no alternative but either to surrender or to die.
釜山 Fǔshān Pusan, second largest city and seaport on the southeastern coast of the Republic of Korea

俛 fǔ *see* "俯" fǔ
see also miǎn

fù

父 fù ❶ father:家～ my father /养～ adopted father; foster father /继～ stepfather /认贼作～ take the foe for one's father ❷ male relative of a senior generation:祖～ grandfather /叔～ uncle /岳～ father-in-law /舅～ uncle
see also fǔ
父辈 fùbèi people of father's generation; elder generation:不辜负～的期望 be worthy of (*or* live up to) the elder generation's expectations
父本 fùběn 〈植物〉male parent:～植株 paternal plant
父党 fùdǎng father's kinsfolk
父老 fùlǎo elders (of a country or district):家乡～ elders at home/～乡亲 fellow countrymen /以更大的成绩告慰～兄弟 gladden the elders and brethren with even greater achievements
父母 fùmǔ father and mother; parents:幼年～双亡 lose both parents when a child /～双全。Both their father and mother are still living.
父母官 fùmǔguān 〈旧语〉father-mother official — magistrate of a county or prefecture (regarded by local people as a parent)
父母之邦 fùmǔzhībāng mother country; native land
父母之命,媒妁之言 fùmǔ zhī mìng, méishuò zhī yán 〈旧语〉command of the parents and good offices of a matchmaker — the old practice of arranging a marriage
父亲 fùqin father:亲生～ own father; biological father
父权制 fùquánzhì patriarchy
父系 fùxì ❶ paternal:～亲属 relatives on the paternal side; paternal relatives ❷ paternal line; patrilineal:～家族制度 patrilineal fami-

ly system /～氏族公社 patrilineal clan commune /～社会 patrilineal (*or patriarchal*) society

父兄 fùxiōng ❶ father and elder brothers ❷ head of a family

父执 fùzhí 〈书面〉 father's friends:董老先生是我的～。Mr. Dong is a friend of my father.

父子 fùzǐ father and son:～都是篮球国手。Both father and son have been on the national basketball team.

赙 fù 〈书面〉 present a gift to a bereaved family

赙金 fùjīn 〈书面〉 money presented to a bereaved family

赙仪 fùyí 〈书面〉 present sent to a bereaved family; gift to a bereaved family

赙赠 fùzèng 〈书面〉 present a gift to a bereaved family

傅[1] fù ❶ 〈书面〉 teach; instruct:～之德义 teach morality and righteousness ❷ teacher; instructor:师～ master; teacher ❸ (Fù) a surname

傅[2] fù 〈书面〉 ❶ attach; stick to; adhere to:为虎～翼 give wings to a tiger — assist an evildoer ❷ lay on; apply:～彩 lay on colours

傅粉 fùfěn put powder on; powder (one's face)

傅会 fùhuì *also* "附会" fùhuì draw wrong conclusions by false analogy; strain one's interpretation

傅科摆 fùkēbǎi Foucault pendulum

傅里叶 Fùlǐyè Jean-Baptiste-Joseph Fourier (1768-1830), French mathemetician:～变换 Fourier transform /～分析 Fourier analysis /～级数 Fourier series

傅立叶 Fùlìyè Francois-Marie Charles Fourier (1772-1837), French sociologist and socialist:～主义 Fourierism

缚 fù tie up; bind fast:作茧自～ spin a cocoon around oneself — get enmeshed in a web of one's own spinning /手无～鸡之力 lack the strength to truss a chicken

富 fù ❶ rich; wealthy:首～ richest person /豪～ powerful and wealthy /致～ get rich /为～不仁 be rich and cruel /～国和穷国 "haves" and "havenots"/国～民安。The country is rich and the people live in peace. ❷ enrich: *see* "～国强兵" ❸ wealth; resource:财～ wealth; riches ❹ rich; abundant:～于水分 rich in moisture /～于幻想 full of imagination /～于表情 with vivid expression /～于独创性 abound in originality /年～力强 in the prime of life ❺ (Fù) a surname

富布赖特奖学金 Fùbùlàitè jiǎngxuéjīn (US) Fulbright scholarship

富富有余 fùfù-yǒuyú have more than needed; have enough and to spare:这些粮食,一家人吃一月也～。The grain is more than a family's monthly consumption.

富贵 fùguì riches and honour; wealth and rank:荣华～ honour and splendour /～人家 wealthy and influential family /～骄人 be arrogant because of one's wealth

富贵病 fùguìbìng rich man's disease (which needs a long period of rest and plenty of nourishment)

富贵不能淫 fùguì bùnéng yín not to be corrupted by riches or rank; be impervious to the temptation of wealth and high position; be incorruptible:～,贫贱不能移,威武不能屈 not to be corrupted by riches or honours, not to depart from principle despite poverty or humble origin, and not to submit to force or threat (Confucian criteria for a scholar's integrity)

富贵浮云 fùguì-fúyún regard wealth and honours as insignificant as floating clouds:不义而富且贵,于我如浮云。To me, ill-gotten riches and honours are but floating clouds.

富国 fùguó ❶ make one's country rich:发展经济以～ develop the economy to make one's country wealthy ❷ rich country:旧的国际经济秩序使～越富,穷国越穷。Thanks to the old economic world order, the rich countries are growing richer and the poor countries poorer.

富国富民 fùguó-fùmín make one's country rich and its people prosperous:顺应～的历史要求 suit the historical needs of making the country strong and the people prosperous

富国强兵 fùguó-qiángbīng make one's country rich and build up its military might:以～为己任 take it as one's responsibility to make one's country rich and its military forces strong

富豪 fùháo rich and powerful people:本城的一大～ one of the richest and most influential people in the city

富集 fùjí enrichment; concentration

富矿 fùkuàng 〈矿业〉 rich ore; high-grade ore

富矿体 fùkuàngtǐ oreshoot

富里酸 fùlǐsuān fulvic acid

富兰克林 Fùlánkèlín Benjamin Franklin (1706-1790), US statesman, writer, inventor and scientist

富丽 fùlì splendid; gorgeous:陈设～的客厅 luxuriously furnished parlour /庄严～的宫殿 imposing and splendid palace /～的江南景色 enchanting scenery south of the Yangtze River

富丽堂皇 fùlì-tánghuáng sumptuous; gorgeous; splendid; grand:～的歌剧院 magnificent opera house/大厅装饰得～。The hall is sumptuously decorated.

富民 fùmín make the people rich:～政策 policy of enriching the people

富农 fùnóng rich peasant; (Russian) kulak

富铅玻璃 fùqiān bōli 〈化工〉 crystal glass

富强 fùqiáng rich and powerful; prosperous and strong:我们的国家已经走上繁荣～的道路。Our country has embarked on the road to prosperity and strength.

富饶 fùráo fertile; abundant:川西平原的～是尽人皆知的。Sichuan Province is well known for its richly endowed western plains.

富人 fùrén rich people; the rich

富商 fùshāng rich merchant:～大贾 wealthy merchants

富士山 Fùshìshān Mount Fuji or Fujiyama, a dormant volcano which is Japan's highest peak

富士银行 Fùshì Yínháng (Japan) Fuji Bank Ltd.

富实 fùshi plentiful; abundant; well-off

富庶 fùshù rich and prosperous:我的家乡美丽而～。My hometown is both beautiful and prosperous.

富岁 fùsuì 〈书面〉 bumper harvest year; good year

富态 fùtai 〈婉词〉〈方言〉 plump; stout:她挺～的。She is inclined to plumpness. /这老太太长得真～。What a full figure the old lady has!

富翁 fùwēng rich man; man of wealth

富锌涂料 fùxīn túliào 〈化工〉 zinc-rich paint; zinc-rich primer

富有 fùyǒu ❶ rich; affluent; wealthy:这位华人很～。This overseas Chinese is very rich. /他出生在一个～的家庭。He was born with a silver spoon in his mouth. ❷ rich in; replete with; full of:～活力 full of vigour /～才华 talented /～个性 of strong personality /～生活情趣 replete with the interests and delights of life /～时代的特色 characteristic of the times

富于 fùyú rich in; full of:～心计 adept at scheming; very calculating /～变化 changeable; capricious /～正义感 with a strong sense of justice /～表现力的语言 vivid and expressive language

富裕 fùyù ❶ prosperous; well-to-do; well off:走上～之路 on the way to prosperity /他家的日子过得挺～。His family is quite well-off. /我的时间比较～,可以帮你抄写。I have some time to spare and can help you copy it. /共同～不等于完全平等,也不等于同时同速～起来。Common prosperity does not mean absolute egalitarianism or simultaneous prosperity. *or* Common prosperity does not mean complete equality or everyone getting rich at the same time and at the same pace. ❷ make rich or prosperous; enrich:发展生产,～人民。Develop production to enrich the people.

富裕中农 fùyù zhōngnóng well-to-do middle-peasant

富余 fùyu have more than needed; have enough and to spare:家家户户的粮食都有～。Every household has a surplus of grain. /他把～的钱存入银行。He deposited the spare money in the bank.

富源 fùyuán natural resources

富足 fùzú affluent; plentiful; abundant; rich:生活～ affluent life /工农业产品～得很。There's an abundance of agricultural and industrial products.

副[1] fù ❶ deputy; assistant; vice-:～总统 vice-president /～总理 vice-premier /～司长 deputy director of the department /～处长 deputy section (*or* division) chief /～代表 deputy representative (*or* delegate) /～经理 assistant manager /～系主任 associate dean of the department ❷ assistant post or position:大～ first mate /二～ second mate /排～ auxiliary platoon leader /队～ secondary captain; deputy team leader /团～ subsidiary regimental commander ❸ complementary; auxiliary; secondary:从事～业 en-

gage in a side occupation; work at a sideline ❹ correspond to; fit: 名~其实 title corresponding with reality; in reality as well as in name /盛名之下,其实难~。It is rather difficult to live up to a great reputation.

副[2] fù 〈量词〉❶ set; pair: 一~眼镜 a pair of glasses /一~中药 a set of Chinese herbal medicines /一~对联 a pair of antithetical couplets ❷ *used to indicate facial expression*: 一~凶相 fierce look /一~可怜相 pitiful look /一~笑脸 smiling face /一~黑里透红的脸膛 sun-tanned ruddy face /一~惊疑的神气 bewildered expression

副本 fùběn duplicate; transcript; copy: 经济合同的~ copy of an economic contract /这是文件的~。It's a duplicate of the document.

副标题 fùbiāotí subheading; subtitle

副产品 fùchǎnpǐn *also* "副产物" by-product

副赤道带 fùchìdàodài 〈气象〉subequatorial belt

副词 fùcí 〈语言〉adverb

副低压 fùdīyā 〈气象〉secondary depression

副高 fùgāo (short for 副高级职称) secondary senior position (such as associate professor, associate research fellow, etc.)

副歌 fùgē 〈音乐〉refrain

副官 fùguān aide-de-camp; adjutant

副虹 fùhóng 〈气象〉secondary rainbow

副驾驶员 fùjiàshǐyuán 〈航空〉copilot; second pilot

副检察长 fùjiǎncházhǎng deputy chief procurator; deputy procurator-general

副交感神经 fùjiāogǎn shénjīng 〈生理〉parasympathetic nerve

副教授 fùjiàoshòu associate professor; adjunct professor

副经理 fùjīnglǐ assistant manager; deputy manager

副井 fùjǐng 〈矿业〉auxiliary shaft

副净 fùjìng painted-face actor skilled in movements and postures in traditional Chinese operas

副句 fùjù 〈语言〉clause

副刊 fùkān supplement: 这份报纸每周有好几种~。This newspaper has several supplements every week.

副科 fùkē minor subject; secondary course: 学生不能重主科,轻~。Students should not be encouraged to overstress the major courses while overlooking the minor ones.

副林带 fùlíndài by-forest belt

副领事 fùlǐngshì vice-consul

副流感 fùliúgǎn 〈医学〉parainfluenza

副秘书长 fùmìshūzhǎng deputy secretary-general: 联合国~ Under Secretary-General of the United Nations

副品 fùpǐn substandard goods; seconds

副区长 fùqūzhǎng deputy district head or chief

副热带 fùrèdài *also* "亚热带" yàrèdài subtropical zone; subtropics; subtropical belt /~高压 subtropical high /~无风带 horse latitudes

副伤寒 fùshānghán 〈医学〉paratyphoid (fever)

副神经 fùshénjīng 〈生理〉accessory nerve

副肾 fùshèn *also* "肾上腺" shènshàngxiàn 〈生理〉adrenal gland

副省长 fùshěngzhǎng deputy provincial governor

副食 fùshí non-staple food: ~供应 supply of non-cereal foodstuffs

副食品 fùshípǐn non-staple food or foodstuffs: ~公司 non-staple food company /~加工厂 non-staple food processing factory /这几年市场上的~越来越丰富。In recent years, non-staple foods are becoming more diversified on the market.

副食商店 fùshí shāngdiàn grocery; grocer's

副市长 fùshìzhǎng deputy mayor

副室 fùshì 〈旧语〉concubine

副手 fùshǒu assistant; helper: 前几年我在他手下当~。In the last few years, I worked as his assistant.

副署 fùshǔ countersign

副题 fùtí *also* "副标题" subtitle; subheading

副县长 fùxiànzhǎng deputy county magistrate

副线圈 fùxiànquān *also* "次级线圈" cìjí xiànquān 〈电工〉secondary coil

副乡长 fùxiāngzhǎng deputy township head or chief

副性征 fùxìngzhēng secondary sex character

副修 fùxiū minor (in a subject): ~课 minor courses

副研究员 fùyánjiūyuán associate research fellow

副业 fùyè sideline; side occupation: 家庭~ household sideline production; family sideline /发展农~生产 develop agriculture and sideline (*or* subsidiary) production

副译审 fùyìshěn associate reviser (in translation)

副翼 fùyì 〈航空〉aileron

副油箱 fùyóuxiāng 〈航空〉auxiliary tank; drop tank

副载波 fùzàibō 〈物理〉subcarrier

副职 fùzhí position of a deputy (to the chief of an office, department, etc.): ~人员 staff in deputy positions

副轴 fùzhóu 〈机械〉countershaft; layshaft

副总工程师 fùzǒnggōngchéngshī deputy chief engineer

副总领事 fùzǒnglǐngshì deputy consul-general

副作用 fùzuòyòng ❶ side effect; by-effect: 这种药品因发现有~而停止出售。This medicine was withdrawn from the market when it was found to have a harmful side effect. ❷ 〈机械〉secondary action

讣 fù ❶ announce sb.'s death ❷ obituary

讣告 fùgào ❶ announce sb.'s death: 立即~亲友 announce sb.'s death to his relatives immediately ❷ obituary: ~栏 obituary column (in a newspaper)

讣闻 fùwén *also* "讣文" obituary (notice): 草拟~ draft an obituary

赴 fù ❶ go to; be bound for; attend: 赶~工地 hurry to the worksite /开~前线 leave for the front /~美留学 go to study in the United States ❷ swim: ~水 swim ❸ *see* "讣" fù

赴敌 fùdí 〈书面〉go to the battlefront: 团结一致,共同~。United as one, they went to the front to fight the enemy.

赴会 fùhuì attend a meeting; meet sb. by appointment

赴难 fùnàn go to the rescue of one's country; go to help save the nation from danger: 共赴国难 join in a united effort to save the nation (*or* for national salvation)

赴任 fùrèn (of an official) go to one's post; be on the way to one's post: 克日~ go to one's post right away

赴汤蹈火 fùtāng-dǎohuǒ be ready to jump into boiling water and plunge into raging fire — go through hell and high water; be ready to risk one's life: ~,在所不辞 not hesitate to face all difficulties and dangers; won't flinch from the most hazardous task

赴席 fùxí go to a banquet

赴宴 fùyàn *see* "赴席"

赴约 fùyuē meet sb. by appointment; keep an appointment

洑 fù swim: ~过河去 swim across the river
see also fú

洑水 fùshuǐ swim

赋[1] fù bestow on; endow with; vest with: 天~ natural endowments

赋[2] fù ❶ 〈旧语〉agricultural tax: 田~ land tax /轻徭薄~ reduce corvée and tax ❷ 〈书面〉levy; impose: 烟酒~以重税。Levy heavy taxes (*or* duties) on cigarettes and liquors.

赋[3] fù ❶ descriptive prose interspersed with verse (a literary form very much in vogue from the Han Dynasty to the period of Northern and Southern Dynasties); rhyme prose; poetic prose; prose poem: 辞~ poetry and rhyme prose ❷ compose (verse); write (poetry): 即席~诗 compose a poem impromptu

赋格曲 fùgéqǔ 〈音乐〉fugue

赋课 fùkè *see* "赋税"

赋敛 fùliǎn levy taxes

赋税 fùshuì land and other taxes; taxes and levies

赋闲 fùxián (of an official, etc.) be unemployed; be out of office: 他~在家,过起卖文的生活来。Unemployed, he had to make a living by his pen.

赋形剂 fùxíngjì 〈药学〉excipient

赋性 fùxìng inborn nature: ~刚强 unyielding by nature; of firm (*or* strong) character

赋役 fùyì taxes and corvée

赋有 fùyǒu possess (naturally); be endowed with; be gifted with: 他温文尔雅,~学者风度。Gentle and cultivated, he had the natural bearing of a scholar.

赋予 fùyǔ entrust; bestow; give: ~他更大的权力 confer more

power on him /这是时代～我们的伟大使命。This is the great mission our age has entrusted to us. /一些古老的风俗习惯被～了崭新的内容。Some ancient customs and habits have assumed brand-new meanings.

赋值 fùzhí 〈信息〉bind

复[1](複) fù ❶ repeat; duplicate: 山重水～ where mountains multiply and rivers double back — at the end of one's hope ❷ compound; complex; complicated: ～分数 complex fraction

复[2](復) fù ❶ turn round; turn over: 反～无常 chop and change; behave capriciously /在脑子里反～考虑 turn over and over in one's mind; mull over ❷ answer; reply: 回～ answer /电～ reply by wire; cable a reply /批～ give an official, written reply (to a subordinate, ect.)

复[3](復) fù ❶ recover; resume: 光～ recover /收～ recover; recapture /修～ repair; restore /万劫不～ be beyond redemption ❷ revenge: 报～ avenge; retaliate

复[4](復) fù again; repeatedly: 年～一年 year after year/死灰～燃 dying embers glowing again; resurgence; revival /不可～得 cannot be obtained again

复摆 fùbǎi 〈物理〉compound pendulum

复背斜 fùbèixié 〈地质〉anticlinorium; compound anticline

复本 fùběn duplicate (copy)

复本位制 fùběnwèizhì 〈金融〉bimetallism

复比 fùbǐ 〈数学〉compound ratio; double ratio

复辟 fùbì restore a dethroned monarch; restore the old order: 妄图使旧制度～ vainly attempt to restore the old system

复波 fùbō 〈物理〉complex wave

复查 fùchá check again; reexamine: 住院～ be in hospital for reexamination /对各单位的卫生状况进行～ check the hygienic conditions of all units again

复仇 fùchóu revenge; avenge: ～心理 vindictiveness; desire for revenge /为死难的同胞～ avenge one's dead compatriots /无时无刻不想～。Not for a minute was revenge forgotten.

复仇主义 fùchóuzhǔyì revanchism: ～者 revanchist

复出 fùchū resume one's official post after rehabilitation; make a comeback

复聪 fùcōng regain or recover one's lost hearing

复电 fùdiàn telegram in reply (to one received): 收到～ receive a reply by telegram /～支持 cable one's support in reply

复调音乐 fùdiào yīnyuè polyphony

复发 fùfā have a relapse; recur: 心脏病～ suffer a relapse of a heart ailment /他的病可能～。His illness is likely to recur. /他的哮喘病～了。He is suffering from asthma again.

复发率 fùfālǜ recurrence rate

复返 fùfǎn come back; return: 去而～ go and come back /青春一去不～。Youth comes but once. *or* Youth's gone, never to return.

复方 fùfāng ❶〈中医〉prescription composed of two or more recipes of herbal medicines ❷ medicine made of two or more ingredients; medicinal compound

复方阿司匹林 fùfāng āsīpǐlín 〈药学〉aspirin compound (APC)

复方甘草合剂 fùfāng gāncǎo héjì 〈药学〉brown mixture

复分解 fùfēnjiě 〈化学〉double decomposition

复分解反应 fùfēnjiě fǎnyìng double decomposition reaction

复辅音 fùfǔyīn 〈语言〉consonant cluster

复根 fùgēn 〈化学〉compound radical

复工 fùgōng return to work (after a strike or layoff): 罢工的工人已经～。The workers on strike have returned to work.

复古 fùgǔ restore old customs, traditions, etc; return to the ancients

复古主义 fùgǔzhǔyì doctrine of "back to the ancients"

复归 fùguī return to the original state; be back to a former condition: 咆哮了一天的大海, 此时～平静。The sea, which roared for the whole day, now has calmed down again.

复果 fùguǒ *also* "聚花果" jùhuāguǒ 〈植物〉multiple fruit; collective fruit; compound fruit

复合 fùhé compound; complex; composite: ～判断 compound judgment /～求偿 composite claim /～国际人格 composite international person /～国 composite state /～条约 composite treaty /～税 compound (*or* mixed) duty /～增长率 compound growth rate /～概率 composite probability /～需求 composite demand /～供给 composite supply

复合材料 fùhé cáiliào composite; composite or complex material: 陶瓷－塑料～ ceramic-and-plastic composite /玻纤～ glass fibre reinforced composite

复合词 fùhécí 〈语言〉compound (word)

复合电路 fùhé diànlù compound circuit

复合肥料 fùhé féiliào compound fertilizer

复合句 fùhéjù 〈语言〉compound or complex sentence

复合量词 fùhé liàngcí 〈语言〉compound classifier

复合元音 fùhé yuányīn 〈语言〉compound vowel; diphthong or triphthong

复合杂交 fùhé zájiāo compound hybridization

复合装甲 fùhé zhuāngjiǎ 〈军事〉composite armour

复核 fùhé ❶ check; cross-check: 把报告中的数据～一下 check the data in the report ❷〈法律〉(of the Supreme People's Court) review a case in which a death sentence has been passed by a lower court

复会 fùhuì resume (a session or sitting): 谈判经过五天休息后再次～。The negotiations resumed after five days of adjournment.

复婚 fùhūn restoration of a marriage; resumption of matrimonial relations; reunion of a couple after divorce

复活 fùhuó ❶ come back to life; revive: 他竟死而～。To our surprise, he came back to life. ❷ bring back to life; resuscitate; resurrect; revive: 军国主义～ resurgence (*or* revival) of militarism ❸〈基督教〉Resurrection

复活节 Fùhuójié 〈基督教〉Easter: ～星期一 Easter Monday /～彩蛋 Easter egg

复激 fùjī 〈电学〉compound excitation: ～发电机 compound generator

复交 fùjiāo ❶ restore friendship; resume relations ❷ reestablish or resume diplomatic relations: 两国将于年底～。The two countries will resume their diplomatic relations at the end of the year.

复旧 fùjiù ❶ restore old ways; return to the past: 主张～ advocate the revival of old ways and traditions ❷ restore; rehabilitate: ～如初 be restored (to one's original state or status)

复句 fùjù 〈语言〉sentence of two or more clauses; complex or compound sentence

复卷机 fùjuǎnjī (of papermaking) rewinding machine; rewinder

复刊 fùkān (of newspaper or magazine) resume publication

复课 fùkè resume classes: 实习完毕, 明日～。The field work is completed, and classes will begin again tomorrow.

复理层 fùlǐcéng 〈地质〉flysch

复利 fùlì 〈经济〉compound interest

复萌 fùméng relapse: 故态～ slip back into one's old ways; revert to type

复名数 fùmíngshù 〈数学〉compound number

复明 fùmíng regain one's eyesight; recover lost eyesight

复命 fùmìng report (to one's superiors) on completion of a task: 这一轮谈判已经结束, 可以回国～了。Having completed this round of negotiations, we are returning to our country to report.

复捻 fùniǎn 〈纺织〉second twist

复任 fùrèn 〈书面〉(of government official) resume one's post

复赛 fùsài 〈体育〉intermediary heat; semi-finals

复色光 fùsèguāng multiple beam; multicolour light

复审 fùshěn ❶ reexamine; re-check ❷〈法律〉review a case: 这个案子有～的可能。It's possible that the case will be reviewed.

复生 fùshēng bring back to life; revive: 死而～ revive; come back to life; return to life after death /人死不能～, 你我还是节哀吧。It would be better for us two to control our grief, as we cannot bring the deceased back to life.

复食 fùshí (of a person after a period of fasting or of a patient who did not feel like eating because of illness) resume eating

复市 fùshì reopen a shop, market, etc. (after a stoppage): 参加罢市的店铺已陆续～。The shops, which were on strike, have reopened one after another.

复式 fùshì 〈会计〉double entry

复式编制 fùshì biānzhì double establishment

复式车床 fùshì chēchuáng 〈机械〉double lathe

复式气缸 fùshì qìgāng multiple cylinder

复式桥牌 fùshì qiáopái duplicate bridge

复试　fùshì　reexamination; second round of examinations
复视　fùshì　〈医学〉double vision
复述　fùshù　❶ repeat: 请你～刚才说过的话。Please repeat what you said just now. ❷ retell (in language learning): 让学生～课文内容 ask the students to retell the text
复数　fùshù　❶〈语言〉plural (number) ❷〈数学〉complex number
复丝　fùsī　〈纺织〉multifilament
复苏　fùsū　❶ come back to life or consciousness; resuscitate: 死而～ resurrection after death / 病人昏迷三天后才～。The patient came back to life after lying unconscious for three days. ❷〈经济〉recovery: 经济～ economic recovery
复透镜　fùtòujìng　compound lens
复位　fùwèi　❶ reset; reduce: 关节～ reset a joint ❷ (of a monarch who has lost power) be restored to the throne; resume power
复位术　fùwèishù　〈医学〉reduction: 骨折～ reduction of a fracture
复胃　fùwèi　complex stomach (of a ruminant); ruminant stomach; *stomachus compositus*
复习　fùxí　review; revise: ～功课 review one's lessons / ～提纲 outline for review / ～材料 material for review
复现　fùxiàn　(of past things) happen again; recur; reappear: 往事一幕幕在脑海～。Scene after scene of past events flashed across my mind.
复线　fùxiàn　〈交通〉double or dual track; multiple track: ～列车 multiple-track train / 京广～ Beijing-Guangzhou double-track railway
复向斜　fùxiàngxié　〈地质〉synclinorium; compound syncline
复写　fùxiě　duplicate; make carbon copies: 把报告～一份 duplicate the report
复写纸　fùxiězhǐ　carbon paper
复信　fùxìn　❶ write a letter in reply; reply ❷ letter in reply; reply
复兴　fùxīng　revive; reinvigorate; rejuvenate: ～国家 rejuvenate the nation / ～国民经济 reinvigorate the national economy / ～民族工业 revitalize the national industry / 文艺～ Renaissance
复姓　fùxìng　compound surname; two-character surname
复学　fùxué　go back to school (after absence); resume one's interrupted studies: "希望工程"使许多失学的农村少年儿童得以～。Project Hope has enabled many drop-outs in the countryside to go back to school.
复盐　fùyán　〈化学〉double salt
复眼　fùyǎn　〈动物〉compound eye (of insects)
复业　fùyè　❶ take up one's old occupation; reestablish one's business ❷ (of a shop) resume business after a close-down; reopen
复叶　fùyè　〈植物〉compound leaf
复议　fùyì　reconsider (a decision): 这个结论当时下得太仓促, 有必要～。The conclusion was reached in a hurry and needs reconsideration.
复音　fùyīn　〈物理〉complex tone
复音词　fùyīncí　〈语言〉disyllabic or polysyllabic word
复印　fùyìn　〈印刷〉duplicate; copy; photocopy; xerox
复印机　fùyìnjī　duplicator; xerox copier; photocopier; copier
复印件　fùyìnjiàn　xerox (copy); duplicate copy
复印纸　fùyìnzhǐ　duplicating paper; copy paper
复元　fùyuán　*see* "复原❶"
复员　fùyuán　❶ return to peacetime condition ❷ demobilize; demob: ～回乡 return to one's home town after demobilization
复员费　fùyuánfèi　demobilization pay
复员军人　fùyuán jūnrén　demobilized soldier; ex-serviceman
复员令　fùyuánlìng　demobilization order
复原　fùyuán　❶ *also* "复元" recover from an illness; be restored to health: 病体～ recover one's health from a disease ❷ restore; rehabilitate: 政府已拨出专款对这座古寺进行～修缮。The government has alloted special funds to restore and repair the old temple. / 文物的～是十分复杂的技术。The restoration of cutural relics requires very complicated technology.
复圆　fùyuán　〈天文〉fourth contact (of a total eclipse); last contact (of a partial eclipse); end of an eclipse
复杂　fùzá　complicated; intricate; complex: ～动荡的国际局势 complex and volatile (*or* turbulent) world situation / 这是多么～的一套程序! What a complicated program it is! / 我怀着～的心情离开办公室。I left the office with mixed feelings. / 你不要使问题～化。Don't complicate matters. / 应该把事情想得～一些。We should not over-simplify things.
复杂劳动　fùzá láodòng　complex labour
复照　fùzhào　〈外交〉note in reply; note of reply; reply note
复诊　fùzhěn　further consultation (with a doctor); subsequent visit (to a doctor)
复职　fùzhí　resume one's post; be reinstated: 他四处活动, 谋求～。He was busy trying to get himself reinstated (in his former position).
复制　fùzhì　duplicate; reconstruct; reproduce; make a copy of: ～模型 reconstructed model / 经过鉴定, 这幅画是～的。According to the appraisal this painting is a copy (*or* replica).
复制片　fùzhìpiàn　duplicated film; copy of a film
复制品　fùzhìpǐn　replica; reproduction
复种　fùzhòng　〈农业〉multiple cropping
复种面积　fùzhòng miànjī　multiple cropping area
复种指数　fùzhòng zhǐshù　multiple crop index
复壮　fùzhuàng　〈农业〉rejuvenation: ～品种 rejuvenated seed strain

覆

fù　❶〈书面〉cover; envelop: 被～ cover / 天～地载 covered by heaven and carried by earth — all-embracing ❷〈书面〉overturn; capsize; upset: 翻天～地 overturning heaven and earth — world-shaking / 翻来～去 toss and turn; toss about ❸ *see* "复[2]" fù
覆败　fùbài　(of an empire, nation, etc.) fall; be thoroughly defeated; lose (a war, etc.)
覆被　fùbèi　cover; overspread; screen: 森林～率占全省面积三分之一以上。More than one third of the province's total area is covered by forests.
覆蔽　fùbì　〈书面〉cover; screen: 为浓云～的月亮 moon that hides behind thick cloud
覆瓿　fùbù　〈书面〉〈谦词〉(of works) of little value; worthless
覆巢无完卵　fù cháo wú wánluǎn　when the nest is overturned no egg stays unbroken — when a family meets ruin, no member can hope to escape unscathed; in a great disaster, no one can escape safe and sound
覆车之戒　fùchēzhījiè　warning taken from the overturned cart ahead; lesson drawn from others' mistakes
覆盖　fùgài　❶ cover: 积雪～着大地。The earth is blanketed with snow. / 刘海儿～着前额。The bang covers the forehead. ❷ plant cover; vegetation
覆盖层　fùgàicéng　〈地质〉overburden
覆盖面　fùgàimiàn　❶ covered area: 森林的～日益减少。Forests have been shrinking. ❷ coverage: 电视台的～ coverage of a TV station / 此项社会保险计划～很大。The social insurance scheme covers an extensive sector (of society).
覆灭　fùmiè　destruction; ruin; total collapse: 难逃～的命运 cannot escape the fate of utter destruction
覆没　fùmò　❶〈书面〉(of ships) sink: 此海域常有过往船只～。The passing boats often sink in this sea area. ❷ (of troops) be overwhelmed; be destroyed: 全军～。The whole army was wiped out. ❸〈书面〉fall into enemy hands; come under enemy occupation: 中原～ fall of the Central Plains
覆盆之冤　fùpénzhīyuān　grievous wrong that has little hope of being redressed; irredeemable wrong: 我这～谁与雪之? Who will avenge my irredeemable wrong?
覆盆子　fùpénzǐ　〈中药〉Korean raspberry
覆水难收　fùshuǐ-nánshōu　spilt water can't be gathered up — what has been lost cannot be retrieved; what is done can't be undone
覆土　fùtǔ　cover up with soil: 种子播下后～约三寸厚。Cover the seeds up with three *cun* of soil after they are sown.
覆亡　fùwáng　(of an empire, nation, etc.) fall; downfall; collapse: 吸取前朝～的教训 draw lessons from the fall of the preceding dynasty
覆辙　fùzhé　track of an overturned cart: 重蹈～ take the track of the overturned cart; repeat the same mistakes

蝮

fù
蝮蛇　fùshé　Pallas pit viper

馥

fù　〈书面〉fragrance: 草～ fragrance of grass / 流香吐～ send out fragrance
馥馥　fùfù　〈书面〉strongly scented; richly fragrant: 花香～, 招引来

一群群蜂蝶。Sweet smelling flowers attracted throngs of bees and butterflies.

馥郁 fùyù 〈书面〉strong fragrance; heavy perfume:鲜花～ flowers with rich sweet scent /～芬芳 fragrant and beautiful

腹

fù ❶ belly; abdomen; stomach:下～部 underbelly /大～便便 pot-bellied; big-bellied /食不果～ have little food to eat ❷ heart; innermost feelings:～悲 grieve; feel grief /～有鳞甲 have scales and shells of reptiles and arthropods in the heart — be evil; be sinister ❸ empty and protruding part in the middle of a vessel or a vase:壶～ belly of a pot

腹案 fù'àn ❶ scheme being hatched; mental plan:他正在盘算～。He is figuring out a plan. ❷ plan that has not been made known to the public:他们对这个问题早有了～。They have already made a plan, though it has not yet been made public.

腹背受敌 fùbèi-shòudí be exposed to attacks from the front and the rear:从～的困境中解脱出来 extricate oneself from a predicament where one is attacked front and rear

腹壁疝 fùbìshàn 〈医学〉ventral hernia; abdominal hernia

腹地 fùdì hinterland:亚洲～ hinterland of Asia

腹诽 fùfěi *also* "腹非"〈书面〉consider sth. wrong in one's mind without saying it; harbour unspoken criticism:在封建时代,～也是要招罪的。In feudal times, even unspoken criticism could invite disaster.

腹稿 fùgǎo draft worked out in one's mind; mental notes:打～ make mental notes

腹股沟 fùgǔgōu *also* "鼠蹊" shǔxī 〈生理〉inguina; groin:～区 inguinal region; iliac region /～淋巴结 inguinal gland /～淋巴结炎 bubo /～疝 inguinal hernia /～管 inguinal canal (*canalis inguinalis*)

腹肌 fùjī 〈生理〉abdominal muscle

腹疾 fùjí 〈书面〉diarrhoea

腹绞痛 fùjiǎotòng 〈医学〉eilema

腹面 fùmiàn abdominal side of an animal

腹鸣 fùmíng borborygmus; intestinal gurgle; "talking tummy"

腹膜 fùmó 〈生理〉peritoneum

腹膜炎 fùmóyán peritonitis

腹膜粘连 fùmó zhānlián 〈医学〉peritoneal adhesion

腹鳍 fùqí 〈动物〉ventral fin

腹腔 fùqiāng 〈生理〉abdominal cavity

腹腔镜 fùqiāngjìng 〈医学〉peritoneoscope

腹水 fùshuǐ 〈医学〉ascites:抽～ tap the abdomen

腹痛 fùtòng abdominal pain

腹吸盘 fùxīpán 〈动物〉ventral sucker

腹泻 fùxiè *also* "水泻" shuǐxiè diarrhoea

腹心 fùxīn ❶ belly and heart — vital organs; key parts:～要地 important place; strategic area ❷ trusted subordinate; reliable agent; crony:他把自己的～之人安插在关键岗位。He placed his cronies at vital posts. ❸ true thoughts and feelings:敢布～ venture to air my opinions

腹心之患 fùxīnzhīhuàn disease in one's vital organ; serious hidden trouble or danger:吏治腐败是该国的～。Official corruption was a hidden scourge for that country.

腹议 fùyì 〈书面〉keep one's criticism or opinion (of sb.) to oneself

腹胀 fùzhàng abdominal distension

腹足 fùzú 〈动物〉abdominal foot or leg; proleg

腹足类 fùzúlèi 〈动物〉gastropod

鳆

fù

鳆鱼 fùyú abalone

付[1]

fù ❶ hand or turn over; commit; give:托～他人保管 commit sth. to sb.'s care /交～使用 turn over for use /～诸实施 put into practice; carry out /见条～书 give the book to the bearer on receiving the note ❷ pay:～邮资 pay postal fee /～现金 pay cash /缴～水电费 pay for water and electricity /费用～讫 charges paid ❸ (Fù) a surname

付[2]

fù *see* "副[2]" fù

付丙 fùbǐng *also* "付丙丁"〈书面〉burn (a letter, etc.):阅毕,即请～。After reading the letter, please burn it immediately.

付出 fùchū pay; expend:～二百万元 pay two million *yuan* /～牺牲 make sacrifice /～血汗 (get sth.) by the sweat of one's brow/为了保卫国家主权,我们将不惜～任何代价。We'll defend the sovereignty of our country at any cost.

付方 fùfāng *also* "贷方" dàifāng 〈会计〉credit side; credit

付刊 fùkān hand over (a manuscript) for printing; send to the press

付款 fùkuǎn pay a sum of money; make payment:货到～ cash on delivery (COD) /凭单～ cash against documents /立即～ instant payment /～不足 insufficient payment /～条件 terms of payment

付款凭证 fùkuǎn píngzhèng payment voucher; payment certificate

付款人 fùkuǎnrén payer; drawee

付排 fùpái 〈印刷〉send to the compositor

付讫 fùqì (of a bill) paid:～支票 paid check; cancelled check /邮资～ postage paid

付清 fùqīng pay in full; pay off; pay up; clear (a bill or cheque):～账款 account squared /货款一次～。Payment for goods should be made in full.

付托 fùtuō put (sth.) in sb.'s charge; put in trust (of sb.); entrust:把孩子～给保姆照管 leave one's child in the nurse's care /你的～我将尽力完成。I'll do what you've entrusted to me.

付息 fùxī payment of interest:还本～ pay back the capital plus interest

付现 fùxiàn pay in cash; make cash payment:～折口 cash discount /～自运〈商业〉cash and carry

付型 fùxíng 〈印刷〉turn the type plate into paper mould after composing and proofreading; make paper moulds or matrices

付印 fùyìn ❶ send to the press ❷ turn over to the printing shop (after proofreading):校对完毕,可以～了。It has been proofread and can now be turned over to the printing shop.

付邮 fùyóu take to the post; send by mail; post; mail

付与 fùyǔ give; pay:～相当的报酬 give reasonable pay

付账 fùzhàng pay a bill; foot a bill

付之一炬 fùzhī-yījù *also* "付诸一炬" commit to the flames; set on fire; burn:外国侵略者把这座皇家园林掠劫一空,然后～。The foreign invaders looted the imperial garden and then committed it to the flames. /他所有的藏书已被～。His whole book collection is burnt up.

付之一笑 fùzhī-yīxiào laugh away; dismiss sth. with a smile:对这些无端指责他只是～。He dismissed these unfounded charges with a mere smile.

付诸东流 fùzhū-dōngliú *also* "付之东流";"付之流水" be gone with the eastward-flowing streams — have all one's efforts wasted; come to naught:数年心血,～。Years of strenuous effort all came to naught.

付梓 fùzǐ 〈书面〉turn over (a manuscript) for printing; send to press

咐

fù *see* "吩咐" fēnfu; "嘱咐" zhǔfu

祔

fù ❶ ancient sacrificial rite ❷〈书面〉bury in the same grave; bury together

鲋

fù 〈古语〉crucian carp

see also "涸辙之鲋" hézhézhīfù

附(坿)

fù ❶ add; attach; append; enclose:药方另纸～上。The prescription is attached hereto on a separate piece of paper. /随信～寄近照一张。With this letter I enclose a recent photograph. *or* Enclosed please find a recent photo. ❷ get close to; be close by; be near:把耳朵～在窗口,听听里面的动静 get close to the window to eavesdrop on what is happening inside ❸ attach oneself to; depend on; comply with:皮之不存,毛将焉～? With the skin gone, what can the hair adhere to?

附白 fùbái appended note:书正付印,错讹只好在书后～订正。The book has been sent to the press. All we can do is to add an errata at the end of the book.

附笔 fùbǐ additional note; postscript (PS):这个文件上另有～。There was a postscript to the document.

附从 fùcóng comply with; yield to; agree to:～合同 contract of adhesion

附带 fùdài ❶ in passing; incidentally; by the way: ~补充一点。By the way, I'd like to add one more point. /这个问题也~讨论一下。This issue can be discussed in passing. ❷ attach; append: 不~条件的援助 assistance (*or* aid) with no strings attached; unqualified aid/书后~着答案。The answers are placed at the end of the book. ❸ subsidiary; supplementary; additional: ~的劳动 supplementary labour /~的任务 subsidiary task /~的损失 incidental damage /~条款 institute clause

附点 fùdiǎn 〈音乐〉dot: ~音符 dotted note

附耳 fù'ěr move close to sb.'s ear: 他们俩在墙角~低语。The two were whispering in the corner.

附凤攀龙 fùfèng-pānlóng *also* "攀龙附凤" curry favour with people of power and position; seek the patronage of influential people

附睾 fùgāo 〈生理〉epididymis; parastata

附睾炎 fùgāoyán epididymitis

附和 fùhè chime in with; echo; parrot: 随声~ chime in with others /她总是~她母亲的话。She is always echoing what her mother says.

附会 fùhuì *also* "傅会" fùhuì draw wrong conclusions by false analogy; make an irrelevant comparison: 牵强~ draw a forced analogy /穿凿~ give strained interpretations and draw farfetched analogies /神话故事是绝对不能~为史实的。Stories in mythology can not be interpreted as historical facts.

附骥 fùjì *also* "附骥尾" win fame by attaching oneself to a bigwig; ride to success on sb.'s coattails; bask in reflected glory: 名人、要人的子孙多有~而显者。Children of eminent or influential people often bask in the reflected glory of their ancestors.

附加 fùjiā ❶ add; append; attach: 协议后面还~有几项说明。A few explanatory notes are attached at the end of the agreement. /还得~几句话以免误解。Some further explanations are needed to avoid possible misunderstanding. ❷ additional; appended; attached: 请注意备忘录后面~的说明。Please take note of the instructions appended to the memorandum.

附加费 fùjiāfèi surcharge; extracharge; additional charge

附加福利 fùjiā fúlì fringe benefit

附加工资 fùjiā gōngzī supplementary wage; extra wage

附加股息 fùjiā gǔxī extra dividend; supplementary dividend

附加税 fùjiāshuì surtax; supertax; additional tax; additional duty

附加条款 fùjiā tiáokuǎn additional article or clause; memorandum clause

附加文件 fùjiā wénjiàn 〈外交〉appended document

附加险 fùjiāxiǎn additional risk; accessory risk

附加刑 fùjiāxíng 〈法律〉accessory punishment

附加议定书 fùjiā yìdìngshū 〈外交〉additional protocol

附加资本 fùjiā zīběn additional paid-in capital

附件 fùjiàn ❶ appendix; annex: 这个文件有三个~。This document has three appendixes. /参看~二。Refer to Annex Two. ❷ enclosure (in a document, etc.) ❸〈机械〉accessory; attachment: 车床~ lathe accessories /计算机~ computer attachments (*or* peripherals)

附件炎 fùjiànyán 〈医学〉adnexitis; annexitis

附近 fùjìn ❶ nearby; adjacent; neighbouring: ~城镇 neighbouring (*or* adjacent) towns /~公共场所 nearby public places /~影剧院 nearby cinemas and theatres /敌机正在轰炸~一座桥梁。The enemy plane was bombing a bridge close by. ❷ close to; in the vicinity of: ~没有旅店。There is no hotel in the vicinity. /他就住在学校~。He lives close to school. /我家地处闹市区,~都是大商店。My home is in the downtown area, with big stores all about. /公共汽车站就在~,走几分钟就可以到了。The bus stop is not far from here, and you can get there in a few minutes.

附丽 fùlì 〈书面〉rely on; attach oneself to; adhere to: 无所~ have nothing to count on /~权贵 attach oneself to persons in power

附录 fùlù appendix: 正文后有两个~。There are two appendixes (*or* appendices) to the text.

附逆 fùnì throw in one's lot with the rebels

附上 fùshàng enclosed herewith: ~征订单一份。An order sheet is enclosed herewith. /~使用说明书一份。Enclosed please find a sheet of specifications.

附设 fùshè have as an attached institution: 商店~家电维修部。A department of maintenance for household appliances is attached to the shop.

附身 fùshēn 〈迷信〉(of ghost, demon, or evil spirit) bedevil a human body; (of person) be possessed (by ghosts or spirits)

附生 fùshēng (of a plant) grow on another plant but not be parasitic on it: 石斛多~在树杈或岩石上。Noble dendrobium mostly grows on the crotch of a tree or rocks.

附生兰 fùshēnglán 〈植物〉tropical orchid; epiphytic orchid; epidendrum; epidendron

附生植物 fùshēng zhíwù epiphyte

附属 fùshǔ subsidiary; auxiliary; attached; affiliated: ~机构 subsidiary body /~工厂 auxiliary factory /这所学院~于经贸部。This institute is affiliated with (*or* attached to) the Ministry of Foreign Trade and Economic Cooperation (MOFTEC).

附属地 fùshǔdì dependent territory; dependency

附属国 fùshǔguó dependency; dependent state

附属品 fùshǔpǐn accessory; appendage

附属小学 fùshǔ xiǎoxué *see* "附小"

附属协定 fùshǔ xiédìng collateral agreement

附属债券 fùshǔ zhàiquàn subordinated debt

附属账户 fùshǔ zhànghù adjunct account; auxiliary account; absorption account

附属中学 fùshǔ zhōngxué *see* "附中"

附送 fùsòng give complimentary gifts: 购买收录机一台,~录音带一盘。Buy a cassette recorder and you'll get a cassette tape for free.

附随 fùsuí ❶ attached; subsidiary; supplementary: ~因素 supplementary factor ❷ depend on; attach oneself to; adhere to; stick to

附体 fùtǐ 〈迷信〉(of ghost, demon, evil spirit, etc.) bedevil a human body; (of person) be possessed (by ghosts or spirits): 吓得魂不~ be scared out of one's wits

附图 fùtú attached map or drawing; figure: 具体位置,详见~。See the diagram below for its specific location.

附息 fùxī cum dividend

附小 fùxiǎo (short for 附属小学) attached or affiliated primary school

附言 fùyán postscript (PS)

附议 fùyì second a motion; support a proposal: 这个提案有五十多位代表~。More than fifty delegates supported (*or* seconded) the motion.

附议者 fùyìzhě seconder

附庸 fùyōng ❶ dependency; vassal: ~国 vassal state /处于~地位 in the position of a dependency ❷ appendage; hanger-on

附庸风雅 fùyōng-fēngyǎ (of officials, landlords, merchants, etc.) mingle with men of letters and pose as a lover of culture; behave like a connoisseur of art and literary works when one is really not

附载 fùzǎi subsidiary note; appendix

附则 fùzé supplementary article (appended to a treaty, decree, etc.)

附肢 fùzhī 〈动物〉appendage

附识 fùzhì note appended to an article, book, etc.; supplementary note

附中 fùzhōng (short for 附属中学) attached or affiliated secondary school: 北师大二~ No. 2 Secondary School attached to the Beijing Normal University

附注 fùzhù note appended to a book, etc.; annotation

附赘悬疣 fùzhuì-xuányóu tumours and wens — redundant and useless things; superfluities: 这部小说提炼不够,从语言到情节~不少。The novel is lacking in refinement and has quite a few superfluities in terms of both language and plot.

附着 fùzhuó adhere to; cling to; stick to: 晶莹的露珠~在花和叶上。The glittering dews shone on the flowers and leaves.

附着力 fùzhuólì 〈物理〉adhesive force; adhesion

附子 fùzǐ 〈中药〉monkshood

驸

fù horse harnessed by the side of a team

驸马 fùmǎ emperor's son-in-law

阜

fù 〈书面〉❶ earthen mound ❷ abundant: 百物殷~。There is plenty of everything. /物~民丰。Products abound and the people live in clover.

服

fù (of Chinese medicine) dose: 他吃了三~药病就好了。He was fully recovered after taking three doses of Chinese medicine.

see also fú

F

负 fù ❶ carry on the back or shoulder; shoulder: ～土筑堤 carry earth to build an embankment /背～伤员 carry the wounded on one's back /肩～重物 shoulder a heavy object ❷ bear; take up: 肩～重托 bear (*or* shoulder) severe burden /～法律责任 undertake legal responsibility ❸ rely on; have at one's back: 自～ conceited /～贵好权 take to scheming on the strength of one's high position ❹ suffer; sustain: 身～重伤 suffer (*or* sustain) serious injuries; get wounded severely ❺ enjoy: 久～盛名 have long enjoyed a good reputation; have long been famous ❻ owe; be indebted: *see* "～债" ❼ fail (in one's duty, obligation, etc.); disappoint; betray: 忘恩～义 be ungrateful /有～厚望 fail to come up to others' expectations; let sb. down ❽ lose (a battle, game, etc.); be defeated: 一胜一～ win a round and lose one /以二比三～于对方 lose the match 2:3 /胜～尚在未知之数。The result is uncertain. ❾〈数学〉minus; negative: ～分数 negative fraction /～八点八 minus eight point eight (－8.8) ❿〈电学〉negative: *see* "～电"

负才使气 fùcái-shǐqì conceited and self-willed; opinionated and wayward

负戴 fùdài 〈书面〉carry things on the back or head — do physical labour

负担 fùdān ❶ bear; carry; shoulder: ～全部医疗费用 bear all the medical expenses /～不起 can not afford /办公室的杂务可由我来～。I can take all the chores in the office. /母亲～全部家务劳动。Mother does all the housework. ❷ burden; load; weight; strain; encumbrance: 经济～ economic burden /精神～ mental strain /沉重的思想～ sth. weighing heavily on one's mind /减轻农民～ lighten the peasants' load /儿子结婚的费用成了全家最大的～。The expenditure of the son's marriage became the greatest encumbrance to the family.

负电 fùdiàn *also* "阴电" yīndiàn negative electricity

负电荷 fùdiànhè negative (electric) charge

负电极 fùdiànjí cathode; negative electrode

负电子 fùdiànzǐ electron; negatron

负反馈 fùfǎnkuì negative feedback; inverse feedback; reverse feedback

负贩 fùfàn pedlar or hawker who carries his goods on a shoulder pole or on his back

负号 fùhào 〈数学〉negative sign (－)

负荷 fùhè ❶〈书面〉bear; shoulder: ～重任 shoulder an important responsibility ❷ *also* "负载"; "载荷" zàihè load; performance capacity: 低～ underload; under capacity /满～ fullload; at full capacity /超～ overload; above capacity

负极 fùjí 〈电学〉negative pole

负笈 fùjí 〈书面〉carry a case of books — leave home to seek knowledge; be away from home pursuing studies: ～从师 be away from home to study under a master /～游学 pursue one's studies in a place far away from home

负加速度 fùjiāsùdù 〈物理〉negative acceleration

负荆请罪 fùjīng-qǐngzuì proffer a birch and ask for a flogging — make a humble and heartfelt apology: 这件事情很对不起你们，我特意来～。I'm very sorry about what happened. I've come here especially to offer my humble apology.

负疚 fùjiù 〈书面〉feel conscience-stricken; be apologetic; feel guilty: 他托付的事没有办好，我很有～之感。I felt profoundly apologetic to him for failing to do well what he had entrusted to me.

负累 fùlěi ❶ burden; load: 我们家里人口多，～大。There are many mouths to feed in our family and the burden is heavy. ❷ implicate; involve; get sb. into trouble

负离子 fùlízǐ *also* "阴离子" yīnlízǐ 〈物理〉anion

负利率 fùlìlǜ negative interest rate

负利息 fùlìxī negative interest

负面 fùmiàn negative: ～影响 unfavourable influence /分析事情正面和～ analyse the positive and negative aspect of a matter

负片 fùpiàn 〈摄影〉negative

负气 fùqì (do sth.) in a fit of pique: ～离座而去 leave one's seat angrily /～出走 leave home in a fit of pique

负情 fùqíng unfaithful in love: ～的人 unfaithful lover

负屈 fùqū suffer a grievance or injustice

负屈衔冤 fùqū-xiányuān *also* "负屈含冤" be wronged on a false charge and have no hope of redress

负伤 fùshāng sustain an injury; be wounded: 在战斗中～ be wounded in a battle

负手 fùshǒu clasp one's hands behind one's back: ～散步 take a walk (*or* stroll) with one's hands clasped behind one's back

负鼠 fùshǔ 〈动物〉opossum (*Didelphis lanigera*)

负数 fùshù 〈数学〉negative number

负透镜 fùtòujìng 〈物理〉minus lens; negative lens

负像 fùxiàng 〈物理〉negative image

负心 fùxīn untrue (esp. in love); ungrateful; heartless: ～薄幸 be inconstant (*or* fickle) in love

负薪救火 fùxīn-jiùhuǒ carry firewood to put out a fire — adopt a wrong method to deal with a situation and end up by making it worse

负薪之忧 fùxīnzhīyōu 〈婉词〉be ill; be indisposed: 刘子闲居，有～。Mr Liu was ill and stayed at home to recuperate.

负暄 fùxuān 〈书面〉get warm by taking the sun in winter: ～北窗下 get warm from sunning oneself under the north window

负压 fùyā negative pressure: ～铸造 〈冶金〉V-process

负隅顽抗 fùyú-wánkàng *also* "负嵎顽抗" (of an enemy) put up desperate resistance with one's back to the wall: 这股敌军～，死不投降。The enemy put up a frantic struggle and refused to surrender.

负约 fùyuē break a promise; go back on one's word: 第一次见面，千万不要～。Don't break a promise, especially for the first appointment.

负载 fùzài *also* "负荷" 〈电学〉load: 高峰～ peak load /工作～ operating load /～调整 load regulation /～功率 bearing power

负责 fùzé ❶ be responsible for; be in charge of; bear responsibility for: 他～这里的工作。He is in charge of the work here. /出了事谁～? Who will be responsible if anything happens? /警方应对公众～。The police should be accountable to the public. /由此产生的一切后果由你方～。Your side will be held responsible for all the consequences arising therefrom. ❷ conscientious: 工作认真～ be conscientious in one's work

负责干部 fùzé gànbù cadre in a leading position; responsible cadre; cadre in charge

负责人 fùzérén person in charge; leading official

负增长 fùzēngzhǎng 〈经济〉negative growth: ～率 negative growth rate

负债 fùzhài ❶ be in debt; incur debts: ～累累 be heavily in debt; be over head and ears in debt /～四千元 owe a debt of 4,000 *yuan* ❷ liabilities: 资产与～ assets and liabilities

负债管理 fùzhài guǎnlǐ liability management

负债净额 fùzhài jìng'é net indebtedness

负债率 fùzhàilǜ debt ratio

负债准备金 fùzhài zhǔnbèijīn liability reserve

负值 fùzhí 〈数学〉negative value; negative

负指数 fùzhǐshù 〈数学〉negative exponent

负重 fùzhòng ❶ bear a (heavy) load or weight: ～行军 loaded march ❷ shoulder an important task

see also "忍辱负重" rěnrǔ-fùzhòng

负重训练 fùzhòng xùnliàn weight training

负重致远 fùzhòng-zhìyuǎn walk a long way carrying a heavy burden — be able to shoulder heavy responsibilities

负阻抗 fùzǔkàng 〈电子〉negative impedance: ～变换器 negative impedance converter /～放大器 negative impedance amplifier

负罪 fùzuì 〈书面〉plead guilty to the charge or accusation; bear the blame

蝜 fù

蝜蝂 fùbǎn legendary little insect, keen on carrying heavy weights

妇(婦) fù ❶ woman ❷ married woman: 新～ newly married woman /主～ housewife, hostess /农～ peasant woman /孕～ pregnant woman ❸ wife: 夫～ man and wife /夫唱～随 harmony between husband and wife

妇产科 fùchǎnkē department of gynaecology and obstetrics: ～医生 gynaecologist

妇产医院 fùchǎn yīyuàn hospital for gynaecology and obstetrics

妇代会 fùdàihuì (short for 妇女代表大会) conference of women representatives; women's conference

妇道 fùdào 〈旧语〉female virtues; rules of proper female behaviour

妇道 fùdao 〈旧语〉women; womenfolk

妇道人家 fùdao-rénjia 〈贬义〉women; womenfolk
妇弟 fùdì younger brother of one's wife; brother-in-law
妇姑勃豀 fùgū-bóxī squabble between mother-in-law and daughter-in-law; domestic row; petty wrangle
妇科 fùkē (department of) gynaecology: ～疾病 gynaecological disease / ～检查 gynaecological check-up
妇科病房 fùkē bìngfáng gynaecological ward
妇科医生 fùkē yīshēng gynaecologist
妇联 fùlián (short for 妇女联合会) Women's Federation: 全国～ All-China Women's Federation
妇女 fùnǚ woman: ～组织 women's organization / ～半边天 women hold up half the sky; women are just as essential as men
妇女病 fùnǚbìng women's disease; gynaecological disease
妇女节 Fùnǚjié (short for 国际劳动妇女节) International Working Women's Day
妇女解放运动 fùnǚ jiěfàng yùndòng women's liberation (movement); women's lib
妇女联合会 fùnǚ liánhéhuì *see* "妇联"
妇人 fùrén married woman
妇人之仁 fùrénzhīrén 〈贬义〉woman's soft nature; mawkish sentimentality: 有～，无丈夫之决 have a woman's sentimentality while lacking a man's resolve
妇孺 fù-rú women and children: 此事～皆知。Even women and children are well aware of it.
妇婴 fù-yīng women and infants or babies
妇幼 fù-yòu women and children: ～卫生 maternity and child hygiene / ～保健 maternity and child care / ～保健站 health centre for women and children

G

gā

夹(夾) gā
see also jiā; jiá
夹肢窝 gāzhiwō *also* "胳肢窝" gāzhiwō armpit

嘎 gā 〈象声〉screech: 汽车～地一声刹住了。The car stopped with a screech.
see also gá; gǎ
嘎巴 gābā 〈象声〉crack; snap: 枯干的树枝～一声断了。A dry twig snapped.
嘎巴 gāba 〈方言〉form into a crust; crust: 瞧，浆糊都～在你裤腿上了。Look; the paste has crusted on your trouser leg. /饭粒都～在锅底上了。The bottom of the pot is all covered with rice crust.
嘎巴儿 gābar 〈方言〉(of porridge, paste, etc.) crust (on utensils, etc.): 衣裳上有粥～。There were porridge crusts on the clothes.
嘎嘣 gābēng 〈象声〉crunch: 铁蚕豆嚼得～响。He was crunching roasted broad beans noisily.
嘎嘣脆 gābēngcuì *also* "嘎巴脆"〈方言〉❶ crisp: 锅巴吃起来～。Crust of cooked rice is crunchy to eat. ❷ clear-cut; forthright; straightforward: 他说话办事一向是～。He is always straightforward in whatever he says or does.
嘎噔 gādēng 〈象声〉crack; snap: 突然听到～一声，麻绳断了。The jute rope broke with a snap. /他的回答使我心里～一震。His reply gave me a start.
嘎嘎 gāgā *also* "呷呷" gāgā 〈象声〉sound made by ducks or wild geese; honk; quack: 雁鸣～，打破了沉寂。The honking of the wild geese broke the silence.
see also gága
嘎啦 gālā 〈象声〉rumbling sound: ～一声响雷 loud crash of thunder /北风呼呼地刮着，刮得窗户～～山响。The windows were rattling in the fierce north wind. /一辆马车～～地迎面驶来。A horse-drawn carriage came rumbling up.
嘎然 gārán ❶ loud noise; ringing sound: 一群大雁～飞鸣而过。A flock of wild geese flew whistling past. ❷ (of a sound) stop abruptly: 电话～中断。The line was disconnected abruptly. /笑声～而止。The laughter ended all of a sudden.
嘎渣儿 gāzhar 〈方言〉❶ scab; crust ❷ crust of cooked rice; rice crust
嘎吱 gāzhī 〈象声〉creak: 独轮车在山路上～～地走着。The wheelbarrow was creaking along the mountain path. /他翻来覆去，弄得床板～作响。The bed squeaked as he tossed from side to side.

呷 gā
see also xiā
呷呷 gāgā *see* "嘎嘎" gāgā
呷西 gāxī bottom-most slave in the Liangshan (凉山) region, Sichuan Province, in the old days

胳 gā
see also gē; gé
胳肢窝 gāzhiwō *see* "夹肢窝" gāzhiwō

旮 gā
旮旮旯旯儿 gāga-lálár 〈方言〉every nook and crany; all the corners: ～都找遍了。Every corner of the room has been searched.
旮旯儿 gālár 〈方言〉❶ nook; corner: 墙～ corner of a wall ❷ out-of-the-way place: 背～ inaccessible recess

咖 gā
see also kā
咖喱 gālí curry: ～鸡 curried chicken /～牛肉 beef curry
咖喱粉 gālífěn curry powder

伽 gā
see also jiā; qié
伽利略 Gālìlüè Galileo Galilei (1564-1642), Italian astronomer, mathematician and physicist: ～望远镜 Galilean telescope /～卫星 Galilean satellites (the four largest moons of Jupiter discovered by Galileo in 1610)
伽马 gāmǎ gamma, third letter (Γ, γ) of the Greek alphabet
伽马放射疗法 gāmǎ fàngshè liáofǎ 〈医学〉gammatherapy
伽马射线 gāmǎ shèxiàn *also* "γ射线"〈物理〉gamma ray

gá

轧 gá 〈方言〉❶ press hard against each other; squeeze: 这儿太～了。It's too crowded here. ❷ make (friends): ～朋友 make friends with sb. ❸ check: ～账 check the accounts
see also yà; zhá
轧轧 gágá 〈象声〉(of machine, wheel, etc.) creak: 这辆车不行了，骑着～响。This bike is no good any more, for it creaks when ridden.
轧姘头 gá pīntou 〈方言〉have sex with sb. other than one's spouse; cohabit with sb.

噶 gá
噶举派 Gájǔpài Kargyupa, usu. called the White Sect, of Lamaism in the Tibet Autonomous Region
噶伦 gálún high official in Tibetan local government in former times
噶厦 gáxià local government of Tibet before 1959, made up of four high officials (噶伦)

嘎 gá
see also gā; gǎ
嘎调 gádiào very high pitch in Beijing opera singing
嘎嘎 gága *see* "尜尜" gága
see also gāgā

钆 gá 〈化学〉gadolinium (Gd)

尜 gá
尜尜 gága *also* "嘎嘎" gága ❶ *also* "尜儿" top-like toy ❷ shaped like tops; top-shaped: ～汤 *gaga* soup (cooked with maize flour sections)

gǎ

嘎 gǎ *see* "生" gǎ

see also gā; gá

嘎七马八 gǎqī-mǎbā *also* "嘎七杂八"〈方言〉odds and ends; medley; mess:棚里面堆放着～的一大堆农具。There is an odd lot of farm implements in the shed. /他～地买回一大堆食物。He bought back a hotchpotch (*or* hodgepodge) of food.

嘎杂子 gǎzázi *see* "生杂子" gǎzázi

嘎子 gǎzi *see* "生子" gǎzi

生 gǎ *also* "嘎" gǎ〈方言〉❶ eccentric; odd; bad-tempered: 那人特～。That fellow is very freakish indeed. ❷ naughty:～小子 naughty boy

生古 gǎgu〈方言〉strange; peculiar; eccentric:老太太脾气特～。The old lady is an eccentric.

生杂子 gǎzázi *also* "嘎杂子" gǎzázi〈方言〉eccentric and scoundrelly person

生子 gǎzi *also* "嘎子" gǎzi〈方言〉naughty boy:听这名字,瞧这模样,一准是个小～。Judging by his name and appearance he must be a mischievous boy.

尕 gǎ〈方言〉small; little:～娃 small child

gà

尬 gà *see* "尴尬" gāngà

gāi

该[1] gāi ❶ ought to; should:你这么大了,～懂事一些。At your age you ought to know better. /本～如此。That's just as it should be. /你太累了,～好好休息一下。You need a good rest, as you're tired out (*or* dog-tired). /～出发了。It's time we were leaving (*or* starting off). ❷ fall to sb.; be sb.'s turn (to do sth.):～你试了。It's your turn to try now. /下次～着你值班。You'll be on duty next time. ❸ deserve;merit:他认为自己～享受这种荣誉。He thought he fully deserved the honour. /活～! 偷鸡不成反蚀把米。It serves him right! He went for wool and came home shorn. ❹ probably; most likely; it is expected:明年这个时候,这条高速公路就～完工了。By this time next year, this express highway will have been completed. /再过半年,我就～毕业了。I'm due to graduate in six months. ❺ *used in exclamatory sentences for emphasis*:我要能跟你一块儿去,那～多好哇! If only I could go with you! /她给病人动手术已连续好几个小时了,～多累呀! She must be exhausted having been operating on the patient for several hours running.

该[2] gāi owe:我～你多少钱? How much do I owe you? /这笔钱我先～着。I'll pay back the money later on.

该[3] gāi this; that; above-mentioned; said:～项 this item /～处 that place /～工厂是本地最大的。The said factory is the biggest in this locality. /～大学有二十多个专业。The (above-mentioned) university has over 20 disciplines. /～地区经济落后。The area in question is backward economically.

该[4] gāi *see* "赅" gāi

该班儿 gāibānr〈方言〉be on duty in turn; be on shift:今天晚上我～。I'll be on night shift today.

该博 gāibó *see* "赅博" gāibó

该当 gāidāng ought to; should:～如此。That's as it should be. /我们～多为祖国做些贡献。We should make a greater contribution to our motherland. /～何罪? What punishment do you think you deserve?

该欠 gāiqiàn owe sb. sth.; be in debt:我量入为出,从来不～别人的。I live within my means, never contracting any debt.

该死 gāisǐ〈口语〉*used to express resentment or anger*:～的! Bastard! *or* Son of a bitch! / 你这～的笨蛋! You damn fool! /～的天气! What abominable weather! /～! 我又忘带出入证了。Oh, blast! I've forgotten my pass again. /～的,这班人又来了。Oh, drat! It's these people again.

该应 gāiyīng〈方言〉❶ *also* "应该" should; ought to ❷ *see* "该着"

该账 gāizhàng be in debt

该着 gāizháo as luck would have it; be destined; be decreed by fate:出门就摔跤,～我倒霉。As luck would have it, I tripped and fell as soon as I stepped out.

垓[1] gāi〈古语〉one hundred million

垓[2] gāi *see* "垓下"

垓下 Gāixià name of an ancient place in today's Lingbi (灵璧) County, Anhui Province:～之战 Battle of Gaixia, 202 BC, final battle between Chu and Han, won by the latter

垓心 gāixīn〈旧语〉centre or middle of a battleground

赅 gāi〈书面〉❶ serve as (sth. else);include:举一～百 give one instance to illustrate a hundred; infer the rest from what is already known; to name only a few /以偏～全 know the part and you know the whole ❷ complete; comprehensive; all-inclusive:言简意～ brief but sufficient;concise; succinct

赅备 gāibèi〈书面〉complete; perfect

赅博 gāibó *also* "该博" gāibó〈书面〉broad and profound; erudite

赅括 gāikuò〈书面〉summarise; generalize

gǎi

胲 gǎi〈书面〉cheek flesh

改 gǎi ❶ change; convert; transform:～塑料包装为纸包 switch from plastic to paper packaging /脾气～好了 become better-tempered /作息时间～了。The work schedule has changed. /她的发型～了。She has altered (*or* changed) her hair style. /这间房子～成仓库了。The room has been converted into a warehouse. ❷ alter; revise;polish:把这件大衣～瘦点儿。Make this coat a bit tighter. /文章～得很简练。The article (*or* essay) has become very concise after the polishing. ❸ correct; rectify; remedy;put right:～作业 correct and grade the students' homework /痛～前非 sincerely mend one's ways; thoroughly rectify one's errors /口吃的毛病很难～。It's difficult to get rid of stammering. ❹ (followed by a verb) change or switch over to:由火车～乘轮船 change from a train to a steamboat /时间紧迫,我们～乘飞机。Since we were pressed for time, we travelled by plane instead. ❺ (Gǎi) a surname

改版 gǎibǎn〈印刷〉❶ change the layout of a printed sheet ❷ change or correct a set page

改扮 gǎibàn disguise oneself as:为了侦察敌情,他～成一个走街串巷的算命先生。To gather intelligence about the enemy he disguised himself as a fortune-teller going from street to street.

改编 gǎibiān ❶ adapt; rearrange; revise:把小说～成电视剧 adapt a novel for TV /这部电影根据同名小说～。The film is adapted from a novel of the same name. /这支民歌～成了轻音乐。The melody of this folk song has been rearranged as a composition of light music. /这部词典已彻底～。The dictionary has been completely revised. ❷ reorganize; redesignate:～军队 reorganize an army /这个师正～为加强旅。The division was redesignated as a reinforced brigade.

改变 gǎibiàn change; alter; transform:～工作作风 change the style of work /人们的工作态度～了。People's attitude towards work has changed. /狼的本性是～不了的。The natural instincts of a wolf are unalterable. *or* The leopard cannot change its spots. /我们花了好些年才～这里的落后面貌。It took us years to rid this locality of its backwardness.

改变符号 gǎibiàn fúhào reindex;change signs

改产 gǎichǎn manufacture products other than those being produced:～销路好的产品 switch to the manufacture of marketable goods

改常 gǎicháng unusual; abnormal; perverse; strange:他今天有点儿～,不像以往那么沉稳。He is a bit abnormal today, without his usual composure.

改朝换代 gǎicháo-huàndài change of dynasty or regime; dynastic change:我看那个国家是到了～的时候了。I think that country is on the threshold of a new dynasty.

G

改称 gǎichēng change the name or title; rename

改窜 gǎicuàn alter; tamper with; falsify: ~文件 tamper with documents

改道 gǎidào ❶ change one's route; reroute: 他们决定~西行。They decided to change their route and head west. ❷ (of a river) change its course: 历史上, 淮河曾几次~。The Huaihe River has changed its course several times over the centuries.

改点 gǎidiǎn change a timetable or schedule: 这趟火车~了。The train has been rescheduled.

改掉 gǎidiào change; give up; discard: ~奢侈习惯 rid oneself of lavish habits /~官僚主义作风 shake off one's bureaucratic style of work

改订 gǎidìng reformulate; revise; rewrite: ~规章制度 draw up new rules and regulations /~价格政策 revise the price policy/ ~税则 alter the tariff /~计划 redraft a plan

改定 gǎidìng change and decide on; amend; revise; change (a previously set instruction or plan): ~工作程序表 revise the work (*or* project) schedule /文章题目是老师~的。The new title of the essay is decided on by the teacher.

改动 gǎidòng change; polish; alter; modify: 规定没有任何~。The rules remain unchanged. /你的论文稍作~便可出版。With some modification your dissertation will be fit for publication.

改恶从善 gǎi'è-cóngshàn abandon evil and do good; atone for one's crime and turn over a new leaf; mend one's ways: 只要他们~, 都有自己的前途。Provided that they give up evil and return to good, they will have a future before them.

改革 gǎigé reform: ~不合理的规章制度 reform irrational rules and regulations /经济体制~ reform of the economic structure; restructuring of the economy /土地~ land (*or* agrarian) reform /文字~ reform of a writing system /民主~ democratic reforms /彻底~ make a thorough reform; reform from top to bottom /进行政治~ institute political reforms /~教育制度 revamp the system of education /~开放政策 the policy of reform and opening to the outside world (*or* opening-up); the reform and open policy

改革派 gǎigépài reformers; reformists

改观 gǎiguān change in appearance; take on a new look: 有了新的领导, 局面就会~。With the new leaders at the helm, things are sure to improve (*or* look up). /自从修了水电站, 这里面貌大为~。This area has taken on a new look since the hydroelectric power station was built.

改过 gǎiguò mend one's ways; correct one's mistakes: 勇于~ be ready to correct one's mistakes; not hesitate to overcome one's errors

改过自新 gǎiguò-zìxīn correct one's errors and make a fresh start; mend one's ways; turn over a new leaf: 大家希望你~, 做个有益于社会的人。We all hope you'll mend your ways and become a useful person to society.

改行 gǎiháng change one's profession or occupation, or trade: 由工人~经商 quit one's job as a worker and go into business /我年纪大了, 不便~。I am much too old to switch over to another profession.

改换 gǎihuàn change; replace; substitute one for another: ~地点 change the place; move away; move to a new place (*or* address)/~名称 rename /有轨电车~成了无轨电车。Trolleybuses have replaced trams.

改换门庭 gǎihuàn-méntíng ❶ change one's family status: 他总想捞个一官半职, ~。He tried hard to become an official so that he could elevate his family status. ❷ switch allegiance to a new master or patron: 你何不~, 另找靠山呢? Why don't you find a new patron?

改悔 gǎihuǐ repent: 不自~ refuse to repent; be unrepentant /死不~的罪犯 die-hard (*or* incorrigible) criminal

改嫁 gǎijià (of a woman) remarry

改建 gǎijiàn reconstruct; rebuild: ~校舍 reconstruct a school building

改醮 gǎijiào 〈旧语〉 *see* "改嫁"

改进 gǎijìn ❶ improve; make better; better: ~工作作风 improve one's work style /街道卫生大有~。The streets are much cleaner than before. ❷ 〈机械〉 modify: ~型火箭 modified version of a rocket /~型气冷反应堆 〈原子能〉 advanced gas-cooled reactor

改口 gǎikǒu ❶ correct oneself (in conversation); withdraw or modify one's previous remark; change one's tune: 他发现说漏了嘴, 连忙~。He hastened to correct himself the moment he discovered he had made a slip of the tongue. /他正说得起劲, 见老王进来, 便~说别的了。He had been holding forth on the subject, but changed the topic when he saw Lao Wang come in. ❷ address sb. in a different way: 小兰已和你哥哥结婚, 你应~称嫂子。You should call Xiao Lan sister-in-law now that she has married your brother.

改良 gǎiliáng ❶ improve; ameliorate: ~农机具 improve farm implements ❷ reform: ~派 reformists ❸ 〈冶金〉 modify: ~合金 modified alloy /~式等温淬火 modified austempering /~树脂 〈化工〉 modified resin

改良主义 gǎiliángzhǔyì reformism: 在清末, ~的道路没有走通。The road of reformism proved to be an impasse in the late Qing Dynasty.

改名换姓 gǎimíng-huànxìng change one's name and surname; disguise oneself under an alias: 逃犯~, 潜伏起来。The escaped convict went into hiding with an assumed name.

改抹 gǎimǒ alter; tamper: 信上有几处~的痕迹。There are a few traces of alteration in the letter.

改判 gǎipàn 〈法律〉 change the original sentence; commute; amend a judgement: 由六个月监禁~驱逐出境。Imprisonment for six months was commuted to deportation.

改平 gǎipíng level off; make flat and even

改平位置 gǎipíng wèizhì level-off position

改期 gǎiqī change the date; reschedule: 研讨会~举行。The seminar has been postponed. /交易会~了。The date set for the trade fair has changed.

改任 gǎirèn change to a new post; have a new appointment: 他~航天工业部部长。He has been transferred to his new post as Minister of Astronautics Industry.

改日 gǎirì *also* "改天" another day; some other day: 咱们~再谈吧。Let's talk it over some other day.

改色 gǎisè ❶ change colour: 秋末冬初, 树木~。The woods change colour at late autumn and early winter. ❷ change countenance; reveal one's feelings: 大敌当前, 面不~ remain calm (*or* keep one's countenance) when confronted with a formidable enemy

改善 gǎishàn improve; better; ameliorate: ~受到损害的形象 spruce up a tarnished image /两国关系开始~。Relations between the two countries have taken a turn for the better. /居住条件一时难有大的~。It takes time to fundamentally improve housing conditions.

改天 gǎitiān *see* "改日"

改天换地 gǎitiān-huàndì transform heaven and earth; change the world; remake nature: 以~的精神全力以赴地建设贫困山区 go all out to develop the poor mountain areas in the spirit of reshaping nature

改头换面 gǎitóu-huànmiàn 〈贬义〉 change the appearance but not the substance; dish up something old in a new form: 这班人~以合法商人身分出现。These people have camouflaged themselves as lawful merchants.

改图 gǎitú 〈书面〉 change a plan: 为了生存, 我们必须~。We must change the plan in order to survive.

改途 gǎitú change a method: 只有~, 才能发展。Only by adopting new approaches can there be development.

改土 gǎitǔ 〈农业〉 improve the soil: 治水~ water control and soil improvement

改土归流 gǎitǔ-guīliú (in the Ming and Qing dynasties) bring the aboriginal chieftains in Yunnan, Guizhou, and Sichuan provinces under the jurisdiction of the central government by giving them regular official titles

改弦更张 gǎixián-gēngzhāng change the string of a musical instrument to make the music more melodious — change over to new ways; make a fresh start; start afresh: 他必须~, 不然将一事无成。He needs to have a new approach to things, otherwise he will get nowhere.

改弦易辙 gǎixián-yìzhé change one's course; strike out on a new path: 他翻然悔悟, ~。He repented and mended his ways.

改线 gǎixiàn alter a (telephone, bus, etc.) line; alter course; reroute

改邪归正 gǎixié-guīzhèng give up evil and return to good; turn over a new leaf: ~, 重新作人 break clean with evil and begin one's life anew /他将~, 更始一新。He will make a new start, turning from wrongdoing to the true path. /我们还会欢迎她, 只要她~。We'll welcome her back, so long as she's willing to see her sins and repent.

改写 gǎixiě ❶ rewrite; adapt: 这篇文章必须~才行。This essay will have to be rewritten. ❷ adapt: 歌剧是根据话剧~的。The opera is adapted from the play.

改写本 gǎixiěběn adapted version; adaptation
改型 gǎixíng retrofit: 将飞机～，以减轻噪音 retrofit the plane to make it quieter
改性 gǎixìng 〈化学〉 modify: ～剂 modifier / ～树脂 modified resin
改修 gǎixiū ❶ renovate: ～庙宇 renovate the temple ❷ alter: ～一条棉裤 alter a pair of padded trousers
改选 gǎixuǎn (hold) a new election: ～班长 elect a new monitor / 这次～，他连任工会主席。He was reelected president of the trade union.
改削 gǎixuē delete and change; shorten and improve; revise: ～原稿 revise and shorten the original draft
改样 gǎiyàng change; alter; change the appearance; change the shape: 几年没回家，家乡完全～了。My hometown has changed completely since I left a few years ago.
改业 gǎiyè change one's occupation, profession, or trade: ～行医 change over to practising medicine
改易 gǎiyì 〈书面〉 change; modify; alter: 这条街道的名称几度～。The name of this street has been altered several times.
改用 gǎiyòng substitute sth. for sth. else: 不用食糖，～蜂蜜 replace sugar with honey
改元 gǎiyuán change the designation of an imperial reign; change the title of a reign
改造 gǎizào transform; reform; remould; remake: ～大自然 remake nature / ～低产田 transform low-yield land / ～旧企业 refurbish old plants / 在～客观世界的同时～主观世界 remould one's subjective world while changing the objective world / 到21世纪，中国的面貌将～一新。By the twenty-first century, China will have taken on a completely new look.
改辙 gǎizhé change over to new methods; change one's ways
改正 gǎizhèng correct; amend; rectify; put right: ～错误 correct one's mistakes / ～缺点 overcome one's shortcomings / ～错案 redress miscarriage of justice
改正片 gǎizhèngpiàn (in optics) corrector plate; correcting plate or lens
改正液 gǎizhèngyè correction fluid
改制 gǎizhì change the political or economic system; change over to a new system
改铸 gǎizhù 〈冶金〉 remould
改装 gǎizhuāng ❶ change one's costume or dress: 她一日三～。She changes her dress three times a day. ❷ repackage; repack: ～费用 repacking charge; reconditioning expense ❸ reequip; refit: ～一架收音机 refit a radio
改锥 gǎizhuī also "螺丝刀" luósīdāo screwdriver
改组 gǎizǔ reorganize; reshuffle; restructure: ～内阁 reshuffle the cabinet / 行政机构业已～。The administration has been restructured.
改嘴 gǎizuǐ 〈口语〉 see "改口"

gài

盖[1]（蓋） gài ❶ lid; cover; cap: 茶壶～ teapot lid / 锅～ pot cover / 鳃～ gill cover / 瓶～ cap of a bottle / 膝～ knee-cap / 轴承～ 〈机械〉 bearing cap (*or* cover) / 天灵～ top of the skull; crown of the head / 引擎～ bonnet (*or* hood) of an engine / 舱口～ hatch door; hatch cover ❷ shell; carapace: 乌龟～ shell of a tortoise / 指甲～儿 fingernail ❸ canopy: 华～ 〈书面〉 canopy (as over an ancient carriage) / 亭亭如～ (of a tree) stand towering with a canopy of leaves ❹ cover; put (over...): 桌子上～着一块布。The table is covered with a cloth. / 孩子睡着了，给他～个毯子。The child has fallen asleep. Pull a blanket over him. / 被子没～好。The bedclothes aren't tucked in properly. / 丑事你想～也～不住。You can't cover up a scandal even if you want to. ❺ affix (a seal): ～钢印 affix the steel (*or* embossing) seal (to sth.) / ～公章 put the official seal(on sth.); apply the official seal (to sth.) ❻ overwhelm; surpass; drown: 欢呼声～过了起哄声。Cheers drowned the booing and hooting. ❼ 〈方言〉 excellent; terrific; tops: 这个电影真叫～。The film is tops (*or* simply superb). / 这魔术玩儿得真～。This jugglery held us spellbound. ❽ build; put up (housing): ～礼堂 build an auditorium / ～个小棚子 put up a shed ❾ rectangular harrow ❿ (Gài) a surname

盖[2]（蓋） gài 〈书面〉 ❶ approximately; about; around: 此书之印行～在1902年。This book was probably first published in 1902. ❷ for; because; in fact: 文章错误甚多，～作者不学之故。The essay teems with errors, because the author is but an indifferent scholar.
see also Gě

盖板 gàibǎn blind flange; butt plate; spear plate: ～接合 concealed joint / ～接头 strap joint
盖杯 gàibēi tea cup with a cover
盖菜 gàicài *also* "芥菜" gàicài 〈植物〉 leaf mustard
盖层 gàicéng 〈石油〉 cap rock
盖戳 gàichuō affix a seal; put a stamp on
盖饭 gàifàn *also* "盖浇饭" rice served with meat and vegetables on top
盖棺论定 gàiguān-lùndìng only when a person is dead, or only when the lid is laid on a person's coffin, can final judgment be passed on him; no final verdict can be pronounced on a person until after his death
盖合碗 gàihéwǎn bowl with a fitted cover
盖火 gàihuo stove lid; burner cap
盖建 gàijiàn build; construct: 几座宿舍楼已在～之中。A few apartment buildings are being built (*or* under construction).
盖韭 gàijiǔ cold-bed chives
盖帘 gàilián round vat lid made of sorghum stalk
盖洛普民意测验 Gàiluòpǔ mínyì cèyàn Gallup poll, an assessment of public opinion devised by George Horace Gallup (1901-1984)
盖帽 gàimào ❶ (of basketball) shot blocking ❷ *also* "盖了帽儿了" 〈方言〉 extremely good; tops; topping: 这场球踢得盖了帽儿了。The football match was topping.
盖然性 gàiránxìng 〈逻辑〉 probability
盖世 gàishì unrivalled; unsurpassed; matchless; peerless: ～英雄 peerless hero / ～无双 unrivalled anywhere in the world; second to none
盖世太保 Gàishìtàibǎo Gestapo, German secret police under Nazi rule
盖柿 gàishì a species of persimmon
盖头 gàitou bridal veil (red silk veil with which to cover the head of a bride at the wedding — an old Chinese custom)
盖碗 gàiwǎn teabowl with a cover
盖造 gàizào build; construct: ～体育馆 build a gymnasium
盖章 gàizhāng affix one's seal; seal; stamp: 由本人签字～ to be signed and sealed by the recipient or applicant / 病假条要医院～才有效。A sick-leave certificate is valid only when it carries the seal of the hospital.
盖虫儿 gàizhōngr *see* "盖杯"
盖子 gàizi ❶ lid; cover; cap; top: 饭盒儿～ lid of a lunch box / 瓶～ bottle top / 捂～ try to hide (*or* cover up) the truth; keep the lid on / 揭～ lift up the lid; uncover; expose ❷ shell (of a tortoise, etc.)

芥 gài
see also jiè

芥菜 gàicài *also* "盖菜" gàicài 〈植物〉 leaf mustard
see also jiècài
芥蓝 gàilán 〈植物〉 cabbage mustard

丐 gài 〈书面〉 ❶ beg ❷ beggar: 乞～ beggar ❸ give; grant; bestow: ～施贫民 give relief to the poor

钙 gài 〈化学〉 calcium (Ca): 缺～ calcium-deficient / 富～食品 high calcium food
钙长石 gàichángshí anorthite
钙代谢 gàidàixiè 〈生理〉 calcium metabolism
钙沸石 gàifèishí scolecite
钙过敏 gàiguòmǐn 〈医学〉 calciphylaxis
钙华 gàihuá 〈地质〉 travertine
钙化 gàihuà 〈医学〉 calcifu
钙化不全 gàihuà bùquán hypocalcification
钙化醇 gàihuàchún 〈生化〉 calciferol
钙化作用 gàihuà zuòyòng calcification
钙镁磷肥 gàiměi línféi calcium magnesium phosphate
钙片 gàipiàn calcium tablet

G

钙球蛋白 gàiqiúdànbái 〈生化〉calcoglobulin
钙缺乏 gàiquēfá calcium deficiency
钙生植物 gàishēng zhíwù calcicole
钙铀云母 gàiyóu yúnmǔ autunite
钙质土 gàizhìtǔ calcium soil

匄 gài 〈书面〉*see* "丐" gài

戤 gài 〈方言〉❶ counterfeit sth. in order to make a profit: ～牌 counterfeit trademark ❷ *see* "隑" gài

溉 gài 〈书面〉water; irrigate: 灌～ irrigate

概[1](**槩**) gài ❶ general; approximate: ～言之 generally speaking; all told /大～ main idea; general outline /梗～ broad outline; gist; synopsis ❷ without exception; absolutely; categorically: 一～而论 treat all alike; be lumped together /至亲好友～莫能外 admit of no exception, not even close relatives and friends /食物出门，～不退换。Food items sold may not be returned. /未经允许，～不许探视病人。No one is allowed to visit the patient without permission.

概[2] gài ❶ manner of carrying oneself; bearing; deportment: 气～ mettle; manner; spirit ❷ 〈书面〉scene; situation; circumstances: 胜～ beautiful scenery

概差 gàichā probable error

概而不论 gài'érbùlùn not care a pin; cannot care less; take no heed of: 他对这类事一向～，淡然置之。As usual, he won't care a damn about such matters.

概观 gàiguān general survey: 中国医学～ survey of traditional Chinese medicine

概见 gàijiàn 〈书面〉see a general outline (of sth.): 其惨败情况可以～。You can have a general idea of what a disastrous defeat they must have suffered. *or* You can well imagine how disastrous the defeat must have been.

概况 gàikuàng brief account (of sth.); general situation; survey: 介绍一下公司～ give a succinct account of the firm /《各国～》*A Brief Survey of the Countries of the World*

概括 gàikuò ❶ sum up; summarize; generalize; epitomize: ～起来说 to sum up /从个别～一般 generalize from particulars /我们可以把大家的建议～为以下几类。We might categorize the proposals as follows. ❷ briefly; in broad outline: ～地说 to put it briefly; to put it in a nutshell /他把剧本的情节～地说了一遍。He described the play in broad outline. *or* He gave a brief account of the plot.

概括性 gàikuòxìng ability to generalize or summarize; quality of being concise and to the point: 他总结发言～很强。His ability to generalize is quite obvious in his concluding speech.

概览 gàilǎn general survey: 《香港～》*A General Survey of Hong Kong*

概率 gàilǜ *also* "几率" jīlǜ 〈数学〉probability: ～分析 probability analysis /～空间 probability space /～流量 probability current /～误差 probable error

概率论 gàilǜlùn 〈数学〉probability theory; law of probability

概略 gàilüè ❶ outline; summary: 这只是故事的～，详细情节可以看原书。This is only a brief summary of the story. For details you may consult the work in the original. ❷ brief; succinct: ～说明 brief account

概略图 gàilüètú skeleton diagram

概论 gàilùn (often used as the title of a book) outline; introduction; survey: 《外交学～》*An Introduction to Diplomacy* /《欧洲文学～》*A Survey of European Literature*

概貌 gàimào general outline; overall picture: 这部书反映了亚洲人民生活的～。This book gives a general picture of the life of the Asian people.

概莫能外 gàimònéngwài admit of no exception whatsoever; be without exception: 矛盾存在于一切事物之中，这是普遍规律，古今中外，～。It is a general principle that contradictions exist in all things. There is no exception to this in modern times or ancient, in China or elsewhere.

概念 gàiniàn concept; conception; notion; idea: 基本～ fundamental conception; basic concept /形成～ form a concept /这件事情我一点～也没有。I haven't the faintest idea of this matter. /办事不能从抽象的～出发。One must not proceed from abstract notions in whatever one does.

概念化 gàiniànhuà conceptualize; write or speak in abstract terms: 这些作品太公式化、～了。These literary works tend too much to formularize and generalize.

概述 gàishù outline; give a brief account: 报告～了最近事态的发展。The report gave a brief account of recent developments.

概数 gàishù approximate number; round number

概算 gàisuàn 〈经济〉budgetary estimates

概要 gàiyào (often used as the title of a book) essentials; outline: 《法学～》*Essentials of Jurisprudence*

隑(**隑**) gài 〈方言〉❶ lean against; lean on: 把梯子～在墙上 lean a ladder against a wall ❷ count on; rely on

gān

漧 gān 〈书面〉dry; desiccated

干[1] gān ❶〈古语〉shield ❷ (Gān) a surname

干[2] gān ❶〈书面〉offend; affront: *see* "～犯" ❷ have to do with; be concerned with; be preoccupied with; be implicated in: 这事与我无～。It's none of my business. ❸〈书面〉seek (official position, official's salary, etc.); pursue: ～进 seek a position

干[3] gān ❶〈书面〉edge of a body of water: 江～ riverside; river bank ❷〈量词〉(usu. used in the early vernacular) *used of people*: 若～ several /那一～子人 that gang; those people

干[4] gān (ten) Heavenly Stems: ～支 Heavenly Stems and Earthly Branches

干[5](**乾**) gān ❶ dry; arid: 风～ air-dry /烘～ stoving /烤～ dry by (*or* over) a fire /阴～ dry in the shade /口～ thirsty; parched /～柴 dry firewood /油漆未～。Wet paint. ❷ without resort to water: *see* "～洗" ❸ dried food: 牛肉～ dried beef; jerked beef /豆腐～ dried bean curd /香～ smoked bean curd /笋～ dried bamboo shoots /萝卜～ dried radish /饼～ biscuit; cracker /面包～ rusk /葡萄～ raisin ❹ empty; hollow: 外强中～ outwardly strong but inwardly weak /水缸～了。The water vat is empty. /钱都花～了。I've spent all the money *or* I'm broke. ❺ without substance; empty; dry: *see* "～号"; "～笑" ❻ taken into nominal kinship; (relatives) not linked by blood: *see* "～亲"; "～妈" ❼ futile; in vain; of no avail: 我们坐在那里～等着他回来。We sat there idly waiting for him to return. ❽〈方言〉rude; blunt; impolite: 你说话别那么～，要不，他会生气的。Don't be so blunt when you speak to him. He might get offended. ❾〈方言〉embarrass or annoy by complaining or making offensive remarks: 我刚才～了他一顿。I put him in a real fix just now. ❿〈方言〉cold-shoulder; slight; leave out in the cold: 主人走了，把他们～起来了。The host strode off, leaving them out in the cold.

see also gàn

干碍 gān'ài ❶ connection; relation: 我看不出这两件事有什么～。I don't see any connection between these two events. ❷ hinder; impede: 恶劣的气候～了军事行动。Bad weather hindered the military operation.

干巴 gānbā 〈方言〉salted and dried (beef, etc.): 牛肉～ dry salted beef

干巴 gānba ❶ dried up; shrivelled; wizened: 苹果都～了。The apples have all dried up. /他成了个瘦～老头儿。He became a wizened old man. ❷ (of skin) desiccated; dry ❸ dry and dull; insipid: 这篇文章写得太～。The article is flat.

干巴巴 gānbābā ❶ dried up; wizened; parched: 雨水不足，地里～的。The land was parched as a result of insufficient rainfall. ❷ dull and dry; insipid; vapid: 文章写得～的。The essay is written in a vapid style. *or* The article is dull as ditchwater. /他说话～的，没人爱听。His droning speech bored everyone.

干巴呲咧 gānbacīliē ❶ dry; dried up; desiccated: 这馒头～的，我

吃不下。I have no appetite for these dry buns. ❷ dull and dry; insipid; flat:这篇散文写得～的,没看头。The prose is very dull. It's not worth reading.

干板 gānbǎn *also* "硬片"yìngpiàn 〈摄影〉photographic plate

干板 X 射线照相术 gānbǎn àikèsī-shèxiàn zhàoxiàngshù 〈医学〉xeroradiography

干梆戏 gānbāngxì 〈方言〉local (*bangzi*) opera arias sung without instrumental accompaniment

干杯 gānbēi drink a toast:我提议为两国人民的友谊～! I propose a toast to the friendship between our two peoples! /为你的健康～! Here's to your health! /～! Cheers! *or* Bottoms up!

干贝 gānbèi dried scallop (adductor):～鱼翅 shark's fin cooked with scallops

干笔 gānbǐ 〈美术〉dry-brush stroke, a technique in traditional Chinese brush painting

干瘪 gānbiě ❶ shrivelled; wizened:～的脸 wizened face /水果～了。The fruit shrivelled up. ❷ dull and dry; insipid; uninteresting:这篇论文太～了。The dissertation is very flat.

干冰 gānbīng 〈化学〉dry ice

干菜 gāncài dried vegetable

干藏法 gāncángfǎ dry storage

干草 gāncǎo hay:晒～ make hay /～垛 haystack; hayrick /～杈 hay-fork

干草原 gāncǎoyuán steppes

干柴烈火 gānchái-lièhuǒ ❶ dry wood and a raging fire:当时情况犹如～,一触即发。The situation then was explosive like dry faggots near a blazing fire. / 移干柴近烈火,难怪其燃。When dry wood is placed near a raging fire, it is not strange that it should start burning immediately. ❷ (of a man and a woman) caught in a burning passion

干城 gānchéng 〈书面〉shield and city wall — defending soldiers; defenders:为国～ defenders of the country

干城章嘉峰 Gānchéngzhāngjiāfēng Kanchengjunga or Kinchinjunga, world's third-highest mountain in the Himalayas on the border between Nepal and Sikkim

干船坞 gānchuánwù dry dock

干醋 gāncù jealousy about something that is none of one's business; vicarious jealousy:吃～ experience uncalled-for (*or* vicarious) jealousy

干脆 gāncuì ❶ frank and straightforward; candid; clear-cut:他为人爽快,办事～。He is straightforward and acts with decision. /我们大家都～点吧,没有必要吞吞吐吐。Let's be frank. There is no need to mince words. /把问题～摆开谈一谈不是更好吗? Wouldn't it be better to put all the cards on the table? ❷ simply; just; altogether:他～一言不发。He simply refused to talk. /这事他们～置之不理。They just ignored the matter, for better or for worse.

干打雷,不下雨 gān dǎléi, bù xiàyǔ all thunder but no rain — much cry and little wool; much noise but no action:大家都嚷着要修一座少年宫,但～,始终没见着少年宫的影子。There has been a public clamour for building a children's palace, but nothing tangible has happened.

干打垒 gāndǎlěi rammed-earth construction; house with walls of rammed earth

干瞪眼 gāndèngyǎn 〈口语〉watch anxiously but be unable to help; look on in despair:眼看见渔船在风暴中沉没,他们只有～,毫无办法。They watched helplessly as the fishing boat sank in the storm.

干电池 gāndiànchí dry cell:～组 dry battery

干爹 gāndiē nominally adoptive father; godfather

干儿子 gān'érzi nominally adoptive son; godson

干法 gānfǎ dry process:～成型 dry-press process /～钻进 dry drilling /～纺丝 dry spinning /～开采 dry mining

干犯 gānfàn offend; encroach upon; infringe (upon):～法规 break the law and regulations /～外交人员的特权与豁免权 infringe upon diplomatic privileges and immunities

干饭 gānfàn cooked rice (as distinct from porridge)

干纺 gānfǎng dry spinning:～纱 dry-spun yarn

干肥 gānféi dried manure

干粉 gānfěn dried vermicelli or noodles made from bean or sweet potato starch

干粉灭火器 gānfěn mièhuǒqì dry-chemical fire extinguisher

干粉气溶胶 gānfěn qìróngjiāo dust aerosol

干腐病 gānfǔbìng 〈植物〉dry rot:果蔬～ dry rot of fruit and vegetables /木材～ dry rot of wood

干戈 gāngē weapons of war; arms; war:动～ take up arms; go to war /～入库,偃武修文 store away weapons of war and encourage the arts of peace /～四起。Fighting broke out all over the country. *or* Civil war erupted nationwide.

干戈扰攘 gāngē-rǎoráng turmoil of war

干股 gāngǔ unpaid-for share; gratuitous share:他凭什么拿百分之二十的～? Why on earth should he have 20% of the shares without paying for them?

干果 gānguǒ ❶ nuts ❷ dried fruit

干寒 gānhán arid and frigid; dry and cold:～的山区 arid and cold mountain area

干旱 gānhàn (of weather or soil) arid; droughty; dry:～地区 arid area /此地连年～。This area has been afflicted by drought for years on end.

干号 gānháo *also* "干嚎" howl without tears; cry aloud but shed no tears

干涸 gānhé dry up; run dry:池塘～。The pond is running dry.

干花 gānhuā dehydrated flower

干荒盆地 gānhuāng péndì playa (a dried lake basin in the desert)

干灰 gānhuī 〈方言〉plant ash used as fertilizer

干货 gānhuò ❶ dried food and nuts (as merchandise);dry cargo:～船 dry cargo ship ❷〈比喻〉real stuff (with no frills or padding):这项计划水分太大,～不多。There's too much empty talk and too little substance in the project.

干急 gānjí feel anxious and helpless:好几个月没有她的消息了,他整天呆在家～。As he had not heard from her for several months, he felt anxious and helpless, shutting himself up at home all day.

干季 gānjì *also* "旱季" hànjì dry season

干将 gānjiāng name of a famous ancient sword; double-edged sword
see also gànjiàng

干胶印 gānjiāoyìn dry offset

干脚气 gānjiǎoqì 〈医学〉dry beriberi

干结 gānjié dry and hard:大便～ get constipated

干尽 gānjìn *also* "净尽" jìngjìn completely; utterly

干净 gānjìng ❶ clean; neat and tidy:把桌子擦～ wipe the table clean /小客厅里收拾得真叫～爽利。The small parlour was impeccably tidy. /孩子们都穿得干干净净的。The kids are all neatly dressed. ❷ (of speech, action, etc.) neat; tidy; straightforward:他文笔～。He writes a concise, straightforward style. /体操动作讲究规范、～。Gymnastic exercises should be accurate and neat. ❸ completely; entirely; totally:我把这事忘了个～。I clean forgot about this. /他把事故责任推了个～。He denied all responsibility for the accident.

干净核弹 gānjìng hédàn clean nuclear bomb

干净利落 gānjìng-lìluo neat and tidy; smart; efficient:这件事他处理得～。He handled the matter with great competence. /谁都知道他办事～。He is well known for his efficiency.

干酒 gānjiǔ dry wine

干咳 gānké dry cough; tussiculation

干渴 gānkě thirsty:我嘴～得要冒烟。I'm fearfully thirsty as if my mouth were burning.

干刻法 gānkèfǎ drypoint

干枯 gānkū ❶ dry up; wither; shrivel; wizen:～的皮肤 wizened skin /古井～了。The old well dried up. /秋天,山上落满了～的树叶。The autumn hills are covered all over with dry fallen leaves. ❷〈医学〉kraurosis

干哭 gānkū cry or wail but shed no tears; cry tearlessly

干酪 gānlào cheese

干酪素 gānlàosù casein

干酪样病变 gānlàoyàng bìngbiàn 〈医学〉caseation

干冷 gānlěng dry and cold:这里的冬天～～的。In winter, it is dry and cold here. /阴冷比～更难受。Wet cold is even worse than dry cold.

干礼 gānlǐ present money as a gift

干连 gānlián involve; implicate:这事～到他的儿子。His son is involved in the affair.

干粮 gānliang solid food; field rations; rations for a journey:明天远足,带足～。Take enough food with you for tomorrow's outing.

干粮袋 gānliangdài haversack; ration bag

干裂 gānliè ❶ (of parched earth, skin, lips, etc.) crack; chap:旱灾严重,地都～了。As a result of the severe drought, there were

cracks all over the fields. ❷〈林业〉seasoning crack
干馏 gānliú *also* "碳化" tànhuà 〈化学〉dry distillation
干禄 gānlù 〈书面〉be after or seek official position
干炉 gānlu *also* "缸炉" gānglu baked sweet cake
干罗音 gānluóyīn 〈医学〉rhonchus; dry rale
干妈 gānmā nominally adoptive mother; godmother
干妹子 gānmèizi 〈方言〉sister (used affectionately to address a young woman of one's own generation)
干媚 gānmèi beg for mercy; curry favour
干面 gānmiàn 〈方言〉wheat flour
干名采誉 gānmíng-cǎiyù seek fame by hook or by crook
干没 gānmò swallow up; embezzle; misappropriate:这笔钱本来是大伙儿的,却被他一个人~了。He gobbled up the money that belonged to all of us.
干磨 gānmò 〈机械〉dry grind:~机 dry grinder / ~削 dry grinding
干娘 gānniáng ❶ nominally adoptive mother; godmother ❷ wet nurse
干呕 gān'ǒu 〈医学〉retch
干皮病 gānpíbìng 〈医学〉xeroderma; ichthyosis
干汽 gānqì net gas
干亲 gānqīn nominally adoptive kinship:认~ take sb. as one's nominally adoptive kinsman or kinswoman
干卿底事 gānqīngdǐshì *also* "干卿何事" what has it to do with you; it's none of your business
干球温度 gānqiú wēndù 〈物理〉dry-bulb temperature:~计 dry-bulb thermometer
干扰 gānrǎo ❶ disturb; interfere:他正聚精会神地写论文,我不便去~他。I hate disturbing him when he is concentrating on his essay. / 要不是受他~,我可以干得更好。I could have done better but for his obstruction. ❷〈物理〉interference; jam:~无线电广播节目 jam a radio programme / ~太大,收音机听不清楚。You can't hear distinctly over the radio; there is too much interference. *or* The broadcast is indistinct because of the jamming. / 电视图像受到了电脑的~。The TV picture is affected by interference from the computer.
干扰波 gānrǎobō interference wave
干扰场 gānrǎochǎng interference field
干扰倒相器 gānrǎo dàoxiàngqì interference inverter
干扰器 gānrǎoqì interference unit
干扰区 gānrǎoqū range or zone of interference
干扰素 gānrǎosù 〈生化〉interferon
干扰台 gānrǎotái jamming station
干扰图 gānrǎotú interference paltern
干扰现象 gānrǎo xiànxiàng 〈医学〉interference phenomenon; cell-blockade phenomenon
干扰源 gānrǎoyuán interference source
干热焚风 gānrè fénfēng zonda (hot dusty north wind in the Argentine pampas)
干人 gānrén 〈方言〉poor people; pauper
干鞣法 gānróufǎ 〈皮革〉dry tannage
干涩 gānsè ❶ puckery because it is dry; dry and puckery:~的嘴唇 dry and puckery lips / 慢慢睁开~的眼皮 slowly open one's dry and puckery eyes ❷ (of voice) hoarse; husky:嗓音~ husky voice; gravel-voiced ❸ affected; not natural:~地一笑 with an affected smile
干砂 gānshā 〈冶金〉dry sand:~型 dry sand mould / ~造型 dry sand moulding / ~铸造 dry sand casting / ~铸件 dry sand cast
干烧鱼 gānshāoyú braised fish with chilli sauce
干涉 gānshè ❶ interfere; intervene; meddle:~别国内政 interfere in the internal affairs of other countries / ~别人私事 meddle in (*or* poke one's nose into) other people's private affairs / 互不~内政 non-interference in each other's internal affairs / 外来~ external interference / 武装~ armed intervention ❷ be related; be connected:二者了无~。Neither of them has anything to do with the other. ❸〈物理〉interference:相长~ constructive interference / 相消~ destructive interference
干涉波痕 gānshè bōhén interference ripple mark
干涉光谱 gānshè guāngpǔ interference spectrum
干涉色 gānshèsè interference colour
干涉条纹 gānshè tiáowén interference fringe
干涉图 gānshètú ❶ interferogram ❷ interference figure
干涉显微镜 gānshè xiǎnwēijìng interference microscope
干涉现象 gānshè xiànxiàng 〈电学〉interference
干涉仪 gānshèyí interferometer
干尸 gānshī mummy
干湿表 gānshībiǎo 〈气象〉psychrometer
干式 gānshì dry-type; dry:~变压器 dry-type (*or* air-immersed) transformer / ~收尘设备 dry-type dust collection system / ~真空泵 dry vacuum pump
干瘦 gānshòu skinny; bony; emaciated:他显得十分~。He looks emaciated. *or* He is just a bag of bones.
干爽 gānshuǎng ❶ (of weather) dry, fresh, and cool ❷ (of roads, etc.) dry:到处都是雨水,找不到~的地方。Rainwater everywhere! You can hardly find a dry spot.
干丝 gānsī 〈方言〉shredded dried bean curd:烧~ braised shredded bean curd with pork
干饲料 gānsìliào dry forage
干松 gānsong 〈方言〉dry and soft:躺在~的草地上 lie on the dry and velvety lawn
干嗽 gānsòu *see* "干咳"
干洗 gānxǐ dry-clean:~店 dry-cleaner's (shop) / 送大衣去~ send an overcoat to the dry-cleaner's
干系 gānxi responsibility; implication:如果出了问题,我们谁也逃脱不了~。If anything happens, none of us can escape the responsibility. / 他同此案有重大~。He is deeply implicated in the case.
干舷 gānxián freeboard
干笑 gānxiào hollow laugh:他~了一声。He gave a hollow laugh (*or* forced smile).
干薪 gānxīn ❶ salary drawn for a sinecure:领~ hold a sinecure ❷ (net) salary:她每月~五百元,还可拿八百元奖金。She receives a salary of 500 *yuan* per month, plus a bonus of 800 *yuan*.
干芯电缆 gānxìn diànlǎn 〈通信〉dry-core cable
干性坏疽 gānxìng huàijū 〈医学〉dry gangrene; senile gangrene
干性罗音 gānxìng luóyīn *see* "干罗音"
干性油 gānxìngyóu drying oil; siccative oil
干选 gānxuǎn 〈矿业〉dry separation
干血浆 gānxuèjiāng desiccated plasma
干血痨 gānxuèláo 〈中医〉type of tubercular disease found in women, usu. characterized by menostasis, recurrent low fever, and general debility
干眼症 gānyǎnzhèng 〈医学〉xerophthalmia
干咽 gānyè sob without tears
干谒 gānyè 〈书面〉seek an audience with a person in power to court his favour
干印术 gānyìnshù 〈印刷〉xerography
干预 gānyù *also* "干与" interfere; intervene; interpose; meddle:~他人家事是很不明智的。It's unwise to interfere in other people's family matters. / 他们争吵得太凶了,我们不得不进行~。They argued so heatedly that we had to intervene.
干预个人隐私 gānyù gèrén yǐnsī 〈法律〉invasion of privacy
干哕 gānyue feel sick; retch:他一起床就~,难受极了。He felt unbearably sick and retched the moment he got up. / 一闻到汽油味就~。The smell of petrol always nauseates me.
干云蔽日 gānyún-bìrì (of tall trees and buildings) reach up to the skies and shut out the sun
干燥 gānzào ❶ dry; arid:气候~ arid climate / 结膜~ xerosis conjunctivae / 口腔~ xerostomia / 大便~ costive; constipated ❷ dull; uninteresting:~无味 dry as dust (*or* a bone); dull as ditchwater ❸ seasoning (of timber):~裂纹 seasoning crack
干燥病 gānzàobìng xerosis
干燥法 gānzàofǎ desiccation; drying
干燥机 gānzàojī dehydrator; drier; exsiccator
干燥剂 gānzàojì drier; drying agent; desiccating agent
干燥炉 gānzàolú 〈冶金〉drier; batch drier
干燥率 gānzàolǜ 〈气象〉index of aridity
干燥膜 gānzàomó desiccator diaphragm
干燥器 gānzàoqì 〈化工〉desiccator; exsiccator; water extractor
干燥箱 gānzàoxiāng dry box; dry oven; drying cabinet
干着急 gānzháojí *also* "干急" be anxious but to no avail; be helplessly worried:他忘了带戏票,~进不去剧院。To his frustration he was denied entry into the opera house because he had forgotten his ticket.
干证 gānzhèng witness concerned (in a case)
干政 gānzhèng meddle in state affairs:这位总统夫人好~。The first lady (*or* The wife of this president) has a liking for meddling

in government affairs.
干支 gānzhī Heavenly Stems and Earthly Branches (two sets of signs, with one being taken from each set to form 60 pairs, designating years, months and days, now mostly years)
干枝梅 gānzhīméi twig or branch (of a plum tree) which bears flowers before leaves come out
干皱 gānzhòu (of skin) shrivelled and wrinkled: 面皮～ wizened face
干贮 gānzhù store up dried greenfeed or green fodder: 秋天农民将白薯藤～起来作饲料。In autumn farmers store up dried sweet potato vines as fodder.
干铸法 gānzhùfǎ 〈冶金〉 dry casting
干租 gānzū *also* "力租" lìzū rent in the form of service; labour rent

玕

gān *see* "琅玕" lánggān

杆

gān pole; staff: 旗～ flagstaff; flagpole / 标～ surveyor's pole / 测～ measure staff; surveying rod / 电线～ pole (for telephone or electric power lines, etc.) / 斜～ slanting pole / 吊～ boom; jib / 桅～ mast
see also gǎn
杆沸石 gānfèishí 〈矿业〉 thomsonite
杆塔 gāntǎ pole; tower; pylon; lattice-type tower
杆子 gānzi ❶ pole; staff ❷ 〈方言〉 rebel ❸ 〈方言〉 robber; bandit: 拉～ organize a band of robbers
see also gǎnzi

酐

gān 〈化学〉 anhydride: 醋酸～ acetic anhydride / 碱～ basic anhydride / 碳～ carbonic anhydride / 亚硫～ sulphurous anhydride

矸

gān
矸石 gānshí 〈矿业〉 waste (rock); gangue
矸子 gānzi *see* "矸石"

竿

gān pole; staff; rod: 竹～ bamboo pole / 钓鱼～ fishing rod / 马～ blind man's staff / 滑～ (a kind of) litter / 爬～ climbing a pole; pole-climbing
竿子 gānzi bamboo or wooden pole: 一～插到底 see that a task or directive is carried out right down to the grass-roots level

肝

gān liver; hepar
肝癌 gān'ái 〈医学〉 cancer of the liver
肝病 gānbìng hepatopathy: ～患者 hepatopath
肝肠 gāncháng liver and intestines
肝肠寸断 gāncháng-cùnduàn afflicted with profound grief; deeply grieved; heartbroken: 目睹这幕人间惨剧, 谁能不～? One cannot but feel heart-rending sorrow at the sight of such a human tragedy.
肝胆 gāndǎn ❶ liver and gall: ～俱裂 feel as if one's liver and gall were torn up — be overwhelmed by grief or terror; be heart-broken or terror-stricken ❷ true heart; open-heartedness; sincerity: 披肝沥胆 lay bare one's heart — be open and sincere; be loyal and faithful ❸ heroic spirit; courage: 英雄～ heroic spirit / ～过人 unsurpassed in valour
肝胆楚越 gāndǎn-chǔyuè (close friends) become estranged; turn hostile to each other
肝胆相照 gāndǎn-xiāngzhào show utter devotion to sb.; treat each other with an open heart: ～, 荣辱与共 treat each other with all sincerity and share weal and woe
肝胆照人 gāndǎn-zhàorén be exceedingly sincere or loyal: 他是条～的血性汉子。He is an upright man, exceedingly loyal to his friends.
肝毒素 gāndúsù 〈医学〉 hepatotoxin
肝风 gānfēng 〈中医〉 disease with such symptoms as dizziness, headache, tinnitis, twitches, etc.
肝功能 gāngōngnéng 〈生理〉 liver function: ～试验 〈医学〉 liver function test / ～障碍 dyshepatia
肝花 gānhua 〈口语〉 liver
肝昏迷 gānhūnmí 〈医学〉 hepatic coma
肝火 gānhuǒ irascibility; spleen: 动～ vent one's spleen; get worked up / ～旺 hot-tempered; irascible
肝精 gānjīng liver extract
肝乐 gānlè 〈药学〉 diisopropylamine dichloroacetate (DADA)
肝瘤 gānliú 〈医学〉 hepatoma
肝脑涂地 gānnǎo-túdì be ready to dash one's brains out or scatter one's innards on the ground — be ready to lay down one's life for a cause; be willing to repay a favour with extreme sacrifice: ～, 在所不惜 would grudge nothing, not even one's life
肝宁 gānníng 〈药学〉 proheparin
肝破裂 gānpòliè 〈医学〉 hepatorrhexis
肝气 gānqì ❶ 〈中医〉 disease with such symptoms as costal pain, vomiting, diarrhoea, etc. ❷ irritability
肝切开术 gānqiēkāishù 〈医学〉 hepatotomy
肝儿 gānr liver (of pig, sheep, ox, etc., used as food): 我们今天吃炒猪～。We'll have fried pork liver today.
肝儿颤 gānrchàn 〈方言〉 one's liver trembles — be terrified; be panick-stricken: 一提起那事就～。The mere mention of that incident sends shivers down my spine (*or* gives me the shivers).
肝肾综合征 gānshèn zōnghézhēng 〈医学〉 hepatorenal syndrome; Heyd's syndrome
肝石 gānshí 〈医学〉 hepatolith: ～病 hepatolithiasis / ～切除术 hepatolithectomy
肝素 gānsù 〈药学〉 heparin
肝泰乐 gāntàilè 〈药学〉 glucurolactone; glucurone
肝糖 gāntáng *also* "糖原" tángyuán glycogen
肝痛 gāntòng 〈医学〉 hepatalgia
肝吸虫 gānxīchóng 〈动物〉 liver fluke: ～病 〈医学〉 hepatic distomiasis; clonorchiasis (*or* clonorchiosis)
肝下垂 gānxiàchuí 〈医学〉 hepatoptosis
肝炎 gānyán 〈医学〉 hepatitis: 丙型～ hepatitis C / 慢性～ chronic hepatitis / 暴发型～ fulminant hepatitis / 中毒性～ toxic hepatitis
肝样变 gānyàngbiàn 〈医学〉 hepatization: 红色～ red hepatization / 灰色～ grey hepatization
肝硬变 gānyìngbiàn 〈医学〉 cirrhosis (of the liver); hepatocirrhosis
肝硬化 gānyìnghuà 〈医学〉 cirrhosis (of the liver)
肝脏 gānzàng 〈生理〉 liver: ～病 hepatopathy / ～病学 hepatology / ～病学家 hepatologist
肝掌 gānzhǎng 〈医学〉 liver palms, as a symptom of cirrhosis
肝蛭 gānzhì *see* "肝吸虫"
肝肿大 gānzhǒngdà 〈医学〉 hepatomegaly
肝周炎 gānzhōuyán 〈医学〉 perihepatitis

甘

gān ❶ sweet; honeyed; pleasant: ～言美语 honeyed words ❷ willingly; voluntarily; readily; of one's own accord: 心～情愿 of one's free will; willingly / ～做人民的老黄牛 be a willing horse for the people; serve the people heart and soul / ～为教育事业献身 dedicate oneself to the cause of education / ～守清贫 be ready to lead a poor but honest life / 自～落后 be resigned to lagging behind / 自～堕落 give oneself up as lost; become degenerate / 不～落后 refuse to trail behind ❸ (Gān) (short for 甘肃) Gansu Province ❹ (Gān) a surname
甘氨酸 gān'ānsuān glycine
甘拜下风 gānbàixiàfēng candidly admit or concede defeat (in a friendly competition, etc.); sincerely acknowledge sb.'s superiority: 先生棋艺高超, 我等～。We gladly bow to your superiority in chess.
甘草 gāncǎo 〈中药〉 licorice root
甘醇 gānchún glycol
甘脆 gāncuì ❶ sweet and crisp: 这种瓜吃起来～爽口。This kind of melon is sweet, crisp, and refreshing. ❷ *also* "甘毳" 〈书面〉 delicacies; choice food
甘丹寺 Gāndānsì Ghadan or Gyaden, Buddhist monastery (first built in 1409) in Tibet Autonomous Region
甘当 gāndāng ❶ be willing to accept (punishment): ～重罚 be ready to accept a heavy penalty ❷ be willing or ready: ～小学生 be willing to learn as a humble student
甘地 Gāndì Mohandas Karamchand Gandhi (1869-1948), leader and symbol of the Indian nationalist movement, called Mahatma reverently
甘地夫人 Gāndì fūren Indira Gandhi (1917-1984), Indian Prime Minister (1966-1977, 1980-1984), not related to Mahatma Gandhi

甘芳 gānfāng sweet and fragrant：蜜枣的滋味，十分～。The candied dates are sweet and fragrant.
甘汞 gāngǒng 〈化学〉calomel；mercurous chloride：～电池 calomel cell /～电极 calomel electrode
甘瓜苦蒂 gānguā-kǔdì a sweet melon or fruit may have a bitter base；honey is sweet，but the bee stings — nothing is perfect
甘贵 gānguì 〈方言〉precious：他把独生女儿看得比啥都～。He regards his only daughter as the apple of his eye.
甘蕉 gānjiāo banana
甘结 gānjié 〈旧语〉written pledge to government authorities：具～ submit a written pledge
甘居 gānjū be content (usu. to be in a lower position)：～人下 be content to be below others；be contented to occupy an inferior position /～中游 be content with the middling state；be resigned to mediocrity
甘苦 gānkǔ ❶ joys and sorrows；weal and woe：同～，共患难 share weal and woe；go through thick and thin together /同甘共苦 share joys and sorrows ❷ hardships and difficulties experienced in work：～自知。One knows best what one has gone through. /没有亲身经历，就不知其中～。You do not realize how difficult it is without personal experience.
甘蓝 gānlán 〈植物〉wild cabbage
甘洌 gānliè sweet and refreshing：～的泉水 sweet and refreshing spring water
甘霖 gānlín good rain after a long drought；timely rain：～普降。A timely rain fell all over the region.
甘露 gānlù ❶ sweet dew ❷〈医学〉manna
甘露醇 gānlùchún mannitol
甘露糖 gānlùtáng mannose；mannitose
甘露子 gānlùzǐ 〈植物〉Chinese artichoke (*Stachys sieboldii*)
甘美 gānměi sweet and refreshing：～的果汁 sweet and refreshing fruit juice
甘泉 gānquán sweet and refreshing spring water
甘柿 gānshì persimmon ripened on the tree without the puckery taste；ripe persimmon
甘受 gānshòu accept willingly；be resigned to：他不是那种～屈辱的人。He is not the kind of person to take an insult lying down.
甘薯 gānshǔ sweet potato：～黑斑病 sweet potato black rot /～软腐病 sweet potato soft rot
甘肃 Gānsù Gansu (Province)
甘遂 gānsuì 〈中药〉root of *gansui* (*Euphorbia kansui*)
甘甜 gāntián sweetness；joy：他们尝到了新社会的～。They have tasted the joys (*or* sweetness) of the new society.
甘味 gānwèi 〈书面〉❶ delicious food；delicacy ❷ appetite for food：食不～ eat without relish；have no appetite (as in a troubled state of mind)
甘心 gānxīn ❶ willing；ready：～为国效劳 be ready to serve one's country /我～到边远山区工作。I am going to work in a remote mountain area of my own accord. ❷ be content with；resign oneself to；be reconciled to：他～身居陋室，写诗作画。He was content to live in a small and simple house，writing poems or painting pictures. /她不～接受命运的摆布。She refused to resign herself to fate. /敌人决不～自己的失败。The enemy will never take their defeat lying down.
甘心情愿 gānxīn-qíngyuàn *also* "心甘情愿" willingly and gladly：我～放弃对财产的要求。I willingly and gladly relinquish all my claims to the property.
甘休 gānxiū be willing to give up；take it lying down：不达目的，决不～。We will never give up until our purpose is achieved. /除非她自己确信错了，她决不会～的。She won't let the matter rest unless she is convinced of her own error.
甘言 gānyán 〈书面〉sweet words；flattering words：～蜜语 sweet words and honeyed phrases；sweet talk；oiling one's tongue
甘油 gānyóu 〈化学〉glycerine；glycerin；glycerol：粗～ crude glycerine /合成～ synthetic glycerine /硝化～ nitroglycerine (explosive)
甘油基 gānyóujī glyceryl
甘油胶 gānyóujiāo glycerin cement
甘油醛 gānyóuquán 〈化学〉glyceraldehyde
甘油三酸酯 gānyóu sānsuānzhǐ 〈化学〉triglyceride；nitroglycerine
甘油酸 gānyóusuān 〈化学〉glyceric acid
甘油酯 gānyóuzhǐ 〈化学〉glyceride
甘于 gānyú be willing to；be ready to；be happy to：作为一名乡村教师，她～默默无闻。As a village teacher，she chooses to remain obscure. /或许你能够～寂寞，但是我不行。Well，perhaps you don't mind solitude，but I do.
甘雨 gānyǔ timely rain：久旱逢～。We had a good rain after a long drought.
甘愿 gānyuàn willingly；readily；gladly：～效劳 be glad to offer one's services；be only too glad to do what one can；be ready to place oneself at sb.'s disposal /～冒此风险 be ready to take the risk /不完成任务，～引退。I will resign if I fail.
甘蔗 gānzhe sugarcane：～板〈建筑〉cane fibre board /～蜡 sugarcane wax /～收割机 cane cutter；cane cutting machine /～装载机 cane loader /～压榨机 cane crusher；cane press /～渣 bagasse /～渣浆厂 bagasse-pulp mill
甘蔗没有两头甜 gānzhe méiyǒu liǎngtóu tián a sugarcane is never sweet at both ends — you cannot eat your cake and have it
甘之如饴 gānzhī-rúyí enjoy sth. bitter as if it were malt sugar — gladly endure hardships for a noble cause：即使历尽千辛万苦，也是～。I will undertake the task gladly for all the hardships it entails.
甘旨 gānzhǐ 〈书面〉delicacies：～之奉 offering of delicacies /饿之于食，不待～。When famished，one will not wait for delicacies. *or* Hunger is the best spice (*or* sauce).
甘紫菜 gānzǐcài 〈植物〉laver

泔 gān

泔脚 gānjiǎo 〈方言〉kitchen waste；hogwash
泔水 gānshui swill；slops；hogwash

疳 gān

〈中医〉infantile malnutrition due to digestive disturbances or intestinal parasites
疳积 gānjī *see* "疳"

坩 gān

〈书面〉earthenware
坩埚 gānguō 〈化学〉crucible：石墨～ graphite (*or* carbon) crucible /～法 crucible process /～炉〈冶金〉crucible furnace
坩埚钢 gānguōgāng pot steel
坩埚黏土 gānguō niántǔ pot clay
坩埚窑 gānguōyáo 〈化工〉pot furnace
坩子土 gānzitǔ 〈方言〉porcelain clay；china clay

苷 gān

see "糖苷" tánggān

柑 gān

mandarin orange
柑橘 gānjú oranges and tangerines；citrus：～酱 marmalade
柑子 gānzi mandarin orange

尴(尷、尲) gān

尴尬 gāngà ❶ in a predicament；cornered；in a dilemma：他进退两难，实在～。He was in a real dilemma as to how to act. /他感到非常～。He was in a quandary. ❷〈方言〉uneasy；embarrassed；unnatural：神态显得很～ look very unnatural；look not quite oneself /这一连串的斥责，使他十分～。This barrage of stern rebuke disconcerted him acutely.

gǎn

赶(趕) gǎn

❶ run after；chase；pursue；catch up：追～ run after；chase after /警车～过了路上所有的汽车。The police car overtook all the cars on the road. ❷ try to catch；make a dash for；rush for；hurry：～末班车 try to catch the last bus /～任务 rush through one's job /～拍电影 shoot a movie to beat a deadline /他连夜～写出了发言稿。He dashed off the text of his speech that very night. /～调更多部队到前线。More troops were rushed to the front. /飞机早上八点起飞，我们能～得上。The plane takes off at 8:00 a.m. I'm sure we'll make it. ❸ go (to a place)：*see* "～集" ❹ drive：～马车 drive a horse-drawn waggon /把猪～入猪圈 herd the pigs into the pigsty ❺ drive out；drive away；expel：把侵略者～出国门 drive the invaders out of the country /那和尚被～出山门。The monk was expelled from the temple. /他们～走了殖民者。They sent the colonialists packing. /独裁者被～下了台。The dictator was toppled from

感光 gǎnguāng 〈摄影〉sensitization:～度 (light) sensitivity
感光计 gǎnguāngjì sensitometer
感光片 gǎnguāngpiàn sensitive sheet
感光性树脂板 gǎnguāngxìng shùzhībǎn 〈印刷〉photopolymer plate
感光纸 gǎnguāngzhǐ sensitive paper
感荷 gǎnhè 〈书面〉be sincerely grateful; be thankful:不胜～ be extremely grateful /～无既。Thank you ever so much.
感化 gǎnhuà reform a misguided person through persuasion, etc.; help an erring person to remould himself or herself:～教育 reformatory education /～院 reformatory
感怀 gǎnhuái ❶ bring back to mind with emotion:～往事 recall past events with nostalgia ❷ reflections; thoughts; recollections:登高～ thoughts on ascending a height
感激 gǎnjī feel grateful; be thankful; feel indebted:不胜～ be deeply grateful; feel very much indebted /～不忘 always remember with gratitude /～之至 be extremely grateful /～莫名。My gratitude beggars description. *or* I'm more grateful than words can express.
感激涕零 gǎnjī-tìlíng be moved to tears of gratitude:落水的孩子被救起,家长～。The parents were moved to tears of gratitude when their drowning child was rescued.
感旧 gǎnjiù think of old acquaintances and past events with emotion or nostalgia
感觉 gǎnjué ❶ feeling; sense perception; sensation:～与概念不同。Sense perception is different from conception. /经过几天修整,我们有一种轻松的～。After several days' rest, we felt relaxed./一登上香山,你马上就会有一种幽美、清爽的～。You will be struck by the elegant beauty and freshness of the place the moment you reach the top of Fragrant Hill. ❷ feel; perceive; realize; become aware of:～很别扭 feel awkward (*or* uncomfortable) /我～浑身无力。I feel weak all over. /我们～此人很文雅。We realized that he was a man of elegant taste. /我～他的病情好像减轻了一些。It seems to me that he is getting better.
感觉过程 gǎnjué guòchéng sense process
感觉过敏 gǎnjué guòmǐn 〈医学〉hyperaesthesia
感觉减退 gǎnjué jiǎntuì 〈医学〉hypaesthesia
感觉论 gǎnjuélùn 〈哲学〉sensualism
感觉器官 gǎnjué qìguān sense organ
感觉神经 gǎnjué shénjīng *also* "传入神经" chuánrù shénjīng 〈生理〉sensory nerve
感觉特性 gǎnjué tèxìng sense quality
感觉异常 gǎnjué yìcháng 〈医学〉paresthesia
感觉阈限 gǎnjué yùxiàn 〈心理〉sense limen; sense threshold
感觉中枢 gǎnjué zhōngshū 〈生理〉sensorium
感慨 gǎnkǎi sigh with emotion:～万千 be full of myriad emotions /～流涕 be moved to tears
感慨万端 gǎnkǎi-wànduān all sorts of feelings well up in one's mind:参观之后,我不禁～。After seeing the exhibition, I felt all sorts of emotions surging up within me. /我站在甲板上观看奔腾的江水,心里～。I could hardly contain myself as I stood on deck and gazed with awe at the turbulent, roaring waves of the river.
感慨系之 gǎnkǎi-xìzhī sigh with deep emotion:一个伟大的国家就这样分崩离析了,这不能不令人～。People can not help sighing with deep emotion at the disintegration of such a great country.
感抗 gǎnkàng 〈电学〉inductive reactance; positive reactance
感愧 gǎnkuì feel deeply indebted to sb. and ashamed of oneself:～交加 with a mixed feeling of gratitude and shame
感喟 gǎnkuì 〈书面〉sigh with feeling:他的不幸经历使我～不已。I sighed deeply over his misfortune.
感冒 gǎnmào *also* "伤风" shāngfēng ❶ cold; flu:流行性～ flu (influenza) /患～ catch cold; have a touch of flu /这是～特效药。The medicine is an effective cure for colds. ❷ catch cold:小心别～。Take care not to catch cold.
感念 gǎnniàn remember with gratitude; recall with deep emotion:～五中 feel grateful from the bottom of one's heart /我将永远～他的好处。I shall always remember his kindness to me.
感佩 gǎnpèi be filled with gratitude and admiration:衷心～。I admire you and feel very grateful to you.
感泣 gǎnqì be moved to tears
感情 gǎnqíng ❶ emotion; feeling; sentiment:动～ be carried away by one's emotions; get worked up /伤～ hurt sb.'s feelings; be offensive to sb. /～流露 betray one's emotions /～不能代替政策。Emotion is no substitute for policy. ❷ affection; love; fondness; attachment:夫妻俩～破裂,只好离婚。As the couple do not love each other any more, they had better divorce. /我对中国文明的摇篮 — 黄河怀有深厚的～。I cherish a deep affection for the Yellow River, the cradle of Chinese civilization.
感情冲动 gǎnqíng chōngdòng be carried away by one's emotions; act on impulse
感情投资 gǎnqíng tóuzī emotional investment (in the form of showing solicitude for colleagues, friends or people at the grass roots, etc. and helping them overcome difficulties in life)
感情洋溢 gǎnqíng-yángyì exuberance of feeling; overflowing with emotion
感情用事 gǎnqíng-yòngshì give way to one's feelings; be swayed by one's emotions; give oneself over to blind impulse; be sentimental:要冷静,不要～。Keep a cool head; don't act impetuously.
感染 gǎnrǎn ❶ infect; taint:细菌～ bacterial infection /手术后～ postoperative infection /轻度～ light infection /预防～ take precautions against infection /防止再～ avoid reinfection /因～伤口发炎。The wound was inflamed by infection. ❷ arouse; inspire; infect; affect:她的乐观情绪～了周围的人。She infected everyone with her optimism. *or* Her optimism was infectious to all. /要用必胜的信念去～战士。One must try to inspire the rank and file with one's own confidence in victory.
感染力 gǎnrǎnlì appeal; power to influence:有生动艺术形象的作品,才能产生强烈的～。Only artistic works with vivid imagery can appeal to people.
感人 gǎnrén moving; stirring; inspiring:～至深 move one profoundly /这一～的场面,真是无法用笔墨来形容。It is impossible to describe this heart-stirring scene.
感人肺腑 gǎnrénfèifǔ touch one to the heart; touch one to the depths of one's soul; tug or pull at one's heartstring:一部～的电影 a soul-stirring film
感纫 gǎnrèn 〈书面〉(usu. used in letter-writing) feel grateful; be thankful
感伤 gǎnshāng sad; sorrowful; maudlin; sentimental:～喜剧 sentimental comedy /～小说 sentimental novel /过分～ mawkish /～自己不幸的身世 feel sad about (*or* lament) one's bad lot
感生 gǎnshēng 〈电学〉induced
感生电流 gǎnshēng diànliú *see* "感应电流"
感世 gǎnshì sigh with regret at the prevailing corrupt public morals:那是一部～之作。The book expresses the author's bitterness about the bad ways of the world.
感受 gǎnshòu ❶ be affected by; catch:～风寒 be affected by the cold; catch a chill ❷ experience; feel; be impressed:父母去世后,他～到了生活的艰辛。He experienced the hardships of life after his parents' death. /我一回到故里,就～到了家乡的温暖。I felt the warmth of my hometown the moment I set foot on its soil. /这次参观中所见所闻使我～很深。I was deeply impressed by what I saw and heard during this visit.
感受器 gǎnshòuqì 〈生理〉receptor
感受性 gǎnshòuxìng receptivity; ability to sense or feel
感受作用 gǎnshòu zuòyòng sensory reception
感叹 gǎntàn sigh over sth. that strikes a chord; sigh with feeling:发出了无可奈何的～ sigh helplessly /家乡的变化使他～不已。He sighed with wonder at the changes of his hometown.
感叹词 gǎntàncí interjection; exclamation
感叹号 gǎntànhào exclamation mark; exclamation point (!)
感叹句 gǎntànjù exclamatory sentence
感天动地 gǎntiān-dòngdì even the heaven and the earth are moved:他的英雄事迹可谓～。His heroic exploits are deeply moving.
感同身受 gǎntóngshēnshòu feel as though one experiences sth. in person; feel indebted as if the favour were received in person; appreciate sth. as a personal favour (said when making a request on behalf of one's friend):你对他的帮助,我～。I regard your help to him as a personal favour.
感物伤怀 gǎnwù-shānghuái feel sad when seeing sth. that reminds one of old acquaintances or past events
感悟 gǎnwù come to realize; become aware (of sth.)
感想 gǎnxiǎng impressions; reflections; thoughts:参观了这个美术展览之后,你有何～? What do you think of the art exhibition you've just visited? *or* What are your impressions of the art exhibition you've just visited? /对你刚才的讲话,我想谈谈自己的～。I would like

G

to say a few words on what you have said.

感谢 gǎnxiè thank; be thankful; be grateful: ～信 letter of thanks / 表示衷心的～ express heartfelt thanks / 他写信来～我们对他的帮助。He wrote to express his gratefulness for our help. / 非常～你及时把情况告诉了我们。Thank you very much for telling us about this in time.

感兴 gǎnxìng feeling or interest aroused by sth.: 蝉声触发了他的～。The chirping of cicadas aroused his interest.

感性 gǎnxìng perception; perceptiveness: 认识的～阶段 perceptual stage of cognition

感性认识 gǎnxìng rènshi perceptual knowledge: 由～到理性认识有时要经过一个很长的阶段。Sometimes it takes a long time to proceed from perceptual knowledge to rational knowledge.

感性运动 gǎnxìng yùndòng 〈植物〉 nastic movement

感性知觉 gǎnxìng zhījué 〈心理〉 sense impression

感言 gǎnyán words to express one's feelings or thoughts; written thoughts or reflections: 建国四十五年～ thoughts on the occasion of the 45th anniversary of the founding of the People's Republic of China

感应 gǎnyìng ❶ response; reaction; interaction; 〈生物〉 irritability ❷ 〈电学〉 induction: 电磁～ electromagnetic induction / 静电～ electrostatic induction / ～干扰 inductive interference / ～式话筒 inductor microphone / ～淬火 induction hardening

感应场 gǎnyìngchǎng 〈电学〉 induction field

感应电动机 gǎnyìng diàndòngjī induction motor

感应电疗法 gǎnyìng diànliáofǎ 〈医学〉 faradism; faradization

感应电流 gǎnyìng diànliú *also* "感生电流"; "应电流" induced current; induction current; faradic current

感应计 gǎnyìngjì induction meter

感应炉 gǎnyìnglú induction furnace

感应率 gǎnyìnglǜ inductivity

感应热 gǎnyìngrè induction heat

感应水雷 gǎnyìng shuǐléi 〈军事〉 influence mine

感应线圈 gǎnyìng xiànquān induction coil; inductor

感遇 gǎnyù 〈书面〉 ❶ be thankful for the favourable treatment received ❷ lament one's hard lot; sigh over one's bitter experience: ～诗 poem depicting one's personal vicissitudes

感召 gǎnzhào move and inspire; impel; influence: 在政府正确政策的～下，他决心弃旧图新。Under the influence of the government's correct policy, he was determined to turn over a new leaf.

感知 gǎnzhī ❶ 〈哲学〉 perception ❷ feel; be aware; sense: 他对自己病情的严重性有所～。He seems to be aware of his serious illness.

鳡

gǎn *also* "黄钻" huángzuàn 〈动物〉 *Elopichthys bambus*

敢[1]

gǎn ❶ brave; bold; courageous; daring: 果～ courageous and resolute; brave and decisive / 勇～ bold; brave; courageous ❷ dare: ～攀高峰 dare to scale the heights / 这事我想都不～想。I even dare not think of it. / 他胆～在我面前撒谎。He had the nerve (*or* impudence) to lie to me. ❸ be sure; be certain: 我～说你是同情他的。I'm certain that your sympathy is with him. / 我不～肯定他是否会接受我们的邀请。I'm not sure whether or not he will accept our invitation. ❹ 〈书面〉〈谦词〉 make bold; take the liberty; venture: ～问家住何方? May I ask where you live?

敢[2]

gǎn 〈方言〉 can it be that: *see* "～是"; "～莫"

敢保 gǎnbǎo surely; assuredly; certainly: 要是这事叫他知道，～要闹翻。He will surely fall out with us if he knows about this.

敢待 gǎndài (often used in the early vernacular) be about to; be on the point of

敢当 gǎndāng ❶ dare to accept responsibility for; have the courage to: ～大任 dare to take heavy responsibilities ❷ 〈谦词〉 (usu. used in the negative) presume (to do sth.); dare: 不～。I do not presume to have such an honour. *or* I feel flattered. / 叫我如何～。This is indeed much more than I'm entitled to.

敢莫 gǎnmò 〈方言〉 can it be that; is it possible that: ～你认识他? Can it be that you know him?

敢怒而不敢言 gǎn nù ér bùgǎn yán be forced to keep one's resentment to oneself; suppress one's rage; choke with silent fury; hold one's tongue with pent-up indignation: 他横行霸道，无法无天，老百姓～。He took the law into his own hands and tyrannized (over) the people so that they could only rage in silence. / 他虽很恼火，但～。He was furious, but he dared not show it.

敢怕 gǎnpà (often used in the early vernacular) perhaps; maybe

敢情 gǎnqing 〈方言〉〈副词〉 ❶ why; so; I say: 哟! ～夜里下了大雪啦。Why! There was a heavy snow last night. ❷ of course; indeed; really: 去长城? 那～好! Going to the Great Wall? That'll be fine (indeed). *or* That's really great.

敢是 gǎnshi 〈方言〉 can it be that; is it possible that: 他们早该到了。～走错道啦? They should be here long ago. Is it possible that they have taken the wrong road?

敢死队 gǎnsǐduì dare-to-die corps; suicide squad: 日本空军～队员 kamikaze

敢想敢干 gǎnxiǎng-gǎngàn dare to think (of sth. extraordinary) and dare to act; be bold of vision and courageous in action

敢许 gǎnxǔ maybe; perhaps: 这块地种上山药，～有好收成。Maybe we'll be able to get a good crop of Chinese yam on this piece of land.

敢于 gǎnyú dare to; be bold in; have the courage to: ～承担责任 dare to shoulder a responsibility / ～面对现实 have the guts to face reality squarely

敢自 gǎnzi 〈方言〉 indeed; really: 你亲自去一趟，那～好。It would be nice indeed if you go there in person.

敢作敢当 gǎnzuò-gǎndāng be bold enough to do sth. and take the consequences

敢作敢为 gǎnzuò-gǎnwéi dare to take action; be afraid of no difficulties

橄

gǎn

橄榄 gǎnlǎn 〈植物〉 ❶ *also* "青果" qīngguǒ Chinese olive (*Canarium album*); fruit of the canary tree ❷ (oil) olive

橄榄绿 gǎnlǎnlǜ olive green

橄榄球 gǎnlǎnqiú 〈体育〉 rugby: 十三人制～ rugby league football; Northern Union football / 十五人制～ rugby; rugby football; rugby union football / 美式～ American football

橄榄石 gǎnlǎnshí 〈矿业〉 olivine

橄榄岩 gǎnlǎnyán 〈地质〉 peridotite

橄榄油 gǎnlǎnyóu olive oil

橄榄陨铁 gǎnlǎn yǔntiě pallasite

橄榄枝 gǎnlǎnzhī olive branch — symbol of peace

gàn

干[1]（幹、榦）

gàn ❶ trunk; stem; main part: 树～ tree-trunk; trunk / 躯～ 〈生理〉 trunk; torso / 骨～ backbone; hard core; mainstay / 基～民兵 core members of the militia ❷ (short for 干部) cadre: 高～ senior cadre; ranking cadre / 提～ promote a soldier or a worker to the rank of a cadre / 审～ examine the cadres' personal histories

干[2]（幹）

gàn ❶ do; act; work: 夜以继日地～ work day and night; work round the clock / 肯～ ready to work; willing to do sth. / 巧～ work skilfully; do sth. in a clever way / 愣～ 〈口语〉 do things recklessly; persist in going one's own way / 蛮～ act rashly; be reckless; be foolhardy / ～尽坏事 do all kinds of evil things; stop at no evil / 埋头苦～ immerse oneself in hard work; be hardworking / ～得很漂亮。Well done! / 今天我有好多事要～。I have a lot on hand today. ❷ competent; capable; able; talented: 才～ ability; competence / 精～ keen-witted and capable; crack / 这人精明强～。He is a man of great ability. ❸ undertake (a job, etc.); hold the post of; assume the office of: 他～过会计。He was once an accountant. ❹ 〈方言〉 go bad; what a mess: 这事眼看要～。This is going to be a disaster. *or* It's going to the dogs.

see also gān

干部 gànbù cadre; public functionary or servant; government or Party employee: 各级领导～ leading cadres at all levels / ～带头 cadres standing in the van / ～政策 policy towards cadres; cadre policy / ～路线 guidelines on cadres; basic principles and methods for selecting cadres / ～下放 arrange for cadres to go to work at grass-roots units or participate in physical labour / ～责任制 cadres respon-

sibility system — a system that stipulates the responsibilities of cadres and the terms for their reward and punishment /～服 *also* "中山装" cadre suit; Sun Yat-sen jacket (called wrongly Mao jacket in the West)
干部学校 gànbù xuéxiào school for cadres; cadre school
干不过 gànbuguò be inferior to sb. (in doing sth.); cannot get the better of sb.: 论打铁，谁都～他。Nobody can surpass him in forging iron.
干才 gàncái ❶ ability; capability: 这个人颇有点～。He is a man of considerable ability. ❷ capable or able person
干道 gàndào artery; main road; trunk line
干得过 gàndeguò be superior to sb. (in doing sth.); can get the better of sb.; beat: 你跟他比割麦，～他吗? Can you beat (*or* outdo) him (*or* get the better of him) in cutting wheat?
干得过儿 gàndeguòr be worth doing; be worthwhile: 这笔生意～。The deal is worth making.
干掉 gàndiào 〈口语〉 kill; get rid of; put out of the way: 他给黑社会歹徒～了。He was bumped off by an underworld thug.
干活儿 gànhuór work; work on a job: 他们都下地～了。They all went to work in the fields. *or* They are all at work in the fields.
干济 gànjì 〈书面〉 capable and experienced: ～之才 competent person
干家 gànjiā ❶ (often used in the early vernacular) manage household affairs ❷ capable or able person: 他是本地有名的～。His exceptional ability is well-known in this area.
干架 gànjià 〈方言〉 ❶ quarrel; squabble: 那两口子老～。The couple often quarrel. ❷ come to blows: 今早你儿子和他班上的同学干了一架。Your son picked a fight with one of his classmates this morning.
干将 gànjiàng capable person; go-getter
see also gānjiāng
干劲 gànjìn drive; vim; vigour; enthusiasm: 鼓～ rouse one's enthusiasm /～十足 brim over with vigour (*or* drive) /这人很有～，工作肯定能做好。He has plenty of go and is sure to do well in his job.
干警 gànjǐng cadres and policemen of the public security office; police officers and constables
干了 gànle 〈方言〉 too bad; what a mess: ～! 这两人又吵起来了! Too bad! The two started quarreling again.
干练 gànliàn capable and experienced: 精明～的人 keen-witted and capable person
干流 gànliú *also* "主流" zhǔliú trunk stream; mainstream
干路 gànlù *see* "干道"
干吗 gànmá 〈口语〉 ❶ why; whatever for: ～这么认真? Why take it so seriously? /～不去试试? Why not go and have a try? ❷ what to do: 这礼拜天咱们～? What are we going to do this Sunday? /你想～? What do you want? *or* What are you up to?
干渠 gànqú 〈水利〉 trunk canal; main canal
干群 gàn-qún public servants in the Party and government organisations and people at the grass roots level; cadres and the masses: 加强～关系 strengthen the relations between the cadres and the masses
干上了 gànshangle be at it; start quarreling: 这对老冤家又～! The two old foes are squabbling again.
干什么 gàn shénme *see* "干吗"
干事 gànshi secretary or clerical worker in charge of sth.: 文娱～ person in charge of recreational activities; officer of recreations /宣传～ person in charge of publicity work
干头儿 gàntour be worth doing; be worthwhile: 这种吃力不讨好的事没～。That's a thankless job. It's not worth the candle.
干细胞 gànxìbāo 〈生物〉 stem cell
干线 gànxiàn main line; trunk line; main; artery: 公路～ arterial or main highway /铁路～ arterial railways; trunk line; trunk railway /交通～ main lines of communication /沿～城镇 main-line towns /～网 arterial grid /供电～ supply mains; main supply /输电～ electric main; trunk transmission line /～电缆 main cable; trunk cable
干校 gànxiào (short for 干部学校) school for cadres; cadre school (school that specializes in training cadres): 五七～ May 7 cadre school (term used in the Cultural Revolution for a farm, etc. where cadres were supposed to re-educate themselves)
干休所 gànxiūsuǒ cadres' sanatorium (establishment for retired and invalid cadres to rest and receive medical treatment); home for retired cadres
干训班 gànxùnbān class for in-service training of government and Party officials
干员 gànyuán 〈旧语〉 capable official
干仗 gànzhàng 〈方言〉 *see* "干架"

旰 gàn 〈书面〉 at night: 宵衣～食 get up before dawn and have meals after dark — be immersed in state affairs

骭 gàn 〈书面〉 ❶ shank; lower leg ❷ rib

绀 gàn dark purple: 发～〈医学〉 cyanosis
绀青 gànqīng *also* "绀紫" dark purple; prune purple

赣 Gàn ❶ Ganjiang River (in Jiangxi Province) ❷ another name for Jiangxi (江西)
赣剧 gànjù one of the local operas in Jiangxi
赣语 Gànyǔ dialect spoken mostly in Jiangxi and partly in Hubei

gāng

江 Gāng a surname

杠 gāng 〈书面〉 ❶ bridge ❷ flagpole; flagstaff
see also gàng

矼 gāng 〈书面〉 stone bridge

扛 gāng ❶ lift with both hands: 力能～鼎 powerful enough to lift a *ding*; as strong as a horse ❷ 〈方言〉 (of two or more people) carry sth. together
see also káng

釭 gāng 〈书面〉 oil lamp

缸(甌) gāng ❶ vat; jar; bowl; crock: 水～ water vat /酒～ wine jar /染～ dyejigger; dye vat /金鱼～ goldfish bowl /一～咸菜 a jar of salted vegetables ❷ compound of sand, clay, etc. for making earthenware: *see* "～盆"; "～瓦" ❸ sth. shaped like a jar or vat: 汽～ cylinder /烟灰～ ashtray
缸管 gāngguǎn earthen pipe
缸径 gāngjìng bore; cylinder diameter
缸炉 gānglu *also* "干炉" gānlu baked sweet cake
缸盆 gāngpén glazed earthen basin
缸式磨机 gāngshì mójī jar mill
缸瓦 gāngwǎ compound of sand, clay, etc. for making earthenwares
缸瓦器 gāngwǎqì *also* "粗陶器" cūtáoqì stoneware
缸用铸铁 gāngyòng zhùtiě cylinder iron
缸砖 gāngzhuān clinker (tile); quarry tile
缸子 gāngzi mug; bowl: 茶～ (tea) mug /糖～ sugar bowl /搪瓷～ enamel mug

肛 gāng anus: 脱～ prolapse of the anus (*or* rectum)
肛表 gāngbiǎo anal or rectal thermometer
肛道 gāngdào *also* "肛管" proctodaeum; anal canal
肛裂 gāngliè 〈医学〉 anal fissure; Allingham's ulcer
肛瘘 gānglòu *also* "漏疮" lòuchuāng; "痔漏" zhìlòu 〈医学〉 anal fistula; *fistula in ano*
肛门 gāngmén 〈生理〉 anus
肛门闭锁 gāngmén bìsuǒ imperforate anus; ectopic anus; anal atresia; *atresia ani*
肛门成形术 gāngmén chéngxíngshù anoplasty
肛门镜 gāngménjìng anoscope: ～检查 anoscopy
肛门神经 gāngmén shénjīng nervi anales
肛门狭窄 gāngmén xiázhǎi stricture of anus
肛门炎 gāngményán anusitis
肛门肿瘤 gāngmén zhǒngliú anus neoplasm

罡 gāng

罡风 gāngfēng *also* "刚风" gāngfēng ❶〈道教〉wind in the empyrean, the highest heaven ❷ high wind; strong wind

冈(岡) gāng (low and flat) ridge (of a hill):山～ low hill; hillock /景阳～ Jingyang Ridge

冈比亚 Gāngbǐyà the Gambia:～人 Gambian

冈比亚河 Gāngbǐyàhé Gambia River

冈底斯山 Gāngdǐsīshān Gandise Mountains, a mountain range in the Tibet Autonomous Region

冈阜 gāngfù hillock; low hill

冈禾 gānghé 〈方言〉upland rice; dry rice

冈陵 gānglíng ridges and hills:～起伏 undulating ridges and hills

冈峦 gāngluán chain of hills

㭎(棡) gāng *see* "青㭎" qīnggāng

㧴(掆) gāng 〈书面〉*see* "扛" gāng

刚[1](剛) gāng ❶ firm; strong; hard; staunch:血气方～ (of young men) full of sap /以柔克～ overcome hardness by softness /柔中有～ strength in gentleness ❷ (Gāng) a surname

刚[2](剛) gāng 〈副词〉❶ just; exactly; precisely:～合适 just right /这件大衣我穿上～好。This overcoat fits me perfectly. ❷ barely; just; no more than:这块布料～够做一件衬衣。This piece of cloth is just (*or* barely) enough for a shirt. /～到六点。It's just six o'clock. *or* It's six sharp. ❸ just; only a short while ago:会议～开始。The meeting has just begun. /他～来过。He was here just now. /～出虎口,又入狼窝 come out of the tiger's mouth only to step into the wolf's lair — be dogged by frequent misfortunes ❹ (used in a compound sentence with 就 following in the second clause to indicate immediacy) hardly ... when ...; no sooner than; just as; only at this moment:我～想给他打电话,他就来了。He came just as I was about to call him. /我～进屋,就下起雨来。I had hardly entered the room when it began to rain. /他～来就发牢骚。No sooner had he arrived than he began to complain. *or* He started to complain the moment he arrived. /他们天～亮就起身了。They set out as soon as dawn began to break.

刚愎 gāngbì stubborn; intractable; unbending:～不仁 headstrong and unkind

刚愎自用 gāngbì-zìyòng self-willed; opinionated; headstrong; bent on having one's own way:他这样～,早晚要碰壁。His obstinacy and conceit will get him into trouble sooner or later.

刚才 gāngcái just now; a moment ago:别把～跟你说的事告诉他。Don't tell him what I told you just now. /他～还在这儿呢。He was around a moment ago.

刚肠 gāngcháng (of character) upright and outspoken:～侠骨 upright and chivalrous

刚虫 gāngchóng fierce birds and beasts

刚瘅 gāngdàn evil spirit; devil; demon

刚度 gāngdù stiffness; rigidity; severity:～常数 stiffness constant /～系数 stiffness coefficient /～条件 rigidity condition /～准则〈航空〉stiffness criterion

刚风 gāngfēng *see* "罡风" gāngfēng

刚刚 gānggang *same as* 刚[2]:他考试～及格。He barely passed the examination. /我参军～一个月。It's only a month since I joined the army. /邮件～到。The mail came just now. /不要打扰他,他～躺下。Don't disturb him. He went to bed only a moment ago.

刚果 Gāngguǒ the Congo:～河 the Congo (River) /～人 Congolese /～语 Congolese (language)

刚果红 gāngguǒhóng Congo red:～试验 Congo red test

刚果胶 gāngguǒjiāo 〈化学〉Congo copal; Congo gum

刚好 gānghǎo ❶ no more, no less; just (right); exactly:人数～够。There're just enough people. /时间～。The time is just about right. /说到他,他～就来了。Talk of the devil, here he comes. ❷ happen to; it so happens that; as luck would have it:两个舞蹈演员～一般高。The two dancers happened to be of the same height. /我～在剧院门口碰见他。It so happened that I met him by the gate of the theatre.

刚架 gāngjià 〈建筑〉rigid frame; stiff frame:～结构 rigid-framed structure /～梁 rigid-frame beam

刚健 gāngjiàn (of character, style, bearing, etc.) vigorous; forceful; dynamic; robust:身姿～ robust physique /～的舞蹈 spirited dance /迈着～的步伐前进 march forward with firm and vigorous steps

刚介 gāngjiè 〈书面〉unyielding and upright; steadfast and honest:这位先生一生～。He is staunch and upright, and remains so all his life.

刚晶 gāngjīng crystallon

刚劲 gāngjìng (of handwriting, bearing, style, etc.) forceful and vigorous; bold; sturdy:那～潇洒的字体让人们赞不绝口。The forceful and elegant brushstrokes won the great admiration of many people.

刚决 gāngjué 〈书面〉staunch and resolute; firm and decisive

刚口 gāngkou *also* "钢口" gāngkou 〈方言〉have a glib tongue; have the gift of the gab:这人好～。That man has a ready tongue.

刚棱 gāngléng upright and sharp-witted

刚烈 gāngliè (a person of) strong character and moral integrity:～女子 woman of strong character and integrity

刚毛 gāngmáo bristle; seta; chaeta

刚毛藻属 gāngmáozǎoshǔ 〈植物〉*Cladophora*

刚气 gāngqì ❶ mettle:他眉宇间露着一股～。His broad forehead shows that he is a man of mettle. ❷ tough; staunch; unyielding:这个人真～,那么重的伤一哼也不哼。He was such a tough guy that he did not give a groan despite his serious wound.

刚强 gāngqiáng firm; steadfast; staunch; unyielding:～铁汉 man of steel /意志～ strong- (*or* iron-)willed /他用～的毅力克服了各种困难,终于取得成功。He succeeded in the end after overcoming many difficulties with great willpower.

刚巧 gāngqiǎo *see* "刚好❷"

刚韧 gāngrèn (of character) firm and unyielding; tenacious:～的性格 strong and tenacious character

刚柔 gāng-róu hard and soft; tough and gentle; firm and flexible

刚柔相济 gāngróu-xiāngjì combine firmness and flexibility; temper toughness with gentleness

刚石 gāngshí *also* "刚玉"〈矿业〉corundum; alundum

刚体 gāngtǐ 〈物理〉rigid body:～动力学 rigid-body dynamics

刚性 gāngxìng 〈物理〉rigidity:～轴 rigid axle; rigid shaft /～拱〈建筑〉rigid arch /～管 rigid pipe /～支架 rigid support /～结构 rigid structure

刚性 gāngxing strong character:一个男子汉应该有～。A man should have a strong character (*or* will).

刚毅 gāngyì resolute and steadfast:～果断 resolute and decisive

刚硬 gāngyìng ❶ firm; unbending; unyielding:性格～ strong character ❷ strong; tough:～的口气 uncompromising tone ❸ hard; solid:～的工具 hard tools

刚勇 gāngyǒng strong-willed and courageous:外柔顺而内～ outwardly gentle and pliable but inwardly strong-willed and courageous

刚玉 gāngyù 〈矿业〉*see* "刚石"

刚玉岩 gāngyùyán emery rock

刚正 gāngzhèng staunch and upright; principled

刚正不阿 gāngzhèng-bù'ē upright and never stooping to flattery; keeping to principles and not yielding to pressure

刚直 gāngzhí upright and outspoken

刚竹 gāngzhú a kind of tough bamboo (*Phyllostachys viridis*), often used for handicraft wares

岗(崗) gāng *see* "冈" gāng

see also gǎng; gàng

钢(鋼) gāng steel:扁～ flat steel /槽～ channel (iron)/轴承～ bearing steel /结构～ structural steel /弹簧～ spring steel /淬火～ quenched steel /工具～ tool steel /软～ mild steel; soft steel /高速～ high-speed steel /不锈～ stainless steel /优质～ high quality steel /铸～ cast steel /铬～ chromium steel /硅～ silicon steel /锰～ manganese steel /合金～ alloy steel /高碳～ high-carbon steel /炼～ steelmaking /轧～ steel rolling /冷轧～ cold-rolled steel /人无志,刀无～。A man without aspirations is like a knife without steel.

see also gàng

钢板 gāngbǎn ❶ steel plate; plate:薄～ steel sheet; sheet steel /厚～ steel plate /成型～ shaped steel plate /网眼～ perforated plate /抗低温～ low temperature resistant steel plate /锅炉～ boiler plate /造船～ ship plate ❷ spring (of a motorcar, etc.) ❸ stencil steel board

钢包 gāngbāo *also* "钢水包" pig iron or crude iron ladle
钢镚儿 gāngbèngr *also* "钢镚子"〈口语〉coin
钢笔 gāngbǐ *also* "自来水笔" zìláishuǐbǐ pen; fountain pen:～尖 pen nib /～帽 pen cap
钢笔画 gāngbǐhuà pen-and-ink drawing
钢笔水 gāngbǐshuǐ 〈口语〉ink
钢笔套 gāngbǐtào ❶ sheath of a pen (made of thread, cloth or silk) ❷〈方言〉cap of a pen; pen cap
钢鞭 gāngbiān iron staff (used as a weapon in ancient China)
钢箔 gāngbó steel foil
钢材 gāngcái steel products; steels; rolled steel
钢城 gāngchéng steel city (a city famous for steel production):鞍山是我国的～。Anshan is our nation's steel city.
钢尺 gāngchǐ steel rule
钢锉 gāngcuò steel file
钢带 gāngdài steel band; steel belt; steel strip
钢刀 gāngdāo knife (made of steel):～虽快,不斩无罪之人。A knife, however sharp, is not to be employed to kill an innocent person. *or* The innocent need have no fear of the law.
钢锭 gāngdìng steel ingot
钢构件 gānggòujiàn steel member; steel part
钢箍 gānggū steel hoop
钢骨 gānggǔ reinforcing (steel) bar
钢骨水泥 gānggǔ shuǐní reinforced concrete
钢鼓 gānggǔ steel drum
钢管 gāngguǎn steel tube or pipe:无缝～ seamless steel tube /异形～ chapped pipe /焊接～ welded steel pipe
钢轨 gāngguǐ *also* "铁轨" tiěguǐ rail:～钢 rail steel /～钳 rail tongs /～探伤仪 rail flaw detector /～连接板 joint fastening /～铝热剂 railroad thermit
钢号 gānghào 〈冶金〉steel grade
钢花 gānghuā spray or spark of molten steel:～飞舞 sparks of molten steel flying about (*or* around)
钢化玻璃 gānghuà bōli toughened glass
钢婚 gānghūn eleventh anniversary of a marriage (observed by Europeans and Americans)
钢架 gāngjià steel frame:～厂房 steel frame (mill) building; steel frame mill or plant /～结构 steel frame structure
钢结构 gāngjiégòu 〈建筑〉steel structure; steel construction
钢筋 gāngjīn *also* "钢骨" reinforcing (steel) bar; steel reinforcement:高强度～ high strength steel /～混凝土 reinforced concrete /～网 wiremesh reinforcement; fabric reinforcement /网状～ steel mesh reinforcement /～工 steel bender; steel fixer /弯～机 steel bender
钢筋铁胆 gāngjīn-tiědǎn have iron nerves and steel sinews — be tough and courageous
钢筋铁骨 gāngjīn-tiěgǔ have muscles of steel and bones of iron — be extremely tough
钢精 gāngjīng *also* "钢种" aluminium (as used for utensils):～锅 aluminium pan
钢锯 gāngjù hacksaw:～架 hacksaw frame /～条 hacksaw blade
钢卷尺 gāngjuǎnchǐ steel (measuring) tape
钢筘 gāngkòu 〈纺织〉reed
钢口 gāngkou ❶ quality of the edge (of a knife, sword, etc.):这把刀～儿不错。The knife has a sharp edge. ❷ have a glib tongue; have the gift of the gab *see also* "刚口" gāngkou
钢盔 gāngkuī (steel) helmet
钢梁 gāngliáng steel girder
钢炮 gāngpào modern cannon or gun:小～ small calibre gun
钢坯 gāngpī 〈冶金〉billet; steel feed; steel billet:大～ bloom /～轧机 billet mill
钢片 gāngpiàn steel disc
钢片琴 gāngpiànqín 〈乐器〉celesta
钢瓶 gāngpíng steel cylinder
钢钎 gāngqiān drill rod; drill steel
钢枪 gāngqiāng rifle
钢琴 gāngqín piano:大～ grand piano /竖式～ upright piano /自动～ pianola /弹～ play the piano /～四重奏 piano quartet /～五重奏 piano quintet /～家 pianist
钢砂 gāngshā steel emery
钢水 gāngshuǐ 〈冶金〉molten steel:～包 steel ladle; pig iron ladle
钢丝 gāngsī (steel) wire:走～〈杂技〉walk the wire; walk a tightrope; high-wire walking
钢丝床 gāngsīchuáng spring bed
钢丝垫子 gāngsī diànzi spring mattress
钢丝锯 gāngsījù fret saw; scroll saw; wire saw
钢丝录音机 gāngsī lùyīnjī wire recorder
钢丝钳 gāngsīqián combination pliers; cutting pliers
钢丝绳 gāngsīshéng steel cable; wire rope; wire cable; wire line
钢丝刷 gāngsīshuā steel brush; steel wire brush; wire brush
钢丝网 gāngsīwǎng steel wire gauze
钢索 gāngsuǒ cable wire; steel rope; wire rope
钢条 gāngtiáo steel bar; steel ribbon
钢铁 gāngtiě ❶ iron and steel; steel:～厂 steelworks; steel mill; iron and steel plant /～工业 iron and steel industry /～公司 iron and steel company /～联合企业 integrate iron and steel works; iron and steel complex ❷ strong and tough as iron and steel:～汉 man of steel; strong (*or* tough) guy /～意志 iron will; indomitable will /～运输线 unbreakable transport line
钢铁长城 gāngtiě-chángchéng great wall of steel (referring to the Chinese People's Liberation Army)
钢芯铝线 gāngxīn lǚxiàn steel-cored aluminium cable or wire; steel-reinforced aluminium cable
钢芯铜线 gāngxīn tóngxiàn steel-cored copper wire
钢印 gāngyìn ❶ steel seal; embossing seal ❷ embossed stamp:上面盖了学院的～ bear the embossed stamp of the College
钢渣 gāngzhā slag
钢蒸馏罐 gāngzhēngliúguàn 〈化工〉steel retort
钢纸 gāngzhǐ vulcanized fibre (paper)
钢制反应釜 gāngzhì fǎnyìngfǔ 〈化工〉steel bomb
钢种 gāngzhǒng *see* "钢精"
钢珠 gāngzhū steel ball (in a ball bearing); ball bearing; ball
钢字 gāngzì steel letter

纲(綱)

gāng ❶ headrope of a fishing net:撒网要抓～ take the net by the headrope when fishing — grasp the heart of the matter when trying to solve a problem ❷ key link; guiding principle; outline; programme:以…为～ with... as the key link; take... as the guiding principle /大～ outline /政～ political programme; platform /党～ party constitution; party platform /全书总～ general outline of the book ❸〈生物〉class:哺乳动物～ class of mammals /亚～ subclass ❹〈旧语〉organization for transporting certain goods in large quantities (sometimes under convoy):盐～ organization for transporting salt in large quantities /～盐 salt transported by such an organization
纲常 gāngcháng three cardinal guides and five constant virtues *see also* "三纲五常" sāngāng-wǔcháng
纲纪 gāngjì 〈书面〉order and discipline:～废弛 become lax about rules and regulations /整顿～ restore order and strengthen discipline
纲举目张 gāngjǔ-mùzhāng once you pull up the headrope of a fishing net, all its meshes open — once you seize hold of the key link, everything falls into place
纲领 gānglǐng ❶ programme:最高～ maximum programme (of a government, political party, etc.) ❷ guiding principle; guidelines:～性文件 programmatic document
纲目 gāngmù (usu. used as the title of a book) detailed outline (of a subject); outline:《本草～》*Compendium of Materia Medica* (written in 1578 by Li Shizhen)
纲要 gāngyào ❶ outline; sketch:先写成～,再写全文。Make an outline before you write the article. ❷ (usu. used as the title of a book or document) essentials; compendium:《中国历史～》*Essentials of Chinese History*

gǎng

港

gǎng ❶ port; harbour:海～ seaport; harbour /军～ naval port /内河～ inland port /商～ commercial port /渔～ fishing port (*or* harbour) /深水～ deep-water port /不冻～ ice-free port; open port /避风～ harbour; haven /自由～ free port /天然～ natural harbour /出发～ port of departure /到达～ port of arrival /目的～ port of destination /装货～ port of shipment; port of loading /交货～ port of delivery /停靠～ port of call /船籍～ port of registry /进口～ port of entry /出～ clear a port; leave port ❷ airport:飞机离～。The plane has taken off. ❸ tributary of a river:常山～ Changshangang,

G

a river in Zhejiang Province ❹ (Gǎng) (short for 香港) Hong Kong; HK: ～英当局 (before 1 July, 1997) British authorities in Hong Kong ❺ Hong Kong style: 她这一身儿多～! How she is dressed in Hong Kong fashion!
港澳 Gǎng-Ào Hong Kong and Macao
港澳办 Gǎng-Àobàn (short for 港澳事务办公室) Hong Kong and Macao Affairs Office
港澳台同胞 Gǎng-Ào-Tái tóngbāo compatriots in Hong Kong, Macao, and Taiwan
港胞 Gǎngbāo compatriot in Hong Kong
港币 gǎngbì Hong Kong currency; Hong Kong dollar
港埠 gǎngbù port; quay port: 国际～ international port
港汊 gǎngchà branching stream
港督 Gǎngdū (before 1 July, 1997) governor of Hong Kong
港府 Gǎngfǔ (before 1 July, 1997) Hong Kong government
港规 gǎngguī harbour regulation
港警 gǎngjǐng port police
港客 gǎngkè guest or customer from Hong Kong
港口 gǎngkǒu port; harbour: 沿海～ coastal port /～泊位 seaport berth /～设施 port facilities /～费用 port charges; port dues /～建筑线 pierhead line /～吞吐量 traffic (of a port) /～河段 〈地理〉 harbour reach
港口税 gǎngkǒushuì port dues
港龙 Gǎnglóng Dragonair, a Hong Kong-based airline corporation
港人治港 Gǎngrén zhì Gǎng Hong Kong people administering Hong Kong (China's policy vis-à-vis Hong Kong)
港商 gǎngshāng merchant or businessman from Hong Kong
港式 gǎngshì Hong Kong fashion
港湾 gǎngwān harbour: ～沉积 estuarine deposit /～泥 estuarine mud
港务 gǎngwù harbour administration: ～代表 representative of port authorities
港务费 gǎngwùfèi harbour dues; port rate
港务监督 gǎngwù jiāndū harbour superintendency administration
港务局 gǎngwùjú port office; harbour authority
港纸 gǎngzhǐ Hong Kong money
港资 gǎngzī Hong Kong capital

G

䒩(䲈) gǎng 〈书面〉 salt marsh

岗(崗) gǎng ❶ hillock; mound: 山～ low hill; hillock /沙～ sand hill /乱坟～ unmarked common graves; unmarked burial-mounds /～峦起伏 undulating hills ❷ ridge; welt; wale ❸ sentry; post: 站～ stand sentry; keep guard /布～ post a sentinel /下～ come off sentry duty; (of workers) be made redundant; be laid off /换～ relieve a sentry (*or* guard) /门～ gate sentry /交通～ traffic police post
see also gāng; gàng
岗村宁次 Gǎngcūnníngcì Yasuji Okamura (1884-1966), one of the top commanders of the Japanese aggressor forces in China in World War II, condemned as war criminal
岗地 gǎngdì farm land on low hills
岗警 gǎngjǐng policeman on point duty
岗楼 gǎnglóu watchtower
岗坡 gǎngpō hillside; mountain slope: ～地 farm land on hillside
岗卡 gǎngqiǎ outpost of the tax office; checkpoint
岗哨 gǎngshào ❶ sentry post ❷ sentry; sentinel: 设置～ post sentries /流动～ person (*or* soldier) on patrol duties; patrol
岗台 gǎngtái sentry stand; police stand
岗亭 gǎngtíng sentry box; police box
岗位 gǎngwèi post; station; job: ～津贴 job subsidy /～培训 on-the-job training /离开～ quit a post /走上新的～ take up a new post; take on a new job /在平凡的～上, 干出了不平凡的成绩 have extraordinary achievements to one's credit at an ordinary post
岗位责任制 gǎngwèi zérènzhì system of post responsibility; system of responsibility for the work done by each individual at his post: 企事业单位都应实行～。The system of post responsibility should be established in all enterprises and institutions.
岗子 gǎngzi ❶ mound; hillock: 土～ (earthen) mound ❷ ridge; wale; welt

gàng

戆 gàng 〈方言〉 foolish; silly; reckless; foolhardy: 这个人～头～脑的。That's a silly fellow.
see also zhuàng
戆大 gàngdà 〈方言〉 fool; blockhead; simpleton; patsy
戆头 gàngtóu 〈方言〉 fool; idiot; nitwit

杠(槓) gàng ❶ thick stick or club: 顶门～ thick staff used to prop up the door leaf from the inside ❷ 〈体育〉 bar: 单～ horizontal bar /双～ parallel bars /高低～ uneven (parallel) bars; asymmetric bars ❸ rod-shaped spare part (of a machine): 丝～ guide screw; leading screw /保险～ bumper ❹ stout poles used to carry a coffin ❺ thick line drawn beside or under words as a mark: 在主要的地方画了两条～ mark the important places (in a article) with 2 thick lines ❻ cross out; delete: 把稿中的病句和错字～掉 cross (*or* strike) out all the faulty sentences and wrongly written characters in the draft ❼ standard; criterion: 他们的做法过了～儿。They have gone beyond the limit of propriety in their action.
see also gāng
杠棒 gàngbàng stout carrying pole
杠荡 gàngdang 〈方言〉 ❶ rock; shake; sway: 不要～新栽培的小树。Don't shake the newly-planted saplings. ❷ hesitate; waver: 这事不能再～了, 要赶快定下来。Stop dilly-dallying. We've got to make a decision on the matter at once.
杠房 gàngfáng 〈旧语〉 old-fashioned undertaker's
杠夫 gàngfū 〈旧语〉 professional coffin bearer
杠杆 gànggǎn ❶ lever; heaver; pry bar: ～臂 lever arm /～支点 balance pivot; lever fulcrum /～作用 leverage; lever action ❷ leverage: 经济～ economic leverage
杠杆定律 gànggǎn dìnglǜ lever law
杠杆率 gànggǎnlǜ leverage
杠杆收购 gànggǎn shōugòu 〈金融〉 leveraged buy-out
杠杆原理 gànggǎn yuánlǐ lever principle
杠杠 gànggang ❶ rules; regulations: 退休要有个年龄～。There should be age limits for retirement. ❷ criterion; standard: 划出几道政策～ define certain policy criteria
杠铃 gànglíng 〈体育〉 barbell: ～片 disc (of a barbell)
杠人 gàngrén *see* "杠夫"
杠头 gàngtóu 〈方言〉 ❶ chief of a group of professional coffin bearers ❷ person who argues for the sake of arguing; incorrigible wrangler: 那人是个～。He is fond of wrangling. ❸ 〈方言〉 a kind of baked bread made of a mixture of leavened and unleavened dough and flattened with a rolling pin: ～大饼 mixed-dough pancake
杠子 gàngzi ❶ thick stick; stout carrying pole ❷ 〈体育〉 bar ❸ thickline marking errors, etc.

岗(崗) gàng
see also gāng; gǎng
岗尖 gàngjiān 〈方言〉 ❶ be full to the brim: ～满 filled to overflowing; full to the brim /～一碗米饭 a full bowl of cooked rice ❷ excellent; superb: 这是一批～儿的大苹果。These are extra-fine big apples.
岗口儿甜 gàngkǒurtián 〈方言〉 extremely sweet

钢(鋼) gàng ❶ sharpen; grind; whet; strop: ～菜刀 sharpen a kitchen knife /～剪刀 grind scissors/～镰刀 whet a sickle/～剃刀 strop a razor ❷ reinforce the edge (of a knife, etc.) by adding steel and retempering
see also gāng
钢刀布 gàngdāobù (razor) strop

gāo

高 gāo ❶ tall; high: ～山大川 high mountains and great rivers /从～处往下看 look down from a height /他比我～一头。He is a head taller than I. /站得～, 看得远。Stand high and you'll see far. /树～万丈, 落叶归根。A tree may grow a hundred thousand feet high,

but its fallen leaves will return to the roots. ❷ height:跳～ high jump /台～三米。The platform is 3 metres high. ❸ advanced; superior:～质量 superior (*or* top) quality /～水平 advanced level /价格太～ exorbitant price /声望～ of a high prestige /～技术 sophisticated technology /这主意真～! What a brilliant idea! ❹ of a high or higher rank:～年级学生 students of higher (*or* senior) grades ❺ loud:嗓门儿～ have a loud (*or* big) voice /～喊 shout at the top of one's voice /调儿起～了。The tune was pitched too high. ❻〈敬词〉your; his; their: *see* "～论";"～见" ❼〈化学〉containing one more oxygen atom in an acid or a chemical compound: *see* "～锰酸钾" ❽〈数学〉altitude:三角形的～线 altitude of a triangle /测～仪 altitude gauge ❾ (Gāo) a surname

高矮 gāo'ǎi height:兄弟俩～差不多。The two brothers are about the same height. /～不一。Some are tall and some short.

高氨血 gāo'ānxuè 〈医学〉hyperammonemia

高昂 gāo'áng ❶ hold high (one's head, etc.) ❷ high; elated; jubilant;exalted:斗志～ have high morale /情绪～ be in great spirits /歌声～ inspiring strains of a song ❸ dear; costly;expensive; exorbitant:为此我们付出了～的代价。It cost us dearly.

高傲 gāo'ào supercilious; conceited; arrogant; haughty:～自大 self-important

高保真度 gāobǎozhēndù high-fidelity; hi-fi

高爆炸弹 gāobào zhàdàn high-explosive bomb

高倍 gāobèi high-powered:～望远镜 high-powered binoculas

高倍显微镜 gāobèi xiǎnwēijìng high-powered microscope

高边疆 gāobiānjiāng 〈军事〉high frontier

高标号 gāobiāohào high grade:～水泥 high-grade cement

高拨子 gāobōzi 〈音乐〉plectrum

高不成,低不就 gāo bù chéng, dī bù jiù be unfit for a higher post but unwilling to take a lower one; can't have one's heart's desire but won't accept less; be unable to attain the best yet unwilling to make do with the second best:他家大小子挑来挑去,～,三十多岁了还没找上对象。His eldest son was so choosy (*or* picky) that he had not yet found a partner in marriage even though he was already over thirty.

高不可攀 gāobùkěpān too high to reach; far beyond one's reach; unattainable:在他的心目中,她是个～的千金小姐。To him she is a wealthy young lady beyond (*or* out of) his reach.

高才 gāocái ❶ remarkable ability; superb talent or gift:～远识 (of a person) superb gift and farsightedness /～硕学 (person) of great talent and scholarship ❷ person of remarkable ability or superb talent:这工作我实在不能胜任,另请～吧。I'm afraid I'm not qualified for the job, so please find someone more suitable.

高才捷足 gāocái-jiézú *also* "高才疾足" capable and efficient:此人～,事事皆居人先。The person is knowledgeable and efficient, and well ahead of others in everything.

高才生 gāocáishēng brilliant student; whiz kid; top of a class

高参 gāocān ❶ senior staff officer ❷ competent adviser; capable counsellor

高层 gāocéng high level:～会议 summit meeting; summit /～建筑 high-rise building; high-rise

高层云 gāocéngyún 〈气象〉altostratus

高层住宅 gāocéng zhùzhái 〈建筑〉high-rise apartment building

高差 gāochā relative altitude

高差计 gāochājì cathetometer

高产 gāochǎn high yield; high production:创～ achieve high yield /～稳产 high and stable yield /～作物 high-yield crop; highly productive crop; heavy yielder /～品种 high-yield variety /～土壤 highly productive soil /～田 high-yield field /～井 high-yield well; prolific well /～轮伐期 high-yield rotation (as of timber cutting) /～优质高效农业 high-yield, high-quality and high-efficiency agriculture

高敞 gāochǎng high and vast; tall and spacious:地势～ open, high terrain /屋宇～ tall and commodious house

高唱 gāochàng ❶ sing loudly; sing with spirit:～战歌向前进 march forward, singing battle songs /～赞歌 sing the praises (of sb. or sth.) ❷ prate; talk glibly about; call out loudly for:他们一面～"和平",一面疯狂备战。They are prating about "peace" but frenziedly preparing for war.

高唱入云 gāochàng-rùyún sing with a resounding voice; sing or write with great spirit

高超 gāochāo superb; outstanding; excellent:见解～ brilliant ideas /技艺～ superb skill

高超声波学 gāochāoshēngbōxué 〈物理〉praetersonics

高超音速 gāochāoyīnsù 〈物理〉hypersonic speed:～飞机 hypersonic aircraft

高潮 gāocháo ❶ high tide; high water:～面 high-water level ❷ upsurge; high tide:社会主义建设的新～ new upsurge in socialist construction ❸ climax:这个故事情节～迭起。The story reaches one climax after another.

高潮线 gāocháoxiàn high-water mark or line

高程 gāochéng altitude; elevation; height:～测量 height measurement /～水头〈水利〉elevation head

高矗 gāochù stand tall and upright; towering:～的山岭挡住了寒风。The towering mountains keep off the cold wind.

高纯度 gāochúndù high purity:～物质 high purity material

高次方程 gāocì fāngchéng equation of higher degree

高醋 gāocù top-quality vinegar

高大 gāodà ❶ tall and big; high:身材～ be of great stature /～的建筑物 high-rise building; high-rise /～明亮的厂房 bright, high-ceilinged workshop ❷ lofty; noble:人们为英雄人物～的形象所鼓舞。People are inspired by the lofty image of the heroes. ❸ (often used in the early vernacular) aged; advanced in years

高待 gāodài 〈方言〉treat with great courtesy; give generous treatment:新女婿头次登门,受到格外～。The new son-in-law was treated with extraordinary courtesy because this was the first time he visited his parents-in-law.

高蛋白 gāodànbái high protein:～食品 high-protein food /富含～ with high-protein content

高档 gāodàng top grade; superior quality:～商品 high-grade goods; expensive commodities of high quality /～产品市场 upmarket /～信贷份额 higher credit tranche (bond for sale abroad)

高蹈 gāodǎo 〈书面〉❶ go on a long journey ❷ live in seclusion; withdraw from society and live in solitude; be a hermit

高等 gāoděng higher; senior; advanced:～数学 higher mathematics /～代数 higher algebra /～化学 advanced chemistry /～哺乳动物 higher mammal /～细菌 higher bacteria /～师范 senior normal school

高等裁判所 Gāoděng Cáipànsuǒ (Japan) High Court

高等动物 gāoděng dòngwù higher animal

高等法院 gāoděng fǎyuàn high court; high court of justice

高等教育 gāoděng jiàoyù higher education; tertiary education

高等学校 gāoděng xuéxiào institutions of higher learning; colleges and universities

高等植物 gāoděng zhíwù higher plant

高低 gāodī ❶ height:建筑物的～ height of a building /～不平的地面 accidented ground;uneven ground /声调的～ the pitch of a voice /小伙子身材～如何? How tall is that young man? ❷ relative superiority or inferiority; difference in degree:何必与他争～。There is no point in vying with him to see who is superior. ❸ sense of propriety; appropriateness:他说话不知～。He had no sense of discretion when he started to talk. ❹〈方言〉on any account; just; simply:嘴都说破了,他～不答应。I talked myself hoarse, but he just wouldn't say yes. ❺〈方言〉at long last:这本书找了好几天,～找到了。We've been looking for the book for several days and now find it at last.

高低杠 gāodīgàng 〈体育〉uneven (parallel) bars; asymmetric bars

高低角 gāodījiǎo 〈军事〉angle of site

高低射界 gāodī shèjiè 〈军事〉vertical field of fire

高低压炮 gāodīyāpào high-low pressure gun

高地 gāodì ❶ highland; upland; elevation:～田 upland field ❷〈军事〉height:无名～ nameless height /抢占三三二～ capture Height 332

高碘酸 gāodiǎnsuān 〈化学〉periodic acid:～盐 periodate

高调 gāodiào lofty tone; high-sounding words:唱～ say fine-sounding things; affect a high moral tone

高度 gāodù ❶ altitude; elevation; height:塔的～ height of a tower /飞行～ flying altitude /要把引进先进技术提高到战略～来认识。We should look at the question of importing advanced technology from the high plane of strategy. ❷ highly; to a high degree:～赞扬 speak highly of; pay high tribute to /～责任感 deep sense of responsibility /～概括 succinct generalization /给予～重视 attach great importance to; set store by /～发展的工业国 highly developed industrial power or country /～集中的统一管理 high degree of centralized and unified management /～机动的部队 hypermobile force /～机密的位置〈军事〉

highly sensitive position
高度表 gāodùbiǎo altimeter
高度差 gāodùchā altitude difference
高度规 gāodùguī height gauge
高度计 gāodùjì see"高度表"
高度角 gāodùjiǎo 〈测绘〉angle of elevation
高额 gāo'é huge amount; great number:~利润 huge profit /~租金 rack-rent /~纳税人 upper-bracket tax-payers /~大众消费时代 age of high mass-consumption
高尔夫球 gāo'ěrfūqiú ❶ golf:~场 golf course; golf links /~棒 golf club /~球袋 golf bag ❷ golf ball
高尔基 Gāo'ěrjī Maxim Gorky, pseudonym of Alexei Maximovich Peshkov (1868-1936), Russian novelist, playwright and revolutionary
高尔基体 gāo'ěrjītǐ 〈生理〉golgiosome
高发 gāofā ❶〈旧语〉pass the imperial examination ❷ high incidence of a disease:食道癌~地区 district with a high incidence of cancer of the esophagus
高飞远走 gāofēi-yuǎnzǒu *also*"远走高飞" fly high and far; be off to distant places
高沸点 gāofèidiǎn high-boiling point:~化合物 high-boiling compound
高沸点溶剂 gāofèidiǎn róngjì high boiler
高分辨率 gāofēnbiànlǜ high-resolution:~仪器 high-resolution instrument
高分低能 gāofēn-dīnéng good at taking exams but poor in practice
高分子 gāofēnzǐ high polymer; macromolecule:~化学 (high) polymer chemistry
高分子化合物 gāofēnzǐ huàhéwù macromolecular compound; high-molecular compound
高分子聚合物 gāofēnzǐ jùhéwù high polymer
高风 gāofēng ❶ wind from the highland ❷ noble character; moral integrity:久仰先生之~。I've admired your noble character for a long time.
高风亮节 gāofēng-liàngjié *also*"亮节高风" exemplary conduct and nobility of character; sterling integrity
高峰 gāofēng ❶ peak; summit; height:1960年5月25日中国登山队胜利地登上了世界第一~珠穆朗玛峰。On 25 May 1960 Chinese mountaineers reached the summit of Mount Qomolangma, the world's highest peak. ❷〈比喻〉peak; height; summit:攀登科学的~ scale the heights of science /~交通量 peak traffic /~时间的交通堵塞令人难以忍受。Traffic jam at peak (*or* rush) hours is really exasperating.
高峰会议 gāofēng huìyì summit meeting; summit
高峰期 gāofēngqī peak period
高浮雕 gāofúdiāo high relief
高秆作物 gāogǎn zuòwù long-stalked crop
高干 gāogàn high-ranking official; senior cadres:~病房 wards (in hospital) for high-ranking officials (*or* cadres) /~子弟 children of senior cadres
高高在上 gāogāo-zàishàng set oneself high above the masses; be divorced from the masses and reality:我们不需要那种~,做官当老爷的干部。We have no use for those cadres who are divorced from the masses and act as overbearing bureaucrats.
高高手儿 gāogaoshǒur show mercy; be lenient:看在我的面上,请诸位对他~。Please let him off for my sake.
高歌 gāogē sing loudly; sing with a resounding voice:~一曲 raise one's voice to sing a song /引吭~ sing joyfully in a loud voice; sing heartily
高歌猛进 gāogē-měngjìn forge ahead singing songs of triumph; advance triumphantly:在新长征路上~ advance triumphantly along the road of the new Long March
高阁 gāogé ❶ high building:~临江。The building is towering over the river. ❷ shelf:束之~ be shelved (*or* pigeonholed)
高个儿 gāogèr *also*"高个子" tall person
高铬钢 gāogègāng 〈冶金〉high chrome steel
高根 gāogēn 〈植物〉coca
高跟鞋 gāogēnxié high-heeled shoes
高工 gāogōng (short for 高级工程师) senior engineer
高古 gāogǔ (of writings) elegant and classic in style
高官 gāoguān high-ranking official; senior official:~会谈 talks by senior officials
高官厚禄 gāoguān-hòulù high office and fat salary; high position with salary to match:只知~,不晓民间疾苦。They care nothing but high position with great remuneration, shutting their eyes to the sufferings of the people.
高官显爵 gāoguān-xiǎnjué (be honoured with) high official titles
高贵 gāoguì ❶ noble; exalted; high:~品质 noble quality ❷ very expensive:服饰~ extravagantly expensive dress ❸ highly privileged; elitist:他出身~的家族。He came from an exalted family.
高寒 gāohán high and frigid; severely cold:~地区 frigid zone
高喊 gāohǎn shout at the top of one's voice
高呼 gāohū shout loudly:振臂~ raise one's arm and shout loudly
高胡 gāohú high pitched two-stringed musical instrument (a kind of 二胡)
高唤 gāohuàn see"高呼"
高积云 gāojīyún 〈气象〉altocumulus
高级 gāojí ❶ senior; high-ranking; high-level; advanced:~工程师 senior engineer /~干部 senior (*or* high-ranking) cadre /~将领 ranking military officer /~官员 high-ranking official /~律师 (UK) barrister /最~会议 summit meeting /~党校 higher party school /~研究 advanced studies (*or* research) ❷ high-grade; high-quality:~消费品 high-grade consumer goods /~墨水 high-quality ink /~化妆品 de luxe cosmetics /这个旅馆真~! This hotel is really first-class.
高级人民法院 Gāojí Rénmín Fǎyuàn Higher People's Court
高级人民检察院 Gāojí Rénmín Jiǎncháyuàn Higher People's Procuratorate
高级社 gāojíshè (short for 高级农业生产合作社) advanced agricultural producers' cooperative (formed in 1955-1957, in which the land and other chief means of production were collectively owned by the co-op and income was distributed according to the principle of "from each according to his ability, to each according to his work")
高级神经活动 gāojí shénjīng huódòng 〈生理〉higher nervous activity
高级神经中枢 gāojí shénjīng zhōngshū 〈生理〉high nerve centre
高级小学 gāojí xiǎoxué higher primary school
高级研究员 gāojí yánjiūyuán senior research fellow
高级移动电话系统 gāojí yídòng diànhuà xìtǒng advanced mobile phone system (AMPS)
高级知识分子 gāojí zhīshifènzǐ higher intellectual
高级职称 gāojí zhíchēng senior academic or professional rank
高级职员 gāojí zhíyuán senior staff member (in an enterprise)
高级智能网 gāojí zhìnéngwǎng advanced intelligent network (AIN)
高级中学 gāojí zhōngxué senior secondary school; senior high school
高级专员 gāojí zhuānyuán high commissioner:~公署 high commission (embassy of one British Commonwealth country in another) /联合国难民事务~办事处 Office of the United Nations High Commissioner for Refugees (UNHCR)
高技术 gāojìshù high technology; high-tech:~开发区 high technology development zone /~的商品化和产业化 commercialization and industrialization of high technologies
高技术园 gāojìshùyuán high-tech park
高加索 Gāojiāsuǒ Caucasus; Caucasia:~山脉 Caucasus Mountains /~人种 Caucasian race /~语系 Caucasian language family /外~ Transcaucasia /北~ Ciscaucasia
高甲戏 gāojiǎxì *also*"戈甲戏" gējiǎxì;"九角戏" jiǔjiǎoxì local opera popular in Fujian and Taiwan provinces
高价 gāojià high price; excessive price:~货物 expensive goods /~耐用消费品 high-priced durable consumer goods /~出售 sell at a fancy price /~收购文物 buy cultural relics at a high price /~收盘 closing high
高架桥 gāojiàqiáo viaduct
高架铁道 gāojià tiědào overhead railway; elevated railway
高见 gāojiàn 〈敬词〉brilliant idea; your, his, or their opinion:愿闻~。I'd like to hear your views. /不知~如何? I wonder if you would be kind enough to enlighten us on this matter. /他的这番~,实在不敢苟同。In fact, I just can't bring myself to agree with his view.
高教 gāojiào ❶ (short for 高等教育) higher education ❷ (short for 高等教师) senior teacher (in a primary or secondary school)
高洁 gāojié noble and unsullied:~的品德 noble and unsullied

G

character
高精度 gāojīngdù 〈机械〉high accuracy; high precision; pinpoint accuracy: ～光学比较仪 omtimeter / ～雷达 high accuracy radar / ～数据传输系统 high accuracy data transmission system
高精尖 gāo-jīng-jiān high-grade, precision and advanced (industrial product, etc.): 这家工厂拥有一百五十多台～设备。This factory boasts over 150 pieces of sophisticated equipment of high grade and precision.
高就 gāojiù (find a) better job: 另有～ have landed a better job / 另请～。You may leave and have a better job elsewhere.
高举 gāojǔ hold high; hold aloft: 游行中～标语牌 hold placards high during a parade
高举远蹈 gāojǔ-yuǎndǎo *also* "高举远引" seclude oneself and avoid all worldly cares
高聚物 gāojùwù 〈化学〉high polymer
高踞 gāojù stand above; set oneself above; lord it over: 干部要和群众打成一片，不要～于群众之上。Cadres should identify themselves with the people and must never lord it over them.
高峻 gāojùn high and steep: 山势～。The mountains are high and steep.
高看 gāokàn overestimate: 您这是～我了。我这点小手艺算不了什么。You're overestimating my ability. I really have not much skill to speak of. / 承蒙～，敢不效力。Since you trust me, I am more than willing to place my services at your disposal.
高亢 gāokàng ❶ loud and sonorous; resounding: 歌声～激越 loud and sonorous singing ❷ (of land) high: 平整～地三十亩 level out (*or* off) more than 30 *mu* of high land ❸ 〈书面〉arrogant; haughty: 生性～ arrogant by nature / ～不群 haughty and not gregarious
高考 gāokǎo university entrance examination: 参加～ take part in the university entrance examination
高空 gāokōng high altitude; upper air: 飞临八千米～ fly at an altitude of 8,000 metres / ～飞行 high-altitude flight / ～缺氧 high-altitude anoxia / ～核试验 high-altitude nuclear test / ～爆炸 high air burst (*or* explosion) / ～适应 high-altitude adaptation
高空病 gāokōngbìng altitude sickness
高空槽 gāokōngcáo high-level trough
see also "低压槽" dīyācáo
高空大气物理学 gāokōng dàqì wùlǐxué aeronomy
高空飞行服 gāokōng fēixíngfú pressure suit; pressurized suit
高空风 gāokōngfēng upper wind; wind-aloft
高空脊 gāokōngjǐ 〈气象〉ridge of high pressure; pressure ridge
高空气候学 gāokōng qìhòuxué aeroclimatology
高空气象学 gāokōng qìxiàngxué aerology
高空作业 gāokōng zuòyè work high above the ground
高跨比 gāokuàbǐ 〈建筑〉rise-span ratio; rise-to-span ratio
高旷 gāokuàng ❶ tall and spacious: ～的厂房 tall and spacious workshop / 月夜清朗～ clear and immense moonlit night ❷ free and natural; unconventional and open: 意境～ originally conceived / 天性～ broad-minded by nature; free and unconventional
高栏 gāolán 〈体育〉high hurdles: 男子一百一十米～ men's 110m high hurdles
高朗 gāolǎng ❶ open and clear: 襟怀～ be open and above board / 风格～ be straightforward in style ❷ (of sound) loud and clear: ～的笑声 ringing laughter ❸ bright and clear: ～的晴空 bright and clear sky
高丽 Gāolí 〈旧语〉Korea
高丽参 gāolíshēn Korean ginseng
高丽王朝 Gāolí Wángcháo Koryo Dynasty, which ruled the Korean Peninsula in 918-1392
高丽纸 gāolízhǐ a kind of white tissue paper
高利 gāolì high interest: ～盘剥 practise usury; exploit by usury / ～外债 high-interest foreign loans / ～政策 dear (*or* tight) money policy
高利贷 gāolìdài usury; usurious loan: 放～ practise usury / ～者 usurer; loan shark; vampire / ～资本 usurer's capital
高良姜 gāoliángjiāng 〈植物〉(lesser) galangal (*Alpinia officinarum*)
高粱 gāoliang *also* "蜀黍" shǔshǔ *kaoliang*; Chinese sorghum: ～酒 liquor made from Chinese sorghum
高粱米 gāoliangmǐ husked *kaoliang*
高粱蚜 gāoliangyá *kaoliang* aphid or aphis
高粱饴 gāoliangyí sweets or candy made of sorghum syrup; sorghum candy
高龄 gāolíng ❶ 〈敬词〉(of people over sixty) advanced age; venerable age: ～老人 senior citizen / 您今年～? May I know your age? ❷ older than usual: ～学员 students above the average age
高龄社会 gāolíng shèhuì *also* "老龄社会" lǎolíng shèhuì aged society
高岭石 gāolǐngshí kaolinite
高岭土 gāolǐngtǔ kaolin: ～型风化壳 residuum of kaolin type
高硫 gāoliú 〈化学〉high sulphur: ～钢 high-sulphur steel / ～煤 high-sulphur coal / ～原油 high-sulphur crude oil; sour crude
高楼大厦 gāolóu-dàshà high buildings and large mansions; high-rise: 如今的北京城，～随处可见。There are skyscrapers and high-rises everywhere in Beijing nowadays.
高楼综合征 gāolóu zōnghézhēng sick building syndrome (SBS)
高炉 gāolú blast furnace: ～煤气 blast furnace gas / ～自动化 automation of blast furnace / ～利用系数 capacity factor of a blast furnace / ～燃气轮机发电厂 blast-furnace gas-turbine power plant
高氯酸 gāolǜsuān 〈化学〉perchloric acid: ～锂 lithium perchlorate / ～钾 potassium perchlorate; potassium hyperchlorate / ～盐 perchlorate
高轮车 gāolúnchē high wheeled car
高论 gāolùn 〈敬词〉enlightening remarks; brilliant views: 卑之无甚～ regard as just a few commonplace remarks
高买 gāomǎi 〈方言〉❶ shop-lifting ❷ shop-lifter
高迈 gāomài 〈书面〉❶ advanced in years: ～之人，精力不济了。Being advanced in age, I am wanting in vigour. ❷ unconventionally graceful; free and natural: 风神～ natural and graceful
高慢 gāomàn arrogant; haughty; supercilious
高帽子 gāomàozi *also* "高帽儿" ❶ empty title or honour; flattery: 他喜欢戴～。He takes to flattery. ❷ tall paper hat (worn as a sign of humiliation); dunce cap
高门 gāomén tall gate — a rich and powerful family: ～大户 rich and powerful family / ～望族 wealthy and influential clan; rich and distinguished family
高锰钢 gāoměnggāng 〈冶金〉high manganese steel
高锰酸钾 gāoměngsuānjiǎ potassium permanganate
高密度 gāomìdù high density: ～存储(器) high density storage / ～电子束 high density electron beam / ～数据系统 high density data system
高棉人 Gāomiánrén Khmer
高棉王国 Gāomián Wángguó Kingdom of Khmer, an ancient kingdom in southeast Asia with Angkor as its capital, which reached the peak of its power in the 11th century
高棉语 Gāomiányǔ Khmer language
高妙 gāomiào ingenious; masterly; skilful: 手艺～ masterly craftsmanship / 笔法～ skilful calligraphy (*or* drawing)
高名 gāomíng great reputation: 少有～ be well known when young
高明 gāomíng ❶ brilliant; smart; wise: 见解～ brilliant idea / 医术～ have superb medical skill / 他自以为比别人～。He considered himself wiser than others. / 他并不怎么～。He was not all that smart. ❷ wise or skilful person: 另请～。Find someone better qualified (than myself for the job).
高难 gāonán (of skill) difficult of attainment; highly difficult: 这套自由体操有几个～动作。There are several highly difficult movements in this set of free callisthenics.
高能 gāonéng high-energy: ～环境 high-energy environment
高能电子 gāonéng diànzǐ high-energy electron; hard electron
高能辐射 gāonéng fúshè high-energy radiation
高能激光 gāonéng jīguāng superlaser
高能加速器 gāonéng jiāsùqì high-energy accelerator
高能粒子 gāonéng lìzǐ high-energy particle; energetic particle: ～反应 high-energy reaction
高能燃料 gāonéng ránliào high-energy fuel
高能物理学 gāonéng wùlǐxué high energy physics
高能质子同步稳相加速器 gāonéng zhìzǐ tóngbù wěnxiàng jiāsùqì bevatron
高年 gāonián ❶ the aged; old people: 赡养～ support the aged ❷ old; advanced in years: ～医生经验丰富。Old doctors have rich experience. ❸ (of wine, etc.) mellow: ～好酒 good wine of early vintage
高黏度 gāoniándù 〈化工〉high-viscosity: ～指数 high-viscosity in-

G

dex
高攀 gāopān 〈套语〉make friends or claim ties of kinship with someone of a higher social position:～不上 be beyond one / 不敢～。I dare not aspire to such an honour.
高朋满座 gāopéng-mǎnzuò with many guests of exalted rank present; a galaxy of distinguished guests
高频 gāopín high frequency: 超～ ultra-high-frequency (UHF) / 甚～ very high frequency (VHF) / 极～ extremely high frequency (EHF)
高频变压器 gāopín biànyāqì 〈电工〉high-frequency transformer
高频磁带录像机 gāopín cídài lùxiàngjī high band VTR
高频淬火 gāopín cuìhuǒ 〈冶金〉high-frequency quenching or hardening
高频电波 gāopín diànbō high-frequency radio wave
高频电缆 gāopín diànlǎn high-frequency cable
高频电疗 gāopín diànliáo 〈医学〉arsonvalization
高频电流 gāopín diànliú 〈电学〉high-frequency current
高频电炉 gāopín diànlú 〈冶金〉high-frequency furnace (an electrical furnace)
高频放大器 gāopín fàngdàqì 〈电子〉high-frequency amplifier
高频干扰 gāopín gānrǎo 〈通信〉high-frequency interference
高频感应电炉 gāopín gǎnyìng diànlú 〈冶金〉high-frequency induction furnace
高频焊接 gāopín hànjiē 〈冶金〉high-frequency soldering
高频继电器 gāopín jìdiànqì 〈电工〉high-frequency relay
高频塑料热合器 gāopín sùliào rèhéqì 〈化工〉high-frequency plastic welder
高频通信 gāopín tōngxìn high-frequency communication
高频外科 gāopín wàikē 〈医学〉high-frequency surgery
高频扬声器 gāopín yángshēngqì 〈电子〉tweeter
高频载波电话 gāopín zàibō diànhuà high-frequency telephone
高气压 gāoqìyā high atmospheric or barometric pressure
高气压区 gāoqìyāqū high-pressure area; region of high barometric pressure
高腔 gāoqiāng vocal music in Chinese opera characterized by high-pitched singing accompanied by percussion instruments only
高强 gāoqiáng excel in; be master of: 武艺～ excel in martial arts
高强度 gāoqiángdù 〈冶金〉high tension; high strength; high intensity: ～低合金钢 high-strength low-alloy steel (HSLA); high-yield low-alloy steel / ～钢 high-strength steel; high-tensile steel; high-duty steel
高强度部件 gāoqiángdù bùjiàn 〈冶金〉high-strength part
高强度磁场 gāoqiángdù cíchǎng 〈电学〉high-intensity magnetic field
高强度电流 gāoqiángdù diànliú high-intensity current
高强度合金 gāoqiángdù héjīn 〈冶金〉high-strength alloy
高强度热处理 gāoqiángdù rèchǔlǐ maraging
高强度铸铁 gāoqiángdù zhùtiě high-strength cast iron
高跷 gāoqiāo stilts: 踩～ walk on stilts
高峭 gāoqiào (of mountains) high and steep
高清晰度电视 gāoqīngxīdù diànshì high definition television (HDTV)
高情 gāoqíng great kindness; boundless hospitality: ～雅意 your great kindness
高擎 gāoqíng hold high; hold aloft
高秋 gāoqiū cool, clear autumn days
高球 gāoqiú 〈体育〉high ball; lob: 放～ lob
高热 gāorè *see* "高烧"
高人 gāorén ❶〈书面〉*see* "高士" ❷ great scholar; master craftsman; masterhand; distinguished personage
高人一等 gāorényīděng a cut above other people; a notch above or higher than others: 他老以为自己～。He always thinks he's superior to others.
高僧 gāosēng eminent monk: 有道～ eminent and learned monk
高山病 gāoshānbìng mountain sickness
高山反应 gāoshān fǎnyìng altitude sickness
高山滑雪 gāoshān huáxuě 〈体育〉alpine skiing
高山景行 gāoshān-jǐngxíng high mountain and broad road — exalted virtue; great moral integrity
高山流水 gāoshān-liúshuǐ *also* "流水高山" lofty mountains and flowing rivers — referring to a person who appreciates one's talents, a bosom friend, or elegant music
高山植物 gāoshān zhíwù alpine plant
高山族 Gāoshānzú Gaoshan or Kaoshan national minority, living in Taiwan Province
高尚 gāoshàng ❶ noble; lofty: ～的品德 noble character / ～的理想 lofty ideals (*or* aspirations) / 读书会使人变得～。Reading makes one rise above vulgar interests. ❷ refined; elegant; cultivated: 谈吐～ refined speech
高烧 gāoshāo *also* "高热" high fever: 发～ have (*or* run) a high fever
高射机关枪 gāoshè jīguānqiāng antiaircraft machine gun
高射炮 gāoshèpào antiaircraft gun or artillery; ack-ack gun: ～火力 antiaircraft fire; ack-ack; flak / ～火力网 flak barrage / ～手 antiaircraft gun crew; antiaircraft gunner
高深 gāoshēn advanced; profound; abstruse; recondite: ～的造诣 of great attainments / 莫测～ unfathomable; abstruse / ～的学问 erudite scholarship
高升 gāoshēng ❶ advance from a lower to a higher position; be promoted: 他最近得到～。He got a promotion recently. ❷〈方言〉a kind of firecracker
高师 gāoshī (short for 高等师范) higher normal school; teachers training college
高士 gāoshì 〈书面〉hermit; recluse; person of moral integrity
高视阔步 gāoshì-kuòbù carry oneself proudly; swagger; strut; prance: 他～地走了过来。He strutted up. / 这位演员～走到室外。The actor swaggered out of the room.
高适 Gāo Shì Gao Shi (formerly translated as Kao Shih, 702-765), poet of the Tang Dynasty
高手 gāoshǒu past master; expert; master-hand; ace: 象棋～ master (Chinese) chess player / 网球～ tennis ace / 这儿～如云，我算得了什么? In this gathering of master-hands, I'm nobody.
高寿 gāoshòu ❶ longevity; long life: 祝您～。Wishing you a long life! ❷〈敬词〉your venerable age
高爽 gāoshuǎng high and open; fresh and cool: 地势～ high and open terrain / 秋日的晴空，～洁净。The autumn sky is clear, clean and crisp.
高水头 gāoshuǐtóu 〈水利〉high-head: ～水力发电厂 high-head hydro-power station / ～水力枢纽 high waterhead hydraulic system
高水位 gāoshuǐwèi high water level; high flood level: ～线 high-water mark (HWM)
高斯 Gāosī Karl Friedrich Gauss (1777-1855), German mathematician, astronomer and physicist
高斯定律 Gāosī dìnglǜ Gauss' theorem
高斯函数 Gāosī hánshù Gauss' function
高耸 gāosǒng stand tall and erect; tower: ～入云 reach to the clouds / 纪念碑～在广场上。The monument towers over the square.
高速 gāosù high speed: ～发展 develop at top speed; grow by leaps and bounds / ～切削 high-speed cutting
高速车 gāosùchē high-speed car
高速挡 gāosùdǎng top gear; high gear
高速钢 gāosùgāng high-speed steel; rapid steel
高速公路 gāosù gōnglù expressway; superhighway
高速缓冲存储器 gāosù huǎnchōng cúnchǔqì 〈信息〉cache
高速列车 gāosù lièchē (US) metroliner; bullet train
高速印刷机 gāosù yìnshuājī high-speed press; high-speed printer
高速阅读器 gāosù yuèdúqì high-speed reader
高塑性钢 gāosùxìnggāng high-ductility steel
高台定车 gāotái dìngchē 〈杂技〉bicycle balancing act on an elevated stand
高抬贵手 gāotái-guìshǒu 〈套语〉be generous; be lenient; not be too hard on sb.: 请您～，让我们进去参观参观。Please be kind enough to let us in for a look. / 如果他得罪了你，万望～，饶了他。If he has offended you in some way, I hope you will overlook it and let him go.
高谈阔论 gāotán-kuòlùn indulge in loud and empty talk; talk volubly or bombastically; harangue: ～的年轻人 group of young people revelling in bombast (*or* shooting the bull)
高弹性 gāotánxìng high elasticity: ～材料 highly elastic material / ～合成纤维 spandex
高碳钢 gāotàngāng high-carbon steel
高汤 gāotāng ❶ (meat or chicken) soup-stock ❷ thin soup
高堂 gāotáng ❶ great hall; big hall ❷〈书面〉parents: ～老母 aged mother
高挑儿 gāotiǎor 〈方言〉(of stature) tall and thin: 那人是细～。

That man is tall and thin.
高头大马 gāotóu-dàmǎ ❶ big strong horse ❷ (of people) tall and big:～的小伙子 tall and strong young man
高头 gāotou 〈方言〉❶ boss; superior:这是～的命令,你必须照办。You must carry it out since it's an order from your superior. ❷ top:他爬到山顶～去了。He has reached the top of the mountain.
高徒 gāotú outstanding disciple:严师出～。A strict teacher produces outstanding students. *or* Capable are disciples trained by strict masters.
高纬度 gāowěidù high latitude; circumpolar latitude
高位 gāowèi ❶〈书面〉prominent position ❷ upper part (of a limb):～截肢手术 amputate a limb at the upper part; perform high amputation
高温 gāowēn high temperature:～消毒 high-temperature sterilization /～气候 megathermal climate /～气冷反应堆 high-temperature gas-cooled reactor /最近几天持续～。The temperature has been high for days.
高温场 gāowēnchǎng high-temperature field
高温超导 gāowēn chāodǎo high-temperature superconductivity
高温淬火 gāowēn cuìhuǒ quench hot
高温堆肥 gāowēn duīféi high temperature compost
高温反应堆 gāowēn fǎnyìngduī high-temperature reactor
高温分解 gāowēn fēnjiě pyrolysis
高温合成 gāowēn héchéng pyrosynthesis
高温化学 gāowēn huàxué pyrochemistry
高温计 gāowēnjì pyrometer
高温切削 gāowēn qiēxiāo high-temperature machining
高温试验 gāowēn shìyàn hot test
高温氧化 gāowēn yǎnghuà high temperature oxidation (HTO)
高温植物 gāowēn zhíwù megatherm; megistotherm
高温作业 gāowēn zuòyè high-temperature operation
高文典册 gāowén-diǎncè 〈书面〉court documents, registers and imperial decrees
高卧 gāowò ❶ rest one's head on a high pillow ❷〈比喻〉live in seclusion; withdraw from society and live in solitude; be a hermit:诸葛亮～隆中。Zhuge Liang lived as a hermit in Longzhong.
高屋建瓴 gāowū-jiànlíng pour water off a steep roof — sweep down irresistibly from a commanding height; operate from a strategically advantageous position:～,势如破竹 press on irresistibly like splitting a bamboo
高下 gāoxià *see*“高低 ❷”
高下在心 gāoxià-zàixīn 〈书面〉take measures suited to the circumstances; (of a powerful person) act according to one's will; do as one pleases
高香 gāoxiāng best joss stick (burned before an idol):烧～ burn the best incense before the idol of a god — pray for a god's or somebody's blessing
高消费 gāoxiāofèi high or excessive consumption:～社会 high consumption society
高小 gāoxiǎo (short for 高级小学) higher primary school
高校 gāoxiào (short for 高等学校) institution of higher learning
高效 gāoxiào highly effective; highly efficient:～杀虫剂 highly effective pesticide /～肥料 concentrated fertilizer /～政府 highly efficient government
高薪 gāoxīn high salary; high pay:～聘请 engage (sb.) at a high salary
高行 gāoxíng 〈书面〉noble conduct; exalted behaviour
高兴 gāoxìng ❶ glad; happy; pleased; cheerful:见到你很～。I'm glad to see you. /看来他非常～。It seems that he is in high spirits. /你怎么一脸的不～? Why? You do look so glum. /他们谈得很～。They seemed to enjoy their conversation. /孩子们高高兴兴地上学去了。The children cheerfully went off to school. ❷ be willing to; be happy to:你不～去看戏,就去看电影好了。If you don't like going to the theatre, you can go to the cinema instead.
高性能 gāoxìngnéng 〈机械〉high performance:～发动机 high performance engine /～飞机 high performance aircraft
高悬秦镜 gāoxuán-qínjìng *also*“高悬明镜” strict enforcement of law; impartial administration of justice
高血糖 gāoxuètáng 〈医学〉hyperglycemia; hyperglycosemia; hyperglykemia
高血压 gāoxuèyā hypertension; high blood pressure
高压 gāoyā ❶〈电学〉high tension; high voltage:～电缆 high-tension cable /～电流 high-tension current /～电力网 high-tension network /～电器 high-voltage electrical apparatus ❷〈物理〉〈气象〉high pressure:～锅炉 high-pressure boiler /～云室 high-pressure cloud chamber /～风 high-pressure blast ❸〈医学〉maximum pressure ❹ high-handed:～手段 high-handed measures /～政策 high-handed policy
高压泵 gāoyābèng high-pressure pump
高压电 gāoyādiàn high-voltage electricity
高压锅 gāoyāguō *also*“压力锅” yālìguō pressure cooker
高压核电池 gāoyā hédiànchí high-voltage nuclear battery
高压脊 gāoyājǐ *also*“高空脊”;“高压楔” ridge of high pressure; pressure ridge
高压灭菌器 gāoyā mièjūnqì autoclave; high-pressure sterilizer
高压水龙 gāoyā shuǐlóng water cannon
高压线 gāoyāxiàn high-tension line or wire
高雅 gāoyǎ elegant and in good taste; refined and graceful:格调～ elegant and graceful style /神态举止,～文静 refined, gentle and quiet in manner
高研 gāoyán (short for 高级研究员) senior research fellow
高眼 gāoyǎn farsighted; having a broad field of vision
高眼鲽 gāoyǎndié 〈动物〉plaice
高扬 gāoyáng ❶ raise; go up:情绪～ be in high spirits /士气～ high morale /汽车开过,尘土～。A cloud of dust was raised as the car passed by. ❷ vigorously carry forward; fully develop:～爱国主义精神 vigorously foster patriotism
高扬程 gāoyángchéng high-lift:～水泵〈水利〉high-lift pump
高谊 gāoyì ❶ lofty friendly sentiments; exalted friendship:深情～ profound friendship ❷ *also*“高义” righteous and just conduct
高音 gāoyīn 〈音乐〉high pitch; high-pitched voice:男～ tenor /女～ soprano /～符号 treble clef
高音喇叭 gāoyīn lǎba tweeter
高音调节器 gāoyīn tiáojiéqì 〈无线电〉high pitch regulator
高雨云 gāoyǔyún 〈气象〉altonimbus
高原 gāoyuán plateau; highland; tableland:青藏～ Qinghai-Tibet Plateau /～冰川 plateau glacier /～湖 plateau lake /～沼泽 highland moor
高原反应 gāoyuán fǎnyìng altitude reaction or sickness
高远 gāoyuǎn high and boundless:志趣～ have lofty aspirations /蓝天～。The blue sky looks high and boundless.
高云 gāoyún high cloud; high-level cloud
高燥 gāozào 〈地理〉high and dry
高增益 gāozēngyì 〈电子〉high gain
高瞻远瞩 gāozhān-yuǎnzhǔ stand high and see far; take a broad and long-term view; show great foresight; be farsighted:在这关键时刻,他～,统观全局。At the critical juncture, he showed great foresight and had the overall situation in mind.
高涨 gāozhǎng ❶ rise; upsurge; run high:群众热情空前～。The enthusiasm of the masses is rising to an unprecedented height. /物价日益～。Commodity prices are running high with each passing day. ❷〈经济〉boom
高招 gāozhāo *also*“高着儿”〈口语〉clever move; brilliant idea; smart trick:看他还有什么～。Let's see what bright ideas he has. /我看他没有什么～了。I don't think he has (got) anything up his sleeve.
高真空 gāozhēnkōng high vacuum:～泵 high vacuum pump /～瓶 high vacuum jar /～整流器 high vacuum rectifier; high vacuum rectifier tube; high vacuum valve
高枕而卧 gāozhěn'érwò lay one's head on one's pillow and sleep without any worries — relax one's vigilance:强敌尚在,我等岂可～! How can we lower our vigilance when strong enemies are still around?
高枕无忧 gāozhěn-wúyōu shake up the pillow and have a good sleep; sit back and relax; sleep soundly without any worries:嫌疑犯并未抓获,目下还不是～的时候。It's no time to sit back and relax when the suspects are still at large.
高枝儿 gāozhīr 〈口语〉higher branches — men of high position; one's superiors:攀～ curry favour with one's betters
高知 gāozhī (short for 高级知识分子) intellectuals with senior professional titles
高脂血 gāozhīxuè 〈医学〉hyperlipoidemia; hyperlipemia
高致 gāozhì 〈书面〉noble character; good taste
高中 gāozhōng (short for 高级中学) senior secondary school

高中　gāozhòng　〈旧语〉pass imperial examinations
高姿态　gāozītài　❶ lofty stance (showing oneself capable of tolerance and generosity)：你要～，不要与他计较。Be generous and tolerant. Let him off. ❷ high profile
高足　gāozú　〈敬词〉your brilliant disciple; your pupil：～弟子 one's best pupil
高阻抗　gāozǔkàng　〈电工〉high impedance：～电缆 high-impedance cable / ～光敏电阻 high-impedance photoresistor / ～转子 high-impedance motor
高祖　gāozǔ　❶ (paternal) great-great-grandfather ❷ first ancestor; earliest ancestor
高祖母　gāozǔmǔ　(paternal) great-great-grandmother

膏

gāo　❶ fat; grease; oil：脂～ fat; grease / 民脂民～ people's fat and marrow — people's wealth earned by hard labour / 春雨如～。Rain in spring is as precious as oil. ❷ paste; cream; ointment; plaster：牙～ toothpaste / 烟～ prepared opium paste / 雪花～ vanishing cream / 修面～ shaving cream / 软～ ointment / 药～ ointment; salve ❸ fertile：～壤 fertile land
see also gào
膏肓　gāohuāng　vital organs (of a body)：～之疾 disease that is beyond cure
see also "病入膏肓" bìngrùgāohuāng
膏火　gāohuǒ　〈书面〉lamp (that burns oil) — cost for burning midnight oil (usu. referring to school expenses)
膏火自煎　gāohuǒ-zìjiān　*also* "膏火自焚" fat burns and fries itself — one who has talent or money incurs misfortune
膏剂　gāojì　medicinal extract; electuary
膏粱　gāoliáng　fat meat and fine grain; rich food
膏粱子弟　gāoliáng zǐdì　children of wealthy families
膏沃　gāowò　〈书面〉(of land) fertile
膏血　gāoxuè　fat and blood (of a human being) — fruits of the people's labour：劳动人民的～被他们吸干了。They have bled the labouring people white.
膏药　gāoyao　plaster：狗皮～〈中药〉dogskin plaster;〈比喻〉shoddy goods / 贴～ apply a plaster
膏腴　gāoyú　〈书面〉fertile：～之地 fertile land
膏泽　gāozé　〈书面〉❶ timely rain (for crops) ❷ grant a favour：～下民 grant favours to people under one's rule
膏子　gāozi　(medicinal) syrup or paste

篙

gāo　punt-pole：竹～ bamboo punt-pole / 杉～ fir pole
篙竿　gāogan　*also* "篙杆"〈方言〉punt-pole
篙工　gāogōng　punter
篙头　gāotou　〈方言〉punt-pole
篙子　gāozi　❶〈方言〉punt-pole ❷ pole (for drying clothes in the sun)

羔

gāo　lamb; kid; fawn：小羊～ lamb; kid / 鹿～儿 fawn / 产～ lambing; kidding
羔皮　gāopí　lambskin; kidskin; kid：～手套 kid gloves; kids
羔羊　gāoyáng　❶ lamb; kid：～痢疾 lamb dysentery ❷ innocent and helpless person：替罪的～ scapegoat
羔羊肉　gāoyángròu　lamb
羔子　gāozi　lamb; kid; fawn

糕(餻)

gāo　cake; pudding：蛋～ cake (enriched with eggs) / 发～ steamed sponge cake / 蜂～ steamed sponge cake (made of wheat or rice flour) / 丝～ steamed corn cake / 年～ New Year cake (made of glutinous rice)
糕饼　gāobǐng　〈方言〉cake; pastry
糕点　gāodiǎn　cake; pastry：～厨师 pastry cook
糕干　gāogan　sweetened rice flour (as a substitute for powdered milk)：～粉 powdered rice-cereal

櫜

gāo　〈书面〉❶ case for armour bows, arrows, etc. ❷ store away

皋(臯)

gāo　❶〈书面〉highland on the riverside：江～ river bank ❷ (Gāo) a surname
皋比　gāopí　〈书面〉tiger's skin; seat made of tiger's skin on which a master sits — teacher's chair

槔(槹)

gāo　*see* "桔槔" jiégāo

睾

gāo
睾囊　gāonáng　scrotum
睾丸　gāowán　*also* "精巢" jīngcháo　testis; testicle：～粘连 synorchidism / ～炎 orchitis / ～肥大 orchdauxe / ～切除术 orchiectomy

gǎo

槁(槀)

gǎo　withered
槁枯　gǎokū　〈书面〉withered; haggard
槁木　gǎomù　withered or dead tree：形如～ look like a withered tree; look haggard
槁木死灰　gǎomù-sǐhuī　dead trees and cold ashes — complete apathy：心如～，不问世事 be sunk in apathy and take no interest in the outside world

搞

gǎo　❶ do; go in for; carry on; be engaged in：～调查研究 do some investigation and study / ～计划生育 carry on family planning / ～副业生产 engage in sideline production / ～阴谋诡计 go in for intrigue and conspiracy / ～投机 play the market / 他是～建筑的。He's in building (*or* construction). / 你在～什么名堂? What are you up to? / 这工作不好～。That's a difficult job. ❷ make; produce; work out：～几个菜 prepare a few dishes / ～个计划 draw up a plan / 这个厂在～新产品。The plant is trying to produce a new product. / 你先～个日程安排。Please work out a schedule first. ❸ make sb. suffer; fix sb.：他俩合起来～我。The two of them joined hands in making things difficult for me. ❹ set up; start; organize：～个实验室 set up a laboratory / 我们想～水果蔬菜生意。We are thinking of starting up in the fruit and vegetable trade. ❺ get; get hold of; secure; wangle：我去～点水来。I'll go and fetch some water. / 给我～两张音乐会票。Get me two tickets for the concert, please. ❻ (followed by a complement) produce a certain effect or result; cause to become：事情给～糟了 make a mess of things / 把人～糊涂了 confuse people / 他连最简单的数学题都～不清楚。He balled up even on the simplest math problem.
搞臭　gǎochòu　discredit; humiliate：他一心要把对手～。He is bent on discrediting his opponent.
搞掉　gǎodiao　get rid of; do away with; remove：把这堆垃圾～ get rid of this rubbish dump / 把鞋子上的泥巴～ remove mud from your shoes / 把某人～ put someone out of the way
搞对象　gǎo duìxiàng　(of a man and woman) go steady; keep steady company; date
搞法　gǎofǎ　method; way of doing things：你这种～，我不同意。I can't agree to your way of doing things.
搞鬼　gǎoguǐ　play tricks; scheme in secret; be up to mischief：谨防敌人～。Beware of the enemy's tricks. / 此人专会暗中～。That man is good at scheming.
搞好　gǎohǎo　make a good job of; do well：～与邻居的关系 foster good relations with one's neighbours / ～救灾工作 do a good job of disaster relief / 这件事只能～，不能搞坏。You must make the thing a sure success. It brooks no failure. / 这块地～了，每亩可以收一千斤。If handled well, this plot can yield 1,000 *jin* per *mu*.
搞活　gǎohuó　invigorate; enliven; rejuvenate：～企业 rejuvenate an enterprise / 实行对外开放，对内～的政策 implement the policy of opening to the outside world and invigorating the domestic economy
搞通　gǎotōng　come to understand：～思想 straighten out one's ideas (*or* thinking) / ～基本道理 grasp the fundamentals
搞头　gǎotou　have a point (in doing sth.); be worth doing：这事没～。There's no point in doing that.

暠

gǎo　〈书面〉white

镐

gǎo　pick; pickaxe：电～ electric pick / 风～ air pick; pneumatic pick / 丁字～ T-shaped pick / 十字～ pick; pickaxe; mattock / 鹤嘴～ pick; pickaxe; mattock
see also Hào
镐头　gǎotou　pick; pickaxe

稿[1]**（稾）** gǎo 〈书面〉stalk of cereal crops; straw: *see* "～荐"

稿[2]**（稾）** gǎo draft; sketch; manuscript: 初～ first draft /修改～ revised draft /腹～ draft worked out in one's mind; mental notes /拟～ make a draft /先打个～儿再画 make a sketch before painting /手～ original (*or* holograph) manuscript; manuscript /原～ original manuscript; master copy /来～ contributed article; contribution /约～ (of editors) make an arrangement in advance with sb. for his contribution /定～ finalize a text /遗～ literary remains; posthumous papers

稿本 gǎoběn manuscript: ～目录 written catalogue

稿酬 gǎochóu *see* "稿费"

稿底 gǎodǐ *also* "稿底子" original manuscript; draft; original sketch (of a painting)

稿费 gǎofèi payment for an article or book written; contribution fee; author's remuneration

稿秆 gǎogǎn 〈方言〉stalk of cereal crops; straw

稿件 gǎojiàn manuscript; contribution

稿荐 gǎojiàn straw mattress; pallet

稿拳 gǎoquán *also* "划拳" huáquán 〈书面〉finger-guessing game (a drinking game at feasts)

稿约 gǎoyuē notice to contributors

稿葬 gǎozàng 〈书面〉get through with the burial hastily

稿纸 gǎozhǐ squared or lined paper for making drafts or copying manuscripts

稿子 gǎozi ❶ draft; sketch: 起个～ make a draft ❷ manuscript; contribution: 这个～是谁写的? Whose manuscript is this? *or* Who wrote this article? /下一期还缺三篇～。The editor is short of 3 contributions for the next issue. ❸ idea; plan: 没个准～ no definite plan

缟 gǎo thin white silk used in ancient China

缟玛瑙 gǎomǎnǎo onyx

缟素 gǎosù white mourning dress: 一身～ be dressed in deep mourning

杲 gǎo ❶ 〈书面〉bright: 如日之～ as bright as sunlight ❷ (Gǎo) a surname

杲杲 gǎogǎo 〈书面〉(of the sun) bright: ～出日。The sun is rising, shining brightly. /秋阳～。The sun shines brightly in the autumn day.

gào

膏 gào ❶ lubricate; grease; oil: 车轴上该～点油了。It's time to lubricate the axle of the cart. ❷ dip a brush in ink and smooth it on an inkstone before writing

see also gāo

告 gào ❶ tell; inform; report; notify: 电～ inform by telegraph /无可奉～。No comment. /此事勿须～人。Don't tell anyone about it. ❷ sue; bring an action or a case against; accuse: ～到法院 sue sb. for sth.; bring a case against sb. /上～ complain to the higher authorities; appeal to a higher court /诬～ bring a false charge; lodge a false accusation ❸ ask for; request; solicit: *see* "～饶"; "～假" ❹ declare; announce: 不～而别 go away without taking leave; leave without saying goodbye; go AWOL; take French leave /自～奋勇 volunteer for the job ❺ announce or declare the completion of sth.: 工作～一段落。The first phase of the work has been completed. /讨论暂～结束。The discussion is temporarily closed.

告哀 gào'āi 〈书面〉pour out one's grievances

告白 gàobái ❶ public notice ❷ profess; explain; express: ～内心的忧虑 express one's worries ❸ 〈经济〉bill

告帮 gàobāng 〈方言〉ask for financial help; beg for material assistance: 他再穷也不愿向别人～。Poor as he is, he would not beg for help.

告便 gàobiàn 〈婉词〉excuse oneself: 请予～。May I be excused? *or* May I go somewhere?

告别 gàobié ❶ take leave of; leave; part from: 他们～故乡，启程北上。They left their hometown and set out for the north. /他～了亲友，奔赴新的工作岗位。He went to take up a new post after taking leave of his relatives and friends. ❷ bid farewell to; say goodbye to: 她向学生们亲切～。She bade her pupils a loving farewell. /我昨晚向他～去了。I went to say goodbye to him last night. ❸ pay one's last respects (to the deceased): 向遗体～ pay one's last respects to the deceased

告别词 gàobiécí farewell speech; valediction

告别演出 gàobié yǎnchū farewell performance

告别宴会 gàobié yànhuì farewell banquet

告别仪式 gàobié yíshì farewell ceremony

告禀 gàobǐng *also* "禀告" report to one's senior or superior

告病 gàobìng ask for sick leave: 他～未出席会议。He was not present at the meeting on account of illness.

告成 gàochéng accomplish; complete: 大功～。The great task is accomplished. *or* The work is crowned with success.

告吹 gàochuī fizzle out; fall through; fail: 两国谈判～了。Negotiations between the two countries fizzled out. /这项工程最终～了。Eventually the project fell through.

告辞 gàocí take leave (of one's host): 天色已晚，就此～。It's getting dark. I'm afraid I must be off now.

告贷 gàodài ask for a loan: ～无门 have nowhere to turn for loans /四处～ try to borrow money right and left

告倒 gàodǎo sue sb. (in court) or complain to authorities against sb. and win the case

告地状 gào dìzhuàng write one's misfortunes on the pavement in order to beg from passers-by

告发 gàofā inform against (sb. to the police); accuse sb. (of an offence); denounce: ～走私犯 inform against a smuggler to the police; denounce sb. as a smuggler /～同案犯 split (*or* rat, *or* squeal) on an accomplice

告乏 gàofá *see* "告罄"

告负 gàofù be defeated; lose: 决赛中客队～。The visiting team lost the finals.

告官 gàoguān lodge a complaint against sb. with the authorities

告急 gàojí ❶ be in an emergency; be critical: 前方～。The situation at the front is critical. /台风将临，大坝～。The dam was in danger with the approaching typhoon. ❷ report an emergency; ask for emergency help: ～的电报 cable asking for emergency help

告假 gàojià ask for leave: ～一周 ask for a one-week leave / 告事假 ask for leave of absence to attend to private affairs; ask for compassionate leave

告讦 gàojié 〈书面〉expose sb.'s dark secrets

告捷 gàojié ❶ win victory; be victorious: 首战～ win the first battle /全线～ be victorious on all fronts ❷ report a victory: 立即打电话向国内～ immediately call back home to report the victory

告竭 gàojié be exhausted: 这种矿储量有限，由于长期开采，今已～。This kind of mineral deposit, with limited ore reserves, is now exhausted after years of mining.

告解室 gàojiěshì 〈基督教〉confessional

告诫 gàojiè *also* "告戒" warn; caution; exhort; admonish: ～手下干部廉洁自律 exhort the cadres working under oneself to be honest and clean /妈妈～我不要过于自信。Mother warned me against being over-confident. /老师经常～大家要谦虚谨慎。Our teacher often admonishes us to be modest and prudent.

告借 gàojiè go and borrow money

告警 gàojǐng ❶ report an emergency ❷ give or sound an alarm: ～系统 warning system /～阀 alarm valve

告绝 gàojué be stamped out; be eliminated: 匪患～。Bandits are wiped out. /去年又有几种稀有动物～。Last year there were reports of the extinction of several species of rare animals.

告竣 gàojùn be completed: 大会准备工作～。We've got everything ready for the conference. *or* Preparations for the conference have been completed.

告劳 gàoláo tell about one's hard work: 不敢～ dare not pride oneself on one's hard work

告老 gàolǎo 〈旧语〉retire on account of age: 他曾做过两朝宰辅，如今～还乡。After serving as prime minister under two emperors, he retired in his old age and returned to his native place.

告满 gàomǎn be full; be completed: 本校今年招生人数～。The enrolment of students at the school this year has already been filled.

告密 gàomì inform against sb.:他做地下工作时,曾因叛徒～而被捕。When he was doing underground work, he was arrested because a renegade informed on (*or* against) him.
告密者 gàomìzhě informer
告罄 gàoqìng run out; be exhausted:弹药～。Ammunition has run out. /市面上纯棉内衣～。Pure cotton underwear has been sold out in the market.
告饶 gàoráo beg for mercy; ask pardon; throw oneself on sb.'s mercy:那恶棍被打翻在地,连声～。That scoundrel was knocked to the ground and was repeatedly begging for mercy.
告扰 gàorǎo sorry to disturb or bother sb.
告舌 gàoshé 〈旧语〉gossip; idle talk
告身 gàoshēn 〈旧语〉certificate of appointment
告示 gàoshi ❶ official notice; bulletin; placard:出安民～ put up a notice to reassure the public; give plenty of advance notice /～牌 billboard ❷〈旧语〉slogan:墙上贴满了红绿～。There are slogans on red and green paper all over the wall.
告送 gàosong *also* "告诵"〈方言〉tell; inform
告诉 gàosù (of an injured party) go to court against sb.; sue: 我将以抢劫罪～他。I shall sue him for robbery.
告诉 gàosu tell; let know:请～我你的电话号码。Please tell me your telephone number. /有用着我的地方,请～一声。In case you need my help, do let me know.
告退 gàotuì ❶ ask for leave to withdraw from a meeting, etc.:你同意的话,我就先～。With your permission, I am leaving now. ❷ withdraw (from an organization):他于去年挂靴～,离开了球队。He left the team last year, thus ending his career as a football player. ❸〈旧语〉hand in one's resignation
告慰 gàowèi take comfort from; comfort; console:我必办成此事,以～老父的在天之灵。I must get it done so that my late father may rest in peace.
告语 gàoyǔ 〈书面〉tell; let know:互相～ tell each other
告谕 gàoyù 〈书面〉(of seniors or superiors) make known; give instructions:～百姓 proclaim to the people of the country
告御状 gào yùzhuàng accuse sb. before the emperor; complain or report to the higher authorities (over one's immediate bosses, etc.)
告枕头状 gào zhěntouzhuàng complain (about sb. or sth.) to one's spouse when in bed; pillow-talk; give a curtain lecture
告知 gàozhī inform; notify; tell:此事我毫无了解,因为一直无人～。I know nothing about the matter, because nobody ever informed me of it.
告终 gàozhōng come to an end; end up:以失败～ end in failure; come to grief in the end /以损人开始,以害己～ start with the aim of harming others and end up by harming oneself
告状 gàozhuàng ❶ bring a lawsuit (against sb.); bring an action or a case (against sb.); sue:向地方法院～ bring an action against sb. in the local court ❷ lodge a complaint against sb. (with one's superior):他在老师那里告了我一状。He complained about me to the teacher.
告准 gàozhǔn 〈方言〉bring a lawsuit that is accepted by the court
告罪 gàozuì 〈谦词〉beg pardon; ask forgiveness:我承认这件事办得不妥,现在向诸位～。I must admit that I've not done the job properly. I am now asking for your forgiveness.

诰 gào ❶〈书面〉order; enjoin ❷〈古语〉written admonition ❸ imperial mandate
诰封 gàofēng confer honorary titles by imperial mandate:～三代 confer honorary titles on three generations
诰诫 gàojiè *see* "告诫" gàojiè
诰命 gàomìng ❶ imperial mandate:皇封～ imperial mandate ❷〈旧语〉women on whom titles were conferred by imperial mandate:～夫人 lady with an honorary title conferred by imperial mandate

锆 gào zirconium (Zr)
锆灯 gàodēng zirconium lamp
锆鞣 gàoróu zirconium tanning:～革 zirconium-tanned leather
锆石 gàoshí *also* "锆英石";"风信子石" fēngxìnzǐshí zircon
锆酸 gàosuān 〈化学〉zirconic acid:～盐 zirconate
锆碳合金 gàotàn héjīn 〈冶金〉zirten
锆锡合金 gàoxī héjīn 〈冶金〉zircaloy

郜 Gào a surname

gē

割 gē ❶ cut; sever; mow:～稻 cut (*or* reap) rice /～草 cut grass; mow grass /收～ reap; harvest /～开 cut open; rip open /～破 cut; gash; slash /～掉 cut off; get rid of ❷ divide; give up:切～ sever; divide /～膏腴之地 cede fertile land /心如刀～ feel as if a knife were piercing one's heart
割爱 gē'ài give up what one treasures; part with some valued or cherished possession:忍痛～ part reluctantly with what one treasures /～见遗 give away one's valued things to another; part with what one holds dear and make a present of it
割臂之盟 gēbìzhīméng *also* "割臂盟";"割臂盟公" swear an oath by making a cut on the arm — secret engagement between lovers
割草机 gēcǎojī lawn mower; grass cutter
割除 gēchú cut off; cut out; excise; remove:～扁桃体 cut out the tonsils; remove the tonsils /～肿瘤 excise a tumour
割地 gēdì cede territory:～赔款 cede territory and pay indemnities /～求和 sue for peace by ceding territory
割肚牵肠 gēdù-qiāncháng feel deep anxiety; be very much worried; be deeply concerned; be on tenterhooks
割断 gēduàn sever by cutting; cut off:不小心～手指 inadvertently cut off one's finger /～联系 sever relations; break off ties /我们不能～历史看问题。We mustn't consider a question out of its historical context.
割鸡焉用牛刀 gē jī yān yòng niúdāo why use an ox-cleaver to kill a chicken; why break a butterfly on the wheel; no need to waste talent on a petty job
割胶 gējiāo rubber tapping
割接法 gējiēfǎ grafting
割炬 gējù 〈机械〉cutting torch; acetylene torch
割据 gējù set up a separatist regime by force of arms; carve out a vast track of land and establish an independent regime:封建～ feudal separatist rule /诸侯～称雄的封建国家 feudal state torn apart by rival principalities /军阀～ nation carved up into a number of separate regimes by rival warlords /工农武装～ independent regime of armed workers and peasants (during the Second Revolutionary Civil War in China, 1927-1937)
割捆机 gēkǔnjī 〈农业〉self-binder; binder; reaper-binder
割礼 gēlǐ 〈宗教〉circumcision
割裂 gēliè cut apart; sever; separate; isolate:引证时～文义 quote (sth.) out of context /形式是不能和内容～开来的。Form and content cannot be separated. *or* Form cannot be separated from its content. /民主和法制密切相关,不能～开来。Democracy is closely bound up with legality, and the two must not be taken in isolation.
割蜜 gēmì cut off the honey comb in order to get honey
割袍断义 gēpáo-duànyì cut the robe and sever ties of friendship; break off all relations with a friend
割漆 gēqī cut the bark of the lacquer tree and let flow the lacquer; tap a lacquer tree
割弃 gēqì throw away; give up; discard; part with:与主题思想无关的东西,必须坚决～。Things that have nothing to do with the main theme must be left out without hesitation.
割枪 gēqiāng *also* "割炬" burning torch
割切 gēqiē *also* "切割" cut metal by lathe, etc.
割青 gēqīng cut green grass:～沤肥 cut green grass to make compost
割情 gēqíng break off friendly relations with sb.; give up what one treasures
割让 gēràng cede:～领土 cede territory /行政～ cession of the administration /租借～ cession in lease /～国 cessionary state; ceding state
割肉机 gēròujī 〈机械〉meat flenser
割晒机 gēshàijī 〈农业〉swather; windrower
割舍 gēshě give up; part with (sth.); give away:难以～ find it difficult to part with (sth.) /忍痛～ give up very reluctantly
割尾巴 gē wěiba eliminate old practices or remnants of certain unsound ideology; make a clean break with what is out-of-date and undesirable:割资本主义尾巴 (used in the Cultural Revolution) make a clean break with capitalism; do away with remnants of capitalism
割席 gēxí *also* "割席绝交" sever friendship; break off friendly re-

G

lations with sb.; break up an old friendship:~分座 separate the seats and break off friendly relations with each other

割线 gēxiàn 〈数学〉secant; secant line

割圆 gēyuán 〈数学〉cyclotomy

割治 gēzhì cure by excision:~痔疮 cure piles by excision /~息肉 cure by excising polyp

哥 gē ❶ elder brother:大~ eldest brother /三~ third elder brother ❷ form of address for the elder male relative of one's generation:表~ elder cousin ❸ friendly way of addressing males of approximately one's age:张大~ Brother Zhang

哥白尼 Gēbáiní Nicolaus Copernicus (1473-1543), Polish astronomer

哥白尼体系 Gēbáiní tǐxì 〈天文〉Copernican System (heliocentric system)

哥本哈根 Gēběnhāgēn Copenhagen, capital of Denmark

哥瓷 Gēcí *Ge* porcelain with crackled glaze; crackle-china

哥德巴赫 Gēdébāhè Christian Goldbach (1690-1764), German mathematician:~问题 Goldbach problem

哥德巴赫猜想 Gēdébāhè cāixiǎng 〈数学〉Goldbach's conjecture

哥德堡 Gēdébǎo Goteborg or Gothenburg, second largest city and seaport in southwest Sweden

哥哥 gēge ❶ elder brother:他有两个~。He has two elder brothers. /亲~ elder blood brother /同父异母或同母异父的~ elder half brother ❷ form of address for elder male of the same generation or same clan:叔伯~ first or second cousin on the paternal side;cousin /远房~ cousin several times removed; distant cousin

哥老会 Gēlǎohuì Society of Brothers, name of a secret society in the early Qing Dynasty:他早年曾参加过~。He once joined a secret society known as the Society of Brothers when he was very young.

哥伦比亚 Gēlúnbǐyà ❶ Colombia (The Colombian Republic):~人 Colombian ❷ Columbia:~特区 District of Columbia / ~大学 Columbia University /~河 Columbia River

哥伦比亚广播公司 Gēlúnbǐyà Guǎngbō Gōngsī (US) Columbia Broadcasting System (CBS)

哥伦比亚号航天飞机 Gēlúnbǐyàhào Hángtiān Fēijī (US) Space Shuttle Columbia

哥伦布 Gēlúnbù Christopher Columbus (1451-1506), Italian navigator

哥罗仿 gēluófǎng 〈化学〉chloroform

哥们儿 gēmenr *also* "哥儿们"〈口语〉❶ brothers ❷ buddies; cronies;pals:要讲原则,不能讲~义气。We must go by principles, not by cronyism. /都是~,你有困难大家还能袖手旁观吗? We are all good buddies. How can we stand idly by while you are having trouble? /嘿,~,你脖子上挂着啥玩意儿? Hi, buddy. What's that on your neck?

哥儿 gēr ❶ brothers (including oneself):我们一共~俩。There are only us two boys in my family. ❷ boy from families of rich people or high officials:公子~ pampered son of a wealthy or influential family

哥儿们 gērmen *see* "哥们儿"

哥萨克人 Gēsàkèrén Cossack

哥斯达黎加 Gēsīdálíjiā Costa Rica:~人 Costa Rican

哥特式 gētèshì 〈建筑〉Gothic:~建筑 Gothic architecture /~家具 Gothic chippendale /巴黎圣母院是一幢~教堂。Notre Dame in Paris is a Gothic cathedral.

哥特式艺术 gētèshì yìshù Gothic art

哥特体 gētètǐ 〈印刷〉gothic (print); black letter

哥窑 Gēyáo *also* "哥瓷" *Ge* porcelain ware with crackled glaze popular in the Song Dynasty

哥子 gēzi 〈方言〉(form of address among close friends) buddy; mate; pal:你~帮帮忙吧! Give me a hand, mate! /老~,这块地是你的吗? Buddy, is this plot yours?

诃 gē 〈书面〉*see* "歌" gē

歌 gē ❶ song:校~ school or college song /民~ folk song /恋~ love song /国~ national anthem /圣诞颂~ Christmas carol /赞美~ hymn /颂~ ode /挽~ elegy /哀~ mournful song; dirge /儿~ children's song, nursery rhymes /凯~ song of triumph; paean /牧~ madrigal /渔~ fisherman's song /战~ battle song; fighting song /主题~ theme song /组~ suite of songs ❷ sing; chant: 高~一曲 chant a melody /能~善舞 good at both singing and dancing /可~可泣 (of heroic deeds) moving one to song and tears; heroic and moving /讴~ sing the praise of; celebrate in song; eulogize /踏~ go step-dancing accompanied by singing

歌本 gēběn songbook:他喜欢收集~。He is fond of collecting songbooks.

歌唱 gēchàng ❶ sing (a song):纵情~ sing heartily /高声~ sing loudly /为人民~ sing for the people /~演员 singer; singing performer; vocalist ❷ sing the praises of; eulogize:~我们幸福的新生活 sing in praise of our happy new life /~伟大的祖国 extol our great motherland /~友谊 laud friendship /~真、善、美,抨击假、恶、丑 eulogize the true, good, and beautiful while stigmatizing the fake, evil, and ugly

歌唱家 gēchàngjiā singer; vocalist

歌词 gēcí words of a song; libretto (of an opera):这首歌的~是一位著名诗人创作的。The words of this song were written by a famous poet.

歌单儿 gēdānr song sheet

歌德 Gēdé Johann Wolfgang Von Goethe (1749-1832), German writer and scholar

歌德派 gēdépài (short for 歌功颂德派) people who always sing the praises of the powers that be

歌调 gēdiào tune of a song; tune

歌功颂德 gēgōng-sòngdé eulogize sb.'s virtues and achievements; sing the praises of sb. (usually one's superior):禁止给党的领导者祝寿,制止~现象。Ban the sending of birthday congratulations to Party leaders, and put a stop to flattery and exaggerated praises.

歌喉 gēhóu (singer's) voice; singing voice:嘹亮的~ resonant singing voice /音质良好的女高音~ soprano voice of fine quality

歌后 gēhòu most accomplished female singer; singing queen

歌会 gēhuì gathering for singing performance; singsong; community-sing

歌姬 gējī singing-girl; female entertainer: ~舞女 singing and dancing girls

歌集 gējí collection of songs; songbook

歌伎 gējì singing girl:~舞娘 female singer and dancer

歌剧 gējù opera:小型~ operetta /~剧本 libretto /~演员 opera performer

歌剧团 gējùtuán opera troupe or company

歌剧舞剧院 gējù-wǔjùyuàn opera and ballet theatre; theatre of opera and dance drama

歌剧院 gējùyuàn opera house

歌诀 gējué formulas or directions put into verse:汤头~ (handbook of) Chinese herb prescriptions in verse

歌鹛 gēméi 〈动物〉song-babbler

歌迷 gēmí song fan or devotee

歌女 gēnǚ female professional singer; singsong girl; singing girl

歌片儿 gēpiānr song sheet:抄~ copy a song sheet /看着~唱 sing from a song sheet

歌谱 gēpǔ music of a song:填写~ set a song to music /照着~练唱 practise singing according to the music of a song

歌鸲 gēqú 〈动物〉nightingale; robin

歌曲 gēqǔ song:流行~ popular song /校园~ campus song /电影~ film song /革命~ revolutionary song

歌声 gēshēng singing voice; vocal part in a performance; singing:~嘹亮。The singing is loud and clear. /~盈耳。The singing continues to ring in my ear. /~绕梁。The voice of singing lingers in the air for days on end.

歌手 gēshǒu singer; vocalist:来自青藏高原的~ singers from the Qinghai-Tibet Plateau /擅长流行歌曲的~ pop singer

歌诵 gēsòng 〈书面〉❶ *see* "歌颂" ❷ sing or chant; read aloud in measured tones

歌颂 gēsòng sing the praises of; laud; extol; eulogize:齐声~ extol in unison /大力~ laud sb. to the skies /~革命先辈的丰功伟绩 sing the praises of the glorious deeds and tremendous achievements of the old generation of revolutionaries

歌台舞榭 gētái-wǔxiè *also* "舞榭歌台" stages for performing songs and dances; places of amusement; singsong houses and dancehalls

歌坛 gētán song circles:~新秀 new stars in song circles

歌舞 gēwǔ song and dance; singing and dancing:~厅 song and dance hall /~晚会 evening party of singing and dancing /~节目

song and dance programme
歌舞伎 gēwǔjì kabuki, popular traditional Japanese drama performed by male actors
歌舞剧 gēwǔjù song and dance drama
歌舞片 gēwǔpiàn musical film; musical
歌舞升平 gēwǔ-shēngpíng extol the good times by singing and dancing — put on a fake or exaggerated show of peace and prosperity
歌舞团 gēwǔtuán song and dance ensemble; song and dance troupe
歌星 gēxīng star singer; singing star; accomplished vocalist:青年～ young star singer;young songster
歌行 gēxíng a flexible form of classical poem that can be set to music and sung
歌谣 gēyáo ballad; folk song; nursery rhyme:教孩子们唱～ teach children to sing nursery rhymes
歌艺 gēyì art of singing:～大进 greatly improve one's singing
歌吟 gēyín sing; chant; recite in cadence
歌咏 gēyǒng singing:～队 singing team; glee club; singing group; chorus /～比赛 singing contest /～会 singsong meeting; singsong; songfest /～活动 singing activity
歌仔戏 gēzǎixì *also* "芗剧" xiāngjù *Gezai* opera, local opera popular in Taiwan and Fujian provinces
歌赞 gēzàn sing the praises of:～延安 sing the praises of Yan'an
歌子 gēzi song:唱支～ sing a song /嘴里哼着～ hum a song

戈 gē
❶ ancient Chinese weapon with a long shaft and a horizontal blade; dagger-axe:兵～ weapons; arms /动干～ resort to arms /倒～ change sides in a war; be a turncoat /反～一击 turn one's weapon around and strike /枕～待旦 lie with one's head pillowed on a spear, waiting for day to break — be combat-ready ❷ (Gē) a surname
戈比 gēbǐ kopeck; kopek; copeck (fractional currency in Russia and some other countries)
戈壁 gēbì 〈地理〉gobi; Gobi Desert
戈登 Gēdēng Charles George Gordon (1833-1885), British colonialist known for the role he played in suppressing the Taiping Revolution and later killed in Khartoum by Sudanese nationalists
戈甲戏 gējiǎxì *also* "高甲戏" gāojiǎxì local opera popular in Fujian and Taiwan provinces
戈兰高地 Gēlán Gāodì Golan Heights (Syrian territory occupied by Israel)

疙 gē
疙疤 gēba 〈方言〉scab; crust
疙瘩 gēda *also* "疙疸" ❶ swelling on the skin; pimple; wart; lump:胳臂上长了几个～。There are some swellings on the arm. /脸上尽是～。The face is dotted with pimples. *or* Pimples have come out all over the face. ❷ lump; knot:面～ small round lumps of dough /芥菜～ rutabaga /线结成了～。The thread has got tangled. ❸ knot in one's heart; hang-up:他帮我解开了心中的～。He helped me rid myself of my hang-up. /他俩之间的～终于解开了。The misunderstanding between the two of them was finally dispelled. ❹ 〈方言〉〈量词〉:一～石头 a piece of stone ❺ 〈方言〉trouble; embarrassment
疙瘩汤 gēdatāng dough drop soup
疙疙瘩瘩 gēge-dādā *also* "疙里疙瘩" 〈口语〉rough; knotty; bumpy:路上净是石子儿,～的,很不好走。The road was rocky, and it was a bumpy (*or* rough) ride. /这事情～的,真难办。This is a knotty problem.
疙渣儿 gēzhar *also* "嘎渣儿" gāzhar scrab; crust

圪 gē
圪垯 gēda ❶ *see* "疙瘩" gēda ❷ *also* "圪塔" mound; knoll
圪节 gējie 〈方言〉❶ point of rice, wheat, or sorghum stalk where it branches ❷ part between two such points ❸ part or section of any elongate thing:断成三～ break into three pieces
圪蹴 gējiu 〈方言〉squat; crouch:老人们喜欢～在树下聊闲天。Aged people like to squat under the tree chatting.
圪捞 gēlao 〈方言〉corner (also used in place names)
圪梁 gēliáng 〈方言〉hill ridge
圪囊 gēnang 〈方言〉crushed beanstalk
圪针 gēzhen 〈方言〉thorn on the stalk of certain plants:枣～ date thorn

屹 gē
see also yì
屹嶝 gēda ❶ *see* "疙瘩" gēda ❷ mound; knoll

仡 gē
see also yì
仡佬语 Gēlǎoyǔ Gelao language
仡佬族 Gēlǎozú Gelao or Kelao nationality, living in Guizhou Province

纥 gē
see also hé
纥繨 gēda lump; knot:线～ thread knot

鸽 gē
pigeon; dove:白～ white pigeon /野～ wild pigeon; dove /信～ homing pigeon; carrier pigeon /和平～ peace dove /～棚 pigeon shed or loft; dovecote /放～ release pigeons /养～ raise pigeons
鸽派 gēpài dovish:～观点 dovish view /～人物 dove /鹰派与～ hawks and doves
鸽哨 gēshào pigeon whistle
鸽子 gēzi pigeon; dove:～笼 dovecote;pigeon house; loft

搁 gē
❶ put; place; lay:整整齐齐地把东西～好 put things in a neat and tidy way /不要随便～东西。Don't leave things about. /这屋子太热,蔬菜～不住。This room is too hot; the vegetables won't keep. /窗台上～了一盆花。There is a pot of flowers on the windowsill. /屋子小,～不下那么多家具。The room is too small to hold so many pieces of furniture. ❷ add; put in:多～点儿糖。Put in more sugar. /～一勺醋。Add a spoonful of vinegar. ❸ put aside; leave over; shelve:耽～ delay; hold up /延～ procrastinate; put off /这件事得～～再办。The matter has to be put aside for the time being. /这件事她总～不下。She is unable to put the matter out of her mind. /这项计划被～起来了。The plan has been pigeonholed. /这些稿子已经～得太久了,应该抓紧清理一下。These manuscripts have been shelved for too long and should be sorted out immediately.
see also gé
搁板 gēbǎn shelf:搭～ put up a shelf
搁笔 gēbǐ lay down the brush; stop writing or painting:～沉思 lay down the pen lost in thought
搁车 gēchē 〈方言〉(of car) pull up; park a car; come to a halt
搁放 gēfàng lay; place:几件衣服～在沙发上。Some clothes have been placed on the sofa.
搁脚板 gējiǎobǎn footrest
搁脚凳 gējiǎodèng footstool
搁浅 gēqiǎn ❶ run aground; get stranded:小船在沙滩～了。The boat was stranded on the beach. ❷ held up; at a deadlock:谈判～了。The negotiations have come to a deadlock. /事情～了。The matter is being held up.
搁物架 gēwùjià rack
搁心 gēxīn be careful; be prudent; take care:环境很复杂,你要多搁点儿心。You must exercise great care under such complicated circumstances.
搁置 gēzhì shelve; put aside; lay aside; pigeonhole:～一项动议 shelve a motion /～脑后 put sth. out of mind /～争议,共同开发 put aside disputes and engage in joint exploitation. /此事关系重大,千万不能～。The matter is too important to be delayed.

袼 gē
袼褙 gēbei pieces of old cloth or rags pasted together to make cloth shoes:糊～ paste pieces of old cloth or rags together

格 gē
see also gé
格登 gēdēng *see* "咯噔" gēdēng
格格 gēgē *also* "咯咯" gēgē 〈象声〉❶ chuckle; giggle:她～地笑着,开心极了。She was chuckling, extremely delighted. ❷ sound

of gritting one's teeth:～地咬牙 knash one's teeth ❸ (of a machine-gun) rattle ❹ cry of certain birds
格格 gēge form of address used by people of the Manchu nationality for princesses and young ladies

咯

gē
see also kǎ; lo; luò
咯哒 gēda *also*"咯嗒" *see*"疙瘩" gēda
咯噔 gēdēng *also*"格登" gēdēng 〈象声〉click; clump:～～的皮靴声 clump of boots (on the floor) /心～～地跳个不停 heart keeps thumping in the chest /耳边传来了～～的皮鞋声。We heard the tramp of a pair of leather shoes.
咯咯 gēgē 〈象声〉 *see*"格格" gēgē
咯吱 gēzhī 〈象声〉creak; groan:地板被他踩得～～响。The floor creaked under his heavy steps.

胳(肐)

gē
see also gā; gé
胳臂 gēbei arm:粗壮的～ brawny arm /紧紧挽着他的～ hold his arm tightly
胳膊 gēbo arm:举起～ raise one's arms
胳膊拧不过大腿 gēbo nǐngbuguò dàtuǐ the arm is no match for the thigh — the weak cannot contend with the strong; the wagon must go whither the horses draw it:这些事得忍就忍着，～，又有什么办法呢? Kings have long arms, so we have to put up with it, or what else can be done?
胳膊腕子 gēbo wànzi *also*"胳膊腕儿" wrist
胳膊肘儿往外拐 gēbozhǒur wǎng wài guǎi *also*"胳膊肘朝外拐" one's elbow turns to the wrong side; side with outsiders instead of one's own people
胳膊肘子 gēbo zhǒuzi *also*"胳膊肘儿"〈口语〉elbow

饹

gē
see also le
饹馇 gēcha a kind of flat cake made of bean powder:绿豆～ green bean cake

gé

革[1]

gé ❶ leather; hide:～制品 leather goods /面～ upper leather /磨面～ buff /绒面～ suede (leather) /坯～ crust leather /皮～ hide; leather /漆～ patent leather /粗鞣～ rough-tanned leather; crust leather /皱纹～ shrink leather /人造～ imitation leather; artificial leather /制～ process hides; tan /制～厂 tannery ❷ (Gé) a surname

革[2]

gé ❶ change; alter; transform:改～ reform /变～ transform; change /鼎～ change of dynasty /兴～ initiate (the new) and abolish (the old); start reforms /沿～ course of change and development; evolution ❷ remove from office; expel; get rid of:斥～ dismiss sb. from office
see also jí
革翅目 géchìmù 〈动物〉dermaptera
革出 géchū expel; dismiss:～教会 excommunication
革除 géchú ❶ abolish; do away with; get rid of; eliminate:～陈规陋习 abolish outmoded regulations and irrational practices /～弊端 get rid of (*or* do away with) malpractices ❷ expel; dismiss; discharge; remove from office:～主任职务 dismiss sb. from the post of dean (*or* director) /～公职 discharge from public service /～军籍 remove one's name from the army roll
革干 gégàn (short for 革命干部) revolutionary cadre
革故鼎新 gégù-dǐngxīn abolish the old and introduce the new; discard the old ways of life in favour of the new; reform the old rules and establish a new order of things:此事虽小，但意在～，是应该支持的。Though far from being important in itself, the change deserves our support for it aims to replace what is old with something new.
革胡 géhú 〈音乐〉four-metal-stringed bowed instrument
革兰氏染色法 Gélánshì rǎnsèfǎ 〈生物〉Gram's staining
革兰氏阳性 Gélánshì yángxìng 〈生物〉Gram positive
革兰氏阴性 Gélánshì yīnxìng 〈生物〉Gram negative
革履 gélǚ leather shoes:西装～ in Western dress and leather shoes
革面洗心 gémiàn-xǐxīn *also*"洗心革面"turn over a new leaf; thoroughly reform oneself
革命 gémìng ❶ revolution:资产阶级～ bourgeois revolution /社会主义～ socialist revolution /参加～ join the revolution /干～ do revolutionary work /将～进行到底 carry the revolution through to the end /农民起来革地主的命。The peasants rose in revolt against the landlords. /～是历史的火车头。Revolution is the locomotive of history. ❷ revolutionary:～高潮 climax of revolution /～利益 revolutionary interest /～干劲 revolutionary impetus /～气概 revolutionary stamina (or mettle) /～气节 revolutionary integrity /～热情 revolutionary fervour (*or* zeal) /～意志 revolutionary will /～精神 revolutionary spirit /～豪情 revolutionary sentiments /～群众歌曲 revolutionary popular song ❸ radical change; transformation; revolution:产业～ industrial revolution /技术～ technical (technological) revolution /思想～ ideological revolution
革命传统 gémìng chuántǒng revolutionary tradition:～教育 education in revolutionary tradition
革命导师 gémìng dǎoshī teacher of revolution
革命发展阶段论 gémìng fāzhǎn jiēduànlùn theory of the development of revolution by stages
革命干部 gémìng gànbù revolutionary cadre
革命公墓 gémìng gōngmù cemetery for revolutionaries
革命化 gémìnghuà revolutionize; do things in a revolutionary way:干部队伍要实行～，年轻化，知识化，专业化 make our cadres more revolutionary, younger, better educated and more professionally competent
革命回忆录 gémìng huíyìlù reminiscences of earlier revolutionary times
革命家 gémìngjiā revolutionary; revolutionist:缅怀老一辈～的功勋 cherish (*or* recall) the meritorious service of revolutionaries of the older generation
革命军人 gémìng jūnrén revolutionary armyman
革命军人委员会 gémìng jūnrén wěiyuánhuì revolutionary armymen's committee (a mass organization of a company in the PLA, elected by its members)
革命浪漫主义 gémìng làngmànzhǔyì revolutionary romanticism:这是～的代表作。This is a representative work of revolutionary romanticism.
革命乐观主义 gémìng lèguānzhǔyì revolutionary optimism
革命烈士 gémìng lièshì *also*"革命先烈"revolutionary martyr
革命领袖 gémìng lǐngxiù leader of a revolution
革命派 gémìngpài revolutionary
革命人道主义 gémìng réndàozhǔyì revolutionary humanitarianism
革命圣地 gémìng shèngdì sacred place of a revolution
革命晚节 gémìng wǎnjié revolutionary integrity in one's later life
革命委员会 gémìng wěiyuánhuì (shortened as 革委会) revolutionary committee, (name for local government at various levels during the Cultural Revolution, 1966-1976)
革命现实主义 gémìng xiànshízhǔyì revolutionary realism:伟大的～著作 great works of revolutionary realism
革命性 gémìngxìng revolutionary character, or quality, or spirit:发扬无产阶级的～ develop (*or* carry forward) the revolutionary spirit of the proletariat
革命英雄主义 gémìng yīngxióngzhǔyì revolutionary heroism
革囊 génáng leather bag
革新 géxīn innovation; renovation:具有重大意义的技术～ technological innovation of great significance /～思想 innovative ideas /技术～者 technical innovator /传统的手工艺技术不断～。Traditional handicraft techniques are being steadily improved (*or* renovated).
革职 gézhí remove from office; cashier; dismiss:～留用 be dismissed from one's official post but kept on as an employee /～查办 discharge sb. from his post and prosecute him /他受到了～的处分。He was punished with dismissal.

葛

gé ❶ (popularly known as 葛麻) ko-hemp; kudzu; *Pueraria lobata* or *thunbergiana*:野～ elegant jassamine (*Gelsemium elegans*) ❷〈纺织〉poplin
see also Gě
葛布 gébù ko-hemp cloth

G

葛粉 géfěn edible starch obtained by grinding the roots of kudzu vine; kudzu starch
葛根 gégēn 〈中药〉root of kudzu vine:～素 puerarin
葛巾 géjīn scarf or kerchief made of a coarse yellowish hemp cloth:～布袍 scarf made of ko-hemp and robe made of cloth
葛藟 gélěi 〈植物〉*Vitis flexuosa*
葛麻 gémá *see* "葛❶"
葛藤 géténg 〈比喻〉tangled or complicated relations

镉

gé *see* "镠镉" jiāogé

槅

gé ❶ latticed door or partition board; lattice ❷ set of latticed shelves:多宝～ lattice framework for curios or bric-a-bracs; curio shelves
槅门 gémén latticed door; lattice
槅扇 géshan partition board

塥

gé 〈方言〉sandy field; sandlot (often used as part of a place name)

嗝

gé ❶ belch:饱～ belch; burp /一连打了几个～儿 keep belching ❷ hiccup; hiccough

镉

gé cadmium (Cd):～灯 cadmium lamp
镉电池 gédiànchí cadmium cell or battery
镉合金 géhéjīn cadmium metal
镉化合物 géhuàhéwù cadmium compound
镉污染 géwūrǎn cadmium pollution
镉中毒 gézhòngdú cadmium poisoning

膈

gé diaphragm
see also gè
膈膜 gémó diaphragm:横～ diaphragm
膈疝 géshàn diaphragmatocele; diaphragmatic hernia
膈食病 géshíbìng 〈医学〉pleurodynia; pleuralgia
膈炎 géyán 〈医学〉diaphragmatitis; diaphragmitis

隔

G

gé ❶ separate; partition; divide; stand or lie between:分～ separate; divide /阻～ separate; cut off; block /～着一条河 be separated by a river /两国～海相望。Our two countries are on the opposite sides of the sea. /龟蛇二山～江相望。Tortoise and Snake Hills face each other across the river. /～一座山就是我们的目的地。Our destination is just on the other side of the hill. /用帘子把一间房～成了两间。The room is partitioned into two with a curtain. ❷ at a distance; after or at an interval:间～ setting apart; interval of space or time; intermission /相～很远 at a great distance from each other /每盏路灯要～开二十米。The lamp-posts should be spaced twenty metres apart. /他每～一天就去医院看她。He went to visit her in the hospital every other day.
隔岸观火 gé'àn-guānhuǒ watch a fire from the other side of the river — look on at sb.'s trouble with indifference; show no concern for another's trouble:这事对他至关重要,你可不能～呀! The matter is of vital importance to him. You can't stand by and look unconcerned at his trouble.
隔板 gébǎn ❶ partition board ❷〈机械〉division plate; baffle plate
隔板式输送带 gébǎnshì shūsòngdài 〈机械〉cell belt
隔壁 gébì next door:住在一家饭馆的～ live next door to a restaurant /～第二间 next door but one /我们两家住～。We are next-door neighbours.
隔壁戏 gébìxì 〈杂技〉a kind of vocal mimicry with the performer imitating the sounds of birds, animals, etc. behind the curtain which stands between him and the audience
隔别 gébié separate; part with:～多年 be separated for years
隔舱 gécāng 〈航天〉bay
隔层 gécéng interlayer
隔代遗传 gédài yíchuán 〈医学〉reversion; atavism
隔断 géduàn cut off; sever; separate; obstruct:同外面的联系完全～ completely cut off from the outside /万水千山隔不断我们之间的情谊。Mountains and rivers cannot sever the friendly ties between us.
隔断 géduan partition (wall, board, etc.)
隔房 géfáng not of the same branch of a family:～兄弟 brothers of different branches of a family
隔行 géháng ❶ of different professions or trades:～如隔山。Difference in profession makes one feel worlds apart. ❷ interlace; interleave:～打印 double space /～书写 write in alternate lines
隔阂 géhé estrangement; barrier; misunderstanding:制造～ foment feelings of estrangement /产生～ cause estrangement; create misunderstanding /消除～ remove (*or* clear up, *or* dispel) misunderstanding; end estrangement /语言上的～ language barrier /兄弟间因争吵而产生～。The quarrel alienated (*or* estranged) him from his brother.
隔火墙 géhuǒqiáng fire division wall; fire wall
隔绝 géjué cut off completely; isolate:与世～ be cut off from the outside world; live in seclusion /音信～ (with) all news blocked off/ ～噪音 insulation of noise /降低温度和～空气是灭火的根本方法。Lowering temperature and cutting off the air are the basic ways of extinguishing fire.
隔离 gélí ❶ separate; keep apart; isolate; segregate:种族～ racial segregation; apartheid /～审查 be taken into custody and under investigation ❷ isolate (the sick, etc.); quarantine:检疫～ place in (*or* under) quarantine /解除检疫～。The quarantine is removed. /传染病人必须～。All patients with contagious diseases must be isolated.
隔离病房 gélí bìngfáng isolation ward
隔离层 gélícéng separation layer
隔离阀 gélífá section valve
隔离饲养 gélí sìyǎng isolated rearing
隔离物 gélíwù spacer; separator
隔离线 gélíxiàn isolation wire
隔离栅 gélízhà isolation fencing
隔凉 géliáng keep warm; keep away cold:把这件雨衣穿上还能隔点凉。Put on the raincoat to keep yourself a bit warmer. /这种褥子不～。This kind of cotton-padded mattress doesn't keep away cold.
隔邻 gélín neighbour; next-door:～屋子里住着一位画家。A painter lives next door.
隔路 gélù *also* "格路" gélù 〈方言〉peculiar; eccentric
隔膜 gémó ❶ lack of mutual understanding; estrangement:他们之间有些～。They are rather estranged from each other. /两人长期不来往,彼此都感到有些～。They have been out of touch for a long time and feel alienated from each other. /经过谈心,他们之间的～终于消除了。They finally cleared up their misunderstanding after a heart-to-heart talk. ❷ unfamiliar; not versed:我对这种方法并不～。I'm no stranger to this method. ❸ diaphragm:阴道～ (contraceptive) diaphragm /～泵 diaphragm pump; bellows pump
隔年黄历 génián-huánglì calendar of the past year — sth. outdated; yesterday's newspaper:～看不得。We shouldn't be bound by those old rules.
隔片 gépiàn 〈机械〉spacer
隔墙 géqiáng ❶ separated by a wall; on the other side of a wall:～有一棵杏树。There is an apricot tree on the other side of the wall. ❷〈建筑〉partition wall:用一道～把大屋一分为二。The big room is divided into two by a partition wall.
隔墙有耳 géqiáng-yǒu'ěr people may be listening on the other side of the wall; walls have ears; beware of eavesdroppers:～,你说话可得当心啊! Be careful (of) what you say, for walls have ears. /他们惟恐～,说话的声音小极了。Afraid of being overheard, they spoke in very low voices.
隔热 gérè 〈建筑〉heat insulation:～材料 thermal insulation material; heat-barrier material /～性能 heat-proof quality /这房顶很厚,既能防寒又能～。The roof is so thick that it can keep out both the heat and the cold.
隔日 gérì day after the next; every other day:我们～再开会。Let's meet again the day after tomorrow.
隔三差五 gésān-chàwǔ *also* "隔三岔五" every now and then; time and again:他～给树苗浇水。He waters the saplings from time to time.
隔山 géshān relationship between siblings of different mothers:～兄妹 half brothers and sisters (by the same father)
隔扇 géshan partition board
隔声 géshēng 〈建筑〉sound insulation:～板 sound insulating board /～材料 sound insulator /～墙 sound-proof wall /～装置 sound arrester
隔世 géshì world in the remote past:恍如～ there seems to be an

interval of a whole generation (said on finding things greatly changed); as if it had happened in the remote past
隔世之感 géshìzhīgǎn feel as if a whole generation has elapsed
隔宿 gésù of the previous night; overnight:家无～粮。There is no food left for tomorrow in the house. /桌上没有～的公文,都及时处理了。There are no leftover official documents on the desk, for they have all been dealt with in time.
隔外 géwài 〈方言〉❶ regard sb. as an outsider:不要～,常来玩儿。Don't feel like a stranger. Do drop in often. ❷ besides; in addition:这儿不好,可～又没处去。It's not very nice here, but there is no other place to go.
隔心 géxīn estrangement; misunderstanding:他俩从没有因为什么～的事闹过别扭。The two of them have never been at odds because of misunderstanding.
隔靴搔痒 géxuē-sāoyǎng scratch an itch from outside one's boot; fail to strike home; be irrelevant; take ineffective measures:你的建议～,没有多少用处。Your suggestion is not very helpful as it fails to get to the root of the matter.
隔厌 géyan 〈方言〉disagreeable; disgusting:妖里妖气,让人～。Her coquetry is disgusting.
隔夜 géyè of the previous night; last night:～菜 last night's leftovers /夏天饭菜最好别～。In summer, it is better not to leave any food for the next day.
隔音 géyīn ❶ sound insulating;soundproof:～设备 sound insulating equipment /这房子～不错。The house is impervious to sound. ❷〈语言〉syllable-dividing
隔音板 géyīnbǎn acoustic celotex board; acoustic septum
隔音符号 géyīn fúhào 〈语言〉syllable-dividing mark
隔音室 géyīnshì soundproof room
隔音纸 géyīnzhǐ sound insulating paper
隔远 géyuǎn 〈方言〉❶ far away ❷ drift apart; become estranged:两人开始～了。The two became estranged. *or* The two began to drift apart.
隔振 gézhèn vibration isolation:～器 isolator
隔肢 gézhi *also* "胳肢" gézhi tickle; titillate

阁

gé 〈书面〉❶ small side door ❷ *see* "阁" gé ❸ (Gé) a surname

颌

gé 〈书面〉mouth
see also hé

蛤

gé ❶ clam ❷ *see* "蛤蚧"
see also há
蛤灰 géhuī lime obtained by burning sea-shells
蛤蚧 géjiè gecko
蛤蜊 gélí ❶ a kind of mollusc ❷ clam
蛤蛎 gélì a kind of bivalve

搿

gé 〈方言〉embrace tightly
搿犋 géjù 〈方言〉(of small farmers) pool livestock, ploughs, etc., and farm cooperatively

阁

gé ❶ pavilion (usu. two-storeyed):楼台亭～ pavilions, terraces, and towers ❷〈旧语〉woman's chamber; boudoir:闺～ boudoir /出～ (of a woman) get married; marry ❸ cabinet:受命组～ be entrusted to form a cabinet /～僚 member of a cabinet /改组内～ reshuffle a cabinet /倒～ bring down a cabinet /入～ become a cabinet minister ❹〈书面〉rack; shelf:束之高～ tie sth. up and place it on the top shelf — shelve; pigeonhole
阁道 gédào 〈书面〉❶ plank road built along the face of a cliff ❷ name of a constellation *see also* "二十八宿" èrshíbāxiù
阁老 gélǎo senior officials of various departments in feudal times
阁楼 gélóu attic; garret; loft:租了一间～ rent a garret
阁下 géxià 〈敬词〉Your Excellency; His or Her Excellency; Honourable (a title used before the names of certain officials, including members of parliament and in England the children of certain nobles); Right Honourable (a title used before the names of certain senior officials, certain nobles, and privy councillors); Your Honour (a title used in speaking to a judge, mayor, governor, senator, etc.); Your Lordship (a title used in speaking to or of a man having the rank of Lord):大使～ Your Excellency Mr. Ambassador; His Excellency the Ambassador; Her Excellency the Ambassadress /敬请～光临。Your Excellency's presence is cordially requested.
阁员 géyuán member of a cabinet:内阁～ cabinet member
阁子 gézi ❶ small wooden house:板～ small wooden house ❷〈方言〉attic:～间 attic

茖

gé
茖葱 gécōng a kind of wild onion (*Allium victorialis*)

格[1]

gé ❶ square (formed by crossed lines); check:在纸上打～儿 square off the paper /画方～ draw squares /表～ form; table /离～儿 be out of place; go beyond what is proper ❷ standard; rule; pattern; style:合～ up to standard /规～ standard; specification /及～ pass (a test or an examination) /降～ lower one's standard or status; be demoted (*or* downgraded) /破～ make an exception; break a rule /升～ promote; upgrade /自成一～ have a style of one's own ❸ character; manner; style:人～ character; personality /风～ manner; style ❹〈书面〉resist; hinder; obstruct; impede:阻～ be an impediment /～于成例 be barred by accepted practice ❺ (Gé) a surname

格[2]

gé 〈语言〉case:主～ nominative case /宾～ objective case /所有～ possessive case

格[3]

gé 〈书面〉probe; delve into; study thoroughly: *see* "～物"

格[4]

gé fight; hit:激烈～斗 be locked in a fierce fight
see also gē
格但斯克 Gédànsīkè Gdansk, industrial port and shipbuilding centre in northern Poland
格调 gédiào ❶ (literary or artistic) style; ethos; quality:～豪放 vigorous and flowing style /～优雅 elegant style /伤感的～ sentimental ethos (*or* quality) /与众不同的～ unique ethos (*or* quality) ❷〈书面〉one's style of work; one's moral quality:～高尚的人 person of integrity and lofty ideals
格斗 gédòu grapple; wrestle; fistfight:勇敢地与歹徒～ bravely grapple with a ruffian
格尔木 Gé'ěrmù Golmud, a city in Qinghai Province
格格不入 gégé-bùrù incompatible; alien; out of tune; like a square peg in a round hole:与时代～ be out of tune with the times /不改变心态他就会和他的同事们～。Without a change of heart he would be a misfit among his colleagues. /她和大家总显得有些～。She does not get along well with others.
格构 gégòu 〈建筑〉lattice:～梁 lattice girder; open-web girder; lattice beam /～桥 lattice bridge
格局 géjú pattern; layout; setup; structure:世界多极化的～ multipolar structure of the world /这个饭店的～与别处不同。This restaurant has a different setup from others. /文章的～显得很乱。The article seems to be poorly organized.
格兰德河 Gēlándéhé Rio Grande, a river of North America that flows southeast to the Gulf of Mexico and forms the US-Mexican frontier from EL Paso to the sea
格雷格速记法 Gēléigé sùjìfǎ Gregg shorthand
格雷杭得公司 Géléihángdé Gōngsī *also* "灰狗公司" Huīgǒu Gōngsī Greyhound Corporation, an inter-city long-distance bus corporation in the United States and Canada
格楞 géleng 〈方言〉stammer; stutter:说话不打～ speak without any stutter /机器发生故障,光打～。There is something wrong with the machine for it keeps sputtering.
格里历 Gélǐlì Gregorian calendar
格林纳达 Gélínnàdá Grenada:～人 Grenadian /～岛 Grenada Island
格林尼治 Gélínnízhì (formerly 格林威治) Greenwich, London borough and former site of the Royal Observatory which was moved to Herstmonceux in East Sussex in 1958
格林尼治恒星时 Gélínnízhì héngxīngshí Greenwich sidereal time (GST)
格林尼治时间 Gélínnízhì shíjiān *also* "格林尼治平时" Greenwich

mean time (GMT)
格林尼治时间间隔 Gélínnízhì shíjiān jiàngé Greenwich interval
格林尼治子午线 Gélínnízhì zǐwǔxiàn Greenwich Meridian (adopted in 1884 as the zero of longitude)
格林童话集 Gélín Tónghuàjí Grimm's Fairy Tales (1812-1822), edited by Jakob Ludwig Karl Grimm and Wilhelm Karl Grimm
格林兄弟 Gélín xiōngdì Jacob Ludwig Karl Grimm (1785-1863) and Wilhelm Karl Grimm (1786-1859), remembered for the anthology of German fairy-tales they compiled
格陵兰 Gélínglán Greenland
格令 gélìng grain, the smallest unit of weight in the troy system equivalent to 0.065 gram
格鲁吉亚 Gélǔjíyà Georgia (name of a country):～人 Georgian /～语 Georgian
格鲁派 Gélǔpài Gelugpa, Yellow Sect of Lamaism in the Tibet Autonomous Region
格路 gélù *also*"隔路"gélù 〈方言〉〈贬义〉peculiar; bizarre; eccentric:脾气～ odd temperament /今年气候真～,已经初冬了,还这么暖和。The temperature this year is really unusual. It is still warm in early winter.
格律 gélǜ rules and forms of classical poetic composition (with respect to tonal pattern, rhyme scheme, etc.):诗词～ poetical meter; metrical pattern of poetry; set rules for versification /～诗 poem with a strict tonal pattern and rhyme scheme
格木 gémù 〈植物〉*Erythrophloeum ferdii*
格涩 gésè *also*"格色"〈方言〉〈贬义〉odd; unusual; strange:这人真～,大家都去就他不去。He is really odd; everyone is going except him.
格杀 géshā fight to kill (with weapons at close quarters):～不贷 kill on the spot without mercy
格杀勿论 géshā-wùlùn kill on sight (without fear of prosecution):军阀政府下令对抗拒复工的工人～。The warlord government issued the order that those workers who refused to return to work be killed on sight without mercy.
格式 géshi form; pattern;〈信息〉format:公文～ form of an official document; documentary form /书信～ form of a letter /按规定的～写 write in the set form /固定的～ fixed form (*or* pattern) / 请将这个软盘～化。Please format this floppy.
格套 gétào conventional method or pattern:要提倡科学种田,凭老～种地不行。We must not fall into a rut but should encourage scientific farming.
格外 géwài ❶ especially; particularly; all the more; extraordinarily:印象～深 especially deep impression /山村里～清静 particularly quiet in a mountain village /今天天气～热。It is exceptionally hot today. /如果能够得到外界帮助,工作将完成得～迅速。If we can get help from the outside, the work will be completed all the more quickly. ❷ extra; additional; added:减少中间环节之后,消费者减去了～的负担。With fewer intermediate links, consumers rid themselves of the extra burden. /手提箱装不下了,只得～找了一个提包。The suitcase is full, and we have to find an additional bag to pack the rest of the things.
格物 géwù 〈书面〉study physical nature; study the world
格物致知 géwù-zhìzhī (theory of cognition in ancient China) knowledge comes from the study of the physical world
格形构造 géxíng gòuzào 〈建筑〉cellular construction
格言 géyán maxim; motto; aphorism
格言诗 géyánshī gnomic poetry
格栅 gézhà grid; grill; grillage
格正 gézheng 〈方言〉smooth and straight; neat and tidy:他的衣服总是那么～。His dress is always well pressed.
格致 gézhì 〈书面〉❶ (short for 格物致知) study the physical world in order to acquire knowledge ❷ used by late 19th century reformers as a generic term for physics, chemistry, etc.
格子 gézi check; chequer:～纸 squared (*or* graph) paper /～布 checked fabric; check /～窗 lattice window /～花呢〈纺织〉tartan /～呢 plaid woolen cloth
格子梁 géziliáng 〈建筑〉gridwork girder

搁

gé bear; stand; sustain; endure
see also gē
搁不住 gébuzhù can't bear; can't stand:丝巾～搓揉。Silk scarves won't stand rubbing.
搁得住 gédezhù able to put up with; able to stand:他体质好,这点小病能～。He has a good constitution and won't go under for this minor illness.

骼

gé *see*"骨骼"gǔgé

胳

gé
see also gā; gē
胳肢 gézhi 〈方言〉tickle; tintillate:～得她格格儿地笑个不住 tickle her so that she keeps chuckling

gě

盖(葢)

Gě a surname
see also gài

葛

Gě a surname
see also gé
葛洪 Gě Hóng Ge Hong (formerly translated as Ko Hung, 284-363), Taoist theoretician and doctor of medicine of the Eastern Jin Dynasty
葛仙米 gěxiānmǐ 〈植物〉nostoc (fresh-water algae)
葛洲坝水利枢纽工程 Gězhōubà Shuǐlì Shūniǔ Gōngchéng Gezhouba Key Water Control Project, on the Yangtze River in Hubei Province

舸

gě 〈书面〉barge:百～争流 all barges vying to be the first

哿

gě 〈书面〉approve; regard as worthy

合

gě ❶ unit of dry measure for grain (= 1 decilitre) ❷ measuring container for 1 decilitre of grain
see also hé

个(個)

gě *see*"自个儿"zìgěr
see also gè

各

gě 〈方言〉〈贬义〉unusual; peculiar:这人真～。This man is quite peculiar.
see also gè

gè

虼

gè
虼螂 gèláng dung beetle
虼蚤 gèzao flea:被～咬了 bitten by fleas; fleabitten /这儿～真多。The place is bursting with fleas.

个[1](個、箇)

gè ❶〈量词〉(a) *usually used before a noun having no particular classifier*:一～西瓜 a watermelon /两～馒头 two steamed buns /三～字 three characters /第四～年头 fourth year /几～月 several months /摔一～跟头 have a fall /人人是英雄,～～是好汉。Each and everyone is a hero. /大家一～一～地走,别挤。Don't push. Leave one by one. (b) *used before an approximate figure*:每周都要来～一两趟 come once or twice every week /这工作看来还需要～两三天才能结束。It seems that the work will take a couple of days to finish. (c) *used after a verb which is followed by an object*:讨～吉利 invite luck /有～什么差错 in case there is a mistake /上了～大当 be grievously deceived (*or* taken in) /吃了～大亏 suffer a great loss /他就喜欢画～画儿,写～字什么的。He is fond of drawing pictures and practising calligraphy. (d) *used between a verb and a complement*:砸～稀巴烂 smash sth. to smithereens /忙～不停 be as busy as a bee /问～明白 ask for clarification /看～仔细 have a careful look /玩～痛快 play to one's heart's content /把敌人打得～落花流水 put the enemy to rout; send the enemy fleeing helter-skelter /雨下～不停。Rain keeps falling. ❷ individual: *see*"～体";"～人"

个[2](個、箇)

gè ❶ *as suffix to the classifer* 些:那

么些～书要看多久才能看完哪! How long will it take to finish reading so many books! ❷〈方言〉*used after* 昨儿,今儿,明儿,*etc.*:昨儿～你去哪儿了? Where did you go yesterday? /赶明儿～让他请客。Ask him to treat us to dinner tomorrow.
see also gě

个案 gè'àn (individual or special) case:～研究 case study / 这件事暂作～处理。This case should be dealt with individually for the time being.

个把 gèba *also* "个把子" about one; one or two:相处了～月 be together for about a month /增加～人 add a person or two

个别 gèbié ❶ individual; specific; particular:～辅导 individual coaching /～谈话 private talk /提倡～谈心 encourage heart-to-heart talk /一般号召与～指导相结合 combine the general call with particular guidance /对她应该～帮助。She should be given specific help. ❷ very few; one or two; exceptional:～情况 isolated cases; exceptional cases /他迟到是很～的情况。It's rare for him to be late. /～人的意见也应该尊重。Even opinions of a few people should be respected. / 这种观点绝不是～的。This kind of view is not at all exceptional.

个别差异 gèbié chāyì 〈心理〉individual difference

个个 gègè each and every one; all:在场的人～束手无策。No one present had any plan or suggestion to offer. /孩子们一～都是那么可爱。All the children are so lovely.

个儿 gèr ❶ size; height; build; stature:瞧这棉桃的～! Look, what huge bolls these are! /他是个大高～。He is a big guy. /他各方面条件都够,就是～太矮。He is qualified for the job in all aspects but one — he is too short. ❷ persons or things taken singly; each:挨～握手 shake hands with each one /卖鸡蛋论斤不论～。Eggs are sold by the *jin* (*or* catty), not by item. /大家挨～自我介绍。All people took turns to introduce themselves. ❸〈方言〉qualified person or rival; match:跟我打架,你还不是～。You're no match for me in a fistfight.

个人 gèrén ❶ individual (as contrasted with the collective); personal:～会员 individual member /～简历 curriculum vitae (CV); personal resume; biographical note /～野心 one's own wild (*or* insensate) ambition /～专断 arbitrary decisions by the individual /～财产 personal property /～得失 personal gains and losses /～防卫 private defence /～卫生 personal hygiene /～隐私 privacy /～责任 personal liability (*or* responsibility) /～账户 personal account /～作用 role of an individual; part played by an individual /～利益服从集体利益 subordinate one's personal interests to those of the collective /以～的名义 in one's own name ❷(used on formal occasions to refer to oneself) I:～认为 in my view (*or* opinion) /～表示赞同。I am for (*or* in favour of) the idea.

个人电脑 gèrén diànnǎo 〈计算机〉personal computer (PC)

个人迷信 gèrén míxìn *also* "个人崇拜" personality cult; cult of the individual

个人密码 gèrén mìmǎ 〈金融〉personal identification number (PIN)

个人手持电话系统 gèrén shǒuchí diànhuà xìtǒng personal handphone system (PHS)

个人所得税 gèrén suǒdéshuì personal income tax

个人通信系统 gèrén tōngxìn xìtǒng personal communication system (PCS)

个人问题 gèrén wèntí personal problem, mostly referring to one's marriage problem

个人项目 gèrén xiàngmù 〈体育〉individual event

个人英雄主义 gèrén yīngxióngzhǔyì individualistic heroism:好逞～ like to be in the limelight

个人主义 gèrénzhǔyì me-first mentality; egoism; (of philosophy) individualism:～思想 always think of oneself first

个体 gètǐ ❶ individual:～农业经营 individual farming /～生产者 individual producer /～商业 business run by individuals /～经营执照 licence for individually-run enterprise ❷ individual or household engaged in small-scale businesses:干了几年～,他挣了一些钱。He was self-employed (*or* ran his own business) for several years and made some money.

个体繁殖 gètǐ fánzhí individual reproduction

个体分析 gètǐ fēnxī ontoanalysis

个体工商业 gètǐ gōngshāngyè industry and trade run by individuals; private industry and commerce

个体户 gètǐhù individual or household engaged in small-scale business; small-scale privately- or individually-owned business

个体经济 gètǐ jīngjì individual economy:扶植～ help develop individual economy

个体经营 gètǐ jīngyíng individually-owned business

个体劳动者 gètǐ láodòngzhě person who works on his own; self-employed labourer:～协会 association of self-employed labourers

个体商贩 gètǐ shāngfàn small retailer; pedlar

个体所有制 gètǐ suǒyǒuzhì individual ownership

个体心理学 gètǐ xīnlǐxué individual psychology

个条 gètiáo 〈方言〉figure; shape:瘦长的～ tall and slender figure

个头儿 gètóur 〈方言〉size; height:这瓜～大。The melon is huge. /几年不见,他就长成一个大～了。He has grown into a tall man since I saw him several years ago.

个位 gèwèi 〈数学〉unit; digit:～数的加减法 addition and subtraction of digits

个性 gèxìng individual character; personality; individuality:～特征 individual characteristics /～解放 liberation of individual personality; liberation of the self /矛盾的共性和～ general and individual character of contradiction; universality and particularity of contradiction /他～很强。He is a man of strong character (*or* personality).

个展 gèzhǎn one-man exhibition (of calligraphy, painting, sculpture, etc.); individual exhibition:在刚刚举办的～中,他的画作受到广泛好评。In the one-man art exhibition held recently, his works were well received.

个中 gèzhōng 〈书面〉therein:～奥妙 inside story; secret of it /～老手 expert in a given field; old hand; past master /～三昧 secret known only to experts; what is experienced only by the initiated /～原因 the whys and wherefores (of sth.)

个中人 gèzhōngrén person in the know; insider:不是～,谁解个中味! Outsiders could not possibly comprehend its essence.

个子 gèzi ❶ height; stature; build:高～ tall person /小～ small fellow; short person /大～ person of large build; big guy ❷ bundle; bunch; bale:谷～ bundle of millet

各

gè ❶ all; every:～部委 all ministries and commissions / ～机关 all government offices /～民主党派 all the democratic parties /全国～地 all parts of the country /～族人民 people of all nationalities /～兵种 all arms of the services ❷ various; different:～方面代表 representatives of different fields /～条战线都频传捷报。Reports of new successes keep pouring in from various fronts. ❸ each; either:～不相同 differ from each other; have nothing in common with each other /～怀鬼胎 each with his or her own axe to grind / 三篇文章～有优点。Each of the three essays has its own merits. / 城墙两头,～有一座塔楼。There is a tower at either end of the city wall.
see also gě

各半 gèbàn half and half; fifty-fifty:～对分 divide it up fifty-fifty; divide it up on a fifty-fifty basis /我们班男女生～。Half of the students in our class are girls.

各奔前程 gèbèn-qiánchéng each pursues his own course; each goes his own way:欢聚至半夜而散,明日～。The happy gathering lasted till midnight and they went in pursuit of their different careers the following day.

各别 gèbié ❶ distinct; different:～对待 treat differently; treat each on its (*or* his, etc.) own merits ❷〈方言〉out of the ordinary; unusual; novel:这件衣服的样式很～。The style of this dress is quite unusual. ❸〈贬义〉odd; funny; freakish; eccentric:这个人真～! What a freak! *or* What a funny fellow!

各别另样 gèbié-lìngyàng unusual; extraordinary:他那种脾气,也是～! He is quite peculiar in temperament.

各不相让 gèbùxiāngràng neither is willing to yield; each is trying to excel the other

各持己见 gèchí-jǐjiàn *also* "各执己见" each sticks to his own view:他俩～,争论不休。Each of the two held fast to his own view and kept on arguing without end.

各吹各的号,各唱各的调 gè chuī gède hào, gè chàng gède diào each blows his own bugle and sings his own song — each does things in his own way; each goes his own way

各打五十大板 gè dǎ wǔshí dàbǎn blame both sides without discrimination; punish the innocent and the guilty alike:你这样不分青红皂白地～,能解决问题吗? How can you settle the dispute if you blame the wronged and the wrongdoer alike?

各得其所 gèdé-qísuǒ each is in his proper place; each is properly provided for; each has a role to play:我们的方针就是统筹兼顾,～。

Our policy is one of overall planning and all-round consideration so that everyone is provided for.
各个 gègè ❶ each; every; various:～单位 each unit /～厂矿 various factories and mines /～朝代 every dynasty ❷ one by one; separately:～解决 piecemeal solution /集中优势兵力，～歼灭。Concentrate a superior force to destroy (*or* wipe out) the enemy forces one by one.
各个击破 gègè-jīpò crush or tackle one by one; divide and conquer
各个儿 gègěr 〈方言〉oneself:你甭管了，我～去找。Never mind, I'll look for it myself.
各…各… gè…gè… ❶ each... his own...:各顾各的 each taking care of himself / 分好了工，就各干各的去吧。Now that the work has been divided up, let each get on with his own job. /各有各的用处。Each has its own use. ❷ all kinds of; all:各省各市 all provinces and municipalities /各种各样的货物 goods of all kinds
各国议会联盟 Gèguó Yìhuì Liánméng Inter-Parliamentary Union
各行各业 gèháng-gèyè all walks of life; all trades and professions
各级 gèjí all or various levels:～政府 governments at all levels /～人民代表大会 people's congresses at all (*or* different) levels /～党组织 party organizations of all (*or* various) levels
各界 gèjiè all walks of life; all circles:～人士 personalities (*or* personages) of various circles; public figures from various circles /～代表 representatives from all walks of life
各尽所能 gèjìn-suǒnéng from each according to his ability:这位厂长善于调动积极性，让大家～。The director knows how to bring every positive factor into play and let each person do his best.
各尽所能，按劳分配 gè jìn suǒ néng, àn láo fēnpèi from each according to his ability, to each according to his work — the socialist principle of distribution
各尽所能，按需分配 gè jìn suǒ néng, àn xū fēnpèi from each according to his ability, to each according to his needs — the communist principle of distribution
各就各位 gèjiù-gèwèi 〈军事〉man your posts;〈体育〉on your marks; take your marks
各取所需 gèqǔ-suǒxū each takes what he needs:冷餐会食品异常丰富，大家可以～。There was a great variety of food at the buffet, so one could take whatever one liked.
各人 gèrén each one; everyone:～的情况不同，应区别对待。As every case is different, they have to be treated differently.
各人自扫门前雪 gèrén zì sǎo mén qián xuě each sweeps the snow from his own doorstep — mind one's own business:～，莫管他人瓦上霜。Each sweeps the snow before his own door and ignores the frost on his neighbour's roof.
各色 gèsè ❶ of all kinds; of every description; assorted:～人等 people of all descriptions /商店里～货物，一应俱全。The shop is well stocked with goods of all kinds. ❷〈方言〉〈贬义〉eccentric; odd; unusual:这人太～。What an odd person! *or* What a freak!
各式各样 gèshì-gèyàng of various kinds or styles:～的服装 dresses of all styles
各抒己见 gèshū-jǐjiàn each airs his own views; everyone speaks up:会上大家～，气氛异常活跃、热烈。The atmosphere was particularly vivid and warm with everyone expressing their views freely at the meeting.
各司其职 gèsī-qízhí each does his or her duty; each performs his or her own functions
各位 gèwèi ❶ everybody (a term of address):请～注意，会议开始了! Attention please, everybody! The meeting is now called to order. /～请入坐。Be seated please, everybody. ❷ every:～代表 fellow delegates /～女士、～先生 ladies and gentlemen
各显神通 gèxiǎn-shéntōng each shows his or her own prowess; each tries for all he or she is worth
各向同性 gèxiàngtóngxìng 〈物理〉isotropy
各向异性 gèxiàngyìxìng 〈物理〉anisotropy
各行其是 gèxíng-qíshì each does what he or she thinks is right; each goes his or her own way:必须统一行动，不得～。There must be unified action, and no one is allowed to do things in his own way.
各有千秋 gèyǒu-qiānqiū each has sth. to recommend him or her; each has his or her strong points; each has its own merits
各有所长 gèyǒu-suǒcháng each has its strengths or advantages:演员们～，各有所短，应互相学习。Actors and actresses have their weaknesses as well as strengths, so they should learn from each other.
各有所好 gèyǒu-suǒhào each has his or her likes and dislikes; each follows his or her own bent
各有一本难念的经 gè yǒu yīběn nánniànde jīng each has a difficult scripture to chant — each has his or her own troubles or vexations; no one is entirely free from worries or anxieties
各执一词 gèzhí-yīcí each sticks to his own version or argument:双方～，互不相让。Both disputants stick to their own arguments and neither would give way.
各种各样 gèzhǒng-gèyàng all kinds of; all manner of:～的理由 all kinds of excuses /～的观点 diverse views /大家的要求～，一时难以满足。It's hard to satisfy everybody all at once (*or* to suit the varied needs of all people for the time being).
各自 gèzì each; respective; individual:根据他们～的需要 according to their respective needs /既要～努力，也要彼此帮助。There must be both individual efforts and mutual help.
各自为政 gèzì-wéizhèng each administers its affairs regardless of the overall interest; each does things in his or her own way:～的局面必须予以制止。We must put an end to divided authority in administration.

硌

gè (of sth. hard or bulging) press or rub against one:褥子没有铺平，躺在上面～得难受。The rumpled mattress stuck into me most uncomfortably. /菜没洗干净，有点～牙。The vegetables were not washed clean so they hurt my teeth.
see also luò
硌窝儿 gèwōr cracked or broken (egg):～蛋 broken egg; damaged egg

铬

gè *also*"克罗米" kèluómǐ 〈化学〉chromium (Cr):～镍线 chrome-nickel wire
铬肠线 gèchángxiàn 〈医学〉chromic catgut
铬镀层 gèdùcéng 〈冶金〉chromium or chrome plating; chromium coating
铬钢 gègāng chromium steel; chrome steel
铬化 gèhuà 〈冶金〉chromium impregnation; chromizing or chromising:～处理 chromizing
铬黄 gèhuáng chrome yellow
铬矿 gèkuàng 〈矿业〉chromite brick
铬锰钢 gèměnggāng chromador; chromium-manganese steel
铬钼钢 gèmùgāng chrome molybdenum steel
铬镍钢 gèniègāng chrome-nickel steel
铬铅矿 gèqiānkuàng crocoite
铬染料 gèrǎnliào 〈化工〉chromic colour
铬鞣 gèróu 〈皮革〉chrome tanning:～革 chrome leather
铬酸 gèsuān 〈化学〉chromic acid:～铅 lead chromate /～盐 chromate /亚～盐 chromite /～盐钝化处理〈冶金〉chromate treatment; chromatizing
铬碳钢 gètàngāng chrome-carbon steel
铬铁 gètiě ferrochrome
铬铁矿 gètiěkuàng chromite
铬铜合金 gètóng héjīn chrome copper

膈

gè
see also gé
膈应 gèying 〈方言〉be disgusted; loath; detest:看他那溜须拍马的样子，我起心里～他。I am disgusted with the way he fawns on people. *or* His flattering manner disgusts me.

gěi

给

gěi ❶ give; present; grant:～他一个铅笔盒 give him a pencil-box /～每个难民发救助款五百元 grant each refugee 500 *yuan* as relief /～以沉重的打击 deal a telling blow /～了他两小时来考虑这个问题。He was allowed two hours to think over the question. /这本书是～你的。This book is for you. /这次旅游～我留下了很深的印象。This trip left a deep impression on me. ❷ (used after a verb to indicate the handing over of sth.) to; with:交～他一封信 hand a letter to him; hand him a letter /把全部力量贡献～祖国和人民 dedicate

oneself to one's motherland and people /我把东西留～你。I'll leave the things with you. /请把盐递～我。Pass me the salt, please. ❸ for; for the benefit of:她～外宾当翻译。She interpreted for the foreign guests. /她～他家看孩子。She babysat for his family. ❹ *used to introduce the recipient of an action, same as* 同:你应该～他道歉。You should apologize to him. /她～我使了一个眼色。She tipped me a wink. ❺ let; allow (a) *used to ask the other party to do sth.*:留出一点时间～职工锻炼身体 give the employees some time for physical exercises /家里寄钱～他买书。His family sent him money for buying books. (b) *used to indicate permission*:这种电影不能～小孩儿看。Children are not allowed to watch such films. (c) *used to show what has happened*:衣服～雨淋湿了。Clothes got wet in the rain. /饭菜都～他吃光了。He's eaten up the food. ❻〈助词〉*used directly before the verb of a passive sentence, etc. to show emphasis*:你快把房间～收拾一下。Please tidy up the room quickly. /茶杯叫他～摔碎了。The cup was broken by him. /托你的事你可～记着点! Please remember what I asked you to do. /坏的水龙头怎么没人来～修一修。How come no one comes to repair the tap that is out of order?
see also jǐ

给出路 gěi chūlù give sb. a way out

给定值 gěidìngzhí given value

给脸 gěiliǎn save sb.'s face; try not to embarrass; do sb. a favour:不知好歹,～不要脸。He doesn't know what is good for him and is fool enough to reject a face-saving offer.

给面子 gěi miànzi *also* "给脸" save sb.'s face; do sb. a favour:都是老朋友了,你不能不～吧? Since we are old friends, you will do me the favour, won't you?

给小鞋穿 gěi xiǎoxié chuān give sb. tight shoes to wear — make things difficult for sb. by abusing one's power; make sb. feel the pinch:你敢提意见,老板就给你小鞋儿穿。If you dare to make a complaint the boss will give you a hard time.

给颜色看 gěi yánsè kàn make it hot for sb.:你如果不安分,他就要～。If you go on making trouble, he'll show (*or* tell) you a thing or two.

给以 gěiyǐ (often used with abstract things) give; allow; grant:～法律制裁 mete out punishment according to law /～充分的重视 pay full attention /～适当照顾 show due consideration /给造谣者以沉重打击 deal rumour-mongers a heavy blow /不给敌人以喘息的机会 give the enemy no breathing space

gēn

根 gēn ❶ root (of a plant):树～ root of a tree /块～ root-tuber /须～ fibrous root /支撑～ buttress root /直～ tap root /侧～ lateral root /主～ main root; taproot /生～ take root /连～拔 pull up by the roots; uproot; root up (*or* out) /盘～错节 with twisted roots and gnarled branches; deep-rooted /本是同～生,相煎何太急。We sprang from the self-same root, why should you try to kill me with hot anger? ❷ offspring; progeny:单～独苗 sole male offspring /他是他家的独～儿。He is the only son of his family. ❸ root; foot; base:舌～ root of the tongue; base of the tongue /齿～ root of a tooth /耳～ base of ears /城墙～儿 foot of a city wall /云出山～。A cloud arose from the foot of a hill. ❹ cause; origin; source; root:病～ cause of illness /祸～ root-cause of trouble or disaster /除～ dig up the roots; do away with the root cause; cure once and for all /刨～问底 get to the bottom of sth. /彼此知～知底 know each other through and through /到大陆来寻～ come to the Chinese mainland to trace one's (family) roots /止水不波,浮云无～。Stagnant water has no waves and a floating cloud has no roots. ❺ thoroughly; completely; entirely: *see* "～治";"～除" ❻ foundation; basis:无～之谈 groundless talk; sheer nonsense ❼〈量词〉long thin piece:几～粉笔 several pieces of chalk /几～头发 several strands of hair /一～木柴 a piece of firewood ❽〈数学〉(short for 方根) root:立方～ cube root /平方～ square root /方程式的～ roots of an equation /虚～ imaginary root ❾〈数学〉solution of an algebraic equation ❿〈化学〉radical:酸～ acid radical /复～ compound radical

根癌病 gēn'áibìng crown gall

根本 gēnběn ❶ source; base; foundation; root:从～上解决问题 tackle the problem at the root; solve the problem once and for all /从～上来说 fundamentally speaking; in the final analysis /水、土是农业的～。Water and soil are the foundation of agriculture. ❷ basic; fundamental; essential; cardinal:～问题 fundamental question (*or* issue); basic problem /～原因 basic reason; root cause /～原则 cardinal principle /～变化 fundamental change; radical transformation /～分歧 essential (*or* fundamental) difference /政策的～立足点 corner-stone of a policy /～出发点 basic point of departure /第三世界国家之间没有～的利害冲突。There is no conflict of fundamental interests among third world countries. ❸ (often used in the negative) at all; ever; simply:我～没有说过这种话。I have never made such remarks. /～就没有这种问题。The problem simply doesn't exist. /他～不认识我。He didn't know me at all. ❹ (often used in the negative) completely; radically:～对立的两种学说 doctrines diametrically opposite to each other /这～行不通。This is wholly impracticable. ❺ thoroughly:必须～改变这一地区的落后面貌。We must thoroughly overcome the backwardness of this region. /这些陈规陋习必须～废除。These outmoded regulations and irrational practices must be done away with root and branch.

根本法 gēnběnfǎ ❶ constitution; fundamental or basic law ❷ (in some countries) basic or fundamental laws in specific fields

根鞭虫 gēnbiānchóng rhizomastigote

根插 gēnchā root planting; root cutting:采用～法 use the method of root cutting

根除 gēnchú eradicate; uproot; root out; eliminate thoroughly:～贩毒吸毒 eliminate drug taking and trafficking /～一切形式的殖民主义 root out all forms of colonialism /～弊端 stamp out (*or* eradicate) malpractice

根代 gēndài〈方言〉descendant; posterity; offspring

根底 gēndǐ ❶ foundation; groundwork:数学～好 well-grounded in mathematics /他的英文～很好。He has a solid foundation in English. /他的～比较差。He is rather weak in basic training. ❷ what lies at the bottom or back of sth.; origin; root; cause:追问～ inquire into the cause of the matter /你知道事情的～吗? Do you have any idea what lies at the bottom of the matter? /这个人的～我不太清楚。I'm not quite clear about the background of this person.

根蒂 gēndì ❶ root and base of plants ❷ cause; origin; root:不知事物～,如何正确分析判断? Without knowing the taproot of the matter, how could one make sound analysis and judgment?

根雕 gēndiāo tree-root sculpture; tree-root carvings:他从事～只有三年。He has been engaged in tree-root carving for only three years.

根腐病 gēnfǔbìng〈农业〉root rot

根荄 gēngāi〈书面〉roots of trees and grass — foundation of things

根痼 gēngù〈书面〉chronic disease; lasting illness:～渐剧 one's chronic disease getting worse

根冠 gēnguān〈植物〉root cap

根函数 gēnhánshù〈数学〉radical function

根号 gēnhào〈数学〉radical sign

根基 gēnjī ❶ foundation; groundwork; basis:打好～ build up (*or* lay) a solid foundation /～稳固 firm foundation (*or* groundwork) /～不牢 shaky foundation ❷ family property; resources:底子薄、～差 poor in foundation and scanty (*or* meagre) in resources

根脚 gēnjiao ❶ foundation of a building:这房子的～很牢固。The foundation of this house is very solid. *or* The house has a solid foundation. ❷ (often used in the early vernacular) family background; origin; past history:这个人～不正。This man has a dubious history.

根接 gēnjiē〈植物〉graft on root

根茎 gēnjīng *also* "根状茎"〈植物〉rhizome or rhizoma:～插 rhizome cutting /～洗涤机 rhizome tuber washer

根究 gēnjiū make a thorough investigation of; get to the bottom of; probe into; scrutinize:～缘由 probe into the cause; inquire into the origin (of a thing) /～事故发生的原因 get to the bottom of the accident /事实真相,必须～。A thorough investigation of the matter must be made.

根据 gēnjù ❶ on the basis of; in conformity with; according to; in the light of; in line with:～人民的利益和愿望 in accordance (*or* conformity) with the interests and desires of the people /～具体情况 in the light of specific conditions; on the merit of each case /～同样理由 for the same reason; by the same token /～"一个中国"的原则 on the principle of "one China" /～同名小说拍摄的电影 film based on a novel of the same title ❷ basis; grounds; foundation:毫无～ utterly groundless /有充分的理论～ have a thorough theoretical base (*or* foundation) /没有科学～ without any scientific basis /说话要以事实作

～。Any statement should be based on facts. /没有充分的～，不要下结论。Don't draw conclusions without sufficient grounds.

根据地 gēnjùdì base area; base:红色～ red base /～军民 soldiers and civilians of a base area; army and people of a base area

根绝 gēnjué stamp out; uproot; eradicate; eliminate:～剥削童工 eliminate the exploitation of child labour /～腐败 stamp out corruption

根瘤 gēnliú 〈植物〉root nodule

根瘤菌 gēnliújūn nodule bacteria:～肥料 nodule bacteria fertilizer

根毛 gēnmáo 〈植物〉root hair

根苗 gēnmiáo ❶ root and shoot:～肥壮 stout and strong root and shoot /长出了～ put out shoots ❷ source; root:铲除罪恶的～ eliminate the root of evil ❸〈旧语〉(male) offspring; posterity; progeny:他是孙家惟一的～。He is the only offspring of the Suns.

根攀植物 gēnpān zhíwù 〈植物〉root climber

根盘节错 gēnpán-jiécuò *also* "盘根错节" with twisted roots and gnarled branches; complicated and difficult to deal with; deep-rooted

根深蒂固 gēnshēn-dìgù *also* "根深柢固" deep-rooted; ingrained; inveterate; firmly established:～的偏见 deep-seated prejudice; ingrained bias /结束了～的封建统治 put an end to the deeply entrenched feudal rule

根深叶茂 gēnshēn-yèmào have deep roots and thick foliage — be well established and flourishing

根生土长 gēnshēng-tǔzhǎng *also* "土生土长" tǔshēng-tǔzhǎng indigenous; native born:～的中国人 Chinese born and bred in the country

根式 gēnshì 〈数学〉radical (expression)

根外施肥 gēnwài shīféi *also* "叶面施肥" yèmiàn shīféi foliage dressing; foliage spray

根蔓 gēnwàn root and stem — cause; origin

根问 gēnwèn cross-examine; interrogate; make detailed inquiries

根系 gēnxì 〈植物〉root system; descending axis

根性 gēnxìng basic character; inherent nature:劣～ inveterate bad habits; inherent weakness /～难改。It is difficult to alter one's character. *or* The leopard cannot change its spots.

根须 gēnxū root hair; fibrous root

根芽 gēnyá root bud; radicle:移植～ transplant root buds /培育～ breed root buds

根用作物 gēnyòng zuòwù 〈农业〉root crop

根由 gēnyóu cause; origin:追查～ find out the whys and wherefores /这事的～非同寻常。The cause of the matter is quite out of the ordinary.

根原 gēnyuán source; origin; root; cause:祸有～。Every disaster has a cause.

根源 gēnyuán ❶ source; origin; cause; root:找出犯错误的～ find out why the error was made /战争是大灾荒、大瘟疫的～。War is the root cause of famine and plague. ❷ originate; stem from; come from:这些现象～于传统文化。These phenomena stem from traditional culture.

根值 gēnzhí 〈数学〉root

根值数 gēnzhíshù 〈数学〉radix

根植 gēnzhí (often used figuratively) take root; strike root:只有～于人民群众中的艺术，才会有生命力。Only when art is rooted among the masses will it have vitality.

根指数 gēnzhǐshù 〈数学〉radical exponent; index of the root

根治 gēnzhì effect a radical cure; cure once and for all; bring under permanent control:～肺结核 effect a radical cure of tuberculosis; eradicate TB /～手术 radical operation (*or* surgery) /～淮河 permanently harness the Huaihe River /～虫害 bring insect pests under permanent control

根轴 gēnzhóu 〈数学〉radical axis

根轴系 gēnzhóuxì 〈植物〉root system

根追 gēnzhuī get to the root of sth:～到底 make a thorough investigation

根子 gēnzi 〈口语〉❶ root (of a plant):这棵树的～扎得很深。The tree is deep-rooted. *or* The tree has struck deep roots in the soil. ❷ antecedent; source; origin; root:要找出犯错误的思想～。The ideological roots of the mistake must be found out.

跟

gēn ❶ heel:左脚～ heel of the left foot; left heel /鞋后～ heel of a shoe /平～鞋 flat-heeled shoes /高～鞋 high-heeled shoes; (high) heels ❷ follow:紧～ follow on (*or* at) one's heels /步步紧～ follow closely step by step /紧～形势 keep abreast of the current situation /请～我走。Please follow me. /快～上，别掉队! Hurry up! Don't lag behind! ❸ (of a woman) marry sb.:因为穷，她只好～了他。She was poor and had to marry him. ❹ (used as a preposition to introduce the recipient of an action) with; and; to; from:～工人农民交朋友 make friends with workers and peasants /～坏人坏事作斗争 fight against evildoers and evildoings /～他学手艺 learn craftsmanship from him /重要的事情要～群众商量。Consult the masses on important matters. /要～群众打成一片。We must identify ourselves with the masses. /快～大伙说说。Tell us all about it. ❺ (used as a preposition to show comparison) as; from:他～你一样高。He is as tall as you. /她～姐姐长得几乎一个样。She looks the same as her sister. *or* She and her sister are as like as two peas. /你的话怎么～他说的不一样? How come your words are different from his? /大家待她就～亲姐妹一样。People treat her as their own sister. ❻ (used as a conjunction to join two or more items) and; with:种子～农药都准备好了。The seeds and the pesticide are both ready. /一楼～三楼的电灯都坏了。Lamps on the first and third floors are all out of order.

跟班 gēnbān ❶ join a regular shift or class; work (together) with a group, team or class:～劳动 (as of a manager) go to work in a workshop for a specified period of time /～听课 audit a class ❷ *also* "跟班的"〈旧语〉footman; attendant:此次出巡，他只带了两个贴身～。He only brought along two personal attendants on the inspection tour.

跟包 gēnbāo 〈旧语〉❶ look after the costumes, etc. for an actor or entertainer ❷ attendant of an actor or entertainer

跟不上 gēnbushàng ❶ fail to keep pace with; be unable to catch up with:～形势的需要 fall short of the demands of the times ❷ be inferior; be not as good as:他的身体还～我呢。His health is not so good as mine.

跟差 gēnchāi 〈旧语〉attendant (especially of an official); footman; flunkey

跟从 gēncóng ❶ follow; obey; comply with ❷〈旧语〉(of a girl) get married ❸〈旧语〉attendants; suite; retinue

跟单信用证 gēndān xìnyòngzhèng documentary credit

跟得上 gēndeshàng ❶ keep pace with; be able to catch up with:～时代 keep pace with the times ❷ be as good as; can be compared with:他的身高都～他哥哥了。He is as tall as his elder brother.

跟丁 gēndīng 〈旧语〉*see* "跟差"

跟斗 gēndou *also* "跟头"〈方言〉❶ fall; somersault:翻～ turn a somersault /他摔了一个～。He had a fall. ❷ setback; frustration; failure:咱们栽～了。We have come a cropper.

跟骨 gēngǔ 〈生理〉calcaneus; calcaneum:～炎 calcaneitis

跟腱 gēnjiàn 〈生理〉Achilles tendon:～反射 Achilles jerk; Achilles tendon reflex /～痛 achillodynia

跟脚 gēnjiǎo 〈方言〉❶〈旧语〉wait upon the master when out on a journey ❷ (of children) follow elders and be unwilling to leave ❸ (of shoes) fit well:这双鞋大小正好，很～。This pair of shoes is exactly my size and fits well. ❹ close upon sb.'s heels:你刚出去，他～儿就来找你了。He came to see you the moment you left.

跟进 gēnjìn follow up; follow suit:前沿已经突破，后续部队源源～。The forward position had been broken through and the follow-up units came pouring in. /老板敬酒，别人也就～。The boss proposed a toast and the others readily followed.

跟劲 gēnjìn 〈口语〉competent; fit for use:这件事他办得挺～。He handled the matter well. /当翻译，他的英语跟不上劲儿。He is not a good translator because of his poor English.

跟屁虫 gēnpìchóng 〈方言〉〈贬义〉persistent follower; shadow; pest

跟前 gēnqián ❶ in front of; close to; near:他把我叫到～。He told me to come closer. /请你到我～来。Please come over here. /桌子～靠着一根钓鱼竿。A fishing rod leans against the table. /小家伙挤到了首长的～。The kid pressed forward to be near the commanding officer. ❷ just before:新年～ shortly before New Year's Day

跟前 gēnqian (of one's children) living with one:孩子们都不在她～。None of the children live with her.

跟人 gēnrén ❶〈口语〉(of women) get married ❷〈方言〉serve as a servant ❸〈旧语〉attendant; servant

跟上 gēnshang keep pace with; catch up with; keep abreast of:～时代的步伐 keep pace with the times /～迅速发展的形势 keep abreast of the fast developing situation /快～! Close up!

跟梢 gēnshāo tail; shadow; follow:有人～ be shadowed

跟摄 gēnshè 〈影视〉❶ follow shot ❷ make a follow shot

跟手 gēnshǒu 〈方言〉❶ conveniently; without additional trouble:离开房间时别忘～关灯。Don't forget to turn off the light when you leave the room. ❷ immediately; at once:她接到护士的电话,～就去医院了。She went to the hospital as soon as she received the call from the nurse.

跟随 gēnsuí ❶ follow; come after; go after:～着革命前辈的足迹前进 follow in the footsteps of the revolutionary forerunners/她从小就～着母亲做针线活儿。She learnt to do the needlework from her mother since childhood. ❷ retinue; entourage:由大批～陪同 accompanied by a large entourage

跟趟儿 gēntàngr 〈方言〉❶ keep pace with; catch up with:他的认识有点儿跟不上趟儿。His understanding is a little behind the times. ❷ in time for:吃完饭再去看电影还～。You still have time for a meal before going to the movie.

跟头 gēntou *also*"斤斗" jīndǒu fall; somersault:小孩摔了一个～,腿受了伤。The child fell and injured his leg./杂技演员一口气翻了五个～。The acrobat did five somersaults at a stretch.

跟头虫 gēntouchóng wiggler; wriggler

跟尾儿 gēnyǐr 〈方言〉right away; at once; close upon sb.'s heels:你先去吧,我～就来。You go first and I'll be there in a moment.

跟着 gēnzhe ❶ follow:～感觉走 follow one's own inclination; follow one's hunch/他在前边走,我在后边～。He walked ahead and I followed./情况变化了,计划也要～改变。When the situation changes, the plan must be changed accordingly. ❷ following; right after:我一到家～就开始做饭。I start cooking as soon as I come back home./暴雨刚过,～就出太阳了。Hardly had the storm stopped when the sun reappeared.

跟追 gēnzhuī track and pursue:～匪徒 be in hot pursuit of the bandits

跟踪 gēnzōng ❶ follow the tracks of; tail:～猎物 track game/～追击 pursue and attack; go in hot pursuit/被特务～了很久 be shadowed (*or* tailed) by a special agent for a long time/一直～罪犯到他藏匿的地方 trail a criminal to his hiding place ❷〈自控〉follow-up; following; tracking:手控～ manual following/自动～ automatic tracking/～调节 follow-up control/光～ optical tracking/电子～ electronic tracking

跟踪搜索 gēnzōng sōusuǒ 〈电子〉track-while-scan

跟踪信号 gēnzōng xìnhào tracking signal

跟踪站 gēnzōngzhàn tracking station

跟踪装置 gēnzōng zhuāngzhì follow-up device; tracking apparatus; tracker

gén

哏 gén 〈方言〉❶ amusing; comical; farcical; funny:他说话的样子真～。The way he speaks is really amusing. ❷ clownish speech or behaviour; clowning; antics:逗～(of the main role in a cross talk) make the audience laugh by saying sth. funny or by playing the fool/捧～(of the supporting role in a cross talk) help the leading role make the audience laugh with words or gestures

gěn

艮[1] gěn 〈方言〉(of character or speech) brusque; blunt; stiff; sharp:这孩子真～。The child is really blunt./说话别太～。Don't put it too sharply.

艮[2] gěn 〈方言〉(of food) tough; hard:发～ turn tough/～萝卜不好吃。Leathery turnips taste bad.
see also gèn

gèn

亘(亙) gèn extend; stretch; span:绵～数百里 (of a mountain range) extend for hundreds of *li*/横～ lie across; span/连～ be continuous/盘～ (of mountains, etc.) stretch in an unbroken chain

亘古 gèngǔ from ancient times; in the remote past:～以来 from time immemorial

亘古及今 gèngǔ-jíjīn *also*"亘古通今" from time immemorial down to the present day

亘古未有 gèngǔ-wèiyǒu never since ancient times; unprecedented; unheard-of:～的奇迹 unprecedented (*or* unheard-of) wonder/这种盛事～。Such a great event has no parallel in history.

艮 gèn ❶ one of the forms of the Eight Trigrams for divination ❷ (Gèn) a surname
see also gěn

茛 gèn *see*"毛茛" máogèn

gēng

庚 gēng ❶ seventh of the ten Heavenly Stems:夏至三～ third day bearing the seventh of the ten Heavenly Stems (in combination with one of the Earthly Branches) after the Summer Solstice, marking the beginning of the first *fu* (伏), or "dog days" *see also*"干支" gānzhī ❷ age:贵～〈敬词〉your age/年～ date of birth/他二人同～。The two of them are of the same age. *or* They two were born in the same year. ❸(Gēng) a surname

庚齿 gēngchǐ 〈书面〉age:交友不必问～,忘年亦可成知音。You don't have to ask how old a person is when you make friends with him, as persons of great disparity in age can also become bosom friends.

庚醇 gēngchún 〈化学〉heptanol

庚醛 gēngquán 〈化学〉heptaldehyde; heptanal

庚日 gēngrì any day designated by the combination of the seventh of the ten Heavenly Stems with one of the Earthly Branches

庚酸 gēngsuān 〈化学〉heptylate

庚帖 gēngtiě 〈旧语〉document with one's horoscope (usu. that of a boy or girl sent as a proposal for betrothal):两家给孩子互换了～。The two families exchanged the documents of their children's horoscopes for the proposed betrothal.
see also"八字帖儿" bāzìtiěr

庚烯 gēngxī 〈化学〉heptene; heptylene

庚信 gēngxìn 〈书面〉menses; menstruation; period

庚子赔款 Gēngzǐ Péikuǎn Indemnity for the 1900 War, known in the West as Boxer Indemnity (a huge sum of money extorted from China by eight imperialist powers after its defeat in the 1900 War or Boxer War, the year of *gengzi* in traditional Chinese chronology)

赓 gēng ❶〈书面〉continue; go on ❷ (Gēng) a surname

赓酬 gēngchóu 〈书面〉exchange poems among friends (usually on the same subject)

赓续 gēngxù 〈书面〉continue:～旧好 continue (*or* resume) an old friendship

赓韵 gēngyùn 〈书面〉write poems using the same rhyme as that of the poems sent to you

鹒 gēng *see*"鸧鹒" cānggēng

羹 gēng thick soup; jelly-like food (such as custard):鸡蛋～ egg custard/莲子～ custard of lotus seeds/羊～ a kind of cake made from red bean flour, sugar, agar, etc./分我一杯～ give me a share of the spoils or profits/飨以闭门～ slam the door in one's face; keep (*or* shut) sb. out

羹匙 gēngchí soup spoon; tablespoon:用～给病人喂饭 feed the sick with a spoon

羹汤 gēngtāng thick soup; broth

耕 gēng ❶ plough; till; cultivate:春～ spring ploughing/中～ intertill/备～ make preparations for ploughing and sowing/免～ no till; no tillage/粗～ extensive cultivation/代～ do farming for sb. else/机～ tractor-ploughing/深～细作 deep ploughing and intensive cultivation ❷ work (for a living); do:笔～ make a living by writing; take up writing/舌～ make a living by teaching

G

耕畜 gēngchù farm animal; draught animal: ～肥壮 stout and strong farm animals /饲养～ raise draught animals
耕地 gēngdì ❶ plough; till: 帮烈军属～ do farm work for a soldier's family or a revolutionary martyr's family ❷ cultivated land: 可～ arable land /未～ uncultivated land /休～ fallow land /～面积 area under cultivation; cultivated area
耕读 gēngdú part-time study, part-time farming: ～小学 part-time primary school in the countryside /～教师 part-time teacher in the countryside
耕翻 gēngfān plough; till; turn the soil over: 播种之前,把土地～一遍。Plough the land once before sowing.
耕夫 gēngfū 〈书面〉 farmer
耕稼 gēngjià 〈书面〉 farming; agriculture
耕具 gēngjù tillage implement; farm-tool: ～齐备 complete set of tillage implements /缺少足够的～ be short of farm-tools
耕牛 gēngniú farm cattle; ox used in farming: ～曾经是农民的命根子。Oxen used to be the lifeline of peasants.
耕绳 gēngshéng rope for harnessing farm animals to farm-tools
耕田 gēngtián plough; till
耕云播雨 gēngyún-bōyǔ command the clouds and rain — reform nature: 为文艺园地百花盛开而～ work hard to create favourable conditions for the flourishing of art and literature
耕耘 gēngyún plough and weed; cultivate: 到了～的季节 be in the ploughing and weeding season /勤于～ work hard at cultivation /一分～,一分收获。The more ploughing and weeding, the better the crop. *or* No pains, no gains.
耕耘机 gēngyúnjī power tiller
耕凿 gēngzáo till land and drill wells
耕者有其田 gēngzhě yǒu qí tián (slogan for land reform raised by Dr. Sun Yat-sen) land to the tiller
耕织 gēngzhī farming and weaving: 男耕女织 men tilling the land and women weaving — idyllic division of labour and life pattern in ancient times
耕植 gēngzhí 〈书面〉 till; cultivate; farm
耕种 gēngzhòng till; cultivate; raise crops: ～农作物 cultivate crops /布置水稻的～工作 make arrangements for the cultivation of rice
耕作 gēngzuò tillage; cultivation; farming: ～方法 methods of cultivation; farming method
耕作机械 gēngzuò jīxiè tillage machinery; farming equipment
耕作技术 gēngzuò jìshù farming technique
耕作园田化 gēngzuò yuántiánhuà garden-style cultivation of farmland; gardenization of farming
耕作制度 gēngzuò zhìdù cropping system

畊

gēng 〈书面〉 *see* "耕" gēng

更[1]

gēng ❶ change; alter; replace: 变～ change; alter; modify /除旧～新 replace the old with the new /～杯易箸 bring clean cups and chopsticks; renew the feast /改弦～张 change over to new ways; make a fresh start ❷ 〈书面〉 experience: *see* "～事"

更[2]

gēng 〈旧语〉 one of the five two-hour periods into which the night was divided; watch: 打～ beat the watches /巡～ keep (night) watch /定～ beat the first watch at 8 p.m. /三～半夜 in the dead of night /五～鸡 chicken simmered for a whole night /起五～,睡半夜 get up before dawn and go to bed late at night
see also gèng
更梆 gēngbāng 〈旧语〉 night watchman's clapper
更变 gēngbiàn change; alter: ～计划 change the plan
更筹 gēngchóu *also* "更签" 〈旧语〉 bamboo slips used by night watchmen for counting the watches of the night
更次 gēngcì 〈旧语〉 period of a night watch, about two hours: 约有一个～ about two hours
更代 gēngdài 〈书面〉 replace; substitute; take turns: 以他人～他的经理职务 find another person to replace him as manager
更递 gēngdì *see* "更迭"
更迭 gēngdié change; alternate: 政府～ reshuffle of government /董事会～频繁 frequent change of the board of directors /丰年和歉年～。Good years alternate with bad (*or* lean).
更订 gēngdìng amend; revise: 本书重印时进行了～。The book was revised when reprinted.
更定 gēngdìng reformulate; revise: ～规章制度 revise rules and regulations
更动 gēngdòng change; modify; alter: 人事～ personnel changes /～计划 modify the plan /时间表～一下 make some alterations in the timetable
更番 gēngfān alternately; by turns; take turns: ～值勤 be on duty by turns /～主持会议 take turns in chairing the meeting; preside over the meeting alternately
更夫 gēngfū 〈旧语〉 night watchman
更赋 gēngfù 〈旧语〉 tax paid to the government in lieu of frontier service
更改 gēnggǎi change; alter: ～时间 alter the time /～路线 change a course; change a route /无法～的事实 unalterable facts /这个决定不能～。This decision must stand as it is.
更鼓 gēnggǔ 〈旧语〉 night watchman's drum
更倌 gēngguān 〈方言〉〈旧语〉 night watchman
更互 gēnghù 〈书面〉 take turns; do in turn: ～服役 be on active service by turns
更换 gēnghuàn change; alter; replace; renew: ～姓名 change one's name; change of name /～零件 renewal (*or* replacement) part /他讲授的内容从来都不～。The content of his lectures remained the same all the time.
更居 gēngjū 〈书面〉 change one's dwelling place; move house
更阑 gēnglán 〈书面〉 in the dead of night; in the still of the night
更阑人静 gēnglán-rénjìng *see* "更深人静"
更楼 gēnglóu 〈旧语〉 night watch tower: 古老的～ age-old night watch tower
更漏 gēnglòu 〈旧语〉 hourglass; sandglass
更名 gēngmíng change one's name: ～改姓 change one's given name and alter the surname; change one's name
更年期 gēngniánqī 〈生理〉 climacteric; climacterium; menopause; change of life: 早发～ 〈医学〉 climacterium praecox /～关节炎 menopausal arthritis; climactic arthritis /～精神病 involutional psychosis /～忧郁症 involutional melancholia; involutional depression
更仆难数 gēngpú-nánshǔ too many to count; innumerable; countless: 他的罪行～。He has committed innumerable crimes. /街上过往的车辆～。There was an endless stream of traffic on the street.
更嬗 gēngshàn 〈书面〉 replace
更深 gēngshēn deep in the night: 夜到～,万籁俱寂,四周安静极了。Late into the night, silence reigned supreme, far and near.
更深人静 gēngshēn-rénjìng deep is the night and not a soul is stirring; all is quiet in the dead of night; silence reigns in the still of the night: ～,秋雨潇潇。The night is deep and silent; the autumn rain drizzles and sighs. /～,只有寒星还在闪烁。In the dead of night only stars twinkled in the cold sky.
更生 gēngshēng ❶ regenerate; revitalize; revive: 自力～ regeneration through one's own efforts; self-reliance ❷ renew; reclaim; recycle: ～布 regenerated cloth /～产品 reclaimed products /可～和不可～资源 renewable and nonrenewable resources
更生稻 gēngshēngdào ratooning rice
更生霉素 gēngshēng méisù 〈药学〉 actinomycin D
更始 gēngshǐ 〈书面〉 discard the old and begin the new; start all over again: 与民～ (pledge to) make a new beginning together with the people
更事 gēngshì 〈书面〉 ❶ experienced in the affairs of the world: 少不～ young and green (*or* inexperienced) /～不多 with little experience in practical affairs ❷ ordinary thing; common occurrence
更替 gēngtì interchange; alternate; replace: 相互～ alternate (*or* replace) each other /季节～ change of season; alternation of seasons; replacement of one season by another /领导人的～ replacement (*or* supersession) of leaders
更头 gēngtóu 〈方言〉 time of one night watch; about two hours: 睡了一个～ sleep for about two hours
更柝 gēngtuò 〈书面〉 watchman's clapper
更香 gēngxiāng 〈旧语〉 joss stick used by night watchmen to mark time, which lasted for about two hours when burnt
更新 gēngxīn ❶ renew; update; replace: 设备～ renewal (*or* updating) of equipment /～产品 renew products /～器 〈自控〉 updater /～数据 transaction tape/岁序～ beginning of a new year /万象～。Everything takes on a new look. *or* Everything looks new and

fresh. ❷ regenerate; renew; restore; renovate:品种～〈林业〉renovation of variety /树的～ renewal of trees /～修剪 rejuvenating pruning; renewal pruning

更新伐 gēngxīnfá 〈林业〉regeneration felling or cutting

更新换代 gēngxīn-huàndài replace the old by the new; upgrade: 采用先进技术,促进产品的～ use advanced technique to update older products

更新世 Gēngxīnshì 〈地质〉Pleistocene Epoch

更新造林 gēngxīn zàolín reforestation

更姓 gēngxìng 〈书面〉❶ change one's surname ❷ change of dynasty or regime; dynastic change

更衣 gēngyī ❶ change one's clothes: 上楼～ go upstairs to have a change ❷〈婉词〉go to the lavatory

更衣室 gēngyīshì locker room; changeroom: 女～ lady's changeroom

更易 gēngyì change; alter; revise: ～习俗 change customs /这篇草稿～过两三次。This draft has been revised several times.

更张 gēngzhāng tune a stringed instrument — change; reform: 改弦～ change policy (*or* plan, practice, etc.); make a fresh start

更正 gēngzhèng emend; make corrections (of errors in published statements or articles): ～凭单 correction voucher / 作必要的～ make necessary corrections /文内谬误之处,务请予以～。It is my earnest hope that you would rectify any error in the article.

更卒 gēngzú 〈旧语〉night watchman

絙(縆、絚) gēng 〈方言〉hawser; cable

絙索 gēngsuǒ 〈方言〉thick rope

gěng

耿 gěng ❶〈书面〉bright; brilliant: ～光 bright light ❷ honest and just; upright: *see* "～直" ❸ (Gěng) a surname

耿饼 gěngbǐng dried and pressed persimmons

耿耿 gěnggěng ❶ bright; brilliant: ～星河 bright Galaxy (*or* Milky Way) ❷ devoted; staunch; dedicated: 忠心～地为人民服务 be dedicated heart and soul to serving the people /～此心,惟有天知。Only God knows my devotion. ❸ have on one's mind; be troubled: ～不寐 lose sleep over sth. /～在心 have sth. on one's mind

耿耿于怀 gěnggěngyúhuái nurse a grievance; bear a grudge; smoulder with resentment: 二十年来,他对此事一直～。Twenty years has passed, but he still has it on his mind. *or* He has nursed a grudge over the matter for two decades.

耿介 gěngjiè 〈书面〉honest and straightfoward; upright: ～拔俗 above the vulgar many /生性～ upright by nature

耿直 gěngzhí *also* "梗直" gěngzhí; "鲠直" gěngzhí honest and frank; candid and outspoken; upright: 为人～ person of moral integrity /性情～ be of honest disposition; be candid and outspoken

埂 gěng ❶ low bank: 田～ low bank of earth between fields; ridge /土～ footpath in the fields; earth dike ❷ long, narrow mound: 前面不远处,是一道光秃秃的小山～。Not far away is a barren mound. ❸ earth dike or embankment: 堤～ earth dike (*or* embankment) /～堰 earth embankment

埂子 gěngzi footpath or ridge in the fields: 地～ low bank of earth between fields; ridge

梗 gěng ❶ stalk; stem: 菠菜～ spinach stalk /花～ stem of a flower; pedicel /茶叶～ tea stalks /玉米～ cornstalk /枝～ stem and branches ❷ straighten; stiffen; hold stiff: ～着脖子一句话也不说 stiffen one's neck without saying a word ❸ straightforward; frank: *see* "～直" ❹〈书面〉obstinate; stubborn: 强～ firm and stubborn /顽～ obstinate ❺ hinder; obstruct; block: 阻～ block; obstruct /从中作～ place obstacles in the way; put a spoke in sb.'s wheel by design

梗概 gěnggài broad outline; main idea; gist; summary: 故事的～ outline of a story; synopsis /只知此事的～ only have a rough idea of this matter /这篇小说的～ gist of the novel

梗塞 gěngsè ❶ block; obstruct; choke; clog: 交通～ traffic jam / 河道～ clog of a river course ❷ *see* "梗死"

梗死 gěngsǐ 〈医学〉*also* "梗塞" infarct: ～形成 infarction /心肌～ myocardial infarction

梗咽 gěngyè *see* "哽咽" gěngyè

梗直 gěngzhí *see* "耿直" gěngzhí

梗滞 gěngzhì be at a standstill; block; hold up

梗子 gěngzi branch or stem of a plant

梗阻 gěngzǔ ❶ block; separate: 山川～ be separated by mountains and rivers; be far away and out of touch ❷ obstruct; hamper; hinder: 横加～ unreasonably obstruct /肆意～ wantonly hamper (*or* hinder) ❸〈医学〉obstruction: 肠～ intestinal obstruction /不完全～ partial obstruction /幽门～ pyloric obstruction

梗阻性肺气肿 gěngzǔxìng fèiqìzhǒng obstructive emphysema

梗阻性痛经 gěngzǔxìng tòngjīng obstructive or mechanical dysmenorrhoea

哽 gěng ❶ choke: 吃饭～着了 be choked by food (*or* choke over food) ❷ choke with emotion; feel a lump in one's throat: 他直觉得喉头发～,一句话也说不出来。He felt a lump in his throat, unable to utter a single word.

哽塞 gěngsè (voice) choke; stop up: 她才说了两个字,话便～在嗓子眼儿里了。She was choked up after saying only a few words.

哽噎 gěngyē ❶ food blocking up the esophagus ❷ *see* "哽咽"

哽咽 gěngyè *also* "梗咽" gěngyè choke with sobs: 她～难言。She was choked with sobs and words failed her.

哽阻 gěngzǔ (of the throat) choke; block; obstruct: 咽喉～ obstruction in the throat

鲠(骾) gěng ❶〈书面〉fishbone: 如～在喉,不吐不快。Like a fishbone stuck in the throat, one won't feel at ease unless one is out with what is on one's mind. ❷ (of a fishbone) get caught in one's throat: 他吃得太快,被鱼刺～住了。He ate so fast that a fishbone got stuck in his throat. ❸〈书面〉upright: *see* "～直"

鲠直 gěngzhí *also* "耿直" gěngzhí honest and frank; candid and outspoken; upright

绠 gěng 〈书面〉rope for drawing up water (from a well, stream, etc.); well rope

绠短汲深 gěngduǎn-jíshēn 〈谦词〉short rope for a deep well — not up to a given task or job: ～,此事实在心有余而力不足。I cannot measure up to the job. As the saying goes, "The spirit is willing, but the flesh is weak."

颈(頸) gěng *see* "脖颈儿" bógěngr

see also jǐng

gèng

堩(堩) gèng 〈书面〉road

暅(晅) gèng 〈书面〉(often used in personal names) shine upon

更 gèng 〈副词〉❶ more; even more; still more: ～少 less; fewer /～坏 worse /争取～大的胜利 win still greater victories /要～好地为人民服务。We should serve the people even better. /我佩服他的学问,～敬重他的品德。I admire him for his learning, but respect him even more for his moral integrity. ❷〈书面〉further; furthermore; what is more: ～进一步 go a step further /～有甚者 what is more /～添新愁 add to one's worries

see also gēng

更加 gèngjiā 〈副词〉more; still more; even more: 你的办法比他的～容易,～好。Your method is easier and better than his. /这样解释～能说明问题。This gives a better explanation of the problem. *or* This explanation gives a clearer picture of the problem.

更其 gèngqí more; still more; even more: 这儿的江水比下游～湍急。The river here is even more torrential than in the lower reaches.

更上一层楼 gèng shàng yī céng lóu climb one storey higher; attain yet better results; scale new heights: 抓好农田管理,力争生产～。Pay more attention to field management and strive for higher crop yield.

更胜一筹 gèngshèng-yīchóu go one better; be even better; be a

G

notch above others：你的棋艺比他～。You are a cut above him in chess playing.
更为 gèngwéi even more；still more：意义～深远 of still greater significance／他比以往～认真学习。He is studying even more earnestly than before.

gōng

工[1] gōng ❶ worker；workman；labourer；working class：女～ woman worker／矿～ miner／技～ skilled worker；technician／水暖～ plumber／电～ electrician／钳～ benchwork；fitter／童～ child labourer／短～ seasonal labourer ❷ work；labour：上～ go to work／收～ stop work；knock off／费～ labour-consuming／计件～ piece work／散～ day labour／加～ process；polish／勤～俭学 part-work and part-study system；work-study programme／别只图省～不顾质量。Don't try to save labour at the cost of quality. ❸（construction）project；construction；building：动～ begin a project；start construction／竣～ complete a project；finish construction／大楼正在施～中。The building is under construction.／工厂开～了。The factory has gone into operation. ❹ industry：化～ chemical industry／军～ war industry；defence industry／～交系统（system of）industry and communications ❺ engineer：高～（short for 高级工程师）senior engineer ❻ man-day：这项工作需要十个～。This work requires ten man-days. ❼ skill；craftsmanship；workmanship：基本～ basic skills／异曲同～ different tunes rendered with equal skill／做～ workmanship；tailorship；acting／美～ art designing／她的唱～极佳。She is a skillful singer. ❽ be expert in or at；be versed in；be good at：～诗善画 be well versed in painting and poetry ❾ exquisite；excellent；delicate：*see*“～稳”；“～巧”

工[2] gōng 〈音乐〉note of the scale in *gongchepu*（工尺谱），corresponding to 3 in numbered musical notation
see also“工尺”
工班 gōngbān workers' team：先进～ advanced workers' team
工本 gōngběn cost（of production）；expense：不惜～ spare no expense；do sth. whatever the cost／～费 cost of production
工笔 gōngbǐ 〈美术〉traditional Chinese realistic painting characterized by fine brushwork and close attention to detail：～画 drawing made with fine，delicate strokes；meticulous painting
工兵 gōngbīng （army）engineer：坑道～ sapper／轻～ pioneer／～连 engineer company／～部队 engineering corps
工部 Gōngbù 〈历史〉ministry of public works in dynastic China
工厂 gōngchǎng factory；mill；plant；works：钢铁～ iron and steel works／化～ chemical works／汽车～ automobile plant／～区 factory district／～废料 factory waste／～厂长 factory manager／现代化～ modernized plant
工场 gōngchǎng workshop；shop：手工业～ handicrafts workshop
工场手工业 gōngchǎng shǒugōngyè workshop handicraft
工潮 gōngcháo workers' demonstration or protest movement；strike movement：闹～ stage a strike；go on strike
工尺 gōngchě *gongche*，traditional Chinese musical scale：～谱 *gongchepu*，traditional Chinese notation
工程 gōngchéng ❶ engineering：土木～ civil engineering ❷ project；programme：建筑～ construction project／水利～ water conservancy project／安居～ housing project／菜篮子～ shopping-basket programme（for increasing vegetable production）／～进度与质量 progress and quality of a project／按～进度分阶段付款 progress payment
工程标准 gōngchéng biāozhǔn engineering standards
工程兵 gōngchéngbīng *also*“工兵”（army）engineer：～部队 engineering troops（*or* units）；engineering corps／铁道～ railway engineering corps／～司令部 headquarters of the engineering corps
工程传热学 gōngchéng chuánrèxué engineering heat transfer
工程地震学 gōngchéng dìzhènxué engineering seismology
工程地质学 gōngchéng dìzhìxué engineering geology
工程电物理学 gōngchéng diànwùlǐxué engineering electrophysics
工程队 gōngchéngduì construction brigade
工程管理 gōngchéng guǎnlǐ engineering management
工程技术人员 gōngchéng jìshù rényuán engineers and technicians
工程经济学 gōngchéng jīngjìxué value engineering；engineering economics
工程师 gōngchéngshī engineer：总～ chief engineer／建筑～ architectural engineer／高级～ senior engineer／助理～ assistant engineer
工程塑料 gōngchéng sùliào engineering plastics
工程图样 gōngchéng túyàng engineering drawing
工程学院 gōngchéng xuéyuàn college of engineering
工程验收 gōngchéng yànshōu 〈建筑〉acceptance of work
工程语言学 gōngchéng yǔyánxué engineering linguistics
工大 gōngdà ❶（short for 工业大学）polytechnical university ❷（short for 工人大学）workers' university
工党 gōngdǎng Labour Party：英国～ British Labour Party
工地 gōngdì building site；construction site：～负责人 man in charge of a construction site／视察核电厂～ inspect a nuclear power plant under construction
工读 gōngdú ❶ study through work；work on a job in order to finance one's study or education：半工半读 part-time work，part-time study；work one's way through school ❷ *see*“工读教育”
工读教育 gōngdú jiàoyù education for juvenile offenders against the law
工读生 gōngdúshēng juvenile offenders against the law who are enrolled as students of a reform school
工读学校 gōngdú xuéxiào reform school；reformatory：～是挽救失足青年的一种有效的教育机构。Reform schools are institutions of effective education for juvenile offenders against the law.
工段 gōngduàn ❶ section of a construction project ❷ workshop section
工段长 gōngduànzhǎng section chief
工房 gōngfáng 〈方言〉❶ living quarters for workers：单身女工～ dormitory for unmarried female workers ❷ factory building；workshop
工分 gōngfēn workpoint（a unit indicating the quantity and quality of labour performed in rural people's communes as basis for payment）：～值 cash value of a workpoint／记～ record workpoints
工蜂 gōngfēng worker（bee）
工夫 gōngfū 〈旧语〉seasonal or casual labourer；odd-job man
工夫 gōngfu *also*“功夫”gōngfu ❶ time：白费～ waste one's time and energy／他只用了两天～就完成了任务。It took him only two days to finish the task.／他们没多大～就回来了。It was not long before they came back.／这工作很费～。This is a time-consuming job. ❷ free time；spare time；leisure：明天有～再来吧！Come again if you have time tomorrow.／你现在有～吗？Are you free now？／沉重的学习负担累得她抽不出一点玩儿的～。The heavy study load deprived her of all her leisure. ❸〈方言〉during the time（when sth. happens）；when；as：正在说话的～，他就来了。He came as I was talking.／上大学那～，我还当过乒乓球冠军呢！I was once the table-tennis champion in my college. ❹ workmanship；skill；effort；work：苦练硬～ practise hard to master the skill／花了好大～ put in a lot of work；make great efforts／只要～深，铁杵磨成针。〈谚语〉If you work at it hard enough，you can grind an iron rod into a needle.／他的诗画都很有～。He showed great attainments in both poetry and painting.
工夫茶 gōngfuchá *see*“功夫茶”gōngfuchá
工服 gōngfú working clothes；work clothes；boiler suit；overalls
工会 gōnghuì trade union；labour union：～会员证（union）membership card／～会费（union）membership dues／公司～ company union（one controlled by the management）／黄色～ scab union／中华全国总～ All-China Federation of Trade Unions
工会主义 gōnghuìzhǔyì unionism；syndicalism
工价 gōngjià labour cost；wages
工架 gōngjià *also*“功架”gōngjià （actor's）movements and postures；gesture：～优美，气度不凡 graceful postures and refined manners
工间 gōngjiān break during working hours：～休息 break during working hours；coffee break；tea break
工间操 gōngjiāncāo work-break exercises
工件 gōngjiàn workpiece；work：～夹具 workpiece holder；（work）fixture／～架 work rest
工匠 gōngjiàng craftsman；artisan：～师傅 master artisan
工交 gōngjiāo （short for 工业和交通运输业）industry and communications：～战线职工 staff and workers of industrial and communication sectors
工缴费 gōngjiǎofèi *also*“工缴”fee that a state-owned company

pays to a private producer with whom it has contracted for processing work; processing fee

工纠队 gōngjiūduì (short for 工人纠察队) workers' pickets; pickets

工具 gōngjù tool; implement; instrument; means: 木工～ carpenter's tools /测量～ measuring instrument /生产～ implements of production /运输～ means of transport /～改革 improvement of tools /参考～ (in a library) reference tools; finding aids /充当帝国主义的～ serve as an instrument of imperialism /语言是人们交流思想最重要的～。Language is the most important means by which people communicate with each other.

工具车床 gōngjù chēchuáng toolmaker lathe

工具袋 gōngjùdài kit bag; workbag

工具房 gōngjùfáng tool storeroom; toolhouse

工具钢 gōngjùgāng tool steel

工具磨床 gōngjù móchuáng 〈机械〉cutter and tool grinding machine; cutter grinder

工具书 gōngjùshū reference book; dictionary: 文史～ reference books on literature and history /好的～畅销不衰。Good reference books are always in great demand.

工具箱 gōngjùxiāng toolbox; toolkit; workbox

工具主义 gōngjùzhǔyì instrumentalism

工绝 gōngjué 〈书面〉refined; exquisite: 所画花鸟山水，并皆～。The paintings of flowers and birds, of mountains and waters — all showed fine brushwork and skilful craftsmanship.

工竣 gōngjùn 〈书面〉completion of a project

工楷 gōngkǎi (in Chinese calligraphy) neat regular script: 他写得一手漂亮的～。He writes a beautiful regular script.

工科 gōngkē engineering course: ～学生 student of engineering; engineering major /报考～ take entrance examinations for an engineering college

工科大学 gōngkē dàxué engineering university

工科学院 gōngkē xuéyuàn engineering college

工矿 gōng-kuàng (short for 工业和矿业) industry and mining: ～企业 enterprises engaged in industrial production and mining; industrial and mining enterprises

工力 gōnglì ❶ expertise; skill; craftsmanship: ～深厚 superb craftsmanship /颇见～ show the hand of a master /～不够 lacking in skill ❷ manpower; labour: ～短缺 be short of manpower

工力悉敌 gōnglì-xīdí 〈书面〉be equally matched in expertise or skill; rival each other in artistry or craftsmanship; be equally skilful: 两件雕塑作品～，难分伯仲。The two sculptures are on a par in craftsmanship. It is hard to tell which is better.

工丽 gōnglì 〈书面〉delicate and beautiful; exquisite: 彩绘～ exquisite coloured drawing

工联主义 gōngliánzhǔyì *see* "工会主义"

工料 gōngliào ❶ labour and materials (used when drawing up a plan or calculating the cost): ～成本 flat cost ❷ materials for a construction project

工龄 gōnglíng length of service; standing; seniority: 有十年～的工人 worker of ten years' standing /考虑～因素 take seniority into consideration

工龄工资 gōnglíng gōngzī pay based on years of service; seniority pay

工龄津贴 gōnglíng jīntiē seniority allowance

工贸 gōng-mào (short for 工业和贸易) industry and trade: ～结合 combination of industry and foreign trade

工帽 gōngmào work hat; hard hat; helmet

工妙 gōngmiào exquisite; fine: ～的技术 sophisticated skill

工农 gōng-nóng workers and peasants: ～大众 broad masses of workers and peasants /～干部 cadres of worker-peasant origin; worker-and-peasant cadres /～出身 be of worker or peasant origin /～子弟 children of workers and peasants /～子弟兵 workers' and peasants' own troops /～武装 worker-peasant armed forces /～苏维埃政府 Workers' and Peasants' Soviet Government

工农兵 gōng-nóng-bīng workers, peasants and soldiers: 为～服务 serve the workers, peasants and soldiers /～学员 worker-peasant-soldier students (during the Cultural Revolution) /～代表 representatives of the workers, peasants and soldiers

工农差别 gōng-nóng chābié difference between industry and agriculture

工农联盟 gōng-nóng liánméng alliance of workers and peasants; worker-peasant alliance

工农业总产值 gōng-nóngyè zǒngchǎnzhí gross output value of industry and agriculture: ～比前一年增长了百分之五。The gross output value of industry and agriculture increased by five per cent over the previous year.

工女 gōngnǚ 〈旧语〉women engaged in sericulture, weaving, sewing, etc.

工棚 gōngpéng builders' temporary shed; work shed: 简易～ simply constructed builders' shed /搭～ put up a work shed

工票 gōngpiào original record of production quota and schedule; work ticket

工期 gōngqī time limit for a project; schedule or deadline for a project: 延误～ behind schedule /缩短～ shorten the time limit for a project /该项目～定为两年。The project is scheduled to be completed in two years.

工钱 gōngqian ❶ money paid for odd jobs; charge for a service: 做一套家具要多少～? How much do you charge for making a suite of furniture? /做一条裙子的～是十元。It costs ten *yuan* to have a skirt made. ❷〈方言〉wages; pay: 克扣～ dock part of the workers' pay /店主给他的～太少。The shopowner paid him too little for his work.

工巧 gōngqiǎo exquisite; superb; fine: ～的玉雕 exquisite jade sculpture /这幅画用笔～。The painting shows fine and skilful brushwork.

工青妇 gōng-qīng-fù (short for 工会、青年团和妇联) Trade Union, Youth League and Women's Federation

工区 gōngqū work area (a grass-roots unit of an industrial enterprise)

工人 gōngrén worker; working man; workman: 产业～ industrial worker /～干部 worker-cadre /～技术员 technician of worker origin; worker-technician /农业～ farm worker /技术～ technical worker /～领袖 workers' leader /煤矿～ miner

工人贵族 gōngrén guìzú labour aristocracy

工人阶级 gōngrénjiējí working class: ～的杰出领袖 outstanding leader of the working class

工人纠察队 gōngrén jiūcháduì workers' pickets

工人俱乐部 gōngrén jùlèbù workers' club

工人日报 Gōngrén Rìbào *Workers' Daily*

工人体育场 Gōngrén Tǐyùchǎng Workers' Stadium (in Beijing)

工人体育馆 Gōngrén Tǐyùguǎn Workers' Gymnasium (in Beijing)

工人运动 gōngrén yùndòng labour movement; workers' movement: ～的盛衰 ebb and flow of the labour movement

工日 gōngrì man-day

工善 gōngshàn 〈书面〉be versed in; be expert or skilful at; be good at: ～刺绣 be good at embroidery; be a skilful embroiderer

工伤 gōngshāng injury suffered on the job; industrial injury: 因～致残 become disabled because of industrial injury

工伤事故 gōngshāng shìgù industrial accident

工商管理 gōngshāng guǎnlǐ business administration; business (management): ～学院 business school / 主修～ major in business administration

工商管理学硕士 gōngshāng guǎnlǐxué shuòshì Master of Business Administration (MBA)

工商会 gōngshānghuì chamber of commerce and industry

工商界 gōngshāngjiè industrial and commercial circles; business circles: ～著名人士 well-known figure in business circles /他代表～发言。He made a speech on behalf of the business community.

工商局 gōngshāngjú *see* "工商行政管理局"

工商科 Gōngshāngkē (HK) Trade and Industry Branch

工商联 gōngshānglián (short for 工商业联合会) association of industry and commerce

工商所 gōngshāngsuǒ administrative office of industry and commerce

工商行政管理局 gōngshāng xíngzhèng guǎnlǐjú administrative bureau for industry and commerce: 国家～ State Administration of Industry and Commerce

工商业 gōngshāngyè industry and commerce: 私营～ privately owned industrial and commercial enterprises /～者 owner of industrial and business company (*or* undertaking)

工商业联合会 gōngshāngyè liánhéhuì *see* "工商联"

工商业统一税 gōngshāngyè tǒngyīshuì industrial and commercial consolidated tax

工舍 gōngshè living quarters for workers

工时 gōngshí man-hour; labour
工事 gōngshì fortifications; defence works: 构筑～ erect fortifications; build defence works/～极其坚固 impregnable defence works / 简易～ improvised fortifications
工属 gōngshǔ family member of a worker
工钿 gōngtián 〈方言〉 wages; pay
工头 gōngtóu foreman; overseer
工徒 gōngtú ❶ apprentice ❷〈书面〉 craftsman; artisan
工团主义 gōngtuánzhǔyì syndicalism: ～者 syndicalist
工委 gōngwěi (short for 工作委员会) working committee
工稳 gōngwěn (of literary works, esp. poetry) neatly organized and well worded: 造句～ well-organized sentences; apt expressions / 这首诗用词典雅, 对仗～。This poem is refined in diction and balanced in structure.
工务科 Gōngwùkē (HK) Works Branch
工细 gōngxì exquisite; fine; refined: 刺绣～ exquisite embroidery
工效 gōngxiào work efficiency: 提高～ improve work efficiency
工效学 gōngxiàoxué ergonomics
工薪 gōngxīn salary; wages; pay: ～微薄 earn low wages; be meagrely paid
工薪阶层 gōngxīn jiēcéng salaried workers; wage-earners
工薪族 gōngxīnzú wage-earners
工休 gōngxiū ❶ regular holiday: 今天我们～。We have a day off today. ❷ break; work break: ～时坚持做工间操 do work-break exercises every day
工休日 gōngxiūrì day off; holiday: 今天是这个工厂的～。Today is a holiday in the factory.
工序 gōngxù working procedure; process: 产品从生产到完工共有十三道～。The product goes through a thirteen-step process from start to finish.
工宣队 gōngxuānduì (short for 工人宣传队) workers' propaganda team (sent to various units to supervise the work during 1968-1976 in the Cultural Revolution)
工业 gōngyè industry: 轻～ light industry /采矿～ mining industry /电力～ power industry /飞机制造～ aircraft industry /服装～ clothing industry /化学～ chemical industry /机械制造～ machine building industry /基础～ basic industry /加工～ processing industry /汽车制造～ automobile industry /燃料～ fuel industry /石油～ petroleum industry /手～ handicraft /塑料～ plastics industry /冶金～ metallurgical industry /原材料～ raw material industry
工业病 gōngyèbìng occupational disease of industrial workers
工业成本制度 gōngyè chéngběn zhìdù industrial cost system
工业电视 gōngyè diànshì industrial television (ITV): ～装置 utiliscope
工业废料 gōngyè fèiliào industrial waste
工业粉尘 gōngyè fěnchén industrial dust
工业革命 Gōngyè Gémìng Industrial Revolution (occurring in western Europe in the late 18th and early 19th centuries)
工业国 gōngyèguó industrial country; industrialized country
工业化 gōngyèhuà industrialization
工业基地 gōngyè jīdì industrial base
工业间谍 gōngyè jiàndié industrial espionage; industrial spy
工业酒精 gōngyè jiǔjīng industrial alcohol
工业品 gōngyèpǐn industrial product; manufactured goods
工业企业 gōngyè qǐyè industrial enterprise
工业气压 gōngyè qìyā industrial atmosphere
工业券 gōngyèquàn manufactures coupon (for manufactured consumer goods in short supply in 1960's and 1970's)
工业生态系统 gōngyè shēngtài xìtǒng industrial ecosystem
工业体系 gōngyè tǐxì industrial system
工业无产阶级 gōngyè wúchǎnjiējí industrial proletariat
工业心理学 gōngyè xīnlǐxué industrial psychology
工业园 gōngyèyuán *also* "工业园区" industrial park: 苏州～ Suzhou Industrial Park
工业噪声 gōngyè zàoshēng industrial noise
工业总产值 gōngyè zǒngchǎnzhí gross value of industrial product
工衣 gōngyī working clothes; work clothes; boiler suit
工蚁 gōngyǐ worker (ant); ergate
工艺 gōngyì ❶ technology: ～复杂 sophisticated technology ❷ craft; handicraft: 手～ handicraft (art) /～超群 superb craft
工艺流程 gōngyì liúchéng technological process
工艺美术 gōngyì měishù industrial art; arts and crafts: ～学院 college of arts and crafts
工艺品 gōngyìpǐn handicraft article; handiwork; handicraft: 手～ handicrafts /民间～ folk craft /一件～ a piece of handiwork; a handicraft piece
工艺设计 gōngyì shèjì technological design
工艺水平 gōngyì shuǐpíng technological level
工艺要求 gōngyì yāoqiú technological requirement or specification
工役 gōngyì ❶〈旧语〉 manual worker; office boy; servant ❷ labour; service: 服～ do corvée labour /派～ assign people to manual labour
工友 gōngyǒu ❶ manual worker (such as janitor, cleaner, etc.); blue-collar worker ❷〈旧语〉 worker; fellow worker
工于 gōngyú be versed in; be adept at; be good at: 他～书法。He is a good calligrapher.
工于心计 gōngyú-xīnjì adept at scheming; very calculating; machiavellian
工余 gōngyú spare time; afterhours; leisure: 他利用～时间学文化。He learned to read and write in his spare time. /～读书使他眼界大开。Afterhours reading widened his horizons.
工欲善其事,必先利其器 gōng yù shàn qí shì, bì xiān lì qí qì a workman must first sharpen his tools if he is to do his work well; success in a job presupposes ready tools
工运 gōngyùn (short for 工人运动) workers' movement; labour movement
工贼 gōngzéi scab; blackleg: 他被资本家收买当了～。He was bought over by the capitalists and became a strikebreaker.
工长 gōngzhǎng section chief (in a workshop, or on a building site); foreman
工整 gōngzhěng orderly; neat: 字迹～ neatly lettered /他的字写得又漂亮又～。He writes a neat and beautiful hand.
工致 gōngzhì neat and refined; delicate; exquisite: 这枝牡丹画得很～。This peony is drawn with a delicate touch. /这个枕套刺绣～, 色彩艳丽。This pillow case is brightly coloured and exquisitely embroidered.
工种 gōngzhǒng type of work in production: 这个工厂有车工、铸工、钳工等不同～。Turning, foundry, and benchwork are among the various jobs in this factory.
工转干 gōngzhuǎngàn change of one's status from worker to cadre
工装 gōngzhuāng working clothes; work clothes; boiler suit
工装裤 gōngzhuāngkù overalls
工拙 gōngzhuō skilfulness or clumsiness: 把两幅画放在一起, 立显～。The different qualities of the two paintings show when they stand next to each other.
工资 gōngzī wages; salary; pay: 基本～ basic wages /附加～ supplementary wages /货币～ money wages /计件～ payment by the piece; piece-rate wage /计时～ payment by the hour; time wage /名义～ nominal wage /实际～ real wage /实得～ take-home wage /浮动～ floating wages /～冻结 wage freeze /领～ draw one's salary; get one's pay /发～ pay (out) wages /从～中扣除 deduct from one's salary
工资表 gōngzībiǎo payroll; pay sheet
工资袋 gōngzīdài pay packet
工资改革 gōngzī gǎigé reform of the wage system
工资级别 gōngzī jíbié wage scale
工资理论 gōngzī lǐlùn wage theory
工资率 gōngzīlǜ wage rate
工资偏差 gōngzī piānchā wage drift
工资调节税 gōngzī tiáojiéshuì wage regulation tax
工资指数 gōngzī zhǐshù wage index
工资制 gōngzīzhì wage system
工资总额 gōngzī zǒng'é total payroll; total wage bill: ～与经济效益挂钩 (system of) linking total payroll with economic performance
工字钢 gōngzìgāng I-steel
工字形 gōngzìxíng I-shaped: 教学大楼呈～。The classroom building is I-shaped.
工作 gōngzuò ❶ work; operation: 努力～ work hard /～速度 operating rate ❷ job; work; career: 找～ look for a job; job hunting / 分配～ assign (*or* allocate) jobs /调动～ transfer sb. to another post / 她是做会计～的。She works as an accountant. ❸ task; work: 科研～ scientific research /经济～ economic work /社会～ community

G

work /我能力有限，承担不了这项～。It is beyond my ability to do the work. /人人都应做好本职～。Everyone should do his own job well.
工作报告 gōngzuò bàogào work report
工作本 gōngzuòběn working copy
工作表现 gōngzuò biǎoxiàn (work) performance
工作存储器 gōngzuò cúnchǔqì working storage; working memory
工作单位 gōngzuò dānwèi organization in which one works; place of work; work unit
工作电压 gōngzuò diànyā working voltage; operating tension
工作队 gōngzuòduì work team; work force
工作服 gōngzuòfú work clothes; boiler suit：进车间必须穿～。When in the workshop, one must wear work clothes.
工作负荷 gōngzuò fùhè working operating load
工作会议 gōngzuò huìyì working conference
工作键 gōngzuòjiàn job key
工作量 gōngzuòliàng amount of work; workload
工作面 gōngzuòmiàn ❶〈矿业〉face; work range：采煤～ coal face / 回采～ stope /～运输机 face conveyor ❷〈机械〉working surface
工作母机 gōngzuò mǔjī *also*“机床” jīchuáng;“工具机”machine tool
工作评估 gōngzuò pínggū job evaluation
工作人员 gōngzuò rényuán working personnel; staff member; functionary
工作日 gōngzuòrì ❶ work hours per day; working day：完成这项任务至少需要十个～。It needs at least ten working days to complete this task. ❷ day for work; workday：我们每周五个～。We work 5 days every week.
工作台 gōngzuòtái operating platform or floor; working table; staging; workbench
工作午餐 gōngzuò wǔcān working lunch
工作许可证 gōngzuò xǔkězhèng work permit
工作样片 gōngzuò yàngpiàn 〈影视〉rushes
工作语言 gōngzuò yǔyán working language
工作站 gōngzuòzhàn 〈计算机〉workstation
工作者 gōngzuòzhě worker：电影～ film worker /教育～ educational worker /美术～ art worker; artist /文艺～ literary and art workers; writers and artists /翻译～ translator; interpreter /新闻～ journalist /音乐～ musician
工作证 gōngzuòzhèng employee's card; identity card; ID card：出示～ produce one's ID card
工作制 gōngzuòzhì (working) day：争取八小时～ fight for the 8-hour working day
工作周 gōngzuòzhōu (working) week：四十五小时～ 45-hour working week
工作周期 gōngzuò zhōuqī action cycle
工作组 gōngzuòzǔ special working group
工作作风 gōngzuò zuòfēng style of work; work style

攻 gōng ❶ attack; assault; take or go onto the offensive：火～ fire attack /进～ attack; assault /围～ besiege; lay siege to /佯～ feign attack; make a feint /总～ general offensive /～入敌阵 storm the enemy position /主～方向 main direction (*or* thrust) of attack (*or* offensive) /全～型选手 all-out attack player /反守为～ turn defensive into offensive /～不进去。The attack hit a snag and made no headway. ❷ accuse; refute; charge：～人之短 attack someone at his or her weakest point /群起而～之。Everyone points an accusing finger at him. ❸ study; specialize in：专～法学 specialize in jurisprudence; major in jurisprudence
攻城打援 gōngchéng-dǎyuán attack a city while preparing to strike at the reinforcements
攻城略地 gōngchéng-lüèdì take cities and seize territories
攻错 gōngcuò 〈书面〉remedy one's own defects by learning from others' virtues; overcome one's own shortcomings by learning from others' strong points：他山之石，可以～。Stones on other hills are good for working jade — one can benefit from other people's advice.
攻打 gōngdǎ attack; assault：～敌人的桥头堡 attack the enemy's bridgehead
攻读 gōngdú ❶ study assiduously; work diligently：刻苦～ study hard /～博士学位 work for a doctorate ❷ specialize in; major in; read：他是～地质学的。He is reading geology.
攻伐 gōngfá attack; send an expedition against
攻防 gōng-fáng offence and defence：研究～战术 study strategies of offence and defence
攻关 gōngguān ❶ storm a strategic pass：前军～未克。The task force failed to seize the pass. ❷ tackle a key problem：～小组 task team /对于重点科研项目我们必须协作～。We must make joint efforts to tackle key research projects.
攻击 gōngjī ❶ attack; assault; launch an offensive：发起总～ launch a general offensive /～敌军阵地 assail the enemy's position / 我军受到意外的～。Our army was surprised by an enemy attack. ❷ accuse; charge; vilify; let fly at：蓄意～ deliberately attack (*or* accuse) /无端的～ groundless accusation /人身～ personal attack /受到报界的～ be vilified by the press
攻击点 gōngjīdiǎn point of attack
攻击机 gōngjījī attack plane; attacker
攻歼 gōngjiān attack and destroy; wipe out：～敌人一个团 wipe out an enemy regiment
攻坚 gōngjiān ❶ storm fortifications; assault fortified positions：～部队 assault troops /～战术 tactics of storming fortifications ❷ tackle a thorny problem：地震预报是科学～的重要项目。Earthquake forecasting is an important but difficult problem for scientists to tackle.
攻坚战 gōngjiānzhàn storming of heavily fortified positions
攻讦 gōngjié 〈书面〉attack sb. by raking up his past; expose sb.'s past misdeeds
攻克 gōngkè capture; seize; take：～城市 capture a city /～难关 resolve (*or* surmount) a serious difficulty; solve a thorny problem
攻苦食淡 gōngkǔ-shídàn working assiduously and living frugally; industry and simple life
攻掠 gōnglüè attack and loot：遭受异国～ be attacked and ransacked by foreign aggressors
攻略 gōnglüè 〈书面〉storm and capture; attack and seize：～要地 seize a key position
攻难 gōngnàn 〈书面〉censure; blame：文中对此书多有～之言。The article contains quite some censures of the new book.
攻剽 gōngpiāo 〈书面〉seize by force; plunder：贼兵溃退之时，沿途～。The routed bandits plundered along the way.
攻破 gōngpò make a breakthrough; breach：～敌军要塞 break through (*or* penetrate) the enemy stronghold /堡垒最容易从内部～。The easiest way to capture a stronghold is from within. /谣言自会被事实～。Rumours will always be exploded by facts.
攻其不备 gōngqíbùbèi strike where or when the enemy is unprepared; launch a surprise attack; take sb. by surprise; catch sb. unawares：出其不意，～。Do the unexpected; attack the unprepared.
攻其一点，不及其余 gōng qí yī diǎn, bù jí qí yú attack sb. for a single fault without considering his other aspects; seize upon one point and ignore all others
攻取 gōngqǔ strike and capture; storm and occupy; attack and seize：～城池 storm and capture a city
攻势 gōngshì offensive; offence：采取～ take the offensive /展开秋季～ start off the autumn offensive /发动猛烈的～ launch a vigorous offensive /遏制住敌人的～ check the enemy offensive /政治～ political offensive /和平～ peace offensive /贸易～ trade offensive /广告～ advertising campaign /宣传～ publicity campaign
攻势防御 gōngshì fángyù offensive defence
攻势作战 gōngshì zuòzhàn offensive operation
攻守 gōng-shǒu offence and defence：篮球赛一开始，双方～都很积极。At the very beginning of the basketball game, both sides were active in offence and defence. /双方互有～。The two sides acted on the offensive by turns.
攻守同盟 gōng-shǒu tóngméng ❶ offensive and defensive alliance; military alliance ❷ agreement between partners in crime not to give each other away; pact to shield each other：订立～ reach an understanding not to give each other away; promise not to betray each other
攻书 gōngshū 〈书面〉gain book knowledge; study：入学～ go to school; study at school
攻丝 gōngsī 〈机械〉tapping：～机 tapping machine
攻无不克 gōngwúbùkè carrying everything before one; all-conquering; ever-victorious：正义之师～。The army for a just cause triumphs over all enemies.
攻袭 gōngxí launch a surprise attack：～城堡 mount a surprise at-

tack on a citadel
攻下 gōngxià capture; take; overcome:～碉堡 capture a stronghold /～这道难题,其他问题就迎刃而解了。Once this difficulty is overcome, other problems will be readily solved.
攻陷 gōngxiàn capture; seize:起义军势如破竹,一连～了好几座城池。The insurrectionary army smashed all resistance and captured a number of cities in succession.
攻心 gōngxīn ❶ mount a psychological attack; try to win over:政策～ try to win over sb. or persuade sb. to confess by explaining the Party's policy ❷〈中医〉fall into a coma or remain in a stupor because of sorrow or anger; be attacked by internal heat:怒气～ be burnt by pent-up anger
攻心翻 gōngxīnfān 〈方言〉Keshan disease
攻心为上 gōngxīn-wéishàng psychological offensive is the best of tactics; the best way is to win over people's heart:用兵之道,～。In war, the best tactic is to win the enemy over (*or* to demoralize the enemy soldiers).
攻心战 gōngxīnzhàn war of nerves; psychological warfare
攻研 gōngyán study intensively:～诗文 make an in-depth study of poetry and prose
攻占 gōngzhàn attack and occupy; storm and capture:～敌人据点 attack and capture an enemy stronghold

功

gōng ❶ meritorious service or deed; achievement; merit; exploit:立大～ render outstanding service /立一等～ be awarded a first class merit; win merit citation class I /二等～ merit citation class II /立新～ win new merits /记～ cite sb. for meritorious service; record a merit /军～ military exploits /卖～ parade one's merits; show off one's achievements /评～ appraise sb.'s merits /庆～ celebrate a victory /邀～ take credit for what is not one's achievement /居～ claim credit for oneself /立～受奖 receive awards for one's meritorious service /无～不受禄 deserve no reward without achievement /劳苦～高 have worked hard and rendered laudable service ❷ effect; success; result:好大喜～ crave greatness and success /徒劳无～ make a futile effort /事倍～半 get half the result with twice the effort /事半～倍 yield twice the result with half the effort /大～告成 be crowned with success ❸ skill; technique:练～ do exercises in gymnastics, acrobatics, etc.; practise one's skill /唱～ vocal technique; skill in singing; art of singing /内～ exercises to benefit the internal organs; internal energy or power /武～ skill in marshal arts; skill in acrobatics in Chinese opera /基本～ basic skill /她唱～好,做～亦佳。She sings well and acts gracefully. ❹ *qigong* or qi-energy, system of deep breathing exercises:练～ practise *qigong* /鹤翔～ Hexiang *gong*; Crane Dance exercise /他声称能发～给人治病。He claims to be capable of treating patients with the power of *qigong*. ❺ effort;〈物理〉work:机械～ mechanical work
功败垂成 gōngbài-chuíchéng fail on the verge of success; suffer defeat when victory is within one's grasp; fall through when success is in sight
功碑 gōngbēi memorial tablet
功不补过 gōngbùbǔguò demerits outweighing merits
功臣 gōngchén person who has rendered outstanding service; hero:以～自居 give oneself the airs of a hero /他是灾区人民的大～。He has rendered outstanding service to people in the disaster area.
功成不居 gōngchéng-bùjū claim no credit for one's service:他～,对自己的要求仍然那么严格。Claiming no credit for his outstanding service, he remains strict with himself.
功成名就 gōngchéng-míngjiù *also*"功成名立";"功成名遂" achieve success and win recognition; be successful and famous:他自觉～,再也不思进取了。He rests on his laurels, thinking that he has won recognition and fame.
功成身退 gōngchéng-shēntuì retire after achieving success; withdraw from public life when the task is accomplished
功成业就 gōngchéng-yèjiù be crowned with success
功垂竹帛 gōngchuí-zhúbó one's meritorious deeds will go down in history
功大于过 gōngdàyúguò one's achievements exceed errors; merits outweigh demerits
功到自然成 gōng dào zìrán chéng constant effort yields sure success:这是～的事情,着急不得。This is something that requires a great deal of steady (*or* sustained) efforts. Impatience certainly doesn't help.
功德 gōngdé ❶ merits and virtues:不可忘记先辈造这个大湖的～。We should not forget our ancestors for the great pains they took in building this big lake for us. ❷〈佛教〉merit; benefaction; beneficence; good deeds or works:积～ accumulate virtue; do good deeds
功德无量 gōngdé-wúliàng one's kindness knowing no bounds; boundless beneficence; great service:他为当地人民修桥补路,～。Building bridges and repairing roads, he rendered great service to the local people.
功德圆满 gōngdé-yuánmǎn achieve perfect virtues and merits; come to a successful conclusion:我这一任能把这件事办好,就算～了。If I can get these things done, I will have fulfilled my mission in office.
功底 gōngdǐ basic training; foundation:天赋好,～差 be talented but lacking in basic training /她语言～扎实。She has a good grounding in language.
功法 gōngfǎ power of one's *qigong*; (in martial arts) exercise of power or energy:内家～ the exercise of internal power
功夫 gōngfu ❶ workmanship; skill; art:练出了一手硬～ master skills through repeated practice /～不负苦心人。Those who work hard will be rewarded. ❷ *see*"工夫" gōngfu
功夫茶 gōngfuchá *also*"工夫茶" gōngfuchá kung fu tea (a kind of black tea originated in Guangdong and Fujian provinces and popular in southern China)
功夫片儿 gōngfupiānr 〈口语〉*see*"功夫片"
功夫片 gōngfupiàn kung fu film; action movie
功过 gōng-guò merits and demerits:～相抵。Merits neutralize demerits. /～不分。No distinction is made between achievements and errors. /～自有后人评说。Later generations will make fair evaluation of one's contributions and mistakes.
功耗 gōnghào power dissipation or consumption
功过是非 gōngguò-shìfēi merits and demerits, right and wrong:按其～,进行评判 pass judgment according to the merits of each case
功绩 gōngjì merits and achievements; meritorious deeds; service; contribution:为教育事业建立了不可磨灭的～ make indelible contributions (*or* service) to the educational cause /革命先烈的～永远留在我们记忆之中。The heroic deeds of the revolutionary martyrs will live forever in our memory.
功架 gōngjià *also*"工架" gōngjià performer's gestures and movements on stage
功课 gōngkè ❶ schoolwork; lesson; course:复习～ review one's lessons /～好 learn one's lessons well; be a good student /每门～都是优秀 get straight As for all the courses; be a straight-A student ❷ homework:做～ do homework ❸〈佛教〉(monks) recite or chant scriptures
功亏一篑 gōngkuīyīkuì fail to build a mound for want of one final basket of earth — fall short of success for lack of a final effort:为山九仞,～。In raising a mound of 20-odd metres one fails to finish the work for lack of just one basket of earth.
功劳 gōngláo contribution; meritorious service; credit:立下汗马～ have performed deeds of great valour; have rendered great service /～属于人民。The credit should go to the people. /这是大家的～,不能记在我一人头上。Everyone has contributed to the success, and I cannot claim all the credit for myself.
功劳簿 gōngláobù record of merits:躺在自己的～上 rest on one's laurels /不要把别人的功劳也记在自己的～上。Don't claim credit for somebody else's achievements.
功力 gōnglì ❶ efficacy; effectiveness; efficiency:讲求～ strive for efficiency ❷ skill; ability:在书法方面有很深的～ be well grounded in calligraphy /～很深的歌唱家 singer of high calibre
功利 gōnglì ❶ utility; use; efficacy:～显著 be of great utility ❷ official position and material gain:热衷于～ be keen on fame and wealth
功利主义 gōnglìzhǔyì utilitarianism:～者 utilitarian
功烈 gōngliè 〈书面〉merits and achievements; contribution:～卓著 outstanding contributions /～盖世 unparalleled achievements
功令 gōnglìng 〈旧语〉laws and decrees; decree
功率 gōnglǜ 〈物理〉power:额定～ rated power /输出～ output rating; rated output /总～ total output
功率表 gōnglǜbiǎo power meter; wattmeter
功率放大器 gōnglǜ fàngdàqì power amplifier
功率计 gōnglǜjì dynamometer
功名 gōngmíng scholarly honour and official rank (in feudal

times)：博取～ seek official position
功名富贵 gōngmíng-fùguì fame and fortune
功名利禄 gōngmíng-lìlù official position and wealth; rank, fame and fortune
功能 gōngnéng ❶ function: ～锻炼 functional training /语法～ grammatical function /肾～正常。The kidneys function normally. ❷〈通信〉functionality
功能键 gōngnéngjiàn function key
功能团 gōngnéngtuán 〈化学〉functional group
功能性疾病 gōngnéngxìng jíbìng functional disease
功能性障碍 gōngnéngxìng zhàng'ài functional disorder
功能性子宫出血 gōngnéngxìng zǐgōng chūxuè functional uterine bleeding
功能元件 gōngnéng yuánjiàn 〈计算机〉functional element
功能主义 gōngnéngzhǔyì functionalism
功效 gōngxiào efficacy; efficiency; effect: ～比原来提高了三倍。The efficiency has increased threefold. /阿司匹林有治头痛的～。Aspirin is effective relieving headaches.
功勋 gōngxūn exploit; feat; meritorious service: 立下了不朽的～ have performed immortal feats /英雄们的盖世～将永载史册，光耀千秋。The valiant exploits of the heroes gave eternal glory to the pages of history.
功业 gōngyè exploits; feats; achievements: ～彪炳 splendid achievements
功用 gōngyòng function; use: 这些机器各有各的～。Each of these machines has its own use (*or* function).
功照日月 gōngzhào-rìyuè one's achievements outshine the sun and the moon — glorious achievements
功罪 gōng-zuì merits and demerits: 应该客观地评价历史人物的～。We should make an objective assessment (*or* evaluation) of the contributions and defects of a historical figure. /千秋～，谁人曾与评说? Who has passed judgement on the good and ill You have wrought these thousand autumns?

红

gōng *see* "女红" nǚgōng
see also hóng

龚(龔)

Gōng a surname
龚开 Gōng Kāi Gong Kai (formerly translated as Kung K'ai, 1222- c.1304), painter and writer of the late Song and early Yuan dynasties
龚自珍 Gōng Zìzhēn Gong Zizhen (formerly translated as Kung Tzu-chen, 1792-1841), Chinese writer and thinker of the Qing Dynasty

供

gōng ❶ supply; furnish; provide: ～不上 run out; be in short supply / 出钱～他上学 provide financial support for his education /他们原料快～不上了。Their raw material supply was running low. ❷ for (the use or convenience of): 仅～参考 for your reference only /～孩子们读的书 books meant for children; children's books / 这个健身房可～五十人同时活动。This gymnasium can accommodate fifty people at a time.
see also gòng
供不应求 gōngbùyìngqiú supply falls short of demand; demand exceeds supply: 电脑～。The supply fails to meet the demand for computers.
供电 gōngdiàn power supply: ～调度员 load dispatcher /～干线 supply line /提前～。Power was supplied ahead of schedule.
供电局 gōngdiànjú power supply bureau
供电系统 gōngdiàn xìtǒng power network; power-supply system; feed system
供稿 gōnggǎo contribute; send manuscripts for publication: 本栏文章由北京大学～。The articles in this column were contributed by Peking University.
供过于求 gōngguòyúqiú supply exceeds demand
供给 gōngjǐ supply; provide; furnish: 发展经济，保障～ develop the economy and ensure the supply /～生活必需品 provide daily necessities /出版单位必须保证小学课本的～。Publishers must ensure the supply of textbooks for primary schools.
供给制 gōngjǐzhì supply system — a system of payment in kind (in operation during China's revolutionary wars and in the early days of the People's Republic, providing working personnel and their dependants with the primary necessities of life)
供暖 gōngnuǎn 〈建筑〉heating: 热水～ hot water heating /蒸汽～ steam heating /～设施 heating facilities /～散热片 heating radiator
供暖系统 gōngnuǎn xìtǒng heating system: 中央～ central heating system
供气 gōngqì 〈机械〉air feed; gas supply: ～管 air supply pipe /保证按时～ ensure air feed on time; guarantee the timely supply of gas
供求 gōng-qiú supply and demand: ～关系 relations between supply and demand; supply-demand situation /～平衡 balance between supply and demand /～价格 price based on supply and demand
供求律 gōng-qiúlǜ 〈经济〉law of supply and demand
供求率 gōng-qiúlǜ supply-demand ratio
供体 gōngtǐ *also* "给体" jǐtǐ 〈医学〉〈化学〉donor
供销 gōng-xiāo supply and marketing: ～情况良好。Both supply and marketing are brisk.
供销合作社 gōng-xiāo hézuòshè *also* "供销社" supply and marketing cooperative
供需 gōng-xū ❶ supply and demand: 避免～脱节 avoid the divorce of supply from demand ❷〈书面〉supply what one needs
供需矛盾 gōng-xū máodùn imbalance between supply and demand
供养 gōngyǎng provide for (one's parents or elders); support: ～祖母 provide for one's grandmother
see also gòngyǎng
供应 gōngyìng supply; provide: 食品～ food supply /市场～ supply of commodities; market supplies /汽油定量～ rationing on gasoline / ～充足 be in abundant supply /计划～ planned supply /免费～ supply free of charge (*or* gratis) /蔬菜～充足。There is a good supply of vegetables. /副食品敞开～。Non-staple foodstuffs can be bought without any restriction.
供应点 gōngyìngdiǎn supply centre
供应舰 gōngyìngjiàn depot ship; tender; supply ship
供应线 gōngyìngxiàn supply line
供应学派 gōngyìng xuépài 〈经济〉supply-side economics

鸩

gōng 〈动物〉tinamou; *Rhynchotus rufescens*

恭

gōng respectful; courteous; reverent: 洗耳～听 listen with respectful attention /不～ disrespectful; irreverent /谦～ modest and courteous; polite and modest
恭凳 gōngdèng stool used by the disabled and the aged for a bowel movement
恭贺 gōnghè congratulate: ～新禧。Happy New Year! *or* With best wishes for a happy New Year! /～新春。I wish you a happy Spring Festival. /～寿辰。Many happy returns (of the day)!
恭候 gōnghòu 〈敬词〉await respectfully: ～光临。We request the pleasure of your company. /我们全家已经～多时了。All my family have been awaiting you for quite a while.
恭谨 gōngjǐn respectful and cautious: 态度～ show respect and caution
恭敬 gōngjìng respectfully; with great respect: 对老人们十分～ be respectful towards old people /恭恭敬敬地行了一个礼 salute with all respect
恭敬不如从命 gōngjìng bùrú cóngmìng the best way of showing respect is to do as you say; it is better to accept deferentially than to decline courteously
恭楷 gōngkǎi neat regular script
恭请 gōngqǐng invite respectfully; invite sincerely: ～光临。The pleasure of your company is requested.
恭顺 gōngshùn respectful and submissive: 一副～的样子 look respectful and compliant
恭肃 gōngsù 〈书面〉respectful and grave
恭桶 gōngtǒng commode; nightstool
恭维 gōngwei *also* "恭惟" flatter; compliment: 说了不少～话 utter a lot of flattering remarks; pay many compliments /他～我英文说得好。He complimented me on (*or* for) my English.
恭喜 gōngxǐ 〈套语〉congratulate: ～你们大功告成。We congratulate you on the success of your work. /～! ～! Congratulations! / ～发财! May you be prosperous! *or* Wish you all the best!
恭迎 gōngyíng welcome respectfully: 列队～ line up to give sb. a respectful welcome

恭正 gōngzhèng ❶ respectful and proper; reverent:大家都～地脱下帽子行鞠躬礼。Everyone took off his hat and made a profound, respectful bow. ❷ carefully and neatly done:他写的字很～。He writes a neat hand.

恭祝 gōngzhù respectfully congratulate:～诞辰 many happy returns (of the day); congratulations on sb.'s birthday

公[1] gōng ❶ public; state-owned; collective:交～ turn (*or* hand) over to the government (*or* community) /出于～心 act in the interest of the public; have no selfish considerations /归～ make sth. a public possession /假～济私 use public office for private gain /全部财产充～ confiscate all the property ❷ common; general:*see* "～比";"～分母" ❸ international; metric:*see* "～顷";"～斤";"～尺" ❹ make public:*see* "～之于世" ❺ equitable; impartial; fair; just:秉～办理 handle affairs equitably or impartially; be evenhanded /不～ unjust; unfair /大～无私 unselfish; selfless /秉～执法 enforce the law with impartiality ❻ public affairs; official business:因～外出 be away on official business /办～时间 office hours /因～致残 be disabled by work-related injury ❼ (Gōng) a surname

公[2] gōng ❶ duke:大～ grand duke /～侯 dukes and marquises /王～ princes and dukes; the nobility ❷ respectful term of address for an aged or elderly man:师～ master's master; teacher's teacher /天～ ruler of heaven; God /李～ revered Mr. Li /诸～请稍候。Will you gentlemen please wait here for a while? ❸ husband's father; father-in-law:外～ mother's father; (maternal) grandfather ❹ (of animals) male:这只兔子是～的。This is a male rabbit. /这只小狗是～的吗? Is the puppy a he?

公安 gōng'ān public security:～机关 public security agency/～人员 public security officer /～侦察机关 public security inspectorate /～派出所 public security station /～部门 public security sector

公安部 Gōng'ānbù Ministry of Public Security

公安部队 gōng'ān bùduì public security troops

公安干警 gōng'ān gànjǐng public security police

公安局 gōng'ānjú public security bureau

公安厅 gōng'āntīng public security department

公案 gōng'àn ❶〈旧语〉court desk used by a judge;judge's desk:大堂摆着三张～。Three desks are placed in the courtroom. ❷ complicated legal case:无头～ intricate case without a clue ❸ controversial issue; strange affair; mystery

公案小说 gōng'àn xiǎoshuō *gong'an* story — story of a clever magistrate settling complicated cases of crime in dynastic times; detective story

公办 gōngbàn government administered; state-run:～企业 government run enterprise /～学校 state school

公报 gōngbào communiqué; bulletin:新闻～ press communiqué /政府～ (government) bulletin /上海～ Sino-US Joint Communiqué (1972) (known as Shanghai Communiqué) /中美建交～ Joint Communiqué on the Establishment of Diplomatic Relations Between the United States of America and the People's Republic of China (1979) /中美八·一七～ Sino-US Joint Communiqué of August 17, 1982 (on the reduction of US arms sales to Taiwan)

公报部 Gōngbàobù (ROK) Ministry of Information:～长官 Minister of Information

公报私仇 gōngbào-sīchóu *also* "官报私仇" guānbào-sīchóu avenge a personal wrong in the name of public interests; abuse public power to retaliate against a personal enemy; use one's official position to punish sb. for a private grudge

公倍数 gōngbèishù 〈数学〉common multiple:最小～ least (*or* lowest) common multiple

公比 gōngbǐ 〈数学〉common ratio

公便 gōngbiàn 〈旧语〉(used often at the end of an official document) for the benefit of all parties concerned:实为～。That is for the benefit of all concerned.

公表 gōngbiǎo make public; publish; announce:此事尚未～。This matter has not yet been made public.

公禀 gōngbǐng 〈旧语〉petition

公布 gōngbù promulgate; announce; publish; make public; issue:～法令 promulgate laws and decrees /～罪状 announce sb.'s crimes /～名单 publish a name list /～命令 issue an order /～方案 lay one's plan before the public; unfold a plan /～名次 announce the winners in the order of their places in a competition /～于众 be made known to the public /账目要定期～。The account should be made public on a regular basis.

公厕 gōngcè (short for 公共厕所) public convenience; public lavatory; restroom

公差 gōngchā ❶〈数学〉common difference ❷〈机械〉tolerance; allowable error:制造～ manufacturing tolerance /安装～ location tolerance

公差 gōngchāi ❶ public errand; official business:出～ go on a public errand; go on official business /派～ assign jobs ❷〈旧语〉runner or bailiff in a *yamen*:他在县衙里当了三年～。He was a runner in the county *yamen* for three years.

公产 gōngchǎn public property:私吞～ take possession of public property; embezzle public property

公娼 gōngchāng licensed prostitute

公车上书 Gōngchē Shàngshū Joint Petiton of Imperial Examination Candidates to the Emperor (led by Kang Youwei 康有为 in 1895 to oppose signing of the Treaty of Shimonoseki 马关条约 and institute reforms, marking the beginning of the Reformist Movement)

公称 gōngchēng of specifications or standards (of a machine, etc.); nominal:～尺寸〈机械〉nominal dimension

公呈 gōngchéng 〈旧语〉petition

公尺 gōngchǐ metre (m)

公出 gōngchū be away on official business

公畜 gōngchù male animal (kept for breeding); stud:良种～ stud of fine breed

公垂线 gōngchuíxiàn common vertical line

公寸 gōngcùn decimetre

公石 gōngdàn hectolitre

公担 gōngdàn weight of 100 kg.; quintal (q.)

公祷书 Gōngdǎoshū *Book of Common Prayer*, official service book of the Church of England

公道 gōngdào justice:主持～ uphold justice /讨一个～ ask for (*or* demand) justice

公道 gōngdao fair; just; evenhanded; reasonable; impartial:待人～ treat people with fairness /买卖～ be fair in business transaction /办事～ be evenhanded; be impartial /价钱～ reasonable price; fair price

公道自在人心 gōngdào zì zài rénxīn people naturally have a sense of justice; a sense of justice is common to all people

公道话 gōngdaohuà impartial remarks:说句～ to be fair; in all fairness; to do sb. justice

公道钱 gōngdaoqián honest money:凭技术挣～ use one's expertise to make honest money

公德 gōngdé public morality, social ethics:有～心 be publicly-spirited /讲～ have a strong sense of public morality /没有一点～心 be completely egoistic

公敌 gōngdí public enemy:人民～ enemy of the people; public enemy /头号～ public enemy number one

公地 gōngdì public land; common

公爹 gōngdiē 〈方言〉husband's father; father-in-law

公丁香 gōngdīngxiāng 〈植物〉cloves (*Flos Caryophylli*)

公牍 gōngdú 〈书面〉official correspondence; official document

公断 gōngduàn ❶ arbitrate:对争端进行～ arbitrate a dispute/～人 arbitrator; umpire ❷ make an impartial judgment

公吨 gōngdūn metric ton (MT)

公而忘私 gōng'érwàngsī be so devoted to public service as to forget one's own interests; keep public interests in mind all the time; be selfless:～,国而忘家。Think of public interests and not private ones, of the state and not the family.

公法 gōngfǎ 〈法律〉❶ public law; *jus publicum* ❷ international law; law of nations:国际～ public international law

公方 gōngfāng state ownership (in a joint state-private enterprise):～代表 representatives of state ownership (in a joint state-private enterprise)

公房 gōngfáng ❶ public housing:强占～ seize housing; squat in a publicly owned house ❷ public place of recreation and sociability for unmarried young people in some minority nationality regions

公费 gōngfèi at public or state expense:～留学 study abroad on state scholarship

公费吃喝 gōngfèi chīhē wining and dining at public expense;

junketing
公费旅游 gōngfèi lǚyóu go on a sightseeing tour at public expense; be off on a junket
公费医疗 gōngfèi yīliáo free medical service or care; public health service:享受～ be provided with free health service or medical care
公分 gōngfēn ❶ centimetre (cm.) ❷ gram (g.)
公分母 gōngfēnmǔ 〈数学〉common denominator
公份儿 gōngfènr 〈方言〉gift that friends club together to buy
公愤 gōngfèn public indignation; popular anger:引起～ arouse public wrath
公服 gōngfú 〈书面〉formal dress of a government official
公干 gōnggàn (official) business:有何～? What important business has brought you here? /他将于近日来京～。He is soon coming to Beijing on business.
公告 gōnggào ❶ inform (the public); announce:以上通令,～全体公民周知。The above circular order is hereby made known to all citizens. ❷ public notice; announcement; proclamation:张贴～ put up (*or* post) an announcement
公告板服务 gōnggàobǎn fúwù 〈信息〉bulletin board service (BBS)
公告栏 gōnggàolán bulletin board
公根 gōnggēn 〈数学〉common root
公共 gōnggòng public; common; communal:～财产 public property /～场所 public places /～建筑 public buildings /～事务 public affairs /～道德 public morality /～福利 public welfare
公共厕所 gōnggòng cèsuǒ public convenience; public latrine; comfort station
公共电话 gōnggòng diànhuà pay phone; public telephone
公共关系 gōnggòng guānxi public relations (PR)
公共积累 gōnggòng jīlěi common accumulation; accumulation fund
公共基金 gōnggòng jījīn public fund
公共交换电信网 gōnggòng jiāohuàn diànxìnwǎng public switched telecoms network (PSTN)
公共交通 gōnggòng jiāotōng mass transit; public transit; public transport
公共课 gōnggòngkè common required course
公共企业 gōnggòng qǐyè government enterprise
公共汽车 gōnggòng qìchē (public) bus:～线路 bus line /～站 bus stop /上～ get on the bus /下～ get off the bus /乘323路～进城 take Bus No. 323 to town
公共食堂 gōnggòng shítáng canteen; mess; cafeteria
公共投资 gōnggòng tóuzī public investment
公共卫生 gōnggòng wèishēng public health
公共域 gōnggòngyù 〈信息〉public domain
公共秩序 gōnggòng zhìxù public order
公共租界 gōnggòng zūjiè 〈旧语〉International Settlement (as in Shanghai)
公公 gōnggong ❶ husband's father; father-in-law:～婆婆待她如同亲生女儿一样。Her parents-in-law treat her as their own daughter. ❷〈方言〉father's father; (paternal) grandfather ❸〈方言〉mother's father; (maternal) grandfather ❹〈敬词〉grandpa; grandad:老～,请问到动物园怎么走? Grandpa, could you tell me how to get to the zoo? ❺〈旧语〉form of address for a eunuch
公股 gōnggǔ government share (in a joint state-private enterprise)
公关 gōngguān (short for 公共关系) public relations; PR:～业务 public relations business /～手法 public relations ploy (*or* gimmick)
公关部门 gōngguān bùmén public relations department
公关人员 gōngguān rényuán public relations officer
公关小姐 gōngguān xiǎojie public relations miss; public relations lady
公馆 gōngguǎn residence (of a rich or important person); mansion:张～ Mr. Zhang's residence
公国 gōngguó duchy; dukedom; principality:卢森堡大～ Grand Duchy of Luxembourg /列支敦士登～ Principality of Liechtenstein
公海 gōnghǎi high seas; open sea:～自由 freedom of the high seas /～渔业 high seas fishery
公害 gōnghài ❶ social effects of pollution; public hazard:环境污染成了一大～。Environmental pollution has become a serious public hazard. ❷ public plague; public scourge:赌博已成～。Gambling has become a public plague.
公函 gōnghán official letter; official correspondence:来往～ official correspondence /到外地出差必须带着～。Official references are a must for one to travel on business.
公会 gōnghuì trade association; trade council; guild
公鸡 gōngjī cock; rooster:一毛不拔的铁～ out-and-out miser
公积金 gōngjījīn accumulation fund; public reserve fund:要把～用在扩大再生产上。The accumulation funds must be used for the expansion of reproduction.
公祭 gōngjì public memorial ceremony:各界人士为牺牲的烈士举行了～。People from all walks of life held a memorial ceremony for the martyrs.
公家 gōngjia 〈口语〉the state; the public; organization; enterprise:爱护～的东西 take good care of public (*or* state) property /损害～的利益 harm public interests /禁止以～的名义请客送礼。No one is allowed to entertain guests and offer gifts at public expense.
公检法 gōng-jiǎn-fǎ public security organs, procuratorial organs and people's courts
公交 gōngjiāo (short for 公共交通) public transport:～路线 public transport route; bus line
公教人员 gōng-jiào rényuán government employees and teachers
公斤 gōngjīn kilogram (kg.); kilo
公举 gōngjǔ choose by the public; recommend by general acclaim:我们大家～他为代表。All of us elected him (to be) our representative.
公决 gōngjué decide by the majority:全民～ public or general referendum /这事需经大家讨论～。The final decision should be made by all present after a thorough discussion.
公爵 gōngjué duke:～夫人 duchess /爱丁堡～ (UK) Duke of Edinburgh
公开 gōngkāi ❶ open; overt; public:～露面 make public appearance /～发表 publish /～出版物 public printings /～的秘密 open secret /～的和暗藏的敌人 overt and covert enemies /我没有什么不能～对人讲的事情。I have nothing that may not be cried from the housetops. *or* I've nothing to hide from the public. /他们之间的矛盾已经～了。Their disagreement is already in the open. /我们～表示不赞成他们的行为。We went public with our disapproval of their behaviour. /她在～场合总感到紧张。She feels nervous in public. ❷ make public; make known to the public:～账目 make the account known to the public /～内幕 divulge the inside story /把秘密～出来 disclose the secret
公开化 gōngkāihuà make public; come out into the open; be brought into the open
公开论战 gōngkāi lùnzhàn public polemic
公开赛 gōngkāisài open tournament
公开审判 gōngkāi shěnpàn public or open trial
公开投票 gōngkāi tóupiào disclosed ballot; open ballot
公开外交 gōngkāi wàijiāo open diplomacy
公开信 gōngkāixìn open letter:致全国人民的～ open letter to the whole nation
公开性 gōngkāixìng glasnost (a term used by former Soviet leader Mikhail S. Gorbachov); openness; transparency
公开招标 gōngkāi zhāobiāo competitive bidding; public bidding; open tender
公筷 gōngkuài chopsticks for serving food; serving chopsticks
公款 gōngkuǎn public money; public fund:贪污～ embezzle public money /挪用～ misappropriate public funds
公厘 gōnglí millimetre (mm.)
公里 gōnglǐ kilometre (km.)
公理 gōnglǐ ❶〈数学〉axiom ❷ generally acknowledged truth; self-evident truth; justice:～战胜强权。Right prevails over might.
公理会 Gōnglǐhuì 〈基督教〉Congregational Church
公历 gōnglì ❶ Gregorian calendar ❷ *see* "公元"
公立 gōnglì established and maintained by the government; public:～学校 public schools /～图书馆 public library
公例 gōnglì general rule:按～处理 handle (it) according to the general rule
公廉 gōnglián 〈书面〉just and upright; fair and honest
公粮 gōngliáng agricultural tax paid in grain; grain delivered to the state; public grain:交～ hand in grain tax; deliver grain to the state
公了 gōngliǎo settle according to law or policy:这件事还是～为好。

We'd better settle it in court.

公路 gōnglù highway; road: 高速～ express highway; expressway /信息高速～ information superhighway /～工程 highway engineering /～交通 highway communication (*or* traffic) /～运输 highway (*or* road) transport /超级～ superhighway /分道行驶～ dual highway /干线～ arterial highway; main-line highway /四车道～ four-lane highway /这儿的～四通八达。Highways here radiate in all directions.

公路立体交叉 gōnglù lìtǐ jiāochā highway grade separation

公路桥 gōnglùqiáo highway bridge

公路容量 gōnglù róngliàng highway capacity

公路支线 gōnglù zhīxiàn feeder road; feeder line

公论 gōnglùn public opinion; verdict of the people: 是非自有～。The people will decide which is right and which is wrong. *or* Public opinion is the best judge.

公买公卖 gōngmǎi-gōngmài be fair in buying and selling; buy and sell at reasonable prices; do honest business

公门 gōngmén 〈旧语〉❶ government office ❷ palace gate

公民 gōngmín citizen: 中国～ Chinese citizen /～道德 civic virtue /～地位 civil status /～身分 citizenship /～的权利和义务 rights and duties of a citizen; civil rights and duties /二等～ second-class citizen /所有香港中国同胞，不论其是否持有"英国属土～护照"，都是中国～。All Hong Kong Chinese compatriots, whether they are holders of "British Dependent Territories Citizens Passport" or not, are Chinese nationals.

公民权 gōngmínquán civil rights; citizenship: 剥夺～ deprive a citizen of his or her rights

公民投票 gōngmín tóupiào referendum; plebiscite

公民意识 gōngmín yìshi awareness of the obligations of citizens

公民自由 gōngmín zìyóu civil liberties

公明党 Gōngmíngdǎng (Japan) *Komeito*; Komei Party

公亩 gōngmǔ arc (a.) (equivalent to 100 square metres)

公墓 gōngmù cemetery

公母俩 gōngmuliǎ 〈方言〉husband and wife: 老～相敬如宾，感情好极了。The old couple respected and loved each other.

公牛 gōngniú bull: 种～ bull kept for covering calving; stud bull

公派 gōngpài be government sponsored: ～出国留学 study abroad on a government scholarship

公判 gōngpàn ❶ openly pronounce a judgment or verdict: ～大会 judgment pronouncement rally ❷ verdict of the public

公平 gōngpíng fair; just; evenhanded; impartial; equitable: ～合理 fair and reasonable /～的判决 just judgment /～解决 equitable solution (*or* settlement) /～待人 deal fairly with sb.; play fair and square /～贸易 fair trade /～定价 arm's length pricing /领导对他不够～。The leaders are somewhat biased against him. /～地说，他并没想伤害你。To be fair to him, he didn't mean to hurt you.

公平秤 gōngpíngchèng fair scales (used in a market as standard scales)

公平尺 gōngpíngchǐ fair yardstick

公平交易 gōngpíng jiāoyì fair deal; arm's length transaction

公平竞争 gōngpíng jìngzhēng fair play; fair competition

公平市价 gōngpíng shìjià fair value

公评 gōngpíng ❶ comment by the public: 我把我的计划说出来，付之～吧。Let me lay my plan before the public for comment. ❷ fair comment

公婆 gōng-pó ❶ husband's father and mother; parents-in-law: 伺候～ wait upon one's parents-in-law ❷〈方言〉couple; husband and wife: 他们两～相亲相爱，日子过得很舒坦。Deeply attached to each other, the couple lived a happy life.

公仆 gōngpú public servant: 社会～ servant of the society

公仆意识 gōngpú yìshi attitude of a public servant

公启 gōngqǐ 〈书面〉❶ letter signed by a number of people ❷ open letter

公切线 gōngqiēxiàn 〈数学〉common tangent

公勤人员 gōng-qín rényuán service personnel in an office; office attendants; members of the service staff

公顷 gōngqǐng hectare (ha.)

公请 gōngqǐng ❶ invite by everybody; recommend by all: 我们～他做司仪。We all asked him to be the master of ceremonies. ❷ pool money to invite sb. to dinner: 我们三人～他，为他饯行。The three of us invited him to a farewell dinner.

公然 gōngrán 〈贬义〉openly; undisguisedly; flagrantly; brazenly; outright: ～撕毁协议 brazenly tear up an agreement /对祖国的～背叛 openly betray one's motherland /～践踏国际法准则 impudently trample on the norms of international law/～破坏停战协定 make a barefaced breach of the armistice agreement /～造谣诬蔑 unabashedly spread rumours and slanders

公认 gōngrèn generally acknowledged; (universally) accepted; established: ～的国际法准则 generally recognized (*or* accepted) principles of international law /～的国际惯例 universally recognized (*or* established) international practice /～的专家 acknowledged expert /～的行为准则 established rules of conduct /举世～的科学家 scientist who has won worldwide recognition /大家～他是全厂最优秀的工人。He is generally acclaimed as the best worker in the factory.

公认会计原则 gōngrèn kuàijì yuánzé generally accepted accounting principles (GAAP)

公认审计准则 gōngrèn shěnjì zhǔnzé generally accepted auditing standards (GAAS)

公人 gōngren 〈旧语〉petty official or servant in a government office

公山羊 gōngshānyáng he-goat; billy goat

公伤 gōngshāng injury suffered on the job; industrial injury: ～事故 industrial accident

公社 gōngshè commune: 原始～ primitive commune /巴黎～ Paris Commune / 人民～ people's commune

公社化 gōngshèhuà be organized into people's communes

公设 gōngshè 〈数学〉postulate

公审 gōngshěn 〈法律〉public trial; open trial: ～大会 public trial meeting /举行～ hold a public trial

公升 gōngshēng litre

公使 gōngshǐ minister; envoy: ～馆 legation /～衔参赞 counsellor with the rank of minister; minister-counsellor/ 特命全权～ Envoy Extraordinary and Minister Plenipotentiary

公式 gōngshì formula: 硬套～ apply the formula mechanically /数学～ mathematical formula

公式化 gōngshìhuà ❶ formulism (in art and literature): ～的写作方法 stereotyped writing /小说人物性格不突出，显得有些概念化、～。Stereotyped and generalized, the characters in the novel lack distinct individuality. ❷ formulistic; stereotyped: 处理问题绝不能～。We must not take a formulistic approach in solving problems.

公式主义 gōngshìzhǔyì formulism

公事 gōngshì ❶ public affairs; official business or duties: 处理～ attend to official duties /～第一。Public affairs come first. /他整天忙于～。Official business keeps him busy all day long. ❷〈方言〉official document: 上午看～，下午写摘要 read documents in the morning and write a summary in the afternoon /批阅～ pore over official papers

公事包 gōngshìbāo briefcase; portfolio

公事房 gōngshìfáng 〈旧语〉office

公事公办 gōngshì-gōngbàn discharge official duties strictly according to rules; not let personal considerations interfere with one's execution of public duties: 要～，不能徇私情。Business is business. One must not be swayed by personal considerations. /他摆出一副～的样子。He assumed the air of one who would handle the matter strictly according to rules.

公输 Gōngshū a surname

公署 gōngshǔ government office: 地区专员～ prefectural commissioner's office

公说公有理，婆说婆有理 gōng shuō gōng yǒulǐ, pó shuō pó yǒulǐ each says he is right: ～，莫衷一是。Everyone says he has the right answer and no consensus is possible.

公司 gōngsī company; corporation; firm: 钢铁～ iron and steel company /进出口～ import and export corporation /保险～ insurance company /经营皮货的～ firm dealing in furs /～律师 corporation lawyer /～所得税 corporate income tax; corporation tax /～信贷 company credit /～章程 corporation by-laws; articles of association/ 跨国～ transnational corporation /多国～ multinational corporation/ 波音～ Boeing Company /可口可乐～ Coca-Cola Co. /百事可乐～ Pepsi Co. Inc. /大宇～ (ROK) Daewoo Corporation /大发工业～ (Japan)Daihatsu Motor Co. Ltd. /朝日啤酒～ (Japan)Asahi Breweries Ltd. /日立～ (Japan) Hitachi Ltd. /松下电气工业有限～ (Japan) Mastsushita Electric Industrial Co. Ltd. /国泰航空～ (HK) Cathay Pacific Airways Ltd. /太古～ (HK) Swire Pacific Ltd. /太古股份有限～ (HK) Butterfield & Swire / 新鸿基地产～ (HK) Sun

Hung Kai Properties Ltd. /怡和有限～(HK) Jardine Matheson & Co. Ltd. /奥利维蒂～(Italy) Ing. C. Olivetti & C.S.P.A. /巴斯夫～(Germany) BASF AG.

公司标识 gōngsī biāoshí corporate logo

公司法 gōngsīfǎ company act; law of corporation; corporation law

公司化 gōngsīhuà corporatisation; incorporation: 美国的～ incorporation of America

公司前景分析 gōngsī qiánjǐng fēnxī swot analysis

公司实体 gōngsī shítǐ corporate entity

公司特征 gōngsī tèzhēng corporate identity

公司战略 gōngsī zhànlüè corporate strategy

公私 gōng-sī public and private: ～分明 be scrupulous in separating public from private interests /～两便 be beneficial (*or* advantageous) to both public and private interests

公私合营 gōng-sī héyíng joint state-private ownership (the principal form of state capitalism adopted during the socialist transformation of capitalist enterprises in China): ～企业 joint state-private enterprise; enterprise under joint public and private management

公私兼顾 gōng-sī jiāngù take into consideration both the public and private interests: 我这一趟出去，～。This is a trip that will attend to both business and personal matters.

公诉 gōngsù 〈法律〉 public prosecution: 提起～ institute prosecution; bring a public charge; institute (*or* start) legal proceedings

公诉权 gōngsùquán right of prosecution

公诉人 gōngsùrén public prosecutor; the prosecution

公诉书 gōngsùshū bill of indictment; bill of prosecution; public indictment

公孙 Gōngsūn a surname

公孙龙 Gōngsūn Lóng Gongsun Long (formerly translated as Kungsun Lung, c. 320-250 BC), philosopher of the Warring States Period

公孙树 gōngsūnshù gingko (tree)

公所 gōngsuǒ public office

公摊 gōngtān (of expenses) be shared equally by all: 旅行费用由我们大家～。We will share the travelling expenses.

公堂 gōngtáng ❶ law court; tribunal: 私设～ set up a clandestine tribunal (*or* a kangroo court) /在～上，她吓得浑身发抖。She was trembling with fear in court. ❷ ancestral hall; memorial temple

公帑 gōngtǎng 〈书面〉 public money; public fund: 糜费～ squander public money

公听并观 gōngtīng-bìngguān listen to all sides and take stock of the overall situation

公庭 gōngtíng ❶ courtyard in front of the imperial ancestral shrine ❷ law court: 对簿～ confront (each other) in court

公同 gōngtóng common; general: ～议定 jointly decide

公推 gōngtuī recommend by general acclaim: 大家～他当车间主任。He was recommended by all his fellow workers to be the workshop director. /小组长由群众～。The group leader is to be elected by all the members of the group.

公文 gōngwén official document: ～程式 forms and formulas of official documents /传送～ deliver official documents /～务求简明扼要。Official documents must be brief and to the point.

公文包 gōngwénbāo briefcase; portfolio

公文袋 gōngwéndài official envelope

公文旅行 gōngwén lǚxíng travel of documents; (bureaucratic) red tape

公文纸 gōngwénzhǐ paper for copying official documents

公务 gōngwù public affairs; official business: ～通信 official communication (*or* correspondence) /执行～ on official duty (*or* business) /～繁冗 be overburdened with official duties /～羁身 be tied down by one's duties /处理～ handle (*or* deal with) public affairs

公务护照 gōngwù hùzhào service passport

公务签证 gōngwù qiānzhèng service visa

公务人员 gōngwù rényuán government functionary

公务员 gōngwùyuán ❶ orderly: 他当～已经三年了。He has been an orderly for three years. ❷ public servant; civil servant; civil service: ～法 public servant law /～考试 civil service examination/ ～考绩制 merit system /国际～制度委员会 International Civil Service Commission (ICSC)

公务员事务科 Gōngwùyuán Shìwùkē (HK) Civil Service Branch

公务员叙用委员会 Gōngwùyuán Xùyòng Wěiyuánhuì (HK) Public Service Commission

公物 gōngwù public property: 爱护～ take good care of public property

公弦 gōngxián 〈数学〉 common chord

公廨 gōngxiè government office or building

公心 gōngxīn ❶ fair-mindedness: 凭～办事 be fair-minded in handling things ❷ public spirit; selflessness: 出以～ in the public interest; without selfish considerations

公休 gōngxiū general holiday; official holiday; public holiday

公选 gōngxuǎn choose by the general public

公鸭 gōngyā drake

公鸭嗓 gōngyāsǎng *also* "公鸭嗓子" sharp and hoarse voice

公演 gōngyǎn perform in public; give a performance: 该剧将于下周首次～。The play is premièring next week. /那部歌剧将再次～。The opera will be put on stage again.

公学 gōngxué public school: 陕北～ Northern Shaanxi Public School (in Yan'an, 1937-1941)

公羊 gōngyáng ❶ male sheep; ram ❷ (Gōngyáng) a surname

公羊传 Gōngyángzhuàn *Spring and Autumn Annals with Commentaries by Gongyang Gao* (公羊高, a scholar of the Warring States Period)

公爷 gōngye 〈旧语〉 respectful form of address for a duke

公议 gōngyì public or mass discussion: 自报～ self-assessment and public discussion /交由群众～ pass on to the rank and file for discussion

公议儿 gōngyìr 〈方言〉 gift bought by clubbing money together (on the occasion of a wedding, etc.): 随～ share the expenses in buying a gift for a friend

公役 gōngyì 〈旧语〉 manual worker in a government office; office attendant

公益 gōngyì public good; public welfare: 热心～ public-spirited / ～劳动 volunteer labour

公益金 gōngyìjīn public welfare fund: 每年都提取利润的百分之五作为厂里的～。Each year the factory sets aside five per cent of its profit for the public welfare fund.

公益事业 gōngyì shìyè public service; public welfare undertaking

公意 gōngyì will of the public; public will: 不能违背～ must not go against the will of the public

公因式 gōngyīnshì 〈数学〉 *see* "公因子"

公因数 gōngyīnshù 〈数学〉 *see* "公约数"

公因子 gōngyīnzǐ 〈数学〉 common factor: 最大～ greatest common factor (*or* divisor)

公英 gōngyīng 〈中药〉 dandelion (used as herbal medicine)

公营 gōngyíng publicly-owned; publicly-operated; public: ～经济 public sector of the economy; public economy /～企业 public enterprise

公营部门 gōngyíng bùmén public sector

公映 gōngyìng (film) be shown to the public: 这部影片即将～。The film is coming soon.

公用 gōngyòng for public use; communal: ～天线 common antenna /厨房由几家～。The kitchen is shared by several families.

公用电话 gōngyòng diànhuà public telephone; pay phone

公用事业 gōngyòng shìyè public utilities; public service: ～局 bureau of public utilities /～公司 public-service corporation

公用网 gōngyòngwǎng 〈通信〉 public network

公有 gōngyǒu publicly owned: ～财产 public property; communal property

公有化 gōngyǒuhuà transfer to public ownership; socialize

公有土地 gōngyǒu tǔdì public land

公有制 gōngyǒuzhì public ownership (of means of production): ～企业 public enterprise

公余 gōngyú after-office hours; spare time; leisure hours: 利用～时间学外语 learn a foreign language during one's spare time

公寓 gōngyù ❶ 〈旧语〉 lodging house; room or suite in a hotel rented by the month ❷ flat; apartment house; apartment: ～大楼 apartment building /两间一套的～ two-room flat /外交～ diplomatic compound

公元 gōngyuán Christian era: 汉朝建立于公元前 206 年，亡于公元 220 年。The Han Dynasty was founded in 206 BC and came to an end in 220 AD.

公园 gōngyuán park: 国家～ national park /这是一个供孩子游戏玩耍的～。This is a park for children.

G

公约 gōngyuē ❶ convention; pact; convenant; treaty: 北大西洋～ North Atlantic Treaty / 日内瓦～ Geneva Convention / 签订～ sign a convention / 缔结～ conclude a pact ❷ joint pledge: 卫生～ public health pledge / 服务～ service pledge (given by workers in the service trades) / 治安～ public security pledge

公约数 gōngyuēshù 〈数学〉 common divisor: 最大～ greatest common divisor

公允 gōngyǔn just and sound; fair and equitable; impartial; even-handed: 持论～ be just and fair in argument / 貌似～ pretend to treat all sides alike; put on an appearance of impartiality / 执法～ enforce law evenhandedly

公债 gōngzhài public or government bonds: 经济建设～ economic construction bonds / 发行～ issue bonds / 购买～ buy bonds / 认购～ subscribe to bonds / 三年期～ three-year bonds

公债券 gōngzhàiquàn public or government bonds

公展 gōngzhǎn exhibit to the public; hold an exhibition

公章 gōngzhāng official seal: 在文件上加盖～ affix an official seal to a document

公账 gōngzhàng accounts of an organization; public accounts

公正 gōngzhèng fair; just; impartial; even-handed: ～的裁决 impartial verdict / ～持久的和平 just and lasting peace / 赏罚～ be fair in meting out rewards and punishments / ～的法官 fair-minded judge / ～的待遇 equitable treatment; fair play / 裁判不～。The judge is unfair (*or* biased).

公证 gōngzhèng notarize; attest: ～事务 notarial affairs / ～遗嘱 notary testament / ～监督 notary supervision / 这份结婚证书是经过～的。This marriage certificate has been notarized.

公证处 gōngzhèngchù notary office

公证会计师 gōngzhèng kuàijìshī certified public accountant

公证人 gōngzhèngrén notary; notary public (NP)

公证委托书 gōngzhèng wěituōshū letter of commitment

公证证明 gōngzhèng zhèngmíng certification by a notary; notarial certification

公证证书 gōngzhèng zhèngshū notarial certificate; notarial document

公之于世 gōngzhīyúshì make public; reveal to the world: 把事情～ make a matter public; publicize a matter

G

公直 gōngzhí fair-minded; fair; just and upright: ～无私 just and selfless

公职 gōngzhí government office; official post; public employment: 开除～ discharge from public employment; strike sb.'s name off the official list / 担任～ hold a public office

公职人员 gōngzhí rényuán government employee; public servant

公制 gōngzhì metric system: ～尺寸 metric size / ～螺纹〈机械〉 metric thread / 折成～ convert to the metric system / ～化 metrication

公忠体国 gōngzhōng-tǐguó be loyal to one's country

公冢 gōngzhǒng 〈书面〉 (public) cemetery

公众 gōngzhòng the public: ～舆论 public opinion / ～领袖 leader of the public / ～集会 public rally; public gathering / 这个博物馆对～开放。This museum is open to the public.

公众人物 gōngzhòng rénwù public figure

公诸同好 gōngzhū-tónghào share enjoyment with those having the same taste: 他急切地把刚买来的名画～。He was unable to hold himself back from showing his friends the famous painting he had just bought.

公猪 gōngzhū male pig; boar

公主 gōngzhǔ princess: 长～ princess royal

公助 gōngzhù ❶ public subsidy or aid: 社会～ financial assistance by society ❷ government subsidy: 这是一所民办～的小学。This is a private primary school subsidized by government funds.

公转 gōngzhuàn 〈天文〉 revolution: ～周期 period of revolution

公子 gōngzǐ son of a prince or high official; 〈敬词〉 sb.'s son: 富家～ son of a rich family / 李～ son of the Lis; Young Mr. Li; Master Li

公子哥儿 gōngzǐgēr pampered son of a wealthy or influential family; dandy; beau: 这个年轻人是个典型的～。The young man is a typical playboy. / 他生活朴素，一点也不像个富商的～。He lives a simple life and shows no sign of being a rich merchant's son.

公子王孙 gōngzǐ-wángsūn sons of princes and nobles; sons of the rich and influential

蚣

gōng *see* "蜈蚣" wúgōng

肱

gōng 〈书面〉 upper arm; arm: 曲～而枕 bend one's arm and rest one's head on it / 股～ right-hand man; able and reliable assistant / ～动脉 brachial artery / ～静脉 brachial vein

肱骨 gōnggǔ 〈生理〉 humerus

肱二头肌 gōng'èrtóujī 〈生理〉 (brachial) biceps

肱梁 gōngliáng 〈建筑〉 cantilever beam; 〈比喻〉 pillar of society

肱木 gōngmù bolster

肱三头肌 gōngsāntóujī 〈生理〉 (brachial) triceps

觥

gōng ancient wine vessel made of bronze

觥筹交错 gōngchóu-jiāocuò wine cups and gaming chips lie about in disarray; dinner party at which wine flows freely; boisterous party where cups go gaily around; wine and dine

觥觥 gōnggōng 〈书面〉 upright and outspoken

弓

gōng ❶ bow: 弩～ crossbow / 强～ heavy bow / 张～搭箭 with bows drawn and arrows set / 左右开～ shoot first with one hand, then with the other; use both hands successively / 弹～ catapult; slingshot ❷ anything bow-shaped: 小提琴的～ bow of a violin / 弹棉花的绷～儿 bow for teasing cotton; cotton-teasing ❸ ancient wooden bow-shaped divider for measuring land ❹ 〈旧语〉 unit of length for measuring land, equal to five *chi* (尺) ❺ bend; arch; bow: ～着腰走路 walk with one's back bent forward / ～腰驼背 hunchbacked ❻ (Gōng) a surname

弓背 gōngbèi ❶ arch one's back; bend low: 老人弓着背走出来。The aged man came out bending low. ❷ back of a bow ❸ hunchbacked ❹ winding road, river, or arched bridge: 顺着公路走，净走～，远多了。The many detours of the highway would make the journey much longer. / 马正走在一座小桥的～上。The horse was walking on the hump of an arched bridge.

弓袋 gōngdài bow case

弓箭 gōngjiàn bow and arrow

弓箭步 gōngjiànbù forward lunge (in *wushu* or gymnastics)

弓弩 gōngnǔ bow and crossbow; bow and arrow: ～手 crossbowman; bowman; archer

弓身 gōngshēn bend oneself; bow: ～哈腰 humble oneself; be obsequious / 他～扶起摔倒的孩子。He stooped to help the fallen child up.

弓弦 gōngxián ❶ bowstring ❷ straight road; direct way: 顺着小路走，净走～，近便多了。We can take a shortcut by the small path that leads directly to the destination.

弓弦乐器 gōngxián yuèqì bowed stringed instrument; bowed instrument; bowed string instrument

弓鞋 gōngxié 〈旧语〉 small, bow-shaped shoe worn by women with bound feet

弓形 gōngxíng ❶ 〈数学〉 arc; segment of a circle: ～角 angle at the segment ❷ bow-shaped; arched; curved

弓形足 gōngxíngzú 〈医学〉 talipes arcuatus

弓腰 gōngyāo arch one's body; stoop; bend over

弓子 gōngzi ❶ bow (of a stringed instrument): 胡琴～ bow of *huqin* ❷ anything bow-shaped

弓钻 gōngzuàn bow drill

躬(躳)

gōng ❶ oneself; in person; personally: 反～自问 examine oneself; introspect ❷ bend forward; bow; stoop: ～身 bend at the waist / ～身下拜 bow down and worship; bend the knee in obeisance

躬逢其盛 gōngféng-qíshèng 〈书面〉 be present in person on the grand occasion; live in times of prosperity

躬耕 gōnggēng do farming; till the soil: 臣本布衣，～于南阳。I used to be a commoner engaged in farming at Nanyang.

躬亲 gōngqīn 〈书面〉 attend to personally: 事必～ attend to everything in person; see to everything oneself

躬行 gōngxíng 〈书面〉 practise personally; do sth. oneself: ～实践 practise what one preaches

宫[1]

gōng ❶ palace: 故～ Imperial Palace; Forbidden City / 行～ imperial palace for short stays away from the capital / 皇～ impe-

rial palace /后～ imperial harem /东～ crown prince's palace; crown prince /寝～ imperial burial place; mausoleum; emperor's or king's resting place ❷ (celestial) palace; residence of immortals: 天～ heavenly palace /月～ palace on the moon; moon /水晶～ Crystal Palace of the Dragon King ❸ temple (used in a name): 雍和～ Lama Temple of Peace and Harmony ❹ place for cultural activities and recreation: 劳动人民文化～ Working People's Cultural Palace /少年～ children's palace ❺〈生理〉 womb; uterus: 子～ uterus; womb /刮～ dilatation and curettage (D. and C.); uterine curettage ❻ (Gōng) a surname

宫[2] gōng 〈音乐〉 note of the ancient Chinese five-tone scale, corresponding to 1 in numbered musical notation
see also "五音" wǔyīn

宫爆鸡丁 gōngbào jīdīng stir-fried diced chicken with chilli and peanuts

宫城 gōngchéng ❶ palace walls in the capital city ❷ imperial capital

宫灯 gōngdēng palace lantern: 门口挂着一对大红～。A pair of red palace lanterns hung by the gate.

宫殿 gōngdiàn palace: ～式建筑 palatial architecture /大楼建得像～一样。The building is modelled on a palace.

宫调 gōngdiào 〈音乐〉 modes of ancient Chinese music

宫娥 gōng'é maid in an imperial palace; maid of honour; maid-in-waiting: 垂泪对～。I shed tears before my palace maids!

宫观 gōngguàn ❶ temporary dwelling place of an emperor when away from the capital ❷ Taoist temple

宫禁 gōngjìn ❶ emperor's living quarters; palace precincts ❷ palace taboos; palace prohibitions

宫颈 gōngjǐng *also* "子宫颈" zǐgōngjǐng uterine neck; cervix uteri: ～癌 cervical cancer /～糜烂 cervical erosion/～钩 cervical tenaculum /～炎 cervicitis

宫内节育器 gōngnèi jiéyùqì intrauterine device (IUD)

宫女 gōngnǚ *also* "宫娥" maid in an imperial palace; maid in-waiting: 后宫的～ maid in the empress's palace; maid in the palace of the empress

宫阙 gōngquè 〈书面〉 imperial palace: 天上～ heavenly palace; palace on high

宫人 gōngrén *see* "宫女"

宫纱 gōngshā light and transparent silk fabric; decorating gauze

宫扇 gōngshàn round or circular fan, originally used by court attendants

宫室 gōngshì ❶ dwelling house; mansion ❷ palace

宫廷 gōngtíng ❶ imperial palace: ～侍卫 imperial bodyguard ❷ royal or imperial court; court

宫廷政变 gōngtíng zhèngbiàn palace revolution; palace coup

宫外孕 gōngwàiyùn 〈医学〉 ectopic pregnancy; extrauterine pregnancy

宫闱 gōngwéi 〈书面〉 palace chambers: ～秘闻 palace secrets

宫刑 gōngxíng castration (a form of punishment in ancient China): 施以～ perform castration (on sb.); castrate
see also "五刑" wǔxíng

宫掖 gōngyè palace chambers

宫苑 gōngyuàn imperial or royal garden

宫泽喜一 Gōngzéxǐyī Miyazawa Kiichi (1919-), Japanese Prime Minister (1991-1993)

宫装 gōngzhuāng *also* "宫妆" dress of a maid of honour

gǒng

巩(鞏) gǒng ❶ consolidate; strengthen; solidify: *see* "～固" ❷ (Gǒng) a surname

巩固 gǒnggù consolidate; strengthen; enhance; solidify: ～国防 consolidate national defence /～地位 strengthen one's position /～三方联盟 strengthen the tripartite alliance /～统治地位 solidify one's rule /建立～的政权 build strong political power/安定团结的局面必将更加～。Stability and unity will surely be further enhanced. /这所楼房的地基很～。The base (*or* foundation) of this new house is solid.

巩膜 gǒngmó 〈生理〉 sclera: ～沟 scleral groove; sulcus sclerae /～膨胀 sclerectasia; sclerectasis

巩膜炎 gǒngmóyán scleritis

巩皮病 gǒngpíbìng *also* "硬皮病" yìngpíbìng scleroderma

汞 gǒng *also* "水银" shuǐyín 〈化学〉 mercury; hydrargyrum (Hg): 甘～ calomel; mercurous chloride /红～ mercurochrome /硫化～ mercuric sulphide /氯化～ mercuric chloride /雷～ mercury fulminate

汞灯 gǒngdēng mercury lamp

汞干电池 gǒnggāndiànchí mercury cell

汞弧 gǒnghú 〈电子〉 mercury arc: ～整流器 mercury-arc rectifier; mercury-vapour rectifier

汞弧灯 gǒnghúdēng 〈电学〉 mercury-arc lamp

汞化 gǒnghuà 〈化学〉 mercuration; mercurization: ～物 mercuride

汞化合物 gǒnghuàhéwù mercury compound

汞控恒温器 gǒngkòng héngwēnqì mercury thermostat

汞齐 gǒngqí *also* "汞合金" amalgam: 合金～ alloy amalgam /～蒸馏罐〈冶金〉 amalgam retort

汞汽 gǒngqì 〈电子〉 mercury-vapour: ～灯 mercury-vapour lamp /～管 mercury-vapour tube

汞污染 gǒngwūrǎn mercury pollution

汞溴红 gǒngxiùhóng *also* "红汞" hónggǒng; "红药水" hóngyàoshuǐ 〈药学〉 mercurochrome

汞中毒 gǒngzhòngdú 〈医学〉 mercurialism; hydrargyrism

汞中毒性肾病 gǒngzhòngdúxìng shènbìng 〈医学〉 mercurial nephrosis

汞柱 gǒngzhù mercury column; mercury

珙 gǒng 〈书面〉 a kind of jade

珙桐 gǒngtóng *also* "空桐树" kōngtóngshù 〈植物〉 dove tree

栱 gǒng *see* "枓栱" dǒugǒng

拱[1] gǒng ❶ cup one hand in the other before the chest (as a form of salutation): *see* "～手" ❷ encompass; encircle; surround: 四山环～的村寨 village encircled by mountains /众星～月。A myriad of stars surround the moon. ❸ hunch up; hump up; arch: 他把腰～了～。He arched (*or* hunched up) his back. ❹ arch: ～式涵洞 arch culvert /～道 archway /把门建成～形 build an arch-shaped door

拱[2] gǒng ❶ (of people) push with one's body; (of pigs, etc.) dig with the snout; (of earthworms, etc.) wriggle through: 以身～门 push open the door with one's body /他～出人群跑了。He elbowed through the crowd and ran away. /猪～土找食。Pigs root in the ground for food. ❷ sprout up through the earth: 苗儿～出土了。The shoots are springing up from the earth.

拱坝 gǒngbà 〈水利〉 arch dam

拱抱 gǒngbào surround; encircle; embrace: 众山～的天然牧场 natural pasture surrounded by mountains

拱璧 gǒngbì 〈书面〉 large piece of jade; treasure: 此物收藏家珍如～。Collectors cherish this as priceless treasure.

拱别 gǒngbié 〈书面〉 take leave by saluting with both hands folded and raised in front: ～众人, 转身上轿。He bid farewell to everyone respectfully and got into his sedan chair.

拱点 gǒngdiǎn 〈天文〉 apsis; apse

拱顶 gǒngdǐng dome; vault

拱服 gǒngfú 〈书面〉 have respect for; admire; esteem: 倾心～ be in respectful admiration

拱火 gǒnghuǒ 〈口语〉 make sb. even more angry; pour oil on the fire: 他已经生了气, 你就别再～了。He is already angry. Please don't fan the flames.

拱肩缩背 gǒngjiān-suōbèi (as in cold weather, or an expression of obsequiousness) hunch (up) one's shoulders and bow one's back

拱立 gǒnglì stand while cupping one hand in the other before one's chest — stand in a reverent posture

拱门 gǒngmén 〈建筑〉 arched door

拱门式冲床 gǒngménshì chòngchuáng 〈机械〉 arch press

拱棚 gǒngpéng arched shed

拱桥 gǒngqiáo 〈建筑〉 arch bridge: 双曲～ double-curvature arch bridge

拱让 gǒngràng *see* "拱手让人"

拱手 gǒngshǒu (usu. used in greeting or saying farewell) fold

G

one's hands in a bow; make an obeisance by cupping one hand in the other before one's chest: ～道别 bid farewell in a respectful manner /～称谢 join one's hands together in salute to express one's thanks /～致礼 salute with joined hands; salute with the hands folded

拱手让人 gǒngshǒu-ràngrén give up submissively; hand over on a silver platter: 把国土～ surrender a country's territory without even a show of fight /你不该将那幅名画～。You shouldn't have handed that famous painting over on a silver platter.

拱瓦 gǒngwǎ pantile; curved tile (for roofing)

拱卫 gǒngwèi surround and protect; defend; guard: ～着首都 guard (*or* protect) the capital on all sides

拱形建筑 gǒngxíng jiànzhù arch; arched construction

拱形隧道 gǒngxíng suìdào arched tunnel

拱形屋顶 gǒngxíng wūdǐng 〈建筑〉arch roof

拱形支架 gǒngxíng zhījià arch support

拱券 gǒngxuàn *also* "券" xuàn 〈建筑〉arch

gòng

贡 gòng ❶ tribute: 进～ pay tribute (to an imperial court) /朝～ present tribute; pay tribute ❷ recommend a person to the imperial court: ～士 person recommended for national service ❸ (Gòng) a surname

贡茶 gòngchá tribute tea; fine quality tea

贡缎 gòngduàn tribute silk; satin

贡奉 gòngfèng pay tribute; present tribute: 地方向朝廷～方物。Local governments presented special local products to the imperial court.

贡举 gòngjǔ ❶ recommend suitable persons to the imperial court for national service ❷ imperial examination system

贡品 gòngpǐn article of tribute; tribute: 琳琅满目的～ a rich variety of tribute

贡生 gòngshēng scholar recommended by local government for further studies at the national capital

贡税 gòngshuì *also* "贡赋" tribute and taxes: 交纳～ pay tribute and taxes

贡献 gòngxiàn ❶ contribute; dedicate; devote: 为革命～一份力量 do one's bit for the cause of revolution /为教育事业～出自己的一生 dedicate (*or* devote) one's life to education /他自觉地把所有的钱财～给慈善事业。He voluntarily gave all his money and property to charities. ❷ contribution; dedication; service: ～卓著 make outstanding contributions /北京猿人的发现是对古人类学的重大～。The discovery of Peking man was an important contribution to paleoanthropology.

贡院 gòngyuàn place where imperial examination at the provincial level was held; provincial imperial examination centre

共 gòng ❶ common; general; universal: 公～ public; common; communal ❷ share: 同呼吸，～命运 share a common fate; throw in one's lot with sb. /～患难 go through hardships together /同甘～苦 share weal and woe; share joys and sorrows ❸ doing the same thing; in company; together: ～存亡 live or die together /和平～处 peaceful coexistence ❹ altogether; in all; all told: 总～ in all; altogether; in the aggregate /年利润～五万元。The annual profit totalled 50 thousand *yuan*. /全家～八人。There are eight people in the family. ❺ (short for 共产党) Communist Party: 中～ Communist Party of China (CPC) /日～ Communist Party of Japan

共边角 gòngbiānjiǎo 〈数学〉coterminal angles

共餐 gòngcān dine together: 同桌～ dine together at one table; eat at the same table

共产党 gòngchǎndǎng Communist Party: ～人 Communist/～员 member of the Communist Party; Communist /～是无产阶级的先锋队。The Communist Party is the vanguard of the proletariat.

共产党宣言 Gòngchǎndǎng Xuānyán *Communist Manifesto* (1848) by Karl Marx and F. Engels

共产风 gòngchǎnfēng "go communist" trend — the wrong practice of infringing upon the fruits of other people's labour during the "Great Leap Forward" in the late 1950's

共产国际 Gòngchǎn Guójì Communist International (1919-1943); Comintern

共产主义 gòngchǎnzhǔyì communism: ～道德 communist morality (*or* ethics) /～精神 communist spirit /～风格 communist style /～觉悟 communist consciousness /～理想 communist ideal /～运动 communist movement /～者 communist

共产主义青年团 gòngchǎnzhǔyì qīngniántuán Communist Youth League

共处 gòngchǔ coexist: 和平～五项原则 Five Principles of Peaceful Coexistence / 和睦～ live in harmony

共存 gòngcún exist side by side; coexist

共大 Gòngdà (short for 江西共产主义大学) Communist Labour University of Jiangxi

共电 gòngdiàn 〈通信〉common battery: ～电话机 common battery telephone set

共电路 gòngdiànlù 〈电学〉cocircuit

共电制 gòngdiànzhì 〈通信〉common-battery system; CB system

共度 gòngdù spend or pass the time together; celebrate together: ～中秋佳节 celebrate the Mid-Autumn (*or* Moon) Festival together

共轭 gòng'è 〈数学〉conjugate

共轭点 gòng'èdiǎn 〈数学〉conjugate point

共轭根 gòng'ègēn 〈数学〉conjugate root

共轭角 gòng'èjiǎo 〈数学〉conjugate angle

共轭面 gòng'èmiàn 〈数学〉conjugate surface

共轭像 gòng'èxiàng 〈物理〉conjugate image

共轭性 gòng'èxìng conjugacy; conjugation

共轭轴 gòng'èzhóu conjugate axis

共发射极 gòngfāshèjí 〈电子〉common emitter

共犯 gòngfàn 〈法律〉❶ commit a crime together; collaborate in a criminal act: 此案由两人～。The two of them joined hands in this crime. ❷ accomplice

共赴国难 gòngfù-guónàn strive together for national salvation when the fate of the country is at stake; unite to meet the national crisis

共管 gòngguǎn ❶ join hands in doing sth.; make joint efforts in managing sth.: 社会治安要全社会齐抓～。Maintaining public order requires the concerted efforts of the entire society. ❷ 〈外交〉(short for 国际共管) condominium

共和 gònghé ❶ *see* "共和行政" ❷ republicanism; republic

共和党 Gònghédǎng (US) Republican Party

共和国 gònghéguó republic: 中华人民～ the People's Republic of China

共和行政 Gònghé Xíngzhèng Joint Administration by Two Dukes in the Zhou Dynasty or Regency by Count Gonghe in lieu of the exiled King, 841-828 BC, beginning of precise contemporary chronology in Chinese history

共和制 gònghézhì republicanism

共话 gònghuà talk together

共基极 gòngjījí 〈电子〉common base

共计 gòngjì ❶ amount to; add up to; total: 面积～三万平方公里 with a total area of 30,000 square kilometres /两个项目的开支～三百万元。The expenditure for the two projects amounted to three million *yuan*. /全班～十五人。Altogether there are fifteen people in the class. ❷ discuss together; plan together: ～国家大事 discuss state affairs together

共价 gòngjià 〈化学〉covalence

共价键 gòngjiàjiàn 〈化学〉covalent bond

共焦反射镜 gòngjiāo fǎnshèjìng confocal mirror

共晶 gòngjīng 〈冶金〉eutectic: ～合金 eutectic alloy /～体 eutectic evaporate /～组织 eutectic structure

共居 gòngjū (mostly of abstract things) coexist

共聚 gòngjù 〈化学〉copolymerization: ～物 copolymer

共聚一堂 gòngjù-yītáng gather in the same hall; come together: 大家～，庆祝母校成立一百周年。Gathering together in the hall we were celebrating the centenary of the founding of our alma mater.

共勉 gòngmiǎn encourage each other (in sth.); make joint efforts: 愿与大家～。Let us encourage each other in our endeavours.

共鸣 gòngmíng ❶ 〈物理〉resonance: ～器 resonator /发生～现象。Acoustic resonance occurs. ❷ sympathetic response: 引起～ arouse sympathy; strike a sympathetic chord /诗人的爱国主义思想引起了读者的～。The patriotism of the poet got a ready response among the readers.

共栖 gòngqī 〈生物〉commensalism: ～现象 commensalism

共青城 Gòngqīngchéng Gongqingcheng — Communist Youth League City, in north Jiangxi Province

共青团 gòngqīngtuán (short for 共产主义青年团) Communist Youth League: ～员 member of the Communist Youth League; League member /～支部 branch of the Communist Youth League; League branch

共生 gòngshēng ❶〈地质〉intergrowth; paragenesis ❷〈生物〉symbiosis: ～细菌 symbiotic bacteria

共生次序 gòngshēng cìxù paragenesis

共生光谱 gòngshēng guāngpǔ symbiotic spectra

共生矿 gòngshēngkuàng mineral intergrowth

共生学 gòngshēngxué symbiotics

共识 gòngshí common understanding; consensus: 寻求～ seek common understanding /达成～ reach agreement (*or* consensus) /在这个问题上我们两方是有～的。We share our view on this matter.

共事 gòngshì work together (in the same organization); be fellow workers: 我俩在一个医院～。We two work in the same hospital. /我们～多年,彼此很熟悉。We have been colleagues for many years and know each other very well.

共通 gòngtōng ❶ universal; applicable to both or all: ～的原则 principles applicable to all; universally applicable principles ❷ common; shared: 性情急躁是两个人～的毛病。Hot temper is the common weakness of the two. *or* Both of them are hot-tempered.

共同 gòngtóng ❶ common; shared; joint: ～边界 common boundary /～行动 act in concert /～被告 joint defendant; codefendant /～账户 joint account /～关心的问题 matters of common concern; issues of common interest /毫无～之处 have nothing in common at all /～点 common ground /～的理想把我们大家紧紧地联在一起。A common ideal united all of us as one. ❷ together; jointly; in conjunction: ～战斗 fight side by side /～富裕 common prosperity /～努力 make joint efforts /～对敌 join forces to oppose the enemy /～负责 share the responsibility /～担保 joint guarantee /～主持会议 cochair a meeting

共同纲领 Gòngtóng Gānglǐng (short for 中国人民政治协商会议共同纲领) Common Programme of the Chinese People's Political Consultative Conference (1949)

共同社 Gòngtóngshè (Japan) Kyodo News Service

共同市场 Gòngtóng Shìchǎng Common Market, an informal name for the European Economic Community (EEC)

共同体 gòngtóngtǐ community: 欧洲经济～ European Economic Community (EEC)/加勒比～ Caribbean Community (CARICOM)/西非国家经济～ Economic Community of the West African States (ECOWAS) / ～法 community law

共同语言 gòngtóng yǔyán common language: 缺少～ lack common language; have different views

共析 gòngxī 〈冶金〉eutectoid: ～钢 eutectoid steel

共享 gòngxiǎng enjoy together; share: ～胜利的喜悦 share the joys of victory /～天伦之乐 enjoy family happiness together /有福～,有祸同当 share joys and sorrows; share weal and woe; stick together through thick and thin /两人～重逢的欢乐。The two of them were immersed in the happy reunion.

共享软件 gòngxiǎng ruǎnjiàn shareware

共享原则 gòngxiǎng yuánzé mutuality principle

共性 gòngxìng general character; generality: ～存在于个性之中。Generality resides in particularity.

共议 gòngyì discuss or deliberate together: ～国是 discuss state policies together

共用 gòngyòng common; shared: ～天线 common antenna /～信道 share channel /～操作系统〈计算机〉share operating system /～程序 shared routine /～存储器 shared storage; common memory /～处理机 shared processor

共用天线电视系统 gòngyòng tiānxiàn diànshì xìtǒng *also* "共天线电视系统" community antenna television system (CATV)

共有人 gòngyǒurén co-owner

共有制 gòngyǒuzhì co-ownership

共运 gòngyùn (short for 共产主义运动) communist movement

共振 gòngzhèn 〈物理〉resonance: ～器 resonator /～腔 resonant cavity /～示波器 resonoscope /～灯 resonance lamp /～态 resonances

共轴 gòngzhóu coaxial: ～圆柱〈数学〉coaxial cylinder /～圆锥 coaxial cone

共总 gòngzǒng altogether; all told; in all: 全厂～有两千人。The factory has two thousand people all told. /这几笔账～有多少? How much do all these accounts add up to?

供[1] gòng ❶ lay (offerings): 把新鲜瓜果～在灵位前 lay fresh fruits in front of the memorial tablet ❷ offerings: 蜜～ honeyed pastery as offerings /上～ lay offerings on the altar

供[2] gòng confess; admit; own up: 逼～ extort a confession; extract a confession by torture /诱～ trap a person into a confession; induce a person to make a confession /串～ act in collusion to make each other's confessions tally /翻～ withdraw a confession; take back one's testimony /口～ statement made by the accused under examination / 招～ make a confession of one's crime; confess /录～ take down a confession or testimony during an interrogation /他～出了主犯的名字。He gave the name of the chief culprit.

see also gōng

供案 gòng'àn altar table; altar

供菜 gòngcài sacrificial dish; sacrificial food

供称 gòngchēng confess; own up; admit: 该犯～作案多次。The culprit confessed that he had committed a number of crimes. /据俘虏～,敌军开小差的很多。According to the captive, many enemy soldiers have deserted.

供词 gòngcí statement made under examination; confession: 在～记录上签字 sign on the recorded confession

供奉 gòngfèng ❶ enshrine and worship; consecrate ❷ attendants, actors, etc., in the imperial palace

供果 gòngguǒ sacrificial fruit

供花 gònghuā sacrificial flower

供尖儿 gòngjiānr 〈方言〉sacrificial candied fruit (arranged in the shape of a pyramid)

供具 gòngjù sacrificial vessel

供品 gòngpǐn offerings: 桌上摆满了～。The table is loaded with offerings.

供认 gòngrèn confess: ～不讳 confess without hiding anything; candidly confess /拒不～ refuse to confess /彻底～ make a clean breast of one's crime

供事 gòngshì hold office

供献 gòngxiàn ❶ sacrifice; lay (offerings) ❷〈方言〉offerings: 菜案上摆着酒肉,这是祭神用的～。On the table are wine and meat, presented as offerings for consecration.

供香 gòngxiāng joss stick

供养 gòngyǎng make offerings to; offer sacrifices to; enshrine and worship; consecrate: ～祖先 enshrine and worship one's ancestors; offer sacrifices to one's ancestors

see also gōngyǎng

供帐 gòngzhàng 〈书面〉furnishings and curtains (for a shrine)

供职 gòngzhí hold office: 在市政府～ work in the city government

供状 gòngzhuàng written confession; deposition: 录写～ copy a written confession

供桌 gòngzhuō altar (table)

gōu

鞲 gōu

鞲鞴 gōubèi *also* "活塞" huósāi piston

篝 gōu 〈书面〉cage

篝火 gōuhuǒ bonfire; campfire: 燃起一堆～ make a bonfire/～晚会 evening party by a campfire; campfire party

篝火狐鸣 gōuhuǒ-húmíng plot a rebellion or an uprising

句 gōu

see also jù

句践 Gōujiàn Goujian (? -465 BC), king of the State of Yue (越) during the Spring and Autumn Period, known for his tenacity in adversity

枸 gōu

see also gǒu; jǔ

枸橘 gōujú *also* "枳" zhǐ trifoliate orange

G

佝 gōu

佝偻 gōulóu 〈口语〉with arched shoulder and back:～着背 hunch-backed

佝偻病 gōulóubìng rickets; rachitis:得了～ suffer from rickets

勾[1](句) gōu

❶ tick off; check ; cross out; strike out:～出正确答案 check the correct answer/把最精彩的段落～出来 tick off the most interesting passage /把他的名字～掉 cross out his name; strike his name off the register /～了这笔账 cancel the debt ❷ delineate; sketch; draw:～一个轮廓 draw an outline /～了两条曲线 draw two curves /用铅笔～出平面图 sketch (*or* trace, *or* rough out) a plan with a pencil ❸ fill up the joints of brickwork with mortar or cement; point:～墙缝 point a brick wall ❹ thicken:汤里～了点芡 add some corn starch to thicken the soup ❺ induce; evoke; arouse; call to mind:～起一腔愁绪 arouse great sorrow /～起对往事的回忆 evoke memories of the past /这句话竟～出了一大段故事来。Unexpectedly, this remark prompted a long story. ❻ collude with; gang up with; entice; inveigle:她又～上了一个男人。She has seduced yet another man. /他们臭味相投,很快就～在一起了。Birds of a feather, they soon flocked together. ❼ (Gōu) a surname

勾[2](句) gōu

〈数学〉〈古语〉shorter leg of a right triangle

see also gòu

勾扯 gōuchě 〈方言〉*see* "勾搭"

勾除 gōuchú tick off; cross off; write off; cancel

勾串 gōuchuàn collude with; gang up with:～官府 be in collusion with the local authorities

勾搭 gōuda ❶ gang up with; be in collusion with:他们是怎么～上的? How did they gang up with each other? /那家伙跟一些恶棍勾勾搭搭。That fellow works hand in glove with some gangsters. ❷ seduce; carry on (an affair) with:她和经理～上了。She has been carrying on with the manager.

勾刀 gōudāo 〈方言〉big, crooked knife

勾动 gōudòng stir up (sb.'s feeling); move; arouse; cause:～食欲 arouse (*or* whet) one's appetite /～思乡之情 make sb. homesick

勾兑 gōuduì mix different types of wine; blend

勾缝 gōufèng 〈建筑〉pointing

勾股定理 gōugǔ dìnglǐ 〈数学〉Pythagorean theorem or proposition

勾股形 gōugǔxíng 〈数学〉〈古语〉right triangle

勾挂 gōuguà drag in; involve; implicate; tie up with:这种事情怎么能跟他～起来呢? How could he get involved in such matters?

勾画 gōuhuà draw (the outline of); trace; delineate; sketch:他只用几笔就～出了一只老鹰的形象。He sketched an eagle with only a few strokes. /寥寥数语,就把山村的美丽夜色～出来了。These few sentences give a fascinating picture of a night at the mountain village. /他～了一幅工厂发展的蓝图。He drafted a blueprint for the development of the factory.

勾绘 gōuhuì draw an outline

勾魂 gōuhún bewitch; enchant; fascinate:勾掉了魂儿 be bewitched; be captivated

勾魂摄魄 gōuhún-shèpò (of a woman) have the power to bewitch men; cast a spell (on); lay an enchantment (on)

勾稽 gōujī *also* "钩稽" gōujī ❶ examine ❷ business accounting

勾践 Gōujiàn *see* "句践" Gōujiàn

勾结 gōujié act in collusion with; collude with; collaborate with; gang up with:既～又争夺 both collude and contend with each other/不法商人和贪污分子相～ lawbreaking businessmen in collusion with embezzlers /～走私犯进行文物倒卖活动 traffic in cultural relics hand in glove with smugglers

勾栏 gōulán *also* "勾阑"〈古语〉❶ theatre ❷ brothel:～女子 prostitute /沦落～ become a fallen woman

勾勒 gōulè ❶ draw the outline of; sketch the contours of; delineate:～出群山的轮廓 draw the contours of the mountains ❷ give a brief account of; sketch out; outline:～出游子思归的情怀 succinctly depict the homesickness of those travelling (*or* staying) abroad

勾连 gōulián *also* "勾联" ❶ gang up with; collude with:暗中～ be in secret collusion /这些人～在一起干坏事。These people ganged up to do evil. ❷ drag in; involve; implicate:这件抢劫案与他有～。He was involved in the robbery.

勾脸 gōuliǎn (in traditional Chinese opera) paint the face; make up the face

勾留 gōuliú stop over; break one's journey; stay:在京～数日 stop over in Beijing for several days; have a stopover of several days at Beijing

勾描 gōumiáo draw the outline of; sketch; delineate:用细线条把景物的轮廓～出来 outline the landscape with fine lines

勾芡 gōuqiàn thicken (with starch):用淀粉给汤～ use starch to thicken the soup

勾曲 gōuqū winding; crooked; bending:他的鼻子有点儿～。His nose is a little bit crooked.

勾惹 gōurě offend; provoke; tease:你别～他。Don't rub him the wrong way. *or* Don't provoke him.

勾摄 gōushè 〈书面〉order the accused to appear in court; summon; arrest:～入狱 put in prison; send to jail

勾手 gōushǒu 〈方言〉gang up with each other:他们早就勾了手了。They have long been working in collusion.

勾通 gōutōng collude; work hand in glove:两个学生在考场上～作弊。The two students worked together to cheat in the examination.

勾头 gōutóu (of rice's or wheat's ripe ears) droop

勾销 gōuxiāo cancel; write off; strike out; nullify:～欠款 cancel a debt /一笔～ write off at one stroke /～宿怨 sink a feud; bury the hatchet

勾心斗角 gōuxīn-dòujiǎo *also* "钩心斗角" gōuxīn-dòujiǎo scheme against each other

勾乙 gōuyǐ tick off; check; mark

勾引 gōuyǐn ❶ tempt; entice; seduce; lure:～无知的少女 seduce innocent girls ❷ induce; evoke; call to mind:他的话～起我的伤心事。His words evoked memories of my past miseries.

勾针 gōuzhēn *also* "钩针" gōuzhēn crochet hook

沟(溝) gōu

❶ ditch; drain; channel; trench:排水～ drainage ditch; drain /交通～ communication trench /水～ ditch; drain /阴～ sewer; sewerage; covered drain /明～ ditch; open sewer /挖了一道很深的～ dig a very deep ditch ❷ groove; rut; gutter; furrow:开～播种 make furrows for sowing /垄～ field ditch /～～坎坎的 rugged and rough /大车在泥路上碾出了两道～。The cart made two ruts in the muddy road. ❸ waterway; gullet; gully:乱石～ boulder-strewn gully /山～ gully; ravine; (mountain) valley /小溪～ brook

沟播 gōubō 〈农业〉trench sowing; gutter-sowing:～机 lister planter /～中耕机 lister cultivator

沟渎 gōudú 〈书面〉irrigation ditch:开通～ dredge an irrigation canal

沟沟坎坎 gōugōu-kǎnkǎn 〈口语〉setback; reverse:人一辈子总得遇到一些～。One's path in life will not always be smooth (*or* strewn with roses).

沟谷 gōugǔ ravine; valley

沟灌 gōuguàn 〈农业〉furrow irrigation

沟壕 gōuháo trench; ditch

沟壑 gōuhè gully; ravine:～纵横 crisscross gullies

沟坎 gōukǎn ditch; trench:跳过一道～ jump over a ditch

沟堑 gōuqiàn ditch; trench

沟渠 gōuqú irrigation canals and ditches:～交错 crisscross of irrigation canals and ditches

沟施 gōushī *also* "条施" tiáoshī 〈农业〉apply fertilizer in furrows

沟蚀 gōushí deep gully cut by flowing water

沟鼠 gōushǔ 〈动物〉*Rattus norvegicus*

沟通 gōutōng link up; connect; join:～南北的铁路 railway connecting the south and the north /～思想 get to know each other's viewpoints better; exchange ideas /～感情 cultivate friendship /～信息 exchange information; facilitate the flow of information /～两国文化的使者 envoy who promotes cultural exchanges between two countries

沟洫 gōuxù 〈书面〉ditch; irrigation canal

沟沿儿 gōuyánr bank of a ditch or canal

沟眼 gōuyǎn mouth of a channel; open end of a ditch

沟栽 gōuzāi 〈农业〉trench transplanting

沟圳 gōuzhèn 〈方言〉ditch; irrigation canal

沟植 gōuzhí 〈农业〉trench planting

G

沟子 gōuzi 〈方言〉ditch; gutter; gully
沟作 gōuzuò 〈农业〉trench culture

钩(鉤) gōu ❶ hook:鱼～ fishhook /挂衣～ clothes-hook /秤～儿 steelyard hook /火～儿 poker /吊～〈机械〉hook; hanger /窗～ window catch /鱼上～了。The fish has swallowed (*or* taken) the bait. ❷ hook stroke (in Chinese characters, e.g. 亅、乛、㇂、乚) ❸ check; mark; tick:给正确答案打上～儿 check the correct answer /按名单在人名前一一打～ check off the names on the list /在表格的方块处打～ tick (*or* check) the box on the form ❹ secure with a hook; hook:～肩搭背 bend one's arm round sb.'s shoulder /他的裤脚给钉子～住了。The bottom of his trouser leg caught on a nail. /他弯脚～住小凳,把它挪到身旁。He hooked his foot under the stool, drawing it nearer to himself. ❺ explore; search after:～深致远 seek the profound truth ❻ crochet:～花边 crochet lace; tat ❼ sew with large stitches:～贴边 sew on an edging ❽ spoken form of the numeral 九 ❾ (Gōu) a surname

钩编 gōubiān crocheting:～织品 crocheting
钩沉 gōuchén seek a profound truth; try to find what has been lost (as a book, etc.):《古小说～》*Rediscovering Lost Ancient Novels*
钩秤 gōuchèng steelyard
钩尺 gōuchǐ a kind of calipers, used to measure the small end of a log
钩虫 gōuchóng hookworm:～病 hookworm disease; ancylostomiasis
钩虫性贫血 gōuchóngxìng pínxuè ancylostomo-anemia
钩端螺旋体病 gōuduān luóxuántǐbìng leptospirosis
钩稽 gōujī *also* "勾稽" gōujī ❶ examine; try to ascertain:～文坛故实 try to find out about past events in literary circles ❷ business accounting
钩接式仪表 gōujiēshì yíbiǎo hook-on instrument; hook-on type meter
钩链 gōuliàn hook chain; hook link chain
钩式运输机 gōushì yùnshūjī hook conveyer
钩头螺栓 gōutóu luóshuān hooked bolt
钩吻 gōuwěn 〈植物〉gelsemium; elegant jessamine
钩心斗角 gōuxīn-dòujiǎo *also* "勾心斗角" gōuxīn-dòujiǎo intrigue against each other; jockey for position:两党～之事层出不穷。Schemes and intrigues were a common occurrence between the two political parties.
钩形扳手 gōuxíng bānshou hook key; hook spanner; hook wrench
钩玄 gōuxuán 〈书面〉seek profound truth; explore the essence:～提要 explore the essence and explain the gist
钩针 gōuzhēn *also* "勾针" gōuzhēn crochet hook
钩子 gōuzi ❶ hook ❷ hook-shaped thing:蝎子的～有毒。A scorpion's sting is poisonous.
钩嘴 gōuzuǐ hooked bill; beak
钩嘴鹛 gōuzuǐméi 〈动物〉scimiter babbler

缑 gōu ❶〈书面〉string round the hilt of a sword or knife ❷ (Gōu) a surname

gǒu

苟[1](❷茍) gǒu ❶ casual; careless; thoughtless; negligent:一丝不～ be scrupulous about every detail; be conscientious and meticulous /不～言笑 be discreet in speech and manner; be solemn and prudent /不敢～同 can hardly agree ❷ (Gǒu) a surname

苟[2] gǒu 〈书面〉provided; if:～不努力,必将落后。If you do not exert yourself, you will surely lag behind. /～能幸免于死,则将终生铭感。Should you spare my life, I will remain deeply grateful to you for the rest of my life.

苟安 gǒu'ān seek momentary peace; be contented with temporary ease and comfort; live in a fool's paradise:～一时 seek security for a time /只图～,不思进取 seek temporary ease with no idea of making further progress
苟存 gǒucún 〈书面〉just manage to survive:幸得～,已成残废。He made a narrow escape, but was disabled for life.
苟得 gǒudé 〈书面〉obtain without effort or justification; gain easy possession of:临财毋～。Don't accept easy money.
苟合 gǒuhé illicit sexual relations
苟合取容 gǒuhé-qǔróng echo other people's view in order to curry favour with them
苟活 gǒuhuó drag out an ignoble existence; live on in degradation:隐忍～ bear the burden of an ignoble life
苟简 gǒujiǎn 〈书面〉slipshod; unduly brief or simple:文章写得过于～。The article is crude and hastily written.
苟利子 gǒulìzi 〈方言〉❶ puppet show; puppet play ❷ puppet; marionette:耍～的 person who manipulates a puppet; person who gives a puppet show; puppeteer
苟免 gǒumiǎn 〈书面〉seek temporary security; seek escape from immediate danger:临难毋～。Don't shy away from your duty when in danger.
苟且 gǒuqiě ❶ drift along; muddle on; be resigned to circumstances:～度日 muddle along /因循～ follow the beaten path and live a purposeless life ❷ perfunctorily; casually; carelessly:～了事 dispose of sth. perfunctorily /他一向工作认真,分毫不肯～。Serious and precise, he has never done any shoddy work. ❸ illicit (sexual relations):～结合 illicit love affair; liaison
苟且偷安 gǒuqiě-tōu'ān rest content with temporary ease and comfort; seek a moment's peace without any thought of the future:大敌当前,切不可～。Faced with a strong enemy, we should not try to seek an ignoble peace.
苟且偷生 gǒuqiě-tōushēng live merely for the sake of living; live in shame; drag out an ignoble existence:生命诚然可贵,但不可～。Life is precious, but one should not live just for the sake of remaining alive.
苟全 gǒuquán preserve (one's own life) without any sense of purpose
苟全性命 gǒuquán-xìngmìng just manage to survive:～于乱世,不求闻达于诸侯 merely try to preserve one's life in times of turbulence and have no intention of seeking fame and position from princes
苟同 gǒutóng 〈书面〉(often used in the negative) agree without giving serious thought; readily subscribe to (other people's views):你的意见我未敢～。I could hardly agree with you.
苟延 gǒuyán prolong with difficulty:～生命 prolong (*or* drag out) one's feeble existence
苟延残喘 gǒuyán-cánchuǎn be on one's last legs; drag out a feeble existence; linger on in a steadily worsening condition:在这种情况下～,比死更可怕。Under such circumstances, death is better than a wretched existence.

枸 gǒu
see also gōu; jǔ
枸骨 gǒugǔ 〈植物〉Chinese holly
枸骨叶 gǒugǔyè 〈中药〉holly leaf
枸杞 gǒuqǐ Chinese wolfberry (*Lycium chinensis*)
枸杞子 gǒuqǐzǐ 〈中药〉fruit of Chinese wolfberry

岣 gǒu
岣嵝 Gǒulǒu (another name for 衡山) Hengshan Mountain (in Hunan Province)

笱 gǒu 〈方言〉basket trap for fish

狗 gǒu *also* "犬" quǎn dog:猎～ hunting dog; hound /丧家～ homeless dog; stray dog /哈巴～儿 Pekingese /疯～ mad dog /狼～ wolfhound /癞皮～ mangy dog /走～ running dog /狼心～肺 rapacious as a wolf and savage as a cur /～东西 cur; son of a bitch /城市不宜养～。It isn't advisable to raise dogs in cities.

狗宝 gǒubǎo 〈中药〉stone of a dog's gallbladder, kidney or bladder
狗蹦子 gǒubèngzi 〈方言〉❶ flea ❷ mischievous person
狗不嫌家贫 gǒu bù xián jiā pín dogs do not shun a poor home:～,子不嫌娘丑。As a dog does not shun a home however poor, a son does not loathe his mother, however plain.
狗吃屎 gǒuchīshǐ 〈戏谑〉fall flat on the face; fall down heavily:跌了个～ stumble and fall flat on one's face

G

狗胆包天 gǒudǎn-bāotiān monstrous audacity; sheer impudence: 这小偷儿～，竟敢到公安局里去行窃。The thief must be as bold as brass to steal from the public security bureau.
狗颠屁股 gǒudiān-pìgu dog wagging its behind — be obsequious; fawn; toady
狗窦 gǒudòu hole in the wall for a dog to get in and out
狗吠不惊 gǒufèi-bùjīng no one is alarmed when dogs bark — social stability and peace
狗吠之惊 gǒufèizhījīng *also* "狗吠之警" alarm at the barking of dogs — social unrest: 国中无～。The country remains peaceful and stable.
狗苟蝇营 gǒugǒu-yíngyíng *also* "蝇营狗苟" ingratiate oneself with sb. to gain one's ends; shamelessly seek personal gains: ～事可羞。It is a shame to seek personal gains without scruple.
狗獾 gǒuhuān *also* "獾" badger
狗急跳墙 gǒují-tiàoqiáng a dog will leap over a wall in desperation; a cornered beast will turn at bay; despair gives courage even to a coward: 俗话说，～，人急造反。As the saying goes, a cornered beast will turn at bay and a cornered person will rise in rebellion.
狗脊蕨 gǒujǐjué 〈植物〉chain fern (*Woodwardia japonica*)
狗木 gǒumù dogwood (*Cornus*)
狗拿耗子，多管闲事 gǒu ná hàozi, duō guǎn xiánshì like a dog trying to catch mice — poke one's nose into other people's business; be a busibody; be too meddlesome
狗刨 gǒupáo *also* "狗爬式" dog paddle
狗碰头 gǒupèngtóu 〈方言〉coffin of poor quality
狗皮膏药 gǒupí gāoyao ❶〈中药〉dogskin plaster (for curing rheumatism, strains, contusions, etc., formerly spread on dogskin, but now usu. on cloth) ❷ quack medicine; fake stuff: 卖～ fob things off on people; practise quackery
狗屁 gǒupì 〈粗话〉boloney; bullshit; rubbish; nonsense: 放你的～! Stop that nonsense! *or* Cut the crap! /～! Bullshit! *or* Shit!
狗屁不通 gǒupì-bùtōng unreadable rubbish; mere trash: 文章～。The article is a load of garbage.
狗屁文章 gǒupì wénzhāng stodgy and worthless article: 他写了点～，就自诩为作家。It is presumptuous of him to proclaim himself a writer on the basis of some unreadable trash of his.
狗气杀 gǒuqìshā 〈方言〉container used to feed chickens (which is somewhat like a birdcage making it difficult for a dog to take food from it)
狗屎 gǒushǐ dog's droppings — worthless stuff: ～不如 utterly worthless /一堆臭～ a pack of disgusting (*or* revolting, *or* repulsive) people
狗屎堆 gǒushǐduī heap of dog's droppings; pile of dog's dung: 不齿于人类的～ filthy and contemptible as dog's dung; spurned by the people as utterly reprehensible
狗头军师 gǒutóu-jūnshī person who offers bad advice; inept adviser; villainous adviser
狗腿子 gǒutuǐzi 〈口语〉hired thug; lackey; flunkey; henchman
狗尾草 gǒuwěicǎo *also* "莠" yǒu 〈植物〉green bristlegrass (*Setaria viridis*)
狗尾续貂 gǒuwěi-xùdiāo dog's tail joined to a marten — a wretched sequel to a fine literary work
狗窝 gǒuwō kennel; doghouse; 〈谦词〉one's humble home: 金窝，银窝，不如家里～。A house built of gold or silver cannot compare with my own humble home. *or* East or west, home is best.
狗血喷头 gǒuxuè-pēntóu *also* "狗血淋头" pour invective upon sb.'s head: 骂得～ let loose a stream of abuse against sb.; pour out a torrent of invective against sb.; heap curses on sb.
狗熊 gǒuxióng ❶ black bear ❷ coward; good-for-nothing: 你真～，占理的事儿也不敢说! What a coward you are! You backed off even when you were right. *or* You were too much of a coward to say it even when right was on your side.
狗眼看人低 gǒuyǎn kàn rén dī 〈贬义〉be damned snobbish; act like a snob: 人不可貌相，你别～。You cannot judge people by their appearance. Don't be snobbish.
狗咬狗 gǒuyǎogǒu dog-eat-dog: 资本主义社会是～的社会。It is a dog-eat-dog society under capitalism.
狗咬吕洞宾 gǒu yǎo Lǚ Dòngbīn snarl and snap at Lü Dongbin (one of the eight immortals in Chinese mythology) — mistake a good man for a bad one: ～，不识好人心。Like the dog that bit Lü Dongbin, you bite the hand that feeds you.
狗蝇 gǒuyíng dog louse fly
狗鱼 gǒuyú 〈动物〉pike (*Esox reicherti*)
狗杂种 gǒuzázhong 〈粗话〉bastard
狗崽子 gǒuzǎizi ❶〈粗话〉pup; puppy ❷ son of a bitch
狗蚤 gǒuzǎo dog flea
狗占马槽 gǒuzhànmǎcáo 〈比喻〉dog in the manger
狗仗人势 gǒuzhàngrénshì 〈粗话〉like a dog threatening people on the strength of its master's power — be a bully with the support of a powerful person: 这些爪牙们～，横行乡里。Backed by their powerful master, these thugs are playing the bully in the village.
狗彘 gǒuzhì dogs and swine
狗彘不若 gǒuzhì-bùruò *also* "狗彘不如" worse than a cur or swine; utterly despicable
狗子 gǒuzi 〈方言〉❶ dog ❷〈贬义〉bastard: 特务～ that bastard of a spy
狗嘴里吐不出象牙 gǒuzuǐlǐ tǔbuchū xiàngyá no ivory can come out of a dog's mouth; a filthy mouth can't utter decent language; what can you expect from a dog but a bark: 别听他的，～，他还能有什么好话? Don't listen to him. You can't expect anything nice from his foul mouth.

耇(耈) gǒu 〈书面〉old age; long life; longevity

gòu

菁 gòu 〈书面〉depths of a mansion or a palace

遘 gòu 〈书面〉meet; come across; encounter: ～患 meet one's misfortune; get into trouble

搆 gòu

搆陷 gòuxiàn frame (sb.) up
see also "构陷" gòuxiàn

覯 gòu 〈书面〉meet: 罕～ rarely seen

媾 gòu 〈书面〉❶ wed: 婚～ marriage ❷ reach agreement; make peace; become reconciled: *see* "～和" ❸ coition: 交～ copulate

媾合 gòuhé 〈书面〉copulation; sexual intercourse
媾和 gòuhé make peace: 单独～ make a separate peace /双方都有～的愿望。Both sides had the wish to make peace.
媾疫 gòuyì 〈兽医〉(as of horses) dourine

彀[1] gòu draw a bow to the full

彀[2] gòu *see* "够" gòu

彀中 gòuzhōng 〈书面〉shooting range; snare; trap: 天下英雄尽入吾～。The talented people of the country have all come under my control (*or* fallen into my trap).

诟 gòu 〈书面〉❶ shame; disgrace; humiliation: ～耻 shame; humiliation ❷ rebuke; reprimand; talk abusively: 世人～之 be reviled by the public

诟病 gòubìng 〈书面〉censure; denounce; condemn; castigate: 为世～ become an object of public condemnation
诟厉 gòulì 〈书面〉scold; censure
诟詈 gòulì 〈书面〉abuse; insult; berate
诟骂 gòumà 〈书面〉revile; bawl out; abuse; vilify: 当众～ vilify in public /竟敢～上司 even dare to abuse one's boss
诟辱 gòurǔ 〈书面〉insult; humiliate

垢 gòu ❶〈书面〉soiled; dirty; filthy: 蓬头～面 with dishevelled hair and dirty face /藏～纳污 shelter evil people and countenance evil practice ❷ dirt; filth; stain: 牙～ dental calculus; tartar /满身油～ with grease stains all over one's clothes /尘～ dust and dirt; dirt /耳～ earwax /水～ scale; incrustation ❸〈书面〉insult; disgrace; humiliation: 含～忍辱 endure humiliation and insult; swallow insults /受天下之～ be humiliated by the public

垢泥 gòuní deposit of sweat, dirt and oil on the skin; dirt; filth

垢腻 gòunì ❶ dust; dirt; grease:墙上满是～。The wall is covered with dirt and grease. ❷ dirty; filthy

垢污 gòuwū filth; dirt:清除～ get rid of the dirt

姤 gòu 〈书面〉❶ meet; encounter ❷ virtue; benevolence

雊 gòu 〈书面〉crowing of a male pheasant

够(夠) gòu ❶ enough; sufficient; adequate:你们那里人力～不～? Have you got enough manpower? /这些钱～他养家的。The money is adequate (*or* sufficient) to support his family. /这房间我们俩住,～大的了。The room is big enough for the two of us. /材料～我们用一阵子了。These materials will last us for a while. /分量～不～? Did you give me full measure? ❷ quite; rather; really:这部电影～刺激的。It's really an exciting film. /房间～大的。The room is quite spacious. /我累得真～受的。I'm tired out. /天～热的。What a hot day! ❸ reach (sth. by stretching):你能～得着书架上那本字典吗? Can you reach the dictionary on the shelf? /我站在桌子上才能～到天花板。I can't reach the ceiling unless I stand on the desk. ❹ reach or be up to (a certain standard, etc.):他当兵～条件。He is eligible for military service. /这些学员当数学教师还不～资格。These trainees are not yet qualified to be teachers of mathematics.

够本 gòuběn ❶ make enough money to cover the cost; break even; get one's money's worth:这个价格还不～呢。The price is not high enough to cover the cost. /这件衬衣我可穿～儿了。I've got my money's worth out of this shirt. ❷ gains and losses balance each other; be quits or even:我豁出去了,杀一个鬼子～,杀两个就赚了。I'm ready to risk everything. If I kill one enemy soldier, then we are even; if I kill two, I'll make a profit.

够不上 gòubushàng be not qualified; be not up to the standard; fall short of:模范教师他还～。He falls short of the requirements of a model teacher.

够不着 gòubuzháo cannot reach; be unable to get:衣服挂得太高,我～。Hanging high, the clothes were out of my reach.

够得上 gòudeshàng be qualified; be up to the standard:他～一个出色的企业家。He has all the qualifications of an outstanding entrepreneur.

够得着 gòudezháo be able to reach:我站在椅子上才能～那扇窗子。I could reach that window only if I stood on a chair.

够格 gòugé be qualified; be up to standard:产品改进后,出口～了。The improved products met the requirements for export. /我当教练不～。I'm not qualified to be a coach.

够过儿 gòuguòr just enough to make both ends meet:他凑合着～。He managed to scrape a living.

够交情 gòu jiāoqing ❶ profound friendship ❷ *see* "够朋友"

够缴裹儿 gòu jiǎoguor 〈方言〉make enough money to cover daily expenses:他这点收入哪够全家缴裹儿。He couldn't make enough money to support his family.

够劲儿 gòujìnr ❶ (of an onerous task, etc.) almost unbearable; too much:最近工作太多,他忙得～。He really has a hard time recently for having such a heavy work load. /她身单力薄,搬这么个大箱子,我看～。She is thin and weak. I don't think she can manage to carry the big box. ❷ strong (in taste, strength, etc.):这酒真～。The liquor is really strong. /这菜辣得真～。The food is really hot. /天冷得～。It's biting cold.

够面子 gòu miànzi enjoy due respect or honour:他这事办得～。He handled the matter in style.

够派 gòupài ❶ stylish; impressive; cool:他出门非坐小汽车才觉得～。To be impressive, he has to ride in a car whenever going out. /她找的那个对象还真～。Her boyfriend looks real cool. ❷ be qualified:坐软卧你还不～。You are not yet qualified to travel in a sleeping carriage with soft berths.

够朋友 gòu péngyou be worthy of the name of a true friend; be a friend indeed:他一点小事也不帮忙,真不～! He didn't even lift a finger to help. How can we call him a friend?

够呛 gòuqiàng *also* "够呛"〈方言〉quite the limit; unbearable; terrible:累得～ dog tired /热得～ excessively hot; unbearably hot /吃的东西真～ appalling food /天气真～。What awful weather! /我这几天忙得～! I have been terribly busy these days.

够瞧的 gòuqiáode awful; really too much:天闷热得真～。What a sultry day! /两口子又吵起来了,真～。It's awful to see the couple quarrelling again. /雨真大,淋得我～! What a pouring rain! I was drenched to the skin.

够受的 gòushòude quite an ordeal; hardly endurable:他这一跤摔得真～。He had a really bad fall. /早饭吃得少,现在饿得真～! I had a light breakfast and feel famished now.

够数 gòushù ❶ enough to make up the required number; sufficient in quantity; enough:你领的铅笔还不～。You didn't get enough pencils to go round. ❷〈方言〉be up to a certain standard:这孩子机灵得～。The child is really smart.

够损的 gòusǔnde (of words) bitterly sarcastic; (of behaviour) tart and mean:他这人说话真～。His remarks are caustic. /这人真～。What a mean fellow!

够味儿 gòuwèir just the right flavour; just the thing; quite satisfactory; really good:她京剧唱得很～。The way she sings Beijing opera is just superb. /龙井茶喝起来真～。Dragonwell tea is exactly to my taste. /这酒不太～。This wine tastes somewhat insipid. /这部小说写得挺～。This novel is really fascinating. /这首诗可不～。This is a rather mediocre poem.

够意思 gòu yìsi ❶ up to a high standard; really something; quite good; terrific:这篇评论说得头头是道,真～。This well-argued commentary is really excellent. /今晚的节目～! Tonight's show is terrific. ❷ generous; friendly; really kind:你这人可真不～! You are not much of a friend (*or* a gentleman), are you?

勾(句) gòu ❶〈旧语〉*see* "够" gòu ❷ (Gòu) a surname

see also gōu

勾当 gòudang 〈贬义〉business; transaction; deal:罪恶～ criminal activities /肮脏～ dirty deal /卑鄙～ shameful (*or* mean) trick /不可告人的～ business under the counter; unseemly dealings /违法乱纪的～ illegal undertakings

构[1](構) gòu ❶ construct; form; build; compose:～词 form a word /结～ structure; composition; construction /～木为巢 construct a wooden hutch on a tree ❷ fabricate; invent; make up:纯属虚～ sheer (*or* downright) fabrication ❸ literary composition:佳～ good piece of writing

构[2](構) gòu 〈植物〉paper mulberry

构兵 gòubīng 〈书面〉resort to arms; be at war; fight:两国～。The two countries are at war.

构成 gòuchéng constitute; form; compose; pose; make up:～威胁 pose a threat /～多数 make up a majority /～对别国内政的干涉 constitute an interference in the internal affairs of other countries /～不安定因素 be a distabilizing factor /土壤的～ composition of the soil /整个建筑由三个部分～。The whole building comprises three parts. /研究所的人员～不尽合理。The research institute is not well-structured in terms of its staff members.

构成主义 gòuchéngzhǔyì 〈美术〉constructivism; constructionism

构词法 gòucífǎ 〈语言〉word-building; word-formation

构架 gòujià structural frame; framework; skeleton; frame:钢筋水泥～ framework of reinforced concrete /这个计划的～很好。This plan is well-framed.

构件 gòujiàn (structural) member; component part:优质～ quality component / 尚需部分～ still need some component parts

构建 gòujiàn (usu. used in connection with abstract things) set up; establish; construct:～新的教育体系 establish a new educational system

构思 gòusī work out the plot of a literary work or the composition of a painting; conceive; construct:～长篇小说 construct a novel /～得相当精巧 be ingeniously conceived /文章～新颖。The article is original in conception.

构图 gòutú 〈美术〉composition (of a picture):～完美 perfect composition /灵巧新奇的～ ingenious and novel composition

构陷 gòuxiàn *also* "搆陷" gòuxiàn make false charges (against sb.); frame (sb.) up; set up:～忠良 make false charges against loyal officials /～好人 frame up innocent people /受人～ be set up

构想 gòuxiǎng ❶ work out the plot of a literary work or the composition of a painting; conceive; construct:这部小说,～和行文都不高明。The novel is mediocre in both conception and execution. ❷ idea; concept; plan; scheme:提出体制改革的～ put forward a plan for structural reforms /"一国两制"的～ concept of "one country,

two systems"
构象 gòuxiàng 〈化学〉conformation
构衅 gòuxìn 〈书面〉provoke a quarrel; start a feud; engender enmity
构型 gòuxíng configuration：～作用 configuration interaction
构怨 gòuyuàn 〈书面〉feud with; incur hatred：两家～很深。The two families have been at feud with each other for a long time.
构造 gòuzào structure; construction;〈地质〉tectonism：分子～ molecule structure / 句子～ sentence construction / 人体～ structure of the human body / ～要素 structural element / ～次序 structural generation / 地质～ geological structure / 地层～ stratigraphic structure / 这种机器～精密。This machine is precise in construction.
构造板块 gòuzào bǎnkuài tectonic plate
构造地震 gòuzào dìzhèn tectonic earthquake
构造地质学 gòuzào dìzhìxué structural geology; tectonics
构造物理学 gòuzào wùlǐxué tectonophysics
构造学 gòuzàoxué tectonics
构造运动 gòuzào yùndòng tectonic movement; tectogenesis
构造主义 gòuzàozhǔyì 〈心理〉structuralism
构置 gòuzhì ❶ arrange; decorate; lay out：精心～的店铺 ingeniously decorated shop ❷ compose; design; construct：～情节 weave a plot
构筑 gòuzhù construct; build：～碉堡 build a fort / ～工事 construct field works (*or* fortifications); build defences; dig in
构筑物 gòuzhùwù 〈建筑〉structure

购(購) gòu purchase; buy：～粮 purchase grain / 赊～ buy on credit / 采～ make purchases for an organization or enterprise; purchase / 代～ buy on sb.'s behalf / 函～ purchase by mail / 套～ illegally buy up / 统～ (of the state) monopolize the purchase (of grain, cotton, etc.) / 预～ purchase in advance / 订～ place an order / 抢～ be on a rush to purchase; panic buying / 认～国库券 subscribe for state treasury bonds / ～进大批化肥 buy a lot of chemical fertilizer
购办 gòubàn purchase; buy：～家具 purchase furniture
购备 gòubèi purchase in advance; buy beforehand：～旅途用品 buy necessities for one's travel
购货本 gòuhuòběn ration book or card for purchase of non-essential food stuffs (under a command economy)
购货单 gòuhuòdān order form; order：～应妥为保存。The order forms should be properly kept.
购货券 gòuhuòquàn ration coupon
购粮证 gòuliángzhèng grain supply book or card (for purchase of grains under a command economy)
购买 gòumǎi purchase; buy：～书籍 buy books / ～文具 buy stationery / ～房地产 purchase real estate / ～公债 purchase government bonds / ～信号 buying signal
购买力 gòumǎilì purchasing power：机关～ institutional purchasing power / 实际～ real purchasing power / 提高～ raise the purchasing power
购买力平价 gòumǎilì píngjià purchasing power parity (PPP)：～论 purchasing power parity doctrine / 以～计算 in terms of purchasing power parity
购买税 gòumǎishuì purchase tax
购募 gòumù 〈书面〉offer a reward (for sth.)
购物袋 gòuwùdài (UK) carrier bag; (US) shopping bag
购物赠券 gòuwù zèngquàn trading stamp
购物中心 gòuwù zhōngxīn shopping centre
购销 gòu-xiāo purchase and sale; buying and selling：～两旺 brisk buying and selling / ～持平 balanced purchase and sale / ～失调 imbalance of buying and selling
购置 gòuzhì purchase (durables)：～家电 purchase electrical household appliances / ～田产 buy real estate

gū

家 gū *see* "阿家阿翁" āgū-āwēng
see also jiā; jie

毂 gū
see also gǔ
毂辘 gūlu *see* "轱辘" gūlu

沽[1] gū 〈书面〉❶ purchase; buy：～酒待客 buy wine to entertain a guest ❷ sell：待价而～ wait to sell at a good price; wait for the highest bid

沽[2] Gū another name for Tianjin
沽名钓誉 gūmíng-diàoyù fish for fame and compliments：～之徒 people who angle for fame (*or* court publicity)

辜 gū ❶ guilt; crime：滥杀无～ indiscriminately kill innocent people / 罪大恶极，死有余～ deserve more than death for one's heinous crimes ❷〈书面〉abandon; betray：～恩背义 perfidious; unfaithful ❸ (Gū) a surname
辜负 gūfù let down; fail to live up to; be unworthy of; disappoint：不～人民的期望 live up to the expectations of the people / ～群众的信任 be unworthy of the trust the masses place in one; let the masses down / 看来我只有～你们的好意了。I'm afraid I have to decline your kind offer. / 你怎么能～大家的一片心意呢? How could you disappoint the hopes we place in you? / 我觉得自己～了他的一片苦心。I felt I had failed him.

酤 gū 〈书面〉❶ weak wine ❷ buy (wine) ❸ sell (wine)：女主人当垆～酒。The hostess sells the wine herself in the wineshop.

轱 gū
轱辘 gūlu *also* "轱轳"; "毂辘" gūlu ❶〈口语〉wheel：车～ wheel of a vehicle / 汽车坏了一个～。One of the car's wheels is out of order. ❷ turn; roll：～～转 turn over and over / 油桶～远了。The oil drum rolled a long way.
轱辘鞋 gūluxié roller skates

咕 gū 〈象声〉(of hens, etc.) cluck; (of turtledoves, etc.) coo
咕哧 gūchi ❶〈象声〉squelch：他在泥地里～～地走着。He was squelching in the mud. ❷〈方言〉talk in a low voice：他们俩悄悄地～了半天。The two of them have been whispering to each other for a long time.
咕嗒 gūda 〈象声〉gurgle; gulp：他～一下子就把一杯酒喝下去了。He gulped down a glass of wine.
咕叨 gūdao ❶ talk on and on; chatter away：她总是没完没了地～。She never stops chattering. ❷ talk to oneself; think aloud：我心里在～，他准是不在家。I figured that he couldn't be at home.
咕噔 gūdēng 〈象声〉thud; plump; thump：他一时心头火起，～跺了一下脚。He flew into a temper and stamped his foot on the floor. / 他拎起小水桶，～～喝了一顿。Holding the small bucket, he began to gulp down the water in it.
咕咚 gūdōng 〈象声〉thud; splash; plump：大石头～一声掉到水里去了。The rock fell into the water with a splash.
咕嘟 gūdū 〈象声〉bubble; gurgle; gulp：锅里的粥～～响。The porridge bubbled in the pot. / 他～～地喝完了一碗水。He drank up a bowl of water at a few gulps.
咕嘟 gūdu ❶ boil or stew for a long time：海带早就～烂了。The kelp is overcooked. / 肉～了半天也没烂。The meat is still very tough though stewed for quite some time. ❷ purse (one's lips); pout：她生气了，～着嘴。She pursed her lips in a sulk.
咕咕 gūgū 〈象声〉(of hens, etc.) cluck; (of turtledoves, etc.) coo：鸽子～地叫。The pigeons were cooing. / 我肚子饿得～地响。I'm so hungry that my stomach keeps rumbling.
咕咕 gūgu ❶ speak or say in a low voice; whisper：这是别人在你耳朵底下瞎～的吧? You have heard it from a whisper, haven't you? ❷ instigate; incite; abet：受人～做错事 be incited to wrongdoing
咕唧 gūjī *also* "咕叽"〈象声〉squelch：他～～地走在泥泞的路上。He was squelching down the muddy road.
咕唧 gūji *also* "咕叽" whisper; murmur; mumble (to oneself)：两个小家伙在一起～了半天。The two boys whispered to each other for quite some time. / 他边走边～。He mumbled while he was walking.
咕隆 gūlōng *also* "咕隆隆"〈象声〉rumble; rattle; roll：大车～～地在公路上走着。The cart rattled along the road. / ～～的雷声响个不停。Thunder kept rumbling.

G

咕噜 gūlū *also* "咕噜噜"〈象声〉rumble; roll: 饥肠～～地响 stomach rumbling with hunger /～～地漱口 gargle one's mouth /一块大石头～～地滚到山下去了。A big rock went rolling down the mountain.
咕噜 gūlu *see* "咕哝"
咕哝 gūnong murmur; mutter; grumble: 他～了几句话，我也没听懂。He mumbled a few words, which I didn't quite catch. /你～什么呢? What are you muttering about? /他为提职的事在我面前～了好半天。He grumbled to me for quite some time about his promotion.
咕容 gūrong 〈方言〉(of a snake, etc.) wriggle: 小蛇慢慢地向前～。The small snake slowly wriggled its way forward.

蛄

gū *see* "蝼蛄" huìgū; "蝼蛄" lóugū
see also gǔ

估

gū estimate; assess; appraise; reckon: ～一～损失多少 assess the damages /低～市场的潜力 underestimate the potential of the market /评～ judge and assess /你能～一～这箱苹果有几斤吗? Can you tell how many *jin* of apples there are in this box?
see also gù
估产 gūchǎn ❶ estimate the yield (of a crop) ❷ appraise the assets; assess
估堆儿 gūduīr estimate the number or value of commodities in a heap: 这些土豆可以～卖。These potatoes could be sold by the heap.
估划 gūhua 〈方言〉estimate; appraise; reckon: 我～他来不了了。I don't think he will be able to come.
估计 gūjì estimate; appraise; take into account; calculate; reckon: 乐观的～ optimistic estimate/保守的～ conservative estimate/错误～ miscalculate /事情的结局很难～。It is hard to anticipate the outcome of the affair. /把对方实力～得过高 overestimate the strength of the opposite side /这种可能性我们必须～到。We must take that possibility into account. *or* That is a possibility to be reckoned with. /我～我们能超额完成任务。I think (*or* reckon) we can overfulfil our task.
估计成本 gūjì chéngběn estimated cost
估计风险 gūjì fēngxiǎn calculated risk
估计误差 gūjì wùchā evaluated error
估价 gūjià ❶ estimated or appraised price: ～表 schedule of prices /～单 list of cost estimates /这幅画～三千元。The appraised price for this picture is three thousand *yuan*. /请你给这件玉雕估估价。Please estimate the price of this jade sculpture. ❷ appraise; evaluate: 对历史人物的～应当结合当时的历史条件。In evaluating historical figures one should take into account the historical conditions of their times. /要正确地～自己。One must take a proper measure of oneself.
估量 gūliang appraise; estimate; assess: 正确地～各种力量的对比 correctly assess the balance of various forces /充分～群众的积极性 take the enthusiasm of the masses into full consideration /事情的最新发展同他的～完全相反。The latest developments are contrary to his estimation.
估摸 gūmo 〈口语〉reckon; suppose; guess: 我～着他这几天就能回来。I reckon he'll be back in a few days. /我～这场球北京队能胜。I guess the Beijing team will win this match.
估税人 gūshuìrén tax assessor
估算 gūsuàn estimate; calculate; consider: ～产量 estimate the yield /～了几种可能出现的结果 consider several possible outcomes /～利息 imputed interest /～收入 imputed income
估损 gūsǔn appraisal of damage; assessment of loss
估值 gūzhí assessment; estimated value

鸪

gū *see* "鹁鸪" bógū; "鹧鸪" zhègū

姑[1]

gū ❶ father's sister; aunt: 大～ eldest aunt /三～ third aunt ❷ husband's sister; sister-in-law: 大～子 husband's elder sister ❸〈书面〉husband's mother; mother-in-law: 翁～ husband's parents ❹ nun; priestess: 尼～ Buddhist nun /道～ Taoist priestess; Taoist nun

姑[2]

gū 〈书面〉just; for the time being: ～置勿论 leave it for the time being
姑表 gūbiǎo relationship between the children of a brother and those of a sister (as viewed by the brother's family); cousinship: ～姊妹 female cousins (daughters of a brother and a sister) /～亲戚 cousinship
姑爹 gūdiē 〈方言〉*see* "姑父"
姑父 gūfu *also* "姑夫" husband of father's sister; uncle
姑姑 gūgu father's sister; aunt
姑舅 gūjiù *also* "姑舅亲" relationship between the children of a brother and a sister; cousinship
姑宽 gūkuān indulge; tolerate: ～谬误 be indulgent towards errors and mistakes
姑老爷 gūlǎoye ❶ (respected form of address for a man used by family members of his wife) son-in-law ❷ husband of one's mother's paternal aunt
姑姥姥 gūlǎolao paternal aunt of one's mother
姑妈 gūmā 〈口语〉father's married sister; aunt
姑母 gūmǔ father's sister; aunt
姑奶奶 gūnǎinai 〈口语〉❶ sister of one's paternal grand father; great-aunt: 老～ old great-aunt ❷ (form of address for a married woman used by members of her family) married daughter ❸〈粗话〉I, your great-aunt (used by a woman in a row)
姑娘 gūniáng 〈方言〉❶ father's sister; aunt ❷ husband's sister; sister-in-law
姑娘 gūniang ❶ girl: 乡下～ country girl ❷ daughter: 她只生了一个～。She has only one daughter.
姑娘儿 gūniangr 〈方言〉〈旧语〉prostitute
姑婆 gūpó 〈方言〉❶ husband's paternal aunt ❷ grandfather's sister
姑且 gūqiě 〈副词〉tentatively; for the moment: ～不论 leave sth. aside for the moment /这是他第一次犯错误，～原谅他。Forgive him this time, since he has never made such mistakes before.
姑嫂 gū-sǎo woman and her brother's wife; sisters-in-law: ～相处很好。The sisters-in-law are on very good terms.
姑妄听之 gūwàngtīngzhī might as well hear sb. out; see no harm in hearing what sb. has to say: 我说得不一定对，你就～吧! I may not be right in what I say, but please hear me out.
姑妄言之 gūwàngyánzhī venture an opinion or a remark; tell sth. for what it's worth: 对这问题，我缺乏研究，只能～。I haven't made a thorough study of this problem, so what I'm going to say is quite tentative.
姑息 gūxī appease; placate; indulge; tolerate: 对侵略行为的～迁就无助于世界的和平与稳定。Indulgence towards aggression will not help world peace and security. /不应该～自己的错误。We shouldn't be soft on our own mistakes.
姑息剂 gūxījì alleviating medicine; palliative
姑息疗法 gūxī liáofǎ 〈医学〉palliative treatment
姑息养奸 gūxī-yǎngjiān to tolerate evil is to abet it; over-indulgence nurtures evil: ～，无异犯罪。It's criminal to tolerate evil.
姑爷爷 gūyéye paternal great-aunt's husband; great-uncle
姑爷 gūye *see* "姑老爷❶"
姑嫜 gūzhāng 〈书面〉husband's parents; parents-in-law
姑丈 gūzhàng husband of father's sister; uncle
姑子 gūzi 〈口语〉Buddhist nun

菇

gū mushroom: 香～ straw mushroom /春～ spring mushroom /冬～ dried mushroom

骨

gū
see also gǔ
骨朵儿 gūduor 〈口语〉flower bud: 这棵月季花结了十多个～。There are a dozen buds on this Chinese rose.
骨碌碌 gūlūlū roll round and round; move rapidly: 小家伙的眼睛～地到处看。The little child's eyes roved about.
骨碌 gūlu roll: 钢蹦从桌上～下去了。The coin rolled under the table. /球在地上～转。The ball is turning round and round on the ground.

菁

gū
菁葖 gūtū 〈植物〉❶ follicle ❷ flower bud

箍

gū ❶ fasten round; bind fast; hoop: 用铁丝～桶 bind a bucket with iron wire /他头上～着条毛巾。He had a towel round his head. /他用皮带把腰～得紧紧的。He wore a leather belt tightly

G

round the waist. ❷ hoop; band:卡～ band; clamp /铁～ iron hoop; hoop iron /胳膊上带着红袖～儿 have a red band round one's arm
箍钢 gūgāng 〈冶金〉hoop iron; banding steel:～带 hoop steel /～轧机 hoop mill
箍节儿 gūjier 〈口语〉〈量词〉piece; passage; section; part:两～木头 two pieces of wood /一～公路 a section of a highway /他话只说了一～,就不再讲了。He stopped halfway and said no more.
箍筋 gūjīn 〈建筑〉stirrup; hoop:～柱 hooped column
箍桶匠 gūtǒngjiàng cooper; hooper
箍眼 gūyan 〈方言〉blinkers (for a horse, donkey, etc.)
箍子 gūzi 〈方言〉(finger) ring:金～ gold ring /针～ thimble
箍嘴 gūzui 〈方言〉muzzle:给马带上～ put a muzzle on a horse; muzzle a horse

苽

gū 〈书面〉*see* "菰" gū

呱

gū
see also guā; guǎ
呱呱 gūgū 〈书面〉cry of a baby
see also guāguā
呱呱坠地 gūgū-zhuìdì (of a baby) be born; come into the world:产儿～ come into the world with a cry

罛

gū 〈书面〉big fishnet

觚

gū ❶〈考古〉wine vessel; goblet; beaker ❷〈古语〉wooden writing tablet:操～ write articles ❸〈书面〉edges and corners

孤

gū ❶ (of a child) fatherless; orphaned:托～ entrust an orphan to sb.'s care /遗～ orphan /怜～惜～ have pity on the orphaned ❷ lone; solitary; isolated; alone:～雁 solitary wild goose /～身一人 all alone; all by oneself ❸ I (used by a king or emperor):称～道寡 call (*or* style) oneself emperor
孤哀子 gū'āizǐ 〈旧语〉(generally used in obituary notices) man bereaved of both his parents; (used in self-reference) this bereft son
孤傲 gū'ào proud and aloof; standoffish and arrogant:一身～的习气 full of aloofness and arrogance /生性～ be proud and reserved by nature /～不群 too haughty to get along with others
孤拔 gūbá ❶ lofty; towering:奇峰～。Fantastic peaks tower aloft. ❷ proud and aloof; supercilious:他流露出一种～自大的情绪。He appears high-and-mighty.
孤本 gūběn only copy extant; only existing copy:海内～ only existing copy in the country
孤臣孽子 gūchén-nièzǐ minister with little influence at court and prince born of a concubine fallen from grace — loyal person who is out of favour; person in disgrace
孤雏腐鼠 gūchú-fǔshǔ solitary nestling and rotten rat — person or thing of no consequence
孤雌寡鹤 gūcí-guǎhè (usu. of a woman) one who has lost one's spouse; widow
孤雌生殖 gūcí shēngzhí 〈生物〉parthenogenesis:～世代 parthenogenesis generation /～体 pathenote
孤单 gūdān ❶ lonely; friendless; solitary; alone:～的少女 friendless girl /～的生活 solitary life /～一人 all alone; all by oneself /老人很～。The old man feels very lonely. ❷ weak; inadequate:要编纂这样一部大词典,仅靠两个人,力量太～了。To compile such a big dictionary, a team of two is far from adequate.
孤胆 gūdǎn (fight the enemy) singlehanded or all alone:～英雄 hero who fights all on his own
孤岛 gūdǎo isolated island
孤丁 gūdīng *also* "孤仃" lonely; solitary; alone:他父母早逝,～一人。His parents died long ago, leaving him all alone in this world.
孤丁 gūding sudden and unexpected development; unexpected problem or difficulty:平地里起～ bolt out of the blue
孤独 gūdú lonely; solitary:～无偶 all alone without a mate /～无援 alone and with no help; all on one's own /～寒微 solitary and poor /他感到异常～和苦闷。He felt extremely lonely and depressed.
孤独症 gūdúzhèng autism
孤儿 gū'ér ❶ fatherless child ❷ orphan:那次大地震后,他成了～。He was orphaned by the terrible earthquake.
孤儿寡母 gū'ér-guǎmǔ *also* "孤儿寡妇" orphans and widows; unprotected women and children:欺人～ bully a widow and her child
孤儿院 gū'éryuàn orphanage
孤芳自赏 gūfāng-zìshǎng solitary flower in love with its own fragrance; lone soul admiring its own purity; indulging in self-admiration; narcissism:～,顾影怜形。He stood alone and aloof, thinking highly of himself and lamenting his own lot.
孤愤 gūfèn 〈书面〉disillusionment with the world
孤负 gūfù *also* "辜负" gūfù let down; fail to live up to; be unworthy of
孤高 gūgāo 〈书面〉proud and aloof; supercilious:～自许 indulge in self-admiration
孤寡 gūguǎ ❶ widows and orphans:老弱～ the old and the weak, and widows and orphans ❷ solitary; lonely; lone:～老婆儿 lone old woman
孤拐 gūguai 〈方言〉❶ cheekbone ❷ ball of the foot
孤寒 gūhán 〈书面〉solitary and poor:～之家 humble family
孤寂 gūjì solitary; lonely:他感到异常～。He felt extremely lonely.
孤家寡人 gūjiā-guǎrén person in utter isolation; person without any friend:关门主义的～策略 closed-doorism of the regal isolationists /我又没牵肠挂肚的家小,～的,怕个啥? I'm a bachelor and have no family responsibilities, so I have nothing to fear.
孤孑 gūjié 〈书面〉lonely; alone; all by oneself:～特立 stand aloof from the mundane world
孤介 gūjiè 〈书面〉honest and upright; unwilling to go along with corrupt people
孤军 gūjūn isolated force:～奋战 fight single-handed; fight a lone battle
孤军薄旅 gūjūn-bólǚ isolated and small force
孤军深入 gūjūn-shēnrù isolated force penetrating deep into enemy territory
孤军作战 gūjūn-zuòzhàn fight in isolation; fight with all outside aid cut off
孤苦 gūkǔ poor and helpless; friendless and wretched:～无依 helpless and alone
孤苦伶仃 gūkǔ-língdīng *also* "孤苦零丁" orphaned and helpless; friendless and uncared for; forlorn and alone:～的弱女子 poor and helpless woman /父母去世后,就剩下她～的一个人。Her parents died, leaving her in the world without kith and kin.
孤老 gūlǎo ❶ lonely and aged ❷ old, childless person:赡养～ support the old and childless ❸〈旧语〉(often used in the early vernacular) lover; whoremaster
孤老院 gūlǎoyuàn old folks' home; home for the aged
孤立 gūlì ❶ isolated; on one's own; helpless:不能～地看待问题。One must not look at problems in isolation. /她感到异常～。She felt forsaken. ❷ isolate:～敌人 isolate the enemy
孤立木 gūlìmù 〈林业〉isolated tree
孤立无援 gūlì-wúyuán isolated and cut off from help:在强敌包围下,这支部队处于～的境地。Surrounded by the formidable enemy, the army found itself in utter isolation.
孤立语 gūlìyǔ *also* "词根语" cígēnyǔ 〈语言〉inflectionless language
孤立主义 gūlìzhǔyì isolationism:～者 isolationist
孤零零 gūlínglíng solitary; lonely; all alone:～地站在河边 stand by the river-side all alone
孤陋寡闻 gūlòu-guǎwén ignorant and ill-informed:～之徒 ignorant person; ignoramus /独学而无友,则孤陋而寡闻。Studying alone without companions, one is bound to be limited in one's horizons.
孤女 gūnǚ orphan girl
孤僻 gūpì unsociable and eccentric:性情～ of an uncommunicative and eccentric disposition /生性～ of an odd and unsociable temperament
孤凄 gūqī lonely and dreary; solitary and desolate:～的感觉 feel lonely and miserable
孤峭 gūqiào 〈书面〉proud and aloof, not complying with current convention
孤弱 gūruò 〈书面〉❶ lonely and weak:～的女子 weak and friendless woman ❷ orphan
孤山 gūshān 〈地质〉monadnock
孤身 gūshēn all on one's own; all alone:他～一人生活多年。He has remained single for years.

孤孀 gūshuāng ❶ orphans and widows ❷ widow
孤耸 gūsǒng *also*“孤竦”lofty；towering：奇峰～。A grotesque peak towers to the skies.
孤行 gūxíng be bent on having one's own way；cling obstinately to one's own course：一意～ act in disregard of other people's objection；act wilfully
孤行己见 gūxíng-jǐjiàn *also*“孤行己意”stubbornly stick to one's own view；be opinionated；be bigoted
孤雄生殖 gūxióng shēngzhí 〈生物〉patrogenesis
孤云野鹤 gūyún-yěhè *also*“野鹤孤云”（move about）like a lonely cloud or a wild crane — free and above worldly cares：野鹤孤云并自闲 carefree like a fleeting cloud
孤掌难鸣 gūzhǎng-nánmíng it's impossible to clap with one hand；it's difficult to achieve anything without support：他深感个人力量有限，真是～啊！He felt keenly that the effort of an individual did not amount to much.
孤证 gūzhèng 〈法律〉solitary evidence
孤植 gūzhí 〈农业〉isolated planting
孤峙 gūzhì stand by oneself；be alone：巍然～ stand lofty and alone
孤注一掷 gūzhù-yīzhì stake everything on a single throw；risk everything on a single venture；put all one's eggs in one basket；venture all in one bottom：决不能采取～的办法。In no case should one stake all on a single throw. /事到如今，别无他法，只好～了。Such being the case, we have no other way but to run this risk.
孤子 gūzǐ ❶ fatherless child ❷ *see*“孤哀子”

菰 gū ❶ wild rice whose stem is eaten as vegetable ❷ mushroom

gǔ

鼓 gǔ ❶ drum：铜～ kettle-drum /腰～ waist drum /敲锣打～ beat drums and strike gongs /隆隆～声 roll of drums ❷ drum-shaped object：石～ drum-shaped stone block /耳～ eardrum；tympanic membrane /货郎～ drum-shaped rattle（used by pedlars or as a toy）；rattle-drum ❸ beat；strike；play；sound：～瑟 play the *se*（ancient Chinese plucked instrument）；play the Chinese harp /～翼（of a bird）flap its wings；wing its way /一～作气（get sth. done）in one sustained effort；at one stroke ❹ blow with a bellows；fan：*see*“～风”❺ rouse；agitate；stir up：～起精神 pluck up（*or* summon）one's spirit ❻ bulge；swell：包里书装得～～的。The schoolbag bulged with books. /墙壁有好几处～出来了。The wall bulged out at several places. /她～起了嘴儿。She pursed up（*or* pouted）her lips.
鼓板 gǔbǎn 〈乐器〉clappers
鼓包 gǔbāo swelling；bump；lump：他的头上碰了个～。A lump has formed on his head. *or* There is a lump on his head.
鼓绷绷 gǔbēngbēng bulging：挎包装得～的。The satchel was bulging. /孩子的肚子胀得～的。The child's belly was swollen.
鼓吹 gǔchuī ❶ advocate；promote；espouse：～和平 espouse peace /～男女平等 advocate the equality of men and women ❷〈贬义〉preach；trumpet：～空洞的裁军计划 trumpet an empty disarmament programme /～实力政策 preach the policy of proceeding from a position of strength
鼓槌 gǔchuí drumstick
鼓荡 gǔdàng agitate；surge；excite；stir：～人心的消息 exciting news /春风～着红旗。Red flags fluttered in the spring wind.
鼓捣 gǔdao 〈方言〉❶ tinker with；fiddle with：他小时候爱～无线电。As a child, he liked to tinker with radios. /小家伙正专心致志地～航模。The child was absorbed in fiddling with a model airplane. ❷ egg on；stir up；incite：暗中～ pull strings behind the scenes /这些坏事都是别人～他干的。Somebody egged him on to do all these evil deeds.
鼓点子 gǔdiǎnzi *also*“鼓点”❶ drumbeats：～越敲越急。The drumbeats grew more and more insistent. ❷ clapper beats which set the tempo for the orchestra in traditional Chinese opera
鼓动 gǔdòng ❶ flap：鸟儿～翅膀。The bird is flapping its wings. ❷ agitate；arouse；stir up；incite：～群众 arouse the masses /～学潮 stir up student unrest /～作战情绪 spur the soldiers on to battle；arouse the fighting spirit /～工人罢工 agitate the workers for a strike；incite the workers to strike /进行政治～ engage in political agitation /他立刻被这个倡议～起来了。He was immediately excited by the proposal.
鼓风 gǔfēng 〈冶金〉strong influx of air；（air）blast：富氧～ oxygen-enriched（air）blast /预热～ blast heating /～冷却 blast cooling
鼓风焙烧法 gǔfēng bèishāofǎ 〈矿业〉blast roasting；roast sintering
鼓风化铁炉 gǔfēng huàtiělú blast cupola furnace
鼓风机 gǔfēngjī *also*“风机”fēngjī blast blower；blast fan；wind machine；blow engine；air-blower；blower：～阀 blower valve /～叶 blower vane
鼓风炉 gǔfēnglú blast furnace：～装料 blast furnace charge
鼓风嘴 gǔfēngzuǐ 〈冶金〉air-blast nozzle
鼓腹 gǔfù 〈书面〉❶ have a full stomach；be well-fed：～而歌 sing with a full stomach；be well-fed and happy ❷ beat one's belly to keep time
鼓鼓囊囊 gǔgu-nāngnāng bulging：包里装满了水果，～的。The bag was bulging with fruit.
鼓惑 gǔhuò *also*“蛊惑”gǔhuò poison and bewitch；instigate；incite
鼓角 gǔjiǎo battle drum and horn used in ancient times：～齐鸣 beat the drums and blare the horns all at once /山下旌旗在望，山头～相闻。Below the hills fly our flags and banners, Above the hilltops sound our bugles and drums.
鼓劲 gǔjìn boost the morale；pluck up one's courage；stir up sb.'s enthusiasm or spirit：互相～ encourage each other/鼓实劲，不鼓虚劲 exert genuine and not sham efforts；work hard in earnest instead of going through the motions
鼓揪 gǔjiu *see*“鼓秋”
鼓浪 gǔlàng raise waves；make waves：巨轮～前进。The huge ship ploughed its way through the waves.
鼓励 gǔlì encourage；urge；spur（on）：～的话 encouraging words /～他刻苦学习 urge（*or* encourage）him to study hard /精神～和物质～相结合 combine moral encouragement with material rewards /他的榜样～我们奋勇前进。His example spurs us on.
鼓励生育政策 gǔlì shēngyù zhèngcè pronatalist policy
鼓励性价格 gǔlìxìng jiàgé incentive price
鼓溜溜 gǔliūliū full and bulging；plump：～的麦粒 full or plump grains of wheat /睁着～的眼睛 with bulging eyes；with one's eyes wide open
鼓楼 gǔlóu drum-tower
鼓轮 gǔlún 〈机械〉drum wheel；drum：～轴 drum axle
鼓膜 gǔmó *also*“耳鼓”ěrgǔ；“耳膜”ěrmó 〈生理〉tympanic membrane；myringa；eardrum
鼓膜穿孔 gǔmó chuānkǒng perforation of the tympanic membrance
鼓膜截除术 gǔmó jiéchúshù tympanectomy
鼓膜镜 gǔmójìng myringoscope
鼓膜炎 gǔmóyán myringitis
鼓弄 gǔnong 〈口语〉fiddle with；tinker with；play with：这孩子就喜欢～积木。The child is fond of playing with blocks.
鼓盆 gǔpén 〈书面〉（Zhuangzi beat an earthen basin and sang when his wife died, and the beating of an earthen basin was later used to refer to the death of one's wife）death of one's wife：～之戚 grief of being bereaved of one's wife
鼓气 gǔqì 〈方言〉feel wronged and act rashly；act out of spite；throw a tantrum：她躺在床上～。She was lying in bed, throwing a tantrum.
鼓丘 gǔqiū 〈地质〉drumlin
鼓秋 gǔqiu *also*“鼓揪”〈方言〉❶ fiddle with；tinker with：～钟表 tinker with clocks and watches ❷ instigate；incite；abet；stir up：有话当面讲，不要背后～。Lay all cards on the table and do not stir up trouble from behind the scenes.
鼓儿词 gǔrcí words sung to the accompaniment of a drum *see also*“鼓书”
鼓煽 gǔshān instigate；incite；stir up；egg on
鼓舌 gǔshé wag one's tongue：摇唇～ wag one's tongue in honeyed talk or malicious gossip /鼓其如簧之舌 give play to one's glib tongue；talk glibly
鼓师 gǔshī （in traditional Chinese opera）musician who keeps time for the band by beating the drum with two thin drumsticks
鼓式磁选机 gǔshì cíxuǎnjī 〈矿业〉drum cobber
鼓室 gǔshì 〈生理〉tympanum：～盖 roof of the tympanum/～炎

tympanitis /～神经 tympanic nerve

鼓手 gǔshǒu drumbeater; drummer

鼓书 gǔshū *also* "大鼓" dàgǔ versified story sung to the accompaniment of a small drum and other instruments: 说～ perform *dagu* /～艺人 *dagu* singer

鼓腾腾 gǔtēngtēng full and bulging; plump: ～的书包 bulging schoolbag

鼓筒式拌和机 gǔtǒngshì bànhuòjī drum mixer

鼓凸 gǔtū bulging; protruding; jutting out: 肌肉～ with bulging muscles; muscular

鼓舞 gǔwǔ encourage; hearten; inspire: 令人～ heartening; inspiring /深受～ feel very much encouraged (*or* heartened) /～士气 boost (*or* enhance) the morale (of soldiers, etc.) /～农民的生产积极性 arouse the farmers' enthusiasm for production /喜讯传来，人人欢欣～。Everyone was elated at the good news.

鼓舞人心 gǔwǔ-rénxīn inspiring; heartening: ～的讲话 inspiring speech (*or* talk) /～的消息 heartening news

鼓形磨床 gǔxíng móchuáng 〈机械〉 drum sander

鼓形铣床 gǔxíng xǐchuáng 〈机械〉 drum miller; drum milling machine; drum-type milling

鼓乐 gǔyuè (strains of) music accompanied by drumbeats: ～喧天。There is a great din of drums and pipes. *or* Loud music fills the air. /～齐鸣，万众欢腾。The jubilant crowds gave loud cheers amid crescendos of music.

鼓噪 gǔzào make an uproar; kick up a din; raise a hubbub; clamour: ～而进 move ahead (*or* in) uproariously /～四起 rise up with a great clamour; rise in a hubbub /群蛙～。A host of frogs are croaking. /会场上一人发难，其他人便跟着～起来。One person made trouble at the meeting and some others joined him in raising a hubbub.

鼓掌 gǔzhǎng clap one's hands; applaud: ～欢迎 clap one's hands (*or* applaud) to welcome/起立～ give a standing ovation /～通过 approve by acclamation /向演员热烈～ warmly applaud the performers; give the performers a big hand

鼓胀 gǔzhàng ❶ bulge; bloat: 橡皮船又～了起来。The rubber boat again bulged with air. /他手背上青筋～。His hands are bulging with blue veins. *or* Blue veins stand out on his hands. ❷ *also* "臌胀" gǔzhàng bloating (of the abdomen, etc.); tympanites; meteorism: 得了～病 suffer from tympanites

G

鼓胀胀 gǔzhàngzhàng bulging; expanding; swelling; ballooning: ～的豆荚 bulging pods /衣服被风吹得～的。The wind swelled the dress as though it were a sail.

鼓棹 gǔzhào 〈书面〉 pull an oar; row: ～前进 row one's way forward; row a boat forward

鼓铸 gǔzhù 〈书面〉 melt metal to mint coins or cast utensils

鼓子词 gǔzicí a kind of *dagu* in the Song Dynasty, consisting mainly of singing mixed with narration, accompanied by the beating of a drum

鼓足干劲 gǔzú gànjìn go all out; exert one's utmost: ～，力争上游，多快好省地建设社会主义。(slogan formulated in 1958) Go all out, aim high and achieve greater, faster, better and more economical results in building socialism. *or* Build socialism with greater, faster, better and more economical results.

瞽

gǔ 〈书面〉 ❶ blind: ～者 blind person ❷ lacking in discernment; stupid: ～说 stupid theory; foolish idea; wild talk

瞽言 gǔyán 〈书面〉 unreasonable and groundless remarks: ～刍议 〈谦词〉 (our) humble views which may reflect lack of discernment

臌

gǔ tympanites: 气～ distension of the abdomen caused by accumulation of gas due to dysfunction of the spleen or to emotional factors /水～ ascites

臌胀 gǔzhàng *also* "鼓胀" gǔzhàng 〈中医〉 distension of the abdomen caused by accumulation of gas or fluid due to dysfunction of the liver and spleen; tympanites; meteorism

古

gǔ ❶ ancient; age-old: ～庙 ancient temple; old temple /怀～ meditate on the past; reflect on an ancient event /远～ remote antiquity /仿～ imitate the style of the ancients; pseudo-archaic /复～ restore ancient ways; return to the ancients /厚～薄今 stress the past, not the present /食～不化 swallow ancient learning without digesting it /博～通今 conversant with things past and present /借～讽今 use the past to disparage the present /从～到今 from ancient times to the present /万～流芳 be remembered throughout the ages ❷ of ancient style: *see* "～朴" ❸ 〈书面〉 simple and sincere: 人心不～。People nowadays are no longer simple and honest. ❹ form of classical poetry that originated before the Tang Dynasty and usu. having four to seven characters to each line, without strict tonal patterns or rhyme schemes: 五～ classical poem with five characters to a line ❺ (Gǔ) a surname

古奥 gǔ'ào archaic and abstruse: 文字～ archaic and abstruse writing (*or* language)

古巴 Gǔbā Cuba: ～人 Cuban /～导弹危机 Cuban missile crisis (1962)

古板 gǔbǎn old-fashioned and inflexible; outmoded and rigid: 性情～ be old-fashioned and inflexible in disposition/思想～ have an outmoded and rigid way of thinking /古古板板的人 prim and proper person

古堡 gǔbǎo castrum; (ancient) castle

古本 gǔběn book of ancient printing; ancient version or edition

古刹 gǔchà ancient temple

古磁学 gǔcíxué palaeomagnetism

古代 gǔdài (referring to the period in Chinese history before the mid-19th century, and sometimes, esp. to the age of slave society) ancient times; antiquity: ～史 ancient history /～文化 ancient culture /～社会 ancient society /～文明 ancient civilization /～流传下来的神话 myths handed down from antiquity

古道 gǔdào ❶ ancient ways; ancient rules and methods: ～可风。Ancient ways may be adopted as models. *or* Ancient ways are worth emulating. ❷ kind; considerate; generous: 忠厚～ honest and kind ❸ ancient road: 踏上石子铺的～ step on a stone-paved ancient road

古道热肠 gǔdào-rècháng considerate and warm-hearted; honest and compassionate: 他一向～，待人诚恳。He is always sincere, considerate and warm-hearted.

古地质学 gǔdìzhìxué paleogeology

古典 gǔdiǎn ❶ classical allusion: 引用～ quote a classical allusion /查～ find chapter and verse for a classical allusion ❷ classical: ～学派 classical school /～决策理论 classical theory on decision-making /～作品 classics

古典芭蕾 gǔdiǎn bālěi classical ballet

古典建筑 gǔdiǎn jiànzhù ❶ classical architecture ❷ classical building

古典经济学 gǔdiǎn jīngjìxué classical economics

古典式摔跤 gǔdiǎnshì shuāijiāo 〈体育〉 Graeco-Roman style wrestling

古典文学 gǔdiǎn wénxué classical literature: 西洋～ classical Western literature /～研究 study of classical literature /～的精华 cream (*or* essence) of classical literature

古典舞 gǔdiǎnwǔ classical dance

古典艺术 gǔdiǎn yìshù classical art

古典音乐 gǔdiǎn yīnyuè classical music

古典主义 gǔdiǎnzhǔyì classicism: 新～ neo-classicism

古董 gǔdǒng *also* "骨董" gǔdǒng ❶ antique; curio; curiosity: 收集～ collect antiques (*or* curios) /～鉴赏家 connoisseur of curios ❷ old fogey; outdated stuff; anachronism: 不折不扣的老～ unmitigated old fogey /这些～，早该处理掉了。All this old stuff should have been disposed of long ago.

古董店 gǔdǒngdiàn antique shop

古董商 gǔdǒngshāng antiquary; antiquarian

古动物学 gǔdòngwùxué palaeozoology

古都 gǔdū ancient capital: 六朝～ capital of six dynasties / ～洛阳 ancient capital of Luoyang

古尔邦节 Gǔ'ěrbāngjié *also* "宰牲节" Zǎishēngjié 〈伊斯兰〉 *'Id al-Kurban*; *'Id al-Adha*

古方 gǔfāng ancient (medical) recipe; classical prescription

古风 gǔfēng ❶ ancient customs; antiquities: ～遗俗 old customs /这儿～依旧。Ancient customs remain unchanged here. ❷ form of classical poetry originated before the Tang Dynasty: 擅长～ be versed in pre-Tang poetry

see also "古体诗"

古怪 gǔguài eccentric; bizarre; odd; strange: ～的名字 strange name /～的模样 odd appearance /稀奇～ rare and queer /性情～ eccentric character

construction; framework; frame construction
骨胶 gǔjiāo 〈化工〉bone glue
骨节 gǔjié 〈生理〉joint:周身~酸痛 ache in all the joints
骨结核 gǔjiéhé *also* "骨痨" bone tuberculosis
骨臼 gǔjiù 〈医学〉bones socket
骨科 gǔkē 〈医学〉(department of) orthopaedics: ~医生 orthopaedist /~专家 specialist in orthopaedics
骨刻 gǔkè 〈工美〉bone sculpture; bone carving
骨库 gǔkù bone storage cabinet
骨痨 gǔláo 〈中医〉tuberculosis of bones and joints; bone tuberculosis
骨力 gǔlì ❶ (as in Chinese calligraphy) strength or force of strokes:这条幅写得很有~。The scroll is written with forceful strokes. ❷ unbending integrity; indomitable spirit
骨力 gǔli 〈方言〉strong; sturdy; tough; durable:这把伞真~。This umbrella has a durable frame. /这老头儿八十了,身子骨还挺~。The old man is already eighty, but he is still hale and hearty.
骨立 gǔlì 〈书面〉bony; angular:憔悴~ haggard and bony
骨料 gǔliào 〈建筑〉aggregate:合成~ combine aggregate /灰浆~ mortar aggregate /矿渣~ cinder aggregate; breeze aggregate /轻~ light aggregate /粗~ thick aggregate /~粒径 aggregate size
骨瘤 gǔliú 〈医学〉osteoma:她的腿病已确诊是长了~。She has been diagnosed as suffering from an osteoma in the leg.
骨螺 gǔluó 〈动物〉murex (*Muricidae*)
骨膜 gǔmó 〈生理〉periosteum:~炎 periostitis /~瘤 periosteoma
骨囊肿 gǔnángzhǒng 〈医学〉bone cyst
骨牌 gǔpái domino:多米诺~理论 domino theory /多米诺~效应 domino effect
骨盆 gǔpén 〈生理〉pelvis:~板 pelvic plate /~畸形 deformity of pelvis
骨盆镜 gǔpénjìng 〈医学〉pelviscope
骨气 gǔqì ❶ strength of character; moral integrity; probity; backbone:中国人有~。The Chinese people have backbone. /别看他穷,但穷得有~。Though he is poor, he is a man of integrity. ❷ vigour and force shown in calligraphy:他的字~清奇。His calligraphy displays elegance and vigour.
骨器 gǔqì bone object; bone implement
骨肉 gǔròu flesh and blood; kindred:情同~ as close to each other as flesh and blood /~之亲 blood relations /海峡两边的中国人都是~同胞。The people on both sides of the Taiwan Straits are the same flesh and blood of the Chinese nation.
骨肉离散 gǔròu-lísàn *also* "骨肉分离" separation of parents and children; family separation
骨肉团圆 gǔròu-tuányuán *also* "骨肉团聚" reunion of parents and children; family reunion
骨肉未寒 gǔròu-wèihán *also* "尸骨未寒" shīgǔ-wèihán while the body of the dead is not cold yet — immediately after sb.'s death:父亲~,儿子们就开始争夺家产了。Hardly had their father breathed his last when the sons began to fight for the family property.
骨肉相残 gǔròu-xiāngcán fratricidal fighting
骨肉相连 gǔròu-xiānglián linked together by flesh and blood
骨肉之情 gǔròuzhīqíng ties of blood; kindred feelings
骨肉至亲 gǔròu-zhìqīn flesh and blood; blood relations
骨软化 gǔruǎnhuà 〈医学〉osteomalacia
骨殖 gǔshi skeleton (of a dead body)
骨瘦如柴 gǔshòu-rúchái thin as a lath; worn to a shadow; mere skeleton; bag or pack of bones:~的孩子 bony child /两月不见,老人已病得~了。The disease has reduced the old man to skin and bones since I saw him two months ago.
骨髓 gǔsuǐ 〈生理〉bone marrow:抽~ draw marrow
骨髓病 gǔsuǐbìng 〈医学〉myelopathy
骨髓瘤 gǔsuǐliú 〈医学〉myeloma
骨髓腔 gǔsuǐqiāng 〈生理〉marrow cavity
骨髓炎 gǔsuǐyán 〈医学〉osteomyelitis
骨髓硬化 gǔsuǐ yìnghuà 〈医学〉myelosclerosis
骨碎补 gǔsuìbǔ 〈中药〉rhizome of darallia (*Davallia mariesii*)
骨炭 gǔtàn bone black; animal charcoal
骨痛热 gǔtòngrè *also* "登革热" dēngérè 〈医学〉dengue fever
骨头 gǔtou ❶ bone:他瘦得皮包~了。He is all skin and bone (*or* a bag of bones). ❷ character:懒~ lazybones /软~ spineless creature /他可真是个硬~。He is a man of unyielding integrity. ❸〈方言〉sarcasm; resentment:他的话里有~! There is a sting in his words.
骨头架子 gǔtou jiàzi 〈口语〉❶ skeleton ❷ very thin person:瘦得只剩~了 be reduced to a skeleton; be all skin and bone
骨头节儿 gǔtoujiér 〈方言〉joint
骨突 gǔtū 〈医学〉apophysis
骨萎缩 gǔwěisuō 〈医学〉bone atrophy
骨细胞 gǔxìbāo 〈生理〉osteocyte
骨学 gǔxué *also* "骨骼学"〈医学〉osteology
骨血 gǔxuè flesh and blood; offspring:自己的亲~ one's own flesh and blood /他是我姑母留下的惟一的~。He is the only child of my deceased aunt.
骨炎 gǔyán 〈医学〉osteitis:变形性~ osteitis deformans
骨硬化 gǔyìnghuà 〈医学〉osteosclerosis:~病 osteopetrosis; ivory bones; marble bones; chalky bones
骨折 gǔzhé fracture:大腿~ fracture in the thigh /粉碎性~ comminuted fracture /开放~ open (*or* compound) fracture /~复位 reduction of a fracture; setting of a fracture /~固定 fracture fixation
骨蒸 gǔzhēng 〈中医〉hectic fever (symptom of consumptive disease)
骨质 gǔzhì 〈生理〉sclerotin
骨质软化 gǔzhì ruǎnhuà 〈医学〉osteomalacia
骨质疏松 gǔzhì shūsōng 〈医学〉osteoporosis
骨质增生 gǔzhì zēngshēng 〈医学〉osteoproliferation
骨赘 gǔzhuì 〈医学〉osteophyma; osteophyte:~病 osteophytosis
骨子 gǔzi frame; ribs:扇~ ribs of a fan /钢条扎成的~ frame made of steel bars
骨子里 gǔzilǐ *also* "骨子里头" ❶〈贬义〉in one's bones; in one's innermost nature; in reality; at bottom:从~仇恨某人 hate sb. to the marrow of one's bones /这人~很狡猾,虽然表面上看不出来。The man was in reality very crafty, though he did not look so. /她嘴里未说什么,但~却是很不满的。Though she didn't say anything, she was very resentful at heart. ❷〈方言〉personal; private:这是他们~的事,你不用管。This is their private affair. You just mind your own business.

榾 gǔ

榾柮 gǔduò 〈方言〉wood block; stump

谷[1] gǔ

❶ valley; ravine; gully; gorge:峡~ gorge; canyon /河~ river valley /幽~ secluded ravine or valley /断层~ fault valley /悬~ hanging valley /槽~ trough valley /裂~ rift valley /万丈深~ fathomless ravine ❷ (Gǔ) a surname

谷[2](穀) gǔ

❶ cereal; grain:打~ thresh grain /五~丰登 abundant harvest of all cereal crops ❷ millet:~穗儿 ears of millet ❸〈方言〉unhusked rice:稻~ unhusked rice; paddy
see also yù
谷氨酸 gǔ'ānsuān 〈生化〉glutamic acid; glutamate:~钾 potassium glutamate /~盐 glutamate /~钙 calcium glutamate
谷胺酸钠 gǔ'ànsuānnà *also* "味精" wèijīng monosodium glutamate (MSG)
谷丙转氨酶 gǔbǐng zhuǎn'ānméi glutamic-pyruvic transaminase (GPT)
谷仓 gǔcāng granary; barn:~机械 barn machinery /丰收之后,~都装满了。All the granaries (*or* barns) were bursting with grain after the bumper harvest. /昔日的"北大荒",如今已成为东北的又一个~。The former "Great Northern Wilderness" has now become another granary (*or* breadbasket) of Northeast China.
谷草 gǔcǎo ❶ millet straw:~垛 stack of millet straw ❷〈方言〉rice straw:~灰 ashes of rice straw
谷蛋白 gǔdànbái 〈生化〉glutelin; gluten
谷底 gǔdǐ bottom of a valley:这次衰退已经到达~。The present recession has touched bottom.
谷底田 gǔdǐtián *also* "坝田" bàtián flat land surrounded (usu. on two or three sides) by hills
谷地 gǔdì valley:他们在~里种上了庄稼。They planted crops in the valley.
谷蛾 gǔ'é 〈动物〉grain moth:~科昆虫 tineid
谷坊 gǔfáng 〈水利〉check dam
谷风 gǔfēng daytime upward draught in the valley; wind coming through the valley floor

谷贱伤农 gǔjiàn-shāngnóng low prices for grain hurt the farmers
谷糠 gǔkāng bran of grain
谷壳 gǔké husk (of paddy, etc.); chaff
谷枯病 gǔkūbìng 〈农业〉glumes blight
谷类 gǔlèi cereal:～食物 cereal (food) /～学家 cerealist
谷类作物 gǔlèi zuòwù cereal crop:扩大～的种植面积 expand the acreage under cereal crops
谷粒 gǔlì grain (of rice, millet, etc.):小鸡啄食地上的～。The chicks were pecking grains of corn on the ground.
谷粒干燥机 gǔlì gānzàojī grain drier
谷粒清选机 gǔlì qīngxuǎnjī grain cleaner; grain separator
谷米 gǔmǐ 〈方言〉(unhusked or husked) rice; paddy
谷神星 Gǔshénxīng 〈天文〉Ceres
谷维素 gǔwéisù 〈药学〉oryzanol
谷物 gǔwù ❶ cereal; grain:～播种机 grain drill (*or* seeder) /～干燥设备 grain-drying plant (*or* unit); grain-drying equipment /～联合收割机 grain harvester combine /～取样器 grain sampler /～湿度计 grain moisture meter ❷ cereal crop
谷物法 gǔwùfǎ (in British history) Corn Law of 1815, repealed in 1846
谷物交易所 gǔwù jiāoyìsuǒ corn exchange :芝加哥～ Chicago Corn Exchange
谷象 gǔxiàng 〈动物〉grain weevil; granary weevil
谷雨 Gǔyǔ ❶ Grain Rain, 6th seasonal division point, marking the sun's position at 30° on the ecliptic ❷ day marking such a seasonal division point, usu. falling on the 20th or 21st of April ❸ period lasting from such a seasonal division point till the next one (Beginning of Summer 立夏)
see also "节气" jiéqì;"二十四节气" èrshísì jiéqì
谷值点 gǔzhídiǎn 〈电学〉valley point
谷值电压 gǔzhí diànyā 〈电学〉valley point voltage
谷子 gǔzi ❶ *also* "粟" sù millet:～面窝窝头 steamed bread of millet flour /金黄的～真叫人喜爱。The golden millet is really lovely. ❷〈方言〉unhusked rice; paddy:把～碾成大米 husk rice
谷子白发病 gǔzi báifàbìng downy mildew of millet
谷租 gǔzū land rent paid in grain

鹄

gǔ 〈书面〉target (for archery):一箭中～ hit the target with one arrow
see also hú

G

鹄的 gǔdì 〈书面〉❶ bull's eye:三箭均中～。All the three arrows hit the bull's eye. ❷ aim; target; purpose

羖(羜)

gǔ 〈书面〉ram

股[1]

gǔ ❶ thigh ❷ section (of an office, enterprise, etc.):财务～ financial (*or* accounting) section /后勤～ logistics section ❸ strand; ply:三～的绳子 rope of three strands /把线捻成～儿 twist the threads into a strand ❹ share of stock (in a company); one of several equal parts:A～ A share / B～ B share / H～ H share /入～ buy a share; become a shareholder /招～ raise capital by floating shares/ 炒～ speculate in stocks /普通～ common stock /优先～ preferred stock /法人～ legal-person share /公～ government share (in a joint state-private enterprise) /私～ private share /合～公司 joint stock company /控～公司 holding company; controlling company /将遗产分为三～ divide the inheritance into three equal parts ❺〈量词〉(a) *used to indicate sth. long and narrow*:一～清泉 a stream of clear spring water /一～棉线 a skein of cotton thread /上山有两～道。There are two paths leading to the mountain top. (b) *used for gas, smell, strength, etc.*:一～劲 a burst of energy /一～热气 a stream (*or* puff) of hot air /一～冷风 a gust of cold wind /一～臭味 a whiff of offensive odor /一～浓烟 a column of heavy smoke /一～怜悯之情 a sentiment of sympathy /一～凛然正气 an air of awe-inspiring righteousness (c)〈贬义〉*used to indicate a group of people*:一～土匪 a band (*or* gang) of bandits /小～敌军 small groups (*or* bands) of enemy troops

股[2]

gǔ longer leg of a right triangle:勾～定理 Pythagorean theorem; Pythagorean proposition
股白肿 gǔbáizhǒng 〈医学〉thrombotic phlegmasia; milk leg; white leg
股本 gǔběn capital stock; equity:～折价 discount on capital stock /～短缺 short of capital /～定额不足 under-capitalisation
股本油 gǔběnyóu 〈经济〉equity oil
股东 gǔdōng shareholder; stockholder:～产权 stockholder's equity
股东基金 gǔdōng jījīn shareholders' fund
股东权益 gǔdōng quányì equity
股动脉 gǔdòngmài femoral artery
股匪 gǔfěi band of robbers; horde or gang of bandits:全歼～ wipe out the entire gang of bandits
股份 gǔfèn *also* "股分" share; stock:～转让 stock transfer/～资本 share capital /～红利 stock bonus /～银行 joint-stock bank /他拥有全公司～的三分之一。He holds one-third of the company's shares (*or* stock).
股份公开公司 gǔfèn gōngkāi gōngsī public company
股份公司 gǔfèn gōngsī joint-stock company; stock company
股份经济 gǔfèn jīngjì economy that employs share holding system
股份期权 gǔfèn qīquán share option
股份无限公司 gǔfèn wúxiàn gōngsī unlimited company
股份溢价 gǔfèn yìjià share premium
股份有限公司 gǔfèn yǒuxiàn gōngsī limited-liability company; limited company (Ltd.)
股份制 gǔfènzhì joint-stock system; stock-holding system:有些国有企业已经转为～。Some state-owned enterprises have been converted to joint-stock ones (*or* have adopted the joint-stock system).
股肱 gǔgōng 〈书面〉right-hand man:～之臣 most trustworthy minister (of a ruler)
股骨 gǔgǔ 〈生理〉thighbone; femur:～骨折 fracture of the thighbone; femur fracture
股金 gǔjīn money paid for shares (in a partnership, cooperative or company); capital:交～ pay for one's share /缺少～ short of share capital /凑集～ raise capital; float shares
股静脉 gǔjìngmài 〈生理〉femeral vein
股利 gǔlì interest on shares; dividend
股栗 gǔlì 〈书面〉tremble with fear
股民 gǔmín person who buys and sells stocks
股票 gǔpiào share certificate; share; stock:发行～ issue stocks; issue shares /购买～ buy stocks (*or* shares) /出售～ offer shares (*or* stocks) for sale; sell shares (*or* stocks) /～买进价 bid price /～卖出价 asked price/～过户 stock transfer; share transfer /～面值 face value of shares (*or* stocks) /炒～ buy and sell stocks; speculate in stocks /～升值 appreciation in share value
股票持有人 gǔpiào chíyǒurén shareholder; stockholder
股票分割 gǔpiào fēngē stock split
股票行市 gǔpiào hángshi *also* "股票行情" current prices of stocks; quotations on the stock exchange
股票价格 gǔpiào jiàgé share price:～指数 stock price index/～涨落线 advance-decline line of stocks
股票交易 gǔpiào jiāoyì buying and selling of stocks; trade in stocks
股票交易所 gǔpiào jiāoyìsuǒ stock exchange
股票交易自动报价系统 gǔpiào jiāoyì zìdòng bàojià xìtǒng stock exchange automated quotations (SEAQ)
股票经纪人 gǔpiào jīngjìrén stockbroker; stockjobber
股票期权 gǔpiào qīquán stock option
股票清理公司 gǔpiào qīnglǐ gōngsī stock clearing corporation
股票市场 gǔpiào shìchǎng stock market
股票证券 gǔpiào zhèngquàn share certificate
股票指数 gǔpiào zhǐshù stock index
股权 gǔquán stock ownership; stockholder's right
股权公司 gǔquán gōngsī holding company
股权证 gǔquánzhèng certificate of share; capital stock certificate
股疝 gǔshàn 〈医学〉femoral hernia; femorocele; crural hernia; gluteal hernia
股神经 gǔshénjīng 〈生理〉femoral nerve
股市 gǔshì (short for 股票市场) stock market:香港～ Hong Kong Stock Market /～暴跌。The stock market fell abruptly. /～崩溃。The stock market crashed.
股息 gǔxī *also* "股利" dividend:～收益 dividend yield /这种股票每年可获百分之十的～。These shares yield (*or* pay) ten per cent a year.
股线 gǔxiàn 〈纺织〉plied yarn; folded yarn

股长 gǔzhǎng section chief; head of a section:总务～ chief (*or* head) of the general affairs section
股子 gǔzi *see* "股[1]❺"

毂 gǔ hub of a wheel:肩摩～击 with jamming vehicles and jostling pedestrians
see also gū

榖 gǔ 〈书面〉❶ good; lucky:～旦 auspicious day; lucky day ❷ official's salary

穀 gǔ paper mulberry

汩 gǔ 〈书面〉(of running water) gurgle
汩汩 gǔgǔ gurgle:溪水～流过。The gurgling brook flows by.
汩没 gǔmò 〈书面〉neglect; overlook:不甘～ not contented to be neglected; not resigned to neglect

gù

雇(僱) gù hire; employ; engage:～保姆 hire a maid / ～长工 employ a long-term farm hand /～家教 engage a private tutor/～卡车 hire a lorry (*or* truck) /解～ discharge; dismiss; sack
雇工 gùgōng ❶ hire labour; hire hands ❷ hired labourer (*or* worker); hired hand; farmhand:虐待～ maltreat hired labourers /在地主家当～ work as a live-in farmhand for a landlord
雇脚 gùjiǎo hire a porter
雇农 gùnóng farmhand; farm labourer: 贫～ poor peasants and farm labourers /他是～出身。He was originally a farmhand.
雇请 gùqǐng employ; engage; hire:～律师 employ a lawyer /～保镖 hire a bodyguard
雇佣 gùyōng employ; hire:～人 employer /被～人 employee /～关系 employer-employee relationship /～合同 contract of employment (*or* engagement) /受人长期～ be in sb.'s regular employ /为某一外国所～ be in the employ of a certain foreign country
雇佣兵 gùyōngbīng mercenary (soldier):～兵役制 mercenary system
雇佣观点 gùyōng guāndiǎn hired-hand mentality — the attitude of one who won't do more than he is paid for:抱有～的人,决不可能干好工作。Those with a hire-hand mentality will never do a good job.
雇佣军 gùyōngjūn mercenary army or troops; mercenary
雇佣劳动 gùyōng láodòng wage labour:～者 wage labourer
雇佣奴隶 gùyōng núlì wage slave:～制 wage slavery
雇佣文人 gùyōng wénrén hack writer
雇用 gùyòng employ; hire:～临时工 employ temporary workers / 他是公司～的清洁工。He is a cleaner hired by the company. /你被～了。You have (got) the job.
雇员 gùyuán employee:高级～ senior employee /～考核 employee rating (*or* evaluation)
雇员股票选择权 gùyuán gǔpiào xuǎnzéquán employee share option
雇主 gùzhǔ employer:行使～的权力 exercise the power of an employer /他正在找～。He is hunting for a job.

顾[1](顧) gù ❶ turn round and look at; look at:环～ look around /回～ look back; review /瞻前～后 look ahead and behind /不屑一～ will not even spare a glance ❷ take care of; attend to; take into consideration or account:～大局 take the interest of the whole into account/奋不～身 dash ahead without giving a thought to one's own safety /自～不暇 unable even to fend for oneself /必须兼～双方利益。Consideration must be given to the interests of both sides. /几件事他全能～上。He can attend to all these matters at once. ❸ pay a visit; visit; call on:承蒙光～ be greatly honoured to have you visit us; thank you for visiting (*or* calling on) us; (of a store) thank you for your patronage ❹ customer: 主～ customer; patron; client ❺ (Gù) a surname

顾[2](顧) gù 〈书面〉❶ but; however; nevertheless:彼非不爱其弟,～有所不能忍者也。It is not that he didn't love his younger brother, but that he could not bear some of the things his brother did. ❷ on the contrary; in lieu of; instead:足反居上,首～居下。The feet are on top, whereas the head is at the bottom — the cart is put before the horse.
顾此失彼 gùcǐ-shībǐ attend to one thing and lose sight of another; have too many things to take care of at the same time; be unable to look after everything at once
顾大局,识大体 gù dàjú, shí dàtǐ bear the overall situation in mind and put the general interest above all else
顾闳中 Gù Hóngzhōng Gu Hongzhong, painter of Southern Tang (937-975), whose masterpiece is *Han Xizai Giving an Evening Banquet* (韩熙载夜宴图)
顾及 gùjí take into consideration; attend to; look after; care for: ～各种不同情况 take all possibilities (*or* eventualities) into account / 无暇～个人私事 have no time to attend to personal affairs; be too busy to attend to personal matters
顾忌 gùjì scruple; qualm; misgiving:不能不有所～ have to think twice (before doing sth.); have scruples about sb. or sth. /毫无～地挥霍公款 make no scruple of squandering public money; squander public money with no qualms /无所～地发表意见 air one's views without misgivings; speak one's mind freely
顾家 gùjiā care for one's own family; attend to the family:一心为公不～ devote oneself to public service instead of attending to one's family /这个女儿很～,经常补贴老人家用。She was considerate of her aged parents' needs and often helped them out with money.
顾恺之 Gù Kǎizhī Gu Kaizhi (formerly translated as Ku K'ai-chih, 346-407), painter of the Eastern Jin Dynasty
顾客 gùkè customer; shopper; client; patron:招徕～ attract (*or* draw) customers /～服务台 customer service /～盈门 filled with customers (*or* shoppers, *or* clients) /～就是上帝。The customer is God./ ～至上 customers first /～满意就是最好的广告。A satisfied shopper is the best advertisement.
顾理 gùlǐ 〈方言〉take care of; look after; care for:～家务 take care of household chores
顾怜 gùlián show concern and affection for; feel sympathy and concern for:他得知远在南方的妻子生病,心中不胜～。He was greatly worried when he heard that his wife had become ill far away in the south.
顾脸 gùliǎn be concerned with face; care for one's reputation:他发起怒来从不～。When he flew into a rage, he never bothered about face. *or* He never cared a damn for face when he was angry.
顾恋 gùliàn concern oneself with; care for; be reluctant to part (from sb. or with sth.):～老小 be concerned about one's old parents and little children /～子女 care for one's children; be reluctant to part from one's children
顾虑 gùlǜ misgiving; apprehension; anxiety; worry:产生～ have misgivings (*or* worries); be worried / 家庭～ family cares; considerations of one's family /毫无～ without the slightest misgivings (*or* hesitancy) /他就是～着我的安全。He was concerned (*or* anxious) about my safety.
顾虑重重 gùlǜ-chóngchóng be full of apprehensions; have no end of worries
顾眄 gùmiàn 〈书面〉turn round and look at; look round
顾面子 gù miànzi save face; keep up appearances; spare sb.'s feelings or sensibilities:工作中要讲实效,不要只～。One should strive for actual results in one's work instead of just trying to keep up appearances. /你难道不知道,他这样说是为了顾你的面子? Didn't you know he said that to spare your feelings (*or* to save your face)?
顾名思义 gùmíng-sīyì seeing the name one thinks of its meaning; as the name implies; as the term suggests; by definition:沪剧,～,就是上海的地方戏。Shanghai opera, as the name suggests, is the local opera of Shanghai.
顾命 gùmìng ❶ treasure one's life; save one's skin:奋不～ show no concern for one's own safety (in doing sth.); be ready to lay down one's life (for a cause, etc.) ❷〈书面〉dying emperor's will and testament:～大臣 senior minister entrusted by the dying emperor to assist the young emperor; minister-regent /～之恩 favour bestowed by the deceased emperor on one in entrusting one to assist the young emperor
顾念 gùniàn think about (with concern); concern oneself about: 对老人十分～ show great concern for the aged /她～着年幼的孩子。She kept thinking about her little children.

顾盼 gùpàn 〈书面〉look round:左右～ look right and left /～自如 look round with ease; behave in a free and easy way

顾盼生姿 gùpàn-shēngzī look round in a charming manner

顾盼自雄 gùpàn-zìxióng look about complacently; strut about pleased with oneself; be conceited:小伙子得了个象棋冠军,不免～。Having won the chess championship, the young man felt proud and looked triumphant.

顾前不顾后 gù qián bù gù hòu drive ahead without considering the consequences; attend to the present and leave the future to take care of itself; act rashly /你这样只图一时痛快,～地乱花钱,哪是过日子的样子? How can you get along by spending money like water and seeking momentary satisfaction?

顾全 gùquán show consideration for and take care to preserve; keep in mind:～各方利益 concern oneself with the interests of all sides /～面子 save (sb.'s) face; spare sb.'s sensibilities /～名誉 take care to preserve one's reputation; act for the sake of one's reputation

顾全大局 gùquán-dàjú take the interests of the whole into account; bear the overall or general interest in mind:我们要～,不要搞本位主义。We should bear in mind the general interest and not just the interest of a particular unit or locality.

顾赡 gùshàn look after; give financial assistance to:～亲朋 support one's relatives and friends

顾问 gùwèn adviser; consultant; counsellor:～班子 advisory group (*or* team) /～费 consulting fee /高级～ senior adviser /法律～ legal adviser; legal counsel /私人～ personal adviser /农业～ adviser in agriculture /国家安全～ (US) national security adviser (to the President) /专家～ expert consultant

顾问公司 gùwèn gōngsī consultant firm

顾问委员会 gùwèn wěiyuánhuì advisory board, committee, or commission; consultative committee:中共中央～ Central Advisory Commission of the Communist Party of China

顾惜 gùxī ❶ take good care of; cherish; treasure:～名节 treasure one's name and (moral) integrity /～自己的身子 take care of one's health; look after oneself /过于～ take excessive care of; be indulgent to; pamper ❷ look after sb. with sympathy:大家都很～这个孤儿。Everyone felt sorry for the orphan and tried to help him.

顾绣 gùxiù *Gu* embroidery, a style of embroidery handed down from the Ming Dynasty

G

顾恤 gùxù 〈书面〉care for; sympathize with; pity

顾炎武 Gù Yánwǔ Gu Yanwu (formerly translated as Ku Yen-wu, 1613-1682), scholar and thinker of the late Ming and early Qing dynasties

顾影自怜 gùyǐng-zìlián ❶ look at one's shadow and lament one's lot; feel self-pity ❷ look at one's reflection and admire oneself; admire oneself in the mirror; be narcissistic

顾瞻 gùzhān 〈书面〉look back; turn round and look at

顾主 gùzhǔ customer; client; patron:他尽量满足～的要求。He did his best to satisfy his customers.

顾左右而言他 gù zuǒyòu ér yán tā look left and right, talking about other matters; steer clear of the crucial point; evade the subject under discussion

故[1]

gù ❶ incident; accident:变～ unforeseen event; misfortune /事～ accident /突生大～。A big misfortune strikes. ❷ reason; cause:无缘无～ without rhyme or reason; for no reason at all /借～缺席 find an excuse to be absent /不知何～他不回信。I wonder why he didn't answer my letter. ❸ intentionally; deliberately; on purpose:～甚其辞 exaggerate sth. on purpose; deliberately exaggerate/明知～犯 wilfully violate (a law or rule) /欲擒～纵 leave sb. at large the better to apprehend him ❹ hence; therefore; consequently; for this reason:这一段重复,～删去。We delete this paragraph because it is a mere repetition.

故[2]

gù ❶ of the past; former; old: 依然～我 still one's old self /一见如～ feel like old friends at the first meeting/温～知新 gain new insights through reviewing old material (*or* texts) ❷ friend; acquaintance:沾亲带～ related (to sb.) as relative or friend; connected by ties of kinship or friendship /孤身一人,无亲无～ be all alone, without any relative or friend; be on one's own, without kith or kin ❸ die:病～ die of illness /物～ die; pass away /他的双亲早～。Both his parents died long ago.

故步自封 gùbù-zìfēng stand still and refuse to make progress; hold fast to established ways of doing things; be complacent and conservative:既不随波逐流,也不～ neither drift with the tide, nor stand still and refuse to advance

故常 gùcháng 〈书面〉old practice; precedent; convention:不依～ break away from the convention /囿于～,不思进取 follow the old way and not try to make progress; be stuck in a rut

故城 gùchéng (ruins of a) former city:～面貌,依稀可辨。The shape of the former city is faintly visible.

故此 gùcǐ for this reason; on this account; therefore

故道 gùdào ❶ old road; beaten track ❷ old river course:黄河～ old course of the Yellow River

故地 gùdì place formerly inhabited or frequented by one; former home; old haunt:～重游,思绪万千。When I revisited this old haunt of mine, my mind ran riot with a host of memories and reflections.

故第 gùdì 〈书面〉former residence:恭亲王～ former residence of Prince Gong (of the late Qing Dynasty)

故都 gùdū former capital; onetime capital:沈阳是清朝～。Shenyang was the capital of the Qing Dynasty for a time.

故而 gù'ér *also* "故尔" therefore; hence

故宫 gùgōng ❶ palace of a former dynasty ❷ (Gùgōng) Imperial Palace in Beijing:游览～ tour the Imperial Palace

故宫博物院 Gùgōng Bówùyuàn Palace Museum (of Beijing)

故国 gùguó 〈书面〉❶ ancient land; country of long history ❷ native land; native soil; motherland:～之思 nostalgic memories of one's motherland /～梦重归,觉来双泪垂。To my native land I return in dreams again, Only to awaken with tears streaming. ❸ hometown; native place

故技 gùjì *also* "故伎" stock trick; old dodge; old tactic:只不过是当年～,有何值得夸耀之处? This is nothing but the same old trick you employed years ago. What is there to brag about?

故技重演 gùjì-chóngyǎn be up to one's old tricks again; play one's stock tricks; repeat the same old tactics

故迹 gùjì ruined site; thing of the past:古战场～ ruins of an old battleground

故家 gùjiā 〈旧语〉influential or aristocratic family

故交 gùjiāo 〈书面〉old friend:多年～ friend of long standing

故旧 gùjiù old friends and acquaintances:门生～ students, old friends and acquaintances

故居 gùjū former residence or home:上海宋庆龄～ former residence of Madame Soong Ching Ling in Shanghai

故垒 gùlěi former barracks; former fortress:～西边,人道是,三国周郎赤壁。West of the old fortress, so people say, is Lord Zhou's Red Cliff in the time of the Three Kingdoms.

故里 gùlǐ native place:荣归～ return to one's native place with honours; return home in glory

故庐 gùlú former home

故弄玄虚 gùnòng-xuánxū purposely turn a simple matter into a mystery; be deliberately mystifying:老爷爷素来爱～,故事一讲到关键地方便住了口。Trying deliberately to keep people in suspense, the old man would always stop talking whenever there was an important turn in the plot of his story.

故去 gùqù (usu. of one's elders) die; pass away:外婆～的消息,给全家带来了巨大的悲痛。The news of grandmother's death brought great sorrow to the family.

故人 gùrén ❶ old friend:～情深 deep affection of an old friend /这次去杭州遇见了不少～,真令人高兴。I was happy to meet many of my old friends during my stay in Hangzhou. ❷〈书面〉person who has died; deceased person; the dead:祭奠～ hold a memorial service for the dead /昔日挚友,今成～。An old friend has, alas, departed forever. ❸ former wife; former husband

故杀 gùshā 〈法律〉premeditated murder; wilful murder

故实 gùshí ❶ historical fact; thing of the past:老人知道不少～。The old man knows quite a few anecdotes of the past. ❷ source (of a quotation or allusion):自传所引～,均有依据。All the quotes in the autobiography are well sourced.

故世 gùshì die; pass away:相继～ die one after another

故事 gùshì old practice; convention; routine:奉行～ follow the convention mechanically

故事 gùshi ❶ story; tale:民间～ folktale; folkstory /神话～ myth /讲～ tell a story /编～ make up a story; spin a yarn ❷ plot:

这部电影缺乏～。The movie does not have a vivid plot.
故事会 gùshihuì gathering at which stories are told; storytelling session:开～ hold a storytelling session
故事片儿 gùshipiānr 〈口语〉feature film
故事片 gùshipiàn feature film
故事诗 gùshishī (a kind of) narrative poem
故书 gùshū ❶ ancient book ❷ old book:他从废纸堆中找出了几本～。He picked up a few old books from a heap of waste paper.
故态 gùtài one's old ways:～难改。It is difficult to change one's old ways.
故态复萌 gùtài-fùméng slip back into one's old ways; revert to one's old attitude; revert to type:前两年他的确有一些进步,可是最近赌博的恶习又～了。He did make some progress during the last couple of years but recently slipped back into his old ways and was given to gambling again.
故土 gùtǔ native land; native soil:远离～ be far away from one's native land /日益思念～ become increasingly homesick; miss one's native land more and more
故土难移 gùtǔ-nányí *also* "故土难离" it is hard to leave one's native land:老爷子不随儿子去上海,说是～。The old man did not want to live with his son in Shanghai, saying that he was already part of his native soil.
故习 gùxí old, inveterate habit:一洗～ get rid of old habits, once and for all /～难改。Old habits die hard.
故乡 gùxiāng native place; hometown; birthplace:怀念～ yearn for (*or* miss) one's hometown /生我养我的～ native soil on which I was born and brought up /月是～明。The moon seems to be brighter in one's native place.
故意 gùyì intentionally; wilfully; knowingly; deliberately; on purpose:～撒谎 tell a deliberate lie /～冷落某人 intentionally leave sb. out in the cold; deliberately snub sb. /～捣乱 make trouble on purpose /～犯规 wilfully violate the rules; make a deliberate foul /他说话之前,先～咳嗽两声。He purposely cleared his throat before he spoke.
故意犯罪 gùyì fànzuì calculated crime; intentional offence:～犯 intentional offender
故意过失 gùyì guòshī active negligence; intentional negligence
故意侵权行为 gùyì qīnquán xíngwéi intentional tort
故意杀人 gùyì shārén intentional homicide:～既遂罪 completed offence of intentional homicide
故友 gùyǒu ❶ deceased friend ❷ old friend:～重逢。Old friends meet again.
故园 gùyuán old home; native place; hometown:凭添两行泪,寄向～流。A double stream of tears trickle down my face, And flow away, as it were, to my old home.
故宅 gùzhái former residence or house
故障 gùzhàng ❶ breakdown; fault; failure; stoppage; trouble:严重～ serious breakdown (*or* stoppage) /小～ minor trouble /排除～ trouble-clearing; trouble-shooting /无～运行 trouble-free operation /～信号 breakdown signal; fault signaling /～跟踪 fault recorder /～预测 failure prediction/～诊断 fault diagnosis /～指示器 fault detector /～率 fault rate /出了什么～? What's gone wrong? /发动机出了～。The engine has a breakdown. *or* The engine is out of order. ❷ 〈计算机〉(concerning software program) bug
故辙 gùzhé 〈书面〉old rut; old method or way
故知 gùzhī old friend:～不弃 not desert an old friend /他乡遇～ meet an old friend in a distant land; run into an old friend far away from home
故址 gùzhǐ former site (of an organization, building, etc.)
故纸堆 gùzhǐduī 〈贬义〉heap of musty old books and papers:他整天埋在～里。He buried himself among a heap of musty old books all day long.
故智 gùzhì old strategem; old trick
故作高深 gùzuò-gāoshēn pretend to be erudite and profound
故作镇静 gùzuò-zhènjìng feign composure; strive to maintain an outward calm:他～地说:"这倒值得庆幸。" "It's certainly a great comfort," he remarked with feigned composure.
故作姿态 gùzuò-zītài strike a pose; make a deliberate gesture; put on airs

估

gù
see also gū
估衣 gùyi secondhand or cheap ready-made clothes:～铺 shop for secondhand clothes

固[1]

gù ❶ firm; strong; solid:稳～ firm; stable; steadfast /根深蒂～ deep-rooted; ingrained ❷ hard; solid:凝～ solidify; coagulate ❸ resolutely; persistently; firmly:～请 request sb. resolutely (to do sth.); invite persistently/～留 firmly ask sb. to stay; insist on sb.'s stay ❹ solidify; consolidate; strengthen:～防 strengthen (*or* consolidate) defence /～本 make the stem strong; strengthen the body ❺ 〈书面〉superficial; ignorant:*see* "～陋" ❻ *see* "痼" gù ❼ (Gù) a surname

固[2]

gù 〈书面〉❶ originally; in the first place; just; as a matter of course:～所愿也。It is just what I wish. /人～有一死。Everyone must die. *or* No one can escape death. ❷ admittedly; no doubt:务农～可,经商亦无不可。Farming is all right, but it is just as good to do business.
固步自封 gùbù-zìfēng *see* "故步自封" gùbù-zìfēng
固醇 gùchún 〈生化〉sterol:胆～ cholesterol
固辞 gùcí 〈书面〉refuse firmly; turn down resolutely:～不就 resolutely refuse to take a post /～不受 firmly decline a gift or offer
固氮 gùdàn nitrogen-fixation
固氮菌 gùdànjūn 〈微生物〉nitrogen-fixing bacteria; azotobacter
固氮作用 gùdàn zuòyòng 〈农业〉nitrogen fixation; azofication
固定 gùdìng ❶ fixed; static; regular:～工资 fixed wages /～班次 (of buses, etc.) regular run /～收入 regular income /～职业 permanent occupation /不要用～眼光看问题。Don't take a static view of things. ❷ fix; regularize:把螺丝～一下 fix a screw /把时间表～下来 fix (*or* set) a timetable /把两厂的协作关系～下来 regularize the coordination between the two factories
固定程序 gùdìng chéngxù 〈计算机〉fixed routine
固定程序计算机 gùdìng chéngxù jìsuànjī fixed sequence computer
固定存储器 gùdìng cúnchǔqì 〈计算机〉fixed memory; permanent memory or storage
固定电容 gùdìng diànróng 〈电工〉fixed capacity
固定电台 gùdìng diàntái fixed station
固定电压 gùdìng diànyā fixed voltage
固定蜂窝网 gùdìng fēngwōwǎng 〈通信〉fixed cellular network
固定工资制 gùdìng gōngzīzhì fixed-wage system
固定汇率 gùdìng huìlǜ fixed exchange rate
固定基金 gùdìng jījīn fixed fund
固定机库 gùdìng jīkù permanent hangar
固定价格 gùdìng jiàgé fixed price
固定陆基导弹 gùdìng lùjī dǎodàn fixed land-based missile
固定平价 gùdìng píngjià fixed parity
固定起重机 gùdìng qǐzhòngjī 〈机械〉stationary crane, derrick
固定式翻锭机 gùdìngshì fāndìngjī 〈冶金〉stationary ingot tilting pot
固定式平炉 gùdìngshì pínglú 〈冶金〉stationary open-hearth furnace
固定网络 gùdìng wǎngluò fixed network
固定资本 gùdìng zīběn *also* "固定资金" fixed capital
固定资产 gùdìng zīchǎn fixed assets:～投资 fixed assets investment
固化 gùhuà solidify:～酒精 solidified alcohol /～剂 firming agent; curing agent
固疾 gùjí *also* "痼疾" gùjí chronic or obstinate disease
固件 gùjiàn 〈计算机〉firmware
固结 gùjié ❶ become solidified; solidify ❷ 〈地质〉consolidation; concretion:～沉降 consolidation settlement /～程度 degree of consolidation /～土壤 consolidated soil /～体 induration
固井 gùjǐng 〈石油〉well cementation
固陋 gùlòu ill-informed:～寡闻 ignorant and ill-informed
固然 gùrán (acknowledging a statement before raising one's main argument) no doubt; it is true; admittedly; to be sure:步行～安全,可就是要慢得多。No doubt it would be safer to walk, but it would be much slower. /工作单位离我们的住所远～是远点儿,不过有班车,还算方便。It is true that we live rather far from work, but with the shuttle bus, it is still quite convenient. /这个办法～可以,别的办法也不妨试试。This method is all right, to be sure, but there's no harm

in trying other methods as well.
固溶体 gùróngtǐ 〈冶金〉solid solution:～合金 solid solution alloy
固若金汤 gùruòjīntāng strongly fortified; impregnable; invulnerable:前沿阵地～。The forward position is invulnerable.
固涩 gùsè *also* "收涩" shōusè 〈中医〉astringent or styptic treatment for night sweating, seminal emission, chronic diarrhoea, anal prolapse, uterine bleeding, etc.:～止汗 stop perspiration with astringents
固沙林 gùshālín sand-fixation forest; dune-fixing forest:～带 sand-fixing forest belt
固守 gùshǒu ❶ defend tenaciously; be firmly entrenched in:战士们～在阵地上。The soldiers were firmly entrenched in their positions. ❷ cling to (sth. outmoded or conventional):～成法,不思改进 cling to the accepted practice without thinking of making any improvement; follow the convention and refuse to think of improvement /～过时的规章制度 adhere (*or* cling) to outdated rules and regulations
固态 gùtài 〈物理〉solid state:～激光器 solid-state laser /～键盘 solid-state keyboard
固体 gùtǐ solid body; solid:～物质 solid matter; solid /～肥料 solid fertilizer /～等离子体 solid-state plasma /～原件 solid-state component /～理论 theory of solids
固体潮 gùtǐcháo *also* "地潮" dìcháo solid tide; bodily tide; earth tide:～校正 earth tide correction
固体电路 gùtǐ diànlù solid-state circuit:固体集成电路 solid integrated circuit
固体废物 gùtǐ fèiwù solid waste:～处理 solid waste treatment
固体酱油 gùtǐ jiàngyóu solidified soy sauce
固体酒精 gùtǐ jiǔjīng solidified alcohol
固体力学 gùtǐ lìxué solid mechanics
固体汽油 gùtǐ qìyóu solidified gasoline; gasoline gel
固体燃料 gùtǐ ránliào solid fuel:～发动机 solid propellant engine; solid engine
固体燃料火箭 gùtǐ ránliào huǒjiàn 〈航天〉solid-propellant rocket; solid rocket:～发动机 solid propellant (rocket) engine; solid engine /～助推器 solid propellant booster
固体推进剂 gùtǐ tuījìnjì solid (rocket) propellant
固体物理学 gùtǐ wùlǐxué solid-state physics
固习 gùxí *see* "痼习" gùxí
固相 gùxiàng 〈物理〉solid phase; solidoid:～反应 solid phase reaction /～烧结 solid(-phase) sintering /～酶 immobilized enzyme
固有 gùyǒu intrinsic; inherent; innate:～权利 inherent right /～的性格 intrinsic traits /～的文化 indigenous culture /这个词是本民族～的语言。This word is native to our language.
固执 gùzhi ❶ obstinate; stubborn:脾气～ have an obstinate temper; be stubborn by nature /人太～了,实在也是招祸的事。When one is too self-willed one is looking for trouble. ❷ persist in; stick to; cling to:任何犯错误的人只要他不讳疾忌医,不～错误,就有改正的希望。It is possible for those who have made mistakes to correct them so long as they do not conceal their mistakes or persist in them.
固执己见 gùzhi-jǐjiàn cling or adhere stubbornly to one's own opinion:在讨论问题时,他不盲从,也不～。He was neither opinionated nor blindly followed others in the discussion.
固着 gùzhuó adhere to; stick to:牡蛎～在海水中的岩石上。Oysters stick to the rocks in the sea water.

痼 gù chronic; enduring; inveterate:沉～ serious and protracted illness; deep-rooted bad habit
痼弊 gùbì deep-rooted malpractice; long-standing abuse:一扫～ sweep away all long-standing abuses
痼疾 gùjí *also* "固疾" gùjí chronic or obstinate disease; incurable disease:资本主义制度的～ chronic malady of capitalism /这种新药治好了他的～。This new medicine has cured him of his chronic disease.
痼癖 gùpǐ addiction; inveterate weakness:他七十岁时把吸烟的～戒了。He gave up his addiction to smoking when he was seventy.
痼习 gùxí *also* "固习" gùxí inveterate habit; confirmed habit:～难改。It is difficult to get rid of a confirmed habit.

堌 gù dyke (usu. used in place names):青～集 Qinggguji (Dark Dyke Fair, a place in Shandong Province) /龙～ Longgu (Dragon Dyke, a place in Jiangsu Province)

崮 gù mountain with a flat top surrounded by cliffs (usu. used in place names):孟良～ Mengliangqu (in Shandong Province)

锢 gù ❶ plug with molten metal; run molten metal into cracks ❷〈书面〉hold in custody; imprison; jail:党～〈旧语〉outlawing of a faction or party (barring their members or sympathizers from becoming officials and restricting their activities) /禁～ keep in custody; hold prisoner; imprison
锢蔽 gùbì 〈书面〉close up; stop up; block
锢弊 gùbì 〈书面〉*see* "痼弊" gùbì
锢疾 gùjí 〈书面〉*see* "痼疾" gùjí
锢露 gùlou *also* "锢漏" plug with molten metal; run metal into cracks:～锅 pot for running molten metal into cracks
锢囚 gùqiú 〈气象〉occlusion:～气旋 occluded cyclone /～锋 occluded front; occlusion

鲴 gù ❶ xenocypris argentea ❷ fish intestines

梏 gù ancient wooden handcuffs:桎～ fetters and handcuffs; shackles

牿 gù 〈书面〉❶ cross wood tied to ox horns to prevent them from butting people ❷ cattle shed; horse stable; barn

guā

㖞(緺) guā ❶〈书面〉purple-blue ribbon ❷〈古语〉(of a woman) strand of hair

苦 guā
苦蒌 guālóu *see* "栝楼" guālóu

栝 guā ❶〈古语〉Chinese juniper ❷〈书面〉nock of an arrow
see also kuò
栝楼 guālóu *also* "苦蒌" guālóu snakegourd fruit; Chinese trichosanthes; *Trichosanthes kirilowi*:～皮〈中药〉trichosanthes peel /～子〈中药〉trichosanthes seed

括 guā *see* "挺括" tǐnggua
see also kuò

刮¹ guā ❶ scrape; scratch; shave:～铁锈 scrape (*or* chip) off rust /把锅底～干净 scrape the bottom of the pot clean /～胡子 shave oneself (*or* one's beard) /～破 cut oneself in shaving /倒着～鱼鳞才能～干净。When scaling a fish, one must do it from tail to head. /就～破一点皮。It was only a scratch. ❷ smear with (paste, etc.):～糨子 stiffen (cloth) by spreading paste over it; size ❸ plunder; fleece; rob; extort:搜～钱财 plunder (*or* fleece) people; extort money ❹〈方言〉scold; give a dressing down:挨一通～ get a dressing down /狠狠～了他一顿 give him a good telling-off

刮²(颳) guā (of wind) blow:风～得真大,把树叶都～光了。It blew so hard that the trees were stripped clean of their leaves. /一阵风～走了他的帽子。A gust of wind blew off his cap. /半夜～起了大风。A gale (*or* A high wind) rose at midnight. /什么风把你～来了? To what do I owe the pleasure of your company? *or* What brought you here?
刮板 guābǎn 〈机械〉scraper plate or blade; scraper; drawing template; drag-flight:～运输机 scraper chain conveyer /链式～运输机 scraping transporter
刮板泵 guābǎnbèng scraper pump
刮板式给煤机 guābǎnshì jǐméijī scraper feeder
刮板式平路机 guābǎnshì pínglùjī scraping grader
刮板输送机 guābǎn shūsòngjī scraper conveyor; drag-flight conveyor
刮鼻子 guā bízi ❶ (as punishment for the loser in a card game, etc.) scrape sb.'s nose (with one's forefinger) ❷ scrape one's own

nose to shame other people ❸〈方言〉scold; tell off; haul over the coals:王师傅狠狠地刮了学徒一顿鼻子。Master Wang gave his apprentice a good scolding.

刮匙 guāchí 〈医学〉curet; curette

刮打扁儿 guādabiǎnr 〈方言〉a kind of locust

刮刀 guādāo scraping cutter; scraping knife; scraper:三角～ triangular scraper

刮地皮 guā dìpí 〈比喻〉batten on the fat of the land; bleed the common people white; grow rich by extortion

刮斗刨煤机 guādǒu páoméijī scraper planer

刮斗装载机 guādǒu zhuāngzàijī scraper loader

刮宫 guāgōng 〈医学〉dilatation and curettage (D and C):现在作人工流产可以不必～了。Abortions nowadays can be done without D and C.

刮垢磨光 guāgòu-móguāng scrape the dirt off sth. and make it shine; bring sth. back to resplendence; carefully polish to attain perfection; keep improving:治学要不断～,才能有所长进。In scholarly pursuits, one should make constant improvement in order to move ahead.

刮刮叫 guāguājiào *also*"呱呱叫" guāguājiào excellent; superb

刮痕 guāhén scratching; scratch:～硬度试验〈机械〉scratch test

刮胡子 guā húzi 〈方言〉tell off; scold:小心领导刮你的胡子。Mind that your boss will take you to task!

刮脸 guāliǎn shave (the face):～刀 razor /～膏 shaving cream (*or* soap)

刮脸皮 guā liǎnpí 〈方言〉rub the forefinger against one's own or sb.'s cheek (to shame sb.); point the finger of scorn at sb.:对于好谈这种空洞理论的人,应该伸出一个指头向他～。We should point the finger of scorn at those who are fond of such irrelevant theorizing. /小心人家刮你的脸皮。Beware that you do not give your critics a handle for ridicule.

刮路机 guālùjī drag; planer

刮目 guāmù look at sb. with new eyes:令人～ deserve to be regarded in a new light

刮目相看 guāmù-xiāngkàn *also*"刮目相待" look at sb. with new eyes; regard sb. in a totally different light; treat sb. with increased respect; sit up and take notice:这些年轻人进步真快,真是"士别三日,当～"哪。What rapid progress these young people have made! Just as the saying goes, "a scholar who has been away three days must be regarded in a new light".

刮痧 guāshā 〈中医〉(as treatment for sunstroke) scraping the patient's neck, chest or back:～是一种古老的民间疗法。Scraping is an ancient folk treatment.

刮舌子 guāshézi tongue scraper

刮削 guāxiāo ❶ scrape:～器 scraper ❷ embezzle; exploit:～钱财 squeeze money out of sb.

刮运机 guāyùnjī scraper transporter

鸹

guā *see*"老鸹" lǎogua

瓜

guā 〈植物〉melon; gourd:冬～ white gourd /西～ watermelon /苦～ bitter gourd /丝～ towel gourd; dishcloth gourd /南～ pumpkin /黄～ cucumber /香～ muskmelon /～棚 melon hut /～藤 melon (*or* gourd) vine /种～得～。As a man sows, so shall he reap. /王婆卖～,自卖自夸。There's nothing like the melons one peddles. *or* There's nothing like leather. /鱼儿离不开水,～儿离不开秧。The melon clings to the vine as the fish to water.

瓜氨酸 guā'ānsuān 〈生化〉citrulline

瓜达拉哈拉 Guādálāhālā Guadalajara, second-largest city of Mexico

瓜代 guādài 〈书面〉succeed:他离任后,由谁～? Who will succeed him when he leaves office?

瓜德罗普 Guādéluópǔ Guadeloupe, a group of islands in the Lesser Antilles (in the West Indies) forming an overseas department of France

瓜蒂 guādì 〈中医〉pedicel or stem of a muskmelon:～散〈中药〉ground pedicel of muskmelon

瓜分 guāfēn carve up; divide up; partition:那个小国的领土被列强～了。The territory of that small country was carved up by the big powers. /查获的赃物被他们～了。The recovered loot was divided up among them.

瓜葛 guāgé connection; implication; association:此事与他有些～。He is somehow implicated in this matter. /原来你们之间还有这么一段～,真有意思。How interesting you were once associated before. /我们两家素无～。Our two families have never had anything to do with each other.

瓜葛亲 guāgéqīn distant relative

瓜类 guālèi 〈农业〉melon; gourd; *Cuckmis melo*:～栽培 melon cultivation /～作物 melon crop /～蔬菜 gourd vegetable

瓜连 guālian 〈方言〉involve; implicate:他与这件案子有～。He was implicated in the case.

瓜纽 guāniǔ *also*"瓜纽子" young fruitlet of melon or gourd

瓜农 guānóng melon grower

瓜皮绿 guāpílǜ cucumber green

瓜皮帽 guāpímào skullcap:头戴一顶旧～ wearing an old shabby skullcap

瓜片 Guāpiàn *guapian*, a green tea produced in Anhui Province:六安～,中外驰名。*Guapian*, produced in Lu'an, is a green tea renowned both at home and abroad.

瓜剖豆分 guāpōu-dòufēn partition or carve up sb.'s territory:那时国家几乎被～,哪里谈得上什么人权? As the country was nearly partitioned then, what human rights were there to speak of?

瓜期 guāqī 〈书面〉date on which one's term of office expires

瓜瓤 guāráng pulp of a melon

瓜仁 guārén kernel of a melon seed

瓜熟蒂落 guāshú-dìluò a melon falls (off the stem) when it is ripe — things will easily be settled when conditions are ripe; at the right time, everything comes easily:～,水到渠成。When the melon is ripe, it falls off its stem. When the water flows, a channel is formed. *or* Everything comes easy at the right time. /他们经过两年的恋爱,终于～,结成了终生伴侣。When the time was ripe after two years of courting, they married each other.

瓜藤上长不出茄子 guāténgshang zhǎngbuchū qiézi 〈谚语〉a melon vine can never grow an eggplant — you cannot make a silk purse out of a sow's ear

瓜田 guātián 〈农业〉melon field

瓜田李下 guātián-lǐxià 〈比喻〉in a melon patch or under a plum tree — in suspicious circumstances or surroundings:瓜田不纳履,李下不正冠。Don't bend to pull on your shoes in a melon patch; don't reach to adjust your hat under a plum tree — don't do anything that may arouse suspicion. /～,古今所慎。When in suspicious circumstances, people have always been careful to avoid suspicions. /室中仅他二人,当然难免～之嫌。As they were the only two people in the room, they naturally fell under suspicion.

瓜条 guātiáo ❶ sugar-preserved white gourd slices ❷ sliced cucumber with condiments

瓜蔓 guāwàn vine of melon or gourd

瓜蔓抄 guāwànchāo 〈旧语〉confiscate the property of an official or a subject and kill all those related one way or another

瓜亚基尔 Guāyàjī'ěr Guayaquil, principal Pacific seaport and second-largest city of Ecuador

瓜子 guāzǐ melon seeds (usu. cooked and flavoured):嗑～ crack and eat melon seeds

瓜子脸 guāzǐliǎn oval face:～上经常带着迷人的笑容。There was always a charming smile on her oval face. /她那漂亮的～上长着一对水灵灵的大眼睛。Her beautiful oval face was lit up by two big bright eyes.

呱

guā

see also gū; guǎ

呱嗒 guādā *also*"呱哒" ❶〈象声〉clip-clop; clack; clatter:～～的马蹄声 clatter of horsehoofs /她穿木屐走起路来～～地响。She clip-clops along when she walks in clogs. ❷〈方言〉mock; satirize:你就会～人! What a mocker you are!

呱嗒 guāda *also*"呱哒"〈方言〉❶ pull a long face:他整天～着脸不理人。He pulled a long face all day, caring to speak to nobody. ❷ chatter; talk rubbish:乱～一阵 chatter away foolishly /你～些什么呀? What nonsense are you talking?

呱嗒板儿 guādabǎnr ❶ bamboo clappers; Chinese castanets:他快板说得好,～也打得好。Good at performing clapper-talk, he handles the bamboo clappers well. ❷〈方言〉clogs:她趿拉上～就出门去了。She slipped into the clogs and went out.

呱呱 guāguā 〈象声〉(of ducks) quack; (of frogs) croak; (of crows) caw:～叫喊的鸭群 flocks of quacking ducks /池塘里的青蛙～

～整夜乱叫，吵得我一点儿都睡不着。The frogs croaking in the pond kept me awake all night.
see also gūgū

呱呱叫 guāguājiào *also*“刮刮叫”guāguājiào 〈口语〉tiptop; topnotch; terrific; superb: 他是个～的厨师。He is a topnotch chef. /这衣服的做工～。The suit is made with superb tailoring. /“你看怎么样?”“～!”“What do you think?”“Terrific (*or* Gorgeous, *or* Tops)!”

呱唧 guāji ❶〈象声〉sound of clapping ❷ clap (hands): 他见别人都鼓掌，只好也跟着～了几下。Seeing everybody applauding, he clapped his hands a few times perfunctorily. /现在是刘先生独唱，大家～～。Now Mr. Liu will sing for us. Please give him a big hand.

胍

guā 〈化学〉guanidine: ～胺 guanamine /～基醋酸 glycocyamine /～卡因 acoine; acoin

刮

guā 〈书面〉scrape off

guǎ

寡

guǎ ❶ few; scarce; scant: 曲高和～ highbrow songs find few listeners /以～敌众 pit a few against many; fight against heavy odds /多～不等 vary in number /～见少闻 poorly informed and ignorant ❷ tasteless; thin; bland: 清汤～水 watery soup; sth. insipid ❸ widowed: 守～ live in widowhood

寡白 guǎbái 〈方言〉(of complexion) pale; pallid: 他吓得脸色～。He turned deathly pale in fear.

寡薄 guǎbó 〈书面〉❶ scant; scarce; not abundant: 资源～ poor in natural resources ❷ (of argument, strength, etc.) insufficient; weak; lacking: 论据～ shaky (*or* weak) argument /科学依据～ inadequate scientific evidence

寡不敌众 guǎbùdízhòng the few cannot withstand the many; be hopelessly outnumbered: ～而退 retreat when hopelessly outnumbered /～，孤难胜群，此常理也。It is common sense that the few are no match for the many and a single man can hardly beat a crowd.

寡淡 guǎdàn (of taste, interest, etc.) watery; tasteless; insipid; dull: ～无味的菜肴 tasteless dishes /～乏味的谈话 insipid (*or* dull) conversation /他的生活单调～。He leads a monotonous and uneventful life.

寡断 guǎduàn irresolute; hesitant and indecisive: 优柔～是一个军事指挥员的致命弱点。Irresolution is a fatal weakness in a military commander.

寡恩 guǎ'ēn unkind; harsh; mean: 刻薄～ unkind and mean

寡二少双 guǎ'èr-shǎoshuāng matchless; peerless; outstanding

寡妇 guǎfu widow: ～弱女 widow with a young daughter /～门前是非多。〈俗语〉The widow's house is a starting post of rumour. *or* Gossips always cluster around a widow's house.

寡硅酸 guǎguīsuān 〈化学〉oligosilicic acid

寡合 guǎhé 〈书面〉hard to get along with; unsociable: 他性情孤僻，落落～。He is of an uncommunicative, eccentric disposition, and difficult to get along with.

寡欢 guǎhuān 〈书面〉unhappy: 郁郁～ unhappy

寡基因 guǎjīyīn 〈生物〉oligogene: ～性状 oligogenic character

寡酒 guǎjiǔ drink wine without taking any food: 喝～ drink wine without any food to go with it

寡居 guǎjū 〈书面〉live in widowhood

寡佬 guǎlǎo bachelor; widower

寡廉鲜耻 guǎlián-xiǎnchǐ lost to shame; brazen: 一副～的丑相 very picture of brazenness /他是个～的家伙，求他做什么? He is a shameless bastard. What's the point of begging him?

寡陋 guǎlòu ill-informed and ignorant

寡霉素 guǎméisù 〈微生物〉oligomycin

寡默 guǎmò 〈书面〉taciturn; reticent; of few words: ～之人 man of few words

寡母 guǎmǔ widowed mother; widow with children: 孤儿～ widow with fatherless children

寡妻 guǎqī ❶ widow ❷〈旧语〉primary wife; main wife

寡情 guǎqíng lacking in affection; unfeeling; cold-blooded: ～少义 lacking in friendship and affection; heartless; cold-blooded

寡趣 guǎqù uninteresting; boring: ～之人 bore / 她常为找了个～死板男人而苦恼。She often felt sad for having married a dull and mulish husband.

寡人 guǎrén ❶ (used by a monarch to refer to himself) I, the sovereign; we: 谁能替～分忧? Who can help resolve our worries? ❷ solitary or isolated person; lonely man: 孤家～ be all on one's own; be totally isolated

寡瘦 guǎshòu 〈方言〉very thin; bony: ～的脸 very thin face /马儿长得～～的。The horse is bony.

寡糖 guǎtáng 〈化学〉oligose

寡头 guǎtóu oligarch: 金融～ financial oligarch; financial magnate /～垄断 oligopoly

寡头政治 guǎtóu zhèngzhì oligarchy

寡味 guǎwèi tasteless; dull; uninteresting: 茶饭～ have no appetite (for food) /他的报告索然～。His talk was boring.

寡闻 guǎwén ill-informed: 孤陋～ ignorant and ill-informed /～陋见 ill-informed opinion

寡言 guǎyán taciturn; of few words: 整天沉默～，不知谁得罪了他。I wonder what's troubling him, for he keeps silent all day long.

寡欲 guǎyù curtail or restrain one's desires: 清心～ cleanse the heart and have few desires; control one's passions and curtail one's desires

寡助 guǎzhù enjoy little support: 得道多助，失道～。A just cause enjoys abundant support, while an unjust cause finds little support.

剐(剮)

guǎ ❶ (capital punishment in ancient times) cut to pieces; dismember: 是杀是～，你看着办吧。Behead me, or cut me to pieces, as you please. /舍得一身～，敢把皇帝拉下马。He who fears not being cut to pieces dares to unhorse the emperor. ❷ cut; slit: 他胳臂上～了一个又深又长的大口子。He had a long and deep cut on his arm.

呱

guǎ *see*“拉呱儿”lāguǎr
see also gū; guā

guà

诖

guà ❶〈书面〉deceive; dupe: ～上之罪 crime of deceiving the sovereign ❷ involve; implicate: *see*“～误”

诖误 guàwù *also*“罣误”guàwù (make) suffer by implication; implicate or involve in trouble: ～百姓 involve the people in disastrous consequences; unintentionally make the people suffer /～全家 implicate the whole family in one's wrongdoing

褂

guà traditional-style garment or jacket; gown: 小～儿 short gown; jacket /长～儿 long gown /马～儿 sleeveless mandarin jacket (worn over a gown) /汗～儿 undershirt

褂子 guàzi traditional-style upper garment; short gown; jacket: 蓝布～ blue jacket

挂(掛)

guà ❶ hang; put up; suspend: 请把大衣～在衣架上。Please hang your overcoat on the hat tree. /教师把地图～在黑板上。The teacher put the map on the blackboard. /一轮明月～在天上。A bright moon hung in the sky. /肖像～倒了。The portrait is upside-down. /这事眼下不好办，还是先～一～吧。As this is rather hard to handle for the time being, why don't we suspend (*or* shelve) it for a while? ❷ leave sth. outstanding; be pending: 这几件案子一直～着呢。These cases have remained unsettled (*or* pending). ❸ ring off; hang up: 她把电话～了。She hung up. /请别～电话，我看看他是否在家。Please hold the line while I find out if he's in. ❹〈方言〉call up; ring up; put sb. through to: 有空时给我～个电话。Ring me up when you're free. /请给我～三〇二房间。Please give me Room 302. *or* Put me through to Room 302, please. /先生，你的电话已～通。You are through, sir. ❺ hitch; get caught: 把拖车～上 hitch up the trailer /树枝把她的头巾～住了。Her scarf got caught on a tree branch. ❻ be anxious; be concerned about; have sth. weighing on one's mind: ～在心上 have sth. at heart /牵肠～肚 feel deep anxiety; be very worried /直到最后一刻，他心里只～着群众的安危。He concerned himself solely with the safety of the people until the last moment. ❼ be covered with; be coated with: 身上～了一层土 be covered with dust /脸上～着天真的微笑 wearing an innocent smile /

瓦器外面～了一层釉子。The earthen pot was glazed on the outside. ❽ register (at a hospital); make an appointment (with a doctor):请～皮肤科。Please register for dermatology. /我～的是四号。My registration number is 4. /这个专家号很难～。It is difficult to make an appointment with this specialist. ❾〈量词〉a set or string of:一～珠子 a string of pearls /一～鞭炮 a string of firecrackers /一～竹帘子 a bamboo curtain /一～驴车 a donkey and cart

挂碍 guà'ài worry; care:心中没有～ carefree; free of worries

挂包 guàbāo 〈方言〉satchel

挂表 guàbiǎo 〈方言〉pocket watch:老式～ old-fashioned pocket watch

挂不住 guàbuzhù 〈方言〉be unable to conceal one's embarrassment or agitation; give oneself away:心里虽然已经服输,但脸上还是有些～。Though convinced of his own mistake, he looked a bit embarrassed.

挂彩 guàcǎi ❶ decorate (usu. with coloured silk festoons) in celebration of sth. or for a festive occasion:人们张灯～,为他操办喜事。People were busy decorating the house with coloured silk festoons (*or* streamers) and lanterns for his wedding ceremony. ❷ be wounded in action:护士正在为～的战士包扎伤口。A nurse was dressing the wounds for a soldier. /没想到刚上战场就～了。Little did he anticipate that he would be wounded shortly after he had gone into battle.

挂车 guàchē trailer

挂扯 guàchě ❶ snag; hook and tear:他的衣服被树枝子～得稀烂。His clothes were torn to tatters on the tree branches. ❷〈方言〉involve; implicate:他和这种事怎么～得上呢? How could he have got involed in such matters?

挂齿 guàchǐ mention:区区小事,何足～。Such a trifling matter is not worth mentioning.

挂锄 guàchú put away the hoe (for the season); finish hoeing

挂橱 guàchú wall cabinet

挂搭 guàda 〈方言〉droop; dangle:折了的树枝在树上～着。Broken twigs were drooping from the tree. /父亲整天皱着眉头～着脸。Father knit his brows and pulled a long face all day long.

挂单 guàdān *also* "挂褡" (of a roaming monk) seek accommodation in a temple:前几天倒有一个游方和尚到此～,第二天一清早就走了。A wandering monk did spend the night here a few days ago, but he left early the next morning.

挂挡 guàdǎng put into gear; move into gear:挂高速挡 put (a vehicle) into high gear; change to high gear /挂不上挡 (of a vehicle) refuse to move into gear

挂灯 guàdēng lamp suspended from the ceiling; pendant lamp:枝形～ chandelier /舞厅里各式～发出柔和的光。In the ballroom, various types of pendant lamps shone softly.

挂斗 guàdǒu trailer

挂钩 guàgōu ❶ hook:衣服～ clothes hooks ❷〈交通〉couple (two railway coaches); hook:(火车)自动～器 automatic coupling /卡车后部有拖曳～。The truck has a towing (*or* drag) hook at the rear. ❸ link up with; establish contact with; get in touch with:奖金与工作表现～ link up bonuses with performance /～单位 institution one has regular links with /大学应与科研单位、生产单位紧密～。Universities should establish close contacts with institutions of research and production. /他们俩早已挂上钩了。The two of them have long been in touch with each other.

挂冠 guàguān 〈书面〉resign (one's official position):～封印 hang up one's official hat and seal up one's seal — resign and leave /一怒之下～而去 resign (one's position) and go off in a huff

挂果 guàguǒ (of a fruit tree) bear fruit:三年成林,五年～ (of newly planted trees) grow into an orchard in three years and begin to bear fruit in five /院子里的这棵柿子树今年第一次挂了果。The persimmon tree in the yard bore its first fruit this year.

挂号 guàhào ❶ register (at a hospital, etc.):看病先～,这是常理。It is routine to register before seeing a doctor. ❷ send by registered mail:～邮资 registration charge /这封信很重要,必须～。This letter is important and must be sent by registered mail (*or* must be registered).

挂号处 guàhàochù registration office

挂号费 guàhàofèi registration fee

挂号信 guàhàoxìn registered mail or letter

挂红 guàhóng hang up red streamers or festoons for a celebration

挂花 guàhuā ❶ (of trees) bloom:桃树～时节 time when peach trees are in blossom ❷ be wounded in action:排长～了,班长代替指挥。The squad leader took over the command after the platoon leader was wounded.

挂怀 guàhuái be anxious or worried about; show concern for; have (sth.) weighing on one's mind:这么点小事还劳你～,真有点过意不去。I am really sorry to trouble you with such a trifle.

挂幌子 guà huǎngzi 〈方言〉❶ hang or put up a shop sign ❷ show evidence; betray (oneself):他一定多喝了两口,脸都～了。He must have had a drop too much. It shows on his face.

挂火 guàhuǒ 〈方言〉fly off the handle; flare up:她心中～,气不打一处来。She was boiling with anger and found everything amiss.

挂货 guàhuò 〈方言〉(of a fruit tree) bear fruit

挂货儿铺 guàhuòrpù 〈方言〉secondhand shop; junk shop

挂记 guàji miss; worry about sb. absent:～远方的儿子 miss one's son who is far away

挂家 guàjiā be concerned about one's family; miss one's family:他就是～,不安心工作。He was too concerned about his family to keep his mind on his work.

挂甲 guàjiǎ retire from a military post:～归田 retire from the army and live in the countryside /该队的几名老队员相继～离队。Veteran members of the team have retired one after another.

挂件 guàjiàn pendent ornament or decoration:金银～ gold and silver pendent ornaments

挂浆陶瓷 guàjiāng táocí slipware

挂劲 guàjìn 〈方言〉get furious; be angry:好不容易劝得这位冷静下来,那一位又挂上劲了。It had taken all our persuasion to calm one down when the other flared up again.

挂镜线 guàjìngxiàn *also* "画镜线" huàjìngxiàn picture moulding; picture rail; picture rod

挂驹 guàjū (of a mare, etc.) be in foal; be pregnant

挂靠 guàkào be attached or affiliated to; be subordinate to; be linked with:中国投资学会～于中国建设银行。China Investment Society is affiliated to the Construction Bank of China.

挂拉 guàla 〈方言〉involve; implicate:他们是成心往你身上～。They deliberately tried to implicate you. /他们是一伙不法之徒,你怎能跟他们～上! They are a lawless bunch. You cannot afford to get involved (with them)!

挂兰 guàlán 〈植物〉*Chlorophgtum comosum*

挂落 guàlào *also* "挂络"〈方言〉involve; implicate:吃～ get implicated /事情闹大了,你我都得受～。You and I shall be incriminated if things come to a head.

挂累 guàlěi involve; implicate:这个案子一定不要～无辜。Innocent people must not be implicated in the case.

挂历 guàlì wall calendar

挂连 guàlián involve; implicate

挂镰 guàlián put away the sickle — complete the year's harvesting

挂恋 guàliàn 〈方言〉worry about; miss:你放心出国学习,不要～我和孩子。Please go abroad and pursue your studies with your mind at ease; don't worry about me and the baby.

挂零 guàlíng (used after a round number) odd:七十～ seventy-odd /报名人数五十～。More than fifty people signed up.

挂柳 guàliǔ full-grown willow branches placed upside down in the water along the embarkment to offset pounding by the floods

挂漏 guàlòu *see* "挂一漏万"

挂虑 guàlǜ feel uneasy or anxious; worry about:你对这件事过于～了。I'm afraid you are over-anxious (*or* overly anxious) about this.

挂免战牌 guà miǎnzhànpái hang up a "no battle" sign; refuse battle or debate

挂面 guàmiàn fine dried noodles; vermicelli:西红柿～ vermicelli with tomato flavouring

挂名 guàmíng in name only; titular; nominal; ostensible:～头头 titular (*or* nominal) head; figurehead /～夫妻 husband and wife in name only; nominal couple /～合伙人 nominal partner; ostensible partner /～差事 nominal job; titular position; sinecure /她在公司只挂个名儿,实际上做自己的生意。Nominally on the company's payroll, she actually does business on her own.

挂念 guàniàn worry about (sb. absent); miss:我一切都好,请不要～。Everything's fine with me. Please don't worry. /我们都很～你。We all miss you very much.

挂拍 guàpāi ❶ (of table tennis, tennis or badminton) give up the bat or racket — retire as a player ❷ come to an end; complete:全国

乒乓球擂台赛日前～。The National Table Tennis Championship Tournament came to an end yesterday.

挂牌 guàpái ❶ (usu. of professionals or businessmen) hang out one's shingle; put up one's brass plate; go into practice or business: ～行医 put up one's brass plate and practise medicine; go into practice as a doctor of medicine /这家公司刚刚～营业。The company has only just started business officially. ❷ put up a tag or label; list: ～股票总值 total value of listed shares /这里销售的摩托车、汽车，一律～标价。Every motorcycle and car on sale here has a price tag on it. /中国银行每日～公布各种外币汇率。The Bank of China puts out a bulletin every day listing the exchange rates of foreign currencies. ❸ (of service personnel, office workers, doctors, etc.) wear a name plate on one's breast: ～办公 wear a name plate when in office

挂牌股票 guàpái gǔpiào listed stock

挂牌汇价 guàpái huìjià posted rate

挂牌上市公司 guàpái shàngshì gōngsī listed company; quoted company

挂牌证券 guàpái zhèngquàn quoted securities; listed securities

挂屏 guàpíng vertically-hung mounted scroll; scroll: 一对金漆～ a pair of scrolls in gold-lacquered frames

挂气 guàqì 〈方言〉 get angry; flare up: 何必为这点小事～? Why get angry over such trifles?

挂起来 guàqilai be shelved; lay aside: 对这个问题大家意见分歧很大，建议～。I propose that this question be shelved as there is a wide divergence of opinion.

挂牵 guàqiān be concerned about (sb. absent); worry about (sb. absent); miss: 老人心里总是～着儿女们。Aging parents are always concerned about their children.

挂欠 guàqiàn get on credit; owe: 他入不敷出，在外常有～。As he cannot make both ends meet, he often gets things on credit.

挂伤 guàshāng be wounded: 腿上～ be wounded in the leg

挂神 guàshén 〈方言〉 concern oneself; have at heart; look after

挂失 guàshī report or declare the loss of sth.: 登报～ declare the loss of sth. in the newspapers /到银行～ report the loss of a cheque, etc. to the bank /～止付 (of a bank) stop payment (upon notification of loss of a cheque) /这个存折已经～。The account-book has been reported as lost. /遗失身分证必须立即向派出所～。You must report to the police sub-station immediately if you lose your ID.

G

挂帅 guàshuài be in command; assume or take command; take charge of; assume leadership: 政治～，思想领先 put politics in command and ideological work in the first place /该项目由市长亲自～。The mayor will assume personal command of the project.

挂锁 guàsuǒ padlock

挂毯 guàtǎn tapestry: 优质～ high-quality tapestry

挂头牌 guà tóupái (as in traditional opera) play the leading role; be the leading star; lead the cast

挂图 guàtú wall map; hanging or wall chart: 墙上贴着一张展示生产情况的大～。There is a big chart on the wall indicating developments in production.

挂线疗法 guàxiàn liáofǎ 〈中医〉 ligating method for treating anal fistula; ligation therapy

挂相 guàxiàng show on one's face; wear a look of displeasure, etc.: 他心里不高兴，脸上可从不～。He never shows his displeasure even when he feels upset.

挂孝 guàxiào wear mourning; be in mourning: 他戴着黑纱，为父亲～。He wore a black armband in mourning for his deceased father.

挂笑 guàxiào wear a smile; smile: 满脸～ be all smiles /她脸上挂着迷人的微笑。There was a charming smile on her face.

挂鞋 guàxié *also* "挂靴" (of a football player, skater, etc.) hang up (sports) shoes — say goodbye to one's career as an athlete; retire as a pro.: 他决定决赛后～。He decided to retire as a professional athlete after the finals.

挂心 guàxīn concern oneself with; be on one's mind; worry about; care for: 孩子入托，给老人看病，哪件事不得她～。Finding a kindergarten for the child, taking their old parents to the hospital, and what not — she had to worry about everything.

挂胸式电话机 guàxiōngshì diànhuàjī breast telephone (phone hanging from the neck)

挂羊头卖狗肉 guà yángtóu mài gǒuròu hang out a sheep's head and sell dog-meat; cry up wine and sell vinegar; sell horse-meat as beefsteak: 我看他们上上下下全是～的货色。I know that the whole lot of them are the kind of people who would sell horse-meat as beefsteak.

挂一漏万 guàyī-lòuwàn (often used by an editor, etc. as a self-deprecating formula) list one item while missing ten thousand others; for one thing cited, ten thousand may have been left out; the list is far from exhaustive; leave much to be desired: 限于水平，难免～。Due to my limited knowledge, incompleteness is hardly avoidable.

挂衣钩 guàyīgōu clothes-hook; coat hook

挂意 guàyì 〈方言〉 mind; care; take to heart: 请不用～。Please forget about it. /我抽支香烟你不会～吧。Would you mind if I smoke a cigarette?

挂掌 guàzhǎng nail on horseshoes; shoe a horse

挂账 guàzhàng buy or sell on credit

挂职 guàzhí ❶ take up a temporary post (in order to temper oneself) ❷ serve in a lower level unit for a period while retaining one's position in the previous unit

挂钟 guàzhōng wall clock: 墙上的～正指十点。The clock on the wall said ten sharp.

挂轴 guàzhóu hanging scroll (of Chinese painting or calligraphy)

卦

guà one of the Eight Trigrams as a divinatory symbol: 八～ Eight Trigrams /占～ practise divination; cast a horoscope /变～ 〈比喻〉 go back on one's word; break an agreement

卦辞 guàcí *also* "彖辞" tuàncí commentaries on various combinations of the Eight Trigrams (in *The Book of Changes*)

卦摊儿 guàtānr fortune-teller's stall

罣(罫)

guà be concerned about

罣误 guàwù *also* "诖误" guàwù (make) suffer by implication; implicate or involve in trouble

絓

guà 〈书面〉 cause to stumble; block

guāi

掴(摑)

guāi *also* guó slap; smack: 耳～子 box on the ear; slap across (*or* on) the face /她使劲地～了他一耳光。She slapped him hard on the face.

乖[1]

guāi ❶ well-behaved; obedient; good: 这孩子真～! What a good child! /真是个～孩子。There's a dear. *or* There's a good boy (*or* girl). ❷ clever; smart; alert: 嘴很～ honey-tongued; honey-lipped /学～了 become smarter (*or* wiser) /得了便宜卖～ show off one's cleverness (*or* shrewdness) after taking advantage of sb. or sth.

乖[2]

guāi 〈书面〉 ❶ be contrary (to reason); be at variance; contradict: 有～人情 run counter to human nature /时～命蹇 one's luck is against one; have bad luck ❷ (of one's character, behaviour, etc.) perverse; abnormal; headstrong

乖舛 guāichuǎn 〈书面〉 ❶ falsehood; fallacy; error ❷ not smooth: 仕途～。The official career is full of twists and turns.

乖乖 guāiguāi ❶ well-behaved; compliant; obedient: 我说啥你都得～地听着。Whatever I say, you will have to behave and listen. /孩子们～地坐着听老师讲故事。The children all sat quietly listening to the teacher's story. ❷ little dear; little darling: 快睡吧，妈妈的好～! Sleep, mummy's little dear! /好好亲爷爷一下，小～。Give grandpa a good kiss, little darling.

乖乖 guāiguai gosh; my; boy: ～，外边真冷! Gosh, it is cold out here! /～，这幅画画得真好! Boy, this painting is real fine!

乖哄 guāihǒng 〈方言〉 coax; humour: ～孩子吃药真不容易。It's not easy to coax a child to take medicine. /她知道怎样～小孩。She knows how to handle children. *or* She has a way with children.

乖蹇 guāijiǎn 〈书面〉 (of one's fate) unfortunate; bad: 时运～ one's fortune is against one; be down on luck

乖觉 guāijué alert; quick; smart: 小麻雀真～，一有动静就飞了。Always on the alert, the little sparrow flew away at the slightest sound. /少年注意到爷爷的眼色，～地扭转了话题。Quick and smart, the boy changed the subject when he caught grandpa's glance.

乖剌 guāilà 〈书面〉 *see* "乖戾"

乖离 guāilí 〈书面〉run counter to; go against; violate:上下～,互相埋怨。People above were at odds with those below, laying the blame on each other.

乖戾 guāilì (of character, behaviour, etc.) perverse; recalcitrant; cantankerous:生性～ perverse by nature /举止～ cantankerous in behaviour /～不正 perverse and abnormal /～之气〈中医〉epidemic pathogenic factor

乖谬 guāimiù absurd; abnormal; fallacious:言辞～ absurd (*or* abnormal) in speech /理论～ theoretically fallacious (*or* absurd)

乖僻 guāipì eccentric; bizarre; unnatural:行为～ eccentric in one's conduct; eccentric behaviour /～之学 bizarre theory; heretical theory

乖巧 guāiqiǎo ❶ cute; lovely:小姑娘伶俐～,很讨人喜欢。The little girl is bright and cute; people all like her. ❷ clever; smart:眼看男朋友要生气了,她～地换了个话题。Seeing her boyfriend was about to get angry, she cleverly changed the subject.

乖顺 guāishùn 〈方言〉obedient; compliant:这个顽皮孩子到了老师面前却特别～。Naughty as he was, the boy became extremely obedient before his teachers.

乖违 guāiwéi 〈书面〉❶ abnormal; perverse:寒暑～ abnormal weather (cold when it should be hot and vice versa) ❷ contrary; contradictory; recalcitrant ❸ part with; separate:久相～。It is a long time since we parted.

乖误 guāiwù fallacy; error; absurdity:文字多有～。There are many errors in the text.

乖张 guāizhāng ❶ eccentric and unreasonable; odd; perverse; recalcitrant:性情～ be of an eccentric and unreasonable character; be perverse by nature ❷〈书面〉not smooth:命运～ vicissitudes of life

guǎi

拐[1](❺柺) guǎi ❶ change direction; turn:见红绿灯往左～。Turn left at the traffic light. /～过邮局,不远就到火车站了。Turn round the post office and the railway station is not far away. /汽车～进一条小巷。The car turned into a lane. /咱们～回去吧。Let's turn back. ❷〈方言〉corner; turning:墙～ corner of a house (*or* wall) ❸ limp:走路一瘸一～ walk with a limp; limp along ❹ (used verbally only, as over the telephone) seven:洞洞～(007) zero, zero, seven ❺ crutch:拄着双～练习走路 practise walking with crutches

拐[2] guǎi ❶ swindle; make away with:老太太报案说她被人～走了一个金项链。The old lady reported to the police that she had been swindled out of a gold necklace. /他～了三十万元公款潜逃境外。He fled across the border with 300,000 *yuan* of public money. ❷ kidnap; abduct:～小孩 abduct (*or* kidnap) children

拐棒 guǎibàng bent stick or club

拐脖儿 guǎibór elbow (of a stove pipe, etc.)

拐场 guǎicháng 〈方言〉go wrong; break down; come a cropper:只要细心就不会～的。Nothing can go wrong if you are careful. /收音机才用两天就～儿了。The radio broke down only two days after it was bought.

拐达 guǎida 〈方言〉be lame; limp:他～～地往车站走去。He walked towards the station with a limp. *or* He limped along towards the station.

拐带 guǎidài abduct:～妇女的罪犯终于被抓获了。The criminal who had abducted the woman was captured at last.

拐孤 guǎigu 〈方言〉(of one's temperament, etc.) eccentric; unsociable

拐棍 guǎigùn ❶ walking stick:爷爷虽然年纪大了,可走路从不拄～儿。Old as he is, granddad never uses a walking stick. ❷ sb. or sth. that can be depended on for help or support:秘书成了这位县长作报告离不开的～。The secretary has become indispensable to the county magistrate whenever he wants to make a speech.

拐角 guǎijiǎo corner; turning:我在马路～的电线杆下等你。I'll be waiting for you by the lamp-post at the street corner. /院墙的～放有一个垃圾箱。There is a dustbin in the corner of the yard.

拐拉 guǎila 〈方言〉be lame; limp:～着脚 walk with a lame foot /他～着,艰难地走下山去。He limped downhill with difficulty.

拐卖 guǎimài abduct and sell:～妇女 abduct and traffic in women; engage in white slavery

拐骗 guǎipiàn swindle; abduct; kidnap:～钱财 swindle money (out of sb.) /～幼女 abduct (*or* kidnap) little girls

拐弯 guǎiwān ❶ turn; turn a corner:汽车～的时候,请大家站稳了。Please hold on to something when the bus turns. /朝前走到路口向右一～就到邮局了。Turn right at the crossroads and you'll be at the post office. ❷ turn round (in thinking or speech); pursue a new course; reorient:你怎么说着说着就～了? How come you turned away (*or* strayed) from the subject as you went on? /你讲的都是新观点,我一下子还拐不过弯来呢。As your views are all new, I find it hard to reorient myself for the time being. ❸ turning; corner

拐弯抹角 guǎiwān-mòjiǎo ❶ go or travel in a zigzag manner:上山的小路～的,可不好走了。The path up the mountain is full of twists and turns and hard to follow. /磕磕撞撞,～,又走了半天,才是内堂房屋。Staggering and zigzagging, he walked along for quite a while before he finally reached the inner quarters. ❷ talk in a roundabout way; beat about the bush:你说话怎么老是～的? Why are you always beating about the bush? /乡下人说话喜欢直来直去,不爱～。Country folks are straightforward and do not like to talk in an oblique way.

拐诱 guǎiyòu carry off (a woman) by fraud; abduct; kidnap:她担心总经理在～她。She was worried that the general manager might try to carry her off by fraud.

拐枣 guǎizǎo Japanese raisin tree; honeytree; *Hovenia dulcis*

拐杖 guǎizhàng walking stick:黑漆～ black lacquered walking stick /丁字形～ crutch

拐肘 guǎizhǒu 〈方言〉elbow

拐子 guǎizi ❶〈口语〉cripple:他小时候生病留下后遗症,成了～。He became crippled from the after-effects of an illness he suffered as a child. ❷ I-shaped reel ❸ crutch:他离开～走不了路。He can't walk without crutches. ❹ abductor; swindler:我今天倒霉,碰上～啦。What bad luck! I ran into a swindler today.

guài

怪[1](恠) guài ❶ strange; odd; queer; eccentric:～病 strange (*or* rare) disease /～问题 odd (*or* strange) question /～念头 fantastic idea; whimsical notion; whim /～石嶙峋 queer rocks of rugged beauty /说来也～ oddly enough; strange to say /这件事～得出奇。It is most unusual. /他的性格很～。He has an eccentric character. ❷ find sth. strange; wonder at; be surprised:毫不足～。It's nothing to be surprised at. /真是少见多～! What ignorance! ❸〈口语〉rather; quite:那地方～远的。It is quite far. /看着他那难受的样子,我心里感到～不舒服的。I felt rather bad to see him suffer so much. /小女孩～可怜的! What a pitiable little girl! ❹ monster; fiend; demon; evil spirit:～力乱神 (as avoided by Confucius in his conversations) monsters, force, disorder and deities /妖魔鬼～ demons and ghosts; monsters of every description

怪[2](恠) guài blame; reproach:这不是她的错,不能～她。It's not her fault; she's not to blame. /为什么～到我头上来了? Why do you pick on me? /他考试不及格只能～自己偷懒。He can only blame his own laziness for flunking the exam. /别睡不着觉～床歪。If you can't fall asleep, don't blame your bed. *or* A bad workman always quarrels with his tools.

怪不得 guàibude ❶ no wonder; so that's why; that explains why:～教室这么整齐明亮,原来是你们打扫过了。No wonder (*or* So that's why) the classroom is so bright and tidy. You folks cleaned it up. /夜里下大雪了,～这么冷! It snowed heavily last night! That explains why it's so cold. ❷ not to blame:这件事～任何人,他自作自受。Nobody but himself is to blame for it.

怪诞 guàidàn weird; strange; fantastic; uncanny:～的想法 weird (*or* strange, *or* fantastic) idea /～的行为 strange (*or* weird) behaviour; antics

怪诞不经 guàidàn-bùjīng weird and uncanny; fantastic; crazy; absurd:～的故事 fantastic (*or* strange) story; cock-and-bull story /～的论点 absurd (*or* crazy) argument

怪道 guàidao 〈方言〉no wonder; so that's why; that explains why:天气预报说今晚有雨,～这么闷热呢! The weather forecast says that it will be raining tonight. No wonder it's so sultry now.

怪话 guàihuà cynical remark; grumble; complaint:整天说～ make cynical remarks all the time /～大王 great grumbler; ace cynic /他一

G

切都得到了，还说什么～？He has got everything he wants; what could he grumble about?

怪杰 guàijié person talented in an abnormal or eccentric way; *monstre sacré*

怪谲 guàijué 〈书面〉weird and fantastic; queer and absurd：～地笑了一笑 smile a weird smile /～而不可信 too absurd (*or* fantastic) to believe

怪里怪气 guàiliguàiqì eccentric; peculiar; queer; weird：～的家伙 eccentric (*or* weird) guy; weirdie; wierdo /打扮得～的 be peculiarly dressed up /她～的，跟大家合不到一块儿。Her queer ways alienated her from others.

怪眉怪眼 guàiméi-guàiyǎn glance with sexual interest; ogle：这些家伙见了姑娘便要～。These guys are always ogling girls.

怪模怪样 guàimú-guàiyàng queer in appearance or manners; grotesque：～的装束 (in) grotesque (*or* kinky) dress

怪癖 guàipǐ eccentric habit or behaviour; eccentricity：他有吞吃烟头的～。He has an eccentric habit of eating cigarette butts.

怪僻 guàipì eccentric; peculiar; cranky：性情～的人 eccentric person; crank /他的～之一是从不乘火车。One of his quirks is that he refuses to travel by train.

怪气 guàiqi queer; odd：这人有点儿～，大热天还戴个皮帽子！The man is a bit queer; he has a fur hat on even in the height of summer.

怪圈 guàiquān vicious circle：打破这个～ break the vicious circle

怪人 guàirén eccentric or peculiar person; crank; weirdie or wierdo; sphinx

怪声怪气 guàishēng-guàiqì *also* "怪声怪调"；"怪腔怪调" in a strange or affected voice; in a disagreeable falsetto：她说话～的，听起来真别扭。She speaks in an affected voice, which grates on the ear.

怪事 guàishì strange or peculiar thing; absurdity; rum go：天下第一～ most absurd thing on earth /咄咄～！What a monstrous absurdity! *or* What a rum go! /～年年有，今年尤其多。Although wonders will never cease, they break the record this year. /真是～，文件怎么不见了？How strange! Where did the document disappear to?

怪胎 guàitāi genetic freak; teratism; monster：在某种意义上，纳粹主义可以说是封建军国主义与垄断资本主义相结合的～。In a sense, Nazism was a monster born of feudal militarism and monopoly capitalism.

怪特 guàitè peculiar; odd; singular：～的闪光 singular flash of light /～的旋律 peculiar (*or* odd) melody

怪题 guàití queer or odd question (in an examination)：老师尽出～和难题，班上大多数学生不及格。Most of the students in this class failed in the examination as the teacher had included a lot of odd and catchy questions in the exam paper.

怪味鸡 guàiwèijī chicken with odd taste — Sichuan-style spicy chicken

怪物 guàiwu ❶ monster; monstrosity：传说以前山洞里住着一个～。Legend has it that there once lived a monster in the cave. /新生的羊羔中有个～，长着两条尾巴。One of the new lambs is a monstrosity (*or* freak); it was born with two tails. ❷ eccentric or peculiar person; crank; weirdie or wierdo：这个老～，今天又发怪论了。The cranky old beggar went and made wild remarks again today.

怪象 guàixiàng strange phenomenon：～迭出。Strange phenomena occurred one after another.

怪笑 guàixiào weird laugh; sardonic laugh; laughter that grates on the ear：他听她说后一阵～。He hooted his sardonic laugh after hearing her out.

怪讶 guàiyà surprise; astonishment

怪异 guàiyì ❶ strange; unusual; bizarre; grotesque：感到～ find sth. unusual (*or* strange) /一种～的声音引起了他的注意。A strange (*or* bizarre) sound caught his attention. ❷ unusual phenomenon; strange phenomenon：书上早有过关于湖中各式～的描述。Books have long described various strange phenomena that occurred in and around the lake.

怪怨 guàiyuàn blame; complain：不要一出事就～他人。Don't blame others whenever anything goes wrong.

怪责 guàizé blame; dress down：她担心会被主任～。She was afraid that director might give her a good dressing down.

怪罪 guàizuì reproach; blame; reprove：上边～下来，谁也逃脱不了责任。When reproaches come from the higher authorities, no one will be able to avoid his share of responsibility.

guān

官[1] guān ❶ government official; military officer; office holder：清～ honest and upright official /贪～ corrupt official; venal official /军～ military officer /～与兵 officers and men /外交～ diplomat /将～ general /文～ civil servant; official /升～ promotion; rise in position /罢～ be dismissed from office /封～许愿〈贬义〉offer official posts and promise favours / 倚～仗势 rely on one's power and position (*or* powerful connections) /～儿不大，架子不小 not high in position, but very haughty in manners ❷ official; government-run; state-owned; government-sponsored：～尺〈旧语〉official ruler /～盐〈旧语〉salt sold by the government /～督商办〈旧语〉government-supervised, merchant-run (enterprises) ❸ public：～厕 public toilet; public lavatory ❹ (Guān) a surname

官[2] guān organ：感～ sense organ /消化器～ digestive organ /五～ five sense organs (eyes, ears, nose, lips, and tongue) /五～端正 have pleasant and regular features

官罢 guānbà settle (a dispute) at court：这件事是～还是私休？悉听尊便。It's up to you whether we settle the matter at court or in private.

官办 guānbàn state-run; operated by the government：～企业 state-run enterprise; state enterprise

官报 guānbào official newspaper; official organ of a government

官报私仇 guānbào-sīchóu *also* "公报私仇" gōngbào-sīchóu abuse public power to avenge a private grudge; settle personal scores in the name of public interests

官本位 guānběnwèi official rank or status taken as the only criterion for judging one's social worth; official rank standard

官逼民反 guānbī-mínfǎn people driven to rebellion by tyrannical government

官兵 guānbīng ❶ officers and men：正确处理～关系 correctly handle the relationship between officers and the rank and file ❷〈旧语〉government troops

官舱 guāncāng 〈旧语〉cabin class (on a ship)

官差 guānchāi ❶ official business or duties; public errand ❷〈旧语〉runner; bailiff (in a feudal *yamen*)

官场 guānchǎng 〈贬义〉officialdom; official circles：～得意 rapid rise up the official ladder /混迹～多年 spend years in official circles /～积习 deep-rooted practices of officialdom

官称 guānchēng ❶ official title：他的～是局长。His official title is Bureau Director. ❷ in (official) name; nominally：要我们交五百元，～是"捐助"，实质是变相摊派。We were asked to hand in 500 *yuan*. It was actually apportionment under the official cover of "donation".

官瓷 Guāncí *Guan* porcelain (ware), popular in the Song Dynasty

官倒 guāndǎo ❶ profiteering by governmental organizations or public servants ❷ official speculator or racketeer (who uses his or her official capacity to make huge profits)

官道 guāndào ❶〈旧语〉government-built or public thoroughfare ❷〈方言〉road; highway

官邸 guāndǐ official residence; official mansion：大使～ ambassador's residence

官渡之战 Guāndù Zhī Zhàn Battle of Guandu (in present north Henan), 199 AD, in which Cao Cao (曹操) defeated Yuan Shao's (袁绍) superior force and was thus enabled to unify northern China

官方 guānfāng of or by the government; official：～发言人 official spokesman (*or* spokeswoman, *or* spokesperson) /～报纸 official newspaper; government newspaper /以～身分出席会议 attend a meeting in one's official capacity /～消息 news from official (*or* government) sources /据～人士透露 according to official quarters /他代表～。He represents the government.

官方汇率 guānfāng huìlǜ official exchange rate; official rate

官方牌价 guānfāng páijià official market quotation

官费 guānfèi 〈旧语〉fund from public coffers; government-financed：～留学 studying abroad at state expense

官费生 guānfèishēng 〈旧语〉student studying abroad on government scholarship

官俸 guānfèng 〈旧语〉salaries paid by the government

官服 guānfú 〈旧语〉ceremonial robe or dress of an official

官府 guānfǔ 〈旧语〉❶ local authorities; government: ~勒索 extortion by government / ~和土匪勾结掠夺百姓。The local authorities worked hand in glove with bandits to plunder the people. ❷ officials

官复原职 guānfùyuánzhí restore an official to his original post; be restored to one's former rank or office; be reinstated: 他赋闲多年,直到最近才~。He was out of office for years and was reinstated only recently.

官官相护 guānguān-xiānghù *also* "官官相卫" bureaucrats shield one another: 旧社会~,老百姓有冤无处申。In the old society, officials protected each other, and the ordinary people had no one to turn to for redress of their grievances.

官话 guānhuà ❶〈旧语〉official dialect — Mandarin (old name for 普通话): 她讲一口流利的~。She speaks fluent Mandarin. ❷ official jargon; bureaucratese; language of officialdom: 你们的发言~连篇,没有一点新意。There's nothing original in your address. It's full of official jargon. /少说~、套话! Don't talk like a bureaucrat! Cut out the stereotypes!

官宦 guānhuàn 〈旧语〉government official: ~之家 family of an official

官讳 guānhuì 〈旧语〉official name (of a person)

官家 guānjiā 〈旧语〉❶ court; government ❷ his majesty; emperor ❸ official

官价 guānjià official price or rate: 按~出售 sell at an official price

官架子 guānjiàzi airs of an official; bureaucratic airs: 别摆~! Don't put on bureaucratic airs!

官阶 guānjiē official rank

官爵 guānjué official rank; rank or title of nobility: 封个一官半爵 be awarded an official rank (*or* title)

官军 guānjūn 〈旧语〉government troops

官款 guānkuǎn 〈旧语〉public money; government money

官吏 guānlì 〈旧语〉government official

官僚 guānliáo bureaucrat; bureaucracy: 工会~ trade-union bureaucrat /~习气太浓 be riddled with bureaucratic practices /你这个人太~! What a bureaucrat you are!

官僚机构 guānliáo jīgòu bureaucratic apparatus

官僚买办 guānliáo mǎibàn bureaucrat-comprador

官僚主义 guānliáozhǔyì bureaucratism: ~者 bureaucratist /~作风 bureaucratic style of work; bureaucratic way of doing things; official red tape /犯了~错误 commit an error of bureaucratism

官僚资本 guānliáo zīběn capital owned by the bureaucrat-capitalist class; bureaucrat-capital: ~是垄断资本。Bureaucrat-capital is monopoly capital.

官僚资本主义 guānliáo zīběnzhǔyì bureaucrat-capitalism

官僚资产阶级 guānliáo zīchǎnjiējí bureaucrat-capitalist class

官了 guānliǎo settle according to law; settle in court

官路 guānlù ❶ government-built or public thoroughfare ❷ official career

官迷 guānmí one who is obsessed by the pursuit of government office; office-seeker; careerist: 这个人是个~,想尽办法往上爬。A brazen careerist, he has tried a hundred and one ways to climb up the official ladder.

官面 guānmiàn ❶〈旧语〉government; state ❷ official circles; political circles: ~上人物 political figure

官名 guānmíng ❶〈旧语〉formal name; official name: 他小名二宝,~大成。His pet name is Erbao and his formal name is Dacheng. ❷ official title: 他喜欢人家称他的~。He likes to be called by his official title.

官暮骄娇 guān-mù-jiāo-jiāo bureaucratism, lethargy, haughtiness, and squeamishness — major manifestations of bureaucratic style

官能 guānnéng organic function; sense; physical faculty: 神经~紊乱 neurotic disorder /人体~有五种:视、听、嗅、味、触。There are five organic functions in human beings, namely, the senses of sight, hearing, smell, taste and touch.

官能团 guānnéngtuán *also* "功能团" gōngnéngtuán 〈化学〉functional group

官能心理学 guānnéng xīnlǐxué faculty psychology

官能症 guānnéngzhèng functional disease

官派 guānpài bureaucratic airs; bureaucratism: 他这个人~十足,你少跟他打交道。He is full of bureaucratic pomposity and you'd better keep away from him.

官气 guānqì bureaucratism; bureaucratic airs: 官儿不大,~十足 no more than a petty official, but bursting with bureaucratic airs /他身为政府要员,却毫无~。Important as he is in the government, he has not the slightest touch of bureaucratism.

官腔 guānqiāng bureaucratese; official jargon; bureaucratic tone: 只会打~,不会办实事 speak in a bureaucratic tone without getting down to real business /一派~ full of official jargon

官亲 guānqīn 〈旧语〉relative of an official: 冒认~ falsely claim relation to an official

官人 guānrén ❶〈书面〉person who holds public office; official ❷〈旧语〉mister (Mr.); sir: ~,请用茶。Please take some tea, sir. ❸ (often used in the early vernacular) woman's term of address for her husband

官纱 guānshā 〈旧语〉silk presented as a tribute; tributary silk (for use of the royal family)

官商 guānshāng ❶ state-run business; government commerce ❷ bureaucrat-like personnel in a government enterprise: 改变~作风 change one's bureaucratic ways of doing business ❸ government and private sector: ~合办企业 enterprise jointly run by the government and private citizens

官舍 guānshè official residence

官身 guānshēn *also* "官身子" 〈旧语〉officeholder: ~不自由。An officeholder enjoys little freedom.

官事 guānshì 〈旧语〉public affairs

官守议员 guānshǒu yìyuán (HK before July 1997) official member: 立法会~ official member of the Legislative Council

官书 guānshū 〈旧语〉books compiled and published by the government; official publications

官署 guānshǔ 〈旧语〉government office; government agency

官司 guānsi 〈口语〉lawsuit: 打~ go to law against sb.; take sb. to court; enter or bring in a lawsuit against sb.; engage in a lawsuit /打不完的笔墨~ endless paperwork in controversies; unending written polemics /吃了一场冤枉~ be falsely charged; be unjustly tried /这件案子未经打~就解决了。The case was settled out of court.

官太太 guāntàitai 〈贬义〉wife of an official

官体 guāntǐ 〈旧语〉official decency or decorum; official propriety: 有失~ disgraceful (*or* improper) for an official

官田 guāntián 〈旧语〉public or state-owned land

官厅 guāntīng 〈旧语〉government office

官位 guānwèi official position; office: 贪恋~ reluctant to leave office

官衔 guānxián official title: 他干事不多,挂的~不少。He hasn't done much work but has quite a few official titles.

官廨 guānxiè 〈旧语〉government office (building)

官衙 guānyá 〈旧语〉*yamen*

see also "衙门" yámen

官燕 guānyàn high-quality edible swallow's nest

官样文章 guānyàng-wénzhāng mere formalities; officialese: ~,照抄不误。It's official jargon, so just copy it as it is. /这不过是~,不必过于认真。These are mere formalities; there is no need to take them too seriously.

官窑 Guānyáo *Guan* Kiln, court porcelain kiln of the Song Dynasty

官瘾 guānyǐn craving after office; obsession for official post: 过~ satisfy one's thirst for an official post /他的~极大。He is an addicted office-seeker.

官印 guānyìn seal of a government office; official seal

官员 guānyuán official; officer: 政府~ government official /高级~ senior official /大使馆~ official of the embassy; embassy staff /外交~ diplomatic official /项目~ programme (*or* project) officer /~护照 official passport /~签证 official visa

官运 guānyùn official or political career; fortunes of officialdom

官运亨通 guānyùn-hēngtōng have a successful official or political career; advance smoothly in officialdom: ~,连升三级 be successful in official career with three rapid promotions

官长 guānzhǎng 〈旧语〉❶ official; your honour: 地方~只知搜刮民财,哪管百姓死活! The local officials only knew how to rob the people, not giving a damn about their welfare. /~老爷,请饶他一命。Your honour, please spare him his life. ❷ army officer

官箴 guānzhēn 〈书面〉maxim for government officials

官职 guānzhí official position; office: 这是个一心谋求~的人。He is

G

an eager office hunter (*or* seeker). /他担任什么～? What's his government post?
官制 guānzhì civil service system; bureaucratic establishment
官秩 guānzhì ranking of officials; official ranks and grades
官中 guānzhōng ❶ government authorities ❷ public-owned:拿着～的钱做人情 do sb. a favour at the expense of the public treasury
官佐 guānzuǒ 〈旧语〉military officer; army officer

棺 guān coffin:盖～论定 the final verdict can not be passed on a person until the lid is placed on his coffin (i.e. until his death)
棺材 guāncai coffin:～铺 coffin shop /进～ die /棺材里伸手—死要钱 reach out a hand for money even in one's coffin—be greedy unto death; be a money-grubber
棺材瓤子 guāncai rángzi 〈粗话〉old vegetable
棺床 guānchuáng coffin platform
棺盖 guāngài lid or cover of a coffin
棺椁 guānguǒ inner and outer coffins
棺架 guānjià bier
棺木 guānmù coffin:众人凑钱给死者买了一副～。They pooled their money and bought the deceased a coffin.

倌 guān ❶ stockman; herdsman; livestock keeper; keeper of domestic animals:羊～儿 shepherd /猪～儿 swineherd /牛～儿 cowherd /马～儿 groom ❷〈旧语〉hired hand (in certain trades):堂～儿 waiter /磨～儿 flour-miller

关(關、関) guān ❶ shut; close:～抽屉 shove in the drawer /这扇窗户～不上。This window doesn't shut. ❷ turn off; switch off:～灯 turn off the light; switch off the light ❸ lock up; shut in:笼子里～着一只小鸟。A bird is shut in the cage. /她外出时把孩子～在屋里。She locks the child in the house when she goes out. /他被～进了牢房。He was jailed. *or* He was put behind bars. ❹ close down; shut down:由于经营不善,连年亏本,他只好～了这家店铺。Due to poor management, he was losing money year after year and had to close down the store. ❺ mountain pass:雄～ impregnable pass /边～ frontier pass /一夫当～,万夫莫开。With one man guarding the pass, ten thousand men cannot get through. ❻ area just outside the city gate:酒店在北～的大街上。The wineshop is located on the street outside the northern gate of the city. ❼ (door) bolt; (door) bar:斩～落锁 cut down the door bar and padlock ❽〈中医〉*short for* "关上" ❾ tax-collector's checkpoint; customs; customs house:过海～ go through customs /这条公路沿线设～,～～上税。There are numerous checkpoints along the road, and a tax must be paid at each. ❿ barrier; critical juncture:突破技术难～ break through a technical barrier /技术攻～小组 team for technical breakthrough /渡过难～ tide over the crisis ⓫ gear; joint; key: *see* "～键"; "～节" ⓬ involve; implicate; concern:休戚相～,患难与共 be bound by a common cause and tide over difficulties together /生死攸～ (a matter) of life and death; (a matter) of vital importance /无～紧要 of no consequence; insignificant /有～部门 department (*or* authority) concerned /事～全局 have a bearing on the situation as a whole /此事与你无～。That does not concern you. ⓭〈旧语〉pay (salary or wage):～饷 get paid /～饷的日子 pay day ⓮ (Guān) a surname
关爱 guān'ài concern and care; love and care:老师们的深切～,使她很受感动。The love and care shown by the teachers moved her greatly.
关隘 guān'ài 〈书面〉(mountain) pass:扼守～ guard a pass
关碍 guān'ài hinder; hamper; impede; obstruct; handicap:无大～ not much of an obstacle
关白 guānbái 〈书面〉report (to one's superior); inform sb. of sth.:不相～ do not inform each other
关板 guānbǎn 〈方言〉(of a store) close:下班时间已到,要～了。Business hours are over and the store will soon close.
关闭 guānbì ❶ close; shut:～城门 close the city gate /～窗户 shut the windows ❷ (of a shop, factory, etc.) close down; shut down:雾太大,机场～了。The airport is closed down because of the heavy fog. /部分工厂因产品滞销而被迫～。Some of the factories shut down because of the sluggish sales of their products.
关尺 guānchǐ 〈旧语〉unit of length used by the custom house, equal to 0.358 metres
关刀 guāndāo long-hilted broadsword; knife with a long handle for fighting on horseback
关岛 Guāndǎo Guam, an island administered as an unincorporated territory of the United States
关帝 Guāndì deified title for Guan Yu (关羽) as god of war, as well as patron guardian of business:～庙 Guandi Temple
关东 Guāndōng ❶ east of Shanhaiguan Pass; the Northeast; northeast China:闯～ go and seek a livelihood in northeast China ❷ Kanto, a region of Japan on the island of Honshu
关东糖 guāndōngtáng a kind of malt candy (first made in northeast China)
关防 guānfáng ❶ measures against divulgence of secrets; security measures:～严密 tight (*or* strict) security measures ❷〈旧语〉government or army seal:～印信 official seal ❸〈书面〉military position at a strategic point; fort; fortress
关服 guānfú customs uniform
关公 Guāngōng reverent term of address for Guan Yu (关羽,160-219) a general in the period of the Three Kingdoms, renowned for his loyalty and later deified as Guandi (关帝)
关顾 guāngù care and concern:感谢你对我们不时～。Thank you for the constant care and concern you've shown for us.
关汉卿 Guān Hànqīng Guan Hanqing (formerly translated as Kuan Han-ching), playwright of the Yuan Dynasty
关乎 guānhū concern; involve; relate:～国计民生 bear on the national economy and people's livelihood /预防疾病是～人民健康的一件大事。Disease-prevention is a matter of great importance that concerns the people's health.
关怀 guānhuái show loving care for; show concern or solicitude for:～教育事业 be concerned about the cause of education /～残疾人福利事业 show solicitude for the welfare of the handicapped /学校～每个学生的健康成长。The school pays great attention to the healthy growth of every pupil.
关怀备至 guānhuái-bèizhì show or express the greatest solicitude for; be extremely considerate of:连长对我们这些新战士～。The company commander has shown the utmost solicitude for us new recruits.
关徽 guānhuī customs emblem or insignia
关键 guānjiàn ❶ door bolt; door bar ❷ hinge; key; crux:～人物 key figure /这便是问题的～所在。This is the crux of the matter. /在这～时刻,你可得顶住。At this crucial (*or* critical) moment, you'll have to stand firm. /～是要把人力组织好。What counts is the optimal organization of manpower (*or* human resources). /今年是实现我们目标的～的一年。It is a year of decisive importance for realizing our goal. /经济要发展,科技是～。Economic growth hinges on science and technology.
关键代码 guānjiàn dàimǎ 〈经济〉key code
关键字 guānjiànzì 〈信息〉key word
关节 guānjié ❶〈生理〉joint:膝～ knee joint /～发硬 stiff joints /～红肿 inflammation of the joint /～肿大 arthrocele /～僵硬 anchylosis /浑身～疼痛。I ache all over at every joint. ❷ key link; crucial point:这是一个要害的～,千万不可忽视。This is a crucial link that you overlook at your peril. /抓住足以影响全局的几个～不放。Firmly grasp the few key links that have a vital bearing on the overall situation. ❸ bribery; clandestine dealings:要促成此事,有些～还需要打通。To get the business done, someone's palm must be greased.
关节固定术 guānjié gùdìngshù 〈医学〉arthrodesia
关节截除术 guānjié jiéchúshù 〈医学〉arthrectomy
关节水肿 guānjié shuǐzhǒng 〈医学〉hydrarthrosis
关节痛 guānjiétòng 〈医学〉arthralgia
关节弯曲 guānjié-wānqū 〈医学〉anthrogryposis
关节学 guānjiéxué 〈医学〉arthrology
关节炎 guānjiéyán 〈医学〉arthritis:他的～又发作了。He had another fit of arthritis.
关金 guānjīn ❶ (during the rule of the Northern Warlords and the Kuomintang government) tariff unit of measure ❷ securities (issued by the Central Bank in 1931 and later used as banknotes):～券 *guanjin* notes
关津 guānjīn pass and ferry; checkpoint (at a pass or ferry crossing)
关紧 guānjǐn 〈方言〉important; significant:这件事十分～。This is a matter of vital importance.
关禁 guānjìn put in confinement; hold in custody:凶手暂时被～在派出所。The murderer (*or* assailant) was temporarily held in cus-

tody in the local police station.

关禁闭 guān jìnbì lock up (as a form of punishment in the army); put in confinement:这个士兵被关了两个月的禁闭。The soldier was locked up for two months.

关口 guānkǒu ❶ strategic pass; checkpoint:把住各个～ guard every checkpoint /～盘查得很厉害。Passengers were strictly checked at the pass. ❷ juncture:在这紧要～,他突然病倒了。He fell ill at this critical juncture.

关里 Guānlǐ see "关内"

关连 guānlián see "关联"

关联 guānlián be linked; be related; be connected:密切～ closely connected /这个段落在全文起着十分重要的～作用。This paragraph functions as a very important link in the text. /工农业生产是相互密切～的。Agriculture and industry are closely interrelated.

关联词 guānliáncí 〈语言〉connective

关贸总协定 Guānmào Zǒngxiédìng (short for 关税及贸易总协定) General Agreement on Tariffs and Trade (GATT), an international treaty signed in 1947 with the object of lowering tariffs and expanding world trade, replaced now by the WTO (World Trade Organization)

关门 guānmén ❶ close (the door):图书馆下午五点～。The library closes at 5 p.m. ❷ close; shut; stop operation:公司生意月月亏本,实在难以维持,只好～了。Losing money every month, the company could hardly carry on and had to close down. /商店今天盘货,～一天。The store is closed today for stocktaking. ❸ close or slam the door; refuse discussion, consideration or negotiation, etc.:他们关上了谈判的大门。They shut the door on negotiations. /商店在价钱上没有～,还可以讨价还价。There's room for further bargaining as the store has left the matter of price open. ❹ last:～弟子 last disciple (of a master) ❺ behind closed doors:我们主张开门办学,反对～办学。We are for open-door schooling and against running schools behind closed doors. ❻ gate of a stronghold; city gate:赶到城楼前,天色还没有破晓,～尚未打开。It was before dawn when we arrived at the gate tower, and the city gate was still shut.

关门打狗 guānmén-dǎgǒu bolt the door and beat the dog — block the retreat of enemy troops and mop them up

关门大吉 guānmén-dàjí 〈讽刺〉(of a business, etc.) wind up; close down for good

关门主义 guānménzhǔyì closed-doorism; exclusionism; policy of keeping out external people, ideas, etc.

关内 Guānnèi inside the Great Wall — areas to the west of Shanhaiguan (山海关)and to the east of Jiayuguan (嘉峪关):从～流落到关外谋生 go north of the Great Wall for a living

关念 guānniàn miss; care about:～子女 miss one's children

关牛棚 guān niúpéng (a term used during the Cultural Revolution) shut (people) up in a cowshed — put (people) in confinement

关卡 guānqiǎ outpost or checkpoint (for taxation or security):～林立。There are checkpoints everywhere.

关切 guānqiè ❶ kind; considerate; thoughtful:～备至 very thoughtful /他态度和蔼,对别人的困难十分～。He is amiable and very considerate to people who are in difficulty. ❷ be deeply concerned about; show concern over:～地注意到 note with concern /话中流露出对管理不善的严重～。In his remarks, he showed grave concern over poor management. /中国政府对此事件十分～。The Chinese Government is greatly concerned about the incident.

关塞 guānsài fortress on a strategic pass

关山 guānshān mountains and frontier passes:～阻隔 separated by mountains and passes /雨后复斜阳,～阵阵苍。The sun returns slanting after the rain And hill and pass grow a deeper blue.

关上 guānshàng 〈中医〉one of the three places at the wrist (*cun*, *guan* and *chi*) where the pulse is usually taken

关涉 guānshè involve; concern; have to do with; affect:这件事～到全体职工的福利,必须抓紧办好。The matter affects the welfare of all our employees and must be attended to without delay.

关市 guānshì frontier fair; border market

关书 guānshū 〈旧语〉letter of appointment

关税 guānshuì customs duty; tariff:保护～ protective tariff /特惠～ preferential tariff /免征～ exempt sb. from customs duties; be duty-free /报复性～ retaliatory tariff

关税壁垒 guānshuì bìlěi tariff wall; customs barrier

关税地区 guānshuì dìqū tariff area

关税豁免 guānshuì huòmiǎn exemption from customs duties

关税率 guānshuìlǜ tariff rate

关税普惠制 Guānshuì Pǔhuìzhì General Preferential Duties

关税同盟 guānshuì tóngméng customs or tariff union

关税限额 guānshuì xiàn'é tariff ceiling

关税优惠 guānshuì yōuhuì tariff preference

关税战 guānshuìzhàn tariff war

关税自主 guānshuì zìzhǔ tariff autonomy

关说 guānshuō 〈书面〉speak on sb.'s behalf; intercede for sb.; put in a good word for sb.

关停并转 guān-tíng-bìng-zhuǎn (of loss-making enterprises) switch to other products, be amalgamated with other enterprises, suspend operations, or close down

关头 guāntóu juncture; moment:生死～ moment of life and death /紧要～ critical moment; moment of truth /危急～方显出英雄本色。The true quality of a hero is revealed at a critical juncture. /这是考验我们每个人的意志的重要～。This is the moment that everyone's will is put to the test.

关外 Guānwài outside the Great Wall — areas to the east of Shanhaiguan and to the west of Jiayuguan

关系 guānxì ❶ relationship:要正确处理政治与业务的～。We should correctly handle the relationship between political and professional work. /这两件事之间没有～。They have nothing to do with each other. ❷ relation(s); tie(s); connection(s):保持友好～ maintain friendly ties; be on good terms; get on very well /建立良好的人际～ establish sound personal relations /建立外交～ establish diplomatic relations (*or* ties) /社会～ social connections /国际～ international relations /公共～ public relations /发生～ have sexual relations; have an affair /暧昧～ dubious relationship /裙带～ nepotism /拉～ trying to establish personal connections (to one's benefit); networking ❸ *guanxi* — personal connections or network:老～ old-comrade network /～是由下列几个方面形成的:学校教育,思想一致,信仰相同或家庭联系。Effective networks are usually formed in one of four ways: at school and university, through shared ideas, through shared beliefs, or through family connections. ❹ bearing; relevance; impact; significance:他与那件事毫无～。He has nothing to do with it. /我们等多久～倒不大,只要能解决问题就好。It doesn't matter how long we have to wait, provided the problem can be solved. ❺ (often used after 由于,因, etc.) because of; since:因为时间～,今天就讲到这里。Since time is almost up, we'll have to stop here today. ❻ membership or personal credentials; organizational connection or identity:党、团～ one's Party or League membership credentials /人员调动要转人事～。When a person is transferred to another post (*or* unit), his personal credentials go with him. /由于战乱,他和组织上的～断了。Because of the war, he lost touch with the Party. ❼ concern; affect; have a bearing on:人才的培养～到国家的长远利益。The training of qualified personnel has a great deal to do with the long-term interests of a country. /这是个直接～到国计民生的大问题。This is a major issue that has a direct bearing on national economy and people's livelihood.

关系户 guānxìhù people who have business dealings with each other on the basis of "Scratch my back and I'll scratch yours"; special connections:他通过～从外省买来一批紧俏商品。Through special connections, he purchased from other provinces large amounts of commodities in short supply. /有～就好办事。It's easy to get things done when you have the right connections.

关系数据库 guānxì shùjùkù 〈信息〉relational database

关系网 guānxìwǎng network of friends; connections:建立～ networking

关系学 guānxìxué art or skill of cultivating good relations with people

关厢 guānxiāng neighbourhood outside a city gate; outside-the-city-gate neighbourhood

关饷 guānxiǎng pay (for soldiers, policemen, etc.):今天～。Today is payday.

关心 guānxīn be concerned with; show solicitude for; be interested in; care for:～群众 care for the masses (*or* ordinary people) /～国家大事 concern oneself with state affairs /大家共同～的问题 matters of common concern; matters of interest to everybody /大家都很～他的健康。All of us are solicitous about his health.

关押 guānyā lock up; put in prison; put behind bars; jail:他因聚赌而遭～。He was locked up for organizing a gambling party. /这座大院是过去～战犯的地方。This compound used to be a prison for war

criminals.

关于 guānyú about; on; concerning; with regard to; as regards: 最近我读了几本～哲学的书。Recently, I have read a few books about philosophy. /昨天听了一个～市场经济的报告。We attended a lecture on market economy yesterday. /～如何改进工作的问题,上级已经作出一定安排。Proper arrangements have already been made by the leadership for improvement of our work.

关张 guānzhāng (of shops) close down; go out of business

关照 guānzhào ❶ look after; take care of: 这里的事请你多～了。I hope you'll spare some time to look after the work here. /多谢你对我的～。Thank you for the trouble you've taken on my behalf. /一路上你们要相互～。Please take care of each other on the journey. ❷ notify by word of mouth: 今天下午开会,请～王教授一声。Please tell Prof. Wang that we'll have a meeting this afternoon. /如果你要离开实验室请～一声。Please let me know if you have to leave the lab.

关中 Guānzhōng Central Shaanxi: ～平原 Central Shaanxi Plain

关注 guānzhù follow with interest; pay close attention to; show concern for: 那个地区近来局势的发展引起了全世界的～。Recent developments in that area have drawn world-wide attention. /全国人民对灾区人民的生活十分～。People all over the country have shown great solicitude for the livelihood of those in the disaster area.

关子 guānzi (of a novel, story, play, etc.) climax; key: 卖～keep people guessing in telling a story; keep sb. in suspense

冠 guān ❶ cap; hat: 二寸免～照片 passport-size bare-headed photo /桂～ laurel /王～ crown /衣～整齐 be neatly dressed /张～李戴 attribute sth. to a wrong person; confuse one thing with another /怒发冲～ bristle with anger; be in a towering rage (*or* passion) ❷ sth. like a cap or at the top of sth. else; corona; crest; comb: 花～ corolla /齿～ crown of a tooth /鸡～ cock's comb /鹰～ crest

see also guàn

冠盖 guāngài 〈书面〉official hats and canopies — officials

冠盖相望 guāngài-xiāngwàng continuous stream of high officials or envoys

冠盖云集 guāngài-yúnjí *also* "冠盖如云" large gathering of ranking officials and dignitaries

冠冕 guānmiǎn ❶ royal crown; official hat ❷ high-sounding; pompous; highfalutin

冠冕堂皇 guānmiǎn-tánghuáng high-toned; high-sounding: ～的理由 high-sounding excuses /在～的旗号下,干着卑鄙龌龊的勾当 resort to dirty tricks under high-sounding pretexts

冠心病 guānxīnbìng 〈医学〉coronary heart disease: ～患者 coronary heart patient /～专家 expert for coronary heart diseases

冠周炎 guānzhōuyán 〈医学〉pericoronitis

冠状动脉 guānzhuàng dòngmài 〈生理〉coronary artery

冠状动脉硬化 guānzhuàng dòngmài yìnghuà 〈医学〉coronary arteriosclerosis

冠状动脉阻塞 guānzhuàng dòngmài zǔsè 〈医学〉coronary artery occlusion

冠状静脉 guānzhuàng jìngmài 〈生理〉coronary vein

冠子 guānzi crest; comb: 鸡～ cockscomb /鹰～ hawkcrest

莞 guān *Scirpus lacustris*, a long-stem water grass

see also guǎn; wǎn

瘝 guān 〈书面〉sickness; pain

鳏 guān wifeless; widowered

鳏夫 guānfū 〈书面〉old wifeless man; bachelor; widower: 这个人七十岁了,当了一辈子～。He is seventy years old and remains a bachelor.

鳏寡孤独 guān-guǎ-gū-dú widowers, widows, orphans and the childless; those who have no kith and kin and cannot support themselves

鳏居 guānjū live as a bachelor or widower; remain wifeless

观(觀) guān ❶ look; see; watch; observe: 袖手旁～ look on (*or* stand by) with folded arms; look on unconcerned /察言～色 weigh up sb.'s words and watch his expression carefully; watch sb.'s every mood /坐～成败 wait to see what will come of sb.'s venture; look on coldly; be a mere onlooker /听其言,～其行 listen to what sb. says and observe what he does /眼～六路,耳听八方 have sharp eyes and keen ears; be observant and alert ❷ sight; spectacle; view: 蔚为大～ present a splendid sight; afford a magnificent view /壮～ grand (*or* magnificent) sight /奇～ wonderful sight (*or* spectacle) /景～ scene; landscape /外～ outward appearance; exterior ❸ outlook; view; concept; conception: 世界～ world outlook /人生～ outlook on life; life outlook /乐～ optimism /悲～ pessimism /唯物史～ materialist conception of history

see also guàn

观测 guāncè ❶ observe and survey: ～洪水涨势 observe and measure the flood tide /～风力的大小 measure the wind-force /气象～ weather observation(s) /～资料 observational data; observations /多年来,他一直在～水土流失情况。He has long been making observations of the soil erosion. ❷ watch and analyse; size up: ～形势 analyse the situation /～敌情 size up the enemy strength (*or* forces); watch enemy movements

观测员 guāncèyuán observer; surveyor

观测站 guāncèzhàn observation station or post

观察 guānchá observe; watch; survey; size up: ～社会 make a social survey /～地形 survey the terrain /～病情 keep a patient under observation /～动静 watch what's going on /～风向 find out which way the wind blows; see how the cat jumps /～国际形势 take stock of the international situation /住院～ be hospitalized for observation

观察病房 guānchá bìngfáng observation or probationary ward

观察机 guānchájī observation plane or aircraft

观察家 guāncháijiā observer (often used by political commentators as a pseudonym): 《人民日报》发表了一篇署名～的重要文章。The *People's Daily* carried an important article by Observer.

观察家报 Guānchájiābào *The Observer*, a British weekend newspaper published since 1791

观察哨 guāncháshào observation post

观察所 guānchásuǒ observation post: 临时～ makeshift observation post /前沿～ forward observation post

观察员 guāncháyuán observer: ～席 observer's seat /～可以列席会议,但无表决权。Observers may attend the conference but have no right to vote.

观场 guāncháng 〈方言〉stand on the sideline and watch what's going on

观潮派 guāncháopài person who takes a wait-and-see attitude; onlooker; bystander

观点 guāndiǎn point of view; viewpoint; standpoint; perspective: 对立～ opposing views /用历史～看问题 look at things from a historical perspective /阐明～ explain one's position /没有正确的政治～,就会迷失方向。Without correct political viewpoints, one is prone to lose one's orientation.

观风 guānfēng be on the lookout; serve as a lookout; watch: 他让同伙在暗处～,自己翻墙而入。He put his partner on the lookout in a dark place while he himself jumped over the wall.

观感 guāngǎn impressions; observations: 谈几点～ make a few observations /此次出访,～如何? What are your impressions of your visit abroad?

观光 guānguāng go sightseeing; see the sights; visit; tour: ～者 sightseer; tourist /～旅行 make a sightseeing tour /～市容 go sightseeing round the city; make a tour round the city

观光客 guānguāngkè tourist

观光团 guānguāngtuán sightseeing party; tour group; tourist group

观过知人 guānguò-zhīrén understand a man by his faults; know a person by observing his or her mistakes

观看 guānkàn look at; watch; view: ～电影 see (*or* view) a film /～电视节目 watch a television show /你们是去参加比赛还是～比赛? Are you going to play the game or watch only?

观客 guānkè 〈方言〉spectator; viewer; audience

观览 guānlǎn 〈书面〉watch; view; browse through: 阅览室的报刊开架陈列,便于读者～。All the newspapers and magazines in the reading-room are displayed on the shelves to make it easy for readers to browse through.

观礼 guānlǐ attend a celebration or ceremony: 他作为国庆特邀代表登上了天安门城楼～。He mounted the rostrum of Tian An Men for National Day celebrations as a specially invited representative.

观礼台 guānlǐtái reviewing stand; visitor's stand

观摩 guānmó view and emulate：～教学 mutual learning among fellow teachers by observing each other's classes; demonstration lecture /～演出 performing before fellow artists for the purpose of discussion and emulation /公司组织了一次售货现场～活动。The company organized an on-the-spot salesmanship demonstration for the sales-clerks.

观念 guānniàn sense; mentality; concept; idea：加强组织～ strengthen one's sense of organization /树立法制～ foster a sense of legality /私有～ private ownership mentality /打破乡土～ do away with provincialism /传统～ traditional concept (*or* view) /陈腐的～ outworn (*or* obsolete) mode of thinking /他在这个问题上有些模糊的～。He has some muddled ideas about this question.

观念形态 guānniàn xíngtài *also*“意识形态”yìshi xíngtài ideology

观赏 guānshǎng view and admire; enjoy the sight of; watch (with appreciation)：～文艺表演 watch theatrical performances /大厅里陈列着许多盆景，供游人～。There are many potted landscapes on display in the hall for the appreciation (*or* pleasure) of visitors.

观赏艺术 guānshǎng yìshù visual arts

观赏鱼 guānshǎngyú fish for display; ornamental fish; pet fish

观赏植物 guānshǎng zhíwù ornamental or decorative plant

观世音 Guānshìyīn *also*“观音”；“观自在”；“观音大士”〈佛教〉*Guanyin*, goddess of mercy; *Avalokitesvara*, *Bodhisattva* of infinite compassion and mercy：大慈大悲的～菩萨 the great merciful Avalokitesvara /救苦救难的～菩萨！May Guanyin protect and preserve us!

观通站 guāntōngzhàn 〈军事〉observation and communication post

观望 guānwàng ❶ wait and see; look on (from the sidelines)：～徘徊 look on hesitatingly /～不前 look on and make no move /采取～的态度 take a wait-and-see attitude ❷ look about; look around：四下～ look around

观无量寿经 Guānwúliàngshòujīng 〈佛教〉*Amitayur-Dhyana Sutra*

观象台 guānxiàngtái ❶〈天文〉observatory：古～ ancient observatory ❷ Terrace for Astronomical Observation (in Beijing, now used to exhibit ancient astronomical instruments)

观音 Guānyīn *see*“观世音”

观音土 guānyīntǔ *also*“观音粉”a kind of white clay (which famine victims used to eat to appease their hunger)

观音竹 guānyīnzhú *also*“凤凰竹”fènghuángzhú 〈植物〉fern-leaf hedge bamboo (*Bambusa multiplex*)

观瞻 guānzhān ❶ appearance of a place; sight; view; image：有碍～ be unsightly; be repugnant to the eye; offend the eye /以壮～ to make a better sight (*or* view) ❷ look; see; view; watch

观战 guānzhàn follow the developments of a war as an onlooker; watch a war; watch a fight; watch a match or game：下棋的只有两个，～者却围了一大堆。There were only two players at the chess-board, but many were watching (the match).

观者如堵 guānzhě-rúdǔ spectators stand around like a wall; there is a big crowd of onlookers

观阵 guānzhèn watch a fight, match, game, or contest

观止 guānzhǐ *also*“叹观止矣”tànguānzhǐyǐ thing of perfection never seen before

观众 guānzhòng audience; spectator; viewer：电视～ TV viewer /戏剧～ theatre goer /～如潮 wave upon wave of spectators /～掌声雷动。The thunderous applause from the audience was deafening.

观众席 guānzhòngxí auditorium (of a theatre); grandstand (of a stadium)

矜

guān 〈书面〉❶ *see*“鳏”guān ❷ *see*“瘝”guān

see also jīn; qín

纶(綸)

guān

see also lún

纶巾 guānjīn blue-ribboned silk kerchief

纶巾羽扇 guānjīn-yǔshàn *also*“羽扇纶巾”wear a scarf and wave a feather fan — ease and natural poise of a scholar strategist

guǎn

莞

guǎn *used in*“东莞”(Dongguan City of Guangdong Province)

see also guān; wǎn

筦

guǎn ❶ *see*“管”guǎn ❷ (Guǎn) a surname

痯

guǎn 〈书面〉tired; sick

琯

guǎn 〈乐器〉jade flute：吹～ play the jade flute

辖(錧)

guǎn 〈书面〉iron coating of the hub; hub sleeve

管[1]

guǎn ❶ tube; pipe; conduit; duct：水～ water pipe /钢～ steel pipe (*or* tube) /油～ oil pipe /输油～ oil pipeline /导～ conduit; pipe; duct /胶～ rubber tube /血～ blood vessel /瘘～ fistula ❷ wind instrument：黑～ clarinet /铜～乐器 brass wind /单簧～ clarinet /双簧～ oboe ❸〈电子〉valve; tube：电子～ electron tube /显像～ picture tube /晶体～ transistor /硅晶体～ silicon transistor /二极～ diode /三极～ triode ❹〈量词〉：一～笔 a pen /一～猎枪 a shotgun /一～牙膏 a tube of toothpaste ❺ (Guǎn) a surname

管[2]

guǎn ❶ manage; run; control：～生产 manage production /～三台机器 run three machines /她～账，我～卖货。She takes care of the accounts and I do the business. /她把家～得井井有条。She keeps her house in good order. ❷ have jurisdiction over; administer：铁路局～八个分局。The railway bureau has eight sub-bureaus under its jurisdiction. /司法机关不归我们～。We have no control over judicial organs. ❸ subject sb. to discipline：这孩子需要好好～一～了。The boy needs discipline. /现在的独生子女真难～！The only child of a family is really hard to take in hand! ❹ be in charge of; undertake：他～礼宾，小王～后勤事务。He is in charge of protocol, while Xiao Wang heads the rear service office. /这工作责任重大，我实在～不了。The matter is very important and beyond my power. ❺ concern oneself with; bother about; mind; care about：大家的事大家～。Everybody's business, everybody's care. /产品质量，领导不～谁～？Who looks after the quality of the products if the leadership doesn't? /别～闲事！Mind your own business! *or* Don't poke your nose into others' business! /别～我，抢救伤员要紧。Don't bother about me! It's urgent to rescue the wounded. ❻ provide; ensure; guarantee：～吃～穿 provide food and clothing /产品有质量问题～修～换。We guarantee to repair or exchange substandard products. ❼ (used in the pattern 管…叫…) call：大家～这间屋子叫俱乐部。People call this room "the club". *or* This room is known as "the club". ❽〈方言〉〈介词〉from; to; towards：～我借东西 borrow something from me /～政府要救济款 ask the government for relief funds ❾〈方言〉no matter who, etc.; despite：～他是谁，违反纪律就得批评。Whoever violates the regulations shall be criticized. /～它下雨不下雨，今天都得出发。Rain or shine, we must set out today. /～你怎么解释，我都不信。For all your explanation, I don't believe it. ❿〈方言〉involve; concern：我爱怎么干就怎么干，不～你的事。I'll do it my own way. It's none of your business.

管扳子 guǎnbānzi *see*“管钳子”

管饱 guǎnbǎo guarantee adequate food：菜不好，饭～。Poor as the food may be, there is enough of it for everyone.

管保 guǎnbǎo ❶ guarantee; assure：我～按时完成任务。I guarantee that I shall fulfil the task in time. /这酒～对健康无害。I assure you that this wine is quite innocuous. ❷ certainly; surely; definitely; you bet：他～不是我的对手。I am sure he's not my match. /"你敢跟她说实话吗？""～敢说。""Dare you tell her the truth?" "You bet (*or* I certainly will)."

管壁 guǎnbì pipe shell; tube wall：～厚度测量仪 pipe wall gauge

管不住 guǎnbuzhù *also*“管不了”be unable to control; cannot manage：自己的孩子自己都～。Even his children refuse to listen to him.

管材 guǎncái tubing; tubular product

管待 guǎndài take care of; entertain; fete; treat or receive cordially

管带 guǎndài 〈旧语〉battalion commander

管道 guǎndào ❶ pipeline; piping; conduit; tubing：安装煤气～ install (*or* fit) gas pipelines /～系统 piping system /纵横交错的地下～ underground network of pipelines /～工 plumber; gas fitter ❷〈方

言〉channel; way:透过各种～来提高幼教水准 seek various ways to improve pre-school education
管定 guǎndìng 〈方言〉sure; certain; no doubt:明天他～来不了。I'm sure he won't show up tomorrow.
管段 guǎnduàn *see* "管片"
管饭 guǎnfàn provide meals gratis or free of charge; include board:除了付工钱之外,还～ provide free meals in addition to wages
管风琴 guǎnfēngqín 〈乐器〉pipe organ; organ:～手 organist
管护 guǎnhù take care of; attend to; care for:一日种树,常年～。A tree is easily planted, but it must be taken care of all the year round.
管家 guǎnjiā ❶〈旧语〉steward; butler:忠实可靠的老～ honest, loyal and reliable steward /他在王家当了几十年的～。He served at the Wang's as a butler for decades. ❷ manager; housekeeper:他的妻子是个节俭的好～。His wife is a thrifty housekeepr. /大家都称赞他是工厂的好～。People praised him as a good manager of the factory. ❸ manage a household; run a house
管家婆 guǎnjiāpó ❶〈旧语〉stewardess; chief female servant ❷ (female) housekeeper; housewife
管见 guǎnjiàn 〈谦词〉my humble opinion; my narrow view; my limited understanding:略陈～。Let me briefly state my humble opinion.
管见所及 guǎnjiàn-suǒjí in my humble opinion; according to my limited understanding (of the matter); as far as I can see
管教 guǎnjiào ❶ certainly; surely; assuredly:只要大家保持一致,～他没法反对。If we all see eye to eye, he'll have no way to object. /～敌人有来无回。We will see to it that the invading enemy won't be able to get away. ❷ discipline; subject (sb.) to discipline:这帮孩子该～～了。These children need discipline. /她从不～自己的孩子。She never corrects her children. ❸ put under surveillance and reeducate through labour
管教干部 guǎnjiào gànbù officer or warden at a reformatory
管教所 guǎnjiàosuǒ reformatory
管界 guǎnjiè ❶ area or land under control; sphere of jurisdiction; jurisdiction zone:事件发生在这个派出所的～内。It took place in an area under the jurisdiction of this police station. ❷ border of a jurisdiction zone
管劲 guǎnjìn 〈方言〉work; be effective:吃这种药～。This medicine is quite efficacious.
管井 guǎnjǐng 〈水利〉tube well
管口鱼 guǎnkǒuyú trumpet fish; flutemouth; *Aulostomidae*
管窥 guǎnkuī look at sth. through a bamboo tube — have a restricted view:～之见 limited understanding (*or* view) /～所及 in my humble opinion /《中国～》*One Man's China*
管窥蠡测 guǎnkuī-lícè look at the sky through a bamboo tube and measure the sea with a calabash — restricted in view and superficial in understanding:～,终乏大观。They do not have a broad vision, as they are shallow in their understanding.
管理 guǎnlǐ ❶ manage; administer; run; supervise:～生产 manage production /～企业 run (*or* manage) an enterprise /～侨务 administer affairs concerning overseas Chinese /市场～ supervise a market /～国家大事 administer (*or* be in charge of) state affairs /经济～ economic administration /商业～ business management (*or* administration) /加强财务～ strengthen the administration (*or* management) of financial affairs ❷ take care of; look after:～宿舍 look after the dorm /～仓库 take care of the warehouse /她把一个八口之家～得井井有条。She kept the house of eight in good order. ❸ watch over; tend; look after:～犯人 watch over prisoners /～牲口 tend draught animals
管理部门 guǎnlǐ bùmén administrative department
管理费 guǎnlǐfèi ❶ management fee ❷ *also* "管理费用" management expenses; costs of administration
管理风格 guǎnlǐ fēnggé management style
管理经济学 guǎnlǐ jīngjìxué managerial economics
管理会计 guǎnlǐ kuàijì management accounting
管理买进 guǎnlǐ mǎijìn management buy-in (MBI)
管理卖出 guǎnlǐ màichū management buy-out (MBO)
管理权 guǎnlǐquán administrative power; right of supervision
管理人员 guǎnlǐ rényuán administrative personnel; managerial staff; administrator:～比率 management ratio
管理水平 guǎnlǐ shuǐpíng level of administration or management
管理委员会 guǎnlǐ wěiyuánhuì administrative or management committee; board of management
管理员 guǎnlǐyuán storekeeper; janitor
管理制度 guǎnlǐ zhìdù administrative regulations; rules of administration
管林员 guǎnlínyuán forest ranger
管路 guǎnlù 〈机械〉pipeline:铺设～ lay pipelines /～输送能力 carrying capacity of a pipeline; delivery capacity
管内 guǎnnèi within one's jurisdiction
管片 guǎnpiàn jurisdiction zone; neighbourhood; department (under sb.'s administration):本～今年头三个月没有重大刑事案件。There was no major criminal report in this neighbourhood during the first quarter of the year.
管卡压 guǎn-qiǎ-yā control, check and suppress (usu. things that should be let alone)
管钳子 guǎnqiánzi *also* "管扳子" pipe wrench; alligator wrench; pipe gripper
管区 guǎnqū district (under sb.'s jurisdiction); jurisdiction zone; pale
管取 guǎnqǔ 〈方言〉sure; certain; no doubt; undoubtedly:他这一去～马到成功。I'm sure he'll succeed this time.
管儿灯 guǎnrdēng 〈口语〉fluorescent lamp; daylight lamp
管纱 guǎnshā 〈纺织〉cop (conical mass of thread on a spindle)
管舌鸟 guǎnshéniǎo Hawaiian honey creeper
管事 guǎnshì ❶ run affairs; be in charge; be responsible:名义上他是厂长,但实际不～。Nominally he is head of the factory, but in reality he is not in charge. ❷ efficacious; effective; of use; useful:治胃病,这药最～儿。This medicine is most effective for stomachache. ❸〈旧语〉steward; butler; manager; person in charge:张家的～ butler of the Zhangs /饭店～ hotel manager
管束 guǎnshù supervise; restrain; check; control:～不严 lax (in) supervision /严加～ keep sb. under strict control /她从小娇生惯养,不受他人～。She was a spoiled girl and defied all restraints.
管委会 guǎnwěihuì (short for 管理委员会) management committee; management board
管辖 guǎnxiá have jurisdiction over; exercise control over; administer:～区 district under the jurisdiction or administration of a larger geopolitical unit /这是省政府～范围之内的事。This is within the jurisdiction of the provincial government. /这个县～的人口有五十多万。This county has jurisdiction over more than half a million people. /北京、天津、上海、重庆直接受国务院～。Beijing, Shanghai, Tianjin and Chongqing are directly under the State Council.
管辖权 guǎnxiáquán jurisdiction
管闲事 guǎn xiánshì meddle in what does not concern one; poke one's nose into others' business:休～! Don't be meddlesome! *or* Mind your own business! /别管他那些闲事。Don't worry over his petty affairs.
管弦乐 guǎnxiányuè orchestral music
管弦乐队 guǎnxián yuèduì orchestra; symphony orchestra
管线 guǎnxiàn piping and wiring; pipes and power lines:～安装 pipelining /在～交错的大城市修建地铁实非易事。It is really no easy job to construct underground railways in a big city with piping and wiring networks.
管押 guǎnyā take sb. into custody; keep sb. in custody; detain:受～的嫌疑犯 suspect held in custody
管用 guǎnyòng efficacious; effective; of use; useful:你说话兴许还～。What you say may have some effect. /光说不～,～的是实际行动。It's not words but deeds that count.
管乐队 guǎnyuèduì wind band; band
管乐器 guǎnyuèqì wind instrument
管账 guǎnzhàng keep accounts; keep books:～的 bookkeeper
管制 guǎnzhì ❶ control:灯火～ blackout /部分灯火～ brownout /军备～ arms control /军事～ military control /交通～ traffic control /实行外汇～ exercise foreign exchange control /加强空中～ strengthen aerial control ❷ put (criminals, etc.) under surveillance:保护性～ protective surveillance /～劳动 labour under surveillance
管中窥豹 guǎnzhōng-kuībào look at a leopard through a tube — see only a part; have a limited view of sth.:我只读了几个片段,对全书算是～。I've read a few passages of the book and can only say I have a rough idea of what it is about.
管中窥豹,可见一斑 guǎn zhōng kuī bào, kě jiàn yībān look at one spot on a leopard and you can visualize the whole animal; get a general idea of the whole thing through seeing a part of it

管仲 Guǎn Zhòng Guanzhong (known reverentially as 管子, Guanzi or Kuan-tzu; ? -645 BC) statesman and prime minister of the State of Qi of the Spring and Autumn Period

管状花 guǎnzhuànghuā *also*“筒状花” tǒngzhuànghuā 〈植物〉 tubular flower

管子 Guǎnzǐ *Guanzi* or *Book of Master Guanzhong*
see also“管仲”

管子 guǎnzi tube; pipe: ～工 plumber; pipe fitter /煤气～ gas pipe /自来水～ tap water pipe

管自 guǎnzì 〈方言〉 ❶ straight away; without consulting anyone: 他不打招呼，～走了。He turned away without saying goodbye. ❷ by all means; merely; simply; just: 他谁都不理，～吃他的饭。He just went on with his meal, not taking heed of anybody. /有问题～问。If you have any questions, don't hesitate to ask.

鳍

guǎn 〈动物〉 *Ochetobius elongatus*

馆(舘)

guǎn ❶ accommodation for guests; mansion; building: 旅～ hotel /国宾～ state guesthouse ❷ embassy, legation or consulate: 大使～ embassy /公使～ legation /总领～ consulate general ❸ term for certain service establishments: 餐～ restaurant /理发～ barber's (shop); hairdresser's /茶～ teahouse /咖啡～ coffee house; café /照相～ photo studio /殡仪～ the undertaker's; funeral parlour (*or* home) ❹ place for cultural activities: 博物～ museum /天文～ planetarium /展览～ exhibition hall /水族～ aquarium /美术～ art gallery /图书～ library /珍宝～ treasures hall /体育～ gymnasium (*or* indoor stadium) /纪念～ memorial hall /文化～ culture centre /文史～ research institute of culture and history /武～ martial arts centre ❺ 〈旧语〉 old-style private school: 坐～ teach at an old-style private school

馆藏 guǎncáng (of a library or a museum) collect; hold: 丰富的～ rich collection of books, paintings, etc.; fine library /学院图书馆～图书百万余册。The college library has a collection of more than one million books. /那幅古画是省博物馆的～。That ancient painting is from the collection of the provincial museum.

馆舍 guǎnshè ❶ 〈旧语〉 inn; hotel; guesthouse ❷ house; building; premises (of an embassy, etc.)

馆子 guǎnzi restaurant; eating house; eatery: 吃～ eat out at a restaurant /四川～ Sichuan restaurant

guàn

冠

guàn ❶ 〈书面〉 wear or put on a hat (formerly as a sign of adulthood): 未～ not wear a hat — not yet an adult; under twenty /沐猴而～ monkey with a hat on — imposing but worthless ❷ precede; crown with: 地方招待所一般都～以所属区县的名称。The name of a local government hostel is usually preceded by that of the district or county. /他唱了几首歌就被～以歌唱家的桂冠。He was crowned with the title of "singer" just for chanting a few songs. ❸ first place; the best; champion: 勇～三军 be the bravest soldier in the army; distinguish oneself by peerless valour /位～群臣 occupy the highest official position; be first among all the officials /本厂啤酒产量居全国各厂家之～。This brewery ranks first in the whole country for beer production. /北京队战胜上海队而夺～。The Beijing team defeated the Shanghai team and won first place. ❹ (Guàn) a surname
see also guān

冠词 guàncí 〈语言〉 article: 定～ definite article /不定～ indefinite article

冠军 guànjūn champion; first-prize winner; gold medallist: 世界～ world champion /获得～ win the first prize (*or* championship, *or* gold medal)

冠军花 guànjūnhuā 〈植物〉 champion; catchfly

冠军赛 guànjūnsài championship(s): 他在那次世界乒乓球～中夺得亚军。He came second in that World Table Tennis Championship.

灌

guàn ❶ irrigate; water: 冬～ winter irrigation /引水～地 channel water to irrigate the fields /排～站 drainage and irrigation station /浇～ watering /喷～ sprinkler irrigation /漫～ flood irrigation /畦～ border irrigation /沟～ furrow irrigation /扩大机～面积 enlarge the pump-irrigated area ❷ fill; pour; cram: ～暖瓶 fill the thermos flask /把牛奶～到瓶里 pour the milk into the bottle /几个瓶子全～满了。The bottles have all been filled up. /北风呼呼地直往屋子里～。The north wind whistled into the house. /可别把他～醉了。Don't get him drunk. /满堂～不是什么好的教学方法。Cramming is not a good teaching method. ❸ record (sound or music on a tape or disc)

灌肠 guàncháng 〈医学〉 give an enema or clyster; clyster

灌肠 guànchang sausage

灌唱片 guàn chàngpiàn make a gramophone record; cut a disc; disc: 这几支歌早就灌成唱片了。These songs were disced (*or* canned) long ago. /给参赛歌星～。Gramophone records will be made for the singers participating in the contest.

灌顶 guàndǐng 〈佛教〉 *abhiseca*

灌溉 guàngài irrigate; water: 机器～ irrigation by pumping /自流～ gravity irrigation /人力～ irrigation by human power /十亩棉田一个上午就～完了。One morning will be enough for watering the ten *mu* of cotton.

灌溉面积 guàngài miànjī area under irrigation; irrigated area

灌溉渠 guàngàiqú *also*“灌渠” irrigation canal or channel

灌溉网 guàngàiwǎng irrigation network

灌溉系统 guàngài xìtǒng irrigation system

灌浆 guànjiāng ❶ 〈建筑〉 grouting: ～泵 grouting pump /～帷幕 grout curtain ❷ 〈农业〉 (of grain) be in the milk: 正值小麦～时节 at a time when the wheat is in the milk; with wheat in the milk ❸ 〈医学〉 form a vesicle (during smallpox or after vaccination) ❹ 〈矿业〉 injection

灌浆成型 guànjiāng chéngxíng slurry molding

灌浆期 guànjiāngqī 〈医学〉 pustulation period

灌录 guànlù make a recording

灌莽 guànmǎng luxuriant vegetation

灌迷魂汤 guàn míhúntāng *see*“灌米汤”

灌米汤 guàn mǐtang bewitch with honeyed words; butter up; lay it on thick; soft-soap: 当面～，背后打黑枪 say nice words to sb.'s face, but defame him maliciously behind his back /你别给我～了，我是不会上当的。Don't flatter (*or* soft-soap) me. I'll not be taken in.

灌木 guànmù bush; shrub: ～丛 brush; brush-wood; shrubbery: 河流两岸～丛生。The river banks were overgrown with shrubs.

灌区 guànqū irrigated area: 红旗渠～ benefited area of the Redflag Irrigation Canal

灌渠 guànqú irrigation canal or channel

灌丧 guànsang 〈贬义〉 drink (alcohol, water, etc.): 别～了! Drink no more!

灌输 guànshū ❶ channel water to another place: 人们用水泵把河水～到干旱的山地。Water was pumped from the river to irrigate the dry land in the hills. ❷ instill into; inculcate; imbue with: ～科学知识 instill scientific knowledge into sb. /不要给孩子们～拜金主义的思想。One should not inculcate children with the idea that money is everything.

灌音 guànyīn have one's voice recorded or canned

灌制 guànzhì tape-record; record: ～唱片 cut a disc /把课文～在磁带上 record the texts on tape

灌注 guànzhù pour: 往木型里～混凝土 pour concrete into a wood mould /把心血全都～在孩子们身上 devote oneself heart and soul to the children

瓘

guàn 〈古语〉 a kind of jade

罐(鑵)

guàn ❶ jar; pot; tin; tank; pitcher: 煤气～ gas tank /储油～ oil storage tank /糖～ sugar bowl /酒～ wine jar /水～ pitcher /果酱～ jar (*or* pot) of jam /一～茶叶 a caddie (*or* caddy) of tea ❷ 〈矿业〉 coal tub

罐车 guànchē tank car; tank truck; tanker

罐笼 guànlóng 〈矿业〉 cage; cage conductor: ～隔间 cage compartment /～间隙 cage clearance /～格 cage way

罐焖羊肉 guànmèn yángròu mutton braised in a pot

罐头 guàntou ❶ 〈方言〉 jar; pot; pitcher; tin ❷ (short for 罐头食品) tinned food; canned food: 水果～ canned fruit /开～刀 tin (*or* can) opener /～厂 cannery

罐装 guànzhuāng canning

罐子 guànzi pot; jar; pitcher; tin; jug: 一～大米 a jarful of rice /瓦～ earthen pot /空～ empty tin /～盛得满满的。The jug is full.

G

鹳 guàn 〈动物〉stork：白～ white stork

观(觀) guàn ❶ Taoist temple：道～ Taoist temple /白云～ White Cloud Temple (in Beijing) ❷ (Guàn) a surname
see also guān

贯 guàn ❶ pass through; penetrate; pierce：横～数省的铁路 railroad that passes through several provinces /学～中西 well versed in both Chinese and Western learning (*or* both oriental and occidental learning) /气～长虹 full of noble aspirations and daring /如雷～耳 reverberate like thunder — resounding fame ❷ be connected; proceed in succession; follow in a continuous line：鱼～而入 coming in succession; enter in single file; file in /前后不连～ inconsistent; incoherent ❸ 〈旧语〉string of 1,000 cash：十五～ (title of a traditional opera) *Fifteen Strings of Cash* ❹ ancestral home; native place：籍～ place of one's birth or origin; native place ❺ 〈书面〉precedent; existing model：一仍旧～ follow the precedent ❻ (Guàn) a surname

贯彻 guànchè carry out or through; implement; execute; put into effect：～政策 carry out a policy /～上级指示 execute instructions of one's superior /～决议 put into effect a resolution /～群众路线 follow the mass line/～十五大精神 act in the spirit of the Fifteenth National Congress of the Communist Party of China /～党的基本路线 implement the Party's basic line

贯穿 guànchuān ❶ run through; penetrate：这条铁路～好几个省市。This railroad runs through several provinces and municipalities. /大运河～南北。The Grand Canal flows north and south. ❷ fill; permeate：实事求是的精神～全文。The article is permeated with the spirit of seeking truth from facts.

贯穿辐射 guànchuān fúshè penetrating radiation

贯串 guànchuàn be permeated with; run through; penetrate：全诗～着强烈的爱国主义精神。A strong patriotic spirit runs through the entire poem.

贯口 guànkǒu 〈戏曲〉rapid verbal exercise

贯气 guànqì 〈迷信〉favourable geomantic omen

贯通 guàntōng ❶ have a thorough understanding of; master (a subject); be well versed in：融会～ achieve mastery through a comprehensive study of the subject /豁然～ suddenly see the light ❷ link up; thread together; join up：～南北 (of railways, etc.) run south and north /武汉长江大桥把京广铁路全线～起来了。The Wuhan Yangtze Bridge links up the entire Beijing-Guangzhou Railway.

贯众 guànzhòng 〈中药〉rhizome of cyrtomium (*Cyrtomium fortunei*)

贯珠 guànzhū string of pearls (often used figuratively to describe the sweet, mellow voice of a singer)：声如～。The sweet and mellow voice rang out like the clink of pearls.

贯注 guànzhù ❶ concentrate on; give full attention to; be absorbed in：他全神～地工作着。He was wholly engrossed in his work. /为了攻克这个技术难关，他～了所有的精力。He concentrated all his energy on this key technical problem. ❷ (of meaning, tone, etc.) connected; consistent：这几句是一气～下来的，十分有力。These sentences are closely connected and very forceful.

惯 guàn ❶ be used or accustomed to; be inured to; be in the habit of：她住～了平房，住不～高楼大厦。She is used to living in one-storey houses and not in tall buildings. /每天早睡早起，他已经～了。He is in the habit of going to bed early and getting up early. /此人说谎话说～了。The man is given to lying. /他对艰苦生活已经过～了。He has become inured to hard life (*or* hardships). ❷ indulge; spoil; pamper; coddle：千万别把孩子～坏了。You mustn't spoil the child. /爷爷奶奶太娇～她。Her grandparents are pampering her.

惯常 guàncháng ❶ habitual; customary：从他那～的动作上，可以看出他是老练的水手。One can judge from his habitual actions that he is a seasoned sailor. ❷ often; frequently：～出门的人，知道旅途上的许多不便。A frequent traveller knows the many inconveniences that may accompany a trip. ❸ usual; normal：他恢复了～的镇定。He recovered his usual composure.

惯盗 guàndào hardened bandit; professional brigand or robber

惯犯 guànfàn habitual offender; hardened criminal; recidivist; repeater：老奸巨滑的～ wily old lag

惯匪 guànfěi hardened bandit; professional brigand

惯技 guànjì 〈贬义〉customary tactic; old trick：他又在施展～。He is playing his old tricks.

惯家 guànjia 〈贬义〉old hand; stager：干这种见不得人的勾当，他可是～了。He is an old hand at such shady deals.

惯例 guànlì ❶ convention; usual practice：按～行事 go by convention /打破～ break free from conventions; break with conventions /国际～ international practice /外交～ diplomatic practice or usage /这已成为～。This has become usual practice. ❷ 〈法律〉precedent：援引～ cite a precedent

惯量 guànliàng 〈物理〉inertia; inertness

惯骗 guànpiàn hardened or professional swindler

惯窃 guànqiè professional or hardened thief

惯熟 guànshú 〈方言〉be familiar with; know well about：她的声音大家听得～的。Her voice is familiar to all of us.

惯偷 guàntōu professional or hardened thief

惯习 guànxí habit：多年的～ long-time habit

惯性 guànxìng 〈物理〉inertia

惯性导航 guànxìng dǎoháng inertial guidance

惯性定律 guànxìng dìnglǜ law of inertia

惯性飞行导弹 guànxìng fēixíng dǎodàn 〈军事〉coaster; coasting missile

惯性矩 guànxìngjǔ moment of inertia

惯性力 guànxìnglì inertial force; mass force

惯用 guànyòng habitually practise; consistently use：～的称呼 customary (*or* habitual) title /人身攻击、造谣诬蔑是他们～的伎俩。Personal attack and slander are their customary tactics. /他～这种卑鄙手法欺骗大家。He consistently uses these mean tricks to deceive people.

惯用法 guànyòngfǎ *also* "惯用语" customary usage; usage：英语～词典 dictionary of English usage /～手册 phrase book

惯于 guànyú be used to; be accustomed to：～海上生活 accustomed to life at sea /他不～在大庭广众面前发言。He is not used to speaking in public.

惯贼 guànzéi *see* "惯窃"

惯纵 guànzòng indulge; spoil; pamper：要不是你～他，这孩子还不至于捅这么大的娄子。The boy might not have got into such big trouble but for your indulgence.

掼 guàn 〈方言〉❶ throw; fling; hurl; toss：～石头 throw stones /他朝窗户上～了两块砖头。He hurled two stones at the window. /她把衣服～在地上。She flung her clothes on the floor. ❷ thresh：～稻 thresh rice ❸ fall; tumble; throw on the ground：老人～了一跟头，一条腿断了。The old man had a fall and broke one of his legs. /我被他～倒了。He threw me on the ground.

掼跤 guànjiāo 〈方言〉❶ wrestling ❷ trip and fall; tumble

掼炮 guànpào torpedo, a kind of firecracker

掼纱帽 guàn shāmào 〈方言〉〈比喻〉cast away one's official hat in anger; resign in resentment; quit office, or give up one's position in a huff：～无助于问题的解决。It won't solve the problem by quitting office. *or* Resignation does not help.

掼桶 guàntǒng *also* "扮桶" bàntǒng 〈方言〉square-shaped wooden pail used for threshing rice

盥 guàn 〈书面〉❶ wash (the hands or face) ❷ toilet articles

盥漱 guànshù wash one's face and rinse one's mouth：我已～完毕，正准备就寝。Having washed up, I am ready for bed.

盥洗 guànxǐ wash one's hands or face; wash up：～用具 toilet articles

盥洗间 guànxǐjiān *also* "盥洗室" washroom

盥洗台 guànxǐtái washstand

涫 guàn 〈书面〉❶ boil ❷ wash one's face and hands

串 guàn 〈书面〉❶ habit ❷ one's dear ones; one's relatives：戚～ one's relatives
see also chuàn

guāng

光 guāng ❶ light; ray：阳～ sunshine; sunlight; sun rays /

星～ star light /月～ moonlight /火～ firelight /可见～ visible light /黑～ black light /曙～ first light of morning; dawn /爱克斯～ X-ray /霞～万道 myriad of sun rays ❷ scenery; landscape; sight:春～明媚 sunlit and enchanting scene of spring; sunny spring scene /观～旅行 sightseeing tour ❸ honour; glory; credit:为国争～ win honour for one's country; do credit to one's country /感到脸上无～ feel ashamed ❹ good; advantage; benefit:这可全是沾了你的～。We've all benefited from you. ❺〈敬词〉*used of what the other party does for one*:请赏～。Please grace us with your presence. *or* Your company is cordially requested. ❻ shine upon; glorify; bring honour to:其精神～于当代,传于后世。His spirit glorifies the contemporary era and will be handed down to posterity. ❼ bright; shiny:与日月齐～ as bright as the sun and the moon /皮鞋擦得油～锃亮。The leather shoes were well polished. ❽ smooth; glossy:两面～ smooth (*or* glossy) on both sides /画画的纸不宜太～。Drawing paper shouldn't be too glossy. ❾ use up; finish:钱花得精～ use up (*or* spend) all one's money /子弹打～了 shoot all one's bullets ❿ bare; naked:～脑袋 bare-headed /～脚丫子 bare-footed /～着上身 be stripped to the waist ⓫ solely; merely; only; alone:～打雷不下雨 all thunder and no rain; all bark and no bite; all words and no action /不要～发牢骚。Don't just grumble. /要脚踏实地,～有热情是不够的。One must set one's feet on solid ground; mere enthusiasm is not enough. ⓬ (Guāng) a surname

光按钮 guāng'ànniǔ light button

光巴 guāngba 〈方言〉(of the human body) bare; naked:～着脊背 be stripped to the waist

光斑 guāngbān 〈天文〉facula; solar flare

光板儿 guāngbǎnr ❶ worn-out fur:穿了几十年的老羊皮袄只剩下～了。After decades of wear and tear, the goat-fur jacket was nothing but a patch of raw hide. ❷〈旧语〉non-engraved copper coin

光膀子 guāng bǎngzi stripped to the waist

光泵 guāngbèng optical pump

光比 guāngbǐ 〈天文〉light ratio

光笔 guāngbǐ 〈计算机〉electronic pen; light pen

光标 guāngbiāo 〈计算机〉cursor:～控制 cursor control /～位置 cursor position /～上下 cursor up and down /～右移 cursor right /～左移 cursor left /～存储器 cursor memory

光波 guāngbō 〈物理〉light wave; optical wave:～长 optical wavelength /～导 optical waveguide; lightguide; fibre waveguide /～干涉 optical interference

光波导探测器 guāngbōdǎo tàncèqì optical waveguide detector

光波干涉仪 guāngbō gānshèyí wavelength interferometer

光波通信 guāngbō tōngxìn 〈通信〉lightwave communication

光彩 guāngcǎi ❶ lustre; splendour; brilliance; radiance:绚丽的～ brilliant lustre /大放～ shine with dazzling splendour ❷ honour; glory:不～的角色 ignominous role /一人立功,全家～。When one member earns a citation, the whole family share in the honour.

光彩夺目 guāngcǎi-duómù dazzlingly bright; brilliant

光彩照人 guāngcǎi-zhàorén brilliant; resplendent:这个女孩～。The girl is a ravishing beauty.

光灿灿 guāngcàncàn bright; shining:～的秋阳 bright autumn sun

光测 guāngcè flash ranging

光测角法 guāngcèjiǎofǎ photogoniometric method

光测距 guāngcèjù light-ranging

光测力学 guāngcè lìxué optical measurement mechanics

光程 guāngchéng optical distance; optical length; optical path:～计算机 optical path computer

光程差 guāngchéngchā optical path difference (OPD)

光尺 guāngchǐ laser range finder; laser ranging device

光赤 guāngchì (of the human body) bare; naked:～着身子游泳 swim naked; go skinny-dipping

光宠 guāngchǒng 〈书面〉favour; honour

光传电话 guāngchuán diànhuà phototelephony

光传输系统 guāngchuánshū xìtǒng optic transmission system

光船租赁 guāngchuán zūlìn bareboat charter; demise charter

光磁性 guāngcíxìng 〈物理〉photomagnetism

光存储器 guāngcúnchǔqì optical memory; optical storage

光大 guāngdà 〈书面〉❶ carry forward; promote; enhance:发扬～爱国主义的优良传统。Carry forward the fine tradition of patriotism. ❷ far and wide; vast

光大实业公司 Guāngdà Shíyè Gōngsī Everbright Industrial Corporation

光带 guāngdài light band; shaft of light

光蛋 guāngdàn 〈方言〉pauper; penniless wretch

光蛋白 guāngdànbái 〈生化〉photoprotein

光刀 guāngdāo laser beam (used as a scalpel); laser scalpel

光导 guāngdǎo 〈物理〉photoconduct:～性 photoconductivity /～管 photoconductive tube; light-pipe; photoconductor; photoresistor

光导电缆 guāngdǎo diànlǎn optical cable

光导电效应 guāngdǎodiàn xiàoyìng photoconductive effect

光导聚合物 guāngdǎo jùhéwù photoconductive polymer

光导器件 guāngdǎo qìjiàn photocon

光导摄像管 guāngdǎo shèxiàngguǎn vidicon

光导纤维 guāngdǎo xiānwéi *also* "光学纤维" light-guide fibre; optical (waveguide) fibre; fibre-optic:～电缆 fibre-optic cable; optical fibre cable /～管 optical fibre tube /～通信系统 optical fibre (*or* fibre-optic) communication system

光点扫描 guāngdiǎn sǎomiáo spot scan; light-spot scanning

光电 guāngdiàn 〈物理〉photoelectricity:～发射 photoelectric emission; photoemission /～二极管 photodiode; photorectifier /～变换器 photoactor

光电报警器 guāngdiàn bàojǐngqì photoelectric alarm

光电材料 guāngdiàn cáiliào photoelectric material

光电测量仪 guāngdiàn cèliángyí photoelectric measuring instrument

光电池 guāngdiànchí photobattery; photocell; photoelectric cell:阻挡层～ barrier-layer cell; barrier-layer photocell /～继电器 photocell relay

光电传感器 guāngdiàn chuángǎnqì photoelectric sensor

光电导 guāngdiàndǎo photoconduction; photoconductance:～体 photoconductor /～效应 photoconductive effect

光电电路 guāngdiàn diànlù photoelectric circuit

光电读出器 guāngdiàn dúchūqì photoreader

光电发生器 guāngdiàn fāshēngqì photocurrent generator

光电管 guāngdiànguǎn phototube

光电光度计 guāngdiàn guāngdùjì photoelectric photometer; electronic photometer

光电计数器 guāngdiàn jìshùqì photoelectric counter

光电继电器 guāngdiàn jìdiànqì photoelectric relay; photoelectric switch

光电晶体管 guāngdiàn jīngtǐguǎn phototransistor; photistor

光电扫描器 guāngdiàn sǎomiáoqì photoelectric scanner (PES)

光电摄像管 guāngdiàn shèxiàngguǎn iconoscope

光电探测器 guāngdiàn tàncèqì photodetector

光电显微镜 guāngdiàn xiǎnwēijìng photoelectric microscope

光电显像管 guāngdiàn xiǎnxiàngguǎn photoelectric viewing tube

光电效应 guāngdiàn xiàoyìng photoelectronic effect

光电钟 guāngdiànzhōng photoelectric clock

光电子 guāngdiànzǐ 〈物理〉photoelectron:～学 photoelectronics; optoelectronics /～电路 optoelectronic circuit /～二极管 optoelectronic diode

光度 guāngdù 〈物理〉luminosity:～分类 luminosity classification /～过大恒星 overluminous star /～过小恒星 underluminous star /～标 photometric scale

光度计 guāngdùjì photometer; luminometer

光发射器 guāngfāshèqì optical emitter

光风霁月 guāngfēng-jìyuè *also* "霁月光风" gentle breeze and clear sky — be broadminded and open-hearted:人品清高,胸怀洒落,一如～。He is a man of integrity and high moral standards, with a broad mind and an open heart.

光伏 guāngfú 〈物理〉photovoltaic:～电池 photovoltaic cell /～计 photovoltaic meter

光符识别 guāngfú shíbié 〈计算机〉optical character recognition

光符阅读机 guāngfú yuèdújī optical character reader (OCR)

光辐射 guāngfúshè (optical) radiation:～伤害 radiation injury

光复 guāngfù recover; regain:～失地 regain lost territory /一连～数座城池。Several cities were recovered in succession.

光复会 Guāngfùhuì 〈历史〉Restoration Society (a revolutionary society active in the early 20th century in China's southeast)

光复旧物 guāngfù-jiùwù *also* "光复旧宗" recover lost territory; restore original institutions

光杆儿 guānggǎnr ❶ bare trunk or stalk:～牡丹 peony bare of leaves; leaveless peony (blossom) ❷ man who has lost his family:父母相继去世,家里就剩他～一个了。When his parents died one after the

G

other, he was left all alone in the world. ❸ leader without a following
光杆司令 guānggǎn sīlìng general with no troops under his command; leader without a following
光跟踪导弹 guānggēnzōng dǎodàn optically tracking missile
光顾 guānggù (usu. used by shopkeepers) patronage: 欢迎～。Your patronage is cordially invited. /您能～敝店，是我们的光荣。Your patronage brings honour to this humble store.
光怪陆离 guāngguài-lùlí grotesque and gaudy; bizarre and motley; fantastic: ～的霓虹灯广告 grotesque and gaudy neon ads (*or* signs) /～的世界 fantastic world /那些贝壳，形状各异，～，好看极了。Bizarre and motley, these variously shaped shells looked most beautiful.
光棍 guānggùn ❶ ruffian; hooligan: 上海滩上有名的～ notorious thug on the Shanghai bund ❷〈方言〉one who is "street-wise"; smart person
光棍不吃眼前亏 guānggùn bù chī yǎnqián kuī a smart man does not fight when the odds are against him
光棍儿 guānggùnr unmarried man; bachelor: 打了一辈子～ remain a bachelor all one's life
光过敏性皮炎 guāngguòmǐnxìng píyán hypericism
光合作用 guānghé zuòyòng 〈植物〉photosynthesis
光华 guānghuá brilliance; lustre; splendour: 日月～ splendour of the sun and moon
光化 guānghuà 〈化学〉❶ actinic: ～性 actinicity; actinism /～射线 actinic ray /～屏幕 actinic screen; sun-screen ❷ photochemical: ～反应 photochemical reaction
光化玻璃 guānghuà bōli actinic glass
光化电池 guānghuà diànchí photochemical cell
光化效应 guānghuà xiàoyìng actinic effect
光化学 guānghuàxué photochemistry: ～发光 photochemiluminescence
光化学烟雾 guānghuàxué yānwù 〈气象〉photochemical smog
光化作用 guānghuà zuòyòng photochemical action
光滑 guānghua smooth; glossy; slick; sleek: ～如玉 as smooth as jade /招牌油漆得明亮～。The shop sign was bright and glossy with paint.
光环 guānghuán ❶ (as of a planet) ring of light: 土星～ Saturn's ring ❷ luminous ring: 霓虹灯组成的五色～ colourful rings of neon light ❸ (as of a god or goddess) halo; aureole
光幻觉 guānghuànjué 〈心理〉pseudophotoesthesia; optical illusion
光辉 guānghuī radiance; brilliance; lustre; glory: ～事迹 glorious deed /～思想 brilliant thoughts /～成就 magnificent achievement /～的一生 glorious life /～形象 illustrious image /～的榜样 shining example / ～夺目 dazzlingly bright; outstandingly brilliant /一滴水能反射出太阳的～。A drop of water may reflect the radiance of the sun. /这一形象给作品增添了艺术的～。This character has added to the artistic brilliance of the work. /这句话闪耀着哲理的～。The remark radiates with philosophic truth. /万里长征是中国革命史上的～篇章。The Long March marked a splendid chapter in the history of the Chinese revolution.
光辉灿烂 guānghuī-cànlàn shining with great splendour; brilliant; magnificent: ～的事业 cause that shines with great splendour; magnificent cause
光辉道路派 Guānghuī Dàolùpài Shining Path, a militant political organization in Peru
光辉霉素 guānghuīméisù 〈药学〉mithramycin
光火 guānghuǒ 〈方言〉get angry; fly into a rage; flare up: 这些话让我～。I flared up at these words.
光激 guāngjī light activated: ～可控硅整流器 light activated SCR (silicon-controlled rectifier)
光计算机 guāngjìsuànjī *also* "激光计算机" jīguāng jìsuànjī laser computer
光检波器 guāngjiǎnbōqì light detector
光降 guāngjiàng 〈书面〉〈敬词〉❶ your gracious presence: ～敝寓 your gracious presence at my humble house ❷ grant; bestow: 承蒙～书札，不胜感激之至。I was extremely grateful to you for writing me the letter.
光接收机 guāngjiēshōujī optical receiver
光洁 guāngjié bright and clean: 大理石桌面～如镜。The table's marble top is as bright and clean as a mirror.
光洁度 guāngjiédù 〈机械〉smooth finish; degree of finish: 高～ high smooth finish /～高 highly polished /～不合标准 below standard in smooth finish
光解 guāngjiě 〈化学〉photolysis: ～质 photolyte
光解作用 guāngjiě zuòyòng 〈化学〉photolysis
光介子 guāngjièzǐ 〈物理〉photomeson
光晶体管 guāngjīngtǐguǎn optotransistor
光景 guāngjǐng ❶ scenery; landscape; scene: 丽日花光，那～实在令人陶醉。It was an intoxicating scene with the sun shining and the flowers in blossom. /一眼望去，疏疏的林，淡淡的月，衬着蔚蓝的天，颇似荒江野渡～。On the horizon were scattered trees and a pale moon against an azure sky — befitting a deserted ferry of a lone river in wilderness. ❷ circumstances; conditions; state of affairs: 如今的～比过去强多了。Conditions (*or* Things) are much better than before. /劳动致富，这几年大家都过上了好～。People have become better-off these days through honest labour. ❸ probably; likely: 很久未遇见她，～是调离了。I haven't seen her for a long time. Probably she's been transferred. /天又阴了，～是要下雪了。It is overcast and looks like snow again. ❹ (usu. used to modify time, quantity, etc.) about; around: 那姑娘约有十六七岁～。That girl was about sixteen. /夜里两点半钟～，他忽然听到了一阵急促的敲门声。Around two-thirty in the morning, he suddenly heard someone knocking urgently at the door. /从这里到车站有三十公里～。It's approximately thirty kilometres from here to the railway station.
光聚作用 guāngjù zuòyòng photopolymerization
光开关 guāngkāiguān optical switch
光刻 guāngkè 〈物理〉photoetching: ～法 photolithography
光控 guāngkòng light-operated; photo-controlled: ～灯泡 light-operated bulb /～开关 photoswitch; light-operated switch
光缆 guānglǎn optical cable: ～组件 optical cable assembly; fibre cable assembly
光雷达 guāngléidá optical direction and ranging; photoradar
光连接器 guāngliánjiēqì optical connector
光亮 guāngliàng ❶ bright; luminous; shiny: ～如新 as bright as new /整洁～的房间 tidy and bright room /皮鞋擦得很～。The leather shoes were shiny with polish. ❷ light: 窗缝里透出一线～。A beam of light came out of a crack in the window.
光量控制 guāngliàng kòngzhì fader control; light control
光量子 guāngliàngzǐ 〈物理〉light quantum; photon
光疗 guāngliáo 〈医学〉phototherapy
光临 guānglín 〈敬词〉presence (of a guest, etc.): 敬请～指导。Your presence and comments are cordially requested. /承蒙阁下～寒舍，鄙人感到十分荣幸。Your excellency's presence at my humble house is a great honour to me.
光溜溜 guāngliūliū ❶ smooth; slippery: ～的冰面 slippery ice /她的头发梳得～的。Her hair was combed smooth. ❷ bare; naked: 院子里～的，没有树，连一棵草都没有。The courtyard was bare with no trees, not even weeds. /孩子脱得～的，正在洗澡。Stripped to the skin, the child is taking a bath.
光溜 guāngliu 〈口语〉slippery; smooth: 这种布面很～，手感好极了。This cloth is very smooth and feels wonderful. /小心点，这段路面太～了。Take care! This part of the road is quite slippery.
光流 guāngliú light stream; luminous flux: ～测量 measurement of luminous flux
光卤石 guānglǔshí carnalite
光路 guānglù optical circuit
光芒 guāngmáng rays of light; brilliant rays; radiance: 金色的太阳～四射。The golden sun was shedding its rays in all directions. /老人的眼里放出智慧的～。The old man's eyes emitted rays of wisdom.
光芒万丈 guāngmáng-wànzhàng shining with boundless brilliance; gloriously radiant; resplendent: 他认为国家的前途～，自己的前途漆黑一团。He thought that although the future of the nation stretched brightly ahead, his own lay in impenetrable darkness.
光密度 guāngmìdù optical density
光密媒质 guāngmì méizhì optically dense medium
光面 guāngmiàn noodles served without meat or vegetables
光敏 guāngmǐn 〈物理〉photosensitive; light-sensitive: ～半导体材料 light-sensitive semiconductor material /～二极管 photosensitive (*or* light-sensitive) diode; photodiode /～三极管 phototriode; phototransistor; photistor /～性 light-sensitivity; photosensitivity
光敏玻璃 guāngmǐn bōli light-sensitive glass; photosensitive glass
光敏电池 guāngmǐn diànchí light-sensitive cell
光敏电子管 guāngmǐn diànzǐguǎn light-sensitive electron tube

G

光敏电阻 guāngmǐn diànzǔ photosensitive resistance; photo resistance:~继电器 photoresistance relay
光敏晶体管 guāngmǐn jīngtǐguǎn phototransistor; photistor
光敏开关 guāngmǐn kāiguān photosensitive switch; light-activated switch
光明 guāngmíng ❶ light:节日的夜晚,广场上一片~。On the festive night, there was light all over the square. /黑暗中仅有的一线~。That was the only streak of light in the darkness. ❷ bright:通体~的水晶球 transparent crystal ball /他顿觉眼前一片~。All of a sudden it was all bright in front of him. ❸ promising; bright:~的出路 bright (*or* promising) future /~的远景 brilliant prospects ❹ openhearted; guileless; aboveboard:只要做事~,就不怕别人说闲话。A guileless man fears no gossip.
光明磊落 guāngmíng-lěiluò open and aboveboard; frank and openhearted:他那~的作风给我留下了不可磨灭的印象。His frank and openhearted manner left an indelible impression on me. /此人有点不够~。This fellow isn't quite honest.
光明日报 Guāngmíng Rìbào *Guangming Daily*, published in Beijing
光明正大 guāngmíng-zhèngdà *also* "正大光明" just and honest; open and aboveboard:这事你做得~,别人爱说什么就让他说吧。What you've done is open and aboveboard. Never mind what people may say.
光能 guāngnéng light energy:~利用率 efficiency of light energy utilization /~测定法 actinography
光年 guāngnián 〈天文〉light-year:这颗恒星距我们有四百万~。The star is 4 million light-years away from us.
光盘 guāngpán (optical) disk
光盘只读存储器 guāngpán zhǐdú cúnchǔqì CD-ROM (compact disk read-only memory)
光票 guāngpiào clean bill; clean draft:~信用证 clean letter of credit
光频 guāngpín light frequency; optical frequency:~放大器 optical frequency amplifier
光谱 guāngpǔ 〈物理〉spectrum:~吸收 spectral absorption /明线~ bright-line spectrum /暗线~ dark-line spectrum /线~ line spectrum /棱镜~ prismatic spectrum /太阳~ solar spectrum /X射线~ X-ray spectrum /原子~ atomic spectrum
光谱比较仪 guāngpǔ bǐjiàoyí spectrocomparator
光谱分辨率 guāngpǔ fēnbiànlǜ spectral resolution
光谱分析 guāngpǔ fēnxī spectral analysis
光谱辐射 guāngpǔ fúshè spectral radiation
光谱化学 guāngpǔ huàxué spectrochemistry
光谱疗法 guāngpǔ liáofǎ 〈医学〉chromotherapy
光谱图 guāngpǔtú spectrum chart; spectrogram
光谱线 guāngpǔxiàn spectral line
光谱学 guāngpǔxué spectroscopy:~家 spectroscopist
光谱仪 guāngpǔyí spectrograph; spectrometer
光气 guāngqì 〈化学〉carbonyl chloride; phosgene
光前裕后 guāngqián-yùhòu (often of people's achievements) glorify one's forefathers and enrich one's descendants; do credit to one's ancestors and good to one's progeny
光强度 guāngqiángdù light-intensity
光球 guāngqiú *also* "光球层" 〈天文〉photosphere
光圈 guāngquān *also* "光孔";"光阑" 〈摄影〉diaphragm; aperture:~快门 diaphragm shutter /~数 f-number /把~定为5.6 set the aperture at 5.6
光荣 guāngróng honour; glory; distinction; credit:~之家 honoured family (usu. in reference to a soldier's family) /~使命 glorious task (*or* mission) /~传统 splendid tradition /~归于人民,归于伟大的祖国。Glory to the people, to the great motherland. /他~牺牲了。He laid down his life with honour. /这位科学家是国家的~。The scientist is a credit to the country.
光荣榜 guāngróngbǎng honour roll:荣登~ appear on the honour roll
光荣花 guāngrónghuā rosette:给劳动英雄戴上~ decorate the labour heroes with rosettes
光润 guāngrùn (usu. of skin) smooth:~的肌肤 smooth skin
光扫描 guāngsǎomiáo photoscanning:~器 optical scanner; photoscanner
光栅 guāngshān 〈物理〉grating; raster:~锐度 grating acuity /~信号 grating signal /~扫描 raster scanning
光闪闪 guāngshǎnshǎn glitter; glisten:~的珍珠 glittering pearl
光身 guāngshēn 〈方言〉❶ single; not with one's family:至今还是~ remain unmarried (*or* single) to this day /他~一人住在北京,家属都在外地。He lives by himself in Beijing with his family living elsewhere. ❷ by oneself; alone:他抛开大伙儿,~回乡去了。He left us and went back to his hometown alone.
光身汉 guāngshēnhàn 〈方言〉bachelor; single man
光渗 guāngshèn 〈物理〉irradiation
光声效应 guāngshēng xiàoyìng 〈物理〉opto-acoustic effect
光声学 guāngshēngxué opto-acoustics
光疏媒质 guāngshū méizhì optically thinner medium
光输入机 guāngshūrùjī optical reader
光束 guāngshù 〈物理〉light beam:参考~ reference beam /像散~ astigmatic (light) beam /相干~ coherent light beam /定向~ directed beam /激光~ laser beam /~半径 beam radius
光束焊机 guāngshù hànjī beam welding machine
光束武器 guāngshù wǔqì beam weapon
光束遥控 guāngshù yáokòng light beam remote control
光速 guāngsù 〈物理〉speed of light; velocity of light:~不变原理 permanent principle of light velocity /~约为每秒三十万公里。The velocity of light is about 300,000 kilometres per second.
光速测距仪 guāngsù cèjùyí geodimeter
光堂堂 guāngtāngtāng bright and clean; smooth; clean:门窗擦得~的。The doors and windows were well cleaned.
光趟 guāngtang *also* "光烫" 〈方言〉smooth; clean:刮得很~的脸 clean shaven face
光天化日 guāngtiān-huàrì in broad daylight; in the light of day; in the open day:把他的嘴脸暴露在~之下 expose his true features to the light of day /~之下你竟敢如此横行! How dare you act so brazenly in broad daylight!
光天线 guāngtiānxiàn light antenna
光通量 guāngtōngliàng 〈物理〉lightflux; luminous flux
光通信 guāngtōngxìn photo-communication; optical communication:~技术 optical communication technique /~纤维 optical communication fibre
光瞳 guāngtóng pupil
光头 guāngtóu ❶ bareheaded; hatless:刮着大风,但他仍然光着头出门了。Although it was blowing hard, he went out bareheaded (*or* without a hat). ❷ shaven head:为了拍电影,他剃了个大~。He had his head shaved clean for the movie. ❸ bald head
光头党 guāngtóudǎng skinheads (a neo-Nazi organization)
光秃 guāngtū barren; bare:~的山岭 bare hills and mountains /开垦~的荒山 reclaim barren hills
光秃秃 guāngtūtū bare; bald:头剃得~的 have one's head shaven clean /山坡上~的,一棵树也没有。The hillside is bare of trees. /树叶都落光了,只剩下~的枝干。There were only bare (*or* naked) branches left, with all the leaves fallen.
光纤 guāngxiān (short for 光学纤维) optical fibre; fibre-optic:~到户 fibre to the home (FTTH)
光纤胆道镜 guāngxiān dǎndàojìng 〈医学〉fibre-optic choledochoscope
光纤电缆 guāngxiān diànlǎn fibre optic cable
光纤化 guāngxiānhuà fiberisation
光纤环路 guāngxiān huánlù fibre in the loop (FITL)
光纤技术 guāngxiān jìshù fibre optics
光纤接头 guāngxiān jiētou fibre-optical splice
光纤声纳 guāngxiān shēngnà optical-fibre sonar
光纤通信 guāngxiān tōngxìn fibre-optical communication
光鲜 guāngxiān ❶ bright and beautiful:衣着~ brightly dressed ❷ 〈方言〉splendid; magnificent:他把这件事情干得~体面,十分出色。He did a splendid job. He is really remarkable!
光线 guāngxiàn light; ray:教室里~充足。The classroom is well lighted. /从门缝里透过一缕~。A beam of light passed through the crack of the door.
光线电话机 guāngxiàn diànhuàjī photophone; phototelephone
光线疗法 guāngxiàn liáofǎ 〈医学〉phototherapy
光效应 guāngxiàoyìng optical effect; luminous effect; photoeffect:~艺术 optical art; op art
光心 guāngxīn optical centre; photocentre
光行差 guāngxíngchā 〈天文〉aberration:~位移 aberration shift
光绪 Guāngxù Guangxu (formerly translated as Kuang-Hsu), title of the reign (1875-1908), of Aisin Gioro Zaitian (爱新觉罗·载湉,

G

1871-1908), 9th emperor of the Qing Dynasty with his aunt the Empress Dowager Cixi (慈禧) actually in control, called reverently Qing Dezong (清德宗) after death

光学 guāngxué optics:几何～ geometrical optics /线性～ linear optics /非线性～ nonlinear optics /～性能 optical property; optical quality /～表面 optical surface /～纯度 optical purity /～介质 optical medium /～测距 optical ranging /～图像 optical image /～透镜 optical lens /～传感器 optical sensor /～分辨率 optical resolution /～模拟计算机 optical analog computer /～全息照相 optical holography /～望远镜 optical telescope

光学玻璃 guāngxué bōli optical glass

光学符号 guāngxué fúhào 〈电子〉(shortened as 光符) optical character:～识别 optical character recognition (OCR) /～识别通用语言 OCR-common language /～阅读机 optical character reader

光学计算机 guāngxué jìsuànjī optical computer

光学技术卫星 guāngxué jìshù wèixīng optical technology satellite (OTS)

光学晶体 guāngxué jīngtǐ optical crystal

光学录音 guāngxué lùyīn optical sound recording:～机 photographic sound recorder

光学容限 guāngxué róngxiàn optical tolerance

光学纤维 guāngxué xiānwéi *also* "光导纤维" optical fibre; fibreoptic

光学显微镜 guāngxué xiǎnwēijìng light or optical microscope

光学像 guāngxuéxiàng optical image

光学仪器 guāngxué yíqì optical instrument

光压 guāngyā light pressure

光艳 guāngyàn bright and beautiful:～的服饰 bright and beautiful dress /～照人 stunningly beautiful

光焰 guāngyàn radiance; flare

光洋 guāngyáng 〈方言〉silver dollar

光耀 guāngyào ❶ brilliant; radiant; splendid; glittering:～夺目 dazzlingly bright /她手上那只～的钻戒吸引了不少人的目光。The glittering diamond ring she wore attracted many eyes. ❷ glory; honour:因成功而感到无比～ take great pride in one's success ❸ bring glory to; win honour for; do credit to:～门楣 win honour and distinction for one's family; bring glory to one's family ❹ shine brilliantly:～史册 shine through the ages /革命烈士的英雄业绩将永载史册,～千秋! The heroic deeds of the revolutionary martyrs shall go down in history and remain glorious for ever!

G

光阴 guāngyīn ❶ time:～冉冉。The years roll on smoothly (*or* slowly). /～荏苒。Time passes by. *or* Time speeds by. /～一去不复返。Lost time is never found again. *or* Time and tide wait for no man. /一寸～一寸金,寸金难买寸～。〈谚语〉An inch of time is an inch of gold, but you can't buy time with gold. *or* Time is gold, but gold can't buy time. ❷〈方言〉life; livelihood:一家三口平安度～。The family of three lead a peaceful life.

光阴似箭 guāngyīn-sìjiàn time flies:～,日月如梭。Time passes like an arrow with the sun and moon moving fast as shuttles. *or* Time flies.

光源 guāngyuán 〈物理〉light source; luminous source; illuminant:～强度 intensity of light source /～效率 source efficiency

光泽 guāngzé lustre; sheen; gloss:墓葬中的珍珠、丝绸和瓷器仍然～鲜明。Pearls, silks and porcelains found in the tomb still retain their lustre (*or* sheen). /他的眼睛已经失去原先的～。His eyes have lost their former lustre.

光照 guāngzhào ❶〈植物〉illumination:～阶段 photostage /～期 light period /～量 quantity of illumination ❷ shine; illuminate:他的功业和品德～人间。His accomplishments and noble character remain resplendent in the world.

光照度 guāngzhàodù *also* "照度"〈物理〉intensity of illumination; illuminance:～计 illumination meter; illuminometer

光照人寰 guāngzhào-rénhuán (of the sun or the moon) shine over the human world

光照日月 guāngzhào-rìyuè shine like the sun and the moon

光照性皮炎 guāngzhàoxìng píyán 〈医学〉photodermatitis

光针 guāngzhēn laser needle (for acupuncture); laser beam (as a needle)

光植物学 guāngzhíwùxué photobotany

光质子 guāngzhìzǐ 〈物理〉photoproton

光制 guāngzhì 〈机械〉finishing:最后～ final finishing /～表面 finished surface /～品 finished product

光致发光 guāngzhì fāguāng photoluminescence

光致裂变 guāngzhì lièbiàn photofission

光致蜕变 guāngzhì tuìbiàn photodisintegration

光中继器 guāngzhōngjìqì optical repeater

光中子 guāngzhōngzǐ 〈物理〉photoneutron

光钟 guāngzhōng photonon

光州 Guāngzhōu Kangju, capital of Chullanam-Dao of the Republic of Korea

光周期 guāngzhōuqī 〈植物〉photoperiod:～反应 photoperiodic reaction

光轴 guāngzhóu optical axis

光柱 guāngzhù light pillar; light cross; light beam:探照灯的～划破了长空。The dark sky was pierced by beams from searchlights.

光子 guāngzǐ *also* "光量子"〈物理〉photon:～层 photon sphere /～束 photon beam /～火箭 photon rocket /～轰击 photon bombardment /～计数 photon counting

光子电子学 guāngzǐ diànzǐxué photoelectronics

光子学 guāngzǐxué photonics

光宗耀祖 guāngzōng-yàozǔ bring honour to one's ancestors:原指望他日后能～,谁知却如此不成材,真令二老伤心。He had been expected to bring honour to his family some day but, quite to the chagrin of his parents, he turned out to be good for nothing.

桄 guāng

see also guàng

桄榔 guāngláng 〈植物〉gomuti palm (*Arenga pinnata*)

珖 guāng

〈书面〉(often used in people's names) a kind of jade

咣 guāng

〈象声〉bang; crash:～的一声,关上了门 slam the door shut; shut the door with a bang

咣当 guāngdāng 〈象声〉bang; crash:卡车走在坎坷不平的山道上,车上的小缸碰得～～响。The jars in the lorry banged against each other as it drove over a bumpy mountain road.

胱 guāng

❶ *see* "胱氨酸" ❷ *see* "膀胱" pángguāng

胱氨酸 guāng'ānsuān cystine:～病〈医学〉cystinosis /～尿〈医学〉cystinuria

胱胺 guāng'àn cystamine

guǎng

广[1](廣) guǎng

❶ (of area, scope, etc.) wide; vast; extensive:经验多,见识～ have rich experience and extensive knowledge /视野宽～ have a broad vision /地～人众 vast and densely populous area /～为流行 be very popular /交游甚～ have many friends; have a large circle of friends ❷ numerous; many:兵多将～ have numerous soldiers and a large number of officers — be rich in manpower; be well-staffed ❸ expand; spread; extend:以～声势 extend one's power and prestige /集思～益 pool the wisdom of the masses /推～先进技术 disseminate (*or* popularize) advanced technology

广[2](廣) Guǎng

❶ (short for 广东 or 广州) Guangdong (Province); Guangzhou (City):两～ Guangdong and Guangxi (the latter shortened as 桂 when used by itself) /老～〈口语〉Guangdong man /京～铁路 Beijing-Guangzhou Railway ❷ (Guǎng) a surname

广板 guǎngbǎn 〈乐器〉*largo*

广播 guǎngbō ❶ broadcast; be on the air:广告已经～多次了。The advertisement was broadcast many times. /小喇叭开始～了。The "Little Trumpet" is now on the air. /这个节目已经停止～。This programme has gone off the air. ❷ radio programme; broadcast:外语～ foreign language broadcast /新闻～ news broadcast /有线～ wired broadcasting; cable broadcasting /实况～ live broadcast; live transmission (over the radio or television) /～天线 broadcast antenna /他经常收听北京电台的～。He often tunes in to Radio Beijing. ❸〈书面〉widely spread; known far and wide:诗名～ well-known poet

广播电视大学 guǎngbō diànshì dàxué radio and television college; university of the air

广播电台 guǎngbō diàntái radio station; broadcasting station:中

央人民～ Central People's Broadcasting Station
广播段 guǎngbōduàn *also*"广播波段" broadcast band; wave band:中波～ medium wave (band) /短波～ short wave (band) /超短波～ ultrashort wave (band) /微波～ microwave (band)
广播发射台 guǎngbō fāshètái broadcast transmitting station
广播稿 guǎngbōgǎo broadcast script
广播讲话 guǎngbō jiǎnghuà broadcast speech; radio talk
广播节目 guǎngbō jiémù broadcast or radio programme
广播剧 guǎngbōjù radio play or drama
广播喇叭 guǎngbō lǎba loudspeaker
广播频道 guǎngbō píndào broadcast channel
广播频率 guǎngbō pínlǜ broadcast frequency
广播摄像机 guǎngbō shèxiàngjī broadcast camera
广播室 guǎngbōshì broadcasting room; studio
广播体操 guǎngbō tǐcāo *also*"广播操" calisthenics with radio music; setting-up exercises to radio music; radio exercises:做～ do exercises to radio music; do radio exercises /～比赛 radio-exercises contest
广播网 guǎngbōwǎng broadcast network; diffusion network
广播卫星 guǎngbō wèixīng broadcasting satellite
广播员 guǎngbōyuán broadcaster; (radio) announcer
广播站 guǎngbōzhàn broadcast station
广播转播车 guǎngbō zhuǎnbōchē outside broadcast vehicle
广博 guǎngbó (of a person's knowledge) extensive; wide:知识～的学者 scholar with extensive knowledge; erudite scholar
广博经 Guǎngbójīng 〈佛教〉 *vyasa-sutra*
广场 guǎngchǎng public square; square:天安门～ Tian'anmen Square /市中心～ city's central square
广大 guǎngdà ❶ vast; wide; extensive:幅员～ vast in territory /～的原野 boundless fields /～的空间 immense space /～农村地区 wide countryside; extensive rural areas ❷ large-scale; widespread; broad:结成～的统一战线 form a broad united front ❸ numerous; many:～体育爱好者 numerous activists in sports; large numbers of sports fans /～人民群众 broad masses of the people /～爱国华侨 vast numbers of patriotic overseas Chinese /～观众 the large audience
广岛 Guǎngdǎo Hiroshima, Japanese city on Honshu Island and target of the first US atomic bomb on 6 August, 1945
广东 Guǎngdōng Guangdong (Province):～话 Guangdong dialect; Cantonese /～人 Guangdong man (*or* woman)
广东戏 guǎngdōngxì Guangdong opera; Cantonese opera
广东音乐 Guǎngdōng yīnyuè Guangdong music; Cantonese music
广度 guǎngdù scope; breadth; range:～不够 not comprehensive enough /你们的科研还要注意～。You must pay attention to widening the scope of your scientific research.
广而告之 guǎng'érgàozhī give extensive publicity; spread far and wide:电视台新节目:"～"。A new TV series "Spread Far and Wide" is now showing.
广而言之 guǎng'éryánzhī speaking generally; in general terms; in a general sense
广泛 guǎngfàn wide; broad; extensive; wide-ranging; widespread:兴趣～ have wide interests /用途～ widely applicable /题材～ a great variety of topics (*or* subjects) /～阅读 read extensively /～影响 widespread influence /～宣传 give wide (*or* extensive) publicity to /～交谈 wideranging conversation /～发动群众 mobilize people on a large scale /～征求意见 solicit opinions from all quarters /～的爱国统一战线 broad patriotic united front /足球是世界上开展最～,影响最大的运动项目之一。Soccer is one of the most widespread and influential sports in the world.
广柑 guǎnggān a kind of orange produced in Guangdong, Sichuan and Taiwan provinces
广告 guǎnggào advertisement; ad:橱窗～ window advertisement /分类～ classified advertisements (*or* ads) /整页～ full-page advertisement /～文字 copy (for an ad) /为新产品大做～ advertise a new product extensively /通过～招聘人员 advertise for help
广告插页 guǎnggào chāyè insert
广告代理人 guǎnggào dàilǐrén advertising agent
广告电话直销 guǎnggào diànhuà zhíxiāo 〈商业〉 direct response advertising
广告费 guǎnggàofèi rate of advertisement; advertising fee
广告公司 guǎnggào gōngsī advertising agency or firm
广告画 guǎnggàohuà poster
广告栏 guǎnggàolán advertisement or ad column
广告牌 guǎnggàopái billboard
广告色 guǎnggàosè poster colour
广告设计 guǎnggào shèjì advertising design
广告心理学 guǎnggào xīnlǐxué advertizing psychology
广告宣传 guǎnggào xuānchuán hype; ad
广告战 guǎnggàozhàn advertising compaign
广告撰稿人 guǎnggào zhuàngǎorén copywriter
广寒宫 guǎnghángōng Moon Palace (mythical palace in the moon)
广货 guǎnghuò articles for everyday use produced in Guangdong; Guangdong goods
广见博识 guǎngjiàn-bóshí have rich experience and extensive knowledge
广交会 Guǎngjiāohuì (short for 广州出口商品交易会) Guangzhou Chinese Export Commodities Fair (held twice a year)
广交四海 guǎngjiāo-sìhǎi make friends extensively
广角 guǎngjiǎo wide angle:～喷嘴 wide-angle nozzle /～望远镜 wide-angle telescope /～扫描 wide-angle scanning /～型照明器 wide-angle lighting fittings; wide-angle luminaire /～漫射〈无线电〉wide-angle diffusion
广角镜 guǎngjiǎojìng ❶ *see*"广角镜头" ❷ sth. that widens one's field of vision; eye-opener:这部书对我来说真是一个～。This book is really an eye-opener to me.
广角镜头 guǎngjiǎo jìngtóu wide-angle lens
广结良缘 guǎngjié-liángyuán perform good deeds everywhere and win universal acclaim
广开才路 guǎngkāi-cáilù open all avenues for people of talent; open broad avenues for able people
广开门路 guǎngkāi-ménlù tap all available channels; explore every possibility:～,发展生产 open all channles for developing production
广开言路 guǎngkāi-yánlù encourage the free airing of views; provide wide opportunities for people to express their opinions:只有～,才能少犯错误。Only by providing wide opportunities for the free airing of views, can one make fewer mistakes.
广阔 guǎngkuò vast; wide; broad; extensive:～的世界 wide world /～的地平线 unbounded horizon /视野～ have a broad view /幅员～ immense territory /胸怀～ broad-minded /～天地,大有作为 vast world where much can be accomplished; vast field for one's talents
广袤 guǎngmào 〈书面〉❶ length and breadth of land:～千里的大草原 vast expanse of prairie a thousand miles across ❷ vast; broad; immense:～无垠的草原 boundless grassland
广漠 guǎngmò vast and bare:～浩瀚的戈壁滩 vast and bare Gobi Desert
广谋博采 guǎngmóu-bócǎi seek advice from all sides
广谋从众 guǎngmóu-cóngzhòng consult and follow the majority
广木香 guǎngmùxiāng 〈中药〉 costusroot (*Saussurea Lappa*)
广宁 Guǎngníng Quang Ninh, a northern Vietnamese Province bordering on China's Guangxi Zhuang Autonomous Region
广谱 guǎngpǔ broad-spectrum:～抗生素 broad-spectrum antibiotic
广求 guǎngqiú 〈书面〉 seek everywhere:～贤圣 seek everywhere for men of virtue; invite men of talent from all walks of life
广厦 guǎngshà 〈书面〉 tall and spacious building; mansion
广式 Guǎngshì Guangdong style; characteristic of Guangdong:～月饼 Guangdong style mooncakes /～香肠 Guangdong sausage
广田弘毅 Guǎngtiánhóngyì Koki Hirota (1878-1948), Japanese Prime Minister and Minister of Foreign Affairs (1936-1937), and a top war criminal
广土众民 guǎngtǔ-zhòngmín vast land and large population:我国素以～著称于世。Our country is noted in the world for her vast territory and large population.
广为 guǎngwéi widely; far and wide; from all quarters:～宣传 publicize (*or* make known) far and wide /～流传 widely circulate or disseminate /～物色 seek from all quarters
广西 guǎngxī Guangxi:～壮族自治区 the Guangxi Zhuang Autonomous Region
广袖 guǎngxiù 〈书面〉broad sleeves:寂寞嫦娥舒～,万里长空且为忠魂舞。The lonely moon goddess spreads her ample sleeves To dance for these loyal souls in infinite space.
广绣 guǎngxiù Guangdong embroidery
广延 guǎngyán 〈物理〉extension:～量 extensive quantity /～参数 extensive parameter

广延宾客 guǎngyán-bīnkè keep an open house

广野 guǎngyě vast fields：平原～ vast plain

广义 guǎngyì ❶ broad sense：～地解释 explain in a broad sense /～的文化 culture in the broad sense of the term ❷〈物理〉generalized；general：～方程 generalized equation /～空间 generalized space /～坐标 generalized coordinate /～相对论 general theory of relativity /～函数〈数学〉distribution；generalized function /～函数论 distribution theory /～积分 improper integral /～级数 generalized series /～逆矩阵 generalized inverse matrix /～实数 extended real number

广宇 guǎngyǔ 〈书面〉❶ spacious hall ❷ space；universe；cosmos

广域网 guǎngyùwǎng 〈信息〉wide area network (WAN)

广域信息服务系统 guǎngyù xìnxī fúwù xìtǒng 〈信息〉wide area information server (WAIS)

广远 guǎngyuǎn far and wide：流传～ spread far and wide

广韵 Guǎngyùn *An Extensive Rhyming Dictionary*, compiled by Chen Pengnian (陈彭年) et al. of the Song Dynasty

广证博引 guǎngzhèng-bóyǐn quote copiously and prove extensively

广众 guǎngzhòng crowd of people；numerous people：稠人～ crowd of people, numerous people /大庭～之下 before a large audience；in public

广种薄收 guǎngzhòng-bóshōu extensive cultivation or farming：这儿地多人少，土质又不好，农民只能～。Due to the vast land, sparse population and poor soil, the farmers here had to rely on extensive cultivation.

广州 Guǎngzhōu Guangzhou (formerly known as Canton)：～人 Cantonese /～出口商品交易会 Guangzhou Chinese Export Commodities Fair

广州起义 Guǎngzhōu Qǐyì Guangzhou Uprising of Dec. 11, 1927 (organized by the revolutionary soldiers and workers of the city, under the leadership of the Communist Party of China — one of the three major uprisings held in that year, the other two being the Nanchang Uprising and Autumn Harvest Uprising)

犷(獷)

guǎng 〈书面〉rustic；uncouth；boorish：粗～ bold and unrestrained；rugged；rough

犷悍 guǎnghàn tough and intrepid；rough and ferocious

G

guàng

桄

guàng ❶ reel (thread or wire) on a revolving frame：快把线～起来。Reel the thread right now. ❷ reel：桌上放着两个线～儿。There are two reels on the table. ❸〈量词〉*used of thread or wire*：两～电线 two reels of wire

see also guāng

桄子 guàngzi reel

逛

guàng stroll；roam；saunter；ramble：到处闲～ roam about /随便～～ take a stroll /～商店 go window-shopping /～公园 visit a park；stroll around a park

逛荡 guàngdang loaf about；loiter：他整日在外边～。He is loafing about all day long.

逛道儿 guàngdàor 〈方言〉〈旧语〉go whoring；visit prostitutes

逛灯 guàngdēng go about town enjoying lantern displays (usu. on the 15th of the 1st lunar month)

逛街 guàngjiē 〈口语〉roam the streets；take a stroll in the streets

逛窑子 guàng yáozi 〈方言〉〈旧语〉visit a brothel；go whoring

逛游 guàngyou saunter；stroll：她星期天喜欢在商场～。She likes to go window-shopping in big malls on sundays.

guī

规(槼)

guī ❶ dividers；compasses：圆～ pair of compasses /两脚～ pair of dividers /分度～ protractor ❷ rule；regulation；convention：家～ family rules /犯～ break the rule(s)；foul /违反校～ violate school regulations /循～蹈矩 conform to convention ❸ admonish；counsel；advise：*see*"～劝"；"～勉" ❹ plan；devise；map out：*see* "～划" ❺〈机械〉gauge：线～ wire gauge /校正～ corrective gauge

规避 guībì evade；shun；dodge；avoid：～战术 evasion tactics /～责任 evade (one's) responsibility /我无法～同他见面。I cannot avoid meeting him. /不要～困难。Don't dodge difficulties.

规程 guīchéng rules；regulations：安全～ safety regulations/操作～ rules of operation /保安～ security rules

规定 guīdìng ❶ stipulate；specify；provide；prescribe：～指标 set a quota /～价格 fix a price /～的格式 prescribed form /法律～的权利和义务 rights and obligations provided for by law /政府～春节放假三天。The government prescribes a three-day holiday for the Spring Festival. /宪法～，保卫祖国是公民应尽的神圣义务。The Constitution stipulates that it is the sacred duty of every citizen to safeguard the motherland. /运动员要在～时间内完成动作。The gymnast is required to finish the exercise within the fixed (*or* prescribed) time. ❷ provisions；stipulations；rules and regulations：违反～ go against the regulations /执行～ carry out the stipulations (*or* provisions) /按上级有关～办。Act according to the relevant rules and regulations prescribed by the senior authorities.

规定电压 guīdìng diànyā assigned voltage

规定动作 guīdìng dòngzuò 〈体育〉compulsory exercise or programme

规定负荷 guīdìng fùhè given load

规定数额 guīdìng shù'é 〈经济〉quota；target

规定语法 guīdìng yǔfǎ 〈语言〉prescriptive grammar

规定载荷 guīdìng zàihè ordinance load；specified load

规范 guīfàn ❶ standard；model；norm：社会～ social norms/道德～ moral standards /行为～ norms of behaviour /技术～ technical standards /质量～ specifications of quality /合乎～ conform to the standards；be up to standard ❷ regular；normal；standard：～科学 normal science /～语法 normative grammar /～语言 normative language /她讲一口～的英语。She speaks standard English. /这种说法不太～。This does not quite conform with regular usage. ❸ regulate；standardize：这是当地为～市场管理制定的做法。These are the measures set by the local authorities to regulate the market management. ❹〈电学〉gauge：～变化 gauge transformation /～不变量 gauge invariant

规范场 guīfànchǎng 〈电学〉gauge field：～论 gauge field theory

规范化 guīfànhuà standardize；normalize：简化字要～。The simplified Chinese characters should be standardized.

规复 guīfù 〈书面〉restore (an organization, system, etc.)

规格 guīgé ❶ specifications；standards；norms：～齐全 complete in (range of) specifications /统一的～ unified standards /不合～ be not up to standard；fall short of specifications/产品的～与说明书中的介绍不太一致。The specifications of the product are not quite in conformity with the technical manual. ❷ requirement；condition：按规定填写统一～的报表。Fill in forms of unified requirements in accordance with the regulations.

规格化 guīgéhuà standardize；normalize

规划 guīhuà ❶ programme；plan：五年～ five-year plan /城市～ city planning /远景～ long-term programme (*or* plan) /制定～ make a plan (*or* programme) ❷ draw up a plan；map out a programme：统一～市区商业网点 draw up a unified plan for the urban commercial network

规诲 guīhuì 〈书面〉admonish；instruct

规谏 guījiàn 〈书面〉admonish；advise

规诫 guījiè 〈书面〉admonish；warn

规矩 guīju ❶ rule；established practice；custom：按老～办事 act according to the established rules /坏了～ violate (*or* go against) established practice /他给自己定下了一条新～。He set (*or* made) a new rule for himself. ❷ well-behaved；well-disciplined；honest：～懂事的姑娘 well-behaved, sensible girl /规规矩矩的生意人 honest (*or* law-abiding) businessman /他的举止行为很～。He is well disciplined in behaviour. *or* He conducts himself very well.

规矩准绳 guīju-zhǔnshéng *also*"规矩绳墨" compass, setsquare, level and plumbline — norms or standards to be followed：法律政令者，吏民～也。Laws and government decrees are the norms of conduct for both officials and commoners.

规例 guīlì rules and customs；precedents and conventions：家乡的～ established rules and customs of one's hometown /处理此类问题有无～可循? Are there any precedents or conventions to go by in handling such matters?

规律 guīlǜ *also*"法则"fǎzé law；regular pattern：必然～ inex-

orable law /普遍～ universal law /供求～ law of supply and demand /自然～ law of nature; natural law /要掌握市场活动的一般～。It is essential to master the general patterns of market activities. /身体要健康,生活就要有～。To maintain physical fitness, one should live a regular life.

规律性 guīlǜxìng regularity; pattern; law:掌握事物发展变化的～。Grasp the law of development and change of things.

规勉 guīmiǎn advise and encourage; urge and admonish:相互～ advise and encourage each other

规模 guīmó scale; scope; dimensions:大～群众活动 mass activity /～宏大 broad in scale (*or* scope) /初具～ begin to take shape /缩小发展～ reduce the scope of development

规模经济 guīmó jīngjì economy of scale

规模生产 guīmó shēngchǎn mass production

规那树 guīnàshù cinchona

规劝 guīquàn admonish; counsel; advise:耐心～ patiently admonish (sb. to do sth.) /好言～ give kind advice /他听不进朋友的好意～。He refused to take the well-intentioned admonitions (*or* advice) of his friends.

规条 guītiáo rule; norm

规限 guīxiàn fixed limit or scope:干什么事都有一定的～和要求。There are certain limits and requirements for everything.

规行矩步 guīxíng-jǔbù ❶ act meticulously in comformity with rules; behave correctly and cautiously:那大嫂虽是乡下人,但～,应酬从容,颇得主人欢心。Though a country woman, the amah was cautious in behaviour and composed in manners, thus winning much favour with her master. ❷ stick to established practice; follow the beaten track:在商战中～必定要吃亏。One would certainly come to grief in business competition if one falls into a rut.

规约 guīyuē ❶ stipulations or rules agreed upon ❷ restrict; restrain:用理智～言行 use reason to keep one's words and deeds within limits

规则 guīzé ❶ rule; regulation:遵守游戏～ abide by the rules of the game /违反交通～ violate traffic regulations /凡有～总有例外。There is no rule without exceptions. ❷ law; rule:自然～ law of nature ❸ regular:～多面体 regular polyhedron /～动词 regular verb /～化 regularization /这条马路弯弯曲曲,有宽有窄,很不～。This road is quite irregular. It zigzags and is not of constant width.

规则式 guīzéshì 〈林业〉formal style:～园林 formal garden

规章 guīzhāng rules; regulations:建立和健全～制度 establish and perfect rules and regulations /遵守法令～ abide by (*or* observe) laws and regulations

规整 guīzhěng ❶ regular; standard; tidy; neat:～的字体 (write a) neat hand ❷ put in order; tidy up:有客人来,得～一下屋子。As some guests are coming, I'll have to tidy up the house.

规正 guīzhèng ❶〈书面〉admonish and correct; put or set right:互相～ correct each other /～风俗 rectify customs; set customs right ❷ regular; tidy; neat:他们围坐成一个不很～的圆圈。They sat in a somewhat irregular circle. ❸〈方言〉rule; regulation

规制 guīzhì ❶ rules and regulations ❷ size and shape:天安门修缮后～未变。After the renovation, the Tian'anmen rostrum retained its original size, shape and style.

圭[1]

guī ❶ tapering jade tablet (held in hand by the nobility on ceremonial occasions in ancient times) ❷ sundial (consisting of an elongated dial and one or two gnomons)

圭[2]

guī ancient measurement of volume, about ten microlitres

圭表 guībiǎo sundial (consisting of an elongated dial and one or two gnomons)

圭角 guījiǎo 〈书面〉point of a jade tablet;〈比喻〉talent displayed:初露～ (make the) first display of one's talent (*or* abilities)

圭臬 guīniè 〈书面〉sundial;〈比喻〉criterion; standard:奉为～ regard as the criterion /适者生存之说,为一些学人视为～。Survival of the fittest remains an established theory in the eyes of some scholars.

圭亚那 Guīyànà Guyana:～人 Guyanese /法属～ French Guyana

圭璋 guīzhāng *also* "珪璋" guīzhāng 〈书面〉precious jade (tablet);〈比喻〉noble character; moral integrity:～之质 noble in character; of high integrity

闺

guī ❶〈书面〉arch-topped door ❷ boudoir:深～ inmost boudoir (of a courtyard house) /待字～中 (of a young girl) not engaged yet

闺范 guīfàn ❶〈旧语〉moral norms for women ❷ (of a woman) demeanour; bearing; poise:一派大家～ poise of a lady of a distinguished family; decorous bearing of a well-bred woman

闺房 guīfáng 〈旧语〉boudoir:后院两间房是小姐的～。The two rooms in the back yard are the young lady's boudoir.

闺阁 guīgé 〈旧语〉boudoir:～名媛 daughter of an illustrious family /～千金 young lady of a distinguished family

闺阃 guīkǔn 〈旧语〉women's quarters:～之内,不容外人随便进出。Outsiders are not allowed in the women's private quarters.

闺门 guīmén door of a boudoir:她是个很少迈出～的娇小姐。She was a pampered young lady who seldom stepped outside of her boudoir.

闺门旦 guīméndàn 〈戏曲〉character role in traditional opera of an unmarried young girl; ingenue:她的拿手好戏是演～。She is excellent in playing the role of young girls.

闺女 guīnü ❶ girl; maiden:黄花～ untouched virgin ❷〈口语〉daughter:张家二～ second daughter of the Zhangs

闺闼 guītà 〈书面〉boudoir

闺秀 guīxiù 〈旧语〉daughter of a rich and powerful family:大家～ daughter of an illustrious family /～淑女 young and virtuous girl

闺怨 guīyuàn 〈书面〉young woman's sorrows and grievances:～诗 lyric poem about a young woman's sorrows

珪

guī *see* "圭" guī

硅

guī 〈化学〉(formerly called 矽) silicon (Si):～单晶 single crystal silicon /多晶～ polycrystalline silicon /可控～ silicon controlled rectifier (SCR) /～尘 siliceous dust; silica dust /二氧化～ silica

硅变压整流器 guībiànyā zhěngliúqì silicoformer

硅存储管 guīcúnchǔguǎn lithicon storage tube; lithocon

硅电池 guīdiànchí silicon cell

硅二极管 guī'èrjíguǎn 〈电子〉silicon diode; silicon diode rectifier

硅肺 guīfèi *also* "矽肺" xīfèi 〈医学〉silicosis; pneumosilicosis:～患者 silicotic

硅肺结核 guīfèi jiéhé 〈医学〉potters' phthisis; grinders' phthisis

硅钢 guīgāng *also* "矽钢" xīgāng 〈冶金〉silicon steel:～薄板 silicon plate

硅铬钢 guīgègāng 〈冶金〉silichrome steel

硅谷 Guīgǔ Silicon Valley, an area with a high concentration of electronics industries southeast of San Francisco:他们决心把高技术开发区建设成中国的～。They are determined to build the high-tech development zone into China's Silicon Valley.

硅光电探测器 guīguāng diàntàncèqì silicon photodetector

硅华 guīhuá *also* "泉华" quánhuá 〈地质〉siliceous sinter; silica sinter; geyserite

硅化 guīhuà silication; siliconization; silicification:～钡 barium silicide /～铀 uranium silicide /～作用 silicification

硅化木 guīhuàmù silicified wood; petrified wood; woodstone

硅化物 guīhuàwù silicide:～敷层 silicide coating

硅胶 guījiāo 〈化学〉silica gel:～填充润滑脂 silica gel grease

硅晶体 guījīngtǐ silicon crystal:～管 silicon transistor /～二极管 silicon diode

硅可控整流器 guīkěkòng zhěngliúqì 〈电学〉silicon controlled rectifier; thyristor

硅铝 guīlǚ 〈矿业〉sial:～层 sial /～带 sial /～土 siallitic soil /～矿物 silica-alumina mineral

硅镁带 guīměidài 〈地质〉sima; simasphere

硅镁石 guīměishí humite

硅锰钢 guīměnggāng silico-manganese steel

硅石 guīshí *also* "二氧化硅" èryǎnghuàguī silica:～玻璃 silica glass /～砂 ganister sand

硅塑料 guīsùliào 〈化工〉silastomer; silicon plastic

硅酸 guīsuān 〈化学〉silicic acid; hydrated silica:～钠 sodium silicate /～钾 potassium silicate /～炉渣 silicate slag

硅酸盐 guīsuānyán 〈化学〉silicate:～工业 silicate industry /～砖 silicate brick /～玻璃 silicate glass /～沉着病〈医学〉silicatosis /～水

泥 portland cement
硅太阳电池 guītàiyáng diànchí 〈电子〉silicon solar cell
硅碳耐火材料 guītàn nàihuǒ cáiliào 〈冶金〉siloxicon
硅铁 guītiě ferrosilicon; silicon iron
硅酮 guītóng 〈化学〉silicone:~聚合物 silicone polymer
硅烷 guīwán silane
硅橡胶 guīxiàngjiāo silicon rubber; silastic
硅藻 guīzǎo 〈植物〉diatom:~土 diatomaceous earth; diatomite
硅砖 guīzhuān silica brick:~炉衬 silica lining
硅铸铁 guīzhùtiě 〈冶金〉silel cast iron

鲑 guī salmon
see also xié
鲑鲈 guīlú trout-perch (*Percopsis*)

归(歸) guī ❶ return; go or come back:衣锦荣~ return home after making good /满载而~ come back fully loaded (with presents, etc.); return from a rewarding journey /放虎~山 allow a tiger to return to the mountains — breed calamity for the future /视死如~ look upon death as going home; face death unflinchingly /无家可~ be homeless ❷ give back; return sth. to sb.:物~原主 return sth. to its rightful owner ❸ converge; come together; group together:百川~海 all rivers flow into the sea /殊途同~ reach the same goal by different routes /众望所~ be the centre of popular confidence; enjoy popular trust /~为几类 classify under several categories; divide into several classes ❹ be in sb.'s charge; put under sb.'s care:~国家所有 be turned over to the state; be owned by the state /这件事~他们管。They are in charge of this. *or* This is their responsibility. /买菜~她,做饭~我。Shopping is her job and cooking mine. ❺ belong to:这一部分遗产~女儿所有。This part of the legacy belonged to the daughter. *or* The daughter inherited this part of the legacy. ❻ *used between identical verbs to indicate uselessness or irrelevance of the action*:批评~批评,咱们还是好朋友,对吧? Despite the criticisms, you and I remain good friends, don't we? /玩笑~玩笑,你欠的钱到期还得还。Never mind the joke, you'll have to repay the debt punctually all the same. ❼〈数学〉divide (on the abacus) with a one-digit divisor:九九~一。Nine divided by nine gives one. ❽ (Guī) a surname

G

归案 guī'àn bring to justice:逮捕~ apprehend and bring to justice /~法办 bring back to court for trial and punishment
归并 guībìng ❶ incorporate into; merge into; amalgamate:有些机构可以~到办公厅。Some institutions can be incorporated into the general office. /已经决定把这两个单位~公司管理。It has been decided to merge these two units and put them under the company's management. ❷ add up; put together; lump together:这四笔账~起来,一共是一百万元。The four accounts add up to one million *yuan*. /几笔资产~起来可以搞个新企业。If you put these assets together, it will be enough to start a new enterprise.
归程 guīchéng return journey:踏上~ start off on one's journey home
归除 guīchú divide (on the abacus) with a divisor of two or more digits
归档 guīdàng place on file; file:~备查 file for future reference /文件已经分类~。The documents have been categorized and filed.
归队 guīduì ❶ rejoin one's unit:伤愈~ return to one's army after one's wound heals ❷ return to the profession one took up before:技术人员学非所用的,要~。Technical staff who are not using their own specialities should be allowed to return to the professions they were trained for.
归服 guīfú 〈书面〉submit to sb.'s authority; pledge allegiance to sb.:~朝廷 submit to the authority of the imperial court; pledge allegiance to the imperial court
归附 guīfù submit to the authority of another; come under:~义军 submit or go over to the side of the righteous (*or* rebel) army /这些农民武装纷纷~了八路军。These armed peasant forces joined the Eighth Route Army one after another.
归根 guīgēn ❶ return to one's native place after a long stay in an alien land; return home:叶落~ a falling leaf settles on the roots — a person residing in a far-away place finally returns to his ancestral home ❷ in a nutshell; in a word; to sum up:~一句话,成败还要看人心向背。To sum up, success or failure depends on the support of the people.
归根结底 guīgēn-jiédǐ *also* "归根结蒂";"归根结柢" in the final analysis; to put it in a nutshell:你说了这么多,~就是一个"钱"字。Although you've said so much, it boils down to nothing more than money.
归公 guīgōng be turned over to the state or the group; be made a public possession:失物三个月无人认领者一律~。Lost properties shall be turned over to the state without exception if not claimed within three months. /一切缴获要~。All captured articles must be turned in (to the army as a whole).
归功 guīgōng give the credit to; attribute the success to:她把自己取得的成绩完全~于集体。She attributed all her achievements to collective efforts. /他谦虚地表示,能拿到金牌,主要~于他的教练和队友。He modestly noted that the credit for obtaining the gold medal should primarily be given to his coach and fellow sportsmen.
归国 guīguó return to one's country:~探亲 return to one's country to visit one's relatives and friends /~观光 return to one's homeland on a sightseeing tour /~证明书 repatriation certificate
归国华侨 guīguó huáqiáo returned overseas Chinese (national)
归国留学生 guīguó liúxuéshēng returned student
归航 guīháng 〈航空〉homing:~飞行 homing flight /~台 homing station; homer /~信标 homing beacon /~附加器 homing adapter /~应答器 homing transponder /~有效距离 homing range
归化 guīhuà ❶〈书面〉submit to the authority of; adopt the customs of; be assimilated by:~中原 submit to the authority of the government of the Central Plains; be assimilated by the Central Plains culture ❷ naturalize:~公民 naturalized citizen
归还 guīhuán give back; return; revert:~原主 return to the rightful owner /按时~ return in time
归还权 guīhuánquán reversion
归回 guīhuí return; go or come back to:~故乡 return to one's homeland /~祖国 back to one's country
归集 guījí gather together; collect:~闲散资金 collect idle (*or* unused) fund
归结 guījié ❶ sum up; conclude; put in a nutshell:问题很多,~起来大体有三种类型。Although there are many problems, they roughly fall into three categories. ❷ conclusion; end (of a story, etc.):这部小说是以大团圆做~的。The novel ends in a happy reunion.
归咎 guījiù impute the blame to; attribute a fault to; put the blame on; blame:他把出事故的责任完全~于他人。He put the blame for the accident entirely on others. /不能将错误~于一个人。It is incorrect to attribute the error to one person only.
归聚 guījù 〈方言〉gather together; put together; collect:把场院的豆子~到一起 gather together the beans on the threshing floor
归客 guīkè one who returns; returnee
归口 guīkǒu ❶ put under centralized management; put under competent authorities:~管理 put under centralized management by specialized departments /~领导 place under the unified leadership of competent departments /~部门 relevant (*or* competent) department (in charge of sth.) ❷ return to the profession one was trained for:他~才一个多月,专业还不够熟悉。It is only a little over a month since he returned to the profession he was trained for; so he hasn't picked up his speciality yet.
归来 guīlái return:国外~ return from abroad
归类 guīlèi sort out; classify; categorize:请将这批文件~存档。Please sort out these documents and place them on file.
归理 guīlǐ tidy up; put in order; sort out:他刚到,连行李还没有来得及~。He has only just arrived and hasn't had time yet to unpack and sort out his luggage.
归里包堆 guīlibāoduī 〈方言〉in total; in all; all together:他们家~只有三口人。There are only three persons all together in his family. /这些苹果~也就是两公斤吧。These apples are no more than two kilos in all.
归零 guīlíng 〈计算机〉return-to-zero (RZ); make zero; zero:~法 return-to-zero method /~代码 return-to-zero code /~系统 RZ system /~元件 RZ element
归拢 guīlǒng put together; gather together:走以前将东西~一下。Put your things together before you leave. /资料、文件太多,一个上午~不完。There are too many reference materials and documents to sort out in just one morning.
归路 guīlù one's way home or back; homeward journey; way of retreat:切断敌人的~ block the enemy's way of retreat
归谬法 guīmiùfǎ reduction to absurdity; *reductio ad absurdum*;

他用～驳斥了这个观点。He refuted the view by reducing it to absurdity.
归纳 guīnà ❶ induce; infer; draw; sum up:这个结论是从大量事实中～出来的。The conclusion was drawn from a great number of facts. ❷ inductive method; induction
归纳法 guīnàfǎ inductive method
归宁 guīníng 〈书面〉(of a married woman) visit one's parents:～父母以尽孝道 visit one's parents to fulfil one's filial duty
归期 guīqī date of return:～未定。The date of return is uncertain. *or* The date of return has not yet been fixed.
归齐 guīqí 〈方言〉❶ in the end; finally:他张罗了好几天,～还是没有去成。He busied himself preparing for the trip for several days but didn't go after all. ❷ altogether; all told; in all:途中往返,～不会超过一个月。The round trip will take less than a month.
归侨 guīqiáo (short for 归国华侨) returned overseas Chinese (national)
归去 guīqù 〈书面〉go back; return home:离家已久,今当～。Having long been away from home, I should go back now.
归趣 guīqù 〈书面〉aim; purpose; objective:做法各异,～却是相近的。Varying in methods, they are similar in objectives.
归人 guīrén 〈书面〉❶ someone who has returned; returnee:倚楼望～。Leaning against the window, she waited for her man to return from afar. ❷ the deceased
归入 guīrù be included in; go under:有些问题可以～甲类,有些则不能。Some questions may go under category A while others may not.
归山 guīshān 〈书面〉❶ (of the sun) set; go down ❷ 〈婉词〉die; pass away
归属 guīshǔ belong to; come under the jurisdiction of; be affiliated to or with:厂方自称～地方。The management of the factory claims to be under the jurisdiction of the local government. /双方在友好的气氛中讨论了该地区的～问题。The two parties discussed the ownership of the area in a friendly atmosphere.
归属权 guīshǔquán 〈法律〉right of attribution
归顺 guīshùn come over and pledge allegiance:～朝廷 surrender and pledge allegiance to the royal court
归思 guīsī 〈书面〉yearnings for home; homesickness:～甚切 acute homesickness
归宿 guīsù home to return to; destination:老人终于有了自己的～。The old man at long last got a home of his own (*or* found his final settling place). /何处才是我的人生～? What is the destination of my life's voyage?
归天 guītiān 〈婉词〉go to one's glory; pass away; die
归田 guītián 〈书面〉resign and return to one's native village:解甲～ retire from military service and return to one's native village; quit military service and resume civilian life
归途 guītú homeward journey; way home; way back:踏上～ set out on one's journey home /～中,他顺道访问了一个阔别多年的朋友。On his way back, he visited a friend he hadn't seen for many years.
归西 guīxī 〈婉词〉go west; pass away; die
归降 guīxiáng surrender; capitulate:被迫～ be compelled to surrender; surrender under force
归向 guīxiàng turning towards (the righteous side); inclination:人心～ inclination of the heart of the people; swing of popular support; trend of popular feeling
归心 guīxīn ❶ desire to return home; homesickness:祖国的兴旺发达使他萌发了强烈的～。His homesickness intensified (*or* grew keener) as the motherland prospered. ❷ sincerely submit (to the authority of sb.); pledge heartfelt allegiance (to sb.):天下～。Sincere allegiance came from all parts of the country.
归心似箭 guīxīn-sìjiàn (want to) speed back home with the swiftness of an arrow; be anxious to return home as soon as possible; be impatient to return home:他～,恨不能插上双翅立刻飞到家中。He was so anxious to return home that he wished he could have wings and fly back at once.
归省 guīxǐng 〈书面〉return and visit one's family; be on family leave:～故里 pay a visit to one's native place /荣国府～庆元宵 Yuanchun Visits Her Parents (at Duke Rong's Mansion) on the Festival of Lanterns (a chapter title from *A Dream of Red Mansions*)
归依 guīyī ❶ *also* "皈依" guīyī be converted to:～佛门 be converted to Buddhism ❷ depend on:无所～的流浪者 vagrant with nothing to live on; homeless vagabond
归因 guīyīn ascribe; attribute:把成功～于运气 attribute (*or* ascribe) the success to luck
归阴 guīyīn leave this world; die
归隐 guīyǐn 〈书面〉withdraw from society and live in solitude; dwell in one's native place in retirement:～故园 retire to one's native village and live in seclusion
归于 guīyú ❶ belong to; be attributed to:光荣～祖国。Glory to the motherland. /不要把一切功劳～自己,一切错误～别人。Don't attribute all merit to yourself and put all blame on others. ❷ tend to; result in; end in:经过充分酝酿,会议对代表名单的意见～一致。After ample deliberation the session finally agreed on the list of delegates. *or* Agreement was reached on the list of delegates after full deliberation at the meeting.
归约 guīyuē 〈数学〉reduction:～算法 reduction algorithm /～证明 proof of reduction /～公式 formula of reduction
归葬 guīzàng (of a deceased person) be taken back and buried in one's native place:～故土 be (taken back and) buried in one's native soil
归赵 guīzhào (of sth. borrowed or lost) return intact to its owner; return in good condition
see also "完璧归赵" wánbì-guīzhào
归着 guīzhe put in order; tidy up:客人来以前把屋里～～。Tidy up the rooms before the guest arrives.
归真 guīzhēn ❶ (of Buddhism and Islamism) die ❷ *see* "归真返璞"
归真返璞 guīzhēn-fǎnpú *also* "返璞归真" (drop all affectation and) return to original purity and simplicity; return to nature; rediscover one's true self
归整 guīzheng put in order; sort out; arrange; tidy up:～家什 put household things in order
归置 guīzhi sort out; arrange; put in order; tidy up:～东西 put things in order /～行李 pack one's luggage /你该～一下房间了。It's time you tidied up your room.
归终 guīzhōng 〈方言〉in the end; finally:我为他们忙上忙下,～倒落了一身不是。I'd been rushed off my feet working for them, only to get nothing but blame in the end.
归舟 guīzhōu returning ship or boat:茫茫湖上,只见一叶～。There was nothing to be seen except a lone returning boat on the vast lake.
归总 guīzǒng put together; put in a nutshell; sum up:～一句话,希望你能顾全大局。To put it in a nutshell, I hope you'll take the overall situation into consideration. /问题太多,来不及～。There isn't enough time to sum up so many questions right now.
归罪 guīzuì put the blame on; impute a fault to:此事与我毫不相干,为什么要～于我? I had nothing to do with this. Why put the blame on me?

皈 guī

皈依 guīyī *also* "归依" guīyī 〈宗教〉❶ ceremony of initiating sb. as a Buddhist ❷ be converted to (Buddhism or some other religion):～天主教 be converted to Catholicism /～三宝 become a Buddhist

瑰 guī

〈书面〉❶ jade-like stone ❷ rare; marvellous; magnificent: *see* "～丽";"～奇"
瑰宝 guībǎo treasure; gem:国之～ national treasure /这些名画是我国古代艺术的～。These renowned paintings are gems of ancient Chinese art.
瑰丽 guīlì surpassingly beautiful; splendid; magnificent:～多姿 elegant and brilliant /～的诗篇 magnificent poem /我站在山头,观赏全城～的夜景。I stood on top of the hill, enjoying the majestic evening scene of the city.
瑰奇 guīqí magnificent; fantastic:～的黄山云海 fantastic (*or* magnificent) clouds of Huangshan Mountain
瑰伟 guīwěi *see* "瑰玮"
瑰玮 guīwěi *also* "瑰伟"〈书面〉❶ (of a person's character) remarkable; unique ❷ (of language or style) ornate
瑰异 guīyì magnificent; fantastic
瑰意琦行 guīyì-qíxíng remarkable ideas and admirable behaviour; outstanding in thought and action

傀 guī

〈书面〉❶ unusual; strange; odd:～奇 unusual; peculiar ❷ stand all by oneself:～然独立,无遮无盖。It stood all by itself

with nothing as a cover.
see also kuǐ

瓌 guī ❶〈书面〉jade-like stone：瑰～玉佩 beautiful jade pendant ❷ *see* "瑰" guī

龟(龜) guī ❶ tortoise；turtle：海～ greenturtle；sea turtle／乌～ tortoise ❷〈口语〉cuckold
see also jūn；qiū

龟板 guībǎn 〈中药〉tortoise plastron；tortoise shell：～胶 tortoise-plastron glue
龟背 guībèi 〈中药〉curvature of the spinal column
龟背石 guībèishí septarium；beetlestone；turtle stone
龟卜 guībǔ tortoise-shell divination；scapulimancy
龟趺 guīfū tortoise-shaped base of a tombstone or stele
龟公 guīgōng cuckold
龟龟琐琐 guīguī-suǒsuǒ dejectedly；listlessly：我再也不要～地过日子了。I won't lead a spiritless life any more.
龟鹤 guīhè turtle and crane (proverbially representing long life)；longevity；long life
龟甲 guījiǎ tortoise-shell：～石 turtle stone／～虫 tortoise beetle
龟鉴 guījiàn *also* "龟镜" oracle and mirror；sth. serving as an object lesson for others or a warning for the future：以作～ draw a lesson from sth.；use sth. as an object lesson or warning
龟龄 guīlíng long life
龟纽 guīniǔ turtle-shaped knob of a seal
龟缩 guīsuō huddle up (like a turtle)；withdraw into passive defence；hole up：吓得～室内 huddle up in fear in the room／敌军都～在碉堡里不敢出来。The enemy soldiers were all holed up in the pillbox and dared not come out.
龟头 guītóu 〈生理〉balanus；glans penis：～炎 balanitis／淋病性～炎 balanoblennorrhea
龟子 guīzi cuckold
龟足 guīzú *also* "石蜐" shíjié 〈动物〉*Pollicipes mitella*, a kind of littoral crustacean

guǐ

庋(庪) guǐ 〈书面〉❶ shelf：倾筐倒～ turn out one's baskets and shelves — give all one has ❷ keep；preserve；shelve：～藏 store up；preserve／～之高阁 have sth. shelved

晷 guǐ ❶〈书面〉shadow cast by the sun；〈比喻〉time：余～ spare time ❷ sundial；gnomon：日～ sundial
晷仪 guǐyí sundial
晷影 guǐyǐng ❶ shadow cast by the sun (on the dial) ❷〈比喻〉time：～易流。How time flows past.

簋 guǐ ancient round-mouthed food vessel with two or four loop handles

鬼 guǐ ❶ ghost；phantom；spirit；apparition：装神弄～ play the ghost／讲～故事 tell a ghost story／镇～ lay a ghost／疑神疑～ be terribly suspicious；be afraid even of one's own shadow／牛～蛇神 ghosts and monsters of all descriptions ❷ derogatory term for a person with a certain vice or problem：胆小～ coward；chicken heart／吸血～ bloodsucker／烟～ chainsmoker／懒～ lazybones／讨厌～ bore／赌～ gambler／冒失～ harumscarum；madcap／馋～ glutton／你这个死～！You devil! ❸ stealthy；clandestine；surreptitious：*see* "～～祟祟"；"～头～脑" ❹ sinister plot；dirty trick：暗中捣～ play tricks in secret／搞～名堂 play dirty tricks (on)／心中有～ have a guilty conscience／其中必定有～。There's something fishy about it. *or* I smell a rat.／这家伙整天不见人影，在搞什么～？He scarcely shows up. What's he up to? ❺ terrible；wretched；damnable：这～天气太热了！What bloody hot weather!／这～地方连个人影都见不着！What a damnable place! Not a single soul is around. ❻〈口语〉clever；smart；quick：这孩子真～！What a clever boy!／这老家伙真够～的。He's an old fox. ❼ one of the twenty-eight lunar mansions or constellations in ancient-Chinese astronomy *see also* "二十八宿" èrshíbāxiù

鬼把戏 guǐbǎxì ❶ sinister plot；treacherous scheme ❷ mischief；monkey trick；monkeyshines；mischievous trick：你们的～只能糊弄别人，骗不了我！Your sly tricks can deceive others but not me!
鬼笔 guǐbǐ 〈植物〉stinkhorn
鬼才 guǐcái person having special talent；special talent：文坛～ person of special talent in literary circles
鬼吹灯 guǐchuīdēng ❶ mischief；monkey trick；monkeyshine；mischievous trick：他又在玩儿什么～？What mischief is he up to this time? ❷ incredible tale；improbable fabrication；cock-and-bull story：我可不信他那些～。I believe none of his cock-and-bull stories. ❸ smash；destroy：把敌人打得彻底～。We completely routed the enemy troops.
鬼聪明 guǐcōngming petty cleverness
鬼打墙 guǐdǎqiáng lose one's way in darkness (as if misled by a ghost)
鬼道 guǐdao 〈方言〉smart；shrewd；clever；sharp：这小孩儿真～，脑瓜儿一转就是一个主意。The boy is really smart and full of brainwaves.
鬼点子 guǐdiǎnzi 〈方言〉wicked idea；trick：你的～可真不少。You do have plenty of tricks up your sleeve.／他想来想去，想出了个～。He thought over and over again and then a devilish idea came to his mind.
鬼风疙瘩 guǐfēng gēda *also* "荨麻疹" xúnmázhěn 〈方言〉nettle rash；urticaria
鬼斧神工 guǐfǔ-shéngōng *also* "神工鬼斧" (of architecture, sculpture, literary works, etc.) uncanny workmanship；prodigious craftsmanship：这工艺之精巧，真所谓～，不可思议。Such delicate and superb craftsmanship is simply incredible (*or* astounding).
鬼怪 guǐguài ghosts and monsters；monsters of all kinds；forces of evil：妖魔～有什么可怕？What's so scary about evil forces?
鬼怪式飞机 guǐguàishì fēijī (US) Phantom (F-4)
鬼鬼祟祟 guǐgui-suìsuì in a hole-and-corner fashion；sneaky；furtive；on the sly：他～站在门外，对她直打手势。He stood furtively outside the door, making gestures to her.／那家伙～地溜进了一座大楼。The man slipped into a building stealthily.／他从来不喜欢这种～的勾当。He never likes this kind of secretive monkey business.
鬼画符 guǐhuàfú ❶ poor handwriting；scrawl：他的签名真像～。His signature is an illegible scrawl. ❷〈比喻〉hypocritical remark：你以为耍个～，人家就相信你了？You thought you could deceive people by those hypocritical words of yours?
鬼话 guǐhuà fake story；falsehood；lie：他这个人，净说～，谁信？Who believes him when he tells nothing but falsehoods?
鬼话连篇 guǐhuà-liánpiān pack of lies
鬼魂 guǐhún ghost；spectre；spirit；apparition：～附体者 medium
鬼混 guǐhùn lead an aimless or irregular life；fool around；hang around；hang about：他不好好学习，整日～。He's fooling around all the time, neglecting his studies.／他近来和几个小流氓～。He has been hanging around with some young hooligans lately.
鬼火 guǐhuǒ *also* "磷火" línhuǒ will-o'-the-wisp；jack-o'-lantern
鬼机灵 guǐjīling 〈口语〉smart；intelligent；clever；sly：这孩子～。The child is very smart.
鬼节 Guǐjié ❶ Ghosts' Festival (15th day of the 7th lunar month) ❷ Halloween, the night of October 31
鬼哭狼嚎 guǐkū-lángháo *also* "鬼哭神号" wail like ghosts and howl like wolves；give bloodcurdling cries and howls：直杀得匪兵～，溃不成军。Fiends wept and demons cried, as the routed enemy soldiers fled helter-skelter.
鬼佬 guǐlǎo 〈方言〉foreign devil；foreigner
鬼脸 guǐliǎn ❶ mask (used as a toy)：戴上～ put on a mask ❷ funny face；grimace；wry face：他伸伸舌头，做个～。He stuck out his tongue and grimaced.
鬼灵精 guǐlíngjīng 〈方言〉❶ most clever；smart ❷ most clever person；unusually smart person：这是个～，谁也不能轻易地骗得了他。He is a knowing card；no one can bluff him.
鬼录 guǐlù 〈迷信〉(on) the nether roll；register or roll of the dead
鬼魅 guǐmèi 〈书面〉ghost and goblins；evil forces；bogey：一切妖狐～都要现出原形。Ghosts and goblins of all descriptions will reveal (*or* betray) their true features.
鬼门关 guǐménguān gate of hell；jaws of death；danger spot；trying moment：他进了～。He got into the jaws of death.
鬼迷心窍 guǐmíxīnqiào be possessed；be obsessed：他～，越输越想赌。Gambling has made him so blind；the more he loses, the more

he gambles.
鬼魔 guǐmó monster; devil; demon
鬼目 guǐmù *also*“凌霄花” língxiāohuā 〈植物〉Chinese trumpet creeper (*Campsis grandiflora*)
鬼伞 guǐsǎn 〈植物〉inky cap
鬼映眼 guǐshǎnyǎn twinkle; glimmer: 黑夜中星星都在～。The stars were twinkling in the night sky.
鬼神 guǐshén ghosts and gods; spirits; supernatural beings
鬼神莫测 guǐshén-mòcè *also*“鬼神不测” beyond the ken of god or devil; extremely mysterious; unfathomable
鬼使神差 guǐshǐ-shénchāi *also*“神差鬼使” doings of ghosts and gods; doing something inexplicably as if manipulated by supernatural beings; unexpected happening; curious coincidence: 真是～，他们俩偏偏在不该会面的时间、不该会面的地点相遇了。As if designed by providence, the two came across each other at the wrong time and in the wrong place. /～，他竟顺着原路又走了回来。As if the spirits made his mind wander, he walked back along the same road he came.
鬼祟 guǐsuì ❶ *see*“鬼鬼祟祟” ❷ ghost; monster
鬼胎 guǐtāi sinister design; dark scheme; ulterior motive; evil plot: 各人都心怀～。Each has an ulterior motive of his own. /不知他心中怀着什么～! I wonder what sinister designs he's been brewing!
鬼剃头 guǐtìtóu (popular term for 斑秃) alopecia
鬼头鬼脑 guǐtóu-guǐnǎo thievishly; in a hole-and-corner fashion; furtively; on the sly: 两个～的人，正在角落里悄悄地说些什么。Two sneaky-looking persons were whispering in the corner.
鬼头 guǐtou 〈口语〉❶ clever and lovely: 这孩子长得怪～的。The child is cute. ❷ clever and lovely child
鬼物 guǐwù ghost; spirit; apparition
鬼黠 guǐxiá sly; cunning; crafty
鬼星团 Guǐxīngtuán 〈天文〉Praesepe
鬼雄 guǐxióng 〈书面〉gallant spirit: 生当作人杰，死亦为～。A brave man when alive; a gallant spirit when dead.
鬼鲉 guǐyóu 〈动物〉devil stinger; lumpfish
鬼蜮 guǐyù ❶ evil spirit; demon: ～为灾。The calamity was caused by evil spirits. ❷ treacherous; sinister
鬼蜮伎俩 guǐyù-jìliǎng devilish stratagem; evil tactics; sinister tricks: 他们就是使尽～，也对我无可奈何。All their sinister tricks could not harm me a bit.
鬼针草 guǐzhēncǎo 〈植物〉beggar-ticks (*Bidens bipinnata*)
鬼主意 guǐzhǔyi evil plan; wicked idea: 他的～真多! He is full of wicked ideas!
鬼子 guǐzi devil (a term of abuse for foreign invaders): 洋～ foreign devil /东洋～ Japanese devil /小～ Japs; Nips
鬼子姜 guǐzijiāng *also*“菊芋” júyù 〈方言〉〈植物〉Jerusalem artichoke

氿

guǐ fountain that gushes sideways; sideway gushed spring

宄

guǐ *see*“奸宄” jiānguǐ

轨

guǐ ❶ rail: 铁～ rail /铺～ lay the rails /电车～道 tramrails ❷ track: 单～ single track /双～ double track /无～电车 trackless tram; trolley (bus) /出～ be derailed ❸ course; orbit; rule; order: 行为不～ act against law (*or* generally accepted norms) /步入正～ take the regular course /纳入正～ put on the right track /越～行为 behaviour against rules (*or* exceeding the bounds); impermissible conduct; transgression ❹ 〈书面〉abide by; adhere to: ～于法令 abide by law
轨道 guǐdào ❶ track: 电车～ tramroad; tramway; tramline /这段～正在抢修。Urgent repair is being made on this part of the track. /两列火车相撞，一列被撞出了～。Two trains collided and one was derailed. ❷ *also*“轨迹” orbit: 抛物线～ parabolic orbit /准椭圆～ quasi-elliptic orbit /绕月～ lunar orbit /送入～ put (a satellite) into orbit /人造卫星进入～。The man-made satellite is now in orbit. ❸ trajectory; path: 这条线表示炮弹的运行～。This is the trajectory of the shell. ❹ course; groove; path; scope: 生产已走上～。Production has got on the right track. /他想把我们纳入他的～。He wants us to follow the path he has designated.
轨道变换 guǐdào biànhuàn 〈航天〉orbital transfer
轨道车 guǐdàochē motor-trolley
轨道导弹 guǐdào dǎodàn orbital missile
轨道衡 guǐdàohéng 〈铁路〉track scale
轨道火箭 guǐdào huǒjiàn orbital rocket
轨道交角 guǐdào jiāojiǎo 〈航天〉inclination of orbit; orbit inclination
轨道空间站 guǐdào kōngjiānzhàn 〈航天〉orbital space station
轨道平面 guǐdào píngmiàn 〈航天〉orbit plane
轨道天文观测卫星 guǐdào tiānwén guāncè wèixīng orbiting astronomical satellite
轨道运动 guǐdào yùndòng 〈天文〉orbital motion
轨度 guǐdù 〈书面〉law; code of conduct
轨范 guǐfàn standard; criterion; yardstick: 道德～ moral code /其书法可为后世～。His calligraphy can serve as a model for later generations.
轨迹 guǐjì ❶〈数学〉locus: 几何～ geometrical locus /双曲线～ hyperbolic locus ❷ orbit; path: 射流～ jet path /涡流～ vortex path ❸ track; footmark: 回首自己的人生～，感慨甚多。All sorts of feelings well up when he looks back at the track of his journey through life. /这部影片真实地反映了近十年我国农村巨变的～。This film portrays the course of great changes in China's rural areas in the past decade.
轨迹函数 guǐjì hánshù locus function
轨迹角 guǐjìjiǎo track angle
轨迹显示 guǐjì xiǎnshì trace display
轨迹线 guǐjìxiàn trajectory
轨距 guǐjù 〈铁路〉gauge: 标准～ standard gauge
轨辙 guǐzhé rut; beaten track
轨枕 guǐzhěn 〈铁路〉sleeper; tie: ～板 concrete slab sleeper /纵向～ longitudinal sleeper /～钢 sleeper bar

匦

guǐ folder; box; casket: 名片～ name-card folder /票～ ballot box

诡

guǐ ❶ deceitful; tricky; sly; cunning: *see*“～称”;“～计” ❷〈书面〉weird; uncanny; eerie: 殊形～制，每各异观。Weirdly shaped, each looked distinctive in its own way.
诡变 guǐbiàn 〈书面〉crafty; treacherous; shifty: ～万端 shifty and treacherous to the extreme; extremely crafty
诡辩 guǐbiàn ❶ sophistry; sophism: ～手法 sophistical reasoning 借助于～ resort to sophistry ❷ quibble: 纯属～ nothing but quibbling
诡辩法 guǐbiànfǎ sophism
诡辩家 guǐbiànjiā sophist
诡辩术 guǐbiànshù sophistry
诡称 guǐchēng falsely allege or claim; pretend; feign: ～失业 falsely claim to be jobless (*or* out of work) /他～自己有病。He pretended to be sick. *or* He feigned sickness.
诡辞 guǐcí *also*“诡词”〈书面〉❶ quibble; give a lame excuse ❷ sophistry; absurd argument; fallacy
诡诞 guǐdàn unfounded and absurd; incredible: 其言～，不可信。Don't believe his absurd remarks.
诡道 guǐdào necromancy; perverse ways
诡道 guǐdao 〈方言〉❶ (of a child) clever; smart ❷ crafty; cunning; foxy
诡怪 guǐguài grotesque; fantastic; supernatural: 行事～ behave in an unnatural manner
诡幻 guǐhuàn fantastic; strange; odd: ～境界 fantastic land
诡计 guǐjì crafty plot; cunning scheme; machination; intrigue; trick; ruse: 耍～ play a trick /中～ be trapped; be taken in /揭穿～ lay bare (*or* expose) a scheme, plot, etc. /他的～被识破了。His crafty plot was seen through.
诡计多端 guǐjì-duōduān have a whole bag of tricks; have a lot of tricks up one's sleeve; be very crafty; be foxy and wily
诡谲 guǐjué 〈书面〉❶ strange and changeable: 技法独树一帜，～多变 with a unique technique, strange and changeful ❷ eccentric; bizarre; enigmatic; mysterious: 此人言语～。He is cryptic in speech. /她～地一笑，朝台上努了努嘴。With an enigmatic smile she pouted her lips at the platform. ❸ cunning; treacherous; sly: 为人～ be of a slippery character
诡雷 guǐléi 〈军事〉booby mine; booby trap
诡秘 guǐmì surreptitious; secretive; furtive: 行踪～ surreptitious in one's movements /言行～ secretive in speech and action

G

诡奇 guǐqí *see* “诡异”
诡笑 guǐxiào pretending to smile; feigned smile
诡异 guǐyì *also* “诡奇” queer; strange; bizarre; odd: ～的情节 bizarre plot (of a story, etc.) /～的笔调 (write) in an odd style /～有趣 fantastic and interesting
诡诈 guǐzhà crafty; cunning; sly; treacherous: 此人～异常。This man is extremely wily.

垝(陒) guǐ 〈书面〉 collapse: ～垣 dilapidated wall; wall in ruins

佹 guǐ 〈书面〉 ❶ perverse; unreasonable ❷ strange; queer; odd ❸ accidental; fortuitous
佹得佹失 guǐdé-guǐshī accidentally gained, accidentally lost

姽 guǐ
姽婳 guǐhuà 〈书面〉 (of a woman) demure and pretty

癸 guǐ last of the ten Heavenly Stems
see also “干支” gānzhī

guì

桂[1] guì ❶ cassia; cinnamon: ～皮 cassia bark; cinnamon ❷ sweet-scented osmanthus ❸ laurel; bay tree: 折～ win the laurel; win victory ❹ cassia-bark tree

桂[2] Guì ❶ Guijiang River in Guangxi (广西) ❷ another name for Guangxi ❸ a surname
桂冠 guìguān laurel: 摘取～ win the laurel; win victory; gain distinction /争夺～ contend for distinction
桂冠诗人 guìguān shīrén poet laureate
桂花 guìhuā 〈植物〉 sweet-scented osmanthus: 八月～满地香。Everywhere in August, osmanthus flowers send forth a delicate fragrance.
桂花酒 guìhuājiǔ wine fermented with osmanthus flowers; osmanthus-flower wine: 问讯吴刚何所有，吴刚捧出～。Wu Gang, asked what he can give, Serves them a laurel brew.
桂剧 guìjù Gui opera, a local opera popular in the Guangxi Zhuang Autonomous Region
桂林 Guìlín Guilin, city and tourist resort in Guangxi: ～山水甲天下。Guilin's scenery is the best in the world. *or* Guilin tops the world in landscape.
桂陵之战 Guìlíng Zhī Zhàn Battle of Guiling of 352 BC (in present Henan) in which the army of Qi (齐) defeated that of Wei (魏) by attacking the latter's rear and waylaying them
桂皮 guìpí ❶ *also* “锡兰肉桂” Xīlán ròuguì cassia-bark tree: ～油 cassia oil ❷ cassia bark; Chinese cinnamon ❸ cinnamon bark
桂系 Guìxì (of) Guangxi faction: ～军阀 Guangxi warlords
桂鱼 guìyú mandarin fish
桂圆 guìyuán 〈植物〉 longan: ～肉 dried longan pulp /～晶 instant longan drink
桂枝 guìzhī 〈中药〉 cassia twig
桂竹 guìzhú *also* “筀竹” guìzhú *Phyllostachys bambusoides*
桂子 guìzǐ 〈书面〉 *see* “桂花”
桂子兰孙 guìzǐ-lánsūn famous descendants; distinguished posterity
桂子飘香 guìzǐ-piāoxiāng fragrance of the osmanthus flowers filling the air — beautiful view around the Mid-autumn Festival

筀 guì
筀竹 guìzhú *see* “桂竹” guìzhú

柜(櫃) guì ❶ cupboard; cabinet: 碗～ kitchen cupboard /书～ bookcase /餐具～ sideboard /床头～ bedside (*or* night) table /衣～ wardrobe /组合式衣～ combined wardrobe and linen cupboard /电视～ TV stand /酒～ cocktail cabinet /多用～ multi-purpose cabinet /保险～ safe/五斗～ chest of drawers ❷ cashier's office; cashier's desk; cashier's: 掌～的 shop-owner /全部现金都已交～。All cash has been submitted (*or* handed in) to the cashier's. /请到～上取钱。Please cash at the cashier's.
see also jǔ
柜橱 guìchú cupboard; cabinet: 这～式样虽已过时，却很适用。Though old-fashioned, the cupboard is quite serviceable.
柜房 guìfáng cashier's office; cashier's desk; shop cashier
柜榴石 guìliúshí 〈矿业〉 cinnamon stone; hessonite
柜上 guìshang ❶ cashier's; shop cashier: ～存款不多了。There isn't much cash at the cashier's. ❷ shop; store: ～盘点，暂停营业一天。The store's closed for the day for stock-taking (*or* inventory).
柜台 guìtái counter; bar: 站～ serve behind the counter /玻璃～ showcase /～值班经理 executive sales manager /他在旧社会是个站～的。He was merely a shop assistant in the old society.
柜台承包 guìtái chéngbāo concession (in a shop)
柜子 guìzi cupboard; cabinet

贵 guì ❶ high-priced; expensive; costly; dear: 昂～ costly /丝绸比棉布～得多。Silks are much more expensive than cotton. /春雨～如油。Spring rains are as valuable as oil. ❷ valuable; highly valued; precious: 十分珍～ priceless /名～ famous and precious; rare /难能可～ commendable for rare achievements /兵～神速。Speed is crucial in war. ❸ of high rank; exalted; noble: 显～ high in office; powerful and influential /权～们 influential officials; bigwigs /他出身高～。He was of blue blood. ❹ 〈敬词〉 your: ～国 your country /～校 your school /～姓? May I know your name? ❺ (Guì) (short for 贵州) Guizhou: 云～高原 Yunnan-Guizhou Plateau ❻ (Guì) a surname
贵宾 guìbīn honoured guest; distinguished guest: 设宴招待～ give a banquet in honour of the distinguished guest(s)
贵宾席 guìbīnxí seats for distinguished guests; distinguished visitors' gallery
贵宾休息室 guìbīn xiūxishì VIP lounge or room
贵耳贱目 guì'ěr-jiànmù treasure what one hears and belittle what one sees; readily place trust in hearsay; be credulous
贵妃 guìfēi *guifei* — highest-ranking imperial concubine: ～醉酒 “Drunken Beauty” (a well-known Beijing opera) /她被封为～。She was made a highest-ranking imperial concubine. *or* The title of *guifei* was conferred on her.
贵干 guìgàn 〈敬词〉 your business: 有何～? What auspicious business brings you here?
贵庚 guìgēng 〈敬词〉 your age
贵贱 guìjiàn ❶ cheap or expensive: ～不等 be of different prices; sell at different prices / 买菜先问问～。You should ask for the price before you buy the vegetable. ❷ high or low social status: 不论～，一律以礼相待。Treat everyone courteously, whatever their social status. ❸ 〈方言〉 in any case; at any rate; at all events; anyway: ～有人留下看家，那我就留下罢。Someone must stay to keep the house anyway, so let me stay.
贵介 guìjiè 〈书面〉 ❶ respected; honourable: ～公子 honourable young gentleman ❷ 〈敬词〉 your (brother): ～弟 your younger brother
贵金属 guìjīnshǔ noble or precious metal
贵客 guìkè distinguished guest; honoured guest
贵客盈门 guìkè-yíngmén the house is full of distinguished guests
贵戚 guìqī emperor's relatives; relatives of the monarch
贵人 guìrén ❶ man of eminence: 王公～ princes, dukes and men of eminence; the nobility ❷ 〈旧语〉 high-ranking imperial concubine
贵人多忘事 guìrén duō wàng shì (often used with mild sarcasm) men of eminence have short memories; great men easily forget: 你可真是～，连当年的挚友都忘记了。As a highly placed person is apt to have a poor momory, so you've forgotten even your bosom friend of old days?
贵阳 Guìyáng Guiyang City, capital of Guizhou Province
贵恙 guìyàng 〈敬词〉 your illness or malady: 不知～痊愈否? I wonder if you have fully recovered from your ailment.
贵要 guìyào powerful and influential: 京中～ people of power and influence in the capital
贵重 guìzhòng valuable; precious; costly: ～首饰 valuable jewelry /～物品 valuables /～药品 costly medicine /～礼品 expensive gift /这些文物比黄金还要～。These cultural relics are more precious than gold.
贵州 Guìzhōu Guizhou (Province)

贵胄 guìzhòu 〈书面〉descendants of a noble family: 出身～ be of noble descent; come from an aristocratic family
贵子 guìzǐ 〈敬词〉(your) child: 愿你们早生～。We hope you'll have a baby soon.
贵族 guìzú noble; aristocrat; peer; patrician: 封建～ feudal nobility / ～习气 aristocratic ways / 工人～ labour aristocrat / 精神～ intellectual aristocrat / 英国的～分为公、侯、伯、子、男五个等级。There are in Britain five noble ranks — duke, marquis, earl, viscount and baron.
贵族院 guìzúyuàn House of Lords, upper house of the British parliament

炅 Guì a surname
see also jiǒng

炔 Guì a surname
see also quē

跪 guì kneel; go down on one's knees: 下～ drop on one's knees; kneel down / 长～不起 kneel a long time; remain on one's knees for a long time
跪拜 guìbài worship on bended knees; kowtow: 行～礼 kowtow to sb.; perform the kowtow; salute sb. on bended knees; prostrate oneself (before a king, etc.)
跪倒 guìdǎo throw oneself on one's knees; fall to one's knees; prostrate oneself; grovel: ～在地 go down on one's knees / ～在石榴裙下 prostrate oneself before a pomegranate-red skirt — be infatuated with a woman / 他表示决不在征服者面前～。He said he would never grovel before a conqueror.
跪垫 guìdiàn hassock
跪伏 guìfú crouch; cower
跪叩 guìkòu kowtow: 行～之礼 perform the kowtow
跪乳 guìrǔ filial piety
跪射 guìshè 〈军事〉kneeling fire
跪姿 guìzī kneeling position: ～射击 shooting from a kneeling position; kneeling fire

刿(劌) guì 〈书面〉wound; cut; stab

鲑(鱥) guì 〈动物〉minnow

桧(檜) guì *also*“刺柏”cìbǎi〈植物〉Chinese juniper (*Juniperus chinensis*)
see also huì

刽(劊) guì 〈书面〉cut off; chop off
刽子手 guìzishǒu ❶ executioner; headsman ❷ slaughterer; butcher: 他是双手沾满人民鲜血的～。He is a butcher whose hands are stained with the blood of the people.

鳜 guì *also*“花鲫鱼”huājìyú〈动物〉mandarin fish

gǔn

衮(袞) gǔn ceremonial dress for royalty: ～冕 emperor's ceremonial dress and hat
衮服 gǔnfú emperor's ceremonial dress; imperial robe
衮衮 gǔngǔn 〈书面〉❶ continual; endless ❷ numerous; many
衮衮诸公 gǔngǔn-zhūgōng 〈讽刺〉high-ranking officials: 国难当头，脑满肠肥的～意当何为? At a time of national peril, what are those big-bellied high-ranking officials going to do? / 请问～，你们能面对平民大众的呼声而充耳不闻吗? Your excellencies, can you turn a deaf ear to the cries of the populace?

滚(滾) gǔn ❶ roll; trundle; tumble: 从楼梯上～下来，摔断了腿 tumble from the staircase and break one's leg / 泪珠从她脸颊上～了下来。Tears coursed down her cheeks. / 孩子在地上直打～儿。The child rolled back and forth on the floor. / 有个小男孩在小路上～铁环。A boy was trundling a hoop on the path. ❷〈贬义〉get away; beat it: ～出去! Get out (of here)! / 你给我～! To hell with you! ❸ boil; seethe: 壶里的水～了。The water is boiling in the kettle. / 泡茶要用～水。Use boiling water to make tea. ❹ roll along or about (in snow or flour); get bigger and bigger; snowball: 利～利。The interest keeps snowballing. ❺ bind; trim: 领口～了一道花边。There was an embroidered hem on the collar. ❻ (Gǔn) a surname
滚边 gǔnbiān *also*“绲边”gǔnbiān (of a dress, etc.) border; edging: ～的衣袖 cuffs trimmed with lace
滚边机 gǔnbiānjī edge knurling machine
滚边器 gǔnbiānqì binding apparatus; binder
滚槽机 gǔncáojī 〈机械〉channelling machine
滚齿法 gǔnchǐfǎ generating process
滚齿机 gǔnchǐjī gear-hobbing machine; hobbing machine; hobber
滚存 gǔncún 〈会计〉(usu. day to day) accumulation: ～盈余 accumulated surplus / ～资金 deferred assets
滚蛋 gǔndàn 〈粗话〉get out; scram; beat it
滚荡 gǔndàng roll; toss; tumble: 湖水～。Waves were rolling in the lake. / 麦浪～。The wheat waved in the field. / 雷声在空际～。Thunder rumbled in the sky.
滚刀 gǔndāo 〈机械〉hobbing cutter; hob
滚刀肉 gǔndāoròu *also*“滚刀筋”〈方言〉unreasonable troublemaker; annoying person; nuisance
滚地传球 gǔndì chuánqiú 〈体育〉(of football) rolling pass
滚地龙 gǔndìlóng *also*“滚地棚”〈方言〉low shabby straw hut; straw shed; thatched shack
滚动 gǔndòng roll; trundle: 坦克履带～着从战壕上碾过去。The tank trundled over the trench. / 眼里～着泪珠。Tears were welling up in her eyes.
滚动摩擦 gǔndòng mócā 〈物理〉rolling friction
滚动投放 gǔndòng tóufàng 〈经济〉〈商业〉rolling launch
滚动轴承 gǔndòng zhóuchéng 〈机械〉rolling bearing
滚翻 gǔnfān 〈体育〉roll: 侧～ sideward roll / 后～ backward roll / 前～ forward roll
滚肥 gǔnféi (usu. of an animal) fat; corpulent: 农场的马都喂得～～的。The farm's horses were all strong and fleshy.
滚沸 gǔnfèi (of liquid) boiling: 一锅～的汤 pot of boiling soup
滚瓜烂熟 gǔnguālànshú be extremely fluent; have at one's fingertips; master thoroughly; know pat: 课文背得～ memorize the text thoroughly; know the text by heart / 他解说这一套已经达到～的程度。He could explain all this as smoothly as a melon rolls out of a cart. / 他这一套太极拳打得～。He has thoroughly mastered this set of *taiji* boxing.
滚瓜溜圆 gǔnguāliūyuán (as of an animal) fat and round
滚瓜流油 gǔnguāliúyóu (as of an animal) fat and glossy
滚滚 gǔngǔn ❶ roll; billow; surge: 波涛～ waves surge / 浓烟～ smoke billows / ～车轮 trundling (*or* rolling) wheels / 心潮～ one's mind being in tumult; feel an upsurge of emotion / ～思绪 surging (*or* tumultuous) thoughts / 历史车轮～向前。The wheel of history rolls on and on. ❷ come or occur continuously; roll: 雷声～ rolls of thunder / 财源～。Wealth (*or* Money) keeps rolling in.
滚锅 gǔnguō 〈方言〉boiling pot
滚剪机 gǔnjiǎnjī 〈机械〉slitting mill; slitting roller
滚净筒 gǔnjìngtǒng cleaning cage; cleaning mill
滚开 gǔnkāi (of liquid) boiling; boiling hot: ～的水 boiling hot water
滚开 gǔnkai 〈贬义〉beat it; scram; clear out: 快给我～! Beat it! *or* Get out! / 你要是看着不顺，你可以～。If you don't like it, you can clear out.
滚雷 gǔnléi ❶〈军事〉rolling mine ❷〈军事〉roll over a mined area ❸ rolling thunder
滚轮 gǔnlún 〈体育〉gyro wheel; hoop
滚木 gǔnmù battle log (used as a projectile or thrown weapon in ancient days): ～礌石 battle logs and rocks (thrown or rolled down a wall or slope at attacking enemy soldiers)
滚木比赛 gǔnmù bǐsài birling; logrolling
滚热 gǔnrè boiling hot; piping hot; burning hot: 一杯～的牛奶 cup of boiling hot milk / 他的额头～，可能发烧了。His forehead is burning hot; he may have a temperature.
滚水 gǔnshuǐ boiling water: ～沏茶 make tea with boiling water
滚水坝 gǔnshuǐbà *also*“溢流坝”yìliúbà overflow dam
滚汤 gǔntāng 〈方言〉boiling water
滚淌 gǔntǎng (of sweat, tears, etc.) roll; stream: 热泪从她脸上～

下来。Hot tears rolled down her cheeks.
滚烫 gǔntàng boiling hot; burning hot:别让～的汤把嘴烫坏了。Take care not to scald your mouth with that boiling hot soup.
滚筒 gǔntǒng 〈机械〉cylinder; roll; bowl
滚筒板 gǔntǒngbǎn roller plate
滚筒式 gǔntǒngshì drum-type
滚筒式烘干机 gǔntǒngshì hōnggānjī cylindrical or drum-type drier
滚筒印花 gǔntǒng yìnhuā roller printing
滚筒印刷机 gǔntǒng yìnshuājī cylinder press
滚筒油印机 gǔntǒng yóuyìnjī mimeograph
滚筒轴 gǔntǒngzhóu roller spindle
滚雪球 gǔn xuěqiú roll a snowball; snowball:～式地发展会员 enrol members like a snowball /他的财富像～～样越滚越多。His wealth snowballed.
滚圆 gǔnyuán round as a ball; perfectly round:小猪崽～～的。The piglets are fat and round. /她的腰身～。She is plump in the middle. *or* She has no waist.
滚轧 gǔnzhá 〈机械〉rolling:～机 rolling mill
滚针轴承 gǔnzhēn zhóuchéng needle bearing
滚珠 gǔnzhū *also* "钢珠" gāngzhū 〈机械〉ball
滚珠轴承 gǔnzhū zhóuchéng *also* "球轴承" qiúzhóuchéng ball bearing
滚柱轴承 gǔnzhù zhóuchéng roller bearing
滚装船 gǔnzhuāngchuán roll-on-roll-off ship; ro-ro
滚子 gǔnzi roller; running pulley:～链 roller-chain

磙(磙)

gǔn ❶ roller:石～ stone roller ❷ level (ground) with a roller:～马路 roll the road /～地 roll the ground
磙子 gǔnzi ❶ stone roller ❷ roller ❸ any round-shaped rolling implement

辊

gǔn *also* "罗拉" luólā 〈机械〉roller
辊筒印花 gǔntǒng yìnhuā 〈纺织〉roller printing
辊压淬火 gǔnyā cuìhuǒ rolled hardening
辊压接合 gǔnyā jiēhé roll bonding
辊子 gǔnzi roller:～输送机 roller conveyor

绲

gǔn ❶ band; ribbon; tape ❷〈书面〉string; rope; cord ❸ trim; hem; bind:袖口上～一条边 bind the cuffs /衣领上～了一道蓝边。The collar is trimmed with a blue lace.
绲边 gǔnbiān *also* "滚边" gǔnbiān embroidered border

鲧(鮌)

Gǔn Gun, father of Yu (禹, legendary ruler whose son set up the Xia Dynasty)

gùn

棍[1]

gùn rod; stick; cane; cudgel:木～儿 wooden rod /竹～儿 bamboo stick; cane /拐～儿 (walking) stick /三节～ three-section cudgel (in martial arts) /～术 art (*or* skill) of cudgel playing

棍[2]

gùn scoundrel; rascal; ruffian:恶～ rascal; ruffian/赌～ gambler /淫～ licentious man; libertine; wolf /党～ party hack; unprincipled politician
棍棒 gùnbàng ❶ club; cudgel; quarterstaff; bludgeon:手持～ with a club in one's hand /他从小就喜欢舞弄～。He's been fond of cudgeling since his boyhood. ❷ stick or staff used in gymnastics:～操 stick exercises
棍骗 gùnpiàn defraud; swindle:不法之徒乘机～,取款潜逃。Those lawbreakers seized the opportunity to swindle people out of their money and abscond with it.
棍儿茶 gùnrchá low quality tea made of tealeaf stalks
棍子 gùnzi stick; club; cudgel; bludgeon; staff:又粗又长的～ thick and long club /不打～,不扣帽子 without resorting to big sticks (i.e. unfair criticism) and sticking political labels on people

guō

郭

guō ❶ outer wall of a city:城～ inner and outer city walls ❷ rim; frame:耳～ auricle ❸ (Guō) a surname
郭沫若 Guō Mòruò Guo Moruo (formerly translated as Kuo Mo-jo, 1892-1978), writer, poet, historian, and archaeologist
郭守敬 Guō Shǒujìng Guo Shoujing (formerly translated as Kuo Shou-ching, 1231-1316), mathematician and astronomer of the Yuan Dynasty
郭熙 Guō Xī Guo Xi (formerly translated as Kuo Hsi), painter of the Northern Song Dynasty
郭象 Guō Xiàng Guo Xiang (formerly translated as Kuo Hsiang, 252-313), philosopher of the Western Jin Dynasty
郭子仪 Guō Zǐyí Guo Ziyi (formerly translated as Kuo Tzu-i, 697-781), general of the Tang Dynasty

聒

guō noisy
聒耳 guō'ěr grate on one's ears; abominably noisy
聒噪 guōzào 〈方言〉noisy; clamorous; long-winded:他～不休,实在烦人! What a bore! He never stops wagging his tongue.

过(過)

Guō a surname
see also guò

蝈(蟈)

guō
蝈蝈儿 guōguor 〈动物〉katydid; long-horned grasshopper:～笼子 grasshopper cage

埚(堝)

guō *see* "坩埚" gānguō

锅(鍋)

guō ❶ pot; pan:饭～ rice pot /炒菜～ frying pan; wok /煎～ frying pan /沙～ earthenware (cooking) pot; clay pot /铝～ aluminium pot (*or* pan) /长柄(有盖)平底～ saucepan /长柄炖～ stewpan /双耳炖～ stewpot /大～ cauldron ❷ cooker:气～ steamer /蒸～ steamer /压力～ pressure cooker /火～ chafing dish ❸ bowl (of a pipe, etc.):烟袋～儿 bowl of a pipe; pipe
锅巴 guōbā ❶ crust of cooked rice; rice crust ❷ dish made of rice crust:～肉片 rice crust with pork slices /～海参 sea cucumber with rice crust
锅饼 guōbing (large, thick) wheat cake
锅铲 guōchǎn slice (a kitchen utensil); spatula
锅房 guōfáng *also* "锅屋"〈方言〉kitchen
锅盖 guōgài lid of a cooking pot
锅垢 guōgòu boiler scale
锅鼓 guōgǔ kettledrum
锅伙 guōhuo 〈旧语〉(simple, temporary) boarding house:搭～ board with (sb.)
锅焦 guōjiāo 〈方言〉*see* "锅巴"
锅盔 guōkui hard wheat cake:白糖～ sweet wheat cake
锅里有碗里才有 guōli yǒu wǎnli cái yǒu *also* "锅里满才有碗里满"〈俗语〉the bowl is full only when the pot is full — the interest of the individual is closely bound up with that of the collective or state
锅炉 guōlú boiler:火管～ fire tube boiler /水管～ water tube boiler /～用水 boiler feedwater /烧～ heat the boiler; tend the boiler /～压 boiler pressure /～效率 boiler efficiency /～性能 boiler performance
锅炉防垢剂 guōlú fánggòujì boiler compound
锅炉房 guōlúfáng boiler room
锅台 guōtái top of a kitchen range; kitchen:妇女只能围着～转的日子一去不复返了。The days when women were tied to the kitchen stove are gone forever.
锅贴儿 guōtiēr lightly fried dumpling:烙～ fry dumplings /羊肉馅儿的～ fried dumpling with mutton filling
锅驼机 guōtuójī 〈机械〉portable steam engine; locomobile
锅烟子 guōyānzi soot on the bottom of a pan; pan soot
锅灶 guōzào pot and stove
锅庄 guōzhuāng Tibetan folk dance
锅子 guōzi ❶〈方言〉pot; pan ❷ bowl (of a pipe, etc.):烟袋～ bowl of a pipe ❸ chafing dish:全家人聚在一起吃～。The whole family sat around, eating from the chafing dish.

彉(彍、彉)

guō 〈书面〉draw or bend a bow

guó

国(國、囯) guó ❶ country; state; nation: 爱～ love the country /救～ save the nation /殉～ die for one's country /外～ foreign country /邻～ neighbouring country /祖～ one's own country; motherland /帝～ empire /王～ kingdom /公～ dukedom; principality /大公～ grand duchy /交战～ belligerent (country) /共和～ republic ❷ of the state; national: ～旗迎风飘扬 national flag fluttering in the breeze ❸ best in the country: *see* "～手" ❹ of China; Chinese: *see* "～学" ❺ (Guó) a surname

国宝 guóbǎo national treasure: 大熊猫被视为中国的～。The giant panda is seen as China's national treasure. /这几位卓越的科学家都是～,要特殊照顾。These outstanding scientists are national treasures and should be given preferential treatment.

国本 guóběn national foundation; cornerstone of a nation: 经济乃是～。Economy is the foundation of a country.

国变 guóbiàn 〈书面〉 national misfortune: 身遭～,创剧痛深。He was in deep distress over the national misfortune.

国别史 guóbiéshǐ history of a particular country

国宾 guóbīn state guest: 设宴招待～ give a banquet in honour of state guests

国宾馆 guóbīnguǎn state guesthouse: 钓鱼台～ Diaoyutai State Guesthouse (in Beijing)

国柄 guóbǐng 〈书面〉 state power; helm of the state: 执掌～ be at the helm of the state; wield state power /～在握 possess (*or* wield) state power

国步 guóbù 〈书面〉 national destiny; fate of a nation: ～艰难。The nation is beset by difficulties.

国策 guócè basic policy of a state; state policy: 改革开放是我国的基本～。Reform and opening up are China's basic national policy.

国产 guóchǎn made in China; home-made: ～品 national product; domestic product /～影片 Chinese-made movie; Chinese film /～彩电 Chinese-made colour TV set /我要买件～货。I wish to buy a Chinese make. *or* I wish to buy Chinese goods.

国朝 guócháo 〈旧语〉 this dynasty

国耻 guóchǐ national humiliation: ～纪念日 day in remembrance of national humiliation /誓雪～ swear to wipe out a national humiliation

国仇 guóchóu national enmity: ～家恨 national enmity and family hatred

国粹 guócuì quintessence or best of Chinese culture: ～派 proponent of the quintessence of Chinese culture; adherent to traditional Chinese culture

国道 guódào national road; national highway

国典 guódiǎn 〈书面〉 laws and institutions of a state

国都 guódū national capital; capital: 定～于北京 make Beijing the capital

国度 guódù country; state; land: 在我们这个伟大的～里,人人都是平等的。People are all equal in this great country.

国法 guófǎ law of the land; national law; law; *lex terrae*: 党纪～ party discipline and state law /～难容 not to be tolerated by law /～无情 the law gives no quarter (to anyone)

国防 guófáng national defence: 加强～ strengthen national defence

国防部 guófángbù ministry of defence; (China) Ministry of National Defence; (US) Department of Defense

国防部长 guófáng bùzhǎng minister of defence; (China) Minister of National Defence; (US) Secretary of Defense

国防大臣 guófáng dàchén (UK) Secretary of State for Defense

国防工业 guófáng gōngyè (national) defence industry

国防建设 guófáng jiànshè building up of national defence

国防军 guófángjūn national defence forces; (of Nazi Germany) *Wehrmacht*

国防科学技术工业委员会 Guófáng Kēxué Jìshù Gōngyè Wěiyuánhuì Commission of Science, Technology and Industry for National Defence

国防力量 guófáng lìliàng defence capability

国防前哨 guófáng qiánshào national defence outpost

国防生产 guófáng shēngchǎn defence production

国防委员会 guófáng wěiyuánhuì national defence council

国防卫星通讯系统 guófáng wèixīng tōngxùn xìtǒng defence satellite communications system (DSCS)

国防现代化 guófáng xiàndàihuà modernization of national defence

国防线 guófángxiàn national defence line

国防支出 guófáng zhīchū expenditure on national defence; defence spending

国风 guófēng ❶〈文学〉folksongs of ancient principalities, part of *The Book of Songs* (诗经) ❷ general mood of a nation; ethos: ～淳正 the national customs are simple and honest

国父 guófù father of a republic (used in the past to refer to Dr. Sun Yat-sen); *pater patriae*

国富民殷 guófù-mínyīn *also* "国富民丰"; "国富民康" prosperous country and well-off people

国歌 guógē national anthem

国格 guógé nation's dignity; national prestige: 不做有损～人格的事 do nothing that may harm one's personal integrity and the dignity of one's country.

国共合作 Guó-Gòng Hézuò cooperation between the KMT and CCP (1923-1927, 1937-1946)

国故 guógù ❶ national cultural heritage; classical learning: 整理～ sort out our national cultural heritage ❷〈书面〉national calamity (such as famine, plague, war, etc.)

国光 guóguāng 〈书面〉 glory of the country

国号 guóhào title of a reigning dynasty, such as Han (汉), Tang (唐) and Song (宋)

国后岛 Guóhòudǎo Kunashiri, one of the four islands under Russian jurisdiction but claimed by Japan

国花 guóhuā national flower: 什么花是中国的～? What is the national flower of China?

国画 guóhuà traditional Chinese painting: 收藏～ collect Chinese paintings /～家 traditional Chinese painter

国徽 guóhuī national emblem

国会 guóhuì (UK) Parliament; (US) Congress; (Japan) Diet; (Israel) Knesset; (Germany) Reichstag: ～山 (US) Capitol Hill; the Hill /～纵火案 Reichstag Fire (1933) /～议员 congressman; member of parliament (MP) /～制 parliamentarism

国会图书馆 Guóhuì Túshūguǎn Library of Congress, the largest library in the United States

国魂 guóhún national spirit; soul of a nation

国货 guóhuò national or domestic goods; China-made goods; Chinese goods: 买～ buy domestic goods

国籍 guójí ❶ nationality; citizenship: 双重～ dual nationality /无～ statelessness /出生～ nationality by birth /根据血统取得的～ citizenship by descent /选择～ choose one's nationality /～所属国 state of nationality /保留中国～ retain one's Chinese nationality /剥夺～ be deprived of nationality /取得～ acquire nationality /申请～ apply for naturalization /加入某国～ be naturalized as the citizen of a country /～不明 of uncertain nationality /放弃～ renounce one's nationality /自动丧失～ lose one's nationality automatically /恢复～ restore one's nationality /凡具有中华人民共和国～的人都是中华人民共和国公民。All persons holding the nationality of the People's Republic of China are citizens of the People's Republic of China. ❷ (of a plane, ship, etc.) national identity: ～不明的飞机 unidentified aircraft

国籍法 guójífǎ law of nationality; nationality law

国计民生 guójì-mínshēng national economy and people's livelihood: 事关～ matters that concern (*or* have direct bearing on) the nation's economy and the people's livelihood

国际 guójì international; foreign; world: ～形势 international situation /～合作 cooperation among nations; international cooperation /～友人 foreign friend /～军备控制与裁军 international arms control and disarmament /建立～政治经济新秩序 establish a new international political and economic order

国际奥林匹克委员会 Guójì Àolínpǐkè Wěiyuánhuì International Olympic Committee (IOC)

国际笔会 Guójì Bǐhuì International Pen (P = poets, playwrights; E = editors; essayists; N = novelists)

国际标准化组织 Guójì Biāozhǔnhuà Zǔzhī International Standards Organization (ISO)

国际标准期刊编号 guójì biāozhǔn qīkān biānhào International Standard Serial Number; ISSN

国际标准书号 guójì biāozhǔn shūhào International Standard Book Number; ISBN

G

国际博览会 guójì bólǎnhuì international fair
国际裁判 guójì cáipàn international referee
国际单位 guójì dānwèi international unit (IU)
国际单位制 guójì dānwèizhì international system of units; international unit system
国际地球物理年 guójì dìqiú wùlǐnián international geophysical year
国际电报电话咨询委员会 Guójì Diànbào Diànhuà Zīxún Wěiyuánhuì International Consultative Committee for Telegraphy and Telephone (CCITT)
国际电话电报公司 Guójì Diànhuà Diànbào Gōngsī (US) International Telephone and Telegraph Corporation (ITT)
国际电信联盟 Guójì Diànxìn Liánméng International Telecommunication Union (ITU)
国际儿童节 Guójì Értóngjié *also* "六一儿童节" Liù-Yī Értóngjié International Children's Day (June 1)
国际法 guójìfǎ (short for 国际公法) international law; law of nations:～委员会 International Law Commission (ILC)/～学派 school of international jurists /～主体 subject of international law
国际法院 Guójì Fǎyuàn International Court of Justice; World Court
国际扶轮社 Guójì Fúlúnshè Rotary International
国际妇女节 Guójì Fùnǚjié *see* "国际劳动妇女节"
国际复兴开发银行 Guójì Fùxīng Kāifā Yínháng International Bank for Reconstruction and Development (IBRD)
国际歌 Guójìgē *The Internationale*
国际个人电脑存储卡协会 Guójì Gèrén Diànnǎo Cúnchǔkǎ Xiéhuì Personal Computer Memory Card International Association (PCMCIA)
国际公法 guójì gōngfǎ public international law; law of nations
国际公制 guójì gōngzhì metric system
国际共产主义运动 guójì gòngchǎnzhǔyì yùndòng international communist movement
国际共管 guójì gòngguǎn (international) condominium
国际关系 guójì guānxì international relations:～基本准则 basic norms of international relations
国际惯例 guójì guànlì international practice
国际广播电视组织 Guójì Guǎngbō Diànshì Zǔzhī International Radio and Television Organization (OIRT)
国际海事卫星组织 Guójì Hǎishì Wèixīng Zǔzhī INMARSAT (International Maritime Satellite Organization)
国际航道 guójì hángdào international waterway or sealane
国际合作社联盟 Guójì Hézuòshè Liánméng International Cooperative Alliance (ICA)
国际红十字会 Guójì Hóngshízìhuì International Red Cross
国际互联网 guójì hùliánwǎng *also* "因特网" yīntèwǎng Internet
国际化 guójìhuà internationalize
国际货币 guójì huòbì international currency; convertible foreign exchange
国际货币基金组织 Guójì Huòbì Jījīn Zǔzhī International Monetary Fund (IMF)
国际机场 guójì jīchǎng international airport
国际驾驶执照 guójì jiàshǐ zhízhào (shortened as 国际驾照) international driving license
国际经济开发合作银行 Guójì Jīngjì Kāifā Hézuò Yínháng International Bank of Economic Co-operation (IBEC)
国际军事法庭 Guójì Jūnshì Fǎtíng International Military Tribunal
国际会计师联盟 Guójì Kuàijìshī Liánméng International Federation of Accountants
国际会计准则委员会 Guójì Kuàijì Zhǔnzé Wěiyuánhuì International Accounting Standards Committee
国际劳动妇女节 Guójì Láodòng Fùnǚjié International Working Women's Day (March 8)
国际劳动节 Guójì Láodòngjié *also* "五一劳动节" Wǔ-Yī Láodòngjié International Labour Day (May 1)
国际劳工组织 Guójì Láogōng Zǔzhī International Labour Organization (ILO)
国际礼让 guójì lǐràng comity of nations; international comity or courtesy; *courtoisie internationale*; *staateugunst*
国际联盟 Guójì Liánméng (shortened as 国联) League of Nations (1920-1946)
国际列车 guójì lièchē international train
国际贸易 guójì màoyì international trade or commerce; world trade
国际民用航空组织 Guójì Mínyòng Hángkōng Zǔzhī International Civil Aviation Organization (ICAO)
国际排球联合会 Guójì Páiqiú Liánhéhuì International Volleyball Federation (IVBF)
国际乒乓球协会 Guójì Pīngpāngqiú Xiéhuì International Table Tennis Federation (ITTF)
国际清算银行 Guójì Qīngsuàn Yínháng Bank for International Settlements (BIS)
国际日期变更线 guójì rìqī biàngēngxiàn international date line
国际商会 Guójì Shānghuì International Chamber of Commerce (ICC)
国际商业机器公司 Guójì Shāngyè Jīqì Gōngsī (US) International Business Machines Corporation (IBM)
国际社会 guójì shèhuì international community; family of nations:呼吁～谴责霸权主义行径 call on the international community to denounce acts of hegemonism
国际市场 guójì shìchǎng international market:进入～ access to the international market; find the way into the world market
国际世界语协会 Guójì Shìjièyǔ Xiéhuì Universal Esperanto Association (UEA)
国际事务 guójì shìwù international affairs; world affairs
国际收支 guójì shōuzhī balance of (international) payments:～不平衡 disequilibrium of balance of payments /～顺差 international payments surplus; favourable balance of payments /～逆差 international payments deficit; unfavourable balance of payments /～危机 international payments crisis
国际水道 guójì shuǐdào international watercourse or waterway:～系统 international watercourse system
国际水域 guójì shuǐyù international waters
国际私法 guójì sīfǎ private international law
国际体操联合会 Guójì Tǐcāo Liánhéhuì International Gymnastic Federation (FIG)
国际通讯卫星组织 Guójì Tōngxùn Wèixīng Zǔzhī *also* "国际卫星组织" International Telecommunications Satellite Organization (INTELSAT)
国际问题研究所 Guójì Wèntí Yánjiūsuǒ Institute of International Studies
国际无线电咨询委员会 Guójì Wúxiàndiàn Zīxún Wěiyuánhuì International Consultative Committee for Radiocommunications (CCIR)
国际习惯法 guójì xíguànfǎ customary international law
国际先驱论坛报 Guójì Xiānqū Lùntánbào (US) International Herald Tribune
国际宪兵 guójì xiànbīng international gendarme
国际象棋 guójì xiàngqí chess:～大师 master of chess
国际新闻工作者协会 Guójì Xīnwén Gōngzuòzhě Xiéhuì International Organization of Journalists (IOJ)
国际协议 guójì xiéyì 〈信息〉internet protocol (IP)
国际刑法 guójì xíngfǎ international penal law
国际刑警组织 Guójì Xíngjǐng Zǔzhī International Criminal Police Organization (Interpol)
国际译联 Guójì Yìlián (short for 国际翻译工作者联合会) International Federation of Translators; *Fédération Internationale des Traducteurs* (FIT)
国际音标 guójì yīnbiāo 〈语言〉international phonetic symbols or alphabet:课本采用～注音。The international phonetic symbols are used in the phonetic notation of the textbook.
国际舆论 guójì yúlùn world (public) opinion
国际语 Guójìyǔ Interlingua
国际原子能机构 Guójì Yuánzǐnéng Jīgòu International Atomic Energy Agency (IAEA)
国际债券交易商协会 Guójì Zhàiquàn Jiāoyìshāng Xiéhuì Association of International Bond Dealers
国际战略研究所 Guójì Zhànlüè Yánjiūsuǒ (UK) International Institute for Strategic Studies (IISS)
国际争端 guójì zhēngduān international dispute
国际证券市场协会 Guójì Zhèngquàn Shìchǎng Xiéhuì International Securities Market Association (ISMA)
国际证券委员会组织 Guójì Zhèngquàn Wěiyuánhuì Zǔzhī Inter-

national Organization of Securities Commissions (IOSCO)
国际直拨 guójì zhíbō IDD (International Direct Dialing)
国际制 guójìzhì *see* "国际单位制"
国际制裁 guójì zhìcái international sanction
国际主义 guójìzhǔyì internationalism: ～者 internationalist/～义务 internationalist obligation /～战士 internationalist fighter
国际自行车联盟 Guójì Zìxíngchē Liánméng International Cyclists Union; *Union Cycliste Internationale* (UCI)
国际纵队 Guójì Zòngduì International Brigade (in the Spanish Civil War of 1936-1939)
国际足球协会联合会 Guójì Zúqiú Xiéhuì Liánhéhuì (shortened as 国际足联) International Federation of Football Associations; *Fédération Internationale de Football Associations* (FIFA)
国际组织 guójì zǔzhī international organization
国家 guójiā state; country; nation: 民族～ nation state /友好～ friendly country /敌对～ hostile or enemy country /发达～ developed country /发展中～ developing country /第三世界～ Third World countries /地大物博、人口众多、历史悠久的～ country with rich natural resources, a large population and a long history /台湾是我们～不可分割的一部分。Taiwan is an integral part of our country.
国家安全部 Guójiā Ānquánbù Ministry of State Security
国家版权局 Guójiā Bǎnquánjú State Copyright Bureau
国家裁判 guójiā cáipàn 〈体育〉national judge (for track and field); national umpire (for volleyball, badminton, tennis, baseball, table tennis, etc.); national referee (for basketball, football, boxing, etc.)
国家测绘局 Guójiā Cèhuìjú State Bureau of Surveying and Mapping
国家出入境检验检疫局 Guójiā Chū-rùjìng Jiǎnyàn Jiǎnyìjú State Administration for Entry-Exit Inspection and Quarantine
国家大事 guójiā dàshì state or national affair
国家导弹防御系统 guójiā dǎodàn fángyù xìtǒng *also* "全国导弹防御系统"〈军事〉(US) NMD (National Missile Defense)
国家地震局 Guójiā Dìzhènjú State Seismological Bureau
国家电信和信息管理机构 Guójiā Diànxìn Hé Xìnxī Guǎnlǐ Jīgòu (US) National Telecommunications and Information Administration
国家杜马 Guójiā Dùmǎ State Duma or Russian Council of State, lower house of the Russian Parliament
国家队 guójiāduì national team
国家发展计划委员会 Guójiā Fāzhǎn Jìhuà Wěiyuánhuì State Development Planning Commission
国家法 guójiāfǎ law of the state; state law; constitutional law
国家纺织工业局 Guójiā Fǎngzhī Gōngyèjú State Bureau of Textile Industry
国家工商行政管理局 Guójiā Gōngshāng Xíngzhèng Guǎnlǐjú State Administration of Industry and Commerce
国家公园 guójiā gōngyuán national park
国家广播电影电视总局 Guójiā Guǎngbō Diànyǐng Diànshì Zǒngjú State Administration of Radio, Film and Television
国家国内贸易局 Guójiā Guónèi Màoyìjú State Bureau of Internal Trade
国家海洋局 Guójiā Hǎiyángjú State Oceanic Administration; National Bureau of Oceanography
国家航空和航天局 Guójiā Hángkōng Hé Hángtiānjú (US) National Aeronautics and Space Administration (NASA)
国家核安全局 Guójiā Hé'ānquánjú National Nuclear Safety Administration
国家环境保护总局 Guójiā Huánjìng Bǎohù Zǒngjú State Environmental Protection Administration (SEPA)
国家机关 guójiā jīguān ❶ state agency or organ; government office: ～工作人员 personnel of state agencies; government functionaries ❷ central government office: ～党委 Party Committee of the Central Government Offices
国家机密 guójiā jīmì state secret: 严守～ strictly guard state secrets
国家机器 guójiā jīqì state machine or apparatus
国家机械工业局 Guójiā Jīxiè Gōngyèjú State Bureau of Machine-Building Industry
国家计划生育委员会 Guójiā Jìhuà Shēngyù Wěiyuánhuì State Family Planning Commission
国家计量局 Guójiā Jìliàngjú State Bureau of Metrology
国家建材局 Guójiā Jiàncáijú (short for 国家建筑材料工业局) State Administration of Building Materials Industry
国家教委 Guójiā Jiàowěi (short for 国家教育委员会, now changed to 教育部) State Education Commission (Ministry of Education from March, 1998)
国家经济贸易委员会 Guójiā Jīngjì Màoyì Wěiyuánhuì State Economic and Trade Commission
国家决算 guójiā juésuàn final accounts of state revenue and expenditure; final state accounts
国家科委 Guójiā Kēwěi (short for 国家科学技术委员会, now changed to 科学技术部) State Science and Technology Commission (Ministry of Science and Technology from March, 1998)
国家恐怖主义 guójiā kǒngbùzhǔyì state terrorism
国家粮食储备局 Guójiā Liángshi Chǔbèijú State Bureau of Grain Reserve
国家林业局 Guójiā Línyèjú State Forestry Bureau
国家垄断资本主义 guójiā lǒngduàn zīběnzhǔyì national or state monopoly capitalism
国家旅游局 Guójiā Lǚyóujú National Tourism Administration
国家煤炭工业局 Guójiā Méitàn Gōngyèjú State Bureau of Coal Industry
国家民族事务委员会 Guójiā Mínzú Shìwù Wěiyuánhuì (shortened as 国家民委) State Ethnic Affairs Commission
国家气象局 Guójiā Qìxiàngjú State Meteorological Administration
国家轻工业局 Guójiā Qīnggōngyèjú State Bureau of Light Industry
国家权力 guójiā quánlì state power: ～机关 agencies or organs of state power
国家社会主义 guójiā shèhuìzhǔyì national or state socialism, another name for Nazism
国家石油和化学工业局 Guójiā Shíyóu Hé Huàxué Gōngyèjú State Bureau of Petroleum and Chemical Industries
国家税务总局 Guójiā Shuìwù Zǒngjú State Taxation Administration
国家所有制 guójiā suǒyǒuzhì state ownership: ～部门 state-owned sector or department
国家体育总局 Guójiā Tǐyù Zǒngjú (formerly 国家体育运动委员会) State Physical Culture Administration
国家统计局 Guójiā Tǒngjìjú State Statistics Bureau
国家图书馆 guójiā túshūguǎn national library
国家外国专家局 Guójiā Wàiguó Zhuānjiājú State Bureau of Foreign Experts Affairs
国家外汇管理局 Guójiā Wàihuì Guǎnlǐjú State Administration of Foreign Exchange
国家文物局 Guójiā Wénwùjú State Cultural Relics Bureau
国家物价局 Guójiā Wùjiàjú State Bureau of Commodity Prices
国家兴亡，匹夫有责 guójiā xīng-wáng, pǐfū yǒu zé the rise and fall of the nation is the concern of every citizen; all men share (in) the responsibility for the fate of their country
国家行为 guójiā xíngwéi act of state; state act
国家行政学院 Guójiā Xíngzhèng Xuéyuàn National School of Administration; (France) *L'École Nationale d'Administration* (ENA)
国家学说 guójiā xuéshuō theory of the state
国家烟草专卖局 Guójiā Yāncǎo Zhuānmàijú State Tobacco Monopoly Bureau
国家药品监督管理局 Guójiā Yàopǐn Jiāndū Guǎnlǐjú State Drug Administration (SDA)
国家冶金工业局 Guójiā Yějīn Gōngyèjú State Bureau of Metallurgical Industry
国家意志 guójiā yìzhì state or national will
国家银行 guójiā yínháng state bank; national bank
国家邮政局 Guójiā Yóuzhèngjú State Post Bureau
国家有色金属工业局 Guójiā Yǒusè Jīnshǔ Gōngyèjú State Bureau of Nonferrous Metal Industry
国家语言文字工作委员会 Guójiā Yǔyán Wénzì Gōngzuò Wěiyuánhuì State Language Work Committee
国家预算 guójiā yùsuàn state budget
国家元首 guójiā yuánshǒu head of state
国家政权 guójiā zhèngquán state power
国家知识产权局 Guójiā Zhīshi Chǎnquánjú State Intellectual

Property Office
国家职能 guójiā zhínéng functions and powers of the state
国家质量技术监督局 Guójiā Zhìliàng Jìshù Jiāndūjú State Bureau of Quality and Technical Supervision
国家中医药管理局 Guójiā Zhōngyīyào Guǎnlǐjú State Administration of Traditional Chinese Medicine
国家主权 guójiā zhǔquán state or national sovereignty: ~豁免原则 principle of sovereign immunity
国家主席 guójiā zhǔxí president (head of state of PRC)
国家主义 guójiāzhǔyì nationalism; etatism: ~者 nationalist; etatist / ~的 nationalistic; nationalist
国家资本主义 guójiā zīběnzhǔyì state capitalism
国家宗教事务局 Guójiā Zōngjiào Shìwùjú State Bureau of Religious Affairs
国交 guójiāo diplomatic relations between nations
国脚 guójiǎo 〈口语〉 player of the national football team; footballer of the national team
国教 guójiào state religion: 英国~ Church of England (Anglican Church)
国界 guójiè national boundary or border
国境 guójìng ❶ national territory: 出入~ leave and enter a country ❷ national border or boundary: 偷越~ illegally cross the border / ~卫生检疫规定 national border health and quarantine regulations
国境线 guójìngxiàn boundary (line) of a country; frontier: 划定~ delimit the boundaries of a country
国境站 guójìngzhàn 〈铁路〉 (national) transit border station; frontier station
国舅 guójiù brother of a queen or empress, or of a queen mother or empress dowager
国剧 guójù ❶ popular traditional opera of a country: 京剧是我国的~。Beijing opera is one of the popular traditional operas of China. ❷〈方言〉Beijing opera
国君 guójūn monarch: 开明~ enlightened monarch
国库 guókù national or state treasury; exchequer: ~证券 exchequer bills; treasury notes; treasury certificate / ~充实 augmentation of the national treasury / ~空虚 depletion of the national treasury / 上交~ hand in to the exchequer
国库券 guókùquàn treasury bond (TB); treasury bill; T-bill; treasury stock: 发行~ issue treasury bonds / 兑换~ convert TB into (*or* exchange TB for) cash
国力 guólì national power or strength; national capabilities: 综合~ comprehensive (*or* overall) national power (*or* strength) / ~雄厚 have solid national strength (*or* strong national power) / ~增强了。The national power has been enhanced. / 经济建设规模超过~。The scale of economic construction goes beyond the national capabilities (*or* nation's capability).
国立 guólì state-maintained; state-run: ~大学 national university
国联 Guólián see "国际联盟"
国脉 guómài 〈书面〉 national lifeline: ~民命 national lifeline(s) and the people's livelihood
国门 guómén 〈书面〉 gateway of a country; border: 拒敌于~之外 keep the enemy beyond the national borders
国民 guómín people of a nation; national: ~待遇(条款) national treatment (clause) / 英国~ British national / 本生的~ natural-born national / 归化的~ naturalized national
国民大会 guómín dàhuì national congress: ~党 (India) Congress Party
国民党 Guómíndǎng Kuomintang (KMT); Nationalist Party: ~党部 head office of the KMT; KMT head office
国民革命军 Guómín Gémìngjūn National Revolutionary Army, first organized in 1925 during the first KMT-CCP cooperation (1923-1927)
国民核算总额 guómín hésuàn zǒng'é national accounting aggregate
国民经济 guómín jīngjì national economy: ~计划 national economic plan / ~持续增长 sustained growth of the national economy
国民生产净值 guómín shēngchǎn jìngzhí net national product
国民生产总值 guómín shēngchǎn zǒngzhí gross national product (GNP)
国民收入 guómín shōurù national income: 国民平均收入 per capita national income
国民议会 guómín yìhuì national assembly
国民政府 guómín zhèngfǔ National Government, set up first in Guangzhou under Dr. Sun Yat-sen, later used as a term for China's central government until 1949
国母 guómǔ ❶ empress; empress dowager ❷ first lady
国难 guónàn national crisis or calamity (caused by foreign aggression): ~当头，一切从简。At this time of national crisis, all unnecessary formalities should be dispensed with.
国内 guónèi internal; domestic; home: ~汇兑 domestic exchange / ~立法 internal legislation; domestic legislation / ~贸易 domestic trade / ~市场 domestic market / ~通信卫星 domestic satellite (DOMSAT) / ~新闻 home news / ~治安 internal security
国内法 guónèifǎ domestic law; national law
国内生产总值 guónèi shēngchǎn zǒngzhí gross domestic product
国内战争 guónèi zhànzhēng civil war; internecine warfare
国鸟 guóniǎo national bird
国破家亡 guópò-jiāwáng with one's country subjugated and family wrecked
国戚 guóqī 〈旧语〉 kinsman of the emperor or relative on the queen's side: 皇亲~ emperor's relatives; very influential people
国旗 guóqí national flag: 中国的~是五星红旗。China's national flag is the five-star red flag.
国情 guóqíng condition or state of a country; national conditions: 从中国的~出发 proceed from China's actual conditions / 合乎中国的~ conform to the reality in China
国情咨文 guóqíng zīwén (US) state of the union message
国庆 guóqìng National Day (in China): ~节 National Day (1 Oct.) / ~活动 National Day celebrations / ~游园会 National Day garden party / 欢度~ celebrate National Day
国人 guórén 〈书面〉 compatriots; fellow countrymen; countrymen: 为~所不耻 be held in contempt by one's fellow countrymen
国丧 guósāng state obsequies; national mourning
国色 guósè 〈书面〉 most beautiful maiden in the country: 具有~之姿 of matchless (*or* peerless) beauty / 这女子堪称~。The young woman was universally recognized as the lady of the land.
国色天香 guósè-tiānxiāng *also* "天香国色" of ravishing beauty and heavenly fragrance (referring to the peony or a beautiful woman)
国色天姿 guósè-tiānzī *also* "天姿国色" unsurpassed beauty; woman of great beauty; celestial beauty
国殇 guóshāng 〈书面〉 fallen heroes of the nation; martyrs to the national cause; elegy of the nation: 身死为~。He fell for his country.
国史 guóshǐ ❶ history of a country or dynasty: 撰写~ write (*or* compose) a national history ❷ 〈旧语〉 official historian; historiographer
国史馆 guóshǐguǎn department of national history; Academia Historica
国士 guóshì 〈书面〉 nationally prominent figure; outstanding personage of a country
国士无双 guóshì-wúshuāng outstanding talent without parallel
国事 guóshì state affairs; national affairs: 关心~ concern oneself with state affairs
国事访问 guóshì fǎngwèn state visit: 正在我国进行~ be in our country on a state visit
国势 guóshì ❶ national power: ~强大 great national power / 蒸蒸日上的~ ever-growing national strength ❷ state of affairs in the country: ~日危。The domestic situation is deteriorating.
国是 guóshì 〈书面〉 matter of vital importance to the state; state policy: 共商~ gather together to discuss matters of national importance / 莫谈~。〈旧语〉 No talking about state affairs.
国手 guóshǒu topnotch person in the country (in chess, medicine, etc.); member of the national team: 青年队里有五名~。Five players in the youth team are from the national team. / 今天是两名~对弈。Both of today's players are among China's masters in chess.
国书 guóshū letter of credence; credentials; letter of commission (for high commissioners): 递交~ present credentials / 接受~ accept credentials / 辞任~ *lettre de recreance* / ~副本 (working) copy of credentials
国术 guóshù traditional Chinese boxing and fencing; traditional Chinese martial arts

国泰航空公司 Guótài Hángkōng Gōngsī (HK) Cathay Pacific Airways

国泰民安 guótài-mín'ān the country enjoys prosperity and the people live in peace: 风调雨顺，～。The weather is favourable, the country prosperous and the people happy.

国帑 guótǎng 〈书面〉 national fund; state finances: 盗用～ embezzlement of national funds

国体 guótǐ ❶ state system: ～是决定国家性质的体制。A state system is a system which determines the fundamental nature of a state. ❷ national prestige or dignity: 有失～ impair national prestige

国统区 guótǒngqū KMT-controlled areas (during the Anti-Japanese War, 1937-1945 and the War of Liberation, 1946-1949)

国土 guótǔ territory; land: 保卫～人人有责。Every citizen has the duty to defend the territory of his or her country.

国土资源部 Guótǔ Zīyuánbù Ministry of Land and Resources

国外 guówài external; overseas; abroad; foreign: ～事务 external affairs / ～来信 letter from abroad / ～市场 overseas (*or* foreign, *or* external) market / ～代理 foreign agency / ～投资 investment in foreign countries; investment overseas (*or* abroad) / ～资产 assets abroad / 侨居～ live abroad / 他厌倦了～的侨居生活，盼望能早日返回祖国。He is fed up with the life of an expatriate and yearns to return to his motherland.

国王 guówáng king; monarch

国威 guówēi international prestige of a state; national power and influence: 大振～ greatly enhance (*or* boost) a country's national power and influence (*or* international prestige)

国文 guówén ❶ national language ❷ 〈旧语〉 Mandarin; Chinese as the national language: 研习～ study Chinese / ～系 Chinese Department / ～课 Chinese (as a subject) / 他的～程度不错。He writes good Mandarin. *or* He is proficient in Chinese.

国务 guówù state affairs: 他日夜为～操劳。He is busy (*or* occupied) with a myriad of state affairs day and night.

国务部长 guówù bùzhǎng minister of state

国务大臣 guówù dàchén minister of state

国务会议 guówù huìyì state conference: 最高～ supreme state conference

国务卿 Guówùqīng (US) Secretary of State: 副～ deputy Secretary of State / 助理～ assistant Secretary of State

国务委员 guówù wěiyuán member of the State Council; state councillor

国务院 guówùyuàn ❶ State Council: ～总理 Premier of the State Council; Prime Minister / ～秘书长 Secretary-General of the State Council ❷ cabinet (in the early years of the Chinese Republic) ❸ (US) State Department: ～发言人(US) spokesperson for the State Department

国务院办公厅 Guówùyuàn Bàngōngtīng General Office of the State Council

国务院参事室 Guówùyuàn Cānshìshì Counsellors' Office of the State Council

国务院发展研究中心 Guówùyuàn Fāzhǎn Yánjiū Zhōngxīn Development Research Centre of the State Council (DRC)

国务院法制办公室 Guówùyuàn Fǎzhì Bàngōngshì Office of Legislative Affairs under the State Council

国务院港澳办公室 Guówùyuàn Gǎng-Ào Bàngōngshì Hong Kong and Macao Affairs Office under the State Council

国务院机关事务管理局 Guówùyuàn Jīguān Shìwù guǎnlǐjú Government Offices Administration of the State Council

国务院经济体制改革办公室 Guówùyuàn Jīngjì Tǐzhì Gǎigé Bàngōngshì Office for Economic Restructuring under the State Council

国务院侨务办公室 Guówùyuàn Qiáowù Bàngōngshì Office of Overseas Chinese Affairs under the State Council

国务院台湾事务办公室 Guówùyuàn Táiwān Shìwù Bàngōngshì Office of Taiwan Affairs under the State Council

国务院特区办公室 Guówùyuàn Tèqū Bàngōngshì Office of Special Economic Zones under the State Council

国务院外事办公室 Guówùyuàn Wàishì Bàngōngshì Office of Foreign Affairs under the State Council

国务院研究室 Guówùyuàn Yánjiūshì Research Office of the State Council

国玺 guóxǐ ❶ imperial or royal seal ❷ seal of the state; national seal; great seal

国学 guóxué ❶ studies of Chinese culture (including history, philosophy, literature, classical Chinese, etc.); Chinese national culture ❷ Imperial College (in ancient China)

国宴 guóyàn state banquet: 设～招待贵宾 give a state banquet in honour of distinguished guests

国药 guóyào Chinese herbal medicine: ～店 store of traditional Chinese medicines

国医 guóyī traditional Chinese medical science; traditional Chinese medical doctor

国音 guóyīn 〈旧语〉 standard Chinese pronunciation (as officially adopted by the state)

国营 guóyíng state-run; state-operated: ～牌价 state-set prices / ～工商业 state-run industry and commerce

国营经济 guóyíng jīngjì *also* "国有经济" state sector of the economy

国营农场 guóyíng nóngchǎng *also* "国有农场" state farm

国营企业 guóyíng qǐyè state-run enterprise

国用 guóyòng expenditure of the state; state or national expenditure

国优 guóyōu (of a product, achievement, etc.) best in the country; national best; top-quality home product: 创～ develop a top-quality home product / ～产品 best product in the country; top-quality home product

国有 guóyǒu state-owned: 收归～ be nationalized / 土地是～的。The land is owned by the state.

国有国法，家有家规 guó yǒu guófǎ, jiā yǒu jiāguī 〈俗语〉 a state has its laws and a family its rules

国有化 guóyǒuhuà nationalize: ～政策 nationalization policy/ 非～ denationalize

国有企业 guóyǒu qǐyè state-owned enterprise (SOE); state enterprise: ～改革 restructuring of state-owned enterprises

国有资产 guóyǒu zīchǎn state(-owned) assets; state property: ～流失 loss of state assets (*or* property) / ～增值 appreciation (in value) of state assets / ～管理局 Administrative Bureau of State-Owned Assets

国语 guóyǔ ❶ national language of a country; Mandarin Chinese ❷ 〈旧语〉 Chinese (as taught in school): ～教员 teacher of Chinese ❸ (Guóyǔ) *Guoyu*, or *Remarks of Monarchs*, history of late Western Zhou and major states in the Spring and Autumn Period, attributed to Zuoqiu Ming (左丘明)

国乐 guóyuè traditional Chinese music

国运 guóyùn 〈书面〉 national destiny or fortunes; fate of a nation: ～兴隆。Fate smiles at the nation.

国葬 guózàng state funeral

国贼 guózéi national traitor; scum of a nation: 声讨～ denounce (*or* condemn) a national traitor

国债 guózhài ❶ national debt ❷ *also* "国库券" treasury bond; government bond

国丈 guózhàng emperor's father-in-law

国之干城 guózhīgānchéng valiant guardian of the nation

国子监 Guózǐjiàn Imperial College (the highest educational administration in dynastic China); Directorate of the Imperial Academy

掴(摑)

guó *see* "掴" guāi

帼(幗)

guó *see* "巾帼" jīnguó

腘(膕)

guó 〈生理〉 hollow or back of the knee

腘窝 guówō 〈生理〉 hollow of the knee; popliteal space

馘(聝)

guó (of ancient wars) count of severed left ears (of enemies as battle achievements)

虢

Guó ❶ Dukedom of Guo, a state in the Zhou Dynasty ❷ a surname

漍

guó 〈书面〉 murmuring sound of flowing water: 溪水～～ babbling of a stream

guǒ

椁(槨) guǒ outer coffin:棺～ inner and outer coffins

果[1] guǒ ❶ fruit; nut:水～ fruit /干～ dried fruit /浆～ berry /野～ wild fruit /开心～ pistachio /腰～ cashew (nut) /开花结～ blossom and bear fruit ❷ result; consequence; outcome; effect:成～ achievement; gain /效～ effect /恶～ disastrous outcome; dire consequences /因～分析 cause and effect analysis /前因后～ cause and effect; entire process /因～报应〈佛教〉*karma*; preordained fate; retribution for sin; punitive justice /劳动成～ fruits of one's labour ❸ (Guǒ) a surname

果[2] guǒ strong-willed; resolute; determined:言必信,行必～。Be true in word and resolute in deed.

果[3] guǒ really; as expected; sure enough:如～ if; in case /～如其言 if this is true; if such is the case /～有意见,不妨实说。Tell me frankly what you have in mind.

果阿 guǒ'ā Goa, a district on India's west coast recovered by India in 1961 from Portuguese rule

果报 guǒbào 〈佛教〉*karma*; retribution for sin; judgment; punitive justice:～之日 day of judgment

果不其然 guǒbuqírán *also* "果不然" indeed; just as expected; I told you so:我早说要下雨,～,下了吧! I said it would rain. Wasn't I right? /大家都说她要出国学习,～,让大家说中了。Everybody said she would go abroad for further study, and to no one's surprise she's gone now.

果菜 guǒcài fruit and vegetable

果虫 guǒchóng fruitworm

果丹皮 guǒdānpí thin sheets made of haw or apple jelly; haw sheets

果冻 guǒdòng jelly; jello:～粉 jelly powder

果断 guǒduàn resolute; decisive:为人精明～ be intelligent and decisive /行为～ be resolute in action /采取～措施 take definitive measures

果饵 guǒ'ěr candies and pastry

果粉 guǒfěn powder on the outer skin of some fruit (such as apple or wax gourd)

果脯 guǒfǔ preserved fruit; candied fruit:什锦～ assorted candied fruit

果腹 guǒfù 〈书面〉satisfy or appease one's hunger; fill one's stomach (usually with poor food):衣不蔽体,食不～ not have enough to wear or eat; suffer both cold and hunger

果干儿 guǒgānr dried fruit

果敢 guǒgǎn determined and daring; courageous and resolute:我佩服他的见识和～。I admire him for his broad vision and resoluteness. /她～地冲向歹徒,全力与他搏斗。She charged at the thug and fought him tooth and nail.

果戈理 Guǒgēlǐ Nikolay Gogol (1809-1852), Russian writer

果核分离机 guǒhé fēnlíjī 〈机械〉fruit stone extractor

果盒 guǒhé compartmentalized box for holding assorted fruits and candies to be sent out as gift

果酱 guǒjiàng *also* "果子酱" jam:自制～ jam made by oneself; home-made jam /橘皮～ marmalade

果胶 guǒjiāo 〈生化〉pectin:～酶 pectase; pectinase /～质 pectic substance/～酸 pectic acid /～糖 pectinose; pectose

果酒 guǒjiǔ *also* "果子酒" fruit wine

果聚糖 guǒjùtáng 〈生化〉levan; fructose

果决 guǒjué firm and resolute; decisive:他办事十分～,从不拖泥带水。He's always decisive in work and never sloppy.

果料儿 guǒliàor raisins, kernels, melon seeds, etc., used in making cakes:～面包 bread with raisins, etc.

果林 guǒlín fruit-bearing forest

果绿 guǒlǜ light green

果木 guǒmù fruit tree:～成林。There are rows and rows of fruit trees.

果木园 guǒmùyuán orchard

果农 guǒnóng fruit grower; orchard worker; orchardman

果盘 guǒpán ❶ fruit tray ❷ *see* "果盒"

果皮 guǒpí skin of fruit; peel; rind:～刀 peeler /请不要乱丢～纸屑。Please don't litter.

果皮箱 guǒpíxiāng litterbin; litterbox; garbage can

果品 guǒpǐn fruit:干鲜～ fresh and dried fruit /～店 fruit store

果品学 guǒpǐnxué descriptive pomology

果儿 guǒr 〈方言〉chicken egg:卧～ poached egg /甩～ scrambled egg

果然 guǒrán ❶ really; as expected; sure enough; indeed:味道～不错。It tastes very nice indeed. /她～没有露面。She did not show up just as expected. /他～名不虚传。His reputation is really well deserved. *or* He really deserves the reputation he enjoys. ❷ if indeed; if really:～是这样的话,事情就好办多了。If that is indeed the case, things would be much easier.

果仁儿 guǒrénr meat of a nut; kernel:～巧克力 nut chocolate

果肉 guǒròu flesh of fruit; pulp

果实 guǒshí ❶ fruit:～累累 laden with fruit /丰硕的～ rich fruit /沉甸甸的～结满枝头。Fruit was hanging heavy on the trees. ❷ gains; fruits:劳动～ fruits of labour /革命的～ fruits of the revolution; revolutionary gains

果蔬干燥机 guǒshū gānzàojī fruit-vegetable drier

果蔬加工厂 guǒshū jiāgōngchǎng fruit-and-vegetable processing plant

果熟期 guǒshúqī fructescence

果树 guǒshù fruit tree:～嫁接 fruit tree graft /～学家 orchardist /～园艺 fruit gardening /～栽培 orcharding; fruit farming; fruit culture; fruit growing; pomiculture/～栽培学 pomology

果松 guǒsōng Korean pine

果酸 guǒsuān tartaric acid

果穗 guǒsuì ear of grain; spike; corn cob

果糖 guǒtáng 〈化学〉fructose; levulose; fruit sugar

果谐 guǒxié Sgor-gzhas song and dance, popular among the Tibetan nationality

果芽 guǒyá fruit bud

果毅 guǒyì 〈书面〉courage and resoluteness; determination and fortitude

果蝇 guǒyíng fruit fly; vinegar fly

果园 guǒyuán fruitery; orchard

果真 guǒzhēn ❶ really; indeed; sure enough; as expected:这次他～获得头奖。He did win first prize this time. ❷ if indeed; if really:～如此,岂不妙哉! If this is really true, it would be wonderful indeed!

果汁 guǒzhī fruit juice:～机 juicer /～甜酒 shrub; rum-shrub

果汁软糖 guǒzhī ruǎntáng marshmallow

果枝 guǒzhī ❶ fruit-bearing shoot; fruit branch ❷ boll-bearing branch (of the cotton plant)

果子 guǒzi ❶ fruit:野～ wild fruit /摘～ pick fruit /～大丰收 bumper harvest of fruit ❷ deep-fried doughnut; pastry

果子酱 guǒzijiàng jam

果子节 Guǒzijié Fruit Festival, celebrated by the Bai nationality in Yunnan Province on the 16th day of the 8th lunar month

果子酒 guǒzijiǔ fruit wine

果子狸 guǒzilí *also* "花面狸" huāmiànlí 〈动物〉masked or gem-faced civet

果子露 guǒzilù fruit syrup

果子盐 guǒziyán 〈药物〉fruit salt

裹 guǒ ❶ tie up; wrap; bind:～起来 wrap up /用绷带～好伤口 bind up the wound; dress the wound /～好包裹 tie up a parcel /马革～尸 wrap the dead body in horsehide /当地人喜欢在头上～一条白毛巾。The local folks like to wrap (*or* bind) their heads with a white towel. *or* The local folks like to wear a white towel turban. ❷ bundle; parcel; package:他大包小～背了好几个。He carried on his back quite a few bundles, big and small. ❸ press into service; round up; pressgang; make away with:土匪撤离时,～走了几个村民。The bandits pressed several villagers into their service when they retreated. /此公离开时～走了我的闹钟。He made away with my alarm clock when he left. ❹〈方言〉suck:小孩一生下来就会～奶。A baby is able to suck at his mother's breast right after it is born.

裹肚 guǒdu waist wrapper

裹脚 guǒjiǎo foot-binding — a vile feudal practice which crippled women physically

G

裹脚 guǒjiao *also* "裹脚布" cloth for foot-binding; bandages used in binding women's feet in feudal China
裹乱 guǒluàn 〈方言〉 confuse; mess up; throw into disorder; disturb:他正在写文章,不许去～。He is writing his paper. Don't disturb him.
裹头巾 guǒtóujīn head wrapper; turban
裹腿 guǒtui puttee; leggings
裹胁 guǒxié *also* "裹挟" force to take part (in evildoing); coerce: 被～而当了土匪 be pressed to join the bandits; become a bandit under duress
裹挟 guǒxié ❶ (of wind, current, etc.) carry away:黄河～着泥沙向东流去。The Yellow River flows east, carrying along mud and sand. ❷ involve; sweep along; be caught up in:形势把他～进去,他也就只好随大流了。He was swept along by the force of circumstances and had to drift with the tide. ❸ *see* "裹胁"
裹扎 guǒzā wrap up; dress (a wound):～伤口 dress a wound
裹足不前 guǒzú-bùqián hesitate to move forward; mark time:我们不能在困难面前～。We must not be afraid to advance in face of difficulties.

菓 guǒ fruit:水～ fruit /红～ haw; hawthorn fruit

蜾 guǒ

蜾蠃 guǒluǒ parasitic wasp (which is a natural enemy of the bollworm)

馃 guǒ deep-fried doughnut

馃子 guǒzi *also* "果子" guǒzi ❶ deep-fried doughnut ❷ 〈方言〉 traditional pastry

guò

过(過) guò ❶ go through or across; cross; pass:通～ go through /～河 cross a river /汽车刚刚～去。The bus has just passed. /阳光穿～云彩。The sun shines through the clouds. ❷ spend (time); pass (time):他愉快地度～晚年。He spent the evening of his life in happiness and contentment. /一眨眼三年～去了。Three years passed like a wink. /～一个星期再给我打电话。Ring me up again in a week's time. /～了冬天,他的健康才有好转。He did not begin to recuperate until winter was over. /春节～得怎样? How did you enjoy your Spring Festival? ❸ transfer; adopt:小女孩～给叔父了。The little girl has been adopted by her uncle./这笔开支没有～到我们的账上。This expenditure has not been transferred to our account. ❹ undergo; go through; go over: *see* "～筛子";"～油" ❺ go over (with one's eyes or in one's mind); read over; call to mind:～名单 go over the name list /交卷前他把答案又～了一遍。He checked his answers again before he handed in his examination paper. /他把昨天听的报告在脑子里～了一遍又一遍。He recalled again and again the lecture he listened to yesterday. ❻ exceed; go beyond; be over: 勇力～人 peerless in strength and valour /言～其实 overstate; exaggerate /水深～腰。The water was waist-deep. /开饭时间已～。Dinner time is over. *or* It's past dinner time. /你坐～了站。You have already gone past your station. /今年雨水～多了。This year's rainfall is excessive. *or* There has been too much rain this year. /这样做太～了。That is really too much. ❼ 〈书面〉 visit: *see* "～访" ❽ 〈方言〉 pass away; die:老爷子是昨儿晚上～的。The old man died last night. ❾〈化学〉〈物理〉 per-; super-; over-:～熔 superfusion /～氧化物 peroxide /～硼酸盐 perborate /～磷酸盐 superphosphate ❿ fault; mistake; demerit:改～ mend one's ways; correct one's mistakes /记～ record sb.'s demerit /知～必改。Mistakes, once discovered, must be rectified. ⓫ *used after a verb plus* 得 *or* 不 *to indicate superiority or inferiority, success or failure, etc.*:我说不～她。I can't outargue her. /一台拖拉机胜得～几十个人。One tractor out-performs dozens of men. /你这么干群众通得～吗? Can you win popular support by doing so? /这样的干部我们信不～。We have no confidence in such cadres. ⓬ 〈方言〉 infect; be contagious:这种病容易～人。This disease is highly contagious.

过(過) guo ❶ *used after a verb to indicate the completion of an action*:账已经付～了。The bill has been paid. /吃～饭了吗? Have you had your lunch? /会已经开～了。The meeting is over. ❷ *used after a verb to indicate past action or experience*:组长说～,这事我们不要再争议了。The group leader told us not to argue about the matter any more. /他当～水手、教员和医生。He has been a sailor, a school-teacher and a doctor. /老人走南闯北,去～的地方很多。The old man travelled widely and visited many places.
see also Guō

过半 guòbàn more than half; over half:任务完成～。More than half of the work has been accomplished.
过半数 guò bànshù more than half; majority:本厂～的工人来自农村。The majority of the workers of this factory are from the countryside.
过磅 guòbàng weigh (on the scales):登机之前行李要～。The luggage must be weighed before boarding.
过饱 guòbǎo have a surfeit of food; overeat (oneself):我吃得～。I am much too full. *or* I've overeaten myself. *or* I've eaten more than my fill.
过饱和 guòbǎohé oversaturation; supersaturation:～溶液 supersaturated solution
过不去 guòbuqù ❶ cannot get through; be unable to get by; be impassable:前方正在修桥,车辆～。As the bridge ahead is under repair, vehicles can't get through. ❷ be hard on; make things difficult for; embarrass:他有意跟我～。He's deliberately making things difficult (*or* making it hot) for me. /你干吗跟他～呢? Why should you try to embarrass him? /别跟这个小孩～! Don't be hard on the boy! ❸ feel sorry:让他白跑一趟,我心里有点～。I'm sorry for having caused him to make a fruitless trip. /不要感到～嘛。Don't take it to heart.
过不着 guòbuzháo not hit it off (with); not be on intimate terms
过场 guòchǎng ❶ 〈戏曲〉 cross the stage ❷ 〈戏剧〉 interlude ❸ show a superficial observance of the rules; do sth. as a mere formality; go through the motions; act in mock seriousness:今天的征求意见只是走～而已。Today's solicitation of opinions was a mere formality (*or* was just for show).
过程 guòchéng course; process:制作～ process of manufacture /我们在执行～中对计划作了修改。We modified our plan in the process of carrying it out. /他们在讨论～中提出了许多重要意见。In the course of the discussion, they put forward a number of important views.
过程控制 guòchéng kòngzhì process control; process monitoring
过程增益 guòchéng zēngyì process gain
过秤 guòchèng weigh (on the steelyard or scale); take the weight of:～员 scalesman /行李还没有～。The luggage hasn't been weighed yet.
过从 guòcóng 〈书面〉 be in frequent contact; associate:两人～甚密。They are on close terms with each other.
过错 guòcuò fault; error:我不是因自身的～受到批评的。I took the blame for no fault of mine.
过当 guòdàng exceed the proper limits; be improper; be inappropriate:防卫～ exceed the proper limits of self-defence
过道 guòdào ❶ corridor ❷ passageway; passage; doorway; driveway
过得去 guòdequ ❶ be able to pass; can get through:前边有哨卡,我们～吗? There's a checkpoint ahead. Can we pass it? ❷ (of living conditions) not hard; passable:她的日子还～。She can get by (*or* manage). ❸ tolerable; Okay; not too bad:他的字还～。His handwriting is presentable. /他的嗓子还～。His voice is not too bad. /准备几个菜招待一下也就～了。It would be good enough to treat them to a few dishes. ❹ (often used in rhetorical questions) feel at ease: 叫大家等这么久,我心里怎么～呢? I am terribly sorry to have kept you all waiting for so long.
过得硬 guòdeyìng be truly proficient; have superb skill:他的医术真是～。His medical skill is superb. /他终于成了一名～的神枪手。He eventually became a marksman of unfailing accuracy (*or* a crack shot).
过得着 guòdezháo be on close terms (with); be familiar (with): 他俩～。The two of them hit it off well.
过电 guòdiàn electrify; get shocked (by electricity)
过电压 guòdiànyā 〈电工〉 overtension; overvoltage:～保护装置 overvoltage protection /～继电器 overvoltage relay
过电影 guò diànyǐng 〈比喻〉 go over past scenes in one's mind; recall; recollect; bring to mind:早上发生的事情在他脑海里一幕一幕～。He went over in his mind what happened this morning.

过冬 guòdōng pass the winter; winter:黑瞎子在哪儿～呢? Where does the black bear winter? /这些大雁要飞到温暖的地方去～。These wild geese are flying to a warmer climate for the winter. /妈妈给我缝制了～的棉衣。Mother has made warm winter clothes for me.

过冬作物 guòdōng zuòwù *also* "越冬作物" yuèdōng zuòwù winter crop; overwintering crop

过度 guòdù excessive; inordinate; undue; over-:饮酒～ drink to excess; take to excessive drinking /劳累～ be overworked; be fatigued /～开采 over-exploitation /～敏感 oversensitive; hypersensitive /酒色～ debauchery

过度杀伤 guòdù shāshāng 〈军事〉 overkill:核～力 overkill nuclear capability; nuclear overkill

过渡 guòdù transition; interim; stopgap:～措施 interim measure /～性贷款 stopgap loan /我把他看作～性人物。I regard him as a transitional figure.

过渡流 guòdùliú 〈航空〉 transition flow

过渡内阁 guòdù nèigé *also* "过渡政府" interim cabinet; caretaker cabinet or government

过渡时期 guòdù shíqī period of transition; transition; transitional period:这所学校目前处于领导班子新老交替的～。The school is in a transition period with the new leadership replacing the old.

过渡时期总路线 guòdù shíqī zǒnglùxiàn general line for the transition period (put forward by Mao Zedong in 1953, basically to accomplish China's industrialization and the socialist transformation of agriculture, handicrafts and capitalist industry and commerce over a fairly long period of time)

过渡性条文 guòdùxìng tiáowén transitional provision

过渡性元素 guòdùxìng yuánsù 〈化学〉 transition element

过端 guòduān (of the Shui Nationality 水族) New Year's Day (which falls late in the 8th month and lasts till early in the 10th month of the lunar year)

过耳之言 guò'ěrzhīyán hearsay; overheard remarks:～,不可听信。Words overheard are not to be trusted. *or* Hearsay is not reliable.

过伐 guòfá 〈林业〉 overcutting; excessive felling

过犯 guòfàn 〈方言〉 error; mistake

过房 guòfáng 〈方言〉 adopt a young relative; have one's child adopted by a relative

过访 guòfǎng 〈书面〉 make a visit; pay a call:有客～。We have a visitor.

过费 guòfèi 〈方言〉 go to undue expense; overspend:他因出差～而受到批评。He was criticized for his overspending while away on business.

过分 guòfèn going too far; excessive; undue; over-:这未免太～了。This is going too far. /～谦虚就近于虚伪了。Excessive modesty verges on hypocrisy. /这个问题你怎样强调都不算～。You cannot overemphasize the problem. /说他们在搞全球霸权主义一点也不～。It's no exaggeration to say that they are trying to establish global hegemony. /把这幅画说得一钱不值也未免太～了。I'm afraid it would be too sweeping to dismiss this picture as completely worthless.

过风儿 guòfēngr 〈口语〉 be ventilated; be draughty; have fresh air blowing in:这里～,坐在这儿凉快多了。It's much cooler to sit over here with fresh air coming in (*or* through).

过福 guòfú 〈方言〉 enjoy excessive ease and comfort; indulge in pleasures

过付 guòfù pay through a go-between; make business deals through a broker

过共晶合金 guògòngjīng héjīn 〈冶金〉 hyper-eutectic alloy

过共析钢 guògòngxīgāng 〈冶金〉 hyper-eutectoid steel

过关 guòguān ❶ cross a mountain pass:一～就可以看见我们村。Our village will come in sight as soon as you cross the mountain pass. ❷〈比喻〉pass a test; come through well; reach a standard:他想蒙混～。He tries to get by under false pretences. /我怕这次口试他难以～。I'm afraid he won't be able to pass the oral test. /质量不～。The quality is not up to standard.

过关思想 guòguān sīxiǎng attitude of trying just to get by or scrape through

过关斩将 guòguān-zhǎnjiàng get through the strategic passes by killing the garrison generals in battles — beat one's adversaries or opponents one by one; overcome one difficulty after another; win a series of matches, etc.

过过风儿 guòguofēngr 〈口语〉 take some fresh air; enjoy the cool:屋里闷热,出来～吧。It's too stuffy in the room. Come out for some fresh air.

过河拆桥 guòhé-chāiqiáo *also* "过河抽板" demolish the bridge as soon as the river's crossed; kick down the ladder; be ungrateful to one's benefactor:他们目的达到,要把我一脚踢开,这是～! Now that they have got what they want, they would kick me out without the least scruple!

过后 guòhòu afterwards; then; later on:这件事暂且这么决定,有什么问题～再议。We will make a temporary decision now and will take it up again afterwards if problems crop up. /贵宾们先参观故宫,～才去了天坛。The distinguished guests visited the Palace Museum and then went to the Temple of Heaven.

过户 guòhù 〈法律〉(of bonds, stocks, property, etc.) transfer of ownership from one person to another; change the name of the owner in a register:这辆小轿车已办理了～手续。The ownership of the car has been transferred.

过户代理机构 guòhù dàilǐ jīgòu transfer agent

过户税 guòhùshuì duties on transfers

过话 guòhuà 〈方言〉 ❶ exchange words; converse; talk with one another:我们不常见面,平时～不多。We see little of each other and seldom talk. ❷ send word; tell; pass on a message:请你替我过个话,明天我要去找他。Would you mind sending him word that I'll call on him tomorrow?

过活 guòhuó make a living; eke out a living:靠过去节省下来的钱～ live on the money saved in the past (*or* on one's savings) /他靠卖蔬菜～。He earned his living by selling vegetables.

过火 guòhuǒ go too far; go to extremes; overdo; go beyond the proper limit:～的行为 excesses /这事儿你做得有点儿～。You are carrying things a bit too far on this question. /这玩笑开得～了。This is going beyond a joke.

过激 guòjī exceedingly drastic; extremist; radical:～言论 radical (*or* extremist) remarks /～行动 excessive action

过激分子 guòjīfènzǐ extremist; radical

过继 guòjì (of a heirless person) adopt a young relative; have one's child adopted by a relative:他从小就～给二叔了。He was adopted by his second uncle while a child.

过家家儿 guò jiājiar *also* "过家景" (children's game) play house

过江之鲫 guòjiāngzhījì shoal of crucian carps crossing the river — numerous; a great deal; a great many

过奖 guòjiǎng 〈谦词〉overpraise; undeserved compliment; flatter:您～了。You flatter me. /～! ～! I feel flattered! *or* I wish I deserved your compliment. /承蒙～,当之有愧。Thank you for the compliment. But I really don't deserve it.

过街老鼠 guòjiē-lǎoshǔ rat crossing the street — person hated by everyone; much-hated person:他成了～,人人喊打。He became like a rat scurrying across a street, with everybody shouting, "Kill it!"

过街柳 guòjiēliǔ 〈植物〉 fontanesia (*Fontanesia fortunei*)

过街楼 guòjiēlóu overhead projection spanning a lane; overhead lane-spanning projection

过街天桥 guòjiē tiānqiáo *also* "过街桥" overhead pedestrian crossing; overpass

过节 guòjié ❶ celebrate a festival:今年他打算回南方～。He's going back to the south for the festival. ❷ festive occasion; festival:节前工作太多,那件事等～后再说。We are too busy before the festival and have to leave that matter till after it.

过节儿 guòjier 〈方言〉 ❶ rituals and formalities:他小心翼翼,生怕错了～。He is very careful not to act contrary to rituals and formalities. ❷ grudge; ill will; hard feelings:听说他们之间有点～。I hear there is a feeling of animosity between them. ❸ detail; trifle:故事中间的一些小～,我就不细说了。I'll omit some minute details of the story.

过劲 guòjìn ❶ go beyond or exceed the limit; overdo:他准饿～了。He must be much too hungry. /你说～了。You overstated the case. ❷〈方言〉(of capability, strength, etc.) great; strong; superb:这衣服缝制得真～,销路准好! These dresses are of excellent tailoring and will surely have a ready market!

过景 guòjǐng past (the time, etc.):赛车赛马是年轻人干的事,我早已过了景了。Car and horse races are for young people, and I'm too old for them.

过境 guòjìng cross the frontier; pass through the territory of a country; be in transit:～放牧 trans-frontier pasture /～耕种 trans-frontier cultivation /～自由 freedom of transit /促进铁路货运～的国

际公约 International Convention to Facilitate the Crossing of Frontiers for Goods Carried by Rail; TIF Convention (1952)

过境报关单 guòjìng bàoguāndān transit declaration

过境国 guòjìngguó transit country or state

过境贸易 guòjìng màoyì transit trade

过境签证 guòjìng qiānzhèng transit visa

过境权 guòjìngquán right of passage; right of transit

过境税 guòjìngshuì transit duty

过客 guòkè passing traveller; transient guest; sojourner:匆匆的～ guest arriving and leaving hastily; traveller coming and going hurriedly /政治舞台上匆匆来去的～ passing traveller in the political arena; transient politician

过来 guòlai come over; come up:车来了,赶快～吧。The car has arrived. Please come over, quick. /那边有个老太太～了。An old woman was coming up from there.

过来 guolai *used after a verb to give an additional meaning* ❶ (often used with 得 or 不)can manage; can handle; can deal with:这么多事,她一个人忙得～吗? There's so much to attend to; can she manage alone? /病人太多,医生照顾不～。There are too many patients for the doctor to take care of. ❷ towards;over; up; in:一个老人正朝我走～。An old man is coming towards me. /捷报从四面八方飞～。News of victory came in thick and fast from all quarters. ❸ turn round; go round:他转过身来对我说话。He turned round and spoke to me. /李明转过脸来,我才认出是他。Only when Li Ming turned back his head did I recognize him. ❹ come round; come to:把坏习惯改～ get rid of one's bad habit /医生把他救～了。The doctor brought him back to life. /她昏迷很久,终于苏醒了～。She finally came round from a long coma. /他真固执,简直劝不～。He is stubborn as a mule, and no amount of persuasion can bring him around.

过来人 guòlairén person who has had the experience; old hand:要知水深浅,须问～。He knows the water best who has waded through it. /我是～,对此事的重要性深有体会。As a person who has gone through it, I fully understand the importance of this matter. /你是～,当然明白其中的道理。As an experienced person, you ought to know why.

过礼 guòlǐ ❶〈旧语〉deliver betrothal gifts from the groom's family to the bride's ❷ pay respects to; greet:几个学生一一上前向老师～。The several students paid their respects in person to their teacher one by one.

过梁 guòliáng 〈建筑〉lintel

过量 guòliàng excessive; over; immoderate:烟酒～ drink and smoke to excess /安眠药千万不可服用～。Never take an overdose of sleeping pills.

过磷酸铵 guòlínsuān'ǎn 〈化学〉ammonium superphosphate

过磷酸钙 guòlínsuāngài 〈化学〉calcium superphosphate

过磷酸盐 guòlínsuānyán 〈化学〉superphosphate

过淋 guòlìn filter; filtrate:把煎好的中药～一下。Please filtrate the decocted medicinal herbs.

过硫化物 guòliúhuàwù 〈化学〉persulfide

过硫酸 guòliúsuān 〈化学〉persulfuric acid:～钾 potassium persulfate; potassium peroxydisulfate /～钠 sodium persulfate; potassium peroxydisulfate /～盐 persulfate

过录 guòlù copy from one notebook or account to another

过路 guòlù pass by on one's way:～人 passer-by /我是～的,口渴了,讨碗水喝。I am just passing by here and dying of thirst. Can you kindly give me some water?

过路财神 guòlù-cáishén temporary god of wealth; one who handles large sums of money for a short time:别看他手里钞票多,他不过是个～罢了。Despite the large sums of money he handles, he is only a vicarious Croesus.

过路黄 guòlùhuáng *also* "金钱草" jīnqiáncǎo 〈植物〉*Lysimachia christinae*

过虑 guòlǜ be over-anxious; worry unnecessarily:有我在,不必～。With me standing by, you have no cause for worry. /儿女都已长大成人,他们的事我们不要～。Now that the children have all come of age, there's no need for us to be over-anxious about them.

过氯化物 guòlǜhuàwù 〈化学〉perchlorhydria

过氯酸 guòlǜsuān 〈化学〉perchloric acid:～盐 perchlorate

过滤 guòlǜ filter; filtrate:～器 filter; filtrator /～设备 filter plant /～材料 filter material

过滤嘴 guòlǜzuǐ filter tip:～香烟 filter-tipped cigarette /超长～香烟 king size filter-tipped cigarette

过卖 guòmài 〈旧语〉(of a restaurant, teahouse, etc.) waiter; waitress; boy

过门 guòmén (of a girl) move into the husband's house upon marriage; marry:她十八岁～,刚二十岁就守寡了。She got married at the age of eighteen and became widowed at twenty.

过门儿 guòménr 〈音乐〉opening bars; short prelude or interlude

过敏 guòmǐn ❶〈医学〉allergy:青霉素～ be allergic to penicillin /药物引起的～ drug-caused allergy /嗅觉～ hyperosmia /触觉～ hyperpselaphesia /听觉～ hyperacusis /痛觉～ hyperalgesia ❷ over-sensitive:别神经～! Don't be hypersensitive!

过敏反应 guòmǐn fǎnyìng *also* "过敏性反应"〈医学〉anaphylaxis; anaphylactic reaction

过敏性 guòmǐnxìng sensitivity; anaphylaxis; hypersensitivity; hypersusceptibility

过敏性鼻炎 guòmǐnxìng bíyán 〈医学〉allergic rhinitis; anaphylactic rhinitis

过敏性皮炎 guòmǐnxìng píyán 〈医学〉allergic dermatitis

过敏性休克 guòmǐnxìng xiūkè 〈医学〉anaphylactic shock; allergic shock

过敏原 guòmǐnyuán 〈医学〉anaphylactogen; sensitinogen

过目 guòmù look over (papers, draft documents, etc.) so as to approve; glance through or over; check:这里有一份备忘录,请～。Here's a memo for you. /名单等总经理～后即可宣布。The name-list shall be announced after being approved by the general manager.

过目不忘 guòmù-bùwàng not forget after reading sth. just once; be gifted with a very retentive memory:她～,记性特好。She has an excellent memory, she only needs one reading to learn something by heart.

过目成诵 guòmù-chéngsòng be able to recite after reading it once; memorize a passage with one reading; have a photographic memory

过年 guònián celebrate or spend the New Year:王小二～,一年不如一年。Things get worse with each passing year. *or* Things go from bad to worse. /年前太忙,～后再说吧。My hands are full with the approaching of the New Year. Let's talk about the matter after it.

过年 guònian 〈口语〉next year:我儿子～该大学毕业了。My son is going to graduate from university next year.

过硼酸 guòpéngsuān perboric acid:～盐 perborate

过期 guòqī exceed the time limit; be overdue; pass the deadline; expire:～作废 invalid after the expiry date /～胶卷 expired film /～票据 overdue bill /～支票 stale (*or* expired) cheque /～杂志 back numbers of a magazine /你借的书已～了。The book you borrowed is overdue for return. *or* your book is overdue. /这个干部一脑子"有权不用,～作废"的思想。He is a functionary who makes the most of his power while in office.

过谦 guòqiān too modest:您太～了。You are really too modest.

过钱 guòqián 〈方言〉pay or take the bill; pay

过桥米线 guòqiáo mǐxiàn rice-flour noodles *à la* Yunnan

过去 guòqù past; former; previous; bygones:～的安排 previous arrangement /请不要再提～。Let's forget about the past. *or* Let the dead bury the dead. /～的事就让它过去吧。Let bygones be bygones. /这个地区～很穷。This used to be a poverty-stricken area. /她英语讲得比～好多了。She speaks much better English than before.

过去 guòqu ❶ go over; pass by:他～把她叫醒。He walked over to wake her up. /我～看一看。Let me go over and have a look. /刚才～两辆公共汽车。Two buses went by just now. ❷〈婉词〉pass away; die:祖父昨天～了。Grandpa passed away yesterday. /人都～了,光哭管啥用呢? Now that he is dead, what's the use of weeping?

过去 guoqu ❶ *used after a verb to indicate motion away from the speaker*:把书给他扔～。Toss the book over to him. /警察沿马路向劫匪追了～。The policemen pursued the robbers down the street. ❷ *used after a verb to indicate turning the other side to the speaker*:她转过身去哭泣。She turned away and wept. /她把纸袋翻了～。She turned the paper-bag inside out. /请转～,我要看看另一面。Please turn it round so that I may see the reverse side. ❸ *used after a verb to indicate loss of normalcy or of original state*:她晕～了。She fainted. /他已昏迷～十分钟了。He's been in a coma for ten minutes. ❹ *used after a verb to indicate success of the action*:挤～ push one's way through; squeeze in /大家对他了如指掌,他是混不～的。People know him only too well to be fooled (*or* confused) by him. ❺ *used after an adjective plus* 得 *or* 不 *to indicate superiority or*

G

inferiority:鸡蛋还能硬得过石头去? How can you expect an egg to be harder than a rock? /这天再冷,也冷不过三九天去。Cold as the day was, it could not be colder than the third nine-day period after the winter solstice (*or* the coldest days in winter).

过儿 guòr 〈方言〉times:这电影我已看了三~了。I've seen the film three times.

过热 guòrè ❶ overheated:经济发展~ overheated economic growth /那几个城市里股票炒得~。There has been wild speculation in stocks in those cities. ❷〈物理〉superheat; overheat; overtemperature:~器 overheater

过人 guòrén ❶ outstanding; excellent:~的记忆力 remarkable memory /精力~ extraordinarily energetic /勇气~ excel in valour /这孩子聪明~。The boy is unusually intelligent. ❷ (of sports) get past; get round:带球~ break through; dribble past an opponent

过日子 guò rìzi pass one's life; live; get along:不会~ not know how to lead a frugal life /小两口挺会~。The young couple are good at housekeeping. /全村三百户人家已经过上了小康日子。All the 300 households in the village have been living in moderate comfort.

过筛子 guò shāizi ❶ sift; sieve; sift out:小麦磨成粉后要~,去掉麸皮,才能成为面粉。The flour is sifted from the bran after the wheat is ground. ❷ carefully select; go over carefully; scan:先把问题过一下筛子,看哪个最重要。Let's go over the questions first, and see which one is the most important.

过山车 guòshānchē roller coaster (in an amusement park)

过山蕨 guòshānjué 〈植物〉walking fern

过山龙 guòshānlóng (common name for 虹吸管) syphon

过山炮 guòshānpào 〈旧语〉mountain gun or artillery

过山跳 guòshāntiào 〈旧语〉long gangplank (from a ship to a coal heap on the dock)

过山瑶 guòshānyáo 〈旧语〉ethnic Yao vagrant

过晌 guòshǎng 〈方言〉afternoon; after 12 a.m.:快~了,怎么还不送饭来? It's after twelve o'clock already. Why haven't they sent the lunch yet?

过身 guòshēn 〈方言〉❶ pass (by); go by; go through:你回来打这里~的时候,到我这里来一下。Please drop in when you pass here on your way back. ❷ die; pass away:父母~后,他离开了北京。He left Beijing after his parents died.

过甚 guòshèn exaggerate; overstate; overdo:言之~ exaggerate (sth.); blow (sth.) up /~其词 overstate a case; give an exaggerated account; stretch the truth

过生日 guò shēngri celebrate one's birthday; hold birthday celebrations

过剩 guòshèng ❶ excess:人口~ overpopulation /精力~ excessively energetic ❷ surplus:资本~ surplus of capital /商品~ glut of goods /劳动力~ oversupply of labour /~农产品 surplus agricultural products /~商品 surplus goods (*or* commodities)

过失 guòshī fault; error; blunder; negligence:偶然~ accidental mistake /这次失败全是你的~造成的。It was all your fault that we failed this time.

过失犯罪 guòshī fànzuì *also* "过失性犯罪" negligent offence; criminal negligence; unpremeditated crime

过失杀人 guòshī shārén involuntary homicide; manslaughter

过失伤害 guòshī shānghài corporal wound by mistake; negligent injury

过失行为 guòshī xíngwéi act of negligence; negligent act

过失责任 guòshī zérèn liability for fault; neglect of duty

过时 guòshí ❶ out-of-date; outdated; outmoded; obsolete; out of fashion:~的机器 outmoded machine /~的观点 obsolete views /衣服式样早已~了。These dresses have long been out of fashion. /这种观念早已~,没有人理会它了。These ideas are completely out-of-date and nobody takes them seriously now. ❷ past the appointed time

过时不候 guòshí-bùhòu no waiting after the set time:我们五点半走,~。We will leave punctually at 5:30 and won't wait.

过时效 guòshíxiào 〈冶金〉overaging

过世 guòshì die; pass away

过事 guòshì ❶〈书面〉error; mistake ❷〈书面〉overact; overdo:~张扬 publicize out of all proportion; ballyhoo ❸〈方言〉marry; wed:当初他们过了事才半个月,丈夫就参了军。Her husband joined the army after they were married for only half a month.

过手 guòshǒu take in and give out (money, etc.); receive and distribute; handle; manage:银钱~,当面点清。Count the money on the spot. /经他~的案子少说也有百余件,还没听说弄错过。He's handled at least over one hundred cases without making a single mistake, so far as I know.

过寿 guòshòu 〈方言〉celebrate one's birthday

过熟 guòshú ❶〈植物〉overmature; overripe:~蔬菜 overripe vegetable ❷〈化工〉overcure:~化 overcuring

过熟林 guòshúlín 〈林业〉overmature forest; old stand

过熟木 guòshúmù overmature timber

过数 guòshù count:这是两千元钱,请你过个数儿。Here's 2,000 *yuan*; please count it.

过水面 guòshuǐmiàn water cooled noodles

过税 guòshuì ❶〈方言〉pay tax ❷〈旧语〉transit tax

过宿 guòsù spend the night; pass the night; put up for the night:昨晚他在外边~了。He spent the night away from home yesterday.

过酸 guòsuān 〈化学〉peracid:~酯 perester

过堂 guòtáng 〈旧语〉appear in court to be tried; be tried; be interrogated:她又被带去~。She was tried again in court. /两天中他过了三次堂。He was interrogated three times within two days.

过堂风 guòtángfēng draught:你坐在~里,要着凉的。You're sitting in the draught. I'm afraid you'll catch cold.

过天 guòtiān 〈方言〉some other day:今天太忙,~再谈吧! I have a very busy schedule today. Let's talk about it some other time.

过厅 guòtīng hallway; lobby

过头 guòtóu ❶ go beyond the limit; exceed:这个月费用太大,开支~了。We overspent our income this month. /花消~要倒霉的。One will come to grief if one spends beyond one's means. ❷ overdo; over-:表演~ overact (in a play or film, etc.) /反应~ overreact /聪明~ be too clever by half /肉煮~了。The meat is overdone. /他也许说了~话。Perhaps he overstated the case.

过屠门而大嚼 guò túmén ér dàjué start munching when passing the butcher's — feed oneself on illusions; hanker for things one cannot get:~,虽不得肉,亦且快意。Illusions may give one pleasure, though nothing in substance.

过往 guòwǎng ❶ come and go; pass:~车辆 passing vehicles; vehicular traffic /~行人 pedestrians; pedestrian traffic ❷ have friendly contact with; associate with:他们是邻居,~甚密。They are neighbours and are on very close terms.

过望 guòwàng more than expected; beyond one's expectation:大喜~ be delighted that things have turned out better than expected; be overjoyed

过为已甚 guòwéi-yǐshèn overdo; overstep the limits:~就会失去人心。If you overdo it, you will lose popular support.

过问 guòwèn concern oneself with; take an interest in; bother about:省长亲自~救灾的事。The governor attended to the work of disaster relief personally. /此事长期无人~。This has been left neglected for a long time. /此事与你无关,你就别~了。It has nothing to do with you. Just ignore it. /这是他的私事,我不打算~。This is his private affair. I am not going to poke my nose into it.

过午 guòwǔ afternoon:她上午不在家,请你~再打电话吧。She is not at home in the morning. Could you ring up again this afternoon?

过五关,斩六将 guò wǔ guān, zhǎn liù jiàng (said of Guan Yu 关羽, a famous general in the Three Kingdoms Period) force five passes and slay six generals — surmount numerous difficulties or obstacles; perform a whole series of heroic exploits or feats of bravery

过误 guòwù mistake; fault; error:我这一年工作中~不少。I've made quite a few mistakes in my work this year.

过细 guòxì meticulous; careful:工作要~ must work with meticulous care /做~的思想工作 do painstaking ideological work (*or* work of persuasion)

过夏 guòxià spend the summer; stay away from the summer heat:他今年到青岛去~。He will go to Qingdao this summer to stay away from the heat.

过小年 guò xiǎonián Minor New Year Celebration, a festival of Gelao nationality in Guizhou Province on the 6th day of the 7th lunar month

过心 guòxīn 〈方言〉❶ suspicious:我是随便说的,谁知她就~了。I mentioned it casually, unaware that she was so suspicious. ❷ be on close terms with:在车间里,就数她俩最~。The two of them are bosom friends in the workshop. /今儿我跟你说点儿~话。I'd like to confide something to you today.

过眼 guòyǎn *also* "过目" read; look over; glance through or over

过眼云烟 guòyǎn-yúnyān as transient as a fleeting cloud; like a

puff of smoke; ephemeral:这一切都将如～,顷刻间化为乌有。All this will vanish like a fleeting cloud. /论起荣华富贵,原不过是～。Fame and wealth are just a flash in the pan.

过氧化氢 guòyǎnghuàqīng 〈化学〉hydrogen peroxide; perhydrol

过氧化物 guòyǎnghuàwù 〈化学〉peroxide

过夜 guòyè ❶ pass the night; put up for the night; stay overnight:昨晚他在朋友家～。He spent the night at a friend's yesterday. ❷ of the previous evening or night:～茶 tea made the previous evening /～菜要热一下再吃。Warm up last night's leftovers before eating them.

过一天,算一天 guò yī tiān, suàn yī tiān muddle along with no thought of tomorrow; while away the time

过意不去 guòyìbùqù *also* "不过意" feel guilty; feel sorry; feel apologetic:这事给您添了不少麻烦,真～。I'm very sorry to have put you to so much inconvenience. *or* I feel rather guilty about having caused you so much trouble.

过阴 guòyīn 〈迷信〉(of a sorceress) act as if possessed by a ghost and able to communicate with the nether world

过瘾 guòyǐn satisfy an urge; enjoy oneself to the full; do sth. to one's heart's content; have a good time:今天晚上玩得真～。We had a wonderful time tonight. /我要抽支雪茄过过瘾。I want to smoke a cigar to satisfy my craving (*or* urge).

过硬 guòyìng be a past master; have a perfect command (of sth.); be really up to the mark; be truly proficient (in sth.):过得硬 be well up to the standard; be able to stand all tests /苦练一身～本领 strive to master true skills through hard practice; practise hard to master true skills /他的操作技术还远不是～的。His operational skill is still far from perfect.

过犹不及 guòyóubùjí going too far is as bad as not going far enough; going beyond is as wrong as falling short; too much is as bad as too little:～,过于苛责也不见得好。Excess is just as bad as deficiency. Too much excoriation is not a good thing.

过于 guòyú too; unduly; over; excessively:～迁就 too accommodating; overlenient /～着急 over-anxious /～啰嗦 too long-winded; over-elaborate

过鱼孔 guòyúkǒng fish pass; fish way

过誉 guòyù 〈谦词〉overpraise; undeserved compliment:承蒙～,不胜感激。I am very grateful to you for the praise you have lavished on me. /我实在并未作出什么成绩,您对我太～了。I really haven't done much and don't deserve your compliment. /您如此～,倒叫我不好意思了。Your overpraise made me feel guilty.

过逾 guòyu excessive; too much:饮酒～,有伤身体。Excessive drinking (*or* Too much drinking) is harmful. /小心没～。You can't be too careful.

过云雨 guòyúnyǔ passing shower

过载 guòzài ❶ overload:～电流 overload current; overcurrent /～容量 overload capacity /～特性 overload characteristic /～系数 overload factor /～装置 overload device /这车白菜～,千万注意不要开太快了。As the truck is overloaded with vegetables, you must take care not to drive too fast. ❷ transship

过载失真 guòzài shīzhēn 〈通信〉blasting

过儎 guòzài *see* "过载❷"

过早搏动 guòzǎo bódòng *also* "早搏" zǎobó 〈医学〉premature beat

过则勿惮改 guò zé wù dàn gǎi if you have faults, do not fear to correct them; know your wrongs and amend them with a good grace

过账 guòzhàng 〈会计〉transfer items (as from a daybook to a ledger); post

过重 guòzhòng (of luggage, letters, etc.) overweight:～加费 overweight charge /行李～ overweight luggage

G

H

hā

哈[1] hā ❶ breathe out (with the mouth open); blow one's breath:～了一口气 breathe out a breath /先往镜子上～几口气再擦。Breathe on the mirror before you wipe it. ❷〈象声〉*usu. reduplicated and used to describe laughter*:～～大笑 roar with laughter; laugh heartily /引得大家～～大笑 draw peals of laughter from everybody ❸〈叹词〉*usu. reduplicated and used to indicate complacency or satisfaction*:～～,我说对了。Aha, so I was right. /～,球进了! Aha, it's in! *or* Aha, he's scored a goal!

哈[2]**(鰕)** hā *see* "哈腰"
see also hǎ; hà

哈巴罗夫斯克 Hābāluófūsīkè *also* "伯力" Bólì Khabarovsk, Russian city on the Amur or Heilongjiang River
哈定 Hādìng Warren Gamaliel Harding (1865-1923), 29th president of the United States (1921-1923)
哈尔滨 Hā'ěrbīn Harbin, capital of Heilongjiang Province
哈佛大学 Hāfó Dàxué Harvard University, oldest American university founded in 1636 at Cambridge, Massachusetts and named after English settler and donor John Harvard (1607-1638)
哈哈镜 hāhājìng distorting mirror
哈哈 hāha (usu. used in the phrase 打哈哈) ❶ make fun of; tease:这个人总是爱打～。The guy is always cracking jokes. /你可别拿我打～。Don't you tease me! ❷ laugh perfunctorily:我跟你说正事,打什么～? I'm talking about a serious matter. Don't you try to laugh it off.
哈哈儿 hāhar 〈方言〉sth. funny; ridiculous matter; joke:别让人家瞧～。Don't make yourself a laughing stock. *or* Don't make a fool of yourself. /这里头～可大着呢! There's much in it that is ridiculous! *or* You just can't imagine what a joke this is!
哈吉 hājí 〈伊斯兰〉*haji* (title of honour for a Muslim who has made a pilgrimage to Mecca)
哈拉雷 Hālāléi Harare, capital of Zimbabwe
哈喇子 hālázi 〈方言〉dribble; drivel; drool:流～ slobber; dribble/馋得他直流～。The food was so tantalizing (*or* tempting) as to make his mouth water.
哈喇 hāla ❶ rancid:这黄油一股～味儿。The butter smells rancid. ❷ (often used in the early vernacular) kill; put to death:把他～了 kill him; have him killed
哈雷彗星 Hāléi Huìxīng 〈天文〉Halley's Comet; the Halley Comet, named after English astronomer Edmond Halley (1656-1742)
哈里发 hālǐfā ❶〈伊斯兰〉caliph; calif; kalif; khalif (chief Muslim civil and religious ruler, regarded as successor of Muhammad) ❷ Chinese Muslim title for those studying Islamic scriptures at a mosque
哈密 Hāmì Kumul or Hami, city in the east of the Xinjiang Uygur Autonomous Region
哈密瓜 hāmìguā Hami melon (a variety of muskmelon produced in Hami)
哈乃斐派 Hānǎifěipài 〈伊斯兰〉Hanafite school
哈尼族 Hānízú Hani nationality, one of the Chinese minority nationalities living in Yunnan Province; Hanis
哈气 hāqì ❶ breathe out (with the mouth open); gasp; pant:累得他直～。He was breathing hard (*or* panting) after heavy labour. ❷ breath (through the open mouth):我感觉到了他的～。I can feel his breath. ❸ steam that forms on a window, etc.:窗子上全都是～,我什么也看不见。I can't see through the window, for it's covered with steam.
哈欠 hāqian yawn:打～ give a yawn; yawn /他一面打～一面伸懒腰。He stretched himself with a yawn. /一人打～,人人都跟着打～。Yawns are catching.
哈萨克斯坦 Hāsàkèsītǎn Kazakhstan:～人 Kazakh /～语 Kazakh (language)
哈萨克族 Hāsàkèzú Kazak nationality (one of China's minority nationalities distributed over Xinjiang, Gansu and Qinghai)
哈失 hāshi 〈方言〉*see* "哈欠"
哈瓦那 Hāwǎnà Havana, capital of Cuba:～雪茄 Havana (cigar)
哈腰 hāyāo ❶ bend one's back; stoop:他腰扭了,没法～。He cannot bend over, as he has strained his back. /那门洞儿要哈着腰才能进去。You have to stoop to go through the door. ❷ bow slightly (as a form of greeting):点头～ bow unctuously; bow and scrape /见到领导,他总要曲背～地打招呼。He always greets his superior with a deferential bow.

铪 hā 〈化学〉hafnium (Hf):～板 hafnium plate /～锭 hafnium ingot
铪锆石 hāgàoshí hafnian zircon

há

虾(蝦) há
see also xiā
虾蟆 háma *see* "蛤蟆" háma

蛤 há clam:～壳 clamshell
see also gé
蛤庑 háhù clamshell bucket
蛤蟆 háma *also* "虾蟆" háma ❶ frog ❷ toad
蛤蟆夯 hámahāng frog rammer, a kind of power-driven walking rammer or tamper
蛤蟆镜 hámajìng frog sun glasses
蛤耙 hápá clam rake
蛤耙网 hápáwǎng clam dredge

hǎ

哈 hǎ ❶〈方言〉scold:妈妈～了他们一顿。Mother gave them a good scolding. ❷ (Hǎ) a surname
see also hā; hà
哈巴狗 hǎbagǒu ❶ *also* "狮子狗" shīzigǒu; "巴儿狗" bārgǒu Pekinese (a breed of pet dog) ❷ toady; sycophant
哈达 hǎdá *hada*, long piece of silk used as greeting gift among Tibetan and Mongolian nationalities:献～ present a *hada*

hà

哈 hà
see also hā; hǎ

H

哈巴 hàba 〈方言〉bend one's knees outward while walking
哈撒 hàsa 〈方言〉shake; sway; rock: 这个小伙子坐没坐样，老～椅子。The young man has got no manners, rocking back and forth in his chair all the time.
哈什蚂 hàshimǎ Chinese forest frog (*Rana temporaria chensinensis*)
哈什蚂油 hàshimǎyóu 〈中药〉dried oviduct fat of the forest frog

hāi

嗨 hāi
嗨嗨调 hāihāidiào (usu. called 耍孩儿) local opera popular in northern Shanxi and Inner Mongolia
嗨哟 hāiyō 〈叹词〉heave ho; yo-heave-ho; yo-ho

咳 hāi 〈叹词〉*used to express sorrow, regret, surprise, etc.*: ～，他怎么病成这个样子？Good heavens! How sick he is! /～，我怎么忘得一干二净！Dammit! How could I have forgotten all about it! /～，真有这么巧的事儿！My, what a coincidence!
see also ké
咳咳腔 hāihāiqiāng (usu. called 耍孩儿) local opera popular in northern Shanxi and Inner Mongolia
咳声叹气 hāishēng-tànqì *also* "唉声叹气" āishēng-tànqì heave deep sighs; moan and groan: 为妻子的病他成天～的。He sighs all the time over his wife's illness.

咍 hāi 〈书面〉❶ laugh at; ridicule: 为众人所～ lay oneself open to ridicule ❷ laugh happily; rejoice ❸ *see* "咳" hāi

hái

骸 hái ❶ bones of the body; skeleton: 尸～ dead body /残～ remains; wreckage /四肢百～ all the limbs and bones ❷ body: 形～ human body /病～ ailing body /遗～ (dead) body; corpse; remains
骸骨 háigǔ human bones (usu. of the dead); skeleton

孩 hái child: 小～儿 child; kid /小女～儿 little girl /她生了一个男～儿。She gave birth to a boy.
孩儿 hái'ér child (usu. used in the early vernacular by parents in addressing their children or by children in reference to themselves when talking to their parents)
孩儿参 hái'érshēn *also* "太子参" tàizǐshēn 〈中药〉caryophyllaceous ginseng (*Pseudostellaria heterophylla*)
孩提 háití 〈书面〉early childhood; infancy: ～时代 early childhood
孩童 háitóng child: 一群～在玩耍。A group of children are playing.
孩子 háizi ❶ child: 男～ boy /女～ girl ❷ son or daughter; child: 他俩有一个女～。The couple has a daughter. /～离开娘，瓜儿离开秧。When a child leaves its mother, it is like a melon torn off the vine.
孩子话 háizihuà silly childish talk; baby talk
孩子气 háiziqì childishness: 他不小了，但一脸的～。He looks childish for his age. /别这么～。Don't be so childish.
孩子头 háizitóu ❶ adult who likes to play with children ❷ leader of a group of children ❸ (often used in a jocular or derogatory way) primary school or kindergarten teacher

还(還) hái ❶ still; yet; nevertheless: ～来得及。There's still time. /飞机～没起飞。The plane has not yet taken off. ❷ even more; still more: 他弟弟比他～要高。His brother is even taller than he is. /今天比昨天～暖和。It is even warmer today than yesterday. ❸ also; too; as well; in addition: 我们不但参观了水族馆，～乘船游了海湾。We not only visited the aquarium, but also went on a pleasure cruise in the bay. /光说不行，～得干。Words must be matched by deeds. ❹ passably; fairly; rather: 他歌唱得～可以。He sings fairly well. /公园不大，树木倒～茂密。The park is small but well-wooded. ❺ (used in the first half of a sentence to set off the inference or extrapolation contained in the second half) even: 老师～听不懂，何况我们呢？Even our teacher cannot understand it, how can we? ❻ *used for emphasis*: 他～真有办法。He is really resourceful. *or* How resourceful he is! /～不快来吃饭！Hurry up! You don't want to miss your dinner, do you? /这～假得了！It can't be a fake! *or* There isn't the slightest doubt that it's true (*or* genuine). ❼ *used to indicate that sth. quite unexpected has happened*: 下这么大雪，你～骑车来了。We did not expect that you would come by bike in such heavy snow. ❽ as early as: ～在几年以前，我们就研究过这个方案。We discussed the plan several years ago.
see also huán
还好 háihǎo ❶ not bad; passable: "你今天考得怎么样?" "～。" "How did you do in today's exam?" "Not so bad." ❷ fortunately: ～，飞机安全着陆了。Fortunately, the plane touched down safely. /～，他们都及时赶到了火车站。They were all lucky enough to get to the train station in time.
还是 háishi ❶ still; yet; nevertheless; all the same: 他失败多次，不过最后～成功了。Though he failed time and again, nevertheless, he succeeded in the end. /我怕去不了，但～要谢谢你邀请我。I'm afraid I won't be able to make it, but thank you all the same for the invitation. ❷ unexpectedly; beyond expectation: 我没想到他这个人～真难对付。I didn't expect him to be so difficult. /那项议案～真通过了！That proposal was adopted after all! ❸ had better: 你～亲自去一趟好。You'd better go there in person. ❹ 〈连词〉or: 你同意～不同意？Do you agree to it or not? /我们上午去，～下午去？Shall we go in the morning or in the afternoon? /不管刮风～下雨，咱们不见不散。Rain or shine, we will not fail to meet at the appointed place.

hǎi

海 hǎi ❶ sea; lake: 出～ put out to sea /公～ high seas /领～ territorial waters (*or* sea) /内～ inland sea /南～ South China Sea /乌梁素～ Wuliangsu Lake (in Inner Mongolia) /北～ Beihai Lake (in Beijing) /～阔凭鱼跃，天高任鸟飞。The sea's vastness allows the fish to leap; the sky's loftiness lets the birds fly. ❷ great number of people or things coming together; expanse; sea: 人～ sea of people; human sea; crowds of people /林～ vast stretch (*or* expanse) of forest /火～ sea of fire /血～ sea of blood; bloodbath /苦～ sea of bitterness; abyss of misery /红旗如～ sea of red flags ❸ extra large; of great capacity; immense: *see* "～碗" ❹ 〈旧语〉(used to indicate the origin of certain plants, etc.) from overseas; foreign: *see* "～棠"; "～枣" ❺ 〈方言〉(usu. followed by 了, 啦, etc.) numerous; countless: 看世界杯足球赛的人可～了去啦。Countless people watched the World Cup (soccer) games. ❻ 〈方言〉at random; aimlessly; everywhere: 她丢了钥匙，～找。She lost her key and has been looking for it everywhere. ❼ 〈方言〉with no limit or restraint: ～吃～喝 eat and drink to one's heart's content ❽ (Hǎi) a surname
海岸 hǎi'àn seacoast; coast; seashore: ～图 coast chart; coast map /～工事 coastal fortifications /～沉积 coast deposit /～地貌 coastal landform; coastal features /～地衣 marine lichen /～林 littoral forest /～外有无数的岛屿。There are numerous islands off the coast.
海岸带 hǎi'àndài coastal zone
海岸警备队 Hǎi'àn Jǐngbèiduì *also* "海岸警卫队" (US) Coast Guard
海岸炮 hǎi'ànpào coast gun: ～兵 coast (*or* seacoast) artillery /～台 coast battery
海岸平原 hǎi'àn píngyuán coastal plain
海岸松 hǎi'ànsōng 〈植物〉maritime pine (*Pinus maritima*)
海岸线 hǎi'ànxiàn coastline: 曲折的～ rugged coastline
海鳌虾 hǎi'áoxiā *also* "龙虾" lóngxiā lobster
海拔 hǎibá *also* "拔海" height above sea level; elevation: ～三千米 3,000 metres above sea level; with an elevation of 3,000 metres /～高度 altitude
海白菜 hǎibáicài *also* "石莼" shíchún sea lettuce
海百合 hǎibǎihé *also* "五角百合" wǔjiǎo bǎihé; "鸡足" jīzú 〈动物〉sea lily; crinoid
海报 hǎibào playbill; notice: 电影～ film (*or* movie) bill /篮球赛～ notice for a basketball match /出～ put up a playbill (for a performance); put up a notice (for a lecture)
海豹 hǎibào seal: ～繁殖场 seal rookery /～皮 sealskin; seal /～捕猎 sealing
海贝壳 hǎibèiké seashell
海笔 hǎibǐ *see* "海鳃"
海标 hǎibiāo seamark; navigation beacon

H

海滨 hǎibīn seashore; seaside: ～城市 seaside city / ～胜地 seaside resort / ～带 shore zone / ～浴场 bathing beach / ～盐沼 marine salina / ～木本群落 littoral woodland / 去～避暑 go to the beach for the summer
海冰 hǎibīng sea ice
海波 hǎibō (common name for 大苏打) 〈化学〉 hyposulfite; hypo
海捕 hǎibǔ 〈旧语〉 issue a warrant to arrest a criminal at large: ～文书 official warrant to arrest a criminal at large
海不扬波 hǎibùyángbō the sea is calm — there is peace in the country: 天下太平, ～。The whole country is at peace.
海部俊树 Hǎibùjùnshù Kaifu Toshiki (1931-), Japanese Prime Minister (1989-1991)
海菜 hǎicài edible seaweed
海槽 hǎicáo oceanic trough
海草 hǎicǎo seaweed
海产 hǎichǎn ❶ marine products ❷ obtained from or produced in the sea: ～植物 marine plant / ～皮革 marine leather; sea leather
海昌蓝 hǎichānglán 〈纺织〉 hydron blue
海潮 hǎicháo (sea) tide
海成湖 hǎichénghú marine lake
海程 hǎichéng distance travelled by sea; voyage: 再有半天的～, 我们就可到达目的地了。Half a day's voyage more and we'll arrive at our destination.
海船 hǎichuán seagoing vessel or ship; oceanliner
海床 hǎichuáng seabed: ～区域 seabed area
海葱 hǎicōng sea onion (*Urginea*)
海错 hǎicuò 〈书面〉 marine products; choice seafood: 山珍～ delicacies from mountains and seas; rare dainties of every kind
海带 hǎidài 〈植物〉 kelp
海胆 hǎidǎn 〈动物〉 sea urchin
海岛 hǎidǎo island (in the sea): ～居民 islander
海岛棉 hǎidǎomián (sea) island cotton (*Gossypium barbadense*)
海盗 hǎidào pirate; sea rover: ～行为 piracy / ～活动猖獗的海峡 strait infested with pirates
海盗船 hǎidàochuán pirate ship; sea rover
海盗旗 hǎidàoqí Jolly Roger; skull-and-crossbones
海盗时代 hǎidào shídài 〈历史〉 Viking period (5th-10th centuries)
海道 hǎidào sea lane
海堤 hǎidī sea wall; sea embankment
海底 hǎidǐ bottom of the sea; seabed; sea floor: ～地形 sea floor relief; submarine morphology / ～矿 submarine mine
海底采矿 hǎidǐ cǎikuàng submarine mining; undersea mining; offshore mining
海底电报 hǎidǐ diànbào submarine telegraph; cablegram
海底电缆 hǎidǐ diànlǎn submarine cable
海底断裂带 hǎidǐ duànlièdài submarine fracture zone
海底反射声纳 hǎidǐ fǎnshè shēngnà bottom bounce sonar
海底高原 hǎidǐ gāoyuán oceanic plateau
海底火山 hǎidǐ huǒshān submarine volcano
海底勘察 hǎidǐ kānchá submarine exploration
海底扩展说 hǎidǐ kuòzhǎnshuō 〈地质〉 sea-floor spreading theory
海底捞月 hǎidǐ-lāoyuè *also* "海中捞月" try to fish out the moon from the bottom of the sea — strive for the impossible or illusory; cry for the moon: 到头来就像～, 空忙一场。It'll all be a fruitless effort (*or* futile attempt) in the end. / 你这样做不过是～罢了。I'm afraid you're attempting the impossible.
海底捞针 hǎidǐ-lāozhēn fish for a needle in the ocean; search for a pin in a haystack: 现在要想找到他, 那还不是～呀! Trying to locate him now is like searching for a needle in a haystack!
海底平顶山 hǎidǐ píngdǐngshān 〈地质〉 guyot
海底山 hǎidǐshān seamount
海底生物 hǎidǐ shēngwù benthos; benthon
海底实验室 hǎidǐ shíyànshì (US) Sealab
海底水雷 hǎidǐ shuǐléi ground mine or torpedo
海底峡谷 hǎidǐ xiágǔ submarine canyon; ocean canyon
海底信标 hǎidǐ xìnbiāo subsea beacon
海底养殖 hǎidǐ yǎngzhí bottom culture
海底油田 hǎidǐ yóutián offshore oilfield
海底资源 hǎidǐ zīyuán seabed resources; submarine resources
海底钻探 hǎidǐ zuāntàn offshore drilling
海地 Hǎidì Haiti: ～人 Haitian
海蛾鱼 hǎi'éyú dragonfish; sea moth (*Pegasus laternarius*)
海防 hǎifáng ❶ coast defence: ～前哨 outpost of coastal defence / ～前线 coastal front ❷ (Hǎifáng) Haiphong, major port in northern Vietnam
海防部队 hǎifáng bùduì coastal defence force
海防舰 hǎifángjiàn coastal defence ship
海防林 hǎifánglín shelter belt for protecting sea coasts
海匪 hǎifěi *see* "海盗"
海风 hǎifēng sea breeze; sea wind
海甘蓝 hǎigānlán sea kale (*Crambe maritima*)
海港 hǎigǎng seaport; harbour: ～设备 harbour installations / ～出口货物量 〈外贸〉 export cargo at all harbours
海鸽 hǎigē guillemot
海沟 hǎigōu oceanic trench; submarine trench: ～坡折(带) trench slope break
海狗 hǎigǒu fur seal; ursine seal
海狗肾 hǎigǒushèn 〈中药〉 testiset penis phocae
海谷 hǎigǔ submarine valley; canyon
海关 hǎiguān customhouse; customs: 通过～ go through customs; clear customs / ～登记 customs entry / ～缉私船 revenue cutter / ～缉私官员 customs revenue officer / ～人员 customs officer / ～申报单 customs declaration / ～通行证 customs pass / ～税务司 (now ～税务司长) (HK) Commissioner of Customs / ～总署 customs head office; (China) General Administration for Customs
海关放行 hǎiguān fàngxíng customs clearance: ～货物 goods cleared by customs / ～证 customs clearance certificate; cocket
海关监管 hǎiguān jiānguǎn customs supervision: ～区 customs supervision zone
海关检查 hǎiguān jiǎnchá customs inspection (*or* examination): ～站 customs inspection post / ～人员 surveyor of customs; customs examiner; landing waiter; landwaiter
海关检疫 hǎiguān jiǎnyì customs quarantine control
海关手续 hǎiguān shǒuxù customs formalities
海关税收 hǎiguān shuìshōu customs revenue
海关税则 hǎiguān shuìzé customs tariff; tariff schedule
海关退税 hǎiguān tuìshuì (customs) drawback; rebate: ～凭证 debenture
海龟 hǎiguī green turtle (*Chelonia mydas*); sea turtle; marine turtle
海国 hǎiguó island country; coastal country
海涵 hǎihán 〈敬词〉 be magnanimous enough to forgive or tolerate (one's errors or shortcomings): 此事处理欠妥, 万望～。May I crave your forgiveness for inadequacy in dealing with the matter?
海话 hǎihuà 〈方言〉 big talk; boast; bragging: 他喜欢在众人面前说～。He loves to talk big in front of an audience.
海魂衫 hǎihúnshān sailor's striped shirt or pullover
海货 hǎihuò marine product; sea food
海基会 Hǎijīhuì (short for 海峡交流基金会) Strait Exchange Foundation (of Taiwan, China); SEF: ～董事长 President of the Strait Exchange Foundation
海脊 hǎijǐ sea ridge; submarine ridge
海鲫 hǎijì Japanese seaperch; surfperch
海疆 hǎijiāng coastal areas and territorial seas: 驻守～ be garrisoned in a coastal area / ～防区 coastal defence zone / 万里～ vast territorial seas
海椒 hǎijiāo 〈方言〉 hot pepper; chilli
海礁 hǎijiāo reef
海角 hǎijiǎo cape; promontory
海角天涯 hǎijiǎo-tiānyá *also* "天涯海角" corners of the sea and ends of the sky — ends of the earth; remotest corners of the world: ～心相连。Heart to heart, though far apart.
海进 hǎijìn *also* "海侵" 〈地质〉 transgression of sea; advance of the sea: ～沉积物 transgressive deposit / ～超覆 transgressive overlap / ～陆退。When the sea advances, the land recedes.
海禁 hǎijìn ban on maritime trade and intercourse with foreign countries (as during the Ming and Qing dynasties): 开～ lift the ban on maritime trade and intercourse with foreign countries
海景 hǎijǐng seascape: ～画 seascape / ～画家 seascape artist; seascapist
海鸠 hǎijiū 〈动物〉 guillemot
海军 hǎijūn navy; naval forces: ～服 navy uniform / ～部 (US) Department of the Navy / ～实力 naval strength (*or* power); sea

power /～军官 naval officer /～飞机 naval aircraft /～巡逻机 maritime patrol plane /～战斗机 fleet fighter /～演习 naval manoeuvre (*or* exercise)
海军岸防兵 hǎijūn ànfángbīng naval coastal defence force
海军航空兵 hǎijūn hángkōngbīng naval air force; naval air service:～基地 naval airbase
海军基地 hǎijūn jīdì naval base
海军蓝 hǎijūnlán navy blue
海军陆战队 hǎijūn lùzhànduì marine corps; marines:～员 marine
海军呢 hǎijūnní navy cloth
海军旗 hǎijūnqí naval flag
海军水面舰艇 hǎijūn shuǐmiàn jiàntǐng naval surface vessel:～部队 naval surface fleet (*or* force)
海军武官 hǎijūn wǔguān 〈外交〉 naval attaché
海军学院 hǎijūn xuéyuàn *also* "海军学校" naval academy
海客 hǎikè 〈书面〉 ❶ mariner; navigator; sailor ❷ wanderer; vagabond:天涯～ wanderer; uprooted person
海口 hǎikǒu ❶ mouth of a river where it flows into the sea; estuary:这是长江的～。This is the mouth of the Yangtze River. ❷ seaport ❸ bragging; boasting (used mostly in the following phrase):夸下～ boast about what one can do; talk big ❹ (Hǎikǒu) capital of Hainan Province
海枯石烂 hǎikū-shílàn (usu. in an oath expressing firm will or unchanging fidelity) even if the seas should run dry and the rocks crumble:～,此心不移。Though the seas may run dry and the rocks may crumble, our hearts will always remain loyal. *or* I will always be true to you even when the seas dry up and the rocks turn to dust.
海况 hǎikuàng ❶ state of the sea; sea conditions (such as temperature, plankton composition, etc.) ❷ wave motion on the sea
海葵 hǎikuí 〈动物〉 actinia; sea anemone:～毒素〈医学〉 actinocongestin
海阔天空 hǎikuò-tiānkōng as boundless as the sea and sky; unrestrained and far-ranging:到～的大世界去闯荡 temper oneself in the wide world; brave the world /退一步～〈俗语〉 take a step back and a boundless world appears before you; give in for the time being and you'll find much leeway afterwards /他俩碰到一起,准会～地聊个没完。Whenever they met, they would shoot the bull endlessly.
海拉尔 Hǎilā'ěr Hailar, seat of Hulun Buir League (呼伦贝尔盟) and biggest processing base for the livestock industry in Inner Mongolia
海蓝 hǎilán sea blue
海蓝宝石 hǎilán bǎoshí aquamarine
海浪 hǎilàng sea wave:～发电 seawave power generation
海狸 hǎilí (now called 河狸)〈动物〉 beaver
海狸鼠 hǎilíshǔ 〈动物〉 coypu; nutria
海里 hǎilǐ nautical mile (=1,852 metres); sea mile
海力蒙 hǎilìméng 〈纺织〉 (transliteration) herring bone cloth
海力司粗呢 hǎilìsī cūní 〈纺织〉 Harris tweed
海蛎子 hǎilìzi *also* "牡蛎" mǔlì oyster
海鲢 hǎilián ladyfish; tenpounder (*Elopssaurus*)
海量 hǎiliàng ❶〈敬词〉 magnanimity:怠慢之处,望您～包涵。I hope you will be magnanimous enough to forgive any lack of attention on my part. ❷ enormous capacity for alcoholic drinks:我知道您是～,多喝几杯不碍事。I know you can hold your liquor. A few more drinks will not put you down.
海岭 hǎilǐng ocean ridge
海流 hǎiliú ocean current:～发电 current power generation
海龙 hǎilóng ❶〈口语〉 sea otter (*Enhydra lutris*) ❷ pipefish
海鲈 hǎilú sea bass
海路 hǎilù sea route; sea-lane; seaway:走～ travel by sea /～运费 maritime transit charge
海绿石 hǎilǜshí glauconite
海伦 Hǎilún Helen, daughter of Zeus and Leda in Greek mythology, whose abduction by Paris led to the Trojan War
海轮 hǎilún seagoing or oceangoing vessel
海萝 hǎiluó 〈植物〉 *Gloiopeltis*, a kind of seaweed
海螺 hǎiluó conch
海洛因 hǎiluòyīn heroin:～瘾 heroinism; heroin-addiction
海马 hǎimǎ ❶ sea horse (*Hippocampus*):日本～ *Hippocampus japonicus* /冠～ *Hippocampus coronatus* /三斑～ *Hippocampus trimaculatus* /～沟〈生物〉 sulcus hippocampus ❷ *also* "海象" walrus (*Odobenus rosmarus*)
海鳗 hǎimán conger pike
海米 hǎimǐ dried shrimps
海绵 hǎimián ❶ sponge:～动物 spongia /～组织 spongy tissue ❷ foam rubber or plastic; sponge:～底球鞋 sponge-insoled shoes
海绵垫 hǎimiándiàn foam rubber cushion
海绵球拍 hǎimián qiúpāi foam-rubber or sponge (table-tennis) bat; foam-rubber or sponge (ping pong) paddle:正贴～ outward pimpled rubber bat /反贴～ inward pimpled rubber bat
海绵田 hǎimiántián sponge soil (usu. level and soft with a deep layer of mellow soil and high content of humus); mellow-soil field
海绵铁 hǎimiántiě sponge iron
海绵橡皮 hǎimián xiàngpí sponge rubber
海面 hǎimiàn sea surface; sea level:～目标 sea surface target /～反射 sea surface reflection
海面升降 hǎimiàn shēngjiàng *also* "海面进退" eustacy; eustasy:～升降运动 eustatic movement
海鸣 hǎimíng sea noise
海南 Hǎinán Hainan:～省 (from 1988) Hainan Province /～行政区 (till 1988) Hainan Administrative Area
海南戏 hǎinánxì *also* "琼剧" qióngjù Hainan opera
海难 hǎinàn perils of the sea; marine or maritime perils; shipwreck:～例外条款 perils of the sea exception /～条款 perils clause /～救助 salvage at sea /～救援公司 salvage company
海内 hǎinèi within the four seas; throughout the land:～孤本 only extant copy (of a book) in the country /～人望 be held in general esteem throughout the land; be the cynosure of the whole country/～外 at home and abroad /～晏如。Peace reigns throughout the land. *or* There is peace and order in the country. /～存知己,天涯若比邻。A bosom friend afar brings a distant land near.
海鲇 hǎinián 〈动物〉 sea catfish
海鸟 hǎiniǎo seabird; seafowl
海鸟粪 hǎiniǎofèn guano
海涅 Hǎiniè Heinrich Heine (1797-1856), German poet
海牛 hǎiniú 〈动物〉 manatee (*Trichechus manatus*); sea cow
海鸥 hǎi'ōu sea gull; sea mew
海鸥效应 hǎi'ōu xiàoyìng 〈物理〉 seagull effect
海派 hǎipài ❶ Shanghai school of Beijing opera (as represented by Shanghai singers who lay emphasis on acting as well as singing) ❷ Shanghai style:～时装 Shanghai fashion /～文化 subculture of Shanghai
海盘车 hǎipánchē 〈动物〉 starfish
海螃蟹 hǎipángxiè sea crab
海泡石 hǎipàoshí 〈矿业〉 sepiolite; sea-foam; meerschaum
海盆 hǎipén 〈地质〉 sea basin; ocean basin
海蓬子 hǎipéngzi 〈植物〉 glasswort; froggrass
海螵蛸 hǎipiāoxiāo 〈中药〉 cuttlebone
海平面 hǎipíngmiàn sea level:～订正 sea-level correction /～气压 sea-level pressure
海旗 hǎiqí maritime flag
海鞘 hǎiqiào 〈动物〉 ascidian; sea squirt
海侵 hǎiqīn *see* "海进"
海丘 hǎiqiū 〈地理〉 oceanic rise
海区 hǎiqū 〈军事〉 sea area
海雀 hǎiquè 〈动物〉 auk; puffin; guillemot
海群生 hǎiqúnshēng 〈药学〉 hetrazan
海人草 hǎiréncǎo *also* "海仁草" (formerly misnamed 鹧鸪菜) *Digenea simplex*, a kind of alga which may be used as medicine for roundworm
海鳃 hǎisāi 〈动物〉 sea pen; sea feather; pennatula
海扇 hǎishàn *also* "扇贝" shànbèi 〈动物〉 sea fan; scallop
海鳝 hǎishàn 〈动物〉 moray; moray eel
海商法 hǎishāngfǎ maritime law:～规 commercial maritime code/～上的债权要求 maritime claim /～外交会议 diplomatic conference on maritime laws
海商旗 hǎishāngqí maritime flag
海上 hǎishàng at sea; on the sea; offshore; maritime; marine:～风暴 storm at sea /～事故 accident at sea; maritime accident /～救助 assistance and salvage at sea /～搜查 search at sea /～霸权 maritime (*or* naval) hegemony /～飞行 oversea flight /来自～的入侵 sea-borne invasion /～无鱼虾自大 in the absence of fish, the shrimp is big and powerful — among the blind the one-eyed man is king

海上保险 hǎishàng bǎoxiǎn maritime or marine insurance:～诉讼 marine insurance action /海上货运保险 marine cargo insurance
海上避撞规则 hǎishàng bìzhuàng guīzé rules of the road at sea
海上补给 hǎishàng bǔjǐ seaborne supply; sealift:～船 marine supply ship
海上导航 hǎishàng dǎoháng marine celestial navigation
海上封锁 hǎishàng fēngsuǒ sea blockade; naval blockade
海上机场 hǎishàng jīchǎng seadrome
海上交通 hǎishàng jiāotōng maritime traffic:～线 sea-lane; sea route
海上开采 hǎishàng kāicǎi offshore production or exploitation:～平台 offshore production platform /海上石油开采 offshore oil production (*or* exploitation)
海上勘探 hǎishàng kāntàn offshore exploration
海上贸易 hǎishàng màoyì maritime trade or commerce
海上幕僚长 Hǎishàng Mùliáozhǎng (Japan) Chief of Maritime Staff
海上飘流物 hǎishàng piāoliúwù flotsam
海上平台 hǎishàng píngtái offshore platform
海上通道 hǎishàng tōngdào *also* "海上航道" sea-lane; seaway
海上丝绸之路 hǎishàng sīchóu zhī lù silk road of the sea
海上巡逻机 hǎishàng xúnluójī maritime patrol aircraft
海上遗弃物 hǎishàng yíqìwù maritime derelict
海上油田 hǎishàng yóutián offshore oilfield
海上遇险信号 hǎishàng yùxiǎn xìnhào *also* "海难信号" signal of marine distress; GMDSS (formerly SOS)
海上运输 hǎishàng yùnshū marine transport
海上自卫队 Hǎishàng Zìwèiduì (Japan) Maritime Self-Defence Force
海上钻井 hǎishàng zuànjǐng offshore drilling:～平台 offshore drilling platform /～船 offshore drilling ship
海上作业 hǎishàng zuòyè offshore operation; operation on the sea
海蛇 hǎishé sea snake
海参 hǎishēn sea cucumber; sea slug; trepang; *beche-de-mer*
海参崴 Hǎishēnwǎi (Chinese name for 符拉迪沃斯托克) Vladivostok:～会谈 Vladivostok Talks
海肾 hǎishèn 〈动物〉 sea pansy
海生元素 hǎishēng yuánsù thalassophile element
海生植物 hǎishēng zhíwù marine plant; thalassophyte
海狮 hǎishī sea lion
海石蕊素 hǎishíruǐsù roccellin
海石蕊酸 hǎishíruǐsuān roccellic acid
海蚀 hǎishí marine or sea erosion; marine abrasion:～阶地 abrasion (*or* marine-cut) terrace /～平原 marine plain; plain of marine denudation /～台地 abrasion platform
海蚀地貌 hǎishí dìmào abrasion geomorphy
海蚀洞 hǎishídòng *also* "海蚀穴" sea cave
海市蜃楼 hǎishì-shènlóu ❶〈气象〉 mirage:勘探队员说,远处的绿洲只是～而已。The surveyor said that the oasis in the distance was only a mirage. ❷〈比喻〉 castle in the air; illusion:你的理想不过是～罢了。Your ambition may prove to be a castle in the air.
海事 hǎishì ❶ maritime affairs:～保险 maritime insurance /～纠纷 marine (*or* admiralty) dispute /～咨询委员会 Maritime Advisory Committee (MAC) /～惯例 custom of the sea ❷ accident or disaster on the sea: *see* "～救助"
海事裁判权 hǎishì cáipànquán maritime jurisdiction; admiralty jurisdiction
海事处 Hǎishìchù (HK) Marine Department
海事法 hǎishìfǎ admiralty law; maritime law
海事法庭 hǎishì fǎtíng maritime court; admiralty court
海事救助 hǎishì jiùzhù salvage at sea:～报酬担保留置权〈法律〉 liens securing claims in respect of assistance on salvage
海事仲裁 hǎishì zhòngcái maritime arbitration:～委员会 maritime arbitration commission
海誓山盟 hǎishì-shānméng lover's pledge of eternal loyalty; solemn pledge of love; vow of eternal love:～,永不变心 make an oath of eternal love and fidelity
海兽 hǎishòu sea animal; marine mammal:鲸鱼是地球上最大的～。The whale is the largest marine mammal on earth.
海黍子 hǎishǔzi a kind of marine alga
海水 hǎishuǐ seawater; brine; sea:～采样 seawater sampling /～自净 self-purification of seawater
海水不可斗量 hǎishuǐ bùkě dǒu liáng the sea cannot be measured with a bushel — great minds cannot be fathomed by common measure:人不可貌相,～。People should not be judged by their appearance and the sea not measured with a bushel.
海水淡化 hǎishuǐ dànhuà sea water desalting; desalination of seawater:～器 desalting kit /～厂 seawater desalting plant
海水工业 hǎishuǐ gōngyè marine industry
海水面 hǎishuǐmiàn level of seawater; sea level
海水温差发电 hǎishuǐ wēnchā fādiàn ocean temperature differential power
海水养殖 hǎishuǐ yǎngzhí marine culture; seawater aquaculture:～场 marine aquaculture park /～面积 marine aquaculture area
海水浴 hǎishuǐyù *also* "海水澡" seawater bath; sea bathing:洗～去 go seabathing
海水皂 hǎishuǐzào marine soap
海松 hǎisōng *also* "红松" hóngsōng; "果松" guǒsōng sea pine; Korean pine
海松树脂 hǎisōng shùzhī galipot
海松酸 hǎisōngsuān pimaric acid
海损 hǎisǔn 〈商业〉 average; sea damage; marine loss:共同～ general average /单独～ particular average /～合约 average agreement /～货物 goods damaged by sea /～理算 average adjustment /～理算人 average adjuster /～保险 marine insurance
海笋 hǎisǔn 〈动物〉 piddock; pholas
海索草 hǎisuǒcǎo hyssop
海獭 hǎitǎ sea otter
海滩 hǎitān seabeach; beach:～砾石 beach gravel /～纹理 beach lamination /～崖 beach scarp
海棠 hǎitáng *also* "海棠果" 〈植物〉 Chinese flowering crab-apple (*Malus spectabilis*)
海塘 hǎitáng seawall
海天一色 hǎi-tiān yīsè the sea melted into the sky; the sea and the sky merged into one
海田 hǎitián marine field (an enclosed area in bay for cultivating marine products)
海桐 hǎitóng *also* "海桐花" tobira (*Pittosporum tobira*)
海图 hǎitú sea or marine chart; nautical chart:～室 chart room (*or* house) /～集 naval atlas /对某一海域编制～ chart a given sea area /在～上绘出舰队的航行路线 chart the route of a fleet
海涂 hǎitú tidal flat; tidal marsh; tidal land:围垦～ reclaim a tidal flat (*or* marsh) by building a seawall
海兔 hǎitù 〈动物〉 sea hare
海退 hǎituì 〈地质〉 regression; recession (of the sea):～超覆 regressive overlap /～相 regressive phase
海豚 hǎitún 〈动物〉 dolphin:～油 dolphin oil /～馆 dolphinarium
海豚星座 Hǎitún xīngzuò 〈天文〉 Delphinus; Dolphin
海豚泳 hǎitúnyǒng *also* "海豚式" 〈体育〉 dolphin butterfly; dolphin fishtail; dolphin
海外 hǎiwài overseas; abroad:居住～ reside (*or* live) abroad /名传～ spread one's name abroad; become known the world over /～华人 overseas Chinese /～华侨 overseas Chinese nationals (*or* citizens); Chinese nationals residing overseas /～同胞 compatriots (*or* countrymen) residing abroad /～市场 overseas market /～投资 overseas investment /～贸易 overseas trade /从～归国定居 return from abroad to settle in the country
海外版 hǎiwàibǎn overseas edition:这本词典很快即出～。This dictionary will soon publish its overseas edition.
海外关系 hǎiwài guānxi relatives residing abroad; overseas connections:利用～打开销路 utilize one's overseas connections to find a market for a product /他过去因～受过迫害。He was persecuted because he had relatives overseas.
海外奇谈 hǎiwài-qítán strange story from over the seas; traveller's tale; tall story:他说的纯属～,绝不可信。He tells nothing but tall tales, and you mustn't trust him.
海湾 hǎiwān ❶ bay; gulf ❷ (short for 波斯湾)(Persian) Gulf:～地区 Gulf area
海湾国家 Hǎiwān guójiā Gulf state — state bordering on the Persian Gulf
海湾战争 Hǎiwān Zhànzhēng Gulf War (between allied forces led by the US, and Iraq over the latter's invasion of Kuwait, 1991)
海碗 hǎiwǎn extra-big bowl; huge bowl

H

海王星 Hǎiwángxīng 〈天文〉Neptune
海卫二 Hǎiwèi Èr 〈天文〉Nereid, satellite of Neptune
海卫一 Hǎiwèi Yī 〈天文〉Triton, satellite of Neptune
海味 hǎiwèi choice seafood; seafood:山珍～ rare dainties from the mountains and the seas; all sorts of delicacies
海屋添筹 hǎiwū-tiānchóu put a counter in a room whenever a cataclysmic change occurs in the world (in addition to the ten roomfuls of such counters already stored) — add more years to your already long life; wish you a long, long life
海峡 hǎixiá strait; channel:对马～ Tsushima Strait / 台湾～ Taiwan Strait / 马六甲～ Strait of Malacca / 英吉利～ English Channel
海峡两岸 Hǎixiá-liǎng'àn two or both sides of the Taiwan Strait
海峡群岛 Hǎixiá Qúndǎo (UK) Channel Islands
海鲜 hǎixiān seafood
海相 hǎixiàng 〈地质〉marine or sea facies
海相沉积 hǎixiàng chénjī 〈地质〉marine deposit; marine sediment
海象 hǎixiàng walrus; whale-horse
海啸 hǎixiào seismic sea wave; *tsunami*
海协会 Hǎixiéhuì (short for 海峡两岸关系协会) Association for Relations Across the Taiwan Strait (on the mainland); ARATS:～会长 President of the Association for Relations Across the Taiwan Strait
海蟹 hǎixiè sea crab
海星 hǎixīng 〈动物〉starfish; sea star
海熊 hǎixióng *also* "海狗" fur seal; ursine seal
海寻 hǎixún nautical fathom (=1.852 metres)
海鸦 hǎiyā murre
海牙 Hǎiyá The Hague (of Holland):～公约 Hague Conventions (1899, 1907) / ～规则 Hague Rules / ～议定书 Hague Protocol / ～维斯培规则 Hague Visby Rules / ～仲裁常设委员会 Permanent Court of Arbitration (The Hague)
海牙国际法庭 Hǎiyá Guójì Fǎtíng International Court at the Hague
海盐 hǎiyán sea salt
海蜒 hǎiyán 〈动物〉anchovy
海晏河清 hǎiyàn-héqīng *also* "河清海晏" the sea is tranquil and the (Yellow) River clear — times of peace; there is peace and tranquility throughout the country
海燕 hǎiyàn (storm) petrel
海洋 hǎiyáng seas and oceans; ocean:～霸权 maritime hegemony/ ～国家 maritime state / ～食物链 marine food chain / ～鱼类种群 marine fish population / ～倾废 marine dumping / ～虹 sea (*or* marine) rainbow / ～气象自动浮标站 automatic meteorological oceanographic buoy / ～热能转换 ocean thermal energy conversion
海洋保护区 hǎiyáng bǎohùqū marine preserve
海洋测深学 hǎiyáng cèshēnxué bathymetry
海洋地球物理学 hǎiyáng dìqiú wùlǐxué marine geophysics
海洋地质学 hǎiyáng dìzhìxué marine geology
海洋调查 hǎiyáng diàochá oceanographic survey or research; undersea exploration:～船 oceanographic (research) vessel
海洋动物 hǎiyáng dòngwù marine animal
海洋法 hǎiyángfǎ law of the sea:～公约 Convention of the Law of the Sea / ～宣言 (Montevideo) Declaration of the Law of the Sea (1970)
海洋工程 hǎiyáng gōngchéng ocean engineering; oceanographic engineering:～测量 ocean engineering survey
海洋公约 hǎiyáng gōngyuē maritime convention
海洋化学 hǎiyáng huàxué marine chemistry
海洋环境 hǎiyáng huánjìng maritime environment:～污染 maritime environmental pollution
海洋经济学 hǎiyáng jīngjìxué marine economics
海洋矿业 hǎiyáng kuàngyè ocean or oceanic mining
海洋牧场 hǎiyáng mùchǎng aquafarm; sea or oceanic pasture
海洋气象船 hǎiyáng qìxiàngchuán ocean weather ship
海洋气象学 hǎiyáng qìxiàngxué marine meteorology
海洋权 hǎiyángquán maritime rights
海洋生态系统 hǎiyáng shēngtài xìtǒng marine eco-system
海洋生物 hǎiyáng shēngwù marine organism; halobiont:～带 marine biocycle / 海洋浮游生物 marine plankton / ～资源 living marine resources
海洋生物地理学 hǎiyáng shēngwù dìlǐxué marine biogeography
海洋生物声学 hǎiyáng shēngwù shēngxué marine bioacoustics
海洋生物学 hǎiyáng shēngwùxué marine biology
海洋石油 hǎiyáng shíyóu offshore oil:～平台 offshore oil extraction platform / ～勘探 offshore oil exploration / ～资源 offshore petroleum resources / ～钻井船 offshore drilling rig
海洋特别保护区 hǎiyáng tèbié bǎohùqū special marine protection area; special marine reserve
海洋卫星系统 hǎiyáng wèixīng xìtǒng MARISAT (marine satellite) system
海洋物理学 hǎiyáng wùlǐxué marine physics
海洋性冰川 hǎiyángxìng bīngchuān marine glacier
海洋性气候 hǎiyángxìng qìhòu maritime or marine climate
海洋学 hǎiyángxué oceanography; oceanology; oceanics
海洋渔场 hǎiyáng yúchǎng offshore fishing ground
海洋渔业 hǎiyáng yúyè sea fishery; marine fishery
海洋资源 hǎiyáng zīyuán marine resources
海洋自然资源保护区 hǎiyáng zìrán zīyuán bǎohùqū marine nature conservation area; marine nature reserve
海妖 hǎiyāo siren; sea monster
海涌 hǎiyǒng swell:风暴带来了强烈的～。The storm brought a powerful swell in its wake.
海鱼 hǎiyú sea fish; marine fish; saltwater fish
海隅 hǎiyú 〈书面〉coastal areas; coastland
海域 hǎiyù sea area; maritime space:黄海～ Yellow Sea waters
海域侦察卫星 hǎiyù zhēnchá wèixīng ocean area satellite
海渊 hǎiyuān 〈地理〉ocean deep
海员 hǎiyuán seaman; sailor; mariner:～船 crewboat / ～俱乐部 seamen's club / ～留置权〈法律〉seamen's lien / ～用语 nautical expression
海源湖 hǎiyuánhú marine lake
海月水母 hǎiyuè shuǐmǔ 〈动物〉aurelia
海运 hǎiyùn sea or marine transport; ocean shipping:～承运人 ocean carrier / ～代理商 ocean shipping agent / ～单据 marine document / ～保险单 marine insurance policy (MIP) / ～提单 ocean bill of lading / ～协定 maritime agreement / ～运费 ocean freight / ～中的货物 goods in transit by sea
海葬 hǎizàng sea-burial
海枣 hǎizǎo 〈植物〉date palm; date
海藻 hǎizǎo marine alga; seaweed; thalassophyte:～产品 seaweed product / ～丛 seaweed bed / ～黏质 seaweed mucilage
海战 hǎizhàn sea warfare; naval battle:特拉法尔加～ Battle of Trafalgar (21 October 1805)
海蜇 hǎizhé jellyfish
海震 hǎizhèn 〈地质〉submarine earthquake; seaquake; sea shock
海蜘蛛 hǎizhīzhū sea spider
海猪 hǎizhū (popular name for 海豚) dolphin
海子 hǎizi 〈方言〉lake

浔 hǎixún *also* xún (formerly used for 海寻) nautical fathom

胲 hǎi 〈化学〉hydroxylamine

醢 hǎi 〈书面〉❶ minced fish or meat paste ❷ cut to small pieces

浬 hǎilǐ *also* lǐ (formerly used for 海里) nautical mile

hài

害 hài ❶ harm; injury; damage; evil:霜～ frost damage; frost injury / 灾～ calamity; disaster / 病虫～ plant diseases and insect pests / 为民除～ rid the people of a scourge / 吸烟有～。Smoking is harmful to health. / 有利必有～。Advantage is always accompanied by disadvantage. *or* Harm goes hand in hand with good. ❷ harmful; destructive; injurious:～草 (harmful) grass ❸ do harm to; cause trouble to; impair:危～国家 do harm to the country; be detrimental to the interests of one's country / 她这种"爱"到头来会～了你。Her "love" will eventually bring harm to you. / 你哪儿去了? ～得我找了你大半天。Where have you been? I've spent a long time looking for you! ❹ kill; murder:暗～ kill secretly; stab in the back / 遇～ be murdered or assassinated ❺ contract (an illness); suffer from:～了

一场大病 contract a serious illness; be seized with a severe illness; fall seriously ill /～疟疾 suffer from malaria; be taken ill with malaria ❻ feel (ashamed; afraid; etc.):～怕 feel afraid
害病 hàibìng fall ill; be sick
害虫 hàichóng injurious or destructive insect; pest
害处 hàichu harm; injury; damage:这对你没～。It will do you no harm. /冰雹对庄稼很有～。Hailstones do a lot of damage to crops.
害肚子 hài dùzi 〈方言〉suffer from diarrhoea; have loose bowels
害口 hàikǒu 〈方言〉suffer from morning sickness
害命 hàimìng take sb.'s life; kill; murder:谋财～ murder sb. for his money
害鸟 hàiniǎo harmful or destructive bird
害怕 hàipà be afraid; be scared; be frightened:～得要命 be scared to death; be mortally afraid; be overcome with fear /不要～困难。Don't be afraid of difficulties. *or* Fear no difficulties. /她显出很～的样子。She looked terribly scared.
害群之马 hàiqúnzhīmǎ evil horse which does harm to the herd; one who brings disgrace on or constitutes a danger to one's group; rotten apple in the barrel; black sheep
害人不浅 hàirén-bùqiǎn do people great harm:这种活动必须禁止，否则在社会上～。This kind of activity must be banned, or else it will cause great harm to society.
害人虫 hàirénchóng evil creature; pest; vermin:扫除一切～。Away with all pests.
害人之心不可有，防人之心不可无 hài rén zhī xīn bùkě yǒu, fáng rén zhī xīn bùkě wú One should never intend to harm others; nor should one forget to guard against others' evil intentions.
害人终害己 hài rén zhōng hài jǐ *also* "害人反害己" be hoist with one's own petard; (a trick, etc.) boomerang (against the schemer); come home to roost; harm set, harm get; harm watch, harm catch:他玩了这么多阴谋，到头来都是～。All his schemes boomeranged against him in the end.
害臊 hàisào feel ashamed; be bashful or shy:见生人～ be shy with strangers /做这种事，你就不感到～? Aren't you ashamed of yourself for what you've done? /真不～! Have you no sense of shame? *or* You've got some nerve!
害兽 hàishòu harmful or destructive animal
害喜 hàixǐ suffer from morning sickness
害羞 hàixiū be shy; be bashful:这位青年教师是第一次上讲台讲课，有些～。The young teacher was a bit shy, as it was the first time he had stood on the rostrum giving a lecture.
害眼 hàiyǎn have eye trouble
害月子 hài yuèzi 〈方言〉suffer from morning sickness

嗐 hài 〈叹词〉*used to express sorrow or regret*:～，想不到他没通过这次考试。Well, I didn't expect him to fail the examination. /～，你怎么不早点告诉我! Oh, why didn't you tell me earlier?

亥 hài last of the twelve Earthly Branches
see also "干支" gānzhī
亥时 hàishí 〈旧语〉period of the day from 9 p.m. to 11 p.m.

恢 hài 〈书面〉pain; unhappiness; misery

氦 hài 〈化学〉helium (He):～族 helium group /～龄 helium age /～闪 helium flash /～循环 helium cycle
氦层 hàicéng heliosphere
氦灯 hàidēng helium lamp
氦弧 hàihú heliarc:～焊 heliarc welding /～焊机 heliarc welder /～切割 heliarc cutting
氦化物 hàihuàwù 〈化学〉helide
氦冷却剂 hàilěngquèjì helium coolant
氦氖激光器 hàinǎi jīguāngqì helium-neon laser
氦年代测定法 hài niándài cèdìngfǎ 〈考古〉helium dating
氦气 hàiqì (common name for 氦) helium:～飞艇 helium airship
氦星 hàixīng helium star
氦液化器 hàiyèhuàqì helium liquifier
氦致冷器 hàizhìlěngqì helium refrigerator

骇 hài frighten; shock; astonish; amaze:惊～万分 be very much frightened; be panic-stricken /惊涛～浪 frightening billows
骇怪 hàiguài be shocked; be astonished:他的表现令人～。We were shocked at his behaviour.
骇惧 hàijù be frightened; be terrified
骇怕 hàipà be scared; be frightened
骇然 hàirán gasp with astonishment; be struck dumb with amazement:～失色 turn pale with astonishment; be flabbergasted /敌军已兵临城下，人人莫不～。All were struck dumb by the news that the city was already under siege.
骇人听闻 hàirén-tīngwén shocking; appalling; horrifying:～的事故 appalling (*or* shocking) accident /～的暴行 horrifying (*or* horrendous) atrocities
骇异 hàiyì be shocked; be astonished:不胜～ be greatly shocked; be astounded

hān

顸 hān 〈方言〉thick:这铁丝太细了，有～点的吗? This iron wire is too fine. Have you got anything thicker? /那年头，谁胳膊～，谁有理。In those years, whoever had a strong arm made law. *or* In those years, might made right.
顸实 hānshi 〈方言〉thick and sturdy:～的棍子 thick and sturdy stick

鼾 hān snore:打～ snore
鼾声 hānshēng sound of snoring:～如雷 snore thunderously /隔壁传来的～，使我久久不能入睡。The snoring that came from the next room kept me awake for a long time.
鼾睡 hānshuì sound, snoring sleep:卧榻之侧岂容他人～! Who will quietly let another man snore beside his own bed! — Nobody will ever allow anybody else to intrude on his turf.
鼾音 hānyīn 〈医学〉sonorous rale

犴 hān 〈方言〉〈动物〉elk; moose

憨 hān ❶ foolish; silly:～头～脑 with a stupid head and a dull brain; foolish-looking ❷ naive; ingenuous; innocent:娇～ sweet and naive; guileless ❸ (Hān) a surname
憨痴 hānchī stupid; idiotic:～的话 stupid remark /～的小儿 idiotic child
憨憨 hānhan ❶ idiotically; simply; unaffectedly:人家劝他，他只是～地一笑。When others tried to dissuade him, he just gave a simple smile. ❷〈方言〉blockhead; simpleton:村里人都管他叫～。Everybody called him "idiot" in the village.
憨厚 hānhou simple and honest; straightforward and good-natured:他为人～。He is frank and honest.
憨乎乎 hānhūhū (of one's appearance, manner, etc.) simple and honest; ingenuous:他那～的样子，又天真，又可笑。His ingenuous manner was at once innocent and funny.
憨傻 hānshǎ honest but simple-minded; fatuous:她不知该说什么，只是～地笑了一笑。Not knowing what to say, she put on a fatuous smile.
憨实 hānshí straightforward and good-natured; simple and honest:～可爱的小伙子 likeable simple and honest young man
憨态 hāntài air of charming naivety:一脸～ look naive and innocent
憨态可掬 hāntài-kějū charmingly naive:那熊猫～，着实令人喜爱。With an air of charming naivety, the panda looks lovely indeed.
憨笑 hānxiào smile artlessly or guilelessly; smile fatuously:姑娘有些害臊，一个劲儿～不说话。Shy to speak, the girl just smiled guilelessly.
憨直 hānzhí honest and straightforward:他兄弟为人太精，而他又～得不懂人情世故。Unlike his brother who is over-smart, he is too honest and straightforward to understand the ways of the world.
憨子 hānzi 〈方言〉blockhead; simpleton

酣 hān ❶ (drink) to one's heart's content:酒半～〈书面〉half drunk; somewhat tipsy ❷ heartily; merrily; to one's heart's content:～歌 sing lustily; sing to one's heart's content
酣畅 hānchàng ❶ merry and lively (with drinking) ❷ sound (asleep) ❸ (of writing, calligraphy, painting, etc.) with ease and

verve; fully:以～的笔墨 (write or paint) with ease and verve
酣畅淋漓 hānchàng-línlí heartily; fully; to one's heart's content:这篇文章把作者对美好的新世界的憧憬抒写得～。The essay fully expressed the author's yearning for a better and brighter new world.
酣梦 hānmèng sweet dream:～正浓 be sleeping soundly
酣眠 hānmián be fast asleep; sleep soundly
酣然 hānrán to one's heart's content; merrily (drunk); sound (asleep):～大醉 be merrily drunk; be as drunk as a lord /～入梦 fall into a sound sleep
酣适 hānshì content and comfortable:睡眠～ sleep soundly and comfortably; be in a sound and sweet sleep
酣熟 hānshú sound (asleep):睡得～ sleep soundly
酣睡 hānshuì sleep soundly; be fast asleep; sleep like a log:隆隆的炮声把战士们从～中惊醒。The roar of cannons roused the soldiers from their deep sleep.
酣甜 hāntián (usu. of sleep) sound and sweet:进入了～的梦境 fall into a sound, sweet sleep
酣饮 hānyǐn drink one's fill; drink to one's heart's content; carouse:～不知醉 drink heavily, without realizing that one is already drunk
酣战 hānzhàn hard-fought battle:势均力敌的～ pitched (*or* fierce) battle between well-matched adversaries
酣醉 hānzuì be dead drunk; become intoxicated:～在幸福之中 be intoxicated with happiness

蚶 hān 〈动物〉blood clam:毛～〈方言〉blood clam
蚶田 hāntián field for raising blood clams; clam-raising ground; clam-bed
蚶子 hānzi 〈动物〉blood clam

hán

寒 hán ❶ cold; frigid; chilly:春～ cold spell (*or* weather) in spring; cold spring /受～ catch cold; catch a chill /～烟衰草 chilly mists and fading plants /～月照窗。The cold moonlight streamed in through the window. ❷ be stricken with terror; tremble with fear:胆～ be terrified; be stricken with panic ❸ poor; needy:贫～ poverty-stricken; impoverished /清～ poor; in straitened (*or* indigent) circumstances /～儒 needy scholar ❹〈谦词〉my humble: *see* "～舍"; "～门"
寒痹 hánbì 〈中医〉arthritis (aggravated by cold)
寒不择衣 hánbùzéyī one who is suffering from cold is not choosy about clothing; beggars can't be choosers
寒蝉 hánchán ❶ cicada in cold weather:噤若～ as silent as a cicada in cold weather — keep quiet out of fear /～凄切 plaintive droning of a cicada in cold weather ❷ a kind of small black cicada
寒潮 háncháo 〈气象〉cold wave; cold-air outbreak
寒伧 hánchen *see* "寒碜"
寒碜 hánchen *also* "寒伧";"寒尘";"寒颤" ❶ ugly; unsightly; shabby:长得～ bad-looking; plain; unsightly /穿得～ be badly (*or* shabbily) dressed ❷ disgraceful; shameful; disreputable:为公家省钱有什么～的。There's nothing disgraceful (*or* shameful) in being frugal with public money. /穷并不～,懒就可耻了。Poverty is no disgrace while indolence is a shame. /你干这事也不嫌～。Aren't you ashamed of yourself for doing that? ❸ ridicule; put to shame:拿话～人 make caustic remarks about sb.; ridicule sb. /他敢当我面吹牛皮,我就得～～他。If he brags in my presence, I'll put him in his place.
寒窗 hánchuāng cold window — hard conditions under which a poor scholar studies:十年～ study under hard conditions (*or* in straitened circumstances) for ten years /～苦读 persevere in one's studies in spite of hardships
寒带 hándài 〈地理〉frigid zone
寒冬 hándōng cold winter; winter:穿这点衣服,耐不过～。You could not survive the severe winter in such light clothes.
寒冬腊月 hándōng-làyuè severe winter; freezing winter; dead of winter
寒风 hánfēng cold wind:～刺骨。The cold wind chills one to the bone (*or* cuts one to the marrow). /～凛冽。The wind is piercingly (*or* bitterly) cold.
寒光 hánguāng light or gleam that makes one feel chilly (usu. in reference to moonlight, a sword, etc.):～闪闪 (of a sword, etc.) gleam coldly /星星闪着～。Stars shine coldly. /刺刀闪着～。The bayonets gleamed with death.
寒号虫 hánhàochóng *also* "狐蝠" húfú; "果蝠" guǒfú 〈动物〉fruit bat; flying fox
寒极 hánjí 〈气象〉cold pole
寒悸 hánjì 〈方言〉shiver or shake with cold
寒家 hánjiā *see* "寒门"
寒假 hánjià winter vacation
寒贱 hánjiàn *see* "寒微"
寒螿 hánjiāng 〈古语〉a kind of cicada
寒噤 hánjìn shiver (with cold or fear); tremble:打～ have (*or* get) the shivers /使人打～ send shivers down sb.'s spine (*or* back)
寒荆 hánjīng 〈谦词〉〈旧语〉my wife
寒苦 hánkǔ destitute; poverty-stricken:出身～ be born of a poor family
寒来暑往 hánlái-shǔwǎng as summer goes and winter comes; as time passes; with the passage of time
寒冷 hánlěng cold; frigid:～的天气 cold weather /山顶上格外～。It was ice-cold (*or* frigid) on the mountaintop.
寒栗 hánlì shiver (with cold or fear):一阵冷风刮来,令人感到～。A gust of cold wind sent shivers through us.
寒凉 hánliáng cold; chilly
寒冽 hánliè 〈书面〉cold; frigid; icy:雪后～。It was icy-cold (*or* frigid) after the snow.
寒流 hánliú ❶ cold (ocean) current ❷〈气象〉cold wave
寒露 Hánlù ❶ Cold Dew, 17th seasonal division point, marking the sun's position at 195° on the ecliptic ❷ day marking such a seasonal division point, usu. falling on the 8th or 9th of October ❸ period lasting from such a seasonal division point till the next one (Frost's Descent 霜降)
see also "节气" jiéqi; "二十四节气" èrshísì jiéqì
寒露风 hánlùfēng (as in southeastern China) cold spell before or after the Cold Dew
寒毛 hánmao fine hair on the human body:老爷爷的"鬼"故事听得我们～直竖,可是谁也不舍得离开。Although the old man's ghost stories made our hair stand on end (*or* scared us stiff), they also held us spellbound.
寒门 hánmén *also* "寒家"〈书面〉❶〈谦词〉〈旧语〉my family:～不幸,遭此大难。My family is so unfortunate as to have incurred this catastrophe. ❷〈旧语〉humble family; lowly family:出身～ be born in a humble family; be of lowly origin
寒漠 hánmò 〈地理〉cold desert:～土 cold desert soil
寒疟 hánnüè 〈中医〉shivering malaria
寒气 hánqì ❶ cold air; cold draught; cold:～逼人。There is a nip in the air. ❷ chill one feels as a result of exposure to cold weather:喝口酒去去～。Drink some liquor to take the chill off the body.
寒峭 hánqiào 〈书面〉chilly; icy:～的西北风 icy northwesterly
寒秋 hánqiū cold autumn; late autumn:独立～ stand alone in the autumn cold
寒热 hánrè ❶〈中医〉chill and fever:～往来 alternating spells of fever and chill ❷〈方言〉run a fever:发～ run (*or* have) a fever; have (*or* run) a temperature
寒色 hánsè *also* "冷色" lěngsè cold or cool colour
寒森森 hánsēnsēn cold; icy; frigid:～的剑气 cold gleam of a sword /～的地窖 icy cellar /虽然已经立春了,但夜里还是～的。There was still a nip in the air at night though spring had set in.
寒舍 hánshè 〈谦词〉my humble home; my humble abode:请二位光临～一叙。May I invite you two to come to my humble home and have a chat?
寒食 Hánshí ❶ festival beginning on the day before Pure Brightness (清明, usu. falling on the 5th or 6th of April) when only cold food was served for three days in ancient times ❷ (another name for 清明 in some areas) Pure Brightness
寒士 hánshì 〈旧语〉poor scholar
寒暑 hánshǔ ❶ cold and heat ❷ winter and summer; whole year:经历十几个～ go through more than a dozen years (*or* through a dozen years or so)
寒暑表 hánshǔbiǎo thermometer
寒丝丝 hánsīsī somewhat chilly:身上～的 feel a bit chilly
寒素 hánsù 〈书面〉❶ poor; destitute; in straitened circumstances:家世～ be from a poor (*or* impoverished) family ❷ person

of scanty means or humble origin:拔擢~ promote people of humble origin ❸ simple; crude; plain:~的院落 unadorned (*or* plain) courtyard

寒酸 hánsuān ❶ (as of a poor scholar) shabby and miserable:一副~相 look shabby and miserable /工资低微的~小职员 sorry underpaid clerk ❷ too simple to be decent; too meagre to be handsome:你出席宴会,穿得不能太~了。When you go to a banquet, you must be decently dressed. /既然要送礼,就不能过于~。If you want to give people a gift, it should be a handsome one.

寒腿 hántuǐ rheumatism in the legs

寒威 hánwēi severity of the cold:抵挡不住冬天的~ cannot resist the severe cold (*or* severity) of winter

寒微 hánwēi 〈书面〉of low station; humble:出身~ of humble origin

寒武纪 Hánwǔjì 〈地质〉Cambrian (Period)

寒武系 Hánwǔxì 〈地质〉Cambrian system

寒心 hánxīn ❶ be bitterly disappointed; be disillusioned:他的堕落令父母~。His degeneration bitterly disappointed his parents. /如此忘恩负义,真让人~。Such ingratitude came as a great blow. ❷ be afraid; be fearful:这部恐怖片看着令人~。This horror movie made one's hair stand on end.

寒星 hánxīng cold-night star:~闪烁。Stars were twinkling in the freezing cold night.

寒暄 hánxuān exchange conventional greetings; exchange amenities or compliments; pass the time of day:她同客人~了几句就开始做饭。She exchanged a few words of greeting with the guests before she started cooking. /~了一阵之后,他就匆匆忙忙地走了。After the usual polite small-talk, he left in a hurry.

寒鸦 hányā 〈动物〉jackdaw

寒衣 hányī winter clothing

寒意 hányì nip or chill in the air:冷风吹来,颇有~。There was quite a nip in the air as the cold wind rose.

寒战 hánzhàn *also* "寒颤" shiver with cold or fear:他打了个~。A shiver ran over his body. *or* A chill shot through him.

寒症 hánzhèng 〈中医〉symptoms caused by cold factors (e.g. chill, loose bowels, slow pulse, etc.)

汗

hán (short for 可汗) Khan:成吉思~ Ghenghis Khan

see also hàn

邯

hán

邯郸 Hándān city in Hebei Province and formerly capital of the State of Zhao (赵, 475-222 BC)

邯郸学步 Hándān-xuébù try to learn the Handan walk — imitate others slavishly only to lose one's own individuality; attempting to walk like a swan, the crow loses its own gait:学习外国经验要切忌~。We must avoid blind imitation when we learn from the experience of other countries.

韩(韓)

Hán ❶ name of a state in the Warring States Period covering present central Henan and southeastern Shanxi provinces ❷ (short for 韩国) Republic of Korea:~刊 journal (*or* magazine) of the Republic of Korea; South Korean journal (*or* magazine) ❸ a surname

韩宝集团 Hánbǎo Jítuán (ROK) Chaebol

韩非 Hán Fēi *see* "韩非子"

韩非子 Hánfēizǐ Hanfeizi (formerly translated as Han-Fei-Tzu, c. 280-233 BC), respectful title for Hanfei, Legalist statesman and thinker of the late Warring States Period

韩幹 Hán Gàn Han Gan (formerly translated as Han Kan), painter of the Tang Dynasty

韩国 Hánguó Republic of Korea (ROK)

韩国广播公司 Hánguó Guǎngbō Gōngsī Korea Broadcasting System (KBS)

韩国日报 Hánguó Rìbào *Korean Daily News*

韩国时报 Hánguó Shíbào *Korean Times*

韩国新闻社 Hánguó Xīnwénshè Korean Information Press

韩信 Hán Xìn Han Xin (formerly translated as Han Hsin, ? -196 BC), strategist in the Qin and Han dynasties:~将兵,多多益善。"The more, the better", as Han Xin said about the number of troops he could command. *or* "The more, the better", like Han Xin commanding troops.

韩愈 Hán Yù Han Yu (768-824), writer and philosopher of the Tang Dynasty

含

hán ❶ keep or hold in the mouth:~一口水 hold some water in the mouth /~一粒水果糖 have a fruit drop in the mouth /~毫吮墨 moisten the tip of the writing brush with one's lips — pause to think while writing /此药须~服。This medicine is to be sucked, not swallowed. ❷ contain; bear:~多种维生素 contain many kinds of vitamins /~泪告别 say goodbye with tears in one's eyes /~硫合金 sulphur-containing alloy /~煤地层 coal-bearing stratum /~油岩石 oil-bearing rock /~铀废水 uraniferous waste water /~尘气体 dusty gas /~氯量 chlorinity /~水分多的水果 juicy fruit ❸ nurse; cherish; harbour: *see* "~恨"; "~怒"

含苞 hánbāo 〈书面〉in bud

含苞待放 hánbāo-dàifàng (of a bud) ready to burst; (of a girl, etc.) in early puberty:~的玫瑰花儿 roses ready to break out into blossom

含悲 hánbēi be filled with deep sorrow:他~忍泪。He fought back his tears though he was filled with deep sorrow.

含尘量 hánchénliàng 〈环保〉dust content; dust load; dustiness

含愤 hánfèn be filled with indignation or resentment:~而死 die in resentment

含垢忍辱 hángòu-rěnrǔ endure contempt and insults; bear or swallow shame and humiliation; eat dirt; eat humble pie:奴隶们不能再~,终于起而反抗了。Unable to stand the humiliation and oppression any longer, the slaves rose in rebellion at last.

含恨 hánhèn cherish resentment; nurse a grievance or hatred:~在心 harbour (*or* nurse) a hatred in one's heart /~终天 die with a deep regret; die unavenged

含胡 hánhu *see* "含糊"

含糊 hánhu *also* "含胡" ❶ ambiguous; vague:说话~ speak in ambiguous terms; equivocate; prevaricate /她回答得很~。She gave an equivocal (*or* a noncommittal) reply. ❷ careless; perfunctory:这可是大事,~不得。This is a matter of vital importance and must be handled with meticulous care. ❸ (usu. used in the negative) show weakness or cowardice:要比就比,我绝不~。Let's have a contest if you will. I'm not the one to turn tail. /你可别小看她,她那手乒乓球打得可真不~。Don't you belittle her. She's not half bad at table tennis.

含糊其辞 hánhu-qící *also* "含糊其词" talk evasively; equivocate; hem and haw:他一时不好实说,只得~地敷衍了几句。He had to skirt the issue as he could not very well tell the truth then.

含混 hánhùn unclear; indistinct; ambiguous:发音~ unclear pronunciation (*or* articulation) /言词~ ambiguous wording /概念~不清。The concept is confused.

含金量 hánjīnliàng ❶ gold content:矿石的~ gold content of ore ❷ real worth or value:同是奖牌,足球冠军比有些球的~可大多了。As first prize, the championship for soccer is worth much more than those for some other ball games.

含矿岩 hánkuàngyán 〈地质〉pay rock

含蜡原油 hánlà yuányóu 〈矿业〉wax-bearing crude (oil)

含殓 hánliàn ❶〈古语〉put a pearl or a jade piece in the mouth of the deceased and encoffin the body ❷〈书面〉put a corpse in a coffin; encoffin:亲视~ supervise in person the process of encoffining the deceased

含量 hánliàng content:净~ net content /维生素 E 的~ content of vitamin E /油的酯~ ester content of oil /含氮量 nitrogen content

含蓼问疾 hánliǎo-wènjí (of a ruler) ask about the people's sufferings with deep concern

含硫原油 hánliú yuányóu sour crude (oil)

含氯氟烃 hánlǜfútīng 〈化学〉perflurocarbons

含能量 hánnéngliàng energy content

含怒 hánnù be in anger:~不语 hold one's tongue in fury /脸上~ one's face betrays anger; look angry

含片 hánpiàn lozenge:止咳~ cough lozenge

含泣吞声 hánqì-tūnshēng choke down one's tears:在丈夫面前,你一味~是不行的。In your relations with your husband, it won't do to be always submissive and swallow endless insults.

含铅玻璃 hánqiān bōli flint glass; lead glass

含铅玻璃纤维 hánqiān bōli xiānwéi lead-containing glass fibre

含铅汽油 hánqiān qìyóu leaded gasoline or petrol:不~ unleaded

H

gasoline; lead-free gasoline
含铅橡胶 hánqiān xiàngjiāo lead rubber
含情 hánqíng cherish affection or tender feelings (for sb. or sth.); exude love:笑脸～。One's smiling face exudes (*or* expresses) love.
含情脉脉 hánqíng-mòmò exude tenderness and love:～的秀目 pretty eyes that bespeak tenderness and love /～地看着美丽的姑娘 make sheep's eyes at a beautiful girl
含忍 hánrěn tolerate; put up with:～而不言 put up with sth. without saying a word
含沙射影 hánshā-shèyǐng attack by innuendo; make insinuating remarks:～、恶语中伤 defame with vicious, insinuating remarks /这篇文章～地攻击新政策。The article attacked the new policy by innuendo.
含生草 hánshēngcǎo rose of Jericho; resurrection plant (*Anastatica hierochuntica*)
含漱剂 hánshùjì 〈药学〉gargle; collutorium
含水层 hánshuǐcéng 〈地质〉water-bearing stratum; aquifer:～等压线 isopiestic line of aquifer
含水量 hánshuǐliàng *also* "含水率" water content; moisture content
含碳量 hántànliàng 〈冶金〉carbon content
含笑 hánxiào have a smile on one's face:～相迎 meet sb. with a smile /～谢绝 decline politely with a smile
含笑九泉 hánxiào-jiǔquán smile in the underworld — one has nothing to regret in life; die happy:沉冤终于昭雪,他可以～了。Since he was finally rehabilitated after having been a victim of gross injustice for years, he would have nothing to regret in life (*or* he could now rest in peace in his grave).
含辛茹苦 hánxīn-rúkǔ endure all kinds of hardships; suffer hardships and privations:丈夫去世后,她～,把孩子们拉扯大。She endured no end of hardships, struggling to bring up her children after her husband's death.
含羞 hánxiū with a shy look; bashfully:～不语 feel too shy to speak /～娇嗔 pout prettily in embarrassment /～自尽 commit suicide from shame
含羞草 hánxiūcǎo 〈植物〉sensitive plant; mimosa
含蓄 hánxù *also* "涵蓄" hánxù ❶ contain; embody:他的话里～着无限的辛酸。There was a tone of untold sadness in his words. ❷ implicit; veiled:～的批评 implicit criticism /～地表示反对 express one's objection in a veiled manner /他在声明中～地承认自己犯了错误。His speech contained an implicit acknowledgement of his mistake. ❸ reserved:态度～ reserved manner /他为人～。He is a man of reserve.
含血喷人 hánxuè-pēnrén make slanderous or vicious accusations against sb.; throw dirt at sb.:想不到他竟然信口胡说,～。I never expected him to be such a shameless liar and vicious slanderer.
含饴弄孙 hányí-nòngsūn (of old people) play with one's grandchildren while chewing maltose — spend one's remaining years happily in the company of one's grandchildren; enjoy happy old age
含义 hányì *also* "涵义" hányì meaning; implication:这篇声明有什么～? What are the implications of this statement? /一个词可以有几种不同的～。A word can have several meanings.
含意 hányì implied meaning; implications:他这样说的～是什么? What did he mean by saying so? *or* What was he driving at with these remarks?
含英咀华 hányīng-jǔhuá study and grasp the essence of sth.; relish the beauty and joy of literature
含油层 hányóucéng 〈地质〉oil-bearing formation or stratum
含油气地区 hányóuqì dìqū 〈地质〉oil-gas bearing area
含油气远景 hányóuqì yuǎnjǐng 〈地质〉oil-gas bearing prospect
含油树脂 hányóu shùzhī oleoresin
含冤 hányuān suffer an injustice; be victim of a false charge:～莫白 suffer a wrong with no hope of being cleared; bear an injustice one cannot clear up /～终天 die uncleared of a false charge; die with one's name uncleared
含冤负屈 hányuān-fùqū suffer wrongs and bear injustices; be wronged on a false charge:～无处申 suffer wrongs and find no redress anywhere
含怨 hányuàn bear a grudge; nurse a grievance:～离去 depart nursing one's grievance; leave in resentment
含蕴 hányùn contain; embody:生活中～着丰富的哲理。There is plenty of philosophy in life.

焓

hán 〈物理〉enthalpy; total heat:～差 enthalpy difference

琀

hán 〈书面〉piece of jade or other jewel put in the mouth of the dead upon burial

晗

hán 〈书面〉dawn is on the point of breaking

函(凾)

hán ❶〈书面〉case; casket; envelope:石～ stone casket /镜～ case for a mirror /填料～ stuffing box ❷ letter:便～ informal letter /公～ official letter /贺～ letter of congratulation /唁～ letter (*or* message) of condolence /专～ special letter /修～ write a letter /致～ send a letter; write (to sb.)
函大 hándà (short for 函授大学) correspondence university
函电 hándiàn letters and telegrams; correspondence
函调 hándiào investigation conducted through correspondence
函牍 hándú 〈书面〉letters; correspondence:～往返 letters and replies; exchange of correspondence
函复 hánfù reply by letter; write a letter in reply:我们对此事的意见将于近日～。We shall send you a letter soon to present our views on this matter.
函告 hángào inform by letter:请～行期。Please inform us by letter about the date of your departure.
函购 hángòu purchase by mail; mail order:～部 mail-order department
函馆 Hánguǎn Hakodate, city in Southern Hokkaido, Japan
函件 hánjiàn letters; mail; correspondence:往来～ incoming and outgoing mail /～摘要 extract of a letter
函件分发器 hánjiàn fēnfāqì mail exploder
函聘 hánpìn engage or employ by letter
函商 hánshāng consult by letter
函授 hánshòu teach by correspondence; give a correspondence course:～部 correspondence department (of a school) /～作业 correspondence exercises (*or* homework) /～辅导 correspondence coaching
函授大学 hánshòu dàxué correspondence university
函授教材 hánshòu jiàocái correspondence textbook
函授教育 hánshòu jiàoyù education by correspondence
函授学校 hánshòu xuéxiào correspondence school
函数 hánshù 〈数学〉function:～变元 function variable /～符号 functional symbol; symbol of function /～运算 functional operation /生产～ production function /消费～ consumption function /正弦～ sine function /余弦～ cosine function /周期～ periodic function
函数表 hánshùbiǎo function table
函数常数 hánshù chángshù function constant
函数方程 hánshù fāngchéng functional equation
函数微分 hánshù wēifēn differential of function
函数值 hánshùzhí functional value
函索 hánsuǒ request by letter:～即寄 be sent on application; be available on request
函询 hánxún inquire by letter; apply by letter
函子 hánzǐ 〈数学〉functor:～范畴 category of functor /～分析 functorial analysis /～扩张 extension of functor

涵

hán ❶ contain; embody:海～ magnanimity of mind (in forgiving one's error); generous forgiveness /这首诗蕴～着深刻的思想。The poem embodies profound ideas. ❷ culvert:桥～ bridges and culverts
涵洞 hándòng culvert
涵盖 hángài contain; cover; embody:这部书～了美学的主要理论。This book contains the leading theories in aesthetics.
涵管 hánguǎn ❶ culvert pipe ❷ pipe-shaped culvert
涵容 hánróng 〈书面〉excuse; forgive; bear with:不周之处,尚望～。Please excuse us for any carelessness or oversight. *or* Please forgive us for being poor hosts.
涵蓄 hánxù *see* "含蓄" hánxù
涵养 hányǎng ❶ ability to control oneself; self-restraint:他很有～。He never loses self-control. *or* He never allows himself to be provoked. /我佩服他的～。I admire him for his self-restraint. ❷ conserve:改良土壤以～地力 conserve soil fertility through soil im-

H

provement
涵义 hányì meaning; implication
see also "含义" hányì
涵闸 hánzhá culvert and sluice

hǎn

罕 hǎn ❶ rarely; seldom: 人迹～至 show little trace of human habitation ❷ (Hǎn) a surname
罕百理派 Hǎnbǎilǐpài 〈伊斯兰〉Hanbalite school
罕觏 hǎngòu 〈书面〉meet rarely; seldom encounter
罕见 hǎnjiàn seldom seen; rare: ～的严重干旱 exceptionally serious drought / 人迹～ with little human trace; hardly inhabited
罕事 hǎnshì rare event; rare thing: 天下之～ sth. rare in the world
罕闻 hǎnwén (sth.) seldom heard of
罕物 hǎnwù rare and valuable thing: 此等～，自是先睹为快。It certainly is a great pleasure to be among the first to take a look at this rare treasure.
罕言寡语 hǎnyán-guǎyǔ (of a person) reticent; taciturn
罕有 hǎnyǒu rare; unusual; exceptional: ～的机会 rare opportunity / ～的现象 uncommon phenomenon

铪 hǎn 〈化学〉hahnium (Ha)

㘎(㘎) hǎn 〈书面〉(of a tiger) roar; growl

喊 hǎn ❶ shout; cry out; yell: ～救命 cry "Help! Help!" / ～声震天 make the air re-echo with shouts; make the welkin ring / 贼～捉贼 thief crying "Stop thief!" / 把嗓子～哑了 shout oneself hoarse / ～价成交的市场 outcry market / 他～了许久，也没有人理睬。He shouted for quite some time, but nobody answered. ❷ call (a person): 出发前～我一下。Call me before you set off. / 有人～我接电话。Somebody called to me to answer the phone. ❸ 〈方言〉call; address: 你～我老王就行了。Just call me Lao Wang.
喊话 hǎnhuà ❶ shout propaganda (at enemy troops across the front line): 阵前～ shout propaganda at enemy troops across the lines ❷ communicate by tele-equipment: 向总部～ communicate with the headquarters by radio
喊魂 hǎnhún also "叫魂" jiàohún 〈迷信〉yell to bring sb.'s soul back (when sb.'s critically ill)
喊叫 hǎnjiào shout; cry out: 请不要～。Please don't shout. / 足球迷们激动地大声～。Greatly excited, the soccer fans shouted at the tops of their voices.
喊门 hǎnmén call at the door
喊嗓子 hǎn sǎngzi ❶ shout loudly; yell: 他高兴得忍不住喊了一嗓子。He gave a yell out of sheer joy. ❷ (of traditional opera singers) practise or exercise one's voice by shouting or singing aloud
喊冤 hǎnyuān cry out about one's grievances: 给了他处分，他直～。He kept complaining about the punishment imposed on him.
喊冤叫屈 hǎnyuān-jiàoqū cry out about one's grievances; complain loudly about an alleged injustice

hàn

汗 hàn sweat; perspiration: 冷～ cold sweat / 出～ sweat; perspire / 发～ induce perspiration (as by medicine) / 盗～ 〈医学〉night sweat / 虚～ abnormal sweating due to general debility / 自～ 〈中医〉spontaneous perspiration (*or* sweating) / ～如雨下 dripping with perspiration
see also hán
汗斑 hànbān ❶ sweat stain ❷ 〈医学〉tinea versicolour
汗背心 hànbèixīn sleeveless undershirt; vest; singlet
汗臭 hànchòu bad smell of perspiration; stink of sweat
汗褂儿 hànguàr 〈口语〉undershirt
汗碱 hànjiǎn sweat stain
汗脚 hànjiǎo feet that sweat easily; sweaty feet
汗津津 hànjīnjīn moist with sweat; somewhat sweaty: 头发～的 hair moist with sweat
汗孔 hànkǒng also "毛孔" máokǒng 〈生理〉pore (of a sweat gland)
汗淋淋 hànlínlín also "汗漉漉" wet with sweat; dripping with sweat: 他跑得浑身～的。He was wet with sweat from running.
汗流浃背 hànliú-jiābèi streaming with sweat (from physical exertion or fear); soaked with sweat; sweating all over: 他干得～了，还不肯休息。He wouldn't take a rest, though he was sweating all over.
汗漉漉 hànlùlù see "汗淋淋"
汗马功劳 hànmǎ-gōngláo distinctions won on the battlefield; war exploits; great contributions or services: 立下～ perform exploits of valour (in battle); render great services; make great contributions; distinguish oneself
汗漫 hànmàn 〈书面〉❶ wide-ranging but irrelevant; wide of the mark; rambling: ～之言 irrelevant remarks; rambling talk / ～不可收拾 hopelessly irrelevant; wide of the mark ❷ (of waters) vast and mighty: 湖海～ vast expanses of water
汗毛 hànmáo fine hair on the human body
汗牛充栋 hànniú-chōngdòng enough books to make the ox carrying them sweat or to fill a house to the rafters — immense number of books; multitude: 坊间关于文化学的著作可谓～，但真正传世之作仍然罕见。Although books on cultural studies are as numerous in the market today as seashells on a beach, few of them are of real lasting value.
汗青 hànqīng 〈书面〉❶ complete a literary work or undertaking, as one would "sweat" the green bamboo strips before writing on them in ancient times: 这部书稿何日～，颇难预料。It's difficult to predict when the book will be completed. ❷ historical records; chronicles; annals: 名留～ carve a name in history / 人生自古谁无死，留取丹心照～。What man was ever immune from death? Let me but leave a loyal heart shining in the pages of history.
汗衫 hànshān ❶ undershirt; vest ❷ 〈方言〉shirt
汗生成 hànshēngchéng also "汗分泌" 〈生理〉hidropoiesis
汗水 hànshuǐ sweat; perspiration: ～湿透了衣衫 with one's shirt soaked in sweat
汗酸 hànsuān hidropoietic acid
汗禢儿 hàntār 〈方言〉Chinese-style singlet or vest
汗腾格里峰 Hànténggélǐfēng Mount Hantengri, one of the peaks of the Tianshan Mountains (天山) in Xinjiang
汗腺 hànxiàn 〈生理〉sweat gland
汗颜 hànyán 〈书面〉blush with shame; feel deeply ashamed: 工作做成这个样子，能不～吗？Who wouldn't blush (*or* be chagrinned) for making such a mess of the job?
汗液 hànyè sweat; perspiration
汗疹 hànzhěn also "痱子" fèizi heat rash; prickly heat; sudamen; miliaria
汗珠子 hànzhūzi beads of sweat: 他脸上的～直往下滚。Beads of sweat rolled down his face.
汗渍渍 hànzīzī 〈方言〉moist with sweat; sweaty: 他用手帕不断地擦着～的脑门儿。He constantly wiped his sweaty forehead with a handkerchief.
汗渍 hànzì sweat stain: ～的旧军服 old, sweat-stained army uniform / 他满脸是灰尘与～。His face was covered with dust and sweat.

闬 hàn 〈书面〉❶ gate to a lane or an alley ❷ wall

扞[1] hàn see "捍" hàn

扞[2] hàn see "扞格"
扞格 hàngé 〈书面〉conflict; contradict: ～不入 be contradictory; be ill-fitting

旱 hàn ❶ dry spell; drought: 受～ suffer from drought; be drought-stricken / 抗～ combat (*or* fight) drought / 庄稼～了。The crops are stricken by drought. / 久～逢甘雨。A soothing rain falls on the parched earth. ❷ *used in contrast with* 水: *see* "～冰"; "～伞" ❸ dryland; land: ～三角洲 dry delta ❹ on land; by land: 起～ take an overland route (usu. on foot)
旱魃 hànbá demon of drought; drought: ～施虐。The demon of drought ran amok. *or* There was a severe drought.
旱冰 hànbīng 〈体育〉roller-skating: 滑～去 go roller-skating
旱冰场 hànbīngchǎng roller-skating rink

旱冰鞋 hànbīngxié roller skates
旱成土 hànchéngtǔ 〈地质〉aridisol
旱船 hànchuán ❶〈方言〉boat-shaped waterside house in a garden ❷ "land boat", a model boat used as a stage prop in some folk dances:跑～ dance the "land boat" dance (with the dancer standing in a boat-shaped float and carrying it forward in her or his dance)
旱道 hàndào 〈方言〉overland route:经～赴京 go to the capital overland
旱稻 hàndào upland rice; dryrice
旱地 hàndì nonirrigated farmland; dryland:～作物 dry crop /～农业 dryland farming
旱谷 hàngǔ 〈地质〉arroyo; wadi
旱季 hànjì dry season:～攻势 dry-season offensive
旱金莲 hànjīnlián *also* "旱莲花"; "金莲花" jīnliánhuā 〈植物〉nasturtium (*Tropaeolum majus*)
旱井 hànjǐng ❶ water-retention well ❷ dry well (used to store vegetables in winter)
旱涝保收 hànlào-bǎoshōu ensure stable yields despite drought or excessive rain; make gains no matter what happens; ensure a safe income:～、高产稳产 give high and stable yields irrespective of drought or excessive rain /承包后的工资不能像以前那样～了。Under the contract system, one can no longer expect a guaranteed salary as before.
旱莲草 hànliáncǎo 〈植物〉*Eclipta prostrata*
旱莲花 hànliánhuā *see* "旱金莲"
旱柳 hànliǔ dryland willow (*Salix matsudana*)
旱路 hànlù overland route:走～ travel by land
旱年 hànnián year of drought
旱桥 hànqiáo viaduct; overpass; flyover
旱芹 hànqín (popularly known as 芹菜) celery (*Apium graveolens*)
旱情 hànqíng drought; damage caused by a drought; ravages of a drought:该地区～严重。The area is afflicted with severe drought. /～已趋缓和。The drought has eased up.
旱伞 hànsǎn parasol
旱生动物 hànshēng dòngwù xerophilous animal
旱生植物 hànshēng zhíwù xerophyte
旱獭 hàntǎ *also* "土拨鼠" tǔbōshǔ 〈动物〉marmot:藏～ Himalayan marmot
旱田 hàntián ❶ nonirrigated farmland ❷ dry land
旱象 hànxiàng signs of drought:～萌生。Signs of drought appeared.
旱鸭子 hànyāzi 〈戏谑〉person who cannot swim; non-swimmer:你们去游泳吧,我可是个～。You folks go swimming; I'm a non-swimmer.
旱烟 hànyān tobacco (smoked in a long-stemmed Chinese pipe)
旱烟袋 hànyāndài long-stemmed Chinese pipe
旱秧田 hànyāngtián dry nursery (for rice seedlings)
旱叶草 hànyècǎo bear grass
旱灾 hànzāi drought
旱作 hànzuò dry farming

悍

hàn ❶ doughty; dauntless; bold:强～ intrepid; valiant; dauntless ❷ fierce; ferocious; unreasonable:刁～ cunning and fierce; wicked and ferocious /凶～ fierce (*or* ferocious) and tough
悍匪 hànfěi ferocious bandit
悍妇 hànfù termagant (woman); shrew
悍然 hànrán outrageously; brazenly; flagrantly:～发动侵略战争 outrageously launch a war of aggression /～镇压人民起义 flagrantly suppress the people's uprising /～宣布 brazenly declare
悍然不顾 hànrán-bùgù in gross defiance or disregard of; fly in the face or teeth of:～国际关系准则 in defiance of norms of international relations /～中国政府的严正警告 utterly disregard the stern warning by the Chinese government
悍勇 hànyǒng 〈书面〉intrepid; dauntless:～好斗 intrepid and bellicose

焊(銲、釬)

hàn weld; solder:点～ spot (*or* point) welding /电～ electric welding /冷～ cold welding /气～ gas welding /软～ soft soldering /铜～ braze welding /电渣～ electroslag welding /对接～ butt welding
焊点 hàndiǎn welding spot; soldered dot
焊缝 hànfèng welding seam; weld line:～加厚 reinforcement of weld /～裂纹 weld metal crack (*or* cracking) /～量规 weld gauge
焊膏 hàngāo soldering paste
焊工 hàngōng ❶ welding; soldering ❷ welder; solderer
焊弧 hànhú 〈冶金〉welding arc:～电压 welding arc voltage
焊花 hànhuā sparks of welding
焊机 hànjī welding machine; welder
焊剂 hànjì welding flux; flux; solder
焊件 hànjiàn weldment:高强度～ high-strength weldment
焊接 hànjiē weld; solder:电弧～ (electric) arc welding /～操作 welding operation /～变形 welding deformation /～车间 welding shop /～钢管 welded steel pipe /～翼缘 welded flange
焊镴 hànlà ❶ welding flux ❷〈方言〉tin solder
焊料 hànliào welding or soldering flux; solder
焊钳 hànqián electrode-holder or pliers
焊枪 hànqiāng welding torch; (welding) blowpipe; welding gun
焊丝 hànsī solder wire; welding stick
焊条 hàntiáo welding rod; solderstick
焊锡 hànxī soldering tin; tin solder
焊药 hànyào welding agent or flux
焊液 hànyè welding fluid; soldering fluid
焊油 hànyóu soldering paste

蔊

hàn
蔊菜 hàncài 〈植物〉marsh cress (*Roripa montana*)

捍

hàn defend; guard
捍蔽 hànbì 〈书面〉protect; guard:～东南 guard the southeast
捍拒 hànjù 〈书面〉defend against; resist
捍卫 hànwèi defend; guard; protect:～领海 defend territorial waters /～民族利益 protect national interests /～祖国尊严 defend national dignity; vindicate national honour
捍御 hànyù 〈书面〉defend; guard:～祖国的边疆 defend the frontiers of one's country

睅

hàn 〈书面〉(of eyes) wide-open and protruding

汉[1](漢)

Hàn ❶ Han Dynasty (206 BC-220 AD):西～ Western Han Dynasty (206 BC-25 AD) /东～ Eastern Han Dynasty (25-220 AD) /～墓 Han Dynasty tomb ❷ Later Han Dynasty (后汉, 947-950 AD) during the period of the Five Dynasties ❸ regime (1360-1363 AD) established by the peasant uprising led by Chen Youliang (陈友谅) in the late Yuan Dynasty ❹ Han nationality:～蒙杂居区 area inhabited by Hans and Mongolians ❺ Chinese (language):～法词典 Chinese-French dictionary ❻ (hàn) man:老～ old man /穷～ poor man /大～ big fellow /好～ brave man; true man; hero /钢铁～ man of iron; person with strong will

汉[2](漢)

hàn Milky Way:银～ Milky Way /河～〈书面〉Milky Way;〈比喻〉starry talk; empty words
汉白玉 hànbáiyù white marble
汉堡 Hànbǎo Hamburg, major city and port in northwestern Germany:～牛排 hamburger steak
汉堡包 hànbǎobāo hamburger
汉城 Hànchéng Seoul, capital of the Republic of Korea
汉调 hàndiào 〈旧语〉Hubei opera
汉奸 hànjiān traitor (to China):～卖国贼 traitor and collaborator; quisling
汉剧 hànjù *also* "汉调" Hubei opera, popular in Hubei and parts of Henan, Shaanxi and Hunan
汉隶 hànlì ❶ Han script, written form of the Chinese language current in the Han Dynasty ❷ calligraphy in the style of Han script
汉民 Hànmín Han people; Han:我老婆是～,我是回民。My wife is a Han but I'm a Hui Muslim.
汉人 Hànrén ❶ Han; Han people ❷ person or people of the Han Dynasty
汉森病 hànsēnbìng 〈医学〉Hansen's disease; leprosy
汉莎航空公司 Hànshā Hángkōng Gōngsī Lufthansa, German civil aviation company
汉书 Hànshū *Han Shu* or *History of Han*, chronicle of the Han Dynasty between 206 BC and 23 AD written by Ban Gu (班固, 32-

H

92)

汉文 Hànwén ❶ Chinese language (usu. written): 译成～ translate into Chinese ❷ Chinese character

汉显 hànxiǎn (short for 汉字显示)〈通信〉showing Chinese Characters on the screen (of a pager): ～呼机 pager which shows Chinese characters on it

汉姓 hànxìng ❶ Han surname ❷ Han surname adopted by people of other nationalities: 许多满人现在都有～。Many Manchus now have Han surnames.

汉学 Hànxué ❶ Han school of classical learning; Han learning (as a variety of Confucian scholarship) ❷ Sinology: ～家 Sinologist

汉语 Hànyǔ Chinese (language): ～方言 dialect of the Chinese language

汉语拼音方案 Hànyǔ Pīnyīn Fāng'àn Pinyin or Scheme for the Chinese Phonetic Alphabet, officially adopted in 1958

汉语拼音字母 Hànyǔ pīnyīn zìmǔ Chinese phonetic alphabet

汉语水平考试 Hànyǔ shuǐpíng kǎoshì HSK — Chinese language proficiency test

汉藏语系 Hàn-Zàng yǔxì Sino-Tibetan family of languages

汉字 Hànzì Chinese character: 简化～ simplified Chinese characters /～显示 Chinese character display /～注音 phonetic transcription of Chinese characters /～处理软件 Chinese character processing software /～输入装置 Chinese (character) input unit /～数据库 Chinese character database /～字盘 Chinese selecting board /日语～ kanji; honji

汉字编码 Hànzì biānmǎ encodement of Chinese characters

汉字简化方案 Hànzì Jiǎnhuà Fāng'àn Scheme for Simplifying Chinese Characters

汉字库 hànzìkù Chinese character library

汉子 hànzi ❶ man; fellow ❷〈方言〉husband

汉族 Hànzú Han nationality, China's main nationality, distributed all over the country

熯

hàn 〈方言〉❶ bake over a slow fire ❷ fry in shallow oil; sauté ❸ steam

暵

hàn 〈书面〉❶ dry by exposing to the sun; sun ❷ dry; withered

翰

hàn 〈书面〉❶ writing brush: 挥～ wield one's writing brush; write (with a brush) ❷ writing; letters: 华～〈敬词〉your letter /书～ writings and letters

翰林 hànlín member of the Imperial Academy (from the Tang Dynasty onward): 前清～ member of the Imperial Academy of the former Qing Dynasty

翰林院 Hànlínyuàn 〈旧语〉Imperial Academy

翰墨 hànmò 〈书面〉brush and ink — writing, painting or calligraphy: 名家～ painting or calligraphy of a famous master

瀚

hàn 〈书面〉vast; immense: ～～ vast; boundless /浩～ vast; immense

瀚海 hànhǎi 〈书面〉vast desert

菡

hàn

菡萏 hàndàn 〈书面〉lotus

憾

hàn regret: 抱～ regret; repent (of sth.) /引以为～ consider sth. a matter for regret; deem sth. regrettable /死而无～ die without regret; die contented

憾然 hànrán disappointed: ～而返 return in disappointment

憾事 hànshì matter for regret: 引为～ regard sth. as a matter for regret; consider sth. regrettable /终身～ regret for life

撼

hàn shake: 摇～ shake violently /震～世界 shake the world /蚍蜉～树 an ant trying to topple a tree — ridiculously overrating oneself

撼动 hàndòng shake; vibrate

撼天动地 hàntiān-dòngdì shake heaven and earth: ～的革命风暴 earthshaking revolutionary storm /战场上喊杀声～。Shouts of "charge forward" shook the battlefield.

颔

hàn 〈书面〉❶ chin ❷ nod

颔联 hànlián third and fourth lines of a *lüshi* (律诗) poem forming a symmetrical couplet

颔首 hànshǒu 〈书面〉nod: ～示意 beckon with a nod /～赞许 give an approving nod; nod approvingly

hāng

夯(碎)

hāng ❶ rammer; tamper: 石～ stone rammer (*or* tamper) /木～ wooden rammer (*or* tamper) /机动～ power rammer (*or* tamper) ❷ ram; tamp: ～地 ram the ground ❸〈方言〉pound; buffet; thrash: 用拳头～人 pound (*or* buffet) sb. with fists ❹〈方言〉carry on one's shoulder with effort

夯板 hāngbǎn tamping plate

夯锤 hāngchuí tamper; rammer: 气动～ air rammer

夯镐 hānggǎo tamping pick

夯歌 hānggē rammers' chant

夯棍 hānggùn tamping bar or rod

夯具 hāngjù rammer; tamper

夯路机 hānglùjī roadpacker

夯土 hāngtǔ 〈建筑〉rammed earth: ～坝 rammed earth dam

夯土机 hāngtǔjī ramming or tamping machine; power rammer or tamper

夯砣 hāngtuó heavy end of a rammer (usu. made of stone or metal)

háng

亢

háng *see* "吭" háng

see also kàng

迒

háng 〈书面〉❶ (of animals or wheels) track ❷ path; trail

杭

Háng ❶ (short for 杭州) Hangzhou: 沪～线 Shanghai-Hangzhou railway ❷ a surname

杭纺 hángfǎng soft plain-weave silk fabric made in Hangzhou

杭剧 hángjù Hangzhou opera

杭育 hángyō 〈象声〉(chanted by groups of manual workers when doing hard work) heave ho; yo-heave-ho; yo-ho: 上山的路上不断响着挑夫们～、～的声音。Porters were heard to chant "Heave ho! Heave ho!" all the way up the mountain.

杭州 Hángzhōu Hangzhou, capital of Zhejiang Province

杭州湾 Hángzhōuwān Hangzhou Bay

颃

háng *see* "颉颃" xiéháng

吭

háng throat: 引～高歌 sing at the top of one's voice; sing lustily

see also kēng

绗

háng

绗绗 hángyuàn *see* "行院" hángyuàn

航

háng ❶ boat; ship: 夕阳西下，两三～靠在岸边。The sun was setting; a couple of boats were riding at anchor off the river bank. ❷ navigate; sail; fly: 出～ set out on a voyage (*or* flight); set sail; take off /远～ go on a long voyage; sail or fly to a faraway place /首～ maiden voyage (*or* flight) /通～ be open to navigation (*or* air traffic)

航班 hángbān scheduled flight; flight (number): ～号 flight number /3201～失去联系。Flight 3201 is out of contact.

航标 hángbiāo navigation mark; buoy: ～灯 navigation light; beacon

航测 hángcè (short for 航空测量) aerial survey: ～摄影机 aerial surveying camera /～平面图 aerophotographic plan /～飞机 air-mapping aircraft

航程 hángchéng voyage; flight; distance travelled: ～万里 voyage

H

(*or* flight) of ten thousand *li*
航程记录器 hángchéng jìlùqì odograph
航船 hángchuán ❶ (in Jiangsu and Zhejiang) wooden boat that plies regularly between inland towns ❷ steamboat or ship (that sails in a river or on the sea)
航次 hángcì ❶ sequence of voyages or flights; voyage or flight number ❷ number of voyages or flights made
航道 hángdào channel; sea-lane; fairway; course: 开辟新～ open an air (*or* a sea) route / 国际～ international sea-lane / 主～ main channel / ～标 navigable channel mark / ～水深 fairway depth / 船被大风吹得偏离了～。The vessel was blown off course by the gale.
航海 hánghǎi navigation: ～家 navigator; voyager
航海多项运动 hánghǎi duōxiàng yùndòng navigational sports
航海法规 hánghǎi fǎguī navigation law
航海雷达 hánghǎi léidá marine radar
航海罗盘 hánghǎi luópán mariner's compass
航海日志 hánghǎi rìzhì logbook; log
航海术 hánghǎishù navigation; seamanship
航海天文历 hánghǎi tiānwénlì nautical almanac
航海天文学 hánghǎi tiānwénxué nautical astronomy
航海图 hánghǎitú nautical chart
航海仪器 hánghǎi yíqì nautical instrument
航海用语 hánghǎi yòngyǔ nautical term
航徽 hánghuī emblem of an airline
航迹 hángjì (of an airplane, ship, rocket, torpedo, etc.) flight path; track; wake: ～角 flight-path angle / ～轴 flight-path axis / ～分析器 flight-path analyzer
航空 hángkōng aviation: 民用～ civil aviation / ～安全 aviation safety / ～货运 airfreight / ～联运 through air transport / ～器材 air material / ～燃料 aviation (*or* aircraft) fuel
航空版 hángkōngbǎn (of a newspaper, etc.) airmail edition
航空包 hángkōngbāo airline bag
航空保险 hángkōng bǎoxiǎn aviation insurance
航空标塔 hángkōng biāotǎ airway beacon
航空兵 hángkōngbīng ❶ air arm; air force: 海军～ naval air force / ～部队 air unit / ～基地 air base ❷ airman
航空病 hángkōngbìng aeropathy
航空测量 hángkōng cèliáng *also* "航测" aerial survey
航空磁测 hángkōng cícè aeromagnetic survey
航空地图 hángkōng dìtú aeronautical chart; aerial map
航空电子学 hángkōng diànzǐxué avionics
航空法 hángkōngfǎ aviation law; law of the air
航空港 hángkōnggǎng air harbour; airport
航空工程 hángkōng gōngchéng aeronautical engineering
航空工业 hángkōng gōngyè aviation or aircraft industry
航空公司 hángkōng gōngsī airline company; airlines; airways: 中国国际～ Air China / 联合～ China United Airlines; (US) United Airlines / 英国～ (UK) British Airways
航空管制 hángkōng guǎnzhì air traffic control
航空航天工业 hángkōng hángtiān gōngyè aerospace industry
航空航天医学 hángkōng hángtiān yīxué aerospace medicine
航空和航天局 Hángkōng Hé Hángtiānjú (US) National Aeronautics and Space Administration (NASA)
航空力学 hángkōng lìxué aeromechanics
航空模型 hángkōng móxíng model airplane
航空母舰 hángkōng mǔjiàn aircraft carrier; flattop: ～战斗群 aircraft-carrier battle group / 不沉的～ unsinkable aircraft carrier (used by some imperialists in reference to China's Taiwan)
航空幕僚长 Hángkōng Mùliáozhǎng (Japan) Chief of Air Staff (of the Defence Agency)
航空气象台 hángkōng qìxiàngtái air weather station; aeronautical meteorological station
航空气象学 hángkōng qìxiàngxué aeronautical meteorology
航空汽油 hángkōng qìyóu aviation gasoline
航空器 hángkōngqì aerial craft; airborne craft; aircraft: ～噪音 aircraft noise / 不明国籍的～ unidentified aircraft
航空日志 hángkōng rìzhì aircraft logbook
航空摄影 hángkōng shèyǐng aerophotography; aerial photography: ～机 air (*or* aerial) camera; airborne camera; aerocamera / ～学 aerophotography
航空探矿 hángkōng tànkuàng mineral exploration aviation; aerial prospecting
航空体育运动 hángkōng tǐyù yùndòng air sports; flying sports
航空天文历 hángkōng tiānwénlì air almanac
航空通用标准 hángkōng tōngyòng biāozhǔn Aircraft General Standard (AGS)
航空小姐 hángkōng xiǎojie air hostess; stewardess
航空协定 hángkōng xiédìng air transport agreement
航空信 hángkōngxìn airmail letter; air letter; airmail
航空学 hángkōngxué aeronautics; aviation
航空学校 hángkōng xuéxiào aviation or flying school
航空学院 hángkōng xuéyuàn aeronautical engineering institute
航空邮件 hángkōng yóujiàn airmail
航空云 hángkōngyún *also* "凝结尾迹" níngjié wěijì condensation trail; contrail; vapour trail
航空运动 hángkōng yùndòng air sports; flying sports
航空运输 hángkōng yùnshū air transport; carriage by air
航空站 hángkōngzhàn airport
航空照相 hángkōng zhàoxiàng *see* "航空摄影"
航空自卫队 Hángkōng Zìwèiduì (Japan) Air Self-Defence Force
航路 hánglù air or sea route: ～标志 route markings / ～指示 (air) traffic guidance / ～畅通。The air (*or* sea) route is clear.
航模 hángmó ❶ (short for 航空模型) model airplane ❷ model ship
航母 hángmǔ (short for 航空母舰) aircraft carrier; flattop
航摄 hángshè (short for 航空摄影) aerial photography; aerophotography: ～地面标志 ground marks for aerial photography
航摄飞机 hángshè fēijī photoplane; air-mapping plane
航速 hángsù speed of a ship or plane: ～为二十节 sail at a speed of 20 knots
航天 hángtiān spaceflight; astronautic flight; aerospace: ～飞行器 aerospacecraft; cosmoplane / ～环境模拟实验室 space environmental simulation laboratory
航天舱 hángtiāncāng space capsule
航天动力学 hángtiān dònglìxué astrodynamics
航天飞船 hángtiān fēichuán spaceship; spacecraft
航天飞机 hángtiān fēijī space shuttle; shuttlecraft
航天服 hángtiānfú space suit
航天港 hángtiāngǎng *also* "航天站" spaceport
航天工业 hángtiān gōngyè space industry; astronautical industry: ～部 ministry of space industry
航天火箭 hángtiān huǒjiàn spacerocket; astrorocket
航天技术 hángtiān jìshù space technology
航天模拟器 hángtiān mónǐqì space flight simulator
航天器 hángtiānqì spacecraft; aerospacecraft: ～对接 spacecraft docking / ～回收 spacecraft recovery (*or* retrieval) / ～着陆 spacecraft landing
航天探测器 hángtiān tàncèqì space probe
航天通信 hángtiān tōngxìn space communication (SPACECOM)
航天学 hángtiānxué astronautics; cosmonautics; space science
航天遥感 hángtiān yáogǎn space remote sensing
航天员 hángtiānyuán astronaut
航天站 hángtiānzhàn spaceport; space station
航图 hángtú chart
航务 hángwù navigational matters: ～局 shipping administration bureau
航线 hángxiàn air or shipping line; route; course: 传统～ customary route / 内河～ inland navigation line / 国际～ international air line / 远洋～ ocean navigation line
航向 hángxiàng course (of a ship or plane): 改变～ change course; tack / 右～ starboard tack / 左～ port tack / ～误差 course error / 指引～ point out the way forward; provide guidance / 拨正～ correct the course
航向方位指示器 hángxiàng fāngwèi zhǐshìqì course-and-bearing indicator
航向陀螺 hángxiàng tuóluó directional gyroscope; azimuth gyro
航行 hángxíng ❶ navigate by water; sail: 内河～ inland navigation / 逆风～ sail against the wind; sail to windward / 顺风～ sail before the wind; sail downwind ❷ navigate by air; fly: 空中～ aerial navigation; flight
航行半径 hángxíng bànjìng navigation radius
航行灯 hángxíngdēng navigation light
航行规则 hángxíng guīzé navigation rules
航行权 hángxíngquán right of navigation

H

航行事故 hángxíng shìgù navigation accident
航运 hángyùn shipping：～业 shipping industry /～市场 shipping market /～会 shipping conference
航运保险 hángyùn bǎoxiǎn shipping insurance
航运法 hángyùnfǎ law of navigation
航运公司 hángyùn gōngsī shipping company
航运权 hángyùnquán navigation right

行 háng ❶ line; row：提～ (as in typing, etc.) begin a new line /第五～ fifth line /排成四～ fall into four lines /字里～间 between the lines /一目十～ take in ten lines at a glance — read very fast ❷ seniority among brothers and sisters：大排～ seniority among siblings of a clan /"你～几？""我～二。""Where do you come among your brothers and sisters?" "I'm the second." ❸ trade; profession; line of business：懂～ know the business; know the ropes /改～ change one's profession; switch to a new profession /各～各业 all trades and professions; different walks of life /当～出色 be outstanding in one's own field ❹ business firm：粮～〈旧语〉wholesale grain shop /商～ trading company; commercial firm /车～ car dealer; bicycle dealer /拍卖～ auctioneer's /委托～ commission shop; commission house ❺〈量词〉*used to refer to anything that forms a line*：两～杨树 two rows of poplars /两～眼泪 two streams of tears
see also hàng; héng; xíng
行帮 hángbāng 〈旧语〉trade association; guild
行辈 hángbèi seniority in the family or clan; position in the family hierarchy：他的～比我大。He ranks as my senior in the clan.
行播 hángbō 〈农业〉row planting
行播机 hángbōjī row planter
行车 hángchē 〈方言〉overhead travelling crane; shop traveller
see also xíngchē
行当 hángdang ❶ trade; profession; line of business：他喜欢环卫这个～。He likes his job as an environmental sanitation worker. ❷〈戏曲〉type of role：他攻京剧中武生这一～。He specializes in playing *Wusheng*, or the martial role in Beijing opera.
行道 hángdao 〈方言〉trade; profession
see also xíngdào
行东 hángdōng 〈旧语〉owner of a trading company, workshop, mill, etc.
行贩 hángfàn pedlar
行规 hángguī guild regulations
行行出状元 hángháng chū zhuàngyuan every profession produces its own leading authority; one may distinguish oneself in any trade
行话 hánghuà jargon; cant：黑道～ cant of the underworld /法律界的～ legal jargon /外交～ diplomat-speak
行会 hánghuì guild：～制度 guild system /～师傅 guild master /～工人 journeyman
行货 hánghuò crudely-made goods; common stock
行纪 hángjì broker house; middleman
行家 hángjia ❶ expert; connoisseur; specialist：老～ old hand /～里手 experts and master hands /～不说外行话。A professional would not speak in the lay language. ❷〈方言〉(used in the affirmative) be expert (at sth.)：您对种树挺～呀。You're quite an expert at planting trees.
行间 hángjiān ❶〈书面〉ranks of the army：出身～ rise from the ranks ❷ between lines or rows：～锄草 hoeing between the rows (of crops); inter-row hoeing /看懂字里～的意思 read between the lines
行间追肥机 hángjiān zhuīféijī 〈农业〉row applicator
行距 hángjù space between rows; spacing; row spacing：$1\frac{1}{2}$～ (of typing) one-and-half spacing /种这种庄稼～一定要宽。Be sure to leave a wide space between rows when planting this crop.
行款 hángkuǎn format of lines in writing or typesetting
行列 hángliè ranks：队伍～整齐 be drawn up in orderly ranks /进入先进企业的～ join the ranks of advanced enterprises
行列式 hánglièshì 〈数学〉determinant：～方程 determinantal equation /～论 theory of determinants
行频 hángpín line frequency
行情 hángqíng quotations (on the market); prices; market conditions：～分析 market analysis /～看跌。The market is weak (*or* bearish). /～看涨。The market is strong (*or* bullish). /～坚守原盘。The market remains unchanged.
行情表 hángqíngbiǎo quotations list; tabulated quotations
行市 hángshi quotations (on the market); prices：～趋高 higher in quotation /～下降 lower in quotation /摸准～ find out which way the market is going /～看好。The market is picking up. /～变化不定。Prices fluctuate constantly.
行式打印 hángshì dǎyìn 〈计算机〉line printing：～机 line printer
行手 hángshǒu expert; veteran; old hand：庄稼老～ experienced farmer
行首 hángshǒu 〈旧语〉courtesan
行伍 hángwǔ the ranks：～出身 rise from the ranks /投身～ join the army; enlist
行业 hángyè trade; profession; industry：服务～ service trades /旅游～ tourist industry; tourism /建筑～ building (*or* construction) industry /广告～ advertising profession /～联合组织 trade confederation /～概况 industrial profile
行业工会 hángyè gōnghuì craft union
行业公会 hángyè gōnghuì craft guild; trade association (of businessmen in the same trade or industry)：航运～ shipping conference
行业亏损 hángyè kuīsǔn 〈经济〉loss incurred by an industry; industry loss：减少～ reduce industry losses
行业语 hángyèyǔ professional jargon; cant
行佣 hángyòng 〈方言〉commission; brokerage; middleman's fee
行院 hángyuàn *also* "衏衏" hángyuàn 〈旧语〉❶ (in the Jin and Yuan dynasties) house of prostitutes; house of actresses ❷ prostitute; actress
行栈 hángzhàn broker's storehouse
行长 hángzhǎng president (of a bank); governor (usu. of an official bank)：中国人民银行～ governor of the People's Bank of China
行子 hángzi 〈方言〉sb. or sth. one doesn't like

绗 háng sew with long stitches：～被子 sew on a quilt cover with long stitches

hàng

沆 hàng 〈书面〉vast expanse of water
沆瀣 hàngxiè 〈书面〉evening mist
沆瀣一气 hàngxiè-yīqì 〈贬义〉like attracts like; birds of a feather flock together; act in collusion; wallow in the mire together：跟侵略者～ work hand in glove with the aggressors

巷 hàng tunnel
see also xiàng
巷道 hàngdào 〈矿业〉tunnel：～壁 wall (of a tunnel) /～掘进 tunnelling
巷道掘进机 hàngdào juéjìnjī tunnelling machine

行 hàng *see* "树行子" shùhàngzi
see also háng; héng; xíng

hāo

蒿 hāo 〈植物〉wormwood; artemisia
蒿草 hāocǎo wormwood
蒿莱 hāolái 〈书面〉overgrown weeds
蒿里之歌 hāolǐzhīgē funeral scroll of an elegy written on the death of a friend
蒿目 hāomù 〈书面〉look as far as the eye can see; gaze into the distance
蒿目时艰 hāomù-shíjiān regard the world's troubles with great anxiety; watch one's troubled country with deep concern：他因～而辞官回乡。Gravely troubled about the ills of the country, he resigned his official post and returned to his native village.
蒿素 hāosù artemisin
蒿子 hāozi wormwood; artemisia
蒿子秆儿 hāozigǎnr tender leaves and stem of crown daisy chrysanthemum (eaten as a vegetable)

嚆 hāo
嚆矢 hāoshǐ 〈书面〉❶ arrow with a whistle attached ❷ forerun-

ner; harbinger; precursor:人造卫星的成功发射是人类星际旅行的～。The successful launching of man-made satellites was a harbinger of man's inter-stellar travel.

薅 hāo ❶ pull up (weeds, etc.); weed by hand:～西红柿地 weed a tomato plot /把杂草～干净。Pull up all the weeds. ❷〈方言〉pull; tug; grab:把某人从椅子里～起来 pull sb. up from the chair /他想跑,我一把～住了他。Seeing that he was trying to get away, I grabbed him instantly.

薅草 hāocǎo weeding

薅锄 hāochú weeding hoe

háo

豪 háo ❶ person of extraordinary powers or endowments: 文～ literary giant /富～ rich and powerful person; tycoon /英～ hero; outstanding figure ❷ bold and unconstrained; magnanimous and forthright; unrestrained:粗～ crude and forthright; untrammelled ❸ rich and powerful: *see* "～门";"～富" ❹despotic; bullying; coercive:土～劣绅 local despots and evil gentry

豪侈 háochǐ excessively luxurious; extravagant:～的生活 live in excessive luxury

豪宕 háodàng 〈书面〉uninhibited; bold and unconstrained

豪夺 háoduó take by force:巧取～ take by force or trickery; seize by hook or by crook

豪放 háofàng uninhibited; bold and unconstrained:性情～ be bold and uninhibited by nature /文笔～ bold and unrestrained penmanship

豪放不羁 háofàng-bùjī unconventional and uninhibited; vigorous and unrestrained:他为人～,热情达观。Bold and uninhibited, he is at once warm-hearted and broad-minded.

豪放派 háofàngpài (usu. of *ci* poetry) powerful and freestyle; school of heroic abandon

豪富 háofù ❶ powerful and wealthy:他家世代～。His family had been powerful and wealthy for generations. ❷ the rich and powerful; plutocrat:他是镇上的～。He is the most powerful and wealthiest person in town.

豪贵 háoguì ❶ wealthy and influential:～公子 son of a wealthy and influential family ❷ wealthy and influential people:干犯～ offend the rich and powerful

豪横 háohèng despotic; bullying:～跋扈 despotic and domineering

豪横 háoheng 〈方言〉of uncompromising integrity; staunch; unyielding:好姑娘,真～! What a steadfast girl!

豪华 háohuá ❶ (of living) extravagant; luxurious:生活～ lead an extravagant life; live in luxury ❷ (of buildings, furniture, ornaments, etc.) sumptuous; splendid; lavish: 衣着～ be dressed in splendid clothes /～小轿车 luxury (*or* de luxe) car

豪华版 háohuábǎn de luxe edition

豪家 háojiā *see* "豪门"

豪杰 háojié person of exceptional ability; hero:江山如画,一时多少～! Mountains and rivers make a vivid picture — what a host of heroes there were then!

豪举 háojǔ bold move; munificent or magnificent act; extravagance:倾家兴学的～ munificent act of selling all one's property to set up schools /一掷千金的～ extravagance of spending one thousand ounces of gold without batting an eyelid

豪客 háokè 〈书面〉robber; bandit

豪迈 háomài bold and generous; heroic:～的事业 heroic cause; splendid undertaking /～的情怀 valiant sentiments /～地宣告 declare with pride /他昂头挺胸,～地向前走去。Head held high, he marched forward gallantly.

豪门 háomén rich and powerful family; wealthy and influential clan:出身～ be from a rich and influential family /～大族 powerful families and great clans

豪奴 háonú servant who bullies people on the strength of his rich and powerful master

豪气 háoqì heroic spirit; heroism:～十足 full of dash

豪强 háoqiáng ❶ arrogant; despotic; tyrannical:逞～ give free rein to one's arrogance; have a free hand in doing what one wishes ❷ despot; bully:剪除该地～ suppress local despots and bullies

豪情 háoqíng lofty sentiments:～逸致 lofty sentiments and unconventional spirit

豪情满怀 háoqíng-mǎnhuái full of pride and enthusiasm; full of spirit:面对困难,他～。In the face of difficulties, he remains in high spirits.

豪情壮志 háoqíng-zhuàngzhì lofty sentiments and high aspirations:他们心中充满建设边疆的～。With hearts overflowing with lofty sentiments and high aspirations they dedicated themselves to the development of the border regions of their country.

豪萨人 Háosàrén Hausa, people of West Africa and the Sudan

豪萨语 Háosàyǔ Hausa (language)

豪商 háoshāng merchant having abundant funds; wealthy merchant; merchant prince

豪奢 háoshē excessively luxurious; extravagant

豪绅 háoshēn despotic gentry

豪士 háoshì person of outstanding talent

豪爽 háoshuǎng bold and unconstrained; uninhibited and straightforward; forthright:性情～ forthright by nature /谈吐～ outspoken and straightforward in speech

豪侠 háoxiá ❶ courageous and chivalrous; gallant:～之士 gallant man ❷ gallant man; man of courage and chivalry:自古燕赵多～。North China has been known for its men of courage and chivalry since time immemorial.

豪兴 háoxìng ebullient high spirits; exhilaration; keen interest:～不减当年 maintain one's ebullient high spirits as always; keep as keen an interest as ever

豪言壮语 háoyán-zhuàngyǔ brave or proud words; heroic remarks or words:这些～激励我们去夺取更大的胜利。These heroic words will encourage us to win still greater victories. /他们发出～:不达目的,誓不罢休! They vowed bravely that they would not stop until they reached their goal.

豪饮 háoyǐn drink lustily; drink heavily; drink with abandon:你我今日作一～。Today, let's drink to our hearts' content.

豪右 háoyòu 〈书面〉*see* "豪族"

豪雨 háoyǔ torrential rain:热带～ tropical downpour /一夜～。The rain came down in buckets the whole night.

豪语 háoyǔ heroic words; brave words; bold promise:～惊人 startling brave remarks

豪猪 háozhū *also* "箭猪" jiànzhū porcupine

豪壮 háozhuàng grand and heroic:～的誓言 grand and heroic oath (*or* pledge) /气势～ with great force or momentum; powerful

豪纵 háozòng bold and unconstrained:赋诗～ compose a poem in a bold and unrestrained style /～狂放的笔墨 bold and unconstrained calligraphy (*or* writing)

豪族 háozú wealthy and influential clan

濠 háo moat:城～ city moat

壕 háo ❶ moat:城～ (city) moat ❷ trench:战～ trench; entrenchment /交通～ communication trench /防空～ air-raid dugout /掘～固守 dig trenches for resistance; dig in

壕沟 háogōu ❶〈军事〉trench ❷ ditch

壕堑 háoqiàn trench; entrenchment:～战 trench warfare

嚎 háo ❶ howl; yell; bawl:狼～ howl of a wolf ❷ wail; cry loudly:～天哭地 weep and wail

嚎春 háochūn howl for mating; be in heat:这猫在～。The cat is howling for a mate.

嚎叫 háojiào *see* "号叫" háojiào

嚎哭 háokū *see* "号哭" háokū

嚎丧 háosāng *see* "号丧" háosāng

嚎丧 háosang *see* "号丧" háosang

嚎啕 háotáo *also* "嚎咷" *see* "号啕" háotáo

毫 háo ❶ fine tapering hair:羊～ fine goat's hair (used to make writing brushes) /秋～ autumn hair (*or* down) (of newly moulted birds or animals); minutest detail /狼～笔 writing brush made of weasel's hair ❷ writing brush:挥～疾书 wield one's writing brush and write quickly ❸ loop for balancing a steelyard (from the user's hand):头～ first loop (on the steelyard, for *liang* measurement) /二～ second loop (on the steelyard, for *jin* measurement) ❹ (used in the negative only) least bit; slightest degree:～不犹豫

H

without the slightest hesitation /～无诚意 without the least sincerity /～无可能 out of the question /～无疑问 as sure as eggs are eggs /～不逊色 not the least bit inferior; by no means worse; every bit equal; second to none /～不迟延 without (the slightest) delay; immediately; at once /这事他～不在乎。He doesn't care a cuss (*or* farthing) about that. *or* He couldn't care less about that. ❺ a thousandth of certain units of measurement: *see* "～米"; "～升"; "～克" ❻ *hao*, a unit of measure $\frac{1}{10}$ of *li* (厘), (a) in weight, equivalent to 0.005 grams (b) in length, equivalent to $\frac{1}{3}$ of a decimillimetre ❼〈方言〉*jiao*, $\frac{1}{10}$ of *yuan*

毫安 háo'ān 〈电学〉milliampere (mA or ma): ～计 milliammeter

毫巴 háobā 〈气象〉millibar (mb)

毫不利己，专门利人 háo bù lì jǐ, zhuānmén lì rén utter devotion to others without any thought of oneself: 学习白求恩～的精神。Learn from Dr. Bethune his spirit of selflessness.

毫法 háofǎ *also* "毫法拉"〈电学〉millifarad

毫发 háofà 〈书面〉(mostly used in the negative) hair; least bit; slightest: ～不差 not deviating a hair's breadth; without the least difference

毫发不爽 háofà-bùshuǎng *also* "毫厘不爽" not deviate a hair's breadth; be perfectly accurate: 他所言与事实～。What he said tallied perfectly with the facts.

毫分 háofēn least; minute; slightest: 不差～ be not different in the least

毫伏 háofú 〈电学〉millivolt: ～安 millivoltampere /～计 millivoltmeter

毫克 háokè milligramme (mg)

毫厘 háolí least bit; iota: 失之～，谬以千里。An error the breadth of a single hair can lead you a thousand *li* astray. *or* The least bit of deviation may eventually result in great divergence.

毫毛 háomáo soft hair on the body; down: 你敢动他一根～! Don't you dare to touch a single hair on his head! /所有这些诬蔑无损于我们一根～。All these calumnies cannot do us the slightest harm.

毫米 háomǐ millimetre (mm)

毫米波 háomǐbō 〈无线电〉millimetre wave: ～段 millimetre-wave band /～通信 millimetre-wave communication

毫秒 háomiǎo millisecond (ms): ～爆破 millisecond blasting /～雷管 millisecond detonator

毫末 háomò 〈书面〉tip of a fine hair — minutest quantity or detail: ～之利 least profit /合抱之木，生于～。Great oaks from little acorns grow.

毫欧 háo'ōu 〈电工〉milliohm: ～计 milliohmmeter

毫升 háoshēng millilitre (ml)

毫宋 háosòng 〈物理〉$\frac{1}{1,000}$ of a sone; millisone

毫瓦 háowǎ 〈电工〉milliwatt: ～表 milliwattmeter

毫微 háowēi ($=10^{-9}$) millimicro-; nano-: ～电路 nanocircuit /～程序 nanoprogramme

毫微安 háowēi'ān millimicroampere; nanoampere

毫微法 háowēifǎ millimicrofarad; nanofarad

毫微伏特 háowēi fútè millimicrovolt; nanovolt

毫微技术 háowēi jìshù nanotechnology

毫微米 háowēimǐ nanometre (nm); millimicron; nanon

毫微秒 háowēimiǎo nanosecond (ns); millimicrosecond: ～处理机 nanoprocessor /～脉冲技术 nanosecond pulse technique

毫微微 háowēiwēi femto ($=10^{-15}$)

毫微微微 háowēiwēiwēi avo ($=10^{-21}$)

毫无二致 háowú-èrzhì without a fraction of difference; as like as two peas; identical: 两者间～。There is not the slightest difference between the two. *or* The two are every bit the same.

毫洋 háoyáng 〈旧语〉monetary unit used in Guangdong and Guangxi prior to 1938 (for Guangdong) and 1939 (for Guangxi): ～券 *haoyang* note

毫针 háozhēn filiform needle in acupuncture; acupuncture needle

毫子 háozi ❶〈方言〉〈旧语〉silver coin of small denominations used in Guangdong and Guangxi prior to 1938 and 1939 respectively ❷ *jiao*, $\frac{1}{10}$ of a *yuan*

蚝(蠔) háo oyster

蚝豉 háochǐ dried oyster meat

蚝油 háoyóu oyster sauce

号(號) háo ❶ howl; yell; bawl: 呼～ yell and cry /啼饥～寒 cry out from hunger and cold /北风怒～。A north wind is howling. ❷ wail: 哀～ cry piteously; wail

see also hào

号呼 háohū cry out; yell: 为正义而～ cry out for justice

号叫 háojiào yell; scream; howl: 疼得～ scream (*or* yell) with pain; cry out with pain /她一面哭，一面～着。She wailed and screamed.

号哭 háokū wail: 在丈夫的坟上～ wail at one's husband's grave

号丧 háosāng howl or scream at a funeral: 抬起棺材的时候，众人一起～。When the coffin was being raised, all started howling in mourning for the deceased.

号丧 háosang 〈方言〉〈贬义〉howl as if at a funeral; cry; wail: 你～什么呀! What the hell are you bawling (*or* crying) for!

号啕 háotáo *also* "号咷"; "嚎啕" háotáo; "嚎咷" háotáo cry loudly; wail: ～痛哭 cry one's eyes (*or* heart) out; cry with abandon /她一发～不已。She wailed even more passionately.

嚎(嘷) háo (of a jackal or wolf) howl: 鬼哭狼～ wail like ghosts and howl like wolves; let loose a stream of wild shrieks and cries

嚎叫 háojiào (usu. of jackals and wolves) howl: 荒野之中，群狼～。Packs of wolves were howling in the wilderness.

貉 háo

see also hé

貉绒 háoróng fine raccoon dog fur (with all the bristles pulled)

貉子 háozi (popular term for 貉 hé) raccoon dog

hǎo

好 hǎo ❶ good; fine; nice: ～消息 good news /～天气 nice weather /～榜样 fine example /～的开始是成功的一半。Well begun, half done. /这话说得太～了。That is a very apt remark. ❷ be in good health; be or get well: 他身体很～。He is in the pink of health. *or* He is very well. /你母亲病～了吗? Is your mother all right now? *or* Has your mother recovered from her illness? ❸ friendly; kind: ～朋友 great (*or* good) friend /他们俩很要～。They are bosom friends. /邻居对她都很～。Her neighbours are all very kind to her. ❹ be easy (to do); be convenient: 这问题～解决。The problem can be easily solved. /这地方真不～找。It was difficult to find the place. ❺ *used before a verb to indicate an aspect that gives satisfaction*: *see* "～吃"; "～看" ❻ *used after a verb to indicate the completion of an action*: 计划订～了。The plan has been drawn up. /请大家排～队。Please line up. /我穿～衣服就去。I'll go after I get dressed. /电视机修～了吗? Have you had the TV set fixed? ❼ *used to express approval, agreement, conclusion, etc.*: ～，你说得完全正确。Yes, you're perfectly right. /～，就照你的意见做吧。OK, let's do it according to your suggestion. /～，今天就到此为止。Well, let's call it a day. ❽ *used ironically to express dissatisfaction*: 你要爬上去，～，看你怎么爬? So you want to climb it; well, let us see how you do it. /～啊，看你还往哪里跑! Now, where else can you go? ❾ *used as a polite formula*: 你～! How do you do? *or* Hello! *or* Hi! /～睡! Good night! /你～走。Good-bye! ❿ for the purpose of; in order to; so that: 平整土地～浇水 level the land for irrigation (*or* watering) /你留个电话，有事我～跟你联系。Give me your telephone number so that I can contact you when necessary. /别忘了带伞，下雨～用。Don't forget to take your umbrella in case it rains. ⓫〈方言〉may; can; should; ought to: 我明天～去你家吗? May I come to your house tomorrow? /东西都已准备停当，你～动身了。Everything is ready. You ought to get going now. ⓬ *used before certain time or numeral indicators to suggest a large number or a long time*: 我等了你～半天。I've been waiting for you for quite a while. /今天下午～几个人来找过你。Quite a few people came in looking for you this afternoon. ⓭ *used before adjectives or verbs for emphasis and with exclamatory force*: 今天～热! How hot it is today! /街上～热闹。What a bustling (*or* busy) street! /你这个人～糊涂! You are such a fool! /原来你躲在这儿，害得我～找! So you've been hiding here. You sure gave me a hard time looking for you! ⓮ (used before adjectives) to

what extent; how:新机场离这儿有～远? How far is the new airport from here? /电影要放～长时间? How long will the film last?
see also hào

好办 hǎobàn easy to handle or cope with:他认为那件事不大～,而这件事比较～。He thinks that is a hard nut to crack, but this is fairly easy.

好比 hǎobǐ can be compared to; may be likened to; be just like:我们当前的工作～一场战斗。Our present work can be compared to a battle. /光阴～河中水,只能流去不能回。Time flies just like flowing water, and it'll never return.

好不 hǎobù (used before bi-syllabic words with exclamatory force) how; what; so:跟他一起打网球,～高兴。How glad I was to play tennis with him. /老同学聚会,～热闹。What a joyous scene it is when former schoolmates get together!

好不容易 hǎobù róngyì *see* "好容易"

好吃 hǎochī tasty; delicious; nice:我觉得这道菜～。I find this dish tasty. /这种苹果不好看,可是～。This kind of apple does not look nice but it is delicious.

好丑 hǎochǒu 〈方言〉❶ good and bad; what's good and what's bad:评论～ comment on what is good and what is bad /不识～ be unable to tell good from bad; not know what's good for one ❷ in any case; at any rate; anyhow:你～去一趟吧,要不怎么办呢? You'll have to go there anyhow, or else what can you do?

好处 hǎochu ❶ benefit; advantage:对人民有～ be of benefit to the people /戒烟～多。There are many advantages in giving up smoking. /经常锻炼身体大有～。It does one a world of good to do exercises regularly. ❷ gain; profit; mileage:从争端中获得最大的～ get maximum profit (*or* mileage) out of a dispute /他没捞到任何～。He has gained nothing out of this.

好处费 hǎochufèi favour fee; kickback:多给～向客户推销不合格产品 sell inferior products to middlemen by giving generous kickbacks

好歹 hǎodǎi ❶ good and bad; what's good and what's bad:不知～ be unable to tell what's good for one; not know chalk from cheese; not appreciate a favour /～人心久后知。A person's heart, good or evil, will be revealed in time. ❷ mishap; disaster:万一他有个～,我们必须立即组织抢救。Should something happen to him, we must come to his rescue immediately. ❸ in a makeshift manner; somehow or other; somehow:时间很紧,～收拾收拾上路吧。As we are pressed for time, let's just pack a few things and get going. ❹ no matter in what way; at any rate; anyhow:～你得去一趟。You should go there anyhow. /你马上就去,～把她叫回来。Go at once and get her back one way or another.

好端端 hǎoduānduān in perfectly good condition; when everything is all right:刚才还～的,怎么一下子就晕倒了? How come he fainted all of a sudden? He was perfectly all right a moment ago. /瞧,～的菜园子,全给野猪祸害了! Look, what havoc the boars have played with this beautiful vegetable garden!

好多 hǎoduō ❶ good or great many; good deal; lots of:她有～朋友。She has a lot of (*or* a great many) friends. /他们准备了～饭菜来款待我们。They prepared a great deal of food to entertain us. ❷〈方言〉how many; how much:剩下～? How much is left? /今天报名的人有～? How many applicants are there today?

好感 hǎogǎn favourable impression; good opinion:博得～ win (*or* earn) the good opinion of others /对某某有～ be well disposed towards sb.; have a good opinion of sb. /听众对他的发言毫无～。His speech made quite an unfavourable impression on the audience.

好钢用在刀刃上 hǎogāng yòng zài dāorènshang 〈谚语〉use the best steel to make the knife's edge — use material where it is needed most; use the best material at the key point:目前顶用的技术人员少,更应该～。As competent technicians are rather scarce these days, they must be used where they are most needed.

好狗不挡道 hǎogǒu bù dǎng dào 〈俗语〉(abusive or jocular) good dogs don't get in the way; do not stand in the way

好过 hǎoguò ❶ have an easy time; be in easy circumstances:日子很不～ have a hard time /日子越来越～。Life is getting better and better. ❷ feel well:他休息了一会儿,觉得～些了。He felt a bit better after taking a rest.

好汉 hǎohàn brave man; true man; hero:～惜～。Heroes are attached to heroes. /不到长城非～。He who doesn't reach the Great Wall is no true man. *or* He is no true man who does not carry something through to the end. /～流血不流泪。A brave man would rather shed blood than tears.

好汉不吃眼前亏 hǎohàn bù chī yǎnqiánkuī 〈俗语〉a wise man will not fight when the odds are obviously against him; a wise man knows when to retreat:～,这帮人不好惹,目前别去碰他们。As wise men never fight when the odds are against them, we'd better leave these vicious people alone.

好汉不提当年勇 hǎohàn bù tí dāngnián yǒng 〈俗语〉a true hero is silent about his past glories:～,这些"光荣史"还说它干吗? Since a true man never dwells on the glories of bygone days, what is the point of raking up one's illustrious past?

好汉一言,快马一鞭 hǎohàn yī yán, kuàimǎ yī biān 〈俗语〉a true man needs no reminder to keep his word, as a swift horse needs no spurring

好汉做事好汉当 hǎohàn zuòshì hǎohàn dāng 〈俗语〉a true man has the courage to accept the consequences of his own actions:～,我不牵连别人。As a true man faces up to the consequences of his own actions, I will certainly not implicate others.

好好儿 hǎohāor ❶ in perfectly good condition; when everything is all right:～的一栋楼房,干吗要拆掉? Why should a building be pulled down when it is still in good shape? /这录音机还～的呀,用不着换。This recorder is still in good order and there is no need to have it replaced. ❷ all out; to one's heart's content; try one's best:～干 do one's best /～想一想 give (the matter) careful thought; mull it over /咱俩～地谈谈心。Let the two of us have a heart-to-heart talk. /这些锅、碗、瓢、盆都得～地擦洗擦洗了。All these pots and pans need a good scouring.

好好先生 hǎohǎo xiānsheng one who tries not to offend anybody; one who never says no; Mr. Please-all:让这位～来评理,这不是瞎子点灯 — 白费蜡? It is utterly futile to ask Mr. Please-all to pass judgment on the matter?

好话 hǎohuà ❶ good words; well-meant advice; useful words:～不说二遍。Good words are never repeated (lest they should be taken lightly). /你要永远记住他的这一番～。You should never forget his well-meant advice. ❷ words of praise; pleasant words:爱听～ be fond of praise /这个人听了～就喜形于色。This fellow brightened up upon hearing the compliments. ❸ words of persuasion; plea; apology:我妈跟人家说了许多～,这事儿才算了结。The matter was put to rest only after my mother had made repeated pleas for reconciliation. /说了一大堆～,他还是无动于衷。He remained unmoved by all our apologies.

好话说尽,坏事做绝 hǎohuà shuōjìn, huàishì zuòjué say every fine word and do every foul deed; stop at no crime for all one's fine words; be a sinner under the guise of a saint:这人阴险狠毒,向来是～。Vicious and malicious by nature, the man is always doing foul deeds even when he mouths fine words.

好坏不分 hǎohuài-bùfēn do not distinguish the good from the bad; not distinguish between those who do a good job and those who do shoddy work

好坏参半 hǎohuài cānbàn partly good and partly bad; ambivalent:～的事物 curate's egg

好几 hǎojǐ ❶ *used after a round number to indicate that the fractional amount is considerable*:他都五十～了,看起来还像个四十岁的人。He looks a man of forty, though he is actually well over fifty. /一袋大米就值一百～。A bag of rice costs much more than a hundred *yuan*. ❷ (used before measure words, time words, and round numbers) quite a few; several:～倍 quite a few times /～千元钱 several thousand *yuan* /修了水库以后,这条河已有～十年没决堤了。Quite a few decades have passed without the river overflowing its banks, since the construction of the reservoir.

好家伙 hǎojiāhuo 〈叹词〉good lord; good heavens; good gracious; gosh:～,这台机器真沉。Good heavens, the machine is really heavy. /～,你们干得真快啊! Gosh, you do work fast.

好价 hǎojià good price:卖个～ get a good price (for sth.) /出个～ offer a good price

好借好还 hǎojiè-hǎohuán 〈俗语〉make it a point to return or repay what one has borrowed:～,再借不难。It's easy to get a loan again if one returns (*or* repays) what one has borrowed in time. *or* Return (*or* repay) what you borrow in time and you'll be welcome the next time.

好景 hǎojǐng good times:但愿～长存。If only good times would stay for ever!

好景不长 hǎojǐng-bùcháng *also* "好景不常" good times don't last long; not every day is Sunday; pleasant hours fly fast:小俩口婚后生

活美满幸福，可惜～，不久就爆发了战争。The young couple lived in harmony and happiness after marriage. But good times don't last long: war soon broke out. (*or* But the pity is: it was not long before war broke out.)

好久 hǎojiǔ ❶ for a long time; long: 我站在这儿等他～了。I've been waiting here for him for quite a long time. /～没有收到他的来信了。We haven't heard from him for quite some time now. ❷〈方言〉how long: 这要～才能学会? How long will it take to learn this?

好看 hǎokàn ❶ good-looking; pretty; interesting; attractive: ～的小说 interesting novel /～的电影 attractive movie /这个小女孩很～。The little girl is really pretty. /这裙子你穿准～。The skirt would look nice on you. /～的花不一定香。Beautiful flowers may not necessarily be fragrant. ❷ honoured; proud: 儿子得了世界冠军，全家脸上都～。The whole family felt greatly honoured when the son won a world championship. ❸ in an embarrassing situation; on the spot: 你这不是赶鸭子上架，成心要我的～吗? You are bent on embarrassing me by asking me to do the impossible, aren't you? /你难道不明白他们是要我的～? Can't you see that they want me to make a fool of myself?

好莱坞 Hǎoláiwū Hollywood, centre of US movie industry located close to Los Angeles: ～明星 Hollywood star

好赖 hǎolài *see* "好歹 ❶❸❹"

好了疮疤忘了疼 hǎole chuāngbā wàngle téng *also* "好了伤疤忘了疼"〈俗语〉forget the pain as soon as the wound has healed; once on shore, one prays no more

好离好散 hǎolí-hǎosàn (of a divorced couple, etc.) part from each other peacefully; part friends

好力宝 hǎolìbǎo *also* "好来宝" a kind of folk singing, sometimes combined with recitation, popular in Inner Mongolia

好脸 hǎoliǎn beaming or smiling face; happy expression (on the face): 你一天到晚没个～，是谁得罪你啦? You've worn (*or* pulled) a long face all day. Who offended you?

好马不吃回头草 hǎomǎ bù chī huítóucǎo 〈俗语〉a spirited horse will not turn back to graze on an old pasture — a true man will not pick up what he has discarded: ～，我既已离开那个单位，就不打算再回去。As a good steed never turns back to graze on a trodden pasture, I do not plan to return to my former employer now that I have left him.

好男不跟女斗 hǎonán bù gēn nǚ dòu 〈俗语〉〈旧语〉a gentleman or decent man doesn't fight women: ～，你跟这些娘儿们吵个什么劲儿! Since a decent man never picks quarrels with women, what's the point of your wrangling with these females?

好孬 hǎonāo 〈方言〉❶ good and bad; what's good and what's bad: ～不分 not distinguish good from bad ❷ in any case; anyhow: 你好不容易来了，我～不能让你就走。Since it is rare to have you here, I will on no account let you go so soon.

好评 hǎopíng favourable comment or reception; high opinion; acclaim: 获得观众～ win acclaim from the audience /博得读者～ be well received by the readers; have a good reception among the readers / 报界对他的发言予以～。The press made favourable comments on his address. *or* His address had a good press.

好气儿 hǎoqìr 〈口语〉(usu. used in the negative) good mood or temper; good humour: 老头儿看见别人浪费公共钱财，就没～。The old man would be upset to see people squander public money.

好球 hǎoqiú (spectator's enthusiastic comment on a ballplayer's performance) well played; good shot; bravo

好儿 hǎor 〈口语〉❶ favour; kindness: 人家过去对咱有～，咱不能忘记。We should never forget their past kindness to us. ❷ benefit; advantage; gain: 这事要是让他知道了，还会有你的～? Do you think you have anything to gain if he should get to know about this? ❸ good wishes; regards; greetings: 见着你母亲，给我带个～。Please give my best wishes to your mother when you see her. *or* Please say "Hello" for me when you see your mother. ❹ praise; acclamation; cheers: 连声叫～ break into repeated cheers /他本想讨个～，没想倒挨了顿骂。Fishing for praise, he got a scolding for his pains.

好人 hǎorén ❶ good or fine person; decent person: ～难当。It is difficult to be a decent person. /～终有好报。Good people will eventually be rewarded. /～说不坏，好酒搅不酸。〈俗语〉Malicious remarks cannot defame a good man, as stirring cannot turn good wine sour. ❷ healthy person: 这活儿～干都费劲，你怎么能让一个病号去干! How can you let an invalid do such work? It's too heavy even for a healthy person. ❸ person who tries to get along with everyone (often at the expense of principle); Mr. Please-all: 他只想当～，说话干事都生怕得罪了谁。As he wants to please everybody, he's mortally afraid of offending anyone in what he says or does.

好人好事 hǎorén-hǎoshì good people and good deeds; fine people and fine deeds: 这个居民小区里的～真不少。There are lots of fine people and fine deeds in the residential quarter (*or* district).

好人家 hǎorénjiā ❶ decent family; respectable family ❷〈书面〉woman from a decent family; respectable woman ❸〈方言〉wealthy family: 她一心要给女儿找个～，也不管女儿情愿不情愿。Bent on finding a wealthy family for her daughter to marry into, she totally disregarded the girl's own sentiments.

好人主义 hǎorénzhǔyì seeking good relations with all and sundry at the expense of principle

好日子 hǎorìzi ❶ auspicious day: 村里人挑了个～庆祝丰收。The villagers chose an auspicious day to celebrate their good harvest. ❷ wedding day: 今儿是你们俩的～，晚上我们也去热闹热闹。Today is your wedding day and we'll join you in the celebrations in the evening. ❸ good days; happy life; comfortable life: 现在大家都过上了～。Today, we are all enjoying a happy life.

好容易 hǎoróngyì *also* "好不容易" manage with great difficulty; have a hard time (doing sth.): 我～才得到了那本词典。It was with great difficulty that I finally managed to get hold of that dictionary. /这孩子高烧两天，～才退了热。The boy's temperature finally dropped after a high fever for two days.

好商量 hǎoshāngliang can be settled through consultation: 你不就这点事儿吗? ～。Is this all you want? It's no problem.

好生 hǎoshēng 〈方言〉❶ quite; so; exceedingly: 你叫我～为难。You made it quite difficult for me. /为这事他～不快。He was so displeased over this. ❷ carefully; properly: 有话～说。Speak properly if you have anything on your mind. /你要～照料双亲。You should take good care of your parents.

好声好气 hǎoshēng-hǎoqì in a gentle voice; in a kindly or friendly manner; gently: ～地说话 speak in a gentle voice /～地商量 talk it over in an amicable manner

好使 hǎoshǐ be convenient to use; work well: 这架照相机不太～。The camera doesn't work properly. /这个牌子的热水器很～。Water heaters of this brand are quite reliable.

好事 hǎoshì ❶ good deed; good turn: 他走到哪里，～就做到哪里。He is always ready to do people a good turn wherever he goes. ❷ (of monks and Taoist priests) perform religious rituals; conduct a service: 王先生请僧人做了几天～。Mr. Wang had monks to perform religious rituals in his house for a few days. ❸〈旧语〉act of charity; good works: 修桥补路，历来视为～。Building bridges and repairing roads have always been regarded as good works. ❹〈书面〉happy event; occasion for celebration: ～从天降。It's a godsend.

see also hàoshì

好事不出门，恶事传千里 hǎoshì bù chūmén, èshì chuán qiānlǐ 〈俗语〉good news never goes beyond the gate while bad news spreads a thousand *li* away; misdeeds spread far and wide while good deeds are relegated to obscurity: ～。没出三天，他这桩丑事就闹得满城风雨了。As good deeds are hedged in and bad deeds make quick rounds, his scandal spread all over town in less than three days.

好事多磨 hǎoshì-duōmó good things never come easy; the course of true love never runs smooth: 这个老年活动站费了好几年时间才建起来，真是～啊! It took quite a few years to set up this recreational centre for the aged. As an old saying goes, good things never come easy.

好手 hǎoshǒu good hand; expert; past master: 烹调～ expert in cooking; good cook /他是木工行中的～。He is a good hand at carpentry.

好受 hǎoshòu feel good; feel well; feel comfortable: 心里不～ feel bad /她睡醒一觉后，感到～多了。She felt much better after a sound sleep. /一身臭汗，真不～。It feels awful to be wet through with sweat.

好说 hǎoshuō ❶〈套语〉*used as a polite response to expressions of gratitude or compliments*: ～，～! 您过奖了。It's very kind of you to say so, but I really don't deserve the compliment. /～，～，这点事算不了什么。Don't mention it. What I did was not much. ❷ *used to express agreement or possible agreement*: 关于参观的事，～。The visit could be arranged. Don't worry. /东西只要您想买，价钱～。Prices will not be a problem if you really want to buy them.

好说歹说 hǎoshuō-dǎishuō use every possible means of persua-

sion; try in every possible way to persuade sb.:大家～,他才同意去休养。He agreed to take a vacation only after we had pleaded with him in every possible way.

好说话儿 hǎoshuōhuàr good-natured; open to persuasion; obliging; complaisant:你们别看我～就想占便宜。Don't you try to take advantage of my good nature. /还是厂长～,批了三万元办俱乐部。The factory director was obliging enough to approve a budget of thirty thousand *yuan* for the club.

好死 hǎosǐ natural death:他不得～! May he die a horrible death!

好死不如赖活 hǎosǐ bùrú làihuó 〈俗语〉 it is better to live a wretched life than to die a comfortable death

好似 hǎosì seem; be like:长城～一条巨龙,蜿蜒在华北到西北的大地上。The Great Wall winds its way across north and northwestern China like a huge dragon. /他小小年纪,说话做事却～大人一般。He speaks and acts just like an adult though he is a mere boy.

好天儿 hǎotiānr fine day; bright, sunny day:大伙儿都趁着～外出郊游了。On a bright sunny day like this, everybody is out on an excursion.

好铁不打钉,好男不当兵 hǎotiě bù dǎ dīng, hǎonán bù dāng bīng 〈旧语〉 as good iron is not used for making nails, so a good man will not serve in the army

好听 hǎotīng ❶ (of sound or voice) pleasant to hear; pleasant to the ear:这支曲子很～。The melody is very sweet (*or* pleasant to the ear). ❷ (of language) satisfactory; palatable; fine:他说得～,做起来就大不一样了。What he says sounds fine, but what he does is another matter. /～的话说了一大箩,但不能兑现又有什么用呢? What's the use of all these fine words if they are only empty talk?

好玩儿 hǎowánr interesting; amusing:这儿没什么～的,我不想呆下去了。I don't feel like staying any longer: there's nothing interesting here. /从三层楼上掉下来可不是～的! It's no joking matter falling from the third floor. /这孩子胖乎乎的,真～。What a chubby, cute child!

好望角 Hǎowàngjiǎo Cape of Good Hope (in South Africa)

好闻 hǎowén smell good or sweet; be pleasant to smell:有的花好看不～。Some beautiful flowers have an unpleasant smell. /真～,你准是做什么好吃的来着。What a sweet smell! You must have cooked something delicious.

好戏 hǎoxì ❶ good play or drama:～不厌百回看。A really good drama is worth seeing a hundred times. /～在后头。The good show comes at the end. *or* The best fish swims near the bottom. ❷ (used ironically) fun:我等着看他的～呢! I'm waiting to see him make a fool of himself.

好像 hǎoxiàng seem; be like:听口音,他～是广东人。Judging from his accent, he seems to be a native of Guangdong. /我们～见过面。It looks as though we have met before. *or* We seem to have met somewhere. /他～一头牛,吃的是草,挤出来的是牛奶。He is like a cow eating grass and offering milk in return.

好笑 hǎoxiào laughable; funny; ridiculous:她幼稚得～。She is ridiculously naive. /这个人说话怪声怪气,真～。It is really funny that he speaks in such an affected manner.

好些 hǎoxiē *also* "好些个" quite a lot; quite a few; a good deal:这书在库里还有～。There are many more copies of the book in the warehouse.

好心 hǎoxīn kind heart; good intention:～也许反而坏事。Good intention may spoil the game. /～自有好报。Good-heartedness is sure to be rewarded. *or* One good turn deserves another.

好心不得好报 hǎoxīn bù dé hǎobào 〈俗语〉 get no thanks for one's good intentions; kind-heartedness may not meet with good recompence:我劝他戒烟,反被他挖苦一顿,真是～。I tried to talk him out of smoking only to be ridiculed by him. That's what I got for my kindness!

好心当作驴肝肺 hǎoxīn dāngzuò lǘgānfèi 〈俗语〉 take sb.'s good will for ill intent:你怎么如此不识好歹,把她的一片好心全当成了驴肝肺。How could you be so ungrateful as to treat her good intentions as ill will?

好心好意 hǎoxīn-hǎoyì with the best of intentions; good-willed and well-intentioned:我～劝他,他却当耳边风。He turned a deaf ear to all my well-intentioned advice.

好心人 hǎoxīnrén well-wisher; good soul:你要相信刘先生,他可是个～。You should place your trust in Mr. Liu; he wishes you well.

好性儿 hǎoxìngr good-tempered; good-natured:他这么不讲理,再～的人也会生气的。He was so unreasonable as to make the best-tempered person angry.

好言 hǎoyán well-meant words; sincere words; kind words:～相劝 admonish in well-intentioned words; plead with sb. earnestly /～相慰 comfort sb. in kind words

好样儿的 hǎoyàngrde 〈口语〉 great fellow; regular guy:他是个～。He's a regular guy. *or* He's a good sort. /～都跟我来灭火。All those who are men enough, come with me to fight the fire.

好一个 hǎoyīge (used in an exclamatory sentence, sometimes ironically) what a:～幽静的去处! What a serene retreat! /～人权卫士! A human rights champion indeed!

好意 hǎoyì good intention; kindness:出于～ out of good intentions; well-intentioned /不怀～ ill-intentioned; with ulterior motives /您的～我心领了,但礼物不能收。I appreciate your kindness, but I can't accept your gift.

好意思 hǎoyìsi have the nerve or face, or cheek:他真～开口让我替他当枪手。He had the cheek to ask me to serve as his cat's paw. /在老人面前,我怎～推托? How could I shirk it in the presence of my elders?

好友 hǎoyǒu close friend; bosom friend:至亲～ close relatives and bosom friends /心腹～ trusted friend /良书即～。A good book is a helpful friend.

好在 hǎozài fortunately; luckily:～他是本地人,情况熟悉。Fortunately, he is a native here and familiar with the local circumstances. /～我带着伞呢,下雨也没关系。Luckily I have an umbrella with me, so it doesn't matter if it rains.

好转 hǎozhuǎn take a turn for the better; take a favourable turn; improve:病势～。The patient is on the mend. *or* The patient is recovering. /混乱的局面开始～。The chaotic situation has taken a turn for the better.

好自为之 hǎozìwéizhī conduct oneself well; do one's best; look out for oneself:现在一切条件都已具备,你要把握时机,～。Now that all the circumstances are ripe, you must grasp your opportunity firmly and make the best of it.

郝 Hǎo a surname

hào

镐 Hào Hao, early capital of the Zhou Dynasty, to the southwest of present Xi'an, Shaanxi
see also gǎo

耗[1] hào ❶ consume; take; cost:～时的工作 time-consuming job /这辆汽车～油太多。This car is a gas-guzzler. /久旱无雨,塘里的水都～干了。The pond is running dry as a result of the long drought. ❷ 〈方言〉 waste time; dawdle:～时间 waste time; dawdle / 别～着了,快开始吧。Stop dillydallying and get started. /总这么～着怎么行,得想个办法才是。We can't stand idle like this. Something must be done about it.

耗[2] hào bad news:噩～ sad news of the death of a friend, relative or person one loves and respects

耗电量 hàodiànliàng power consumption; power input

耗费 hàofèi expend; cost; consume:～时间 consume time /～人力物力 expend both human and material resources /组织这项活动～太大。It took too much money and time to organize this activity.

耗功 hàogōng 〈物理〉 wasted work

耗竭 hàojié exhaust; use up; deplete:资源～ be drained (*or* depleted) of natural resources /敌人兵力已经～。The military strength of the enemy is exhausted. /他奄奄一息,生命就要～了。He was on the verge of death. *or* His life was fading out.

耗尽 hàojìn exhaust; use up; deplete:～国力 exhaust the strength of a country /～青春 wear out one's youth /～精力 consume all one's energies /他几年坐吃山空,把家产都～了。He dissipated all his fortune in a few years of idling and heavy spending.

耗尽区 hàojìnqū depletion region; exhaustion region

耗能 hàonéng consume energy:～型产业 energy-consuming industry

耗热量 hàorèliàng 〈物理〉 heat consumption

耗散 hàosàn 〈物理〉 dissipate:功率～ power dissipation /～功率

wasted power /能量～ energy dissipation /热～ thermal (*or* heat) dissipation
耗散网络 hàosàn wǎngluò dissipative network
耗散尾迹 hàosàn wěijì dissipation trail; distrail
耗散因数 hàosàn yīnshù dissipative factor
耗神 hàoshén exhaust one's vigour:～费力 use up one's vigour and strength
耗损 hàosǔn consume; waste; lose:～精力 wear sb. down /机器～ wear and tear of machinery /减少粮食在加工中的～ reduce the wastage of grain in processing
耗损电阻 hàosǔn diànzǔ loss resistance
耗损范围 hàosǔn fànwéi exhaustion range
耗血 hàoxuè 〈医学〉hematozemia
耗氧量 hàoyǎngliàng consumed oxygen; oxygen consumption; oxygen uptake
耗油量 hàoyóuliàng oil consumption
耗油率 hàoyóulǜ specific fuel consumption; oil consumption rate
耗资 hàozī consume or expend money; cost:～巨万 cost over ten thousand *yuan*
耗子 hàozi 〈方言〉mouse; rat:扒手一见警察就像～见到猫。At mere sight of the police, the pickpocket was as terrified as a mouse facing a cat.
耗子药 hàoziyào ratsbane

颢 hào 〈书面〉white and shining:～气 fresh air

灏 hào ❶ *see* "浩" hào ❷ *see* "皓" hào

昊 hào 〈书面〉❶ vast and boundless ❷ sky; heaven

淏 hào 〈书面〉(of water) clear

号[1](號) hào ❶ name; title:绰～ nickname /徽～ title of honour; good name /代～ code name /国～ name of a dynasty /年～ title of an emperor's reign /旗～ banner; flag ❷ alias; assumed name; alternative name:别～ alias ❸ business house; firm:分～ branch (of a firm, etc.) /商～ shop; store /银～ banking house ❹ mark; sign; signal:记～ mark /符～ sign; mark /击掌为～ clap as a singal ❺ order; sequence:编～ serial number /型～ model; type /对～ check the number /挂～ register (at a hospital) ❻size:中～ medium size /头～新闻 top news /五～铅字 No. 5 type ❼ kind; sort; type:跟这～人打交道得小心, 别上当受骗。Watch out for cheating when you deal with people of this sort. /这～买卖可做不得, 要犯法的。Don't get involved in this kind of business or you'll break the law. /干我们警察这～工作的, 难得正点上下班。People like us policemen seldom work regular hours. ❽ person of a given type:病～ patient; person on the sick list; sick personnel /伤～ (of military personnel) the wounded ❾ (used mostly after numericals) ordinal number: (a) *ordinarily*:第三～简报 Bulletin No. 3 /门牌～ street number; house number (b) *for date of month*:五月一～ May 1st ❿ 〈量词〉*used to indicate numbers*: (a) *of people*:有三百多～人在这个食堂用餐。Over three hundred people eat in this canteen. (b) *of business deals*:一会儿工夫, 就做了几～买卖。Several deals were made in no time. ⓫ put a mark on; give a number to:～房子 mark out houses (as billets, etc.) /把这些东西都～一～。Please mark out all these things. ⓬ feel (the pulse): *see* "～脉"

号[2](號) hào ❶ order; verbal command:发～施令 issue orders ❷ anything used as a horn:螺～ conch-shell trumpet; conch ❸ any brass wind instrument:军～ bugle /小～ trumpet /圆～ French horn ❹ bugle call; any call made on a bugle:冲锋～ bugle call to charge /熄灯～ lights-out; taps /吹起床～ sound the reveille
see also háo
号兵 hàobīng trumpeter; bugler
号称 hàochēng ❶ be known as:景德镇～瓷都。Jingdezhen Township is known as the porcelain capital. ❷ claim to be:他拥兵八千, ～一万。With a troop of eight thousand, he claimed to be ten thousand strong.
号灯 hàodēng navigation light
号房 hàofáng 〈旧语〉❶ janitor's room; reception office ❷ janitor ❸ dormitory for students of the Imperial College (国子监) ❹ cubicle in the imperial examination compound (贡院) for each of the candidates of the imperial examination
号服 hàofú livery
号角 hàojiǎo ❶ bugle; horn ❷ bugle call:吹响了冲锋的～ sound the bugle call to charge /吹响了向21世纪进军的～ sound the clarion call to march towards the 21st century
号坎儿 hàokǎnr 〈旧语〉numbered singlet worn by coolies
号控机 hàokòngjī number switch; numerical switch
号令 hàolìng ❶ verbal command:～三军 issue orders to the three armed services ❷ order soldiers to go into action:发布～ issue battle orders
号码 hàomǎ number:电话～ telephone number /～表 directory /～查询 directory enquiries
号码机 hàomǎjī numbering machine
号脉 hàomài 〈中医〉feel the pulse
号牌 hàopái numberplate; check:车辆～ vehicle registration plate; licence plate; number plate (on a vehicle)
号炮 hàopào signal gun
号旗 hàoqí signal flag
号声 hàoshēng trumpet call:～四起。Clarion calls were sounded from all sides.
号手 hàoshǒu trumpeter; bugler
号数 hàoshù number
号筒 hàotǒng 〈旧语〉brass-wind instrument used to transmit orders in the army
号头 hàotóu ❶ number:你的电话～是多少? What's your telephone number, please? ❷ 〈方言〉date of a month:每月五日是我们发工资的～。The fifth of every month is our pay day. *or* We are paid on the fifth of each month.
号外 hàowài extra (of a newspaper):《人民日报》～ extra to the *People's Daily*
号衣 hàoyī 〈旧语〉livery; army uniform
号型 hàoxíng size (of shoes, clothes, etc.)
号召 hàozhào call; appeal:发出～ call for; call on /响应国家的～ respond to the call of the country; answer the call of the country /战斗的～ call to battle /～大家参加植树活动 appeal to everyone to take part in the tree-planting activity
号召书 hàozhàoshū (written) appeal
号志灯 hàozhìdēng red signal lamp used by railway workers
号子 hàozi ❶ 〈方言〉mark; sign; signal ❷ jail; prison cell:他是进过～的人。He has been behind bars. ❸ labour song sung to sychronize movements with one person leading; work chant:打夯的工人们在喊～。The rammers were singing a chant.

浩 hào ❶ great; vast; grand ❷ many; much; numerous
浩博 hàobó plentiful; abundant; extensive:征引～ quote copiously from many sources
浩大 hàodà very great; huge; vast:声势～的庆祝活动 grand celebrations /～的规模 huge in scale /工程～。It's a project of great magnitude.
浩荡 hàodàng ❶ vast and mighty; expansive:～的洞庭湖水 vast and mighty Dongting Lake /碧波～ vast expanse of water ❷ mighty; immense:军威～ mighty army /～的人群 large crowds of people /浩浩荡荡的革命队伍 mighty revolutionary contingents
浩繁 hàofán vast and numerous:典籍～ voluminous work; vast collection of books /这个机构承担着～的科研任务。This institution is entrusted with a heavy load of scientific research work.
浩歌 hàogē sing in a loud voice; sing heartily
浩瀚 hàohàn ❶ (of water) vast; expansive:～的海洋 vast expanse of ocean ❷ numerous; immense:古籍～ large numbers of classic works /～的宇宙 boundless universe /～的资料 huge masses of data
浩浩 hàohào ❶ vast; wide; extensive:～的天空 immensity of the sky ❷ vast and mighty:～的江水 mighty river
浩劫 hàojié disaster; calamity; catastrophe:战争～ scourge (*or* holocaust) of war /历史～ historical catastrophe /遭到～ suffer a calamity
浩茫 hàománg 〈书面〉vast; extensive; boundless:～的大地 vast land /心事～ be weighed down with boundless care and concern
浩淼 hàomiǎo *also* "浩渺" (of water) extending into the distance; vast:烟波～ vast expanse of misty, rolling waters
浩气 hàoqì noble spirit:～凛然 awe-inspiring noble spirit /～凌云 soaring noble spirit /～长存。Imperishable is the noble spirit. *or* A

noble spirit will never perish.
浩然 hàorán 〈书面〉❶ vast; expansive; mighty: 江流～ mighty river / 洪波～ huge waves ❷ just and upright; righteous: ～正气 awe-inspiring righteousness
浩然之气 hàoránzhīqì noble spirit; moral force
浩如烟海 hàorúyānhǎi (of data, literature, etc.) as vast as the open sea; tremendous amount of: 历代典籍～ vast accumulation of ancient literature / 在～的资料中查找 search in a sea of data
浩叹 hàotàn heave a deep sigh; sigh deeply
浩特 hàotè (Mongolian) village or town inhabited by herdsmen

皓(皜) hào ❶ white: ～髯 white beard / 明眸～齿 bright eyes and white teeth ❷ bright; luminous: 月出～兮。The rising moon sheds a great brilliance.
皓白 hàobái white: 须发～ white hair and beard
皓齿蛾眉 hàochǐ-éméi white teeth and pretty eyebrows
皓矾 hàofán 〈化学〉 zinc sulphate
皓首 hàoshǒu hoary head: ～穷经 study hard even when one is very old
皓月 hàoyuè bright moon: ～千里。A glorious moon shone over a vast land. / ～当空, 引吭高歌。With a bright moon hung in the sky, he sang at the top of his voice.

皞 hào 〈书面〉 bright; luminous

好 hào ❶ like; love; be fond of: ～读书 be fond of reading / ～动 be active (*or* restless) / ～静 be inactive; prefer quietness / ～钻牛角尖 enjoy splitting hairs / 投其所～ cater to sb.'s likes (*or* tastes) ❷ be liable to: ～晕船 easily get seasick / ～发脾气 apt (*or* liable) to lose one's temper / 鲜菜～烂。Fresh vegetables rot easily. / 马路狭窄, ～堵车。Traffic often jammed those narrow streets.
see also hǎo
好吃 hàochī enjoy eating good food; be greedy: 这小伙子太～, 挣的钱都吃光了。Fond of good food, the young fellow spends all he earns on eating.
好吃懒做 hàochī-lǎnzuò be fond of eating and averse to working; be gluttonous and lazy: 两口子都～, 没法儿不穷。The couple was both greedy and lazy and could not but be flat broke.
好出风头 hàochū-fēngtou like to be in the limelight; be fond of being the focus of public attention
好大喜功 hàodà-xǐgōng have a passion for the grandiose; crave grandeur and success: 他～, 不切实际。Because of his obsession with greatness and success he is never realistic. *or* He is overambitious and unrealistic.
好斗 hàodòu bellicose; combative: ～的公鸡 fight-happy cock / ～分子 militant
好高务远 hàogāo-wùyuǎn *also* "好高骛远" aim too high; reach for what is beyond one's grasp; bite off more than one can chew: 办事情要循序渐进而不要～, 急于求成。Instead of setting our sights too high and being overanxious for success we should proceed systematically with our work. / 他有点～的劲头。He seems to be trying to run before he can walk.
好管闲事 hàoguǎn-xiánshì be fond of meddling in others' business; enjoy poking one's nose in other people's affairs; be meddlesome: 这件事与你无关, 不要做～的人。You have nothing to do with the matter. Don't be a meddler.
好客 hàokè be hospitable; keep open house: 小镇上的人殷勤～, 远近闻名。People in the small town are known for their hospitality.
好奇 hàoqí be curious; be full of curiosity: 出于～, 他特意去那条街上看了看。He made a special trip to that street merely out of curiosity. / 他从农村乍到大城市, 对许多事情都～。As he has just come to a big city from the country, he is curious about many things.
好奇心 hàoqíxīn curiosity: 这孩子的～很强。The child is full of curiosity.
好强 hàoqiáng eager to put one's best foot forward; eager to do well in everything: 他很～, 从来不肯服输。He is eager to do well (*or* excel) in whatever he does and never admits defeat.
好色 hàosè (of a man) be lecherous; be fond of women; indulge in sensual pleasure: ～之徒 lecher; libertine; womaniser: 吾未见好德如～者也。I have never come across any man who pursues virtue more than sensual pleasure.
好善乐施 hàoshàn-lèshī *also* "乐施好善" enjoy helping those in need; be generous in one's charity; be philanthropic: 老先生以～而闻名遐迩。The old gentleman was renowned far and wide for his philanthropic generosity.
好尚 hàoshàng one's likes or preferences; what is valued or held in esteem: 各有～。People vary in their preferences.
好胜 hàoshèng eager to excel in everything; keen to outdo others: 争强～ strive to outdo others in everything / ～心切 be eager to outshine others
好事 hàoshì meddlesome; interfering; officious: ～者 busybody / 改改你那～的毛病吧。You'd better get rid of your bad habit of meddling in others' affairs. / 谁让你～, 惹祸了吧! Now you are on the spot. That's what you get for meddling in other people's business.
see also hǎoshì
好事之徒 hàoshìzhītú busybody; meddler
好为人师 hàowéirénshī be fond of teaching others; like to lecture other people: 人之患, 在～。It's a human failing to love to tell others what to do.
好恶 hàowù likes and dislikes; taste: 不能凭个人～评品人物。We should not judge a man by our own liking. / 各人～不一。People have different tastes.
好学 hàoxué be fond of learning; be eager to learn: 他虽年事已高, 但仍～如前。Though advanced in age, he is still as fond of learning as he used to be.
好学不倦 hàoxué-bùjuàn never tire of learning
好逸恶劳 hàoyì-wùláo love ease and comfort but hate to work: 他从小养成了～的毛病。He fell in the bad habit of detesting work and seeking after comforts in his childhood.
好战 hàozhàn bellicose; warlike: ～分子 hawkish elements; warmongers / ～成性 warlike
好整以暇 hàozhěngyǐxiá remain calm and composed while handling pressing business; take things easy: 任何情况下他总能～, 令人佩服。He is much admired for being able to keep calm in handling pressing matters under any circumstances.

hē

诃¹ hē scold

诃² hē *see* "诃子"
诃子 hēzǐ *also* "藏青果" zàngqīngguǒ 〈植物〉 myrobalan (*Terminalia chebula*)

呵¹ hē breathe out (with the mouth open): ～手 breathe on one's hands (to warm them) / ～一口气 breathe out; exhale / 一气～成 get sth. done at one go

呵²(訶) hē scold: 叱～ shout at; scold loudly

呵³ hē *see* "嗬" hē
呵斥 hēchì *also* "呵叱"; "喝叱" hēchì; "喝斥" hēchì scold loudly; berate; excoriate: 厉声～ scold severely / 他把儿子～了一顿。He gave his son a dressing-down.
呵呵 hēhē 〈象声〉 guffaw; laugh loudly: 笑～ laugh heartily; guffaw / 他～地笑个不停。He couldn't help guffawing.
呵喝 hēhè 〈书面〉 shout loudly (to reprimand, intimidate, etc.): 他一声～, 把大伙儿吓了一跳。Shouting loudly, he gave us a start.
呵护 hēhù 〈书面〉 ❶ bless: 愿神灵～ God bless ❷ cherish; take good care of: ～备至 cherish most dearly; treat with profound love and care
呵欠 hēqian 〈方言〉 yawn
呵责 hēzé scold severely; give sb. a dressing-down: 他无缘无故地～我, 使我不能忍受。I can't put up with being scolded by him for no reason.

嗬 hē (used to indicate astonishment) ah; oh: ～, 真棒! Oh, it's terrific! / ～, 真烫! Wow, it's scalding!

喝¹(欱) hē ❶ drink: ～水 drink water / ～汤 eat soup /

他病得厉害，～口水都吐。He is so seriously ill that he vomits even when he takes a sip of water. ❷ drink alcoholic liquor：大吃大～ eat and drink extravagantly /～得酩酊大醉 get dead (*or* blind) drunk / 这人一～多，话就没完没了。He becomes very talkative when he has a few drinks too many.

喝[2] hē *see* "嗬" hē
see also hè

喝叱 hēchì *also* "喝斥" *see* "呵斥" hēchì

喝闷酒 hē mènjiǔ drink alone in depression

喝墨水 hē mòshuǐ drink ink — study in a school：喝过洋墨水 have studied abroad /他是家中唯一喝过点墨水的人。He was the only one in the family who had received some education. /高先生墨水喝得多，还是请他先谈吧。Mr. Gao has read a great deal. Let's ask him to talk first.

喝水不忘掘井人 hēshuǐ bù wàng juéjǐngrén when you drink the water, think of those who dug the well

喝西北风 hē xīběifēng drink the severe northwest wind — suffer from cold and hunger; starve：那会儿我们穷得揭不开锅，只有～的份儿。In those days of extreme poverty we had nothing to eat but the northwest wind. /不种粮食，吃什么？难道～吗？What do we eat if nobody plants crops? Can we live on air?

蠚 hē 〈方言〉(of bees, wasps, etc.) sting

hé

阂 hé cut off from; not in communication with：语言隔～ language barrier

核[1] hé ❶ pip; stone：枣～ stone of a date /无～葡萄 pipless grapes; seedless grapes /无～蜜橘 pipless tangerine; seedless orange ❷ nucleus：细胞～ cell nucleus /菌～ sclerotium ❸ atomic nucleus; nuclear energy; nuclear weapon：无～区 nuclear-free zone

核[2]（**覈**） hé ❶ examine; check：审～ examine /复～ check ❷〈书面〉faithful; true; real：其文直，其事～。His writings are straight-forward and true to the facts.
see also hú

核安全 hé'ānquán nuclear security, nuclear safety：～标准 nuclear safety standard /～保障 nuclear safeguard

核按钮 hé'ànniǔ nuclear button (for nuclear war)

核保护伞 hébǎohùsǎn nuclear umbrella

核爆炸 hébàozhà nuclear explosion：～探测卫星 nuclear (blast) detection satellite

核不扩散条约 Hébùkuòsàn Tiáoyuē Nuclear Non-proliferation Treaty

核裁军 hécáijūn nuclear disarmament

核查 héchá examine; check; verify：～手段 means of verification / 由联合国监督小组对撤军进行～ verification of the troop withdrawal by a UN supervisory mission /～出一处运算错误 find a calculating mistake by checking /审计小组～了这家公司的固定资产。The auditing team verified the fixed assets of the company.

核尘 héchén nuclear dust

核磁共振 hécí gòngzhèn nuclear magnetic resonance：～探测器 nuclear magnetic resonance detector /～谱 nuclear magnetic resonance spectrum /～波谱仪 nuclear magnetic resonance chemical analyser

核磁子 hécízǐ nuclear magneton

核打击力量 hédǎjī lìliàng nuclear strike capability or force：第二次～ second nuclear strike capability

核大国 hédàguó nuclear power

核蛋白 hédànbái 〈生化〉nucleoprotein

核弹 hédàn *also* "核炸弹" nuclear bomb; N-bomb

核弹头 hédàntóu nuclear warhead; uranium warhead：模拟～ simulated nuclear warhead /热～ thermonuclear warhead /～导弹 nuclear-armed missile; nuclear-capability missile; nuclear-tipped missile; nuclear missile

核当量 hédāngliàng nuclear equivalent

核导弹 hédǎodàn nuclear missile

核岛 hédǎo nuclear island

核电厂 hédiànchǎng nuclear power plant

核电荷 hédiànhè nuclear charge

核电站 hédiànzhàn nuclear power plant

核定 hédìng check and ratify; appraise and decide：～地价 appraise and fix land prices /～资本 approved capital

核冬天 hédōngtiān (as aftermath of nuclear war) nuclear winter

核动力 hédònglì nuclear power：～导弹 nuclear-powered missile / ～卫星 nuclear powered satellite

核对 héduì check; verify; identify or examine：～账目 check accounts /～笔迹 identify sb.'s handwriting /～事实 verify the facts / 我们一一～了群众举报的情况。We checked the offences reported by the masses one by one.

核讹诈 hé'ézhà nuclear blackmail

核发 héfā approve and issue：～驾驶执照 approve and issue a driving licence

核反应 héfǎnyìng *also* "核子反应" nuclear reaction
see also "链式反应" liànshì fǎnyìng; "热核反应" rèhé fǎnyìng

核反应堆 héfǎnyìngduī nuclear reactor

核防护 héfánghù nuclear protection

核防卫 héfángwèi nuclear defence

核废料 héfèiliào nuclear waste：～处理 nuclear waste disposal

核风险 héfēngxiǎn nuclear risk

核辐射 héfúshè ❶ radiate or emit α, β, γ or neutron rays ❷ nuclear radiation

核苷 hégān 〈生化〉nucleoside：～酸 nucleotide

核感应 hégǎnyìng nuclear induction

核工程 hégōngchéng nuclear engineering

核工业 hégōngyè nuclear industry

核光磁效应 héguāngcí xiàoyìng nuclear photomagnetic effect

核果 héguǒ 〈植物〉drupe

核合成 héhéchéng nucleosynthesis

核黄疸 héhuángdǎn kernicterus

核黄素 héhuángsù 〈药学〉riboflavin; lactoflavin：～缺乏症 ariboflavinosis

核火箭 héhuǒjiàn nuclear rocket

核计 héjì assess; calculate：～选票 count the vote /～成本 assess the cost

核减 héjiǎn trim (a budget, etc.)：～经费 cut (*or* reduce) a budget

核俱乐部 héjùlèbù nuclear club

核聚变 héjùbiàn nuclear fusion

核扩散 hékuòsàn nuclear proliferation

核理论 hélǐlùn nuclear theory

核力 hélì nuclear force

核裂变 hélièbiàn nuclear fission：～火箭 fission rocket

核垄断 hélǒngduàn nuclear monopoly

核门槛 héménkǎn nuclear threshold

核能 hénéng *also* "核子能" nuclear energy

核起搏器 héqǐbóqì 〈医学〉nuclear pacemaker

核潜艇 héqiántǐng nuclear-powered submarine

核燃料 héránliào nuclear fuel

核仁 hérén ❶〈生物〉nucleolus ❷ kernel (of a fruit-stone)

核审 héshěn examine and verify：～生产计划 examine and approve the production plan

核失控 héshīkòng nuclear runaway

核实 héshí verify; check：～数据 verify the data /这份材料未经～，仅供参考。These are unverified materials and are for your reference only. /顾客反映的情况需要调查～。The complaints of the customers need to be verified.

核事故 héshìgù nuclear accident

核试验 héshìyàn nuclear test：大气层～ atmospheric nuclear test / 高空～ high-altitude nuclear test /地下～ underground nuclear test

核数署署长 Héshùshǔ shǔzhǎng (HK) Director of Audit

核衰变 héshuāibiàn nuclear disintegration

核素 hésù ❶〈生化〉nuclein ❷〈核物理〉nuclide

核酸 hésuān 〈生化〉nucleic acid：～酶 nuclease /～内切酶 endonuclease /～外切酶 exonuclease

核算 hésuàn examine and calculate; assess; accounts：成本～ cost accounting /独立～ keep separate accounts /～劳动成本 work out the cost of labour

核算单位 hésuàn dānwèi accounting unit：基本～ basic accounting

unit /独立～ independent accounting unit
核糖 hétáng 〈生化〉ribose:～霉素 ribostamycin /～酸 ribonic acid
核糖核酸 hétáng hésuān 〈生化〉ribonucleic acid; RNA:脱氧～ deoxyribonucleic acid; DNA /信息～ messenger ribonucleic acid; m-RNA /～病毒 ribovirus /～酶 ribonuclease
核桃 hétao *also*"胡桃" hútáo walnut:～酪 walnut cream
核桃虫 hétaochóng *also*"蛴螬" qícáo 〈方言〉〈动物〉grub
核桃仁 hétaorén walnut kernel; walnut meat
核桃酥 hétaosū walnut cake
核蜕变 hétuìbiàn nuclear disintegration; nuclear destruction
核威慑 héwēishè 〈军事〉nuclear deterrence
核威慑力量 héwēishè lìliàng nuclear deterrent (power)
核威胁 héwēixié nuclear threat
核微粒污染 héwēilì wūrǎn contamination from nuclear fallout
核污染 héwūrǎn nuclear or radioactive pollution
核武库 héwǔkù nuclear arsenal
核武器 héwǔqì *also*"原子武器" yuánzǐ wǔqì nuclear weapon; N-weapon; nuke:～试验 nuclear weapons test /～储备 stockpiling of nuclear weapons /～致胜论 theory of victory by nuclear weapons
核物理 héwùlǐ nuclear physics
核物探 héwùtàn nuclear geophysical prospecting
核销 héxiāo cancel after verification
核心 héxīn nucleus; core; kernel; heart of the matter:领导～ core of leadership /～人物 key person; key figure /～力量 force at the core /～问题 heart of the matter /～部门 key department /～小组 core group; inner circle
核心家庭 héxīn jiātíng nuclear family
核心科目 héxīn kēmù core subject
核芯 héxìn nuclear core (of a reactor)
核医学 héyīxué nuclear medicine
核议 héyì examine and discuss
核优势 héyōushì nuclear superiority
核灾难 hézāinàn nuclear catastrophe; nuclear holocaust
核战争 hézhànzhēng nuclear war or warfare
核震 hézhèn 〈天文〉corequake
核证无误 hézhèng wúwù certified:经～的副本将分发各签字国和参加国。Certified copies shall be distributed to each of the signatory and acceding states.
核周期 hézhōuqī nuclear cycle
核装置 hézhuāngzhì nuclear device
核准 hézhǔn examine and approve; check and ratify; confirm; ratify:～书 instrument of approval /待～ *ad referendum* /部长～了盖楼计划。The minister approved the building plan. /该项目经有关部门～后可上马。The project can start after examination and approval by the department concerned.
核资 hézī verify capital or asset:清产～ check-up of assets
核子 hézǐ nucleon:～靶 nucleon target
核子反应 hézǐ fǎnyìng *see*"核反应"
核子能 hézǐnéng nucleonic energy
核子武器 hézǐ wǔqì nucleonic weapon; nuclear weapon
核子学 hézǐxué nucleonics

劾 hé expose sb.'s misdeeds or crimes:弹～ impeach

盍(盇) hé 〈书面〉why not:夫子～行邪? Why not get away?

阖(阇) hé 〈书面〉❶ entire; whole:～城 entire city /～村 whole village ❷ shut; close:～门 close the door
阖府 héfǔ *also*"阖第"〈敬词〉your whole family:敬请～光临。The presence of your whole family is cordially requested.
阖家 héjiā whole family:祝您～健康幸福。Wish your family good health and happiness.
阖家团圆 héjiā-tuányuán reunion of all family members; the whole family is reunited
阖眼 héyǎn close the eyes; sleep

翮 hé ❶ shaft of a feather; quill ❷〈书面〉wing (of a bird):施～起高翔 stretch the wings and soar skyward

河 hé ❶ river:江～ rivers /内～ inland river (waterway) /运～ canal /冰～ glacier /界～ boundary river ❷ Milky Way system:～外星系 extragalactic nebula ❸ (Hé) Yellow River
河岸 hé'àn river bank
河浜 hébāng 〈方言〉creek; streamlet
河蚌 hébàng freshwater mussel; clam
河北 Héběi Hebei (Province)
河北梆子 Héběi bāngzi Hebei clapper opera
see also"梆子腔" bāngziqiāng
河北杨 héběiyáng *also*"椴杨" duànyáng Chinese linden (*Tilia*)
河边 hébiān river bank
河滨 hébīn riverside
河伯娶妇 Hébó-qǔfù 〈迷信〉ancient custom of sacrificing a young beautiful girl to be the wife of the river god so as to please him and make sure that there is no flood in the area
河槽 hécáo riverbed
河汊子 héchàzi branch of a river
河川 héchuān rivers and creeks
河川水力学 héchuān shuǐlìxué fluvial hydraulics
河床 héchuáng *also*"河漕";"河身" riverbed
河道 hédào river course:疏通～ dredge waterways
河堤 hédī river embankment
河东狮吼 Hédōng-shīhǒu (used to describe the fear of a henpecked husband) roar of the lioness from the east side of the river — the shrew scolds her husband; a bad-tempered domineering wife flies into a rage
河段 héduàn section of a river
河防 héfáng ❶ flood-prevention work done on rivers, esp. the Yellow River:～工程 flood-prevention works on the Yellow River ❷ (military) defence on the Yellow River:～部队 defending troops on the Yellow River /～主力 main force defending the Yellow River
河肥 héféi river silt used as manure
河粉 héfěn rice noodles
河港 hégǎng river port
河工 hégōng ❶ river conservancy works (esp. for the Yellow River) ❷ river conservancy workers
河工学 hégōngxué river engineering
河沟 hégōu brook; stream
河谷 hégǔ river valley
河海沉积 héhǎi chénjī 〈地理〉fluviomarine deposit
河汉 héhàn 〈书面〉❶ Milky Way; galaxy ❷〈比喻〉farfetched words; statements too farfetched to gain credulity; disbelief:幸毋～斯言。I hope you will not take this as wild talk.
河涸渔竭 héhé-yújié the river dries up and the fish in it die
河湖港汊 héhú-gǎngchà rivers, lakes and their branches
河积平原 héjī píngyuán 〈地理〉fluvial plain
河麂 héjǐ *also*"獐" zhāng river deer; water deer
河口 hékǒu river mouth; stream outlet; estuary; ria
河口湾 hékǒuwān firth; frith; estuary
河狸 hélí beaver (*Castor fiber*)
河狸鼠 hélíshǔ nutria; coypu (*Myocastor coypus*):～皮毛 nutria
河流 héliú river:多国～ multinational river /通航～ navigable river
河流沉积 héliú chénjī fluvial or fluviatile deposit
河流袭夺 héliú xíduó 〈地质〉river capture; river piracy
河柳 héliǔ *also*"旱柳" hànliǔ dryland willow (*Salix matsudana*)
河漏 hélou *hele*, a kind of noodles made from buckwheat or sorghum flour
see also"饸饹" héle
河鲈 hélú common perch; freshwater bass
河卵石 héluǎnshí cobble; pebble; shingle
河马 hémǎ hippopotamus; hippo; river horse
河鳗 hémán river eel
河漫滩 hémàntān washland; alluvial flat; valley flat; river flat
河南 Hénán Henan (Province)
河南梆子 Hénán bāngzi Henan clapper opera
see also"豫剧" yùjù;"梆子腔" bāngziqiāng
河南坠子 Hénán zhuìzi ballad singing to the accompaniment of the *zhuiqin* (坠琴), popular in Henan Province
河内 Hénèi Hanoi, capital of Vietnam
河泥 héní river silt; river mud
河螃蟹 hépángxiè fresh-water crab
河清海晏 héqīng-hǎiyàn *also*"海晏河清" the Yellow River is

H

clear and the sea is calm — the world is at peace; it is time of peace and prosperity:现如今国泰民安，～。Today the people live in peace and the country enjoys prosperity.

河清难俟 héqīng-nánsì it is hard to wait till the Yellow River becomes clear — the time would be too long to wait for sth. to happen; it takes too long to wait, and life is short

河曲 héqū bend (of a river)

河渠 héqú rivers and canals; waterways:～纵横 be crisscrossed by rivers and canals

河山 héshān rivers and mountains; land; territory:大好～ beautiful rivers and mountains (of a country); land of beauty /锦绣～ land of enchanting beauty /重整～ rebuild one's country /祖国～，无比壮丽 magnificent and glorious landscape of our beloved motherland

河身 héshēn riverbed

河水 héshuǐ river water:～净化 river water cleaning

河水獭 héshuǐtǎ common, fresh-water otter; otter

河滩 hétān flood land

河塘 hétáng river embankment

河套 hétào ❶ bend of a river ❷ (Hétào) Great Bend of the Yellow River

河套地区 Hétào Dìqū *also* "河套平原" Hetao Area (at the top of the Great Bend of the Yellow River in Inner Mongolia and Ningxia)

河套人 Hétàorén 〈考古〉 Hetao man, *Homo sapiens* living at the top of the Great Bend of the Yellow River about 35,000-50,000 years ago

河豚 hétún *also* "鲀" tún globefish; balloonfish; puffer:～中毒 fuguism; tetrodotoxism

河外空间 héwài kōngjiān 〈天文〉 extragalactic space

河外星系 héwài xīngxì *also* "河外星云"〈天文〉 anagalactic nebula; extragalactic nebula

河湾 héwān ancon; cove; river bend

河网 héwǎng network of waterways:～化 build a network of waterways /～平原 river plain

河乌 héwū 〈动物〉 dipper; water ouzel

河西走廊 Héxī Zǒuláng Hexi or Gansu Corridor (in northwestern Gansu, so called because it lies to the west of the Yellow River)

河系 héxì river system

河鲜 héxiān freshwater fish, shrimp, etc.

河相 héxiàng 〈地理〉 fluviatile facies

河蟹 héxiè freshwater crab

河沿 héyán river bank; riverside

河鱼 héyú freshwater fish; river fish

河鱼之疾 héyúzhījí 〈婉词〉 have loose bowels; suffer from diarrhea or stomach ailment:近日苦于～。I've been suffering from a stomach ailment for days.

河源 héyuán river head or source

河岳 héyuè rivers and mountains; land; territory:光耀史册，气壮～ leave a glorious and magnificent page in history

河运 héyùn river transport

何 hé ❶ *used in specific questions* (a) what; which; who: ～人 who; whom /～事 what /～时 what time; when /有～见教? Is there anything you want to see me about? /有～不同? What is the difference? (b) where:～处 what place; where /～方而来 where from; whence /家住～方? Where do you live? /意欲～往? Where are you going? *or* Whither? (c) why:～出此言? Why did you utter such remarks? ❷ *used in rhetorical questions*:有～不可? Why not? /～济于事? Of what avail is it? /～颜见人? How can I show myself before anyone again? /～至于此? How did it come to such a pass? /谈～容易! But that is by no means easy. *or* It's easier said than done. ❸ (Hé) a surname

何必 hébì *used in rhetorical questions or statements to indicate that there is no need for sth.*:我们是老朋友了，～客气。There's no need for old friends like us to stand on ceremony. *or* Why such formality between old friends like us? /一点小事儿，～为之烦恼? Why get upset over such a trifle? /你～替他开脱呢? There is no need for you to plead for him. *or* Why should you plead for him? /～大惊小怪? What is there to be surprised at? /～当真。Why take it so seriously?

何不 hébù *used in rhetorical questions to emphasize or suggest sth.*:～再试一下? Why not try again? /他是行家，～向他请教? He is an expert. Why don't we (*or* you) ask him for advice?

何曾 hécéng *used in rhetorical questions to emphasize negation of sth. in the past*:天哪! 我～知道此事? Good gracious! I never knew this. /这么些年来，她～提起过想出国留学的事? In all these years, when did she ever mention her desire to study abroad?

何尝 hécháng *used in rhetorical questions or statements to emphasize negation*:事实真相，我～知道。When did I ever know the truth? *or* I never knew the truth. /这些教训人们～忘记过? Never has anyone forgotten these lessons. /我～没劝过他，只是他听不进去。Not that I had not warned him, but he just wouldn't listen.

何啻 héchì 〈书面〉 *used in rhetorical questions or statements for emphasis*:～万千 more than tens of thousands; virtually myriads /～天壤之别 no less than the difference between heaven and earth; world of difference /该国的贫民窟～人间地狱。The slums in that country are literally a living hell.

何等 héděng ❶ what kind:他是～人物? What kind of person is he? /你是～人，敢来干涉我的事? Who are you to interfere with me? ❷ (used in exclamations) what; how:这孩子～聪明! What a clever boy (he is)! *or* How clever the boy is! /能用我的知识为祖国服务，是～的光荣! How glorious it is to use my knowledge in the service of my own country!

何妨 héfáng *used in rhetorical questions to suggest sth.*:这些意见说说又～? Why not speak up? *or* There is no harm in making our suggestions.

何干 hégān *used in rhetorical questions to show that there is no connection whatever*:这事与我～? What has that got to do with me? *or* What business is it of mine?

何故 hégù why; what for; what is the reason for:他～至今未到? Why hasn't he come yet?

何厚铧 Hé Hòuhuá Edmund Ho Hau-wah (1955-), first chief executive of the Macao Special Administrative Region (from 20 Dec. 1999)

何苦 hékǔ *also* "何苦来" why take the trouble; why bother; why:～自寻烦恼? Why worry yourself sick? /这事与你无干，～为它劳神? Why bother your head about something that is not your concern? /为这点小事争吵，～呢? Arguing over such trifles — is it worth it? /你这是～来? Why bring all this trouble on yourself?

何况 hékuàng much less; let alone; moreover; furthermore:牺牲尚且不怕，～这些困难。We fear no death, let alone these difficulties. /她连饮料都不愿喝一杯，更～留下吃饭了。She wouldn't take a drink, much less stay for dinner. /这个建议本身就不够周全，～实施起来费用也太大。The proposal was not well thought out; moreover, it would have been too expensive.

何乐而不为 hé lè ér bù wéi why not go ahead with it; why not do it; be only too glad to do it:这是一本万利的事，你～呢? The project cannot fail to bring enormous returns for your investment. Why not go ahead with it?

何其 héqí (usu. with a note of disapproval) how; what:～毒也! How malicious (*or* vicious)! /～愚蠢! What a fool! /～相似乃尔! What a striking likeness (*or* similarity)! /此等人～多也! There are just too many of them.

何去何从 héqù-hécóng what course to follow:两条道路摆在面前，你～? There are two roads before you; which one would you take (*or* follow)?

何如 hérú 〈书面〉 ❶ how about:再下一盘棋，～? How about another game of chess? ❷ what kind of:陈先生～人也? What kind of person is Mr. Chen? ❸ (often used together with 与其 in rhetorical questions) wouldn't it be better:与其求人，～求己? Wouldn't it be better to rely on oneself than on others? /与其临渊羡鱼，～退而织网。Rather than stand on the verge of a lake and covet the swimming fish, one would do well to go back home and weave a fishing net.

何首乌 héshǒuwū *also* "首乌"〈中药〉 tuber of multiflower knotweed (*Polygonum multiflorum*)

何谓 héwèi 〈书面〉 ❶ what is:～大学? What is a university? ❷ what is meant by; what is the meaning of:阁下此言～也? What do you mean by that?

何仙姑 Hé Xiāngū He Xiangu (formerly translated as Ho Hsien-ku), one of the Eight Immortals in Taoist mythology

何消 héxiāo *used in rhetorical questions or statements to show there is no need for sth.*:这～你替她做。There is no need for you to do it for her. *or* You don't have to do it for her. /～说，我明天一定会去的。It goes without saying that I'll go tomorrow. *or* Certainly,

I'll go tomorrow.

何须 héxū *used in rhetorical questions or statements to show something is not necessary*：我都知道了，～再说! I know all about it. You don't have to say anything more. /～如此匆忙，骑车去那里只要五分钟。There is no hurry. It takes only 5 minutes to get there by bike. /这事～这么多人? 我一个人就能干了。This job does not require so many people. I can handle it by myself.

何许 héxǔ 〈书面〉what place; what kind of; what:此君～人也? What sort of person is this gentleman? *or* What place is this gentleman from?

何以 héyǐ ❶〈书面〉with what; how:君～教我? What are you going to enlighten me about? /此等情况～解释? How can you explain all this? /不杀此贼，～谢天下? How can the people be pacified if this traitor is not executed? ❷ for what reason; why:～他要提前离开? Why does he want to leave earlier? /昨日已然说定，～变卦? You agreed to this yesterday. What made you change your mind?

何在 hézài 〈书面〉where:原因～? What is the reason for it? *or* For what reason? /公道～? Where can one find justice? /症结～? What is the crux of the matter?

何止 hézhǐ *used in rhetorical questions to indicate a number or extent far greater than the one given*:方圆～百里 extend far more than a hundred *li* in periphery /近年来的好作品～这些? There are far more fine works produced in recent years than I have mentioned. *or* These are merely a few of the fine works produced in recent years.

何足 hézú *followed by a verb or verbal phrase to form a rhetorical question or statement indicating negation*:～挂怀 not worth thinking about; not worthy of mention /～为奇 *also* "～为怪" nothing to wonder at; nothing wonderful or surprising /～与论国家大事 not worth discussing state affairs with; nobody to share concerns about the state with

何足道哉 hézúdàozāi not worth talking about:写这等小文章，～! Such petty articles are two a penny!

何足挂齿 hézúguàchǐ be not worth mentioning:区区小事，～。Such a trifle is not worth mentioning. *or* Please don't mention such a trifle. /一点薄礼表敬意，～。This unworthy gift is only a small token of my esteem for you. Please don't mention it.

荷[1]

hé lotus

荷[2]

Hé (short for 荷兰) the Netherlands; Holland:～属圭亚那 Dutch Guyana (now independent and renamed Surinam) /中～两国于1954年建立外交关系。Diplomatic relations were established between the People's Republic of China and the Netherlands in 1954.

see also hè

荷包 hébao ❶ small bag (for carrying money and odds and ends); pouch:绣～ embroider a pouch (for a man one loves) ❷ pocket (in a garment)

荷包蛋 hébaodàn fried egg; poached egg

荷尔蒙 hé'ěrméng 〈生理〉(now called 激素) hormone

荷花 héhuā lotus:《～舞》*Lotus Dance* /～虽好，也要绿叶扶持。With all its beauty, the lotus needs the green leaves to set it off.

荷花生日 héhuā shēngrì 〈方言〉Lotus Festival (24th day of the 6th lunar month)

荷兰 Hélán the Netherlands; Holland:～人 Dutch; Dutchman; Hollander /～语 Dutch (language) /～干酪 Dutch cheese

荷兰合金 Hélán héjīn 〈冶金〉Dutch metal

荷兰金 hélánjīn 〈冶金〉Dutch gold

荷兰麻布 Hélán mábù 〈纺织〉hollands

荷兰牛 hélánniú Holstein (cattle)

荷兰式拍卖 Hélánshì pāimài Dutch auction, a sale of goods in which the price is gradually reduced until a buyer is found

荷兰水 hélánshuǐ 〈方言〉aerated water; soda water

荷兰猪 hélánzhū (popular term for 豚鼠) guinea-pig; cavy

荷马 Hémǎ Homer (c.9th century BC), ancient Greek poet, and author of the epics *Iliad* (伊利亚特) and *Odyssey* (奥德赛):～时代 Homeric Age

荷塘 hétáng lotus pond:《～月色》*Lotus Pond in the Moonlight* (celebrated essay by Zhu Ziqing 朱自清, 1927)

荷叶 héyè lotus leaf:～粉蒸肉 pork slices with rice flour steamed in lotus leaves /～珠露 dewdrops sparkling on lotus leaves /～饼 thin pancake

荷叶边 héyèbiān (of woman's dress, etc.) flounce; furbelow; falbala; flouncing:镶着～的裙子 flounced skirt

曷

hé 〈书面〉❶ how; why ❷ when

鞨

hé *see* "靺鞨" Mòhé

鹖

hé a kind of fighting bird in ancient books

鹖鸡 héjī *see* "褐马鸡" hèmǎjī

涸

hé 〈书面〉dry up; run dry:～井 dry well

涸竭 héjié dry up; run dry:溪水～。The brook dried up.

涸泽而渔 hézé'éryú *also* "竭泽而渔" jiézé'éryú drain the pond to get all the fish; kill the goose that lays the golden eggs:这种～的事傻瓜才会干。Only idiots would kill the goose that lays the golden eggs.

涸辙之鲋 hézhézhīfù fish trapped in a dry rut — person in a desperate situation who needs immediate relief

合[1]

hé ❶ close; shut:～上眼 close one's eyes /缝～伤口 sew up (*or* suture) a wound /笑得前仰后～ rock with laughter /请把书～上。Close your books please. ❷ come together; join; combine:～为一体 combine (*or* merge) into one /～住一套房子 share a flat (*or* an apartment) ❸ whole; entire:～族 whole clan /～村 entire (*or* whole) village /～家大小 whole family ❹ conform with; suit; agree:～规矩 conform with the rules; follow the convention /～胃口 suit one's taste; be to one's taste /～则留，不～则去 stay if the conditions are suitable, or quit if they are not /正～我意。It suits me fine. ❺ be equal to; add up to:一米～三市尺。A metre is equal to 3 *chi*. /货款加运费～多少钱? How much was the payment for the goods plus shipping expenses? ❻〈书面〉proper; appropriate:理～如此。We deem it appropriate to do so. ❼〈量词〉(of passages at arms) round; bout:大战三十余～ fight thirty-odd rounds ❽〈天文〉conjunction ❾ (Hé) a surname

合[2]

hé 〈音乐〉note of the scale in *gongchepu* (工尺谱), corresponding to 5 in numbered musical notation

see also gě

合办 hébàn operate or run jointly:～一家企业 run (*or* set up) an enterprise jointly; operate a joint venture

合瓣 hébàn 〈植物〉sympetalous; gamopetalous

合瓣花 hébànhuā sympetalous flower:～类 metachlamydeae; sympetalae

合瓣花冠 hébàn huāguān gamopetalous corolla

合抱 hébào (of a tree, etc.) so big that one can just get one's arms around:三人～的大树 tree so big that it takes three people to embrace it with outstretched arms

合抱之木，生于毫末 hébào zhī mù, shēngyú háomò a huge tree grows from a tiny seedling; great oaks from little acorns grow

合璧 hébì (of two different things) combine harmoniously; match well:中西～ harmonious combination of Chinese and Western elements /诗画～ painting matched with poetry; painting with a poem inscribed on it

合编 hébiān ❶ compile in collaboration; co-edit:这本字典是他们～的。They jointly compiled the dictionary. ❷ merge and reorganize (army units, etc.):两军～后，战斗力大为增强。The merger of the two armies greatly strengthened their combat effectiveness.

合并 hébìng ❶ merge; amalgamate:把十个委员会～成三个 amalgamate ten committees into three /那两家商行去年～了。The two firms merged last year. /两案将～处理。The two cases will be handled together. ❷ (of an illness) be complicated by another illness:麻疹～肺炎 measles complicated by pneumonia

合并症 hébìngzhèng *also* "并发症" bìngfāzhèng 〈医学〉complication

合不来 hébulái not get along well; be incompatible:性格～ not compatible in temperament /我们俩就是～。The two of us just can't get along.

合不着 hébuzháo 〈方言〉not worthwhile:这件事太～了。It is not at all worthwhile. /这么好的地，种饲料～。It doesn't pay to grow feed crops on such fertile soil.

合槽 hécáo feed (draught animals) from the same trough; raise (draught animals) together: ～喂养 feed (draught animals) from the same trough

合唱 héchàng chorus: 混声～ mixed chorus / 无伴奏～ unaccompanied chorus / 女声～ female chorus / 男声～ male chorus / 童声～ childrens chorus

合唱曲 héchàngqǔ (music for) chorus

合唱团 héchàngtuán *also* "合唱队" chorus; choir: ～指挥 chorus master

合成 héchéng ❶ compose; compound: ～一种药 compound a medicine / 由两部分～ be composed of two parts / ～军队 combined arms unit / 录音～ dubbing / ～镜头 process shots / 加速度～〈物理〉 composition acceleration / 这根绳子由三股～。This is a rope of three strands (braided together). ❷〈化工〉 synthetize; synthesize: ～材料 synthetic material / ～醇 synthol / ～钢 synthetic steel / ～燃料 synthol; synfuel; synthetic fuel / ～汽油 synthetic gasoline / ～润滑油 syntholube / ～烃类 synthin

合成氨 héchéng'ān 〈化学〉 synthetic ammonia

合成词 héchéngcí 〈语言〉 compound word

合成代谢 héchéng dàixiè 〈生理〉 anabolism

合成革 héchénggé synthetic leather

合成函数 héchéng hánshù 〈数学〉 composite function

合成琥珀 héchéng hǔpò ambroin; amberoid

合成结晶牛胰岛素 héchéng jiéjīng niúyídǎosù 〈药学〉 synthetic crystalline bovine insulin

合成酶 héchéngméi 〈生化〉 synthetase; synzyme

合成染料 héchéng rǎnliào synthetic dye

合成石油 héchéng shíyóu synthetic petroleum

合成树脂 héchéng shùzhī 〈化工〉 synthetic resin: ～胶合板 resin-bonded plywood / ～结合剂 cycleweld

合成数 héchéngshù 〈数学〉 composite number

合成塔 héchéngtǎ 〈化工〉 synthetic tower

合成图像 héchéng túxiàng composite image; composograph

合成图像摄像装置 héchéng túxiàng shèxiàng zhuāngzhì vistascope

合成洗涤剂 héchéng xǐdíjì synthetic detergent; syndet

合成洗衣粉 héchéng xǐyīfěn synthetic washing powder

合成纤维 héchéng xiānwéi synthetic fibre; synthon

合成橡胶 héchéng xiàngjiāo synthetic rubber; synthal

合成照片 héchéng zhàopiàn 〈摄影〉 composite photograph

合当 hédāng (often used in the early vernacular) be fated: 那天～他们有事。They were fated to get into trouble that day.

合得来 hédelái get along well; be compatible: 你应该挑个同你～的人作组友。You should choose a partner you can get along with.

合得着 hédezháo 〈方言〉 worthwhile: 这些东西很贵，但～。They are expensive, but worth what you pay for them.

合订本 hédìngběn one-volume edition; bound volume: 《毛泽东选集》～ one-volume edition of the *Selected Works of Mao Zedong* / 《人民日报》～ bound volume of *People's Daily* / 《中国日报》～ file of *China Daily*

合度 hédù right, proper; appropriate: 长短～ of the right length / 安排～ proper arrangements / ～的体育活动有利健康。An appropriate amount of physical exercise is good for one's health.

合恩角 Hé'ēnjiǎo (Chile) Cape Horn, at the southernmost tip of South America

合二而一 hé'èr'éryī 〈哲学〉 two combine into one

合法 héfǎ legal; lawful; legitimate; rightful: ～地位 legal status / ～行为 lawful action (*or* conduct) / 唯一～政府 sole legal government / ～婚姻 lawful marriage; licit marriage / ～要求 lawful claim; rightful claim / ～收入 lawfully earned income / ～身份 legal status / ～权益 legitimate rights and interests / ～居住权 lawful right of residence / ～继承权 legitimate right of inheritance; rightful inheritance / ～继承人 rightful heir

合法化 héfǎhuà legalize; legitimize: 在有些国家和地区，赌博被～了。Gambling is legalized in some countries and areas.

合肥 Héféi Hefei, capital of Anhui Province

合该 hégāi should; ought to: ～受到尊敬 ought to be honoured / ～如此。That is as it should be.

合格 hégé qualified; up to standard: ～的教师 qualified teacher / 保证产品质量～ vouch for the quality of the products / 这批进口仪器大都不～。Most of these imported instruments are not up to standard.

合格率 hégélǜ acceptance rate

合格证 hégézhèng certificate of inspection; certificate of quality

合共 hégòng altogether; in all; all told: ～二万元捐款 donations of 20,000 *yuan* in all; total of 20,000 *yuan* in donations

合股 hégǔ ❶ pool capital; form a partnership: 与某人～ enter into partnership with sb. / ～企业 joint stock enterprise ❷〈纺织〉 plying: ～线 ply (*or* plied) yarn; twine

合股人 hégǔrén co-partner

合乎 héhū conform with or to; correspond to; accord with; tally with: ～实情 accord with the actual situation / ～群众的利益 conform with the interests of the people / ～自然规律 be in conformity (*or* accordance) with the law of nature / ～要求 meet the requirements / ～读者的需要 cater to the needs of readers / ～情理 stand to reason; be reasonable / ～逻辑 be logical / ～规格 be up to the specifications / ～题裁的文体 style appropriate to the subject matter

合欢 héhuān ❶ (of man and woman) enjoy (sexual) bliss together; make love ❷ *also* "马缨花" mǎyīnghuā 〈植物〉 silk tree

合会 héhuì 〈旧语〉 a kind of mutual loan club whose members contribute a fixed amount of money at regular intervals for the use of one member on a rotating basis

合婚 héhūn 〈旧语〉 exchange of horoscopes of the two parties before formal betrothal to see whether they are compatible or not

合伙 héhuǒ form a partnership (with sb.); enter into partnership (with sb.): ～经营 run a business in partnership / ～打劫 gang up in robbery / 双方决定自明年起～。The two sides have decided to enter into partnership as of next year. / 李先生让他～办公司。Mr. Li has taken him into partnership in his company.

合伙公司 héhuǒ gōngsī partnership

合伙企业 héhuǒ qǐyè partnership

合伙人 héhuǒrén partner: 资深～ senior partner

合击 héjī make a concerted or joint attack: 分进～ concerted attack by converging columns / 司令部决定各师于次日拂晓～敌军。The headquarters decided that all the divisions under its command were to make a concerted attack on the enemy at dawn the following day.

合计 héjì amount to; add up to; total: 这次旅行的各项费用～约五千元。The expenses for the trip amounted to about 5,000 *yuan*. / 把全部数字～一下。Add up all the figures. / 上周参观展览的人数～达一万五千。Visitors to the exhibition totalled 15,000 last week.

合计 héji ❶ think over; mull over; figure out: 我心里一直在～这件事。I have been thinking it over. / 让我～～下一步该怎么办。Let me figure out what is to be done next. ❷ consult: 大家～～，看哪个方案比较切实可行。Let's put our heads together and see which of the plans is the most feasible.

合剂 héjì 〈药学〉 mixture: 复方甘草～ brown mixture

合家 héjiā whole or entire family: ～团圆 reunion of the whole (*or* entire) family / 祝～欢乐。I wish you and your family happiness.

合家欢 héjiāhuān family group photo: 照一张～ take a family group photo

合脚 héjiǎo (of shoes or socks) fit: 我穿这双鞋特别～。These shoes fit me perfectly.

合金 héjīn alloy: 二元～ binary alloy / 三元～ ternary alloy / ～铸铁 alloy cast iron / ～添加剂 alloying additive / ～工艺 alloying technology

合金钢 héjīngāng alloy steel: 高～ high-alloy steel / ～结构钢 structural alloy steel / ～工具钢 alloy tool steel

合金结晶体管 héjīn jiéjīngtǐguǎn 〈电子〉 alloy-junction transistor; fused-junction transistor

合金元素 héjīn yuánsù alloying element

合卺 héjǐn 〈书面〉 (of bride and bridegroom) drink the nuptial cup — go through the wedding ceremony

合犋 héjù *also* "插犋" chājù (of peasants) pool draught animals and bigger farm tools, and do farmwork together

合刊 hékān combined issue (of a periodical): 《人民文学》九、十月份～ combined September and October issue of *People's Literature*

合口 hékǒu ❶ (of a wound) heal; heal up: 这伤要十天才能～。It will take ten days for the wound to heal up. ❷ (of food, etc.) be to one's taste: 母亲做的菜更～。The food mother prepares is more to my taste.

合口呼 hékǒuhū 〈语言〉 syllables ending in u or a final (韵母) beginning with u (e.g. 古 gǔ, 团 tuán)
see also "四呼" sìhū

合饹 héle *also* "饸饹" héle *hele*, a kind of noodles made from buckwheat or sorghum flour

合理 hélǐ rational; reasonable; equitable; sensible: ~安排 rational (*or* proper) arrangement /~的建议 sensible suggestion /~收费 reasonable charge /~轮作〈农业〉proper rotation of crops /~密植 rational close planting /~冲撞〈体育〉fair charge /社会财富的~分配 equitable distribution of social wealth /凡是存在的，都是~的。(as a philosophical thesis) Whatever is, is right.

合理化 hélǐhuà rationalize: ~建议 rationalization proposal

合力 hélì ❶ join forces; concert efforts: 同心~ unite and make a concerted effort; work together with one mind /我们~把门弄开了。Together we forced the door open. ❷〈物理〉resultant (of forces)

合流 héliú ❶ flowing together; confluence: 嘉陵江和长江在重庆~。The Jialing and the Yangtze rivers meet at Chongqing. ❷ collaborate; work hand in glove: "宁汉~" merger of the Nanjing and Wuhan regimes (1927) ❸ merge into one: 儒、道~而生玄学。*Xuanxue* was born of the merger of Confucianism and Taoism.

合流河 héliúhé confluent (river)

合龙 hélóng 〈建筑〉close a dam, dyke, etc. built from two ends; join the two sections of a bridge built from two ends: 大坝~ closing of a dam /河流~ damming of a river

合拢 hélǒng come together; join together; gather: 用绳子把柴禾~到一起，打成捆儿 gather the firewood and tie it in a bundle

合霉素 héméisù 〈药学〉syntomycin

合谋 hémóu conspire; plot together: ~不轨 plot sedition together /三人~ conspiracy of three people /盗贼与用人~偷窃珠宝。The thieves conspired with the servants to steal the family's jewels.

合拍 hépāi ❶ in time; in step; in harmony: 与时代潮流不~ be out of step with the trend of the times /与现代都市生活的节奏~ (keep) in step with the tempo of modern city life /他的意见常和大家不~。His opinions were often out of harmony with those of others. ❷ collaborate (on a film, etc.); shoot a film in collaboration: 这是一部中、日~的影片。This film was jointly produced by Chinese and Japanese studios. ❸ take a group photo or picture

合浦珠还 Hépǔ-zhūhuán *also* "合浦还珠" pearls returned to Hepu (from the story that in the Han Dynasty pearl clams in Hepu, a pearl-producing area in today's Guangdong and Guangxi, migrated to other areas as a result of corrupt administration and indiscriminate fishing but came back when the administration improved) — recovery of sth. or return of sb. after an absence: 此乃家父遗物，早年被窃，今日幸得~。This article belonged to my late father. It is so nice to recover it after it was stolen years ago.

合情合理 héqíng-hélǐ fair and reasonable; fair and square: ~的要求 reasonable demand /这样解决问题是~的。It is fair and square to settle the issue this way.

合群 héqún ❶ get on well with others; be sociable or gregarious: ~的性格 sociable disposition /此人不太~。He does not mix well with others. *or* He is a bad mixer. ❷ form a group or society for mutual aid; gang up

合扇 héshàn 〈方言〉hinge

合身 héshēn (of clothing) fit: 这件上衣很~。This jacket fits well.

合十 héshí put or hold the palms together before one (as a Buddhist greeting): ~相迎 put together one's palms in greeting

合时 héshí fashionable; in vogue: 穿戴~ dress fashionably

合式 héshì ❶ up to standard; in agreement with the forms and formulas: 这个青年老生的唱做均~。This young *laosheng* actor sings and dances in the proper style. ❷ *see* "合适"

合适 héshì suitable; appropriate; becoming; right: 她穿蓝衣服看上去很~。Blue looks very becoming on her. /他做这工作是再~不过了。He was the right man for the job. /你认为怎样~就怎样做吧。Do as you see fit. /哪个日子对你最~? Which date suits you best?

合手 héshǒu ❶〈方言〉be congenial; cooperate (with each other): 眼下他俩好像有点不大~。Right now they don't seem to be getting on too well in their collaboration. ❷〈书面〉put the palms together before one in salutation

合署 héshǔ (of related offices) handle official business together in the same building: 海关与边境检查站在这间大厅里~办公。The Customs and the Border Inspection Bureau work side by side in this hall.

合数 héshù *also* "合成数"〈数学〉composite number

合算 hésuàn ❶ paying; worthwhile: 选用好料子做一套衣服是~的。It pays to choose quality material for a suit. /在这上面花这么多时间不~。It isn't worthwhile to spend so much time on it. ❷ reckon; calculate: ~一下你一共有多少钱，看到底够不够。Reckon up all your money and see if you have enough.

合榫 hésǔn matchjoint; matching joint

合题 hétí 〈哲学〉synthesis

合体 hétǐ ❶ (of clothing) fit: 她的旗袍非常~。Her cheongsam (*or* mandarin gown) fits her beautifully. ❷〈语言〉composite character (i.e. composed of two or more elements, such as 明 composed of 日 and 月)

合同 hétong contract: 销售~ sales contract /合资~ joint venture contract /雇用~ contract of employment /抵押~ mortgage contract /奖惩~ bonus-penalty contract /包销~ exclusive sales contract /承兑~ acceptance contract /代理~ agency contract /附加~ accessory contract /"开口"~ open(-ended) contract /可以撤消的~ voidable contract /"交钥匙"~ turnkey contract /签订~ sign a contract /撕毁~ tear up a contract /履行~ carry out a contract /~期限 contract period /~期满 expiration of a contract /按~行事 act ex contract /~条款 contract terms /~纠纷 contract dispute /~规定利率 contractual (*or* contracted) interest rate /~当事人 contracting party; party to a contract

合同法 hétongfǎ 〈法律〉contract law

合同工 hétonggōng contract worker; contract labour: ~制 contract labour system

合同医院 hétong yīyuàn assigned hospital (under medical insurance or public medicine)

合同制 hétongzhì contract system

合围 héwéi ❶ (in battle or hunting) surround; encircle: 分进~ surround by converging columns ❷〈书面〉*see* "合抱"

合宪性 héxiànxìng 〈法律〉constitutionality

合心 héxīn suit; be to one's liking or taste: 这件衣服挺~。This dress is quite to my taste.

合眼 héyǎn ❶ close one's eyes; sleep: ~安睡 go to sleep /一夜没~ not get a wink of sleep all night ❷ die; pass away: 老太太是今天凌晨合的眼。The old lady passed away early this morning.

合演 héyǎn appear in the same play or performance; perform together; co-star: 父女俩~小品。Father and daughter put on skits together.

合叶 héyè *also* "合页" hinge: ~片 hinge strap

合一 héyī combine into one; merge into a single whole

合宜 héyí suitable; appropriate; becoming; right: 朴素的衣服在学校里穿很~。Plain, simple clothes are appropriate for school wear.

合议庭 héyìtíng 〈法律〉collegiate bench (of judges, or of a judge and people's assessors); collegial panel: ~通常由审判员一人，人民陪审员二人组成。A collegiate bench usually consists of one judge and two people's assessors.

合议制 héyìzhì 〈法律〉collegiate system (judicial system under which justice is administered by a collegiate bench of judges, or by a judge and people's assessors)

合意 héyì suit; be to one's liking or taste: 一切都合你意吗? Is everything to your liking?

合营 héyíng jointly operate; run (business) in partnership: ~期满 expiration of an agreement for a joint venture /中外~公司 jointly-run Chinese-foreign company

合营企业 héyíng qǐyè joint venture or enterprise: 公私~ enterprise under joint public-private ownership

合影 héyǐng ❶ have a photo or picture taken together; take a group photo or picture: 会见后宾主~留念。After the meeting the guests and the host posed for a group photo to mark the occasion. ❷ group photo or picture: 毕业班~ group picture of the graduating class

合用 héyòng ❶ share: 电话~线 (telephone) party line /两个学生~一台电脑。Two students share a computer. ❷ fit for use; of use: 这东西好看，但不~。It may look pretty, but it is not fit for use. /对我们来说，这房间太大了，不太~。The room is too large to suit our purpose.

合于 héyú accord with; tally with; conform to: ~国情 accord with (*or* conform to) the conditions of a country /~价值规律 be consistent with (*or* tally with) the law of value

合约 héyuē contract: 签订~ sign (*or* conclude) a contract

合葬 hézàng (esp. of husband and wife) be buried in the same grave: 她死后遗体迁回故乡，与丈夫~。Her body was carried back to her native village and buried with her husband's remains in the

H

same grave. /这里～着三十多位烈士。More than thirty revolutionary martyrs were buried together here.
合闸 hézhá switch on; switch in:～顺序 switch order /～继电器 closing relay
合掌 hézhǎng put the palms together before one (as a Buddhist greeting):～礼拜 hold the palms together in worship
合账 hézhàng ❶〈口语〉figure out or add up accounts; make up accounts ❷〈方言〉be worthwhile; pay
合照 hézhào ❶ take a group photo ❷ group photo
合辙 hézhé ❶ be in agreement; be on the same wavelength:咱俩的意见～。We see eye to eye. ❷ in rhyme; rhythmical:快板～儿,容易记。Clapper talk is rhythmical and easy to memorize.
合着 hézhe 〈方言〉*used to express surprised discovery*:～你是不喜欢吃我烤的饼啊。So you don't like the cake I baked.
合趾猿 hézhǐyuán 〈动物〉siamang (*Hylobates syndactylus*)
合众国际社 Hézhòng Guójìshè United Press International (UPI), a US news agency
合著 hézhù write in collaboration; co-author:这本专著是由三位硕士生～的。The monograph is co-authored by three MA candidates.
合资 hézī invest or own jointly; pool capital; enter into partnership:中外～企业 joint venture involving both Chinese and foreign investment; jointly-owned Chinese-foreign enterprise; Chinese-foreign joint venture /～各方 parties to a joint venture /陈家兄弟～经营了一家豪华餐馆。The Chen brothers ran a luxury restaurant as a joint partnership.
合资经营 hézī jīngyíng joint venture:～企业 joint venture; joint venture enterprise
合子 hézǐ 〈生物〉zygote:～形成 zygogenesis
合子 hézi ❶ a kind of fried pie with meat or vegetable filling ❷ *also* "盒子" hézi box; case
合纵连横 hézòng-liánhéng (during the Warring States Period) opposite strategic theories of vertical (north-south) or horizontal (east-west) alliance of states against or with the State of Qin; strategic manoeuvring of all kinds
合奏 hézòu instrumental ensemble:民乐～ ensemble of traditional folk instruments /木管乐～ ensemble of woodwinds
合作 hézuò cooperate; collaborate; work together:分工～ share out the work and cooperate with each other /友好～关系 relations of friendship and cooperation /北南～ North-South cooperation /～生产大型民航飞机 co-produce large civilian aeroplanes /这尊塑像是由一位著名的雕刻家和他的两名学生～完成的。This statue was made by a famous sculptor and two of his students.
合作化 hézuòhuà (movement to) organise cooperatives:农业～ cooperative transformation of agriculture
合作经济 hézuò jīngjì cooperative economy; cooperative sector of the economy
合作经营 hézuò jīngyíng jointly run or operate; manage in cooperation; run a cooperative business operation:～企业 cooperatively managed enterprise (*or* business)
合作社 hézuòshè cooperative; co-op
合作医疗 hézuò yīliáo cooperative medical service or care; cooperative medicine; community-sponsored medical service:～保险制度 system of community-sponsored medical treatment /这个乡已经普及了～。All the inhabitants of the township are now covered by a co-operative medical service.
合作银行 hézuò yínháng cooperative bank

颌 hé jaw:上～ upper jaw /下～ lower jaw /～畸形 jaw abnormality
see also gé
颌裂 héliè 〈医学〉gnathoschisis
颌痛 hétòng 〈医学〉gnathodynia
颌下点 héxiàdiǎn 〈生理〉gnathion
颌下腺 héxiàxiàn *also* "唾液腺" tuòyèxiàn 〈生理〉submaxillary gland
颌炎 héyán 〈医学〉gnathitis
颌针鱼 hézhēnyú 〈动物〉needlefish
颌指数 hézhǐshù *also* "颌突度" gnathic index

盒 hé ❶ box; case:饭～儿 lunch box; messtin /铅笔～ pencil box; pencil case /糕点～儿 pastry box ❷ box-shaped fireworks
盒带 hédài (short for 盒式磁带) cassette tape
盒饭 héfàn box lunch
盒式磁带 héshì cídài cassette tape:～录音机 cassette tape recorder
盒式存储器 héshì cúnchǔqì cassette memory; cartridge memory
盒式录像带 héshì lùxiàngdài videocassette; video-cartridge
盒式照相机 héshì zhàoxiàngjī box camera
盒子 hézi ❶ box; case; casket ❷ box-shaped fireworks ❸ *see* "盒子枪"
盒子菜 hézicài 〈方言〉cooked food sold in boxes
盒子花 hézihuā fireworks in the shape of a box
盒子枪 héziqiāng *also* "盒子炮"〈方言〉Mauser pistol

禾 hé ❶ standing grain (esp. rice) ❷〈古语〉foxtail millet
禾本科 héběnkē 〈植物〉grass family:～植物 grass /～绿肥 graminaceous green manure
禾草 hécǎo 〈植物〉grass
禾草学 hécǎoxué agrostology
禾场 hécháng 〈方言〉threshing floor
禾苗 hémiáo seedlings of cereal crops
禾木胶 hémùjiāo grass tree gum; acaroid gum

和[1](龢) hé ❶ gentle; mild; kind:天气晴～ warm and fine /风～日丽 gentle breeze and bright sun /性情温～ have a gentle disposition /对敌狠,对己～ ruthless to one's enemy and kind to one's own people ❷ harmonious; on good terms:～为贵 harmony is most precious; nothing is more precious than peace /天时、地利、人～ favourable climatic, geographical and human conditions /两家失～。The two families are at odds (*or* at loggerheads) with each other. *or* They have fallen out with each other. ❸ peace:讲～ *also* "媾～" make peace; negotiate for peace /主～ advocate peace; favour peaceful settlement /劝～ mediate; persuade sb. to make peace ❹〈体育〉draw; tie ❺ (Hé) a surname

和[2] hé ❶ together with:这药丸要～姜汤一起服下。The pills are to be swallowed with ginger water. ❷〈介词〉*used to indicate relationship, comparison, etc.*:～群众打成一片 become one with the masses /这件事～他无关。It has nothing to do with him. /我～他意见相同。I agree with him. ❸ and:丈夫～妻子 man and wife /粮食～棉花的产量 output of grain and cotton ❹〈数学〉sum:二加三的～为五。The sum of two and three is five. *or* Two and (*or* plus) three makes five.

和[3] Hé Japan; Japanese:汉～词典 Chinese-Japanese dictionary
see also hè; hú; huó; huò
和蔼 hé'ǎi kindly; affable; amiable:～的老师 kindly teacher /～的老人 amiable (*or* genial) old man /待人～ be amiable (*or* affable) to people
和蔼可亲 hé'ǎi-kěqīn gentle and affable; genial; amiable:我感到她是一位～的人。I find her gentle and affable.
和畅 héchàng (of a wind) gentle and pleasant:春风～ gentle and pleasant spring breeze
和道 hédao 〈方言〉gentle; kindly; amiable:待人～ be kindly
和法 héfǎ 〈中医〉counteraction and harmonization — counteracting the disease by adjusting the functional relation of the internal organs
和风 héfēng ❶ soft or gentle breeze:～习习。A gentle breeze is blowing. /～,艳阳,鸟语,花香 — 春天又降临了大地。A balmy breeze, a radiant sun, birdsong, fragrant flowers — spring is here again. ❷〈气象〉moderate breeze
和风细雨 héfēng-xìyǔ like a gentle breeze and light rain — in a gentle and mild way:思想工作要～ ideological work should be done in the manner of "a gentle breeze and mild rain"; do ideological work in a gentle and mild way
和服 héfú (Japanese) kimono:～腰带 obi (for women and children)
和光同尘 héguāng-tóngchén conceal one's brilliance and be as humble as dust; refrain from showing one's ability and not vie with others:～,与世浮沉 conceal one's ability and drift with the tide
和好 héhǎo ❶ harmony; concord; amity:邻里关系～。The neighbours live in harmony. ❷ become reconciled:～如初 become recon-

ciled; be on good terms again; restore good relations /小两口像孩子似的，一会儿吵架，一会儿又～了。The young couple behaved just like children, quarrelling one moment and making it up again the next.

和合 héhé ❶〈书面〉harmonious:阴阳～ harmony between *yin* and *yang* /～文化 culture of harmony /他们夫妻关系不太～。The couple aren't quite compatible with each other. ❷ (Hé-Hé) (commonly called 和合二仙) twin genii He-He

和合二仙 Hé-Hé èrxiān twin genii He-He, legendary gods of harmonious union with one holding a lotus and the other holding a box, both symbols of harmony, whose pictures used to be displayed at wedding ceremonies

和缓 héhuǎn ❶ gentle; mild:语气～ in a gentle voice; in a mild tone /态度～ adopt (*or* take) an easy attitude /这药药性～。This medicine is quite mild. ❷ ease up; relax:～紧张气氛 relieve the tension /该地区的紧张局势趋于～。Tension in the region is easing up.

和会 héhuì (short for 和平会议) peace conference:巴黎～ Paris Peace Conference (1919; 1946)

和奸 héjiān adultery by consent

和解 héjiě become reconciled:～的态度 conciliatory attitude /表示愿意～ show a willingness to conciliate /双方～了。They are reconciled.

和局 héjú drawn game; draw; tie:比赛以～结束。The game ended in a draw. /他们俩人下棋，经常是～。The two usually tie with each other in chess games.

和乐 hélè harmonious and happy:一家人甚是～。The family live in harmony and happiness.

和美 héměi harmonious and happy:～的家庭 happy family /和和美美过日子 live happily together; live in happy harmony

和睦 hémù harmony; concord; amity:～相处 live in harmony; coexist in peace and harmony /夫妻～ conjugal harmony /家庭～ family harmony; domestic peace /邻里关系～ good neighbourly relations /民族～ national concord /友好～ friendly and harmonious relations

和暖 hénuǎn pleasantly warm; warm and genial:～宜人 pleasantly warm /天气～ warm, genial weather /～的春天 pleasantly warm spring; genial spring

和盘托出 hépán-tuōchū make a clean breast of everything; hold nothing back:把自己的所作所为～ make a clean breast of everything one has done /开始他矢口否认，但终于～。At first he denied everything, but eventually he came clean.

和平 hépíng ❶ peace:～运动 peace movement /保卫～ defend (*or* safeguard) peace /～倡议 peace proposal /～力量 forces of peace /～统一祖国 peaceful reunification of the motherland /～友好条约 treaty of peace and friendship /～外交政策 foreign policy of peace /～麻痹思想 false sense of peace and security /～利用原子能 peaceful utilization of atomic energy; use of atomic energy for peaceful purposes /～解决国际争端 peaceful settlement of international disputes; settlement of international disputes by peaceful means /爱好～的国家 peace-loving country /持久～ lasting peace /永久～ eternal peace /维持～行动 peace keeping operation ❷ mild:熊猫性情～。The giant panda is mild by nature. /一般来说，中药药性～。Generally speaking, Chinese herbal medicine is mild. ❸ peaceful; tranquil; calm:心境～ peaceful mind; ease of mind

和平岛 hépíngdǎo 〈方言〉traffic island

和平队 Hépíngduì (US) Peace Corps

和平鸽 hépínggē dove of peace

和平攻势 hépíng gōngshì peace offensive

和平共处 hépíng gòngchǔ peaceful coexistence

和平共处五项原则 hépíng gòngchǔ wǔxiàng yuánzé Five Principles of Peaceful Coexistence (first introduced in a Sino-Indian agreement in April, 1954: mutual respect for territorial integrity and sovereignty, mutual non-aggression, non-interference in each other's internal affairs, equality and mutual benefit, and peaceful coexistence)

和平过渡 hépíng guòdù peaceful transition

和平解放 hépíng jiěfàng peaceful liberation

和平竞赛 hépíng jìngsài peaceful competition

和平门 Hépíngmén Gate of Peace, Beijing

和平谈判 hépíng tánpàn peace negotiations; peace talks

和平统一，一国两制 hépíng tǒngyī, yīguó liǎngzhì peaceful reunification and one country, two systems (a policy of the Chinese government on the Taiwan question)

和平演变 hépíng yǎnbiàn peaceful evolution (usu. referring to an outside attempt to subvert a socialist state by peaceful means)

和平战略 hépíng zhànlüè strategy of peace

和平中立政策 hépíng zhōnglì zhèngcè policy of peace and neutrality

和平主义 hépíngzhǔyì pacifism:～者 pacifist

和棋 héqí draw or tie in chess or other board games

和气 héqi ❶ gentle; kindly; courteous; polite:态度～ be courteous in manner /语气谦恭～ be polite and modest in speech /说话～ speak politely (*or* gently); be soft-spoken /待人～ be kind (*or* friendly) to people /那位长官倒还～。The officer looked pretty even-tempered. ❷ harmonious; friendly; amiable:和和气气地过日子 live harmoniously and amiably /他们彼此很～。They are very friendly with each other. ❸ friendship; harmony:别为这事伤了～。Don't let this hurt our friendship. *or* Let's remain friends despite that unpleasantness.

和气生财 héqi-shēngcái (as a motto for business people) amiable temper brings wealth; amiability begets riches; do business with a smile, and you will make a pile (of money)

和洽 héqià harmonious; on friendly terms:他俩关系～。Their relations are harmonious.

和亲 héqīn (of some dynasties) attempt to pacify rulers of minority nationalities in the border areas by marrying daughters of the Han imperial family to them:～政策 policy of pacification through (such) marriage

和软 héruǎn gentle; soft; mild:～的语调 soft tone

和善 héshàn kind and gentle; kindly; genial:～的面容 kindly face /心地～ kind-hearted /～寿长。Kindliness makes for longevity.

和尚 héshang Buddhist monk:大～ (as a polite form of address to a Buddhist monk) master

和尚打伞，无法无天 héshang dǎsǎn, wú fǎ wú tiān like a Buddhist monk holding an umbrella, there is no hair (发, a homophone for 法 law) nor heaven — defy laws human and divine; be absolutely lawless; run wild:他的做法真是～。He is simply flouting all laws.

和尚头 héshangtóu 〈口语〉❶ shaven head:剃个～ have one's head shaved ❷ male; man; boy:那时我们班上全是～。Our class then consisted of boys entirely.

和声 héshēng ❶ soft voice; mild tone:说话～细气 speak softly ❷〈音乐〉harmony:～练习 harmonic exercise /为歌曲配～ harmonize a song /～小音阶 harmonic minor scale

和声学 héshēngxué 〈音乐〉harmonics; harmony

和事老 héshìlǎo peacemaker or mediator (esp. one who is more concerned with stopping the bickering than settling the issue):一有争执，他总是做～。He was always ready to play the peacemaker whenever there was a dispute.

和数 héshù 〈数学〉sum:～校验 sum check /～累计器 sum accumulator

和顺 héshùn gentle and amiable:性情～ of gentle and amiable disposition

和谈 hétán peace talks; peace negotiation:板门店～ Pamunjon Talks (for ending hostilities in Korea, 1951-1953)

和田 Hétián Hotan, county in southern Xinjiang:～地毯 Hotan rugs /～河 Hotan River

和调 hétiáo 〈书面〉harmonize; mix:～上下 harmonize relations between superiors and inferiors (higher authorities and grass-roots, etc.) /～五味 mix the five flavours (in cooking) /这两种颜色配得很～。These two colours are well matched.

和头 hétóu both ends of a coffin; front end of a coffin

和婉 héwǎn (of speech) mild and roundabout; tactful:语气～ in a mild tone /他批评得很～。He made his criticism very tactfully.

和文 Héwén Japanese (language)

和息 héxī 〈方言〉pacify; conciliate; reconcile:～纷争 pacify a dispute

和弦 héxián 〈音乐〉chord:～风琴 chord organ

和祥 héxiáng kindly; genial; amiable:～的面容 kindly look

和谐 héxié harmonious:～一致 in perfect harmony /音调～ melodious; tuneful /音符～ accord of notes /～融洽的气氛 cordial and harmonious atmosphere /那几种颜色配在一起十分～。Those colours blend well together. /宾主谈得很～。The host and guest had a most cordial conversation.

和煦 héxù pleasantly warm; genial:～的冬阳 genial winter sun /春风～。The spring breeze is warm and pleasant.

H

和颜悦色 héyán-yuèsè have a kind face; have a genial expression; be kindly and affable: 孩子错了，要～地给他讲道理。When a child makes a mistake, one should explain it to him or her in a kindly and affable manner.

和衣 héyī (sleep) with one's clothes on; (sleep) in one's clothes: ～而眠 sleep with one's clothes on

和议 héyì peace talks; peace negotiations: 达成～ reach a peace agreement /～破裂。The peace talks broke up.

和易 héyì gentle and unassuming; amiable: ～近人 amiable and easy of approach

和约 héyuē peace treaty: 缔结～ conclude a peace treaty

和悦 héyuè kindly; affable; amiable: 表情～ wear an amiable look; have a genial expression

和衷共济 hézhōng-gòngjì work together with one accord (in time of difficulties); make concerted efforts to overcome difficulties: 大难当前，大家必须～。In the present crisis it is essential that we should be loyal to each other and stand together.

盉 hé (used in ancient China) bronze tripod for warming wine

齕 hé 〈书面〉 bite: 食其肉而～其骨 eat the flesh and munch away at the bones

纥 hé *see* "回纥" Huíhé

see also gē

貉 hé (generally called 貉子 or 狸) raccoon dog (*Nyctereutes procyonoides*)

see also háo

饸 hé

饸饹 héle *also* "合饹" héle；"河漏" hélou a kind of noodles made from buckwheat or sorghum flour (with a special press): ～床子 press for making *hele* noodles /压～ make *hele* noodles with a press

hè

鹤 hè crane: 丹顶～ red-crowned crane /～年 crane's age — longevity

鹤顶红 hèdǐnghóng red fleshy knot on the crane's head (supposed to be poisonous)

鹤发鸡皮 hèfà-jīpí *also* "鸡皮鹤发" (of old people) white hair and wrinkled skin; hoary head with wrinkled skin; aged: 年过七旬而无～之状。Though over 70 years old, he doesn't look aged at all.

鹤发童颜 hèfà-tóngyán *also* "童颜鹤发" (of old people) white hair and youthful complexion; healthy in old age; hale and hearty: 他虽已八十高龄，但～，非常健康。At the age of 80, he still had ruddy cheeks and enjoyed excellent health.

鹤立 hèlì 〈书面〉 stand expectantly; wait eagerly

鹤立鸡群 hèlì-jīqún (of a person) be like a crane standing among chickens; be a triton among the minnows; stand head and shoulders above others; be the pick of the bunch: 自以为～ think oneself cream of the crop /他和这些人共事，自然是～。Working among these people, he is easily the pick of the bunch. /凭他的人品才学，在这个小山村里，可谓～了。With his personality and learning, he undoubtedly stands head and shoulders above all others in this small mountain village.

鹤虱 hèshī 〈植物〉 *Lappula echinata*

鹤鸵 hètuó *also* "食火鸡" shíhuǒjī cassowary (*Casuarius casuarius*)

鹤膝风 hèxīfēng 〈中医〉 arthroncus of the knee

鹤嘴镐 hèzuǐgǎo pickaxe; pick; mattock

赫[1] hè ❶ conspicuous; distinguished; grand: 地位显～ occupy a distinguished position (in a hierarchy, etc.); be powerful; be influential ❷ (Hè) a surname

赫[2] hè (short for 赫兹) 〈电学〉 hertz: 千～ kilohertz /兆～ megahertz

赫尔辛基 Hè'ěrxīnjī Helsinki, capital of Finland

赫赫 hèhè illustrious; impressive: 声威～ be of great renown /～战功 outstanding (*or* impressive) military exploit

赫赫有名 hèhè-yǒumíng distinguished; very famous: ～的将军 illustrious general /～的英雄 renowned hero

赫鲁晓夫 Hèlǔxiǎofū Nikita Sergeyevich Khrushchev (1894-1971), leader of the former Soviet Union for 11 years after Stalin's death until he was deposed in 1964

赫然 hèrán ❶ unexpectedly and shockingly: 一只黑熊～出现在他的面前。To his consternation, a black bear suddenly appeared before him. ❷ terribly (angry): 天子～而怒。The emperor got terribly angry all of a sudden (*or* flew into a violent rage).

赫哲族 Hèzhézú Hezhen nationality, living in Heilongjiang Province

赫兹 hèzī hertz (Hz); Hertz: ～波 Hertz wave /～振荡 Hertz oscillation /～天线 Hertz antenna

荷 hè ❶ carry on one's shoulder or back: ～担而行 carry a load on a shoulder-pole ❷ 〈书面〉 bear; take on: 身～重任 bear heavy responsibilities ❸ burden; responsibility: 重～ heavy burden; heavy responsibility ❹ 〈书面〉 (usu. used in letter writing) obliged; grateful: 感～ be obliged /为～ will be appreciated

see also hé

荷负 hèfù 〈书面〉 bear; shoulder: ～重任 shoulder heavy responsibilities

荷枪实弹 hèqiāng-shídàn (of a soldier or policeman) carry a loaded rifle on one's shoulder; be ready for emergencies: 出事那天，满街都是～的士兵。The streets were lined with soldiers carrying loaded rifles on the day of the accident.

荷载 hèzài ❶ carry a load ❷ load: ～分布 load distribution /～馈线 load feeder /～系数 load factor /～变形曲线 load-deformation curve

荷重 hèzhòng weight a building can bear; weight load: ～系数 load factor

壑 hè gully; big pool: 沟～ gully; ravine /丘～ hills and valleys /以邻为～ use neighbours' land as a drain; shift one's troubles (*or* problems) onto others

吓(嚇) hè ❶ threaten; intimidate: 威～ threaten /恫～ intimidate ❷ 〈叹词〉 *used to express disapproval or resentment*: ～，你也太不像话了! Humph, how impudent you are! /～，他怎能这样呢? Tut-tut, how could he act like that?

see also xià

愒 hè 〈书面〉 scare; frighten: 恐～ terrorize; intimidate; threaten

see also kài; qì

褐 hè ❶ 〈书面〉 coarse cloth or clothing: 短～ short jacket made of coarse cloth ❷ brown: ～色上衣 brown coat

褐斑 hèbān (of paper) foxing; brown stain

褐斑病 hèbānbìng 〈植物〉 brown spot or rot

褐变 hèbiàn (of vegetables and fruits) brown stain

褐腐病 hèfǔbìng 〈植物〉 brown rot

褐黄斑 hèhuángbān 〈医学〉 chloasma

褐家鼠 hèjiāshǔ *also* "沟鼠" gōushǔ; "大家鼠" dàjiāshǔ; "褐鼠" brown rat (*Rattus norvegicus*)

褐马鸡 hèmǎjī *also* "鹖鸡" héjī 〈动物〉 *Crossoptilon mantchuricum*, rare variety of pheasant indigenous to north China with blackish brown plumage and silvery to bluish tail feathers

褐煤 hèméi *also* "褐炭" brown coal; lignite

褐色 hèsè brown; tan: ～腐植酸 brown humic acid

褐色产品 hèsè chǎnpǐn 〈商业〉 brown goods (referring to electrical appliances such as TV sets, radios, VCRs, etc., which used to be painted brown on the outside)

褐色土 hèsètǔ drab soil

褐蛇 hèshé brown snake

褐铁矿 hètiěkuàng brown iron ore; limonite

褐云母 hèyúnmǔ anomite

褐藻 hèzǎo 〈植物〉brown alga

喝

hè shout loudly:吆～ call; cry out /厉声大～ shout angrily
see also hē

喝彩 hècǎi cheer; acclaim:众人鼓掌～。The crowd applauded in unison. /他们的精彩表演博得全场～。Their brilliant performance brought the house down.

喝倒彩 hè dàocǎi boo; hoot; make catcalls:她唱得太差劲,难怪观众～。She sang so poorly that the audience booed.

喝道 hèdào 〈旧语〉(of *yamen* runners, lictors, etc.) shout out to pedestrians to make way for an approaching official

喝令 hèlìng shout (out) a command:警察～围观的人们走开。The policemen shouted to the crowd of onlookers to move on.

喝六呼幺 hèliù-hūyāo *also* "呼幺喝六" shout when throwing the dice (in hopes of the winning number); gamble with the dice

喝问 hèwèn shout (out) a question or interrogation:严词～ question (sb.) sternly

猲

hè 〈书面〉❶ gasping with fear ❷ threaten; intimidate
see also xiè

和

hè ❶ join in the singing:附～ chime in (with others) /一唱一～ sing in duet; echo each other ❷ compose a poem of the same theme and rhyme scheme as one by someone else; write a poem in reply (to sb.'s poem):《～柳亚子先生》*Reply to Mr. Liu Yazi*
see also hé; hú; huó; huò

和诗 hèshī poem (written) in reply:～一首 write a poem in reply

翯

hè (of bird's feather) white and sleek

翯翯 hèhè 〈书面〉(of bird's feather) shiningly white

贺

hè ❶ congratulate; felicitate; celebrate:电～ cable a message of congratulations; send a congratulatory telegram /共～新春 celebrate the Spring Festival together ❷ (Hè) a surname

贺匾 hèbiǎn horizontal congratulatory plaque

贺词 hècí speech or message of congratulation:致～ give (*or* deliver) a speech of congratulation /新年～ New Year message; New Year greetings

贺电 hèdiàn congratulatory telegram or cable; message of congratulation

贺函 hèhán *also* "贺信" letter of congratulation; congratulatory letter

贺卡 hèkǎ greeting card:生日～ birthday card /圣诞～ Christmas card

贺兰石 hèlánshí *Helan* jade

贺礼 hèlǐ congratulatory gift:生日～ birthday present (*or* gift) /结婚～ wedding present

贺联 hèlián congratulatory couplet (written on scrolls, etc.):大厅里挂满了～。The hall was covered with scrolls inscribed with congratulatory couplets.

贺年 hènián extend New Year greetings; pay a New Year call:电话～ extend New Year greetings by phone

贺年片 hèniánpiàn New Year card

贺片 hèpiàn greeting card:新年～ New Year card /生日～ birthday card; greeting card for one's birthday /祝愿早日康复的～ get-well card

贺喜 hèxǐ congratulate sb. on a happy occasion; offer congratulations or felicitations:同事们纷纷前来向他～。His colleagues came one after another to offer him their congratulations.

贺信 hèxìn *also* "贺函" congratulatory letter; letter of congratulation

贺仪 hèyí 〈书面〉congratulatory gift

贺幛 hèzhàng large oblong sheet of silk with a congratulatory message written on it

hēi

黑

hēi ❶ black:～疤 black scar /把衣服染～ dye the dress black ❷ dark; dusk:起早贪～ work from dawn to dusk /天～以前 before dark /屋子里～得伸手不见五指。It was so dark in the room that you couldn't see your hand before you. /这孩子怕～。The kid is afraid of the dark. ❸ secret; shady; clandestine; unlawful: *see* "～会"; "～仓" ❹ wicked; evil; vicious:心～手狠 evil-minded and ruthless /有些买卖人真～。Some traders are just infamous. ❺ reactionary:～指示 reactionary orders (*or* instructions) ❻〈口语〉do sth. unlawful or unethical:～了他 kill him; do him in /他把那笔钱～了。He pocketed the money. /咱们是朋友,你可不能～我呀。Since we're chums, you won't cheat me, will you? ❼ (Hēi) (short for 黑龙江) Heilongjiang ❽ (Hēi) a surname

黑癌 hēi'ái 〈医学〉melanotic cancer; melanocarcinoma; melanoscirrhus

黑暗 hēi'àn ❶ dark:～的冬夜 dark winter night /洞里一片～。It was pitch-dark in the cave. ❷ corrupt; evil; reactionary:～的旧社会 dark old society /～统治 reactionary (*or* evil) rule /～的官场 corrupt officialdom /揭露～ expose evils; show up the seamy side; rake muck

黑暗大陆 Hēi'àn Dàlù Dark Continent (the continent of Africa because formerly little was known about it)

黑白 hēibái ❶ black and white:～相间 black alternating with white; in black and white stripes (*or* chequers) /～花儿 black-and-white pattern ❷ right and wrong; good and evil:混淆～ confound right and wrong; juggle with facts

黑白电视 hēibái diànshì black-and-white television:～机 black-and-white TV set /～显像管 monochrome picture tube

黑白分明 hēibái fēnmíng black-and-white; black contrasted with white; in sharp contrast:他看问题就是～,不是好就是坏。He thinks in black-and-white terms, of either-or.

黑白胶卷 hēibái jiāojuǎn black-and-white film:一卷～ a roll of black-and-white film

黑白片儿 hēibáipiānr 〈口语〉black-and-white movie or film

黑白片 hēibáipiàn black-and-white film or movie

黑斑病 hēibānbìng 〈植物〉black rot; black spot

黑斑蚊 hēibānwén *also* "伊蚊" yīwén 〈动物〉aedes; yellow-fever mosquito

黑板 hēibǎn blackboard:擦～ clean (*or* erase) the blackboard

黑板报 hēibǎnbào blackboard newspaper

黑板擦 hēibǎncā (blackboard) eraser

黑帮 hēibāng (member of) a reactionary gang; sinister gang:～分子 member of a reactionary (*or* sinister) gang; gangster

黑豹党 Hēibàodǎng Black Panther Party (a US Black organization of the 60's and 70's):～党员 Black Panther

黑变病 hēibiànbìng ❶〈医学〉melanosis; melanism:巩膜～ melanosis sclerae /结肠～ melanosis coli ❷〈植物〉melanose (*Septoria ampelina*)

黑不唧 hēibujī 〈贬义〉black; dark:你满手～的,快去洗洗。Your hands are black. Go and wash them.

黑不溜秋 hēibuliūqiū 〈方言〉dark; black; swarthy:长得～的 be swarthy; be dark-complexioned /她穿着～的衣服,神情黯然。Dressed in black, she looked depressed.

黑黪黪 hēicāncān (usu. of skin or hair) swarthy; dark; black:～的脸盘儿 swarthy face

黑潮 hēicháo 〈地理〉*Kuroshio*; Japan Current or Stream

黑车 hēichē ❶ unlicensed taxi ❷ car without registration

黑沉沉 hēichénchén (of the sky, etc.) dark; overcast:天色～的。The sky was overcast.

黑瓷 hēicí black porcelain

黑刺李 hēicìlǐ 〈植物〉blackthorn; sloe (*Prunus spinosa*)

黑疸 hēidǎn *see* "黑穗病"

黑道 hēidào ❶ unlighted road (at night):咱们这里尽是～,出去时带上电筒。There aren't any road lamps here. Take an electric torch with you when you go out. ❷ illegal activity:～买卖 shady trade ❸ underworld; banditry:～人物 underworld figure; gangster

黑道日子 hēidào rìzi 〈迷信〉unlucky day; unauspicious day

黑灯瞎火 hēidēng-xiāhuǒ *also* "黑灯下火" dark and unlighted:一停电,～,什么事也干不成。When power is cut and it is pitch dark, you have to call it a day.

黑地 hēidì (a piece of) unregistered land

黑点 hēidiǎn 〈比喻〉blemish; smirch; disgrace

黑店 hēidiàn (often used in the early vernacular) inn run by outlaws

黑貂 hēidiāo *also* "紫貂" zǐdiāo sable:～皮 sable fur; sable

黑鲷 hēidiāo *also* "乌颊鱼" wūjiáyú black porgy (*Sparus macrocephalus*)
黑洞洞 hēidōngdōng pitch dark; pitch black: 隧道里～的。It was pitch black in the tunnel.
黑洞 hēidòng *also* "坍缩星" tānsuōxīng 〈天文〉 black hole; collapsed star; collapsar: ～学说 theory of black holes
黑豆 hēidòu black soya bean
黑非洲 Hēi Fēizhōu Black Africa
黑粉病 hēifěnbìng *see* "黑穗病"
黑粪 hēifèn 〈医学〉 melaena
黑钙土 hēigàitǔ *also* "黑土" black earth; chernozem
黑格尔 Hēigé'ěr Georg Wilhelm Friedrich Hegel (1770-1831), German idealist philosopher: ～主义 Hegelianism / ～辩证法 Hegelian dialectics
黑更半夜 hēigēng-bànyè 〈口语〉 in the dead of night; in the still of the night: ～, 咱们能到哪去呢? Where can we go in the dead hours of the night?
黑咕隆咚 hēigulōngdōng 〈口语〉 very dark; pitch-dark: 山路上～的, 她会不会走丢? It's pitch-dark on the mountain path. Won't she get lost?
黑管 hēiguǎn 〈乐器〉 (popular term for 单簧管) clarinet
黑光 hēiguāng ultraviolet rays; black light
黑光灯 hēiguāngdēng black light lamp
黑锅 hēiguō scapegoat: 背～ be made a scapegoat (*or* whipping boy)
黑果 hēiguǒ huckleberry; blackberry
黑海 Hēihǎi Black Sea: ～舰队 Black Sea Fleet (of Russia and the Ukraine)
黑黑实实 hēihei-shīshī (of a person) swarthy and sturdy: ～的小伙子 swarthy, sturdy young man
黑糊糊 hēihūhū *also* "黑忽忽"; "黑乎乎" ❶ black; blackened; blackish: ～的陶罐 blackish pottery urn / 他满手都是油泥, ～。His hands are blackened with grease. ❷ dim; dusky; darkish: 树林里～的。It was rather dark in the woods. ❸ indistinct in the distance; blurred: ～的人影 blurred figure / 路旁～的一片人。A crowd of people loomed by the roadside.
黑胡椒 hēihújiāo black pepper (*Piper nigrum*)
黑胡桃 hēihútáo black walnut (*Juglans nigra*)
黑户 hēihù ❶ household or person without residence registration; unregistered family or resident: 报不上户口, 他岂不成了～? Without official registration, isn't his residence illegal? ❷ shop or firm without a business licence
黑话 hēihuà ❶ (thieves') cant; (bandits') argot: 他们说的是～, 你听不懂。You won't understand the cant they use. ❷ malicious, obscure words; double-talk: ～连篇 full of double-talk
黑桦 hēihuà 〈植物〉 *Betula dahurica*
黑鲩 hēihuàn *also* "青鱼" qīngyú 〈动物〉 black carp
黑会 hēihuì clandestine or unlawful meeting
黑货 hēihuò contraband (goods); smuggled goods: 买卖～ trade in contraband / 他的那批～已经出手。He had got that batch of smuggled goods off his hands.
黑家鼠 hēijiāshǔ *also* "黑鼠" black rat (*Rattus rattus rattus*)
黑麂 hēijǐ 〈动物〉 tufted deer (*Elaphodus cephalophus*)
黑间 hēijian 〈方言〉 night: ～外面凉。It's rather cold outside at night.
黑胶布 hēijiāobù 〈电工〉 black tape; friction tape
黑胶绸 hēijiāochóu *also* "拷绸" kǎochóu; "茛绸" liángchóu rust-coloured variety of summer silk; gambiered Guangdong silk
黑角 Hēijiǎo Pointe-Noire, largest seaport of the Republic of Congo (Brazzaville)
黑家 hēijie 〈方言〉 night: ～白日 day and night; every day
黑金钢石 hēijīngāngshí carbonado
黑晶 hēijīng smoky quartz
黑晶晶 hēijīngjīng black and bright; jet-black: ～的眼睛 sparkling black eyes / ～的头发 jet-black hair
黑颈鹤 hēijǐnghè black-necked crane
黑净 hēijìng (in *Kunqu* opera) black painted-face role
see also "黑头"
黑胫病 hēijìngbìng *also* "黑茎病" 〈植物〉 black shank
黑克尔管 hēikè'ěrguǎn 〈乐器〉 heckelphone
黑客 hēikè hacker (person who tampers with other people's computers through the Internet): 电脑～ computer hacker / 该国的军事情报网络曾被～渗透。The military information networks of the country were penetrated (*or* breached, *or* broken into) by hackers. / 该商业网址上月遭～用"拒绝服务"的方式攻击。The commercial Internet site was hacked last month by a "denial-of-service" attack.
黑口 hēikǒu black-border format (of a traditional thread-bound book) — a format with a black border or line printed along the middle of the block-printed sheet, presenting a black edge when the sheet is folded into two pages and bound at the opposite edges: 大～ broad black-border format / 小～ slender black-border format
see also "白口❶" báikǒu
黑牢 hēiláo dark dungeon; black hole: 打入～ put (sb.) in a dark dungeon
黑鹂 hēilí blackbird
黑里康大号 hēilǐkāng dàhào 〈乐器〉 helicon
黑里俏 hēiliqiào black beauty
黑栎 hēilì black oak (*Quercus velutina*)
黑亮 hēiliàng jet-black; glossy black; shiny black: 她有一头～的头发。She has glossy (*or* shiny) black hair. *or* She is raven-haired.
黑溜溜 hēiliūliū shiny black; jet-black: 一双～的眼睛 sparkling black eyes
黑瘤 hēiliú *also* "黑色素瘤" 〈医学〉 melanoma: 恶性～ melanoepithelioma / ～病 melanomatosis
黑龙江 Hēilóngjiāng ❶ Heilongjiang River (called the Amur in Russia) ❷ Heilongjiang Province
黑鲈 hēilú black bass (*Micropterus*)
黑鹿 hēilù 〈动物〉 sambar; sambhur (*Cervus unicolor*; *Rusa unicolor*)
黑马 hēimǎ dark horse — little-known person who unexpectedly becomes successful or prominent: 这次竞选中, 除了目前领先的候选人以外, 还可能出现一两名～。Apart from the front-runners, there may yet appear one or two dark horses in the election campaign.
黑马产品 hēimǎ chǎnpǐn 〈商业〉 FAD, product whose sales soar for a time and then drop almost as quickly
黑麦 hēimài rye
黑麦草 hēimàicǎo ryegrass
黑茫茫 hēimángmáng (mostly of night) boundless darkness: 眼前是～的一片, 简直无法辨认方向。We were greeted by such boundless darkness that we simply couldn't make out where we were.
黑眉乌嘴 hēiméi-wūzuǐ blackened and dirty: ～的水壶 blackened dirty kettle / 他脸让烟熏得～的。His face was blackened by soot.
黑莓 hēiméi blackberry
黑霉 hēiméi black mould
黑蒙蒙 hēimēngmēng dark and indistinct; indistinct in the darkness: 林子里～的一片, 什么也看不见。The woods are wrapped in impenetrable darkness. / 战士们趁着～的夜色爬进了围墙。Under cover of night the soldiers climbed over the wall.
黑锰矿 hēiměngkuàng hausmannite
黑面 hēimiàn flour not completely separated from bran; coarse flour
黑面包 hēimiànbāo rye bread; black or brown bread
黑名 hēimíng bad reputation: 为人担～ be held in ill repute on sb. else's account; be a scapegoat for sb.
黑名单 hēimíngdān blacklist: 上了～ be on a blacklist; be blacklisted
黑木耳 hēimù'ěr (same as 木耳) edible black fungus
黑幕 hēimù (sinister) inside story; shady deal: 揭穿～ disclose the inside story; show up a shady deal; expose a sinister scheme / ～重重 shrouded in sinister secrecy
黑尿 hēiniào *also* "黑蛋白尿" 〈医学〉 melanuria; melanuresis
黑奴 hēinú black slave: 《～吁天录》 (early translation of) *Uncle Tom's Cabin*
黑皮病 hēipíbìng 〈医学〉 melanoderma: 老年～ senile melanoderma
黑啤酒 hēipíjiǔ dark beer; stout
黑漆 hēiqī 〈化工〉 black varnish; black japan: 涂～ japanning
黑漆寥光 hēiqī-liáoguāng 〈方言〉 very dark; pitch dark: 屋里没有灯, ～。It was pitch dark in the unlit room.
黑漆漆 hēiqīqī pitch dark: ～的夜晚 pitch-dark night
黑钱 hēiqián money obtained by unlawful means (e.g. bribery, etc.); ill-gotten money: 收～ accept or extract illegal money; take bribery / 洗～ money laundering
黑枪 hēiqiāng ❶ concealed firearms ❷ shot fired treacherously from a hiding place: 打～ fire a shot treacherously from a hiding-

place; snipe treacherously / 挨～ be sniped at
黑黢黢 hēiqūqū pitch black; pitch dark: ～的天 pitch-black sky
黑雀麦 hēiquèmài rye brome grass (*Bromus secalinus*)
黑热病 hēirèbìng 〈医学〉 kala-azar
黑热病原虫 hēirèbìng yuánchóng 〈医学〉 Leishman-Donovan body
黑人 Hēirén Black; Negro: 美国～ Afro-American; Black American / ～领袖 Black leader / ～音乐 Black music / ～权力 Black power / ～英语 Black English; Ebonics
黑人 hēirén ❶ person without residence registration; unregistered resident: 他的签证早过期了，是个～。His visa has long expired, so his residence is illegal. ❷ person in hiding
黑肉瘤 hēiròuliú 〈医学〉 melanosarcomatosis
黑色 hēisè black: ～颜料 black pigment / ～绝缘胶布 black tape / 你穿这身～西服很精神。You look smart in this black suit.
黑色火药 hēisè huǒyào black powder
黑色金属 hēisè jīnshǔ ferrous metal: ～矿床 ferrous metal deposit / ～合金 ferrous alloy
黑色经济 hēisè jīngjì 〈经济〉 black economy (that part of the GDP, not covered by official statistics and hence not subject to taxation)
黑色人种 hēisè rénzhǒng black race; negroid race
黑色素 hēisèsù 〈生化〉 melanin
黑色涂料 hēisè túliào 〈化工〉 blackwash; blacking
黑色喜剧 hēisè xǐjù black comedy
黑色幽默 hēisè yōumò 〈文学〉 black humour: ～作家 black humourist
黑森森 hēisēnsēn ❶ dark and gruesome: ～的城堡 dark ghastly castle / 天～的。The sky was overcast. *or* It was a gloomy day. ❷ black and thick: ～的络腮胡子 thick black whiskers
黑纱 hēishā black armband; mourning band: 带～ wear a mourning band
黑衫党 Hēishāndǎng Blackshirts, another name for the National Fascist Party (Italian fascist party formed in Nov. 1921 after World War I)
黑舌 hēishé 〈医学〉 melanoglosia
黑社会 hēishèhuì underworld: ～头目 chieftain of the underworld; gang leader / ～成员 underworldling; gangster
黑石 Hēishí 〈伊斯兰〉 Black Stone (of Mecca)
黑市 hēishì black market: ～商人 black marketeer / ～汇率 black market exchange rate / ～交易 black market deal; under-the-counter sale / 他在～上买了一台彩电。He bought a colour TV on the black market.
黑市价 hēishìjià black market rate or price
黑市票 hēishìpiào black market ticket; scalping ticket: ～贩 scalper; ticket tout
黑手 hēishǒu wicked man manipulating sb. or sth. from backstage; evil backstage manipulator: 幕后有一只～在操纵。A wicked hand was pulling the strings behind the scenes.
黑手党 Hēishǒudǎng Mafia; Black Hand: ～成员 Mafioso
黑霜 hēishuāng black frost
黑鼠 hēishǔ *see* "黑家鼠"
黑死病 hēisǐbìng *also* "鼠疫" shǔyì black death; the plague
黑松 hēisōng Japanese black pine (*Pinus thunberjii*)
黑素 hēisù 〈生化〉 melanin
黑素癌 hēisù'ái 〈医学〉 melanocarcinoma; melanotic cancer
黑素沉着病 hēisù chénzhuóbìng *also* "黑变病" 〈医学〉 melanosis
黑素瘤 hēisùliú 〈医学〉 melanoma
黑素上皮癌 hēisù shàngpí'ái melanoepithelioma
黑素细胞瘤 hēisù xìbāoliú melanocytoma
黑穗病 hēisuìbìng *also* "黑疸"; "黑粉病" 〈农业〉 smut
黑糖 hēitáng 〈方言〉 brown sugar
黑桃 hēitáo (of cards) spade: ～六 spade six / ～皇后 queen of spades; spade queen
黑陶 hēitáo 〈考古〉 black pottery: ～制品 black pottery artifact
黑陶文化 hēitáo wénhuà *also* "龙山文化" Lóngshān wénhuà black-pottery culture
黑腾腾 hēiténgténg dusky; darkish; blackish: 一团～的烟雾 a cloud of blackish smoke
黑体 hēitǐ ❶ 〈印刷〉 boldface ❷ 〈物理〉 blackbody: ～辐射 blackbody radiation
黑体字 hēitǐzì 〈印刷〉 boldface type
黑天 hēitiān night: ～半夜 late at night; in the middle of the night; in the depth of night / 一直到～他才回来。He was not back until after dark.
黑天白日 hēitiān-báirì *also* "黑间白日"; "黑夜白日" day and night; day in, day out: 经过三个月～的苦干，他终于完成了任务。After working day and night for three months, he eventually managed to accomplish the task.
黑甜甜 hēitiántián (sleep) soundly: 天已大亮，他还睡得～的。It was broad daylight and he was still fast asleep.
黑甜乡 hēitiánxiāng land of dark sweetness; sound sleep; land of Nod: 我正待问他，他却早已进入了～。I was going to question him when I found him already sound asleep.
黑帖 hēitiě 〈口语〉 anonymous note or letter; poison-pen note or letter
黑铁皮 hēitiěpí black sheet iron
黑铜矿 hēitóngkuàng tenorite
黑头 hēitóu (in traditional Chinese opera) "black-face" role; painted face role: 唱～ play the painted-face role
黑土 hēitǔ *also* "黑钙土" black earth; chernozem: ～地 black earth; black earth field
黑腿病 hēituǐbìng 〈畜牧〉 blackleg
黑尾蟒 hēiwěimǎng 〈动物〉 black-tailed python (*Python molurus*)
黑窝 hēiwō nest of illegal activities; gangsters' or criminals' lair; den: 警察一夜之间掏了几处～。The police raided several gangsters' dens overnight.
黑乌乌 hēiwūwū deep black; jet-black: ～的眉毛 thick black eyebrows / ～的钢索 jet-black wire cable
黑钨矿 hēiwūkuàng wolframite
黑瞎子 hēixiāzi 〈方言〉 black bear
黑匣子 hēixiázi 〈航空〉 "black boxes", popular name for "flight data and cockpit voice recorders": 寻找失事飞机的～ search for the black boxes of the crashed airplane
黑下 hēixia 〈方言〉 night; dark: 他～又出去了。He went out again after dark.
黑线 hēixiàn (used in the Cultural Revolution to refer to a "revisionist" or "reactionary" school or system) black line; revisionist line: 文艺～ black (*or* revisionist) line in art and literature / ～人物 person connected with a "black line"
黑线鳕 hēixiànxuě *also* "黑斑鳕" haddock (*Melanogrammus aeglefinus*)
黑心 hēixīn black heart; evil mind: ～的女人 woman with a black heart / 他对她的家财早就起了～。He has long cast covetous eyes on her wealth.
黑信 hēixìn 〈口语〉 poison-pen letter; anonymous letter
黑猩猩 hēixīngxing chimpanzee
黑熊 hēixióng *also* "狗熊" gǒuxióng Asiatic black bear
黑锈病 hēixiùbìng black stalk
黑魆魆 hēixūxū dark: 林中～的，什么也看不见。It was so dark in the wood that they could not see a thing.
黑压压 hēiyāyā *also* "黑鸦鸦" dense mass: ～的人群 dense crowd / 远处～的一片，什么也看不清。One could see nothing but a blurred mass in the distance.
黑眼镜 hēiyǎnjìng sunglasses
黑眼珠 hēiyǎnzhū black pupil (of the eye); dark iris
黑曜岩 hēiyàoyán 〈矿业〉 obsidian
黑夜 hēiyè night: 当～来临时 as darkness is setting in / 他们是昨天～动身的。They set out last night. / ～笼罩着小城。The little town is shrouded in the darkness of night. / ～已经过去，曙光就会到来。When night is gone, dawn is near at hand.
黑衣修士 hēiyī xiūshì 〈宗教〉 Black Friars
黑蝇 hēiyíng black-fly
黑油油 hēiyōuyōu shiny black; jet-black: ～的头发 shiny (*or* glossy) black hair
黑黝黝 hēiyōuyōu ❶ *see* "黑油油" ❷ dim; dark: 一片～的松林 a dark mass of pine trees / 四周～的。It was dark all around.
黑鱼 hēiyú (popular term for 乌鳢) snakeheaded fish; snakehead
黑云母 hēiyúnmǔ 〈矿业〉 black mica; biotite
黑运 hēiyùn bad luck; misfortune: 走～ have bad luck; be down on one's luck; be out of luck
黑灾 hēizāi extensive drought in a pastoral area
黑早 hēizǎo 〈方言〉 dawn: 他每天～就下地干活儿。He set out to work in the fields at dawn every day.

H

黑枣 hēizǎo ❶ *also* "软枣" ruǎnzǎo dateplum persimmon (*Diospyros lotus*) ❷〈比喻〉bullet; shot: 像他这样的魔王，该给他个～吃。A tyrant like him deserves to be shot.
黑藻 hēizǎo black alga (*Hydrilla verticillata*)
黑账 hēizhàng secret account; private record: 查公司的～ investigate into the secret account of a company
黑芝麻 hēizhīma *Semen sesami nigrum*
黑种 hēizhǒng black race; negroid race: ～人 Black
黑竹 hēizhú *also* "紫竹" zǐzhú 〈植物〉black bamboo
黑子 hēizǐ ❶〈书面〉black mole (on the skin): 她眉心有一～。She has a black mole between her eyes. ❷〈天文〉sunspot

嘿(嗨) hēi 〈叹词〉❶ *used as a form of greeting or to call attention*: ～，你准备停当了吗? Hey! Are you all set? /～，你倒是上啊! Hey, you! Go ahead! /～，小心点儿，别滑倒了! Mind your step. It's slippery! ❷ *used to express satisfaction or self-congratulation*: ～，咱们这篇文章写得真不错呀! Hey! Our article is really well-written. ❸ *used to express surprise*: ～，下雨了! Why, it's raining! /～，原来你在这儿! Ah, there you are!
see also mò
嘿嘿 hēihēi 〈象声〉(of laughter) ha ha

hén

痕 hén mark; trace: 斑～ mark or scar /泪～ tear stain /裂～ crack; rift /伤～ scar; bruise
痕迹 hénjì mark; trace; vestige: 车轮的～ ruts; wheel tracks /作案的～ traces of a crime /衬衣上满是墨水的～。The shirt is dotted with ink spots. /在这个山村里，旧日的～几乎不存在了。This mountain village shows few vestiges (*or* traces) of its old self.
痕量 hénliàng *also* "痕迹量"〈化学〉trace: ～分析 trace analysis /～杂质 trace impurity
痕量元素 hénliàng yuánsù 〈化学〉trace element; tracer element

hěn

很 hěn 〈副词〉very; quite; awfully: ～快 very fast /～聪明 quite (*or* very) clever /～冷 awfully (*or* very) cold /老师～了解我。The teacher knows me very well. /他昨晚的表演精彩得～。The performance he gave last night was wonderful.

狠[1] hěn ❶ ruthless; relentless: 凶～ ferocious and relentless /心～手黑 vicious and ruthless /你对这孩子太～了。You are being cruel to the child. ❷ make a painful effort; harden (one's heart, etc.): ～了～心 steel one's heart (against sth.) /～着劲止住眼泪 fight back one's tears ❸ resolute; firm; stern; vigorous: ～～打击歪风 take resolute measures against unhealthy tendencies; crack down on evil trends firmly /～抓政策落实 pay special attention to the implementation of a policy; implement a policy vigorously

狠[2] hěn *see* "很" hěn
狠巴巴 hěnbābā fierce; ferocious: 他～地盯了她一眼。He gave her a ferocious stare.
狠毒 hěndú vicious; wicked; venomous: 阴险～ vicious and ruthless /心肠～ venomous; black-hearted /～的本性 wicked (*or* vicious) nature
狠辣 hěnlà vicious; ruthless; venomous: 手段～ (by) vicious means
狠命 hěnmìng 〈方言〉do all one can; do one's utmost; make an all-out effort: ～地跑 run for all one is worth /我～把她往上拉。I made a desperate effort to pull her up.
狠心 hěnxīn ❶ harden one's heart; make up one's mind; set one's heart: 狠不下心 cannot harden one's heart (to do sth.) /～钻研新技术 set oneself to the study of new technologies /他只要下了～，什么都难不倒他。Once his mind is made up, no difficulty can hold him back. ❷ heartless; merciless; cruel: 你怎么这么～哪! You've got a heart of stone! /他太～了。He is just heartless.

hèn

恨 hèn ❶ hate; resent: 怀～在心 nurse a hatred; bear a grudge /～得要命 hate with all one's soul /～得咬牙切齿 grind one's teeth with hatred ❷ regret; remorse: 抱～终天 have eternal regret /心中又悲又～ be filled with remorse as well as grief /～不相逢未嫁时。What a pity we didn't meet before you (*or* I) got married. *or* How sorry I am that I met you (my true love) only after my marriage.
恨不得 hènbude *also* "恨不能" be anxious to; be dying or itching to: 我～揍他一顿。I am itching to give him a beating. /孩子们～今天就上新公园去。The kids are dying to go to the new park today. /他～立刻回到家乡。How he wishes he could get back to his hometown right away.
恨人 hènrén 〈方言〉irritating; being a nuisance: 真～! What a nuisance! *or* How irritating! /那家伙可～了。That fellow is a perfect nuisance.
恨入骨髓 hènrùgǔsuǐ *see* "恨之入骨"
恨事 hènshì matter for regret: 终身～ lifelong regret /以此为～ deem it most regrettable
恨铁不成钢 hèn tiě bù chéng gāng wish that iron could turn into steel at once — be anxious for sb. to improve: 我老生他的气，是～啊! I am often exasperated with him simply because I am so anxious for him to make progress. /我父亲对我很失望，他是～。My father is disappointed with me, because I failed to live up to his expectations.
恨恶 hènwù 〈方言〉detest; be disgusted with
恨小非君子，无毒不丈夫 hèn xiǎo fēi jūnzǐ, wúdú bù zhàngfū a man with little power of hatred is no man at all; every real man has his venom
恨之入骨 hènzhī-rùgǔ *also* "恨入骨髓" hate to the marrow of one's bones; hate with every fibre of one's marrow; hate with all one's soul; hate like poison: 我揭露了他的卑劣手段，他便对我～。I exposed his underhand trick, so he hates my guts.

hēng

亨[1] hēng ❶ go smoothly or well ❷ (Hēng) a surname
亨[2] hēng (short for 亨利)〈电学〉henry
亨利 hēnglì 〈电学〉henry: 微～ microhenry /～定律 Henry's law /～计 inductance meter
亨通 hēngtōng go smoothly or well; prosper: 祝君万事～。May everything go well (*or* smoothly) with you. /他一向官运～。He has risen rapidly in the officialdom (*or* official hierarchy).

哼 hēng ❶ snort; groan: 厌恶地～了一声 give a snort of disgust /她痛得～了起来。She groaned with pain. ❷ hum; croon: ～首歌 hum a song /～一首摇篮曲 croon a cradlesong /她每天晚上都一边～着歌一边哄孩子睡觉。Every night she would croon her baby to sleep.
see also hng
哼唱 hēngchàng sing in a low voice; hum: 她在～一首民歌。She was humming a folksong.
哼哧 hēngchī 〈象声〉puff and blow: 他一上楼梯就～～地直喘。He would puff and blow every time he went up the stairs.
哼哈 hēnghā hum and haw: 你到底什么意见? 别哼哼哈哈的! Stop humming and hawing! Out with your opinion.
哼哈二将 Hēng-Hā èrjiàng ❶ Generals Heng and Ha (two fierce-looking divinities guarding a Buddhist temple gate, with Heng, or the "Snorter", ejecting two rays of light from his nostrils, and Ha, or the "Blower", blowing a great gust of yellow gas out of his mouth) ❷ pair of (truculent) men serving one master or working hand in glove with each other
哼哼 hēngheng 〈方言〉groan; snort: 病人疼得～了一夜。The patient groaned with pain all night.
哼哼唧唧 hēngheng-jījī mumble: 别～的，大声点说。Don't mumble. Speak louder, please. /她那么娇气，有一点病痛就～的。She

is so squeamish that a little pain will set her groaning.

哼唧 hēngji murmur; hum; croon:他一个人边走边～着。He murmured to himself while walking.

哼气 hēngqì 〈方言〉utter a sound or word:她起初不～，后来突然哭了起来。She kept silent at first but then all of sudden burst into tears.

哼儿哈儿 hēngrhār 〈象声〉hum and haw; hum and ha:他总是～的，我真够了。I'm really fed up with his hums and ha's. /你别老是～的，我可是认真的。Don't just hum and haw. I'm serious.

哼声 hēngshēng 〈电学〉hum:～调制 hum modulation /～器 hummer

哼唷 hēngyō 〈叹词〉heave ho; yo-heave-ho; yo-ho

脝 hēng *see* "膨脝" pénghēng

啈 hēng 〈叹词〉*used to express prohibition*

see also hèng

héng

恒(恆) héng

❶ lasting; permanent:永～ eternal; everlasting ❷ perseverance; constancy (of purpose):持之以～ persevere in (doing) sth. ❸ usual; common; constant:～态 usual (*or* normal) appearance /人之～情 common failing, feeling or reaction ❹ (Héng) a surname

恒产 héngchǎn real estate

恒齿 héngchǐ *also* "恒牙"〈生理〉permanent tooth; *dentes permanentes*:～系 *also* "～列" permanent dentition

恒等 héngděng 〈数学〉identical; identically equal:～变换 identical transformation /～表示 identity representation /～代换 identical substitution; identity substitution /～公式 identical formula

恒等定理 héngděng dìnglǐ 〈数学〉identical theorem; identity theorem

恒等方程 héngděng fāngchéng 〈数学〉identical equation

恒等函数 héngděng hánshù 〈数学〉identity function

恒等号 héngděnghào identity symbol

恒等式 héngděngshì identical equation; identity

恒等网络 héngděng wǎngluò identical network

恒等于零 héng děngyú líng identically vanishing

恒等元素 héngděng yuánsù identical element

恒定 héngdìng constant:～功率 constant power; firm power /～电压 constant voltage /～项〈数学〉constant term

恒定波 héngdìngbō constant wave (CW)

恒定场 héngdìngchǎng constant field; stationary field

恒定电流 héngdìng diànliú constant current

恒定负载 héngdìng fùzài constant load

恒定马力 héngdìng mǎlì constant horse power

恒定脉冲 héngdìng màichōng isopulse

恒河 Hénghé Ganges River (in South Asia)

恒河鳄 hénghé'è gavial; charial (*Gavialis gangeticus*)

恒河猴 hénghéhóu rhesus monkey (*Macaca mulatta*)

恒河平原 Hénghé Píngyuán Gangetic Plain; plain of the Ganges River

恒河三角洲 Hénghé Sānjiǎozhōu Ganges Delta

恒河沙数 Hénghé-shāshù as numerous as the sands of the Ganges; innumerable; countless:天下的书籍～，你我怎么能读得过来呢? There are innumerable books in the world. How can you or I read every one of them?

恒久 héngjiǔ long lasting; enduring:～不变 eternal; everlasting

恒量 héngliàng 〈物理〉constant

恒流 héngliú (short for 恒定电流)〈电学〉constant-current:～充电 constant-current charge /～放电 constant-current discharge /～配电 constant-current distribution

恒流变压器 héngliú biànyāqì constant-current transformer

恒流电动机 héngliú diàndòngjī constant-current motor

恒流电源 héngliú diànyuán 〈电学〉constant-current supply or source

恒流发电机 héngliú fādiànjī constant-current generator

恒流调节器 héngliú tiáojiéqì constant-current regulator

恒流制 héngliúzhì constant-current system

恒山 héngshān Mount Heng in Shanxi Province, one of the Five Sacred Mountains in China

恒生 Héngshēng (HK) Hang Sang:～银行 Hang Sang Bank /～指数 Hang Sang Index

恒湿 héngshī constant humidity:～箱 constant humidity cabinet /～器 humidistat

恒速 héngsù constant speed or velocity; const-sp:～传动 constant-speed drive /～扫描 constant-speed scanning /～轧制 constant-speed rolling /～调速器 isochronous governor; astatic governor

恒温 héngwēn constant temperature:～车间 constant-temperature workshop /～法 constant-temperature method /保持～ keep the temperature constant

恒温动物 héngwēn dòngwù homoiotherm; homotherm; warm-blooded animal

恒温炉 héngwēnlú constant-temperature furnace

恒温器 héngwēnqì thermostat

恒温室 héngwēnshì thermostatic chamber; constant-heat cabinet; constant-temperature room

恒温箱 héngwēnxiāng 〈医学〉incubator; thermostated container

恒心 héngxīn perseverance; constancy of purpose:有～才能成事。Perseverance leads to success. /他做什么都缺少～，结果一事无成。Without constancy of purpose, he has accomplished nothing.

恒星 héngxīng 〈天文〉(fixed) star

恒星年 héngxīngnián 〈天文〉sidereal year

恒星日 héngxīngrì 〈天文〉sidereal day

恒星时 héngxīngshí 〈天文〉sidereal time

恒星视差 héngxīng shìchā stellar parallax

恒星天文学 héngxīng tiānwénxué 〈天文〉stellar astronomy

恒星物理学 héngxīng wùlǐxué 〈天文〉stellar physics

恒星系 héngxīngxì stellar system; galaxy

恒星月 héngxīngyuè sidereal month

恒星云 héngxīngyún star cloud

恒性 héngxìng perseverance:他缺的就是～。He lacks nothing but perseverance. /干什么都要有～，别这山望着那山高。You must persevere in whatever you choose to do. Don't always think that grass is greener on the other side of the fence.

恒压 héngyā (short for 恒定电压)〈电学〉constant-voltage:～输电 constant-voltage transmission

恒压变压器 héngyā biànyāqì constant-voltage transformer

恒压电池 héngyā diànchí constant cell

恒压器 héngyāqì barostat

恒牙 héngyá permanent tooth; *dentes permanentes*

see also "恒齿"

恒言 héngyán common saying

姮 héng

姮娥 Héng'é *also* "嫦娥" Cháng'é 〈书面〉goddess of the moon

横 héng

❶ horizontal; transverse:划一～道 draw a horizontal line /沟渠纵～ criss-crossed by ditches ❷ from east to west; from west to east; *see* "～贯" ❸ across; crosswise; sideways:～着写 write across the page /一根巨木～放在小路上。A huge log lay across the path. ❹ at a right angle (to sth.):人行～道 pedestrians' crossing; zebra crossing /他闭着眼～躺在床上。He was lying across the bed with his eyes closed. ❺ place crosswise or horizontally:～槊赋诗 place one's spear crosswise while composing a poem; compose a poem in between fighting /～刀夺爱 draw one's sword to seize what sb. cherishes; take away sb.'s woman (*or* valued possession) by force /咱们把长桌子～过来放。Let's turn the long table crosswise. ❻ unrestrained; turbulent:老泪～流 tears streaming down one's aged face ❼ (used in idiomatic expressions or formal language) violently; fiercely; flagrantly; *see* "～加" ❽ horizontal stroke (in a Chinese character):先～后竖。Write the horizontal stroke before the vertical one. ❾〈方言〉in any case; anyhow; anyway:她～不去，你有啥办法? What if she wouldn't go in any case? /今天我～要把这活干完。Anyhow I'm going to finish the job today. ❿〈方言〉probably; (most) likely:天都黑了，她～不来了。It's already dark. She is probably not coming.

see also hèng

横匾 héngbiǎn inscribed horizontal board (over the entrance of a public building, institution, historical structure, etc.)

横标 héngbiāo streamer; banner:巨幅～ huge streamer

横滨 Héngbīn Yokohama, second largest city and seaport on Honshu Island, Japan

横波 héngbō ❶〈书面〉(usu. of a woman) (cast) a glance:～一笑 give sb. a smiling glance ❷〈物理〉transverse wave:～探伤 transverse wave testing

横草不动,竖草不拿 héng cǎo bù dòng, shù cǎo bù ná *also*"横针不拈,竖线不动"〈俗语〉not bother to lift a finger

横插一杠子 héng chā yī gàngzi poke one's nose in (sb. else's business); barge in uninvited; interfere flagrantly; butt into:他干得好好的,你干么要～? Why did you butt into something he was doing so well?

横产 héngchǎn *also*"横位"〈医学〉transverse presentation

横产位 héngchǎnwèi 〈医学〉transverse presentation; torso presentation; trunk presentation

横陈 héngchén lie across:一水～,将城市分成两半。A river runs through the city, cutting it into two parts. /战场上尸体～。The battlefield was strewn with dead bodies.

横冲直撞 héngchōng-zhízhuàng *also*"横冲直闯" dash around like mad; jostle and elbow one's way; barge or charge about; rampage:他在敌阵中～,毫不畏惧。He charged about fearless amidst the enemy battle array. /看到匪徒们在村里～那劲儿,真气死人了! It made my blood boil to see the bandits rampaging in the village.

横穿 héngchuān cross; go across:～马路时要注意来往车辆。Lookout for the traffic when you cross a street. /一条小路～而过。A footpath lay across.

横档 héngdàng (of a table, etc.) crosspiece

横刀跃马 héngdāo-yuèmǎ gallop ahead with sword drawn:国难当前,大丈夫当～,保国于疆场。Confronted with national subjugation, a true man will take up arms and serve his nation on the battlefield.

横倒竖歪 héngdǎo-shùwāi in disorder; in a mess; higgledy-piggledy:桌上～地放着几个空酒瓶。Some empty wine bottles lay higgledy-piggledy across (*or* scattered upon) the table.

横笛 héngdí ❶ *also*"笛子" dízi (Chinese) bamboo flute ❷ transverse flute

横渡 héngdù cross (a river, etc.):～长江 cross the Yangtze River /驾帆船～大西洋 sailing across the Atlantic

横断层 héngduàncéng 〈地质〉cross fault; transverse fault

横断裂 héngduànliè cross fracture

横断面 héngduànmiàn *see*"横剖面"

横断山脉 Héngduàn Shānmài Hengduan Mountains, a series of parallel mountain ranges running in a north-south direction through Sichuan, Yunnan and Tibet

横队 héngduì rank; row:排成五列～ form a five-deep rank; line up five deep

横额 héng'é ❶ inscribed horizontal board ❷ horizontal scroll bearing an inscription (usu. hung over a door and flanked by two vertical scrolls forming a couplet) ❸ streamer (hung over a door or rostrum)

横幅 héngfú ❶ horizontal scroll of painting or calligraphy ❷ streamer; banner:游行者高举着～标语走向广场。The demonstrators marched towards the square, holding high banners with slogans on them.

横杆 hénggān 〈体育〉crossbar;〈机械〉overarm

横格纸 hénggézhǐ lined paper

横隔膜 hénggémó 〈生理〉diaphragm

横亘 hénggèn lie across or between; span:现在已经有十几座大桥～在长江上。There are now more than a dozen bridges spanning the Yangtze River. /两省交界处～着一座东西走向的山脉。Between the two provinces lies a mountain chain running from east to west.

横梗 hénggěng (mostly used with abstract nouns) block; stifle:一种憎恶的感觉～在心头。A feeling of disgust filled his heart.

横贯 héngguàn pass through from east to west or from west to east; traverse:这条铁路～六省。The railway traverses six provinces. /新建的运河从东向西～全县。The newly-built canal runs through the county from east to west.

横巷 hénghàng 〈矿业〉crossdrift; crosscutting

横加 héngjiā wilfully; flagrantly; forcibly:～白眼 look upon (sb.) with unwaranted contempt /～指责 make unfounded charges; hurl abuses /～干涉 interfere wantonly; put one's oar in

横结肠 héngjiécháng 〈生理〉transverse colon

横截面 héngjiémiàn cross-section; transverse section

横锯 héngjù 〈机械〉cross cut:～锯床 cross-cut frame saw

横空 héngkōng across the sky:彩虹～。A rainbow arched across the sky. /～出世,莽昆仑,阅尽人间春色。Far above the earth, into the blue, You, wild Kunlun, have seen All that was fairest in the world of men.

横跨 héngkuà stretch over or across; span:～欧亚大陆 stretch over the Eurasian land mass /一座大桥～江上。A big bridge spans the river.

横梁 héngliáng ❶〈建筑〉crossbeam; cross girder ❷〈汽车〉cross member

横流 héngliú ❶ (of tears) gush; stream:他涕泪～。Tears bathed his cheeks. ❷ (of water) flow in all directions; flood:沧海～,方显出英雄本色。When the seas are in turmoil, Heroes are on their mettle.

横眉 héngméi frown in anger; scowl:两人～相对。Fierce-browed, they glared at each other.

横眉怒目 héngméi-nùmù *also*"横眉努目";"横眉立目" glare hatred (at); dart an angry look (at):面对敌人,他～。He darted angry looks at the enemy. /门里出来一个～的家丁。A fierce-looking servant appeared at the door.

横眉竖眼 héngméi-shùyǎn glare in anger

横楣 héngméi *also*"横楣子" crossbeam (of a door or window frame)

横拍握法 héngpāi wòfǎ 〈体育〉(of table tennis) hand-shake grip; tennis grip

横批 héngpī horizontal scroll bearing an inscription (usu. hung over a door and flanked by two vertical scrolls forming a couplet)

横披 héngpī horizontal scroll of calligraphy or painting

横剖面 héngpōumiàn *also*"横断面";"横切面" transverse section; cross section

横七竖八 héngqī-shùbā in disorder; in a mess; in a clutter; higgledy-piggledy:地上～地躺着几个醉汉。Several drunkards were lying higgledy-piggledy on the floor. /屋子里～堆放着大大小小的纸箱子。The room was cluttered with cartons of all sizes.

横切 héngqiē crosscut

横切锯 héngqiējù crosscut saw

横切面 héngqiēmiàn *see*"横剖面"

横肉 héngròu ugly, ferocious facial muscles (usu. used in the following phrase):满脸～ (of a person) look ugly and ferocious

横扫 héngsǎo ❶ sweep across; sweep away; make a clean sweep of:～一切 sweep everything away; be overwhelming /～残敌 wipe out the remaining enemy troops /～千军如卷席 roll back the enemy as one would a mat; make a clean sweep of numerous enemy troops ❷ glance quickly from side to side:他向大家～了一眼,才开口讲话。He threw a glance across the room before he started to speak.

横生 héngshēng ❶ grow wildly:庭院里蔓草～。The courtyards were overgrown with creepers and weeds. ❷ happen unexpectedly; crop up:～是非。A dispute (*or* quarrel) cropped up. ❸ be overflowing with; be full of:妙趣～ be overflowing with wit; be full of wit

横生枝节 héngshēng-zhījié deliberately complicate a problem by raising side issues; throw obstacles in the way:免得～ avoid possible complications /对方在谈判中～。The opposite party created obstacles in the negotiations.

横是 héngshi 〈方言〉probably; (most) likely:～要下雨了。It looks like rain. /他们现在还没到,～路上塞车了。They are not here yet. Probably they are caught in a traffic jam. /他情绪不好,～出什么事儿了。He looks depressed. There must be something wrong.

横竖横 héngshùhéng 〈方言〉go ahead regardless; be ready to risk everything:这孩子成绩不好,别人又常常笑话他,他就～,逃起学来。Since he was often ridiculed for his poor grades at school, the boy went the whole hog and began to play truant.

横竖 héngshu 〈口语〉in any case; anyhow; anyway:还是我在家等他吧,～我今天不打算出门。Let me stay behind to wait for him; I don't intend to go out today in any case.

横顺 héngshùn 〈方言〉in any case; anyhow; anyway:还是说出来吧,～他总会知道的。You'd better tell him the truth since he'll get to know it anyway.

横说竖说 héngshuō-shùshuō speak over and over again (to convince sb.); exhaust all means of persuasion:妻子～,他就是不听。His wife's repeated efforts at persuasion simply fell on deaf ears.

横躺竖卧 héngtǎng-shùwò (of people) lie here and there:只见孩子们在草地上～。The children were lying here and there on the lawn.

横挑鼻子竖挑眼 héng tiāo bízi shù tiāo yǎn 〈口语〉find fault; pick holes; nitpick:她总是对儿媳～的。She is always finding fault with her daughter-in-law. /这项规划不能出一点差错,欢迎大家～。

H

This plan is so important that it won't permit any mishap; you're most welcome to pick holes in it.

横尾翼 héngwěiyì 〈航空〉tail plane; horizontal stabilizer

横纹肌 héngwénjī 〈生理〉striated muscle

横向 héngxiàng ❶ crosswise; transverse; lateral; horizontal:～协作 cross cooperation /～交流 lateral exchange /～摆动 cross shake; lateral oscillation /～进刀〈机械〉cross (*or* traverse) feed /～扩散 transverse diffusion ❷ from east to west or west to east:这是一条～山路。This mountain path goes from east to west.

横向磁场 héngxiàng cíchǎng transverse magnetic field

横向电波 héngxiàng diànbō transverse electric wave

横向拱 héngxiànggǒng transverse arch

横向剪毛机 héngxiàng jiǎnmáojī cross shearing machine

横向力 héngxiànglì cross, lateral, or transverse force

横向联系 héngxiàng liánxì lateral or horizontal ties:横向经济联系 horizontal economic cooperation (*or* ties) /扩大～ increase horizontal (*or* lateral) ties; expand cooperation between enterprises

横向强度 héngxiàng qiángdù transverse strength

横向扫描 héngxiàng sǎomiáo transverse scanning

横向思维 héngxiàng sīwéi lateral thinking

横向移位 héngxiàng yíwèi lateral displacement or drift

横向应力 héngxiàng yìnglì lateral stress

横心 héngxīn steel oneself; resolve; be determined:横下一条心 steel oneself (to do sth. despite consequences); make a firm resolve /横下心来努力工作 resolve to work hard /下～要自食其力 be determined (*or* make up one's mind) to earn one's own living

横行 héngxíng run wild; run amok; be on a rampage:～一时 run wild for a time /～不法 defy law; act (*or* behave) in total disregard of law; be violent and lawless /土匪～乡里。Bandits ran amok in the country. *or* Banditry was rife in the country. /我不能容他～。I can't leave him unchecked.

横行霸道 héngxíng-bàdào ride roughshod; play the despot or overlord; tyrannize; domineer:～的家伙 domineering fellow /～,为所欲为 play the despot and do whatever one likes /他～的日子不会长了。The day will not be far off when he has to stop playing the tyrant.

横行无忌 héngxíng-wújì do whatever one likes without the least scruple; run amok; run wild:旧社会这地方官匪～,百姓居无宁日。In the old society this area was infested with despotic officials and ruthless bandits, and the people led a most miserable life.

横须贺 Héngxūhè Yokosuka, Japanese seaport on Honshu Island (本州岛) where the United States built a naval base after World War II

横许 héngxǔ 〈方言〉probably; (most) likely:～他不回来了。Probably he won't come back.

横痃 héngxuán 〈医学〉bubo (an inflammatory swelling of lymph nodes, especially in the groin)

横溢 héngyì ❶ (of a river) overflow; brim over:江河～ rivers and streams overflowing their banks /夏日消溶,江河～,人或为鱼鳖。In summer days your melting torrents Flood the streams and rivers, Turning men into fish and turtles. ❷ (of talent, feelings, etc.) brimming; overflowing; abundant:才华～ be brimming (*or* bursting) with talent; have superb talent /热情～ be overflowing with enthusiasm

横越 héngyuè fly across (from east to west or vice versa):～太平洋 fly across the Pacific

横征暴敛 héngzhēng-bàoliǎn extort excessive taxes and levies; levy heavy or exorbitant taxes:百姓不堪～之苦。The populace could not bear the crushing burden of excessive taxes and levies.

横直 héngzhí 〈方言〉in any case; anyway; anyhow:～你得跟我去。Anyhow you must come with me.

横轴 héngzhóu ❶〈机械〉cross axle or shaft; transverse or lateral axis ❷ horizontal scroll (of calligraphy or painting)

横坐标 héngzuòbiāo 〈数学〉abscissa

行

héng *see* "道行" dàoheng

see also háng; hàng; xíng

珩

héng top gem of a girdle-pendant (as worn by aristocrats and high officials in ancient China)

珩床 héngchuáng 〈机械〉honing machine

珩磨 héngmó 〈机械〉honing:～机 hone; honing machine /～轮 honing wheel

桁

héng 〈建筑〉purlin

桁架 héngjià 〈建筑〉truss:～跨度 truss span /～式大梁 trussed girder

桁架桥 héngjiàqiáo truss bridge

桁梁 héngliáng 〈航空〉longeron;〈建筑〉braced girder

桁条 héngtiáo 〈建筑〉purlin; stringer

骱

héng

骱骨 hénggǔ *also* "胻骨" hénggǔ 〈中医〉tibia and fibula; shin bone and splint bone

胻

héng 〈中医〉calf

胻骨 hénggǔ *see* "骱骨" hénggǔ

鸻

héng 〈动物〉plover:金～ golden plover

衡

héng ❶ graduated arm of a steelyard ❷ any weighing apparatus ❸ weigh; measure; judge:权～利弊 weigh the advantages and disadvantages; weigh the pros and cons ❹〈书面〉levelled; balanced:平～ balance /均～ balance; equillibrium ❺ (Héng) a surname

衡量 héngliang ❶ measure; judge:～是非 measure right and wrong; tell right from wrong /不能用金钱来～ can not measure in terms of money; be priceless /不能光以资历来～一个人的贡献。One should not judge a person's contribution by his seniority alone. /考试只是～学习成绩的一种方式。Examinations are only one way to measure one's study. ❷ weigh; consider:～得失 weigh (up) the gains and losses /我左右～了一下,觉得还是不去为好。After weighing the pros and cons, I'm inclined not to go. /别急着做决定,先～～再说。Don't rush to a decision. Give the matter careful consideration first.

衡平法 héngpíngfǎ 〈法律〉law of equity; rules of equity

衡平法庭 héngpíng fǎtíng equity tribunal

衡器 héngqì weighing apparatus

衡情度理 héngqíng-duólǐ consider the circumstances and judge by common sense — all things considered:～,你还是让他一次为好。All things considered, it would be best for you to give in to him this time.

衡山 Héngshān Mount Heng (in Hunan Province, southernmost of China's Five Sacred Mountains)

蘅

héng *see* "杜蘅" dùhéng

hèng

横

hèng ❶ rude; rough; fierce and brutal; harsh and unreasonable:蛮～ rude and unreasonable; arbitrary /强～ brutal and unreasonable; tyrannical /他对人真～。He is fierce and brutal to people. ❷ inauspicious; unexpected:～遭此难 suffer an unexpected misfortune (*or* disaster)

see also héng

横暴 hèngbào violent and unreasonable; perverse and brutal:不畏～ not fear the violent and unreasonable

横财 hèngcái ill-gotten wealth or gains; windfall:发了一笔～ get a windfall; get a fortune by foul means /人无～不富。〈俗语〉No one becomes rich without windfall. *or* No one gets rich by walking the straight path.

横祸 hènghuò unexpected calamity; sudden misfortune:飞来～ bolt from the blue; unexpected disaster /突遭～ suffer an unexpected disaster; meet with sudden misfortune

横蛮 hèngmán rough and unreasonable; tyrannical:态度～ be tyrannical

横逆 hèngnì 〈书面〉perverse and violent behaviour or treatment:某殊不幸,遭此～。How unfortunate I am to have suffered such violent and perverse treatment.

横事 hèngshì untoward accident or happening; unexpected calamity; sudden misfortune:连遭～ suffer a series of unexpected disasters

横死 hèngsǐ die a violent or unnatural death; meet with a sudden death

横议 hèngyì make unreserved comments or unbridled criticisms: 遭人～ be subjected to unbridled criticism and backbiting

横恣 hèngzì tyrannical and unscrupulous; perverse and wanton: 群雄割据，盗匪～。Separatist regimes were established and banditry ran rife.

啈 hèng *used to express determination or indignation*: 他～声说:"我非报复他不可!" "Damn! I must get even with him!" he said angrily.
see also hēng

hm

噷 hm 〈叹词〉 *used to express reproach or displeasure*: ～，你要闹到几时! Humph, when will you stop making this scene! /～，他还骗得了我? Humph, does he think he can fool me?

hng

哼 hng 〈叹词〉 *used to express dissatisfaction or suspicion*: ～，要我为他说话? 他不配! Humph, so he wants me to put in a good word for him? He doesn't deserve it. /～，我就不信她不知情。Humph! I don't believe she is not in the know.
see also hēng

hōng

烘 hōng ❶ dry; warm; bake: ～脚 warm one's feet at a fire /～蛋糕 bake a cake /～湿衬衣 dry a wet shirt by a fire ❷ set off

烘焙 hōngbèi cure (tea or tobacco leaves)

烘衬 hōngchèn *see* "烘托"

烘干 hōnggān ❶ dry over fire or heat: 她在火边把头巾～了。She dried her kerchief at the fire. ❷ 〈化学〉 stoving; oven-dry; kiln-dry: ～法 oven-drying method /～重 oven-dried weight

烘干机 hōnggānjī drying machine; dryer: 电动～ electric dryer

烘缸 hōnggāng (urn-shaped) dryer

烘烘 hōnghōng 〈象声〉 *used to describe the sound of a roaring fire*: 篝火～。The bonfire (*or* campfire) was roaring.

烘烤 hōngkǎo toast; bake: ～小松饼 bake muffins /～油漆 bake paint

烘篮 hōnglán bamboo basket holding a small brazier (for keeping warm)

烘笼 hōnglóng ❶ basketwork frame propped over an oven or a brazier for drying clothes ❷ 〈方言〉 *see* "烘篮"

烘漆 hōngqī baking finish; stoving finish; oven-baked finish

烘染 hōngrǎn emphasize or set off by elaboration; embroider on (sth.): 他把自己所听到的，加上许多～之词，活灵活现地讲给我们听。He elaborated (*or* embroidered) ingeniously on what he had heard and gave us a most vivid presentation.

烘热 hōngrè (usu. of one's feeling) warm: 听了这些话，他心里一阵～。These words sent a wave of warmth through him. /听母亲说起自己的婚事，她觉得脸上有些～。On hearing mother mention her marriage, she felt her cheeks burning slightly.

烘丝机 hōngsījī cut-tobacco dryer

烘托 hōngtuō ❶ (in Chinese painting) add shading around an object to make it stand out; set off by shading ❷ make conspicuous by contrast; throw into sharp relief; set off: ～手法 technique of contrast /蓝天～白云 white clouds against the blue sky /小说中常用次要人物来～主要人物。In novels minor characters often serve as foils to set off the principal ones.

烘箱 hōngxiāng (baking) oven

烘相器 hōngxiàngqì 〈摄影〉 print dryer

烘云托月 hōngyún-tuōyuè paint clouds to set off the moon; provide a foil to set off a character or an incident (as in literary work): 他善用～的手法刻画人物。He is good at portraying his characters through contrast.

烘炙 hōngzhì toast; bake

哄 hōng ❶ 〈象声〉 *used to describe roars of laughter or uproarious talk*: 众人～的一声大笑起来。All burst into uproarious laughter. ❷ hubbub; din
see also hǒng; hòng

哄传 hōngchuán (of rumours) circulate widely: 这个谣言几小时就在村子里～开了。In a matter of hours the rumour spread throughout the village.

哄动 hōngdòng *also* "轰动" hōngdòng cause a sensation; make a stir: 这是去年～全国的十大新闻之一。This was one of last year's top ten news items that caused a nationwide sensation.

哄闹 hōngnào (of a crowd of people) make a lot of noise; hubbub: 只见一帮人在饭馆门口～。A crowd of people were seen making a hubbub in front of the restaurant.

哄抢 hōngqiǎng ❶ (of a crowd of people) making a panic purchase of; panic-buying: ～风 panic purchase by large crowds ❷ scramble for (public property, goods, etc.); engage in mass looting: ～国家物资 open looting of state-owned goods and materials (usu. by a large crowd)

哄然 hōngrán boisterous; uproarious: ～大笑 burst into uproarious laughter; roar with laughter /舆论～。There was a public outcry.

哄抬 hōngtái (of speculators, etc.) drive up (prices): ～物价 force (*or* jack) up prices

哄堂大笑 hōngtáng dàxiào whole room rocking with laughter; all the audience roaring with laughter: 他的话引起～。His remarks set the whole room rocking with laughter. /丑角的表演使观众～。The audience broke into uproarious laughter at the performance of the clown.

哄笑 hōngxiào (of a crowd of people) roar with laughter; burst into laughter: 他说得大伙儿禁不住～起来。Everybody burst into loud laughter at what he said. /他的演说引起听众一阵又一阵～。His speech drew peals of laughter from the audience.

薨 hōng (of feudal lords or high officials) die; pass away: ～逝 die; pass away

轰(轟、❸揈) hōng ❶ 〈象声〉 bang; boom: ～的一声，火就着了起来。The fire broke out with a bang. /～! ～! ～! 礼炮鸣放二十一响。Boom! Boom! Boom! Twenty-one salvoes were fired. ❷ roar; rumble; bombard; explode: 万炮齐～。Ten thousand cannons went off. /巨雷～倒大树。The tall tree was struck (*or* blasted) down by lightning. ❸ shoo away; drive off; drive: ～乌鸦 shoo away the crows /～牲口 drive draught animals /只怕你～我不动。I'm afraid you can't drive me away. /演讲人被～下台。The speaker was booed off the platform.

轰动 hōngdòng *also* "哄动" hōngdòng cause a sensation; make a stir: ～文坛 cause a sensation in the world of letters /听了他的发言，整个会场～了。His speech made a great stir in the audience (*or* in the hall).

轰动效应 hōngdòng xiàoyìng sensational effect

轰动一时 hōngdòng-yīshí create a furore; cause a great sensation; be all the rage: ～的艳闻 sensational affair /这一丑事曾～。The scandal made a big stir at the time. /这是一部曾经～的电视剧。The teleplay was a great hit when it was screened.

轰赶 hōnggǎn shoo away; drive off; drive: ～麻雀 shoo away the sparrows /～牲口 drive draught animals /～苍蝇 whisk the flies off

轰轰 hōnghōng 〈象声〉 rumble; boom; buzz: 蝇子～地乱飞。Flies were buzzing around. /火车～地前进。The train rumbled on.

轰轰烈烈 hōnghōng-lièliè on a grand and spectacular scale; with vim and vigour; vigorous; dynamic: 群众运动～。The mass movement unfolded on a spectacular scale. /救灾活动搞得～。Disaster relief work is going on vigorously.

轰击 hōngjī ❶ shell; bombard; blast: ～敌人工事 shell enemy fortifications ❷ 〈物理〉 bombard: 中子～ neutron bombardment /～感生电导 bombardment-induced conductivity

轰隆 hōnglōng 〈象声〉 rumble; roll: ～的雷声 rolling (*or* rumbling) thunder /远处炮声～～地响。Guns rumbled in the distance. /百米之外就能听见～～的机器声。The humming of machines could be heard a hundred metres away.

H

轰鸣 hōngmíng thunder; roar:礼炮～。Salvoes roared. /雷声～，大地回春。Thunder rolled and spring returned.
轰然 hōngrán with a loud crash or bang; with loud noise:～作响 (of an engine, etc.) make a loud noise /～一声，大楼被夷为平地。The building was levelled to the ground with a deafening crash.
轰嚷 hōngrǎng make a hubbub; make a racket; spread noisily:胜利的消息在这一带很快～开了。News of the victory soon spread throughout the area.
轰响 hōngxiǎng thunder; roar:马达～。Motors roared. /惊雷～。There came a sudden clap of thunder.
轰炸 hōngzhà bomb; bombard:盲目～ blind bombing /定点～ pin-point bombing /俯冲～ dive-bombing /饱和～ saturation bombing /地毯式～ carpet bombing /～任务 bombing mission /～航程 bombing run /连续投弹～ train bombing /全面～ full-scale bombardment /高空～ high-altitude bombing; high-level bombing /密集～ massive bombing /云上～ overcast bombing /他们因遭受～而被迫离开城市。They were bombed out of the city.
轰炸机 hōngzhàjī bomber:战斗～ fighter-bomber /俯冲～ dive-bomber /超音速～ supersonic bomber /舰载～ carrier-based bomber; carrier-borne bomber /喷气式～ jet bomber /无人驾驶～ unmanned bomber; pilotless bomber; robot bomber /重型～ large bomber; heavy bomber /战略～ strategic bomber
轰炸瞄准具 hōngzhà miáozhǔnjù bombsight
轰炸误差 hōngzhà wùchā bombing error

吽 hōng word used in Buddhist incantation

訇 hōng ❶ loud noise:～的一声 with a loud noise /～然 with a loud crash (*or* bang) ❷ *see* "阿訇" āhōng

hóng

鸿 hóng ❶ swan goose; Chinese goose (*Anser cygnoides*):哀～ wild goose crying forlornly (over the death of its mate, etc.) ❷〈书面〉letter:远方来～ letter from afar ❸ great; grand ❹ (Hóng) a surname
鸿博 hóngbó 〈书面〉learned; erudite:～之士 man of great learning; erudite scholar
鸿福 hóngfú *also* "洪福" hóngfú great blessing; great happiness
鸿沟 hónggōu wide gap; chasm:不可逾越的～ unbridgeable gap; impassable chasm
鸿鹄 hónghú ❶ swan ❷〈比喻〉person with noble ideals; person of lofty aspirations
鸿鹄之志 hónghúzhīzhì 〈比喻〉lofty ambition; high aspirations:燕雀安知～? How can a sparrow or swallow imagine the lofty voyages of a swan? *or* Little men can never appreciate the high aspirations of great minds.
鸿毛 hóngmáo 〈书面〉goose feather; sth. very light or insignificant:死有重于泰山，有轻于～。Some deaths are heavier than Mount Tai and some lighter than a feather.
鸿门宴 Hóngményàn banquet at Hongmen — a feast or meeting set up as a trap for the invited (originally a banquet held at Hongmen in 206 BC by Xiang Yu 项羽 in honour of his rival Liu Bang 刘邦, at which an attempt was to be made on the latter's life)
鸿蒙 hóngméng *also* "鸿濛"〈书面〉chaos believed to be the primeval state of the universe before heaven was separated from earth; primeval atmosphere of nature; primeval state:～初辟 when heaven was first separated from earth; when the world was first created
鸿篇巨制 hóngpiān-jùzhì magnum opus; monumental work:这是积十年之功完成的～。This is a monumental work, completed only after ten long years.
鸿儒 hóngrú 〈书面〉man of great learning; erudite scholar
鸿图 hóngtú *also* "宏图" hóngtú great plan; grand prospect:大展～ carry out one's grand plans; fulfil one's lofty ambitions; ride on the crest of success
鸿雁 hóngyàn ❶ *see* "鸿❶" ❷〈书面〉letter
鸿雁传书 hóngyàn-chuánshū mail delivered by swan geese; letter from afar
鸿运 hóngyùn *also* "红运" hóngyùn good luck:～高照 be blessed with good luck; ride on the crest of fortune
鸿爪 hóngzhǎo *also* "雪泥鸿爪" xuění-hóngzhǎo marks left by goose talons in the snow;〈比喻〉traces of past events

黉(黌) hóng 〈古语〉school; academy
黉门 hóngmén 〈古语〉school:～秀才 scholar who passed the imperial examination at the county level (in the Ming and Qing dynasties)
黉宇 hóngyǔ 〈古语〉school building

虹 hóng *also* "彩虹" cǎihóng rainbow
see also jiàng
虹彩 hóngcǎi 〈气象〉iridescence:～云 iridescent cloud
虹膜 hóngmó 〈生理〉iris:～出血 iridemia
虹膜炎 hóngmóyán iritis
虹霓 hóngní rainbow
虹吸 hóngxī *also* "虹吸作用"〈物理〉siphonage:～瓶 siphon bottle
虹吸泵 hóngxībèng siphon-pump
虹吸管 hóngxīguǎn *also* "虹管" siphon
虹吸现象 hóngxī xiànxiàng siphonage
虹雉 hóngzhì 〈动物〉monal
虹鳟 hóngzūn 〈动物〉rainbow trout (*Salmo irideus*)

魟 hóng 〈动物〉stingray

红 hóng ❶ red:～地毯 red carpet /鼻子冻得通～ with one's nose chilled beet-red /因为睡眠不足，他的两眼都～了。His eyes became bloodshot from lack of sleep. ❷ red cloth, bunting, etc., used on festive occasions:披～ wear red sashes (*or* cloth) as a sign of honour, festivity, etc. /挂～ hang up red festoons (*or* bunting) ❸ symbol of success or popularity:开门～ get off to a flying start /满堂～ all-round victory (*or* success) /她是眼下最走～的影星。She is the most popular movie star at the moment. ❹ revolutionary; red:又～又专 be both red and expert; be both socialist-minded and professionally proficient ❺ bonus; dividend:分～ distribute or draw dividends
see also gōng
红案 hóng'àn red (chopping) board — cooking that prepares dishes (as distinguished from "白案" bái'àn, cooking that prepares pasta, pastry and rice):～师傅 chef who prepares dishes
红白喜事 hóng-bái xǐshì *also* "红白事" red and white affairs — weddings and funerals:大办～是一种落后的习俗。It is a backward custom to make much ado about weddings and funerals.
红百合木 hóngbǎihémù lantern tree (*Crinodendron hookeranum*)
红柏 hóngbǎi red cedar
红斑 hóngbān 〈医学〉erythema:结节性～ E nodosum
红斑狼疮 hóngbān lángchuāng 〈医学〉lupus erythematosus
红榜 hóngbǎng honour roll or board:他的名字上了～。His name is in the honour roll.
红包 hóngbāo red envelope or paper bag containing money (usu. given privately as a tip, gift, bonus or bribe):送～ hand (sb.) a red envelope containing money; give (sb.) money in a red envelope /塞～ tuck money wrapped up in a piece of red paper in sb.'s hand; give sb. money in a red envelope
红宝石 hóngbǎoshí ruby:～戒指 ruby ring /～激光器 ruby laser
红宝石婚 hóngbǎoshíhūn ruby wedding anniversary — 40th wedding anniversary
红不棱登 hóngbulēngdēng 〈口语〉(often implying distaste or displeasure) red; reddish:好好的脸，抹得～的，有什么好看! Why on earth did you daub your charming face with so much rouge?
红菜汤 hóngcàitāng borsch
红菜头 hóngcàitóu beetroot
红茶 hóngchá black tea
红茶菌 hóngchájūn *also* "海宝" hǎibǎo tea fungus
红场 Hóngchǎng Red Square (in Moscow)
红潮 hóngcháo ❶ blush; flush:她的脸上泛起～。She was blushing. ❷ menses; menstruation ❸ *also* "赤潮" chìcháo red tide; red water
红尘 hóngchén world of mortals; vanity fair:看破～ see through the vanity of the world; be disillusioned with human society /远离～ far away from human society; away from the madding crowd

红赤赤 hóngchìchì (of eyes or face) very red:妈妈的眼睛因为连日熬夜熬得~的。Mother's eyes became bloodshot as she had been staying up late for several nights on end.
红绸舞 hóngchóuwǔ Red Silk Dance (Chinese folk dancing with long scarves of red silk)
红筹股 hóngchóugǔ "red chips" — stocks of mainland-funded enterprises in Hong Kong:~与国企股一再上扬。The red chips and stocks of state-owned mainland enterprises have been rising constantly.
红大麻哈鱼 hóngdàmáhǎyú sockeye; red salmon (*Oncorhymchus nerka*)
红丹 hóngdān red lead; minium
红丹漆 hóngdānqī red lead paint
红蛋 hóngdàn red eggs (eggs dyed red to celebrate the birth of a child, and distributed among friends and relatives)
红道 hóngdào 〈口语〉 path of ascent in official hierarchy; career as an official
红得发紫 hóngde-fāzǐ (of a person) be extremely popular; (of an official) be at the height of one's power and influence:这位歌星现在正~。The pop star is all the rage at the moment. *or* The singer is now at the height of her (*or* his) popularity. /当时他是政府里一个~的人物。He was one of the most influential figures in that administration.
红灯区 hóngdēngqū red-light district
红灯照 Hóngdēngzhào Red Lanterns League (young women's organization in the *Yihetuan* or Boxers' Movement, so named because its members were dressed in red and held red lanterns)
红澄澄 hóngdēngdēng bright red; scarlet:石榴熟了,满树~的,像挂上串串小灯笼。The tree turned bright red with ripe pomegranates hanging like clusters of red lanterns.
红笛鲷 hóngdídiāo *also* "红鱼" red snapper (*Lutianus erythropterus*)
红电气石 hóngdiànqìshí 〈地质〉 rubellite
红点鲑 hóngdiǎnguī 〈动物〉 char
红点颏 hóngdiǎnké 〈动物〉 (generally known as 红靛颏儿) *Luscinia calliope*
红定 hóngdìng betrothal gifts to the girl's family by her fiancé:下~ offer betrothal gifts
红豆 hóngdòu ❶ red bean shrub (*Abrus precatorius*); Indian licorice; patenoster pea ❷ *also* "相思子" xiāngsīzǐ seeds of this shrub used as token of love; love peas:~寄相思。Red beans are a token of love.
红豆杉 hóngdòushān Chinese yew (*Taxus chinensis*)
红矾 hóngfán 〈方言〉 (white) arsenic
红粉 hóngfěn rouge and powder; cosmetics; 〈比喻〉 woman:~佳人 beautiful young woman /~知己 beautiful woman who is a bosom friend; appreciative female friend /不爱~爱刀枪 (of a girl) keen on (playing with) swords and spears, but not rouge and powder
红封 hóngfēng *see* "红包"
红汞 hónggǒng 〈药学〉 *also* "汞溴红" gǒngxiùhóng mercurochrome
红股 hónggǔ 〈经济〉 bonus stock or share:发行~ bonus issue
红骨顶 hónggǔdǐng 〈动物〉 moorhen
红骨髓 hónggǔsuǐ red (bone) marrow
红鹳 hóngguàn flamingo
红光满面 hóngguāng-mǎnmiàn *also* "满面红光" one's face glowing with health; in ruddy health:他保养得好,总是~的。He is well preserved and always in ruddy health.
红桧 hóngguì 〈植物〉 *Chamaecyparis formosensis*
红果 hóngguǒ 〈方言〉 fruit of large Chinese hawthorn; haw
红海 Hónghǎi Red Sea, long arm of sea separating Africa from the Arabian Peninsula
红河 Hónghé Red River, a river that rises in southern China and flows 1,175 km southeast through northern Vietnam
红鹤 hónghè 〈动物〉 ibis
红红绿绿 hónghóng-lǜlǜ colourful; in gay colours:~的花边图案 colourful lace design /孩子们穿着~的衣裳。The children are dressed in gay colours.
红狐 hónghú *also* "赤狐" chìhú red fox
红花 hónghuā ❶ 〈中药〉 false saffron; safflower (*Carthamus tinctorius*):藏~ saffron (*Crocus sativus*) /~油 safflower oil ❷ red flower:~虽好,也要绿叶扶持。〈俗语〉 Beautiful as the red flower is, it takes the green leaves to set it off.
红花草 hónghuācǎo *also* "紫云英" zǐyúnyīng Chinese milk vetch (*Astragalus sinicus*)
红货 hónghuò 〈旧语〉 valuables; jewelry:~摊子 jewelry booth
红火 hónghuo flourishing; prosperous; thriving:生意~。Business is prospering (*or* booming). /日子~起来了。Life is improving. /谁家办喜事这么~? Who is holding such a grand wedding ceremony? /五月的石榴花开得~。The pomegranate flowers are in full bloom in May.
红极一时 hóngjí-yīshí enjoy great popularity for a time; be all the rage: 30 年代她在戏剧界曾~。In the 1930's she emerged as the celebrity of the hour in theatrical circles.
红胶木 hóngjiāomù Brisbane box (*Tristania conferta*)
红脚鹬 hóngjiǎoyù 〈动物〉 redshank
红教 Hóngjiào (common name for 宁玛教) Red Sect (sect of Tibetan Lamaism prevailing in the 8th and 9th centuries); Red Hat Lamaism
红巾军 hóngjīnjūn ❶ Red Turbans, anti-Jin armed forces of the people in north China during the early Southern Song Dynasty ❷ Red Turbans, peasant rebel army towards the end of the Yuan Dynasty *see also* "红巾起义"
红巾起义 Hóngjīn Qǐyì Red Turbans Uprising (large-scale peasant uprising at the close of the Yuan Dynasty, 1351-1366, with its participants wearing red turbans)
红净 hóngjìng red-face role, painted-face role representing honest officials, brave generals, etc. in traditional Chinese opera, whose make-up is largely in red
红角 hóngjué popular actor or actress:在这一带,她可算一个叫得响的~儿。She is something of a popular actress in this area.
红军 Hóngjūn ❶ (short for 中国工农红军) Red Army; the Chinese Workers' and Peasants' Red Army, 1927-1937:当兵就要当~。Join the Red Army if you want to be a soldier. ❷ Red Army, army of the former Soviet Union before 1946:苏联~ Soviet Red Army
红栲 hóngkǎo *also* "红锥";"刺栲" cìkǎo 〈植物〉 *Castanopsis hystrix*
红口白舌 hóngkǒu-báishé *also* "赤口白舌" chìkǒu-báishé ❶ 〈方言〉 talk nonsense; gossip irresponsibly ❷ misunderstanding or dispute arising over conversation
红利 hónglì bonus; dividend
红利备付比率 hónglì bèifù bǐlǜ dividend cover
红利股 hónglìgǔ *also* "红股" bonus stock; bonus share
红脸 hóngliǎn ❶ blush:她一见生人就~。She blushes every time she meets a stranger. ❷ flush with anger; get angry:我们共同生活三十年,从来没红过脸。We have been living together for 30 years and have never exchanged angry words between us.
红粮 hóngliáng 〈方言〉 *kaoliang*; Chinese sorghum
红磷 hónglín *also* "赤磷" chìlín red phosphorus
红铃虫 hónglíngchóng pink bollworm
红领巾 hónglǐngjīn ❶ red scarf (worn by the Young Pioneers):~是红旗的一角。The red scarf is part of the red flag. /少先队员们把~献给了这位革命老人。The Young Pioneers presented a red scarf to the veteran revolutionary. ❷ Young Pioneer:我们都是~。We are all Young Pioneers.
红领章 hónglǐngzhāng red collar tab (as formerly worn by PLA men)
红柳 hóngliǔ *also* "柽柳" chēngliǔ 〈植物〉 Chinese tamarisk; rose willow; purple willow
红楼梦 Hónglóumèng *also* "石头记" Shítoujì *A Dream of Red Mansions* (*or The Story of the Stone*), novel published in the early Qing Dynasty about 1790 by Cao Xueqin (曹雪芹)
红绿灯 hónglǜdēng traffic lights; traffic signals:过马路要看~。Watch the traffic lights before you cross a street.
红绿色盲 hónglǜ sèmáng 〈医学〉 xanthocyanopsia; red-green blindness:先天性~ Daltonism
红螺 hóngluó 〈动物〉 *Rapana thomasiana*
红麻 hóngmá 〈植物〉 bluish dogbane (*Apocynum venetum*)
红麻料儿 hóngmáliàor *also* "朱雀" zhūquè 〈动物〉 rosefinch
红玛瑙 hóngmǎnǎo red agate; sardonyx
红毛丹 hóngmáodān 〈植物〉 rambutan (*Nephelium lappaceum*)
红毛坭 hóngmáoní 〈方言〉 cement
红帽子 hóngmàozi ❶ red cap; "communist" label (for branding any progressive person or sympathizer to the CPC during the KMT

H

rule)：那时候，～满天飞，动不动就把青年学生抓进牢房。In those days, with the "red cap" bandied about, young students would be arrested and imprisoned at any moment. ❷ (railway) porter; redcap
红梅花雀 hóngméihuāquè avadavat; red munia (*Amandava amandava*)
红媒 hóngméi matchmaker; go-between
红煤 hóngméi 〈方言〉anthracite
红霉素 hóngméisù 〈药学〉erythromycin
红焖 hóngmèn stew in soy sauce：～鸭块 stewed duck pieces with soy sauce
红米 hóngmǐ red rice
红棉 hóngmián *also* "木棉" mùmián silk cotton; kapok
红模子 hóngmúzi sheet of paper with red characters printed on it (to be traced over with a brush by children as initial exercises in learning calligraphy)：描～ trace in black ink over characters printed in red
红木 hóngmù rosewood; mahogany：～家具 mahogany (*or* rosewood) furniture
红男绿女 hóngnán-lǜnǚ gaily dressed young men and women：公园里一对对～，牵手偕行。Gaily dressed young couples walked hand in hand in the park.
红娘 hóngniáng ❶ (Hóngniáng) maid in the play *The West Chamber* (西厢记), whose good offices help bring about the union of the lovers, her mistress Yingying (莺莺) and scholar Zhang (张生) ❷ kind-hearted go-between; well-meaning matchmaker
红娘鱼 hóngniángyú 〈动物〉sea robin; red gurnard
红牌 hóngpái 〈体育〉red card：出示～ show the red card
红盘 hóngpán 〈旧语〉prices listed on the day when shops reopen for business after the Spring Festival (*or* the Chinese New Year); post-New-Year's quotations
红喷喷 hóngpēnpēn red; reddish：～的苹果 reddish apples / 姑娘～的脸颊上挂着微笑。The girl wore a smile on her rosy face.
红砒 hóngpī *also* "砒霜" pīshuāng arsenic
红皮病 hóngpíbìng 〈医学〉erythroderma
红皮书 hóngpíshū red paper; red book
红票 hóngpiào 〈旧语〉❶ complimentary ticket; free ticket ❷ theatre ticket sold at a higher price than usual (usu. alloted by powers that be)
红萍 hóngpíng 〈植物〉red duckweed
红扑扑 hóngpūpū ruddy; rosy：由于兴奋，她脸上～的。Her face is aglow with excitement.
红葡萄藤 hóngpútaoténg 〈植物〉*also* "爬墙虎" páqiánghǔ Boston or Japanese ivy
红旗 hóngqí red flag; red banner (often as a symbol of revolution or as a prize for an advanced work unit)：五星～ Five-Star Red Flag (national flag of the PRC) / 在～下长大 be brought up under the red flag; grow up in the People's Republic of China / 我们车间一直保持着流动～。Our workshop has always kept the mobile red banner with us.
红旗单位 hóngqí dānwèi red-banner unit; advanced unit
红旗渠 Hóngqíqú Hongqi Canal, famous irrigation project built in the 1960's in Henan Province
红旗手 hóngqíshǒu red-banner pacesetter; model worker：她连续三年获得三八～的称号。She won the title of March 8th Red-Banner Pace-setter for three years running.
红契 hóngqì 〈旧语〉officially registered contract or title-deed
红青 hóngqīng *also* "绀青" gànqīng dark purple; plum (colour)
红区 hóngqū Red Area (base area established by the Chinese Communist Party during the Second Revolutionary Civil War, 1927-1937)
红曲 hóngqū red colouring agent for food made from fermented round rice, also used as a Chinese medicine
红壤 hóngrǎng *also* "红土" red soil or earth：～改良工程 red soil improvement project
红热 hóngrè red heat
红人 hóngrén favourite (with sb. in power); fair-haired boy：市长的～ favourite with the mayor / 在那好人受气的日子里，他竟然成了～。In the days when good people suffered, he was actually favoured.
红润 hóngrùn ruddy; rosy：小姑娘～的脸 rosy cheeks of a little girl
红三叶 hóngsānyè *also* "红三叶草" 〈植物〉red clover
红色 hóngsè ❶ red：～是暖色，使人振奋。Red is a warm colour which stimulates people. ❷ revolutionary; red：～政权 red political power / ～根据地 revolutionary base
红色高棉 Hóngsè Gāomián Khmer Rouge, political faction which ruled Cambodia between 1975 and 1979 under the name of Democratic Kampuchea (民主柬埔寨)
红色盲 hóngsèmáng red-blindness
红色资本家 hóngsè zīběnjiā red capitalist — referring to patriotic capitalists after liberation in 1949
红杉 hóngshān ❶ Chinese larch ❷ redwood
红伤 hóngshāng gun or knife wound; bleeding wound
红烧 hóngshāo braise in soy sauce：～鲤鱼 carp braised in brown sauce
红苕 hóngsháo 〈方言〉sweet potato
红参 hóngshēn red ginseng
红生 hóngshēng red-faced young man role in traditional opera *see also* "红净" hóngjìng
红绳系足 hóngshéng-xìzú *also* "赤绳系足" chìshéng-xìzú be engaged to marry (an ancient legend has it that the Old Man of the Moon, god of marriage, attaches a red cord to the feet of a betrothed couple)
红十字会 Hóngshízìhuì Red Cross (Society)
红视症 hóngshìzhèng 〈医学〉erythropsia; erythropia
红事 hóngshì red affair — marriage; wedding
红薯 hóngshǔ (common name for 甘薯) sweet potato
红树 hóngshù 〈林业〉mangrove (*Rhizophora*)
红松 hóngsōng Korean pine
红糖 hóngtáng brown sugar
红桃 hóngtáo heart (in cards)：他叫了四～但没打成。He bid four hearts (in bridge) but did not make it.
红陶 hóngtáo red pottery; terra-cotta
红藤 hóngténg Sargent gloryvine (*Sargentodoxa cuneata*)
红彤彤 hóngtōngtōng *also* "红通通" bright red; glowing：～的晚霞 bright red sunset glow (*or* clouds) / ～的脸 ruddy complexion
红铜 hóngtóng 〈冶金〉❶ *also* "紫铜" zǐtóng red copper ❷ red brass：～合金 red brass alloy
红头文件 hóngtóu wénjiàn 〈口语〉document issued by a Party or government office (usu. with the title printed in red, hence the name); official document
红头蝇 hóngtóuyíng red-eyed fly
红土 hóngtǔ ❶ *see* "红壤" ❷ *see* "红土子"
红土子 hóngtǔzi *also* "铁丹" tiědān; "红土" red oxide (used as a dye)
红外 hóngwài (short for 红外线) infrared ray; infrared
红外报警装置 hóngwài bàojǐng zhuāngzhì infrared warning device
红外成像 hóngwài chéngxiàng infrared imaging：～系统 infrared imaging system / ～照相术 infrared photography
红外导航 hóngwài dǎoháng infrared navigation
红外电视 hóngwài diànshì infrared television
红外发射 hóngwài fāshè infrared emission：～器 infrared transmitter
红外辐射 hóngwài fúshè infrared radiation
红外跟踪 hóngwài gēnzōng infrared tracking
红外光电摄像管 hóngwài guāngdiàn shèxiàngguǎn infrared vidicon
红外光谱 hóngwài guāngpǔ infrared spectrum：～仪 infrared spectrometer
红外光束 hóngwài guāngshù infrared beam
红外激光 hóngwài jīguāng infrared laser：～雷达 coherent infrared radar
红外激射 hóngwài jīshè *also* "红外激射器" iraser (infrared amplification of stimulated emission of radiation)
红外胶卷 hóngwài jiāojuǎn infrared photographic film
红外雷达 hóngwài léidá infrared radar
红外瞄准镜 hóngwài miáozhǔnjìng sniperscope
红外目标 hóngwài mùbiāo infrared target：～识别 infrared identification
红外区 hóngwàiqū infrared：短波～ short infrared / 近～ near infrared / 中～ intermediate infrared / 远～ far infrared
红外全息照相 hóngwài quánxī zhàoxiàng infrared holography
红外扫描 hóngwài sǎomiáo infrared scanning：～装置 infrared scanning device
红外色散 hóngwài sèsàn infrared dispersion

红外摄影 hóngwài shèyǐng infrared photography
红外天文学 hóngwài tiānwénxué infrared astronomy
红外天线 hóngwài tiānxiàn infrared antenna
红外通信 hóngwài tōngxìn infrared communication
红外线 hóngwàixiàn *also* "红外光"; "热线" rèxiàn (shortened as 红外)〈物理〉infrared; infrared ray:～辐射 infrared radiation /～扫描 infrared scanning /～扫描装置 infrared scanner /～探测器 infrared detector /～照相 infrared photography /～电子学 infranics /～电视 nectotelevision (*or* nectovision) /～寻的制导导弹 infrared seeker
红外相片 hóngwài xiàngpiàn infrared photo
红外星 hóngwàixīng〈天文〉infrared star
红外遥感 hóngwài yáogǎn infrared remote sensing:～仪 IR (infrared remote) sensor
红外夜视系统 hóngwài yèshì xìtǒng infrared night vision system
红外预警系统 hóngwài yùjǐng xìtǒng infrared early-warning system
红外照相 hóngwài zhàoxiàng infrared photography:～机 infrared camera
红外制导 hóngwài zhìdǎo infrared guidance
红外自动寻的 hóngwài zìdòng xúndì infrared homing:～导弹 infrared homing missile; infrared homer
红卫兵 Hóngwèibīng Red Guards (mass organization of young people during the Cultural Revolution, 1966-1976):中学～ secondary school Red Guards
红细胞 hóngxìbāo *also* "红血球" red blood cell; red corpuscle; erythrocyte:～计数 red blood cell count
红线 hóngxiàn main thread; red line:"无产阶级文艺～" proletarian red line in art and literature /贯穿全书的一条～ main thread running through the book
红小兵 Hóngxiǎobīng Little Red Guards (school children's organization during the Cultural Revolution to replace the Young Pioneers)
红小豆 hóngxiǎodòu red bean
红小鬼 hóngxiǎoguǐ Little Red Devil (affectionate term of address for teenager soldiers in the Communist-led armies before 1949)
红心 hóngxīn red heart — heart loyal to the cause of proletarian revolution:一颗～为祖国 with a red heart forever loyal to the motherland /一颗～,两手准备 with unchanging devotion to the motherland but prepared for two possible alternatives (concerning one's prospects, etc.)
红锌矿 hóngxīnkuàng zincite
红新月会 Hóngxīnyuèhuì Red Crescent (Society) (in an Islamic country)
红星 hóngxīng red star (often as a symbol of the proletarian revolution):～帽徽 red star cap insignia (of Communist-led armies before and after 1949)
红学 Hóngxué studies of the *Hongloumeng* (《红楼梦》, *A Dream of Red Mansions*); *Hongloumeng* scholarship
红学家 Hóngxuéjiā *Hongloumeng* scholar
红血球 hóngxuèqiú *see* "红细胞"
红殷殷 hóngyānyān bright red:～的杜鹃花 bright red azalea flowers
红颜 hóngyán rosy cheeks; pretty face; beautiful woman:～易老。Beauty is but transient. *or* Beauty is but skin-deep.
红颜薄命 hóngyán-bómìng beautiful women suffer ill fates; beautiful women are ill-fated; a beautiful woman has an unfortunate life:自古红颜多薄命。From time immemorial, beautiful women have often suffered ill fates.
红眼 hóngyǎn ❶ see red; be infuriated or furious:输红了眼 become desperate due to loss in gambling ❷〈方言〉be jealous; be envious; covet:看着有些人富起来,他就～。He is green with envy at seeing some people get rich.
红眼病 hóngyǎnbìng ❶ (popular term for 急性结膜炎) acute conjunctivitis ❷ jealousy; envy; green-eyed monster
红艳艳 hóngyànyàn bright red; brilliant red:～的朝阳 bright red morning sun /山丹丹开花～。The blooming morningstar lily is brilliant red.
红样 hóngyàng red-pencilled proofs; corrected proofs
红药水 hóngyàoshuǐ mercurochrome
红叶 hóngyè red autumnal leaves (of the maple, etc.):沾着露珠的～闪闪发光。The red autumnal leaves are glistening with dewdrops.
红衣主教 hóngyī zhǔjiào cardinal:～团 cardinalate
红移 hóngyí〈天文〉red shift:～公式 red shift formula
红缨枪 hóngyīngqiāng red-tasselled spear
红油 hóngyóu chilli oil:～肚丝 shredded tripe with chilli oil /～鸡丁 diced chicken with chilli oil
红釉 hóngyòu flambé glaze, a type of red porcelain
红鱼 hóngyú *also* "红笛鲷" (red) snapper
红云 hóngyún red cloud;〈比喻〉blush; flush:两颊泛起～。One's face turns red.
红运 hóngyùn *also* "鸿运" hóngyùn good luck:走～ have a spate of good luck; ride on the crest of fortune
红晕 hóngyùn blush; flush:姑娘的脸上泛起了～。The girl's face blushed scarlet.
红糟 hóngzāo red wine dregs (used as seasoning)
红枣 hóngzǎo red date
红藻 hóngzǎo red alga
红涨 hóngzhàng (of a person's face) be swelled by a rush of blood; flush:他～着脸,一时答不出话来。For a moment he was unable to reply, his face all red.
红蜘蛛 hóngzhīzhū〈方言〉red spider (mite); spider mite
红痣 hóngzhì port-wine stain; port-wine mark
红肿 hóngzhǒng red and swollen
红柱石 hóngzhùshí〈地质〉andalusite
红专 hóng-zhuān be red and expert; be socialist-minded and vocationally proficient
红装 hóngzhuāng *also* "红妆"〈书面〉❶ gay feminine attire:阿姊闻妹来,当户理～。Hearing that her younger sister had returned, she dressed up and rouged her face in her boudoir. ❷ young woman:～素裹 young woman clad in white
红锥 hóngzhuī *also* "红椎"; "刺栲" cìkǎo *see* "红栲"

荭 hóng

荭草 hóngcǎo prince's feather (*Polygonum orientale*); prince's plume

洪 hóng

❶ big; vast:～才 great talent ❷ flood:防～ flood control (*or* prevention) /山～ mountain torrents ❸ (Hóng) a surname
洪帮 Hóngbāng〈旧语〉*Hong* Society (secret society derived from Heaven and Earth Society 天地会 and entrenched in the Yangtze and Pearl River valleys in the 19th and early 20th centuries)
洪波 hóngbō great waves; billows:～涌起。Mountainous waves surged (on the sea). /～滚雪。The wind whipped the waves into a snowy foam.
洪大 hóngdà loud:～的涛声 roaring waves
洪都拉斯 Hóngdūlāsī Honduras:～人 Honduran
洪恩 hóng'ēn great favour, kindness or grace:如此～,永生不忘。I will never forget the great kindness (*or* favour) you've done to me.
洪泛区 hóngfànqū floodplain; flooded area
洪峰 hóngfēng flood peak:～流量 peak flood; peak discharge /黄河～今晨已过郑州。The flood peak in the Yellow River passed Zhengzhou this morning.
洪福 hóngfú *also* "鸿福" hóngfú great blessing; great bliss:～齐天 limitless blessing; boundless bliss
洪荒 hónghuāng primeval chaos (of the world); primeval times:～世界 primeval world /～时代 primeval ages; remote antiquity
洪积层 hóngjīcéng *also* "洪积统"〈地质〉diluvium
洪积平原 hóngjī píngyuán diluvial plain
洪积扇 hóngjīshàn〈地理〉proluvial fan
洪积世 Hóngjīshì〈地质〉Diluvial Epoch
洪亮 hóngliàng loud and clear; sonorous:声音～而清晰 clear and sonorous voice /～的钟声 resonant bell
洪量 hóngliàng ❶ magnanimity; generosity ❷ great capacity for liquor
洪流 hóngliú mighty torrent; powerful current:汹涌的～ surging torrents /改革的～ powerful current of reform /游行群众汇成一股浩浩荡荡的～。The demonstrators (*or* marchers) converged into a mighty torrent.
洪炉 hónglú great furnace:革命的～ mighty furnace of revolution
洪脉 hóngmài〈中医〉(powerful and regular) pulse beating like waves; full pulse

洪升 Hóng Shēng Hong Sheng (formerly translated as Hung Sheng, 1645-1704), writer and playwright of the Qing Dynasty
洪水 hóngshuǐ flood; floodwater: 肆虐的～ devastating flood / ～滔滔 surging flood / ～位 flood level / ～季节 flood season
洪水猛兽 hóngshuǐ-měngshòu fierce floods and savage beasts; great scourge: 视为～ regard (sb. or sth.) as a great scourge / 侵略者对人民的危害甚于～。The aggressors did the people more harm than savage beasts. *or* The aggressors savaged the people even more than wild beasts.
洪涛 hóngtāo *also* "洪波" great waves; billows: ～滚滚。Huge waves rolled high.
洪武 Hóngwǔ Hongwu, title of the reign (1368-1398) of Zhu Yuanzhang (朱元璋), founder and 1st emperor of the Ming Dynasty, called reverently Ming Taizu (明太祖) after death
洪宪之役 HóngXiàn ZhīYì Campaign to Defend the (Republican) Constitution against Yuan Shikai (袁世凯) who proclaimed himself emperor on 12 December 1915 and was later forced to renounce the monarchy
洪秀全 Hóng Xiùquán Hong Xiuquan (formerly translated as Hung Hsiu-chuan, 1814-1864), leader of the Taiping Heavenly Kingdom
洪汛 hóngxùn flood information; flood message
洪灾 hóngzāi damages done by flood or inundation: 特大～ great disaster brought by flood or inundation; disastrous flood / 遭受～ be devastated by a big flood
洪钟 hóngzhōng 〈书面〉large bell: 声如～ have a stentorian (*or* sonorous) voice

渶 hóng *see* "荭" hóng

蕻 hóng *see* "雪里蕻" xuělǐhóng
see also hòng

铁 hóng 〈书面〉device on a crossbow for shooting an arrow

宏 hóng ❶ great; grand; magnificent: 宽～ large-minded; magnanimous / ～辩 well-supported argument; eloquent contention / ～变量 macro-variable ❷ (Hóng) a surname
宏病毒 hóngbìngdú 〈计算机〉macro virus
宏博 hóngbó extensive; wide; large-minded: 内容～ extensive (*or* rich) in content / 宽厚～ generous and large-minded
宏敞 hóngchǎng (of a building) spacious; roomy; commodious: ～的大殿 commodious hall
宏程序库 hóngchéngxùkù 〈计算机〉macro library
宏程序设计 hóngchéngxù shèjì 〈信息〉macroprogramming
宏大 hóngdà grand; great: ～的体育场 vast stadium / ～建筑 majestic building / ～的抱负 great aspirations / ～的气魄 boldness of vision / 规模～ grand scale / 音量～ great volume
宏放 hóngfàng 〈书面〉broad-minded; unprejudiced
宏富 hóngfù rich; abundant; plentiful: 采摭～ be a rich collection / 征引～ quote extensively / 学识～ very learned; erudite / 经验～ rich in experience; very experienced
宏观 hóngguān macro; macroscopic: ～对称 macroscopic symmetry / ～观念 macroscopic concept / ～分析 macrocheck / ～研究 macroexamination / ～状态 macrostate / ～组织 macrostructure
宏观管理 hóngguān guǎnlǐ macro-control; macro-administration
宏观结构 hóngguān jiégòu macrostructure
宏观经济 hóngguān jīngjì macro-economy: ～调节 macroeconomic regulation / ～政策 macroeconomic policy / ～效益 macroeconomic result (*or* efficiency)
宏观经济学 hóngguān jīngjìxué macroeconomics
宏观世界 hóngguān shìjiè macro-world; macrocosm
宏观调控 hóngguān tiáokòng macro-adjustment and control
宏观统计学 hóngguān tǒngjìxué macrostatistics
宏观营销 hóngguān yíngxiāo 〈商业〉macromarketing
宏观语言学 hóngguān yǔyánxué macrolinguistics
宏阔 hóngkuò vast; wide; broad: ～的天空 boundless sky
宏朗 hónglǎng (of sound) loud and clear; sonorous: ～的笑声 loud, unrestrained laughter
宏丽 hónglì magnificent; grand; majestic: ～的建筑 magnificent building
宏亮 hóngliàng *also* "洪亮" hóngliàng loud and clear; sonorous: ～的嗓音 sonorous voice
宏论 hónglùn *also* "弘论" hónglùn learned argument; intelligent view; informed opinion: 大发～ argue or hold forth at great length
宏谟 hóngmó 〈书面〉grand project; great plan
宏模块 hóngmúkuài 〈计算机〉macroblock
宏模组件计算机 hóngmú zǔjiàn jìsuànjī macro-modular computer
宏儒 hóngrú *also* "鸿儒" hóngrú learned scholar; erudite person
宏赡 hóngshàn 〈书面〉extensive knowledge: 学力～ have a wide range of knowledge; be learned
宏图 hóngtú *also* "弘图" hóngtú; "鸿图" hóngtú great plan; grand prospect; lofty aspirations: 改造家乡面貌的～ great plans for transforming one's hometown / 一展～ carry out a grand plan; fulfil (*or* realize) one's lofty aspirations
宏伟 hóngwěi magnificent; grand: ～的建筑 magnificent edifice / ～的战略目标 grand strategic goal / ～的史诗 great epic / 我们的事业～壮丽。Ours is a noble cause.
宏扬 hóngyáng *see* "弘扬" hóngyáng
宏愿 hóngyuàn *also* "弘愿" hóngyuàn great aspirations; noble ambition: 中国人民一定会实现使国家现代化的～。The Chinese people will surely achieve their great aspirations to modernize the country.
宏旨 hóngzhǐ *also* "弘旨" hóngzhǐ main theme; leading idea: 无关～ irrelevant to the main theme (*or* topic); insignificant; irrelevant / 掌握这篇文章的～ grasp the main theme (*or* points) of this article
宏指令 hóngzhǐlìng 〈计算机〉macro-instruction; macro-order
宏壮 hóngzhuàng magnificent; majestic: ～的大厦 grand building / 气势～ of great momentum; powerful
宏组件 hóngzǔjiàn 〈计算机〉macroelement

竑 hóng 〈书面〉broad; wide

闳 hóng ❶〈书面〉gate of a lane or alley ❷〈书面〉great; grand; vast ❸ (Hóng) a surname
闳中肆外 hóngzhōng-sìwài (of writing, etc.) rich in substance and graceful (*or* bold) in style

呟 hóng *see* "噌呟" chēnghóng

铉 hóng clink

翃(翝) hóng 〈书面〉fly

纮 hóng lace on a hat in ancient times

弘 hóng ❶ (now often written as 宏) great; grand; magnificent: ～大 grand; great; vast / 气势恢～ of great momentum; imposing / ～济时艰 relieve the difficulties of the times extensively ❷ enlarge; expand: 思～祖业 try to increase the ancestral property ❸ (Hóng) a surname
弘量 hóngliàng large capacity (for tolerance, forgiveness, etc.); magnanimity
弘论 hónglùn *see* "宏论" hónglùn
弘图 hóngtú *see* "宏图" hóngtú
弘扬 hóngyáng *also* "宏扬" hóngyáng 〈书面〉carry forward; develop; enhance: ～祖国文化 develop the national culture; carry forward the cultural heritage / 必须大力～优秀传统道德。Energetic efforts must be made to promote and popularise fine traditional virtues.
弘远 hóngyuǎn far and wide; far-reaching; longlasting: 意义～ of far-reaching and endurable significance
弘愿 hóngyuàn *see* "宏愿" hóngyuàn
弘旨 hóngzhǐ *see* "宏旨" hóngzhǐ
弘治 Hóngzhì Hongzhi, title of the reign (1488-1505) of Zhu Youcheng (朱祐樘), 10th emperor of the Ming Dynasty, called reverently Ming Xiaozong (明孝宗) after death

泓 hóng 〈书面〉❶ (of water) deep ❷〈量词〉*used of clear water*: 一～清泉 a clear spring / 一～潺潺流水 a stream of murmuring water

H

hǒng

哄 hǒng ❶ fool; humbug; kid:我～了他，心中不安。Having fooled him, I felt uneasy. ❷ keep in good humour; coax; humour: ～孩子睡觉 coax a child to sleep /她会～孩子。She knows how to handle children. *or* She has a way with children.
see also hōng; hòng

哄逗 hǒngdòu coax; humour

哄弄 hǒngnong 〈方言〉deceive; make a fool of; fool:你别信他，他专门～人。Don't you trust him. He loves to make a fool of people.

哄骗 hǒngpiàn cheat; humbug; hoodwink

哄劝 hǒngquàn coax:母亲把小男孩搂在怀里～他吃药。Mother held the little boy in her arms and coaxed him to take the medicine.

hòng

澒 hòng

澒洞 hòngdòng 〈书面〉spread all over the place; be boundless

讧 hòng 〈书面〉quarrel; discord:内～ internal strife

蕻 hòng ❶〈书面〉luxuriant; exuberant ❷〈方言〉long stem of certain vegetables
see also hóng

哄(閧) hòng uproar; clamour; horseplay:起～ jointly create a disturbance; start a clamorous jeer or hoot; tease tumultuously /一～而散 break up in an uproar; disperse with great hubbub
see also hōng; hǒng

哄场 hòngchǎng (of an audience) make catcalls; hoot; boo

哄闹 hòngnào uproar; hubbub:会场上一片～声。There was a terrible din at the assembly hall.

hōu

齁[1] hōu snore

齁[2] hōu ❶ sickeningly sweet or salty:少放点糖，要不～死人了。Go easy on sugar, or it will make me sick. ❷〈方言〉(usu. indicating distaste or disapproval) awfully; too; so:这些天～冷。It has been awfully cold these days. /真不想吃这药，～苦! I hate to take this medicine; it tastes so bitter! /这些苍蝇～让人讨厌。The flies are too much of a nuisance.

齁齁 hōuhōu 〈象声〉snore:鼻息～ stertorous breathing /～熟睡 snore away in sound sleep

齁声 hōushēng noise of snoring; snore:～如雷 snore thunderously /～大作 snore loudly

hóu

侯 hóu ❶ marquis; marquess:王～ princes and marquises ❷ nobleman; high official:～门 mansion of the nobility ❸ (Hóu) a surname
see also hòu

侯服玉食 hóufú-yùshí wear noblemen's clothing and eat exquisite food; live in clover:国难当头，这些政客却～，极尽奢侈。At a time of national crisis, these politicians were still rolling in luxury.

侯爵 hóujué marquis:～夫人 marquise; marchioness /女～ marquise; marchioness

侯门如海 hóumén-rúhǎi *also* "侯门似海" the gate of a noble house is like the sea; the mansions of the nobility are inaccessible to the common man

侯氏制碱法 Hóushì zhìjiǎnfǎ *also* "联合制碱法" liánhé zhìjiǎnfǎ process of soda production invented by Hou Debang (侯德榜, 1890-1974)

瘊 hóu wart

瘊子 hóuzi wart

糇(餱) hóu 〈书面〉solid food (prepared for a journey); field rations; rations for a journey:～粮自备。Everyone should bring his own food.

喉 hóu 〈生理〉larynx; throat:咽～ pharynx and larynx; throat /歌～ (singer's) voice; singing voice /～病 laryngeal disease

喉癌 hóu'ái laryngocarcinoma; throat cancer; cancer in the throat

喉痹 hóubì 〈中医〉pharyngitis

喉壁音 hóubìyīn 〈语言〉pharyngeal (sound)

喉擦音 hóucāyīn 〈语言〉guttural fricative

喉颤音 hóuchànyīn 〈语言〉glottal roll or trill

喉成形术 hóuchéngxíngshù 〈医学〉laryngoplasty

喉穿刺术 hóuchuāncìshù 〈医学〉laryngocentesis

喉蛾 hóu'é tonsillitis

喉风 hóufēng 〈中医〉sore throat:～散 throat powder

喉干燥 hóugānzào 〈医学〉laryngoxerosis

喉疳 hóugān ulceration of throat

喉管 hóuguǎn ❶ windpipe; trachea ❷ a kind of reed instrument popular in Guangdong and Guangxi

喉急 hóují *also* "猴急" hóují 〈方言〉worried; anxious:一副～相 anxious look

喉结 hóujié *also* "结喉"〈生理〉Adam's apple; larynx; prominentia laryngea

喉结核 hóujiéhé 〈医学〉laryngophthisis

喉镜 hóujìng 〈医学〉laryngoscope; laryngendoscope:～检查 laryngoscopy

喉科学 hóukēxué laryngology

喉咙 hóulong throat:～充血 have congestion in one's throat /～里冒烟 one's throat burns like fire — very thirsty /他咳嗽一声，清清～。He coughed to clear his throat.

喉麻痹 hóumábì 〈医学〉laryngoparalysis

喉囊肿 hóunángzhǒng 〈医学〉laryngocele

喉切除术 hóuqiēchúshù 〈医学〉laryngectomy

喉切开术 hóuqiēkāishù 〈医学〉laryngotomy

喉清韵雅 hóuqīng-yùnyǎ silver voice and beautiful singing; sing in a sweet and charming voice

喉塞音 hóusèyīn 〈语言〉glottal stop

喉痧 hóushā 〈中医〉scarlet fever

喉舌 hóushé mouthpiece:这份报纸是大资产阶级的～。This newspaper is the mouthpiece of the big bourgeoisie.

喉神经 hóushénjīng laryngeal nerve

喉痛 hóutòng laryngalgia; sore throat:我～。I have a sore throat.

喉头 hóutóu larynx; throat

喉咽 hóuyān 〈生理〉laryngopharynx

喉炎 hóuyán 〈医学〉laryngitis:慢性～ chronic laryngitis; clergyman's sore throat /～患者 laryngitic

喉音 hóuyīn 〈语言〉guttural sound; glottal; laryngal; gutturophony

喉痈 hóuyōng 〈医学〉retropharyngeal abscess

喉阻塞 hóuzǔsè 〈医学〉laryngeal obstruction

睺 hóu *see* "罗睺" luóhóu

篌 hóu *see* "箜篌" kōnghóu

猴 hóu ❶ monkey:金丝～ golden monkey /猕～ macaque /狐～ lemur ❷〈方言〉(usu. of children) smart; clever; mischievous:这孩子多～啊! What a mischievous boy! ❸〈方言〉squat (like a monkey):几个老头～在路边闲唠嗑。A few old men squatted on their haunches, chatting at the roadside.

猴急 hóují *see* "喉急" hóují

猴面包树 hóumiànbāoshù 〈植物〉monkey-bread tree; baobab (*Adansonia digitata*)

猴年马月 hóunián-mǎyuè *also* "驴年马月" lǘnián-mǎyuè impossible date; day that will never come:那要等到～! I'm afraid we'll be waiting for all eternity!

猴皮筋儿 hóupíjīnr *also* "猴筋儿" rubber band:跳～ rubber-band

rope skipping
猴拳 hóuquán 〈体育〉monkey boxing (in *wushu*):打～ play monkey boxing
猴儿精 hóurjīng 〈方言〉❶ astute; shrewd; smart:这小子～的。That fellow is awfully shrewd. ❷ clever and mischievous person; mischief-maker:这孩子是个～。The boy is a mischief-maker.
猴儿快 hóurkuài quick as a monkey:这小子溜得～。He slipped away before anyone noticed it.
猴手猴脚 hóushǒu-hóujiǎo careless; hasty; rash:你已经是大孩子了,不能老那么～的。Now that you are a big boy, you shouldn't behave like a harum-scarum (*or* cut-up).
猴狲 hóusūn monkey:～王〈旧语〉(usu. of a private school master) "king of little monkeys"
猴头 hóutóu 〈植物〉hedgehog hydnum (*Hydnum erinaceus*); bear's head:～菌 hedgehog fungus (*Hericium erinaceus*)
猴头猴脑 hóutóu-hóunǎo look funny and foolish
猴戏 hóuxì ❶ show by a performing monkey; monkey show:看～ go to (*or* watch) a monkey show ❷〈戏曲〉performance with the Monkey King (孙悟空) as the hero
猴枣 hóuzǎo 〈中医〉bezoar or stone from a macaque (used as antipyretic, etc.)
猴子 hóuzi monkey

骺 hóu 〈生理〉epiphysis:～板 epiphyseal plate
骺脱离 hóutuōlí 〈医学〉epiphysiolysis
骺炎 hóuyán 〈医学〉epiphysitis:椎骨～ vertebral epiphysitis

hǒu

吼 hǒu ❶ (of large animals) roar; growl:狮～。The lion roared. /牛～。The ox bellowed. ❷ (of angry or excited people) shout; roar:狂～ shout madly /怒～ roar with anger ❸ (of wind, siren, cannon, etc.) howl; boom:北风怒～。The north wind was howling. /万炮齐发,～声如雷。Thousands of cannons started firing all at once, crashing and rumbling like thunder.
吼喊 hǒuhǎn shout; cry; roar; howl:就算她有错,你也不该这样冲她～。Even if she had been wrong, you shouldn't have shouted (*or* yelled) at her.
吼猴 hǒuhóu howling monkey; howler
吼叫 hǒujiào roar; bellow; howl:老虎～着向山羊扑去。The tiger roared and pounced (*or* sprang) on the goat.
吼鸣 hǒumíng roar; boom; growl:发动机的～声 roar of an engine
吼三喝四 hǒusān-hèsì 〈方言〉act the high-and-mighty; boss people about; throw one's weight about:别对我～的! Don't be so arrogant!
吼声 hǒushēng loud shouts and calls; roar; boom:～震天。The shouts and calls resounded between heaven and earth. *or* The roaring went to the sky.

犼 hǒu legendary dog-like man-eating animal

hòu

厚 hòu ❶ thick:～墙 thick wall /～～的一层沙子 thick layer of sand ❷ thickness:三毫米～的玻璃 glass 3mm thick (*or* in thickness) /雪～三尺。The snow is three *chi* deep. ❸ deep; profound:深情～谊 profound friendship /我俩交情不～。We are not very close. ❹ kind; magnanimous:宽～ kind; lenient /～以待人 be magnanimous to people ❺ large; generous; handsome:待遇优～ handsome reward (*or* remuneration, *or* pay) ❻ rich or strong in flavour:味道浓～ rich flavour /酒味醇～。The wine tastes mellow and strong. ❼ well-off; well-to-do; wealthy:家底儿～ well-to-do family ❽ favour; stress:他待你独～。He treated you with special favour. ❾ (Hòu) a surname
厚爱 hòu'ài 〈敬词〉your favour; your care and support:承蒙～。I'm indebted to you for your care and support. /总有一天要报答您的～。Some day I will reciprocate the favour you have shown to me.
厚壁铸件 hòubì zhùjiàn 〈冶金〉heavy section casting
厚薄 hòubó ❶ thick or thin; thickness:～正好 (be) of the right thickness /～如何? How thick is it? ❷ show favour or disfavour; be intimate or distant:朋友之间何须分～。Among friends, you certainly should not discriminate against one in favour of another.
厚薄规 hòubóguī *also* "塞尺" sāichǐ 〈机械〉feeler (gauge); thickness gauge
厚此薄彼 hòucǐ-bóbǐ favour one and discriminate against the other; make fish of one and flesh of another; treat with partiality:刘老师对学生从不～。Professor Liu never favours some students while neglecting others.
厚待 hòudài treat kindly and generously; give preferential treatment; be munificent:人家这样～咱们,咱们可要对得起人家。As they are so generous to us, we must not disappoint them.
厚道 hòudao honest and kind:他可是个～人。He is a kind and honest man.
厚德载福 hòudé-zàifú great virtue brings happiness
厚度 hòudù thickness:～达三英尺 to a thickness of three feet; three feet thick /～计 thickness gauge
厚墩墩 hòudūndūn very thick:～的羊皮袄 heavy sheepskin jacket
厚恩 hòu'ēn 〈敬词〉your kindness; your generosity; your favour:报答～ requite your kindness; pay you a debt of gratitude
厚帆布 hòufānbù sailcloth; cottonine
厚非 hòufēi (usu. used in the negative, or in a rhetorical question) undue blame; excessive criticism:无可～ above criticism; beyond reproach; blameless
厚古薄今 hòugǔ-bójīn stress the past, not the present; praise the past and belittle the present:对文化史的研究不能～。We must not extol the past and denigrate the present in studying the history of culture.
厚积薄发 hòujī-bófā be so well versed in a subject as to be able to write about any part of it with ease; be well-grounded; be well-prepared:只有对西方哲学做到～,才能写出这样的好论文。Only when well grounded in Western philosophy can one write such an excellent thesis.
厚今薄古 hòujīn-bógǔ stress the present, not the past; value the present and slight the past:在学术研究中要贯彻～的方针。We must stress the present, not the past in academic research.
厚金 hòujīn high pay; large remuneration:～重聘 offer sb. a large salary; recruit sb. at high pay
厚礼 hòulǐ generous gift; munificent present:他不会为～所动。He will not be moved by generous gifts.
厚利 hòulì fat or large profit; high interest:贪图～ be after (*or* seek) fat profit
厚脸皮 hòuliǎnpí *also* "厚脸" cheeky; brazen; thick-skinned:厚着脸皮去求情 have the cheek (*or* nerve) to ask for a favour; summon up one's courage to beg for kindness (*or* mercy) /他可真是～! The nerve of him! /这小子～,说什么他都不在乎。The guy is so thick-skinned as not to know what embarrassment means.
厚禄 hòulù large salary:高官～ high position and huge salary
厚貌深情 hòumào-shēnqíng kindly in appearance but unfathomable at heart:此人～,不可不防。Despite his outward kindness there's something unfathomable about him. We'd better watch out.
厚膜 hòumó thick-film:～电路 thick-film circuit /～微电子学 thick-film microelectronics
厚皮 hòupí thick-skinned; brazen; cheeky; shameless:这个人～,批评无用。He's shameless and it's no use criticizing him.
厚皮菜 hòupícài *also* "牛皮菜" niúpícài 〈方言〉chard; leaf beet (*Beta vulgaris*)
厚皮动物 hòupí dòngwù pachyderm
厚朴 hòupò 〈中医〉bark of official magnolia (*Magnolia officinalis*)
厚生 hòushēng 〈书面〉improve people's livelihood; make people better off:利用～ make good use of everything to secure a better livelihood for people
厚生省 Hòushēngshěng (Japan) Ministry of Health and Welfare
厚实 hòushi ❶ thick:厚厚实实的褥子 thick mattress /又～又暖和的棉大衣 very heavy and warm overcoat ❷ broad; thick and sturdy:～的肩膀 broad and sturdy shoulders ❸ profound and sound; deep and solid:学术基础～ have a solid academic foundation ❹〈方言〉honest and sincere:为人～ be sincere and upright ❺ wealthy; abundant; rich:家底～ well-off family; financially solid family; family with substantial resources
厚硕 hòushuò thick and large:宽大～的叶子 broad and thick leaves

厚望 hòuwàng great expectations; high hopes: 寄予～ place (*or* lay) great hopes on / 有负～ fall short of sb.'s expectations (*or* hopes); let sb. down

厚味 hòuwèi rich or strong flavour

厚谢 hòuxiè thank sb. with a generous gift; bring a generous thankyou present: 事成之后, 定当～。When this gets done, you will be generously rewarded.

厚颜 hòuyán thick-skinned; impudent; brazen: 如此～, 真不知羞耻! What a nerve! He simply has no sense of shame.

厚颜无耻 hòuyán-wúchǐ shameless; past shame; brazen as brass: ～的人 person without the slightest sense of shame / 他～地坐在那儿不走。He sat there as bold as brass and refused to leave. / 你干了那些事还来见我, 真是～。What cheek (*or* nerve) to come to see me after all you have done!

厚谊 hòuyì deep feeling; deep friendship: 深情～ deep affection / 她对我的～永生难忘。I'll never forget her tenderness towards me.

厚意 hòuyì kindness; generosity; kind thought: 多谢众乡亲的～。Many thanks to my townsfolk for their generosity.

厚遇 hòuyù excellent pay and privileges; liberal wages and benefits: 享此～, 我们怎能不努力工作? With such liberal pay and generous benefits, we should put our shoulders to the wheel.

厚葬 hòuzàng elaborate funeral

厚重 hòuzhòng ❶ thick and heavy: ～的棉帘子 heavy cotton-padded curtain / ～织物 heavy fabrics ❷ generous; munificent: ～的礼物 generous gift ❸ 〈书面〉 honest and serious: 他为人～。He is an honest and grave man.

侯 hòu (used in 闽侯) Minhou, name of a county in Fujian Province
see also hóu

堠 hòu 〈古语〉 earthen watchtower

候[1] hòu ❶ wait; await: 请稍～。Please wait a minute. *or* Just a minute, please. ❷ inquire after: 请代我向他致～。Please give him my best regards. *or* Please remember me to him.

候[2] hòu ❶ time; season: 时～ time / 季～ season / 气～ weather ❷ 〈气象〉 period of five days; pentad: *see* "～温" ❸ condition; state: 火～ duration and degree of heating, smelting, cooking, etc. / 征～ symptom; sign

候补 hòubǔ be an alternate; be a candidate (for a vacancy); be a substitute: ～书记 alternate secretary / ～董事 alternate director / 中共中央～委员 alternate member of the Central Committee of the CPC / ～队员 〈体育〉 substitute

候场 hòuchǎng (of an actor or actress) wait one's turn to enter the stage: ～的演员 actor awaiting his turn to enter

候车 hòuchē wait for a bus or a train: ～的时间不会太长。You won't have to wait long before the bus arrives.

候车棚 hòuchēpéng covered bus stop

候车室 hòuchēshì waiting room (in a railway or coach station)

候虫 hòuchóng seasonal insect

候风地动仪 hòufēng dìdòngyí ancient seismograph (invented by Zhang Heng 张衡 in the Han Dynasty)

候光 hòuguāng 〈书面〉〈敬词〉 expect the presence of sb. (at): 今晚洁樽～, 务请驾临。We request the pleasure of your company at dinner tonight.

候机楼 hòujīlóu terminal building; air terminal

候机室 hòujīshì airport lounge; airport waiting room

候教 hòujiào 〈书面〉〈敬词〉 await your instructions: 本星期日下午在舍下～。I'll be awaiting your instructions at my home this Sunday afternoon.

候鸟 hòuniǎo migratory bird; migrant (bird); bird of passage; visitant

候缺 hòuquē 〈旧语〉 wait to fill a vacancy: 在京～ be in the capital waiting to fill a vacant post

候审 hòushěn 〈法律〉 await trial or cross-examination: ～人 suspect for trial / ～期间, 被告不得外出。While awaiting trial, the accused is not allowed outdoors.

候温 hòuwēn 〈气象〉 average temperature of a five-day period; pentad mean (temperature)

候选人 hòuxuǎnrén candidate: 总统～ presidential candidate; candidate for the presidency / ～资格 candidancy; candidature; qualifications for standing for election / ～名单 list of candidates / 提出～ nominate (*or* put up) a candidate

候讯 hòuxùn await court trial or cross-examination

候账 hòuzhàng pay or foot a bill

候诊 hòuzhěn wait to see the doctor: 每天～的病人多达五百人。There are as many as 500 patients every day. / 请按序～。Please wait till called.

候诊室 hòuzhěnshì waiting room (in a hospital)

后[1](後) hòu ❶ back; rear; behind; hind: (汽车)～箱 rear trunk / 房前屋～ in front and at the back of a house; before and behind a house / 敌～ behind enemy lines / 落～ fall (*or* lag) behind ❷ after; afterwards; later: 课前课～ before and after class / 日～ later (on); in (the) future / 不久以～ soon afterwards; before long / 一星期～ in a week; one week after; a week later / 先来～到 in the order of arrival; first come, first served / 按时间先～ in time sequence ❸ last; back: ～十名 last ten persons / 最～一批南飞的雁群 last of the southbound wild geese ❹ offspring; progeny: 绝～ without issue; have no male offspring

后[2] hòu ❶ empress; queen: 皇～ empress / 王～ queen / ～妃 empress and imperial concubines / 皇太～ empress dowager ❷ 〈古语〉 emperor; monarch; sovereign: 夏～ emperor of the Xia Dynasty ❸ (Hòu) a surname

后半 hòubàn latter half; second half: ～辈子 latter half of one's life / ～场比赛 second half of a game (*or* match)

后半晌 hòubànshǎng 〈方言〉 afternoon

后半生 hòubànshēng latter half of one's life

后半天 hòubàntiān afternoon

后半叶 hòubànyè latter half of a century: 18 世纪～ latter half of the 18th century

后半夜 hòubànyè *also* "下半夜" xiàbànyè wee or small hours; after midnight: 我～才入睡。I fell asleep only after midnight.

后备 hòubèi reserve: ～队员 reserves / ～物资 reserve materials / ～系统 back-up system; stand-by system / 留有～ keep sth. in reserve

后备存储器 hòubèi cúnchǔqì 〈计算机〉 backing memory; backing store; look-aside memory; back-up memory

后备电池 hòubèi diànchí back-up battery; battery backup

后备队 hòubèiduì 〈军事〉 reserve force: 总～ general reserve force

后备军 hòubèijūn ❶ reserves: 召集～ call up the reserve(s) / 被编入～ be placed on the reserves (*or* reserve list, *or* backup roster) ❷ reserve force: 产业～ industrial reserve; reserve army of labour

后备软盘 hòubèi ruǎnpán back-up diskette

后背 hòubèi ❶ back (of the human body): ～疼 backache ❷ 〈方言〉 rear; behind: 攻敌人～ attack the enemy from behind

后辈 hòubèi ❶ later generations; descendants; posterity: ～子孙 descendants; later generations / 先人们希望～能超过他们。Our forefathers expected future generations to surpass them. ❷ juniors; younger generation: 在工作中, 咱们～要多向老一辈学习。In our work, we of the younger generation should learn from our elders.

后边 hòubian back; rear; behind: 院子～是一片小松林。At the back of (*or* Behind) the courtyard is a small stretch of pines.

后冰期 hòubīngqī late glacial period

后不僭先 hòubùjiànxiān first come, first served: 难道你连～的道理也不懂? First come, first served. Don't you know that?

后步 hòubù room for manoeuvre; leeway: 说话办事不能不留～。One has to leave enough leeway in whatever one says or does.

后部 hòubù back; hindside; rear; posterior: ～航舱 afterhold

后场扣球 hòuchǎng kòuqiú 〈体育〉 back-court spiking

后尘 hòuchén 〈书面〉 dust raised by someone walking in front: 步人～ follow in sb.'s footsteps; trail along behind others; follow suit / 重蹈前人失败的～ repeat the failures of one's predecessors

后沉 hòuchén (of a cart load, etc.) back-heavy

后成矿床 hòuchéng kuàngchuáng subsequent deposit; epigenetic deposit

后耻骨 hòuchǐgǔ 〈医学〉 postpubis

后冲 hòuchōng 〈机械〉 backlash: ～力 backlash

后处理 hòuchǔlǐ ❶ 〈化学〉 aftertreatment ❷ 〈纺织〉 finishing: ～车间 finishing workshop ❸ 〈机械〉 post-processing; post-treatment

H

后代 hòudài ❶ later periods (in history); later ages ❷ later generations; descendants; posterity:为～造福 benefit (*or* work for the wellbeing of) future generations /打他一死,这家人也就绝了～。His death in effect meant the end of his line of succession.
后挡板 hòudǎngbǎn tailboard; rear apron; backplate
后灯 hòudēng taillight; tail lamp; rear lamp
后殿 hòudiàn back chamber (of a palace); rear chamber; rear hall (of a temple)
后爹 hòudiē 〈口语〉 stepfather
后蝶 hòudié queen butterfly
后端 hòuduān rear end; back end:～数据库 back-end database /～停车灯 rear-end stop lamp /～装载机 end loader
后盾 hòudùn backing; backup (force); support; supporter:有你做我的～,我就什么都不怕了。With your backing, I'm not afraid of anything.
后发制人 hòufā-zhìrén gain mastery by striking only after the enemy or adversary has struck:有的时候,我们可以～。Sometimes we may subdue the enemy by striking after he has struck the first blow.
后方 hòufāng ❶ rear:～补给 rear supply /～医院 rear (*or* base) hospital /～部署 disposition in the rear /插入敌人的～ penetrate the enemy lines /～的工作也很重要。Work in the rear is also very important. ❷ behind; at the back; in the rear:仪仗队的～是小学生队伍。Behind the guard of honour were primary school pupils.
后防 hòufáng rear defence:加强～ strengthen rear defence
后房 hòufáng ❶ rear-room (of a house); posterior chamber ❷ living quarters for one's concubines; concubines
后妃 hòufēi empress and imperial concubines; queen and royal concubines
后夫 hòufū second or third, etc. husband
后福 hòufú good days to come; blessings to follow:～无量 boundless future happiness /大难不死,必有～。A disaster survived is a blessing in store.
后父 hòufù stepfather
后跟 hòugēn heel; heelpiece (of a shoe or sock):～提带 backstrap
后工业化社会 hòugōngyèhuà shèhuì postindustrial society
后宫 hòugōng ❶ living quarters (in the palace) for imperial concubines; imperial harem; seraglio ❷ imperial concubines
后顾 hòugù ❶ turn back (to take care of sth.):无暇～ cannot find time to attend to things one has left behind ❷ look back or upon:青年爱前瞻,老人常～。Young people tend to look ahead into the future while old people are wont to look back upon the past.
后顾之忧 hòugùzhīyōu disturbance in the rear; trouble back at home; family worries:解除教师们的～ relieve teachers of their family worries /他们固守堡垒,无～。They were entrenched in the stronghold without any fear of attacks from behind.
后滚翻 hòugǔnfān 〈体育〉 backward roll
后果 hòuguǒ consequence; aftermath:战争的～ aftermath of war /前因～ cause and effect /～将难以设想。The consequences would be beyond the worst imagination. /由此产生的一切～将由你们承担。You will be (held) responsible for all the consequences arising therefrom.
后海 Hòuhǎi Rear Lake (in Beijing)
后汉 Hòu Hàn ❶ Eastern Han Dynasty (25-220) ❷ Later Han Dynasty (947-950), one of the Five Dynasties
后汉书 Hòu-Hànshū *History of Eastern Han*, one of *The Twenty-Four Histories* (二十四史)
后花园 hòuhuāyuán back garden
后话 hòuhuà sth. to be taken up later (in one's speech or writing):这是～,暂且不提。I'll come to this again later. *or* More of this later.
后患 hòuhuàn future trouble:消除～ remove the cause of future trouble
后患无穷 hòuhuàn-wúqióng no end of trouble for the future; endless trouble in store; fraught with danger ever afterwards:此人不除,～。If this man is not got out of the way, there will be the deuce to pay.
后悔 hòuhuǐ regret; remorse:深深～ be in deep remorse /～不已 be overcome with regret /毫不～ feel no remorse at all /她心里有些～。She felt a tinge of regret.
后悔莫及 hòuhuǐ-mòjí *also* "后悔无及" too late to regret or repent; cry over spilt milk:他一时糊涂,铸成大错,真是～! It was a momentary slip that resulted in such a blunder! And now his remorse is too late.
后悔药 hòuhuǐyào 〈比喻〉 medicine for remorse; remedy for the bygone; regret:吃～ be filled with remorse (*or* regret) /～没处买。There's no medicine for remorse on sale. *or* It's no use crying over spilt milk.
后会有期 hòuhuì-yǒuqī meet again some day; see you again:请多多珍重,你我～。Take good care of yourself! We'll meet again some day.
后婚儿 hòuhūnr 〈旧语〉 remarried divorcee; remarried woman:他又成了家,找了个～。He remarried, and this time, a divorced woman.
后机身 hòujīshēn 〈航空〉 rear fuselage
后脊梁 hòujǐliang 〈方言〉 back (of the human body); backbone; spine; spinal column
后记 hòujì postscript; afterword
后继 hòujì succeed; carry on; follow up:前仆～ carry on the cause of the fallen; advance wave upon wave /～者 successor /～设计 follow-up design
后继无人 hòujì-wúrén have no successor:我们的工作～。There is no successor to our task.
后继有人 hòujì-yǒurén have (worthy or qualified) successors:应该注重培养青年科学家,使基础理论的研究～。We should emphasize the training of young scientists so that there will be qualified successors to carry on research in basic theory.
后稷 Hòujì ❶ legendary founder of the Zhou clan, which was to set up the Zhou Dynasty ❷ God of Agriculture ❸ (hòujì) minister of agriculture under Emperor Shun (舜)
后甲板 hòujiǎbǎn afterdeck; quarterdeck
后焦点 hòujiāodiǎn back focus
后焦距 hòujiāojù back focal length
后脚 hòujiǎo ❶ rear foot (in walking):前脚刚一抬,～就直打哆嗦。When I lifted my front foot, my rear foot started to tremble. ❷ immediately after:他前脚刚走,儿子～就溜出去了。His son slipped out the moment he left.
后街小巷 hòujiē-xiǎoxiàng back street
后金 Hòu Jīn Later Jin Dynasty (1616-1636, later called Qing Dynasty)
后襟 hòujīn back of a Chinese robe or jacket; back of a garment
后进 hòujìn ❶ with less learning; junior in service:提携～ give help and guidance to juniors ❷ less advanced; underdeveloped; lagging behind:～地区 underdeveloped areas (*or* regions) /～企业 less-advanced enterprise; enterprise that lags behind ❸ person or unit lagging behind:变～为先进 help those lagging behind to become the advanced
后进先出 hòujìn-xiānchū last-in first-out
后劲 hòujìn ❶ delayed effect; aftereffect:红葡萄酒～儿大。Red wine has a strong delayed effect. ❷ reserve strength; staying power; stamina:干这活要有～。You need stamina for this kind of work. /长跑要留～。One should conserve one's strength in long-distance running.
后晋 Hòu Jìn Later Jin Dynasty (936-947), one of the Five Dynasties
后景 hòujǐng background:这幅画的～是一片松树林。The background of the painting is a pine wood.
后颈 hòujǐng nape; back of one's neck
后聚焦 hòujùjiāo post-focusing:～式彩色显像管 post-focusing type colour picture tube
后觉 hòujué 〈心理〉 aftersensation
后凯恩斯主义 hòukǎi'ēnsīzhǔyì 〈经济〉 post-Keynesian economics
后空翻 hòukōngfān 〈体育〉 backward somersault
后昆 hòukūn 〈书面〉 descendants; posterity; later generations
后拉力 hòulālì backpull
后来 hòulái ❶ afterwards; later; then; since then:～她怎么样了? What happened to (*or* became of) her afterwards? /他去年三月来过一封信,～就再也没来信了。He has not written to me ever since last March. ❷ newly come; newly arrived:～的各位请坐好。All latecomers please be seated.
后来居上 hòulái-jūshàng *also* "后者居上" the latecomers come out first; successors surpass their predecessors; catch up from behind:～超过先进国家 leapfrog the advanced countries /我们不但要赶上世界先进水平,而且应该～。We must not only catch up with but also sur-

H

pass the world's advanced levels.

后来人　hòuláirén　latecomer; successor: 这项事业不愁没有～。We are sure to have successors to carry on the cause.

后浪推前浪　hòulàng tuī qiánlàng　*also* "后浪催前浪" waves behind drive on those before; each wave pushes at the one ahead — the new generation excels the old: 长江～，世上新人胜旧人。As the Yangtze River surges on wave upon wave, so the new generation surpasses the old.

后脸儿　hòuliǎnr　〈方言〉back (of sb. or sth.): 把镜子的～也擦一擦。Wipe the back of the mirror as well. /看～，那人像是老张。Viewed from behind, the man looked like Lao Zhang.

后梁　hòuliáng　❶ (Hòu Liáng) Later Liang Dynasty (907-923), one of the Five Dynasties ❷〈机械〉back rest; rear spar

后路　hòulù　❶ communication lines to the rear; route of retreat: 抄匪徒的～ outflank the bandits; attack the bandits from the rear /卡住敌人的～ block the enemy's route of retreat ❷ room for manoeuvre; way of escape: 留条～ leave oneself a way out; keep an option open

后掠角　hòulüèjiǎo　〈航空〉sweep angle; sweepback

后掠翼　hòulüèyì　〈航空〉swept-back wing: ～飞机 swept-back wing aircraft

后轮　hòulún　rear wheel; back wheel; trailing wheel

后妈　hòumā　〈口语〉stepmother

后门　hòumén　❶ back door or gate: 他们是从～出的公园。They left the park by the back gate. ❷ back-door or backstairs influence: 走～之风 practice of back-door deals /你为什么给她开～? Why did you make an exception in her favour? /那时候没有～很难办事。It was hard to get things done without pull at the time.

后门交易　hòumén jiāoyì　〈经济〉under the counter or back-door deals

后面　hòumian　❶ at the back; at or in the rear; behind: ～的人能听得见吗? Can you hear me at the back? /大楼～有个小花园。There is a small garden behind the building. ❷ later: 这个问题～将作详细阐述。The question will be dealt with in detail later.

后母　hòumǔ　stepmother

后脑　hòunǎo　〈生理〉hindbrain; rhombencephalon: ～腔 metacoele; epicoele

后脑海　hòunǎohǎi　〈方言〉hindbrain

后脑勺儿　hòunǎosháor　*also* "后脑勺子"〈方言〉back of the head

后年　hòunián　year after next

后娘　hòuniáng　〈口语〉stepmother

后农业社会　hòunóngyè shèhuì　postagricultural society

后怕　hòupà　fear after the event: 事故过后好几个星期，仍感到～。The fear lingered on for weeks after the accident. /那天的事只要一想起来，我还真有些～。I'm still scared whenever I think of what happened the other day.

后排　hòupái　back row: ～坐位 seat in the back row; back row seat /～插上战术〈体育〉back-setter-move-forward play (in volleyball) /我去晚了，只好坐在～。I got there late and had to take a back row seat.

后妻　hòuqī　second or third, etc. wife

后期　hòuqī　later stage; later period: 抗日战争～ (in) the later stage of the War of Resistance Against Japan / 70 年代～ (in) the late 70's /细胞分裂～ anaphase /～管理 final-period management /～追肥 manuring late

后起　hòuqǐ　(of people of talent) up-and-coming; budding: ～的歌手 budding young singer /体坛～好手 promising young sportsman /～的足坛骁将 new generation of valiant footballers

后起之秀　hòuqǐzhīxiù　promising young person; up-and-coming youngster; budding young talent; rising star

后桥　hòuqiáo　rear or back axle (of a car or truck): ～壳 rear axle housing /～传动轴 rear axle propeller

后勤　hòuqín　rear or general service; logistics: ～服务 rear service /～支援 logistic support /～工作人员 logistical (*or* general service) personnel /做好～工作 do a good job in providing rear services (*or* in logistic support)

后勤部　hòuqínbù　rear-service department; logistics department: ～长 director of the logistics department /中国人民解放军总～ General Logistics Department of the PLA

后勤部队　hòuqín bùduì　rear-service unit; rear service

后勤机关　hòuqín jīguān　rear-service establishment

后勤基地　hòuqín jīdì　logistics base; rear supply base

后勤人员　hòuqín rényuán　rear-service personnel

后勤学　hòuqínxué　logistics

后穹窿镜　hòuqiónglóngjìng　〈医学〉culdoscope: ～检查 culdoscopy

后鞧　hòuqiū　harness

后儿　hòur　*also* "后儿个"〈口语〉day after tomorrow: ～早上八点，我在校门口等你。I'll be waiting for you at the school gate at 8:00 a.m. the day after tomorrow.

后人　hòurén　❶ later generations; futurity: 前人栽树，～乘凉。One generation plants trees under whose cool shade another generation rests. ❷ descendants; posterity; offspring: 您也该为～想想。You've got to consider the wellbeing of your children and grandchildren.

后任　hòurèn　successor: 他的～是个中年人。His successor is a middle-aged man.

后日　hòurì　day after tomorrow

后三角队形　hòusānjiǎo duìxíng　〈军事〉V-formation

后厦　hòushà　rear porch; back veranda: 前廊～ front and back verandas

后晌　hòushǎng　〈方言〉afternoon

后晌　hòushang　〈方言〉evening: ～饭 supper

后身　hòushēn　❶ back of a person: 我只看见那个人的～。I only saw the man's back. ❷ back of a garment: 这件衬衣的～上有个洞。There is a hole in the back of this shirt. ❸ at the back of a house, etc.: 房～儿有几棵枣树。There are some date trees behind the house. ❹〈迷信〉reincarnation: 猪八戒据称是天蓬元帅的～。Zhu Bajie (The Pig) is supposed to be an earthly reincarnation of heavenly Marshal Tianpeng. ❺ successor (to an organization or a system): 中国人民解放军是八路军、新四军的～。The PLA is the successor to the Eighth Route and New Fourth armies.

后生可畏　hòushēng-kěwèi　the young deserve to be regarded with awe; a ragged colt may make a good horse; every oak has been an acorn: 小伙子进公司才三个月，已能独当一面，真是～。He entered the company only 3 months ago and is now working on his own. Here's a young man to be looked out for.

后生女　hòushēngnǚ　〈方言〉young woman; lass

后生子　hòushēngzǐ　〈方言〉young man; lad

后生　hòusheng　〈方言〉❶ young man ❷ having a youthful appearance; youthful: 长得～ look young (for one's age) /～家 young man; youth /她都五十多了，还打扮得那么～。She is over fifty, but is dressed like a young woman.

后世　hòushì　❶ later ages; future or later generations: 莎翁的剧作对～文学的影响是巨大的。Shakespeare's plays have had an immense influence upon literature of later ages. ❷ offspring; descendant: 年深日久，这批难民的～已在当地扎了根。After many years the descendants of these refugees took root in those localities. ❸〈佛教〉next life: 前世积德，～享福。Accumulate merit in this life and you will live in ease and comfort in the next.

后事　hòushì　❶ what happened afterwards: 欲知～如何，且听下回分解。(usu. used in a traditional Chinese novel) For what happened later, please turn to the next chapter. /前事不忘，～之师。Past experience, if not forgotten, serves as a guide for the future. ❷ funeral (affairs): 他正忙于料理父亲的～。He is busy making arrangements for his father's funeral.

后视　hòushì　back vision: ～标杆 back hub

后视镜　hòushìjìng　rearview mirror; rear-vision mirror

后视图　hòushìtú　〈机械〉back view; rear view

后手　hòushǒu　❶〈旧语〉successor: 这些事得～接着办。This must be carried on by our successors. ❷〈旧语〉recipient (of a receipt, bill, invoice, etc.) ❸ defensive position (in chess): 一着不慎，就变成～了。A careless move landed one in a defensive position. *or* An ill-thought-of move cost one the initiative (in a chess game). ❹ (～儿) room for manoeuvre; way of escape: 订合同之前，他早已留了～。He had left himself a way out before signing the contract.

后首　hòushǒu　〈方言〉❶ afterwards; later: 我当时没听懂他的意思，～一想才明白了。I didn't get his message at first, but I figured it out later. ❷ behind: 院子的～是条小胡同。Behind the courtyard is a small lane.

后熟　hòushú　afterripening: 青色香蕉不经～不好吃。Green bananas do not taste good without afterripening.

后熟期　hòushúqī　〈农业〉afterripening period

后熟作用　hòushú zuòyòng　〈农业〉afterripening

后嗣　hòusì　descendant; offspring; posterity

后台　hòutái　❶ backstage: 他在～管理道具。He worked backstage

as a property man (*or* master). ❷ backstage supporter; behind-the-scenes backer; patron:我知道他的～硬，要不他不会这么嚣张。I know he had very strong backing (*or* powerful patrons), or he wouldn't have been so high-and-mighty.
后台老板 hòutái lǎobǎn backstage boss; behind-the-scenes backer; wire puller:我不管你的～是谁，这事说不行就是不行！I don't care who is your patron. When I say "no", I mean "no".
后唐 Hòu Táng Later Tang Dynasty (923-936), one of the Five Dynasties
后膛枪 hòutángqiāng breechloader
后膛装填 hòutáng zhuāngtián 〈军事〉breech loading
后天 hòutiān ❶ day after tomorrow:大～是中秋节。We shall celebrate the Moon Festival three days from today. /～晚上七点半，我们火车站见。We'll meet at the railway station at 7:30 p.m. the day after tomorrow. ❷ nurtured; postnatal; acquired:敏捷的头脑有天生的成分，更有～造就的成分。A quick mind is the result of nurture as well as nature.
后天免疫 hòutiān miǎnyì 〈医学〉acquired immunity
后头 hòutou ❶ at the back; in the rear; behind ❷ afterwards; later; then:她先是对我冷淡，～干脆不理我了。She began by giving me the cold shoulder and then, simply cut me dead.
后图 hòutú 〈书面〉plans for the future; future plans
后土 hòutǔ 〈旧语〉(god of) earth:皇天～ heaven and earth
后腿 hòutuǐ hind leg
后退 hòutuì draw or fall back; retreat; back away:光能前进，不能～ can only advance, not retreat /在困难面前～ shrink from difficulties /敌军全面～。The enemy fell back in full retreat. /你现在想～已经太晚了。It is already too late for you to backpedal.
后卫 hòuwèi ❶〈军事〉rear guard:～战斗 rearguard action /～阵地 position of the rear guard; rear-guard position ❷ (in soccer) full back:左～ left back ❸ (in basketball) guard
后现代主义 hòuxiàndàizhǔyì 〈文学〉postmodernism:～诗歌 postmodernistic poetry
后项 hòuxiàng 〈数学〉consequent
后效 hòuxiào aftereffect; future conduct or behaviour:保留学籍，以观～ keep a student on the school roll and see how he behaves in the future
后卸车 hòuxièchē 〈机械〉rear-dump truck or wagon
后心 hòuxīn upper back; centre of one's back; metathorax; metastethidium
后行 hòuxíng then; later; afterwards, etc.:先行减息，～分配土地。Reduction of rent and interest first, and distribution of land second. /上半年先办好这几件事，其他事可～。Let's get these few things done in the first half of the year. The rest will be dealt with later.
后序 hòuxù epilogue
后续 hòuxù ❶ follow up:～会议 follow-up meeting /～成本 after-cost /～部队很快到达了无名高地。In no time the follow-up units had reached the unnamed hill. ❷〈方言〉remarry:去年，他又～了一位夫人。He remarried last year.
后学 hòuxué young scholar; junior student:以劝～ give advice and encouragement to junior scholars
后牙 hòuyá backtooth; molar tooth
后言不接前语 hòuyán bù jiē qiányǔ speaking incoherently; disjointed speech
后仰壳 hòuyǎngké 〈方言〉fall flat on one's back
后腰 hòuyāo small of the back
后遗症 hòuyízhèng ❶〈医学〉sequelae:小儿麻痹～ sequelae of infantile paralysis ❷ after-effect; residual effect; hangover:政治运动的～ after-effects of political movements
后尾儿 hòuyǐr end; rear:船～ stern /排在～ stand at the end of a queue; be at the bottom of a list /他走得慢，落在～了。He fell behind, for he walked at a leisurely pace. /故事的～倒也圆满。The story has a happy ending.
后裔 hòuyì descendant; offspring; posterity:孔子～ descendant of Confucius /男性～ male posterity /名垂～。He will live forever in the hearts of his descendents. *or* His name will go down to posterity.
后印象主义 hòuyìnxiàngzhǔyì postimpressionism
后影 hòuyǐng shape (of a person or thing) as seen from behind; outline of sb.'s back:看～，她好像是玛丽。Viewed from behind, she seemed to be Mary.
后元音 hòuyuányīn 〈语言〉back vowel
后圆线虫 hòuyuánxiànchóng lungworm
后援 hòuyuán reinforcements; backup force; backing:～机构 backup institution; sponsor (institution) /～迟迟不到，形势万分危急。The situation was critical, as reinforcements were slow to come.
后援会 hòuyuánhuì backup institution; (of a sports team) fans' club:上海队～ fans' club for the Shanghai (soccer) team
后院 hòuyuàn ❶ backyard:他早已搬进～。He moved into the backyard long ago. ❷ rear; home:～起火，他心绪不宁。He is upset about (*or* because of) the trouble at home.
后账 hòuzhàng ❶ private accounts ❷ account to be settled later; outstanding score:这件事办得公正妥帖，不怕别人算～。We are fair and square in handling the case, so we don't worry about any later examination.
后罩房 hòuzhàofáng 〈方言〉rear rooms (behind the main rooms in a quadrangle)
后者 hòuzhě the latter:两者中～比前者好得多。Of the two, the latter is far better than the former.
后肢 hòuzhī 〈动物〉hind leg; posterior limb
后置 hòuzhì postposition:～定语 postpositive attributive /～放大器 post amplifier
后周 Hòu Zhōu Later Zhou Dynasty (951-960), one of the Five Dynasties
后轴 hòuzhóu rear axle; aft shaft; backshaft; rearmost axle:～驱动 rear-axle drive
后肘子 hòuzhǒuzi hind shank
后主 hòuzhǔ 〈古语〉last king or emperor of a dynasty
后装载机 hòuzhuāngzàijī 〈机械〉rearloader
后缀 hòuzhuì 〈语言〉suffix; postfix:～表示法 suffix notation; postfix notation
后奏曲 hòuzòuqǔ postlude
后足 hòuzú metapedes; metapodium; pleopod
后坐 hòuzuò 〈军事〉recoil:～指标 recoil indicator
后坐力 hòuzuòlì 〈军事〉recoil; backblow; backlash:无～炮 recoilless gun
后座 hòuzuò backseat; backstand
后座议员 hòuzuò yìyuán backbencher:～席 back benches (in a parliament)

逅

hòu see "邂逅" xièhòu

垕

hòu see "厚❶-❽" hòu

鲎[1] (鱟)

hòu 〈动物〉king or horseshoe crab

鲎[2] (鱟)

hòu 〈方言〉rainbow
鲎虫 hòuchóng *also* "水鳖子" shuǐbiēzi 〈动物〉apus; tadpole shrimp; apodal fetus

hū

糊

hū plaster:用灰～墙 plaster a wall /给院墙再～一层泥。Spread another layer of mud on the yard's walls.
see also hú; hù

屳[1] (膴)

hū 〈方言〉cover:这波斯猫的长毛快把眼睛都～住了。The eyes of the Persian cat are almost covered by its long hair. /雨后杂草长得快，把小苗都～住了。The weed grew so fast after the rain that it had almost choked the seedlings.

屳[2] (膴)

hū 〈书面〉❶ large; spacious ❷ be supercilious; cold-shoulder:～而无礼 arrogant and rude

乎[1]

hū 〈书面〉〈助词〉❶ *used in a question, functioning as* 吗:王侯将相宁有种～? Are kings and generals born to be what they are? /汝知此事～? Are you aware of the matter? /一之为甚，其可再～? Once is more than enough, how can you do it again? ❷ *used in a selective question, functioning as* 呢:然～，否～? Is it right or not? ❸ *used to express supposition, functioning as* 吧:其

是之谓～? Is this what it is about, more or less? /成败兴亡之机,其在斯～? Success or failure, rise or fall, probably depends on this.

乎[2] hū ❶ *used after a verb, functioning as* 于:出～意料 exceed one's expectations; be beyound one's expectations /忘～所以 be carried away (by sth.) /吾又何怨～今之人? Why should I blame people of today? ❷ *used after an adjective or adverb for rhythm's sake*:迥～不同 completely different /郁郁～ lush; luxuriant /断～不可 out of the question; absolutely impossible

乎[3] hū 〈书面〉〈叹词〉(same as 啊) O; oh; alas:天～! My God!; My Lord!; Good Heavens!

烀 hū stew in shallow water:～白薯 stew sweet potatoes

滹 hū

滹沱 Hūtuó name of a river in Hebei Province

嘑 hū 〈书面〉 see "呼" hū

呼[1] hū ❶ breathe out; exhale:～吸 breathe /长长地～了一口气 exhale a long breath ❷ shout; cry out:～口号 shout slogans /大声疾～ shout at the top of one's voice; cry in the highest pitch /～爹叫娘 cry "mamma" in distress /欢～ shout with joy; cheer; hail ❸ call:千～万唤 call repeatedly /一～百诺 hundreds respond to a single call /直～其名 address sb. by name (as a sign of familiarity or disrespect) /他一下火车就～他妻子。He paged his wife (*or* called her on the beeper) as soon as he got off the train. ❹ (Hū) a surname

呼[2] hū 〈象声〉:～～地直喘气 panting; short of breath /～～大睡 snore loudly in one's sleep; snore away /大北风～～地吹。A cold northerly was howling.

呼哱哱 hūbōbō 〈动物〉 hoopoe

呼哧 hūchī *also* "呼蚩" 〈象声〉 puffing:～～直喘粗气 puff and blow /许多老人一到冬天就～带喘的。Many old people pant and breathe hard in winter. /风箱～～地响着。The bellows were wheezing.

呼叱 hūchì *also* "呼斥" shout at; berate; excoriate; scold

呼嗒 hūda see "忽搭" hūda

呼风唤雨 hūfēng-huànyǔ ❶ bid wind and rain to come; summon wind and rain — control the forces of nature; exercise magic powers:那妖怪来无影,去无踪,～,本事了得。The monster is really powerful. It comes and goes without trace, summoning wind and rain as it likes. ❷ stir up trouble:你不要小看了这个女人。她一旦得势就能～,干出些难以预料的事来。Don't you underestimate this woman. Once in power she will make trouble and you don't know what will come next.

呼庚呼癸 hūgēng-hūguǐ *also* "庚癸之呼" gēngguǐzhīhū beg for financial help; ask for a loan:军中粮草尚无～之需。There is no shortage of provisions for the army yet.

呼喊 hūhǎn call out; shout:大声～ raise a cry; cry out /高兴得～起来 exclaim with delight

呼号 hūháo wail; cry out in distress:仰天～,悲痛欲绝 lament to heaven and wail with deep sorrow /青年学生奔走～,力图挽救国家危亡。The young students went around campaigning to save the country from subjugation.

呼号 hūhào ❶ 〈通信〉 call sign; call letters:～分配 assignment of call signs ❷ catchword (of an organization); motto; slogan:少先队的～是:"准备着,为共产主义事业而奋斗!" The Young Pioneer's motto is: "Be prepared and struggle for the cause of communism."

呼号机 hūhàojī call signal apparatus

呼号指令 hūhào zhǐlìng calling order

呼和浩特 Hūhéhàotè Huhhot or Huhehot, capital of the Inner Mongolia Autonomous Region

呼喝 hūhè shout; bawl; berate; excoriate:～威胁 shout threateningly at sb. /别这样穷～,我没聋! Don't bawl at me like that. I am not deaf.

呼吼 hūhǒu scream; roar; howl:北风～。The north wind was howling (*or* wailing). /猛虎～。A fierce tiger was roaring.

呼唤 hūhuàn ❶ call:美好的未来正在～青年一代。A bright tomorrow is calling the young people. /听从人民的～,全力报效国家。Answer the call (*or* summons) of the people and serve the country heart and soul. ❷ shout; call out:大声～ call out loudly /她觉得有人在～她。She could hear someone calling out her name.

呼唤系统 hūhuàn xìtǒng 〈通信〉 paging system

呼饥号寒 hūjī-háohán *also* "啼饥号寒" tíjī-háohán cry for lack of food and clothing; be in abject poverty

呼机 hūjī *also* "呼叫机"; "寻呼机" xúnhūjī pager; beeper

呼叫 hūjiào ❶ 〈通信〉 call; ring:～信号 calling signal /～局 calling station /～声 ring tone /～灯 calling lamp /～表 calling list /船长,总部在～我们。Captain, the headquarters is calling us. ❷ call out; shout:他拼命挣扎,大声～。He struggled desperately, calling out for help.

呼叫等待 hūjiào děngdài 〈通信〉 call waiting

呼叫接通信号 hūjiào jiētōng xìnhào 〈通信〉 call-connected signal

呼叫率 hūjiàolǜ 〈通信〉 calling rate

呼叫转移 hūjiào zhuǎnyí 〈通信〉 call forwarding

呼叫装置 hūjiào zhuāngzhì 〈通信〉 calling device

呼救 hūjiù call or cry for help; send out GMDSS signals:我听见有个女人在～。I heard a woman crying out for help. /失事的船在～。A wrecked ship is sending out GMDSS signals.

呼救信号 hūjiù xìnhào distress signal; signal for help; GMDSS (formerly SOS):～频率 distress frequency

呼拉圈 hūlāquān hula hoop

呼拉舞 hūlāwǔ *also* "草裙舞" cǎoqúnwǔ hula; hula-hula

呼啦 hūlā *also* "呼喇"; "呼啦啦" 〈象声〉:旗子在大风中～～直响。The flags are flapping in the wind. /他一梭子打过去,敌人～倒下一大片。He fired a clip of bullets at the enemy and felled them in large numbers.

呼喇 hūlā see "呼啦"

呼来挥去 hūlái-huīqù order or boss around; have at one's beck and call:干吗～的总想使唤别人? Why are you always in the habit of ordering people about?

呼噜 hūlū 〈象声〉 wheeze:爷爷一犯气喘病,喉咙里老是～直响。Grandpa becomes wheezy each time he has an attack of asthma.

呼噜 hūlu 〈口语〉 snore:打～ snore /～声 snoring; snore

呼伦贝尔草原 Hūlúnbèi'ěr cǎoyuán Hulun Buir grassland (in northeastern Inner Mongolia)

呼牛呼马 hūniú-hūmǎ call me a bull, I am a bull; call me a horse, I am a horse — be indifferent to people's praise or blame:几十年来,李先生任人～,一心只在学术研究上下功夫。For decades, Mr. Li has immersed himself in academic research, paying no attention to people's praise or blame.

呼朋引类 hūpéng-yǐnlèi *also* "引类呼朋" gang up with people of the same stripe; summon one's pals and followers:～,合伙结帮 gather one's cronies around one to form a gang

呼扇 hūshan *also* "唿扇" hūshan ❶ (of a flat or thin object) shake; quiver; tremble:我想给棚子换个硬顶,这个软顶一遇风就直～。I want to build a hard roof for the shed. The soft one flaps too much in the wind. ❷ fan (with a thin or flat object):他跑得满头大汗,摘下草帽不停地～。Sweating all over from running, he took off his straw-hat to fan himself continuously.

呼哨 hūshào *also* "唿哨" hūshào whistle:打～ give a whistle /只听见一声～,苇丛中荡出一只小船来。With a whistle, a boat emerged from behind the reeds.

呼声 hūshēng ❶ cry; voice:良心的～ voice of conscience /撕心裂肺的～ heart-breaking cry /在这次选举中谁的～最高? Who is likely to win most votes in the election? ❷ voice of the people; *vox populi*:群众的正义～ just demand of the masses /倾听人民的～ listen to the voice of the people

呼天抢地 hūtiān-qiāngdì lament to heaven and knock one's head on earth; utter cries of anguish:她看见儿子的尸首时,～,痛不欲生。On seeing the dead body of her son, she cried her eyes out, wishing herself dead as well.

呼图克图 hūtúkètú 〈宗教〉(in the Qing Dynasty) title given to a Living Buddha

呼吸 hūxī ❶ breathe; respire:屏住～ hold one's breath /口对口～ mouth-to-mouth respiration /人工～ artificial respiration /早晨～新鲜空气 breathe in fresh air in the morning /病人～急促,病情有变。The patient's condition was worsening as he became short of breath. ❷ 〈书面〉 single breath — an instant; moment:成败就在～之间。Success or failure hinges on a single moment.

H

呼吸瓣 hūxībàn breathing valve
呼吸道 hūxīdào 〈生理〉respiratory tract
呼吸分析器 hūxī fēnxīqì breathalyser (for measuring the alcoholic content of one's breath)
呼吸急促 hūxī jícù tachypnea
呼吸计 hūxījì respirometer
呼吸痉挛 hūxī jìngluán respiratory spasm
呼吸困难 hūxī kùnnan (respiratory) dyspnea; difficult breathing: ～综合征 respiratory depress syndrome
呼吸疗法 hūxī liáofǎ respiratory therapy
呼吸率 hūxīlǜ respiratory rate
呼吸麻痹 hūxī mábì respiratory paralysis
呼吸器 hūxīqì respirator
呼吸器官 hūxī qìguān respiratory organ or apparatus
呼吸衰竭 hūxī shuāijié respiratory failure
呼吸停止 hūxī tíngzhǐ apnea; respiratory arrest
呼吸系统 hūxī xìtǒng respiratory system: ～疾病 respiratory system disease; disease of the respiratory system
呼吸相通 hūxī-xiāngtōng be of the same mind; have identical views; have common interests: ～,患难与共 share feelings and sentiments and go through thick and thin together
呼吸性碱中毒 hūxīxìng jiǎnzhòngdú respiratory alkalosis
呼吸性酸中毒 hūxīxìng suānzhòngdú respiratory acidosis
呼吸抑制中枢 hūxī yìzhì zhōngshū respiratory depress centre
呼吸障碍 hūxī zhàng'ài disorder of respiration; respiratory disorder
呼吸正常 hūxī zhèngcháng eupnea; normal breathing
呼吸中枢 hūxī zhōngshū 〈生理〉apneustic centre; respiratory centre
呼吸周期 hūxī zhōuqī respiratory cycle
呼啸 hūxiào whistle; scream; whizz: 寒风～。A cold wind was howling. /炮弹～着落下来。The shells came whistling down. /一列火车～而过。A train thundered past.
呼延 Hūyán a surname
呼幺喝六 hūyāo-hèliù *also* "喝六呼幺" ❶ play at dice; shout for the top number to come up; gamble noisily ❷〈方言〉domineering; arrogant: 小小一个村长,居然也～,神气活现。A mere village head, he swaggered and adopted an imperious bearing.
呼应 hūyìng echo; work in concert with: 群芳争艳,百鸟～。Flowers are vying for beauty; birds are singing in concert. /有人发难,有人呐喊助威,遥相～。Some started the trouble, and others echoed by shouting encouragement.
呼吁 hūyù appeal; call on: 紧急～ urgent appeal /～和平 appeal for peace /向全世界～ appeal to the whole world /～社会各界捐献 call on people from all walks of life to contribute (*or* donate)
呼吁书 hūyùshū letter of appeal; appeal
呼噪 hūzào shout noisily: 众人～向前,桥上堵得水泄不通。Crowds of people moved on noisily blocking up the bridge completely.
呼之即来,挥之即去 hū zhī jí lái, huī zhī jí qù be at sb.'s beck and call: 衙门里的听差,对老爷俯首贴耳,一个个都是～。Docile and obedient, all the runners in the *yamen* were at the beck and call of the magistrate.
呼之欲出 hūzhīyùchū (of a lifelike figure in a picture or a character in a novel) seem ready to come out at one's call; be vividly portrayed: 小说中的几个主要人物,写得活灵活现,～。The main characters in the novel are graphically portrayed and true to life.

忽[1]

hū neglect; overlook; ignore: 疏～ overlook

忽[2]

hū suddenly: ～明～暗 now bright, now dim; bright one minute and dim the next /气温～高～低。The temperature fluctuates a lot. /大风里,火光～明～暗。The fire kept flickering in the wind.

忽[3]

hū ❶ one hundred thousandth of a unit ❷ unit of length (＝0.00001 metre) ❸ unit of weight (＝0.00001 gram): 十～等于一丝。Ten *hu* makes a *si*.
忽必烈 Hūbìliè Kublai Khan (1215-1294), statesman, military strategist and first emperor of the Yuan Dynasty, who officially established the capital in Dadu (大都), today's Beijing, in 1272
忽布 hūbù *also* "啤酒花" píjiǔhuā (transliteration) hop
忽搭 hūda *also* "呼嗒" hūda flap; flutter: 门上的破席被风吹得直～。The torn mat curtain over the door flapped in the wind.
忽地 hūdì suddenly; abruptly: ～刮起了大风。Suddenly it began to blow hard. /油灯～灭了。The oil lamp went out all of a sudden.
忽而 hū'ér now..., now...: 他～皱眉,～微笑。He frowned one minute and smiled the next. /歌声～高,～低,如泣如诉,凄婉动人。Now high, now low, the singing went on as if someone was telling a touching story.
忽忽 hūhū ❶ (of time) pass quickly: 离开故乡,～又是一年了。Another year has flown by since I left my hometown. ❷ confused; dazed: ～如有所失 look perplexed and lost
忽忽不乐 hūhū-bùlè be absent-minded and depressed; look distracted and unhappy: 这几天姐姐一直神色黯然,～。My elder sister has been in low spirits these days.
忽…忽… hū…hū… now..., now...: 忽高忽低 now high, now low; fluctuate in tune /忽左忽右 now left, now right — go from one extreme to another /忽哭忽笑 cry one minute and laugh the next /生意忽好忽坏。Business fluctuates from one day to the next.
忽克 hūkè centimilligram (cmg: $\frac{1}{100,000}$ gram)
忽冷忽热 hūlěng-hūrè sometimes hot and sometimes cold; blow hot and cold; now hot, now cold: 这两天天气～,容易感冒。The weather is changeable these days. It's easy to catch cold. /他俩的关系～。Their relationship is now good, now bad. /工程～,断断续续,进展很慢。Going by fits and starts the construction has made little headway.
忽律 hūlǜ *see* "猢猡" hūlǜ
忽略 hūlüè neglect; overlook; lose sight of: ～不计 overlook; not take into account /这些问题虽小,但千万不可～。Though of minor importance, these matters should in no case be neglected.
忽米 hūmǐ centimillimetre (cmm: $\frac{1}{100,000}$ metre)
忽然 hūrán suddenly; all of a sudden: ～听到有人在外面叫他。Suddenly he heard someone calling him outside.
忽闪 hūshǎn (of a light) flash; sparkle: 闪光弹～一亮,又～一亮。The flare sent out a flash and then another flash. /流星拖着长长的尾巴,最后～一亮,消失在夜空。The meteor with its long bright streak of light flashed the last flash before it disappeared into the dark sky.
忽闪 hūshan (of eyes, etc.) flash; glitter; sparkle: 她～着又大又黑的眼睛,天真无邪地看着他。Her big black eyes sparkling, she looked at him innocently.
忽视 hūshì ignore; overlook; disregard; neglect: 渐被～ fall into neglect /一支不可～的力量 force not to be trifled with; force to be reckoned with /朋友的忠告不可～。A friend's advice must not be ignored. /即使是问题的次要方面,我们也不能～。We must by no means overlook even the secondary aspects of a problem.
忽微 hūwēi 〈书面〉tiny amount: 其量～,不足道也。Minuscule in weight, it is really insignificant.
忽悠 hūyou 〈方言〉rock; sway; flicker: 长长的扁担在他肩上直～。The long carrying-pole swayed on his shoulder. /夜色中,江面的渔火～～的。In the darkness of the night, lights flickered on the fishing boats on the river.

滹

hū
滹浴 hūyù 〈方言〉have or take a bath; bathe

惚

hū *see* "恍惚" huǎnghū

唿

hū
唿扇 hūshan *see* "呼扇" hūshan
唿哨 hūshào *see* "呼哨" hūshào

猢

hū
猢猡 hūlǜ *also* "忽律" hūlǜ crocodile; alligator

戏(戲、戱)

hū *see* "於戏" wūhū
see also xì

hú

壶(壺)

hú ❶ kettle; pot; can: 水～ kettle /茶～ teapot /

H

酒～ wine pot /油～ oil can /喷～ watering can; sprinkling can /夜～ chamber pot ❷ bottle; flask: 行军～ water bottle; canteen /暖～ thermos bottle (*or* flask) ❸ (Hú) a surname
壶腹 húfù 〈生理〉ampulla
壶口瀑布 Húkǒu Pùbù Hukou falls, well-known cataract on the Yellow River in Shanxi Province
壶穴 húxué *also* "瓯穴" ōuxué pit or hole in the rocky bottom of a waterfall, or under a whirlpool in a river

胡[1] Hú ❶ Hu, general term for non-Han nationalities living in the north and west of China in ancient times: ～人 national minorities in north and west China; northern and western minority Chinese /五～十六国〈历史〉five minority nationalities and sixteen kingdoms ❷ (hú) introduced from northern or western nationalities or from abroad: ～服 *hu* dress ❸ a surname

胡[2] hú recklessly; wantonly; outrageously: ～干 do things recklessly; go it blindly

胡[3] hú 〈书面〉why: 田园将芜, ～不归? My field and garden are lying neglected. Why not return?

胡[4]**(鬍)** hú moustache; beard; whiskers: 络腮～ whiskers; full beard /大～子 heavily-bearded /八字～子 moustache
胡编乱造 húbiān-luànzào cook up (a tale); fabricate; concoct: 纯属～。It's sheer fabrication. /干吗给我～? Why did you cook up (*or* invent) stories about me?
胡缠 húchán harass; pester; squabble endlessly (over trivialities): 一味～ keep on pestering people
胡扯 húchě ❶ talk nonsense; drivel: 莫要～! Don't you talk rubbish! ❷ chat; chitchat: 大家～了一通, 也就慢慢散去了。After shooting the bull (*or* breeze) for a while, we gradually dispersed.
胡臭 húchòu *also* "狐臭" húchòu body odour; bromhidrosis
胡床 húchuáng *also* "交椅" jiāoyǐ; "交床" jiāochuáng; "绳床" shéngchuáng a kind of folding stool
胡吹 húchuī boast outrageously; talk big: ～瞎说 talk through one's hat /他把自己的过去～了一通。He made a wild boast about his past.
胡达 Húdá Allah; Khuda (in Persia)
胡登洲 Hú Dēngzhōu Hu Dengzhou (1522-1597), Islamic scholar of the Ming Dynasty
胡蝶 húdié *see* "蝴蝶" húdié
胡豆 húdòu *also* "蚕豆" cándòu broad bean
胡匪 húfěi *also* "胡子" bandit
胡蜂 húfēng 〈动物〉wasp; hornet; vespid: ～科 *Vespidae*
胡佛 Húfó Herbert Clark Hoover (1874-1964), 31st President of the United States (1929-1933)
胡搞 húgǎo ❶ mess up; meddle with: 这孩子, 躲在厨房里～些什么? What is the child up to in the kitchen? ❷ carry on an affair with; be promiscuous: ～男女关系 be promiscuous /～女人 carry on affairs with women
胡瓜 húguā *also* "黄瓜" huángguā cucumber
胡话 húhuà ravings; wild talk: 夜里, 这孩子烧得直说～。The child was delirious from fever during the night.
胡黄连 húhuánglián 〈中药〉*also* "胡连"; "假黄连" jiǎhuánglián *radix picrorrhizae*
胡笳 hújiā 〈乐器〉reed pipe, instrument used by the northern tribes in ancient China
胡椒 hújiāo pepper: ～粉 ground pepper /白～ white pepper /黑～ black pepper
胡椒薄荷 hújiāo bòhe peppermint
胡椒鲷 hújiāodiāo 〈动物〉grunt (*Plectorhynchus cinctus*)
胡椒碱 hújiāojiǎn piperine
胡椒酸 hújiāosuān piperic acid
胡椒中毒 hújiāo zhòngdú piperism
胡搅 hújiǎo ❶ pester sb.; be mischievous: 别跟爷爷～了。Stop pestering grandpa. /这儿本来就乱, 你就别在这儿～了。It's already chaotic here. Don't you add to it. ❷ argue tediously and vexatiously; wrangle: 要讲理, 不要～。Be reasonable and don't wrangle.
胡搅蛮缠 hújiǎo-mánchán harass sb. with unreasonable demands; pester sb. endlessly; wrangle: ～是没用的。Pestering people will get you nowhere.
胡克 Húkè Robert Hooke (1635-1703), English scientist: ～定律 Hooke's law, a law of elasticity
胡来 húlái ❶ mess up; fool with: 不会修电灯, 千万别～! If you do not know how to fix an electric light, don't fool with it. ❷ run wild; make trouble; commit all kinds of outrages: 别在公众场所～。Don't behave recklessly in a public place.
胡连 húlián *see* "胡黄连"
胡芦巴 húlúbā 〈植物〉fenugreek (*Trigonella foenumgraecum*)
胡噜 húlu 〈方言〉❶ stroke; caress; rub: 他～了一下孩子的头发。He stroked (*or* caressed) the child's hair. ❷ sweep (away); scrape together: ～到一起 sweep (*or* scrape) together /地不脏, ～几下得了。As the floor is not dirty, a couple of sweeps will do. /她这么三下两下一～, 事儿就干完了。With a couple of quick and neat motions, she got things done in a jiffy. ❸ manage; cope with; deal with: 这么多事, 他一个人怕～不过来。He alone may not be able to cope with so much work.
胡乱 húluàn ❶ carelessly; casually; perfunctorily: 他～擦了一把脸就上床了。He gave his face a careless rub with a towel and went to bed. /他～扒拉了几口饭, 又出去了。He ate a hasty meal (*or* grabbed a quick bite) and went out again. ❷ at will; at random; groundlessly; unreasonably: 此事重要, 不能～作出决定! This is very important, and no decision should be made offhandedly. /咱们不了解内情, 最好别～猜测。We'd better not make any wild guesses since we are not in the know.
胡抡 húlūn 〈方言〉act recklessly; do rashly; be foolhardy: 办事要考虑好了, ～可不行。Think things over and do not act recklessly.
胡萝卜 húluóbo carrot: "～加大棒"政策 carrot and stick policy
胡萝卜素 húluóbosù *also* "叶红素" yèhóngsù 〈生化〉carotene; beta-carotene
胡麻 húmá flax: ～籽 flaxseed; linseed
胡闹 húnào act wildly; make trouble; do mischief: 你们就知道～! All you know is to get up to mischief all the time. /不要为一丁点儿小事去～。Don't kick up a row about such trifles. /叫孩子们别～了。Tell the children to calm down.
胡吣 húqìn 〈口语〉speak groundlessly or unreasonably; talk nonsense or rubbish: 别听这小子～! Don't pay any heed to the guy's nonsense!
胡琴 húqin 〈乐器〉*huqin*, two-stringed bowed instrument (including *erhu* 二胡, *jinghu* 京胡, etc.)
胡人 húrén member of a northern tribe in ancient China
胡哨 húshào whistle
胡说 húshuō talk nonsense; drivel: 信口～ talk nonsense /他～些什么? What was he drivelling about? /我才不信你这些～。Don't expect me to believe your absurd stories.
胡说八道 húshuō-bādào *also* "胡说白道"; "胡说乱道" talk nonsense; twaddle: 别～! Don't talk rot! /让你的～见鬼去吧! Away with your baloney! /你满嘴～什么? What is all this rubbish you're giving us?
胡思乱想 húsī-luànxiǎng imagine things; go off into wild flights of fancy; let one's imagination run away with one: 他开始～起来。He began to indulge in wild fancies. /不要～, 只顾放心去。Don't imagine things. Just go and stop worrying. /她坐在院子里又～起来。Sitting in the garden, she was sunk in reverie.
胡荽 húsui 〈植物〉coriander
胡桃 hútáo walnut: ～壳 walnut shell /～木 walnut
胡桐 hútóng 〈植物〉poon; poon tree: ～木 poon
胡同 hútong lane; alley
胡图人 Hútúrén Hutu, ethnic community in Rwanda and Burundi
胡涂 hútu *also* "糊涂" hútu confused; muddle-headed; stupid: ～官判～案。A muddle-headed judge passed a silly verdict.
胡颓子 hútuízǐ *also* "沙枣" shāzǎo 〈植物〉thorny elaeagnus (*Elaeagnus pungens*)
胡须 húxū beard and moustache; beard; moustache
胡言 húyán nonsense; ravings; wild talk: 一派～ arrant nonsense; pack of lies /满口～ full of idiotic drivel
胡言乱语 húyán-luànyǔ talk nonsense; rave: 她常常在梦中～。She often babbles in her dreams. /我不要听你这～! None of your rubbish! /不要～。Don't shoot off your mouth. /她有时～, 人家听不懂。She sometimes raved unintelligible gibberish.
胡杨 húyáng 〈植物〉diversiform-leaved poplar (*Populus euphratica*)

胡支 húzhī 〈口语〉❶ give irresponsible directions or advice; misguide:你可别~我,让我走冤枉路。Don't show me the wrong way. ❷ prevaricate; equivocate:问他在这儿干什么,这家伙跟我~。When I asked the guy what he was up to here, he quibbled.

胡枝子 húzhīzǐ 〈植物〉shrub lespedeza (*Lespedeza bicolor*)

胡志明 Húzhìmíng Ho Chi Minh (1890-1969), leader of the Communist Party of Viet Nam

胡志明市 Húzhìmíngshì Ho Chi Minh City, major city in southern Viet Nam, formerly known as Saigon (西贡)

胡诌 húzhōu fabricate (wild tales); cook up:你瞧你都~了些什么! Gee, what a wild yarn you have spun! /你明明来晚了,又何必~一大堆理由呢? You've come late. Why cook up so many excuses?

胡诌乱道 húzhōu-luàndào *also*"胡诌乱扯" fabricate wild tales; cook up stories:他回家时已是后半夜,只好对妻子~了一通。He came back home after midnight and had to tell his wife some cock-and-bull story.

胡子 húzi ❶ beard; moustache; whiskers:白~老头 white-bearded old man ❷ 〈方言〉*see*"胡匪"

胡子工程 húzi gōngchéng project that drags on for years; unduly long project

胡子拉碴 húzilāchā stubbly beard; bristly unshaven chin:看你~的,还不刮刮脸! Look at that stubbly beard of yours. You need (to have) a shave right now!

胡子鲇 húzinián *also*"塘虱"tángshī 〈动物〉*Clarias fuscus*, a kind of catfish

胡子蛙 húziwā *also*"髭蟾"zīchán 〈动物〉*Vibrissaphora boringii*

胡走游飞 húzǒu-yóufēi loaf about; wander around:他整天~,不着家。He dilly-dallies all day long without returning home.

胡作非为 húzuò-fēiwéi act wildly in defiance of the law or public opinion; commit all kinds of outrages; run amuck:他因~而被捕入狱。He was arrested and put behind bars for his evil deeds.

湖 hú ❶ lake:~水 lake water /咸水~ saltwater lake /淡水~ freshwater lake /西~ West Lake /~上人家 lake-dwellers /~上泛舟 boating on the lake /~光岚影 shimmering light of the lake and hazy atmosphere of the mountain ❷ (Hú) (short for 湖州) Huzhou (now Wuxing 吴兴, Zhejiang Province) ❸ (Hú) Hunan or Hubei:两~ Hunan and Hubei

湖北 Húběi Hubei (Province)

湖笔 húbǐ writing brush produced in Huzhou, Zhejiang Province; Huzhou brush

湖滨 húbīn lakeside:~新建了一幢楼房。A new building has been put up at the lakeside (*or* on the lake).

湖吃海喝 húchī-hǎihē indulge in extravagant eating and drinking:非~办不成事么? Is wining and dining the only way to get things done?

湖荡 húdàng lake:~地区 lake area /~里盛产鱼虾。Fish and shrimp abound in the lake.

湖光山色 húguāng-shānsè landscape of lakes and mountains; natural beauty:~,交相辉映。The lake and hills add radiance and beauty to each other.

湖广 Húguǎng Hunan and Hubei as one province during the Ming Dynasty; Hunan, Hubei, Guangdong and Guangxi as one province during the Yuan Dynasty:~总督 governor-general of Hunan and Hubei /~熟,天下足。When crops are good in Hunan and Hubei, the whole country will not be short of grain.

湖积平原 hújī píngyuán lacustrine plain

湖剧 hújù Wuxing opera popular in Zhejiang Province

湖蓝 húlán bright blue; light blue:~色的轿车 bright blue car

湖绿 húlǜ light green:~的绸子 light green silk

湖南 Húnán Hunan (Province)

湖盆 húpén lake basin

湖泊 húpō lake:~地貌 lake geomorphy /~地区 lakeland /~水资源 water resources in lakes /~污染 lake pollution /~养鱼 fish culture in lake /~渔业 lake fishery /~运输 lake transport /~志 record of a lake /~效应 lake effect

湖区 húqū lake region or district

湖色 húsè light green:她身穿~裙子,更显得淡雅不俗。She looked specially graceful in a light green skirt.

湖石 húshí (short for 太湖石) stone from the Taihu Lake; Taihu stone, famous for its cavities and unique shape, and good for rockery in landscaping

湖滩 hútān lake beach; lake shoal

湖田 hútián land reclaimed from a lake; shoaly land

湖蛙 húwā marsh frog (*Rana ridibunda*)

湖心亭 húxīntíng pavilion in the middle of a lake; mid-lake pavilion

湖鸭 húyā duck (raised in a lake)

湖盐 húyán lake salt

湖羊 húyáng 〈动物〉*Huyang*, a breed of fine wool sheep raised in Zhejiang Province

湖泽 húzé lakes and marshes:江河~ rivers, lakes and marshes /~地区 marshy land

湖沼 húzhǎo lakes and marshes

湖沼浮游生物 húzhǎo fúyóu shēngwù eulimnoplankton

湖沼学 húzhǎoxué limnology

湖沼植物 húzhǎo zhíwù lacustrine plants

湖震 húzhèn *also*"湖啸"〈地质〉seiche

湖绉 húzhòu 〈纺织〉crepe silk produced in Huzhou (now Wuxing), Zhejiang Province; Huzhou crepe silk

糊[1] hú stick (paper, cloth, etc.) with paste; paste:~墙 paste paper on a wall; paper a wall:~窗户 paste a sheet of paper over a lattice window; seal the cracks around a window with paper /~风筝 make a kite

糊[2] hú *see*"煳" hú

糊[3] hú *see*"餬" hú

see also hū; hù

糊粉 húfěn 〈生化〉aleurone

糊糊 húhu 〈方言〉❶ gruel made of ground maize, flour, etc.; mush:稀~ thin gruel; mush /棒子~ cornmeal gruel; mush ❷ disturbance; trouble; disorder:再这样乱折腾,是要闹出~来的。If we continue to act as everybody pleases, we'll end up in trouble.

糊精 hújīng 〈生化〉dextrin; starch gum:~酶 dextrinase

糊口 húkǒu *also*"餬口"húkǒu keep body and soul together; eke out a living:养家~ support (*or* maintain) one's family; provide for one's family /以种菜~ eke out a living by growing vegetables /那几年家里穷,勉强能~。My family was poor in those years and was barely able to keep body and soul together.

糊里糊涂 húlihútū muddle-headed; mixed up; foolish; confused:~地犯了错误 make a mistake with one's mind in a haze; commit an error without knowing how

糊料 húliào thickener

糊墙纸 húqiángzhǐ wall paper

糊涂 hútu *also*"胡涂"hútu ❶ muddled; confused; bewildered:~人 muddled person; muddle-head /装~ pretend not to know; feign ignorance /聪明一世,~一时。Every man has a fool in his sleeve. /你越说我越~。The more you spoke, the more confused I became. ❷ confusion:一塌~ utter confusion ❸ 〈方言〉blurred; indistinct; dim; vague:天已黄昏,远处的村落看起来~不清。In the dim light of dusk, the village looked blurred in the distance.

糊涂虫 hútuchóng *also*"糊涂蛋";"糊涂鬼" blunderer; bungler; idiot; blockhead:你这个~,竟然把这么一件重要的事情忘了! How could you forget such an important thing, you dolt!

糊涂账 hútuzhàng chaotic accounts; mess:全是一笔~。A total mess. *or* Everything is in disorder.

糊嘴 húzuǐ *also*"糊口" eke out a living; make both ends meet

煳 hú burnt:饼烙~了。The pancake is burnt. /别把鞋子烤~了! Don't scorch the shoes.

瑚 hú *see*"珊瑚" shānhú

葫 hú

葫芦 húlu bottle gourd; calabash:酒~ wine calabash /油~ oil gourd /也不知道他~里卖的是什么药。I don't know what he has got up his sleeve.

葫芦科植物 húlukē zhíwù cucurbit

葫芦瓢 húlupiáo gourd ladle

葫芦提 húlutí *also*"葫芦蹄";"葫芦题" muddled; confused:那老家

H

伙被我～瞒过了。I pull the wool over that old man's eyes.
葫蔓藤 húmànténg *also*“钩吻”gōuwěn;“断肠草”duànchángcǎo 〈植物〉elegant jessamine (*Gelsemium elegans*)
葫蒜 húsuàn 〈植物〉rocambole (*Allium scorodoprasum*)

醐
hú *see*“醍醐”tíhú

蝴
hú
蝴蝶 húdié *also*“胡蝶”húdié butterfly
蝴蝶阀 húdiéfá 〈水利〉butterfly valve
蝴蝶果 húdiéguǒ 〈植物〉*Cleidiocarpon cavaleriei*
蝴蝶花 húdiéhuā ❶〈植物〉fringed iris ❷ bow tie ❸ butterfly loop (as a decoration, etc.):把丝带打成一个～ tie a silk ribbon into a butterfly loop
蝴蝶结 húdiéjié bow; bow-tie:把鞋带打成～ tie one's shoelaces in a bow /小姑娘头上扎了一个～。The little girl wore a bow on her head. /他穿黑西装,打黑～,显得有些拘谨。A black suit and a black bow-tie made him look a bit reserved.
蝴蝶树 húdiéshù *Tarrietia parvifolia*
蝴蝶瓦 húdiéwǎ small green tile
蝴蝶鱼 húdiéyú butterfly fish
蝴蝶装 húdiézhuāng butterfly binding, a Chinese form of book-binding in which two pages are printed on one sheet that is folded to form the verso and recto sides of uncut pages

衚
hú
衚衕 hútong *see*“胡同”hútong

鹕
hú *see*“鹈鹕”tíhú

猢
hú
猢狲 húsūn a variety of macaque; monkey:树倒～散。When the tree falls, the monkeys scatter — when the boss falls from power, his lackeys disperse.
猢狲人布袋 húsūn rù bùdài *also*“猢狲入袋”the monkey goes into the bag — lose one's freedom:编修辞书是苦差事,主编常以“～”自嘲。It's hard work editing and revising a dictionary. The chief editor often derides himself as a monkey in a bag.

餬
hú gruel; porridge; congee:玉米～ maize gruel; mush /小米～ millet gruel
餬口 húkǒu *also*“糊口”húkǒu keep body and soul together; eke out a living; keep the pot boiling:靠摆小摊儿～ set up a stall for one's keep /父亲终年劳累,仅得～。Father worked all the year round and was barely able to support the family.

核
hú *same as*“核❶”hé, *used in certain colloquial collocations*
see also hé
核儿 húr 〈口语〉❶ stone; pit; core:樱桃～ cherry stone /李～ plum stone /桃～ peach stone /杏～ apricot stone /梨～ pear core /苹果～ core of an apple ❷ sth. resembling a fruit stone:煤～ partly burnt coals (*or* briquettes); cinders /冰～ ice nucleus

搰
hú 〈书面〉❶ dig ❷ stir up; make muddy

鹘
hú *also*“隼”sǔn falcon
鹘突 hútu muddled; confused; bewildered:～梦 confused dream /～尚书 muddle-headed minister

囫
hú
囫囵 húlún whole:～而食 gobble up whole; swallow whole /～尸首 complete corpse
囫囵吞枣 húlún-tūnzǎo swallow a date whole — gulp down without chewing; lap up information without digesting it; read hastily without thinking:学习要反复思考,不能～。One must mull over what one has learned, and not take it in without discrimination.
囫囵个儿 húlungèr 〈方言〉❶ whole; complete:由于家里穷,他小时候没穿过一件～的衣裳。A child from a poor family, he never wore a single complete piece of clothing. ❷ sleep without undressing; sleep in one's clothes:他累极了,刚往床上一歪,就～睡着了。He was so tired that he fell asleep in his clothes as soon as he lay down in bed.
囫囵觉 húlunjiào sound sleep without interruption; sleep like a log; sleep like a top:她每天夜里起来给孩子喂奶,换尿布,没睡过一个～。She never had a whole night's sleep for she had to get up at midnight to breastfeed her baby and change the nappies (*or* diapers).

鹄
hú swan:鸿～ swans and wild geese
see also gǔ
鹄发 húfà white or grey hair:～童颜 (with) hoary hair and a boy's countenance — hale and hearty
鹄候 húhòu 〈书面〉await respectfully; expect:～回音。I am humbly looking forward to your reply. /她每天都倚窗～,盼望丈夫归来。She leaned by the window everyday, awaiting her husband's return.
鹄立 húlì 〈书面〉stand straight up:～瞻望 standing upright and looking into the distance
鹄面菜色 húmiàn-càisè be haggard and pale; look emaciated and famished
鹄面鸟形 húmiàn-niǎoxíng thin, pale and famished:贫病交加,他变得～,简直不像人样儿了。Pale and haggard from poverty and sickness he was just a skeleton.
鹄望 húwàng 〈书面〉eagerly look forward to:延颈～ crane one's neck and look with eager expectation
鹄形鸠面 húxíng-jiūmiàn *also*“鸠形鹄面”thin and gaunt; haggard and emaciated; sickly looking

和
hú win in a game of mah-jong or cards
see also hé; hè; huó; huò

狐
hú ❶ fox:草～ female fox /赤～ red fox /银～ silver fox ❷ (Hú) a surname
狐步舞 húbùwǔ foxtrot:他们在跳～。They are dancing a foxtrot.
狐臭 húchòu *also*“狐臊”;“胡臭”húchòu body odour; bromhidrosis
狐蝠 húfú fox bat:～式战斗机 Foxbat jet fighter
狐猴 húhóu lemur
狐假虎威 hújiǎ-hǔwēi the fox borrows the tiger's ferocity (by walking in the latter's company) — bully people by virtue of sb. else's influence; flaunt one's powerful connections; swagger about in borrowed plumes:他靠着他爹的势力,～,无恶不作。Taking advantage of his father's influence he stopped at nothing in doing evil.
狐狸 húli fox
狐狸狗 húligǒu fox dog; spitz; spitzdog
狐狸精 húlijīng fox spirit — seductive woman; woman of easy virtue; vamp
狐狸尾巴 húli wěiba fox's tail — sth. that gives away a person's real character or evil intentions; cloven hoof:～总是要露出来的。A fox cannot hide its tail. *or* The devil cannot hide his cloven hoof. /在众目睽睽之下,这个狡猾的老家伙终于露出了～。The sly old fox eventually revealed his true colours in public.
狐埋狐搰 húmái-húhú the fox buries it and the fox digs it up — be too suspicious and indecisive to achieve anything
狐媚 húmèi bewitch by coquettish cajolery; entice by flirtatious charm:～惑主 entice one's master by coquettish charms
狐媚子 húmèizǐ seductive woman; coquette; vamp
狐朋狗友 húpéng-gǒuyǒu evil associates; dissolute company; pack of rogues; gang of scoundrels:他在外面结交了一帮～。He ganged up with a bunch of ruffians.
狐潜鼠伏 húqián-shǔfú *also*“狐凭鼠伏”lie low; be in hiding:匪徒白天在草丛中～,不敢露面。During the day the bandits hid in the thicket, not daring to make their appearance.
狐肷 húqiǎn skin of a fox's chest, belly and armpits
狐裘 húqiú fox-fur robe
狐裘羔袖 húqiú-gāoxiù fox-fur coat with lamb's-wool sleeves — it is good on the whole but still leaves sth. to be desired:他办事还算妥当,虽然有时略有～之憾。On the whole he can handle things quite well, although sometimes he is not entirely free of blemishes.
狐犬 húquǎn fox dog
狐群狗党 húqún-gǒudǎng *also*“狐朋狗党”pack of rogues; bad lot; gang of scoundrels:那些人不过是～而已。Those people are just a

pack of rogues after all.
狐臊 húsāo body odour; bromhidrosis
狐死首丘 húsǐ-shǒuqiū when a fox dies, it lies with its head towards the hillock where it was born — yearn for one's native place; cherish tender sentiments for one's birthplace
狐死兔泣 húsǐ-tùqì when the fox dies, the hare cries (for its kind):～,李氏灭,夏氏宁独存? The hare mourns the death of the fox. If the Li's are ruined, can the Xia's survive alone?
see also "兔死狐悲" tùsǐ-húbēi
狐兔之悲 hútùzhībēi strong feeling of fellowship; sympathy for someone like oneself
狐尾草 húwěicǎo foxtail
狐仙 húxiān fairy fox; fox immortal (the superstitious belief that the fox can assume the human form and behave as a human after long years of Taoist worship)
狐疑 húyí doubt; suspicion:心中不免～ can not but feel suspicious / 听了这一番话,他不禁满腹～。He couldn't help having misgivings at hearing these remarks.
狐疑不决 húyí-bùjué wavering and unable to decide; indecisive; suspicious and hesitating:此事令我～。This matter made me hesitant.
狐鼬 húyòu 〈动物〉tayra; taira

弧

hú ❶〈数学〉arc ❷ bow (in ancient times):弦木为～ make a bow by stretching a string on a tree branch
弧度 húdù *also* "弪" jìng ❶〈数学〉radian ❷ circular measure; radian measurement
弧度波长 húdù bōcháng radian length
弧度测量 húdù cèliáng arc measurement
弧段 húduàn 〈数学〉segment of a curve
弧光 húguāng arc light; arc:～发生器 arc generator /～放电 arc discharge /～谱 arc spectrum /～谱线 arc line /～照明 arc lighting
弧光灯 húguāngdēng *also* "炭精灯" tànjīngdēng arc lamp; arc light:～用直流发电机 arc dynamo
弧焊 húhàn *also* "弧焊接" arc welding:～发电机 arc welding generator /～焊缝 arc weld /～机 arc welding set /～面罩 arc welding helmet
弧菌 hújūn vibrio:霍乱～ *Vibrio cholerae*; cholera vibrio /腐败～ *Vibrio septicus*
弧菌病 hújūnbìng vibriosis
弧面 húmiàn cambered surface
弧铅焊 húqiānhàn 〈冶金〉arc brazing
弧圈球 húquānqiú 〈体育〉loop drive
弧线 húxiàn arc; curve; curved line:供求关系～ demand and supply curves /～运动 movement in a curve /流星在夜空中画出一条～。The meteor left a bright arc in the dark sky.
弧形 húxíng arc; curve:～避雷器 arc-arrester /～构造 arc structure
弧形失真 húxíng shīzhēn 〈影视〉arc distortion
弧形闸门 húxíng zhámén 〈水利〉radial gate

斛

hú 〈旧语〉dry measure, originally equal to 10 *dou* (斗), later 5 *dou*:一～米 a *hu* of rice

槲

hú 〈植物〉Mongolian oak (*Quercus dentata*)
槲果 húguǒ *also* "橡子" xiàngzǐ; "栎子" lìzǐ acorn
槲寄生 hújìshēng 〈植物〉mistletoe (*Viscum coloratum*)
槲栎 húlì *also* "青冈" qīnggāng 〈植物〉oriental white oak (*Quercus aliena*)

嘝

hú (old term for 蒲式耳) bushel

觳

hú
觳觫 húsù 〈书面〉tremble with fear; shake in one's shoes:我不忍心看着它～的样子。I couldn't bear the sight of the animal trembling with fear.

縠

hú 〈书面〉crêpe gauze

hǔ

浒

hǔ waterside:在河之～ by the side of a river /《水～》*Water Margin*; *Heroes of the Marshes*

虎[1]

hǔ ❶ tiger:小～ tiger cub /母～ tigeress /猛～ fierce tiger /驯～ tame (*or* train) a tiger ❷ brave; vigorous:～狼之兵 ferocious soldiers (*or* troops) ❸〈方言〉put on a fierce or angry look:他～起脸来的样子真让人害怕。When he turned angry, he would look frightening. ❹ (Hǔ) a surname

虎[2]

hǔ *see* "唬" hǔ
see also hù
虎背熊腰 hǔbèi-xióngyāo broad-shouldered and thick-waisted; of a powerful build; muscular and sturdy:他虽未成年,却长得～,身强力壮。Although not yet a grown-up, he is already of a stocky and imposing build.
虎贲 hǔbēn brave and strong man; brave warrior:～之士 valiant warrior
虎彪彪 hǔbiāobiāo sturdy and imposing; robust and impressive:～的小伙子 strapping young man
虎步 hǔbù ❶ vigorous and broad steps:这个战士一弓身,几个～就蹿到小高地上。Bending low the soldier leapt up the hillock in a few vigorous strides. ❷〈书面〉carry oneself with dignity:龙行～ of a majestic bearing ❸ exercise rule (over a region):～关中 dominate the central Shaanxi plain
虎伥 hǔchāng (legend has it that the ghost of a man killed by a tiger helped the tiger kill other human beings) helper of an evildoer; accomplice
虎胆 hǔdǎn ❶ tiger's gallbladder ❷〈比喻〉as brave as a tiger:～英雄 lion-hearted hero
虎毒不食子 hǔ dú bù shí zǐ *also* "虎毒不食儿" even a hungry tiger doesn't eat its own cubs — kindred feelings are irresistable
虎耳草 hǔ'ěrcǎo 〈植物〉saxifrage
虎伏 hǔfú 〈体育〉gyro wheel; hoop
虎符 hǔfú 〈历史〉tiger-shaped tally issued to generals as imperial authorization for troop movement; tiger tally:铜～ copper tiger tally /盗～ steal a tiger tally
虎骨酒 hǔgǔjiǔ 〈中药〉tiger-bone liquor
虎虎 hǔhǔ mighty; powerful; forceful; vigorous:拳打得～生风 strike powerful blows (in boxing)
虎虎有生气 hǔhǔ yǒu shēngqì brim over with vigour and vitality; be vigorous and energetic; be full of vim and vigour:老人年岁虽大,但要起大刀来,仍～。Although advanced in years he is still vigorous when he gives a performance of swordplay.
虎将 hǔjiàng brave general
虎劲 hǔjìn dauntless drive; dash:有一股子～ full of drive and daring; have plenty of dash; with a lot of push
虎鲸 hǔjīng killer whale (*Orcinus orca*)
虎踞龙盘 hǔjù-lóngpán *also* "虎踞龙蟠";"龙盘虎踞" like a coiling dragon and crouching tiger — a forbidding strategic point:～今胜昔,天翻地覆慨而慷。The City, a tiger crouching, a dragon curling, outshines its ancient glories; In heroic triumph heaven and earth have been overturned.
虎克定律 Hǔkè dìnglǜ 〈物理〉Hooke's law
虎口 hǔkǒu ❶ tiger's mouth — jaws of death:～脱险 have a narrow escape; have a close shave /才离～,又入狼窝 fall into the wolf's den right after one gets out of the tiger's mouth; out of the frying pan into the fire ❷ part of the hand between the thumb and the index finger:医生在～处的合谷穴给我扎了一针。The doctor put a needle into the acupoint between my thumb and index finger.
虎口拔牙 hǔkǒu-báyá pull a tooth from the tiger's mouth — brave the greatest danger; beard the lion in his den
虎口余生 hǔkǒu-yúshēng *also* "虎口逃生" escape from the tiger's jaws — extricate oneself from a dangerous situation; escape by the skin of one's teeth; have a narrow escape:我是～,凡事都已看破了。Having survived quite a few disasters I am totally disillusioned with worldly things now.
虎狼 hǔláng like tigers and wolves; ferocious and ruthless;

H

fiendish and savage：～之辈 (of a person) ferocious like a tiger
虎狼之国 hǔlángzhīguó country like a hungry tiger and predatory wolf — aggressor or aggressive country：～不可信。An aggressive country must not be trusted.
虎狼之威 hǔlángzhīwēi imposing like a tiger and wolf — impressive and dignified manner；prowess
虎里虎气 hǔlihǔqì strong and mighty；robust and forceful：～的小伙子 strong and robust young man
虎落平阳被犬欺 hǔ luò píngyáng bèi quǎn qī a tiger on level ground may be bullied by a dog；a man who has lost power or influence may be insulted by an underling
虎猫 hǔmāo *also*"豹猫" bàomāo〈动物〉margay；tiger cat (*Felis wiedii*)
虎门条约 Hǔmén Tiáoyuē Treaty of Humen (supplement to the Treaty of Nanking) signed at Humen, Guangdong on 8 October 1843 between Great Britain and the Qing court, enabling the former to establish settlements in Chinese seaports
虎皮宣 hǔpíxuān light-striped coloured rice paper
虎皮鹦鹉 hǔpí yīngwǔ budgerigar；parakeet
虎魄 hǔpò *also*"琥珀" hǔpò amber
虎气 hǔqi of imposing manner：小伙子方脸大眼，瞧着挺～。Square-faced and big-eyed, the young man looks quite impressive.
虎钳 hǔqián vise；jaw vise：万能～ universal vise /～台 vise bench /～口 vise jaw
虎丘 Hǔqiū Tiger Hill in Suzhou(苏州)，Jiangsu Province
虎入羊群 hǔrùyángqún tiger among a flock of sheep — the strong riding roughshod over the weak：这队生力军冲进敌阵，如～，锐不可当。Like a tiger dashing into a flock of sheep, the reinforcements swept into the enemy's position carrying everything before it.
虎鲨 hǔshā〈动物〉horned shark (*Heterodontus*)
虎蛇 hǔshé tiger snake (*Notechis scutatus*)
虎生生 hǔshēngshēng vigorous and mighty；dynamic and forceful：～的大眼睛 radiant big eyes /～的年轻人 vigorous young people
虎狮 hǔshī tiglon
虎视 hǔshì ❶ glare at with avarice and malice；eye covetously：敌寇～中原。The invading enemy cast covetous eyes at the central plains. ❷ awe-inspiring gaze：战士们在阵前～敌人，待命出击。The soldiers at the front line glared at the enemies, waiting for the order to charge.
虎视眈眈 hǔshì-dāndān glare like a tiger eyeing its prey；eye greedily or menacingly：他们对邻国～。They cast menacing eyes on the neighbouring countries.
虎势 hǔshi *also*"虎实"〈方言〉healthy and strong；robust：小伙子膀大腰粗的，长得挺～。The lad is strong and healthy, with broad shoulders and a thick chest.
虎瘦雄心在 hǔ shòu xióngxīn zài be poor but ambitious；live in poverty but cherish lofty ideas：～，人贫志气存。Poor as he is, he is a man of lofty aspirations.
虎头虎脑 hǔtóu-hǔnǎo (mostly used of a child) naive and healthy：这孩子～的，真逗人喜爱。This robust naive child is so lovely.
虎头牢房 hǔtóu láofáng〈旧语〉death row
虎头牌 hǔtóupái tiger-head tablet (made of wood and erected in front of *yamen* during the Qing Dynasty to show its authority)：衙门口立着～，两旁站立着凶神恶煞的衙役。A tiger-head tablet was set up in front of the *yamen* and on both sides of the gate stood fiend-like *yamen* runners.
虎头蛇尾 hǔtóu-shéwěi with a tiger's head but a snake's tail — in like a lion, out like a lamb；fine start and poor finish：干什么工作都不能～。In whatever we do, we should not let the work tail off once it gets started. /这会～，开幕式那么隆重，结尾却那么草率。After a grand opening, the hasty closing session of the conference is a bit anticlimactic.
虎头捉虱 hǔtóu-zhuōshī try to catch lice on a tiger's head — provoke unwisely：你为什么要惹她呢？这不是～吗？Why provoke her? Aren't you inviting (*or* courting) trouble?
虎威 hǔwēi (of a general) power and prestige；majestic bearing：冒犯～ offend against sb.'s power
虎尾春冰 hǔwěi-chūnbīng tread on the tiger's tail or on spring ice — be in a dangerous or precarious situation；tread on thin ice；be in peril
虎啸风生 hǔxiào-fēngshēng tigers howl and the wind rises — time to give full play to one's talents：彼时天下大乱，正是英雄乘势，～之日。The whole country being in disorder, great men rose to the call of the times.
虎穴 hǔxué tiger's den：～追踪 track a tiger to its lair；track the enemy to its base /～除奸 eliminate a traitor in his stronghold /不入～，焉得虎子？How can you catch tiger cubs without entering the tiger's lair? *or* Nothing ventured, nothing gained.
虎穴龙潭 hǔxué-lóngtán *also*"龙潭虎穴" tiger's den and dragon's pool — dangerous place；precarious situation；enemy stronghold
虎牙 hǔyá〈口语〉protruding canine tooth
虎眼石 hǔyǎnshí tiger's-eye
虎疫 hǔyì〈中医〉cholera
虎鼬 hǔyòu〈动物〉tiger weasel (*Vormela peregusna*)
虎跃龙腾 hǔyuè-lóngténg *also*"龙腾虎跃" dragons rising and tigers leaping — a scene of bustling activity：他的自由体操动作有～之势。His floor performance was powerful and graceful. /他深信自己必有～之时。It was his deep conviction that he would one day have a chance to display his talents.
虎杖 hǔzhàng〈中药〉giant knotweed (*Polygonum cuspidatum*)
虎帐 hǔzhàng〈古语〉general's tent：～谈兵 discuss military affairs in the general's tent

琥 hǔ

琥珀 hǔpò *also*"虎魄" hǔpò amber：～项链 amber necklace /～玻璃 amber glass /～色 amber
琥珀树脂 hǔpò shùzhī kochenite
琥珀酸 hǔpòsuān〈化学〉succinic acid
琥珀油 hǔpòyóu amber oil

唬(虎) hǔ

bluff：别～人，我才不信呢。Stop bluffing. I don't believe it. /不是我～人，我真看见狼了。I'm not trying to scare you. I did see wolves.
see also xià

hù

户 hù

❶ door：夜不闭～ not bolt the door during the night；feel safe without locking up /小心门～ mind the doors；be sure that the doors are locked ❷ household；family：挨家挨～ from house to house；from door to door /小家小～ small family (*or* household)；common (*or* poor) family /困难～ hard-up-families /这楼里住了多少～？How many households are there in the building? ❸ family status：门当～对 be well matched in social and economic status (for marriage) ❹ (bank) account：账～ account /立～ open an account with the bank /存～ (bank) depositor ❺ (Hù) a surname
户部 Hùbù〈历史〉Ministry of Revenue in dynastic China：～尚书 Minister of Revenue in the Ming and Qing dynasties
户次 hùcì household time — one household counted once：去年，村委会为村民解决生产急需共三十多～。Last year the village committee helped various households to meet their urgent needs in production more than thirty times.
户籍 hùjí ❶ census register；household register：～科 household registration section ❷ registered permanent residence
户籍法 hùjífǎ law of population registration
户籍警 hùjíjǐng policeman in charge of household registration
户均 hùjūn per household (average)：去年全村～收入一万元。Last year, per household income of the village averaged 10,000 *yuan*. /这个村子全年～售猪八头多。Every household of the village sold an average of eight pigs for the whole year.
户口 hùkǒu ❶ number of households and population：这个小村子～不多。There are not many households and people in this small village. ❷ registered residence：报～ register one's residence；apply for residence /销～ cancel one's residence registration /查～ check residence cards；check on household residents /申请转～ (to the local authorities) for change of domicile /临时～ (registered) temporary residence /长期～ (registered) permanent residence /～证件 household registry document
户口簿 hùkǒubù *also*"户口本儿" (permanent) residence booklet
户口管制 hùkǒu guǎnzhì domicile control
户口普查 hùkǒu pǔchá census

H

户口清册 hùkǒu qīngcè census record
户内 hùnèi indoor; indoors:～活动 indoor activity /～电缆 inside cable /～设备 indoor equipment /供～使用 for indoor use /在～工作 work indoors
户枢 hùshū door hinge; door axis
户枢不蠹 hùshū-bùdù a door-hinge is never worm-eaten — constant activity staves off decay:俗话说"流水不腐,～",事物总是在自身不断的运动中葆其活力和生命的。As the saying goes, running water is never stale and a door-hinge never worm-eaten. Thus things preserve their vigour and vitality through constant activity.
户庭 hùtíng 〈书面〉door and courtyard — within the house:足不出～ never step out of doors; confine oneself within doors
户头 hùtóu (bank) account:他新开了一个～。He has just opened an account.
户外 hùwài outdoor; outdoors:～有一片草坪。There is a lawn outdoors. /每日应有一定的～活动。It is necessary to do some outdoor exercises every day.
户限 hùxiàn 〈书面〉threshold:小儿尚幼,犹不能过～。The young son was too small to be able to cross the threshold.
户限为穿 hùxiànwéichuān one's threshold is worn low by visitors — endless flow of visitors:每天宾客盈门,～。There is an endless stream of visitors and the house is full every day.
户养 hùyǎng be raised or reared by individual households (as distinct from collective raising):今年,本村～的牲畜达数百头。This year the number of livestock raised by private households in the village has reached several hundred.
户牖 hùyǒu 〈书面〉door; door and windows:～紧闭。The door and windows are shut tight.
户长 hùzhǎng 〈方言〉head of a household
户主 hùzhǔ head of a household (as registered on the residence card)
户子 hùzi 〈方言〉household; family:种地～ farming household

戽

hù ❶ bailing bucket (for irrigation):风～ wind-driven bailing bucket ❷ bail:～水抗旱 bail water to combat the drought
戽车 hùchē noria
戽斗 hùdǒu 〈农业〉bailing bucket; bailer:～板 bucket board
戽水机 hùshuǐjī scooping machine; bailing machine

沪(滬)

Hù (another name for 上海) Shanghai:京津～ Beijing, Tianjin and Shanghai /～宁线 Shanghai-Nanjing Railway
沪剧 hùjù Shanghai opera

护(護)

hù ❶ protect; guard; shield:守～ guard /爱～ cherish; treasure; take good care of /维～ safeguard; defend; uphold /养路～路 maintain, patrol and guard a road (*or* railway) /用手遮～眼睛 shield one's eyes with one's hand ❷ be partial to; shield; shelter:庇～ shelter; shield; put under one's protection /官官相～ bureaucrats shield one another /～孩子不好。It's bad to be partial to one's own child.
护岸 hù'àn 〈水利〉bank revetment:～工程 bank protection work
护岸林 hù'ànlín protective belt (of trees) along an embankment; bank protection belt
护板 hùbǎn backplate; fender apron; guard board
护壁 hùbì *also* "墙围子" qiángwéizi;"墙裙" qiángqún 〈建筑〉 wainscot; dado
护臂 hùbì archer's forearm protector; bracer
护庇 hùbì 〈口语〉shelter; shield; screen; cover:你和她好,就该～她吗? Should you shield her just because she is your friend?
护兵 hùbīng military guard; escort
护城河 hùchénghé city moat
护持 hùchí ❶ shield and sustain:～交通要道 guard and maintain a traffic juncture /父亲死后,店里的买卖全靠舅父一人～。After father's death, it was uncle who managed the shop. ❷ look after; take care of:她像姐姐似地～我。She looked after me like my own sister.
护从 hùcóng ❶ follow around as bodyguard; escort ❷ guard; bodyguard
护犊子 hù dúzi *also* "护驹子"〈口语〉be partial to one's child; shield one's child:不是我～,我们家孩子怎么你了? I'm not shielding my own child, but what has he done to you after all?
护短 hùduǎn shield a shortcoming or fault:为孩子～只能害了他。You'll only do harm to your child, trying to shield his errors.
护耳 hù'ěr earflap; earmuff:老人头上光着,却带了一副皮～。Although bare-headed the old man wore a pair of leather earmuffs.
护法 hùfǎ ❶〈宗教〉protect the Buddha dharma or Buddhist doctrine ❷ protector of the Buddha dharma or Buddhist doctrine; alms giver; benefactor ❸ uphold the constitution, a slogan raised by Dr. Sun Yat-sen in 1917 against the Northern Warlords
护法运动 Hùfǎ Yùndòng Campaign to Uphold the Provisional Constitution, led by Dr. Sun Yat-sen in 1917-1918 against the Northern Warlords
护发 hùfà capilliculture; hair care:～用品 hair care articles /～素 hair conditioner /～膏 hair ointment
护封 hùfēng (book) jacket
护肤霜 hùfūshuāng face cream; body lotion
护符 hùfú *see* "护身符"
护盖 hùgài protective cover or hood
护官符 hùguānfú amulet for (maintaining and elevating one's) official position:～上写的皆是本地大族名宦之家。On the promotion amulet were written the names of all the influential local families and officialdom.
护轨 hùguǐ guardrail:枕木～ guard sleeper
护国运动 Hùguó Yùndòng Campaign to Defend the Republic, a movement launched in December 1915 by Cai E (蔡锷), Tang Jiyao (唐继尧) and Li Liejun (李烈钧) against would-be emperor Yuan Shikai (袁世凯) till the latter's death in June 1916
护航 hùháng escort; convoy:～机 escort aircraft /～舰队 escort flotilla; convoy /～舰 convoy ship /～任务 escort mission /总统座机由五架喷气战斗机～。The president's plane was escorted by five jet fighters.
护驾 hùjià escort the emperor; defend the king
护肩 hùjiān 〈方言〉shoulder pad
护颈 hùjǐng 〈体育〉neck guard; padded neck flap
护胫 hùjìng 〈体育〉shin-guard
护驹子 hù jūzi *see* "护犊子"
护具 hùjù 〈体育〉protective appliance (used in bayonet charging or fencing); pad:他俩披上～,端起木枪对刺起来。Pads all over, the two started charging at each other with wooden spears.
护栏 hùlán guardrail; railings; rail fence
护理 hùlǐ ❶ nurse; tend:医务～人员 medical and nursing staff /～病人 nurse a patient /感谢你的～,使我恢复了健康。I am grateful to you for nursing me back to health. ❷ protect; take care of:棚栽培,关键在于～。Care and attention is the key to greenhouse gardening.
护林 hùlín protect the forest:～防火 protect the forest and guard against fire; forest protection and fire prevention
护林员 hùlínyuán forest ranger
护领 hùlǐng *also* "衬领" chènlǐng detachable collar
护路 hùlù ❶ patrol and guard a road or railway:～斗争 struggle to protect railways ❷〈交通〉road maintenance:～队 road maintenance crew
护路工 hùlùgōng ❶〈铁路〉trackman; trackmaster; track walker ❷ road maintenance worker
护路林 hùlùlín shelter belt (along a road)
护面 hùmiàn *also* "护脸"〈体育〉face guard; mask
护目镜 hùmùjìng goggles
护坡 hùpō 〈水利〉〈交通〉slope protection:～墙 slope wall
护墙板 hùqiángbǎn 〈建筑〉panel; dado; wainscot:这屋子装有～。The room is wainscotted.
护青 hùqīng 〈方言〉keep watch over ripening crops
护秋 hùqiū keep watch over ripe crops
护身符 hùshēnfú *also* "护符" ❶ amulet; protective talisman:他身挂一串念珠,作为～。He wore a string of beads as a protective talisman. ❷ person or thing that protects one from punishment or censure; shield:他以合法的经营作为～,掩盖其走私活动。He was engaged in smuggling under the cover of licenced business.
护士 hùshi (hospital) nurse:白衣～ white-robed nurse /实习～ student nurse /夜班～ night nurse /男～ male nurse /～节 Nurses' Day
护士学校 hùshi xuéxiào nurses' school
护士长 hùshizhǎng head nurse
护手 hùshǒu *also* "护手盘"〈体育〉handguard (of a fencing sword); coquille; cup guard
护守 hùshǒu guard; defend:～大桥 guard a big bridge

护送 hùsòng escort; convoy: 军用品～车队 escort vehicles carrying army provisions /一路有人～ be escorted all the way
护田林 hùtiánlín farmland shelter belt
护腿 hùtuǐ 〈体育〉shin-guard; shin-pad
护腕 hùwàn 〈体育〉bracer
护卫 hùwèi ❶ protect; guard: 营房周围,日夜有哨兵～。There were sentries guarding the barracks around the clock. /一路上幸亏有人～,这才没出事。Thanks to protection throughout the journey, we arrived safe and sound. ❷ bodyguard: 几个～远远地跟在后面。Several bodyguards followed at a distance.
护卫舰 hùwèijiàn escort vessel; frigate; corvette
护卫艇 hùwèitǐng *also* "炮艇" pàotǐng gunboat
护膝 hùxī 〈体育〉kneepad; kneecap
护校 hùxiào (short for 护士学校) nurses' school
护心镜 hùxīnjìng round metal piece on armour to protect the chest; chest plate
护胸 hùxiōng 〈体育〉chest protector; chest pad
护袖 hùxiù 〈方言〉oversleeve
护养 hùyǎng ❶ cultivate; nurse; raise; rear: ～秧苗 nurse young plants; cultivate seedlings /～仔畜 raise (*or* tend) newborn animals /在她的精心～下,几只羊羔都救活了。Under her careful nursing, the lambs were all brought back to life. ❷ maintain: ～铁路 maintain a railway line
护佑 hùyòu protect; safeguard; bless and protect: ～一方 safeguard a locality /愿老天～你! God bless you!
护渔 hùyú patrol and protect fisheries and fishing resources on the sea; provide fishery protection
护渔船 hùyúchuán fishing patrol boat; fishing protection vessel
护院 hùyuàn 〈旧语〉❶ guard the courtyard (for a wealthy and powerful family) ❷ courtyard guard
护运 hùyùn armed escort: ～车队 convoy escort /黄金由武装人员～至银行金库。The gold reached the bank's vault under armed escort.
护照 hùzhào ❶ passport: 普通～ ordinary passport /公务～ service passport /官员～ official passport /外交～ diplomatic passport /办理～签证 process passport and visa applications /拒发～ withhold a passport /本～前往世界各国有效。This passport is valid for travel to all countries. /～有效期延长至… the validity of this passport is extended to... ❷ 〈旧语〉official permit for a business trip or transport of merchandise
护罩 hùzhào shield; mask; hood; cover: 安全～ (protective) hood; guard /电焊工头戴～正在焊接钢筋。Wearing a head shield, the welder is welding a reinforcing bar.
护桩 hùzhuāng fender pile

扈 hù ❶ 〈书面〉retinue ❷ (Hù) a surname
扈跸 hùbì 〈书面〉*see* "扈驾"
扈从 hùcóng 〈书面〉❶ retinue; entourage; retainer ❷ accompany; attend: 随车～ go along in the car (*or* train) as escort, etc.
扈驾 hùjià 〈书面〉emperor's retinue or entourage (carriages)

鄠 hù *see* "鄠鄠" méihù

怙 hù 〈书面〉rely on: 失～ have nobody to rely on, one's father being dead; have lost one's father
怙恶不悛 hù'è-bùquān persist in evil and refuse to repent; be steeped in iniquity and refuse to reform; remain impenitent: ～的战争罪犯 incorrigible war criminals /～者,将绳之以法。Those who remain impenitent will be brought to justice.
怙恃 hùshì 〈书面〉❶ count on; rely on; depend on: ～权势作威 abuse power to ride roughshod over the people /无父何怙,无母何恃! Who can an orphan rely on? ❷ father and mother (used in the third person): 少失～ become an orphan; lose one's parents when young

祜 hù 〈书面〉blessing; bliss: 受天之～ be blessed by God

楛 hù 〈古语〉〈植物〉plants of the chaste tree type, the stems of which can be used to make arrow shafts
see also kǔ

岵 hù 〈书面〉mountain covered by vegetation

糊 hù paste: 面～ paste /芝麻～ sesame paste /玉米～ (cornmeal) mush
see also hū; hú
糊弄 hùnong 〈方言〉❶ fool; deceive; palm off: 这孩子尽～人! The child is always trying to deceive people. /别再～大家了! Don't you fool us any more! ❷ go through the motions; be slipshod in work: 这套家具人家结婚用,不能瞎～! This set of furniture is made specially for a wedding, and the work mustn't be done in a sloppy way.
糊弄局 hùnongjú 〈方言〉shoddy work; trashy things: 这活儿～,经不起细看。It's shoddy workmanship that won't bear close examination. /他这个人干什么事都是～,一点儿也不牢靠。He does everything perfunctorily and is not at all reliable.

鹱 hù *also* "剪水鹱" jiǎnshuǐhù 〈动物〉shearwater

鳠 hù 〈动物〉*Hemibagrus*: 斑点～ *Hemibagrus guttatus* /大鳍～ *H. macropterus*

瓠 hù a kind of edible gourd
瓠果 hùguǒ pepo
瓠子 hùzi a kind of edible gourd

互 hù mutual; each other; one another: ～致问候 extend greetings to each other /相～帮助 help one another /～不退让 neither side is willing to retreat /～派大使 exchange of ambassadors /～不侵犯 mutual non-aggression /～不干涉内政 non-interference in each other's internal affairs
互帮互学 hùbāng-hùxué help and learn from each other
互补 hùbǔ mutually complementary: ～性 complementarity /我们两国经济是～的。Our two countries are mutually complementary in economy.
互补电路 hùbǔ diànlù complementary circuit
互补分配 hùbǔ fēnpèi 〈电学〉complementary distribution
互补色 hùbǔsè complementary colours
互不侵犯条约 hùbùqīnfàn tiáoyuē (mutual) non-aggression treaty or pact
互不相交 hùbùxiāngjiāo 〈数学〉mutually disjoint
互不相容 hùbùxiāngróng mutually repellent
互斥 hùchì mutual exclusion; mutual repulsion
互导 hùdǎo 〈电学〉mutual conductance; transconductance
互访 hùfǎng exchange visits: 高层人士的～标志着两国间友好关系的新发展。The high-level exchanges marked a new stage of development of friendly relations between the two countries.
互感 hùgǎn *also* "互感应"〈电工〉mutual inductance: ～器 mutual inductor /～线圈 mutual inductor
互…互… hù…hù… mutual; each other: 互敬互爱 love and respect each other; show mutual respect and love /互让互利 mutual accommodation and benefit /互依互存 depend on each other for existence; be interdependent /互问互答 take questions from each other
互换 hùhuàn exchange; swap: ～批准书 exchange instruments of ratification /～照会 exchange of notes /～备忘录 exchange of memoranda /～协定 swap agreement
互惠 hùhuì mutually beneficial; mutually preferential; reciprocal: 平等～ equality and mutual benefit /贸易～ reciprocity in trade /～关系 mutually beneficial relations /～原则 principle of reciprocity
互惠待遇 hùhuì dàiyù reciprocal preferential treatment
互惠法 hùhuìfǎ law of reciprocity
互惠共生 hùhuì-gòngshēng 〈生物〉mutualistic symbiosis; reciprocal symbiosis; mutualism
互惠关税 hùhuì guānshuì mutually preferential tariff
互惠条约 hùhuì tiáoyuē reciprocal treaty
互惠信贷 hùhuìxìndài mutual credit loans; mutual credit facilities; swap credits
互兼董事 hùjiān dǒngshì interlocking directorship
互见 hùjiàn ❶ (of writings) (in two or more places) mutually explanatory and supplementary ❷ both have; exist at the same time: 瑕瑜～ have defects as well as merits; contain both strong and weak points
互利 hùlì mutually beneficial; of mutual benefit: 平等～ equality and mutual benefit /双方本着互惠～的原则,签订了一项贸易协定。The

two sides signed a trade agreement in the spirit of reciprocity and mutual benefit.

互联 hùlián ❶〈电工〉interconnect:～电力系统 interconnect electric power system ❷〈通信〉interconnection

互联网 hùliánwǎng ❶ *also*"互连网" internet; internet-work; interconnected network ❷ Internet
see also"因特网" yīntèwǎng

互联网空间 hùliánwǎng kōngjiān cyberspace

互联网销售商 hùliánwǎng xiāoshòushāng cyberseller

互联网协议 hùliánwǎng xiéyì 〈信息〉Internet Protocol (IP)

互谅互让 hùliàng-hùràng mutual understanding and mutual accommodation:本着～的原则,两国顺利地解决了边界问题。The boundary issue between the two countries was smoothly settled in accordance with the principle of mutual understanding and accommodation.

互免 hùmiǎn mutual exemption:～签证协议 agreement on mutual exemption of visas

互让 hùràng mutual accommodation or concession; give and take; meet each other half way:他们缺乏～的精神,所以总谈不拢。They couldn't come to an agreement because neither wanted to accommodate the other.

互溶 hùróng be intersoluble:～性 intersolubility /酒精和水～。Alcohol and water are intersoluble.

互生 hùshēng alternate phyllotaxy:叶椭圆形,～,粉红色。The leaves are oval, alternate and pink-coloured.

互市 hùshì 〈旧语〉trade between countries in the border area or harbour:边民出入国界～,是这里的传统习惯。It has been a custom here for border inhabitants to cross the boundary and do trade.

互诉 hùsù 〈法律〉cross claim; cross action

互通 hùtōng communicate with each other; exchange:～消息 exchange information /～边市 open border markets to each other /～姓名 introduce each other

互通有无 hùtōng-yǒuwú each supplies what the other needs; meet each other's needs; exchange needed goods

互为表里 hùwéibiǎolǐ be interlinked; supplement each other; work hand in glove

互为条件 hùwéitiáojiàn each is the condition of the other; be mutually conditional

互为因果 hùwéiyīnguǒ interact as both cause and effect; act on and reinforce each other

互相 hùxiāng mutual; each other:～标榜 eulogizing and boosting each other /～拆台 cut the ground (*or* pull the rug) from under each other's feet; hinder each other's work /～扯皮 argue over trifles; bicker /～渗透 infiltrate into each other; interpenetrate /～掣肘 hamstring each other; make things difficult for each other /～关联 be interrelated /～排斥 be mutually exclusive /～勾结 work in collusion /～依存 be interdependent

互相确保毁灭论 hùxiāng quèbǎo huǐmièlùn 〈军事〉theory of MAD (mutually assured destruction)

互训 hùxùn (of writings) (in two or more places) mutually explanatory

互余 hùyú 〈数学〉complementarity:～角 complementary angle /～律 complementarity law; complementary law

互质 hùzhì 〈数学〉relatively prime:3 和 11～。Three and eleven are prime to each other.

互质数 hùzhìshù 〈数学〉prime number

互助 hùzhù help each other:团结～ unity and mutual help /～合作 mutual aid and cooperation /～小组 mutual aid group /～储蓄银行 mutual savings bank

互助会 hùzhùhuì mutual help club or society

互助基金 hùzhù jījīn mutual fund

互助组 hùzhùzǔ ❶ mutual aid group:我们同在一个学习～。We are in the same mutual help study group. ❷ mutual aid team (an elementary form of organization in China's agricultural cooperation):组织～ organize a mutual aid team

沍(冱) hù 〈书面〉❶ freeze:～寒 freezing cold; icy cold ❷ stop up; close up; block:～涸 be worried and pent-up

虎 hù
see also hǔ

虎不拉 hùbulā 〈方言〉〈动物〉shrike

笏 hù *also*"朝笏" cháohù;"手板" shǒubǎn tablet (held before the chest by officials when received in audience by the emperor)

huā

砉 huā 〈象声〉swish:老鹰～的一声从树上腾空飞起。With a swishing sound, the eagle flew up from the tree and into the blue.
see also xū

化 huā (same as 花[2]) spend; expend:～时间 spend time /乱～钱 squander money; spend money unnecessarily
see also huà

化子 huāzi *also*"花子" huāzi beggar

花[1] huā ❶ flower; blossom; bloom:雌～ female flower /雄～ male flower /两性～ hermaphrodite flower /家～ cultivated flower /野～ wild flower /苹果～ apple blossom /桃～ peach blossom /梅～ plum flower /荷～ lotus flower/百合～ lily /杜鹃～ azalea /兰～ orchid /菊～ chrysanthemum; mum /丁香～ lilac /茉莉～ white jasmine /牡丹～ peony /赏～ appreciate flowers; admire the beauty of flowers /采～ pick flowers /献～ present flowers /玫瑰～盛开。The roses are in full bloom. ❷ ornamental or decorative plant:种～ cultivate (*or* plant, *or* grow) flowers /浇～ water flowers ❸ anything resembling a flower:灯～儿 snuff (of a candlewick) /钢～ spark of molten steel /雪～儿 snowflakes /浪～儿 spray /冰～儿 ice flower ❹ fireworks:放～ let (*or* shoot) off fireworks /看礼～ watch fireworks display ❺ pattern; design:白地蓝～儿 blue flowers on a white background /这件毛衣的～儿很大方。The pattern of this knitting is elegant. ❻ decorated with flowers or decorative patterns:绣～被面 embroidered quilt cover /雕～家具 furniture with carvings /～衣服 bright-coloured clothes ❼ multicoloured; coloured; variegated:小～猫 spotted kitten /～蝴蝶 variegated butterfly ❽ blurred; dim; bleary:看～了眼 one's eyes get blurred /老眼昏～ dim-sighted from old age ❾ threadbare:上衣袖子都磨～了。The jacket is threadbare at the sleeves. ❿ showy; tricky; false: *see*"～招";"～架子";"～言巧语" ⓫ flower; cream; essence; quintessence:文艺之～ cream of art and literature /革命之～ flower of the revolution ⓬〈比喻〉young, pretty woman:校～ campus belle /交际～ social butterfly ⓭ prostitute; be related to prostitutes:烟～女 prostitute /寻～问柳 visit places of ill fame; frequent brothels; go whoring ⓮〈方言〉romantic (in love); promiscuous; lascivious:～女人 promiscuous woman /～～事儿(extramarital) affair; sex scandal /这人看起来老成,其实可～了。Priggish as he may appear, he is something of a womanizer. ⓯ cotton:废～ waste cotton /轧～ gin cotton /弹～ fluff cotton (with a bow) ⓰ particles; drops:泪～儿 tears /葱～儿 chopped spring onion ⓱ young of certain animals:鱼～ fish fry ⓲ smallpox:天～ smallpox /种～儿 vaccinate /这孩子正在出～儿。The child is suffering from smallpox. ⓳ wound:他在突围时挂～了。He got wounded when breaking out of the encirclement. ⓴ (Huā) a surname

花[2] huā spend; expend:～功夫 take time; be time-consuming /～钱如流水 spend money like water; be most extravagant /到那儿～了三个小时。It took me three hours to get there. /该～的一定要～。Spend as you should.

花把势 huābǎshi *also*"花把式" experienced flower grower or gardener; skilled flower grower; florist

花白 huābái grey; grizzled:两鬓～ become grey at the temples /～胡子 grey (*or* grizzled) beard

花斑 huābān piebald:～马 piebald horse /～猫 spotted cat

花斑癣 huābānxuǎn *also*"汗斑" hànbān 〈医学〉tinea versicolour

花瓣 huābàn petal

花苞 huābāo bud:长出～ put out buds

花被 huābèi 〈植物〉perianth; floral envelope

花绷子 huābēngzi *also*"绷子" embroidery frame; hoop; tambour

花边 huābiān ❶ decorative border:盘子上有一道金色～。The plate is bordered with a golden pattern. *or* There is a golden floral border round the edge of the plate. ❷〈纺织〉cording; fancy lace:带～的女式衬衫 woman's shirt trimmed with lace /装饰着～的窗帘 (win-

H

dow) curtain with lace trimmings /袖口镶～。The ends of the sleeves are laced. ❸〈印刷〉fancy borders in printing:～文学 short, snappy newspaper (*or* magazine) article set off in borders ❹〈方言〉silver dollar

花边新闻 huābiān xīnwén titbits (of news); interesting sidelights

花柄 huābǐng stalk; authocaulus

花布 huābù cotton print; print

花不棱登 huābulēngdēng 〈口语〉of jumbled colours; variegated: 这件外衣～的,太俗气了。This variegated coat is of poor taste.

花彩 huācǎi festoon; streamer:～装饰 festoonery /在房间里挂上～。Hung up festoons in the room.

花菜 huācài 〈方言〉cauliflower

花残月缺 huācán-yuèquē flowers wither and the moon wanes — a scene of decline; estrangement between husband and wife or between lovers:一夜秋风,后园～,草木零落,令人伤情。A night of autumn wind had left a desolate scene in the back garden — a sad sight to see. /昔日恩爱夫妻,如今～,恩断义绝,究竟是谁的过错? Who is to blame for the estrangement of a once affectionate couple?

花草 huācǎo (ornamental) flowers and plants; herbal flowers:退休后,老人家爱养个～什么的。After retirement, granddad liked growing flowers, plants and what not.

花插 huāchā ❶ flower pad (usu. kept in a shallow water basin) ❷ bottles of various shapes for inserting cut flowers:案头、床头和墙角都放着～,插着各色时令鲜花。On the desk, at bedside, and in the corners of walls are placed bottles of various shapes with seasonal fresh flowers in them.

花插座 huāchāzuò pinholder

花插着 huāchazhe interspersed; mixed:大人、孩子～坐在树阴下听说书。Adults and children sat interspersed in the shade, listening to storytelling. /教书之余,他也～写点文章,搞点翻译。In addition to teaching, he also does some writing and translating for a change.

花茶 huāchá *also* "香片" xiāngpiàn scented tea:茉莉～ jasmine tea

花铲 huāchǎn trowel; scoop

花厂 huāchǎng *also* "花厂子"〈旧语〉shop raising and selling flowers

花车 huāchē festooned vehicle; float (decorated vehicle in a procession)

花晨月夕 huāchén-yuèxī blossoming morning and moonlit evening — peaceful and delightful moment:多少个～,我们在树林里漫步、谈心。For many a peaceful and delightful time, we had heart-to-heart talks while strolling in the woods.

花池子 huāchízi flower bed

花虫 huāchóng 〈方言〉pink bollworm; flower bug

花蝽 huāchūn flower bug

H

花丛 huācóng flowering shrubs; flowers in clusters:～穿蝶 butterflies flit from flower to flower; butterflies flutter about among the flowers

花簇 huācù flowers in clusters; inflorescence:～烂漫 clusters of bright flowers in full bloom

花大姐 huādàjiě (colloquial term for 瓢虫)〈动物〉ladybird; ladybug

花搭着 huādazhe interspersed; diversified:各种蔬菜～吃 diversify one's diet by eating various kinds of vegetables

花旦 huādàn 〈戏曲〉*huadan*, female role in Chinese opera

花道 huādào Ikebana, art of Japanese flower arrangement

花灯 huādēng festive lantern (as displayed on the Lantern Festival); colourful lantern:看～ watch festive lanterns /正月十五闹～ display of colourful lanterns on the Lantern Festival (which falls on the 15th of the first month of the lunar year)

花灯戏 huādēngxì 〈戏曲〉Huadeng opera, popular in Yunnan, Sichuan and other provinces

花颠 huādiān *also* "花颠癫" ❶〈医学〉erotomania ❷ erotomaniac

花点子 huādiǎnzi ❶ trick; deceitful idea:他骗人的～真不少。He is really full of gimmicks. ❷ fancy but impractical idea:他尽出些～。He has come up with all sorts of unrealistic ideas.

花店 huādiàn florist's (shop); flower shop

花钿 huādiàn ornament worn on a woman's head in former times

花凋叶落 huādiāo-yèluò flowers wither and leaves fall off — a scene of decline

花雕 huādiāo high-grade Shaoxing (绍兴) rice wine

花缎 huāduàn figured satin; brocade; damask:～刺绣 brocade embroidery

花朵 huāduǒ flower; blossom:儿童是祖国的～。Children are the flowers of our motherland.

花萼 huā'è calyx:～瓣化性 calycanthemy /～管 calyx tube

花儿 huā'ér *hua'er*, a folk song popular in Gansu, Qinghai and Ningxia

花房 huāfáng greenhouse

花肥 huāféi ❶ fertilizer or manure applied at the time of florescence for more flowers and fruits ❷ fertilizer or manure applied to potted plants

花费 huāfèi spend; expend; cost:老师～了不少时间帮助我补课。The teacher spent a lot of time helping me make up for the lessons I had missed. /公司大量的钱都～在应酬上了。Much of the firm's money has been used for entertainment and receptions. /父亲在我的身上～了不少心血。Father took great pains with my education.

花费 huāfei money spent; expenditure; expense:～大 with great expense /他结婚的～可不小。His wedding cost him almost a fortune.

花粉 huāfěn ❶〈植物〉pollen:采集～ collect pollen /～管 pollen tube /～孢子 pollen spore /～过敏反应 pollen hypersensitivity /～传染 pollen transmission /～粒 pollen grain ❷〈中药〉powder made of Chinese trichosanthes' root

花粉病 huāfěnbìng 〈医学〉pollen allergy; hay fever; pollinosis; pollenosis

花粉抗原 huāfěn kàngyuán pollen-antigen

花粉食品 huāfěn shípǐn pollen food; beebread food

花府绸 huāfǔchóu poplin broche

花岗闪长岩 huāgāng shǎnchángyán granodiorite

花岗岩 huāgāngyán ❶ granite:～冲积物 granite wash /～化 granitization /～纹纸 granite paper /～质层 granite layer ❷ granite-like; incorrigibly obstinate

花岗岩脑袋 huāgāngyán nǎodai *also* "花岗石脑袋" granite-like skull; ossified thinking:他那个～,恐怕难得开窍了。With his ossified thinking, perhaps he will never be able to embrace any new ideas.

花糕 huāgāo cake with sugar and raisin filling

花格 huāgé lattice:～大梁〈建筑〉lattice girder /～呢 woolen check /窗～ tracery

花格墙 huāgéqiáng lattice wall

花梗 huāgěng pedicel; flower stalk or stem; peduncle

花骨朵 huāgūduo (flower) bud

花鼓 huāgǔ flower-drum, a folk dance popular in the Yangtze Valley:正月十五晚,四乡表演～的民间艺人都在镇上汇齐。On the night of the 15th of the first month of the lunar year, all flower-drum dancers gathered in town.

花鼓戏 huāgǔxì 〈戏曲〉flower-drum opera, popular in Hunan, Hubei, Jiangxi and Anhui provinces

花冠 huāguān ❶ corolla:合瓣～ gamopetalous corolla /离瓣～ choripetalous corolla ❷ wreath; sumptuous hat worn by a woman on her wedding day in former times:新娘子头戴～,哭哭啼啼地登上花轿。Wearing a gorgeous hat the bride got onto the bridal sedan chair weeping and wailing endlessly.

花光柳影 huāguāng-liǔyǐng colourful and lustrous flowers and drooping green willows — advent of spring:湖边～,春色宜人。It is a pleasant spring scene, with bright flowers all around and weeping willows overhanging the lake.

花棍舞 huāgùnwǔ *also* "霸王鞭" bàwángbiān rattle stick dance

花好月圆 huāhǎo-yuèyuán (mostly used as complimentary address for the newly married) blooming flowers and full moon — perfect conjugal bliss:～人长寿 complete happiness and longevity

花和尚 huāhéshang ❶ unconventional monk (who does not observe the Buddhist commandments not to drink wine, not to eat meat, not to womanize, etc.) ❷ monk with a tattooed back:～鲁智深 Tattooed Monk Lu (one of the outlaws of *Water Margin*《水浒》)

花盒 huāhé fireworks:放～ let off fireworks

花红 huāhóng ❶ *also* "林檎" línqín;"沙果" shāguǒ 〈植物〉Chinese pear-leaved crab apple (*Malus asiatica*) ❷ gift for a wedding betrothal or such festive occasion:～彩礼 wedding gift ❸ bonus:分～ share out bonus; draw extra dividends (*or* profits) ❹ tip; gratuity; gift of money

花红柳绿 huāhóng-liǔlǜ ❶ red blossoms and green willows — luxuriant vegetation:～艳阳天 bright spring day with red blossoms

and green willows ❷ gorgeously dressed; colourful:姑娘们一个个打扮得～。All the girls were colourfully dressed.
花候 huāhòu flowering season
花户 huāhù ❶〈旧语〉household:通知各家按～摊钱。Notify every family that the contribution will be apportioned by the household. ❷ family vending flowers for a living; florist household
花花点点 huāhuā-diǎndiǎn (of spots) interlocked and tangled; dappled:～的蹄印 tangled (*or* overlaid) hoof prints /阳光透过干枯的树枝～地照在雪地上。Sunshine filtered through the dry tree branches and cast its dappled light on the snow ground.
花花公子 huāhuā-gōngzǐ dandy; swinger; playboy; fop:他年轻时是个～,只知道吃喝玩乐。He was a dandy when young and knew nothing but pleasure-seeking.
花花绿绿 huāhuā-lǜlǜ brightly coloured; multicoloured; colourful:～的气球 colourful balloons /穿得～的姑娘们 girls (dressed) in reds and greens; girls in rich colours /柜台上摆满了～的布匹。The counter was full of multicoloured cloth.
花花世界 huāhuā-shìjiè merry and material world; dazzling world with its myriad temptations; world of sensual pleasures; vanity fair:他从乡下来到这个～,怎么也不习惯。A country lad, he just couldn't get used to the ways of this dazzling human world.
花花太岁 huāhuā-tàisuì lascivious despot or bully; king of lechers:～式的人物 lewd man /人们管他叫～。People nicknamed him "king of lechers".
花花肠子 huāhua-chángzi 〈方言〉scheme; trick; craft; crafty person:这个人～可多了。This person is full of tricks (*or* craft). /今后可别理那些～了,留神再上当。Keep away from those crafty people and take care not to be duped again.
花花搭搭 huāhua-dādā ❶ interspersed; diversified:米饭、面食,咱们～地换着样儿吃。We will diversify our diet by having both rice and pasta. ❷ be irregular in size and density:地上～地长着几棵树苗。A few saplings grew here and there in the fields.
花环 huāhuán ❶ garland; lei; floral hoop:～舞 garland dance ❷ wreath
花卉 huāhuì ❶ flowers and plants:～栽培 floriculture; floristry /～展览 flower show /～装饰 flower decoration /禁止采摘～ no plucking of flowers or plants ❷〈美术〉painting of flowers and plants in traditional Chinese style:擅长～ be good at painting flowers and plants
花会 huāhuì ❶ (flower) fair mostly held during the Spring Festival with various folk art and sport performances ❷ flower display where commodities and local produce are also sold or exchanged:赶～ go to a flower display
花鲫鱼 huājìyú 〈方言〉mandarin fish
花甲 huājiǎ sixty years of age:年近～ nearly sixty years old; approaching sixty
花架 huājià pergola:搭～ build a pergola
花架子 huājiàzi ❶ showy but useless martial arts movements ❷ good in appearance but useless in practice; fancy but of no practical value; show piece; mere form:不搞浮夸,不搞～ neither engage in exaggeration nor seek form at the expense of substance /练兵是为了打仗,不是专搞～给人看。We train troops not as show, but with a view to fighting battles.
花笺 huājiān fancy stationery paper
花剑 huājiàn 〈体育〉foil
花键 huājiàn 〈机械〉spline:～轴 spline shaft /～座 splined hub /～铣床 spline miller /～铣刀 spline cutter /～拉刀 spline broach /～滚刀 spline hob /～滚齿机 spline hobbing machine
花匠 huājiàng gardener; florist; floriculturist
花娇柳媚 huājiāo-liǔmèi charming flower and enchanting willow — (usu. of girl) charming and slender
花椒 huājiāo 〈植物〉❶ Chinese prickly ash:院墙四周种了一圈～。Chinese prickly ashes were planted around the wall of the courtyard. ❷ seeds of such plant:～粉 seed powder of Chinese prickly ash
花轿 huājiào bridal sedan chair:大姑娘坐～,第一回 like a maiden mounting a bridal sedan chair — very first time
花秸 huājiē chopped straw
花街柳巷 huājiē-liǔxiàng red-light district; disreputable quarters
花金龟子 huājīnguīzǐ flower chafer
花茎 huājīng see "花轴"
花镜 huājìng presbyopic glasses:老～ presbyopic glasses
花酒 huājiǔ drink and make merry accompanied by courtesans:吃～ eat, drink and make merry accompanied by courtesans
花卷 huājuǎn steamed twisted roll
花开并蒂 huākāi-bìngdì two flowers growing from the same base — symbol of conjugal luck
花枯病 huākūbìng blossom blight
花葵 huākuí 〈植物〉tree mallow
花魁 huākuí ❶ queen of flowers; most beautiful flower (usu. in reference to the Chinese plum flower):她是傲霜斗雪的～。She is like the Chinese plum flower defying frost and snow. ❷ celebrated prostitute; leading courtesan:卖油郎独占～。The young oil vendor won the heart of the leading courtesan.
花篮 huālán ❶ flower basket:死者灵前放着几只～。Several baskets of flowers were placed in front of the coffin of the deceased. ❷ gaily decorated basket:姑娘手里提着一只小巧美丽的～。The girl had in her hand a small and beautifully decorated basket.
花蕾 huālěi (flower) bud:～初绽 with first buds shooting out /～脱落 flower abscission /枝头点缀着数点～。The branches were embellished with a few swelling buds.
花梨木 huālímù see "花榈木"
花里胡哨 huālihúshào 〈口语〉❶ gaudy; garish:她打扮得～的,俗不可耐。Gaudily dressed, she looked unbearably vulgar. ❷ showy; without solid worth; not reliable:他不像隔壁那个～的小子,人可实在哩! Unlike the superficially clever boy next door, he was truly a young man of solid worth.
花鲢 huālián variegated carp
花脸 huāliǎn male character in traditional Chinese opera with a darkish painted face
花翎 huālíng peacock feather (on a mandarin's hat):夺去顶戴～ deprive sb. of his official position; dismiss sb. from office
花令 huālìng season of florescence:养蜂必须随着～迁移蜂箱。Beehives must be moved with the season of florescence.
花柳病 huāliǔbìng venereal disease (VD); sexually-transmitted disease (STD)
花露 huālù 〈中药〉(medicinal) liquid distilled from honeysuckle flowers or lotus leaves
花露水 huālùshuǐ toilet water or lotion; cologne water
花榈木 huālúmù also "花梨木"〈植物〉*Onmosia henryi*
花麻 huāmá also "枲麻" xǐmá male plant of hemp
花马掉嘴 huāmǎ-diàozuǐ 〈方言〉speak sweet words; use blandishments; talk glibly:你不用和我～的,有话就实说吧! Don't use honeyed words with me; out with it!
花蜜 huāmì 〈植物〉nectar:～酵母 nectaromycetes
花面狸 huāmiànlí also "果子狸" guǒzilí; "青猺" qīngyáo masked civet (cat); gem-faced civet (cat)
花苗 huāmiáo ❶ seedlings of ornamental plants:花圃中的～都长出半寸长了。The seedlings in the flower nursery are half a *cun* tall. ❷〈方言〉seedlings of cotton
花名 huāmíng ❶〈旧语〉name of a person (used for household registration) ❷ name of a prostitute
花名册 huāmíngcè register (of names); membership roster; muster roll
花明柳暗 huāmíng-liǔ'àn also "柳暗花明" blooming flowers and dark willows — a beautiful scene
花木 huāmù flowers and trees (in parks and gardens); flowering tree:～商店 flower shop; florist's /不许攀折～! Don't pick the flowers!
花呢 huāní fancy suiting
花鸟 huāniǎo 〈美术〉painting of flowers and birds (in traditional Chinese style):专攻～ specialize in flower-and-bird painting
花农 huānóng flower grower
花盘 huāpán ❶〈植物〉flower disc ❷〈机械〉disc chuck; faceplate:～夹爪 faceplate jaw /～轧头 dog for faceplate
花炮 huāpào fireworks and firecrackers:放～ let off fireworks and firecrackers /点～ light fireworks and firecrackers
花盆 huāpén flowerpot:～架 jardinière
花苹果 huāpíngguǒ 〈植物〉flowering crab; crab apple
花瓶 huāpíng flower vase; vase:～钟 vase clock
花瓶儿 huāpíngr ❶ see "花瓶" ❷ woman employed not for her ability but for her good looks; ornament
花圃 huāpǔ ❶ flower nursery ❷ parterre; flower garden
花谱 huāpǔ florilegium

花期 huāqī florescence of plants; flowering season: ～已过 pass out of bloom /～喷剂 bloom spray /～不遇。Flowers bloom at different times. /寒冬腊月,梅花正当～。Severe winter is just the florescence of plums. /今年～将要推迟。Flowering will be late this year.
花旗 Huāqí Stars and Stripes; Star-Spangled Banner; USA
花旗参 huāqíshēn American ginseng
花旗松 huāqísōng 〈林业〉Douglas fir; spruce fir (*Pseudotsuga taxifolia* or *menziesii*): ～油 Douglas fir oil
花旗银行 Huāqí Yínháng (US) First National City Bank of New York
花扦儿 huāqiānr fresh flower with twig; silk flower; paper flower: 她把买回来的～插在瓶内。She inserted into the bottle the flowers she had bought.
花前月下 huāqián-yuèxià among flowers and under the moon — ideal place for people in love: 多少次～,我们依偎低语。Many a time, we snuggled together talking softly among moonlit flowers.
花枪 huāqiāng ❶ short spear (used in ancient times): 那员小将手执～,左冲右突,如入无人之境。Holding a short spear in his hands, the young warrior dashed around as if he had entered no man's land. ❷ trickery: 耍～ play tricks
花腔 huāqiāng ❶ florid ornamentation in opera singing; coloratura ❷ guileful talk: 你少在我跟前耍～,我不吃这一套! Cut out your blandishments. They don't work on me.
花腔女高音 huāqiāng nǚgāoyīn coloratura (soprano)
花墙 huāqiáng tracery wall; lattice wall
花俏 huāqiào (of clothes) bright-coloured and fashionable: 她不爱穿那些～的衣服。She is not fond of gaudy dresses.
花青 huāqīng 〈化学〉cyanine: ～染料 cyanine dyes
花青素 huāqīngsù anthocyanidin
花楸 huāqiū *also* "山梨" shānlí 〈植物〉sorb; rowan; *Sorbus alnifloria*; *Sorbus aucuparia*
花圈 huāquān (floral) wreath; garland: 献～ place (*or* lay) a wreath /扎～ wreathe flowers into a garland; make a wreath /～舞 garland dance /丧礼～ funeral wreath
花拳 huāquán flowery or fancy boxing (that has no practical value): 他也曾学过几路～,不过是装装样子。He once learned some sort of fancy boxing, just for show.
花拳绣腿 huāquán-xiùtuǐ dazzling or fancy martial arts without practical use; useless fancy boxing; mere ostentation: 像这种～、华而不实的人,有什么用处? What's the use of showy persons without genuine abilities?
花雀 huāquè bramble finch; brambling
花儿洞子 huārdòngzi semi-underground flower greenhouse or cold frame; hothouse for growing flowers
花儿匠 huārjiàng ❶ gardener; florist ❷ artificial flower maker
花儿样子 huāryàngzi embroidery pattern
花儿针 huārzhēn embroidery needle
花容月貌 huāróng-yuèmào *also* "花容玉貌" (of a woman) fair as a flower and beautiful as the moon; (of one's looks) as pretty as a flower and as lovely as the moon; extremely beautiful: 她长得～,美如天仙。She is extremely beautiful and looks like a fairy girl.
花蕊 huāruǐ 〈植物〉stamen; pistil
花色 huāsè ❶ pattern and colour: ～入时 fashionable colours and patterns /这套连衣裙的～很美。This woman's dress is beautiful in both pattern and colour. ❷ (of merchandise) variety of designs, sizes, colours, etc.: 最新～ latest designs /～齐备 have a rich (*or* large) assortment of goods
花色品种 huāsè-pǐnzhǒng variety of colours and designs: ～齐全 rich (*or* whole) variety of colours and designs
花色素 huāsèsù anthocyanidin: ～酶 anthocyanase
花纱布 huāshābù cotton, cotton yarn and cloth
花衫 huāshān 〈戏曲〉one of the female characters, more vivacious than *qingyi* (青衣) but less so than *huadan* (花旦)
花哨 huāshao ❶ (of decoration, ornament) garish; gaudy; showy: 会客室的装饰过于～。The decoration in the drawing room is a bit too flashy. ❷ full of flourishes; flowery; fancy: 电视里的广告越来越～。TV ads are getting more and more fancy. /你少来这些～点子,就你聪明! Cut out your fancy ideas! Don't try to be smart.
花舌子 huāshézi 〈方言〉❶ pleasant but insincere remarks; sweet talk; honeyed words ❷ sweet talker; honey-lipped or honey tongued person
花生 huāshēng peanut; groundnut: ～收获机 peanut harvester /～衣 peanut coat /～蛋白酶 arachain
花生饼 huāshēngbǐng 〈农业〉peanut cake
花生豆儿 huāshēngdòur 〈方言〉shelled peanut or groundnut
花生黑斑病 huāshēng hēibānbìng cercospora black spot of peanut
花生酱 huāshēngjiàng peanut butter
花生壳 huāshēngké peanut shell
花生米 huāshēngmǐ *also* "花生仁" shelled peanut; peanut kernel
花生糖 huāshēngtáng peanut brittle
花生油 huāshēngyóu peanut oil
花石纲 huāshígāng transporting ornamental rocks and rare plants for the enjoyment of the emperor in the late Northern Song Dynasty — a cause of popular misery and revolt
花市 huāshì flower market or fair
花事 huāshì blooming of flowers: ～已过。The florescence has passed. /当年,～最盛的去处就数西山了。In those years the Western Hills was the best place to go for the full bloom.
花饰 huāshì floriation; ornamental design: 新式女套装辅以浅蓝色的～,又大方又好看。Complemented by the light blue ornamental design, the new-style two-piece looked both beautiful and in good taste.
花鼠 huāshǔ Siberian chipmunk; chipmunk
花束 huāshù bunch of flowers; bouquet
花说柳说 huāshuō-liǔshuō 〈方言〉insincere sweet words; flowery words: 经不住他～,她终于答应了婚事。Unable to resist his honeyed words, she finally consented to the marriage.
花丝 huāsī ❶ 〈植物〉filament ❷ 〈工美〉filigree: ～工 filigree work /～镶嵌 filigree inlaying
花丝绒 huāsīróng velvet brocade; brocade velvet
花坛 huātán *also* "花台" (raised) flower bed; flower terrace; parterre
花天酒地 huātiān-jiǔdì indulge in dissipation; live in the world of wine and women; be (out) on the tiles; lead a decadent and dissolute life: 十里洋场上,达官贵人过的是～的生活。The powerful and wealthy led a life of debauchery in the metropolis.
花厅 huātīng (of some large residences) drawing room (mostly built between courtyards or in a garden)
花筒 huātǒng cylindrical fireworks
花头 huātou 〈方言〉❶ decorative pattern; figure: 面料～优美,手感也好。The dress material has an elegant pattern, and feels good as well. ❷ trick; ruse; stratagem: 你少给我出～,谁还会上你的当! Stop your little tricks. They could fool no one. ❸ new ideas: 哥儿几个数他～多。Among the several brothers he is the one who always has new ideas up his sleeve. ❹ knack: 这种游戏看似简单,其实～不少。The game seems easy, but actually there are quite a few tricks in it.
花团锦簇 huātuán-jǐncù *also* "花攒锦簇"; "花簇锦攒" bouquets of flowers and piles of brocade — rich multicoloured decorations; very splendid and beautiful: ～之乡,荣华富贵之地 land of splendour, wealth and power /新房布置得～,艳丽非凡。The bridal chamber was most gorgeously decorated. /那文章写得～一般。The article was brilliantly written.
花托 huātuō 〈植物〉receptacle
花纹 huāwén decorative pattern; figure: 羽毛的～ marking of a bird plumage /～玻璃 figured glass /～钢板 riffled plate (*or* sheet) /～图案 floral design /瓷瓶上有浅蓝色的～。These porcelain vases have light blue designs on them. /她一双巧手,能织各种～的地毯。With her dab (*or* quick and clever) hands she is able to weave carpets of various patterns.
花坞 huāwù sunken flower-bed
花无百日红 huā wú bǎirì hóng no flowers can bloom for a hundred days — good times do not last long: 人无千日好,～。No one can remain friendly for a thousand days, nor can flowers be in bloom for a hundred.
花媳妇儿 huāxífur *also* "二十八星瓢虫" èrshíbāxīng piáochóng potato ladybug or ladybird
花线 huāxiàn ❶ 〈电工〉flexible cord; flex ❷ coloured thread
花香鸟语 huāxiāng-niǎoyǔ *also* "鸟语花香" singing birds and fragrant flowers — a lovely spring scene
花项 huāxiang 〈方言〉item to spend money on: 出门在外,～多,你多带点钱。Take some more money. You may need it on your trip.
花消 huāxiao *also* "花销" ❶ spend; expend (money): 他的工资还不够他一个人～。He cannot even support himself on his meagre

wages. ❷ cost; expense; spending:这几个月的～太大。The expenses have been far too large for these past few months. ❸〈旧语〉commission, taxes and levies:市面不景气,各种～又重,这爿店子只怕开不下去了。As business is slack and the various costs are heavy, I am afraid it'll be difficult for the shop to carry on.

花鞋 huāxié 〈方言〉embroidered shoes

花信 huāxìn florescence: ～风 winds that usher in florescence, supposed to occur 24 times from spring to early summer /～年华 (said of a woman) twenty-four years of age /～尚早。It is too early for the florescence. *or* The florescence is still far away.

花须 huāxū 〈口语〉stamen; pistil

花序 huāxù 〈植物〉inflorescence:穗状～ spike /伞形～ umbel

花絮 huāxù titbits (of news); interesting sidelights:大会～ (interesting) sidelights on the conference /乒坛～ sidelights of the table tennis world

花癣 huāxuǎn 〈医学〉pityriasis simplex on the face

花熏 huāxūn 〈工美〉jade vessel for perfuming; jade perfumer

花押 huāyā 〈旧语〉signature:画～ put one's signature (on a document, etc.); sign (a document, etc.)

花芽 huāyá 〈植物〉(flower) bud:～形成 flower bud formation /～孕育 flower bud initiation

花言巧语 huāyán-qiǎoyǔ sweet words; honeyed words; slick talk; blandishments:你小子惯会人前～! What a sweet-talker you are before people! /今天不许你～。No banana oil today.

花眼 huāyǎn presbyopia

花样 huāyàng ❶ (floral) design; pattern; variety:该店展销的旅游鞋～繁多、号码齐全。The sneakers on display in the shop are of various designs and all sizes. /你这件衣料和我的一样,只是～不同。Your dress is made of the same material as mine. They are different only in pattern. ❷ embroidery patterns:她的～挺多,你去借两样来用用。She has many embroidery patterns. Why don't you go and borrow one or two from her? ❸ trick:耍～ play pranks (on sb.) /你又闹什么～? What new tricks are you up to? /你少给我们玩～! None of your monkey tricks.

花样刀 huāyàngdāo ice skates (for figure skating)

花样翻新 huāyàng-fānxīn ❶ change pattern or design; change methods and ways of doing things:近年来,女装花样在不断翻新。There have been constant innovations in the design of women's dress in recent years. ❷ put old stuff in a new guise; ring changes (on sth.):尽管他们的骗术～,我自有一定之规,决不上当。I am determined not to fall into their traps even though they may ring changes on their old tricks.

花样滑冰 huāyàng huábīng 〈体育〉figure skating:～男舞伴 carrying partner

花样滑水 huāyàng huáshuǐ figure or acrobatic water skiing

花样跳伞 huāyàng tiàosǎn skydiving:～运动员 skydiver

花样游泳 huāyàng yóuyǒng *also* "水上芭蕾" shuǐshàng bālěi 〈体育〉synchronized swimming; water ballet

花药 huāyào ❶〈植物〉anther:～培养 anther culture ❷ flower pesticide

花椰菜 huāyēcài *also* "花菜" cauliflower

花叶 huāyè 〈植物〉floral leaf

花叶病 huāyèbìng 〈农业〉mosaic (disease):甜菜～ beet mosaic /～毒 mosaic virus

花蝇 huāyíng flowerfly

花用 huāyòng 〈口语〉spend; expend; cost:袋里的钱不多了,不敢～。With little money in my pocket, I dare not spend any.

花园 huāyuán *also* "花园子" flower garden; garden:屋顶～ roof garden /～城市 garden city /～公寓 garden apartment

花展 huāzhǎn flower show

花账 huāzhàng padded accounts or bills:造～ make out a padded account; pad accounts

花障 huāzhàng flower coiled fence: ～之内是半亩大小的草坪。Within the flower-coiled fence was half a *mu* of lawn.

花招 huāzhāo *also* "花着" ❶ showy movement in *wushu* (武术); flourish:设计武打动作时,尽量少用～,以造成真实感。In action designing, minimize showy movements so as to give a sense of reality. ❷ trick; ruse; stratagem:耍政治～ resort to political chicanery /他这个人哪,尽耍～。This man is a past master at trickery.

花朝 huāzhāo Flowers' Day, birthday of flowers, the 12th day of the 2nd lunar month: ～之夕,我们相约去看花会。On the eve of Flowers' Day, we promised each other to go to the flower fair.

花朝戏 huāzhāoxì local opera popular in the counties of Zijin (紫金), Wuhua (五华), Longchuan (龙川) and Huiyang (惠阳) in Guangdong Province

花朝月夕 huāzhāo-yuèxī ❶ beautiful flowered morning and light moonlit night — charming scene on a fine day: ～,与二三挚友促膝而谈,其乐何如? Wouldn't it be a great pleasure to have a heart-to-heart talk with a few close friends on a fine day? ❷ 15th day of the 2nd and 8th lunar months

花枝招展 huāzhī-zhāozhǎn (of a woman) be gorgeously dressed:舞会上引人注目的是那几个～的女郎。Several sumptuously dressed girls were the centre of attention at the ball.

花钟 huāzhōng flower clock

花轴 huāzhóu *also* "花茎" floral axis

花烛 huāzhú bridal or wedding candles (usu. with dragon and phoenix designs to be lit in the bridal chamber):洞房～夜 wedding night

花烛夫妻 huāzhú fūqī formally married couple; legitimate husband and wife

花柱 huāzhù 〈植物〉style; stylus; stylet

花砖 huāzhuān tile (flooring); tileboard:～地 tile floor

花子儿 huāzǐr ❶ flower or plant seed ❷〈方言〉cotton seed:～油 cotton-seed oil

花子 huāzi *also* "化子" huāzi beggar:～头 chief beggar /老～ old begger

哗(嘩)

huā 〈象声〉:～～流淌的小溪 brawling (*or* babbling) stream /河水～～直淌。The river gurgled on. /只听见～的一声,大铁门拉上了。With a clang the iron gate was pulled to.

see also huá

哗啦 huālā *also* "哗啦啦"〈象声〉:暴雨～～下了整整一天。The torrential rain kept going all day. /～一声,旧屋倒塌了。The dilapidated house fell heavily to the ground.

huá

搳

huá

搳拳 huáquán *see* "划拳" huáquán

豁

huá

see also huō; huò

豁拳 huáquán *see* "划拳" huáquán

划[1]

huá paddle; row:～舢板 row a sampan /～桨 paddle; row /往上水～ paddle upstream

划[2]

huá be to one's profit; pay:～得着 it pays; it's profitable

划[3](劃)

huá scratch; cut the surface of:～玻璃 cut a piece of glass /树枝～了他的脸。A twig scratched his face. /火柴湿了～不着。Wet matches cannot ignite. /上衣～破了。The jacket got torn. /一颗流星～过夜空。A meteor streaked (*or* flashed) across the evening sky.

see also huà; huai

划不来 huábulái it doesn't pay; it's not worthwhile:为这种人卖命,真是～。It's not worthwhile to sweat for people like him.

划得来 huádelái it pays:花五十元买这双鞋～。It pays to buy this pair of shoes for fifty *yuan*.

划船运动 huáchuán yùndòng boating

划拉 huála 〈方言〉❶ whisk away or off; brush lightly; sweep:你给我～～身上的雪。Please brush (*or* whisk) the snow off my coat. /抽空把院子里的脏东西～～。Please find time to sweep up the garbage in the courtyard. /她把顶柜上的浮土～了几下。She gave the top of the cupboard a quick dust. ❷ seek; look for; ask for:你从哪儿～来这些破烂玩意儿? Where did you get all this rubbish? ❸ gather; collect; scoop:～柴火 collect firewood /我去打工,～点钱花。I am going to do some part-time work to earn some extra money. ❹ scrawl; scribble:你随便～两笔也比我强。Even your scrawl is better than my writing. /你这叫写字? 纯粹是乱～! Do you call this handwriting? It's sheer scribble.

划拳 huáquán *also* "搳拳" huáquán; "豁拳" huáquán finger-

guessing game — a drinking game at feasts：他们几个～行令，直闹了半宿。They played a drinking game until midnight.
划水 huáshuǐ 〈体育〉make strokes with one's arms：他刚学游泳，还不大会～。As he was just learning how to swim, he could only make a few strokes with his arms (*or* paddle a bit with his arms).
划算 huásuàn ❶ calculate; weigh：～来，～去，他整夜没合眼。He was wide awake the whole night weighing the pros and cons. ❷ be to one's profit; pay：这园子还是种瓜～。It pays to grow melons in this garden.
划艇 huátǐng 〈体育〉regatta; rowboat; Canadian canoe; canoeing：～运动 canoeing /皮～ kayak /单人～ single; Canadian single /双人～ double; Canadian pair
划行 huáxíng paddle; row：有节奏地～ paddle rhythmically
划子 huázi small rowboat：木～ small wooden rowboat

滑 huá ❶ slippery; smooth; glossy：光～的石板 smooth stone slab /路陡苔～ steep path and slippery moss /这只猫有一身光～乌亮的毛。The cat has glossy black fur. ❷ slip; slide; glide：从山坡上～下去 slide down the hillside ❸ cunning; crafty; oily; slippery：油腔～调 have a glib tongue /奸～小人 treacherous villain; crafty mean person /偷奸耍～ treacherous and slippery /这次查得严，你休想～过去。You simply can not hope to slip through since the inspection this time is really strict. ❹ (Huá) a surname
滑板 huábǎn ❶〈机械〉slide ❷〈体育〉(of table tennis) feint play ❸〈体育〉skateboard
滑冰 huábīng ❶〈体育〉ice-skating; skating：～运动员 skater /速度～ speed skating /花样～ figure skating /单人～ single skating /双人～ pair skating; pairs /风帆～ skate sailing /～艇 ice-canoe /～鞋 skate ❷ glide or skate on ice：小时候，我们常去后海坐在小木橇上～。We often went to the Rear Lake when I was a kid to glide on the ice on little wooden sleds.
滑冰场 huábīngchǎng skating rink
滑不唧溜 huábujīliū *also* "滑不唧"; "滑不唧唧"〈方言〉slippery：路上～的，摔了好几跤。The road was so slippery that I tumbled several times.
滑草坡运动 huácǎopō yùndòng grass skiing
滑肠 huácháng 〈中医〉lientery
滑车 huáchē ❶〈机械〉pulley; block：～组 block and tackle; pulley block ❷〈生理〉trochlea
滑车神经 huáchē shénjīng 〈生理〉trochlear nerve(s)
滑尺 huáchǐ slide rule
滑道 huádào chute; slide; ski run; ski track：～运输 chuting /一条～从山顶直达山下。A ski track (*or* chute) goes from the top all the way down to the foot of the mountain.
滑动 huádòng slide; glide; slip：～齿轮 sliding gear /～接触 sliding contact /～开关 slide switch /～离合器 sliding clutch /～磨损 skimming wear /～凸轮 sliding cam /～闸门 slide gate
滑动关税 huádòng guānshuì sliding tariff
滑动摩擦 huádòng mócā 〈物理〉sliding friction：～系数 coefficient of sliding friction
滑动轴承 huádòng zhóuchéng 〈机械〉sliding bearing
滑阀 huáfá 〈机械〉guiding valve; slide valve：～装置 slide valve gear
滑竿 huágān a kind of litter (usu. made of bamboo poles)：那几个抬～的老乡路上唱起了山歌。The villagers carrying the litter began to sing folk songs.
滑规 huáguī 〈物理〉sliding gauge
滑旱冰 huá hànbīng roller skate：流行～。Roller skating is popular nowadays.
滑稽 huájī ❶ funny; amusing; comical：～故事 funny story /～表演 comic performance /滑天下之大稽 be the biggest joke in the world; be the object of universal ridicule; be absurd (*or* ludicrous) to the extreme; be the height of absurdity /他觉得这件事又～又可气。He found the matter both amusing and annoying. ❷〈戏曲〉comic talk (popular in Shanghai, Suzhou, Hangzhou and their adjacent areas, similar to comic dialogue or cross talk in nothern China)
滑稽剧 huájījù ❶ *see* "滑稽戏" ❷ ridiculous performance; farce; absurdity
滑稽戏 huájīxì *also* "滑稽剧"〈戏曲〉a kind of farce, popular in Shanghai and some parts of Jiangsu and Zhejiang provinces
滑降 huájiàng ❶〈体育〉glissade (i.e. sliding down a snow-covered mountain side in mountaineering) ❷〈航空〉glide down; descend：飞机～安全着陆。The plane glided down to a safe landing. ❸〈体育〉(of skiing) descent：直线～ straight descent /斜线～ traverse /犁式～ snowplough
滑跤 huájiāo slip and fall：我出门就滑了一跤。I slipped and fell the moment I stepped outside.
滑精 huájīng 〈中医〉involuntary emission; spermatorrhoea
滑扣 huákòu slide fastener
滑浪 huálàng *also* "冲浪" chōnglàng surfing：～板 surfboard /～者 surfer
滑利 huáli ❶ smooth; glossy; sleek ❷ cause to limber up：按摩可以疏通经络，～关节。Massage can unclog the main and collateral channels in the human body and limber up the joints.
滑裂 huáliè slip crack
滑溜 huáliū stir-fry with thick gravy; sauté with starchy sauce：～里脊 sauté fillet with thick gravy /～鱼片 sauté fish slices with thick gravy
滑溜 huáliu silky; smooth (with the implication of fondness)：这条裤子又～又凉快。This pair of trousers is smooth and cool.
滑轮 huálún *also* "滑车"〈机械〉pulley; block：定～ fixed (*or* fast) pulley /动～ movable pulley /～组 block and tackle; pulley block; block and falls
滑脉 huámài 〈中医〉slippery pulse; smooth pulse
滑面 huámiàn 〈机械〉sliding surface; slide face
滑膜 huámó 〈生理〉synovial membrane; synovium
滑膜炎 huámóyán 〈医学〉synovitis
滑腻 huánì (of the skin) satiny; velvety; creamy：光洁、～的皮肤，如同婴儿一样。The skin is smooth and creamy like that of a baby.
滑片式压缩机 huápiànshì yāsuōjī rotary sliding vane compressor
滑坡 huápō ❶〈地质〉landslide; landslip; downslide：～体 slip mass /雨季中，这一段路面多次出现～。Several landslides occurred in this section of road during the rainy season. ❷ decline; slump; deteriorate：质量～。There has been a decline in quality. /国民经济出现严重～。The national economy has slumped.
滑橇 huáqiāo skid; sled：～式起落架 landing skid; landing sled; skid (*or* sled) landing gear /～着陆 skid landing
滑润 huárùn smooth; well-lubricated：～剂 lubricant /他躺在一块～的大青石上。He was lying on a huge smooth grey stone.
滑沙运动 huáshā yùndòng 〈体育〉sand surfing
滑石 huáshí 〈矿业〉talcum; talc
滑石粉 huáshífěn talcum powder
滑爽 huáshuǎng smooth and comfortable：～添加剂 slip additive /这种纺织品具有挺括、～等特点。This textile is characterized by its firmness and smoothness.
滑水 huáshuǐ 〈体育〉water ski：～板 hydro-ski; aquaplane /～运动 water skiing /～运动员 water skier; aquaplaner
滑胎 huátāi 〈中医〉habitual abortion
滑膛炮 huátángpào smoothbore cannon; smoothbore
滑膛枪 huátángqiāng smoothbore (gun); musket
滑梯 huátī (children's) slide
滑铁卢 Huátiělú Waterloo, place near Brussels, Belgium, and scene of Napoleon's defeat in 1815：～战役 Battle of Waterloo
滑头 huátóu ❶ slippery fellow; sly customer：老～ old sly fellow; old fox /小～ petty slicker ❷ slippery; shifty; slick：耍～ try to shirk work (*or* responsibility); act in a slick way
滑头滑脑 huátóu-huánǎo crafty; slick; sly; cunning：张家二小子～的，你少跟他往来。You must keep away from the second son of the Zhang's as far as possible since he is so cunning.
滑翔 huáxiáng glide：～着陆 glide landing /飞机顺着山谷～。The plane was gliding along the mountain valley.
滑翔道 huáxiángdào glidepath：～信标 glidepath beacon /～指示设备 glidepath equipment
滑翔机 huáxiángjī glider; sailplane：初级～ primary glider /中级～ secondary glider /简易～ hang-glider /～机场 gliderport /～驾驶员 volplanist
滑翔器 huáxiángqì 〈航天〉glider：航天～ space glider /火箭～ rocket glider; rocket-assisted glider
滑翔式炸弹 huáxiángshì zhàdàn glide bomb
滑行 huáxíng ❶ slide; coast：下坡～ coast down a slope /在冰道上～ glide along an ice track ❷ taxi：飞机降落并～到位。The plane comes in and taxis up to its place.
滑行道 huáxíngdào 〈航空〉taxi strip; taxiway; taxi track：～灯 taxi-track lights

滑雪 huáxuě ski; skiing:上山～ go skiing in the mountains /～上山吊车 ski lift /～旅行 ski touring /～者 skier /～运动 skiing
滑雪板 huáxuěbǎn skis
滑雪场 huáxuěchǎng ski run
滑雪车 huáxuěchē skibob:～运动 skibobbing
滑雪摩托 huáxuě mótuō snowmobile
滑雪衫 huáxuěshān ski suit
滑雪鞋 huáxuěxié ski boots
滑雪休息处 huáxuě xiūxichù ski lodge
滑雪杖 huáxuězhàng ski pole or stick
滑音 huáyīn ❶〈语言〉glide ❷〈音乐〉portamento
滑泽 huázé smooth; well-lubricated
滑脂 huázhī 〈化工〉grease; grease lubricant:～盒 grease-box
滑脂枪 huázhīqiāng 〈机械〉grease gun

鲋

huá 〈动物〉*Hemibarbus maculatus*

猾

huá cunning; crafty; sly
猾吏 huálì fraudulent or cunning official:～贪赃枉法,无所不为。Perverting justice for a bribe, the cunning official stopped at nothing to do evil.

华[1](華)

huá ❶ radiance; magnificence; splendour:光～ brilliance; splendour; radiance /～服 splendid dress; magnificent clothes ❷ corona:日边之～,其美无比。The corona around the sun is most beautiful. ❸ prosperous; flourishing:繁～ flourshing; bustling /荣～富贵 wealth and rank; glory; splendour ❹ best part; cream:英～ cream; best part /才～ literary (*or* artistic) talent /含英咀～ relish the joys of literature ❺ luxurious; extravagant; flashy:豪～ luxurious; sumptuous; splendid /浮～ showy; ostentatious; flashy; flowery /朴实无～ simple and unadorned ❻ time; years:韶～ beautiful springtime; glorious youth /年～ time; years ❼ grizzled; grey: *see* "～发" ❽〈书面〉〈敬词〉your:～宗 your namesake

华[2](華)

huá matter formed by sediment of mineral in spring water:钙～ travertine /矽～ siliceous sinter; silica sinter

华[3](華)

Huá ❶ China:驻～使节 diplomatic envoys to China; heads of diplomatic missions in China ❷ Chinese (language):～俄词典 Chinese-Russian Dictionary ❸ (Hua, pronounced as Huà and also Huá in recent years) a surname
see also Huà
华北 Huáběi north China, area including Hebei, Shanxi and the municipalities of Beijing and Tianjin:～平原 North China Plain
华表 huábiǎo ornamental column erected in front of a palace, tomb, etc.
华彩 huácǎi ❶ gorgeous, resplendent or rich colour:妙笔着～ gorgeously painted by an artistic hand ❷ magnificent; multi-coloured; bright and colourful:～的衣料 bright and colourful dress material
华彩段 huácǎiduàn 〈音乐〉cadenza
华达呢 huádání 〈纺织〉gabardine
华诞 huádàn 〈书面〉〈敬词〉your birthday:六十～ (your) sixtieth birthday
华灯 huádēng colourfully decorated lantern; (coloured) light:～初上 when the evening lights are lit /广场上春风拂面,～溢彩。On the square a spring breeze was stroking the face and the lights were bright and colourful.
华东 Huádōng east China, consisting of one municipality and seven provinces: Shandong, Jiangsu, Zhejiang, Anhui, Jiangxi, Fujian and Taiwan, and Shanghai Municipality
华而不实 huá'érbùshí flashy and without substance; superficially clever:办事要讲实效,不要搞形式主义、～的那一套。Whatever one does, one should strive for better practical results instead of going for ostentation.
华尔街 Huá'ěrjiē Wall Street, a street at the southern end of Manhattan, New York, where the New York Stock Exchange and other leading financial institutions are located:～财阀 Wall Street magnate /～老板 Wall Streeters
华尔街日报 Huá'ěrjiē Rìbào (US) *The Wall Street Journal*, a business and financial newspaper founded in 1889
华尔兹 huá'ěrzī waltz:跳～ dance a waltz /施特劳斯～圆舞曲 Strauss waltz
华发 huáfà 〈书面〉grey hair:满头～的老人 grey-haired old man (*or* woman) /早生～ have grey hair at an early age (*or* prematurely)
华夫饼干 huáfū bǐnggān waffle
华盖 huágài ❶ (as over an imperial carriage) canopy; baldachin ❷〈天文〉aureole ❸〈迷信〉*Huagai*, a constellation believed in ancient times to cause bad luck:交～运 be in bad luck; have bad luck /运交～欲何求? What can one ask for when luck is against him? ❹〈中医〉*Huagai*, an acupuncture point
华工 huágōng 〈旧语〉indentured Chinese labourer working abroad
华冠丽服 huáguān-lìfú fine hat and beautiful clothes — be gorgeously dressed:几位～的男子走进宾馆大厅。Several magnificently dressed men walked into the hall of the guesthouse.
华贵 huáguì ❶ gorgeous and precious:～的家具 sumptuous furniture /外形～,质地优良 be of magnificent appearance and excellent quality /这位女子衣着～,谈吐大方。This lady is elegantly dressed and has a great deal of poise in her speech. ❷ luxurious and wealthy:～之家 wealthy (*or* opulent) family
华衮 huágǔn ceremonial dress of emperors, princes and nobility in ancient China
华翰 huáhàn 〈书面〉〈敬词〉your letter:喜奉～ pleased to receive your letter
华航 Huáháng (short for 中华航空公司) China Airlines (of Taiwan, China)
华居 huájū 〈书面〉〈敬词〉your residence
华里 huálǐ Chinese *li*, a unit of distance ($= \frac{1}{2}$ kilometre)
华丽 huálì magnificent; resplendent; gorgeous:～的外表 resplendent exterior /宏伟、～的宫殿 magnificent (*or* splendid) palace /室内陈设相当～。The room was sumptuously furnished. /作者早年的诗作,词藻～。The author's early poems were written in flowery (*or* ornate) language.
华美 huáměi magnificent; resplendent; gorgeous:衣着～ beautifully dressed
华纳兄弟影片公司 Huánà Xiōngdì Yǐngpiàn Gōngsī (US) Warner Bros. Picture, Inc.
华南 Huánán south China, i. e. the Pearl River valley including Guangdong and Guangxi
华年 huánián one's best years; youthful years; youth
华侨 huáqiáo overseas Chinese nationals; Chinese residing abroad; overseas Chinese:～政策 policy towards overseas Chinese nationals /归国～ returned overseas Chinese /～领袖 overseas Chinese leader /～学校 school for overseas Chinese
华侨日报 Huáqiáo Rìbào *Wah Kiu Yat Po*, a Hong Kong newspaper
华清池 Huáqīngchí Huaqing Pool in Xi'an, Shaanxi (a spa favored by the Tang Imperial Concubine Yang Guifei 杨贵妃)
华人 huárén ❶ Chinese ❷ foreign citizens of Chinese origin or descent:美籍～ Chinese American
华润集团 Huárùn Jítuán China Resources Group, mainland-funded corporation based in Hong Kong
华沙 Huáshā Warsaw, capital of Poland
华沙条约 Huáshā Tiáoyuē Warsaw Treaty or Pact, signed at Warsaw in 1955 by the then East European countries and the former Soviet Union, in response to the creation of NATO, and dissolved in 1991:～组织 Warsaw Treaty Organization
华盛顿 Huáshèngdùn George Washington (1732-1799), first President of the United States (1789-1797)
华盛顿(哥伦比亚特区) Huáshèngdùn (Gēlúnbǐyà Tèqū) Washington, D.C., capital of the United States
华盛顿邮报 Huáshèngdùn Yóubào *The Washington Post*, leading US newspaper since 1877
华氏 Huáshì Fahrenheit:～温度计 Fahrenheit thermometer /～80度 eighty degrees Fahrenheit; 80°F
华丝葛 huásīgé 〈纺织〉type of jacquard silk fabrics of fine and thin texture, mostly used for making lined clothes
华文 Huáwén Chinese (language):～学校 Chinese language school /～报纸 Chinese language newspaper
华屋山丘 huáwū-shānqiū *also* "华屋丘墟" majestic and magnificent building reduced to a mound of earth; prosperity and decline; vicissitudes; ups and downs:数十年间变化之大,如同～,沧海桑田,令人

H

不胜感慨。The vast changes over those past decades make one feel sad about the vicissitudes of life.

华西 Huáxī west China, an area covering the upper reaches of the Yangtze River including Sichuan Province and Chongqing Municipality

华夏 Huáxià *Huaxia*, an ancient name for China; Cathay:～古国 ancient nation of China /～子孙 descendants of Cathay

华夏系构造 Huáxiàxì gòuzào 〈地质〉Cathaysian (structural) system

华兴会 Huáxīnghuì Society for the Revival of China, a revolutionary organization set up in 1904 in Hunan and united in 1905 with Revive China Society (兴中会) and others to form the United League (同盟会)

华严寺 Huáyánsì Huayan Temple, one of China's major temples in Datong (大同), Shanxi Province

华严宗 Huáyánzōng Huayan Sect of Buddhism in China

华艳 huáyàn gorgeous; ravishing: 文辞～ flowery (*or* embellished, *or* ornate) diction

华裔 huáyì ❶〈书面〉China and the neighbouring countries ❷ foreign citizen of Chinese origin or descent: ～人士 foreign personages of Chinese origin / ～社区 Chinese community

华语 Huáyǔ Chinese (language): ～国家 Chinese-speaking country / ～广播 broadcast in Chinese; Chinese broadcast

华约 Huáyuē (short for 华沙条约组织) Warsaw Treaty Organization (May 1955-July 1991)

华簪之家 huázānzhījiā noble family

华章 huázhāng 〈书面〉〈敬词〉your beautiful writing; your brilliant work: 拜读～，感慨万分。I was greatly moved to read your brilliant writing.

华枝睾吸虫 huázhīgāoxīchóng 〈医学〉clonorchis sinensis

华中 Huázhōng central China, area covering the middle reaches of the Yangtze River including Hubei and Hunan provinces

华胄 huázhòu 〈书面〉❶ descendants of a noble family: 承籍～，为非作歹 indulge in ill-doing by dint of one's family influence ❷ Chinese; Chinese people; people of Chinese ancestry

华柱 huázhù 〈建筑〉candelabrum

华滋 huázī 〈书面〉luxuriant; flourishing: 白露凋～。Luxuriant plants wither away under autumn frost.

哗(嘩、譁) huá

noise; clamour: 喧～ confused noise; commotion; hubbub / 寂静无～ silent and still; very quiet / 舆论大～。There was a public outcry.

see also huā

哗变 huábiàn mutiny: 卫戍部队～投入叛军。The garrison force mutinied and joined the rebels. /～的士兵包围了总统府。The mutinous soldiers surrounded the presidential palace.

哗然 huárán in an uproar; in commotion: 听众～。The audience kicked up a din (*or* burst into an uproar).

哗笑 huáxiào uproarious laughter: 旁观者不禁发出阵阵～。The onlookers could not help bursting into peals of uproarious laughter.

哗噪 huázào clamour; hubbub; din; racket: 孩子们听说这场电影看不成了，立刻～起来。Hearing that they could not see the film, the children raised a terrible clamour.

哗众取宠 huázhòng-qǔchǒng curry favour by claptrap; try to please the public with claptrap; seek popularity by doing or saying sth. sensational; play to the gallery: ～者 demagogue / 他的发言，意在～，讨好听众。His speech was intended to please the audience with claptrap.

铧(鏵) huá

ploughshare: 双轮双～犁 double-wheeled and double-shared plough; double-wheeled and double-furrow plough

铧式犁 huáshìlí mouldboard plow; turnplow; bottomplow

骅(驊) huá

骅骝 huáliú 〈书面〉red fine horse; red steed; roan

huà

话 huà

❶ word; talk: 空～ empty (*or* idle) talk / 废～ nonsense; rubbish / 套～ stereotyped expression / 捧场～ compliment; flattery / 客气～ words of courtesy; polite remarks / 土～ local, colloquial expressions; local dialect / 洋～ foreign (*or* alien) expression / 家常～ small talk; chitchat / 心里～ one's innermost thoughts and feelings / 告别～ farewell remark / 俗～说 as the saying goes / 把文章中的这几句～删去。Please delete these sentences in the article. ❷ talk about; speak about: 茶～会 tea party / 共～往事 talk together about past events

话把儿 huàbàr *also* "话靶儿" subject for ridicule; handle: 抓别人的～做文章 seize sb.'s mistake to make an issue of it

话白 huàbái ❶〈戏曲〉monologue; dialogue; spoken part ❷ prelude monologue (by a storyteller); prologue

话本 huàběn storyteller's script (in folk literature during the Song and Yuan dynasties); text of a story: 宋元～ script for storytelling in Song and Yuan folk literature / ～小说 vernacular novel

话别 huàbié say a few parting words; bid good-bye: 依依～ bid farewell reluctantly / 临行前与友人～，直至深夜。He went to say goodbye to his old friend, and they talked deep into the night.

话柄 huàbǐng subject for ridicule; loophole; handle: 你说话一定要小心，别让人拿作～。You must be careful when you speak so as not to give people a handle (*or* an opening).

话不投机 huàbùtóujī can't see eye to eye with; have a disagreeable conversation: ～半句多。When the conversation gets distasteful, to say one word more is a waste of breath. *or* A disagreeable conversation is a waste of time.

话茬儿 huàchár 〈方言〉❶ thread of discourse or conversation: 我接着他的～，把有关情况给大家伙说说。I will continue from where he left and tell you some relevant facts. ❷ tone of one's speech: 他已露出～，似乎不同意你的条件。His tone of speech suggested that he did not agree to your terms.

话到舌尖留半句 huà dào shéjiān liú bànjù 〈俗语〉hold sth. back when one is just about to say it all; one should not speak one's mind too freely

话锋 huàfēng thread of discourse; topic of conversation: 她见来了外人，有意把～一转。Seeing some outsiders coming in, she deliberately switched the conversation to some other subject. / 我看他是成心避开～，不敢把事情挑明了。I think he avoids the topic on purpose, not daring to put all the cards on the table.

话家常 huà jiācháng chitchat; exchange small talk: 他担任区长以来，难得与老母～了。He has seldom chatted with his old mother since he was appointed head of the district government.

话旧 huàjiù talk over old times; talk about the good old days; reminisce: 清茶一杯，故友数人，我们何时还能相聚～？A cup of tea, and some longtime friends, well, when could we gather again to talk over old times?

话剧 huàjù modern drama; stage play: 演～ perform (*or* stage) a modern drama / 排～ rehearse a modern drama

话剧团 huàjùtuán modern drama troupe; theatrical company

话口儿 huàkǒur 〈方言〉tone; note; implied meaning: 听她的～，好像有些不乐意。From what she said, she seemed a bit reluctant.

话里有话 huàlǐ-yǒuhuà *also* "话中有话" words mean more than they say; there's more to it than meets the ear: 人家～，他没有听出来。He failed to realize the implications of these words.

话料 huàliào 〈口语〉material of conversation or chat

话篓子 huàlǒuzi 〈方言〉talkative or long-winded person; chatterbox; windbag: 这姑娘可是个～。The girl is really a chatterbox.

话梅 huàméi preserved plum

话说 huàshuō ❶ (often used to begin a story, etc.) (The story) says...: ～母子二人一路辛苦，终于来到京城。As the story has it, the mother and son braved all kinds of difficulties and arrived at the capital at long last. ❷ talk; narration; account: ～中国 talk about China

话题 huàtí subject of a talk; topic of conversation: 热门～ popular topics of conversation / 谈着谈着，～就转了。They shifted their subject (of conversation) unawares.

话亭 huàtíng telephone box or booth; kiosk: 附近有座～。There is a telephone box just round the corner.

话筒 huàtǒng ❶ telephone transmitter ❷ microphone: ～噪声 microphone noise ❸ *also* "传声筒" chuánshēngtǒng megaphone

话头 huàtóu thread of discourse: 你不要打断我的～。Don't interrupt me (*or* cut me short). / 她接着他的～，又说开了。She took up the thread of his conversation and went on.

话务员 huàwùyuán (telephone) operator:～代号 operator's number

话匣子 huàxiázi 〈方言〉❶ gramophone ❷ radio (receiving set):老人晚上爱听个～。The old man liked listening to the radio in the evening. ❸ chatterbox:她是个关不住的～。She is an incorrigible chatterbox.

话绪 huàxù mood for or interest in talking:酒把他的～引出来了。Liquor helped arouse (*or* spark) his interest in conversation.

话言话语 huàyán-huàyǔ one's words or remarks; what one says or speaks:从他～中透露,这件事似乎不太好办。From what he said it seems that the matter is a hard nut to crack.

话音 huàyīn ❶ one's voice in speech:听～,你是上海人? Judging from your accent, you are from Shanghai, aren't you? /村长～一落,大家就议论开了。As soon as the village head finished speaking the villagers started arguing about the matter. ❷ tone; implication:听他的～儿,他们准是又想变卦了。His tone suggests that they are going to change their minds again.

话语 huàyǔ speech; remark; utterance:他～不多,可是说得很中肯。He didn't say a lot but very much to the point.

话中有刺 huàzhōng-yǒucì (there are) hidden barbs in one's words; have a sting in the tail; sarcastic remark:他听出她～,不觉脸带愠色。He could not help looking annoyed when he detected there was a catch in her remarks.

画[1](畫) huà ❶ draw; paint:～画儿 draw a picture /～油画 paint in oils /～水彩画 paint in watercolours /～素描 sketch; draw a sketch /～水墨画 paint in Chinese ink /～山水 make a traditional Chinese painting of mountains and waters; draw a landscape /～草图 make a sketch /～人像 make a portrait ❷ drawing; painting; picture:风景～ landscape (painting) /人物～ figure painting /山水～ mountains-and-waters painting; landscape painting /壁～ mural (painting); fresco /水彩～ watercolour (painting) /水墨～ ink and wash; wash painting /宣传～ publicity poster /招贴～ poster /版～ engraving ❸ be decorated with paintings or pictures: *see* "～屏"; "～堂"

画[2](畫、劃) huà ❶ draw a line or write a character as a mark:～线 draw a line ❷ stroke (of a Chinese character):笔～ strokes of a Chinese character /一笔一～ write neatly /"天"字四～。The character "天" has four strokes. ❸〈方言〉horizontal stroke (in Chinese characters)

画板 huàbǎn 〈美术〉drawing board

画报 huàbào illustrated magazine or newspaper; pictorial

画笔 huàbǐ 〈美术〉painting brush; brush

画饼 huàbǐng pie in the sky; Barmecide feast; soap bubble:不料情况突然变化,他的希望也就成了～。Unexpectedly, things took a sudden turn and his hopes were completely dashed.

画饼充饥 huàbǐng-chōngjī draw cakes to allay hunger — feed on illusions:望梅止渴,～ quench one's thirst by imaginary plums and allay one's hunger by painted cakes — console oneself with false hopes

画布 huàbù canvas (for painting)

画册 huàcè album of paintings; picture album:～纸板 album board

画策 huàcè *see* "划策" huàcè

画叉 huàchā long-handled fork (used for hanging or taking off scroll of painting)

画船 huàchuán gaily-painted pleasure boat

画到 huàdào register one's attendance at a meeting or an office; sign in:八点准时～。Sign in at eight sharp.

画地为牢 huàdì-wéiláo draw a circle on the ground to serve as a prison — restrict sb.'s activities to a designated area or sphere:一个作家如若把自己限在一个小圈子里,无异于～。If a writer confines himself to a small circle, it is no different from serving in prison.

画栋雕梁 huàdòng-diāoliáng *also* "雕梁画栋" painted pillars and carved beams (of a magnificent building)

画法 huàfǎ 〈美术〉technique of painting or drawing:这幅山水的～自有独到之处。This way of painting mountains and waters is quite original.

画舫 huàfǎng gaily-painted pleasure boat:湖边停靠着数只～。There are several gaily-painted pleasure boats anchored along the bank of the lake.

画符 huàfú (of a Taoist priest) draw a magic figure to invoke or exorcise spirits and bring good or ill fortune:～念咒 draw magic figures and recite incantations

画幅 huàfú ❶ picture; painting ❷ size of a picture:方寸～竟表现出十分丰富的内容。Much is expressed in the tiny space of a picture.

画稿 huàgǎo ❶ approve a draft (of an official document):按规定,文件主管领导～之后,才能付印。As a rule, an official document cannot be printed until approved by the competent authorities. ❷ rough sketch (for a painting):对照～,可以看出,画家构思曾几经变动。A comparison of the rough sketches shows that the painter made several alterations in the composition of the picture.

画格 huàgé 〈影视〉frame

画舸 huàgě 〈书面〉*see* "画舫"

画工 huàgōng ❶ (professional) painter ❷ *also* "画功" technique of painting:～精细 refined technique of painting

画供 huàgòng 〈法律〉sign on a written confession:他在严刑拷打之下画了供。He signed on the written confession under cruel torture.

画鬼容易画人难 huà guǐ róngyì huà rén nán 〈俗语〉it's easier to draw a ghost than a human — it's easier to engage in groundless and irresponsible talk than to stick to facts

画虎不成反类犬 huà hǔ bù chéng fǎn lèi quǎn *see* "画虎类狗"

画虎画皮难画骨 huà hǔ huà pí nán huà gǔ *see* "画龙画虎难画骨"

画虎类狗 huàhǔ-lèigǒu *also* "画虎类犬"; "画虎不成反类犬" set out to draw a tiger and end up with the likeness of a dog — aim high but achieve little; make a poor imitation:旧体诗不易学,青年人勉强为之,往往～,不伦不类。Old-style poetry is not easy to learn. Young people who try their hand at it often end up with a poor imitation, neither fish nor fowl.

画夹 huàjiā painting folder

画家 huàjiā painter; artist

画架 huàjià easel:～背 easelback

画匠 huàjiàng ❶ artisan-painter ❷〈贬义〉inferior painter

画角 huàjiǎo 〈古语〉painted military bugle

画境 huàjìng picturesque scene:沿三峡乘舟而下,如入～,目不暇接。Going down the Three Gorges of the Yangtze by boat, one feels as if one became part of the picturesque scene which is a feast for the eyes.

画镜线 huàjìngxiàn picture string

画具 huàjù 〈美术〉painter's paraphernalia

画卷 huàjuàn ❶ picture scroll:这几幅山水～,皆出自名家之手。These scrolls of mountains and waters are all by master painters. ❷ magnificent scenery; moving spectacle:西湖胜景犹如一幅天然的～。The beautiful West Lake is just a magnificent spectacle of nature. /作者用充满激情的笔触,描绘了一幅动人的战争～。The artist, with his fervent brush strokes, portrayed a moving battle scene.

画绢 huàjuàn silk for drawing on; drawing silk

画刊 huàkān ❶ pictorial section of a newspaper ❷ pictorial

画框 huàkuàng frame (for a picture)

画廊 huàláng ❶ painted corridor:沿湖～逶迤,亭榭相连,别具特色。With a long painted corridor winding along the lake linking up the pavilions and kiosks, the scenery is unique. ❷ (picture) gallery:二楼～上展出了山水画轴。The painted scrolls of landscape are on display in the gallery on the second floor.

画梁雕栋 huàliáng-diāodòng painted beams and carved pillars

画龙点睛 huàlóng-diǎnjīng bring the painted dragon to life by putting in the pupils of its eyes — add the touch that brings a work of art to life; add the finishing touch; add a word or two to clinch the point:结尾处对现状的抨击,是全文～之笔。The criticism levelled against the existing state of affairs at the end of the article is what clinches the point.

画龙画虎难画骨 huà lóng huà hǔ nán huà gǔ *also* "画虎画皮难画骨"〈俗语〉in drawing a tiger or dragon, it is easy to show its skin or scales, but not its bones:～,知人知面不知心。As you can draw a tiger's skin but not its bones, so you can know a man's face but not his heart.

画眉 huàméi ❶〈动物〉*Garrulax canorus*, a kind of song bird ❷ draw or paint eyebrows

画眉草 huàméicǎo love grass

画面 huàmiàn ❶ general appearance of a picture; tableau:这幅山水长轴～奇特,画法新颖,深受行家好评。The peculiar tableau and novel technique of the long scroll landscape won high commendation from

experts. ❷〈影视〉frame:影片中这几幅内容相关的～,表现了人物复杂的内心世界。The related frames of the film revealed the complex inner world of the characters.

画诺 huànuò 〈旧语〉sign approval on an official document by a government functionary

画皮 huàpí disguise or mask of an evildoer:剥掉这个伪善者的～ strip the mask off (*or* unmask) this hypocrite /这个内心邪恶的人,却披了一张善良的～。This man hid his wickedness under a mask of benevolence.

画片儿 huàpiānr 〈口语〉*see* "画片"

画片 huàpiàn miniature reproduction of a painting; printed picture; picture postcard:风景～ landscape postcard /明星～ picture of a star

画屏 huàpíng painted screen:大厅用～隔成两半。The hall is partitioned off with a painted screen.

画谱 huàpǔ ❶ picture copybook *see also* "画帖" ❷ book on the art of drawing or painting:他对历代的～,有过深入的研究。He has made a thorough study of books on the art of drawing that were handed down from past generations.

画圈 huàquān draw a circle with a pen; draw a circle on an official document acknowledging approval or having read it:有些领导同志只知道画圈圈、批条子,严重脱离群众。Some leading comrades do nothing but draw circles on official documents and write out instructions, thus totally divorcing themselves from the masses.

画蛇添足 huàshé-tiānzú draw a snake and add feet to it — ruin the effect by adding sth. superfluous; do sth. entirely unnecessary:剧作者最后加了一个美满的结局,实在是～。By adding a "tail" of a happy ending the playwright only ruined the effect of the play.

画师 huàshī ❶ master in painting; painter ❷ one who earns his keep by painting; professional painter:宫廷～ painter for the royal (*or* imperial) court / 旅游点常有一些民间～当众献艺。At the tourist sites, there are often some popular professional painters showing their painting skills in public.

画十字 huà shízì ❶ make one's cross or "X" as signature:父亲被逼无奈,只好在契约上画了十字。Father was forced to make his cross on the contract. ❷〈宗教〉make the sign of the cross; cross oneself:她跪在耶稣像前,一边祷告,一边虔诚地画着十字。On bended knees in front of Christ's portrait, she piously crossed herself while praying.

画室 huàshì studio

画坛 huàtán painting or drawing world; painting or drawing circles

画帖 huàtiè book of model paintings or drawings:他从三岁起,就开始临摹～。He started copying model paintings when he was three years old.

画图 huàtú ❶ draw designs, maps, etc.: ～员 draftsman; draughtsman; designer /～室 studio ❷ picture:作者善于描绘农村生活的多彩～。The author is good at drawing colourful pictures of country life. /沿湖一带,风景美如～。The lake side is very picturesque.

画外音 huàwàiyīn 〈影视〉offscreen voice; voice-over; narrator; narration

画像 huàxiàng ❶ draw or paint a portrait; portray:让人～ sit for one's portrait /这位老画师专给名人～。The old painter draws portraits specially of celebrities. ❷ portrait; portrayal:领袖～ portrait of a leader /客厅墙上挂着老人青年时代的自～。On the wall of the hall is the old man's self-portrait as a young man.

画像石 huàxiàngshí 〈考古〉stone relief (on an ancient tomb, shrine, etc.):～墓 tomb with stone relief

画行 huàxíng 〈旧语〉sign OK (on an official document by a responsible person):请速呈总长～。Please submit the document to the chief of general staff for approval right away.

画押 huàyā make one's cross or mark; sign:签字～ sign; affix one's signature

画页 huàyè page with illustrations (in a book or magazine); plate:书中～的设计和印制都很精美。Both the designs and printing of the book's illustrations are exquisite.

画一 huàyī *also* "划一" huàyī standardized; uniform

画苑 huàyuàn gathering place of artists or painters; fine arts circles; painting world

画苑冠冕 huàyuàn-guānmiǎn prominent position or person in the circle of fine arts:齐白石老人,可称得上是～。The old man Qi Baishi deserved the title of master in the painting world.

画院 huàyuàn ❶ imperial art academy, notably that during the reign of Emperor Huizong (徽宗) of the Song Dynasty, whose paintings were characterized by delicate brushwork and close attention to detail:宫廷～ imperial art academy ❷ art academy:江苏～ Art Academy of Jiangsu

画展 huàzhǎn art exhibition; exhibition of paintings; art show:名人～ art exhibition by eminent painters /儿童～ exhibition of paintings by children

画知 huàzhī acknowledge receipt of invitation

画脂镂冰 huàzhī-lòubīng draw on butter or carve ice — futile undertaking; vain attempt:你休要做这种～的蠢事。You'd better give up your futile attempt.

画纸 huàzhǐ paper for painting or drawing; drawing paper

画中人 huàzhōngrén beautiful painted girl; ideal beauty; dream girl:这位小娘子出落得像～。The young lady looks like the beautiful girl in the picture.

画中有诗 huàzhōng-yǒushī there is poetry in the painting; the painting has a poetic quality:像这样～的山水精品,近年来已不多见。Fine landscape paintings with poetic ambience like these have been rare in recent years.

画轴 huàzhóu painted scroll; scroll painting:山水～ scroll painting of landscape /仕女～ traditional Chinese scroll painting of beautiful women

画字 huàzì 〈方言〉make one's cross or mark; sign:刘、王两家均在契约上画了字。The two families of Liu and Wang both signed the contract.

嫿(嫿) huà *see* "婳嫿" guīhuà

划[1](劃) huà ❶ delimit; differentiate:～范围 delimit the sphere /～清界线 make a clear distinction between; make a clean break with sb. /～成右派 be stigmatized as a rightist ❷ transfer; assign:～账 transfer accounts /银行已将那笔贷款～给我厂。The bank transferred the loan to our factory. ❸ plan:筹～ plan and prepare /策～ plan; plot; scheme; engineer

划[2](劃) huà *see* "画[2]" huà

see also huá; huai

划拨 huàbō ❶ transfer:按合同规定,工程所需款项于本年底前由银行～。According to the contract, the money for the project will be transferred through the bank before the end of the year. ❷ allocate:下季度,由公司～的钢材将增加百分之三十。The rolled steel allocated by the company for the next quarter of the year will increase by 30%.

划策 huàcè *also* "画策" huàcè offer advice; give counsel; plan; scheme:此次成功,全仗老兄幕后～。The success is entirely due to your backstage planning.

划等号 huà děnghào equate one thing with another:这两种错误的性质不同,不能～。The two mistakes, different in nature, must not be mentioned in the same breath.

划地为牢 huàdì-wéiláo *see* "画地为牢" huàdì-wéiláo

划定 huàdìng delimit; designate:～作业区 designate the area of operation /两国重新～边界。The two countries re-delimited the boundary line.

划分 huàfēn ❶ divide; partition:～卫生责任区 divide into zones of sanitation responsibility /战后,大国重新～势力范围。After the war the big powers carved out spheres of influence all over again. /机构改革后,这几个部门应重新～权限。After the organizational reform, these departments should redefine their competence. ❷ differentiate; distinguish:～阶级成分 determine class status /～不同性质的矛盾 distinguish between different kinds of contradictions /该书各篇,哪些是作者本人所写,哪些是后学者所加,实在难以～。It is rather hard to determine which parts of the book were written by the author himself and which were added to it by later scholars.

划粉 huàfěn tailor's chalk

划杠杠 huà gànggang (originally) draw a line; set limits:你别先～,把自己排除在外。You must not try to set limits and count yourself out.

划归 huàguī put under (sb.'s administration, etc.); incorporate into:近郊几个县,已经～直辖市了。The suburban counties have been incorporated into the centrally administered municipality. /转产的大

型企业,一律～地方管理。Big enterprises that have changed their lines of production will all be put under local administration.

划价 huàjià (of hospital pharmacy) calculate medical expenses for a patient:患者先～,后付款。Patients must have their medical expenses calculated before paying.

划句号 huà jùhào put in a period or full stop:划上完满的句号 bring sth. to a successful conclusion

划框框 huà kuàngkuang set limits; place restrictions:～,定调调 place restrictions and set the tone

划清 huàqīng draw a clear line of demarcation; make a clear distinction; differentiate clearly:跟敌人～界限 make a clean break with the enemy; draw a clear line of demarcation between ourselves and the enemy /是非界限是个原则问题,一定要认真～。The distinction between right and wrong is a matter of principle, and we must tell them apart meticulously.

划然 huàrán 〈书面〉clear and neat; clearly different:～分开 clearly disparate (*or* separate)

划时代 huàshídài epoch-making:～的事件 epoch-making event /～的历史文献 landmark historical document; momentous historical document

划一 huàyī ❶ standardized; uniform:尺寸～ be of uniform size /整齐～的公文格式 standardized format of official documentation ❷ standardize; make consistent:～体例 make the style (of writing) consistent

划一不二 huàyī-bù'èr ❶ fixed; unalterable:价格～。As priced. *or* No bargaining. ❷ rigid; cut and dried:这类文章可长可短,没有～的要求。There is no rigid requirement (*or* no hard and fast rule) for the length of this type of article.

化[1]

huà ❶ change; turn; transform:变～ change; alter /千变万～ myriads of changes; ever-changing /顽固不～ stubbornly resisting any change; obdurate /～悲痛为力量 turn sorrow (*or* grief) into strength /～敌为友 convert an enemy into a friend ❷ convert; influence:教～ educate and influence /潜移默～ exert a subtle influence on sb.'s character, thinking, etc. ❸ melt; dissolve:冰消雪～。The ice and snow have melted away. /冻肉先在水里～一～。First put the frozen meat in the water to defrost for a while. ❹ digest; eliminate; dispel; remove:～食 help digestion ❺ burn up:焚～ burn up; incinerate /烧～ burn (paper, etc. as an offering to the dead) /火～ cremate /～尸炉 cremator; cinerator ❻ (of monks and priests) pass away; die:坐～ pass away in a sitting posture /羽～ (of Taoists) ascend to heaven and become immortal; die ❼ (short for 化学) chemistry:理～ physics and chemistry /生～ biochemistry ❽ *used as a suffix to a noun or an adjective to indicate sth. or sb. is becoming or made to have that attribute*:绿～ make (a place) green by planting trees, flowers, etc.; afforest /美～ beautify; prettify; embellish /丑～ blacken; discredit /恶～ worsen; aggravate; deteriorate /深～ deepen /机械～ mechanize /现代～ modernize /沙漠～ desertification /园林～ make a place green with parks and woods

化[2]

huà 〈宗教〉(of Buddhist monks or Taoist priests) beg alms:募～ collect alms

see also huā

化除 huàchú clear up; dispel; remove:～成见 dispel prejudices /～隔阂 clear up misunderstandings; end estrangement

化冻 huàdòng thaw; defrost

化肥 huàféi (short for 化学肥料) chemical fertilizer

化废为宝 huàfèiwéibǎo turn waste materials into things of value; turn waste into assets

化粪池 huàfènchí septic tank

化腐朽为神奇 huà fǔxiǔ wéi shénqí *also* "化腐为奇" turn the foul and rotten into the rare and ethereal; make the rotten things miraculous; make the useless useful; turn bad into good

化干戈为玉帛 huà gāngē wéi yùbó cease hostilites and make peace; bury the hatchet; turn hostility into friendship:双方只要有诚意,就不难～,和平解决彼此的争端。It will not be difficult to resolve disputes and make peace provided the two sides have good faith. /如今两国～,建立了友好睦邻关系。The two countries have buried the hatchet and become friendly neighbours.

化工 huàgōng (short for 化学工业) chemical industry:～机械 chemical machinery /～生产 chemical production /～系统 departments of chemical industry and affiliated organizations /～原料 industrial chemicals /～产品 chemical products

化工厂 huàgōngchǎng chemical plant:～废水 chemical plant wastewater

化公为私 huàgōngwéisī turn public property into private property; line one's pocket with public funds; embezzle public property

化合 huàhé 〈化学〉chemical combination:～反应 combination reaction /氢与氧～而成水。The combination of hydrogen and oxygen produces water.

化合价 huàhéjià *also* "原子价" yuánzǐjià valence

化合量 huàhéliàng combining weight

化合物 huàhéwù 〈化学〉chemical compound:高分子～ high polymer; highly polymerized compound /～合成 synthesis of compounds

化剑为犁 huàjiànwéilí beat swords into ploughshares; disarm and make peace

化解 huàjiě resolve; eliminate:～矛盾 resolve contradictions /她心中的疑虑难以～。It's difficult to dispel her misgivings.

化境 huàjìng sublimity; perfection:已入～ reach perfection /她的表演艺术已臻～,自有独特的风格。Her performance is superb, and she has a distinctive style of her own.

化疗 huàliáo chemotherapy:～专家 chemotherapist

化零为整 huàlíngwéizhěng gather parts into a whole; assemble the parts into a whole:小股部队～,经过整编后,又派赴前线。The small detachments were merged and sent to the front after reorganization.

化名 huàmíng ❶ use an assumed name:～刘玉 go by the alias Liu Yu ❷ assumed name; alias:他写文章用的是～。He writes under a pseudonym. /他用阿兰这个～来遮人耳目。He passed by the name of Alan.

化募 huàmù (of Buddhist monks or Taoist priests) collect alms; beg alms

化脓 huànóng fester; suppurate:子宫～ pyometra /～的伤口 festering wound

化脓球菌 huànóng qiújūn pyococcus

化脓性皮炎 huànóngxìng píyán 〈医学〉pyoderma; pyodermatitis

化脓性肾炎 huànóngxìng shènyán 〈医学〉pyonephritis

化身 huàshēn ❶ incarnation:佛经故事中的鹿王,正是菩萨的～。The deer king in the stories of Buddhist scripture was the incarnation of Bodhisattva. ❷ embodiment:真理的～ embodiment of truth /旧小说中把包公、海瑞等清官,描写成正义的～。Honest and upright officials like Bao Gong and Hai Rui were often described in old novels as justice incarnate. /她是欢乐的～。She was phantom of delight.

化生 huàshēng ❶〈生理〉metaplasia ❷〈书面〉give birth and foster growth:天地～万物。From heaven and earth come all things in this world.

化石 huàshí 〈考古〉fossil:变为～ fossilize; become fossilized /标准～ index fossil /指相～ facies fossil /微体～ microfossil /～作用 fossilification; fossilization /古生物～ paleobiofossil /恐龙～ dinosaur fossil /～带 fossil zone /修整～ dress fossil /～组合 assemble a fossil

化痰 huàtán 〈中医〉reduce phlegm:清热～ alleviate fever and reduce phlegm /～利咽 reduce phlegm and soothe the pharynx /～平喘 resolve sputum and relieve asthma /～散结 reduce phlegm and resolve hard masses /～生津 good for expectoration /～生津剂 expectorant /～止咳 reduce phlegm and stop coughing

化痰药 huàtányào 〈医学〉apophlegmatisant

化铁炉 huàtiělú 〈冶金〉cupola furnace; blast cupola; cupola; iron-melting furnace

化外 huàwài 〈旧语〉outer fringes of civilization; place of cultural backwardness:～之地 region of cultural wilderness (*or* beyond the pale of civilization) /～之民,不知礼数。Uncivilized beings do not know what courtesy means.

化为灰烬 huàwéi-huījìn turn to dust and ashes; crumble to dust; be consumed by fire; be reduced to ashes:一场大火使大片森林～。A big fire burnt out a vast tract of forest.

化为泡影 huàwéi-pàoyǐng vanish like soap bubbles; melt into thin air; come to naught:她多年美梦～。Her fond dream for many years went down the drain.

化为乌有 huàwéi-wūyǒu pass into nothingness; vanish into thin air; go up in smoke:一场豪赌把他十年的积蓄～。All his savings over a decade vanished after the gambling spree.

化纤 huàxiān (short for 化学纤维) chemical fibre:～厂 chemical fibre factory /～织品 chemical textile

H

化险为夷 huàxiǎnwéiyí turn danger into safety; get out of the jaws of danger; head off a disaster:他终于～，反败为胜。Finally, he turned the tables on his opponent and won the game. /船遇狂风暴雨，多亏船长镇定指挥，始得～。The ship was caught in a violent storm, but it weathered the crisis thanks to the captain's guidance and presence of mind.
化形 huàxíng (of demons and ghosts) change of appearance; metamorphosis:老水怪～后，变作一个美丽的姑娘。The old water monster turned itself (*or* metamorphosed) into a beautiful girl.
化学 huàxué ❶ chemistry:有机～ organic chemistry /无机～ inorganic chemistry /分析～ analytical chemistry /应用～ applied chemistry /物理～ physical chemistry /理论～ theoretical chemistry /放射～ radiochemistry /生物～ biochemistry /～专业 chemistry major /～研究所 institute of chemistry ❷〈口语〉celluloid:这套餐具是～的。This set of tableware is made of celluloid.
化学爆炸 huàxué bàozhà chemical explosion
化学变化 huàxué biànhuà chemical change
化学玻璃 huàxué bōli chemical glass:～器皿 chemical glassware
化学成分 huàxué chéngfen chemical composition
化学除草剂 huàxué chúcǎojì chemical herbicide
化学除莠 huàxué chúyǒu chemical weed control
化学当量 huàxué dāngliàng chemical equivalent
化学电池 huàxué diànchí chemical battery
化学动力学 huàxué dònglìxué chemical kinetics
化学镀 huàxuédù chemical plating
化学惰性 huàxué duòxìng chemical inertness
化学发光 huàxué fāguāng chemiluminescence
化学反应 huàxué fǎnyìng chemical reaction:～物 chemical reaction product
化学方程式 huàxué fāngchéngshì chemical equation
化学仿生学 huàxué fǎngshēngxué chemical bionics
化学肥料 huàxué féiliào chemical fertilizer
化学废物 huàxué fèiwù chemical waste
化学分类学 huàxué fēnlèixué chemotaxonomy
化学分析 huàxué fēnxī chemical analysis
化学符号 huàxué fúhào chemical symbol
化学工程 huàxué gōngchéng chemical engineering
化学工业 huàxué gōngyè chemical industry:国家石油和～局 State Bureau of Petroleum and Chemical Industries
化学合成 huàxué héchéng chemosynthesis
化学激光器 huàxué jīguāngqì chemical laser
化学计量学 huàxué jìliàngxué stoichiometry
化学键 huàxuéjiàn chemical bond
化学疗法 huàxué liáofǎ chemotherapy
化学能 huàxuénéng chemical energy
化学平衡 huàxué pínghéng chemical equilibrium
化学溶蚀 huàxué róngshí chemolysis
化学杀菌 huàxué shājūn chemosterilization
化学渗透 huàxué shèntòu chemosmosis
化学式 huàxuéshì chemical formula
化学试剂 huàxué shìjì chemical reagent
化学水文学 huàxué shuǐwénxué chemical hydrology
化学脱水 huàxué tuōshuǐ chemical dehydration
化学稳定性 huàxué wěndìngxìng chemical stability
化学武器 huàxué wǔqì chemical weapon
化学系统工程 huàxué xìtǒng gōngchéng chemical system engineering
化学纤维 huàxué xiānwéi chemical fibre
化学性质 huàxué xìngzhì chemical property
化学烟雾 huàxué yānwù chemical smog
化学冶金学 huàxué yějīnxué chemical metallurgy
化学抑制剂 huàxué yìzhìjì chemical inhibitor
化学育种 huàxué yùzhǒng breeding by chemical induction
化学元素 huàxué yuánsù chemical element:～周期表 periodic table of chemical elements
化学运动性 huàxué yùndòngxìng chemokinesis
化学战争 huàxué zhànzhēng chemical warfare
化学制版 huàxué zhìbǎn chemical type
化学作用 huàxué zuòyòng chemical reaction; chemism
化验 huàyàn chemical or physical examination; laboratory test:～单 laboratory test report /～结果 result of laboratory test /～室 laboratory /～员 laboratory technician (*or* assistant); analyst /～证明 analysis certificate /血常规～ ordinary blood test
化蛹 huàyǒng 〈生物〉pupate:～进度 pupation progress
化油器 huàyóuqì 〈机械〉carburetor
化淤 huàyū 〈中医〉eliminate stasis:～消肿 eliminate stasis and swelling
化雨春风 huàyǔ-chūnfēng *also* "春风化雨" life-giving breeze and rain — salutary influence of education, etc.
化育 huàyù bring up; rear:阳光雨露，～万物。Sunlight, rain and dew nourish all things on earth.
化缘 huàyuán (of Buddhist monks or Taoist priests) beg alms:托钵～ hold an bowl and beg alms /～的行脚僧 alms-begging itinerant monk
化斋 huàzhāi *also* "打斋" dǎzhāi;"打斋饭" dǎzhāifàn (of a monk) beg a (vegetarian) meal; beg alms from door to door
化整为零 huàzhěngwéilíng break up the whole into parts:部队～，分散突围。The troops organized themselves into small units and broke out of the encirclement separately.
化妆 huàzhuāng put on make-up; make up; apply cosmetics:对镜～ put on make-up before a mirror /～后，她显得更美了。After the make-up she looked even more attractive.
化妆品 huàzhuāngpǐn cosmetics:女性～ female cosmetics /进口～ imported cosmetics /～专柜 cosmetics counter/ 整套～ dressing set /～工业 cosmetics industry /～制造商 cosmetician /滥用～ lavishly cosmeticize
化妆师 huàzhuāngshī visagiste; make-up man
化妆室 huàzhuāngshì ❶ dressing room ❷〈方言〉toilet; lavatory
化妆台 huàzhuāngtái dressing-table; dresser
化装 huàzhuāng ❶ (of actors) make up:她～演一名歌手。She made up for the part of a singer. ❷ disguise; disguise oneself:～侦察 go reconnoitering in disguise /他们俩常～成夫妻执行任务。They often performed missions disguised as man and wife.
化装室 huàzhuāngshì dressing-room
化装舞会 huàzhuāng wǔhuì costume ball; fancy dress ball; masquerade

华(華)

Huà ❶ Mount Hua (in Shaanxi Province) ❷ a surname
see also huá
华山 Huàshān Mount Hua in Shaanxi Province, one of the Five Sacred Mountains in China
华佗 Huà Tuó Hua Tuo (141-203), noted surgeon and physician at the end of the Han Dynasty
华佗再世 Huà Tuó zàishì rebirth of the great surgeon Hua Tuo; present-day Hua Tuo
华嵒 Huà Yán Hua Yan (formerly translated as Hua Yen) (1682-1756), painter of the Qing Dynasty

桦(樺)

huà 〈植物〉birch:白～ white birch /黑～ black birch /～木 birch wood

huái

淮

Huái Huaihe River
淮北 Huáiběi Huaibei, region north of the Huaihe River, esp. northern Anhui Province:～平原 Huaibei Plain
淮海 Huáihǎi Huai-Hai, area north of the Huaihe River with Xuzhou (徐州) as the hub and Haizhou (海州)
淮海戏 huáihǎixì 〈戏曲〉Huaihai opera, a local opera popular in areas around Huaiyin (淮阴) and Xuzhou in northern Jiangsu Province
淮海战役 Huáihǎi Zhànyì Huai-Hai Campaign (6 Nov. 1948-10 Jan. 1949), second of the three decisive battles fought between the People's Liberation Army, led by the CPC, and the Kuomintang Armies in the Chinese People's War of Liberation
淮河 Huáihé Huaihe River, major river between the Yellow River and the Yangtze
淮剧 huáijù 〈戏曲〉Huai opera, popular in northern Jiangsu
淮南 Huáinán Huainan, region between the Huaihe and the Yangtze rivers, esp. central Anhui Province
淮南子 Huáinánzǐ *Huainanzi*, a work of eclectic learning compiled by Prince Huainan and others of the Western Han Dynasty

怀(懷) huái ❶ chest; bosom: 敞胸露～ bare one's chest (*or* breast); have one's jacket (*or* shirt) unbuttoned /婴儿偎在母亲的～里。The baby nestled in its mother's arms. ❷ mind; heart: 壮～激烈 be filled with righteous indignation; be lofty-minded /虚～若谷 be humble and open-minded /开～畅饮 drink to one's heart's content /正中下～ be just what one wants; fit in exactly with one's wishes ❸ think of; yearn for; miss: ～乡之情 yearning for one's native place; homesickness; nostalgia /追～往事 recall past events; reminisce about the old days ❹ conceive (a child): ～了双胞胎 be expecting twins ❺ keep in mind; cherish; harbour; nurse: ～有私心 have selfish motives /～有杀机 have a thirst for blood; harbour an intention to kill /心～仇恨 nurse a hatred /～着远大的理想 cherish high aspirations /满～激情 be filled with ardour ❻ (Huái) a surname

怀宝迷邦 huáibǎo-míbāng keep one's talents to oneself and not serve one's country; render no service to one's country, though talented: 我们不能学旧时代的隐士, ～, 不去报效祖国。We should not imitate hermits of the past and refuse to use our talents in the service of our country.

怀抱 huáibào ❶ hold or carry in one's arms; embrace: ～婴儿的女人 woman with a baby in her arms ❷ bosom; embrace: 睡在母亲的～里 sleep in one's mother's arms /我如今又回到了故乡的～。I have now returned to the embrace of my home town. ❸ cherish: ～着治国安邦的远大志向 cherish the lofty ideal of bringing peace and prosperity to one's country ❹〈书面〉ambition; ideal; wish: 他的～未必能够实现。He may not be able to realize his ambition (*or* ideal). ❺〈方言〉babyhood: 在这姑娘～儿时我就见过她。I saw the girl when she was still a baby.

怀璧其罪 huáibì-qízuì the precious jade lands its innocent possessor in jail; an innocent man gets into trouble because of his talents: 这种～的现象并不少见。It is no rare thing that innocent people get persecuted for their talents.

怀表 huáibiǎo pocket watch

怀才不露 huáicái-bùlù refrain from showing one's abilities; sheathe or hide one's talents; be modest about one's learning: 大智若愚, ～。A really wise man looks slow-witted and does not show his abilities.

怀才不遇 huáicái-bùyù have had no opportunity to use one's talents; be unrecognized for all one's talents: 他一辈子～, 穷困潦倒而死。He never had an opportunity to use his talents and died in frustration and poverty.

怀春 huáichūn〈书面〉(of young girls) yearn for the opposite sex; be lovesick: 少女～ lovesick young girl

怀古 huáigǔ meditate on the past; reflect on an ancient event: ～诗 poem meditating on the past, or reflecting on an ancient event /～凭吊 evoke a sense of the past when visiting historical ruins /发～之幽情 express one's nostalgia for the past

怀鬼胎 huái guǐtāi〈比喻〉harbour evil designs; have ulterior motives; have a bad conscience: 谁知道你心里怀着什么鬼胎! Who knows what ulterior motives you have!

怀恨 huáihèn cherish hatred; bear ill will; nurse grievances; be resentful: 对别人的批评～在心 bear a grudge against sb. for his criticism /事情过去很久了, 何必总是～在心? Why nurse grievances over something long past? /她心里～, 嘴上却不说什么。She said nothing, though feeling resentful.

怀旧 huáijiù recall past events or old friends (with kindly thoughts); be nostalgic for old times or friends: 老人爱～。Old people tend to be nostalgic for the past. /经常～是衰老的表现。It is a sign of aging (*or* senility) to be given to recalling one's good old days.

怀恋 huáiliàn think fondly of (past times, old friends, etc.); look back nostalgically; miss: ～旧时的情人 think fondly of (*or* miss) one's old flame /心中的～向谁诉说? Who could I tell my nostalgic (*or* lovesick) feelings?

怀念 huáiniàn cherish the memory of; think of longingly; miss: ～故乡 think of one's hometown with nostalgic longing; miss one's hometown; be homesick /往事的～ memories of the past (*or* a past event) /深情地～着某人 cherish sb.'s memory with deep affection

怀妊 huáirèn be pregnant; be in the family way

怀柔 huáiróu control through mollification or conciliation: 这种～政策, 正是霸道政策的补充。The policy of conciliation (*or* placation) serves as a complement to hegemonism.

怀素 Huáisù Huaisu (725-785), Buddhist monk and calligrapher of the Tang Dynasty, esp. known for his wild cursive handwriting

怀胎 huáitāi be pregnant; conceive (a baby): 调查就像"十月～", 解决问题就像"一朝分娩"。Investigation may be likened to long months of pregnancy and solving a problem to the day of birth.

怀想 huáixiǎng cherish the memory of; think about with affection; yearn for: 往事辛酸, 令人～不已。Past miseries brought back countless memories.

怀疑 huáiyí ❶ doubt; scepticism; suspicion: 表示～ cast doubts (*or* suspicions)(on sb. or sth.) /消除～ dispel doubts; clear up suspicions /毫不～ without the slightest suspicion; without a shadow of doubt /持～态度 take a sceptical attitude /我对他的能力表示～。I am doubtful (*or* sceptical) about his ability. /谁也没有～你的话。Nobody doubts your word. ❷ suspect: 我～他今天不会来了。I suspect that he'll not show up today. /他～林中埋有伏兵。He suspected an ambush in the woods.

怀疑对象 huáiyí duìxiàng suspect

怀疑论 huáiyílùn *also* "怀疑主义"〈哲学〉scepticism: ～者 sceptic

怀怨 huáiyuàn cherish hatred; bear ill will; have complaints; be resentful: 有话好说, 不必如此～。Out with what you have in mind, and stop being resentful.

怀孕 huáiyùn be pregnant; be with child; conceive; be expecting: 妇女～期保健措施 health precautions during a woman's pregnancy /他妻子～了。His wife is expecting.

耰 huái

耰耙 huáiba〈农业〉a kind of harrow used in northeast China

槐 huái ❶〈植物〉Chinese scholartree (*Sophora japonica*): 刺～ locust tree /洋～ acacia ❷ (Huái) a surname

槐蚕 huáicán inchworm; geometer; looper (living on a Chinese scholartree)

槐豆 huáidòu Chinese scholartree seeds; sophora beans

槐黄 huáihuáng sophora yellow, a dye made from sophora flowers and beans

槐角 huáijiǎo *also* "槐实"〈中药〉seed pod of the Chinese scholartree; sophora pod

槐米 huáimǐ〈中药〉sophora bud

踝 huái〈生理〉ankle; malleolus: 内～ internal malleolus /外～ external malleolus /～宽 ankle breadth

踝骨 huáigǔ anklebone; malleolus

踝关节 huáiguānjié ankle

踝子骨 huáizigǔ〈口语〉ankle; anklebone

徊 huái *see* "徘徊" páihuái

see also huí

huài

坏(壞) huài ❶ bad; poor; defective: ～影片 bad (*or* harmful) film /～习气 bad habit /比想像的要～ worse than expected /越来越～ go from bad to worse /这事办得不～。That was pretty well done. *or* That was not bad at all. ❷ evil; wicked: 为人太～ such an evil person; so wicked ❸ go bad; break down: 米饭～了。The rice went bad. /自行车～了。The bike broke down. /我有一颗牙～了。One of my teeth has decayed. /玩具摔～了。The toy crashed and broke. /他不小心吃～了肚子。Careless eating spoiled his stomach. ❹ spoil; ruin: 成事不足, ～事有余 unable to accomplish anything but liable to spoil everything /电视看多了, ～眼睛。Watching too much TV will ruin (*or* spoil) your eyesight. ❺ badly; awfully; very: 疼～了(of a wound, etc.) hurt badly; (of a person) feel a great deal of pain /饿～了 be very hungry; be famished /累～了 be dog-tired; be dead tired /渴～了 be dying of thirst /忙～了 be terribly busy /这件事可把他气～了。That threw him into a rage. ❻ evil idea; dirty trick: 使～ play a dirty trick; do a mischief; resort to trickery /一肚子～ full of evil ideas (*or* dirty tricks)

坏包儿 huàibāor〈口语〉rascal; rogue; bad egg: 这小子是有名的～, 什么事都干得出来。He is a notorious rascal capable of anything.

坏处 huàichu harm; disadvantage: 对你有什么～呢? What harm

H

will that do you? /赌博的～太大。Gambling is a great scourge. /凡事多往～着想，以免临时措手不及。Keep the disadvantages in mind so as not to be caught unprepared.

坏蛋 huàidàn rascal; scoundrel; bastard; bad egg:把这个～抓起来，谁也不感到意外。No one was surprised when the rascal was thrown into prison.

坏东西 huàidōngxi rogue; rascal; scoundrel; bastard:有几个～专门造谣生事。There are a few bastards who make a living by spreading rumours and stirring up trouble.

坏分子 huàifènzǐ bad element; evildoer

坏话 huàihuà ❶ unpleasant words:好话～都要听。One must hear people out, whether their words sound pleasant or not. ❷ malicious remarks; vicious talk:他的一个毛病是爱在背后说别人～。One of his weaknesses is that he often speaks ill of others behind their backs.

坏疽 huàijū 〈医学〉gangrene:伤口～，病人生命垂危。As gangrene has set in the wound, the patient's life is in immediate danger.

坏疽性肺炎 huàijūxìng fèiyán 〈医学〉gangrenous pneumonia

坏人 huàirén bad or wicked person; evildoer; scoundrel:～不臭，好人不香。Bad people are not despised and good people not respected. /～当道，好人受气。Bad people hold sway while good people are pushed around. /这条小路上常有～拦劫单身妇女。Women on their own are often mugged in this back-alley.

坏事 huàishì ❶ ruin sth.; spoil sth.; make things worse:这样做非～儿不可。It will only make things worse that way. /他一看试卷就知道要～。One look at the test paper and he knew he was in for it. ❷ bad thing; evil deed:～做绝 stop at nothing in doing evil /～变好事 turn bad things to good account /干～的人决不会有好下场。Evildoers will come to no good end.

坏水 huàishuǐ 〈口语〉〈比喻〉evil trick; deceit; craft and guile:使～ play evil tricks; use deceit /蔫不唧儿地冒～ be full of tricks though quiet /别信她! 这个女人可是一肚子～! Don't trust her. She's full of craft and guile.

坏死 huàisǐ 〈医学〉necrosis:局部～ local necrosis /渐进性～ necrobiosis /肌肉～ necrosis of muscle /骨～ necrosis of bone /～组织 slough

坏心眼儿 huàixīnyǎnr 〈口语〉evil intention; dirty or mean trick:你为什么老是跟我们使～? Why are you always playing mean tricks against us? /自打同她见面后，他就存了～。He began to harbour evil intentions against her after their first meeting.

坏血病 huàixuèbìng 〈医学〉scurvy; vitamin C deficiency; scorbutus:婴儿～ infantile scurvy

坏账 huàizhàng bad debt or loan

huai

H

划(劃) huai *see* "刵划" bāihuai
see also huá; huà

huān

欢(歡、懽) huān ❶ joyous; merry; happy:悲～离合 joys and sorrows, partings and reunions /不～而散 part in discord /～叙友情 renew a friendship happily; have a happy reunion with friends /寻～作乐 seek pleasure; make merry; have a good time /(一晌)贪～ indulge in pleasure (for a moment) ❷ lover; sweetheart:另有新～ have a new sweetheart; love someone else /非其所～〈书面〉not what one fancies (*or* likes, *or* loves) /男～女爱 mutual love between man and woman; love between the sexes /求～ seek sexual pleasure; ask (usu. a girl) for sex /偷～ have illicit sexual pleasure; have an affair ❸ 〈方言〉vigorously; with great drive; with a vengeance; in full swing:干得～ get into the swing of one's work; work vigorously /这几个孩子玩得正～。These children are having a hell of a good time. /鸟儿叫得真～。The birds are chattering incessantly.

欢蹦乱跳 huānbèng-luàntiào *also* "活蹦乱跳" huóbèng-luàntiào dancing and jumping with joy; healthy-looking and vivacious; alive and kicking:～的青年人 young people overflowing with vigour; exuberant young people /我看着这些～的孩子们，连自己也觉得年轻了许多。Looking at those healthy and vivacious kids, I felt much younger myself.

欢忭 huānbiàn 〈书面〉happy; joyous; joyful

欢畅 huānchàng elated; joyous:大病已愈，她心中感到分外～。Fully recovered from the serious illness, she was elated.

欢唱 huānchàng sing merrily:尽情～ sing to one's heart's content

欢度 huāndù spend (an occasion) joyfully:～新春佳节 celebrate the Spring Festival (*or* the Chinese Lunar New Year) (with jubilation) /～晚年 spend one's remaining years in happiness; live out one's last years a contented person

欢歌 huāngē sing merrily:～曼舞 sing merrily and dance gracefully /远处传来姑娘们的阵阵～。The girl's happy singing was heard from a distance.

欢好 huānhǎo happy and harmonious:两情～。The two love each other dearly. *or* The couple live happily and harmoniously together.

欢呼 huānhū hail; cheer; acclaim:～试验成功 hail the success of an experiment /三次向他～ give him three cheers /代表们全体起立，鼓掌～。The delegates gave him a standing ovation.

欢呼雀跃 huānhū-quèyuè shout and jump for joy; be elated:听到这消息后，人们～，奔走相告。People were elated to hear the news and passed it round quickly.

欢聚 huānjù happy get-together; happy reunion:合家～ happy family reunion /一个偶然的机会，分别多年的老同学又～在一起。Chance brought together old schoolmates who had not seen one another for years.

欢聚一堂 huānjù-yītáng get together joyously in the same hall; gather happily under the same roof; be together on a happy occasion:代表们～，畅谈形势，交流心得。The delegates happily gathered under the same roof, freely exchanging their views and ideas on state affairs.

欢快 huānkuài cheerful and light-hearted; lively:奏起～的乐曲 strike up a lively tune /她踏着～、急骤的舞步，在大厅里旋转着。She danced with light and quick steps, whirling around the hall.

欢乐 huānlè happy; merry; joyous; gay:～的歌声 merry songs (*or* singing) /～的时光 happy days /～的景象 scene of great joy (*or* gaiety) /～的场合 joyous occasion /外国马戏团的来访，更给山城增添了节日的～气氛。The visit of a foreign circus added to the festive gaiety of the mountain city.

欢眉喜眼 huānméi-xǐyǎn *also* "欢眉笑眼";"欢眉大眼"〈方言〉be all smiles; beam with joy:他～的，像有什么喜事似的。He was all smiles, as if on a most joyous occasion.

欢闹 huānnào ❶ play joyfully; gambol; romp:孩子们在门外～。The children are romping (about) outside the gate. ❷ noise and excitement; bustle:～的锣鼓声 joyful sound of gongs and drums

欢洽 huānqià happy and friendly:两人谈得十分～。They had a very happy and friendly talk.

欢庆 huānqìng celebrate joyously:～节日 celebrate (*or* observe) a festival

欢声 huānshēng cheers; applause:～达九霄 cheer to high heaven /个个笑逐颜开，处处～一片。There is a smile on every face and cheers everywhere.

欢声雷动 huānshēng-léidòng cheers resound like rolls of thunder; give a thundering ovation:演员谢幕时，全场～，掌声经久不绝。When the actors and actresses responded to the curtain call, the audience broke into a deafening ovation and prolonged cheers.

欢声笑语 huānshēng-xiàoyǔ cheers and laughter:房间里洋溢着一片～。The room was full of cheers and laughter.

欢实 huānshi *also* "欢势"〈方言〉cheerful; vigorous; lively:你看，幼儿园的孩子们多～啊! Look, how lively the children are in the kindergarten! /半夜时分，大家还玩得正～呢。Midnight found everybody at the height of enthusiasm.

欢送 huānsòng see off; send off; bid farewell:～仪式 farewell (*or* send-off) ceremony /列车徐徐开动，他们挥手告别了～的人群。As the train pulled out they waved goodbye to the crowd who had come to see them off.

欢送会 huānsònghuì farewell party; farewell or send-off meeting

欢腾 huānténg great rejoicing; jubilation:举国～ nationwide jubilation /他的话音一落，人们立刻～起来。People rejoiced as soon as he finished speaking. /喜讯传来，全校一片～。The good news turned the whole school into a scene of jubilation.

欢天喜地 huāntiān-xǐdì wild with joy; overjoyed:～迎新春 greet the Spring Festival with boundless joy /他一接到入学通知书，就～地跑回家中报信。No sooner had he received the college admission than

he ran back home, wild with joy, to tell his family about it.
欢慰 huānwèi pleased and gratified; happy and contented
欢喜 huānxǐ ❶ joyful; happy; delighted:皆大～ to the satisfaction of all; with every one feeling happy /～欲狂 be rapt (*or* wild) with joy /欢欢喜喜迎新年 celebrate a happy New Year ❷ like; be fond of; delight in:节假日,他～郊游。He likes to go on excursions on holidays. /我～游泳。I am fond of swimming. *or* I am keen on swimming.
欢喜冤家 huānxǐ-yuānjia quarrelsome and loving couple; quarrelsome lovers:真是一对～! What a couple, loving and quarrelling at the same time!
欢笑 huānxiào laugh heartily; laugh merrily:他们一边议论,一边高声～。They laughed heartily while arguing over something. /她虽然心中极度痛苦,但还得强颜～。Although she was in great agony, she had to force a smile (*or* force herself to look happy).
欢心 huānxīn favour; liking; love:他每天送去一束鲜花,以博取姑娘的～。He had a bunch of flowers sent to the girl every day in order to win her heart (*or* favour). /小狗很可爱,颇得主人的～。The lovely puppie is its owner's pet.
欢欣 huānxīn joyous; elated; happily encouraged:你的成功令我～。I'm filled with joy at your success.
欢欣鼓舞 huānxīn-gǔwǔ filled with exultation; jubilant:～地迎接新世纪的到来 usher in the new century with great rejoicing; hail the new century with elation /科研出了新成果,大家～。People were jubilant over the new achievements in scientific research.
欢颜 huānyán 〈书面〉joyous expression; smile:强作～ force oneself to look happy
欢宴 huānyàn give a banquet or dinner in honour of sb.; fete:～来宾 hold a dinner in honour of the visitor; fete the visitor
欢迎 huānyíng ❶ welcome; greet; meet:夹道～贵宾 line the street to welcome a distinguished guest /到机场～客人 meet a guest at the airport /～兄弟单位莅临参观、指导。Visitors from other units are welcome and their suggestions and criticisms appreciated. /～惠顾。Welcome to our shop (*or* restaurant, etc.)! /～你来北京! Welcome to Beijing! /～你到这里来。We're glad to have you here (with us). /～你在中国多看些地方。We hope you'll see more of China (*or* more places in China). /～你,哈雷彗星! Hello, Halley's Comet! ❷ receive favourably:话剧《雷雨》一上演即深受观众的～。The drama *Thunderstorm* was warmly received by the audience as soon as it was staged. /这种小型农具很受农民～。These farm tools are popular among farmers.
欢迎词 huānyíngcí welcoming speech; address or speech of welcome:致～ deliver a welcoming speech
欢迎会 huānyínghuì party or meeting to welcome sb.
欢娱 huānyú 〈书面〉happy; joyous; gay:万方～。People were happy and gay throughout the country.
欢愉 huānyú happy; joyous; joyful:人们都沉浸在节日的～之中。Everybody was in a happy festive mood.
欢悦 huānyuè joyous; merry:～的笑声 merry laughter /他俩心情～,不禁唱起歌来。They were both so happy together that they could not help singing.
欢跃 huānyuè jubilation; joy:举国～。Jubilation prevailed in the country. /开学后,寂静的校园又～起来。At the beginning of the new semester, life with its joyous bustle returned to the quiet campus.

讙(嚾)
huān 〈书面〉❶ hubbub; uproar:举座尽～。The entire room was in an uproar. ❷ *see* "欢" huān

獾(貛)
huān *also* "狗獾" gǒuhuān badger
獾臭鼬 huānchòuyòu 〈动物〉hog-nosed skunk
獾式轰炸机 huānshì hōngzhàjī 〈军事〉Badger (bomber)
獾油 huānyóu badger fat (for treating burns)

huán

瓛(瓛)
huán a kind of jade ornament

萑
huán 〈植物〉a kind of violet, used as herbal medicine

桓
Huán a surname

貆
huán 〈书面〉❶ cub of the racoon dog ❷ porcupine

还(還)
huán ❶ go or come back; return; restore:～家 go back home; return home /生～ come back alive; survive /返老～童 recover one's youthful vigour ❷ give back; return; repay:～书 return a book /～钱 repay; pay back /～清债务 pay off one's debt /到期该～了 be due for return (*or* repayment) ❸ give or do sth. in return:以牙～牙,以眼～眼 an eye for an eye and a tooth for a tooth; tit for tat ❹ (Huán) a surname
see also hái
还报 huánbào repay; requite; reciprocate:做好事不图～ do good to others without expecting any return
还本 huánběn repayment of principal or capital:～付息 repay capital with interest
还魂 huánhún ❶〈迷信〉revive after death; return from the grave:人死岂能～? How can one revive after death? *or* How can life return to a corpse? ❷〈方言〉reclaim; recycle; reprocess:～纸 recycled paper /～橡胶 reclaimed rubber
还击 huánjī ❶ fight back; return fire; counterattack:奋力～ do all one can to counterattack /英勇～ fight back bravely /自卫～ return fire in self-defence ❷〈体育〉riposte (in fencing)
还价 huánjià counter-offer; counter-bid; bargain:讨价～ bargain (*or* haggle) over prices; bargain /明码标价,请勿～。(sign in a shop) All prices as marked. No bargaining.
还口 huánkǒu answer back; retort:骂不～ not retort when sworn at
还款信用状 huánkuǎn xìnyòngzhuàng 〈经济〉reimbursement letter of credit
还礼 huánlǐ ❶ return a salute:将军一边快步走着,一边举手～。The general strode along rapidly, returning the salute. ❷ give a gift in return:你收人重礼,咱们拿什么～呀? Now that you have accepted such an expensive gift, what shall we give in return?
还情 huánqíng repay or return a favour:人家帮了咱的忙,咱应当～才是。We should repay him for the help he gave us.
还手 huánshǒu strike or hit back:打不～ not hit back when struck
还俗 huánsú (of Buddhist or Taoist priests) resume or return to secular life:小和尚不甘寺中寂寞,常有～之心。Unable to bear the ascetic life of the temple, the young monk often thought of resuming secular life.
还席 huánxí give a return banquet or dinner:礼尚往来嘛,对他的盛情,我们自当～。Courtesy demands reciprocity, so we shall certainly invite him to dinner in return for his hospitality.
还乡 huánxiāng return to one's native place:告老～ retire and return to one's native village (*or* town) /游子～,睹物伤情,他不禁流下了两行热泪。Back in his native place after a long absence, he was seized with emotion, with tears rolling down his cheeks.
还乡团 huánxiāngtuán "home-going legion" — armed vigilante corps organized by runaway landlords to return and restore their power over peasants during the civil war of 1946-1949; landlords' restitution corps
还醒 huánxing regain consciousness; come to; come round:他终于～了过来。He came to at last.
还言 huányán reply; answer; retort:他唠唠叨叨了一阵子,见老伴没有～的意思,就主动收了兵。He chattered on for quite some time and then, seeing that his wife made no attempt to retort, stopped on his own.
还阳 huányáng 〈迷信〉come back to life; revive after death
还阳参 huányángshēn 〈植物〉*Crepis capillaris* (used as herbal medicine)
还原 huányuán ❶ restore to the original state or shape:他把翻乱的东西都～了,又仔细地检查了一遍。He put everything back in place and double-checked carefully. ❷〈化学〉reduction:～剂 reducing agent; reductant; reducer /～炉 reduction furnace /～酶 reductase
还原染料 huányuán rǎnliào vat dye; vat colour
还原焰 huányuányàn reducing flame; inner flame
还愿 huányuàn ❶〈迷信〉redeem a vow (as to the Buddha):老太太为了～,守了整整一年的斋。To redeem her vow to the Buddha, the old lady fasted for a whole year. ❷〈比喻〉fulfil one's promise:许了愿就得～。If one makes a promise, one has to keep it.
还债 huánzhài pay one's debt; repay a debt:借债容易～难。It is easier to run into debt than get out of it. /为了～,母亲将家里稍值几

个钱的东西典当一空。To repay the debt, mother pawned everything that was worth a penny.

还账 huánzhàng pay one's debt; pay one's bill; repay a loan:赖着不～ procrastinate over debt repayment; drag one's feet in paying a debt (*or* bill, *or* loan) /这笔钱是用来～的。This sum is set aside for the repayment of debts.

还政于民 huánzhèngyúmín hand (state) power back to the people; restore or establish democracy

还嘴 huánzuǐ 〈口语〉answer back; talk back:你这个死丫头,还敢～! How dare you talk back, you bad girl!

环(環) huán ❶ ring; hoop; loop:吊～〈体育〉ring /耳～ earring /门～ knocker /花～ (flower) wreath /滚铁～ bowl (*or* trundle) the hoop ❷〈体育〉ring:射中八～ hit the 8-point ring /命中十～ hit the centre of the target; hit the bull's eye /打了个零～ miss the target /射击总成绩为 189～ score 189 points in marksmanship ❸ link:关键的一～ key link; essential link /～～相扣 each linked with another; closely linked with one another ❹ surround; encircle; hem in:～湖公路 road winding round a lake /四面～水 be surrounded by water on all sides; be hemmed in by water /三～路 Third Ring Road; Third Loop; Third Beltway ❺〈化学〉cyclic; cyclo-:～醇 cyclic alcohol; ring alcohol; cyclitol /～酮 cyclic ketone; cyclone /～胺 cyclammonium; cyclamine ❻ (Huán) a surname

环靶 huánbǎ 〈体育〉round target

环保 huánbǎo (short for 环境保护) environmental protection:～部门 departments of environmental protection /～型汽车 environment-friendly car

环抱 huánbào surround; encircle; embrace:青山～的小村庄,那是我度过童年时光的地方。That hamlet nestling among the green hills is where I spent my childhood.

环比指数 huánbǐ zhǐshù 〈经济〉chain index

环剥 huánbō *also* "环割"〈林业〉ring-cut

环衬 huánchèn *also* "衬页" chènyè 〈印刷〉lining paper

环城 huánchéng round the city:～线 round-the-city route /～赛跑 round-the-city race /～路 round-the-city road; ring road; loop; beltway

环带 huándài ❶ ring of light; halo ❷〈动物〉clitellum

环岛 huándǎo *also* "环形岛"〈交通〉traffic circle; roundabout; rotary

环地轨道 huándì guǐdào 〈航天〉earth orbit:进入～ (of a satellite) enter into earth orbit /～会合 (make an) earth orbital rendezvous

环锭纺纱机 huándìng fǎngshājī 〈纺织〉ring spinner

环锭细纱机 huándìng xìshājī 〈纺织〉ring frame

环堵萧然 huándǔ-xiāorán 〈比喻〉with hardly anything within the four walls; poorly furnished; poverty-stricken:老先生家中除了几箱旧书外,～,别无长物。Except for a few boxes of old books, there was nothing of value in the home of the old man.

环肥燕瘦 Huánféi-Yànshòu (usu. of beautiful women) plump or slim each has a beauty of her own;〈比喻〉each has her or its own style of beauty:这几位名家的书法艺术自成一格,真是～,各擅其美。These renowned masters have evolved their unique calligraphic styles, each graceful and beautiful in its own way.

环顾 huángù 〈书面〉look about:～左右而言他 look around and evade the issue /～四周,满目萧然。Looking about, one sees a desolate scene all round.

环海 huánhǎi surrounded or hemmed in by sea:小岛四周～。The islet is surrounded by sea on all sides.

环合 huánhé (used usu. in describing natural environment) surround; encircle:四面树木～,仅一小径相通。There were trees on all sides, with just a footpath leading to the outside.

环化 huánhuà 〈化学〉cyclization:～橡胶 cyclized rubber; cyclorubber /～橡胶树脂 cyclized rubber resin

环化聚合 huánhuà jùhé 〈化学〉cyclopolymerization; cyclic polymerization

环化脱氧 huánhuà tuōyǎng 〈化学〉dehydrocyclization

环礁 huánjiāo 〈地质〉atoll

环节 huánjié ❶〈动物〉segment ❷ link:薄弱～ weak link /主要～ key link /生产中的每一个～都要认真考虑。All links in the production process (*or* chain) should be carefully considered.

环节动物 huánjié dòngwù annelid:～门 Annelida

环颈雉 huánjǐngzhì 〈动物〉ring-necked pheasant

环境 huánjìng ❶ environment:～管理 environmental management /～危机 environmental crisis /～质量评价 environmental quality assessment /世界～日 World Environment Day (June 5) /联合国～规划署 United Nations Environmental Programme (UNEP) /自然～ natural environment /保护～ protect the environment /改良～ improve the environment /学校地处郊区,周围～不错。Situated in the suburbs, the school boasts a good environment. /他工作的地方～优美如画。The place where he works is very picturesque. ❷ surroundings; circumstances; conditions:～恶劣 harsh conditions /社会～ social surroundings /换换～ have a change of air /我努力适应陌生的～。I do my best to adapt myself to the new circumstances. /孩子们需要幸福的家庭～。Children need a happy home environment.

环境保护 huánjìng bǎohù environmental protection:～法 law of environmental protection; environmental law /～标准 environmental protection standards /～工作者 environmentalist /～总局 Environmental Protection Administration

环境地质学 huánjìng dìzhìxué environmental geology

环境调查卫星 huánjìng diàochá wèixīng ESS; environmental survey satellite:～网 ESS network

环境改良 huánjìng gǎiliáng environmental improvement

环境工程学 huánjìng gōngchéngxué environmental engineering

环境规划 huánjìng guīhuà environmental planning

环境监测 huánjìng jiāncè environmental monitoring:～系统 environmental monitoring system

环境决定论 huánjìng juédìnglùn environmentalism

环境科学 huánjìng kēxué environmental science

环境空气 huánjìng kōngqì ambient air

环境生态学 huánjìng shēngtàixué environmental ecology

环境卫生 huánjìng wèishēng environmental sanitation or hygiene:～学 environmental hygiene /～工程 environmental hygiene project; environmental hygiene engineering /搞好～,防止疾病蔓延。Do a good job in environmental sanitation to prevent the spread of disease.

环境污染 huánjìng wūrǎn pollution of the environment; environmental pollution; environmental contamination:～源 environmental pollutant; source of environmental pollution (*or* contamination) /～病 pollution disease

环境医学 huánjìng yīxué environmental medicine

环境应力场 huánjìng yìnglìchǎng ambient stress field; in-place stress field

环境噪音 huánjìng zàoyīn environmental noise; ambient noise

环列 huánliè stand or arrange in a circle:士兵左右～。Soldiers were standing in a semicircle (round sb.).

环流 huánliú 〈气象〉circulation; circulating current:大气～ atmospheric circulation /～型 circulation pattern /～理论 circulation theory

环幕电影 huánmù diànyǐng Circarama

环佩 huánpèi (jade) pendant:～丁东。The jade pendants jingled.

环球 huánqiú ❶ round the world:～旅行 round-the-world tour /～飞行 flying round the world; circumnavigation /～两周 go round the world twice ❷ Earth; whole world

环球航空公司 Huánqiú Hángkōng Gōngsī (US) Transworld Airways (TWA)

环球网 huánqiúwǎng World Wide Web (WWW) *see also* "万维网" wànwéiwǎng

环球卫星通讯 huánqiú wèixīng tōngxùn global satellite communication

环球影片公司 Huánqiú Yǐngpiàn Gōngsī Universal Pictures Co., US film studio since 1912

环球邮报 Huánqiú Yóubào *The Globe and Mail*, Canadian newspaper since 1844

环绕 huánrào surround; encircle; revolve round:红绿掩映,清流～。The red buildings were shaded by green trees and surrounded by clear brooks. /孩子们手拉着手,～着一棵大榕树又唱又跳。Hand in hand, the children sang and danced round a big banyan tree.

环绕速度 huánrào sùdù 〈天文〉circular or orbital velocity; first cosmic velocity

环山 huánshān ❶ round a hill or mountain:～公路 road (*or* highway) going round a mountain /～而行 move (*or* go) round a hill ❷ surrounded by hills or mountains:三面～,一面临水 surrounded by hills on three sides and by water on the fourth (side)

环蛇 huánshé krait

环生 huánshēng happen one after another; occur in quick succes-

H

sion：险象～ signs of danger appearing everywhere
环食 huánshí *also*"日环食" rìhuánshí 〈天文〉annular eclipse (of the sun)
环视 huánshì look around：他～了一下在座的听众，开始作报告。He looked around at those present and then began his speech. /～周围，但见青山夕照，茅舍生烟。All around, there was nothing but the green hills in the setting sun and thatched huts with rising chimney smoke.
环伺 huánsì watch closely from all round：列强～于外。The imperialist powers were watching (China) closely from the outside.
环太平洋 huán-Tàipíngyáng circum-Pacific：～地区 circum-Pacific region; Pacific Basin /～地震带 circum-Pacific seismic belt /～构造带 circum-Pacific tectonic belt
环眺 huántiào look (far) round：～四周 look round
环烃 huántīng 〈化学〉cyclic hydrocarbon
环烷 huánwán 〈化学〉cycloalkane; cycloparaffin; naphthene：～基 cycloalkyl; naphthenic base /～酸 naphthenic acid /～烃 cycloalkane
环卫 huánwèi ❶ (short for 环境卫生) environmental sanitation：～部门 public sanitation department /～工人 sanitation worker ❷ 〈书面〉palace guards; imperial guards
环烯 huánxī 〈化学〉cycloalkene; cycloolefin
环线 huánxiàn ring route; circular route：地铁～ circular underground railway; circular subway route; belt subway
环行 huánxíng going in a circle; make a circuit：～地铁 belt subway; circuit underground /～公共汽车 bus with a circular route /绕岛～一周，要用三十分钟。It takes 30 minutes to go round the island.
环行岛 huánxíngdǎo *see*"环岛"
环行公路 huánxíng gōnglù ring road; beltway; belt highway
环行铁路 huánxíng tiělù circuit railway; belt railway line
环形 huánxíng annular; ring-like; loop-like：～日光灯管 annular fluorescent lamp /～晶体管 annular transistor /～锯 annular saw; bandsaw /～齿轮 ring gear /～开关 ring switch /～网络 loop network; ring network /～线圈 loop coil; toroid
环形计算机网络 huánxíng jìsuànjī wǎngluò loop computer network
环形交叉 huánxíng jiāochā 〈交通〉roundabout; traffic circle; rotary
环形山 huánxíngshān 〈天文〉lunar crater; ring structure
环形天线 huánxíng tiānxiàn ring antenna; loop antenna; coil antenna：～测向仪 loop direction finder /～调整误差 loop alignment error /环形辨向天线 loop sense antenna
环氧树脂 huányǎng shùzhī 〈化学〉epoxide resin; epoxy resin; epoxy：～黏合剂 epoxy (resin) adhesives /～合金〈冶金〉epoxy alloy /～铸模〈冶金〉epoxy resin pattern
环氧树脂漆 huányǎng shùzhīqī epoxy resin coating
环游 huányóu travel or tour round：～世界 travel (*or* tour) round the world; make a round-the-world trip
环宇 huányǔ *also*"寰宇" huányǔ entire world：轰动～ raise a worldwide sensation
环轧 huánzhá 〈冶金〉looping channel：～法 loop mill rolling /～机 looping mill; looping type rolling mill
环志 huánzhì ring mark
环状 huánzhuàng cyclic; annular; ring-like; loop-like：～低聚物〈化学〉cyclic oligomer /～高聚物〈化学〉cyclic polymer /～二聚物〈化学〉cyclic dimer /～分子〈物理〉ring molecule /～星系〈天文〉ring galaxy; annular galaxy /～扩散 encircling diffusion /～剥皮〈林业〉girdling
环状软骨 huánzhuàng ruǎngǔ 〈生理〉cricoid：～切开术 cricotomy
环状珊瑚礁 huánzhuàng shānhújiāo atoll reef
环状星云 huánzhuàng xīngyún ring nebula
环状芽接法 huánzhuàng yájiēfǎ annular budding
环子 huánzi ring; link：门～ knocker /铁～ iron hoop /耳～ earring

寰

huán extensive region：尘～ this world; this mortal life /惨绝人～ tragic beyond compare (in this human world)
寰球 huánqiú *also*"环球" huánqiú Earth; whole world：～同享太平。Peace prevails all over the world.
寰宇 huányǔ *also*"环宇" huányǔ 〈书面〉Earth; whole world：声震～ enjoy a high reputation in the world

阛

huán
阛阓 huánhuì 〈书面〉market; business district

鬟

huán (of women's hair style) bun; rings or coils of hair：云～ high rings /～髻 bun (of woman's hair)

圜

huán *see*"转圜" zhuǎnhuán
see also yuán

鹮

huán 〈动物〉ibis

嬛

huán *see*"琅嬛" lánghuán

缳

huán 〈书面〉❶ noose：投～ hang oneself (with a noose) ❷ hang：～首 be hanged /～首之罪 crime punishable by hanging

锾

huán ancient unit of weight, about 0.3 kilogram：罚～ fine

郇

Huán a surname
see also Xún

huǎn

缓

huǎn ❶ slow; unhurried; sluggish：迟～ slow; tardy /舒～ slow and unhurried; leisurely /迂～ slow in movement; dilatory /从～ go slow; take one's time /性子～ sluggish by nature ❷ delay; postpone; put off：～付 delay (*or* defer) payment /暂～ postpone; put off; defer /刻不容～ brook no delay; be of great urgency /死～ (short for 死刑缓期执行) death penalty with reprieve (*or* suspended execution) /我～些日子还你钱。I'll return the money to you a few days later. ❸ relaxed; not tense：紧张局势业已弛～。The tense situation has eased off. ❹ revive; recuperate; come to：花都蔫了，再不浇水就～不过来了。The withering flowers will not revive if they are not watered at once. /老人一口气没～过来，归天了。The old man failed to come to and died. /他休息了好一阵子才～过劲儿来。He felt refreshed only after a long rest.
缓兵之计 huǎnbīngzhījì stratagem to gain a respite; trick to gain time; stalling tactics：敌军要求谈判，明显是～。The enemy's request for negotiations was an obvious trick to gain time. /我们不妨先来个～，暂时不去理他。We may just as well resort to stalling tactics and leave him alone for the time being.
缓不济急 huǎnbùjìjí slow action cannot save a critical situation; a slow remedy cannot meet an urgency; too slow in coming is of no help：临渴掘井，～。When you start digging a well to quench your thirst, the solution is too slow to be of any help.
缓步 huǎnbù walk slowly; stroll：～而去 walk away unhurriedly; stroll away /他～穿过草地，消失在林中。He sauntered across the lawn and disappeared behind the trees.
缓步代车 huǎnbù-dàichē *also*"缓步当车" stroll or walk in a leisurely way instead of going by car：路不算远，我们不如～吧。As it's not much of a distance, we may just as well take a stroll to get there.
缓冲 huǎnchōng buffer; cushion：～作用 buffer effect; cushioning effect /～库存 buffer stock /他在争执双方之间，起到一种调和、～的作用。He functions as a mediator and buffer between the disputing parties. /形势急迫，看来难有～的余地。The situation became so critical that there seemed to be hardly any room for mitigation.
缓冲存货 huǎnchōng cúnhuò 〈商业〉buffer stock
缓冲地带 huǎnchōng dìdài *also*"缓冲区" buffer zone; buffer area：在交战双方之间建立～ establish a buffer zone between the belligerent parties
缓冲国 huǎnchōngguó buffer state
缓冲剂 huǎnchōngjì 〈化学〉buffer
缓冲气袋 huǎnchōng qìdài 〈汽车〉air bag
缓冲器 huǎnchōngqì 〈机械〉buffer; bumper cushion
缓冲债券 huǎnchōng zhàiquàn 〈金融〉cushion bond
缓冲装置 huǎnchōng zhuāngzhì buffer unit; cushioning device
缓发 huǎnfā 〈物理〉delay：～辐射 delayed radiation /～中子 delayed neutron /～衰变 delayed decay /～质子 delayed proton
缓和 huǎnhé ❶ relax; ease off or up：～与裁军 détente and disarmament /国际紧张局势有所～。The international tension relaxed (*or*

eased off). /大雨下了两天，仍不见～。It poured for two days with no sign of subsiding. ❷ alleviate; mitigate; defuse: ～边境一触即发的局势 defuse the explosive situation at the border /双方都要尽力克制，以～矛盾。Both should exercise restraint and mitigate their contradictions.

缓和剂 huǎnhéjì 〈化学〉moderator; mollient; modifier

缓和曲线 huǎnhé qūxiàn 〈铁路〉easement curve; adjustment curve; transition curve

缓化剂 huǎnhuàjì 〈化学〉negative catalyst; moderator

缓急 huǎnjí ❶ pressing or otherwise; of greater or lesser urgency: 处理问题要有轻重～。Matters should be handled according to their importance and urgency. /是缓是急，你总该把它放在心上。Pressing or not, you will have to keep it in mind. ❷ emergency; difficulty: 储粮以解～。Store up grain to meet emergencies.

缓急相助 huǎnjí-xiāngzhù help each other in time of need or in an emergency

缓颊 huǎnjiá 〈书面〉intercede (on sb.'s behalf); put in a good word (for sb.): ～之功永世不忘。I shall never forget your kind intercession on my behalf.

缓建 huǎnjiàn postpone or delay construction

缓缰 huǎnjiāng give (a horse) the reins; loosen the reins

缓解 huǎnjiě alleviate; allay; improve; ease up: ～痛苦 alleviate (*or* allay) a pain /～药 alleviant /病情～ improvement of a patient's condition /癌症～ remission (*or* lysis) of cancer /马路加宽后，交通阻塞现象有所～。Traffic congestion was alleviated after the road was broadened. /危机已明显～。The crisis has clearly eased.

缓慢 huǎnmàn slow; sluggish: 动作～ slow in movement; slow-moving; sluggish /～行进的游行队伍 slow-moving (*or* sluggish) procession /大桥工程进展～。The construction of the bridge is making slow (*or* little) progress.

缓辔 huǎnpèi give (a horse) the reins; loosen the reins: ～徐行 loosen the reins and slow down to a leisurely pace

缓坡 huǎnpō gentle slope: 一过山口，就是～，路好走多了。Beyond the mountain pass there was a gentle slope and it became much easier to walk.

缓期 huǎnqī postpone a deadline; suspend; put off; delay: 判处有期徒刑五年，～两年执行 sentence to five years in prison with a two-year reprieve /按合同规定，不得～付款。The contract stipulates no delayed (*or* deferred) payment.

缓气 huǎnqì get a breathing space; have a respite; take a breather: 不给对手以～的机会 give no respite to one's adversary /干了许久，缓口气吧。We've been working quite a long time now. Let's have (*or* take) a breather. /经过急救，她终于缓过气来了。After first aid was applied, she came to at last.

缓图 huǎntú plan slowly and carefully: 容～之。Allow me some time to plan (*or* achieve) this.

缓限 huǎnxiàn postpone the deadline; extend the time limit: ～三天 postpone the deadline for three days

缓效肥料 huǎnxiào féiliào 〈农业〉slow-release fertilizer

缓泻 huǎnxiè *also* "轻泻" qīngxiè 〈医学〉mild purgation: ～药 mild purgative

缓行 huǎnxíng ❶ move, drive or walk slowly: 拄杖～ walk slowly with a stick (*or* cane) /弯道～。(road sign) Zigzag ahead, drive slowly. ❷ put off; postpone: 计划～。The programme has been postponed.

缓刑 huǎnxíng 〈法律〉temporary suspension of a sentence; reprieve; probation: ～制度 probationary system /～判决 probationary sentence /判处死刑，～两年 sentence to death with a two-year reprieve /～期间重新犯罪 commit new crimes during the probationary period /处以～ put an offender on probation

缓刑犯 huǎnxíngfàn 〈法律〉probationer: ～监督官 probation officer

缓性 huǎnxìng phlegmatic temper; slow effect: ～药 medicine that produces slow effects /他是个～子，你急他不急。He is a man of phlegmatic temper. However impatient (*or* pressed) you may be, he always takes his time.

缓醒 huǎnxing 〈方言〉come to; regain consciousness: 他这一跤摔得太重，半天才～过来。He fell so heavily that he did not come to until much later.

缓役 huǎnyì 〈军事〉deferment (of military service); deferral

缓悠悠 huǎnyōuyōu slowly; at a leisurely pace: 他一边～地擦窗户，一边轻轻地哼着歌儿。While cleaning the windows slowly, he was humming a tune.

缓征 huǎnzhēng postpone the imposition of a tax or levy: 对灾区实行～或免征政策，以利休养生息。The policy of tax postponement or exemption was implemented in the calamity-stricken areas to facilitate rehabilitation.

huàn

浣(澣) huàn 〈书面〉❶ wash; rinse: ～衣 wash clothes /～纱 rinse yarn /《～溪沙》(title of a tune for *ci* poetry) *Wash Stream Sands* ❷ any of the three 10-day periods of a month: 下～ last ten days of a month /争取下月中～完成项目 strive to finish the project between the 11th and 20th of next month

浣熊 huànxióng racoon

睆 huàn 〈书面〉❶ bright ❷ beautiful; lovely

鲩 huàn (popularly known as 草鱼) grass carp

宦 huàn ❶ official: 官～人家 family of high officials ❷ hold a public office; be an official: 仕～ have an official career /始～至今，清贫如洗。Since he first became an official, he has remained poor as a church mouse. ❸ eunuch: ～者当道，国运必衰。With the eunuchs holding real power, the nation would certainly suffer. ❹ (Huàn) a surname

宦场 huànchǎng officialdom; official circles

宦官 huànguān *also* "太监" tàijiàn eunuch

宦海 huànhǎi 〈比喻〉(sea of) officialdom; official circles: ～沉浮 ups and downs in officialdom; vicissitudes of an official life; chequered official career

宦门 huànmén 〈书面〉family of officials: ～公子 young man from a family of officials; son of an official

宦囊 huànnáng 〈书面〉savings accumulated during one's official career: ～清苦 have meagre savings as an official; accumulate little money during one's term of office

宦情 huànqíng 〈书面〉desire or aspiration for an official career: 少无～。As a young man, he had no desire to become an official.

宦途 huàntú 〈书面〉official career: ～坎坷 official career full of frustrations

宦游 huànyóu 〈书面〉office-hunting: ～四方 go hither and thither in pursuit of an official position /～者 office-seeker (*or* -hunter)

逭 huàn 〈书面〉escape; flee: 罪不可～。One's crime is too great to be pardoned.

豢 huàn feed; groom; keep

豢养 huànyǎng feed; groom; keep: ～家禽 feed poultry; raise poultry /敌人～的走狗 running dog (*or* lackey) in the enemy's pay

患 huàn ❶ trouble; peril; disaster: 水～ flood /外～ foreign aggression /～至呼天 〈书面〉cry to Heaven for help only when a calamity occurs; never pray until it is too late /心腹之～ serious hidden trouble (*or* danger) /养痈遗～ to leave evil unchecked spells ruin /有备无～。Preparedness averts peril. ❷ anxiety; worry: 忧～无穷 endless worries; unending trouble /忧～意识 (sense of) concern for the fate of one's country; sense of crisis (*or* insecurity) (as in business competition) /欲加之罪，何～无辞? If one wants to frame somebody, one never need worry how to find the pretext. *or* He who has a mind to beat his dog will easily find his stick. ❸ contract; suffer from (an illness): ～乙型肝炎 contract (*or* suffer from) hepatitis B /～感冒 catch cold

患病 huànbìng fall ill; be ill

患处 huànchù affected part (of a patient's body): ～疼痛异常 be terribly painful in the affected part; the affected part hurts very much /涂于～ apply (the medicine) to the affected part

患得患失 huàndé-huànshī worry about personal gains and losses; be swayed by considerations of gain and loss: 整天为私利而～，这种人能不愁容满面吗? When people are swayed by selfish consideration how can they look free of worry?

患难 huànnàn trials and tribulations; adversity; trouble: 同甘苦，共～ share joys and sorrows; share weal and woe

患难夫妻 huànnàn-fūqī husband and wife who have been through thick and thin together

患难见知己 huànnàn jiàn zhījǐ *also* "患难见真情" a friend is best found in adversity; a friend in need is a friend indeed

患难与共 huànnàn-yǔgòng share hardships and dangers; go through trials and tribulations together:～的战友和夫妻 couple who are comrades-in-arms and have gone through trials and tribulations together

患难之交 huànnànzhījiāo friend in adversity; friend in need; tested friend

患者 huànzhě patient; invalid; sufferer:～须知 information for patients /肺结核～ TB patient /精神病～ neuropathic; psychopath

漶 huàn *see* "漫漶" mànhuàn

擐 huàn 〈书面〉wear; put on:～甲执兵 be clad in armour and hold a weapon

轘 huàn (ancient form of torture and execution) tearing the body apart with horse-drawn carts

奂(奐) huàn 〈书面〉❶ mumerous; plentiful:美轮美～。(of a house, etc.) How magnificent! ❷ (of writing or diction) bright; brilliant:～其丽饰。What beautiful decorations!

涣 huàn dissolve; dissipate; vanish

涣涣 huànhuàn 〈书面〉(of water, etc.) torrential; over-flowing; vast:水～ vast expanse(s) of water

涣然 huànrán melt away; dissipate; vanish:听了他的一席话,我心中的气～无存。My anger melted away after hearing his words.

涣然冰释 huànrán-bīngshì melt away (like ice); vanish like air; clear up:他们之间的误会～。The misunderstanding between them was cleared up. /我的疑虑～。My misgivings vanished like thin air.

涣散 huànsàn lax; slack; demoralized:纪律～ be lax in discipline /士气～ have a deflated (*or* failing) morale /精神～ be demoralized; be distraught /队伍～ be undisciplined and poorly organized /～斗志 sap sb.'s morale (*or* fighting will); demoralize

痪 huàn *see* "瘫痪" tānhuàn

焕 huàn shining; glowing

焕发 huànfā ❶ shine; glow; irradiate:英姿～ dashing and spirited /他大步走来,精神～,红光满面。He came over in big strides, full of vim and vigour and in ruddy health. ❷ display vigour; cheer up:～精神 call forth one's vigour; cheer up

焕发青春 huànfā-qīngchūn (of old people, etc.) radiate the vigour of youth; have a new lease of life; rejuvenate:老人～,又投身于科研事业了。The old man displayed the vigour of his youth again and threw himself into scientific research. /这些民间手工艺品,重新～,受到中外游客的喜爱。These folk handicraft products had a new lease of life and found favour again with both Chinese and foreign tourists.

焕然 huànrán bright; splendid; brilliant; lustrous:容光～ (one's face) glowing with health

焕然一新 huànrán-yīxīn take on an entirely new look; look brand new:经过修整、粉刷,大殿的面貌～。After repairs and whitewashing, the temple took on an entirely new look.

换 huàn ❶ exchange; barter; trade:～俘 exchange prisoners (of war) /互～国书 exchange letters of accreditation /用家用电器～木材、兽皮 barter home appliances for timber and hides /以辛勤的劳动～来的幸福生活 happy life earned by honest labour ❷ change; substitute:～衣服 change one's clothes /～～环境 have a change of air (*or* scene) /以次～好 substitute inferior stuff for fine material /～句话说 in other words /旧貌～新颜。A new look replaced the old one. ❸ convert:把人民币～成美元 convert (*or* change) Renminbi (RMB) into US dollars

换班 huànbān ❶ change shifts; take over the duty or work; relieve a person on duty:白班和夜班的～时间是下午六点。The night shift takes over from the day shift at 6 p.m. /这活儿我干了三十年,该～了。As I've been on this job for thirty years already, it's time for me to be relieved. ❷〈军事〉changing of the guard:夜里放哨的士兵两个钟头一～。The change of sentries occurred every two hours during the night.

换边 huànbiān 〈体育〉change sides

换步 huànbù 〈军事〉change step

换茬 huànchá 〈农业〉change of crops:～种白薯 change the crop to sweet potatoes; plant sweet potatoes instead (of a previous crop)

换车 huànchē change trains or buses; transfer:从这里去省城,途中要换两次车。One must change buses twice to get to the provincial capital from here.

换乘 huànchéng change; transfer:在动物园～332 路 change to bus No. 332 at the zoo /火车到达终点站后,～长途公共汽车。Transfer (*or* Change) to a coach when the train reaches its destination.

换代 huàndài ❶ (of a dynasty or regime) change:改朝～ dynastic changes ❷ (of a product, etc.) replace; regenerate:～产品 new model (of product) /加速产品的更新换代 accelerate the development of new models and new products (*or* the upgrading of products)

换挡 huàndǎng 〈机械〉shift gears:自动～ shift gears automatically /～变速装置 power-shift gear box

换发球 huànfāqiú 〈体育〉change of service

换防 huànfáng 〈军事〉relieve a garrison:部队～,临行前附近老乡都来送别。When the relieved garrison troops were ready to depart, nearby villagers all came to bid them farewell.

换房 huànfáng exchange housing:两家～ exchange of housing between two families /房管部门在公园举办～大会。The housing authorities held a housing exchange fair in the park.

换俘协定 huànfú xiédìng agreement for exchange of prisoners; cartel

换岗 huàngǎng relieve a sentry; change the guard:趁哨兵～的时候,他们溜出了营房。They stole out of the barracks while the sentry was being relieved. /每天清晨四时～。The guard is changed at four o'clock in the morning.

换个儿 huàngèr 〈口语〉exchange positions:咱们换个个儿,你靠窗户坐吧。Let's exchange our seats so that you may sit by the window. /这两个抽屉大小不同,不能～。As these two drawers are different in size, they are not interchangeable.

换工 huàngōng exchange labour:咱家没有拖拉机,这几年要不是同张家～,这块地早荒了。As we have no tractor, this field would have lain waste but for our exchange of labour with the Zhangs.

换购 huàngòu purchase by way of barter:用农产品～生产资料 barter farm produce for means of production

换汇 huànhuì earn foreign exchange:制成品的～率要比原材料高得多。Manufactures earn much more foreign exchange than raw materials.

换货 huànhuò exchange goods; barter:易货～ barter; trade by barter /～协定 barter agreement /～和付款协定 goods exchange and payments agreement

换季 huànjì change (garments) with the season; put on different clothes for a new season:临走前,她把～的衣服都为丈夫收拾好了。Before she left, she had taken out for her husband all the clothes to be worn for the new season.

换肩 huànjiān shift the load (one is carrying) from one shoulder to the other:会挑担子的人～时不用停歇。Those who are accustomed to carrying loads on a shoulder-pole do not stop to shift the pole from one shoulder to the other.

换届 huànjiè replace or re-elect when a term of office expires:～选举 re-election (when the current term expires) /今年年底,市人大将～。The municipal people's congress will stand for re-election by the end of the year.

换景 huànjǐng 〈戏剧〉scene shifting

换流器 huànliúqì 〈电工〉changer

换马 huànmǎ 〈比喻〉〈贬义〉change horses (half way); have sb. replaced (before his term is over):不要中途～。Don't change (*or* swap) horses in mid-stream. /一个月之间,军人集团首领已数次～。The military junta had to recast its leadership several times within a single month.

换毛 huànmáo moult:小鸡在～。The chicks are moulting.

换脑筋 huàn nǎojīn 〈比喻〉change one's way of thinking:如今搞市场经济,不换换脑筋就会走投无路了。Now that we've a market economy, we won't be able to manage unless we change our way of thinking.

换能器 huànnéngqì 〈物理〉transducer; transverter

H

换谱 huànpǔ *see* "换帖"

换气 huànqì take a breath (in swimming):船老大水性好,能在水中憋很久不～。The boatman was a good swimmer who could remain submerged for a long time without breathing.

换气扇 huànqìshàn *also* "排风扇" páifēngshàn ventilation fan

换钱 huànqián ❶ change money; break a bill or note:大票找不开,请给换一下钱。This bill is too big; please break it for me. ❷ sell:编两只竹篮子～买米 weave two bamboo baskets and sell them to buy rice /揭不开锅的时候,母亲总是把家里的东西拿去典当～。When there was no food in the house, mother would pawn what she could find at home for some money.

换亲 huànqīn exchange daughters in marriage to each other's sons:有的山区兴～的陋习,不知坑害了多少年轻女子。It is a bad custom in some mountainous areas to exchange daughters in marriage to each other's sons, and it is a plague on many young girls.

换取 huànqǔ exchange or barter for; get in return:以辛勤的劳动～幸福的生活 earn a happy life by the sweat of one's brow /他把山货拉到集市上去～日用品。He carried mountain products to the market town, which he bartered for everyday necessities.

换热器 huànrèqì heat exchanger

换人 huànrén 〈体育〉substitution (of players):甲队～,10号上,7号下。Substitution for Team A: No. 7 out; No. 10 in.

换算 huànsuàn conversion:～表 conversion table /～公式 conversion formula /～因数 conversion factor /把英里～成公里 convert miles into kilometres

换汤不换药 huàn tāng bù huàn yào 〈比喻〉same old stuff with a different label; old wine in a new bottle; change in name only:新政府上台又能怎样? 只不过是～! What difference does a new government make? Nothing but old wine in a new bottle!

换帖 huàntiě (become sworn brothers by) exchange of papers bearing each other's name, age, place of origin and other personal details:～兄弟 sworn brothers

换位 huànwèi 〈数学〉conversion

换位思考 huànwèi sīkǎo put oneself in another's shoes and think in his or her terms; think in sb. else's perspective

换文 huànwén exchange of notes or letters:就发展两国贸易关系问题～ exchange notes on the development of trade between the two countries /通过～达成谅解 reach understanding through an exchange of letters

换席更酌 huànxí-gēngzhuó food and wine are served afresh:老友登门,全家人～,热烈欢迎。When the old friend arrived, food and wine were served afresh with the whole family showering warm attention upon him.

换洗 huànxǐ change and wash (clothing, sheets, etc.):衣服勤～是好习惯。It is a healthy habit to change and wash one's clothes frequently. /出门要多带几套～的衣服。One should take several changes of clothes with one while travelling.

H

换向 huànxiàng 〈电学〉commutation:～磁极 commutating pole /～电流 current of commutation /～电容器 commutating capacitor (*or* condenser) /～开关 commutator switch; change-over switch; reversing switch /～时间 commutating period; turn-around time /～试验 commutation test /～器 commutator

换血 huànxiě blood transfusion; 〈比喻〉reorganization by introducing fresh personnel; recast:该足球队刚刚进行了大～。The soccer team has just had a major transfusion of talent. *or* It has just had a wholesale change of players.

换心 huànxīn 〈方言〉heart-to-heart; intimate:～朋友 intimate friend; bosom friend

换牙 huànyá (of a child) grow permanent teeth:这孩子快～了。The child will grow permanent teeth soon.

换言之 huànyánzhī 〈书面〉in other words; that is; namely; viz

换样 huànyàng change in pattern, style or form; take on a different look:屋子内外粉刷一新,完全～了。Freshly whitewashed in and out, the house has had a facelift.

换药 huànyào redress (a wound, etc.):每三天换一次药 redress the wound once every three days

换羽 huànyǔ (of birds) moult:这种候鸟大都在春夏之交～。These migratory birds moult mostly in late spring and early summer.

换约 huànyuē exchange treaty texts or instruments of ratification

换装站 huànzhuāngzhàn 〈铁路〉trans-shipment station

唤

huàn call (out); summon:呼～求援 call out loud for help /响应祖国的召～ answer the call of the motherland /千呼万～始出来,犹抱琵琶半遮面。She appeared only after repeated summons, Holding in her arms a *pipa* which half shielded her face.

唤起 huànqǐ ❶ arouse:～人们的热情 kindle people's enthusiasm (*or* fervour) /～民众,共御外患。Arouse the masses of the people in a common effort to resist foreign aggression. ❷ call; draw; recall:～人们的注意 call (*or* draw) attention (to sth.) /此情此景,不由～他对往事的回忆。What he saw evoked past memories.

唤头 huàntou percussion tool (used by itinerant grinders, barbers, etc. to attract customers):黄昏的街灯,北风卷着翻飞的雪花,卖熟食的小贩敲着～,这些儿时的印象再也追寻不到了。Dim street lights, snowflakes dancing in the northerly wind, percussion from the delicatessen stands and so forth — all were fresh in my childhood memories but none was anywhere to be found.

唤醒 huànxǐng wake up; awaken; arouse:春雷～了冬眠的大地。The spring thunder seemed to wake up the land from its wintry sleep. /这本书～了不少沉沦的青年人。This book aroused many young people from despondency.

幻

huàn ❶ unreal; imaginary; illusory:梦～ illusion; dream; reverie /虚～ unreal; illusory; visionary /致～作用 hallucinatory (*or* hallucinogenic) effect ❷ change or conjure magically:变～莫测 change unpredictably

幻灯 huàndēng ❶ slide show:放～ show slides /～是一种视听教育手段。The slide show is a means for audio-visual teaching. ❷ slide projector

幻灯机 huàndēngjī slide projector:自动对焦～ automatic focussing slide projector /反射～ episcope /透反射两用～ epidiascope

幻灯片 huàndēngpiàn (lantern) slide; filmstrip:～盒 slide magazine /放关于中国的～ show slides of China

幻方 huànfāng *also* "纵横图" zònghéngtú 〈数学〉magic square

幻化 huànhuà change magically:雪后的花园～成一片神话般的水晶世界。The snow turned the garden magically into a crystal fairyland.

幻景 huànjǐng illusion; mirage:人类昔日的～,如今已变成现实。Scenes that existed only in dreams have now turned into reality.

幻境 huànjìng dreamland; fairyland:走进这鸟语花香、绿树成荫的山谷,如同走进了童话中的～。Once in this luxuriantly green valley where birds were singing and flowers giving off perfume, one felt as if in a fairyland.

幻觉 huànjué hallucination; illusion:产生～ hallucinate /～症 hallucinosis /～剂 hallucinogen /病人出现这些～是常有的事情。It is nothing uncommon that a patient has these illusions.

幻梦 huànmèng dream; fantasy; illusion:从～中醒悟过来 wake up from a dream

幻灭 huànmiè disillusion:多年的希望一朝～,能不使他悲痛万分? How could he keep from deep grief when his long-cherished hopes were dashed?

幻日 huànrì 〈气象〉parhelion; mock sun; sun dog

幻视 huànshì 〈医学〉photism; visual hallucination:～镜 pseudoscope /～效应 pseudoscopic effect

幻术 huànshù magic; conjuring

幻数 huànshù 〈数学〉magic numbers

幻听 huàntīng 〈医学〉phonism; acousma; auditory hallucination:病人有～、幻视现象。The patient is hearing and seeing things. *or* The invalid suffers from auditory and visual hallucination.

幻想 huànxiǎng ❶ fancy; dream; imagine:眼望星空,他～着自己也变成了天边的一颗小星。Looking up into the star-lit sky, he fancied himself to be a small star out there. ❷ illusion; fantasy:对诸如此类的事情,他从不抱～。He never cherished any illusions about such things. /丢掉～,准备斗争。Cast away illusions and get prepared for struggle. /她沉湎于～之中,离现实越来越远。Indulging in fantasies, she drifted further and further away from reality.

幻想曲 huànxiǎngqǔ 〈音乐〉fantasia

幻象 huànxiàng phantom; phantasm; mirage:他脑子里充满了种种奇异的～。His mind was full of fantastic phantoms. /所谓"佛光",实际上是特定气象条件下出现的一种～。The so-called "Buddha's halo" is actually a kind of mirage that appears under given meteorological conditions.

幻嗅 huànxiù 〈医学〉olfactory hallucination

幻影 huànyǐng unreal image; phantom:这种仙境不过是一种～。The fairyland is nothing but an unreal image.

幻影式战斗机 huànyǐngshì zhàndòujī Mirage, a series of fighter

planes made in France
幻月 huànyuè 〈气象〉paraselene; mock moon:～环 paraselenic circle
幻肢 huànzhī 〈医学〉phantom limb:～痛感 phantom (limb) pain

huāng

肓 huāng see“病入膏肓”bìngrùgāohuāng
荒 huāng ❶ waste; uncultivated:土地抛～。The land is left uncultivated. *or* The land lies waste. /田园尽～，饿殍遍野。The farms had all gone to rack and ruin, and bodies of the starved were strewn everywhere. ❷ desolate; wild; barren: see“～岛”;“～山” ❸ famine; crop failure:饥～ famine /逃～ flee from famine ❹ wasteland; uncultivated land:开～ reclaim (*or* open up) wasteland /生～ virgin soil /碱～ alkaline wasteland /沙～ sandy wasteland ❺ neglect; be out of practice:别把学习～了。Don't neglect your lessons (*or* studies)./多年不摸画笔，都～了。It's a long time since I last used a paint brush; I'm out of practice. /我的法文丢～了。My French is rusty. ❻ shortage; scarcity:粮～ grain shortage; scarcity of grain /师资～ shortage of teachers ❼ unreasonable; absurd: see“～谬”;“～诞” ❽〈方言〉uncertain; unverified: see“～信”;“～数” ❾〈书面〉indulge; be addicted:～于游乐 indulge in pleasure-seeking
荒草 huāngcǎo weeds:～丛生 overgrown with weeds
荒村 huāngcūn out-of-the-way village or hamlet:～僻壤 far-off hamlet in a remote region
荒诞 huāngdàn ❶ absurd; preposterous; fantastic:行为～ absurd behaviour /～的主意 fantastic idea /～离奇 absurd and incredible; weird and uncanny ❷〈哲学〉〈文学〉the absurd:～哲学 philosophy of the absurd /～主义 absurdism
荒诞不经 huāngdàn-bùjīng (incredibly) fantastic; preposterous; absurd:～之谈 preposterous statement; cock-and-bull story; tall story (*or* tale)
荒诞派 huāngdànpài 〈文学〉the absurd:～戏剧 theatre of the absurd; absurd theatre /～作家 absurdist /～的黑色幽默 black humour of the absurd
荒诞无稽 huāngdàn-wújī preposterous and groundless; fantastic and absurd:～的谬说 preposterous argument; absurd theory
荒岛 huāngdǎo deserted island; uninhabited island:不毛的～ barren island
荒地 huāngdì wasteland:开垦～ open up (*or* reclaim) wasteland /～造林 afforestation of wasteland /连年战乱，到处都是～。Due to successive years of war, land lay waste everywhere.
荒废 huāngfèi ❶ leave uncultivated; lie waste:男人们大多进城找工作了，不少农田都已～。With most men hunting for jobs in town, much of the land was left uncultivated. ❷ neglect; be out of practice:～学业 neglect one's studies /球艺～ be out of practice in basketball, football, etc. ❸ fall into disuse or disrepair; waste (time):长期～不用的一幢楼房 long-abandoned building /水库～已久。The reservoir has long fallen into disuse. /他年轻时不务正业，～了宝贵的年华。He was not interested in honest work when he was young and wasted the prime years of his life.
荒古 huānggǔ remote antiquity:～世界 world of remote antiquity
荒寒 huānghán desolate and cold:～地带 desolate frigid area
荒旱 huānghàn drought:遭了～ suffer from drought; be stricken by drought /～之年 year of drought and famine
荒秽 huānghuì 〈书面〉lie waste; go out of cultivation:田地～。The land was left uncultivated.
荒火 huānghuǒ bush fire; prairie fire:严防～! Guard against bush fires!
荒货 huānghuò 〈方言〉old stuff; waste; scrap:收～ buy scrap /拾～ collect scrap /～店 salvage shop
荒瘠 huāngjí bleak and barren:～的土地 wild, barren land
荒寂 huāngjì bleak and quiet:四周空旷～。It is bleak and quiet open country all round.
荒郊 huāngjiāo desolate outskirts (of a town); wild country; wilderness:横尸～ die (*or* lie dead) in the wilderness /～野外，坟冢累累。Grave mounds strewed the desolate country.
荒凉 huāngliáng bleak and desolate; wild:～的山野 bleak and desolate mountainous country /～的沼泽地 wild marsh /一片～ bleak and desolate scene; scene of desolation /～寥落 lonely and pathetic sight (*or* scene)
荒乱 huāngluàn in great disorder; in turmoil:～的年代 year of social upheaval (*or* turmoil)
荒落 huāngluò ❶ wild and deserted:～的古寺 deserted old temple ❷〈书面〉out of practice; rusty
荒谬 huāngmiù absurd; preposterous:～的论调 ridiculous formulation (*or* statement) /～的观点 preposterous point of view/～透顶 sheer absurdity; height of absurdity
荒谬绝伦 huāngmiù-juélún absolutely preposterous; absurd to the extreme
荒漠 huāngmò ❶ desolate and vast:他走在这～的草原上，感到无比的孤寂。He was overwhelmed by a feeling of loneliness as he trudged along on the vast desolate prairie. ❷ desert; wilderness:～土 desert soil /～化 desertification /这个地区长期受风沙侵袭，已逐渐变成了～。The region is gradually turning into desert as a result of prolonged erosion by sandy wind.
荒年 huāngnián year of crop failure; famine year; lean year:～无六亲。In a famine year, people would even leave their relatives in the lurch. /每逢～，农民们只好离乡背井，出外谋生。In a year of crop failure, peasants had to leave their native place to seek survival elsewhere.
荒僻 huāngpì wild and remote; desolate and out-of-the-way:～的山村 desolate and out-of-the-way mountain village /这地方虽然～，却具有开发价值。Wild and remote as it is, it is a place good for development.
荒弃 huāngqì lie waste; leave uncultivated:～的土地 land left uncultivated; wasteland
荒歉 huāngqiàn crop failure; famine:～岁月 famine years
荒腔走板 huāngqiāng-tuǒbǎn also“荒腔走调”sing out of (time and) key; sing out of tune:我唱起歌来常常～。I often sing out of key.
荒山 huāngshān barren hill:在～上面植树造林 plant trees on a barren hill; afforestate a barren hill
荒山野岭 huāngshān-yělǐng barren hills and wild mountains:就在那～之中盘踞着一股残匪。A band of remnant bandits were entrenched in those wild mountains.
荒时暴月 huāngshí-bàoyuè time of dearth; lean year; hard time:咱家全无积蓄，遇上～如何是好? As there are no savings in the family, what shall we do when we fall upon hard times?
荒疏 huāngshū out of practice; rusty:多年不上讲台，教学～了。As I haven't taught for quite some time, I'm afraid I am rather out of practice. /她的英文有些～了。Her English is a bit rusty.
荒数 huāngshù 〈方言〉rough figure; approximate number:亩产量只能先报个～儿。We can only give rough figures for yields per *mu* at present.
荒率 huāngshuài 〈书面〉careless; rash; perfunctory:他做事～。He is a rash man.
荒滩 huāngtān barren beach; uncultivated beach:开发～ develop an uncultivated beach /～造林 plant trees on uncultivated beaches; afforestate barren beaches
荒唐 huāngtang ❶ absurd; preposterous; fantastic; ridiculous:～的要求 preposterous (*or* absurd) demand /～故事 old wives' tale; cock-and-bull story /这种说法～可笑。This remark is simply ridiculous. /事情办得太～。The matter was handled in an extremely foolish way. ❷ dissolute; dissipated; loose:～的生活 dissipated (*or* loose) life /～了一辈子 live fast all one's life /他年轻时颇为～，后来终于变得本分了。He settled down at last after sowing his wild oats.
荒颓 huāngtuí desolate and rundown:～的古寺 dilapidated old temple
荒无人烟 huāngwúrényān desolate and uninhabited:～的原野 wilderness
荒芜 huāngwú lie waste; be overgrown with weeds:土地～，民不聊生。The land lay waste and the people lived in dire poverty. /昔日～的洼地变成了绿色的稻田。What used to be low-land overgrown with weeds has been turned into green rice fields.
荒信 huāngxìn 〈方言〉unconfirmed news or information; rumour:别让～给搞迷糊了。Don't be misled by rumours.
荒墟 huāngxū waste open land; debris; ruins
荒野 huāngyě wilderness; wild country; the wilds:～之地 wild country /一片～ vast expanse of wilderness
荒淫 huāngyín dissolute; licentious; debauched:～无道的暴君 dissipated and unprincipled tyrant /～无度导致他的毁灭。Unbridled de-

bauchery led to his ruin.

荒淫无耻 huāngyín-wúchǐ dissipated and shameless; openly given to debauchery：此人生活糜烂，～。This person leads the life of a libertine.

荒原 huāngyuán desolate open country; wild country; wilderness：他们在无边无际的～上建起了自己的家园。They built their homes in the boundless wilderness.

荒政 huāngzhèng ❶〈旧语〉relief policy or measure adopted by the government in years of famine ❷〈书面〉neglect public duties or state affairs

荒置 huāngzhì leave unused; desert; abandon：有些设备一次未用就被～在露天里。Some equipment was dumped in the open and never used.

荒冢 huāngzhǒng desolate and uncared-for grave; nameless grave：～埋骨 bury sb.'s bones in a desolate uncared-for graveyard; be buried in a nameless grave

慌 huāng flurried; confused; panicky：心～意乱 alarmed and confused / 不要～！Don't panic! / 面对那么多人，她一下子就～了。She was scared out of her wits when she faced such a big audience. / 阴谋被揭露后，他们～了手脚。When their plot was exposed, they got flustered and did not know what to do.

慌 huang〈口语〉(used after 得 as a modifier) unbearably; awfully：饿得～ be awfully hungry; be famished / 累得～ be tired out; be completely exhausted; be dog-tired; be played out / 心里闷得～ be bored to death; be bored stiff

慌不择路 huāngbùzélù flee along any path one stumbles upon; seize on any solution when hard pressed：～，饥不择食。You take any road when you're panicky and any food when you're hungry.

慌促 huāngcù with unseemly haste; in a flurry; in a hurry：他～地出了家门。He left his house in a flurry. / ～之间我竟把手提包落在出租车上了。I was in such a hurry that I left my handbag in the taxi.

慌慌 huānghuang flurried; hurried; hasty：时间还早，你～什么？What's the hurry? There's plenty of time.

慌急 huāngjí flustered and hasty; anxious and flurried：他心里～，被脚下的什么东西绊倒在地。Anxious and flurried, he stumbled over something and fell down.

慌里慌张 huānglihuāngzhāng *also*"慌慌张张" in a hurried and confused manner; all in a fluster; in a flurry：这个小伙子总是～的，老叫人不放心。The young man is always in a fluster and doesn't seem to be very dependable.

慌乱 huāngluàn flurried; alarmed and confused：～得手足无措 be so alarmed and confused that one does not know what to do / 一想到马上就要出门，姑娘的心里十分～。The thought of the imminent long journey put the girl in a great tizzy.

慌忙 huāngmáng in a great rush; in a hurry; hurriedly：～赶到医院 rush to the hospital / ～离去 leave in a hurry / 他说话总是那样不慌不忙的。He always speaks in a poised manner (*or* with composure).

慌神儿 huāngshénr be scared out of one's wits; panic：进考场不能～。Be sure to remain coolheaded in the examination room.

慌手慌脚 huāngshǒu-huāngjiǎo in a (great) flurry or tizzy; hurry-scurry：～的年轻人 hurry-scurry young man / ～出了门 leave home in a flurry; go off hurry-scurry

慌张 huāngzhāng flurried; flustered; confused：脸上透出～的神色 look flustered / 别～！没有任何危险！Don't panic! There's no danger! / 他做事总是慌慌张张的。He is always flurried in doing things.

慌作一团 huāngzuòyītuán be thrown into utter confusion; be totally at a loss; be in a great flutter：一听到这消息，他们便两腿筛糠，～。The news sent shudders through their bodies and threw them into utter confusion.

塃 huāng〈方言〉ore

huáng

黄[1] huáng ❶ yellow; sallow; xanthic：～屋顶 yellow roof / ～银矿 xanthoconite / 面～肌瘦 look sallow; be lean and baggard ❷ gold：～白之物 gold and silver; money ❸ yolk：双～蛋 egg with two yolks; double-yolked egg ❹ pornography：～毒 evil of pornography; pornography / ～源 source of pornography; supplier of pornography / 扫～ wipe out pornography and prostitution ❺ (Huáng) (short for 黄河) Yellow River：治～工程 projects to harness the Yellow River ❻ (Huáng) (short for 黄帝) Huangdi; Yellow Emperor：炎～子孙 descendants of Yandi and Huangdi — the Chinese people ❼ (Huáng) a surname

黄[2] huáng〈口语〉fizzle out; fall through; be off：他虽尽了力，但计划还是～了。The plan fell through despite his efforts. / 明天的聚会恐怕要～，因为我妻子病了。I'm afraid tomorrow's party's off because my wife's ill.

黄埃 huáng'āi〈书面〉yellowish dust：狂风怒吼，～弥漫。The wind was howling, blurring the sky with yellowish dust.

黄矮病 huáng'ǎibìng〈农业〉yellow dwarf; yellow stunt：水稻～ yellow dwarf virus of rice

黄巴巴 huángbābā〈方言〉yellowish; sallow：这女人脸上～的，嘴唇一点血色都没有。She looked so sallow that even her lips were colourless.

黄斑 huángbān ❶〈生理〉yellow spot; macula lutea retinae ❷ yellow stain; fox mark：旧报纸上满是～。The old newspaper was full of fox marks.

黄包车 huángbāochē〈方言〉rickshaw; ricksha：～夫 rickshaw man

黄宝石 huángbǎoshí oriental topaz

黄骠马 huángbiāomǎ white-spotted yellow horse

黄表纸 huángbiǎozhǐ〈迷信〉yellow paper (for sacrificial use)

黄宾虹 Huáng Bīnhóng Huang Binhong (formerly translated as Huang Pin-hung, 1864-1955), Chinese traditional painter

黄病 huángbìng〈口语〉jaundice

黄菠萝 huángbōluó〈中药〉bark of the cork tree (*Bhelodendron*)

黄柏 huángbò *see*"黄檗"

黄檗 huángbò *also*"黄柏" ❶〈植物〉armur cork; cork tree ❷〈中药〉bark of the cork tree (*Bhelodendron*)

黄菜 huángcài〈方言〉scrambled eggs：摊～ scrambled eggs; omelette / 溜～ stir-fried eggs

黄灿灿 huángcàncàn bright yellow; golden：～的金锭 bright yellow gold ingots / ～的麦浪 golden waves of wheat

黄巢起义 Huáng Cháo Qǐyì Huang Chao Uprising, a peasant uprising starting in 875 AD, under Huang Chao's leadership, which eventually toppled the Tang Dynasty

黄刺玫 huángcìméi〈植物〉yellow rose (*Rosa xantina*)

黄带子 huángdàizi〈旧语〉yellow ribbon worn by member of the Qing royal clan; member of the Qing royal clan

黄丹 huángdān yellow lead

黄疸 huángdǎn *also*"黄疸病";"黄病"〈医学〉jaundice; icterus：肝原性～ hepatogenous jaundice / 阻塞性～ obstructive jaundice / ～指数 icterus index / 新生儿～ icterus neonatorum

黄疸性贫血 huángdǎnxìng pínxuè icteroanemia

黄道 huángdào〈天文〉ecliptic：～光 zodiacal light / ～星座 zodiacal constellation / ～坐标 ecliptic coordinate / ～流星 ecliptic meteor

黄道带 huángdàodài zodiac

黄道吉日 huángdào-jírì *also*"黄道日" propitious or auspicious date; lucky day：老头子迷信，出远门要选个～。The old man was so superstitious (that) he would choose a propitious date for a long journey.

黄道婆 Huángdàopó Huang Daopo (c. 1245-?), woman innovator of textile technique of the Yuan Dynasty

黄道十二宫 huángdào shí'èrgōng (in ancient astronomy) 12 signs of the zodiac; zodiacal signs

黄澄澄 huángdēngdēng glistening yellow; golden：～的广柑 golden orange / ～的金质奖章 glistening gold medal / 热腾腾，～的玉米糕馋得人直流口水。My mouth watered at the sight of the steaming golden corn cakes.

黄帝 Huángdì Huangdi or Yellow Emperor — legendary ruler and ancestor of the Chinese nation：～陵 Mausoleum of the Yellow Emperor in Huangling County, Shaanxi Province / ～庙 Temple of the Yellow Emperor in Huangling County, Shaanxi Province

黄帝内经 Huángdì Nèijīng *also*"内经" *Classic of Internal Medicine*, China's earliest classic work on medicine completed between 403-221 BC of the Warring States Period and preserved to this day

黄碘 huángdiǎn 〈化学〉iodoform
黄鲷 huángdiāo 〈动物〉yellow porgy
黄豆 huángdòu soya bean; soybean:～芽 soya bean sprouts
黄泛区 huángfànqū area formerly flooded by the Yellow River
黄蜂 huángfēng wasp:～毒 wasp venom /大～ hornet
黄蜂巢 huángfēngcháo vespiary
黄蜂蜡 huángfēnglà cera flava
黄公望 Huáng Gōngwàng Huang Gongwang (formerly translated as Huang Kung-wang, 1269-1354), painter of the Yuan Dynasty
黄姑鱼 huánggūyú spotted maigre (*Nibea albiflora*)
黄骨髓 huánggǔsuǐ yellow marrow; medulla ossium flava; ossium flava medulla
黄瓜 huánggua cucumber:酸～ pickled cucumber /～色拉 cucumber salad
黄瓜香 huángguaxiāng *also* "地榆" dìyú garden burnet
黄冠 huángguān ❶ yellow hat (of a Taoist priest) ❷ Taoist priest:遁迹～ withdraw from worldly affairs and become a Taoist priest
黄果树瀑布 Huángguǒshù Pùbù Huangguoshu Falls, biggest falls in China located in Guizhou Province
黄海 Huánghǎi Yellow Sea, off the east coast of China
黄河 Huánghé Yellow River (5,464 km. long, second longest river in China):～流域 Yellow River Valley /～故道 former course of the Yellow River; abandoned course of the Yellow River /～三角洲 Yellow River Delta /《～大合唱》*Yellow River Cantata*
黄河象 huánghéxiàng 〈考古〉Yellow River stegodon
黄褐斑 huánghèbān 〈医学〉chloasma
黄褐色 huánghèsè yellowish-brown; tawny
黄鹤楼 Huánghèlóu Yellow Crane Tower in Wuhan(武汉), Hubei Province
黄花 huánghuā ❶ chrysanthemum ❷ (popular term for 金针菜) day lily ❸ without sexual experience; virgin:～闺女 virgin /～后生 virgin boy
黄花菜 huánghuācài day lily
黄花地丁 huánghuā dìdīng 〈植物〉dandelion
黄花岗起义 Huánghuāgǎng Qǐyì Huanghuagang Uprising of 27 April 1911 led by Huang Xing (黄兴) and others against the Manchu Government, which hastened the downfall of the Qing Dynasty
黄花苜蓿 huánghuā mùxu 〈植物〉(California) bur clover
黄花女儿 huánghuānǚr *also* "黄花闺女" 〈口语〉virgin (girl)
黄花晚节 huánghuā-wǎnjié moral integrity in one's later life or old age:保持～ maintain one's moral integrity in one's later years
黄花鱼 huánghuāyú yellow croaker
黄化 huánghuà 〈植物〉yellowing; actiolation; etiolation:～病 yellows /～现象 actiolation
黄桦 huánghuà yellow birch; silver birch; swamp birch (*Betula alleghaniensis*)
黄昏 huánghūn dusk; twilight; gloaming:～时分 at dusk /夕阳无限好,只是近～。Beautiful as the setting sun looks, It is the last glow before dusk.
黄昏恋 huánghūnliàn love between old people; twilight love
黄祸 huánghuò Yellow Peril or Scourge, the so-called threat of Asian peoples, especially the Chinese, to White supremacy
黄鹡鸰 huángjílíng yellow wagtail
黄麂 huángjǐ 〈动物〉muntjac
黄酱 huángjiàng salted and fermented soya paste
黄教 Huángjiào Yellow Hat Lamaism, largest sect of Tibetan Lamaism
黄巾起义 Huángjīn Qǐyì Yellow Turbans Uprising, a large-scale peasant uprising which broke out at the end of the Eastern Han Dynasty (from 184 AD onwards) with its participants wearing yellow turbans
黄金 huángjīn gold:～饰品 gold ornament /～储备 gold reserve /～市场 gold market /～水道 most profitable waterway /～未为贵,安乐值钱多。Enjoyment and comfort is worth more than gold.
黄金分割 huángjīn fēngē *also* "中外比" zhōngwàibǐ 〈数学〉golden section; extreme and mean ratio
黄金海岸 Huángjīn Hǎi'àn Gold Coast, changed to Ghana when the country won independence in 1957
黄金时代 huángjīn shídài ❶ golden age:当时是大唐帝国的～。That period was the golden age of the Tang Empire. ❷ prime of one's life:他一生的～都献给了教育事业。He devoted the prime of his life to the cause of education.
黄金时间 huángjīn shíjiān (as on TV) prime time; peak viewing time:～节目 prime time item
黄荆 huángjīng 〈植物〉five-leaved chaste tree (*Vitex negundo*)
黄猄 huángjīng 〈动物〉muntjac
黄晶 huángjīng citrine; topaz
黄精 huángjīng 〈中药〉sealwort (*Polygonatum sibiricum*)
黄酒 huángjiǔ yellow rice wine; yellow millet wine; Shaoxing wine
黄口小儿 huángkǒu-xiǎo'ér *also* "黄口孺子" sucking baby;〈贬义〉callow young fellow
黄葵 huángkuí musk mallow (*Hibiscus moschatus*)
黄蜡蜡 huánglālā (mostly of facial complexion) sallow; colourless:他病重得很,脸色～的。He was seriously ill, with his face colourless.
黄蜡 huánglà beeswax; cera flava
黄老 Huáng-Lǎo (short for 黄帝与老子) Huangdi and Laozi (honoured by the Taoists as their patriarchs):～之学 teachings of the Huangdi and Laozi; Taoist philosophy as taught by Laozi and his immediate disciples /～学派 philosophical school of the Huangdi and Laozi; classical Taoist school /～思想 classical Taoist thinking; classical Taoist concept
黄鹂 huánglí *also* "黄莺";"鸧鹒" cānggēng oriole:黑枕～ black-naped oriole /～唤春。When the oriole calls, spring is returning.
黄历 huángli *also* "皇历" huángli 〈旧语〉(lunar) almanac
黄连 huánglián 〈中药〉rhizome of Chinese goldthread (*Coptis Chinensis*); coptis:哑巴吃～,有苦难言 a dumb person eating bitter herbs — suffering in silence /～树下弹琴 — 苦中作乐 seek joy amidst sorrow; try to enjoy oneself despite one's suffering
黄连木 huángliánmù 〈植物〉Chinese pistache
黄连素 huángliánsù 〈药学〉berberine
黄楝树 huángliànshù *also* "苦木" kǔmù *Picrasma quassioides*
黄梁木 huángliángmù *Anthocephalus chinensis*
黄梁梦 huángliángmèng *also* "黄粱美梦";"一枕黄粱" yīzhěn-huángliáng Golden Millet Dream (from the story of a discontented poor scholar who fell asleep while waiting for his lunch and dreamed that he became a high official and enjoyed a life of wealth and comfort, only to wake up and find that the pot of millet was still cooking on the fire for him); daydream; pipe dream:事到如今,他还在做着发财的～呢。To this day he is still daydreaming about becoming rich.
黄磷 huánglín yellow phosphorus
黄鳞 huánglín〈植物〉yellow scales; shore lichen (*Xanthoria parietina*)
黄龙 huánglóng ❶ (Huánglóng) *also* "黄龙府" capital of the Kingdom of Jin (金), main rival for the Southern Song Dynasty; enemy capital:直捣～ defeat the enemy and capture his capital /痛饮～ drink to one's heart's content when one captures the enemy capital ❷ yellow dragon — dust storm; sandstorm:征服～ conquer dust storms ❸ yellow dragon — chain of yellow smoke (from chimneys):锁住～ lock up the "yellow dragon" — prevent chimneys from belching out yellow smoke; eliminate yellow smoke pollution
黄栌 huánglú 〈植物〉smoke tree (*Cotinus coggygria*)
黄麻 huángmá (roundpod) jute:～纸 jute paper /～袋 gunnysack; gunny bag; gunny /～袋布 gunny (cloth)
黄毛丫头 huángmáo yātou 〈戏谑〉〈贬义〉chit of a girl; saucy miss:你这个～! 瞧我治不了你! Saucy miss! See how I shall make you pay for this!
黄梅季节 huángméi jìjié *also* "黄梅天" rainy season (usu. April and May in the middle and lower reaches of the Yangtze River)
黄梅戏 huángméixì Huangmei opera, popular in central Anhui Province
黄梅雨 huángméiyǔ *also* "梅雨";"霉雨" méiyǔ prolonged intermittent drizzles characteristic of the rainy season in the middle and lower reaches of the Yangtze River
黄焖 huángmèn braised in brown sauce:～鸭块 braised duck cubes with brown sauce
黄米 huángmǐ glutinous millet
黄明胶 huángmíngjiāo 〈中药〉oxhide gelatin
黄鸟 huángniǎo (popular term for 金丝雀) canary
黄牛 huángniú ❶ ox; cattle:为孩子们当老～ be a willing horse for

children ❷〈方言〉tout; scalper: ～票 scalper's ticket ❸〈方言〉(act like a) person who fails to keep promises; unreliable person: 你可不许～。Now, don't you go back on your word!

黄排 huángpái *also* "胭脂鱼" yānzhiyú 〈方言〉*Myxocyprinus asiaticus*

黄牌 huángpái 〈体育〉yellow card: 吃了一张～ get a yellow card; 〈比喻〉get a serious warning

黄袍加身 huángpáo-jiāshēn be draped with the imperial yellow robe (by one's supporters) — be acclaimed emperor; be made or make oneself emperor

黄皮寡瘦 huángpí-guǎshòu 〈方言〉sallow and skinny; thin and pale: 看他～的样子，病得不轻。He must be very ill, for he looks terribly thin and sallow.

黄皮书 huángpíshū ❶ yellow book — International Certificate of Vaccination ❷ Yellow Paper — official statement or document of a government or congress (called White Paper in most countries)

黄皮症 huángpízhèng 〈医学〉xanthosis

黄皮子 huángpízi *also* "黄鼬"〈方言〉yellow weasel

黄漂 huángpiāo (short for 黄河漂流) floating down (certain sections) of the Yellow River

黄浦江 Huángpǔjiāng Huangpu River (formerly translated as Whangpoo River), a tributary of the Yangtze River, which flows through Shanghai

黄埔军官学校 Huángpǔ Jūnguān Xuéxiào Huangpu or Whampoa Military Academy, established in Guangzhou in 1924 by Dr. Sun Yat-sen with the help of the Soviet Union and the Chinese Communist Party

黄埔军校 Huángpǔ Jūnxiào *see* "黄埔军官学校"

黄埔条约 Huángpǔ Tiáoyuē Treaty of Huangpu, first unequal treaty signed at Huangpu, Guangdong on 24 October 1844 between China and France

黄芪 huángqí 〈中药〉root of membranous milk vetch (*Astragalus membranaceus*)

黄芩 huángqín 〈中药〉root of large-flowered skullcap (*Scutellaria baicalensis*)

黄曲霉毒素 huángqūméi dúsù aflatoxin

黄曲霉菌 huángqūméijūn 〈微生物〉*Aspergillus flavus*

黄曲霉素 huángqūméisù aflatoxin; flavacin; flavacol: 产～菌株 aflatoxigenic strain

黄曲霉素中毒症 huángqūméisù zhòngdúzhèng 〈医学〉aflatoxicosis

黄泉 huángquán netherworld: 命归～ go to the netherworld; die / ～之下 in the netherworld; in one's grave / ～路上无老少。Death may fall on the young as well as the old. *or* Every one is equal in death.

黄雀 huángquè siskin: 螳螂捕蝉，～在后。The mantis stalks the cicada, unaware of the siskin behind. *or* When one covets gains ahead one is often unaware of dangers behind.

黄壤 huángrǎng yellow earth; yellow soil

黄热病 huángrèbìng yellow fever

黄色 huángsè ❶ yellow: ～上衣 yellow jacket / ～氧化汞 yellow mercury oxide / ～蛋白 xanthoprotein ❷ decadent; vulgar; pornographic: ～新闻 salacious news; sex news / ～歌曲 lewd song / ～音乐 decadent music / ～书刊 obscene publication / ～电影 pornographic movie; sex film; blue film / ～录像 pornographic video; blue video

黄色工会 huángsè gōnghuì blackleg union; scab union

黄色瘤 huángsèliú 〈医学〉*also* "黄疣" xanthoma

黄色人种 huángsè rénzhǒng yellow race

黄色文学 huángsè wénxué pornography

黄色炸药 huángsè zhàyào ❶ trinitrotoluene (TNT) ❷ (popular term for 苦味酸) picric acid

黄山 Huángshān Huangshan Mountains, in southern Anhui Province

黄杉 huángshān Douglas fir or spruce

黄鳝 huángshàn *also* "鳝鱼" shànyú rice-field eel; finless eel

黄石国家公园 Huángshí Guójiā Gōngyuán Yellowstone National Park, largest national park of the United States since 1872

黄熟 huángshú 〈农业〉yellow maturity; yellow ripeness: ～期 stage of yellow maturity (*or* ripeness) / 小麦已经～。The wheat is ripe and yellow.

黄鼠 huángshǔ ground squirrel; suslik

黄鼠狼 huángshǔláng *also* "黄鼬" yellow weasel: ～拖鸡，越拖越稀 like a coop of chickens preyed upon by a weasel — draining away each day

黄鼠狼单咬病鸭子 huángshǔláng dān yǎo bìngyāzi weasels single out lame ducks to catch — the worst problems always seem to plague those already in trouble

黄鼠狼给鸡拜年 huángshǔláng gěi jī bàinián a weasel makes a courtesy call to a chicken — harbour evil intentions; have ulterior motives: ～，没安好心。When a weasel makes a courtesy call to a chicken, he harbours no good intentions.

黄水疮 huángshuǐchuāng *also* "脓疮病" nóngchuāngbìng 〈医学〉impetigo: 治～的良药是降汞软膏。Ammoniated mercury ointment is the best cure for impetigo.

黄檀 huángtán 〈植物〉*Dalbergia hupeana*

黄汤 huángtāng 〈贬义〉rice wine; liquor: 他～灌多了，满嘴胡说八道。Having had a drop too much, he was all drunken talk.

黄糖 huángtáng 〈方言〉brown sugar

黄体 huángtǐ 〈生理〉corpus luteum: ～激素 corpus luteum hormone

黄体瘤 huángtǐliú 〈医学〉xanthofibroma

黄体酮 huángtǐtóng 〈生理〉progesterone

黄天荡之战 Huángtiāndàng Zhī Zhàn Battle of Huangtiandang in 1130 (near present-day Nanjing, Jiangsu Province), in which the Song forces led by Han Shizhong (韩世忠) defeated the invading Jin (金) army, thus preserving the Southern Song Dynasty

黄铁矿 huángtiěkuàng pyrite

黄庭坚 Huáng Tíngjiān Huang Tingjian (formerly translated as Huang Ting-chien, 1045-1105), poet of the Northern Song Dynasty

黄铜 huángtóng brass: ～丝 brass wire / ～制品 brass work / ～管 brass pipe (*or* tube)

黄铜矿 huángtóngkuàng chalcopyrite

黄土 huángtǔ 〈地质〉loess: ～地 loessland / ～化 loessification

黄土高原 huángtǔ gāoyuán loess plateau

黄烷 huángwán 〈生化〉flavane: ～醇 flavanol / ～酮 flavanone

黄萎病 huángwěibìng 〈农业〉verticillium wilt: 棉花～ verticillium wilt of cotton

黄兴 Huáng Xīng Huang Xing (1874-1916), democratic revolutionary and main military assistant to Dr. Sun Yat-sen

黄锈病 huángxiùbìng *also* "黄疸"〈农业〉yellow rust

黄癣 huángxuǎn 〈医学〉favus; tinea favosa

黄烟 huángyān 〈方言〉tobacco (smoked in a long-stemmed pipe)

黄羊 huángyáng Mongolian gazelle

黄杨 huángyáng 〈植物〉Chinese littleleaf box

黄杨木 huángyángmù boxwood: ～雕 boxwood carving

黄猺 huángyáo *also* "青鼬" qīngyòu *Martes flavigula*, a kind of dark brown weasel

黄莺 huángyīng oriole

黄油 huángyóu ❶ grease: ～枪 grease gun ❷ butter: ～面包 bread and butter / 人造～ artificial butter; margarine / 给烤面包片抹上～ butter one's toast

黄鼬 huángyòu *also* "黄鼠狼" yellow weasel

黄鱼 huángyú ❶ *also* "黄花鱼" yellow croaker ❷〈旧语〉stowaway passenger who pays the driver or sailor ❸〈方言〉gold bar: 大～ big gold bar (ten taels) / 小～ small gold bar (one tael)

黄玉 huángyù 〈矿业〉topaz

黄藻 huángzǎo yellow-green algae

黄账 huángzhàng 〈方言〉bad debt

黄纸板 huángzhǐbǎn *also* "马粪纸" mǎfènzhǐ strawboard

黄种 huángzhǒng yellow race; Mongoloid race: ～人 Mongoloid; yellow man

黄宗羲 Huáng Zōngxī Huang Zongxi (1610-1695), thinker and historian of the late Ming and early Qing dynasties

黄遵宪 Huáng Zūnxiàn Huang Zunxian (1848-1905), poet of the late Qing Dynasty

潢¹

huáng 〈书面〉pond; pool

潢²

huáng dye or colour paper: 装～ decoration; mounting; packing

潢纸 huángzhǐ (used for painting and calligraphy in ancient times) paper in dyed cork-tree-juice

癀

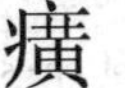
huáng

H

癀病 huángbìng 〈方言〉anthrax

璜

huáng 〈书面〉semicircular jade pendant

磺

huáng sulphur:硝～ nitre and sulphur /～内酯 sultone /～酰 sulphonyl; sulfuryl

磺胺 huáng'àn 〈药学〉sulphanilamide (SN); sulfanilamide:长效～sulfamethoxypyridazine (SMP) /～药 sulfa drug; sulphonamide/～甲基嘧啶 sulfamerazine /～醋酰 sulphacetamide (SA) /～嘧啶 sulphadiazine (SD) /～异呋喃唑 sulphafurazole; gantrisin

磺胺脒 huáng'ànmǐ *also* "黄胺胍" sulphaguanidine (SG)

磺胺噻唑 huáng'àn sāizuò sulphathiazole (ST)

磺化 huánghuà sulphonating:～剂 sulphonating agent /～反应 sulphonating reaction /～煤 sulphonated coal /～作用 sulfonation

磺基 huángjī sulpho-; sulfo-:～水杨酸 sulfosalicylic acid /～苯酸 sulfobenzoic acid

磺酸 huángsuān sulphonic acid; sulfonic acid; mahogany acid

磺酸盐 huángsuānyán sulphonate

磺酰胺 huángxiān'àn 〈化学〉sulphonic acid amide; sulphamide

蟥

huáng *see* "蚂蟥" mǎhuáng

簧

huáng ❶ reed (in a musical instrument):口琴～ mouth organ reed /巧舌如～ have a glib tongue ❷ spring:锁～ lock spring /锁～舌 spring bolt /锁～片 tumbler spring; flat spring /弹～ spring /圈～ coil(ed) spring /拉～ tension spring /板～ flat spring

簧风琴 huángfēngqín 〈乐器〉reed organ; harmonium

簧片 huángpiàn reed (in a musical instrument)

簧乐器 huángyuèqì reed instrument

锽

huáng *see* "簧" huáng

皇

huáng ❶〈书面〉grand; magnificent:堂～ grand; magnificent ❷ emperor; sovereign:女～ empress /教～ pope /玉～大帝 Jade Emperor /太上～ emperor's father; backstage ruler; overlord ❸ (Huáng) a surname

皇朝 huángcháo dynasty

皇城 huángchéng imperial city (usu. within the capital)

皇储 huángchǔ crown prince

皇带鱼 huángdàiyú oarfish

皇帝 huángdì emperor:～也有草鞋亲。〈俗语〉Even an emperor has poor relations. /～的女儿不愁嫁。〈俗语〉A princess need not worry about her marriage. *or* A scarce item has no lack of demand.

皇恩 huáng'ēn imperial beneficence; imperial favour:～浩荡。How beneficent (*or* magnanimous) His Imperial Majesty is!

皇甫 Huángfǔ a surname

皇宫 huánggōng imperial palace:～御苑 imperial palaces and gardens

皇冠 huángguān imperial or royal crown:～上的明珠 pearl on the crown

皇后 huánghòu empress; queen

皇皇 huánghuáng ❶ *see* "惶惶" huánghuáng ❷ *see* "遑遑" huánghuáng ❸ magnificent; splendid:～巨著 voluminous work; masterpiece

皇家 huángjiā imperial house or family:出身～ be born in an imperial family; be born to (*or* in) the purple /～园林 imperial garden /～卫士 imperial (*or* royal) guard

皇家航空公司 Huángjiā Hángkōng Gōngsī KLM (*Koninklijke Luchtvaart Maatschappij*), a Dutch airline

皇历 huángli *also* "黄历" huángli 〈口语〉(lunar) almanac

皇粮 huángliáng ❶〈旧语〉public grain; grain tax to the government:交～ pay grain tax ❷ funds, goods, etc. provided by the government:他是吃～的。He is paid by the government. *or* He is a government employee.

皇陵 huánglíng imperial mausoleum

皇亲 huángqīn kinsman or relative of the emperor

皇亲国戚 huángqīn-guóqì kinsman or relative of the emperor:端的是～也不须怕他。Even if he truly belonged to the royal family I wouldn't be afraid of him.

皇权 huángquán imperial power or authority

皇上 huángshang (reigning) emperor; His Majesty; Your Majesty:～并不知有此事。His Majesty knows not of the matter. /～驾崩了。The emperor has departed this life.

皇室 huángshì ❶ imperial family; royal house:～贵胄 scion of the imperial family; scion of royal stock ❷ royal court; imperial government:效忠～ be loyal to the imperial government

皇太后 huángtàihòu empress dowager:两宫～ two main wives of the late emperor; both empress dowagers

皇太极 Huángtàijí Huangtaiji (1592-1643), 2nd emperor of the Manchus before the Qing Dynasty unified China, called reverently Qing Taizong (清太宗) after death

皇太子 huángtàizǐ crown prince

皇天 huángtiān Heaven; Great Heaven:～在上 (used when taking an oath) with Heaven watching me from above /～无亲,惟德是辅。〈书面〉Great Heaven is impartial; it helps only the virtuous.

皇天不负苦心人 huángtiān bù fù kǔxīnrén Heaven helps those who help themselves; Providence doesn't let down a man who does his best; keep thy shop and thy shop will keep thee

皇天后土 huángtiān-hòutǔ Heaven and Earth:～,可鉴我心。Heaven and Earth may witness my intention.

皇位 huángwèi throne:继承～ succeed (*or* accede) to the throne

皇协军 Huángxiéjūn "Imperial Subsidiary Army" (one of the quisling forces fighting alongside the Japanese army in north China during the War of Resistance Against Japanese Aggression, 1937-1945)

皇庄 huángzhuāng imperial or royal estate

皇子 huángzǐ emperor's son; prince

皇族 huángzú royal or imperial clan; people of imperial lineage

湟

Huáng

湟水 Huángshuǐ Huangshui River, originating in Qinghai Province and joining the Yellow River in Gansu Province

湟鱼 huángyú *also* "裸鲤" luǒlǐ 〈动物〉*Gymnocypris przewalskii*, a kind of carp found in the Qinghai Lake

惶

huáng fear; dread; trepidation:惊～ panic; be alarmed

惶惶 huánghuáng *also* "皇皇" huánghuáng in a state of anxiety; on tenterhooks, alarmed:人心～ popular anxiety /～然如丧家之犬 be frightened as a stray cur

惶惶不可终日 huánghuáng bùkě zhōngrì be in a constant state of anxiety; be on tenterhooks all the time

惶惑 huánghuò perplexed and alarmed; apprehensive:～不解 be puzzled /～不安 perplexed and uneasy /～的脸色 apprehensive look

惶急 huángjí scared and anxious:～的神情 frightened and distressed look /人心～。People are alarmed and anxious.

惶悸 huángjì alarmed; frightened:～不安 be on tenterhooks

惶窘 huángjiǒng 〈书面〉seized with fear; panic-stricken

惶惧 huángjù scared; terrified:～失色 blanch with fear; be thoroughly terrified

惶遽 huángjù 〈书面〉alarmed; frightened; scared:神色～ look scared (*or* frightened)

惶恐 huángkǒng scared; terrified:万分～ be seized with fear; be scared out of one's wits /他两眼盯住冲着自己的枪口,心里～极了。Staring at the barrel of the pistol, he was petrified.

惶恐不安 huángkǒng-bù'ān be in a state of alarm; be on tenterhooks:她整日～,不知怎样来应付这突如其来的灾难。She was on tenterhooks all day, completely at a loss how to deal with the unexpected disaster.

惶愧 huángkuì be afraid and ashamed:～交集 have a mixed feeling of fear and shame

惶然 huángrán frightened and uneasy; alarmed:～不知所措 be alarmed and confused; be frightened out of one's senses

惶悚 huángsǒng 〈书面〉scared; terrified:～不安 be on tenterhooks

煌

huáng bright; brilliant:灯火辉～ brightly lit /辉～的胜利 brilliant victory

煌斑岩 huángbānyán 〈地质〉lamprophyre

煌煌 huánghuáng bright; brilliant:金～的勋章 glittering golden decoration (*or* medal) /明星～。The stars are sparkling.

遑

huáng 〈书面〉leisure:不～ have no leisure; be occupied

遑遑 huánghuáng *also* "皇皇" huánghuáng 〈书面〉in haste:～欲何

之？Where are you hastily heading for?

遑论 huánglùn 〈书面〉 out of the question; much less：衣食无着，～其他。Without shelter and food, you cannot even begin to talk about anything else.

喤 huáng

喤喤 huánghuáng 〈书面〉 ❶ sonorous and harmonious sound of bells and drums：钟鼓～ harmonious chiming of bells and beating of drums ❷ (of child) loud crying

蝗 huáng

locust：灭～ wipe out locusts／食～鸟 locust bird

蝗虫 huángchóng locust：～遮天蔽日 cloud of locusts

蝗蝻 huángnǎn *also* "跳蝻" tiàonǎn nymph of a locust

蝗灾 huángzāi plague of locusts

篁 huáng

bamboo grove; bamboo：幽～ secluded bamboo grove／修～ tall bamboo／新～ young bamboo

锽 huáng

锽锽 huánghuáng sound of bells and drums

徨 huáng

see "彷徨" pánghuáng

艎 huáng

see "艅艎" yúhuáng

凰 huáng

see "凤凰" fènghuáng

鳇 huáng

Huso dauricus

偟 huáng

see "怅偟" zhānghuáng

隍 huáng

dry moat outside a city wall

huǎng

怳 huǎng

see "惝怳" chǎnghuǎng

谎 huǎng

lie; falsehood：撒～ lie; tell a lie／弥天大～ monstrous lie; outrageous lie; barefaced lie

谎报 huǎngbào make a false report (about sth.); give false information; lie：～粮食产量 lie about the grain output／～成绩 give a false account of one's achievements

谎报军情 huǎngbào-jūnqíng make a false report about the (military) situation：这个村向上级～，夸大水灾损失。The village made a false report to the higher authorities, exaggerating the damage caused by the flood.

谎称 huǎngchēng falsely claim：有人～税务人员，向个体户敲诈钱财。Somebody pretended to be a tax collector and extorted money from small stall owners.

谎花 huǎnghuā 〈植物〉 staminate flower; fruitless flower

谎话 huǎnghuà lie; falsehood：说～ tell a lie; lie／～连篇 tell a pack of lies; lie like a gas-meter; lie in one's throat (*or* teeth)

谎价 huǎngjià excessive price; exorbitant price; extortionate price

谎骗 huǎngpiàn deceive：这简直是～小孩子的伎俩。This is nothing but a trick to deceive innocent children.

谎信 huǎngxìn 〈方言〉 unproved information; unconfirmed news; rumour

谎言 huǎngyán lie：拆穿～ expose a lie／揭穿某人的～ give the lie to sb.／驳斥～ refute a lie／捏造～ invent a lie／散布～ spread a lie／纯属～ sheer (*or* gross) lie／一派～ a pack of lies／无耻～ impudent (*or* outrageous) lie／显系～ transparent lie／～总是站不住脚的。Lies have short legs. *or* Lies are always lame.

谎语癖 huǎngyǔpǐ 〈心理〉 mythomania; pseudologia：～患者 mythomaniac; pseudologue／幻想性～ pseudologia fantastica

恍 huǎng

❶ all of a sudden; suddenly ❷ (used in combination with 如，若) seem; as if：这一切～如梦境。All this happened as if in a dream.

恍惚 huǎnghū *also* "恍忽" ❶ in a trance; absent-minded：神情～ look absent-minded ❷ dimly; faintly; seemingly：～记得 faintly remember／我～回到了童年时代。I seemed to be back in my childhood.

恍然 huǎngrán all of a sudden; suddenly：～醒悟 wake up to the truth in an instant／～若失 feel lost; find oneself at sea; feel that one has lost one's bearings

恍然大悟 huǎngrán-dàwù realize all of a sudden; suddenly see the light：他一句话使我～。His words opened my eyes instantly.

恍如隔世 huǎngrúgéshì it seems as if a whole generation had passed; feel as if cut off from the outside world for ages; it seems as if sth. had happened in the remote past

恍悟 huǎngwù wake up to reality suddenly; suddenly come to realize the truth：她说她要退学，我听了一愣，后来才～过来。When she said she was quitting school, it was quite a while before I realized what was on her mind.

晃 huǎng

❶ dazzle：明～～的招牌 shining signboard／阳光把我的眼睛～花了。The shining sun dazzled me. ❷ flash past：人群里有一个熟悉的身影～了一下就不见了。A familiar figure flashed past and disappeared into the crowd.／一～暑假就过完了。The summer vacation passed in a flash.／他左手虚～一招，右掌击中对手面颊。Feinting with his left hand, he hit his adversary's face with his right.

see also huàng

晃眼 huǎngyǎn ❶ dazzling：灯光～，能调暗些吗？The light is dazzling; will you please turn it down? ❷〈比喻〉 in a flash; in a split second; in a wink：刚才还见他在这里，怎么一～就不见了？I saw him here just now. How could he have disappeared in a wink? *or* How could he vanish into thin air?

幌 huǎng

〈书面〉 heavy curtain

幌子 huǎngzi ❶〈旧语〉 shop sign; signboard：小酒铺外高挑着一面酒～。Hoisted high outside the wineshop was a sign bearing the word "WINE". ❷ pretence; cover; front：骗人的～ facade; front／在和谈的～下加紧备战 intensify war preparations under the cover (*or* pretence) of peace talks

huàng

晃(搌) huàng

shake; sway：～落树上的枣子 shake down dates from a tree／摇头～脑 wag one's head (smugly) — look pleased with oneself／坐着～腿是坏习惯。It's a bad habit to shake one's leg while sitting.／树枝在风里不停地～着。The branches kept swaying in the wind.

see also huǎng

晃荡 huàngdang ❶ rock; sway; swing：来回～ swing (*or* sway) to and fro／一瓶子不响，半瓶子～ the half-filled bottle sloshes, the full bottle remains quiet — the dabbler in knowledge chatters away, the wise man stays silent; silent water runs deep／风很大，小船在水里直～。The small boat was rocking in the strong wind. ❷ saunter; loaf：成天在外面～ loaf around all day long

晃动 huàngdòng shake; rock; sway：路灯在风中不停地～。The road lantern kept swaying in the wind.／请不要～椅子！Don't rock the chair, please!／我的牙齿有点儿～。One of my teeth wobbles a bit.

晃梯 huàngtī 〈杂技〉 balancing on an upright ladder

晃摇 huàngyao rock; shake; sway; swing：～摇篮 rock a cradle

晃悠 huàngyou shake from side to side; wobble; stagger：走道儿直～ stagger along／这小树经不起你～。The young tree can't stand your shaking.／我踩得桌子直～。The table wobbled under my feet.／他把药瓶～了几下，倒出几滴棕色的药水来。He shook the bottle several times and poured out a few drops of brown mixture.

滉 huàng

〈书面〉 (of water) deep and wide

榥 huàng

〈书面〉 curtain; screen

huī

麾 huī

❶〈古语〉 standard of a commander ❷〈书面〉 command：～军向敌人进击 command an army to attack the enemy

麾下 huīxià 〈书面〉❶ troops under sb.'s command: 王将军～的十万大军 hundred thousand men (*or* soldiers) under General Wang's command / 我在刘总～任职。I serve (*or* have a job) under General Manager Liu. ❷〈敬词〉general; commander; your excellency

珲 huī *see* "瑷珲" Àihuī
see also hún

挥 huī ❶ wave; brandish; shake; wield: ～旗示意 wave a flag as a signal / ～刀舞枪 brandish swords and rifles / ～拳 shake one's fist (at sb.) / ～之即去 leave (*or* depart) at a motion of one's hand ❷ wipe off: ～汗 wipe off one's sweat ❸ command (an army): ～军前进 command an army to march forward; order one's army to push forward ❹ scatter; disperse: *see* "～发"; "～金如土"

挥斥 huīchì 〈书面〉❶ criticize; reproach; scold ❷ bold and unrestrained; untrammelled; uninhibited: 书生意气, ～方遒。Filled with student euthusiasm, Boldly we cast all restraints aside.

挥动 huīdòng brandish; wave; shake: ～手臂 wave one's arm / ～老拳 shake one's fists (at sb.) / ～皮鞭 wield a whip / 他～板斧, 冲了过来。Wielding a pair of hatchets, he charged over.

挥发 huīfā volatilize: ～元素 volatile element / ～作用 volatilization / ～煅烧 volatilizing roasting / ～损失 volatilization loss / 汽油容易～。Gasoline is volatile. / 这种药必须密封, 免得～。This medicine must be hermetically sealed to prevent volatilization.

挥发性 huīfāxìng volatility; volatileness: ～化合物 volatile compound / ～油漆 volatile paint (*or* varnish) / ～溶剂 volatile solution / ～物质 volatile matter / ～蒸发 volatile evaporation

挥发油 huīfāyóu volatile oil; (sometimes) gasoline

挥戈 huīgē brandish one's weapon (while marching); advance boldly: ～跃马 brandish one's weapon on horseback — march with great élan / ～南下 (of a general) command one's army to march south; (of an army) march south

挥汗如雨 huīhàn-rúyǔ *also* "挥汗成雨" (of weather) so hot that perspiration falls like rain; (of people) dripping with sweat; wet through: 到达半山腰时, 我们已经气喘吁吁、～了。Half way up the hill, we were already wet through and breathing hard.

挥翰 huīhàn 〈书面〉wield one's writing brush; write (with a brush)

挥毫 huīháo 〈书面〉wield one's brush; write or paint (with a brush): ～泼墨 take up a brush and paint (*or* write) / ～赋诗 take up one's brush and write poetry / 对客～ write with a brush in the presence of a guest

挥霍 huīhuò ❶ spend freely; squander: ～浪费 spend extravagantly / ～无度 spend without restraint; squander wantonly ❷〈书面〉lively; free and easy: 生性～ have a free and easy character

挥金如土 huījīn-rútǔ throw gold about like dirt; spend money like water; play ducks and drakes with one's money: 想当初我～, 他不知用了我多少钱。Just think how much he had from me when I was spending money like water!

挥泪 huīlèi wipe off one's tears; shed tears: ～而别 wipe off one's tears as one parts from sb.; part (*or* depart) in tears / ～斩马谡 (originally of Zhuge Liang) wipe off his tears as he orders Ma Su's execution — steel oneself to do sth. painful but necessary

挥洒 huīsǎ ❶ sprinkle or spray (water); shed (tears): 将水～在草坪上 sprinkle water over a lawn / ～热血 shed one's blood (for a worthy cause) ❷ paint or write with ease: 手执画笔, ～自如 wield a painting brush with facility and freedom ❸〈书面〉free and unrestrained: 风神～ free and graceful demeanour

挥师 huīshī command an army: ～东渡黄河 command an army to march eastward across the Yellow River

挥手 huīshǒu wave one's hand; wave: ～告别 wave farewell; wave good-bye / 马路对过有人向我～。Somebody waved to me from across the street. / 他不停地～, 示意我不要再说。He kept waving to me, motioning me to say no more.

挥舞 huīwǔ wave; brandish; shake: ～拳头 shake one's fist (at sb.) / ～手臂 wave one's arms about; saw the air / ～彩旗迎佳宾 wave colourful banners to welcome distinguished guests / ～指挥棒 brandish the baton; order people about

辉(煇) huī ❶ radiance; splendour; glow: 光～ radiance; lustre; glow / 增～ add to the splendour; do credit (to sb.) / 落日余～ last rays of the setting sun; evening glow ❷ shine; glow: 与江河同在, 与日月同～ flow like the river and shine like the sun; (of one's reputation, feats or works) last for ever and ever

辉安岩 huī'ānyán 〈地质〉auganite

辉长岩 huīchángyán 〈地质〉gabbro

辉沸石 huīfèishí stilbite

辉钴矿 huīgǔkuàng *also* "辉砷钴矿" cobaltite; cobaltine

辉光 huīguāng ❶ radiance; splendour; glow: 夕阳的～ splendour of the setting sun; evening glow ❷〈电学〉glow: ～灯 glow lamp / ～电流 glow current / ～放电 glow discharge / ～放电开关 glow switch / ～放电管 glow discharge tube / ～显示 glow visualization / ～阴极 glow cathode

辉煌 huīhuáng brilliant; splendid; glorious; magnificent: ～成就 outstanding (*or* splendid, *or* remarkable) achievement / ～灿烂的文化 illustrious culture (*or* civilization) / ～的前景 bright prospect / ～的时代 glorious age / 灯火～ brightly lit; brilliantly illuminated; ablaze with lights / 金碧～ dazzlingly magnificent

辉菌素 huījūnsù lustericin; lystericin

辉绿岩 huīlǜyán 〈地质〉diabase

辉煤 huīméi glossy coal; glance coal

辉钼矿 huīmùkuàng molybdenite

辉镍矿 huīnièkuàng polydymite; beyrichite

辉砷钴矿 huīshēn gǔkuàng cobaltite

辉石 huīshí 〈地质〉pyroxene; augite

辉锑矿 huītīkuàng antimony glance; stibnite

辉铜矿 huītóngkuàng chalcocite; copper glance

辉耀 huīyào shine; glow; glisten: 晨光～。The morning sun shines brightly.

辉银矿 huīyínkuàng argentite

辉映 huīyìng *also* "晖映" huīyìng shine; reflect: ～成趣 shine upon each other to mutual advantage; present a beautiful picture together / 湖光山色, 交相～。The lake and hills add radiance and beauty to each other.

辉照 huīzhào shine; glow: 月光～着幽静的田野。The moon shone upon the serene fields.

晖 huī sunshine; sunlight: 春～ spring sunshine / 朝～ glow of the rising sun; dawning / 斜～ slanting rays of the sun / 夕阳的金色余～ golden rays of the setting sun

晖映 huīyìng shine; reflect

翚 huī ❶〈书面〉fly; soar ❷ (used in ancient books) pheasant of multicolour feathers

袆(禕) huī 〈古语〉sacrificial robe for the queen or empress

灰 huī ❶ ash: 炉～ ashes from a stove / 烟～ tobacco ash; cigarette ash / 香～ incense ash / 草木～ plant ash (as fertilizer) / 火山～ volcanic ash / 骨～ bone ash (as fertilizer or for cleansing); ashes of the dead / 死～ dying embers ❷ dust; powder: 青～ graphite powder / 这房间里～大得很。The room is very dusty. ❸ lime; (lime) mortar: ～墙 plastered wall / 抹～ apply mortar ❹ grey: ～色上衣 grey jacket / 穿一身～ dressed in grey / 淡～ light grey / 深～ dark grey / 铁～ iron-grey / 银～ silver-grey ❺ disheartened; discouraged: 万念俱～ be totally disillusioned; lose all hope; abandon oneself to despair

灰暗 huī'àn murky grey; gloomy: 天色～ gloomy sky; murky grey sky / 脸色～ ashen look / 房间的格调太～了。The tone of the room seems a bit too gloomy.

灰白 huībái greyish white; ashen; pale: ～的月色 pale moonlight / 两鬓～ greying temples

灰白质 huībáizhì 〈生理〉*also* "灰质" grey matter; cinerea

灰败 huībài dingy; dreary: 斑驳而～的墙壁已经粉刷一新。The dingy and spotty wall has been whitewashed.

灰不喇唧 huībulājī 〈贬义〉grey and dull: 这种布～的, 穿在你身上真难看。This grey and dull cloth looks so ugly on you.

灰不溜丢 huībuliūdiū *also* "灰不溜秋" 〈方言〉❶〈贬义〉gloomily greyish; grey and dull: 这衣服～的, 你穿太不合适了。The suit is grey and dull; it doesn't become you at all. ❷ dispirited; down-hearted; crestfallen: 他挨了批评, 觉得～的。He was criticized and crestfallen.

灰菜 huīcài *also* "灰灰菜"(popular term for 藜) lamb's-quarters; goosefoot
灰尘 huīchén dust; dirt:掸掉衣服上的～ dust one's clothes /灯罩上落满了～。The lampshade was covered with dust.
灰尘肺 huīchénfèi 〈医学〉pneumoconiosis
灰尘监测器 huīchén jiāncèqì dust monitor
灰沉沉 huīchénchén (usu. of the sky) dull grey; dull; gloomy:天空～的,像是要下雨的样子。It's gloomy and looks like rain.
灰顶 huīdǐng mortared or plastered roof:～小屋 mortar-roofed hut
灰斗 huīdǒu ash bucket; hod
灰飞烟灭 huīfēi-yānmiè *also* "烟飞灰灭" become ashes and smoke; vanish like so much smoke:谈笑间,樯橹～。Amid talking and laughing, He put the enemy fleet to ashes and smoke.
灰分 huīfēn 〈矿业〉ash content:～物质 ash substance /～改良剂 ash modifier
灰粪 huīfèn ❶ ash compost; ash manure:给庄稼上一些～ apply ash compost to the crop ❷〈方言〉ashes of burnt grass on wasteland
灰膏 huīgāo slaked lime; plaster
灰姑娘 Huīgūniang Cinderella, heroine of a famous folk tale
灰光 huīguāng 〈天文〉grey light
灰鹤 huīhè 〈动物〉grey crane
灰糊糊 huīhūhū *also* "灰乎乎" ❶ greyish; dull grey:～的影子 greyish shadow ❷ dim; unclear:～的远山 dim mountains on the horizon; distant dim hills
灰化土 huīhuàtǔ *also* "灰壤"〈地质〉podzol
灰桦 huīhuà grey birch; oldfield birch; poplar-leaved birch (*Betula populifolia*)
灰黄琥珀 huīhuáng hǔpò 〈矿业〉ambrite
灰黄霉素 huīhuángméisù 〈药学〉griseofulvin; grisovin; fulcin
灰浆 huījiāng mortar; plaster:～槽 mortar-trough /～桶 mortar bucket
灰烬 huījìn ashes:几间草屋在大火中顷刻化为～。Several thatched houses were burnt to ashes in no time.
灰鲸 huījīng grey whale (*Eschrichtius robustus*)
灰口铁 huīkǒutiě *also* "灰铁"〈冶金〉grey (pig) iron
灰冷 huīlěng discouraged; downhearted; depressed:他满腔的热情逐渐～下来。Gradually, his fervour turned into depression.
灰领工人 huīlǐng gōngrén grey collar worker
灰溜溜 huīliūliū ❶ dull grey; dingy:快脱掉这件～的衣服吧。You'd better take off this dull grey jacket at once. /这间屋子～的颜色,住在里面不舒服。The room is dingy and uncomfortable to live in. ❷ gloomy; dejected; crestfallen:他总是～的。He always looked dejected. /不要把他弄得～的,抬不起头来。We must not dampen his spirits so that he won't be able to hold his head up.
灰霉 huīméi grey mold:～病 grey mold /～素〈药学〉grisein /～酸 grisic acid /～胺 grisamine
灰蒙蒙 huīmēngmēng dusky; overcast:天刚破晓,远处的山峦～的。The distant mountain peaks looked dusky in the early dawn (*or* when dawn was breaking). /天色～的,使人感到一种无以名状的忧伤。The sky was overcast and was weighing down upon me with an unaccountable depression.
灰锰氧 huīměngyǎng 〈药学〉potassium permanganate
灰泥 huīní plaster:～板 plasterboard /给(墙、天花板等)抹～ plaster (a wall, ceiling, etc.)
灰棚 huīpéng 〈方言〉❶ straw ash shed ❷ mortar-roofed hut
灰雀 huīquè bullfinch
灰壤 huīrǎng 〈农业〉podzol
灰色 huīsè ❶ grey; ashy:深～ dark grey; Oxford grey /～房屋 grey house; drab house /～调 grey tone ❷ pessimistic; gloomy; dispirited:～的作品 pessimistic (*or* grey) work /心情～ feel dejected (*or* dispirited) ❸ obscure; ambiguous:他对改革的态度是～的。He is ambiguous about reforms.
灰色大袋鼠 huīsè dàdàishǔ forester; grey kangaroo
灰色散 huīsèsǎn 〈药学〉grey powder (*Hydrargyrum cum creta*)
灰色市场 huīsè shìchǎng 〈金融〉grey market (unofficial market in shares before regular distribution)
灰色收入 huīsè shōurù grey income
灰色系统 huīsè xìtǒng grey system:～理论 grey system theory
灰沙 huīshā dust and sand:～蔽天 dust and sand blocking the sun
灰沙燕 huīshāyàn sand martin
灰市 huīshì *see* "灰色市场"
灰鼠 huīshǔ (another name for 松鼠) squirrel
灰陶 huītáo grey pottery
灰铁 huītiě grey (pig) iron
灰头土脸儿 huītóu-tǔliǎnr 〈方言〉❶ (of head or face) covered with dust:每次扬场,他都弄成～的。He got himself dirty all over each time he went winnowing. ❷ gloomy; downhearted; crestfallen:他满怀高兴去帮忙,倒闹了个～地被轰了出来。He went gladly to give a helping hand, only to get thrown out crestfallen.
灰土 huītǔ dust:卡车开过,扬起一片～。The truck raised a cloud of dust as it drove by.
灰心 huīxīn lose heart; be discouraged; be disheartened:我的考试成绩总上不来,真有点儿～。I really feel a bit depressed that my test scores have remained poor.
灰心丧气 huīxīn-sàngqì very much disheartened; (down) in the dumps; dejected and crestfallen:别～的,失败了再干嘛! Don't lose heart. Start anew after your failure!
灰熊 huīxióng grizzly bear; silvertip
灰衣修士 huīyī xiūshì 〈宗教〉Grey Friar
灰莺 huīyīng whitethroat (*Sylvia communis*)
灰指甲 huīzhǐjia 〈医学〉ringworm of the nails; onychomycosis
灰质 huīzhì 〈生理〉grey matter; cinerea:脑～炎 polioencephalitis /脊髓～炎 (popularly known as 小儿麻痹症) poliomyelitis; polio
灰子 huīzi 〈方言〉opium:抽～ opium-smoking

恢 huī broad; vast; extensive

恢诞 huīdàn 〈书面〉(of language or writing) fantastic; absurd; preposterous:此说～不典。The theory is fantastic and absurd.
恢复 huīfù ❶ renew; resume; return to normal:交通秩序已～正常。Transport services are now back to normal. ❷ retake; recover; regain; resume:～失地 retake (*or* recover) lost territory /～知觉 regain consciousness; come to one's senses /～健康 recover one's health; recuperate /～名誉 rehabilitate one's reputation /～原职务 reinstate sb. in his former office /～传统作风 renew traditional work style /～权威 reassert one's authority /～对香港行使主权 resume the exercise of sovereignty over Hong Kong /萧条过去后,公司花了好长时间才～元气。It took a long time for the company to get on its feet again after the depression.
恢复期 huīfùqī convalescence; recovery; recuperation period
恢复系 huīfùxì 〈农业〉restorer line
恢复原状 huīfù yuánzhuàng resume the original shape; return to the original state; restore the original state; 〈法律〉*restitutio in integrum* (rescinding of contract or transaction on the ground of fraud, etc., so as to return to the original position)
恢弘 huīhóng *also* "恢宏"〈书面〉❶ extensive; vast; great:气势～ with tremendous momentum; of great momentum /～的事业 great cause; vast undertaking ❷ carry forward; develop; enhance:～士气 boost the morale
恢恢 huīhuī 〈书面〉extensive; vast:～有余 be more than spacious; have plenty of space /天网～,疏而不漏。The net of heaven has large meshes, but it lets nothing through. *or* Justice has long arms.
恢廓 huīkuò 〈书面〉❶ broad; wide; vast:～的胸襟 broad-minded; large-hearted; magnanimous ❷ expand; extend:～祖业 expand one's ancestral estate (*or* wealth) /～领地 extend one's manor (*or* fiefdom)

诙 huī 〈书面〉❶ banter; tease good-humouredly ❷ mock; ridicule

诙谐 huīxié humorous; jocular:～的故事 humorous story /～百出 be full of humour; crack no end of jokes /谈吐～ witty in speech
诙谐曲 huīxiéqǔ 〈音乐〉scherzo; humoresque
诙嘲 huīzhāo 〈书面〉be humorous; banter:席间～ crack jokes at a dinner table

咴 huī

咴儿咴儿 huīrhuīr 〈象声〉(of a horse) neigh; whinny:母马在～地唤叫着小马。The mare whinnied for her colt.

虺 huī *see* "喧虺" xuānhuī

虺 huī

see also huǐ

虺隤 huītuí *also* "虺隤"〈书面〉(of horses) fall ill due to exhaus-

tion

撝(撝、撝) huī 〈书面〉command; order

徽[1] huī ❶ emblem; badge; insignia:国～ national emblem /校～ school badge /帽～ cap insignia /团～ Youth League badge /军～ military insignia; insignia of the armed forces ❷ fine; glorious

徽[2] Huī Huizhou, former prefecture with its seat at today's Shexian County (歙县) in Anhui

徽标 huībiāo emblem; insignia:这个足球队有自己的～。The football team has its own insignia.

徽调 huīdiào ❶ tunes of Anhui opera, which had a strong influence on the shaping of Beijing opera ❷ 〈旧语〉Anhui opera

徽号 huīhào glorious title; title of honour:影迷们送给她"电影皇后"的～。She was called "Movie Queen" by her fans.

徽记 huījì mark; sign; logo; insignia:这架飞机不带任何～。The plane has (*or* carries) no insignia on it.

徽剧 huījù Anhui opera

徽墨 huīmò Hui inkstick produced in Huizhou (徽州) of Anhui

徽章 huīzhāng badge; insignia:他往我胸前别上一枚～。He put a badge on my chest.

徽帜 huīzhì 〈书面〉flag (as a symbol or sign)

隳(隓) huī 〈书面〉destroy; ruin:～人城池 destroy a city /～节败名 ruin sb.'s integrity and reputation

huí

回[1](囘、囬、❶迴、廻) huí ❶ circle; wind:巡～ go the rounds; make the circuit (of sth.) /迂～ circuitous; winding; roundabout /峰～路转。The path winds along mountain ridges. ❷ return; go or come back:～到原处 go back to the starting point; be back to square one ❸ turn round:他～过身去跟大家打招呼。He turned round to greet all of us. ❹ answer; reply; respond:～他一份礼。Send him a gift in return. /我～过他一次电话。I rang him back once. ❺ report (to higher authorities, etc.):头儿提出的问题已经～了。I've already reported back to the boss on what he asked. ❻ decline; cancel; dismiss:～掉邀请 decline an invitation /～掉预订的旅馆房间 cancel a hotel reservation /～掉雇员 dismiss an employee /我最近太忙,只好～了那次约见。As I am far too busy these days, I have called off that appointment. ❼ 〈量词〉*used to indicate frequency of occurrance*:我去过他们家两～。I've been to their home twice. /原来是这么～事。So that's how the things stand. ❽ 〈量词〉chapter; section; session:这部小说共有一百～。The novel has one hundred chapters. /欲知后事如何,请听下～分解。(formula used at the end of each session in traditional storytelling or a novel) If you want to know what happened next, please read the following chapter.

回[2](囘、囬) Huí ❶ Hui nationality:孙中山曾提出汉满蒙～藏"五族共和"的主张。Dr. Sun Yat-sen proposed the establishment of a republic based upon the five major ethnic groups of the Hans, Manchus, Mongolians, Huis and Tibetans. ❷ (Huí) a surname

回拜 huíbài pay a return visit or call:择日～ choose a date for a return call

回报 huíbào ❶ report back (to sb. on sth.):你任务完成后向领导～。You should report back to the leadership after you finish your work. ❷ repay; requite; reciprocate:～主人的盛情 repay the host for his hospitality /承蒙救援,他日将有所～。We will certainly reciprocate your help some day. ❸ retaliate; get one's own back:行恶者,必遭～。One will have to pay for one's evildoings. *or* Retribution is certain to overtake the evildoer.

回避 huíbì ❶ evade; dodge; avoid; shun:～矛盾 dodge contradictions /～问题 evade a question; beg the question /～要害 sidestep the crux of the matter /～实质性讨论 steer clear of any substantive discussion /不可～的争论 unavoidable (*or* inevitable) dispute /他像躲避鬼魂似地～我。He shunned me as if I were a ghost. /发言人巧妙地～作出任何明确回答。The spokesman tactfully avoided giving any definite answer (*or* committing himself). ❷ (as of a judge or witness) avoidance; challenge; recuse:要求证人～ challenge (*or* recuse) a witness /与本案涉嫌对象有亲朋关系的最好统统～。Avoidance is the best policy for anyone who has an intimate relationship with the suspect of the case. /在我姻兄的提升问题上我必须～。I must stay out of the matter concerning my brother-in-law's promotion.

回避制度 huíbì zhìdù avoidance system; challenge system; system of withdrawal

回禀 huíbǐng 〈旧语〉report back (to one's elder or superior)

回波 huíbō 〈电学〉echo; return wave:雷达～ radar echo /～脉冲 echo pulse; returning echo; return wave /～检验 echo checking /～失真 echo distortion /～效应 echo effect /～测高计 echo altimeter; Alexanderson altimeter /～消除器 echo eliminator

回驳 huíbó refute:当面～ refute sb. to his (*or* her) face /据理～ rebut sb. on just grounds

回采 huícǎi 〈矿业〉stoping; extraction; recovery:快速～ fast extraction /～工作面 stope /～率 percentage (*or* rate) of recovery; recovery /～损失 mining loss

回茬 huíchá second crop (in the year):～小麦 wheat as second crop in the year

回肠 huícháng ❶ 〈生理〉ileum:～炎 ileitis ❷ 〈书面〉worried; agitated

回肠荡气 huícháng-dàngqì *also* "荡气回肠" (of music, poetry, etc.) soul-stirring; thrilling; inspiring:这首诗令人～。This poem is soul-stirring.

回肠九转 huícháng-jiǔzhuǎn one's mind burning with anxiety and agitation:这件事使他～,焦急万分。This matter filled him with great anxiety and distress.

回潮 huícháo ❶ get damp or moist:雨天东西容易～。Things easily get moist in the rainy season. /地下室～得厉害。It's very damp in the cellar. ❷ (of old customs, etc., that have once disappeared) resurgence; reversion:封建迷信活动有所～。There has been a resurgence of feudalistic and superstitious activities.

回潮率 huícháolǜ 〈纺织〉(moisture) regain

回嗔作喜 huíchēn-zuòxǐ (one's) anger turns into joy; fury changes into smiles:丈夫的一番解释使她～,高高兴兴地上班去了。Her husband's explanation turned her anger into joy, and she went to work happily.

回程 huíchéng ❶ return trip:～路上 on the way back /～大约需要三天。The return trip will take about three days. ❷ 〈机械〉return stroke:～速度 return speed /～损耗 return loss

回春 huíchūn ❶ return of spring:大地～,万紫千红。The return of spring has made the land a riot of colour. ❷ bring back to life:妙手～ (of a doctor) bring the dying back to life /～妙药 miraculous cure; wonderful remedy /～乏术。There is no way to bring the patient back to life.

回窜 huícuàn flee back; turn round and run:敌军绕道～。The enemy took a detour and fled back.

回答 huídá answer; reply; response:满意的～ satisfactory answer (*or* response) /～问题 answer (*or* reply to) a question /新闻发言人的～有理有节。The spokesperson's responses to the questions were well-reasoned and measured.

回单 huídān note acknowledging receipt of sth.; receipt

回荡 huídàng resound; reverberate; echo:庄严的国歌在礼堂里～。The auditorium resounded with the solemn national anthem. /火车的轰鸣声在隧道中～。The roar of the train reverberated in the tunnel. /欢呼声在我耳边～。The shouts of joy echoed in my ears.

回电 huídiàn ❶ wire back:未及～ fail to wire a reply /即予～ immediately cable a reply ❷ return cable:三十日～悉。Return cable of 30th instant received.

回跌 huídiē (of prices) drop or fall back:物价开始～。Prices began to fall back.

回动 huídòng 〈机械〉reverse:～机制 reversing mechanism

回返 huífǎn come or go back; get back; return:～家园 return to one's native place /～路程走了三天。It took three days to get back.

回访 huífǎng pay a return visit or call:我明日～张经理。I'll pay Manager Zhang a return visit tomorrow.

回风 huífēng 〈矿业〉return air:～道 air return way /～巷 return airway

回奉 huífèng return:～赠礼 make a present in return; present a return gift

H

回复 huífù ❶ reply (to a letter):急待～ wait anxiously for a reply; demand an immediate reply ❷ restore; return to:～原状 return to the original state (*or* status quo ante) /肿胀的伤口日渐～。The swollen wound healed gradually.
回购 huígòu buy back; counter-purchase:～价 repurchase price /～交易 buy-back deal
回顾 huígù look back; review; pass over in review:经济形势～ review of the economic situation /昔日的～ review of the past /梦一般的～ dreamy retrospections /～往事,浮想联翩。As I looked back on the past, my mind thronged with thoughts. /～起来,那真是一段有趣的经历啊。In retrospect, that was really an interesting experience.
回顾展 huígùzhǎn review; retrospective exhibition:三十年代优秀影片～ review of the best movies of the 30's /毕加索作品～ retrospective exhibition of Picasso's paintings
回光返照 huíguāng-fǎnzhào last glow of the setting sun — temporary clearing up of mind or momentary recovery of consciousness before death; sudden spurt of activity prior to death or collapse:老人那天精神很好,说话也多,可谁知道这原来是～啊? The old man seemed to be in good spirits and spoke more than usual that day. Who could have known that it was just a momentary recovery before his death?
回光镜 huíguāngjìng reflector
回归 huíguī ❶ return:～自然 return to nature; go back to nature /～祖国 return to one's motherland; revert to the sovereignty of the country /认同～ acknowledge a common ancestry and motherland ❷〈统计〉regression:～方程 regression equation /～分析 regression analysis /～函数 regression function /～模型 regression model
回归带 huíguīdài *also* "热带" rèdài tropical zone
回归年 huíguīnián 〈天文〉tropical year
回归热 huíguīrè 〈医学〉relapsing fever
回归线 huíguīxiàn 〈地理〉tropic:南～ Tropic of Capricorn /北～ Tropic of Cancer
回锅 huíguō cook again:这菜要回回锅。The dish must be heated up. /隔夜饭菜要～才能食用。Food left over from the previous day should be recooked before it is served.
回锅肉 huíguōròu stir-fried boiled pork slices in hot sauce; twice-cooked pork
回国 huíguó return to one's country or native land:～留学生 student who has returned from abroad; returned student /～述职 return to one's country and report on one's work /代表团定于23日～。The delegation is scheduled to return home on the twenty-third.
回航 huíháng 〈航空〉〈航海〉return to base; return to port:飞机不及～,因燃油用尽,中途坠落海中。The plane ran out of fuel and crashed into the sea before making base.
回合 huíhé round; bout:第五个～,他被对方一个上钩拳击倒在地。He was knocked out by an uppercut in the fifth round.
回纥 Huíhé *also* "回鹘" Huíhú ancient name for the Uygur nationality
回护 huíhù defend; shield:不要～孩子的错误。Don't shield mistakes of your children.
回话 huíhuà ❶ (usu. used by a junior to a senior in reply to the latter's inquiry, etc.) reply:回大人的话,小人生于杭州,不是苏州。In reverent reply to your inquiry, sir, I was born in Hangzhou, not Suzhou. ❷ reply; answer; confirm:带个～ take (*or* bring) a message by way of reply /她究竟来不来,请给个～。Please confirm whether she will come or not.
回还 huíhuán return:壮士一去不～。The warrior went away, never to return.
回环 huíhuán winding; zigzagging:青山逶迤,道路～。Green mountains undulate like waves and roads wind in zigzags and loops.
回黄转绿 huíhuáng-zhuǎnlǜ *also* "回黄倒绿" leaves turning from yellow to green and green to yellow — the succession of seasons; the vicissitudes of life
回回 Huíhui 〈旧语〉Hui (nationality)
回火 huíhuǒ 〈冶金〉❶ tempering:～炉 tempering furnace /～脆性 temper bristleness /～裂纹 temper crack /～硬度 tempering hardness ❷ (of an oxyacetylene blow pipe) backfire
回火温度 huíhuǒ wēndù 〈冶金〉drawback temperature; temper temperature:～范围 tempering range
回击 huíjī fight back; return fire; counterattack:给敌人以无情的～ hit back at the enemy ruthlessly; make a merciless counterattack upon the enemy
回家 huíjiā go or come home; return home:在～的路上 on one's way (back) home
回见 huíjiàn 〈套语〉see you later; cheerio; see you soon; good-bye
回交 huíjiāo 〈生物〉backcross:～亲本 backcross parent /～子代 backcross progeny
回教 Huíjiào Islam; Mohammedanism:他信～。He believes in Islam.
回敬 huíjìng ❶ return a compliment or gift:举杯～ drink a toast in return ❷ do or give in return; retaliate; give tit for tat; give as good as one gets:如果你们先开枪,我们就加倍～。If you fire the first shot, we shall retaliate with redoubled power. /"那全是你的错。"他～了一句。"It's entirely your fault," he retorted.
回绝 huíjué decline; refuse; reject:我提出愿意帮忙,被他～了。I offered to help, yet he declined. /他的要价太高,被我一口～。He asked for too much, and I flatly refused.
回空 huíkōng (of a lorry, ship, etc.) return unloaded:～车 unloaded lorry on a return trip
回口 huíkǒu 〈方言〉answer back; talk back; retort:看你再敢～! I dare you to talk back again!
回扣 huíkòu *also* "回佣" (sales) commission; kickback:吃～ take a commission (for what one buys as an agent or for a deal one helps make) /拿～ accept a kickback
回来 huílai come back; return; get back:他还没有～。He hasn't come back yet. *or* He isn't back yet. /我刚从国外～。I've just returned from abroad.
回来 huilai (used after a verb) back:可把你盼～了! Thank God, you are back at last! /他买～一辆汽车。He bought a car.
回廊 huíláng winding corridor:一条～通向湖心小亭。A winding corridor led to the pavilion on the lake.
回老家 huí lǎojiā (usu. jocular or mocking) die; be no more:再不老实就送你～。I'll send you to the next world, if you don't behave yourself.
回礼 huílǐ ❶ return a salute:军长一边走,一边～。The army commander returned the salute while walking. ❷ give a gift in return: 吩咐手下人～ order one's subordinate to give a gift in return ❸ return gift:这份～太重了。The return gift was too expensive.
回历 Huílì Islamic calendar
回磷 huílín 〈冶金〉rephosphoration:～钢 rephosphorized steel
回流 huíliú ❶ backflow; return:河水～ backflow of a river /人才～ return of talents (to their native place or country) ❷ reflux; backflow; return:～比 reflux ratio /～波痕 backflow ripple /～阀 reflux valve; return valve /～电路 return circuit /～管 return pipe /～式风洞 return circuit wind tunnel
回笼 huílóng ❶ steam again; resteam:包子要～热一下再吃。These buns should be steamed again before they are served. ❷ withdraw (currency) from circulation:货币～的手段之一是抛售商品。One way to withdraw currency from circulation is to increase sales of commodities.
回笼觉 huílóngjiào sleep again after waking up in the morning:睡个～挺舒服。It's cosy to go to sleep again after waking up in the morning.
回炉 huílú ❶ melt down:废铁～ melt down scrap iron; use scrap iron for melting /这个部件必须～重造。This part must be melted down and recast. ❷ bake again:～烧饼 rebaked sesame-seed cake ❸ retrain by taking a refresher course:裁下来的人都要～培训。All those who are laid off must be retrained by taking refresher courses.
回禄 Huílù 〈书面〉Huilu, name of the legendary god of fire:～之灾 fire disaster /惨遭～ be burnt down
回路 huílù ❶ retreat; way back:～已被切断。The retreat was cut. ❷〈电学〉return circuit; return; loop:～电流 loop current /～增益 loop gain /～传递函数 return transfer function
回銮 huíluán (of an emperor) return (from a trip outside the capital)
回落 huíluò (of water level, price, etc.) fall after a rise; drop:金价～。The gold price dropped. /猛涨的河水开始～。The fast-rising water in the river began to fall. /股市行情～。The stock prices are going down (*or* declining).
回马枪 huímǎqiāng back thrust:杀他个～ give sb. a backthrust; fire a Parthian shot /他们冷不防给敌人个～。They swung back and caught the enemy off guard.

回门 huímén (of a man) visit one's inlaws with one's newly-wed wife (usu. a few days after the wedding); (of a newly-wed wife) visit one's own family with one's husband:那天小两口～,一路上有说有笑,可高兴了。The day the newly-wed couple visited the bride's family, they were very happy together, talking and laughing all the way.

回描 huímiáo *see* "回扫"

回民 Huímín Hui people; Hui:～餐馆 Moslem restaurant /他是～。He is a Hui.

回明 huímíng (to one's seniors) explain; make clear:～青天大老爷,此事纯属子虚乌有。May I make clear to your most upright worship: this is nothing but a frame-up.

回眸 huímóu (usu. of a woman) look back; glance back:～一笑 glance back and smile

回目 huímù (of a traditional novel) chapter subtitle

回念 huíniàn think back; recall; call back to mind:～往事 think of past events /学校生活～起来似乎比现实还要快乐得多。School life seems much happier in retrospect than in reality.

回娘家 huí niángjia (of a newly-wed woman) visit one's parents; 〈比喻〉 return to one's place of origin or former place of work:新媳妇～。The newly-wed woman visited her parents. /学成之后我还要～。I will go back to my former place of work when I have finished my studies.

回暖 huínuǎn get warm again after a cold spell:寒流过去,天气逐渐～。With the cold current over, the weather was getting warmer and warmer.

回聘 huípìn *also* "返聘" fǎnpìn re-engage (usu. retirees) for work; re-employ:～退休人员 re-engage retirees

回棋 huíqí *also* "悔棋" huǐqí retract a false move:跟他下棋没劲,他老是～。He is a spoilsport for playing chess as he's always retracting his moves.

回迁 huíqiān (of those who have been removed to make way for a project, or evacuated during an emergency) move back; return:新楼盖好后,居民又～了。The inhabitants moved back when the new building was completed.

回青 huíqīng 〈方言〉(of winter crops or transplanted seedlings) turn green:一场小雨,地里的麦苗开始～了。The young wheat shoots turned green after a drizzling rain.

回请 huíqǐng return hospitality; give a return banquet:我在和平饭店～王先生。I gave a return banquet in Mr. Wang's honour at the Peace Hotel.

回去 huíqu return; go back; be back:听说你明天就要～了。I hear you will return (*or* go back) home tomorrow.

回去 huiqu (used after a verb) back:拿～ take (sth.) back /把手缩了～ draw back one's hand /滚～! Go back home!

回绕 huírào winding; zigzagging:这里,清泉～,古木参天。There are winding brooks and towering old trees all around.

回热 huírè 〈机械〉regenerate:～器 regenerator /～式汽轮机 regenerative steam turbine

回扫 huísǎo *also* "回描"〈电子〉flyback; retrace:～电路 flyback circuit /～脉冲 flyback pulse; kickback pulse /～线 flyback line; return line; retrace line /～变压器 kickback transformer

回煞 huíshà 〈迷信〉return of soul of the deceased (to former home) a few days after death

回身 huíshēn turn round:他放下信,～就向自己的房间走去。He put the letter on the table, turned round and made for his room.

回神 huíshén 〈口语〉recover from shock, fright, panic or absent-mindedness; realize what has happened:还未等他回过神儿来,那个蒙面人已越墙逃走了。Before he realized what had happened, the masked man had disappeared over the wall.

回升 huíshēng rise again (after a fall); pick up:气温开始～。The temperature is beginning to go up again. /出生率～。There is an up-turn in the birth rate. /产量正在～。Production is picking up. /购买力再次～。Purchasing power surged once again.

回生 huíshēng ❶ return to life; bring back to life:起死～ bring the dying back to life /～乏术 know no way to bring sb. back to life ❷ (of people) be out of practice; (of skills, etc.) get rusty:学了外文不常用是要～的。If you learn a foreign language but do not use it often, you'll soon be out of practice.

回声 huíshēng echo:山谷～ echoes in a valley /～测距 echo ranging /～定位 echo location /老人咳嗽时,空屋发出一种令人难受的～。The uninhabited house echoed discomfortingly as the old man coughed.

回声测深 huíshēng cèshēn echo depth sounding:～仪 sonic echo depth finder; acoustic depth finder; fathometer

回声探测仪 huíshēng tàncèyí sonic echo sounder; acoustic sounder; echo-sounding gear

回声学 huíshēngxué catacoustics

回师 huíshī (of a commander) bring back the troops; (of an army) go back:三万大军明明正在准备南下过江,一夜之间却又～北上。Having demonstrated a clear intention to cross the river towards the south, the 30,000 men turned round overnight and marched north.

回事 huíshì 〈旧语〉(as by a servant to his master) report

回收 huíshōu ❶ recycle; recover; retrieve:～废物 recycle waste /～贵重金属 retrieve rare metals /～余热 recover waste heat ❷ take back; retrieve; recover:～贷款 recover loans /卫星～ retrieval (*or* recovery) of a satellite /～区域 recovery zone

回收舱 huíshōucāng 〈航天〉recovery capsule

回收率 huíshōulǜ rate of recovery

回收期 huíshōuqī 〈经济〉payback period

回收塔 huíshōutǎ 〈化学〉recovery tower

回收站 huíshōuzhàn (waste matter) collection depot

回收装置 huíshōu zhuāngzhì retrieving device

回手 huíshǒu ❶ turn round and stretch out one's hand:他走了出去,又～把灯关上。He went out and turned back to turn off the light. ❷ hit back; return a blow:打不～ not hit back when hit

回首 huíshǒu ❶ turn one's head; turn round:他～发现有个人尾随着自己。When he turned round he found someone tailing (after) him. /惊～,离天三尺三。I turn my head startled, The sky is three foot three above me! ❷〈书面〉look back; recollect:不堪～话当年 can not bear to talk about the past /～往事,老泪纵横。Recollections brought tears streaming down the old man's cheeks.

回书 huíshū 〈书面〉reply; letter in reply

回赎 huíshú redeem:～当物 redeem sth. pawned; redeem sth. from the pawnshop

回水 huíshuǐ 〈水利〉backwater; return water:～曲线 backwater profile /～管 return pipe (*or* piping)

回丝 huísī 〈纺织〉waste yarn

回思 huísī recall; bring back to the mind:～往事 recall (*or* think of) past events

回苏灵 huísūlíng 〈药学〉dimefline

回溯 huísù recall; recollect; look back upon:～艰难的岁月 recollect (*or* look back upon) the difficult years /～过去,展望未来 recall the past and look into the future /此事可以～到三十年前的一个下午。This can be traced back to an afternoon thirty years ago.

回天 huítiān reverse a hopeless situation:无力～ incapable of reversing a hopeless situation

回天乏术 huítiān-fáshù know no way to save the situation:政局不可收拾,看来谁也是～了。The political situation was so desperate that nobody was able to save it.

回天之力 huítiānzhīlì power to reverse a desperate or hopeless situation; tremendous power:虽有复兴国家之志,却无～。Despite his determination to revive the nation, he had no power to turn the tide.

回填 huítián 〈建筑〉backfill:～土 backfill /～时要层层夯实。The backfill should be rammed tight layer after layer.

回条 huítiáo note that acknowledges receipt of sth.; receipt:你把这包东西送到王大爷家,请他写个～。Take this parcel to Uncle Wang and ask him for a receipt.

回帖 huítiě 〈旧语〉receipt (for postal remittance)

回头 huítóu ❶ turn one's head; turn round:他头也不回地径直离去。He strode away without even turning his head. ❷ come back; return:一去不～ go away and never return ❸ repent; mend one's way:看来他是不会～了。It seemed that he would never repent. /浪子～金不换。A prodigal son who has mended his way is more precious than gold. *or* Broken bones well set become stronger. ❹ later; some other time:～再说好吗? Shall we talk about it some other time? /请先休息,～再谈公事。Please take a rest before we talk business.

回头见 huítóujiàn see you later; cheerio:我先走一步,咱们～! I must get going now. See you later!

回头客 huítóukè regular customer; frequenter; repeat customer:来这个商店购物的多是～。Customers of the shop are mostly its frequenters.

H

回头路 huítóulù 〈比喻〉road back to where one started; road of retrogression:决不能走～ never take the road of retrogression; never backtrack
回头人 huítóurén 〈方言〉remarried widow
回头是岸 huítóu-shì'àn 〈比喻〉turn from one's evil ways; repent and be saved:苦海无边,～。〈佛教〉The sea of bitterness has no bounds; repent, and the shore is at hand.
回味 huíwèi ❶ aftertaste:这玩意儿刚吃时不怎么样,～起来倒真是不赖。The stuff is not so tasty when first eaten but leaves a great aftertaste. ❷ call to mind and ponder over; ponder retrospectively; ruminate over:这文章耐人～。The article gives us plenty of food for thought.
回味无穷 huíwèi-wúqióng leave prolonged aftertaste; afford much food for thought:这橄榄吃起来～。These olives leave a lingering sweet aftertaste in the mouth. /这些寓言让人～。These fables are very thought-provoking.
回文 huíwén palindrome, a word or phrase that reads the same backwards or forwards
回文诗 huíwénshī circular poem or "two-way" poem, which makes sense both when read in the usual way and when read backwards; palindromic poem
回席 huíxí invite sb. to dinner in return for his or her hospitality; give a return banquet
回戏 huíxì (of an opera troupe, etc.) cancel a performance offhand
回乡 huíxiāng return to one's home village or town:～务农 return to one's home village and take up farming
回乡知识青年 huíxiāng zhīshi qīngnián educated youth who has returned to do farm work in his home village
回乡证 huíxiāngzhèng home visit permit (for the residents of Hong Kong, etc.)
回翔 huíxiáng circle round; wheel:海鸥在船上空～。The seagulls were circling over the ship.
回响 huíxiǎng reverberate; echo; resound:枪声在山谷中～。The shots reverberated in the valley. /她的话语久久在我耳边～。Her words rang in my ears for a long time. /这一倡议在全国青年人中激起了强烈的～。The proposal evoked strong repercussions among young people all over the country.
回想 huíxiǎng think back; recall:那次事故～起来,心有余悸。It gives me shudders to recall the accident. /他的话使我～起童年时代。What he said brought back to my mind memories of my childhood. /～此事,甚觉可笑。It was really absurd in retrospect.
回销 huíxiāo (of the state) resell (to the place of production)
回心转意 huíxīn-zhuǎnyì change one's mind; come round; think better (of sth.):叫她趁早～,这是为她好。The sooner she changes her mind the better for her. /如果她妈妈不能～,她便不能再读书了。If her mother did not relent, she would be unable to continue her studies.
回信 huíxìn ❶ write in reply; write back; reply:还未给大哥～呢。I haven't written back to my elder brother yet. /望及早～。Looking forward to hearing from you soon. ❷ letter in reply; reply:至今未见～。I haven't received any reply. ❸ verbal message in reply; reply:究竟能否光临,请给个～儿。Please let me know whether you'll be able to come.
回形针 huíxíngzhēn (paper) clip
回醒 huíxǐng 〈口语〉wake up to the reality:听了这番话,他终于～过来了。After hearing these words, he finally shook off his illusion.
回修 huíxiū return for repairs:～商品 commodity returned for repairs /～活儿 repairs (for commodities returned)
回叙 huíxù ❶ flashback:这篇小说～太多,情节过于繁复。The plot of the story is too involved as it contains a lot of flashbacks. ❷ recount; recall:～往事 recount past events
回旋 huíxuán ❶ circle round; wheel:老鹰在峰顶～。The eagle was wheeling over the peak. /为避开敌人主力,我们一直在山区～。In order to avoid the enemy's main forces, we had been circling round in the mountains. ❷ (room for) manoeuvre:话已说绝,再也没有什么可～的了。The last word was said, and no room was left for manoeuvre. /留点儿～之地,别把话说死了。Don't make it so definite — allow a little latitude.
回旋加速器 huíxuán jiāsùqì 〈物理〉cyclotron:同步～ synchrocyclotron
回旋炮 huíxuánpào flexible gun; swivel gun
回旋曲 huíxuánqǔ 〈音乐〉rondo
回旋余地 huíxuán-yúdì room for manoeuvre; leeway; latitude; flexibility:事已至此,看来难有～了。As things have come to such a pass, there doesn't seem to be any room for manoeuvre at all.
回忆 huíyì call to mind; recall; recollect:沉浸在甜蜜的～里 lost in sweet memories of the past /～往事,心潮澎湃。Memories of past events (*or* the past) brought an upsurge of emotion.
回忆对比 huíyì-duìbǐ recall the past or past misery and contrast it with the present or today's happiness
回忆录 huíyìlù reminiscences; memoirs; recollections:《艾登～》*Eden's Memoirs* /《战争～》*Reminiscences of the War Years*
回译 huíyì back or reverse translation; retroversion
回音 huíyīn ❶ echo; resound; reverberate:这屋子～太大。The house echoes too loudly. ❷ reply; response:未获～ receive no reply (*or* response) /立盼～ look forward to an immediate reply ❸ 〈音乐〉turn:逆～ inverted turn
回音壁 Huíyīnbì Echo Wall (in the Temple of Heaven, Beijing)
回应 huíyìng reply; answer; response:我叫了半天门也无人～。I knocked at the door for a long time but nobody answered. /他的讲话包含了对贵方建议的～。His speech contained a response to the proposal made by your side.
回映 huíyìng (of light, etc.) reflect:湖面～出五颜六色的灯光,煞是好看。The coloured lights, reflected on the lake, made a wonderful scene.
回佣 huíyòng *also* "回扣"〈方言〉(sales) commission; kickback
回油泵 huíyóubèng 〈机械〉scavenging pump; oil scavenger pump
回油器 huíyóuqì 〈机械〉oil scavenger
回游 huíyóu *see* "洄游" huíyóu
回援 huíyuán (of an army) turn round to reinforce or rescue (a friendly army)
回赠 huízèng give (sb. a present) in return:～一束鲜花 present sb. with a bouquet of flowers in return
回涨 huízhǎng (of water level, etc.) rise again; swell again:物价～。The prices have gone up again.
回执 huízhí note acknowledging receipt of sth.; receipt
回注 huízhù 〈石油〉reinjection
回柱 huízhù 〈矿业〉prop drawing:～机 prop drawer; post puller
回转 huízhuǎn ❶ go back; return:～故里 return to one's native place ❷ turn round:他～车头向原地开去。He wheeled his car round and drove back. ❸ rotate; revolve; gyrate:～发射机 rotary transmitter (RS)
回转半径 huízhuǎn bànjìng 〈航海〉radius of gyration; gyroradius
回转泵 huízhuǎnbèng rotary pump
回转电动机 huízhuǎn diàndòngjī slewing motor
回转工作台 huízhuǎn gōngzuòtái 〈机械〉rotary or rotating table
回转炉 huízhuǎnlú 〈冶金〉rotary furnace
回转罗盘 huízhuǎn luópán gyrocompass
回转式钻床 huízhuǎnshì zuànchuáng rotary drill
回转体 huízhuǎntǐ 〈数学〉solid of revolution
回转窑 huízhuǎnyáo rotary kiln
回转仪 huízhuǎnyí gyroscope; gyro
回族 Huízú Hui nationality, inhabiting the Ningxia Hui Autonomous Region mainly, but also distributed over other parts of China
回嘴 huízuǐ 〈口语〉answer or talk back; retort:过去,孩子受到长辈责骂是不许～的。In the past, children were not supposed to talk back when they were taken to task by their seniors.

洄 huí 〈书面〉(of water) whirl

洄游 huíyóu *also* "回游" huíyóu 〈动物〉migration:产卵～ spawning migration /觅食～ feeding migration /生殖～ breeding migration /季节～ seasonal migration /～性鱼类 migratory fish

茴 huí

茴芹 huíqín anise
茴香 huíxiāng 〈植物〉❶ fennel:～油〈药学〉fennel oil /～液 fennel water ❷ 〈方言〉aniseed:～豆 beans flavoured with aniseed
茴鱼 huíyú grayling (*Thymallus*)

蛔(蚘、蛕) huí roundworm

蛔虫 huíchóng roundworm; ascarid:～病 roundworm disease; as-

cariasis

徊 huí see "低徊" dīhuí
see also huái

huǐ

悔 huǐ regret; repent: 忏～ be penitent; repent; confess (one's sins) /追～莫及 too late to regret /～之无益 no use crying over spilt milk

悔不当初 huǐbùdāngchū regret not having pursued a different course; regret having done sth.: 早知今日，～。If one had known then what it was to be like now, one wouldn't have done as one did.

悔改 huǐgǎi repent and mend one's ways: 不思～ have no intention of mending one's ways; be unwilling to repent

悔过 huǐguò repent one's error; be repentant: ～从善 repent and return to the path of virtue /毫无～之心 have (*or* show) no intention to repent

悔过书 huǐguòshū written statement of repentance; written confession

悔过自新 huǐguò-zìxīn repent and turn over a new leaf; repent and make a fresh start: 他决心～，重新做人。He was determined to atone for his wrongdoing and make a fresh start.

悔恨 huǐhèn deeply regret; be filled with remorse: ～莫及 be filled with useless remorse; regret in vain /～交加 be stung by remorse and shame; have a mixed feeling of remorse and shame /对此你将～终身。You will spend the rest of your life regretting this.

悔婚 huǐhūn break an engagement (for marriage)

悔棋 huǐqí *also* "回棋" huíqí retract a false move in a chess game

悔痛 huǐtòng regret and agony: 他自知有错，～地低头不语。He realized his mistake, and hung his head in silent remorse.

悔悟 huǐwù realize and regret one's error; repent: 似有～ seem to realize and regret one's mistake; seem to repent /虽经反复教育，但仍无～。Despite repeated talks to help him, he showed no sign of repentance.

悔之无及 huǐzhī-wújí *also* "悔之晚矣"; "悔之莫及" it is too late to repent; it is no use regretting it now: 祸根不除，必将～。You would regret it to the end of your life if the bane is not removed now.

悔罪 huǐzuì show penitence (for a crime, etc.); show repentance: 他有～之意。He has shown some inclination for repentance.

虺 huǐ 〈古语〉 a kind of poisonous snake
see also huī

虺虺 huǐhuǐ 〈书面〉 crash or roll of thunder; thunder clap

虺蜴 huǐyì 〈书面〉 poisonous lizard; 〈比喻〉 vicious person: ～之性不可改也。A venomous nature will never change.

虺蜮 huǐyù 〈书面〉 poisonous snake and aquatic monster; 〈比喻〉 insidious or sinister person

毁(❷燬、❸譭) huǐ ❶ destroy; ruin; demolish: 撕～ tear to pieces; tear up /捣～ smash; demolish /销～ destroy (by melting or burning) /～了庄稼 ruin a crop /自～长城 destroy one's own defence /～了某人的前程 ruin sb.'s career ❷ burn up: 烧～ burn down; destroy by fire ❸ defame; slander: 诋～ vilify; slander /～人名声，不择手段 employ every means to defame sb. ❹ 〈方言〉 refashion; make over: 我要把这条裙子给孩子～一条长裤。I want to have a pair of trousers made for the boy out of this skirt.

毁败 huǐbài destroy; ruin; damage: 小庙～不堪。The small temple was practically in ruins.

毁谤 huǐbàng slander; malign; calumniate: ～他人 malign sb. /乞灵于～ resort to slandering /揭穿敌人的～ lay bare the enemy's calumnies

毁害 huǐhài destroy; damage; ruin: 这里野猪出没，常常夜间出来～庄稼。The country was frequented by wild boars, which would come out at night and damage the crops.

毁坏 huǐhuài destroy; damage; ruin: ～文物古迹 destroy archeological sites and relics /～他人名声 ruin sb.'s reputation /～公物 vandalize public property

毁家纾难 huǐjiā-shūnàn sell one's family estate to relieve the distress of the country; spend one's fortune to aid the country during a crisis; offer all one has to help in charity: 当年父亲～，在这一带是有名声的。At that time, my father was known far and wide for offering all he had in charity.

毁林 huǐlín deforest; disafforest: ～辟田 reclaim land by deforestation

毁馏 huǐliú 〈化学〉 destructive distillation

毁灭 huǐmiè destroy; exterminate; wreck: ～物证 destroy material evidence /～性地震 ruinous earthquake /自我～ self-destruction /给以～性打击 deal a crushing (*or* devastating) blow at /战争、疾病和灾荒～了这个民族。War, diseases, and famine wrecked this nation.

毁圮 huǐpǐ 〈书面〉 ruin; collapse: 庙宇～。The temple was in ruins.

毁弃 huǐqì ruin; scrap; annul: 条约已被～，战争迫在眉睫。With the treaty scrapped, war was imminent.

毁容 huǐróng disfigure: 遭暴徒～的姑娘正在进行整容手术。The girl who was disfigured by a thug is undergoing plastic surgery.

毁伤 huǐshāng injure; damage: ～半径 〈军事〉 radius of damage; radius of rupture /～名誉 character assassination; damaging sb.'s reputation

毁损 huǐsǔn damage; impair: 经过这次风暴，岛上房屋建筑～严重。The storm did great damage to the houses and buildings on the island.

毁于一旦 huǐyú-yīdàn be destroyed in a day; be destroyed in a moment: 多年辛苦经营的事业～，他怎能不痛心疾首? How could he help feeling great agony when the undertaking he took pains to build over the years was ruined overnight?

毁誉 huǐyù praise or blame; acclamation or censure: 不计个人的荣辱～ be indifferent to praise or blame /～失当 apportion praise and blame inappropriately

毁誉参半 huǐyù-cānbàn (of a person) get both praise and censure; be as much censured as praised; (of a book, etc.) have a mixed reception: 他自认一生～，功过任人评说。He believed he had both successes and failures in his life, which must be left to others to comment on.

毁约 huǐyuē annul a contract or treaty; go back on one's word: ～行为 breach of contract /随便～会严重影响公司的信誉。It will adversely affect the company's credibility to annul a contract groundlessly. /君子焉能任意～? How could a gentleman go back upon his promise?

毁约诉讼 huǐyuē sùsòng breach-of-promise suit

毁訾 huǐzǐ 〈书面〉 slander; defame; vilify; calumniate: ～朝政 vilify the government

huì

汇[1](滙、匯、❷❸彙) huì ❶ converge: 三江交～之处 where three rivers converge (*or* meet) /细流～成大川。Small streams converge into a mighty river. ❷ gather together; collect: ～制成册 have (articles, pictures, etc.) collected and printed in book form ❸ things collected; assemblage; collection: 词～表 vocabulary; word list /总～ aggregate; complete inventory (*or* collection)

汇[2](滙、匯) huì ❶ remit: 邮～ postal remittance /电～ telegraphic transfer (TT); money draft telegram /～付 pay by remittance /货款已经～出。Payment for goods has been remitted already. ❷ foreign exchange: 创～ earn foreign exchange

汇报 huìbào report; give an account of: 书面～ written report /口头～ verbal (*or* oral) report /思想～ (give an) account of one's ideological progress and problems /～工作 report to sb. on one's work /～会 report-back meeting /关于上半年业务工作的～ report on the business operations of the first half of the year

汇报演出 huìbào yǎnchū (of a dramatic troupe back from a tour in the countryside or abroad) (give a) report-back performance

汇编 huìbiān ❶ compile; collect: ～成册 collect in book form /～参考资料 compile reference materials ❷ compilation; collection; corpus; compendium: 文件～ collection of documents /资料～ corpus of data ❸ 〈计算机〉 assembly: ～过程 assembly process /～控制 assembler control /～系统 assembly system; assemble system; assembler system /～程序 assembly program (*or* routine); assembler program (*or* routine)

H

汇编语言 huìbiān yǔyán 〈计算机〉assembly language; assembler language: ～加工程序 assembly language processor
汇编指令 huìbiān zhǐlìng 〈计算机〉assembler directive; assembler instruction; assembler command
汇拨支付 huìbō zhīfù payment by remittance
汇单 huìdān money order; remittance slip
汇兑 huìduì ❶ remittance: 国内～ domestic remittance / ～网 remittance network ❷ exchange: ～率 rate of exchange / ～平价 par of exchange / ～损失 exchange loss / ～银行 exchange bank / ～价变动 exchange movement / ～价换算表 exchange table
汇兑管制 huìduì guǎnzhì exchange control
汇费 huìfèi *also* "汇水" remittance fee
汇丰银行 Huìfēng Yínháng Hongkong and Shanghai Banking Corporation
汇合 huìhé converge; join: ～成一股洪流 join (*or* unite) to form a gigantic current / 各种力量的～ convergence of various forces / 这里是汉水与长江的～处。This is the confluence of the Hanshui and Yangtze rivers. *or* This is where the Hanshui River joins the Yangtze.
汇集 huìjí *also* "会集" huìjí collect; compile; converge; assemble: ～资金 collect funds / ～资料 collect data / 人群在广场～。Crowds (*or* Throngs) of people gathered at the square.
汇寄 huìjì remit: 他按月向家里～生活费。He remits a living allowance to his family every month.
汇价 huìjià exchange rate; conversion rate: ～上扬 exchange rate appreciation / ～下跌 exchange rate depreciation
汇聚 huìjù *see* "会聚" huìjù
汇款 huìkuǎn ❶ remit money: 他到邮局～去了。He's gone to remit some money at the post office. ❷ remittance: 邮政～ postal remittance / ～方式 method of remittance / ～收款人 beneficiary of remittance / ～收据 receipt for remittance
汇款单 huìkuǎndān money order; remittance slip
汇款人 huìkuǎnrén remitter: ～简短附言 sender's remarks
汇流 huìliú converge; flow together: 小溪～成河。Little creeks converge into a river.
汇流平原 huìliú píngyuán confluence plain
汇流条 huìliútiáo 〈电学〉busbar
汇拢 huìlǒng gather together; converge; assemble: ～各方意见 gather together comments and suggestions from all sides / 人群在旗杆周围～。People gathered round the flag pole. / 两支游行队伍在市政府前～。The two processions converged at the city hall.
汇率 huìlǜ exchange rate; conversion rate: 固定～ fixed exchange rate / 浮动～ floating exchange rate / 中心～ central rate
汇率调节制 huìlǜ tiáojiézhì exchange rate regulating system
汇票 huìpiào draft; bill of exchange; money order: 银行～ bank draft / 邮政～ postal money order / 即期～ demand draft / 定期～ time draft / 见期～ bill at sight; sight bill / ～贴现(率) discount (rate) of bill / 承兑～ honour (*or* accept) a bill / 拒绝承兑～ dishonour a bill / 取～ cash a money order
汇融 huìróng converge; mix together; merge: 各种力量～在一起。Various forces merged into one.
汇水 huìshuǐ *also* "汇费" remittance fee
汇算 huìsuàn collect and square up; settle an account: 请将这次展销会的收支账目～一下。Please square up the income and expenditure accounts of the sales show.
汇演 huìyǎn *also* "会演" huìyǎn joint performance (by a number of theatrical troupes)
汇展 huìzhǎn joint exhibition: 名牌时装～ joint exhibition of brand-name fashions
汇注 huìzhù ❶ converge and flow into: 两条河在此～入海。The two rivers converge here before flowing into the sea. ❷ variorum: ～本 variorum edition; variorum
汇总 huìzǒng gather; collect; pool: ～读者意见 gather together readers' comments / ～后再缴纳 pay on a consolidated basis / 各组意见正在～。Ideas from various groups are being pooled.

讳(諱)

huì ❶ avoid as taboo: 隐～ cover up; gloss over / 为贤者～ avoid anything that may compromise a sage's name / 直言不～ speak bluntly; call a spade a spade ❷ taboo; forbidden word: 他没想到犯了头头儿的～。Little did he realize that he had said something that was taboo with his boss. ❸ 〈旧语〉name of emperor, high official, head of a family, or elder of a clan, regarded as taboo by his subjects or juniors
讳疾忌医 huìjí-jìyī seek no medical advice lest one should be known as victim of a disease; hide one's illness for fear of treatment; 〈比喻〉refuse to face up to one's troubles or problems: 任何犯错误的人，只要他不～，我们就应帮助他。Whoever has erred deserves our assistance if he does not conceal his error for fear of criticism.
讳忌 huìjì taboo: 不知～ know no taboo / 毫不～ avoid nothing as taboo; hold nothing back
讳莫如深 huìmòrúshēn carefully avoid mentioning sth.; not utter a single word about sth.; guard a secret closely: 他们对关键的技术～，外人是打听不出的。They are clam-like about the key techniques, and no outsiders can draw them out.
讳饰 huìshì avoid and cover up; whitewash: 如实描写，毫无～。The description is true to life without the least whitewash.
讳言 huìyán dare not or would not speak up: 无可～ there's no denying (*or* hiding) the fact; be undeniable / 毫不～ make no attempt to cover up the truth; make no bones about telling the truth; speak straight from the shoulder

彗(篲)

huì 〈书面〉broom
彗尾 huìwěi 〈天文〉tail of a comet
彗星 huìxīng 〈天文〉comet

慧

huì intelligent; bright; clever: 智～ wisdom; intelligence / 聪～ clever; bright / 早～ early maturity (of one's intelligence)
慧根 huìgēn 〈佛教〉talent to thoroughly comprehend Buddhist teachings; innate intelligence
慧黠 huìxiá 〈书面〉clever and sly; shrewd: 他～过人，办事极为机敏。He is unusually clever and smart in getting things done.
慧心 huìxīn enlightened mind; wisdom: 姑娘如此～，实在难得。It is really rare for a girl (like you) to have such an enlightened mind.
慧眼 huìyǎn eye of wisdom; discerning eyes; penetrating insight: 独具～ see what others can not / ～识英才。It takes discerning eyes to find a man of great talent.
慧中秀外 huìzhōng-xiùwài *also* "秀外慧中" intelligent within and beautiful without; both intelligent and beautiful

蔧

huì *see* "王蔧" wánghuì

嘒

huì 〈书面〉tiny: ～彼小星。How tiny and dim that star is.

恚

huì 〈书面〉hate; resentment; grudge: 既愧且～ both ashamed and resentful
恚愤 huìfèn 〈书面〉anger; wrath; indignation
恚恨 huìhèn 〈书面〉hatred; resentment; enmity; malice
恚怒 huìnù 〈书面〉anger; wrath

卉

huì (usu. decorative) grass: 花～ flowers and grasses / 奇花异～ rare flowers and exotic grasses

惠

huì ❶ favour; kindness; benefit: 恩～ favour / 互～ mutual benefit / 优～ preferential treatment / 施～ bestow a favour (*or* kindness) / 受～之人 beneficiary / ～我良多 you have been very kind to me; you have conferred much kindness on me; you have benefited me greatly ❷ *used in complimentary reference to the other party's action or behaviour*: ～书 your letter ❸ (Huì) a surname
惠存 huìcún 〈敬词〉please keep (this as a souvenir); to so-and-so: 王文先生～ — 李义敬赠 (written on a souvenir or present) To Mr. Wang Wen — with compliments from Li Yi
惠而不费 huì'érbùfèi bestow a favour which would cost very little; do a kind act which does not cost much; be of great profit without costing much: 这是～的事，我们何乐而不为呢？We will be only too glad to do things that benefit others with little cost to ourselves.
惠风 huìfēng 〈书面〉gentle breeze: ～和畅。A gentle breeze is blowing.
惠顾 huìgù 〈敬词〉your patronage: 承蒙～，不胜感激。We are really grateful for your patronage.
惠及 huìjí 〈书面〉be of benefit to; bring benefit to: ～远方 one's kindness extends to remote places

惠鉴 huìjiàn please be kind enough to read (the following letter)
惠临 huìlín 〈敬词〉your gracious presence：敬请～。Your presence is requested. /日前～，失迎为歉。I must apologize for failing to welcome you personally the other day when you honoured us with your visit.
惠灵顿 Huìlíngdùn Wellington, capital of New Zealand
惠灵顿公爵 Huìlíngdùn Gōngjué first Duke of Wellington (1769-1852), British field marshal who defeated Napoleon at Waterloo, and prime minister (1828-1830)
惠能 Huìnéng Huineng (638-713), eminent monk of the Tang Dynasty and founder of the southern sect of *Chan* or Zen Buddhism
惠然 huìrán friendly; kind; generous：～莅临 your kind presence：～肯来 (of a host welcoming guests) your gracious presence is most appreciated
惠山泥塑 Huìshān nísù Huishan clay figures, a kind of coloured sculpture made in Wuxi (无锡), Jiangsu Province
惠施 Huì Shī Hui Shi (c.370-c.310 BC), philosopher and logician of the Warring States Period
惠予 huìyǔ kindly; be kind enough to：请～协助。Your kind assistance is requested. *or* You are kindly requested to give assistance.
惠允 huìyǔn 〈敬词〉your generous permission or consent：承蒙～ with your generous (*or* kind) permission
惠泽 huìzé 〈书面〉favour; benefit：～播于海内 be of benefit to people far and wide
惠赠 huìzèng 〈敬词〉kind gift of money or material help：年来多受～，不胜感谢。I am most grateful to you for the kind assistance you rendered me over the year.

蕙 huì 〈植物〉orchid

蕙兰 huìlán *Cymbidium faberi*, a kind of orchid
蕙心 huìxīn 〈书面〉(of a woman) pure heart; heart of gold
蕙质兰心 huìzhì-lánxīn *also* "蕙心兰质" pure in heart and spirit; pure-hearted and charming

蟪 huì

蟪蛄 huìgū a kind of cicada

阓 huì *see* "阛阓" huánhuì

靧 huì 〈书面〉wash one's face

殨 huì (of a sore) run; fester：伤口～脓。The wound festered and ran with pus.

哕(噦) huì 〈书面〉(of birds) chirp; cry

see also yuě
哕哕 huìhuì 〈书面〉jingling (of bells)：鸾声～。The bells of the horse-drawn carriage jingled on.

秽(穢) huì ❶ dirty：污～ filthy ❷ ugly; abominable：自惭形～ feel unworthy (*or* inadequate) (beside sb.); have a sense of inferiority /淫～ obscene; salacious; bawdy

秽德 huìdé 〈书面〉filthy behaviour; evil conduct
秽恶 huì'è filthy; nasty; dirty
秽迹 huìjì 〈书面〉dirty or unsavoury record; (trace of) filth：～斑斑 patches of filth; stained record /这个女人过去有～。This woman has an unsavoury past.
秽乱 huìluàn promiscuous; debauched; licentious：～宫闱 make the (imperial) palace filthy with one's promiscuity
秽气 huìqì bad smell; offensive smell; stink：～冲天 stink to high heaven
秽土 huìtǔ rubbish; refuse; dirt：院子里～成堆。There were piles of filth (*or* rubbish) in the courtyard.
秽闻 huìwén 〈书面〉ill repute (usually in referrence to promiscuous behaviour)：～四播 be ill reputed far and wide
秽亵 huìxiè 〈书面〉❶ filth; dirt：不避～ avoid no filth (*or* dirt) ❷ obscene; salacious; bawdy：～的语言 obscene language /～的玩笑 bawdy (*or* dirty) joke
秽行 huìxíng 〈书面〉abominable behaviour; promiscuous conduct
秽语 huìyǔ vulgar remarks; dirty words; obscene language：市井～ marketplace vulgarisms and obscenities /厕所～涂鸦 vulgar graffiti in the loo
秽浊 huìzhuó dirty; filthy：空气～，令人窒息。The filthy air is suffocating.

翙(翽) huì

翙翙 huìhuì 〈书面〉flapping sound (of birds)

喙 huì 〈书面〉❶ bill; beak (of a bird); snout (of an animal)：鸟～ beak of a bird ❷ mouth：不容置～ not allow anybody to butt in; brook no intervention /百～莫辩 a hundred mouths (*or* tongues) could not explain it; it takes more than eloquence to make this clear

喙长三尺 huìcháng-sānchǐ have a tongue three feet long — have a smooth tongue; have the gift of the gab：此人～，巧言善辩。Born with the gift of gab, this man is clever and eloquent in speech.

贿 huì ❶〈书面〉money and property ❷ bribe：行～ practise bribery; give bribes; bribe

贿赂 huìlù bribe：～罪 bribery /～手段 means of bribery /～品 boodle /拒收～ reject a bribe /因接受～而受到起诉 be sued for accepting (*or* taking) bribery /～成风。Bribery has become a common practice. *or* Corruption is the order of the day.
贿赂公行 huìlù-gōngxíng people give and accept bribes openly; corruption is rife
贿买 huìmǎi buy with bribery; buy over; suborn：～选票 buy votes
贿通 huìtōng bribe; buy over：～门卫 bribe the guards
贿选 huìxuǎn practise bribery at an election; rig an election by bribery：～丑闻 election scandal

会[1](會) huì ❶ get together; assemble; meet：聚～ get-together; party; meeting /约～ date; appointment ❷ meet; see：与…相～ meet sb. /我一定要～～此人。I must see this man. ❸ meeting; party; conference; convention：欢迎～ welcoming party /欢送～ farewell (*or* send-off) party /运动～ sports meet; athletic meeting; games /舞～ ball; dance; dancing party /晚～ evening party /英语晚～ English evening /群众集～ mass rally /讨论～ symposium /报告～ speech; public lecture /研讨～ seminar /吹风～ briefing /例～ regular meeting /年～ annual meeting ❹ association; society; union; foundation：学生～ student union (*or* federation) /工～ trade union /农～ peasant association /帮～ secret society /协～ association /商～ business association; chamber of commerce /教～ church /国～ congress; parliament /联谊～ friendship association; fraternity; brotherhood /代表大～ congress; assembly /分～ branch; chapter /委员～ committee; commission /董事～ board of trustees /理事～ council /联合～ federation /学～ (academic) society /研究～ (research) institute /基金～ foundation; fund /互助～ mutual assistance fund ❺ temple fair：赶庙～ go to the fair ❻ pilgrimage; religious festival; village thanksgiving festival：迎神赛～ idolatrous procession ❼ association of people who contribute regularly to a common fund and draw from it by turns; rotatory credit club：幸福～ joy-luck club ❽ major city; large city; capital：大都～ big city; metropolis /省～ provincial capital ❾ opportunity; occasion：机～ opportunity /适逢其～ happen to be present at the occasion ❿〈书面〉happen to：～天大雨，道不通。It happened to rain, and the road became impassable. ⓫〈书面〉surely; with certainty：长风破浪～有时。There will be a day when we will be riding the wave of successes (*or* victories).

会[2](會) huì ❶ understand; comprehend; grasp：心领神～ understand tacitly; readily take a hint /难以领～ difficult to comprehend; cannot see the point /只可意～，不可言传 can be sensed but not explained in words /误～ misunderstand ❷ be acquainted with; have knowledge of：他～两门外语。He knows two foreign languages. ❸ can; be able to：我不～骑自行车。I can't ride a bike. /这孩子刚～走路。The child has just learnt to walk. ❹ well versed in; good at; conversant：能说～道 have a smooth (*or* glib) tongue /能写～画 be good at calligraphy and painting /很～这一套 be a past master in this sort of game /他～修各种电器。He is skilful in repairing all kinds of electronic appliances. ❺ be likely to; be sure to：我～告诉你的。I am sure to let you know. *or* I'll let you know. /他不～不来。He is bound to show up. /十有八九他是不～干的。He is very likely to turn it down.

H

会³(會) huì foot or pay the bill：今天我请客，由我来～。Let me pay the bill today. *or* It's on me today.

会⁴(會) huì *see* "会儿"
see also kuài

会标 huìbiāo symbol of an event or a gathering; emblem of an association; logo：亚运会的～ Asian Games' symbol (*or* logo)

会餐 huìcān dine together; have a dinner or luncheon party：元旦～ New Year dinner /～用具 mess kit; mess gear

会操 huìcāo joint drilling; concerted exercises：明天各校～，市长将亲临检阅。Students of various schools will take part in joint exercises tomorrow, and the mayor will be present at the review.

会场 huìchǎng conference or assembly hall; meeting place; site of a conference

会钞 huìchāo pay the bill; foot the bill：今天由我～。I'll pay the bill today. *or* It's on me today. /还是各会各的钞为好。It's better to go Dutch.

会车 huìchē (of vehicles) cross; pass by each other：咱们俩将在前边～。Our cars will cross each other somewhere ahead.

会当 huìdāng 〈书面〉should; ought to：大丈夫～战死疆场，何以隐匿山林耶? A real man should die on the battlefield rather than live in seclusion among the mountains.

会党 huìdǎng 〈旧语〉secret society (in the late Qing Dynasty)：～蜂起。Secret societies mushroomed.

会道门 huì-dàomén superstitious sects and secret societies

会典 huìdiǎn collections of imperial laws and regulations：《明～》*Laws and Regulations of the Ming Dynasty*

会费 huìfèi membership dues or fees：联合国～ assessed contribution (to the UN) /会员要按期交纳～。Members are obliged to pay membership fees regularly.

会风 huìfēng style of meeting：～不正 unhealthy style of meeting

会攻 huìgōng concerted attack; combined onslaught

会馆 huìguǎn 〈旧语〉guild hall; provincial or county guild：湖南～ Hunan Guild (Hall)

会海 huìhǎi sea of meetings — numerous meetings：文山～ piles of official papers and endless meetings

会合 huìhé join; meet; converge; assemble：两军胜利～。The two armies joined forces in victory. /两条河在山那边～。The two rivers converge beyond the hill. /同学们在学校门口～之后出发去市中心。The students assembled at the school gate and then started off for downtown.

会合点 huìhédiǎn meeting point; rallying point; rendezvous

会合周期 huìhé zhōuqī 〈天文〉synodic period

会话 huìhuà conversation：英语～手册 handbook of English conversation /一段～ conversation piece

会徽 huìhuī emblem of an organization; society or association emblem; logo

会集 huìjí *see* "汇集" huìjí

会籍 huìjí membership (of a society, association, etc.)：开除～ expel sb. (from an association, etc.)

会见 huìjiàn meet; meet with; have a meeting with：总统今晨在总统府～了来访的外长。The president met with the visiting foreign minister in his offical residence this morning.

会剿 huìjiǎo take joint or concerted action to suppress (bandits); jointly quell or put down

会聚 huìjù *also* "汇聚" huìjù assemble; meet; flock together：我们约定在王教授家～。We decided to gather at Prof. Wang's.

会聚透镜 huìjù tòujìng 〈物理〉convergent lens

会刊 huìkān ❶ proceedings of a conference, etc. ❷ journal of an association, society, etc.

会考 huìkǎo standard examination (for students from various schools in a locality)：全省～ examination for students in the whole province

会客 huìkè receive a visitor or guest：～时间 visiting hours /开会时间，恕不～。No visitors. Meeting in session. /厂长正在～。The factory manager is receiving a visitor. /～占去他很多时间。Visitors take a great deal of his time.

会客室 huìkèshì reception room

会猎 huìliè 〈书面〉❶ hunt together ❷〈比喻〉be at war; fight

会门 huìmén superstitious sects and secret societies

会盟 huìméng (of monarchs in ancient China) meet to form alliances

会面 huìmiàn meet：他们约好中午～。They've made an appointment to meet at noon. /我们不常～。We don't see much of each other.

会票 huìpiào 〈旧语〉cheque issued by an old-style Chinese private bank payable in other localities

会期 huìqī ❶ time fixed for a conference; date of a meeting：确定～ fix a date for a meeting /推迟～ postpone (*or* put off) a meeting ❷ duration of a meeting：～初步定为五天。The conference is initially scheduled to last five days.

会齐 huìqí gather; assemble：大家明天早晨八时在火车站门前～。We shall gather in front of the railway station at eight o'clock tomorrow morning.

会旗 huìqí flag of a conference; conference flag or standard

会签 huìqiān countersign; countersignature：这个报告等各兄弟单位～后上报中央。This report will be sent to the central government after being countersigned by other departments concerned.

会亲 huìqīn 〈旧语〉mutual visit between a newly-wedded couple's in-laws

会儿 huìr 〈口语〉moment：请稍等一～。Please wait a moment. /我一～就回来。I won't be a minute. /他一～就来。He'll be here shortly (*or* presently).

会商 huìshāng hold a conference or consultation; negotiate：这事要～有关单位。We should consult the departments concerned about the matter. *or* The matter will have to be referred to departments concerned. /经多次～，这个问题已经解决。The problem has been solved after repeated consultations.

会社 huìshè ❶ association; society ❷ commercial firm, especially in Japan：株式～ limited company

会审 huìshěn ❶ joint hearing; joint trial：举行～ conduct a joint trial (*or* hearing) ❷ make a joint checkup：～工作计划 check the work plan jointly

会师 huìshī join forces; effect a junction：两军胜利～。The two armies joined forces triumphantly.

会试 huìshì 〈旧语〉general examination (for the successful candidates of all the provincial civil examinations, held once every three years in the capital during the Ming and Qing dynasties)

会首 huìshǒu *also* "会头" initiator or chief of society, association, etc.

会水 huìshuǐ be able to swim：我不～。I can't swim. /淹死～的，打死卖拳的。A swimmer may get drowned, and a martial boxer may get killed.

会说 huìshuō have the gift of gab; have a glib tongue：我们之中数他最～。He is the one among us who has a facile tongue.

会所 huìsuǒ headquarters or office building of a nongovernmental organization：商会～ headquarters of the chamber of commerce

会谈 huìtán talks; negotiation：双边～ bilateral talks /中美大使级～ Sino-US ambassadorial talks /中英～第二阶段第一轮 first round of the second phase of the Sino-British negotiations /～纪要 minutes of talks; notes of talks; record of discussions; summary of a conversation; memcon (memorandum of conversation)

会堂 huìtáng meeting hall; assembly hall; conference hall; hall：人民大～ Great Hall of the People

会通 huìtōng 〈书面〉achieve mastery through a comprehensive study of the subject

会同 huìtóng together with; jointly with：质量问题由信息产业部～国内贸易局共同解决。The problem of quality shall be tackled by the Ministry of Information Industry in conjunction with the Bureau of Internal Trade.

会务 huìwù day-to-day work of a conference; routine affairs of a conference：～费 registration fee for a conference /主持～ be in charge of the conference's day-to-day work

会悟 huìwù 〈书面〉realize; come to understand; see the light：你按我说的向他示意，他定能～。Give him a hint of what I said; he'll surely see the point.

会晤 huìwù meet：双方代表秘密～。Representatives of both sides met secretly. /两国外长将在边境～。The foreign ministers of the two countries will confer at the border.

会衔 huìxián countersign (a document)：这道文由三个部级单位～。This document shall be countersigned by three ministries.

会心 huìxīn understanding; knowing：露出～的微笑 give an under-

H

standing smile /～地点点头 nod understandingly /彼此～地眨了眨眼。They winked knowingly at each other.

会须 huìxū 〈书面〉shall; will; should:共庆胜利,～一醉。We shall drink to our hearts' content to celebrate the victory.

会穴 huìxué 〈中医〉crossing point (a point where two or more channels cross each other)

会演 huìyǎn *also* "汇演" huìyǎn joint performance (by a number of theatrical troupes, etc.):京剧现代戏～ modern Beijing opera festival

会厌 huìyàn 〈生理〉epiglottis:～切除术 epiglottectomy /～炎 epiglottitis

会厌软骨 huìyàn ruǎngǔ 〈生理〉*cartilago epiglottica*

会要 huìyào book of economic and political institutions and regulations of a dynasty:《唐～》*Institutions and Regulations of the Tang Dynasty*

会议 huìyì ❶ meeting; conference; convention:首脑～ summit conference; summit /圆桌～ round-table conference /工作～ working conference /生产～ production meeting /预备～ preparatory meeting /正式～ official meeting /非正式～ unofficial meeting /全体～ plenary session (*or* meeting); plenum /特别～ special meeting; extraordinary session /限制性～ restricted meeting /公开～ open meeting /秘密～ secret session; closed meeting; meeting in camera /开放性～ open-ended meeting /紧急～ urgent meeting /小组～ group meeting /定期～ periodic meeting /例行～ regular meeting /部长级～ ministerial meeting /～地点 venue; meeting place /～日程 daily agenda of a conference (*or* meeting) /～室 meeting (*or* conference) room /～厅 conference (*or* assembly) hall /召开～ call (*or* hold) a meeting; hold (*or* convene) a conference /取消～ cancel (*or* call off) a meeting /中止～ suspend a meeting /出席～ attend a meeting /列席～ attend a meeting as a non-voting delegate (*or* non-voting participant) /宣布～开始 declare the meeting open; call a meeting to order; the meeting is declared open; the meeting is called to order /～到此结束。The meeting is closed. /～休会吃午餐。The meeting is adjourned (*or* recessed) for lunch. /～不定期休会。The meeting is adjourned *sine die*. /～延期举行,何时召开,另行通知。The meeting is postponed until further notice. ❷ council; conference (as an organization):部长～ council of ministers /中国人民政治协商～ Chinese People's Political Consultative Conference (CPPCC)

会意 huìyì ❶〈语言〉combined meaning; associative compounds, one of the six categories under which Chinese characters are constituted:"信"字是由"人"字和"言"字合成的～字,表示人说的话有信用。The Chinese for "faith" is "信", a combination of "person" and "word", which means "keeping one's word". ❷ understanding; knowing:两个姑娘交换了一下眼色,～地笑了。The two girls exchanged glances and smiled knowingly. /大家～地点点头。People nodded understandingly.

会阴 huìyīn 〈生理〉perineum:～破裂 rupture of perineum /～体 perineal body /～切开术 perineotomy /～缝合术 perineorrhaphy

会饮 huìyǐn drink together

会友 huìyǒu ❶ fellow members of a society, club, etc.:我们是写作协会的～。We are members of the same writers' association. ❷〈书面〉make friends:君子以文～。Gentlemen make friends through literary (*or* academic) exchanges.

会元 huìyuán candidate who came out first in the general examination during the Ming and Qing dynasties

会员 huìyuán member:正式～ full (*or* full-fledged) member /非正式～ associate member /列席～ non-voting member /～银行 member bank /～权利及特权 rights and privileges of membership /～人数 membership

会员国 huìyuánguó member state or nation; member:非～ non-member state /出席并参加表决的～ member present and voting

会员证 huìyuánzhèng membership card

会员资格 huìyuán zīgé status of a member; membership

会战 huìzhàn ❶〈军事〉meet or engage in a decisive battle:斯大林格勒～ Battle of Stalingrad /两军～中原。The two armies were engaged in a decisive battle in central China. ❷ join in a battle; launch a mass campaign:煤炭大～ great battle for coal; join forces to mine coal /用搞～的办法解决不了思想问题。Mass campaigns are no cure for ideological lapses.

会章 huìzhāng ❶ charter; constitution (of an association, society, etc.):制定～ draft a constitution (of a society) /～精神 spirit of the charter ❷ emblem (of an association, society, etc.):小旗上印着该会～。The society's emblem is printed on the pennant.

会长 huìzhǎng president (of a society or association):对外友协～ President of Chinese People's Association for Friendship with Foreign Countries /商会～ Chairman of the Chamber of Commerce

会账 huìzhàng *also* "会钞" pay or foot a bill

会诊 huìzhěn (of doctors) group consultation; multi-speciality consultation:中西医～ hold group consultations of doctors practising Chinese and Western medicine /经专家～才找出了他的病因。The cause of his disease was not found until after the consultations of specialists.

会址 huìzhǐ ❶ site of an association or society ❷ site of a conference or meeting:遵义会议～ site of the Zunyi Meeting

会众 huìzhòng ❶ audience (at a meeting); participants ❷〈旧语〉members (of a secret society)

会子 huìzi ❶ period of time; some time; a while; a moment:说～话儿 chat for a while /来了好一～了,该回家了。I've been here for quite some time and should go home now. ❷ *huizi*, paper money issued in the Southern Song Dynasty

烩(燴) huì

❶ braise:肉末～白菜 braised minced meat and Chinese cabbage /～豆腐 bean curd braised in soy sauce ❷ cook (rice, etc.) with meat, vegetables and water:～饼 shredded pancakes cooked with meat, vegetables and water

荟(薈) huì

〈书面〉luxuriant growth (of plants)

荟萃 huìcuì (of distinguished people or exquisite objects) gather together; assemble:人才～ galaxy of talent /～一堂 gathering together in one hall; distinguished gathering /博物馆里珍宝～。The museum has a fine collection of treasures.

荟集 huìjí gather; assemble; collect:这是人才～的地方。This is a place where talented people gather.

桧(檜) huì

used as a personal name:秦～ Qin Hui, a treacherous court official of the Southern Song Dynasty

see also guì

绘(繪) huì

paint; draw:描～ depict; describe; portray

绘画 huìhuà drawing; painting:～室 studio /～颜料 tempera (*or* gouache) colour; tempera; gouache; colour /～台 painting table /～板 wooden board /～布 canvas

绘声绘色 huìshēng-huìsè *also* "绘影绘声" vivid; lively:～的描述 graphic description /人们～地谈论着这件事,仿佛都亲自经历过一样。People talked about it vividly, as if they had all experienced it themselves.

绘事 huìshì 〈书面〉matters concerning painting; painting business

绘图 huìtú mapping; plotting; sketch:～板 drawing board; field plotter; plotting table /～笔 border pen; plot pen; mapping pen /～机 draught machine; plotter /～室 drawing room /～员 draftsman; mapper; draughtsman /～纸 drafting paper; drawing paper

绘像 huìxiàng draw portraits

绘影绘声 huìyǐng-huìshēng *also* "绘声绘影" *see* "绘声绘色"

绘制 huìzhì draw:～图表 draw charts and diagrams /～地图 draw a map; map /～草图 draw a sketch; make a rough drawing /～社会主义建设的蓝图 draw up a blueprint for socialist construction

诲 huì

teach; instruct:教～ instructions

诲人不倦 huìrén-bùjuàn be tireless in teaching; teach with tireless zeal:学而不厌,～ have never grown tired of learning, nor wearied of teaching others what one has learnt

诲淫诲盗 huìyín-huìdào propagate sex and violence; stir up base passions:～的录像 video-show full of sex and violence /严禁出版发行～的黄色书刊。The publication and circulation of pornographic books and periodicals are strictly forbidden.

晦 huì

❶ last day of a lunar month ❷ dark; dim; obscure; gloomy:隐～ obscure; veiled ❸ night:风雨如～。It was windy and raining, dark as night. ❹ cover up; hide:韬光养～ hide one's capacities and bide one's time

晦暗 huì'àn dark and gloomy:面色～ look glum /心情～ feel distressed; feel down

晦迹 huìjì 〈书面〉live in seclusion; withdraw from society and live

H

in solitude：埋名～ lead a secluded, anonymous life /～山林 live like a hermit in remote areas

晦明 huì-míng 〈书面〉❶ day and night：何～之若岁？Why do the days wear on like years? ❷ bright or dark

晦溟 huìmíng *also* "晦冥"〈书面〉dark；dim：风雨～。It was dark with wind and rain.

晦气 huìqì ❶ unlucky：自认～ be resigned (*or* reconciled) to one's bad luck /真～，刚出门就摔了一跤！Damned unlucky! (*or* What rotten luck!) A fall right outside the house! ❷ pale and gloomy look：一脸～ unhealthy look that threatens ill luck

晦涩 huìsè obscure；hard to understand：语言～难懂。The language is obscure and almost unintelligible. /别把问题搞得复杂而～。Don't complicate and confuse the issue.

晦朔 huìshuò 〈书面〉from the last day of a lunar month to the first day of the next one；from dusk to dawn

hūn

荤 hūn ❶ meat or fish：～素搭配 balanced diet of meat and vegetables /开～ break a vegetarian diet；start eating meat /冷～ cold meat；cold buffet ❷〈佛教〉odorous vegetables：五～ garlic, scallion, onion, leek, etc. ❸ filthy；indecent：～笑话 dirty joke
see also xūn

荤菜 hūncài meat dish：他每顿饭都是三菜一汤，两个素菜，一个～。For lunch or dinner, he always has one soup and three dishes, including two vegetables and one meat.

荤话 hūnhuà obscene language；dirty words

荤口 hūnkǒu coarse language；vulgarism

荤腥 hūnxīng meat or fish：他只吃素食，不沾～。He is a vegetarian and eats no meat at all.

荤油 hūnyóu lard：这菜是用～炒的。This dish is cooked in lard.

昏 hūn ❶ dusk：黄～时分 at dusk；in the twilight /晨～ at dawn and dusk ❷ dark；dim；murky：天～地暗 murky sky over a dark earth；dark all round /天～～，地冥冥。Heaven and earth were one thick pall of murkiness. ❸ confused；muddled；dizzy：头～眼花 dizzy and giddy /利令智～ be blinded by lust for gains ❹ lose consciousness；faint：～倒 fall into a swoon；go off into a faint；fall unconscious；faint /她又～过去了。She fainted again. *or* She once more fell unconscious.

昏暗 hūn'àn dim；dusky：～的天色 gloomy skies /～地域 twilight zone /屋里的光线非常～。It is quite dusky (*or* dim) in the room. /东方的天边渐渐～下来。Dusk crept over the sky on the eastern horizon.

H

昏沉 hūnchén ❶ murky：暮色～ murky twilight /～的月色 dim moonlight ❷ dazed；befuddled：头脑～ be dazed /一夜未睡，今天脑子昏昏沉沉的。After a sleepless night, I feel befuddled (*or* in a daze) now.

昏呆 hūndāi stupor

昏定晨省 hūndìng-chénxǐng 〈旧语〉wait upon (one's parents) at bedtime and greet (them) in the morning — duties of a filial child in old times

昏黑 hūnhēi dusky；dark：眼前一片～。It was pitch dark all round.

昏花 hūnhuā dim-sighted：老眼～ dim-sighted from old age /我日渐～的眼睛看不清小字了。With my failing sight, I can hardly read small print.

昏话 hūnhuà absurd remark；nonsense；preposterous talk：这个可怜的白痴～连篇。The poor idiot was babbling nonsense.

昏黄 hūnhuáng pale yellow；faint；dim：～的月色 pale moon；faint moonlight /暮色～。It was dim twilight. /这里道路坑洼，路灯～。The roads here were full of potholes and the street lights dim.

昏昏欲睡 hūnhūn-yùshuì drowsy；sleepy：他多喝了点儿，只觉得～。With a drop too much, he felt quite sleepy. /他整天一副懒洋洋、～的样子。He is lackadaisical and looks drowsy all day long. /他的报告枯燥乏味，听得人～。His boring speech (*or* steady drone) always sends listeners to sleep.

昏惑 hūnhuò dazed and confused；dazed and puzzled：心神～ befuddled state of mind

昏厥 hūnjué *also* "晕厥" yūnjué faint；swoon：～过去 fall into a coma；faint away /接二连三的～使她虚弱到极点。Successive fainting fits (*or* swoons) made her extremely weak.

昏君 hūnjūn fatuous and self-indulgent ruler：～无道，坏人当政，国将不国。With a debauched monarch on the throne and wicked people in power, the days of the dynasty were numbered.

昏聩 hūnkuì decrepit and muddle-headed：～无能 decrepit and incompetent /～无知 addleheaded and ignorant

昏乱 hūnluàn ❶ dazed and confused；befuddled：脑子里一片～ be totally befuddled ❷〈书面〉confusion and disorder：政治～ political chaos /世道～ social disarray

昏茫 hūnmáng dim and hazy：雾霭中只见一片～。All appeared as a blur in the mist.

昏眊 hūnmào 〈书面〉dim-sighted：双目～ be dim-sighted in both eyes

昏昧 hūnmèi 〈书面〉❶ dim；hazy；obscure ❷ dark or despotic rule

昏蒙 hūnméng 〈书面〉❶ muddle-headed；confused in thinking；with one's mind in a haze or daze ❷ dark；dull：～欲雪的天气 dull sky threatening snow

昏迷 hūnmí stupor；coma；shock：处于～状态 in a coma；comatose /创伤引起的～ traumatic shock /孩子终于从长时间的～中苏醒了过来。The child had at last come to from a long coma. /老人已～了一整天。The old man has remained unconscious for a whole day.

昏睡 hūnshuì lethargic sleep；lethargy：处于～状态 in a lethargic state

昏睡病 hūnshuìbìng 〈医学〉sleeping-sickness；lethargy：非洲～ African lethargy

昏死 hūnsǐ faint；swoon；coma：～过去 faint away；fall into a coma

昏天黑地 hūntiān-hēidì ❶ pitchdark：山区夜晚，～的，走路可不容易。It was pitchdark at night in the mountain areas, and this made our journey rather difficult. ❷ dizzy：突然我眼前一黑，只觉得～的，什么也不知道了。I felt everything went black and then fell unconscious and knew nothing. ❸ perverted；decadent；wanton：～的生活 dissipated life /他整天～地泡在赌场和妓院里胡混。Debauched and decadent, day after day he indulged himself in gambling and whoring. ❹ complete chaos：人们在走廊里吵了个～。Fierce wrangling turned the corridor into chaos. ❺ dark rule and social disorder：～的旧社会 dark and lawless old society

昏头昏脑 hūntóu-hūnnǎo *also* "昏头胀脑" with one's mind numb；addleheaded；muddle-headed；confused and dizzy：我怎么～的，把我妈的大衣给穿来了！How addleheaded I am! I've put on my mother's coat by mistake. /她整天在厂家和客户之间穿梭，跑得～。She shuttled nonstop between producers and customers until her head was reeling. /他喝醉了，～地撞进了别人的办公室。He was drunk and fumbled into others' offices.

昏头转向 hūntóu-zhuànxiàng *also* "晕头转向" yūntóu-zhuànxiàng confused and disoriented

昏星 hūnxīng 〈古语〉evening star (Venus or Neptune that appears in the western sky after sunset)

昏眩 hūnxuàn dizzy；giddy：突然一阵～，她再也支持不住，栽倒在地。She was overcome by a sudden fit of giddiness and fell on the ground in spite of herself.

昏夜 hūnyè dark night

昏庸 hūnyōng fatuous；muddle-headed；stupid：～无能 fatuous and incompetent /老朽～之辈 stupid old vegetable

昏晕 hūnyūn faint；feel dizzy：巨大的爆炸声把他震得～了过去。He was badly shocked by the deafening explosion and fainted.

惛 hūn 〈书面〉muddle-headed；fatuous

惛惛 hūnhūn muddled；incoherent

阍 hūn 〈书面〉❶ tend or guard the door：司～ doorkeeper；gatekeeper ❷ palace gate：叩～ knock at the palace gate /帝～九重。The imperial palace is heavily guarded.

阍者 hūnzhě 〈书面〉doorkeeper；gatekeeper；janitor

棔 hūn 〈古语〉〈植物〉albizzia

婚 hūn wed；marry：已～ married /未～ unmarried /晚～ marry late /早～ marry too young；get married early /再～ remarry /重～〈法律〉bigamy /离～ divorce /定～ be engaged (*or* betrothed) to sb. /新～夫妇 newly-weds /指腹为～ be wedded to each other

through parental arrangements before birth /男大当～，女大当嫁。A boy will have to take a wife and a girl a husband when they grow up.

婚变 hūnbiàn divorce; extramarital affair (that disrupts a marriage):不久有了～，两人分手了。Their marriage broke up not long after. They each went their own way.

婚假 hūnjià wedding leave

婚嫁 hūnjià marriage:～之事 marriage; wedding

婚检 hūnjiǎn physical check-up before marriage

婚礼 hūnlǐ wedding ceremony; wedding:举行～ hold a wedding ceremony /传统～ traditional wedding /～蛋糕 wedding cake

婚恋 hūnliàn fall in love and get married:这些民族有着不同的～风情。These ethnic groups all have their own customs of courtship and marriage.

婚龄 hūnlíng ❶ years of marriage:他俩的～已有三十年。They've been married for thirty years now. ❷ (legally) marriageable age:他俩今年刚够～。They just reached the legal age for marriage this year.

婚配 hūnpèi married:小女年方二十，尚未～。My daughter is 20 years old and not yet married.

婚期 hūnqī wedding day:推迟～ postpone one's wedding /～一天天临近了。The wedding day is drawing near.

婚娶 hūnqǔ (of a man) marry

婚丧喜庆 hūnsāng-xǐqìng marriage and funeral — important occasions of a family:方圆数十里的～,没有不请他去帮忙的。His help is sought by every family around here on important occasions such as weddings and funerals.

婚纱 hūnshā (lady's) wedding garment

婚生子女 hūnshēng zǐnǚ 〈法律〉children born in wedlock; legitimate children:非～ children born out of wedlock; illegitimate children

婚事 hūnshì marriage; wedding:父母包办的～ marriage arranged by one's parents /你们什么时候办～啊? When will you have your wedding?

婚书 hūnshū 〈旧语〉marriage certificate:一纸～ marriage certificate

婚俗 hūnsú customs of marriage

婚外恋 hūnwàiliàn extramarital love; extramarital sex; affair:他有～的绯闻。There have been rumours about his having an affair with some woman.

婚筵 hūnyán wedding feast

婚姻 hūnyīn marriage; matrimony:～自主 marry of one's own free will /包办～ arranged marriage /买卖～ mercenary marriage /权宜～ marriage of convenience /不门当户对的～ *mésalliance* /匹配的～ well-matched marriage /～关系 wedlock /～大事 important matters like marriage /～登记 marriage registration /他俩的～十分美满。Their marriage is a very happy one.

婚姻法 hūnyīnfǎ marriage law:按～的规定办事 act according to the provisions of the marriage law

婚姻介绍所 hūnyīn jièshàosuǒ matrimonial agency

婚姻劝拢，祸祟劝开 hūnyīn quàn lǒng, huòsuì quàn kāi 〈俗语〉bring together estranged couples and dispel misfortune:～。明知无效，我们也要做到仁至义尽。As the saying goes, "One should try to bring estranged couples together and avert misfortune." Even if we know the attempt may fail, we must still do our best.

婚姻状况 hūnyīn zhuàngkuàng marital status

婚育期 hūnyùqī marriageable and childbearing age

婚约 hūnyuē marriage contract; engagement:订立～ make a marriage contract; make an arrangement to marry /解除～ break off one's engagement

hún

浑 hún ❶ muddy; murky; turbid:刚下过雨，河水很～。The river is muddy after the rain. /井水变～，可能要来地震。The water has turned turbid in the well; it may portend a possible earthquake. ❷ addle-brained; foolish; stupid:真是个～虫! What an idiot! /从未见过像他那样～的人! Never seen anyone more addle-brained than he is! ❸ simple and natural:他的歌声雄～自然。He has a rich and natural voice. ❹ whole; full; complete; all over:～身是胆 be full of guts /～身是血 bleed all over ❺ (Hún) a surname

浑蛋 húndàn *also* "混蛋" húndàn 〈粗话〉wretch; skunk; bastard; son of a bitch:这个～今天不知要闹出什么花样来呢! I wonder what the son of bitch is up to today! /你这个～还不给我滚! You bastard! Get out of here!

浑噩 hún'è ignorant; simple-minded; muddle-headed:～麻木 ignorant and insensitive

浑古 húngǔ of primitive simplicity; simple and unsophisticated:这枚印章刻得疏密有致，～有力。The seal's strokes are well spaced, simple and vigorous.

浑厚 húnhòu ❶ simple and honest:天性～ simple and honest by nature ❷ (of writing, painting, etc.) simple and vigorous:他的山水画～有力。His landscape painting is characterized by bold and vigorous strokes. ❸ (of voice) deep and sonorous:～的音色 full and sonorous voice /～的男低音 deep and resonant bass

浑话 húnhuà nonsense; fatuous talk; impudent remark

浑浑噩噩 húnhún-è'è fatuous and ignorant; simple-minded; muddle-headed:青年人要有所作为，不应该～地活着。Young people shouldn't muddle along, but should do something worthwhile.

浑家 húnjiā (usu. used in the early vernacular) wife

浑金璞玉 húnjīn-púyù *also* "璞玉浑金" jade and gold in natural state; uncut jade and unrefined gold; unadorned beauty:她像～一样，丝毫也没有沾染世俗习气。Her beauty is unadorned, and she is entirely free of worldliness.

浑括 húnkuò all in all; in a word; long and short; in a nutshell:～全书，我认为写得不错。All in all, I consider the book a success. /他找了许多借口，～起来，就是不想帮忙。He gave many excuses; in a nutshell, he didn't want to help.

浑名 húnmíng *also* "诨名" hùnmíng nickname; agnomen

浑朴 húnpǔ simple and honest:性格～ simple and honest in nature; of simple and honest character /画风～ paint in a plain and simple style /～的语言 plain and simple language

浑球儿 húnqiúr *also* "混球儿" húnqiúr 〈方言〉rascal; wretch; skunk; son of a bitch

浑然 húnrán ❶ integrated; unified; integral:～天成 integral whole ❷ completely; fully; entirely:～不觉 be entirely unaware /～不理 completely ignore

浑然一体 húnrán-yītǐ integrated mass; unified entity; integral whole:情景交融，～。One's feelings and the scene are in perfect harmony and form an integral whole.

浑人 húnrén unreasonable person

浑如 húnrú very much alike; exactly like:蜡像都十分逼真，～真人一般。Ingeniously done, the wax figures are all lifelike.

浑身 húnshēn from head to heel; from top to toe; all over:～冰凉 ice-cold all over /～上下都是土 covered with dust from top to toe /～上下，一丝不挂 be stark naked; have nothing on at all /～都是力气 brimming (*or* bursting) with energy /使出～解数 do one's level best; do all one can

浑身是胆 húnshēn-shìdǎn be every inch a hero; be filled with guts; be the very embodiment of valour

浑实 húnshi ❶ sturdy; thickset; brawny; robust:浓眉大眼，高大～的小伙子 tall and sturdy young man with thick eyebrows and big eyes ❷ (of a child) innocent:这小男孩真～可爱! What an innocent and lovely boy! ❸ dependable; steady and sure

浑水摸鱼 húnshuǐ-mōyú fish in troubled waters; try to gain advantage out of other people's troubles:他挑拨离间，制造混乱，以便～。He tried to sow discord and create confusion so as to fish in troubled waters.

浑说 húnshuō (talk) rubbish; (make) an impudent remark; drivel:信口～ wag one's tongue too freely; shoot one's mouth off; talk irresponsibly

浑似 húnsì *also* "浑如" exactly like:这小伙子长相～其父。The young lad looks exactly like his father. *or* The young man is a chip of (*or* off) the old block.

浑天仪 húntiānyí 〈古语〉❶ armillary sphere ❷ celestial globe

浑象 húnxiàng *also* "浑天仪"〈古语〉celestial globe

浑仪 húnyí *also* "浑天仪"〈古语〉armillary sphere

浑圆 húnyuán perfectly round:一颗颗～的珍珠 perfectly round pearls /～的月亮 full moon

浑浊 húnzhuó muddy; turbid:河水～ turbid waters of the river /病房里～的空气对她很不适宜。The foul air in the ward is very bad for her.

珲

hún 〈书面〉a kind of jade
see also huī

魂

hún ❶ soul：祭忠～ offer a sacrifice to the loyal soul (of) / 招～ call home the soul of the dead /阴～不散 the ghost lingers on ❷ mood; spirit：神～颠倒 be infatuated /失～落魄 be distracted; have the jitters ❸ lofty spirit of a nation; army, etc.：国～ national spirit /军～ spirit of the army; army spirit

魂不附体 húnbùfùtǐ feel as if one's soul had left one's body; be shaken to the depths of one's soul：吓得她～，脸色惨白。She was scared out of her wits, looking deadly pale.

魂不守舍 húnbùshǒushè ❶ in a trance; absent-minded：他整天～，做什么也打不起精神。He has been in a trance these days and has no heart for anything. ❷ be panic-stricken; be terrified：他终日惶惶然，一副～的样子。He was seized with fear all day, looking panic-stricken.

魂飞魄散 húnfēi-pòsàn be panic-stricken; go out of one's mind; be half dead with fright：吓得～ be frightened out of one's wits

魂灵 húnlíng soul; soul of the dead

魂魄 húnpò soul

魂牵梦萦 húnqiān-mèngyíng miss very much; pine for：这便是他日夜思念，～的恋人。She is the woman he has been yearning for by day and dreaming about at night.

混

hún *see* "浑❶❷" hún
see also hùn

混蛋 húndàn *see* "浑蛋" húndàn

混球儿 húnqiúr *see* "浑球儿" húnqiúr

混水摸鱼 húnshuǐ-mōyú *see* "浑水摸鱼" húnshuǐ-mōyú

馄

hún

馄饨 húntun wonton; dumpling soup：～皮儿 dumpling (*or* ravioli, *or* wonton) wrappings /一碗～ a bowl of dumpling (*or* ravioli) soup /包～ make dumplings

hùn

混

hùn ❶ mix; mingle; confuse：稻谷里～了不少沙子。The rice is mixed with a lot of sand. /鱼龙～杂，良莠难分。The good and the bad are mixed up, and it is difficult to tell one from the other. /这是对双胞胎，我老是给弄～了。They are twins. I often confuse one with the other. /那个坏蛋～在人群中。That bastard mingled with the crowd. ❷ pass for; pass off as; palm off as：鱼目～珠 pass off fish eyes as pearls — pass off the sham as genuine ❸ muddle along; muddle on; drift along：他在这儿实在～不下去了，只好远走高飞。Being unable to muddle on here, he had to hit the road. ❹ get along with：她和工人们～得很熟。She hit it off with the workers. ❺ carelessly; at random; irresponsibly：～出主意 put forward irresponsible suggestions /～说 speak thoughtlessly
see also hún

混编 hùnbiān mixed grouping：男女～的班级 mixed class

混成旅 hùnchénglǚ 〈军事〉mixed brigade

混充 hùnchōng pass oneself off as; palm sb. or sth. off as：他挂出牌子来～医生。He put up a business sign and passed himself off as a doctor. /小贩以假货～珍珠蒙骗顾客。The pedlar palmed fake pearls off onto customers.

混沌 hùndùn ❶ chaos (the primeval state of the universe according to Chinese legend)：～初开 when earth was first separated from heaven; at the dawn of civilization ❷ innocent; simple-minded and ignorant：思想～ muddle-headed /～无知 simple-minded and ignorant; naive like a child

混饭 hùnfàn *also* "混饭吃" ❶ make a living as best one can; work just to get by：我不过是～，谈不上好不好。I just get by; there's nothing wonderful about it. /工作失去了意义，岂不成了～而已！If your work doesn't mean anything to you, then it is merely a way to earn your bread. ❷ 〈方言〉eat at another's expense

混纺 hùnfǎng 〈纺织〉❶ blending：～织物 blend fabric; union /这种纱是用百分之四十的毛和百分之六十的棉～而成的。This yarn is a blend of 40% wool and 60% cotton. ❷ blend fabric：棉毛～ fabric of wool and cotton

混号 hùnhào *see* "诨号" hùnhào

混合 hùnhé mix; blend; mingle：男女生～编班 have mixed classes of boys and girls /把奶粉和面粉～在一起 blend milk powder and flour /这趟车是客货～列车。This is a mixed train. /这几样东西不能～。These things mustn't be mixed up.

混合编队 hùnhé biānduì 〈军事〉composite formation

混合贷款 hùnhé dàikuǎn mixed loan

混合经济 hùnhé jīngjì mixed economy

混合面儿 hùnhémiànr 〈旧语〉flour mixed with earth and other adulterants (sold in the Japanese-occupied areas during the War of Resistance Against Japanese Aggression); mixed flour

混合器 hùnhéqì 〈化学〉mixer

混合色 hùnhésè secondary colour

混合授粉 hùnhé shòufěn 〈农业〉mixed pollination

混合双打 hùnhé shuāngdǎ 〈体育〉mixed doubles

混合台 hùnhétái *also* "自然台" zìrántái standard horse power unit (for tractors)

混合委员会 hùnhé wěiyuánhuì mixed commission; mixed committee

混合物 hùnhéwù mixture：空气是氧、氢、氮等多种气体的～。The air is a mixture of oxygen, hydrogen, nitrogen and various other gases.

混合岩 hùnhéyán 〈地质〉migmatite

混混儿 hùnhunr 〈方言〉scoundrel; street rowdy; conniving idler; loafer

混迹 hùnjì unworthily mix with：～于士林 unworthily occupy a place among scholars

混交 hùnjiāo 〈林业〉trees of two or more species growing together; mixed growth of different trees

混交林 hùnjiāolín mixed forest：松、栎～ mix forest of pines and oaks

混进 hùnjìn *also* "混入" infiltrate; sneak into; worm one's way into：～革命队伍的敌特分子 enemy spies who have wormed their way into the revolutionary ranks /有些不三不四的人～会场来了。Some dubious characters have sneaked into the conference hall.

混料机 hùnliàojī 〈机械〉blender

混流 hùnliú mixed flow; mixed-phase flow：～式水轮机 mixed-flow turbine /～式涡轮机 mixed turbine

混乱 hùnluàn confusion; chaos; disorder：思路～ confused train of thought /交通～ traffic tangles /思想～ ideological confusion; muddled thinking /管理～ confusion in management /～局面 chaotic state (*or* situation) /会场秩序十分～。The meeting was in great disorder. /他的讲话在人群中引起了一片～。His speech threw the audience into disarray.

混茫 hùnmáng ❶ indistinct; hazy：天气阴沉，江面上一片～。It was cloudy and a pall of mist hung over the river. ❷ 〈书面〉ignorant; benighted

混蒙 hùnméng ❶ 〈方言〉deceive; cheat; mislead：别让他～过去。Don't let him get by under false pretences. ❷ 〈书面〉ignorant; benighted

混名 hùnmíng *see* "浑名" húnmíng; "诨名" hùnmíng

混凝剂 hùnníngjì 〈化学〉coagulant

混凝土 hùnníngtǔ 〈建筑〉concrete：预应力～ prestressed concrete / 预制～ precast concrete /～搅拌机 concrete mixer /～结构 concrete structure /～振捣器 (concrete) vibrator

混凝纸浆 hùnníng zhǐjiāng papier-mâché

混频 hùnpín 〈电子〉frequency mixing：～器 mixer /～线 mixer line

混频管 hùnpínguǎn mixed tube; mixer tube

混日子 hùn rìzi muddle along; drift along; scrape by：糊里糊涂地～ muddle along (*or* on) without any clear purpose in life /这小子不好好工作，成天～。The young man has no interest in his work and simply scrapes by.

混声合唱 hùnshēng héchàng mixed chorus

混世魔王 hùnshì mówáng devil incarnate; fiend in human shape; monster：臭名昭著的～ notorious villain

混事 hùnshì scrape a living; muddle along：～而已 scrape a living / 他在外企里混过几天事。He did some kind of job at a foreign firm for a short time.

混水摸鱼 hùnshuǐ-mōyú *also* "浑水摸鱼" húnshuǐ-mōyú fish in troubled waters：谨防有人～。Watch out for those who try to muddy the waters for their own benefit.

H

混同 hùntóng confuse; mix up:注意他们两人的区别，不可将他们～起来。You must take note of the differences between the two and not mix them up. /一个共产党员不能把自己～于一般群众。A Party member should set a higher demand on himself than an ordinary person.

混为一谈 hùnwéiyītán lump or jumble together; confuse sth. with sth. else:不要把自由与放纵～。Don't confuse liberty with licence. /政治问题与学术问题要严格区分开来，千万不能～。We should strictly separate political from academic matters and must not lump them together.

混响 hùnxiǎng 〈物理〉reverberation:～传输系数 reverberation transmission coefficient

混淆 hùnxiáo obscure; mix up; confuse; confound:～敌我 confuse friend with foe /真假～ the sham (*or* false) is mixed up with the genuine (*or* true) /我把人名～了。I have mixed their names up. /是非界限～不清。The distinction between right and wrong is blurred.

混淆黑白 hùnxiáo-hēibái mix up black and white; confuse right and wrong

混淆视听 hùnxiáo-shìtīng mislead the public; befuddle or confuse public opinion

混淆是非 hùnxiáo-shìfēi confuse right and wrong

混血儿 hùnxuè'ér person of mixed blood; half-breed:那小孩是个～。That kid is of mixed blood.

混一 hùnyī amalgamation

混杂 hùnzá mix; mingle; confound:泥沙俱下，鱼龙～。The waters were muddied, and the bad became mixed with the good. /在他的发言中，表扬里～着某些责怪。Praises were mingled with some blame in his speech.

混战 hùnzhàn tangled warfare; tangled fighting:军阀～ tangled warfare among warlords; tangled fighting between warlords /～一场 engage in a free-for-all

混账 hùnzhàng 〈粗话〉scoundrel; rascal; bastard; son of a bitch:你这个不通人性的～东西! You scandalous bastard! /～透顶，没人怜的狗东西! That incestuous, wretched son of a bitch!

混账话 hùnzhànghuà vile rubbish; impudent language

混浊 hùnzhuó muddy; turbid:～无神的眼睛 dull (*or* lacklustre) eyes /屋里的空气十分～。The air is quite foul (*or* stale) in the room. /被污染的河水显得～不清。The polluted river looks muddy and turbid.

混子 hùnzi person unworthy of his title; quack; imposter

混作 hùnzuò 〈农业〉mixed cropping; mixed cultivation

诨 hùn joke; jest:打～ make gags; crack jokes /插科打～ jesting; buffoonery

诨号 hùnhào nickname

诨名 hùnmíng nickname:小学生也会相互起～。Even pupils know how to nickname each other.

圂 hùn 〈书面〉lavatory; privy

溷 hùn 〈书面〉❶ confusion; chaos; disorder:～浊 filthy and muddy ❷ lavatory; WC

溷厕 hùncè 〈书面〉toilet; lavatory

溷浊 hùnzhuó *see* "混浊" hùnzhuó

恩(慁) hùn 〈书面〉❶ suffering; misery ❷ disturb; create trouble

huō

豁[1] huō split; crack; breach:裤子上～了个大口子。There is a big split in the trousers. /船体～了个大裂口。The ship's hull had a huge crack in it.

豁[2] huō pay a high price (for sth. one must do); give up; sacrifice:～出性命也要把溺水的孩子救起来。I would even give up my life to save a drowning child. /学外语得～时间。It takes lots of time to learn a foreign language.

see also huá; huò

豁出去 huōchuqu go ahead at any price; be ready to risk everything:这次他真的是～了。He is ready to risk everything this time. /为了孩子，她得～，哪还顾得上自己的身体呢? For her child's sake, she would go ahead at any price even at the cost of her own health.

豁口 huōkǒu opening; breach; crack:城墙～ opening (*or* breach) in the city wall /水缸边上有个～。There is a crack in the edge of the water jar. /北风从山的～吹过来。The north wind blows in through the mountain pass.

豁命 huōmìng risk one's life; be ready to pay any price:～也得把事情办好。I will get the job done even at the expense of my life.

豁子 huōzi 〈方言〉❶ opening; breach; crack:碗口上有个～。The bowl has a chip at the rim. ❷ harelipped person:人们背后都叫他～。People called him "harelip" behind his back.

豁嘴 huōzuǐ ❶〈口语〉harelip:～的学名是"腭裂"。The technical term for harelip is cleft palate. ❷ harelipped person

耠 huō hoeing:～地 hoe the earth; do hoeing

耠子 huōzi hoe:用～翻地 break up the soil with a hoe; hoe the earth /他会使～，也会使犁。He knows how to use a plough as well as a hoe.

劐 huō 〈口语〉❶ slit or cut with a knife:把鸡肚子～开洗净 cut open the chicken's breast, hollow it out and wash it clean ❷ *see* "耠" huō

嚄 huō 〈叹词〉wow:～! 这么多水果呀! Wow! Such a lot of fruit!

see also huò; ǒ

攉 huō shovel (coal, ore, etc.) from one place to another:～土 shovel earth /～煤机 coal shovel /～煤工人 coal shoveller

锪 huō ream:～刀 countersink

騞(剨) huō 〈书面〉crashing sound

huó

活[1] huó ❶ live:～一百岁 live to (be) one hundred /苟～ live on in degradation /～到老，学到老 learn as long as one lives; one is never too old to learn /复～ come back to life; revive /生龙～虎 full of vim and vigour /为吃而～，还是为～而吃? Live to eat, or eat to live? ❷ alive; living; live:生吞～剥 swallow alive; copy mechanically /～鱼 live fish /～着的人比死人更重要。The living are more important than the dead. ❸ save (the life of a person); feed; keep alive:养家～口 support (*or* provide for) a family /药可～人。Medicine can save people's lives. /一个农民能养～几口人? How many persons can a farmer feed? ❹ movable; flexible; moving:～水 flowing water /灵～ flexible ❺ vivid; lively; quick:对内搞～经济 enliven (*or* invigorate) domestic economy /他的脑子真～。He has a quick mind. /要把思想工作做～。Ideological work should be done in a lively way. /他们把生意做～了。They are very resourceful in doing business. ❻ exactly; simply; *see* "～现"; "～像"

活[2] huó ❶ work; job:木工～儿 woodwork; carpentry /抢挑重～儿 be ready to do heavy work /庄稼～儿 farm work; farming /体力～儿 physical work; manual labour (*or* work) /脏～儿累～儿 messy and tiring work /请给咱找件～儿干干。Please find a job for me. ❷ product; finished product:不出～儿 not productive; not efficient /这批～儿干得快，质量也好。This batch of products has been made quickly and is of good quality.

活靶 huóbǎ 〈军事〉moving or manoeuvring target:练习打～ practise shooting at moving targets

活靶子 huóbǎzi live target:他的理论被当作～来批判。His doctrine served as a live target of criticisms.

活扳手 huóbānshou diagonal wrench; clyburn spanner

活版 huóbǎn 〈印刷〉typography; letterpress

活版印刷 huóbǎn yìnshuā typographic printing; typography; letterpress printing:～机 letterpress (printing) machine

活瓣 huóbàn 〈生理〉valve; flap

H

活宝 huóbǎo bit of a clown; funny fellow:他是个大～，尽在众人面前出洋相。He is quite a bit of a clown, often making an exhibition of himself in public.
活报剧 huóbàojù living newspaper; skit:街头～ street skit
活蹦蹦 huóbēngbēng lively and full of vitality; vivacious; active; sprightly:在她的笔下个个人物都～的富有情趣。Every character she portrayed was full of life and human appeal.
活蹦乱跳 huóbèng-luàntiào skip and jump about; be alive and kicking:～的鲜鱼虾 live fish and shrimps that are still skipping and jumping about /幼儿园里的孩子一个个～的。The children in the kindergarten are full of life.
活便 huóbian 〈方言〉❶ flexible; nimble; agile:他手脚还算～。He is still agile. /这把折椅不怎么～，多年不用了吧? This folding chair is not flexible enough, I guess it's not been used for years, has it? ❷ convenient; handy:这么办就～多了。It'll be more convenient to do it this way. /出门身上带点旅行支票就会感到～些。Traveller's cheques may come in handy on trips.
活冰川 huóbīngchuān 〈地理〉active glacier
活茬 huóchá 〈方言〉farm work:秋后地里的～儿不多了。At the end of autumn, there is not much to do in the fields.
活地图 huódìtú walking map:老人是～，对这一带地形熟极了。The old man is such a competent guide, familiar with every nook and cranny of this area.
活地狱 huódìyù hell on earth; living hell
活动 huódòng ❶ move about; exercise:久坐后要站起来～～。After sitting for a long time, one should stretch one's legs. /我这就下楼散散步，～～筋骨。I'm going downstairs to limber up the joints (*or* limber myself up). ❷ shaky; unsteady:钉了两颗钉子，桌子腿不再～了。With two nails in the leg, the table is no longer rickety. /门牙有些～，不能咬东西。My front teeth are a bit loose and cannot bite. ❸ mobile; movable; flexible:条文要规定得比较～些。The regulations should be fairly flexible. /他的心思渐渐～了，语气也不那么坚决了。He began to relent a little and sounded less adamant. ❹ activity; manoeuvre:秘密～ secret activities /集体～ collective activities /派别～ factional activities; sectarian activities /体育～ sports; exercise /科研～ scientific pursuits /～范围 sphere of activities; scope of operation /老干部～室 recreation room for retired cadres /你这样做使我没有一点～的余地。By doing so you've left me with no alternative. /有一股土匪在这一带～。A group of bandits are operating around here. ❺ use personal influence or irregular means; manoeuvre; wangle: 为升官而四处～ manoeuvre (*or* jockey) for one's promotion /请你帮他～一下。Will you put in a word for him, please? *or* Use your influence on his behalf, please.
活动坝 huódòngbà 〈水利〉movable dam
活动扳手 huódòng bānshou 〈机械〉adjustable spanner or wrench
活动床 huódòngchuáng adjustable bed
活动房屋 huódòng fángwū mobile home; Nissen hut
活动分子 huódòngfènzǐ activist:体育～ sports activist /文娱～ activist in art and cultural pursuits
活动家 huódòngjiā activist; public figure:工会～ union activist /党务～ Party affairs activist /政治～ political figure /社会～ public figure; personage
活动起重机 huódòng qǐzhòngjī runabout crane
活动桥 huódòngqiáo movable bridge; swing bridge
活动舞台 huódòng wǔtái revolving stage
活动资本 huódòng zīběn movable or liquid capital
活度 huódù 〈化学〉activity:～系数 activity coefficient
活泛 huófan *also*"活分"❶ nimble; agile; flexible; good at adaptation:心眼～ adaptable; resourceful /我年岁不大，手脚却不够～。I am not nimble enough for my age. /他为人勤奋，就是脑筋不～。He is hard-working but not quick-minded. ❷ have money to spare or lend; have spare money:所借的钱等你手头～些再还不晚。You may return the money I lent you when you have some to spare.
活佛 huófó ❶〈宗教〉Living Buddha:～转世 reincarnation of a Living Buddha ❷ (in classical novels) Buddhist monk or lay person who assists people in distress and saves people from danger:济公～ Divine Monk Ji Gong
活该 huógāi ❶ serve sb. right:～如此! He got what he deserved! *or* It served him right! ❷〈方言〉should; be decreed by fate:我是～受罪的命! I'm predestined to suffer in my life. /碰上好医生，我～有救。With such a good doctor, I should be saved.
活工资 huógōngzī unfixed wage; conditional wage
活荷载 huóhèzài 〈交通〉〈建筑〉live load
活化 huóhuà 〈化学〉activation:～剂 activator /～吸附 activation absorption /～能 activation energy
活化石 huóhuàshí *also*"孑遗生物"jiéyí shēngwù living fossil
活话 huóhuà indefinite, vague, or open-ended remark; non-committal words:说～ not commit oneself in speech; make non-committal remarks /他临走前留下一句～，说可能还会回来。He left, right before departure, a vague message, saying that he might come back later.
活活 huóhuó ❶ while still alive:～打死 be beaten to death ❷ simply; completely; almost:那匹马是～累死的。That horse simply died of overwork. /瞧他那个样，～是个疯子。He looked as if he had gone completely mad.
活火山 huóhuǒshān active volcano
活计 huóji ❶ handicraft work; manual labour:她的针线～做得很好。She is very good at needlework. /今天的～要重新安排。Today's work assignment must be rearranged. ❷ handiwork; work:她一边给我看她做的～，一边和我聊天。She showed me her work while chatting with me.
活检 huójiǎn (short for 活组织检查)〈医学〉biopsy
活见鬼 huójiànguǐ it's sheer fantasy; you're imagining things; how preposterous:你几时见到我上舞台了，真是～! You were just imagining things when you said that you saw me acting on the stage!
活校 huójiào proof-reading that checks the original as well as the proofs
活教材 huójiàocái vivid example for education; object lesson:反贪斗争的～ vivid example for education in the struggle against corruption; object lesson in fighting against corruption
活结 huójié slipknot; bowknot:打了个～ make a slipknot
活局子 huójúzi 〈方言〉trap; snare; fraud; hoax
活口 huókǒu ❶ living witness to a crime; survivor of a murder attempt:证人中只剩下这唯一的～，一定要尽力抢救。This is the only witness that has survived the murder and must be saved by all means. ❷ prisoner or criminal who can furnish information ❸ support oneself or one's family ❹ flexible tone; open-ended remark:他的话有点～，达成协议的希望还是有的。He spoke in a somewhat flexible tone so there's still hope for us to reach agreement.
活扣 huókòu *see*"活结"
活劳动 huóláodòng human labour; living labour
活力 huólì vigour; vitality; energy:浑身充满～ full of vigour /增强经济～ revitalize the economy /集贸摊点给首都市场增添了～。Fairs, retailers and venders have added to the flourishing of the capital's market.
活灵活现 huólíng-huóxiàn *also*"活龙活现"vivid; lifelike:他把整个事件说得～，就像亲眼见到似的。He gave a vivid account of the incident as if he had seen it with his own eyes.
活溜 huóliu 〈方言〉❶ shaky; unstable; loose:门柱有些～，该修一修了。The door frame is a bit shaky and needs repair. ❷ flexible; nimble; agile:我的膝关节不够～。My knees are a bit stiff.
活路 huólù ❶ thorough path:往左拐是条～，一直通到车站。The road after you turn left will take you all the way to the station. ❷ workable method; feasible approach:问题难办，没有什么现成～。It's a hard nut and there's no easy way of cracking it. ❸ means of subsistence; way to keep alive:没有其他～，我不得不这么干。I had to do it because there was no other way out. /眼下，我真是一点～也没有了! I just have no way to make a living now!
活路 huólu manual or physical labour
活络 huóluò 〈方言〉❶ loose; shaky:老年人牙齿～是常有的事。It is very common that aged people's teeth become loose. ❷ flexible; non-committal; indefinite:头脑～ nimble mind /她说得很～，不知究竟同意了没有。She was rather non-committal, and I wonder if she agreed. ❸ (of a person) smart; clever
活络丹 huóluòdān 〈中药〉bolus for activating energy flow in channels and collaterals
活埋 huómái bury alive
活卖 huómài sale of estate with the seller reserving the right to redeem it
活门 huómén 〈机械〉valve
活命 huómìng ❶ earn a bare living; scrape along; eke out an existence:他在旧社会靠拉洋车～。He scraped along by pulling a rickshaw in the old society. /全家就靠妈妈给人家洗衣服～。The mother eked

out a living for the family by doing laundry for other people. ❷〈书面〉save sb.'s life; survive:感谢您的～之恩。I am indebted to you for saving my life. ❸ life:求你留他一条～。I beg you to spare his life.

活命哲学 huómìng zhéxué philosophy of survival; keeping oneself alive at all costs

活泼 huópo ❶ lively; vivacious; vivid:短小～的节目 short and lively items (of performance) /天真～的女孩 vivacious girl /～风趣的语言 vivid and humorous language /生动～的政治局面 dynamic political atmosphere ❷〈化学〉reactive:单体～度 monomer reactivity

活菩萨 huópúsa Buddha incarnate; saviour; person who is full of compassion for the needy and the suffering

活期 huóqī current:～储蓄 current deposit; demand deposit /～存款 current deposit /～存款账户 current account /～放款 demand loan /这笔钱存～。This sum of money is to be deposited in our current account.

活棋 huóqí ❶ *weiqi* or go game with two traps or more; chess game in which there is plenty of room for manoeuvring ❷ agreeable and invigorating atmosphere; move that creates such an atmosphere:厂长的一着～,使工厂起死回生。The clever move of the director has saved the factory from bankruptcy.

活气 huóqì lively atmosphere:工地上人来车往,热火朝天,充满～。With men and vehicles hurrying back and forth, the construction site was bustling with activity, and a lively atmosphere prevailed. /会议开得死气沉沉,毫无～。The meeting was spiritless.

活契 huóqì conditional (real estate) sales contract, one that allows the seller to redeem the real estate within a given period of time

活钱儿 huóqiánr ❶ cash; ready money:手头上没有什么～。I have no ready money on hand. ❷ non-salary income; extra income:除工资外,我没有什么～。I earn no other income except my salary.

活塞 huósāi *also*"鞴鞴" gōubèi〈机械〉piston:～泵 piston pump /～杆 piston rod /～圈 piston ring /空气压缩机～ air compressor piston /后～ back piston /内～ inner piston /～发声仪 pistonphone /～发动机 piston engine

活色生香 huósè-shēngxiāng 〈口语〉lifelike; to the life; vividly:人人都想看看电影明星如何～地出现在自己面前。Everybody would like to see how a movie star looks and behaves in real life.

活神仙 huóshénxian man noted for his longevity; person supposed to have clairvoyance

活生生 huóshēngshēng ❶ real; living; in real life:～的现实教育了她。The living reality taught her a lesson. ❷ while still alive:敌人用坦克把人～地碾死了。The enemy's tanks ran people over and killed them.

活食 huóshí live earthworms, insects, rabbits, fish, etc., used to feed bigger animals

活受罪 huóshòuzuì have a hell of a life or time:大热天穿一身厚西服简直是～。I was having a hell of a time in a warm suit in the heat of summer.

活水 huóshuǐ flowing water; running water:源头～ flowing water at the source;〈比喻〉inexhaustible inspiration (as from life, etc.)

活死人 huósǐrén 〈方言〉〈粗话〉living corpse; blockhead; slowcoach

活似 huósì *see*"活象"

活体 huótǐ living body:～鉴定〈法律〉identification of the living

活体检查 huótǐ jiǎnchá 〈医学〉biopsy

活体解剖 huótǐ jiěpōu vivisection

活头儿 huótour will to live; interest in life:你这么不争气,我还有什么～! You are such a disappointment to me. What's there for me to live for?

活脱儿 huótuōr (of looks and behaviour) look exactly like; be the spit and image of; be an exact replica of:兄弟俩长得像极了,～是一个模子倒出来的。The two brothers look very much alike, and each is an exact replica of the other.

活物 huówù (usu. of a pet) living thing

活鲜鲜 huóxiānxiān ❶ vivid; of real life; living:～的现实 actual fact; reality; true reality /～的情景 vivid scene (*or* picture) ❷ fresh; vigorous; energetic:～的树苗 fresh sapling

活现 huóxiàn appear vividly; come alive:活龙～ exactly like the real one; lifelike /神气～ cocksure; high and mighty /临行前乡亲们送我的那一幕动人情景又～在眼前了。The scene of country folks seeing me off upon my departure once again appeared vividly in my mind's eye.

活像 huóxiàng look exactly like; as like as two peas; be the spit of:她长得～她母亲。She is a chip off the old block. /小姑娘说话、做事都有条有理,～个大人。The little girl speaks and acts methodically, just like a grown-up. /这个蜡像～真的一样。This wax statue is lifelike.

活性 huóxìng 〈化学〉active; activated; activity:水泥的～ activity of cement /抗氧～ antioxygenic activity /～化 activation

活性染料 huóxìng rǎnliào reactive dye

活性炭 huóxìngtàn 〈化学〉active or activated carbon

活血 huóxuè 〈中医〉invigorate blood circulation:当归可以～。*Danggui* (*or* Chinese angelica) can improve blood circulation.

活血丹 huóxuèdān 〈中药〉blood-activating pellet

活阎王 huóyánwang devil incarnate; demon king; tyrannical ruler:谁不骂他是个杀人不眨眼的～! Everybody called him a bloodthirsty tyrant!

活页 huóyè loose-leaf; detachable leaf:～本 loose-leaf notebook /～夹 loose-leaf binder; spring binder /～文选 loose-leaf selections /～纸 paper for a detachable leaf notebook

活用 huóyòng apply in a creative way; make flexible use of

活跃 huóyuè ❶ dynamic; active; brisk; lively:思想～ dynamic thinking; untrammelled thinking; active mind /学术空气～ lively academic atmosphere /～的文化生活 active cultural life /市场～。Business is brisk. /会场空气顿时～了起来。The atmosphere in the meeting room became lively at once. /他长期以来一直～在新闻战线上。He has long been active on the journalistic front (*or* in the forefront of journalism). ❷ enliven; animate; invigorate; stimulate:发展经济,～市场 develop the economy and enliven the market /～农村经济 stimulate (*or* activate) the rural economy /～业余文娱生活 liven up spare-time cultural and recreational activities

活质 huózhì *also*"原生质" yuánshēngzhì bioplasm

活捉 huózhuō capture alive:～敌高级军官十五人。Fifteen senior enemy officers were captured alive.

活字 huózì 〈印刷〉movable type or letter; type font:～盘 type case; letter board

活字版 huózìbǎn movable type; original font

活字典 huózìdiǎn walking dictionary:老先生是有名的～,没有他不认识的字。The old man is noted as a walking dictionary, there is hardly any word he does not know.

活字合金 huózì héjīn *also*"铅字合金" qiānzì héjīn type metal

活字印刷 huózì yìnshuā movable-type printing; letter press

活组织检查 huózǔzhī jiǎnchá 〈医学〉biopsy

活罪 huózuì (endure) hardships, tortures, etc., while alive; bitter sufferings:生前受够了～ suffer great hardships in one's life /死罪可免,～难逃 exemptible from the death penalty but hardly from punishment

和 huó mix with water:～一点水泥把墙窟窿堵上。Prepare some cement to fill the hole on the wall.

see also hé; hè; hú; huò

和面 huómiàn mix flour with water; make or knead dough

和面机 huómiànjī flour-mixing machine; flour mixer

huǒ

火 huǒ ❶ fire:炉～ fire (in the stove) /篝～ camp fire /点～ make fire /着～ be on fire /放～ set fire to (a house, etc.); set (sth.) on fire /救～ fight a fire; engage in fire fighting /烤～ warm oneself by a fire /灭～ put out (*or* extinguish) a fire /纵～ commit arson /文～ slow (*or* soft) fire /微～ small fire /玩～ play with fire /刀耕～种 slash-and-burn cultivation /救～队 fire team; fire brigade /一场大～把他家烧得精光。His house was razed to the ground in a big fire. /战士们接受了血与～的洗礼。The soldiers went through the test of blood and fire. ❷ firearms; ammunition; firing; fire:军～ firearms and ammunition /交～ exchange fire; exchange shots; fire at each other /开～ open fire; fire /停～ stop firing; cease-fire /(枪)走～ (of firearms) discharge accidentally /战～ fire of war /炮～连天 gunfire licks the heavens ❸〈中医〉internal heat, one of the six causes of disease:上～ suffer from excessive internal heat /败～ relieve internal heat; relieve inflammation /肝～旺 rather irascible ❹ red as fire; fiery; flaming: *see*"～红";"～鸡" ❺ urgent; pressing:他风风～～地闯了进来。He butted in, in a feverish haste. ❻ anger;

H

temper:怒～(flames of) fury /发～ lose temper; get angry /窝～ simmering rage; pent-up fury /我一见孩子逃学就～了。I flared up (*or* flew into a rage) at the sight of my truant son. /此时此刻千万别惹他发～。You mustn't rub him up the wrong way just now. ❼ prosperous; thriving; flourishing:买卖红～。Business is brisk. ❽ *see* "伙" huǒ ❾ (Huǒ) a surname

火拔子 huǒbázi *also* "拔火罐儿" báhuǒguànr 〈方言〉〈中医〉cup

火把 huǒbǎ torch:点燃～ light a torch /举起～ hold up a torch /～游行 torchlight procession

火把节 Huǒbǎjié Torchlight Festival, traditionally observed by Yi (彝), Bai (白) and other national minorities in China towards the end of the 6th month of the lunar calendar

火伴 huǒbàn *also* "伙伴" huǒbàn partner

火棒 huǒbàng 〈杂技〉lighted torch:他可以同时抛接多至十六枝～。He can juggle up to sixteen lighted torches.

火暴 huǒbào *also* "火爆" 〈方言〉❶ fiery; impetuous:脾气～ have a fiery temper ❷ vigorous; exuberant; prosperous; exciting:日子过得越来越～。Our life is becoming more and more prosperous. /石榴花开得真～。The pomegranate is in full blossom. /这场戏的场面很～。The scene of the play is one of bustle and excitement.

火并 huǒbìng open fight between factions; open fight among partners, associates or confederates; intramural strife:～王伦 (of Wang's associates in the novel *Heroes of the Marshes*《水浒》) get rid of Wang Lun /昨天夜间的枪战原来是流氓团伙之间的～。The gunfire yesterday evening turned out to be a fight between two gangs.

火柴 huǒchái match:～盒 matchbox /～梗 match stick /～厂 match factory /擦～ strike a match

火场 huǒchǎng scene of a fire

火车 huǒchē train:～票 railway (*or* train) ticket /～时刻表 railway (*or* train) schedule; railway timetable /～司机 engine driver; (locomotive) engineer /～站 railway station /～站台 railway platform /～车厢 railway coach (*or* car) /电气～ electric locomotive /～卧铺 sleeping berth (in a train); couchette /乘～ go by train /～上交货价 free on rail; FOR /昨天有一列～出轨了。A train derailed yesterday.

火车轮渡 huǒchē lúndù train ferry

火车头 huǒchētóu ❶ (railway) engine; locomotive:这是一台老掉牙的蒸汽～。This is a steam engine that has become a museum piece. ❷ person or thing which plays a leading role:王队长是我们这个钻井队里不知疲倦的～。Director Wang, always working untiringly, has set a good example for everyone in the drilling team. /革命是历史的～。Revolution is the locomotive of history.

火成喷出岩 huǒchéng pēnchūyán 〈地质〉extrusive igneous rock

火成侵入岩 huǒchéng qīnrùyán 〈地质〉intrusive igneous rock

火成碎屑岩 huǒchéng suìxièyán 〈地质〉pyroclastic igneous rock

火成岩 huǒchéngyán 〈地质〉igneous rock; petrosilex

火炽 huǒchì vigorous; flourishing; bustling with noise and excitement:销售～ sell like hot pies /比赛到了最～的阶段。The race has reached the most exciting phase. *or* The competition has reached its peak. /他们厂的生产这两年搞得很～。Production has been growing vigorously in their factory in the last couple of years.

火冲冲 huǒchōngchōng impetuous; anxious; irritated; furious:她～地对我大声叫嚷。She yelled at me angrily.

火铳 huǒchòng firelock

火刀 huǒdāo 〈方言〉steel (for flint):～火石 flint and steel

火地岛 Huǒdìdǎo Tierra del Fuego, archipelago separated from the southern tip of South America by the Strait of Magellan

火电 huǒdiàn (short for 火力发电) thermal power; thermo-power generation

火电厂 huǒdiànchǎng thermal power plant; heat-engine plant

火电站 huǒdiànzhàn thermal power station:～设备 thermo-power generating equipment

火毒 huǒdú burning; scorching:～的太阳 scorching sun

火法冶金 huǒfǎ yějīn 〈冶金〉pyrometallurgy

火夫 huǒfū 〈旧语〉❶ fireman; stoker ❷ *also* "伙夫" huǒfū mess cook:他曾在军阀的军队里当过～。He once served as a cook in a warlord army.

火攻 huǒgōng attack with fire; fire attack:风高天旱宜～。High wind and dry weather are good conditions for launching a fire attack.

火钩子 huǒgōuzi fire hook; poker

火管锅炉 huǒguǎn guōlú 〈机械〉fire-tube boiler

火罐儿 huǒguànr 〈中医〉cupping jar or glass:拔～ cupping

火光 huǒguāng flame; blaze; firelight:～烛天。The flames lit up the sky. /～照得大地一片通红。The land was reddened by the blaze.

火锅 huǒguō chafing dish; hotpot; instant boiled dish:紫铜～ copper hotpot /四川～ Sichuan chafing dish /海鲜～ seafood chafing dish /涮～ have chafing dishes (*or* instant boiled dishes)

火海 huǒhǎi sea of fire:眼前一片～。There's a sea of fire before my eyes. *or* I saw nothing but fire.

火海刀山 huǒhǎi-dāoshān *also* "刀山火海" sea of flames and mountain of swords:刀山敢上,火海敢闯 dare to cross a mountain of swords and a sea of fire — ready to undergo any severe trials

火红 huǒhóng ❶ red as fire; fiery; flaming; scarlet:～的钢水 flaming molten steel /～的朝霞 fiery morning glow /～的晚霞 flaming red sunset /～的心〈比喻〉honest and warm heart /～的太阳在远方的地平线上沉下去了。The sun went down in flames on the far horizon. /春天的山坡上杜鹃花一片～。The hillsides in spring flamed with azaleas. ❷ prosperous; thriving:生意～ thriving (*or* brisk) business

火候 huǒhou ❶ duration and degree of heating, cooking, smelting, etc.:炼钢得看～。Steelmaking depends largely on the smelting duration and temperature. /这道菜的～恰到好处。This dish was done to a turn. /不到～不揭锅。Don't open the pot before it's properly done. *or* Don't do things prematurely. ❷ level of attainment:别看他人小,戏艺上已有相当～。Young as he is, he is quite accomplished in theatrical art. ❸ crucial moment:我们人手正紧,你来得是～。You've come at the right moment as we're short of hands.

火狐 huǒhú red fox

火呼呼 huǒhuhu breathe hard with anger; pant with fury

火花 huǒhuā ❶ spark:～飞溅 sparks flying off in all directions /冒出灿烂的～ burst forth in bright sparks /迸发出青春的～ beam with the vigour of youth /～放电 spark discharge ❷ matchbox picture:～收藏家 collector of matchbox pictures

火花室 huǒhuāshì 〈物理〉spark chamber; combustion chamber

火花塞 huǒhuāsāi 〈机械〉sparking plug; sparkplug; ignition plug

火化 huǒhuà cremate:～场 crematorium; crematory /～工 cremator /提倡～ encourage cremation /她的遗体将于后日～。Her remains will be cremated the day after tomorrow.

火浣布 huǒhuànbù asbestos cloth

火鸡 huǒjī turkey:雄～ turkey cock /雌～ turkey hen /小～ turkey pullet /美国感恩节主要吃～。Turkey is the main dish on Thanksgiving (Day) in the States.

火鸡舞 huǒjīwǔ turkeytrot

火急 huǒjí urgent; pressing:十万～ most urgent; extra-urgent /～文电 flash message /情况～,速作处理! It's most pressing. Immediate measures (shall) be taken!

火急火燎 huǒjí-huǒliǎo be extremely worried; be terribly anxious

火棘 huǒjí 〈植物〉fire-thorn

火祭 huǒjì 〈宗教〉agnihotra

火剪 huǒjiǎn ❶ *also* "火钳" fire-tongs; tongs ❷ (of hairdressing) curling tongs; curling irons

火碱 huǒjiǎn caustic soda

火箭 huǒjiàn rocket:发射～ fire (*or* launch) a rocket /～部队 rocket troops /～发射场 rocket launching site /～发射台 rocket launching pad /～发射架 rocket launching mount /～发射系统 rocket-firing system /～技术 rocketry /穿甲～ armour-piercing rocket /单级～ one-stage rocket /多级～ multi-stage rocket /捆绑式～ rocket with strap-on boosters /弹道～ ballistic rocket /液体燃料～ liquid-fuelled rocket /～固体推进剂 solid propellant (for rocket) /机载～ aircraft rocket /同温层～ stratospheric rocket /信号～ signal rocket /制动～ brake rocket; retro-rocket

火箭弹 huǒjiàndàn rocket; rocket projectile:穿甲～ armour-piercing rocket /反坦克～ antitank rocket

火箭干部 huǒjiàn gànbù cadre who has been skyrocketed to a high position; highflier

火箭炮 huǒjiànpào rocket gun

火箭筒 huǒjiàntǒng rocket launcher or projector; bazooka

火井 huǒjǐng gas well

火警 huǒjǐng fire alarm:～灯 firewarning light /～电话 fire number /～系统 fire alarm system /～装置 pull station /～自动警报器 pyrostat

火镜 huǒjìng convex lens

火酒 huǒjiǔ 〈方言〉(ethyl) alcohol

火居道士 huǒjū dàoshi one who practises Taoism at home
火具 huǒjù *also* "火工品" ignition apparatus or equipment
火炬 huǒjù torch; torchlight: ～赛跑 torch race / ～游行 torchlight parade / ～接力赛 torch relay race / 奥运会～交接仪式 hand-over ceremony of the Olympic torch
火炬计划 Huǒjù Jìhuà Torch Programme, a plan to develop new and high technology
火炕 huǒkàng heated *kang*; heated brick bed: 睡～对治风湿性关节炎有好处。The heated brick bed is good for rheumatoid arthritis.
火坑 huǒkēng fiery pit; pit of hell; abyss of suffering: 推入～ push sb. into an abyss of suffering / 我们要设法把她救出～。We must try all we can to get her out of that living hell.
火口 huǒkǒu 〈地质〉 crater: ～底 crater floor
火口湖 huǒkǒuhú crater lake
火筷子 huǒkuàizi fire-tongs; tongs
火辣辣 huǒlālā ❶ burning; scorching: ～的骄阳 scorching sun ❷ hurt; burn: 我脖子上的伤口～地作痛。The wound in my neck hurts badly. / 碘酒涂在伤口上引起～的疼痛。The iodine burns on the wound. ❸ anxious; thrilled; flushed: 他心里～, 差点儿不能自制。He was burning with anxiety, almost beside himself. / 她羞得不敢抬头, 脸上～的。She blushed scarlet, without the courage to look up. ❹ (of a person, character, etc.) bold and resolute; (of language) acerbic; sharp: ～的批评 sharp criticism / 她～的性格, 敢说敢干。Bold and resolute, she is unafraid in her words and actions.
火老鸦 huǒlǎoyā 〈方言〉 leaping flames; tongues of fire: ～闪电般窜上一垛干草, 顷刻间便烧为灰烬。The flames darted onto a rick of straw, and burnt it to ashes in no time.
火犁 huǒlí 〈方言〉 tractor
火力 huǒlì ❶ thermal power ❷ 〈军事〉 firepower; fire: ～控制 control of fire; fire control / ～配系 organization of fire; fire system / ～突击 fire assault / ～网 network of fire; fire net / ～掩护 fire cover / ～侦察 reconnaissance by firing / ～支援 supporting fire; fire support / 集中～ concentrate the fire (on) / 交叉～ cross-fire / ～分散 fire dispersion / ～基地 fire base / ～伏击 fire ambush ❸ cold-resistant capacity of the human body: 年轻人～旺。Young people could better resist cold.
火力点 huǒlìdiǎn *also* "发射点" fāshèdiǎn firing point: ～隐蔽在山洞里。The firing points were hidden in caves.
火力发电 huǒlì fādiàn thermo-power generation: ～厂 thermal power station (*or* plant) / ～设备 thermo-power generating equipment
火力圈 huǒlìquān field of fire: 敌军完全进入了我～之内。All enemy troops had entered our field of fire.
火力群 huǒlìqún (dense) concentration of firing positions
火镰 huǒlián steel (for flint): 他打着了～。He made a fire by striking the steel on the flint.
火亮 huǒliàng ❶ 〈方言〉 spark: 炉子里一点～也没有了。All sparks died out in the stove. ❷ bright; illuminated
火烈鸟 huǒlièniǎo flamingo
火流星 huǒliúxīng 〈天文〉 bolide; fireball
火龙 huǒlóng ❶ fiery dragon — lantern or torchlight procession: 大堤上的灯笼火把宛如一条～。The lanterns and torchlights on the dike looked like a fiery dragon. ❷ 〈方言〉 air channel (from brick kitchen stove to chimney); flue ❸ 〈方言〉 red spider ❹ red wheat mite
火笼 huǒlóng 〈方言〉 basketed heater; basketed firepan; brazier
火炉 huǒlú *also* "火炉子" (heating) stove: ～用具 fire irons
火轮船 huǒlúnchuán *also* "火轮" 〈旧语〉 steamship; steamer
火冒三丈 huǒmào-sānzhàng fly into a rage; fly into a towering passion; flare up: 你的行为真叫我～。Your acts made my blood boil.
火帽 huǒmào 〈军事〉 detonating cap; percussion cap
火煤 huǒméi *also* "火媒" firelighter; kindling: 抽水烟斗离不开～。A paper spill is needed to light a water pipe.
火门 huǒmén 〈军事〉 vent; nipple
火棉 huǒmián guncotton; pyroxylin
火苗 huǒmiáo *also* "火苗子" tongue of flame; flame: 炉子里的～直往上窜。The flames darted up in the stove.
火磨 huǒmò power driven mill; electric mill
火泥 huǒní fire clay
火捻 huǒniǎn ❶ firelighter; kindling ❷ fuse: 别把鞭炮的～子弄湿了。Don't get the firecrackers' fuses wet.
火奴鲁鲁 Huǒnúlǔlǔ *also* "檀香山" Tánxiāngshān Honolulu, capital and principal port of Hawaii, USA
火炮 huǒpào cannon; gun; artillery piece: ～发射阵地 gun position
火盆 huǒpén fire pan; brazier: 南方人冬天取暖常用～。In the south, a brazier is commonly used for heating in winter.
火票 huǒpiào 〈旧语〉 urgent dispatch (sent from capital to province during the Qing Dynasty)
火拼 huǒpīn *see* "火并"
火漆 huǒqī *also* "封蜡" fēnglà sealing wax: ～印 wax seal / 用～加封 seal a letter with wax; be wax sealed
火气 huǒqì ❶ anger; temper: 你的～真大。You really have a bad temper. / 他实在压不住心头的～。He tried in vain to hold back his anger. ❷ heat in human body; cold-resistant capacity: 年轻人～足。Young people are full of vim and vigour. ❸ 〈中医〉 internal heat: ～盛 have high internal heat / 败～ reduce internal heat
火器 huǒqì 〈军事〉 firearm
火钳 huǒqián *also* "火剪" fire-tongs; tongs; fire-poker
火枪 huǒqiāng firelock: 他常年使用这枝～打猎。He hunted with this firelock all year round.
火墙 huǒqiáng ❶ wall with flues for space heating; hot wall ❷ fire net: 交叉火力形成一道难以跨越的～。The crossfire formed an impenetrable wall of fire.
火情 huǒqíng state of a fire: ～严重。The losses caused by the fire are very serious.
火球 huǒqiú fireball
火雀 huǒquè fire finch
火热 huǒrè ❶ burning hot: 太阳～～的, 路上没有一个人。The sun was scorching, and there was not a soul in sight on the road. ❷ fervent; fiery; passionate: ～的恋情 passionate love / ～的眼光 fiery eyes / ～的欲望 fervent (*or* passionate) desire ❸ intimate: 打得～ carry on intimately (with sb.); be as thick as thieves / 谈得～ be in the middle of an intimate conversation ❹ fierce; intense: ～的斗争 fierce fight
火绒 huǒróng kindling fibre; tinder: ～盒 tinderbox
火绒草 huǒróngcǎo edelweiss (*Leontopodium alpinum*)
火肉 huǒròu 〈方言〉 ham
火伞高张 huǒsǎn-gāozhāng scorching sunlight in summer
火色 huǒsè 〈方言〉 condition of fire; duration and degree of heating, cooking, smelting, etc.; strength of fire: 拿稳～ make sure that the fire is just right
火山 huǒshān volcano: 活～ active volcano / 死～ extinct volcano / 休眠～ dormant volcano / ～喷发 volcanic eruption / ～作用 volcanism
火山岛 huǒshāndǎo volcanic island
火山地震 huǒshān dìzhèn volcanic earthquake
火山湖 huǒshānhú crater lake
火山灰 huǒshānhuī volcanic ash; cinerite; tephra: ～暴 ash shower / ～层 volcanic ash bed
火山口 huǒshānkǒu crater
火山砾 huǒshānlì lapillus
火山熔岩 huǒshān róngyán lava
火山学 huǒshānxué volcanology
火山岩 huǒshānyán volcanic rock
火山渣 huǒshānzhā cinder; scoria; slag: ～沉积 cinderite / ～块 blob of slag; lump of slag
火山锥 huǒshānzhuī (volcanic) cone
火伤 huǒshāng burn (caused by fire)
火上加油 huǒshàng-jiāyóu *also* "火上浇油" pour oil on the fire; add fuel to the flames: 他怒气未消, 你这几句话正好～。He was still in a rage and you chose this moment to pour oil on the flames.
火烧火燎 huǒshāo-huǒliǎo 〈比喻〉 ❶ feel terribly hot; feel very painful: 肩上的伤口～地疼。The wound in the shoulder ached terribly. ❷ be restless with anxiety: 急得他心里～的。He was restless with anxiety.
火烧眉毛 huǒshāo-méimao the fire is singeing the eyebrows — extremely urgent; pressing: 这是～的事, 得赶快办才行。This is a matter of utmost urgency, so we must hurry up.
火烧油层 huǒshāo yóucéng 〈石油〉 combustion (of oil) *in situ*
火烧云 huǒshāoyún morning glow; evening glow; crimson clouds at sunrise or sunset
火烧 huǒshao ❶ destroy by fire; burn ❷ baked wheaten cake: 糖～ sweet baked cake / 卤煮～ baked cake in meat soup
火舌 huǒshé tongues of fire; licking flame: 炉子吐出的～蹿得老高老高的。The tongues of fire in the stove flicked (*or* shot, *or*

darted) high up.
火绳 huǒshéng kindling rope; rope of plaited plants burnt as a mosquito repellent: ～枪 harquebus; matchlock
火石 huǒshí ❶ flint ❷ artificial flint: 打火机的～要换了。The cigarette lighter needs a new flint.
火势 huǒshì intensity or state of fire; fire: 风助～，火借风威，越烧越大。As the wind blew, the fire grew wilder and wilder.
火势 huǒshi bustling; exciting; thrilling: 晚会开得挺～的。The evening party was full of fun and excitement.
火树石 huǒshùshí flint
火树银花 huǒshù-yínhuā fiery trees and silver flowers — display of fireworks and a sea of lanterns (on a festival night); brilliantly lighted place: 国庆之夜，天安门前～，绚丽多姿，吸引了成千上万的游人。On the night of the National Day, tens of thousands of people were attracted by the display of fireworks and sea of lanterns in front of Tian An Men.
火速 huǒsù at top speed; posthaste: ～电告 cable back immediately /～前往 go there posthaste /～向前线增援 rush up (*or* speed) reinforcements to the front
火损 huǒsǔn fire damage
火炭 huǒtàn live charcoal; burning wood
火塘 huǒtáng 〈方言〉 fire pit: ～里只剩下一点儿余火。There were only some embers left in the fire pit.
火烫 huǒtàng ❶ burning hot; boiling hot; fiery: ～～的前额 fiery forehead /水泥混凝土路面被炎日晒得～。The concrete road surface was burning hot under the scorching sun. ❷ have one's hair permed with hot curling tongs
火头 huǒtóu ❶ flame; fire: ～太小，该添燃料了。The fire is too low and needs to be replenished. ❷ duration and temperature of heating, smelting, cooking, etc.: ～不到，菜就不够味儿。Dishes won't taste good if not cooked for the right time and at the right temperature. ❸ place where a fire started: ～在三楼。The fire started somewhere on the 2nd (*or* 3rd) floor. ❹ fit of anger; blaze of anger; flare-up: 你先压压～，有话再说。Hold (*or* Control) your temper before you speak.
火头军 huǒtóujūn 〈戏谑〉 army cook; mess sergeant
火头上 huǒtóushang at the height of one's anger: 他正在～，别理他! Leave him alone. He is having a fit.
火腿 huǒtuǐ ham; gammon: 云南～ Yunnan ham /金华～ Jinhua ham /～月饼 ham-stuffed moon cake
火腿蛋 huǒtuǐdàn ham and egg
火网 huǒwǎng *also* "火力网" 〈军事〉 cross fire; interlocking pattern of fire
火卫 Huǒwèi (short for 火星卫星) 〈天文〉 Martian satellite: ～二 Deimos, smaller and slower satellite of Mars /～一 Phobos, inner satellite of Mars
火匣子 huǒxiázi 〈方言〉 coffin (of inferior quality and painted red)
火险 huǒxiǎn ❶ fire insurance: 保～ buy fire insurance ❷ fire danger: ～预警仪 fire-danger meter /～季节 fire season
火线 huǒxiàn ❶ battle line; frontline; battlefield; firing line: ～救护 frontline first aid /上～ go to the front /～立功 render meritorious service in the battlefield /轻伤不下～ remain at the front with minor wounds /他上过～，打过仗。He has fought at the battlefront. ❷ 〈电学〉 live wire; power line
火巷 huǒxiàng narrow strip of open space between houses; firebreak
火硝 huǒxiāo 〈化学〉 nitre; saltpetre: ～纸 touch paper
火蝎子 huǒxiēzi 〈方言〉 young scorpion
火星 huǒxīng ❶ (Huǒxīng) 〈天文〉 Mars: ～人 Martian /～探测器 Mars probe /～大气层 Mars atmosphere ❷ spark: ～四溅 shower of sparks; throwing off sparks in all directions /发出～ emit sparks /打出～ strike out sparks /她气得两眼直冒～。She was simply furious (*or* mad with anger).
火星卫星 Huǒxīng wèixīng Martian satellite
火星学 huǒxīngxué areology
火刑 huǒxíng execution by fire; the stake: 处以～ condemn (sb.) to the stake
火性 huǒxìng *also* "火性子" hot or quick temper: 他是个～子，一点就着。He has a quick temper and flares up at the slightest irritation.
火眼 huǒyǎn 〈医学〉 pinkeye: 害～ have pinkeye
火眼金睛 huǒyǎn-jīnjīng piercing eye; penetrating insight: 他有一对专门识别真假的～。He is a man of penetrating insight, capable of telling the true from the false.
火焰 huǒyàn *also* "火苗" flame: ～层 zone of flame /～切割 flame cutting /～中心 flame kernel /扑不灭的～ unquenchable fire /熊熊的～ blazing flames /她心中的爱情～被重新点燃了。The flames of love were rekindled in her heart.
火焰光度计 huǒyàn guāngdùjì flame photometer
火焰光谱 huǒyàn guāngpǔ flame spectrum
火焰喷射器 huǒyàn pēnshèqì flamethrower
火药 huǒyào gunpowder; powder: 黑～ charcoal gunpowder /～棉 guncotton /～库 powder magazine /～是我国古代四大发明之一。Gunpowder is one of the four great inventions in ancient China.
火药桶 huǒyàotǒng powder keg; danger spot: 坐在～上 sit on a powder keg /东南欧的～ danger spot of southeastern Europe
火药味 huǒyàowèi smell of gunpowder: 充满了～儿 have a strong smell of gunpowder; be bellicose /不知怎么搞的，他这两天说话总带点儿～。I wonder why his speech smacks so heavily of gunpowder these days.
火蚁 huǒyǐ fire ant
火疫 huǒyì 〈农业〉 fire blast
火因 huǒyīn cause of fire: 调查～ investigate into the cause of a fire
火引子 huǒyǐnzi material for starting a fire
火印 huǒyìn mark made by burning; brand: 盖～ burn a mark on; mark with brand /这些马身上都有我家的～。These horses have my family's brand on them.
火油 huǒyóu 〈方言〉 kerosene
火源 huǒyuán source of combustion; fire starter; that which may start a fire
火灾 huǒzāi fire (as a disaster); conflagration: 毁灭性的～ devastating fire; fatal fire /森林～ forest fire /～保险 fire insurance /～监测 fire monitoring /～探测设备 fire detection equipment /这场～的起因是自燃。The cause of the fire is spontaneous combustion.
火葬 huǒzàng cremation: ～炉 cremator
火葬场 huǒzàngchǎng crematorium; crematory
火躁 huǒzào 〈方言〉 hot-tempered; impetuous; fire-eating: 此人性情～。He is a fire-eater.
火针 huǒzhēn *also* "燔针" fánzhēn; "淬针" cuìzhēn; "烧针" shāozhēn 〈中医〉 hot-needle acupuncture: ～疗法 red-hot needle therapy /～术 ignipuncture
火蜘蛛 huǒzhīzhū 〈方言〉 red spider
火纸 huǒzhǐ ❶ nitropaper; touch paper ❷ 〈方言〉 paper burnt at a memorial ceremony for the dead
火中取栗 huǒzhōng-qǔlì pull chestnuts out of the fire; be a cat's paw: 利用别人替你～ use others as your cat's paw
火种 huǒzhǒng kindling material; kindling; tinder: 科学～ sparks of science /播下革命的～ sow the seeds of revolution
火烛 huǒzhú anything that may cause a fire: 小心～! Be careful about fires!
火主 huǒzhǔ resident of a house where a fire started; person responsible for the starting of a fire
火柱 huǒzhù column of fire: ～冲天。The flames shot up into the sky.
火箸 huǒzhù 〈方言〉 fire-tongs; tongs
火砖 huǒzhuān firebrick; furnace brick

钬

huǒ 〈化学〉 holmium (Ho)
钬激光器 huǒjīguāngqì holmium laser

伙[1](火)

huǒ mess; board; meals; food: 包～制 meals at a fixed rate; board /搭～ eat regularly in a mess (*or* family) /单独开～ cook one's own food (*or* meals); do one's own cooking /在单位入～ board at the canteen of one's unit

伙[2](火、夥)

huǒ ❶ partner; mate: 他们是同～。They are partners. ❷ partnership; company: 自愿入～ enter into partnership on a voluntary basis /成群结～ band together; in throngs; in crowds /三人合～办了一家公司，两三年后又散了～。The three of them set up a firm in partnership, but parted company a couple of years later. ❸ 〈量词〉 group (of people); band; gang: 一～青年人 a group of young people /一～强盗 a band of robbers /三个一

群，五个一～ in twos and threes; in small groups ❹ combine; join; club: 他们两人合～办了一家小吃店。The two of them clubbed together to start a snack bar. /几户农民～买了一台拖拉机。Several peasants pooled their money and bought a tractor.

伙伴 huǒbàn partner; companion; pal: 小～们一起唱歌跳舞。The young pals sang and danced together.

伙犯 huǒfàn accomplice: ～证词 testimony of an accomplice

伙房 huǒfáng kitchen (in a school, factory, etc.): 他定期到～去帮厨。He helps with the preparation of food in the kitchen regularly.

伙夫 huǒfū *also* "火夫" huǒfū 〈旧语〉 mess cook

伙耕 huǒgēng club to cultivate; cultivate as partners

伙计 huǒji ❶ partner; business associate ❷〈旧语〉 hired hand; salesman: 给地主家当～ work as a hired hand for a landlord /他曾在一家绸布店当过几年～。He was hired as a salesman by a silk store for several years. ❸〈口语〉 fellow; mate: ～，搭个手! Give me a hand, mate!

伙食 huǒshi mess; food; meals; board: ～费 board expenses; money spent on meals /～补助 food allowance (*or* subsidies) /～节余 mess savings /～管理 mess management /～尾子 mess savings /这里的～很好。The food here is very good.

伙食科 huǒshikē mess section; catering office

伙食团 huǒshituán mess

伙同 huǒtóng act in league or collusion with; gang up with: 他～会计贪污公款。He embezzled public money in collusion with the accountant. /他们～坏人扰乱社会治安。They ganged up with bad elements to disrupt law and order.

伙友 huǒyǒu partner; companion; mate

伙种 huǒzhòng *see* "伙耕"

伙子 huǒzi group; band; gang: 他们是一～! They are of the same gang! /他们是一～地痞流氓! They are a band of thugs.

夥[1]

huǒ 〈书面〉 much; many; a great deal of; numerous: 成绩甚～ numerous achievements

夥[2]

huǒ partnership; company: 搭～ work in company; form a partnership

huò

豁

huò ❶ open; clear; open-minded; generous: 开～ open and clear; broad-visioned; open-minded /显～ clear; obvious; manifest; distinct /醒～ clear; explicit; manifest ❷ exempt; remit: ～其赔偿 exempt from compensation

see also huá; huō

豁达 huòdá be generous and open-minded: 心胸～ be open-minded and magnanimous

豁达大度 huòdá-dàdù be bighearted and open-minded: 此人～，有将帅之才。Fair and magnanimous, he is a born commander.

豁朗 huòlǎng sanguine; optimistic; cheerful: 面对一望无际的大草原，他觉得心里格外～。Standing on the prairie that stretched to the horizon, he felt especially light-hearted and cheerful.

豁亮 huòliàng ❶ roomy and bright; open and clear: ～的大厅 spacious and bright hall /听了他的一席话，心里顿觉～了许多。I felt quite enlightened by his words. ❷ (of one's voice) loud and clear; sonorous; resonant: 嗓音～ have a sonorous voice

豁免 huòmiǎn exempt (sb. from sth.); remit; make immune: ～捐税 exempt sb. from taxes; remit taxes /放弃～ waive immunity /档案～ immunity of archives /关税～ immunity from duties /捐税～ immunity from taxation; tax exemption(s) /民事管辖～ immunity from civil jurisdiction /行政管辖～ immunity from administrative jurisdiction /刑事管辖～ immunity from criminal jurisdiction /刑事责任～ immunity from criminal liability /诉讼～ immunity from suit /司法程序～ immunity from judicial process /外交～权 diplomatic immunity /外交房舍～ immunity of diplomatic premises /有限制～ restrictive immunity /无限制～ unqualified immunity /职能～ functional immunity /主权～ sovereign immunity /住所～ immunity of the domicile /作证～ immunity from giving testimony /～法 immunity act /～区 exempt zone /联合王国国家～法 United Kingdom State Immunity Act /美国外国主权～法 United States Foreign Sovereign Immunity Act

豁然 huòrán clear; open; thorough: ～大悟 be fully awakened /～开悟 be thoroughly enlightened

豁然贯通 huòrán-guàntōng see the whole thing in a clear light: 反复细读十来遍，忽然～，竟悟出其中的道理来。I read it carefully a dozen times and, all of a sudden, came to realize it all and got the point.

豁然开朗 huòrán-kāilǎng see the light clearly; be fully enlightened: 穿过弯弯曲曲的山洞，眼前～，竟是一片没有见过的胜境。Having zigzagged through the cave, I found myself in a bright open space, a charming scene I had never seen before. /读了这本书，心里～，对前途有了信心。After reading the book, I felt fully enlightened and became confident about the future.

祸(禍)

huò ❶ misfortune; disaster; calamity: 灾～ disaster; calamity; misfortune /战～ scourge of war /天灾人～ natural and man-made calamities /车～ road (*or* traffic, *or* car) accident /大～临头 imminent catastrophe /惨～ horrible disaster; frightful calamity /横～ unexpected calamity; sudden misfortune /惹～ ask for (*or* invite) trouble; court disaster /嫁～于人 shift the misfortune onto others; put the blame on sb. else ❷ bring disaster upon; ruin; injure; damage: ～及百姓 play (*or* wreak) havoc among the people

祸不单行 huòbùdānxíng misfortunes never come singly; when sorrows come, they come not single spies; mishaps always come in battalions; it never rains but it pours: 俗话说，福无双至，～。As the saying goes, happiness comes alone while misfortune loves company.

祸不妄至 huòbùwàngzhì woes never come without reason; disaster never strikes without cause

祸不旋踵 huòbùxuánzhǒng misfortune is not far off; trouble is brewing; danger is imminent

祸从口出 huòcóngkǒuchū misfortunes come from the mouth; disaster results from careless talk; a loose tongue is a source of evil: 病从口入，～。Disease goes in by the mouth and disaster comes out of it.

祸从天降 huòcóngtiānjiàng disaster comes like a bolt from the sky

祸端 huòduān 〈书面〉 source of the disaster; cause of ruin

祸福无门 huò-fú wúmén disaster or happiness knows no doors — one brings it upon oneself

祸根 huògēn root of trouble; cause of ruin; apple of discord; bane: 铲除～ root out (*or* uproot, *or* eradicate) the source of disaster /边界问题是两国不和的～。The boundary question was the apple of discord between the two countries. /他的小聪明成了～。His petty smartness proved a curse to him.

祸国殃民 huòguó-yāngmín wreck the country and ruin the people; cause grave harm to the state and the people: ～的卖国贼 traitor who has brought calamity to the nation

祸害 huòhai ❶ disaster; calamity; ruin: 引起～ cause a misfortune; bring ruin /眼病是当地居民的一大～。Eye diseases have always been a major trouble among the local inhabitants. ❷ bane; curse; scourge: 这小子是个～，早晚要出点事。He is such a scourge. He'll cause trouble sooner or later. ❸ damage; destroy; ruin: 牲口～了大片庄稼。The cattle have damaged a large stretch of crops. /自己走邪路，还要～别人。Not only is he leading a depraved life but he is also ruining others.

祸患 huòhuàn disaster; calamity; trouble: ～频仍 successive calamities /～不断 incessant disasters /～无穷 endless trouble /极大的～ grave curse

祸乱 huòluàn disaster and turmoil; calamity and chaos: 连年～，民不聊生。The people lived in dire poverty through calamities over the years.

祸起萧墙 huòqǐ-xiāoqiáng troubles start from within the family; misfortunes befall the house from within its walls; there is internal strife afoot

祸事 huòshì disaster; calamity; mishap: 家里出了大～。A grave disaster has fallen on the family.

祸首 huòshǒu chief culprit: 罪魁～ chief offender; ringleader; arch criminal: 二次大战的～ chief culprit of World War II

祸水 huòshuǐ person (esp. a woman) or thing that brings trouble; bane; peril: 旧社会常把女人叫做～。In the old society women were often called the "bane of men". /他们想把～引向东方。They tried to divert the peril to the east.

祸祟 huòsuì 〈迷信〉 ghost-afflicted disaster

H

祸胎 huòtāi root of trouble; cause of disaster: 埋下～ sow the seeds of misfortune
祸兮福所倚，福兮祸所伏 huò xī fú suǒ yǐ, fú xī huò suǒ fú also "祸福倚伏" good fortune lieth within bad, bad fortune lurketh within good; from sorrow comes happiness, in happiness lurks sorrow
祸心 huòxīn evil intent: 包藏～ harbour malicious intentions /～毕露 betray one's evil intent
祸殃 huòyāng disaster; calamity; scourge; curse: 招致～ court (or invite) disaster
祸种 huòzhǒng source of trouble; cause of disaster

霍 huò ❶ suddenly; quickly ❷ (Huò) a surname
霍地 huòdì suddenly: ～闪开 dodge quickly /～冲了出去 dash (or rush) out all of a sudden
霍尔木兹海峡 Huò'ěrmùzī Hǎixiá Strait of Hormuz, a strait separating Iran from the Arabian Peninsula and linking the Persian Gulf with the Gulf of Oman
霍霍 huòhuò ❶〈象声〉sound of grinding knives, etc.: 磨刀～向牛羊 sharpen one's knife to slaughter cattle /镰刀磨得～作响。The sickle scraped on the whetstone. ❷ flash: 电光～。The lightning flashed. /他两眼～闪光。His eyes flashed (or sparkled).
霍拉舞 huòlāwǔ hora, lively Romanian and Israeli folk dance
霍乱 huòluàn ❶〈医学〉cholera: 流行性～ epidemic cholera /轻性～ cholerine /假～ cholera morbus /～疫苗 cholera vaccine /正在流行～。Cholera is (running) rampant at the moment. ❷〈中医〉acute gastroenteritis
霍奇金氏病 huòqíjīnshìbìng also "淋巴网状细胞瘤" línbā wǎngzhuàng xìbāoliú〈医学〉Hodgkin's disease; lymphoreticuloma
霍去病 Huò Qùbìng Huo Qubing (140-117 BC), general of the Western Han Dynasty
霍然 huòrán ❶ suddenly; quickly: ～云消。Quickly the clouds dispersed. /远方～打过一道闪电。All of a sudden, lightning flashed in the distance. ❷〈书面〉(of an illness) be cured quickly: 一剂中药，病体～而愈。The patient got well quickly after one dose of Chinese herbal medicine.
霍闪 huòshǎn〈方言〉lightning: 一道～从半空中打下。A lightning bolt shot down from the sky.

藿 huò〈书面〉leaves of pulse plants
藿香 huòxiāng〈中药〉wrinkled giant hyssop (*Agastache rugosus*)

嚯 huò ❶〈叹词〉oh; wow: ～，你穿这套衣服真漂亮！Oh, how smart you look in this suit! /～！真是天下第一神射手！Wow! He's really the best marksman I've ever seen! ❷〈象声〉: ～～大笑 guffaw /他～地站了起来。He jumped to his feet like a flash.

H

臛 huò〈书面〉meat soup

獾 huò
獾狮狓 huòjiāpí〈动物〉okapi

嚄 huò〈书面〉❶ shout or laugh loudly: 他～的一声喝起彩来。He cheered loudly. ❷〈叹词〉(showing surprise) oh; wow: ～，好凉的水呀！Wow! Such cold water!
see also huō; ǒ

蠖 huò see "尺蠖" chǐhuò

镬 huò ❶〈方言〉pot; pan; boiler ❷〈古语〉huge pot; cauldron: 斧锯鼎～ hatchet, saw, cooking tripod and cauldron — ancient instruments of torture
镬子 huòzi〈方言〉pot; pan; boiler; cauldron

雘 huò〈书面〉red or black mineral paint; high-quality colours

获(❶❷獲、❸穫) huò ❶ capture; catch; seize: 捕～ seize one's prey; capture /破～ uncover; unearth /拿～ apprehend (a criminal) /俘～敌军 capure enemy soldiers /查～走私物品 seize smuggled goods /抓～逃犯 arrest (or apprehand) an escaped convict ❷ get; obtain; win: ～冠军 win the championship (or gold medal) /如～至宝 as if one had found sth. priceless ❸ harvest; reap: 收～晚稻 harvest (or gather in) the late rice /收～量 harvest yield
获得 huòdé get; gain; acquire; win: ～满足 get satisfaction /～金质奖章 win a gold medal /～巨大成就 score great achievements; achieve great success /～经济效益 gain economic benefits /～博士学位 obtain (or get, or receive) a doctoral degree /～观众好评 win acclaim from the audience /～经验 acquire (or gain) experience /～全胜 sweep the board /早稻～了丰收。We had a bumper harvest of early rice. /罪犯在狱中～了新生。The criminal got a new lease of life in the penitentiary.
获得性 huòdéxìng〈生物〉acquired character
获得性免疫 huòdéxìng miǎnyì acquired immunity
获得性免疫缺损综合征 huòdéxìng miǎnyì quēsǔn zōnghézhēng (popularly known as 艾滋病) acquired immune deficiency syndrome (AIDS)
获奖 huòjiǎng win a prize; receive an award: ～电影 prize-winning film
获救 huòjiù be saved; be rescued: 溺水的孩子～了。The drowning child was rescued.
获利 huòlì earn profit; make a profit: ～年度 profit-making year /他每卖一件衣服～五十元。He obtained a profit of 50 *yuan* for each dress sold.
获取 huòqǔ acquire; obtain; gain; win: ～知识 acquire knowledge /～养分 obtain nourishment /～荣誉和地位 gain fame and position
获胜 huòshèng win; be victorious; triumph: 上海队以五比一～。The Shanghai team won the match five to one. /今年以来我们首次～。This was our first win this year.
获胜率 huòshènglǜ average of wins
获释 huòshì be released; be set free; be freed: ～出狱 be released from the jail /有两名战犯提前～。Two war criminals got off before their sentences expired.
获悉 huòxī learn (of an event); get to know: ～您即将归国，我们无比欣喜。We were all elated to learn that you are coming back from abroad.
获知 huòzhī see "获悉"
获致 huòzhì see "获得"
获准 huòzhǔn secure approval; get permission: 开业申请业已～。Our application for opening the business has been approved (or granted). /经过一番口头交涉，我们～参观某空军基地。After some verbal representations, we obtained permission to visit the airbase.

或 huò ❶ perhaps; maybe; probably: 马上动身，～能赶上末班车。Set out right now and you'll probably be able to catch the last train. ❷ or; either... or...: 你～他，谁都可以。You or he, either will do. /～你来，～我去，怎么都行。Either you come over, or I go to your place, as you please. ❸〈书面〉somebody; some one; some people: ～曰 it is said that...; some say /人固有一死，～重于泰山，～轻于鸿毛。Man will die sooner or later, but some deaths are as heavy as Mt. Tai, and some are as light as a feather. ❹〈书面〉slightly; a little bit: 不可～缓 cannot wait any longer; cannot be postponed at all; brook no delay
或…或… huò…huò… or; either... or...: 或去或留 go or stay /或胜或负 either win or lose /或高或矮 tall or short; high or low /或早或晚 whether early or late /或迟或早 sooner or later
或然 huòrán probably: ～性 probability /～误差 probable error
或然率 huòránlǜ also "概率" gàilǜ probability
或许 huòxǔ perhaps; maybe; probably: 他～将要退休。Perhaps he will retire. /快点走！我们～还能赶上他。Hurry up! We may be able to catch up with him. /他～来，～不来。He may or may not come.
或则 huòzé or; either... or...: 每天清晨公园里都有很多人锻炼，～跑步，～打拳，～练气功，～跳舞，有趣极了。It is interesting to watch lots of people doing exercises in the park early in the morning. They either go jogging, practise boxing, work on *qigong*, or dance.
或者 huòzhě ❶ perhaps; maybe: 你的建议～对改进工作有所助益。Your suggestion may prove to be of help in improving our management. ❷ or; either... or...: ～赞成，～反对，～弃权，你必须表明态度。For, against, or abstain — you must take a stand.

惑 huò ❶ be puzzled; be bewildered: 惶～ perplexed and alarmed; apprehensive /困～不解 be greatly puzzled ❷ delude; mis-

lead:妖言～众 spread fallacies to hoodwink people /蛊～人心 confuse and poison people's minds; resort to demagogy /诱～青少年犯罪 seduce teenagers into committing crimes

惑乱 huòluàn confuse; befuddle:～人心 confuse people's minds

惑然 huòrán puzzled; bewildered:～不解 feel quite puzzled; feel confused

惑众 huòzhòng delude or confuse people:造谣～ fabricate rumours to mislead people

鱤 huò a genus of sea fish

和[1] huò mix; blend:～面 mix flour with water; prepare dough /水泥里～点沙子 mix sand into cement /把白糖、面粉和鸡蛋～在一起。Blend sugar, flour and eggs (together).

和[2] huò 〈量词〉(number of) rinses;〈中医〉(ordinal number of) boilings:床单已经洗了三～。The bed-sheet has been given three rinses. /一剂药要煮两～。Each dosage of herbal medicine should be boiled twice. /头～药跟二～药装在一起分三次喝。The first two decoctions should be mixed and divided into three doses.

see also hé; hè; hú; huó

和弄 huònong 〈方言〉❶ mix; blend; play with:小家伙在地上～沙子玩。The little child played with sand on the ground. ❷ sow discord:肯定有人在中间～。Someone must have deliberately driven a wedge between us.

和稀泥 huò xīní 〈比喻〉try to paper things over; mediate differences at the sacrifice of principle; patch things up:这个人不错,就是有时爱～。He is a good man, except that he sometimes tries to paper over differences.

货 huò ❶ currency; money:通～ currency /硬通～ hard currency ❷ goods; commodity; product:国～ home (*or* domestically) produced goods; domestic products /山～ mountain products; household utensils made of wood, bamboo, clay, etc. /现～ merchandise on hand; spots; goods in stock /缺～ in short supply; out of stock /洋～ foreign goods /次～ inferior goods /年～ special purchases (*or* goods) for the Chinese Spring Festival /鲜～ fresh fruit (*or* vegetables); fresh aquatic food /大路～ popular goods; ordinary products /小百～ small articles of daily use /交～ deliver goods /接～ receive goods /理～ tally goods /盘～ taking stock; stock-taking /点～ count (*or* check) goods /卸～ discharge (cargo); unload /～好客自来。First-rate goods advertise themselves. *or* Good wine needs no bush. ❸〈粗话〉*used in reference to a person*:好吃懒做的～ lazybones /蠢～! Blockhead! *or* Idiot! /骚～! Bitch! *or* Whore! /贱～! Whore! *or* Slut! ❹〈书面〉sell:～卖 sell

货比三家 huòbǐsānjiā comparison of different offers:如今买东西要～。One should compare the prices at various shops (*or* suppliers) before buying something.

货币 huòbì money; currency:～浮动 currency float /～信用 confidence in the currency /～信用危机 monetary and credit crisis /～理论 monetary theory /～发行 issuance of paper money /储备～ reserve currency /法定～ legal tender /可兑换～ convertible currency /周转～ vehicle currency /辅助～ subsidiary note; subsidiary coin

货币贬值 huòbì biǎnzhí (currency) devaluation; (currency) depreciation:通货膨胀的涵义就是～,就是钱不值钱。Inflation means the devaluation of currency. In other words, a unit of money is not worth as much as it used to be.

货币单位 huòbì dānwèi monetary unit

货币地租 huòbì dìzū 〈经济〉money rent

货币工资 huòbì gōngzī money wages

货币供给 huòbì gōngjǐ money supply

货币化 huòbìhuà monetization

货币回笼 huòbì huílóng currency recovery; withdrawal of currency from circulation

货币集团 huòbì jítuán monetary bloc; currency bloc

货币交换 huòbì jiāohuàn exchange through money

货币经济 huòbì jīngjì monetary economy:～学 monetary economics

货币流通量 huòbì liútōngliàng currency in circulation; money supply

货币平价 huòbì píngjià currency parity; par value of currency

货币升值 huòbì shēngzhí (currency) revaluation; (currency) appreciation

货币市场 huòbì shìchǎng money market

货币同盟 huòbì tóngméng monetary union

货币危机 huòbì wēijī monetary crisis

货币性资产 huòbìxìng zīchǎn monetary assets

货币学派 huòbì xuépài monetary school

货币战 huòbìzhàn currency war; monetary war

货币政策 huòbì zhèngcè monetary policy

货币制度 huòbì zhìdù monetary system

货币主义 huòbìzhǔyì monetarism

货币资本 huòbì zīběn money capital

货驳 huòbó freight barge

货仓 huòcāng warehouse; freight house

货舱 huòcāng (cargo) hold; cargo bay (of a plane):(轮船)前～ forward hold /(轮船)后～ after hold /～装卸工 holdman

货差 huòchā cargo loss or damage (during the course of transport)

货场 huòchǎng goods or freight yard:～承运人 haulier /～里堆满了各类货物。The freight yard is full of goods of various descriptions.

货畅其流 huòchàngqíliú free flow of materials and products

货车 huòchē ❶ freight train; goods train ❷ goods van or wagon; truck; lorry:～司机 truck driver /用～跑运输 trucking /～挂车 trailer

货船 huòchuán freight or cargo ship; cargo vessel:不定期～ tramp steamer /定期～ cargo liner /一艘运煤的～ coal vessel /这艘～装满了煤。The ship is freighted with coal.

货单 huòdān manifest; waybill; shipping list:发～ dispatch list /按～发货 dispatch (goods) by shipping list

货到付款 huòdào fùkuǎn *also* "货到支付" cash on delivery (COD):双方讲定～。Both sides agreed to cash on delivery.

货到即提 huòdào jítí delivery on arrival

货店 huòdiàn 〈方言〉store; shop

货柜 huòguì ❶ goods counter; counter ❷〈方言〉container:～列车 container freightliner /～运输 container shipment /～码头 container terminal

货机 huòjī 〈航空〉air freighter; cargo plane or aircraft

货价 huòjià commodity price; price of goods:～看涨。Prices of goods are expected to rise. /～回升。Commodity prices are picking up. /～不稳。Prices fluctuate.

货架子 huòjiàzi ❶ goods shelves:～上陈列着各式鞋帽。Various kinds of hats and shoes are displayed on the shelves. ❷ luggage-carrier or carrier (of a bicycle)

货款 huòkuǎn money for buying or selling goods; payment for goods

货郎 huòláng street vendor; itinerant pedlar:～仍然起着方便山区民众生活的作用。Itinerant pedlars still play an important role in the life of those living in mountainous areas.

货郎担 huòlángdàn itinerant pedlar's load (carried on a shoulder pole)

货郎鼓 huòlánggǔ rattle-drum (used by pedlars):～的响声招来了一大群小孩。The pedlar's rattle-drum beats attracted a throng of children.

货流 huòliú flow of goods or freight

货轮 huòlún freighter; cargo ship; cargo vessel

货棚 huòpéng goods shed; covered stall:春节前,沿街搭起了不少大～。Many goods stalls were put up along the streets before the Spring Festival.

货票 huòpiào invoice; delivery order:凭～提货 pick up goods by delivery order

货品 huòpǐn kinds or types of goods:～检验证 certificate of inspection /商店不大,但经营的～也有数千种。Small as it is, the shop trades in thousands of kinds of goods.

货色 huòsè ❶ goods; kinds and quality of goods:这些布都是上等～。These rolls of cloth are all first-class goods (*or* quality goods). /本店～齐全。Goods of every description are available in this store. ❷〈贬义〉stuff; trash; rubbish:谁都知道他那篇文章究竟是什么～! Everybody knows his article is mere trash. /兄弟俩是同一路～! The two brothers are birds of a feather.

货声 huòshēng hawk:我怀念老北京小贩走街串巷的～。I miss the hawker's cries in the lanes of old Beijing.

货损 huòsǔn freight damage; cargo damage:～严重 heavy freight

H

damage /禁止野蛮装卸，减少~。There must be no careless loading and unloading and a reduction in cargo damage.

货摊 huòtān stall; stand: ~一个接一个地摆满了街道两旁。The street is lined up with stalls and stands on either side.

货梯 huòtī freight elevator; freight or goods lift

货位 huòwèi ❶〈铁路〉〈量词〉car load ❷ storage space: 所有的~都放满了。There's no space left for storage.

货物 huòwù goods; commodity; merchandise: ~名称 description of goods /~种类 kinds (*or* types) of merchandise /~检查 examination of cargo /~残损检验 inspection of damaged cargo /~托运 consignment of goods /~吞吐量 port's volume of freight traffic /商店里面琳琅满目的~吸引了众多顾客。The superb display of goods in the store attracted large numbers of customers.

货物税 huòwùshuì excise tax

货箱 huòxiāng packing box; container: ~运输 containerized shipping

货样 huòyàng sample goods; sample: ~卡 sample card /~室 sample room /你先看看~，再决定是否买的问题。Take a look at the samples before you decide to buy or not.

货源 huòyuán source of goods; supply of goods: ~不足 inadequate supply of goods /开辟新~ look for new source(s) of goods /扩大~ increase the supply of commodities

货运 huòyùn freight transport; shipment of commodities: ~码头 cargo terminal /~业务 cargo service /~公司 transport company

货运单 huòyùndān waybill

货运费 huòyùnfèi shipping cost; freight (charges)

货运量 huòyùnliàng volume of rail freight; volume of road haulage

货运列车 huòyùn lièchē goods or freight train

货运周转量 huòyùn zhōuzhuǎnliàng rotation volume of goods or freight transport

货栈 huòzhàn warehouse

货真价实 huòzhēn-jiàshí ❶ quality goods at a fair price: ~，童叟无欺。Genuine goods and fair prices, and no cheating. ❷ through and through; out-and-out; dyed-in-the-wool: 他是个~的骗子手! He is a downright crook!

货殖 huòzhí 〈书面〉engage in commerce, mining, etc.; engage in trade; be in business; ply a trade

货主 huòzhǔ owner of cargo; consignor or consignee of cargo

臛

huò meat broth

J

激 jī ❶ (of water, etc.) swash; splash; dash:一石～起千层浪。A stone tossed into water raises (*or* dashes up) a thousand ripples. /险些～起一场风波。It almost caused a commotion. ❷ (cause to) fall ill from getting wet; (cause to) catch a chill:他这个身子如何禁得骤雨一～。With so weak a constitution, he couldn't but fall ill from being caught in such a storm. ❸〈方言〉chill (by putting in ice water, etc.):把瓜放在冷水里～一会儿。Chill the melon in the ice water awhile. ❹ arouse; evoke; stimulate; incite:刺～stimulate; excite ❺ (feeling) stirred or moved:感～涕零 be moved to tears of gratitude; shed grateful tears /～于义愤 be stirred by righteous indignation. ❻ radical; drastic; fierce; violent:过～ too radical; extremist / 偏～ extreme /～辩 heated argument

激昂 jī'áng excited and impassioned; vehement; roused:～地发表演说 deliver an impassioned speech /消息传来,群情～。People were all wrought up (*or* roused) at the news. *or* Public feeling ran high on hearing the news. /军乐队奏起雄壮～的国歌。The military band played the inspiring national anthem.

激昂慷慨 jī'áng-kāngkǎi *also*"慷慨激昂" vehement; rousing; passionate:～的歌曲 stirring song

激变 jībiàn ❶ violent or radical change; cataclysm:战场形势～。The war situation has taken a radical turn. ❷〈书面〉enrage people and give rise to a turmoil:～良民 infuriate law-abiding citizens and cause a social upheaval

激波 jībō 〈物理〉shock wave

激磁 jīcí *also*"励磁" lìcí 〈物理〉excite (an electric magnetic field):～换能器 exciting transducer /～机 exciter; exciting dynamo

激磁磁铁 jīcí cítiě field magnet

激磁线圈 jīcí xiànquān drive coil; magnetizing coil

激荡 jīdàng ❶ surge; rage:江涛～。The river is surging. /胸中～着无法抑制的愤怒。Our hearts are overflowing with irrepressible anger. ❷ agitate; toss:浪花～着小船。The small boat was tossed by the waves. / 歌声～人心。People's hearts were agitated by the song.

激动 jīdòng ❶ excite; stir (up); agitate; inspire:他们～得长时间拥抱在一起。They were so moved that they embraced each other for a long time. / 他～地说着。He was speaking in an agitated tone. / 这个戏十分～人心。This drama is very moving. ❷ *see*"激荡"

激动素 jīdòngsù 〈植物〉kinetin

激发 jīfā ❶ arouse; stimulate; spur:～创造的灵感 stimulate one's creative inspiration /～人们的美感 arouse one's sense of beauty; awake sb. to a sense of beauty /～青年的上进心 trigger youth's desire to do better /教师的鼓励会～他进一步地努力。The teacher's encouragement will spur him on to further efforts. ❷〈物理〉excite:热～ thermal excitation /～机制 excitation mechanism /～波 excitation wave /～能级 excitation level /～能 excitation energy

激发态 jīfātài 〈物理〉excited state

激奋 jīfèn be roused to action; be stirred into activity:～人心的场面 stirring scene

激愤 jīfèn *also*"激忿" wrathful; indignant; enraged:群情～。Popular feelings are running high.

激光 jīguāng *also*"莱塞" láisè laser (an acronym from light amplification by stimulated emission of radiation):～发射机 laser transmitter /～干涉仪 laser interferometer /～接受机 laser receiving set /～束 laser beam /～波束制导武器 laser beam riding weapon /～导弹跟踪系统 laser missile tracking system /～源 lasing light emitter/～转换器 lasecon /～自导导弹 laser-seeker /～显微光谱分析仪 laser microspectral analyser /～测量 laser gauge

激光测距 jīguāng cèjù laser ranging:卫星～ satellite laser ranging / ～轰炸系统 laser ranging bombing system /～仪 laser range finder; laser distance measuring instrument

激光测云仪 jīguāng cèyúnyí laser ceilometer

激光唱机 jīguāng chàngjī laser disc player; compact disc player

激光唱片 jīguāng chàngpiàn laser disc; compact disc (CD)

激光打印机 jīguāng dǎyìnjī laser printer

激光导波通信 jīguāng dǎobō tōngxìn laser wave guide communication

激光导航 jīguāng dǎoháng laser navigation

激光干涉仪 jīguāng gānshèyí laser interferometer

激光光谱学 jīguāng guāngpǔxué laser spectroscopy

激光光纤 jīguāng guāngxiān laser fibre; lasing fibre:～传输系统 laser fibre-optic transmission system

激光化学 jīguāng huàxué laser chemistry

激光加工 jīguāng jiāgōng laser processsing (e.g. 激光焊 laser welding and 激光切割 laser cutting)

激光聚变 jīguāng jùbiàn laser fusion

激光雷达 jīguāng léidá lidar detection; optical laser radar

激光器 jīguāngqì *also*"莱塞" láisè laser; laser device

激光枪 jīguāngqiāng laser gun

激光手术刀 jīguāng shǒushùdāo laser scalpel

激光通信 jīguāng tōngxìn laser communication; laser device

激光诱发核聚变 jīguāng yòufā héjùbiàn laser-induced fusion

激光照明器 jīguāng zhàomíngqì laser illuminator

激光制导 jīguāng zhìdǎo 〈航空〉laser guidance /～导弹 laser (guided) missile

激光准直仪 jīguāng zhǔnzhíyí laser collimator

激弧管 jīhúguǎn 〈电工〉excitron

激化 jīhuà sharpen; intensify; aggravate; become acute:矛盾的～ sharpening of contradictions /国内各种矛盾日趋～。Various kinds of contradictions in the country are intensifying. /争权夺利的斗争进一步～。The struggle to scramble for power and gain is becoming even more acute.

激活 jīhuó 〈物理〉activate:～剂 activator /～媒质 active medium /～能 activation energy /某些植物成分能～细胞免疫反应。Some plant elements can activate cellular immunization response.

激将 jījiàng goad or prod sb. into action /请将不如～。It's better to prod a person into action than to implore him to do something.

激将法 jījiàngfǎ (method of) prodding sb. into action (as by ridicule, sarcasm, etc.); (method of) goading sb. into doing sth.:对他这个人只能使用～。A person like him has to be spurred on.

激进 jījìn radical; militant:～分子 radical /～思想 radical ideology/～主义 radicalism /采取～措施 take drastic means

激进派 jījìnpài radicals; militants

激剧 jījù ❶ intense; sharp; fierce; acute:看样子他是在进行～的思想斗争。It appears that he is having an intense soul-searching at the moment. ❷ rapid:病情～恶化。His condition is rapidly deteriorating.

激浪 jīlàng turbulent waves; torrential waters:金沙江水～滔滔。The Golden Sand River surges forward rapidly. *or* The Jinsha surges on in torrents.

激冷 jīlěng 〈冶金〉shock chilling; chill:～层 chill /～轧辊 chilled roll /～铁 chilled iron

激励 jīlì ❶ encourage; impel; urge; inspire:～斗志 inspire one's fighting will /～士气 boost the morale of the army /孩子们对她的信赖～她尽力为他们服务。The children's faith put her on her mettle to

do her best for them. /伟大的理想会~人们奋勇前进。A lofty ideal will impel people to advance courageously. ❷〈电子〉drive; excite; stimulate:~变压器 exciting transformer /~管 excitron; exciter tube /~器 exciter; stimulator /~整流器 exciter rectifier

激烈 jīliè ❶ intense; fierce; sharp; violent:~的冲突 sharp conflict /~的语言 strong language /互相~指责 exchange acrimonious remarks /一场~的风暴就要卷来了。A violent thunderstorm is bearing down upon us. /整个比赛异常~。It was an extraordinarily gruelling match. ❷ (of character, feeling, etc.) uplifting; upright and unyielding:壮怀~ with lofty aspirations

激灵 jīling *also* "机灵" jīling 〈方言〉shock; startle:吓了他一~ give him a shock (*or* start) /听到一点儿响声,他~一下就坐起来了。He sat up with a start on hearing the sound.

激流 jīliú torrent; rapids; turbulent current:闯过~ shoot the rapids /山下的~发出轰轰的巨响。The turbulent current down the mountain is rumbling loudly.

激论 jīlùn pungent remarks; sharp words; radical saying

激酶 jīméi 〈生化〉kinase

激恼 jīnǎo provoke so as to enrage:他是有意用这话来~你的。He purposely used these words to provoke you.

激怒 jīnù provoke; enrage; infuriate; exasperate:看他那~的样子,我真有点害怕。I'm really a bit frightened at his infuriated manner. /他们的罪恶行径~了群众。Their criminal moves enraged the masses.

激起 jīqǐ arouse; evoke; cause; stir up:~观众感情上的共鸣 evoke an emotional response from the audience /~对新生活的憧憬 stimulate one's longing for a new life /~众怒 arouse popular indignation; stir up public wrath /获得头等奖的可能性~了他的劲头。The possibility of winning first prize set his energies afire.

激切 jīqiè 〈书面〉(of language) vehement and forthright; impassioned:我这番话也许说得过于~。I may have said something too strong.

激情 jīqíng intense emotion; passion; fervour; ardour; enthusiasm:她的歌声充满了火一样的~。Her singing is full of fiery passion. /他满怀~地走上新的工作岗位。He took up his new post with great enthusiasm. /他的演出充满了~。His performance was full of fervour.

激赏 jīshǎng 〈书面〉highly appreciate; greatly admire:这首小诗得到评论家们的~。This little poem has received acclaim from critics.

激素 jīsù *also* "荷尔蒙" hé'ěrméng 〈生理〉hormone:黄体~ luteal hormone /生长~ growth hormone /性~ sex hormone /催~药 hormonagogue /~疗法 hormonotherapy; endocrinotherapy

激肽 jītài 〈生化〉kinin:~酶 kininase

激湍 jītuān 〈书面〉torrential currents; turbulent waters:河水~ turbulent river

激扬 jīyáng ❶ drain away the mud and bring in fresh water; drive out evil and usher in good:指点江山,~文字,粪土当年万户侯。Pointing to our mountains and rivers, Setting people afire with our words, We counted the mighty no more than muck. ❷ excited and high-spirited; vehement:~的歌声 spirited singing ❸ encourage; urge:~士气 boost the morale

激涌 jīyǒng (water) roll turbulently; toss tempestuously:怒涛~ furious raging billows /心潮~,思绪万千。His mind is in a tumult with a multitude of thoughts.

激元 jīyuán 〈物理〉excimer

激越 jīyuè (of sound, feeling, etc.) loud and strong; intense; vehement:雄浑~的军号声 loud and ringing bugle sound / 感情~ intense emotion /音乐时而低沉,时而高昂~。The music is sometimes low, sometimes loud and spirited.

激增 jīzēng increase sharply; rise steeply; soar; shoot up:产量~ steep rise in output /人口~ sharp increase of population /这种产品的销量~。The sales volume of this product is soaring. /转口贸易~。Transit trade has shot up.

激战 jīzhàn fierce fighting; pitched battle:~竟日。A bitter battle raged the whole day. /一场唇舌~过后,两人谁也不服谁。After a fierce battle of words, neither side is convinced.

激浊扬清 jīzhuó-yángqīng *also* "扬清激浊" drain away the mud and bring in fresh water; eliminate vice and exalt virtue

激子 jīzǐ 〈物理〉exciton:~学 excitonics

齑(齏)

jī 〈书面〉❶ finely chopped ginger, garlic, etc. ❷ fine; powdery

齑粉 jīfěn 〈书面〉fine powder; broken bits:转眼间便被碾成~ be ground to dust in the twinkle of an eye /化为~ reduce to broken bits; reduce to fine powder

跻(躋)

jī 〈书面〉ascend; climb (up); mount:~于体育强国之列 rank among the powerful sports countries of the world

跻攀 jīpān 〈书面〉climb; clamber; scale

跻身 jīshēn ascend; mount; go up to a higher position or level:我国的计算机技术一定能~于世界先进行列。Our computer technology will certainly rise to the advanced level of the world.

襀

jī 〈书面〉wrinkle (on one's clothes); crease

积(積)

jī ❶ amass; gather; store up; accumulate:堆~ pile up; accumulate; heap up /山~ pile mountain high /囤~ corner the market; hoard for speculation /蓄~ store up; save up /日~月累 accumulate over the years /防止房间~下灰尘 prevent the room from gathering dust ❷ accumulated; long-standing; long pending; age-old:郁~ pent-up /沉~ deposit ❸〈中医〉indigestion:奶~ (of babies) indigestion due to improper milking /食~ dyspepsia; indigestion /痞~ lump in the abdomen /捏~ method of treating children's digestive disorder by kneading or massaging the muscles along the spine; chiropractic ❹〈数学〉product:乘~ product /求~ find the product by multiplication

积案 jī'àn long-pending case:清理~ clear the docket

积弊 jībì accumulated malpractice; long-standing abuse:~难除。It's difficult to get rid of age-old malpractice. *or* Accumulated evil practices are difficult to eradicate.

积不相能 jībùxiāngnéng 〈书面〉have always been at variance; have never been on good terms; there has been no love lost (between the two); be always at odds:二人~,很难共事。These two persons will have a hard time working together for they always disagree with each other.

积层电池 jīcéng diànchí packed cell

积储 jīchǔ store up; lay up:把每月的余钱~起来 store (*or* lay) up spare money every month

积存 jīcún store up; stockpile:库中~颇多。There are too many goods in stock. /这是多年~下来的一笔钱。This is a sum of money that has been saved for years.

积德 jīdé do good deeds (for one's own salvation):~行好 do good deeds and dispense charities /积阴德 do good deeds to one's credit in the next world

积淀 jīdiàn sediments accumulated over the years:传统文化的~ inertia of traditional culture

积恶 jī'è ❶ do one wicked deed after another; do evil time and again ❷ accumulated evildoings:查抄逆产,以清~。Make an inventory of a criminal's possessions and confiscate them so as to punish accumulated evildoings.

积非成是 jīfēi-chéngshì repeated lies become truths:众口铄金,~。Public clamour can confound right and wrong, and incessant repetition can turn lies into truths.

积肥 jīféi collect (farmyard) manure; store compost

积分 jīfēn ❶〈数学〉integral:定~ definite integral /不定~ indefinite integral /~微分方程 integrodifferential equation /~变换 integral transforms ❷ accumulated points:足球联赛中,两队~相同。The two teams have the same number of accumulated points in the league football matches.

积分电动机 jīfēn diàndòngjī integrating motor

积分方程 jīfēn fāngchéng integral equation

积分放大器 jīfēn fàngdàqì integrating amplifier

积分学 jīfēnxué integral calculus

积分仪 jīfēnyí integrator

积愤 jīfèn pent-up indignation:倾吐~ pour out one's pent-up grievances

积复励 jīfùlì 〈电工〉cumulative compound excitation:~电动机 cumulative compound motor /~发电机 cumulative compound generator

积垢 jīgòu accumulated filth; gathered dirt

积谷防饥 jīgǔ-fángjī store up grain against famine:常言道:养儿防老,~。As the saying goes, raise children to provide against old age and store up grain against famine.

积毁销骨 jīhuǐ-xiāogǔ accumulated defamation melts the bones

— repeated slanders may cause one's ruin; calumny destroys：那些阴险小人很懂得～的道理。Those insidious, base people know well that defamation may spell ruin for its victim.

积极 jījí ❶ positive：～因素 positive factors /有～意义 of positive significance /～平衡 positive balance /～中立 positive neutrality ❷ active; forceful; energetic; vigorous：～防御 active defence /～威慑 active deterrent /～支持 support vigorously; give active support /～响应号召 enthusiastically answer a call /～工作 work hard /～推动 promote energetically /他游泳很～。He is very keen on swimming.

积极分子 jījífènzǐ ❶ activist; active element; stalwart：党的～ Party activist /在技术革命中涌现出大批的～。Large numbers of activists have come to the fore in the course of the technological revolution. ❷ enthusiast; devotee; fan; buff：社区活动的～ community enthusiast /科学工作的～ scientific work devotee

积极性 jījíxìng zeal; ardour; initiative; enthusiasm：革命的～ revolutionary zeal /妇女参政的～ women's enthusiasm for participation in government and political affairs /充分调动广大教职员工的～ bring into full play the initiative of the teaching, administrative and supporting staff

积渐 jījiàn gradually; by degrees：～养成的习惯 form a habit gradually

积久 jījiǔ accumulate in the course of time; form over the years：～成习 form a habit or custom over the years /省吃俭用，～致富 make a fortune by skimping and saving for a long time /说谎对他来说已～成习，不下决心是难改掉的。Lying has already become his second nature, and it would be hard for him to give it up without making a determined effort.

积聚 jījù gather; amass; accumulate; build up：～力量 build up strength; gather strength /资本～ accumulation of capital /～起大量的财富 amass a great deal of wealth

积劳 jīláo 〈书面〉be overworked for a long period of time：他周身的病痛，乃是～所致。All his diseases are caused by sustained overwork.

积劳成疾 jīláo-chéngjí 〈书面〉break down from constant overwork; fall ill through prolonged overwork; be run down：他～，过早地离开了人世。He fell ill through constant overwork and died too young.

积累 jīlěi ❶ accumulate; gather：～了丰富的教学经验 have gained a great deal of teaching experience; have accumulated a wealth of teaching experience ❷〈经济〉accumulation (for reinvestment)：原始～ primitive accumulation /资本～ capital accumulation /正确处理～和消费的关系 correctly handle the relationship between accumulation and consumption

积累基金 jīlěi jījīn accumulation fund

积漏器 jīlòuqì 〈机械〉leak collector

积木 jīmù building blocks; toy bricks

积木化 jīmùhuà 〈自控〉modularize：～设计 modular design

积木式 jīmùshì cordwood system; building block system (BBS)：～原理 building block principle

积木式计算机 jīmùshì jìsuànjī model computer; modularized computer

积木式信息处理设备 jīmùshì xìnxī chǔlǐ shèbèi 〈信息〉modular information processing equipment

积年 jīnián 〈书面〉for many years; year after year：～旧案 law cases piled up over the years

积年累月 jīnián-lěiyuè for months and years：～，辛勤耕耘，才有了著作等身的成果。Only after making strenuous efforts for years on end has he become an accomplished writer with a wealth of works published.

积脓 jīnóng 〈医学〉empyema

积怒 jīnù pent-up indignation：深怨～ deep hatred and pent-up anger

积欠 jīqiàn ❶ have one's debts piling up：还清了～的债务 have paid off one's debts ❷ outstanding debts; arrears：无力偿还～ unable to clear up all outstanding debts

积弱 jīruò decline and weakness that came about over the years：～不振 be broken down because of continued ill health

积善 jīshàn accumulation of good deeds; performance of one good deed after another

积善余庆 jīshàn-yúqìng *also* "积善之家，必有余庆" those who do good deeds will be blessed with fortune

积少成多 jīshǎo-chéngduō accumulate little by little; amass gradually; many a little makes a mickle：他多年收集火花，～，如今林林总总，不下千种。He has been collecting matchbox drawings (*or* pictures) for years, and little by little, he has now collected more than a thousand kinds of them.

积食 jīshí 〈方言〉indigestion

积愫 jīsù genuine feeling that has been kept deep in one's bosom：倾吐～ pour out one's innermost feelings

积土成山，积水成川 jī tǔ chéng shān, jī shuǐ chéng chuān heaped-up earth becomes a mountain, accumulated water becomes a river; many a little makes a mickle

积威 jīwēi power and influence built up over a long period of time

积温 jīwēn sum of the difference between average temperature and given temperature over a given period of time; cumulative temperature

积习 jīxí deep-rooted habit; long-standing practice：～成俗。A long-standing practice becomes a custom.

积习难改 jīxí-nángǎi old weaknesses or ingrained habits are hard to change; old habits die hard

积蓄 jīxù ❶ put aside; accumulate; save：～力量 accumulate strength /～一笔钱 save a sum of money /他每月都可以从工资中～一部分钱。He is able to salt away part of his salary every month. /他们正在～，准备下月结婚。They are saving up for the wedding next month. ❷ savings：辛辛苦苦得来的～ hard-earned savings /他有一笔为数不少的～。He has a handsome deposit.

积雪 jīxuě accumulated snow; snow：地上的～很厚。The snow lay thick on the ground. *or* There is a thick layer of snow on the ground.

积压 jīyā keep long in stock; overstock：～物资 materials kept too long in stock /商品～ overstocking of goods /～的资金 funds tied up by overstock /～资金 let funds lie idle /处理～多时的事情 clear off arrears of work /一批稿件～在这位编辑桌上。Manuscripts have been piling up on this editor's desk. /～在心头的怒火，此刻总爆发了。The pent-up anger now burst out.

积淤 jīyū ❶ silt up; deposit ❷ build up; accumulate：～在心底的忧愤 worry and indignation built up deep in one's heart

积余 jīyú ❶ lay up; save：他长期省吃俭用，已～了不少的钱。He has been living frugally for a long time and has saved quite a handsome amount of money. ❷ savings：近些年来，他手头儿有了一点～。He has built up some savings in recent years.

积羽沉舟 jīyǔ-chénzhōu enough feathers can sink a boat; small things may gather into a mighty force; offences, however minor, will bring disaster if unchecked：～，群轻折轴，我们怎么能轻视积累的作用呢? As enough feathers can sink a boat and a load of light things can break the axle of a cart, we should in no way belittle the effect of accumulation.

积雨 jīyǔ spell of rainy days：～初霁。It begins to clear up after a spell of rainy days. /～成灾。The incessant rain has caused a flood.

积雨云 jīyǔyún 〈气象〉cumulonimbus

积玉堆金 jīyù-duījīn mountains of jade and gold; enormous wealth

积郁 jīyù smouldering; pent-up;〈医学〉stasis：～成疾 fall ill from stasis /发泄～在心中的不满 pour out pent-up grievances

积怨 jīyuàn accumulated rancour; piled-up grievances：～甚多 have incurred a great deal of resentment

积愿 jīyuàn long-cherished wish; long-standing aspiration：倾吐～ express one's long-cherished wish without reservation

积云 jīyún 〈气象〉cumulus：层～ straocumulus /卷～ cirrocumulus/高～ altocumulus

积蕴 jīyùn lie hidden and undeveloped; be latent

积载因素 jīzài yīnsù stowage factor

积攒 jīzǎn 〈口语〉save bit by bit; collect piecemeal：这几年老人家～了一点点钱。The old man has saved money bit by bit these years.

积重难返 jīzhòng-nánfǎn bad old practices die hard; ingrained or inveterate habits are difficult to get rid of：这些～的陋规，谁也不能一下子革除。No one is able to get rid of these bad old practices at one stroke.

积铢累寸 jīzhū-lěicùn *also* "铢积寸累" save every tiny bit; accumulate bit by bit

积贮 jīzhù store up; stockpile; lay in：～粮食 store grain; lay in grain

积祖 jīzǔ (often used in the early vernacular) for many generations; generation after generation：～就是个有名的财主 be from a

family that has been wealthy for generations

击(擊) jī ❶ beat; hit; knock; strike: ～鼓助兴 beat a drum to add to the festive atmosphere /在他肩上重重地～了一拳 strike him a heavy blow on the shoulder /反戈一～ rebel and hit back /他轻轻地一～桌子。He tapped on the desk. ❷ attack; assault; assail: 出～ launch an attack /反～ strike back; beat back; counter-attack /夹～ attack from both flanks /突～ make a sudden and violent assault /追～ pursue and attack /伏～ ambush /迎头痛～ deal a head-on blow /不堪一～ cannot withstand a single blow ❸ come in contact with; bump into; collide with: 冲～ pound against; charge /目～ witness; see with one's own eyes

击败 jībài defeat; beat; vanquish; crush: ～对手 beat one's opponent /～敌军 defeat the enemy force /～一切来犯之敌 rout (*or* crush) all the invaders

击毙 jībì shoot dead; strike dead: 一名抢劫犯被当场～。A robber was shot dead on the spot.

击沉 jīchén bombard and sink; send (a ship) to the bottom: ～一些旧军舰 sink some old warships /在那次海战中,有三艘敌舰被～。In that sea battle, three enemy warships were sent to the bottom.

击穿 jīchuān 〈电学〉 puncture; breakdown: ～试验 breakdown (*or* puncture) test

击打 jīdǎ beat; lash: 骤雨～水面。A heavy shower is beating down on the river.

击发 jīfā ❶ pull the trigger ❷ 〈军事〉 percussion: ～装置 percussion lock (*or* mechanism)

击毁 jīhuǐ smash; demolish; shatter; destroy: ～坦克数辆 destroy several tanks /～敌机数十架 smash scores of enemy planes

击剑 jījiàn 〈体育〉 fencing: ～运动员 fencer /～场 fencing strip; fencing terrain; piste /～服 fencing clothes /～技术 sword play; swordsmanship /～裤 fencing breeches

击节 jījié beat time: ～称赏 clap and applaud; beat time and applaud enthusiastically

击节叹赏 jījié-tànshǎng show appreciation (of a poem or a piece of music) by beating time with one's hand; admire immensely

击溃 jīkuì rout; thoroughly defeat; put to flight: ～敌军 put the enemy to flight /～强敌 send the crack enemy army fleeing helter-skelter

击落 jīluò shoot down; bring down; down: ～敌军两架侦察机 shoot (*or* bring) down two enemy reconnaissance planes

击破 jīpò break up; destroy; smash; rout: 各个～ destroy one by one; destroy in detail /堡垒最容易从内部～。A fortress is most vulnerable when attacked from within.

击球 jīqiú 〈体育〉 (as in baseball) batting: ～员 batter; batsman

击伤 jīshāng wound (a person); damage (a plane, tank, etc.); injure: 被流弹～ be wounded by stray bullets

击赏 jīshǎng 〈书面〉 appreciate: 他的作品得到几位作曲名家的～。His works have won acclaim from several famous composers.

击水 jīshuǐ ❶ pat or flap on the water: 举翼～ flap the wings on the water ❷ swim: 到中流～ venturing into midstream, we struck the waters; we swam to mid-stream

J

击退 jītuì beat back; push back; repel; repulse: ～敌军的进攻 repulse the enemy attack /～来犯之敌 repel invaders

击弦乐器 jīxián yuèqì 〈乐器〉 hammered string instrument (such as a hammer dulcimer)

击以猛掌 jīyǐměngzhǎng give sb. a shove — give a serious warning

击乐器 jīyuèqì percussion instrument

击掌 jīzhǎng ❶ clap one's hands; applaud: ～为号 give the signal by clapping one's hands ❷ strike sb.'s palms with one's own (to make a vow): ～为盟 clap each other's hands to vow alliance

击中 jīzhòng hit: ～目标 hit the target /～痛处 hit one where it hurts /八次～,两次未中 eight hits and two misses

击中要害 jīzhòng-yàohài strike home; hit home; hit the bull's-eye; hit sb.'s vital point: 他举剑击中了要害。He raised his sword and struck home. /他的分析～,我很赞赏。I admire his analysis which hits the nail on its head. /你批评得对,击中了我们的要害。You're right in your criticism; you've pinpointed our main weakness.

墼 jī *see* "炭墼" tànjī

基 jī ❶ base; foundation: 坝～ base of a dam /路～ road bed; bed /房～ foundations (of a building) /奠～ lay a foundation ❷ basic; fundamental; primary; cardinal: *see* "～调" ❸ 〈化学〉 radical; base; group: 自由～ free radical /石蜡～ paraffin base /氨～ amino; amino-group /羟～ hydroxyl (group) /羧～ carboxyl (group) /乙烯～ vinyl /盐～ alkali

基本 jīběn ❶ base; foundation: 人民是国家的～。People are the foundation of a country. ❷ basic; fundamental; primary; cardinal: 四项～原则 four cardinal principles /～观点 basic concept; fundamental view /～纲领 basic programme /～核算单位 basic accounting unit /～利率 prime rate /他想收集一些～资料。He wanted to collect some "meat-and-potato" information. /他介绍了计划的～点。He explained the nuts and bolts of his plan. /你能谈谈打乒乓的～要领吗? Can you talk about the ABC of playing ping-pong (*or* the fundamentals of ping-pong)? ❸ main; chief; essential: 工作的～条件 primary working conditions /～特征 essential features /～力量 main force ❹ basically; in the main; on the whole; by and large: 这部电影～是好的。This film is good on the whole. /演出～是成功的。The performance was successful by and large.

基本词汇 jīběn cíhuì 〈语言〉 basic vocabulary; basic word-stock

基本单位 jīběn dānwèi basic unit

基本电荷 jīběn diànhè 〈物理〉 elementary charge

基本法 jīběnfǎ basic law: 香港特别行政区～ Basic Law of the Hong Kong Special Administrative Region

基本工资 jīběn gōngzī basic salary or wage

基本功 jīběngōng basic training; basic skill; essential technique; fundamentals: 苦练～ practise hard in basic skills /练好～ have a thorough training in basic skills; master the basic skills /写作的～ essential technique in writing (*or* composition)

基本国策 jīběn guócè basic policy of the state; basic state policy: 计划生育是我国的一项～。Family planning is a basic policy of our country.

基本建设 jīběn jiànshè ❶ capital construction: ～投资 investment in capital construction ❷ undertaking of primary importance: 教材建设是提高教学质量的一项～。Compilation of teaching materials is of primary importance to the quality of teaching.

基本粒子 jīběn lìzǐ *also* "粒子" 〈物理〉 elementary particle

基本路线 jīběn lùxiàn basic line

基本矛盾 jīběn máodùn 〈哲学〉 basic contradiction

基本上 jīběnshang ❶ principally; mainly: 这项任务,～要靠你们队来完成。We are mainly depending on your team to finish (*or* complete) this task. ❷ on the whole; in the main; by and large: 大桥～建成了。The bridge has been constructed in the main.

基本速率接入 jīběn sùlǜ jiērù 〈通信〉 basic rate access (BRA)

基波 jībō 〈物理〉 fundamental wave; fundamental harmonic: ～失真 fundamental component distortion

基槽 jīcáo *also* "基坑" foundations

基层 jīcéng basic level; primary level; grass roots: ～单位 unit at the grass-roots level; grass-roots unit; basic unit /～干部 cadre at the basic level; official at the grass roots /～领导 leading body at the basic level; basic-level leadership /～选举 elections at the basic level /～组织 organization at the basic level; primary organization /～代表 representative from the grass roots /～行政机构 administrative organ at the basic level

基础 jīchǔ ❶ foundation: 这座大楼的～很牢固。This building has got a solid foundation. ❷ base; foundation; basis: ～工作 spade work /～教材 basic teaching material /打好～ lay a solid foundation /在普及的～上提高 raise standards on the basis of popularization /他的英语语法～比较扎实。He has a fairly solid grounding in English grammar. ❸ economic base

基础处理 jīchǔ chǔlǐ 〈水利〉 foundation treatment

基础代谢 jīchǔ dàixiè 〈生理〉 basal metabolism

基础工业 jīchǔ gōngyè basic industry

基础教育 jīchǔ jiàoyù elementary education

基础金融工具 jīchǔ jīnróng gōngjù plain vanilla

基础科学 jīchǔ kēxué basic science

基础课 jīchǔkè basic course (of a college curriculum)

基础理论 jīchǔ lǐlùn basic theory

基础设施 jīchǔ shèshī infrastructural facilities; infrastructure

基础知识 jīchǔ zhīshi elementary, rudimentary, or basic knowledge

基底负载 jīdǐ fùzài 〈电工〉 base load: ～发电厂 base load electric station; base load power station; base load station /～发电机 base

load generator
基底细胞癌 jīdǐ xìbāo'ái 〈医学〉basal-cell carcinoma
基地 jīdì base: 军事～ military base / 导弹～ missile base / 工业～ industrial base / 原料～ source of raw material / 能源～ energy base; source of energy / 商品粮～ commodity grain base / 城市的蔬菜～ vegetable base for the cities
基点 jīdiǎn ❶ base; centre: 建立电化教学～ set up audio-visual education centres / 以集镇为～, 发展农村商品经济 develop rural commodity economy centring (*or* based) on the town ❷ basis; point of departure; starting point: ～价格 basic point pricing / 我们的友谊以互相信任为～。Our friendship is based on mutual trust. ❸〈测绘〉base point (BP)
基调 jīdiào ❶〈音乐〉fundamental key; main key ❷ keynote: 定下会议的～ set the keynote for a conference / 发扬实事求是精神是这篇讲话的～。The gist of the speech was to encourage the spirit of seeking truth from facts.
基督 Jīdū 〈宗教〉Christ
基督复临会 Jīdū Fùlínhuì Advent Christian Church
基督纪元 Jīdū jìyuán Christian era
基督教 Jīdūjiào ❶ Christianity; Christian religion ❷ *also* "耶稣教" Yēsūjiào Protestantism
基督教科学箴言报 Jīdūjiào Kēxué Zhēnyánbào *Christian Science Monitor*, a US newspaper first published in 1908
基督教女青年会 Jīdūjiào Nǚqīngniánhuì Young Women's Christian Association (YWCA)
基督教青年会 Jīdūjiào Qīngniánhuì Young Men's Christian Association (YMCA)
基督教世界 Jīdūjiào Shìjiè Christendom
基督复临安息日会 Jīdū Fùlín Ānxīrìhuì Seventh Day Adventists
基督论 Jīdūlùn 〈宗教〉Christology
基督徒 jīdūtú Christian
基多 Jīduō Quito, capital of Ecuador
基尔特 jī'ěrtè (transliteration) guild: ～社会主义 guild socialism
基肥 jīféi *also* "底肥" dǐféi 〈农业〉base manure; base fertilizer
基辅 Jīfǔ Kiev or Kyiv, capital of Ukraine
基干 jīgàn ❶ backbone; (hard) core: ～民兵 primary militia; core members of the militia / ～队伍 hard core ranks ❷ cadres at the basic level; grassroots cadres
基荷机组 jīhè jīzǔ 〈电工〉base load unit
基极 jījí 〈电工〉base electrode: ～接地 base earth / ～电流 base current
基加利 Jījiālì Kigali, capital of Rwanda
基价 jījià base price
基建 jījiàn (short for 基本建设) capital construction: ～工程 capital construction project / ～战线 capital construction line; capital construction front
基脚 jījiǎo foot of a wall; foundation: 砌～ build the foot of a wall by laying bricks or stones
基金 jījīn fund: 积累～ accumulation fund / 外汇平准～ exchange stabilization fund / 福利～ welfare fund / 教育～ education fund / 大修～ fund for major overhaul / 生产～ production fund / 流通～ circulation fund
基金会 jījīnhuì foundation
基坑 jīkēng *also* "基槽" foundations
基里巴斯 Jīlǐbāsī Kiribati, an island country in the western Pacific
基流 jīliú 〈电工〉base current
基诺 jīnuò keno, a gambling game somewhat like lotto, in which players cover numbers on their cards
基诺族 Jīnuòzú Jino nationality, a Chinese national minority in Yunnan Province
基片 jīpiàn 〈电工〉substrate: ～座 substrate holder
基期 jīqī 〈统计〉base period
基色 jīsè *also* "原色" yuánsè primary colour
基生 jīshēng sprout from the bottom part of a stem: ～叶〈植物〉basal leaf; bathyphyll / ～细胞〈植物〉basilar cell
基石 jīshí ❶ foundation stone: 为博物馆开工奠定～ lay a foundation stone for the construction of a museum ❷〈比喻〉cornerstone: 维护和平是我国外交政策的～。The maintenance of peace is the cornerstone of our country's foreign policy.
基数 jīshù ❶ cardinal number ❷〈统计〉base: 以今年第一季度的贸易额为～ take the volume of trade of the first quarter of this year as the base
基态 jītài 〈物理〉ground state: 原子的～ atomic ground state
基体 jītǐ substance constituting the major part of a compound; 〈冶金〉matrix: 金属～ metallic matrix / ～材料 base material
基团 jītuán (a generic term for) atomic groups and radicals
基线 jīxiàn ❶〈数学〉base ❷〈测绘〉datum line
基辛格 Jīxīngé Henry Alfred Kissinger (1923-), American diplomat and Secretary of State (1973-1977)
基性岩 jīxìngyán basic rock (black or dark grey rock of volcanic origin such as basalt, consisting chiefly of sodium or potassium alumino-silicates, with some iron, basic in character, supposed to constitute the bulk of the earth beneath its solid crust, and found as extrusions at the surface in some places)
基岩 jīyán bedrock
基业 jīyè (of an enterprise) foundation; base: 创立～ lay the foundation of one's enterprise, etc.
基因 jīyīn 〈生理〉gene: ～型 genotype / ～流动 gene flow / ～变异 genovariation / ～突变 gene mutation / ～中心 gene-centre / 显性～ dominant gene / 隐性～ recessive gene / ～谷 gene valley / 结构～ structural gene / 操纵～ operator gene / 控制～ control gene / 调节～ regulator gene / 等位～ allele
基因病 jīyīnbìng genophathy
基因复制 jīyīn fùzhì gene duplication
基因工程 jīyīn gōngchéng *also* "遗传工程" yíchuán gōngchéng genetic engineering
基因库 jīyīnkù gene bank; gene pool
基因疗法 jīyīn liáofǎ gene therapy
基因移植 jīyīn yízhí gene transplantation
基因组 jīyīnzǔ genome; genom: 人类～ human genome
基音 jīyīn 〈音乐〉fundamental tone; ground note
基于 jīyú because of; in view of; on account of: ～以上种种原因,我们不准备参加这次会议。For all the above-mentioned reasons, we are not going to take part in the conference. / ～这种严重情况,建议采取果断措施,制止事态进一步扩大。In view of the serious situation, it is suggested that resolute measures be taken to prevent aggravation of the incident.
基址 jīzhǐ ❶ foundations of a ruined palace, etc.; ruins: 唐代宫殿～ ruins of a Tang palace ❷〈书面〉foundation; cornerstone; quitessence
基质 jīzhì 〈生物〉stroma; substrate; substratum; matrix: ～蛋白 stromatin
基准 jīzhǔn ❶〈测绘〉datum: ～点 datum point / ～面 datum plane / ～线 datum line ❷ standard; criterion: ～兵 guide; base marker / 制定生产指标,不能把～定得过高或过低。To set a production target, it is not advisable to have the criterion fixed too high or too low.

箕

jī ❶ dustpan ❷ loop (of a finger print): 斗～ fingerprint ❸ winnowing basket; winnowing fan: 筲～ rice-washing basket ❹〈天文〉one of the 28 constellations in ancient Chinese astronomy ❺ (Jī) a surname
箕伯 Jībó Jibo, god of wind in ancient Chinese mythology
箕斗 jīdǒu ❶〈书面〉constellations; stars ❷〈书面〉false reputation: 徒具～虚名 have an undeserved reputation (of being an expert, etc.) ❸〈书面〉fingerprint ❹〈矿业〉skip
箕踞 jījù 〈书面〉sit (on the floor) with one's legs stretched out — sit in an impolite, casual manner

錤

jī *see* "镃錤" zījī

期(朞)

jī 〈书面〉one whole year or month
see also qī
期年 jīnián 〈书面〉one whole year
期月 jīyuè 〈书面〉one whole month

赍(齎)

jī 〈书面〉❶ cherish; harbour: *see* "～志而殁" ❷ give as a present: ～盗粮 give robbers grain
赍发 jīfā 〈书面〉give sb. money etc.; aid sb.: ～盘缠 give sb. money to cover travelling expenses
赍恨 jīhèn 〈书面〉have a gnawing regret; feel regretful: ～而终 die full of regrets

J

赍赏 jīshǎng grant a reward; bestow a reward
赍志而殁 jīzhì'érmò die with one's ambition unfulfilled:～,长恨无已。It's a matter of eternal regret to die without realizing one's aspirations.

奇
jī ❶ odd (number):～偶 odd and even numbers /～日 odd-numbered days (of a month) ❷〈书面〉fractional amount; odd lots:八十有～ eighty odd
see also qí
奇函数 jīhánshù 〈数学〉odd function
奇零 jīlíng *also*"畸零"jīlíng 〈书面〉fractional amount; odd lots
奇偶校验 jī-ǒu jiàoyàn 〈信息〉parity
奇数 jīshù 〈数学〉odd number
奇蹄动物 jītí dòngwù 〈动物〉perissodactyle (animal)
奇宇称 jīyǔchēng 〈物理〉odd parity
奇整数 jīzhěngshù 〈数学〉odd integer

剞
jī
剞劂 jījué 〈书面〉❶ knife used for carving; graver ❷ cut blocks; block-print (book)

畸
jī ❶ lopsided; unbalanced: *see*"～轻～重"❷ irregular; eccentric; abnormal: *see*"～形"❸〈书面〉fractional amount; odd lots
畸变 jībiàn ❶ abnormal change ❷〈物理〉distortion
畸零 jīlíng ❶ *see*"奇零"jīlíng ❷ all alone:～无侣 companionless
畸轻畸重 jīqīng-jīzhòng attaching too much weight to one and too little weight to another; now too much, now too little; unbalanced:中学生不可重理轻文,～。Secondary school students should not attach too much weight to natural science and too little weight to liberal arts.
畸胎 jītāi 〈生理〉monster; monstrosity; teras:多毛～ hairy monster /～瘤 teratoma /～学 teratology
畸形 jīxíng ❶ deformity; malformation:先天～ congenital malformation /肢体发育～ have a deformed limb /～手 clubhand; talipomanus /～学 teratology ❷ lopsided; uneven; unbalanced:～发展 lopsided development

犄
jī
犄角 jījiǎo 〈方言〉corner:桌子～ corner of a table /嘴～儿 corners of the mouth /墙～ corner formed by two walls /从眼～流下两滴泪珠儿来。Two big teardrops came down from the corners of the eyes.
犄角 jījiao 〈方言〉horn:牛～ ox horn /鹿～ antler /羊～ sheep horn

觭
jī *also*"奇"jī 〈书面〉odd number

乩
jī *see*"扶乩"fújī

咭
jī *see*"叽"jī

畟
jī
畟奸 jījiān *also*"鸡奸"jījiān sodomy; buggery

唧
jī spurt; squirt:～了他一身水。The water squirted all over him. /血～地从伤口冒出。Blood spurted from the wound.
唧咕 jīgu whisper; mutter
see also"叽咕"jīgu
唧唧 jījī 〈象声〉(of insects) chirp:虫声～ with insects chirping
唧唧鹬 jījīyù 〈动物〉peep
唧唧嘎嘎 jīji-gāgā *also*"叽叽嘎嘎"jīji-gāgā 〈象声〉creak; crackle; giggle:姑娘们～地笑起来。The girls giggled.
唧唧喳喳 jīji-zhāzhā *also*"叽叽喳喳"jīji-zhāzhā chirp; twitter:小鸟～地叫。The birds are chirping (*or* twittering). /几个姑娘站在屋子犄角～说个没完。Several girls are standing in the corner of the room, chattering continuously.
唧啾 jījiū 〈象声〉chirp
唧溜 jīliū ❶ clever; quick-witted:不～ not clever; clumsy ❷ (often used in the early vernacular) beautiful ❸ (often used in the early vernacular) strong and healthy
唧哝 jīnong talk in a low voice; whisper; talk under one's breath:他们俩在隔壁唧唧哝哝商量了好半天。The two of them spent a lot of time in the next room, discussing something in a whisper.
唧筒 jītǒng pump

羁(覊)
jī 〈书面〉❶ bridle; headstall; halter:无～之马 horse without a bridle (*or* halter); unbridled horse ❷ control; restrain; restrict:放荡不～ unconventional and uninhibited /豪放不～ bold and unconstrained ❸ stay; delay; hamper; detain:俗事～身 be tied up with routine business
羁绊 jībàn 〈书面〉trammels; fetters; shackles; yoke:摆脱旧传统的～ break the fetters of obsolete tradition; smash the shackles of outmoded convention; shake off the yoke of old custom /近来被一些琐事～着,不能出门。I have been detained by some trivial matters lately and unable to go out.
羁泊 jībó 〈书面〉stay away from home; stop; remain:～异乡 stay in an alien land
羁愁 jīchóu nostalgia; homesickness:客居异国起～。Residing in a foreign land one cannot help being nostalgic.
羁缚 jīfù tie; bind up; fetter:摆脱～ shake off the bonds (*or* fetters)
羁勒 jīlè 〈书面〉control; restraint:冲破旧思想的～ smash the shackles of the old ideas
羁留 jīliú ❶ stay; stop over:短期～上海 short sojourn at Shanghai /我一刻也不想在此地～。I don't feel like stopping over here at all. ❷ keep in custody; detain:～审查 be kept in custody for interrogation; detain for interrogation
羁旅 jīlǚ 〈书面〉stay long in a strange place; live in an alien land:～天涯 live in the remotest corner of the world
羁縻 jīmí 〈书面〉❶ win over; draw over; rope in ❷ *see*"羁留"
羁囚 jīqiú imprison; put in jail; put behind bars
羁束 jīshù *also*"羁约"〈书面〉keep within bounds; restrain
羁押 jīyā 〈书面〉detain; take into custody:～候审 committed for trial
羁滞 jīzhì stay in a strange place for a long period of time:～异乡 stay far away from one's hometown for a long period of time /～海外 remain long overseas

笄
jī large pin that women used to hold their hair in ancient China:及～ (of a girl) come of age

嵇
Jī a surname
嵇康 Jī Kāng Ji Kang (formerly translated as Hsi K'ang, 223-262), scholar and thinker of the Three Kingdoms

稽[1]
jī ❶ check; examine; scrutinize; investigate:有案可～ be on record; be verifiable /无～之谈 nonsense; baseless talk ❷ argue; dispute:反唇相～ retort like for like; argue back ❸ (Jī) a surname

稽[2]
jī 〈书面〉delay; linger; procrastinate:令出不～。The order is to be enforced without delay.
see also qǐ
稽查 jīchá ❶ check (to prevent tax evasion, etc.); investigate:严格～走私活动 strictly check on cases of smuggling ❷ inspector; customs officer:他担任过铁路～。He was once a railway inspector.
稽迟 jīchí 〈书面〉stop; delay; procrastinate:～不进 mark time
稽核 jīhé audit; check; examine:这批账目尚未～。These accounts have not yet been checked (*or* audited).
稽考 jīkǎo 〈书面〉ascertain; verify:对有关史实加以～ verify some historical facts /无可～ be unverifiable (*or* unascertainable)
稽留 jīliú 〈书面〉hold up; delay; detain:因事～ be detained by business /这笔钱支付不了在这里～数日的花消。The money we have can hardly cover the expenses of staying here for several days.
稽留热 jīliúrè 〈医学〉continued fever
稽延 jīyán 〈书面〉postpone; put off:～时日 stall; drag one's feet /事情紧急,不得～。The matter is urgent and brooks no delay.

几[1]
jī small table:茶～儿 tea table; teapoy /窗明～净 (used to describe a scholar's study) bright windows and clean tables

几[2](幾)
jī 〈书面〉❶ close to; nearly; almost; practi-

cally:～近于零 virtually nothing /～为骗子所欺 almost taken in by cheats /缺席者～半。Nearly half the people are absent. ❷ slight sign or trace: *see* "～微"

see also jǐ

几案 jī'àn long narrow table; table

几丁质 jīdīngzhì 〈生化〉 chitin

几乎 jīhū ❶close to; nearly; all but; practically:高兴得～跳起来 be so excited that one nearly jumps /头发～全白了。The hair has almost all turned grey (*or* white). /这个村子～每家都有电视机。Practically every family in this village has a TV. /他跟我打乒乓球～总是赢的。When he played ping-pong with me, he won ninety-nine times out of a hundred. ❷ *also* "几几乎"hardly; almost:他们在森林里～迷了路。They were almost lost in the forest. /我听到这个消息,～不敢相信。I could hardly believe my ears when I heard the news. /那个职业拳击手被打得～丧了命。The prize fighter was beaten to within an inch of his life. /我昨天遭车祸～遇难。I had a narrow escape from a car accident yesterday.

几几乎 jījīhū *see* "几乎❷"

几近 jījìn be on the brink or verge of; be close to:你的行为～荒唐。What you have done borders on the absurd.

几率 jīlǜ 〈数学〉 probability

几微 jīwēi 〈书面〉 ❶ minute; tiny:～之差 minute difference; subtle difference ❷ sign; omen; indication

几维鸟 jīwéiniǎo kiwi, a flightless New Zealand bird with hair-like feathers and a long bill

几希 jīxī 〈书面〉 hardly any; very few; scarcely any:彼此相差～ not much difference between the two /人活百岁者～。Few people live to a hundred years.

几至 jīzhì almost; nearly:勤奋读书,～忘食 be so diligent in one's study as to almost forget to eat

讥(譏)

jī ridicule; deride; mock; satirize:行为不端,为人所～ be ridiculed for improper behaviour /冷言相～ make sarcastic comments

讥嘲 jīcháo ridicule; satirize; gibe:她常恶意地～他。She often ridicules him out of malice.

讥刺 jīcì 〈书面〉 ridicule; satirize; deride:冷语～ deride people by cutting remarks

讥讽 jīfěng ridicule; deride; mock:你怎么能像别人一样～他,嘲笑他呢? How could you join the others in ridiculing and sneering at him?

讥骂 jīmà ridicule and fling abuses:肆无忌惮地～ wantonly ridicule and fling abuses

讥评 jīpíng ridicule and criticize:～时政 make satirical comments on government affairs

讥诮 jīqiào 〈书面〉 sneer at; scoff; deride:冷漠、～,都不是与人交往的应有态度。Indifference or sneering is not the proper attitude to take in our dealings with others.

讥讪 jīshàn 〈书面〉 ridicule; deride; mock

讥弹 jītán ridicule and attack:～时弊 satirize and attack current malpractices

讥笑 jīxiào scoff at; sneer at; jeer; mock:他依然我行我素,毫不理睬某些人的～。Completely ignoring some people's sneers, he persists in his old ways. /她～那个以富自傲的杂货店老板娘。She scoffed at that purse-proud grocer's wife. /小张喜欢～别人的缺点。Xiao Zhang is given to laughing at others' shortcomings.

讥议 jīyì make sneering comments (on sth.); ridicule and reproach:他常常无原则地～厂方的某些举措。He often irresponsibly ridicules and takes exception to the measures adopted by the plant leadership.

礼(禨)

jī 〈书面〉 fortune; good luck

玑(璣)

jī 〈书面〉 ❶ pearl that is not quite round:珠～ pearls ❷ ancient astronomical instrument:璇～ ancient astronomical instrument; armillary sphere

靰(鞿)

jī 〈书面〉 reins; halter

机(機)

jī ❶ machine; engine:挖泥～ dredging machine; dredge /内燃～ internal-combustion engine /印刷～ printing machine; printer /计算～ computer /录音～ tape recorder /起重～ hoist; crane /发电～ generator ❷ aircraft; aeroplane; plane:客～ passenger plane /班～ airliner; regular air service; scheduled flight /专～ special plane; private plane /轰炸～ bomber /战斗～ fighter plane /直升～ helicopter; copter /侦察～ reconnaissane plane; scout /滑翔～ glider /舰载～ carrier-borne (*or* carrier-based) aircraft /僚～ wing plane /长～ lead plane; pilot plane ❸ crucial point; pivot; key link:转～ turning point; turning for the better /生～ lease of life /事～ situation; circumstances; trend of events /危～ crisis ❹ chance; occasion; opportunity:趁～ take advantage of the situation; seize the opportunity /时～ opportunity; opportune moment /战～ combat opportunity /随～应变 act according to circumstances /有～可乘 opening to take advantage of; loophole that can be exploited /坐失良～ let an opportunity slip; miss the boat ❺ organic:无～化学 inorganic chemistry /有～体 organism ❻ important affairs:日理万～ handle numerous state affairs every day ❼ intention; idea:动～ motive /杀～ murderous intentions ❽ flexible; quick-witted; clever:灵～ sudden inspiration; brain-wave /神～妙算 superb strategy and wonderful foresight

机变 jībiàn 〈书面〉 act according to the changing situation; adapt oneself to circumstances:善于～ good at adapting oneself to changing circumstances; flexible

机播 jībō sow by machine; machine sowing:全县～小麦二十万亩。Two hundred thousand *mu* were sown with wheat by machines in the county.

机不可失 jībùkěshī can't afford to lose the opportunity; not let the opportunity slip through one's fingers:～,时不再来。Don't let slip the opportunity, it may never come again. *or* Opportunity knocks but once. /兵贵神速,～。Speed is precious in war; time lost will never be regained.

机舱 jīcāng ❶ engine room (of a ship) ❷ passenger compartment (of an aircraft); cabin

机铲 jīchǎn mechanical shovel

机场 jīchǎng airport; airfield; aerodrome:国际～ international airport /临时～ makeshift airfield /简易～ airstrip /军用～ military airfield /～标志 aerodrome markings /～灯标 airport beacon /～行李传送带 carousel

机车 jīchē (popularly called 火车头) locomotive; engine:内燃～ diesel locomotive /电力～ electric locomotive /蒸汽～steam locomotive /～牵引力 hauling capacity of a locomotive /～司机 locomotive engineer; engine driver

机车车辆厂 jīchē chēliàngchǎng rolling stock plant

机车组 jīchēzǔ locomotive crew

机船 jīchuán motor vessel

机床 jīchuáng machine tool:重型～ heavy machine tool /精密～ precision machine tool /自动程序控制～ automatic program-controlled machine tool /木工～ woodworking machine tool /金属切削～ metal cutting machine tool /数字程序控制～ numerically controlled machine tool /～工业 machine tool industry /～厂 machine tool plant; machine tool works

机电 jīdiàn electromechanical:～换能器 electromechanical transducer /～设备 electromechanical equipment; electromechanical device /～产品 mechanical and electrical products /～公司 mechanical and electrical products company; mechanical and electrical company

机电学 jīdiànxué electromechanics

机顶盒 jīdǐnghé 〈影视〉 digital set-top box, a device that links a TV set to the Internet and shows Internet programmes on the TV monitor

机动 jīdòng ❶ motor-driven; motorized:～车辆 motor-driven vehicle; motor vehicle /～脚踏两用车 moped ❷ flexible; adaptable; expedient; mobile:～灵活的战略战术 flexible strategy and tactics /要给各车间一点～的余地。Each workshop should be allowed some room for decision making. ❸ in reserve; for emergency use:～时间 time kept in reserve /留百分之二十作～开支 keep back 20% for extras /～床位 emergency beds /～财力 stand-by financial resources

机动力量 jīdòng lìliàng reserve force

机动粮 jīdòngliáng grain reserve for emergency use

机动性 jīdòngxìng mobility; flexibility; manoeuvrability

机读目录 jīdú mùlù 〈信息〉 machine-readable catalogue (MARC); machine-readable bibliographic records

机断 jīduàn act on one's own judgment in an emergency; make a prompt decision:～行事 act promptly at one's discretion

机帆船 jīfānchuán motor sailboat; motorized junk

J

机房 jīfáng ❶ generator or motor room ❷ engine room (of a ship)
机锋 jīfēng (Buddhist phraseology) witty and penetrating remarks:论辩颇具～。The debate is full of witty and incisive remarks.
机耕 jīgēng 〈农业〉tractor-ploughing; tractor-ploughed: ～面积 area ploughed by tractors; acreage under mechanized farming / ～队 mechanized ploughing team
机耕船 jīgēngchuán wet-field tractor; boat tractor
机工 jīgōng mechanic; machinist
机工车间 jīgōng chējiān machine shop
机构 jīgòu ❶ mechanism: 传动～ transmission mechanism / 分离～ disengaging mechanism / 液压～ hydraulic pressure mechanism / 变速～ gearshifting mechanism ❷ organ; organization; institution; structure; setup: 金融～ financial setup / 科研～ scientific research institute / 治安～ security apparatus / 新闻宣传～ media and information setup / 政府～ government organization / 管理～ the management / 军事～ military establishment / 教育～ educational institution ❸ internal structure of an organization: 精简行政～ streamline the administrative structure / ～调整 adjust the organizational structure/ ～臃肿,层次重叠 unwieldy (*or* overstaffed) and overlapping organizations
机构改革 jīgòu gǎigé structural reform; reorganization; structural streamlining; restructuring
机构投资者 jīgòu tóuzīzhě institutional investor
机栝 jīguā *also* "机括" ❶ mechanism of a crossbow for shooting the arrow ❷ 〈书面〉administrative power; administrative authority
机关 jīguān ❶ mechanism; device; gear: 打开～,车床就开动起来。The lathe will run when the gear is started. ❷ machine-operated: ～布景 machine-operated stage scenery ❸ office; agency; organ; body: 领导～ leading bodies / 党政～ Party and government organizations / 文化教育～ cultural and educational institutions / 公安～ public security organs / 行政～ administrative offices / 执法～ law-enforcing agencies / 税务～ tax bureau / ～工作 office work ❹ stratagem; scheme; trick: 布下～ lay a scheme / 识破～ see through a trick
机关报 jīguānbào organ; offical newspaper (of a party, government, etc.)
机关党委 jīguān dǎngwěi Party membership committee (in a government organ)
机关干部 jīguān gànbù government functionary; office staff
机关刊物 jīguān kānwù organ; official publication (of a party, government, etc.)
机关炮 jīguānpào cannon
机关枪 jīguānqiāng *also* "机枪" machine-gun
机关算尽 jīguān-suànjìn *also* "机关用尽" do much plotting and scheming; use every stratagem: 他～,害人害己。He did great harm to others as well as to himself by incessant plotting and scheming.
机关算尽太聪明,反误了卿卿性命 jīguān suànjìn tài cōngmíng, fǎn wùle qīngqīng xìngmìng all your clever calculations and intrigues have resulted only in your doom; too much cunning and plotting is the cause of your undoing; be hoist with one's own petard
机灌 jīguàn motor-pumped irrigation: ～田 pump-irrigated field
机化 jīhuà 〈生化〉organize
机徽 jīhuī plane emblem
机会 jīhuì chance; opportunity; opening: 大好～ golden opportunity / 经商的好～ good opening for business / 错过～ lose (*or* miss) a chance / ～难得 rare opportunity; chance of a lifetime / 抓住～ seize a chance / 利用～ make use of the opportunity / 趁此～讲几句话 take this opportunity to say a few words
机会成本 jīhuì chéngběn opportunity cost
机会均等 jīhuì jūnděng equal opportunity for all: ～原则 principle of equal opportunity
机会主义 jīhuìzhǔyì opportunism: "左"、右倾～ Right and "Left" opportunism / ～路线 opportunist line / ～者 opportunist
机加工 jījiāgōng machinework: 可～性 machinability
机件 jījiàn 〈机械〉parts; works: 钟表～ works of a clock or watch/ 车床的～ parts of a machine tool / 汽车的～出了毛病。Something is wrong with the vehicle's works.
机井 jījǐng motor-pumped well
机警 jījǐng alert; watchful; vigilant; sharp-witted: ～的战士 vigilant soldier / ～的回答 sharp-witted reply (*or* retort) / 异常的沉着和～ extraordinarily calm and alert / 他～地留意着对方的一举一动。He is keeping a close watch on the other side's movements.
机具 jījù machines and tools: 农业～ farm implements; agricultural implements
机库 jīkù 〈航空〉airplane hangar; hangar
机理 jīlǐ mechanism: 分娩～〈医学〉mechanism of labour / 腐蚀～ corrosion mechanism / 结晶～ crystalization mechanism
机灵 jīling ❶ *also* "机伶" clever; bright; smart; intelligent: ～的孩子 clever child; intelligent child / 很～的年轻人 very smart young man / 动作～得像只猫 as agile as a cat / 海狸这一次变得十分～,它很小心地走近他们。The beaver now being completely aware approaches them cautiously. ❷ *also* "激灵" jīling give a start; start up
机灵鬼 jīlingguǐ smart fellow; clever person: 他是个～儿,谁也不容易欺骗得了他。He is very smart; no one can bluff him easily.
机率 jīlǜ probability
机米 jīmǐ ❶ machine-processed rice ❷ *also* "籼米" xiānmǐ polished long-grained non-glutinous rice
机密 jīmì ❶ secret; classified; confidential: ～文件 classified papers; confidential documents / 商讨～大事 discuss important confidential affairs / 露出一副很～的样子 put on an air of secrecy ❷ secret: 国家最高～ top state secret / 泄露～ leak a secret; let out a secret; divulge a secret
机敏 jīmǐn alert and resourceful; quick-witted; dexterous: ～过人 uncommonly resourceful / 他们在战斗中既～又勇敢。They were brave and resourceful in battle. / 只要你工作～,就会得到提拔。You will be promoted if you keep your eye on the ball.
机谋 jīmóu 〈书面〉stratagem; manoeuvre; artifice; scheme: 这人忠实肯干,但缺少～。He is honest and willing to work hard, but lacks resourcefulness.
机能 jīnéng 〈生理〉function; faculty: 心～不全 cardiac insufficiency / ～亢进〈医学〉erethism / 人体器官的～ functions of human organs
机器 jīqì machine; machinery; apparatus: 安装新～ install new machinery / 国家～ state apparatus; state machine / 战争～ war machine / ～保养和维修 machine maintenance and repair / ～打包 machine press-packing / ～造型 machine moulding / ～制造 machine building / 宣传～ mass media; 〈贬义〉propaganda machine
机器翻译 jīqì fānyì machine translation
机器脚踏车 jīqì jiǎotàchē 〈方言〉motorcycle
机器人 jīqìrén *also* "机械人" robot: 这个～已经达到了 20 世纪 80 年代国际先进水平。This robot is up to the advanced international standards of the 1980's.
机器人学 jīqìrénxué robotics
机器油 jīqìyóu lubricating oil; lubricant
机枪 jīqiāng machine-gun: 轻～ light machine-gun / 重～ heavy machine-gun / 高射～ anti-aircraft machine-gun / 多管～ multiple barrelled machine-gun / 手提～ light automatic gun / 圆盘～ drumfed gun
机枪手 jīqiāngshǒu machine-gunner
机巧 jīqiǎo adroit; deft; dexterous; ingenious: 他的回答很～。He answered ingeniously. *or* He gave a clever reply.
机权 jīquán ability to act according to circumstances; stratagem; scheme
机群 jīqún group or flight of planes: 大～ air armada; air fleet
机身 jīshēn fuselage
机师 jīshī ❶ engineer ❷ 〈方言〉pilot
机手 jīshǒu machine operator
机体 jītǐ ❶ 〈生理〉organism ❷ 〈航空〉airframe
机头 jītóu nose (of an aircraft)
机头炮 jītóupào nose gun
机微 jīwēi *also* "几微" jīwēi sign; omen; indication: 识～,通谋虑 can detect the slightest sign and know how to cope
机尾 jīwěi tail (of an aircraft)
机务 jīwù machine operation and maintenance: ～工 maintenance man / ～工作 maintenance work
机务段 jīwùduàn maintenance section; 〈交通〉(locomotive) depot
机务人员 jīwù rényuán ❶ maintenance personnel ❷ 〈航空〉ground crew
机先 jīxiān 〈书面〉sign or harbinger of coming events: 制敌于～ check the enemy before they take any action / 要行动于～。It's better to take preventive measures.
机械 jīxiè ❶ machinery; machine; mechanism: ～故障 mechanical failure; mechanical breakdown / ～试验 mechanical testing / ～零件

machine components ❷〈比喻〉mechanical; inflexible; rigid:～的观点 mechanical approach /～地搬用别人经验 mechanically copy another's experience /～的战术 inflexible tactics /你这样做,未免太～。Your approach is rather mechanical (*or* rigid).
机械波 jīxièbō mechanical wave
机械厂 jīxièchǎng machinery plant:纺织～ textile machinery plant /建筑～ building machinery plant /矿山～ mining machinery plant /农业～ agricultural machinery plant /重型～ heavy machinery plant
机械动力学 jīxiè dònglìxué mechanical kinetics
机械工程学 jīxiè gōngchéngxué mechanical engineering
机械工业 jīxiè gōngyè machine building industry
机械功 jīxiègōng mechanical work
机械化 jīxièhuà mechanize:农业～ mechanization of agriculture
机械化部队 jīxièhuà bùduì mechanized forces; mechanized troops; mechanized unit
机械加工 jīxiè jiāgōng machining
机械利益 jīxiè lìyì machine benefit; mechanical advantage
机械论 jīxièlùn *see*"机械唯物主义"
机械能 jīxiènéng〈物理〉mechanical energy
机械人 jīxièrén robot
机械师 jīxièshī machinist
机械手 jīxièshǒu〈机械〉mechanical arm; manipulator:仿效～ master-slave manipulator /万能～ general-purpose manipulator
机械唯物主义 jīxiè wéiwùzhǔyì *also*"机械论"〈哲学〉mechanical materialism
机械效率 jīxiè xiàolǜ mechanical efficiency
机械运动 jīxiè yùndòng mechanical movement
机械制图 jīxiè zhìtú mechanical drawing
机心 jīxīn ❶〈书面〉mind given to deception or trickery:外似木讷,内存～。Seemingly simple and slow, but actually deceptive and tricky. ❷ movement (of a watch or clock):～骨架 skeleton movement
机型 jīxíng ❶ type (of an aircraft) ❷ model (of a machine)
机修 jīxiū machine maintenance; machine repair; mechanical repair:～工 maintenance man /～车间 machine repair shop; mechanical repair shop
机绣 jīxiù machine embroidery
机要 jīyào confidential:～工作 confidential work /掌握～ in control of confidential matters
机要部门 jīyào bùmén department in charge of confidential work
机要秘书 jīyào mìshū confidential secretary
机要员 jīyàoyuán cipher officer; cryptographer
机宜 jīyí principles of action; guidelines:请示～ ask for guidelines from one's superior /面授～ brief sb. on how to act
机翼 jīyì〈航空〉wing (of an aircraft)
机引 jīyǐn motor-drawn
机油 jīyóu engine oil; machine oil
机遇 jīyù〈书面〉favourable circumstance; luck; opportunity:把握～ seize an opportunity /挑战与～并存。Challenges and opportunities exist side by side. /这样的～不完全出于偶然。This kind of favourable circumstance is by no means accidental. /应该承认,我的～不错。I must admit I do have some luck.
机缘 jīyuán good luck; good fortune; lucky chance:～凑巧 as luck would have it; by chance; by lucky coincidence /我们的相识,是由于一个偶然的～。We became acquainted by accident.
机缘论 jīyuánlùn occasionalism
机运 jīyùn ❶ opportunity; chance:偶然的～ lucky chance ❷ fate:他把失败的原因归结为～。He attributed his failure to fate.
机载导弹 jīzài dǎodàn air-launched missile
机载火箭 jīzài huǒjiàn aircraft projectile rocket
机载计算机 jīzài jìsuànjī airborne computer
机载警报与控制系统 jīzài jǐngbào yǔ kòngzhì xìtǒng airborne warning and control system (AWACS)
机载雷达 jīzài léidá airborne radar
机载小口径火箭 jīzài xiǎokǒujìng huǒjiàn subcaliber aircraft rocket (SCAR)
机诈 jīzhà〈书面〉crafty; cunning; sly
机长 jīzhǎng〈航空〉aircraft or crew commander; captain (of an aeroplane)
机罩 jīzhào〈机械〉bonnet; hood:发动～ engine bonnet; engine hood; hood
机制 jīzhì ❶ machine-processed; machine-made:～糖 machine-processed sugar /～纸 machine-made paper /～煤球 machine-processed (*or* -made) briquet /～水饺 machine-made dumplings ❷ mechanism:激发～〈物理〉excitation mechanism /计算机～ computer mechanism /结晶～ crystallization mechanism /分娩～〈医学〉mechanism of labour or childbirth /动脉硬化～ mechanism of arteriosclerosis /引入竞争～,激发了各商场搞活经营的积极性。The introduction of competition gave an incentive to all department stores for improving their management.
机智 jīzhì quick-witted; resourceful:勇敢～ brave and quick-witted /他～老练,能够承担这项任务。Being resourceful and experienced, he is quite up to the task.
机助翻译 jīzhù fānyì machine-aided translation
机杼 jīzhù ❶〈书面〉loom ❷〈比喻〉conception (of a piece of writing):他的散文自出～,别具一格。Being original in conception, his prose has a distinctive style of its own.
机子 jīzi〈口语〉❶ loom ❷ small machine (e.g. a sewing machine, a telephone) ❸ trigger
机组 jīzǔ ❶〈机械〉unit; set:水轮发电～ hydraulic generating set/液压～ hydraulic unit ❷ aircrew; flight crew:在飞机失事中,六名～人员及三十名乘客同时遇难。Six members of the crew and thirty passengers died in the plane crash.

矶(磯)

jī rock projecting over the water:钓～ projecting rock for angling
矶沙蚕 jīshācán palolo worm
矶蟹 jīxiè kelp crab

叽(嘰)

jī〈象声〉sharp sound of small birds:小鸟～～叫。Little birds chirp.
叽咕 jīgu *also*"唧咕" jīgu talk in a low voice; whisper; mutter:这两个凑在一块儿又～什么呢? What are these two people up to, talking to each other in such low voices the minute they are together? /她一边嘴里～着,一边舒舒服服地坐在沙发上。She prattled on, as she settled comfortably down on the sofa.
叽叽嘎嘎 jīji-gāgā *also*"唧唧嘎嘎" jīji-gāgā〈象声〉creak; cackle:老牛拉着破车,一路～地响。The aged ox pulled a worn-out cart, creaking all the way. /听他这么一说,大家～地笑起来。Everybody started cackling on hearing his remarks.
叽叽喳喳 jīji-zhāzhā *also*"唧唧喳喳" jīji-zhāzhā〈象声〉chirp; twitter:只见人们交头接耳,好像在～议论什么。People are seen whispering in each other's ears; it seems they are jabbering about something.
叽里旮旯儿 jīligālár〈方言〉corners (of a house, etc.):我～都找到了,就是不见这东西。I simply can't find this object, though I have searched every nook and cranny.
叽里咕噜 jīligūlū〈象声〉❶ gabble; jabber:那个外国人～地连说带比画,他也没搞清楚是个什么意思。He failed to understand that foreigner, who was gabbling and gesticulating all the time. ❷ rumble:巨大的岩石顺着山坡～滚下山去。Huge rocks went tumbling down the hill. /在高低不平的路上,大车～地响着。The cart rumbled along the rough road. /我饿得肚子～地叫。I am hungry; my stomach's rumbling.
叽里呱啦 jīliguālā〈象声〉talk noisily:～地说个没完 talk noisily without end

肌

jī muscle:随意～ voluntary muscle /腹～ abdominal muscle /胸～ pectoral muscle /横纹～ striated muscle /平滑～ smooth muscle /骨骼～ skeletal muscle /三角～ deltoid muscle/二头～ biceps /心～ cardiac muscle; myocardium /面黄～瘦 pale and emaciated
肌氨酸 jī'ānsuān〈生化〉methyl aminoacetic acid; methyl glycocoll; sarcosine
肌病 jībìng〈医学〉myopathy
肌颤搐 jīchànchù〈医学〉myopalmus; myoseism
肌醇 jīchún〈生化〉inositol
肌蛋白 jīdànbái〈生化〉myogen
肌动蛋白 jīdòng dànbái〈生化〉actin
肌肤 jīfū〈书面〉(human) skin:～之亲 blood relations; intimate relations between man and woman /～若冰雪 skin as smooth as ice and as white as snow; a tender and white skin
肌肤甲错 jīfū jiǎcuò〈中医〉scaly dry skin, a symptom of blood

J

stasis; pellagra
肌苷 jīgān 〈生化〉inosine:～酸 inosinic acid
肌红蛋白 jīhóngdànbái 〈生化〉myoglobin
肌坏死 jīhuàisǐ 〈医学〉myonecrosis
肌腱 jījiàn 〈生理〉tendon:～炎〈医学〉myotenositis
肌痉挛 jījìngluán 〈医学〉myospasm:～病 myospasmia
肌理 jīlǐ 〈书面〉skin texture:～细腻 fine-textured skin
肌瘤 jīliú 〈医学〉myoma:多发性～ myomatosis /～切除术 myomectomy; myomotomy; myectomy /子宫～切除术 myomohysterectomy
肌麻痹 jīmábì 〈医学〉myoparalysis
肌囊虫 jīnángchóng sarcocystis
肌强直 jīqiángzhí 〈医学〉myotonia; myotone
肌球蛋白 jīqiúdànbái 〈生化〉myoglobulin
肌肉 jīròu *also*"筋肉" jīnròu muscle:～发达 muscular; brawny /～疾病 muscle disease /～系统 muscle systems /脸颊上的～抽搐了一下 have a cramp in the cheek
肌肉肿瘤 jīròu zhǒngliú muscle tumor
肌肉注射 jīròu zhùshè intramuscular injection
肌酸 jīsuān 〈生化〉creatine:～酶 creatinase
肌体 jītǐ human body; organism:不能让歪风邪气侵害政府机关的～ must not allow corrupt practices to contaminate the government apparatus
肌萎缩 jīwěisuō 〈医学〉muscular distrophy; amyotrophy amyotrophiar
肌细胞 jīxìbāo muscle cell
肌纤维 jīxiānwéi 〈生理〉muscle fibre
肌炎 jīyán myitis; myositis:进行性骨化性～ progressive ossifying myositis /流行性～ epidemic myositis
肌硬化 jīyìnghuà myosclerosis
肌原细胞 jīyuánxìbāo myofibril
肌注 jīzhù (short for 肌肉注射)〈医学〉intramuscular injection
肌组织 jīzǔzhī 〈生理〉muscular tissue

饥[1]

jī hungry; starving; famished:半～半饱 be underfed /充～ allay one's hunger /忍～挨饿 endure the torments of hunger /如～似渴 be eager (*or* keen); thirst after /饱一顿,～一顿 eat one meal and skip the next — can hardly keep body and soul together

饥[2](饑)

jī famine; crop failure:是年大～。That was a year of great famine.
饥饱劳碌 jībǎo-láolù *also*"饥饱劳役" slave all day long with no guarantee against hunger:～的日子已经一去不复返了。Gone are the days when people slaved all the time and did not know where the next meal was to come from.
饥不择食 jībùzéshí a hungry person is not choosy about his food; all food is delicious to the starving; hunger is the best sauce:～,寒不择衣。When one's hungry one eats what there is; when one's cold one wears what one has.
饥餐渴饮 jīcān-kěyǐn eat while hungry and drink while thirsty:一路上～,夜住晓行,不几日就来到了山海关。Travelling all day and stopping only for food and sleep, we soon arrived at Shanhai Pass.
饥肠 jīcháng 〈书面〉empty stomach:夜来～如转雷。When night fell, the rumblings of an empty stomach sounded like rolling thunder.
饥肠辘辘 jīcháng-lùlù one's stomach rumbling with hunger; rumblings of an empty stomach:这座旧兵营里住着数千～的难民。The old barracks housed several thousand hungry refugees.
饥饿 jī'è be hungry; starve:～难挨 suffer from unbearable hunger
饥饿病 jī'èbìng 〈医学〉hunger or hungry disease
饥饿线 jī'èxiàn on the verge of starvation:挣扎在～上 struggle along on the verge of starvation
饥寒 jīhán hunger and cold:流落街头,～难耐 can hardly stand the hunger and cold while wandering about the streets
饥寒交迫 jīhán-jiāopò suffer from hunger and cold; live in hunger and cold; be poverty-stricken:陷入～的困境 be reduced to utter penury /挣扎在～的死亡线上 struggle for survival in the face of starvation and cold /伸出同情的手来支援～的人们 lend a helping hand to suffering people
饥荒 jīhuang ❶ famine; crop failure:闹～ be famine-stricken ❷ be hard up; be hard pressed for money; be short of money:近几月,店里生意清淡,闹～。As business has been slack these months, the shop is running short of money. ❸ debt:他拉了不少～。He has run into a heavy debt.
饥馑 jījǐn 〈书面〉famine; crop failure:那年月,军阀混战,～荐臻。In those years, warlords fought against each other and there were no end of famines.
饥渴 jīkě hunger and thirst:爬上山顶,大家顿觉疲乏～。On reaching the mountain top, we were all overcome with fatigue, hunger and thirst.
饥民 jīmín famine victim; famine refugee
饥馁 jīněi 〈书面〉hunger; starvation
饥歉 jīqiàn 〈书面〉poor harvest; crop failure
饥色 jīsè malnourished look (on one's face):面有～ look pallid because of hunger

畿

jī capital city and its environs:京～ capital city and its surrounding areas
畿辅 jīfǔ 〈书面〉capital city and its environs

圾

jī *see*"垃圾" lājī

芨

jī
芨芨草 jījīcǎo 〈植物〉splendid achnatherum (*Achnatherum splendens*)

鸡(鷄、雞)

jī chicken; fowl:雏～ chick; chicken /公～ cock; rooster /母～ hen /珍珠～ guinea fowl /骨顶～ coot /铁公～ iron cock; miser /烧～ roast chicken /养～场 chicken farm /～食 chicken feed /～汤 chicken broth /手无缚～之力 lack the strength to truss up a chicken; be very weak
鸡巴 jība 〈口语〉cock; penis
鸡肠鼠肚 jīcháng-shǔdù *also*"鼠肚鸡肠";"小肚鸡肠" xiǎodù-jīcháng narrow-minded; petty
鸡虫得失 jīchóng-déshī fight over inconsequential matters; argue over things of little importance:为了一些～闹得天翻地覆 kick up a big row over some trivial matters
鸡雏 jīchú chick; chicken
鸡蛋 jīdàn (hen's) eggs:炒～ scrambled eggs /煎～ fried eggs /煮～ hard-boiled eggs /～煎饼 egg pancake
鸡蛋糕 jīdàngāo (sponge) cake
鸡蛋羹 jīdàngēng steamed egg custard
鸡蛋里挑骨头 jīdànli tiāo gǔtou *also*"鸡蛋里找骨头" look for a bone in an egg; look for a flaw where there is none; find fault; nit-pick
鸡蛋碰石头 jīdàn pèng shítou like an egg striking a rock — attack sb. far stronger than oneself:这种军队跟我们碰,好比～。Pitting their army against ours is like throwing eggs at a rock.
鸡多不下蛋 jī duō bù xiàdàn too many hens won't lay; too many cooks spoil the broth:别看他们眼下挺热闹,～,将来不定怎么样。They're having a jolly time now, but since too many cooks spoil the broth, it's hard to see how they'll fare in future.
鸡飞蛋打 jīfēi-dàndǎ the hen has flown away and the eggs in the coop are broken — all is lost; fall between two stools:你别想得太美了,只怕～,人财两空。Don't indulge in fancy. I'm afraid you will fall between two stools and lose everything.
鸡飞狗走 jīfēi-gǒuzǒu *also*"鸡飞狗跳";"鸡飞狗窜" hens flying and dogs running — mass confusion; great disorder
鸡公 jīgōng 〈方言〉cock; rooster
鸡公车 jīgōngchē 〈方言〉wheelbarrow
鸡骨支床 jīgǔ-zhīchuáng laid up in bed emaciated; reduced to a bag of bones
鸡冠 jīguān *also*"鸡冠子" cockscomb
鸡冠菜 jīguāncài *also*"黑白菜" hēibáicài a variety of cabbage
鸡冠花 jīguānhuā 〈植物〉coxcomb; cockscomb
鸡冠石 jīguānshí 〈矿业〉realgar
鸡冠子 jīguānzi cockscomb
鸡黄 jīhuáng 〈方言〉chick
鸡霍乱 jīhuòluàn fowl cholera
鸡尖 jījiān 〈植物〉*Terminalia hainanensis*
鸡奸 jījiān *also*"鸡奸" jījiān sodomy; buggery
鸡口牛后 jīkǒu-niúhòu *also*"鸡尸牛从" chicken's head and cow's rump:宁为鸡口,无为牛后 better be a chicken's head than a cow's

J

rump — better reign in hell than serve in heaven
鸡口田 jīkǒutián *also*"鸡口地"〈方言〉chicken-haunted field (near the edge of a village); chicken haunts
鸡肋 jīlèi 〈书面〉chicken ribs — things of small value：有如～，食之无味，弃之可惜。It's like chicken ribs. You don't want to eat them, because they are tasteless, but you hesitate to throw them away.
鸡零狗碎 jīlíng-gǒusuì in bits and pieces; fragmentary：～的事 odds and ends; petty matters
鸡毛 jīmáo chicken feather：拿着～当令箭 take a chicken feather for a warrant to give commands; treat one's superior's casual remark as an order and make a big fuss about it /～堵着耳朵 have chicken feathers in one's ears — be unable to hear anything
鸡毛掸子 jīmáo dǎnzi feather duster
鸡毛店 jīmáodiàn 〈旧语〉small and crude inn
鸡毛上天 jīmáo-shàngtiān a chicken feather flies up to heaven; a seemingly impossible thing has been done; pigs might fly
鸡毛蒜皮 jīmáo-suànpí chicken feathers and garlic skins; trifles; trivialities：像这样～的小事不必操心。There is no need to worry about such trifles.
鸡毛信 jīmáoxìn message with a feather attached as a sign of urgency
鸡毛帚 jīmáozhǒu 〈方言〉feather duster
鸡鸣而起 jīmíng'érqǐ rise at cockcrow — diligent; industrious：～，孜孜焉亦不为利 rise early and work diligently without any thought of personal gain
鸡鸣狗盗 jīmíng-gǒudào (ability to) crow like a cock and snatch like a dog — play small tricks：～之徒 mean people who play petty tricks
鸡内金 jīnèijīn 〈中药〉membrane of a chicken's gizzard
鸡皮疙瘩 jīpí gēda goose pimples; gooseflesh; goose bumps：吓得浑身都起了～ so terrified that one's flesh creeps /冻得我直起～。It was so cold that I had gooseflesh all over. /一提起那件事，他就起～。The mere mention of that event raised goosebumps on his skin. /他身上起了一层～。He couldn't help breaking out in goose pimples.
鸡皮鹤发 jīpí-hèfà *also*"鹤发鸡皮" wrinkled skin and white hair — advanced in age
鸡婆 jīpó 〈方言〉hen
鸡犬不惊 jīquǎn-bùjīng even fowls and dogs are not disturbed — excellent army discipline; peace and tranquility：大军过处，～，万民拥护。All the people support the army, which keeps excellent discipline wherever it goes.
鸡犬不留 jīquǎn-bùliú even fowls and dogs are not spared — ruthless mass slaughter：这一带的很多村庄，当年被侵略军杀得～。In those areas all were slaughtered ruthlessly by the invaders, not sparing even fowls and dogs.
鸡犬不宁 jīquǎn-bùníng even fowls and dogs are not left in peace — general disturbance or turmoil：闹得家里～ throw the whole family into confusion /害得老百姓～ wreak havoc among the people
鸡犬升天 jīquǎn-shēngtiān even fowls and dogs ascend to heaven (together with the person who has achieved immortality); relatives and followers of a high official easily get promoted
鸡犬相闻 jīquǎn-xiāngwén live nearby or in the neighbourhood：鸡犬之声相闻，老死不相往来 people do not visit each other all their lives, though the crowing of their cocks and the barking of their dogs are within hearing of each other; live within hail but never visit each other; live in seclusion and autarky
鸡茸 jīróng minced chicken：～鱼翅 shark's fin with minced chicken
鸡肉 jīròu chicken (as food)
鸡舍 jīshè chicken coop; henhouse; roost
鸡尸牛从 jīshī-niúcóng *see*"鸡口牛后"
鸡虱 jīshī chicken louse
鸡松 jīsōng fried chicken floss
鸡素烧 jīsùshāo sukiyaki, a Japanese dish of sliced meat simmered with vegetables and sauce
鸡头米 jītóumǐ 〈植物〉Gorgon fruit
鸡尾酒 jīwěijiǔ cocktail：～会 cocktail party; cocktail reception
鸡瘟 jīwēn chicken pest
鸡窝 jīwō chicken coop; henhouse; roost
鸡窝里飞出金凤凰 jīwōli fēichu jīnfènghuáng 〈俗语〉a phoenix soars out of a chicken coop — a miraculous event：山村里出了个世界冠军，真是～。A girl from this mountain village has become a world champion. Isn't it a miracle?
鸡心 jīxīn ❶ heart-shaped：～领 V-neck ❷ heart-shaped pendant
鸡新城疫 jīxīnchéngyì 〈畜牧〉Newcastle disease
鸡胸 jīxiōng 〈医学〉pigeon breast; chicken breast
鸡血石 jīxuèshí bloodstone; heliotrope; oriental jasper
鸡血藤 jīxuèténg 〈植物〉reticulate millettia (*Milletia reticulata*)
鸡鸭鱼肉 jī-yā-yú-ròu chicken, duck, fish or meat — rich food
鸡眼 jīyǎn *also*"肉刺" ròucì 〈医学〉corn; clavus：～膏 corn plaster
鸡杂 jīzá chicken giblets
鸡爪枫 jīzhǎofēng 〈植物〉full-moon maple (*Acer palmatum*)
鸡爪疯 jīzhǎofēng 〈中医〉chicken claws; rheumatic hands
鸡子儿 jīzǐr 〈方言〉(hen's) egg
鸡子 jīzi 〈方言〉chicken
鸡㙡 jīzōng *Collybia albuminosa*, a kind of edible fungus

屐

jī ❶ clogs：木～ clogs ❷ shoes in general：草～ straw sandals
屐履 jīlǚ shoes

姬

jī ❶ complimentary term for women in ancient China：美～ beautiful woman ❷ name used in ancient China for a concubine：侍～ concubine ❸〈旧语〉professional female singer：歌～ singing girl; female entertainer ❹ (Jī) a surname
姬蜂 jīfēng 〈动物〉ichneumon wasp
姬妾 jīqiè concubine：～成群 have a whole harem (*or* troop) of concubines
姬鼠 jīshǔ a kind of rat

缉

jī seize; arrest; apprehend：通～逃犯 order the arrest of a criminal at large /巡～ patrol in order to seize thieves and smugglers /侦～ track down and arrest
see also qī
缉捕 jībǔ seize; catch; arrest：～人员 arresting officer; hound of law /罪犯已～归案。The criminal has already been apprehended and brought to justice.
缉查 jīchá search; ransack：挨户～ make a house-to-house search
缉毒 jīdú ❶ crack down on drug trafficking ❷ arrest drug traffickers
缉访 jīfǎng search and make inquiries
缉获 jīhuò succeed in seizing or arresting; capture：～在逃罪犯 capture a fleeing criminal /～走私货物 seize smuggled goods
缉拿 jīná seize; arrest; apprehend：～凶手 apprehend a murderer /～归案 bring (a criminal) to justice /～逃犯 arrest an escaped criminal
缉私 jīsī seize smugglers or smuggled goods; suppress smuggling; crack down on smuggling：～船 anti-smuggling patrol boat; coast guard vessel /～人员 anti-contraband personnel /～队 anti-smuggling squad

jí

疾[1]

jí ❶ disease; malady; sickness; illness：恶～ foul disease /宿～ chronic complaint; old malady /沉疴痼～ serious and lingering disease /残～ disability /眼～ eye trouble /积劳成～ fall ill from overwork ❷ suffering; pain; distress; difficulty：*see*"～苦" ❸ hate; loathe; abhor：痛心～首 with bitter hatred

疾[2]

jí swift; fast; quick; vigorous：手～眼快 sharp-eyed and swift-handed; with quick hands and keen eyes /～似流星 swift as a shooting star; very quick /大声～呼 make a loud appeal
疾病 jíbìng disease; sickness; illness：控制～的发生和蔓延 control the outbreak and spread of a disease /～丛生 be infested with all kinds of diseases /传染性～ infectious (*or* contagious) disease
疾步 jíbù at full speed; with quick steps：～而行 move at full speed; go swiftly /～向前 step forward quickly
疾驰 jíchí gallop away; go by quickly; whirl off：～的火车 train running at full speed /群马～。A herd of horses were galloping away.
疾恶如仇 jí'è-rúchóu hate evil like an enemy; hate the wicked

like enemies; detest evil:他一生光明磊落,~。He has been open and aboveboard all his life and detests all sorts of evil.

疾风 jífēng ❶〈气象〉moderate gale; force 7 wind ❷ strong wind; gale:~迅雨 strong wind and swift rain /~暴雨 violent storm; tempest; hurricane

疾风劲草 jífēng-jìngcǎo the force of the wind tests the strength of the grass — strength of character is tested in a crisis; adversity is the touchstone of man:疾风知劲草,烈火见真金。Sturdy grass withstands high winds; true gold stands the test of fire. /~,危难时方显英雄本色。Crisis reveals the true character of a man as high winds prove the sturdiness of the grass.

疾风扫落叶 jífēng sǎo luòyè strong wind sweeping away fallen leaves — carry everything before one; be irresistible

疾患 jíhuàn 〈书面〉disease; illness; ailment:注重卫生,免生~。Pay heed to hygiene so as to avoid disease.

疾进 jíjìn (troops) march forward at full speed:部队沿着公路连夜~。The troops marched forward at full speed along the highway throughout the night.

疾苦 jíkǔ sufferings; hardships:关心群众的~ be concerned about the distress of the people /关心民间~ show concern for the sufferings of the people /时时把群众的~挂在心上 always have the afflictions of the masses at heart

疾雷不及掩耳 jíléi bùjí yǎn ěr *also*“迅雷不及掩耳” xùnléi bùjí yǎn ěr as sudden as a flash of lightning

疾忙 jímáng in a hurry; in haste; hurriedly

疾趋 jíqū 〈书面〉move swiftly:~而过 go past swiftly

疾驶 jíshǐ speed past; whirl away:小汽车~而去。The car whirled off.

疾首蹙额 jíshǒu-cù'é with aching head and knitted brows — frown in disgust; express deep abhorrence:小民~而无处控诉。Though filled with disgust, a common person could find no place to lodge complaints.

疾书 jíshū write swiftly:挥笔~ put pen to paper and write swiftly

疾速 jísù very fast; at high speed; rapidly:~行车 drive a car at high speed

疾恶 jíwù hate; abhor:~黑暗势力 loathe the evil forces

疾行 jíxíng walk quickly:队伍在林间公路上~。The troops marched quickly along the highway in the woods.

疾言厉色 jíyán-lìsè harsh words and stern looks; angry or stern look:老人在世时对手下人从不~。The old gentleman was never brusque with his subordinates. /老师昨天~地训斥了他。Stern-faced, the teacher gave him a good dressing down yesterday.

疾疫 jíyì 〈书面〉disease; illness

疾走 jízǒu go swiftly:见他铁青着脸,在村外的小路上~着。He was seen going swiftly along the path outside the village with his face turned ashen.

疾足先登 jízú-xiāndēng *also*“捷足先登” jiézú-xiāndēng the quick footed mounts first; he that runs fastest gets the ring; the early bird catches the worm

蒺 jí

蒺藜 jíli *also*“蒺藜”〈植物〉puncture vine:铁~〈军事〉caltrop

嫉 jí

❶ jealous; envious; covetous:~才 be jealous of a talented person ❷ hate; detest:愤世~俗 detest the world and its ways

嫉妒 jídù be jealous of; envy:~在折磨她,使她难以入睡。She can't fall asleep for she is burning with jealousy. *or* She is so consumed with jealousy that she can't get to sleep.

嫉恶如仇 jí'è-rúchóu *see*“疾恶如仇” jí'è-rúchóu

嫉富 jífù be jealous of the rich; envy the better-off

嫉恨 jíhèn envy and hate; hate out of jealousy

嫉视 jíshì look upon with hatred

嫉贤妒能 jíxián-dùnéng envy the good and be jealous of the capable:我们的干部切不可狭隘自私,~。Our officials must never be so narrow-minded and selfish as to be jealous of people of worth and ability.

嫉羡 jíxiàn envy and admire:~的目光 look with envy and admiration

瘠 jí

〈书面〉❶ lean; emaciated; thin and weak:瘦~的年轻女子 skinny young girl ❷ barren; poor:贫~的土地 poor soil; barren land

瘠薄 jíbó barren; unproductive:土质~ infertile land; poor soil /村外有一片~的荒丘。There is a barren hillock outside the village.

瘠人肥己 jírén-féijǐ impoverish others to enrich oneself:~的行为是不道德的。It is immoral to enrich oneself at others' expense.

瘠瘦 jíshòu ❶ (of body) lean; thin and weak ❷ (of land) barren; poor; lean

瘠田 jítián barren land

踖 jí

〈书面〉small step

踖踽 jíjǔ 〈书面〉cautious and afraid; nervous

嵴 jí

ridge of a mountain or hill

鹡 jí

鹡鸰 jílíng 〈动物〉wagtail

吉 jí

❶ lucky; auspicious; felicitous; propitious:凶多~少 bode ill rather than well /择~成婚 choose an auspicious day for the wedding / 万事大~。All is well. ❷ (Jí) a surname

吉贝树 jíbèishù kapok tree; silk cotton tree

吉比特 jíbǐtè *also*“吉伽比特”〈信息〉gigabit

吉卜赛人 Jíbǔsàirén *also*“茨冈人” Cígāngrén;“吉普赛人” Gipsy; Gypsy

吉布提 Jíbùtí Djibouti:~人 Djiboutian

吉达 Jídá Jidda, chief port of Saudi Arabia on the coast of the Red Sea

吉大港 Jídàgǎng Chittagong, a seaport in southeast Bangladesh on the Bay of Bengal

吉旦 jídàn 〈书面〉auspicious day

吉尔吉斯斯坦 Jí'ěrjísīsītǎn Kirghizstan:~人 Kirghizstani

吉光片羽 jíguāng-piànyǔ fragment of a highly treasured relic:~,弥足珍贵。A fragment of a highly treasured relic is invaluable.

吉伽 jíjiā giga (= thousand million, or 10^9)

吉剧 jíjù Jilin opera

吉利 jílì lucky; fortunate; auspicious; propitious:图个~ hope for good luck; do sth. for good luck /大吉大利 extremely fortunate /~年头 auspicious years; lucky times

吉林 Jílín Jilin (Province)

吉隆坡 Jílóngpō Kuala Lumpur, capital of Malaysia

吉尼斯 Jínísī (short for ~世界纪录大全) *Guinness* (*Book of Records*):载入《~世界纪录大全》get into the *Guinness Book of Records*

吉普车 jípǔchē jeep

吉期 jíqī wedding day:~定在下月十六日。The wedding is to be held on the sixteenth of next month.

吉庆 jíqìng auspicious; propitious; happy:平安~ safe and happy / 今天双喜临门,是~的日子。It is a happy day since a double blessing has descended upon the house.

吉庆有余 jíqìng-yǒuyú auspicious happiness in superabundance

吉人天相 jírén-tiānxiàng *also*“吉人自有天相”;“吉人天佑” heaven helps a good man; heaven assists the virtuous; heaven helps the good out of harm's way :他两次遇上飞机失事,但~,都安然无恙。He was in two airplane accidents, but nothing happened to him; he had a charmed life.

吉日 jírì auspicious day; happy day:~良辰 lucky day; happy day

吉时 jíshí good time; auspicious or propitious time:~良辰 propitious time; lucky time

吉他 jítā 〈乐器〉guitar

吉田茂 Jítiánmào Yoshida Shigeru (1878-1967), Japanese Prime Minister (1946-1947 and 1948-1954)

吉祥 jíxiáng lucky; auspicious; propitious:~如意 be as lucky as one wishes; auspicious

吉祥物 jíxiángwù mascot:作为2000奥运会~的是:鸭嘴兽“西德”,食蚁针鼹“米利埃”和笑翠鸟“奥利”。The official mascots of the 2000 Olympic Games are “Syd” the duck-billed platypus, “Millie” the spiny ant-eating echidna, and “Olly” the laughing kookaburra bird.

吉星 jíxīng lucky star

吉星高照 jíxīng-gāozhào one's star is rising or in the ascendant

吉凶 jí-xiōng good or ill luck:此去~难断。It is difficult to foretell whether this trip of mine will be a success or not.

吉凶未卜 jí-xiōng wèibǔ no one knows how it will turn out; one's fate is in the balance
吉言 jíyán auspicious remarks; blessing:借你的～,这件事我干了! With your blessing I shall go ahead with it.
吉兆 jízhào good omen; propitious sign:此非～。This is not at all a good omen. *or* It doesn't augur well.

诘

jí
see also jié
诘屈聱牙 jíqū-áoyá *see* "佶屈聱牙" jíqū-áoyá

佶

jí 〈书面〉robust and sturdy
佶屈聱牙 jíqū-áoyá *also* "诘屈聱牙" jíqū-áoyá full of difficult, unpronounceable words; sth. of a tongue-twister:有些译文,尤其是所谓直译的文字,写得～。Some translations especially literal translations, are full of difficult, unpronounceable words.

姞

Jí a surname

藉

jí ❶〈书面〉tread on; trample underfoot; insult:人皆～之 be trodden upon by everyone ❷ (Jí) a surname
see also jiè
藉藉 jíjí *see* "籍籍" jíjí

籍

jí ❶ book; record; register:典～ ancient codes and records; ancient classics /古～ ancient books /史～ historical records; history books /秘～ secret records /簿～ account books, records, etc. /图～ maps of territory and census registers /户～ household register; population register ❷ place of origin; native place; hometown:祖～ ancestral home; land of one's ancestors /原～ ancestral home; original family home ❸ membership:党～ party membership /国～ nationality /学～ one's name on the school roll; one's status as a student /会～ membership (of an association) /外～ (of) foreign nationality ❹ (Jí) a surname
籍贯 jíguàn place of one's birth or origin; native place:我的～是河南省郑州市。Zhengzhou City in Henan Province is my home town.
籍籍 jíjí *also* "藉藉" jíjí 〈书面〉❶ (sound) noisy; tumultuous:人言～。People are talking in a noisy and confusing way. ❷ crisscross:尸骨～ with bodies scattered about
籍没 jímò register and confiscate (sb.'s property)

踖

jí *see* "踧踖" cùjí

革

jí 〈书面〉(of wound or illness) fatal; critical:夫子之病～矣。The master was suffering from a fatal illness.
see also gé

楖

jí 〈古语〉China cypress

棘

jí ❶ sour jujube ❷ thorn bushes; brambles:荆～ thistles and thorns; brambles ❸ prick; puncture: *see* "～手"
棘刺 jícì ❶ bristle (on a porcupine's back, etc.) ❷ prickle or thorn (grown on an animal or plant)
棘轮 jílún 〈机械〉ratchet (wheel)
棘皮动物 jípí dòngwù echinoderm
棘手 jíshǒu thorny; sticky; knotty; troublesome:这件事大家都感到～。Everyone thinks this is a sticky business. /他没想到竟会遇到这样～的问题。He never thought of coming across such a thorny problem. /这确实是个～的问题。This is indeed a tough problem. *or* It's really a hard nut to crack.
棘爪 jízhuǎ 〈机械〉pawl; detent:止回～ check pawl

楫

jí 〈书面〉oar:舟～〈书面〉vessels

辑

jí ❶ collect; gather; compile; edit:编～ edit; compile /剪～ cut and edit /纂～ edit and compile /选～ compile; edit ❷ part; volume; division:这套丛书分为五～,每～十本。This set of books has five parts, each consisting of ten volumes (*or* books).
辑录 jílù compile; collect:～成册 be compiled into books
辑睦 jímù 〈书面〉peaceful; harmonious; in amity
辑要 jíyào summary; abstract:会议事项～ abstract of the proceedings of the meeting
辑佚 jíyì *also* "辑逸" ❶ compile scattered writings (ancient or comtemporary) ❷ book thus compiled:《唐诗～》*A Collection of Scattered Poems of the Tang Dynasty*
辑印 jíyìn collect scattered materials or works of an author and have them printed

戢

jí ❶〈书面〉hide; conceal ❷〈书面〉restrain; put away (arms):～兵 cease hostilities; store up arms and declare armistice /愿将军少～雷霆。It is sincerely hoped that the general would refrain from flying into a rage. ❸(Jí) a surname
戢怒 jínù 〈书面〉restrain one's anger; take hold of oneself; become placated
戢翼 jíyì 〈书面〉(of a bird) fold its wings;〈比喻〉retire
戢影 jíyǐng 〈书面〉retire from public life; disappear from the scene:～家园 retire from public life and stay at home

蕺

jí
蕺菜 jícài *also* "鱼腥草" yúxīngcǎo cardate houttuynia (*Houttuynia cordata*)

集

jí ❶ gather; collect; assemble:聚～ gather together /百感交～ be overwhelmed with mingled feelings /游泳好手云～上海。Ace swimmers all assembled in Shanghai. ❷ market; fair:赶～ go to a country fair; go to market /逢～ on market day ❸ collection; anthology:诗～ collection of poems /画～ album of paintings /地图～ atlas /歌曲～ songbook /文～ collected (literary) works /全～ complete works; collected works /续～ sequel /经史子～ Confucian classics, history, philosophy, and literary writings ❹ volume; book; part:他的经济论文分五～出版。His essays on economics will be published in five volumes. /这部电影片分上、中、下三～。This film is in three parts. /那部电视剧共有二十五～。That TV soap opera is a 25-part serial. ❺ (short for 集合❹) set; assemblage ❻ (Jí) a surname
集部 jíbù literary works, one of the major categories in ancient Chinese book collections
集材 jícái 〈林业〉logging; skidding; yarding:索道～ cable logging /～道 skid road /～绞盘机 yarder
集尘器 jíchénqì 〈机械〉dust arrester; dust collector; duster
集尘设备 jíchén shèbèi dust collecting equipment
集成 jíchéng ❶(usu. used in book titles) collection:《论语注疏～》*Collected Annotations and Glossaries on the Analects* ❷〈电子〉integration:计算机～制造 CIM (computer integrated manufacturing) /～半导体器件 integrated-semiconductor /～磁存储器 integrated magnetic memory
集成电路 jíchéng diànlù 〈电子〉integrated circuit:～晶体管 integrated circuit transistor /～块 integrated circuit block /～设备 integrated circuitry
集成光路 jíchéng guānglù integrated optical circuit; optical integrated circuit
集大成 jí dàchéng be a comprehensive expression; be an agglomeration; be the culmination; epitomize:他是这一派思想的～者。He epitomized the thought of this school. /韩非子集先秦法家思想之大成。Pre-Qin Legalist thought finds its finest expression in the writings of Han Fei Zi.
集电杆 jídiàngān trolley pole
集电弓 jídiàngōng bow collector; bow trolley
集电极 jídiànjí 〈电子〉collecting electrode; collector
集电靴 jídiànxuē collector shoe
集股 jígǔ raise capital; form a stock company
集管 jíguǎn 〈机械〉header
集合 jíhé ❶ assemble; gather; muster; rally; call together:～地点 assembly place or point; rendezvous /～部队,准备出发 muster (*or* rally) the troops and get ready to start out /下令紧急～ call an emergency muster /去参观展览会的人在大门口～。Those going to visit the exhibition please assemble at the gate. ❷ (used as a word of command) fall in:～! Fall in! ❸ gather together; collect:～材料 collect materials /～全村劳动力修水利 gather together all the village's labour force to build water conservancy projects ❹ (shortened as 集)〈数学〉set; assemblage; collection; aggregation
集合号 jíhéhào bugle call for fall-in

集合论 jíhélùn 〈数学〉set theory

集合名词 jíhé míngcí 〈语言〉collective noun

集合体 jíhétǐ 〈矿业〉aggregate

集会 jíhuì assembly; rally; gathering; meeting: 举行群众～ hold a mass rally /宪法保障公民～结社自由。The constitution protects the citizens' freedom of assembly and association. /像这样盛大的～, 在本市还是第一次。Such a grand gathering is unprecedented in this city.

集结 jíjié mass; muster; concentrate; build up: ～力量 muster forces; build up strength /我军主力～在张村一带。The main force of our army is assembled around Zhang Village.

集结地域 jíjié dìyù assembly area

集解 jíjiě (usu. used in book titles) collected annotations or commentaries:《史记～》*Collected Commentaries on the Historical Records*

集锦 jíjǐn a collection of choice specimens: 风景照～ outstanding examples of landscape photoes /图片～ collection of fine (*or* superb) pictures /各国邮票～ collection of choice stamps from all countries

集居 jíjū live in a compact community: 过去这里是贫民～的地方。This used to be the slum where poor people lived densely together.

集句 jíjù poem made up of lines from various poets

集聚 jíjù gather; collect; assemble: ～一堂 assemble together in one hall /操场上～着一群人。A crowd of people gathered (*or* assembled) in the playground.

集刊 jíkān collected papers (of an academic institution): 方言研究～ collected papers on the research of dialects

集流环 jíliúhuán 〈电工〉slip ring

集拢 jílǒng gather (together): 场院中～了一大群人。A large crowd of people gathered in the courtyard.

集录 jílù collect and compile: 他正在～去年发表的语言学论文。He is collecting and compiling all the linguistic papers published last year.

集贸市场 jímào shìchǎng fair trade market — a town or country market at which various products are sold and bought

集纳 jínà collect and compile; collect and sum up: 这些字体是从宋版书上～起来的。These styles of calligraphy are collected and compiled from books published in the Song Dynasty.

集权 jíquán centralization of state power: ～统治 centralized rule / ～政治 centralized politics (*or* political authority)

集群 jíqún group together: 青蛙～迁徙。Frogs move in groups. /搞好打坦克～的训练。Strengthen the training for attacking tank groups.

集日 jírì market day

集散 jísàn (of goods, passengers, etc.) collect and scatter

集散地 jísàndì collecting and distributing centre; distributing centre: 这个城市水陆交通方便, 是本省东南部农副产品的～。Boasting easy land and water transport, the city is the collecting and distributing centre of agricultural and sideline products in the southeastern part of our province.

集散市场 jísàn shìchǎng terminal market

集少成多 jíshǎo-chéngduō every little bit helps; it all adds up; accumulate little by little; many a little makes a mickle

集市 jíshì country fair; market; marketplace: 本城有好几个～。There are several markets in this city.

集市贸易 jíshì màoyì country fair trade

集释 jíshì *see*“集解”

集束 jíshù bundle up: ～手榴弹 bundled hand grenades; bundled-up hand grenades

集束炸弹 jíshù zhàdàn 〈军事〉cluster bomb (unit); CBU cluster

集水 jíshuǐ 〈水利〉catchment: ～工程 catchwork /～井(沟、管) collector well (drain, pipe)

集水面积 jíshuǐ miànjī catchment area

集水区 jíshuǐqū catchment area; catchment district

集思广益 jísī-guǎngyì draw on collective wisdom and absorb all useful ideas; pool the wisdom of the masses; draw on all useful opinions: 这件工作最好同大家商量一下, 以便～。As for this work, it's best to pool our wisdom by consulting all people concerned. /我们在这个问题上要尽可能地～。We should try our best to solicit opinions extensively on this matter.

集体 jítǐ collective: ～观念 collective spirit /战斗的～ militant collective /荣立～一等功 gain a Collective Award of Merit, First Class/ ～财产 collective property /～企业 collective enterprise /～行为 collective behaviour /～治疗 group therapy /～创作 collective creative work /～福利事业 collective welfare cause /关心～ show concern for the collective /～婚礼 group wedding — a wedding ceremony attended by a number of couples

集体安全 jítǐ ānquán collective security

集体防卫 jítǐ fángwèi collective defence

集体户 jítǐhù ❶ people engaging in collective management of agriculture, industry or business enterprises ❷ communal housing of several singles

集体化 jítǐhuà collectivization: 农业～ the collectivization of agriculture /坚持走～的道路 stick to the road of collectivization

集体经济 jítǐ jīngjì collective economy

集体领导 jítǐ lǐngdǎo collective leadership

集体农庄 jítǐ nóngzhuāng collective farm

集体生产劳动 jítǐ shēngchǎn láodòng collective productive labour

集体宿舍 jítǐ sùshè dormitory

集体所有制 jítǐ suǒyǒuzhì collective ownership

集体舞 jítǐwǔ group dancing

集体英雄主义 jítǐ yīngxióngzhǔyì collective heroism

集体主义 jítǐzhǔyì collectivism

集团 jítuán group; clique; circle; bloc: 军事～ military bloc /军人～ junta /统治～ ruling clique; ruling circle; the establishment /小～ coterie; small clique /～犯罪 organized crime /七十七国～ Group of 77 /社会～ social group /垄断～ monopoly group /盗窃～ gang of robbers

集团购买力 jítuán gòumǎilì group purchasing power; institutional purchasing power: 压缩～ cut down institutional purchasing power

集团军 jítuánjūn group army; army group

集训 jíxùn assemble for training: ～班 class for training athletes; training class /干部轮流～。Cadres take turns to receive training.

集训队 jíxùnduì team of athletes in training

集腋成裘 jíyè-chéngqiú the finest fragments of fox fur, sewn together, will make a robe — many a little makes a mickle; little drops of water make a mighty ocean; every little bit helps

集邮 jíyóu stamp collecting; philately: ～簿 stamp-album

集邮爱好者 jíyóu àihàozhě stamp-collector; philatelist

集邮册 jíyóucè *also*“集邮簿”;“插册”chācè stamp album; stamp book

集约 jíyuē intensive: ～农业 intensive farming; intensive agriculture /～饲养〈农业〉intensivism / ～投资〈经济〉intensive investment

集约化 jíyuēhuà intensification: ～经营 intensive management

集运 jíyùn ❶ (of goods, materials, etc.) gather together and transport: ～木材 transport timber in large quantity ❷ containerized transport

集镇 jízhèn town; market town

集中 jízhōng concentrate; centralize; assemble; focus: ～听讲 focus one's attention on the lecture; listen to the lecture attentively /火力～ concentration of fire (on a target)/民主～制 democratic centralism /～指挥 centralized command /思想不～ be absent-minded / ～反映 concentrated expression (*or* manifestation) /～正反两方面的意见 sum up all opinions, both positive and negative /～优势兵力 muster superior forces /他的全部精力都～到这项工作上了。He has devoted himself entirely to this work. /这个单位的职工住得很～。Employees of this unit live close together. /警察的注意力～到一家餐馆, 那里来来往往顾客不少。The police finally zeroed in on a restaurant where they saw many incoming and outgoing patrons.

集中供暖 jízhōng gōngnuǎn 〈建筑〉central heating

集中轰炸 jízhōng hōngzhà mass bombing

集中数据处理 jízhōng shùjù chǔlǐ 〈自控〉centralized data processing

集中营 jízhōngyíng concentration camp

集注 jízhù ❶ focus; concentrate: 人们把目光～到老卢身上。Every eye was focused on Lao Lu. /他的心思又完全～到那件事情上了。He has concentrated his attention on that matter again. ❷ *also*“集解”;“集释” variorum:《楚辞～》*Variorum of the Poetry of Chu*

集注本 jízhùběn variorum edition: 我手头没有这部古籍的～。I don't have the variorum edition of this ancient work at hand.

集装箱 jízhuāngxiāng *also*“货柜”huòguì 〈交通〉container: ～船 container ship /～运输 containerized traffic /～车 container car /～堆放场 container pool; container yard /～化 containerization /～码头 container terminal

集资 jízī raise money or fund; collect money; pool resources: 这座教学楼是群众～修建的。This classroom building was constructed with money collected from the people.

集子 jízi collection; collected works; anthology:这个～收有他的近作十篇。This collection included ten of his latest writings.

集总 jízǒng 〈电子〉lumped:～电容 lumped capacitance

及[1] jí ❶ reach; come up to; attain:不～ unequal to; not up to; inadequate /力所能～ to the best of one's ability /财力所～ within one's means /悔之不～ too late to repent; too late for regrets /由表～里 proceed from the outside to the inside /波～ spead to; involve /过犹不～。Going too far is as bad as not going far enough. ❷ catch up with; be in time for:～到 by the time; as soon as / 望尘莫～ be too far behind to catch up ❸ match; be equal to:我的棋艺远不～他。He plays chess far better than I do. ❹〈书面〉think of by analogy; take into account; give consideration to: 推己～人 treat other people as you would like to be treated yourself; be considerate / 攻其一点,不～其余 attack someone for a single fault while ignoring his or her other aspects ❺ (Jí) a surname

及[2] jí 〈连词〉*used to join two or more nouns or nounphrases, usu. with the one following* 及 *subordinate in meaning*:张氏夫妇～子女 the Zhangs and their children /阳台上、屋檐下～走廊两旁,摆满了各种盆花。Flowerpots are placed everywhere, on the balcony, under the eaves and along the two sides of the corridor.

及第 jídì pass an imperial examination:状元～ be the Number One Scholar in the highest imperial examination /进士～ be a successful candidate in the highest imperial examination

及锋而试 jífēng'érshì wield the sword when it is sharp; use troops when the morale is high; take action when the moment is opportune; strike when the iron is hot

及格 jígé pass a test, examination, etc.; pass:入学考试～ pass the entrance examination /考试不～ fail (in) the examination

及格赛 jígésài 〈体育〉qualifying contest

及冠 jíguàn (of a boy) come of age (at 20 in ancient times); attain full age; become an adult:未到～之年 not yet of age

及笄 jíjī 〈书面〉(of a girl) reach the hairpin age (at 15 in ancient times when she was ready to get married):年已～ have reached the age of 15 (*or* the marriageable age)

及龄 jílíng reach a required age:～儿童均已入学。All school-age children have been sent to school.

及门 jímén 〈书面〉be directly taught by a master (who formally acknowledges one as disciple):～弟子 pupil directly taught by a master; first-generation disciple

及时 jíshí ❶ timely; in time; seasonable:～到达 arrive in time /～播种 sow in good time /～的行动 well-timed move /来得太～了 come at just the right time; arrive in the nick of time /这场雨下得～。This rain is quite timely. *or* It's raining at an opportune moment. ❷ promptly; at once:司机～采取了有效措施。The driver took effective measures without delay. /发现问题,～研究解决。Problems, once discovered, should be studied and solved promptly.

及时行乐 jíshí-xínglè seize every opportunity to enjoy life; eat, drink and be merry:～的思想不足取。It is ill-advised just to enjoy worldly pleasures as much as one can.

及时雨 jíshíyǔ ❶ timely rain when the crops need it most; auspicious rain ❷ timely help:谢谢你送来了～,要不我今天无论如何完不成任务。Thank you for your timely help or I would never have accomplished the task today.

及物动词 jíwù dòngcí 〈语言〉transitive verb

及于 jíyú ❶ reach (the region, area, etc.); spread to:其影响～全国。Its influence has spread all over the country. ❷ as regards; in respect of

及早 jízǎo at an early date; as soon as possible; before it is too late:～改正错误 correct one's mistakes before it is too late; mend one's ways without delay /你们要～动身赶往车站。You should lose no time starting off for the station.

及至 jízhì by (a given time); up to; until:～上星期我才得到他的消息。I didn't hear from him until last week.

伋 jí *see* "急" jí

庋 jí 〈书面〉door bolt

汲 jí ❶ draw (water):～水浇园 draw water for the garden ❷ (Jí) a surname

汲汲 jíjí 〈书面〉be anxious; hunger for; hanker after:～于富贵 crave wealth and power

汲取 jíqǔ draw; derive:～营养 derive nourishment from

汲引 jíyǐn 〈书面〉draw water;〈比喻〉recommend for promotion; promote

极(極) jí ❶ utmost point; extreme:无所不用其～ go to every extreme; stop at nothing /愚蠢之～ be the height of folly /登峰造～ reach the peak; reach the acme; reach the summit /登～ ascend the throne ❷ pole:南～ South Pole; Antarctic Pole /北～ North Pole; Arctic Pole /阳～ positive pole /阴～ negative pole ❸ do one's utmost; reach the limit:～诽谤之能事 spare no slander whatsoever; stop at nothing to slander /物～必反。Things turn into their opposites when they go to the extreme. /乐～生悲。Joy at its height engenders sorrow. ❹ last; ultimate; highest:罪大恶～ be guilty of the most heinous crimes ❺〈副词〉extremely; exceedingly; utterly:可笑～了 be extremely ridiculous /～困难的问题 exceedingly difficult problem /～不愉快的事情 most unpleasant thing /～少数 tiny minority; only a handful /～耐人寻味 afford much food for reflection /他的记忆力～好。He has got a very good memory.

极板 jíbǎn 〈电子〉plate

极大 jídà 〈数学〉maximum:～原理 principle of the maximum /～值 maximum (value) / ～化 maximation

极地 jídì polar region:～航空 polar aviation /～航行 arctic navigation; polar air navigation /～气候 polar climate

极低频 jídīpín 〈电子〉extremely low frequency (ELF)

极点 jídiǎn ❶ the limit; the extreme; the utmost:荒谬到～ be absurd in the extreme; be the height of absurdity /宽大到了～ reach the limit of leniency; be extremely lenient /混乱到了～ in a state of utmost confusion /高兴到了～ be extremely happy ❷〈数学〉vertex; pole:～配置 pole allocation

极顶 jídǐng ❶ peak; top of a mountain:泰山～ summit of Mount Tai ❷ extreme:他对你佩服到～。He simply adores you. ❸ extremely; utterly:～聪明 extremely clever /～糊涂 be foolish to the extreme

极度 jídù ❶ extremely:～悲哀 be extremely sorrowful /～努力 exert oneself to the utmost /～疲劳 be tired out; be exhausted; be overcome with fatigue ❷ extreme; utmost; limit: 到了～reach the limit (*or* extreme)

极端 jíduān ❶ extreme:从一个～走到另一个～ go from one extreme to the other /不要走～。Don't go to extremes. ❷ extreme; utter; exceeding:～仇恨 be extremely hostile; show extreme hatred / ～腐化 corrupt to the core /～负责 have a boundless sense of responsibility /～贫穷 dire poverty; abject poverty /～愚蠢 height of stupidity /～个人主义者 out-and-out egoist /～民主化 ultrademocracy /～分子 extremist /他是一个～种族主义者。He is a dyed-in-the-wool racist. /我们从前要组织一个俱乐部,他是～反对的。When we first wanted to organize a club, he was dead set against it.

极而言之 jí'éryánzhī if the worst comes to the worst; talking in extreme terms;我说这个话是～,把问题讲透。I am talking in extreme terms and putting it bluntly.

极高频 jígāopín 〈电子〉extremely high frequency (EHF)

极冠 jíguān 〈天文〉polar cap

极光 jíguāng 〈天文〉aurora; polar lights: 北～ aurora borealis; northern lights /南～ aurora australis; southern lights /～千米辐射 auroral kilometric radiation

极光弧 jíguānghú 〈天文〉auroral arc

极光扫描光度计 jíguāng sǎomiáo guāngdùjì auroral scanning photometer

极化 jíhuà polarization:～张量 polarization tensor /～强度 polarization intensity /～子 polaron /～电池 polarization cell /～开关 polarization switch /～陶瓷 polarized ceramics /～线圈 polarizing coil

极口 jíkǒu (praise, speak, condemn, etc.) highly:观众对这部影片～称道。The audience all speak highly of this film.

极乐鸟 jílèniǎo *also* "风鸟" fēngniǎo bird of paradise

极乐世界 jílè shìjiè *also* "西天" xītiān 〈佛教〉Sukhavati; Pure Land; Western Paradise:这些国家不是什么～,人间天堂。These countries are by no means a paradise on earth (*or* a land of milk and honey). /细观此景,与我大唐何异! 所谓～,诚此之谓也。On close examination it is no different from our Great Tang. This must be what is meant by paradise.

极力 jílì exert oneself to the utmost; spare no effort:～帮助 do one's best to help /～吹捧 laud sb. to the skies /～渲染 paint a glowing picture of (sth.)/～夸大 blow sth. up out of all proportion/～劝说 try very hard to convince /～宣扬 energetically advertise /～赶先进 spare no effort to catch up with the advanced /～提前完成任务 exert oneself to the utmost to fulfill the task ahead of schedule/她～讨好他,但他感兴趣的却是另一个姑娘。She threw herself at his head, but he was interested in another girl.

极量 jíliàng ❶〈药学〉maximum dose ❷ maximum:潜力已经发挥到了～。The potential has been tapped to the full.

极面 jímiàn 〈数学〉polar face:～绕组〈电工〉pole-face winding; compensated winding

极目 jímù look as far as the eye can see:～远眺 gaze into the distance /～四望 take a panoramic view (from some vantage point)/登高～ climb high to look farther /～望去,雪后的草原真是一片银装世界。Looking afar, I found the prairie after snow to be a vast expanse of silver.

极品 jípǐn 〈书面〉❶ highest grade; best quality:～花茶 best quality jasmine tea /酒中～ best among wines or spirits /～狼毫 best quality writing brush made of hair from weasel's tail /关东人参号称～。Ginseng from China's northeastern provinces is ranked among the highest grade. ❷ highest ranking (official):官居～ be an official of the highest rank

极谱 jípǔ 〈物理〉polarogram:～仪 polarograph /～分析 polarographic analysis /～学 polargraphy

极其 jíqí most; extremely; profoundly; exceedingly:～光荣而艰巨的任务 most glorious and arduous task /留下～深刻的印象 leave a profound impression (on sb.)/态度～严肃 with an extremely serious attitude; in all seriousness

极圈 jíquān 〈地理〉polar circle:北～ Arctic Circle /南～ Antarctic Circle

极权 jíquán totalitarian:～政府 totalitarian government

极权主义 jíquánzhǔyì totalitarianism:～者 totalitarian

极盛 jíshèng heyday; zenith; acme:～时期 golden age; heyday; zenith /明清两代,制瓷工艺达到了～期。Porcelain technology reached its acme during the Ming and Qing dynasties. /二十年前,我还是个小伙子,精力～。Twenty years ago, I was still a young man in the prime of life.

极天际地 jítiān-jìdì reach to the high heavens and pervade the earth; be very high

极为 jíwéi extremely; exceedingly; most:～勇敢 extremely brave /～不满 most dissatisfied /～贫困 exceedingly poor

极限 jíxiàn the limit; the maximum; the ultimate:无～ limitless; open-ended /～负荷〈电学〉limit load /～压力〈物理〉limiting pressure /～承载量 ultimate bearing capacity /～设计 limit design /～分布 limiting distribution /达到每小时 150 英里的最高～ reach a maximum of 150 miles per hour

极限量规 jíxiàn liánggūi limit gauge; external limit range

极小 jíxiǎo 〈数学〉minimum:～原理 principle of the minimum

极小口径终端 jíxiǎo kǒujìng zhōngduān 〈信息〉very small aperture terminal (VSAT)

极刑 jíxíng capital punishment; death penalty:处以～ sentence to capital punishment

极性 jíxìng polarity:～换向器 polarity reverser /～继电器 polarity relay /～转换开关 polarity-reversing switch

极夜 jíyè polar night

极意 jíyì try one's best; rack one's brains:～模仿 try hard to imitate

极右 jíyòu ultra-right:～分子 ultra-rightist

极值 jízhí 〈数学〉extreme value; limit value

极致 jízhì of highest attainments; of greatest accomplishment

极轴 jízhóu 〈数学〉polar axis

极昼 jízhòu polar day

极左 jízuǒ ultra-left:～思潮 ultra-left trend of thought /～分子 ultra-leftist

极坐标 jízuòbiāo polar coordinate:～曲线 polar curve /～图 polar diagram /～导航系统〈航海〉polar-coordinate navigation system

岌

jí 〈书面〉(of a mountain) high; lofty; towering:白浪若山～。White waves look like a towering mountain.

岌岌 jíjí 〈书面〉❶ (of a mountain) towering ❷ precarious:～不可终日 live in constant fear; live precariously/于斯时也,天下殆哉,～乎! At this juncture, there is great danger under heaven (*or* across the land).

岌岌可危 jíjí-kěwēi in imminent danger; in a precarious situation; in great peril; in a critical condition:国势～ country being in great danger /河堤～。The embankment is in great peril. /病情～。The patient's condition is critical. /这个多党联合政府～。The multi-party coalition government is hanging by a thread.

笈

jí 〈书面〉❶ book chest:负～游学 carry a book chest and leave home to pursue studies ❷ book; record:古～ ancient books

级

jí ❶ level; rank; grade:高～官员 senior (*or* ranking) official /各～领导干部 leading cadres at all levels /三～工 grade-3 worker/一～战备 No. 1 alert; maximum alert; red alert /六～地震 earthquake of magnitude 6 (on the Richter scale) /五～风 force 5 wind (on the Beaufort scale) /一～茶叶 grade A tea; first-class tea /八～工资制 eight-grade wage scale (*or* system) /省～机关 (Party and government) organizations at the provincial level /大使～会谈 talks at ambassadorial level /最高～会议 top-level talks; summit talks; summit /越～提拔 be promoted more than one grade at a time /中～英语教材 intermediate English textbook /低～趣味 vulgar interest; bad taste ❷ (of a school) course; grade; class; form:留～ fail to go to the next grade; repeat the year's work; stay down /升～ go up one grade /升留～制度 system of promoting or holding back students /同～不同班的几个女生 several girl students from different classes of the same grade ❸ step:石～ stone steps ❹〈量词〉step; stage:二十～的梯子 ladder of 20 steps /多～火箭 multistage rocket /七～浮屠 seven-storeyed tower ❺〈语言〉degree:比较～ comparative degree /最高～ superlative degree

级别 jíbié rank; level; grade; scale:干部～ rank of a cadre /外交～ diplomatic rank /工资～ wage scale; grade on the wage scale /棉花的～ grade of cotton

级差 jíchā differential:文官机构的工资～ salary differentials in the civil service /～收入调节税 tax for regulating differential incomes

级差地租 jíchā dìzū differential (land) rent

级差佣金 jíchā yòngjīn graded commission

级间 jíjiān 〈电工〉interstage:～变压器 interstage transformer /～耦合 interstage coupling

级间分离 jíjiān fēnlí 〈航天〉stage separation

级联 jílián 〈电子〉〈电工〉cascade (connection):～管 cascade tube/～补偿 series compensation; cascade compensation /～放大器 cascade amplifier /～电动机 cascade motor /～冷凝器 cascade condenser /～液化 cascade liquefaction

级任 jírèn *also* "级任老师" (of primary and secondary schools) teacher in charge of a grade or form

级数 jíshù 〈数学〉progression; series:等比～ geometric progression /等差～ arithmetic progression /～渐进法求解 series approximation to solution

急

jí ❶ impatient; anxious; restless; hasty:～着要答复 be anxious to get a reply /等～了 be impatient of (*or* at) waiting /干吗这么～? Why all this haste? ❷ make restless or anxious; worry:他的病不见好,真～人! He's getting no better. I am worried to death about him. ❸ irritable; annoyed; nettled:开句玩笑,没想到他真～了。I was joking. I didn't expect him to get angry (*or* nettled). ❹ fast; rapid; sudden; violent:～雨 pelting rain /～转弯 sudden turnabout /炮声甚～ violent rumbling of guns /水流湍～。The current is swift. /她讲话太～。She speaks too fast. /他病来得很～。He was taken ill all of a sudden. ❺ urgent; compelling; pressing:～待解决 call for immediate solution /十万火～ most urgent /～不容缓 too urgent to allow of delay /病～乱投医 turn to whatever doctor is available when critically ill /需要甚～,必须尽快满足。The need is urgent (*or* pressing) and must be met promptly. ❻ urgent matter; urgency; exigency; emergency:当务之～ urgent task at present; urgent matter confronting us today /告～ appeal for emergency help /应～措施 measures to meet exigencies /救～ help sb. to cope with a contingency; help meet an urgent need /燃眉之～ pressing need; matter of extreme urgency ❼ be eager to help:～人之难 be eager to help those in need /～群众之所急 be keen on meeting the needs of the masses

急案 jí'àn urgent case; case demanding immediate attention

急巴巴 jíbābā hasty; in a hurry: ～地跑来 come running in great hurry
急板 jíbǎn 〈音乐〉presto
急暴 jíbào impatient and irascible; impetuous and violent
急变 jíbiàn abrupt change; unexpected crisis; sudden about-turn: 要有应付～的准备 be prepared to cope with sudden changes
急病 jíbìng acute disease: 害～ contract an acute disease /～忙请医。In case of serious illness, a doctor is hurriedly sent for.
急不可待 jíbùkědài be too impatient to wait; be extremely anxious; can scarcely wait: 他～地抢着发言。He is very anxious to speak before others.
急步 jíbù walk with quick steps; go swiftly: ～走向教室 walk quickly towards the classroom
急茬儿 jíchár 〈方言〉urgent matter; emergency case: 这是～, 得赶紧办。This is an emergency case and must be attended to immediately.
急驰 jíchí whirl away; speed past: 一转脸, 我看见一辆车～而过。Turning around, I saw a car speeding past.
急赤白脸 jíchibáiliǎn *also* "急扯白脸" 〈方言〉face turning red, or pale because of too much anxiety: 两个人～地吵个没完。Faces turning red, the two were arguing without end.
急匆匆 jícōngcōng hurriedly; in a hurry
急促 jícù ❶ hurried; rapid: 号声～高昂 rapid and high bugling (sound) /～跃进〈军事〉rush; advance by rushes /呼吸～起来 gasp for breath /我的心在～跳动。My heart was beating rapidly. /我被一阵～的脚步声惊醒。I was suddenly woken up by a patter of footsteps. ❷ (of time) short; pressing: 时间很～, 我们快动手吧。Since time is short, let's get to work at once. /抢修桥梁的期限十分～。The time alloted for repairing the bridge was most pressing.
急电 jídiàn urgent telegram; urgent cable
急方 jífāng 〈中医〉emergency prescription
急风暴雨 jífēng-bàoyǔ violent storm; hurricane; tempest: 黑云骤起, ～随之而来。A violent storm came on in the wake of the swiftly gathering dark clouds. /革命的～来势迅猛。The revolutionary tempest surged swift and violent.
急腹症 jífùzhèng 〈医学〉acute abdominal disease; acute abdominal pain
急公好义 jígōng-hàoyì zealous for public welfare; public-spirited: 这项工程得到几位～的企业家的捐助。 Some public-spirited entrepreneurs contributed to the project.
急功近利 jígōng-jìnlì eager for quick success and instant benefit; anxious to get quick results and instant profits: 这都是些目光短浅、～的做法。These are all short-sighted acts aimed at quick results and instantaneous gains.
急管繁弦 jíguǎn-fánxián *also* "繁弦急管" orchestral music with quick rhythm and rich melody
急猴猴 jíhóuhóu 〈方言〉in a great hurry; hastily: 干吗这么～的? Why so much hurry?
急火 jíhuǒ ❶ quick fire; high heat: ～煸炒 stir-fry with high heat/～煮不好饭。Rice will not be well cooked with high heat. ❷ pent-up fury caused by anxiety: ～攻心 burning with anxiety and fury
急急风 jíjífēng ❶〈戏曲〉way of playing a percussion instrument in rapid rhythm, used often to accompany tense and rapid movements in opera ❷ hurriedly; in a hurry: 他～地赶到了。He came in a hurry.
急急如律令 jíjí rú lǜlìng act quickly as instructed, used as a magic formula by Taoist priests to exorcise evil spirits
急急巴巴 jíji-bābā in a hurry; hurriedly: 你让我～地赶回来干什么? Why did you make me come back in such a hurry?
急急惶惶 jíji-huánghuáng hurry in fright: 黑暗中有几个人～跑过。Several figures ran past in the dark in fright.
急煎煎 jíjiānjiān be worried: 他怕赶不上这次演出, 心里～的。He was rather worried as he was afraid of missing the performance.
急件 jíjiàn urgent document or dispatch
急进 jíjìn ❶ *also* "激进" jījìn radical: ～派 radical party; radical /～情绪 radical feeling /～做法 radical way of doing things ❷ quick or rapid movement: 大队人马向城里～。A large number of troops moved towards the city swiftly.
急惊风 jíjīngfēng 〈中医〉accute infantile convulsions: ～遇到了慢郎中 a case of acute disease being treated by a procrastinating doctor — deferred action where prompt medical attention is needed; urgent case receiving slow treatment
急救 jíjiù first aid; emergency treatment: 采取～措施 take first-aid measures /进行～ give first-aid (to sb.)
急救包 jíjiùbāo first-aid dressing
急救车 jíjiùchē (emergency) ambulance; breakdown van; emergency vehicle
急救人员 jíjiù rényuán first-aid personnel
急救药品 jíjiù yàopǐn first-aid medicine
急救药箱 jíjiù yàoxiāng first-aid kit
急救站 jíjiùzhàn first-aid station
急救中心 jíjiù zhōngxīn first-aid centre; emergency centre
急就章 jíjiùzhāng hurriedly-written essay; hasty work; improvisation: 我这篇文章是～, 经不起推敲。My article was written in great hurry and won't bear scrutiny.
急剧 jíjù rapid; drastic; sharp; sudden: ～增加 rapid increase /～上涨 steep rise; sharp rise; sky-rocketing /～下降 sudden drop; sharp decline; plummet /天气～的变化 sudden change of weather /形势发生～的变化 abrupt turn in the situation /他～地喘息起来。He gasped for breath. /她的心～地跳动。Her heart is beating fast.
急遽 jíjù rapid; quick; swift; sharp: 一阵～的敲门声, 把他从梦中惊醒。Rapid knocks at the door woke him up from a dream.
急口令 jíkǒulìng 〈方言〉tongue twister
急来抱佛脚 jí lái bào fójiǎo 〈俗语〉clasp Buddha's feet when in trouble — seek help at the last moment; make a frantic last-minute effort: 平时不烧香, ～ never burn incense when all is well but clasp Buddha's feet when in distress — do nothing until the last minute
急溜溜 jíliūliū in a hurry; anxious: 他放下饭碗, ～地出去了。Putting down his bowl, he went out in a hurry.
急流 jíliú ❶ strong current; torrent; rapid stream; rapids: ～险滩 rapids and shoals /～滚滚 surging torrents /～划艇竞赛〈体育〉white-water racing ❷ jet stream; jet flow
急流勇进 jíliú-yǒngjìn forge ahead against a swift current; advance against heavy odds; press on in the teeth of difficulties
急流勇退 jíliú-yǒngtuì resolutely retire at the height of one's (official) career; extricate oneself from a difficult situation in good time: 尊大人精神正旺, 何以就这般～? Your father is still in his prime, why should he be so eager to retire?
急脉缓灸 jímài-huǎnjiǔ handle a tense situation calmly; make haste slowly
急忙 jímáng in a hurry; in a rush; in haste: 他～走了。He hurried off. /大家这样急急忙忙干什么? Why is everybody in such a hurry? /他接到父亲病重的电报后, ～打点行李, 连夜赶回家去。On receiving the telegraph saying that his father was seriously ill, he immediately packed his bags and rushed back home that very night.
急难 jínàn ❶〈书面〉be anxious to help (those in danger): 急人之难 be eager to help those in distress ❷ misfortune; adversity; grave danger: 人有～, 则倾力相助 do all one can to help those in dire straits
急迫 jípò urgent; critical; pressing; imperative: 最～的任务 most pressing task; task of the greatest urgency /任务～, 须立即行动。Immediate action should be taken since it is an urgent task.
急起直追 jíqǐ-zhízhuī rouse oneself to catch up; strive to overtake: 不甘落后的人们都要～。Those who do not want to lag behind should do their utmost to catch up.
急切 jíqiè ❶ eager; impatient; urgent; imperative: ～的需要 imperative need /语气～ impatient tone /～地盼望 eagerly look forward to ❷ hurriedly; in haste: ～间我也拿不出什么好办法。I cannot come up with any good idea on the spur of the moment. /在这～忙乱中, 她越发慌了手脚。She was all the more at a loss what to do in such hurried confusion.
急如星火 jírúxīnghuǒ in a frantic hurry; extremely pressing; most urgent; posthaste: 运送救济物资～。Relief must be sent posthaste. /他～, 日夜兼程地赶了回来。Travelling day and night, he came back in great haste.
急三火四 jísān-huǒsì 〈方言〉in a hurry; in great haste: 没等我说完, 他就～地把话打断了。He cut me short without waiting for me to finish.
急刹车 jíshāchē ❶ slam the brakes on (a car, etc.) ❷ bring to a halt; stop abruptly: 不知他们听到了什么风声, 来了个～。I wonder what has brought them to a sudden halt.
急射 jíshè 〈军事〉rapid or quick fire
急事 jíshì matter in need of immediate attention; urgent matter: 我有～, 得先走一步。I have to leave now, for I have something urgent to attend to.

J

急速 jísù very fast; at high speed; rapidly; quickly: 部队～地向前行进。The troops marched quickly. /情况变化是～的。The situation is changing fast. /病情～恶化。The patient's condition deteriorated rapidly.

急湍 jítuān ❶ swift current; rapids: ～似箭,猛浪若奔。Swift currents are like arrows released; violent waves are like galloping horses. ❷ swift; rapid: 溪流～ swift stream

急弯 jíwān sharp turn: 前方有个～。Sharp turn ahead. /车子向左拐了个～。The car turned sharply to the left.

急务 jíwù pressing work or business; urgent task: 有～在身 have some urgent work on hand /解决能源问题,是当前的～。The pressing task facing us today is to solve the energy problem.

急先锋 jíxiānfēng one or those eager to take the lead (in doing sth.); daring vanguard; shock force: 他们是现代化建设的～。They are the daring vanguard in the modernization drive.

急行军 jíxíngjūn rapid march; forced march: 部队一夜～来到了火车站。The troops came to the train station after a rapid march all night.

急性 jíxìng ❶ acute: ～脑膜炎 acute meningitis /～阑尾炎 acute appendicitis /～肺炎 acute pneumonia /～肠炎 chordapsus /～发炎 acute inflammation /～流行病 acute epidemic ❷ impetuous; impatient: ～人 impetuous person

急性病 jíxìngbìng ❶〈医学〉acute disease ❷ impetuosity: 犯～ become impetuous or impatient (where patience or prudence is called for)

急性呼吸道疾病 jíxìng hūxīdào jíbìng acute respiratory disease (ARD)

急性子 jíxìngzǐ 〈中药〉seed of garden balsam

急性子 jíxìngzi ❶ impatient; impetuous ❷ impetuous person: ～容易吃亏。Impatient people are liable to come to grief.

急需 jíxū ❶ be badly in need of; need urgently: 购置～的器材 purchase the much-needed equipment / 老人～照料。The old man is in need of immediate care. /该厂～原料。The factory needs raw material badly. ❷ urgent need: 以满足顾客的～ meet the pressing (*or* crying) need of the customers

急眼 jíyǎn 〈方言〉❶ get angry; fly into a rage: 人家这么两句就惹你～啦。How can you get angry just because others have made these remarks? ❷ be worried; be anxious: 他一～,连话都说不出来了。His words fail him when he gets worried. ❸ urgent; pressing; imperative: ～的事 pressing work or business; sth. urgent

急要 jíyào critical; vital: ～事 matter of great urgency /～工作 work of vital importance; urgent work

急用 jíyòng urgent need: 这批物资暂存,以备～。This lot of materials will be stored up for emergency need. /这是留着～的钱,你不能拿走。You are not allowed to take this money away as it is kept for a rainy day.

急于 jíyú eager; keen; anxious; impatient: ～知道发生了什么事 be impatient to know what has happened /别～下结论。Don't jump to conclusions. /许多条件不具备,何必～开工! Why start the project in such a hurry when a number of conditions are still lacking?

急于求成 jíyú-qiúchéng overanxious for quick results; impatient for success: ～往往导致失败。Undue haste often leads to failure. *or* Haste makes waste.

急躁 jízào ❶ irritable; hot-tempered; irascible: 性情～ of irritable temperament /你不要～,要冷静。Don't get worked up. Cool it! ❷ impetuous; rash; impatient: 反对～冒进 be against rashness and premature advance /别～,等研究完了再干。Be patient, please. We'll take the matter up when we have studied it thoroughly.

急诊 jízhěn emergency call; emergency treatment: 挂～ register as an emergency case

急诊病人 jízhěn bìngrén emergency case

急诊室 jízhěnshì emergency ward

急症 jízhèng sudden attack or onset of an illness or disease; acute disease

急智 jízhì nimbleness of mind in dealing with emergencies; ability to make quick and intelligent decisions in time of crisis; quick-wittedness: 他颇有～,能够应付各种突然情况。He is quick-witted and able to deal with all kinds of emergency.

急中生智 jízhōng-shēngzhì suddenly hit upon a way out of a predicament; show resourcefulness in an emergency: 他突然～,把枪托猛地朝那人的胸口一撞。He had a sudden flash of inspiration; he jabbed the man hard in the chest with the butt of his gun.

急骤 jízhòu rapid; hurried; hasty: ～的脚步声 hurried footsteps

急转直下 jízhuǎn-zhíxià (of a situation, etc.) take a sudden turn and then develop rapidly: 那年秋天,国内的局势～。The situation in the country took a sudden turn that autumn. *or* That autumn, the nation's situation turned sharply. /病情～,意外地恶化了。The patient took an unexpected turn for the worse.

即[1]

jí ❶ approach; reach; be close to; be in contact: 可望不可～ within sight but beyond reach /若～若离 keep sb. at arm's length / 不～不离 be neither too close nor too distant ❷ attain; assume; undertake: *see* "～位" ❸ presently; at present; in immediate future: ～将成行 about to start off (*or* set out) /成功在～。Success is in sight. ❹ prompted by the occasion: *see* "～兴"; "～席"

即[2]

jí 〈书面〉❶ be; mean; that is: 荷花～莲花 lotus, that is (*or* namely) lotus flower /非亲～友 if not a relative, then a friend / 在旧社会,毕业～失业。In the old society graduation meant unemployment. /承认错误～改正错误之起点。Admitting one's mistake marks the starting point of its correction. ❷ at once; immediately; in no time: 招之～来 come at the first call /一触～发 touch-and-go / 稍纵～逝 transient; fleeting /稍加修改～可使用 can be used immediately after slight revision /问题的症结～在于此。Herein lies the crux of the question. ❸ even if; even though; though: ～遇困难,亦应尽量设法如期完成。You should try your best to meet the deadline even if there are difficulties.

即便 jíbiàn even; even if; even though; though: ～跟我没有关系,我也要管。I'm going to take up the matter even though it is none of my business.

即发电雷管 jífā diànléiguǎn instantaneous detonator

即或 jíhuò even; even if; even though; though: 你就大胆干吧,～走一点弯路也不要紧。Be brave and get down to work at once. It doesn't matter even if you have to take a roundabout course.

即将 jíjiāng be about to; soon; be on the point of: 会议～开始。The meeting is about to begin. /展览会～闭幕。The exhibition will soon be closed. /春节～来临。The Spring Festival is drawing near. /暑假～到来。Summer vacation is at hand. /北京四环路～竣工。The Fourth Ring Road in Beijing is nearing completion. /他告诉他们商业的繁荣～来临。He told them that a business boom was just round the corner.

即景 jíjǐng 〈书面〉(of a literary or artistic work) the scene rouses one's creative impulse; be inspired by what one sees: 西湖～ West Lake Vistas (title of a poem, etc.)

即景生情 jíjǐng-shēngqíng the scene brings back memories; the scene touches a chord in one's heart: ～,他想起了自己的不幸遭遇。What he saw reminded him of his unfortunate past. /他～,赋诗一首。The scene moved him to compose a poem. *or* Drawing inspiration from the scene, he composed a poem.

即景诗 jíjǐngshī extempore verse or poem

即刻 jíkè at once; immediately; promptly; instantly: ～向工地出发 start right away for the worksite /他～就到。He'll be here in no time.

即令 jílìng even; even if; even though; though: ～这次试验失败了,我们也不应气馁。We are not going to lose heart even if this experiment fails.

即期 jíqī 〈经济〉immediate; spot; at sight: ～付现 immediate cash payment; prompt cash payment /～汇价 spot rate /～价格 spot price / ～外汇 spot exchange /～交货 delivery on the spot /～汇票 demand bill; demand draft /～票据 demand note; note at sight /～经营净利概念 current operating concept of net income

即日 jírì ❶ this or that very day; today: 本协定自～起生效。The present agreement takes effect as from today. /本条例自～起施行。The regulations come into force as of today. ❷ within the next few days; soon: 录取通知书～可以发出。The admission notice will be dispatched within a few days. /大米～投放市场。The rice will be marketed soon.

即如 jírú as; like: ～你所说,她是个有胆识的开拓者。As you say, she is a trailblazer full of courage and insight.

即若 jíruò 〈书面〉even; even if; even though; although: ～小学生亦知此。Even school children know this well.

即时 jíshí immediately; forthwith; at once; instantly: ～付款 immediate payment /～交货 prompt delivery /～管理情报系统 real time

management information system /～信息处理系统 real time information-processing system /～制度 real time system /命令下达,～起程。Set out at once after the announcement of the order.

即时速度 jíshí sùdù instantaneous velocity

即食 jíshí (of food) instant:～面 instant noodles

即使 jíshǐ even; even if; even though; though:～你当时在场,恐怕也没有办法。Even if you were there, I'm afraid you could do nothing about it. /～取得很大成绩,他也不该自满。However great his success is, he shouldn't feel conceited.

即世 jíshì 〈书面〉pass away; die

即事 jíshì write with deep feeling about what one sees; write out of inspiration:～诗 poem written to express one's feelings on the occasion; extempore (*or* impromptu) poem

即位 jíwèi ❶ take one's seat ❷ ascend the throne

即席 jíxí 〈书面〉❶ impromptu; extemporaneous; offhand:～赋诗 improvise a poem /～录音 instantaneous recording /他的～讲话总是很出色的。He is always at his best when he speaks off the cuff. /尽管毫无准备,他仍能～演唱一首民歌。Though quite unprepared, he was nevertheless able to sing a folk song on the spur of the moment. ❷ take one's seat (at a dinner table, etc.):宾主～ hosts and guests taking their seats

即行 jíxíng put into practice immediately; carry out right away; implement at once:～召开大会 hold a meeting immediately /～枪决 carry out the execution right away; execute by shooting at once

即兴 jíxìng impromptu; extemporaneous:～之作 improvisation /他是～出去旅行的。He had not planned to take the trip; he just left on the spur of the moment.

即兴曲 jíxìngqǔ 〈音乐〉impromptu

即兴诗 jíxìngshī extempore verse

即以其人之道,还治其人之身 jí yǐ qí rén zhī dào, huán zhì qí rén zhī shēn deal with a man as he deals with you; pay a person back in his own coin:我党的方针便是"～",以打对打,以拉对拉。The policy of our Party is to "do unto them as they do unto us", stick for stick and carrot for carrot.

亟

jí 〈书面〉urgently; promptly; anxiously; earnestly:～待解决 have to be settled urgently; demand prompt solution /～盼复函 earnestly look forward to your reply /～须纠正 must be speedily put right /～欲成行 desire most ardently to make the journey; want very much to set out /～须注意 call for immediate attention /此缺点～应纠正。The shortcoming must be overcome (*or* rectified) without delay.

see also qì

亟亟 jíjí 〈书面〉in a hurry; in haste:～奔走 go on errands in a hurry /不必～。Take it easy. *or* Take your time.

殛

jí 〈书面〉kill:雷～ be struck dead by lightning

jǐ

脊

jǐ ❶ spine; backbone; vertebra: *see* "～椎" ❷ sth. like a spine; ridge:山～ ridge of a hill or mountain /屋～ ridge of a roof /书～ spine of a book /高压～ ridge of high pressure; pressure ridge /海～ ridge on an ocean bottom

脊背 jǐbèi back (of a human being or any other vertebrate)

脊梁 jǐliang 〈方言〉back (of a human body)

脊梁骨 jǐlianggǔ backbone; spine:活像个断了～的癞皮狗 just like a mangy dog with a broken back (a term of contempt for renegades, etc.) /戳～ criticize sb. behind him; backbite

脊檩 jǐlǐn *also* "大梁" dàliáng; "正梁" zhèngliáng 〈建筑〉ridgepole; ridgepiece

脊鳍 jǐqí 〈动物〉dorsal fin

脊神经 jǐshénjīng spinal nerve

脊髓 jǐsuǐ spinal cord:～孔 myelopore

脊髓灰质炎 jǐsuǐ huīzhìyán (popularly called 小儿麻痹症)〈医学〉poliomyelitis; polio; infantile paralysis:～疫苗 poliomyelitis vaccine; poliovirus vaccine

脊髓脊膜炎 jǐsuǐ jǐmóyán 〈医学〉meningomyelitis

脊髓痨 jǐsuǐláo 〈医学〉myelanalosis

脊髓麻痹 jǐsuǐ mábì 〈医学〉myeloparalysis; spinal paralysis

脊髓痛 jǐsuǐtòng 〈医学〉myelalgia

脊髓炎 jǐsuǐyán 〈医学〉myelitis

脊索 jǐsuǒ 〈动物〉notochord

脊索动物 jǐsuǒ dòngwù chordate (animal)

脊瓦 jǐwǎ 〈建筑〉ridge tile

脊柱 jǐzhù spinal or vertebral column; backbone; spine; rachis:～裂 bifid spine; spina bifida; rachischisis /～强直 rigid spine; poker spine /～缘 vertebral margin; margo vertebralis

脊柱病 jǐzhùbìng 〈医学〉rachiopathy

脊柱炎 jǐzhùyán 〈医学〉rachitis

脊椎 jǐzhuī ❶ vertebra; back:～抽液 spinal tap ❷ spine; backbone

脊椎病 jǐzhuībìng 〈医学〉spondylopathy; spinal disease

脊椎动物 jǐzhuī dòngwù vertebrate

脊椎骨 jǐzhuīgǔ vertebra; spine

脊椎结核 jǐzhuī jiéhé 〈医学〉spondylocace

脊椎炎 jǐzhuīyán 〈医学〉spondylitis

济(濟)

Jǐ name of an ancient river which rose in present Henan and flowed through northern Shangdong into the Bohai Sea, and whose channel was later taken over by the Yellow River

see also jì

济楚 jǐchǔ 〈书面〉well-dressed; handsome:衣冠～ well-dressed; decently dressed; in full dress

济济 jǐjǐ (of people) many; abundant; numerous:人才～ abundance of capable people; galaxy of talent

济济跄跄 jǐjǐ-qiāngqiàng numerous and well-behaved:会议期间各方代表～,一时称盛。During the meeting representatives of all walks of life gathered together, and it was a grand spectacle.

济济一堂 jǐjǐ-yītáng gathering of many people; gathering together under the same roof:各国科学家们～,商讨世界环保问题。Scientists from all countries gather together to discuss the world environmental problem.

济南 Jǐnán Jinan, capital of Shandong Province

挤(擠)

jǐ ❶ crowd; throng; cram; pack:～满了人 be crowded with people /～作一团 huddle together; be packed like sardines /大厅已经～满。The hall is filled to capacity. /这几天特别忙,许多事儿都～在一块儿了。I have been very busy recently, having to attend to several matters at the same time. ❷ jostle; push; squeeze:～进去 force one's way in; squeeze in /从人群中～过去 push through a crowd; elbow one's way through a crowd /你推我～ hustle and bustle /别～! Don't push. /大家再往中间～～。Please move a bit to the centre. ❸ squeeze; press:～掉水 squeeze water out /～橘子汁 squeeze juice from an orange /～时间学习 find time to study ❹ exclude; squeeze out; push out:他被～出了董事会。He was excluded from the board of directors.

挤兑 jǐduì run on a bank

挤对 jǐdui 〈方言〉force sb. to submit or yield:他不愿意,就别～他了。Don't force him to do it if he is unwilling.

挤咕 jǐgu 〈方言〉wink:眼睛里进去了沙子,一个劲儿地～。The eye kept winking when a grain of sand got into it. /我朝他直～眼儿,叫他别开腔。I winked at him to keep quiet.

挤挤插插 jǐji-chāchā 〈方言〉very crowded; crammed; packed tight or full; packed like sardines:～坐了一屋子人。The house is filled to capacity. *or* The house is packed full.

挤落 jǐluo 〈口语〉shove aside; push out; squeeze out:别～人。Don't push me out.

挤眉弄眼 jǐméi-nòngyǎn make eyes; wink:大家丢纸团,扔砖头,～,无所不为。They were up to every conceivable trick: passing notes, throwing bricks, winking and making signs to one another. /调皮的小伙子,躲在我背后～做怪脸。Some of the mischievous ones, hiding themselves behind me, wrinkled their noses in a grimace.

挤奶 jǐnǎi milk (a cow, etc.)

挤奶机 jǐnǎijī milking machine; milker

挤破门 jǐpòmén the door breaks down with overcrowding — too many visitors:来谈生意的～。Business negotiators flocked to the office.

挤塞 jǐsè crowd and block; jam:这一地段最热闹的街道,被人群～得水泄不通。The bustling streets of this area are all jam-packed with people.

挤压 jǐyā extrude; press:～机〈冶金〉extrusion press; extruder /

(从模型内)～出管子 extrude tubing /～载荷 extrusion load /～模塑法 extrusion moulding /～应力 extrusion stress /当心脏骤停跳动时，要～心脏，使它复跳。When the heart stops beating all of a sudden, you must press it and make it beat again.

挤牙膏 jǐ yágāo squeeze toothpaste out of a tube — be forced to tell the truth bit by bit：赶紧痛痛快快都说出来，不要这样～！Make a clean breast of it. Don't talk like squeezing toothpaste out of a tube.

挤轧 jǐyà engage in internal strife or infighting：互相～ try to put each other down (*or* do each other in)

挤眼 jǐyǎn wink at sb.：他俩彼此挤了挤眼儿。They winked at each other.

挤占 jǐzhàn squeeze in and forcibly occupy; squat; commandeer：～私房 forcibly occupy private houses; squat (in) a private house /挪用～教育经费 misappropriate educational funds

戟

jǐ ❶ halberd ❷〈书面〉stimulate; excite

戟指 jǐzhǐ 〈书面〉point one's fingers angrily at：～怒目 point one's fingers and look daggers at sb. /～顿足 stamp one's feet and point one's fingers angrily at sb.

掎

jǐ 〈书面〉❶ pull; pin down ❷ tow; pull; draw

掎角之势 jǐjiǎozhīshì tactic or posture of dividing one's forces to pin down the enemy or joining one's forces to mount a pincer's attack on the enemy：取～ adopt the tactic of dividing one's forces to pin down the enemy or mounting a pincer's attack on him /为～ present such a posture

掎摭 jǐzhí 〈书面〉❶ condemn; denounce：～弊病 criticize malpractices ❷ pick

几(幾)

jǐ ❶ how many; what; to what extent or degree：你来～天了？How many days (*or* How long) have you been here? /今天星期～？What day is today? /～点钟？What's the time? /你的座位是～号？What's your seat number? /离这儿有～里地？How far is it from here? /这孩子～岁啦？How old is the child? ❷ a few; several; some：～天 several days /过～天 in a couple of days /～十 tens; dozens; scores /十～岁的孩子 teenagers /三十～ thirty-odd; over thirty; more than thirty /所剩无～ not much left /每隔～分钟 every few minutes /经过～百次试验才获得成功。The experiment succeeded after having failed hundreds of times.

see also jī

几曾 jǐcéng (used in a rhetorical question to indicate negation) at what time in the past; when：在他生病期间，我～安睡过一夜？During his illness, when did I have a good night's sleep?

几次三番 jǐcì-sānfān time and again; repeatedly：～地前来寻衅 come repeatedly to pick a quarrel /～来看我 come to visit me time and again

几多 jǐduō 〈方言〉how many; how much; how：这袋米有～重？How much does this sack of rice weigh? /从这里到县城～里？How far (*or* How many *li*) is it from here to the county town? /这孩子～聪明！How clever the kid is! /父母在孩子身上不知花了～精力。The parents devoted endless energy to the care of their children.

几分 jǐfēn a little; a bit; somewhat; rather：回答问题时有～紧张 rather nervous in answering questions /让他～ humour him a little; cut him some slack /他有～艺术家气质。He is something of an artist. /警察对他的举止有～怀疑。The police were somewhat suspicious of his behaviour.

几何 jǐhé ❶〈书面〉how much; how many：人生～！Life is but transient. *or* For tomorrow we die. /这点东西能值～，何必认真。These things are not worth much. Why so serious about it? ❷〈数学〉geometry：～光学 geometrical optics /～分布 geometric distribution /～规划法 geometric programming /～平均数 geometric mean; geometric average

几何动力学 jǐhé dònglìxué geometrodynamics

几何概率 jǐhé gàilǜ geometric probability

几何级数 jǐhé jíshù 〈数学〉geometric progression; geometric series：马尔萨斯认为，人口按～增长，生活资料按算术级数增长。According to T. R. Malthus, population increases with geometrical progression and subsistence increases with arithmetical progression.

几何体 jǐhétǐ *also* "立体" lìtǐ solid

几何图形 jǐhé túxíng geometric figure

几何学 jǐhéxué geometry：解析～ analytic(al) geometry /立体～ solid geometry /平面～ plane geometry

几何作图法 jǐhé zuòtúfǎ geometrograph

几经 jǐjīng experience several times：～波折 experience ups and downs /～变换 experience changes several times; go through several changes

几内亚 Jǐnèiyà Guinea：～人 Guinean

几内亚比绍 Jǐnèiyà-Bǐshào Guinea-Bissau

几内亚湾 Jǐnèiyàwān Gulf of Guinea, a large inlet of the Atlantic Ocean bordering on the coast of Guinea

几起几落 jǐqǐ-jǐluò up again and down again; on-and-off; off-and-on：修楼的事～，至今仍未动工。The building project has been taken up and put down several times, and there is no sign yet of its execution.

几儿 jǐr 〈方言〉what date：今儿是～？What's the date today? /大哥～走的？When did the elder brother leave?

几儿个 jǐrge 〈方言〉what time：小张～结婚？When will Xiao Zhang get married?

几时 jǐshí what time; when：你们～见他马虎过？When did you ever find him doing things carelessly? /你～有空～来。Drop in whenever you are free.

几许 jǐxǔ ❶〈书面〉how much; how many：这类作品，能传世的又有～？How many of these writings can last for generations? /庭院深深深～？Deep is the mansion's court yard, but who knows how deep? ❷ a little; a few：他祖上也曾留下～薄产，足以度日。He inherited a small property from his ancestors and could make do.

麂

jǐ 〈动物〉muntjac

麂皮 jǐpí chamois (leather); chammy

麂子 jǐzi 〈口语〉muntjac

虮(蟣)

jǐ

虮子 jǐzi egg of a louse; nit

己

jǐ ❶ self; oneself; one's own：舍～为人 sacrifice oneself for others /损人利～ benefit oneself at others' expense /据为～有 make sth. one's own /排除异～ get rid of those who are not one's own people ❷ sixth of the ten Heavenly Stems (天干)

己二酸 jǐ'èrsuān adipic acid

己方 jǐfāng one's own side

己见 jǐjiàn one's own opinion：各抒～。Each airs his or her own views.

己任 jǐrèn one's own duty or responsibility：以天下为～ deem it one's own responsibility to concern oneself with the affairs of the country

己所不欲，勿施于人 jǐ suǒ bù yù, wù shī yú rén do not do to others what you would not have them do to you; do unto others as ye would be done by：中国古话说："～。"我们反对外来干涉，为什么我们会去干涉别人的内政呢？As the old Chinese saying goes "Do not impose on others what you would not like others to impose on you". Since we are opposed to interference from outside, why should we try to interfere in the internal affairs of other countries?

己欲立而立人 jǐ yù lì ér lì rén wishing to establish oneself, one should help others to do likewise

鱾

jǐ 〈动物〉*Girella punctate*

纪

Jǐ *also* Jì a surname

see also jì

给

jǐ ❶ supply; provide; furnish：补～ supplies /自～自足 self-sufficiency; autarky /这段时间，他连零用钱也仰～于父兄。In those days, he depended on his father and elder brothers even for pocket money. ❷ ample; abundant; well-provided for：家～户足。Every household is well provided for.

see also gěi

给付 jǐfù pay money owed to; pay：按章～ pay according to rule

给水 jǐshuǐ supply water; provide feedwater：～工程 water-supply engineering /～站 water-supply station /锅炉～ boilerfeed water /～器 water feeder /～管 feed pipe /～箱 feed-tank

给体 jǐtǐ *also* "供体" gōngtǐ donor：～受体共聚物 donor-acceptor

J

给养 jǐyǎng provisions; victuals: 自筹～ try to provide for oneself/上级及时给小岛上的驻军送去了～。The higher authorities timely sent provisions to the troops stationed on the small island.

给予 jǐyǔ *also* "给与"〈书面〉give; render; offer: ～补助 give subsidies /～折扣 grant a discount /～忠告 offer some advice /～热烈欢迎 accord a warm welcome /～帮助 extend (*or* render) assistance (*or* help) /～礼遇 show hospitality /～积极评价 make a positive appraisal; comment favourably /～表扬 praise; speak highly /对于这些谬论，我们必须～有力的驳斥。We must refute these fallacies forcefully.

jì

寂 jì ❶ still; quiet; calm; silent: 万山沉～。All mountains are dead quiet and still. /江边阒～无人。There is no sign of human beings; it is all quiet along the river bank. ❷ lonely; lonesome; solitary: 枯～ bored and lonely /孤～ lonesome; all alone /幽～ secluded and lonely /冷～ quiet and solitary

寂寂 jìjì quiet; still; noiseless: ～荒山 quiet barren mountain /四周～无声。No sound is heard all around.

寂静 jìjìng quiet; silent; still: ～无声 dead still; all quiet /～的街道 quiet street; quiet neighbourhood /在～的深夜里 in the still (*or* dead) of night /货车过去了，一切又都～下来。With the passing of the truck, all returns to peace and quiet.

寂苦 jìkǔ lonely and distressed: ～的心情 feel lonely and sorrowful

寂寥 jìliáo 〈书面〉solitary; lonesome: ～无人 feel lonesome having no one in sight

寂灭 jìmiè ❶ perish; die out: 楼下的人声渐渐～。Noises downstairs died out gradually. ❷〈佛教〉nirvana

寂寞 jìmò ❶ lonely; lonesome: 他一个人住在海边相当～。He led a solitary life, living all by himself in this seaside house. /老人～凄凉，令我难过。The old man looked so forlorn that I felt really sorry for him. ❷ quiet; still: 这条小巷，白天少有人行，夜晚更加～。The small lane is almost deserted during the day and becomes even quieter at night.

寂默 jìmò quiet; still; silent

寂然 jìrán 〈书面〉silent; still; quiet; soundless: 他凝神静听，却又～无声。He listened attentively for some time, but there was not a single sound.

齐（齊） jì 〈书面〉❶ seasoning; flavouring; condiment ❷ alloy
see also qí

济（濟） jì ❶ ferry; cross a river; go across a stream: 和衷共～ work as one man to cross a river — pull together to overcome difficulties ❷ relieve; aid; help: 接～ give material or financial help / ～人之急 relieve sb. from distress; aid (*or* help) sb. in his hour of need /～弱扶倾 help the weak and the distressed /缓不～急。Slow action can't meet urgent need. ❸ be helpful; benefit: 无～于事 not help matters; be of no help
see also Jǐ

济急 jìjí give urgent relief; relieve sb. in need; meet the emergency: 这笔钱权为你～。This sum of money will help you tide over difficulties.

济困扶危 jìkùn-fúwēi *also* "扶危济困" help the distressed and succour those in peril; assist the poor and help those in trouble: 他一生仗义疏财，～。He contributed money to good causes and assisted people in distress all his life.

济贫 jìpín relieve the poor: 劫富～ rob the rich to relieve the poor

济世 jìshì be of help to the people and society: 行医～ practise medicine to help people /～安民 bring prosperity to the country and a better life to the people /～之才 person capable of managing state affairs

济事 jìshì (often used in the negative) be of help; be of use: 怨天尤人不～。Complaining is of no avail (*or* doesn't help matters). /老人叹道："人老了，不～了！" The old man sighed: "I'm getting old and am no longer of any use!"

济州岛 Jìzhōudǎo Cheju-do, islands south of the Korean Peninsula

济助 jìzhù give material or financial help

霁（霽） jì 〈书面〉❶ clear up after rain or snow: 雨～。The rain is over and the sky is clearing up. ❷ calm down after being angry: 色～ calm down after being angry; appear mollified

霁红 jìhóng *also* "祭红" jìhóng bright red colour used in glazing pottery

霁色 jìsè blue colour similar to that of the sky after rain

霁威 jìwēi 〈书面〉cease to be angry

霁月光风 jìyuè-guāngfēng *also* "光风霁月" bright moon and gentle breeze after rain — openhearted; open and aboveboard: 待人如～，律己则严霜烈日 kind and generous to others but strict with oneself (like the severe frost and scorching sun)

荠（薺） jì
see also qí

荠菜 jìcài 〈植物〉shepherd's purse

荠苧 jìníng 〈植物〉Chinese mosla (*Mosla chinensis*)

剂（劑） jì ❶ pharmaceutical or chemical preparation: 汤～ decoction (of herbal medicine) /搽～ liniment /催醒～ analeptic /滴鼻～ nasal drops /滴眼～ eye drops /丸～ pill; bolus /片～ tablet /酊～ tincture /锭～ lozenge /合～ mixture /冲～ medicine to be taken after being mixed with boiled water, wine, etc. /膏～ medicinal extract /糊～ paste /浸～ infusion /乳～ emulsion /散～ powder medicine /漱～ gargle /栓～ suppository /吸入～ inhalation /洗～ lotion /洗眼～ eye lotion /消毒～ disinfectant /针～ injection /麻醉～ anaesthetic; narcotic ❷〈化工〉agent: 催化～ catalyst; catalytic agent /干燥～ drying agent; desiccant /防腐剂～ preservative; antiseptic /冷冻～ refrigerant /试～ reagent /杀虫～ insecticide; pesticide ❸ a small piece of dough ❹〈量词〉*used of concoctions of herbal medicine*: 一～中药 a dose of Chinese herbal medicine /连服三～ take three doses in a row

剂量 jìliàng 〈药学〉dosage; dose: 有效～ effective dosage

剂量计 jìliàngjì 〈化学〉dosimeter

剂量学 jìliàngxué 〈化学〉dosimetry

剂型 jìxíng 〈药学〉form of a drug (e.g. liquid, powder, pill)

剂子 jìzi small piece of dough

哜（嚌） jì 〈书面〉taste

哜哜嘈嘈 jìjì-cáocáo 〈象声〉talk noisily and confusingly; clatter: 屋子里～，不知他们在说些什么。They are talking noisily and confusingly in the room, and I find it difficult to make out what they are saying.

鲚（鱭） jì 〈动物〉long-tailed anchovy; anchovy

计 jì ❶ count; compute; calculate; number: 不～其数 countless; innumerable /数以万～ by the tens of thousands; numbering tens of thousands /按质～价 price sth. according to its quality /不～成本 whatever the cost; not concerned about the cost /去年赢利额共～五百万元。All told, the profit of last year is 5 million *yuan*. ❷ meter; gauge: 体温～ clinical thermometer /压力～ piezometer; pressure gauge /雨量～ rain gauge /硬度～ sclerometer /气温～ thermograph /风向～ anemometer; wind gauge /湿度～ (hair) hygrometer /速度～ speed indicator /血压～ sphygmomanometer /电压～ voltmeter /光度～ photometer /吸力～ suction gauge ❸ idea; ruse; stratagem; plan: 眉头一皱，～上心来 knit the brows and a stratagem comes to one's mind /缓兵之～ stalling tactics; stratagem to gain respite /中～ fall into a trap /苦肉～ ruse of inflicting an injury on oneself to win the confidence of the enemy /将～就～ turn sb.'s trick against himself /无～可施 at one's wits' end; at the end of one's tether ❹ make plans; design; aim; intend: 设～ design; make plans / 为提高效率～ with a view to increasing efficiency /为国家利益～ in the interest of the country /为长远～ from a long-term point of view ❺ consider; concern oneself; care; bother about: 不～成败 not care if one succeeds or fails /无暇～及 have no time to bother about sth. ❻ (Jì) a surname

计步器 jìbùqì 〈体育〉pedometer

计策 jìcè stratagem; plan; ruse; device: 中了他人的～ fall into others' trap /用～把敌人调进包围圈 use a stratagem to lure the ene-

J

my into the encirclement
计尘器 jìchénqì konimeter
计程表 jìchéngbiǎo taximeter
计程车 jìchéngchē taxi
计程仪 jìchéngyí 〈航海〉log:电~ electric log
计酬 jìchóu calculate the sum of payment; pay:~方法 way of calculating the payment /按时~ pay by the hour /按劳~ to each according to his or her labour
计出万全 jìchū-wànquán foolproof plan or scheme:这种事情,在眼下是很难~的。It's difficult to make a surefire plan for matters like that at the moment. /贾琏只顾贪图二姐美色,听了贾蓉一篇话,遂为~。Jia Lian was so infatuated by Second Sister's beauty that he felt Jia Rong's plan was foolproof.
计费 jìfèi 〈通信〉billing
计工 jìgōng assessment of work done:~单 time ticket
计划 jìhuà ❶ plan; project; programme:综合性~ comprehensive project (*or* plan) /工作~ work plan /科研~ science and research programme /制定~ make a plan; draw up (*or* work out) a plan /~编制 plan formulation; planning /~控制系统 project control system/ ~期 plan period; planning period /~指标 indicators for plan; plan target /人造地球卫星按预定~返回地面。The man-made satellite returned to earth as scheduled (*or* planned). ❷ map out; plan:明天~干什么? What do you intend to do tomorrow? /我~先到上海,然后去杭州。I plan to go to Shanghai first and then to Hangzhou.
计划采购 jìhuà cǎigòu scheduled purchasing or procurement
计划产量 jìhuà chǎnliàng designed output; scheduled production
计划单列市 jìhuà dānlièshì city specifically designated in the state plan
计划法 jìhuàfǎ law on planning
计划供应 jìhuà gōngyìng planned supply
计划经济 jìhuà jīngjì planned economy; command economy
计划生产 jìhuà shēngchǎn planned production:~能力 planned productive capacity
计划生育 jìhuà shēngyù family planning; birth control; planned parenthood:实行~,是中国的一项基本国策。It is one of China's basic policies to carry out family planning.
计划体制 jìhuà tǐzhì planning system
计划外产品 jìhuàwài chǎnpǐn non-planned product
计价 jìjià valuation:~过低 undervaluation /~过高 over-valuation
计价器 jìjiàqì fee register
计件 jìjiàn reckon by the piece:~合同 agreement by piece /~奖励工资 piecework premium wage; piecework incentive wage /~管理方案 piecework management plan /~制 piece rate (system) /~折旧法 unit depreciation method
计件工人 jìjiàn gōngrén piece-worker; rate worker; man paid by the job
计件工资 jìjiàn gōngzī piece rate wage; piecework wage; piece wage:~制 piecework system /~率 piece rate; piecework rate
计件工作 jìjiàn gōngzuò piecework
计较 jìjiào ❶ bother about; haggle over; fuss about:此类小事,何需~。Don't be so particular about such trifles. /何必斤斤~于一己的得失。Why concern oneself so much with personal gains or losses? /不要~几角钱的零头! Let's not haggle over a few coins (*or* small change). ❷ argue; dispute:我现在不同你~。I won't argue with you now. /他这个人从不与人家~。He is the kind of person who never picks a quarrel with others. ❸ think over; consider; mull over:日后再作~。Let's think it over later. /如何做才好,要好好~~。We must consider carefully (*or* mull over) what's the best way to do it.
计量 jìliàng count; calculate; measure:~耕地 measure the cultivated land /用脚步~一下两人之间的距离 step off the distance between two persons /~检定 metrological verification /~信息 metrical information /~技术 measurement technique /~法制 metrological legislation /~器具 measuring instrument /遭到无法~的损失 suffer immeasurable damage; suffer inestimable losses
计量经济学 jìliàng jīngjìxué econometrics
计量心理学 jìliàng xīnlǐxué psychometrics
计量学 jìliàngxué metrology
计虑 jìlǜ ❶ scheme; stratagem ❷ plan; map out; think over:他正~着怎样进行春耕。He is thinking over the spring ploughing.
计略 jìlüè 〈书面〉scheme; stratagem:长于~ good at stratagems
计谋 jìmóu stratagem; scheme; trap:巧设~ cleverly map out a scheme /他定了~,单等对方入圈套。Having laid a trap, he is just waiting for the opponent to fall into it.
计穷力竭 jìqióng-lìjié come to the end of one's tether; have shot one's last bolt; be at one's wits' end:我已~,只能听你的了。I'm at my wits' end, so I can only rely on you.
计日程功 jìrì-chénggōng estimate exactly how much time is needed to complete a project; have the completion of a project well in sight; be certain of success in time:中国的兴盛是可以~的。The day is not far off when China will attain prosperity.
计生委 jìshēngwěi (short for 计划生育委员会) family planning commission
计时 jìshí reckon by time:~成本 hour cost /~日工 measured day-work /~研究 time study /~制度 time system /~卡片 time-card
计时工资 jìshí gōngzī payment by the hour; hourly rate; time-rate wage
计时工作 jìshí gōngzuò timework
计时器 jìshíqì hourmeter; hour counter
计时赛 jìshísài 〈体育〉timetrial
计时员 jìshíyuán 〈体育〉timekeeper
计数 jìshǔ count; calculate:难以~ hard to calculate; countless /一一~ count one by one
计数 jìshù count:~控制 counting control /~管理 management through figures
计数器 jìshùqì counter:盖革~ Geiger counter /闪烁~ scintillation counter
计算 jìsuàn ❶ count; calculate; compute; reckon:~选票 count the votes /~生产成本 calculate (*or* estimate) the cost of production/ 把损耗~在内 reckon the spoilage in /~圆柱体的体积 compute the volume of a cylinder ❷ consideration; planning:他做什么事都有~。He did everything according to plan. ❸ trick; scheme:互相~ try to harm each other /他专能~人。He is a past master at tricking others.
计算尺 jìsuànchǐ slide rule
计算机 jìsuànjī computer; calculating machine:电子~ electronic computer /数字控制~ digital control computer /模拟~ analogue computer /微型~ microcomputer /个人~ personal computer (PC) /~编目系统 computerized catalogue system /自动程序控制~ automatic sequence-controlled calculator /超高速巨型~ giant ultra-high-speed computer /自动数字跟踪分析~ automatic digital tracking analyser computer /~机房 computer room /~科学 computer science
计算机病毒 jìsuànjī bìngdú *also* "电脑病毒" diànnǎo bìngdú computer virus
计算机程序 jìsuànjī chéngxù computer program:~设计 computer programming /~编制员 computer programmer
计算机存储器 jìsuànjī cúnchǔqì computer memory; computer storage
计算机代码 jìsuànjī dàimǎ computer code
计算机断层扫描 jìsuànjī duàncéng sǎomiáo *also* "CT扫描" computerized tomography
计算机辅助软件设计 jìsuànjī fǔzhù ruǎnjiàn shèjì computer-aided software design (CASD)
计算机辅助设计 jìsuànjī fǔzhù shèjì computer-aided design (CAD)
计算机辅助语言教学 jìsuànjī fǔzhù yǔyán jiàoxué computer-assisted language learning (CALL)
计算机辅助制造 jìsuànjī fǔzhù zhìzào computer-aided manufacturing (CAM)
计算机工艺 jìsuànjī gōngyì computer art
计算机监控系统 jìsuànjī jiānkòng xìtǒng computer supervisory control system
计算机控制 jìsuànjī kòngzhì computer control
计算机模拟 jìsuànjī mónǐ computer simulation
计算机排字 jìsuànjī páizì computer typesetting
计算机配置 jìsuànjī pèizhì computer configuration
计算机情报检索 jìsuànjī qíngbào jiǎnsuǒ information retrieval by computer
计算机全息术 jìsuànjī quánxīshù computer holography
计算机软件 jìsuànjī ruǎnjiàn computer software
计算机数据 jìsuànjī shùjù computer data:~处理装置 computer data processing unit /~存贮装置 computer data memory unit
计算机数据检索系统 jìsuànjī shùjù jiǎnsuǒ xìtǒng computerized data retrieval system
计算机通讯系统 jìsuànjī tōngxùn xìtǒng computer communica-

tion system
计算机网络 jìsuànjī wǎngluò computer network:～设备 computer network facilities /～制 computer network system
计算机现金 jìsuànjī xiànjīn cyber cash
计算机效率 jìsuànjī xiàolǜ computer efficiency
计算机应用 jìsuànjī yìngyòng computer application; computer utility
计算机硬币 jìsuànjī yìngbì cyber coin
计算机硬件 jìsuànjī yìngjiàn computer hardware
计算机语言 jìsuànjī yǔyán computer language
计算机元件 jìsuànjī yuánjiàn computer component
计算机站 jìsuànjīzhàn computer installation
计算机指令 jìsuànjī zhǐlìng computer instruction
计算机制图 jìsuànjī zhìtú computer graphics
计算器 jìsuànqì calculator
计算数学 jìsuàn shùxué numerical or computational mathematics
计算语言学 jìsuàn yǔyánxué computational linguistics
计算中心 jìsuàn zhōngxīn computer centre
计议 jìyì deliberate; consider; talk over; consult:从长～ take one's time in coming to a decision; think sth. over carefully /和同事们～过 have consulted with one's colleagues /评比如何进行尚未～好。It is not yet settled how to make a public appraisal.

髻 jì hair worn in a bun or coil; chignon:抓～ one of the twisted knots of hair on either side of the head /蝴蝶～儿 butterfly-shaped hair bun

惎 jì 〈书面〉❶ hate ❷ instruct; enlighten

蓟[1] jì 〈植物〉setose thistle

蓟[2] Jì place in ancient times (close to present-day Beijing), capital of the State of Yan (燕) during the Zhou Dynasty
蓟马 jìmǎ 〈动物〉thrips, a kind of insect:烟～ tobacco thrips

檵 jì
檵木 jìmù 〈植物〉*Loropetalum chinense*

芰 jì 〈古语〉water caltrop; water chestnut

技 jì skill; ability; trick:绝～ unique skill /特～ stunt; trick/雕虫小～ insignificant skill /献～ make a display of one's feats /一～之长 what one is skilled in; skill /黔驴～穷 at one's wits' end /使敌人无所施其～ make it impossible for the enemy to play any tricks
技法 jìfǎ technique; skill and method:这位画家很讲究～。This painter paid special attention to technique.
技改 jìgǎi (short for 技术改造) technical transformation or innovation:～方案 scheme for technical innovation (*or* renovation)
技工 jìgōng ❶ skilled worker ❷ mechanic; technician
技工学校 jìgōng xuéxiào *see* "技校"
技击 jìjī art of attack and defence in *wushu*
技能 jìnéng technical ability; mastery of a technique; skill:～训练 skill training /写作的基本～ basic writing technique /在计算机操作上有较好的～ be skilful at operating a computer /～考试 trade test
技巧 jìqiǎo ❶ skill; technique; craftsmanship:刺绣～ one's skill at embroidery /电气～ cinematic technique /艺术～ artistry /高超的美发～ superb skill in hairdressing ❷ *see* "技巧运动"
技巧运动 jìqiǎo yùndòng 〈体育〉acrobatic gymnastics; sports acrobatics; tumbling
技穷 jìqióng at one's wits' end; at the end of one's resources
技师 jìshī technician
技士 jìshì junior technician
技术 jìshù ❶ technology; technique; skill; expertise:科学～ science and technology /采用先进～ adopt advanced techniques (*or* technology) /～熟练 be skilful; be proficient /～操作规程 regulations for technical operations /～合作 technological (*or* technical) cooperation /～交流 exchange of technical know-how; technical exchange/～援助 technical assistance /提高～水平 increase technical competence /～要求很高 demand high-level technology /宇宙飞行～ space technology /作精彩的～表演 give a brilliant display of skill ❷ technical plant or equipment
技术兵种 jìshù bīngzhǒng technical forces; technical military services
技术储备 jìshù chǔbèi technological reserve
技术犯规 jìshù fànguī 〈体育〉technical foul
技术服务 jìshù fúwù technical service:～专业户 household specialized in technical service
技术改造 jìshù gǎizào technical innovation; technological transformation
技术革命 jìshù gémìng technological revolution:～运动 drive for technological revolution
技术革新 jìshù géxīn *also* "技术改革" technological or technical innovation:～小组 technological innovation cell /～周期 technical innovation cycle
技术工人 jìshù gōngrén skilled worker
技术规范 jìshù guīfàn technical or technological specification
技术鉴定 jìshù jiàndìng technical appraisal or evaluation
技术经济学 jìshù jīngjìxué techno-economics
技术开发 jìshù kāifā technological development
技术科学 jìshù kēxué applied sciences
技术恐惧症 jìshù kǒngjùzhèng technophobia (fear of the negative effect of science and technology on society and environment)
技术狂 jìshùkuáng technomania
技术力量 jìshù lìliàng technical force; technical personnel
技术密集产品 jìshù mìjí chǎnpǐn technology-intensive product
技术名词 jìshù míngcí technical term
技术情报 jìshù qíngbào technical intelligence
技术人员 jìshù rényuán technical personnel or staff
技术社会 jìshù shèhuì technopolis
技术市场 jìshù shìchǎng technical market — place where technique and technical materials are bought and sold
技术手册 jìshù shǒucè technical or technological manual
技术推广站 jìshù tuīguǎngzhàn technical dissemination station:农业～ agrotechnical station
技术性 jìshùxìng technical; of a technical nature:～问题 technical matter /～的层次 technical level
技术学校 jìshù xuéxiào technical school
技术研究所 jìshù yánjiūsuǒ technological research institute
技术员 jìshùyuán technician:农业～ agronomist
技术知识 jìshù zhīshi technical expertise; technological know-how
技术职称 jìshù zhíchēng titles for technical personnel
技术指导 jìshù zhǐdǎo ❶ technological guidance; technical guidance:～费 fee for technical advice ❷ technical adviser
技术转让 jìshù zhuǎnràng technology transfer; transfer of technical know-how
技术装备 jìshù zhuāngbèi technical plant; technological plant:～故障控制 engineering casualty control
技术咨询 jìshù zīxún technical advice
技术资料 jìshù zīliào technical or technological data
技术作物 jìshù zuòwù *also* "经济作物" jīngjì zuòwù cash crop; industrial crop
技校 jìxiào technical school — a school where secondary-level technical personnel and skilled workers are trained:这些工人都在～培训过三年。All these workers were trained in technical schools for three years.
技痒 jìyǎng itch to display one's skill:他看见别人下棋,不觉～。Seeing some people playing chess, he itched to have a go.
技艺 jìyì skill; skillfulness; artistry; feat:～精湛 highly skilled; masterly /～高超 superb skill

伎 jì ❶ *also* "技" jì skill; ability; trick:故～重演 be up to one's old tricks again; play the same old trick ❷〈古语〉professional female dancer or singer:歌～ professional singer
伎俩 jìliǎng trick; ruse; intrigue; manoeuvre:玩弄卑劣～ play a dirty trick /惯用的～ one's favourite gimmick /鬼蜮～ devilish intrique /骗人的～ deceptive ploy; ruse /贼喊捉贼的～ the tactic of "a thief crying 'stop thief'"

妓 jì prostitute; whore:狎～ go whoring
妓女 jìnǚ prostitute; whore; streetwalker
妓院 jìyuàn brothel:逛～ visit a brothel

J

寄

jì ❶ send by post; post; mail: ~印刷品 send printed matter /把书~给他 post him the book /~钱 remit money /~信 post a letter; mail a letter /~航空信 send a letter by airmail ❷ entrust; deposit; place; park: 把某物~在某人处 deposit sth. with sb. /把钥匙~在我处 entrust the key to me /她把婴儿~在姑母家。She parked her baby at her aunt's. *or* She left her baby with her aunt. /父母在我身上~了很大希望。My parents have placed great hopes on me. ❸ depend on; attach oneself to: *see* "~食"; "~居" ❹ adopted: ~儿 adopted son /~父母 foster parents

寄殡 jìbìn lay a coffin in a place temporarily

寄存 jìcún deposit; leave; check: ~行李 deposit one's luggage; check one's luggage /把大衣~在衣帽间 check one's overcoat at the cloakroom /行李~处 left-luggage office; checkroom /自行车~处 bicycle park /~费 deposit charge /我把书~在他那里了。I've left my books in his keeping. *or* I've left my books with him.

寄存器 jìcúnqì 〈计算机〉 register: 变址~ index register /进位~ carry storage register

寄递 jìdì deliver (a letter)

寄顿 jìdùn leave (with sb.); leave in the care of: 我把孩子~在她处。I left my child in her care. *or* I entrusted her with the care of my child.

寄放 jìfàng leave (with sb.); leave in the care of: 行李全部~在亲戚的家中。All the luggage is left with my relative.

寄费 jìfèi postage

寄父 jìfù *also* "寄爹" fosterfather

寄怀 jìhuái *also* "寄情" 〈书面〉 express one's feelings: 赋诗~ compose poems to vent one's feelings

寄籍 jìjí stay away from home: ~上海 stay in Shanghai (for quite some time)

寄迹 jìjì 〈书面〉 stay in a place for the time being: ~桂林 sojourn in Guilin

寄件人 jìjiànrén sender

寄居 jìjū live away from home; live with a relative, etc. (because of one's straitened circumstances): ~在叔父家 live with one's uncle/多年~海外 live overseas for years

寄居蟹 jìjūxiè hermit crab

寄卖 jìmài *also* "寄售" consign for sale on commission; put up for sale (in a secondhand shop): 把旧钢琴放在信托商店里~ place (*or* leave) an old piano in a secondhand shop for sale

寄卖品 jìmàipǐn consignment merchandise

寄卖商行 jìmài shānghóng commission shop; secondhand shop

寄名 jìmíng former superstitious practice of having a monk as a child's master or someone as his god father so as to ensure his long life

寄母 jìmǔ *also* "寄娘" fostermother

寄女 jìnǚ adopted daughter

寄情 jìqíng express one's feelings: ~山水 write about (*or* paint) mountains and rivers to vent one's feelings

寄人篱下 jìrén-líxià live under another's roof; depend on sb. for a living; depend on another person for support: 他过不惯这种旅居国外、~的生活。He does not like living abroad, under someone else's roof. /他想起那岫烟住在贾府园中,终是~。He thought to himself, Xiuyan was simply a dependant living in the Jias' house.

寄身 jìshēn 〈书面〉 stay in a place temporarily; have a sojourn in some place: ~海外 stay overseas for a time

寄生 jìshēng ❶ 〈生物〉 parasitism ❷ parasitic: ~生活 parasitic life; living off others /~阶级 parasitic class

寄生虫 jìshēngchóng ❶ parasite: ~病 parasitic disease; parasitosis ❷ person who leads a parasitic life; parasite

寄生动物 jìshēng dòngwù parasitic animal

寄生蜂 jìshēngfēng parasitic wasp

寄生物学 jìshēngwùxué parasitology

寄生振荡 jìshēng zhèndàng 〈电学〉 parasitic oscillation

寄生植物 jìshēng zhíwù parasitic plant

寄食 jìshí live with a relative (because of one's straitened circumstances): 他只身到此,暂时~在亲戚家。Coming here all alone, he had to live with a relative for the time being.

寄售 jìshòu *see* "寄卖"

寄宿 jìsù ❶ lodge; put up: ~在某处 lodge with sb.; put up at sb.'s house ❷ (of students) board

寄宿生 jìsùshēng resident student; boarder

寄宿学校 jìsù xuéxiào boarding school; residential college

寄托 jìtuō ❶ entrust (to the care of sb.); leave (with sb.): 把自行车~在邻居家里 entrust one's bike to the care of a neighbour /孩子没人照料,我把她~在朋友家里。Having no person to look after the child, I left her with a friend. ❷ place (hope, etc.) on; find sustenance in; repose: 精神有所~ have sth. to repose one's trust in; have spiritual sustenance /把希望~在年轻的一代人身上 place one's hope on (*or* repose one's hope in) the young generation

寄销 jìxiāo consignment (sale): ~品 consignment merchandise

寄信人 jìxìnrén sender

寄秧 jìyāng raise rice seedlings temporarily in a field (so as to transplant them in other fields when the right time comes)

寄养 jìyǎng entrust one's child to the care of sb.; ask sb. to bring up one's child: 她从小就~在姑妈家。She was brought up by her aunt.

寄意 jìyì send one's regards

寄予 jìyǔ *also* "寄与" ❶ place (hope, etc.) on: 做父母的总是对儿女~期望。Parents always pin their hopes on the children. ❷ show; give; express: ~关怀 show solicitude for sb. /他对中国人民~同情。He expressed sympathy for the Chinese people.

寄语 jìyǔ 〈书面〉 send word: ~故人 send a message to friends /~亲人报喜讯 send happy news to one's dear ones

寄寓 jìyù ❶ 〈书面〉 lodge; live away from home: ~他乡 stay away from home ❷ place (hope, etc.); carry: 这首诗~了诗人的思乡之情。The poem conveys the poet's nostalgia for his hometown.

寄主 jìzhǔ *also* "宿主" sùzhǔ 〈生物〉 host (of a parasite)

寄住 jìzhù live away from home: 从小就~在外祖父家里 live in grandpa's house from childhood

寄子 jìzǐ adopted son

徛

jì 〈方言〉 stand up

冀[1]

jì 〈书面〉 hope; long for; yearn for; look forward to: 希~ hope for; look forward to /心有所~ long for sth.

冀[2]

Jì ❶ another name for Hebei Province ❷ a surname

冀求 jìqiú hope to get or gain

冀图 jìtú hope; desire; long for: ~重振家业 hope to rebuild the family fortune

冀望 jìwàng 〈书面〉 hope; look forward to: 她~从火柴的光焰中得到一点温暖。She was hoping to get some warmth from the burning match.

骥

jì 〈书面〉 ❶ thoroughbred horse: 老~伏枥,志在千里 an old steed in the stable still aspires to cover a thousand *li* a day — a veteran with high aspirations ❷ virtuous and competent person

罽

jì 〈书面〉 felt; rug

觊(覬)

jì 〈书面〉 hope for; try to get

觊觎 jìyú 〈书面〉 covet; cast greedy eyes on: ~别国领土 covet another country's territory

稷

jì ❶ (broomcorn) millet ❷ god of grains worshipped by ancients: 社~ god of the land and god of grains — state or country

季

jì ❶ season: 春~ spring /夏~ summer /秋~ autumn /冬~ winter /换~ change of seasons /四~ four seasons of a year; at all seasons ❷ period of time that has a distinctive characteristic; season: 雨~ rainy season /旱~ dry season /旺~ busy season /淡~ slack season ❸ last period of (a dynasty): 清~ end of the Qing Dynasty ❹ last month of a season: *see* "~春"; "~冬" ❺ fourth or youngest among brothers: ~弟 fourth or youngest brother /伯仲叔~ eldest, second, third and youngest of brothers ❻ (Jì) a surname

季报 jìbào quarterly (bulletin or report)

季春 jìchūn last month of spring

季冬 jìdōng last month of winter

季度 jìdù quarter (of a year): 第一~ first quarter of a year /~预算 quarterly budget /~指标 quarterly quota /这次会议安排在今年第四~。The meeting is scheduled to be held in the fourth quarter of

the year.
季风 jìfēng *also*“季候风”〈气象〉monsoon:冬季～ dry monsoon / 夏季～ wet monsoon
季风林 jìfēnglín monsoon forest
季风气候 jìfēng qìhòu monsoon climate
季风雨 jìfēngyǔ monsoon rain
季父 jìfù 〈书面〉uncle; youngest uncle
季候 jìhòu 〈方言〉season:隆冬～ in the depths of winter (season)
季节 jìjié season:春耕～ spring ploughing season / ～指数 seasonal index number / ～变化 seasonal variation / ～差价 seasonal price differences; seasonal variations in price / ～关税 seasonal duties / ～迁徙 seasonal migration; transhumance / 北京这时候正是百花盛开的好～。Beijing is now in its golden season, with hundreds of flowers in bloom.
季节工 jìjiégōng seasonal worker
季节洄游 jìjié huíyóu seasonal migration (of fish, etc.)
季节性 jìjiéxìng seasonal:～储备 seasonal reserve / ～趋势 seasonal trend / ～工作 seasonal work; seasonal jobs / ～路线 seasonal route / ～行业 seasonal trade / ～折扣 seasonal discount / 蔗糖生产的～很强。Sugar production is very seasonal.
季军 jìjūn third place in a contest or sports match
季刊 jìkān quarterly publication; quarterly
季肋 jìlèi *also*“软肋”ruǎnlèi;“橛肋”juélèi 〈生理〉hypochondrium
季母 jìmǔ 〈书面〉aunt; youngest aunt
季秋 jìqiū last month of autumn
季世 jìshì 〈书面〉last phase of an age; last period of a dynasty:殷周～ last years of the Shang Dynasty and the Zhou Dynasty
季夏 jìxià last month of summer
季相 jìxiàng natural scene of a particular season in a particular region:深秋的草原呈现一片枯黄的～。The pastures are a vast scene of withered grass in late autumn.
季子 jìzǐ 〈书面〉youngest brother
季子 jìzi 〈方言〉period of about two or three months:这～都忙些什么? What have you been doing for the last couple of months?

悸

jì 〈书面〉(of the heart) throb with terror; 惊～ palpitate with terror / 心～ palpitate (with anxiety and fear) / 心有余～ have a lingering fear
悸动 jìdòng (of heart) throb with terror:忽然听到一声巨响,我的心怦怦地～着。My heart began to throb with terror when I heard a loud noise.
悸栗 jìlì tremble with fear

偈

jì libretto in Buddhist scripture
see also jié

洎

jì 〈书面〉up to (a point or period of time):自古～今 from ancient times up to the present / ～乎近世 by modern times

垍

jì 〈书面〉solid earth

祭

jì ❶ offer sacrifices to:～祖宗 offer sacrifices to one's ancestors / ～天 offer a sacrifices to Heaven; worship Heaven ❷ hold a memorial ceremony for:公～死难烈士 hold a public memorial service for martyrs ❸ wield (sth. magic):～起法宝 wield a magic wand
祭典 jìdiǎn ceremony to offer sacrifices
祭奠 jìdiàn hold a memorial ceremony for:～阵亡将士 hold a memorial ceremony for officers and soldiers killed in action
祭红 jìhóng *also*“霁红”jìhóng bright red colour used in glazing pottery
祭礼 jìlǐ ❶ sacrificial rites; memorial ceremony ❷ sacrificial offerings
祭灵 jìlíng hold a memorial ceremony in a mourning hall or in front of a coffin containing the dead
祭品 jìpǐn sacrificial offering; oblation
祭器 jìqì sacrificial utensil or vessel
祭扫 jìsǎo sweep a grave and pay respects to the dead; hold a memorial ceremony for a dead person at his or her tomb:～烈士陵园 hold a memorial ceremony in the martyrs cemetery
祭祀 jìsì offer sacrifices (to gods or ancestors)
祭台 jìtái *see*“祭坛”
祭坛 jìtán sacrificial altar
祭文 jìwén funeral oration; elegiac address:一篇凄楚动人的～ a sad and moving funeral oration
祭享 jìxiǎng offer sacrifices (to a god); worship (a god) by offering sacrifices
祭仪 jìyí 〈书面〉❶ sacrificial offerings; oblations ❷ ceremony of offering sacrifices; sacrificial rites
祭灶 jìzào 〈旧语〉offer sacrifices to the kitchen god on the 23rd or 24th of the 12th lunar month
祭幛 jìzhàng large, oblong sheet of silk with inscriptions, presented at a funeral

漈

jì 〈书面〉water's edge; waterside

穄

jì broomcorn millet
穄子 jìzi *also*“糜子”méizi broomcorn millet

鰶

jì 〈动物〉gizzard shad

际(際)

jì ❶ border; boundary; edge:边～ border; boundary / 天～ horizon / 无边无～ boundless / 一望无～的大海 vast expanse of ocean stretching to the horizon ❷ in; inside:脑～ in one's head / 胸～ in one's mind ❸ between; among:春夏之～ between spring and summer / 国～ international; among nations / 厂～交流 exchange between factories / 校～合作 intercollegiate cooperation / 星～旅行 interplanetary travel / 洲～导弹 intercontinental missile / 人～关系 relationship between people; interpersonal relationship ❹ occasion; moment; time:危急之～ at a critical moment / 本校教学改革进行之～ at the time when the school is carrying out education reform ❺ on the occasion of:～此盛会 on the occasion of this grand gathering / ～此佳节 on this festive occasion ❻ one's experiences or lot; circumstances:遭～ vicissitudes in one's life; one's lot
际逢 jìféng 〈书面〉meet by chance; happen to be:～盛世 happen to live in a flourishing age
际会 jìhuì come across; run into; meet:～风云 face to face with a turbulent time
际涯 jìyá 〈书面〉boundary:渺无～ vast; boundless
际遇 jìyù 〈书面〉(mostly good) opportunity; favourable turn in life; spell of good fortune

鲫

jì 〈动物〉crucian carp
鲫瓜 jìguā *also*“鲫瓜子”〈口语〉crucian carp; crucian
鲫鱼 jìyú crucian carp; crucian

系(繫)

jì tie; fasten; do up; button up:～围裙 wear (*or* put on) an apron / ～鞋带 tie shoe laces / ～衣服扣子 button up a jacket / ～好安全带 fasten the safety belt
see also xì
系泊 jìbó moor (a boat):～浮筒 mooring buoy
系船索 jìchuánsuǒ mooring rope; mooring line
系留 jìliú moor (a balloon or airship)
系留塔 jìliútǎ mooring mast; mooring tower

既

jì ❶ already:保持～有的荣誉 keep (*or* maintain) the acquired reputation / 一言～出,驷马难追 a word once spoken cannot be taken back even by a team of four horses — what has been said cannot be unsaid ❷ as; since; now that:你～来了,就住下吧! Please stay with us now that you are already here. / 他～如此坚决,我也不便多说。I won't say anything more since he is so determined. ❸〈书面〉finished; done; over:语未～,有老氓笑于旁。An old man started laughing before I finished my words. ❹ both... and...; as well as:～懂英语又懂德语 know both English and German / 这孩子～健康又活泼。The child is lively as well as healthy. / 文体～简明又有力。The style is as concise as it is vigorous.
既成事实 jìchéng shìshí accomplished fact; fait accompli:给我们造成了～ present us with a fait accompli / 承认～ accept a fait accompli
既得利益 jìdé lìyì vested interest:维护～ protect one's vested interest
既得利益集团 jìdé lìyì jítuán (group or faction with) vested in-

terests

既定 jìdìng set; fixed; established: ～目标 set objective; fixed goal / ～方案 existing plan / ～方针 established policy

既而 jì'ér 〈书面〉afterwards; later; subsequently: ～雨住, 欣然登山。Soon afterwards the rain stopped and we began to climb up the mountain with delight.

既决犯 jìjuéfàn 〈法律〉convicted prisoner; convict

既来之, 则安之 jì lái zhī, zé ān zhī since one is here, one may as well stay and make the best of it; take things as they come: ～。反正谁在这里也呆不长, 能忍则忍吧。Let's make the best of it. (*or* We might as well take things as they come.) Since we won't be here long, we'd better put up with it.

既然 jìrán 〈连词〉since; as; now that: ～如此 since it is so; such being the case; under these circumstances / ～这种方式不行, 我们就试试别的方式吧。Since this doesn't work, let's try another way. / 我～恢复了健康, 就可以继续工作了。Now that I am well again, I can go on with my work.

既是 jìshì since; as; now that: 事情～如此, 也只好作罢了。Such being the case, we can only give up.

既遂 jìsuì 〈法律〉accomplished offence: ～犯 accomplished offender; consummate offender / ～罪 accomplished offence; completed offence; consummated crime

既往 jìwǎng ❶ past: 一如～ as always; as in the past ❷ past affairs; what one has done in the past: 不究～ let bygones be bygones

既往不咎 jìwǎng-bùjiù *also* "不咎既往" forgive sb.'s past misdeeds; let bygones be bygones: ～, 以后办起事来, 审慎点就是了。What is past is past. Be more cautious next time about what you do. / 他们决定～, 言归于好。They decided to wipe the slate clean and be friends again. / 此事不必多说了。君子～。Please don't bring the matter up any more. A gentleman doesn't bear a grudge.

既望 jìwàng 〈书面〉16th day of a lunar month, the day after the full moon

既约分数 jìyuē fēnshù 〈数学〉fraction in the lowest terms; irreducible fraction; reduced fraction

既在矮檐下, 怎敢不低头 jì zài ǎiyán xià, zěn gǎn bù dītóu you have to bow your head under low eaves — one has to yield to the inevitable; one has to bow to the circumstances: 这是"～!"三藏只得双手合着, 与他见个礼。As the saying goes, "You have to bow your head under low eaves", Sanzang was obliged to put his palms together and greet him.

塈

jì 〈书面〉❶ spread plaster on the roof ❷ take a rest; rest ❸ take; fetch

暨

jì ❶〈书面〉and; as well as; with: 诸弟～诸侄均安好。All the brothers and nephews are fine. ❷〈书面〉to; up to: 从古～今 from ancient times to the present ❸ (Jì) a surname

穊

jì 〈书面〉dense; close: 深耕～种 plough deep and plant closely

鱀

jì 〈动物〉white-flag dolphin

记

jì ❶ remember; recall; bear in mind; commit to memory: ～清楚 remember clearly / ～生词 learn the new words by heart / 死～硬背 learn by rote / ～得快忘得也快 soon learnt, soon forgotten / 如果我没有～错的话 if I remember right; if my memory serves me; if my memory doesn't fail me / 我～不起他的名字。I can't recall his name. / 此人博闻强～。The man has wide learning and a retentive memory. ❷ write down; record; jot down; take down: ～笔记 take notes / ～日记 keep a diary / ～邮编号码 jot down the postal code (*or* zip code) / ～地址 write down the address / 把结果～下来 record the results / 给他～大功一次 award him a citation for merit / 登～ register; enter one's name / 摘～ take notes / 速～ shorthand; stenography ❸ note; record; narrative; account: 大事～ chronicle of major events / 游～ travel notes / 传～ biography ❹ mark; stamp; sign: 标～ sign / 印～ print; mark / 暗～儿 secret mark ❺ birthmark: 他右手背上有块黑～。He has a black birthmark on the back of his right hand. ❻〈方言〉〈量词〉*usu. used of certain actions*: 一～耳光 a slap in the face / 一～重扣 a forceful smash (in volleyball)

记仇 jìchóu bear grudges; harbour resentment: 她～记一辈子。She would harbour any resentment for all her life. / 他好在从不～。His strong point is that he never bears a grudge.

记得 jìde remember; recall; call back to mind; keep in memory: 我完全不～了。I have clean forgotten. / 我～告诉过他了。I remember having told him so. / 你还～学生时代的情形吗? Can you recall your school days? / 你～住这么多数字吗? Can you carry all these figures in your head?

记分 jìfēn ❶ keep the score; record the points (in a game) ❷ register a student's marks: ～册 (teacher's) markbook ❸ (as in a production team) record workpoints

记分牌 jìfēnpái scoreboard

记分员 jìfēnyuán scorekeeper; scorer; marker

记工 jìgōng record workpoints (earned by a commune member): ～单 work sheet

记工本 jìgōngběn workpoint registration book

记工员 jìgōngyuán workpoint recorder

记功 jìgōng cite for meritorious service; record a merit: 给排长记一等功。Award the platoon leader a citation for Merit, First Class.

记挂 jìguà 〈方言〉be worried about; be concerned about; keep thinking about; miss: 离家后他一直～着双亲。After leaving home, he kept thinking about his parents. / 我们都～着他的病。We are all concerned about his illness. / 我们多么～你! We missed you terribly. *or* How we missed you!

记过 jìguò record a demerit: 记大过一次 record a serious demerit / 违反纪律的人要～。Those who break discipline will have their infractions put on record.

记号 jìhào mark; sign: 在衣服上做个～ mark one's clothes; make a mark on one's clothes / 联络～ contact sign / ～阅读机 mark-reader / ～感应读打卡机 mark-sensing reader; puncher

记恨 jìhen bear grudges; bear ill will: 他俩经常争吵, 但从不～。The two often quarrel with each other, but never bear ill will.

记录 jìlù *also* "纪录" jìlù ❶ take notes; keep the minutes; note down; record: ～在案 be on record; go on record; be put on record / 把主席发言的主要内容～下来 note down the gist of the chairman's speech / 把这项决议～下来 make a minute of the decision ❷ minutes; notes; record; transcript: 会议～ minutes of a meeting / 会谈～ transcript of talks / 小组讨论～ notes of a group discussion / 正式～ official record / 逐字～ verbatim record / 摘要～ summary record / 原始～ original records / 列入会议～ place on record; place in the minutes; minute ❸ notetaker; recorder: 担任会议～ be the notetaker of a meeting ❹ record: 国家～ national record / 少年～ junior record / 亚洲～ Asian record / 保持～ hold a record / 保持不败～ keep a perfect record / 平～ equal a record; match a record / 打破～ break a record / 刷新一项世界～ set a new world record

记录本 jìlùběn minute book

记录片儿 jìlùpiānr 〈口语〉*see* "记录片"

记录片 jìlùpiàn *also* "纪录片" jìlùpiàn documentary film; documentary: 大型～ full-length documentary film / 电视～ televised documentary

记录员 jìlùyuán notetaker; stenographer

记名 jìmíng put down one's name (on a cheque, etc. to indicate responsibility or claim); sign: 无～投票 secret ballot / ～投票 vote by open ballot / ～支票 order cheque / 不～支票 bearer cheque / ～债券 registered bonds / ～股票 registered shares

记念 jìniàn *see* "纪念" jìniàn

记念 jìnian keep thinking of; miss: 她时时～着在国外学习的儿子。She keeps thinking of her son, who is studying abroad.

记谱法 jìpǔfǎ 〈音乐〉musical notation

记起 jìqǐ recall; recollect; call to mind: ～解放前的苦难生活 recall the miserable days before liberation / 我记不起这件事了。It has escaped my memory.

记取 jìqǔ remember; bear in mind: ～过去的教训 bear in mind the lessons of the past / ～正反两方面的经验 draw on experiences both positive and negative

记认 jìrèn ❶ identify; distinguish: 他的字迹我能～。I can identify his handwriting. ❷〈方言〉mark; sign: 借来各家的椅子要做个～, 将来不要还错了。Mark those borrowed chairs so that you won't make mistakes when returning them.

记时仪 jìshíyí 〈天文〉chronograph

记事 jìshì ❶ keep a record of events; make a memorandum: ～本 notebook / 刻木结绳～ (ancient way of) keeping records by notching

J

wood or tying knots ❷ account or record of events; annal; chronicle
记事儿 jìshìr (of a child) begin to remember things:那时我太小,还不~。I was too small then to remember things.
记述 jìshù record and narrate; give an account of:这篇文章~了作者的童年生活。This article gives an account of the author's childhood.
记诵 jìsòng commit to memory; memorize; learn by heart:~名句 memorize well-known sentences or passages /~一些范文,对写作大有帮助。It would greatly help your writing if you learn some model essays by heart.
记协 jìxié (short for 记者协会) journalists' association
记性 jìxing memory:~坏 have a poor memory /~特差 have a memory like a sieve /人老了,~不好。I'm getting old and my memory is failing me.
记叙 jìxù narrate:~简练 be concise in narration; narrate concisely/ ~体 narration; narrative (style)/~生动 give a graphic narration
记叙文 jìxùwén narration; (written) narrative
记要 jìyào see "纪要" jìyào
记忆 jìyì ❶ remember; recall:很值得~的往事 past events well worth remembering /就~所及 so far as I can remember (or recollect); to the best of my memory /这事我~不起来了。It has slipped my memory. ❷ memory:单凭~可能出错。You might go wrong if you rely on your memory alone. /这里的一切,给我留下了美好的~。Everything here has left me a very good impression.
记忆储存 jìyì chǔcún 〈信息〉memory storage
记忆广度 jìyì guǎngdù memory span
记忆库 jìyìkù memory bank
记忆力 jìyìlì faculty of memory; memory:~衰退 one's memory is failing; failing memory
记忆曲线 jìyì qūxiàn memory curve
记忆缺失 jìyì quēshī 〈医学〉amnesia
记忆犹新 jìyì-yóuxīn remain fresh in one's memory:当时的情景,至今~。What happened then still remains fresh in my memory.
记载 jìzǎi ❶ put down in writing; record:把事实忠实地~下来 record the facts truthfully /有文字~的历史 recorded history ❷ record; account:历史~ historical records; annals /《春秋》里就有关于陨石的~。There are accounts of aerolites in *The Spring and Autumn Annals*.
记账 jìzhàng keep accounts; keep books; charge to an account:~买卖 transaction for account /把它记在某人账上 charge (or put) it to sb.'s account /~程序 accounting process; accounting programme /~计算机 billing machine /~价格 account price /~制业务 credit system service /每人要了一杯啤酒,他把酒钱记在账上。Each one ordered a glass of beer and he chalked it up (or put it on their tab).
记账卡 jìzhàngkǎ debit card
记者 jìzhě reporter; correspondent; newsman; journalist:采访~ reporter /常驻~ resident correspondent /随军~ war correspondent/特派~ special correspondent /体育新闻~ sports reporter /通讯~ correspondent /新华社~ reporter of the Xinhua News Agency; Xinhua correspondent /美联社~ reporter of the Associated Press /法新社~ reporter of AFP (*Agence France-Presse*) /答~问 news briefing
记者席 jìzhěxí press gallery
记者协会 jìzhě xiéhuì journalists' association
记者招待会 jìzhě zhāodàihuì press conference; news conference
记者证 jìzhězhèng press card
记住 jìzhu learn by heart; bear in mind:把暗语~ learn the watchwords by heart /我会~这件事。I shall keep this in mind.

忌

jì ❶ be jealous of; envy:猜~ be envious; envy /疑~ be suspicious and resentful /~贤妒能 be jealous of the worthy and able ❷ fear; dread; scruple:投鼠~器 hesitate to pelt a rat for fear of smashing the dish it is on — hold back from taking action against an evildoer for fear of involving or harming good people /讳疾~医 avoid seeing a doctor in order to conceal one's illness; hide one's sickness for fear of treatment /他们对你有所顾~。They have scruples about you. ❸ avoid; shun; abstain from; refrain from:~辛辣 avoid bitter and hot food /婴儿~服 not to be taken by babies /百无禁~ all taboos in abeyance; no prohibitions of any kind /医生要病人~荤腥。The doctor told the patient to abstain from meat and fish. ❹ quit; give up:~酒 give up alcohol; abstain from wine
忌辰 jìchén anniversary of the death of a parent, ancestor, or anyone else held in esteem
忌惮 jìdàn 〈书面〉dread; be afraid; fear; scruple:肆无~ stop at nothing; be unscrupulous /毫无~地做某事 make no scruple to do (or of doing) sth.
忌妒 jìdu be jealous of:十分~ consumed by jealousy; green with envy /对你,他很羡慕,可没有~的意思。He admires you but is by no means jealous.
忌恨 jìhèn hate; detest; harbour hatred (for sb.); bear a grudge (against sb.):互相~ bear grudges against each other
忌讳 jìhui ❶ taboo:犯~ violate a taboo; break a taboo /他最~人家揭他的短儿。He bitterly resents any attempt to rake up his shortcomings. ❷ avoid as harmful; abstain from:做学问最~浅尝辄止。In studies one must avoid feeling satisfied with superficial knowledge. ❸ 〈方言〉vinegar
忌戒 jìjiè give up; drop; stop:一切陋习均在~之列。All bad customs must be stamped out.
忌刻 jìkè *also* "忌克" envious and mean; jealous and malicious:此人性多~,听不得不同意见。Being jealous and malicious, the man won't tolerate differing views.
忌口 jìkǒu *also* "忌嘴" avoid certain food (as when one is ill); be on a diet:他飞禽走兽,什么肉都吃,从不~。He eats all kinds of meat, whether of birds or beasts, and never avoids anything.
忌日 jìrì ❶ see "忌辰" ❷ 〈迷信〉date on which certain things should be avoided
忌食 jìshí ❶ avoid certain food for health reasons or because of medical treatment:~生冷 avoid cold and uncooked food ❷ avoid certain food out of religious beliefs:印度教徒~牛肉。Hindus avoid beef.
忌嘴 jìzuǐ see "忌口"

跽

jì 〈书面〉sit on one's knees and heels with the upper part of the body erect

迹(跡、蹟)

jì ❶ mark; trace:足~ footmark; footprint /踪~ trace; track /血~ bloodstain /字~ handwriting; writing /蛛丝马~ clues; traces /航~ track; flight path /真~ authentic work /油~ oil stain /墨~ ink mark; sb.'s writing or painting /袭~ follow in another's footsteps; follow suit /绝~ disappear; be stamped out ❷ remains; ruins; vestige:残~ vestige; trace or sign of sth. that once existed /古~ historic site; place of historic interest /陈~ thing of the past /古战场的遗~ remains of an ancient battlefield ❸ outward sign; indication:~近违抗 almost a sign of defiance
迹地 jìdì 〈林业〉slash
迹象 jìxiàng sign; indication; straw in the wind:这一带出现了将要地震的某些~。There are some signs of a possible earthquake in this area. /两国关系有松动的~。There are indications that a thaw is likely in the relations between the two countries.

纪[1]

jì discipline:军~ military discipline /法~ law and discipline /纲~ law and order /党~ party discipline /违法乱~ break the law and violate discipline /遵~守法 abide by the law and discipline

纪[2]

jì ❶ put down in writing; write down; record: *see* "~念";"~元" ❷ 〈古语〉twelve years' cycle or period; (now of longer period) age; epoch:世~ century /中世~ the Middle Ages ❸ 〈地质〉period:震旦~ Sinian Period /侏罗~ Jurassic Period /石炭~ Carboniferous Period /泥盆~ Devonian Period /奥陶~ Ordovician Period

see also Jǐ
纪纲 jìgāng 〈书面〉❶ law:~不肃 law not being strictly enforced ❷ moral standard
纪检 jìjiǎn (short for 纪律检查) inspect discipline:~部门 discipline inspection department /~工作 work of inspecting discipline; discipline inspection work
纪录 jìlù see "记录" jìlù
纪录片儿 jìlùpiānr see "记录片儿" jìlùpiānr
纪录片 jìlùpiàn see "记录片" jìlùpiàn
纪律 jìlǜ discipline:遵守~ abide by (or keep, or observe) disci-

J

pline /违反～ violate discipline /～严明 be strict in discipline; enforce rigid discipline; be highly disciplined /～教育 education in discipline /加强～性 strengthen discipline /给某人～处分 take disciplinary actions (*or* measures) against sb.; discipline sb. /～制裁 disciplinary sanction /劳动～ labour discipline /课堂～ class discipline

纪律检查委员会 jìlǜ jiǎnchá wěiyuánhuì commission for inspecting discipline

纪年 jìnián ❶ way of numbering the years:公元～ Christian era /阴历用干支～。In the lunar calendar, the years are designated by the Heavenly Stems and Earthly Branches. ❷ chronological record of events; chronicles; annals:～体 chronological order /《中国历史大事～》*Annals of Important Events in Chinese History*

纪念 jìniàn *also* "记念" jìniàn ❶ pay tribute to; commemorate; mark:值得～的日子 memorable day /～活动 commemorative activities /举行～大会 hold a commemoration meeting /为了～中华人民共和国的成立 in commemoration of the founding of the People's Republic of China /修建一座医院以～某人 build a hospital in memory of sb. /～建校五十周年 mark (*or* observe) the 50th anniversary of a school /银婚～ silver wedding anniversary /这座纪念碑是～秋收起义的。This monument commemorates the Autumn Harvest Uprising. ❷ souvenir; keepsake; memento:送一本书作个临别～ offer (sb.) a book as a souvenir at parting /把它留作我们友谊的～。Keep it as a memento of our friendship.

纪念碑 jìniànbēi monument; memorial:人民英雄～ Monument to the People's Heroes /独块巨石～ monolithic monument /为～揭幕 unveil a monument /建立革命烈士～ erect a memorial to the revolutionary martyrs

纪念币 jìniànbì commemorative coin

纪念册 jìniàncè commemorative or autograph book; commemorative or autograph album:题词～ autographic album

纪念封 jìniànfēng commemorative envelope

纪念馆 jìniànguǎn memorial hall; museum in memory of sb.:鲁迅～ Lu Xun Museum /徐悲鸿～ Xu Beihong Memorial Hall

纪念品 jìniànpǐn souvenir; keepsake; memento:她参观故宫时,买了许多～。She bought a lot of souvenirs when visiting the Palace Museum.

纪念日 jìniànrì commemoration day:抗日战争胜利～ commemoration day of the victory of the War of Resistance Against Japanese Aggression; day commemorating the victory of the War of Resistance Against Japanese Aggression

纪念塔 jìniàntǎ memorial tower; monument:华盛顿～ (US) Washington Monument

纪念堂 jìniàntáng memorial hall; commemoration hall:毛主席～ Chairman Mao Memorial Hall /中山～ Dr. Sun Yat-sen's Memorial Hall

纪念邮票 jìniàn yóupiào commemorative stamp

纪念章 jìniànzhāng souvenir badge:交换～ exchange souvenir badges

纪实 jìshí record of actual events; on-the-spot report:北京亚运会开幕式～ on-the-spot report of the opening ceremony of the Beijing Asian Games

J

纪实文学 jìshí wénxué documentary writing

纪事 jìshì ❶ record facts; narrate:～诗 narrative poem /～文 narrative writing; narration ❷(usu. used in book titles) record of facts or historical events; account:《唐诗～》*Some Facts About Tang Poems*

纪事本末体 jìshì běnmòtǐ history presented in separate accounts of important events

纪委 jìwěi (short for 纪律检查委员会) commission for inspecting discipline; discipline commission:～成员 member of the commission for inspecting discipline; commissioner for inspecting discipline; commissioner for discipline inspection

纪行 jìxíng travel notes:《欧洲～》*Notes on a Trip to Europe* /《海南～》*A Trip to Hainan*

纪要 jìyào *also* "记要" jìyào summary of minutes; summary:会谈～ summary of talks; summary of conversations /座谈会～ summary of a forum (*or* panel discussion)

纪元 jìyuán ❶ beginning of an era (e.g. an emperor's reign) ❷ epoch; era:第一颗人造卫星的上天,开辟了宇宙探索的新～。The launching of the first man-made satellite ushered in a new era for space exploration.

纪传体 jìzhuàntǐ history presented in a series of biographies:二十四史,都是～史书。The Twenty-Four Histories are all written in the form of a series of biographies.

勣

jì 〈书面〉 achievement; accomplishment; attainment; merit

绩

jì ❶ twist hempen thread:纺～ twist flax (*or* hemp) fibres and weave ❷ achievement; accomplishment; contribution; merit:功～ merits and achievements; contributions /战～ military achievement; military exploit /成～ achievement; success /考～ check on work performance /劳～ merits and achievements /伟～ great feats; glorious achievements /勋～ meritorious service; outstanding contributions /业～ outstanding accomplishment /政～ achievements in one's official career /败～ defeat; reverse

绩效 jìxiào performance; achievement; success:～显著 marked achievements

继(繼)

jì ❶ continue; succeed; inherit; follow:嗣～ succeed; inherit /后～有人 be followed by qualified successors /前赴后～ advance wave upon wave /日以～夜 day and night /相～落成 be built in succession /相～去世 die one after another /子～父业 son inheriting father's profession ❷ then; afterwards:才离去,～又返回 left a moment ago and then returned

继承 jìchéng ❶ inherit; succeed:～财产 inherit property /～王位 succeed to the throne /他从父亲那里～了一份家业。He inherited a family property from his father. ❷ carry on or forward; advance:～革命传统 carry on (*or* forward) the revolutionary tradition /～某人衣钵 step into the shoes of sb.; take over the mantle of sb. ❸ carry on sb.'s unfinished work; continue the work left by the deceased

继承法 jìchéngfǎ law of succession; succession act; inheritance law

继承国 jìchéngguó successor; succeeding state

继承权 jìchéngquán right of succession; right of inheritance; heirship:剥夺～ disinherit (sb.) /长子～ primogeniture

继承人 jìchéngrén heir; successor; inheritor:直系～ lineal successor; heir of the body /法定～ heir at law; legal heir /当然～ heir apparent /假定～ heir presumptive /限定～ heir in tail /王位～ successor to the throne

继承税 jìchéngshuì inheritance tax

继电控制系统 jìdiàn kòngzhì xìtǒng relay control system

继电器 jìdiànqì 〈电工〉 relay:～开关 switch

继电设备 jìdiàn shèbèi relay equipment

继电随动系统 jìdiàn suídòng xìtǒng on-off servo

继而 jì'ér then; afterwards:对于他的一套做法,起初是反对,～将信将疑,最后终于服了。At first I opposed his way of doing things, then I gave him the benefit of the doubt, and finally I was persuaded.

继父 jìfù stepfather

继后 jìhòu then; afterwards:他先满口说是要去,～又说不去了。At first he readily promised to go, and then he said he thought better of it.

继进 jìjìn continue to advance

继母 jìmǔ stepmother

继女 jìnǚ stepdaughter

继配 jìpèi *also* "继室" 〈旧语〉 second wife (taken after the death of one's first wife)

继任 jìrèn succeed (sb.) in a post:～首相 succeed sb. as prime minister /他辞职后由副手老黄～。After his resignation, his assistant Lao Huang succeeded him in his post. /他于去年～工党领袖。He took over as leader of the Labour Party last year. /谁将～联合国秘书长? Who is the next secretary general of the UN?

继室 jìshì *see* "继配"

继嗣 jìsì 〈书面〉 ❶ be adopted ❷ adopted son:那个青年人就是张先生的～。That young man is Mr. Zhang's adopted son.

继往开来 jìwǎng-kāilái carry forward the cause and forge ahead into the future:改革开放是一项～的伟大事业。The reform and opening policy is a great cause pioneered by our predecessors that has ushered in a new era.

继位 jìwèi succeed to the throne

继武 jìwǔ 〈书面〉 follow close on sb.'s heels:～前贤 carry on the noble cause of the previous generations

继续 jìxù ❶ continue; remain; go on; keep on:～有效 remain

valid; remain in force /～执政 continue in office; remain in power /～保险 continued insurance /～成本 continuing cost /～审计 continuous audit /～教育 further education /明天～开会。The meeting will resume tomorrow. /大雨～了三昼夜。The heavy rain fell for three days on end. /不能～容忍这种状况存在下去。We can no longer put up with the situation. ❷ continuation; sequal:退却是防御的～;而追击则是进攻的～。Withdrawal is a continuation of defence while pursuit is a continuation of attack.

继子 jìzǐ ❶ adopted son ❷ son of one's spouse by previous marriage; step-son

jiā

家¹ jiā ❶ family; household:养～ support one's family /阖～团聚 family reunion /成～立业 get married and embark on one's career /他们一～四口。They are a family of four. /张～和李～是亲戚。The Zhangs and Lis are relatives. /他全～都是工人。They are all workers in his family. /这个村有十几户人～。There are over a dozen households in this village. /～有万贯不如薄技在身。To learn a skill is worth more than ten thousand strings of cash. ❷ home:这儿就是我的～。Here is my home. *or* This is my home. /有空请去我～坐坐。Drop in whenever you are free. /我准备寒假回～过春节。I am going home for the Spring Festival in the winter vacation. /他不在～。He is not in (*or* is out). ❸ place where one belongs (e.g. officer at a barracks, official in his office, etc.):校长刚出去开会了,不在～。The principal is not in his office as he has just left for a meeting. /我找到营房,刚好连长不在～。The company commander was not in the barracks when I got there. ❹ person or family engaged in a certain trade:船～ boatman /渔～ fisherman's family /农～ peasant family /酒～ wineshop /店～ shopowner /东～ master; boss ❺ specialist in a certain field; expert:作曲～ composer /作～ writer /画～ painter /专～ expert /行～ expert; connoisseur /语法学～ grammarian /文学～ man of letters /语言学～ linguist /音乐～ musician /科学～ scientist / 法学～ jurist /计算机专～ computer expert /军事～ strategist /政治～ statesman /艺术～ artist /社会活动～ social activist ❻ school of thought; school:法～ legalist school /儒～ Confucian school /道～ Taoist school /诸子百～ various schools of thought /一～之言 views of one school or a particular individual /百～争鸣。A hundred of schools of thought contend. ❼ *refering to one of the opposite parties*:公～ state; the public /两～下成和棋。The chess game ended in a draw. ❽〈谦词〉my:～父 my father /～兄 my elder brother /～母 my mother /～姐 my elder sister ❾ domestic; tame; cultivated:～兔 rabbit /～蝇 housefly ❿〈方言〉tamed; domesticated; broken:马戏团的老虎已经养～了。The tigers of the circus have already been tamed. ⓫〈量词〉*used of families or enterprises*:四～人家 four families /三～饭馆 three restaurants /五～商店 five shops /几～邻居相处得很好。These neighbours are on good terms with each other. *or* These neighbours get along very well. ⓬ (Jiā) a surname

家² jia ❶ *used after certain nouns, indicating the category they come under*:姑娘～ girls /女人～ women /小孩子～别插嘴! You kids, stop cutting in! ❷〈方言〉*used after a man's name, refering to his wife*:祥子～ Xiangzi's wife /老二～ second son's wife

see also gū; jie

家财 jiācái family property:万贯～ family property worth ten thousand strings of cash; wealthy family

家蚕 jiācán *also* "桑蚕" sāngcán silkworm

家产 jiāchǎn family property or fortune:颇有～ have quite a handsome family fortune /变卖～ sell off one's family property /～处分〈法律〉family arrangement

家长里短 jiācháng-lǐduǎn 〈方言〉domestic chitchat; gossip:几位老大娘凑到一块儿尽谈些～。These old women gossip whenever they are together.

家常 jiācháng daily life of a family; domestic trivia:跟老乡们拉起～来 engage in small talk with villagers /～饼 simple cake; family cake

家常便饭 jiācháng-biànfàn *also* "家常饭" ❶ home cooking; homely or plain food; simple meal:上我家吃顿～吧! Come and have potluck with us. ❷ common occurrence; routine; all in the day's work:打架斗殴成了～。Scuffles and clashes became a matter of daily occurrence. /站几小时对她来说是～。For her, several hours on her feet was hardly anything novel. /腐败在那儿是～的现象。Corruption is a common practice there.

家常菜 jiāchángcài home cooking; home-style dish

家常话 jiāchánghuà small talk; chitchat:两人谈了一阵～。The two chitchatted for some time.

家仇 jiāchóu family feud; family hatred (for the invader):国难～ nation's calamity and family hatred against the enemy

家丑 jiāchǒu family scandal; skeleton in the cupboard or closet:不怕亮～ not be afraid to make known one's family scandal; dare wash dirty linen in public

家丑不可外扬 jiāchǒu bùkě wàiyáng domestic shame should not be made public; don't wash dirty linen in public; it's an ill bird that fouls its own nest:他想不出该找谁说说家里的事,才不至于惹人笑。～呀。He couldn't think of anyone he could confide in without fear of being laughed at. Family troubles were not a thing to be talked about in public!

家畜 jiāchù domestic animal; livestock:～保险 livestock insurance

家传 jiāchuán ❶ handed down from older generations of the family; sth. that runs in the family:～手艺 trade handed down in the family ❷ spread from one family to another:～户诵 widely known among the families

see also jiāzhuàn

家祠 jiācí ancestral temple or shrine; clan hall

家慈 jiācí 〈书面〉〈谦词〉my mother

家当 jiādang 〈口语〉family belongings; property:没有什么值钱的～ no valuable family belongings to speak of /我离开北京时,全部～就是一只箱子。When I left Beijing, all I had was one suitcase.

家道 jiādào family financial situation:～小康 be comfortably off; be well off /～中落 decline in family financial situation /～衰微 straitened family circumstances

家底 jiādǐ family property accumulated over a long time; resources:～薄 without substantial resources; financially shaky /这个厂的～儿厚。This factory has many resources.

家电 jiādiàn (short for 家用电器) household appliance; household electric appliance

家丁 jiādīng 〈旧语〉private soldier-cum-family servant

家法 jiāfǎ ❶ theory and methods of academic studies handed down from a master to his disciples ❷ domestic discipline exercised by the head of a clan or household ❸ rod or stick for punishing children or servants in a traditional household

家翻宅乱 jiāfān-zháiluàn house being turned upside down; domestic confusion; turmoil in the house:你们是怎么着,又这么～起来。What are you doing? Turning the whole house upside down again!

家访 jiāfǎng visit to the parents of schoolchildren or young workers

家风 jiāfēng family custom and style; family tradition

家父 jiāfù 〈谦词〉my father

家鸽 jiāgē pigeon; homing pigeon:养～ raise pigeons /～以爱家著称。Pigeons are well known for their intense love of home.

家馆 jiāguǎn 〈旧语〉family school (for children of rich parents)

家规 jiāguī family rules:高府的～很严。The Gaos have very strict family rules. /国有国法,家有～。As each country has its law, so each family has its rules.

家和万事兴 jiā hé wànshì xīng if the family lives in harmony, all affairs will prosper; harmony in the family leads to prosperity in all undertakings

家户 jiāhù 〈方言〉family; household:这个小村子,～不算多。This small village doesn't have a lot of families.

家伙 jiāhuo *also* "傢伙" jiāhuo 〈口语〉❶ tool; utensil; weapon:锣鼓～ gongs and drums /带上梳洗的～。Take your toilet articles with you. /吃完饭可得把～刷出来。Wash clean your bowls, etc., after a meal. /这把～挺好使。This is a very handy tool. /这伙人手里都有～。These people are all armed. ❷ fellow; chap; guy:小～ little chap; kid /坏～ scoundrel; villain /你这个～真啰嗦! What a fussy guy you are! /我们这群老～还有什么用? What's the use of a bunch of old fellows like us? ❸ domestic animal; livestock:这会儿,得喂喂这群～啦! It's time I fed these animals.

家给人足 jiājǐ-rénzú each family is provided for, and every person is well fed and well clothed; all live in plenty

家计 jiājì family livelihood:那年头,～艰难,哥哥不得不到外地去谋生。In those years, we lived a very hard life and my elder brother had to leave home to make a living.

家祭 jiājì family ceremony held in memory of the dead
家家 jiājiā every or each family：本村～有人在外经商。Every family in this village has someone engaged in trade outside.
家家户户 jiājiā-hùhù every family; every household：～贺新年。All families are celebrating the New Year.
家家有本难念的经 jiājiā yǒu běn nánniànde jīng each family has its own problems; every family has some sort of trouble
家教 jiājiào ❶ family education; upbringing：缺～ not properly brought up; ill-bred /～严 be strict with one's child /这孩子讲文明，懂礼貌，很有～。Being well brought up, this child is refined and polite. ❷ private tutor (for a school child, etc.); private tutoring：请～ engage a private tutor
家景 jiājǐng *see* "家境"
家境 jiājìng *also* "家景" family financial situation; family circumstances; family conditions：～清寒 of a poor family /～好 from a well-off family /幼时～清贫。The family was in straitened circumstances in his childhood. /她的～越来越坏。Her family financial situation is going from bad to worse.
家居 jiājū stay at home without any job：～三年，手艺也生疏了。His craft is getting rusty since he has stayed at home idle for three years.
家具 jiājù *also* "傢具" jiājù furniture：两件～ two pieces of furniture /一套～ a set of furniture /组合～ suite of furniture /红木～ mahogany furniture /～工业 furniture industry
家眷 jiājuàn ❶ wife and children; one's family：去年他领着～定居在济南。Last year he brought his family to Jinan and settled there. ❷ wife：他三十多岁了，还没有～。He is over thirty and is not yet married.
家君 jiājūn 〈书面〉〈谦词〉 my father：谢谢您的关心，～身体尚可。I deeply appreciate your kindness. My father is still in fairly good health.
家口 jiākǒu members of a family; number of people in a family：这一户住房不小，但～不多。This family has a spacious house but only a few members.
家累 jiālěi family burden; family cares：～重 be encumbered with a large family /这几年他的～不轻。In recent years he has been shouldering a heavy family burden.
家里 jiāli ❶ in the family; at home：～来了客人。There is a guest in my home. /～事，～了。What happens in the family can be settled in the family. ❷ 〈口语〉 one's wife：～病啦，我刚陪她上了医院。My wife is ill and I have just accompanied her to the hospital. ❸ *used to refer to the unit one works in when away from it on business*：出来半年多了，不知道～的技术改革进行得怎么样。Having been away from my unit for half a year on business, I wonder how things are going with technological innovations there.
家里的 jiālide *also* "家里人" 〈口语〉 my wife
家门 jiāmén ❶ house gate; home：好多天没出～ have not stepped out of the house for days; have been staying indoors for days ❷ 〈书面〉 family：有辱～ bring disgrace to the family ❸ 〈方言〉 member of the same clan：他是我的～堂兄弟。He is my cousin and we are of the same clan. ❹ family background：自报～ give one's family background; tell about one's family
家庙 jiāmiào ancestral temple or shrine; clan hall
家母 jiāmǔ 〈谦词〉 my mother
家娘 jiāniáng 〈方言〉 husband's mother; mother-in-law
家奴 jiānú bond servant; house slave
家贫如洗 jiāpín-rúxǐ clean broke; destitute; penniless：他已落得～。He is as poor as a church mouse.
家破人亡 jiāpò-rénwáng *also* "家败人亡" with one's family broken up, some gone away, some dead; with a family broken up and destroyed：六十年前那次大水灾，害得多少人～，妻离子散。Innumerable families were broken up by that flood sixty years ago, with wives separated from their husbands and children from their parents.
家谱 jiāpǔ family tree; genealogical tree; genealogy; pedigree：查～ trace the family tree /修～ compile a genealogy
家雀儿 jiāqiǎor 〈方言〉 sparrow
家禽 jiāqín domestic fowl; poultry：～饲养场 poultry farm /～饲养员 poultryman
家去 jiāqu 〈口语〉 return home; go back home：孩子吓得不敢～。The child was so scared that he dared not go home.
家人 jiārén ❶ family member：～团聚 family members getting together; family reunion ❷〈旧语〉 servant

家舍 jiāshè house; room：清扫～ clean the house
家神 jiāshén family god
家生 jiāshēng ❶ 〈方言〉 utensils; tools; furniture：锣鼓～ gongs and drums /红木～ rosewood furniture ❷ 〈书面〉 family livelihood ❸ *see* "家生子"
家生子 jiāshēngzǐ *also* "家生"；"家生孩儿" 〈旧语〉 servant born of servant parents
家声 jiāshēng family reputation; family fame：败坏～ ruin family reputation /重振～ reestablish (*or* regain) family fame
家乘 jiāshèng 〈书面〉 record of family or household affairs; family tree; genealogical tree
家史 jiāshǐ family history：血泪～ family history of blood and tears
家世 jiāshì 〈书面〉 family background; family social status：～寒微 be of plebeian origin /这位大臣出身豪门，～显赫。The minister was born of rich parents with a distinguished family background.
家事 jiāshì ❶ household affair：他很忙，～都由妻子操心。He is very busy and leaves household affairs in the charge of his wife. ❷ 〈方言〉 family financial situation; family circumstances
家室 jiāshì ❶ family：无～之累 have no family to support; have no family to provide for ❷ wife：已有～ have a wife ❸ 〈书面〉 house
家什 jiāshi *also* "傢什" jiāshi 〈口语〉 utensils, tools, furniture, etc.：开办饭馆的～都齐了。Everything needed for the opening of a restaurant is ready.
家书 jiāshū letter to or from home：修～一封 write a letter to one's family /烽火连三月，～抵万金。With turmoil of battle three months on end, A letter from home is worth a fortune in gold.
家塾 jiāshú 〈旧语〉 family school
家属 jiāshǔ family member; (family) dependent：军人～ armymen's families /职工～ families of workers and staff members /随军～ family members that live in the barracks; families that follow the army /～宿舍 living quarters for families; family dormitory
家属工厂 jiāshǔ gōngchǎng factory run by family members of workers, cadres, armymen, etc.
家数 jiāshù academic or artistic group in which knowledge and technique are handed down by the masters from one generation to another
家私 jiāsī 〈口语〉 family property or fortune：～万贯 with a large amount of family property
家天下 jiātiānxià concept that regards the whole country as one's (family) property
家庭 jiātíng family; household：大～ extended family /核心～ nuclear family /血亲～ consanguine family /姻亲～ conjugal family /～服务 domestic service /～负担 family responsibilities (*or* burden) /～破裂 breakdown of a family
家庭背景 jiātíng bèijǐng family background
家庭病床 jiātíng bìngchuáng home sickbed; hospital bed set up in the patient's house：30 年前，天津市首创了第一张～，而今已发展到 30 万张。The first hospital bed set up in a patient's house was initiated in Tianjin 30 years ago, and now the total has gone up to 300,000 beds.
家庭成员 jiātíng chéngyuán family member
家庭出身 jiātíng chūshēn family origin; class status of one's family：我是工人～。I was born of working-class parents.
家庭妇女 jiātíng fùnǚ housewife
家庭副业 jiātíng fùyè household sideline production
家庭工业 jiātíng gōngyè household industry
家庭观念 jiātíng guānniàn attachment to one's family; strong sense of family
家庭教师 jiātíng jiàoshī private teacher; (private) tutor：越来越多的家长请～来辅导孩子的功课。An increasing number of parents engage private tutors to help their children with their studies.
家庭教育 jiātíng jiàoyù family education; home education
家庭经济 jiātíng jīngjì family or home economics
家庭纠纷 jiātíng jiūfēn family quarrel; domestic discord; family dispute
家庭劳动服务介绍所 jiātíng láodòng fúwù jièshàosuǒ domestic service agency
家庭联产承包责任制 jiātíng liánchǎn chéngbāo zérènzhì 〈经济〉 contracted responsibility system based on the household with remuneration or income linked to output; household contract responsibility system with remuneration linked to output
家庭生活 jiātíng shēnghuó home life; family life

J

家庭手工业 jiātíng shǒugōngyè domestic handicraft
家庭学 jiātíngxué family studies
家庭作业 jiātíng zuòyè homework
家童 jiātóng 〈旧语〉boy servant
家徒四壁 jiātúsìbì *also* "家徒壁立" have nothing but the bare walls in one's house — live in miserable penury:她望着空荡荡的屋子,茫然地笑笑:"真是~呀!"。Looking round the empty room, she told herself with a wry smile, "Nothing but four bare walls."
家蚊 jiāwén *also* "库蚊" kùwén culex
家屋 jiāwū (residential) house
家无担石 jiāwúdànshí *also* "家无儋石" not even a picul of grain in the house — impoverished family
家无二主 jiāwú'èrzhǔ a house can't have two masters
家无隔宿之粮 jiā wú gésù zhī liáng not know where the next meal comes from; live from hand to mouth:三四年工夫,竟落得~,穿的衣服也都是千补万衲的。In three or four years his family was reduced to penury, with nothing but rags to wear.
家务 jiāwù household duties:~劳动 housework; household chores / 料理~ keep house / 减轻妇女的~负担 reduce women's burden of household chores
家系 jiāxì genealogy:~学家 genealogist
家下 jiāxia (often used in the early vernacular) in the family; in the house:~人 family member; of the same family
家弦户诵 jiāxián-hùsòng (of poems and essays) be read in every family and chanted in every house; be widely known and liked; be a household word
家乡 jiāxiāng hometown; native place:~菜 food from one's hometown; food cooked in hometown style / ~小调 popular tune of one's native place / ~风味 flavour of the cooking of one's hometown
家乡话 jiāxiānghuà native dialect
家小 jiāxiǎo ❶ wife and children ❷ wife
家信 jiāxìn letter to or from one's family:平安~ letter to or from one's family saying that everything is well
家兄 jiāxiōng 〈谦词〉my elder brother:~嘱我问候您。My elder brother asked me to give you his regards.
家学 jiāxué ❶ knowledge passed on from generation to generation in a family ❷ family school
家学渊源 jiāxué-yuānyuán (benefit from) a line of scholars in the family:他在史学上的成就出于~。His achievements in historical studies came from the long tradition of learning in his family.
家训 jiāxùn 〈书面〉parental instruction
家严 jiāyán 〈书面〉〈谦词〉my father
家宴 jiāyàn family dinner; family reception
家燕 jiāyàn *also* "燕子" yànzi swallow
家养 jiāyǎng tame; domesticate; cultivate
家业 jiāyè ❶ family property; property:继承~ inherit the family property ❷〈书面〉undertaking or learning handed down from one's ancestor
家用 jiāyòng ❶ family expenses; housekeeping money:贴补~ supplement housekeeping money; help pay family expenses ❷ for household use; domestic:~冰箱 domestic refrigerator; domestic cabinet / ~电灶 domestic induction heater
家用电器 jiāyòng diànqì household appliance; household electric appliance
家有千口,主事一人 jiā yǒu qiān kǒu, zhǔshì yī rén a family has many people but only one master; a house can't have more than one master:~,村里办啥事情总得有个头哇! A village needs one man to call the shots, just like a family.
家鱼 jiāyú cultivated fish
家喻户晓 jiāyù-hùxiǎo known to every household; on everbody's lips; known to all:宣传法律知识要做到~。Knowledge of law should be made known to every household. / 这口号已~。This slogan has already become a household word. / 他的名字~。His name is on everyone's lips.
家园 jiāyuán ❶ home; homeland:重建~ rebuild one's home; rebuild one's village or town / 重返~ return to one's hometown ❷〈方言〉grown in a home garden:~茶叶 homegrown tea
家院 jiāyuàn ❶ courtyard:~里练不出千里马,花盆里栽不出万年松。A steed will not be trained in a courtyard; a pinetree will not be raised in a flowerpot. ❷〈旧语〉servant
家贼 jiāzéi thief in the family; one who commits an in-house theft:有迹象表明,这家银行被盗,可能有~。Signs indicate that the bank robbery was an inside job.
家贼难防 jiāzéi-nánfáng a thief in the family is hard to detect; it's most difficult to defend against a thief within the house or company
家宅 jiāzhái house; residence; home
家长 jiāzhǎng ❶ head of a family; patriarch ❷ parent or guardian of a child:开~会 hold a parents' meeting
家长式 jiāzhǎngshì patriarchal:~统治 paternalism; arbitrary rule as by a patriarch
家长制 jiāzhǎngzhì patriarchal system:书记要善于集中大家的意见,不要搞"一言堂","~"。The secretary should be good at summing up the ideas of the masses and must not have the only say or behave like a patriarch.
家长作风 jiāzhǎng zuòfēng highhanded way of dealing with people; patriarchal behaviour
家珍 jiāzhēn family heirloom:如数~ as if enumerating one's family treasures — have an intimate knowledge of the subject
家政 jiāzhèng household management; home economics
家政学 jiāzhèngxué home economics
家种 jiāzhòng ❶ cultivated:~人参 cultivated ginseng / 把野生药材改为~ bring wild medicinal herbs under cultivation ❷ grown in one's own garden:这些蔬菜都是~的。These vegetables are all from our own garden.
家主 jiāzhǔ head of a family; patriarch
家传 jiāzhuàn household biography; record of the affairs of family members meant to set an example for descendents
see also jiāchuán
家资 jiāzī family property:~耗尽 squander all one's family property
家子 jiāzi 〈口语〉family; household:这~有八口人。There are eight members in this family. / 我们村好几~都有电视机了。Quite a few households in our village have TV sets.
家族 jiāzú clan; family:~公司 family firm / 吴姓是本镇的大~。The Wu family is a big clan in this town.

镓

jiā 〈化学〉gallium (Ga)
镓酸 jiāsuān 〈化学〉gallic acid:~盐 gallate
镓烷 jiāwán 〈化学〉gallane

傢

jiā
傢伙 jiāhuo *see* "家伙" jiāhuo
傢具 jiāju *see* "家具" jiāju
傢什 jiāshi *see* "家什" jiāshi

夹(夾、❷挾)

jiā ❶ press from both sides; clip; pinch:把文件~在一起 clip papers together / 门~了她的手指头。The door squeezed (*or* pinched) her fingers. / 他的车~在两辆卡车中间。His car was sandwiched between two trucks. ❷ carry (sth.) under one's arm:他~起皮包走了。Carrying a briefcase under his arm, he left. ❸ place or stay in between:把邮票~在集邮册里 put the stamps in a stamp-album ❹ mix; mingle; intersperse:风声~着雨声 whistle of wind intermingled with (*or* accompanied by) the patter of rain / 白话~文言 mixture of vernacular and literary styles / 孩子们~在大人中间。The children mingle with the adults. ❺ clip; clamp; folder:纸~ paper clip / 发~ hairpin / 钱~ wallet / 文件~ folder / 报~ newspaper holder / 弹~ cartridge clip / 活页~ loose-leaf bind
see also gā; jiá
夹板 jiābǎn ❶ boards for pressing or holding sth. together ❷〈医学〉splint:石膏~ plaster splint / 给受伤的腿上~ splint the broken leg
夹板气 jiābǎnqì under crossfire from two opposing sides; attacked or blamed by two opposing sides; whipsawed:受~ be caught in the crossfire from two opposing sides; get blamed by both sides
夹壁墙 jiābìqiáng *also* "夹壁";"夹墙" hollow wall
夹层 jiācéng 〈建筑〉mezzanine; sandwich:~板 sandwich plate / ~结构 sandwich construction
夹层玻璃 jiācéng bōli sandwich glass
夹叉射击 jiāchā shèjī 〈军事〉bracketing fire; bracket
夹缠 jiāchán 〈方言〉harass; nag; worry; pester:他天天到我这里~,真讨厌! He comes to harass me every day. How annoying!
夹带 jiādài ❶ carry secretly; smuggle:不能~鞭炮上车。Don't smuggle the firecrackers onto the train. ❷ notes smuggled into an

J

examination hall ❸ mix; mingle:～私心 motivated partly by selfishness

夹当 jiādāng 〈方言〉at the very moment; when:在我很困难的～,他帮助了我。He offered me help when I needed it most.

夹道 jiādào ❶ narrow lane; passageway:穿过这两座楼房中间的～,向左一拐就是我的家。Passing through this passageway and turning left at the corner, you'll find my house. ❷ line both sides of the street:～欢迎贵宾 line the street to welcome a distinguished guest / 公园的后部,小桥流水,浓荫～。At the back of the park, there is a small bridge over running water, with trees lining both sides of the path.

夹缝 jiāfèng narrow space between two adjacent things; crack; crevice:书掉在两张桌子的～里。The book dropped into the narrow space between the two desks.

夹肝 jiāgān 〈方言〉food made from animal's pancreas, especially from pigs, oxen, sheep, etc.

夹攻 jiāgōng attack from both sides; converging attack; pincer attack:受到两面～ be under a two-pronged attack; be caught in a two-way squeeze /前后～ attack from the front and the rear simultaneously /～敌人 make pincer attacks on the enemy; hold the enemy in pincers /左右～ under crossfire from left and right /内外～ attack from inside and outside

夹棍 jiāgùn 〈旧语〉clamping rods, an instrument of torture applied to a criminal's legs

夹击 jiājī converging attack; pincer attack:从东西两端～ make a pincer attack from east and west

夹剪 jiājiǎn cross-shaped clamping tool; tongs; tweezers

夹角 jiājiǎo 〈数学〉included angle

夹紧 jiājǐn clamp:～器 clamp check /～装置 clamp device; clamping mechanism

夹具 jiājù 〈机械〉vise; clamp; fixture; jig

夹克 jiākè *also* "茄克" jiākè;"甲克" jiǎkè jacket:皮～ leather jacket

夹盘 jiāpán 〈机械〉chuck; chuck plate:～外圆磨床 chucking grinding machine external /～转塔车床 chucking capstan and turret lathe

夹批 jiāpī annotations and comments made in between the lines of writings

夹七夹八 jiāqī-jiābā incoherent; confused; cluttered (with irrelevant remarks):～地述说了一遍 make a confusing account /他～说了一大段,这才落到主题上。He rambled for quite a while before coming to the point.

夹钳 jiāqián 〈机械〉clam; clamp; clamp frame

夹生 jiāshēng half-cooked; half-baked:这饭吃起来有点～。This rice is not properly cooked.

夹生饭 jiāshēngfàn ❶ half-cooked rice ❷ task difficult to perform because it has not been done properly at the outset

夹丝玻璃 jiāsī bōli wired glass

夹尾巴 jiā wěiba ❶ dejected; crestfallen; depressed:敌人～逃跑了。The enemy troops ran away with their tails between their legs. ❷ prudent and modest:夹起尾巴做人 be modest and prudent

夹馅 jiāxiàn stuffed (pastry, etc.):～烧饼 stuffed sesame seed cakes

夹心 jiāxīn ❶ with filling:巧克力～糖 sweets with chocolate centres /～蛋糕 sandwich cake ❷ 〈冶金〉sandwiched-in; sandwiching:～焊接 sandwich braze /～钢 sandwich steel /～轧制 sandwich rolling

夹心饼干 jiāxīn bǐnggān sandwich biscuit or cookie

夹叙夹议 jiāxù-jiāyì narration interspersed with comments

夹杂 jiāzá be mixed up with; be cluttered with; be mingled with:脚步声和笑声～在一起。The sound of footsteps mingled with laughter. /红色条纹中～着蓝色条纹。Red stripes alternate with blue ones. /他说话～着南方口音。He speaks with a slight southern accent. /文章里～着许多不成熟的想法。The article is interlarded with half-baked ideas.

夹杂物 jiāzáwù 〈冶金〉inclusion

夹渣 jiāzhā 〈冶金〉slag inclusion:～生铁 cinder pig; cinder pig iron

夹峙 jiāzhì stand erect facing each other:江水在山崖的～中滚滚地流着。The river water is rolling between two towering cliffs.

夹竹桃 jiāzhútáo 〈植物〉(sweet-scented) oleander

夹注 jiāzhù interlinear notes:这本古文选本有～。There are interlinear notes in this selection of classical writings.

夹子 jiāzi clip; tongs; folder; wallet:不锈钢～ stainless steel clip / 点心～ cake tongs /头发～ hairpin /文件～ folder; binder /皮～ wallet; pocketbook /讲义～ teaching-materials binder

浃(浹) jiā 〈书面〉soak through; spread all over:汗流～背 soaked with sweat

筴(筴、梜) jiā chopsticks

see also cè

葭 jiā 〈书面〉young shoot of a reed; young reed

葭莩 jiāfú 〈书面〉membrane of a reed stem; 〈比喻〉distant relative:～之亲 distant relative; person of distant relationship

佳 jiā ❶ good; fine; excellent; beautiful:风景绝～ extremely beautiful scenery /健康状况尚～ be in fairly good health; be in good shape /心情欠～ be in a bad mood; feel dejected /政绩不～ have little to one's credit in one's official career ❷ *used together with a numeral to refer to a group of outstanding people or things*:今年的十～民歌手 this year's top ten folk song singers /这种电冰箱名列去年的十～之一。This refrigerator was among the best ten brands last year.

佳宾 jiābīn *also* "嘉宾" jiābīn honoured guest; welcome guest

佳话 jiāhuà deed praised far and wide; story on everybody's lips; much-told tale:传为～ become a fine story on everybody's lips /给后人留下一段～ leave behind a much-told tale

佳节 jiājié happy festival time; festival:新春～ happy Spring Festival /张灯结彩庆～ celebrate the joyous festival with lanterns and decorations /每逢～倍思亲。On every festive occasion I think all the more of my dear ones far away.

佳境 jiājìng ❶ beautiful place; scenic spot:这里树木葱茏,曲径通幽,真乃～。The place is really a Shangri-La with luxuriant trees and winding paths leading to secluded spots. ❷ most pleasant stage or state:渐入～ become more and more interesting

佳句 jiājù beautiful line (in a poem); well-turned phrase:他的诗中每有～。He often has beautiful lines in his poems.

佳丽 jiālì ❶ (of looks, scene, etc.) good; beautiful:江南～地,金陵帝王州。Southern Jiangsu is a beautiful place and Nanjing an imperial abode. ❷ 〈书面〉beautiful woman; beauty:后宫～三千人。There are thousands of beauties in the palace.

佳美 jiāměi good; nice; beautiful:滋味～ nice taste /～的菜肴 delicious food

佳妙 jiāmiào wonderful; superb:文辞～ elegant language; refined writing

佳酿 jiāniàng 〈书面〉vintage wine:绍兴～ Shaoxing vintage rice wine

佳偶 jiā'ǒu 〈书面〉❶ happy married couple:～天成 ideal marriage divinely arranged ❷ ideal spouse

佳品 jiāpǐn product of excellent quality among its kind:调味～ excellent seasoner /哈密瓜是瓜中～。Hami melon is the best of all melons.

佳期 jiāqī ❶ wedding day; nuptial day ❷ dating time for lovers; lover's time for rendezvous

佳趣 jiāqù good taste and charm:山谷幽邃,别有～。The mountain valley, deep and quiet, has a charm of its own.

佳人 jiārén 〈书面〉beautiful woman:南国～ beautiful woman from the South /二八～ girl of sweet sixteen

佳肴 jiāyáo delicious food; delicacy:～美酒 delicious food and vintage wine

佳音 jiāyīn welcome news; glad tidings; favourable reply:喜闻～。I am delighted to hear the news of your success.

佳作 jiāzuò fine piece of writing; excellent literary work:这个短篇小说是近几年难得的～。This short story is an excellent work rarely seen in recent years.

加 jiā ❶ add; plus:把这些数字～在一起 add these figures together /风雪交～ raging snowstorm /好上～好 be better still /七～八等于几? How much is seven plus eight? /桌子～椅子共九件。All told, there are nine desks and chairs. ❷ increase; rise; raise; augment:要求～工资 ask for a wage increase (*or* rise) /～多 add; in-

crease /～高 heighten /～厚 thicken /添砖～瓦 contribute one's bit / 添枝～叶 exaggerate ❸ put in; add; append:～上标点符号 put in the proper punctuation marks /～把劲 exert oneself in one's work /给自己～上新的头衔 confer a new title on oneself /给他～了许多罪名 level many charges against him /给汽车～点油。Fill the car with some petrol. /在裙子上～上花边儿。Trim the dress with lace. ❹ *same as* 加以 *but used generally after a monosyllabic adverb*:不～干涉 not interfere / 严～管制 exercise strict control /横～阻挠 wilfully obstruct / 不～思索 without giving it much thought /有则改之,无则～勉。Correct mistakes if you have committed any, and guard against them if you have not. ❺ (Jiā) a surname

加班 jiābān work overtime; work an extra shift:～时间 overtime; overhours /～奖金 overtime bonus /～限度 limit of overtime

加班费 jiābānfèi overtime pay; overtime wages; call-back pay; overtime cost

加班加点 jiābān-jiādiǎn be on overtime; work extra shifts; put in extra hours:～津贴 overtime premium; overtime allowance /为了如期完成任务,他们只得～。They had to work longer hours and extra shifts to accomplish the task on schedule.

加保 jiābǎo additional insurance:～费 additional premium (AP)

加倍 jiābèi ❶ double; be twice as much:～奉还 repay twice as much /～余额递减法 double-declining balance method /产量加了一倍。The output has been doubled. ❷ double; redouble:～努力 redouble one's efforts; pull up one's socks /～小心 be doubly careful /～用功 be extremely hardworking at one's studies

加餐 jiācān add a snack; have an extra meal; eat (much) more: 努力～ eat as much as one can /课间～关系到孩子的成长。A snack in between classes has a direct bearing on the growth of children.

加车 jiāchē (put on) extra buses or trains

加成 jiāchéng 〈化工〉addition:～化合物 additive compound; addition compound /～反应 addition reaction

加成定价 jiāchéng dìngjià mark-up pricing

加大 jiādà increase; augment; enlarge:～药量 increase the dose /～范围 enlarge the scope /～油门 open the throttle; step on the gas

加德满都 Jiādémǎndū Kathmandu, capital of Nepal

加点 jiādiǎn extra time; overtime

加碘盐 jiādiǎnyán iodized salt

加尔各答 Jiā'ěrgèdá Calcutta, second largest city and important port of India

加法 jiāfǎ 〈数学〉addition:～交换率 commutative law by addition/～器 adder; adding device; adding machine

加封 jiāfēng ❶ paste a paper strip seal on (doors, drawers, etc.); seal off:仓门已～。A paper strip seal has been pasted on the storehouse door. ❷ confer another title on sb.:受到了皇帝的～ be conferred another title by the emperor

加感 jiāgǎn 〈电工〉loading inductance:～天线 loaded antenna /～线路 loadline /～线圈 loading coil

加工 jiāgōng ❶ process:～厂 processing factory /木材～ wood processing /艺术～ artistic treatment /来样～ processing according to investor's samples /来料～部 processing department for sent-in materials /食品～ food processing /～工业 processing industry /～能力 processing ability /～程序 job arrangement; job sequence /～单 working order /～材料 worked (*or* processed, *or* finished) materials /粗～ first stage of processing /精～ refined processing /～验收 acceptance of work /冷～ cold working /～周期 process cycle; processing cycle /～自动化 process automation ❷ polish; finish; refine:这篇文章需要～。This article needs polishing.

加工订货 jiāgōng-dìnghuò place orders (with enterprises) for processing materials or supplying manufactured goods

加固 jiāgù reinforce; consolidate; strengthen:～堤坝 reinforce dykes and embankment /～工事 improve defence works /对危旧房屋进行改建或～ have dilapidated houses rebuilt or consolidated

加官 jiāguān 〈旧语〉be promoted in rank; be made a higher official

加官进爵 jiāguān-jìnjué receive official promotion; advance in rank and position

加害 jiāhài injure; do harm to:～于人 do harm to sb.; do sb. an injury /他～的人太多了。Too many people have been his victims.

加害方 jiāhàifāng 〈法律〉party causing the injury; injuring party

加害人 jiāhàirén 〈法律〉author of the injury; person causing the injury; injuring person; inflictor; injurer

加号 jiāhào 〈数学〉plus sign (+)

加厚剂 jiāhòujì 〈摄影〉intensifier

加急 jiājí ❶ become rapid and violent; intensify:枪声又突然地～起来。Gunfire became rapid and intensive all of a sudden. ❷ urgent: ～电 urgent telegram; urgent cable

加加林 Jiājiālín Yuri Alekseevich Gagarin (1934-1968), Russian cosmonaut who in 1961 made the first manned space flight

加价 jiājià raise the price; hike the price:～出售 sell at a higher price

加紧 jiājǐn step up; speed up; intensify:～训练 intensify training /～治疗 speed up medical treatment /这个问题要～解决。The problem must be solved as soon as possible.

加劲 jiājìn ❶ put more energy into; redouble one's efforts:～学习 study harder /这项工程需要加把劲儿才能按期完成。Greater efforts are needed if the project is to be completed according to schedule. ❷〈建筑〉stiffen:～梁 stiff (*or* stiffening) girder /～角钢 stiffening angle /～肋 stiffening rib

加剧 jiājù aggravate; sharpen; intensify; exacerbate:～国际紧张局势 aggravate international tension /他们之间的权力斗争又～了。Their power struggle has again intensified. /裂痕正在～。The rift is widening. /疼痛～。The pain sharpens (*or* becomes more acute).

加聚物 jiājùwù 〈化学〉addition polymer

加快 jiākuài ❶ quicken; speed or step up; accelerate; expedite: ～精神文明建设的步伐 step up the building (*or* development) of spiritual civilization /～建设速度 quicken the tempo of construction /～新技术的推广和应用 accelerate the spread and application of the new technology /～信息传递 speed up information transmission /火车～了速度。The train picked up speed. ❷ procedure for the holder of a slow train ticket to take a fast train:我这张票要～。I'd like to have this ticket exchanged for (*or* made into) an express train ticket.

加快轴 jiākuàizhóu accelerating axle

加宽 jiākuān broaden; widen:～衣服的腰身 widen the waist measurement of a dress /桥面比原设计～了一米。The bridge floor is one metre wider than its former design.

加拉加斯 Jiālājiāsī Caracas, capital of Venezuela

加勒比共同体 Jiālèbǐ Gòngtóngtǐ Caribbean Community (CARICOM)

加勒比海 Jiālèbǐhǎi Caribbean Sea

加里曼丹 Jiālǐmàndān Kalimantan, Indonesian part of the island of Borneo

加里宁 Jiālǐníng Mikhail Ivanovich Kalinin (1875-1946), head of state of Soviet Russia (1919-1938) and of the Soviet Union (1938-1946)

加力 jiālì 〈航空〉thrust augmentation; afterburning

加力发动机 jiālì fādòngjī boost engine

加力俯冲 jiālì fǔchōng afterburning dive

加力装置 jiālì zhuāngzhì augmentor

加利福尼亚 Jiālìfúníyà (shortened as 加州) California, a state on the Pacific coast of the United States:～大学 University of California

加料 jiāliào ❶ feed in raw material:自动～ automatic feeding /～工人 feeder ❷ reinforced:～药酒 reinforced tonic wine /～狼毫 writing brush reinforced with superfine weasel hair

加榴炮 jiāliúpào gun-howitzer

加仑 jiālún gallon

加码 jiāmǎ ❶〈旧语〉raise the price of commodities; overcharge: 解放前夕,粮价不断～,日子实在难熬。On the eve of liberation, grain prices kept rising, making life extremely difficult for common people. ❷ raise the stakes in gambling ❸ raise the quota:今年的生产任务～了。The production quota of this year has been raised.

加煤机 jiāméijī firing machine; stoking machine

加盟 jiāméng ally oneself to;〈比喻〉join (a sports team, etc.):他后来～北京京剧团。He later joined the Beijing Opera Troupe.

加密 jiāmì 〈通信〉encrypt:～电路 encrypted circuit /～机 encryptor

加冕 jiāmiǎn coronation; crowning:～典礼 coronation; coronation ceremony

加冕日 jiāmiǎnrì (UK) Coronation Day

加拿大 Jiānádà Canada:～人 Canadian

加拿大广播公司 Jiānádà Guǎngbō Gōngsī Canadian Broadcasting Corporation (CBC)

加拿大航空公司 Jiānádà Hángkōng Gōngsī Air Canada

加那利群岛 Jiānàlì Qúndǎo Canary Islands, Spanish provinces

off northwestern Africa
加纳 Jiānà Ghana:~人 Ghanaian
加捻 jiāniǎn 〈纺织〉 twisting
加农榴弹炮 jiānóng liúdànpào howitzer
加农炮 jiānóngpào cannon; gun
加派 jiāpài dispatch more (people, etc.):~岗哨 send more sentinels; designate more sentinels
加蓬 Jiāpéng Gabon:~人 Gabonese
加气 jiāqì 〈建筑〉 air entrainment
加气混凝土 jiāqì hùnníngtǔ aerocrete
加气水泥 jiāqì shuǐní air entraining cement
加强 jiāqiáng strengthen; intensify; enhance; reinforce:~法制 strengthen the legal system /~战备 enhance combat readiness /~管理 improve (*or* tighten up) the management /~警戒 heighten (military) vigilance /~体育锻炼 intensify sports training /~生产第一线 reinforce the production front /~排〈军事〉 reinforced platoon /~军事力量 augment military strength /双方允诺在谈判进行期间不~兵力。Each side promised not to beef up its forces while negotiations are under way.
加强肋 jiāqiánglèi reinforcing rib; strengthening rib
加强外胎 jiāqiáng wàitāi reinforced tyre
加强原料 jiāqiáng yuánliào reinforced material
加氢 jiāqīng 〈化工〉 hydrogenization; hydrogenation:~处理 hydrotreatment; hydroprocessing /~精制 hydrofining; hydrofinishing /~裂化 hydrocracking /~气化 hydrogasification /~脱硫 hydrodesulfurizing /~预处理 hydropretreating
加氢汽油 jiāqīng qìyóu 〈化工〉 hydrogasoline
加权平均法 jiāquán píngjūnfǎ 〈数学〉 weighted averages method
加权平均值 jiāquán píngjūnzhí 〈数学〉 weighted average
加热 jiārè heating:~器 heater /~炉 heating furnace /水~到 100 度就沸腾。Water boils when heated to one hundred degrees.
加人一等 jiārén-yīděng be superior to ordinary people; stand head and shoulders above others
加入 jiārù ❶ add; mix; put in:~一点佐料 add some condiments ❷ join; accede to:~条约 accede to a treaty /~工会 join the trade union /~中国国籍 acquire Chinese citizenship /申请~中国作家协会 apply for membership of the Chinese Writers' Association
加入国 jiārùguó acceding state
加入书 jiārùshū instrument of accession
加塞儿 jiāsāir 〈口语〉 push into a queue out of turn; jump a queue; butt in line:请排队,别~! Please line up. Don't jump the queue.
加赛 jiāsài 〈体育〉 additional tie-breaking match or game
加色法 jiāsèfǎ 〈影视〉 additive process
加沙地区 Jiāshā Dìqū Gaza Strip, a strip of coastal territory in the southeast Mediterranean administered by Egypt
加上 jiāshang ❶ add; plus:饭菜~酒水共八十元。All the dishes plus drinks add up to 80 *yuan*. ❷ moreover; in addition; furthermore
加深 jiāshēn deepen; enhance; aggravate:~对祖国的热爱 deepen one's love for one's motherland /~裂痕 widen a rift /~水井 deepen a well /~艺术修养 enhance one's artistic accomplishment /这个国家经济危机日益~。The economic crisis of this country has been worsening.
加湿器 jiāshīqì humidifier
加时赛 jiāshísài 〈体育〉 play-off:在足球的~中,以先进一球的队为胜者。In the play-off of a soccer (*or* football) game, whichever team scores the first goal wins the game.
加试 jiāshì add (more items) to an examination:今年高考要~体育。Physical education has been added to this year's college entrance examination.
加数 jiāshù 〈数学〉 addend
加速 jiāsù quicken; speed up; accelerate; expedite:~步伐 quicken one's steps (*or* pace) /~我国建设 accelerate our country's construction /~我国军队的现代化建设 speed up the modernization of our army /~商品周转 expedite the turnover of commodities /汽车~行驶。The car has picked up (speed). /错误政策~政府的垮台。The wrong policies hastened the downfall of the government.
加速度 jiāsùdù 〈物理〉 acceleration:重力~ acceleration of gravity
加速度计 jiāsùdùjì accelerometer
加速器 jiāsùqì 〈物理〉 accelerator:静电~ electro-static accelerator /回旋~ cyclotron /粒子~ particle accelerator /同步~ synchrotron /直线~ linear accelerator /微波~ microwave accelerator /稳相~ synchrocyclotron
加速运动 jiāsù yùndòng 〈物理〉 acclerated motion
加速折旧 jiāsù zhéjiù accelerated depreciation
加添 jiātiān increase; add; put in; augment
加委 jiāwěi 〈旧语〉 carry out the formalities of appointment; appoint:他的理事长一职已由省府~。He has been appointed director-general by the provincial government.
加温 jiāwēn raise the temperature; heat (up)
加线 jiāxiàn 〈音乐〉 ledger line; leger line
加线台球 jiāxiàn táiqiú 〈体育〉 balkline billards
加楔儿 jiāxiēr 〈方言〉 jump a queue
加薪 jiāxīn increase the salary; raise the pay
加压 jiāyā pressurization; compression; pressure:~淬火 pressure quenching /~气焊 pressure-gas welding /~铸焊 pressure thermite welding /~密封〈机械〉 pressure seal /~蒸煮器〈化工〉 pressure-cooker /~蒸馏器 pressure-still /~氧化 pressure oxidation
加压舱 jiāyācāng pressurized module
加压釜 jiāyāfǔ *also* "热压釜" rèyāfǔ; "高压釜" gāoyāfǔ compression cauldron
加一 jiāyī increase ten per cent:这些布头~出售。These odd bits of cloth are sold with ten per cent thrown in.
加以 jiāyǐ ❶ *used before disyllabic verbs to indicate how to deal with the matter mentioned above*:对某事~分析 make an analysis of sth. /发现错误时请及时~纠正。In case you find any mistake, please correct it immediately. /有一个问题必须~说明。There is a problem that needs explanation. ❷ in addition; moreover:她本来就聪明,~特别用功,所以进步很快。She is very clever, and moreover she studies exceptionally hard, so she has made rapid progress.
加意 jiāyì with special care; with close attention:~提防 be particularly watchful /对贵重仪器要~保护 protect valuable instruments with special care
加油 jiāyóu ❶ oil; lubricate:这台机器该~了。This machine needs oiling. ❷ refuel:空中~ air refueling; inflight refueling /这条国际航班的飞机中途要降落~两次。This international airliner needs to land twice for fueling during its flight. ❸ make an extra effort:~干 work with added vigour /小王,~! Come on, Xiao Wang! /观众给运动员~。The spectators cheered the players (on). /观众朝运动员们喊道:"~!~!" "Play up! Play up!" (*or* "Go! Go! Go!") the spectators shouted to the athletes.
加油车 jiāyóuchē fuel truck; refueling truck; refueller
加油飞机 jiāyóu fēijī tanker aircraft
加油添醋 jiāyóu-tiāncù *also* "加油加醋" embellish (a story); add inflammatory details (to a story); exaggerate:他在叙述自己的经历时,总爱~。When recounting his experiences, he is fond of adding colour and emphasis to them.
加油站 jiāyóuzhàn filling station; petrol station; gas station
加枝添叶 jiāzhī-tiānyè *also* "添枝加叶" exaggerate; add highly coloured details (to a story)
加重 jiāzhòng ❶ make or get heavier; increase the weight:~思想负担 increase one's worries /~自行车 heavy-weight-bearing bike /~语气 in an emphatic tone ❷ make or become more serious; aggravate:~困难 aggravate the difficulty /危机日益~ deepening crisis /伤势~。The wound was getting worse.

痂 jiā scab; crust:疮~ scab /结~ form a scab; crust /焦~ eschar /嗜~之癖 have a particular liking for scab; have a depraved taste

袈 jiā

袈裟 jiāshā *kasaya*, a patchwork outer vestment worn by a Buddhist monk

麚 jiā 〈书面〉 stag; buck

珈 jiā ornament worn by ancient Chinese women

嘉 jiā ❶ good; nice; fine:~言 nice words /~礼 wedding ceremony /~谋善政 excellent achievements in one's official post ❷ praise; laud; commend:~纳 praise and accept /其志可~。His noble aspirations deserve commendation. ❸ (Jiā) a surname

嘉宾 jiābīn *also*"佳宾" jiābīn honoured guest; welcome guest:～席 seats for honoured guests
嘉惠 jiāhuì 〈书面〉❶〈敬词〉(with) your favour; (thanks to) your kindness ❷ benefit; profit; give favour:～士林 benefit academic circles
嘉奖 jiājiǎng commend; cite:～有功人员 cite those who have performed meritorious service /受到上级的～ receive a citation from one's superior
嘉奖令 jiājiǎnglìng citation
嘉靖 Jiājìng Jiajing (formerly translated as Chia-Ching), title of the reign (1522-1566) of Zhu Houcong (朱厚熜, 1507-1567), 12th emperor of the Ming Dynasty, called reverently Ming Shizong (明世宗) after death
嘉勉 jiāmiǎn 〈书面〉praise and encourage:给这个连记集体二等功,以示～。Award the company a citation for Merit, Second Class by way of praise and encouragement.
嘉名 jiāmíng 〈书面〉good reputation
嘉庆 Jiāqìng Jiaqing (formerly translated as Chia-Ch'ing), title of the reign (1796-1820) of Aisin Gioro Yongyan (爱新觉罗·颙琰, 1760-1820), 5th emperor of the Qing Dynasty, called reverently Qing Renzong (清仁宗) after death
嘉耦 jiā'ǒu happily married couple
嘉尚 jiāshàng 〈书面〉praise; approve:深可～ be worthy of high praise; be very praiseworthy
嘉慰 jiāwèi 〈书面〉praise and comfort:表示～ show praise and comfort
嘉许 jiāxǔ 〈书面〉praise; approve:他脸上露出～的笑容。A smile of approval appeared on his face.
嘉言懿行 jiāyán-yìxíng wise words and noble deeds:外祖父的～,在我的心灵里留下了深刻的烙印。Grandpa's fine words and deeds left a deep impression on me.
嘉峪关 Jiāyùguān Jiayu Pass, at the western end of the Great Wall in Gansu Province

茄 jiā ❶〈古语〉stem of lotus ❷ *see* "雪茄" xuějiā
see also qié
茄克 jiākè *also* "夹克" jiākè; "甲克" jiǎkè jacket

枷 jiā cangue — wooden yoke for a prisoner:披～带锁 be in chains
枷锁 jiāsuǒ bond; yoke; chains; shackles; fetters:带着～ be in fetters; be in chains /砸碎～ smash shackles /摆脱封建主义(殖民主义、帝国主义)的～ shake off the yoke of feudalism (colonialism, imperialism)

跏 jiā
跏趺 jiāfū 〈宗教〉sit cross-legged

笳 jiā *see* "胡笳" hújiā

伽 jiā 〈物理〉gal
see also gā; qié
伽倻琴 jiāyēqín plucked stringed instrument, used by the Korean nationality

迦 jiā *see* "獾迦狓" huòjiāpí

jiá

夹(夾、裌、袷) jiá double-layered; lined:～袄 lined jacket /～被 double-layered quilt
see also gā; jiā

荚(莢) jiá pod:结～ bear pods; pod /豌豆～ pea pods/榆～ fruit of elm /皂～ Chinese honey locust
荚果 jiáguǒ pod; legume
荚蒾 jiámí 〈植物〉*Viburnum dilatatum*

颊(頰) jiá cheek:双～凹陷 (with) sunken cheeks /酒后～红 cheeks flushed with drinking
颊骨 jiágǔ 〈生理〉cheekbone
颊肌 jiájī 〈生理〉buccinator
颊囊 jiánáng *also*"颊嗛"〈动物〉cheek pouch
颊上添毫 jiáshàng-tiānháo make a portrait come alive by adding some hair on the cheeks — add the punch line
颊腺 jiáxiàn 〈生理〉buccal gland

蛱(蛺) jiá
蛱蝶 jiádié a kind of butterfly harmful to crop plants; vanessa

铗(鋏) jiá 〈书面〉❶ pincers; pliers; tongs:火～ fire tongs /铁～子 iron tongs /剪票～ conductor's punch ❷ sword; sabre:长～ long sword ❸ handle of a sword; hilt

恝 jiá 〈书面〉be indifferent
恝然 jiárán 〈书面〉indifferent; apathetic:～置之 be indifferent and ignore sth. /～而去 leave without paying any heed
恝置 jiázhì 〈书面〉ignore; neglect

戛(戞) jiá 〈书面〉knock gently; tap:～玉敲金 sonorous and pleasant tone
戛戛 jiájiá 〈书面〉❶ difficult; hard going:惟陈言之务去,～乎其难哉! How difficult it is to get rid of hackneyed phrases in writing! ❷ original; unique:～独造 of great originality
戛然 jiárán 〈书面〉❶〈象声〉loud cry of a bird:～长鸣 cry loud for a long time ❷ stop abruptly; stop suddenly:汽车～而止。The car stopped all of a sudden. /突然汽笛尖鸣,火车～煞住了。Suddenly a shrill whistle sounded and the train screeched to a halt.

跲 jiá 〈书面〉trip and fall

jiǎ

贾 Jiǎ a surname
see also gǔ
贾思勰 Jiǎ Sīxié Jia Sixie, born in present Shangdong, agronomist of the Northern Wei Dynasty and author of *Important Arts for the People's Welfare* (齐民要术)
贾宪三角 Jiǎ Xiàn sānjiǎo *also* "杨辉三角" Yáng Huī sānjiǎo;帕斯卡三角 Pàsīkǎ sānjǎo Pascal's triangle
贾谊 Jiǎ Yì Jia Yi (200-168 BC), versatile scholar and writer of early Han Dynasty, famous for his *fu* prose and political essays

槚 jiǎ 〈古语〉Chinese catalpa or tea tree

榎 jiǎ ❶ *see* "槚" jiǎ ❷ *see* "～草"
榎草 jiǎcǎo *also* "铁苋菜" tiěxiàncài 〈植物〉〈中药〉*Alcalypha australis*

甲[1] jiǎ ❶ first of the ten Heavenly Stems ❷ A; first:～等 first-rate; first class /～级牛奶 grade A milk /富～天下 richest on earth ❸ *used to refer to an unspecified person or thing*:～方与乙方 party A and party B ❹ (Jiǎ) a surname

甲[2] jiǎ ❶ shell; carapace:龟～ tortoise shell /鳞～ scale and shell (of reptiles and arthropods) /鳖～ turtle shell ❷ nail:手指～ fingernail /趾～ toenail /灰指～ ringworm of the nails; onychomycosis ❸ armour:装～车 armoured car; armoured vehicle /丢盔卸～ throw away one's helmet and coat of mail — flee pell-mell /披～ put on a suit of armour /解～归田 take off one's armour and return to country life; be demolized; retire

甲[3] jiǎ 〈旧语〉administrative unit of 10 households
see also "保甲" bǎojiǎ
甲胺 jiǎ'àn 〈化学〉methylamine
甲板 jiǎbǎn deck:前～ foredeck /后～ after deck; quarter deck /上～ upper deck /下～ lower deck /～值勤 deck duty
甲苯 jiǎběn 〈化工〉toluene; methylbenzene
甲兵 jiǎbīng 〈书面〉❶ armour and weaponry; military equip-

J

ment:修我~ keep our armour and weaponry in good order ❷ soldier in armour
甲病 jiǎbìng 〈医学〉onychopathy; onychosis
甲部 jiǎbù major division of traditional bibliography, consisting of classics; category of Chinese classics
甲虫 jiǎchóng beetle
甲床 jiǎchuáng 〈生理〉hyponychium
甲床炎 jiǎchuángyán onychia; onychitis
甲醇 jiǎchún 〈化工〉methyl alcohol; methanol
甲醇中毒 jiǎchún zhòngdú methyl alcohol poisoning
甲第 jiǎdì 〈书面〉❶ house of a rich and influential family ❷ highest rank in imperial examinations
甲酚 jiǎfēn 〈化学〉cresol:~树脂 cresol resin /~塑料 cresol plastics /~盐 cresylate
甲肝 jiǎgān (short for 甲型肝炎) hepatitis A:一种能迅速有效杀灭~病毒的新型消毒剂已在北京出售。A new disinfectant, which is quick and effective in killing hepatitis A virus, is now on sale in Beijing.
甲睾酮 jiǎgāotóng 〈药学〉methyltestosteróne
甲沟炎 jiǎgōuyán 〈医学〉paronychia
甲骨文 jiǎgǔwén inscriptions on tortoise shells or animal bones of the Shang Dynasty (c. 16th-11th centuries BC); ancient Chinese characters carved on tortoise shells or animal bones; oracle bone inscriptions; language used in such inscriptions
甲基 jiǎjī methyl:~溴〈化工〉methyl bromide /~纤维素〈药学〉methylcellulose /~砷酸 methyl-arsinic acid /~氨基酸〈生化〉methylamino acid /~麦角新碱〈药学〉methylergonovine
甲级股 jiǎjígǔ 〈金融〉Alpha Stock
甲级战犯 jiǎjí zhànfàn top war criminal
甲克 jiǎkè also "茄克" jiākè; "夹克" jiākè (transliteration) jacket; informal jacket:~衫 informal jacket /男式紧身短~ shell jacket
甲壳 jiǎqiào crust; shell:~纲动物 crustacea
甲壳动物 jiǎqiào dòngwù crustacean:~学 crustaceollogy; carcinology
甲壳质 jiǎqiàozhì also "壳质" qiàozhì 〈生化〉chitin
甲醛 jiǎquán 〈化学〉formaldehyde:~尿素 urea formaldehyde /~水 formalin; formadehyde solution
甲酸 jiǎsuān 〈化学〉formylic acid; formic acid; methanoic acid:~低铁 iron formate /~高铁 ironic formate /~盐 formate; formiate
甲烷 jiǎwán 〈化工〉methane
甲萎缩 jiǎwěisuō 〈医学〉onychatrophia
甲午战争 Jiǎwǔ Zhànzhēng Sino-Japanese War of 1894-1895 (launched by Japanese imperialists to annex Korea and invade China)
甲酰胺 jiǎxiān'àn 〈化学〉formamide:~酶 formamidase
甲型肝炎 jiǎxíng gānyán see "甲肝"
甲癣 jiǎxuǎn 〈医学〉ringworm of the nails; onychomycosis
甲氧胺 jiǎyǎng'àn 〈药学〉methoxamine
甲氧基 jiǎyǎngjī 〈化学〉methoxyl
甲夜 jiǎyè early evening (about eight p.m.)
甲鱼 jiǎyú soft-shelled turtle
甲仗 jiǎzhàng 〈书面〉❶ armour and weaponry ❷ soldier in armour
甲种粒子 jiǎzhǒng lìzǐ also "阿耳法粒子" ā'ěrfǎ lìzǐ 〈物理〉alpha particle
甲种射线 jiǎzhǒng shèxiàn also "阿耳法射线" ā'ěrfǎ shèxiàn 〈物理〉alpha ray
甲周炎 jiǎzhōuyán 〈医学〉perionychia
甲胄 jiǎzhòu 〈书面〉armour
甲状旁腺 jiǎzhuàng pángxiàn 〈生理〉parathyroid gland; parathyroid
甲状软骨 jiǎzhuàng ruǎngǔ 〈生理〉thyroid cartilage; cartilago thyroidea
甲状腺 jiǎzhuàngxiàn 〈生理〉thyroid gland; thyroid
甲状腺功能亢进 jiǎzhuàngxiàn gōngnéng kàngjìn 〈医学〉hyperthyroidism
甲状腺机能减退 jiǎzhuàngxiàn jīnéng jiǎntuì 〈医学〉hypothyreosis; hypothyroidism
甲状腺机能障碍 jiǎzhuàngxiàn jīnéng zhàng'ài 〈医学〉dysthyreosis
甲状腺切除术 jiǎzhuàngxiàn qiēchúshù 〈医学〉thyroidectomy
甲状腺素 jiǎzhuàngxiànsù thyroxine
甲状腺炎 jiǎzhuàngxiànyán 〈医学〉thyreoitis; thyroiditis; strumitis
甲状腺肿 jiǎzhuàngxiànzhǒng 〈医学〉goitre
甲子 jiǎzǐ cycle of sixty years in traditional Chinese chronology
see also "干支" gānzhī
甲紫 jiǎzǐ gentian violet

岬 jiǎ ❶ cape; promontory; headland; ness ❷ space between two mountains; narrow passage between mountains; col
岬角 jiǎjiǎo cape; promontory

钾 jiǎ 〈化学〉potassium (K):氯化~ potassium chloride /溴化~ potassium bromide /硫酸~ potassium sulphate /氯酸~ potassium chlorate /硝酸~ potassium nitrate
钾肥 jiǎféi potash fertilizer
钾碱 jiǎjiǎn potash
钾镁硫酸盐 jiǎměi liúsuānyán 〈化学〉Sul-Po-Mag; sulphate of potassium-magnesia; potassium magnesium-sulphate
钾硝 jiǎxiāo 〈化学〉potassium nitrate
钾氩法 jiǎyàfǎ 〈考古〉potassium-argon dating; K-Ar
钾盐 jiǎyán sylvite

胛 jiǎ
胛骨 jiǎgǔ 〈生理〉shoulder blade
胛子 jiǎzi 〈方言〉shoulder

斝(斚) jiǎ 〈考古〉round-mouthed three-legged wine vessel

瘕 jiǎ 〈书面〉lump in the abdomen

椵 jiǎ *see* "椵" gǔ

假 jiǎ ❶ false; fake; bogus; counterfeit; sham; phoney:~和平 phoney peace /搀~ adulterate /以~乱真 create confusion by passing off the spurious as genuine /弄虚作~ play false /真~难分 difficult to tell true from false /弄~成真。What was make-believe turns out to be reality. ❷ suppose; presume; assume: *see* "~设" ❸ if; in case: *see* "~使" ❹ borrow; avail oneself of; make use of:~革命之名 usurp the name of revolution /狐~虎威 the fox borrowing the ferocity of the tiger /不~思索 without taking time to think; offhand
see also jià
假案 jiǎ'àn case based on false charges; trumped-up case
假扮 jiǎbàn pass oneself off as; dress up as:~圣诞老人 dress up as Father Christmas; disguise oneself as Santa Claus
假币 jiǎbì counterfeit money; fake money; forged money
假裁军 jiǎcáijūn phoney or sham disarmament
假钞 jiǎchāo counterfeit note; forged bank note
假充 jiǎchōng pretend to be; pose as:~内行 pretend to be an expert /~英雄 pose as a hero /他企图~医生。He tried to pass himself off as a doctor.
假传圣旨 jiǎchuán-shèngzhǐ deliver a false imperial edict — give a fake order
假慈悲 jiǎcíbēi crocodile tears:算了,别在我面前猫哭老鼠~了。Well, don't shed crocodile tears in front of me.
假大空 jiǎ-dà-kōng engage in lying, boasting and empty talk; talk big and utter hollow words:党风不正反映在文风上,突出表现为~。Lying, boasting and empty talk that characterize the style of writing are a concentrated expression of the unhealthy style of Party work.
假道 jiǎdào via; by way of:~巴黎去非洲 go to Africa via Paris /我~日本去美国。I went to United States by way of Japan.
假道学 jiǎdàoxué sanctimonious person; hypocrite:这人是个~,惯于欺世盗名。The man is a hypocrite and is used to fishing for undeserved fame.
假定 jiǎdìng ❶ suppose; assume; hypothesize; presume:~成本 assumed cost; hypothetical cost /~负债 nominal liability /~利息 assumed interest; hypothetical interest /~他知道这回事 suppose he knew what happened /~你说的都是真理,也不必如此骄傲。You don't have to be so arrogant even if what you have said is true. ❷ hypothesis

假动作 jiǎdòngzuò 〈体育〉deceptive movement; feint
假发 jiǎfà wig; hairpiece:戴～ wear a wig; be bewigged
假分数 jiǎfēnshù 〈数学〉improper fraction
假根 jiǎgēn 〈植物〉rhizoid
假公济私 jiǎgōng-jìsī use public office for private gain; exploit public office for private ends; job:借职权之便～ take advantage of one's position (*or* public office) to feather one's own nest /他～,把弟弟安排到一个高工资的岗位上。He jobbed his brother into a well-paid post.
假果 jiǎguǒ 〈植物〉pseudocarp; spurious fruit
假合金 jiǎhéjīn 〈冶金〉pseudo-alloy
假花 jiǎhuā artificial flower
假话 jiǎhuà lie; falsehood:全是～ sheer fabrication; pack of lies
假黄连 jiǎhuánglián artificial rhizome of Chinese goldthread
假借 jiǎjiè ❶ make use of (sb. else's name, etc.); use false pretences:～外力搞竞选 make use of outside forces to enter into an election contest /他～他叔父的名义到处招摇。He goes about cheating people in the name of his uncle. /这个人～名义向许多人借钱。The man was borrowing money from many people under false pretences. ❷〈语言〉phonetic loan characters; characters adopted to represent homophones — one of the six categories of Chinese characters (六书) ❸〈书面〉be tolerant towards; bear with:针砭时弊,不稍～ show no tolerance whatever in criticizing current evils
假令 jiǎlìng 〈书面〉in case; in the event that
假冒 jiǎmào disguise oneself as; pose as; palm off (a fake as genuine):～签名 forged signature /～商标 counterfeit trademark /～产品 knock-offs of others' products /～名牌商品 imitations of brand-name goods /～伪劣产品 fake and inferior goods; counterfeit and shoddy goods /谨防～。Beware of fakes.
假眉三道 jiǎméi-sāndào 〈方言〉put on an act or show:你别～地骗人了。Don't put on an act to deceive people.
假寐 jiǎmèi 〈书面〉catnap; doze:凭几～ lean on a tea table to doze / ～片刻 doze off a while
假门假事 jiǎmen-jiǎshì *also* "假门假氏" pretend to be serious; put on an act; feign sincerity:他～地说了几句冠冕堂皇的话。He said some high-sounding words insincerely (*or* in an affected manner).
假面 jiǎmiàn mask; false front
假面具 jiǎmiànjù ❶ mask; false front:本店为小朋友们准备了各式各样的～,欢迎选购。Our shop has prepared all kinds of masks for children. Please come and buy them. ❷ hypocrisy; pretence; mask:揭穿某人的～ expose sb.'s hypocrisy; tear the mask off sb.; unmask sb.
假面舞会 jiǎmiàn wǔhuì masked ball; masquerade
假民主 jiǎmínzhǔ bogus democracy; sham democracy; mock democracy
假名 jiǎmíng ❶ pseudonym; alias; false name:～托姓 pass off sb.'s name as one's own ❷ kana, a Japanese syllabary:片～ katakana /平～ hiragana
假模假式 jiǎmo-jiǎshì *also* "假模假样" put on an act; pretend to be serious:我看不惯他那个～。I cannot stand his hypocritical manners.
假票据 jiǎpiàojù false bill
假撇清 jiǎpiēqīng 〈方言〉feign innocence
假漆 jiǎqī varnish
假情假意 jiǎqíng-jiǎyì unctuous; affected:他～地送给我这件礼物。He presented me with this gift affectedly.
假球 jiǎqiú rigged ball game or match:打～ rig a ball game or match; play foul (in football game, etc.)
假仁假义 jiǎrén-jiǎyì pretended benevolence and righteousness; hypocrisy:～之人 hypocrite /我看他说这些好话只不过～而已。In my opinion, he was merely paying lip service by those words of praise./ 他～地表示十分抱歉。He affected deep regret.
假如 jiǎrú if; supposing; in case:～明天下雨,我就不来了。I won't come if it rains tomorrow. /～他来的话,告诉我一声。In case he comes, let me know. /～出了问题,我们该怎么办? Suppose (*or* Supposing) something should go wrong, what shall we do?
假若 jiǎruò if; suppose; in case:～他的病早发现,不至于到这个地步。If his illness had been discovered earlier, it would not have come to such a pass.
假嗓子 jiǎsǎngzi falsetto
假山 jiǎshān rockery
假设 jiǎshè ❶ suppose; assume; grant; presume:～这件事发生在你们单位,你将如何处置? Suppose this happens in your unit, what will you do about it? ❷ fiction:故事情节是～的。The plot is purely fictitious. ❸ hypothesis:新的发现已证明那个～不能成立。The new discoveries have given the lie to that hypothesis.
假设成交 jiǎshè chéngjiāo assumptive close (of a deal)
假声 jiǎshēng 〈音乐〉falsetto
假使 jiǎshǐ if; in case; in the event that:～气候正常,早稻可望丰收。We are in for a good early rice harvest if the weather is fine.
假释 jiǎshì 〈法律〉release on parole; release on probation
假释犯 jiǎshìfàn 〈法律〉parolee
假手 jiǎshǒu ❶ do sth. through sb. else; make a cat's-paw of sb.:他们～雇佣军向一个主权国家发动了武装入侵。They used mercenaries to launch an armed invasion of a sovereign state. ❷ artificial hand
假手于人 jiǎshǒuyúrén (achieve one's end) through the instrumentality of sb. else; make sb. else do the work:他想～排挤我。He is trying to squeeze me out through someone else.
假说 jiǎshuō hypothesis
假死 jiǎsǐ ❶〈医学〉suspended animation; asphyxia ❷ play possum, play dead; pretend to be dead; feign death
假瘫 jiǎtān 〈医学〉pseudoparalysis
假途灭虢 jiǎtú-mièguó subjugate the state of Guo by asking for the right of way across its territory:此乃"～"之计也,虚名收川,实取荆州。This is the ruse known as "borrow a road to subjugate Guo". Under the pretence of attacking Sichuan in the west they are actually trying to capture Jingzhou.
假托 jiǎtuō ❶ on the pretext of; on the pretence of:他～有病,不去参加会议。He didn't go to the meeting on the pretext of illness. ❷ under sb. else's name; pass oneself off as:这本书显然是别的学派的人所～的。No doubt this book was written by someone who passed himself off as a proponent of this school. ❸ by means of; through the medium of:～古事以喻今 use ancient events to comment on present affairs by innuendo
假脱机 jiǎtuōjī 〈计算机〉spool
假戏真唱 jiǎxì-zhēnchàng *also* "假戏真做" do sth. seriously after starting it as a joke, ruse, etc.; what was make-believe turns out to be reality:同台演罗米欧与朱丽叶的两个演员～,后来结成了夫妻。The actor and actress who played Romeo and Juliet on stage together turned fiction into reality and got married afterwards.
假想 jiǎxiǎng imagination; hypothesis; supposition; fiction:～对手 imaginary opponent /那仅仅是～。It's a mere conjecture. /科学上有许多～需要证实。Many hypotheses in science need to be verified. /我曾～这件婚事能够成功。I once imagined that the marriage would be a success.
假想敌 jiǎxiǎngdí 〈军事〉imaginary enemy; hypothetical foe
假相 jiǎxiàng *see* "假象"
假象 jiǎxiàng ❶ false appearance:造成一种～ create a false impression; put up a false front /不要被～所欺骗。Don't be taken in by appearances. ❷〈地质〉pseudomorph
假小子 jiǎxiǎozi tomboy
假惺惺 jiǎxīngxing hypocritically; unctuously; insincerely:～地宣布 declare unctuously /他～地和我套起近乎来。He insincerely tried to cotton up to me. /他本来就讨厌我,现在又～地为我离开而悲伤。He never liked me, and now he sheds crocodile tears over my leaving.
假性近视 jiǎxìng jìnshì 〈医学〉pseudomyopia:近来患～的儿童越来越多。More and more children have been suffering from pseudomyopia recently.
假性斜视 jiǎxìng xiéshì 〈医学〉pseudostrabismus
假性心绞痛 jiǎxìng xīnjiǎotòng 〈医学〉pseudoangina
假牙 jiǎyá dental prosthesis; false tooth; denture
假眼 jiǎyǎn ocular prosthesis; artificial eye; glass eye
假洋鬼子 jiǎyángguǐzi 〈贬义〉(of a Chinese) mock foreign devil; fake foreigner
假药 jiǎyào imitation medicine; fake medicine
假以辞色 jiǎyǐcísè speak to someone kindly and encouragingly
假意 jiǎyì ❶ unction; insincerity; hypocrisy:虚情～ hypocritical show of cordiality ❷ pretend; put on:～应承 pretend to promise / ～奉承 cheap flattery
假孕 jiǎyùn 〈医学〉pseudocyesis
假造 jiǎzào ❶ forge; counterfeit:～的文件 forged document /～的护照 counterfeit passport /这张票据是～的。This bill is a forgery. *or* This is a forged bill. /不用说这消息完全是～的。No doubt, this

piece of news is sheer fabrication. ❷ invent; fabricate; cook up:～罪名 cook up a charge against; frame up /～理由,骗取金钱 invent (*or* work out) an excuse so as to cheat others out of their money
假招子 jiǎzhāozi assume airs; strike a pose
假正经 jiǎzhèngjing hypocrisy; prudery:装什么～? Why put on an air of respectability? /我看他是个～。It seems to me that he is a hypocrite.
假肢 jiǎzhī artificial limb
假植 jiǎzhí 〈农业〉heel in
假装 jiǎzhuāng pretend; feign; make a show of:～有兴趣 make a show of interest /～恼怒 feign annoyance /～是一个天真无邪的女孩 play the ingenue /这位母亲对儿子的犯罪行为～不知道。The mother pretended to know nothing about her son's crime. /我再三盘问,他却～不知。I asked him again and again, but he affected ignorance.
假装疯魔 jiǎzhuāng-fēngmó 〈方言〉put on an air of being out of one's senses; feign madness
假座 jiǎzuò use (a place) for a certain purpose:～俱乐部举办联谊会 hold a get-together at a club

jià

稼 jià ❶ sow (grain):耕～ ploughing and sowing; farm work ❷ cereals; crops:庄～ crops; standing grain
稼穑 jiàsè 〈书面〉sowing and reaping; farming; farm work:不到农村不知～之艰难。You don't know how hard farm work is until you go to the countryside.

嫁 jià ❶ (of a woman) marry:终身不～ remain single all one's life /婚～喜事 wedding /出～ be married to a man /改～ remarry /再～ remarry /他把女儿～给一个外国人。He married his daughter to a foreigner. ❷ (of blame, loss, etc.) shift; transfer:转～ shift; transfer
嫁出去的女儿,泼出去的水 jiàchuqude nǚ'er, pōchuqude shuǐ a married daughter is like spilt water — a married daughter is no longer a member of the family:俗语说的"～",叫我能怎么样? As the saying goes, "A married daughter is like spilt water". So what can I do about it?
嫁祸 jiàhuò shift the misfortune (onto others)
嫁祸于人 jiàhuòyúrén shift the misfortune onto sb. else; put the blame on sb. else; lay one's own fault at sb. else's door:使出了～的惯技 apply the habitual tactics of laying the fault at sb. else's door /他自己捅了娄子,却～。He himself made a blunder but tried to put the blame on somebody else.
嫁鸡随鸡,嫁狗随狗 jià jī suí jī, jià gǒu suí gǒu 〈旧语〉(of a woman) marry a cockerel and follow a cockerel, marry a dog and follow a dog — throw in one's lot with one's husband
嫁接 jiàjiē 〈植物〉graft:～亲和力 grafting affinity /～杂种 graft hybrid
嫁妆 jiàlián dowry; trousseau
嫁娶 jiàqǔ marriage:各民族都有自己的～风俗。Each nationality has its own marriage customs.
嫁人 jiàrén 〈口语〉(of a woman) get married; marry:她已～了,叫你不要等她了。She asks you to forget her as she's already married.
嫁妆 jiàzhuang *also* "嫁装" dowry; trousseau:给女儿一份～ dower a daughter /置办～ purchase dowries

价(價) jià ❶ price:零售～ retail price /批发～ wholesale price /高～ high-priced /廉～ low-priced /无～之宝 priceless treasure /单～ unit price /基～ basic price /集市贸易～ rural fair price /牌～ price /实～ net price /市～ market price /议～ negotiated price /变相涨～ price hike (*or* rise) in disguise /要～ ask a price /削～ reduce the price; reduced price /压～ force prices down /出厂～ price offered by the producing factory; ex-factory price /货真～实 genuine goods at a fair price ❷ value:等～交换 exchange of equal values /估～ estimate the value of; evaluate /评～ evaluate; appraise ❸〈化学〉valence:电～ electrovalence /共～ covalence /原子～ atomic valence /多～元素 element of multivalence /氢是一～元素。Hydrogen is a one-valence element. /氧是二～元素。Oxygen is a two-valence element.

see also jiè; jie
价带 jiàdài 〈物理〉valence band
价电子 jiàdiànzǐ 〈化学〉valence electron
价格 jiàgé price:商品～ commodity price /定～ set (*or* fix) a price /～公道 fair price /～偏高 relatively high price /标明～ mark with a price tag; have goods clearly priced /～管制 price control /～波动 price fluctuation /～稳定 price stability /～体系 price system /最低～ bedrock (*or* bottom, *or* floor) price /最高～ ceiling price /收盘～ closing price /开盘～ opening price /浮动～ floating price /垄断～ monopoly price /～弹性 price elasticity /～冻结 price freeze /～变动 price fluctuation
价格标签 jiàgé biāoqiān price tag
价格补贴 jiàgé bǔtiē price subsidy (from the state); state subsidy to offset price in crease
价格差别 jiàgé chābié price discrimination
价格倒挂 jiàgé dàoguà selling prices going below purchasing prices; price distortions
价格法 jiàgéfǎ pricing law
价格剪刀差 jiàgé jiǎndāochà price scissors
价格结构 jiàgé jiégòu 〈经济〉price mechanism or structure
价格敏感性 jiàgé mǐngǎnxìng price sensitivity
价格收益率 jiàgé shōuyìlǜ price-earnings ratio; P/E (ratio)
价格双轨制 jiàgé shuāngguǐzhì two-tier or two-track pricing system (where official and market prices are different)
价格体制 jiàgé tǐzhì 〈经济〉price system
价格战 jiàgézhàn price war
价格政策 jiàgé zhèngcè price policy; pricing policy:稳定～ price stabilization policy
价格指数 jiàgé zhǐshù 〈经济〉price index:～化 indexation of prices; price indexation
价键 jiàjiàn 〈化学〉valence bond:～晶体 valence crystal
价款 jiàkuǎn money paid for sth. purchased; money received for sth. sold; cost:～已付 cost paid; money paid /～收讫 money received
价廉物美 jiàlián-wùměi (of a commodity) cheap but good; inexpensive but of fine quality:我也正想买一件～的皮背心。I happened to want a good inexpensive fur jacket. /这家饭店的清炖牛肉,二十元一大盘,可谓～。The stewed beef in this restaurant costs only 20 *yuan* for a large portion. The dish is not only delicious but also cheap.
价码 jiàmǎ 〈口语〉(market) price:店里的货都标有～。All the goods in the shop are priced (*or* have prices marked on them).
价目 jiàmù marked price; price:～表 price list /～单 price list
价签 jiàqiān price tag
价钱 jiàqian price:讲～ bargain (with sb. for sth.); haggle over the price /～公道 fair price; decent or reasonable price /菠菜什么～? What's the price of spinach? *or* How much is the spinach? /不管～多少,我们都得买来。We must get it at any price.
价位 jiàwèi price level; price:无可挑剔的高品质,不可思议的低～。(used in advertisement) Impeccable quality; reasonable price. /近年来该商品始终在低～徘徊。The commodity has been hovering at a low price level in recent years.
价值 jiàzhí ❶ value:经济～ economic value /票面～ face value /交换～ exchange value /剩余～ surplus value /使用～ use value /商品～ commodity value /～尺度 measure of value /～保证 value assurance/～效果 value effect /～改善 value improvement ❷ worth; cost; value:～五万元的精密仪器 fifty thousand *yuan* worth of precision instruments /一项有很大～的发明 an invention of great worth /这台电视机～五千元。This television set costs (*or* is worth) 5,000 *yuan*.
价值尺度 jiàzhí chǐdù measure of value
价值分析 jiàzhí fēnxī value analysis
价值工程 jiàzhí gōngchéng value engineering
价值观 jiàzhíguān *also* "价值观念" values:西方的～ Western values
价值规律 jiàzhí guīlǜ law of value
价值连城 jiàzhí-liánchéng worth several cities — invaluable; priceless:这柄古剑～。This ancient sword is priceless. /最近出土了几件～的稀世珍宝。Several invaluable rare treasures have been unearthed recently.
价值量 jiàzhíliàng magnitude of value
价值属性 jiàzhí shǔxìng 〈经济〉property of value
价值形式 jiàzhí xíngshì *also* "价值形态"〈经济〉form of value
价值学 jiàzhíxué 〈哲学〉axiology

价值指数 jiàzhí zhǐshù value index

假

jià ❶ holiday; vacation: 暑～ summer vacation / 寒～ winter vacation / 例～ official holiday / 节～日 festive occasion (*or* day) / 度～ spend one's vacation / 放～ have a holiday or vacation ❷ leave of absence; furlough: 病～ sick leave / 事～ leave of absence to attend to personal affairs / 超～ overstay one's leave of absence / 请～ ask for leave / 休～ be on leave (*or* furlough) / 续～ extend one's leave of absence / 销～ report back after one's leave of absence *see also* jiǎ

假期 jiàqī ❶ vacation; holiday: 学校的～ school holidays / ～什么时候开始? When will the holidays begin? ❷ period of leave

假日 jiàrì holiday; day off: ～饭店 Holiday Inn

假条 jiàtiáo ❶ application for leave: 你递上～了吗? Have you sent in your application for leave? ❷ leave permit; absence slips: 事～ personal business leave slip / 医生给我开了三天的病～。I've got a doctor's certificate for three days' sick leave.

架

jià ❶ frame; shelf; hanger; stand; rack: 车～ frame of a cart; bicycle rack / 书～ bookshelf / 笔～ rack or stack for holding Chinese brushes; pen-stand / 脸盆～ washstand / 篮球～ basketball stand / 工具～ tool rack / 行李～ luggage-rack / 衣～ clothes hanger / 葡萄～ grape trellis / 钢～桥 steel-framed bridge / 闭～式 closed stacks; closed shelves / 开～ (in a library) open stacks; (in a shop) open shelves / 衣帽～ clothes tree / 脚手～ scaffold / 支～ support; stand / 画～ easel ❷ prop up; put up; erect: ～桥 put up (*or* build) a bridge / 把梯子～起来 prop up a ladder / 把炮～在炮架上 mount a gun on a gun carriage / ～电话线 set up telephone lines / ～起双拐 walk by supporting oneself with a pair of crutches / 鼻子上～着一副眼镜 a pair of glasses supported by the bridge of the nose; a pair of glasses on the nose ❸ fend off; ward off; withstand: 用铁棍～住了砍来的刀 use the iron rod to fend off the sword thrust / 敌军来势凶猛, 他们有点招～不住。The enemy attacked fiercely and they found it hard to withstand them. ❹ kidnap; abduct; take sb. away forcibly: 绑～银行家 kidnap a banker ❺ support; help along: ～着老人回家 help an old man home (by supporting him) ❻ fight; quarrel: 打～ fight; come to blows / 吵～ quarrel; have a row / 骂～ quarrel; wrangle / 拉～ try to stop people from fighting each other / 劝～ step in and patch up a quarrel; mediate between quarrelling parties ❼ 〈量词〉 (a) *used of sth. with a stand or mechanism*: 一～飞机 an airplane / 两～钢琴 two pianos / 一～葡萄 a cluster of grapes; a trellis of grapes (b) 〈方言〉 *used of mountains, etc.*: 一～大山 a large mountain

架不住 jiàbuzhù 〈方言〉 ❶ cannot sustain (the weight); cannot stand (the pressure); cannot withstand: ～这样大的损失 cannot sustain such heavy loss / ～这样的高压 can't stand such high pressure / ～这么大的浪费 can't afford such waste ❷ be no match for; cannot vie with: 你再有钱也～她能花。Your money is no match for her extravagance.

架次 jiàcì sortie: 一天共出动飞机二百～。All told, the planes made 200 sorties within one day.

架得住 jiàdezhù 〈方言〉 can put up with; can stand: 这么多作业孩子～吗? How could children cope with so much homework?

架豆 jiàdòu kidney bean

架构 jiàgòu ❶ build; construct ❷ framework; scaffold: 钢～ steel framework ❸ structure; pattern; layout: 市场～ market structure

架锯 jiàjù buck-saw

架空 jiàkōng ❶ built on stilts; overhead; aerial: ～铁路 overhead railway / 沿河的那排房子是～的。The row of houses along the river are built on stilts. ❷ impracticable; impractical; unpractical: 缺少实际材料的～议论 impractical argument without any substantiated materials ❸ make (sb.) a mere figurehead; kick upstairs: 把他由团长提升为副师长, 是明升暗降, 将他～。When promoted from regiment commander to assistant division commander, he was kicked upstairs and reduced to a mere figurehead.

架空电缆 jiàkōng diànlǎn aerial cable

架空管道 jiàkōng guǎndào overhead pipe

架空索道 jiàkōng suǒdào cable way

架票 jiàpiào kidnap

架设 jiàshè erect (above ground or water level, as on stilts or posts); put up; set up: ～电话线 set up telephone lines; lay telephone lines / ～高压线 erect high-tension lines (*or* cables) / 市内～了许多座过街桥。Many overpasses have been built within the city.

架势 jiàshi *also* "架式" ❶ posture; air; manner: 摆出高人一等的～ assume a posture of superiority / 装出电影明星的～ put on the air of a movie star; pose as a movie star ❷ 〈方言〉 (judging by) the appearances of things; trend: 看她病的～是不行了。She seems to be sinking fast and has little hope of recovery.

架秧子 jiàyāngzi 〈方言〉 instigate; stir up; incite: 起哄～ stir up trouble

架子 jiàzi ❶ frame; stand; rack; shelf: 花盆～ flowerpot stand / 货～ goods shelf / 骨头～ skeleton / 床～ bedstead ❷ framework; outline: 筹备组经过一年的努力, 把这所大学的～搭起来了。After a year's work, the preparatory group set up the framework of this university. ❸ airs; arrogance; haughty manner: 官僚～ bureaucratic airs / 摆～ put on airs / ～十足 overbearing; on one's high horse / 放下～ throw off one's airs; get rid of one's haughtiness / 没有～ be easy of approach; be modest and unassuming ❹ posture; stance: 他拉开～, 唱起了京剧。He adopted a stance and began to sing an aria from a Beijing opera. / 一看～, 就知道他是个好木匠。Judging from the way he works, you can tell that he is a good carpenter.

架子车 jiàzichē man-drawn two-wheel cart

架子工 jiàzigōng 〈建筑〉 ❶ scaffolding ❷ scaffolder

架子花 jiàzihuā 〈戏曲〉 male character with painted face in Chinese operas

架子猪 jiàzizhū 〈畜牧〉 feeder pig

驾

jià ❶ harness; draw or pull (a cart, etc.): ～起两头牛耕田 yoke a pair of oxen to plough the fields / 两匹马～着的大车 cart harnessed with two horses / 并～齐驱 keep abreast of each other ❷ drive; pilot; sail; ride: ～车 drive a car / ～飞机 pilot a plane / ～舟 sail a boat / 腾云～雾 ride the clouds — levitate ❸ vehicle; carriage; 〈敬词〉 you: 车～ vehicle or carriage / 屈～ be kind enough to make the journey / 劳～ excuse me ❹ emperor's carriage; emperor: 御～ imperial carriage; emperor / 保～ escort the emperor

驾崩 jiàbēng (of an emperor) pass away; die

驾到 jiàdào 〈敬词〉 arrive: 阁下～, 蓬荜生辉。Your Excellency's arrival has lent lustre to my humble house.

驾临 jiàlín 〈敬词〉 your arrival; your esteemed presence: 敬备菲酌, 恭候～。Your presence is kindly requested at my humble dinner.

驾凌 jiàlíng *also* "凌驾" override; surpass

驾轻就熟 jiàqīng-jiùshú drive a light carriage on a familiar road; handle a job with ease due to previous experience; do a familiar job with ease: 以他的生活积累和艺术修养, 演这个人物自然～。With his rich experience and artistic accomplishments, he is able to play this part with facility.

驾驶 jiàshǐ drive (a vehicle); pilot (a ship or plane): ～汽车 drive a car / 无人～飞机 pilotless aircraft / ～技术 driving technique / 小心～! Drive with care.

驾驶舱 jiàshǐcāng 〈航空〉 control cabin; cockpit; pilot's compartment

驾驶舱声音记录器 jiàshǐcāng shēngyīn jìlùqì 〈航空〉 cockpit voice recorder, popularly called "black box"

驾驶杆 jiàshǐgǎn 〈航空〉 control stick; control column; joystick

驾驶盘 jiàshǐpán steering wheel

驾驶室 jiàshǐshì driver's cab; wheel house; pilot house

驾驶台 jiàshǐtái 〈航海〉 bridge; (as of a tractor) driver's cab

驾驶仪 jiàshǐyí 〈航空〉 pilot

驾驶员 jiàshǐyuán driver; pilot

驾驶执照 jiàshǐ zhízhào (shortened as 驾照) driving licence; driver's licence

驾束式导弹 jiàshùshì dǎodàn beam rider

驾校 jiàxiào (short for 驾驶学校) driving school

驾御 jiàyù *also* "驾驭" ❶ drive (a horse, cart, etc.): 这匹烈马很难～。It is very difficult to control this mettlesome horse. ❷ control; tame; master: ～局势 control the situation; have the situation in hand / ～自然 tame nature / ～语言的能力很强 have an aptitude for the language; have a good command of the language

驾辕 jiàyuán pull a cart or carriage from between the shafts; be hitched up: ～马 wheel horse; pole horse; thill-horse; thiller / 用一匹骡子～ harness a mule in the shafts

驾云 jiàyún ❶ fly in the air by magic; levitate ❷ walking on air; treading on air; self-satisfied: 你越抬举他, 他还越～。The more you praise him, the more self-complacent he will become.

J

jiān

菅 jiān ❶〈植物〉villous themeda (*Themeda gigantea* var. *villosa*), a kind of coarse grass which can be used for papermaking:草~人命 treat human life as if it were not worth a straw; act in utter disregard of human life ❷ (Jiān) a surname

煎 jiān ❶ fry in shallow oil:~鱼 fry fish /~馒头片 fry slices of steamed bread ❷ simmer in water; decoct:~药 decoct medicinal herbs /~茶 simmer tea in water ❸〈量词〉decoction:头~药 first decoction (of herb medicine)

煎熬 jiān'áo suffering; distress; torture; torment:受尽苦难和~ suffer from all kinds of hardships and torments

煎逼 jiānbī force; compel; coerce:纠缠~ badger and coerce /他被种种苦恼~着。He is under the strain of all kinds of worries.

煎饼 jiānbing thin pancake made of millet flour, etc.:~果子 fried Chinese doughnut wrapped in thin mungbean flour pancake; fried pancake rolled up with egg filling

煎堆 jiānduī〈方言〉fried ball of glutinous rice flour

煎剂 jiānjì (of herbal medicine) decocta; decoction

煎迫 jiānpò force; compel; coerce:贫困~ suffer from privation /内忧外患,交相~ be repeatedly beset with domestic trouble and foreign aggression

煎心 jiānxīn be extremely worried; be overwhelmed with worry and anxiety

煎灼 jiānzhuó burning with anxiety; deeply worried

湔 jiān〈书面〉cleanse

湔祓 jiānfú〈书面〉do away with (filth, bad habits, etc.)

湔洗 jiānxǐ〈书面〉❶ cleanse; wash ❷ get rid of (disgrace, stain, etc.):~前耻 wipe out an old disgrace

湔雪 jiānxuě〈书面〉clear (sb.) of a false charge; redress a wrong:十载冤情,一朝~。A ten-year-old wrong was redressed overnight.

兼 jiān ❶ double; twice:轻兵~道以出,掩其不意。The army marched at double speed with light packs and took the enemy by surprise. ❷ simultaneously; concurrently; cum:总理~外交部长 premier and concurrently minister of foreign affairs /身~数职 hold several posts simultaneously /~作卧室的书房 study-cum-bedroom; study that doubles as a bedroom /~管 be also in charge of /二者不可得~ can't have both at the same time

兼爱 jiān'ài (Mozi's ideal during the Warring States Period) universal love

兼备 jiānbèi have both... and...; as well as:德才~ have both political integrity and ability; combine professional competence with political integrity /文武~ be well versed in civilian as well as military affairs

兼并 jiānbìng annex (territory, property, etc.); acquire:被某国~ be annexed by a certain country /土地~ annexation of land /企业~ amalgamation of enterprises /~几家小公司 acquire a few small companies

兼并成本 jiānbìng chéngběn〈经济〉acquisition cost

兼并国 jiānbìngguó〈法律〉annexing state

兼差 jiānchāi〈旧语〉concurrent post; part-time job

兼程 jiānchéng travel at double speed:~前进 advance at the double /日夜~ travel day and night /~奔丧 hasten home posthaste for the funeral of a parent

兼而有之 jiān'éryǒuzhī have both at the same time:基础科学、应用科学的研究~。It covers the research of both the basic and the applied sciences.

兼顾 jiāngù give consideration to two or more things; take account of two or more things:公私~ give consideration to both public and private interests /~双方利益 take into account the interests of both sides /统筹~ make an overall (*or* a comprehensive) plan by taking all factors into consideration

兼毫 jiānháo Chinese writing brush made of a mixture of weasel's and goat's hair

兼课 jiānkè ❶ do some teaching in addition to one's main occupation ❷ hold two or more teaching jobs concurrently

兼权熟计 jiānquán-shújì give careful consideration to all aspects of a problem; weigh things with great care:利害得失,~ carefully weigh the gains and losses (*or* the pros and cons)

兼人 jiānrén〈书面〉one person who is equal to two:~之量 have the capacity of two persons combined; have two men's strength /~之勇 very courageous

兼任 jiānrèn ❶ hold a concurrent post:~秘书和打字员 be a secretary and typist concurrently ❷ part-time:~教师 part-time teacher /~几个单位的法律顾问 part-time legal adviser to several units

兼容 jiānróng ❶ embrace all; be compatible with each other; be tolerant:善恶不能~。Virtue and evil are not compatible with each other. ❷〈物理〉compatible:~型单片集成电路 compatible monochrome integrated circuit /~制彩色电视系统 compatible colour TV system /~制电视 compatible television

兼容并包 jiānróng-bìngbāo tolerant; all-embracing; all-inclusive:~的政策 liberal (*or* tolerant) policy /这位先生学问渊博,中西文化~。The gentleman has great learning in both eastern and western cultures.

兼容机 jiānróngjī〈计算机〉compatible computer

兼容性 jiānróngxìng compatibility; compatibleness:声频视频~ audio-visual compatibility

兼施 jiānshī apply diverse methods simultaneously:软硬~ resort to both soft and hard tactics; combine the carrot and the stick; use both persuasion and coercion /~并用 employ various methods at the same time

兼收并蓄 jiānshōu-bìngxù incorporate things of diverse nature; take in everything:这个绘画馆对历代不同风格、流派的名画~。This gallery takes in all the famous paintings of different ages, different styles and different schools.

兼祧 jiāntiāo〈书面〉be made heir to one's uncle as well as to one's father; be appointed heir to two families

兼听则明,偏信则暗 jiān tīng zé míng, piān xìn zé àn listen to both sides and you will be enlightened, and heed only one side and you will be benighted; a clear head comes from an open mind

兼旬 jiānxún twenty days:无~之粮 grain in store won't last twenty days; not have much grain left

兼优 jiānyōu be good in more than one field:品学~ (of a student) of good character and scholarship; (of a person) of integrity and learning

兼之 jiānzhī〈书面〉what is more; furthermore; besides; in addition; moreover:工期甚紧,~连阴雨,其困难可以想见。You could well imagine how difficult it is for us when the project is hard pressed for time, and what's more, we have an unbroken spell of wet weather.

兼职 jiānzhí ❶ hold two or more posts concurrently:身兼三职 hold three posts concurrently /领导干部不宜~过多。It is not advisable for leading cadres to hold many posts at the same time. ❷ concurrent post; part-time job:辞去~ resign one's concurrent (*or* part-time) job /~法医 adjunct medical examiner

兼职教师 jiānzhí jiàoshī part-time teacher

蒹 jiān〈古语〉sth. like reed

搛 jiān pick up (with chopsticks):~菜 pick up vegetables with chopsticks /把鱼刺~出来 pick out a fishbone

鹣 jiān pair of lovebirds — fabulous birds each with one eye and one wing and always having to fly together

鹣鲽 jiāndié〈书面〉〈比喻〉an affectionate couple

鹣鹣 jiānjiān legendary lovebirds

鳒 jiān〈动物〉spiny-rayed flounder; big-mouthed flounder

缣 jiān〈书面〉fine silk

缣帛 jiānbó fine silk

缣素 jiānsù fine white silk for painting or writing

间(間) jiān ❶ between; among:朋友~ among friends /彼此~的差别 difference between them ❷ within a definite

time or space：乡～ in the countryside /瞬～ in no time /夜～ at night; in the evening /民～ popular; among the people /期～ during the time or period /此～ here; around here ❸ room：里～ inner room /外～ outer room /盥洗～ washroom /套～ suite; apartment; flat ❹〈量词〉*used of smallest units of housing*：两～卧室 two bedrooms /一～阅览室 a reading room /三～办公室 three offices
see also jiàn
间冰期 jiānbīngqī 〈地质〉interglacial stage; interglacial
间不容发 jiānbùróngfà not a hair's breadth in between — the situation is extremely critical：此事～，我们一定要争取早日解决。The matter is extremely critical. We must try to resolve it at the earliest possible time.
间级 jiānjí 〈电工〉interpole：～电动机 interpole motor /～电机 interpole machine
间架 jiānjià ❶ framework or structure of a house ❷ form of a Chinese character：这字～匀称，笔锋有力。This character is written symmetrically and with firm strokes. ❸ structure of an essay
间距 jiānjù distance between：从足迹的～可以知道动物四肢或躯体的长短。One can tell the length of an animal's limbs or body by the distance between its footprints.
间量 jiānliang 〈方言〉area of a room; floor space：你这间卧室比我的～儿大。Your bedroom is more spacious than mine.
间脑 jiānnǎo 〈生理〉diencephalon
间皮 jiānpí 〈生理〉mesothelium：～瘤 mesothelioma /～细胞 mesothelial cell
间质 jiānzhì 〈生理〉mesenchyme; interstitium：～肺炎〈医学〉interstitial pneumonia /～肝炎〈医学〉interstitial hepatitis /～心肌炎〈医学〉interstitial myocarditis /～细胞 interstitial cell
间奏曲 jiānzòuqǔ 〈音乐〉intermezzo; entr'acte

熸

jiān 〈书面〉❶ (of fire) die out ❷ be routed

肩

jiān ❶ shoulder：耸～ shrug one's shoulder /歇～ take the load off one's shoulder for a rest /并～而行 walk side by side /～不能挑，手不能提 unable to shoulder or carry; not used to manual labour ❷ undertake; shoulder; sustain; bear：身～大任 undertake an important position; bear (*or* shoulder) heavy responsibilities ❸〈方言〉carry on the shoulder; shoulder：他～起麻包就走。He threw the sack on his shoulder and carried it away.
肩膀 jiānbǎng shoulder：硬～ have broad shoulders (for responsibilities) /溜～ have round shoulders — shirk responsibilities; be irresponsible
肩垂病 jiānchuíbìng 〈医学〉drop shoulder
肩负 jiānfù undertake; shoulder; take on; bear：～重荷 bear a heavy burden; shoulder heavy loads /～重大的责任 shoulder heavy responsibilities /我们～着祖国的希望。The country places its hope on us. /这样艰巨的任务，我恐怕～不起。I'm afraid I am unable to take on this difficult task.
肩挂式喷雾器 jiānguàshì pēnwùqì 〈农业〉shoulder-hung sprayer
肩关节炎 jiānguānjiéyán 〈医学〉omarthritis
肩荷 jiānhè 〈书面〉shoulder; undertake; bear：～重任 shoulder a heavy responsibility
肩胛 jiānjiǎ 〈书面〉shoulder
肩胛骨 jiānjiǎgǔ 〈生理〉scapula; shoulder blade
肩摩毂击 jiānmó-gǔjī *also*"摩肩击毂" shoulder to shoulder and hub to hub — crowded with people and vehicles：大街上熙来攘往，～。The street is a scene of hustle and bustle.
肩摩踵接 jiānmó-zhǒngjiē *also*"摩肩接踵" be crowded with people：那天街上人特别多，真是～，川流不息。That day the street was a steady stream of people coming and going all the time.
肩扭伤 jiānniǔshāng wrenched shoulder; shoulder-joint sprain
肩披 jiānpī shoulderette; capelet
肩挑背负 jiāntiāo-bèifù carry on the shoulder and back
肩痛 jiāntòng 〈医学〉omalgia; omodynia：～风 omagra
肩头 jiāntóu ❶ on the shoulder：压在～ be shouldered with a burden ❷〈方言〉shoulder：～不一般高 uneven shoulders
肩窝 jiānwō hollow part of the shoulder
肩先露 jiānxiānlù 〈医学〉shoulder presentation
肩炎 jiānyán 〈医学〉omitis
肩舆 jiānyú sedan chair
肩章 jiānzhāng ❶ shoulder-strap; shoulder loop ❷ epaulette
肩周炎 jiānzhōuyán 〈医学〉periarthritis

戋（戔）

jiān small
戋戋 jiānjiān 〈书面〉minute; slight; small; tiny：～微物 minute things /为数～ few in number /～之数 tiny bit; very small amount

浅（淺）

jiān
see also qiǎn
浅浅 jiānjiān *also*"溅溅" jiānjiān 〈书面〉〈象声〉sound of flowing water：石濑～ river rapids babbling

笺（箋、❷❸牋）

jiān ❶ annotation; commentary：*see*"～注" ❷ writing paper：信～ letter paper; writing paper /便～ notepaper ❸ letter：投～求职 send application letters looking for jobs
笺牍 jiāndú 〈书面〉letter; correspondence
笺札 jiānzhá 〈书面〉letter; correspondence
笺纸 jiānzhǐ writing paper; letter paper
笺注 jiānzhù 〈书面〉notes and commentary on ancient texts

溅（濺）

jiān
see also jiàn
溅溅 jiānjiān *see*"浅浅" jiānjiān

鞯（韉）

jiān *see*"鞍鞯" ānjiān

渐

jiān 〈书面〉❶ soak; be saturated with; imbue：淇水汤汤，～车帷裳。The Qi River overflowed and the carriage curtain was soaked wet. ❷ flow into：南～于江 flow south and empty into the Yangtze River
see also jiàn
渐冉 jiānrǎn *also*"渐苒"〈书面〉(pass) gradually; by degrees
渐染 jiānrǎn 〈书面〉❶ be imperceptibly influenced：日～而不自知 be influenced daily without realizing it; not be conscious of being subtly influenced little by little ❷ pass gradually
渐渍 jiānzì 〈书面〉be tinted gradually; be contaminated little by little：～邪恶 be gradually given to evil ways

槛

jiān 〈书面〉wooden wedge

歼（殲）

jiān annihilate; wipe out; destroy：～敌三千 annihilate 3,000 enemy troops /聚而～之 round up so as to wipe out
歼轰机 jiānhōngjī 〈军事〉strike fighter
歼击 jiānjī attack and destroy：敌军一个师遭我包围～。We encircled, attacked and destroyed an enemy division.
歼击机 jiānjījī fighter plane; fighter
歼灭 jiānmiè annihilate; exterminate; wipe out; destroy：～毒枭 annihilate drug barons /～一切敢于入侵之敌 wipe out any enemy that should dare to invade /给予～性的打击 strike a crushing blow; deal a mortal blow /集中优势兵力，各个～敌人 concentrate a superior force to destroy the enemy forces one by one
歼灭射击 jiānmiè shèjī annihilation fire
歼灭战 jiānmièzhàn war or battle of annihilation：集中力量打～ concentrate forces to fight a campaign of annihilation

瑊

jiān 〈书面〉jade-like stone
瑊玏 jiānlè 〈书面〉jade-like stone

缄

jiān 〈书面〉seal; close：广州陈～ (as written on an envelope) from Chen in Guangzhou
缄封 jiānfēng seal a letter
缄口 jiānkǒu 〈书面〉keep one's mouth shut; hold one's tongue; say nothing; keep silent：～不语 hold one's tongue; keep silent /三缄其口 with one's lips sealed — be extremely cautious in one's words
缄口结舌 jiānkǒu-jiéshé keep silent with one's mouth shut — not daring to say anything：百姓～，非国家之福也。It is not good for the country if people dare not say anything.
缄密 jiānmì firmly sealed; shut tight：文件严加～，不得开视。The document is firmly sealed, and no one is allowed to open it.
缄默 jiānmò keep silent; be reticent：保持～ remain silent /大家纳闷，他在会上何以～不语。People are wondering why he doesn't utter

a word at the meeting.
缄札 jiānzhá 〈书面〉letter; correspondence

监(監) jiān ❶ supervise; inspect; watch; control:总~ chief inspector; general supervisor ❷ prison; jail:收~ put sb. into jail; imprison /探~ visit a prisoner /女~ women's prison
see also jiàn

监测 jiāncè monitor; observe and measure:环境~ monitoring the environment; observation and survey of the environment /空气污染~ monitoring air pollution /地震~ earthquake observation and measurement /~标准 monitoring standard
监测器 jiāncèqì monitor:污染~ contamination monitor /自动~ automatic monitor
监测卫星 jiāncè wèixīng monitoring satellite
监察 jiānchá supervise; inspect; examine; control:对政府各级工作人员进行~ supervise government officials at all levels
监察部 jiānchábù Ministry of Supervision
监察委员会 jiānchá wěiyuánhuì control commission; supervisory committee
监察员 jiāncháyuán supervisor; controller
监察院 Jiāncháyuàn Control *Yuan* (China before 1949):~院长 President of the Control *Yuan*
监察制度 jiānchá zhìdù supervisory system
监场 jiānchǎng invigilate or monitor at an examination hall or room
监督 jiāndū ❶ supervise; superintend; control:~部门 supervisory department; superintendent office /在政府严格的~下 under strict government supervision /在联合国~下举行选举 hold an election under the supervision of the United Nations /~劳动改造 reform through labour under surveillance /长期共存,互相~ long-term coexistence and mutual supervision ❷ supervisor:他是产品质量~。He is the inspector of the quality of products.
监督劳动 jiāndū láodòng do penal work under surveillance; labour under guard
监督权 jiāndūquán authority to supervise
监犯 jiānfàn prisoner; convict
监房 jiānfáng prison; jail
监工 jiāngōng ❶ supervise work; oversee:~员 job supervisor; factory superintendent; overseer ❷ overseer; supervisor
监管 jiānguǎn keep watch on; supervise and control (e.g. prisoners, etc.)
监规 jiānguī prison regulations
监护 jiānhù ❶〈法律〉guardianship; tutelage:被~人 ward ❷ observe, tend and nurse:这个病人须二十四小时~。This patient needs nursing round the clock.
监护权 jiānhùquán 〈法律〉guardianship:孩子的~ guardship over a child
监护人 jiānhùrén guardian:孩子的~ guardian to a child
监禁 jiānjìn take into custody; imprison; put in jail; put behind bars:~处罚 punishment of imprisonment /被判处~三年 be sentenced to three years' imprisonment
监考 jiānkǎo ❶ monitor; invigilate:这个考场由他~。This examination hall is under his invigilation. ❷ monitor; invigilator:他是这个考场的~。He is the invigilator of the examination hall.
监控 jiānkòng ❶ monitor and control:~台 control and monitor console /~程序 monitor routine /~器 monitor unit /~信息 monitor message ❷ supervise and control:对副食品价格实行~ supervise and control the prices of non-staple foodstuffs
监牢 jiānláo prison; jail
监理 jiānlǐ inspect and handle; supervise; manage:交通~员 traffic control personnel /工程~公司 construction supervision company
监票 jiānpiào examine ballots
监票人 jiānpiàorén ballot examiner; scrutineer; scrutator
监舍 jiānshè prison house
监事 jiānshì supervisor; member of a supervisory committee:~会 supervisory committee; (Germany) *Aufsichtsrat*
监视 jiānshì keep watch on; keep a lookout over:~作案嫌疑分子 watch the suspects; keep watch on the suspects /~某人 place sb. under surveillance /电子~ electronic surveillance /暗中~ keep watch in secret
监视居住 jiānshì jūzhù 〈法律〉live at home under surveillance
监视控制程序 jiānshì kòngzhì chéngxù supervisory control programme
监视控制台 jiānshì kòngzhìtái supervisory control desk
监视雷达 jiānshì léidá surveillance radar
监视器 jiānshìqì monitor
监视人 jiānshìrén guard; sentinel
监视哨 jiānshìshào 〈军事〉supervisor
监守 jiānshǒu have custody of; guard; take care of
监守自盗 jiānshǒu-zìdào steal what is entrusted to one's care; embezzle; defalcate:~,罪加一等 be doubly guilty for embezzlement (of what is entrusted to one's care)
监听 jiāntīng monitoring:电台~员 monitor operator /~台 monitors' desk /~系统 monitoring system /~装置 monitoring device
监听器 jiāntīngqì audiomonitor; monitor
监听无线电台 jiāntīng wúxiàn diàntái monitoring station
监外执行 jiānwài zhíxíng serving sentence or time outside the prison under surveillance; parole
监押 jiānyā ❶ imprison; take into custody; put in jail ❷ send away under escort:法警~犯人去受审。The bailiff took the criminal under escort for a trial.
监狱 jiānyù prison; jail:被关进~ be put in prison; be imprisoned
监狱法 jiānyùfǎ 〈法律〉prison law
监狱看守 jiānyù kānshǒu (prison) guard
监狱学 jiānyùxué penology
监狱长 jiānyùzhǎng warden
监证 jiānzhèng check and affirm; examine and certify
监制 jiānzhì ❶ supervise the manufacture of ❷ supervise the shooting of (films, etc.)

坚(堅) jiān ❶ solid; hard; firm; strong:~城 strongly defended city /其~无比 as hard as a brick; adamant /船~炮利 armoured ships with big guns; superior weaponry /~不能破 impregnable ❷ armour; heavily fortified point; fortification; stronghold:攻~ storm strongholds /无~不摧 destroy all fortifications; be all-conquering /披~执锐 wear armour and hold weapons ❸ firmly; flatly; determinedly; resolutely:~拒 flatly refuse; categorically reject /意志不~ be irresolute; be wavering /困难越大志越~ be all the more resolute in face of mounting difficulties ❹ (Jiān) a surname
坚壁 jiānbì hide supplies to prevent the enemy from seizing them; place in a cache; cache:撤退前把粮食和物资统统~起来 cache all grain and materials before evacuation
坚壁清野 jiānbì-qīngyě strengthen defence works, evacuate non-combatants, and hide provisions and livestock; strengthen the defences and clear the fields:对敌人~,封锁消息 keep food and other supplies out of the reach of the enemy and block his channels of information
坚不可摧 jiānbùkěcuī indestructible; invulnerable:众志成城,~。Unity of will is an impregnable stronghold.
坚持 jiānchí persist or persevere in; uphold; insist on; stick or adhere to:~团结,反对分裂 uphold unity and oppose a split /~武装斗争 persevere in armed struggle /~自力更生的政策 abide by the policy of self-reliance /~原来的计划 adhere (*or* stick) to the original plan /~到底 stick it out; stick through thick and thin; carry through to the end /~真理 hold firmly to the truth /~错误观点 cling to (*or* persist in) one's mistaken views /~天天看报 make a point of reading newspapers every day /~己见 hold on to one's own view; be opinionated /~下去就是胜利。Perseverance means victory. /他~说他是无罪的。He insisted that he was innocent. *or* He insisted on his innocence. /你这种习惯要是~下去,一定会增强体质。This habit of yours, if kept up, will certainly improve your health.
坚持不懈 jiānchí-bùxiè unremitting; unswerving; persistent:进行~的斗争 carry on the struggle perseveringly /作~的努力 make unremitting efforts /~地工作下去 carry on the work unflaggingly /只要~,你自会成功。Keep at it and you'll succeed.
坚定 jiāndìng ❶ firm; resolute; staunch; steadfast:立场~ take a firm stand /意志~ constancy of purpose /态度~ maintain a resolute attitude /意志~的人 man of will /~的目光 unflinching look; steadfast gaze ❷ strenghten; fortify:~信念 fortify one's conviction /~信心 strenghen one's confidence /~了自己的决心 harden one's resolve
坚定不移 jiāndìng-bùyí firm and unshakable; unswerving; un-

flinching; adamant:不因为困难而退缩,要～地干下去。Don't shrink back before difficulties. Carry on unflinchingly. /罢工的工人们～,老板最后不得不作出让步。The workmen on strike stood firm and the boss finally had to give in.

坚固 jiāngù strong; firm; solid:～的要塞 strong fortress /～的阵地 firm position /～的基础 solid foundation /～耐用 sturdy and durable /～的堤坝 strong dykes and dams /码头修得很～。The wharf is solidly built.

坚固呢 jiāngùní 〈纺织〉 denim

坚果 jiānguǒ 〈植物〉 nut

坚甲利兵 jiānjiǎ-lìbīng strong armour and sharp weapons; good armour and weapons; armed prowess or strength:巩固的国防不能没有～。Armed strength is indispensable to a strong national defence.

坚劲 jiānjìng strong and powerful

坚决 jiānjué firm; resolute; determined; adamant:采取～的措施 take resolute measures /意志～ of adamant (*or* strong) will /～的表情 determined look /～取缔 rigorously suppress (*or* ban) /～反对 firmly oppose; set oneself against; put one's foot down /～改正错误 not hesitate to correct one's mistakes /～完成任务 fulfil one's task without fail /～、彻底、干净、全部地消灭敌人 annihilate the enemy resolutely, thoroughly, wholly and completely /他说话的口气很～。He spoke in an uncompromising tone.

坚苦 jiānkǔ arduous; difficult; hard; tough:翻译是～的工作。Translation is an arduous task.

坚苦卓绝 jiānkǔ-zhuōjué showing the utmost fortitude; tireless and indomitable:～的精神 indomitable and tireless spirit /～的战斗 hard-fought battle /进行了～的工作 carry on a most trying task

坚牢 jiānláo solid; strong; firm; fast:这座桥是钢筋混凝土的结构,非常～。This bridge, with its reinforced concrete structure, is very solid.

坚牢度 jiānláodù 〈纺织〉 fastness:耐酸～ fastness to acids /耐日光～ fastness to sunlight; sunfastness /耐洗～ washfastness

坚强 jiānqiáng ❶ strong; firm; staunch; indomitable:～的意志 strong will; unyielding will /～的领导 firm leadership /～的战士 staunch fighter /～不屈的精神 dauntless spirit /～的后盾 powerful backing /～的毅力 iron will ❷ strengthen:这一年的锻炼,～了我们的队伍。This year's training has strengthened us.

坚强不屈 jiānqiáng-bùqū firm and unyielding; staunch and unbending:他一生～。He remained firm and unyielding to the end of his days.

坚确 jiānquè 〈书面〉 resolute and steadfast; firm and unshakable; unswerving:～的信念 firm and unshakable belief

坚忍 jiānrěn steadfast and persevering; firm and unbending:从他们脸上,我看到了农民的朴实和～。I read farmers' honesty, steadfastness, and perseverance on their faces.

坚忍不拔 jiānrěn-bùbá firm and indomitable; stubborn and unyielding; tenacious:～的精神 indomitable spirit; tenacious and dauntless spirit /～的意志 unyielding will

坚韧 jiānrèn tough and tensile; tenacious:这种皮革很～,有多种用途。This leather, being tenacious, has a lot of uses (*or* is useful in many ways).

坚韧不拔 jiānrèn-bùbá *also* "坚忍不拔" firm and unflinching; persistent and dauntless:有了～的精神,才能战胜困难。It is only with indomitable spirit that one can overcome difficulties.

坚如磐石 jiānrúpánshí solid as a rock; rock-firm:我国各族人民的团结,～。The unity of the people of all nationalities in our country is as firm as a rock.

坚实 jiānshí ❶ solid; steady; sturdy; substantial:打下～的基础 lay a solid foundation /～的树干 sturdy trunk /迈出～的步伐 take firm and steady steps ❷ strong; sturdy:～的身体 strongly built body /肌肉～、富有弹性的长腿 pair of muscular, resilient long legs

坚守 jiānshǒu stick to; hold fast to; stand fast:～岗位 stick to one's post /～阵地 hold fast to one's position; hold one's ground; dig in /～待援 hold on (*or* out) till the reinforcements arrive /～信念 abide by one's conviction

坚挺 jiāntǐng ❶ strong and powerful; stiff and straight:～的身架 strong and erect body ❷ 〈金融〉 strong:目前金融市场上日元～。At present the Japanese yen is strong (*or* robust) in the money market.

坚信 jiānxìn firmly believe; be deeply convinced; be fully confident of; have infinite faith in:～能赢得最后胜利 be certain of final victory /～这种学说 have implicit faith in this doctrine /我～胜利是属于我们的。I am convinced that the victory will be ours.

坚信不移 jiānxìn-bùyí firmly believe; be without a shadow of doubt; have profound faith:对于达到这个目标,他～。He felt certain that he could achieve the goal.

坚毅 jiānyì firm and persistent; staunch and determined; with inflexible will:神色～ look determined

坚硬 jiānyìng hard; rigid; solid:～的土壤 hard soil /～的金属板 rigid metal plate /～的花岗石 solid granite /老汉的骨头是～的,没有一丝的奴颜婢膝。He is an intrepid old man, not in the least obsequious.

坚贞 jiānzhēn faithful; staunch; constant:在这种考验面前,可以看出他的品格是多么～。One can see how faithful he is in the face of this test.

坚贞不屈 jiānzhēn-bùqū remain faithful and unyielding; stand firm and unbending; be staunch and indomitable:～,视死如归 remain faithful and unyielding, and face death unflinchingly /～的民族气节 indomitable national spirit

坚贞不渝 jiānzhēn-bùyú be always faithful; remain loyal forever:～的爱情 remaining faithful to one's love; faithful love

坚执 jiānzhí stick to; cling to; persist in:～己见 stubbornly stick to one's own opinion /～不允 firmly refuse to permit

坚致 jiānzhì 〈书面〉 solid, fine and dense:石质～。The stone is solid, fine and dense.

鲣(鰹)

jiān 〈动物〉 oceanic bonito; skipjack (tuna)

鲣鸟 jiānniǎo booby

尖

jiān ❶ pointed; tapering; sharp:长而～的手指 long, tapering fingers /削～铅笔 sharpen a pencil /这种东西两头～,中间粗。It has two pointed ends and a thick middle part. ❷ shrill; sharp; piercing:～嗓子 sharp voice /嗓门儿又～又脆。The voice was shrill and crisp. ❸ sharp; acute; keen:耳朵～ have sharp ears; be sharp-eared /鼻子～ have an acute sense of smell; be sharp-nosed /他眼睛很～。He has a sharp eye. *or* He is sharp-sighted. ❹ make (one's voice, etc.) shrill or sharp:～着嗓子 in a shrill voice ❺ point; tip; tapering end:钢笔～儿 tip of a pen; point of a pen; pen-point /针～ point of a needle or pin; pinpoint /牛角～儿 tip of a horn /塔～ pinnacle of a pagoda; spire ❻ best of its kind; pick of the bunch; cream of the crop:拔～儿的 top-notch; pick of the bunch /冒～儿 stand out; be conspicuous; be in the limelight ❼ 〈方言〉 stingy; miserly; calculating:这人太～,一丁点儿亏都不吃。He is a meanie, always trying to profit at others' expense. ❽ sharp-tongued; caustic:这姑娘嘴太～,跟谁都搞不好关系。The girl is too sharp-tongued to get along with others.

尖兵 jiānbīng ❶ 〈军事〉 point; vanguard:～连 point (*or* vanguard) company /～班 advance squad ❷ trailblazer; pathbreaker; pioneer; vanguard:改革开放的～ pioneers in reform and opening to the outside world /石油工业的～ pathbreaker in the petroleum industry /地质勘测人员,是工业战线的～。Geological prospecting team members are trailblazers on the industrial front.

尖脆 jiāncuì (of sound or voice) sharp; clear and crisp:深夜传来一声～的枪声。A sharp shot was heard in the late evening.

尖担两头脱 jiāndàn liǎngtóu tuō lose both ways; fall between two stools

尖刀 jiāndāo sharp knife; dagger:～连 〈军事〉 dagger company /她这话似～穿我心。Her words were a dagger to my heart.

尖顶 jiāndǐng pinnacle; acme; tip; top:主峰的～直插霄汉。The top of the highest peak pierced into the sky.

尖端 jiānduān ❶ pointed end; tip; peak:标枪的～ point of a javelin /这种笔的～有一个小圆珠。There is a small ball at the pointed end of the pen. ❷ sophisticated; most advanced:～产品 most advanced product /～技术 most sophisticated technology

尖端放电 jiānduān fàngdiàn 〈电学〉 point discharge

尖端科学 jiānduān kēxué most advanced branch of science; frontier of science

尖端武器 jiānduān wǔqì sophisticated weapon

尖阁群岛 Jiāngé Qúndǎo Senkaku Islands, Japanese name for China's Diaoyu Islands (钓鱼岛)

尖叫 jiānjiào shriek; scream; yell; whoop:到处是～声,掌声和口哨声。There were whooping, clapping and whistling everywhere.

尖晶石 jiānjīngshí 〈矿业〉 spinel

尖刻 jiānkè acrimonious; caustic; cutting; biting:～的批评 caustic

J

criticism /说话~ speak with bitter sarcasm; be sharp-tongued /~的讽刺 poignant satire /你用词多么~! How venomous your words are!

尖口钳 jiānkǒuqián *also* "尖嘴钳" needlenosed pliers: 一把~ a pair of needlenosed pliers

尖括号 jiānkuòhào angle brackets (〈 〉)

尖冷 jiānlěng biting cold; piercing cold: ~的西北风 biting northwest wind

尖厉 jiānlì (of voice or sound) high-pitched and piercing; shrill: 朔风~。The north wind is whistling.

尖利 jiānlì ❶ sharp; biting; keen; cutting: ~的匕首 sharp dagger/笔锋~ poignant writing /这些话过于~。These words are too acrimonious. ❷ shrill; piercing: ~的叫声 shrill cry

尖溜溜 jiānliūliū 〈方言〉very sharp: 他总把铅笔削得~的。He always sharpens his pencil to the full. /她那小嗓子唱起歌来~的。She has a shrill voice when she sings.

尖嫩 jiānnèn (of voice) thin and delicate: 她的嗓音~。She has got a tender, piping voice.

尖劈 jiānpī wedge

尖脐 jiānqí ❶ narrow triangular abdomen of a male crab ❷ male crab

尖峭 jiānqiào ❶ (of a mountain) tall and steep: ~的山峰 tall, steep mountain peak ❷ *also* "尖俏" (of a voice) piercing; shrill

尖锐 jiānruì ❶ sharp-pointed: 长剑~的锋刃在月光下闪着寒光。The sharp edge of the sword glinted coldly in the moonlight. ❷ sharp; keen; penetrating; incisive: ~地指出工作上的错误 point out sharply the error in sb.'s work /他目光~, 看问题很深刻。Having a keen eye, he looks at problems with great insight. ❸ shrill; piercing: ~的汽笛声 shrill whistle /飞机掠空而过, 啸声~刺耳。The plane swept past, leaving an unpleasant piercing sound. ❹ intense; sharp; potent; acute: ~的思想斗争 intense soul-searching /~对立 be diametrically opposed to each other /~的批评 sharp (*or* incisive) criticism /斗争复杂~ acute and complicated struggle

尖锐化 jiānruìhuà sharpen; intensify; aggravate; become more acute: 局势更加~。The situation was further aggravated.

尖酸 jiānsuān acrid; harsh; acrimonious; tart: 说话~ speak with bitter sarcasm

尖酸刻薄 jiānsuān-kèbó tart and mean; bitterly sarcastic; scathing: ~的小人 tart mean guy

尖头 jiāntóu pointed end; sharp point; tip

尖头蝗 jiāntóuhuáng a kind of locust

尖团音 jiāntuányīn 〈语言〉term for *jianyin* (the combination of z, c and s with i, ü or compound vowels beginning with i, ü) and *tuanyin* (the combination of j, q and x with i, ü or compound vowels beginning with i, ü)

尖吻鲈 jiānwěnlú 〈动物〉Nile perch (*Lates niloticus*)

尖细 jiānxì (of a voice) small and shrill: ~的嗓音 small shrill voice

尖啸 jiānxiào shriek; scream: ~的寒风 howling cold wind

尖削 jiānxuē sharp-cut: ~的面孔 sharp angular face /笔直~的山峰高耸云霄。The straight sharp-cut mountain peak shoots up into the sky.

尖音 jiānyīn *jianying*, the combination of z, c and s with i, ü or compound vowels beginning with i, ü

尖子 jiānzi ❶ point; tip ❷ best of its kind; pick of the bunch; cream of the crop: 重视培养~运动员 pay attention to training top-notch athletes /航空驾驶员中的~ ace among the airmen /青年演员中的~ pick of the young performers ❸ sudden rise in pitch (in opera singing)

尖子班 jiānzibān class of top students; class of talents

尖嘴薄舌 jiānzuǐ-bóshé have a caustic and flippant tongue: 那些年轻人~, 老拿她取笑。Those young people have very sharp tongues and always make fun of her.

尖嘴猴腮 jiānzuǐ-hóusāi pointed mouth and monkey's cheek — thin angular face; ugly appearance

尖嘴钳 jiānzuǐqián *see* "尖口钳"

艰(艱) jiān

difficult; arduous; hard: 步履维~ walk with great difficulty; have difficulty in walking

艰窘 jiānjiǒng difficult (situation); poverty-stricken: ~的生活 impoverished life

艰巨 jiānjù onerous; arduous; formidable: 交给某人~任务 entrust sb. with an onerous task /~的工程 formidable project /付出~的劳动 make strenuous efforts /~的斗争 hard struggle

艰苦 jiānkǔ arduous; difficult; hard; tough: ~创业 pioneer an enterprise with arduous efforts /在~的环境里锻炼 temper oneself under tough conditions /~的岁月 hard times; hard days; in times of trial and tribulation /~备尝 have experienced all hardships; have suffered untold hardships

艰苦奋斗 jiānkǔ fèndòu arduous struggle

艰苦朴素 jiānkǔ-pǔsù hard work and plain living

艰苦卓绝 jiānkǔ-zhuójué extreme hardship and difficulty: ~的斗争 most arduous and bitter struggle /歌颂了~的革命英雄主义精神 sing the praises of the indomitable spirit of revolutionary heroism

艰困 jiānkùn hard; difficult; tough

艰难 jiānnán difficult; arduous; hard: ~岁月 hard times; difficult days /处境~ find oneself in straitened circumstances; be in a predicament /~的使命 difficult mission /~的工作 strenuous work; tough job /克服人生道路上数不清的~ overcome countless barriers in one's life

艰难竭蹶 jiānnán-jiéjué hard-pressed and destitute: 于~之中, 存有聊以卒岁之想 hoping to tide over the year in the midst of hardship and destitution

艰难困苦 jiānnán-kùnkǔ difficulties and hardships; trials and tribulations: 不论在任何~的场合, 只要还有一个人, 这个人就要继续战斗下去。Whatever the difficulties and hardships, so long as a single man remains, he will fight on.

艰难曲折 jiānnán-qūzhé difficulties and setbacks: ~的一生 checkered life

艰难险阻 jiānnán-xiǎnzǔ *also* "险阻艰难" difficulties and obstacles: 战胜了许多~ conquer (*or* surmount) innumerable difficulties and obstacles /备尝~ suffer (*or* experience) all kinds of hardships /长征路上遇着了说不尽的~。We encountered untold difficulties and dangers on the Long March.

艰涩 jiānsè involved and abstruse; intricate and obscure: 这篇文章写得~费解。This article is very obscure and hard to understand.

艰深 jiānshēn difficult to comprehend; abstruse: ~的哲学理论 abstruse philosophical theory /~的词句 unfathomable sentences

艰危 jiānwēi difficulties and dangers; hardships and perils: 饱受~ undergo a lot of difficulties and dangers /把民族从~和灾难中拯救出来 save the nation from a disastrous situation

艰险 jiānxiǎn hardships and dangers; perils: 不畏~ brave hardships and dangers /征途上充满了~。The journey is full of perils.

艰辛 jiānxīn distress; hardships: 历尽~, 方有今日。He has got where he is after having gone through all those hardships.

艰虞 jiānyú 〈书面〉difficulties and worries

艰贞 jiānzhēn unswerving in face of dangers and difficulties: ~不拔 firm and unflinching in face of difficulties

鞬 jiān

case for bow and arrows on horseback

犍 jiān

bullock; castrated bull: 老~ bullock

犍牛 jiānniú bullock

犍子 jiānzi 〈方言〉bullock

奸[1] jiān

❶ wicked; evil; false; treacherous: 洞烛其~ see through sb.'s treachery ❷ betray one's country or monarch; traitorous: *see* "~臣" ❸ traitor: 内~ hidden traitor (*or* enemy agent) /为国除~ rid the country of traitors (*or* collaborators) ❹ crafty; self-seeking and wily: 藏~耍滑 hide the evil intention by acting in a slick way

奸[2](姦) jiān

illicit sexual relations; adultery: 通~ commit adultery /捉~ catch adultery in the act /强~ rape; violate /轮~ rape by turns; gang rape

奸不厮瞒, 俏不厮欺 jiān bù sī mán, qiào bù sī qī *also* "奸不厮欺, 俏不厮瞒" have never concealed from you my bad as well as good side

奸臣 jiānchén treacherous court official; treacherous courtier: 卖国~ treacherous courtier who betrays the country /结党弄权的~ treacherous court officials who gang together and abuse power for private ends /那时朝廷~当道, 谗佞专权。Wicked ministers and sycophants held sway in the imperial court.

奸党 jiāndǎng clique or people disloyal to the country or monarch; cabal: ~弄权, 天下大乱。As a wicked clique held power,

J

the land was thrown into turmoil.

奸刁 jiāndiāo treacherous and sly:为人～ of treacherous and sly character

奸恶 jiān'è 〈书面〉crafty and evil; treacherous

奸夫 jiānfū adulterer; intrigant; inamorata

奸妇 jiānfù adulteress; paramour

奸宄 jiānguǐ 〈书面〉evildoers; malefactors

奸猾 jiānhuá *also* "奸滑" treacherous; crafty; deceitful; sly; cunning:～的对手 treacherous adversary /～的笑脸 deceitful smiling face /十分～的人 sly old fox /这个经纪人很是～。This broker is very cunning (*or* crafty).

奸计 jiānjì evil scheme or plot:中了敌人的～ fall into the enemy's trap

奸狡 jiānjiǎo treacherous; crafty; cunning; wily; sly:～的商人 wily merchant

奸佞 jiānnìng 〈书面〉❶ crafty and fawning:～的权臣 crafty and ingratiating powerful official ❷ crafty sycophant:～当道 with treacherous sycophants in power

奸情 jiānqíng adulterous affair

奸人 jiānrén evildoer; malefactor

奸商 jiānshāng unscrupulous merchant; profiteer

奸尸 jiānshī necrophilia

奸私 jiānsī sinister activities in secret; sinister secrets:揭发～ expose the covert sinister activities

奸徒 jiāntú perfidious person

奸污 jiānwū rape; violate; seduce:～妇女 rape (*or* violate, *or* seduce) a woman /～处女 defloration

奸细 jiānxi spy; enemy agent:敌人派来的～ spy sent by the enemy; enemy spy /混入内部的～ agent infiltrating an organization

奸险 jiānxiǎn wicked and crafty; treacherous; sinister; malicious:～毒辣 wicked and venomous /～的用心 sinister motive

奸笑 jiānxiào sinister smile; villainous smile:一脸～ wear a villainous smile on one's face

奸邪 jiānxié 〈书面〉❶ crafty and evil; treacherous:～本性 (sb.'s) treacherous nature ❷ crafty and evil person:～当道,残害忠良。When a wily and evil person was in power, good honest people were persecuted.

奸凶 jiānxiōng 〈书面〉treacherous and ferocious people:攘除～ get rid of evil and ruthless people

奸雄 jiānxióng person who climbs to a high position through unscrupulous scheming; arch-careerist:乱世之～ treacherous pretender in times of turmoil

奸淫 jiānyín ❶ illicit sexual relations; adultery ❷ rape; seduce:～烧杀 rapes, murders and arson

奸淫掳掠 jiānyín-lǔlüè rape and loot:入侵者杀人放火,～,无恶不作。The aggressors commited murder, arson, rape and every crime imaginable.

奸淫罪 jiānyínzuì 〈法律〉carnal intercourse

奸贼 jiānzéi traitor; conspirator; treacherous court official

奸诈 jiānzhà fraudulent; crafty; deceitful; treacherous:为人～ person of perfidious character /～之徒 trickster /心怀～ harbour treacherous motives /再～的狐狸也骗不了好猎手。No fox is cunning enough to deceive a good hunter.

jiǎn

謇 jiǎn 〈书面〉❶ stutter; stammer:因～而徐言 stutter out slowly ❷ upright:外似～正,内实谄谀 be upright in appearance but obsequious at heart

謇谔 jiǎn'è 〈书面〉upright and bold in one's speech

蹇 jiǎn ❶〈书面〉lame; crippled:～驴 lame donkey ❷〈书面〉not smooth-going; unlucky; hapless:命运多～ unlucky (*or* hapless) lot ❸〈书面〉donkey; inferior horse:策～赴前程 spur on the donkey ❹ (Jiǎn) a surname

蹇吃 jiǎnchī 〈书面〉stutter; stammer

蹇涩 jiǎnsè 〈书面〉❶ difficult; unlucky; hapless:命运～ hard lot ❷ not smooth-going

蹇运 jiǎnyùn unlucky or hapless lot

蹇滞 jiǎnzhì 〈书面〉difficult; unfortunate

蹇拙 jiǎnzhuō 〈书面〉obscure and clumsy

瀽 jiǎn 〈方言〉sprinkle (water); pour (liquid)

裥 jiǎn 〈方言〉folds (in clothes, etc.):打～ make folds

简[1] jiǎn ❶ simple; succinct; terse; brief:～而言之 in short; in brief; in a nutshell /一切从～ make everything as simple as possible /删繁就～ simplify sth. by cutting out the superfluous /～短 brief; terse; succinct ❷ simplify; abridge; make sth. simpler:精兵～政 better troops and simpler administration; streamlined administration ❸ (Jiǎn) a surname

简[2] jiǎn ❶ bamboo slip (used for writing on in ancient times):竹～ bamboo slips /断编残～ stray fragments of text ❷ note; letter:书～ letters; correspondence /手～ informal personal note to a friend

简[3] jiǎn 〈书面〉select; choose: *see* "～拔"; "～任"

简拔 jiǎnbá 〈书面〉select and promote

简板 jiǎnbǎn 〈音乐〉a kind of percussion instrument consisting of two flat wood or bamboo pieces

简报 jiǎnbào bulletin; brief report:新闻～ news bulletin (*or* briefing) /会议～ conference bulletin; brief reports on conference proceedings /工作～ brief work report

简本 jiǎnběn abridged or concise edition:《现代汉语小词典》是《现代汉语词典》的～。*Pocket Modern Chinese Dictionary* is an abridged edition of *A Dictionary of Modern Chinese Language*.

简笔画 jiǎnbǐhuà sketch

简编 jiǎnbiān (often used in book titles) short course; concise edition; abridged edition:《中国文学史～》*A Brief History of Chinese Literature* /《中国通史～》*A Concise Edition of General Chinese History*

简便 jiǎnbiàn simple and convenient; handy:～的方法 simple and convenient method; handy way /这种办法～易行。This method is simple and easy to apply.

简并星 jiǎnbìngxīng 〈天文〉degenerate star

简策 jiǎncè *also* "简册"〈书面〉bamboo slips strung together; book

简称 jiǎnchēng ❶ acronym; abbreviated form of a name or title; abbreviation:政协是政治协商会议的～。CPPCC is the abbreviation for the Chinese People's Political Consultative Conference. ❷ be called sth. for short:首都钢铁公司～首钢。The Capital Iron and Steel Company is call "Shougang" (Capital Steel) for short.

简单 jiǎndān ❶ simple; brief; uncomplicated:～明了 simple and clear; concise and explicit /头脑～ simple-minded /～地说,我不同意。To be brief, I disagree. /他～地说明了这件事。He put the matter in a nutshell. /他～地讲了事情的经过。He gave a brief account of what happened. /事情没有看起来那么～。There is more to it than meets the eye. /这些字笔画～,容易写,容易认。These characters are easy to write and recognize as they have few strokes. ❷ (often used in the negative) commonplace; ordinary:这个案子涉及许多人,可不～。The case involves many people. It is really quite complicated. /这工作可并不～。This is no ordinary job. /八岁的孩子画得这么好,真不～! The eight-year-old draws so well; he's a marvel! ❸ oversimplified; cursory; casual; offhand:～从事 do things in a casual way /处理事情过于～ handle things in an oversimplified way /这篇文章我只是～地看了看。I only glanced over this article.

简单报酬率 jiǎndān bàochóulǜ 〈经济〉simple rate of return

简单动作研究 jiǎndān dòngzuò yánjiū simple motion study

简单多数 jiǎndān duōshù simple majority

简单化 jiǎndānhuà oversimplification

简单计分法 jiǎndān jìfēnfǎ straight point method

简单劳动 jiǎndān láodòng 〈经济〉simple labour

简单连续制造程序 jiǎndān liánxù zhìzào chéngxù continuous simple process

简单平均法 jiǎndān píngjūnfǎ simple average method

简单商品生产 jiǎndān shāngpǐn shēngchǎn *also* "小商品生产" xiǎoshāngpǐn shēngchǎn small commodity production

简单数字法 jiǎndān shùzìfǎ simple numerical system

简单算术平均指数 jiǎndān suànshù píngjūn zhǐshù simple arithmetic index number

J

简单行销组合模式 jiǎndān xíngxiāo zǔhé móshì simple marketing mix model
简单优先技术 jiǎndān yōuxiān jìshù simple precedence technique
简单再生产 jiǎndān zàishēngchǎn simple reproduction
简牍 jiǎndú 〈书面〉❶ bamboo slip (used for writing on in ancient times); books ❷ letter; correspondence
简短 jiǎnduǎn brief; terse; concise; short: ～的发言 concise speech / 他的反驳～有力。His refutation was brief and forceful. / 这个学术报告很～。This academic report is very succinct.
简断截说 jiǎnduàn-jiéshuō brief and to the point; straightforward: ～吧,那件事办不成了。To be quite blunt, that matter can't be done.
简而言之 jiǎn'éryánzhī make a long story short; put it in a nutshell; in brief; in short: ～,我一定去。In short, I am going.
简分数 jiǎnfēnshù 〈数学〉common fraction; simple fraction
简古 jiǎngǔ 〈书面〉brief and archaic: 文笔～ archaic and terse style of writing
简化 jiǎnhuà simplify: ～工序 simplify working processes
简化汉字 jiǎnhuà Hànzì ❶ simplify Chinese characters (i. e. reduce the number of strokes and eliminate complicated variants) ❷ simplified Chinese character
简化字 jiǎnhuàzì simplified Chinese character
简洁 jiǎnjié succinct; terse; pithy; concise: ～有力的文笔 in a pithy and vigorous style / 表述～ describe in a terse language / 文章应该比口语～。Writings should be more concise than spoken language.
简捷 jiǎnjié ❶ *also* "简截" simple and direct; forthright: 这篇小说描写～,可是新鲜有味。The description of this short story is quite simple and direct, but very refreshing. ❷ simple and quick: 这种办法要～得多。This method is simple and can get the job done quickly.
简捷法 jiǎnjiéfǎ 〈数学〉simplex algorithm
简截 jiǎnjié *see* "简捷❶"
简介 jiǎnjiè ❶ introduce briefly: ～这本书的内容 give a brief account of the contents of the book ❷ brief introduction; synopsis: 剧情～ synopsis of a play / 《高校～》*A Brief Introduction to Institutes of Higher Learning*
简劲 jiǎnjìng (writing) succinct and powerful: 笔墨～ terse and forceful writing
简况 jiǎnkuàng brief account; short introduction
简括 jiǎnkuò brief but comprehensive; compendious: 《老子》一书～而富有哲理。*Classic of the Way and Virtue* is a compendious and highly philosophical work.
简历 jiǎnlì biographical note; curriculum vitae (CV); résumé; concise biography: 填写～ fill in the curriculum vitae form
简练 jiǎnliàn terse; concise; succinct; pithy: 文字～,寓意深刻 be succinct in language and pregnant with meaning / 把自己的感受尽可能准确而～地表达出来 express one's feeling as precisely and tersely as possible
简陋 jiǎnlòu simple and crude: ～的房间 shabby room / 室内的摆设很～。The room is sparely furnished.
简略 jiǎnlüè simple (in content); compact; brief; sketchy: ～的序言 very brief preface / 报告稍嫌～,但内容可靠。The report is a bit sketchy, but it is reliable.
简码 jiǎnmǎ brevity code; simplified code
简慢 jiǎnmàn negligent (in attending to one's guest); slighting: 招待～,请多包涵。Please excuse us for any negligence in the reception.
简明 jiǎnmíng simple and clear; succinct; concise: 《～英汉词典》*A Concise English-Chinese Dictionary* / ～技术规范 condensed specifications / ～损益表 condensed profit and loss statement / ～资产负债表 condensed balance sheet / 这篇评论～而流畅。This commentary is succinct and well written.
简明不列颠百科全书 Jiǎnmíng Bùlièdiān Bǎikē Quánshū *Concise Encyclopaedia Britannica*
简明扼要 jiǎnmíng-èyào terse and clear; brief and to the point; concise: 这部词典的释义～。The explanations in this dictionary are concise and to the point. / 我们的时间不多,所以要求他说得～。We didn't have much time, so we asked him to make it short.
简明新闻 jiǎnmíng xīnwén news in brief
简朴 jiǎnpǔ simple and unadorned; plain: 语言～ plain language / ～的陈设 modest furnishings / 衣着～ simple and unadorned clothing / 这件木雕,线条～而优美。The lines of this wooden sculpture are simple and beautiful.
简谱 jiǎnpǔ 〈音乐〉numbered musical notation
简切 jiǎnqiè simple and to the point
简任 jiǎnrèn 〈旧语〉second rank in the four-echelon officialdom of China before 1949
简省 jiǎnshěng simplify; use sparingly; economize: ～手续 simplify procedures / ～费用 economize on expenses
简师 jiǎnshī (short for 简易师范) junior normal school
简率 jiǎnshuài 〈书面〉❶ simple and straightforward: 为人～ simple and honest person ❷ rough; sketchy: 记录～ sketchy minutes
简素 jiǎnsù ❶ simple and plain ❷ bamboo slips and white silk for writing on in ancient times
简缩 jiǎnsuō simplify; cut; reduce: 人员数量应该～。The (number of) staff should be reduced.
简体 jiǎntǐ ❶ simplified (after reducing the number of strokes) ❷ *see* "简体字"
简体字 jiǎntǐzì simplified Chinese character
简帖 jiǎntiě 〈旧语〉letters; correspondence
简图 jiǎntú sketch; diagram; abbreviated drawing; simplified scheme
简谐运动 jiǎnxié yùndòng 〈物理〉simple harmonic motion
简写 jiǎnxiě ❶ write a Chinese character in simplified form ❷ simplify (a book for beginners, etc.)
简写本 jiǎnxiěběn simplified edition
简亵 jiǎnxiè 〈书面〉negligent (in attending to one's guest); slighting
简讯 jiǎnxùn news in brief: 新闻～ news in brief
简雅 jiǎnyǎ simple and refined; plain and elegant: 记叙～ give a simple and refined account; describe in a simple and elegant way
简要 jiǎnyào brief and to the point; concise: 写个～的提纲 make a brief outline / 回答十分～ give a laconic answer / 我们很忙,所以我只～地把情况告诉你。We are in a hurry, so I'll give you the story in a nutshell.
简仪 jiǎnyí 〈天文〉abridged armilla
简易 jiǎnyì ❶ simple and easy: 汉语拼音字母用法～,便于学习。The Chinese phonetic alphabet is simple and easy to learn. ❷ simply constructed or equipped; unsophisticated: ～沙发 simply-structured sofa / ～住房 simply-equipped house / ～行军床 simple camp bed
简易病房 jiǎnyì bìngfáng simply equipped ward
简易电子计算机 jiǎnyì diànzǐ jìsuànjī simple electronic computer
简易读物 jiǎnyì dúwù easy reader
简易法庭 jiǎnyì fǎtíng summary court
简易公路 jiǎnyì gōnglù simply-built highway; makeshift road
简易机场 jiǎnyì jīchǎng airstrip
简易楼 jiǎnyìlóu economically constructed building; economical building
简易师范 jiǎnyì shīfàn junior normal school
简约 jiǎnyuē ❶ brief; concise; sketchy: 这个古文选本的注释过于～。The annotation of this selection of classical writings is much too brief. ❷ frugal; thrifty: 生活～ live frugally
简则 jiǎnzé brief rules
简札 jiǎnzhá 〈书面〉letters; correspondence
简章 jiǎnzhāng general regulations: 招生～ general regulations for enrolling students; general rules of (college) admission
简政放权 jiǎnzhèng-fàngquán streamline administration and delegate powers to lower levels
简直 jiǎnzhí ❶ simply; just; at all: ～荒谬得很 simply ridiculous / ～难以想像 virtually unimaginable / ～跟新的一样 as good as new; practically new / 天冷得～可以把你冻僵。It was literally cold enough to freeze you. / 这种菜～没法吃。This food is not edible at all. / 出版这种书～是浪费纸张。The publication of such books is just so much waste of paper. / 三个月就建成了这座工厂,～是个奇迹。The setting up of this plant in three months is nothing short of a miracle. ❷ 〈方言〉may just as well: 雨下得这么大,你～别回去了。It is raining cats and dogs. You may just as well stay here instead of going home.
简质 jiǎnzhì 〈书面〉simple and plain: 叙述～ simple and plain description (*or* account)
简装 jiǎnzhuāng plainly-packed or -packaged: ～烟 plainly-packed cigarettes / ～货 plainly-packed goods

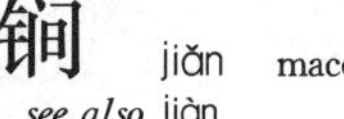

see also jiàn

鬋 jiǎn 〈书面〉❶ hanging hair on the temples ❷ shave

揃 jiǎn 〈书面〉cut off; separate

翦 jiǎn ❶ *see* "剪" jiǎn ❷ (Jiǎn) a surname

剪 jiǎn ❶ scissors; shears; clippers: 王麻子刀~ Wang Mazi-brand knives and scissors ❷ scissor-shaped tool: 夹~ scissor-shaped clamping tool / 火~ firetong; tongs ❸ cut (with scissors); clip; trim: ~掉 cut off; scissor off / ~断 cut off; nip; snip / ~开 cut open / ~发 have one's hair cut / ~鞋样 cut out a shoe pattern / ~窗花 cut paper for window decoration / ~羊毛 shear a sheep / 把纸边~齐 have the paper edge trimmed / 修~圣诞树 trim a Christmas tree ❹ wipe out; exterminate: *see* "~灭"; "~除"

剪报 jiǎnbào ❶ cut out (useful information) from newspapers ❷ newspaper cutting; newspaper clipping: ~材料汇编 compilation of newspaper cuttings

剪裁 jiǎncái ❶ cut out (a garment); tailor: ~衣服 cut out a dress / 母亲夜夜~缝补。Mother tailors and mends night after night. ❷ cut out unwanted material (from a piece of writing); prune: 这部电影在对原著的~上很下了一番功夫。This is a well-pruned film, cutting out all the unwanted materials of the original work.

剪彩 jiǎncǎi cut the ribbon (as at an opening ceremony): ~仪式 ribbon-cutting ceremony / 为大桥通车~ cut the ribbon for the opening of the bridge to traffic

剪草除根 jiǎncǎo-chúgēn *also* "斩草除根" zhǎncǎo-chúgēn cut the weeds and dig up the roots — remove the root of trouble: 去恶务尽, ~ uproot the evil and eliminate the cause of trouble

剪草机 jiǎncǎojī grass mower; grass-mowing machine; lawn mower

剪除 jiǎnchú wipe out; weed out; annihilate; exterminate: ~凶顽 wipe out confirmed evildoers / ~贼寇 get rid of bandits and robbers

剪床 jiǎnchuáng 〈机械〉shearing machine

剪创 jiǎnchuàng clip wound

剪刀 jiǎndāo scissors; shears: 一把~ a pair of scissors

剪刀差 jiǎndāochā scissors movement of prices; scissors differential or difference; price scissors: 缩小~ narrow the price scissors / 扩大~ widen the price scissors

剪辑 jiǎnjí ❶〈影视〉montage; film editing: 电影~机 motion-picture editing machine / 这部电影~得很成功。This film is well edited. ❷ recut; re-edit: ~照片 re-edit photos / 电影录音~ highlights of a live recording of a film

剪接 jiǎnjiē montage; film editing

剪径 jiǎnjìng (often used in the early vernacular) waylay; hold up

剪毛 jiǎnmáo 〈畜牧〉shearing; clipping: ~机 shearing machine / 一~ first shearing

剪灭 jiǎnmiè wipe out; annihilate; exterminate: ~群雄 subdue independent warlords

剪票 jiǎnpiào punch a ticket: ~口 ticket-punching entrance

剪票铗 jiǎnpiàojiá conductor's punch

剪切 jiǎnqiē 〈机械〉shearing: ~刀具 shearing tool / ~机 shearer / ~模 shearing die / ~作业线 cutting line; shear line

剪切力 jiǎnqiēlì 〈物理〉shearing force

剪切形变 jiǎnqiē xíngbiàn 〈物理〉shearing deformation

剪秋萝 jiǎnqiūluó 〈植物〉senno campion (*Lychnis senno*)

剪贴 jiǎntiē ❶ clip and paste (sth. out of a newspaper, etc.) in a scrapbook or on cards: 这本书是剪剪贴贴拼凑而成的。The book is a scissors-and-paste affair. ❷ cutout: 举办幼儿~展览 hold an exhibition of children's cutouts

剪贴簿 jiǎntiēbù scrapbook

剪形绿篱 jiǎnxíng lǜlí clipped or trimmed hedge

剪形树 jiǎnxíngshù clipped tree

剪影 jiǎnyǐng ❶ paper-cut silhouette: 浪迹异国, 靠在街头给人~过生活。Roaming about overseas, I lived on cutting paper silhouettes for people. ❷ outline; sketch: 根据考古材料写成的原始人生活的~ sketch describing primitive people's life, based on the results of archaeological researches

剪应力 jiǎnyìnglì 〈机械〉shearing stress

剪枝 jiǎnzhī 〈林业〉lopping; pruning; trimming: ~刀 lopping shears / ~工具 pruning implements / ~剪 lopping shears

剪纸 jiǎnzhǐ 〈工美〉paper-cut; scissor-cut: 春节前, 村儿里家家户户的门窗上都换上了新~。Before Spring Festival, every family in the village had new paper-cuts pasted on doors and windows.

剪纸片儿 jiǎnzhǐpiānr 〈口语〉〈影视〉*see* "剪纸片"

剪纸片 jiǎnzhǐpiàn 〈影视〉a kind of cartoon and puppet film

剪烛西窗 jiǎnzhú-xīchuāng *also* "西窗剪烛" friends and relatives get together and talk intimately

剪子 jiǎnzi scissors; shears; clippers: 理发~ barber's clippers / 医用~ scissors for medical use / 羊毛~ shears

谫(譾) jiǎn 〈书面〉shallow; superficial; meagre: 能薄而才~ have meagre talent

谫陋 jiǎnlòu 〈书面〉shallow; superficial; meagre: 学识~ have little learning

戬 jiǎn 〈书面〉❶ get rid of; wipe out ❷ lucky; propitious: ~縠 perfect happiness; bliss

茧[1](繭) jiǎn cocoon: 蚕~ silkworm cocoon / 作~自缚 spin a cocoon round oneself; get enmeshed in a web of one's own spinning

茧[2](蠒) jiǎn callus: 老~ thick callus / 重~ callosity; thick callus

茧巴 jiǎnbā 〈方言〉callus

茧绸 jiǎnchóu pongee; tussah silk

茧花 jiǎnhuā 〈方言〉callus

茧子 jiǎnzi ❶〈方言〉silkworm; cocoon ❷ callus

柬 jiǎn card; note; letter: 请~ invitation card / 书~ letters; correspondence / 贺~ congratulatory letter

柬埔寨 Jiǎnpǔzhài Cambodia: ~人 Cambodian

柬帖 jiǎntiě note; short letter

柬邀 jiǎnyāo invite (sb.) by writing

睐 jiǎn 〈书面〉bright (usu. used in personal names)

拣[1](揀) jiǎn choose; select; pick: ~便宜的买 select and buy the cheaper ones / ~容易的题先做 choose the easier problems to tackle first / 挑肥~瘦 pick the fat or choose the lean — choose whatever is good for one; be choosy

拣[2](揀) jiǎn (same as 捡) collect; gather

拣佛烧香 jiǎnfó-shāoxiāng burn incense to the Buddha of one's own choice — favour one person rather than another; treat with partiality: 同是至亲, 他为何~? They are both his own flesh and blood. Why does he favour one more than the other?

拣了芝麻丢了西瓜 jiǎnle zhīma diūle xīguā *also* "捡了芝麻丢了西瓜" jiǎnle zhīma diūle xīguā pick up the sesame seeds but overlook the watermelons; be mindful of minor matters to the neglect of major ones; be penny wise and pound foolish

拣便宜 jiǎn piányi buy on the cheap; get the better of a bargain: 兄弟相斗, 让外人拣了便宜。While the brothers are at loggerheads with each other, outsiders stand to benefit. / 你别想在我身上~。Don't you try to take advantage of me.

拣选 jiǎnxuǎn select; choose; pick: ~上等药材配制成新药 select the best quality medicinal herbs and make them into a new drug

拣择 jiǎnzé choose; pick; select: ~吉日 select an auspicious day (for a wedding, etc.)

减(減) jiǎn ❶ subtract; deduct; minus: 八~四 subtract four from eight / 从总收入中~去成本 deduct costs from total receipts / 削~ slash; lower / 裁~ cut down; reduce / 偷工~料 scamp work and stint (on) materials / 八~二等于六。Eight minus two is equal to six. *or* Two from eight is six. ❷ reduce; diminish; decrease; cut: 饭量~了许多 have sharply lost one's appetite / 雄心不~当年 be as ambitious as ever / 学汽车驾驶的人有增无~。The number of people learning driving is growing. / 非生产人员要逐步~下来。The number of nonproductive personnel should be reduced step by step.

减编 jiǎnbiān staff reduction
减并 jiǎnbìng 〈物理〉degenerate:～半导体 degeneracy semiconductor
减产 jiǎnchǎn reduction of output; fall or decline in production:烟草～百分之十。The output of tobacco fell by ten per cent. /今年粮食因灾～。The crop yields showed a drop this year because of natural disasters.
减除 jiǎnchú wipe out; get rid of:～人民的痛苦 relieve the people of their sufferings
减低 jiǎndī reduce; lower; diminish; slow down:～速度 slow down; lower (*or* slacken) speed /～价格 lower the price /～标价 mark down /～运费 freight cutting /～造价 lessen the cost /～能耗 bring down energy consumption /房租～了百分之十。The house rent is reduced by ten percent.
减法 jiǎnfǎ 〈数学〉subtraction
减肥 jiǎnféi reduce fat; slim; lose weight:设法～ try to lose weight /～操 slimming exercises /对中老年来说,慢跑不失为一种～运动。Jogging can be a fat-reducing exercise for the middle-aged and old people.
减幅 jiǎnfú range of decrease; decrease; amount of cut:燃料价格～在一成以上。The price of fuel will be cut more than 10%.
减号 jiǎnhào 〈数学〉minus sign (-)
减河 jiǎnhé 〈水利〉distributary
减缓 jiǎnhuǎn retard; slow down; reduce; decelerate:～车速 slow down; reduce speed /～衰老 decelerate ageing /～作物生长速度 retard the growth of crops
减活化 jiǎnhuóhuà 〈化学〉deactivation:～剂 deactivator
减价 jiǎnjià reduce the price; mark down:～百分之十 reduce the price by ten percent; make a ten percent reduction in price /积压品～出售 sell overstocked goods at a reduced price; sell old stock at reduced prices /清仓大～ clearance sale /药品～了。The price of medicine has come down.
减免 jiǎnmiǎn ❶ mitigate or annul (a punishment) ❷ reduce or remit (taxation, etc.):～学费 reduce or remit tuition (fees); enjoy a partial or total tuition waiver
减摩 jiǎnmó 〈机械〉antifriction
减摩合金 jiǎnmó héjīn 〈机械〉antifriction alloy; antifriction metal
减摩涂层 jiǎnmó túcéng 〈机械〉friction coat
减摩轴承 jiǎnmò zhóuchéng 〈机械〉antifriction bearing
减轻 jiǎnqīng lighten; lessen; allay; alleviate; mitigate:～处分 mitigate a punishment /～怨恨 allay enmity /～疼痛 alleviate pain /～某人的负担 lessen the burden of sb.; ease sb. of his burden /～惩罚 commute (*or* reduce) punishment /～家庭的负担 lighten the burden of one's family /～劳动强度 reduce labour intensity /～责任 diminish responsibility /～罪行 extenuate a crime /～压力 relieve pressure /体重～ lose weight /药物奏效,症状～了。As the medicine took effect, the symptoms lessened.
减却 jiǎnquè drop; go down; reduce; decrease
减弱 jiǎnruò weaken; relax; subside; abate:风势～了。The wind has abated (*or* subsided). /长期生病,体质～了。He was debilitated by a protracted disease. /进攻的势头～了。The momentum of the offensive diminished (*or* was weakened). /洪峰穿过三峡,水势逐渐～。After passing through the Three Gorges, flood water started to slow down.
减色 jiǎnsè lose lustre; impair the excellence of; detract from the merit of:这一缺陷使这幅画大大～。The defect detracts greatly from the value of the painting. *or* The defect makes the painting lose much of its lustre. /情节拖沓使这篇小说～不少。The loose plot spoils the novel.
减色法 jiǎnsèfǎ 〈影视〉subtractive process:～印片 subtractive printing
减杀 jiǎnshā weaken; lessen; reduce:这些设施,是为了～洪峰期的水势。The facilities are designed to reduce the torrents of water during the peak flood period.
减少 jiǎnshǎo reduce; decrease; diminish; lessen:～开会时间 reduce the time for meetings /～危险 lessen the danger /～百分之十 cut down by ten percent /～误差 commit fewer errors /给他～一些工作 relieve him of some of his work /伤亡人数大大～了。The number of casualties has greatly diminished. /次品的数量大大～。The quantity of defective goods has fallen off considerably.
减声器 jiǎnshēngqì 〈机械〉silencer; muffler
减湿 jiǎnshī dehumidify:～器 dehumidifier
减数 jiǎnshù 〈数学〉subtrahend
减数分裂 jiǎnshù fēnliè 〈生物〉meiosis
减税 jiǎnshuì reduce the rate of tax; make a tax reduction
减税让利 jiǎnshuì-rànglì reduce tax on enterprises and allow them to retain more profits
减速 jiǎnsù slow down; decelerate; retard:汽车～了。The car was decelerating. *or* The car was slowing down. /快到十字路口时要～。Slow up before you reach the crossroads.
减速度 jiǎnsùdù deceleration
减速副翼 jiǎnsù fùyì 〈航空〉deceleron
减速火箭 jiǎnsù huǒjiàn 〈航天〉retro-rocket
减速剂 jiǎnsùjì 〈物理〉moderator
减速器 jiǎnsùqì 〈机械〉reduction gear or device; parabrake
减速伞 jiǎnsùsǎn 〈航空〉drag parachute; deceleration parachute
减速运动 jiǎnsù yùndòng 〈物理〉retarded motion
减损 jiǎnsǔn reduce; decrease; lessen; cut down:增益～ increase profit and reduce loss
减缩 jiǎnsuō reduce; cut down; retrench:～编制 reduce the staff
减退 jiǎntuì go down; subside; abate; decline:病人的热度已～了。The patient's fever has abated. /洪水已～。The flood has subsided. /他视力逐渐～。His eyesight is declining. /我的记忆力～。My memory is failing. /他的那股热情正在～。His enthusiasm is on the decline.
减薪 jiǎnxīn reduce salary:裁员～ cut down the number of employees and reduce the salary
减刑 jiǎnxíng 〈法律〉reduce a penalty; commute a sentence; mitigate punishment
减削 jiǎnxuē cut down; reduce:这个研究所的经费,未经政府同意,任何人不得～。No one is allowed to cut down the funds for this institute without the permission of the government.
减压 jiǎnyā reduce pressure; decompress:～器 pressure reducer; decompressor /～室 decompression chamber
减员 jiǎnyuán ❶ depletion of numbers (usually in the armed forces); personnel reduction:战斗～ depletion of combat strength /非战斗～ depletion of noncombat strength ❷ cut down the number of personnel:这个机关正在～。The organization is reducing its staff.
减灾 jiǎnzāi reduction of natural disasters
减震 jiǎnzhèn shock absorption; damping:～器〈机械〉shock absorber; damper; snubber
减租减息 jiǎnzū-jiǎnxī reduction of rent for land and of interest on loans (CPC's agrarian policy during the War of Resistance Against Japanese Aggression, 1937-1945); reduction of rent and interest

碱(鹼、堿) jiǎn

❶ alkali base; 强～ alkali; strong base /弱～ weak base /烧～ caustic soda ❷ soda:纯～ soda (ash):洗涤～ washing soda ❸ alkalinize; base:这堵墙都～了。This wall has been basified.
碱草 jiǎncǎo *also* "羊草" yángcǎo 〈植物〉*Aneurolepidium chinense*
碱测定法 jiǎncèdìngfǎ 〈化学〉alkalimetry
碱地 jiǎndì alkaline land
碱电池 jiǎndiànchí 〈电工〉alkaline-manganese cell; alkaline cell
碱度 jiǎndù 〈化学〉alkalinity; basicity:～计 alkalimeter
碱化 jiǎnhuà alkalinization; basification
碱荒 jiǎnhuāng alkaline wasteland:改造～ transform alkaline wasteland
碱金属 jiǎnjīnshǔ alkali or alkaline metal
碱尿症 jiǎnniàozhèng 〈医学〉alkaluria:高空～ altitude alkaluria
碱溶液 jiǎnróngyè 〈化学〉aqueous alkali
碱式盐 jiǎnshìyán 〈化学〉basic salt
碱土 jiǎntǔ 〈农业〉alkali soil:白～ white alkali soil /黑～ black alkali soil /盐～ saline-sodic soil; saline-alkali soil /～滩 alkali flat /～法制浆 alkali pulping process
碱土金属 jiǎntǔ jīnshǔ alkaline-earth metal
碱洗 jiǎnxǐ 〈化学〉caustic wash; alkaline cleaning:～塔 alkali scrubber /～装置 alkaline cleaner
碱性 jiǎnxìng alkalinity; basicity:～土 alkaline soil /～染料 basic dyes /～法〈冶金〉basic process /～氧气炼钢法 basic oxygen process /～长石 alkali feldspar
碱性反应 jiǎnxìng fǎnyìng alkaline reaction
碱性岩 jiǎnxìngyán alkaline rock
碱性转炉 jiǎnxìng zhuànlú 〈冶金〉basic converter; basic-lined

converter; Bessemer steel converter; Thomas converter: ～钢 Thomas steel; basic Bessemer steel; basic converter steel /～铸铁 basic Bessemer cast iron
碱血病 jiǎnxuèbìng 〈医学〉alkalaemia
碱液 jiǎnyè lye
碱中毒 jiǎnzhòngdú 〈医学〉alkalosis; alkali poisoning

趼(繭) jiǎn callus:重～ callosity; thick callus /老～ callosity; thick callus
趼子 jiǎnzi *also* "茧子" jiǎnzi; "老趼" lǎojiǎn callus:手上磨出了～ work out a callus of the hand; have one's hand callused

枧[1] jiǎn *also* "笕" jiǎn conduit made of long bamboo

枧[2] jiǎn 〈方言〉soap:香～ toilet soap

笕 jiǎn long bamboo pipe for channeling water:檐下安有水～。A long bamboo pipe is fixed under the eaves for channeling rainwater.

觃 jiǎn 〈书面〉*see* "茧" jiǎn

囝 jiǎn 〈方言〉❶ son ❷ child

检(檢) jiǎn ❶ check up; inspect; examine:翻～ look through (books, papers, etc.) /～字 find a word in a dictionary /体～ medical check-up ❷ restrain oneself; be careful in one's conduct: 行为不～ depart from correct conduct; behave improperly /言语不～ be careless about one's words; speak indiscreetly /自～ restrain oneself ❸ (same as 捡) pick up; collect ❹ (Jiǎn) a surname
检波 jiǎnbō 〈通信〉detection:～管 detection tube /～器 detector
检测 jiǎncè test and determine: ～点 control point; monitoring point /～时间 testing time
检查 jiǎnchá ❶ check up; inspect; examine; investigate:～工作 inspect work /体格～ have a physical examination; have a health check; have a medical check-up /～证件 examine one's certificates /～人数 count the number of people /～账目 check the account; audit the account /～产品质量 check on the quality of the product /新闻～ press censorship /思想～ ideological self-examination /卫生～ sanitary inspection /钡餐～ barium meal examination /常规～ routine examination /全身～ general check-up /透视～ examine by fluoroscopy /邮件～ postal inspection ❷ review; reference; check:对上学期工作进行全面～ make a comprehensive review of our work last term /这些材料要保存起来,以便日后～。These materials should be kept for later reference (*or* check). ❸ self-criticism:认真～自己的错误 earnestly criticize one's own mistakes
检查哨 jiǎncháshào checkpost
检查团 jiǎnchátuán inspection party
检查员 jiǎncháyuán inspector; examining officer
检查站 jiǎncházhàn checkpoint; checkpost; inspection station
检察 jiǎnchá procuratorial work:～工作 procuratorial work /～案卷 prosecuting files /～人员 procuratorial personnel
检察官 jiǎncháguān public procurator; public prosecutor; prosecuting attorney
检察机关 jiǎnchá jīguān procuratorial organ
检察院 jiǎncháyuàn procuratorate:～院长 procurator-general /最高人民～ Supreme People's Procuratorate /军事～ military procuratorate
检察长 jiǎncházhǎng chief procurator; public procurator-general
检场 jiǎnchǎng 〈旧语〉arrange or collect stage property with the curtain up
检点 jiǎndiǎn ❶ examine; check:～行李 check the luggage ❷ be discrect or cautious (about what one says or does):你近来行为很失～。You have been very indiscreet in your conduct lately. /糖尿病人对饮食不可不～。The diabetics must be very careful about their food.
检定 jiǎndìng examine and check; inspect:药品～ examine and check medicines /～商用计量器具 inspect the calculating appliances /～假设论 theory of testing hypothesis
检校 jiǎnjiào examine and check
检斤 jiǎnjīn weigh things on a scale
检举 jiǎnjǔ report (an offence) to the authorities; inform against (an offender):～电话 telephone number for reporting a case / ～贪污分子 inform against an embezzler /～某人的盗窃行为 report sb. to the authorities for theft
检举人 jiǎnjǔrén informant; accuser
检举箱 jiǎnjǔxiāng box for accusation letters
检举信 jiǎnjǔxìn letter of accusation; written accusation:向司法部门写～ send a letter of accusation to the judicial departments
检漏 jiǎnlòu 〈电工〉leak hunting:～器 leak detector; leak localizer
检录 jiǎnlù 〈体育〉call the roll and guide sportsmen into the arena:～员 person who calls the roll and guides sportsmen into the arena /径赛～员 clerk of course /～长 chief clerk of course /田赛～员 clerk of field
检票 jiǎnpiào examine tickets or ballots
检审 jiǎnshěn test and examine:进行机动车、驾驶员～工作 have motor vehicles and drivers tested and examined
检视 jiǎnshì check up; examine:地勤人员正在～将要起飞的飞机。Ground personnel are examining the plane that is going to take off.
检试 jiǎnshì (of machines, facilities, installations, etc.) test; examine; inspect
检束 jiǎnshù examine and restrain (oneself):公共场所,观瞻所系,应当自行～。We must behave ourselves in public so as not to offend the eye.
检数单 jiǎnshùdān tally sheet
检索 jiǎnsuǒ look up sth. (in books, references, etc.); retrieve; search:电脑～ search by computer /目录～ catalogue-search /资料按音序排列便于～。Written materials are arranged in alphabetical order for easy reference. /这个图书馆开始使用一种超高速标题～系统。This library has begun to use an extra-efficient subject index searching system.
检讨 jiǎntǎo ❶ self-criticism:作～ make a self-criticism /认真～自己的缺点和不足 sincerely examine one's own mistakes and shortcomings /开生活～会 hold a meeting to help each other through criticism and self-criticism ❷〈书面〉review; inspect; study:对于前人的学术成果,我们必须进行深入地～。We must have an in-depth study (*or* review) of the academic achievements of our predecessors.
检修 jiǎnxiū examine and repair; overhaul; maintenance:定期～汽车 overhaul cars at regular intervals /～工 maintenance man /～成本 cost of overhaul /～范围 scope of repair /～费用 recondition expense / ～规则 regulations of inspection and repair /～手册 overhaul manual /～停机 maintenance outage /这台发动机要全面～。This engine needs a complete overhaul. /雨季前对旧房要～一遍。Old houses must be examined and repaired before the rainy season.
检寻 jiǎnxún check and look for:～遗物 check and look for things left behind by the deceased
检验 jiǎnyàn test; examine; inspect:商品～ commodity inspection / ～产品 test a product /～程序 check routine; check problem; test program; test routine /～分析 examination and analysis /～负载 proof load /～工具 inspection instruments /实践是～真理的唯一标准。Practice is the sole criterion of truth.
检验单 jiǎnyàndān check list; inspection sheet
检验飞行 jiǎnyàn fēixíng test flight
检验费 jiǎnyànfèi survey fee
检验员 jiǎnyànyuán inspector; inspecting officer
检验证 jiǎnyànzhèng certificate of inspection; testing certificate
检疫 jiǎnyì quarantine:～范围 quarantine range /～动植物 quarantine of animals and plants
检疫锚泊地 jiǎnyì máobódì quarantine anchorage
检疫旗 jiǎnyìqí quarantine flag; yellow flag
检疫员 jiǎnyìyuán quarantine officer
检疫站 jiǎnyìzhàn quarantine station
检疫证明书 jiǎnyì zhèngmíngshū quarantine certificate; vaccination certificate; yellow book
检阅 jiǎnyuè ❶ review (troops, etc.); inspect: ～军队 inspect troops; review troops /～三军仪仗队 review a guard of honour from the three armed services /～群众游行队伍 inspect contingents of mass paraders /这次展览是对近期发明创造的一次～。The exhibition is a review of recent inventions. ❷ browse; look over; glance over; leaf through:～书报 glance over books and newspapers /～国内外的有关资料 look over relevant references, domestic and foreign
检阅台 jiǎnyuètái reviewing stand
检字表 jiǎnzìbiǎo word index:汉语拼音～ Pinyin (*or* phonetic)

J

index of Chinese characters
检字法 jiǎnzìfǎ 〈语言〉 way in which Chinese characters are arranged (as in a dictionary); indexing system for Chinese characters: 音序～ alphabetic order indexing /部首～ indexing system by radicals /四角号码～ Chinese characters' four-corner decimal indexing

硷(礆、鹼)

jiǎn *also* "碱" jiǎn alkali; soda: 番木鳖～ strychnine /山梗菜～ lobeline /氨茶～ aminophylline /毒扁豆～ physostigmine; eserine /吐根～ emetine /麻黄～ ephedrine

捡(撿)

jiǎn pick up; collect; gather: ～柴 gather firewood /～麦穗儿 pick up ears of wheat; glean a wheat field /在海边～贝壳 collect sea shells on the seashore /～到一个钱包 find a purse /把地上的破纸～进垃圾箱 pick up the pieces of paper and leave them in the dustbin
捡了芝麻丢了西瓜 jiǎnle zhīma diūle xīguā pick up the sesame seeds but overlook the watermelons
see also "拣了芝麻丢了西瓜" jiǎnle zhīma diūle xīguā
捡漏 jiǎnlòu 〈建筑〉 repair the leaky part of a roof; plug a leak in the roof
捡漏儿 jiǎnlòur 〈方言〉 find fault (with sb.); nitpick: 他总爱～。He is always trying to nitpick.
捡破烂儿 jiǎn pòlànr pick odds and ends from refuse heaps: 你从哪儿捡来这么多破烂儿? Where did you get all that rubbish?
捡拾 jiǎnshí pick up; collect; gather
捡拾压捆机 jiǎnshí yākǔnjī 〈农业〉 pick-up baler; pick-up press
捡洋落儿 jiǎn yánglàor 〈方言〉 get a windfall: 村儿里有的人想到城里去～。Some villagers wanted to go to the city to seek windfalls.

睑(瞼)

jiǎn eyelid: 眼～ eyelid
睑瘤 jiǎnliú 〈医学〉 blepharoncus
睑痉挛 jiǎnjìngluán 〈医学〉 blepharism; blepharospasm
睑皮松垂 jiǎnpí sōngchuí 〈医学〉 blepharochalasis
睑腺炎 jiǎnxiànyán 〈医学〉 sty; stye
睑炎 jiǎnyán 〈医学〉 blepharitis

俭(儉)

jiǎn thrifty; frugal: 节～ thrifty; frugal /勤～ hardworking and thrifty; diligent and frugal /省吃～用 eat sparingly and spend frugally; be economical in everyday spending /克勤克～ be industrious and frugal /勤工～学 study on a work-study basis
俭朴 jiǎnpǔ thrifty and simple; economical: 平日里衣着很～ dress simply in daily life /中国农民勤劳～。Chinese farmers are hardworking and frugal.
俭省 jiǎnshěng economical; thrifty: 过日子～ live a thrifty life; live economically /用钱～ spend one's money sparingly
俭约 jiǎnyuē 〈书面〉 frugal; economical; thrifty

剸

jiǎn 〈书面〉 *see* "剪" jiǎn

jiàn

箭

jiàn ❶ arrow: 弓～ bow and arrow /毒～ poisoned arrow/ 放～ shoot (*or* let loose) an arrow /一束～ a sheaf of arrows /冷～ arrow shot from hiding; sniper's shot /令～ arrow-shaped token of authority used in the army in ancient China /响～ whistling arrow / 袖～ arrow worked by a spring concealed in a sleeve /火～ rocket / ～不虚发 every shot tells /一～双雕 shoot two hawks with one arrow; kill two birds with one stone /～搭上弓 fit an arrow to the bow; get everything prepared /～离弦。The arrow has left the string. *or* The die is cast. /～如雨下。Arrows rained down thick and fast. ❷ distance covered by a flying arrow
箭靶子 jiànbǎzi target for archery
箭步 jiànbù sudden big stride forward: 一个～蹿上去 dash forward with a sudden big stride
箭窗 jiànchuāng small window on an embrasured watchtower over a city gate for watching and shooting arrows
箭毒 jiàndú curare; curari
箭垛子 jiànduǒzi ❶ parapet; battlements ❷ target for archery
箭杆 jiàngǎn arrow shaft
箭楼 jiànlóu embrasured watchtower over a city gate
箭石 jiànshí 〈考古〉 belemnite
箭筒 jiàntǒng quiver
箭头 jiàntóu ❶ arrowhead; arrow tip; arrow point ❷ arrow (as a sign)
箭托 jiàntuō arrow rest
箭鱼 jiànyú swordfish
箭在弦上 jiànzàixiánshàng like an arrow on the bowstring — there can be no turning back; reach the point of no return: ～,不得不发。The arrow on the bowstring has to be shot. *or* When the arrow is on the string, it must go.
箭猪 jiànzhū porcupine
箭竹 jiànzhú 〈植物〉 arrow bamboo (*Sinarundinaria nitida*)
箭镞 jiànzú metal arrowhead

间(間)

jiàn ❶ space or time in between; break; opening: 客厅当～儿 in the middle of the living room /乘～抽烟 have a smoke during a break ❷ enmity; estrangement; discord: 团结无～ united as one /两人多～。The two of them are often in discord. ❸ separate; intersperse: 晴雨相～ wet days alternated with fine days / 多云～晴 cloudy with occasional sun /室内铺着红白相～的地板砖。The room is decorated with floor brick chequered with red and white. ❹ sow discord: 反～ set one's enemies at odds /挑拨离～ sow dissension; set people by the ears ❺ thin out (seedlings): ～菜秧 thin out vegetable seedlings
see also jiān
间壁 jiànbì next door; next-door neighbour: 张家就住在～。The Zhangs live next door.
间厕 jiàncè 〈书面〉 be intermingled; be mixed: ～其间 get mixed up in it
间道 jiàndào 〈书面〉 bypath; shortcut: 从～而返 come back by a shortcut
间谍 jiàndié spy: ～活动 espionage /～战 spy war /双重～ double agent / 色情～案 case of sex espionage
间谍飞机 jiàndié fēijī spy plane
间谍网 jiàndiéwǎng espionage network; spy ring
间谍卫星 jiàndié wèixīng spy satellite
间断 jiànduàn be disconnected; be interrupted: 他坚持学外语,三年从来未～。He has kept on learning English for three years without interruption. /他从十二岁起开始学画,一直没有～过。Not for a moment has he stopped painting since he started at the age of twelve.
间断性 jiànduànxìng 〈哲学〉 discontinuity: 不～ continuity
间伐 jiànfá 〈林业〉 intermediate cutting — cutting down some trees to speed up the growth of a forest or to prevent diseases and pests: ～强度 intensity of intermediate cutting
间隔 jiàngé ❶ interval; intermission: 楼与楼之间～十五米 space out the buildings fifteen metres apart /～均匀 evenly spaced /每两行玉米之间留出适当的～。There should be a proper space between each two rows of maize. /～五年后,我才又一次踏上了故乡的土地。I came back to my hometown after an interval of five years. ❷ separate: 两个院落之间有一堵墙～。The two courtyards are separated by a wall.
间隔号 jiàngéhào 〈语言〉 separation dot — punctuation mark separating the day from the month, as in 一二·九运动 (the December 9th Movement), or separating the parts of a person's name, as in 埃德加·斯诺 (Edgar Snow)
间或 jiànhuò occasionally; now and then; sometimes; from time to time; once in a while: ～空中飞过一颗流星。A meteor shoots across the sky once in a while. /我每天步行上班,下雨天～坐公共汽车。I go to work on foot every day, but occasionally by bus on rainy days.
间接 jiànjiē indirect; secondhand: 这只是造成塌方的～原因。This is only the indirect cause for the collapse. /这个消息,我只是～听来的,所以并不完全相信。Since I only got the news secondhand, I took it with a grain of salt.
间接宾语 jiànjiē bīnyǔ 〈语言〉 indirect object
间接成本 jiànjiē chéngběn indirect cost
间接传染 jiànjiē chuánrǎn indirect infection
间接电弧焊 jiànjiē diànhúhàn indirect electric arc welding
间接电弧炉 jiànjiē diànhúlú 〈冶金〉 indirect electric arc furnace; indirect arc furnace: 摇动式～ indirect arc rocking furnace
间接犯罪 jiànjiē fànzuì consequential crime
间接肥料 jiànjiē féiliào indirect fertilizer

间接费用 jiànjiē fèiyòng overheads
间接分裂 jiànjiē fēnliè *also* "有丝分裂" yǒusī fēnliè 〈生物〉mitosis
间接负债 jiànjiē fùzhài indirect liabilities
间接汇兑 jiànjiē huìduì indirect exchange
间接汇率 jiànjiē huìlǜ indirect rate
间接接触 jiànjiē jiēchù 〈医学〉mediate contact
间接经验 jiànjiē jīngyàn indirect experience
间接贸易 jiànjiē màoyì indirect trade
间接输血 jiànjiē shūxuè indirect transfusion
间接税 jiànjiēshuì indirect tax
间接投资 jiànjiē tóuzī indirect investment
间接推理 jiànjiē tuīlǐ 〈逻辑〉mediate inference
间接消费 jiànjiē xiāofèi indirect consumption
间接选举 jiànjiē xuǎnjǔ indirect election
间接引语 jiànjiē yǐnyǔ 〈语言〉indirect speech
间接证据 jiànjiē zhèngjù circumstantial evidence
间苗 jiànmiáo 〈农业〉thin out seedlings or young shoots: ～机 gapper; gapping machine /～器 thinner; gapper
间日 jiànrì 〈书面〉every other day: ～一至 come every other day /～疟〈医学〉tertian fever; tertian malaria
间色 jiànsè secondary colour
间隙 jiànxì ❶ interval; gap; space: 利用工作～学习 study in intervals of one's work /劳动～ work break /教练在比赛～面授机宜。The coach briefed his team during time-out. ❷〈机械〉clearance: 齿轮～ gear clearance
间歇 jiànxiē intermittence; intermission; interval: 脉搏～ intermittence of the pulse /～反应〈化学〉intermittent reaction /～性精神病 intermittent insanity; periodic insanity /～训练 interval training /～放电 intermittent discharge /～油润 intermittent oiling /这台机器的旋转，每隔半分钟～一次。The rotation of this machine has an intermittence once every half a minute.
间歇泉 jiànxiēquán *also* "间歇喷泉"〈地质〉geyser; intermittent spring
间歇热 jiànxiērè 〈医学〉intermittent fever
间杂 jiànzá be intermingled; be mixed: 五色～ with five colours mixed together /红黄～ mixture of red and yellow /～其间 get mixed up in it
间阻 jiànzǔ 〈书面〉separate; cut off: 山川～ be separated by mountains and rivers
间作 jiànzuò *also* "间种"〈农业〉intercropping: 实行～能比较充分地利用耕地。Intercropping can ensure better utilization of cultivated land.

涧

jiàn ravine; gully; mountain cleft: 山～ mountain stream /溪～ mountain brook

瞷(瞯)

jiàn 〈书面〉peep

锏

jiàn iron protection for a wheel axle
see also jiǎn

谏

jiàn 〈书面〉expostulate with (one's superior or friend); admonish: 进～ remonstrate with the monarch /诤～ criticize (sb.'s faults) frankly; admonish /劝～ plead with sb. not to do sth.; admonish against sth. /拒～饰非 reject criticisms and gloss over errors /从～如流 follow advice eagerly
谏官 jiànguān official whose duty is to remonstrate with the emperor
谏劝 jiànquàn admonish; advise: 剀切～ earnestly give advice
谏诤 jiànzhèng 〈书面〉criticize sb.'s faults frankly: 对友人多所～ often criticize friend's faults frankly
谏阻 jiànzǔ dissuade sb. from (doing sth.); advise sb. not to (do sth.)

谫(譾)

jiàn 〈书面〉be eloquent; have a silver tongue

践(踐)

jiàn ❶ trample; tread: 勿～草地。Keep off the grass. ❷ act on; carry out; execute: 实～ put into practice; carry out /～言 keep one's promise; keep one's word
践履 jiànlǚ 〈书面〉❶ trample; tread ❷ carry out; act on
践诺 jiànnuò 〈书面〉keep one's promise; keep one's word: 这是早就说定了的事，你必须～。This has long been fixed, and you mustn't break your promise.
践踏 jiàntà ❶ tread on: 防止牲畜～庄稼 prevent the animals from treading on the crops ❷ trample underfoot; ride roughshod over; violate; devastate: ～人民的民主权利 trample on the democratic rights of the people /～百姓 ride roughshod over the common people /～真理 trample upon truth /国际关系准则遭到～。Principles guiding international relations have been violated.
践行 jiànxíng carry out; implement: ～诺言 keep one's promise; keep one's word
践约 jiànyuē keep a promise; keep an appointment: 他准时～。He kept the appointment on time.
践祚 jiànzuò 〈书面〉ascend the throne; be enthroned

贱(賤)

jiàn ❶ low-priced; inexpensive; cheap: ～卖三天 hold a sale for three days; sell cheap for three days ❷ lowly; common; humble: 微～ humble; lowly /贫～ poor and lowly /卑～ mean and low ❸ low-down; mean; base; despicable: 下～ low-down; base /轻～ mean and worthless /～脾气 despicable temper (such as preferring rough living to comfort, hard work to ease, etc.) ❹ look down upon; despise; contemn: 人皆～之。People all despise him. ❺〈谦词〉my: ～恙 my illness /～躯尚在。I'm still in good health.
贱骨头 jiàngǔtou ❶〈粗话〉miserable wretch; contemptible wretch ❷〈戏谑〉self-imposed sufferer; trouble seeker: 你这个～，有福不会享，老了还要为儿女操劳。You poor wretch! You never know how to enjoy life and are still toiling at this age for your children.
贱货 jiànhuò ❶ cheap or shoddy goods; things of little value ❷〈粗话〉miserable wretch; good-for-nothing
贱货贵德 jiànhuò-guìdé despise material goods and value virtue
贱民 jiànmín ❶〈旧语〉person of a lower social status ❷ Pariah, the lowest caste in India; untouchable
贱内 jiànnèi 〈谦词〉my wife
贱人 jiànrén (usu. used in old novels) contemptible woman; slut
贱视 jiànshì look down upon; despise

溅(濺)

jiàn splash; spatter; splatter: 钢花四～。Sparks of molten steel were flying in all directions. /他～了一身水。The water splashed all over him. *or* He was splashed with water all over. /卡车开过时，～了我们一身泥。As the truck went by, it spattered us with mud. /他讲得激动时，唾沫四～。He sputtered when talking exictedly.
see also jiān
溅落 jiànluò splash down: 在太平洋中成功～ make a successful splash-down in the Pacific /陨石～海中。Stony meteorites fell into the sea.
溅落点 jiànluòdiǎn splash point

饯¹(餞)

jiàn give a farewell dinner

饯²(餞)

jiàn candy (fruit): 蜜～ candied fruit; preserved fruit
饯别 jiànbié give a farewell dinner: ～亲友 give a farewell dinner to a relative; give a relative a farewell dinner /殷勤～ give a solicitous farewell dinner
饯行 jiànxíng give a farewell dinner: 给他们～ give a farewell dinner in their honour

荐¹(薦)

jiàn ❶ recommend; introduce: 向校长举～教员 recommend a teacher to the school principal /毛遂自～ volunteer one's services ❷〈书面〉sacrifice; devote: 我以我血～轩辕。I am determined to give my life to my motherland.

荐²(薦)

jiàn 〈书面〉❶ grass; straw: 麋鹿食～。David's deer feed on grass. ❷ straw mat: 草～ straw mat
荐拔 jiànbá 〈书面〉recommend sb. for promotion
荐骨 jiàngǔ *also* "骶骨" dǐgǔ sacrum
荐举 jiànjǔ propose sb. for an office; recommend: 发现和～年轻的优秀管理人才 discover and recommend excellent young managers

J

荐任 jiànrèn 〈旧语〉third rank in the four-echelon officialdom of China before 1949
荐头 jiàntou 〈方言〉〈旧语〉employment agent:～店 employment agency
荐贤 jiànxián recommend persons of virtue and ability
荐引 jiànyǐn 〈书面〉recommend:经他～,我在这家工厂的技术科谋到了职务。With his recommendation, I got a post in the technological section of this factory.
荐椎 jiànzhuī *also* "骶骨" dǐgǔ 〈生理〉sacrum
荐擢 jiànzhuó 〈书面〉recommend sb. for promotion:～他为医院副院长。He was promoted to the post of deputy director of the hospital on recommendation.

渐 jiàn gradually; little by little; by degrees:天气～暖。The weather is growing warm. *or* The weather becomes warmer and warmer. /夜色～浓。It's getting dark. /他的名字～被忘却。His name has fallen into oblivion.
see also jiān
渐变 jiànbiàn ❶ gradual change:天色～。The weather changes gradually. ❷〈生物〉anamorphism; anamorphosis
渐次 jiàncì 〈书面〉gradually; one after another:远山近树～融化在夜色中。Faraway mountains and nearby trees are gradually lost in the dusk of the night. /戴首饰的人～多起来了。More and more people are wearing jewellery.
渐渐 jiànjiàn 〈副词〉gradually; by degrees; little by little:脚步声～消失了。The sound of footsteps gradually died away. /出国旅游的人～多起来了。More and more people go abroad as tourists. /这位妇女的头发随着年龄的增长～灰白了。The woman's hair was turning grey as age crept up on her.
渐进 jiànjìn advance gradually; progress step by step:循序～ advance step by step in due order; progress in orderly sequence
渐进主义 jiànjìnzhǔyì incrementalism; gradualism
渐近 jiànjìn 〈数学〉asymptotics:～线 asymptote /～学 asymptotology /～值 asymptotic value
渐开线 jiànkāixiàn 〈机械〉involute:～齿轮 involute gear /～花键 involute spline
渐露端倪 jiànlù-duānní things begin to show their true colours:事情的真相～。The truth of the matter begins to emerge.
渐入佳境 jiànrù-jiājìng (of a situation, etc.) be improving; become better and better:过了亭阁,～。As they went through a hall and pavillion the scene was getting increasingly attractive.
渐衰期 jiànshuāiqī autumn
渐缩管 jiànsuōguǎn 〈机械〉reducing pipe
渐悟 jiànwù gradual awakening to the truth (in Buddhist doctrine)
渐显 jiànxiǎn 〈影视〉fade in
渐新世 Jiànxīnshì 〈地质〉Oligocene Epoch
渐隐 jiànyǐn 〈影视〉fade out

僭 jiàn 〈书面〉exceed one's responsibility of office; usurp:～号 adopt an illegal title /～位 usurp the throne /～越 overstep one's authority; go beyond proper bounds
僭妄 jiànwàng 〈书面〉go beyond one's bounds and act recklessly

鉴(鑒、鑑) jiàn ❶ ancient bronze mirror:以铜为～,可正衣冠。With bronze as a mirror, one can set right one's clothes and hat. ❷ reflect; mirror:光可～人 so shining and bright that it can serve as a looking glass ❸ inspect; survey; scrutinize; examine:赏～ appreciate (an artistic work, etc.) /请～核。Please examine (this). ❹ warning; forewarning; object lesson:借～ use for reference; draw lessons /殷～ setback which serves as a warning to others /引以为～ take warning from it; take it as an object lesson /前车之覆,后车之～。The overturning of the cart in front is a warning to the carts behind. ❺〈套语〉form of address at the very beginning of a letter:惠～ be kind enough to read /钧～ (I) wish to draw your attention
鉴别 jiànbié discern; distinguish; differentiate; discriminate:～能力 ability to differentiate; power of discrimination; discernment /～真伪 discern the false from the genuine /～古玩字画 make an appraisal of antiques and ancient paintings /～是非的能力 ability to distinguish right from wrong /在比较中～ distinguish by comparison
鉴别器 jiànbiéqì 〈电子〉discriminator
鉴察 jiànchá 〈书面〉scrutinize; examine; inspect
鉴定 jiàndìng ❶ appraisal (of a person's strong and weak points); (overall) evaluation:毕业～ graduation appraisal /内行～结论 expert conclusion ❷ appraise; identify; authenticate; determine:请专家～这幅画是否赝品 invite experts to determine the authenticity of this painting /在产品～会上评为优质品 be judged to be of excellent quality at the product appraising meeting
鉴定人 jiàndìngrén identifier; surveyor; appraiser
鉴定书 jiàndìngshū 〈商业〉testimonial; written appraisal:专家～ expert's report
鉴戒 jiànjiè warning; object lesson:过去的错误应当引为～。We should take warning from past mistakes.
鉴谅 jiànliàng 〈书面〉〈套语〉*used to ask for understanding or forgiveness*:招待不周,务乞～。We sincerely hope you'll excuse us for any negligence in our service.
鉴貌辨色 jiànmào-biànsè try to read sb.'s mind by observing the expression on his face:这些生意人真能～。These businessmen are really good at reading people's minds by watching their facial expression.
鉴赏 jiànshǎng appreciate:～能力 connoisseurship /～家 connoisseur /对艺术的～能力 ability to appreciate works of art /他对中国画有很高的～力。He has a keen eye for traditional Chinese painting.
鉴往知来 jiànwǎng-zhīlái foresee the future by reviewing the past; infer from the past to predict the future:有知识和实践的人才有～的本领。Only knowledgeable and experienced people are able to predict the future by reviewing the past.
鉴于 jiànyú in view of; seeing that; considering:～情况有了发展,我建议修改计划。In view of the new development, I suggest that we should revise our plan. /～任务紧迫,他们立刻开始了工作。As the task was urgent, they got down to work at once.
鉴原 jiànyuán 〈书面〉excuse; forgive; pardon:尚希～为幸。I sincerely hope you'll forgive me.
鉴真和尚 Jiànzhēn héshang Monk Jianzhen or Ganijin Wajo (688-763), eminent Chinese monk of the Tang Dynasty who travelled to Japan in 753 to preach Buddhism
鉴证 jiànzhèng ❶ distinguish and confirm:该地出土的文物,考古专业人员～为西周时代殉葬品。After careful examination and identification, the archaeologists found that the cultural relics unearthed here were funerary objects of the Western Zhou Dynasty. ❷ confirm the authenticity, legality and feasibility of a contract

监(監) jiàn ❶ imperial office:国子～ Imperial College, the highest educational administration in feudal China ❷ (Jiàn) a surname
see also jiān
监本 jiànběn books printed by successive Imperial Colleges
监生 jiànshēng 〈旧语〉Imperial College students or those who passed the entrance examination for the Imperial College and qualified to study there

槛(檻) jiàn ❶ banister; balustrade ❷ cage:～车 prisoner's cage-van (used in ancient times) /兽～ animal cage; wooden railings for animals
see also kǎn

见[1](見) jiàn ❶ see; behold; witness; catch sight of:亲眼所～ see with one's own eyes; see for oneself /世所罕～ seldom seen in this world; rare sight on earth /一～如故 feel like old friends at first sight /刚才我～他匆匆走过。I caught sight of him hurrying away a moment ago. ❷ meet with; be exposed to:糖～水即溶。Sugar dissolves in water. /她的眼睛～风就流泪。Her eyes watered when exposed to wind. ❸ show evidence of; appear or seem to be:～诸明文 be expressed in writing; be put down in black and white /～之于行动 be translated into action /商情已～好转。Trade (*or* Business) appeared to be picking up. ❹ refer to; see; vide:～第三页 see page 3 /不～经传 not to be found in the classics — not authoritative ❺ meet; receive; call on; see:～客 receive guests /～上级 call on one's superiors /去～老朋友 meet one's old friend /避而不～ avoid meeting sb. /明天～。See you tomorrow. /～了他替我问好。Send my regards when you see him. ❻ view; opinion:依我之～ in my opinion; to my

mind /政～ political view /偏～ prejudice; bias /英雄所～略同。Heroes hold similar views. *or* Great minds think alike. ❼ (Jiàn) a surname

见²(見) jiàn 〈书面〉〈助词〉❶ *used before a verb to express the passive idea*：～弃 be rejected; be discarded /～重于当时 be held in esteem by his contemporaries ❷ *used before a verb to express the request that others would do sth. for one*：～教 ask to benefit from sb.'s advice /即希～告。Hope to be informed immediately. *or* Please let me know at once.

见爱 jiàn'ài be liked or loved; be regarded highly：承蒙～。I'm greatly honoured by your high opinion of me. /承此间一个商人～，叫我在他家中做个主管。Here, a merchant took a liking to me and appointed me his steward.

见报 jiànbào appear in the newspapers：这条消息明天～。This piece (*or* item) of news will be published in the newspaper tomorrow.

见背 jiànbèi 〈书面〉〈婉词〉(of an elder) pass away：慈父～。My dear father passed away.

见不得 jiànbude ❶ not to be exposed to; unable to stand：这种药～潮。This kind of medicine is not to be exposed to damp. *or* This medicine will be spoiled if exposed to damp. /病人～风。The patient can't stand the wind. ❷ not fit to be seen or revealed：～人的勾当 scandal; shameless deed ❸ 〈方言〉unable to put up with; unable to tolerate：我～偷懒。I can't stand people being lazy.

见财起意 jiàncái-qǐyì harbour evil intentions at the sight of money

见长 jiàncháng be good at; be expert in：他以音乐～。He is good at music. /他的散文以平易自然～。He is a past master at writing simple and natural prose.
see also jiànzhǎng

见称 jiànchēng 〈书面〉be praised; be known：以球艺精湛～ be praised for one's mastery of the ball game /～于世 be well-spoken-of

见得 jiànde (used in the negative and interrogative) seem; appear：怎～明天会下雨? Why do you think it's going to rain tomorrow? /何以～? How so? /这种说法不～准确。This argument might (*or* may) not be correct. /这些人不～都行。Not all these people are capable. /何以～他没有说? How do you know that he didn't say so?

见地 jiàndì insight; judgment：这篇文章颇有～。The article shows remarkable insight.

见多识广 jiànduō-shíguǎng experienced and knowledgeable：老陆走南闯北，～。Travelling extensively, Lao Lu is experienced and knowledgeable. /你是老教员，～。You're a veteran teacher with wide experience.

见方 jiànfāng 〈口语〉square：一米～ one metre square

见访 jiànfǎng 〈书面〉〈套语〉your call; your visit：承蒙～，不胜荣幸。I'm greatly honoured by your visit.

见分晓 jiàn fēnxiǎo be clear; be sorted out; clear up (a matter or doubts); find a solution：事情明日即～。The outcome of the whole affair will be clear tomorrow.

见风使舵 jiànfēng-shǐduò *also*"见风转舵"；"看风使舵" kànfēng-shǐduò trim one's sails to the wind; be a weathercock：他看出了老张的意思，便～，马上改口。Sensing Lao Zhang's real intention, he trimmed his sails and made a sharp turnabout. /他是一个～的人。He is the kind of person who swims with the tide. *or* He's a weathercock.

见风是雨 jiànfēng-shìyǔ take wind as a sure sign of rain — jump to conclusions

见风转舵 jiànfēng-zhuǎnduò *see*"见风使舵"

见缝插针 jiànfèng-chāzhēn stick in a pin wherever there's room — make use of every bit of time or space：小伙子～地学习数学。The lad is making use of every bit of his time to study mathematics.

见缝就钻 jiànfèng-jiùzuān seize every opportunity to curry favour with sb. in authority for personal gain; seize every chance to seek personal advantage

见告 jiàngào 〈书面〉〈套语〉keep me informed; let me know

见功 jiàngōng be effective; produce the desired result：这药服了三剂，仍不～。This medicine has not yet produced the desired effect though I have taken three doses.

见怪 jiànguài mind; take offence：对我的讲话可别～! I hope you will not take offence at my words. /若不～，当直言相告。I'll tell you quite frankly, if you don't mind.

见怪不怪 jiànguài-bùguài not be surprised by anything unusual; be used to sth. uncommon：这种事多了，也就～了。You won't be surprised by such things when you become inured to them.

见怪不怪，其怪自败 jiàn guài bù guài, qí guài zì bài fear not the fearful, and its fearfulness disappears："～"。不用管它，随它去就是了。"Ignore a monster and it will defeat itself." Just let it be; there's no need to take any notice of it.

见鬼 jiànguǐ ❶ fantastic; ridiculous; preposterous; absurd：你又在～了! You're imagining things again. /真是见了鬼了，剪子怎么转眼就不见了? That's funny! How come the scissors disappear in the twinkling of an eye? ❷ go to hell; go to the devil; to hell with it：让种族歧视～去吧。To hell with racial discrimination! /见你的鬼去吧! 我才不接受你的条件呢。I'll see you dead before I accept your terms.

见好 jiànhǎo (of a patient's condition) get better; mend：我的胃病～。My stomach trouble is getting better now.

见好就收 jiànhǎo-jiùshōu leave well enough alone; stop before going too far; stop at the right time; leave while the going's good

见后 jiànhòu see below; *vide post*; *vide infra*

见惠 jiànhuì 〈书面〉〈套语〉be presented with a gift：蒙兄以佳酿～，感谢莫名。I am really indebted to you for the wonderful wine you've sent me.

见机 jiànjī as the opportunity arises; as befits the occasion; according to circumstances：～而行 act according to circumstances; decide on the spot; do as one sees fit /屋里吵作一团，他～悄悄地溜走了。Seeing the house was in a mess, he seized the opportunity to sneak away.

见机行事 jiànjī-xíngshì act according to circumstances; do as one sees fit; use one's discretion：他来的时候我会～的。I'll play it by ear when he comes. /要是遇到意外，你们可以～。If anything untoward should happen, you may use judgment and do what you deem best.

见教 jiànjiào 〈套语〉favour me with your advice; instruct me：阁下有何～? Is there something you want to enlighten me about? /谬误之处，务望～。I sincerely hope you will point out my mistakes.

见解 jiànjiě view; opinion; idea; understanding：～不同 hold different views; have different opinions /提出新的～ put forward some new ideas /他对这个问题有独到的～。He has some original notions on this problem.

见景生情 jiànjǐng-shēngqíng *also*"触景生情" chùjǐng-shēngqíng one's emotion is roused by the scene; be moved by what one sees; recall old memories at familiar sights：古诗词中有不少是～之作。Many ancient poems are works of nostalgia.

见老 jiànlǎo (of appearance) ageing：他比前两年～多了。He looks much older than he was two years ago.

见棱见角 jiànléng-jiànjiǎo edges and corners are clearly visible — display one's ability and drive

见礼 jiànlǐ salute; greet：主客～，然后落座。The host and guests greeted each other and then took their seats.

见利思义 jiànlì-sīyì remember what is right at the sight of money; maintain one's integrity when tempted by money：国家干部要～。Government cadres must bear honour and integrity in mind when tempted by money.

见利忘义 jiànlì-wàngyì forget what is right at the sight of money; forsake good for the sake of gold; sacrifice principle for profit：我不干～的事。I'll do nothing to sacrifice principle for profit. /他是一个～的小人。He is a mean person who is not above selling his honour for money. /他被～的朋友出卖了。He was betrayed by a friend blinded by the lust for gain.

见谅 jiànliàng 〈书面〉〈套语〉excuse me; forgive me：我有急事不能与会，务请～。Please forgive me for not being able to come to the meeting, for I have some urgent business to attend to.

见猎心喜 jiànliè-xīnxǐ thrill to see one's favourite sport and itch to have a go：街角上一群老人在下棋，他不免～，挤进去援支了几招。He couldn't help feeling thrilled at the sight of a group of old men playing chess at a street corner, and he elbowed his way in eagerly giving advice concerning the moves.

见马克思 jiàn Mǎkèsī (often used by Chinese revolutionary veterans) go to see Marx — breathe one's last; pass away：他已去～了。He has breathed his last.

见面 jiànmiàn meet; see：初次～ meet for the first time /我们分别以后，很少～。We have seldom seen each other since we parted. /领导应当经常和群众～。It's necessary for leading cadres to keep close

contact with the masses. /这部电影从明日起和观众～。The film will be released tomorrow. /彼此思想要～。Each should state frankly what's on his mind.

见面礼 jiànmiànlǐ present given to sb. (usu. one's junior) at first meeting

见面熟 jiànmiànshú 〈口语〉hail-fellow-well-met

见票即付 jiànpiào-jífù 〈商业〉payable at sight; payable on demand; payable to bearer:这是一张～的票据。This bill is payable on demand.

见弃 jiànqì be discarded or rejected:以品行不端～于亲朋好友 be rejected by friends and relatives because of bad behaviour

见前 jiànqián see above; *vide ante*; *vide supra*

见钱眼开 jiànqián-yǎnkāi open one's eyes wide at the sight of money:像他这种贪婪的人,怎不～? Being greedy, how can he not jump at the chance of making money?

见俏 jiànqiào sell well; be in high demand; be salable

见轻 jiànqīng (of illness) get better:吃药以后,病势～。After he took the medicine, his condition improved.

见情 jiànqíng be grateful:你给他帮忙,可是他不见你的情。You are doing him a favour but he doesn't seem to be grateful to you.

见人说人话,见鬼说鬼话 jiàn rén shuō rénhuà, jiàn guǐ shuō guǐhuà be all things to all men; doublespeak; be two-faced; speak with a forked tongue:这人八面圆通,善于～。The guy is smooth and slick, being all things to all men.

见仁见智 jiànrén-jiànzhì different people have different views; opinions differ:这个戏艺术上的得失,历来～,看法不一。So far as the artistic strengths and weaknesses of this play are concerned, different people have always held different views.

见上 jiànshàng see above; *vide supra*

见上帝 jiàn shàngdì go to see God — go the way of all flesh; die:如果我听你们的,成天躺着,恐怕早就～去了。If I had listened to your advice and stayed in bed all day long, I would have left this world long ago.

见神见鬼 jiànshén-jiànguǐ be terribly suspicious; be even afraid of one's own shadow:你们别～的,他不是那种人! Don't be so suspicious! He's not that kind of person.

见世面 jiàn shìmiàn see the world; enrich one's experience:经风雨,～ face the world and brave the storm; see life and stand its tests /他阅历广,见过世面。He has seen something of the world and is well experienced. /这回到深圳去参观,可见了世面了。The trip to Shenzhen was a real eye-opener.

见事风生 jiànshì-fēngshēng create trouble with very little cause

见识 jiànshi ❶ widen one's knowledge; enrich one's experience:到处走走,～～也是好的。It will do you good to travel around and widen your horizons. ❷ knowledge; experience:有～的人 person of rich experience; person of extensive knowledge /～短浅 lacking in knowledge and experience; shallow; superficial /～广博 with wide experience; of extensive experience /她说话没轻重,你千万别跟她一般～。She doesn't know how to say things properly so don't take offence at her words.

见树不见林 jiàn shù bù jiàn lín not see the wood for the trees; fail to see the wood for the trees

见死不救 jiànsǐ-bùjiù see someone in mortal danger without lifting a finger to save him:你们不能～。You can't just watch people die and not lend a helping hand.

见所未见 jiànsuǒwèijiàn see what one has never seen before; have never seen before; be unprecedented:许多奇事,则～,闻所未闻。I saw and heard of many strange things of which I had not the slightest inkling before.

见天 jiàntiān 〈口语〉every day:～儿操练 have drills every day /他～早上出去散步。He goes out and takes a stroll every morning.

见天见 jiàntiānjian 〈方言〉every day:他～练气功。He practises *qigong* or deep breathing exercise every day.

见头知尾 jiàntóu-zhīwěi orderly and thorough:他做事～。He is orderly and thorough in what he does.

见兔放鹰 jiàntù-fàngyīng release the hawk when seeing the hare — take action only when one is sure of personal gain

见兔顾犬 jiàntù-gùquǎn look at one's dog when seeing the hare — not yet too late to take action in an emergency

见外 jiànwài regard sb. as an outsider:你对我这么客气,倒有点～了。Please don't go to so much trouble about me, or I'll feel I'm being treated as a stranger. /请不要～。Don't bother please. *or* Make yourself at home.

见危授命 jiànwēi-shòumìng be ready to die for one's country when it is in danger:他～,算得上真英雄。He is a real hero, ready to sacrifice his life for his country.

见微知著 jiànwēi-zhīzhù from the first small beginnings one can see how things will develop; from one small clue one can see what is coming; a little straw shows which way the wind blows:好的领导者能～,防患于未然。A good leader is able to foresee what is coming and take preventive measures.

见闻 jiànwén what one sees and hears; knowledge; information:～不广 have limited knowledge /以广～ widen one's knowledge; enrich one's experience /这次旅游增长了不少～。I have learned a lot from the journey.

见物不见人 jiàn wù bù jiàn rén see things but not people; see only material factors to the neglect of human ones

见习 jiànxí learn on the job; be on probation:在工厂～ work on probation at a factory /一年～期 (on) one-year probation

见习技术员 jiànxí jìshùyuán technician on probation; probationary technician

见习领事 jiànxí lǐngshì student consul

见习生 jiànxíshēng intern; probationer

见习医生 jiànxí yīshēng intern

见下 jiànxià see below; *vide infra*

见贤思齐 jiànxián-sīqí emulate those better than oneself:我这样做,只不过是～,向别人学习罢了。What I did was just keep up with those better than myself and learn from them.

见效 jiànxiào become effective; produce the desired result:上这种肥料～快。This kind of fertilizer took effect quickly. /他的方法很～。His method produced the desired result.

见笑 jiànxiào ❶〈谦词〉incur ridicule (by one's poor performance):文章写得不好,～,～。Excuse my poor writing. /诗写得不好,真是～了。The poem is not well-written; hope you won't mind. ❷ laugh at (me or us):好久没弹钢琴了,弹得不好,请大家别～。I haven't played the piano for ages, so please don't laugh at me if I fail to make the grade.

见笑大方 jiànxiào-dàfāng *also* "贻笑大方" yíxiào-dàfāng make a laughing stock of oneself before experts; incur the ridicule of experts

见新 jiànxīn 〈方言〉make over; refurbish; renew:要辆新的自行车,不要旧车～的。I want a new bike, not one which is made over. *or* I want a new bike, instead of a made-over one.

见血封喉 jiànxuèfēnghóu ❶〈植物〉upas (*Artiaris toxicaria*):～箭毒 antiar ❷ (of a poison, etc.) kill instantly when soaked in (the victim's) blood

见义勇为 jiànyì-yǒngwéi be ready to take up the cudgels for a just cause; have the courage to do what is right:这位老工人一向热情耿直,～。This senior worker has always been warm-hearted and honest, ready to help a just cause.

见异思迁 jiànyì-sīqiān change one's mind the moment one sees something new; be inconstant or irresolute:这对于一班～的人,对于一班鄙薄技术工作以为不足道、以为无出路的人,也是一个极好的教训。His example is an excellent lesson for those people who wish to change work the moment they see something different and for those who despise technical work as of no consequence or as promising no future. /～者将一无所获。A rolling stone gathers no moss.

见于 jiànyú (used to indicate a source or reference) appear; be seen:这个成语～《论语》。This proverb appears in *The Analects of Confucius*.

见责 jiànzé 〈书面〉be blamed; be reprimanded; be reproached

见长 jiànzhǎng grow perceptibly:这孩子怎么老不～? How come the child doesn't seem to be growing?

see also jiàncháng

见证 jiànzhèng ❶ be a witness to; be qualified to bear witness to:这件事我可以～。I can bear witness to this affair. ❷ witness; testimony:丝绸之路是中国同亚欧各国人民友好交往的历史～。The Silk Road is a historical witness to the friendly exchange between the Chinese people and the peoples in Asia and Europe.

见证人 jiànzhèngrén eyewitness; witness

见罪 jiànzuì 〈书面〉take offence:我直话直说,请勿～。I won't mince my words and hope you will take no offence.

J

舰(艦) jiàn warship; naval vessel; man-of-war:战～ warship /军～ warship; naval vessel /旗～ flagship /布雷～ mine layer /扫雷～ mine sweeper /航空母～ aircraft carrier; carrier /护航～ convoy ship /装甲～ armoured ship /战列～ battleship /驱逐～ destroyer /巡洋～ cruiser /导弹驱逐～ guided missile destroyer /导弹巡洋～ guided missile cruiser /登陆～ landing ship /供应～ supply ship; tender /指挥～ control vessel /主力～ capital ship

舰船 jiànchuán ships (including naval and civil ships)

舰队 jiànduì fleet; naval force:南海～ Nan Hai Fleet; South China Sea Fleet /第七～(US) 7th Fleet /特混～(naval) task force /～司令 admiral /～卫星通信系统 fleetsatcom (fleet satellite communications)

舰队街 Jiànduìjiē Fleet Street, a London street where many leading British newspapers have their offices, hence the allusive reference to the British press

舰对岸导弹 jiànduì'àn dǎodàn ship-to-shore missile

舰对地导弹 jiànduìdì dǎodàn ship-to-ground missile

舰对舰导弹 jiànduìjiàn dǎodàn ship-to-ship missile

舰对空导弹 jiànduìkōng dǎodàn ship-to-air missile

舰桥 jiànqiáo commanding bridge on a warship; bridge (of a naval ship)

舰日 jiànrì day a warship spends at sea

舰首 jiànshǒu bow

舰首炮 jiànshǒupào bow chaser

舰艇 jiàntǐng naval ships and boats; naval vessels:两栖作战～ amphibious vessel /作战～ combat ship /水面～ surface vessels

舰尾 jiànwěi stern

舰尾炮 jiànwěipào stern chaser

舰位 jiànwèi (of a warship) location (on high seas); berth (in a harbour)

舰载 jiànzài carrier-borne; carrier-based; ship-based:～导弹 ship-based missile /～飞机 shipboard aircraft; deck-landing aircraft

舰长 jiànzhǎng captain (of a warship)

舰只 jiànzhī warship; naval vessel:海军～ naval vessels /海岸巡逻～ coastal patrolling vessels

剑(劍、劒) jiàn sword; sabre:短～ stiletto /宝～ double-edged sword /轻～ rapier /重～ epee /花～ foil /双刃长～ rapier /佩～ sabre /仗～ hold a sword /击～ fence /舞～ perform a sword-dance /刀光～影 glint and flash of cold steel

剑拔弩张 jiànbá-nǔzhāng with swords drawn and bows bent; at daggers drawn:两国～,大战爆发在即。A war is imminent with both countries rattling their sabres. /他们两个人你一言我一语的,有点～的阵势。They continued bandying words with one another as if they might come to blows.

剑柄 jiànbǐng handle of a sword; hilt

剑齿虎 jiànchǐhǔ 〈考古〉sabre-toothed tiger; machairodont

剑齿象 jiànchǐxiàng 〈考古〉stegodon

剑道 jiàndào (Japan) kendo

剑及履及 jiànjí-lǚjí *also* "履及剑及" resolute and quick action

剑客 jiànkè swordsman:小孩很喜欢听人讲～的故事。The boys are fond of listening to the tales of swordsmen.

剑兰 jiànlán 〈植物〉gladiolus (*Gladidus gandavensis*)

剑麻 jiànmá 〈植物〉sisal hemp

剑眉 jiànméi straight eyebrows slanting upwards and outwards; dashing eyebrows

剑桥 Jiànqiáo Cambridge, city in Cambridgeshire, England, on the River Cam and seat of a major English university:～郡 Cambridgeshire /～大学 University of Cambridge

剑鞘 jiànqiào scabbard; sheath

剑术 jiànshù art of fencing; swordsmanship

剑突 jiàntū 〈生理〉ensiform process; xiphoidprocess

剑尾鱼 jiànwěiyú 〈动物〉swordtail (fish)

剑吻鲸 jiànwěnjīng 〈动物〉beaked whale

剑吻鲨 jiànwěnshā 〈动物〉goblin shark (*Scapanorhynchus owstoni*)

剑舞 jiànwǔ sword-dance

剑侠 jiànxiá (used in kung fu novels) knight-errant or swordsman who champions the cause of the downtrodden

剑仙 jiànxiān (used in kung fu novels) immortal swordsman who levitates and wields magic power

剑鱼 jiànyú 〈动物〉swordfish

垈 jiàn ❶ prop up; support:打～拨正 support and right sth. ❷ keep off water with earth and stone

件 jiàn ❶〈量词〉piece:一～衬衫 a shirt /两～上衣 two coats /三～家具 three pieces of furniture ❷ *things that can be counted*:案～ law case /锻～ forged piece; forging /工～ workpiece /零～ spare parts /配～ fittings of a machine /信～ mail; letters /证～ credentials; certificate /稿～ manuscript; contribution /邮～ postal matter; mail /大～儿 big piece /快～儿 express letter; express mail /慢～儿 slow mail /急～ urgent dispatch or document ❸ letter; correspondence; paper; document:密～ confidential documents; classified papers /要～ important document /抄～ duplicate; copy /附～ annex

件子 jiànzi 〈方言〉piece

建[1] jiàn ❶ build; construct; erect:新～一片楼房 erect a number of new buildings /兴～居民点 start building a residential area /扩～ extend; expand /改～ reconstruct; rebuild /修～ build; construct ❷ establish; set up; found:创～ found; create /筹～歌舞团 prepare to set up a song and dance ensemble ❸ propose; put forward; advocate:～策 offer advice; give counsel

建[2] Jiàn Fujian Province

建安 Jiàn'ān Jian'an, title of the reign (190-220) of Liu Xie (刘协,181-234), 12th and last emperor of the East Han Dynasty, reverently entitled Han Xiandi (汉献帝) after death:～文学 Literature of the Jian'an Period (noted for its vigour and power, as represented by the work of Cao Cao 曹操, Cao Pi 曹丕, Cao Zhi 曹植 and the Seven Talented Writers) /～风骨 the vigorous and powerful style of Jian'an Literature

建安七子 Jiàn'ān Qīzǐ Seven Talented Writers of the Jian'an Period (The seven writers are: Kong Rong 孔融, Chen Lin 陈琳, Wang Can 王粲, Xu Gan 许幹, Ruan Yu 阮瑀, Ying Yang 应玚, and Liu Zhen 刘桢)

建白 jiànbái 〈书面〉put forward (a proposal); express (one's views):一年来政协向政府～甚多。The CPPCC has put forward quite a number of proposals to the government over the past year.

建柏 jiànbǎi *also* "福建柏" fújiànbǎi 〈植物〉*Fokienia hodginsii*

建材 jiàncái (short for 建筑材料) building materials:～工业 building materials industry

建党 jiàndǎng ❶ found or form a political party ❷ Party-building:～路线 line for Party-building

建档 jiàndàng place (sth.) on file; set up a (new) file

建都 jiàndū found a capital; make (a place) the capital:很多王朝曾在西安～。Many dynasties set their capital in Xi'an. /明清～北京。The Ming and Qing dynasties made Beijing their capitals.

建盖 jiàngài construct; build:～住宅楼 build residential (*or* apartment) buildings

建功 jiàngōng do a deed of merit; perform meritorious service:～立业 render meritorious service and make a distinguished career

建馆 jiànguǎn set up an embassy, a museum, etc.

建国 jiànguó ❶ found a state; establish a state:中华人民共和国～五十周年 fiftieth anniversary of the founding of the People's Republic of China /～初期 in the early days of our republic ❷ build up a country:勤俭～ build up our country through diligence and frugality /～方略 plan for national development

建交 jiànjiāo establish diplomatic relations:～联合公报 joint communique on the establishment of diplomatic relations /～国 country having diplomatic relations (with China) /～谈判 negotiation for establishing diplomatic relations

建醮 jiànjiào perform a Taoist ritual for departed souls

建军 jiànjūn ❶ found an army ❷ army building:～路线 line for army building /～原则 principles of army building

建军节 Jiànjūnjié Army Day (1 August)

建兰 jiànlán *also* "兰花" lánhuā 〈植物〉sword-leaved cymbidium (*Cymbidium ensifolium*)

建立 jiànlì ❶ build; start; found; set up:～家庭 set up a family /～实验室 build a laboratory /～新的生活 start a new life /～起一支教学队伍 organise a contingent of teaching staff /～统一战线 form a

J

united front /～一座革命烈士纪念碑 erect a monument to revolutionary martyrs ❷ establish; build up:～独立完整的工业体系 establish an independent and integrated (*or* comprehensive) industrial system /～胜利的信心 build up confidence in victory /～功勋 perform meritorious deeds /～威信 foster one's prestige /～各项规章制度 work out rules and regulations of all kinds /～生产责任制 initiate a system of production responsibility

建漆 jiànqī ❶ Fujian lacquer ❷ Fujian lacquerware

建绒 jiànróng velvet; velour

建设 jiànshè build; construct:经济～ economic construction /～社会主义 build socialism /加强国防～ strengthen national defence /～一支人数众多的科学技术队伍 build up a large contingent of scientific and technical personnel /大搞四化～ make an all-out effort for the four modernizations /城乡～ urban and rural development /～成本 construction cost /～周期 construction cycle / ～银行 Construction Bank

建设部 jiànshèbù Ministry of Construction

建设省 Jiànshèshěng (Japan) Ministry of Construction

建设性 jiànshèxìng constructive; positive:～批评 constructive criticism /～意见 positive idea /这次会谈是坦率和友好的,也是富有～的。This talk is very constructive as well as frank and cordial.

建树 jiànshù make a contribution; contribute:对发展人文科学有所～ contribute to the development of humanistic studies / 颇有～ have many attainments to one's credit /他在生物工程学方面的～很多。He has made a great contribution in genetic engineering.

建团 jiàntuán build up the League (i. e. the Communist Youth League)

建文 Jiànwén Jianwen, title of the reign (1399-1402) of Zhu Yunwen (朱允炆), 2nd emperor of the Ming Dynasty, entitled Ming Huidi (明惠帝) after death: ～帝 Emperor Jianwen

建言 jiànyán 〈书面〉 state (one's views and proposals); offer advice or suggestions:听众常对办好广播事业～。Listeners often offer their views on how to improve broadcasting.

建窑 Jiànyáo *Jianyao*, a well-known darkish porcelain of the Song Dynasty

建议 jiànyì propose; suggest:合理化～ rationalization proposal /反～ counterproposal /～参观博物馆 suggest a visit to the museum /～尽早开始 propose an early start /～成立老干部俱乐部 propose to set up a veterans' club /大夫～我休养一个时期。The doctor suggested that I rest for a period. /采纳了他的～ accept his suggestion /拒绝考虑一项～ turn down a suggestion /根据他的～ at his suggestion; on his suggestion /三点～ three-point proposal

建议价格 jiànyì jiàgé recommended price

建元 jiànyuán ❶ first reign title after the founding of a dynasty ❷ founding of a state

建造 jiànzào build; construct; make:～这条公路花了三年时间。It took three years to construct this highway.

建账 jiànzhàng keep accounts

建政 jiànzhèng build up political power

建制 jiànzhì organizational system:部队～ organizational system of the army /县级～ organizational system of a county /～部队〈军事〉 organic unit

建置 jiànzhì set up; install

建筑 jiànzhù build; construct; erect:～高速公路 construct a superhighway /～铁路 build a railway /～法规 building law /～公司 building company /～标准化 standardization of construction /～材料定额 building material consumption norm /～工程定额 construction project quota /宏伟的～ magnificent structure /唐代～ building of the Tang Dynasty /～群 architectural complex /上层～ superstructure /人民大会堂是首都最宏伟的～之一。The Great Hall of the People is one of the most magnificent buildings in Beijing.

建筑材料 jiànzhù cáiliào building materials

建筑工程学 jiànzhù gōngchéngxué architectural engineering

建筑工地 jiànzhù gōngdì construction site

建筑工人 jiànzhù gōngrén construction worker

建筑红线 jiànzhù hóngxiàn property line

建筑设计 jiànzhù shèjì architectural design

建筑物 jiànzhùwù building; structure:这一～具有历史意义。This building is of historical importance.

建筑学 jiànzhùxué art of architecture:他主修～学。He majored in architecture.

建筑业 jiànzhùyè building industry

建筑装饰 jiànzhù zhuāngshì architectural ornament or decoration

楗 jiàn 〈书面〉 ❶ door bar; door bolt ❷ materials (e. g. bamboo, wood, stone, earth, etc.) used to stop the breaching of a dike

踺 jiàn

踺子 jiànzi 〈体育〉 somersault:～后空翻 backward somersault in the air

毽 jiàn shuttlecock

毽子 jiànzi shuttlecock:踢～ kick the shuttlecock (as a game)

键 jiàn ❶〈机械〉 key:轴～ shaft key ❷〈书面〉 metal bolt (of a door) ❸ key (of a typewriter, piano, etc.):琴～ key (on a musical instrument) /按～ press the key; press the button /电～ button; telegraph key ❹〈化学〉 bond:电价～ electrovalent bond /共价～ covalent bond

键槽 jiàncáo 〈机械〉 keyway; key slot; key seat:～插刀 key-way tool /～铣床 keyseater

键合 jiànhé 〈化学〉 bonding

键控 jiànkòng keying; key-drive:～继电器〈电工〉 key relay /～开关〈电工〉 detachable key switch /～器〈电子〉 keyer /～管〈电子〉 keyer tube

键盘 jiànpán keyboard; fingerboard:打字机～ keyboard of a typewriter /计算机～ computer keyboard /钢琴～ piano fingerboard

键盘乐器 jiànpán yuèqì keyboard instrument

健 jiàn ❶ healthy; robust; strong:康～ healthy; in good health /雄～ robust; vigorous; energetic /刚～ strong and energetic; robust /保～ health protection; health care ❷ strengthen; toughen; fortify; invigorate:～脑 be good for the brain /～肾 invigorate the function of the kidney ❸ be strong in; be good at:～饭 healthy appetite /～羡 admire very much

健步 jiànbù (walk with) vigorous strides:～登上主席台 mount the rostrum with vigorous steps

健步如飞 jiànbù-rúfēi walk as if on wings; walk quickly and vigorously:年过七旬,依然～。Though he is over seventy, he still walks vigorously.

健存 jiàncún (of a person of advanced age) be still living and in good health:许多同辈相继去世,～的屈指可数。Many of his contemporaries died one after another, and the number of those still living can be counted on the fingers of one hand.

健啖 jiàndàn 〈书面〉 have an enormous appetite; be fond of eating

健斗 jiàndòu be good at fighting

健儿 jiàn'ér ❶ valiant fighter:在战火里锻炼出来的～,是不知什么叫疲劳的。Dauntless fighters tempered in war make nothing of fatigue. ❷ good athlete:体育～为祖国争得了荣誉。Good athletes have won honour for the motherland.

健将 jiànjiàng ❶ master; expert:文坛～ master in the world of letters /这位经理手下有几员～。There are several experts working under this manager. ❷ master of a sport; master sportsman; ace player:体操～ master gymnast /足球～ top-notch footballer /网球～ ace tennis player

健捷 jiànjié vigorous and swift:～的步伐 (in) vigorous and quick steps

健康 jiànkāng ❶ health; physique:～检查 health check-up /提高～水平 improve one's health condition /我近来身子～多了。I'm in much better shape (*or* health) recently. /那老翁虽已八十五岁高龄,但仍很～。The man is still sound in mind and limb even though he is eighty-five. /让我们举杯祝李教授～长寿! Let's drink to the health of Professor Li! ❷ healthy; fit; sound:～的思想 sound idea; wholesome thought /～的生活方式 healthy life style /～高尚的娱乐 healthy and noble recreation /为祖国语言的纯洁～而斗争 strive for the purity and soundness of the mother tongue

健康证明书 jiànkāng zhèngmíngshū health certificate

健朗 jiànlang hale and hearty; healthy and strong:他已经七十开外了,可是还很～。Though already on the wrong side of seventy, he is still hale and hearty.

健美 jiànměi strong and handsome; vigorous and graceful:体型～ graceful figure /～的青春 vigorous and lovely youth

健美操 jiànměicāo callisthenics; body-building exercise:优美的～表演 graceful performance of callisthenics

健美运动 jiànměi yùndòng body-building:越来越多的人渐渐喜欢上了～。More and more people have come to like body-building.

健全 jiànquán ❶ sound; sane; healthy; perfect:身心～ sound in mind and body /头脑～ right mind /～的发展 healthy development /制度不～ irregular system /有～的体魄,才有～的头脑。A sound mind dwells in a sound body. /他神经不～。He is out of his mind. /没有～的法制,不可能有～的民主。Without a sound legal system, there can't be sound democracy. ❷ strengthen; improve; amplify; perfect:～法制 perfect the legal system /～管理制度 improve the management system /～民主集中制 strengthen democratic centralism /建立和～人民调解组织 establish and amplify people's mediating organizations

健身 jiànshēn keeping fit; body-building:每天清晨,孩子们都做～操。The children do their daily dozen early in the morning.

健身房 jiànshēnfáng gymnasium; gym; fitness centre:我们学院～设备不够。There is a lack (*or* shortage) of equipment in the college gymnasium.

健身器 jiànshēnqì 〈体育〉fitness or body-building equipment

健身球 jiànshēnqiú ball for health — a kind of small ball used by aged people to improve health (by putting two such balls on one palm and using the five fingers to cause them to rotate and revolve either clockwise or counter-clockwise)

健身运动 jiànshēn yùndòng body-building

健实 jiànshí sturdy; strong and healthy; robust:～的身躯 of sturdy build

健讼 jiànsòng 〈书面〉be litigious

健谈 jiàntán be a good talker; be a brilliant conversationalist:这位老人说古论今,很是～。The elderly gentleman is a good talker, speaking on a variety of subjects, past and present.

健忘 jiànwàng forgetful; having a bad memory:我真～! I have such a bad memory! /这才几天的事? 想不到老兄如此～! This happened only a couple of days before! I'm surprised you seem so forgetful. /我要把这些事记下来,因为我很～。I'll write those things down, as I have a memory like a sieve.

健忘症 jiànwàngzhèng 〈医学〉amnesia

健旺 jiànwàng healthy and vigorous:青少年时期正是身体、精力～时期,要努力学习。Young people are in the healthy and vigorous period of their lives and should therefore study hard.

健胃药 jiànwèiyào stomachic tonic

健在 jiànzài 〈书面〉(of a person of advanced age) be still living and in good health:参加那次会议的各国领导人,现在只有这一位还～。Of those national leaders who attended the international meeting, he is the only one who is still living and enjoys good health.

健壮 jiànzhuàng healthy and strong; robust:～的运动员 robust athlete /～的体魄 strong body /～的胳膊 sinewy arm /～粗大的手 big horny hands

腱

jiàn 〈生理〉tendon:肌～ tendon /筋～ tendon

腱瘤 jiànliú 〈医学〉tenontophyma

腱膜 jiànmó 〈生理〉aponeurosis

腱鞘 jiànqiào 〈生理〉tendon sheath

腱鞘囊肿 jiànqiào nángzhǒng 〈医学〉ganglion

腱鞘切除术 jiànqiào qiēchúshù 〈医学〉tenosynovectomy

腱鞘炎 jiànqiàoyán 〈医学〉tenosynovitis

腱撕裂 jiànsīliè 〈医学〉pulled tendon

腱炎 jiànyán 〈医学〉tenonitis; tenontitis; tenositis

腱子 jiànzi (beef or mutton) shank:他爱吃牛～肉。He likes to eat beef shank.

jiāng

将(將)

jiāng ❶〈书面〉support; take; bring:携～家属 bring one's family /挈妇～雏 take along the woman and child ❷ take care of (one's health): *see* "～息" ❸〈方言〉(animals) give birth to; breed:～羔 bear a kid /～驹 give birth to a foal ❹〈书面〉do sth.; deal with; handle (a matter): *see* "～事" ❺ (in chess) check:～死 checkmate /打～ corner the check /吃～ discover check; beat and check; capture the check ❻ put sb. on the spot:我们把他～住了。We've got him there. ❼ incite; challenge; spur; prod:只需几句话一～,他就会干。Just a few words will incite him to action. /他很有主意,你再～他也没用。He knows his own mind. It is useless trying to egg him on. ❽〈介词〉(often used in idioms or dialects) with; by means of; by:～功折罪 expiate one's crime by good deeds /恩～仇报 requite kindness with enmity /～鸡蛋碰石头 dash an egg against a stone ❾〈介词〉*used to introduce the object before the verb*:～书拿来 bring the book; have the book brought here /～门关上 shut the door; have the door shut /～精华与糟粕分开 separate the essence from the dross ❿ be going to; be about to; will; shall:行～就木 have one foot in the grave /天～下雨。It's going to rain. /会议～开始。The meeting is about to begin. /天～黄昏。It's getting dark. /计划～提前完成。The plan will be finished ahead of schedule. ⓫ besides; and; also: *see* "～信～疑" ⓬〈助词〉*used between a verb and an objective complement*:做～起来 start to work; get going /拿～出去 bring out /哭～起来 begin to weep /走～进去 get into the room ⓭ (Jiāng) a surname

see also jiàng; qiāng

将才 jiāngcái just now; a moment ago:他～还在这里,怎么一会儿就不见了? He was here a moment ago, how come he disappeared all of a sudden?

see also jiàngcái

将次 jiāngcì 〈书面〉be about to; be going to:正当此项工作～完成之际,又交来了另一项工作。When this task was about to be completed, another one was assigned.

将错就错 jiāngcuò-jiùcuò leave a mistake uncorrected and make the best of it; leave an error alone:这条信息有误,可他还是～地传给了我。Although fully aware that the information was not quite reliable, he passed it on to me without warning me of the fact.

将功补过 jiānggōng-bǔguò make amends for one's faults by good deeds:他想要～,报效国家。He wants to work off a demerit, so as better to serve his country.

将功赎罪 jiānggōng-shúzuì *also* "将功折罪" atone for a crime by meritorious acts; expiate one's crime by good deeds:凡是已经做过坏事的人们,赶快停止作恶,悔过自新,准其～。Those who have been doing evil should immediately stop, repent and start anew, and we will give them a chance to make amends for their crimes by good deeds. /对于罪犯,我们的方针是立功者可以～。Our policy concerning the criminals is that those who have performed meritorious deeds can have their crimes mitigated.

将护 jiānghù 〈书面〉take good care of

将计就计 jiāngjì-jiùjì turn sb.'s trick against him; beat sb. at his own game:何不～,诱敌上钩? Why not try to turn the enemy's ruse to advantage and lure him into the trap?

将将 jiāngjiāng 〈方言〉just:不多不少,～装满一瓶 not more, not less, just enough to fill up a bottle /这次考试他～及格。He just passed the examination.

将近 jiāngjìn close to; nearly; approximately; almost:～完成 near completion /～半夜了。It was almost midnight. /他～七十岁了。He is close to (*or* on) seventy. /～年底,街上人来人往,特别热闹。Towards the end of the year, the streets are a scene of hustle and bustle.

将就 jiāngjiu make do with; make the best of; put up with:我这件棉袄可以～着再穿一个冬天。I can make do with this cotton-padded coat for another winter. /～着在这里过一夜吧,明天给你找别的地方。Put up with this for one night and I'll try to find you another place tomorrow. /在家里的时候,母亲事事～她,把她娇养惯了。At home, mother used to pamper and spoil her.

将军 jiāngjūn ❶ (in chess) check ❷ put on the spot; embarrass; discomfit; challenge:他们将了我一军,要我当众唱歌。They put me in a fix by asking me to sing in public. ❸ general ❹ high-ranking military officer

将军肚 jiāngjūndù 〈戏谑〉pot-belly; big belly; beer belly

将来 jiānglái future:美好的～ bright future /在可以预见的～ in the foreseeable future /在不远的～人们生活会更幸福。In the near future (*or* in the not too distant future) people will lead an even happier life. /这里～是本市的商业区。Our city's business centre will be here.

将勤补拙 jiāngqín-bǔzhuō make up for lack of skill with or by industry

将事 jiāngshì 〈书面〉handle affairs; deal with matters:慎重～ manage (*or* conduct) affairs carefully

将息 jiāngxī rest; recuperate:我劝他安心～,待康复后再去上班。I advised him to stay at home to have a good rest and not to go to work until fully recovered.

将心比心 jiāngxīn-bǐxīn put oneself in another's place or shoes: ~,你说,我应该怎么办? Put yourself in my place, and tell me what I should do.
将心换心 jiāngxīn-huànxīn win the hearts of others by sincerity: 我们应该推诚相见,~。We must open our hearts to each other in all sincerity.
将信将疑 jiāngxìn-jiāngyí half believing, half doubting; hover between doubt and belief: 对他的话,我~。I take him half seriously and half skeptically. *or* I only half believe what he says.
将养 jiāngyǎng rest and recuperate; convalesce: 你刚做完手术,还需~~。You need a good rest after the operation.
将要 jiāngyào be going to; will; shall: 我们~开会讨论那个问题。We are going to call a meeting to discuss the problem. /他不久~毕业了。He will soon finish school.
将欲取之,必先与之 jiāng yù qǔ zhī, bì xiān yǔ zhī give in order to take: 关于丧失土地的问题,常有这样的情形,就是只有丧失才能不丧失,这是"~"的原则。As for loss of territory, it often happens that only by loss can loss be avoided; this is the principle of "give in order to take".

螿(蟼) jiāng *see* "寒螿" hánjiāng

鳉(鱂) jiāng 〈动物〉 killifish

浆(漿) jiāng

❶ thick liquid: 豆~ soya-bean milk /泥~ mud; slurry /岩~ megma /血~ blood plasma /脑~ brains /糖~ syrup /纸~ paper pulp /~皮子 skin (*or* skim) of the milk ❷ starch: ~床单 starch bedsheets /上~〈纺织〉 sizing; starching /把衬衫领子~一下 have the shirt's collar starched
see also jiàng
浆板 jiāngbǎn (of papermaking) pulp board
浆度 jiāngdù (of papermaking) degree of beating (in making pulp)
浆果 jiāngguǒ 〈植物〉 berry
浆膜 jiāngmó 〈生理〉 serosa; serous coat
浆膜炎 jiāngmóyán 〈医学〉 scrositis
浆砌 jiāngqì build by laying bricks or stones one layer after another
浆纱 jiāngshā 〈纺织〉 sizing: ~机 sizing machine; slasher
浆洗 jiāngxǐ wash and starch: 靠~度日 live on washing and starching /衣服~得很干净。The clothes are washed and starched clean.
浆液 jiāngyè ❶〈纺织〉 size ❷ serum
浆纸机 jiāngzhǐjī (of papermaking) coating machine

江 jiāng

❶ river: 在~心 in the middle of a river /领~ navigate a ship on a river /沿~ along the river; littoral; riparian ❷ (Jiāng) the Changjiang or Yangtze River: 下~ lower reaches of the Yangtze River /~淮 Yangtze-Huaihe Valley /~汉 Yangtze-Hanshui Valley ❸ (Jiāng) a surname
江岸 jiāng'àn river bank
江北 Jiāngběi ❶ areas north of the lower reaches of the Yangtze River ❷ north of the Yangtze River
江潮 jiāngcháo tide at a river mouth
江东 Jiāngdōng 〈旧语〉 lower reaches of the Yangtze River : ~父老 elders of one's native region (*or* place); old country folks
江段 jiāngduàn section of a river
江防 jiāngfáng ❶ preventive project or works against flood along a river, esp. along the Yangtze River ❷ defence along the Yangtze River: ~工事 defence works along the Yangtze
江干 jiānggān 〈书面〉 river bank; along the river
江河日下 jiānghé-rìxià go from bad to worse; be on the decline: 国力衰微,令人有~之感。The decline of national power made one feel that the country was going to the dogs.
江湖 jiānghú ❶ rivers and lakes ❷ all corners of the country: 流落~ lead a vagrant life /走~ tramp from place to place /闯~ make a living wandering from place to place as an acrobat, etc. ❸ itinerant entertainers, quacks, etc.: ~郎中 quack; mountebank
江湖好汉 jiānghú hǎohàn valorous man of the wide world; Robin Hood (of the rivers and lakes)
江湖骗子 jiānghú piànzi swindler; charlatan
江湖气 jiānghúqì ❶ be loyal to a brotherhood or fraternity ❷ given to braggadocio ❸ slick; wise in the ways of the world
江湖医生 jiānghú yīshēng quack; mountebank
江湖艺人 jiānghú yìrén itinerant entertainer
江郎才尽 Jiāngláng-cáijìn Jianglang written out — a writer whose creative powers are exhausted: 这位作家如今已是~了。The writer has exhausted his creative powers by now.
江蓠 jiānglí ❶〈植物〉 *Gracilaria confervoides* ❷〈古语〉 a kind of vanilla
江流 jiāngliú river; waters; current; flow: 湍急的~ rapid current /滚滚~ surging waters
江轮 jiānglún river steamer
江米 jiāngmǐ polished glutinous rice
江米酒 jiāngmǐjiǔ *also* "酒酿" jiǔniàng; "醪糟" láozāo fermented glutinous rice
江米纸 jiāngmǐzhǐ paper made of glutinous rice
江南 Jiāngnán ❶ areas south of the lower reaches of the Yangtze River ❷ south of the Yangtze River
江南机器制造总局 Jiāngnán Jīqì Zhìzào Zǒngjú Jiangnan Arsenal, a military enterprise established in Shanghai in 1865
江山 jiāngshān ❶ rivers and mountains; land; landscape: ~如画 picturesque landscape; beautiful scenery /~不老 eternity of rivers and mountains — wishing sb. a long life /~如此多娇,引无数英雄竞折腰。The land so rich in beauty Has made countless heroes bow in homage. ❷ country; state power: 打~ fight for state power /保~ defend the country /~美人 the throne and the beauty /人民的~人民坐。The country belongs to the people and the people are its masters.
江山易改,秉性难移 jiāngshān yì gǎi, bǐngxìng nán yí *also* "江山易改,本性难移" it's easy to change rivers and mountains but hard to change a person's nature; what's bred in the bone will not go out of the flesh; a leopard cannot change his spots
江苏 Jiāngsū Jiangsu (Province)
江天 jiāngtiān vast sky over a river: ~一色 river and sky blending into one colour /热风吹雨洒~。A hot wind spatters raindrops on the sky-brooded waters.
江豚 jiāngtún *also* "江猪" 〈动物〉 black finless porpoise
江西 Jiāngxī Jiangxi (Province)
江西腊 jiāngxīlà general term for China aster
江心补漏 jiāngxīn-bǔlòu repair a leak in mid-stream — belated action when a good opportunity has already been let slip: 你是~,烦恼怨谁? Who else but yourself can you blame for missing such a good opportunity?
江鳕 jiāngxuě 〈动物〉 burbot (*Lota lota*)
江洋大盗 jiāngyáng dàdào notorious robber or pirate
江珧 jiāngyáo 〈动物〉 pen shell
江珧柱 jiāngyáozhù dried adductor of a pen shell; dried scallop
江右 Jiāngyòu old name for Jiangxi Province
江猪 jiāngzhū *see* "江豚"
江孜 Jiāngzī Gyangze, a county in the south of the Tibet Autonomous Region
江左 Jiāngzuǒ 〈旧语〉 south of the lower reaches of the Yangtze River: 偏安~ be content to maintain a regime much reduced in territory in areas south of the lower reaches of the Yangtze River

茳 jiāng

茳芏 jiāngdù *also* "咸水草" xiánshuǐcǎo 〈植物〉 *Cyperus malaccensis* var. *brevifolius*

豇 jiāng

豇豆 jiāngdòu cowpea
豇豆红 jiāngdòuhóng peach bloom glaze, a rare porcelain in the Qing Dynasty

礓 jiāng ❶ *see* "礓礤儿" ❷ *see* "砂礓" shājiāng

礓礤儿 jiāngcǎr 〈方言〉 flight of steps; stairs

僵(❶殭) jiāng

❶ stiff; rigid; numb: ~直 stiff and rigid /手脚冻~了。Hands and feet were numb with cold. ❷ deadlock; impasse; stagnation: 把关系搞~了 have the relations strained /双方的态度都很强硬,谈判有点~。With both sides sticking to their

guns, the negotiation is somewhat deadlocked. ❸〈方言〉stop smiling; look stern:他～着脸。He kept a straight face.

僵巴 jiāngba 〈口语〉stiff; rigid; numb:手都冻～了。Hands were stiff with cold.

僵板 jiāngbǎn 〈方言〉❶ stiff; rigid; inflexible:～的面孔 straight face /他～地坐在椅子上,一动不动。He sits on the chair motionless with a stiff back. ❷ harden:～田 hardened field /～地 hardened land

僵瓣 jiāngbàn 〈植物〉stiff petal

僵持 jiāngchí (of both parties) neither is willing to give in; refuse to budge; be at a deadlock:想办法打破～局面 attempt to break the deadlock /两种意见～不下。Neither would yield to the other in their views. /两国关系不能老这样～下去。Relations between the two countries should not remain locked forever in a stalemate.

僵化 jiānghuà become rigid; ossify:头脑～ ossified way of thinking; stereotyped thinking /它的肢体已经～。Its limbs are already rigid. /骄傲自满只会使思想～。Arrogance and conceit will ossify one's thinking.

僵局 jiāngjú deadlock; impasse; stalemate:裁军谈判陷入～。The disarmament negotiations have reached an impasse.

僵冷 jiānglěng numb with cold:在雪地里站了半天,手脚～。After I stood in the snowy field for quite a long while, both my hands and feet were numb with cold.

僵仆 jiāngpū (body) become stiff and fall down

僵尸 jiāngshī (rigid) corpse:政治～ political mummy

僵死 jiāngsǐ dead; rigid; ossified:～的教条 ossified dogma

僵卧 jiāngwò lie stiff and rigid:～的死尸 corpse lying stiff and rigid

僵硬 jiāngyìng ❶ stiff:手指～ feel stiff in the fingers /～的冻土 hardened frozen earth ❷ rigid; hidebound; inflexible:～的公式 rigid formula /～的态度 inflexible attitude /保守～ conservative and hidebound /～的规定 hard and fast rules /他的舞蹈动作～。His dance movements are stiff and awkward.

僵直 jiāngzhí stiff and rigid; unbending

僵滞 jiāngzhì dull and rigid; inflexible:～的眼光 glassy stare /他平时灵活的舌头,这会儿变得～了。How come his glib tongue is tied now?

疆

jiāng ❶ boundary; border; frontier:边～ border area; frontier region /海～ coastal areas and territorial waters /无～ boundless ❷ (Jiāng) (short for 新疆) Xinjiang

疆场 jiāngchǎng battlefield:驰骋～ gallop across the battlefield; perform outstanding exploits on the battlefield /久历～的老将军 senior battle-hardened general /战死～ die a hero on the battlefield (*or* in battle)

疆界 jiāngjiè boundary; border:划分～ delimit the boundary

疆土 jiāngtǔ territory:～辽阔 vast territory /边防部队严守～。Frontier guards keep close watch over the country's territory.

疆埸 jiāngyì 〈书面〉❶ (of fields) ridge ❷ border region

疆域 jiāngyù territory; domain:～广大,资源丰富 vast territory and rich resources

缰(繮)

jiāng reins; halter:脱～之马 runaway horse; 〈比喻〉uncontrollable; out of hand /信马由～ ride with lax reins

缰绳 jiāngsheng reins; halter:收紧～ draw (*or* pull on) reins

姜[1](薑)

jiāng ginger

姜[2]

Jiāng a surname

姜花 jiānghuā ginger lily; garland flower

姜黄 jiānghuáng ❶〈植物〉turmeric ❷ (of facial colour) gingerish; sallow:病人脸色～,气息微弱。The patient's face was gingerish, and he was breathing weakly.

姜夔 Jiāng Kuí Jiang Kui (formerly translated as Chiang K'ui, c.1155-c.1221), *ci* poet and musician of the Southern Song Dynasty

姜片虫 jiāngpiànchóng fasciolopsis:～病 fasciolopsiasis

姜是老的辣 jiāng shì lǎode là old ginger is hotter than new — old hands are better than greenhorns:俗话说"～",这位老干部考虑问题的确沉稳周到得多。True to the saying that old hands are better than novices, this veteran cadre considered problems with far greater prudence and thoughtfulness.

姜太公 Jiāng Tàigōng Jiang Taigong or Grandpa Jiang, popular name for Jiang Ziya (姜子牙), legendary character modelled upon Lü Shang (吕尚), or Lü Wang (吕望), statesman and strategist who became adviser and prime minister to King Wen of Zhou (周文王), at the age of 80 (hence the popular name 太公), and helped the young King Wu (周武王) overthrow the Shang Dynasty and establish the Zhou Dynasty:～在此,百无禁忌。〈俗语〉With Jiang Taigong here, all taboos are invalid — you can now say or do whatever you want to.

姜太公钓鱼,愿者上钩 Jiāng Tàigōng diàoyú, yuànzhě shànggōu fish like Jiang Taigong, who cast a hookless and baitless line for the fish that wants to be caught — ask for willing victim or collaborator

姜汤 jiāngtāng ginger tea

姜芋 jiāngyù 〈植物〉*Canna edulis*

姜汁啤酒 jiāngzhī píjiǔ ginger beer

jiǎng

蒋(蔣)

Jiǎng a surname

蒋帮 Jiǎngbāng 〈贬义〉Chiang clique

蒋介石 Jiǎng Jièshí Chiang Kai-shek (1887-1975), leader of the Kuomintang (KMT)

蒋经国 Jiǎng Jīngguó Chiang Ching-kuo (1910-1988), leader of the KMT on Taiwan and son of Chiang Kai-shek

蒋宋孔陈 Jiǎng-Sòng-Kǒng-Chén Chiang Kai-shek (蒋介石), T.V. Soong (宋子文), H.H. Kung (孔祥熙), Chen Kuo-fu (陈果夫) and Chen Li-fu (陈立夫) (C.C.), representing the four ruling families of the KMT from the 1930's to 1949

桨(槳)

jiǎng oar:荡起双～ pull on two oars; go boating

奖(獎)

jiǎng ❶ praise; commend; encourage; reward:嘉～ commend; praise /褒～ praise and honour /过～ overpraise; make an undeserved compliment /～某人勋章一枚 award sb. a medal ❷ award; bonus; prize; reward:颁～ hand out prizes /受～ receive a prize /得～人 prize-winner; award-winner /评～ decide on awards through discussion or evaluation /特等～ top grade award /有～销售 prize sale /有～储蓄 prize deposit /有～购物 prize purchase /他在比赛中得一等～。He won first prize in the tournament. /她得本年度最佳编剧～。She received an award for the best scenario of the year.

奖杯 jiǎngbēi cup (as a prize):赢得～ win the cup

奖惩 jiǎngchéng rewards and punishments:～制度 system of rewards and penalties /～严明 strictly abide by the regulations concerning rewards and disciplinary sanctions

奖金 jiǎngjīn money award; bonus; premium:发放～ distribute bonuses /年终～ year-end bonus /～制度 bonus system; premium system /质量～ bonus for quality /季度～ season bonus /～工资 bonus wages /～额 amount of bonus /～税 tax on bonuses

奖励 jiǎnglì encourage and reward; award; reward:～先进生产者 reward advanced workers; give awards to advanced workers /受到～ be encouraged and rewarded /物质～ material incentive /精神～ moral encouragement /超产～ reward for overfulfilling the production quota /～工资 premium (*or* reward) wages; incentive pay /～建议制度 incentive-suggestion system

奖牌 jiǎngpái medal (as an award)

奖品 jiǎngpǐn prize; award; trophy

奖旗 jiǎngqí (silk) banner (as an award)

奖勤罚懒 jiǎngqín-fálǎn reward the diligent and punish the lazy

奖劝 jiǎngquàn encourage and advise:诱掖～ guide and help, encourage and reward

奖券 jiǎngquàn lottery ticket:出售～ sell lottery tickets /购买～ purchase lottery tickets

奖赏 jiǎngshǎng award; reward; premium:～有功人员 award those who have performed meritorious deeds

奖饰 jiǎngshì 〈书面〉praise; commend:过于～,愧不敢当。It is a praise I don't very well deserve.

奖售 jiǎngshòu ❶ sales incentive; prize sale; reward sale:现在商店里作兴～。Nowadays reward sales are quite popular in shops and stores. ❷ sell (sth. in short supply or at reduced prices) as a re-

J

ward:把粮食卖给国家的农民可以～低价化肥。The farmers who sell their grain to the state can buy chemical fertilizer at a discount.

奖台 jiǎngtái temporary platform or stage on which prizes are awarded to the winners; presentation stage or platform

奖许 jiǎngxǔ praise; give encouragement

奖学金 jiǎngxuéjīn scholarship; (student) grant; exhibition

奖掖 jiǎngyè 〈书面〉reward and promote; encourage by promoting and rewarding:～后进 encourage and promote one's juniors

奖挹 jiǎngyì 〈书面〉reward and promote:大加～ reward profusely

奖优罚劣 jiǎngyōu-fáliè *also* "奖优惩劣" reward the good and punish the bad

奖誉 jiǎngyù ❶ honour:授予他以人民艺术家的～。Award him the honour (*or* Honour him with the title) of People's Artist. ❷ praise; award:深受～ be highly praised

奖章 jiǎngzhāng medal; decoration:金质～ gold medal /银质～ silver medal /铜质～ bronze medal /纪念～ commemorative medal /～获得者 medalist

奖状 jiǎngzhuàng certificate of merit or award; citation; honorary credential; diploma:他一生得了不少～。He has been awarded quite a number of certificates of merit during his lifetime.

讲(講) jiǎng ❶ speak; talk; say; tell:～事情的经过 tell what has actually happened /～笑话 crack a joke /～成绩,也～缺点 talk about shortcomings as well as achievements /一本～中国古代文学的书 a book dealing with ancient Chinese Literature /～几点意见 make a few remarks /～心里话 bare one's heart; open one's heart /背后～别人的坏话 speak ill of others behind their backs /用英语来～吧。Say it in English. /他对那一点～得特别详细。He dwelt upon that point in great detail. ❷ explain; make clear; interpret:把道理～清楚 state the reasons clearly /你能把这条规则给我～一下吗? Can you explain this rule to me? /这段话可以有两种～法。This passage can be interpreted in two ways. ❸ discuss; negotiate:～条件 negotiate the terms /接受工作不～条件 accept a task unconditionally ❹ as far as sth. is concerned; as to; concerning; with regard to:从效果来～ with regard to effect /～能力,我不如你。As to ability, I am not your match. *or* I can't match your ability. /～质量,这家工厂的产品是信得过的。When it comes to the quality of product, you can trust that factory. ❺ stress; pay attention to; consider; be particular about:～团结 stress unity /～质量 pay attention to quality /不～情面 have no consideration for anyone's sensibilities; be inexorable /不～政策 in disregard of policy /～吃～穿 be particular about food and clothing /～交情 do things for the sake of friendship

讲道 jiǎngdào preach; sermonize:听牧师～ listen to (*or* attend) a minister's sermon

讲法 jiǎngfa ❶ way of saying things; wording; diction; term:"吝啬鬼"换一个～就是"守财奴"。Another term for "miser" is "niggard". ❷ opinion; understanding; version; statement:关于埃及金字塔怎么建成的问题,现在～不一。People have different opinions concerning the building of Egypt's pyramids.

讲稿 jiǎnggǎo draft or text of a speech; lecture notes:写～ make a draft of a speech /念～ read out lecture notes /说话不用～ speak without notes

讲古 jiǎnggǔ tell legends in the past:孩子们最爱听老辈～。Children love to listen to older people telling stories about legendary heroes.

讲和 jiǎnghé make peace; settle a dispute; become reconciled; be conciliated:停战～ cease fire and make peace /使战争双方～ help the two warring sides reach a settlement /经过劝解,两人～了。The two became reconciled after mediation.

讲话 jiǎnghuà ❶ speak; talk; address:讲心里话 speak one's mind /讲老实话 tell the truth /敢～ dare to air one's views /在群众大会上～ address the mass rally/孩子在学～。The baby is learning to speak. /他很会～。He's a good talker. *or* He has a ready tongue. ❷ blame; censure:你这样搞特殊,难怪人家要～了。You're so keen on seeking personal privileges. Small wonder people take you to task for this. ❸ speech; talk:鼓舞人心的～ stirring speech /令人昏昏欲睡的～ droning talk ❹ (often used in book titles) talks; guide; introduction:《在延安文艺座谈会上的～》 *Talks at the Yan'an Forum on Literature and Art* /《政治经济学～》 *A Guide to Political Economy* /《语法～》 *An Introduction to Grammar*

讲价 jiǎngjià bargain; haggle over prices:同厂家～ bargain with the manufacturer over prices /在集市上买东西要会～儿。You need to be good at haggling if you buy things at a fair.

讲价钱 jiǎng jiàqian ❶ haggle over prices ❷ negotiate terms:为人民服务不能～。It must be unconditional to serve the people.

讲解 jiǎngjiě explain; expound; explicate:这位老师～课文十分耐心。The teacher is very patient in explaining the text.

讲解员 jiǎngjiěyuán guide; interpreter; commentator; announcer

讲究 jiǎngjiu ❶ be particular about; be fussy or fastidious about; pay attention to; stress:～吃穿 be fastidious about one's food and clothing /～质量 stress quality /用词要～分寸。Pay attention to the proper choice of words. ❷ careful study:教学法大有～。Teaching methods need careful study. *or* Teaching is quite an art. /这里面的～可不是一眼就能看穿的。There's more to it than meets the eye. ❸ exquisite; superb; tasteful:～的早餐 excellent breakfast /～的服装 elegant dress /客厅的陈设很～。The lounge is tastefully furnished. /港口有几家很～的电影院。There are some splendid cinemas at the port.

讲课 jiǎngkè teach; lecture:他在我女儿学校～。He teaches in my daughter's school. /他在给甲班讲化学课。He is lecturing to Class A on chemistry. /他上午给我们讲了三堂英语课。He gave us three English lessons this morning.

讲理 jiǎnglǐ ❶ reason (with sb.); argue:你最好心平气和地同他～。You'd better reason with him calmly. ❷ listen to reason; be reasonable; be sensible:蛮不～ be impervious to reason /你不能这样不～。You mustn't be so unreasonable. /这一家人是～的。The family are quite amenable to reason.

讲论 jiǎnglùn ❶ talk about; discuss:不要在背地里～别人。Don't talk about other people behind their backs. /大家都在～这件事。The matter is on everyone's lips. ❷ deal with:这是一本～哲学的书。This is a book on philosophy.

讲面子 jiǎng miànzi care about sb.'s sensibilities:他不大～。He has no consideration for anyone's sensibilities.

讲明 jiǎngmíng explain; make clear; state explicitly:～我们的意图 explain our intention /～我们的观点 make clear our views /这一点非～不可。This point must be made quite explicit.

讲排场 jiǎng páichang put up a show; go in for ostentation and extravagance; be ostentatious; go in for pomp:结婚不要～。One should not hanker after pomp and extravagance in a wedding. /这家商场开张时大讲了一通排场。This department store put up an extravagant show on its opening day.

讲盘儿 jiǎngpánr *also* "讲盘子"〈方言〉negotiate about the price and terms

讲评 jiǎngpíng comment on; appraise:作文～ comment on students' compositions

讲情 jiǎngqíng intercede; plead (for sb.); put in a good word (for sb.):为儿子～ intercede (with sb.) for one's son /托人～ ask sb. to plead for one

讲求 jiǎngqiú be particular about; pay attention to; stress; strive for:～文明礼貌 strive for good manners /～经济效益 lay emphasis on better economic results; stress economic benefits; underline economic performance /不要太～外表。Don't pay too much attention to appearances. /产品应～质量。Stress must be placed on the quality of the products.

讲师 jiǎngshī lecturer

讲史 jiǎngshǐ 〈旧语〉telling historical stories as a folk art

讲授 jiǎngshòu lecture; impart; instruct; teach:～经史 teach classics and histories /～知识 impart knowledge /～马克思主义哲学 give lectures on Marxist philosophy

讲书 jiǎngshū explain a text; teach; lecture:学生专心地听老师～。Students are listening attentively to the teacher's explanation of the text.

讲述 jiǎngshù tell about; give an account of; recount; relate:～英雄故事 tell about heroic exploits /～家乡的巨大变化 give an account of the great changes that have happened to one's home town /她把故事详详细细地～了一番。She related the story in great detail.

讲说 jiǎngshuō explain; tell; talk about:大家坐在场院上听老张头～三国故事。People were sitting in the courtyard, listening to Lao Zhang tell stories of the Three Kingdoms.

讲台 jiǎngtái platform; dais; rostrum

讲坛 jiǎngtán ❶ platform; rostrum ❷ forum:这个博物馆是传播自然科学知识的好～。This museum is a good forum for spreading knowledge of natural science.

讲堂 jiǎngtáng lecture room; classroom

讲题 jiǎngtí ❶ explain the exercise problems:老师,您给讲讲题吧! Teacher, please explain to us the exercise problems. ❷ subject of a

lecture; topic of a speech

讲习 jiǎngxí ❶ lecture and study ❷ study; research: ～学问 academic research

讲习班 jiǎngxíbān study group

讲习所 jiǎngxísuǒ institute (for instruction or training): 农民运动～ Peasant Movement Institute (for training peasant leaders)

讲信修睦 jiǎngxìn-xiūmù keep good faith and promote amicable relations: 两国～,各保疆土。Keeping good faith with each other, the two countries are on friendly terms, each maintaining order within its own territory.

讲叙 jiǎngxù tell about; give an account of; narrate: ～他童年的经历 give an account of his childhood

讲学 jiǎngxué give lectures; deliver lectures; discourse on academic subjects: 出国～ give lectures overseas / 来华～ come to China on a lecture tour

讲演 jiǎngyǎn lecture; speech; talk: 登台～ mount the rostrum to deliver a speech / 英语～比赛 English speech contest

讲义 jiǎngyì lecture sheets; teaching materials: 他在写～。He is preparing his lecture sheets.

讲义气 jiǎng yìqi set store by personal loyalty or friendship: 他太～,损害了原则。He values personal loyalty at the expense of principles.

讲座 jiǎngzuò lecture; course of lectures: 计算机知识～ computer lessons / 电视台举办日语～。The TV station is giving lectures on Japanese.

耩

jiǎng sow with a drill: ～地 sow the land with a drill / ～豆子 sow beans with a drill

耩子 jiǎngzi 〈方言〉 drill

膙

jiǎng

膙子 jiǎngzi 〈方言〉 callosity; callus: 他手上起了～。Calluses appeared on his hands.

jiàng

酱(醬)

jiàng ❶ thick sauce or paste made from soya beans, flour, etc.: 黄～ salted and fermented soya paste / 甜面～ thick sweet paste made from fermented flour / 炸～ fried soya paste ❷ things cooked or pickled in soya sauce: ～黄瓜 pickled cucumber / ～萝卜 pickled radish / ～鸭 braised duck flavoured with soybean sauce / ～鸡 jellied chicken cooked in soy sauce ❸ cook or pickle things in soy sauce: 把鸡～一～ have the chicken cooked in soy sauce / ～点萝卜 have the radishes pickled in soy sauce ❹ sauce; paste; jam: 草莓～ strawberry jam / 蕃茄～ tomato sauce; ketchup / 辣～ hot sauce / 芝麻～ sesame butter (*or* paste) / 豆瓣～ soybean paste / 虾～ shrimp sauce / 花生～ peanut butter

酱爆鸡丁 jiàngbào jīdīng stir-fried diced chicken with soybean paste

酱菜 jiàngcài vegetables pickled in soy sauce; pickles

酱豆腐 jiàngdòufu fermented bean curd

酱坊 jiàngfáng (traditional) shop making and selling sauce, pickles, etc.; sauce and pickle shop

酱缸 jiànggāng jar or vat for making or keeping soybean paste, pickled vegetables, etc.

酱肉 jiàngròu pork cooked in soy sauce; braised pork seasoned with soy sauce

酱色 jiàngsè dark reddish brown: 我喜欢～。Dark reddish brown is my favourite colour. *or* I go for dark reddish brown.

酱油 jiàngyóu soy sauce; soy: 辣～ pungent sauce; Worchester sauce

酱园 jiàngyuán shop making and selling sauce, pickles, etc.; sauce and pickle shop

酱紫 jiàngzǐ dark reddish purple: ～色的大衣 overcoat in dark reddish purple

将(將)

jiàng ❶ general; commander; military officer: 主～ chief commander; commanding general / 良～ good general / 骁～ valiant general / 宿～ veteran general / 上～ general / 中～ lieutenant general / 少～ major general / 准～ brigadier (general) / 损兵折～ suffer heavy casualties ❷ 〈书面〉 command; lead: 韩信～兵,多多益善。When Han Xin was in command, the more troops, the better. ❸chief piece in Chinese chess

see also jiāng; qiāng

将才 jiàngcái ❶ ability to lead or command troops ❷ man with military talent; born general

see also jiāngcái

将官 jiàngguān general: 他由上校升为～。He has been promoted from colonel to general.

将官 jiàngguan high-ranking military officer: 众～到大帐听令。All high-ranking military officers, go to the commander's tent to take orders.

将领 jiànglǐng high-ranking officer; general: 三军高级～出席了今天的军事会议。High-ranking officers from the three armed services attended today's conference on military affairs.

将令 jiànglìng order (issued by the commanding general): 传～ issue the commanding general's order; pass on the commanding general's order / 领～ take orders from the commanding general

将门 jiàngmén family of a general: 出身～ come from a general's family

将门出将 jiàngmén-chūjiàng *also* "将门有将" the family of a general is bound to turn out more generals

将门虎子 jiàngmén-hǔzǐ valiant son from a general's family; capable young man of distinguished parentage

将门无犬子 jiàngmén wú quǎnzǐ 〈俗语〉 a general's family will not produce a coward of a son

将门之子 jiàngménzhīzǐ descendant of a general; person coming from a line of generals

将棋 jiàngqí *shogi*, Japanese chess

将士 jiàngshì 〈书面〉 officers and men; commanders and fighters: 全体～奋勇杀敌。All the officers and men fought bravely against the enemy.

将帅 jiàngshuài high cammanding officer: ～之才 (man with) talent to be a good general; makings of a good commander

将相 jiàngxiàng generals and ministers: ～出寒门。Generals and ministers often come from lowly families. / ～本无种,男儿自当强。Ministers or generals may not be born of distinguished ancestries; a true man should strive for self-realization. *or* No man is born to greatness; he achieves it by his own efforts.

将校 jiàngxiào collective term for generals and field officers; high-ranking military officers

将遇良材 jiàngyùliángcái meet one's equal; find one's own match; diamond cuts diamond: 棋逢对手,～。As an ace chess player meets his peer, so a general finds his own match in military talent.

将在外,君命有所不受 jiàng zài wài, jūn mìng yǒusuǒ bù shòu a general at the front may even refuse an emperor's order: 这就叫"～"。As the saying goes, when the general is out campaigning, sometimes he has to use his own discretion.

将指 jiàngzhǐ 〈书面〉 ❶ middle finger ❷ big toe

将佐 jiàngzuǒ 〈书面〉 high-ranking military officers

浆(漿)

jiàng *see* "糨" jiàng

see also jiāng

匠

jiàng ❶ craftsman; artisan: 铁～ blacksmith / 石～ stonemason / 工～ craftsman / 花～ floriculturist; gardener / 画～ artisan-painter / 小炉～ tinker / 篾～ craftsman who makes articles from bamboo strips; bambooware craftsman / 油漆～ painter / 首饰～ jeweler / 泥水～ bricklayer; tiler / 箍桶～ cooper; hooper / 泥瓦～ bricklayer; tiler; plasterer / 成衣～ tailor / 银～ silversmith / 皮～ cobbler / 漆～ lacquerware worker / 锁～ locksmith / 铜～ coppersmith / 锡～ tinsmith / 鞋～ shoemaker / 能工巧～ skilled craftsman ❷ 〈书面〉 person of remarkable achievements in a particular field; master: 文学巨～ literary giant

匠气 jiàngqì (of sculpture or painting) mediocre with no originality

匠人 jiàngrén artisan; craftsman

匠心 jiàngxīn 〈书面〉 ingenuity; craftsmanship: 独具～ show ingenuity; have great originality / 颇具～ display a lot of imagination

匠心独运 jiàngxīn-dúyùn (in art and literature) exercise one's inventive mind; give play to one's own ingenuity or creativity: 他的小说～,篇篇有特色。Each of his novels shows great originality and has

distinctive features of its own.

弶 jiàng 〈书面〉❶ trap; snare:装～捕鼠 set a trap to catch rats ❷ catch in a trap; trap:～鸟 trap a bird

虹 jiàng another pronunciation of 虹 (hóng) when it is used separately
see also hóng

洚 jiàng 〈书面〉overflow; inundate:～水 overflow of water; flood

降 jiàng ❶ go down; fall; drop; lose:升～ go up and down; rise and fall /～雪 fall of snow /气温骤～ sudden drop of temperature /体重下～ lose weight /飞机～在二号跑道上。The plane landed on runway two. ❷ lower; reduce: *see* "～温";"～雨";"～低" ❸ (Jiàng) a surname
see also xiáng

降班 jiàngbān ❶ send (a student) to a lower grade ❷ (of students) stay behind; repeat the year's work

降半旗 jiàng bànqí hoist a flag at half-mast:～致哀 fly a flag at half-staff as a sign of mourning

降尘 jiàngchén *also* "落尘" luòchén dust fall; fallen dust

降低 jiàngdī reduce; cut down; drop; lower:～成本百分之二十 reduce the cost by 20 per cent /～血压 bring down the blood pressure /～材料消耗 cut down the consumption of materials /～了声音说话 talk in a lowered voice /～要求 moderate one's demands /声音～了一点。The voice lowered a little. /气温突然～到华氏二十度。The temperature suddenly dropped to twenty degrees Fahrenheit. /他感到自己在亲友心目中的地位～了。He felt that he had been diminished in the eyes of his relatives and friends.

降调 jiàngdiào 〈语言〉falling tone; falling tune

降幅 jiàngfú (of prices, profits, income, etc.) range of decrease:今年蔬菜价格～很大。The prices of vegetables have fallen by a big margin this year.

降格 jiànggé 〈书面〉lower one's standard or status:～录取 admit sb. by lowering the standard /两国的外交关系已由大使级～为代办级。The diplomatic relations between the two countries were demoted from the level of ambassador to that of charge d'affaires.

降格以求 jiànggéyǐqiú fall back on sth. inferior to what one originally wanted; settle for a second best:他买不到卧铺票,只好～,买硬座了。He had to settle for a hard-seat ticket since no sleeper ticket was available.

降号 jiànghào 〈音乐〉flat

降级 jiàngjí ❶ reduce to a lower rank; demote:～处分 punish by demotion; impose a demotion penalty ❷ send (a student) to a lower grade:～学生 student sent to a lower grade

降价 jiàngjià lower or reduce the price; cut down the price:滞销货物～处理 sell unsalable goods at reduced prices; get rid of unmarketable goods by cutting down the price

降阶相迎 jiàngjiē-xiāngyíng go down the steps to meet (a guest); go out of one's way to welcome:他觉得对这位颇有名望的作家应该～。He felt that he should go out of his way to greet the renowned writer.

降结肠 jiàngjiécháng 〈生理〉colon descendens; descending colon

降解 jiàngjiě 〈化学〉degradation:～性 degradability /可～塑料 degradable plastic /～塔 degradation tower /～物 catabolite

降临 jiànglín 〈书面〉befall; arrive; come:夜幕～。Night fell. /严冬～。Severe winter is drawing near. /希望好运能～到自己头上。Hope that good luck might befall me.

降落 jiàngluò descend; land; alight:作紧急～ make an emergency landing /强迫～ forced landing /垂直～ vertical landing /～辅助设备 landing aid /～设备 landing equipment /一只鸟～在树枝上。A bird alighted on a branch. /灾难～人间。Disaster befell the world. /飞行员跳伞～。The pilots parachuted.

降落场 jiàngluòchǎng landing field

降落区 jiàngluòqū drop zone; dropping zone

降落伞 jiàngluòsǎn parachute

降幂 jiàngmì 〈数学〉descending power:～次序 descending order of power /～级数 series of decreasing powers

降旗 jiàngqí lower a flag

降生 jiàngshēng 〈书面〉(as of the founder of a religion, etc.) be born:公元始于传说耶稣～的那一年。The Christian era starts with the year in which Christ was said to be born.

降水 jiàngshuǐ 〈气象〉precipitation:人工～ artificial precipitation /自南至北有一～过程。There will be precipitation from the south to the north.

降水概率 jiàngshuǐ gàilǜ 〈气象〉precipitation probability

降水量 jiàngshuǐliàng (amount of) precipitation

降水区 jiàngshuǐqū precipitation area

降温 jiàngwēn ❶ lower the temperature (as in a workshop):防暑～ lower the temperature for headstroke (*or* sunstroke) prevention ❷〈气象〉drop in temperature:气象台预报今天大风～。The meteorological observatory reports a strong wind and a drop in temperature today. ❸〈比喻〉cool down; decrease:经济过热现象需要～。The economy is overheated and needs to be cooled. /旅游热已经～。The travel craze has already waned.

降香 jiàngxiāng *also* "降真香"〈植物〉*Acronychia pedunculata*

降心相从 jiàngxīn-xiāngcóng subject one's own will to the dictates of others; yield against one's own will:严峻的客观形势使这一派不得不～。The grim situation compelled the faction to submit against their will.

降雪 jiàngxuě snowfall

降雪量 jiàngxuěliàng snowfall

降血脂药 jiàngxuèzhīyào 〈药学〉antilipemic agent

降压 jiàngyā ❶〈电工〉reducing voltage; step-down:～变电站 step-down substation /～变压器 step-down transformer ❷ bring down the blood pressure:～药 hypotensive (medicine)

降压片 jiàngyāpiàn 〈药学〉hypertension pill

降雨 jiàngyǔ fall of rain; rainfall

降雨量 jiàngyǔliàng rainfall:年～ annual rainfall

降雨云带 jiàngyǔ yúndài rainbelt

降职 jiàngzhí demote

降旨 jiàngzhǐ issue an imperial edict

降志辱身 jiàngzhì-rǔshēn lower and humiliate oneself:这种～的事情我不干。I won't do anything degrading.

绛 jiàng deep red; crimson

绛紫 jiàngzǐ dark reddish purple:天边出现一片～色的云霞。A dark reddish purple cloud appears in the horizon.

强(強、彊) jiàng stubborn; obdurate; unyielding:倔～ unbending; obdurate /死～ extremely stubborn /跟他妈～个没完 keep talking back to his mother
see also qiáng; qiǎng

强嘴 jiàngzuǐ reply defiantly; answer back; talk back:不要和老人～! Don't talk back to your elders!

糨(糡) jiàng thick:粥太～。The porridge is too thick.

糨糊 jiànghu paste:打～ make paste

糨子 jiàngzi 〈口语〉paste:用～把窗户糊上 have the window pasted (with paper)

犟(勥) jiàng obstinate; stubborn; self-willed; headstrong:脾气～ headstrong /他～得很,不听劝。He is very opinionated and impervious to persuasion.

犟劲 jiàngjìn tenacious will

犟嘴 jiàngzuǐ *see* "强嘴" jiàngzuǐ

jiāo

浇[1](澆) jiāo ❶ pour (liquid on sth.); sprinkle (water on sth.):～水 sprinkle water /把火～灭 put out a fire by pouring water on it /～粪 apply manure to the fields /凉水～头 pour cold water on the head /大雨～得他全身都湿透了。He was drenched to the skin in the rain. ❷ irrigate; water:车水～地 lift water (by waterwheel) to irrigate fields /～菜 water vegetable plots ❸ cast:～铁水 cast molten iron /～铅字 type casting; type founding

浇[2](澆) jiāo 〈书面〉unkind; harsh; mean: *see* "～薄"

浇柏油机 jiāobǎiyóujī tar-dressing machine

J

浇版 jiāobǎn 〈印刷〉casting:～机 casting machine
浇包 jiāobāo 〈冶金〉casting ladle:～结瘤 ladle heel
浇薄 jiāobó 〈书面〉(of customs, manners, etc.) mean; unkind; harsh:世风～ harsh (*or* snobbish) ways of the world /人情～ unfeeling towards other people; indifferent to the feelings of others
浇补 jiāobǔ 〈冶金〉casting-on
浇灌 jiāoguàn ❶ pour; mould:～混凝土 pour concrete ❷ water; irrigate:用水库的水～稻田 use water in a reservoir to irrigate rice fields /烈士的鲜血～了这片土地。This land has been fostered by the blood of martyrs.
浇焊 jiāohàn 〈冶金〉flow welding
浇口 jiāokǒu 〈冶金〉pouring head; runner; runner pipe; running head:～杯 pouring bush or basin; runner bush or basin; runner cup /～箱 pouring box
浇冷水 jiāo lěngshuǐ *also* "泼冷水" pō lěngshuǐ pour cold water on — dampen enthusiasm; discourage:人家正在兴头上,你可别～。He is in high spirits. Don't spoil his mood.
浇漓 jiāolí 〈书面〉(of customs, manners, etc.) sophisticated and unnatural:世风～ moral degeneration of the world
浇头 jiāotou 〈方言〉gravy; sauce; dressing:～面 noodles with sauce /鸡丝～ sauce made of shredded chicken meat /牛肉～ beef sauce /排骨～ spareribs sauce
浇注 jiāozhù ❶〈冶金〉pouring; teeming; casting:开放型～ casting in open /低温～ cast cold /冷硬～ case-hardend casting /离心～ centrifugal casting /～车间 pouring hall /～钢水 pour steel /～工 pourer; caster /～块 castable /～铸型 casting molds; running castings ❷ devote; dedicate; give:他把全部心血～在教育事业上。He devoted himself heart and soul to the cause of education.
浇筑 jiāozhù 〈建筑〉pour (concrete, etc.):～的大坝 concrete-poured dam
浇铸 jiāozhù 〈冶金〉casting; pouring:～机 casting machine /金属～ metal founding /砂型～ sand casting /～版〈印刷〉cast

交[1] jiāo ❶ hand in; hand or turn over; pass on; deliver:～作文 hand in one's composition /～税款 pay tax /面～ deliver in person /把一项任务～给某人 entrust sb. with a task /～还所借用品 give back or return borrowed articles /～活 turn over a finished item /货已～齐。All goods are delivered. /把枪～出来! Hand over the gun! ❷ reach; set in; come:～了好运气 have good luck /今年～春早。Spring set in early this year. /快～冬至了。The Winter Solstice is approaching. /等～秋后,她的病可能会好转。Her condition might improve when autumn comes. ❸ meet; join:夏秋之～ when summer is changing into autumn /位于两条铁路之～ be located at the junction of two railways /这个县在三省之～。This county stands where three provinces meet. ❹ cross; intersect:AB 和 CD 两线～于 E 点。Line AB intersects line CD at E. /两条铁路在这里相～。These two railways cross here. ❺ associate with; befriend:～朋友 make friends /此人不可～。This is not the person to associate with. ❻ friend; acquaintance; friendship; relationship; relation:点头之～ nodding acquaintance /一面之～ passing (*or* casual) acquaintance /忘年～ friendship between people of different age groups /多年之～ friendship of many years (*or* long standing) /患难之～ tested friend /建～ establish diplomatic relations /绝～ sever relations; break off relations /初～ new acquaintance /故～ old friend; close friend /私～ personal friendship /邦～ diplomatic relations ❼ have sexual intercourse; copulate; mate; breed:杂～ crossbreed ❽ mutual; reciprocal; each other:水乳～融 as well blended as milk and water; in complete harmony ❾ together; simultaneous:内外～困 be beset with difficulties at home and abroad /风雪～加 snowing and blowing hard /悲喜～集 mixed feelings of grief and joy ❿ deal; bargain; business transaction:成～ strike a bargain; conclude a transaction; make (*or* clinch) a deal

交[2] jiāo *see* "跤" jiāo

交白卷 jiāo báijuàn ❶ hand in a blank examination paper:一个问题都回答不出来,他只好～了。Being unable to answer any of the questions, he could do nothing but hand in a blank examination paper. ❷ completely fail to accomplish a task; prove wholly unsuccessful; lay an egg:摸清情况,以免回去～。We must find out exactly how things stand here, or we'll have nothing to report back.
交拜 jiāobài 〈旧语〉bride and bridegroom salute each other at a wedding ceremony:夫妻～ man and wife salute each other
交班 jiāobān hand over to the next shift; change shift:下午五点～ hand over to the next shift at five p.m.
交办 jiāobàn entrust (sth. to one's subordinates); send (sb.) on an errand:～任务,克日完成 assign a task and set the date for its completion
交半 jiāobàn half and half:新旧～ half new and half old
交保 jiāobǎo bail:～释放 allow bail; accept bail; take bail /不准～ refuse bail
交杯酒 jiāobēijiǔ mutual toasting by bridegroom and bride by drinking from each other's cup at a wedding ceremony
交臂 jiāobì 〈书面〉❶ cross one's arms; cup one hand in the other before one's chest to make an obeisance ❷ being so close that arms of two people touch each other; rub shoulders:～擦肩 pass each other so close that their shoulders almost rub ❸ have one's hands tied behind one's back
交臂失之 jiāobì-shīzhī *also* "失之交臂" just miss the person or opportunity:这样好的机会便～了。Such a good opportunity was thus let slip.
交变 jiāobiàn alternate:～梯度理论〈物理〉alternating-gradient theory /～部件〈机械〉alternate block /～压力 alternate pressure /～振动试验机 alternating impact test
交变磁场 jiāobiàn cíchǎng 〈物理〉alternating magnetic field
交变电场 jiāobiàn diànchǎng 〈电学〉alternating electric field
交变电流 jiāobiàn diànliú *also* "交流电" alternating current (AC)
交变电压 jiāobiàn diànyā alternating voltage
交兵 jiāobīng 〈书面〉(of two or more parties) be at war; wage war:自古以来,两国～,不斩来使。From time immemorial, two countries at war would not kill each other's envoys.
交并 jiāobìng appear simultaneously:悲喜～ mixed feelings of grief and joy; grief and joy intermingled /饥寒～ suffer cold and hunger at the same time
交叉 jiāochā ❶ cross; intersect; crisscross:～进给系统 cross feed system /～控制系统 crossed controls /～需求弹性 cross elasticity of demand /平面～ crossing at grade; grade crossing; level crossing /立体～ flyover crossing; overhead crossing /直角～ crossing at right angles /菱形～ diamond crossing /公路和铁路在这儿～。The highway crosses the railway here. *or* The highway and the railway intersect here. ❷ overlap:这两门学科有～的地方。There are overlapping areas in these two branches of learning. *or* The two disciplines overlap in certain areas. ❸ alternate; stagger:口头作业和笔头作业～进行 do oral and written homework alternately
交叉承认 jiāochā chéngrèn 〈外交〉cross recognition
交叉点 jiāochādiǎn intersection
交叉感染 jiāochā gǎnrǎn 〈医学〉cross-infection
交叉汇率 jiāochā huìlǜ 〈经济〉cross rate
交叉火力 jiāochā huǒlì crossfire
交叉控股 jiāochā kònggǔ cross-holding
交叉学科 jiāochā xuékē interdisciplinary science
交叉遗传 jiāochā yíchuán 〈医学〉crisscross inheritance
交差 jiāochāi report to the leadership after accomplishing a task; report on the fulfilment of one's duty:完不成任务,我们无法～。There is no way for us to account for our mission if we fail to fulfil it.
交钞 jiāochāo paper currency issued in the Jin and Yuan dynasties
交出 jiāochū surrender; hand over:～赃物 surrender one's booty /～违禁品 hand over contraband
交瘁 jiāocuì 〈书面〉be tired out simultaneously:心力～ be mentally and physically exhausted
交存 jiāocún deposit; hand in for safekeeping:～批准书 deposit instruments of ratification
交错 jiāocuò ❶〈书面〉interlock; interlace; crisscross:～的树枝 interlaced branches /～抽样 zigzag sampling /工厂里管道纵横～。Ducts and pipes crisscross in the factory. /交界处,两县的农田犬牙～。The farmland of the two counties interlocks each other at the border. ❷〈机械〉staggered:～气缸 staggered cylinders /～布置 staggered arrangement
交错存储器 jiāocuò cúnchǔqì 〈自控〉interlaced storage; interleaving memory
交代 jiāodài ❶ hand over; turn over; transfer:～工作 hand over work to one's successor; brief one's successor on handing over work /办～ transfer duties ❷ tell; leave word; order:已～得清清楚

J

楚 have given clear-cut orders /老师～我们这样做的。The teacher told us to do it this way. /他没有～一声就走了。He went away without leaving a word. /我就要走了，你还有什么话要～吗？I'm going to leave. Do you have anything more to say? ❸ *also* "交待" explain or clarify to people concerned; brief; account for; confess: ～政策 explain (*or* elucidate) a policy /～任务 brief sb. on his or her assignment /坦白～ confess; own up (to) /～问题 give an account of one's wrongdoings /彻底～ make a clean breast (of sth.) /无法向中国人民～ find it difficult to account for it to the Chinese people; be unable to account for oneselves to the Chinese people /～不过去 be unable to justify an action

交待 jiāodài ❶ *see* "交代❸" ❷ end (usu. used to refer to an unhappy situation): 我这条命差点在车祸中～。I was almost killed in the traffic accident.

交道 jiāodào dealings; contact: 打～ have dealings with

交底 jiāodǐ tell (sb.) what one's real intentions are; put all one's cards on the table; give the bottom line: 互相～ tell each other the bottom line

交点 jiāodiǎn ❶〈数学〉point of intersection ❷〈天文〉node: ～月 nodical month

交电 jiāodiàn transport equipment and electrical household appliances: ～公司 communications and electrical company

交锋 jiāofēng cross swords; engage in a battle or contest; have a trial of strength: 与敌人～ fight a battle with the enemy; engage the enemy in battle /思想～ confrontation of ideas; clash of views /双方在这个问题上已多次～。The two sides have crossed swords several times on this issue. /两支足球队明日第一次～。The two football teams will meet (*or* face each other) for the first time tomorrow.

交付 jiāofù ❶ pay: ～定金 down payment /～现金 payment in cash /～房租 pay house rent ❷ hand over; turn over; deliver; consign: ～表决 put to the vote /～审查 hand over for investigation /～审判 commit for trial; submit to trial /～日期 due date; date of delivery /～使用 commissioning of a project /新建楼房将于月底～使用。The new building will be made available at the end of the month. /这里的一切事我已全权～给你。I have entrusted you with all the work here.

交感神经 jiāogǎn shénjīng 〈生理〉sympathetic nerve: ～系统 sympathicus /～瘤〈医学〉sympatheticoma; sympathoma /～系统病 sympathicopathy /～炎 sympathiconeuritis

交割 jiāogē ❶ complete a business transaction: ～期 date of completing a business transaction ❷ transfer; delivery; hand over: 工作都～清了。The work has already been handed over. /货物正在～。The goods are just being turned over.

交给 jiāogěi leave (with or to sb.); entrust to sb.'s care: 请把钥匙～我。Please leave me the key. *or* Leave the key with me. /把这事～他。Leave the matter to him. /我在国外时，女儿的教育工作便～了她姑姑。When I was abroad, I entrusted the education of my daughter to her aunt.

交工 jiāogōng hand over a completed project: 提前～ hand over a completed project ahead of schedule

交公 jiāogōng hand over to the collective or the state

交媾 jiāogòu sexual intercourse; copulation; coitus

交关 jiāoguān ❶ be related; have to do with: 性命～ (a matter) of life and death; of vital importance ❷〈方言〉very; extremely: 上海今年冬天～冷。It is extremely cold this winter in Shanghai. ❸〈方言〉many; a lot of: 公园里人～。There are a lot of people in the park.

交好 jiāohǎo (of people or states) be on friendly terms: ～有年 be on friendly terms for a long time /两国～。The two countries befriend each other.

交合 jiāohé ❶ link together: 悲喜～ joy mingled with sadness ❷ sexual intercourse; copulation

交黑 jiāohēi 〈方言〉dusk; about to turn dark: 天～的时候，雨下得很大。It was raining heavily when night was about to fall.

交厚 jiāohòu on very good terms with: 他们与我～。I'm on intimate terms with them.

交互 jiāohù ❶ each other; mutual: ～评改习作 correct and comment on each other's writings /～分配法 distribution on a reciprocal basis ❷ alternately; in turn: 他两手～地抓住绳索往上爬。Holding on to the rope, he climbed up hand over hand. /两种方式可～使用。The two methods can be used in turn.

交互式 jiāohùshì 〈通信〉interactive: ～多媒体电视 interactive multimedia television (IMTV)

交欢 jiāohuān 〈书面〉make friends (with sb.); win sb.'s friendship: 握手～ shake hands and be friends

交还 jiāohuán return; give back; hand back; restore: 按时～报刊杂志 return borrowed newspapers and magazines in time /迷失的孩子已～给他的父母。The lost child has been restored to his parents. /二次大战后，台湾岛已～给中国。Taiwan Island was returned to China after the Second World War.

交换 jiāohuàn ❶ exchange; interchange; swap: ～战俘 exchange war prisoners /～意见 interchange opinions; compare notes /与某人～座位 swap seats with sb. /～条件 give-and-take conditions; quid pro quo /～场地〈体育〉exchange of courts, goals or ends /～纪念品 exchange souvenirs /～队旗 exchange team flags /～庚帖 exchange notes bearing each other's horoscopes ❷ business exchange: 商品～ exchange of commodities /用小麦～大米 barter wheat for rice /用钢材～石油 swap steel for oil /等价～ exchange of equal value

交换齿轮 jiāohuàn chǐlún 〈机械〉change gear

交换机 jiāohuànjī (telephone) exchange; switchboard: 最新式的～ up-to-date switchboard

交换价值 jiāohuàn jiàzhí 〈经济〉exchange value: 这种产品没有～。This kind of product is of no exchange value.

交换律 jiāohuànlǜ 〈数学〉commutative law

交换器 jiāohuànqì 〈电工〉converter

交换群 jiāohuànqún 〈数学〉commutative group

交换照会 jiāohuàn zhàohuì 〈外交〉exchange of notes

交辉 jiāohuī add radiance and beauty to each other: 楼台殿阁，金碧～。High towers and pavilions add splendour and magnificence to each other.

交汇 jiāohuì (current) converge; meet; join: 长江口因为咸水和淡水～，鱼类资源极为丰富。The mouth of the Yangtze River is rich in fish resources because salty and fresh water meet there.

交会 jiāohuì meet; converge; intersect: 郑州是京广、陇海铁路的～点。Zhengzhou is the intersection of the Beijing-Guangzhou and Long-Hai railways. *or* The Beijing-Guangzhou and Long-Hai railways intersect in Zhengzhou.

交混 jiāohùn mix; mingle; blend: 这一林区，桦树和橡树～在一起。In this forest area, birches are mingled with oaks. /屋子里各种气味～，令人窒息。The mixture of various smells in the house is suffocating.

交火 jiāohuǒ open fire; exchange fire; fight: 两国军队在边境～。Fighting broke out between troops of the two countries in the border area.

交货 jiāohuò deliver goods: 即期～ prompt delivery /近期～ near delivery /远期～ forward delivery /船上～ ex ship delivery /铁路旁～ ex rail delivery /仓库～ ex warehouse delivery /分批～ delivery by instalments; partial delivery /～不足 short delivery /～期限控制 delivery control

交货单 jiāohuòdān delivery order

交货付款 jiāohuò fùkuǎn cash on delivery (COD)

交货港 jiāohuògǎng port of delivery

交货率 jiāohuòlǜ delivery ratio

交货期 jiāohuòqī date of delivery

交货收据 jiāohuò shōujù delivery receipt

交货证明书 jiāohuò zhèngmíngshū certificate of delivery

交集 jiāojí (of different feelings) be mixed; occur simultaneously: 惊喜～ mixed feelings of surprise and joy; surprise and joy intermingled /百感～ all sorts of feelings well up in one's heart

交际 jiāojì social intercourse; communication: ～很广 have a large circle of acquaintances; be well-connected /～应酬 business entertainment /语言是人类重要的～工具。Language is an important means of human intercourse (*or* communication). /他善于～。He is a good mixer. *or* He's socially active. /平日里他不大同人～。He generally does not like to have contacts with people.

交际处 jiāojìchù protocol division; public relations office

交际费 jiāojìfèi allowance for entertainment; (as of a manager) expense account

交际花 jiāojìhuā 〈贬义〉social butterfly; social beauty: 她年轻时是一朵～。She was a social butterfly when she was young.

交际舞 jiāojìwǔ *also* "交谊舞" ballroom dancing; social dancing: ～曾经十分流行。Ballroom dancing was once all the rage.

交加 jiāojiā (of two things) accompany each other; occur simultaneously: 贫病～ be dogged by both poverty and illness /拳足～ give (sb.) punches as well as kicks; punch and kick (sb.) /风雨～的夜晚 night of raging rainstorm /内忧外患～ beset with domestic trouble

and foreign invasion

交角 jiāojiǎo ❶〈航天〉inclination ❷〈数学〉angle of intersection

交接 jiāojiē ❶ join; connect:现在正是冬春～的季节。Now is the time when winter is changing into spring. ❷ hand over and take over:～班 relieve a shift /办理～手续 go through a handing over formality (*or* procedure) /参加赠书的～仪式 attend a book-presentation ceremony ❸ associate with; make friends with:他～了不少志趣相同的朋友。He has made friends with quite a few people who share his aspiration and interest.

交结 jiāojié ❶ associate with; make friends with:他在文艺界～很广。He has a large number of friends in art and literary circles. ❷〈书面〉interconnect:～盘错 interconnect and crisscross

交睫 jiāojié upper and lower eyelashes meeting each other — be asleep:目不～ be awake

交界 jiāojiè (of two or more places) have a common boundary:三省～ place where three provinces meet; juncture of three provinces /福建北面与浙江～。Fujian is bounded on the north by Zhejiang. /中国东北和朝鲜～。China's northeast borders on Korea.

交颈 jiāojǐng neck-to-neck, as two mandarin ducks; neck; fondle and kiss:～而眠 sleep neck to neck

交警 jiāojǐng (short for 交通警察) traffic police; traffic policeman

交九 jiāojiǔ enter the nine periods (of nine days each) following the winter solstice:～的天气 very cold weather

交卷 jiāojuàn ❶ hand in an examination paper ❷ complete one's task; carry out an assignment:这事交给他办,三天准能～。Give him the task and he is sure to finish it in three days.

交口 jiāokǒu ❶ speak in unison ❷〈方言〉talk with each other; converse; chat:他们久未～。They have not been talking to each other for a long time.

交口称誉 jiāokǒu-chēngyù praise unanimously; be praised by one and all; receive unanimous acclaim:政府的这些措施,全国人民～。The people throughout the country are unanimous in praising these policies of the government.

交困 jiāokùn be in difficulties:内外～ be beset with difficulties both at home and abroad

交联 jiāolián 〈化学〉cross link:～结构 cross-linked structure /～聚合物 cross-linked polymer /～聚苯乙烯树脂 cross-linked polystyrene resin

交流 jiāoliú ❶ flow simultaneously:涕泪～ shed tears and have a runny nose ❷ exchange; interflow; interchange:～工作经验 exchange work experience; draw on each other's experience in work /城乡物资～ flow of goods and materials between city and country /经济和技术～ economic and technological interchange /人材～ exchange of qualified personnel /学术～ academic exchanges /思想～ exchange of views (*or* ideas) /信息～ exchange of information /两国人民之间的文化～,源远流长。The cultural exchange between the two peoples is of long standing.

交流电 jiāoliúdiàn alternating current

交流发电机 jiāoliú fādiànjī alternating current generator; alternator

交流式 jiāoliúshì of an interactive nature:～教学法 interactive teaching method

交流学者 jiāoliú xuézhě exchange scholar; visiting scholar (on an exchange programme)

交纳 jiāonà pay (to the state or an organization); hand in:～房租 pay rent /～税金 pay tax /～所得税 pay income tax /～水电费 pay charges for water and electricity

交派 jiāopài assign sth. to sb.; leave with (a subordinate):这是县里～下来的任务。This is the task assigned by the county authorities.

交配 jiāopèi mating; copulation:～期 mating season /～唤叫 mating call

交朋友 jiāo péngyou make friends:与约翰～ make friends with John / 我们交了许多新朋友。We have made a lot of new friends.

交迫 jiāopò (of pressures) come from all sides:饥寒～ suffer from hunger and cold /老人终年过着贫病～、半饥半饱的日子。Beset by poverty and illness, the old man was half-starved all year round.

交契 jiāoqì 〈书面〉(of people or states) be on friendly terms; have friendly relations

交浅言深 jiāoqiǎn-yánshēn have a hearty talk with a casual acquaintance; give sincere advice to people one knows only slightly:我与你初会,～,幸勿见怪。Please excuse me if I have spoken too bluntly at our very first meeting.

交情 jiāoqing friendship; friendly relations:与某人有～ be on friendly terms with sb. /他是个讲～的人。He is always ready to do things for the sake of friendship.

交融 jiāoróng blend; mix; mingle:情景～ (of literary work) feelings fitting happily with the scene

交涉 jiāoshè negotiate; take up (sth. with sb.); make representations (to sb. about sth.):向有关当局进行～ make representations to the authorities concerned /经过多次～,事情终于解决了。The problem was finally settled through repeated negotiations. /这个问题要继续～。We'll pursue the matter further. /我向他～过几次了。I've taken up the matter with him on several occasions.

交手 jiāoshǒu fight hand to hand; be engaged in a hand-to-hand combat; come to grips:与敌人～ engage the enemy in hand-to-hand combat /他们不仅对骂,而且交起手来了。They not only cursed each other but actually came to blows. /近几年,两队多次～,互有胜负。The two teams have met several times in recent years, each having victories and defeats.

交售 jiāoshòu sell (to the state):向国家多～粮棉 sell more grain and cotton to the state /完成今年的～任务 fulfil this year's selling quota

交税 jiāoshuì pay tax:他从不误～。He is never late for paying tax.

交绥 jiāosuí ❶〈书面〉be at war ❷ meet; converge:四月至六月,冷暖空气在华南～。Between April and June, cold and warm air meet in south China.

交泰 jiāotài union; convergence; harmony:日月～ union (*or* harmony) of the sun and the moon / ～殿 Hall of Union, in the Palace Museum in Beijing

交谈 jiāotán talk with each other; converse; chat:用英语～ talk in English /亲切～ heart-to-heart talk /自由～ free chat /他们就共同关心的问题进行了友好的～。They held a friendly conversation on matters of common concern.

交替 jiāotì ❶ give place to; replace; supersede:新旧～。The new replaces the old. *or* The old gives place to the new. /在这春夏～之际,很容易闹病。It is very easy to get ill at the time when spring is changing into summer. ❷ alternately; one after another; in turn:～演奏两国国歌 play the national anthems of the two countries respectively /昼夜～。Day alternates with night. /近来家中孩子们～着生病。Recently children fell ill one after another.

交替存储器 jiāotì cúnchǔqì 〈自控〉interleaving memory

交调 jiāotiáo 〈无线电〉intermodulation:～失真 intermodulation distortion

交通 jiāotōng ❶ communication:阡陌～ crisscrossing paths on farmland ❷ traffic; communications:～不便 have poor transport facilities; be inconveniently located /～繁忙 heavy traffic /公路～ highway traffic /空中～ air traffic /市内～ urban traffic ❸ (of secret underground work, esp. during the War of Resistance Against Japanese Aggression and the War of Liberation) liaison:跑～ do liaison work ❹ liaison man; underground messenger:地下～ underground liaison man; underground messenger ❺〈书面〉associate with; collude with:与权贵～ try to make friends with bigwigs

交通安全 jiāotōng ānquán traffic safety:～法规 traffic safety code

交通标线 jiāotōng biāoxiàn traffic marking

交通标志 jiāotōng biāozhì traffic sign

交通部 jiāotōngbù Ministry of Communications:中华人民共和国～ Ministry of Communications of the PRC

交通车 jiāotōngchē office bus; shuttle bus

交通岛 jiāotōngdǎo traffic island

交通干线 jiāotōng gànxiàn main line of communications; trunk road; main artery of traffic

交通高峰 jiāotōng gāofēng traffic peak

交通工具 jiāotōng gōngjù means of transport:缺少～ lack means of transport

交通管理 jiāotōng guǎnlǐ traffic control

交通管理色灯 jiāotōng guǎnlǐ sèdēng traffic lights

交通规则 jiāotōng guīzé traffic regulations:违反～ commit a traffic offence; break traffic regulations

交通壕 jiāotōngháo *also* "交通沟"〈军事〉communication trench

交通警 jiāotōngjǐng traffic police:～中队 detachment of traffic police

交通量 jiāotōngliàng volume of traffic

交通事故 jiāotōng shìgù traffic accident; road accident:～现场

scene of a traffic accident
交通网 jiāotōngwǎng network of communication lines
交通线 jiāotōngxiàn lines of communication; communication lines
交通信号 jiāotōng xìnhào traffic signal
交通要道 jiāotōng yàodào vital communication line
交通员 jiāotōngyuán liaison man; underground messenger *see also* "交通❸"
交通运输 jiāotōng yùnshū communications and transport
交通站 jiāotōngzhàn liaison station; liaison place *see also* "交通❸"
交通指挥台 jiāotōng zhǐhuītái police stand
交通阻塞 jiāotōng zǔsè traffic hold-up; traffic jam; traffic block; traffic snarl
交头接耳 jiāotóu-jiē'ěr speak in each other's ears; whisper to each other:前面椅子里的一对情侣,~谈得很入神。The two lovers are whispering to each other in the front chairs, totally absorbed in their conversation. /次日,寨中三三五五,~,议论纷纷。Next day men in small groups were to be seen everywhere in the fortress, some talking, others listening, heads together and ears stretched out. /门卫不许擅离岗位,不许~。The guards must on no account absent themselves and must maintain strict silence.
交往 jiāowǎng associate; contact:~甚密 have an intimate association; have close contact /在与世界各国的~中,我们遵循和平共处的五项原则。In our contacts with countries the world over, we adhere to the Five Principles of Peaceful Coexistence. /他喜欢与要人~。He likes to rub elbows (*or* shoulders) with important people.
交尾 jiāowěi mating; pairing; coupling:现在是鱼的~期。It is the mating season for fish.
交午 jiāowǔ ❶ up to noontime; by noon:天已~。It's already noontime. ❷〈书面〉crisscross
交恶 jiāowù fall foul of each other; be at odds; become enemies:两国~。The two countries became hostile to each other. / 两人素来~。There was no love lost between the two.
交相辉映 jiāoxiānghuīyìng add radiance and beauty to each other; enhance each other's beauty:湖光山色,~。The lake and the hills enhance each other's beauty.
交响曲 jiāoxiǎngqǔ 〈音乐〉symphony:我最喜欢贝多芬的第五~。Beethoven's Fifth Symphony is my favourite.
交响诗 jiāoxiǎngshī 〈音乐〉symphonic poem; tone poem
交响乐 jiāoxiǎngyuè 〈音乐〉symphony; symphonic music
交响乐队 jiāoxiǎng yuèduì symphony orchestra; philharmonic orchestra
交卸 jiāoxiè hand the duties of office over to one's successor
交心 jiāoxīn lay one's heart bare; open one's heart:向好友~ unbosom oneself to one's close friend /他是我能够~的朋友。He is one that I can confide in.
交学费 jiāo xuéfèi pay a tuition fee;〈比喻〉regard a loss as the necessary price of learning a lesson:对于那些造成了巨大浪费还以"~"来搪塞的人,人民有权追究他的责任。The people have the right to call to account those who try to explain away their enormous waste on the pretext of "paying a tuition fee".
交验 jiāoyàn hand over for inspection:~护照 hand over a passport for inspection
交钥匙项目 jiāoyàoshi xiàngmù turn-key project
交椅 jiāoyǐ ❶ ancient folding chair:坐头把~ occupy the highest post; be in command ❷〈方言〉armchair
交易 jiāoyì business; bargain; deal; trade; transaction:做成一笔~ make a deal; conclude a transaction; strike a bargain /现金~ cash transaction /赊账~ credit transaction /黑市~ black market bargain / ~额 volume of trade /~券 trading stamp /定期~ trade on term /期货~ forward (*or* futures) business /拿原则做~ barter away principles
交易会 jiāoyìhuì commodities fair; trade fair:中国春季出口商品~ China's Spring Export Commodities Fair (at Guangzhou)
交易所 jiāoyìsuǒ exchange:证券~ stock exchange; security exchange /商品~ commodity exchange
交谊 jiāoyì 〈书面〉friendship; friendly relations:两人有很深的~。The two share a deep friendship.
交谊舞 jiāoyìwǔ "friendship dance" — social dance; ballroom dance
交映 jiāoyìng add lustre and beauty to each other:园中花木繁多,红绿~。The garden is bursting with flowers and trees, a brilliant scene of red and green.
交游 jiāoyóu 〈书面〉make friends:~甚广 have many friends /他性格豪爽,爱~。He is a man of straightforward character and is fond of making friends.
交运 jiāoyùn have good luck:今天真~! What good luck today!
交杂 jiāozá mix; intermingle:爱与恨~在他的心头。Love and hatred are intermingled in his heart.
交战 jiāozhàn be at war; fight a war:~理由 casus belli /两国~。The two countries are at war. /~两方各派全权代表签订和约。Each of the two belligerent sides has sent plenipotentiaries to sign the peace treaty.
交战国 jiāozhànguó belligerent country; belligerent state; belligerent power; belligerent nation:共同~ co-belligerent; co-belligerent powers (*or* states) /~已经坐到了谈判桌前。The belligerent nations have already been at the negotiating table.
交战团体 jiāozhàn tuántǐ belligerent; belligerent community; party to a war
交战行为 jiāozhàn xíngwéi 〈法律〉belligerent act
交战状态 jiāozhàn zhuàngtài 〈法律〉belligerency; state of war
交账 jiāozhàng ❶ hand over accounts:向新接手的会计~ hand over accounts to a new accountant ❷ account for:如果完不成任务,我们回去怎么向领导~? If we fail to fulfil the task, what are we going to say to our superiors (*or* how are we going to report back)?
交织 jiāozhī ❶ interwine; mingle:欢呼声和锣鼓声~在一起。Thunderous ovation mingled with beating of drums and gongs. ❷ interweave:棉麻~ interweave cotton with flax /~绸 mixed silk-rayon piece goods /黑白~ interwoven of black and white /腈涤~混纺 blend of chinlon and terylene
交直流发电机 jiāo-zhíliú fādiànjī double-current generator
交趾支那 Jiāozhǐ Zhīnà Cochin China, former name for the southern region of Vietnam
交子 jiāozǐ first paper currency of China, appearing in the early years of the Northern Song Dynasty
交子 jiāozi 〈方言〉fall; tumble:跌~ have a fall
交嘴雀 jiāozuǐquè 〈动物〉crossbill
交作 jiāozuò appear or occur simultaneously:雷电~ lightning accompanied by thunder

茭 jiāo 〈书面〉dry grass as fodder
茭白 jiāobái 〈植物〉wild rice stem
茭笋 jiāosǔn 〈方言〉wild rice stem

蛟 jiāo flood dragon, a mythical creature capable of invoking storms and floods
蛟龙 jiāolóng flood dragon:~得水 the flood dragon goes into water —be in the most congenial surroundings; get a good opportunity to display one's talent /~之志 great ambitions

跤 jiāo tumble; fall:摔了一~ have a fall

鸡 jiāo
鸡鶄 jiāojīng 〈古语〉a kind of aquatic bird

胶(膠) jiāo ❶ glue; gum:树~ gum /鱼~ fish glue /鳔~ isinglass; fish glue /骨~ bone glue /乳~ emulsion /桃~ peach gum /皮~ hide glue /植物~ vegetable gum /动物~ animal size (*or* glue) /酪素~ cascin glue /鹿角~ deerhorn glue ❷ stick with glue; glue:镜框坏了,把它~上。The picture frame is broken, so glue it. ❸ gluey; sticky; gummy: *see* "~泥" ❹ rubber:~底鞋 rubber-soled shoes /~包电缆 rubber-insulated cable
胶版 jiāobǎn 〈印刷〉offset plate
胶版打样机 jiāobǎn dǎyàngjī offset proof press
胶版复印 jiāobǎn fùyìn hectograph
胶版印刷 jiāobǎn yìnshuā offset printing; offset; offset lithography:~机 offset press
胶版纸 jiāobǎnzhǐ offset paper
胶布 jiāobù ❶ rubberized fabric:绝缘~ friction-tape; tape ❷〈口语〉adhesive plaster; sticking plaster; adhesive tape
胶布带 jiāobùdài rubberized tape; adhesive tape
胶带 jiāodài rubberized tape; adhesive tape
胶冻 jiāodòng jelly

J

胶合 jiāohé glue together; veneer; cement; bond: ～金属板 plymetal
胶合板 jiāohébǎn plywood; veneerboard; veneer wood
胶合剂 jiāohéjì glue bond
胶化 jiāohuà gelatinate; gelatinize; colloidize: ～剂 gelatinizing agent; gelling agent / ～物 gelatinizer
胶结 jiāojié *also* "胶接" glue; cement: ～绝缘接头 glued insulation joint
胶结材料 jiāojié cáiliào cementing material
胶结剂 jiāojiéjì cementing agent
胶卷 jiāojuǎn roll of film; film: 三个～ three rolls of film / 黑白～ black and white film / 彩色～ colour film / 冲～ have one's film developed; develop film / 电影～ cinefilm; motion-picture film / 全色～ panchromatic film / ～暗盒 cassette; film cassette
胶卷阅读机 jiāojuǎn yuèdújī film reader
胶粒 jiāolì micelle; colloidal particle
胶料 jiāoliào sizing material; size
胶轮 jiāolún rubber tyre: ～大车 rubber-tyred cart
胶姆糖 jiāomǔtáng *also* "口香糖" kǒuxiāngtáng chewing gum
胶木 jiāomù bakelite
胶囊 jiāonáng 〈药学〉capsule
胶泥 jiāoní ❶ clay ❷〈建筑〉mastic cement: 沥青～ asphalt cement
胶黏 jiāonián 〈方言〉gluey; sticky; gummy
胶凝 jiāoníng gelate: ～剂 gelatinizing agent; gelling agent / ～体 gelation
胶凝作用 jiāoníng zuòyòng gelation
胶皮 jiāopí ❶ (vulcanized) rubber ❷〈方言〉rickshaw
胶皮电缆 jiāopí diànlǎn 〈电工〉india-rubber cable
胶片 jiāopiàn *also* "软片" ruǎnpiàn film: 彩色～ colour film / 正色～ orthochromatic film / 全色～ orthopan film / 缩微～ microfiche / 缩微～摄影机 microfilm camera / 缩微～阅读机 film reader / ～光学读取装置 film optical-sensing device / ～记录器 film recorder; film register / ～显影冲洗机 film (*or* plate) processor
胶乳 jiāorǔ ❶〈植物〉latex ❷〈化学〉latex: 硫化～ vulcanized latex; vultex
胶水 jiāoshuǐ mucilage; glue
胶态 jiāotài 〈物理〉colloidal state: ～发射物 colloidal propellant / ～悬浮 colloidal suspension / ～运动 colloidal movement
胶体 jiāotǐ 〈化学〉colloid
胶体化学 jiāotǐ huàxué colloid chemistry
胶体溶液 jiāotǐ róngyè colloid solution
胶鞋 jiāoxié ❶ rubber overshoes; galoshes; rubbers ❷ rubber-soled shoes; tennis shoes; sneakers
胶性 jiāoxìng colloidal property; colloidality
胶靴 jiāoxuē high rubber overshoes; galoshes
胶压 jiāoyā compregnate: ～木材 compregnated wood; compreg
胶印 jiāoyìn offset printing; offset lithography; offset: ～机 offset press; offset machine; printing machine
胶原 jiāoyuán 〈生化〉collagen: ～酶 collagenase / ～性疾病〈医学〉collagenosis
胶原病 jiāoyuánbìng 〈医学〉collagenosis; collagen disease
胶粘剂 jiāozhānjì adhesive: 这种～很有效。This kind of adhesive is very effective.
胶质 jiāozhì gel
胶质水泥 jiāozhì shuǐní gel-cement
胶柱鼓瑟 jiāozhù-gǔsè play the *se* (an ancient zither-like instrument) with the pegs glued — stubbornly stick to old ways in the face of changed circumstances: 此人～, 过于固执了。That fellow is really too strait-laced and stubborn.
胶着 jiāozhuó deadlocked; stalemated: 战斗处于～状态。The war is now in a stalemate.

鲛

jiāo shark
鲛人 jiāorén a fish-like person in ancient tales who lived in the South Sea and whose tears turned into pearls
鲛绡 jiāoxiāo silk woven by the fish-like person in the South Sea; thin yarn

郊

jiāo suburbs; outskirts: 京～一带 suburban areas of Beijing / 东～ eastern suburbs; eastern outskirts / 近～ near suburbs / 远～ outer suburbs; remote outskirts of a city / ～县 suburban county of a city
郊寒岛瘦 jiāohán-dǎoshòu Jiao is cold and Dao is lean (Jiao is Meng Jiao 孟郊 and Dao is Jia Dao 贾岛, both poets of the Tang Dynasty) — descriptive of literary and poetic works which describe poverty and deprivation in life
郊区 jiāoqū suburban district; suburbs; outskirts: ～居民 suburban; suburbanite / 大城市的～要建设一些卫星城镇。Some satellite towns should be built in the outskirts of metropolitan cities.
郊外 jiāowài country around a city; outskirts: ～多有名胜古迹。There are quite a number of scenic spots and historical sites in the outskirts.
郊野 jiāoyě outskirts; countryside
郊游 jiāoyóu outing; excursion: 到湖滨去～ go on an outing to the lakeside; go for an excursion to the lakeside
郊原 jiāoyuán open country in the suburbs

姣

jiāo 〈书面〉beautiful; handsome: 天下之至～。She is the most beautiful woman on earth.
姣好 jiāohǎo beautiful; graceful: ～的姿容 beautiful appearance
姣丽 jiāolì beautiful; good-looking
姣美 jiāoměi beautiful; graceful: ～的天鹅 graceful swan
姣妍 jiāoyán beautiful; pretty: ～的景色 lovely scenery

教

jiāo teach; instruct: 互～互学 teach and learn from each other / ～人识字 teach sb. how to read and write / 他～他们数学。He instructs them in mathematics. *or* He teaches them mathematics. / ～然后知不足。Teaching others will make you realize your own ignorance.
see also jiào
教书 jiāoshū teach school; teach: ～先生 teacher / 他在这所中学教了三十年书了。He has been teaching in this middle school for thirty years.
教书匠 jiāoshūjiàng 〈贬义〉pedagogue
教书育人 jiāoshū-yùrén impart knowledge and educate people: ～是老师的天职。It is the bounden duty of a teacher to pass on knowledge and enlighten people.
教学 jiāoxué teach; teach school: 他全神贯注地进行～。He is engrossed in teaching.
see also jiàoxué

艽

jiāo *see* "秦艽" qínjiāo

椒

jiāo any of several hot spice plants: 辣～ chilli; red pepper / 青～ green pepper / 胡～ pepper / 番～〈中医〉hot pepper; chilli / 花～ Chinese prickly ash / 秦～ a kind of thin and long hot pepper / 柿子～ sweet bell pepper; sweet pepper
椒房 jiāofáng imperial concubine's residence; imperial concubine
椒目 jiāomù dark seeds of pepper fruit
椒盐 jiāoyán condiment made of roasted prickly ash and salt; spiced salt: ～排骨 spareribs with spiced salt / 软炸里脊上放点～ add some spiced salt to the soft-fried tenderloin

镠

jiāo
镠辐 jiāogé 〈书面〉interlock; crisscross

娇(嬌)

jiāo ❶ tender; delicate; lovely; charming: 嫩红～绿 tender blossoms and delicate leaves / 撒～ act like a pampered child / 江山多～ gorgeous land ❷ squeamish; finicky; fragile; frail: 她工作不到一小时就叫苦, 未免太～了。She started grumbling after working for less than an hour; she's really too soft. ❸ pamper; spoil: 小孩别太～了。Don't spoil children!
娇爱 jiāo'ài indulge (a child); spoil; pamper: 母亲～自己的孩子。A mother often indulges her child lovingly.
娇嗔 jiāochēn (young woman) be coquettishly angry: 她故作～地顶了一句。She talked back, pretending coquettishly to be angry.
娇痴 jiāochī artless but lovely; naive but charming: ～的小姑娘 naive but lovely little girl
娇宠 jiāochǒng indulge; pamper; spoil: 父母对孩子不能过于～。Parents shoudn't indulge their children too much.
娇脆 jiāocuì (of a woman's voice) tender and pleasing; pleasantly delicate: 她用～的声音欢快地歌唱。She gaily sings in a tender and

sweet voice.

娇翠 jiāocuì (of flowers and grass or scenery) charming; fresh and green:雨后的湖山分外~。Lakes and mountains are extremely charming and fresh after the rain.

娇滴滴 jiāodīdī ❶ delicately pretty; affectedly sweet:~的声音 affectedly sweet voice /这少女生就一副~的标致模样。This young girl is delicately pretty. ❷ too delicate; frail:她把女儿惯得~的。She spoiled her daughter so much that the little girl was overdelicate.

娇惰 jiāoduò charming and sluggish; pretty and indolent:她似乎刚睡醒,带着十分~的神气。Charmingly indolent, she seems to have just waked up.

娇儿 jiāo'ér ❶ darling son ❷lovely young son or daughter

娇惯 jiāoguàn pamper; spoil; coddle:~孙子 coddle (*or* dote on) one's grandson /~有余,管教不足 over-indulged and under-disciplined

娇贵 jiāogui ❶ enervated (by good living); pampered:别那么~孩子。Don't pamper children that way. ❷ fragile; frail; delicate; easy to break:~的玻璃器皿 fragile glassware /这仪器很~。This instrument is very delicate.

娇憨 jiāohān childish but lovely; naive and charming:女儿~的一声笑,使他板不起脸来。His daughter's artless but lovely laughter made it difficult for him to resume a straight face.

娇好 jiāohǎo (as of a young girl) tender and graceful; charming and beautiful

娇红 jiāohóng bright red; crimson:两颊~ rosy cheeks

娇黄 jiāohuáng light yellow:麦苗葱绿,菜花~。Wheat seedlings are pale green and rapeflowers light yellow.

娇客 jiāokè ❶ son-in-law ❷ pampered person

娇蓝 jiāolán sky blue; azure:天空真像~~的海面。The sky is very much like the blue sea.

娇丽 jiāolì dazzlingly beautiful:遍山野花,~多姿。Bright-coloured and beautiful wild flowers are all over the mountain.

娇绿 jiāolǜ light green:远处是一片~的草坪。In the distance, there is a stretch of verdant lawn.

娇美 jiāoměi tender and beautiful; sweet and charming:~动人 charming and touching /~的风姿 graceful bearing

娇媚 jiāomèi ❶ coquettish; flirtatious ❷ sweet and charming:~的牡丹,在百花丛中最鲜艳。The sweet and charming peony is the most beautiful among the flowers.

娇嫩 jiāonen fragile; delicate; tender and lovely:~的玫瑰花 tender and lovely rose blossom /粉红~的小脸蛋 rosy and lovely small face /他的身体太~。He is much too delicate.

娇娘 jiāoniáng beautiful young lady

娇女 jiāonǚ beloved daughter; pretty little girl

娇娜 jiāonuó (of young ladies) graceful bearing

娇妻 jiāoqī young and pretty wife

娇气 jiāoqi ❶ delicate; squeamish; finicky:~十足 full of finicky airs /你的身体也太~了,说感冒就感冒。You're really too delicate, catching cold so easily. /去掉~ get rid of squeamishness /一看她那娇里娇气的样子就够了。The sight of her squeamish manner is more than enough. ❷(of things) easily broken or damaged; fragile

娇娆 jiāoráo 〈书面〉enchantingly beautiful:海棠花~异常。The Chinese flowering crabapple is ravishingly beautiful.

娇柔 jiāoróu gentle and charming; delicate and lovely:河畔~的垂柳 tender and charming weeping willow on the river bank

娇弱 jiāoruò tender and delicate; frail and delicate:~的姑娘 frail and delicate girl /~的声音 tender and weak voice

娇生惯养 jiāoshēng-guànyǎng be pampered and spoiled:他绝不是~的孩子。He was no mama's boy. /她自小~,何尝受过一点委屈。Living in luxury ever since childhood, she has never been put to any inconvenience. /独生子女经常是~的。An only child is usually brought up in easy circumstances by doting parents.

娇声 jiāoshēng tender and sweet voice; gentle and charming voice:~软语 sweet voice and soft words /~媚气 silky voice and coquettish manner /~娇气 speak in a seductive tone

娇态 jiāotài sweet and charming manner:故作~ put on a sweet and charming air

娇娃 jiāowá ❶ pretty young girl ❷〈方言〉pampered child:这帮大城市来的~从来没有经受过艰苦的考验。These pampered children from large cities have never experienced any hardship.

娇婉 jiāowǎn tender and sweet (voice)

娇小 jiāoxiǎo small and delicate; petite:~的女孩子 petite young girl

娇小玲珑 jiāoxiǎo-línglóng delicate and exquisite; petite and charming:这女孩身材~,一对乌亮的眼珠左顾右盼。Petite and delicate, the girl glanced right and left with her bright black eyes. /这姑娘长得~。She is a cute little girl.

娇羞 jiāoxiū (of young girls) bashful; shy; blushing:她现在大方多了,没有从前那种~的姿态了。Her manner is much more open with her girlish shyness gone.

娇艳 jiāoyàn delicate and charming; tender and beautiful:~绝伦 be delicate and charming beyond compare /一丛丛~的红玫瑰花 clumps of dazzling red rose

娇养 jiāoyǎng coddle; pamper; spoil:她在家里给母亲~惯了。At home, mother used to pamper her.

娇慵 jiāoyōng 〈书面〉(of females) sluggish; negligent; indolent

娇纵 jiāozòng indulge (a child); pamper; spoil:~孩子不是爱他而是害他。To indulge a child is the way to ruin him, not to cherish him.

骄(驕) jiāo

❶ proud; arrogant; supercilious; conceited:戒~戒躁 guard against arrogance and rashness /胜而不~ not be dizzy with success /~者必败。Pride goes before a fall. ❷〈书面〉intense; fierce; violent; vigorous: *see* "~阳"

骄傲 jiāo'ào ❶ arrogant; haughty; conceited:~矜夸 haughty and boastful /虚心使人进步,~使人落后。Modesty helps one make progress; conceit makes one lag behind. ❷ be proud; take pride:我们为有这样的成就而~。We are proud of our achievements. *or* We take pride in the achievements we have scored. ❸ pride:万里长城是我们民族的~。The Great Wall is the pride of our nation.

骄傲自大 jiāo'ào-zìdà conceited and arrogant; self-important; swollen with pride:我们班有那么两三个~的小伙子。In our class there are two or three guys who are terribly puffed up.

骄傲自满 jiāo'ào-zìmǎn conceited and self-satisfied; arrogant and complacent:~,不思进取 be self-complacent and have little mind to move ahead

骄兵 jiāobīng ❶ army which is puffed up with pride ❷ soldiers not obeying orders:~悍将 unruly commanders and soldiers

骄兵必败 jiāobīng-bìbài an arrogant army is bound to lose:~,古今中外概莫能外。It is without exception anywhere and any time that an arrogant army is doomed to defeat.

骄横 jiāohèng arrogant and tyrannous; overbearing:~不法 presumptuous and unlawful /~残暴 overbearing and cruel

骄横跋扈 jiāohèng-báhù arrogant and overweening; lordly and imperious; throw one's weight about:他手下有一群~的将领。He has quite a number of arrogant and unruly generals under him.

骄蹇 jiāojiǎn 〈书面〉arrogant; conceited:~不逊 be arrogant and rude /~自负 be arrogant and conceited

骄矜 jiāojīn 〈书面〉self-important; arrogant; haughty:不因学业有成而~ not feel proud (*or* not put on airs) for having achieved success in one's study

骄狂 jiāokuáng arrogant and brazen:~自是 be arrogant and opinionated

骄慢 jiāomàn high and mighty; haughty:~不谨 be imprudent and arrogant

骄气 jiāoqi overbearing airs; arrogance; haughtiness:不可有点成绩就~十足。Don't be swell-headed when you have made some progress.

骄人 jiāorén ❶ villain holding sway ❷ treat others overbearingly; be haughty towards others:稍有成绩,便以此~ treat others condescendingly when having some achievement to one's credit

骄奢淫逸 jiāoshē-yínyì lordly, luxury-loving, loose-living and idle; wallowing in luxury and pleasure; extravagant and dissipated:~之徒 people who are given to dissipation and debauchery

骄阳 jiāoyáng 〈书面〉blazing or scorching sun:~似火 scorching sun /六月的~炙烤着大地。The blazing sun in June baked the earth.

骄盈 jiāoyíng 〈书面〉conceited and self-satisfied; arrogant and complacent

骄躁 jiāozào arrogant and impetuous:~的情绪 feel arrogant and impulsive

骄子 jiāozǐ favoured or favourite son;〈比喻〉spoiled son:天之~ God's favoured one; unusually lucky person /时代的~ favourite (*or* choice) of the time

骄恣 jiāozì 〈书面〉arrogant and wilful:~无节 be arrogant and

J

wilful to the extreme /居功～ claim credit for oneself and become arrogant
骄纵 jiāozòng arrogant and headstrong：～酷虐的暴君 wilful tyrant /～放恣 overbearing and debauched

焦[1] jiāo ❶ burnt; scorched; charred：～味 smell of burning; burnt smell /舌敝唇～ talk till one's tongue and lips are parched /饭烧～了。The rice is burnt. /椅子给火烧～了。The chair was charred by the fire. /你把我的衬衣烫～了。You scorched my shirt in ironing it. /他靠火太近，把眉毛烧～了。He got too near the fire and singed his eyebrows. ❷ coke：炼～ coking /结～ coke ❸ worried; anxious：心～ worried ❹〈中医〉certain parts of the body：三～ three visceral cavities housing the internal organs /上～ part of the body cavity above the diaphragm housing the heart and lungs /下～ part of the body cavity below the umbilicus housing the bladder, kidneys and bowels /中～ part of the body cavity between the diaphragm and the umbilicus housing the spleen, stomach, etc. ❺ (Jiāo) a surname

焦[2] jiāo (short for 焦耳)〈物理〉joule
焦比 jiāobǐ 〈冶金〉coke ratio
焦愁 jiāochóu worried; depressed：母亲为他的病昼夜～。Mother is worrying about his illness day and night.
焦脆 jiāocuì ❶ (of food) turn crisp after being baked or fried：～的麻花 crisp fried dough twist ❷ (of a voice, sound, etc.) clear; crisp：～的枪声 clear shots
焦点 jiāodiǎn ❶〈数学〉〈物理〉focal point; focus：主～ principal focus /虚～ virtual focus /实～ real focus ❷〈比喻〉central issue; focus; crux; point at issue：斗争的～ focus of the struggle /矛盾的～ focal points of contradictions /问题的～ crux (*or* heart) of the matter /争论的～所在。Here lies the point at issue.
焦度 jiāodù focal power
焦耳 jiāo'ěr 〈物理〉(transliteration) joule, a measure of energy
焦烦 jiāofán irritable; fidgety; agitated：你别叨叨了，叫人～得很。Stop nagging, as you are setting my nerves on edge.
焦干 jiāogān extremely dry：～的树叶，一点就着。The extremely dry leaves will catch fire the moment they are lit. /烈日下的前沿战士，嘴唇都～了。The lips of frontier guards have become parched under the scorching sun.
焦黑 jiāohēi be burned black; blacken with fire：被烧得～的土地 land blackened with fire /～的食物 burnt food
焦糊糊 jiāohūhū be burned black; blacken with fire
焦化 jiāohuà 〈化学〉coking; coal carbonization：延迟～ delayed coking /～厂 coking plant /～设备 coker
焦黄 jiāohuáng sallow; brown：脸色～ sallow face /把面包片头烤得～ toast slices of bread brown /煎得～的荷包蛋 eggs fried brown
焦急 jiāojí anxious; agitated; worried：～的神色 agitated look; perturbed look /为儿子的健康而～ be anxious about a son's health; worry over a son's health /～地在屋里走来走去 flutter about the room nervously /～不安 be on pins and needles; be in a flutter; be in a swivet /那位老人～万分。The old man was all anxiety.
焦痂 jiāojiā 〈医学〉eschar; scar
焦距 jiāojù 〈物理〉focal distance; focal length
焦渴 jiāokě terribly thirsty; parched：～难挨 unable to put up with the terrible thirst
焦枯 jiāokū shrivelled; dried up; withered：大旱之年，草木～。Grass and trees withered in the prolonged drought.
焦苦 jiāokǔ worried; depressed：他的前半生在～中度过。He lived the first half of his life in anxiety.
焦辣辣 jiāolālā ❶ irritating or acrid smell of sth. burnt：镇上一片火海，到处都能闻到～的气味。The town is a sea of fire and is pervaded by an irritating smell of burnt things. ❷ scorching or blazing hot：～的太阳 blazing sun; scorching sun ❸ burning with anxiety and remorse：听了这些话，他只觉得脸上～的不自在。Hearing these words, he felt uneasy, and his cheeks burned.
焦烂 jiāolàn burnt and worn out：衣服烧得～。The dress is burnt beyond recognition.
焦劳 jiāoláo 〈书面〉worry and trouble about：为国～ be deeply concerned about the country's affairs
焦雷 jiāoléi thunderclap; loud peal of thunder：打了一个大～。There was an earsplitting clap of thunder.
焦沥青 jiāolìqīng pyrobitumen
焦裂 jiāoliè split apart or crack because of a serious shortage of water：～的土地 cracked (*or* rent) ground; ground split apart because of a serious shortage of water; parched ground
焦溜鱼片 jiāoliū yúpiàn fried fish slices with sauce
焦炉 jiāolú coke oven
焦虑 jiāolǜ feel anxious; be troubled; have worries and misgivings：～不安 sit (*or* be) on thorns /他为父亲的健康而～。He is anxious about his father's health. /～有什么用呢？What's the use of worrying? /他感到～不安。His mind misgave him. /她的语调带着一点～。There was a note of concern in her voice.
焦煤 jiāoméi *also* "主焦煤" zhǔjiāoméi coking coal
焦墨 jiāomò thick ink; dried up ink
焦念 jiāoniàn worry about sb. who is absent; be very concerned about：她～着远方的儿子。She is full of concern for her son who is far away from home.
焦切 jiāoqiè anxious and impatient; restless with anxiety：～的心情 feel anxious and impatient
焦圈儿 jiāoquānr crisply fried ring of dough (for breakfast)
焦热 jiāorè extremely hot; scorching hot：～的日光 scorching daylight /他急得浑身～。He was burning with anxiety.
焦思 jiāosī rack one's brains; feel anxious：～苦虑 think very hard; cudgel one's brains
焦炭 jiāotàn coke：沥青～ pitch coke /～置换法 coke replacement ratio
焦糖 jiāotáng caramel
焦头烂额 jiāotóu-làn'é badly battered; in a terrible fix; in a sorry plight：敌军被打得～，狼狈逃窜。Badly battered, the enemy fled helter-skelter. /他起早摸黑，忙得～。He started work early and knocked off late, up to his neck with work.
焦土 jiāotǔ scorched earth — ravages of war：一片～ with everything burned down and lying in ruins /一场战乱，把这座城市变成了～。The war razed the city to the ground.
焦土政策 jiāotǔ zhèngcè scorched earth policy (in warfare)
焦萎 jiāowěi shrivelled; withered：被烤得～的树木又恢复了生气。The burnt and withered trees returned to life again.
焦心 jiāoxīn 〈方言〉feel terribly upset：等得～ feel terribly worried by (*or* from) waiting /孩子们挤在一间小房子里，看着就～。It really got me down to see the children cooped up in a tiny room.
焦忧 jiāoyōu feel anxious; be worried：他昼夜～，茶饭都觉得寡味。He is worried day and night, having no appetite for food or drink.
焦油 jiāoyóu 〈化学〉tar：煤～ coal tar /木～ wood tar
焦枣 jiāozǎo crisp date; fire-dried, stoned date
焦躁 jiāozào restless with anxiety; impatient：～不安 fidgety; on pins and needles; like a cat on hot bricks
焦炙 jiāozhì extremely anxious：她～得彻夜不眠。She was so anxious that she lay wide awake all night.
焦灼 jiāozhuó 〈书面〉deeply worried; extremely anxious：他眼里闪过一种～、痛苦的神情。There is a flash of anxiety and distress in his eyes.
焦子 jiāozi 〈方言〉coke

蕉 jiāo any of several broadleaf plants：香～ banana /芭～ *bajiao* banana; plantain /美人～ canna; Indian shot
see also qiáo
蕉柑 jiāogān *also* "招柑" zhāogān a kind of late-maturing orange
蕉麻 jiāomá *also* "马尼拉麻" mǎnílámá 〈植物〉abaca; Manila hemp; *Musa textilis*
蕉农 jiāonóng banana producer; banana farmer
蕉藕 jiāo'ǒu *also* "蕉芋"; "姜芋" jiāngyù 〈植物〉*Canna edulis*

礁 jiāo reef; rock：触～ strike a reef; run up on a rock /暗～ submerged reef /珊瑚～ coral reef /环～ atoll
礁湖 jiāohú lagoon surrounded by atolls
礁石 jiāoshí reef; rock

嶕 jiāo
嶕峣 jiāoyáo 〈书面〉stand tall and erect

僬 jiāo
僬侥 jiāoyáo 〈古语〉legendary dwarfs

J

鷦 jiāo

鷦鷯 jiāoliáo 〈动物〉wren

鷦莺 jiāoyīng 〈动物〉wren warbler

jiáo

嚼 jiáo

masticate; chew; munch: 细～慢咽 chew carefully and swallow slowly; chew one's food well before swallowing it /味同～蜡 like chewing wax — insipid /咬文～字 pay too much attention to wording; play with words; mince words

see also jiào; jué

嚼谷 jiáogu daily expenses

嚼裹儿 jiáoguor *also* "缴裹儿" jiǎoguor 〈方言〉daily expenses: 我挣的这点钱哪够～呀! How can my small earnings possibly cover the daily expenses?

嚼口 jiáokou bit (of a bridle): 拉住马～的绳环。Get hold of the bit of the bridle.

嚼蛆 jiáoqū 〈方言〉talk nonsense or rubbish: 走! 干活去, 别听他瞎～。Come off it! Go to work and don't listen to his nonsense.

嚼舌 jiáoshé *also* "嚼舌头"; "嚼舌根" ❶ wag one's tongue; chatter; blabber; gossip: 别在背后～。Don't gossip behind people's backs. /不要～。Don't wag your tongue. ❷ argue meaninglessly; squabble: 跟这种人～白费时间。You're wasting your time arguing with such people.

嚼烟 jiáoyān chewing tobacco

嚼用 jiáoyong 〈口语〉daily expenses: 人口多, ～大, 不节省点怎么行呢? With so many people in the family to provide for, how can I manage if I don't economize?

嚼子 jiáozi bit (of a bridle)

矫(矯) jiáo

argumentative; contentious; quarrelsome

see also jiǎo

矫情 jiáoqing 〈方言〉quarrelsome; contentious; unreasonable: 有理说理, 不要～。Be reasonable, if you think you are in the right. Stop quibbling. /这人太～。This person is too contentious.

see also jiǎoqíng

jiǎo

湫 jiǎo

〈书面〉low-lying

see also qiū

湫隘 jiǎo'ài narrow and low-lying: 街巷～ narrow and low-lying streets and lanes

筊 jiǎo

〈书面〉bamboo rope

铰 jiǎo

❶ 〈口语〉cut with scissors: ～条裤子 cut out a pair of trousers /～成两半 cut in two; cut into halves; cut in half /把绳子～断 cut the rope /把包装袋～开 cut open the packing bag ❷ *also* "绞" bore with a reamer; ream: *see* "～床"; "～孔" ❸ hinge: *see* "～接"

铰床 jiǎochuáng 〈机械〉reamer

铰刀 jiǎodāo ❶ 〈机械〉reamer ❷ 〈方言〉scissors

铰接 jiǎojiē 〈机械〉join with a hinge; articulate: ～框架 hinged frame /～式大客车 articulated bus /～无轨电车 articulated trolleybus

铰孔 jiǎokǒng 〈机械〉ream; reamed hole; reaming: ～车床 reaming lathe /～机 reaming bench; reaming machine; broaching machine; broacher /～钻床 reaming drill press

铰连叶片泵 jiǎolián yèpiànbèng 〈机械〉articulated vane pump

铰链 jiǎoliàn hinge: ～销 hinge pin /～接合 hinge joint

佼 jiǎo

〈书面〉beautiful; handsome; pretty: ～人 beauty /面目～好 of beautiful appearance

佼佼 jiǎojiǎo 〈书面〉above average; outstanding: 庸中～ outstanding among the mediocre; better than the common run of people

皎 jiǎo

❶ 〈书面〉clear and bright; white and luminous: ～月东升。A luminous moon is rising in the east. ❷ (Jiǎo) a surname

皎白 jiǎobái (of moonlight) bright and clear; white and luminous: ～银河 glistening white Milky Way /～的月光 bright and clear moonlight

皎皎 jiǎojiǎo very clear and bright; glistening white: ～者易污。The immaculate stains easily. *or* The immaculate is easily sullied.

皎洁 jiǎojié bright and clear: 一尊晶莹～的玉佛 a sparkling and crystal-clear jade statue of Buddha /今天的月亮显得格外～。The moonshine is unusually bright and clear tonight.

狡 jiǎo

crafty; foxy; cunning; sly

狡辩 jiǎobiàn argue without reason; quibble; resort to sophistry: 无理～ sheer sophistry /很会～ be good at quibbling

狡猾 jiǎohuá *also* "狡滑" sly; wily; crafty; cunning: 像狐狸一样～ (as) cunning as a fox /脸上露出～的微笑。A sly smile appears on the face.

狡计 jiǎojì tricky plot; crafty trick; wily trap: 谨防中了敌人的～ guard against falling into the enemy's trap

狡捷 jiǎojié 〈书面〉agile; swift; nimble

狡谲 jiǎojué 〈书面〉sly and treacherous

狡狯 jiǎokuài 〈书面〉crafty; deceitful; cunning: 此人～多变, 要多加小心。The man is capricious and deceitful; you've to be very careful with him.

狡赖 jiǎolài deny (by resorting to sophistry); cunningly disavow: 证据确凿, 不容～。The conclusive evidence admits of no denial.

狡兔三窟 jiǎotù-sānkū a wily hare has three burrows — a crafty person has more than one hideout: 俗话说"～", 总该多有儿条对策才好。As "A wily hare has three burrows", so we have to prepare several alternatives under the persent circumstances.

狡兔死, 良狗烹 jiǎotù sǐ, liánggǒu pēng *also* "狡兔死, 走狗烹" after the cunning hare is killed, the hound is boiled — get rid of those who help one seize power so one's success is assured: ～; 敌国灭, 谋臣亡。As the hound is boiled after the hare is killed, so the emperor's counsellor is doomed when the enemy state is destroyed.

狡黠 jiǎoxiá 〈书面〉sly; crafty; cunning: 她～地笑了笑, 没有马上回答他的问题。She smiled slyly, instead of giving him an immediate reply.

狡诈 jiǎozhà deceitful; crafty; cunning; tricky: 为人～ of deceitful temperament /玩弄～的手法 play tricks

狡展 jiǎozhan 〈方言〉deny (by resorting to sophistry); quibble: 他做了亏心事, 再～也无用。He has a bad conscience, and it's no use denying his part in it.

饺 jiǎo

a kind of dumpling: 水～ boiled dumplings (with meat and vegetable stuffing) /烫面～ steamed dumplings (with its dough mixed with boiling water)

饺子 jiǎozi dumpling (with meat and vegetable stuffing): ～皮 dumpling wrapper /～馅 filling for dumplings; stuffing /包～ make dumplings /煮～ boil dumplings in water

绞 jiǎo

❶ (of two or more strands) twist into one; entangle: 两股线～在一起了。Two strands of strings got entangled. /不要把这两个问题～在一起。Don't mix up (*or* confuse) these two questions. ❷ twist; wring: ～毛巾 wring (*or* twist) a towel /把床单～干 wring out a wet bed sheet /把那衣服～一把。Give those clothes a wring. /她心如刀～。She felt as if a knife were being twisted in her heart. /他们衣服湿透了, 可以～出水来。Their clothes are wringing wet. ❸ 〈机械〉reaming: ～孔 ream a hole ❹ hang by the neck: 把他～死! Hang him! ❺ wind: 用绞盘机把锚～起来 wind (*or* raise) the anchor up by turning the capstan ❻ 〈量词〉skein; hank: 一～纱 a hank of yarn /一～毛线 a skein of woollen yarn

绞包针 jiǎobāozhēn big needle (for sewing sacks, etc.)

绞缠 jiǎochán ❶ twist; plait; bind; wind: 小姑娘脑袋后面垂着～的发辫。The little girl has a plaited braid hanging at the back of her head. ❷ entangle; worry; harass: 这个问题紧紧～着他的心。He is very much harassed by this problem.

绞肠痧 jiǎochángshā 〈中医〉dry cholera

绞车 jiǎochē winch; windlass

绞刀 jiǎodāo 〈机械〉reamer

绞架 jiǎojià gallows: 他被送上了～。He was sent to the gallows.

绞结 jiǎojié twist; bind; wind; entangle: 他的心绪像千丝万缕, ～在一起。His mind, like a thousand and one threads twisted (*or*

twined) together, is in an awful tangle.
绞决 jiǎojué execute by hanging
绞脸 jiǎoliǎn (of a married woman) have the fine hair on her face removed by twisting and untwisting thin threads alternately to pull it out
绞脑汁 jiǎo nǎozhī rack one's brains; task one's mind:我绞尽脑汁回想究竟把书放到哪里去了。I cudgelled my brains trying to remember where I had left the book.
绞盘 jiǎopán capstan:推杆～ bar capstan
绞肉机 jiǎoròujī meat mincer or grinder; mincing machine:这种～非常好使。This kind of meat mincer works well.
绞杀 jiǎoshā ❶ hang (sb.) ❷ strangle; throttle:～于摇篮中 strangle in the craddle; nip in the bud /文化～ cultural strangle
绞纱 jiǎoshā 〈纺织〉 skein:～染色 skein dyeing
绞纱络筒机 jiǎoshā luòtǒngjī 〈纺织〉 drum hank winder
绞索 jiǎosuǒ (hangman's) noose:把～套在了他们自己的脖子上 have nooses tied round their own necks
绞滩 jiǎotān winch a ship across rapids
绞痛 jiǎotòng 〈医学〉 angina:肚子～ abdominal angina; colic /心～ angina pectoris
绞心 jiǎoxīn ❶ extremely sad; harrowing:娘儿俩为失去亲人而流着～的眼泪。Both the mother and child shed sad tears for the loss of their dear ones. ❷ rack one's brains:这无疑是他的多年～杰作，发表后定会得到读者的好评。Obviously this is his masterpiece after years of painstaking effort; it is sure to win the acclaim of readers when it is published.
绞刑 jiǎoxíng death by hanging; be condemned to be hanged; sentence to the gallows:～架 gallows (tree) /判处～的犯人 gallows bird /他这种人应处以～。People of his type are gallows-ripe.

搅(攪)

jiǎo ❶ stir; mix; mingle:把面粉和水～匀 mix up flour and water /～馅儿 mix the stuffing /把粥～凉了再喝 stir cool the porridge and then take it /我们只听见桨在湖里～得水响。The only sound we could hear was the splash of oars in the lake. /你和那些二流子～在一起，能搞出什么名堂来？It won't do you any good if you hang around with those loafers. ❷ disturb; upset; annoy:推土机的噪音～得人睡不着觉。The noise of the bulldozer is so annoying that people can hardly sleep.
搅拌 jiǎobàn stir; mix:放在水里，不停地～，使之溶解 put it in the water and keep on stiring until it is dissolved.
搅拌机 jiǎobànjī mixer:这是一种新型的～。This is a new-model mixer.
搅拌器 jiǎobànqì stirrer; agitator
搅拌箱 jiǎobànxiāng mixing box
搅缠 jiǎochán entangle and worry; pester; disturb:他顾不得和孩子～，急匆匆地走了。He left in a hurry, tearing himself from the children who were pestering him.
搅动 jiǎodòng ❶ stir; mix:～沉在水底的石灰 stir the lime at the bottom of the water /用筷子在碗里～ use chopsticks to stir what remains in the bowl ❷ disturb; mess up:～四邻 disturb the neighbours
搅街 jiǎojiē 〈方言〉 (of prostitutes) walk in the street to solicit patrons
搅哄 jiǎohong stir up trouble; create a disturbance:不许这帮人在这儿瞎～! They are forbidden to gather together here to create disturbances.
搅浑 jiǎohún stir into a muddy state; stir into a mess:把水～ stir water into a muddy state — create a disturbance; throw into turmoil
搅混 jiǎohun 〈口语〉 mix; blend; mingle:把水泥，沙和石子～在一起 mix cement, sand and pebbles /把好米和次米～到一块儿 blend high quality and low quality rice
搅和 jiǎohuo 〈口语〉 ❶ mix; mingle; involve:这是我们自己的事，你们别往里头～。This is our own business. Don't try to butt in. /你书念得太多，全～在一块儿啦。You have read too many books and have got all of them mixed up. ❷ mess up; ruin; spoil:昨天的会让他们几个～了。They spoiled yesterday's meeting.
搅局 jiǎojú upset the apple cart; make a mess of sth.:这个人爱～，谁都不愿同他共事。As he is a troublemaker, no one likes to work together with him.
搅炼 jiǎoliàn 〈冶金〉 puddling:～钢 puddled steel /～炉 puddle furnace; puddling furnace; puddler /～铁 puddled iron
搅乱 jiǎoluàn cause trouble; throw into disorder; mess up; disturb:要维持好秩序，防止有人～。It is imperative to maintain public order and prevent anyone from causing trouble. /她常～我的工作。She always pokes her nose into my affairs and makes a mess of my work. /警惕敌人～我们的阵线。We must be on our guard against any attempt of the enemy to create confusion in our ranks.
搅闹 jiǎonào make a din; raise roughhouse; disturb; harass:是谁在外面～? Who is making that noise outside?
搅扰 jiǎorǎo disturb; annoy; upset:对不起，～你了。Sorry to have disturbed you. *or* Sorry to have given you so much trouble.
搅乳 jiǎorǔ churnmilk:～机 churn

挢(撟)

jiǎo 〈书面〉 ❶ lift; raise:～首远望 raise one's head and look afar ❷ *see* "矫[1]❶" jiǎo

矫[1](矯)

jiǎo ❶ rectify; remedy; straighten out; correct:～俗 rectify a bad practice /～邪归正 turn over a new leaf ❷ (Jiǎo) a surname

矫[2](矯)

jiǎo strong; powerful; brave: *see* "～健"; "～捷"

矫[3](矯)

jiǎo pretend; feign; counterfeit:～诏 counterfeit an imperial edict; take unauthorized action in the name of an emperor
see also jiáo
矫激 jiǎojī 〈书面〉 ❶ rectify and encourage:～流俗 rectify a bad practice and encourage a good one ❷ (of writing and speech) go to extremes:～的愤世嫉俗的诗篇 poem which expresses extreme detestation of the world and its ways; poem which holds the world and its ways in utter contempt
矫健 jiǎojiàn strong and vigorous; brisk and dynamic; sturdy:身姿～，神采飞扬 glowing with health and radiating with vigour /～敏捷 sturdy and nimble /她勉强才跟上哥哥～的步伐。She was barely able to keep up the brisk pace of her brother.
矫矫 jiǎojiǎo 〈书面〉 ❶ brave and strong; chivalrous:～英姿 valiant and heroic in bearing ❷ superb; outstanding:～不群 out of the ordinary; preeminent /～不凡 out of the common run; prominent and distinguished
矫捷 jiǎojié vigorous and nimble; agile; brisk:他爬起树来，像猿猴那样～。When climbling a tree, he was nimble as a monkey.
矫命 jiǎomìng 〈书面〉 counterfeit an order; issue false orders
矫平 jiǎopíng 〈冶金〉 flattening; roll flattening; leveling:～机 leveling machine
矫情 jiǎoqíng 〈书面〉 be affectedly unconventional; pretend to be uncommon:～立异 contrive to be different /～干誉 hide one's true feeling to go after fame
see also jiáoqing
矫揉造作 jiǎoróu-zàozuò affected; artificial:～的笑容 artificial smile /她那～的姿态令人难以忍受。Her affectations are insufferable (*or* unbearable). /这位演员的表演有点～。This actor's performance is a bit affected.
矫若游龙 jiǎoruòyóulóng *also* "矫若惊龙" as dynamic as a flying dragon; as strong and brave as a lion:他的字飘若浮云，～。His handwriting has the flowing grace of the floating clouds and the brilliant vigour of a flying dragon.
矫饰 jiǎoshì feign in order to conceal sth.; dissemble; dissimulate:毫无～之处 free from (*or* without) any affectation /美是不能～的。It is impossible to dissemble beauty.
矫顽磁力 jiǎowán cílì 〈物理〉 coercive force:～表 coercimeter
矫枉过正 jiǎowǎng-guòzhèng exceed the proper limits in righting a wrong; overcorrect:矫枉必须过正，不过正不能矫枉。Proper limits have to be exceeded in order to right a wrong, or else the wrong cannot be righted. /你这样做未免有～之失。I'm afraid you've overdone it in righting the wrong.
矫味 jiǎowèi cover up a nasty smell; change an ugly taste:中药里，甘草可用来～。Liquorice root can be used to change the nasty taste of some traditional Chinese medicine.
矫形 jiǎoxíng 〈医学〉 orthopaedic
矫形术 jiǎoxíngshù 〈医学〉 orthopaedics:机械～ orthopraxy
矫形外科 jiǎoxíng wàikē 〈医学〉 orthopedic surgery; plastic

surgery:～学 orthopaedics (*or* orthopedics)
矫形医师 jiǎoxíng yīshī orthopaedist; orthopod
矫正 jiǎozhèng correct; remedy; put right; rectify:～偏差 rectify a deviation /～口吃 correct a stammer /～视力 remedy defects of vision /～学习方法 improve methods of study
矫直 jiǎozhí 〈冶金〉 flattening:拉伸～ stretcher leveling; straightening /～模 flattening die
矫直机 jiǎozhíjī 〈冶金〉 flattener unit; flattening machine; straightening machine; straightener
矫治 jiǎozhì correct and cure (such defects as strabismus, stammer, etc.):～口吃 correct and cure stammer /对视力减退的学生进行药物～。Give medical treatment to those students whose eyesight is failing.
矫作 jiǎozuò deliberate affectation:这篇小说人物塑造得很自然，毫无～之感。Characters depicted in this novel are all quite natural without any affectation.

侥(僥) jiǎo

see also yáo
侥幸 jiǎoxìng lucky; by luck; by a fluke:～心理 idea of leaving things to chance; trusting to luck /～得免 escape by good fortune /～考试及格 pass the examination by a fluke /子弹没有打着我，但我只是～脱险。The bullet missed me, but it was a close shave (*or* close call).

僬 jiǎo

僬倖 jiǎoxìng *see* "侥幸" jiǎoxìng

皦 jiǎo

❶〈书面〉(of jade, pearls, etc.) pure white; brilliant:～日 bright sun ❷〈书面〉pure; clean; clear ❸ (Jiǎo) a surname

徼 jiǎo

〈书面〉beg; request:～福 beg good fortune; request a blessing
see also jiào
徼倖 jiǎoxìng *see* "侥幸" jiǎoxìng

缴 jiǎo

❶ pay; hand over; hand in:～电话费 pay a telephone bill /～工会会费 pay trade union membership dues ❷ capture (arms):～了他们的武器 have captured their arms; have them disarmed
see also zhuó
缴付 jiǎofù pay:～水电费 pay the water and electricity bill
缴裹儿 jiǎoguor living expenses
see also "嚼裹儿" jiáoguor
缴获 jiǎohuò capture; seize:从敌人手里～的文件 documents seized from the enemy /一切～归公。Turn in everything captured.
缴纳 jiǎonà *also* "交纳" jiāonà pay:～学费 pay tuition /～税金 pay taxes
缴枪 jiǎoqiāng ❶ (of enemy) hand over arms; surrender:～不杀! Lay down your arms and we'll spare your lives! ❷ capture the enemy's guns:缴了十支枪 have captured ten rifles
缴税 jiǎoshuì *also* "交税" jiāoshuì pay taxes:他能自觉～。He pays taxes conscientiously.
缴销 jiǎoxiāo hand in for cancellation:汽车报废时要不要～原牌照? When a car is discarded as useless, should its licence plate be handed in for cancellation?
缴械 jiǎoxiè ❶ disarm:敌人被包围～。The enemy have been encircled and disarmed. ❷ (of enemy) surrender one's weapons; lay down one's arms:～投降 lay down one's arms and capitulate

脚(腳) jiǎo

❶ foot:赤～ barefoot /手～ (movement of) hands and feet /失～ lose one's footing /腿～ legs and feet /小～ bound feet /轻手轻～ gently; softly /手忙～乱 in a flurry ❷ base; foot:墙～ foot of a wall /山～ foot of a hill /裤～ bottom of a trouser leg ❸ *used in connection with carrying and transporting manually*:赶～〈旧语〉(of a porter) serve with a donkey or mule (for transport) /捎～ give sb. a lift (*or* ride) ❹〈方言〉dregs; residue:滓～ dregs /茶～ leftover tea and tea leaves
see also jué
脚板 jiǎobǎn sole (of the foot):山里人有一副铁～。People living in the mountains have a pair of toughened feet.
脚背 jiǎobèi *also* "脚面" instep
脚本 jiǎoběn script; scenario:电影～ scenario /相声～ crosstalk script
脚脖子 jiǎobózi 〈方言〉ankle:扭了～ sprain (*or* twist) one's ankle
脚步 jiǎobù ❶ step; pace; stride:～大 big step ❷ footstep; pace; walking movement:放慢～ slow down one's pace /噔噔的～声 stomping sound of one's footsteps /～踉跄 stagger; walk with unsteady step /听出某人的～声 recognize sb.'s footfalls /奇怪的是姐妹俩怎么这样不同:姐姐像大象一样重步慢行，妹妹却～轻快，有如舞蹈演员。It is curious that the two sisters should be so different; the elder stamps about like an elephant, the younger is light of foot as a dancer.
脚踩两只船 jiǎo cǎi liǎng zhī chuán *also* "脚踏两只船" straddle two boats — have a foot in either camp; hedge one's bets:～，两边买好儿 straddle two boats and curry favour with both sides
脚灯 jiǎodēng ❶ footlights ❷ night light
脚蹬子 jiǎodēngzi pedal; treadle
脚底 jiǎodǐ *also* "脚底板" sole (of the foot):～抹油 — 溜之大吉 rub oil on one's sole — sneak away; be as slippery as an eel /～起了茧。There are calli on the sole of the foot. *or* The sole of the foot has been calloused.
脚地 jiǎodì 〈方言〉floor (of a house or building):砖墁～。The floor is bricked.
脚店 jiǎodiàn 〈方言〉inn
脚垫 jiǎodiàn callus on the sole of the foot
脚法 jiǎofǎ skill in playing football or kicking the shuttlecock; footwork:～细腻 fine skill in sports, playing football, or kicking the shuttlecock, etc.; nimble footwork
脚夫 jiǎofū 〈旧语〉❶ porter:解放前他是个～。He used to be a porter before liberation. ❷ person who hires out his donkey or mule and accompanies it on foot
脚杆 jiǎogǎn *also* "脚杆子"〈方言〉leg:两条～都跑断了还没有到达目的地。I have been run off my legs, and yet the destination is not in sight.
脚跟 jiǎogēn *also* "脚根" heel:用～传球 pass the ball with his heel / 站稳～ stand firm; gain a firm foothold
脚孤拐 jiǎogūguai 〈方言〉metatarsal bone
脚行 jiǎoháng 〈旧语〉❶ agent or firm rendering service in transporting goods ❷ porter
脚痕 jiǎohén footprint; footmark; track
脚后跟 jiǎohòugen heel
脚户 jiǎohù 〈方言〉porter
脚花 jiǎohuā ❶ cotton of low quality ❷ cotton dregs (in a textile mill)
脚踝 jiǎohuái 〈生理〉malleolus; ankle
脚迹 jiǎojì footprint; footmark; track:森林里多处见到大象的～。Elephants' tracks are seen at quite a few places in the forest.
脚价 jiǎojià *also* "脚价钱"〈方言〉payment to a porter
脚尖 jiǎojiān tip of a toe; tiptoe:踮着～走 walk on tip-toe; tiptoe/他踮着～向前看。He looked forward by standing on tiptoe.
脚劲 jiǎojìn 〈方言〉strength of the legs:他～好，能走能跑。He has got strong legs and is able to walk and run easily.
脚扣 jiǎokòu climbers; climbing iron; grapnel
脚力 jiǎolì ❶ strength of one's legs:我～不行，走不得长路。I haven't got strong legs and can't walk a long distance. ❷〈旧语〉porter:雇个～ hire a porter ❸ payment to a porter:～已付。The porter has already been paid. ❹〈旧语〉tips paid to errand men who came to deliver gifts
脚镣 jiǎoliào fetters; shackles
脚炉 jiǎolú foot warmer; foot stove
脚路 jiǎolù 〈方言〉social connections (for securing jobs, etc.); pull
脚驴 jiǎolǘ donkey that is hired for transport
脚轮 jiǎolún caster; roller (small wheels fixed to the bottom of handbags, suitcases, sofa legs, bed legs, etc.)
脚马 jiǎomǎ *also* "马子" mǎzi; "脚马子" straw of rope, etc. worn over ordinary shoes to prevent sliding
脚门 jiǎomén *also* "角门" jiǎomén side gate
脚面 jiǎomiàn instep
脚牛 jiǎoniú 〈方言〉stud bull

J

脚盆 jiǎopén basin for washing one's feet
脚片 jiǎopiàn 〈方言〉foot
脚蹼 jiǎopǔ flipper (for swimming):他带上~,潜游到深水去。With flippers on, he dived into the deep water.
脚气 jiǎoqì 〈医学〉❶ beriberi ❷ athlete's foot
脚钱 jiǎoqian 〈旧语〉payment to a porter:他挣的~不够养家餬口。What he earned as a porter was not enough to make ends meet.
脚刹车 jiǎoshāchē foot brake:踩~ apply the foot brake
脚手架 jiǎoshǒujià 〈建筑〉scaffold; scaffolding
脚踏 jiǎotà foot-operated:~开关 foot-switch
脚踏板 jiǎotàbǎn treadle (of a sewing machine)
脚踏泵 jiǎotàbèng foot pump
脚踏车 jiǎotàchē *also*"自行车" zìxíngchē 〈方言〉bicycle
脚踏两只船 jiǎo tà liǎng zhī chuán *see*"脚踩两只船"
脚踏实地 jiǎotà-shídì have one's feet planted on solid ground — earnest and down-to-earth:~地干几年,准能干出点成绩来。Get down to earnest work for several years and you are sure to get somewhere.
脚踏脱粒机 jiǎotà tuōlìjī pedal thresher
脚踏制动 jiǎotà zhìdòng foot brake; pedal brake
脚梯 jiǎotī ladder fixed on a train for people to get on and alight
脚头 jiǎotóu ❶〈方言〉leg movement; pace:~快 fast-paced ❷ foot; footwork:~有功夫 have excellent footwork ❸〈旧语〉those who oversee the work of the porters and exploit them; overseer
脚腕子 jiǎowànzi *also*"脚腕儿" ankle
脚窝 jiǎowō 〈方言〉rather deep footprint or footmark:雪地上留着三个人的杂乱的~。Three men's deep footmarks were left in confusion on the snowy ground.
脚下 jiǎoxià ❶ under one's feet:~是一片草地。There is a lawn underfoot. ❷〈方言〉at present; right now:~是农忙季节,劳力比较紧张。As it is harvesting season, manpower is in short supply. ❸〈方言〉near; close; about:大年~ close to the Spring Festival
脚心 jiǎoxīn underside of the arch (of the foot); arch
脚癣 jiǎoxuǎn *also*"脚气"〈医学〉ringworm of the foot; tinea pedis; athlete's foot
脚丫子 jiǎoyāzi *also*"脚鸭子";"脚巴丫子"〈方言〉foot:光着~ barefooted/忙得~朝天 be up to one's neck in work
脚叶 jiǎoyè tobacco or vegetable leaves that are close to the root
脚印 jiǎoyìn footprint; footmark; track:踏着先辈的~前进 follow in the footsteps of one's predecessors/几个行人匆匆走过,在雪地上留下了一串串~。Several people walked past in a hurry, leaving behind lines of footprints on the snow.
脚鱼 jiǎoyú 〈方言〉soft-shelled turtle
脚闸 jiǎozhá backpedalling brake; coaster brake
脚掌 jiǎozhǎng sole (of the foot)
脚爪 jiǎozhǎo 〈方言〉paw; claw; talon
脚正不怕鞋歪 jiǎo zhèng bùpà xié wāi a straight foot is not afraid of a crooked shoe — an innocent person fears nothing:让他们去说三道四吧,我是~。Let them gossip. I have done nothing wrong and therefore have nothing to fear.
脚指甲 jiǎozhǐjia toenail
脚指头 jiǎozhǐtou 〈口语〉toe
脚趾 jiǎozhǐ toe
脚踵 jiǎozhǒng 〈书面〉heel
脚猪 jiǎozhū 〈方言〉stud pig; stud boar; breeding male pig
脚注 jiǎozhù footnote
脚镯 jiǎozhuó ankle bracelet; anklet
脚资 jiǎozī payment to a porter
脚踪 jiǎozōng footprint; footmark; track

角[1]

jiǎo ❶ horn:牛~ oxhorn/鹿~ antler/羊~ sheep horn/凤毛麟~ phoenix feathers and unicorn horns — precious and rare things ❷ bugle; horn:号~ bugle/鼓~ drum and horn (used in the army) ❸ horn-shaped thing:豆~ fresh kidney beans/皂~ Chinese honey locust/菱~ water caltrap/触~ antenna; feeler ❹ cape; promontory; headland:好望~ Cape of Good Hope/非洲之~ Horn of Africa ❺ corner:墙~ corner of a wall/眼~ corner of the eye/额~ frontal eminence/鬓~ hair on the temples/东北~ northeast corner/天涯海~ ends of the earth/英语~ English corner ❻〈数学〉angle:补~ complementary angle/对~ opposite angle/钝~ obtuse angle/锐~ acute angle/内~ interior angle/外~ exterior angle/多面~ polyhedral angle/反射~ reflex angle/邻~ adjacent angle/同位~ corresponding angle/二面~ dihedral angle/直~ right angle/三面~ triangle ❼〈量词〉quarter:一~饼 a quarter of a pancake ❽ first of the 28 constellations *see also*"二十八宿" èrshíbāxiù

角[2]

jiǎo *jiao*, fractional unit of money in China ($=\frac{1}{10}$ of a *yuan* or 10 *fen*):五元六~ five *yuan* and six *jiao*

角[3]

jiǎo *see*"饺" jiǎo
see also jué

角暗里 jiǎo'ànli 〈方言〉in the corner; in remote places:躲在~ hide oneself in a corner
角斑病 jiǎobānbìng 〈农业〉angular leaf spot
角刨 jiǎobào 〈机械〉angle plane
角材 jiǎocái 〈冶金〉angle section
角尺 jiǎochǐ angle square
角蛋白 jiǎodànbái 〈生化〉keratin
角动量 jiǎodòngliàng 〈物理〉angular momentum
角豆树 jiǎodòushù 〈植物〉carob
角度 jiǎodù ❶ angle; degree of angle:这个抽油烟机安装的~不合适。This cooker hood is not fixed at the proper angle. ❷ point of view; angle:从不同的~来看 view sth. from a different angle/不能光从个人的~来看问题。One shouldn't approach a problem only from one's personal point of view.
角度计 jiǎodùjì goniometer; angle gauge
角阀 jiǎofá 〈机械〉corner valve
角钢 jiǎogāng *also*"三角铁" sānjiǎotiě L-steel; angle iron or steel:~矫正机 angle straightener; angle straightening machine
角弓反张 jiǎogōng fǎnzhāng 〈医学〉opisthotonos
角管式锅炉 jiǎoguǎnshì guōlú 〈机械〉corner tube boiler
角规 jiǎoguī angle gauge
角果 jiǎoguǒ 〈植物〉seed composed of two carpels, with the pod cracking from base up when ripe
角花 jiǎohuā corner design (of a vessel or a piece of furniture); corner decoration
角化 jiǎohuà 〈生理〉cornification; keratinization:~组织 keratized tissue
角化癌 jiǎohuà'ái 〈医学〉cancroid
角化病 jiǎohuàbìng keratosis; keratoma:皮肤~ keratoderma/老年~ keratoma senile
角加速度 jiǎojiāsùdù 〈物理〉angular acceleration
角巾私第 jiǎojīn-sīdì live in retirement:老先生功在社稷,今日~,口不言功,真古名将风度! Sir, after performing meritorious deeds for your country, you now live in retirement and remain reticent about your exploits. This is the way of great generals of old!
角距 jiǎojù angle pitch; angular distance
角砾岩 jiǎolìyán 〈地质〉breccia
角楼 jiǎolóu watchtower at a corner of a citywall; corner tower; turret
角落 jiǎoluò ❶ corner:院墙内四个~都种上了果树。Fruit trees are planted in all the four corners of the courtyard. ❷ nook; remote place:躲在阴暗的~里搞阴谋诡计 plot in a dark corner/把家里的每个~都搜遍了,也没找到这件东西。We searched every nook and cranny of the house, but failed to recover the object.
角马 jiǎomǎ 〈动物〉gnu
角门 jiǎomén *also*"脚门" jiǎomén side gate:本医院职工多从~出入。Staff members of our hospital come and go through the side gate.
角膜 jiǎomó 〈生理〉cornea:~病〈医学〉keratopathy/~虹膜炎 keratoiritis; corneoitis/~结膜炎 keratoconjunctivitis/~切开术 keratotomy/~软化 keratomalacia
角膜混浊 jiǎomó hùnzhuó corneal opacity
角膜炎 jiǎomóyán 〈医学〉corneitis; keratitis; keratoiditis
角膜移植术 jiǎomó yízhíshù 〈医学〉keratoplasty; corneal transplantation
角票 jiǎopiào *also*"毛票" máopiào banknotes of one, two, or five *jiao* denominations
角球 jiǎoqiú 〈体育〉corner kick
角鲨 jiǎoshā 〈动物〉spiny dogfish
角闪石 jiǎoshǎnshí 〈矿业〉hornblende
角速度 jiǎosùdù 〈物理〉angular velocity
角台 jiǎotái frustum of a pyramid

角铁 jiǎotiě 〈冶金〉angle block; angle-iron; corner iron:～剪床 angle shear /～压直机 angle-iron straightening /～折弯机 angle-iron bending machine
角宿 jiǎoxiù 〈天文〉Spica
角压机 jiǎoyājī 〈冶金〉angle press
角岩 jiǎoyán 〈矿业〉hornstone
角页岩 jiǎoyèyán 〈矿业〉hornfels
角轧 jiǎozhá 〈冶金〉angular rolling
角质 jiǎozhì 〈生物〉cutin; keratin:～层〈植物〉cuticle
角雉 jiǎozhì 〈动物〉tragopan
角柱 jiǎozhù ❶ prism ❷ corner pillar
角柱体 jiǎozhùtǐ prism
角锥 jiǎozhuī *also* "角锥体" pyramid
角子 jiǎozi 〈方言〉〈旧语〉silver coin of one or two *jiao*
角坐标 jiǎozuòbiāo 〈数学〉angular coordinate

剿(勦) jiǎo send armed forces to suppress; put down; quell:清～ clean up; suppress /围～ encircle and annihilate /追～ pursue and wipe out
see also chāo
剿除 jiǎochú wipe out; exterminate; annihilate:～各路残敌 annihilate remnants of various enemy forces
剿匪 jiǎofěi suppress bandits
剿灭 jiǎomiè exterminate; wipe out:～残余土匪 exterminate the remnants of the bandits /派兵～ send troops to wipe out (bandits)

jiào

窖 jiào ❶ cellar or pit for storing things; cellar:地～ cellar / 菜～ vegetable cellar; clamp /冰～ icehouse /酒～ wine cellar /青贮～ ensilage cellar ❷ store (sth.) in a cellar or pit:～冰 store ice in a cellar
窖藏 jiàocáng store (things) in a cellar or pit:保存鲜薯的最好办法是～。The best way to keep sweet potatoes is to store them in a root cellar.
窖肥 jiàoféi 〈方言〉make compost (in a pit)
窖穴 jiàoxué cellar or pit for storing things
窖子 jiàozi 〈口语〉cellar or pit for storing things

滘 jiào 〈方言〉tributary of a river (often used in place names):道～ Daojiao (in Guangdong Province)

窌 jiào 〈书面〉cellar

觉(覺) jiào sleep:睡～ sleep /午～ afternoon nap; noontime snooze; siesta /今天睡了一大～。I had a sound sleep today.
see also jué

珓 jiào *also* "杯珓" bēijiào 〈书面〉divination implement (made of shells, bamboo or wooden pieces)

校 jiào ❶ check; proofread; collate:二～ second proof; proofread for the second time /～稿子 proofread manuscripts ❷ compare; contest: *see* "～场"
see also xiào
校本 jiàoběn collated edition (of a book)
校测 jiàocè calibrate and test:～功率 calibrate and test power
校场 jiàochǎng *also* "较场" jiàochǎng 〈旧语〉drill ground:～比武 hold a contest in military skills on the drill ground /～操练 military training in the drill ground
校雠 jiàochóu 〈书面〉collate:聚书数千卷,皆自～。He had several thousand volumes of books and collated them all himself.
校次 jiàocì number of times a proof is read before publishing:第三～ the third proof; proofread for the third time
校点 jiàodiǎn collate and punctuate:《史记》～本 collated and punctuated text of *Historical Records*
校订 jiàodìng check against the authoritative text:这本书的错讹之处较多,须重新～出版。There are many errors in this book, and it should be checked against the authoritative text and republished.
校对 jiàoduì ❶ check against a standard; calibrate:这台计量器已～合格。This measuring instrument has been calibrated. ❷ proofread; proof:这本书已印出样张,正在～。The specimen pages are already printed and are being proofread. ❸ proofreader:他在出版社当～。He works as a proofreader in a publishing house.
校对符号 jiàoduì fúhào proofreader's mark
校改 jiàogǎi read and correct proofs:这篇文章已经作者本人～。The proof of this article has been read and corrected by the author himself.
校核 jiàohé proofread; check against a standard; calibrate
校勘 jiàokān collate:～古书 collate ancient books /这个本子经过～,比较可靠。This book is fairly reliable after collation.
校勘学 jiàokānxué textual criticism
校猎 jiàoliè 〈旧语〉hunt animals by erecting wooden fences
校书 jiàoshū ❶ collate books ❷ 〈旧语〉another name for prostitute
校验 jiàoyàn calibrate and check:～控制台〈计算机〉checkout console /～员 check operator /～线路 checking circuit
校样 jiàoyàng proof sheet; proof:二～ second proof /长条～ galley proof /同意按～付印 pass the proofs for press /在～上修改 make corrections in proof
校阅 jiàoyuè ❶ read and revise:这本译著已经名家～。This translation has been read and revised by experts. ❷ 〈书面〉review:～三军 review troops of the three armed services
校正 jiàozhèng proofread and correct; correct; rectify:～错字 correct misprints /～仪器 rectify an instrument /重新～炮位 rectify the emplacement again /～补偿装置〈机械〉correction and compensation device /～控制模型 corrective control model
校注 jiàozhù check against the authoritative text and annotate:《水浒》～本 (checked and) annotated edition of *Water Margin*
校准 jiàozhǔn 〈机械〉calibration:方位～ bearing calibration /～器 calibrator /～设备 line-up test

较[1] jiào ❶ compare:～一～劲儿 have a trial of strength; compete /有一个～为清楚的概念 have a comparatively clear idea /我厂产量～去年增加百分之三十。The output of our factory has increased by 30 per cent as compared with last year. /任务～前更为繁重了。The task is more arduous than before. ❷ 〈书面〉haggle; quibble; dispute:锱铢必～ quibble over every penny; bicker about every trifle /斤斤计～ haggle over every ounce

较[2] jiào 〈书面〉clear; obvious; marked; evident:彰明～著 obvious; conspicuous /二者～然不同。The two are clearly different. *or* There is a marked difference between the two.
较比 jiàobǐ 〈方言〉comparatively; fairly; quite:这间屋子～宽绰。This room is relatively more spacious.
较场 jiàochǎng drill ground
see also "校场" jiàochǎng
较劲 jiàojìn *also* "叫劲" jiàojìn ❶ match one's strength with; have a contest with:暗中～ have a tacit contest with (*or* against) sb. /看来他决心跟我～。It seems he is determined to have a trial of strength with me. ❷ set oneself against; be at odds with:这两天天气真～,连水缸都结冰了。The weather is dreadful. Even the water vat is frozen over. ❸ require special effort:眼下是三夏时期,正是～的时候。Now is the busy summer season and we must put our shoulders to the wheel.
较量 jiàoliàng ❶ measure one's strength; have a contest; have a trial or test of strength; compete:暗地里在互相～ compete against each other in secret /综合国力的～ contest of comprehensive national power /经过反复的～,我们终于胜利了。After repeated trials of strength, we won out at last. /这是一场高水平的～。This is a high-level contest. /这场比赛,是一场技术和意志的～。This match is a test of skill and will. ❷ 〈方言〉haggle; argue; dispute:为了赶班机,他便不再和过去那样～车价。He did not haggle over the taxi fare as before since he had to catch a plane.
较为 jiàowéi a little more:现在他觉得～舒服些。Now he feels a bit more comfortable.
较真 jiàozhēn *also* "叫真" jiàozhēn 〈方言〉serious; earnest:老王干活可～儿啦,你可别马马虎虎的。Lao Wang is very serious with work, so don't be lackadaisical. /你较什么真儿啊! 他就是这么随便一说。Don't take it seriously. He just said it casually.
较著 jiàozhù 〈书面〉evident; obvious

see also "彰明较著" zhāngmíng-jiàozhù

斠 jiào ❶〈古语〉strickle ❷〈书面〉check against the authoritative text

教[1] jiào ❶ teach; instruct: 言传身~ teach by precept and example /管~ subject sb. to discipline; discipline /调~ guide (children) /家~ family education; upbringing /因材施~ teach students in accordance with their aptitude /请~ ask for advice; consult /孺子可~。The child is worth teaching. ❷ religion: 基督~ Christianity /佛~ Buddhism /道~ Taoism /伊斯兰~ Islam /信~ believe in a religion /传~ do missionary work /在~ be a follower (of a religion, etc.) ❸ (Jiào) a surname

教[2] jiào see "叫[2]" jiào
see also jiāo

教案 jiào'àn ❶ teaching plan; lesson plan ❷ case involving foreign missionaries in the last days of the Qing Dynasty

教本 jiàoběn textbook

教鞭 jiàobiān (teacher's) pointer: 他执~已有三十余年了。He has been teaching for more than thirty years.

教材 jiàocái teaching material; textbook: 编写~ compile teaching materials /辅导~ guidance teaching material; guidance material /大学英语~ college English textbook

教程 jiàochéng (often used in book titles) course of study; (published) lectures: 《对外关系史~》*A Course in History of Foreign Relations*

教导 jiàodǎo instruct; teach; give guidance: 在老师的~下 guided by the teacher /~有方 teach in the right way /接受师长的~ accept the teacher's guidance /有背家长的~ go against the guidance (*or* teaching *or* instructions) of one's parents

教导队 jiàodǎoduì training unit; officer-training corps (of an army)

教导团 jiàodǎotuán officer-training corps (of an army): ~团长 commandant of the officer-training corps

教导员 jiàodǎoyuán (battalion) political instructor

教德 jiàodé moral quality of a teacher; teaching ethics

教范 jiàofàn 〈军事〉manual: 兵器~ manual of arms; manual /射击~ manual of shooting (*or* marksmanship) /维修~ manual of maintenance

教坊 jiàofāng 〈旧语〉❶ office in charge of imperial music first set up during the Tang Dynasty ❷ prostitutes for government officials

教父 jiàofù ❶〈基督教〉theologian of the period from the second century AD to twelfth century AD who had the authoritative power in working out and interpreting creed ❷ godfather

教父教母 jiàofù-jiàomǔ godparents

教改 jiàogǎi (short for 教育改革) education(al) reform: ~组 education(al) reform group /这次会议是为了总结和推广~新成果。The meeting was held to sum up and publicize achievements of the educational reform.

教工 jiàogōng teaching and administrative staff (of a school)

教官 jiàoguān drillmaster; instructor

教管 jiàoguǎn subject to discipline: ~不严 not strict with sb.; lax in imposing discipline

教规 jiàoguī 〈宗教〉canon

教化 jiàohuà 〈书面〉educate; train in good manners; cultivate; edify: 古人重视诗歌的~作用。Ancient people paid attention to the educational role of music and poetry.

教皇 jiàohuáng 〈基督教〉pope; pontiff: ~自动诏书 *motu proprio*

教皇国 Jiàohuángguó 〈历史〉Papal States; States of the Church

教皇通谕 jiàohuáng tōngyù 〈基督教〉encyclical letter; literae encychlical; papal encyclical

教皇诏书 jiàohuáng zhàoshū 〈基督教〉papal bull

教会 jiàohuì (Christian) church: 东正~ Eastern Orthodox Church /~法规 canon law /~教育 parochial education

教会论 jiàohuìlùn 〈宗教〉church doctrine

教会学校 jiàohuì xuéxiào missionary school

教诲 jiàohuì 〈书面〉teaching; instruction: 长辈的谆谆~，我们永远也不会忘记。We will always bear in mind the earnest instructions of our elders.

教具 jiàojù teaching aid: 直观~ aids to object teaching; audio-visual aids

教科书 jiàokēshū textbook: 英语~ English textbook

教练 jiàoliàn ❶ train; drill; coach: 持枪~ drill with weapons /徒手~ drill without weapons /他~出了一批优秀的篮球运动员。He has trained a group of excellent basketball players. ❷ coach; instructor: 足球~ football coach /体操~ gymnastic coach /排球~ volleyball coach /~兼队员 playing coach /领队兼~ team leader and coach /~面授机宜。The coach gave a confidential briefing.

教练车 jiàoliànchē learner-driven vehicle

教练船 jiàoliànchuán training ship

教练弹 jiàoliàndàn practice projectile; dummy shell; dummy

教练机 jiàoliànjī trainer aircraft; trainer

教练员 jiàoliànyuán coach; instructor; trainer

教龄 jiàolíng years that a teacher spends in teaching; length of service as a teacher: 这所学校有五名三十多年~的老教师。The school boasts five veteran teachers of over 30 years' standing.

教令 jiàolìng 〈军事〉manuel of instruction: 飞行~ flight manual

教门 jiàomén ❶ Islam; Mohammedanism ❷ religious sect; denomination

教母 jiàomǔ godmother

教女 jiàonǚ goddaughter

教派 jiàopài religious sect; denomination

教区 jiàoqū 〈基督教〉parish: ~牧师 rector; vicar /主教~ diocese (a district under the pastoral care of a bishop); bishopric

教权主义 jiàoquánzhǔyì 〈宗教〉clericalism

教师 jiàoshī teacher; schoolteacher: 兼职~ part-time teacher /专职~ full-time teacher /中小学~ primary and secondary school teacher /历史~ history teacher

教师节 Jiàoshījié Teachers' Day (Sept. 10 in China)

教士 jiàoshì 〈基督教〉priest; clergyman; Christian missionary

教室 jiàoshì classroom; schoolroom: 视听~ audio-visual classroom /大~ lecture room; lecture hall /阶梯~ lecture theatre

教授 jiàoshòu ❶ professor: 副~ associate professor /客座~ visiting professor; guest professor /晋升为~ be promoted to professor ❷ instruct; teach: ~得法 teach with a correct approach /~历史 teach history

教授法 jiàoshòufǎ teaching method; pedagogics

教唆 jiàosuō instigate; abet; put sb. up to sth.: ~犯罪 instigate sb. to crime /~者 abettor /被~犯罪 subornation /这孩子让别人~坏了。The child has been put up to evil. *or* The child has been instigated to do evil.

教唆犯 jiàosuōfàn abettor; instigator

教唆罪 jiàosuōzuì instigation to a crime; solicitation

教坛 jiàotán teaching circles; teaching world: 蜚声~ be renowned in the teaching world

教堂 jiàotáng church; cathedral: 大~ abbey; cathedral /威斯敏斯特大~ Westminster Abbey /~长凳 pew

教条 jiàotiáo ❶〈宗教〉creed; canon; tenet ❷ dogma; doctrine; tenet: 不能把理论当成~。Theories must not be taken as dogmas. /你这个人对事情的看法太~。You are too dogmatic in your views. ❸ dogmatism

教条主义 jiàotiáozhǔyì dogmatism; doctrinairism: ~者 dogmatist; doctrinaire

教廷 jiàotíng (of Roman Catholicism) the Vatican; the Holy See

教廷大使 jiàotíng dàshǐ nuncio

教廷公使 jiàotíng gōngshǐ internuncio

教廷使节 jiàotíng shǐjié pontifical legate

教廷特使 jiàotíng tèshǐ papal legate

教头 jiàotóu drill master; instructor

教徒 jiàotú believer or follower of a religion: 基督~ Christian /耶稣~ Protestant /天主~ (Roman) Catholic /回~ Muslim; Moslem; Islamite; believer of Islamic faith /佛~ Buddhist /道~ Taoist /喇嘛~ Lamaist /公谊会~ Quaker /公理会独立派~ Independent /卫理公会派~ Methodist /再洗礼派~ Anabaptist

教委 jiàowěi (short for 教育委员会) Commission of Education (now Ministry of Education)

教务 jiàowù educational administration

教务处 jiàowùchù dean's office

教务长 jiàowùzhǎng dean of studies; academic dean

教习 jiàoxí ❶〈旧语〉school teacher ❷〈书面〉teach; train: ~书法 teach sb. calligraphy /~水师 train a naval force

教学 jiàoxué teaching; education: ~方法 teaching method /~内容

J

content of courses /～计划 teaching plan /～实习 teaching practice / 课堂～ teaching in classroom; classroom teaching /～医院 teaching hospital /～机器 teaching machine

see also jiāoxué

教学大纲 jiàoxué dàgāng teaching programme; syllabus

教学法 jiàoxuéfǎ pedagogy; teaching method:～研究 pedagogical research /教员应该研究～。Teachers should study pedagogy.

教学方针 jiàoxué fāngzhēn principle of teaching

教学改革 jiàoxué gǎigé *see* "教改"

教学人员 jiàoxué rényuán teaching staff; faculty

教学相长 jiàoxué-xiāngzhǎng teaching benefits teacher and student alike: 通过教学实践,青年教员懂得了～的道理。Through teaching, young teachers came to understand the meaning of "teaching benefits teachers as well as students."

教训 jiàoxun ❶ chide; teach sb. a lesson; give sb. a talking-to or dressing-down; lecture sb. (for wrongdoing, etc.):他喜欢～人。He is fond of lecturing others. /我要好好地～她一顿! I'll give that woman a piece of my mind. /老师～了我一番,因为我在课堂上不守纪律。The teacher told me off for lack of discipline in the classroom. /我永远忘不了我母亲经常～我的一句话,"一个人可以不做官,但要做人。" I'll never forget my mother's often-repeated admonition:"A person can live without being a high official, but he must live as a decent person." ❷ lesson; moral:血的～ lesson paid for with blood; lesson written in blood /吸取～ draw a lesson (*or* moral) from sth.; take warning from sth. /历史的～ lessons of history

教言 jiàoyán 〈书面〉words of admonition; instructions

教研室 jiàoyánshì teaching and research section; teaching and research division

教研组 jiàoyánzǔ teaching and research group

教养 jiàoyǎng ❶ bring up; teach; train; educate:父母有～子女的责任。Parents have the duty to educate their children. ❷ breeding; upbringing; education; culture:缺乏～ lack breeding; be uncouth / 这小伙子很有～。This young man is well educated. ❸〈法律〉correction; reeducation:劳动～ reeducation through labour

教养员 jiàoyǎngyuán kindergarten teacher

教养院 jiàoyǎngyuàn house of correction; reformatory; workhouse

教义 jiàoyì religious doctrine; creed; tenet

教益 jiàoyì 〈书面〉benefit gained from sb.'s wisdom; enlightenment; benefit from advice or instruction:希望你能从他的批评中得到～。I hope you'll benefit from his criticisms.

教友 jiàoyǒu 〈基督教〉fellow; brother; sister

教友会 Jiàoyǒuhuì *also* "公谊会" Gōngyìhuì Society of Friends; Quakers

教育 jiàoyù ❶ education; schooling:学龄前～ pre-school education /初等～ primary education; elementary education /中等～ secondary education /高等～ higher (*or* tertiary) education /职业技术～ professional and technological education /业余～ spare-time education /在职～ on-the-job education; mid-career education /成人～ grown-up (*or* adult) education /提高～质量 raise educational quality /～学院 college of education; normal college /～基金 education fund /我国的～事业在稳步发展。Education in our country is developing steadily. ❷ teach; educate; inculcate:～孩子尊重长者 teach children to respect their elders /～大家节约用水 inculcate in everybody the importance of saving water; inculcate everybody with the need to be economical in using water /思想～ ideological education / 用说服～的方法解决问题 solve problems through persuasion and education /这些事情～了我。These facts have enlightened me.

教育部 jiàoyùbù Ministry of Education

教育程度 jiàoyù chéngdù level of education

教育电视 jiàoyù diànshì instructional televison; education TV station or programme

教育方针 jiàoyù fāngzhēn policy for education; educational policy:我们的～,应该使受教育者在德育、智育、体育几方面都得到发展,成为有社会主义觉悟的、有文化的劳动者。It's our educational policy to enable everyone who receives an education to develop morally, intellectually and physically and become a worker with both socialist consciousness and culture.

教育革命 jiàoyù gémìng revolution in education

教育家 jiàoyùjiā educationist; educator

教育界 jiàoyùjiè educational circles; educational world

教育统筹司 Jiàoyù Tǒngchóusī (HK) Secretary for Education and Manpower (before July 1997)

教育心理学 jiàoyù xīnlǐxué educational psychology

教育学 jiàoyùxué pedagogy; pedagogics; education

教育制度 jiàoyù zhìdù system of education

教谕 jiàoyù ❶ teaching; instruction:谨遵～ carefully follow the instructions ❷ religious instructions

教员 jiàoyuán teacher; instructor:一位有经验的～ an experienced teacher /充当反面～ play the role of a negative teacher; serve as a teacher by negative example

教员休息室 jiàoyuán xiūxishì staff room; common room

教泽 jiàozé enlightenment received from a teacher:难忘老师多年的～。I shall always remember my teacher for the benefits he has given me over the years.

教长 jiàozhǎng 〈伊斯兰〉imam;〈基督教〉dean

教长国 jiàozhǎngguó 〈伊斯兰〉imamate

教正 jiàozhèng 〈书面〉〈套语〉instruct and correct; give advice and comment:送上拙著一册,敬希～。With the compliments of the author.

教职员 jiào-zhíyuán teaching and administrative staff

教主 jiàozhǔ founder of a religion; patriarch

教子 jiàozǐ godson

滶

jiào *see* "滘" jiào

酵

jiào ferment; leaven:引～ leaven /发～ ferment; leaven

酵母 jiàomǔ *also* "酵母菌";"酿母菌" niàngmǔjūn yeast:鲜～ yeast cake

酵母菌 jiàomǔjūn saccharomycete

酵素 jiàosù 〈化学〉ferment; enzyme

酵子 jiàozi 〈方言〉leaven

藠

jiào

藠头 jiàotou 〈植物〉Chinese onion (*Allium chinense*)

斠

jiào 〈方言〉if only; provided

叫[1](呌)

jiào ❶ cry; shout; yell:大～一声 give a loud cry; yell /尖～ scream; shriek /嗥～ *also* "嚎～" howl /吼～ roar / 狗～ bark /鸡～ crow /猫～ mew; miaow /驴～ bray /羊～ bleat /马～ neigh /大喊大～ shout at the top of one's voice /拍手～好 clap and shout "bravo" /她兴奋得～了起来。She gave a shout of excitement. / 汽笛在～。The steam whistle is blowing. ❷ greet; call; ask:她在隔壁房间,请～她过来。She is in the next room; please ask her over. / 你去～他们快来。Go and ask them to come quickly. /老张～你。Old Zhang is calling you. /你的电话～通了。Your call has been put through. /这孩子认生,不爱～人。The child shies at strangers and doesn't like to greet people. /谁～门呢? Who's knocking at the door? ❸ hire; order; get:～出租车 hire a taxi; call a taxi /～了一车蜂窝煤 order a cartload of honeycomb briquetes /～几个人来帮忙。Get some people to help. ❹ name; call; designate:我们～他老王。We call him Old Wang. /这盘棋下得真～棒。This is a really exciting chess game. ❺〈方言〉male (animal or fowl): *see* "～驴";"～鸡"

叫[2](呌)

jiào ❶ make; order; ask:～人为难 make one feel embarrassed /医生～我好好休息。The doctor ordered me to have a good rest. /这件事很～她伤心。She was saddened by this affair. /～我怎么办? What shall I do? ❷ allow; permit; let:他不～我去,我只好不去。I can do nothing but stay since he doesn't allow me to go. ❸〈介词〉*used to introduce the doer of an action*:玻璃杯～儿子打碎了。The glass was broken by my son. /所有的对手都～他一个一个给打败了。All the opponents were beaten by him one after another. /我～雨淋了。I was caught in the rain.

叫板 jiàobǎn 〈戏曲〉rhyme the last sentence of a spoken part to introduce a singing part; use movements as a prelude to singing

叫菜 jiàocài order dishes:他一下子～了四个菜。He ordered four dishes at once.

叫春 jiàochūn (of cats) mating call

叫哥哥 jiàogēge 〈方言〉〈动物〉katydid; long-horned grasshopper

叫喊 jiàohǎn shout; yell; howl:你在公共场所这样大声～,岂不影响了别人? You are shouting at the top of your voice in public places. Won't that disturb other people?

J

叫号 jiàoháo shout loudly; cry out loudly; yell
叫好 jiàohǎo applaud; shout "Bravo!"; shout "Well done!":他的精彩表演，博得全场～。His excellent performance brought the house down.
叫号 jiàohào ❶ call a number:看病的人都坐在门外等候护士～。Registered patients are all waiting outside of the door for the nurse to call their numbers. ❷〈方言〉sing a work song to synchronize movements, with one person leading:几个小伙子叫着号把大木头抬起来。Several young fellows managed to lift the big woodblock by chanting a work song. ❸〈方言〉provoke by words; challenge:他这样说简直是在～。He is deliberately trying to kick up a row.
叫横 jiàohèng say harsh and unreasonable words:你没有本事就得认输，不必跟我～。You have to admit defeat since you are not up to the job. Don't try to pick on me.
叫吼 jiàohǒu roar; bawl:汽笛一声～，车轮慢慢启动了。With the blowing of the steam whistle, the wheels started moving.
叫呼 jiàohū shout; yell:你～个啥呀? 他上街买东西去了。Why all this shouting? He is out shopping.
叫花子 jiàohuāzi *also*"叫化子"〈口语〉beggar:～照火，只往自己怀里扒。Like beggars trying to get warm by a fire, everyone wants to get near it — be concerned with one's own interest only.
叫花子鸡 jiàohuāzijī beggar's chicken (whole chicken baked in a mud coating)
叫唤 jiàohuan ❶ cry out; call out:肚子疼得直～ cry out with stomachache／已经是大人了，这点苦也不能吃，～什么! A grownup like you should be able to stand this pain. Come on, stop yelling.／天一亮，妈妈就～我们起床。Mother would call us to get up the minute the sun rose. ❷ (of animals) cry; shout:小鸟在树上叽叽喳喳地～。Small birds are chirping in the tree.
叫魂 jiàohún *also*"喊魂" hǎnhún〈迷信〉call back the spirit of the sick
叫鸡 jiàojī〈方言〉cock; rooster:天不亮～就打鸣。The rooster crows just before dawn.
叫街 jiàojiē beg food by shouting along the street:～的 beggar
叫劲 jiàojìn *see*"较劲" jiàojìn
叫绝 jiàojué applaud as the very best (one has seen, etc.); shout "Bravo!":拍案～ applaud by thumping the table; thump the table and shout "Bravo!"
叫苦 jiàokǔ complain of hardship:～叫累 complain of hardship or fatigue／她只有暗暗～。She could do nothing but groan inwardly.
叫苦不迭 jiàokǔ-bùdié pour out endless grievances; complain incessantly:物价飞涨，老百姓～。With soaring prices there are no end of complaints among the ordinary people.
叫苦连天 jiàokǔ-liántiān complain to high heaven; ventilate one's bitter grievance:苛捐杂税层出不穷，弄得老百姓～。The ever-increasing taxes and levies caused widespread discontent among the people.／那些跟去的人，谁是愿意的? 不免心中抱怨，～。None of the servants escorting them wanted to go. Simmering with resentment they cursed their fate.
叫驴 jiàolǘ〈方言〉jackass
叫骂 jiàomà shout curses:他突然～起来，别人怎么也劝不住。He started to shout curses all of a sudden, and people failed to dissuade him, however hard they tried.
叫卖 jiàomài cry one's wares; peddle; hawk:沿街～ hawk one's wares in the streets／楼下不时传来小贩的～声。Peddlers' cries came time and again from downstairs.
叫门 jiàomén call at the door (to be let in):你听听，好像有人在～。Listen, it seems someone's calling at the door.
叫名 jiàomíng ❶ name; term; designation:这只是当地的～。This is only a local name for it. ❷〈方言〉nominal; existing in name or word, not in fact:这孩子～七岁，其实还不到六岁。The kid is said to be seven; in fact he is not six yet.
叫鸣 jiàomíng (of cocks) crow
叫牌 jiàopái bid (at bridge):该你～了。It's your bid now.
叫屈 jiàoqū complain of being wronged; protest against an injustice:喊冤～ cry out about one's grievances
叫嚷 jiàorǎng shout; howl; clamour:胡乱～ shout and scream madly／歇斯底里地～ yell hysterically／你们别～了好不好? 屋里有病人。Stop shouting, will you? There is a sick person in the house.
叫天子 jiàotiānzi〈方言〉〈动物〉skylark
叫条子 jiào tiáozi〈旧语〉write on a slip of paper to call for prostitutes or courtesans
叫响 jiàoxiǎng win applause; be successful and acknowledged:在全国～的名牌产品 brand-name product which has become famous all over the country／买卖～了。Our business has made a good start.
叫嚣 jiàoxiāo clamour; raise a hue and cry:拼命～ raise a terrific hue and cry; raise a hullabaloo; kick up a din／据理反击各种污蔑和战争～ justly rebut all kinds of slanders and war clamour
叫啸 jiàoxiào whistle; scream:一颗颗的子弹～而来。Shots came whistling one after another.
叫歇 jiàoxiē〈旧语〉go on a strike:聚众～ gather a crowd for a strike
叫醒 jiàoxǐng wake up; awaken:快～他，马上就要出发了。Wake him up quickly. We are going to set out immediately.
叫真 jiàozhēn *also*"较真" jiàozhēn〈方言〉be earnest; be serious:说一说就算了，干吗那么～儿呀? It's enough to make him aware of the matter. Why do you take it so seriously?
叫阵 jiàozhèn challenge an opponent to a fight; throw down the gauntlet
叫字号 jiào zìhao ❶〈旧语〉good name; name of a famous shop; name of a shop with a good reputation:在这一带，他的商号很～。His shop is of good repute in this area. ❷ flaunt one's superiority; throw one's weight about:这件事办砸了，他就别再～了。If he doesn't do this well, he will no longer be in a position to throw his weight about.
叫子 jiàozi〈方言〉whistle
叫座 jiàozuò draw a large audience; appeal to the audience; be a box-office success:这位演员在青年观众中最～。This actor draws the largest audience among the youngsters.／这部电影很～。This film is quite a box-office success.
叫做 jiàozuò *also*"叫作" be called; be known as:我们的组织原则～民主集中制。Our organizational principle is known as democratic centralism.／通常把中秋节～八月节。Mid-Autumn Festival is generally called August Festival.

嚼

jiào *see*"倒嚼" dǎojiào
see also jiáo; jué

皭

jiào〈书面〉pure white; spotlessly clean

轿(轎)

jiào sedan (chair); litter:彩～ bridal sedan chair／花～ bridal sedan chair／山～ mountain litter／驮～ sedan (chair) carried on an animal's back
轿车 jiàochē ❶〈旧语〉(horse-drawn) covered carriage ❷ bus or car:大～ bus; coach／小～ car; limousine; sedan／三排座小～ limousine
轿夫 jiàofū one who lives by carrying sedans; sedan carrier
轿子 jiàozi sedan (chair):抬～ carry a sedan;〈比喻〉sing the praises of (influential people)／坐～ sit on sedan; go by sedan chair

峤(嶠)

jiào〈书面〉mountain path
see also qiáo

醮

jiào ❶〈旧语〉libation at wedding ceremony:再～ (of a woman) remarry ❷ Taoist sacrificial ceremony:打～ perform a Taoist ritual／斋～ go fasting

噍

jiào〈书面〉chew; eat:倒～ chew the cud; ruminate／齿以～食。Teeth are for chewing food.
噍类 jiàolèi〈书面〉living beings; human beings:一城无～ no living human beings in the whole city

嗷

jiào〈书面〉cry; yell

徼

jiào〈书面〉❶ boundary:边～ boundary ❷ patrol:～巡京师 patrol the capital city
see also jiǎo

jiē

秸(稭)

jiē grain stalk after threshing; straw:麦～ wheat straw／豆～ bean stem (*or* stalk)／花～ chopped straw／秫～

J

gaoliang stalk; sorghum stalk

秸秆 jiēgǎn straw; crop stalks after threshing:～还田 use plant stalks as fertilizer for the fields

秸子 jiēzi 〈方言〉crop stalks after threshing:包米～ corn stem; maize stalk

结 jiē bear (fruit); form (seed); produce:～了不少葡萄 have borne quite a lot of grapes /只开花不～果 blossom without bearing fruit /这种花不～子。This flower doesn't produce (*or* form) seeds. *or* This flower doesn't go to seed.

see also jié

结巴 jiēba ❶ stammer; stutter:～得厉害 stammer badly /他结结巴巴地找了个借口。He stammered out an excuse. /我只好用结结巴巴的广东话和他交谈。I could only stutter (out) a conversation with him in Cantonese. ❷ stammerer; stutterer:他是个～。He is a stammerer (*or* stutterer).

结巴颏子 jiēbakēzi 〈方言〉stammerer; stutterer

结果 jiēguǒ bear fruit; fructify:开花～ blossom and bear fruit; produce positive results /～期 fructescence /～树 fruiter /这些树每年～。These trees fruit annually.

see also jiéguǒ

结实 jiēshí bear fruit; fructify:苹果树今年～特早。The apple trees are fruiting early this year.

结实 jiēshi ❶ solid; sturdy; stout; durable:～的椅子 solid chair /～的布 strong (*or* sturdy, *or* tough) cloth /～的合成纤维织物 hard-wearing synthetic fabrics /～的绳子 stout rope /这种料子不太～。This kind of material is not very durable. /他的手脚都被捆了个～。Both his hands and feet are tied fast. ❷ strong; sturdy; tough; robust:身体～的人 sturdily built man /～的肌肉 firm muscles; strong muscles /～的拳头 iron fist /你的身子骨比我～多了。You're much stronger than I am.

节(節) jiē

see also jié

节骨眼 jiēguyǎn 〈方言〉critical juncture; vital link:他正在～上赶了回去。He arrived in the nick of time! /在目前这个～上,咱们可不能大意! We cannot afford to be careless at this critical moment.

节子 jiēzi knot (of wood)

疖(癤) jiē

疖子 jiēzi ❶〈医学〉furuncle; boil:手上长了个～。There is a boil on the hand. ❷ knot (in wood)

接 jiē ❶ come into contact with; come close to; be in touch with:短兵相～ hand-to-hand fight; fighting at close quarters; close-range fighting /交头～耳 speak in each other's ears /待人～物 the way one gets along with people ❷ connect; join; link up; put together:把两根电线～上 connect the two pieces of wire /～管子 join two pipes together /～线头 tie broken threads; join two threads together /上气不～下气 be out of breath /一个～一个的胜利 succession of victories; one victory after another /～上页末行 continued from the last line of preceeding page /请～2175 分机。Extension 2175 please. /请～英语系。Put me through to the English Department, please. /天线地线都～好了。Both the aerial and the ground wire are fixed. /这个片子剪～得很好。This film is well edited. ❸ catch; take hold of:用脸盆～漏 use basins to catch leaking water /你先把箱子～一下。Please take hold of the box for a moment first. /这种刁球我～不好。I am not good at receiving such a tricky service. ❹ receive; take; accept:～到上级指示 receive instructions from higher authorities /～电话 answer the phone; receive a phone call; take (*or* accept) a phone call /我们好久没～到他的来信了。We haven't heard from him for quite some time. /你的钱我不能～。I can't take (*or* accept) your money. ❺ meet; welcome:到机场～人 go to the airport to meet sb. /把客人～进大厅 welcome the guests to the hall; usher the guests into the hall ❻ take over; succeed:～李老师的课 take over Professor Li's class /你走后谁～所长的职务? Who will succeed you as the institute director after you leave? ❼ (Jiē) a surname

接班 jiēbān take one's turn on duty; take over from; carry on:～的时间到了。It is time to change shifts. /我这就去～。I'm going to take a turn on duty right now. /我今天接夜班。I'll be on the night shift today. /局长要退休了,我想你会接好班的。The bureau chief is going to retire, and I believe you will be his qualified successor.

接班人 jiēbānrén successor:当好社会主义建设事业的～ be worthy successors to the socialist cause

接茬儿 jiēchár 〈方言〉❶ pick up the thread of a conversation; chime in:我就讲这些,谁～说? I'll stop here. Who will speak next? ❷ after that; and then:他们～把明天的工作商量了一下。After that they began to discuss next day's work.

接产 jiēchǎn midwiving; helping female animals to deliver their young

接长不短 jiēcháng-bùduǎn 〈方言〉often; frequently:这个人～地捅娄子。This man often makes blunders.

接触 jiēchù ❶ come into contact with; get in touch with:与群众保持～ keep in touch with the masses /～语言环境 be exposed to a (foreign) language /竹竿太短,～不到房檐。The bamboo stick is too short to reach the eaves. /会议期间我们～了许多外国代表。During the session, we came into contact with a good number of foreign delegates. ❷ engage:两支舰队已脱离～。The two fleets have disengaged. /午夜时分,与敌军主力～。We engaged the main force of the enemy at about midnight. ❸〈电工〉contact:～不良 loose contact; poor contact /～故障 contact fault /～断路器 contact breaker /～放电加工 electro-arc contact machining

接触传染 jiēchù chuánrǎn 〈医学〉contagion:～病 contagious disease

接触炉 jiēchùlú 〈化学〉contact furnace

接触性皮炎 jiēchùxìng píyán 〈医学〉contact dermatitis

接触眼镜 jiēchù yǎnjìng *also* "隐形眼镜" yǐnxíng yǎnjìng contact lenses

接触政策 jiēchù zhèngcè 〈外交〉policy of engagement:奉行积极接触的政策 pursue a policy of active engagement

接待 jiēdài receive; admit:热情地～顾客 warmly receive customers /～中心 reception centre /这个招待所可～三百人。This guest house accommodates three hundred people. /这个展览会已开始～观众。This exhibition is now open for (*or* to) visitors.

接待单位 jiēdài dānwèi host organization

接待人员 jiēdài rényuán reception personnel; receptionist

接待日 jiēdàirì reception day (when a leader of an organization receives visitors to listen to their suggestions, complaints, etc.)

接待团 jiēdàituán reception committee:～团长 chairman of the reception committee; head of the host team

接待站 jiēdàizhàn reception centre

接敌 jiēdí 〈军事〉close with the enemy; engage the enemy:～队形 approach formation

接地 jiēdì ❶〈电工〉ground connection; grounding earthing:～线 ground wire; earth lead ❷〈航空〉touchdown; ground contact:～迎角 landing angle

接点 jiēdiǎn 〈电工〉contact

接二连三 jiē'èr-liánsān one after another; in quick succession; repeatedly:～地遭受挫折 suffer repeated setbacks /最近厂里～地出事故。Accidents happened in quick succession recently in the factory. /此方人家都用竹篱木壁,于是～,牵五挂四,将一条街烧得如"火焰山"一般。Since most of the nearby buildings had bamboo fences and wooden walls, the fire spread from house to house until the whole street was ablaze like a flaming mountain.

接防 jiēfáng relieve a garrison; relieve:～部队 relieving unit

接风 jiēfēng give a dinner for a visitor from afar; give a welcome dinner:～洗尘 give a dinner of welcome

接羔 jiēgāo 〈畜牧〉deliver lambs:～房 lamb-delivery room /～季节 lambing season

接骨 jiēgǔ set a (broken) bone; set a fracture

接骨术 jiēgǔshù 〈医学〉osteopathy; coaptation; bonesetting

接管 jiēguǎn take over (control):～倒闭的企业 take over a bankrupt enterprise /他退休后,部分工作由我～。I'll take over part of his work after his retirement.

接轨 jiēguǐ ❶ connect the rails:兖石铁路全线～铺通。The whole Yanzhou-Shijiazhuang railway has been laid and connected. ❷ get onto the track; switch over to; integrate:与世界经济～ get integrated into the world economy / 与国际惯例～ follow international practice

接合 jiēhé 〈机械〉joint:气密～ airtight joint /水密～ watertight joint /～器〈机械〉adapter

接合部 jiēhébù *also* "接合点"〈军事〉junction point

接活 jiēhuó accept work; receive an order

接火 jiēhuǒ ❶ start to exchange fire:小分队在桥头与敌人~。The squad started to exchange fire with the enemy at the end of the bridge. ❷〈电工〉energize:这座楼刚盖好,就~了。The building was connected to the electric mains immediately after its completion.

接济 jiējì give material assistance to; give financial aid to;supply:~物资 supply relief goods and materials /受到亲友的~ get pecuniary help from relatives /大雪封山, 有的哨所粮食一时~不上。As all mountain passes had been sealed by the heavy snow, some sentry posts could not be supplied in time.

接驾 jiējià greet an emperor; welcome an emperor

接见 jiējiàn receive; give an interview to:~记者 give an interview to correspondents /~外交使节 receive foreign diplomats /~来访的外国贵宾 meet visiting foreign dignitaries

接界 jiējiè have a common border; have a common boundary; border

接近 jiējìn be close to; be near; approach; approximate:~世界先进水平 approach the advanced world level /~群众 be in close contact with the masses /易于~ be easy of approach (*or* access) /难以~ be difficult to approach; be stand-offish /~完工 be near completion /~正常 be close to normal /~点 point of proximity /~权 right of approach /意见非常~ have almost identical views; see pretty much eye to eye

接颈交臂 jiējǐng-jiāobì be neck to neck and arm in arm; be very intimate: 他们青梅竹马, ~。They have been together since childhood and are very intimate with each other.

接境 jiējìng have a common border; border:鲁南与苏北~。Southern Shandong borders on northern Jiangsu.

接客 jiēkè ❶ receive guests ❷ (of a prostitute) receive or entertain a client

接口 jiēkǒu ❶ continue the conversation; cut in:大妈马上接上口说:"有不到的地方请多多担待。" The old lady immediately cut in, "Please pardon us if we've done anything wrong." ❷ join; junction:这里正是新沟与旧沟~的地方。This is the junction of the new and old channels. ❸ opening that is cut when grafting:用芽接刀来~ use a bud grafting knife to cut an opening ❹〈信息〉interface

接口信息处理机 jiēkǒu xìnxī chǔlǐjī interface message processor (IMP)

接力 jiēlì relay:四百米~ 400-metre relay /火炬~ torch relay /混合泳~ (in swimming) medley /自由泳~ crawl relay /~运输 relay transport /异程~ medley relay /~练习 relay practice /~运动员 relay member

接力棒 jiēlìbàng relay baton

接力赛跑 jiēlì sàipǎo relay race; relay:~队 relay team

接连 jiēlián on end; in a row; repeatedly; in succession:~两次获得锦标赛冠军 win the championship twice in a row /~两个星期 for two weeks on end /~几年获得丰收 reap bumper harvests for years running /~不断 continuously; incessantly; in rapid succession /~打了几次电话 make repeated phone calls /~写了几封信 write several letters at a stretch

接邻 jiēlín border on; be next to; adjoin:中国与许多国家~。China borders on quite a number of countries.

接龙 jiēlóng (in cards or dominoes) build a sequence or run

接木 jiēmù graft woody plants

接目镜 jiēmùjìng eyepiece; coular; lens

接纳 jiēnà ❶ admit (into an organization);accept (as a member):讨论~会员问题 discuss the question of admitting new members /她被~为工会会员。She was accepted as a member of the trade union. ❷ adopt; accept; take:他~了大家的意见。He took our advice.

接盘 jiēpán *also* "受盘" shòupán accept what is offered for sale and continue the management; buy (a business, etc.)

接片 jiēpiàn 〈影视〉splicing:~机 splicer

接气 jiēqì coherent; consistent:这些报道前后不~。These reports lack consistency. /这两段文章不太~。These two paragraphs are not quite coherent.

接洽 jiēqià take up (a matter); arrange or talk (business, etc.); consult:同某人~业务 arrange business with sb.; talk business with sb. /与有关单位~ consult with the department concerned; take up the matter with the department concerned /本店办理邮购,望来函~。Our shop provides mail-order service. Please write to us for further information. /这件事由我跟他们~。Let me talk the matter over with them.

接腔 jiēqiāng answer; respond; take up (a cue, etc.):队长追问干私活儿的事, 大家谁也没有~。The team leader inquired about moonlighting, but no one replied.

接亲 jiēqīn 〈口语〉(of the bridegroom) go to the bride's home to escort her to the wedding

接取 jiēqǔ ❶ receive:通过电讯~命令 receive orders through telecommunications ❷ meet; greet:请假回乡,~家眷 ask for leave to go back to one's home town and bring one's family members (*or* wife and children)

接壤 jiērǎng border (on); be contiguous (to); be bounded (by):~地区 contiguous areas /吉林省的东南部与朝鲜~。Jilin is bounded on the southeast by Korea.

接任 jiērèn take over a job; replace; succeed:~主席 take over the chairmanship /继某人~议长 succeed sb. as the speaker; replace the present speaker

接三 jiēsān *also* "送三" sòngsān 〈旧语〉three days after a person died, the deceased's family would invite Buddhist monks, Taoist priests, etc. to pray for the soul of the deceased

接墒 jiēshāng 〈农业〉(of soil) well moistured

接生 jiēshēng deliver a child; practise midwifery:这位医生~的经验很丰富。The doctor is experienced in midwifery.

接生婆 jiēshēngpó (traditional) midwife

接生员 jiēshēngyuán (modern-style) midwife

接事 jiēshì accept a post and start to work:新院长今天到任~。The new director took up his post and started to work today.

接收 jiēshōu ❶ receive; accept:不~礼物 refuse gifts or presents /~订货 receive orders /~无线电信号 receive radio signals /~来稿 receive manuscripts /~机 receiver /~天线 receiving antenna; receiving aerial / 对方~了我们释放的两批战俘。The other side accepted the two batches of prisoners of war released by us. ❷ take over (property, etc.); expropriate:~企业 take over a business /~仪式 take-over ceremony /政府已~了这座旧领事馆的房屋。The government has already taken over the premises of the former consulate. ❸ admit; recruit:不~插班生 refuse anyone who wants to join a class in the middle of a course /球队~新队员。The ball team has recruited new players.

接手 jiēshǒu ❶ take over (duties, etc.):他调走后,工作由我~。I took over his work after he was transferred. ❷〈体育〉catcher

接受 jiēshòu accept;take;learn:~任务 accept a task /~勋章 accept a medal /~委托 take on a trust; accept a commission /~某人的劝告 take sb.'s advice /~教训 learn a lesson /~定货 take an order; accept an order /~考验 face up to a test /~遗产 inherit a legacy /~教育 be educated /~新鲜事物 absorb what is new /~保证人 guarantee /~承诺人 acceptee /~赔偿人 indemnitee /~处罚 acceptance of punishment /~抗诉 acceptance of a protest /~判决 acceptance of a judgment /单纯~ acceptance simpliciter /附保留~ acceptance under reserve (*or* with reservations)

接受国 jiēshòuguó accepting state; receiving state; recipient country

接受书 jiēshòushū instrument of acceptance

接受条款 jiēshòu tiáokuǎn acceptance clause

接穗 jiēsuì 〈植物〉scion

接榫 jiēsǔn ❶ connect tenons ❷ (as of literary writings) coherent;joining:有些材料从长篇作品里节选, 前后~的地方不得不稍稍变动一下。As some materials are adapted from long writings, some changes have to be made to render them coherent.

接谈 jiētán meet and talk with sb.:这笔交易是副经理~的。This business was taken up by the assistant manager. /我几次去找他~,他总是扯些不着边际的题外话。I went to talk business with him several times, but he always put me off by some vague excuses.

接替 jiētì take over; succeed; replace:~某人当大使 succeed sb. as ambassador /上级命令他~二旅旅长的职务。The higher authorities ordered him to take over the command of the second brigade.

接通 jiētōng put through:~电话 switch through to /你刚才要的长途已经~。The long distance call you wanted is now through.

接头 jiētóu ❶ connect; join:电线~的地方要用胶布缠好。The joined wires should be tied fast with adhesive plaster. ❷ contact; get in touch with; meet:~地点 contact point; rendezvous /关于购买设备的事, 我们已派人去与厂方~。As for the purchase of equipment, we have already sent someone to contact the factory. ❸ know about; be familiar with; have knowledge of:我刚到这所学校, 许多事不~。I am new to this college and know little about it. ❹〈纺织〉piecing; tying-in

接头儿 jiētour connection; joint; junction:四通~〈机械〉four-way connection /万向~〈机械〉universal joint
接吻 jiēwěn kiss:~道别 kiss sb. goodbye
接物 jiēwù 〈书面〉❶ get along with people:处事~ attend to matters and deal with people /~待人 the way one gets along with people ❷ come face-to-face with reality
接物镜 jiēwùjìng objective lens; objective
接线 jiēxiàn ❶〈电工〉wiring:~图 wiring diagram; connection diagram ❷ connecting cord, line or cable
接线插座 jiēxiàn chāzuò connector socket
接线生 jiēxiànshēng 〈旧语〉telephone operator
接线箱 jiēxiànxiāng *also* "接线盒" junction box (JB)
接线员 jiēxiànyuán telephone operator
接线柱 jiēxiànzhù 〈电工〉terminal; binding post
接续 jiēxù continue; follow:他把刚才中断了的话~说下去。He continued from where he had left off.
接引 jiēyǐn ❶ meet; greet:上级派两人来~我们。The higher authorities sent two persons to meet us. ❷ receive and guide:~后学 receive and guide (*or* instruct) later learners
接应 jiēyìng ❶ come to sb.'s aid; back up; reinforce:派一个连去~ send a company to reinforce ❷ give material assistance; supply:我们粮食充足,可随时~你们。We have plenty of grain and can supply you whenever you need it.
接遇 jiēyù 〈书面〉receive:~宾客 receive guests and visitors
接援 jiēyuán reinforce and aid:派去~的部队已经和敌人交火了。The reinforcements have already engaged the enemy.
接站 jiēzhàn meet at the railway station or bus stop
接着 jiēzhe ❶ catch(hold of sth.):我往下扔,你~。I'll throw it down for you to catch hold of. ❷ follow; carry on:她读完课文,~就逐句解释。She read over the text and went on to explain it sentence by sentence. /他到了上海,~又到了杭州。He went to Shanghai and then to Hangzhou. /今天下午~讨论。The discussion will be resumed this afternoon.
接枝 jiēzhī branch grafting
接旨 jiēzhǐ receive (and accept) an imperial edict
接踵 jiēzhǒng 〈书面〉follow on sb.'s heels:摩肩~ jostle each other in a crowd
接踵而来 jiēzhǒng'érlái *also* "接踵而至" on sb.'s heels; in the wake (of sth.):战争方告结束,饥荒又~。Famine followed on the heels of war. /应征稿件~。A steady stream of contributions came in.
接种 jiēzhòng 〈医学〉have an inoculation; inoculate:~牛痘疫苗 be vaccinated /~防伤寒疫苗 be inoculated against typhoid /~卡介苗 have a BCG vaccine
接嘴 jiēzuǐ answer; respond; follow sb.'s cue:老王不~,只顾坐在那里看电视。Absorbed in watching TV, Lao Wang gave no answer.

揭 jiē ❶ tear off; remove; take off:~膏药 take off a plaster /~邮票 remove a stamp /~去商标 tear off a trade mark ❷ uncover; lift (the lid, etc.):~面纱 unveil /~被子 lift the quilt ❸ expose; show up; make public; bring to light:~内幕 make public the inside story /~隐私 bring shameful secrets into the open /把他的老底儿~出来 drag the skeleton out of his closet ❹〈书面〉raise; hoist:~竿为旗 raise a bamboo pole to serve as a standard of revolt ❺ (Jiē) a surname
揭榜 jiēbǎng ❶ announce the results of an examination ❷ tear off or take off a notice inviting applications for jobs, etc., from a wall as a sign of accepting the invitation
揭裱 jiēbiǎo remove the old mount of a picture and mount it anew
揭不开锅 jiēbukāiguō have nothing in the pot; have nothing to eat; go hungry:他们昨晚上就~了。They have run out of food since last night.
揭穿 jiēchuān expose; lay bare; disclose; show up:~谎言 expose a lie /~秘密 disclose (*or* expose) a secret /~阴谋 uncover a plot /~他们宣传的虚伪性 give the lie to their propaganda /他们的阴谋必须~。It is imperative to lay bare their evil plot. /这些政治暴发户的真面目被~了。The political upstarts were cut down to size.
揭疮疤 jiē chuāngbā pull the scar right off sb.'s sore; cut sb. to the quick; rub salt in sb.'s old wounds:他最忌讳别人揭他的疮疤。He bitterly resents being touched on the raw.
揭底 jiēdǐ reveal the inside story; lay bare; expose:他当场揭了那个骗子的底儿。He exposed that cheat on the spot.
揭短 jiēduǎn rake up sb.'s faults; disclose sb.'s shortcomings:她专爱揭别人短处。She was always ready to rub people on the raw.
揭发 jiēfā expose; unmask; lay bare; bring to light:~暴行 expose atrocities /~犯罪事实 bring a criminal fact to light /~检举 expose and denounce /根据已经~的材料 according to facts already revealed /对以前的错误一定要~。The mistakes of the past must be laid bare. /新闻记者~了这一丑闻的真相。The journalists blew the lid off the cover-up of the scandal.
揭盖子 jiē gàizi take off the lid; bring to light; bring into the open:这伙腐败官员的盖子刚刚揭开。The malpractices of these corrupt officials are being brought to light.
揭竿 jiēgān raise the standard of revolt; start an uprising
揭竿而起 jiēgān'érqǐ rise in rebellion; start an uprising; raise the standard of revolt:被压迫得走投无路的农民不得不~。The peasants, oppressed and driven to the wall, were forced to rise in rebellion.
揭根子 jiē gēnzi expose sb.'s secrets and failings
揭锅 jiēguō ❶ (when food is done) open the lid of the pot to take out the food:米饭还没~,孩子就吵着要吃。Children are crying for food before the rice is ready. ❷ bring out in the open when the time is ripe:这是机密,不到~的时候,不能乱说。This is a secret, so don't blurt it out until the right time.
揭举 jiējǔ put forward in public
揭开 jiēkāi uncover; reveal; lay bare; make public:~内幕 reveal the inside story; get to the bottom /~事实的真相 lay bare the fact of the matter /~序幕 ring up (*or* raise) the curtain /~历史的新纪元 usher in a new era in history /~科技史上的新一页 turn over a new page in the history of science and technology /今天,这个哑谜的谜底终于~了。Today, the mystery has at last been solved.
揭老底 jiē lǎodǐ reveal the inside story; disclose sb.'s unsavoury past; dredge up embarrassing facts about sb.'s past:老板尽可能地避开他的前妻,生怕她~儿。The boss goes out of his way to avoid his ex-wife for fear that she might disclose his unsavoury past.
揭露 jiēlù expose; unmask; bring to light; lay bare; unveil:~帝国主义的真面目 expose imperialism in its true colours; show the imperialists up for what they are /~事物的本质 uncover the essence of things /~阴谋 lay bare a plot /~伪君子 unmask a hypocrite /~暗藏的敌特分子 ferret out hidden enemy agents /~时弊 bring current malpractices to light /报界~了市长的丑行,致使他竞选失败。The press pulled the plug on the mayor, and he lost his election.
揭秘 jiēmì break a secret; unveil a mystery:由于有人~,丑闻才暴露于光天化日之下。The scandal did not see the light of day until somebody disclosed some secret dealings.
揭幕 jiēmù ❶ unveil (a monument, etc.); inaugurate:为展览会~ inaugurate an exhibition /举行烈士纪念碑的~典礼 unveil a monument to the martyrs ❷ the curtain rises (on a big event); begin; start:大选~。The general election starts.
揭幕式 jiēmùshì unveiling ceremony
揭破 jiēpò unveil; unmask; lay bare; bring to light:说到这儿我们不妨~他的一件秘密。Now, we might as well bring a secret of his to light.
揭示 jiēshì ❶ announce; make public; promulgate:~牌 notice board /~板 notice board ❷ reveal; disclose; bring to light:~真理 reveal the truth /~生活真谛 point out (*or* reveal) the true meaning of life /~内心矛盾 bring the contradictions of one's inner world to light /~人类社会发展的客观规律 shed (*or* cast) light on the objective laws governing the development of human society
揭挑 jiētiao 〈方言〉rake up sb.'s faults; disclose sb.'s shortcomings
揭帖 jiētiě 〈旧语〉notice put up on the wall (usually concerning personal affairs)
揭晓 jiēxiǎo announce; make known; publish:乒乓球赛的结果已~。The result of the table tennis match has been announced. /考试~,她得了第一名。She got first place according to the announcement of the examination results. /名单~,他们三人均在其中。The three of them were all in the name list just published.
揭载 jiēzǎi 〈书面〉publish (in newspapers, etc.)
揭橥 jiēzhū 〈书面〉reveal; bring to light; indicate; mark

皆 jiē 〈书面〉all; each and every:四邻~知 known to all the neighbours /老幼~宜 applicable to the old and the young alike
皆大欢喜 jiēdàhuānxǐ everybody is happy; all are satisfied:他做了

J

一件功德无量、～的善事。To the satisfaction of all he did a good work of boundless beneficence.

皆伐 jiēfá 〈林业〉clear felling

湝 jiē

湝湝 jiējiē 〈书面〉(of water) running; flowing

楷 jiē 〈方言〉〈植物〉Chinese pistache

see also kǎi

喈 jiē

喈喈 jiējiē 〈书面〉❶ (of sound) harmonious: 钟鼓～。Bells and drums sounded harmoniously. ❷ chirp; twitter: 鸟鸣～ chirping of the birds

阶(階、堦) jiē ❶ steps; stairs: 台～ flight of steps / 石～ stone steps ❷ rank: 军～ military rank / 官～ official rank

阶层 jiēcéng ❶ (social) stratum: 社会各～ social strata / 中间～ intermediate stratum ❷ class: 劳动者～ labouring class; working people / 高薪～ high-salary class / 特权～ privileged class; vested interests / 工薪～ wage-earning class; wage earners / 知识～ intelligentsia

阶乘 jiēchéng *also* "析因" xīyīn 〈数学〉factorial

阶地 jiēdì 〈地理〉terrace

阶段 jiēduàn ❶ stage; phase; period: 发展的新～ new stage (*or* phase) of development / 过渡～ transitional stage / 历史～ historical period / 现～的任务 present task / 疾病的严重～ critical phase of an illness / 这项工程要分～进行。This project will proceed by stages. / 从目前这个～来看, 他的表现是好的。As things now stand, his performance is quite good. ❷ 〈矿业〉level: ～高度 level interval

阶段性成果 jiēduànxìng chéngguǒ result or product of one phase of a project; initial result or product

阶级 jiējí ❶ 〈书面〉steps ❷ 〈旧语〉official ranks ❸ (social) class: ～冲突 class conflict / ～警惕性 class vigilance / ～内容 class content / 深厚的～友爱 deep class love; strong class solidarity / 有产～ propertied class / 自在～ class in itself / 自为～ class for itself / 剥削～ exploiting class / 被剥削～ exploited class / 官僚资产～ bureaucrat bourgeoisie / 垄断资产～ monopoly bourgeoisie / 买办资产～ comprador bourgeoisie / 流氓无产～ lumpenproletariat / 民族资产～ national bourgeoisie / 无产～ proletariat / 小资产～ petty bourgeoisie / 我们都是～兄弟。We are all brothers of the same class. *or* We are all class brothers.

阶级报复 jiējí bàofu class vengeance

阶级本能 jiējí běnnéng class instinct

阶级本质 jiējí běnzhì *also* "阶级本性" class nature

阶级成分 jiējí chéngfèn class status

阶级斗争 jiējí dòuzhēng class struggle

阶级队伍 jiējí duìwu class ranks

阶级分化 jiējí fēnhuà class polarization

阶级分析 jiējí fēnxī class analysis

阶级感情 jiējí gǎnqíng class feelings: 朴素的～ simple class feelings

阶级根源 jiējí gēnyuán class origin

阶级观点 jiējí guāndiǎn class viewpoint

阶级基础 jiējí jīchǔ class basis

阶级教育 jiējí jiàoyù class education

阶级觉悟 jiējí juéwù class consciousness; class awareness

阶级烙印 jiējí làoyìn brand of a class

阶级立场 jiējí lìchǎng class stand

阶级利益 jiējí lìyì class interests

阶级路线 jiējí lùxiàn class line

阶级矛盾 jiējí máodùn class contradiction

阶级社会 jiējí shèhuì class society: 我们处在一个～。We are now in a class society.

阶级性 jiējíxìng class character; class nature

阶级异己分子 jiējí yìjǐ fènzǐ alien-class element

阶级阵线 jiējí zhènxiàn class alignment

阶梯 jiētī flight of stairs; ladder: 进身的～ stepping stone / ～成本 stair-step cost; step cost / ～分配法 step-ladder method; step distribution method / 找到了向上爬的～ have found a stepping stone; have found a ladder of promotion

阶梯教室 jiētī jiàoshì lecture theatre; terrace classroom

阶下囚 jiēxiàqiú prisoner; captive: 昔日座上客, 今日～。An honoured guest in the past, he is a prisoner now.

嗟 jiē 〈书面〉sigh; lament: ～何及! It's too late to lament. *or* What is the use of lamentations now?

嗟悔 jiēhuǐ 〈书面〉regret; lament: 他们没有抓紧时间办成这件大事, 令人～。It is regrettable that they have failed to take the opportunity and accomplish the important task.

嗟悔无及 jiēhuǐ-wújí too late for sighs and regrets: 否则, 因循坐误, 责有攸归; 全国丧亡, ～。Otherwise, the responsibility will fall on those who procrastinate and allow the situation to deteriorate. Once the country's doom is sealed, it will be too late for regrets and lamentations.

嗟来之食 jiēláizhīshí food handed out in contempt; handout: ～, 吃下去肚子要痛的。He who swallows food handed out in contempt will get a bellyache.

嗟叹 jiētàn 〈书面〉heave a sigh; sigh: ～不已 keep sighing

镙 jiē 〈方言〉sickle

街 jiē ❶ street: 大～ avenue; boulevard / 大～小巷 streets and lanes / 上～购物 go shopping; go downtown to do some shopping ❷ 〈方言〉country fair; market: 赶～ go to a fair; go to market

街道 jiēdào ❶ street: 穿过～ cross a street ❷ residential district; neighbourhood: ～工作 neighbourhood service; community work

街道办事处 jiēdào bànshìchù subdistrict office

街道服务站 jiēdào fúwùzhàn neighbourhood service centre

街道工厂 jiēdào gōngchǎng neighbourhood factory

街道居民委员会 jiēdào jūmín wěiyuánhuì neighbourhood committee

街道派出所 jiēdào pàichūsuǒ neighbourhood police substation

街道企业 jiēdào qǐyè neighbourhood enterprise

街道食堂 jiēdào shítáng neighbourhood or community canteen

街道医院 jiēdào yīyuàn neighbourhood hospital

街灯 jiēdēng street lamp: 几个老头在～下下棋。Several old men were playing chess under a street lamp.

街坊 jiēfang 〈口语〉neighbour: 老～ longtime neighbours / 街里～ close neighbours

街坊会 jiēfanghuì (HK) Kai Fong association

街坊四邻 jiēfang-sìlín neighbours; neighbourhood: 他一家吵得～不安。His family were so noisy that everyone in the neighbourhood was terribly disturbed.

街垒 jiēlěi street barricade: 他们用树木设～。They used felled trees to throw up barricades across the street.

街门 jiēmén courtyard door facing the street; street door (of a house): 记住夜里关～。Remember to close the front courtyard door.

街面儿上 jiēmiànrshang 〈方言〉❶ (activities) in the street: 过去冷清的～, 如今车水马龙, 热闹异常。The street, which used to be lonely and deserted, is now full of traffic and bustling with excitement. / 哥们儿, 都是～的朋友, 有话好说。Mates, we are all good buddies in the street, so why can't we talk things over? ❷ neighbourhood: ～都很熟悉他。Everybody in the neighbourhood knows him well.

街衢 jiēqú street; avenue

街市 jiēshì downtown street: 城里的～十分繁华。The downtown streets in the city are quite prosperous.

街谈巷议 jiētán-xiàngyì street gossip; talk of the town: 我初到长沙时, 会到各方面的人, 听到许多的～。Soon after my arrival in Changsha, I met all sorts of people and picked up a good deal of gossip.

街头 jiētóu street corner; street: 十字～ (at the) crossroads / ～叫卖 hawk one's wares in the street / ～做小买卖的多是乡下人。Most of the peddlers in the city are from the countryside.

街头剧 jiētóujù street-corner skit; street performance: 节假日走在街上, 可以欣赏一些～。Walking along the street on holidays, one may come across and enjoy street performances.

街头卖艺 jiētóu màiyì perform in the street; busk

街头诗 jiētóushī poems posted on street walls or distributed in leaflet form

街头巷尾 jiētóu-xiàngwěi streets and lanes: ～, 议论纷纷。You hear all sorts of talk on the street corner everywhere.

街心 jiēxīn city centre

街心公园 jiēxīn gōngyuán garden in the centre of the city; park at an intersection
街子 jiēzi 〈方言〉❶ street:小～ small lane ❷ market; fair:赶～ go to a fair; go to market

jié

讦 jié 〈书面〉chide (sb. for his faults); expose (sb.'s hidden misdeeds):攻～ rake up sb.'s muck; attack

絜 jié 〈书面〉*see* "洁" jié
see also xié

洁(潔) jié clean; pure; clear:纯～ pure; clean /高～ noble and unsullied; noble and pure /简～ terse; succinct /光～ bright and clean /皎～ (of moonlight) bright and clear /廉～ honest /贞～ chaste and undefiled /整～ clean and tidy; neat
洁白 jiébái spotlessly white; pure white:～的牙齿 pure white teeth /穿一身～的衣服 be in a spotlessly white dress /～无瑕 spotless and flawless; pure and innocent; untarnished and flawless
洁净 jiéjìng clean; spotless; neat and tidy:这饭馆虽小，但很～。Small as it is, the restaurant is neat and tidy.
洁具 jiéjù sanitary equipment
洁菌素 jiéjūnsù 〈药学〉jiemycin
洁癖 jiépǐ ❶ fastidiousness about cleanliness; mysophobia:人人知道她有～。As is known to everyone, she is fastidious about cleanliness. ❷ (as of one's character) refusing to be contaminated and keeping aloof from worldly things
洁身自好 jiéshēn-zìhào ❶ refuse to be contaminated by evil influence; preserve one's purity:他是一位和蔼可亲，～的老人。He is an amiable old man, who keeps away from anything immoral. ❷ mind one's own business (in order to keep out of trouble); stand aloof (out of self-interest):我们怎么能对周围事物不闻不问，而～呢? How can we be indifferent to affairs around us and mind only our own business?
洁牙剂 jiéyájì dentifrice
洁莹 jiéyíng clean and sparkling; spotless and crystal-clear
洁治 jiézhì 〈医学〉scaling:～器 tooth scaler
洁樽 jiézūn 〈书面〉clean the wine vessel:～候光 have all the wine vessels cleaned and cordially wait for your presence

诘 jié 〈书面〉closely question; interrogate:反～ counter with a question /究～ ask for an explanation /盘～ cross-examine; question
see also jí
诘难 jiénàn 〈书面〉censure; blame; condemn
诘问 jiéwèn 〈书面〉closely question; interrogate; cross-examine:～他为何出尔反尔。I closely questioned him why he went back on his word.
诘责 jiézé 〈书面〉censure; rebuke; reprimand; denounce:对他的无理取闹进行～ rebuke him for his troublemaking
诘朝 jiézhāo 〈书面〉morning; next morning

袺 jié 〈书面〉hold or carry sth. in the front of one's jacket

桔 jié
see also jú
桔槔 jiégāo well sweep; sweep for drawing water out of a well
桔梗 jiégěng 〈中药〉root of balloon flower (*Platycodon grandiflorum*)

拮 jié
拮据 jiéjū in straitened circumstances; short of money; hard pressed for cash; hard up:手头～ be short of money /家里的景况日渐～。The family is living in reduced circumstances.

鲒 jié 〈古语〉〈动物〉a kind of clam

劼 jié 〈书面〉❶ prudent; cautious ❷ hard-working; diligent

结 jié ❶ tie; knit; knot; weave:～鞋带 tie one's shoe laces; lace up one's shoes; do up one's shoes /～领带 knot one's tie /把两根绳子～在一起 knot two ropes together /～毛衣 knit wool into a sweater; knit a sweater out of wool /～鱼网 weave a fishing net ❷ tie a knot; knot:活～ slip-knot /死～ fast knot /蝴蝶～ bowknot; bow tie /在绳子上打个～ tie a knot in a cord; tie a cord into a knot /打得不牢固的～ fool's (*or* granny) knot /平～ reef knot /同心～ true knot /把～打紧一点 make a tight knot; make a knot tight /把～打松一点 make a knot loose /解～ untie a knot; undo a knot /～松了。The knot has slipped. ❸ congeal; form; forge; associate:成群～队 in crowds; in throngs / ～为夫妻 be tied in wedlock /湖水冻～。The lake was frozen over./罪犯常常～为团伙。Criminals often form gangs./他在这里交～了许多朋友。He has formed a large circle of friends here. ❹ settle; finish; conclude:终～ end; finish /完～ finish; be over /～账 settle accounts ❺〈旧语〉written guarantee; affidavit:具～ give a written guarantee /保～ understanding (written to the government) to stand guarantee for sb. ❻〈电子〉junction: p-n ～ p-n junction /生长～ grown junction ❼〈生理〉node:淋巴～ lymph node /喉～ Adam's apple (*pomum adami*)
see also jiē
结案 jié'àn wind up a case; close a case; settle a lawsuit:这件民事纠纷已经～。This civil lawsuit has already been settled.
结疤 jiébā scab; become scarred:伤口已经～了。A scab has formed over the wound.
结拜 jiébài become sworn brothers or sisters:～为生死弟兄 become sworn brothers
结伴 jiébàn go together; do (sth.) together; work in company:～而行 go or travel together /我们和他们～游湖。We joined them in touring the lake (together).
结冰 jiébīng freeze; ice up; ice over:水摄氏零度～。Water freezes at 0°C. *or* Ice forms at 0°C. /池塘～了。The pond was frozen over. *or* The pond was iced up (*or* over).
结彩 jiécǎi adorn or decorate with festoons:大厅上张灯～。The hall was adorned with lanterns and streamers (*or* festoons).
结草衔环 jiécǎo-xiánhuán *also* "衔环结草" show gratitude even after one's death; return sb.'s kindness:我当～，以报大德。I will be deeply grateful and repay you for your great kindness.
结肠 jiécháng 〈生理〉colon:乙状～ sigmoid colon
结肠病 jiéchángbìng 〈医学〉colonopathy
结肠镜 jiéchángjìng 〈医学〉colonoscope
结肠炎 jiéchángyán 〈医学〉colitis
结肠下垂 jiécháng xiàchuí 〈医学〉coloptosis
结肠造口术 jiécháng zàokǒushù 〈医学〉colostomy
结成 jiéchéng form; forge; establish:～同盟 form an alliance; become allies /～深厚的友谊 forge a profound friendship /同某人～一伙 gang up with sb. /～终身伴侣 form a lifelong companionship /～生死之交 become sworn friends /～统一战线 form (*or* establish) a unified front /～贸易伙伴 enter into a trade partnership
结仇 jiéchóu start a feud; become enemies; incur hatred:因为一点小事而结了仇 start a feud over sth. trivial /两家～。The two families became enemies.
结存 jiécún ❶ cash on hand; balance:你银行账户上～一百元。The balance standing to your credit is 100 *yuan*. *or* You have a balance of 100 *yuan* in the bank. /现款～已经不多了。There isn't much cash on hand. ❷ goods on hand; inventory
结党营私 jiédǎng-yíngsī form a clique to pursue selfish interests; gang up for selfish purposes:一群～的政客 gang of self-seeking politicians /那个封建王朝末期，官吏～，无人不贪。In the last days of that feudal dynasty, government officials were greedy without exception and ganged up for selfish purposes.
结缔组织 jiédì zǔzhī 〈生理〉connective tissue
结缔组织瘤 jiédì zǔzhīliú 〈医学〉mesocytoma
结缔组织炎 jiédì zǔzhīyán 〈医学〉inflamation of connective tissue (ICT)
结发夫妻 jiéfà fūqī husband and wife by the first marriage
结构 jiégòu ❶ structure; composition; construction:经济～ economic structure /原子～ atomic structure /土壤～ soil structure /技术～ technological makeup /人体～ structure of the human body /产品～ product mix /价格～ price mechanism /语言的～ language structure /组织～ framework of an organization /进口～ import mix /～严密的文章 well-organized essay ❷〈建筑〉structure; framework; construction:钢～ steel structure /钢筋混凝土～ reinforced concrete structure /轻质混凝土～ light-concrete structure /焊接～

welded construction /铆合～ riveted construction /钢～桥梁 bridge with a steel framework ❸〈地质〉texture:斑状～ porphyritic texture /致密～ compact texture

结构钢 jiégòugāng structural steel

结构工资制 jiégòu gōngzīzhì composite wage system

结构力学 jiégòu lìxué structural mechanics

结构式 jiégòushì 〈化学〉structural formula

结构图 jiégòutú structural drawing

结构心理学 jiégòu xīnlǐxué structural psychology

结构语言学 jiégòu yǔyánxué structural linguistics

结构主义 jiégòuzhǔyì structuralism

结构主义学派 jiégòuzhǔyì xuépài structuralist school

结构主义语法 jiégòuzhǔyì yǔfǎ structural grammar

结关 jiéguān customs clearance:～货物 cleared goods

结棍 jiégùn 〈方言〉❶(body) muscular; sturdy; strong:这小伙子身体长得多～! How strongly built this young man is! ❷ heavy; awful; terrible:这一记打得很～。This is a hefty blow (*or* punch).

结果 jiéguǒ ❶ result; outcome; fruit:在一定条件下,坏的东西可以引出好的～。Under given conditions, a bad thing can lead to good results. /锅炉爆炸,～他受伤了。He was injured as a result of a boiler explosion. /那场悲剧是嫉妒的～。The tragedy is the outcome of jealousy. /～,我们打赢了。Finally, we won the game. /谈判毫无～。The negotiation was fruitless. ❷ kill; finish off:野猪林这个险恶去处,不知～了多少英雄好汉。One wonders how many heroes have met their deaths in such a dangerous place as Yezhulin.
see also jiēguǒ

结果管理 jiéguǒ guǎnlǐ management by results; results management

结合 jiéhé ❶ combine; identify; integrate; link:与群众相～ identify oneself with the masses; become one with the masses /把理论与实践～起来 link (*or* combine, *or* integrate) theory with practice /中西医～ combine Chinese traditional medicine and Western medicine; integrate Chinese traditional medicine and Western medicine /科研同生产～ couple scientific research with production /劳逸～ strike a proper balance between work and rest /制定计划要～具体情况。Plans should be made in the light of specific conditions. ❷ be united in wedlock or marriage

结合酶 jiéhéméi 〈生化〉desmoenzyme

结合膜 jiéhémó 〈生理〉*see*"结膜"

结合能 jiéhénéng 〈物理〉binding energy

结核 jiéhé ❶〈医学〉tubercule; tuberculosis; consumption:肺～ pulmonary tuberculosis (TB)/骨～ bone tuberculosis /淋巴～ tuberculosis lymphadenitis; scrofula /肠～ enterophthisis; intestinal tuberculosis ❷〈矿业〉nodule:锰～ manganese nodule /钙质～ calcium nodule /铁质～ iron nodule

结核病 jiéhébìng tuberculosis; TB:～医院 tuberculosis hospital (*or* sanatorium)

结核杆菌 jiéhé gǎnjūn tubercle bacillus

结核菌素 jiéhéjūnsù tuberculin

结喉 jiéhóu 〈生理〉Adam's apple (*pomum adami*)

结汇 jiéhuì 〈经济〉settlement of exchange

结婚 jiéhūn marry; get married:～年龄 age for marriage; matrimonial or marriageable age /～礼物 wedding present; wedding gift /他们将于元旦～。They are going to be married on New Year's Day.

结婚登记 jiéhūn dēngjì marriage registration

结婚仪式 jiéhūn yíshì wedding ceremony

结婚证书 jiéhūn zhèngshū marriage certificate; marriage lines

结伙 jiéhuǒ ❶ form a gang; gang up:～成队 gang up; group together ❷〈法律〉complicity

结集 jiéjí ❶ collect articles, etc. into a volume:把自己这几年写的散文～付印 compile a collection of prose items written in recent years and send it to the press ❷ assemble; concentrate:～兵力 concentrate troops /沿海～了十个师。Ten divisions have been massed along the coast.

结记 jiéjì 〈方言〉❶ miss; worry about:你走吧!这里有大娘照顾,不用～。You can leave now! As granny is looking after us here, you don't have to worry about anything. ❷ remember:以后出去～着关门。Remember to close the door behind you when you go out next time.

结痂 jiéjiā eschar; crust; scab

结茧 jiéjiǎn cocooning

结交 jiéjiāo make friends with; associate with; mix with:在文艺界～了许多朋友 have a large circle of friends in the world of art and literature

结焦 jiéjiāo coke; coking

结节 jiéjié 〈医学〉tuber; tubercle; node:麻风～ leproma /坐骨～ sciatic tuber /～病 sarcoidosis /～性麻风 lepromatous leprosy; cutaneous leprosy /～性脑硬化 tuberous sclerosis /～性皮炎 lumpy skin disease

结节虫 jiéjiéchóng nodular worm

结晶 jiéjīng ❶ crystallize:～断面〈化学〉crystalline fracture /～岩石 crystalline rock /～固体 crystalline solid /烧瓶中的液体里慢慢～出白色的小颗粒。Small white grains were crystallized slowly from the liquid in the flask. ❷ crystal:盐～ salt crystals /明矾是无色透明的～。Alum is a colorless transparent crystal. ❸ crystallization:智慧的～ crystallization of wisdom /知识的～ quintessence of knowledge /两国人民友谊的～ product of the friendship between the people of two countries

结晶化学 jiéjīng huàxué crystallography

结晶水 jiéjīngshuǐ water of crystallization; crystal water

结晶体 jiéjīngtǐ *also*"晶体" crystal

结晶学 jiéjīngxué crystallography

结局 jiéjú final result; upshot; outcome; ending:悲惨的～ tragic results; sad denouement /好的～ happy ending /事件的～ outcome of an event; upshot of the matter /必然～ inescapable fate /～如何,很难预料。It's hard to foresee how it will turn out.

结块 jiékuài agglomerate; curdle

结蜡 jiélà 〈石油〉paraffin precipitation; wax precipitation:～事故 paraffin accident

结缡 jiélí 〈旧语〉get married; marry:他俩～三十年,相敬如宾。They have treated each other with respect in the thirty years of their married life.

结庐 jiélú 〈书面〉build a simple house or hut:～隐居 live a retired (*or* reclusive) life in a simple house

结缕草 jiélǚcǎo *also*"巴根草" bāgēncǎo 〈植物〉*Zoysia japonica*

结论 jiélùn ❶ *also*"断案" duàn'àn 〈逻辑〉conclusion (of a syllogism); deduction ❷ conclusion; verdict:得出错误的～ reach a wrong conclusion /让历史去作～ let history deliver the judgment /对某人的历史作～ reach a conclusion on sb.'s personal history; pass (official) judgment (*or* verdict) on sb.'s history /科学的～建立在对客观事物正确认识的基础上。A scientific conclusion is based on the correct understanding of reality. /不要忙于下～。Don't jump to conclusions.

结脉 jiémài 〈中医〉slow and intermittent pulse

结盟 jiéméng form an alliance; ally; align:不～国家 nonaligned country /不～政策 nonaligned policy /不～运动 the nonaligned movement /两国～。The two countries formed (*or* entered into) an alliance.

结膜 jiémó *also*"结合膜"〈生理〉conjunctiva:～反应 conjunctival reaction

结膜腺 jiémóxiàn conjunctival glands

结膜炎 jiémóyán 〈医学〉conjunctivitis

结末 jiémò ❶ ending:这本小说的～很平淡。The ending of the novel is too commonplace. ❷ in the end; at last:～他还是采纳了我们的建议。At last he took our advice.

结幕 jiémù ❶ last act (of a play) ❷ ending; finale:事情刚刚开始,～还早着呢! This is just the beginning; the ending is still far away.

结纳 jiénà make friends with; associate with:深相～ strive for close friendships; become close friends

结契 jiéqì 〈书面〉become friends through finding each other very congenial

结欠 jiéqiàn balance due:去年～三百元。The balance due of last year is 300 *yuan*. /所有～已全部还清。All balance due has been paid up.

结亲 jiéqīn ❶ marry; get married:这小两口是去年春上结的亲。The young couple got married last spring. ❷ (of two families) become related by marriage

结清 jiéqīng settle; square up; liquidate:～账目 square accounts (with sb.) /～债务 settle a debt

结球 jiéqiú (of vegetables) ball up:花椰菜不～。Cauliflowers don't ball up.

结球甘蓝 jiéqiú gānlán cabbage

J

结舌 jiéshé unable to say anything because of terror or lack of argument; tongue-tied: 瞠目～ stare tongue-tied; stare dumbfounded / 张口～ be agape and tongue-tied; be at a loss for words / 钳口～ shut one's mouth and keep silent

结社 jiéshè form an association

结社自由 jiéshè zìyóu freedom of association

结绳 jiéshéng tie knots: 目前在一些原始部落中, ～记事仍是常事。In some primitive tribes, it is still a common practice to keep records by tying knots.

结石 jiéshí 〈医学〉stone; calculus: 肾～ kidney stone / 胆～ gall stone / 泌尿道～ urinary calculus / 排出～ discharge stones; pass stones

结识 jiéshí get acquainted (with sb.); get to know (sb.); make friends with: ～了一些县区干部 get to know some county and district cadres / 有幸～了这位老画家。I have the pleasure of getting acquainted with this old painter. / 此行～了许多朋友。I've made a lot of new friends on this trip.

结束 jiéshù ❶ end; complete; conclude; wind up; close: ～讲话 wind up a speech / ～争论 terminate a controversy / ～访问 conclude a visit / ～混乱状态 put an end to a chaotic situation / 主席宣布会议～。The chairman declared the meeting closed. / 这项工程什么时候～? When will this project be completed? / 全国人口普查基本～。The nationwide (*or* national) census is almost at an end. / 幸福的童年生活是那样的短暂, 一闪就～了。Happy childhood life is so short that it flashes past quickly. ❷ (often used in the early vernacular) style of dressing; makeup

结束语 jiéshùyǔ concluding speech; concluding remarks

结驷连骑 jiésì-liánqí stream of coaches — the ostentation of high officials and noble lords when going out

结素 jiésù (short for 结核菌素) tuberculin

结算 jiésuàn settle accounts; close an account; wind up an account: 用硬通货～ use hard currency for quoting prices and settling accounts / 每月与银行～一次 settle with the bank once a month / 到财务科去～差旅费 go to the finance section to settle the business travelling expenses / ～贷款 loan for the settlement of accounts / ～单据 document of settlement / ～价格 settlement price / ～业务自动化 clearing automation / ～账户 close an account / ～资金 settlement fund / ～银行 settlement bank / 记账～ settlement on account / 非现金～ settlement through accounts

结算日 jiésuànrì account day

结体 jiétǐ structure of Chinese characters

结头 jiétóu 〈方言〉knot: 打了一个～ tie a knot

结托 jiétuō 〈书面〉make friends and depend on each other: 深相～ become good friends and rely on each other for support

结尾 jiéwěi ❶ ending: 小说的～ ending of a novel / 以 *-ness* ～的名词 nouns ending in *-ness* / ～阶段 final stage; winding-up stage / ～写得好。The ending is well written. ❷ 〈音乐〉coda

结习 jiéxí 〈书面〉ingrained habit; inveterate habit: 此人咬文嚼字, 大有书生～。The man likes to mince words, thus betraying an ingrained habit of a pedant.

结嫌 jiéxián bear a grudge against each other: 他们两人因一些小事～。They two fell out with each other through some trifling matters.

结穴 jiéxué write the last few lines of an article, a story, etc.; conclude: 善于～ be good at writing the conclusion (of a story, etc.) / 此文～有力。The article ends forcefully.

结业 jiéyè complete a course; finish one's studies: ～证书 certificate for completing a course / 英语短训班七月底～。The short-term English course is going to end in July.

结义 jiéyì 〈旧语〉become sworn brothers or sisters: ～弟兄 sworn brothers

结余 jiéyú cash surplus; surplus; balance: 经费～ balance of funds / 这是～下来的钱。This is the surplus saved. / 收支两抵, 略有～。After balancing income and expenses, there is a little cash surplus. / 这笔～暂不动用。This balance will be kept for the time being.

结语 jiéyǔ concluding remarks: 这几句～十分精彩。These concluding remarks are brilliant indeed.

结冤 jiéyuān start a feud; become enemies; incur hatred

结缘 jiéyuán form ties (of affection, friendship, etc.); take a liking; become attached: 他自幼便与绘画结了缘。He took a fancy to painting from childhood.

结怨 jiéyuàn bear grudges; contract enmity; incur hatred: 两人～甚深。The two of them nursed intense hatred against each other. / 因为遗产分配问题, 他与弟弟～, 多年不来往。He bore grudges against his younger brother because of quarrels over inheritance, and they had not visited each other for years.

结扎 jiézā 〈医学〉ligation; ligature: ～血管 ligature (*or* tie up) blood vessels / 输卵管～术 ligation of oviduct / 输精管～术 vasoligation

结渣 jiézhā 〈冶金〉slag-bonding

结账 jiézhàng settle accounts; square accounts; balance the books: ～记录 closing entries / 年底～ settle accounts at the end of the year / 请服务员～ ask the waiter (*or* waitress) to bring the check (*or* bill) / ～符号法 symbol system of account / 这家百货店每月25日～。The department store closes its books on the 25th of each month. / 小姐, ～! Bill, please.

结症 jiézhèng (of animals) disease such as obstruction or indigestion

结撰 jiézhuàn theme and structure of a writing

结子 jiézi knot: 把绳子打个～ make a knot in a rope; tie a knot in a rope / 把～解开 loosen a knot; undo a knot; untie a knot

结组 jiézǔ 〈体育〉roped party (in mountaineering)

截

jié ❶ cut; separate; sever: 从中～开 cut in the middle / ～头去尾 cut off both ends / 斩钉～铁 resolute and decisive ❷ 〈量词〉section; chunk; length: 一～儿绳子 a (length of) rope / 一～水管 a section of pipe / 话说了半～儿 break off half way; finish only half of what one has to say / 裤子短了半～。The trousers are a little bit too short. ❸ stop; check; intercept; stem: ～球 intercept a pass / 堵～ block and obstruct / 快去～住那辆车。Go and stop that car immediately. ❹ by (a specified time); up to: *see* "～至"

截长补短 jiécháng-bǔduǎn take from the long to add to the short; draw on the strength of each to offset the weakness of the other; even up scarcity and plenty: 我们要彼此～共同提高。We must learn each other's good points and make common progress.

截道 jiédào highway robbery

截断 jiéduàn ❶ cut off; block; obstruct: ～各种联系 cut off all means of communication / ～敌人的退路 block the enemy's retreat / 一座大坝, 把河水拦腰～。A big dam cut the river in the middle. ❷ cut short; interrupt: ～某人的讲话 cut sb. short / 交通为暴风雪所～。Traffic was interrupted by a heavy snowstorm.

截断球 jiéduànqiú 〈体育〉intercept; steal (in basketball)

截夺 jiéduó waylay; hold up

截稿 jiégǎo stop accepting incoming articles or contributions: ～日期 closing date

截光盘 jiéguāngpán episcotister

截光器 jiéguāngqì optical chopper; light chopper; chopper

截获 jiéhuò intercept and capture: ～情报 intercept information / ～一艘海上走私船 intercept a smuggling ship at sea / ～了那名逃犯 capture the criminal at large

截击 jiéjī intercept: ～敌人的轰炸机 intercept the enemy's bombers / ～任务 intercept mission

截击导弹 jiéjī dǎodàn interceptor or interception missile

截击机 jiéjījī interceptor

截击卫星 jiéjī wèixīng anti-satellite satellite; killer-satellite

截句 jiéjù ❶ take a sentence from an article: 断章～ quote out of context ❷ poem of four lines, each containing five or seven characters, with a strict tonal pattern and rhyme scheme *see also* "绝句" juéjù

截流 jiéliú dam a river: ～工程 project of damming a river / 新建小水库四座, 塘坝～三十一处。Four small reservoirs were built together with thirty-one dikes to dam up rivers and streams.

截流井 jiéliújǐng 〈建筑〉catch basin

截流式排水系统 jiéliúshì páishuǐ xìtǒng intercepted drain system

截留 jiéliú hold back; withhold; retain: ～国家财政收入 hold back state revenue / ～税款 keep back tax payment / ～利润 retain profits / 凡是规定下放到城市和企事业的权力, 各中间层次不得～。No intermediate administrative units are allowed to withhold any of the powers delegated to cities, enterprises and institutions.

截煤机 jiéméijī 〈矿业〉coalcutter; cutter

截门 jiémén pipe valve

截面 jiémiàn section: 横～ cross section / 正～ normal section / ～图 sectional drawing

截取 jiéqǔ cut out; cut sth. into sections and take from them: ～

一段铁丝 cut out a section of iron wire /短篇小说，一般只～生活的一个横断面。A short story is usually based only on one segment of life.

截然 jiérán sharply; distinctly; completely: 两种～相反的意见 two contrary opinions; two opinions diametrically opposed to each other /两人对孩子的教育方法～对立。The two of them held totally different views on how to educate their child. /文章内容与形式不能～分开。The form and content of an article cannot be separated. /这里的天气可以～分为两季：雨季和旱季。The weather here can be distinctively divided into the rainy season and drought season.

截然不同 jiérán-bùtóng poles apart; completely different; different as black and white; as alike as chalk and cheese: 你现在的说法，与先前～。What you are saying now is totally different from what you said before. /他俩的性格是～的。The two of them are poles apart in character. /孩子的世界，与成人～。The child's world is completely different from that of an adult.

截水沟 jiéshuǐgōu catchwater-drain; interceptor drain; crown ditch

截瘫 jiétān 〈医学〉paraplegia: 痉挛性～ spastic paraplegia / 高位～ high paraplegia / 他是个～病人。He is suffering from paraplegia. *or* He is a paraplegic patient.

截听 jiétīng 〈通信〉intercept: ～接收机 intercept receiver /～器 interceptor /～站 intercept station

截枝林 jiézhīlín 〈林业〉stem-shoot forest

截肢 jiézhī 〈医学〉amputation: 高位～high amputation

截止 jiézhǐ ❶ end; close: 预订杂志～期 closing day for subscription of the magazine /报名的～日期是五月底。The closing date for signing up is the end of May. /削价销售早已～，你来晚啦。The sale ended quite a while ago, and you are too late for it. ❷ 〈电工〉cut-off: ～电平 cut-off level

截趾适履 jiézhǐ-shìlǚ cut your feet to fit shoes; stretch on the Procrustean bed

截至 jiézhì by (a specified time); up to: ～年底 up to the end of the year; by the end of the year /～昨日，报考者已逾三千。Up to yesterday, the number of people who signed up for the examination surpassed three thousand.

截子 jiézi 〈量词〉section; stretch; chunk; length: 活儿干了半～ work being half done /走了一大～山路 have covered a long stretch of mountain road /他的英语可不如你，差一大～哪。His command of English is far inferior to yours.

劫[1]（刦、刧、刼）

jié ❶ rob; loot; plunder; raid: 抢～ rob; loot /打家～舍 loot; plunder /洗～一空 loot the place empty ❷ coerce; compel: *see* "～持".

劫[2]

jié (short for 劫波) calamity; adversity; disaster; misfortune: 浩～ great calamity /遭～ meet with catastrophe /在～难逃。If you're doomed, you're doomed. *or* There's no escape from fate.

劫波 jiébō ❶〈佛教〉(transliteration) *kalpa*; predestined disaster or trial ❷ natural and man-made calamities: 度尽～兄弟在，相逢一笑泯恩仇。We remain kith and kin despite all the vicissitudes and drown our enmity in a broad smile when we meet face to face.

劫持 jiéchí kidnap; hold under duress; hijack; abduct: ～飞机 hijack an aeroplane /～人质 hijack hostages /遭人～ be abducted; be kidnapped /～者 hijacker; abductor

劫道 jiédào waylay; hold up; mug: 他被～了。He was waylaid by bandits. *or* He was mugged.

劫夺 jiéduó seize (a person or his property) by force: 侵略者～我财物，杀戮我边民。The invaders seized our people's property and slaughtered our frontier citizens.

劫匪 jiéfěi highwayman; robber: 他是个作案多起的～。He is a highwayman of many crimes.

劫富济贫 jiéfù-jìpín rob from the rich and give to the poor

劫后余烬 jiéhòu-yújìn signs or indications of a disaster

劫后余生 jiéhòu-yúshēng be a survivor of a disaster; have been through the fire: 我是那次空难的～者。I'm a survivor of that air disaster.

劫灰 jiéhuī ashes; war remains

劫机 jiéjī air piracy; hijacking of aircraft

劫机者 jiéjīzhě hijacker; skyjacker

劫掠 jiélüè plunder; loot; maraud: ～一空 ransack completely; make a clean sweep /解放前，此地常有土匪～村子。Before liberation, villages in this area were often plundered by bandits.

劫难 jiénàn disaster; calamity: 屡遭～ have experienced many disasters

劫数 jiéshù 〈佛教〉inexorable doom; predestined fate: ～已定。One's doom is sealed.

劫洗 jiéxǐ loot; sack: ～者 looter

劫营 jiéyíng make a surprise attack on the enemy camp

劫余 jiéyú 〈书面〉❶ leftover of the loot ❷ after a disaster

劫狱 jiéyù break into a jail and rescue a prisoner: 对这个毒枭要严加看守，以防～。Keep a close watch on the drug baron so as to prevent anyone from breaking into the jail to rescue him.

劫运 jiéyùn adversity; misfortune: ～难逃 impossible to escape one's misfortune; unavoidable hard lot

劫寨 jiézhài attack the enemy camp by surprise

劫制 jiézhì 〈书面〉threaten by force: 受到绑架者的～ be forced into submission by the kidnappers

蜐

jié *see* "石蜐" shíjié

节[1]（節）

jié ❶ joint; node; knot: 骨～ joint (of bones) /脱～ out of joint /竹～ bamboo joint /藕～ node of lotus root /枝～ branches and knots; trivialities /关～ joint /盘根错～ with twisted roots and gnarled branches; deep-rooted ❷ division; section; part: 音～ syllable /季～ season /时～ season; time /章～ chapters and sections /这一章分为四～。The chapter falls into four sections (*or* parts). ❸〈量词〉section; length: 第三章第二～ Section Two, Chapter Three /十八～车厢 eighteen railway coaches /四～课 four periods; four classes /一～钢管 a length of steel tube /一～甘蔗 a section of sugarcane /三～粉笔 three pieces of chalk ❹ festival; red-letter day; holiday: 过～ celebrate a festival; observe a festival /端午～ Dragon Boat Festival /建军～ Army Day /三八～ International Working Women's Day /中秋～ Mid-Autumn Festival /儿童～ Children's Day ❺ abridge: 对原文略有删～。This is a slightly abridged version of the original. ❻ economize; save; restrain; control: ～电 save electricity; economize on electricity /～水 save water /有理有利有～ on just grounds, to our advantage and with restraint ❼ item: 细～ details /礼～ courtesy; ceremony /不拘小～ not bother about trifles ❽ moral integrity; chastity: 气～ moral integrity /保持晚～ keep one's integrity in one's later years /变～ turn one's coat ❾ (Jié) a surname

节[2]

jié 〈航海〉knot: 船速为十～。The ship is making 10 knots.

see also jiē

节哀 jié'āi restrain one's grief: 务望～保重。I sincerely hope you will restrain your grief and take good care of yourself.

节哀顺变 jié'āi-shùnbiàn restrain one's grief and be reconciled to the inevitable loss

节疤 jiébā *also* "节巴" bulging part of the bamboo and reed; scar of a tree; joint

节本 jiéběn abridged edition; abbreviated version: 《红楼梦》～ abridged edition of *A Dream of Red Mansions*

节操 jiécāo high moral principle; moral integrity: 此人谦恭好学，有～。He is a person of moral integrity, unassuming and eager to learn.

节点 jiédiǎn 〈电工〉panel point; nodal point; node

节度 jiédù 〈书面〉control; supervise; check; restrain: ～三省兵力 command the armed forces of the three provinces

节度使 jiédùshǐ local official in charge of the military and administrative affairs of several prefectures during the Tang Dynasty; governor

节妇 jiéfù 〈旧语〉woman who keeps her chastity or widowhood

节概 jiégài 〈书面〉high moral principle; moral integrity

节根 jiégēn on the eve of a big festival

节候 jiéhòu season and climate: 现在正是寒冷的冬天～。It is now the cold winter season.

节徽 jiéhuī emblem of a certain holiday: 植树节～ tree-planting emblem; emblem for tree-planting day

节汇 jiéhuì save foreign exchange: 由于更多地使用国产零部件，北京今年预计可～两亿美元。It's estimated that 200 million US dollars of foreign exchange will be saved this year in Beijing due to the increasing use of home-made parts.

J

节货 jiéhuò goods supplied at festival time：办～ shop for a festival

节假日 jiéjiàrì festivals and holidays

节俭 jiéjiǎn thrifty；frugal；economical：生活～清淡 live a simple and frugal life / 日子好了，也要勤劳，也要～。People should be industrious and thrifty even when life is getting better.

节减 jiéjiǎn reduce；decrease：～开支 reduce expenses；cut down expenditure；reduce spending

节节 jiéjié successively；continuously；steadily：～抵抗 resist the enemy at every step / ～后退 make one retreat after another / ～推进 keep on moving (*or* pushing) forward / 芝麻开花～高〈俗语〉a sesame stalk puts forth flowers notch by notch；make steady progress / 生活质量～提高。The quality of life is improving.

节敬 jiéjìng 〈旧语〉money or present given to employees on a festival

节口 jiékǒu 〈书面〉economize on food：缩衣～ economize on clothing and food

节口 jiékou 〈方言〉critical moment：眼下正是早稻快熟、中稻要扬花的～，田里的水一滴也少不得。At this critical moment when the early rice is maturing and semi-late rice flowering, the field needs a lot of water and not a single drop should be stinted.

节劳 jiéláo be moderate in using labour；avoid over-exertion：年岁不饶人，您要注意～。You are no longer young. Please take things easy.

节礼 jiélǐ present given on a festival

节理 jiélǐ 〈地质〉joint：倾向～ dip joint / 走向～ strike joint

节烈 jiéliè 〈旧语〉(of a woman, esp. a widow) rigorously chaste

节令 jiélìng climate and other natural phenomena of a season：～不正 not in the right season / ～不等人。The seasons wait for no man. *or* Time and tide wait for no man. / 元宵节吃些元宵以应～。Let's eat some sweet dumplings at the Lantern Festival, as befits the occasion.

节流 jiéliú ❶ reduce expenditure：开源～ broaden sources of income and reduce expenditure ❷〈机械〉throttle：全～ full throttle

节流阀 jiéliúfá 〈机械〉throttle valve

节录 jiélù extract；excerpt：从一篇文章中～几段 excerpt some passages from an essay / 社论～ extracts from an editorial / 这本书我只读过～。I have only read excerpts of the book.

节律 jiélǜ rhythm and law：保持生产运行的正常～ maintain the normal rhythm of production

节略 jiélüè ❶ capsule；excerpt；extract：演讲稿的～ excerpt of a speech / 这是 20 世纪《名人实录》一书的～版。This is an encapsulation of *Who's Who* in the 20th century. ❷ reduce and save；omit；leave out：文章的后一部分～了。The latter part of the article has been deleted (*or* left out). ❸〈外交〉memorandom；aide-memoire

节目 jiémù ❶ programme；item (on a programme)；number：戏剧～ theatre programme / 广播～ broadcasting programme / 电视～ television programme / 第一个～ first item (*or* number) on the programme / 演出什么～？What's on the programme? ❷ item；list：外国代表团日程中有个～是参观宝山钢铁厂。One of the items on the itinerary of the foreign delegation is to visit Baoshan Iron and Steel Company.

节目单 jiémùdān programme；playbill

节目主持人 jiémù zhǔchírén host (of a radio or TV show)；compère；anchorperson

节能 jiénéng economize on energy；save energy：～月 energy conservation month / 国家将建设一批～骨干项目。The government will build a number of key energy-saving projects.

节能灯 jiénéngdēng energy-saving lamp

节能灶 jiénéngzào energy-saving stove

节拍 jiépāi 〈音乐〉metre；tempo；tact：合着～ keep time / ～程序设计 beat-time programming / ～装配生产方式 tact-system production

节拍器 jiépāiqì 〈音乐〉metronome

节气 jiéqi ❶ one of the twenty-four seasonal division points by which the solar year is divided under the traditional Chinese calendar according to the sun's apparent movement on the ecliptic (黄经), with the Vernal Equinox (春分) marking 0° on this imaginary line and each of the twenty-four points spaced by 15° from the next. The traditional Chinese calendar, however, starts the solar year with the Beginning of Spring (立春) marking the sun's position at 315°, to suit seasonal changes in the North China Plain and the Lower Yangtze Basin ❷ day marking such a seasonal division point ❸ period lasting from such a seasonal division point till the next one；solar term

see also "二十四节气" èrshísì jiéqì

节钱 jiéqian 〈旧语〉money reward given to servants on a festival

节日 jiérì commemoration day；festival；red-letter day；holiday：庆祝～ celebrate a festival (*or* holiday) / 祝你～愉快。Wish you happiness on this festive occasion. / 广场披上了～的盛装。The square is in gala decorations.

节赏 jiéshǎng *see* "节钱"

节省 jiéshěng economize；save；use sparingly；cut down on：～资金 reduce funds / ～原材料 economize on raw materials / ～开支 cut down expenses；reduce spending / 父母亲过日子很～。My parents have lived a frugal life. / 我们还是可以对付过去的，只不过暂时要～点。We'll make it all right. We will just have to tighten the purse strings for a while.

节食 jiéshí eat moderately；reduce the amount of food；go on a diet：缩衣～ save on clothing and food / ～减肥 go on a diet to reduce weight

节水器 jiéshuǐqì water-saving device

节外生枝 jiéwài-shēngzhī *also* "节上生枝" ❶ side issues or new problems crop up unexpectedly ❷ raise obstacles；deliberately complicate an issue：你方提出这个问题，明明是～。You're obviously raising an issue which has nothing to do with the matter at hand. / 他们不但对和平谈判毫无贡献，而且在不断地～。They have not only contributed nothing towards peace negotiations, but have in fact caused complications.

节下 jiéxia 〈口语〉on and around holidays and festivals：～出门，要注意交通安全。You must pay attention to traffic safety when going out on holidays.

节选 jiéxuǎn excerpts；extracts：一本书的～ extracts (*or* excerpts) from a book

节要 jiéyào main points of an extract；abstract：论文～ gist of the extract from an essay

节衣缩食 jiéyī-suōshí economize on food and clothing；tighten one's belt：两口子～，攒钱为女儿买了一架钢琴。The couple lived frugally, saving every penny to buy a piano for their daughter. / 他自己～，尽力帮助有困难的人。He economized on food and clothing in order to help people in need. / 父亲失业时，我们不得不～。When father was out of a job (*or* out of work), we had to tighten our belts.

节译 jiéyì abridged translation：我读过《复活》的～本。I've read an abridged translation of *Resurrection*.

节用 jiéyòng reduce spending；cut down expenses：兴利～ promote what is beneficial and cut down expenses

节油器 jiéyóuqì fuel economizer

节余 jiéyú ❶ save：今年～了一些钱留到明年用。We've saved some money this year for next year's use. ❷ surplus (as a result of economizing)；saving；money or material saved：这是上年的～。This is last year's surplus.

节育 jiéyù birth control：我们要认真做好宣传教育和～服务，把计划生育工作抓紧抓好。We should conscientiously persuade and educate the masses and provide good service in birth control so as to make a success of family planning.

节育环 jiéyùhuán intrauterine device (IUD)；the loop

节育手术 jiéyù shǒushù birth control surgery

节欲 jiéyù restrain one's carnal desires；check one's selfish desire

节约 jiéyuē practise thrift；cut costs；economize；save：～费用 reduce expenses / ～开支 reduce spending；cut down expenses；retrench (expenditure) / ～用水 economize on water；save on water / 勤俭～ hardworking and thrifty / 增产～ increase production and practise economy / ～奖 bonus for economizing / ～劳动的机械 labour-saving machinery / ～资本 capital-saving

节支 jiézhī economize on expenditure；cut down expenses；reduce expenses：各地都在深入开展增产节约、增收～运动。The campaign to increase production and practise economy, raise revenue and reduce expenditure is deepening in all parts of the country.

节肢动物 jiézhī dòngwù arthropod

节制 jiézhì ❶ command and manage：这个师由你～。This division is under your command. ❷ control；check；be moderate in：～饮食 be moderate in eating and drinking / ～生育 birth control / ～开支 control spending / ～性成本 regulated cost / ～资本 control capital ❸ temperance；abstinence

J

节制闸 jiézhìzhá 〈水利〉check gate

节奏 jiézòu rhythm; tempo: ~轻快 (play) in quick rhythm /随着音乐的~跳起舞来 dance to the rhythm of music /心脏有~地跳动。The heart beats rhythmically. /希望你工作的~稍微徐缓一些。I hope you will slow down the tempo of your work a little bit.

蛣(蠘) jié also "竹节虫" zhújiéchóng; "麦秆虫" màigǎnchóng 〈动物〉stick insect; walkingstick: ~是一种节肢动物。The walkingstick is an arthropod.

疌 jié 〈书面〉very fast; quickly; rapidly

捷[1](捷) jié prompt; agile; nimble; quick: 敏~ quick; nimble; agile /迅~ agile; quick; prompt /矫~ vigorous and agile; brisk

捷[2](捷) jié victory; triumph; success: 大~ great victory /奏~ win a battle; score a success /首战告~ be victorious in the first battle; win the first battle /连战连~ win one battle after another /祝~大会 meeting to celebrate a victory

捷报 jiébào news of a victory; report of a success

捷报频传 jiébào-pínchuán news of victory keeps pouring in: 工业战线~。Reports of success keep flooding in on the industrial front.

捷乘法 jiéchéngfǎ 〈数学〉abridged multiplication

捷除法 jiéchúfǎ 〈数学〉short division; abridged division

捷近 jiéjìn short and direct: ~的路 shortcut; royal road

捷径 jiéjìng shortcut; royal road: 走~ take a shortcut; cut corners /另寻~ find another royal road /这是上山的~。This is the shortcut to the mountain top.

捷克 Jiékè Czech: ~共和国 Czech Republic /~语 Czech (language)/~斯洛伐克〈旧语〉Czechoslovakia (now as two independent countries)

捷书 jiéshū 〈书面〉written victory report; written report on a success

捷速 jiésù quickly and promptly: 他渴望的水终于找到了,他~地走近水边。He finally found the water he was dying for and hurried to it.

捷音 jiéyīn news of a victory; report of a success

捷足先登 jiézú-xiāndēng the swift-footed arrive first; the race is to the swiftest; it's the early bird that catches the worm: 此次全国锦标赛,上海队~,先我夺魁。In the national championship, the Shanghai Team grabbed the first prize before we had a chance to. /我正要申请那个工作时,发现已有人~了。I found that someone had beaten me to it when I was going to apply for the job.

睫 jié eyelash; lash: 目不交~ not sleep a wink

睫毛 jiémáo eyelash; lash

睫毛油 jiémáoyóu mascara

睫状肌 jiézhuàngjī 〈生理〉ciliary muscle

睫状体 jiézhuàngtǐ 〈生理〉ciliary body: ~分离术〈医学〉cyclodialysis /~切除术〈医学〉cyclectomy; ciliectomy /~炎〈医学〉cyclitis

倢 jié 〈书面〉❶ see "捷[1]" jié ❷ see "婕" jié

倢伃 jiéyú see "婕好" jiéyú

婕 jié

婕妤 jiéyú also "倢仔" jiéyú 〈古语〉official title for an imperial concubine

竭 jié ❶ exhaust; use up; 精疲力~ exhausted; worn out; tired out /取之不尽,用之不~ with an inexhaustible supply ❷〈书面〉(run) dry: 枯~ dry up

竭诚 jiéchéng wholeheartedly; with all one's heart: ~拥戴 give wholehearted support /~帮助 go all out to help; give help in all sincerity /~为大众服务 serve the masses heart and soul

竭尽 jiéjìn use up; exhaust: ~所能 work to the best of one's ability; do the best one can

竭尽全力 jiéjìn-quánlì spare no effort; do everything one can; exhaust all one's strength: ~进行抢救 spare no effort to save; do one's utmost to save; do all one can to rescue /他~地跑,但还是输了。He ran for all he was worth, but didn't manage to win the race. /他们~与干旱作斗争,终于获得了丰收。They battled the drought with might and main and were rewarded with a bumper harvest.

竭蹶 jiéjué 〈书面〉destitute; impoverished: 艰难~ hardship and destitution /经济~ economically impoverished /~状态 be in straitened circumstances

竭力 jiélì do one's utmost; use every ounce of one's energy; go all out: ~支持 give all-out support /~抵赖 do one's utmost to deny /~控制传染病的流行 try by every possible means to control the spreading of infectious diseases /~鼓吹 loudly trumpet /~反对 energetically oppose /~宣传 assiduously propagate /~抗拒 stubbornly resist /~装出若无其事的样子 try one's best to appear as if nothing has happened /他~反对那项法案。He opposed the bill with all his might.

竭泽而渔 jiézé'éryú drain the pond to get all the fish; kill the goose that lays the golden eggs: 不可不顾人民的困难,~,诛求无已。Do not "drain the pond to catch the fish", making endless demands on the people and disregarding their hardships.

羯[1] jié see "羯羊"

羯[2] Jié Jie or Chieh, an ancient ethnic group derived from the Xiongnu or Huns

羯布罗香 jiébùluóxiāng 〈植物〉dipterocarp

羯鼓 jiégǔ drum said to have come from the Jie nationality in ancient times

羯羊 jiéyáng 〈动物〉wether

楬 jié 〈书面〉stake used as a mark; marking stake

碣 jié stone tablet: 墓~ tombstone /残碑断~ remains of a stone tablet

偈 jié 〈书面〉valiant: 其人晖且~。The man is sanguine and valiant.

see also jì

杰(傑) jié ❶ outstanding person; hero: 豪~ gallant man /俊~ person of uncommon talent /人~ outstanding personality /英~ hero; valiant man ❷ outstanding; prominent; distinguished: 人~地灵 remarkable place turning out outstanding men

杰出 jiéchū outstanding; distinguished; remarkable; splendid: ~的战士 outstanding fighter /~的作家 distinguished writer /~的音乐才能 remarkable talent (*or* aptitude) for music /~的艺术成就 splendid artistic achievements /~功勋 renowned exploits /~的社会活动家 celebrated social activist

杰斐逊 Jiéfěixùn Thomas Jefferson (1743-1826), 3rd President of the United State (1801-1809) and author of *The Declaration of Independence* (1776)

杰作 jiézuò masterpiece: 这是一篇浪漫主义的~。This is a masterpiece of romanticism.

桀 jié name of the last ruler of the Xia Dynasty, traditionally considered a tyrant: ~傲不逊 arrogant and unyielding /~黠暴戾 cruel and ferocious

桀骜 jié'ào 〈书面〉wild and stubborn: ~不轨之徒 wild and unruly person

桀骜不驯 jié'ào-bùxùn 〈书面〉stubborn and intractable; obstinate and unruly: ~的烈马 stubborn and unruly steed /他还是那么~。He's still as bigoted and intractable as ever.

桀犬吠尧 jiéquǎn-fèiyáo the tyrant Jie's cur yaps at the sage-king Yao — the zeal of an unscrupulous lackey to please its master

桀纣 Jié-Zhòu tyrants Jie and Zhou (the last rulers of the Xia and Shang dynasties respectively, both standing for unbridled tyranny)

榤 jié 〈书面〉roost (where chickens rest)

孑 jié 〈书面〉lonely; all alone: ~影孤单 all alone with only one's own shadow for company

孑孓 jiéjué 〈动物〉wiggler; wriggler

J

孑立 jiélì lonely with no one to depend on：茕茕～，形影相吊 remain all alone, with only body and shadow comforting each other

孑然 jiérán 〈书面〉solitary; lonely; alone：～无依 be left alone with no one to rely on /众叛亲离，～无党 alienated from the people and deserted by one's followers

孑然一身 jiérán-yīshēn all alone in the wide world; with no relatives and friends：离乡背井，～ be away from home and all alone in the world

孑身 jiéshēn 〈书面〉solitary; alone：～远遁 flee far away by oneself

孑遗 jiéyí 〈书面〉survivor of a natural disaster or war：无有～ no one surviving the disaster; no survivor

孑遗生物 jiéyí shēngwù live fossile

jiě

解（觧）jiě ❶ separate; divide; split：溶～ dissolve /瓦～ disintegrate /融～ melt; thaw /迎刃而～（of bamboo）split all the way down once it meets the edge of the knife; be easily solved ❷ untie; undo; unbutton：～上衣 unbutton the jacket /～结 untie a knot /～腰带 undo the waistbelt /～麻袋 unbind the sack ❸ relieve; remove; dispel; dismiss：～痛 alleviate pain /～疑心 dispel doubts (*or* suspicions) /～困 relieve sleepy feeling /调～ mediate; make peace /排～ divert oneself (from loneliness *or* boredom) /～油腻 cut the grease of a rich meal (as with a cup of tea, etc.) ❹ explain; construe; clear up; interpret：注～ (explanatory) notes; annotation /题～ key to exercises or problems /剖～ analyse; dissect /详～ explain in detail; detailed explanation /劝～ ease sb.'s anxiety; persuade /讲～ explain /辩～ try to justify ❺ understand; comprehend; be clear：费～ hard to understand; obscure /误～ misunderstand /理～ understand; comprehend /大惑不～ be extremely perplexed /一知半～ have a smattering of knowledge /不～其意 not know what he means ❻ relieve oneself：小～ go to the lavatory (to urinate) /大～ go to the lavatory (to defecate) ❼〈数学〉solution：求～ find the solution /～题 solve (a mathematical, etc.) problem /你这个～法不对。Your way of solving it is not correct.

see also jiè; xiè

解饱 jiěbǎo 〈方言〉allay or satisfy one's hunger：不论吃什么，能～就行。Anything that could appease my hunger will do. /北方人认为吃面食比吃大米～，而南方人却认为米饭比面食经饿。Northerners think that cooked wheaten food is better than rice in satisfying one's hunger, while southerners think just the opposite (*or* the other way round).

解表 jiěbiǎo 〈中医〉inducing sweat; diaphoresis

解表药 jiěbiǎoyào diaphoretic

解馋 jiěchán satisfy a craving for good food：搞点红烧肉～ get some braised pork to satisfy one's craving for delicacies

解嘲 jiěcháo try to explain things away when ridiculed; console oneself：聊以～ serve somehow to relieve embarrassment /他这样做不过是～而已。He was merely finding excuses to console himself.

解酲 jiěchéng 〈书面〉relieve sb. of drunkenness：酽茶～。Strong tea can relieve one of drunkenness.

解愁 jiěchóu free from worries; relieve depression：借酒～ try to dispel depression or melancholy by drinking /他们找了个耍把戏的来～释闷。They got a conjuror to make them forget their worries.

解除 jiěchú free; relieve; remove; lift; dispel：～烦恼 dispel worries /～宵禁 lift the curfew /～思想顾虑 free one's mind of all misgivings (*or* apprehensions) /～职务 remove sb. from his post; relieve sb. of his office /～合同 terminate (*or* dissolve) a contract /～婚约 renounce an engagement /～扣押〈法律〉release of distress /～精神枷锁 shake off the mental shackles /～痛苦 kill the pain /危险终于～了。The danger was finally removed.

解除警报 jiěchú jǐngbào ❶ sound the all-clear ❷ all-clear

解答 jiědá answer; explain; solve：～在实践中提出来的新问题 solve new problems arising from practical work /这些问题请你～。Please answer these questions.

解冻 jiědòng thaw; unfreeze：～季节 thawing season /～资产 unfreeze assets /～银行信贷 unfreeze bank loans /地面～了。The ground has thawed out. /两国关系～。There was a thaw (*or* relaxation) in the relations between the two countries.

解毒 jiědú ❶〈医学〉detoxify; detoxicate：～药 antidote ❷〈中医〉relieve internal heat or fever：这种药丸～消炎。This pill can relieve internal heat and reduce inflammation.

解饿 jiě'è satisfy or appease one's hunger; stay one's stomach：吃些糕点～ take some cake to appease (*or* satisfy) one's hunger

解乏 jiěfá recover from fatigue; refresh oneself：他休息了两天，～了。He has got over his fatigue after two day's rest. /洗个热水澡解解乏。You should take a hot bath to refresh yourself.

解法 jiěfǎ 〈数学〉solution：这道题有好几种～。There are several solutions to this problem.

解放 jiěfàng ❶ liberate; emancipate; free：～生产力 liberate the productive forces; unfetter the productive forces /民族～运动 national liberation movement /妇女～运动 women's liberation movement; women's lib /中国人民要求～的斗争 the Chinese people's struggle for liberation ❷ (esp. referring to the overthrow of KMT rule in China in the late 1940's) liberation：～前 before liberation; pre-liberation /～后 after liberation; post-liberation

解放脚 jiěfàngjiǎo liberated feet — half-bound feet; bound feet unbound

解放军 jiěfàngjūn ❶ liberation army ❷ (short for 中国人民解放军) the Chinese People's Liberation Army; the PLA ❸ PLA man

解放军报 Jiěfàngjūnbào *Liberation Army Daily*, organ of the Central Military Commission of the Communist Party of China, first published in 1956

解放区 jiěfàngqū (esp. in contrast to KMT-controlled areas) liberated area

解放日报 Jiěfàng Rìbào *Liberation Daily*, organ of the Communist Party of China in Yan'an from 1941 to 1947

解放思想 jiěfàng sīxiǎng emancipate the mind; free oneself from outmoded ideas：～，实事求是 emancipate the mind and seek truth from facts

解放战争 jiěfàng zhànzhēng ❶ war of liberation ❷ China's War of Liberation (1946-1949)

解纷 jiěfēn settle a dispute：排难～ mediate a dispute; pour oil on troubled waters

解疙瘩 jiě gēda solve a problem that is on sb.'s mind; get rid of a hang-up：郭主任这回可没解开她心头上的疙瘩。Director Guo failed to cut (*or* untangle) the knot in her mind this time.

解雇 jiěgù discharge; dismiss; sack; fire：被～ be dismissed; get the sack /上星期一老板把我～了。My boss gave me the axe last Monday.

解寒 jiěhán dispel the cold：喝碗姜汤，解解寒。Drink a bowl of ginger soup to dispel the cold.

解和 jiěhé 〈方言〉settle a dispute; make peace：不要吵了，我来给你们～。Stop arguing, and let me mediate your dispute.

解恨 jiěhèn vent one's hatred; have one's hatred slaked：为百姓～ slake the masses' hatred /杀了那个恶霸方解我心头之恨。Only the execution of that local tyrant can give vent to my hatred.

解惑 jiěhuò explain difficulties; clear up doubts or questions：发蒙～ teach a child to read and write, and answer his or her questions

解甲 jiějiǎ ❶ take off one's armour：～而息 take off one's armour to have a rest ❷ leave the army; surrender：十四万人齐～。One hundred and forty thousand soldiers all surrendered.

解甲归田 jiějiǎ-guītián take off one's armour and return to one's native place; be demobilized：老王～后，仍保持着当年工作时的那股劲头。Retired from office, Lao Wang is still as full of drive as he was at his post.

解胶 jiějiāo dispergation：～剂 dispergator

解教 jiějiào be released from the reeducation-through-labour camp

解禁 jiějìn lift a ban：～期间 open season; open time

解痉 jiějìng 〈中医〉spasmolysis

解酒 jiějiǔ relieve or neutralize the effect of alcohol：喝醋不能～。Vinegar cannot relieve the effect of alcohol.

解救 jiějiù save; rescue; deliver：～某人脱险 save sb. from danger /～溺水儿童 rescue a drowning child /解放以后西藏农奴才从苦难的深渊中～出来。It was after liberation that the Tibetan serfs were delivered from the abyss of misery.

解聚 jiějù 〈化学〉depolymerization or depolymerisation：～酶 depolymerase /～橡胶 depolymerized rubber

解决 jiějué ❶ solve; resolve; overcome; settle：～难题 solve difficult problems /～边界争端 settle a border dispute /～矛盾 resolve contradictions /～赔偿 settle a claim /～困难 overcome a difficulty;

find a way out of a difficulty /～麻烦问题的能手 trouble-shooter /为了～本市用水紧张的问题，已经动工修建一座大水库。In order to relieve the water shortage, a big reservoir is under construction. ❷ dispose of; finish off; eliminate:～敌人一个连 wipe out a company of enemy troops /据守在山头的敌人已被我军～。The enemy troops holding the mountain top were finished off by our army.

解开 jiěkāi untie; undo; unfold:～包裹 untie a package; undo a parcel; unfold a parcel /～鞋带 unlace the shoes /～纽扣 undo a button; unbutton /～行李 unpack /～一团乱线 unravel the threads of a tangled skein /～一个谜 solve (*or* read) a riddle; solve (*or* find a clue to) a mystery /～疙瘩 get rid of a hang-up /解不开的谜 insoluble mystery

解渴 jiěkě quench or satisfy one's thirst:喝凉茶～ drink cold tea to quench one's thirst /汽水解不了渴。Soft drinks won't satisfy your thirst.

解扣 jiěkòu 〈电工〉trip:自动～ automatic trip

解扣儿 jiěkòur ❶ unbutton; undo a button ❷〈比喻〉sink a feud; get rid of a hang-up; remove ill will; overcome difficulties

解缆 jiělǎn untie the mooring rope — set sail

解理 jiělǐ 〈矿业〉cleavage:～面 cleavage surface (*or* plane) /～脆性 cleavage brittleness /～断裂 cleavage fracture

解铃系铃 jiělíng-xìlíng *also*"解铃还需系铃人" let him who tied the bell on the tiger take it off — whoever started the trouble should end it:～,这些次品是你买进来的,现在还是由你退回去。As the saying goes, whoever started the trouble should end it. You should return the defective goods you bought.

解码 jiěmǎ decipher; decode:～器 decoder

解闷 jiěmèn divert (oneself from boredom); amuse:读点闲书可以～。Light reading can divert you from boredom. /你想个什么法子,给她解解闷儿。Can you think of some way to amuse her? /我知道她的用意无非给我～。I knew she was trying to cheer me up.

解密 jiěmì declassify:这些五十年代的外交文件已经～。These diplomatic documents of the 1950's have now been declassified.

解民倒悬 jiěmín-dàoxuán relieve people of their worries and sufferings; help people out of their misery:农民起义的领袖们懂得,要想得天下,必须～。Leaders of the peasant uprisings knew full well that they had to relieve people of their sufferings in order to seize power.

解难 jiěnán relieve sb. of difficulties; explain difficult points; solve problems:为民～ help the people overcome difficulties /释疑～ remove doubts and solve puzzles

解难 jiěnàn rescue sb. from danger or disaster:消灾～ get rid of calamities and remove dangers

解囊 jiěnáng 〈书面〉open one's purse:慷慨～ make generous contributions of money /别人有难处,他总是乐于～相助的。He is always willing to put his hand in his pocket for anyone in financial straits.

解聘 jiěpìn dismiss from employment; sack; fire:他因工作态度不好被公司～。He was dismissed by the company for a poor work attitude.

解剖 jiěpōu ❶ dissect; anatomize; autopsy:尸体～ autopsy; post-mortem examination /活体～ vivisection /～青蛙 dissect a frog /人体～图 human body dissection view; cutaway view ❷〈比喻〉analyse; examine; critique:～一篇文章 critique an article /他经常自我反省,自我～。He often engages in ideological introspection and self-examination.

解剖刀 jiěpōudāo scalpel; dissecting knife

解剖麻雀 jiěpōu-máquè (method of) "dissecting a sparrow" — analysing a typical case

解剖学 jiěpōuxué anatomy:人体～ human anatomy

解气 jiěqì vent one's spleen; work off one's anger:我真想痛骂他一顿解解气儿。How I wish to give him a good scolding to work off my anger.

解劝 jiěquàn soothe; mollify; placate; comfort:他～了半天,她才消了气。After he spent a long time trying to mollify her, she finally cooled down. /这两口子常闹别扭,邻居总是耐心～。The couple was often at odds, and their neighbour always tried to soothe them patiently.

解热 jiěrè 〈中医〉relieve internal heat or fever:～止咳 relieve internal heat and stop the cough

解热药 jiěrèyào antifebrile; antipyretic; antithermic

解人 jiěrén 〈书面〉understanding and sensible person

解任 jiěrèn 〈书面〉be relieved of one's office

解散 jiěsàn ❶ dismiss (as a command):～! Dismiss! *or* Dismissed! /现在～,大家自由活动,一小时后还在这里集合。Go now, and assemble here one hour later. In the meantime, you can do as you like. ❷ break up; dissolve; disband:～国会 dissolve a parliament /～组织 break up an organization /～俱乐部 disband a club /市政府～了两个办事机构。The city government has closed down two of its offices.

解事 jiěshì understanding; intelligent; thoughtful; sensible

解释 jiěshì explanation; interpretation; construction; exposition:得到了科学的～ receive a scientific explanation /作了正确的～ give a correct interpretation /作出错误的～ put a false construction (on sth.) /反复～ explain time and again; repeatedly explain /～意图 make clear one's intention /～性备忘录 explanatory memorandom /～性法规 declaratory statute /～性发言 explanatory statement /这个词你作何～? How do you account for this word? /对他的沉默你怎么～? How do you interpret his silence? /这个理论他～得很透彻。He has expounded this theory thoroughly.

解释权 jiěshìquán power of interpretation; right of interpretation

解释图 jiěshìtú key drawing

解手 jiěshǒu ❶ relieve oneself; go to the toilet; go to the rest room:厕所在哪儿,我想去解个手。Where is the toilet? I want to relieve myself. /我去解个手儿就来,你稍微等一会儿。Please wait a moment, I'll be back right after I wash my hands. ❷〈书面〉part company

解绶 jiěshòu return the office seal and resign:他从总理处回来后～而去。He resigned after coming back from the prime minister's office.

解说 jiěshuō explain orally; comment:我们一边参观,一边听向导的～。We toured the place while listening to the guide's explanation.

解说词 jiěshuōcí commentary; caption

解说员 jiěshuōyuán commentator; announcer; narrator; guide (to an exhibition, park, etc.)

解溲 jiěsōu relieve oneself; go to the toilet; go to the washroom

解算器 jiěsuànqì 〈数学〉solver

解题 jiětí ❶ solve a (mathematical, etc.) problem:这种～法已经落伍了。This way of solving a problem is out of date. ❷ (often used in book titles) explanatory remarks on the author, content, etc. of a book or article; introductory note

解体 jiětǐ ❶ decompose; split up ❷ disintegrate; collapse:原苏联的～ disintegration of the former Soviet Union /封建社会的～ breakup of the feudal system /这个国家已经～。This country has already crumbled (*or* fallen apart).

解调 jiětiáo 〈电子〉demodulate:～器 demodulator

解脱 jiětuō ❶〈佛教〉*mukti*; *vimukta* ❷ free oneself; extricate oneself; get rid of:～窘境 extricate oneself from a predicament (*or* embarrassment) /～烦恼 free oneself from worries /～苦难 relieve misery ❸ exonerate; absolve:为某人～ absolve sb. from responsibility; plead for sb. /她认为老者是蒙了不白之冤,觉得应该仗义执言,替他～。She thought the old man had been wronged, and it was her duty to speak out from a sense of justice to exonerate him.

解围 jiěwéi ❶ raise or lift a siege; rescue sb. from a siege:敌人援军纷至,我军只得～而去。With the enemy enforcements coming in large numbers, we had to leave and lift the siege. ❷ help sb. out of a predicament; save sb. from embarrassment; come to sb.'s rescue:在我下不来台的时候,多亏大姐过来替我解了围。Luckily my elder sister came to my rescue when I was in a spot.

解慰 jiěwèi comfort; soothe; console

解悟 jiěwù come to understand; realize:～捷疾 quick to understand

解吸 jiěxī 〈化学〉desorb; release the absorbed gas or solute

解析 jiěxī 〈数学〉analyze:～法 analytics

解析几何学 jiěxī jǐhéxué analytic geometry

解析数论 jiěxī shùlùn 〈数学〉analytic theory of numbers

解像力 jiěxiànglì (image) resolution (ability to distinguish between contiguous details of an image in television, usually expressed as the number of lines per screen)

解消 jiěxiāo remove; relieve; get rid of:～疑虑 remove doubts and suspicions (*or* misgivings); clear one's mind of doubt

解严 jiěyán declare martial law ended; lift a curfew:～令 order of lifting a curfew /宣布～ declare martial law ended

解颜 jiěyán 〈书面〉break into a smile; smile; beam

解衣 jiěyī undress; take off one's clothes

解衣推食 jiěyī-tuīshí remove one's own garment to clothe sb. else and give him the food from one's own plate — treat sb. with great kindness:他对我有～之恩。I'm greatly indebted to him for his unselfish generosity.

解颐 jiěyí 〈书面〉smile:小孙子在那里学狗叫，老爷爷为之～。The grandpa is smiling at his grandson who is mimicking a dog's bark.

解疑 jiěyí ❶ dispel doubts and misgivings; clear up a doubt:～释惑 dispel doubts and clear up perplexities ❷ explain a difficult point; solve a puzzle

解忧 jiěyōu assuage sorrow; dispel worry:～排难 relieve sb. from anxiety

解郁 jiěyù relieve melancholy:何以～? What is there to ease melancholy?

解约 jiěyuē terminate an agreement; cancel or rescind a contract

解约金 jiěyuējīn cancellation money

解约权 jiěyuēquán right of rescission

解约书 jiěyuēshū letter of cancellation

解职 jiězhí dismiss from office; relieve sb. of his post:～金 compensation for removal; severence pay

姐

jiě ❶ elder sister; sister:二～ second elder sister /胞～ full elder sister; own sister ❷ elder female relative:表～ elder female cousin (on the maternal side) /堂～ elder female cousin (on the paternal side) ❸ general term for young women:刘三～ third sister of the Liu family; Third Sister Liu

姐夫 jiěfu elder sister's husband; brother-in-law

姐姐 jiějie ❶ elder sister:他有两个～。He has two elder sisters. ❷ elder female cousin:叔伯～ elder first cousins (on the paternal side)

姐妹 jiěmèi ❶ sisters:同胞～ sisters of the whole blood; full sisters /异父～ half sisters /她是独生女，没有兄弟～。She is an only child without any brothers and sisters. ❷ brothers and sisters:你们～几个? How many brothers and sisters do you have?

姐妹城市 jiěmèi chéngshì sister cities; twin cities:北京和东京结成～。Beijing has formed sister-city ties with (*or* is twinned with) Tokyo.

姐妹学校 jiěmèi xuéxiào sister schools; sister universities

姐儿 jiěr 〈方言〉sister:你看他们～几个多亲热。See how affectionate (*or* close) these sisters are.

姐儿们 jiěrmen 〈口语〉sisters:自打～成家以后，一年也难得聚上一次。After the sisters married, it was difficult for them to meet, even once a year.

姐丈 jiězhàng *see*"姐夫"

毑

jiě *see*"媄毑" āijiě

jiè

褯

jiè

褯子 jièzi 〈方言〉diaper:快给孩子换～。Diaper the child quickly.

戒

jiè ❶ guard against; be on the alert against; be prepared against:警～ be on the alert /～骄 guard against arrogance ❷ exhort; admonish; caution; warn:引以为～ take warning from sth.; take sth. as an object lesson /累～不改 refuse to mend one's ways despite repeated admonitions ❸ give up; drop; stop:～烟 give up smoking /～赌 stop gambling /～荤腥 go on a vegetarian diet ❹ abstinence; taboo:酒～ abstinence from drinking /杀～ abstinence from killing /开～ break an abstinence ❺ Buddhist monastic discipline; religious precept or commandment:受～ attain the full status of a monk or nun /犯～ violate a religious discipline (*or* commandment) /传～ initiate sb. into monkhood or nunhood /破～ break a religious precept /斋～ abstain from meat, wine, etc.; fast ❻ (finger) ring:钻～ diamond ring

戒备 jièbèi guard; take precautions; be on the alert:时刻～着 be always on the alert; keep a sharp lookout all the time /早有～ have long taken precautions /～松懈 lax security /你们先把这三个人～起来! First keep these three people under guard!

戒备森严 jièbèi sēnyán enforce tight security; guard heavily:总统府四周～。The presidential palace was heavily guarded on all sides.

戒尺 jièchǐ 〈旧语〉teacher's ruler for beating students; ferule

戒饬 jièchì *also*"戒敕"〈书面〉warn; admonish; exhort:～将士 exhort generals and soldiers

戒除 jièchú give up; drop; stop:～恶习 give up (*or* rid oneself of) a bad habit /～烟酒 stop smoking and drinking

戒刀 jièdāo Buddhist monk's knife

戒牒 jièdié *also*"度牒" dùdié ordination diploma (for Buddhist monks)

戒方 jièfāng *see*"戒尺"

戒忌 jièjì ❶ taboo:杀生是他的～。He has a taboo against killing living things. ❷ avoid; abstain from; guard against:他对违法的事一向十分～。He always abstains from illegal actions.

戒骄戒躁 jièjiāo-jièzào guard against arrogance and rashness; be on guard against conceit and impetuosity:～，永远保持谦虚进取的精神。Guard against conceit and rashness, always remain modest and keep forging ahead.

戒惧 jièjù vigilance and fear:引起邻国的～ arouse the vigilance and fear of neighbouring countries

戒绝 jièjué give up; stop; get rid of:抽烟有百害而无一利，以～为宜。Since smoking is harmful without a single redeeming feature, you'd better give it up.

戒律 jièlǜ *also*"戒条"〈宗教〉religious discipline; commandment:清规～ regulations and taboos /各种宗教都有自己的～。Each religion has its own commandments.

戒慎 jièshèn 〈书面〉be vigilant and prudent

戒坛 jiètán altar where people are initiated into monkhood or nunhood

戒条 jiètiáo *see*"戒律"

戒心 jièxīn vigilance; wariness:人们对他显然存有～。People obviously keep a wary eye on him. /对拍马的人要怀有～。Be wary of sycophants.

戒严 jièyán enforce martial law; impose a curfew; cordon off (an area):～地区 district under martial law /宣布～ declare (*or* proclaim) martial law /实行～ enforce (*or* impose) a curfew /撤销～ call off (*or* lift) a curfew /全城～。The whole city is cordoned off. /下午十时至次晨五时～。Curfew was imposed from 10 p.m. to 5 a.m.

戒严法 jièyánfǎ martial law

戒严令 jièyánlìng order of martial law; curfew

戒严状态 jièyán zhuàngtài state of siege:宣布国家进入～ declare the country under a state of siege

戒指 jièzhi (finger) ring:金～ gold ring /翡翠～ jadeite ring /结婚～ wedding ring /订婚～ engagement ring

诫

jiè warning; admonish; advise:规～ warn; admonish /训～ admonish; rebuke; reprimand

藉

jiè ❶〈书面〉pad; cushion; mat:以茅草为～ use thatching as a mattress ❷ fill up; pad:枕～ lying on top of each other; lying in disorder /～地而坐 sit on the ground ❸ *see*"借[2]" jiè

see also jí

介[1]

jiè ❶ be situated between; interpose:媒～ intermediary; medium /～于两大国之间 be between two powerful countries ❷ introduce:简～ short introduction ❸ remain; have in mind:毫不～意 not mind at all ❹ (Jiè) a surname

介[2]

jiè armour; shell:～虫 beetle /鳞～ scale and shell

介[3]

jiè 〈书面〉upright; high-minded:耿～ honest and frank; upright

介[4]

jiè 〈戏曲〉stage direction for certain movements:饮酒～ drinking wine /相见～ (of two persons) meeting each other /张生笑～ Zhang smiles (*or* laughs)

介[5]

jiè ❶〈量词〉*used of persons*:一～书生 a scholar ❷〈方言〉so; such:～许多 so many; so much /像煞有～事 seem as if one had done sth. important (*or* one were a big shot); be swaggering

介词 jiècí 〈语言〉preposition
介弟 jièdì 〈书面〉〈敬词〉your brother
介电常数 jièdiàn chángshù 〈电学〉dielectric constant
介电塑料 jièdiàn sùliào plastic dielectric
介电体 jièdiàntǐ dielectric substance; dielectrics
介电系数 jièdiàn xìshù 〈电学〉dielectric coefficient
介夫 jièfū 〈书面〉soldier in armour; warrior
介怀 jièhuái take offence; mind: 毫不～ not mind at all; not take the least offence
介介 jièjiè 〈书面〉❶ have sth. on one's mind; be troubled: ～于怀 brood on (an injury, one's neglected duty, etc.); take sth. to heart ❷ separate; cut off
介立 jièlì 〈书面〉not pander to the fashion; be independently minded: 孤行～ go one's own way in defiance of popular fashions; refuse to bow to fashions
介壳 jièqiào shell (of oysters, snails, etc.)
介壳虫 jièqiàochóng scale insect
介然 jièrán 〈书面〉❶ firm and steadfast; unswerving; staunch: ～不挠 indomitable; unyielding ❷ have sth. on one's mind; be troubled: ～于怀 brood over what people say or do; take sth. seriously ❸ extraordinary; unusual
介入 jièrù intervene; interpose; get involved; butt in: ～无原则纠纷 get involved in petty disputes / ～诉讼当事人 intervening party / ～行为 intervening act / 别～他人私事。Don't intervene in others' private affairs. / 公司和工会双方都不愿政府～。Neither the management nor the labour union wanted the government to step in.
介绍 jièshào ❶ introduce; present: 自我～ introduce oneself / ～性条款 introductory provisions / ～对象 introduce sb. to a potential marriage partner; find sb. a boy or girl friend / 请给我们两个～～。Please introduce us. ❷ recommend; introduce; sponsor: ～某人入党 recommend sb. for party membership; sponsor sb. to be a member of a party / 为某人～工作 recommend sb. for a post / ～一种新的工作方法 initiate (*or* introduce) a new method of work / 她由张先生～加入民盟。She joined the Democratic League under the sponsorship of Mr. Zhang. / 京剧已被～到许多国家。Beijing opera has been introduced into many countries. ❸ let know; brief; give an account of: ～情况 brief sb. on the situation; put sb. in the picture; fill sb. in / ～他的模范事迹 make known his exemplary deeds / ～最新科技发展 give an account of the latest scientific and technological developments
介绍人 jièshàorén ❶ one who introduces or recommends sb.; sponsor: 我是小张的入团～。I was Xiao Zhang's sponsor when he applied for Youth League membership. ❷ matchmaker; go-between
介绍信 jièshàoxìn recommendation; letter of introduction; reference
介形虫 jièxíngchóng mussel-shrimp
介意 jièyì (often used in the negative) take offence; mind: 她刚才那句话不是有心的,你可千万别～。She didn't say that on purpose, so don't take it to heart. / 这点小事他从不～。He never minds such trifles. / 我对此事毫不～。I have put the matter entirely out of my mind.
介音 jièyīn (in Chinese pronunciation) head vowel, any of the three vowels i, u and ü used in compound vowels (as i in iang)
介原子 jièyuánzǐ 〈物理〉mesic atom
介质 jièzhì ❶ *also* "媒质" méizhì 〈物理〉medium: 工作～ actuating medium ❷〈电学〉dielectric; insulating medium or substance: ～加热 dielectric heating / ～强度 dielectric strength
介质晶体 jièzhì jīngtǐ dielectric crystal
介质调谐 jièzhì tiáoxié dielectric tuning
介质透镜 jièzhì tòujìng di-lens
介质增益系数 jièzhì zēngyì xìshù gain coefficient of medium
介胄 jièzhòu 〈书面〉armour and helmet: ～之士 men in armour; ancient warriors
介子 jièzǐ 〈物理〉meson; mesotron: ～工厂 meson factory

疥

jiè scabies
疥虫 jièchóng 〈医学〉sarcoptic mite
疥疮 jièchuāng 〈医学〉scabies
疥蛤蟆 jièháma toad
疥螨 jièmǎn itch mite; sarcoptic mite
疥螨病 jièmǎnbìng psoroptic mange; sarcoptic mange
疥癣 jièxuǎn 〈兽医〉mange: 长～的狗 mangy dog / 羊～ sheep scab
疥癣之疾 jièxuǎnzhījí minor trouble; immaterial illness: ～,何足挂齿! Such minor troubles are not worth worrying about.

玠

jiè 〈书面〉large elongated tablet of jade (held in the hands by ancient rulers on ceremonial occasions)

芥

jiè ❶ mustard ❷ small grass — tiny and trivial things: 草～ trifle; mere nothing / 纤～ thin and slender / 尘～ rubbish; garbage; refuse
see also gài
芥菜 jiècài leaf mustard
see also gàicài
芥菜疙瘩 jiècài gēda rutabaga
芥蒂 jièdì 〈书面〉ill feeling; unpleasantness; grudge: 不存～ harbour no grudge; nurse no ill feelings / ～于心 take sth. amiss / 你和叔叔之间,真是没有一点～了吗? Are there really no ill feelings between you and uncle?
芥末 jièmo *also* "芥黄" mustard: ～鸭掌 duck webs with mustard
芥子 jièzǐ mustard seed
芥子气 jièzǐqì 〈化学〉mustard gas
芥子油 jièzǐyóu mustard oil

骱

jiè 〈方言〉joint: 脱～ dislocation

界

jiè ❶ boundary; border: 疆～ boundary of a country; national boundary / 越～ cross the border / 边～争端 border dispute / 地～ boundary of a piece of land / 省～ boundary between provinces / 两国以河为～。The boundary between the two countries is the river. ❷ scope; range; extent: 境～ extent reached; state / 管～ scope of jurisdiction / 眼～ field of vision / 租～ foreign concession ❸ walks of life; circles: 各～人民 all sections of the people; people of all walks of life / 学术～ academic circles / 科技～ world of science and technology / 妇女～ women's circles / 外交～ diplomatic circles ❹ primary division in nature; kingdom: 动物～ animal kingdom / 植物～ vegetable kingdom / 矿物～ mineral kingdom / 有机～ organic kingdom / 无机～ inorganic kingdom ❺ primary division in stratigraphy; group: 古生～ Palaeozoic Group / 元古～ Proterozoic Group / 无生～ Azoic Group ❻〈数学〉bound: 上～ upper bound / 下～ lower bound
界碑 jièbēi boundary tablet; boundary marker; survey marker
界标 jièbiāo boundary mark
界尺 jièchǐ ungraduated ruler
界定 jièdìng specify the limits; delimit; define: 这个词的含义缺少精确的～。There is no clear definition for the meaning of this word. / 两个单位的职权范围必须有明确的～。The terms of reference of the two organizations must be specified.
界河 jièhé boundary river
界湖 jièhú boundary lake
界划 jièhuà draw a line; demarcate: 渭河和它的支流～着远处的平原。The Wei River and its tributaries line the distant plain.
界画 jièhuà (in traditional Chinese painting) technique of drawing lines with the aid of a ruler in painting palatial buildings
界面 jièmiàn interface: ～分配系数 interface distribution coefficient / ～张力〈物理〉interfacial tension
界内球 jiènèiqiú 〈体育〉in bounds; in
界山 jièshān boundary mountain
界石 jièshí boundary stone or tablet
界说 jièshuō 〈旧语〉definition: 关于分子的～ definition of molecule; molecular definition
界外球 jièwàiqiú 〈体育〉out-of-bounds; out
界限 jièxiàn ❶ demarcation line; dividing line; limits; bounds: 划清新思想和旧思想的～ draw a clear line between old and new ideas / 这对青年人的关系已经超过一般朋友的～。The relationship between the young man and woman has gone beyond the limits of ordinary friendship. / 这项科研,要打破一些学科～。This scientific research project entails breaking the bounds among several academic disciplines. ❷ limit; end: 他的贪欲是没有～的。His greed knows no limit.
界限量规 jièxiàn liángguī *also* "界限塞规"; "极限量规" jíxiàn liángguī; "量规" limit gauge
界线 jièxiàn ❶ boundary line: 再过去二三里地就到了两国国境的～了。Two or three *li* further ahead stands the boundary line of the

two countries. ❷ dividing line; demarcation line; limits; bounds:他的发言混淆了是非～。His speech confused (the dividing line between) right and wrong. ❸ edge; verge:这一带满山满坡都是杉树林,望不到～。The Chinese firs on the mountains and slopes here stretch as far as the eye can see.

界域 jièyù boundary; border area

界约 jièyuē border agreement (between two neighbouring countries)

界址 jièzhǐ location of a dividing line (of land):清查～ find out where the dividing line lies

界纸 jièzhǐ squared paper for brush writing

界桩 jièzhuāng boundary marker

蚧 jiè *see* "蛤蚧" géjiè

价 jiè 〈书面〉messenger; errand boy:所嘱之序文草拟完毕,已付来～。I have drafted the preface you asked me to write and given it to your errand boy.
see also jià; jie

借[1] jiè ❶ borrow:～笔 borrow a pen /我想把这张图～回去看看。I want to take the map home to have a detailed look (*or* study). ❷ lend; loan:～书给某人 lend sb. a book; loan sb. a book /～出 be in circulation; be out /续～ renewal (of a loaned book) /这本书是孤本,不外～。As this is the only copy, the book is not for lending.

借[2]**(藉)** jiè ❶ use as a pretext:～批评之名,行诽谤之实 use criticism as a pretext for slander /假～维护人权的名义,干涉别国内政 interfere in the internal affairs of other countries on the pretext of defending human rights (*or* in the name of upholding human rights) ❷ make use of; take advantage of; rely on:～星星辨别方向 tell direction by the stars /～此机会表达谢意 take the opportunity to express one's thanks /船～风势向对岸急驶。Driven by the wind, the ship sailed swiftly towards the other bank.

借词 jiècí 〈语言〉loan word; loan; borrowed word

借代 jièdài 〈修辞〉rhetorical devices such as metonymy

借贷 jièdài ❶ borrow or lend money:～利息 loan interest /～合同 "borrow and loan" contract /这个工厂靠～维持生产。This factory depends on loans to keep production going. ❷ debit and credit sides:～记账法 debit-credit bookkeeping method

借贷资本 jièdài zīběn loan capital

借单 jièdān *also* "借单子" receipt for a loan; IOU

借刀杀人 jièdāo-shārén murder with a borrowed knife — make another person to get rid of an adversary; kill by another's hand:要能够～,让敌人干掉他,倒省了我们好多事。If we can use the enemy as a cat's paw to get rid of him, we'll be spared a lot of trouble.

借调 jièdiào temporarily transfer; loan; second:他已～到文化部工作。He was on loan to the Ministry of Culture. /回国后,他被上级机关～了。After returning from abroad, he was seconded to a higher leading body.

借读 jièdú ❶ study at a school away from one's registered permanent residence; study at a school on a temporary basis ❷ study at a school without entering one's name in the school roll

借端 jièduān 〈书面〉use as a pretext; make an excuse of; find an excuse:～滋事 find an excuse to stir up trouble /～讹诈 find a pretext for blackmailing /～寻衅 pick quarrels on some pretext or other

借方 jièfāng 〈会计〉debit side; debit:把一百元的账记入某人～ enter 100 *yuan* to sb.'s debit; debit sb. with 100 *yuan*; debit 100 *yuan* against sb.

借风使船 jièfēng-shǐchuán *also* "借水行舟" sail before the wind — attain one's own end through the agency of sb. else:今见金桂所为,先已开了端了,她便乐得～,先弄薛蝌到手。Now that her mistress had made the first move, she saw it as a good chance to get Xue Ke first.

借古讽今 jiègǔ-fěngjīn use the past to disparage the present; borrow an ancient lesson to criticize an current practice:这是一篇～的作品。It is a piece of writing using the past to ridicule the present.

借故 jiègù find an excuse; seize a pretext:～生端 make use of anything as a pretext for kicking up a row /～推辞了他的邀请。Find an excuse to turn down his invitation.

借光 jièguāng ❶ benefit from association with sb. or sth.:能去那座古庙参观是借了他哥哥的光。Thanks to his brother's help, we were able to visit that ancient temple. ❷〈套语〉〈口语〉excuse me:～,上火车站怎么走? Excuse me, but could you show me the way to the railway station? /～,几点了? What time is it now, please?

借花献佛 jièhuā-xiànfó present Buddha with borrowed flowers — borrow sth. to make a gift of it:今天是老孟请客,我～,敬你们一杯吧。Though it's Lao Meng's treat today, I'd like to take the opportunity to toast you.

借火 jièhuǒ ask for a light:对不起,向您借个火儿。Excuse me, would you mind giving me a light?

借鉴 jièjiàn use for reference; draw on the experience of; draw on:这方面的外国经验可供我们～。We can draw on the experiences of foreign countries in this regard. /这篇报告文学～了意识流手法。This reportage used the technique of stream of consciousness.

借景 jièjǐng borrow or use the scenery outside a garden to harmonize with that within

借镜 jièjìng use for reference; draw lessons from; draw on the experience of

借酒浇愁 jièjiǔ-jiāochóu drown care in the wine cup; drink sorrow down; drown one's worries in drink:～愁更愁。Trying to drink down your sorrow only makes it worse. /你今晚若不肯来陪我,我就只好呆在家里～了。If you won't come with me tonight, I'll just have to stay home and cry in my beer.

借据 jièjù receipt for a loan; IOU; debt on bond; evidence of debt

借考 jièkǎo take part in an entrance examination away from one's registered permanent residence

借口 jièkǒu use as an excuse; use as a pretext:他～头痛走了。He went away on the pretext of a headache. /他想找～把责任推脱掉。He wanted to find an excuse to shirk responsibility.

借款 jièkuǎn ❶ borrow or lend money; ask for or offer a loan:向银行～ ask for a loan from the bank /～给厂家 offer a loan to a factory /～人 borrower /～单 loan agreement; loan contract /～股份 debenture stock /～企业 borrowing enterprise; borrowing venture /～手续 borrowing procedures /～日期 borrowing date ❷ loan:收回一笔～ recall a loan

借契 jièqì loan agreement; loan contract

借取 jièqǔ borrow:～别人的钱物必须尽早偿还。You must return as soon as possible the money or things borrowed from others.

借券 jièquàn 〈书面〉receipt for a loan; IOU

借如 jièrú 〈书面〉provided; if; in case

借入资本 jièrù zīběn borrowed capital; debenture capital

借尸还魂 jièshī-huánhún (of a dead person's soul) find reincarnation in another's corpse — (of sth. evil) revive in a new guise:这本书以宣扬科学为名,让封建迷信思想～。This book revived feudal superstition in the name of promoting science.

借使 jièshǐ 〈书面〉provided; if; in the event of

借是友,讨是敌 jiè shì yǒu, tǎo shì dí 〈俗语〉He that does lend will lose his friend.

借势 jièshì take advantage of sb. else's power and influence:～压人 bully people on the strength of one's powerful connections

借书处 jièshūchù (of a library) loan desk; circulation desk

借书证 jièshūzhèng library card

借水行舟 jièshuǐ-xíngzhōu *see* "借风使船"

借宿 jièsù stay overnight at sb. else's place; put up for the night:我可以在这里～一夜吗? May I put up here for the night? /我昨夜在这位农民家～。I stayed overnight in this farmer's house yesterday.

借题发挥 jiètí-fāhuī make use of the subject under discussion to put over one's own ideas; seize on an incident to expatiate on sth. else:他的文章,往往～,讽刺当时的世态。In his articles he often seized on some incidents to hold up the ways of the world to ridicule. /我～地教训了他几句。I took the opportunity to vent my feelings and give him a talking-to.

借条 jiètiáo receipt for a loan; IOU:打个～ make out (*or* write) a receipt for a loan

借位 jièwèi 〈数学〉borrow

借问 jièwèn 〈敬词〉may I ask:～去北京图书馆怎么走? Could you tell me the way to the Beijing Library? /～酒家何处有,牧童遥指杏花村。May I ask where I can find a pub? The shepherd boy pointed to the distant Xinghua Village.

借香敬佛 jièxiāng-jìngfó borrow joss-sticks and burn them before Buddha — do favours or make gains at others' expense：修桥补道，尽摊人家官工，你这叫～。You contracted for the building of bridges and repairing of roads for the common good, but you forced poor men to work without pay. That was using public works to feather your own nest.

借以 jièyǐ so as to; with a view to; by way of：进行调查～了解真相 make inquiries so as to find out the truth; find out the truth through investigation／举这几个例子，无非是～说明他的为人。These examples are cited simply for the purpose of shedding light on his character.

借用 jièyòng ❶ borrow：～一下你的自行车行吗？May I borrow your bike? ❷ use sth. for another purpose：我不能饮酒，只能～清茶一杯来祝贺你的成功。I'm a teetotaller and have to toast your success with a cup of tea.

借喻 jièyù 〈修辞〉 borrowed analogy; borrowed figure of speech; metonymy

借约 jièyuē loan agreement; loan contract

借阅 jièyuè borrow (books or reference materials) for reading：～报纸 borrow newspapers for reading

借债 jièzhài borrow money; raise or contract a loan：～度日 live by borrowing／～抵押品 security for a loan／～还债，窟窿还在。By incurring one debt to repay another, what you owe still remains.

借账 jièzhàng borrow money; raise a loan; contract a loan

借支 jièzhī ask for an advance on one's pay; obtain an advance on one's salary

借重 jièzhòng rely on (for support); enlist (sb.'s help)：今后我们对您还要多所～。We'll count on you for more help (*or* support) in the future.

借住 jièzhù stay at sb. else's place temporarily; put up for the time being：他有三个月都在邻居家～。He stayed in his neighbour's house for three months.

借助 jièzhù ❶ have the aid of; draw support from：～显微镜检察细菌 examine bacteria with the aid of a microscope／他可以～双拐行走了。He can walk with the support of two walking-sticks. ❷ give financial aid：他穷得两手空空，连旅费还是友人～的。He's penniless and even his travelling expenses are defrayed by his friends.

借箸 jièzhù 〈书面〉 devise plans for others：愿为先生～一筹。I'm ready to work out a plan for you.

借箸代筹 jièzhù-dàichóu make a plan for someone else

借字 jièzì (of Chinese characters) be interchangeable; borrow one homophone to stand for another

借字儿 jièzìr 〈口语〉 IOU; loan chit

解(觧)

jiè carry or take under guard; escort：～款 take money (to a bank)／起～ send a criminal (*or* captive) under escort／把犯人押～到省城 escort a criminal to the capital city of the province
see also jiě; xiè

解差 jièchāi 〈旧语〉 one who escorts criminals or captives

解送 jièsòng escort or take under guard：～犯罪嫌疑人去法院 escort a suspect to the court for trial

解元 jièyuán (during the Ming and Qing dynasties) scholar who won the first place in provincial imperial examinations

解子 jièzi *see* "解差"

届

jiè ❶ fall due：*see* "～时" ❷ 〈量词〉 session; class：九二～毕业生 class of 1992／本～毕业生 this year's graduates／上～联大 last session of the UN General Assembly／第七～全国人民代表大会 Seventh National People's Congress／本～市人民代表大会 present city (*or* municipal) people's congress

届满 jièmǎn at the expiration of one's term of office：任期～ at the expiration of one's term of office／这位处长没等～就被免职了。This section head was removed from his post (*or* was relieved of his duties) before his term of office expired.

届期 jièqī when the day comes; on the appointed date：～未归 fail to return on the appointed date

届时 jièshí when the time comes; at the appointed time; on the occasion：～参加 be present at the appointed time／欢迎～光临指导。It is hoped that you will honour us with your presence and advice on that occasion.

jie

家

jie *see* "价" jie
see also gū; jiā

价(價)

jie ❶〈方言〉 *used for emphasis after a negative adverb*：不～。No!／别～。Don't!／甭～! Don't! *or* Stop it! ❷ *used as a suffix to certain adverbs*：成天～忙 be busy all day long／震天～响 noise so loud as to shake the skies; deafening sound
see also jià; jiè

jīn

津[1]

jīn ❶ saliva：望梅生～ quench one's thirst by thinking of plums — feed on hopes ❷ sweat：遍体生～ sweat or perspire all over ❸ moist; humid; damp

津[2]

jīn ❶ ferry crossing; ford：要～ powerful and influential position; key post／问～ ask the way to the ford; make inquiries (as about price or the situation)／迷～ maze ❷ (Jīn) (short for 天津) Tianjin

津巴布韦 Jīnbābùwéi Zimbabwe：～人 Zimbabwean

津逮 jīndài 〈书面〉 ❶ reach by way of a ferry crossing：这水中的险要处，世上少有～者。Very few people have ever reached the perilous places in the river. ❷ way for pursuing academic studies

津渡 jīndù 〈书面〉 ferry crossing

津筏 jīnfá 〈书面〉 ❶ raft for ferry crossing; ferry raft ❷ access; way

津津 jīnjīn ❶ tasty; interesting：甜～ pleasantly sweet; quite pleasing ❷ (of water or sweat) flow; come out：汗～ sweaty; moist with sweat／水～ moist with sweat or water

津津乐道 jīnjīn-lèdào take delight in talking about; dwell upon with great relish; talk with great relish：对此～ prattle on this to one's heart's content／她那样～地谈论她的孩子，我看不惯。I can't stand the way she gushes over her children.／这便是有些人常～的事。This is the very event often cited with great gusto by some people.

津津有味 jīnjīn-yǒuwèi with relish; with gusto; with great enjoyment; with keen pleasure：听得～ listen with keen interest／他愉快地跟我闲谈，～地回忆他小学时代的生活。He chatted cheerfully with me, relishing the memory of his school days.

津梁 jīnliáng ferry crossing and bridge; 〈比喻〉 guide (to learning)：英语～ guide to English learning

津润 jīnrùn 〈书面〉 moisten; be moist

津贴 jīntiē ❶ allowance; subsidy：给予～ grant an allowance; grant a subsidy／残废～ disability allowance／出差～ travel allowance／生活～ living allowance／～制度 allowance system ❷ grant an allowance; subsidize：每月～他一些钱。He is granted a monthly allowance.

津要 jīnyào 〈书面〉 ❶ place of strategic importance on land or water ❷ powerful and influential position：久踞～ long hold a key post

津液 jīnyè ❶〈中医〉 body fluid ❷ saliva

琎(璡)

jīn jade-like stone

禁

jīn ❶ bear; stand; endure：弱不～风 too weak to stand a gust of wind; frail／涤纶～洗。Polyester bears a lot of washing.／尼龙袜～穿。Nylon socks wear well. ❷ hold back; contain oneself; restrain oneself：不～流下眼泪 can't hold back one's tears／情不自～ can't refrain from; can hardly restrain oneself／不～大笑 can't help laughing loudly
see also jìn

禁不起 jīnbuqǐ (usu. of people) be unable to stand (tests, trials, etc.) or withstand (an attack, etc.)：～考验 fail to stand a test／～风浪 cannot weather a storm／～糖衣炮弹的攻击 cannot withstand an attack with sugar-coated bullets

禁不住 jīnbuzhù ❶ be unable to bear or endure; can't stand：晚稻～霜冻。The late rice can't stand frost.／这柱子～屋顶的重量。The pillars can't hold up the roof.／地毯～长期磨损。The carpet can't

J

stand up to the wear and tear of prolonged use. /这座木桥~大卡车。This wooden bridge won't bear the weight of a heavy truck. ❷ can't help (doing sth.); can't refrain from: 一阵冷风吹过, 他~打了个寒噤。He couldn't help shivering with cold when a gust of chill wind blew over.

禁得起 jīndeqǐ (usu. of people) be able to stand or withstand: ~长期斗争的考验 be able to stand the test of a protracted struggle /我相信再大的挫折他也~。I believe he is strong enough to brave any setback.

禁得住 jīndezhù be able to stand or endure; can bear: 这座建筑~强地震。The building can withstand sharp earthquakes. /再熬两夜我也~。I am able to put up with two more sleepless nights.

禁受 jīnshòu bear; stand; sustain; endure: ~考验 withstand a test

襟

jīn ❶ front of a garment: 前~ front part of a Chinese garment /小~ smaller or inner piece on the right side of a Chinese garment which buttons on the right /对~ a kind of Chinese-style garment with buttons down the front /衣~ one or two pieces making up the front of a Chinese garment /正~危坐 straighten one's clothes and sit properly ❷ brothers-in-law whose wives are sisters: ~兄 husband of one's wife's elder sister; brother-in-law /~弟 husband of one's wife's younger sister; brother-in-law

襟抱 jīnbào 〈书面〉breadth of mind; aspiration; ambition

襟度 jīndù 〈书面〉breadth of mind; tolerance; forbearance

襟怀 jīnhuái 〈书面〉bosom; heart; (breadth of) mind: ~坦荡 magnanimous heart /他缺少一个领导者应有的~。He lacks the breadth of vision essential for a leader.

襟怀坦白 jīnhuái-tǎnbái have a broad mind; be honest and above board: 现如今, 像他这样~的人不多见了。Very few people nowadays are as unselfish and upright as he is.

襟山带河 jīnshān-dàihé cloaked with hills and girdled by rivers

襟翼 jīnyì 〈航空〉flap

巾

jīn piece of cloth (used as a towel, scarf, tie, muffler, kerchief, etc.): 餐~ table napkin /茶~ tea cloth /领~ scarf, neckerchief /毛~ towel /纱~ gauze kerchief /头~ scarf; kerchief /网~ net-like scarf /围~ muffler; scarf /浴~ bath towel /枕~ towel used to cover a pillow

巾帼 jīnguó 〈书面〉❶ ancient women's headdress ❷ woman: ~须眉 manly woman

巾帼英雄 jīnguó yīngxióng heroine: 本县出了一位全国闻名的~。Our county produced a heroic woman who won nationwide fame.

巾箱本 jīnxiāngběn small-sized ancient book; pocket book

今

jīn ❶ modern; present-day; now: 当~ now; at present /至~ up to now /而~ nowadays /迄~ to this day; until now /于~ nowadays; today; now /如~ nowadays; these days /古~中外 ancient and modern, Chinese and foreign /古往~来 through the ages ❷ today: ~明两天 today and tomorrow ❸ this 〈书面〉: ~次 this time

今不如昔 jīnbùrúxī the present is inferior to the past: 在守旧派看来, 世间的一切都~。To conservatives, things nowadays are inferior to those in the past. /鲁迅的《风波》中所描写的九斤老太就是一个以为~的典型人物。The Nine-jin Granny, depicted in *Tempest* by Lu Xun, was a typical character who claimed that "the present is not as good as the past".

今草 jīncǎo style of cursive hand of Chinese calligraphy, evolved in the 3rd-6th centuries

今晨 jīnchén this morning

今番 jīnfān this time

今非昔比 jīnfēixībǐ the past cannot be compared with the present; the present is vastly different from the past: 姑老爷~, 老有人跟在他后面溜须拍马。Now my honorable son-in-law is not the man he was. There are always people bowing and scraping to him.

今古奇观 Jīn-Gǔ Qíguān *Wonderous Tales Old and New*, collection of short stories of the Ming Dynasty

今古奇谈 jīn-gǔ qítán modern and ancient strange tales; tall story

今后 jīnhòu from now on; in the days to come; henceforth; henceforward; hereafter; in future: 在~年月里 in the years to come; in the coming years /两国的经贸关系~一定会更密切。The economic and trade relations between the two countries will surely become closer in the days to come. /你对~有什么打算? What do you plan to do in the future? /~的路也许更艰难曲折。Perhaps the road ahead is much more difficult and tortuous.

今年 jīnnián this year: ~夏天 this summer; last summer /~的雨水太多。We had too much rain this year.

今儿 jīnr *also* "今儿个"〈方言〉today: ~是我的生日。It is my birthday today.

今人 jīnrén modern people; moderns: 古人的某些幻想, ~已把它变成现实。Modern men have turned many ancient people's fantasies into reality.

今日 jīnrì ❶ today: ~事, ~毕。Today's work must be done today. *or* Don't put off till tomorrow what should be done today. ❷ present; now: ~的社会制度 present social system

今日中国 Jīnrì Zhōngguó *China Today*, a monthly magazine in Chinese and many foreign languages

今生 jīnshēng this life: 但愿你我~还有相会之日。I hope we will have a chance to meet again in our lifetime.

今生今世 jīnshēng-jīnshì this life; this very life: 这一教训我~永不忘。I will never forget this lesson as long as I live. *or* I will bear this lesson in mind for the rest of my life.

今胜于昔 jīnshèngyúxī the present is superior to the past; the present outshines the past

今是昨非 jīnshì-zuófēi realize now that one has been wrong in the past; be in the right now but not in the past: 他认真回顾前半生经历, 深感~。Looking back at the first half of his life, he was keenly aware that he had been wrong in the past.

今世 jīnshì ❶ this age; contemporary age ❷ this life: ~难忘救命之恩。I'll never forget your kindness in saving my life.

今岁 jīnsuì this year: ~多雨。We had too much rain this year.

今天 jīntiān ❶ today: 一年前的~ a year ago today /~的报纸 today's newspapers /~运气不佳。Today just isn't my day. ❷ present; now: ~的年轻人 young men of today /~的国际形势 present international situation /在~的条件下 under the current conditions

今晚 jīnwǎn this evening; tonight

今文 jīnwén *also* "隶书" lìshū modern script (of the Han Dynasty)

今夕 jīnxī this evening; tonight

今昔 jīn-xī present and past; today and yesterday: 北京的~ Beijing, past and present; Beijing's yesterday and today

今昔对比 jīn-xī duìbǐ contrast the past with the present: 对本县工作~, 感慨良多。Various feelings were welling up in my mind as I compared my county's today with its yesterday.

今宵 jīnxiāo tonight

今夜 jīnyè tonight; this evening: ~月色分外明。The moon appears extraordinarily bright tonight.

今译 jīnyì modern translation; modern-language version: 古诗~ ancient poems rendered into modern Chinese /《史记~》*The Historical Records in Modern Chinese*

今音 jīnyīn 〈语言〉modern (as distinct from classical) pronunciation of Chinese characters

今雨 jīnyǔ 〈书面〉〈比喻〉new friend

今朝 jīnzhāo ❶〈方言〉today: ~有酒~醉 today's wine I drink today; enjoy while one can ❷〈书面〉the present; now: 数风流人物, 还看~。For truly great men Look to this age alone.

衿

jīn ❶ *see* "襟" jīn ❷〈书面〉belt; girdle

矜

jīn ❶ pity; sympathize with; have compassion for: ~恤 show sympathy and consideration /哀~ feel compassion for; pity /~贫救厄 sympathize with and aid the poor and suffering people ❷ self-conceited; self-important; singing one's own praise: ~功自伐 be fond of bragging about one's contributions; ring one's own bell; blow (*or* sound) one's own horn /骄~ self-important; domineering; haughty /自~有功 claim to have performed meritorious deeds ❸ prudent; restrained; reserved: ~而不争 firm but not quarrelsome

see also guān; qín

矜持 jīnchí restrained; reserved: 显出~之态 put on airs /他~地笑了笑。He gave a restrained smile.

矜贵 jīnguì 〈书面〉❶ self-conceited; arrogant; singing one's own praise: 恃才~ be inordinately proud of one's own talent ❷ precious; valuable: 此书刊印精美, 且为海内孤本, 弥足~。This book is extremely

J

valuable as it is a rare copy and exquisitely printed.

矜娇 jīnjiāo self-important; arrogant

矜夸 jīnkuā conceited and boastful:～自大 conceited and arrogant / 力戒～ guard against conceit and haughtiness

矜悯 jīnmǐn 〈书面〉sympathize with; pity; have compassion for: ～无辜 sympathize with (*or* have compassion for) innocent people

矜恃 jīnshì 〈书面〉conceited and arrogant

矜惜 jīnxī have pity on; sympathize with; show tender affection for

矜恤 jīnxù ❶ pity; take pity on; have compassion for:他心中对这个病人有无限的～。He had boundless compassion for the patient. ❷ comfort and compensate (a bereaved person):～孤苦的老人 comfort and compensate the bereaved old man

矜重 jīnzhòng restrained and dignified; reserved:过于～ be far too reserved

约 jīn 〈书面〉ribbon that fastens up the two pieces making up the front of a Chinese jacket

金[1] jīn ❶ metal:合～ alloy /五～店 hardware store /冶～ metallurgy ❷ money:现～ cash; ready money /资～ funds; capital /酬～ monetary reward; remuneration /薪～ salary; pay /押～ cash pledge; deposit /奖～ money award; bonus /罚～ fine; forfeit /养老～ old-age pension /奖学～ scholarship /基～会 foundation; fund /拾～不昧 not pocket the money one picks up ❸ ancient metal percussion instrument; gong:鸣～收兵 strike a gong to withdraw troops ❹ gold :～戒指 gold ring /纯～ pure gold /～首饰 gold jewellery /镀～ gold plated /烫～ gild; bronze /淘～ pan gold /沙～ placer gold ❺ precious; dignified:～诺 unbreakable promise; promise that can be relied on /乌～墨玉 coal ❻ golden:～发 golden hair /黑底～字 golden characters on a black background /～发女郎 blonde ❼ (Jīn) a surname

金[2] Jīn Jin Dynasty (1115-1234)

金榜 jīnbǎng 〈旧语〉list of successful candidates in the final imperial examination:～题名 find one's name on the list of successful candidates; succeed in official examinations

金镑 jīnbàng another name for pound; sterling:～汇兑 sterling exchange

金宝 jīnbǎo gold and treasure

金杯 jīnbēi golden cup; gold cup

金本位 jīnběnwèi 〈金融〉gold standard

金笔 jīnbǐ fountain pen with a gold nib; (quality) fountain pen

金币 jīnbì gold coin

金碧 jīnbì gold and green; golden paint:～山水 gold-and-green landscape

金碧辉煌 jīnbì-huīhuáng (of a building, etc.) looking splendid in green and gold; resplendent and magnificent; glorious:～的故宫 magnificent Palace Museum /他们望着城内万家烟火,那长江如一条白练,琉璃塔～,照人眼目。They gazed at the smoke from the thousands of houses in the city, the Yangtze River like a white silk girdle, and the golden glitter of the glazed pogoda. /新近修缮好的天安门更加显得雄伟壮丽,～。The newly renovated Tian An Men looks more grand and splendid than ever.

金边 Jīnbiān Phnom Penh, capital of Cambodia

金边证券 jīnbiān zhèngquàn gilt-edged securities

金伯利岩 jīnbólìyán 〈矿业〉kimberlite

金箔 jīnbó goldleaf; gold foil

金不换 jīnbuhuàn not to be exchanged even for gold; invaluable; beyond price; priceless:浪子回头～。A returned prodigal is more precious than gold.

金灿灿 jīncàncàn glittering like gold; golden bright and dazzling: 春天的太阳,～的。The spring sun is golden bright and dazzling.

金蝉脱壳 jīnchán-tuōqiào slip out of a predicament like a cicada sloughing its skin; escape by cunning manoeuvring; get away by putting sb. off the scent:～之计 escape by the trick of a "golden cicada shedding its skin"

金城汤池 jīnchéng-tāngchí ramparts of metal and a moat of boiling water — impregnable fortress:我们的阵地是～,敌人插上翅膀也过不来! Ours is a strongly fortified position and the enemy will never be able to penetrate even if they have wings.

金翅雀 jīnchìquè 〈动物〉greenfinch (*Carduelis sinica sinica*)

金疮 jīnchuāng 〈中医〉metal-inflicted wound; incised wound

金错 jīncuò 〈书面〉inlaying gold:～器皿 gold-inlaid ware /宝刀～鞘 treasured sword with a gold-inlaid scabbard

金达莱 jīndálái (translated from Korean) azalea

金殿 jīndiàn imperial palace

金雕 jīndiāo golden eagle

金额 jīn'é 〈书面〉amount or sum of money:您买的这几样东西,总～为五百五十元。All told, the things you want to buy amount to five hundred and fifty *yuan*.

金饭碗 jīnfànwǎn well-paid job:他这工作可真是个～。His is a lucrative post indeed.

金粉 jīnfěn ❶ lead powder ❷ pollen ❸ gold bits

金风 jīnfēng 〈书面〉autumn wind:～送爽 cooling autumn wind / ～习习。Autumn wind is blowing gently.

金刚 jīngāng ❶〈方言〉pupa:挖～,消灭苍蝇 wipe out flies by digging up the pupas ❷ (Jīngāng) Buddha's warrior attendant:四大～ Buddha's four great warrior attendants; four guardian warriors

金刚经 Jīngāngjīng 〈佛教〉*Vajracchedika-sutra*

金刚努目 jīngāng-nǔmù *also* "金刚怒目" glare like a temple door god — be fierce of visage:这个人～地冲我大喝一声。Glaring fiercely, this guy shouted at me at the top of his voice.

金刚砂 jīngāngshā *also* "钢砂" gāngshā 〈机械〉emery; corundum; carborundum:～磨床 emery grinder

金刚石 jīngāngshí *also* "金刚钻" diamond:～砂轮〈机械〉diamond wheel /～钻头 diamond bit; diamond drill /～钻机〈矿业〉diamond drill

金刚石婚 jīngāngshíhūn (as a European custom) 60th or 75th anniversary of a marriage

金刚钻 jīngāngzuàn diamond:没有～,别揽瓷器活。〈俗语〉Don't try to mend porcelain wares unless you have a diamond cutter. *or* Don't undertake a difficult job if you don't have the necessary skills for it.

金糕 jīngāo haw jelly

金戈铁马 jīngē-tiěmǎ shining spears and armoured horses — a symbol of war; gallant, formidable warriors

金革 jīngé 〈书面〉❶ swords, armour and helmets, etc. ❷ war:无～之事 no such thing as war; free from hostilities

金工 jīngōng metalworking; metal processing:～机械 metalworking machinery /～工人 metalworker

金箍棒 jīngūbàng golden cudgel (weapon used by the Monkey King in the novel *Pilgrimage to the West*)

金股 jīngǔ 〈金融〉golden share

金鼓齐鸣 jīngǔ-qímíng all the gongs and drums are beating — prelude to intense and fierce fighting:山背后～,乃将军亲自引军来到。The sound of gongs and drums was heard behind the hill, and there was the general in person with a large army.

金瓜 jīnguā ❶ a kind of pumpkin ❷ long club with one end shaped like a longish golden melon, an ancient weapon which was later carried by a guard of honour

金光 jīnguāng golden light; golden ray:～闪闪 glittering; glistening /一轮朝阳,万道～。The rising sun radiates myriad golden rays.

金光大道 jīnguāng-dàdào golden road; bright broad highway

金龟 jīnguī tortoise

金龟婿 jīnguīxù rich son-in-law

金龟子 jīnguīzǐ 〈动物〉scarab

金贵 jīngui 〈口语〉precious; valuable:这里没有水源,吃水比吃香油还～。Water is scarce here and more precious than sesame oil.

金合欢 jīnhéhuān 〈植物〉sponge tree

金衡 jīnhéng troy (weight):～制 troy weight; troy /三～盎司 three ounce troy

金红 jīnhóng red and light yellow:晚霞的颜色自淡而浓,自～而碧紫。The colour of sunset glow is deepening, from red yellow to dark purple.

金红石 jīnhóngshí 〈矿业〉rutile

金花菜 jīnhuācài (California) bur clover

金环蛇 jīnhuánshé (banded) krait (*Bungarus fasciatus*)

金煌煌 jīnhuānghuāng *also* "金晃晃" golden bright:～的琉璃瓦 golden bright glaze tile

金黄 jīnhuáng golden yellow; golden:～色的秀发 golden hair; blonde hair / 秋天,漫山遍野,一片～。In autumn the mountains and open country are a sea of golden yellow.

J

金黄色葡萄球菌 jīnhuángsè pútao qiújūn staphylococcus aureus: ~肺炎 staphylococcal pneumonia
金汇兑本位 jīnhuìduì běnwèi 〈金融〉gold exchange standard
金婚 jīnhūn golden wedding, 50th wedding anniversary
金鸡 jīnjī golden pheasant: ~报晓。The crow of a cock heralds the break of day.
金鸡独立 jīnjī-dúlì stand on one foot as the cock does: 你站在地上~,那一条腿不许放下来。You stand on the ground on one leg and keep the other leg up.
金鸡奖 Jīnjījiǎng Golden Rooster Award, annual film award by the China Film Association
金鸡纳树 jīnjīnàshù cinchona
金鸡纳霜 jīnjīnàshuāng 〈药学〉quinine
金鸡纳素 jīnjīnàsù cinchonine
金甲 jīnjiǎ 〈书面〉armour and helmet
金浆玉醴 jīnjiāng-yùlǐ ❶ wine of the best quality ❷ elixir of life
金奖 jīnjiǎng gold medal; highest award; first prize
金交椅 jīnjiāoyǐ 〈贬义〉extremely important post or position: 勾心斗角二十年,他才爬上了这把极有权势的~。Only after twenty years' jockeying for power did he attain this position of great influence.
金酒 jīnjiǔ gin
金橘 jīnjú 〈植物〉kumquat
金卡 jīnkǎ 〈金融〉gold card
金科玉律 jīnkē-yùlǜ golden rule and precious precept: 封建时代奉儒家经典为~。In the feudal times, Confucian classics were taken as infallible precepts./不能把他的话当做~。You mustn't think his words are impeccable.
金壳郎 jīnkéláng 〈方言〉〈动物〉scarab
金口 jīnkǒu highly esteemed words: 敬聆~ listen to sb.'s advice respectfully / 依你~。Let things be as you say. *or* We'll do as you say.
金口玉言 jīnkǒu-yùyán *also* "金口玉音" emperor's words; pearls of wisdom; golden saying: 难道他的话就是~,不能改变? Are his words oracular and unchangeable (*or* fixed)?
金库 jīnkù *also* "国库" guókù national treasury; state treasury; exchequer
金块 jīnkuài gold bullion
金矿 jīnkuàng goldmine: ~区 goldfield
金兰 jīnlán sworn brothers: ~之友 sworn friends / 义结~ be sworn brothers
金兰谱 jīnlánpǔ 〈旧语〉genealogical records of sworn brothers, each keeping a copy
金兰湾 Jīnlánwān (Vietnam) Cam Ranh Bay
金兰之交 jīnlánzhījiāo intimate friendship; sworn brotherhood
金兰之契 jīnlánzhīqì lasting friendship
金莲 jīnlián 〈旧语〉lily feet — women's bound feet: 三寸~ three-inches-long bound foot
金莲花 jīnliánhuā 〈植物〉nasturtium
金铃子 jīnlíngzǐ 〈植物〉chinaberry
金缕玉衣 jīnlǚ-yùyī 〈考古〉jade clothes sewn with gold thread
金绿宝石 jīnlǜ bǎoshí *also* "金绿玉" 〈矿业〉chrysoberyl
金銮殿 jīnluándiàn Hall of Golden Chimes (a popular name for the emperor's audience hall); throne room
金马玉堂 jīnmǎ-yùtáng Imperial Academy
金猫 jīnmāo 〈动物〉golden cat (*Felis temminckii*)
金霉素 jīnméisù 〈药学〉aureomycin
金门岛 Jīnméndǎo Jinmen Islands (formerly translated as Quemoy Islands), of Fujian Province
金门桥 Jīnménqiáo Golden Gate Bridge, a suspension bridge in San Francisco, US
金门绣户 jīnmén-xiùhù golden gates and embroidered screens — the house of the extremely rich: 怨不得姑娘不认得,你们在这~里,哪里认得木头? I'm not surprised you don't know, miss. Living behind golden gates and embroidered screens, what should you know about wood?
金迷纸醉 jīnmí-zhǐzuì *also* "纸醉金迷" live an extravagant life; be given to sensual pleasures; indulge in a wanton life
金牛座 Jīnniúzuò 〈天文〉Taurus
金瓯 jīn'ōu 〈书面〉golden bowl symbolizing national territory: 收拾~一片,分田分地真忙。We have reclaimed part of the golden bowl And land is being shared out with a will.
金瓯无缺 jīn'ōu-wúquē golden bowl remaining intact; unimpaired territorial integrity
金牌 jīnpái 〈体育〉gold medal: ~得主 gold medalist
金瓶梅 Jīnpíngméi *Plum in the Gold Vase*, first novel written entirely by an individual author in China (who called himself Xiaoxiaosheng 笑笑生), probably in the late 16th century, with the first extant edition in 1617
金瓶掣签 jīnpíng chèqiān (traditional practice for deciding on the final choice of the soulboy of Dalai or Panchen Lama in Tibet) draw slips or lots from a gold urn: 以~确定十世班禅的转世灵童 draw lots from a gold urn to decide who is the reincarnation of the late 10th Panchen Lama
金漆 jīnqī 〈工美〉gold lacquer; Ningpo varnish: ~镶制品 inlaid gold lacquerware / ~盒子 casket of gold lacquer; gold lacquer casket
金器 jīnqì gold vessel
金钱 jīnqián money: ~万能 money is almighty; money talks / ~至上 value money above everything else / ~主义 money worship
金钱板 jīnqiánbǎn ❶ clappers used in ballad-singing and storytelling to beat time ❷ a kind of musical art popular in Sichuan, Guizhou, etc.
金钱豹 jīnqiánbào leopard
金钱草 jīnqiáncǎo 〈植物〉❶ *Herba lysimachiae* ❷ *Lysimachia christinae*
金钱松 jīnqiánsōng 〈植物〉golden larch (*Pseudolarix amabilis*)
金枪仙人掌 jīnqiāng xiānrénzhǎng 〈植物〉tuna (*Opuntia tuna*)
金枪鱼 jīnqiāngyú tuna; tunny (*Thunnus thynnus*): ~船 tuna boat
金秋 jīnqiū autumn
金曲 jīnqǔ great hit; popular song
金阙 jīnquè 〈书面〉imperial palace
金日成 Jīnrìchéng Kim Il Sung (1912-1994), leader of DPRK
金融 jīnróng finance; banking: ~机关 financial institution / ~交易 financial transaction / ~呆滞 financial stringency / ~公司 finance company / ~紧缩 tight money policy; deflationary policy / ~投机 monetary speculation / ~危机 financial crisis / ~制裁 financial sanction
金融工具 jīnróng gōngjù financial instrument
金融寡头 jīnróng guǎtóu financial oligarch; financial magnate
金融行 jīnrónghámg finance house
金融界 jīnróngjiè financial circles
金融巨头 jīnróng jùtóu financier; financial tycoon; shark of high finance
金融时报 Jīnróng Shíbào *The Financial Times*, a British newspaper published since 1888
金融市场 jīnróng shìchǎng money market; financial market
金融事务科 Jīnróng Shìwùkē (HK) Monetary Affairs Branch
金融司 Jīnróngsī (HK before July 1997) Secretary for Monetary Affairs
金融体制 jīnróng tǐzhì monetary system
金融中介 jīnróng zhōngjiè financial intermediary
金融中心 jīnróng zhōngxīn financial centre; banking centre
金融资本 jīnróng zīběn financial capital
金三角 Jīnsānjiǎo Golden Triangle, an area between Burma, Thailand and Laos, notorious for its drug production and trafficking
金嗓子 jīnsǎngzi beautiful voice; sweet, mellow voice: 她天生一副~,从小就喜欢唱歌。Born with a sweet voice, she has liked singing from childhood.
金色 jīnsè golden: ~的麦浪 golden waves of wheat / 我们披着~的朝阳走上山顶。Bathed in the golden rays of the morning sun, we climbed towards the mountain top.
金沙萨 Jīnshāsà (called Leopoldville under colonial rule) Kinshasa, capital of the Democratic Republic of the Congo (once called Zaire)
金闪闪 jīnshǎnshǎn golden bright and dazzling; sparkling or glistening with golden light: ~的阳光 golden bright and dazzling sunlight; dazzling sunlight
金身 jīnshēn Buddha's image in gold foil
金石 jīnshí ❶ 〈书面〉metal and stone — a symbol of firmness and strength: ~之交 unbreakable friendship / ~同盟 firm alliance ❷ inscriptions on ancient bronzes and stone tablets
金石为开 jīnshí-wéikāi move even metal and stone: 精诚所至,~。No difficulty is insurmountable if one sets one's mind to it.
金石学 jīnshíxué the study of inscriptions on ancient bronzes and

stone tablets; epigraphy

金饰 jīnshì gold ornament

金属 jīnshǔ metal: 黑色～ ferrous metal / 有色～ non-ferrous metal / 稀有～ rare metal / 轻～ light metal / 重～ heavy metal / 粉末～ powdered metal / ～废料 scrap metal / ～互化物 intermetallic compound / ～制品 metal work / ～成品率 metal yield / ～分布比 metal distribution ratio / ～回收率 metal recovery rate / ～级品位 metal-grade / ～线厂 wire works / ～预制件 metal fabrication

金属本位 jīnshǔ běnwèi metallic standard

金属玻璃 jīnshǔ bōli metal glass

金属分币 jīnshǔ fēnbì coin; small denomination coin

金属工艺品 jīnshǔ gōngyìpǐn metal handicrafts ware

金属加工 jīnshǔ jiāgōng metal processing; metalworking

金属键 jīnshǔjiàn metallic bond

金属结构 jīnshǔ jiégòu metal structure: ～厂 metal structure works

金属膜 jīnshǔmó metal film; metallic membrane: ～荧光屏 metallized screen

金属模 jīnshǔmú metal pattern

金属疲劳 jīnshǔ píláo metal fatigue

金属切削 jīnshǔ qiēxiāo 〈机械〉 metal-cutting; metal removal: ～机床 metal-cutting machine tool / ～率 metal removal factor; metal removal rate; metal removal efficiency / ～能力 metal-cutting capacity

金属探伤 jīnshǔ tànshāng flaw detection: X 射线可以用作～，工程师们用它来查明金属物体的内部结构以确定其中有无疵病。X-rays can function as a flaw detector, which engineers use to find out how metal objects are internally structured in order to check whether there are any flaws in them.

金属陶瓷 jīnshǔ táocí 〈冶金〉 metallized ceramics; metalceramics; metalloceramics: ～烧结制品 metal-ceramic agglomerate

金属涂料 jīnshǔ túliào metallic paint

金属显像管 jīnshǔ xiǎnxiàngguǎn 〈电子〉 metal-Braun tube; metal kinescope

金属型 jīnshǔxíng 〈冶金〉 metal mould; permanent mould: ～铸造 metal mould casting; permanent mould casting / ～铸造机 permanent mould casting machine

金属性 jīnshǔxìng metallicity

金属氧化物半导体 jīnshǔ yǎnghuàwù bàndǎotǐ 〈电子〉 metal oxide semiconductor: ～集成电路 metal oxide semiconductor integrated circuit (MOSIC) / ～器件 metal oxide semiconductor device

金水河 Jīnshuǐhé Golden Water River, in front of Tian An Men, Beijing

金水桥 Jīnshuǐqiáo Golden Water Bridge, marble bridge across the Golden Water River in front of Tian An Men, Beijing

金丝草 jīnsīcǎo 〈植物〉 *Hypericum chinense*; *Hyporicum patulum*

金丝猴 jīnsīhóu golden monkey; snub-nosed monkey

金丝雀 jīnsīquè canary

金丝雀症 jīnsīquèzhèng canary pox

金丝镶嵌 jīnsī xiāngqiàn 〈工美〉 gold filigree

金丝燕 jīnsīyàn 〈动物〉 esculent swift

金丝枣 jīnsīzǎo a variety of Chinese date

金斯敦 Jīnsīdūn ❶ Kingston, capital of Jamaica ❷ Kingstown, capital of St. Vincent

金松 jīnsōng 〈植物〉 *Sciadopitys verticillata*

金粟兰 jīnsùlán 〈植物〉 *Chloranthus spicatus*

金汤 jīntāng (short for 金城汤池) strongly fortified fortress or city: 固若～ strongly fortified; impregnable; invulnerable

金田起义 Jīntián Qǐyì peasant uprising held at Jintian village of Guangxi (广西) in 1851, which marked the beginning of the Taiping Revolution and was led by Hong Xiuquan (洪秀全) and Yang Xiuqing (杨秀清)

金条 jīntiáo gold bar

金童玉女 jīntóng-yùnǚ 〈道教〉 Golden Boy and Jade Maiden; boy and girl attendants of a god or goddess: 而况四小姐蕙芳，七少爷阿萱一对～，也在他身旁。What's more, he had his two precious children, his son Ah Xuan and his daughter Huifang, at his side.

金柝 jīntuò a watchman's clapper

金文 jīnwén also "钟鼎文" zhōngdǐngwén inscriptions on ancient bronze objects; ancient language used in such inscriptions

金窝银窝，不如自家草窝 jīnwō yínwō, bùrú zìjiā cǎowō 〈俗语〉 a poor man treasures his shack more than gold and silver mansions; be it ever so humble, there's no place like home; home is home, be it ever so homely; east or west, home is best

金乌 jīnwū 〈书面〉 Golden Crow — the sun: ～西坠。The sun is setting (*or* sinking) in the west.

金屋藏娇 jīnwū-cángjiāo live with one's young concubine in a plush house; keep a mistress in a love nest; take a concubine

金无足赤 jīnwúzúchì gold can't be hundred percent pure: ～，人无完人。Gold can't be pure and man can't be perfect. *or* There are spots even on the sun. / ～，对人何苦求全责备? As gold can never be pure, how can we demand perfection of man?

金吾不禁 jīnwú-bùjìn lift the curfew: 此地是～，正好夜游。Since the curfew has been lifted here, night is the perfect time for sightseeing.

金线鱼 jīnxiànyú 〈动物〉 red coat; golden thread

金相 jīnxiàng 〈冶金〉 metallographic: ～检验 metallographic examination / ～显微镜 metalloscope

金相学 jīnxiàngxué metallography

金相玉质 jīnxiàng-yùzhì *also* "玉质金相" (of people) sterling qualities; nobility of character; (of literary works) excellent in content and form: ～，百世无匹。It is of such extraordinary quality that nothing will match it for generations to come.

金小蜂 jīnxiǎofēng 〈动物〉 tiny golden wasp; pteromalid

金星 jīnxīng ❶ (Jīnxīng) 〈天文〉 Venus ❷ golden star: ～红旗 flag with a gold star in the centre of a red ground — national flag of Viet Nam ❸ spark; star: 两眼冒～ see stars

金星玻璃 jīnxīng bōli aventurine glass

金言 jīnyán precious words; valuable remarks

金眼鲷 jīnyǎndiāo 〈动物〉 berycoid

金疡 jīnyáng 〈书面〉 metal-inflicted wound; incised wound

金要足赤，人要完人 jīn yào zúchì, rén yào wánrén gold must be pure and man must be perfect; perfectionism: 求全责备，～，是形而上学的表现。To demand perfection, to require gold to be one hundred percent pure and man to be entirely flawless, is a manifestation of metaphysical thinking.

金钥匙 jīnyàoshi golden key — very effective way: 知识是认识世界的～。Knowledge is the golden key to the understanding of the world.

金银财宝 jīnyín-cáibǎo gold, silver and other treasures; treasures

金银花 jīnyínhuā 〈植物〉 honeysuckle

金银花露 jīnyínhuālù 〈中药〉 distilled liquid of honeysuckle

金银炉 jīnyínlú 〈冶金〉 doré furnace

金樱子 jīnyīngzǐ 〈中药〉 fruit of Cherokee rose (*Rosa laevigata*)

金鱼 jīnyú goldfish: 他有一双～眼睛。He has a pair of bulging eyes. *or* He has a pair of protruding eyes.

金鱼草 jīnyúcǎo 〈植物〉 *Antirrhinum magus*

金鱼虫 jīnyúchóng 〈动物〉 water flea

金鱼缸 jīnyúgāng goldfish bowl

金鱼藻 jīnyúzǎo 〈植物〉 species of bornwort (*Ceratophyllum demersum*)

金玉 jīnyù 〈书面〉 gold and jade; precious stone and metals; treasures: ～之言 precious and valued advice

金玉良言 jīnyù-liángyán golden saying; pearls of wisdom; invaluable advice; excellent counsel: 您的～，我将铭之肺腑。Your invaluable advice will be engraved on my mind.

金玉满堂 jīnyù-mǎntáng one's house filled with gold and jade; wealthy with vast riches: ～，莫之能守。Nobody can be sure to keep his wealth forever.

金玉其外，败絮其中 jīnyù qí wài, bàixù qí zhōng rubbish coated in gold and jade; fair without, foul within; rotten interior beneath a fine exterior: 这是一帮～的公子哥儿。This is a gang of pampered sons of wealthy families who are all good-for-nothing.

金元 jīnyuán gold dollar; US dollar: ～外交 dollar diplomacy

金圆券 jīnyuánquàn a kind of paper money circulated in 1948 by the Kuomintang government

金云母 jīnyúnmǔ 〈矿业〉 phlogopite

金盏花 jīnzhǎnhuā 〈植物〉 pot marigold (*Calendula officinalis*)

金针 jīnzhēn ❶ 〈书面〉 needle used in sewing and embroidery ❷ 〈中医〉 acupuncture needle ❸ dried day lily flower ❹ secret of success; tricks of trade; knack; key to success: 处世～ key to worldly success

金针菜 jīnzhēncài 〈植物〉 ❶ day lily ❷ day lily flower

J

金针虫 jīnzhēnchóng 〈动物〉wireworm
金针鲷 jīnzhēndiāo 〈动物〉snapper
金针度人 jīnzhēn-dùrén teach sb. the tricks of trade
金正日 Jīnzhèngrì Kim Chong Il (1941-), son of Kim Il Sung (金日成) and leader of DPRK
金枝玉叶 jīnzhī-yùyè gold branches and jade leaves — descendants of royal families: 他娶了一位皇族的～。His wife was a descendant of the royal family. /你还自以为是～似的小姐吗? So you think you're a fine lady, eh?
金钟儿 jīnzhōngr 〈动物〉click beetle
金字塔 jīnzìtǎ pyramid: 埃及～是世界奇观之一。The Egyptian pyramids are one of the world's wonders.
金字塔报 Jīnzìtǎbào *Al Ahram*, an Egyptian newspaper founded in 1875
金字招牌 jīnzì zhāopái ❶ gold-lettered signboard of a shop: 你何必总想找个名导师, 给自己挂上～呢? Why should you seek vain reputation by trying to get a famous professor as your mentor? ❷ vain glorious title
金子 jīnzi gold: ～一般的心 heart of gold

筋(觔)

jīn ❶ muscle: 钢～铁骨 steel muscle and iron bone — tough and strong ❷ tendon; sinew: 扭了～ get one's sinew sprained /抽～ have a cramp; pull a tendon /牛蹄～儿 tendons of beef ❸ veins that stand out under the skin: 腿肚子上满是青～。Blue veins stand out on his calves. ❹ anything resembling a tendon or vein: 叶～ ribs of a leaf /钢～ steel bar /面～ gluten /橡皮～儿 rubber band /菜老～多嚼不烂。The vegetables are so old and stringy that no one can chew them.
筋道 jīndao 〈方言〉❶ (of food) tough and chewy: 抻面吃到嘴里挺～。Hand-pulled noodles are very chewy. ❷ sturdy (old man): 这老头儿倒很～。This old man is quite hale and hearty.
筋斗 jīndǒu 〈方言〉❶ somersault; tumble: 翻几个～ make a number of tumbles /这位体操运动员的～翻得又高又飘。This gymnast's somersault is high and graceful. ❷ fall; tumble (over): 摔了个～ have a fall; tumble over; trip and fall /骄傲自满的人容易栽～。Pride goes before a fall.
筋骨 jīngǔ muscles and bones — physique: 锻炼～ develop one's muscles; strengthen the physique /每天早晨跑跑步, 活动活动～。Jogging every morning will limber you up.
筋节 jīnjié ❶ muscles and joints ❷ vital links in a speech or essay: 这些话正说到～儿上。These words are very much to the point.
筋力 jīnlì ❶ physical strength: ～已衰 physical decline ❷ 〈方言〉toughness of food, etc.: 绿豆粉皮的～大。Sheet jelly made from mung beans is quite tough.
筋络 jīnluò 〈中医〉main and collateral channels, regarded as a network of passages, through which vital energy circulates and along which the acupuncture points are distributed
筋脉 jīnmài passages through which vital energy circulates, regulating bodily functions
筋疲力尽 jīnpí-lìjìn *also* "精疲力竭" jīngpí-lìjié exhausted; played out; worn out; tired out: 刚走了一半路, 她已经两腿酸痛, ～了。She was tired out, with aches in both legs, after covering only half the distance. /开车开到～时你必须休息, 不然要出事故。You should stop driving when you feel dead-tired, for that is the time you are likely to have a traffic accident. /干完一天活, 我都～。After a day's work, I would be all tuckered out.
筋肉 jīnròu muscles
筋头麻脑儿 jīntóu-mánǎor *also* "筋头马脑儿" 〈方言〉❶ meat that is tough and not easy to chew; tough meat ❷ things that are good for nothing; worthless things: 要这些～的破烂儿有什么用? What's the use of having all this rubbish?

斤[1](❶觔)

jīn ❶ *jin*, unit of weight ($=\frac{1}{2}$ kilogram) ❷ *added to the name of sth. measured by weight to form a general term*: 煤～ coal / 盐～ salt

斤[2]

jīn ancient instrument or tool for felling trees: 斧～ axe; hatchet
斤斗 jīndǒu *also* "跟头" gēntou 〈方言〉fall; somersault
斤斤 jīnjīn fuss about; haggle over: ～于琐事 bother too much about trifles /不要～于表面形式。Don't fuss about formalities.
斤斤计较 jīnjīn-jìjiào haggle over every ounce; be calculating: 要以大局为重, 对个人的利害得失, 不应～。You should take the interests of the whole into account instead of being engrossed in personal gains and losses.
斤两 jīnliǎng weight: ～不足 short weight; underweight /我人微言轻, 说话缺少～。I'm a low man on the totem pole, and my words carry little weight.

jǐn

堇

jǐn
堇菜 jǐncài *also* "堇堇菜" 〈植物〉violet
堇青石 jǐnqīngshí 〈矿业〉cordierite
堇色 jǐnsè violet

廑(厪)

jǐn 〈书面〉only; merely
see also qín

谨

jǐn ❶ careful; cautious; prudent; circumspect: 恭～ respectful and cautious /拘～ cautious; reserved; not given to rashness /勤～ diligent and prudent /严～ rigorous; strict; meticulous /～守诺言 carefully keep one's promise /～奉法令 scrupulously abide by decrees ❷ solemnly; sincerely: ～启 yours respectfully /我～代表中国政府和中国人民, 对您的正式来访表示热忱欢迎。On behalf of the Chinese government and people, I wish to extend our warmest welcome to you on your official visit to China.
谨饬 jǐnchì 〈书面〉prudent; careful; cautious
谨防 jǐnfáng guard against; beware of: ～有误 caution oneself against possible error /～暗箭。Guard against a hidden attack. /～恶犬。Beware of the vicious dog. /～假冒。Look out for imitations.
谨厚 jǐnhòu be prudent and honest: ～朴实 be simple and honest
谨密 jǐnmì be prudent and circumspect: 办事～ be prudent and circumspect in handling affairs
谨上 jǐnshàng 〈套语〉sincerely yours
谨慎 jǐnshèn prudent; careful; cautious; circumspect: 谦虚～ be modest and prudent /说话～ be guarded in one's speech /～从事 act with caution /言行～ be prudent in one's words and deeds /为人～ be circumspect by nature /过于～ be overcautious /总之你讲话～为好。In short, you'd better keep a careful watch on what you say.
谨小慎微 jǐnxiǎo-shènwēi overcautious in small matters; timid and wary; punctilious: ～的小职员 timid petty clerk /他一向～。He is always cautious in the extreme.
谨严 jǐnyán careful and precise: 防守～ careful and rigorous defence /他做事章法～。He is cautious and methodical in his work. /他写诗极其～。He strictly follows the rules in writing poems.
谨言慎行 jǐnyán-shènxíng speak and act cautiously; be discreet in word and deed: 他是个～的人, 不会和你深谈。Being very discreet, he would not engage in a heart-to-heart talk with you.
谨愿 jǐnyuàn 〈书面〉prudent and faithful; honest
谨赠 jǐnzèng with the compliments of: 外交学院～。With the compliments of the Foreign Affairs College.

瑾

jǐn 〈书面〉beautiful jade: ～瑜匿瑕 flaws are hidden in a beautiful gem; even a beautiful gem has flaw

槿

jǐn
槿麻 jǐnmá 〈植物〉gombo hemp (*Hibiscus cannabinus*)

馑

jǐn *see* "饥馑" jījǐn

仅(僅)

jǐn 〈副词〉only; merely; barely; just: ～够一个月开销 be barely enough for a month's expenses /绝无～有 only one of its kind /～供参考 for reference only /硕果～存 rare survival /～够糊口 live from hand to mouth /～凭记性 from memory /这～是时间问题。It is only a matter of time.
see also jìn
仅见 jǐnjiàn rarely seen: 世所～ have no parallel anywhere /今年的水灾, 为几十年所～。This year's flood is rare in recent decades.
仅仅 jǐnjǐn 〈副词〉only; merely; barely; just: 他写这本书～用了十天时间。It took him only (*or* just) ten days to write the book. /～服

装一项，就获利十万元。A profit of a hundred thousand *yuan* has been gained from the sale of garments alone. /他～为了一点小事就发脾气。He flew into a temper over a mere triviality (*or* trifle).

仅只 jǐnzhǐ only; merely; alone:今年郊区水果大丰收，～苹果的产量就达一千五百万公斤。The suburbs got another bumper harvest in fruit this year, and the apple output alone reached 15 million kilograms.

紧(緊) jǐn ❶ tight; taut; close:拉～弓弦 pull the bowstring taut /眉头皱得～，一脸不高兴 knit one's brows and look unhappy /鼓面绷得非常～。The surface of the drum is stretched tight (*or* to the full). ❷ fast; firm; close:把门关～ close the door fast /捏～笔杆 hold firm the shaft of a pen /身子～贴在山崖上 cling close to the wall of a cliff /城门～闭。The city gate is firmly shut. /眼睛～盯住他。Keep a close watch on him. ❸ tighten; fasten:～～鞋带 tighten (*or* fasten) a shoelace /螺丝～好了。The screw has been tightened up. ❹ close; too tight:抽屉太～，拉不开。The drawer is too close to pull open. /这双鞋子太～。These shoes are too tight. *or* These shoes pinch. /苔藓～贴地面生长。Moss grows close to the ground. ❺ urgent; pressing; following (each other) closely:时间很～。Time is pressing. /情况越来越～。The situation became more and more critical. /雪下得更～了。It is snowing even harder. /战斗正～。The battle was heated. /一个任务～接着一个任务。One task is closely followed by another. ❻ hard up; hard pressed; short of money:手头～ be short of money; be hard up /银根～。Money is tight. /他家孩子多，生活相当～。With too many children, the family is hard pressed for cash.

紧巴巴 jǐnbābā ❶ tight; taut:这件上衣我穿～的。The coat is a tight fit for me. ❷ hard up:那时我们日子过得～的。We were in straitened circumstances then. *or* We were hard up in those days.

紧梆梆 jǐnbāngbāng ❶ tight; taut:膝盖以下，打着～的裹腿。A puttee was tightened taut below the knee. ❷ hard up; short of money:他多年来生活总是～的。He has been hard up for years.

紧绷绷 jǐnbēngbēng ❶ tight; taut:～的绳子 tight (*or* taut) rope /弦拉得～的。The string is stretched tight (*or* taut). ❷ strained; stiffened; sullen:脸上～的 strained look /走进考场，她心里～的。She felt stressed when she entered the examination hall.

紧逼 jǐnbī press hard; close in on:步步～ press on at every stage /全场～ full-court press (in basketball) /半场～ half-court press (in basketball) /他～着我还钱。He pressed me to pay him back. /敌军向我军营房～而来。The enemy troops were closing in on our barracks.

紧称 jǐnchen 〈方言〉❶ small but serviceable:这屋子虽然小点儿，倒挺～。Though it is a little bit too small, the room is quite serviceable. ❷ tight fit; neatly-dressed:她打扮得～利落。She is neatly dressed.

紧凑 jǐncòu compact; terse; succinct; well-knit:讲话～ speak succinctly; make a concise speech /剧情～。The play has a well-knit plot. /文章结构～。The article is well organized. /庭院的格局～，给人一种和谐的美感。The garden is compactly laid out, giving people a sense of harmonious beauty.

紧促 jǐncù hurried; short and pressing; urgent:呼吸～ short of breath; gasp for breath /听到一声～的叫声 hear an urgent cry

紧蹙 jǐncù (brows) tightly knit:听到这好消息，他～的双眉一下舒展开来。On hearing this good news, he lifted his tight-knit brows.

紧跟 jǐngēn follow closely; keep in step with:我～在他的后面进了屋子。I stepped into the house close at his heels. *or* I followed him into the house. /这个戏贴近生活，～形势。This play is true to life and keeps pace with the times.

紧公差 jǐngōngchā 〈机械〉close-tolerance:～锻造 close-tolerance forging

紧箍咒 jǐngūzhòu Incantation of the Golden Hoop, used by the Monk in the novel *Pilgrimage to the West* to keep the Monkey King under control — inhibition:要想调动群众的生产积极性，就必须去掉各种平均主义的～。To arouse people's enthusiasm for production, you must remove equalitarian inhibitions of all descriptions. /维持全家生计的～把他牢牢地套住了。He was weighed down with the burden of supporting his family.

紧关节要 jǐnguān-jiéyào most important; critical:合龙是这项工程～的阶段。Closure is the most important part of this project.

紧急 jǐnjí urgent; emergent; pressing; critical:～的事情 urgent issue (*or* case) /进行～协商 hold immediate consultations /～任务 pressing task /～关头 critical moment /～呼叫 urgent call /～追捕 hot pursuit /～抢救 emergency rescue /～出动 urgent (*or* emergent) dispatch /～支援 emergency aid /～订货 rush order /～停电 emergency power cut /～修理 first-aid repair

紧急出口 jǐnjí chūkǒu emergency exit (as in a theatre or plane)

紧急措施 jǐnjí cuòshī emergency measure

紧急法令 jǐnjí fǎlìng emergency act

紧急故障信号 jǐnjí gùzhàng xìnhào abort light

紧急会议 jǐnjí huìyì emergency meeting; urgent meeting

紧急集合 jǐnjí jíhé emergency muster

紧急警报 jǐnjí jǐngbào emergency alarm

紧急起飞 jǐnjí qǐfēi (of a plane) scramble

紧急特别联大 jǐnjí tèbié Liándà 〈外交〉emergency special session of UN General Assembly

紧急信号 jǐnjí xìnhào emergency signal; distress signal

紧急闸 jǐnjízhá emergency brake

紧急状态 jǐnjí zhuàngtài state of emergency

紧急着陆 jǐnjí zhuólù emergency landing

紧紧 jǐnjǐn closely; firmly; tightly:～盯着 fix one's eyes on the target /～依靠集体智慧 rely firmly on collective wisdom /她把嘴闭得～的。Her mouth was tightly shut. /两队不分上下，比分～咬住。The two teams are equally matched with very close scores.

紧链器 jǐnliànqì chain tightener

紧邻 jǐnlín close neighbour; immediate neighbour:老张家是我家的～。The Zhangs are my next-door neighbours.

紧锣密鼓 jǐnluó-mìgǔ *also* "密锣紧鼓" wildly beating gongs and drums — intense publicity campaign in preparation for some public undertaking:他竞选总统的各项准备正在～地进行着。An intense publicity campaign is going on in preparation for his bid for the presidency.

紧忙 jǐnmáng ❶ tense and busy:这是一年中最～的季节。This is the busiest season in the year. ❷ hurry up; be in a hurry:他刚出去，你～追，还来得及。He has just left and you'll catch up with him if you hurry.

紧密 jǐnmì ❶ close together; inseparable; unseverable:我们团结得更～了。We have further enhanced our unity. /个人的命运和民族的命运～地联系着。Personal fate is closely connected (*or* linked) with that of the nation. ❷ rapid and intense:～的枪声 rapid, intense firing /～的雨点打在窗户上。Rapid raindrops were pattering against the window panes.

紧迫 jǐnpò pressing; critical; urgent; imminent:他感到了事情的严重和～。He realized that the matter was serious and urgent. /时间～，不容多想。Being pressed for time, I can't mull over the matter.

紧迫感 jǐnpògǎn sense of urgency:时间不等人，我们要有～。Time and tide wait for no man. We must have a sense of urgency.

紧俏 jǐnqiào have a ready market; supply falls short of demand:～货 commodities which have a ready market; salable goods /这种料子很～。This kind of material sells like hot cakes. /彩电曾经是众人争购的～家电。Color TV receivers were once in such short supply that people rushed to purchase them.

紧缺 jǐnquē lack; be short of; be in short supply:～商品 commodities that are in short supply /物资～ shortage of goods and materials /政府将通过调整信贷结构等措施，帮助一些企业认真解决资金～的困难。By such measures as readjusting credit structure, the government tries to help some enterprises with their tight funds.

紧身儿 jǐnshenr close-fitting undergarment; undershirt:～胸衣 corset

紧士裤 jǐnshìkù jeans

紧实 jǐnshi tight; close:车上有一筐装得很～的苹果。In that car, there is a tightly packed basket of apples.

紧缩 jǐnsuō reduce; contract; retrench; tighten:～编制 reduce staff /～生产 curtail production /～时期 period of retrenchment /～包围圈 tighten a ring of encirclement /由于收入明显地减少，我们该～开支了。With our income sharply reduced, it is time to draw rein on our expenditures. /目前没有必要执行一种～计划。There is no need to implement an austerity programme at present.

紧缩财政 jǐnsuō cáizhèng 〈经济〉austerity budget

紧缩措施 jǐnsuō cuòshī 〈经济〉austerity measure; retrenchment

紧缩银根 jǐnsuō yíngēn 〈经济〉tight money supply:目前必须～。We must tighten up money supply at present.

紧缩政策 jǐnsuō zhèngcè 〈经济〉deflation policy; policy of retrenchment

紧压茶 jǐnyāchá (tighty-pressed) tea lump or brick

J

紧严 jǐnyán tight; close:房屋四壁和门窗都是~的,冬天冷风进不去。The doors, windows and four walls of the house are sealed tight, keeping out the cold wind in winter.

紧要 jǐnyào critical; crucial; vital:无关~ of no consequence; of no importance /在两国谈判的~关头 at the critical moment (*or* juncture) of the negotiations between the two countries /这个会事关~。This meeting is of vital importance.

紧衣缩食 jǐnyī-suōshí *also* "节衣缩食" jiéyī-suōshí economize on food and clothing; live frugally

紧张 jǐnzhāng ❶ nervous; edgy; keyed up:考试时~ be nervous during an examination /出了什么事,这么~。What happened? You're in quite a state. /他整天神情~,一定有什么心事。There must be something worrying him as he has been on edge (*or* over-wrought) all day. /轮到她口试时,她突然~得不得了。When her turn for the oral test came, she suddenly had butterflies in her stomach. ❷ tense; intense; strained:~的劳动 intense labour /~关系 strained relationship /~动人的情节 exciting and intriguing plot /缓和国际~局势 ease international tension /在战斗~时刻 in the heat of battle /他这一番话使会议的气氛顿时~起来。His words immediately created a tense atmosphere at the meeting. /工程正在~地进行。Construction was in full swing. /今天活动太~。We've had a busy day. *or* We've had a tight (*or* crowded) schedule today. ❸ in short supply; tight:解决住房~问题 ease housing shortage /煤炭供应~,水电都不足。Since there is a shortage of coal, the supply of power and running water is inadequate. /他们人手~。They are short of hands (*or* short-handed). /建筑材料十分~。Construction materials are in great demand.

紧张症 jǐnzhāngzhèng 〈医学〉catatonia; catatony

紧着 jǐnzhe 〈口语〉speed up; press on with; hurry:他~走,连头都不抬。He walked away in such a hurry that he even didn't lift his head. /眼看着就要下雨了,大家要~干。It looks like rain. Let's hurry.

紧追 jǐnzhuī hot pursuit:~恐怖分子 be in hot pursuit of terrorists

紧子 jǐnzi 〈方言〉tight-fitting undergarment

紧自 jǐnzi 〈方言〉always; all the time; invariably:~犹豫 always hesitant /~痛哭 keep crying bitterly

锦

jǐn ❶ brocade:织~ brocade /蜀~ Sichuan brocade /如花似~ as pretty as flower and brocade /衣~还乡 return to one's home town in silken robes (after becoming wealthy and influential) ❷ bright and gorgeous:~笺 exquisite letter paper /~瑟年华 youth, prime of one's life /前程似~ splendid prospects; glorious future

锦标 jǐnbiāo prize; trophy; title:得~ win a prize /夺取~ strive for a title

锦标赛 jǐnbiāosài championship contest; championships:世界乒乓球~ World Table Tennis Championships /世界青年足球~ World Youth Football Championships

锦标主义 jǐnbiāozhǔyì cups and medals mania; everything for the medal

锦簇花团 jǐncù-huātuán *also* "花团锦簇" bouquets of flowers and piles of silk — beautiful and colourful decorations

锦缎 jǐnduàn brocade

锦鸡 jǐnjī 〈动物〉golden pheasant

锦葵 jǐnkuí 〈植物〉high mallow:~科 *Malvaceae*

锦鳞 jǐnlín 〈书面〉colourful fish

锦纶 jǐnlún polyamide fibre

锦囊 jǐnnáng embroidered bag or pouch (used by ancient Chinese poets to keep poems jotted down on scraps of paper)

锦囊佳句 jǐnnáng-jiājù *also* "锦囊佳制" embroidered bag verses — fine verses; beautiful poems

锦囊妙计 jǐnnáng-miàojì stratagems to deal with an emergency; wise counsel:献上一条~ present a clever stratagem /他狡狯地向我射来冷冷的一眼,好像说:"你的~在哪里呢?" He shot me a cold, crafty glance which seemed to say, "What's happened to your beautiful schemes now?"

锦屏 jǐnpíng brocade screen

锦旗 jǐnqí silk banner (as an award or a gift)

锦上添花 jǐnshàng-tiānhuā add flowers to the brocade — make what is good still better:对于他们,最需要的还不是"~",而是"雪中送炭"。For them the prime need is not "more flowers on the brocade" but "fuel in snowy weather". /这幅好画,再配上你这首好诗,真是~。This beautiful picture is made even more beautiful with your excellent poem inscribed on it.

锦心绣口 jǐnxīn-xiùkǒu *also* "锦心绣腹" elegant thoughts and flowery speech; elegant and refined:好一个~的少年! What an elegant and refined youth!

锦绣 jǐnxiù as beautiful as brocade; elegant; splendid; magnificent:~文章 piece of elegant writing /万里江山披~。This land of ten thousand *li* is full of splendour and beauty.

锦绣河山 jǐnxiù héshān land of charm and beauty; beautiful land:收拾好这~ run the beautiful country well

锦绣前程 jǐnxiù qiánchéng glorious or splendid future

锦衣卫 Jǐnyīwèi Guards in Embroidered Coats — a secret service of the Ming Dynasty

锦衣玉食 jǐnyī-yùshí brocades and delicacies — live an extravagant life:世兄是~,无不遂心的。You have all the luxuries you can desire.

尽[1](儘)

jǐn ❶ to the greatest extent or degree possible:~着力气干活 spare no effort in working ❷ within the limits, bounds, or time:~着一周完成 get it finished within a week /~着在本市安排参观活动。Please arrange visits within the bounds of the city. /行期已定,我们~着这几天做准备。As the departure date is fixed, we have to get everything ready before that. ❸ give priority or precedence to:坐位不够,先~客人们坐吧。As there are not enough seats, let visitors be seated first. ❹ (used before phrases indicating direction or location) furthest; most:~底下 at the very bottom /~后头 rearmost; furthest back /路的~南头 at the southern end of the road

尽[2](儘)

jǐn 〈方言〉keep on doing sth.:你整天~闹着玩儿可不行。It won't do if you keep on playing all day long. /这些日子~刮风。We're having an awful lot of wind these days.

see also jìn

尽管 jǐnguǎn ❶ feel free to; not hesitate to:有劲~使 do as much as you can /有意见~提好了。Don't hesitate to make comments or suggestions if you have any. /你~直说。Just speak out. /这事你~放心,一切全在我身上。I'll attend to everything about it. So please don't worry. ❷ 〈方言〉always; all the time:别人问她,她不说,~哭。She was crying all the time, refusing to say anything when asked. /~挑人家的毛病可不好。It's not right to always find fault with others. ❸ though; even though; in spite of; despite:~任务困难,他们仍设法按时完成了。Though the task was difficult, they managed to accomplish it in time. /他~有缺点,可还是一个好学生。For all his shortcomings, he is a good student. /~他一连去了三封信,也还是没有回音。He had sent three letters in a row, but still he didn't get any reply.

尽可能 jǐnkěnéng as far as possible; as best as one can; to the best of one's ability:~早 as early as possible; at the earliest possible date /~好的办法 the best possible means; the best means available /明天的座谈会,我~赶来参加。I'll try my best to come to tomorrow's forum. /处理问题~要考虑得全面些。Be as thoughtful as you can in handling the problem.

尽快 jǐnkuài as quickly as possible; as soon as possible; promptly:请~付房租。Please pay the rent as soon as possible. /问题要~解决,不能再拖了。The problem must be solved at once (*or* promptly). There should be no further delay.

尽量 jǐnliàng to the best of one's ability; as far as possible:~紧缩开支 cut down expenses as far as possible /~利用时间 make the best of one's time /~拿吧! Take as much as you want! /只要我能办到的,~办到。I'll do the best (*or* everything) I can. /他在这篇文章里~做到有所创见。He was straining after originality in his paper.

see also jìnliàng

尽让 jǐnràng 〈方言〉give precedence to others out of courtesy or thoughtfulness; politely or modestly decline (a favour, an offer, etc.):他们相处得很好,凡事都有个~。They are on very good terms, trying to accommodate each other in whatever they do.

尽先 jǐnxiān give priority to; put first:~考虑住房问题 give first priority to the housing problem /~完成这项任务 accomplish this task first

尽早 jǐnzǎo as soon as possible:字典用毕,请~送还。Please return the dictionary as soon as you finish using it. /请~答复。Please give us a reply at your earliest convenience.

尽自 jǐnzi 〈方言〉keep on doing sth.:别~伤心了。Don't keep on

J

feeling sad. *or* Stop feeling sad.

卺 jǐn 〈书面〉nuptial wine cup：合～ drink the wedding cup；get married

jìn

进(進) jìn ❶ advance；move forward；march ahead；press onward：迈～ forge ahead；march forward／挺～ (of troops) boldly drive on；press ahead／猛～ advance by leaps and bounds／奋～ advance bravely／推～ (of troops) move forward；drive on／突～ push forward；press onward／跃～ leap forward；advance with big strides／高歌猛～ stride forward singing militant songs；advance triumphantly／不～则退。Move forward，or you'll fall behind. ❷ enter；come into；go into；get into：～大门 enter the gate／～医院 be sent to hospital；be hospitalized／～球〈体育〉score a goal／走～客厅 walk into the hall／施工重地，闲人免～。Construction site. No admittance except on business.／火车～站。The train is pulling in.／厂里～了一批新工人。The factory has taken on (*or* employed) a batch of new workers. ❸ receive；take：这种买卖～钱。You'll earn a lot of money doing this kind of business. ❹ submit；present：～一言 give a word of advice ❺ eat；drink；take：～药 take medicine／滴水不～ not take even a single drop of water — unable to eat or drink ❻ (used after a verb) into；in：把信投～邮筒 post a letter into a pillar box／把衣服装～箱子 pack clothes into a trunk／买～一批图书 lay in a good supply of books／引～国外的新技术 import new foreign technology／他几个球都没有踢～球门。He missed the goal several times. ❼ any of the several rows of houses within an old-style residential compound：一～三间 three houses in a row (within a residential compound)

进逼 jìnbī close in on；bear down on；advance on；press on towards：步步～ steadily close in／向敌人的右翼～ advance on the right wing of the enemy／游击队～县城。The guerrillas were pressing on towards the county town (*or* seat).

进兵 jìnbīng (of troops) drive on；forge ahead；march towards：向敌占区～ advance on the enemy controlled areas

进补 jìnbǔ take tonic；take extra nourishment：冬令～ take tonic in winter

进步 jìnbù ❶ advance；move forward；progress；improve：他作文有～。His composition has improved.／今年我们各方面都取得了～。Great progress has been made in every field of our work this year.／虚心使人～，骄傲使人落后。Modesty helps one to go forward, whereas conceit makes one lag behind. ❷ (politically) progressive：思想～ have progressive ideas／～书刊 progressive publications／～组织 progressive organization／这些主张是～的。These are forward-looking views.

进餐 jìncān eat；take a meal：按时～ take food at regular time／一同～ eat together／共进晚餐 have supper together

进谗 jìnchán 〈书面〉speak ill (of sb. before elders or superiors)：乘机～ take the opportunities to malign people

进场 jìnchǎng ❶ (as of sportsmen) march into the arena ❷〈航空〉approach：～失败 missed approach／～航向 approach course／～信标 approach-beacon；marker beacon

进呈 jìnchéng 〈书面〉submit；present：～御览 submit for the emperor's perusal

进城 jìnchéng ❶ go into town；go to town：搬到郊区以来多日未～了。I haven't been to town for days since I moved to the suburbs. ❷ enter the big cities (to live and work)：春节后民工大批～。Rural workers swarmed into the big cities after the Spring Festival.

进程 jìnchéng course；process；progress：加快了历史～ advance the course of history／影响工作～ hinder the progress of work／加快试验的～ speed up the (process of) experimentation／技术力量不足，严重影响了本厂技术革新的～。The shortage of technological personnel has seriously affected technological innovation at (*or* in) our factory.

进尺 jìnchǐ 〈矿业〉footage：掘进～ drifting footage／凿岩～ drilling footage／开拓～ tunnelling footage／钻机钻探的年～ year's footage of a drilling machine

进出 jìn-chū ❶ enter and exit；pass in and out：妨碍人们～ block up the way／～时间卡 in-and-out time card／车辆由此～。Vehicles this way!／自行车统由西门～。Bicycles go in and out through the western gate.／这栋楼～只有一个大门。This building has only one door for entrance and exit. ❷ (business) turnover：这个公司去年有十多亿元的～。Last year, this company had a turnover of more than a billion *yuan*.

进出口 jìn-chūkǒu ❶ exits and entrances；exit：剧场的～ exit of a theatre／地下室的～ entrance of a cellar／人防工程的～ entrances and exits of civil air defence works ❷ imports and exports：～业务 imports and exports／～平衡 balance of imports and exports／～税 imports and exports duty／～货物报关单 customs declaration for imports and exports／～申报 import and export declaration／～许可证 license for imports and exports／～专业公司 specialized import and export corporation／～商品交易会 trade fair／中国粮油食品～公司 China National Cereals, Oils, and Foodstuffs Import and Export Corporation

进出口代理制 jìn-chūkǒu dàilǐzhì system of import and export agency

进出口贸易 jìn-chūkǒu màoyì import and export trade；foreign trade

进寸退尺 jìncùn-tuìchǐ advance by one inch but retreat by a foot — lose much more than what one gets

进刀 jìndāo 〈机械〉feed：～装置 feed arrangement；feed gear；feeder

进德修业 jìndé-xiūyè improve one's virtue and refine one's professional ability

进抵 jìndǐ (of troops) arrive (at a certain place)；reach：部队～大沙河一带。The troops have reached the Dashahe region.

进度 jìndù ❶ rate of progress or advance：加快～ quicken the pace；quicken the tempo／加速技术革新的～ step up technical innovation／目前的～ present rate of progress／～报表 progress report；progress sheet (*or* chart)／～估计 progress estimate／～时间表 progress schedule ❷ planned speed；schedule：按～施工 carry out construction according to plan (*or* schedule)

进度表 jìndùbiǎo progress chart

进而 jìn'ér proceed to the next step：他们拟定了计划，～付诸实施。They drew up a plan and then proceeded to carry it out.／先搞试点，～逐步推广。First make experiments at selected units；next, spread the experience step by step.

进发 jìnfā set out；set off；start：向泰山山顶～ head for the top of Mount Tai／汽车向颐和园～。The car started for the Summer Palace.／目标已定，我们就开始～。The destination being decided on, we set out accordingly.

进犯 jìnfàn intrude into；invade：击退～的敌人 repulse the invading enemy／抗击～之敌 resist the aggressor troops／一股敌军～边境。An enemy detachment intruded into the border region.

进风井 jìnfēngjǐng 〈矿业〉downcast (shaft)

进风口 jìnfēngkǒu air intake

进奉 jìnfèng submit；present：～珍宝 present treasures

进港导航 jìngǎng dǎoháng approach navigation

进港航道 jìngǎng hángdào approach channel；port entrance

进攻 jìngōng attack；assail；assault；offensive：向敌发起～ launch an offensive against the enemy／击退敌人的疯狂～ beat back the enemy's fierce assault／重新组织力量～ reorganize forces for another attack／～队形 attack formation／～命令 order to attack／～敌人的侧翼 attack the enemy in the flank／下半时我方加强～，连进两个球。In the second half, our team strengthened its offensive and scored two goals in succession.

进攻性武器 jìngōngxìng wǔqì offensive weapon

进贡 jìngòng ❶ pay tribute (to a suzerain or emperor) ❷ grease or oil sb.'s palm：向上司～ grease one's superior's palm

进化 jìnhuà evolution：生物～的过程 evolutionary process of organisms／人类从猿～到人，经历了一个漫长的时期。It took a long period of time for man to evolve from the anthropoid ape.

进化论 jìnhuàlùn theory of evolution；evolutionism：～者 evolutionist

see also "达尔文主义" Dá'ěrwénzhǔyì

进化树 jìnhuàshù pedigree；genealogical tree；family tree

进货 jìnhuò lay in a new stock of merchandise；replenish one's stock：～渠道 channel to replenish one's stock／～价格 purchasing price；commodity price；price of goods／～成本 purchasing cost／～分类账 purchase ledger；bought ledger／～折扣 purchase discount／～选择权 purchase option

进击 jìnjī advance on (the enemy)；launch an attack：奋勇～敌人

bravely advance on the enemy /向一切恶势力～ launch attacks on all evil forces

进见 jìnjiàn call on (sb. holding high office); have an audience with:～总统 have an audience with the president /～之礼 present upon meeting sb. (for the first time)

进谏 jìnjiàn 〈书面〉 remonstrate with the monarch

进剿 jìnjiǎo advance on to wipe out:～残匪 attack and exterminate the remaining bandits

进京 jìnjīng go to the capital of the country:～开会 go to the capital for a meeting /～上访 go to the capital and appeal to the authorities concerned for help /～公干 go to the capital on business

进境 jìnjìng progress; advance:他近来学习大有～。He has made much progress in his studies recently.

进酒 jìnjiǔ 〈书面〉 urge sb. to drink (at a banquet)

进爵 jìnjué 〈书面〉 be promoted to a higher rank:加官～ receive official promotion; advance in rank and position

进军 jìnjūn march; advance:向沙漠～ go and conquer the desert /向敌人～ march against the enemy /径向敌后～ drive straight into areas behind the enemy lines /～中原 advance on the Central Plains /向四个现代化～ drive for the four modernizations /北伐军胜利～。The Northern Expeditionary Army marched on victoriously.

进军号 jìnjūnhào bugle call to advance

进口 jìnkǒu ❶ enter port; sail into a port:油轮～。The tanker sailed into port. /外轮～。A foreign ship reached (*or* made) port. ❷ import:～订货管理 management of import orders /～商品价格管理 price control of import commodities /限制奢侈品～ limit the import of luxuries /～替代产品 import substitutes /这个国家的粮食靠～。This country depends on imports for its grain. ❸ entrance:火车站～ entrance of a train station /剧场～ entrance of a theatre ❹〈机械〉inlet:鼓风～ blast inlet

进口报单 jìnkǒu bàodān import declaration

进口壁垒 jìnkǒu bìlěi import barrier

进口补贴 jìnkǒu bǔtiē import subsidy

进口代理商 jìnkǒu dàilǐshāng import agent

进口额 jìnkǒu'é volume of import

进口附加税 jìnkǒu fùjiāshuì import surcharge

进口港 jìnkǒugǎng port of entry

进口货 jìnkǒuhuò imported goods; imports:～指定检查 average sampling

进口检疫 jìnkǒu jiǎnyì import quarantine

进口结构 jìnkǒu jiégòu import makeup; import structure

进口商 jìnkǒushāng importer

进口收托 jìnkǒu shōutuō inward collection

进口税 jìnkǒushuì import duty

进口限额 jìnkǒu xiàn'é import quota

进口许可证 jìnkǒu xǔkězhèng import license

进款 jìnkuǎn income; receipts:这个个体户每月有上万元的～。This self-employed businessman has a monthly income of more than ten thousand *yuan*.

进窥 jìnkuī 〈书面〉(of armed forces) close in (to seek battle)

进来 jìnlai come in; get in; enter:请～吧! Please come in! /带他～。Bring him in. /路过时～坐坐。Please drop in any time you're passing by. /从外面～了一位男青年。A young man entered from outside. /门开了,～一股冷风。A gust of cold wind blew in when the door opened.

进来 jìnlai (used after a verb) in; into:走～ walk in /搬～ move in /从外面拿～两把椅子。Two chairs were brought in from outside. /风从窗口吹～。The wind came in through the window. /货物都运进仓库里来了。All the goods have been carried into the warehouse.

进料 jìnliào 〈机械〉feed:～斗 feeding skip /～装置 feeding apparatus; feeder unit /～器 feeder /～泵〈化工〉charging pump

进路 jìnlù access; admission passage; road or way forward:阻挡～ block the way forward

进门 jìnmén ❶ go in; pass the gate:～之前要查看通行证。Your pass will be checked at the gate. ❷ learn the rudiments of sth.; cross the threshold:师傅领～,修行看各人。The master initiates the apprentices, but their skill depends on their own efforts. ❸ (of a woman) get married and move into the bridegroom's family:她是刚～的媳妇。She has just married into the family. *or* She's the new bride.

进迫 jìnpò approach; draw near; close in on:～敌巢 close in on the enemy's den

进汽 jìnqì 〈机械〉(air) admission; (air) admittance; (air) induction; (air) intake:～阀 induction valve; intake valve /～口 admission (*or* admitting) port /～道 air inlet; admission passage /～歧管 induction manifold; inlet manifold; intake manifold

进前 jìnqián move forward:只要有人～,就会踏上地雷。Whoever moves forward will step on the mine.

进取 jìnqǔ keep forging ahead; be eager to make progress; be dynamic; be enterprising:奋发～ be energetic and daring

进取心 jìnqǔxīn enterprising spirit; initiative; gumption; drive

进去 jìnqu go in or into; get in or into; enter:进屋里去 go into the house /进不去 be unable to enter /他刚～,叫你也赶快～。He has just got in there and asked you to join him quickly.

进去 jinqu (used after a verb) in; into:闯～ break in; barge in /把玻璃嵌～ fit a piece of glass in /把手伸～ stretch one's hand in /衣服太小,穿不～。The dress is too small to wear (*or* put on). /别人的意见他听不～。He wouldn't listen to others' opinions.

进入 jìnrù enter; get into:～决赛阶段 enter the finals /～前八名 advance into the last eight; enter the last eight pool /～盛夏季节 be in the midst of high summer /～战斗 go into action /～战备阶段 be in combat readiness /～新的发展时期 enter a new stage of development /～市场 enter a market /火山又～活动期。The volcano has reached its active period. /这几年他们的生活有了转机,～了顺境。In recent years, their life has taken a turn for the better, and things are going smoothly.

进入角色 jìnrù juésè enter into the spirit of a character; live one's part:这位演员似乎还没有～。It seems that the actor hasn't got inside the character that he is playing.

进身 jìnshēn stepping stone:明清士人以八股文作为～的阶梯。Scholars of the Ming and Qing dynasties used the "eight-part essay" as a stepping stone in their official career.

进身之阶 jìnshēnzhījiē stepping stone (in one's offical career):他就在这个营盘里找一个小差事,作为～。He then found a job of some kind in this camp as a stepping stone to some higher position.

进深 jìnshen (of a house or a room) distance from the entrance to the rear; depth:这间屋子的～太小,只能摆下一张床和桌子。This room is so small that it only has space for a bed and a table.

进食 jìnshí take food; eat one's meal:按时～ have one's meals at the fixed time

进士 jìnshì 〈历史〉successful candidate in the highest imperial civil service examination; palace graduate

进水闸 jìnshuǐzhá 〈水利〉intake work; intake

进退 jìntuì ❶ advance and retreat:～自如 be free to advance or retreat (in a battle or game); have plenty of room for manoeuvre /～无门 no way to advance or to retreat — in a dilemma or bind /～狼狈 not knowing what to do; in a predicament ❷ sense of propriety:不知～ have no sense of propriety

进退两难 jìntuì-liǎngnán find it difficult to advance or to retreat; can go neither forward nor back; be in a dilemma:他一时～,真不知道怎么办才好。He felt caught in a dilemma for the moment and did not know which way to turn. /她不愿去打篮球,又没有理由推辞,觉得实在～。She didn't want to play basketball but could find no pretext to refuse. She was in a quandary.

进退失据 jìntuì-shījù nothing to rely on whether one advances or retreats — at an impasse

进退维谷 jìntuì-wéigǔ on the horns of a dilemma; between the devil and the deep blue sea:他现在～,不知所措。Caught in a dilemma, he is now at his wit's end. /正在～的当儿,我们帮他们下了决心。At this moment of indecision, we helped them make up their minds.

进位 jìnwèi 〈数学〉carry (a number, as in adding)

进袭 jìnxí march on and make a surprise attack against (the enemy):乘隙～敌营 seize an opportunity to mount a surprise attack on the enemy encampment

进贤 jìnxián 〈书面〉recommend or recruit an able and virtuous person

进献 jìnxiàn submit; present:～方物 present some local products

进香 jìnxiāng (of Buddhists or Taoists) go on a pilgrimage to a temple; offer incense; worship:近几年,到杭州灵隐寺～的善男信女真不少。These years, there has indeed been a large number of devout men and women going on pilgrimages to the Ling Yin Temple in Hangzhou.

进香客 jìnxiāngkè Buddhist pilgrim

进项 jìnxiang income; receipts:这个养殖场的~可不少。This aquatic farm has quite a handsome income.

进行 jìnxíng ❶ be in progress; be under way; proceed; go on:会议的准备工作正在~。Preparations for the meeting are under way. /会谈在友好的气氛中~。The talks proceeded in a friendly atmosphere. /手术~得怎样? How did the operation go? /音乐会在~之中。The concert is in progress. /讨论~了三个小时。The discussion lasted three hours. /大会明天继续~。The conference will continue tomorrow. ❷ carry on; carry out; conduct: ~详细调查 conduct thorough investigations /~比较 make a comparison /~艰苦的斗争 wage an arduous struggle /~垂死挣扎 put up a desperate or last-ditch struggle /~恶毒攻击 level a virulent attack /~经济封锁 enforce an economic blockade /~讨论 hold a discussion /~刑事诉讼 institute penal proceedings /~投机倒把 engage in speculation and profiting /~报复 make reprisals /~了解 get oneself acquainted with; try to understand /尽管大家千方百计地~劝阻,他还是一意孤行。Although we all tried our best to dissuade him, he was bent on having his own way. ❸ be on the march; march; advance:队伍在~中接到了新的命令。The troops were on the march when they received the new orders.

进行曲 jìnxíngqǔ march:《义勇军~》*March of the Volunteers* /乐队高奏~。The band struck up a march in high spirits.

进修 jìnxiū engage in advanced studies; take a refresher course:在职~ in-service training; on-the-job training /业务~ vocational studies; vocational training /离职~ off-the-job training

进修班 jìnxiūbān class for further studies

进修生 jìnxiūshēng student engaged in further studies

进学 jìnxué 〈历史〉(of scholars in the Ming and Qing dynasties) pass the entrance examination so as to be allowed to continue their studies in the county and prefectural schools

进言 jìnyán offer an opinion; voice or air one's view:大胆~ presume to express one's opinions

进谒 jìnyè 〈书面〉call on (sb. holding high office); have an audience with:大使~驻在国总统。The ambassador called on the president of the country to which he was accredited.

进一步 jìnyībù advance a step; go a step further; further: ~提高产品质量 further improve the quality of the product /作~调查 make further investigation /~扩大缺口 widen a gap /对经济发展规律有了~的了解 have a better understanding of the laws of economic development /他们试图阻止局势的~恶化。They tried to stop the situation from worsening.

进益 jìnyì ❶〈书面〉progress; improvement:学问大有~。Great progress has been made in (one's) learning. ❷ income; earning:你一年有多少~? What's your annual income?

进用 jìnyòng recommend or employ: ~能人 recruit talented people

进展 jìnzhǎn progress; headway:国有企业体制改革取得了~。The structural reform of state enterprises has made headway. /他们的科学研究~顺利。Their scientific researches are progressing smoothly. /事情~如何? How are things going?

进占 jìnzhàn attack and occupy; attack and capture; capture:我军昨天已~该省省城。Our army captured the capital of that province yesterday.

进站 jìnzhàn (as of a train) get in; pull in; draw up at a station:准时~ draw up at the station on time

进账 jìnzhàng income; receipts

进针 jìnzhēn 〈中医〉push in an acupuncture needle

进止 jìnzhǐ 〈书面〉❶ advance and retreat ❷ manners; bearing; deportment; mien

进驻 jìnzhù enter and be stationed in; enter and garrison:部队已~边城。Troops have been stationed in the border city.

晋[1] (晉)

jìn ❶ enter; advance: ~京 go to the capital ❷ promote:连~三级 be promoted three times in succession /加官~爵 set promotion

晋[2] (晉)

Jìn ❶ name of a state during the Zhou Dynasty ❷ Jin Dynasty (265-420) ❸ Later Jin Dynasty (936-946) ❹ another name for Shanxi Province ❺ a surname

晋级 jìnjí 〈书面〉rise in rank; be promoted:他工作作出色,几年内连续~。He has been promoted several times in a few years because of his excellent work.

晋见 jìnjiàn call on (sb. holding high office); have an audience with:这些官员正在等着~总统。These government officials are waiting to have an audience with the president.

晋剧 jìnjù local opera in Shanxi Province

晋升 jìnshēng promote to a higher office: ~为教授 be promoted to professor /职务~ be promoted to a higher post /职称~ be conferred a higher professional title

晋文公 Jìn Wéngōng named Chong'er (重耳, 697-628 BC), monarch of the State of Jin (636-628 BC), and first hegemon of the Spring and Autumn Period

晋谒 jìnyè 〈书面〉call on (sb. holding high office); have an audience with:求职时,父亲带他~一位总经理。When he was looking for a job, his father took him to call on a general manager.

晋职 jìnzhí 〈书面〉be promoted to a higher post

瑨

jìn 〈书面〉jade-like stone

搢

jìn 〈书面〉❶ insert; stick ❷ shake

搢绅 jìnshēn *see* "缙绅" jìnshēn

缙

jìn 〈书面〉red silk

缙绅 jìnshēn *also* "搢绅" jìnshēn 〈旧语〉gentry (with official titles)

墐

jìn 〈书面〉❶ stuff sth. with mud ❷ *see* "殣❶" jìn

殣

jìn ❶ bury; inter; entomb ❷ die of hunger; starve to death:道无~者。No one died of hunger on the road.

觐

jìn ❶ present oneself before (a monarch) ❷ go on a pilgrimage:到麦加去朝~ go on a pilgrimage to Mecca

觐见 jìnjiàn 〈书面〉present oneself before (a monarch); go to court; have an audience with: ~国王 present oneself before the king

仅(僅)

jìn 〈书面〉approaching; approximately; near:士卒~万人。The number of soldiers was near ten thousand. *or* There were nearly ten thousand soldiers.

see also jǐn

禁

jìn ❶ prohibit; forbid; ban:严~走私。Smuggling is strictly forbidden. ❷ put behind bars; imprison; detain:囚~ imprison; put in jail /软~ put sb. under house arrest /拘~ take into custody ❸ what is forbidden by law or custom; taboo:犯~ violate a ban (*or* prohibition) /违~品 contraband (goods) /宵~ curfew /海~ ban on maritime trade or intercourse with foreign countries /门~森严 with the entrances heavily guarded /令行~止 strict enforcement of orders and prohibitions /入国问~。On entering a country ask about its taboos. ❹ forbidden area:宫~ imperial palace

see also jīn

禁闭 jìnbì confinement (as a punishment):关了三天~ be placed in confinement for three days

禁闭室 jìnbìshì guard room

禁兵 jìnbīng imperial guard

禁城 jìnchéng imperial palace wall:紫~ Forbidden City

禁地 jìndì forbidden area; restricted area; out-of-bounds area:这片园林,原是封建皇朝的~。This garden used to be restricted to feudal emperors and their families.

禁毒 jìndú prohibit drug or narcotics

禁赌 jìndǔ prohibit gambling; suppress gambling; ban gambling

禁遏 jìn'è 〈书面〉prohibit; ban; forbid; prevent

禁伐林 jìnfálín forest where tree felling is prohibited; forest preserve

禁方 jìnfāng 〈中医〉secret medicinal recipe

禁宫 jìngōng imperial palace; forbidden palace

禁锢 jìngù ❶〈旧语〉debar from holding office:在封建时代,有些知识分子被~终身。In feudal times, some intellectuals were debarred from holding offices all their lives. ❷ keep in custody; imprison; jail:警察把他~在一个山洞里。The police kept him in a cave. ❸ confine; enthral; shackle:被旧习惯所~ be shackled by old customs /跳出形而上学思想的~ free oneself from the fetters of metaphysical thinking

禁果 jìnguǒ 〈宗教〉forbidden fruit

J

禁毁 jìnhuǐ prohibit and destroy (books, etc., that violate a ban)

禁火 jìnhuǒ fire prohibition — no one was allowed to light a fire to cook food during the "cold food festival" in ancient times

禁忌 jìnjì ❶ taboo:属~之列 under taboo /百无~ no prohibition of any kind /过去此地民间多~。There used to be a lot of taboos in this area. ❷ avoid; abstain from;〈医学〉contraindicate:~生冷 avoid eating anything raw or cold /这药的~很多,服用时要注意。There are many contraindications concerning this medicine, please take it with care.

禁忌症 jìnjìzhèng 〈医学〉contraindication:接种~contraindications to vaccination

禁酒 jìnjiǔ prohibition on alcoholic drinks:~时期 the Prohibition (in American history, 1920-1933)

禁绝 jìnjué totally prohibit; completely forbid:这些不良现象一时尚难~。It is not easy to completely ban these unhealthy tendencies in a short time. /这家商店做到了~伪劣品。This shop has got rid of all fake and shoddy goods.

禁军 jìnjūn 〈历史〉forces that protect the capital city or the imperial palace; imperial guard:~教头 military instructor of the imperial guard

禁例 jìnlì prohibitory regulations; prohibitions:触犯了~要受到严厉的处罚。Anyone who violates prohibitions would be severely punished.

禁猎 jìnliè prohibition on hunting:动物保护区~。Hunting is forbidden in animal protection areas.

禁猎区 jìnlièqū no-hunting area; game preserve or reserve

禁令 jìnlìng prohibition; ban:取消~ nullify a prohibition /解除~ lift (*or* remove) a ban /犯~ break (*or* violate) a ban /下一道~ lay a prohibition; impose a ban

禁律 jìnlǜ prohibitory regulation or decree

禁脔 jìnluán chunk of meat for one's exclusive consumption; one's exclusive domain or preserve:这些关键的技术过去是被师傅看作~的。These key technical skills used to be regarded by the master artisan as his exclusive domain.

禁门 jìnmén 〈计算机〉inhibitory-gate; except gate:~输入 inhibiting input

禁区 jìnqū ❶ forbidden zone; restricted zone; out-of-bounds area:军事~ military restricted zone; military forbidden zone /误入~ enter a restricted zone by mistake /科学无~。There is no out-of-bounds area as far as science is concerned. ❷ (of wildlife or vegetation) preserve; reserve; natural park:这里是森林~,不得砍伐树木或狩猎。This is a forest preserve, and no tree felling or hunting is allowed. ❸〈医学〉forbidden band ❹〈体育〉(of football) penalty area; (of basketball) restricted area

禁赛 jìnsài forbid sb. from participating in a match (due to violation of rules); suspend from competition (as punishment)

禁食 jìnshí fast:一周~期 fast of one week

禁食疗法 jìnshí liáofǎ fasting treatment; starvation cure

禁书 jìnshū banned book:这些书在清代是~。These were banned books in the Qing Dynasty.

禁条 jìntiáo prohibitory regulation; prohibition

禁屠 jìntú prohibition or ban on butchering (animals):~耕牛 ban on butchering farm cattle

禁卫 jìnwèi ❶ guard the capital city and the imperial palace:~森严 heavily guarded ❷ emperor's bodyguard; imperial guard

禁卫军 jìnwèijūn troops that protect the capital city or imperial palace; imperial guard

禁物 jìnwù banned goods and materials; contraband

禁压 jìnyā try one's best to control or stop:~不住自己的悲伤 be unable to repress one's sadness; can't help feeling sad

禁押 jìnyā take into custody

禁烟 jìnyān ❶ *see* "禁火" ❷ ban on opium smoking and trafficking; ban on the planting of opium poppy

禁夜 jìnyè curfew

禁抑 jìnyì 〈书面〉press down; restrain; suppress:她虽然努力~,还是流露出不安的神情。She tried hard to control herself, but she couldn't help betraying her anxiety. *or* She tried in vain to suppress her uneasiness.

禁渔 jìnyú prohibition on fishing; fishing prohibition; fishing ban:~期 fishing prohibition period

禁渔季 jìnyújì closed fishing season; no-fishing season

禁渔区 jìnyúqū forbidden fishing zone; no-fishing area

禁欲 jìnyù suppress sensual enjoyment; be ascetic:过着~生活 lead an ascetic life /~修行 mortify the flesh; mortification /我们提倡艰苦朴素,但决不主张~。We encourage hard work and plain living, but we never advocate asceticism.

禁欲主义 jìnyùzhǔyì asceticism

禁苑 jìnyuàn imperial garden

禁运 jìnyùn embargo:封锁~ blockade and embargo /打破~ break an embargo /对战时违禁品实行~ impose an embargo on contraband of war /~法 embargo law /~物资 contraband goods and materials

禁运品 jìnyùnpǐn contraband

禁止 jìnzhǐ prohibit; ban; forbid:~某人做某事 forbid sb. to do sth. /~拍照。Cameras are forbidden. /这部电影~上演。The film is banned. /~燃放鞭炮。No firecrackers. /~入内。No admittance. /~停车。No parking. /~通行。No thoroughfare. *or* Closed to traffic. /~招贴。Post no bills. /公共场所~吸烟。No smoking in public places. /~喧哗。No uproar. *or* Keep quiet. /已宣布~驻军入村。The village was declared out of bounds for the soldiers posted nearby.

禁止超车区 jìnzhǐ chāochēqū 〈交通〉no-passing zone

禁止脉冲 jìnzhǐ màichōng inhibit pulse

禁止器 jìnzhǐqì 〈计算机〉inhibitor

禁制 jìnzhì restrain; control; check:她~不住内心的感情,哇的一声哭起来了。She couldn't control her feelings and burst into tears.

禁制品 jìnzhìpǐn articles the manufacture of which is prohibited except by special permit; banned products or goods

禁子 jìnzi *also* "禁卒"〈旧语〉jailer

禁阻 jìnzǔ prohibit; ban; forbid; stop:他们都要这么干,我一个人怎么~得住? Since they all want to do it, how can I possibly stop them all by myself?

噤

jìn ❶〈书面〉keep silent:~口不敢复言 keep silent and dare not open one's mouth again ❷ shiver:寒~ shiver with cold

噤闭 jìnbì 〈中医〉lockjaw (caused by an illness); tetanus

噤口痢 jìnkǒulì 〈中医〉severe dysentery (whereby a patient loses appetite utterly and vomits whenever he eats or drinks)

噤若寒蝉 jìnruòhánchán as silent as a cicada in cold weather — keep silent out of fear:可是,当谈话刚接触到正题的时候,他就立即讳莫如深,~了。When we got down to business in our conversation, he would immediately become quiet, not uttering a single word.

噤声 jìnshēng keep silent; not say a word

唫

jìn 〈书面〉remain silent; be tongue-tied

近

jìn ❶ near; close; immediate:在最~的将来 in the near future /~距离射击 fire at close range /舍~求远 seek far and wide for what lies close by /~在眼前 right before one's eyes; near at hand /远水解不了~渴 Distant water cannot quench present thirst. /春节临~了。Spring Festival is drawing near. *or* It'll soon be Spring Festival. /从这里到车站哪条路最~? Which is the shortest way from here to the railway station? ❷ approaching; nearly; approximately; close to:年~不惑 approaching forty; getting on for forty /~于事实 border on the truth /时~午夜。It was close on midnight. /~九点了。It is nearly nine. /谈判已~尾声。The negotiation is drawing to an end. /日~黄昏。It was near dusk. ❸ intimate; closely related:亲~ intimate; closely related /两人关系很~。The two of them are bosom friends. ❹〈书面〉easy to understand; simple and obvious:浅~ simple and easy to understand /言~旨远 simple in language but profound in meaning

近岸 jìn'àn offshore:~海域 offshore area /~结构 offshore structures

近便 jìnbian close and convenient:住在这里上班~多了。It's much more convenient to go to work living here. /这里有条小路走着~。There is a shortcut around here.

近臣 jìnchén 〈旧语〉minister close to an emperor; favourite courtier

近程 jìnchéng short range:~雷达 short-range radar /~火箭 short-range rocket

近程弹道导弹 jìnchéng dàndào dǎodàn 〈军事〉short-range ballistic missile (SRBM)

近程攻击导弹 jìnchéng gōngjī dǎodàn 〈军事〉short-range attack missile (SRAM)

近处 jìnchù vicinity; place nearby:～没有客店。There isn't any inn close by (*or* in the neighbourhood).
近磁极区 jìncíjíqū 〈物理〉polar cusp areas (areas near the magnetic field poles)
近刺 jìncì 〈军事〉short thrust; short lunge
近代 jìndài ❶ modern times (a term used in Chinese history specifically to refer to the period from the middle of the 19th century to 1919):～少见的重大变化 momentous changes seldom witnessed in modern times ❷ capitalist era
近代史 jìndàishǐ modern history:中国的～是一部屈辱史。The modern history of China (i.e. from mid-1800's to 1919) is a history of humiliation.
近道 jìndào shortcut:抄～ take a shortcut /走～ follow a shortcut; take a shortcut; cut corners
近地点 jìndìdiǎn 〈天文〉perigee:～高度 perigee altitude /～角距 perigee angle distance
近点年 jìndiǎnnián 〈天文〉anomalistic year
近点月 jìndiǎnyuè 〈天文〉anomalistic month
近点周 jìndiǎnzhōu 〈天文〉anomalistic revolution
近东 Jìndōng Near East
近拱点 jìngǒngdiǎn 〈航天〉periapsis (the orbital point nearest the focus of attraction)
近古 jìngǔ (in Chinese history) recent antiquity, from the 10th century to the middle of the 19th century (roughly from the Song Dynasty to the Opium wars)
近海 jìnhǎi coastal waters; inshore; offshore:～渔业 inshore fishing /～航运 shipping in coastal waters; offshore shipping /在～勘探石油 offshore oil drilling /利用～养殖海带 make use of the coastal water to raise kelp /～水产资源 offshore aquatic resources
近海工程 jìnhǎi gōngchéng offshore engineering
近海群岛 jìnhǎi qúndǎo offshore archipelago
近红外 jìnhóngwài 〈物理〉near infra-red (region of the electromagnetic spectrum between the visible and the thermal or far infra-red):～光谱 near infra-red spectrum /～线 near infra-red ray
近乎 jìnhu ❶ nearly; close to; almost:～完成 be nearly completed /～不可能 almost impossible /～黑色的黑棕色 brown approaching black /～真丝的人造丝 near silk /～神话的宣传 propaganda little short of a fairy tale /总额～一亿元。The total comes up to approximately 100 million *yuan*. /他的那个笑话～粗俗。That joke of his almost sounded vulgar. ❷〈方言〉intimate; friendly; clubby:套～ try to be friendly with; try to chum (*or* pal, *or* cozy) up with; cotton up to /两个人越来越～。The two of them become more and more chummy with each other.
近畿 jìnjī 〈书面〉capital and its environs
近郊 jìnjiāo outskirts of a city; suburbs; environs:住在～ live on the outskirts of a city /～有几处游览点。There are several scenic spots in the suburbs.
近焦点 jìnjiāodiǎn perifocus
近焦距离 jìnjiāo jùlí 〈天文〉perifocal distance (in an orbit, the distance between the focus containing the primary body and the perigee)
近捷 jìnjié shortcut:～的出海路线 shortcut to the sea
近今 jìnjīn 〈书面〉present; now:～趋势 current tendencies
近景 jìnjǐng ❶ scenery close by ❷〈摄影〉close shot ❸ present situation; current condition; immediate prospect:两国合作的～不错,但远景难料。The cooperation between the two countries is pretty good in the short term, but hard to predict over the long term.
近距离谈判 jìnjùlí tánpàn 〈外交〉proximity talks
近况 jìnkuàng recent developments; current situation; how things stand:东欧～ recent developments in Eastern Europe /不了解她的～ have no idea how things stand with her /～日趋紧张。The current situation is growing increasingly tense. /他的～如何? How is he getting on?
近空间 jìnkōngjiān near space (the region outside the earth's atmosphere but within the earth-moon region)
近来 jìnlái recently; of late; lately:北京～雨水甚多。Beijing has too much rain these days. /他～火气不小。He is in a bad temper lately.
近理 jìnlǐ be reasonable; stand to reason
近邻 jìnlín near or immediate neighbour:远亲不如～。Close neighbours are more helpful than distant relatives.
近路 jìnlù shortcut:走～可以早到二十分钟。You can arrive there twenty minutes earlier if you take the shortcut.
近密 jìnmì close; intimate:这两家倒是挺～的。The two families are very close.
近庙欺神 jìnmiào-qīshén those near the temple make fun of the gods; the nearest to church, the farthest from god; familiarity breeds contempt
近年 jìnnián in recent years:～获奖的影片不少。Quite a few films have won prizes in recent years.
近旁 jìnpáng nearby; near; close to:学校～有一个汽车加油站。There is a filling (*or* gas) station near the school.
近迫作业 jìnpò zuòyè 〈军事〉construction under fire; sapping
近期 jìnqī in the near future:～决策 near-term decision /～展望 near-term prospect /～预报 short-term forecast /此事～必有结果。Results will appear (*or* come) in the near future.
近前 jìnqián 〈方言〉nearby; near; just in front of sb.
近亲 jìnqīn close relative; near relation:～收养 adoption by a close relation /～相奸〈法律〉coitus illicitus
近亲繁殖 jìnqīn fánzhí close breeding; inbreeding:大熊猫的～ inbreeding of giant pandas /学术界也有～的问题。Exclusive practices are also sometimes found in academic circles.
近亲婚姻 jìnqīn hūnyīn consanguineous marriage
近情 jìnqíng reasonable; sensible; rational:作者善文辞,叙事～而生动。The author is a man of literary talent, and his description is at once reasonable and graphic.
近人 jìnrén ❶ modern man:甲骨文是19世纪末才发现的,～对它作了许多考释。Inscriptions on bones or tortoise shells were discovered in the late 19th century, and people thereafter have done a lot of textual research and explanation. ❷〈书面〉close associate or friend:妈妈把巧云看作～,对她说了自己的心里话。Mother took Qiao Yun as a confidante and opened her heart to the woman.
近日 jìnrì ❶ recently; in the past few days:～病情有转机。The condition of the patient has been improving in recent days. ❷ within the next few days:她～来北京。She is coming to Beijing in a few days' time.
近日点 jìnrìdiǎn 〈天文〉perihelion
近世 jìnshì modern times; modern age
近视 jìnshì ❶ myopia; nearsightedness:～散光 myopic astigmatism ❷〈比喻〉shortsightedness:这种做法在政治上是～,在经济上是失算。This move is politically shortsighted and economically injudicious.
近视眼 jìnshìyǎn ❶ myopia; nearsightedness; shortsightedness ❷ myopic or nearsighted person
近视眼镜 jìnshì yǎnjìng spectacles for nearsighted person
近水楼台 jìnshuǐ-lóutái waterside pavilion — advantageous position:他家有人在这家商店工作,买便宜货自然是～。Someone in his family works in this shop. That's why the family always has the advantage of buying goods at bargain prices.
近水楼台先得月 jìn shuǐ lóutái xiān dé yuè a waterfront pavilion gets the moonlight first — the advantage of being in a favoured position:我们是争不过他们的,他们～嘛! We are not their match as they are in a favourable position and enjoy special advantages.
近水知鱼性,近山识鸟音 jìn shuǐ zhī yú xìng, jìn shān shí niǎo yīn he who lives near the water knows the habits of fish, and he who lives near the hill is acquainted with the singing of birds — the environment in which we live and work influences us in much of what we do
近似 jìnsì approximate; near; similar:～估算额 approximate estimate sum /～最佳解 near optimum solution /兄弟俩十分～。The two brothers are as like as two peas. /这两个地方的方音有些～。The dialects of the two localities are somewhat similar to each other.
近似读数 jìnsì dúshù approximate reading
近似法 jìnsìfǎ method of approximation
近似分析法 jìnsì fēnxīfǎ approximate analysis method
近似计算 jìnsì jìsuàn approximate calculation
近似商 jìnsìshāng 〈数学〉approximate quotient
近似值 jìnsìzhí 〈数学〉approximate value
近岁 jìnsuì 〈书面〉in recent years; in the past few years
近体诗 jìntǐshī "modern style" poetry, referring to innovations in classical poetry during the Tang Dynasty, marked by strict tonal patterns and rhyme schemes:～以律诗为代表。Modern style poetry finds best expression in *lüshi* (a poem of eight lines, each containing five or seven characters, with a strict tonal pattern and rhyme

scheme).
近投 jìntóu (of basketball) close-in or quarter-court shot
近卫军 jìnwèijūn ❶ armed escort of a monarch; imperial guards ❷ (esp. in Europe) crack troops; picked troops; Guards
近卫团 jìnwèituán (esp. in Europe) Guards: 十八近卫师团 18th Guards Division
近卫文麿 Jìnwèiwénmí Konoe Fumimaro (1891-1946), Japanese Prime Minister (1937-1939 and 1940-1941)
近闻 jìnwén anecdote of recent years; recent story
近心点 jìnxīndiǎn 〈天文〉pericentre (point of an orbit closest to the primary body)
近星点 jìnxīngdiǎn 〈天文〉periastron (point in the orbit of a double star closest to a companion star)
近幸 jìnxìng 〈书面〉❶ (usually of an emperor) confer favour on ❷ favourite at court; emperor's favoured courtier
近洋 jìnyáng coastal ocean; inshore; offshore: ~捕鱼作业 inshore fishing
近义词 jìnyìcí near-synonym
近因 jìnyīn immediate cause: 两国交恶的~ immediate cause of the enmity between two countries
近音速 jìnyīnsù 〈物理〉near-sonic speed
近影 jìnyǐng picture taken recently; recent photo
近友 jìnyǒu close friend; bosom friend
近于 jìnyú border on; be close to: ~粗暴 border on rudeness /~胡话 little short of ravings /他说的话更~事实。His words are closer to the truth.
近月 jìnyuè in recent months: ~以来，市场繁荣，物价稳定。In the last few months, the market has been brisk and the prices stable.
近月点 jìnyuèdiǎn 〈航天〉perilune
近悦远来 jìnyuè-yuǎnlái people nearby are pleased and those afar are anxious to come over — a policy of benevolence attracts people far and near
近在眉睫 jìnzàiméijié very near as if located right before one's eyelash; near at hand; imminent: 一场灾祸~。A disaster is imminent.
近在咫尺 jìnzàizhǐchǐ close at hand; well within reach; just around the corner: 我军伟大的战功，不在以往而在未来，这未来即~。The greatest exploits of our army are not in the past but in the future, the very immediate future.
近战 jìnzhàn ❶ fight at close quarters ❷ close combat: ~武器 close-in weapons
近战导弹 jìnzhàn dǎodàn 〈军事〉infighting missile
近照 jìnzhào picture taken recently; recent photo
近支 jìnzhī close branch of a clan
近朱者赤，近墨者黑 jìnzhūzhě chì, jìnmòzhě hēi one who stays near vermilion gets stained red, and one who stays near ink gets stained black — one takes on the colour of one's company: ~，你在交朋友时要小心! As what's near cinnabar goes red, and what's next to ink turns black, you must be very careful in choosing your company. /~，你儿子跟那些人混在一起，能学出个好来? As he who lies with dogs will rise with fleas, how could your son learn anything good by mixing with those people?
近紫外线 jìnzǐwàixiàn 〈物理〉near ultra-violet rays
近作 jìnzuò recent work (of a writer)

靳

jìn ❶〈书面〉be stingy; grudge; stint: 悔不小~ regret not having been a bit more tightfisted ❷ (Jìn) a surname

劲(勁、劤)

jìn ❶ strength; powers energy: 用~ put forth strength; exert oneself /手~ (muscular) strength of the hand / 加把~ put on a spurt /费~ entail great effort; be strenuous /浑身一点~儿都没有 feel very weak; be exhausted /白酒~儿大，黄酒~儿小。White liquor is strong while rice wine is weak. *or* White liquor is stronger (*or* more powerful) than rice wine. /他越干越有~。The more he works, the more energetic he becomes. /他的~使完了。His strength gave out. ❷ spirit; mood; gusto; drive: 干~儿十足 full of drive (*or* enthusiasm) /干得非常起~ work with unusual vigour; work with great zeal /他们俩一向很对~儿。These two always get along very well with each other. /年轻人要有一股闯~。Young people need to have the spirit of a pathbreaker. ❸ air; manner; look; expression: 显出一股高兴~儿 look very happy; have a joyful expression on one's face /瞧他那骄傲~儿! How arrogant he looks! /唉呀! 看我这个糊涂~儿，把钥匙锁在屋子里了! How stupid of me to leave the key locked in the house! ❹ interest; relish; savour; gusto: 他对下棋没~儿。He has no interest in chess. *or* He's in no mood for chess. /这场球越看越有~儿。The more you watched the game, the more interesting it became.
see also jìng
劲道 jìndào 〈方言〉strength; energy; effort; vigour
劲力 jìnlì physical strength; power; might: ~充实 be full of physical strength
劲气 jìnqì 〈方言〉strength; energy; vigour: 浑身~ be full of vigour /吃饱了身上有~ feel very energetic after eating one's fill
劲头 jìntóu 〈口语〉❶ strength; energy: 他身体好，~儿大。He is in good health and full of energy. ❷ vigour; vitality; drive; zeal: 工作有~ be full of drive in one's work /他当上了委员，~更足。After he became a committee member, his energy knew no bounds. /他下起棋来可有~儿啦。He is very keen on chess. *or* He is an avid chess player.

浸(❸寖)

jìn ❶ soak; dip; steep; immerse: 将头~入水中 immerse (*or* put) one's head in water /把要炸的花生米先放在水里~一~。Soak the peanuts in water before frying them. /她把手巾沉~在溪水里。She steeped her handkerchief in a brook. ❷ be soaked (in liquid); be steeped; (of liquid) ooze; leak: 衣服让汗~湿了。The clothes were soaked with (*or* in) sweat. /这块岩石一年四季往外~水。This rock oozes water all the year round. ❸〈书面〉gradually; bit by bit: 友谊~厚 friendship growing gradually
浸沉 jìnchén immerse; steep: 血衣~在水里，水都变成红色了。When the bloody clothes were steeped in water, it turned red. /人们都~在欢乐的气氛里。Everyone was immersed in the festive atmosphere.
浸镀 jìndù 〈冶金〉dip plating; immersion plating
浸膏 jìngāo 〈药学〉extract
浸铬钢板 jìngè gāngbǎn 〈冶金〉chromatic dipping sheet
浸灌 jìnguàn ❶ (as of floodwater) come in; spread out; flood: 海水~ sea water spreading over ❷ irrigate: 放水~秧田 irrigate the rice seedling bed
浸焊 jìnhàn dip soldering; solder dipping
浸剂 jìnjì 〈药学〉infusion
浸渐 jìnjiàn 〈书面〉gradually: 由殷红~变为淡赭。The blackish red gradually turned to light reddish brown.
浸礼 jìnlǐ 〈基督教〉baptism; immersion
浸礼会 Jìnlǐhuì 〈基督教〉Baptist Church: ~教友 Baptists
浸没 jìnmò ❶ submerge; flood; immerse: ~透镜〈物理〉immersion lens /~折射计〈物理〉immersion refractometer /~式加热器 immersion heater /整个村庄被洪水~。The whole village was submerged in the flood. ❷ be immersed in; be permeated with: 伟人逝世，人们~在悲痛之中。People were immersed in grief at the passing away of the great man.
浸没铸造 jìnmò zhùzào 〈冶金〉immersion casting
浸泡 jìnpào soak; immerse: 水磨元宵要先把江米在水里~三天后再磨。Glutinous rice must be immersed in water for three days before it can be ground into powder.
浸染 jìnrǎn ❶ be contaminated; be gradually influenced: ~不良习气 be contaminated with bad habits ❷ soak; infiltrate: 烈士的遗嘱虽被血~过，但字迹依然清晰可辨。The martyr's will had been soaked in blood, but the handwriting was still legible. ❸〈纺织〉dip-dye: 毛衣要~成蓝色。The sweater is to be dip-dyed blue.
浸濡 jìnrú 〈书面〉❶ soak; make wet ❷ be contaminated; be tainted
浸润 jìnrùn ❶ soak; steep: 细雨~着脚下的沃土。The fine drizzle was soaking the fertile land under foot. ❷〈书面〉gradually influence; affect little by little ❸〈物理〉adhesion: 水能~玻璃而不能~石蜡。Water can adhere to glass but not wax. ❹〈医学〉infiltration: ~癌 infiltration carcinoma /~进展期 infiltrative progressive stage /~麻醉 infiltrative anesthesia /~型肺结核 infiltrative pulmonary tuberculosis /~性生长 infiltrative growth
浸润之谮 jìnrùnzhīzèn insidious slander which gradually soaks into the mind: 毋听~。Do not listen to false charges.
浸透 jìntòu ❶ soak; saturate; steep; infuse: 半路上遇上一场大雨，衣服被雨水~了。My clothes were soaked with water for I was caught in the rain on the way. /黄豆必须~后才能发芽。Beans will only sprout after being immersed. ❷ infiltrate: 水~了表土。The water has sunk through the topsoil. ❸〈比喻〉immerse; engross: 空

J

气里～着清香。The air is filled with a faint aromatic scent. /一种失望感～了他整个身心。He has sunk into despair.

浸透策略 jìntòu cèlüè 〈商业〉penetration strategy

浸涂 jìntú 〈冶金〉dip-coating:～施工 dip application

浸信会 Jìnxìnhuì 〈基督教〉Southern Baptist Church (of the United States)

浸浴 jìnyù ❶ be bathed in water; be immersed ❷〈比喻〉be bathed:大地上的一切都～在温暖的阳光中。Everything on earth was bathed in the warm sunlight.

浸种 jìnzhǒng 〈农业〉seed soaking (in water):温汤～ hot water treatment

浸渍 jìnzì soak; ret; macerate:亚麻～ flax retting /～剂 soaker /～液 maceration extract /～槽 maceration tank /汗水～了内衣。The underwear is soaked with sweat.

祲

jìn 〈迷信〉evil spirit; sinister atmosphere

尽(盡)

jìn ❶ exhausted; finished; devoid:取之不～ inexhaustible /一网打～ capture all with one haul of the dragnet /丧～天良 utterly devoid of conscience; conscienceless; heartless /精疲力～ tired out; exhausted /弹～粮绝 run out of ammunition and food supplies /有其说不～的好处。Words failed to express fully its advantages. ❷〈书面〉die; pass away:自～ kill oneself; commit suicide /同归于～ perish together; bring about mutual destruction ❸ to the utmost; to the limit:用～力气 exert oneself to the utmost /详～ in every detail /仁至义～ show extreme forbearance /山穷水～ where the mountains and rivers end — at the end of one's rope /他以前受～了苦。He had his fill of sufferings in the past. ❹ use up; exhaust:竭～全力 exert all possible effort /人～其才,物～其用 make the best possible use of human and material resources /各～所能 each according to his ability ❺ try one's best; do all one can; put to the best use:～责任 do one's duty; discharge one's responsibility /～一切办法 seek in every way; by every means possible ❻ all; entire:不可～信 not to be believed word for word; to be taken with a grain of salt /～做坏事 indulge in all kinds of evil-doing /应有～有 have everything that one expects to find / ～信书不如无书 better not to read at all than to believe all one reads /前功～弃。All that has been achieved is spoiled.

see also jǐn

尽处 jìnchù terminal point; end:山峡～,豁然开朗。One suddenly sees broad light at the end of the mountain valley.

尽瘁 jìncuì 〈书面〉exert oneself to the utmost:一生～国事 devote all one's life to state affairs /鞠躬～,死而后已 bend one's back to the task until one's dying day

尽付东流 jìnfù-dōngliú all is thrown into the eastward flowing stream — all is lost; all one's effort is wasted:两人为小事反目,多年情义,～。The two of them fell out over a trifle. Their friendship of many years was thus broken off.

尽欢 jìnhuān enjoy oneself to the utmost:～而散 leave after everyone has thoroughly enjoyed himself

尽节 jìnjié ❶ be loyal (often at the expense of one's life):～劳心 be loyal and hardworking / ～疆场 die loyally on the battlefield (for one's country, etc.) ❷〈旧语〉(of a woman) sacrifice one's life in defence of one's virginity or chastity

尽捐前嫌 jìnjuān-qiánxián forget all past grudges, ill will or enmity; let bygones be bygones

尽力 jìnlì do all one can; try one's best:～相助 do all one can to help /这项工作我会～及时完成的。I'll try my best to finish this job in time. /他们都～在工作中帮助我。They took great pains to help me with my work. /那出戏给人一种～雕琢的印象。The play gave us the impression of straining after effects.

尽力而为 jìnlì'érwéi do one's best; do everything in one's power; exert every effort:这件事看来已难以挽回,不过我～就是了。There seems to be nothing we could do to save the situation, but I'll do the best I can.

尽量 jìnliàng (drink or eat) to the full:～吃饱 eat one's fill; eat to the full

see also jǐnliàng

尽其所长 jìnqísuǒcháng work to the best of one's ability

尽其所有 jìnqísuǒyǒu give everything one has; give one's all

尽其在我 jìnqízàiwǒ do one's best or utmost:不管别人怎么想,我定会～。I'll do my best no matter what other people may think.

尽情 jìnqíng to one's heart's content; as much as one likes:～款待 treat with utmost kindness /孩子们～地唱啊,跳啊,笑啊,闹啊。Children were singing, dancing, laughing, and playing to their hearts' content. /他想～地把积压在心的愤懑发泄出来。He longed to give full vent to his pent-up anger.

尽然 jìnrán (used in the negative) exactly like this:你以为他说的都是真事,恐怕未必～吧! You thought what he said was the truth, but that might not be the case.

尽人皆知 jìnrénjiēzhī be known to all; be common knowledge:这件事已经是～的了,你又何必还那样遮遮盖盖呢? As this matter is known to all (*or* is already an open secret), why do you try to cover it up? /～,多吃青菜对身体健康有好处。It is common knowledge that eating more vegetables is good for health.

尽人事 jìn rénshì do what one can (to save a dying person, etc.); do all that is humanly possible (though with little hope of success):～,听天命 do all that is humanly possible and leave the rest to God

尽日 jìnrì 〈书面〉all day long:激战～。A fierce battle raged the whole day.

尽入彀中 jìnrù-gòuzhōng have all (the gifted men) under one's control:那个国家想凭借其财力,使天下英才～。That country tries to net all talented people everywhere on the strengh of its financial resources.

尽如人意 jìnrú-rényì just as one wishes; entirely satisfactory:哪能事事～? How can you expect everything to turn out just as you wish? /本报有志于版面编排的改进,但尚未能～。This paper has long set its mind on improving the layout, though the result is still not up to expectations.

尽善尽美 jìnshàn-jìnměi acme of perfection:虽然翻译并不～,但他已尽他的力了。Although the translation was by no means flawless, he did it to the best of his ability. /他们的新居,油漆和装饰都～。Their new home was painted and decorated to a queen's taste.

尽释前嫌 jìnshì-qiánxián forget all former grudges or ill will:他们以团结为重,消除误会,～。Setting store by unity, they cleared up misunderstandings and forgot all about their past quarrels.

尽是 jìnshì full of; all; entirely; without exception:你说的～我不知道的。All you said is news to me. /这一带～高楼大厦。This area is full of huge buildings.

尽收眼底 jìnshōu-yǎndǐ have a panoramic view:飞机在重庆上空徐徐降落,美丽的山城～。The entire beautiful mountain city of Chongqing came into view as the plane slowly made its landing.

尽数 jìnshù whole amount; all; total:将所欠款项～归还。Return all the borrowed money.

尽态极妍 jìntài-jíyán (of appearance, manner, decoration, etc.) very beautiful; exquisite

尽头 jìntóu end:长廊的～ end of the long corridor /～路 dead end; cul-de-sac /黑夜到了～,黎明就会出现。After the dark night comes dawn.

尽夕 jìnxī 〈书面〉whole night; all night:～不寐 lie awake all night

尽孝 jìnxiào be filial to one's parents; be a filial son or daughter

尽心 jìnxīn with all one's heart:～照顾 take care of sb. with all one's heart /他对工作很～。He is always conscientious in his work. /他给别人干事,总是那么～尽力。He is always exerting himself to the utmost when doing things for others.

尽心竭力 jìnxīn-jiélì (do sth.) with all one's heart and might; exert one's utmost

尽兴 jìnxìng to one's heart's content; (enjoy oneself) to the full:唱得～ sing to one's heart's content /此次春游,人人～。We fully (*or* heartily) enjoyed ourselves in this spring outing.

尽性 jìnxìng ❶ wilful; wayward:～地哭 keep on crying heedless of others' advice ❷〈书面〉give full scope to one's individuality

尽言 jìnyán 〈书面〉❶ say all one has to say; express oneself fully in words:书不～,言不尽意。Writing cannot fully express what one wants to say, and words cannot fully express what one means. ❷ straightforward advice; plain exhortation

尽义务 jìn yìwù ❶ do one's duty; fulfil one's obligation:既要享受权利,也要～。Fulfilling one's obligation while enjoying one's right. ❷ work without asking for reward; do sth. free:他教我英语是～的。He teaches me English free of charge.

尽意 jìnyì ❶ express fully one's feelings or intentions:他这首诗～地抒发了思乡之情。His poem expressed fully his homesickness. ❷ to one's heart's content; (enjoy oneself) to the full:我星期天～地玩了一天。I enjoyed myself fully this Sunday.

J

尽责 jìnzé try one's best to fulfil one's responsibility; do one's duty

尽职 jìnzhí fulfil or do one's duty

尽止 jìnzhǐ end; stop:他对于钱财的欲望永无～。His lust for money is insatiable.

尽致 jìnzhì reach the extreme:发挥～ bring into full play /淋漓～ incisively and vividly; thoroughly /几句话把这个赌徒的投机心理表现得极为～。These words brought into bold relief the speculative character of this gambler.

尽忠 jìnzhōng ❶ be loyal to:～报国 be loyal and patriotic /～尽孝 be loyal to one's country and filial to one's parents ❷ sacrifice one's life; lay down one's life:他父亲早年为国～,是一位坚强不屈的烈士。His father was a staunch martyr, sacrificing his life for the country in his early years.

烬(燼)

jìn cinder; ashes:灰～ ashes; cinders /余～ ashes; embers /化为灰～ turn to dust and ashes; reduced to ashes

烬余 jìnyú 〈书面〉❶ ashes; embers ❷ after a disaster:～之民 survivors of a disaster; victims of a disaster

荩[1](藎)

jìn *see* "荩草"

荩[2](藎)

jìn 〈书面〉loyal; faithful

荩草 jìncǎo 〈植物〉hispid arthraxon (*Arthraxon hispidus*)

荩臣 jìnchén 〈书面〉faithful or loyal official:王之～ faithful official of the king; king's loyal official

赆(贐、賮)

jìn 〈书面〉money presented at parting:～送一无所取。The money presented at parting was left untouched.

赆行 jìnxíng 〈书面〉present money when seeing people off; present money at parting

赆仪 jìnyí 〈书面〉money presented at parting

妗

jìn

妗母 jìnmǔ 〈方言〉wife of one's mother's brother; aunt

妗子 jìnzi 〈口语〉❶ wife of one's mother's brother; aunt ❷ wife of one's wife's brother:大～ wife of one's wife's elder brother /小～ wife of one's wife's younger brother

jīng

京[1]

jīng ❶ capital of a country:进～赶考 go to the capital to take part in the imperial examination ❷ (Jīng) (short for 北京) Beijing:大会在～举行。The meeting is to be held in Beijing. ❸ (Jīng) a surname

京[2]

jīng 〈古语〉ten million

京白 jīngbái 〈戏曲〉parts in Beijing opera spoken in Beijing dialect

京白梨 jīngbáilí a kind of sweet juicy pear produced in the Beijing region

京报 jīngbào 〈旧语〉official gazette

京菜 jīngcài dishes cooked in the northern taste and style

京城 jīngchéng capital of a country:名满～的老字号 famous shop of long standing in the capital

京都 jīngdū ❶ capital of a country:北宋的～建于开封。The capital of the Northern Song Dynasty was Kaifeng. ❷ (Jīngdū) Kyoto, a city and the ancient capital (794-1868) of Japan

京二胡 jīng'èrhú *also* "嗡子" wēngzi a kind of Chinese violin, similar to the two-stringed Chinese fiddle *erhu*

京官 jīngguān 〈旧语〉government officials in the capital of the country

京国 jīngguó 〈旧语〉capital of a country

京胡 jīnghú *jinghu*, a two-stringed bowed instrument with a high register, used mainly to accompany Beijing opera singing; Beijing opera fiddle

京花 jīnghuā silk flower

京华 jīnghuá 〈书面〉capital:誉满～ be famed all over the capital

京畿 jīngjī 〈书面〉capital city and its environs

京剧 jīngjù *also* "京戏" Beijing opera:～流派 schools of Beijing opera /～现代戏 modern Beijing opera /～唱腔 music for voices in Beijing opera /～行当 type of role in Beijing opera /著名～武生 actor famous for playing martial roles in Beijing opera

京锣 jīngluó a kind of small gong, used to accompany in Beijing opera

京派 jīngpài Beijing school (of Beijing opera)

京腔 jīngqiāng Beijing dialect; Beijing accent:撇～ imitate the Beijing accent

京阙 jīngquè 〈书面〉capital; imperial palace

京师 jīngshī 〈书面〉capital

京师大学堂 Jīngshī Dàxuétáng Capital or Metropolitan University (1898-1912), predecessor of Beijing University

京味 jīngwèi of special Beijing flavour; with Beijing characteristics:～小吃 snacks of Beijing flavour /这个戏的～儿很浓。The play is rich in Beijing ambience (*or* flavour).

京味小说 jīngwèi xiǎoshuō novels written in Beijing vernacular about Beijing people and their ways and customs

京戏 jīngxì Beijing opera:能哼几句～ be able to hum some tunes of Beijing opera

京绣 jīngxiù Beijing embroidery

京油子 jīngyóuzi 〈旧语〉Beijing sharper; frivolous and slippery person who loafs about all day:～,卫嘴子,都是贬义词。Both "Beijing sharper" and "Tianjin wrangler" are derogatory terms.

京韵大鼓 jīngyùn dàgǔ 〈戏曲〉storytelling in Beijing dialect with drum accompaniment

京族 Jīngzú Gin nationality, living in the Guangxi Zhuang Autonomous Region

麖

jīng *also* "马鹿" mǎlù;"水鹿" shuǐlù red deer

惊(驚)

jīng ❶ start; get alarmed; be frightened:受～的孩子 frightened children /～叫 give a cry of alarm; scream with fear /大吃一～ be greatly surprised /大～小怪 be shocked at sth. perfectly normal /心～肉跳 have the jitters /一场虚～ a false alarm /他听到尖叫声心里一～。He started at the shriek. /她被这个消息～呆了。She was stupefied at this news. ❷ surprise; shock; amaze:一声～雷 a sudden clap of thunder /一鸣～人 amaze the world with a single brilliant feat /打草～蛇 beat the grass and frighten away the snake ❸ shy; stampede:畜群～跑 stampede of a herd /大雷雨～了牛群。The thunderstorm stampeded the cattle. /喇叭一响,马～了。The horse shied at the horn.

惊怖 jīngbù alarmed and frightened; terrified:～万分 in a great panic

惊诧 jīngchà 〈书面〉surprised; amazed; astonished:他的突然出现使大家～不止。Everyone was greatly surprised at his sudden appearance. /～莫名。No word can fully express his astonishment.

惊颤 jīngchàn tremble or shiver with fear:刚才的事使她～不已。She kept trembling over what had happened a moment ago.

惊车 jīngchē runaway draught animal pulling the cart behind it

惊怵 jīngchù alarmed and frightened; terrified

惊呆 jīngdāi stunned; stupefied:看到孩子摔得鼻青脸肿,他～了。He was stupefied at the sight of the badly bruised child.

惊动 jīngdòng alarm; startle; alert; disturb:这个消息～了全校。The whole school was startled by the news. *or* The news created a sensation in the school. /病人睡了,不要～他。The patient is asleep. Don't disturb him. /这件事我们自己解决吧,还是不～领导为好。Let's solve the problem ourselves instead of bothering the leaders.

惊愕 jīng'è 〈书面〉shocked; stunned; stupefied:～不已 unable to recover from one's shock; totally stupefied /这也难怪他们个个～得目瞪口呆,事情确是出乎人们的意料之外。It's no wonder that everyone was struck dumb, for the matter was literally a bolt out of the blue.

惊风 jīngfēng 〈中医〉infantile convulsions:急～ acute infantile convulsions

惊风骇浪 jīngfēng-hàilàng *also* "惊涛骇浪" terrifying wind and turbulent waves — perilous situation:小船颠簸在～中。The small boat was rocking along in the howling wind and mounting waves. /从～里走过来的人们才会坚强无比。Only those who have gone through storm and stress can become firm and strong.

惊服 jīngfú be amazed at and admire; be filled with wondering admiration:剧团精湛的表演深为观众所～。The excellent performance of the troupe filled the audience with wondering admiration.

惊弓之鸟 jīnggōngzhīniǎo bird startled by the mere twang of a

bow-string; badly frightened person:在我军的沉重打击下,敌军都已成了~。Badly trounced by our army, the enemy troops were like birds startled by the mere twang of a bowstring. /他已经是~了! He's become a bird that shies at the sight of a bow.

惊怪 jīngguài surprised; amazed; astonished:日食、月食是正常现象,用不着~。The eclipse of the sun or moon is a quite normal phenomenon. There's nothing to make a fuss about.

惊闺 jīngguī noise-makers that a salesman or knife grinder uses to attract (usu. female) customers; clappers

惊骇 jīnghài 〈书面〉frightened; scared; panic-stricken:同伙的被抓,使他无比~。He was extremely frightened after his accomplice had been caught.

惊号 jīngháo loud cry of alarm; scream with fear

惊鸿 jīnghóng startled swan; elegance and grace of a beauty; beauty:翩若~,婉若游龙 as graceful (*or* elegant) as a swan and as supple as a dragon /~一瞥 barely catch a glimpse of a passing beauty

惊鸿艳影 jīnghóng-yànyǐng (glimpse of) lithe and graceful figure of a pretty girl

惊呼 jīnghū cry out in alarm:齐声~ everybody crying out in alarm; give a cry of alarm simultaneously

惊慌 jīnghuāng alarmed; scared; terrified; panic-stricken:~不安 jittery; nervy /神色~ look alarmed /~失色 be so scared as to look pale; pale with fear /那消息引起了~。The news caused a panic. /他们的脸色有点紧张,可是并不~。They were not panic-stricken though they looked a bit nervous.

惊慌失措 jīnghuāng-shīcuò frightened out of one's wits; seized with panic; paralysed with fear:保持冷静,别~! Keep cool. Don't panic.

惊惶 jīnghuáng alarmed; scared; panic-stricken; on tenterhooks:他们~得面面相觑。They were so terrified that they gazed at each other in speechless despair.

惊魂 jīnghún frightened out of one's wits; panic-stricken:~甫定 have just got over the state of terror; have just recovered from fright

惊魂未定 jīnghún-wèidìng not yet recovered from a fright; still badly shaken:参谋长默默地站在~的司令官面前。The chief-of-staff was standing in silence before his shaken superior.

惊惑 jīnghuò alarmed and perplexed; surprised and apprehensive

惊急 jīngjí nervous and worried because of an unexpected or untoward accident:他心脏病突发,妻子~不已。His wife was all nerves after his sudden heart attack.

惊悸 jīngjì 〈书面〉palpitate with fear:两个人同时~地左右望望。The two looked around, palpitating with fear. /她从~的梦中醒过来,听见猫头鹰凄厉的叫声。Awakening from the fearful dream, she heard the sad cry of an owl.

惊搅 jīngjiǎo disturb:我看他睡得正香,便不再去~他。I decided not to disturb him seeing he was in a sound sleep.

惊叫 jīngjiào cry in fear; scream with terror; give a cry of alarm:她的神气是那么阴森可怕,他忍不住~起来。She appeared so terrifying that he couldn't help screaming with fear.

惊惧 jīngjù alarmed and frightened:敌军~,纷纷逃窜。The enemy scurried away in panic.

惊遽 jīngjù 〈书面〉startle; panic:~而起 jump up with a start

惊觉 jīngjué wake up with a start

惊厥 jīngjué ❶ faint from fear:听到哥哥的噩耗,母亲顿时~倒地。My mother fainted and fell to the ground the moment she heard about the death of my elder brother. ❷〈医学〉convulsions

惊恐 jīngkǒng seized with terror; terrified; panic-stricken

惊恐万状 jīngkǒng-wànzhuàng in great panic; convulsed with fear:一只野兔~地向林间飞奔而去。A hare sped towards the woods in great panic. /大街上人人~。On the main streets people milled about nervously.

惊雷 jīngléi frightening thunder; loud clap of thunder; thunderous warning or awakening:一声震天动地的~ sudden clap of a shattering thunder / 于无声处听~。You could hear thunderous warning in that dead silence.

惊乱 jīngluàn alarmed and confused:敌军~,四处逃窜。The enemy troops were in panicky confusion and ran for their lives in all directions.

惊马 jīngmǎ startled horse; runaway horse:拦住 ~ stop a stampeding horse

惊梦 jīngmèng wake up from a dream with a start:《游园~》*Dream in a Garden*

惊慕 jīngmù surprised and envious:~的神色 look of surprise and envy

惊怕 jīngpà scared; frightened:大家要安定下来,不要~。Calm (*or* Cool) down; don't be panicky.

惊佩 jīngpèi be surprised and admire:他这种毅力实在令人~。His strong will is really surprising and calls for admiration.

惊奇 jīngqí wonder; marvel; be surprised; be amazed:他如此放肆,令人~。His rudeness is surprising. /我们都张开了嘴,~万分。We all gaped with amazement. /她向他哭诉着,不顾同车厢的其他乘客~的目光。She sobbed to him, ignoring quizzical looks from other people in the carriage.

惊怯 jīngqiè alarmed and timid; scared and afraid:每到天色黑下来的时候,她孑然独处,更是~。When dark fell, she was left alone and became even more lonely and frightened.

惊群 jīngqún runaway animals; stampeding herd

惊扰 jīngrǎo alarm; agitate; disturb:实在对不起,~您了! Terribly sorry to bother you. /事情本来不大,我们何必自相~? It's really not that serious, why should we raise a false alarm?

惊人 jīngrén astounding; astonishing; amazing; surprising:~的速度 astonishing speed /~的消息 astonishing (*or* shocking) news /~的记忆力 surprising memory /貌不~ ordinary appearance /这件事确实~。This incident is really amazing. /此人虽然干瘦,但却有~的活力。Though thin, he is a man of astounding vigour (*or* vitality). /语不~死不休。I swear not to stop until I find words that will leave people gasping with wonder.

惊人之笔 jīngrénzhībǐ words that leave people gasping with wonder; telling phrases

惊人之举 jīngrénzhījǔ masterstroke; *coup de maître*:他做不出什么~。He won't set the Thames on fire.

惊赏 jīngshǎng be amazed and praise:很多人都~他的伟大成就。Many people are amazed at his great achievements and are full of praise for them.

惊蛇入草 jīngshé-rùcǎo (of Chinese calligraphy) write characters swiftly and with strokes flowing together; write a cursive hand in a vigorous and nimble style

惊师动众 jīngshī-dòngzhòng mobilize many people (for a task); make a tremendous fuss (over sth.):别为这点小事~啦。Don't try to arouse so many people for such a petty cause.

惊世骇俗 jīngshì-hàisú *also* "惊世震俗" astound the world with an extraordinary idea, etc.:你的高见,真可谓~。Your idea was really amazing.

惊悚 jīngsǒng alarmed and frightened

惊叹 jīngtàn exclaim with admiration; wonder; marvel:他~道:"你的成绩真了不起。" "Your success is really wonderful," he exclaimed with admiration. /我深深地为这个国家的文学成就而~。I marvel at the literary achievements of this country.

惊叹号 jīngtànhào exclamation mark (!)

惊堂木 jīngtángmù *also* "惊堂";"惊堂板"〈旧语〉piece of board used by a magistrate in trying a case to frighten the accused (by striking it on the table and making a loud noise)

惊涛骇浪 jīngtāo-hàilàng *also* "惊风骇浪" terrifying waves; stormy sea; perilous situation; hazards in life:你见过大海的~吗? Have you ever seen a stormy sea? /不要怕~,硬着头皮顶住。Don't be afraid of storm and stress; just stand your ground until it blows over. / 他一生不知经历了多少次~。He has gone through countless hazards in his life.

惊天动地 jīngtiān-dòngdì (of sound) extremely loud; earsplitting; earthshaking; world-shaking:~的一声巨响 earsplitting sound / ~的变化 earthshaking change /这样一来,恐怖的空气更浓了,好像真有什么~的大灾祸就要到来一般。This heightened the tension even more, as if some tremendous calamity was just about to happen.

惊悟 jīngwù realize with a shock; wake up with a start:他一下子~过来了。He woke up with a start all of a sudden.

惊悉 jīngxī 〈书面〉be shocked or distressed to learn:~黄先生不幸逝世 be distressed to learn of the passing away of Mr. Huang

惊喜 jīngxǐ pleasantly surprised:~交集 be filled with elation and amazement; have mixed feelings of surprise and joy /~若狂 be madly happy /"是你?!"他露出~的神色。"Oh, it's you!" He looked pleasantly surprised.

惊吓 jīngxià frighten; terrify; scare:这突然的犬吠声~了她。She

J

was scared at the sudden bark of the dog. / 这孩子受了～，大声哭了起来。The child had a shock and began to cry.

惊险 jīngxiǎn alarmingly dangerous; perilous; breathtaking; thrilling: ～的表演 breathtaking performance / ～情节 amazing plot / ～飞行表演 stunt flying / 杂技表演有许多～动作。There were quite a few astounding feats in the acrobatic performance.

惊险片 jīngxiǎnpiàn thriller; adventure film

惊险小说 jīngxiǎn xiǎoshuō thriller (fiction)

惊羡 jīngxiàn wonder; marvel: 这位演员的高超表演令观众～。The audience marvelled at the actor's superb performance.

惊心 jīngxīn be heart-stirring; be surprised at heart; be shocked: 触目～ startling; shocking; horrifying / ～掉胆 tremble with fear; be hair-raising; be scared stiff / ～怵目 strike the eye and rouse awe in the mind; be shocked to witness; be thoroughly frightened / 恨别鸟～。The flitting birds stir my homesick heart.

惊心动魄 jīngxīn-dòngpò soul-stirring; profoundly moving: ～的场面 soul-stirring scene / 然而一阵阵猛烈的呼噪像巨浪迭起，一个比一个高，真有～的力量。Yet spasm after spasm of fierce clamour welled up like huge waves, each higher than the last, a clamour to make even the stoutest heart quail.

惊醒 jīngxǐng ❶ wake up with a start: 近来，她夜里常常从梦中～。Of late she often woke up with a start from her dream. ❷ rouse suddenly from sleep: 敲门声～了刚刚入睡的小刘。The knocking at the door awakened Xiao Liu who had just fallen asleep.

惊醒 jīngxing sleep lightly; be a light sleeper: 睡觉～点儿。Keep alert in your sleep. *or* Don't sleep like a log. / 年纪大的人睡觉很～。Elderly people are likely to be light sleepers.

惊讶 jīngyà surprised; amazed; astonished; astounded: ～得发呆 be dumbfounded; be stunned / 他的话使我们大家感到～。His words astonished us all. / 我着实为他的大胆而～了。I was really surprised at his boldness.

惊疑 jīngyí surprised and bewildered: 他用～的目光看着我。He looked at me, surprised and puzzled.

惊异 jīngyì surprised; taken aback; astonished; amazed: 我睁大了眼睛，～得说不出话来。My eyes wide open, I was so surprised that words failed me.

惊猿脱兔 jīngyuán-tuōtù startled monkeys and fleeing hares — take flight in disorder: 那伙匪徒就像～，漫山越岭地逃散了。That pack of bandits took to their heels in disarray, fleeing helter-skelter all over the hills.

惊蛰 Jīngzhé ❶ Waking of Insects, 3rd seasonal division point, marking the sun's position at 345° on the ecliptic ❷ day marking such a seasonal division point, usu. falling on the 5th or 6th of March ❸ period lasting from such a seasonal division point till the next one (Vernal Equinox 春分)
see also "节气" jiéqì; "二十四节气" èrshísì jiéqì

惊怔 jīngzhèng 〈方言〉 stunned; stupefied

鲸 jīng

whale: 雄～ bull whale / 雌～ cow whale / 蓝～ blue whale / 须～ whalebone whale / 抹香～ sperm whale / 长须～ finback / 捕～炮 whaling gun / 捕～者 whaler / 捕～船 whaling ship; whale catcher (*or* chaser)

鲸波 jīngbō ocean waves

鲸醇 jīngchún 〈生化〉 kitol

鲸蜡 jīnglà spermaceti (wax)

鲸目动物 jīngmù dòngwù cetacean

鲸肉 jīngròu whalemeat

鲸鲨 jīngshā whale shark (large living animal up to 20 metres long)

鲸吞 jīngtūn swallow like a whale; annex (a large tract of territory): 蚕食～ nibble away like a silkworm or swallow like a whale; encroach upon or occupy territory in various ways / 小公司被大公司～。Small companies are annexed by big ones.

鲸须 jīngxū baleen; whalebone; whale fin

鲸油 jīngyóu whale oil; blubber: 割～ flench

鲸鱼 jīngyú whale

鲸仔 jīngzǎi whale calf

猄 jīng

see "黄猄" huángjīng

旌 jīng

❶ ancient type of banner consisting of multicolour plumes or streamers, hoisted to the masthead or peak of a flagpole: ～蔽日兮敌若云。The armies' banners were blotting out the sun and the enemy were overwhelming in number. ❷〈书面〉 confer a memorial archway or horizontal inscribed board on sb.; praise; extol: 以～其美 use it to praise his virtue

旌表 jīngbiǎo (of a feudal ruler) confer a memorial archway or horizontal inscribed board on sb. for loyalty or filial piety; commend: 苟有一介之善，宜在～之例。Every good deed, however small, should be commended.

旌麾 jīnghuī 〈旧语〉 banner or standard of a commander; command of an army: ～南指。The army is driving southwards.

旌旗 jīngqí banners and flags: ～招展。The banners and pennants are fluttering in the wind. / 山下～在望，山头鼓角相闻。Below the hills fly our flags and banners, Above the hilltop sound our bugles and drums.

旌恤 jīngxù 〈书面〉 praise the dead and comfort and compensate the bereaved family

粳(秔、稉) jīng

粳稻 jīngdào round-grained nonglutinous rice

粳米 jīngmǐ polished round-grained rice

精 jīng

❶ refined; polished; picked; choice: ～金 fine gold / ～矿 concentrate / 兵在～而不在多。Troops are valued for quality rather than for numbers. ❷ essence; spirit; concentrate; extract: 柠檬～ lemon extract / 樟脑～ spirits of camphor / 醋～ vinegar concentrate / 鱼肝油～ cod-liver oil extract / 酒～ ethyl alcohol; alcohol / 香～ essence / 糖～ saccharin / 味～ monosodium glutamate (MSG); gourmet powder ❸ perfect; excellent; essential: 去粗取～ discard the dross and select the essence; skin off the best / 取～用弘 select the finest from a vast quantity ❹ fine; delicate; exquisite; superb: 工艺很～ superb or exquisite workmanship / 体大思～ broad in conception and meticulous in details ❺ smart; sharp; astute; shrewd: 生意做得～ be a shrewd businessman; be smart in business dealings / 这孩子～极了，一点亏也不吃。This child is extremely smart and will never be at a disadvantage. ❻ skilled; versed; conversant; proficient: ～于太极拳 be proficient at *taiji* boxing / ～于算术 be skilled in numbers / ～于针灸 be well versed in acupuncture and moxibustion / 博而不～ extensive but superficial in knowledge; Jack of all trades / 业～于勤。Mastery of a subject comes from diligence. ❼ energy; vigour; spirit: 聚～会神 concentrate one's attention; be all attention / 养～蓄锐 conserve strength and store up energy / 无～打采 listless; lackadaisical / 励～图治 exert oneself (*or* strive) to make the country prosperous ❽ sperm; semen; seed: 受～ fertilization / 遗～ seminal emission ❾ goblin; spirit; demon: 白骨～ White Bone Demon / 耗子～ mouse spirit / 害人～ poltergeist; ogre; mischief-maker / 传说有个狐狸成了～。Legend has it that a fox turned into a bewitching woman. ❿〈方言〉 extremely; very; awfully: 他人长得～瘦。He is very thin (*or* a bag of bones). / 外边～凉的。It is extremely cool outside. ⓫〈中医〉 fundamental substance which maintains the functioning of the body; essence of life

精白 jīngbái pure white; snow white: ～米 polished white rice

精薄 jīngbáo extremely thin: ～的被子 extremely thin quilt

精本 jīngběn de luxe edition: 插图～ illustrated de luxe edition / ～书画 de luxe edition of painting and calligraphy

精兵 jīngbīng picked troops; crack troops: ～强将 picked troops and good generals

精兵简政 jīngbīng-jiǎnzhèng better troops and simpler administration; better staff and simpler administration; streamlined administration

精彩 jīngcǎi brilliant; splendid; superb; marvelous; wonderful: ～场面 wonderful scene / ～的舞蹈 marvelous dancing / ～的盆景 splendid potted landscape / ～的发言 excellent speech / 钢琴弹得很～ play brilliantly at the piano / 陈列品真是琳琅满目，～纷呈。The exhibits are a feast for the eyes, each being a wonder. / 他的诗文写得很～。He was particularly accomplished as poet and essayist. ❷〈书面〉 expression; spirit: 她那没有～的眼睛突然发光了。Her expressionless eyes blazed forth all of a sudden.

精巢 jīngcháo 〈生理〉 ❶ animal's gonad ❷ spermary; testis; testicle

精诚 jīngchéng 〈书面〉 absolute sincerity; good faith: 在敌人面前，我们应当～团结。We must unite as one in the face of the enemy.

J

精诚所至,金石为开 jīngchéng suǒ zhì, jīnshí wéi kāi complete sincerity can affect even metal and stone — no difficulty is insurmountable if one sets his mind on it; absolute sincerity can conquer all

精赤 jīngchì ❶ naked; bare; nude:～的肩膀 naked or bare shoulder ❷〈方言〉bare lower part of the body; be naked from the waist down:～赤膊 be stripped bare; be stark naked

精赤条条 jīngchì-tiáotiáo stark naked; nude; completely bare:那些在塘里洗澡的孩子～地爬了上来。The children who had a bath in the pool came out stark naked.

精虫 jīngchóng 〈生理〉spermatozoon

精纯 jīngchún ❶ pure:～的猫睛石 pure cat's eye ❷ exquisite; superb:技艺～ exquisite artistry; superb skill; masterly craft

精醇 jīngchún ❶ mellow; rich:酒味～ mellow wine ❷ *see* "精纯❶"

精萃 jīngcuì cream; pick; choice:世界乒坛的～ pick of the world's table-tennis players /这是全书的～之处。This is the essence of the whole book.

精粹 jīngcuì succinct; pithy; terse; concise:文章要写得短些,～些。Articles should be shorter and more succinct.

精打光 jīngdǎguāng 〈方言〉with nothing left; have nothing at all:满满的一桌菜吃得～。The food which had covered the table was all eaten up.

精打细算 jīngdǎ-xìsuàn careful calculation and strict budgeting:他不论做啥事,事先全都～过。Whatever he does, he makes careful plans and calculations. /为了存钱买房子,他们不得不～。To save money to buy a house, they have to pinch pennies. /这一项目拨款很少,我们必须～。With so little money allocated for the project, we must make every cent count.

精蛋白 jīngdànbái 〈生化〉protamine

精当 jīngdàng precise and appropriate:用词～ precise and appropriate wording; felicitous choice of words /评价极为～ make pertinent (*or* befitting) comments

精到 jīngdào precise and penetrating:他把这个道理阐发得十分～。He elucidated this principle with great precision and insight.

精雕细刻 jīngdiāo-xìkè *also* "精雕细镂" work (at sth.) with the care and precision of a sculptor; work (at sth.) with meticulous care:～的工艺品 artistic work chiselled and carved with delicate touches /他的作品讲究～。He is meticulous about his writing.

精豆子 jīngdòuzi 〈方言〉bright and clever child; smart (small) guy

精读 jīngdú ❶ read carefully and thoroughly:有些重要著作需要～。Some important articles call for careful and thorough reading. ❷ intensive reading (as a course)

精度 jīngdù precision; accuracy:高～ high precision /～检查 accuracy checking; alignment test /～指数 index of precision /这种仪器的～达到世界先进水平。The instrument is up to the advanced world level in precision.

精锻 jīngduàn finish forge

精纺 jīngfǎng spinning:～机 spinning-frame /～羊毛 combing wool /～麦尔登呢〈纺织〉worsted melton

精干 jīnggàn ❶ (of a body of troops, etc.) small in number but highly trained; crack:派出一个～的工作组 dispatch a crack working team ❷ keen-witted and capable; smart and efficient:这个青年人模样儿很～。This young man looked very capable.

精耕细作 jīnggēng-xìzuò intensive and meticulous farming; intensive cultivation

精工 jīnggōng refined; delicate:～的刺绣 exquisite embroidery /制作～ of fine workmanship

精刮 jīngguā 〈方言〉〈贬义〉be good at calculating; be given to scheming

精怪 jīngguài goblin; spirit; demon

精光 jīngguāng ❶ with nothing left:钱用得～ spend all one's money /房子烧得～。The house was burned to the ground. /戏票不到一小时就卖得～。All the tickets were sold out in less than an hour. /我原来学的东西,已经忘得～。I have clean forgotten what I learnt. ❷ shiny; bright:玻璃窗擦得～。The window panes are cleaned bright. /他穿着小皮夹克,下巴刮得～。He is in a tight leather jacket, with his chin shaved smooth.

精悍 jīnghàn ❶ smart and efficient; capable and energetic:人虽矮小,却很～。Short as he is, he is very capable and vigorous. ❷ pithy and poignant:文笔～ pithy and pungent writing

精核 jīnghé 〈书面〉check in detail; examine carefully:～是非 make a careful distinction between right and wrong

精华 jīnghuá ❶ cream; pick; essence; quintessence:～部分 pick of the crop /中国古典文学的～ cream of Chinese classical literature /去其糟粕,取其～ discard the dross and select the essence /他们是一国的～。They are the flower (*or* the best and the brightest) of the nation. ❷〈书面〉brilliance; radiance:日月之～ radiance of the sun and moon

精魂 jīnghún soul; spirit

精加工 jīngjiāgōng 〈机械〉finish machining; precision work:～车床 finish turning lathe /～进给 finishing feed /～留量 allowance for finish /～制成品 highly wrought goods

精荚 jīngjiá 〈动物〉spermatophose

精简 jīngjiǎn retrench; simplify; streamline; cut (down):～节约 simplify administration and practise economy/～课程 cut down the curriculum /～会议 cut meetings to a minimum /～机构 simplify (*or* streamline) administrative structure; downsize management /～报表 slash the number of forms; cut down paperwork /～手续 simplify procedures /～整编 streamline and reorganize an organization /～非生产人员 reduce nonproductive personnel /～下来的工人 redundant factory workers /这篇文章的内容大可～。There is much that can be cut in this article.

精讲 jīngjiǎng teach succinctly:～多练 teach only the essentials and ensure plenty of practice

精洁 jīngjié clean and beautiful:屋宇～ elegant and tidy house

精进 jīngjìn strive for progress; forge ahead:努力～ try one's best to make further progress

精警 jīngjǐng (of articles, remarks, etc.) pithy and penetrating:～的句子 pithy and incisive remark

精镌 jīngjuān chisel and carve with delicate touches; work (at sth.) with meticulous care:～的檀香扇 beautifully carved sandal wood fan

精绝 jīngjué exquisite and ingenious; superb:～的语言艺术 superb language art

精矿 jīngkuàng 〈矿业〉concentrate

精拉 jīnglā 〈冶金〉finish draw:～丝机 fine wire drawing machine

精力 jīnglì energy; vitality; vigour; vim:～不足 be deficient in energy /～过人 exceptional vitality /～充沛 full of vim and vigour; vigorous; energetic /把毕生～献给教育事业 devote the energies of a life to the cause of education /集中～搞科研 concentrate one's effort on scientific research /病好了以后,他～旺盛。He was as fit as a fiddle after recovering from illness.

精练 jīngliàn *also* "精炼" concise; terse; succinct; compact:文章～ compact article /用～的语言表达丰富的内容 use concise language to express rich content

精炼 jīngliàn ❶〈冶金〉refine; purify:火法～ fire refining /真空～ vacuum refining /～期 refining period /～炉 refining furnace /～钢 purified steel; refined steel /～法 purifying method /原油送到炼油厂去～。Crude oil will be sent to an oil refinery to be purified (*or* processed). ❷ *see* "精练"

精良 jīngliáng excellent; superlative; superior; of the best quality:装备～ well-equipped /武器～ highly sophisticated weapons /这批体育器械制作～。This batch of sports equipment is of excellent workmanship.

精量播种 jīngliàng bōzhòng 〈农业〉precise drilling:～机 precision (seed) planter; precision (seed) drill

精料 jīngliào 〈畜牧〉concentrated feed; rich, nourishing feed

精灵 jīngling ❶ spirit; demon:有很多关于小～在月光下跳舞的故事。There are many stories about elves dancing in the moonlight. ❷〈方言〉(of a child) clever; bright; smart; intelligent:这孩子很～。The child is very smart indeed.

精馏 jīngliú 〈化学〉rectification:～酒精 rectified alcohol /～塔 rectifying (*or* fractionating) tower

精煤 jīngméi 〈矿业〉clean coal

精美 jīngměi exquisite; superb; delicate; elegant:～的工艺品 exquisite handicraft article /～的瓷器 delicate porcelain /～的食品 delicacy /～的餐具 fine tableware /包装～ beautifully packaged /装帧～ superb binding and layout /古石桥的栏杆上雕刻着～的图案。There is an elegant design carved on the balustrade of the ancient stone bridge.

精密 jīngmì precise; exact; accurate:～仪器 precision instrument /～铸造 precision casting /～锻造 precision forging /～着陆 precision

J

landing /～天平 precision balance /～光学机械 precision optical machinery /～机床 precision machine tool /他们有～的分工。There was a clear-cut division of labour among them.

精密度 jīngmìdù precision; accuracy

精妙 jīngmiào exquisite and ingenious:广东的牙雕绣球可达十数层，真是～之极。Guangdong carved ivory balls could have more than ten layers. They are really superb and ingenious.

精敏 jīngmǐn 〈书面〉alert and resourceful; quick-witted:～过人 unusually quick-witted and sagacious

精明 jīngmíng astute; smart; bright; shrewd:～的商人 shrewd (*or* astute) businessman /老张做起生意来非常～。Lao Zhang is as sharp as a razor in business. /他在政界有～刚正的名声。He enjoys the reputation of a sagacious and upright politician in politics.

精明强干 jīngmíng-qiánggàn intelligent and capable; able and efficient:她的婆婆倒是个～的女人啊，很有打算。Her mother-in-law is a clever and capable woman, who knows how to drive a good bargain.

精磨 jīngmó 〈机械〉finish grinding; precision grinding

精囊 jīngnáng 〈生理〉gonecyst; seminal vesicle: ～石〈医学〉gonecystolith /～炎〈医学〉gonecystitis

精疲力竭 jīngpí-lìjié *also* "筋疲力尽" jīnpí-lìjìn exhausted; worn out; tired out; spent:这种办法叫"磨菇"战术，将敌人磨得～，然后消灭之。This may be called the tactics of "wear and tear", that is, of wearing the enemy down to complete exhaustion and then wiping them out. /这些事足以使他～了。These things were enough to sap his last ounce of strength.

精辟 jīngpì penetrating; incisive; insightful: ～的见解 penetrating view /～的评论 incisive comment / ～的分析 in-depth analysis /～的谈话 brilliant remarks

精品 jīngpǐn work created with painstaking effort; work of a high order; top-quality product:艺术～ top-notch artistic work; artistic work of excellent quality /花茶中的～ top-quality jasmine tea

精奇 jīngqí exquisite and marvellous; fine and intriguing:这朵花绣得～。The flower is exquisitely embroidered.

精气 jīngqì ❶〈书面〉absolute sincerity; good faith ❷〈书面〉vital *qi* of *yin* and *yang*; vitality ❸〈中医〉vital substance which maintains the functioning of the body

精气神儿 jīngqìshénr 〈口语〉vigour; energy; drive:他睡了一会儿，～又来了。He was refreshed and energetic after a short nap.

精强 jīngqiáng picked and strong:兵马～ picked and powerful troops

精强力壮 jīngqiáng-lìzhuàng full of vitality:一群～的小伙子 group of vigorous and energetic young fellows

精巧 jīngqiǎo fine; exquisite; ingenious:技艺～ fine craftsmanship/ ～的机器 ingenious machine /庭园布局～ exquisite layout of a garden

精切 jīngqiè precise and appropriate; convincing and relevant:论证～ prove with precise and convincing arguments

精禽 jīngqín mythical bird *jingwei*
see also "精卫填海"

精勤 jīngqín be devoted and diligent:治学～ pursue one's study industriously and with undivided attention

J

精穷 jīngqióng 〈方言〉extremely poor:那时他家境还不算～，念过几年书。He had several years of schooling, for at the time his family was not too poor.

精确 jīngquè accurate; exact; precise:～计算 accurate calculation / ～计量 precise measurement /～的时间 exact time /下一个～的定义 give a precise definition /～地说，这段距离恰好三英里。The distance is three miles to an inch.

精确度 jīngquèdù measure of precision

精肉 jīngròu 〈方言〉lean (pork) meat

精锐 jīngruì crack; picked:派出～部队 dispatch crack (*or* picked) troops /这是该国最～的王牌军。This is the élite military unit of the country.

精舍 jīngshè 〈旧语〉❶ study ❷ temple building

精深 jīngshēn deep; profound:博大～ with both extensive knowledge and profound scholarship; erudite /～的理论 abstruse theory / 这位专家对上古史的研究最为～。This expert is particularly specialized in research on ancient history.

精神 jīngshén ❶ spirit; mind; consciousness:共产主义～ communist spirit /进取～ enterprising spirit /一丝不苟的治学～ scrupulous scholarship /～振奋 in fine mettle /～上的满足 intellectual satisfaction /～高度紧张 be extremely nervous /～反常 lose one's mental balance /～正常 have all one's buttons (*or* marbles) /人总是要有点～的。A man needs spirit. ❷ essence; gist; spirit; substance:传达一个重要讲话的～ relay (*or* convey) the essential points of an important speech /报告的主要～ gist of a report /领会原文的～ capture the spirit of the original /理解文章的～实质 understand the thrust of the article /贯彻代表大会的～ act in the spirit of the congress

精神 jīngshen ❶ vigour; energy; vitality; drive:振作～ bestir oneself; summon up one's energy; get up steam /打起～ cheer oneself up /懒洋洋地提不起～ languid and listless /～颓废 dissipated; despirited /～矍铄 hale and hearty /下棋太费～。It is most taxing to play chess. /他七十多岁了，还那么～！He's over seventy and still as sound as a bell! ❷ lively; spirited; vigorous:挺～的小伙子 vigorous young man; lad full of life /夏林从头到脚一身新，显得格外～。Dressed up in new clothes, Xia Lin looks especially impressive.

精神崩溃 jīngshén bēngkuì 〈医学〉psychorrhexis; nervous breakdown

精神变态 jīngshén biàntài 〈医学〉psychopathia; metaphrenia

精神病 jīngshénbìng 〈医学〉mental disease; mental disorder; psychosis:～人 mental patient /～医生 psychiatrist /～病房 psychiatric ward / ～水浴疗法 hydropsychotterapy

精神病学 jīngshénbìngxué psychiatry

精神病院 jīngshénbìngyuàn psychiatric hospital; mental home, hospital, or institution

精神财富 jīngshén cáifù intellectual assets or wealth

精神产品 jīngshén chǎnpǐn intellectual product

精神错乱 jīngshén cuòluàn 〈医学〉amentia;〈心理〉alienation;〈法律〉insanity:他表现得像个～的人。He acted like a man off (*or* out of) his head.

精神抖擞 jīngshén-dǒusǒu brace up; be energetic; be vigorous:～地迈着大步 walk with long, vigorous strides /他们都是～，脸上没有一丝倦容。They were full of vitality, and not a trace of weariness showed in their faces.

精神发育迟缓 jīngshén fāyù chíhuǎn 〈医学〉mental retardation

精神分裂症 jīngshén fēnlièzhèng 〈医学〉schizophrenia; dementia praeacox

精神分析 jīngshén fēnxī psychoanalysis:～医生 psychoanalyst

精神鼓励 jīngshén gǔlì moral encouragement; moral support

精神贵族 jīngshén guìzú intellectual aristocrat

精神焕发 jīngshén-huànfā be in high spirits; one's spirits rise:～地继续向前行进 continue one's advance in a mood of keen exhilaration /她机灵敏锐的眼光投射在他那～的脸上。She shot a keen glance at his animated radiant face. /一想起这些往事，他就～，信心百倍了。When he recalled past events, his confidence and spirits soared.

精神恍惚 jīngshén-huǎnghū absent-minded; listless:～，若有所思 absent-minded and lost in thought /你看上去～，可能医生给你用的药有副作用吧？You looked very spaced-out. Maybe that medication the doctor put you on has some side effects.

精神枷锁 jīngshén jiāsuǒ ideological shackles; mental yoke

精神境界 jīngshén jìngjiè mental outlook; spiritual ethos: ～高尚 have a noble ethos / ～低下 have a lowly mental outlook; have rather vulgar tastes

精神疗法 jīngshén liáofǎ 〈医学〉mental therapeutics; psychotherapy; mind cure

精神面貌 jīngshén miànmào mental attitude or outlook

精神生活 jīngshén shēnghuó cultural life; intellectual life

精神胜利法 jīngshén shènglìfǎ defeat regarded as victory; spiritual victory

精神失常 jīngshén shīcháng have bats in the belfry; have lost one's marbles; have a screw loose; be deranged:每个人都知道这老人～。Everybody knows that the old man has got bats in the belfry. /你居然辞掉这样好的工作，一定是～。You must have a screw loose to quit such a good job. *or* You're out of your mind to quit such a good job.

精神食粮 jīngshén shíliáng nourishment for the mind; spiritual food

精神世界 jīngshén shìjiè inner world; mental world

精神衰弱 jīngshén shuāiruò 〈医学〉psychasthenia

精神损耗 jīngshén sǔnhào invisible waste

精神体 jīngshéntǐ 〈宗教〉spiritual being

精神头儿 jīngshentóur 〈口语〉full of vim and vigour:她一聊起来，～可就大了。She is full of vim and vigour when she starts to gossip.

精神外科 jīngshén wàikē 〈医学〉psychosurgery

精神文明 jīngshén wénmíng cultural and ideological progress; (advanced) culture and ideology; (advanced) culture and ethics; spiritual civilization:物质文明和～一起抓 attend to both spiritual and material civilization /在社会主义社会～建设中,要认真加强和改进思想政治工作。In building a socialist society with advanced culture and ethics, we should strengthen and improve our ideological and political work.

精神污染 jīngshén wūrǎn ideological or moral pollution; spiritual contamination — corrosive influence of decadent ideas

精神鸦片 jīngshén yāpiàn mental or spiritual opium (sth. that corrupts people's mind)

精神药理学 jīngshén yàolǐxué 〈医学〉psychopharmacology

精神哲学 jīngshén zhéxué philosophy of mind

精神支柱 jīngshén zhīzhù ideological prop

精神治疗 jīngshén zhìliáo see "精神疗法"

精神状态 jīngshén zhuàngtài state or frame of mind:～不好 be in low spirits /老人虽患有癌症,但～极佳。Though he suffers from cancer, the old man is the very image of optimism.

精神准备 jīngshén zhǔnbèi mental preparation or readiness:作好～ be mentally prepared

精审 jīngshěn 〈书面〉(of writing, plans, etc.) precise and comprehensive

精湿 jīngshī soaking wet:我全身淋得～。I was soaked to the skin.

精收细打 jīngshōu-xìdǎ careful reaping and threshing:～,颗粒归仓 reap and thresh carefully to bring the entire harvest home

精瘦 jīngshòu skinny; skin and bones:浑身～ bag of bones /饿得～ be bony from hunger /～的小猪 skinny piglet /～的衣裳 extremely slim dress

精梳 jīngshū 〈纺织〉combing:～机 comber /～纱 combed yarn /～工艺 combing /～毛纺 worsted spinning

精熟 jīngshú very skilful:剑术～ excellent swordsmanship

精饲料 jīngsìliào concentrated feed; concentrate; rich nourishing feed

精髓 jīngsuǐ marrow; pith; quintessence:马克思主义的～ pith and marrow of Marxism /古典文学的～ quintessence of classical literature

精镗 jīngtáng 〈机械〉finish boring; precision boring

精调 jīngtiáo 〈机械〉accurate adjustment; fine regulation

精通 jīngtōng be proficient in; be well versed in; have a good command of; master:～数学 be well versed in mathematics /～法律 have an intimate knowledge of law /～音乐 be proficient in music /～世故 be familiar with the ways of the world; know what o'clock it is; be worldly-wise /～在于运用。Use makes mastery. *or* Practice makes perfect. /他～几种语言。He has several languages at his fingertips. /他对中国历史颇为～。He is well posted up in Chinese history.

精透 jīngtòu throughly; through and through:他在大雨中淋了个～。He was soaked through and through in the pouring rain.

精微 jīngwēi profound and abstruse:求索宇宙的～ explore the mystery of the universe

精卫填海 jīngwèi-tiánhǎi *Jingwei* (a mythical bird said to be the reincarnation of the drowned daughter of Yandi) trying to fill up the sea with pebbles — dogged determination to achieve one's purpose

精铣 jīngxǐ 〈机械〉finish milling

精细 jīngxì ❶ meticulous; fine; careful:办事妥贴～ handle matters appropriately and circumspectly /这件事情考虑得十分～。This matter has been carefully thought out. /想不到他盘算得这样～。I didn't think he would have planned it so meticulously. ❷ sharp and careful; shrewd

精娴 jīngxián 〈书面〉extremely skilful; deft

精详 jīngxiáng precise and comprehensive:考证～ precise and comprehensive textual research

精心 jīngxīn take great pains; work painstakingly; be meticulous; be elaborate:～培植的花卉 painstakingly cultivated flowers and plants /她在医护人员的～治疗和护理下脱险。She escaped from the grip of death thanks to meticulous medical treatment and nursing. /感谢主人为了接待我们所作的～安排。We wish to thank our host for the careful arrangements he made for our reception.

精选 jīngxuǎn ❶〈矿业〉concentration ❷ carefully chosen; choice:～的商品 choice commodities /～水稻良种 carefully select the improved varieties of rice

精雅 jīngyǎ exquisite and refined; elaborate and tasteful:～的书房 elegant study /花厅陈设十分～。The drawing room is furnished in good taste.

精严 jīngyán careful and strict:他的文章措辞～,条理分明。His article is exact in wording and clear in presentation.

精研 jīngyán study hard:～外文 study foreign languages diligently; devote oneself to the study of foreign languages

精盐 jīngyán refined salt; table salt

精要 jīngyào succinct and to the point; pithy:内容～ succinct in content

精液 jīngyè 〈生理〉seminal fluid; semen:冻干～〈畜牧〉freeze-dried semen /～分析 semen analysis

精一 jīngyī 〈书面〉single-mindedness; unity of purpose

精义 jīngyì sum and substance; essence; gist

精益求精 jīngyìqiújīng constantly improve sth.; keep improving:业务上～ constantly improve and perfect one's professional skill /一丝不苟、～的治学精神 spirit of being scrupulous about every detail and keeping on improving in one's academic pursuit

精英 jīngyīng ❶ cream; essence; quintessence:很多出土文物,都是我国古代文化的～。Many unearthed historical relics are the cream of our country's ancient culture. ❷ the best and the brightest; elite:象棋～ outstanding chessplayer /当代青年的～ elite of contemporary youth

精于 jīngyú be proficient in; be keen on; be good at:～此道 be well versed in this sort of thing /～风筝制作 be good at making kites

精原细胞瘤 jīngyuán xìbāoliú 〈医学〉seminoma

精蕴 jīngyùn profound content; essentials:探索天体运行的～ probe (into) or find out the fundamental law governing the movement of celestial bodies

精轧 jīngzhá 〈冶金〉finish rolling:～机 finishing mill; finisher

精湛 jīngzhàn consummate; superb; exquisite:技术～ exquisite skill /～的表演艺术 consummate performing art /他的人物、花卉和山水无不～。His technique in painting figures, flowers and landscape is superb without exception.

精整 jīngzhěng 〈冶金〉finishing; sizing:～工段 finishing department /～加工 final finish /～作业线 finishing line

精制 jīngzhì make with extra care; refine:～糖 refined sugar /～品 highly finished products; superfines /这些瓷器都是～而成的。These chinawares are made with extra care.

精致 jīngzhì fine; exquisite; consummate; delicate:～的手工艺品 fine handicrafts wares /～的花灯 delicate flowery lantern /～的花边 exquisite lace /平房后面是一座～的花园。Behind the house there was an exquisite garden. /那幅画装裱得颇为～。The painting is delicately mounted.

精忠 jīngzhōng boundless loyalty (to the country or nation):～报国 serve one's motherland with selfless loyalty

精装 jīngzhuāng ❶ (of books) clothbound; hardback; hardcover:～书籍 hardcover books /绸面～ clothbound with silk /布面～ clothbound with cotton ❷ (commodities) elaborately packed:～商品 elaborately packed commodities /～茶叶 elegantly-packed tea

精装本 jīngzhuāngběn hardback edition; de luxe edition

精壮 jīngzhuàng able-bodied; strong; robust

精子 jīngzǐ 〈生理〉sperm; spermatozoon:～发生 spermatogenesis /～过少 spermacrasia

精仔 jīngzǐ 〈方言〉smarty; smartie

菁

jīng ❶ essence; cream ❷ lush; luxuriant

菁华 jīnghuá essence; cream; quintessence

菁菁 jīngjīng 〈书面〉lush; luxuriant:其叶～ with its lush leaves

睛

jīng eyeball:定～细看 give sth. or sb. a detailed (*or* good) look /目不转～ gaze fixedly /画龙点～ bring the painted dragon to life by putting in the pupils of its eyes

鼱

jīng see "鼩鼱" qújīng

鶄

jīng see "䴔鶄" jiāojīng

腈

jīng 〈化学〉nitrile

腈纶 jīnglún acrylic fibres:～毛线 knitting wool made of acrylic fi-

bres

荆 jīng ❶ chaste tree; vitex:披～斩棘 break through brambles and thorns /～天棘地 thistles and thorns everywhere — a very difficult situation (with one barrier after another in one's path) ❷ (Jīng) a surname

荆笆 jīngbā piece of woven twigs of the chaste tree (used for making a fence, thatched roof, etc.)

荆钗布裙 jīngchāi-bùqún thornwood hairpins and hemp skirt — simple lowly dress of a poor woman

荆棘 jīngjí thistles and thorns; brambles; thorny undergrowth:～丛生 overgrown with brambles — beset with difficulties /那山上～桠杈,薜萝牵绕。The (mountain) ridge was overrun with brambles and creepers.

荆棘铜驼 jīngjí-tóngtuó *also* "铜驼荆棘" dilapidated state of a subjugated nation:～使我悲! The devastation of my country pains my heart!

荆棘载途 jīngjí-zàitú *also* "荆棘塞途" path overgrown with brambles — a path beset with difficulties:他这一生,可说是～,但他始终保持着乐观进取的精神。His life could be compared to a path beset with difficulties, but he always remained optimistic and forward-looking in spirit.

荆芥 jīngjiè 〈中药〉 *jingjie* (*Schizonepeta tenuifolia*)

荆条 jīngtiáo twigs of the chaste tree (used for weaving baskets, etc.):～筐 baskets made of twigs of the chaste tree /～篱笆 fence of twigs of the chaste tree; twig fence

荆榛 jīngzhēn overgrown with grass and bushes:古寺荒凉,～满目。The ancient temple is a scene of desolation, overgrown with grass and bushes.

兢 jīng

兢兢 jīngjīng cautious; fearful:战战～ tremble with fear and trepidation /～于职守 be cautious and circumspect in discharging one's official duty

兢兢业业 jīngjīng-yèyè cautious and conscientious:～地工作一辈子 work conscientiously all one's life

晶 jīng ❶ bright; shiny; glittering:蓝～～ bright and blue ❷ quartz; (rock) crystal:水～ quartz /红～ garnet /紫～ amethyst /茶～ citrine; yellow quartz /墨～ smoky quartz ❸ any crystalline substance:结～ crystallization; crystal /冰～ ice crystal

晶格 jīnggé 〈物理〉(crystal) lattice:面心～ face-centred lattice /体心～ body-centred lattice

晶光 jīngguāng ❶ bright or glittering light:～耀眼 dazzling light /～锃亮 shiny light ❷〈书面〉〈比喻〉expression; look

晶洁 jīngjié crystalline and pure:～的玉石 bright pure jade /～的诗篇 fresh and lucid poem

晶界 jīngjiè 〈物理〉crystal boundary; grain boundary:～腐蚀 grain-boundary corrosion; crystal boundary corrosion

晶晶 jīngjīng 〈书面〉bright; shiny; glittering:～的星光 bright starlight /亮～ glittering; sparkling; glistening

晶粒 jīnglì 〈物理〉(crystalline) grain

晶亮 jīngliàng bright; glittering:～的眼睛 sparkling eyes

晶明 jīngmíng bright; glittering; sparkling:树叶上闪动着～的露珠。Dew drops are glistening on the leaves.

晶片 jīngpiàn 〈电子〉wafer:～加工 wafer process /～开关 wafer switch

晶石 jīngshí 〈矿业〉spar

晶态 jīngtài 〈物理〉crystalline state:～半导体化合物 crystalline semiconduction compound

晶体 jīngtǐ *also* "结晶体" jiéjīngtǐ;"结晶" jiéjīng crystal:单～ monocrystal /多～ polycrystal /～结构 crystal structure /～生长 crystal growth

晶体点阵 jīngtǐ diǎnzhèn 〈物理〉crystal lattice

晶体二极管 jīngtǐ èrjíguǎn transistor diode

晶体发生学 jīngtǐ fāshēngxué crystallogery

晶体管 jīngtǐguǎn transistor:硅～ silicon transistor /锗～ germanium transistor /～收音机 transistor radio

晶体学 jīngtǐxué crystallography

晶体钟 jīngtǐzhōng crystal clock

晶莹 jīngyíng sparkling and crystal-clear; glittering and translucent:～露珠 sparkling dew /泪光～ glistening teardrops /～的眼睛 crystal-clear eyes /～清澈的湖水 glittering and crystal-clear lake water

晶闸管 jīngzháguǎn 〈电子〉thyristor:光控～ light activated thyristor /可关断～ gate-turnoff thyristor

晶状体 jīngzhuàngtǐ crystalline lens:～瘤 phacoma /～炎 phacitis; phacoiditis; crystalloiditis

坙(巠) jīng 〈书面〉network of rivers and streams

泾(涇) jīng ❶〈方言〉brook; stream ❷(Jīng) (short for 泾河) Jing River

泾渭不分 Jing-Wèi bùfēn makes no distinction between the Jing and Wei rivers — fail to distinguish between the good and the bad

泾渭分明 Jing-Wèi fēnmíng as different as the waters of the Jing and Wei rivers — wholly different

茎(莖) jīng ❶ stem (of a plant); stalk:抽～ (of the stem of certain plants) put forth /根～ rhizome /花～ floral axis /块～ stem tuber /直立～ erect stem /鳞～ bulb /球～ corm /缠绕～ vine /地上～ acrial stem of plant /地下～ subterranean stem of plant /草质～ herb stem ❷ anything like a stem or stalk:剑～ sword handle; hilt ❸〈量词〉〈书面〉*used for sth. long and thin*:数～白发 some white hair(s)

茎秆切碎机 jīnggǎn qiēsuìjī 〈农业〉stalk-cutter shredder

茎枯病 jīngkūbìng stem wilt

茎叶植物 jīngyè zhíwù cormophyte

经[1](經) jīng ❶〈纺织〉warp:*see* "～纱" ❷〈中医〉channels:*see* "～络" ❸〈地理〉longitude:东～ east longitude /西～ west longitude ❹ manage; rule; deal in; engage in:～国之才 ability to administer a state ❺〈书面〉hang:自～ hang oneself ❻ constant; regular; normal:不～之谈 preposterous statement; cock-and-bull story /荒诞不～ absurd; fantastic ❼ scripture; canon; classic:圣～ Holy Bible /佛～ Buddhist sutra; Buddhist scripture /金刚～ Diamond Sutra /法华～ Saddharmapundarika Sutra /藏～ Tripitaka; whole collection of Buddhist texts /古兰～ Koran /四书五～ Four Books and Five Classics /取～ go on a pilgrimage for Buddhist scriptures /引～据典 quote the classics; quote authorities /不见～传 not to be found in classics /各有一本难念的～。Each has his own trouble. ❽ menses; menstruation:行～ menstruate /通～ stimulate the menstrual flow /调～ regulate the menstrual function ❾ (Jīng) a surname

经[2](經) jīng ❶ (pass) through; via; by way of:～东京回国 return home via Tokyo /途～广州 pass through Guangzhou /～兰州去乌鲁木齐 go to Ürümqi by way of Lanzhou /身～百战 have fought many battles; be a veteran of many wars /饱～风霜的老人 weather-beaten old man; experienced old man /这个方案已～上级批准。This plan has been approved by higher authorities. ❷ stand; bear; endure:～得起时间的检验 can stand the test of time /这个结论,似乎～不起推敲。It seems that this conclusion doesn't bear scrutiny. *see also* jìng

经办 jīngbàn handle; manage; deal with:这件事是他一手～的。This affair is handled by him alone.

经闭 jīngbì *also* "闭经"〈中医〉amenorrhoea

经编 jīngbiān 〈纺织〉warp knitting:～针织物 warp-knitted fabric /～机 tricot machine

经部 jīngbù general category of writings in ancient times, including the Four Books and the Five Classics and other books concerning characters, phonology and exegetical studies

经产 jīngchǎn 〈医学〉multiparity:～孕妇 multigravida

经产妇 jīngchǎnfù 〈医学〉multipara

经常 jīngcháng ❶ day-to-day; everyday; daily:～工作 routine work /～储备 current reserve /～开支 running expenses /～费用 overhead; ordinary expediture /～收入 regular income /～项目的平衡 balance on current account /～账户 current account /～化 become a regular practice /他们是我店～的顾客。They are regular customers of our shop. ❷ frequently; constantly; regularly; often:～交换意见 regularly exchange ideas /～工作到深夜 often work till the small hours /～出入酒楼舞厅 frequent restaurants and dance parlors /此类

事故～发生。This kind of accident often occurred. /此地春天～下雨。It often rains here in spring. /他～改变主意。He constantly changes his mind.

经幢 jīngchuáng 〈佛教〉stone pillar inscribed with Buddha's name or Buddhist scripture

经典 jīngdiǎn ❶ classics: 儒家～ classics of Confucius and Mencius; Confucian classics /博览～ be well read in classics ❷ scriptures: 道教～ Taoist scriptures ❸ classical: ～著作 classical works

经典力学 jīngdiǎn lìxué 〈物理〉classical mechanics

经典释文 Jīngdiǎn Shìwén *Pronunciation and Meaning of Words in the Classics*, written by Lu Deming (陆德明) of the Tang Dynasty

经典作家 jīngdiǎn zuòjiā author of classics; classic writer: 马克思主义～ authors of Marxist classics

经度 jīngdù longitude

经断 jīngduàn 〈中医〉menopause

经幡 jīngfān sutra streamer

经方 jīngfāng collective name for all the ancient medical works; prescriptions in ancient medical books

经费 jīngfèi fund; outlay: 行政～ administrative expenditure /～转移 transfer of appropriation /科研～不足 shortage of funds for scientific research /改进学校的电教装置，需要一大笔～。It requires a heavy outlay to improve a school's language laboratory facility.

经风雨，见世面 jīng fēngyǔ, jiàn shìmiàn see the world and brave the storms: 让孩子一个人出去闯一闯，经经风雨，见见世面，这对他会有好处的。Let the child leave home to venture out himself. It will do him good to see life and stand its tests.

经管 jīngguǎn be in charge of; steward: ～商务 be in charge of business /～产业 steward a property

经管责任 jīngguǎn zérèn stewardship

经过 jīngguò ❶ process; course: 事情的～尚待调查。The course of the incident remains to be investigated. ❷ pass; go through; undergo: ～人民大会堂西侧 go by the west side of the Great Hall of the People /船只都要～英吉利海峡到达伦敦。All ships have to go through the English Channel to reach London. ❸ continue; go on: 编写这部词典，～了整整十年时间。The compilation of this dictionary has taken exactly ten years. /～了漫长的岁月，地下的生物遗体变成了化石。The remains of living things underground turned into fossiles after a long period of time. ❹ as a result of; after; through: ～认真考虑作出了决定。A decision was made after careful consideration. /我们～共同的努力取得了新成就。We have scored new successes by (*or* through) our common efforts. /合同～双方签字后，立即生效。The contract becomes effective immediately upon the signature of the two parties. /这件事～领导了吗? Have the leaders approved of this matter?

经互会 Jīnghùhuì (short for 经济互助委员会) Council for Mutual Economic Assistance (of the former Soviet Union and her allies, now disbanded); Comecon

经籍 jīngjí 〈书面〉❶ Confucian classics ❷ (usu. ancient) books in general: 北京图书馆收藏有大量宋元本～。The Beijing Library has a large collection of original books of the Song and Yuan dynasties.

经纪 jīngjì ❶ manage (a business): 老于～ experienced in business ❷ manager; broker: 解放前，他在交易所里当～。Before liberation, he was a broker in the exchange. ❸ 〈书面〉handle; look after

经纪人 jīngjìrén broker; middleman; agent: 房地产～ estate agent /商品～ commodity broker

经济 jīngjì ❶ economy: 发展～ develop economy /繁荣～ promote economic prosperity /国有～ state sector of the economy; state-owned economy /社会主义～ socialist economy /资本主义～ capitalist economy /私营～ privately managed economy /个体～ individual economy /工业～ industrial economy /农业～ agricultural economy /国民～ national economy /市场～ market economy /计划～ planned economy; command economy /地下～ underground economy /～群体 economic group /～循环 economic cycle /专属～区 exclusive economic zone /联合国大会～和财政委员会 Economic and Financial Committee of the UN General Assembly /～和社会理事会 (UN) Economic and Social Council (ECOSOC) /总统～咨文 (US) economic report of the president /规模～ economy of scale /～平衡 economic equilibrium /～失调 dislocation of the economy /～地位 economic status; economic position /～成效 economic effect /～封锁 economic blockade /～改革 economic reform /～合作 economic cooperation /～计划 economic planning /～结构 economic structure /～赔偿 economic compensation; financial reimbursement /～衰退 recession /～损失 pecuniary loss /～起飞 economic take-off ❷ of industrial or economic value; economic: *see* "～作物" ❸ financial condition; income: ～宽裕 well-off; well-to-do; comfortably off /～负担 financial burden /～困难 be in financial difficulties; be hard up ❹ economical; frugal; thrifty: ～实用 economical and practical /时间和精力方面都很～ economical of time and energy ❺ 〈书面〉run or manage the country: 有～之才 have the ability to administer the state

经济布局 jīngjì bùjú economic layout

经济舱 jīngjìcāng (of ship or airplane accommodations) economy class; economy cabin

经济成分 jīngjì chéngfen sector of the economy; economic sector

经济承包责任制 jīngjì chéngbāo zérènzhì economic responsibility system with contracted jobs

经济地理学 jīngjì dìlǐxué economic geography

经济地质学 jīngjì dìzhìxué economic geology

经济动物 jīngjì dòngwù economic animal

经济法 jīngjìfǎ economic law

经济法规 jīngjì fǎguī laws and regulations pertaining to the economy; economic statutes

经济法庭 jīngjì fǎtíng economic tribunal

经济犯罪 jīngjì fànzuì economic crime

经济复苏 jīngjì fùsū economic resurgence or recovery

经济杠杆 jīngjì gànggǎn economic lever: 国家在正确运用行政、立法等手段的同时，要更好地运用价格、税收、信贷等各种～，保证国民经济的平稳发展。While properly employing administrative, legislative or other means, the government should make better use of such economic levers as price, tax and credit in order to ensure the stable development of the national economy.

经济规律 jīngjì guīlǜ *also* "经济法则" law of economy; economic law

经济合同 jīngjì hétong economic contract

经济合作与发展组织 Jīngjì Hézuò Yǔ Fāzhǎn Zǔzhī Organization for Economic Cooperation and Development (OECD), an international organization set up in 1961

经济核算 jīngjì hésuàn economic accounting; business accounting: ～单位 business accounting unit

经济互助委员会 Jīngjì Hùzhù Wěiyuánhuì *see* "经互会"

经济环境 jīngjì huánjìng economic environment

经济机制 jīngjì jīzhì economic mechanism; economic regime

经济基础 jīngjì jīchǔ economic base; economic basis: ～和上层建筑 the economic base and the superstructure

经济技术开发区 jīngjì jìshù kāifāqū *also* "经济开发区" economic technological development zone; economic development zone

经济科 Jīngjìkē (HK) Economic Services Branch

经济恐慌 jīngjì kǒnghuāng economic depression; economic panic

经济昆虫 jīngjì kūnchóng economic insect

经济立法 jīngjì lìfǎ economic legislation

经济联合体 jīngjì liánhétǐ economic association; conglomeration; conglomerate; combination

经济林 jīngjìlín economic forest

经济逻辑 jīngjì luóji economic logic

经济命脉 jīngjì mìngmài economic lifeline; economic arteries; key branches of the economy: 掌握了国家的～ gain control of the economic lifelines of a country

经济模式 jīngjì móshì mode or pattern for economic development; economic mould

经济企划厅 Jīngjì Qǐhuàtīng (Japan) Economic Planning Agency

经济企划院 Jīngjì Qǐhuàyuàn (ROK) Ministry of Economic Planning: ～长官 Minister of Economic Planning

经济渗透 jīngjì shèntòu economic infiltration

经济师 jīngjìshī (used in professional ranking) economic administrator

经济实体 jīngjì shítǐ economic entity

经济司 Jīngjìsī (HK before July 1997) Secretary for Economic Services

经济特区 jīngjì tèqū special economic zone: 深圳的发展和经验证明，我们建立～的政策是正确的。The development and experience of Shenzhen has proved the correctness of our policy in establishing special economic zones.

经济体制 jīngjì tǐzhì economic structure: ～改革 reform of the

J

economic structure; economic structural reform; economic restructuring
经济外交 jīngjì wàijiāo economic diplomacy
经济危机 jīngjì wēijī economic crisis
经济萧条 jīngjì xiāotiáo economic slump or depression
经济效益 jīngjì xiàoyì economic efficiency; economic results or effects: 讲究～ stress economic benefits or effects / 以最少的消耗, 取得最大的～ obtain maximum economic results at minimum costs / ～好、有还贷能力的企业 enterprises that excel in economic performance and have the ability to pay debts
经济学 jīngjìxué economics: ～家 economist
经济一体化 jīngjì yītǐhuà economic integration
经济援助 jīngjì yuánzhù economic aid or assistance
经济杂交 jīngjì zájiāo 〈畜牧〉 commercial crossbreeding
经济责任制 jīngjì zérènzhì economic responsibility system: 我们应该在国有企业整顿过程中, 有计划有步骤地推行和完善～。We should promote and perfect the system of economic responsibility step by step and in a planned way in the process of streamlining state-owned enterprises.
经济战 jīngjìzhàn economic warfare
经济制裁 jīngjì zhìcái economic sanctions
经济制度 jīngjì zhìdù economic system
经济秩序 jīngjì zhìxù economic order
经济主义 jīngjìzhǔyì economism
经济作物 jīngjì zuòwù industrial crop; cash crop
经见 jīngjiàn ❶ see with one's own eyes: 你是头一次～这样的暴雨吧。This must be the first time you have seen such a violent thunderstorm with your own eyes. ❷ often see: 山鸡这里～, 很容易猎获。Pheasants are a common sight here, and they are very easy to hunt.
经解 jīngjiě books explaining the meaning of classics; glossaries of the classics
经久 jīngjiǔ ❶ prolonged: 销路～不衰 remain in great demand for a long time ❷ durable; fast: 色泽～不褪。The colour is fast and will not fade.
经久不息 jīngjiǔ-bùxī prolonged; enduring: ～的欢呼声 prolonged ovation
经卷 jīngjuàn scrolls of Buddhist sutras; scrolls of Buddhist scripture: ～雕板 wood block for printing scrolls of Buddhist scripture
经理 jīnglǐ ❶ handle; manage: 这个乡办企业实际上是由他一手～的。This town-run enterprise was in fact managed by him personally. ❷ manager; director: ～负责制 system of the manager assuming full responsibility / ～角色理论 managerial role theory / ～联席会议 joint executive meeting / 他如今是一家大公司的总～。He is now the president of a big company.
经历 jīnglì go through; undergo; experience: ～长期的磨炼 undergo a long process of tempering / ～艰难挫折 experience hardships and setbacks / ～两个阶段 go through two stages / 曲折多变的～ a chequered career / 生活～ life experience / 过去的苦难～ sufferings of the past / 这巍峨的古塔, ～了千年的风雨侵蚀。The lofty ancient tower has been eroded by wind and rain for thousands of years. / 两国人民有遭受帝国主义侵略的共同～。Our two peoples share the same experience of being subjected to imperialist aggression in the past.
经略 jīnglüè ❶ 〈书面〉 manage and manoeuvre: 此人颇见～之才。This man is quite resourceful in military and administrative affairs. ❷ 〈历史〉 high commissioner, generally of frontier areas: ～使 high commissioner of a border area
经纶 jīnglún 〈书面〉 ❶ combed silk threads ❷ statecraft; statesmanship: 满腹～ talent for managing state affairs; encyclopedic mind; profound scholarship / 大展～ put one's statecraft to full use; turn one's statesmanship to full account
经络 jīngluò 〈中医〉 main and collateral channels, regarded as a network of passages, through which vital energy circulates and along which the acupuncture points are distributed
经脉 jīngmài 〈中医〉 passages through which vital energy circulates, regulating bodily functions
经贸 jīngmào economy and trade: 今年上半年, 我国对外～继续发展。In the first half of the year, our economic relations and trade with foreign countries continued to grow.
经贸委 jīngmàowěi (short for 国家经济贸易委员会) State Economic and Trade Commission
经密 jīngmì 〈纺织〉 warp density; ends per inch
经年 jīngnián for one or several years: 卧病～ be laid up for years
经年累月 jīngnián-lěiyuè for years; year in and year out; for years on end: 埋头钻研, ～ bury oneself in study year in and year out / 地质工作者～跋山涉水, 在野外工作。The geology workers scaled mountains and forded streams for years on end to do field work.
经期 jīngqī (menstrual) period: ～正常 regular menstruation / ～不正常 irregular menstruation
经期错后 jīngqī cuòhòu 〈医学〉 delayed menstrual cycle
经期延长 jīngqī yáncháng 〈医学〉 menostaxis
经纱 jīngshā 〈纺织〉 warp: ～和纬纱 warp and weft
see also jìngshā
经商 jīngshāng engage in trade; be in business: 他早年去南洋～。In his early years, he was in business in Southeast Asia.
经师 jīngshī ❶ 〈旧语〉 teacher of Confucian classics: ～易得, 人师难求。It's easier to get a teacher of classics than a teacher of man. ❷ 〈佛教〉 master who expounds the text of Buddhism
经史子集 jīng-shǐ-zǐ-jí Confucian classics, history, philosophy and belles-lettres — the four traditional categories of Chinese writings
经始 jīngshǐ ❶ 〈书面〉 start to build; initiate; pioneer: ～大业 blaze a trail in a great undertaking ❷ 〈军事〉 laying out the ground plan of a fortified work; tracing: ～线 trace
经世 jīngshì 〈书面〉 manage or administer state affairs: ～之才 ability to administer the country / 留心～致用之学 pay attention to the practical knowledge of managing state affairs
经手 jīngshǒu handle; deal with: ～人 person handling a particular transaction, job, etc. / ～费 brokerage; commission / 我～的钱款都有单据可查。I kept for reference all the receipts for the money I handled.
经受 jīngshòu undergo; experience; sustain; stand: ～严峻的考验 experience grim trials; stand up to rigorous tests; withstand trials and tribulations / ～战斗锻炼的士兵 soldiers tempered in battle / ～许多苦难 undergo much suffering / 两位老人～不住丧子的打击。The elderly couple could not stand the blow of the death of their son.
经售 jīngshòu sell on commission; deal in; distribute; sell: 本店～日用杂品。Our shop sells articles of daily use. / 这类物品由化工商店～。These kinds of goods are distributed by chemical shops. / 这家商场～的商品在一万五千种以上。This shopping centre deals in commodities of more than fifteen thousand varieties.
经书 jīngshū Confucian classics
经水 jīngshuǐ ❶ menstruation; menses ❷ 〈旧语〉 river that has its source in the mountains and flows into the sea
经水过多 jīngshuǐ guòduō 〈医学〉 menorrhagia
经水涩少 jīngshuǐ sèshǎo scanty menstruation
经水无定 jīngshuǐ wúdìng irregular menstruation
经堂 jīngtáng hall for keeping or chanting Buddhist scriptures
经天纬地 jīngtiān-wěidì ability to weave the warp and woof of the universe — ability to run the country: ～之才 ability to manage state affairs
经停 jīngtíng stop over; make a stopover: 这个航班～东京。There will be a stopover in Tokyo on this flight.
经痛 jīngtòng 〈医学〉 dysmenorrhoea
经外奇穴 jīngwài qíxué 〈中医〉 extra nerve points, i. e. points not mentioned in the ancient medical classics
经纬 jīngwěi ❶ meridian and parallel (lines) ❷ main threads; orderliness; reason: ～万端 have too many things to attend to / 他如今说话越发没了～。He has become even more senseless in his speech now. / 他把自己从讲台上所听到的一些～讲给别人听。He retold what he heard from the rostrum to others. ❸ 〈书面〉 plan and administer: ～天下 attend to state affairs; order and regulate affairs of state ❹ 〈旧语〉 Confucian classics, etc.
经纬度 jīngwěidù longitude and latitude
经纬仪 jīngwěiyí theodolite; transit: ～测量 transit survey
经文 jīngwén passages from the Confucian classics or religious scriptures
经武 jīngwǔ 〈书面〉 strengthen military preparations: 整军～ consolidate the army and strengthen defences
经线 jīngxiàn ❶ 〈纺织〉 warp ❷ 〈地理〉 meridian (line)
经销 jīngxiāo sell on commission; deal in; distribute; sell: ～处 agency / ～部 distributing department / ～协定 agreement to sell sth. / 这个商店～各种空调设备。This shop deals in all kinds of air-conditioning equipment.

经销品牌 jīngxiāo pǐnpái dealer brand
经销商 jīngxiāoshāng distributor
经心 jīngxīn careful; mindful; conscientious:你干工作不能漫不～。You mustn't be careless with your work./干什么工作都要～。One should be conscientious in whatever one does./近十年,他～于集邮。He has taken great care to collect stamps these ten years.
经行便血 jīngxíng biànxiě blood stool during menstruation
经行浮肿 jīngxíng fúzhǒng edema during menstruation
经行腹痛 jīngxíng fùtòng *also* "痛经" tòngjīng dysmenorrhoea
经行腰痛 jīngxíng yāotòng lumbago during menstruation
经学 jīngxué study of Confucian classics:～家 expert in the study of Confucian classics; Confucian classicist; Confucian scholar /～大师 great master of Confucian studies
经血 jīngxuè 〈中医〉menses; menstruation
经验 jīngyàn ❶ experience:～丰富 have rich experience; be very experienced /缺少工作～ lack work experience; not be sufficiently experienced in work /直接～ direct experience /搬用别人的～ mechanically copy other's experience /教学～ teaching experience /～教训 experiences and lessons /总结～ sum up experience /积累～ accumulate experience /交流～ exchange experience /介绍～ pass on one's experience /～概率 empirical probability /～数据 empirical data /～曲线 experience curve ❷ go through; experience:这样的事情他从来没有～过。He has never experienced this kind of thing. *or* He has never had such experience before.
经验论 jīngyànlùn empiricism:～者 proponent of empiricism; empiricist
经验批判主义 jīngyàn pīpànzhǔyì empiriocriticism
经验之谈 jīngyànzhītán wise counsel of an experienced person:这是多么宝贵的～啊! How precious is the advice of an experienced person!
经验主义 jīngyànzhǔyì empiricism:～者 empiricist
经一事,长一智 jīng yī shì, zhǎng yī zhì whatever one does, one profits by it; in doing we learn; a fall in the pit, a gain in the wit
经义 jīngyì 〈旧语〉❶ meaning and significance of Confucian classics ❷ subject or course of the imperial examination
经意 jīngyì careful; mindful:不～地碰了她一下 touched her inadvertently /这些话说得似不～,其实良有用心。Casual as the remark might seem, it was said on purpose.
经营 jīngyíng ❶ manage; operate; run; engage in:～副业 engage in sideline production /发展多种～ promote a diversified economy /国家～的工商业 state-operated industry and commerce /改善经营管理 improve management and administration /～管理人才 managerial and administrative personnel /～方针策略 management principles and tactics /～合同 operating agreement /～疆域 business boundaries /～目标 management objectives; operational objectives /～和财务报告 operating and financial review /本店～家电产品。The shop deals in household electrical appliances. /这个公司是港商独资～的。This is a firm wholly-owned and run by a Hong Kong businessman. ❷ plan and organize:苦心～ take great pains to build up (an enterprise, etc.) /惨淡～ keep (an enterprise, etc.) going by painstaking effort; carry on a business with strenuous exertion
经营比率 jīngyíng bǐlǜ operating ratio
经营成本 jīngyíng chéngběn operating loss; operation cost; operational cost; handling cost
经营管理学 jīngyíng guǎnlǐxué management science
经营决策 jīngyíng juécè operating decision
经营权 jīngyíngquán power of management; managerial authority
经营性亏损 jīngyíngxìng kuīsǔn loss incurred from operation; operational loss; operating loss
经营周期 jīngyíng zhōuqī operational cycle
经营资金 jīngyíng zījīn operation fund; floating capital
经用 jīngyòng ❶ durable:这种杯子又好看又～。The glass is not only nice-looking but also durable. ❷〈书面〉be often used
经由 jīngyóu via; by way of:～巴黎去伦敦 go to London via Paris
经佑 jīngyòu 〈方言〉look after; attend to; take care of:细心～孤儿 take good care of an orphan
经援 jīngyuán (short for 经济援助) economic aid or assistance
经院哲学 jīngyuàn zhéxué *also* "烦琐哲学" fánsuǒ zhéxué scholasticism
经藏 jīngzàng 〈佛教〉Sutra-Pitka; collection of sutras
经轴 jīngzhóu 〈纺织〉warp beam
经咒 jīngzhòu scripture and mantras of Buddhism, Taoism, etc.
经传 jīngzhuàn ❶ Confucian classics and commentaries on them; Confucian canon ❷ classical works; classics:名不见～ be not well known; be a mere nobody
经传释词 Jīngzhuàn Shìcí *Explication of Words in the Classics*, exegetical study of form words in ancient Chinese, written by Wang Yinzhi (王引之) of the Qing Dynasty
经子 jīngzi 〈方言〉hemp; flax:捻～ twist flaxen thread

jǐng

井[1] jǐng ❶ well:打～ sink (*or* drill) a well /掘～ dig (*or* drive) a well /机～ motor-pumped well /枯～ dry well /坐～观天 look at the sky from the bottom of a well — narrow-minded and bigoted /落～下石 drop a stone on sb. who has fallen into a well — hit sb. when he is down ❷ sth. in the shape of a well:矿～ pit; mine /油～ oil well /盐～ salt well /竖～ (vertical) shaft /天～ small yard /自喷～〈石油〉flush well /抽油～〈石油〉pumping well /废～ abandoned well /风～ air shaft /排水～ pumping shaft ❸ settlement; village:市～ market place /背乡离～ leaving one's home village ❹ one of the lunar mansions *see also* "二十八宿" èrshíbāxiù ❺ (Jǐng) a surname

井[2] jǐng in good order:*see* "～然";"～～有条"
井泵 jǐngbèng 〈矿业〉well pump
井壁 jǐngbì wall of a well:～坍塌 cave-in; caving /～取心〈石油〉side-wall coring /～取样〈石油〉side-wall sampling
井场 jǐngchǎng 〈石油〉well site:～管理费 field overhead
井地 jǐngdì *see* "井田制"
井底 jǐngdǐ ❶ bottom of a well:～样品〈石油〉bottom-hole sample ❷〈矿业〉shaft bottom; pit bottom:～车场 shaft station /～矿仓 shaft pocket
井底之蛙 jǐngdǐzhīwā frog in a well — person with a very limited outlook:～,所见不大;萤火之光,其亮不远。A frog in a well sees a limited world; a firefly sends out a glimmering light. /彼年幼学浅,如～。He is a young man with narrow vision, like a frog at the bottom of a well.
井冈山 Jǐnggāngshān Jinggang Mountains (forming the middle section of the Luoxiao 罗霄 Range straddling Hunan and Jiangxi provinces), where Mao Zedong established China's first peasant revolutionary base area in 1927
井灌 jǐngguàn 〈水利〉well irrigation
井架 jǐngjià ❶〈石油〉derrick:轻便～ portable derrick; portable mast ❷〈矿业〉headframe; headgear; pithead frame
井井有条 jǐngjǐng-yǒutiáo in perfect order; shipshape; methodical; orderly:～地工作 work methodically /货物摆放得～。All the goods were stacked in neat piles. /他喜欢把什么都弄得～。He likes everything to be shipshape and in apple-pie order. /她是一位非常讲究治家的妇女。她家里的一切都安排得～。She was a very meticulous housewife. Everything in her home was just so.
井臼 jǐngjiù well and mortar for drawing water and grinding grain — household chores:亲操～ do household chores oneself
井口 jǐngkǒu ❶ mouth of a well ❷〈矿业〉pithead ❸〈石油〉wellhead:～气 wellhead gas; casinghead gas /～装置 wellhead assembly
井楼 jǐnglóu 〈矿业〉head house; shaft house
井喷 jǐngpēn 〈石油〉blowout
井然 jǐngrán 〈书面〉orderly; neat and tidy; shipshape; methodical; systematic:秩序～ in good order /陈设～ well-arranged
井然有序 jǐngrán-yǒuxù in apple-pie order; orderly; methodical:各项工作安排得～。All aspects of the work were methodically arranged.
井绳 jǐngshéng coiled rope used in drawing water from a well:一朝被蛇咬,十年怕～。Once bitten by a snake, one shies at a coiled rope for the next ten years; once bitten, twice shy
井水不犯河水 jǐngshuǐ bù fàn héshuǐ well water does not intrude into river water — I'll mind my own business, you mind yours:我和他～,怎么就冲了他? I kept as clear of him as well water is from river water. How could my horoscope clash with his? /他干他的,我干我的,彼此～。Let him go his way and I'll go mine. We won't interfere with each other.
井台 jǐngtái wellhead

井田制 jǐngtiánzhì "nine squares" system (of land ownership in China's slave society) with one large square divided into 9 small ones (like the Chinese character 井), the 8 outer ones being allocated to slave families who had to cultivate the central one for the slave owner
井筒 jǐngtǒng ❶ shaft of a well ❷〈矿业〉pit shaft:～隔间 shaft compartment /～掘进 shaft excavation
井蛙 jǐngwā *see* "井底之蛙"
井位 jǐngwèi well location; well-site
井下 jǐngxià in the pit; in the shaft:～作业 operation in a pit; underpit operation /～采煤区 underground coal mining district /～充填工 pillar man; pillar packer; waller; pack builder; packer /～检查灯 inspection lamp
井斜 jǐngxié 〈石油〉well deflection; well deviation:这口井～是1.9度。The well had a deviation of 1.9 degrees from the vertical.
井盐 jǐngyán well salt
井邑 jǐngyì 〈书面〉city; town; market place:～萧条。The town is desolate.

肼 jǐng 〈化学〉bydrazine

阱(穽) jǐng trap; pitfall; pit:陷～ trap; pitfall

警 jǐng ❶ alert; vigilant: *see* "～戒" ❷ sharp; acute; keen:机～ sharp-witted; alert and resourceful ❸ warn; admonish; alarm:鸣枪示～ give a warning by firing a gun; fire a warning shot ❹ alarm; emergency; accident:火～ fire alarm /报～ give an alarm; report (an accident, etc.) to the police /告～ report an emergency ❺ (short for 警察) police; policeman:民～ people's police /门～ guard at an entrance /武～ armed police /骑～ mounted police
警拔 jǐngbá 〈书面〉unexpectedly original; surprisingly unconventional:造语～ surprisingly unconventional wording
警报 jǐngbào alarm; siren; warning; alert:拉～ sound the alarm; sound the siren /空袭～ air-raid alarm /解除～ all clear /战斗～ combat alert /～信号 alarm signal /发布台风紧急～ issue an urgent typhoon warning /降温～ warning of a drop in temperature /～系统 warning system ; alarm system
警报器 jǐngbàoqì siren; alarm
警备 jǐngbèi guard; garrison:～部队 garrison troops /～区 garrison command /～司令部 garrison headquarters /～司令 garrison commander /上海～区 Shanghai Garrison /～森严 tightly garrisoned; heavily guarded /日夜～ be on guard day and night; guard day and night
警跸 jǐngbì 〈书面〉clear the way for the imperial carriage and stop all traffic
警标 jǐngbiāo 〈旧语〉navigation mark; beacon
警策 jǐngcè 〈书面〉❶ whip (a horse) on ❷ (language) concise and penetrating:～之言 pithy and incisive remarks
警察 jǐngchá police; policeman:女～ policewoman /人民～ people's police /便衣～ plainclothes policeman or policewoman; plainclothes /交通～ traffic police /刑事～ criminal police /治安～ security police /武装～部队 armed police troops
警察局 jǐngchájú police station or office
警察巡逻车 jǐngchá xúnluóchē radio car; radio patrol car; patrol car
警车 jǐngchē police car; police van
警笛 jǐngdí ❶ police whistle ❷ siren; alarm
警动 jǐngdòng ❶ attractive, out-of-the-ordinary manner ❷ alarm; disturb
警督 jǐngdū police supervisor (middle category of Chinese police officers):一级～ Police Supervisor, Class I
警服 jǐngfú police uniform
警告 jǐnggào ❶ remind; alert; put on one's guard:他～自己,以后要多加小心。He reminded himself to be more cautious in future. /他不顾大夫的～,又抽起烟来了。Throwing the doctor's advice to the winds, he started smoking again. ❷ warn; caution; admonish:我们～那些贩毒分子,莫要以身试法。We warn the drug traffickers not to run afoul of the law. ❸ warning (as a disciplinary measure):撤消～处分 withdraw (*or* rescind) a disciplinary warning /他受到严重～处分。He was given a serious warning.
警告机制 jǐnggào jīzhì 〈动物〉aposematic mechanism
警告信号 jǐnggào xìnhào 〈交通〉warning signal
警官 jǐngguān police officer:他是现役～,在武警部队干了三年了。He is a police officer on the active list and has served in the armed police for three years.
警棍 jǐnggùn ❶ policeman's baton; truncheon; billyclub ❷〈旧语〉policeman who abused his power to bully people
警号 jǐnghào ❶ warning signal; alarm:那是一口在抗战时期作为全村～用的大铁钟。That was the big iron bell which was used as the warning signal for the whole village during the War of Resistance Against Japanese Aggression. ❷ number-badge a policeman wears on his uniform
警徽 jǐnghuī police emblem:珍视～ treasure the police emblem
警监 jǐngjiān police commissioner (highest category of Chinese police officers):总～ General Police Commissioner /副总～ Deputy General Police Commissioner /三级～ Police Commissioner, Class III
警戒 jǐngjiè ❶ *also* "警诫" warn; admonish:我事先就～过他。I warned him in advance. ❷ be on the alert; guard; keep a close watch:采取～措施 take precautions /在门口布置～ post guards at the gate /行军～ protection on move /宿营～ protection at rest /战斗～ combat security
警戒部队 jǐngjiè bùduì outpost troops; security force; security detachment
警戒地带 jǐngjiè dìdài outpost area
警戒色 jǐngjièsè 〈动物〉warning coloration; aposematic coloration
警戒哨 jǐngjièshào outguard; picket guard
警戒水位 jǐngjiè shuǐwèi warning water level; warning line; warning stage
警戒线 jǐngjièxiàn cordon; security line; warning limit
警戒状态 jǐngjiè zhuàngtài state of alert
警句 jǐngjù aphorism; epigram; witty remark:名言～ famous sayings and pithy remarks /这本书里有许多～。There are many epigrams in this book.
警觉 jǐngjué ❶ vigilance; awareness; consciousness; alertness:政治～性 political alertness (*or* vigilance) /他很～,从不放过任何一个可疑的线索。He is always vigilant, never letting pass any doubtful clue. ❷ sound an alarm; warn against; awaken:用文学作为武器,以～世人。Literature is used as a weapon to awaken the people.
警力 jǐnglì police force; police power; guards:～不足 shortage of police
警铃 jǐnglíng alarm bell
警辟 jǐngpì (of speech, view, etc.) penetrating; incisive:评论～ incisive comments /～的见解 penetrating views
警切 jǐngqiè penetrating and to the point:～之言 trenchant remarks
警犬 jǐngquǎn police dog; patrol dog
警容 jǐngróng policeman's discipline, appearance and bearing
警绳 jǐngshéng police rope (used to bind criminals)
警士 jǐngshì police; policeman or policewoman; police officer; constable
警世 jǐngshì warn or admonish the world:～良言 wise counsel that admonishes the world
警司 jǐngsī police superintendent (lower category of Chinese police officers):二级～ Police Superintendent, Class II
警探 jǐngtàn police and detectives; police detective
警惕 jǐngtì be vigilant; be on guard; watch out; be on the alert:提高～ heighten our vigilance /放松～ relax vigilance /丧失～ drop (*or* lower) one's guard; be off one's guard /～出工伤事故 watch out for industrial accidents /～地监视可疑的人 keep a close and vigilant watch on a suspicious person /有何情况他都会通知我们的,他很～。If anything comes up, he will let us know. He has (*or* keeps) his ear to the ground. /特别警卫～着侵犯者。Special guards were on the qui vive for trespassers.
警惕性 jǐngtìxìng vigilance; alertness
警亭 jǐngtíng police kiosk or post
警卫 jǐngwèi ❶ guard with armed forces:担负～任务 be on guard duty /～室 guardroom /～员 bodyguard /～连 guards company /岗哨林立,～森严。Lookout posts are everywhere and the place is heavily guarded. ❷ guardsman; guard:门口站着两位～。Two guards were standing at the gate.
警卫秘书 jǐngwèi mìshū security secretary
警务 jǐngwù police affairs; police service

J

警务处处长 jǐngwùchù chùzhǎng (HK) Commissioner of Police

警悟 jǐngwù 〈书面〉❶ quick; alert; sagacious:性甚～ very quick-witted ❷ sound an alarm; alert; awaken:促其～ alert (*or* awake) sb.

警衔 jǐngxián police rank:他们有些人改为文职,有些人挂了～。Some of them have become civilian staff, while others have assumed police ranks.

警宪 jǐngxiàn 〈旧语〉police and military police

警械 jǐngxiè police apparatus or instruments (used in carrying out public duties)

警醒 jǐngxǐng ❶ be a light sleeper:我睡觉最～了。I'm a very light sleeper. ❷ *also* "警省" warn; caution; alert; awaken:鉴往知来,值得我们～。Past experience alerts us to future developments.

警讯 jǐngxùn *also* "警信" emergency news; emergency information

警语 jǐngyǔ aphorism; epigram

警员 jǐngyuán ❶ general term for (rank-and-file) police; constable:大批～赶赴现场。Many policemen were rushed to the scene of crime (*or* accident). ❷ police constable (rank and file of Chinese police):一级～ Police Constable, Class I /二级～ Police Constable, Class II

警枕 jǐngzhěn alarm pillow (made of a section of round log)

警钟 jǐngzhōng alarm bell; tocsin:～长鸣。The alarm bell keeps ringing. /这次事故给我们敲起了～,以后一定要更加注意交通安全。This accident has sounded the alarm. We must pay more attention to traffic security from now on.

警种 jǐngzhǒng police services

儆 jǐng warn; admonish:惩一～百 punish one to warn a hundred; make an example of sb. /以～效尤 warn anyone against committing the same mistake

儆戒 jǐngjiè warn people against making mistakes again; warn people to correct mistakes

儆省 jǐngxǐng warn; alert; awaken

景[1] jǐng ❶ view; sight; scene; landscape; scenery:夜～ night view (*or* scene) /山～ mountain scenery /雨～ rainy scene /盆～ potted landscape /奇～ wonderful view; extraordinary sight /情～ scene; sight; circumstances /秋～ autumn scenery /取～ find a view (to picture, paint, etc.) /写～ portray the scenery /全～ full view; panorama /远～ distant view /良辰美～ beautiful scene on a bright day ❷ situation; condition; circumstance:光～ circumstance; condition /晚～ one's circumstances in old age /前～ prospect; future /年～ year's harvest /远～规划 long-range plan /触～生情。The sight strikes a chord in one's heart. /好～不长。Good times do not last. ❸ scenery (of a play or film); setting:背～ background; backdrop /内～ indoor setting /外～ outdoor scene /实～ scene shot on location /吊～ drop scenery ❹ scene (of a play):第二幕第二～ Act II, Scene II ❺ (Jǐng) a surname

景[2] jǐng admire; esteem; revere; respect: *see* "～仰"; "～慕"

景德镇 Jǐngdézhèn Jingdezhen (in Jiangxi Province), famous for its porcelain

景点 jǐngdiǎn scenic spots:这条路线～较多,每年吸引着大批游客。There are numerous scenic spots along this route, so it attracts large crowds of tourists each year.

景观 jǐngguān ❶ landscape:自然～ natural landscape /草原～ pasture landscape /森林～ forest landscape /岩溶～ karst landscape ❷ sights worth seeing:人文～ sights of human interest (e.g. historical relics)

景教 Jǐngjiào Nestorianism

景况 jǐngkuàng situation; condition; circumstances:～富裕 in affluent circumstances /～正在逐步好转。The situation is taking a turn for the better. *or* Things are beginning to pick up.

景慕 jǐngmù 〈书面〉esteem; respect; revere; admire:受人～ be much looked up to; be held in respect /我怀着～的心情瞻仰中山陵。Cherishing a feeling of esteem, I paid my respects at the Sun Yat-sen Mausoleum.

景片 jǐngpiàn piece of (stage) scenery; flat

景颇族 Jǐngpōzú Jingpo nationality, living in Yunnan Province

景气 jǐngqì ❶ prosperity; boom; state of the economy:经济～ economic prosperity; state of the economy /经济不～ economic recession (*or* slump) /市场不～。The market is dull (*or* sluggish). ❷ landscape; scene:眼前呈现一片黄土高原的～。The landscape of a loess plateau unfolded before my eyes (*or* before me).

景区 jǐngqū scenic spot:开辟新～ open (up) new scenic spots

景色 jǐngsè scenery; sight; view; scene; landscape:～迷人 enchanting sight /初春的～ early spring scene /自然～ natural scenery /～如画的山村 picturesque mountain village /锦绣江南,到处是秀丽～。Attractive landscape is seen everywhere in the beautiful land south of the lower reaches of the Yangtze River.

景山 Jǐngshān Coal Hill in Beijing:～公园 Coal Hill Park

景深 jǐngshēn 〈摄影〉depth of field

景胜 jǐngshèng famous scenic spot:我站在桥头远眺西山～。Standing at the bridgehead I enjoyed a distant view of the beautiful Western Hills.

景泰 Jǐngtài Jingtai, title of the reign (1450-1456) of Zhu Qiyu (朱祁钰,1428-1457), 7th emperor of the Ming Dynasty, called reverently Ming Daizong (明代宗) after death

景泰蓝 jǐngtàilán cloisonné enamel; cloisonné

景天 jǐngtiān 〈植物〉red-spotted stonecrop (*Sedum erythrosticum*)

景物 jǐngwù scenery; scene; sight:这里的～引人入胜。The scenery here is alluring.

景象 jǐngxiàng scenery; sight; picture:一派繁华～ one vast panorama of prosperity /一派紧张忙碌的～ a scene of hustle and bustle /这里不再是当年荒凉萧瑟的～。The place is no longer the bleak and desolate sight it used to be. /那～早已变得一片模糊。That picture has long become blurred. *or* The scene has long since dimmed.

景仰 jǐngyǎng respect and admire; hold in deep esteem:～之情 feelings of respect and admiration /他的气节,令人～。His moral courage is indeed worthy of our esteem.

景遇 jǐngyù 〈书面〉situation; circumstances; one's lot:听说他这几年在国外的～不佳。I hear that he is not getting on very well abroad in recent years.

景致 jǐngzhì view; scenery; scene:这里的优美～令我们流连忘返。The scenery here was so lovely that we could hardly tear ourselves away from it. /步入后山,别有一番～。The scene is quite unique at the back of the mountain.

景状 jǐngzhuàng scene; sight; situation; circumstances

憬 jǐng 〈书面〉wake up to reality; come to see the truth

憬然 jǐngrán 〈书面〉become awake; awaken:～猛省 be suddenly awakened; come to realize all of a sudden /闻之～ be awakened (on) hearing it

憬悟 jǐngwù wake up to reality; come to see the truth; come to see one's error, etc.:这些事实使他有所～。These facts served to wake him up to reality.

璟 jǐng 〈书面〉lustre of jade

颈(頸) jǐng ❶ neck:引～受戮 crane one's neck (waiting) to be decapitated /长～鹿 giraffe ❷ anything shaped like the neck:子宫～ cervix (of womb) /曲～甑 retort /管～ tube neck /轴～ neck of shaft

see also gěng

颈动脉 jǐngdòngmài 〈生理〉common carotid artery; carotid artery; jugular:～淋巴结 jugular gland

颈静脉 jǐngjìngmài 〈生理〉jugular vein

颈肋 jǐnglèi 〈生理〉cervical rib

颈联 jǐnglián third antithetical couplet in a *lüshi* poem (the fifth and sixth lines) which asks for a matching of both sound and sense in the two lines, with the matching words in the same part of speech

颈淋巴结炎 jǐnglínbājiéyán 〈医学〉cervical adenitis

颈强直 jǐngqiángzhí 〈医学〉nuchal rigidity

颈缩 jǐngsuō 〈冶金〉necking; necking down

颈项 jǐngxiàng neck

颈椎 jǐngzhuī 〈生理〉cervical vertebra; vertebrae cervicales:～关节强硬〈医学〉cervical spondylosis

颈子 jǐngzi 〈方言〉neck

刭(剄) jǐng 〈书面〉cut the throat:自～〈书面〉cut one's

own throat; commit suicide

jìng

竟[1] jìng ❶ end; finish; complete: 黑暗终有～时。There will always be an end to darkness. ❷ from beginning to end; throughout; whole: ～夜无眠 lay awake the whole night (*or* throughout the night) ❸〈书面〉in the end; finally; eventually: 有志者事～成。Where there's a will there's a way.

竟[2] jìng 〈副词〉*used to indicate unexpectedness or surprise*: 都以为他一定不答应,谁知他～答应了。All had thought he would not agree, but actually he agreed. /雷雨天气,出门怎么～忘了带伞? How could you be so careless as to forget to take an umbrella with you in such stormy weather?

竟而 jìng'ér unexpectedly; to one's surprise; actually: 万没料到他～遭遇了不幸。To my great surprise, he met with misfortune (*or* an accident).

竟敢 jìnggǎn have the audacity; have the impertinence; dare: 你～讲这样的话? How dare you say such a thing! /他～和老人顶嘴。He had the impudence to talk back to his elders.

竟购 jìnggòu scramble to buy: 争相～ fall over each other to buy (sth.)

竟然 jìngrán 〈副词〉*used to indicate unexpectedness or surprise*: ～不顾事实 fly in the face of the facts /这任务～在一周内就完成了。To our surprise, the task was finished in only one week. /真可惜,他～失去这样一个绝好的机会。It is a pity that he should miss such a golden opportunity. /想不到这小小的厂子,～能生产出这样精密的仪器! Who would have thought that such a small factory could produce such precise instruments!

竟日 jìngrì throughout the day; all day long: ～流连不去 linger all day

竟至 jìngzhì go so far as to; go to the length of; have the impudence or effrontery to: 为了一点小事,两人～打起来了。The two went so far as to come to blows over a trifle.

竟自 jìngzì *see* "竟然"

境 jìng ❶ border; boundary: 国～ national boundary /迁移出～ emigrate /移居入～ immigrate /驱逐出～ deport /接～ border on /出～ leave the country /大兵压～。A massive enemy force is bearing down on the border. /入～问俗。On entering a country, inquire about its customs. *or* When in Rome, do as the Romans do. ❷ place; area; land; territory: 仙～ fairyland /渐入佳～ gradually enter a favourable or pleasant stage /身临其～ be personally on the scene /如入无人之～ like entering an unpeopled land — meeting no resistance at all /学无止～。Knowledge is infinite. *or* There is no limit to knowledge. ❸ condition; situation; circumstances: 困～ difficult position; predicament; sorry plight /在逆～中 in adverse circumstances; in adversity /在顺～中 in favourable circumstances /处～ situation one finds oneself in /心～ state of mind /家～ family financial condition /意～ artistic conception /事过～迁。The affair is over and the situation has changed. *or* A lot of water has flowed under the bridge.

境地 jìngdì ❶ condition; circumstances; plight: 处于贫困的～ be in straitened circumstances /处于这样尴尬的～,叫我说些什么好呢? Being in this embarrassing situation, what shall I say? /这家公司的～很糟。The company found itself in a predicament. /第三世界的贫困人民陷于水深火热的～。The impoverished peoples of the third world are in deep waters. ❷ *see* "境界❷"

境界 jìngjiè ❶ boundary: 两省以河为～。The river forms the boundary between the two provinces. ❷ extent reached; plane attained; state; realm: 达到崇高的思想～ attain a lofty realm of thought /开拓新的～ open up a new vista /他的演技已经达到出神入化的～。His performance has reached the acme of perfection.

境况 jìngkuàng condition; circumstances: ～好 well-to-do; well off; comfortably off /～大有改善。Conditions have significantly improved. *or* Things have looked up greatly.

境域 jìngyù ❶ condition; situation; circumstances ❷ area; domain; realm: 进入一个生平未曾涉足过的～ enter a realm one has never set foot on /此地绿草如茵,鸟语花香,别有～。This place is another world, with its carpet of green grass, singing birds and fragrant flowers.

境遇 jìngyù circumstances; one's lot: 悲惨～ miserable lot /晚年～不佳 wretched circumstances in one's twilight years /几十年坎坷艰辛的生活～,炼就了他坚忍不拔的性格。Decades of setbacks and hardships have tempered his indomitable will.

镜 jìng ❶ looking glass; mirror: 铜～ bronze mirror /明～ bright mirror /穿衣～ full-length mirror /哈哈～ distorting mirror /照～ look at oneself in the glass /破～重圆 broken mirror joined together — reunion of husband and wife after separation /波平如～。The lake is as smooth as a mirror. ❷ lens; glass; mirror: 墨～ *also* "太阳～" sunglasses /眼～ glasses; spectacles /花～ presbyopic lenses /凹～ concave mirror /凸～ convex mirror /茶～ spectacles made of citrine or yellow coloured glass /后视～ rearview mirror /望远～ telescope /放大～ magnifying glass; magnifier /显微～ microscope /潜望～ periscope /平光～ plain glass spectacles /分光～ spectroscope /反光～ reflector /聚光～ condensing lens; condenser /物～ objective lens /偏光～ polariscope /荧光～ fluorescope /内窥～ endoscope /接目～ eyepiece; ocular /腹腔～ peritoneoscope /滤色～ (colour) filter /折射～ refractor

镜报 Jìngbào (HK) *The Mirror Post*

镜花水月 jìnghuā-shuǐyuè flowers in a mirror or the moon in the water — illusion

镜框 jìngkuàng picture frame

镜煤 jìngméi 〈矿业〉vitrain

镜面 jìngmiàn mirror face; mirror plane: ～磨削 mirror finish; mirror grinding /～抛光 mirror polish /～探照灯 mirror projector

镜片 jìngpiàn lens

镜频 jìngpín 〈通信〉image frequency

镜台 jìngtái dressing table

镜铁 jìngtiě 〈冶金〉mirror iron; specular iron; specular cast iron; spiegeleisen

镜铁矿 jìngtiěkuàng 〈矿业〉specularite; specular iron ore

镜头 jìngtóu ❶ camera lens: 标准～ standard lens /远摄～ telephoto lens /可变焦距～ zoom lens /广角～ wide-angle lens /加膜～ coated lens /望远～ telescope lens /～遮光罩 lens hood ❷ shot: 几个记者在抢～。Several journalists are vying for the shot. *or* Several reporters are vying in taking pictures. ❸ scene; shot: 特技～ special effects shot; trick shot /特写～ close-up /伪装～ process shot /电影～ cinema scene /有几个～要重拍。Several cinema shots need to be taken again. *or* Several scenes must be re-shot.

镜匣 jìngxiá wooden case with a looking glass and other toilet articles; dressing case; toilet-box

镜箱 jìngxiāng ❶ (of a camera) dark room or chamber ❷ bathroom medicine cabinet whose door is faced with a mirror

镜像 jìngxiàng 〈通信〉image by inversion; mirror image: ～干扰 image interference /～阻抗 image impedance

镜鱼 jìngyú 〈动物〉butterfish; silvery pomfret

镜子 jìngzi ❶ mirror; looking glass ❷〈口语〉glasses; spectacles

竞(競) jìng ❶ compete; contest; contend; vie: 万类霜天～自由。Under freezing skies a million creatures freely contend. /百里江面,千帆～发。A thousand boats set sail on a long stretch of the river. ❷〈书面〉strong; powerful: 南风不～。The southerly wind is gentle.

竞渡 jìngdù ❶ boat race: 龙舟～ dragon-boat regatta; dragon-boat race ❷ swimming race: 游泳健儿～昆明湖。Swimmers are racing (*or* having a swimming meet) in Kunming Lake.

竞技 jìngjì sports; athletics: ～运动 athletic sports /～体育场 sports arena

竞技体操 jìngjì tǐcāo 〈体育〉gymnastics

竞技状态 jìngjì zhuàngtài form (of an athlete): ～良好 in good form (*or* shape); in top form /保持良好的～ maintain good form /～不好 in bad form (*or* shape); out of form; off one's game

竞赛 jìngsài contest; competition; emulation; race: 体育～ athletic contest; athletic competition /～规则 rules of a contest (*or* competition) /～制度 race system /～期 contest period; competition period /～理论 theory of games /～值 value of game /劳动～ labour emulation /军备～ arms race; armament race

竞相 jìngxiāng compete; vie: ～购买 vie in buying /～拆台 compete in pulling the rug from under sb. else's feet

竞销 jìngxiāo compete for the market：这种产品在国际市场上很有～能力。This product is highly competitive in the world market.
竞秀 jìngxiù compete for the beauty crown：群芳～。All the lovely and fragrant flowers are vying with each other for the beauty crown.
竞选 jìngxuǎn enter into an election contest; campaign for (office); stand for; run for：～总统 run for the presidency / ～伙伴 running mate / ～纲领 election programme / ～活动 electioneering; campaigning / ～运动 election campaign / 参加～ run in the election; stand for election / ～演说 election-rally speech; campaign speech / ～旅行 electioneering tour; campaign tour
竞选委员会 jìngxuǎn wěiyuánhuì election committee
竞艳 jìngyàn vie for beauty：百花～。All flowers vie for beauty in full bloom.
竞争 jìngzhēng compete; vie; contend：公开～ open competition / 自由～ free competition / 激烈的～ keen competition; fierce rivalry / ～商品 rival commodities / ～市场 competitive market / ～投资 competitive investment / ～者 vier; competitor; contender; rival / ～阶段 competitive stage / ～能力 competitive strength; competitive power / ～信息 competitive information / ～性工资 competitive wage / 这个工厂参与了国际市场的～。This factory is now competing in the world market. / 今年参加～奖杯的有多少队？How many teams are contending for the cup this year?
竞争机制 jìngzhēng jīzhì competitive mechanism
竞争价格 jìngzhēng jiàgé competitive price
竞争性 jìngzhēngxìng competitiveness：～贬值 competitive devaluation
竞逐 jìngzhú compete and pursue：互相～ compete with each other for (the prize, etc.) / 群雄～ rivalry among great men
竞走 jìngzǒu 〈体育〉(heel-and-toe) walking race：五公里～ five kilometre walking race / 公路～ highway walking race / ～运动员 walker / ～裁判员 walking judge / 长距离～运动员 long distance walker / ～鞋 walking shoes

净[1](淨)

jìng ❶ clean：干～ clean / 窗明几～ with bright windows and clean tables; bright and clean / 这孩子的脸没有洗～。The child's face hasn't been properly washed. ❷ wipe (sth.) clean：用湿布～一～黑板 wipe clean the blackboard with a wet cloth ❸ with nothing left; completely：用～ use up / 吃～ eat up / 烧～ burnt up / 会场上的人散～了。All those attending the meeting have left. / 他将老本儿赔～了。He has lost everything he had. / 把盆里的水倒～了。Empty the basin of its water. ❹ net; pure：～收入 net income / ～出口 net export / ～进口 net import / ～存货 net inventory / ～成本 pure cost ❺ nothing but; only; merely：书架～是科技书籍。There are nothing but science and technology books on the shelf. / 不能～管看书，还得活动活动。It's no good sitting there all day reading. You should stretch your legs from time to time. / ～顾说话，忘了时间。I have kept talking, forgetting all about time. / 他～爱开玩笑。He likes to crack jokes all the time.

净[2](淨)

jìng 〈戏曲〉"painted face", a character type in Beijing opera, etc.
净白 jìngbái pure white：～的牙齿 pure white teeth
净产值 jìngchǎnzhí net output value
净出口国 jìngchūkǒuguó 〈外贸〉net exporting country; net exporter：石油～ net exporter of oil
净吨位 jìngdūnwèi net tonnage
净额 jìng'é net amount
净高 jìnggāo 〈建筑〉clear height
净荷载 jìnghèzài net load
净化 jìnghuà purify; cleanse; clean：～污水 purify sewage water; sewage purification / ～城市空气 purify city air / ～器 purifier / ～塔 purifying column / ～语言 purify the language / 民族～ ethnic cleansing / ～车间 cleaning shop / ～工段 purification section / ～台 clean bench / 对影片作～处理 sanitize a film
净价 jìngjià net price
净街 jìngjiē close a street to traffic
净洁 jìngjié pure and clean; clean
净尽 jìngjìn completely; utterly：楼中的蟑螂消灭～。All the cockroaches in the building have been wiped out. / 这座山上的树木已被砍伐～。This mountain has been denuded of trees.
净角 jìngjué "painted face", a character type in Beijing opera, etc.
净空 jìngkōng ❶ (in navigation) distance between the water surface and the bridge above or the top of a cave; clearance; head room ❷ (in air service) clear airspace with no barrier around the airport ❸〈建筑〉headroom
净口 jìngkǒu purify the language in folk art performance
净跨 jìngkuà 〈建筑〉clear span
净宽 jìngkuān clear width
净亏 jìngkuī net loss; net deficit
净理 jìnglǐ 〈宗教〉ablution
净利 jìnglì net profit (after taxes)：～对净值的比率 ratio of net profit to net worth
净流动资产 jìngliúdòng zīchǎn 〈经济〉net current assets
净马力 jìngmǎlì 〈机械〉net horse power
净面 jìngmiàn wash one's face：清水～ wash one's face with water
净身 jìngshēn (of a man) be castrated
净室 jìngshì clean and tidy house or room (usu. a nun's or monk's)
净手 jìngshǒu ❶〈方言〉clean one's hands ❷〈婉词〉wash one's hands; relieve oneself
净水厂 jìngshuǐchǎng water treatment plant
净素 jìngsù plain and simple：衣着～ be plainly dressed
净桶 jìngtǒng 〈婉词〉chamber pot; nightstool; latrine bucket; commode
净土 jìngtǔ ❶〈佛教〉*Sukhavati*; Pure Land; Paradise of the West ❷ any clean, unpolluted place：这个地区污染严重，难见一方～。The area is so seriously polluted that not a single inch of clean land can be found.
净土经 Jìngtǔjīng 〈佛教〉*Sukhavati-vyuha-sutra*
净土宗 Jìngtǔzōng 〈佛教〉Pure Land Sect
净销价法 jìngxiāojiàfǎ 〈商业〉net selling price method
净效率 jìngxiàolǜ 〈机械〉net efficiency
净心 jìngxīn ❶ free from care：过几天～的日子 free oneself from care for several days ❷ have a peaceful and quiet mind; feel completely at ease：难得有～。It is difficult to have one's mind entirely at peace with itself.
净意 jìngyì 〈方言〉❶ on purpose; by design：别～找事儿。Don't pick a quarrel. ❷ specially; purposely：我是～来请他的。I have come specially to invite him.
净余 jìngyú remainder; surplus：收支相抵，～二十五元。After a balance of revenue and expenditure, there is a surplus of twenty-five *yuan*. / 除去旅费外，～一百元。The balance on hand is one hundred *yuan* after all travelling expenses are deducted.
净院 jìngyuàn 〈旧语〉temple
净增 jìngzēng net increase; net growth
净值 jìngzhí net worth; net value：出口～ net export value / 进口～ net import value
净重 jìngzhòng net weight：～条件 net weight term / ～货运密度 net-ton-kilometres per kilometre of line / 这盒蘑菇罐头～350克。This tin of mushrooms has a net weight of three hundred and fifty grams.
净赚 jìngzhuàn net earnings; net profit

静

jìng ❶ still; calm; motionless：～待时机 lie low and bide one's time ❷ silent; quiet; noiseless：大家谁也不说话，～了好大一阵。It was quiet for quite some time, for no one spoke. / 戏散了，人走光了，厅里～～的。The hall was silent after everyone left at the end of the play. / 他应该～下来思考这个问题。He should calm (*or* cool) down and think over the matter. ❸ calm; quieten：请大家～一～。Please be quiet. ❹ (Jìng) a surname
静鞭 jìngbiān 〈旧语〉whistling whip carried by an imperial guard of honour
静场 jìngchǎng ❶ spectators leaving the cinema or theatre after the film or play ends ❷ silent scene (usu. referring to a short silent scene on the stage during a theatrical performance)
静磁场 jìngcíchǎng 〈物理〉magnetostatic field; static-magnetic field
静等离子体 jìngděnglízǐtǐ 〈物理〉quiescent plasma
静电 jìngdiàn 〈物理〉static electricity; static：～除尘器 electrostatic precipitator / ～纺纱 electrostatic spinning / ～加速器 electrostatic accelerator / ～喷漆 electrostatic paint spraying

静电场 jìngdiànchǎng electrostatic field
静电感应 jìngdiàn gǎnyìng electrostatic induction
静电荷 jìngdiànhè electrostatic charge
静电计 jìngdiànjì electrometer
静电扫描 jìngdiàn sǎomiáo electrostatic scanning
静电学 jìngdiànxué electrostatics
静电印刷 jìngdiàn yìnshuā xerography; electrostatic copying or printing
静观 jìngguān observe calmly:～默察 observe and study things with composure /～情势 take soundings /～自得。Everything comes to him who waits.
静荷载 jìnghèzài 〈建筑〉dead load
静候 jìnghòu quietly await:～佳音 quietly awaiting the good news
静弧 jìnghú 〈物理〉quiet arc
静寂 jìngjì quiet; silent:～的山谷 still mountain valley /清晨江面～。The river is quiet in the early morning.
静街 jìngjiē ❶ close the streets to traffic:城里已经～,显得特别冷清。As the streets are closed to traffic, the city appeared to be deserted. ❷ quiet street
静力学 jìnglìxué 〈物理〉statics:气体～ aerostatics
静脉 jìngmài 〈生理〉vein:～输血法 venous transfusion /～输液法 phleboclysis; venous transfusion
静脉点滴 jìngmài diǎndī 〈医学〉intravenous drip
静脉瘤 jìngmàiliú 〈医学〉phlebangioma
静脉曲张 jìngmài qūzhāng 〈医学〉varix; varicosity
静脉炎 jìngmàiyán 〈医学〉phlebitis
静脉注射 jìngmài zhùshè 〈医学〉intravenous injection
静美 jìngměi gentle beauty:这位欧洲女士颇有一点东方妇女的～。The European lady definitely had something of the gentle beauty of oriental women.
静谧 jìngmì 〈书面〉quiet; calm; still; tranquil:～的月夜 quiet moonlit night /乡间的～生活 tranquil life in the country /海滨的夏夜是～的。Summer evening on the seashore is calm and tranquil.
静摩擦 jìngmócā static friction
静摩擦力 jìngmócālì 〈物理〉static friction force; stiction
静默 jìngmò ❶ become silent:屋子里一阵难堪的～。Another spell of embarrassing silence fell upon the room. /礼堂里一片～。It was all quiet in the auditorium. ❷ mourn in silence; observe silence:～致哀三分钟 observe three minutes' silence /人们肃立在他的遗体前,～致哀。People stood in front of his remains, mourning in silence.
静穆 jìngmù solemn and quiet:灵堂里一片～。It was all solemn and quiet in the mourning hall.
静僻 jìngpì secluded; lonely:～的小路 secluded path /这村庄很～。This is a quiet and out-of-the-way village.
静平衡 jìngpínghéng 〈物理〉static balance; static equilibrium
静悄悄 jìngqiāoqiāo very quiet:四处～,没有一个人影。It was quiet all round, and not even a soul could be seen.
静若处女,动若脱兔 jìng ruò chǔnǚ, dòng ruò tuōtù as quiet as a maiden when at rest and as nimble as an escaping hare when in action; demure as a maiden and quick as a rabbit; deliberate in counsel, prompt in action
静肃 jìngsù solemn silence:～前进 advance in solemn silence
静态 jìngtài ❶ static state:～电阻 static resistance /～报表 static statement /～比率 static ratio /～平衡 static equilibrium /～特性 static characteristic /～分配 static allocation /～电流 static current /～工作点 static working point /～计算 static computation /～控制 static control /～模型 static model /～目标 static object ❷ (observe and study) from the static point of view; static:～研究 study of static state /～分析 static analysis
静听 jìngtīng listen attentively and quietly:屏息～ listen with bated breath
静物 jìngwù still life:～写生 paint a still life
静物画 jìngwùhuà still-life drawing; still life
静物摄影 jìngwù shèyǐng still-life photography
静息 jìngxī still; quiet; motionless:树上的鸟儿都～了。Birds on the trees are all quiet.
静心 jìngxīn ease of mind; peace of mind:～读书 be engrossed in study
静压力 jìngyālì static pressure
静养 jìngyǎng rest quietly to recuperate; convalesce:～几个月 have a rest-cure of a few months /病人需要～康复。The patient needs rest in quietude to recuperate. /我身体不适,在家～。I have been convalescing at home since I fell ill.
静幽幽 jìngyōuyōu quiet; calm; silent:深夜马路上～的,什么响声都没有。In the still of the night, it was all quiet in the street, without so much as a single sound.
静园 jìngyuán close a park (according to scheduled time):～后,不准在园内逗留。No one is allowed to stay in the park after closing time.
静噪 jìngzào clipping or muting of noise:～器 noise clipper; noise killer; noise limiter; damper
静止 jìngzhǐ static; motionless; at a standstill:天地间不存在绝对～的事物。Nothing is absolutely at rest in this world. /不要～地孤立地看待事物。Don't view things as static and isolated. /直到傍晚,风才完全～下来。The wind didn't subside till dusk.
静止锋 jìngzhǐfēng 〈气象〉stationary front
静止能量 jìngzhǐ néngliàng 〈物理〉rest energy
静止质量 jìngzhǐ zhìliàng 〈物理〉rest mass
静坐 jìngzuò ❶ sit quietly; sit still, esp. as a form of therapy:他心里十分不安,哪里～得下来。He was so worried that he could hardly sit still. ❷ sit down; sit in:～罢工 sit-down (strike) /～示威 sit-in (demonstration); sit-down (protest)

靖 jìng ❶ peace; tranquillity:安～ peace and tranquillity /宁～ orderly and tranquil ❷ pacify; suppress:～边 pacify the border regions /平～ suppress a rebellion and stabilize the situation /绥～政策 policy of appeasement ❸ (Jìng) a surname
靖国 jìngguó stabilize the country
靖国神社 Jìngguó Shénshè (Japan) *Yasukuni* Shrine; Japanese shrine for the war-dead built in Tokyo in 1869, including war criminals of WWII:～法案 *Yasukuni* Shrine Bill /参拜～ pay homage to *Yasukuni Jinja*
靖康 Jìngkāng Jingkang, title of the reign (1126-1127) of Zhao Huan (赵桓), 9th emperor of the North Song Dynasty, entitled Song Qinzong (宋钦宗) after death
靖康之变 Jìngkāng Zhī Biàn Catastrophe of Jingkang, when the Jin (金) army marched south in 1126-1127 (year of Jingkang), captured the eastern capital of Song (东京, present Kaifeng), and took both the emperor Qinzong and his father Huizong (徽宗) prisoner, thus putting an end to the Northern Song Dynasty
靖乱 jìngluàn put down a rebellion
靖乱之役 Jìngluàn Zhī Yì Campaign to Restore Order, 1399-1402, when Zhu Di (朱棣), the prince of Yan marched south with his army from Beiping (now Beijing), defeated the emperor Huìdì (惠帝), made himself emperor, and removed the capital of the Ming Dynasty to Beijing
靖卫团 jìngwèituán local armed force organized by landlords and despotic gentry during the Second Revolutionary Civil War (1927-1937)

靓 jìng 〈书面〉decorate; make up:～衣 beautiful dress; beautiful clothing
see also liàng
靓妆 jìngzhuāng 〈书面〉beautiful adornments:丽服～ beautiful clothing and adornments

婧 jìng 〈书面〉talented woman

敬 jìng ❶ respect; honour; esteem; revere:尊～ respect; esteem; honour /致～ pay one's respects; salute /可～ respectable; venerable /肃然起～ be filled with deep veneration /崇～ esteem; venerate; revere /相～如宾 (of man and wife) treat each other with respect ❷ respectfully; reverently:～请光临 request the honour of your presence /～请斧正 please make whatever corrections you like /～请指教 humbly request your advice /失～ sorry I didn't recognize you; sorry ❸ offer politely:～茶 serve tea /回～ return a compliment /孝～ present gifts to one's elders or superiors ❹ (Jìng) a surname
敬爱 jìng'ài respect and love:～的老师 respected and beloved teacher; beloved teacher /人们～他一生做好事。He is held in high esteem for the good deeds he has done all his life.
敬辞 jìngcí term of respect; polite expression
敬而远之 jìng'éryuǎnzhī stay at a respectful distance from (sb.);

hold at arm's length; give (sb. or sth.) a wide berth:不明他们的底细,我想最好是～。Not knowing what they were, I thought I had better keep a distance from them.

敬奉 jìngfèng ❶ piously worship ❷ offer respectfully; present politely:～挂毯一幅,以表谢忱。I'm respectfully offering you a piece of tapestry as a token of my gratitude.

敬服 jìngfú esteem and admire:他为人正直,技术精湛,大家十分～。People all esteem and admire him very much for his rectitude and superb craftsmanship.

敬告 jìnggào 〈敬词〉inform; notify:～读者 notice to readers

敬鬼神而远之 jìng guǐshén ér yuǎn zhī respect spiritual beings but keep them at a distance; keep a person at arm's length (as if he was a deity or ghost)

敬贺 jìnghè 〈敬词〉congratulate (sb. on sth.); offer congratulations

敬候 jìnghòu ❶〈敬词〉await or wait respectfully:～回复 wait to hear from sb. ❷ greet (sb.) respectfully; pay one's homage (to sb.):～起居 inquire after sb.'s health with respect

敬酒 jìngjiǔ propose a toast; toast:宴会上,主人起立～。At the banquet, the host stood up and proposed a toast.

敬酒不吃吃罚酒 jìngjiǔ bù chī chī fájiǔ 〈俗语〉refuse a toast only to drink a forfeit — submit to sb.'s pressure after first turning down his request; be constrained to do what one at first declined:干脆还是痛痛快快地答应了吧,免得～。It's better to agree right away so as to avoid being forced later to do it against one's will.

敬老爱幼 jìnglǎo-àiyòu respect the aged and cherish the young:～是公民的义务。It is the duty of every citizen to show respect to the aged and love for the young.

敬老院 jìnglǎoyuàn home of respect for the aged; old folk's home:约有二百个各种类型的～ about 200 homes of different kinds for the aged

敬老尊贤 jìnglǎo-zūnxián respect the elderly and the virtuous:这里有～的好风气。It's a fine practice here to respect the elderly and honour the virtuous.

敬礼 jìnglǐ ❶ give a salute; salute; send greetings:向老师～ give a salute to the teacher /举手～ raise one's hand to salute /举枪～ lift a rifle to salute /鸣炮～ fire a salute ❷ *used at the end of a letter*:此致～ with high respect; with best wishes

敬慕 jìngmù respect and admire:您一直是我～的师长。You have always been my respected and admired teacher.

敬佩 jìngpèi esteem; admire:我心里充满了对他的～。My heart brims with admiration for him. /我对他的为人,一向是很～的。I always hold him in high esteem for his integrity.

敬启者 jìngqǐzhě 〈旧语〉(used at the beginning of a letter) I beg to inform you

敬若神明 jìngruò-shénmíng *also* "奉若神明" fèngruò-shénmíng worship (sb.) as deity; worship:在上级面前他表现出一副～的样子。He put on a look of pious deference in the presence of his superiors.

敬上 jìngshàng (used at the end of a letter after one's signature) truly yours; yours truly

敬颂 jìngsòng 〈敬词〉earnestly wish:～安康。Wish you good health.

敬挽 jìngwǎn (used in inscribing an elegiac couplet, a floral wreath, etc.) with deep condolences from sb.:张老先生千古。某某～。Eternal repose to venerable Mr. Zhang! With deep condolences from So-and-so.

敬畏 jìngwèi hold in awe and veneration; revere:同僚和部属都～他。He is much revered by his colleagues and subordinates. /她对父亲心存～。She always stood in awe of her father.

敬贤礼士 jìngxián-lǐshì show respect to the virtuous and courtesy to the scholarly

敬献 jìngxiàn 〈敬词〉present politely; offer respectfully:～鲜花 present fresh flowers

敬香 jìngxiāng piously burn joss sticks before the Buddha

敬谢不敏 jìngxiè-bùmǐn 〈套语〉beg to be excused; regret being unable to comply with your request:近日身体不适,对他们的请托只好～。Feeling indisposed lately, I have to turn down their request and beg to be excused.

敬信 jìngxìn respect and trust

敬仰 jìngyǎng revere; venerate:深受人民爱戴和～的伟大政治家 great statesman who commands deep love and reverence among the people /我们院长是位受人～的人。Our principal is a man whom everyone looks up to.

敬养 jìngyǎng respect and support:～老人 respect and provide for aged people

敬业 jìngyè dedicate oneself to work or study:～精神 professional dedication; professional ethics

敬意 jìngyì respect; tribute:对秘书长先生卓有成效的工作表示～ pay sincere tribute to the secretary-general for the outstanding work he has done /薄酒一杯,略表～。I propose a toast to express my respect. /顺致最崇高的～。〈外交〉I avail myself of this opportunity to renew to you the assurances of my highest consideration.

敬语 jìngyǔ words spoken out of respect or courtesy; respectful remarks

敬赠 jìngzèng respectfully presented by:作者～ with the author's compliments /出版社～ with the publisher's compliments

敬重 jìngzhòng deeply respect; revere; esteem; honour:为大家所～ be revered by all /相互～ honour each other /大家都十分～这位老教师。We all have great respect for the senior teacher. /我很～他。He stands high in my esteem.

敬祝 jìngzhù 〈敬词〉sincerely wish:～身体健康。Wish you good health.

倞 jìng 〈书面〉strong

see also liàng

痉(痙) jìng

痉病 jìngbìng 〈中医〉febrile disease with symptoms such as convulsions, opisthotonos, trismus, etc.

痉挛 jìngluán convulsion; spasm; fit:食管～ spasm of the esophagus; esophagospasm /胃～ spasm of the stomach /腓肠肌～ spasm of musculus gastrocnemius /他患羊癫疯病,发病时～不止。He suffers from epilepsy, and is convulsed with cramps when he has a relapse.

痉跳病 jìngtiàobìng 〈医学〉saltatory spasm; dancing spasm

痉笑 jìngxiào 〈医学〉risus sardonicus; cynic spasm; canine spasm

痉语 jìngyǔ 〈医学〉logoklony; logospasm

径(徑、❶❷❸逕) jìng

❶ footpath; path; trail; track:路～ route; way /山～ mountain track /曲～通幽。A winding path led to a secluded spot. ❷ way; road; means:门～ access; key; way /途～ way; channel /捷～ easy way; shortcut /独辟蹊～ open a new path for oneself ❸〈副词〉directly; straight; straightaway:～行处理 dispose of sth. directly; handle sth. straightaway /取道武汉～回广州 go straight back to Guangzhou via Wuhan /来稿请～寄编辑部,不要寄给个人。Please send contributions to the editorial department instead of any individual. ❹ (short for 直径) diameter:半～ radius /口～ bore; calibre /小口～手枪 small-bore pistol

径道 jìngdào 〈书面〉footpath; track; path; trail

径迹 jìngjì 〈物理〉track:蜕变～ decay track /～起点 track origin

径流 jìngliú 〈水利〉runoff:地表～ surface runoff /地下～ groundwater runoff /～调节 runoff regulation

径情直遂 jìngqíng-zhísuì easily win what one desires; be as smooth as one would wish:事情的发展难得有～的时候。Rarely is the course of things as direct and smooth as one would wish.

径赛 jìngsài 〈体育〉track:～项目 track event /～选手 track sportsman; track athlete /～检录员 clerk of course

径庭 jìngtíng 〈书面〉quite different; very unlike:大相～ entirely different; poles apart

径向 jìngxiàng 〈物理〉radial:～间隙 radial clearance /～轴承 radial bearing

径行 jìngxíng (do sth.) without consulting others; (do sth.) on one's own:这笔贷款,厂方不得～处置。The factory is not authorized to deal with the loan itself.

径直 jìngzhí straight; directly; straightaway:～向学校走去 make straight for the school; go rightaway to the school /你可以～飞广州。You can fly nonstop to Guangzhou. /你～去办吧,不必再商量了。You may go ahead with it without further consultation.

径自 jìngzì 〈副词〉without leave; without consulting anyone:他没打招呼,～走了。He went away without so much as a by-your-leave. /下架的复本书,图书馆可～处理。The library could dispose of the duplicate copies that were taken off the shelves.

胫(脛) jìng

shin:不～而走 get round fast; spread like

J

wildfire; sell like hot cakes
胫腓骨 jìngféigǔ 〈生理〉tibiofibula
胫骨 jìnggǔ 〈生理〉shin bone; tibia
胫骨肌 jìnggǔjī 〈生理〉tibialis

劲(勁) jìng strong; vigorous; powerful; sturdy: 强～ powerful; robust /遒～ stalwart; vigorous /刚～ bold and vigorous; sturdy /苍～ old and strong
see also jìn
劲拔 jìngbá 〈书面〉powerful; tall and straight: ～的苍松 tall sturdy pine (tree)
劲草 jìngcǎo strong grass — loyal and virtuous person in face of danger and hardship: 疾风知～。The force of the wind tests the strength of the grass — strength of character is tested in time of adversity.
劲吹 jìngchuī (of the wind) blow fiercely: 北风～。The northern wind is blowing hard.
劲敌 jìngdí formidable adversary; strong opponent or foe: 遇到了～ meet a strong rival
劲风 jìngfēng strong wind
劲悍 jìnghàn intrepid; valiant; dauntless: ～之卒 valiant soldiers
劲急 jìngjí *also* "劲疾" strong and swift: 平原的风夜晚更为～。The evening wind blew even harder and swifter over the plains.
劲健 jìngjiàn strong and energetic; strong and forceful: 笔力～ vigorous calligraphy /一片绚丽的红花～地挺立在原野中。A stretch of gorgeous red flowers are standing unbent in the wilderness.
劲烈 jìngliè strong; forceful: 海风～ strong sea wind
劲旅 jìnglǚ crack troops; strong contingent: 陆军～ crack army troops /这个足球队是南美的一支～。This football team is one of the strongest in South America.
劲峭 jìngqiào strong and sharp: ～的西北风 strong and piercing northwest wind
劲射 jìngshè (in football, etc.) forceful or powerful shot: 他一脚～破门。He sent the ball into the goal with a powerful shot.
劲升 jìngshēng ❶ (of rocket, etc.) rise with a powerful thrust ❷ quick rise in one's position
劲挺 jìngtǐng powerful and straight; tall and majestic: 秀竹～。The bamboo is tall and straight.
劲秀 jìngxiù strong and beautiful; vigorous and graceful: 字迹～ vigorous and graceful hand /～的古松 sturdy and beautiful old pine
劲直 jìngzhí 〈书面〉staunch and honest
劲卒 jìngzú 〈书面〉crack troops; valiant soldiers: 良将～ good commanders and valiant soldiers

弪(弳) jìng *also* "弧度" húdù 〈数学〉radian

经(經) jìng 〈纺织〉warping
see also jīng
经纱 jìngshā warp yarn; make yarn into warp
see also jīngshā

J

jiōng

扃 jiōng 〈书面〉❶ bolt, hook, or bar for fastening a door from outside ❷ door; door leaf: 柴～ door made of firewood ❸ shut a door: ～户 shut the gate

坰 jiōng 〈书面〉open country; outermost suburb

駉 jiōng 〈书面〉❶ (of horses) stout and strong ❷ fine steed

jiǒng

窘 jiǒng ❶ in straitened circumstances; short of money; hard up: 手头～ be hard up; be short of money /他家里很～。His family is in financial straits. ❷ awkward; embarrassed; ill at ease: 非常～ greatly embarrassed /他对问题回答不上来，觉得很～。He felt rather awkward for not being able to answer the question. ❸ embarrass; upset; disconcert: 用尖刻话去～某人 embarrass sb. with scathing remarks /他可把你～住了。He's got you there!
窘促 jiǒngcù 〈书面〉❶ poverty-stricken; in dire straits ❷ embarrassed; hard pressed
窘乏 jiǒngfá be in straitened circumstances; be hard up: 手中～ be short of money; be hard up
窘急 jiǒngjí poverty-stricken; impoverished: 生活～ live in dire poverty
窘境 jiǒngjìng awkward situation; predicament; plight: 处于～ be in a sorry plight /陷于～ be landed in an awkward predicament /摆脱～ free oneself from a predicament; get out of difficulties
窘苦 jiǒngkǔ poverty-stricken; poor and wretched
窘况 jiǒngkuàng predicament; distress: 我已陷入身无分文的～。I have been reduced to utter penury.
窘困 jiǒngkùn embarrassed; awkward; in a difficult position: ～潦倒 miserably poor and frustrated; down and out
窘迫 jiǒngpò ❶ poverty-stricken; very poor: 他家境～。He is in straitened circumstances (*or* unable to make both ends meet). /我眼下的日子十分～。I am now in an economic straight jacket. ❷ hard pressed; embarrassed; in a predicament: 他的处境越来越～了。He found himself increasingly pressed into a corner. /多亏他把我从受人奚落的～中解救了出来。Luckily he got me out of the fix of being taunted.
窘态 jiǒngtài embarrassed look: 露出一副～ show embarrassment; look embarrassed
窘相 jiǒngxiàng embarrassed look: 他显出了～。He looked ill at ease.

炅 jiǒng 〈书面〉❶ sunlight ❷ bright
see also Guì

煛 jiǒng 〈书面〉sunlight

颎 jiǒng 〈书面〉firelight

冋 jiǒng 〈书面〉❶ light ❷ bright: ～～秋月 bright autumn moon

泂 jiǒng 〈书面〉❶ distant; far away ❷ (of water) deep and wide

炯 jiǒng bright; shining
炯戒 jiǒngjiè *also* "炯诫" 〈书面〉apparent warning; obvious object lesson: 着记大过一次，以昭～。It is decided to record a serious demerit as a warning.
炯炯 jiǒngjiǒng 〈书面〉(of eyes) bright; shining: 目光～ sparkling eyes; piercing eyes /两只眼睛～发亮 two bright and shining eyes
炯炯有神 jiǒngjiǒng-yǒushén (of eyes) bright and piercing: 我面前站着一个胸厚肩阔的青年，双目～。Standing before me was a youth of bulky build who had a pair of gleaming and penetrating eyes.
炯然 jiǒngrán ❶ clear; evident: ～不惑 clear and without doubt ❷ bright; shining: 珠翠～ shiny pearls and jade /目光～ sparkling eyes; piercing eyes

迥 jiǒng 〈书面〉❶ remote; far away: 山高路～ high mountains and long road ❷ widely different: ～若两人 look like a different person
迥别 jiǒngbié greatly different: 新城与旧城～。The new city is vastly different from the old.
迥乎 jiǒnghu widely different: 二者～不同。The two are entirely different.
迥然 jiǒngrán far apart; widely different: 目前的国际形势和过去～有别。The international situation today is a far cry from that of the past.
迥然不同 jiǒngrán-bùtóng utterly different; not in the least alike; poles apart: 这两幢大楼风格～。The two buildings are diametrically opposed to each other in architectural style.
迥殊 jiǒngshū 〈书面〉utterly different
迥异 jiǒngyì widely different: 他们二人性情～。The two people are poles apart in temperament.

絅(褧) jiǒng 〈书面〉unlined dustcoat

jiū

究 jiū ❶ study carefully; probe into; investigate: 研～ study; research /查～ investigate and ascertain /穷～ make a thorough inquiry; probe into /追根～底 get to the root (*or* bottom) of the matter /未便深～其事 not in a position to go deeply into the matter /追～责任 investigate a matter to find out who is responsible ❷〈书面〉actually; really; after all: ～非长远之计。After all, this is not a permanent solution. /～属谁的责任? Who should actually be held responsible for all this? /气势汹汹, ～欲何为? What is he really after by striking such a threatening pose?

究办 jiūbàn investigate and deal with: 此案必须依法～。The case should be investigated and dealt with according to law.

究根儿 jiūgēnr 〈口语〉get to the bottom (of sth.); trace (sth.) to its very source; the whys and wherefores: 这事已经了结, 你不必～了。The case is closed. You don't have to get to the bottom of it.

究诘 jiūjié 〈书面〉try to get to the heart of the matter: 不可～ unfathomable /实际情况如何, 难以～。It is difficult to find out what really happened.

究竟 jiūjìng ❶ outcome; truth; whole story: 我想知道个～。I want to know the whole story. *or* I want to know the whole truth. /他们走到门外看个～。They went out of the house to see what had actually happened. ❷ (used in questions for emphasis) actually; exactly: ～是谁说了算? Who exactly has the final say? /你又是这么躲躲闪闪的, 你～同意不同意? You are hedging again. Do you agree or do you not? /今天下午～谁主持会议? Who is actually going to chair the meeting this afternoon? /你大吵大闹～是干什么? What the hell are you howling about? *or* What on earth do you hope to accomplish by making such a fuss? ❸ after all; in the final analysis: 他们～是亲兄弟。After all, they are brothers. /大家不晓得将来～怎么样。Nobody knows what will actually happen. /谎言～不能掩盖事实。In the final analysis, lies cannot cover up the truth.

究问 jiūwèn probe into; investigate thoroughly; cross-examine; interrogate: 我不便～他, 只有把话题另绕一个圈子。I was not in a position to interrogate him, so I talked in a roundabout way.

究细儿 jiūxìr 〈方言〉study in detail; thoroughly investigate: 这事儿大家不过随便说说, 你别～。People are talking about it casually. Don't take it too seriously.

究真儿 jiūzhēnr 〈方言〉study seriously; examine earnestly: 要明了作者的用意, 对于故事情节不一定细～。To find out the author's intention it is by no means necessary to make a detailed study of the plot of his story.

勼 jiū 〈书面〉gather; assemble

鸠 jiū turtledove: 斑～ turtledove /雉～ turtledove /海～ guillemot /绿～ green pigeon

鸠合 jiūhé *see* "纠合" jiūhé

鸠集 jiūjí *see* "纠集" jiūjí

鸠摩罗什 Jiūmóluóshí Kumarajiva (344-413), Indian Buddhist monk born in West Territories (西域, now Xinjiang) and translator of many Buddhist texts into Chinese

鸠山一郎 Jiūshānyīláng Hatoyama Ichiro (1883-1959), Japanese Prime Minister (1954-1956)

鸠形鹄面 jiūxíng-húmiàn haggard; gaunt and emaciated; skin and bones; like a scarecrow: 这些人个个衣不蔽体, 饿得～。These people are in rags and are all skin and bones from starvation.

鸠占鹊巢 jiūzhàn-quècháo *also* "鹊巢鸠占" the turtle-dove occupies the magpie's nest — seize another person's home, etc. for one's own use

阄(鬮) jiū lot: 我们来抓～儿, 抓着的便去做饭。Let's draw lots to decide who's going to prepare the meal.

樛 jiū 〈书面〉(of trees) bend down

鬏 jiū (of hair) bun; knot; chignon: 她把头发梳成了一个～。She wears her hair in a bun.

揪 jiū ❶ hold tight; grab; seize: ～住不放 hold in a tight grip /～住流氓的领子 seize a hooligan by the collar /～头发 grab one's hair /～住绳子往上爬 hold the rope tight and climb up /孩子～着我的衣服, 跟在我身后。The child followed me, gripping the back of my coat. ❷ pull; tug; drag: 把线头～出来 grasp a piece of thread and draw it out /把他～过来。Drag him over.

揪辫子 jiū biànzi *also* "抓辫子" zhuā biànzi seize sb.'s pigtail — seize upon sb.'s faults; capitalize on somebody's weak point: 揪住辫子不放 grasp sb.'s queue and not let go — use sb.'s shortcomings as a handle against him

揪出 jiūchū uncover; ferret out: 公共汽车上～一个小偷。A pickpocket was caught in the bus.

揪揪 jiūjiu 〈方言〉❶ not smooth; have folds, etc.: 你这衣服怎么老～着呀? How come your clothes are always wrinkled? ❷ have a heavy heart: 那件事使他的心一直～着。He felt very upset over the matter.

揪痧 jiūshā 〈中医〉folk treatment for sunstroke or other febrile diseases by repeatedly pinching the patient's neck, back, etc., to achieve congestion and relieve fever

揪心 jiūxīn 〈方言〉anxious; troubled; worried: 这孩子太不听话, 多叫人～。The child is very wilful. How worrisome he is! /母亲一想起父亲的生意来就～。Whenever mother thinks of father's business, she can't help feeling a gnawing worry.

啾 jiū

啾唧 jiūjī 〈象声〉(as of insects and small birds) chirp

啾啾 jiūjiū 〈象声〉chirp; twitter: 林中小鸟～。Birds are chirping in the woods.

啾啁 jiūzhōu 〈书面〉〈象声〉chirp

赳 jiū

赳赳 jiūjiū valiant; gallant: 雄～, 气昂昂 gallant and high-spirited /～武夫, 为国干城。Men of valour (*or* Soldiers of dauntless courage) are pillars of the state.

纠[1] jiū entangle; involve: *see* "～缠"

纠[2] jiū band together; assemble: 收离～散 assemble stragglers and disbanded soldiers

纠[3] jiū ❶〈书面〉inform against (sb.); supervise: ～举要犯 denounce an arch criminal (to the authorities) ❷ correct; rectify; right: ～缪绳违 rectify mistakes and punish law breakers according to law /有错必～。Mistakes once found must be corrected.

纠察 jiūchá ❶ maintain order at a public gathering ❷ picket: 担任～ act as a picket; be on the picket line

纠察队 jiūcháduì pickets

纠察线 jiūcháxiàn picket line

纠缠 jiūchán ❶ get entangled; get involved; be in a tangle: ～纷乱 tangled skein /这个问题很微妙, 你千万不要～进去。The matter is very delicate. Take care not to get involved. /要尽量避免在枝节问题上～不休。Try your best to avoid quibbling over minor issues. ❷ trouble; worry; pester: 我还有事, 别来～。I'm busy. Stop pestering me. /他老是来～她。He is always bothering her. /她～着妈妈给她买一件新衣服。She's been badgering mother to buy her a new dress. /这人被两种互相矛盾的想法所～。The man was torn between two conflicting ideas.

纠缠不清 jiūchán-bùqīng be too tangled up to unravel; get terribly entangled: 几个相关的概念在我的脑子里～。Several mutually related concepts got mixed up in my mind.

纠扯 jiūchě get entangled; be in a tangle

纠纷 jiūfēn dispute; quarrel; issue: 边界～ boundary dispute /调解～ settle a dispute by mediation; mediate a dispute /挑起～ stir up trouble /家庭～ household quarrel /婆媳～ squabble between mother-in-law and daughter-in-law

纠风 jiūfēng get rid of professional malpractices: 深入开展～工作。Expose the work to view so as to rectify professional malpractices.

纠葛 jiūgé entanglement; dispute: 邻里之间的～ quarrel among neighbours /感情～ emotional entanglement /在财产问题上发生了点～。There is some kind of dispute over family property.

纠合 jiūhé *also* "鸠合" jiūhé 〈贬义〉band together; gather together; collect: ～多数 muster (*or* line up) a majority /～一批打手

J

gather together a bunch of thugs /～党羽，图谋不轨 assemble one's followers and attempt a coup /他们～在一起反对他。They are ganging up against him.

纠集 jiūjí *also* "鸠集" jiūjí 〈贬义〉get together; collect; muster: ～一帮歹徒 gather together a band of rogues /～残兵败将 collect the remnants of a routed army /因利害关系～在一起 be drawn together by common interests /敌人～三个师的兵力，向我军阵地发动进攻。The enemy, having mustered together three divisions, launched an offensive on our position.

纠结 jiūjié be entangled; be interwined: 绳子～在一起了。The ropes are entangled. /杂草和瓜藤～到一起。The weeds have interwined with the melon vines. /各种各样的难题～缠绕，理不出个头绪来。All kinds of difficult problems are intertwined with each other, and it is difficult to sort things out.

纠偏 jiūpiān rectify a deviation (in policy or ideology); correct an error in orientation: ～救弊 rectify deviations and remedy defects

纠弹 jiūtán 〈书面〉expose and impeach (government officials for their mistakes or crimes); censure

纠正 jiūzhèng correct; put or set right; rectify; redress: ～不良倾向 rectify unhealthy tendencies /～冤案 redress a wrong; right a wrong /如果我不对，请予～。Don't hesitate to correct me if I'm wrong. /工作中的错误已得到～。The mistake in work has been put to rights.

jiǔ

酒 jiǔ ❶ alcoholic drink; wine; liquor; spirits: 黄～ rice wine /葡萄～ (grape) wine /干～ dry wine /烈性～ liquor; spirits /红葡萄～ red wine; port /白葡萄～ white wine /白～ (white) spirits; liquor /陈～ old wine; mellow wine /桂花～ wine fermented with osmanthus flowers /高粱～ wine made of sorghum /料～ cooking wine /露～ alcoholic drink mixed with fruit juice; punch /江米～ fermented glutinous rice /啤～ beer /黑啤～ stout; dark beer /苹果～ cider; applejack /汽～ light sparkling wine /烧～ spirits; white spirits /甜～ sweet wine /果子～ fruit wine /药～ medicinal liquor /喜～ wine drunk at wedding feast /鸡尾～ cocktail /香槟～ champagne /伏特加～ vodka /金～ gin; dry gin /罗木～ rum /威士忌～ whisky /味美思～ vermouth /雪利～ sherry /白兰地～ brandy /酿～ make wine; brew beer /下～ (of food, etc.) go with wine /行～ serve wine to guests /劝～ urge sb. to drink /伤～ get sick from drinking too much wine /醒～ dispel the effects of alcohol; sober up /祝～ drink a toast /纵～ drink to excess /奠～ wine as offerings to the spirits of the dead /罚～ be made to drink as a forfeit /花天～地 indulge in dissipation; lead a life of debauchery /灯红～绿 red lanterns and green wine; scene of debauchery ❷ (Jiǔ) a surname

酒吧 jiǔbā *also* "酒吧间" bar (room)

酒保 jiǔbǎo 〈旧语〉bartender; barkeeper

酒杯 jiǔbēi wine cup or glass

酒鳖子 jiǔbiēzi ❶〈旧语〉flat leather bag for keeping wine, alcohol, spirits, etc.; flat wine pot ❷ drunkard; sot: 他是一个～，一天也离不开酒。He is a drunkard who can't live one day without alcohol.

J

酒不醉人人自醉 jiǔ bù zuì rén rén zì zuì it's not the wine that intoxicates but the drinker who intoxicates himself

酒菜 jiǔcài ❶ food and drink: 准备～，招待客人 prepare food and drink for the guests ❷ food to go with wine or liquor: 买几个咸鸭蛋给老头子当～儿。Buy some salted duck's eggs to go with wine for the old man.

酒厂 jiǔchǎng brewery; winery; distillery

酒池肉林 jiǔchí-ròulín *also* "肉林酒池" lakes of wine and forests of meat — lead a life of extravagance and dissipation

酒刺 jiǔcì acne

酒德 jiǔdé good drinking habit: 这个人无～。This man knows no propriety in drinking.

酒店 jiǔdiàn ❶ wineshop; public house; pub ❷ hotel

酒饭 jiǔfàn drink and food: 我去拜访他，他每以～相待。Whenever I called on him, he would prepare drink and food for me.

酒疯 jiǔfēng drunken fit; drunken antics: 撒～ throw a drunken fit; be crazy drunk

酒逢知己千杯少 jiǔ féng zhījǐ qiān bēi shǎo among bosom friends, a thousand cups are too few: ～，话不投机半句多。A thousand cups of wine among congenial friends are too few, while one word in disagreeable company is more than enough.

酒缸 jiǔgāng ❶ wine jar ❷〈方言〉wineshop

酒馆 jiǔguǎn *also* "酒馆子" eatery; restaurant

酒鬼 jiǔguǐ drunkard; sot; wine bibber; tippler: 几个～又在小馆儿里撒酒疯。Several sots are in a drunken brawl again in the small restaurant.

酒酣耳热 jiǔhān-ěrrè warmed with wine; mellow with drink: ～，即席赋诗 compose poems offhand at the table when warmed with wine

酒好客自来 jiǔ hǎo kè zì lái 〈俗语〉good wine needs no host

酒后开车 jiǔhòu kāichē drunk driving; driving a car while intoxicated (DWI); driving when under the influence of alcohol

酒后失态 jiǔhòu shītài forget oneself in one's cups; lose self-control when drunk

酒后失言 jiǔhòu shīyán make indiscreet remarks under the influence of alcohol; when the wine is in, the wit is out

酒后失仪 jiǔhòu shīyí discourtesy after drink

酒后吐真言 jiǔhòu tǔ zhēnyán one speaks the truth over the cups; in wine there is truth; wine in, truth out

酒后无德 jiǔhòu-wúdé liquor talks mighty loud when it gets loose from the jug: 这家伙～，一个劲儿地撒泼。The fellow made a lousy scene after the wine had driven his wit out.

酒壶 jiǔhú wine pot; flagon

酒花 jiǔhuā 〈植物〉hops (used for beer)

酒会 jiǔhuì cocktail party

酒家 jiǔjiā ❶ wineshop; restaurant: 广东～ Guandong Restaurant /峨嵋～ Emei Restaurant ❷〈旧语〉waiter in a wineshop; bartender

酒浆 jiǔjiāng 〈书面〉wine; alcohol; drink; spirits

酒窖 jiǔjiào wine cellar

酒酵母 jiǔjiàomǔ *also* "酒母" distiller's yeast (for fermenting beer)

酒精 jiǔjīng ethyl alcohol; alcohol: ～比重计 spirit gauge /～灯 spirit lamp; alcohol burner /～炉 alcohol heater /～温度计 spirit thermometer; alcohol thermometer /～中毒 alcoholism

酒具 jiǔjù drinking utensils

酒坑 jiǔkēng 〈口语〉dimple

酒老味醇，人老识深 jiǔ lǎo wèi chún, rén lǎo shí shēn wine and judgment mellow with age

酒力 jiǔlì ❶ capacity for liquor: 他不胜～，喝一点儿就醉。He can't hold much liquor, and will get drunk after drinking a bit. ❷ stimulating effect of wine; influence of alcohol: 几杯酒下肚，不一会儿～发作，浑身焦热。After drinking several cups of wine, he began to feel its effect and became uncomfortably hot all over.

酒帘 jiǔlián *see* "酒望"

酒量 jiǔliàng capacity for liquor; one's drinking capacity: 很有～ be a heavy drinker; can hold a lot of liquor; drink like a fish /他爱喝酒，可～不大。He likes to drink, but can't hold much liquor.

酒龄 jiǔlíng number of years a wine has been kept or stored; age of a wine: 这瓶葡萄酒～可长了。This is a bottle of really old wine.

酒令 jiǔlìng drinkers' wager game: 行～ play a drinkers' wager game

酒楼 jiǔlóu restaurant

酒垆 jiǔlú ❶〈旧语〉earthen platform for wine jars in a wineshop ❷ wineshop; public house; restaurant

酒母 jiǔmǔ *see* "酒酵母"

酒囊饭袋 jiǔnáng-fàndài wine pot and rice bag — good-for-nothing: 如此简单的事他也办不好，真是个～。He cannot even handle such a simple thing. What a dunce!

酒酿 jiǔniàng *also* "酒娘" fermented glutinous rice

酒气熏人 jiǔqì xūnrén breathe alcohol

酒器 jiǔqì drinking vessel

酒钱 jiǔqian 〈旧语〉tip

酒曲 jiǔqū distiller's yeast

酒肉朋友 jiǔròu-péngyou wine-and-meat friend; fair-weather friend: ～，柴米夫妻 friends while there are wine and food; man and wife while there are firewood and rice /～是不能共患难的。Fair-weather friends cannot go through hardships together.

酒色 jiǔsè ❶ wine and women: 沉湎～ indulge oneself in wine and women; be given to sensual pleasures ❷ the colour of wine: ～很正。The wine looks pretty good. ❸〈书面〉drunken state; drunkenness

酒色财气 jiǔ-sè-cái-qì wine, women, avarice, and pride — the

four cardinal vices
酒色之徒 jiǔsèzhītú one who lusts after wine and women; libertine; debauchee: 我当初以为他人品不错, 却原来是个～。I thought he was quite a good man. Actually, he gives all his time to wine and women.
酒石酸 jiǔshísuān tartaric acid: ～锑钾〈药学〉antimony potassium tartrate
酒食 jiǔshí food and drink
酒食征逐 jiǔshí-zhēngzhú wine-and-meat friends inviting each other to feasts and sensual pleasures
酒水 jiǔshuǐ ❶ drinks; beverages and alcohol: 这一桌饭菜加～共五百元。The meal comes to 500 *yuan*, beverages included. ❷〈方言〉feast; banquet: 办了一桌～ give a feast
酒肆 jiǔsì 〈书面〉wineshop; public house: 茶楼～ teahouses and wineshops
酒嗉子 jiǔsùzi 〈方言〉tin wine cup
酒提 jiǔtí wine dipper
酒徒 jiǔtú drunkard; wine bibber
酒望 jiǔwàng *also* "酒望子"; "酒帘"〈旧语〉streamer hanging in front of a wineshop: ～高挑 streamer hanging high in front of a wineshop
酒涡 jiǔwō *see* "酒窝"
酒窝 jiǔwō *also* "酒涡" dimple: 这小姑娘一笑就露出两个小～, 真讨人喜欢。The little girl shows two charming dimples when she smiles.
酒席 jiǔxí banquet; feast: 为宾客大摆～ entertain guests to a sumptuous banquet
酒醒 jiǔxǐng awake from drunkenness
酒兴 jiǔxìng elation caused by intoxication: ～正浓 at the height of one's drinking bout
酒性 jiǔxìng alcoholic strength: 使～ act on alcoholic strength
酒筵 jiǔyán feast: 洗尘～ feast to welcome sb.
酒宴 jiǔyàn feast; banquet: 丰盛的～ sumptuous banquet / ～已经摆好。The feast is ready.
酒肴 jiǔyáo ❶ wine and food ❷ food that goes with wine or liquor
酒药 jiǔyào yeast for brewing rice wine or fermenting glutinous rice
酒靥 jiǔyè 〈方言〉dimple
酒意 jiǔyì signs of getting tipsy; tipsy feeling: 有点～ be slightly tipsy; have a drop in one's eye; be mellow / 他几杯下肚有了几分～。He had scarcely drunk a few cups of wine when he began to appear tipsy.
酒糟 jiǔzāo distillers' grains
酒糟鼻 jiǔzāobí *also* "酒渣鼻" acne rosacea; brandy nose
酒枣 jiǔzǎo liquor-saturated dates
酒盅 jiǔzhōng *also* "酒钟" small handless wine cup
酒馔 jiǔzhuàn 〈书面〉food and drink: 桌上摆了果品～。There are fruit, food, and drink on the table. *or* Fruit, food, and drink cover the table.
酒资 jiǔzī tip
酒足饭饱 jiǔzú-fànbǎo have drunk and eaten to satiety or to one's heart's content; have eaten and drunk one's fill
酒醉 jiǔzuì ❶ drunkenness: ～失言 say sth. indiscreet when drunk ❷ immerse (food) in liquor: ～螃蟹 liquor-saturated crab

韭(韮)

jiǔ 〈植物〉fragrant-flowered garlic; (Chinese) chives: 青～ young chives; chive seedlings
韭菜 jiǔcài fragrant-flowered garlic; (Chinese) chives
韭葱 jiǔcōng leek (*Allium porrum*)
韭黄 jiǔhuáng hotbed chives

九

jiǔ ❶ nine: ～号楼 Building No.9 / ～层楼 ninth floor / ～成新 ninety percent new / ～年义务教育 nine-year compulsory education / 四加五得～。Four plus five is nine. ❷ beginning from the day of the Winter Solstice, each of the following nine nine-day periods is called a "nine": 数～寒冬 during the nine-day periods; freezing days of winter / 冷在三～。The coldest days are in the third nine-day period after the Winter Solstice. ❸ numerous; many: 三弯～转 many twists and turns / 三六～等 various grades and ranks
九层之台, 起于累土 jiǔ céng zhī tái, qǐ yú lěi tǔ a nine-storey tower begins with a pile of earth; from little acorns oaks do grow
九重 jiǔchóng 〈书面〉❶ ninth heaven: ～天上现星辰。The stars appear in the highest heavens. ❷ imperial residence; imperial palace ❸ nine storeys; nine floors: ～之台 nine-storey tower
九重霄 jiǔchóngxiāo highest of heavens
九大行星 jiǔ dà xíngxīng 〈天文〉nine principal planets (of the solar system: 水星 Mercury, 金星 Venus, 地球 Earth, 火星 Mars, 木星 Jupiter, 土星 Saturn, 天王星 Uranus, 海王星 Neptune, 冥王星 Pluto)
九鼎 jiǔdǐng ❶ legendary nine tripods (made by Emperor Yu of the Xia Dynasty and passed down through Zhou as national treasures) ❷ sth. of heavy weight or great importance: 一言～ a word that carries much weight; word of decisive importance / ～大吕 of influential role or position
九段 jiǔduàn ninth-dan (highest grade in go or *weiqi*)
九二〇 jiǔ'èrlíng *also* "赤霉素" chìméisù 〈生化〉gibberellin (a plant growth stimulant)
九宫 jiǔgōng nine modes of ancient Chinese music
九宫格儿 jiǔgōnggér squared paper for practising Chinese calligraphy, each square crisscrossed with intersecting lines in the shape of 井
九归 jiǔguī rules for doing division with a one-digit divisor on the abacus
九级风 jiǔjífēng 〈气象〉force 9 wind; strong gale
九角戏 jiǔjiǎoxì *also* "高甲戏" gāojiǎxì a kind of local opera in Fujian Province
九节狸 jiǔjiélí 〈动物〉zibet; large Indian civet
九斤黄鸡 jiǔjīnhuángjī Jiujinhuang, a kind of brown large chicken well known for its meat, with the male weighing as much as 9 *jin* or $4\frac{1}{2}$ kilos
九九表 jiǔjiǔbiǎo multiplication table
九九歌 jiǔjiǔgē *also* "小九九" xiǎojiǔjiǔ ❶ multiplication rhymes ❷ scheme; plot
九九归一 jiǔjiǔguīyī *also* "九九归原" when all is said and done; all in all; in the last analysis; in the end: ～, 这种人太危险, 不可与之交游。In the final analysis, such people are too dangerous to associate with. / 这是全国人民的心愿, ～, 台湾是一定要回归祖国的。This is the aspiration of the people of the whole country. After all, Taiwan will return to the motherland.
九流三教 jiǔliú-sānjiào *also* "三教九流" people of all sorts
九龙 Jiǔlóng (HK) Kowloon
九龙壁 Jiǔlóngbì Nine-Dragon Screen (an imperial decoration in Beijing)
九龙敕令 Jiǔlóng Chìlìng 〈历史〉(HK) Kowloon Order in Council
九牛二虎之力 jiǔ niú èr hǔ zhī lì strength of nine bulls and two tigers — herculean effort; utmost exertion: 费尽～ make tremedous effort; exert oneself to the utmost; use every ounce of one's strength; do all one can / 费了～, 还是没把他说动。Although we tried our very best, we failed to persuade him.
九牛一毛 jiǔniú-yīmáo single hair out of nine ox hides — a drop in the ocean: 对他来说, 这点钱只是～而已。For him, this much money is just peanuts.
九派 jiǔpài Nine streams — the numerous branches of the Yangtze River in Hubei and Jiangxi provinces: 茫茫～流中国。Wide, wide flow the nine streams through the land.
九品 jiǔpǐn 〈历史〉❶ nine grades of official rank in dynastic China ❷ ninth grade (official)
九窍 jiǔqiào nine body orifices or openings, consisting of eyes, ears, nostrils, mouth, urethral orifice, and anus
九秋 jiǔqiū ninety days of the autumn season: ～天气 autumn weather
九曲回肠 jiǔqū-huícháng *also* "九回肠" knot in one's stomach; pent up feelings of sadness; melancholy
九曲桥 jiǔqūqiáo zigzag bridge
九衢 jiǔqú 〈书面〉roads which radiate in all directions: ～纵横 crisscross roads which extend in all directions
九泉 jiǔquán 〈书面〉nine springs — grave; nether world: 含笑于～ smile in the underworld; have nothing to regret in life; sink happily into the nether world
九泉之下 jiǔquánzhīxià below in the nine springs — in the nether world; after death: ～, 不能瞑目 would turn in one's grave / ～, 他亦可瞑目。His soul may rest at peace.
九三学社 Jiǔ-Sān Xuéshè Jiusan or September 3 Society, one of the democratic parties in China, formed in 1944 as "Society of

J

Democracy and Science" (民主科学社), changed to present name in 1945

九死一生 jiǔsǐ-yīshēng escape by the skin of one's teeth; miss death by a hair's breadth; narrow escape from death: 天哪! 汽车差点儿撞上他了，那真是～。Heavens! That was a near thing (*or* close shave). The car only just missed him.

九天 jiǔtiān ninth heaven; highest of heavens: ～九地 world of difference; far apart; widely different /～揽月 clasp the moon in the Ninth Heaven — great aspiration

九头鸟 jiǔtóuniǎo ❶ legendary bird with nine heads ❷ cunning man; deceitful man; crafty man

九尾狐 jiǔwěihú nine-tailed fox — crafty and evil person

九五 jiǔwǔ imperial throne: ～之尊 the imperial throne

九锡 jiǔxī nine things, such as clothing, carriages, weapons, etc., bestowed by the emperor on a powerful minister who usu. claimed these honours as a prelude to usurping the throne

九霄 jiǔxiāo highest heavens; sky of the skies: 声震～。The sound reverberated through the sky.

九霄云外 jiǔxiāoyúnwài beyond the highest heavens; immeasurably far away: 把谨慎和克制抛到了～ throw overboard all caution and restraint; cast all caution and restraint to the winds /他把愁闷都撇在～。He soared out of his dark mood to the highest joy. /那种泰然自若的神气早就跑到～去了。There was no trace of his former composure.

九星联珠 jiǔxīng liánzhū nine planets clustering in an arc

九一八事变 Jiǔ-Yībā Shìbiàn September 18th Incident (seizure of Shenyang on September 18, 1931 by the Japanese aggressors, as a step towards their occupation of the entire northeastern China)

九一四 jiǔyīsì 〈药学〉"914" or neosalvarsan (a modification of *liulingliu* 六〇六)

九音锣 jiǔyīnluó nine-toned gong; Chinese gong chimes

九渊 jiǔyuān 〈书面〉abyss

九月 jiǔyuè ❶ September ❷ ninth month of the lunar year; ninth moon

九章算术 Jiǔzhāng Suànshù *Jiuzhang Suanshu* or *Nine Chapters on Mathematical Art*, one of China's early writings on mathematics completed in the first century

九折 jiǔzhé ten percent discount

九折臂 jiǔzhébì *also* "三折肱" sānzhégōng 〈比喻〉rich in experience: 要～才能成为良医。Experience makes a good doctor.

九州 Jiǔzhōu ❶ nine administrative divisions (legend has it that ancient China was divided into nine administrative divisions) ❷ China (often used in poetry or classical prose): 死去原知万事空，但悲不见～同。Fully aware nothing matters after death, I regret not seeing the country unified. ❸ Kyushu, Japan

九族 jiǔzú 〈旧语〉nine degrees or forms of kinship; nine families (including one's own plus father's, grandfather's, great-grandfather's, great-great-grandfather's, son's, grandson's, great-grandson's, and great-great-grandson's); nine families (including four families from the father's side, three families from the mother's side and two families from the wife's side): 祸灭～ bring death penalties upon all of one's relatives

J

久

jiǔ ❶ for a long time; long: 年深日～ with the passage of time; as the years go by /～雨 long spell of rain /蓄谋已～ long premeditated /天长地～ enduring as the universe; everlasting and unchanging /我认识他已有很～了。I've known him for a long time. /他离开这儿很～了。He left here long ago. ❷ of a specified duration: 这本书写了三年之～。It took as long as three years to write the book. /他去了多～了? How long has he been away?

久别 jiǔbié be separated for a long time

久别重逢 jiǔbié-chóngféng meet again after a long separation; reunite after a long parting: 他们～，分外亲热。They were exceptionally warm towards each other when they met again after a long separation.

久病 jiǔbìng be ill for a long time: ～初愈 have just recovered from a long illness

久病成医 jiǔbìng-chéngyī 〈俗语〉prolonged illness makes a doctor of a patient; a patient will become a doctor after a long illness

久病床前无孝子 jiǔbìng chuángqián wú xiàozǐ 〈俗语〉no son would be filial towards a parent long laid up in bed; a constant guest is never welcome

久长 jiǔcháng for a long time

久等 jiǔděng wait for a long time: 叫你～，实在抱歉。I'm extremely sorry for having kept you waiting. /经理让他～，他很恼火。He was furious because the manager let him cool his heels for quite some time.

久而久之 jiǔ'érjiǔzhī in the course of time; after a long time; as time passes: 他每晚做俯卧撑，～，遂成了习惯。He did push-ups every night, and by and by, formed a habit of it. /机器不好好养护，～就要生锈。The machine will get rusty if it is not well maintained.

久旱逢甘雨 jiǔ hàn féng gānyǔ have a welcome rain after a prolonged spell of drought — have a long-felt need satisfied: 人生快事莫如～，他乡遇故知，洞房花烛夜，金榜题名时。The happiest events in one's life were sweet rains after a long drought, meeting an old acquaintance in an alien land, enjoying wedding-night felicities, and passing the imperial examination with distinction.

久航高度 jiǔháng gāodù 〈航空〉altitude for maximum endurance

久航速度 jiǔháng sùdù 〈航空〉speed for maximum endurance

久后 jiǔhòu in the future; long afterwards: ～回忆起这事，也不会感到遗憾。When I think of this in the future, I'll not regret it.

久假不归 jiǔjiǎ-bùguī put off indefinitely returning sth. one has borrowed; appropriate sth. borrowed for one's own use: 我那本词典被人～，只好再买一本应急了。Someone failed to return the dictionary borrowed from me long ago, so I had to buy another for urgent use.

久经 jiǔjīng ❶ experience for a long time; go through repeatedly: ～战斗的人物 people who have gone through many battles ❷ happen long before: ～诀别的故乡 hometown to which one bade farewell long before; hometown which one left long ago

久经锻炼 jiǔjīng-duànliàn well-steeled; well-tempered; long-tested: 这些人都是～的革命家。They are all seasoned revolutionaries.

久经风霜 jiǔjīng-fēngshuāng have experienced all sorts of hardships; be weather-beaten

久经考验 jiǔjīng-kǎoyàn long-tested; seasoned: 他是一个～的战士。He is a seasoned soldier. /新工作中的任何困难都吓不倒他，他是～的。He won't be cowed by anything on the new job. He's gone through the mill.

久久 jiǔjiǔ for a long time: 他～不能成寐。It was quite a while before he fell asleep. /他的话～地回响在我的耳边。His words rang in my ears for a very long time.

久居别家招人嫌 jiǔ jū biéjiā zhāo rén xián to stay in another man's home too long incurs odium; overstay one's welcome; the best fish smell when they are three days old

久旷 jiǔkuàng 〈书面〉❶ neglect for a long time; be vacant for a long time: 此片耕地～。This field has long lain waste. ❷ (of a man) remain single long after one's matrimonial age or long after the death of one's wife: ～无偶 remain single long with no spouse

久阔 jiǔkuò 〈书面〉separate for a long time: 二十年不到北京，～重来，感触很多。When he came back to Beijing after twenty years, all sorts of feelings welled up in his mind.

久炼成钢 jiǔliàn-chénggāng steel is made through prolonged tempering — practice makes perfect

久留 jiǔliú stay long: 我不便～，就此告辞。It was inadvisable for me to stay long, so I stood up to say goodbye. /我们不能在这儿～了。We must not linger here too long.

久慕 jiǔmù 〈套语〉long admire; long look forward to: ～大名。I've long been looking forward to meeting you.

久陪 jiǔpéi accompany sb. for a long time: 不能～了，再见吧! I'm sorry to have to go now. See you later.

久疏音问 jiǔshū yīnwèn 〈书面〉have been negligent in keeping up correspondence (with)

久停 jiǔtíng stay long: 我不能在这儿～，得赶紧走。I must hurry up for I can't stay here long.

久违 jiǔwéi 〈套语〉how long it is since we last met; I haven't seen you for ages: ～了，一向可好? Haven't seen you for ages. How is everything with you?

久闻大名 jiǔwén dàmíng I've heard about you for a very long time: ～，如雷贯耳。I have long heard of your great name, and it thunders in my ears. *or* I have long heard of your resounding name.

久许 jiǔxǔ 〈书面〉for quite a while: 沉思～ be deep in thought for some time

久悬不决 jiǔxuán-bùjué long unsettled; still outstanding: ～的问题

unsettled issue of long standing

久仰 jiǔyǎng 〈套语〉(formerly used at first meeting) I feel it an honour to make your acquaintance; I'm very pleased to meet you:他的道德文章,我是～的。I've long heard of his integrity and literary talent.

久已 jiǔyǐ long ago; long since:这件事我～忘怀。I've long forgotten all about it.

久远 jiǔyuǎn far back; ages ago; of the remote past; time-honoured:碑文年代～,无法辨认。The stone inscriptions are age-old and unrecognizable (*or* illegible). /这是一本可以传之～的书。This is a book that can be handed down from generation to generation.

久在河边走,没有不湿鞋 jiǔ zài hébiān zǒu, méiyǒu bù shī xié *also* "常在河边走,哪能不湿鞋" cháng zài hébiān zǒu, nǎnéng bù shī xié one can hardly avoid wetting one's shoes if one keeps going to the waterside — one who is in constant contact with corrupt practices, etc., is bound to be affected; the pitcher that goes to the well too often is broken at last

灸

jiǔ 〈中医〉moxibustion

灸治 jiǔzhì treat with or by moxibustion

玖[1]

jiǔ nine (used for the numeral 九 on cheques, etc., to avoid mistakes or alterations):贰拾～圆 twenty-nine *yuan*

玖[2]

jiǔ 〈书面〉jade-like black stone

jiù

就[1]

jiù ❶ come near; move towards:～着烛光看书 read by candlelight /～着炉子烘衣服 dry clothes by the fireside /～着宅子周围开了一片菜地 open up a vegetable plot around the house /避重～轻 evade the heavy (burden, responsibility, etc.) and take up the light/删繁～简 simplify sth. by cutting out the superfluous /半推半～ yield with a show of reluctance; give way after making a show of declining ❷ undertake; engage in; embark on:按部～班 follow the prescribed order /驾轻～熟 drive a light carriage on a familiar road — do a familiar job with ease /各～各位〈体育〉On your marks! *or* Each takes his own place! ❸ *used in a passive sentence to introduce an action*: *see* "～歼"; "～擒" ❹ accomplish; attain; make:功成业～ (of a person's career) be crowned with success /一挥而～ flourish a pen and it's done /不堪造～ utterly worthless ❺ take advantage of; accommodate oneself to; suit; fit:你可以～你的方便作出安排。You may make whatever arrangements that suit your convenience. /这件大衣过紧,但是我只好～着穿了。This coat is too tight for me, but I'll have to make do with it. ❻ (of food, etc.) go with:花生米～酒 have peanuts to go with wine /这种鱼是～饭的好菜。This kind of fish goes well with rice.

就[2]

jiù 〈副词〉❶ at once; right away; in a moment:我这～来。I'm coming. *or* I'll be right there. *or* I won't be a minute. /天很快～亮了。It turned light right away. ❷ as early as; already:大风一清早～住了。The strong wind subsided early in the morning. /他在童年时～参加了红军。He joined the Red Army early in his childhood. ❸ as soon as; no sooner... than; right after:他们一下火车,～到联络处去了。They went direct to the liason office as soon as they got off the train. /我刚到家～下起雨来了。No sooner had I reached home than it began to rain. /办完事我～回家。I'll go home right after I finish the work. ❹ (often with 只要,要是,既然, or similar phrase in the conditional clause) *used to indicate that sth. comes natually under certain conditions or circumstances*:只要他办事公正,你～没有理由抱怨了。So long as he handles the matter fairly, you'll have no cause to grumble. /只要质量好,我～想多买一点。I'll buy more if it is of good quality. /既然没事,～多坐一会儿吧。Stay a little longer since you have nothing else to attend to. ❺ as much as; as many as:一个月～节约了十吨煤 save as much as ten tons of coal in one month /他三天才来一次,你一天～来两次。He came here only once in three days, but you came as often as twice in one day. /不要那么多人,我们两个～能干完。Why so many people? The two of us will be able to finish the job. ❻ *used between two identical words or expressions to express tolerance or resignation*:电吹风坏了～坏了吧,再买一个新的。The hair blower is out of order, so be it. Let's go and buy a new one. /去～去,怕什么? I'll go if I must. What's there to be afraid of? ❼ *used to indicate that sth. has been like this all along*:街道本来～不宽,每逢集市更显得拥挤了。The street is narrow as it is, and it gets all the more crowded on market days. /我本来～不想去,是你非拉我去的。I never said I wanted to go. It was you that got me to. ❽ only; merely; just:万事俱备,现在～等他点头了。Everything is ready, and now we have only to wait for his approval. /～要一枚 8 毛邮票。Just an eight-*mao* stamp, please. ❾ *used to express resolve*:我～不信他干这个工作不适合。I just don't believe that he is unfit for the job. /我早晨跟他打招呼,他～不理我。He simply cut me dead when I greeted him this morning. /不去,不去,～不去! I won't go, never! ❿ exactly; precisely; very; right:这～是我最需要的。This is precisely what I want. /办公室～在这里。The office is right here. /工商银行～在附近。The Bank of Industry and Commerce is just round the corner.

就[3]

jiù 〈连词〉even if; ever though:你～闷口不说,他也不会轻易放过你的。Even if you keep your mouth shut, he won't let you off lightly. /～让神医华佗来,也治不好这病了。Even if Hua Tuo, the miracle-working doctor, came, the patient could not be cured.

就[4]

jiù 〈介词〉with regard to; as far as; concerning; on:～目前情况来看 as matters now stand /～我来说 so far as I am concerned/～其本身而言 as far as it goes; as far as it is concerned /～国有企业改造进行讨论 have discussions on reforming state-owned enterprises /双方～共同关心的问题交换了意见。The two sides exchanged views on questions of common concern.

就伴 jiùbàn accompany sb. (on a journey):～同行 travel together/这一次我得先去了,不能跟你～了。I can't accompany you this time for I have to go first.

就便 jiùbiàn at one's convenience; while you're at it:你～把这封信发了。Please post this letter on your way. /～也替我买一份《中国日报》。While you're about it, buy me a copy of *China Daily* too. /下次跟他见面时,～向他解释一下。When you see him next time, please explain this to him.

就捕 jiùbǔ be arrested:～的嫌疑犯 the arrested suspect

就餐 jiùcān have one's meal:顾客请在十二点至下午二点到餐厅～。The guests are kindly requested to have their meals in the dining room from 12:00 to 14:00.

就此 jiùcǐ at this point; here and now; thus:～前往 go ahead from here /他没有获得一等奖,不能～得出结论,说他已经大大落后了。He didn't win the first prize, but it doesn't follow that he is already falling far behind. /送君千里,终须一别,你我～作别吧。We have to part even if you accompany me by walking a thousand *li*. So let's say goodbye here and now. /工作～告一段落。The work has thus come to a close.

就搭 jiùda 〈方言〉make do with; yield to; accommodate:我本来没有想去看电影,为了～你,去看看吧。I hadn't thought of seeing a film, but to accommodate you, let's go and see it.

就逮 jiùdài 〈书面〉be arrested

就道 jiùdào start off; set out on a journey:束装～ pack one's gear to set out on a journey

就地 jiùdì on the spot; on site:～视察〈军事〉on-site inspection /～审判 on-the-spot trial /～调解 on-the-spot mediation /～采购 local procurement /～检验 floor inspection /～生产,～配套 manufacture complete sets of equipment locally /上级命令我队～宿营。The higher echelon ordered us to encamp where we were.

就地取材 jiùdì-qǔcái draw on local resources; make use of indigenous materials; draw on local talents:～,就地使用 draw on local resources and make full use of them; draw on local talents and give them full play

就地正法 jiùdì-zhèngfǎ execute (a criminal) on the spot; execute summarily:该国宣布,毒品走私犯一经捕获,立即～。The authorities of the country proclaimed that drug-smugglers would be executed on the spot immediately upon arrest.

就读 jiùdú attend school; take a course:～于复旦大学 study at Fudan University

就范 jiùfàn submit; give in; conform:强迫～ force sb. to conform; compel to give in /逼人～ force sb. to submit /几经波折,才使他～。He was made to yield only after repeated pressure.

J

就根儿 jiùgēnr 〈方言〉originally; at first:他～干得不错嘛。He hasn't done badly in the first place.

就馆 jiùguǎn 〈旧语〉serve as tutor; be assistant or private adviser to a ranking official or general

就合 jiùhe 〈方言〉❶ comply or yield without reference to principles; make do with; accommodate; humour:对孩子不能总～,该严的地方要严。Don't always humour the child. You must be strict with him whenever necessary. /建筑堤防人命关天,材料可不能～。You must never stint materials in building embankments, for they will have to protect the people's lives. ❷ curl up; huddle up; twist:他的腰和腿都～在一块儿了。His legs were all huddled up to his waist.

就歼 jiùjiān be wiped out; be annihilated; be destroyed:残敌全部～。The remnants of the enemy troops have all been eliminated.

就教 jiùjiào ask for advice; consult:移樽～ seek advice /我很荣幸有机会向大家～。I'm greatly honoured to have the chance to ask all of you for advice.

就近 jiùjìn (do or get sth.) nearby; in the neighbourhood; without having to go far:我们下了火车,～找了住处。We got off the train and found accommodation near the railway station. /我的孩子们都～上学。My children are all going to a nearby school. /几乎所有的东西～都能买到。We can get almost everything in the neighbourhood.

就里 jiùlǐ inside information:不知～ have no inside information

就令 jiùlìng 〈书面〉even if; even:有一分热,发一分光,～是萤火,也可以在黑暗里发一点光。Give as much light as the fuel can produce, for even a firefly can give a little light in darkness.

就木 jiùmù 〈书面〉be laid in a coffin — die:行将～ about to die

就聘 jiùpìn accept an invitation; accept an appointment:他已～为教授。He has already accepted his appointment as professor.

就坡下驴 jiùpō-xiàlǘ 〈俗语〉alight from one's donkey at a rise in ground — accommodate to circumstances; sail with the wind; seize an opportunity (to do sth.):既然对方已经同意我们的条件,我们正好～。Since the other side has agreed to our terms, we may as well take the opportunity and accept its offer.

就擒 jiùqín be arrested; be caught:束手～ allow oneself to be captured (*or* taken) without putting up a fight

就寝 jiùqǐn retire for the night; turn in; go to bed:我们学校晚十一点熄灯～。According to school rules, we all go to bed when the lights are put out at 11 p.m.

就痊 jiùquán about to be cured; near recovery:病渐～ be almost cured (*or* recovered)

就任 jiùrèn take up one's post; take office; assume office:～要职 take up an important post /～临时总统 assume the office of interim president

就食 jiùshí 〈书面〉❶ go somewhere for one's food:分兵～ divide forces and live off the land ❷ make a living:～江南 earn one's living in the southern part of the lower reaches of the Yangtze River

就使 jiùshǐ 〈书面〉even if; even though:～获胜,亦不可轻敌。You must not belittle your enemy even if you win.

就势 jiùshì make use of momentum:我躲过对手的拳头,～一掌把他打倒在地。I evaded a blow from my opponent and took advantage of his momentum to knock him off his feet.

就事 jiùshì 〈旧语〉take up one's post:他在一家公司里谋了个职位,明日去～。He has found a job as an office clerk in a company and is going to take up his post tomorrow.

就事论事 jiùshì-lùnshì consider or judge sth. as it stands; deal with a matter on its merits:～是不行的,因为那是孤立地看待事物。It won't do to consider anything simply as it stands, because that means judging things out of context.

就是 jiùshì ❶ *usually used with* 了 *at the end of a sentence to express affirmation*:错误不大,改了～了。As it is not a serious mistake, all he has to do is to correct it. /我一定照办,你放心～了。You can rest assured that I'll do what you wish. ❷ quite right; exactly; precisely:～,～,你的意见很好嘛。Exactly, your suggestion is quite good. ❸ *used for emphasis*:随你怎么说,我～不愿意。You may say as you like, but I'll never do it. /不懂～不懂,不要装懂。If you don't understand, you don't understand. Don't try to pretend to understand. /这孩子～招人喜欢。The child is very lovely indeed. ❹ only; simply; just:这孩子挺聪明,～有点淘气。The child is quite clever, but he is just a little naughty. /他别的都不喜欢,～喜欢钓鱼。He likes nothing but fishing. ❺ (used together with 也) even if; even:你～不同意,也不能发脾气嘛! Even if you don't agree, you shouldn't lose your temper! /他们哥儿俩长得一模一样,～家里人有时也分不清。The two brothers look very much alike, and even their family members sometimes find it difficult to tell them apart.

就是说 jiùshìshuō that is to say; in other words; namely:我儿子已通过了高考,～,他将被一所大学录取。My son has passed the entrance examination. That is to say, he is going to one of the universities. /今天是春节,～今天是旧历新年。It is Spring Festival today; in other words, it is the Chinese New Year.

就手 jiùshǒu while you're at it; at one's convenience:你洗衣服时～把我的衬衣也洗一洗。Wash my shirt as well when you do washing. /你回家时～儿买点菜回来吧。Please bring some vegetables when you come home.

就算 jiùsuàn even if; granted that:～有困难也不是不可以克服的嘛。Even if there are difficulties, they are not insurmountable. /～我说得不对,你也不该发脾气。You should not have flared up even if I had said something out of place.

就位 jiùwèi take one's place; be seated at the table:审判长、审判员等～后,就正式开庭了。When the presiding judge and judges all have taken their places, the trial formally starts.

就席 jiùxí take one's seat at a banquet; be seated at a dinner table:～畅饮 be seated at the banquet and drink one's fill

就刑 jiùxíng be punished; be executed

就许 jiùxǔ maybe; perhaps:保不住他今儿～来了。It's likely he may come today.

就绪 jiùxù be in order; be all set; be ready:一切布置～。All arrangements have been made. *or* Everything is ready. /本届奥运会已准备～。All the preparations for the Olympic Games are in order (*or* done). /下一期杂志基本编辑～。The next issue of the magazine has almost been edited.

就学 jiùxué go to school:他决定弃商～。He decided to give up business and go to school.

就要 jiùyào near; about to; going to; on the point of:她～掉泪了。She was on the verge of tears. /春节～到了。The Spring Festival is drawing near. /天～黑了,我们赶快走吧! Let's hurry up as night is going to fall. /旅游～结束了。The trip is nearing the end.

就业 jiùyè find employment; take up an occupation; get a job:创造～机会 create opportunities for employment; create more jobs /～登记 employment registration /～率 employment rate /～前培训 pre-job training /百分之五的劳动力不能～。Five per cent of the labour force can not be employed.

就业安置 jiùyè ānzhì outplacement

就医 jiùyī seek medical advice; go to the doctor's; see a doctor; go to hospital:到门诊部去～ go to the clinic to see a doctor /保外～ be bailed out for medical treatment

就义 jiùyì be executed for championing a just cause; die a martyr:英勇～ face execution bravely; die a hero's death /从容～ face death calmly

就诊 jiùzhěn see a doctor; seek medical advice

就枕 jiùzhěn lie down to sleep; go to bed

就正 jiùzhèng solicit comments (on one's writing):～于同行 ask for (*or* solicit) comments from one's colleagues /～于专家学者 invite (*or* request) experts and scholars to offer their criticisms

就职 jiùzhí assume office:宣誓～ take the oath of office; be sworn in /宣布～ announce (*or* make public) one's assumption of office /～视事 assume office and attend to official business

就职典礼 jiùzhí diǎnlǐ *also* "就职仪式" inauguration; inaugural ceremony

就职演说 jiùzhí yǎnshuō inaugural speech

就中 jiùzhōng ❶ between two parties:～调停 mediate a dispute ❷ among; in:～原委他最清楚。As for the whys and wherefores of the matter, he knows best.

就坐 jiùzuò *also* "就座" take one's seat; be seated:围着会议桌～sit round the conference table /会议马上开始,请大家～。The meeting is about to begin. Please be seated. /主席团成员在台上第一排依次～。Members of the presidium took their seats in the front row in due order.

僦

jiù 〈书面〉rent; hire; lease:～屋 rent a house /～费 rent; rental

鹫

jiù *also* "雕" diāo 〈动物〉vulture:秃～ cinereous vulture /兀～ griffon vulture

厩(廐、廏) jiù stable; cattle-shed; pen

厩肥 jiùféi *also* "圈肥" juànféi 〈农业〉 barnyard manure

救(捄) jiù ❶ rescue; save; salvage: 呼～ call out for help; send out an SOS (signal) /把病人从死亡的边缘～了过来 rescue a patient from the jaws of death /只有社会主义能够～中国。Only socialism can save China. ❷ help; relieve; succour: 生产自～ support oneself through work relief (after a natural disaster) /抱有～人济世的宏愿 cherish high aspirations of helping others and remaking the world

救拔 jiùbá 〈书面〉 save; rescue; deliver: 把他从绝望中～出来 deliver him from despair

救兵 jiùbīng relief troops; reinforcements: 搬～ call in or ask for reinforcements /内无粮草，外无～ have no provisions within or reinforcements without — be left utterly helpless

救场 jiùchǎng save the show or performance (as when an understudy steps in to substitute for an absent principal performer): ～如救火。To save a show is as urgent as to put out a fire.

救度 jiùdù (of Buddhism or Taoism) pray for people and preach a religious creed so as to relieve people from suffering: ～众生 save all living creatures from suffering

救焚拯溺 jiùfén-zhěngnì save people from fire and drowning; rescue people from danger or misery

救国 jiùguó save the nation; strive for national salvation: ～阵线 salvation front /～救民 save the country and the people

救护 jiùhù relieve (a sick or injured person); give first-aid; rescue: ～灾区伤员 give first-aid to the injured of the stricken area /战地～工作 rescue work at a battlefield /及时～ timely relief

救护车 jiùhùchē ambulance

救护船 jiùhùchuán ambulance ship

救护队 jiùhùduì ambulance corps

救护飞机 jiùhù fēijī ambulance aircraft

救护所 jiùhùsuǒ first-aid station

救护条款 jiùhù tiáokuǎn sue and labour clause; suing and labouring clause

救护站 jiùhùzhàn first-aid station

救荒 jiùhuāng send relief to a famine area; help to tide over a crop failure: ～运动 campaign to help people tide over a famine /生产～ relieve famine by promoting production

救活 jiùhuó bring (sb.) back to life; revive; resuscitate: ～垂死病人 resuscitate the dying patient; bring the dying back to life /伤势太重，恐怕救不活了。The wound might be too serious to be cured.

救火 jiùhuǒ fire fighting: ～队员 fireman; fire fighter /消防队员正在～。The firemen are putting out the fire.

救火车 jiùhuǒchē fire engine; fire truck

救火队 jiùhuǒduì fire brigade or company

救火投薪 jiùhuǒ-tóuxīn try to put out a fire by throwing firewood on it — take counterproductive measures; add fuel to the flames

救火扬沸 jiùhuǒ-yángfèi pour boiling water to put out the fire — not a basic solution to the problem

救急 jiùjí help cope with an emergency; help meet a pressing need: 救人之急是义不容辞的。It is one's duty to come to the rescue of a person in distress. /调运来的粮食和物品可真～了。The grain and materials sent to us arrived just when we needed them most.

救济 jiùjì relieve; succour: ～费 relief fund /～粮 relief grain /临时～ stop-gap relief /对贫民的～ poor relief /紧急～ emergency relief /社会～事业 social relief facilities; charities /～地震灾民 provide relief to earthquake victims /～难民 relieve refugees /开仓～饥民 open the storehouse to relieve the hungry /有些残疾人依靠政府的～维持生计。Some of the handicapped live on government relief.

救驾 jiùjià save the emperor from danger — 〈戏谑〉 save sb. from an awkward situation: 多亏你救了我的驾！Thanks a lot for rescuing me from embarrassment!

救经引足 jiùjīng-yǐnzú save a person who hangs himself by pulling his feet — take a counter-productive action

救苦救难 jiùkǔ-jiùnàn help the needy and relieve the distressed; help suffering people; relieve people of their sufferings: ～的观世音 benevolent *Avalokitesvara*, Goddess of Mercy /～的好嫂子，五十块总得借给我。Angel of mercy, you must lend me fifty dollars.

救困扶危 jiùkùn-fúwēi relieve and help people in danger: 他一向～。He is always ready to relieve people of their distress and help them.

救民水火 jiùmínshuǐhuǒ help people out of dire misery: 这是一支～的军队。This is an army ready to help people out of an abyss of suffering.

救命 jiùmìng save sb.'s life: ～！ Help! /～之恩 debt one owes to sb. for saving one's life

救命稻草 jiùmìng-dàocǎo straw to clutch at: 在危急关头，他像快要淹死的人那样急于捞～。At the critical moment he was like a drowning man trying desperately to catch a straw.

救命恩人 jiùmìng ēnrén savior: 还不快快来谢谢这位救命大恩人。Come over and thank this gentleman who saved your life.

救难 jiùnàn help sb. out of distress

救难船 jiùnànchuán rescue ship

救人须救彻 jiùrén xū jiù chè to save sb. you must save him fully: 救火须救灭，～。To save a person, you must make sure he is entirely out of danger, just as to put out a fire, you must make sure it is thoroughly extinguished.

救人一命，胜造七级浮屠 jiùrén yī mìng, shèng zào qī jí fútú to save a human life is better than to build a seven-storeyed pagoda; better save one life than build a seven-tiered pagoda

救生 jiùshēng lifesaving: ～索 lifeline /～设备 lifesaving appliance; life preserver

救生带 jiùshēngdài life belt

救生筏 jiùshēngfá life raft

救生圈 jiùshēngquān life buoy; life ring

救生艇 jiùshēngtǐng lifeboat

救生网 jiùshēngwǎng life net; safety net

救生衣 jiùshēngyī *also* "救生服" life jacket

救生员 jiùshēngyuán lifeguard; lifesaver

救世军 Jiùshìjūn 〈基督教〉 Salvation Army

救世主 Jiùshìzhǔ 〈基督教〉 the Saviour; the Redeemer: 以～自居 regard oneself as the Saviour; pose as the Saviour /从来就没有什么～。There has never been any Saviour.

救赎 jiùshú 〈宗教〉 redemption

救赎论 jiùshúlùn 〈宗教〉 doctrine of redemption

救死 jiùsǐ rescue the dying; save (sb. or sth.) from the brink of ruin

救死扶伤 jiùsǐ-fúshāng heal the wounded and rescue the dying: "～"是医务人员的天职。"Heal the wounded and rescue the dying" epitomizes the work ethic of the medical profession.

救亡 jiùwáng save the nation from subjugation; strive for national salvation: 抗日～ resist the Japanese invaders for national salvation /奔赴～第一线 rush to the front of national salvation

救亡图存 jiùwáng-túcún save the nation from subjugation and ensure its survival; fight for the survival and salvation of the nation

救险车 jiùxiǎnchē wrecking truck; wrecking car

救星 jiùxīng any individual or group of individuals who help relieve people of their sufferings; liberator; emancipator: 在旧中国，劳苦大众渴望找到自己的～。In old China, the toiling masses were yearning for a liberator.

救恤 jiùxù relieve; succour: ～灾民 provide relief to victims of disaster

救药 jiùyào (usu. used in the negative) cure; save; rescue: 不可～ incurable; incorrigible; hopeless

救应 jiùying aid and support; reinforce: 我们再派两个班去～他们。Let's send another two platoons to reinforce them.

救援 jiùyuán come to sb.'s rescue; rescue: ～车 rescue vehicle; wrecking truck /～列车 wrecking train /～物资 relief supplies /拂晓前，我们同前来～的部队会师了。Before dawn, we joined forces with the troops that came to our rescue.

救灾 jiùzāi ❶ provide disaster relief; send relief to a disaster area; help the people tide over a natural disaster ❷ obviate disaster

救正 jiùzhèng put right; correct; remedy; redress; set right

救治 jiùzhì treat and cure; bring (a patient) out of danger: 无法～ beyond cure; incurable /悉心～ treat and cure with great care /病人处于昏迷状态，必须迅速～。The patient is in a state of coma and must be given prompt treatment.

救助 jiùzhù help (sb.) in danger or difficulty; succour: ～费用 salvage charges /～基金 relief fund /重要的是予以及时～。The important thing is to give them timely help.

旧(舊) jiù ❶ past; outdated; antiquated; old: ～制度

old system /～杂志 back numbers of a magazine /～风俗 antiquated custom /～章法 outdated ways and regulations /除～布新 get rid of the old to make way for the new /因循守～ stick to old ways; follow the beaten path /不要用～脑筋对待新事物。Do not judge new things by old standards. ❷ used; old; worn; secondhand: ～雨伞 used (*or* old) umbrellas /～车 used car /～家具 timeworn furniture /～的不去,新的不来。If the old is not thrown away the new won't come to hand. ❸ former; onetime: *see* "～居";"～部" ❹ old friendship; old friend; old acquaintance: 怀～ miss the past and old acquaintances; nostalgia /念～ remember old friendship /亲戚故～ relatives and friends

旧案 jiù'àn ❶ case of long standing: 清理积年～ clear up all cases of years' standing ❷ old regulations; former practice: 一切暂照～办理。For the present, handle all cases according to former regulations.

旧病 jiùbìng chronic complaint; old trouble; chronic illness

旧病复发 jiùbìng-fùfā ❶ recurrence of an old illness; have a relapse ❷ slip back into old ways; go back to an old bad habit: 他～,又在吸毒了。He has slipped back into his old bad habit and is again taking drugs.

旧部 jiùbù former subordinate

旧地 jiùdì place where one went or stayed before; once familiar place; old haunt

旧地重游 jiùdì-chóngyóu revisit a once familiar place: ～,不禁有今昔沧桑之感。When revisiting my old haunt, I cannot help feeling a bit sad about the vicissitudes of life.

旧调重弹 jiùdiào-chóngtán *also* "老调重弹" lǎodiào-chóngtán harp on the same string; play the same old tune: 他今天的发言虽说搬了几个新名词,其实不过是～。Despite a few new terms his speech was nothing but a rehash of old ideas.

旧都 jiùdū former capital; old capital

旧恶 jiù'è old grievance; old wrong: 不念～ forgive an old wrong; let bygones be bygones

旧故 jiùgù old friend: ～胜新知。Old friends are better than new acquaintances.

旧观 jiùguān former appearance; old look: 古城今日,迥非～。Today, the old city is vastly different from what it used to be. /引进新工艺,实现技术革新,使这家工厂一改～。The factory has taken on a completely new look with the introduction of new technologies and technical innovations.

旧贯 jiùguàn 〈书面〉old system; old regulations; outmoded ways and regulations: 因仍～ follow outmoded regulations; stick to old ways

旧国 jiùguó old capital

旧好 jiùhǎo 〈书面〉❶ old friendship: 重修～ reestablish an old friendship; restore an old friendship ❷ old acquaintance; old friend

旧恨新仇 jiùhèn-xīnchóu *also* "旧恨新怨" old and new grievances; new hatred piled on old: ～,我一一记心头。I bear in mind all the bitterness, old and new.

旧恨新愁 jiùhèn-xīnchóu old sorrows and new worries

旧话重提 jiùhuà-chóngtí say again what one said before; repeat an old tale

旧货 jiùhuò old or used goods; secondhand goods; junk

旧货店 jiùhuòdiàn secondhand shop; junk shop

旧货市场 jiùhuò shìchǎng flea market

旧货摊 jiùhuòtān secondhand stall

旧疾 jiùjí chronic complaint; illness of long standing

旧迹 jiùjì ❶ past occurrence or event ❷ historic site; place of historic interest

旧家 jiùjiā 〈书面〉old and well-known family: ～子弟 children of an established family

旧交 jiùjiāo old acquaintance: 都是～,彼此熟悉。They know each other very well, for they are old acquaintances.

旧教 Jiùjiào Catholicism

旧金山 Jiùjīnshān *also* "三藩市" Sānfānshì (US) San Francisco

旧居 jiùjū former residence; old home

旧框框 jiùkuàngkuang convention; stereotype: 打破～ break conventions

旧历 jiùlì old Chinese calendar; lunar calendar: ～新年就是春节。The lunar new year is the Spring Festival.

旧历年 jiùlìnián lunar new year; Chinese New Year

旧例 jiùlì outmoded rules and regulations; old practice

旧梦 jiùmèng past experience; good old days: 追忆～之夜 reminiscent night

旧梦重温 jiùmèng-chóngwēn renew a sweet experience of bygone days

旧民主主义革命 jiùmínzhǔzhǔyì gémìng democratic revolution of the old type; old-democratic revolution

旧年 jiùnián ❶ 〈方言〉last year ❷ Spring Festival; Chinese New Year

旧瓶装新酒 jiùpíng zhuāng xīnjiǔ new wine in an old bottle; new content in old form: 京剧现代戏,虽说是～,但还是有创新的。There is some originality in the modern Beijing opera even though it is, so to speak, new wine in an old bottle.

旧前 jiùqián 〈方言〉years ago; before; in the past

旧情 jiùqíng friendship of bygone days: 不忘～ remember an old-time friendship

旧日 jiùrì former days; old days: 依然保持～的丰姿。There are still some traces of the graceful manner of the old days.

旧社会 jiùshèhuì old society (usu. referring to China before 1949)

旧诗 jiùshī classical poetry (with or without strict tonal patterns) as distinct from vernacular poetry (which is usually free verse or verse with comparatively uncertain rhyme schemes)

see also "古体诗" gǔtǐshī; "近体诗" jìntǐshī

旧石器时代 jiùshíqì shídài Old Stone Age; Paleolithic era

旧时 jiùshí old times; old days: 偶翻相册,～的许多事情又重现脑海。When I opened the album by chance, many past events came to my mind again.

旧识 jiùshí ❶ used to know (sb.) ❷ old acquaintance; old friend: ～新交遍天下。We have friends, both old and new, all over the world.

旧式 jiùshì old type; old fashion: ～房子 old-style building /～军队 old-type army /～家庭 old-fashioned family/～婚姻 traditional marriage /～武器 outdated weapons

旧事 jiùshì thing of the past: 这些～不必重提了。You don't have to rake up these matters of the past.

旧书 jiùshū ❶ used book; old book: 我买了一堆～。I bought a pile of secondhand books. ❷ books by ancient writers

旧书店 jiùshūdiàn secondhand bookstore

旧俗 jiùsú old custom

旧损 jiùsǔn old and worn out; timeworn: ～家具 old and worn out furniture

旧态 jiùtài condition of the old days; old self: ～依然。The condition remains as it was. *or* He remains his old self.

旧唐书 Jiù Tángshū *Jiu Tang Shu* or *Old History of Tang*, a huge work on the history of the Tang Dynasty in 200 volumes completed in 945 by a group of scholars headed by Liu Xu (刘昫)

旧套 jiùtào outmoded style; former style; old stereotype: 摆脱～ get rid of the outmoded style; break out of old stereotypes

旧体 jiùtǐ old style: ～诗词 old-style poetry; classical poetry

旧闻 jiùwén ❶ outdated news; old news; old lore; past events ❷ anecdotes: 这本书收集北京文人～,有一定的参考价值。This book has collected anecdotes about Beijing scholars and is of some reference value.

旧物 jiùwù ❶ books and records of our forefathers; old relics: 前朝～ things left behind by the previous dynasty ❷ former territory: 光复～ recover lost territories

旧习 jiùxí old habit and custom: ～难改。It's difficult to change old habits and customs.

旧学 jiùxué old Chinese learning (as distinct from the new or Western learning)

旧业 jiùyè ❶ old trade; predecessors' cause: 重操～ take up one's old (*or* former) trade again ❷ former property: ～荡然无存。His former property is all gone.

旧游 jiùyóu once visited: 苏州是我～之地,离开它已经有六年了。I once visited Suzhou, and that was six years ago.

旧友 jiùyǒu old acquaintance; old friend

旧雨 jiùyǔ old friend: ～重逢。Old friends meet again.

旧雨新知 jiùyǔ-xīnzhī *also* "旧雨新雨"; "旧雨今雨" acquaintances, old and new

旧怨 jiùyuàn old grudge; old scores: 不记～ forgive old grudges; let bygones be bygones

旧约 Jiùyuē 〈宗教〉*The Old Testament*

旧宅 jiùzhái old residence; old house

旧章 jiùzhāng outmoded ways and regulations; old rules:更改～ change the old rules /率由～ follow the beaten track; act in accordance with established rules

旧账 jiùzhàng old debt; old score; old feud:这些陈年～就不要算了。We may just as well forget about those old scores.

旧知 jiùzhī old acquaintance; old friend

旧址 jiùzhǐ former site (of a certain organization, etc., which has either moved out or ceased to exist):北京大学～ former site of Beijing University /这是我们机关的～。This is where our office once was (*or* used to be).

旧制 jiùzhì ❶ old system; old practice:概依～ act in strict accordance with old practices ❷ China's old system of weights and measures:现在市尺和市斤已成～。Nowadays *chi* and *jin* belong to the old system of weights and measures.

臼 jiù ❶ mortar:石～ stone mortar /杵～ mortar and pestle ❷ any mortar-shaped thing: *see* "～齿" ❸ joint (of bones):脱～ dislocation (of joints)

臼齿 jiùchǐ molar

柏 jiù 〈植物〉Chinese tallow tree:乌～ Chinese tallow tree

舅 jiù ❶ mother's brother; uncle:大～ eldest uncle /二～ second uncle ❷ wife's brother; brother-in-law:妻～ brother-in-law ❸〈书面〉husband's father

舅父 jiùfù mother's brother; uncle

舅姑 jiùgū 〈书面〉husband's parents; parents-in-law

舅舅 jiùjiu *also* "舅父"〈口语〉uncle

舅妈 jiùmā *also* "舅母"〈口语〉aunt

舅母 jiùmu wife of mother's brother; aunt

舅嫂 jiùsǎo wife of wife's brother; sister-in-law

舅子 jiùzi 〈口语〉wife's brother; brother-in-law:大～ wife's elder brother /小～ wife's younger brother

疚 jiù 〈书面〉remorse; guilt; compunction:负～ feel guilty /内～于心 have a guilty conscience; have a twinge of remorse /并未感到内～ have no qualms or compunction (about doing sth.) /愧～ be ashamed and uneasy /歉～ apology; regret

疚愧 jiùkuì guilty conscience; compunction:感觉～ feel guilty /～的心情 have a guilty conscience

疚歉 jiùqiàn apologetic; regretful:想到刚才错怪了他,心里不免有些～。I felt regret for having wronged him just now.

疚痛 jiùtòng painful and uneasy; worried:一种没有完成任务的～,使他心情异常烦恼。A painful feeling of failure to fulfil the task gnawed at him.

疚心 jiùxīn feel sorry; feel ill at ease:了却一件使他～的事 get rid of what pricks his conscience

疚责 jiùzé feel guilty and blame oneself for it

柩 jiù coffin with a corpse in it:棺～ coffin with a corpse in it /灵～ coffin that contains a corpse

柩车 jiùchē hearse

咎 jiù ❶ fault; blame:引～辞职 take the blame and send in one's resignation /引～自责 blame oneself for a misdeed; hold oneself responsible for a serious mistake ❷ censure; punish; blame:既往不～ forgive sb.'s past misdeeds; let bygones be bygones /动辄得～ be frequently taken to task; be blamed for whatever one does ❸ ill luck; bad fortune:休～ good luck and misfortune; weal and woe

咎戾 jiùlì 〈书面〉misdeed; crime:免于～ pardon one's crime; free from prosecution

咎由自取 jiùyóuzìqǔ have only oneself to blame; be one's own worst enemy:他落得如此下场,实在是～。He only had himself to blame for falling into such a plight.

咎有应得 jiùyǒuyīngdé get what one deserves:你是～。It serves you right.

jiu

蹴 jiu *see* "圪蹴" gējiu

see also cù

jū

车(車) jū ❶ chariot, one of the pieces in Chinese chess:丢卒保～ give up a pawn to save a chariot — sacrifice minor things to save major ones ❷ (of chess) castle; rook
see also chē

且 jū ❶〈书面〉〈助词〉oh:狂童之狂也～! Oh, young man, you are the most foolish of all fools! ❷ used in persons' names
see also qiě

疽 jū 〈中医〉subcutaneous ulcer; deep-rooted ulcer:鼻～ (of a horse) glanders /瘭～ pyogenic infection of the pad of a finger /疔～ miliary vesicle under the nose or on either side of the mandible /坏～ gangrene /乳～ intramammary abscess /炭～ anthrax /痈～ ulcer /气肿～ blackleg; black quarter

趄 jū *see* "趑趄" zījū
see also qiè

苴 jū

苴麻 jūmá *also* "种麻" zhǒngmá female plant of hemp

雎 jū

雎鸠 jūjiū 〈古语〉turtledove:关关～,在河之洲。The turtledoves' crying sound came from the small islet in the river.

狙 jū ❶〈古语〉a kind of monkey ❷〈书面〉be on watch for; spy:～伺 watch in secret

狙击 jūjī ambush; snipe:～敌人 snipe at the enemy

狙击手 jūjīshǒu sniper

狙击战 jūjīzhàn 〈军事〉sniping action

鞠[1] jū ❶ rear; bring up:～育 rear; bring up ❷〈书面〉bend: *see* "～躬" ❸ (Jū) a surname

鞠[2] jū 〈古语〉a kind of ball:蹴～ kick a ball

鞠躬 jūgōng ❶ bow:～道谢 bow one's thanks /鞠了个九十度的躬 make a deep bow; bow to a 90° angle /全场起立欢呼,于是她风度翩翩地鞠了一躬,以表谢意。Greeted by a standing ovation she gracefully responded by making a bow. ❷〈书面〉in a discreet and scrupulous manner:斯～君子也。This is a scrupulous and respectful gentleman.

鞠躬尽瘁 jūgōng-jìncuì bend oneself to a task and exert oneself to the utmost; spare no effort in the performance of one's duty; be as painstaking as one can be in one's work:～,死而后已 bend one's back to a task until one's dying day; give one's all or one's best till one's heart ceases to beat /为人民～几十年 serve the people wholeheartedly for decades

鞠养 jūyǎng 〈书面〉bring up:～教诲 bring up and educate

掬(匊) jū hold with both hands:双手～米 scoop up some rice with both hands /笑容可～ radiant with smiles /憨态可～ disarmingly naive

掬诚 jūchéng wholeheartedly; with all one's heart:～相待 treat sb. with all sincerity

掬饮 jūyǐn scoop up water to drink:～山泉 scoop up water from a mountain spring to drink

拘 jū ❶ arrest; detain; take into custody:～之以候审 detain sb. for trial ❷ restrain; constrain:无～无束 unconstrained; free and easy /不～小节 be negligent of trivial matters; not bother about trifles /不～礼节 not stand on ceremony /不～形式 be not particular about form ❸ adhere to rigidly; be inflexible: *see* "～泥" ❹ restrict; limit; bound:大小不～ regardless of size /选拔人才不～一格 not stick to one pattern in choosing gifted and talented people

拘板 jūban 〈方言〉(of movement or talk) rigid; awkward; ill at ease; up-tight:动作～ awkward in movement /我和你随便聊聊,不必

这么～。Don't be so uptight; we're only chatting.

拘捕 jūbǔ arrest:～权 power of arrest /依法～ arrest in the name of the law

拘传 jūchuán sign a warrant and summon sb.

拘管 jūguǎn restrain; control; restrict:严加～ keep under strict control

拘魂 jūhún 〈迷信〉arrest one's soul

拘忌 jūjì have scruples (about); have misgivings:恣意妄为,无所～ act wilfully without scruple

拘检 jūjiǎn 〈书面〉examine and restrain oneself; be restrained and cautious:性粗犷,无～。He is bold and straightforward, having no use for restraint.

拘谨 jūjǐn overcautious; reserved; punctilious:为人～ be rather reserved /言谈～ talk in a guarded way /举止～ behave overcautiously /本来很大方的姑娘,一下子变得～了。The girl who used to carry herself with ease and confidence turned out to be ill at ease all of a sudden. /一到正式场合发表意见,大家往往～起来。People often become reserved and withdrawn when it comes to airing their views on formal occasions.

拘禁 jūjìn detain; take into custody:～嫌疑犯 take a suspect into custody

拘礼 jūlǐ be punctilious; stand on ceremony:他显得太～了。He appears to be too punctilious. /这儿一切都很随便,不用～。Things are quite free and easy here. We don't stand on ceremony.

拘留 jūliú ❶ detain; hold in custody; intern:～审讯 detain for interrogation /～方式 form of detention /～期间 duration of detention ❷ (as a form of administrative punishment) detention; provisional apprehension:被处以十五天～ received a punishment of 15 days detention

拘留国 jūliúguó detaining power

拘留所 jūliúsuǒ house of detention; bridewell; lockup

拘留证 jūliúzhèng detention warrant

拘挛 jūluán ❶ cramps; spasms:手足～ have cramps in hands and feet ❷ 〈书面〉rigidly adhere to (formalities, etc.):～章句 rigidly adhere to the wording

拘挛儿 jūluanr 〈方言〉stiff; numb:这天儿真冷,手都冻～了。It's so cold today that my hands have gone numb.

拘拿 jūná arrest; catch:～犯人 arrest criminals

拘泥 jūnì ❶ be a stickler for (forms, etc.); cling to (formalities, etc.); stick fast to:～于形式 stick fast to form; be formalistic /～于小节 be tied down by petty conventions /小说与历史不同,它不必～于细节的真实。Novels are different from history. They don't have to be true to fact in every detail. ❷ restrained; uneasy:举止～ be ill at ease

拘票 jūpiào arrest warrant; warrant

拘牵 jūqiān 〈书面〉tie; bind up; fetter; confine:～于成规 be confined to customary practice

拘囚 jūqiú detain; take into custody; imprison; put in jail:屡被～ be imprisoned repeatedly

拘守 jūshǒu ❶ rigidly adhere to; stick fast to:～陈规 hold fast to old rules and practices /～绳墨 rigidly follow the rules ❷ 〈书面〉put behind bars; imprison

拘束 jūshù ❶ restrain; restrict:他觉得他的活动受到了新规定的～。He felt the new regulations had restricted his activities. ❷ constrained; embarrassed; ill at ease:她谈笑自若,一点～也没有。She chattered on and on, holding nothing back.

拘系 jūxì take into custody

拘押 jūyā detain; take into custody:～逃犯 take an escaped prisoner into custody

拘役 jūyì short term of forced labour under detention

拘囿 jūyòu rigidly keep to; stick to; be confined to:～于成说 confine oneself to the accepted theory or formulation

拘迂 jūyū 〈书面〉stubborn adherence to worn-out rules and ideas

拘着 jūzhe be hindered; be restricted; be obstructed:人家～面子,多少得给点回报。For fear of hurting our feelings, they would at least give us something in return.

拘执 jūzhí be a stickler for (form, etc.); be punctilious:他办事过于～。He is rather rigid in handling things.

拘絷 jūzhí 〈书面〉put in jail; imprison; take into custody

拘滞 jūzhì inflexible; rigid; restrained:他为人比较谨慎～。He is rather cautious and inflexible.

跔

jū 〈书面〉(of hands and feet) cramps (caused by cold weather)

鮈

jū 〈动物〉gudgeon (*Gobio gobio*)

驹

jū ❶ young horse; colt:千里～ winged steed ❷ foal:怀～ be in foal; be with foal

驹光 jūguāng sunbeam — time:～易逝。The sunbeam fades (away) easily. *or* Time flies.

驹子 jūzi foal:马～ foal

居

jū ❶ reside; dwell; live:侨～国外 reside abroad /客～他乡 live in an alien land /深～简出 live in the seclusion of one's own home; live a secluded life /分～ (of members of a family) live apart /同～ live together; cohabit /移～ move one's residence; migrate /杂～ (of two or more nationalities) live together ❷ residence; house; home:迁～ move house; change one's residence /新～ new home; new residence /安～乐业 live and work in peace and contentment ❸ be (in a certain position); occupy (a place):～左 be on the left side /～全国首位 rank first in the country; occupy first place in the country /身～要职 hold an important post /后来～上。The latecomers surpass the old timers. *or* The new generation surpasses the old. /二者必～其一。It must be one or the other. ❹ claim; assert:以老资格自～ flaunt one's seniority; be a self-styled veteran ❺ save; store up; lay by:囤积～奇 hoarding and profiteering /奇货可～ hoarding as a rare commodity; rare commodity worth hoarding ❻ 〈书面〉stay put; be at a standstill:变动不～ mutable; changeable; volatile /岁月不～。Time marches on. ❼ used in the names of some restaurants:同和～ Tonghe Restaurant ❽ (Jū) a surname

居哀 jū'āi observe mourning for one's parent

居安思危 jū'ān-sīwēi think of danger in times of peace; be vigilant in peace time:～,思则有备,有备无患。To be alert to danger in times of peace means mental preparedness, which in turn ensures security.

居处 jūchǔ ❶ live; reside:～的地方 living quarters; lodgings ❷ 〈书面〉living conditions:～益困。The living conditions are getting worse.

居处 jūchù residence; dwelling:他对现在的～很满意。He is quite satisfied with his present residence.

居多 jūduō be in the majority:他买东西以中低档品～。Most of the things he bought were of medium or lower grades. /我们厂女工～。Women workers in our plant are in the majority.

居高临下 jūgāo-línxià occupy a commanding position; take on a condescending air:潼关城～,地势险要。Situated on a commanding height, the city of Tongguan is very important strategically. /她那副～的神态,使人很不舒服。Her condescending (*or* high and mighty) air makes people very uncomfortable.

居功 jūgōng claim credit for oneself:他为这项科研计划的成功贡献最大,但却从不～。He contributed most to the success of this scientific research project, but he never paraded his own merit.

居功自傲 jūgōng-zì'ào claim credit and put on airs; become arrogant because of one's achievements

居官 jūguān 〈书面〉hold a government post; assume a government office:～清廉 be an honest official

居积 jūjī 〈书面〉accumulate wealth; corner (the market); hoard for speculation:～致富 amass a fortune

居家 jūjiā ❶ stay at home:病后～的日子不少。I stayed at home for quite some time after I was taken ill. ❷ run a household; keep house:～勤俭 manage a family economically; be frugal in housekeeping

居间 jūjiān (mediate or work) between two parties:～贸易 intermediary trade /～说合 bring two parties together

居间人 jūjiānrén intermediary; mediator

居里 jūlǐ ❶ (Jūlǐ) Marie Curie (1867-1934) and Pierre Curie (1859-1906), French physicists and chemists, pioneers of radioactivity and winners of the Nobel Prize for Physics (1903):～夫人 Madame Curie ❷ 〈物理〉curie (measure of radioactivity)

居留 jūliú reside:临时～ temporary residence /长期～ permanent residence /～在中国的外国人 foreigner residing in China

居留权 jūliúquán right of residence; right of abode

居留证 jūliúzhèng residence permit：长期～ permanent residence permit
居民 jūmín resident; inhabitant; dweller：城市～ city dwellers; urban inhabitants
居民点 jūmíndiǎn residential area
居民身份证 jūmín shēnfènzhèng resident identity card
居民委员会 jūmín wěiyuánhuì neighbourhood committee; residents' committee
居奇 jūqí store up a scarce commodity for profiteering; corner the market; hoard for speculation：囤积～ hoarding and profiteering /～牟利 seek profits by cornering the market
居然 jūrán ❶ unexpectedly; to one's surprise; (go) so far as：敌人～使用了毒气。The enemy went so far as to use poison gas. /他～会相信这件事！Fancy his believing it! /谁会想到～有这样的事！Who would have thought of such a thing! /事情过了才几天，你～忘了。How could you have forgotten something that happened only a few days ago. /他～有脸说出这样的事来。He had the nerve (*or* gall) to say such a thing. ❷〈书面〉obvious; evident; apparent：乡俗民情，～可见。Local customs and conditions are for all to see.
居人 jūrén inhabitant; resident：巷无～。There is no inhabitant in this lane. *or* There is no one living in this lane.
居丧 jūsāng 〈书面〉observe mourning for one's dead parent
居士 jūshì ❶ lay Buddhist; *upasaka* ❷ retired scholar
居室 jūshì ❶ room：这一户四口人，住着二～一个单元的楼房。This family of four lives in a two-room flat. ❷〈方言〉house：篱内是一个方庭，围在正中的是一个小小的～。Within the fence, there is a square courtyard with a small house in the centre. ❸〈书面〉(of a married couple) live together：男女～。The man and woman cohabit.
居首 jūshǒu occupy the first place; rank first：这个县的工农业总产值在全省～。The total value of this county's industrial and agricultural output ranks first in the whole province. /他的考试成绩～。He came out on top in the exam.
居孀 jūshuāng 〈书面〉live as a widow
居所 jūsuǒ residence; dwelling (place)
居停 jūtíng ❶ stay; take up quarters：他在山上宾馆～一宿，次日下山。He stayed overnight in a hotel on the mountain and came down the following day. ❷〈书面〉landlord; host
居委会 jūwěihuì (short for 居民委员会) neighbourhood committee; residents' committee
居下讪上 jūxià-shànshàng inferiors talking ill of their superiors
居心 jūxīn harbour (evil) intention：～险恶 with evil or vicious intentions
居心不良 jūxīn-bùliáng harbour evil intentions
居心叵测 jūxīn-pǒcè with sinister design; with ulterior motives：他的这番议论总让人觉得～。People felt that he had an axe to grind in making such remarks.
居于 jūyú hold (a post); occupy (a certain position)：～领导地位 be in a leading position
居止 jūzhǐ 〈书面〉❶ live; stay：宅院幽静，颇堪～。With a quiet and secluded courtyard, it's a nice place to live in. ❷ residence：两家～相近。Their residences are quite close to each other. *or* The two families live close to each other.
居址 jūzhǐ 〈书面〉address
居中 jūzhōng ❶ (mediate or work) between two parties：～调停 mediate between two parties; act as a mediator ❷ be placed in the middle：并排三间，这家商店～。There were three shops in a row. This one is in between. /他走近大沙发，～坐定。He went to the sofa and sat down in the middle.
居住 jūzhù live; reside; dwell：～条件 housing conditions /在国外～多年 reside abroad for quite a long time /他自小就～在城里。He has been living in the city since his childhood. /这是个多民族～地区。This is a region inhabited by a number of national minorities.
居住国 jūzhùguó country of residence
居住面积 jūzhù miànjī living space; floor space
居住期限 jūzhù qīxiàn length of residence
居住小区 jūzhù xiǎoqū residential district
居住证 jūzhùzhèng residence permit

裾 jū 〈书面〉❶ full front of a Chinese gown ❷ full front and back of a Chinese gown
裾礁 jūjiāo 〈地质〉fringing reef; shore reef

琚 jū ❶ a kind of jade worn by ancient people ❷ (Jū) a surname

椐 jū small tree with big joints which the ancient people used to make walking sticks

据 jū see "拮据" jiéjū
see also jù

腒 jū 〈书面〉dry preserved bird meat

椇 jū 〈书面〉sedan chair (for use in mountains); litter

挶 jū 〈书面〉❶ tools for carrying earth; basket and pole ❷ take hold of; grasp

锔（锯） jū mend (crockery) with clamps：～碗 mend bowls with clamps /～锅 mend pots with clamps
see also jú
锔碗儿的 jūwǎnrde tinker
锔子 jūzi clamp used in mending crockery

鞫 jū 〈书面〉interrogate; question：～讯 interrogate; question

鵴 jū 〈书面〉scoop up with spoons, ladles, etc.

jú

菊 jú ❶ chrysanthemum：除虫～ Dalmatian chrysanthemum /矢车～ cornflower /雏～ daisy; *Bellis perennis* /翠～ China aster /黄春～ camomile /金鸡～ coreopsis /绣线～ spiraea /赏～ visit a chrysanthemum (flower) show ❷ (Jú) a surname
菊蒿 júhāo *also* "艾菊" àijú 〈植物〉tansy
菊花 júhuā chrysanthemum：～酒 chrysanthemum wine
菊苣 júјù 〈植物〉chicory (*Cichorium intybus*)
菊科 júkē 〈植物〉composite family
菊石 júshí 〈地质〉ammonite
菊坛 jútán theatrical circles; Beijing opera circles
菊芋 júyù *also* "洋姜" yángjiāng 〈植物〉❶ Jerusalem artichoke; girasole (*Helianthus tuberosus*) ❷ stem tubers of Jerusalem artichokes
菊月 júyuè ninth month of the lunar year, named after the chrysanthemum which is in full bloom in the month
菊展 júzhǎn chrysanthemum show：每年秋季北京中山公园都举办～。There is a chrysanthemum show every autumn in the Dr. Sun Yat-sen Memorial Park of Beijing.

桔 jú see "橘" jú
see also jié

橘 jú tangerine; orange：福～ tangerine produced in Fujian; Fujian tangerine /蜜～ tangerine /柑～ oranges and tangerines /枸～ trifoliate orange /金～ kumquat /越～ cowberry /～树 tangerine tree
橘柑 júgān 〈方言〉tangerine
橘红 júhóng ❶ tangerine (colour); reddish orange ❷〈中药〉dried tangerine peel
橘黄 júhuáng orange (colour)
橘络 júluò 〈中药〉tangerine pith
橘农 júnóng tangerine farmer
橘汁 júzhī orange juice
橘子 júzi tangerine

鶪 jú 〈古语〉〈动物〉shrike

局[1] jú ❶ chessboard：棋～ chessboard; chess game ❷ game; set; innings：第二～ (of table tennis, etc.) second game; second set; (of shuttlecock, baseball, etc.) second innings /下一～棋 play a

J

game of chess /和～ drawn game; draw; tie /平～ draw; tie /连胜三～ win three games at a stretch ❸ situation; position; state of affairs: 战～ war situation /政～ political situation /时～ current situation /全～ overall situation; situation as a whole /败～ losing battle; lost game /定～ inevitable outcome; foregone conclusion /僵～ deadlock; stalemate /大～已定。The outcome is certain (*or* indubitable). ❹ breadth of mind; magnanimity; tolerance: 此人通敏有智～。This man is sharp-witted and tolerant. ❺ gathering; party: 饭～ dinner party; banquet /赌～ gambling party ❻ ruse; trap; trick: 骗～ fraud; trap; swindle /糊弄～ duty performed or done in a perfunctory manner ❼ restrain; constrain; restrict: *see* "～促"; "～限"

局[2] jú ❶ part; portion: *see* "～部" ❷ bureau; department: 教育～ bureau of education /税务～ tax bureau /铁路～ railway administration ❸ functional office: 邮～ post office /电话～ telephone exchange ❹ shop: 书～ publishing house; bookshop

局本 júběn books published by the official publishing houses in the Qing Dynasty

局部 júbù part; locality: ～地区 parts of an area; some areas /～现象 local phenomena /～优势 partial superiority /～投标 partial bid /～照明 local illumination; spot lighting /～反应 local reaction /不能只顾～利益 must not consider only partial and local interests

局部存储器 júbù cúnchǔqì local memory

局部解剖 júbù jiěpōu 〈医学〉 topography

局部麻醉 júbù mázuì 〈医学〉 local anaesthesia

局部模拟 júbù mónǐ partial simulation

局部战争 júbù zhànzhēng local war; partial war

局促 júcù *also* "偈促" júcù; "跼促" júcù ❶ narrow; constricted; cramped: 参加会议的人多, 这个会场显得很～。As many people are attending the meeting, the hall seems very cramped. ❷ 〈方言〉 (of time) short: 开工在即, 准备工作尚多, 时间太～。The construction will soon begin, and time is too short to get all the preparatory work done. ❸ feel or show constraint; be ill at ease

局促不安 júcù-bù'ān be ill at ease; feel embarrassed: 她坐在那儿～。She sat there very ill at ease. /她不由得越加～起来了。She felt even more uncomfortable and awkward.

局地 júdì parts of an area; some areas: ～天气预报 weather forecast for parts of an area /～气候异常。The climate of some areas is abnormal.

局度 júdù 〈书面〉 tolerance; magnanimity; forbearance: 此人颇有～。The man is quite broad-minded.

局蹐 jújí *see* "跼蹐" jújí

局量 júliàng 〈书面〉 tolerance; magnanimity; forbearance: ～不能容物 not tolerant towards others

局麻 júmá (short for 局部麻醉) 〈医学〉 local anaesthesia

局面 júmiàn ❶ aspect; phase; prospect; situation: 生动活泼的政治～ lively and dynamic political situation /打开～ open up a new prospect; make a breakthrough /～一新 enter a new phase; take on a new aspect /处于尴尬的～ be in a fix (*or* predicament) /这个国家现在处于分裂和混乱的～。The country is now plagued with division and turmoil. ❷ 〈方言〉 scale; size: 这家商店～虽不大, 货色倒齐全。The shop is of moderate size, but it is well stocked.

局内 júnèi *also* "局中" take part in; be party to

局内人 júnèirén *also* "局中人" one who is among the inner circle; insider: 此事非～不得而知。The affair is known to insiders alone. *or* Only insiders are in the know.

局骗 júpiàn trap; cheat; swindle: ～财物 swindle sb. out of his money or property

局气 júqi 〈方言〉 fair; impartial: 要一碗水端平, 别来不～的。Be fair to all sides. Don't play foul!

局势 júshì situation: 国际紧张～ tense international situation; international tension /～日趋恶化。Things are getting worse and worse. /～有所缓和。The situation is a bit relaxed. *or* The tension has eased a little.

局天蹐地 jútiān-jídì *see* "跼天蹐地" jútiān-jídì

局外 júwài have nothing to do with (sth.); be an outsider: 置身～ keep oneself away from sth.; refuse to be drawn into a matter

局外人 júwàirén outsider: 我们～还是不介入这件事为妙。It's better for us outsiders to keep away from the whole business. /她仿佛是一个～。She doesn't seem to be among the inner circle.

局限 júxiàn limit; confine: 不能把自己～于一个小天地里 must not confine oneself to a small circle; must not shut oneself up within narrow confines /人的认识受到时代的～。A person's understanding (*or* mental horizon) is limited by the times.

局限性 júxiànxìng limitations

局域网 júyùwǎng 〈信息〉 local area network (LAN): ～互联 LAN interconnection

局子 júzi 〈旧语〉 ❶ police station ❷ establishment that used to provide armed guards or *wushu* coaches ❸ trap; snare: 我们险些中了他的～。We had almost fallen into his trap.

焗 jú 〈方言〉 ❶ method of steam cooking: 盐～鸡 salted and steamed chicken ❷ feel suffocated; be stifled

焗油 júyóu ❶ treat hair with cream to make it soft and shiny: 她每两周～一次。She has her hair treated in cream once every two weeks. ❷ hair treatment cream

跼 jú 〈书面〉 (of one's back) bent

跼促 júcù *see* "局促" júcù

跼蹐 jújí *also* "局蹐" jújí 〈书面〉 ❶ ill at ease; nervous: 最近的反贪污斗争使他～不安。The present anti-corruption struggle put him on tenterhooks. ❷ narrow; cramped

跼天蹐地 jútiān-jídì *also* "局天蹐地" jútiān-jídì in straitened circumstances; with hardly any place to live in

锔 jú 〈化学〉 curium (Cm)

see also jū

偈 jú

偈促 júcù *see* "局促" júcù

jǔ

举(舉、擧) jǔ ❶ lift; raise; hold up: 高～ hold high; hold aloft /～义旗 raise the standard of revolt /～枪瞄准猎物 level one's gun at the prey /～杯祝老人健康 raise one's glass and drink to the old man's health /挺～〈体育〉 clean and jerk; jerk /抓～〈体育〉 snatch /推～〈体育〉 press /运动员～起了一百五十公斤的杠铃。The athlete succeeded in lifting the barbell weighing one hundred and fifty kilos. ❷ act; work; deed; move: 豪～ bold action /创～ pioneering work /善～ good deed /壮～ heroic undertaking /轻～妄动 act rashly /多此一～ make an unnecessary move /一～两得 kill two birds with one stone /一～一动 every act and every move ❸ start; begin; initiate; raise: 百端待～。A thousand things remain to be done. ❹ 〈书面〉 give birth (to a child): ～一男 give birth to a boy ❺ elect; choose: 选贤～能 elect the virtuous and choose the gifted /大家～他当业务学习组长。People elected him the leader of their vocational study group. ❻ (short for 举人) successful candidate in the imperial examinations at the provincial level in the Ming and Qing dynasties: 中～ pass the imperial examination at the provincial level ❼ cite; enumerate; take; give: ～典型事例 cite a typical example /列～大量的事实 list large numbers of facts /检～不法行为 report an illegal act to the authorities /再～我们家为例。Next, take our family as an example. ❽ 〈书面〉 all; whole; entire: *see* "～坐"; "～世"; "～国"

举哀 jǔ'āi ❶ 〈旧语〉 wail in mourning ❷ go into mourning: 总统逝世, 全国～。The whole nation was in mourning over the death of the president. /王后病逝, 发丧～。When the queen died, the sad news was proclaimed and the whole country went into mourning.

举案齐眉 jǔ'àn-qíméi hold the tray level with the brows — husband and wife treating each other with courtesy; married couple loving and respecting each other

举办 jǔbàn conduct; hold; run: ～研讨会 hold a seminar /～舞会 hold a ball /～酒会 give a cocktail party /～学术讲座 sponsor a series of academic lectures

举报 jǔbào report (an offence); inform (against an offender): 设立～电话 open an informants' hot-line telephone /设立～中心 set up an informant centre

举杯 jǔbēi raise one's glass (to propose a toast): ～祝贺新郎新娘幸福 drink to (the happiness of) the bride and bridegroom

举兵 jǔbīng 〈书面〉 raise an army: ～出征 send troops on an expedition /～北上 dispatch troops to the north

举不胜举 jǔbùshèngjǔ too numerous to mention: 类似情况～。

Cases like this are too numerous to cite.

举步 jǔbù 〈书面〉step forward; stride forward; walk: ～如飞 walk as if on wings /腿关节疼痛得使他难以～。The leg joints are so painful that he finds it difficult to step forward.

举步维艰 jǔbù-wéijiān (find it) difficult to take a step; hard to start: 学校修建教工宿舍的事～。It was quite difficult to get the housing project for college faculty started.

举措 jǔcuò move; act; measure: 这是一项新～。This is a new move (*or* measure).

举措失当 jǔcuò-shīdàng make an ill-advised or indiscreet move: 该公司在两桩交易中～。The company erred in two business deals.

举鼎绝膑 jǔdǐng-juébìn break one's kneecap while lifting a tripod — be unequal to one's task; do sth. beyond one's power; overestimate one's own strength

举动 jǔdòng movement; move; act; activity: 不同寻常的～ extraordinary move /～灵活 be nimble in movement /她的～令人惊诧。Her conduct was shocking.

举发 jǔfā report (evildoer or evil doings) to the authorties concerned: 向公安机关～ report to the public security bureau

举凡 jǔfán 〈书面〉ranging from... to...; all... such as...: ～琴棋书画,她样样精通。She is good at all such things as musical instruments, chess, calligraphy and painting.

举国 jǔguó whole nation: ～称颂 universal acclaim /～一致抗御外侮。The whole nation is united against foreign aggressors. /伟人逝世,～悲痛。The passing away of the great man left the whole country deep in grief and sorrow.

举国欢腾 jǔguó huānténg the whole nation is jubilant

举国上下 jǔguó shàngxià from the leaders of the nation to the common people; entire nation: ～总动员 general mobilization of the nation /～,同仇敌忾。The entire country was united by a common hatred of the enemy.

举劾 jǔhé 〈书面〉list crimes and mistakes so as to impeach (a public official)

举火 jǔhuǒ 〈书面〉❶ light a fire: ～为号 light a beacon ❷ light a kitchen fire; light a stove: 日中,尚未～。Though it was already noontime, the kitchen fire was still not lit.

举家 jǔjiā whole family: ～老小 all members of the family, old and young /～迁蜀。The whole family moved to Sichuan.

举架 jǔjià 〈方言〉the height of a house: 这间房子～矮。This house is too low.

举荐 jǔjiàn recommend (a person): 无论是自荐,还是～,都要考试试用。Whether recommended by oneself or others, every candidate must pass an examination and be on probation for a time.

举借 jǔjiè borrow (a large amount of money); raise (a loan): ～外债 borrow a large sum from foreign countries; raise foreign loans

举力 jǔlì lift: 气球的～ lift of a balloon

举例 jǔlì give an example; cite an instance: ～说明 illustrate with examples /～来说 for example; for instance /～发凡 give examples in different categories to explain the stylistic rules of the book /不必更多～了。It's needless to multiply examples.

举目 jǔmù 〈书面〉raise the eyes; look: ～千里 look a thousand *li* ahead; look far afield /～远眺,只见这草原与天相接,无边无际。Looking into the distance, one could see a vast expanse of grassland merging with the horizon.

举目无亲 jǔmù-wúqīn have no one to turn to (for help); be a stranger in an alien land: ～的地方 place where there is not a soul one knows

举棋不定 jǔqí-bùdìng hesitate about or over what move to make; be unable to make up one's mind; be irresolute; waver; vacillate; shilly-shally: 到了处理具体问题时,他就～了。When it comes to dealing with specific problems, he becomes hesitant. /正当我～的时候,他的话帮助我下了决心。When I was unable to make up my mind, his words helped me to come to a decision.

举人 jǔrén successful candidate in the imperial examinations at the provincial level in the Ming and Qing dynasties

举世 jǔshì throughout the world; universally: ～皆知 be known to everybody /～无敌 unrivalled (*or* matchless) in the world; second to none /～无伦 unparalleled the world over

举世闻名 jǔshì-wénmíng of world renown; world-famous: ～的万里长城 world-famous Great Wall

举世无双 jǔshì-wúshuāng unrivalled; matchless: 他说他的惊险表演,空前绝后,～。He says he can do a wonderful stunt, the likes of which are not to be found anywhere in the world.

举世瞩目 jǔshì-zhǔmù attract worldwide attention; become the focus of world attention: 我国经济发展取得了～的成就。The achievements of our economic development have captured world attention.

举事 jǔshì 〈书面〉start a revolt; stage an uprising; rise in rebellion

举手 jǔshǒu raise one's hand(s); put up one's hand(s): ～表决 vote by a show of hands /～加额 raise one's hand to the forehead to congratulate /～可得 be within one's grasp /举双手赞成 be totally in favour; fully support /举起手来! Hands up!

举手礼 jǔshǒulǐ hand salute

举手投足 jǔshǒu-tóuzú any move; any action: 她去世多年了,但她的音容笑貌,～,至今还留在我的脑海里。Though she has been dead for years, her lovely voice and smiles, her every move and act are still fresh in my mind.

举手之劳 jǔshǒuzhīláo *also* "一举手之劳" lift a finger: 你不用谢我,这不过是～。No need to thank me; it's nothing.

举坛 jǔtán weightlifting world; weightlifting circles

举头 jǔtóu raise one's head: ～望明月 raise one's head to gaze at the bright moon

举贤荐能 jǔxián-jiànnéng recommend the virtuous and the able; promote gifted people: ～不避亲。When it comes to recommending talented people, you need not deliberately avoid mentioning your relatives and friends.

举行 jǔxíng hold (a meeting, ceremony, etc.); stage; conduct: ～罢工 go on strike /～集会和示威游行 stage rallies and demonstrations /～招待会 host a reception /～结婚典礼 perform a wedding ceremony /明天要～庆祝会。The celebration will take place tomorrow. /双方～了认真会谈。The two sides were engaged in earnest negotiations (*or* discussions).

举眼 jǔyǎn raise the eyes; look: ～一看,遍山红叶。Looking round, one finds the mountain a vast sea of red leaves.

举要 jǔyào (usu. used in book title) essentials: 《唐宋文～》 *Quintessence of Essays of the Tang and Song Dynasties*

举业 jǔyè poems and essays written during the imperial examinations

举一反三 jǔyī-fǎnsān mention one side and think out the other three sides; draw inferences about other cases from one instance: 做学问要善于～,触类旁通。In academic pursuits, one must be able to learn by analogy and judge the whole from the part.

举一赅百 jǔyī-gāibǎi *see* "举一反三"

举义 jǔyì 〈书面〉stage an uprising; rise in rebellion

举隅 jǔyú grasp a typical example and you will grasp the whole category; comprehend by analogy; draw inferences about other cases from one instance

举债 jǔzhài 〈书面〉borrow money: ～度日 live on borrowed money /为大办婚事而～ borrow money for a sumptuous wedding /～成本 cost of debt /～筹资 debt financing

举直错枉 jǔzhí-cuòwǎng recommend and appoint upright people and dismiss crooked people

举止 jǔzhǐ bearing; manner; deportment; mien: ～娴雅 deport oneself gracefully /～不凡 of extraordinary bearing /～粗野 have a rude manner; be fierce of mien /～庄重 conduct oneself in a dignified manner; carry oneself with dignity /～失措 lose one's presence of mind /他的～像军人。He bears himself like a soldier. /她～大方,言语洒脱。She was an outspoken girl with a free and easy manner.

举踵 jǔzhǒng 〈书面〉on tiptoe

举重 jǔzhòng weightlifting: ～运动员 weightlifter; lifter; strongman /～台 weightlifting platform

举子 jǔzǐ students recommended to take part in the imperial examination

举足轻重 jǔzú-qīngzhòng hold the balance; be of crucial importance; prove decisive: 具有～的影响 be of decisive influence /具有～的地位 occupy a pivotal (*or* crucial) position /他在这里可是～的人物。He is a bigshot here.

举坐 jǔzuò *also* "举座" all those present: ～惊骇。All those present were thrown into a panic.

榉(櫸) jǔ *see* "山毛榉" shānmáojǔ

弆 jǔ 〈书面〉collect; preserve: 藏～ collect and preserve

J

柜 jǔ
see also guì
柜柳 jǔliǔ *also* "元宝枫" yuánbǎofēng 〈植物〉 *Pterocarya stenoptera*

矩(榘) jǔ ❶ carpenter's square; square:不以规～,不能成方圆。If compasses and squares are not used, you will not be able to draw squares or circles — no rules, no shape. ❷ rules; regulations:循规蹈～ follow rules, orders, etc., docilely /规行～步 stick to the established practice; behave correctly and cautiously ❸〈物理〉moment:力～ moment of force /惯性～ moment of inertia
矩臂 jǔbì 〈物理〉moment arm
矩尺 jǔchǐ *also* "曲尺" qūchǐ carpenter's square
矩形 jǔxíng *also* "长方形" chángfāngxíng rectangle: ～线圈 square coil
矩矱 jǔyuē 〈书面〉rules and regulations; norms and standards: 合于～ conform to the rules and regulations; be in accord with norms and standards
矩阵 jǔzhèn 〈数学〉matrix
矩阵代数 jǔzhèn dàishù matrix algebra

沮 jǔ ❶〈书面〉stop; check; prevent:见不义而～ stop any act of injustice the moment one detects it ❷ turn gloomy; turn glum; feel dejected:气～ in low spirits
see also jù
沮遏 jǔ'è 〈书面〉check; stop; prevent
沮丧 jǔsàng ❶ dejected; depressed; dispirited; disheartened:神气～ look depressed /心情十分～ in very low spirits /士气～ in low morale /他感到～。He felt disheartened. /她不～,不急躁,不把死神的威胁放在心上。Neither dispirited nor impatient she looks death squarely in the face. ❷ make (sb.) lose hope; make (sb.) feel depressed:这几年的艰苦生活,毁坏了我的健康,～了我的勇气。Hard life in recent years has impaired my health and sapped my morale.

龃 jǔ
龃龉 jǔyǔ *also* "钼铻" jǔyǔ 〈书面〉upper and lower teeth not meeting properly — disagreement; incongruity; discord:双方发生～。The two sides are at loggerheads with each other.

咀 jǔ chew:含英～华 relish the cream of literature; contain the best of the literary tradition
see also zuǐ
咀嚼 jǔjué ❶ masticate; chew:他把东西放在嘴里～了半天,竟也辨别不出是什么滋味来。He failed to tell its taste though he chewed it for a long time. ❷ mull over; ponder; chew the cud; ruminate:她把他刚才讲的话,又前前后后地～一番,才感到事态果然严重。Chewing over the words he just said, she came to realize the gravity (*or* seriousness) of the situation.

钼 jǔ
see also chú
钼铻 jǔyǔ 〈书面〉see "龃龉" jǔyǔ

踽 jǔ
踽踽 jǔjǔ 〈书面〉(walk) alone:他成了一个～独行、孤苦伶仃的人。He turned out to be a person walking all by himself, friendless and wretched.

筥 jǔ 〈书面〉round bamboo basket

蒟 jǔ
蒟酱 jǔjiàng ❶〈植物〉betel pepper ❷ betel pepper sauce
蒟蒻 jǔruò *also* "魔芋" móyù *Amorphophalus rivieri* (*A. konjac*)

枸 jǔ
see also gōu; gǒu
枸橼 jǔyuán *also* "香橼" xiāngyuán 〈植物〉citron
枸橼酸 jǔyuánsuān *also* "柠檬酸" níngméngsuān 〈化学〉citric acid
枸橼酸钠 jǔyuánsuānnà 〈药学〉sodium citrate

椇 jǔ ❶ see "枳椇" zhǐjǔ ❷ rack for sacrificial animals offered to gods or ancestors

jù

聚 jù assemble; gather; get together:欢～ have a happy get-together or reunion /团～ reunite /凝～ condense /物以类～ birds of a feather flock together /～少成多 many a little makes a mickle; a penny saved is a penny earned /那里～了一群人。A crowd of people is gathered there. /我们下星期天～一～好吗? Shall we have a get-together next Sunday?
聚氨酯 jù'ānzhǐ *also* "聚氨基甲酸酯" 〈化学〉polyurethane
聚宝盆 jùbǎopén treasure bowl — place rich in natural resources; cornucopia:柴达木盆地是祖国矿藏资源的～。The Chaidamu Basin is our motherland's treasure bowl, rich in natural resources.
聚苯乙烯 jùběnyǐxī 〈化学〉polystyrene:～塑料 polystyrene plastic
聚变 jùbiàn 〈物理〉fusion:核～ nuclear fusion /受控～ controlled fusion
聚变反应 jùbiàn fǎnyìng fusion reaction:～堆 fusion reactor
聚丙烯 jùbǐngxī 〈化学〉polypropylene
聚丙烯腈 jùbǐngxījīng 〈化学〉polyacrylonitrile
聚餐 jùcān dine together (usu. on festive occasions); have a dinner party:毕业班同学今晚在学校食堂～。Graduating students are having a dinner party tonight in the school canteen.
聚丁烯 jùdīngxī 〈化学〉polybutylene
聚丁橡胶 jùdīng xiàngjiāo butadiene rubber
聚赌 jùdǔ gambling group or party; group gambling:严禁～。Group gambling is strictly forbidden.
聚砜 jùfēng 〈化学〉polysulfone
聚氟乙烯 jùfúyǐxī 〈化学〉polyvinyl fluoride
聚光灯 jùguāngdēng spotlight
聚光镜 jùguāngjìng condensing lens; condenser
聚合 jùhé ❶ assemble; get together:各路人马已经～到一起来了。Troops from various quarters have come together. ❷〈化学〉polymerization:定向～ stereoregular (*or* stereotactic) polymerization /～反应 polyreaction /～管〈化工〉polymerizing pipe
聚合草 jùhécǎo *also* "紫草" zǐcǎo 〈植物〉*Symphy tum officinale*
聚合果 jùhéguǒ *also* "聚生果"〈植物〉*Rosaceae*
聚合物 jùhéwù 〈化学〉polymer:高分子～ high polymers /工程～ engineering polymers
聚花果 jùhuāguǒ *also* "复果" fùguǒ 〈植物〉multiple or compound fruit; collective fruit
聚汇 jùhuì (water currents) flow together; converge:湘江、澧水、沅江、资水都～于洞庭湖。The Xiangjiang, Lishui, Yuanjiang and Zishui rivers all empty into the Dongting Lake.
聚会 jùhuì ❶ gather; assemble; get together; meet:今年春节,有几位高中时的老同学在他家里～。This Spring Festival, some of his high-school classmates got together at his home. ❷ get-together; party:今天这个～很热闹。We had a very exciting reunion today.
聚伙 jùhuǒ gang up:～抢劫 gang robbing
聚积 jùjī accumulate; amass; collect; build up:～力量 build up forces; gather forces; build up strength /～了雄厚的资本 have accumulated (*or* amassed) abundant capital
聚集 jùjí gather; assemble; crowd; collect:江边～了很多人,他们是来看龙舟赛的。A lot of people crowded along the river bank to watch the dragon-boat race. /老师把学生～在她周围。The teacher gathered her pupils round her.
聚甲基丙烯酸甲酯 jùjiǎjībǐngxīsuānjiǎzhǐ 〈化学〉polymethyl methacrylate
聚甲醛 jùjiǎquán 〈化学〉polyformaldehyde
聚歼 jùjiān round up and wipe out; annihilate en masse:～了敌人一个团 round up and liquidate an enemy regiment
聚焦 jùjiāo 〈物理〉focusing:指向～ directional focusing /～成像 focusing and image formation
聚焦器 jùjiāoqì focalizer
聚精会神 jùjīng-huìshén concentrate one's attention; be all attention; be all eyes and ears:～地搞经济建设 concentrate on economic

development / ～地听课 listen attentively in class / 他正在～地读摊在书桌上的报纸。He was engrossed in the newspapers that lay spread across the desk.

聚居 jùjū inhabit a region (as an ethnic group); live in a compact community: 京郊有一个满族～地区。There is a region in the suburbs of Beijing inhabited by the Man nationality.

聚居点 jùjūdiǎn settlement

聚敛 jùliǎn amass wealth (by heavy taxation); levy heavy taxes: ～钱财 amass wealth and property by heavy taxation / 这个统治者搜刮～财富的手段是骇人听闻的。The way the ruler extorted money and amassed wealth was really appalling.

聚拢 jùlǒng gather together: 把自己的东西～在一块儿。Gather together your own belongings. / 她注意到天空的黑云渐渐地～了。She observed that black clouds were piling up in the sky.

聚氯乙烯 jùlǜyǐxī 〈化学〉 polyvinyl chloride (PVC): ～塑料 polyvinyl chloride plastic; PVC plastic

聚落 jùluò village or hamlet; settlement: 这里原本是个荒洲, 后来陆续有人居住, 遂成～。This used to be a desolate area. Since people came to live here it gradually turned into a village.

聚齐 jùqí assemble (at an appointed place): 去春游的人明早七点在学校门口～。Those who want to go on the spring outing, please assemble at the school gate at seven tomorrow morning.

聚醛树脂 jùquán shùzhī 〈化学〉 aldehyde resin

聚伞花序 jùsǎn huāxù 〈植物〉 cyme

聚散 jù-sàn meet and separate: ～匆匆 meet and part with each other hurriedly / 人生～无常。Meetings and partings in life are quite accidental.

聚沙成塔 jùshā-chéngtǎ many grains of sand will pile up into a pagoda — many a little makes a mickle; many littles make a great deal

聚生 jùshēng grow together; cluster

聚生果 jùshēngguǒ *see* "聚合果"

聚首 jùshǒu 〈书面〉 gather; meet: 那年秋天, 我们几个人在南京～。In autumn that year, several of us gathered in Nanjing. / 我等何时再能～? When shall we meet again?

聚四氟乙烯 jùsìfúyǐxī 〈化学〉 polytetrafluoroethylene (PTFE)

聚讼 jùsòng hold different opinions and fail to agree

聚讼纷纭 jùsòng-fēnyún there is a welter of conflicting opinions; people argue back and forth without coming to an agreement; opinions differ widely: ～, 互生疑异。Endless argument leads to suspicion and estrangement.

聚谈 jùtán meet to talk: 一群文学爱好者常在假日～。A group of lovers of literature often met and compared notes among themselves during holidays.

聚碳酸脂 jùtànsuānzhī 〈化学〉 polycarbonate

聚头 jùtóu 〈书面〉 gather; meet: 不是冤家不～。Enemies and lovers are destined to cross paths.

聚蚊成雷 jùwén-chéngléi a swarm of mosquitos sounds like thunder — public clamour can do great harm: ～, 不可不防。Precautions must be taken as many petty noises may create a great disturbance.

聚晤 jùwù 〈书面〉 meet: ～一堂 gather together

聚烯烃 jùxītīng 〈化学〉 polyolefin

聚酰胺 jùxiān'àn 〈化学〉 polyamide: ～塑料 polyamide plastics

聚弦板 jùxiánbǎn tail piece

聚星 jùxīng 〈天文〉 multiple star

聚蓄 jùxù accumulate; build up; save: ～力量 build up forces; build up strength; gather forces

聚乙烯 jùyǐxī 〈化学〉 polyethylene; polythene: ～塑料 polythene plastic

聚乙烯醇 jùyǐxīchún 〈化学〉 polyvinyl alcohol (PVA)

聚义 jùyì 〈旧语〉 gather together in an armed revolt against reactionary rulers: ～英雄 heroes who had gathered in revolt

聚议 jùyì meet for discussion; discuss together: ～大事 discuss important issues together

聚饮 jùyǐn drink together; have a drinking party

聚酯 jùzhǐ 〈化学〉 polyester: ～塑料 polyester plastic / ～薄膜 polyester film / ～纤维 polyester fibre / ～树脂 mylar

聚众 jùzhòng gather a crowd: ～斗殴 incite a crowd to a brawl / ～闹事 incite a mob disturbance or riot

巨(❶钜)

jù ❶ huge; tremendous; colossal; gigantic: ～幅画像 huge portrait / 艰～ arduous; formidable / 超级～星 superstar / 创～痛深 grievous injury; deep distress / 为数甚～ come up to a large number ❷ (Jù) a surname

巨螯蟹 jù'áoxiè 〈动物〉 giant crab (*Macrocheira Kaempferi*)

巨变 jùbiàn great change; sea change; radical change: 面貌～ great change in appearance; facelift

巨擘 jùbò 〈书面〉 ❶ thumb ❷ authority in a certain field: 诗坛～ prince of poets / 医界～ authority in medical circles / 音乐界～ virtuoso in the musical world / 国画～ master in traditional Chinese painting circles

巨齿鲸 jùchǐjīng 〈动物〉 bottlenose whale

巨大 jùdà tremendous; colossal; massive; enormous; immense: ～的胜利 major victory / ～的规模 massive scale / ～的努力 stupendous efforts / ～的进步 prodigious improvement / ～的影响 enormous influence / ～的物质力量 colossal material force / ～的功绩 gigantic achievements / ～的损失 great loss / ～的障碍 big barrier / ～的灾难 catastrophe

巨袋鼠 jùdàishǔ 〈动物〉 diprotodon

巨蠹 jùdù 〈书面〉 big moth — big scoundrel; bad egg

巨憝 jùduì 〈书面〉 very bad person: 大奸～ very wicked scoundrel / 元恶～ arch villain or blackguard

巨额 jù'é huge sum or amount; enormous; immense: ～外汇 large sum of foreign currency / ～利润 enormous profits / ～赤字 gaping financial deficits / ～货币 large amounts of money / 为国家积累～财富 accumulate immense wealth for the country / ～现款 heaps of cash / ～交易 massive transactions

巨富 jùfù ❶ immense amount of wealth ❷ billionaire; magnate: 美国石油～ American oil magnate; American oil baron / 他在股票投机中成为～。He became extremely rich through speculation in stocks.

巨蝮 jùfù 〈动物〉 bushmaster (*Lachesis muta*)

巨构 jùgòu ❶ tall building ❷ great work: 艺术～ masterpiece of art

巨贾 jùgǔ big merchant or businessman

巨猾 jùhuá 〈书面〉 very sly person; old fox: 老奸～ past master of machination and manoeuvre; crafty old scoundrel

巨祸 jùhuò huge disaster; massive calamity: 想不到这么一件小事竟然招来了～。No one thought that such a triviality would lead to a huge disaster.

巨奸 jùjiān 〈书面〉 treacherous person; very malicious person

巨奸大猾 jùjiān-dàhuá wily old fox; crafty old scoundrel; past master of machination and manoeuvre; arrant swindler

巨匠 jùjiàng 〈书面〉 great master; consummate craftsman: 科学～ great scientist / 文坛～ great master in art and literature

巨浸 jùjìn 〈书面〉 big lake

巨款 jùkuǎn large amount of money; immense amount of money: 卷～潜逃 abscond with a huge sum of money

巨浪 jùlàng billow; surge; mountainous waves

巨量 jùliàng large number of; great deal of: ～的鱼虾 vast amount of fish and shrimps

巨灵 jùlíng infinitely resourceful god

巨流 jùliú mighty current: ～滚滚 surging current; rolling current / 时代的～ mighty current of the times

巨轮 jùlún ❶ large wheel: 时代的～ wheel of the age / 历史的～不可逆转。The wheel of history can not be turned back. ❷ large ship: 远洋～ large oceangoing ship / 万吨～ oceanliner of ten thousand tons

巨然 Jùrán Juran (formerly translated as Chu-Jan), Chinese brush painter of the 10th century in the late Five Dynasties and early Song Dynasty period

巨人 jùrén giant; colossus: 泥足～ colossus with feet of clay / ～国 country of giants / ～传 *Gargantua and Pantagruel* (1532-1562, by François Rabelais) / 科学界的～ giant in the scientific world / 文化～ literary giant / 民族的～ great man of the nation / ～和侏儒都属于发育异常。Giants and dwarfs are all humans of abnormal growth.

巨人症 jùrénzhèng 〈医学〉 gigantism

巨商 jùshāng big businessman; business tycoon: 港澳～ big businessmen from Hong Kong and Macao

巨蛇 jùshé 〈动物〉 python

巨石文化 jùshí wénhuà 〈考古〉 megalithic culture

巨室 jùshì ❶ big house ❷ aristocratic family; old and well-known family: 豪门～ powerful aristocratic family

巨噬细胞 jùshì xìbāo 〈生理〉 macrophage

巨头 jùtóu magnate; tycoon: 钢铁～ steel magnate / 石油～ oil baron / 金融～ financial magnate / 该国工业界的～ industrial tycoons

of the country

巨头鲸 jùtóujīng 〈动物〉pilot whale; blackfish (*Globicephalus*)

巨万 jùwàn 〈书面〉millions; tens of thousands: 耗资～ cost a large amount of money / 费用以～计 spend money in tens of thousands

巨蜥 jùxī 〈动物〉monitor (*Varanus salvator*)

巨细 jù-xì big and small: 事无～, 必亲自过问。He took a personal interest in all matters, big and small.

巨细胞 jùxìbāo 〈生理〉giant cell: ～瘤 giant cell tumour

巨蟹座 Jùxièzuò Cancer (one of the twelve zodiacal constellations)

巨星 jùxīng ❶〈天文〉giant star; giant ❷ outstanding person; superstar: 足坛～ super football star

巨型 jùxíng giant; heavy; mammoth; colossal: ～客机 giant airliner / ～喷气客机 jumbo jet / ～运输机 giant transport plane

巨型大学 jùxíng dàxué magaversity

巨型油轮 jùxíng yóulún super (oil) tanker; oilberg

巨眼 jùyǎn 〈书面〉mental discernment; insight; acumen: ～识英雄 have an acumen for talents

巨亿 jùyì huge amount of: ～的资产 colossal amount of assets

巨猿 jùyuán 〈动物〉*Gigantopithecus*

巨制 jùzhì great work; massive work: 鸿篇～ massive work / 这幅狩猎出行图是唐章怀太子墓中的～。This hunting expedition mural painting is a great work from the tomb of Prince Zhanghuai of the Tang Dynasty.

巨著 jùzhù monumental work; magnum opus: 哲学～ magnum opus of philosophy / 史学～ monumental work of historical science

巨子 jùzǐ ❶ honourable title for leader of the Mohist School (770-221 BC) ❷〈书面〉authority; leading figure; tycoon: 文坛～ authority in art and literature / 革命～ revolutionary giant / 实业界～ industrial tycoon

炬 jù torch; flame: 火～ torch / 付之一～ burn down; consign to the flames / 目光如～ eyes blazing like torches; blazing with anger; with a discerning eye

讵 jù 〈书面〉〈副词〉*used to introduce a rhetorical question*: ～料事情生变? Who expected that things would suddenly change?

苣 jù *see* "莴苣" wōjù
see also qǔ

拒 jù ❶ resist; repel; ward off: 抗～ resist; defy / ～敌于国门之外 block the enemy at the gate of our country / 前门～虎, 后门进狼 drive a tiger from the front door and let a wolf in at the back — fend off one danger only to fall prey to another ❷ refuse; reject: ～不交待 refuse to make a confession / 来者不～ refuse nobody; everybody is welcome

拒捕 jùbǔ resist arrest: 罪犯亮出凶器, 公然～。The criminal took out a lethal weapon, brazenly resisting arrest.

拒斥 jùchì resist and repel; defy and reject: ～外来势力的渗入 resist and exclude the penetration of foreign influence

拒付 jùfù 〈经济〉refuse payment; dishonour (a cheque): 全部～ refuse payment in full / 部分～ refuse partial payment

拒贿 jùhuì refuse a bribe

拒谏饰非 jùjiàn-shìfēi reject admonitions and gloss over errors: ～, 必招败损。To reject criticisms and whitewash one's mistakes is to invite defeat and ruin.

拒绝 jùjué refuse; reject; turn down; decline: ～发表评论 refuse to comment / 婉言～ graciously decline / 断然～ flatly refuse / ～谈判 say no to negotiation (*or* talk) / ～有益的劝告 reject a piece of good advice / 我的话深深地伤了他的感情, 因此他～我的任何道歉。He was so hurt by what I said that he closed the door on my attempt to apologize. / 所有熟人都～和他来往。All his acquaintances gave him the cold shoulder.

拒马 jùmǎ barbed barrier to prevent enemy troops or vehicles from passing through

拒命 jùmìng 〈书面〉refuse or defy an order

拒聘 jùpìn decline or turn down an appointment

拒人于千里之外 jù rén yú qiānlǐ zhī wài keep people at a distance of one thousand *li*; be arrogant and unapproachable: 为了一点小事情就～, 实在不好。To cold-shoulder a man for a mere trifle is not advisable.

拒收 jùshōu refuse (to accept)

拒守 jùshǒu 〈书面〉defend; guard: 凭险～ defend by taking advantage of a strategic barrier

拒载 jùzài (of a taxi driver) refuse to take passengers

距[1] jù distance: 株～ distance between two plants / 标～ spacing in the rows / 焦～ focal distance; focal length / 差～ gap; difference / 相～不远 not far from each other / 此地～火车站仅五里。It is only five *li* from here to the train station. / 两家相～一条街。The two families are only one block away from each other. / ～开幕只有一星期了。It is only one week before the opening day.

距[2] jù spur (of a cock, etc.)

距角 jùjiǎo 〈天文〉elongation

距离 jùlí ❶ be apart or away from; be at a distance from: ～远 be at a long distance; be far off / ～近 be at a short distance; be close or near / 这件事～现在已有三十多年。This event occurred some 30 years ago. ❷ distance: 中～赛跑 middle-distance race / 等～ equidistance / 扩大～ increase the distance; widen the gap / 缩小～ reduce (*or* lessen) the gap / 测定目标的～ find out the range of the target / 长～运输 long-haul transport / 与他的期望有很大～ fall far short of his expectation / 行驶的车辆要保持一定的～。There should be a certain distance between driving cars.

秬 jù 〈书面〉black millet

钜[1] jù 〈书面〉❶ hard iron ❷ hook

钜[2] jù *see* "巨❶" jù

遽 jù ❶ hurriedly; speedily; hastily: ～起 stand up hurriedly / 老至何～! How quickly one becomes old! ❷ frightened; agitated; alarmed: 遑～ be panicky

遽尔 jù'ěr 〈书面〉suddenly; unexpectedly: 不料他正当壮年, 竟～作古。Alas, he died so suddenly in the prime of his life.

遽然 jùrán 〈书面〉suddenly; abruptly: ～一声雷鸣 a sudden peal of thunder / 巨祸～而至。Great calamities befell us all of a sudden.

遽色 jùsè 〈书面〉frightened expression

醵 jù 〈书面〉contribute money; pool money: ～金 pool cash; pool money / ～资 pool money; pool funds

镰 jù ancient musical instrument, similar to a bell in shape

沮 jù
see also jǔ

沮洳 jùrù bog; mire

具[1] jù ❶ utensil; tool; implement: 农～ farm tool (*or* implement); agricultural implement / 家～ furniture / 餐～ tableware; dinner service / 茶～ tea set; tea service / 玩～ toy / 道～ stage property; prop for stage / 教～ teaching aid / 文～ stationery ❷〈书面〉talent; ability: 才～ capability ❸〈书面〉〈量词〉: 一～座钟 a desk clock / 一～僵尸 a corpse / 一～石磨 a stone mill

具[2] jù ❶ be endowed with; possess; have: 略～轮廓 have begun to take shape; have begun to show its general outline / 颇～才干 be quite gifted / 独～匠心 show ingenuity; have originality / 各～特色。Each has its own style. ❷〈书面〉provide; furnish; fix: 敬～菲酌 respectfully invite you to a humble dinner (*or* simple meal) / 应用之物毕～。All the things required were ready. ❸〈书面〉state; enumerate; write out: 条～时弊 list (*or* enumerate) current malpratices

具保 jùbǎo (get sb. to) sign a guarantee (for oneself): 联名～ jointly sign a guarantee for sb. / 解放前, 他通过某知名人士出面～, 才得出狱。Before liberation, he was released from prison only after a well-known person signed a guarantee for him.

具备 jùbèi possess; have; be provided with: ～信心 have confidence; be confident / ～有利因素 have advantages / ～作案的可能性 have the possibility (*or* opportunity) to commit the crime / ～入学条

J

件 be qualified to be admitted to a school or college /～必要条件 satisfy the necessary requirements; meet the essential requirements

具结 jùjié 〈旧语〉 sign an undertaking: ～释放 be released on bond / ～领回失物 sign a receipt for restored lost property /责令～悔过 instruct to write a statement of repentance /～完案 sign and close the case

具领 jùlǐng draw; receive: ～失物 receive (*or* get) lost property / ～奖金 draw a bonus

具名 jùmíng put one's name (to a document, etc.); affix one's signature: 这封信首尾均未～。No signature or name is affixed at the beginning or end of this letter.

具体 jùtǐ ❶ concrete; exact; detailed; specific: 描写得很～ describe in (great) detail /～情况要～分析。Concrete conditions require concrete analysis. /你能否说～一些? Could you please elaborate (on it)? *or* Could you be more specific? /这种说法不够～。The remark is a bit vague. ❷ particular; specific; given: ～的人选还没有定下来。The specific candidate is not yet decided. /你不去有什么～理由? What particular reasons do you have for not going? ❸ apply theory or principle to a certain person or thing (followed by 到): 这是就一般而论,～到不同的单位,情况也还有差别。This is a general rule. When it is applied to different units, there is bound to be some difference.

具体而微 jùtǐ'érwēi small but complete; miniature: 这幅画卷～地再现了一千年前繁华的都市生活。This scroll painting is a miniature of bustling city life about a thousand years ago.

具体劳动 jùtǐ láodòng 〈经济〉 concrete labour

具文 jùwén mere formality; dead letter: 此规定成了一纸～。This regulation turned out to be nothing but a scrap of paper.

具有 jùyǒu possess; have; be provided with: ～光荣传统 have a glorious tradition /～高度的责任心 possess a high sense of responsibility /～重大意义 be of great importance /～约束力 be binding /～证人资格 be qualified as a witness /～时代特点 marked by the distinctive features of the times /中国是一个～灿烂的古代文化遗产的国家。China is a country with a splendid heritage of ancient culture.

惧(懼) jù fear; dread; frighten: 有所戒～ have something to fear /无所畏～ intrepid; dauntless; undaunted /临危不～ face danger unflinchingly; betray no fear in (the) face of danger /民不畏死,奈何以死～之? People are not afraid to die, why do you threaten them with death?

惧惮 jùdàn fear; dread; be afraid; be scared

惧内 jùnèi 〈书面〉 henpecked: 我是尊重妻子,而不是～。I think highly of my wife; I'm not a henpecked husband.

惧怕 jùpà be afraid; fear; dread: 我们不～批评和自我批评。We are not afraid of criticism and self-criticism. /像他这样的人,是不会～困难和危险的。Men like him will never dread difficulties or dangers.

惧怯 jùqiè be afraid; be scared: 她露出了愁苦～的面容。She looked worried and scared.

惧色 jùsè look of fear: 毫无～ look undaunted /她面有～。A frightened look came over her face.

犋 jù 〈量词〉 unit of animal power (enough to pull a plough or a similar farm tool)

俱 jù 〈书面〉 all; complete: 声泪～下 shedding tears while speaking; in a tearful voice /事实～在。All the facts are on hand. /万事～备,只欠东风。Everything is ready, and all that we need is an east wind. *or* All is ready except what is crucial.

俱乐部 jùlèbù club: 工人～ workers' club /海员～ seamen's club /体育～ athletic club /～会员 member of a club; clubber

俱全 jùquán complete in all varieties; comprehensive: 这个阅览室中外文语言工具书～。Chinese and foreign language dictionaries are available in all varieties in this reading-room. /麻雀虽小,五脏～。The sparrow may be small, but it has all the vital organs.

飓 jù

飓风 jùfēng hurricane

瞿 jù look at sth. in surprise; look around in consternation
see also Qú

瞿然 jùrán 〈书面〉 be surprised; be shocked: ～惊觉 be surprised to realise; wake up with a start

句 jù ❶ sentence: 破～ pause at the wrong place of a sentence /字～ words and expressions; writing /造～ make sentences /疑问～ interrogative sentence /陈述～ declarative sentence /祈使～ imperative sentence /命令～ imperative sentence /省略～ elliptical sentence /并列～ compound sentence /例～ illustrative sentence; example /警～ aphorism; epigram /名～ famous saying /问～ question /字斟～酌 choose one's words with great care; weigh every word ❷ 〈量词〉 *used of language*: 一～口号 a slogan /写了几～诗 write a few lines of verse /三～话不离本行 can hardly open one's mouth without talking shop; talk shop all the time /这段话共有八～。This paragraph consists of eight sentences.
see also gōu

句点 jùdiǎn full stop; period

句读 jùdòu pause (both at the end of a sentence or of a phrase); sentences and phrases

句法 jùfǎ ❶ sentence structure: 这两句诗的～很特别。The sentence structures of these two lines of verse are very unusual. ❷ 〈语言〉 syntax: ～分析 syntactic analysis

句号 jùhào full stop; full point; period (。) (.)

句型 jùxíng sentence pattern: ～练习 pattern drill

句子 jùzi sentence

句子成分 jùzi chéngfèn sentence element; part of a sentence: 汉语的～一般分为主语、谓语、宾语、定语、状语和补语六种。The elements of a Chinese sentence usually consist of the following six categories: subject, predicate, object, attribute, adverbial, and complement.

据(據) jù ❶ occupy; hold; seize: 占～ occupy /盘～ be entrenched /独～一方 lord it over a district /军阀割～ separatist warlord regimes ❷ rely on; depend on: ～杖而行 walk on a stick /～山险可久守 can defend the place for a long time by taking advantage of a mountain defile ❸ according to; on the basis of; on the grounds of: ～气象台预报 according to the weather forecast from the meteorological observatory /～同名小说改编 adapted from the novel of the same name /～调查 on the basis of the investigation /引经～典 quote from classic authorities ❹ evidence; proof; certificate: 字～ written pledge /证～ evidence; proof; testimony /单～ documents such as receipts, bills, vouchers, invoices, etc. /收～ receipt /数～ data /真凭实～ conclusive evidence; hard evidence /言之有～ speak on good grounds (*or* authority) /查无实～。Investigation reveals no evidence (against the suspect).
see also jū

据称 jùchēng it is said; according to some sources: ～,案情调查已有重大进展。It was alleged that the investigation into the case had made major headway.

据传 jùchuán a story is going around that; rumour has it that; people are saying that: ～金饰品要涨价。Rumour has it that gold ornaments will go up in price.

据此 jùcǐ on these grounds; in view of the above; from this; accordingly: ～我们可得出如下结论。From this we can come to the following conclusion. /仅～尚不足以下判断。It is still too early to pass a judgment on these grounds.

据点 jùdiǎn strongpoint; fortified point; stronghold

据理 jùlǐ according to reason; on just grounds

据理力争 jùlǐ-lìzhēng argue strongly on just grounds: 原则问题必须～。We must argue strongly on matters of principle.

据情 jùqíng according to facts: ～上报 report the facts to one's superior; submit a factual report

据实 jùshí according to reality: ～汇报 report the facts; make a factual report /～招供 tell the facts in court /～招认 make a truthful confession (of one's crime)

据守 jùshǒu defend; guard; be entrenched in: ～无名高地 defend an unnamed hill /～险要 be entrenched in a place strategically located and difficult of access /这一带有重兵～。This area is heavily guarded.

据说 jùshuō it is said; they say; allegedly; reportedly: ～他与此事有牵连。He is allegedly involved in the matter. /到吴家堡～还有五公里。They say it is still five kilos away from Wujiabu. /这种新药～疗效很好。This new medicine is reportedly very effective. /～两国正在秘密谈判。It is said that the two countries are having secret negotiations.

据为己有 jùwéijǐyǒu take forcible possession of; seize by force;

appropriate：将别人的财产～ appropriate others' property /不能将公物～。One should not pocket public property as one's own.
据闻 jùwén see“据说”
据悉 jùxī it is reported：～有关方面对这一问题尚未研究。It is reported that the parties concerned have not yet discussed this problem.
据险 jùxiǎn rely on mountainous or otherwise difficult terrain：～顽抗 stubbornly resist by taking advantage of strategically difficult terrain
据有 jùyǒu occupy；hold；possess；own：～江东（as of the State of Wu of the Three Kingdoms）occupy the area east of the Yangtze River（Bend from Wuxi to Nanjing）

踞

jù ❶ crouch；squat；sit：箕～〈书面〉sit（on the floor）with one's legs stretched /虎～龙盘 tiger crouching and dragon curling — a place of strategic importance（often used to describe the city of Nanjing）/古塔雄～山颠。The ancient tower is imposingly situated at the summit of the mountain. ❷ be entrenched；occupy：高～ stand above；set oneself above /盘～ be entrenched /虎～东南 dominate over the southeast
踞傲 jù'ào arrogant；haughty
踞守 jùshǒu guard；be entrenched in
踞坐 jùzuò 〈书面〉sitting posture, with the arch of feet and one's bottom on the ground or floor and one's knees bent upwards

剧[1]（劇）

jù ❶ drama；play；show；opera：历史～ historical play /现代～ modern drama /肥皂～ soap opera /悲～ tragedy /喜～ comedy /传奇～ melodrama /编～ playwright；screenwriter；scenarist /清唱～ oratorio /京～ Beijing opera /粤～ Guangdong opera /越～ Shaoxing opera /沪～ Shanghai opera /吉～ Jilin opera /楚～ Chu opera /川～ Sichuan opera /滇～ Yunnan opera /赣～ Jiangxi opera /藏～ Zang opera /歌～ opera /笑～ farce /戏～ drama；play /舞～ dance drama /歌舞～ song and dance drama /诗～ drama in verse /话～ modern drama；stage play /街头～ street-corner skit；street performance /独幕～ one-act play /广播～ radio play /惨～ tragedy；calamity /丑～ farce /电视连续～ TV serial ❷（Jù）a surname

剧[2]（劇）

jù acute；sharp；severe；intense：急～ rapid；sharp；drastic /加～ aggravate；intensify；exacerbate /旱情加～。The drought is getting worse. /观众～减。The size of the audience reduced sharply.
剧本 jùběn play；drama；script；scenario；libretto：歌剧～ libretto /话剧～ drama script /电影～ scenario /分镜头～ shooting script /上演新～ stage a new drama /～创作 playwriting；script writing /近十年他编了十几个京剧～。In these ten years, he has compiled dozens of Beijing opera librettos.
剧变 jùbiàn violent or drastic change；radical transformation：病情～。The patient's condition deteriorated sharply. /局势～。There has been a radical change in the situation.
剧场 jùchǎng theatre：露天～ open-air theatre；amphitheatre /木偶～ puppet show theatre
剧跌 jùdiē （of prices, output, etc.）drop violently；plummet
剧毒 jùdú deadly poisonous；highly toxic：～农药 deadly poisonous pesticide
剧改 jùgǎi （short for 戏剧改革）opera reform
剧咳 jùké burst of coughs
剧烈 jùliè violent；acute；severe；fierce：～的爆炸声 violent explosion /～的斗争 fierce struggle /物价的～波动 wild fluctuation in commodity prices /～的疼痛 severe pain /我的心～地跳动着。My heart is beating fast.
剧目 jùmù list of plays or operas；programme of performance：传统～ traditional plays /保留～ repertoire
剧评 jùpíng review of a play or opera；dramatic criticism
剧情 jùqíng story or plot of a play or opera：～简介 synopsis /～简单 simple plot /～复杂 intricate plot /～展开 unfolding of the story /曲折的～对观众很有吸引力。The complicated plot of the drama caught on well with the audience.
剧坛 jùtán theatrical circles：受到～广泛赞誉 widely acclaimed in theatrical circles
剧谈 jùtán 〈书面〉talk freely；speak uninhibitedly：他口吃不能～。He can't speak as much as he would want to, for he is a stammerer.
剧痛 jùtòng acute or severe pain：伤口～起来。There was a gnawing pain in the wound.
剧团 jùtuán theatrical company；opera troupe；troupe：京～ Beijing opera troupe /芭蕾舞～ ballet troupe /歌舞～ song and dance ensemble /业余～ amateur troupe /实验～ experimental theatre /话～ modern drama troupe /此地有各种～。There are all sorts of theatrical companies here.
剧务 jùwù ❶ stage management ❷ stage manager
剧饮 jùyǐn drink to one's heart's content；drink one's fill
剧院 jùyuàn ❶ theatre：到～看戏 go to the theatre ❷ theatrical company；opera troupe；troupe：青年艺术～ Youth Arts Troupe /中国京～ China Beijing Opera Troupe /北京人民艺术～ The People's Arts Theatre of Beijing
剧增 jùzēng increase drastically or sharply
剧涨 jùzhǎng rise rapidly；soar
剧照 jùzhào stage photo；still：电影～ still
剧中人 jùzhōngrén characters in a play or opera；cast of characters；dramatis personae
剧终 jùzhōng the end；curtain
剧种 jùzhǒng ❶ type of traditional opera：地方～ local opera /越剧现今已成为全国性的大～。Shaoxing opera has become a nation-wide traditional opera. ❷ type or genre of drama art
剧组 jùzǔ play staff — a group of people working on the same play including the playwright, director, actors and other workers
剧作 jùzuò drama；play
剧作家 jùzuòjiā playwright；dramatist；librettist

锯

jù ❶ saw：工字～ frame saw /手～ handsaw /圆～ circular saw /拉～ two-handed saw /刀～ knife and saw /钢～ hack saw /电～ electric saw /齿形～ saw /钢丝～ fret saw /油～ chain saw /链～ chain saw ❷ cut with a saw；saw：～树 saw a tree /～铁条 saw an iron strip
锯齿 jùchǐ sawtooth：～形回采法〈矿业〉sawtooth stoping
锯齿草 jùchǐcǎo 〈植物〉alpine yarrow（*Achillea alpina*）
锯床 jùchuáng 〈机械〉sawing machine：圆盘～ circular sawing machine
锯缝 jùfèng saw kerf
锯鳞鱼 jùlínyú 〈动物〉big-eyed soldierfish
锯末 jùmò sawdust
锯木厂 jùmùchǎng sawmill；lumber-mill
锯鲨 jùshā 〈动物〉saw shark
锯条 jùtiáo saw blade
锯屑 jùxiè sawdust
锯子 jùzi 〈方言〉saw

倨

jù 〈书面〉haughty；overbearing；arrogant：前～后恭 first supercilious and then deferential；change from arrogance to humility
倨傲 jù'ào overweening；haughty；arrogant：～无礼 rude and supercilious

窭（窶）

jù 〈书面〉poor；impoverished：贫～ poor；impoverished /～而不能葬 be too poor to bury the dead

屦（屨）

jù ❶ straw sandals：麻～ flax sandals /葛～ sandals of kudzu vine ❷ tread；step on；tramp over
屦及剑及 jùjí-jiànjí *also*“剑及屦及”perform a task with vigour and urgency；take immediate action

juān

蠲

juān ❶〈书面〉remit；exempt；relieve：～减 mitigate（a punishment）；annul（a punishment）/～赋 remit taxation；exempt from tax ❷（often used in the early vernacular）stock；accumulate；store up
蠲除 juānchú 〈书面〉absolve；exempt；relieve：此类繁琐规定，一并～。These overelaborate rules and regulations will be abolished altogether.

J

蠲免 juānmiǎn 〈书面〉reduce; remit (taxation, etc.); mitigate or annul (a punishment): ～农民的不合理负担 remit the unreasonable burdens on the farmers

圈 juān ❶ shut in a pen; pen in: 把猪～起来 pen up the pigs / 把狗～上，别让它咬人。Pen in the dog so as to prevent it from biting people. / 天天～在家里闷得慌。One feels bored being confined to the house day in and day out. ❷〈口语〉lock up: 他把孩子～在家里。He shut the boy up at home.
see also juàn; quān

涓 juān 〈书面〉tiny stream

涓埃 juān'āi 〈书面〉insignificant; negligible: 尽～之力 make what little contribution one can; do one's bit / ～之功 insignificant contribution

涓滴 juāndī 〈书面〉tiny drop; dribble; driblet: ～不漏 with no tiny drop being left out

涓滴归公 juāndī-guīgōng every bit goes to the public treasury: 税收理应～。Every cent of the collected tax should be turned over to the public treasury.

涓涓 juānjuān 〈书面〉trickle sluggishly: ～小溪 trickling brook / ～细流 small stream / ～清泉 trickling clear spring / ～不壅，终为江河。If small streams are not obstructed, they will eventually become mighty rivers.

捐 juān ❶ relinquish; abandon; give up: 细大不～ grab everything, big or small / ～忿弃瑕 forget about past resentment and become reconciled; bury the hatchet ❷ contribute; donate; subscribe: 募～ solicit contributions; appeal for donations / ～寒衣 contribute winter clothing / 为救济灾区～了一笔钱 donate a sum of money to provide relief to the disaster-stricken area ❸ tax; levy: 房～ housing tax / 苛～杂税 exorbitant taxes and levies; multifarious taxes

捐班 juānbān 〈旧语〉get an official post through contributions to the government instead of through the imperial examination during the Qing Dynasty: ～出身 one who gets an official post by contributing money to the government

捐款 juānkuǎn ❶ contribute money: ～办学 contribute money to set up a school ❷ contribution; donation; subscription: 把各地的～分发给灾民。Distribute donations from all areas to the victims of natural disaster.

捐募 juānmù solicit contributions; collect donations

捐纳 juānnà ❶〈旧语〉pay money for an official post ❷ contribute; donate; present

捐弃 juānqì 〈书面〉relinquish; forsake; abandon: ～前嫌，重归于好 cast away past grievances so as to renew cordial relations (*or* friendship)

捐躯 juānqū sacrifice one's life; lay down one's life: 为国～ lay down one's life for one's country / 英勇～ die a hero's death; die a hero

捐生 juānshēng sacrifice one's life; lay down one's life

捐输 juānshū 〈书面〉contribute; donate: 慷慨～ make generous contributions

捐税 juānshuì taxes and levies: 公民有交纳～的义务。It is the citizen's duty to pay taxes and levies.

捐嫌修好 juānxián-xiūhǎo make up with sb.; be reconciled; kiss and be friends: 两国～。The two countries have effected a reconciliation.

捐献 juānxiàn contribute (to an organization); donate; present: ～粮食 contribute grain / ～书籍 donate books / 他把收藏的文物～给国家。He has presented all the cultural relics he collected to the state.

捐赠 juānzèng contribute (as a gift); donate; present: ～一笔巨款 contribute a big sum of money / ～一万元 make a donation of 10,000 *yuan*; present a donation of 10,000 *yuan*

捐助 juānzhù offer (financial or material assistance); contribute; donate: 我靠大家的～渡过了难关。People saw me through the difficulties by offering all kinds of assistance.

捐资 juānzī give financial assistance: ～兴学 donate money to set up a school

鹃 juān *see* "杜鹃" dùjuān

娟 juān 〈书面〉beautiful; graceful: 婵～〈书面〉(used in ancient prose or poetry) graceful or lovely woman; the moon / ～好静秀 beautiful, modest and refined

娟娟 juānjuān (of a person or thing) lovely; beautiful: ～明月 lovely bright moon

娟媚 juānmèi lovely; graceful: 翠竹～ graceful green bamboo

娟秀 juānxiù 〈书面〉beautiful; graceful; elegant: ～流利的字迹 elegant and smooth handwriting / 字体～而遒劲 graceful and vigorous style of calligraphy / 这姑娘容貌～。This girl is goodlooking.

镌(鐫) juān 〈书面〉engrave; carve; inscribe: ～石 engrave a stone / ～心铭骨 be engraved on one's bones and heart — a lasting memory

镌刻 juānkè engrave; carve; inscribe: 石碑上～着那些抗日烈士的名字。Names of those martyrs who sacrificed their lives in the War of Resistance Against Japanese Aggression are engraved on the stone tablet. / 这些话深深～在我的心底。These words are deeply imprinted on my mind.

镌镂 juānlòu 〈书面〉carve; engrave

朘 juān ❶ exploit ❷ reduce: 日削月～ be reduced or impoverished day after day, month after month
see also zuī

朘削 juānxuē 〈书面〉❶ exploit: ～无极 exploit without limit ❷ reduce; cut down

juǎn

卷 juǎn 〈书面〉turn up one's sleeves
see also juàn

卷(捲、④锩) juǎn ❶ roll (up); curl; furl: 把地图～起来 roll up the map / ～头发 curl one's hair / 把舌尖～向上颚 curl the tip of the tongue towards the hard palate / ～帆 furl the sails; take in a reef / ～旗子 furl the flags / 烙饼～大葱 roll green Chinese onions with pancakes / 树叶干得都～起来了。The leaves were dried and curled up. ❷ sweep along, up, or off; pull up; carry along: 风～着雨点劈劈啪啪打在窗子上。The wind sent the raindrops splashing on the window. / 旋风～起一棵大树。The whirlwind pulled up a big tree. *or* The whirlwind uprooted a big tree. ❸ cylindrical mass of sth.; roll: 铺盖～儿 bedding roll; bedroll; roll of bedding / 卫生～纸 toilet-roll / 胶～ roll of film; film / 烟～ cigarette ❹ steamed roll: 花～儿 steamed twisted roll / 春～ spring rolls ❺〈量词〉roll; spool; reel: 一～纸 a roll of paper / 一～布 a roll of cloth / 一～钞票 a roll of banknotes / 一～线 a spool of thread / 一～电缆 a reel of cable
see also juàn

卷巴 juǎnba 〈口语〉roll up; coil; curl; furl: 他把铺盖和零碎东西～～，都拿回了家。He rolled up his bedding, as well as his odds and ends, and took all of them home.

卷笔刀 juǎnbǐdāo pencil sharpener: 电动～ electric pencil sharpener

卷层云 juǎncéngyún 〈气象〉cirrostratus

卷尺 juǎnchǐ tape measure; band tape: 布～ cloth tape; linen tape / 钢～ steel tape

卷动 juǎndòng roll; swirl; whirl: 大风～着雪花。The strong wind sent the snowflakes whirling.

卷发 juǎnfà curly hair; wavy hair; crimped hair

卷发器 juǎnfàqì curler

卷积云 juǎnjīyún 〈气象〉cirrocumulus

卷帘门 juǎnliánmén *see* "卷门"

卷毛狗 juǎnmáogǒu poodle

卷门 juǎnmén *also* "卷帘门" folding door

卷铺盖 juǎn pūgai ❶ pack up and quit: 听说这项工作难度大、报酬低，他卷起铺盖就走。As soon as he heard that the job was difficult and the pay low, he packed up and quit. / 何必在这里受人的气！我马上就～走啦！I've had enough! I'll pack my things and go. ❷ get fired; get the sack: 我已经叫她带着你们一起～滚蛋！I've told her to take you all away, bag and baggage. / 老板叫我～。The boss gave me the boot.

卷曲机 juǎnqūjī 〈纺织〉crimping machine
卷染机 juǎnrǎnjī 〈纺织〉dye jigger
卷绕 juǎnrào 〈纺织〉winding:～机 take-up machine
卷刃 juǎnrèn *also* "锩刃" juǎnrèn (of a knife blade) be turned:这把菜刀剁排骨时～了。This kitchen knife got turned when chopping spareribs.
卷入 juǎnrù be drawn into; be involved in; get mixed up with:～漩涡 be drawn into a whirlpool /～派别斗争 get embroiled in factional strife /～重重困难 be entangled in a web of difficulties /～改革的浪潮 throw oneself into the reform tide /我们反对大国的军事～。We oppose military involvement by big powers.
卷舌辅音 juǎnshé fǔyīn 〈语言〉retroflex consonant
卷舌音 juǎnshéyīn 〈语言〉retroflex
卷舌元音 juǎnshé yuányīn 〈语言〉retroflex vowel
卷缩 juǎnsuō roll up; curl up; huddle oneself up
卷逃 juǎntáo abscond with valuables
卷筒 juǎntǒng reel
卷筒纸 juǎntǒngzhǐ web:～印刷机 web press
卷土重来 juǎntǔ-chónglái stage a comeback:他们要挣扎,他们要变天,他们要～。They would struggle to restore their former ruling position, and they would fight to make a comeback.
卷尾猴 juǎnwěihóu 〈动物〉(weeping) capuchin; weeping monkey
卷吸作用 juǎnxī zuòyòng entrainment; flow of fluids
卷心菜 juǎnxīncài 〈方言〉cabbage
卷须 juǎnxū 〈植物〉tendril
卷烟 juǎnyān ❶ cigarette:～包装机 cigarette packer /～厂 cigarette factory /～工业 cigarette industry /～机 cigarette (making) machine /～纸 cigarette paper /带过滤嘴的～ filter-tipped cigarette ❷ cigar
卷扬 juǎnyáng (of wind) send dust, scraps of paper, etc., flying
卷扬机 juǎnyángjī hoist; hoister
卷叶蛾 juǎnyè'é 〈动物〉leaf roller
卷云 juǎnyún 〈气象〉cirrus
卷轴 juǎnzhóu reel:天线～ aerial reel
see also juànzhóu
卷装货 juǎnzhuānghuò cargo in coil; cargo in roll
卷子 juǎnzi steamed roll
see also juànzi

锩

juǎn (of the edge of a sword or knife) be turned
锩刃 juǎnrèn *see* "卷刃" juǎnrèn

juàn

桊

juàn small wooden stick or iron ring on the ox nose:牛鼻～儿 small wooden stick or iron ring which is fixed on the ox nose

眷(❷睠)

juàn ❶ family dependant:亲～ one's relatives; family dependants /家～ wife and children; one's family /女～womenfolk of a family /侨～ relatives of Chinese nationals living abroad; relatives of overseas Chinese ❷〈书面〉have tender feeling for: *see* "～顾";"～念"
眷爱 juàn'ài have a strong attachment to; have deep affection for; love:～生活 have a strong attachment to life; love life
眷顾 juàngù 〈书面〉show concern for; take care of:承蒙～,感谢不尽。I am really indebted to you for your solicitude.
眷怀 juànhuái cherish the memory of; think of; remember fondly; miss:～亲友 cherish the memory of one's relatives and friends
眷眷 juànjuàn 〈书面〉bear in mind constantly; yearn for:～不忘 will remember forever /～之心 cannot bear to part; be reluctant to part
眷口 juànkǒu 〈书面〉one's family; family dependants
眷恋 juànliàn 〈书面〉be sentimentally attached to (a person or place); have tender thoughts for; have deep affection for:家乡的一切都使他～。He is nostalgic for everything in his hometown..
眷念 juànniàn 〈书面〉think fondly of; feel nostalgic about; have tender thoughts for; think affectionately of:他～祖国的感情是多么强烈啊! How strong is his affection for the motherland!
眷属 juànshǔ ❶ family dependants:携～南下 take one's wife and children along to the south /他孤身一人,没有～。He is single and has no family. ❷ married couple:愿天下有情人都成～。May all lovers on earth become couples.
眷佑 juànyòu 〈书面〉show loving care for and bless
眷注 juànzhù 〈书面〉show loving care for; show solicitude for:深承～ be deeply indebted to sb. for his loving care

帣

juàn 〈书面〉bag
see also juǎn

卷

juàn ❶ book:画～ painting scroll /手不释～ always have a book in one's hand; be an avid reader/掩～叹息 close the book and lament /开～有益。Reading is always profitable. ❷ volume; fasicle:四～本《列宁选集》*Selected Works of Lenin* in four volumes /～一 first volume; book one; volume one /家有藏书万～ boast a collection of ten thousand volumes ❸ examination paper:答～ answer sheet /试～ examination paper /交白～ hand in an unanswered (*or* blank) examination paper /阅～ grade papers /评～ rate papers ❹ file; dossier:调～ draw a file /查～ look through the files /案～ records; files; archives
see also juǎn
卷次 juàncì volume serial number; volume number:按～装订 bind according to the serial numbers
卷柜 juànguì 〈方言〉filing cabinet
卷帙 juànzhì 〈书面〉book (in terms of quantity); volume:～浩繁 vast collection of books
卷轴 juànzhóu 〈书面〉scroll
see also juǎnzhóu
卷轴装 juànzhóuzhuāng way of book-binding (sheets of paper pasted together into a long strip and made into a roll with a wooden stick, ivory or jade as the axis)
卷子 juànzi ❶ examination paper:发～ hand out (*or* distribute) examination papers /看～ read examination papers /她批～很公正。She marks the examination papers fairly. ❷ ancient hand-copied book that could be rolled up
see also juǎnzi
卷宗 juànzōng ❶ file; dossier:机密～ confidential file /把这个问题的～调来查一查。Draw (*or* pull) the file on this problem for a check. ❷ folder

圈

juàn ❶ (of livestock) pen; fold; sty:猪～ pigsty; pigpen; hogpen /羊～ sheepfold; sheep pen /马～ stable /起～ remove manure from a pigsty, sheepfold, etc. /棚～ covered pen (*or* fold, *or* sty) /垫～ bed down the livestock; spread earth in a pigsty, cowshed, etc. ❷ (Juàn) a surname
see also juān; quān
圈肥 juànféi 〈农业〉barnyard manure; muck
圈舍 juànshè livestock's pen, animals' house, etc.
圈养 juànyǎng rear livestock in pens or sties:～牲畜 rear livestocks in pens
圈猪 juànzhū pigs that are raised in sties

倦

juàn ❶ tired; worn out; weary:疲～不堪 be dog tired; be fatigued /困～ sleepy ❷ be weary; be tired; be bored:厌～ be weary of; be tired of /学而不厌,诲人不～ be insatiable in learning and tireless in teaching /孜孜不～ take great pains in doing sth.; work diligently
倦怠 juàndài tired and sleepy:神色～ look tired and sleepy
倦容 juànróng tired appearance:他脸上略带～。There is a slightly tired look on his face.
倦色 juànsè tired appearance or expression:面有～ look tired
倦意 juànyì tiredness; weariness; sleepiness:毫无～ not feel in the least tired
倦游 juànyóu 〈书面〉be weary of wandering and sightseeing:～归来 come back because one is fed up with vacationing and sightseeing

睊

juàn
睊睊 juànjuàn 〈书面〉look through the corners of the eyes; look askance

罥

juàn 〈书面〉hang; put up

狷(獧) juàn 〈书面〉❶ impatient; impetuous:～忿 impatient and irritable ❷ upright; honest:～洁 exercise self-control and keep away from immorality

狷傲 juàn'ào 〈书面〉aloof and supercilious; detached and haughty

狷急 juànjí of impetuous temperament; irritable in temper:～不能从俗 be impatient and refuse to follow customs and conventions

狷介 juànjiè 〈书面〉upright; honest:～之士 honest person; upright person

狷狭 juànxiá 〈书面〉be narrow-minded

绢 juàn thin tough silk

绢本 juànběn silk scroll:两幅～山水画 two silk scrolls of mountains-and-waters (*or* landscape) painting

绢纺 juànfǎng silk spinning

绢花 juànhuā *also*"京花" jīnghuā 〈工美〉silk flower

绢画 juànhuà classical Chinese painting on silk

绢丝 juànsī spun silk (yarn):～薄绸 carbaso /～纺绸 spun silk pongee /～织物 spun silk fabric; schappe

绢网印花 juànwǎng yìnhuā 〈纺织〉screen printing; serigraphy:～法 silk-screen process

绢子 juànzi 〈方言〉handkerchief

隽(雋) juàn ❶〈书面〉meaningful ❷ (Juàn) a surname

隽永 juànyǒng 〈书面〉meaningful; significant; pregnant with implication:诗意～ expressive poem /写景～传神 thoughtful and graphic description of the scene

隽语 juànyǔ pithy remark

juē

撅[1] juē ❶ stick up; pout (one's lips):小辫～着。The pigtail is sticking up. /吃早饭的时候，大家都～着嘴。At breakfast, everyone was sulking. ❷ embarrass (sb.) openly; contradict:～人 embarrass one to one's face /他平白地～我一顿。He contradicted me for no reason at all. ❸ make (a fainted person) come to by massage, etc.:她晕倒了，连～带叫，折腾了半天，才缓醒过来。She fainted, and came to slowly after the others spent quite some time awaking her by giving her massotherapy and what not.

撅[2](撧) juē 〈口语〉break (sth. long and narrow); snap:一～两段 break (sth.) in two /把竿子～断 snap a bamboo pole

撅巴 juēba ❶ break; snap:把那些树枝子～～烧火吧! Let's break those tree branches to make a fire. ❷ give massotherapy to and move the limbs of a fainted person so as to make him or her come to

撅搭 juēda 〈方言〉❶ stick up:两条小辫子～着。Two pigtails are sticking up. ❷ unsteady walking movement:他～～地朝前走去。He staggered forward.

噘 juē stick up; pout (one's lips):～嘴 pout (one's lips); thrust out (one's lips)

屩(屫、蹻) juē 〈书面〉straw sandals

jué

觉(覺) jué ❶ sense; feel; sensation; perception:视～ sight /听～ sense of hearing /色～ color sensation /味～ taste; sense of taste; taste sensation /嗅～ smell; sense of smell; smell perception /知～ perception /触～ touch; sense of touch; tactile sensation /光～ light sensation /错～ illusion /不知不～ unconsciously; unwittingly /～着有点发烧 feel one has a temperature /几乎～不出来 can hardly sense it; can hardly be felt ❷ wake (up); awake:大梦初～ just awake from a long dream ❸ become aware or conscious; become awakened:自～自愿 voluntarily; of one's own free will /先～ one who becomes politically awakened (*or* conscious) earlier than others

see also jiào

觉察 juéchá sense; become aware of; perceive; detect:～态度有变化 perceive a change in attitude /～危险 become aware of danger /～某人的敌意 sense sb.'s hostility /想不到这个秘密竟然被她～到了。It was unexpected that she should have detected this secret.

觉得 juéde ❶ feel:～恶心 feel disgust; feel sick /在生人面前他～不自在。He felt uncomfortable in the presence of strangers. /他的大公无私使我们～羞愧。His unselfishness made us feel small. ❷ think; feel:他～这个计划不妥当。He felt the plan to be unwise. /我～他们俩在谈恋爱。I have a feeling that the two of them are in love. /我～我是正确的。I think I am correct. /警察午夜看到店里还亮灯光时，～有点不对头。When the policeman saw a light on in the store at midnight, he sensed something was wrong.

觉乎 juéhu 〈口语〉feel; sense:这针扎下去不～怎么样。You don't feel much when the needle is stuck (into you).

觉悟 juéwù ❶ consciousness; awareness; understanding:提高～ heighten one's awareness /政治～ political consciousness; political understanding /思想～ ideological understanding /工人的阶级～使他们在为美好未来的斗争中团结一致。The class consciousness of the workers made them unite in the struggle for a bright future. ❷ begin to understand; come to realize; become aware of; become politically awakened:我们希望他能～过来，改正错误。We hope he'll come round and mend his ways. /他近来～了，决不再跟这种人打交道。He has come to realize that he should not get along with such people any longer. ❸〈佛教〉awakening; illumination

觉醒 juéxǐng awaken:世界人民的新～ new awakening of the world's people /～了的工人阶级 awakened working class /一个伟大的、沉睡的民族～了。A great nation is rousing up from a deep sleep.

珏(瑴) jué 〈书面〉two pieces of jade joined together

厥[1] jué faint; swoon; lose consciousness; fall into a coma:昏～ faint; swoon /惊～ faint from fear; convulsions /痰～ coma due to blocking of the respiratory system /晕～ faint; syncope

厥[2] jué 〈书面〉❶ his or her; its; their:～父 his or her father /大放～词 talk a lot of nonsense; spout a stream of empty rhetoric /～功甚伟。Great are his services to the country. ❷ only then:左丘失明，～有《国语》。Only when Zuoqiu Ming lost his sight did he compile *Remarks of Monarches* in the Spring and Autumn Period.

蕨 jué 〈植物〉brake (fern):狗脊～ chain fern

蕨菜 juécài edible tender leaves of brakes

蕨类植物 juélèi zhíwù pteridophyte

橛(橜) jué short wooden stake; wooden pin; peg:小木～儿 short wooden stake

橛肋 juélèi 〈生理〉hypochondrium

橛子 juézi short wooden stake; wooden pin; peg

劂 jué *see*"剞劂" jījué

蹶(蹷) jué fall; setback:一～不振 lose heart after one setback; never recover from a setback

see also juě

獗 jué *see*"猖獗" chāngjué

矍 jué 〈书面〉look surprised:～然失容 look shocked; appear surprised

矍矍 juéjué look around in surprise

矍铄 juéshuò 〈书面〉hale and hearty:精神～的老者 hale and hearty old man

攫 jué seize; snatch; grab:老鹰～兔 an eagle grabbing a hare /他那歌声中的忧伤，紧紧～住了我的心。I was riveted by his melancholy singing.

攫夺 juéduó grab; plunder:～财富 appropriate wealth

攫取 juéqǔ seize; grab; snatch:～权力 seize power /～他人劳动成果 grab the fruit of others' labour /从物价暴涨中～厚利 make fabu-

lous profit out of inflation

镢(鐝) jué 〈方言〉pick; pickaxe

镢头 juétou 〈方言〉pick; pickaxe

噱 jué 〈书面〉loud laughter: 令人一～make one laugh out loud /笑～ loud laughter

see also xué

爵[1] jué rank of nobility; peerage: 封～ confer a title (of nobility) /公～ duke /侯～ marquis /伯～ earl; count /子～ viscount /男～ baron /勋～ lord /卖官鬻～ sell official posts and titles

爵[2] jué ancient wine vessel with three legs and a loop handle

爵禄 juélù 〈书面〉rank of nobility and the emoluments that go with it

爵士 juéshì ❶ knight: 授以～封号 confer the title of a knight ❷ sir: 爱德华～ Sir Edward

爵士舞 juéshìwǔ jazz dance

爵士摇滚乐 juéshì yáogǔnyuè jazz-rock

爵士乐 juéshìyuè *also* "爵士音乐" jazz

爵位 juéwèi rank or title of nobility: 欧洲国家的～,一般分为公侯伯子男五等。The nobility in Europe are divided into five ranks. They are duke, marquis, earl, viscount, and baron.

爝 jué

爝火 juéhuǒ 〈书面〉torch; small fire

嚼 jué masticate; chew: 咀～ chew; masticate; mull over; ruminate /过屠门而大～ pass the butcher's and start munching — feed on illusions

see also jiáo; jiào

脚(腳) jué *see* "角[1]" jué

see also jiǎo

角[1] jué *also* "脚" jué ❶ role; part; character: 主～ leading (*or* principal) role; main character /配～ supporting role; co-star ❷ 〈戏曲〉type of role: 旦～ female role /生～ male character /净～ "painted face" /丑～ clown ❸ actor or actress: 本剧团的名～儿 famous actor or actress of this troupe

角[2] jué contend; struggle; fight: 口～ quarrel; bicker /与人～才智 compete with others in intelligence and wisdom

角[3] jué ancient, three-legged wine cup

角[4] jué 〈音乐〉note of the ancient Chinese five-note scale, corresponding to 3 in numbered musical notation

角[5] Jué a surname

see also jiǎo

角抵 juédǐ ancient wrestling

角斗 juédòu wrestle: 我看出对方的弱点,～时乘其不备,突然把他凌空举起。Having found the opponent's weak point in the wrestling match, I took him by surprise and raised him high above my head.

角斗场 juédòuchǎng wrestling ring

角力 juélì have a trial of strength; wrestle: 他身患绝症,正在咬紧牙关与死神～。He is suffering from a fatal illness and gritting his teeth to wrestle with death.

角色 juésè ❶type of role (in films, drama, TV shows, etc.): 派～ choose the cast /进入～enter into the spirit of a character; live one's part ❷ role; part: 正面～ positive character /反面～negative character /他在这件事里扮演了不光彩的～。He played a contemptible role in this matter. /别瞧不起我们清洁工,这种～哪儿也少不了。Don't look down upon us street cleaners. We are indispensable anywhere.

角逐 juézhú contend; contest; compete; enter into rivalry: 进行～ enter into rivalry /群雄～ tussle among warlords /情场～的失败者 loser in the tournament of love /这一地区成了各种势力的～场所。The region has become an arena of fierce contention among various forces. /两队正在场上展开激烈的～。The two teams are competing fiercely in the game.

桷 jué square rafter

谲 jué 〈书面〉❶ cheat; swindle: 正而不～ honest; upright and never up to cheats or swindles ❷ strange; odd: 诡～ strange and changeful; treacherous /怪～ fantastic

谲诈 juézhà cunning; crafty: 此人很是～。This man is very crafty.

决[1]**(決)** jué ❶ make a decision; decide; determine: 表～ decide by vote; vote /判～ make a court decision; pass judgment /裁～ rule; adjudicate /犹豫不～ hesitate; be in a state of indecision /～一胜负 fight it out /议而不～ discuss sth. without reaching a decision /悬而未～ hanging in doubt; unresolved; outstanding ❷ (used before negatives) definitely; absolutely; certainly; under any circumstances: ～不可能 absolutely impossible; no way /～非偶然 in no case accidental /～无异言 have no disagreement whatsoever /～不退让一步 never yield an inch /～无此事 no such things have ever happened /～不反悔 will under no circumstances go back on one's word /～非长久之计 not at all a permanent solution /此事～难成功。There is not the least chance for its success. ❸ decide the final result; win or lose: ～出冠亚军 decide who is the champion /速战速～ fight a quick battle to force a quick decision ❹ execute (a person): 枪～ execute by shooting /处～ put to death; execute

决[2]**(決)** jué (of a dyke, etc.) be breached; burst: 溃～ (of a dyke or dam) burst

决策 juécè make policy; make a strategic decision: 战略～ strategic decision /英明～ wise decision /重大～ major policy decision /～权 decision-making power /～阶段 decision phase /～行为 decision behaviour /～资料 decision data /～参数 decision parameters /～于帷幄之中。Strategic decisions are devised within a command tent.

决策机构 juécè jīgòu policy-making body; structure or anatomy of decision-making

决策人 juécèrén policy maker; decision maker

决雌雄 jué cíxióng *see* "决一雌雄"

决堤 juédī breach or burst a dyke: 河水暴涨,下游有三处～。The dyke was breached at three points along the lower reaches of the river as it was rising rapidly.

决定 juédìng ❶ decide; resolve; make up one's mind: 她～当一名大夫。She decided to be a doctor. /这事由你～。It's for you to decide. *or* It's up to you. /问题就这样～了。That decides (*or* settles) the question. /他一旦～做某件事,总是不达目的决不罢休的。Once he sets his heart on something, he won't give up till he gets it. ❷ decision; resolution: 通过～ pass (*or* adopt) a decision /起草～ draft a decision (*or* resolution) /这个问题尚未作出～。No decision has been made about this question yet. ❸ determine; decide: 存在～意识。Man's social being determines his consciousness. /内容～形式。Content decides (*or* determines) form. ❹ decisive: ～因素 decisive factor; determinant

决定论 juédìnglùn 〈哲学〉determinism

决定权 juédìngquán power to make decisions: 有最后～ have the final say

决定性 juédìngxìng decisiveness: ～作用 decisive role /～战斗 decisive battle /在争夺冠军那天,当比赛进行到～时刻,我队运动员全都紧张起来了。On the day of the championship game, as the zero hour drew near, the players of our team all tensed up.

决斗 juédòu ❶ duel: 进行～ fight a duel /要求～ challenge sb. to a duel /俄国大诗人普希金是～而死的。The great Russian poet A. S. Pushkin died in a duel. ❷ life-and-death struggle; decisive struggle; duel: 这两种势力展开生死存亡的～。The two forces are locked in a desperate struggle for survival.

决断 juéduàn ❶ make a decision: 大家充分发表意见后,由他～。He made a decision only after everyone had aired their opinions. ❷ resolve; decisiveness; determination; resolution: 英明～ brilliant resolution /他是个有～的人。He is a man of determination. *or* He is a man of great resolve. /在紧急关头,他缺乏～。He was indecisive in the face of an emergency.

决计 juéjì ❶ decide; make up one's mind: 他～出国求学。He de-

cided to leave his country to pursue his studies. /他～提前退休。He made up his mind to retire ahead of time. ❷ definitely; certainly; surely:你照这样办～没有错。You definitely can't go wrong if you do it this way. /坚持下去，～能成功。Perseverance will surely lead to success.

决绝 juéjué ❶ break off; cut off; sever:与世～的情绪 feeling (*or* mood) of having nothing to do with the world any more /二十年前，她毅然与家庭～。She resolutely broke with her family twenty years ago. ❷ firm; resolute:对此，他的态度十分～。He was adamant on the question.

决口 juékǒu (of a dike, etc.) be breached; burst:黄河大堤～breaching of the Yellow River embankment /堵住～ close (*or* stop) up a breach

决裂 juéliè break with;past company with; rupture:与封建主义的传统～ break with the feudal tradition /和旧我～ turn over a new leaf /两国关系一度～。Friendly relations between the two countries once ruptured. /两个好友从此～。The two friends fell out then and there.

决明 juémíng 〈植物〉*Cassia obtusifolia*; *Cassia tora*

决明子 juémíngzǐ 〈中药〉cassia seed; semen cassiae

决然 juérán 〈书面〉❶ firmly; resolutely; determinedly:毅然～resolutely and determinedly; firmly /我们～不同意旨在干涉别国内政的种种做法。We flatly oppose all kinds of practices aimed at interfering in the internal affairs of other countries. ❷ definitely; unquestionably; inevitably; undoubtedly:道听途说，～得不到真实的情况。You will never get to know the truth if you listen to hearsay.

决撒 juésā (often used in the early vernacular) rupture; breach

决赛 juésài finals:半～ semi-finals /四分之一～ quarter-finals /进入～ enter into the finals /～选手 finalist /篮球～ basketball finals

决胜 juéshèng decide the outcome of the battle; determine the victory:运筹于帷幄之中，～于千里之外 devise strategies within a command tent, which will ensure victory a thousand *li* away

决胜局 juéshèngjú 〈体育〉deciding game or set

决死 juésǐ life-and-death:～之战 life-and-death battle; last-ditch fight

决算 juésuàn final accounting of revenue and expenditure; final accounts:国家～ final state accounts /～表 final statement /～审计 audit of returns /～书 final report /～账户 final account /年度～ annual final accounts /年终～ final accounts at the end of the year /～明细表 itemized final accounting of revenue and expenditure

决心 juéxīn determination; resolution:有战胜困难的～ be resolved to surmount the difficulties /动摇他的～ shake (*or* weaken) his determination /下～ resolve; make up one's mind /～加倍努力 be determined to redouble one's efforts /他们～把这一案件追查到底。They made up their minds to pursue the case to a definitive conclusion. /参加奥林匹克运动会—这曾是他～要实现的抱负。To take part in the Olympics — this was an ambition that he had set his mind on achieving.

决一雌雄 juéyīcíxióng fight to see who is stronger; fight it out:两军准备在这里～。The two opposing armies were ready to fight a decisive battle here.

决一死战 juéyīsǐzhàn fight a life-and-death battle; fight to the bitter end; fight to the death:作好了与敌人～的准备。We are prepared to fight the enemy to the finish.

决疑 juéyí dispel doubts; solve difficult problems

决议 juéyì resolution:提出～草案 put forward a draft resolution /撤销～ revoke (*or* cancel) a resolution /通过～ pass (*or* adopt, *or* carry) a resolution /经过反复讨论作出～ accept (*or* approve) a resolution after repeated discussion /贯彻～ carry out a resolution

决意 juéyì set one's mind; have one's mind made up; be determined:他～明天一早就动身。He has decided to set out early tomorrow. /他～在一周内把稿子写好。He made up his mind to finish the article within a week.

决狱 juéyù 〈书面〉try a court case

决战 juézhàn decisive battle; decisive engagement:这是最后的～。This is the last decisive battle.

诀[1]

jué ❶ rhymed formula:口～ pithy formula in rhyme /歌～ formulas put into verse ❷ knack;key to success; tricks of the trade:秘～ secret of success; key to success /妙～ clever way of doing sth.; knack

诀[2]

jué bid farewell; part (when there is little chance of meeting each other again):永～ part never to meet again; part forever; be separated by death

诀别 juébié bid farewell; part:与家人～ part with (*or* bid farewell to) one's family /她母亲的～言词是如此悲凄。Her mother's words at the final parting were replete with sorrow and sadness.

诀窍 juéqiào secret of success; tricks of the trade; knack:成功的～ secret of success /做菜的～ knack of cooking /掌握了新型计算机的～ get the hang of a new-type computer

诀要 juéyào 〈书面〉secret of success; knack; trick

玦

jué penannular jade ring (worn as an ornament in ancient China)

砄

jué 〈书面〉stone; rock

抉

jué 〈书面〉pick out; single out:～目 gouge out sb.'s eyes

抉剔 juétī search and pick out; pick and choose:～精华 pick out the essence; skim the cream

抉瑕擿衅 juéxiá-tīxìn deliberately find fault with; nitpick

抉瑕掩瑜 juéxiá-yǎnyú pick out flaws to cover up the radiance of the jade — comment harshly so as to write off the good points

抉择 juézé 〈书面〉choose:生死～ choose between life and death /他第一次面临人生～的苦恼。For the first time he is faced with the trouble of making a choice in life.

抉摘 juézhāi 〈书面〉❶ choose:～真伪 choose between the true and the fake ❷ expose and condemn:～弊端 expose and castigate malpractices /～细过 uncover and censure minor mistakes

鴂

jué *see* "鶗鴂" tíjué

䴁

jué 〈古语〉shrike

䴁舌 juéshé 〈书面〉(of language) difficult to understand; hardly intelligible

觖

jué 〈书面〉dissatisfied

觖望 juéwàng 〈书面〉feel bitter because of dissatisfaction:每怀～ would often be dissatisfied and feel bitter

駃

jué

駃騠 juétí ❶ hinny; mule ❷ 〈古语〉a kind of fine steed

掘

jué dig; excavate:～地道 dig a tunnel /～通 dig through /采～ excavate /发～ excavate; unearth /～壕据守 dig oneself in; entrench oneself /～地三尺 dig to a depth of three feet; dig deep /临渴～井 not dig a well until one's thirsty — act too late /自～坟墓 dig one's own grave

掘进 juéjìn 〈矿业〉driving; drifting tunnelling:～工作面 driving face /平巷～ drilling /快速～ quick tunnelling /全断面～ full-face tunnelling

掘墓人 juémùrén gravedigger

掘土机 juétǔjī *also* "电铲" diànchǎn excavator; power shovel

崛

jué 〈书面〉rise abruptly

崛立 juélì stand tall and erect:峰峦～ towering ridges and peaks

崛起 juéqǐ 〈书面〉❶ (of a mountain, etc.) stand abruptly; rise suddenly:盆地中央，～一座高耸入云的奇峰。In the middle of the basin an extraordinary peak rises abruptly, towering into the clouds. ❷ rise (as a political force); spring into being:抗日游击队～于广大农村。The anti-Japanese guerrillas rose in the vast rural areas.

倔

jué

see also juè

倔强 juéjiàng *also* "倔犟" stubborn; unyielding; unbending:我喜欢她那股～劲儿。I like her for her tenacity.

孓

jué *see* "孑孓" jiéjué

绝

jué ❶ cut off; break off; sever:隔～ isolate; cut off /拒～

refuse; reject; turn down / ～了生路 cut off sb.'s livelihood / 滔滔不～ pouring out words without end (*or* in a steady flow); hold forth / 谢～参观。Not open to visitors. / 赞颂之辞不～。There was no end of praise and acclamation. ❷ exhausted; spent; used up; finished: 弹尽粮～ have run out of ammunition and provisions / 斩尽杀～ kill all; wipe out the whole lot / 法子都想～了。All possible ways have been explored (*or* tried). *or* All possibilities have been exhausted. / 不要把话说～，要留有余地。Don't go to extremes in what you say; leave some room for manoeuvre. / 做人别那么～! Don't be so uncompromising! ❸ desperate; beyond help; hopeless: *see* "～路"; "～处逢生" ❹ stop breathing; die: 悲痛欲～ be sorrowful to death ❺ unique; superb; matchless: 拍案叫～ express admiration by thumping the table / 她的枪法真～。Her marksmanship was a beauty. / 他的书画可称双～。His calligraphy and painting can both be rated as superb works of art. ❻ extremely; most: ～大错误 grievous mistake; awful blunder / ～好机会 golden opportunity; excellent chance / ～大部分 most part / 深恶痛～ have a deep-seated (*or* an ingrained) hatred; hate bitterly ❼ (used before negatives) absolutely; in the least; in all circumstances; on any account: ～无此意 have absolutely no such intentions / ～不允许 would never permit (*or* allow) / ～非偶然 by no means fortuitous (*or* accidental) / ～不甘心 never reconcile oneself to / ～不同意 would in no circumstances agree / 有这种想法的～非少数。It is definitely not the minority that shares this opinion. / 我们～不能袒护他。We must on no account shield him. ❽ (short for 绝句) *jueju*, a poem of four lines, each containing five or seven characters, with a strict tonal pattern and rhyme scheme: 五～ five-character verse line / 七～ seven-character verse line

绝版 juébǎn out of print: ～书刊 out-of-print publications / 这本书早已～。This book has long been out of print.

绝笔 juébǐ ❶ last words written before one's death: ～信 last letter written before one's death ❷ last work of an author or painter ❸ 〈书面〉 best essay, poem or painting: 集中收集的名家作品，堪称一时～。The pieces in the collection were the cream of the time.

绝壁 juébì precipice: 悬崖～ sheer precipice and overhanging rocks

绝产 juéchǎn ❶ no harvest; crop failure: 那年遭涝灾，庄稼全部～。There was no harvest of any crop at all that year because of the flood. ❷ heirless property or an inheritance the heir wishes to give up

绝唱 juéchàng ❶ acme of perfection: 鲁迅先生称《史记》为史家之～。Mr. Lu Xun ranked *Historical Records* as the zenith in history works. ❷ last singing or song before one's death; swansong: 想不到这支歌成了她的～。I didn't expect it to be her swansong.

绝处逢生 juéchù-féngshēng find one's way out of an impasse; be unexpectedly rescued from a desperate situation: 吉人天相，～。Heaven helps a good man escape from death. / 这封信使他～。The letter gave him a new lease of life. / 家庭有～之感。Hopes revived in the family when all had seemed lost.

绝代 juédài 〈书面〉 unique among one's contemporaries; peerless: 才华～ unrivalled talent / ～佳人 beauty of beauties; incomparable beauty; woman of unsurpassed beauty; matchless beauty

绝倒 juédǎo 〈书面〉 shake one's sides (laughing); roar with laughter: 令人～ split (*or* hold) one's sides; be sidesplitting / 诙谐百出，令人～ make people roar with laughter by one's irrepressible humour

绝地 juédì ❶ extremely dangerous place: 这里左边是峭壁，右边是深渊，真是个～。This is really an extremely dangerous spot with the precipice on the left and the abyss on the right. ❷ hopeless situation: 陷于～ fall into a hopeless situation / 他身处～，视死如归。When in extreme danger, he looked upon death as going home.

绝调 juédiào 〈书面〉 ❶ unrivalled; matchless: ～佳人 matchless beauty; incomparable beauty ❷ peak of poetic perfection: 千古～ poetic masterpiece through the ages

绝顶 juédǐng ❶ extremely; utterly: ～荒谬 utterly ridiculous; height of absurdity / ～机密的事情 extremely confidential matter / 这孩子聪明～。The child was exceptionally intelligent. / 他认为自己是～的天才。He regards himself as a superb man of genius. ❷ 〈书面〉 highest peak: 泰山～观日出 enjoy watching the sunrise at the top of Mount Tai / 会当凌～，一览众山小。Climbing up to the summit (of Mount Tai), I find all the surrounding mountains dwarfed.

绝对 juéduì ❶ absolute: ～优势 absolute predominance; overwhelming superiority / ～多数 absolute majority / ～担保 absolute guarantee / ～禁止 unconditional prohibition / ～禁制品 absolute contraband / 运动是～的。Motion is absolute. / 不要把话说得太～了。Don't be so definitive in what you say. ❷ based on one condition without considering all the others; absolute: ～误差 absolute error ❸ absolutely; perfectly; definitely: ～拒绝 flatly refuse / ～正确 perfectly right / ～不行 categorically not / ～有把握 positively certain of success / ～可信 utterly trustworthy ❹ most; extreme: 拥护的占～大多数。The vast majority of the people were in favour.

绝对地租 juéduì dìzū absolute rent

绝对法 juéduìfǎ binding law; *jus cogens*

绝对高度 juéduì gāodù absolute height; absolute altitude

绝对观念 juéduì guānniàn 〈哲学〉 absolute idea

绝对衡平法 juéduì héngpíngfǎ absolute equity

绝对豁免 juéduì huòmiǎn absolute immunity

绝对量度 juéduì liángdù 〈物理〉 absolute measurement

绝对零度 juéduì língdù 〈物理〉 absolute zero

绝对贫困化 juéduì pínkùnhuà absolute pauperization

绝对平均主义 juéduì píngjūnzhǔyì absolute equalitarianism or egalitarianism

绝对剩余价值 juéduì shèngyú jiàzhí absolute surplus value

绝对湿度 juéduì shīdù 〈气象〉 absolute humidity

绝对唯心主义 juéduì wéixīnzhǔyì absolute idealism

绝对温度 juéduì wēndù 〈物理〉 absolute temperature

绝对星等 juéduì xīngděng 〈天文〉 absolute magnitude

绝对音乐 juéduì yīnyuè absolute music

绝对真理 juéduì zhēnlǐ 〈哲学〉 absolute truth

绝对值 juéduìzhí 〈数学〉 absolute value

绝对中立 juéduì zhōnglì absolute neutrality

绝对主义 juéduìzhǔyì 〈哲学〉 absolutism

绝甘分少 juégān-fēnshǎo *also* "绝少分甘" be strict with oneself and generous towards others; share weal and woe; share comforts and hardships: 在艰苦的年代里，这位将军从来与战士～。In the years of hardship, the general used to share out everything with his men.

绝根 juégēn without offspring; have no descendants

绝后 juéhòu ❶ without offspring or issue; with no descendants ❷ never to be seen again: 空前～ never known before and never to occur again; unique / 虽不能说是～，但至少也是空前的。Though we can't say it will never happen again, it was at least never known before.

绝户 juéhu ❶ without offspring or issue ❷ childless person or family

绝活 juéhuó one's best skill: 内画山水是王师傅的～。In-bottle landscape painting is Master Wang's unique skill.

绝技 juéjì unique skill; consummate skill: 身怀～ with unique skill / 骑马的～ feats of horsemanship

绝迹 juéjì disappear; vanish; be extinct; be stamped out: 该传染病早已～。That kind of epidemic disease has long been stamped out. / 有不少传统产品已经～了。Quite a few traditional specialities have disappeared altogether.

绝交 juéjiāo break off relations (as between friends or countries): 两国早已～。The two countries have long severed relations (with each other). / 两位老朋友就因为一点小事～了。The two old friends parted company because of a mere triviality.

绝经 juéjīng 〈生理〉 menopause

绝景 juéjǐng extremely beautiful scenery or scene

绝境 juéjìng ❶ 〈书面〉 remote and out-of-the-way place ❷ hopeless situation; impasse; dead end; blind alley; cul-de-sac: 困难重重，陷于～ be placed in dire straits, facing mountains of difficulties / 陷侵略者于～ land the aggressors in an impasse

绝句 juéjù *jueju*, a poem of four lines, each containing five or seven characters, with a strict tonal pattern and rhyme scheme *see also* "截句❷" jiéjù

绝口 juékǒu ❶ (used only after 不) cease talking: 赞不～ give unstinted praise; praise profusely / 骂不～ heap endless insults upon sb.; pour out a stream of abuse ❷ keep one's mouth shut: ～不提 never breathe a word about sb. / ～不道前恩 never say a single word about the favours bestowed on others / 他们为何对签订合同的事～不提呢? Why did they avoid all mention of signing the contract?

绝粒 juélì 〈书面〉 run out of food; not take in any grain: 他们被洪水围困，～三日。Besieged by flood they had not taken in any grain for three days in succession.

绝路 juélù ❶ cut off the way out: 办法总是有的，还不至于绝了路。We are not yet at the end of our tether. We'll find a way somehow.

J

❷ road to ruin; blind alley; impasse: 引上～ lead sb. up a blind alley / 走上～ take the road to ruin; head for one's doom / 他说这样做生意是自寻～。He said that this was a suicidal way of doing business.

绝伦 juélún 〈书面〉 unsurpassed; unequalled; unrivalled; peerless; matchless: 聪颖～ incomparably intelligent / 英勇～ peerless bravery / 美妙～ absolutely wonderful / 雄伟～ acme of grandeur / 精美～ exquisite beyond compare; superb / 荒谬～ height of absurdity; utterly preposterous

绝卖 juémài 〈旧语〉 sell off (one's real estate) for good

绝门 juémén ❶ family without offspring: ～绝户 family without offspring ❷ job or trade no one is engaged in: 这个行当快成～了。This trade is going to disappear (*or* die out). ❸ unique skill: 这手是他的～活儿。That is his unique skill. ❹ unexpected; unimaginable: 他在这件事上，做得太～啦。What he did on this matter has gone beyond the limit.

绝密 juémì top-secret; most confidential; (for your) eyes only: ～文件 top-secret papers / ～消息 most confidential information

绝妙 juémiào extremely clever; superb; excellent; perfect: ～的反面教材 excellent material for learning by negative example / ～的讽刺 superb irony / ～的配合 marvellous coordination / ～的景致 wonderful view / ～的画像 exquisite portrait / ～好辞 splendid diction; elegant language / ～的技艺 perfect artistry; admirable skills

绝灭 juémiè become extinct: 濒于～ about to be extinct; on the verge of extinction

绝灭战 juémièzhàn war of extermination

绝命书 juémìngshū ❶ suicide note ❷ note written on the eve of one's execution

绝品 juépǐn peerless work of art; unrivalled work of art

绝棋 juéqí "dead game" of chess (either a checkmate as in chess, or a game of go beyond retrieval)

绝情 juéqíng have no consideration for anyone's sensibility; break off relations; be heartless: ～忘义 be unfeeling and ungrateful

绝群 juéqún towering above the common run; unsurpassed; superb; unequalled

绝然 juérán absolutely; completely; wholly; entirely: ～相反 diametrically opposite

绝热 juérè 〈物理〉 heat insulation: ～材料 heat-insulating material; thermal insulating material / ～变化 adiabatic change (*or* variation) / ～冷却 adiabatic cooling / ～曲线 adiabatic curve; adiabatics / ～压缩 adiabatic compression / ～过程 adiabatic process

绝塞 juésài 〈书面〉 remote frontier fortress

绝色 juésè 〈书面〉 (of a woman) exceedingly beautiful; of unrivalled beauty: 传说西施是古代的一位～佳人。It is said that Xi Shi was a great beauty in ancient China.

绝食 juéshí fast; go on a hunger strike: ～斗争 go on a hunger strike

绝世 juéshì 〈书面〉 ❶ unique among one's contemporaries; peerless: ～之姿 paragon of beauty / ～珍品 peerless treasure / ～佳作 masterpiece; unsurpassed excellent work / ～无双 unequalled; unique ❷ pass away; die

绝收 juéshōu no harvest at all: 秋粮～ no harvest of autumn crops; no autumn grain harvest

绝嗣 juésì 〈书面〉 without offspring; without issue; heirless; childless

绝望 juéwàng giving up all hope; hopelessness; despair: 陷入～的心境 sink into despair / 眼神里透着～ despondent look in the eyes / 事情还没有完全～，你用不着太伤心。You don't have to be so brokenhearted, for the matter is not yet entirely hopeless. / 哀求和反抗都没有用，他陷入了～。Pleas and resistance were of no avail, and he was driven to the brink of desperation.

绝无仅有 juéwú-jǐnyǒu only one of its kind; unique: 这么大的冬瓜，在当地并非～。White gourd that big is by no means rare in this region.

绝响 juéxiǎng 〈书面〉 lost music; anything (e.g. art, skill) lost to the modern world: 这种美妙的古乐，久已～。Such wonderful ancient music has long been lost.

绝续 juéxù dying out or surviving (referring to a critical moment); life or death: 存亡～的关头 critical moment of life and death

绝学 juéxué 〈书面〉 ❶ lost learning ❷ profound learning; unique scholarship

绝艺 juéyì consummate art or skill: 他有一手捏泥人儿的～。He has got a consummate skill in moulding clay figurines.

绝育 juéyù 〈医学〉 sterilization: ～手术 sterilization operation

绝域 juéyù 〈书面〉 out-of-the-way or inaccessible place; remote foreign land

绝缘 juéyuán ❶ be cut off from; be isolated from: 他不是一个与外界完全～的人。He is not the sort of person who entirely cuts himself off from the outside world. ❷ 〈电学〉 insulation: ～材料 insulating material; insulant / ～套管 insulating sleeve; spaghetti (tubing)

绝缘体 juéyuántǐ insulator

绝缘纸 juéyuánzhǐ insulating paper

绝缘子 juéyuánzǐ insulator

绝早 juézǎo extremely early

绝招 juézhāo *also* "绝着" ❶ unique skill: 武术～ unique *wushu* skill ❷ unexpected tricky move: 我们没答应他们的条件，一定要防备他们使出断电的～。We have rejected their terms and must therefore guard against their trick of cutting power supply.

绝症 juézhèng incurable disease; fatal illness

绝种 juézhǒng (of a species) become extinct; die out: 由于大量捕杀，近些年许多动物～了。Many animals have become extinct in recent years because of excessive hunting.

绝子绝孙 juézǐ-juésūn 〈粗话〉 without offspring: 他会～！ May he die heirless!

juě

蹶 juě

see also jué

蹶子 juězi *also* "尥蹶子" liào juězi (of horses, donkeys, etc.) kick backwards (with hind leg)

juè

倔 juè gruff; blunt; surly; irascible: 说话～ be blunt of speech / 这人真～。He's surly enough. / 他深知老人的～脾气。He was well acquainted with the irascible temper of the old man.

see also jué

倔巴 juèba 〈方言〉 gruff; surly; blunt

倔头 juètóu surly man

倔头倔脑 juètóu-juènǎo blunt of manner and gruff of speech: ～的小伙子 blunt young man

jūn

军 jūn ❶ armed forces; forces; army; troops: 常备～ standing army / 后备～ reserves; reserve force / 裁～ disarmament / 参～ join the army / 从～ join the army; enlist / 敌～ enemy troops; hostile forces / 边防～ frontier force; frontier guards / ～民联防 army-civilian joint defence / 国防～ national defence forces; (of Germany) Wermacht / 正规～ regular army / 海～ navy / 空～ air force / 陆～ ground force; army / 禁～ imperial guards / 扩～ arms expansion / 生力～ fresh troops / 主力～ main force / 联～ allied forces; united army / 雇佣～ mercenary army; mercenaries / 义勇～ army of volunteers; volunteers / 野战～ field army / 远征～ expeditionary forces / 驻～ garrison / 娘子～ women soldiers / 建～ found (*or* build) an army / 溃不成～ be utterly routed / 拥～爱民 support the army and cherish the people / 劳动后备～ labour reserves / 劳动大～ labour army; contingent of labour forces ❷ army; corps: ～以上干部 cadres at or above the level of army commander; cadres of army level and above / 这个～下辖三个师。This army has got three divisions under it. *or* This army consists of three divisions.

军备 jūnbèi armament; arms: 扩充～ engage in arms expansion / 裁减～ disarmament / ～费用 military expenditure / ～控制 arms control

军备竞赛 jūnbèi jìngsài armament race; arms race

军兵种 jūn-bīngzhǒng arms and services of the armed forces

军博 Jūnbó (short for 中国人民革命军事博物馆) Military Museum of the Chinese People's Revolution (built in 1959 and located in western Beijing)

J

军部 jūnbù army headquarters:～有令，我们必须立即出发。An order has come from the army headquarters that we set out immediately.
军操 jūncāo military drill
军曹鱼 jūncáoyú 〈动物〉cobia; sergeant fish; crab-eater (*Rachycentron canadum*)
军车 jūnchē military vehicle
军船 jūnchuán naval ship; troop carrier
军代表 jūndàibiǎo military officer put in charge of some government department, enterprise, school, etc. during the Cultural Revolution; representative of the army (at a supplier's, etc.)
军刀 jūndāo soldier's sword; sabre
军地两用人才 jūn-dì liǎngyòng réncái personnel trained for both military and civilian services:培养～，开发了干部战士的智力，强化了部队的战斗力。Through training soldiers for both military and civilian services, the intelligence of officers and men has been developed and their combat effectiveness raised.
军队 jūnduì armed forces; army; troops:～建制 military organization /人民～和老百姓是一家人。The people's army and civilians are members of the same family.
军队标号 jūnduì biāohào military symbol
军队番号 jūnduì fānhào designation of a military unit
军阀 jūnfá warlord; military strongman (who keeps the government under his thumb):反动～ reactionary warlords /～混战 warlords engaging in tangled warfare /～作风 worlord ways; warlord style
军阀割据 jūnfá gējù separatist warlord regime
军阀主义 jūnfázhǔyì warlordism
军法 jūnfǎ military criminal code; military law:触犯～ military offence /～从事 punish by military law
军法审判 jūnfǎ shěnpàn court-martial
军方 jūnfāng the military:他是～的代表。He is a representative from the military.
军费 jūnfèi military expenditure:～开支 military spending /削减～在国家预算中所占的比例 cut down the proportion of military expenditure in the national budget
军分区 jūnfēnqū military subarea; military subregion
军风 jūnfēng military style; military spirit:我们的军队有着良好的～。Our army has got a good military style.
军风纪 jūnfēngjì soldier's bearing and discipline
军服 jūnfú military uniform; uniform
军服呢 jūnfúní army coating
军港 jūngǎng naval port
军鸽 jūngē pigeon for military use; military pigeon:训练～ train military pigeon
军歌 jūngē army song
军工 jūngōng ❶ (short for 军事工业) war industry:～生产 war production /～产品 military industrial products /～系统向天津转让100多项技术成果。Departments of war industry have transferred to Tianjin over 100 technical achievements. ❷ (short for 军事工程) military project
军功 jūngōng military exploit:立～ perform military exploits; render meritorious military service
军功章 jūngōngzhāng medal for military merit
军官 jūnguān officer:空军～ air force officer /～学校 military school; military college (*or* academy) /校级～ field officer /～待遇 officer's remuneration
军管 jūnguǎn military control
军管会 jūnguǎnhuì (short for 军事管制委员会) military control commission
军规 jūnguī military discipline:军人要遵守～。An armyman must observe military discipline.
军棍 jūngùn 〈旧语〉cane for corporal punishment in the army
军国主义 jūnguózhǔyì militarism:～化 militarization /～者 militarist
军号 jūnhào bugle
军徽 jūnhuī army emblem
军婚 jūnhūn marriage of serviceman or servicewoman:他犯有破坏～罪。He is found guilty of disrupting the marriage of a serviceman.
军火 jūnhuǒ munitions; arms and ammunition:～交易 deal in arms; arms deal /～工业 munitions industry; armament industry /～舰 ammunition ship /～走私 munitions smuggling
军火库 jūnhuǒkù arsenal
军火商 jūnhuǒshāng munitions merchant; arms dealer; merchant of death
军火制造商 jūnhuǒ zhìzàoshāng munitioner
军机 jūnjī ❶ military plan:断决～ decide on military plans /贻误～ delay or frustrate the fulfilment of a military scheme ❷ military secret:他因泄露～而受到指控。He is charged with leaking a military secret.
军机处 Jūnjīchù office in the Qing Dynasty that helped the emperor to handle confidential military and political affairs
军籍 jūnjí military status; one's name on the army roll:保留～ retain one's military status /开除～ strike sb.'s name off the army roll; discharge sb. from the army
军纪 jūnjì military discipline:违犯～ breach of military discipline
军舰 jūnjiàn *also* "兵舰" bīngjiàn warship; naval vessel
军阶 jūnjiē (military) rank; grade
军界 jūnjiè military circles; the military:他在～享有很高的声望。He enjoys high prestige in military circles.
军垦 jūnkěn reclamation of wasteland by an army unit
军垦农场 jūnkěn nóngchǎng army reclamation farm; army farm
军控 jūnkòng (short for 军备控制) arms or armament control
军礼 jūnlǐ military salute:行～ give a salute; salute
军力 jūnlì military strength
军粮 jūnliáng army provisions; grain for the army:～库 military grain depot; army granary
军烈属 jūn-lièshǔ family members of active servicemen or of martyrs
军龄 jūnlíng length of military service:他是一位有30年～的老军人。He is a veteran who has served in the army for thirty years.
军令 jūnlìng military order:执行～ carry out a military order
军令如山 jūnlìng-rúshān *also* "军令如山倒" military orders must be obeyed on all accounts; a military order has the force of a landslide
军令状 jūnlìngzhuàng written pledge making oneself liable to punishment by military law in case of failure to execute an order or fulfil a mission:我愿立～保证三个月完成任务。I'm ready to write a pledge to fulfil the task in three months.
军旅 jūnlǚ 〈书面〉army; armed forces; troops:～生涯 military career /～之事 military affairs
军绿 jūnlǜ army green
军马 jūnmǎ ❶ army horse:～场 army horse-breeding farm; army horse ranch ❷ troops; soldiers:各路～ all units; various forces
军帽 jūnmào army cap; service cap
军民 jūn-mín army and people; soldiers and civilians; military and civilian:～关系 relations between the army and the people; army-people relations /～联防 army-civilian joint defence /～一致 harmony between the army and the people /～团结如一人，试看天下谁能敌? If the army and the people are united as one, who in the world can match them?
军民共建 jūn-mín gòngjiàn joint efforts by the army and the people:～两个文明 joint efforts of the army and the people to promote material as well as cultural and ethical progress (*or* both material and spiritual civilizations)
军命 jūnmìng military mission; military order:～在身，不便久留。As I am on a military mission, I can't stay here for long.
军品 jūnpǐn products for military use; military products
军棋 jūnqí military chess
军旗 jūnqí army flag; military banner; colours; ensign
军旗礼 jūnqílǐ colours salute
军器 jūnqì 〈旧语〉ordnance; armament
军情 jūnqíng military situation; war situation:收集～ collect military information /刺探～ spy on military movements /～紧急 critical military situation; critical war situation
军区 jūnqū military region; (military) area command:各大～ greater military areas; major military regions /～司令部 headquarters of a military area command /北京～ Beijing Military Command /省～ provincial military command
军权 jūnquán military power; military leadership:争夺～ struggle for military power; vie for military leadership
军犬 jūnquǎn dog for military use; military dog
军人 jūnrén soldier; serviceman; armyman:现役～ person in active service /复员～ demobilized soldier /～大会 soldiers' conference

(of a company)/～家属 soldier's dependants; armyman's family members
军容 jūnróng soldiers' discipline, appearance and bearing:整饬～ strengthen army discipline and maintain required standards for appearance and bearing /～整肃 keep up military bearing
军师 jūnshi 〈旧语〉imperial official with power to supervise military affairs; military counsellor; army adviser:狗头～ inept adviser; villainous adviser /这盘棋,你下,我当～。You play this game of chess, and I'll give you counsel.
军实 jūnshí 〈书面〉❶ armament and army provisions ❷ booty and captives
军史 jūnshǐ history of an army, esp. the People's Liberation Army:新四军～ history of the New Fourth Army (1937-1946)
军士 jūnshì noncommissioned officer (NCO)
军事 jūnshì military affairs:～表演 display of military skills /～部署 military deployment; disposition of military forces /～路线 military line /～民主 military democracy /～设施 military installation /～素质 military qualities; fighting capability /～训练 military training /～野营 off-base military training; military training in the field /～优势 military superiority /～原则 principle of operation; military principle /～冒险 military adventure (*or* gamble, *or* risk) /～冲突 military clash (*or* conflict) /～干涉 military intervention /～装备 military equipment /～工程学 military engineering /～政变 military *coup d'état* /～医学 military medical science /～技术 military technology /～测绘 military mapping /～地理学 military geography /～检察院 military procuratorate /～占领 military (*or* armed) occupation
军事大国 jūnshì dàguó major military power
军事法庭 jūnshì fǎtíng military tribunal; military court; court-martial:他被～判为犯有泄露军机罪。He was pronounced by the military court guilty of leaking military secrets.
军事分界线 jūnshì fēnjièxiàn military demarcation line
军事革命 jūnshì gémìng revolution in military affairs (RMA), referring to the application of information technology in military affairs
军事工业 jūnshì gōngyè war industry
军事顾问 jūnshì gùwèn military adviser:～团 military advisory group
军事管制 jūnshì guǎnzhì military control
军事管制法 jūnshì guǎnzhìfǎ martial law
军事管制委员会 jūnshì guǎnzhì wěiyuánhuì military control commission
军事化 jūnshìhuà militarize; place on a war footing:经济～ militarization of the economy /非～地区 non-militarized zone /参加野营的学生过着～的生活。The students who went camping followed a military routine.
军事基地 jūnshì jīdì military base:有些国家在海外建有～。Some countries have military bases abroad.
军事集团 jūnshì jítuán military bloc
军事家 jūnshìjiā strategist
军事科学 jūnshì kēxué military science
军事联盟 jūnshì liánméng military alliance
军事情报 jūnshì qíngbào military intelligence
军事实力 jūnshì shílì military might
军事态势 jūnshì tàishì military posture
军事体育 jūnshì tǐyù military sports:世界～五项赛结束,中国获团体冠军。The World Competition of Five Military Sports Events was over and China won the team title.
军事条令 jūnshì tiáolìng military manual
军事条约 jūnshì tiáoyuē military treaty or pact
军事挑衅 jūnshì tiǎoxìn military provocation
军事停战委员会 jūnshì tíngzhàn wěiyuánhuì military armistice commission
军事同盟 jūnshì tóngméng military alliance
军事文学 jūnshì wénxué military literature
军事学院 jūnshì xuéyuàn military academy or institute
军事演习 jūnshì yǎnxí military exercise; war manoeuvre
军事一体化 jūnshì yītǐhuà military integration
军事政府 jūnshì zhèngfǔ military government; junta
军售 jūnshòu arms sale
军书 jūnshū 〈书面〉military documents and registers; military record or account book
军属 jūnshǔ soldier's dependents; armyman's family
军帖 jūntiě 〈旧语〉military proclamation
军统 Jūntǒng Bureau of Military Investigation and Statistics (a secret service agency of the KMT); BMIS:～特务 BMIS special agent
军团 jūntuán army group; (as of Rome) legion:第三～ Third Army Group /古罗马～ Roman legion /外籍～ foreign legion
军团病 jūntuánbìng 〈医学〉legionaires' disease
军屯 jūntún troops engaged in farming as well as garrison duties
军威 jūnwēi military prestige:～大振 greatly boost military prestige; raise military morale immensely /金戈铁马,壮我国威,壮我～。Shining spears and armoured horses added to the prowess of our country and our army.
军委 Jūnwěi (short for 中国共产党中央军事委员会) Military Commission of the Central Committee of the Communist Party of China:国务院、中央～发布命令,嘉奖立功的指战员。The State Council and the Central Military Commission issued an order citing the officers and soldiers for their meritorious service.
军伍 jūnwǔ 〈旧语〉troops; army; armed forces:～生活 army life; military life
军务 jūnwù military affair; military task:督理～ superintend and manage military affairs
军衔 jūnxián military rank:～制度 system of military ranks
军饷 jūnxiǎng soldier's pay and provisions:克扣～ embezzle soldier's pay and provisions
军校 jūnxiào military school; military academy:黄埔～ Whampoa Military Academy (1924-1927)
军械 jūnxiè ordnance; armament:～员 armourer /～修理所 armament maintenance centre
军械处 jūnxièchù ordnance department
军械库 jūnxièkù ordnance depot; arms depot; armoury
军心 jūnxīn soldier's morale:动摇～ sap the army's morale /～不稳 shaky the morale of the troops /振奋～ heighten (*or* boost) the morale of the troops
军需 jūnxū ❶ military supplies:～工厂 military supplies factory ❷ 〈旧语〉quartermaster
军需船 jūnxūchuán storeship; supply ship
军需库 jūnxūkù military supply depot
军需品 jūnxūpǐn military supplies; military stores
军宣队 jūnxuānduì (short for 解放军毛泽东思想宣传队) Mao Zedong Thought propaganda team of the People's Liberation Army (sent to government departments, enterprises, schools, etc., to take overall charge during the Cultural Revolution); PLA propaganda team
军训 jūnxùn military training:参加～ take part in military training /搞好～ make a success of military training; strengthen military training
军衣 jūnyī military uniform; uniform
军医 jūnyī medical officer; military surgeon
军营 jūnyíng military camp; barracks:刚踏进～,我就听到了军号声。Hardly had I stepped into the barracks when I heard a bugle blowing.
军用 jūnyòng for military use; military:～地图 military map /～飞机 warplane; military aircraft /～列车 military train /～物资 military supplies; *matériel* /～警报与探测系统 military warning and detection system /～桥 military bridge /～器械 military equipment /～车辆 military vehicle
军邮 jūnyóu army postal service; army post; army mail
军援 jūnyuán military aid
军乐 jūnyuè martial music; military music:～队 military band /奏起雄壮的～ play majestic martial music
军运 jūnyùn military transport:～任务 military transport task
军长 jūnzhǎng army or corps commander
军政 jūnzhèng ❶ military and political:～大学 military and political college /～训练 military and political training /～当局 civil and military authorities ❷ military administrative work:～人员 military administrative personnel ❸ army and government:～关系 relations between the army and the government
军政府 jūnzhèngfǔ military government
军职 jūnzhí official post in the army; military appointment:久任～ have long held an official post in the army
军制 jūnzhì military system

军中无戏言 jūnzhōng wú xìyán no levity is allowed in the armed forces; no joking in the army
军种 jūnzhǒng (armed) services:各～兵种 all services and arms
军转民 jūnzhuǎnmín (of a factory) switch or convert from manufacturing military products to goods for civilian use
军装 jūnzhuāng military or army uniform; uniform
军资 jūnzī military supplies

皲 jūn

皲裂 jūnliè 〈书面〉(of skin) chap:手足～ hand and foot chaps; chapped hand and foot /嘴唇～ chap in the lip; lip chap

均 jūn

❶ equal; even:分得不～ not evenly divided (*or* distributed) /苦乐不～ uneven share of burdens and comforts /贫富不～ disparity of wealth between the rich and the poor /势～力敌 match each other in strength; be well matched ❷ without exception; every one; all:各项任务～已完成。All the tasks have been finished (*or* completed). /家中～好，请勿挂念。Everything (*or* Everybody) is well in the family. Don't worry. /各界人士～表同意。People from all walks of life agree without exception.
均等 jūnděng equal; impartial; fair:机会～ equal opportunity /势力～ balance of power
均分 jūnfēn divide equally; share out equally:～为三 divide into three equal parts /奖金应按贡献大小分配，不能～。The bonus should be distributed according to one's contribution instead of being shared out equally.
均衡 jūnhéng balanced; proportionate; harmonious; even:饮食～ balanced diet /供求～ equilibrium of supply and demand /～发展 balanced (*or* harmonious) development /～生产 levelling of production; equilibrium in production /参加决赛的四个队在体力和技术上大体～。The four teams entering the finals are roughly even in physical strength and skill.
均衡裁军 jūnhéng cáijūn balanced disarmament
均衡汇率 jūnhéng huìlǜ equilibrium rate of exchange
均衡利率 jūnhéng lìlǜ equilibrium rate of interest
均衡论 jūnhénglùn 〈哲学〉 theory of equilibrium
均拉 jūnlā 〈方言〉 on the average:每亩地～，至少也有五百斤的产量。There should at least be an average output of 500 *jin* per *mu*.
均买均卖 jūnmǎi-jūnmài fair dealings in business
均热 jūnrè 〈冶金〉 soaking:～炉 soaking pit
均势 jūnshì balance of power; equilibrium of forces; balance; equilibrium; parity:使一方与另一方形成～ balance one side with (*or* by) another; keep the two sides in equilibrium /军事～ military parity /核～ nuclear parity /保持～ keep the balance /打破～ break (*or* upset) the balance
均摊 jūntān share equally:损失～ share a loss equally /水电费按户～。Charges for water and electricity will be shared equally on a household basis.
均田制 jūntiánzhì 〈历史〉 equal-field system
均温 jūnwēn average temperature:年～摄氏 26.4 度。The average annual temperature is 26.4°C.
均相 jūnxiàng 〈化学〉 homogeneous phase:～催化剂 homogeneous catalyst /～沉淀法 homogeneous precipitating method
均一 jūnyī even; uniform; homogeneous
均一性 jūnyīxìng 〈化学〉 homogeneity
均夷 jūnyí 〈地质〉 grade:～平原 graded plain
均匀 jūnyún even; well-distributed:呼吸～ even breathing /雨水～ even rainfall (*or* precipatation) /～速度 even speed; uniform velocity /～负载 uniform load /把饲料拌～ get the fodder well mixed up /这儿冷热～，长年都像春天。It is like spring all year round here as it is neither too hot nor too cold. /我国人口众多，分布又不～。The population of our country is large and not well distributed.
均沾 jūnzhān share (interests, etc.) equally; have equal access to (advantages):利益～ even share of benefits
均值法 jūnzhífǎ averaging method
均质性 jūnzhìxìng 〈物理〉 isotropy

钧 jūn

❶ ancient unit of weight (equal to 30 *jin*):千～一发 hundredweight hanging by a hair — an extremely critical situation ❷ potter's wheel; throwing wheel ❸ 〈书面〉〈敬词〉 you; your
钧安 jūn'ān 〈书面〉〈敬词〉 wish you good health
钧鉴 jūnjiàn 〈书面〉〈敬词〉 your attention
钧命 jūnmìng 〈书面〉〈敬词〉 your order:谨尊～ in deference to your instruction
钧启 jūnqǐ 〈书面〉〈敬词〉 Yours sincerely; Sincerely yours
钧陶 jūntáo 〈书面〉 potter's wheel — educate and foster talents (as potters mould clay)
钧谕 jūnyù 〈书面〉〈敬词〉 your written advice
钧轴 jūnzhóu 〈书面〉〈比喻〉important government post; person at the helm of the state
钧座 jūnzuò 〈书面〉〈敬词〉 Your Excellency

麇(麕) jūn

〈古语〉 river deer
see also qún

菌 jūn

❶ fungus:红茶～ tea fungus /真～ fungus ❷ bacterium:病～ pathogenic bacteria; germs /杆～ bacillus /结核～ tubercle bacillus /霉～ mould /球～ coccus /细～ germ; bacterium /杀～ disinfect; sterilize
see also jùn
菌肥 jūnféi (short for 细菌肥料) bacterial manure
菌核 jūnhé sclerotium
菌落 jūnluò 〈微生物〉 colony
菌苗 jūnmiáo 〈医学〉 vaccine
菌丝 jūnsī 〈植物〉 hypha
菌丝体 jūnsītǐ mycelium
菌血症 jūnxuèzhèng 〈医学〉 bacteriemia

龟(龜) jūn

see also guī; qiū
龟裂 jūnliè ❶ (of skin) chap ❷ (of parched earth) be full of cracks:百年不遇的大旱，使大片土地～。The biggest drought in a century made the parched earth full of cracks.

君 jūn

❶ monarch; sovereign; supreme ruler:国～ monarch /储～ crown prince /暴～ tyrant; despot ❷ 〈书面〉 gentleman; Mr.:杨～ Mr. Yang /欢迎诸～远道而来。Welcome to all the gentlemen coming from afar.
君侧 jūncè 〈书面〉 trusted courtiers of a monarch:清～ get rid of the bad people trusted by the monarch (often as an excuse for revolt)
君礼臣忠 jūnlǐ-chénzhōng as the monarch treats his ministers with propriety, so the ministers serve the monarch with loyalty
君临 jūnlín ❶ monarch's rule; govern:～天下 govern (*or* rule) the country /～一切 take charge of everything ❷ approaching; drawing near:在黎明～的前一刻，周围显得特别黑暗。With the approach of dawn, it is becoming particularly dark all around.
君迁子 jūnqiānzǐ 〈中药〉 fruit of date plum (*Diospyros lotus*)
君权 jūnquán monarchical power:～神授论 theory of divine right of kings
君辱臣死 jūnrǔ-chénsǐ when the monarch is humiliated the minister dies:君忧臣劳，～。The minister worked to relieve the monarch's worries, and he would rather die than see his monarch humiliated.
君上 jūnshàng 〈书面〉 monarch; sovereign
君王 jūnwáng monarch; sovereign; emperor
君长 jūnzhǎng ❶ monarch; sovereign ❷ head of a tribe
君之代 Jūnzhīdài *Kimigayo*, or *His Majesty's Reign*, de facto Japanese national anthem legalized in 1999
君主 jūnzhǔ monarch; sovereign:被废黜的～ deposed monarch /退位～ abdicated monarch
君主国 jūnzhǔguó monarchical state; monarchy:现今～多在欧洲。Nowadays most of the monarchical states are to be found in Europe.
君主立宪 jūnzhǔ lìxiàn constitutional monarchy
君主制 jūnzhǔzhì monarchy:立宪～ constitutional monarchy /绝对～ absolute monarchy
君主专制 jūnzhǔ zhuānzhì autocratic monarchy; absolute monarchy
君子 jūnzǐ man of noble character; virtuous man; superior man; gentleman:伪～ hypocrite /正人～ man of moral integrity /谦谦～ modest, self-disciplined gentleman; hypocritically modest person /

J

梁上～ gentleman on the beam — burglar; thief /以小人之心度～之腹 gauge the heart of a gentleman with one's own mean measure

君子报仇，十年不晚 jūnzǐ bàochóu, shínián bù wǎn even ten years isn't a long time for a gentleman to seek vengeance; it's never too late to take one's revenge

君子不念旧恶 jūnzǐ bù niàn jiù'è a gentleman does not bear grudges

君子成人之美 jūnzǐ chéng rén zhī měi a gentleman is always ready to help others attain their goals

君子动口不动手 jūnzǐ dòng kǒu bù dòng shǒu a gentleman uses his tongue, not his fists

君子国 jūnzǐguó (imaginary) land of the virtuous：传说中的～，现实生活中是不存在的。The legendary land of the virtuous is non-existent in reality.

君子和而不同 jūnzǐ hé ér bù tóng a gentleman gets along with others, but not necessarily agrees with them

君子绝交不认仇 jūnzǐ juéjiāo bù rèn chóu a good man terminates a friendship without rancour

君子兰 jūnzǐlán 〈植物〉kaffir lily

君子劳心，小人劳力 jūnzǐ láo xīn, xiǎorén láo lì the gentleman uses his brain and the mean man his brawn

君子坦荡荡 jūnzǐ tǎndàngdàng a gentleman is open and magnanimous

君子协定 jūnzǐ xiédìng gentlemen's agreement：咱们订个～。Let's come to a gentlemen's agreement.

君子一言，快马一鞭 jūnzǐ yī yán, kuàimǎ yī biān a gentleman is as good as his word, as a steed gallops at the first crack of the whip

君子一言，驷马难追 jūnzǐ yī yán, sìmǎ nán zhuī a word spoken is past recalling; what is said can't be retracted

君子忧道不忧贫 jūnzǐ yōu dào bù yōu pín a gentleman fears not poverty but lack of principles

君子喻于义，小人喻于利 jūnzǐ yù yú yì, xiǎorén yù yú lì the superior man is concerned with righteousness and the mean man with gain

君子之交淡如水 jūnzǐ zhī jiāo dàn rú shuǐ the friendship between gentlemen is as pure as crystal; a hedge between keeps friendship green

莙 jūn

莙荙菜 jūndácài 〈植物〉*Beta vulgaris* var. *cicla*

鲪 jūn

〈动物〉sebastodes：黑～ *Sebastodes fuscescens* /汤氏～ *S. thompsoni*

jùn

寯 jùn

〈书面〉*see* "俊" jùn

菌 jùn

mushroom

see also jūn

菌柄 jùnbǐng (of fungus) stem

菌根 jùngēn mycorrhiza; micorhiza

菌伞 jùnsǎn (of fungus) cap

菌子 jùnzi 〈方言〉gill fungus; mushroom

箘 jùn

〈书面〉❶ bamboo shoots ❷ a kind of bamboo mentioned in ancient books

浚(濬) jùn

dredge：～河 dredge a river /疏～ dredge /修～ dredge (a river)

浚泥船 jùnníchuán dredger

浚渫 jùnxiè 〈书面〉dredge

竣 jùn

complete; finish：告～ have been accomplished /完～ (of a project, building, etc.) be completed /～事 be concluded

竣工 jùngōng (of a project) be completed：新铁路全线～。The entire new railway line has been completed.

焌 jùn

〈书面〉burn

see also qū

畯 jùn

〈古语〉official in charge of agriculture

峻 jùn

❶ (of mountains) high：险～ precipitous /巉～ dangerously steep; precipitous /山势高～ high and steep mountains /崇山～岭 high mountain ridges ❷ harsh; hard; severe; stern：严～ stern; severe /冷～ cold (expression); frosty (looks) /严刑～法 harsh law and severe punishment

峻拔 jùnbá (of mountain) high and steep：山势～ high and steep mountains

峻急 jùnjí 〈书面〉❶ (of water currents) rapid; torrential：江流～ rapid river currents ❷ severe and impatient; impetuous; stern：生性～ of impatient disposition

峻节 jùnjié 〈书面〉high moral principle; moral integrity

峻拒 jùnjù 〈书面〉turn down abruptly; refuse sternly

峻刻 jùnkè 〈书面〉severe and harsh

峻厉 jùnlì severe; stern; grim; rigorous：～的目光 grim look; stern look

峻峭 jùnqiào high and steep

峻险 jùnxiǎn precipitous; dangerously steep：～的小路 dangerously steep footpath

峻泻 jùnxiè empty the bowels with drastic purgatives

峻直 jùnzhí high and straight：～的山峰 straight and towering mountain peak

俊(❷隽、儁) jùn

❶ handsome; pretty; beautiful：那个小姑娘长得真～。The girl is quite pretty. /小伙子挺～的，就是有点儿腼腆。The young fellow is rather handsome but a bit shy. ❷ person of outstanding talent：英～有为 eminently talented and promising

俊杰 jùnjié person of outstanding talent; hero：～在位 with the most talented men in office /识时务者为～。Whoever understands the times is a hero.

俊丽 jùnlì beautiful and elegant

俊迈 jùnmài 〈书面〉outstandingly graceful：洒脱～ free, easy and elegant /神情～ look very graceful; wear an elegant expression

俊髦 jùnmáo 〈书面〉person of outstanding talent; extremely talented person

俊美 jùnměi pretty：她比姐姐更～。She is even prettier than her sister.

俊男倩女 jùnnán-qiànnǚ handsome men and beautiful women

俊气 jùnqi pretty; delicate; elegant; fine：那个小姑娘眉清目秀，挺～。Having delicate features, that young girl is very lovely.

俊俏 jùnqiào 〈口语〉pretty and charming：～的小伙子 handsome young man /这姑娘模样儿十分～。This girl looks very pretty and charming.

俊爽 jùnshuǎng 〈书面〉bold and handsome：风姿～ graceful and unrestrained bearing

俊伟 jùnwěi 〈书面〉be gifted with eminent talent and insight：～的人物 person of outstanding ability and talent

俊秀 jùnxiù pretty; of delicate beauty：论面貌～，方圆几十里没有哪个姑娘比得上她。So far as her delicate beauty is concerned, she is matchless for miles around.

俊雅 jùnyǎ 〈书面〉pretty and tasteful：玲珑～的楼阁 exquisite and tasteful pavilions

俊彦 jùnyàn 〈书面〉man of outstanding ability and intellect

俊逸 jùnyì 〈书面〉handsome, free and easy; out of the ordinary：才思～ uncommon talent

馂 jùn

〈书面〉left-over

骏 jùn

fine horse; steed

骏马 jùnmǎ fine horse; steed：～飞奔 galloping steed /～却驮痴汉走。A magnificent steed gets a dolt for a rider.

骏足 jùnzú 〈书面〉fine horse; steed

珺 jùn

〈书面〉a kind of jade

捃(攟、攈) jùn

〈书面〉pick up：～其菁华 grasp the essence; skim the cream

捃摭 jùnzhí 〈书面〉pick up; select; collect

J

郡 jùn ❶〈历史〉prefecture ❷ county (in the UK, Ireland, etc.):牛津～ Oxfordshire

郡县制 jùnxiànzhì 〈历史〉system of prefectures and counties (a system of local administration which took shape during the Eastern Zhou and Qin dynasties)

K

kā

𣑊 kā 〈方言〉❶ place in between; clamp; embed:我鞋跟～在石头缝里。The heel of my shoe was caught in the rock crevice. ❷ corner; nook:山～～ remote mountain recesses ❸ chink; crack; crevice; fissure:木～ chink in wood /石～～ crevice in rock

揢 kā 〈口语〉scrape with a knife:用刀把墙皮～掉 scrape off the wall surface with a knife /把锅盖上的铁锈～一下 scrape away rust on a pot lid /油漆大门前要先把门～干净。You must scrape the door before painting it again.

揢吃 kāchi *also*“揢哧”〈口语〉scrape with a knife:把墙上的标语～掉。Scrape the slogan from the wall.

喀 kā 〈象声〉*indicating noise made in coughing or vomiting*:～的一声,他吐出一口痰。He spat with a loud sound. *or* He coughed up.

喀吧 kābā *also*“咔吧”kābā 〈象声〉snap; crack:～一声,棍子撅成两截。The stick broke into two with a crack. *or* The stick snapped in half.

喀布尔 Kābù'ěr Kabul, capital of Afghanistan

喀嚓 kāchā *also*“咔嚓”kāchā 〈象声〉crack; snap:只听～一声扁担断了。The carrying pole broke with a crack (*or* snapped).

喀哒 kādā *also*“咔哒”kādā 〈象声〉click:～一声,他把电话挂上了。He hung up with a click.

喀尔巴阡山 Kā'ěrbāqiānshān Carpathians, mountain range extending from southern Poland to Romania

喀喇昆仑山 Kālākūnlúnshān Karakorum Mountains, chain of mountains in western China

喀麦隆 Kāmàilóng Cameroon:～人 Cameroonian

喀秋莎 Kāqiūshā (transliteration from Russian) ❶ Katyusha, a girl's name ❷ multi-barrel rocket launcher

喀什 Kāshí Kashgar or Kashi, city in the west of the Xinjiang Uygur Autonomous Region

喀斯喀特山脉 Kāsīkātè Shānmài Cascade Range, mountain range along the west coast of North America

喀斯特 kāsītè *also*“岩溶”yánróng 〈地理〉karst:～地形 karst topography /～溶洞 karst cave

喀土穆 Kātǔmù Khartoum, capital of the Sudan

咔 kā 〈象声〉click; clack:他～的一声关上抽屉。He closed the drawer with a clack.
see also kǎ

咔吧 kābā *see*“喀吧”kābā

咔嚓 kāchā *see*“喀嚓”kāchā

咔哒 kādā *see*“喀哒”kādā

咖 kā
see also gā

咖啡 kāfēi coffee; café:喝一杯～ drink a cup of coffee /清～ black coffee; *café noir* /牛奶～ white coffee; coffee with milk; *café au lait* /速溶～ instant coffee /～精 coffee extract (*or* essence) /～磨 coffee grinder (*or* mill) /～渣 coffee grounds /～树 coffee tree /请把咖啡煮浓点。Please make the coffee stronger.

咖啡杯 kāfēibēi coffee cup

咖啡豆 kāfēidòu coffee bean

咖啡壶 kāfēihú coffee pot

咖啡碱 kāfēijiǎn *also*“咖啡因”〈药学〉caffeine; caffeinum

咖啡色 kāfēisè coffee (colour); dark brown

咖啡厅 kāfēitīng *also*“咖啡馆”coffee bar; coffee house; café; caff

咖啡锈病 kāfēi xiùbìng coffee rust

咖啡因 kāfēiyīn 〈药学〉*see*“咖啡碱”

咖啡中毒 kāfēi zhòngdú caffeinism

咖啡种植园 kāfēi zhòngzhíyuán coffee plantation; cafetal

kǎ

卡 kǎ ❶ (short for 卡路里) calorie:大～ kilocalorie; kcal ❷ card:分类～ classified (*or* classification) card /索引～ index card /信用～ credit card ❸ cassette:双～录音机 double-cassette recorder ❹ truck; lorry:十轮～ ten-wheeled truck (*or* lorry)
see also qiǎ

卡巴迪 kǎbādí 〈体育〉kabaddi, popular folk game of the Indian subcontinent

卡巴胂 kǎbāshèn 〈药学〉carbarsone

卡奔达 Kǎbēndá Cabinda, enclave of Angola at the mouth of the Congo

卡宾枪 kǎbīnqiāng carbine:～手 carbineer; carbinier

卡车 kǎchē truck; lorry:重型～ heavy-duty truck /轻型～ pickup (truck) /军用～ camion /～起重机 truck crane /～运输 truckage /～驾驶员 trucker; truckdriver

卡尺 kǎchǐ 〈机械〉calibre gauge or rule; calliper rule or gauge; vernior calliper

卡带 kǎdài cassette tape

卡丁车 kǎdīngchē 〈体育〉Carting car, a mini Formula-One-styled racing car

卡规 kǎguī measuring tool used to measure axles and convex workpieces; callipers
see also“界限量规”jièxiàn liángguī

卡介苗 kǎjièmiáo 〈药学〉BCG (Bacille Calmette-Guérin) vaccine; TB vaccine:打～ have a BCG vaccine

卡拉 OK kǎlā'ōukèi karaoke, a form of entertainment in which one sings songs against a pre-recorded backing:～酒吧 karaoke bar

卡拉奇 Kǎlāqí Karachi, largest city and major port of Pakistan

卡林顿子午线 Kǎlíndùn zǐwǔxiàn 〈天文〉Carrington meridian

卡龙 kǎlóng kalong, stringed instrument of the Uygur nationality; Uygur dulcimer

卡路里 kǎlùlǐ 〈物理〉caloric

卡那霉素 kǎnàméisù 〈药学〉kanamycin:～链霉菌 streptomyces kanamyceticus

卡盘 kǎpán 〈机械〉chuck:分动～ independent chuck /三爪～ three jaw chuck /～式机床 chucking machine

卡片 kǎpiàn card; fiche:～储存器 card file /～袋 card pocket /～目录 card catalogue /～索引 card index /～库 card base /～容量 card capacity /～分类机 card sorter; card sorting machine /～复制机 card reproducer /～计数器 card counter /～式分类账 card ledger /～输出机 card output unit /～柜 card cabinet /～盒 card case (*or* box) /～译码器 card translator /～调整器 (card) conditioner /资料～ reference card /～存取 card access /～代码 card code /～阅读机 card reader /～簿 rotary file of cards

卡普兰氏综合征 Kǎpǔlánshì zōnghézhēng 〈医学〉Caplan's syn-

drome

卡普伦 kǎpǔlún 〈化工〉capron(e); kapron

卡其 kǎqí *also* "咔叽" kǎjī 〈纺织〉khaki (cotton)

卡钳 kǎqián 〈机械〉callipers：内外～ combination callipers／内～ inside callipers／外～ outside callipers／一只～ a pair of callipers

卡曲 kǎqū *also* "卡装" car coat

卡萨布兰卡 Kǎsàbùlánkǎ Casablanca, seaport and largest city of Morocco

卡式录像机 kǎshì lùxiàngjī video cassette recorder

卡式录音机 kǎshì lùyīnjī audio cassette recorder

卡斯特罗 Kǎsītèluó Fidel Castro (1926-), leader of Cuba since 1959

卡他 kǎtā 〈医学〉catarrh：夏季～ summer catarrh; hay-fever／春季～ vernal catarrh／萎缩性鼻～ atrophic catarrh／鼻～ coryza／～结膜炎 catarrhal conjunctivitis

卡他性 kǎtāxìng 〈医学〉catarrhal：急性～鼻炎 acute catarrhal rhinitis／～鼻炎 coryza／～肺炎 catarrhal pneumonia／～黄疸 catarrhal jaundice／～结膜炎 pinkeye; catarrhal conjunctivitis／～中耳炎 catarrhal otitis media／～胃炎 catarrhal gastritis

卡塔尔 Kǎtǎ'ěr Qatar：～人 Qatari

卡特 Kǎtè Jimmy Carter (1924-), 39th President of the US (1977-1981)

卡特尔 Kǎtè'ěr 〈经济〉cartel：钢铁～ steel cartel／～化 cartelization

卡通 kǎtōng ❶ animated cartoon：～片 animated cartoon (film) ❷ cartoon; comic strip; strip cartoon

卡瓦酒 kǎwǎjiǔ kava, an intoxicating drink made from the crushed roots of a Polynesian shrub

卡翁达 Kǎwēngdá Kenneth Kaunda (1924-), leader of the independence movement and first President of Zambia (1964-1991)

卡扎菲 Kǎzhāfēi Muammar al-Qaddafi (1942-), leader of Libya (1969-)

卡值 kǎzhí 〈物理〉calorific value

咔 kǎ

see also kā

咔叽 kǎjī *also* "卡其" kǎqí 〈纺织〉khaki

咔唑 kǎzuò 〈化学〉carbazole：～胺 carbazolamine

佧 kǎ

佧佤族 Kǎwǎzú old name for the Wa (佤) nationality, living in Yunnan Province

胩 kǎ

also "异腈" yìjīng 〈化学〉carbylamine; isocyanide

咯 kǎ

cough up：他最终还是把鱼刺～出来了。He managed to cough up the fishbone at last.

see also gē; lo; luò

咯痰 kǎtán cough up phlegm

咯血 kǎxiě 〈医学〉spit blood; haemoptysis; haemoptoe

kāi

开[1]（開） kāi

❶ open; turn on; be on：～锁 open a lock; unlock／～瓶子 open a bottle／～盖子 open the lid／～灯 turn (*or* switch) on the light／～电视 turn on the TV／无线电～着呢。The radio is on. ❷ make an opening; open up; reclaim：～矿 open up a mine; exploit a mine／～路 cut out a path; clear (*or* blaze) a path／在墙上～个洞 make an opening in the wall ❸ open out; come loose：花园里的花儿都～了。The flowers in the garden are opening (*or* in bloom).／扣儿～了。The knot has come untied.／粘好的三合板又～了。The glued three-ply board has come loose again. ❹ thaw; become navigable：河～了，我们昨天坐船去了城里。The river thawed and we went to town by boat yesterday. ❺ lift (a ban; restriction, etc.)：*see* "～戒" ❻ start; operate; drive; run：～机器 operate a machine; run a machine／～飞机 pilot (*or* fly) an airplane／轮船马上要～了。The steamboat is about to set sail. ❼ (of troops, etc.) set out; move：昨夜城里～进了两团人马。Two regiments moved into the city last night. ❽ set up; run：～饭馆 run a restaurant／～商店 open (up) a shop ❾ begin; start：～先例 set a precedent; create a precedent ❿ hold (a meeting, exhibition, etc.)：～欢送会 hold (*or* throw) a farewell party／～迎新会 hold a meeting to welcome newcomers ⓫ write out; make out：～收条 make out a receipt／～个单子 make a list／～药方 write a prescription／出发前到人事处去～介绍信。Get a letter of introduction from the personnel department before you set out. ⓬ pay (wages, fares, etc.)：～薪 pay a salary; get one's salary／这笔费用由谁～？Who shall pay the expenses? ⓭ 〈方言〉kick out; fire; sack：随意～掉工人 sack workers at will ⓮ boil：水～了。The water is boiling. ⓯ serve (a meal, banquet, etc.)：～席 serve dinner; serve a meal ⓰〈方言〉finish; eat up：他把十个包子全～了。He finished all the ten steamed stuffed buns. ⓱ *used after a verb or an adjective*：(a) extend; expand; spread：谣言传～了。The rumour has spread far and wide.／这支歌儿很快便流行～了。The song soon became popular. (b) start and continue：一见到我她就哭～了。She began to cry as soon as she saw me.／天一亮大伙就干～了。Everyone started working at daybreak.／头场雪后，天就冷～了。It got cold after the first snow. ⓲ percentage; proportion (in round numbers)：把他的功过说成三七～是公道的。It is a fair assessment to say that his work is 70% achievements and 30% mistakes.／利润按四六～分成。We have to divide the profit in the proportion of four to six. ⓳ 〈印刷〉division of standard size printing paper：对～(纸) folio／四～ quarto／八～ octavo／十六～ sixteenmo; 16mo／三十二～ thirty-twomo; 32mo ⓴ (Kāi) a surname

开[2]（開） kāi

carat：*see* "～金"

开[3]（開） kāi

used after a verb：(a) apart; away：离～ go away／推～窗户 fling the window open／滚～。Get out.／把他俩拉～。Pull (*or* Keep) them apart.／救护车来了，快让～。Here comes the ambulance; hurry and get out of the way. (b) big enough (to contain, hold, etc.)：这张床睡不～两个人。This bed is not big enough for two people.／进来吧，大伙都坐得～。Come on in; there's room enough for everybody.

开拔 kāibá (of troops) move; set out：拂晓前，部队～了。The troops set out before daybreak.

开板 kāibǎn 〈方言〉(of shop) start doing business：商店从前天起提前一小时～儿。The store started doing business an hour earlier from the day before yesterday.

开办 kāibàn open; set up; start：～工厂 start a factory／～新企业 set up a new enterprise／～超级商场 open a supermarket／～一家英文报纸 launch an English newspaper／～一所学校 run a new school

开办费 kāibànfèi opening or initial expenses; preliminary cost

开办税 kāibànshuì organization tax

开本 kāiběn 〈印刷〉format; book size：四～ quarto／八～octavo／十六～ 16mo

开笔 kāibǐ ❶ 〈旧语〉begin learning to write poems and essays：他七岁～学做诗。He began learning to write poems at the age of seven.／～学书 begin to practise calligraphy ❷ 〈旧语〉time for taking up the writing brush in a year：新春～ start writing in the new (lunar) year ❸ start writing a book or an article：他筹划多年的著作昨已～。He set out on the long-projected book yesterday.

开边 kāibiān 〈书面〉expand a country's territory：皇帝久有～之心。The emperor had long craved territorial aggrandizement.

开编 kāibiān start compiling or editing：这本词典，何时～？When will work start on the dictionary?

开标 kāibiāo open sealed tenders; open tenders：～日期 tender opening date

开播 kāibō ❶ (of a radio or TV station) begin broadcasting：有线电视台业已～。The cable network has begun broadcasting. ❷ begin broadcasting a programme：这部电视连续剧是上月～的。This TV serial began to be broadcast (*or* aired) last month. ❸ begin or start sowing：本省冬麦已经～。The seeding of winter wheat has begun in the province.

开步 kāibù take long steps; stride; march：～走 march forward／他刚～就打了个踉跄。He staggered the moment he strode out.

开采 kāicǎi mine; extract; exploit; recover：～铁矿 mine iron ore／～海底天然气 tap (*or* extract) natural gas from the bottom of the sea／～量 yield (of a mine, etc.)／～费用 mining cost／～厚度 working thickness; mining width／～深度 mining depth／～顺序 mining sequence／～速度 mining rate／～损失 exploitation losses／合资～沿海石油 joint recovery of offshore petroleum

开仓济贫 kāicāng-jìpín open granaries to relieve poverty; open the barn to help the impoverished
开舱 kāicāng break bulk; break out (a cargo)
开槽 kāicáo (open a) slot; (make a) notch; (cut a) groove: ～机 groover; groove-cutting machine; notching machine / ～锯 grooving saw / ～线 slotted line
开衩 kāichà vent (at the bottom of a coat at the sides or back); branch; slit: 中间～ centre vent / 旁边～ side vent(s) / 你新做的大衣开不开衩? Do you want any vent in your new overcoat?
开差 kāichāi 〈旧语〉(of troops) move; set out: 明天拂晓～ set out at dawn tomorrow
开场 kāichǎng begin; open; start: 赶快进去, 戏马上就～了。Go on in! The play will begin in a minute. / 他一举打破学校跳高纪录, 给运动会带来了个好～。The sports-meet got off to a very good start with his breaking the school record in the high jump.
开场白 kāichǎngbái ❶ prologue (of a play) ❷ opening speech; introductory remarks: 他在～中介绍了自己的身分。He introduced himself in the opening speech.
开敞 kāichǎng ❶ open: 大门～着。The door is wide open. ❷ spacious: ～的房间 spacious room
开敞式 kāichǎngshì 〈电工〉open type: ～电动机 open motor / ～电机 open type machine
开畅 kāichàng free from worry; happy: 心怀～ open and unworried; happy
开车 kāichē ❶ drive or start a car, train, etc.: 在高速公路上～每小时不得超过九十公里。One should not exceed the limit of 90 kilometres per hour when driving on the expressway. / 酒后不许～。No drunk-driving. ❷ set a machine going; start a machine
开车的 kāichēde 〈旧语〉driver; chauffeur
开诚布公 kāichéng-bùgōng open-hearted; in all sincerity and frankness: 我们双方～地谈一谈。Let's have a frank and sincere talk. / 他～地和我们谈了心里话。He bared his heart (*or* soul) to us.
开诚相见 kāichéng-xiāngjiàn be frank and open; treat open-heartedly; lay one's heart bare; talk from the fullness or bottom of one's heart: 我们彼此应该～, 都不要有所隐瞒。We should be frank and open, and hide nothing from each other.
开城 Kāichéng Kaesong, city of the Democratic People's Republic of Korea to the south of the 38th parallel
开秤 kāichèng (usu. of a purchasing centre for seasonal produce) begin business: 货栈～收购中草药已经三天了。It is three days since the warehouse began purchasing medicinal herbs.
开初 kāichū at the beginning; at first; from the outset: ～我们并不认识, 接触多了也就熟了。At first, we didn't know each other, but gradually we became familiar.
开除 kāichú expel; discharge; dismiss: ～学籍 expel from school / ～公职 discharge sb. from public employment; take sb.'s name off the books / ～以示训戒 dismiss sb. by way of disciplinary punishment / 他因玩忽职守而被～了。He got the sack for neglecting his duties. / 两个学生被～了。Two students were sent down.
开锄 kāichú 〈农业〉start the year's hoeing: ～那天中午, 他才赶回家中。He didn't get home until noon on the day they started the year's hoeing.
开船 kāichuán set sail; sail; weigh anchor: 按期～ sail on time / ～时间 sailing time; hour of sailing / 当他们到达时, 已经～了。When they arrived, the ship had already set sail.
开创 kāichuàng open; initiate; pioneer; found; set up: ～新纪元 open (*or* usher in) a new epoch / ～新局面 create a new situation / ～新事业 pioneer a new cause / 家父～了这所医院。My father founded the hospital.
开创精神 kāichuàng jīngshen initiative; pioneering spirit
开春 kāichūn beginning of spring (usu. referring to the first month of the lunar year); early spring: 赶在～之前把肥料送到地里。Fertilizers should be carted to the fields before the beginning of spring.
开打 kāidǎ 〈戏曲〉(perform) acrobatic fighting: 一阵紧锣密鼓, 台上的黑头和武丑～了。With a wild beating of gongs and drums, the black-faced warrior and the military comedian performed an acrobatic fighting routine.
开大肌 kāidàjī dilator muscle
开裆裤 kāidāngkù open-seat pants; split pants: 孩子出世前, 她把对襟小褂、～都做好了。Before giving birth, she had already prepared a baby's button-down jacket and open-seat pants.
开刀 kāidāo ❶ (usu. used in the early vernacular) behead; decapitate: ～问斩 execute by beheading; behead sb. ❷ make the first target of attack: 干吗单拿我～? Why should you single me out to start with? / 我不愿拿小张～。I didn't want to make an example of Xiao Zhang. ❸ perform or have an operation; operate or be operated on: 连续八小时给病人～ operate on a patient for eight hours running
开导 kāidǎo show sb. what is right or sensible; help sb. to straighten out his mistaken or muddled thinking; give guidance to; enlighten: 孩子小, 有了错误好好～他。He is still a child and needs guidance when he makes a mistake. / 他见我闹情绪, 也常～我。Seeing me sulking (*or* in such low spirits), he would often try to help me put things in the right perspective.
开倒车 kāi dàochē turn back the wheel of history; turn the clock back; return to the past: 别～! Don't backpedal! / 如今提倡婚姻自主, 你们这群老顽固, 要～呀? Nowadays, free marriage is advocated. Are you old mossbacks going to turn back the wheel of history?
开道 kāidào ❶ clear the way: 鸣锣～ beat gongs to clear the way (for officials in feudal times); prepare the public for a coming event / 他带了三千精兵在前面～。He led three thousand crack troops to clear the way ahead. ❷ 〈方言〉make way: 喝令三山五岳～。Let the mountains make way.
开地 kāidì ❶ plough; till; turn up the soil ❷ 〈方言〉open up wasteland ❸ 〈书面〉open up territory: ～千里 enlarge one's territory by one thousand *li*
开奠 kāidiàn (family of the deceased) hold a memorial ceremony for the deceased before a funeral procession; pre-funeral memorial
开吊 kāidiào 〈旧语〉receive visitors who come to offer condolences before a funeral procession; hold ceremonies of condolence
开顶 kāidǐng 〈方言〉be balding: 他三十岁就～了。He became (*or* went) bald at the age of 30.
开顶风船 kāi dǐngfēngchuán sail against the wind; struggle against heavy odds: 他是个讲原则的人, 不怕～, 也不怕丢乌纱帽。He is a man of principle, ready to struggle against heavy odds and not afraid to forfeit his official post.
开动 kāidòng ❶ start; set in motion: ～机车 set the engine in motion / ～马达 start a motor / ～脑筋 use one's brains; think things over ❷ move; march; set out: 前军拂晓～, 大军随后趱行。The vanguard units set out at daybreak, and the main forces followed up after.
开冻 kāidòng thaw: 趁还未～, 我们去溜冰吧! Let's go skating before the thaw sets in. / 天气转暖, 江河～。Rivers unfreeze as it gets warmer.
开端 kāiduān beginning; start; 故事的～ beginning of a story / 这一纠纷是两国交恶的～。The relationship between the two countries began to worsen after the dispute.
开恩 kāi'ēn show or have mercy; bestow or grant a favour
开尔文 kāi'ěrwén 〈物理〉degree Kelvin; kelvin
开发 kāifā ❶ develop; open up; exploit: ～边远地区 develop remote areas / ～矿藏 exploit mineral resources / ～荒山 open up barren mountains / ～公司 development company / ～中心 development centre / ～成本 development cost / ～费用 development expenditure / ～规划 development project / ～周期 construction cycle ❷ bring into play; tap; develop: ～智力 tap intellectual resources / 研究与～先进技术 research and development of advanced technology
开发 kāifa pay; distribute: ～车钱 pay travelling expenses / ～喜钱 distribute luck money (among well-wishers, etc.)
开发计划署 Kāifā Jìhuàshǔ United Nations Development Programme (UNDP)
开发区 kāifāqū Open Economic Zone (OEZ); (investment and) development zone
开发性项目 kāifāxìng xiàngmù exploration project
开发银行 kāifā yínháng development bank: 亚洲～ Asia Development Bank (ADB)
开饭 kāifàn ❶ serve a meal: 大家请入席, 马上～。Please be seated, and the meal will be served in a second. ❷ (of a public canteen) open; be in service: ～时间 dining (*or* service) hours / 饭厅十二时～。The dining-hall opens at 12.
开方 kāifāng ❶ *also* "开方子" write (out) a prescription: ～后, 先划价, 然后交款、取药。With the doctor's prescription, you must first ask the accountant to figure out the amount of money for the medicine and then after paying, get the medicine at the pharmacy.

❷〈数学〉extraction of a root; evolution: ～键 root key /～指令 extract instruction /～法 extraction of root /开立方 extraction of the cube root /开平方 extraction of the square root

开方子 kāi fāngzi see "开方❶"

开房间 kāi fángjiān 〈方言〉rent a room in a hotel: 每到一地, 他都先～, 安顿好后才开始旅游观光。Wherever he goes, he always finds hotel accommodation before sightseeing.

开放 kāifàng ❶ (flowers) come into bloom; blossom: 牡丹～, 空谷生艳。As the peony is in bloom, the deserted valley is a riot of colour. ❷ open to traffic or public use: ～锚位 open berth /～水道 open lead /机场因大雪关闭一天后又～了。After being snowed under for a day, the airport opened again. ❸ be open (to the public): 展览会将于 1 月 1 日起～。The exhibition will open to the public from (*or* as of) 1st January. ❹ lift a ban; lift a restriction; deregulate; open: ～边境贸易 lift the ban on frontier trade /～技术市场 open markets for technology exchanges /改革～ reform and open to the outside world /～政策 opening-up policy; open policy /门户～政策 open-door policy /～经济 open economy /～地区 open area (*or* region) /扩大～范围 expand the open areas; open the country (*or* economy, *or* area) further /农产品价格～势在必行。It is imperative to deregulate (*or* de-control) prices of agricultural produce. ❺ outgoing; uninhibited; open-minded: 为人乐观～ of a sanguine and uninhibited disposition

开放城市 kāifàng chéngshì open city; city open to foreigners

开放大学 kāifàng dàxué open university

开放带 kāifàngdài open zone; open area

开放电路 kāifàng diànlù 〈无线电〉open electric circuit

开放港 kāifànggǎng open port

开放搞活 kāifàng-gǎohuó open and enliven; deregulate and envigorate: ～市场 deregulate and enliven the market

开放骨折 kāifàng gǔzhé *also* "开放性骨折"〈医学〉open or compound fracture

开放式基金 kāifàngshì jījīn open-end fund

开封 kāifēng ❶ break or open a seal; open an envelope; open a parcel ❷ (Kāifēng) Kaifeng, city in Henan Province and capital of the Northern Song and other dynasties

开缝 kāifèng ❶ split; crack: 桌面～儿了。There is a crack in the table. ❷ slotting; slot: ～槽 slot driller ❸〈方言〉have one's ideas straightened out; be enlightened: 听了老王的讲话, 他心里才开了缝儿。He felt enlightened by Lao Wang's words.

开幅 kāifú 〈纺织〉scutch: ～机 scutcher

开赴 kāifù march to; be bound for: ～战场 march to the front /～生产第一线 leave for the first line (*or* forefront) of production

开复 kāifù 〈书面〉❶ recover (lost territory); recapture ❷ restore (one's former office); reinstate: 他先被罢免而后又～。He was dismissed, but was later reinstated (in his former position).

开革 kāigé discharge; dismiss; sack; fire: 他原为警官, ～后开始做小买卖。He used to be a police officer but started up a small business after he was discharged. /厂方～了六十余名工人。More than sixty workers at the factory were sacked.

开工 kāigōng ❶ (of a factory, etc.) go into operation; be put into operation; start operation: ～效率 on-stream efficiency /～不足 be operating under capacity /新厂在鞭炮声中～了。The new factory went into operation amid the sound of firecrackers. ❷ (of a construction project, etc.) start (work): 宾馆已经破土～。The ground has been broken for the construction of a guest house.

开工率 kāigōnglǜ utilization of capacity; operating rate: 上半年, 全厂～达 95%。During the first half of the year, the factory operated at 95% of its capacity.

开弓不放箭 kāi gōng bù fàng jiàn draw the bow but not shoot the arrow — make an empty threat; be swashbuckling

开沟 kāigōu dig a ditch, gutter, or trench: ～机 ditching machine; trench digger /～铲 furrowing blade; furrower /～犁 digger plough; ditch(ing) plough; gutter plough /～排涝 dig trenches to drain waterlogged fields /～平地 dig ditches and level land

开关 kāiguān ❶ *also* "电门" diànmén 〈电工〉switch; switchgear: ～盒 switch box; switchgear cabinet /～厂 switchgear plant /～屏 switchboard /分档～ step switch /通断～ on-off switch /双向～ two-way switch /闸刀～ knife switch ❷ button; knob: 油门～ button for oil; oil button /气门～ button for gas; gas button /～按钮 switch knob; shift knob; switching push-button

开关灯头 kāiguān dēngtóu switch socket

开棺验尸 kāiguān yànshī exhume a corpse for autopsy; open the coffin and examine a corpse

开馆 kāiguǎn ❶ open (a library, museum, etc.) to the public ❷ open a diplomatic or consular mission abroad

开光 kāiguāng ❶ (of cloisonné, carved lacquerware, pottery and porcelain, etc.) leave a space (for additional decorative patterns) ❷〈宗教〉enshrine a Buddha statue ❸〈戏谑〉have one's hair cut; shave

开锅 kāiguō boil: ～后, 把火拧小点。When it boils, turn the fire down.

开国 kāiguó found a state; establish a dynasty (in feudal times): ～大典 founding ceremony (of a state) /～元勋 founding father(s) of a country /～纪念 founding anniversary of a nation; national day

开焊 kāihàn (of welded joint) snap; break

开航 kāiháng ❶ become open for navigation; begin flight service: 一条又一条新航线～了。New air routes were opened up one after another. /运河～后, 交通方便多了。We find travel much easier, now that the canal is open to navigation. ❷ set sail: ～日期 sailing day; date of departure /去上海的班轮上午十一点～。The ship for Shanghai sails at 11 a.m.

开合桥 kāihéqiáo bascule bridge; folding bridge; draw bridge: ～桥孔 draw span /～桥跨 pivot span /～桥墩 pivot pier

开河 kāihé ❶ (of a river) thaw: 眼看春气萌动, 就要～了。As spring is in the air, the river is soon going to thaw. ❷ construct a canal; dig a river course: ～工程在全力进行中。The construction of the canal is in full swing.

开后门 kāi hòumén 〈比喻〉open the back door — offer advantages to one's friends or relations by underhand means; resort to backstair or under-the-counter deals: 利用职务之便～ abuse one's position to secure benefits for one's friends (*or* relations) /要同假公济私, ～的现象作斗争。We must combat any act of jobbery and back-door deals.

开壶 kāihú kettle with hot or boiled water: 服务员提着～为茶客续水。The waitress poured hot water out of a kettle into the customers' teacups.

开户 kāihù open an account; establish an account: 办理～手续 open an account with a bank

开户银行 kāihù yínháng bank of deposit

开花 kāihuā ❶ blossom; bloom: ～时节 blooming period /桃树要～了。The peach trees are beginning to blossom. ❷ explode; break up; open: 这只鞋～儿了。This shoe is unglued. /炸弹在敌人阵地上开了花。The bombs exploded on the enemy's position. ❸ burst with joy; beam with smiles: 乐开了花 burst with joy; feel elated; be in high spirits ❹ (of experience or a cause) spread; bloom: 愿你们的致富经验遍地～。May your experience in bettering yourselves spread to every corner of the land.

开花弹 kāihuādàn fragmentation bullet; high explosive shell

开花结果 kāihuā-jiēguǒ blossom and bear fruit — yield positive results

开花馒头 kāihuā mántou split-top steamed bun

开花期 kāihuāqī 〈植物〉florescence; flowering period

开花炸弹 kāihuā zhàdàn scatter bomb

开化 kāihuà ❶ become civilized: 这一时期, 人类巢居穴处, 尚在不～的状态。At that time, man still lived in nests or caves, lingering in an uncivilized state. ❷ thaw: 冻土～ frozen earth beginning to thaw

开怀 kāihuái to one's heart's content; heartily: ～畅饮 drink to one's heart's content; go on a drinking spree /～大笑 burst into hearty laughter; laugh heartily /我知道你是海量, 且请～吃两盏儿。I know you have a real capacity for liquor, so don't stint on your drinking.

开怀儿 kāihuáir 〈口语〉give birth to the first child: 秋后新媳妇～, 生下了一对双胞胎。After the autumn harvest, the young daughter-in-law gave birth to twins, her firstborns.

开环 kāihuán 〈自控〉open loop: ～控制 open loop control /～机器人 open loop robot

开荒 kāihuāng open up wasteland; reclaim wasteland: ～屯田 open up wasteland and grow food grain /～救灾 help people open up wasteland to tide over natural calamities

开荒垦植 kāihuāng-kěnzhí reclaim wasteland for farming

开会 kāihuì hold or attend a meeting: 我不去～。I'm not going to the meeting. /请安静, 现在～了。Please be quiet. Let's start the meeting now.

K

开荤 kāihūn ❶ begin or resume a meat diet; end a meatless diet ❷ have a novel experience:看这种演出,我可是~了。Watching this kind of show was something new for me.

开荤戒斋 kāihūn-jièzhāi break a vegetarian fast and terminate vows (not to drink, smoke, etc.)

开火 kāihuǒ ❶ open fire; fire:向敌人~! Fire at the enemy! /前线~了! Fire has been exchanged at the front! ❷ attack (in speech or writing); assail (with words):向官僚主义~ combat bureaucratism

开伙 kāihuǒ ❶ run a mess or cafeteria:刚开学,学校还没有~。The new term is only just begun. The school cafeteria is not yet open. ❷ provide food:这个机关的食堂早晚不~。The canteen of this institute only provides food at noon.

开豁 kāihuò ❶ open and clear; bright and clear:走出山口,眼前一马平川,分外~。Out of the mountain pass, I came in view of a flat country, open and boundless. ❷ become broadened or enlightened in mind:听了母亲的一席话,他心里顿感~。Mother's words broadened his vision instantly. *or* He was enlightened by his mother's words.

开饥荒 kāi jīhuang 〈方言〉cope with financial emergencies

开机 kāijī ❶ start a machine ❷ start shooting a film, TV play, etc.

开基 kāijī 〈书面〉initiate an undertaking; lay the foundation of an enterprise:他是本公司的~人之一。He is one of the founders of the corporation.

开霁 kāijì 〈书面〉clear up (after rain or snow):雪后~ clear up after snow

开价 kāijià ❶ charge or ask a price; make a quotation:~过高 over-quote /这架钢琴~三千。They charge $3,000 for the piano. ❷ opening price; asking price

开架 kāijià *also* "开架式" ❶ (of a library, etc.) open-stack:~阅览室 open-stack (reading) room /~借阅 open the stacks to readers; open-stack circulation; open access ❷ (of a store, etc.) open-shelf:~售货 open-shelf selling

开间 kāijiān ❶ 〈方言〉about 3⅓ metres, the standard width of a room in an old-style house:单~ narrow one-room house (of about 3⅓ metres in width) /双~ wide one-room house (of about 6⅔ metres in width) ❷ width of a room:这屋子~很大。The room is quite spacious. ❸ 〈建筑〉bay

开缄 kāijiān 〈书面〉unseal (a letter, etc.); open mail

开疆 kāijiāng 〈书面〉open up territory; push out the boundary line

开讲 kāijiǎng begin lecturing or story-telling:刘教授~民间文学史的那一天,大教室里座无虚席。The day Prof. Liu began lecturing on the history of folk literature, all seats in the auditorium were occupied.

开奖 kāijiǎng draw and announce the winning ticket in a public lottery

开交 kāijiāo (mostly used in the negative) end; resolve:忙得不可~ be up to one's neck in work; be awfully busy /吵得不可~ get into an endless squabble

开胶 kāijiāo come unglued:我的鞋底~了。The sole of my shoe came unglued.

开脚 kāijiǎo at the very beginning; from the outset:工程一~就不顺利。The project went awry at the very beginning.

开解 kāijiě ease the anxiety or sorrow of; console:大家说了许多~的话,她听后心里好受多了。After we said a lot to console her, she felt much better.

开戒 kāijiè break an abstinence (from smoking, drinking, etc.):打那次~之后,他又抽烟又喝酒,谁也劝不了他。Ever since he broke his abstinence (*or* fell off the wagon) he has been smoking and drinking to excess and nobody can dissuade him.

开金 kāijīn (of gold) carat; gold alloy:十八~ 18 carat gold; gold 18 carats fine /~首饰 alloyed gold jewellery

开襟 kāijīn ❶ garment with buttons down the front or the right side:对~ (garment) with buttons down the front /右~ with buttons down the right side ❷ 〈书面〉leave one's jacket or blouse unbuttoned; unbutton one's jacket or blouse

开进 kāijìn (troops) move forward (to engage the enemy):全连徒步~。The whole company marched forward to fight the enemy.

开禁 kāijìn lift a ban; rescind a prohibition:~之后,边境贸易有了很大发展。Since the ban was lifted, frontier trade has developed rapidly.

开镜 kāijìng start shooting a film, TV play, etc.

开局 kāijú ❶ (of a chess or ball game) start; begin:排球比赛~不到20分钟,中国姑娘就拿下了第一局。The Chinese girls won the first set in less than 20 minutes after the volleyball game began. ❷ beginning:~不利 make a bad (*or* an unfavourable) beginning

开具 kāijù prepare or write out (a list, receipt, certificate, etc.); list:~清单 write out (*or* draw up) a detailed list; prepare a detailed inventory /~证明文件 issue a certificate

开卷 kāijuàn ❶ 〈书面〉open a scroll or book; read ❷ *see* "开卷考试"

开卷考试 kāijuàn kǎoshì *also* "开卷" open-book examination:古汉语选读本学期~。There will be an open-book final (*or* terminal) examination for Selected Classical Chinese Readings.

开卷有益 kāijuàn-yǒuyì reading enriches the mind; reading is always profitable

开掘 kāijué ❶ dig:~水井 dig a well /~深海油田 drill in a deep-sea oil field ❷ (of literature) deeply explore and fully express (subject matter, character, etc.):你们要大胆地向生活真实进行~。You must be bold in exploring and portraying real life.

开浚 kāijùn dredge (a river, etc.):~西湖 dredge West Lake

开考 kāikǎo begin an examination or a test

开科 kāikē 〈书面〉hold an imperial examination:~取士 select officials through imperial examinations; enlist talents through the imperial civil service examination system

开课 kāikè ❶ begin school; begin classes:培训班本周五报到,下周一~。Registration for the training course starts this Friday while classes begin next Monday. ❷ (chiefly in college) offer a course; give a course; teach a subject:下学期开什么课? What courses are offered for next term? /谁开国际关系课? Who teaches International Relations?

开垦 kāikěn open up or reclaim (wasteland); bring under cultivation:~荒地 bring barren land under cultivation /~沿海荒滩 open up deserted beaches

开口 kāikǒu ❶ open one's mouth; start to talk:不便~ find it difficult to bring the matter up (*or* to broach the subject) /在这种场合,你最好不~。You'd better hold your tongue on such occasions. /我只得~求人了。I could do nothing but beg for help. ❷ put the first edge on a knife; sharpen (for the first time):这把刀使了半年也没开过口。This knife has not yet been sharpened since it was first put to use half a year ago.

开口扳手 kāikǒu bānshou 〈机械〉open-ended spanner

开口闭口 kāikǒu-bìkǒu every time one opens one's lips; whenever one speaks; say the same thing again and again:这孩子嘴甜,~总是叔叔、阿姨的。This child is smooth-tongued, calling people uncle or aunt whenever she opens her lips. /她一天到晚,~就是这几句话。She did nothing but repeat these words all day long.

开口对焊 kāikǒu duìhàn 〈机械〉open butt weld

开口对接 kāikǒu duìjiē 〈机械〉open butt joint

开口饭 kāikǒufàn 〈旧语〉profession of singing, acting, story-telling, etc.:她八岁就吃上了~。She began to sing and act in traditional operas at the age of eight.

开口呼 kāikǒuhū 〈语言〉syllables with sounds other than i, u and ü as the final *yunmu* (韵母) or as part of it
see also "四呼" sìhū

开口环 kāikǒuhuán split ring; clip ring

开口跳 kāikǒutiào 〈戏曲〉acrobatic comedian; clown skilled in martial arts

开口销 kāikǒuxiāo 〈机械〉split pin

开口笑 kāikǒuxiào open-top steamed bread

开口信件 kāikǒu xìnjiàn unsealed letter

开口子 kāi kǒuzi ❶ (of a dyke) break; burst:一夜暴雨,下游河堤~了。After a night's thunderstorm, the dyke broke somewhere in the lower reaches. ❷ stretch a rule or regulation (in favour of sb. or sth.); give the green light to (illegal activities):私卖粮库存粮,这个口子谁也不能开。No one should ever give the green light to illegal sales of stored rice.

开快车 kāi kuàichē ❶ step on the gas; drive at a high speed; speed:酒后~ drunk driving and speeding /归家时,他心急如火,一路~。He was in a great hurry and sped all the way back home. ❷ hurry through one's work; speed up the work; do quick work at the expense of quality:时间足够了,开什么快车呀? Why do you make such short work of the job while there is ample time?

开旷 kāikuàng wide and spacious:~的原野 open wild country

开矿 kāikuàng open up a mine; exploit a mine:这几年,村民们~采煤,日子富多了。The villagers are much better-off these years by coal mining.

开扩 kāikuò ❶ (of outlook, mind, etc.) open; broad; uninhibited:胸怀~ broad-minded ❷ expand; widen:~眼界 broaden one's outlook (*or* vision, *or* horizons)

开阔 kāikuò ❶ open; wide; vast:~的蓝天 open (*or* boundless) blue sky /一片~地带 a great stretch of open country; a vast expanse of land ❷ tolerant; liberal:心胸~ broad-minded; unprejudiced /他是一位思想~,待人慷慨的长者。He is a tolerant and open-hearted senior. ❸ widen:~路面 widen the road /~眼界 broaden one's outlook (*or* vision, *or* horizons) /~知识面 enlarge one's range of knowledge

开阔地 kāikuòdì open terrain; open ground; unenclosed ground

开阔平原 kāikuò píngyuán open plain

开朗 kāilǎng ❶ open and clear:出了地道,眼前豁然~。Once out of the tunnel, I found myself in broad daylight. ❷ sanguine; cheerful; optimistic:性格~活泼 always lively and cheerful /胸怀~,精神焕发 optimistic and spirited

开犁 kāilí ❶ start the year's ploughing:春上~时,一连下了几天小雨。When spring ploughing started, it drizzled for days running. ❷ *also* "开墒" plough the first furrow as a guideline

开例 kāilì create or set a precedent:大家都应该按章程办事,不能从我这~。Every one should abide by the rules and regulations, and I'll not set a bad precedent.

开镰 kāilián start harvesting:麦熟了,家家户户收拾家什,准备~。The wheat is ripe. Every household is getting the farm tools (*or* implements) ready for the harvest.

开脸 kāiliǎn ❶〈旧语〉(of a girl at the time of getting married) change hair style, clear off the fine hair on the face and neck, and trim the hair on the temples ❷ (in sculpture, etc.) carve the face of a figure

开链 kāiliàn 〈化学〉open chain; open chaining:~烃 chain hydrocarbon

开列 kāiliè draw up (a list); list:~名单 make a list of names /~清单 draw up (*or* make out) a list; make an inventory /请把旅行要带的东西~出来。Please make out a list of things you are going to take with you on your trip. /候选人~如下。The candidates are listed as below (*or* as follows).

开裂 kāiliè crack; burst open; split open:木板~。The board is cracked. /桶底~。The barrel split across the bottom.

开溜 kāiliū 〈方言〉slip (away); sneak or slink off; leave stealthily:半路上有好几个人悄悄地开了溜。Several people slunk off on the way.

开耧 kāilóu start the year's sowing (with an animal-drawn seed plough):~时节,恰好下了一场小雨。It drizzled just at the time of spring sowing.

开颅术 kāilúshù 〈医学〉craniotomy

开路 kāilù ❶ open a way; blaze a trail:逢山~,遇水架桥 cut paths through mountains and build bridges across rivers /部队边~,边行进。The troops were opening a new path while marching. ❷ take the lead; lead the way:他在前面~。He was in the front to lead the way. ❸ *also* "断路" duànlù 〈电工〉open circuit:~插头 open plug /~插孔 open-circuit jack /~电压 open-circuit voltage

开路先锋 kāilù-xiānfēng pathbreaker; trailblazer; pioneer:他是我们厂搞革新的~。He is a pacesetter in our factory's technological innovation.

开绿灯 kāi lǜdēng give the green light; give the go-ahead:为不合格的产品~,必定会损害国家和消费者的利益。Giving the green light to substandard (*or* inferior) products is bound to harm the interests of the state and consumers.

开罗 Kāiluó Cairo, capital of Egypt

开罗会议 Kāiluó Huìyì Cairo Conferences, November-December 1943, two meetings of allied countries for planning major offensives against world fascism in WWII

开罗宣言 Kāiluó Xuānyán Cairo Declaration (1 December 1943)

开锣 kāiluó ❶〈戏曲〉strike the gong to start a performance:~戏 first item (of performance); first play /你怎么来这么晚,戏早~了。You are so late. The play has begun for some time. ❷ (of a game or match) begin; start:篮球联赛月底~。The league basketball matches will start at the end of this month.

开曼群岛 Kāimàn Qúndǎo Cayman Islands (in the West Indies)

开毛机 kāimáojī 〈纺织〉wool opener

开门 kāimén ❶ open the door; keep the door open; do sth. in public:~整党 open-door consolidation of the Party, a campaign aimed to consolidate the Party with the help of the masses /快去~。Hurry up and open the door. ❷ (bank, office, etc.) open; begin business for the day:商店九点~。The shop opens at 9 a.m. /银行~时间是上午 9 点半至下午 3 点半。The banking hours are from 9:30 a.m. to 3:30 p.m.

开门办学 kāimén bànxué open-door schooling

开门红 kāiménhóng make a good beginning; get off to a good or flying start:来一个新年~。Let the beginning of the year be greeted with successes. *or* Let the new year get off to a flying start.

开门见山 kāimén-jiànshān come straight to the point; cut the cackle and come to the horses; speak bluntly; say point-blank:他有点不耐烦了,你最好还是~,谈谈正事吧。He is getting impatient. You'd better cut the cackle and get down to business. /谈话时父亲~,直截了当地指出问题所在。Father came straight to the point when he started talking. /咱们干脆~,有话直说。Let's be frank with each other and say what we have got in mind.

开门七件事 kāimén qījiànshì life necessities:~:柴米油盐酱醋茶。The seven necessities of life are firewood, rice, oil, salt, soy, vinegar and tea.

开门揖盗 kāimén-yīdào open the door to robbers — invite disaster by letting in evildoers; court trouble

开门整风 kāimén zhěngfēng open-door rectification of the style of work, a campaign aimed to rectify the Party's work style with the help of the masses

开蒙 kāiméng 〈旧语〉teach children to learn to read and write (as at an old-style private school); (of children) begin learning to read and write; start schooling:~识字课本 textbook for children to learn characters; primer /小时候,他上过私塾,~老师是一位乡下秀才。When he was young, he went to an old-style private school, where a country scholar taught him to read and write.

开棉机 kāimiánjī 〈纺织〉opener:棉箱~ hopper opener /豪猪~ porcupine opener

开明 kāimíng enlightened; liberal:~人士 enlightened personage /~的思想 liberal ideas (*or* views) /他虽然出身于一个旧家庭,但思想还算~。Though he was born in an old-fashioned (*or* a traditional) family, he was quite liberal-minded.

开明绅士 kāimíng shēnshì enlightened gentry — individual landlords and rich-peasants with democratic leanings who, influenced by the CPC's policy of unity, favoured resistance against Japan, and supported democracy and reduction of land rent and loan interest during the War of Resistance Against Japan (1937-1945), and in the War of Liberation (1946-1949), opposed Kuomintang rule and approved of land reform

开幕 kāimù ❶ curtain rises; begin a performance:~前五分钟我才赶到剧场。I arrived at the threatre five minutes before the play began. ❷ open; inaugurate:展览会~比预期晚了两天。The exhibition opened two days behind schedule. /盼望已久的大会今晨终于~了。The long-awaited conference was at last inaugurated this morning.

开幕词 kāimùcí opening speech or address

开幕式 kāimùshì opening ceremony; inauguration; inaugural ceremony

开年 kāinián ❶ beginning of a year ❷〈方言〉next year

开拍 kāipāi start shooting (a film, TV serial, etc.):~! (used by director) Camera!

开盘 kāipán 〈经济〉opening quotation (on the exchange):~汇率 opening rate /~价格 opening price

开嗙 kāipǎng 〈方言〉exaggerate to show off; brag:听,他又~了! Listen! He's talking big again.

开炮 kāipào ❶ open fire with artillery; fire:几门大炮同时~,震耳欲聋。Several cannons fired at the same time with an ear-shattering (*or* a deafening) roar. ❷ fire or level criticism at; fiercely criticize:向错误~ severely criticize mistakes and errors /向一切腐败现象~ denounce (*or* condemn) corruption of all descriptions

开坯 kāipī 〈冶金〉cogging; blooming:~机 cogging mill; bloomer; blooming mill /~轧机 breakdown mill; big mill

开辟 kāipì ❶ open; start; set up; establish:~航线 open an air (*or* sea) route /~第二战场 open a second front /~专栏 start (*or* launch) a special column /~学术新领域 establish a new branch of learning /~其它税收来源 tap other revenue sources /~一条上山的路

K

cut a path up the hill; hew out a path up the hill /～新路子 blaze new trails ❷ develop; promote; explore:～边疆 develop border areas /～工作 promote work (in a given area, etc.); push work forward /～各种商品流通渠道 explore more avenues for commodity circulation /～新局面 make a breakthrough ❸ (short for 开天辟地) creation of the world:自～以来 since the beginning of history

开篇 kāipiān ❶ introductory song in *tanci* (弹词), etc.:越剧、沪剧等地方曲种和弹词一样通常都有～。Shaoxing and Shanghai operas, like *tanci*, usually begin with an introductory song. ❷ beginning of a literary work

开瓢儿 kāipiáor 〈方言〉(often used humorously) break one's head:他让人给～了。His head was broken (in a fight). *or* He got a cut on his head.

开票 kāipiào ❶ open the ballot box and count the ballots:投票结束后，由监票人负责～，并报告结果。After the vote, the scrutineers will open the ballot box, count the ballots and report the result. ❷ make out an invoice or bill:提货时别忘了～! Don't forget to make out an invoice when you pick up goods!

开屏 kāipíng (of a peacock) spread its tail; display its fine tail feathers:孔雀～ peacock spreading its tail

开瓶费 kāipíngfèi (at a restaurant, etc.) corkage

开普敦 Kāipǔdūn Capetown, port city of South Africa

开启 kāiqǐ ❶ open:这种新式灭火器可以自动～。This new-style fire extinguisher is able to open automatically. ❷ start; begin:～了商文化的先河 mark the beginnings of Shang culture /～一代新文风 set a new style of writing

开启器 kāiqǐqì opener:瓶盖～ bottle opener

开气儿 kāiqìr *also* "开隙儿"〈方言〉vent or slit at the sides of a garment:小～的月白大褂 bluish white unlined long gown that slits on both sides /后边开个气儿 have a vent at the back (of a blouse)

开枪 kāiqiāng fire with a rifle, pistol, etc.; shoot; fire:～还击 return fire /他只要～，没有不中的。He never misses when he shoots. /他们朝天～，驱散人群。They fired into the air in an attempt to disperse the crowd.

开腔 kāiqiāng begin to speak; open one's mouth or lips:他一生气就不～了。He would always keep mum when angry. /等了许久，老头终于～了。We waited a long time before the old man started to talk.

开窍 kāiqiào ❶ have one's ideas straightened out; begin to realize:他总算有点～了，明白一定有谁在跟他过不去。It somehow dawned upon him that someone must be trying to make things difficult for him. /他的一番话使我开了窍。His words have enlightened me. ❷ (children) start to gain knowledge, or understand things:男孩子～往往比女孩子晚。Boys tend to start to understand things at a later age than girls. ❸〈方言〉(used sarcastically) see (the ways of) the world; experience life:乡下后生从未～，他哪里见过这种世面? How could a country boy, who had never seen the outside world, ever have had such experience?

开亲 kāiqīn 〈方言〉become engaged or betrothed; (of two families) become related by marriage

开晴 kāiqíng 〈方言〉(of sky) clear up (after rain); become sunny:雨渐渐住了，但天还没～。It gradually stopped raining but the sky had not yet cleared up.

开球 kāiqiú 〈体育〉(in soccer) kick off; (in basketball) start the game; (in volleyball or tennis) serve

开缺 kāiquē 〈旧语〉(of a position) become vacant:～候补 (of a position) fall vacant /万一～，我即托人与你候补。Once there is a vacancy, I'll manage to put you on the waiting list.

开刃儿 kāirènr put the first edge on (a knife or a pair of scissors); sharpen for the first time:这把刀刚～，快极了。This knife has just got its first edge and is extremely sharp.

开赛 kāisài begin a match, game, or competition:～仅三十秒钟，中国队就射进一球。The Chinese team kicked a goal 30 seconds after the match started. /本市高校演讲比赛～。This city's collegiate speech contest has begun.

开山 kāishān ❶ cut into a mountain (for quarrying, etc.):～取石 blast mountains for rocks /～劈岭 blast the mountains and split the hills /～筑路 cut mountains to construct roads; build roads by cutting through mountains ❷ open the (closed) mountains for grazing or lumbering:这几座岭子秋后～时，才让人进山采伐。Only in autumn will these mountains open for lumbering. ❸〈佛教〉build the first temple on a well-known mountain ❹ *see* "开山祖师"

开山子 kāishānzi 〈方言〉axe; hatchet

开山祖师 kāishān-zǔshī *also* "开山祖";"开山鼻祖" founder of a religious sect or a school of thought; founding father; founder:寺院前有几座古碑，碑文记载了～历经艰险，创建寺庙的事迹。In front of the temple, there are some ancient stone tablets on which are inscriptions recording hardships the founding abbot went through in building the temple. /他是田园诗的～。He was the founder of the pastoral school in poetry.

开衫 kāishān cardigan:男～ cardigan for men; men's cardigan /女～ cardigan for women; women's cardigan

开墒 kāishāng *also* "开犁" plough the first furrow (as a guideline):他顺着地边～，这时，天还没有亮。When he ploughed the first furrow along the side of the field, it was before daybreak.

开烧 kāishāo 〈方言〉sleep in the open wilderness by a campfire; camping:暑期约几个年轻朋友去～。I shall go camping with a few young friends this summer.

开设 kāishè ❶ open (a shop, factory, etc.):～旅馆 open a hotel /～医院 establish a hospital ❷ offer (a course in college, etc.):～中西比较文学课 offer a course of comparative Chinese and Western literatures /这些是本系～的课程。These are our department's course offerings.

开审 kāishěn start the trial; sit at session:～日期 hearing time /本庭明日上午九时～。This law court will be in session at 9 o'clock tomorrow morning.

开始 kāishǐ ❶ start; begin; commence:从头～ begin from the very beginning /重新～ start anew /～生效 take effect; come into effect /以损人～，以害己告终 start with the aim of harming others and end up by harming oneself ❷ start doing; set about doing sth.:～写工作报告 start writing one's work report /一切准备就绪，可以～了。Everything is ready. Let's get started. ❸ initial stage; beginning; outset:一种新的工作，～总是会有不少困难。One is bound to have many difficulties at the beginning of a new job. /～他不同意，但后来让步了。At first he didn't agree, but later he relented.

开驶 kāishǐ (of a vehicle, ship, etc.) go; travel; be bound for

开氏温标 Kāishì wēnbiāo 〈物理〉Kelvin scale

开示 kāishì ❶ write to inform; instruct:～地址 write out one's address ❷ enlighten:弟子愚昧，望祈～。I am uninformed and sincerely hope to be enlightened.

开市 kāishì ❶ (of a shop) reopen after a cessation of business:加工站～那天，他请了吹打，还放了几挂响炮。The day his processing centre reopened, he invited a Chinese wind and percussion ensemble to perform and also fired several strings of firecrackers. ❷ first transaction of a day's business:今天～的一笔买卖，批发了五千件工作服。The first transaction of today's business was the wholesale of 5,000 work jackets.

开市行情 kāishì hángqíng opening quotation

开式循环 kāishì xúnhuán 〈机械〉open-cycle:～发动机 open-cycle engine /～燃气轮机 open-cycle gas turbine /～反应堆系统 open-cycle reactor system

开释 kāishì release (a prisoner); acquit; set free:无罪～ be released as innocent /因证据不足而得以～ be set free on the ground of insufficient evidence

开手 kāishǒu 〈方言〉at the outset; at first

开首 kāishǒu 〈方言〉at the start; at the beginning; at first:凡事～难。Things always look difficult at first. *or* The first step is always difficult.

开涮 kāishuàn 〈方言〉tease; make fun of:你们别拿我～。Don't try to make a fool of me.

开水 kāishuǐ ❶ boiling water:用～沏茶 make tea with boiling water ❷ boiled water:凉～ cool boiled water /白～ plain boiled water

开说 kāishuō 〈方言〉help straighten out sb.'s wrong or muddled thinking; advise; enlighten:他心眼儿窄，你得经常～他。He is narrow-minded, so you have to help him to see the light quite often.

开司米 kāisīmǐ *also* "开士米"〈纺织〉cashmere:～斜纹呢 cut cashmere /～纶 cashmilan /～山羊 down goat

开岁 kāisuì 〈书面〉beginning of a year

开榫 kāisǔn 〈机械〉mortise and tenon; make a mortise and tenon joint:～机 mortising machine; tenoning machine /～凿 mortise chisel

开他敏 kāitāmǐn 〈医学〉ketamine

开台 kāitái begin a theatrical performance:戏已经～了。The performance has already begun.

开台锣鼓 kāitái luógǔ flourish of gongs and drums introducing a

theatrical performance:好在当年在延安的许多同志将著文详加介绍,我的粗枝大叶的东西就算作~好了。Fortunately, many comrades from Yan'an days will write about this at length, so that my rough-and-ready words may serve the same purpose as the beating of the gongs before a theatrical performance.

开堂 kāitáng 〈方言〉❶ open a court session; hold (a) court; call the court to order:~审讯 hold a court session ❷ (of a restaurant) start business ❸ prepare a place for mourning:~吊孝 set up a mourning hall for people to offer condolences

开膛 kāitáng gut; disembowel (poultry, livestock, etc.):~母鸡 disembowelled hen /猪煺毛后就~。The pig will be disembowelled (*or* gutted) right after its hair is removed.

开膛炮 kāitángpào open-chambered gun

开天窗 kāi tiānchuāng ❶ (of a syphilitic) have a rotten nose ❷ 〈旧语〉put in a skylight — leave a blank in a publication (to show that sth. has been censored)

开天辟地 kāitiān-pìdì when heaven was separated from earth — creation of the world; genesis of history; dawn of history:自从盘古~以来,我们不晓得造飞机,造汽车,现在开始能造了。Never since Pan Gu separated heaven and earth have we been able to make planes and cars, but now we are beginning to make them. /~第一回,山村穷孩子上了大学。For the first time in history, a poor child from a mountain village has gone to university.

开庭 kāitíng 〈法律〉open or hold a court session; call the court to order:~审理 (the court) hold hearings (*or* a session); open a court session /~通知 notice of trial /请入座,现在~。Be seated! This court is now in session.

开通 kāitōng ❶ enlighten; inspire; cultivate:~民智 cultivate public intellect; enlighten the people ❷ (of communication lines or routes) be put into use; be open to traffic:~邮路 establish a postal route /这条高速公路已竣工并~使用。The highway has been completed and opened to traffic.

开通 kāitong ❶ open-minded; liberal; broad-minded:思想~的老人 open-minded old man /我看她的思想~得有点过头。I am afraid that she is liberal to a fault. ❷ liberate; liberalize; enlighten:~~某人的思想 liberate sb.'s mind; enlighten sb.

开头 kāitóu ❶ start; begin; get one's feet wet:我们的学习刚~,你很快就能赶上。We've just begun our lessons and you can easily catch up. /跳舞一旦~就不难了。It's not hard to dance once you get your feet wet. ❷ start sth.; make a start; set the ball rolling; set on foot:这件事是谁~搞起来的? Who set that business afoot? /既是你开的头儿,你就得继续下去。As you have started it, you'll have to keep the ball rolling. ❸ beginning:万事~难。Everything is hard in the beginning.

开头炮 kāi tóupào be the first to fire; be the first to make a speech (often critical in nature):今天会上我~,直话直说。I'm going to speak first at the meeting today, without mincing my words.

开脱 kāituō absolve; exonerate; exculpate; vindicate:为人~责任 absolve (*or* acquit, *or* clear) sb. of responsibility; free sb. from responsibility /你不应替他~。You shouldn't have pleaded for him.

开拓 kāituò ❶ open up; pioneer; create:~道路 open up a path /~精神 pioneering spirit /~新的创作路子 create a novel way of writing /时代为青年人的发展~了广阔天地。Our age has provided wide opportunities for young people to realize their ambitions. ❷ 〈矿业〉 developing; opening:~巷道 development opening /~进尺 tunnelling footage

开拓型人才 kāituòxíng réncái pioneering talent; trailblazer

开拓者 kāituòzhě pioneer:两国友好关系的~ pioneers of friendly ties between our two countries

开挖 kāiwā excavate; dig:~运河 excavate a canal /~渠道 dig (*or* hew) a channel /~机械 excavation machinery

开外 kāiwài over; above; beyond:他看上去有六十~了。He looks over sixty. /我院离城五公里~。Our college is more than five kilometres from the town.

开玩笑 kāi wánxiào ❶ crack, or make, or play a joke; joke; make fun of; pull sb.'s leg:人们围炉而坐,抽着烟,开着玩笑。The men sat around the stove, smoking and cracking jokes. /别生气,我只是~而已。Don't be offended, I was only joking. /先生你这可是~。You're pulling my leg, sir. /这个人经不起~。He can't take a joke. ❷ treat casually; regard as a trifling matter:这可不是~的事情,不小心会出人命。This is no joke (*or* trifling matter); if you're not careful, it could cost someone his life.

开往 kāiwǎng (of a train, ship, etc.) leave for; be bound for:连队~新的驻地。The company left for a new barracks. /~伦敦的特快列车昨晚出轨了。The London (bound) express derailed yesterday evening.

开胃 kāiwèi ❶ whet the appetite; stimulate the appetite:~食品 appetizer /吃点儿山楂糕~。Take some slices of haw jelly to stimulate your appetite. ❷ 〈方言〉 amuse oneself (at sb.'s expense); make fun of; pull sb.'s leg

开胃菜 kāiwèicài appetizer; antipasto

开胃酒 kāiwèijiǔ aperitif

开胃药 kāiwèiyào aperitive; appetizer

开悟 kāiwù 〈书面〉wake up to reality; comprehend; realize:霍然~ wake up to reality suddenly

开戏 kāixì play begins; curtain rises:快~了,请入座吧。The play will begin in a minute. Please be seated.

开隙儿 kāixìr 〈方言〉*see* "开衩"

开先 kāixiān 〈方言〉at first; at the beginning:~他也是不同意。At first, he didn't agree either.

开线 kāixiàn come unsewn:裤裆开了线了。The trousers came unsewn (*or* apart) at the crotch.

开饷 kāixiǎng 〈方言〉issue pay; pay wages or salaries

开相 kāixiàng 〈戏曲〉description of a character

开小差 kāi xiǎochāi ❶ (of a soldier) desert; sneak off; go AWOL; take French leave:军心不稳,有许多士兵~了。As the soldiers' morale was low, many of them deserted their regiments. /执法队正四处抓~的逃兵。The law enforcement corps is tracking down the AWOLs (*or* deserters) everywhere. /他俩刚~。The two of them have just skulked (*or* slunk) away. ❷ be absent-minded; be in a brown study:工作时思想不能~。Don't let your mind wander (*or* be woolgathering) while working.

开小会 kāi xiǎohuì talk to each other in a low voice at a meeting:坐在后排的几个,开始低声~了。Those sitting in the back row began to talk to each other under their breath.

开小灶 kāi xiǎozào prepare special food for sb. (as a privilege); give special favour:食堂的大师傅看他们练得辛苦,每晚主动为他们~,包饺子。Seeing that they were practising hard, the cook of the canteen volunteered to make dumplings for them every evening as a special favour. /教练给他"~",一直陪他练到深夜。The coach gave him special training and accompanied him in his practice late into the night.

开销 kāixiao ❶ pay expenses:这几个小钱,够~吗? Is so little money enough to cover the expenses? ❷ expense:日常~ daily (*or* running) expenses /住在乡下,~不大,也还方便。Living in the countryside is cheap, and convenient, too.

开心 kāixīn ❶ feel happy; rejoice; be delighted:今天我很~。I feel very happy today. /她~,我就放心了。Her joy sets my mind at ease. /他滑雪滑得很~。He got a big kick out of skiing. ❷ amuse oneself (at sb.'s expense); make fun of sb.:少拿别人~! Stop amusing yourself at others' expense!

开心斧 kāixīnfǔ soothing persuasion:话是~,不愁他不听劝告。Soothing words are persuasive, so I don't think he'll refuse to listen.

开心果 kāixīnguǒ pistachio

开心丸儿 kāixīnwánr *also* "宽心丸儿" kuānxīnwánr words of comfort

开衅 kāixìn outbreak of hostilities

开行 kāixíng start a car, train, ship, etc.:航船就要~了,祝你一路顺风! The ship is to sail immediately. Bon voyage!

开胸 kāixiōng *also* "开胸术" 〈医学〉 thoracotomy

开学 kāixué school opens; term begins:~的第一天 first day of a new term (*or* semester)

开学典礼 kāixué diǎnlǐ school's opening ceremony

开言 kāiyán (usu. used in traditional opera) speak; talk; tell:心中有事难~。It is difficult to unbosom one's innermost feelings.

开颜 kāiyán smile; beam:三军过后尽~。The three armies march on, each face glowing.

开眼 kāiyǎn open sb.'s eyes; widen sb.'s view or horizon; broaden sb.'s vision:这次去南方几个开放城市转了转,大家可~了。The trip to several open cities in the south was really an eye-opener for all of us.

开演 kāiyǎn (of a play, movie, etc.) begin:晚上七时准时~。The play will begin at 7 p.m. sharp.

K

开眼界 kāi yǎnjiè broaden one's vision：把这些钱给你妈瞧瞧，叫她开开眼界。You can show the money to your mother and that'll be an eye-opener for her! /这次出国考察，使我开了眼界。This study tour abroad expanded my horizon.

开洋 kāiyáng 〈方言〉 dried, shelled shrimps

开洋荤 kāi yánghūn 〈方言〉 taste, see or experience things exotic：什么时候吃顿西餐开个洋荤。I'll have my first taste of Western-style food some day as a special treat.

开业 kāiyè (of a shop, etc.) start business; (of a lawyer, doctor, etc.) open a private practice：私人～ open a private practice /～行医 practise medicine

开夜车 kāi yèchē work late into the night; put in extra time at night; burn the midnight oil：通宵～ stay up all night working /下周考试，这几天同学们都忙着～。As there will be an exam next week, the students are all busy working (*or* cramming) late into the night. /今晚上～也要把稿子赶出来。I must finish the article today even if I have to burn the midnight oil.

开音节 kāiyīnjié 〈语言〉 open syllable

开印 kāiyìn start printing：本报今日三点十分～。We started printing at ten past three today.

开映 kāiyìng (film) start showing：电影下午三点～。The movie starts at 3 p.m.

开元 Kāiyuán Kaiyuan, one of the titles of the reign (712-756) of Li Longji (李隆基，685-772，6th emperor of the Tang Dynasty, called reverently Tang Xuanzong 唐玄宗 after death), covering the years 713-741

开元音 kāiyuányīn 〈语言〉 open vowel

开元之治 Kāiyuán Zhī Zhì Peace and Prosperity of the Kaiyuan Years (713-741), heyday of Li Longji's entire reign (712-756), as well as of the Tang Dynasty

开园 kāiyuán picking starts at an orchard or melon field：来吃西瓜吧！西瓜～了。Come and taste our watermelons. The picking (*or* harvest) has started.

开源节流 kāiyuán-jiéliú open up the source and regulate the flow; tap new resources and economize on consumption; increase income and reduce expenditure：在四化建设中，～是极为重要的。It is imperative to enhance income and cut down cost in our modernization drive.

开云见日 kāiyún-jiànrì disperse the clouds and see the sun — remove misunderstanding; darkness recedes and light dawns; see justice again：听君一席话，犹如～，心胸顿觉豁然。Your words dispelled the clouds in my mind, and I saw the light instantly.

开凿 kāizáo cut (a canal, tunnel, etc.); dig：～隧道 dig a tunnel /～山路 cut a road into the mountain /～渠道 hew a channel

开闸 kāizhá open the sluice gate or valve; let loose the sluice：～放水 open (*or* free) the sluices; let loose the sluices /思绪像开了闸的洪水，一下子奔涌出来。Thoughts gushed out like water from an opened sluice.

开斋 kāizhāi ❶ (of one on a vegetarian diet) resume a meat diet ❷〈伊斯兰〉come to the end of Ramadan

开斋节 Kāizhāijié 〈伊斯兰〉 Lesser Bairam; Festival of Fast-breaking; *'Id al-Fitr*

开展 kāizhǎn ❶ develop; launch; promote; carry out：～课外活动 develop (*or* promote) extracurricular activities /～批评与自我批评 carry out criticism and self-criticism /～增产节约运动 launch a movement for increasing production and practising economy /～反腐败运动 launch an anti-corruption campaign (*or* drive) /开放政策推动了科研工作的～。The policy of opening to the outside world has given impetus to the development of scientific research. ❷ (of an exhibition) open ❸ open-minded; enlightened; politically progressive：思想～ be open-minded /政治上不够～ lagging behind in political understanding; slow in political progress

开战 kāizhàn ❶ make war; open hostilities：极力避免同时在两条战线上～ try one's best to avoid fighting on two fronts at the same time /哪一个国家首先～？Which nation drew the sword first? ❷ battle (against nature, conservative forces, etc.)：向穷山恶水～ battle against barren hills and untamed rivers /向一切腐朽没落思想～ combat (*or* fight) corrupt and decadent ideology

开战理由 kāizhàn lǐyóu 〈法律〉 *casus belli*

开绽 kāizhàn come unsewn：新买的鞋没穿几天就～了。The new shoes split (*or* came unsewn) at the seams soon after I bought them.

开张 kāizhāng ❶ start or open a business; begin doing business：本店明日～。The store will begin doing business tomorrow. ❷ make the first transaction for the day：今天～的这桩买卖不错，一下子收了近千元货款。The first transaction of today's business is not bad. It brought in almost a thousand *yuan* in cash. ❸ beginning; start：重打锣鼓另～ start a new business to the beating of gongs and drums; start all over again ❹〈书面〉open-minded; receptive ❺〈书面〉vast and magnificent：气势～ with great momentum; of magnificent sweep

开张大吉 kāizhāng-dàjí (as of a business) auspicious beginning; flying start：张老板，～！Mr. Zhang, I wish your enterprise an auspicious beginning. *or* May prosperity attend the opening of your business, Mr. Zhang. /这次我们～，一下子就吃掉敌人一个营。We got off to a flying start in this campaign by wiping out an enemy battalion at one stroke.

开仗 kāizhàng ❶ make war; open hostilities：两军重新～。The two armies reopened hostilities. ❷〈方言〉fight; come to blows：他俩昨天下午又～了。They two had a fight again yesterday afternoon.

开账 kāizhàng ❶ make out a bill：她一天到晚～、收款、付款，忙得不可开交。All day long, she is up to her neck making out bills and receiving and paying money. ❷ pay or take the bill (at a restaurant, hotel, etc.)：客人已～离店。The guest has checked out of the hotel.

开诊 kāizhěn (of a doctor, etc.) begin to treat or receive patients

开征 kāizhēng levy (taxes); tax：～所得税 collect income tax /官府只知道～要钱，哪管咱们老百姓的死活！The government cared nothing about the people; all they did was to levy taxes and collect money.

开支 kāizhī ❶ pay; disburse; spend：由国库～ be disbursed by the state treasury /不应当用的钱，坚决不能～。Do not spend a penny more than necessary. ❷ expenses; expenditure; spending：节省～ reduce expenses; retrench /裁减军费～ cut down military spending /诸项～，共计七百万元整。All told, the expenditure comes to seven million *yuan*. ❸〈方言〉pay wages or salaries：你们什么时候～？When do you get your pay? /今天～。你拿到了吗？Today is pay day. Have you got your salary?

开中药铺 kāi zhōngyàopù 〈比喻〉start a Chinese pharmacy — be content with listing phenomena instead of giving a logical analysis in writing or speech：党八股的第五条罪状是：甲乙丙丁，～。The fifth indictment against sterotyped Party writing is that it arranges items under a complicated set of headings, as if starting a Chinese pharmacy.

开宗明义 kāizōng-míngyì make clear the purpose and main theme from the very beginning; state the purpose at the very beginning：这篇文章～，表明了作者的观点。The article presents the author's view at the very beginning.

开足马力 kāizú mǎlì switch to top gear; go full steam ahead; work at full blast; go all out：汽车～，在泥泞中挣扎前进。The car struggled forward in the mud with the throttle wide open. /水利工程正在～进行。The water conservancy project is under full swing.

开钻 kāizuàn 〈石油〉 spud in

开罪 kāizuì offend; displease：无意中，他～了顶头上司。He offended his immediate boss unwittingly.

锎 kāi 〈化学〉 californium (Cf)

揩 kāi wipe; rub：～汗 wipe the sweat away /请用布把玻璃窗～一～。Please wipe (*or* clean) the window with a cloth. /用手绢～～你的鼻子。Wipe your nose on (*or* with) your handkerchief.

揩布 kāibù rag

揩拭 kāishì clean; cleanse：用抹布～桌面 clean a table with a rag; wipe a table with a cloth

揩油 kāiyóu get petty advantages (at the expense of other people or the state); scrounge：贪图小利，到处～ be tempted by small gains and scrounge whatever one can /不要揩女人的油。Don't take liberties with women.

kǎi

慨（❷嘅） kǎi ❶ indignant：我对他的行为感到愤～。I felt indignant at his acts. ❷ deeply touched：感～万分 sigh with strong

K

emotion ❸ generous：慷～ bighearted；unstinting

慨当以慷 kǎidāngyǐkāng *also*“慨以慷”；“慨而慷” high-spirited and vigorous；daring and energetic：他的诗～，读起来令人感发兴起。Vigorous and full of spirit, his poems have an elevating effect upon the reader.

慨诺 kǎinuò consent readily；kindly promise：承蒙～，十分感激。I'm deeply grateful for your kind promise.

慨然 kǎirán ❶ with deep feeling；emotionally：接到作品落选的通知后，他～长叹。He let out a sigh of regret on hearing that his work wasn't selected. ❷ generously；without stint：～相许 promise generously／～相助 help without stint；help readily

慨叹 kǎitàn lament with a sigh；sigh with regret：～再三 repeatedly sigh with regret／为之～不已 keep voicing regret over sth.

慨允 kǎiyǔn consent readily；kindly promise：～捐助 kindly promise to contribute

菅

kǎi 〈化学〉carane

楷

kǎi ❶ model；pattern：为万世之～ be a model of all ages ❷（of Chinese calligraphy）regular script：小～ regular script in small characters／大～ regular script in big characters／正～ regular script／工～ neat regular script

see also jiē

楷范 kǎifàn 〈书面〉model；pattern

楷模 kǎimó model；role model；example；paragon：光辉的～ shining example／廉洁的～ paragon（*or* model）of honesty／引为～ take（*or* regard）as a role model

楷式 kǎishì model；pattern；rule

楷书 kǎishū *also*“正楷”zhèngkǎi regular script

楷体 kǎitǐ ❶（of Chinese calligraphy）regular script；standard style（of handwriting）：他精于书法，尤善～。He is a master in Chinese calligraphy, especially in regular script. ❷ block letter（of phonetic alphabet）

楷则 kǎizé 〈书面〉model；pattern：堪为～ can be regarded as a model

锴

kǎi 〈书面〉iron of good quality

恺（愷）

kǎi 〈书面〉❶ happy；joyful；cheerful and resourceful ❷ triumphant strains

恺切 kǎiqiè 〈书面〉❶ true and pertinent：～晓喻 let it clearly be known to all ❷ earnest；sincere

恺悌 kǎitì 〈书面〉affable；genial：慈祥～ kind and affable／～多智 genial and resourceful

恺悌君子 kǎitì-jūnzǐ amiable gentleman

闿（闓）

kǎi 〈书面〉open

垲（塏）

kǎi 〈书面〉（of terrain）high and dry：山峦相连，其势爽～。High and cool are the endless mountain ranges.

剀（剴）

kǎi

剀切 kǎiqiè 〈书面〉❶ true and pertinent：所举事实，～而又详明。The facts presented are true and clear in every detail. ❷ conscientious；earnest：言辞～ earnest remarks

铠（鎧）

kǎi armour：铁～ armour；mail／首～ helmet

铠甲 kǎijiǎ （suit of）armour：他身披～，手执利斧。He wore a suit of armour and held a sharp axe.

铠仗 kǎizhàng 〈书面〉armour and weapon

铠装 kǎizhuāng 〈电工〉armour；shield；sheath：～电缆 armoured cable／～玻璃 armoured glass／～开关箱 steel-clad switchbox

凯（凱）

kǎi ❶ triumphant（strains）：奏～而归 return in triumph ❷（Kǎi）a surname

凯恩斯 Kǎi'ēnsī John Maynard Keynes（1883-1946），English economist：～效应理论 Keynes effect theory／～主义 Keynesianism；Keynesian economics

凯恩斯集团 Kǎi'ēnsī Jítuán Cairns Group（of 18 agricultural products exporting countries including Australia, Brazil, Argentina and Canada）

凯风 kǎifēng 〈书面〉south wind

凯歌 kǎigē song of victory；song of triumph；paean：壮丽的～ stirring paean／～阵阵，喜报频传。Songs of triumph are heard all round, and good news keeps pouring in.

凯旋 kǎixuán triumphant or victorious return：～柱 triumphal column／～之日 day of triumphant return／参加世界锦标赛的中国体操队昨已～。The Chinese gymnastic team returned from the world championships in triumph yesterday.

凯旋门 Kǎixuánmén ❶ triumphal arch ❷ Arch of Triumph；Arc de Triomphe（in Paris）

kài

欬

kài 〈书面〉cough：謦～ cough

欬唾成珠 kàituò-chéngzhū brilliant comments and remarks；exquisite and elegant diction：才思敏捷，～ quick in wit and elegant in speech

愒

kài 〈书面〉have an insatiable desire for；be greedy

see also hè；qì

忾（愾）

kài 〈书面〉hatred：同仇敌～ common hatred for the enemy

kān

刊（栞）

kān ❶ print；publish：创～（of a newspaper, etc.）start publication；be launched／停～ suspend（*or* stop）publication／复～ resume publication／发～词 foreword（*or* introduction）to a periodical ❷ periodical；publication：期～ journal；periodical／报～ newspapers and magazines／周～ weekly／半月～ semi-monthly；fortnightly／双周～ fortnightly；biweekly／月～ monthly／双月～ bimonthly／季～ quarterly／年～ annual；yearbook／特～ special issue／增～ supplement／合～ combined issue（of a periodical）／画～ pictorial section of a newspaper；pictorial／校～ school magazine；college journal／专～ special issue（*or* column）；monograph／副～ supplement ❸ delete；correct

刊碑立石 kānbēi-lìshí carve and set up a stone tablet

刊本 kānběn block-printed edition：原～ original（*or* master）block-printed edition／宋～ block-printed edition of the Song Dynasty；Song block-printed edition

刊播 kānbō publish and broadcast（an item of news）

刊布 kānbù 〈书面〉print and publish；announce or make public through printed matter：读者对于本文的意见，我们是非常乐于～以公诸社会的。We are very glad to publish our readers' opinions and comments on this article.

刊登 kāndēng publish in a newspaper or magazine；carry：～声明 carry a statement／作品～于创刊号。The article was published in the first issue.

刊定 kāndìng revise and finalize：～谬误 correct errors and mistakes／这本集子是作者亲手～的本子。This collection was revised and finalized by the author himself.

刊发 kānfā publish（in a newspaper or magazine）；carry：大量～农村新面貌的报道 carry a great many reports on the new look of the rural areas

刊刻 kānkè cut blocks；block-print：这部诗稿最早～于清光绪年间。This poem was first block-printed during Guang Xu's reign in the Qing Dynasty.／诗社～的作品，至今流传甚广。Works block-printed by the poets' club are widely read even today.

刊落 kānluò 〈书面〉delete；strike out：～陈言 delete platitudes／～文字 strike out unnecessary words

刊谬补缺 kānmiù-bǔquē correct errors and make up deficiencies；supply errata and supplements

刊授 kānshòu teach through publications；give courses through periodicals：世界语～招生。Students will be enrolled to learn Esperanto mainly through publications.／《中国青年》杂志对全国数十万青年进行～教育。*China Youth* offers courses to tens of thousands of young people through the periodical.

刊授大学 kānshòu dàxué （shortened as 刊大）university offering

courses through periodicals; periodical university:他打算一边工作,一边业余自学,拿一张"~"或"函大"的文凭。He is planning to teach himself in his spare time so as to obtain a certificate from a "periodical university" or "correspondence university".

刊头 kāntóu masthead of a newspaper or magazine:~题字 masthead inscription /设计~ design a newspaper masthead /画~ draw a masthead for a magazine

刊物 kānwù publication:定期~ periodical (publication) /科技~ publication on science and technology; science publication /内部~ restricted publication /发行~ issue a publication /出版~ publish a periodical (*or* journal) /非法~ illegal publication /淫秽~ obscene publication

刊误 kānwù correct errors in printing:再版时已作数处~。A number of corrections were made when it was reprinted.

刊误表 kānwùbiǎo errata; corrigenda

刊行 kānxíng print and publish:向国内外~ publish in and outside China /各省~的报刊、杂志,计有三千余种。There are more than 3,000 newspapers and magazines printed and published in the provinces.

刊印 kānyìn set up and print; block-print:工厂负责~的杂志有三种。The factory sets up and prints three magazines.

刊载 kānzǎi publish (in a newspaper or magazine); carry:这一期月刊上~了几位知名女作家的作品。This month's issue carried writings of several famous women writers.

刊正 kānzhèng proofread and correct; rectify:~碑文 rectify the inscription on a tablet /~旧作之误 correct the errors in a piece of old writing (*or* in a previous article)

堪

kān ❶ may; can:不~设想 cannot be imagined; be dreadful to contemplate /~称典范 set an example; be exemplary; be good enough to serve as a model /他的书画~称双绝。Both his calligraphy and painting can be rated as consummate works of art. ❷ bear; endure:不~回首 can't bear to look back /不~一击 can't withstand a single blow; collapse at the first blow /难~ feel very embarrassed; be intolerable /狼狈不~ in an extremely awkward position; in a sorry plight; in dire straits

堪布 kānbù 〈佛教〉❶ lama in charge of the commandments ❷ head or abbot of a lamasery ❸ title of a monk official in the former Tibetan local government

堪察加半岛 Kānchájiā Bàndǎo Kamchatka Peninsula (in northeast Russia)

堪达罕 kāndáhǎn 〈方言〉elk; moose

堪当重任 kāndāng-zhòngrèn be capable of performing important tasks; can fill a position of great responsibility:此人才德兼备,~。Having both talent and virtue, the man is quite equal to important tasks.

堪堪 kānkān 〈方言〉about to; on the point of; soon:那棒~扫到头顶时,他往后一闪就躲过去了。That bat was about to hit his head, when he ducked by bending back.

堪培拉 Kānpéilā Canberra, capital of Australia

堪萨斯 Kānsàsī Kansas, state in central United States

堪舆 kānyú 〈书面〉geomancy; *feng shui*:~家 geomancer /~先生 one who practises geomancy as a profession; geomancer

戡

kān suppress; put down

戡乱 kānluàn 〈旧语〉suppress or put down a rebellion:"~时期" period of suppressing Communist "rebellion" (declared by KMT reactionaries upon launching civil war in 1946)

戡平 kānpíng succeed in suppressing (a rebellion):~大乱,安邦定国 quell (*or* put down) a great rebellion and bring peace and stability to the land

勘

kān ❶ read and correct the text of; collate:校~ collate ❷ investigate; survey:踏~ make a field survey (of a railway line, construction site, etc.)

勘测 kāncè survey:~水文、地理 survey hydrological and geographical features /~工作 surveying work /地质~ geological survey /地形~ topographical survey /~报告 survey report /~队 survey party /~图 exploration map

勘察 kānchá *also* "勘查" ❶ reconnoitre:~地形 terrain reconnaissance /~敌情 reconnoitre the enemy position; gather intelligence ❷ 〈地质〉prospect; survey:~地下煤层 prospect an underground coal bed /~油田分布情况 prospect the distribution of an oil deposit /实地~ on-the-spot survey /联合~队 joint survey team

勘定 kāndìng ❶ survey and determine:~分界线 survey and determine the boundary (*or* line of demarcation) ❷ 〈书面〉check and ratify; appraise and decide:~税则 check and ratify rules and regulations of taxation

勘核 kānhé check; verify:该文的写作年代已无从~。It is impossible to verify (*or* confirm) when this article was written.

勘校 kānjiào collate; proofread:~经籍 collate classics

勘探 kāntàn exploration; prospecting:磁法~ magnetic prospecting /地震~ seismic prospecting /空中~ aerial exploration /~井 exploratory well /~基地 exploration base; prospecting base /~地区 exploration area /~队 prospecting team /~矿物资源 prospect mineral resources /~者 prospector

勘探地震学 kāntàn dìzhènxué exploration seismology

勘问 kānwèn 〈书面〉question; interrogate

勘误 kānwù correct errors in printing:~之处 corrections made

勘误表 kānwùbiǎo errata; corrigenda

勘验 kānyàn 〈法律〉inspect; examine; hold an inquest:~现场 inspect the scene (of a crime, etc.)

勘正 kānzhèng proofread and correct

龛(龕)

kān 〈迷信〉niche; shrine:佛~ Buddha's niche /神~ shrine (for idols or ancestral tablets) /壁~ niche

龛影 kānyǐng 〈医学〉niche (the location or image of an ulcer as observed in an X-ray)

看

kān ❶ look after; take care of; tend:~病人 look after a patient; attend to a sick person /~小孩 take care of a baby; baby-sit; baby-mind /~一群羊 tend a flock of sheep /~瓜 keep watch in the melon fields /~庄稼 take care of the crops; keep watch on the crops /你不在的时候谁~铺子? Who's tending the shop while you're away? ❷ keep under surveillance; keep watch over; guard:~犯人 keep watch over prisoners /~住对方的得分手 mark the scorer of the rival team /把这几个家伙先~起来。Take these men into custody first. /~住他,别让这家伙给溜掉了。Keep an eye on that fellow. Don't let him sneak off.

see also kàn

看财奴 kāncáinú *also* "守财奴" shǒucáinú miser; skinflint

看场 kāncháng guard or watch the threshing floor (during the harvest season):村长派了几个人~。The village head set several watches on the threshing floor.

看地头 kān dìtóu ❶ keep watch over ripening crops in the fields:每天晚上~,人都累死了。I'm tired out keeping watch in the fields every night. ❷ be buried after death

看管 kānguǎn ❶ guard; watch:~犯人 guard prisoners /这几个人要小心~! Keep a close eye on these people! ❷ look after; attend to; keep in custody:行李一定要留人~。Someone must stay behind to look after the luggage. /谁~这些箱子? Who will attend to these suitcases? /被盗轿车现由警方~。The stolen car is now in police custody.

看护 kānhù ❶ nurse; look after:~病人 nurse the sick; look after a patient /精心~老人 take great pains to care for old people ❷ 〈旧语〉hospital nurse:她母亲曾在教会医院当过~。Her mother used to be a nurse in a missionary hospital.

看家 kānjiā ❶ look after the house; mind the house; sit the house; house-sit:大人们都下地了,留下一个孩子~。All grown-ups have gone to the fields, leaving one child behind to mind the house. /夏天她为一教授~。She house-sat for a professor in the summer. ❷ outstanding (ability); special (skill):~武艺 one's outstanding martial skill

看家本领 kānjiā-běnlǐng one's stock-in-trade; one's special ability:拿出~ make a show of one's special skill

看家狗 kānjiāgǒu watchdog:我早就认识这小子,他是村长的一条~。I've long known this rascal. He's the village head's watchdog (*or* snitch).

看家戏 kānjiāxì play or opera one is particularly good at:他的~是《四郎探母》。*The Fourth Son Returning to Visit His Mother* is the play which shows him at his best.

看林人 kānlínrén forester; ranger

看门 kānmén ❶ look after the house:小心~,别让外人进来。Look after the house with care. Don't let strangers in. /他退休后给单位

K

~。He guards the entrance for his unit after retirement. ❷ doorkeeper; gateman; janitor
看门人 kānménrén gatekeeper; watchman
看青 kānqīng keep watch over ripening crops:几个~的小伙子熬不住夜,都睡着了。The young people who watched over the ripening crops at night hopelessly fell asleep (*or* did not last the night and fell asleep).
看守 kānshǒu ❶ look after; take care of:~财物 take care of the property /~山林 tend the mountain woods ❷ watch; guard; keep under surveillance:~囚犯 guard prisoners (*or* convicts) ❸ jailer; turnkey; warder:女~ wardress /他买通~,给家里捎了一封信。He bribed the jailer and sent a letter home.
看守内阁 kānshǒu nèigé *also* "看守政府"; "过渡内阁" guòdù nèigé;"过渡政府" guòdù zhèngfǔ caretaker cabinet
看守所 kānshǒusuǒ lockup (for prisoners awaiting trial); detention house
看押 kānyā take into custody; detain; keep under detention:~俘虏 detain captives /~罪犯 take criminals into custody
看养 kānyǎng ❶ raise; rear:~牲口 raise livestock ❷ look after; bring up:~孤儿 look after an orphan

kǎn

槛(檻) kǎn threshold
see also jiàn
槛梁 kǎnliáng door sill; sill beam
颇 kǎn
颇颔 kǎnhàn 〈书面〉hungry
轗 kǎn
轗轲 kǎnkě 〈书面〉*see* "坎坷" kǎnkě
侃[1] kǎn 〈书面〉❶ upright and honest; straightforward ❷ joyful; cheerful; amiable
侃[2] kǎn 〈方言〉chat idly; tattle:他特别能~。He is a real talker. /我们一边喝酒,一边瞎~。We gossiped over cups of wine.
侃大山 kǎn dàshān 〈方言〉*also* "砍大山" kǎn dàshān chat idly; gossip; shoot the breeze:我们常到一块儿~。We often get together and shoot the bull.
侃侃 kǎnkǎn 〈书面〉❶ joyful:~如也 in a joyful manner; honest and joyful ❷ upright and straightforward ❸ with ease and composure
侃侃而谈 kǎnkǎn'értán speak with ease and assurance; speak freely and frankly:会上,他理直气壮,~。At the meeting, he spoke with great fervour and perfect assurance.
侃快 kǎnkuài 〈方言〉frank and neat; clear-cut and straightforward:他办事~利索。He is neat and straightforward in doing things.
侃儿 kǎnr *also* "坎儿" kǎnr 〈方言〉code word; enigmatic language:调(diào)~ talk in enigmatic language; speak code words /这些话都是他们那一行的~。These words are the jargon of their trade.
侃爷 kǎnyé 〈方言〉big talker; gossip; tattler:这部电视剧是北京的几位~侃出来的。The plot of this TV play took shape from the idle chatter of a few Beijing gossips.

K

坎[1](❸埳) kǎn ❶ one of the Eight Trigrams (formerly used in divination) representing water *see also* "八卦" ❷ bank; ridge:田~儿 raised path through fields /土~儿 earthen bank /石~ (flood control) stone ridge ❸〈书面〉depression; pit; hole: ❹ critical moment; crux; point of great importance:你要说到~儿上。Please keep to the point. /我国改革正当~儿上。Our country has now reached a critical moment in its reform. ❺ streak of bad luck; predicament:这次可是你的~儿。Your're in for it this time.
坎[2] kǎn (short for 坎德拉)〈物理〉candela
坎德拉 kǎndélā 〈物理〉candela (cd); new candle
坎肩儿 kǎnjiānr sleeveless jacket (usu. padded or lined); vest; waistcoat:西服~ waistcoat /皮~ leather waistcoat /棉~ padded sleeveless jacket
坎井 kǎnjǐng ❶ *also* "坎阱" pit; trap; pitfall:挖~,诱捕猎物 dig pits to trap game /行不义之事,如自蹈~。Doing evil is like setting traps for oneself. ❷ abandoned well
坎坷 kǎnkě ❶ bumpy; rough:山路~ rugged mountain path /道路~不平。The road is rough and bumpy. ❷〈书面〉full of frustrations:~一生,郁郁不得志 lifetime of frustrations and thwarted ambitions
坎壈 kǎnlǎn 〈书面〉in straits; unsuccessful (in one's career):~失志 have an unsuccessful career and be in straitened circumstances /~一生 be frustrated throughout one's life
坎离砂 kǎnlíshā 〈中医〉traditional thermal powder for rheumatism; thermal powder
坎帕拉 Kǎnpàlā Kampala, capital of Uganda
坎炁 kǎnqì 〈中药〉umbilical cord
坎儿 kǎnr ❶ critical moment; important juncture:他说到~上了。He drove the point home (*or* hit the nail on its head). ❷ *see* "侃儿" kǎnr
坎儿井 kǎnrjǐng 〈农业〉karez; kariz; underground channel-connected well system (used in Xinjiang)
坎土曼 kǎntǔmàn *also* "砍土镘" kǎntǔmàn 〈农业〉Uygur mattock
坎子 kǎnzi raised ground:土~ mound
坎子礼儿 kǎnzilǐr (of gang members) etiquette on first meeting sb.; gang greetings
坎子上的 kǎnzishangde 〈方言〉〈旧语〉theatre custodian
莰 kǎn 〈化学〉camphane; bornane:~醇 baras camphor
砍 kǎn ❶ cut; chop; hack; fell:~柴 cut firewood /~树 fell tree ❷ reduce; cut:项目数目被~掉了三分之一。The number of projects was cut by one-third. ❸〈方言〉throw (at sth. or sb.):拿碎砖头~鸟 throw brickbats at birds /不要让那些孩子~石头玩! Stop those kids from throwing stones for fun. ❹ *see* "侃[2]" kǎn
砍大山 kǎn dàshān *see* "侃大山" kǎn dàshān
砍刀 kǎndāo chopper; hacking knife; broadsword
砍伐 kǎnfá fell (a tree); cut down:~木材 fell timber /禁止~森林! Tree felling is prohibited! *or* No tree felling. /这几十亩山林,已被~一空。These dozens of *mu* of mountain slope are denuded of trees.
砍林鸟 kǎnlínniǎo woodcreeper; woodhewer
砍头 kǎntóu chop off the head; behead:~示众 behead in public /~不要紧,只要主义真。I fear no death, since I die for a just cause. *or* My head may be chopped off, but my cause will live on!
砍头疮 kǎntóuchuāng *also* "砍头痈" carbuncle on the neck
砍土镘 kǎntǔmàn *see* "坎土曼" kǎntǔmàn
砍砸器 kǎnzáqì 〈考古〉chopper; chopping tool
欿 kǎn 〈书面〉❶ not self-satisfied; not complacent:~然 not look complacent ❷ frustrated; depressed:~憾 be melancholy; feel frustrated (*or* depressed)

kàn

阚 Kàn a surname
瞰(❷矙) kàn ❶ look down from a height; overlook:鸟~ get a bird's-eye view /俯~ look down at; overlook ❷〈书面〉peep; look:阳货~孔子之亡也 。Yang Huo found Confucius absent.
墈 kàn 〈方言〉(often used in names of places) high embankment:~上 Kanshang (in Jiangxi Province)
磡 kàn 〈方言〉(often used in names of places) cliff:槐花~ Huaihuakan (in Zhejiang Province)
嵌 kàn *used in names of places*:赤~ Chikan (in Taiwan Province)
see also qiàn

看 kàn ❶ look at; see; watch; read: ～照片 look at a photo /～电影 see a film; go to the movies (*or* cinema) /～电视 watch TV /～戏 go to the theatre; see a play, an opera, etc. /～球赛 watch a ball game /～小说 read a novel /～杂志 read a magazine (*or* journal) ❷ think; consider; view; judge: 从实质上～ judging by essentials /你～她能行吗? Do you think she is okay? /去听听他的口气, 他对这件事怎么～。Go to sound him out on this (matter). /我们不能片面地～问题。We must not take a one-sided (*or* lop-sided) view of things. /只有～清形势才能作出正确的判断。Correct judgment comes only after sober assessment of the situation. ❸ call on; visit; go to see: ～朋友 visit (*or* call on) a friend /军长去～伤病员了。The army commander has gone to see the sick and wounded. /有空我会来～你。I'll drop in on you when I can. ❹ look upon; regard; treat: 小～ look down upon sb.; belittle sb. /另眼相～ regard (*or* treat) sb. with special respect ❺ treat (a patient or an illness): ～急诊 treat an emergency patient /郑大夫～糖尿病有办法。Dr. Zheng has a special way of treating diabetes. /我这病恐怕～不好了。I'm afraid my illness won't get cured. ❻ look after; attend to: 照～病人 attend to the sick /～小孩 baby-sit; look after a child ❼ (used to show sth. is going to happen, or as a warning) mind; watch out; look: ～车! Watch out for the traffic! /小心端好碗, ～烫着! Be careful with your bowl. Mind you don't get scalded! /～, 菜快凉了, 别只顾说话了。Look, the food's getting cold! Don't just talk. ❽ (used after a verb or verbal structure to indicate a tentative action) try and see; ... and see what'll happen: 试试～ have a try /等等～ wait and see /摸摸～ just feel it /让我想想～。Let me see (*or* think it over). ❾ depend on; rely on: 这件事全～你了。It all depends on you now. /这件事究竟如何办, 要～情况而定。As to how to go about the matter, it depends on the circumstances. /是否动手术, 要～病人退不退烧。An operation for the patient will hinge on whether his (*or* her) fever goes down or not.

see also kān

看把戏 kàn bǎxi 〈口语〉watch a circus or an acrobatic show; watch some cheap fun; look at a cheap game: 李家小两口一打架, 胡同里那些爱凑热闹～的人们就都出来观看。Whenever the young couple of the Li family came to blows, the gossips and busybodies in the alley would all come and watch the scene.

看白戏 kàn báixì 〈口语〉watch plays, operas, etc., without paying for it; gatecrash (a performance): 门口抓住了几位想～的人。Several gatecrashers were caught at the entrance (to the theatre).

看扁 kànbiǎn underestimate; belittle: 你别把我～了。Don't you underestimate me. /别门缝里看人, 把人家给～了。Don't look at people with a jaundiced eye and make little of them!

看病 kànbìng ❶ (of a doctor) see a patient: 王大夫正在～。Dr. Wang is treating a patient. /赶快请大夫～! Send for a doctor at once! ❷ (of a patient) see a doctor; consult a doctor: 今天下午我将带父亲去～。I'm going to take my father to see the doctor this afternoon. /我找了几家医院也没看好病。I've been to several hospitals but I'm not yet cured (of my illness).

看不出 kànbuchū unable to perceive or detect: ～真假 cannot tell whether sth. is genuine or fake /我～这样做究竟有什么不好。I see nothing wrong in so doing.

看不过 kànbuguò *also* "看不过去"〈口语〉can't bear (to see) any more of; cannot stand by and watch: 这孩子太不礼貌了, 我实在～, 说了他几句。I could bear no more of the child's impertinence and gave him a talking-to. /他太过分了, 真是让人～去了。This is really too much of him, and I can hardly put up with it.

看不起 kànbuqǐ look down upon; belittle; scorn; despise: 尽管有人～, 但他仍然在这个平凡的工作岗位上干了十几年。Though looked down upon by some, he remained at this menial job for more than ten years. /他最～这号人。He's full of disdain for persons of this sort.

看不上眼 kànbushàngyǎn spurn; disdain; hold in contempt: 不要因人家年轻就～。Don't write anybody off just because he or she is young.

看不顺眼 kànbushùnyǎn show disgust for; be disgusted at or with; dislike: 你～就别跟他交往。If you dislike him, just keep away from him. /这里有些事叫人～。You won't like certain things here.

看菜吃饭, 量体裁衣 kàn cài chīfàn, liàng tǐ cáiyī regulate the appetite according to the dishes and cut the dress according to the figure — act according to actual circumstances

看茶 kànchá 〈旧语〉(to the servant when a guest arrives) serve tea; bring tea

看成 kànchéng look upon as; regard as; take as; take for: 我们不应把幻想～事实。We shouldn't regard fantasy (*or* illusion) as reality. /你把我～什么人了? What do you take me for? /她被～全院的标兵。She is considered a pace-setter in the college.

看承 kànchéng 〈书面〉look after; take care of: 一向多蒙～, 心中感激不尽。I am very grateful to you for the solicitude you have always shown me.

看出 kànchū make out; see: ～形势的严重性 see (*or* be aware of) the gravity of the situation /～问题的所在 have found out where the shoe pinches /她一眼就～他来意不善。She saw at first sight that he had come with bad intentions.

看出苗头 kànchū miáotou have discerned symptoms of (a trend); have got the scent of; have felt the pulse of; have found out which way the wind blows

看穿 kànchuān see through: 明眼人不难～其用心之所在。A discerning person will readily see through his ulterior motives.

看待 kàndài look upon; regard; consider; treat: 你怎么能这样～自己的生身父母呢? How can you treat your own parents like that? /我把你当作这方面的行家～。I look upon (*or* regard) you as an expert on such matters. /你如何～这件事情? What do you think of the matter?

看到 kàndào catch sight of; be in view of; see: ～形势的变化 take note of the change in the situation /站在楼顶上, 你就可以～天安门了。You will see Tian An Men (*or* Tian An Men will come into view) when you stand on top of the building. /我这辈子恐怕再也看不到他了。I'm afraid I shall never see him again.

看得过儿 kàndeguòr *also* "看得过去"〈口语〉(performance, sports match, etc.) worth watching

看得起 kàndeqǐ have a good opinion of; think highly of; think much of: 有谁～懒汉? Who thinks anything of a lazybones? /承蒙您～, 我一定不辜负您的期望。I'm honoured by your trust. I will certainly not let you down.

看低 kàndī underestimate: 你太～她的能量了! You have underestimated her capabilities!

看跌 kàndiē (of market prices) be expected to fall: 行情～。Prices are expected to fall. /这几天股市～。The stock market tends to be bearish these days.

看法 kànfa ❶ view; point of view; opinion: 不同的人, ～不同。Views differ from person to person. /关于你上大学的事, 你母亲和我～完全一致。Your mother and I see eye to eye about your going to university. ❷〈口语〉unfavourable opinion or judgment: 大家对他有些～。People don't think highly of him.

看风色 kàn fēngsè *also* "看风头"; "看风向" see or find out which way the wind blows: ～行事 try to find out how the wind blows before taking action

看风使舵 kànfēng-shǐduò *also* "见风使舵" jiànfēng-shǐduò; "见风转舵" jiànfēng-zhuǎnduò trim one's sails to the wind; steer according to the wind; serve the time: ～的人 time-server /她～, 口吻随即变得温和起来。Trimming her sails, she framed her words more amicably. /最后, 商界人士～加入胜方, 而使该候选人以压倒多数当选。Sensing which way the wind blew, the business people finally jumped on the bandwagon, enabling the candidate to win by a landslide.

看风水 kàn fēngshui practise geomancy

看顾 kàngù take care of; look after; attend to: ～老母 look after one's elderly mother /这几位护士～病人都很细心。The nurses are meticulous in attending to the sick.

看官 kànguān 〈旧语〉(as used in traditional Chinese novels) you readers; dear readers

看惯 kànguàn become accustomed to the sight of: 这种事我们早已～了。We have long been used to this kind of things. /～了就好了。You'll get inured to it. /我真看不惯她向他调情那样子。I just cannot bear seeing her flirting with him. /看不惯的事儿多啦! There are plenty of things to be frowned upon!

看好 kànhǎo ❶ look up; get better: 今年外贸形势～。Foreign trade will pick up in the current year. ❷ expect sb. or sth. to win: 今秋～羊绒衫。Cashmere sweaters are expected to be hot (*or* in vogue) this autumn. /这次足球联赛人们～北京队。The Beijing team is the favourite team for the league games.

看花容易栽花难 kàn huā róngyì zāi huā nán flowers are pleasant

to look at but hard to raise

看见 kànjian catch sight of; see:你能从这扇窗户～海。You get a view of the sea from this window. /火车越开越远,最后看不见了。The train moved farther and farther away and was at last lost to view. /～来船时,这些被流放到孤岛上的人异常高兴。When the marooned people sighted a ship coming, they were overwhelmed with joy.

看开 kànkāi accept an unpleasant fact with equanimity; resign oneself (to a hard circumstance); not take to heart:凡事要～些,不要过分悲伤。Whatever happens, don't take it too much to heart and don't let yourself be overcome with grief.

看看 kànkan ❶ look carefully; examine:你好好～,这都是上等的货色。Look carefully. These are all of best (*or* high) quality. /这次远行,打算～各地的风土人情。I plan to have a good (*or* close) look at local conditions and customs on the journey. ❷ soon; in a moment:～天色已晚,只好找了个地方住下。Soon it became dark, so we had to find a place to stay for the night.

看客 kànkè 〈方言〉spectators; viewers; audience

看来 kànlai 〈口语〉it seems; it appears; it looks (as if, as though):今天～我要迟到了。It seems I'm going to be late today. /～我只能依靠自己了。Apparently, I have to rely on myself. /他～很是聪明。He appears to be quite clever.

看破 kànpò ❶ see through:我～了他的骗局,不再和他来往了。Having seen through his swindle, I had no more dealings with him. ❷ become disillusioned; take nothing to heart:这些俗事还是～些好,要不然会把你气死。Don't take such trivial matters to heart or you'll be driven out of your senses.

看破红尘 kànpò-hóngchén see through human vanity; be disillusioned with the ways of the world

看齐 kànqí ❶ dress:向右～! Dress right, dress! ❷ keep up with; emulate:向劳动英雄～ emulate labour heroes /他尽力向班上好同学～。He is trying his best to keep up with the more advanced students in his class.

看起来 kànqilai it looks as though; it appears:～这件事有人支持。It seems that there are people behind all this. /这天气～还得冷几天。It looks as if the cold weather will last a few more days.

看亲 kànqīn 〈方言〉take a look at one's prospective son-in-law or daughter-in-law

看轻 kànqīng underestimate; look down upon; take lightly; belittle:不要把这种工作～了。Don't underestimate the importance of this work. /你未免～了这件事的严重性。You really took the grave matter too lightly. /自己不能～自己。One should never demean oneself.

看清 kànqīng ❶ see clearly; have a clear view of:戴上眼镜,我一切都～了。Wearing glasses, I can see everything clearly. ❷ realize:她～了局势的严重性。She realized the gravity of the situation.

看觑 kànqù (often used in the early vernacular) ❶ look:仔细～ look carefully ❷ look after; take care of

看热闹 kàn rènao ❶ be a looker-on; gloat over:自己的弟弟出了事,当哥哥的真能在一边儿～? Can anyone simply look on with folded arms when his younger brother is in trouble? /这场败局可有人等着～呢! There are people out there gloating over our defeat. ❷ watch the bustling scene; watch the fun:到庙会～去! Let's go to the fair to have some fun.

看人眉睫 kànrén-méijié 〈比喻〉subservient; docile:～的软骨头 mean, despicable yesman

看人挑担不吃力 kàn rén tiāodàn bù chīlì 〈俗语〉none knows the weight of another's burden

看人下菜 kànrén-xiàcài *also* "看人端菜";"看人下菜碟儿"〈比喻〉treat people according to their social status; be snobbish:他这号人～,势利得很。He is a real snob, treating people discriminatorily.

看人嘴脸 kànrén-zuǐliǎn be subservient; live on other's favours:我讨厌那种～,对阔老唯唯诺诺的小人。I hate to see such servile yesmen that fawn on rich people.

看日子 kàn rìzi 〈迷信〉select an auspicious day

看上 kànshang take a fancy to; settle on; fall in love with:你准是～她了。You must have fallen in love with (*or* taken a fancy to) her. /他～了这件上衣。He settled on this jacket./ 这个女生～了老师。The schoolgirl had a crush on one of her teachers.

看手相 kàn shǒuxiàng tell someone's future by examining the lines on the palm of his or her hand; read palms as a means of fortune-telling; practise palmistry

看死 kànsǐ think a person unalterable or unredeemable:不能用固定的眼光把一个犯错误的人～。We should not take a cut-and-dried approach to an erring person and think him incorrigible.

看台 kàntái 〈体育〉stands; bleachers; grandstand:比赛还未开始,～四周早已挤满了观众。The bleachers had been long full of spectators, waiting for the game to start. /～上彩旗挥舞,喊声震天。All over the stands, coloured flags were flying amid deafening shouts.

看透 kàntòu ❶ understand thoroughly; gain an insight into:他这一手我怎么都看不透。I simply don't understand this move of his. ❷ see through:他想愚弄我? 没门儿! 我早就～他了。He wanted to fool me? Not bloody likely! I have long seen through him.

看头 kàntou 〈口语〉worth seeing or reading:这出戏有～吗? Is the play worth seeing? /这种小说毫无～,一钱不值! This kind of novel isn't worth the paper it is written on.

看图识字 kàntú-shízì learn to read with the aid of pictures:她在幼儿～教学方面,总结出了一套经验。She formulated a set of experiences for teaching children to learn to read with the aid of pictures.

看望 kànwang call on; visit; see:～父母 pay a visit to one's parents /～朋友 call on friends

看相 kànxiàng 〈迷信〉tell sb.'s fortune by reading his or her face, etc.:算命～先生 fortune-teller /～术 physiognomy /找人～ visit a physiognomist (*or* fortune-teller)

看笑话 kàn xiàohua watch sb. make a fool of himself or herself; have a good laugh at sb.'s expense; make a mock or mockery of:大家都在看他的笑话。People are all watching him make a fool of himself. /这件事,我们要特别小心,不要给人家～。We must be very careful not to make a laughing-stock of ourselves.

看眼色 kàn yǎnsè take a hint; take one's cue:～行事 act upon a hint

看样子 kàn yàngzi *see* "看来"

看医生 kàn yīshēng 〈方言〉go to see a doctor:孩子发烧了,下午就去～。The child is having a fever, and I'm going to take him to see a doctor this afternoon.

看涨 kànzhǎng (of market prices) be expected to rise; be on the rise:棉纱行情～。The cotton yarn price is expected to rise (*or* is on the rise). /价格～,马上买进。Buy at once for the rise. /期货市场～。The futures market is bullish.

看着办 kànzhebàn do as one pleases; do as one sees fit:这事你就～吧。Do as you see fit. /谈判的总方针已定, 怎么谈你～吧。With the general guidelines set, you can act at your discretion during the negotiation.

看中 kànzhòng *see* "看上"

看重 kànzhòng regard as important; value; set store by:～老师的忠告 value the teacher's advice /我俩都非常～儿时建起的友谊。Both of us set great store by the ties of friendship forged in our childhood.

看朱成碧 kànzhū-chéngbì take red for green — be dazzled; be confused:老眼昏花,～。As my eyesight is failing with age, I often get confused with colours.

看座 kànzuò 〈旧语〉(order issued to a servant or waiter) find a seat for the guest

看做 kànzuò *also* "看作" look upon as; regard as; take as; take for:不要把人家的忍让～软弱可欺。Don't take their forebearance for weakness and try to bully them. /我会把你的事～我自己的事。I'll regard your wish and need as my own.

kāng

康[1] kāng ❶ healthy:安～ safe and sound /健～ healthy; in good health; in the pink ❷ 〈书面〉well-being; abundance; affluence:～年 good year /小～ comparatively well-off ❸ (Kāng) a surname

康[2] kāng *see* "糠" kāng

康拜因 kāngbàiyīn 〈机械〉combine (harvester)

康采恩 kāngcǎi'ēn (transliteration from the German Konzern) 〈经济〉conglomerate

康德 Kāngdé Immanuel Kant (1723-1804), German philosopher:～主义 Kantianism

康狄液 kāngdíyè 〈化学〉Condy's fluid, a disinfectant

康阜 kāngfù 〈书面〉peace and affluence

康复 kāngfù be restored to health; recover; recuperate; rehabilitate:病体～ recover from an illness; recuperate (one's strength) /～车 bus for the disabled /～工程 rehabilitation engineering /祝你早日～。Hope you'll soon be well again. *or* Wish you a speedy recovery.

康复中心 kāngfù zhōngxīn health recovery centre; rehabilitation centre

康健 kāngjiàn healthy; in robust health:身体～ enjoy good health

康乐 kānglè peace and happiness:祝君合家～! May you and your family live in peace and happiness!

康乐球 kānglèqiú *also*“克郎球” kèlángqiú;“克郎棋” kèlángqí caroms

康乐中心 kānglè zhōngxīn recreation centre

康乃馨 kāngnǎixīn 〈植物〉carnation; clove pink (*Dianthus caryophullus*)

康宁 kāngníng 〈书面〉healthy and sound:家父年届八十而极～。Now eighty years old, my father is still hale and hearty.

康平 kāngpíng 〈书面〉peace and stability:海内～。There is peace and stability across the land.

康平纳 kāngpíngnà *also*“联合制” liánhézhì 〈经济〉combine

康强 kāngqiáng 〈书面〉strong and healthy:身体～ strong and healthy; in robust health

康衢 kāngqú 〈书面〉broad road; wide street

康泰 kāngtài 〈书面〉healthy; peaceful:身体～ healthy; in good health /祝全家～。Wish you and your family good health and a peaceful life. *or* May you and your family enjoy good health and live in peace.

康铜 kāngtóng 〈冶金〉constantan

康熙 Kāngxī Kangxi, title of the reign (1662-1722) of Aisin Gioro Xuanye (爱新觉罗·玄烨, 1654-1722), 2nd emperor of the Qing Dynasty, called reverently Qing Shengzu (清圣祖) after death

康熙字典 Kāngxī Zìdiǎn *The Kangxi Dictionary*, a 42-volume Chinese dictionary complied during the reign of Kangxi

康有为 Kāng Yǒuwéi Kang Youwei (formerly translated as Kang Yu-wei) (1858-1927), Chinese scholar and reformist

康庄大道 kāngzhuāng-dàdào broad road; main road:企业从此走上了稳步发展的～。From then on, the enterprise embarked on a broad road of steady development.

慷(忼) kāng

慷慨 kāngkǎi ❶ vehement; fervent:我们的战士那么忠诚、那么～、那么勇敢! Our soldiers are so faithful, enthusiastic and heroic. ❷ generous; liberal; magnanimous:～无私的援助 generous and selfless aid

慷慨悲歌 kāngkǎi-bēigē sing with solemn fervour

慷慨陈词 kāngkǎi-chéncí speak with fervour; speak with righteous indignation; present one's views vehemently:律师～，据理力争。The lawyer presented the case vehemently and strongly on just grounds.

慷慨激昂 kāngkǎi-jī'áng *also*“激昂慷慨” impassioned; vehement; passionate; enthusiastic and fervent:他义正辞严，～地驳斥了对方的污蔑。Upholding justice, he vigorously refuted the slander of the other party. /他的演讲～，激动人心。His speech was impassioned and moving.

慷慨解囊 kāngkǎi-jiěnáng help sb. generously with money; give money freely and generously:他多次～，资助穷困学生。Many times he generously offered financial assistance to needy students.

慷慨就义 kāngkǎi-jiùyì go to one's death like a hero; die a martyr's death:壮士怒斥敌酋，然后面不改色，～。After indignantly denouncing the enemy chieftain, the hero died a martyr's death without blinking an eye.

慷慨仗义 kāngkǎi-zhàngyì act generously to uphold justice; be just and generous

慷他人之慨 kāng tārén zhī kǎi be liberal with other people's money; be generous at the expense of others; cut a large thong of another man's leather

糠(穅) kāng

❶ chaff; bran; husk:秕～ chaff /稻～ paddy chaff /米～ rice bran /谷～ corn husk ❷ (usu. of a radish) spongy:～心儿 be spongy at heart; be spongy in the middle /萝卜～了。The radish has gone spongy.

糠包 kāngbāo bag of chaff; good-for-nothing:他那个～儿子总给他惹祸。His good-for-nothing son often makes trouble for him.

糠秕 kāngbǐ ❶ chaff; bran ❷ worthless stuff:弃之如～ discard as rubbish /～之事，何足挂齿! Such trifles are not worth mentioning!

糠菜半年粮 kāngcài bànnián liáng have nothing to eat but chaff and herbs for half the year — lead a life of semi-starvation:那些年日子艰难，家家都是～。In those years, life was really hard, and almost every family had to live on chaff and herbs half the time.

糠醇 kāngchún 〈化学〉furancarbinol; furfuryl alcohol:～树脂 furfuryl-alcohol resin

糠麸 kāngfū chaff; bran; husk:～类饲料 bran fodder

糠基树脂 kāngjī shùzhī 〈化工〉furfuryl resin

糠醛 kāngquán 〈化学〉furfural:～树脂 furfural resin

糠市 kāngshì slum; shantytown:城东一带，旧称～，住的都是穷人。The east end of the city, which used to be called "shantytown", was where poor people dwelled.

糠酸 kāngsuān 〈化学〉furoic acid:～甲酯 methyl furoate

糠虾 kāngxiā opossum shrimp; possum shrimp; mysis

糠油 kāngyóu oil abstracted from bran; bran oil

糠疹 kāngzhěn 〈医学〉pityriasis:白～ alba pityriasis /头皮～ pityriasis capitis

糠疹癣菌 kāngzhěn xuǎnjūn 〈医学〉pityrosporon

㰠 kāng

see“榔㰠” lángkang

躿 kāng

see“躴躿” lángkāng

鱇 kāng

see“鮟鱇” ānkāng

闶 kāng

see also kàng

闶阆 kāngláng *also*“闶阆子”〈方言〉open space within a structure:这井下面的～真大啊! How spacious it is at the bottom of the well!

káng

扛 káng

carry on the shoulder; shoulder:手拉肩～ pull with hands and carry on the shoulder; pull and shoulder /这个任务你一定要～起来。You have to shoulder this task.

see also gāng

扛长工 káng chánggōng *also*“扛长活” work as a farmhand on a yearly basis:他长大以后就在地主家～。Once he was a grown-up, he went to work as a farm labourer for a landlord.

扛大个儿 káng dàgèr 〈方言〉work as a stevedore or porter:～的 porter at the railway station; stevedore

扛大活 káng dàhuó work as a farm labourer for heavy work

扛竿 kánggān 〈杂技〉acrobatics on a bamboo pole

扛活 kánghuó work as a farm labourer:新来的～的人里头，有一个十几岁的男孩。Among the newly hired farmhands was a teenager boy.

扛肩儿的 kángjiānrde 〈旧语〉porter

扛码头 káng mǎtou 〈方言〉〈旧语〉work as a docker or longshoreman

扛小活 káng xiǎohuó work as a part-time farm labourer

kàng

亢 kàng

❶ high:高～ loud and sonorous; resounding ❷ haughty; arrogant:不～不卑 neither haughty nor humble; neither arrogant nor servile ❸ excessive; extreme ❹ second of the 28 constellations in ancient Chinese astronomy *see also*“二十八宿” èrshíbāxiù ❺ (Kàng) a surname

see also háng

亢奋 kàngfèn stimulated; excessively excited:心情～ be in an excessively excited mood (*or* state)

亢旱 kànghàn severe drought; very dry weather:入夏以来，天气～，滴雨未下。It has been extremely dry and rainless since summer began. /这一带连年～，村民们都逃荒去了。The villagers all fled from famine due to successive years of severe drought.

亢进 kàngjìn 〈医学〉hyperfunction; sthenia:甲状腺机能～ hyperthyroidism

亢礼 kànglǐ 〈书面〉salute each other as equals

亢直 kàngzhí 〈书面〉upright and outspoken:他过于~,得罪了不少人。He offended many people by outspokenness.

闶 kàng 〈书面〉tall and big; lofty
see also kāng

炕 kàng ❶ *kang*, a heatable brick bed:火~ heated *kang*; heated brick bed /土~ heatable adobe bed; adobe *kang* /烧~ heat a brick bed ❷〈方言〉bake or dry by the heat of a fire:炉子边~着白薯。Sweet potatoes are being baked on the side of the stove. /把湿衣服放在炕头上~一~。Dry the wet clothes on the heated *kang*.

炕单儿 kàngdānr *also* "炕单子" (bed) sheet
炕洞 kàngdòng flue of a *kang*
炕柜 kàngguì *also* "炕橱" cupboard on the *kang*
炕琴 kàngqín 〈方言〉*see* "炕柜"
炕梢 kàngshāo further end of a *kang* (from the stove); cooler end of a *kang*:我们娘儿俩在~睡,你睡炕头。You will sleep at the warmer end of the *kang*, and my daughter and I at the other end.
炕头 kàngtóu ❶ warmer end of a *kang*:老婆孩子热~ wife, children and a warm *kang* — old-time farmer's idea of a comfortable life ❷ edge of a *kang*
炕席 kàngxí *kang* mat
炕沿 kàngyán edge of a *kang*
炕桌儿 kàngzhuōr small, low table for use on a *kang*; *kang* table

抗 kàng ❶ resist; combat; fight:~敌 fight the enemy /~寒 resist the cold /抵~ resist; oppose /对~ oppose; contest; confront /顽~ put up a stubborn fight /~地震 earthquake-resistant; anti-seismic /~冲击 shock-resistant /~白蛋白 antialbumin /~菌 antibacterial /~毒药 antidote /~溶血球素 antihemolysin /~催化药 anticatalyst /~白蚁药 termite-proof drug ❷ refuse; defy:~租 stop paying rent /~捐~税 refuse to pay levies and taxes ❸ contend with; be a match for: *see* "~礼"

抗阿米巴药 kàng'āmǐbāyào amebicide
抗癌 kàng'ái anticancer:~新药 new anticancer drug
抗癌霉素 kàng'áiméisù 〈生化〉sarkomycin
抗膀子 kàng bǎngzi 〈方言〉oppose; resist; challenge:谁敢跟我~,我就对谁不客气。I won't be soft on anyone who dares to oppose me.
抗暴 kàngbào fight against violent repression:~斗争 struggle against violent repression
抗爆 kàngbào 〈化工〉antiknock; antidetonation:~剂 antiknock (agent); antidetonant; antiknock compound /~汽油 antiknock gasoline /~建筑 explosive-resistant structure
抗辩 kàngbiàn ❶ contradict; refute; speak in self-defence:直言~,语惊四座 make a blunt contradiction that raises the eyebrows of everyone present ❷〈法律〉counterplea; demurrer:进行~ enter a demurrer; put in a demurrer /~人 pleader; opposing counsel /我们来法院不是应诉,是~。We appear in court not to raise a defence, but to challenge the court's jurisdiction. /他针对指控提出"无罪"~。He entered a plea of "not guilty" to the charges filed against him.
抗病 kàngbìng 〈农业〉disease-resistant:~力 resistance to disease
抗病毒 kàngbìngdú antiviral:~剂 antivirotic; antivirus /~性 antiviral property
抗不育 kàngbùyù antisterility
抗扯强度 kàngchě qiángdù tear resistance; tear strength
抗尘走俗 kàngchén-zǒusú hanker after fame and gain:此等~的势利人,我们还是少同他们来往为好。We'd better keep away from such snobbish people who crave fame and gain.
抗虫害 kàngchónghài 〈农业〉pest-resistant
抗磁 kàngcí 〈物理〉diamagnetism:~材料 diamagnetic (*or* antimagnetic) material /~共振 diamagnetic resonance
抗大 Kàngdà (short for 中国人民抗日军政大学) Chinese People's Anti-Japanese Military and Political University (set up in Yan'an during the War of Resistance Against Japan)
抗代谢物 kàngdàixièwù 〈生化〉antimetabolite
抗倒伏 kàngdǎofú 〈农业〉resistant to lodging; lodging-resistant:~性 lodging resistance
抗稻瘟霉素 kàngdàowēn méisù blastmycin
抗稻瘟品种 kàngdàowēn pǐnzhǒng 〈农业〉rice-blast-resistant variety
抗滴虫药 kàngdīchóngyào antitrichomonal agent
抗丁 kàngdīng fight against press-ganging; resist forcible drafting:~抗粮 resist forcible drafting and grain levy /四乡村民纷纷而起,~风潮此起彼伏。All around the countryside the villagers rose in revolt against press-ganging.
抗冻剂 kàngdòngjì anti-freezing agent
抗毒素 kàngdúsù 〈医学〉antitoxin:~疗法 antitoxin therapy /~原 antitoxigen
抗毒素血清 kàngdúsù xuèqīng 〈医学〉antitoxic serum
抗断应力 kàngduàn yìnglì 〈物理〉breaking strength
抗辐射 kàngfúshè radioresistance; radiation hardening:~工艺 radiation hardening process /~剂 anti-rad
抗腐蚀 kàngfǔshí resistant to corrosion
抗干扰 kànggānrǎo anti-interference; anti-jam; jamproof:~导弹 jamproof guided missile /~电路 anti-jamming circuit; anti-clutter circuit /~防护频带 interference guard band /~滤波器 anti-interference filter /~素 anti-interferon /~装置 anti-jamming unit
抗感染药 kànggǎnrǎnyào anti-infectious agent
抗过敏 kàngguòmǐn antianaphylaxis:~素 antianaphylactin; antisensibilism
抗寒服 kànghánfú cold-proof suit
抗寒植物 kànghán zhíwù cold-resistant plant
抗旱 kànghàn fight a drought; combat a drought:~作物 drought-resistant crop /~性能 drought resistance /这种新品种有较好的~性能。This new drought-resistant breed is effective.
抗衡 kànghéng rival; compete; contend with; match:与敌国相~ vie (*or* contend) with an enemy country /我队具备了与世界冠军~的实力。Our team is now able to challenge the world champion. /小王知道,在姿色、年龄上,自己都不能与她~了。Xiao Wang is aware that she is no match for her in appearance and age.
抗洪 kànghóng fight a flood; combat a flood:~抢险 combat a flood and rush to deal with an emergency /~排涝 fight a flood and drain water-logged areas
抗坏血酸 kànghuàixuèsuān 〈药学〉ascorbic acid; vitamin C:~钠〈化学〉sodium ascorbate
抗婚 kànghūn refuse to marry the person chosen by one's family:~出走 run away from home to escape an arranged marriage
抗击 kàngjī resist; fight back:~入侵之敌 resist (*or* fight) an invading enemy
抗激素 kàngjīsù 〈生化〉antihormone
抗剪强度 kàngjiǎn qiángdù 〈机械〉shearing strength; shear strength
抗结核药 kàngjiéhéyào antitubercular agent; antituberculotic
抗静电 kàngjìngdiàn antistatic electricity; antistatic:~地面材料 antistatic flooring /~天线 antistatic antenna /~涂料 antistatic coating /~剂 antistat
抗拒 kàngjù resist; defy:~搜查 resist search /~法律秩序 defy law and order /~心理 negativism /对方的无理要求,遭到我方坚决~。We categorically rejected the unreasonable demands of the other side.
抗捐 kàngjuān refuse to pay levies:~风潮 unrest (*or* agitation) against taxation
抗菌素 kàngjūnsù 〈药学〉*see* "抗生素"
抗菌血清 kàngjūn xuèqīng 〈药学〉antiseptic serum
抗菌增效剂 kàngjūn zēngxiàojì 〈药学〉antiseptic synergist
抗抗毒素 kàngkàngdúsù antiantitoxin
抗抗体 kàngkàngtǐ antiantibody
抗拉强度 kànglā qiángdù 〈机械〉tensile strength
抗拉试验 kànglā shìyàn tensile test
抗老剂 kànglǎojì 〈化工〉antiager
抗涝 kànglào prevent water-logging:做好防汛~工作 prepare for prevention of flooding and water-logging
抗礼 kànglǐ *also* "亢礼" kànglǐ 〈书面〉salute each other as equals:分庭~ stand up to sb. as an equal
抗粮 kàngliáng refuse to hand in grain:~抗税 refuse to hand in grain and pay taxes
抗麻风药 kàngmáfēngyào antileprotic; anti-leprosy agent
抗酶 kàngméi 〈生化〉antienzyme
抗霉素 kàngméisù 〈生化〉antimycin:~甲 antimycin A
抗美援朝战争 Kàng-Měi Yuán-Cháo Zhànzhēng War to Resist US Aggression and Aid Korea (1950-1953)
抗命 kàngmìng ❶ defy orders; disobey:我等~,实出无奈。We had no choice but to disobey orders. ❷ defy one's destiny

抗磨 kàngmó wear-resistant; antiwear; antifriction: ～材料 abrasion-resistant material; wear-resistant material; anti-abrasion material /～轴承 antifriction bearing

抗逆力 kàngnìlì *also* "抗性"; "抗逆性" resistance: ～品种 resistant variety

抗凝 kàngníng anticoagulate: ～剂 anticoagulant

抗凝疗法 kàngníng liáofǎ 〈医学〉 anticoagulant therapy

抗凝血激酶 kàngníngxuè jīméi 〈生化〉 antithrombokinase; antithromboplastin

抗疟药 kàngnüèyào antimalarial (agent)

抗疲劳 kàngpíláo 〈机械〉 antifatigue: ～剂 antifatigue agent/～性 fatigue resistance

抗强悯弱 kàngqiáng-mǐnruò oppose the strong, sympathize with the weak; resist the bully, side with the underdog

抗球蛋白 kàngqiúdànbái 〈医学〉 antiglobulin

抗燃性 kàngránxìng flame resistance

抗热合金 kàngrè héjīn heat-resisting alloy

抗日民族统一战线 kàng-Rì mínzú tǒngyī zhànxiàn anti-Japanese national united front (1936-1945)

抗日战争 Kàng-Rì Zhànzhēng War of Resistance Against Japanese Aggression (1937-1945)

抗蠕变强度 kàngrúbiàn qiángdù 〈冶金〉 creep strength

抗上 kàngshàng disobey one's superior; act contrary to the will of one's boss; show insubordination

抗蛇毒素 kàngshédúsù antivenin; antivenom

抗神经毒素 kàngshénjīngdúsù antineurotoxin

抗渗 kàngshèn 〈水利〉 impermeable; impervious: ～试验 impermeability test /～性 impermeability; anti-permeability

抗生菌 kàngshēngjūn antibiotic bacteria

抗生菌肥 kàngshēngjūnféi antibiotic fertilizer

抗生素 kàngshēngsù (formerly called 抗菌素) 〈药学〉 antibiotic; microbiotic: ～测定 antibiotic assay /广谱～ broad- (*or* wide-) spectrum antibiotic /窄谱～ narrow-spectrum antibiotic /四环系～ tetracycline antibiotic

抗湿剂 kàngshījì moisture resistant

抗属 kàngshǔ family member of those who took part in the War of Resistance Against Japan under CPC leadership

抗霜 kàngshuāng 〈农业〉 frost-resistant

抗水性 kàngshuǐxìng water-resistance; water-resisting property

抗税 kàngshuì refuse to pay taxes

抗诉 kàngsù 〈法律〉 appeal against a judgment or an arbitration; protest

抗酸 kàngsuān antacid; acid resistant: ～剂 antacid /～添加剂 antacid additive /～菌 acid-fast bacteria

抗体 kàngtǐ 〈医学〉 antibody; antisubstance: ～活性 antibody activity /～特异性 antibody specificity /～缺陷综合征 antibody deficiency syndrome

抗弯强度 kàngwān qiángdù 〈机械〉 bending strength; bend strength; buckling strength

抗违 kàngwéi disobey; defy

抗心律失常药 kàngxīnlǜ shīchángyào antiarrhythmic drug

抗兴奋剂 kàngxīngfènjì 〈药学〉 contrastimulant; contrastimulus

抗性 kàngxìng resistance: ～因子 resistance factor

抗血清 kàngxuèqīng antiserum

抗血栓形成剂 kàngxuèshuān xíngchéngjì antithrombotic agent

抗血吸虫药 kàngxuèxīchóngyào schistosomicide

抗血友病 kàngxuèyǒubìng antihemophilic: ～球蛋白 antihemophilic globulin (AHG) /～药 antihemophilic /～因子 antihemophilic factor (AHF)

抗血脂药 kàngxuèzhīyào antilipemic

抗压强度 kàngyā qiángdù 〈机械〉 compressive strength; compressive resistance: ～试验 compressive strength test

抗压性能 kàngyā xìngnéng 〈物理〉 compressive property

抗氧化 kàngyǎnghuà antioxidant; antioxidation: ～剂 antioxidant /～酶 antioxidase /～作用 antioxidation

抗药性 kàngyàoxìng 〈医学〉 resistance to drugs: 避免产生～ avoid becoming drug-fast

抗胰岛素 kàngyídǎosù 〈生化〉 anti-insulin: ～酶 anti-insulinase

抗议 kàngyì protest; remonstrate; object: 正式～ formal (*or* official) protest /严正～ solemn protest /提出～ lodge a protest (with sb. against sth.) /～集会 protest rally /～书 written protest /学生就伙食问题向学校当局提出～。The students protested to the school authorities about the poor food.

抗议照会 kàngyì zhàohuì note of protest

抗御 kàngyù resist and defend against: ～外侮 resist foreign aggression /～入侵之敌 fight the invading enemy /提高～自然灾害的能力 enhance capabilities to cope with (*or* combat) natural disasters

抗原 kàngyuán 〈医学〉 antigen: ～结构 antigenic structure /～抗体反应 antigen-antibody reaction /～抗体复合物 antigen-antibody complex /澳大利亚～ Australia antigen; hepatitis antigen /～疗法 antigenotherapy /～性 antigenicity /～血 antigenemia

抗灾 kàngzāi fight or combat natural disasters: 动员群众～自救。Mobilize the people in an effort to fight natural disasters and provide for themselves.

抗噪声 kàngzàoshēng antinoise: ～传声器 antinoise microphone /～度 noise immunity /～受话器 antinoise (*or* noise-reducing) headphone

抗战 kàngzhàn ❶ war of resistance against aggression ❷ (Kàngzhàn) (short for 抗日战争) War of Resistance Against Japanese Aggression (1937-1945): ～时期 during the Anti-Japanese War

抗张强度 kàngzhāng qiángdù *see* "抗拉强度"

抗真菌 kàngzhēnjūn antimycotic; antifungal

抗震 kàngzhèn ❶ anti-seismic; anti-quake: ～结构 〈建筑〉 anti-seismic structure /～加固 anti-quake reenforcement (of a building, etc.) /～设计 aseismatic design /～试验 shock (*or* aseismatic) test /～性能 anti-quake capability /～措施 anti-quake measure ❷ take preventive measures to reduce the loss as caused by an earthquake: ～救灾工作 earthquake relief work /防震～ prevent and reduce the loss from an earthquake

抗震建筑 kàngzhèn jiànzhù earthquake-proof construction; earthquake-resistant structure; aseismatic or anti-seismic building

抗争 kàngzhēng make a stand against; resist: 奋起～ rise to resist; rise in resistance /极力～ try one's best to make a stand against /据理～ counter on just grounds /公司太小,无法与大型跨国公司～。The firm is too small to contend with large transnational corporations.

抗肿瘤药 kàngzhǒngliúyào antineoplastic

囥 kàng 〈方言〉 hide: 你把表～哪儿了? Where have you hidden (*or* tucked away) the watch?

钪 kàng 〈化学〉 scandium (Sc)

伉 kàng ❶ 〈书面〉 (of spouse) matching or fit ❷ 〈书面〉 lofty; big and tall ❸ (Kàng) a surname

伉俪 kànglì 〈书面〉 married couple; husband and wife: ～之情 love between husband and wife /情笃～ happily married; couple very much in love /结为～ be married; become man and wife

伉直 kàngzhí 〈书面〉 upright and outspoken: 坚忍～ steadfast and upright

kāo

尻 kāo 〈古语〉 buttocks; bottom; behind: 兔去～, 狐去首。Cut off the hare's behind and the fox's head (before cooking).

尻带 kāodài breeching (for a draught animal)

尻子 kāozi 〈方言〉 buttocks; bottom

kǎo

考[1](攷) kǎo ❶ ask sb. to answer a difficult question; quiz; question: 婚前～夫婿 quiz one's prospective husband before the wedding /你把我～住了。Your question has baffled me. *or* You've got me there. ❷ give or take an examination or test: ～满分 get full marks in an exam /～大学 take college entrance examinations /～语文 have a test in Chinese /应～ sit for an examination; take an examination /补～ make-up exam /统～ unified national (*or* provincial, *or* city) examination /大～ end-of-term examination; final exam /报～ enter oneself for an examination; sign up for an examination; apply for an entrance examination /招～ admit (*or* enrol) students by examination /主～ chief examiner /你的期终考试

~得怎样? How did you do in the final examination? ❸ check; inspect: see "~勤" ❹ study; investigate; verify: 思~ deliberate; mull over /待~ remain to be verified / 参~ consult; refer to

考[2] kǎo 〈书面〉one's deceased father: 先~ my deceased father

考妣 kǎobǐ 〈书面〉deceased parents: 惶惶然如丧~ be on tenterhooks as if one had lost one's parents

考查 kǎochá check; examine: ~学习成绩 check student's work / 认真~前一段工作 make an earnest examination of our previous work

考察 kǎochá ❶ inspect; investigate on the spot: ~基地建设 inspect the building of a base /到各地~ make an inspection tour of various places /组团出国~ organize a group to go abroad on an investigation (*or* study) tour /~报告 findings of an investigation team /~团 study group; inspection team ❷ observe and study: ~问题的实质 go into the crux of the matter /在实际工作中~干部。Cadres are to be tested in practical work.

考场 kǎochǎng examination hall or room

考成 kǎochéng 〈书面〉examine and assess the work and achievements of officials; appraise or judge performance: 年终~ end-of-year assessment

考茨基主义 Kǎocíjīzhǔyì Kautskyism, the views represented by Karl Kautsky (1854-1938) of the Second International

考的松 kǎodìsōng *also* "可的松" kědìsōng 〈药学〉cortisone

考点 kǎodiǎn examination place: 这次考试全国共设二百零一个~, 三千五百三十二个考场。There are a total of 3, 532 examination rooms in 201 sites in the whole country.

考订 kǎodìng examine and correct; do textual research: ~正伪 examine and rectify the false /作者作了大量的~工作。The author has done a lot of textual research.

考分 kǎofēn result of an examination; score or mark of an examination

考工记 Kǎogōngjì *Book of Diverse Crafts*, classic work on science and technologies of ancient China, compiled towards the end of the Spring and Autumn Period

考古 kǎogǔ ❶ engage in archaeological studies: ~测量 archaeological survey /~调查 archaeological investigation /~发掘 archaeological excavation /~发现 archaeological discovery (*or* finding) /~单位 archaeological institution ❷ archaeology: 他在大学所学的专业是~。He majored in archaeology at university.

考古学 kǎogǔxué archaeology: ~家 archaeologist

考官 kǎoguān 〈旧语〉examiner: 主~ chief examiner

考核 kǎohé check; assess; appraise: 工作~ assessment (*or* appraisal) of work /一年一度的~评比 annual check and appraisal /建立定期~制度 set up a routine check-up system /~标准 assessment criteria /企业~ assessment of the performance of an enterprise; appraisal of enterprise performance

考绩 kǎojì assess or appraise staff performance: 按规定, 公司每年~两次。As a rule, the company checks the employees' performance twice a year. /工厂根据~的结果, 决定职工的升降和奖惩。The factory will decide on the promotion or demotion and reward or punishment of its employees according to the results of assessments.

考校 kǎojiào *also* "考较" examine and verify; check: 只是略微看了一眼, 没有细加~。It was only a casual look, and no detailed checking was done.

考究 kǎojiu ❶ observe and study; investigate; examine closely; research: 这本集子中收集的十八篇论文, 是作者多年潜心~的结果。The eighteen papers of this collection are the result of the author's years of research. /要仔细~同义词的差别。We should examine the delicate shades of meaning between the synonyms. ❷ fastidious; particular; choosy: 吃喝不~ not choosy about food /他对衣着一向~得很。He is always very particular about his dress. ❸ exquisite; fine: 用料~ made of high-quality fabric /这条街上有一家装饰~, 环境优雅的咖啡馆。There is on this street an exquisitely decorated coffee house with beautiful surroundings.

考据 kǎojù textual criticism; textual research: 作者在这方面的~, 有一定的深度和广度。The author did quite extensive and thorough textual research in this field.

考卷 kǎojuàn examination paper; test paper

考克 kǎokè *also* "旋塞" xuánsāi 〈机械〉(transliteration) cock

考课 kǎokè 〈书面〉see "考绩"

考拉 kǎolā *also* "树袋熊" shùdàixióng koala

考量 kǎoliang consider; ponder; mull over: 我已经~过了, 迟早得照他的意思办。I have already given it some thought; sooner or later, we'll have to do as he wishes.

考虑 kǎolǜ consider; think over; deliberate: ~成熟后再行动 take action after mature (*or* careful) consideration /出自人道主义的~ out of humanitarian considerations /这种要求不予~。We will not consider such a demand. /他们提出了一个供大家~的方案。They put forward a plan for deliberation. /正在~旅行路线问题。The problem of itinerary is now under study.

考掠 kǎolüè 〈书面〉torture during interrogation: 重加~ subject to severe torture during interrogation

考评 kǎopíng assess and evaluate: 通过~决定官员的聘任 appoint officials based on assessment and evaluation

考期 kǎoqī date of examination: ~临近, 必须加紧准备。The exam date is drawing near, and we must step up our preparation.

考勤 kǎoqín check on work attendance: 记~ register work attendance; record the attendance / ~簿 attendance record / ~卡 attendance card / 车间对~抓得很紧。The workshop is very strict with attendance.

考勤钟 kǎoqínzhōng telltale (clock); time-clock: 上班时工人们都要在~上刷卡。Workers have to punch the clock when they come on shift.

考求 kǎoqiú explore; probe; seek; search after: ~真谛 seek truth

考区 kǎoqū area or regional examination centre; examination division: 成都~ Chengdu Area Examination Centre /计有二十一个考场, 分为三个~。There are 21 examination rooms under three examination divisions.

考取 kǎoqǔ pass an entrance examination; be admitted to school or college (after an examination): 他在国外同时~了两所院校, 而且校方都同意给奖学金。He has been admitted to two colleges abroad with a promise from each to provide a scholarship.

考生 kǎoshēng candidate for an entrance examination; examinee: ~须知 notice to examinees

考试 kǎoshì examination; test: 参加~ take an examination; sit for an examination /举行~ hold an examination /~成绩 examination result; examination score; examination mark /托福~ TOEFL /大学入学~ college entrance examination /期末~ end-of-term examination; final (*or* terminal) exam /期中~ mid-term examination /学年~ year-end examination /~成绩优良 pass an exam with good grades (*or* with distinction)/~及格 pass an examination; get a pass /~刚及格 scrape through (an exam) /~不及格 fail (in) an examination; fall down on an exam; flunk /~制度 examination system /~方法 method of examination /通过~入学 be admitted upon (*or* after an) examination

考试院 Kǎoshìyuàn Examination *Yuan* (China before 1949)

考释 kǎoshì do textual research and make explanations; study and explain textual material: 他潜心于~甲骨文, 成果甚丰。He achieved fruitful results from intensive study of bone and carapace inscriptions.

考题 kǎotí examination question; examination paper: 他们让我负责出~。They asked me to set the examination paper. /~难易适度。The examination questions are framed at an appropriate level of difficulty.

考问 kǎowèn examine orally; question: 仔细~ question sb. closely

考验 kǎoyàn test; trial; ordeal: 久经~的外交官 long-tested (*or* tried-and-true) diplomat /经历可怕的~ pass through a terrible ordeal /经不住时间的~ cannot stand the test of time /他们在革命战争中经受过严峻的~。They have gone through the severe trial of revolutionary wars.

考语 kǎoyǔ 〈旧语〉comments or appraisal remarks (on work)

考证 kǎozhèng ❶ textual criticism; textual research ❷ engage in textual research and criticism; find as a result of research: 这位学者探微发幽, 旁征博引, ~出《红楼梦》的作者是曹雪芹。After painstaking and meticulous research and citing copiously from many sources, the scholar found that Cao Xueqin wrote *A Dream of Red Mansions*.

考中 kǎozhòng pass an examination; be admitted to (a college, etc.) through examination: ~北大数学系 pass the entrance examinations and be admitted to the Department of Mathematics of Peking University

烤 kǎo ❶ bake; roast; toast: ~白薯 bake sweet potatoes /

我喜欢吃～馒头。I like toasted steamed buns. /快把湿衣服脱下～干。Take off your wet clothes and dry them by the fire. ❷ warm oneself (by a fire or some other heat source):太阳热得～人。The sun is scorchingly (*or* baking) hot. *or* The sun is hot enough to fry your hide.

烤钵 kǎobō 〈冶金〉cupel:～冶金法 cupellation

烤茶机 kǎochájī tea dryer

烤电 kǎodiàn 〈医学〉diathermy

烤麸 kǎofū steamed gluten:～烧肉 pork cooked with steamed gluten

烤火 kǎohuǒ warm oneself by a fire:～费 heating fee; heating cost /请进屋烤烤火吧! Please come into the house and warm yourself by the fire!

烤架 kǎojià gridiron

烤蓝 kǎolán *also* "发蓝" fālán 〈工美〉blue baking finish

烤炉 kǎolú oven

烤面包 kǎomiànbāo toasted bread; toast:一片～ a slice of toast / ～架 toast rack /～器 toaster

烤漆 kǎoqī stove varnish

烤肉 kǎoròu barbecue; roast meat; roast:～签 brochette /～叉 skewer; spit /星期日美美地吃上一顿～。Let's have a nice roast (*or* barbecue) for Sunday dinner.

烤乳猪 kǎorǔzhū roast suckling pig

烤箱 kǎoxiāng oven; toaster

烤鸭 kǎoyā roast duck:北京～ roast Beijing duck /～店 roast duck restaurant

烤芽 kǎoyá accelerate the germination of seeds

烤烟 kǎoyān flue-cured tobacco:～卷烟 Virginian-type cigarette / ～叶 flue-cured tobacco

烤羊肉串 kǎoyángròuchuàn mutton shish kebab (a common snack food)

烤炙 kǎozhì (sun or heat) scorch:炎夏的太阳～着大地。The hot summer sun is scorching the earth.

栲 kǎo 〈植物〉evergreen chinquapin

栲胶 kǎojiāo tannin extract:～浸提器 tannin extractor

栲栳 kǎolǎo *also* "筹箸" kǎolǎo; "笆斗" bādǒu wicker basket

拷 kǎo flog; beat; torture

拷贝 kǎobèi (transliteration) copy:～机 copying press /～铅笔 copying pencil

拷贝纸 kǎobèizhǐ copy paper; copying paper

拷绸 kǎochóu *also* "黑胶绸" hēijiāochóu rust-coloured summer silk; gambiered Guangdong silk

拷打 kǎodǎ flog; beat; torture:在狱中,他多次受到～。He was tortured many times while in prison.

拷花 kǎohuā 〈纺织〉embossing:～布 embossed cloth

拷掠 kǎolüè *also* "考掠" kǎolüè 〈书面〉torture during interrogation

拷纱 kǎoshā *also* "香云纱" xiāngyúnshā 〈纺织〉gambiered Guangdong gauze

拷问 kǎowèn torture during interrogation; interrogate with torture:严刑～ subject sb. to severe torture during interrogation

筹 kǎo

筹箸 kǎolǎo *see* "栲栳" kǎolǎo

kào

铐 kào ❶ handcuffs:上～ put handcuffs on sb. /戴着手～脚镣 be shackled in handcuffs and chains ❷ put handcuffs on sb.; handcuff:把他～起来。Handcuff him. *or* Cuff him.

铐子 kàozi 〈方言〉handcuffs

靠[1] kào ❶ (of sb.) lean:～着墙 lean against the wall /我只能～在桌子上休息一会儿。I could only lean on a desk for a rest. /犯人们背～背坐着。The criminals sat back to back. ❷ (of sth.) lean or stand against:把扁担～在门背后 lean the shoulder pole against the back of the door /伞～在椅背上。The umbrella stood against the back of a chair. ❸ keep to; get near; come up to; near:车辆～右行驶。All vehicles keep to the right. /我到的时候,船已经～码头了。The ship had already docked when I arrived. /他们昨天参观了一家～海的工厂。Yesterday they went to visit a factory by the sea. ❹ depend on; rely on:～自己想办法 be left to one's own devices /他～自己的努力读完了大学。He finished college by relying on his own efforts. *or* He worked his way through college. ❺ trust:可～ reliable; trustworthy

靠[2] kào 〈戏曲〉military officer's armour:扎～ armour worn by a military officer

靠岸 kào'àn pull in to shore; draw alongside:～天数 lay days /～条款 shore clause /船～时,已是夜里十点了。It was already 10 p.m. when the ship drew alongside. /船～行驶。The boat hugged the coast.

靠把 kàobǎ *also* "靠背" 〈戏曲〉stage armour:～武生 actor in stage armour playing a martial role in Chinese opera /～戏 performance by such actors

靠傍 kàobàng 〈方言〉rely on; depend on:不～别人 not depend on others

靠背 kàobèi ❶ back (of a chair):椅子的～坏了。The back of the chair is out of order. ❷ 〈戏曲〉*see* "靠把"

靠背轮 kàobèilún *also* "离合器" líhéqì clutch

靠背椅 kàobèiyǐ chair

靠边 kàobiān ❶ keep to the side:车辆～停。All cars should stop along the roadside. /行人～走。Pedestrians should keep to the side (of the road). ❷ 〈方言〉reasonable; sensible; relevant:你这话说得还～儿。Now you've said something sensible. /不～的话,少说! Cut out all irrelevant ranting.

靠边儿站 kàobiānrzhàn stand aside; get out of the way; (be forced to) leave the post; lose power:请～! Please step aside! /他已经～两年了。He was put out to pasture two years ago.

靠泊 kàobó (of a ship) stop; anchor; berth:挖泥船～在码头附近的江面上。The dredger anchored in the river by the dock.

靠不住 kàobuzhù unreliable; undependable; untrustworthy:这话～。This story is unreliable. /这种～的人怎能承担这么重要的工作? How can such an untrustworthy person be given so important a task?

靠常 kàocháng 〈方言〉often; frequently:店里～总住着十来个人。Often there are about a dozen people staying at the inn.

靠得住 kàodezhù reliable; dependable; trustworthy:我认为他这话～。I think what he said is true. /这人～。He is a dependable person.

靠垫 kàodiàn cushion:沙发～ cushion for a sofa /～很厚的坐椅 deep-cushioned chair

靠伏 kàofú lean on; lean against:他～在栏杆上,观赏水中游鱼。Leaning on the railing, he was enjoying the swimming fish in the water.

靠耩 kàojiǎng *also* "靠耧" overlap drill-sowing over the edge of a sown strip

靠接 kàojiē 〈植物〉grafting by approach; inarching:插～ cutting inarching /割裂～ inarching by cleaving

靠近 kàojìn ❶ near; close to; by:动物园～我们学院。The zoo is near our college. /他们俩坐得十分～。The two of them sat very close to each other. ❷ draw near; approach:船正向码头～。The ship was approaching the wharf. /火车已经～车站。The train is pulling into the station.

靠拢 kàolǒng draw close; close up:向我～! Close up! /向左～! Left close! /小船慢慢～过来,船上的人也都看清了。The boat gradually drew close to us and the passengers on board were clearly visible. /你们必须向人民～。You must identify yourselves with the people.

靠耧 kàolóu *see* "靠耩"

靠模 kàomó 〈机械〉profiling; copying:～铣床 profiling (*or* copying) milling machine /～车床 copying lathe /～夹具 profiling attachment /～板 master plate

靠盘儿 kàopánr 〈方言〉feel certain; be reliable:干这种活儿～。I'm sure I can handle the job.

靠谱 kàopǔ reasonable; sound:这人说话不～,不能听他的。What this man said doesn't sound right. Forget it.

靠旗 kàoqí 〈戏曲〉pennants worn at the back of a warrior in Chinese opera

靠山 kàoshān backer; patron; backing:他在公司里有～。He's got strong backing in the company. /那年头,一个人在外混事,不能不找个

K

～。In those days, one had to find a patron in order to get along in society.

靠山吃山，靠水吃水 kào shān chī shān, kào shuǐ chī shuǐ those living on a mountain live off the mountain; those living near the water live off the water — make use of local resources

靠山临水 kàoshān-línshuǐ *also*“依山傍水” yīshān-bàngshuǐ hard by the hills and overlooking the water; with hills at the back and the water in the front：这小村子～，风景秀美。This small village is picturesquely located near between a mountain and a river.

靠身 kàoshēn 〈方言〉❶ sb. to depend on; provider：她养下一个好闺女，老来有了～。Having brought up a good daughter, she will have a provider when she gets old. ❷（～儿）next to the skin; tight：新做的小棉袄紧～儿。The newly-made padded petticoat fits tight.

靠实 kàoshi 〈方言〉❶ really; actually：他连续忙了几天，也～疲倦了。He has been up to his neck in work for several days running and is really tired out. ❷ reliable; dependable; trustworthy：孩子还小，家里得有个～的帮手。As the child is still young, we need a reliable helper in the house. ❸（of mood）composed; assured; at ease：只要他肯担保，我就～了。I'm at ease so long as he is willing to provide sponsorship.

靠手 kàoshǒu （of a chair）armrest; handrest

靠天吃饭 kàotiān-chīfàn depend on Heaven for（one's）food; live at the mercy of the weather or elements

靠头 kàotou backer; patron; backing; support：有了～ find support /没个～ have no backing /找个～ look for a patron

靠托 kàotuō rely on; depend on; expect：圆满完成任务就～这最后的几天。We depend on these last few days to fulfil our task. /有个好邻居，看门户也有～。A good neighbour may help keep watch on your house for you when you are out.

靠椅 kàoyǐ 〈方言〉chair

靠枕 kàozhěn back cushion：新买的～很舒适。The back cushion I bought lately is very comfortable.

靠准 kàozhǔn 〈方言〉reliable; dependable; trustworthy：这条消息不一定～。This information might not be reliable. /我这个朋友很～，你尽可以信任他。This friend of mine is very trustworthy. You can place yourself entirely in his hands.

熇（焅） kào stew a fish or meat dish until the gravy or sauce becomes thick：～大虾 stewed prawns

犒 kào reward with food and drink

犒劳 kàolao ❶ reward with food and drink：沿途的百姓，用好酒好饭～子弟兵。People along the way took out their best wine and food to feast the soldiers who fought for them. ❷ rewarded food and drink：吃～ enjoy rewarded food and drink

犒赏 kàoshǎng reward a victorious army, etc., with bounties：～三军 feast and offer bounties to the army /特加～ give special rewards

犒师 kàoshī 〈书面〉reward an army with food and drink：遣使者～ send an envoy to reward the army with food and drink /献牛酒～ present beef and wine to reward the army

kē

颏 kē （generally known as 下巴 or 下巴颏儿）chin
see also ké

颏勒嗉 kēlesù 〈方言〉Adam's apple

榼 kē 〈古语〉ancient vessel for wine or water

榼藤子 kēténgzǐ *also* “眼镜豆” yǎnjìngdòu 〈植物〉*Entada phaseoloides*, whose vines and seeds are used as herbal medicine

磕（搕） kē ❶ knock（against sth. hard）：～掉了门牙 have one's front teeth knocked out /膝盖～破了皮 graze（*or* scrape）one's knee /脑袋上～了个包 get a bump on one's head /小男孩滑了一跤，头正好～在一块石头上。The little boy slipped, knocking his head right against a rock. /洗这些杯子时小心点儿，别～了边。Mind you don't chip any of the glasses when you wash them. ❷ knock（sth. out of a container）; knock out：～烟斗 knock out one's pipe /～掉鞋底的泥 knock the mud off shoes

磕巴 kēba 〈方言〉❶ stutter; stammer：这孩子说话～。The child speaks with a stutter. ❷ one who stammers; stammerer

磕打 kēda knock; knock out：把提包上的土～掉。Knock the dirt off the handbag.

磕磕绊绊 kēke-bànbàn ❶ stumble; limp; walk with difficulty：他才两岁，走路还～的。The baby is only two years old and still walks unsteadily（*or* toddles）. ❷ bumpy; rough：～的山路 rugged mountain path /这路怎么～的！What a bumpy road! ❸ hindrance; difficulty; setback：工作中免不了～。Difficulties and setbacks are only to be expected in one's work.

磕磕撞撞 kēke-zhuàngzhuàng stagger along; stumble; reel：他喝得半醉，～地回了家。He stumbled home half drunk.

磕碰 kēpèng ❶ knock against; bump against; collide with：玻璃器皿要用纸板垫一下，免得搬运时～了。Pack some cardboard round the glassware so that the pieces will not bump（*or* knock）against each other during transport. /这些碗盘一路上磕磕碰碰的，居然一个也没碎。These plates and bowls have been bumped about all the way. It's a miracle that none of them is broken. /衣架放在过道上，进进出出总是～。The clothes tree stands in the corridor, so people often bump against it when walking by. ❷ clash; squabble：这些人住在一个院子里，生活上出现一些～是难免的。For people living in the same compound, friction over petty matters is hardly avoidable in their everyday life.

磕碰儿 kēpengr 〈方言〉❶ chip in a utensil：小心！酒瓶口上有个～。Take care! There's a chip in the mouth of the wine bottle. ❷ setback; frustration：谁一辈子没有点～！Who can be entirely free from setbacks in life?

磕头 kētóu kowtow; bump one's head to the ground in obeisance：～如捣蒜 *kowtow* again and again（to beg for sb.'s mercy or express one's gratitude）

磕头虫 kētóuchóng *also*“叩头虫” kòutóuchóng snapping beetle

磕头碰脑 kētóu-pèngnǎo ❶ bump against things on every side（when cluttered together）; push and bump against each other（in a crowd）：别担心，这么大的孩子有时候免不了要～的。Don't worry, a child of his age does bump himself sometimes. /一大群人～地挤着看热闹。A big crowd of people pushed and bumped against one another to get a glimpse of the fun. ❷ rub elbows（with each other）; often see; frequently meet：他们都住一个院儿，成天～的。Living in the same courtyard, they are encountering each other all the time. ❸ clash or conflict between people：他是个热心人，街坊邻里有个～的事，他都出面调停。He is a warm-hearted man and often acts as a mediator whenever conflicts occur in the neighbourhood.

磕膝盖 kēxīgài 〈方言〉knee

磕牙 kēyá 〈方言〉chat; banter：闲～ engage in chitchat

嗑 kē 〈方言〉words; talk; chat：唠～ have a chat（*or* talk）/他的嘴老不闲着，～真多！He's holding forth all day long; he never seems to run out of words!
see also kè

瞌 kē

瞌眈 kēchong 〈方言〉sleep; doze：打～ be sleepy; doze off; nod off /～几分钟 doze for a few minutes; take forty winks

瞌睡 kēshuì sleepy; drowsy：打～ be sleepy; doze off; nod off /我昨晚熬夜了，今天～得很。I stayed up late last night and feel terribly sleepy today.

瞌睡虫 kēshuìchóng ❶（as used in traditional stories）sleep-inducing insect：他刚看一会儿书，～就上来了。Hardly had he read for a few minutes when sleep stole over him. ❷ sleepyhead

疴 kē （formerly pronounced ē）〈书面〉illness：养～ recover from an illness; recuperate /沉～不起 unlikely to recover from a severe and lingering illness

珂 kē 〈书面〉❶ jade-like stone ❷ ornament on a bridle

珂罗版 kēluóbǎn *also*“珂啰版” collotype：～印刷 collotype printing

坷 kē
see also kě

坷垃 kēla *also*“坷拉”〈方言〉clod：打土～ break clods

苛 kē ❶ harsh; severe; rigorous; exacting: 对方提出的条件太～了。The terms offered by the other side (*or* party) are much too harsh. ❷ overelaborate; tedious: ～礼 overelaborate ritual

苛暴 kēbào 〈书面〉harsh and cruel; relentless; tyrannical: ～之吏 harsh and cruel official /为政～ rule tyrannically

苛察 kēchá 〈书面〉exacting; faultfinding; overcritical: 他自以为很精明，其实过于～。He considers himself observant and astute; in fact, he is overcritical (*or* too picky).

苛待 kēdài treat harshly; be hard upon: 你太～他了。You are a bit too hard on him.

苛毒 kēdú harsh and vicious; venomous: ～小人 base person; villain

苛化 kēhuà 〈化学〉causticize: ～剂 causticizer; causticizing agent / ～氢化法 caustic hydride process / ～作用 causticization

苛捐杂税 kējuān-záshuì exorbitant taxes and levies; multifarious and onerous taxes

苛刻 kēkè harsh; relentless; mean and exacting: 这样～的条件，我们无论如何不能接受。We can never accept such harsh terms. /不要对下级太～啦。Don't be so hard on (*or* harsh to) your subordinates. / 他这样对待你未免太～了。It was mean of him to treat you so shabbily.

苛酷 kēkù harsh and relentless; ruthless: 为人～ ruthless by nature

苛虐 kēnüè 〈书面〉harsh and cruel; relentless; tyrannical: 政治～ tyrannical politics

苛求 kēqiú make excessive demands; be exacting; be overcritical: 他们都是新手，不能过于～。They are all greenhorns. You shouldn't be so exacting (*or* demanding).

苛求无厌 kēqiú-wúyàn make endless, excessive demands; be insatiably greedy: ～的暴君 tyrant who makes endless, excessive demands; insatiable tyrant /～的贪官 insatiably greedy official

苛细 kēxì 〈书面〉severe and exacting: 这个规则搞得太～。This rule is overelaborate and too exacting.

苛性 kēxìng 〈化学〉causticity

苛性钾 kēxìngjiǎ caustic potash

苛性碱 kēxìngjiǎn caustic alkali

苛性钠 kēxìngnà caustic soda or sodium

苛杂 kēzá 〈书面〉exorbitant taxes and levies: 免除～ repeal exorbitant taxes

苛责 kēzé criticize severely; excoriate: 这个老板脾气急躁，出一点儿小错也要遭到他的～。The boss is irascible. He'll give you a good dressing-down for a petty fault.

苛政 kēzhèng tyrannical or oppressive government: 反抗～ revolt against tyranny

苛政猛于虎 kēzhèng měngyú hǔ oppressive government is fiercer than a tiger; tyranny is worse than a tiger

苛重 kēzhòng (of taxes, etc.) onerous; exorbitant: ～的租税 onerous rents and taxes

柯 kē ❶〈书面〉stalk; branch; bough: 交～错叶 with branches intertwined and leaves touching each other ❷〈书面〉axe-handle; helve ❸ (Kē) a surname

柯尔克孜族 Kē'ěrkèzīzú Kirgiz nationality, living mainly in the Xinjiang Uygur Autonomous Region

柯立芝 Kēlìzhī John Calvin Coolidge (1872-1933), 30th President of the US (1923-1929)

柯西 Kēxī Augustin-Louis Cauchy (1789-1857), French mathematician: ～定理 Cauchy's theorem

柯西金 Kēxījīn Alexsei Nikolayevich Kosygin (1904-1980), Soviet leader who succeeded Khrushchev as Prime Minister in 1964

砢 kē

砢碜 kēchen 〈方言〉❶ ugly; unsightly ❷ disgraceful; shabby ❸ ridicule; make a fool of
see also "寒碜" hánchen

轲 kē *used in personal names*: 孟～ Meng Ke (known in the West as Mencius, c. 372 - c. 289 BC)
see also kě

钶 kē 〈化学〉(now known as 铌) columbium (Cb)

匼 kē 〈旧语〉kerchief

匼匝 kēzā 〈书面〉surround; encircle

窠 kē nest; burrow: 在树上做～ make a nest in a tree /蜂～ beehive

窠巢 kēcháo bird's nest; nest

窠臼 kējiù 〈书面〉set pattern (of writing or other artistic work); convention: 不落～ not be bound by conventions; show originality; be unconventional /我们要摆脱前人的～，独创一格。We must break with old patterns to create a style of our own.

棵 kē 〈量词〉*usu. used of plants*: 一～白菜 a head of cabbage /两～树 two trees /三～树苗 three saplings /一～草 a cluster of grass

棵儿 kēr size (of plants): 我要买那边～大的几棵大白菜。I want to buy those big Chinese cabbages over there.

棵子 kēzi 〈方言〉stem or stalk (of crops): 高粱的～比谷子高多了。Sorghum stalks are much taller than millet stalks. *or* Sorghum grows much taller than millet.

颗 kē 〈量词〉*used of grains and grain-like things*: 一～豌豆 a pea /五～珍珠 five pearls /～～汗珠 drops (*or* beads) of sweat

颗粒 kēlì ❶ anything small and roundish: 粗～的盐 crude salt /这些药丸的～怎么不一样大? How come these pellets are different in size? ❷ (of cereals) each grain: ～归仓 get every grain to the granary; harvest every single grain /～无收 total crop failure

颗粒肥料 kēlì féiliào granulated fertilizer

颗粒物质 kēlì wùzhì particle; particulate matter

颗粒细胞 kēlì xìbāo granular cell

髁 kē 〈生理〉condyle

稞 kē

稞麦 kēmài *also* "青稞" qīngkē highland barley

科[1] kē ❶ branch of academic or vocational activity; subject of instruction or study; discipline; department: 学～ branch of study; discipline /文～ humanities; liberal arts /理～ sciences; natural sciences /工～ engineering; technology /本～ undergraduate programme /专～ vocational study; special course of study /内～ (department of) internal medicine; medical department /外～ (department of) surgery /小儿～ paediatrics department /妇产～ obstetrics and gynecology department /眼～ ophthalmology department /牙～ dental department /耳鼻喉～ ENT (ear-nose-throat) department / 泌尿～ urology department /皮肤～ dermatology department /骨～ orthopedics department /神经～ neurology department /胸外～ thoracic surgery department /心脏外～ department of cardiac surgery / 矫形外～ orthopedic surgery department /创伤外～ traumatology department /麻醉～ anaesthesiology department /百～全书 encyclopedia ❷ administrative section: 人事～ personnel section /财务～ finance section /总务～ general affairs section /～级干部 cadre at the rank of section chief ❸ imperial civil examinations; subject in such examinations: 登～ pass the imperial civil examinations; obtain degrees in the imperial examinations ❹ old-type Chinese opera school; regular professional training: 坐～ undergo professional training at an old-type Chinese opera school ❺〈生物〉family: 蔷薇～ rose family /豆～植物 plant of the bean family; legume /猫～动物 animal of the cat family; feline

科[2] kē 〈书面〉❶ law; rule: 金～玉律 golden rule and precious precept /犯有前～ have a criminal record ❷ impose (a punishment, etc.); pass (a sentence): ～罪 impose a punishment on sb.; punish sb.

科[3] kē (in classical Chinese scenario or libretto) stage directions for actions: 笑～ laughs /饮酒～ drinks wine

科白 kēbái 〈戏曲〉actions and spoken parts

科班 kēbān ❶ old-type traditional opera school ❷ regular professional training

K

科班出身 kēbān chūshēn have received regular professional training; be a professional by training：搞医务工作最好是～。A medical worker should undergo regular professional training.
科场 kēchǎng place where an imperial civil examination was held; imperial examination site：～不利 have no success in the imperial civil examinations
科处 kēchǔ impose (a punishment); sentence：～徒刑 sentence sb. to imprisonment
科第 kēdì grading of successful candidates in the imperial civil examinations
科斗 kēdǒu *also*“蝌蚪”kēdǒu tadpole
科斗文 kēdǒuwén *also*“科斗字”tadpole characters — ancient Chinese script painted on bamboo slips (resembling tadpoles in their top-heavy shape)
科尔沁草原 Kē'ěrqìn Cǎoyuán Horqin Grassland, in the east of the Inner Mongolian Autonomous Region
科罚 kēfá 〈书面〉impose a punishment：违者～。Violators (of a regulation, etc.) shall be punished.
科幻 kēhuàn (short for 科学幻想) science fiction：～小说 science fiction (novel)
科幻片 kēhuànpiàn science fiction film or movie
科诨 kēhùn comic talk or action inserted in a traditional opera
科技 kējì science and technology：～情报 scientific and technological information /～规划 programme (*or* plan) for the development of science and technology /～大学 university of science and technology /～术语 scientific and technical terminology /～人才 scientific research and technological personnel /～界 scientific and technological circles /～工作者 person engaged in science and technology; scientist and technician /～兴农 invigorate agriculture by applying science and technology
科甲 kējiǎ (in the Han and Tang dynasties) top grade in the imperial civil examinations; imperial civil examinations：～出身 have passed the imperial examinations (esp. at the palace or provincial level); hold a degree for passing such examinations
科教 kējiào (short for 科学教育) science and education：～兴国 make the country strong through science and education
科教片 kējiàopiàn (short for 科学教育影片) science education film; popular science film or TV programme
科举 kējǔ imperial civil examinations：废～、办学校 abolish the imperial civil examinations and establish modern schools
科举制度 kējǔ zhìdù imperial civil examination system, introduced during the Sui and Tang dynasties, generally held once every three years with subjects varying from dynasty to dynasty, and officially abolished in 1905
科利尔百科全书 Kēlì'ěr Bǎikē Quánshū Collier's Encyclopedia, published in 24 volumes in 1950 in the United States
科敛 kēliǎn 〈书面〉extort (money, etc.); collect (taxes, etc.)：～钱粮 extort money and grain /～繁重 impose onerous levies and taxes
科伦坡 Kēlúnpō Colombo, capital of Sri Lanka
科伦坡计划 Kēlúnpō Jìhuà Colombo Plan, a development plan started in 1951 covering south and southeast Asia with the participation of some developed countries
科盲 kēmáng person who is ignorant of science; "science-illiterate"：在信息社会里，～如何能经营企业? How can those who have no scientific knowledge run enterprises in an information society?
科名 kēmíng official rank won by a successful candidate in the imperial examinations
科摩罗 Kēmóluó Comoros：～人 Comoran; Comorian /～群岛 Comoros Islands
科目 kēmù ❶ subject (in a curriculum); course：必修～ obligatory (*or* compulsory) course /选修～ elective (*or* optional) course /五个～要进行期末考试。Examinations in five courses will be given at the end of the term. ❷ headings in an account book ❸ grades of successful candidates in imperial civil examinations
科尼亚克酒 kēníyàkèjiǔ cognac, a high-quality brandy distilled in Cognac in western France
科派 kēpài 〈书面〉apportion (levies, etc.); collect (money, etc.) officially：～捐款 collect money through official channels
科普 kēpǔ (short for 科学普及) popular science：～读物 popular science reader (*or* book)
科室 kēshì administrative or technical offices (of a factory or enterprise); units at section or office level：～人员 office staff (*or* personnel) /精简～ reduce and restructure administrative and technical offices
科坛 kētán scientific circles：～新秀 promising young scientist
科特迪瓦 Kētèdíwǎ Côte d'Ivoire (also known as Ivory Coast), francophone West African country
科头跣足 kētóu-xiǎnzú 〈书面〉bareheaded and barefooted
科威特 Kēwēitè Kuwait：～人 Kuwaiti
科西嘉 Kēxījiā Corsica, a French island off the west coast of Italy：～人 Corsican
科协 kēxié (short for 科技协会) association of science and technology
科刑 kēxíng 〈书面〉impose or mete out a punishment; sentence：定罪～ judge (*or* pronounce) sb. guilty (of a crime) and sentence him or her accordingly
科学 kēxué ❶ science：～知识 scientific knowledge /～文献 scientific literature /～研究 scientific research /～实验 scientific experiment /～史 history of science /～技术合作协定 agreement on scientific and technical (*or* technological) cooperation /理论～ pure science /应用～ applied science /自然～ natural (*or* physical) sciences; hard sciences /社会～ social sciences /人文～ humanities /基础～ fundamental (*or* basic) sciences /信息～ information science /软～ soft science /尖端～ top science /边缘～ frontier science ❷ scientific：这种说法很不～。This statement is not at all scientific.
科学城 kēxuéchéng district (in a city) or town for scientific and technological institutions
科学共产主义 kēxué gòngchǎnzhǔyì scientific communism
科学幻想小说 kēxué huànxiǎng xiǎoshuō (popular) science fiction
科学技术 kēxué jìshù science and technology：～是第一生产力。Science and technology are primary productive forces.
科学技术部 kēxué-jìshùbù Ministry of Science and Technology
科学家 kēxuéjiā scientist
科学教育影片 kēxué jiàoyù yǐngpiàn *see*“科教片”
科学社会主义 kēxué shèhuìzhǔyì scientific socialism
科学学 kēxuéxué science studies; scienology
科学院 kēxuéyuàn academy of sciences：中国～ Chinese Academy of Sciences; Academia Sinica /中国社会～ Chinese Academy of Social Sciences
科学哲学 kēxué zhéxué philosophy of science
科研 kēyán (short for 科学研究) scientific research：～规划 plan for scientific research /～成果 findings of scientific research; achievements in scientific research /～机构 scientific research institute /～人员 scientific research personnel /～项目 scientific research project /～课题 research topic /独创性的～ original research /～考察船 research ship /搞～ do research
科员 kēyuán member of an administrative section; section member
科长 kēzhǎng section chief

蝌 kē

蝌蚪 kēdǒu tadpole
蝌蚪文 kēdǒuwén *see*“科斗文”kēdǒuwén
蝌子 kēzi 〈方言〉tadpole

轲 kē

轲垃 kēla *also*“坷垃”kēla clod of earth

ké

颏 ké

see“红点颏”hóngdiǎnké；“蓝点颏”lándiǎnké
see also kē

咳 ké

cough：干～ dry cough /百日～ whooping cough /～了一下 give a cough /～得很厉害 have a bad cough /血都～出来了 cough up blood /～得嗓子都哑了 cough oneself hoarse
see also hāi
咳喘 kéchuǎn asthmatic cough
咳呛 kéqiàng 〈方言〉choking cough; cough
咳嗽 késou cough：～药 cough drops; cough medicine /阵发性～

K

spasmodic cough /令人窒息的～ choking cough /断断续续的～ staccato cough /痉挛性～ convulsive cough /～有痰 bring up phlegm when coughing
咳嗽糖浆 késou tángjiāng cough syrup

壳(殼) ké ❶ shell:花生～ peanut shell /子弹～ bullet shell /脑～ skull ❷〈机械〉housing; casing; case:涡轮～ turbine casing /护～ protective (*or* protecting) case
see also qiào
壳朗猪 kélangzhū 〈方言〉feeder pig
壳体 kétǐ shell:～铸件 shell casting
壳体结构 kétǐ jiégòu shell-structure
壳体理论 kétǐ lǐlùn shell theory
壳型 kéxíng 〈冶金〉shell mould; shell:～造型 shell moulding /～铸件 shell casting

揢 ké 〈方言〉❶ get stuck; wedge:衣柜门～住了,拉不开。The wardrobe door has got stuck. It won't open. /鞋小～脚。The shoes are so small that they pinch my feet. ❷ create difficulties; make things difficult:他总是想法～我。He is always trying to make things difficult for me.

kě

渴 kě ❶ thirsty; dry:口～ be thirsty; be dry (for a drink) /解～ quench one's thirst /饥～难忍 hungry and thirsty beyond endurance; famished and parched /～死了 be dying for a drink; die of thirst /临～掘井 not start digging a well until one is thirsty; not do sth. until it is too late; be lacking in foresight ❷ yearningly; eagerly
渴笔 kěbǐ (in traditional painting or calligraphy) "dry stroke" — stroke drawn with little ink
渴待 kědài expect eagerly or yearningly:大伙儿都瞪大了眼睛,～他开口说话。Everybody was looking wide-eyed and expectantly at him to speak up.
渴慕 kěmù admire greatly:怀着～的心情 with great admiration /我对你～已久。I have admired you greatly for a long time.
渴念 kěniàn yearn for; long for; miss:～你早日归来 yearn for your early return
渴盼 kěpàn look forward to; expect eagerly; hope earnestly for:～家乡早日现代化 look forward eagerly to the time when one's hometown is modernized; hope earnestly for the modernization of one's hometown
渴求 kěqiú hope earnestly for; hunger for; strive for:～帮助 earnestly solicit help /～解放 long for liberation /～知识 hanker after knowledge; have a thirst for knowledge /这是他～已久的职位。This is a position he has long aspired to.
渴睡 kěshuì be sleepy; be drowsy:～时就不要再学习了。Don't study any more if you're sleepy.
渴望 kěwàng long for; thirst for; yearn for:～复仇 thirst for revenge /～已久 have long awaited (sth.) eagerly /老人～返回故乡。The old man yearned to return to his native place. /我～着新年的到来。I was looking forward to the New Year holidays.
渴想 kěxiǎng long for; miss very much:～离家已久的儿子 miss one's long-absent son very much
渴仰 kěyǎng 〈书面〉admire profoundly; look up to

可[1] kě ❶ approve; agree:认～ approve /不置～否 decline to comment; be noncommittal ❷ can; may:～进～退 be free to press forward or back out; can either attack or retreat /～大～小 may be big or small; may be serious or light /～杀而不～辱 you can kill (sb.) but not insult (him); (sb.) would rather die than be humiliated /～意会而不～言传 can be appreciated but not clearly defined; defy analysis (*or* description) /你～把我的想法告诉他。You may as well tell him what I think. /不～这样乱讲。You shouldn't talk such rubbish. ❸ (often used with a monosyllabic verb to form an adjectival phrase) need (doing); be worth (doing):这出戏～看。The play is worth seeing. /我没什么～说的。I have nothing to say. ❹〈书面〉about; some:年～二十 about twenty years of age /长～七尺 some seven *chi* in length ❺〈方言〉go as far as is possible; make the best or most of; make do:～嗓子喊 shout at the top of one's voice /他疼得～地打滚儿。He rolled all over the place in pain. ❻ (usu. used in the early vernacular) be fully recovered (from an illness):待你病～后商量。We won't discuss it until you get well again. ❼ (Kě) a surname

可[2] kě 〈副词〉❶ but; yet:我本想去,～天太冷。I meant to go, but it was too cold. /做得虽不是太好,～她已经尽了最大的努力了。That was not very satisfactory, but she did her best. /～事儿没那么容易。Well, things are not that easy. ❷ *used for emphasis*:他～真是个大好人。He is really kind-hearted. /你～把钱带来了! So you've brought the money with you. /～别忘了。Mind you don't forget it. /～把我给累坏了。I am practically worn out. ❸ *used in a rhetorical question for emphasis*:这么大的北京城,～上哪儿去找他呀? Beijing is such a big city. Where on earth should we find him? ❹ *used in a question to emphasize doubt*:这件事他～同意? Has he really approved of this? /你～曾跟父亲商量过? Have you actually discussed this with father?

可[3] kě fit; suit:～人意 agreeable to one; just what one wants /这回真是～了她的心了。It suited her perfectly this time.
see also kè
可爱 kě'ài lovable; lovely; likeable:清纯～ pure and lovely /～的祖国 beloved motherland /～的婴儿 cute baby/树上的嫩枝绿得～。The tender twigs of the trees are beautifully green.
可悲 kěbēi sad; lamentable; deplorable:～的结局 sad (*or* tragic) ending /～的失败 dismal failure /愚蠢得～! What deplorable stupidity!
可比 kěbǐ comparable:～产品 comparable product
可比价格 kěbǐ jiàgé 〈经济〉comparable price; constant price
可比性 kěbǐxìng comparability:这两件事风马牛不相及,本来就没有～。The two incidents are totally unrelated (to each other) and lack comparability.
可比指数 kěbǐ zhǐshù comparative index
可鄙 kěbǐ contemptible; despicable; mean:自私得～ despicable selfishness /～伎俩 mean trick
可编程序计算器 kěbiān chéngxù jìsuànqì programmable calculator
可编程序只读存储器 kěbiān chéngxù zhǐdú cúnchǔqì 〈信息〉programmable read-only memory (PROM)
可变 kěbiàn variable; changeable:～因素 variable factor /～反差 variable contrast /～性 variability /人心～。Public opinion is changeable.
可变比 kěbiànbǐ variable ratio
可变参数 kěbiàn cānshù *also* "可变参量" variable parameter
可变电容器 kěbiàn diànróngqì variable condenser
可变电压 kěbiàn diànyā variable voltage
可变电阻 kěbiàn diànzǔ variable resistance
可变价格 kěbiàn jiàgé variable pricing; variable price
可变利率 kěbiàn lìlǜ variable (interest) rate
可变翼 kěbiànyì 〈航空〉adjustable wing; swing-wing
可变资本 kěbiàn zīběn variable capital
可补偿性 kěbǔchángxìng compensability:～损失 reparable loss /～伤害 compensable injury
可不 kěbù *also* "可不是" (used to express agreement) right; exactly:"这东西太贵了!""～,有多少人能买得起!" "This is too expensive." "Right you are! I wonder how many people can afford it?" /"她是全班最好的学生。""～,她还得过两个全国奖呢!" "She is the best student in her class." "Exactly. She has also won two national prizes." /"你最近挺忙的吧?""～,忙得团团转。" "You must have been quite busy recently." "You said it! I've been up to my neck in work lately."
可怖 kěbù horrible; frightful:他突然看见一张～的面孔。He suddenly saw a horrible face. /周围一片漆黑,十分～。It was frighteningly dark all around.
可采储量 kěcǎi chǔliàng 〈矿业〉recoverable reserves or deposit
可操左券 kěcāozuǒquàn be sure to succeed; be certain of success; have sth. in the bag:如果我们锲而不舍,一定～。If we persevere, we are bound to succeed.
可拆 kěchāi detachable; removable; collapsible:～部分 detachable (*or* removable) section /这种婴儿推车是～的。This kind of pram is

K

collapsible.

可拆砂箱 kěchāi shāxiāng 〈机械〉 snap flask

可偿还 kěchánghuán redeemable:～股票 redeemable stock /～债券 redeemable bond

可乘之机 kěchéngzhījī opportunity that can be exploited to sb.'s advantage; opening:不给敌人以～ give the enemy no opportunity / 这样,你就给了投机商～。Well, you are playing into the hands of speculators.

可持续发展 kěchíxù fāzhǎn sustainable development

可耻 kěchǐ shameful; disgraceful; ignominious:～的行径 shameful conduct /以～的失败告终 end in ignominious defeat

可待因 kědàiyīn 〈药学〉 codeine

可导炸弹 kědǎo zhàdàn controlled bomb

可的松 kědìsōng 〈药学〉 cortisone

可丁可卯 kědīng-kěmǎo *also* "可钉可铆" ❶ to the exact number; on the exact scale; exactly:～八小时工作 work for eight hours full load /他每月工资总是～,花个精光。He spent every penny of his salary every month. ❷ strictly observant (of rules); meticulous; inflexible:他办事～的,你就别想让他放你一把啦。He is so inflexible that you can't expect him to bend the rules for you.

可读性 kědúxìng readability:这虽是本学术作品,但～很强。Though it is a scholarly work it is quite readable.

可锻 kěduàn 〈冶金〉 ductible; forgeable:～性 forgeability; ductibility; malleability

可锻铸铁 kěduàn zhùtiě *also* "马铁" mǎtiě; "玛钢" mǎgāng 〈冶金〉 malleable (cast) iron

可兑换 kěduìhuàn convertible:～货币 convertible currency (*or* money)/不～货币 inconvertible currency (*or* money)

可兑换性 kěduìhuànxìng 〈经济〉 convertibility

可兑换证券 kěduìhuàn zhèngquàn 〈金融〉 convertible bond

可伐林 kěfálín 〈林业〉 open woods

可纺性 kěfǎngxìng 〈纺织〉 spinnability

可分解性 kěfēnjiěxìng decomposability

可歌可泣 kěgē-kěqì moving one to song and tears; moving; stirring:～的英雄事迹 heroic and moving deed /～的斗争 epic struggle

可耕 kěgēng 〈农业〉 arable; cultivable:～层 arable layer

可耕地 kěgēngdì arable land; cultivable land

可更新资源 kěgēngxīn zīyuán renewable resource:不～ non-renewable resource /利用太阳能等～ exploit renewable resources such as solar energy

可攻可守 kěgōng-kěshǒu be able either to go on the offensive or to hold one's position; be in a position either to attack the enemy or to defend oneself:全队～,球艺高超。The team is composed of excellent players, able to take the offensive or assume the defensive as the situation requires.

可观 kěguān ❶ be worth seeing:这部电影在艺术上大有～。The movie is well worth seeing, artistically speaking. ❷ considerable; sizable; impressive:成绩～ impressive achievement /面积～ sizable area /损失～ substantial loss /取得了～的经济效益和社会效益 achieve significant economic returns and social benefits /申请该科研项目的人为数～。There is a considerable number of applicants for the research project.

可贵 kěguì valuable; commendable; praiseworthy:精神～ praiseworthy spirit /热情～ commendable enthusiasm /这种道义上的支持是难能～的。Such moral support is hard to come by and particularly valuable.

可焊性 kěhànxìng 〈冶金〉 weldability

可好 kěhǎo just at that moment; just then; by happy coincidence:我正想去拜访他,～他来了。I was about to pay him a visit when he turned up.

可恨 kěhèn hateful; detestable; repugnant; abominable:～之至 most hateful /这种人说话不算数,真～! It is detestable for such people to make promises but never keep them.

可互换 kěhùhuàn 〈机械〉 interchangeable:～部件 interchangeable parts /～装配 interchangeable assembling /～性 interchangeability

可回收 kěhuíshōu recoverable; retrievable:～卫星 retrievable (*or* recoverable) satellite /～助推火箭 recoverable booster rocket

可加工性 kějiāgōngxìng 〈机械〉 machinability; workability

可加工永磁材料 kějiāgōng yǒngcí cáiliào workable permanent magnetic material

可嘉 kějiā laudable; praiseworthy:他力图挽回颓局,精神～。He made a laudable effort to save the deteriorating situation. /其志～,其情可悯。While his ambition is worthy of praise, his lot deserves sympathy.

可见 kějiàn ❶ it is thus clear or evident that:由此～,他的动机是好的。It is thus clear that he meant well. /～此人居心不良。This can prove that he harbours evil intentions. ❷ visible; visual:～辐射 visible radiation /～极光 visual aurora

可见度 kějiàndù *also* "能见度" néngjiàndù visibility:雾天～很低。Visibility is low on foggy days.

可见光 kějiànguāng 〈物理〉 visible light:～谱 visible spectrum

可脚 kějiǎo 〈方言〉 (of shoes, etc.) fit well:这双鞋又漂亮,又～。This pair of shoes is pretty and just the right size. /这双袜子大了,他穿着不～。The socks are too big for him.

可劲 kějìn 〈方言〉 exert one's efforts; do one's utmost:要按期完成任务,咱们得～干啊! We must do our utmost (*or* work for all we are worth) if we want to fulfil the task in time. /我～地喊,警告他有危险。I shouted at the top of my voice to warn him of the danger.

可惊 kějīng surprising; startling

可敬 kějìng worthy of respect; respectable; respected:～的老人 venerable old man /～的学者 much respected scholar /他的奉献精神可钦～。His dedication is admirable and worthy of esteem.

可聚变物质 kějùbiàn wùzhì fusionable material

可卡因 kěkǎyīn *also* "古柯碱" gǔkējiǎn cocaine:～瘾 cocaine addiction; cocainism /有～瘾的人 cocaine addict; cocainist

可抗辩条款 kěkàngbiàn tiáokuǎn 〈法律〉 contestable clause

可靠 kěkào reliable; dependable; trustworthy:他的信息不～。His information is not reliable. /他是一个～的人。He is a trustworthy person.

可靠性 kěkàoxìng reliability:材料的～ reliability of material /～技术 reliability engineering /～设计 reliability design

可靠性试验 kěkàoxìng shìyàn fail-test

可可 kěkě *also* "蔻蔻" kòukòu (transliteration) cocoa:～奶 cocoa milk /～粉 cocoa powder /～饮料 cocoa drink /～树 cocoa tree; cocoa /～脂 cocoa butter /～味的糖果 candies with cocoa flavour

可可豆 kěkědòu cocoa beans; cocoa

可可碱 kěkějiǎn 〈化学〉 theobromine

可可儿的 kěkěrde 〈方言〉 just at the moment; as luck or chance would have it:我刚要出门,～就遇着下雨。I was just going out when it began to rain.

可控 kěkòng controllable:～热核反应 controllable thermonuclear reaction /～整流器 controlled rectifier

可控硅 kěkòngguī 〈电子〉 silicon-controlled rectifier (SCR); thyristor:～开关 silicon-controlled switch (SCS)/～整流器 silicon-controlled rectifier

可口 kěkǒu (of food) palatable; tasty; nice:家乡风味的菜,非常～。Food cooked in the style of one's hometown is extremely tasty. /菜肴～了,我的饭量就大了。When the food is delicious, I always have a good appetite.

可口可乐 kěkǒu kělè Coca-Cola; coke

可扩缩性 kěkuòsuōxìng 〈信息〉 scalability

可兰经 Kělánjīng *also* "古兰经" Gǔlánjīng 〈伊斯兰〉 Koran

可乐 kělè ❶ funny; amusing; laughable:看他穿了两只不一样的鞋,真～! It was most funny to see him wearing two odd shoes. ❷ (short for 可口可乐) coke:来一罐～。Give me a coke. ❸ soft drink similar to Coca-Cola:百事～ Pepsi-Cola /天府～ Tianfu Cola

可乐果 kělèguǒ kola nut

可怜 kělián ❶ pitiful; pitiable; poor:他三岁就死了父母,真是个～的孩子。He is indeed a poor child, for he lost both his parents at three. ❷ pity; have pity on:求您～～她。Have some pity on her please. /对这种一贯做坏事的人绝不能～他。We should show no mercy to such a hardened evildoer. ❸ meagre; miserable; wretched:少得～ extremely scanty; very little /穷得～ as poor as a church mouse /他的汉语知识贫乏得～。His knowledge of Chinese is terribly meagre. /今年大旱,收成也很～。There was a severe drought this year and the harvest was miserable.

可怜巴巴 kěliánbābā pitiable; pathetic:儿子眼含着泪,～地望着他。His son, tears in eyes, looked at him pitiably. /你就挣这么～的一点儿钱啊? Is that all you earn? It's really pathetic!

可怜虫 kěliánchóng pitiful creature; miserable wretch:一个向隅而泣的～ a wretch left to grieve in the cold

可怜见 kěliánjiàn deserve one's pity or sympathy:他对父母的那片孝心怪～的。His devotion to his parents is worthy of sympathy. /瞧这小姑娘瘦得～的。See, the little girl is piteously thin.

可裂变物质 kělièbiàn wùzhì 〈物理〉 fissile or fissionable material
可流通金融工具 kěliútōng jīnróng gōngjù 〈金融〉 negotiable instrument
可恼 kěnǎo annoying; irritating:他这个人真～。He's so irritating. *or* He is getting on my nerves.
可能 kěnéng ❶ possible; probable; likely:～范围内 in so far as it is possible; as much as one can /～最大降水量 probable maximum precipitation /双方不大～达成协议。It is not likely for the two parties to reach an agreement. *or* The two parties are not likely to reach agreement. ❷ possibility; probability:这种～几乎等于零。The possibility is practically nil (*or* virtually non-existent). /计划不能完成的～是存在的。It is possible that the plan will not be carried out to completion. ❸ probably; perhaps; maybe:她～回家了。She's probably gone home. /～会采纳他的建议。His suggestion may be accepted. /你～没听懂我的话。Perhaps you didn't quite understand what I said. *or* Probably you didn't catch my meaning.
可能储量 kěnéng chǔliàng 〈矿业〉 probable or possible reserve
可能误差 kěnéng wùchā possible error
可能性 kěnéngxìng possibility; probability; feasibility:缺少～ lack probability (*or* feasibility) /颇有～ be quite possible (*or* probable)
可逆 kěnì reversible:～变化 reversible change /～性原理 reversibility principle /～电动机〈电工〉 reversible motor /～发动机〈机械〉 reversing engine /～轧机 reversing mill /～转向装置 reversible steering /～式水轮机 reversible turbine
可逆反应 kěnì fǎnyìng 〈化学〉 reversible reaction
可怕 kěpà fearful; dreadful; terrible; horrible:～的洪水 terrible flood /～的无知 dreadful ignorance /犯罪现场十分～。The scene of the crime was frightful (*or* terrifying). /这一事件带来了～的后果。The incident was attended by dire consequences.
可欺 kěqī ❶ easily cowed or bullied:他可不是个～的人。He is not a person to be bullied. /不要把我方的克制看作是软弱～。Do not take our restraint for a sign of weakness. ❷ guillible; easily duped:老实～ be simple-minded and gullible
可气 kěqì annoying; exasperating:这孩子真～! The child is very annoying.
可巧 kěqiǎo as luck would have it; by a happy coincidence:我正想到天津去看他,～他却出差来了北京。I was planning to go all the way to visit him in Tianjin, but as luck would have it, he came to Beijing on business. /我们打算去买电影票,～他送来了几张。We were going to buy movie tickets when he came and offered us some.
可亲 kěqīn amiable; affable; genial:和蔼～ amiable; affable /老同学聚在一起,觉得特别～。There was an atmosphere of great geniality at the gathering of old schoolmates.
可取 kěqǔ desirable; advisable:大家认为花点钱给产品作广告是～的。It is considered desirable to spend some money advertising our product. /她的建议颇有～之处。Her suggestion has something to recommend it. /这几幢房子各有～之处。Each of the houses has its own advantages.
可燃 kěrán combustible; inflammable; burnable:～部分 combustible part (*or* component)
可燃物 kěránwù combustible (matter); inflammable (matter)
可燃性 kěránxìng 〈化学〉 combustility; flammability:～试验 inflammability test
可人 kěrén 〈书面〉 ❶ one who has apparent merits or desirable qualities ❷ person one loves; sweetheart:朝思暮想的～ sweetheart that one misses day and night ❸ after one's fancy; pleasant; satisfying:风味～ have a pleasant flavour; be satisfying (*or* agreeable) in taste /楚楚～ (of a girl) of delicate beauty; graceful and charming
可溶 kěróng 〈化学〉 soluble:～于水 be soluble in water /～质 solvent /～磷酸 soluble phosphoric acid
可溶物质 kěróng wùzhì soluble substance
可溶性 kěróngxìng 〈化学〉 solubility:～淀粉 soluble starch /～硫化染料 soluble sulphuric dye /～阳极 soluble anode
可熔 kěróng 〈化学〉 fusible; meltable:～保险丝 electric fuse /～度 *also* "～性" fusibility; meltability
可身 kěshēn 〈方言〉 (of clothing) be a good fit; fit nicely:这件大衣真～! This coat fits me nicely!
可实现利润 kěshíxiàn lìrùn 〈经济〉 realisable profit
可食 kěshí edible:～菌 edible fungus
可视电话 kěshì diànhuà picture-phone; videophone
可视图文 kěshì túwén 〈通信〉 videotext
可是 kěshì ❶ 〈连词〉 but; yet; however:远足回来,大家都累了,～很愉快。Everyone was tired but happy after the excursion. /他嘴上说得好听,心里～老大的不愿意。Despite his agreeable words, he was most reluctant at heart. ❷ 〈副词〉 *used for emphasis*:你～亲眼看见怪兽了? Did you really see the monster with your own eyes? /这事～怪不得我呀! I'm not to blame for this at all! /这人～不简单。He is no sucker. /这一问～把他问倒了。The question put him on the spot.
可赎回股票 kěshúhuí gǔpiào redeemable shares
可塑 kěsù plastic:黏土是一种～物质。Clay is a plastic substance (*or* material).
可塑性 kěsùxìng plasticity; adaptability; malleability:儿童的～很大。Children are most adaptable.
可塑炸药 kěsù zhàyào plastic explosive
可叹 kětàn it is regrettable; it is a pity:～我年事已高,难以相助。It is regrettable that I'm too old to help. /一个有才华的人落到如此地步,殊为～。That a man of talent should have come to such a sorry pass is a matter of great regret.
可体 kětǐ (of clothing) fit nicely; be a good fit
可调 kětiáo 〈机械〉 adjustable; tunable:～扳手 adjustable spanner (*or* wrench) /～杠杆 adjustable lever /～叶片和固定叶片轴式水轮机 adjustable and fixed-blade propeller hydraulic turbine /～变压器〈电工〉 transtat
可望而不可即 kě wàng ér bùkě jí *also* "可望而不可及" within sight but beyond reach; unattainable; inaccessible:这对我们来说是～的。For us, it's something that we may aspire to but can never attain.
可谓 kěwèi 〈书面〉 it may be said; one may well say:他对国事～鞠躬尽瘁。One may well say that he exerted himself to the utmost for his country.
可恶 kěwù hateful; detestable; abominable:～之极 utterly detestable; extremely loathsome /实在是太～! What a curse!
可惜 kěxī unfortunately; it's a pity; it's too bad:～我未能来。Unfortunately I wasn't able to come. /你失去这个机会是很～的。It is a pity that (*or* What a pity) you missed the opportunity. /很～我记不全了。Much to my regret, I cannot remember them all.
可惜了儿的 kěxīliǎorde 〈方言〉 it's too bad; what a pity:大白馒头扔了,怪～。It's too bad that such good steamed buns have been simply thrown away.
可喜 kěxǐ gratifying; heartening:情况发生了～的变化。To our gratification, things have changed for the better. /在学习上她表现出～的进步势头。She has shown encouraging signs of improvement in her study.
可想而知 kěxiǎng'érzhī one can imagine; one may well imagine:第一步一经走出,以后的各步则～了。When the first move has been taken, it's not hard to imagine what is to follow. /他对自己的父母都是这么粗鲁,对别人更～了。He is rude to his own parents, let alone other people.
可笑 kěxiào ❶ ridiculous; ludicrous:幼稚～ ridiculously childish; childish and stupid /～之至 extremely foolish; height of absurdity /～不自量 cut a sorry figure by overrating oneself; make a laughing stock of oneself by overestimating one's ability/你穿这条紧身牛仔裤样子很～。You look ludicrous (*or* ridiculous) in those tight jeans. ❷ funny; amusing; laughable:～的故事 laughable (*or* amusing) story /～的动作 funny gesture
可心 kěxīn after one's heart; satisfying; to one's liking:～人 person after one's heart /这笔用着～。The pen writes well. /她好不容易买了双～的鞋。At last she managed to buy a pair of shoes she really liked.
可信 kěxìn credible:～性 credibility /你看此事～程度如何? How credible do you think the story is?
可行 kěxíng feasible; workable:切实～的计划 feasible (*or* practicable) plan /这条建议不～。This proposal wouldn't work (*or* is not feasible).
可行性 kěxíngxìng feasibility:～研究 feasibility study /～报告 feasibility report
可压缩 kěyāsuō 〈物理〉 compressible:～流体 compressible fluid
可延展性 kěyánzhǎnxìng ductility; extensibility
可研磨性 kěyánmóxìng 〈冶金〉 abradibility
可疑 kěyí suspicious; dubious:形迹～ look suspicious /～分子 dubious character; suspect /我觉得他的话十分～。I feel very suspicious about what he said. *or* His words seem very dubious to me. /这事有些～。There is something fishy about it.
可以 kěyǐ ❶ can; may:～理解 can be understood; be understand-

able /～为鉴 may be taken as an example (*or* warning) /～休矣。It's time that this stops. *or* Enough of it! /你～放心,我们会帮助解决这个问题的。You may rest assured that we will help solve the problem. /我～替你先签草约吗? May I sign the protocol on your behalf? ❷ pretty good; not bad; passable:这部电影还～。This film is not bad. /我考得还～。I didn't do badly at the exam. /他的德语还～。His German can pass muster. /这外套穿上还～吧? Do I look all right in this jacket? ❸ terrible; awful; dreadful:这件皮大衣的标价高得～。The price of this fur coat is terribly high. /他那儿子调皮得实在～。That son of his is awfully naughty. /她那张嘴真够～的,谁都怕她三分! She's got such a dreadful (*or* sharp) tongue that everyone holds her somewhat in awe.

可意 kěyì gratifying; satisfactory:这里的饭菜还～吗? How do you like the food here?

可有可无 kěyǒu-kěwú not essential; not indispensable:录像机是～的东西,就别买了。A video-recorder is not essential. Forget it.

可遇而不可求 kě yù ér bùkě qiú sth. that one may happen to run across but cannot expect to find when one looks for it; sth. so rare that one can only stumble upon it by luck:人生有些机遇是～的。Some opportunities in life come by chance, not through seeking.

可造之才 kězàozhīcái person suitable for training (for a particular skill or job); person with great potential; promising young man or woman

可憎 kězēng hateful; repulsive; detestable:面目～ look repulsive

可折叠机翼飞机 kězhédié jīyì fēijī folding wing airplane

可着 kězhe make the best or most of; go as far as is possible; make do:没有大纸,咱们就～这张纸画吧。Let's make do with this paper for the drawing since we haven't got a bigger piece. /你就～这块料裁吧。You'll have to cut the dress according to the cloth.

可着劲儿 kězhejìnr 〈口语〉 as much as one can; as much as one wishes; to one's heart's content:～干 work with all one's energy; work to the best of one's ability /～唱 sing to one's heart's content /饿久了,千万别～吃东西。When you've been hungry for a long time, be sure to restrain yourself when you start eating.

可支配收入 kězhīpèi shōurù disposable income:个人～ disposable personal income (DPI)

可知论 kězhīlùn 〈哲学〉 theory of the knowability of the universe:不～ agnosticism

可知性 kězhīxìng 〈哲学〉 knowability:宇宙的～ knowability of the universe

可执行文件 kězhíxíng wénjiàn 〈信息〉 EXE

可转换债券 kězhuǎnhuàn zhàiquàn 〈金融〉 convertible loan stock

可转让 kězhuǎnràng ❶ transferable:～权利 transferable right /这种入场券不～。One must not give away such tickets of admission (to others). ❷ negotiable:～提单 negotiable bill of lading /～证券 negotiable securities

可转让定期存单 kězhuǎnràng dìngqī cúndān transferable certificate of deposit

可转让信用证 kězhuǎnràng xìnyòngzhèng transferable credit

坷

kě *see* "坎坷" kǎnkě
see also kē

轲

kě *see* "轗轲" kǎnkě
see also kē

K

kè

刻

kè ❶ carve; engrave; cut:雕～ carve; engrave; sculpt /～图章 engrave a seal /～蜡板 cut stencils /在石碑上～题词 carve an inscription on a stone tablet ❷ unit of time when the water clock or hourglass was used to measure time (with 100 such units in a day) ❸ quarter (of an hour):两点一～ quarter past two /还有三～钟。There are still three quarters of an hour (*or* forty-five minutes) to go. ❹ moment; time:此～ at this moment /顷～ in no time; in an instant /即～便到 arrive in no time /稍等片～ wait a moment; one moment /一～千金 value every minute ❺ in the highest degree:深～ penetrating; profound; in-depth ❻ cutting; biting; harsh:苛～ overly strict; harsh ❼ set a time limit

刻板 kèbǎn ❶ *also* "刻版" cut wood or metal blocks (for printing) ❷ stiff; inflexible; mechanical:他是个正派人,就是太～。He is an upright man, but rather inflexible. /别人的经验是应该学习的,但是不能～地抄袭。Although we should learn from other people's experience, we must never copy anyone blindly (*or* mechanically).

刻版印刷 kèbǎn yìnshuā block printing

刻本 kèběn block-printed edition:元～ Yuan Dynasty block-printed edition

刻薄 kèbó mean; unkind; sarcastic; cynical:～寡恩 be harsh and ungenerous (to one's followers or inferiors) /话别说得这么～。Don't be so sarcastic. *or* Don't make such caustic comments. /他待人十分～。He is very mean to people. *or* He treats people meanly. /你这么说不有点～吗? Wasn't it somewhat unkind of you to say so?

刻不容缓 kèbùrónghuǎn be extremely urgent; demand immediate attention; brook no delay:～的任务 task which brooks no delay; extremely urgent task /组织抢救队,～。Organize a rescue team without a moment's delay. /这事～,得马上行动。There's no time to lose. We must take immediate action.

刻刀 kèdāo graver; burin

刻毒 kèdú venomous; spiteful; malignant:用语～ be spiteful in one's words; make venomous remarks (*or* comments) /～咒骂 hurl spiteful curses (at sb.); heap venomous abuse (on sb.); be full of malignant abuse

刻度 kèdù graduation (on a vessel or instrument); scale division:～杯 graduated glass /～尺 graduated ruler; dividing rule /～器 graduator /～盘 graduated disc; dial scale

刻工 kègōng ❶ carving skill:～精细的雕塑 sculpture with fine workmanship ❷ carver; engraver

刻骨 kègǔ engraved on one's bones; deeply ingrained; deep-seated; deep-rooted:～仇恨 deep-seated hatred; lasting animosity /～相思 (of lovers) miss each other very much; be love-sick

刻骨铭心 kègǔ-míngxīn *also* "镂骨铭心" lòugǔ-míngxīn;"铭心刻骨" be engraved on one's mind or in one's heart; be remembered with gratitude:～之言 words which make an indelible impression /您的恩典～,永志不忘。Your kindness is deeply etched upon my mind. I shall never forget it.

刻鹄类鹜 kèhú-lèiwù try to carve a swan and at least you'll get a duck — the imitation, though imperfect, is not bad; aim reasonably high and you won't fall far short

刻花 kèhuā engraved or carved designs:传统～装饰 engraved traditional designs /～玻璃 cut-glass

刻画 kèhuà ❶ engrave or draw:不要在墙上随意～。Don't scrawl on the wall. *or* No graffiti. ❷ depict; portray:～入微 depict (*or* portray) to the last detail /人物～ characterization /人物～得生动、深刻 give a vivid and in-depth description of the characters

刻记 kèjì ❶ bear in mind:～在心 bear (sth.) in mind ❷ mark engraved on a vessel; engraving

刻刻 kèkè every moment; constantly:时时～ all the time; at every moment; ceaselessly /你离家后,母亲～为你担忧。You have been a constant worry to mother since you left home.

刻苦 kèkǔ ❶ hardworking; assiduous; painstaking:～的精神 spirit of hard work; assiduity /～好学 be studious and diligent /他聪明有余,～不足。He is quite intelligent but does not work hard enough. /她的～努力终于取得了成果。Her painstaking efforts were finally crowned with success. ❷ simple and frugal; thrifty:他过日子一向很～。He has always lived a frugal life.

刻漏 kèlòu *also* "漏刻";"漏壶" lòuhú water clock; hourglass; clepsydra

刻镂 kèlòu carve; engrave:府邸的大门～精致。The gate of the mansion was delicately engraved.

刻露 kèlù 〈书面〉 profound but lucid:文笔～ write in a lucid and penetrating style

刻期 kèqī *also* "克期" kèqī set a time limit; set a date

刻日 kèrì *also* "克日" kèrì set a date; set a time limit

刻深 kèshēn 〈书面〉 ❶ deep; profound:其意～。Its meaning is profound. ❷ severe; harsh; stern:～寡恩 harsh and ungenerous (to one's inferiors, etc.)

刻石 kèshí ❶ carve or engrave characters or designs on a stone ❷ stone engraved with characters or designs

刻丝 kèsī *also* "缂丝" kèsī 〈工美〉 *kesi* weaving (a type of silk weaving done by the tapestry method)

刻下 kèxià at present; right now:～抽不出身 unable to spare any time at the moment; be fully occupied right now

刻线机 kèxiànjī ruling engine; ruling machine

刻写 kèxiě ❶ cut (stencils):我一共～了十张蜡纸。I cut ten stencils altogether. /他脸上～着焦虑。Anxiety and worry were written on his face. ❷〈书面〉carve; engrave

刻削 kèxuē ❶ whittle and carve:～竹木 whittle a piece of bamboo or wood ❷〈书面〉exploit mercilessly:～百姓 (of an official) exploit the people mercilessly ❸〈书面〉harsh; onerous:～之法 harsh laws

刻意 kèyì strive sedulously:～讨好 go out of one's way to please sb.

刻意求工 kèyì-qiúgōng sedulously seek perfection; be scrupulous in one's workmanship:这是诗人的～之作。This is a poem that shows the poet's earnest effort to strive for perfection.

刻印 kèyìn ❶ carve or engrave a seal;以～自娱 amuse oneself by carving seals; make a hobby of seal carving ❷ cut stencils and print:～宣传品 cut stencils and print propaganda material /他的话深深地～在人们心头。His words were engraved deep in the hearts of the people.

刻制 kèzhì make sth. by carving; carve:精工～的盒子 delicately carved box

刻舟求剑 kèzhōu-qiújiàn cut a mark on the gunwale of a moving boat to indicate where one's sword dropped into the river — take measures or act without regard to changing circumstances:缘木求鱼,～,徒劳而无功。It's a futile attempt to climb a tree to catch fish and nick the boat to seek the sword.

刻字 kèzì carve or engrave characters on a seal, tablet, etc.

刻字社 kèzìshè seal-engraving shop

溘 kè 〈书面〉suddenly:～逝 pass away (*or* die) suddenly

溘然 kèrán 〈书面〉suddenly

溘然长逝 kèrán-chángshì suddenly pass away; die a sudden death

嗑(齣) kè crack sth. between the teeth:～瓜子儿 crack melon seeds /老鼠在箱子上～了个洞。Mice gnawed a hole in the chest.
see also kē

嗑牙 kèyá 〈方言〉indulge in idle talk; gossip

克[1](❸❹剋、尅) kè ❶〈书面〉can; be able to:不～分身 cannot get (*or* tear oneself) away ❷ overcome; restrain:以柔～刚 overcome the tough with the mild ❸ capture; conquer; subdue:迭～重镇 capture one strategic town after another /攻无不～ be invincible ❹ digest

克[2](剋、尅) kè set a time limit:～日完工 set a date for completing the work

克[3] kè gram(g):五百～ 500 grams; half a kilogram

克[4] kè ❶ Tibetan unit of dry measure holding about 12.5 kilograms of barley ❷ Tibetan unit of land area equal to about 1 *mu* or $\frac{1}{15}$ of an acre

克当量 kèdāngliàng 〈化学〉gram equivalent

克敌制胜 kèdí-zhìshèng defeat an enemy and win a victory:～的法宝 magical weapon with which to defeat the enemy; best way to defeat the enemy

克分子 kèfēnzǐ ❶〈化学〉gram molecule ❷〈心理〉molar:～行为 molar behaviour

克分子量 kèfēnzǐliàng 〈化学〉gram molecular weight

克分子浓度 kèfēnzǐ nóngdù 〈化学〉molarity (M)

克分子体积 kèfēnzǐ tǐjī 〈化学〉gram molecular volume

克夫 kèfū 〈迷信〉(of a woman) be a jinx to one's husband (so that he dies prematurely, etc.)

克服 kèfú ❶ overcome; surmount; conquer:～重重困难 overcome (*or* surmount) one difficulty after another /～缺点 rectify one's shortcoming /～恶习 correct a bad habit /～各种错误思想 get rid of various erroneous ideas /～私心杂念 do away with selfish considerations ❷ put up with (hardships, inconveniences, etc.); make do; endure:这房间太小,你们今晚就～一点吧。The room is a bit small, but I'm afraid you'll have to make do with it tonight.

克复 kèfù recover; recapture:～失地 recover lost territory

克格勃 Kègébó KGB (Russian acronym for the former Soviet State Security Committee); member of KGB

克化 kèhuà 〈方言〉digest (food):吃太多了,～不了 eat too much to digest

克己 kèjǐ ❶ be strict with oneself; exercise self-denial; be unselfish:～待人 deny oneself but treat others generously ❷ (used by shopkeepers) reasonable:价钱～ reasonable price ❸ frugal:生活～ live a frugal life

克己奉公 kèjǐ-fènggōng deny oneself and work wholeheartedly for the public interest; be unselfishly devoted to public duty:～的好干部 honest official devoted to his (*or* her) duty

克己复礼 kèjǐ-fùlǐ (as a Confucian ethical ideal) exercise self-restraint and return to propriety (i.e. Zhou rites)

克减 kèjiǎn cut down on; dock; divert (sth. for one's own purse):～工钱 (of a foreman, etc.) pocket a portion of workers' pay; dock workers' wages /不得～下拨的经费。No diversion of any part of the appropriation (for other purposes) is permitted.

克捷 kèjié 〈书面〉win a victory; triumph:所向～ win one victory after another in one's advance; be invincible all along the way

克卡 kèkǎ 〈物理〉gram calorie

克扣 kèkòu pocket part of employees' pay; dock:～军饷 dock part of soldiers' pay (for one's own use)

克拉 kèlā carat (about 0.2 gram):五～的钻戒 diamond ring of five carats

克莱斯勒汽车公司 Kèláisīlè Qìchē Gōngsī Chrysler Corporation, major US car manufacturer

克郎球 kèlángqiú *also*"克郎棋" caroms:打～ play caroms

克朗 Kèlǎng ❶ Krona (unit of money in Sweden and Iceland) ❷ Krone (unit of money in Norway and Denmark) ❸ Koruna (unit of money in Czech Republic)

克厘米 kèlímǐ gram-centimetre

克里奥尔 Kèlǐ'ào'ěr Creole:～人 Creole /～语 Creole (language)

克里米亚 Kèlǐmǐyà Crimea, peninsula lying between the sea of Azov and the Black Sea

克里姆林宫 Kèlǐmǔlíngōng Kremlin

克林顿 Kèlíndùn William Jefferson Clinton (1946-), 42nd President of the United States (1993-)

克隆 kèlóng (transliteration) clone:～羊 cloned sheep /～人 clone a human (being) /～技术 cloning technology /许多国家都禁止～人。It is forbidden in many countries to try to clone human beings.

克罗地亚 Kèluódìyà Croatia:～共和国 Republic of Croatia /～语 Croat; Croatian /～人 Croat; Croatian

克罗马努人 Kèluómǎnǔrén 〈考古〉Cro-Magnon man (an Upper Palaeolithic species of man, whose fossils were unearthed at Cro-Magnon in southern France in 1868)

克罗米 kèluómǐ *also*"铬" gè (transliteration) chrominium

克期 kèqī *also*"刻期" kèqī set a time limit; set a date:～开工 set a date for beginning the work /务必～完工 must be completed within the deadline

克勤克俭 kèqín-kèjiǎn be industrious and frugal; practise diligence and thrift:～是一种美德。It is a virtue to be hard working and thrifty.

克丘亚语 Kèqiūyàyǔ Quechua (language), language spoken among Indians of Peru and Ecuador

克日 kèrì *also*"刻日" kèrì set a date or deadline

克山病 kèshānbìng 〈医学〉Keshan disease (endemic disease that was first discovered in Keshan county, Heilongjiang Province)

克绍箕裘 kèshào-jīqiú follow in the footsteps of one's forefathers; carry on what one's forefathers started

克什米尔 Kèshímí'ěr Kashmir:查谟和～ Jammu and Kashmir /～公主号事件 Incident of the Kashmir Princess (1955)

克食 kèshí help the digestion:山楂能～。Haws help digestion.

克式量 kèshìliàng *see*"克分子量"

克丝钳子 kèsī qiánzi combination pliers; cutting pliers

克汀病 kètīngbìng 〈医学〉cretinism

克星 kèxīng jinx; natural enemy:猫头鹰是鼠类的～。The owl is the natural enemy of mice and rats.

克抑 kèyì 〈书面〉restrain; suppress:她的妒忌情绪难以～。She can hardly suppress her jealousy.

克原子 kèyuánzǐ 〈化学〉gram atom

克制 kèzhì restrain; control:～一时的冲动 restrain oneself from

impulsive action /没有~住自己的脾气 fail to control one's temper / 采取~态度 exercise (*or* show) great restraint

氪 kè 〈化学〉krypton (Kr)

可 kè

see also kě

可汗 kèhán 〈历史〉khan: 天~ Heavenly Khan (honorary title given to Li Shimin 李世民, second emperor of the Tang Dynasty, by minority people of China)

课[1] kè ❶ class; lecture: 备~ prepare lessons /讲~ give a lecture / 上~ attend a class; give a class /练习~ practice class /自习~ homework class; class for self-study ❷ subject; course: 开新~ offer a new course /必修~ required course; compulsory (*or* mandatory) course /选修~ elective (*or* optional) course /基础~ basic course /专业~ specialized course /外语~ foreign languages (as a course) /体育~ physical education; physical training /你们有几门~? How many courses (*or* subjects) do you take? ❸ class; period: 一星期教八节~ teach eight periods per week /我今天有一节化学~。I have a chemistry class today. ❹ lesson: 第三~ Lesson Three /本英语教材共有二十~。There are twenty lessons in this English textbook. ❺ subdivision of an administrative unit; section: 会计~ accounting section

课[2] kè ❶〈旧语〉tax: 交~ pay taxes /盐~ salt tax ❷ levy; impose: ~以罚金 impose a fine

课[3] kè divination; fortune-telling: 起~了。The (divination) session is on.

课本 kèběn textbook: 数学~ textbook in mathematics; maths textbook

课表 kèbiǎo school or class schedule

课程 kèchéng course; curriculum: ~设置 curriculum; courses offered /~负担 course-load /~计划 syllabus /~表 school (*or* class) schedule /~进度 teaching schedule

课间 kèjiān break (between classes): ~休息 break; recess

课间餐 kèjiāncān break-time snack (for school children)

课间操 kèjiāncāo setting-up exercises during a break (between classes)

课卷 kèjuàn student's written work

课目 kèmù ❶ subject; course ❷〈军事〉course: 军训~ military training courses

课时 kèshí class hour; period: 英语精读课每周六~。There are six class hours per week for English Intensive Reading.

课室 kèshì classroom

课税 kèshuì ❶ levy taxes; charge duties: ~基准 basis of assessment for taxation /~价值 taxable value ❷ taxes; rates: 受灾区可免部分~。The disaster-afflicted areas may be partially exempted from taxes.

课堂 kètáng classroom: ~教学 classroom instruction (*or* teaching) /~纪律 classroom discipline /~讨论 classroom discussion; seminar /~表现 classroom performance /~作业 classwork

课题 kètí ❶ topic for class discussion: 这是我们今天讨论的惟一~。This is the only topic for today's discussion. ❷ question or topic for study; problem; task: 研究~ research topic /这是我们当前面临的重大~。This is an issue of great importance facing us at present.

课题组 kètízǔ research group (for an assigned topic)

课外 kèwài outside class; after school; extra-curricular: ~活动 extra-curricular activities /~辅导 (as of a teacher) help (a student) outside class; give tutorials /~辅导员 extra-curricular instructor (usu. involved in political or social work) /~学术活动 academic activities after class /~作业 homework

课文 kèwén text: 必须学好~, 才能做对练习。You must learn the text well before you can do the exercises correctly.

课业 kèyè lessons; classwork; schoolwork: 学生不可荒废~, 整天看电视。Students are not supposed to watch TV all day long to the neglect of their lessons (*or* schoolwork).

课椅 kèyǐ schoolroom chair; classroom chair

课余 kèyú after school; after class: 丰富学生的~文体活动 enrich the students' recreational and sports activities after school /他利用~时间学习第二外语。He is learning a second foreign language after class.

课桌 kèzhuō student's desk in school; classroom desk

锞 kè (gold or silver) ingot: 金~ gold ingot

锞子 kèzi small gold or silver ingot (formerly used as money)

骒 kè female (mule or horse): ~骡 female mule

骒马 kèmǎ mare

客 kè ❶ guest; visitor: 来~ guest; visitor /常~ frequent visitor /稀~ rare visitor /远~ visitor (*or* guest) from afar /贵~ guest of honour; distinguished guest /送~ see a guest off /欢迎你到我家来作~。You're welcome to our home. /我喜欢在家里请~。I prefer to entertain friends at home. /你点菜吧,今天我请~。You order the dishes. It's on me today. ❷ passenger; traveller: 旅~ traveller /乘~ passenger ❸ live or settle in a strange place: 独在异乡为异~ live all alone in a strange place ❹ travelling merchant: 珠宝~ travelling jeweler ❺ customer; patron; client: 顾~ customer; patron; client /房~ lodger; boarder /回头~ regular customer ❻ person engaged in some particular pursuit requiring a certain amount of travelling and running around: 香~ Buddhist pilgrim /政~ politician /说~ person whose task it is to persuade sb.; lobbyist/食~ hanger-on (of an aristocrat or a wealthy family) /侠~ person skilled in martial arts and ready to run chivalrous errands for others; knight-errant /剑~ professional swordsman ❼ independent of human consciousness; objective: *see* "~观" ❽〈方言〉〈量词〉*used for food or drinks sold in portions*: 两~冰激凌 two icecreams /五~盒饭 five lunchboxes

客帮 kèbāng 〈旧语〉group of itinerant merchants or pedlars from other localities

客边 kèbiān 〈方言〉alien land; strange land: 他独自一人在~住了二十年。He lived alone in a strange land for twenty years.

客边人 kèbiānrén 〈方言〉person who lives in an alien land; non-native resident

客舱 kècāng passenger cabin (on a ship, plane, etc.): 头等~ first-class cabin

客场 kèchǎng 〈体育〉(in basketball as between two competing teams) other team's home court; (in soccer) other team's home ground: ~比赛 away game — game played on the other team's court or ground /该队主场以3比1胜了对手,~以1比1打平。The team defeated its rival three to one on home ground while tying it one to one in the away game.

客车 kèchē ❶ passenger train; passenger car ❷ coach; bus: 大~ coach

客船 kèchuán passenger ship: 定期~ liner /夜半钟声到~。Late at night the sound of the bell reaches the traveller's boat.

客串 kèchuàn (usu. of an amateur) participate in a show as a guest performer: ~演员 guest actor (*or* actress)

客次 kècì 〈书面〉temporary lodgings away from home

客邸 kèdǐ 〈书面〉residence away from home

客地 kèdì 〈书面〉alien land; place away from home: 身处异乡~ be in a strange land; be away from home

客店 kèdiàn inn

客队 kèduì 〈体育〉visiting team (in a game)

客饭 kèfàn ❶ ordinary meal arranged for a visitor to take at a canteen or cafeteria; visitor's set meal ❷ table d'hote; set meal

客贩 kèfàn trader from outside the area; travelling trader

客房 kèfáng ❶ guest room ❷ room (in a hotel): 这家小店只有五间~。The small inn has only five rooms (for hire).

客观 kèguān objective: ~事实 objective fact; reality /~原因 objective cause /~价值 objective value /~的批评 objective criticism /~的分析 objective analysis /~反应 objective reflection /~地说 objectively speaking /看问题~ view a problem objectively

客观必然性 kèguān bìránxìng objective necessity

客观规律 kèguān guīlǜ objective law

客观实在 kèguān shízài *also* "客观现实" objective reality

客观世界 kèguān shìjiè objective world

客观条件 kèguān tiáojiàn objective condition

客观唯心主义 kèguān wéixīnzhǔyì objective idealism

客观性 kèguānxìng objectivity; objectiveness

客观真理 kèguān zhēnlǐ objective truth

K

客观主义 kèguānzhǔyì objectivism
客官 kèguān 〈旧语〉(usu. used by a waiter, boatman or shopkeeper) patron
客馆 kèguǎn 〈旧语〉guest house
客户 kèhù ❶〈旧语〉tenant (farmer):这些庄稼人都是本地地主的～。These peasants all rented land from the local landlords. ❷〈旧语〉non-native resident; immigrant:村边山坡上住的是几家～。On the slope near the village lived a few immigrant families. ❸ customer; client:国内外～ domestic and foreign customers /大～ major customer or client
客户服务器 kèhù fúwùqì 〈信息〉client server:～计算 client server computing
客话 kèhuà ❶ polite words; polite formula ❷ (often used in book titles) record of one's life in an alien land ❸ Hakka (dialect)
客货船 kè-huòchuán passenger-cargo vessel or ship
客机 kèjī passenger plane; airliner
客籍 kèjí ❶ province into which a settler has moved:山东只是我的～,我原籍山西。I am really a native of Shanxi. Shandong is only my second home. ❷ settler from another province:填表时请注明是否～。Please indicate whether you are a native or a settler.
客家 Kèjiā Hakka:～人 Hakka (people)
客家话 Kèjiāhuà Hakka (dialect):～在广东、福建、广西、台湾等省都很流行。Hakka is widely spoken in Guangdong, Fujian, Guangxi, Taiwan, and other provinces.
客居 kèjū live abroad; live away from home:～他乡 live away from one's native place /他现在～美国。He lives in the United States now.
客军 kèjūn 〈旧语〉troops moved in from other provinces
客来客往 kèlái-kèwǎng customers or visitors come and go — be thronged with customers or visitors:父亲在世时,家中总是～的。When father was alive, our house was frequented by visitors.
客里空 kèlǐkōng (transliteration from Russian) ❶ Krikon — person who is always fabricating and exaggerating things; person bent on hyperbole and empty talk ❷ hyperbolic language; empty talk
客流 kèliú volume of passenger traffic; passenger flow:春节～量最大。The volume of passenger traffic reaches its climax before and after the Chinese New Year.
客轮 kèlún passenger ship
客满 kèmǎn (of theatre, hotel, etc.) be filled to capacity; have a full house:今晚歌剧院已～。Tickets for tonight's opera are all sold out.
客票 kèpiào passenger ticket
客气 kèqi ❶ polite; courteous:～话 polite words /～的称呼 polite form of address /毫不～地加以回绝 refuse bluntly /你太～了。You're very kind. *or* It's very kind of you. ❷ modest:这个称号你当之无愧,就别～了。You deserve this title. Don't be too modest. ❸ speak or behave politely; stand on ceremony:自己拿吧,～什么! Take what you want, and don't stand on ceremony. *or* Come on, help yourself. /他～了一番才转入正题。He came to the topic after a few words of courtesy.
客卿 kèqīng 〈书面〉〈旧语〉person from one feudal state serving in the court of another
客人 kèren ❶ guest; visitor:今晚我们有～。We have company tonight. ❷ guest (at a hotel, in a restaurant, etc.); patron; customer:这家旅馆服务好,～总是很多。As the hotel offers excellent service, it attracts a lot of guests (*or* it is patronized by many guests). ❸ passenger; traveller
客商 kèshāng itinerant or visiting businessman; travelling trader:各国～云集广交会。Business people from various countries came to the Guangzhou Export Commodities Fair.
客舍 kèshè 〈书面〉guesthouse; lodging house; hostel
客室 kèshì *also* "客屋" guestroom; guest chamber
客水 kèshuǐ floodwater coming in from other areas:此处地势低,是～汇流之所。This place is so low that floodwater comes in from many other areas.
客死 kèsǐ die in a strange land; die abroad
客随主便 kèsuízhǔbiàn the guest must suit the convenience of the host; the guest must comply with the wishes of the host:我是客人,自然是～。As a guest, I naturally did what the host thought fit.
客岁 kèsuì 〈书面〉〈旧语〉last year
客堂 kètáng 〈方言〉parlour; drawing room
客套 kètào ❶ polite formulas; civilities:二人初次见面,免不了要讲几句～。Since it was the first time they had met each other, they exchanged a few words of greetings. ❷ make polite remarks; exchange courtesies:他站起身,又～了几句,然后出门而去。He stood up, made some polite remarks and then went out of the door.
客套话 kètàohuà polite formulas; civilities:待人接物,总得会一些～。Polite greetings are necessary for social occasions.
客梯 kètī 〈航空〉airstairs:随机～ airsteps; built-in airstairs; self-contained airstairs
客体 kètǐ 〈哲学〉〈心理〉〈法律〉object:～依恋〈心理〉object attachment /犯罪～〈法律〉object of crime
客厅 kètīng parlour; drawing room; sitting room; lounge
客土 kètǔ ❶〈农业〉earth brought in from elsewhere to improve the soil ❷〈书面〉place or land where one lives away from home; foreign country; strange land:侨居～ reside in a strange land; live abroad
客位 kèwèi seats reserved for guests or passengers
客席指挥 kèxí zhǐhuī guest or visiting conductor
客星 kèxīng 〈旧语〉comet
客姓 kèxìng surname of a non-native person:王家庄只有两三家～。There are only a couple of families with different surnames in Wang Village.
客寓 kèyù ❶ inn; hostel ❷ live in an alien land; reside away from home
客源 kèyuán source of tourists; potential customers or tourists:～丰富 have no lack of potential customers or tourists
客运 kèyùn passenger transport:～量 volume of passenger transport /～高峰期 peak time for passenger transport
客运列车 kèyùn lièchē passenger train
客栈 kèzhàn inn (sometimes with warehouse and trans-shipment service)
客站 kèzhàn ❶ railway station ❷ bus stop
客座 kèzuò ❶ seat or place for a guest or client:～单间 private room for a client ❷ professional person invited to work temporarily in an institution:～研究员 visiting research fellow /～演员 guest star
客座教授 kèzuò jiàoshòu guest or visiting professor

恪

kè 〈书面〉scrupulously and respectfully; meticulously:～尽职守 be whole-heartedly devoted to one's duty
恪守 kèshǒu 〈书面〉scrupulously abide by (a promise, treaty, etc.):～中立 observe strict neutrality /我国一向～和平共处五项原则。Our country has always adhered faithfully to the Five Principles of Peaceful Coexistence.
恪守不渝 kèshǒu-bùyú consistently abide by:老老实实做人是他一生～的信条。The maxim he has observed all his life is "Be an honest man."
恪遵 kèzūn scrupulously obey (laws, orders, traditions, etc.):～旨意 act in strict conformity with sb.'s desire

缂

kè
缂丝 kèsī *also* "刻丝" kèsī 〈工美〉❶ *kesi* weaving, a type of silk weaving done by the tapestry method ❷ *kesi* fabric or ware

kēi

剋(尅)

kēi ❶ beat; fight:被～得鼻青脸肿 be beaten black and blue /两人动手～起来了。The two of them came to blows. ❷ scold; curse:挨～ get a scolding /他妈～了他一顿。His mother gave him a dressing down.
剋架 kēijià 〈方言〉have a fist fight

kěn

肯[1](肎)

kěn flesh sticking to the bone:中～ draw blood; hit the nail on the head; be to the point

肯[2]

kěn ❶ agree; consent:我们做了半天工作,他才～了。We had talked for quite a while before he finally agreed. /此事已得局长首～。It has won approval by the director. /他不～接受这个任务。He refused to (*or* would not) accept the task. ❷ be willing or ready

(to do sth.); be agreeable (to doing sth.):～卖力气 be willing to do hard work; be hardworking /～学习 be eager to learn /～帮助人 be always ready to help others /他～来吗? Will he come? ❸〈方言〉be liable to; frequently occur:这里冬天～下雨。It often rains here in winter.

肯定 kěndìng ❶ affirm; confirm; regard as positive; approve:应该～成绩,克服缺点。It is necessary to affirm our achievements and overcome our shortcomings. /我们还不能～手术是否对他有必要。We have yet to affirm whether an operation is necessary for him. /他们对此既不～,也不否认。They neither confirmed nor denied it. /我可以～他的话是真的。I can testify to what he said. /医生～他是得了癌症。The doctor is positive that he has got cancer. ❷ affirmative; positive:～的回答 affirmative answer /～的评价 positive assessment ❸ doubtless; certain; sure:～是出了什么事。Something must have gone wrong. /我知道你～会帮我的。I knew you would be kind enough to help me. /他的口气很～。He said this with great certainty. ❹ definite; clear; unambiguous:会不会涨价,我不敢～。I cannot say for sure whether the price will go up or not. /他的态度不那么～。His attitude isn't very clear-cut.

肯尼迪 Kěnnídí John Fitzgerald Kennedy (1917-1963), 35th President of the United States (1961-1963)

肯尼亚 Kěnníyà Kenya:～人 Kenyan /～古猿〈考古〉Kenyapithecus (living about 14-20 million years ago)

肯綮 kěnqìng 〈书面〉❶ joint (in an animal body) ❷ most important juncture or place; crux; key point:深中～ get to the heart of the matter

肯塔基 Kěntǎjī Kentucky, state in central southeastern United States

肯雅塔 Kěnyǎtǎ Jomo Kenyatta (1891-1978), Kenyan nationalist leader

啃(齦) kěn gnaw; nibble:～干馒头 nibble at a dried bun /～大部头 delve into big volumes (of books) /老鼠把木箱子～穿了。Mice nibbled their way through the wooden chest.

啃骨头 kěn gǔtou gnaw at a bone; crack a hard nut; work painstakingly at a difficult task

啃啮 kěnniè *also* "啃噬" gnaw; nibble:马蜂～花叶。Wasps were nibbling at the flowers. /巨大的悲痛～着她的心。Tremendous grief was gnawing her heart.

啃青 kěnqīng 〈方言〉❶ (of people) reap green or unripe crops for food ❷ (of sheep, draught animals, etc.) nibble green crops

恳(懇) kěn ❶ sincerely; earnestly:～谢 thank sincerely /～劝 persuade (*or* admonish) earnestly /～祈 beg fervently ❷ request; entreat; beg:敬～ respectfully request

恳辞 kěncí decline in all sincerity; beg off earnestly:他对主席一职,一再～。He earnestly declined the position of president time and again.

恳切 kěnqiè sincere; earnest:～地期待 earnestly expect /语调～ speak in a sincere tone /～的要求 earnest (*or* ardent) request

恳亲会 kěnqīnhuì 〈旧语〉social meeting arranged for students' parents

恳情 kěnqíng plead; intercede (on sb.'s behalf):～话 pleading words

恳请 kěnqǐng earnestly request; cordially invite:～光临。Your gracious presence is cordially requested. *or* You are cordially invited to the party. /～予以协助。Your assistance is earnestly requested.

恳求 kěnqiú beg sincerely; implore; entreat; beseech:我们只得～你替我们作最后一次努力。We cannot but implore you to make a final effort on our behalf. /由于各方的～,学校已同意重新考虑这个决定。In response to earnest requests from various quarters, the school authorities agreed to reconsider the decision.

恳谈 kěntán have a heart-to-heart talk; talk sincerely:～会 get-together where participants are engaged in free and cordial conversation

恳托 kěntuō make a sincere request; earnestly entrust:～别人照顾自己的孩子 earnestly entreat sb. to take care of one's child

恳挚 kěnzhì 〈书面〉earnest; sincere:情意～ show great sincerity /言语～动人 express oneself in sincere and moving terms; make a sincere and moving appeal

垦(墾) kěn turn up (soil); cultivate (land); reclaim (wasteland):～田 cultivate farmland /开～荒地 reclaim wasteland /军～农场 army reclamation farm

垦复 kěnfù open up land that has gone out of cultivation; recultivate or reclaim land that has lain waste:～荒地百余亩 open up more than one hundred *mu* of land that has lain waste

垦覆 kěnfù make furrows between rows of trees, plant green manure crops, and plough them under in order to enrich the soil for the trees

垦荒 kěnhuāng reclaim wasteland; open up virgin soil; bring wild country under cultivation

垦区 kěnqū reclamation area; reclaimed area

垦殖 kěnzhí cultivate wasteland

垦种 kěnzhòng reclaim and plant; open up and cultivate:大片可以～的荒地 large tracts of arable wasteland

kèn

裉(褃) kèn seam between the body and the sleeve (of a jacket):抬～ measurement from the shoulder to the armpit /煞～ sew a sleeve on to the body of a jacket

掯 kèn 〈方言〉❶ push down hard; press:～住牛脖子 press hard at the ox's neck ❷ deliberately make things difficult:勒～ be hard on sb. ❸ (of eyes) contain; hold:她～着泪花。Her eyes welled with tears.

kēng

坑 kēng ❶ pit; depression; hollow:在地上刨个～ dig a pit (*or* hole) in the ground /粪～ manure pit; cesspool /弹～ shell pit /水～ puddle /沙～ jumping pit; sandpit /火～ fire pit; living hell; abyss of suffering /满脸麻～ face pitted with smallpox /一个萝卜一个～ one turnip, one hole — each has his own task, and there is nobody to spare ❷ tunnel; hole; pit:矿～ pit /煤～ coal pit /～口 pithead ❸〈古语〉bury alive:～杀 bury alive (usu. in a pit) /焚书～儒 (of Qin Shi Huang, the first Emperor of the Qin Dynasty) burn the books and bury Confucian scholars alive ❹ harm by cunning or deceit; cheat; hoodwink:他被人～了。He was hoodwinked. /你这样做可～了我们了。Acting the way you did, you got us into a fix. ❺ (Kēng) a surname

坑道 kēngdào ❶〈矿业〉pit; gallery ❷〈军事〉tunnel:～战 tunnel warfare /～工事 tunnel defences; tunnel fortifications /～作业 tunnelling

坑害 kēnghài entrap; ensnare; do harm to (by scheming, cunning, deception, etc.):～人民 do harm to the people; bring disasters to the people; make the people suffer /～顾客(of a trader) cheat (*or* swindle) customers /他是受人～才落到了这个地步。He has come to such a pass because he fell into the trap set for him.

坑井 kēngjǐng (in mining) gallery and pit; tunnel; pit

坑坑洼洼 kēngkeng-wāwā *also* "坑坑坎坎" full of bumps and hollows; full of pits and holes; bumpy:～的一生 life full of setbacks and frustrations /这条路～的,不好骑车。This road is too bumpy for cycling.

坑口电站 kēngkǒu diànzhàn power plant at the pithead; power station at a coal mine

坑炉 kēnglú 〈冶金〉pit furnace

坑蒙 kēngmēng *also* "坑蒙拐骗" swindle; cheat:他用这种方法～了不少人。He cheated quite a few people this way.

坑木 kēngmù 〈矿业〉pit prop; mine timber

坑骗 kēngpiàn cheat; defraud; swindle:用假冒伪劣产品～顾客 cheat customers with shoddy (*or* counterfeit) products /他受了奸商的～,经营小本生意破了产。Swindled by profiteers, he went bankrupt and lost his small business.

坑气 kēngqì *also* "沼气" zhǎoqì methane

坑人 kēngrén cheat; deceive; trick:他决不干～的事。He would never stoop to cheating. /花一百元买这么个不中用的东西,真～坑到家了! A hundred *yuan* for this worthless stuff? It's downright rob-

K

bery!

坑洼 kēngwā ❶ hole; hollow; depression: 填平～ fill up holes ❷ low-lying; depressed: ～不平的小路 path full of holes and bumps

坑子 kēngzi 〈口语〉pit; hole; puddle: 水～ water puddle; pool of water

吭

kēng utter a sound or word; speak: 一声不～ not say a word; remain silent / 这么半天, 他连～都没有～一声。He never said a single word all the while.

see also háng

吭哧 kēngchi ❶ puff; puff and blow: 他抱着一大摞书～～地走上楼去。He walked upstairs with a big stack of books in his arms, puffing hard from the strain. ❷ work hard; toil: 我在这儿～了半天了, 报告还没憋出来。I've been wrestling for quite a long time over the report but all in vain. ❸ hem and haw: 你～了半天, 究竟什么意思? Stop hemming and hawing! What exactly do you mean?

吭唧 kēngji ❶ snivel: 别～了! 要什么说就是了。Stop sniveling! Just tell me what you want. ❷ hem and haw: 他吭吭唧唧了半天, 我什么也没听明白。I couldn't get anything out of his hemming and hawing. ❸ work with great effort; strain; toil: 他～了好几天才写出这篇文章。He toiled for quite a few days to get the article out.

吭气 kēngqì *see* "吭声"

吭声 kēngshēng *also* "吭气" utter a sound; breathe a word: 你怎么不～? Why don't you say something? / 不管你怎么问, 他反正是不～。He kept mum no matter what questions you put to him. / 她虽受了冤枉, 也不吭一声。She did not utter a word, though she was wronged.

阬

kēng 〈书面〉*see* "坑" kēng

硁(硜、磤)

kēng 〈书面〉sound of striking stones; clangour

硁硁 kēngkēng 〈书面〉shallow and bigoted: ～自守 be stubborn and refuse to change / ～之见〈谦词〉my humble and shallow view

铿(鏗)

kēng 〈象声〉clang; clatter: 压路机～～地碾过石子层。The road-roller clattered over the cobblestones.

铿锵 kēngqiāng (of gongs, cymbals, *pipa*, or similar instruments) rhythmic and sonorous; sonorous and forceful: ～有力的讲话 ringing and powerful speech / 歌声～ rhythmic and resonant singing / 这首诗读起来音调～。This poem is characterized by the rhythm and resonance of its diction.

铿然 kēngrán 〈书面〉sonorous and forceful; loud and clear: 溪水奔流, ～有声。The brook runs on, gurgling loud and clear down its course.

kōng

空

kōng ❶ empty; hollow; void; unoccupied: ～抽屉 empty drawer / ～位子 unoccupied seat / ～招牌 mere signboard; all appearance but no substance / 赤手～拳 with bare hands; unarmed / 虫把屋梁都蛀～了。The beam has been eaten hollow by worms. / 你不能～着肚子喝酒。You mustn't drink on an empty stomach. / 院子里的人都走～了。The courtyard is deserted. *or* There isn't a single soul in the yard. / 没有群众支持, 你再说也是～的! Without popular support, your words mean nothing, though you may repeat them for the umpteenth time. ❷ air; sky: 天～ sky / 晴～万里 vast clear sky / 领～ territorial air (space) / 半～ in mid-air / 对～射击 fire into the air / 高～ at a high altitude / 真～ vacuum / 太～ outer space ❸ in vain; for nothing; to no avail: ～忙一阵 bestir oneself in vain; make fruitless efforts; be busy for nothing / ～跑一趟 make a trip in vain; make a futile journey / ～欢喜 rejoice too soon; rejoice only to be let down / 我们的希望都落～了。All our hopes were dashed to pieces.

see also kòng

空靶 kōngbǎ air, aerial, or airborne target

空包弹 kōngbāodàn 〈军事〉blank cartridge

空瘪 kōngbiě empty and shrunken; hollow and withered: ～的麦穗 withered ears of wheat / ～的皮球 shrunken ball / 三日未进餐, 肚已～。As he hadn't had any food for three days, he felt as if his stomach had all shrivelled up.

空舱费 kōngcāngfèi 〈交通〉dead freight

空肠 kōngcháng 〈生理〉jejunum

空肠炎 kōngchángyán 〈医学〉jejunitis

空敞 kōngchǎng open and vast; spacious: ～的草地 open and vast grassland

空城计 kōngchéngjì empty-city stratagem (bluffing the enemy by keeping the gates of a weakly defended city open as if a trap were laid for him inside); presenting a bold front to conceal a weak defence: 我们总得留个人在后面照料, 不能唱～啊! It won't do for us all to pack up and go. We'll have to leave somebody behind to keep an eye on things.

空船吃水 kōngchuán chīshuǐ 〈交通〉light draught

空船重量 kōngchuán zhòngliàng 〈交通〉light weight

空挡 kōngdǎng 〈机械〉neutral gear: 挂～ put (a car, etc.) in neutral gear

空荡荡 kōngdàngdàng *also* "空落落" empty; deserted: 午夜时刻, 街上～的。It was midnight, and the street was deserted. / 广场上～的。The square was spacious and empty.

空洞 kōngdòng ❶ empty; hollow; devoid of substance: ～的文章 empty article; article without substance / 这个计划太～。The plan is too vague and general. ❷ cavity: 肺～ pulmonary cavity / 两肺均有～。There are cavities in both lungs.

空洞洞 kōngdòngdòng empty; deserted: 店堂里～的, 一个顾客也没有。The shop was empty of customers.

空洞无物 kōngdòng-wúwù empty; windy; devoid of content

空对地导弹 kōngduìdì dǎodàn air-to-surface guided missile (ASM); air-to-ground missile

空对空 kōngduìkōng air-to-air: ～激光测距 air-to-air laser ranging / ～雷达截获 air-to-air radar acquisition / ～识别 air-to-air identification

空对空导弹 kōngduìkōng dǎodàn air-to-air guided missile; air-to-air missile (AAM)

空对潜导弹 kōngduìqián dǎodàn air-to-underwater missile (AUM)

空乏 kōngfá ❶ poverty-stricken ❷ empty and dull: ～的生活 dull and meaningless life

空翻 kōngfān 〈体育〉somersault; flip: 前～ forward somersault; forward flip / 后～ backward somersault; back flip

空泛 kōngfàn vague and general; not specific: ～的议论 vague and general opinions; generalities / 内容～ devoid of content / 你这不过是一个～的愿望。This is just an idle hope of yours. / 写文章要力求具体, 切忌～。It is essential to be specific and avoid platitudes in one's writing.

空防 kōngfáng 〈军事〉air defence: ～部队 air defence force (*or* troops)

空房 kōngfáng ❶ empty room ❷ house in which a wife lives while her husband is away: 独守～ be a grass widow

空腹 kōngfù ❶ on an empty stomach: ～服用 to be taken on an empty stomach / 明早～来抽血。Come and have your blood test on an empty stomach tomorrow morning. ❷ 〈书面〉ignorant; without learning: ～高心 have little learning but think highly of oneself

空港 kōnggǎng (short for 航空港) airport

空谷足音 kōnggǔ-zúyīn footsteps one hears in a deserted mountain valley — valuable information or opinion that is difficult to come by; sth. rare and precious

空喊 kōnghǎn clamour without taking action; loud and empty talk: ～现代化是不会使家乡富裕起来的。Loud, empty talk about modernization will not bring prosperity to our native village.

空耗 kōnghào waste: ～精力 waste one's energy / ～资源 squander natural resources

空话 kōnghuà empty or idle talk; lip service; hollow words: 他一天什么事也不干, 尽讲～。He does nothing but indulge in idle talk all day long. / 把文章中的～、废话统统去掉。Cross out all the hollow and meaningless words from the article. / 这种恭维, 只不过是～, 千万不可当真。Such compliments are nothing but lip service. You mustn't take them seriously.

空话连篇 kōnghuà-liánpiān long-winded empty talk; reels of empty verbiage

空怀 kōnghuái 〈畜牧〉non-pregnant; barren: 想尽办法使所有适龄母畜都不～。Every effort must be made to impregnate all female animals without exception.

空幻 kōnghuàn visionary; illusory: 这对年轻人担心他们珍视的幸福也许会是～。The young couple feared that the happiness they cher-

ished so much might be illusory.

空基 kōngjī air-based:～巡航导弹 air-based cruise missile

空际 kōngjì in the sky; in the air:广场上掌声和欢呼声洋溢～。On the square, the air was filled with applause and shouts of joy.

空寂 kōngjì open and silent; deserted and quiet:～的山野 open and silent mountainous country /小街上～无人。There was not a soul in the deserted lane.

空架子 kōngjiàzi mere skeleton; bare outline; framework without substance:这个处其实是个～,只有官没有兵。This office is a mere skeleton, with somebody in charge but no staff running the show. /母亲尽力支撑着周家这个～。Mother struggled to keep up appearances for the Zhou family.

空间 kōngjiān space:生存～ living space; *lebensraum* /外层～ outer space /～战 space war /～构架 space frame /～防御 space defence /～节省装置 space saver /～成像 aerial imaging /～磁暴 interplanetary magnetic storm /以～换时间〈军事〉exchange space for time; gain time by giving up territory

空间病 kōngjiānbìng space syndrome

空间波 kōngjiānbō space or spatial wave

空间点阵 kōngjiān diǎnzhèn *also* "晶体点阵" jīngtǐ diǎnzhèn 〈物理〉space lattice; crystal lattice

空间电荷 kōngjiān diànhè 〈电子〉space charge

空间法 kōngjiānfǎ 〈法律〉space law

空间感受 kōngjiān gǎnshòu *also* "空间知觉"〈心理〉space perception

空间技术 kōngjiān jìshù space technology

空间科学 kōngjiān kēxué space science

空间垃圾 kōngjiān lājī space junk

空间曲线 kōngjiān qūxiàn 〈数学〉space curve

空间实验室 kōngjiān shíyànshì skylab

空间速度 kōngjiān sùdù space velocity

空间天文学 kōngjiān tiānwénxué space astronomy

空间通信 kōngjiān tōngxìn space communication

空间图形 kōngjiān túxíng ❶ *also* "几何图形" jǐhé túxíng spatial pattern; geometric pattern ❷ three-dimensional image; stereopicture

空间行走 kōngjiān xíngzǒu space walk

空间遥测 kōngjiān yáocè space telemetry

空间医学 kōngjiān yīxué space medicine; aeromedicine

空间站 kōngjiānzhàn *also* "航天站" hángtiānzhàn 〈航天〉space station

空间知觉 kōngjiān zhījué 〈心理〉space perception

空舰导弹 kōngjiàn dǎodàn air-to-ship missile

空降 kōngjiàng airborne:～部队 airborne force /～袭击 airborne raid /～点 landing area; airborne area /～作战 airborne war

空降兵 kōngjiàngbīng airborne force; paratroops; parachutists

空姐 kōngjiě 〈口语〉(short for 空中小姐) air hostess; stewardess

空晶石 kōngjīngshí 〈矿物〉chiastolite

空军 kōngjūn air force:～补给站 air force station /～部队 air force; air (force) unit; air component /～后备队 air force reserve (AFRES) /～基地 air base; air force base (AFB) /～司令部 general headquarters of the air force; air command /～司令员 commander of the air force /～试验场 air proving ground /～特遣部队 air task force /～战斗序列 air order of battle

空军武官 kōngjūn wǔguān air attaché

空壳铸件 kōngké zhùjiàn 〈冶金〉slush casting

空空导弹 kōngkōng dǎodàn air-to-air missile

空空如也 kōngkōngrúyě completely empty; all empty:肚子里～ have an empty stomach; be hungry;〈比喻〉have an empty head /她不断地支取自己的储蓄,如今已是～。She constantly nibbled at her savings until she had practically nothing left.

空口 kōngkǒu ❶ eat dishes without rice or wine; eat rice or drink wine with nothing to go with it:～喝酒容易醉。One gets drunk easily when one has nothing to go with the wine. ❷ merely give a verbal statement; pay lip service:这事～是和他说不明白的。You cannot clarify this to him merely by talking.

空口说白话 kōngkǒu shuō báihuà pay lip service; make empty promises

空口无凭 kōngkǒu-wúpíng a mere verbal statement is no guarantee; words of mouth are no guarantee; talk is cheap:～的话我不信。I won't trust mere words of mouth.

空旷 kōngkuàng open and spacious; wild:一片～原野,了无人烟 a vast stretch of open country with no trace of human habitation /孩子们喜欢到工厂后面那片～的地方去玩。Children loved to play in the open space behind the factory. /昔日繁忙的码头如今～萧条。The once bustling dock is now a scene of desolation.

空匮 kōngkuì scarce; scanty; empty:国库～。The national treasury is almost empty.

空阔 kōngkuò open and vast; spacious:海天～ vast ocean and sky

空廓 kōngkuò open; spacious; vast

空雷 kōngléi aerial mine

空寥 kōngliáo *see* "空寂"

空灵 kōnglíng indescribably free; free and natural:～的笔触 (in) an indescribably free style /我的笔写不出这～的妙景。It's just beyond me to describe such a natural and graceful scene.

空论 kōnglùn idle talk; empty talk:不切实际的～ irrelevant remarks; empty talk /少发～,多干实事! Less talk, more action!

空落 kōngluò empty and desolate; quiet and deserted:都去上班了,家里～无人。Everyone had gone to work and the house was empty and quiet.

空落落 kōngluòluò empty; deserted; in desolation:他送走妻子回到家来,心里觉得～的。He felt a touch of emptiness when he came back home after seeing his wife off. /叶子落光了,树林里显得～的。Stripped of foliage, the woods looked bare and forlorn.

空门 kōngmén ❶〈佛教〉Buddhism:遁入～ become a Buddhist monk or nun; take a monastic vow ❷ (of football) unguarded gate

空濛 kōngméng 〈书面〉hazy; misty:山色～ hills hidden (*or* shrouded) in mist /烟雾～ vast expanse of drifting mist /细雨～。A fine drizzle blurred the view.

空名 kōngmíng ❶ empty title; titular position; mere figurehead:他挂了个主任的～,实际一点主也作不了。He is director only in name and has no say in anything. ❷ undeserved reputation:不务～ seek no vain glory; live up to one's reputation /说她唱歌唱得好,不过是个～。She is said to be a good singer, but she doesn't really deserve the reputation.

空漠 kōngmò *also* "空寞" ❶ empty and quiet:～的原野 desolate champaign (*or* plain); open wild country ❷ void and confused:～的心田 emptiness and confusion in one's heart

空难 kōngnàn air disaster; air crash; plane crash:这次～中有五十人丧生。Fifty people died in the air crash.

空炮 kōngpào empty talk; idle boasting:放～ talk big; spout hot air; make unrealistic promises

空气 kōngqì ❶ air:新鲜～ fresh air /潮湿～ moist air /压缩～ compressed air /～流通 (air) ventilation /～传染〈医学〉air-borne infection /～电池〈电工〉air dry cell; air battery /～断路器 air circuit breaker; air break /～开关 air-break switch; air switch /～绝缘 air insulation /～过滤器 air-filter; air cleaner /～涡轮 air turbine ❷ atmosphere:热烈友好的～ warm and friendly atmosphere /政治～ political atmosphere (*or* climate)/紧张的～ tense atmosphere; tension /这里学术～浓厚。One feels great enthusiasm in academic studies here.

空气泵 kōngqìbèng air pump

空气锤 kōngqìchuí *also* "气锤" qìchuí pneumatic hammer; air hammer

空气弹道 kōngqì dàndào aeroballistic or atmospheric trajectory

空气动力试验 kōngqì dònglì shìyàn aerodynamic experiment or test

空气动力弹性 kōngqì dònglì tánxìng aeroelasticity

空气动力学 kōngqì dònglìxué aerodynamics

空气加湿器 kōngqì jiāshīqì humidifier

空气间隙光纤 kōngqì jiànxì guāngxiān air-supported fiber

空气净化 kōngqì jìnghuà air purification; air-cleaning:～器 air-purifier

空气冷却 kōngqì lěngquè air-cooling:～器 air-cooler

空气力学 kōngqì lìxué aeromechanics

空气调节 kōngqì tiáojié air-conditioning:～器 (often shortened as 空调) air conditioner

空气透视法 kōngqì tòushìfǎ aerial perspective

空气污染 kōngqì wūrǎn air pollution:～指数 air pollution index (API)

空气压缩机 kōngqì yāsuōjī air compressor

空气浴 kōngqìyù air bath

空气轴承 kōngqì zhóuchéng air bearing

空前 kōngqián unprecedented; unparalleled:～浩劫 unprece-

dented catastrophe /～的规模 unprecedented (*or* unheard-of) scale /～的盛况 extraordinarily grand occasion /～高涨 be at an all time high /这五年来取得的成绩在我国历史上是～的。The achievements scored over the past five years are without parallel in the history of our country. /他们正处在一个～困难的时期。Never before have they seen more difficult days.

空前绝后 kōngqián-juéhòu unprecedented and unrepeatable; unique:～的奇闻 most bizarre story in history /成吉思汗的征服在历史上恐怕是～的。Genghis Khan's conquests probably are historically unique.

空腔 kōngqiāng 〈物理〉cavity:～电路 cavity circuit /～加速器 cavity accelerator /～波导(管)〈电子〉hollow-pipe waveguide; hollow-type guide /～振荡器 hollow-space oscillator

空勤 kōngqín air duty:～人员 aircrew; flight crew

空情 kōngqíng (usu. in reference to the enemy's presence in the air) conditions in the air; aviation circumstances

空阒 kōngqù 〈书面〉empty and quiet:～的古寺 tranquil ancient temple

空人儿 kōngrénr ❶ empty-handed:他进了一趟城什么都没买,～回来了。He didn't buy anything when he went to town, and came back empty-handed. ❷ one without any family or other burden:这钱你拿着,我～一个,怎么也好对付。Take this money. I don't have any family to support and can manage all right.

空射导弹 kōngshè dǎodàn 〈军事〉air-launched guided missile (ALMS):～系统 air-launched missile system

空身 kōngshēn carry no luggage; carry nothing:你还是～进去不为人注意。To escape notice, you'd better not carry anything when you walk in.

空身人儿 kōngshēnrénr ❶ *see* "空身" ❷ *see* "空人儿❷"

空驶 kōngshǐ 〈交通〉travel empty; deadhead:～的货车 deadhead freight train /～卡车返回车库 deadhead a truck back to the depot /～去上海接货 deadhead to Shanghai to carry back the goods

空室清野 kōngshì-qīngyě *also* "空舍清野" (in war times) hide all belongings and provisions, and clear the fields, so as to leave nothing for the invading enemy
see also "坚壁清野" jiānbì-qīngyě

空手 kōngshǒu ❶ empty-handed; with bare hands:～而归 return empty-handed /你～怎么能打得过他们? How could you fight them with bare fists? ❷ (usu. used in painting or embroidery) without a model or a sample:～画的画儿 painting based on one's imagination

空手道 kōngshǒudào 〈体育〉karate

空疏 kōngshū 〈书面〉empty; scanty; lacking in substance:学问～ have scanty and unsubstantial learning (*or* knowledge)

空速 kōngsù 〈航空〉air speed:飞行～ flight airspeed; flying airspeed

空胎 kōngtāi (of female animals) fail to conceive after mating or insemination; remain non-pregnant:～率 rate of non-pregnancy (of female animals)

空谈 kōngtán ❶ empty or idle talk; prattle; windy abstractions:纸上～ empty abstractions on paper /～无济于事。Empty talk won't help. ❷ talk without doing anything; indulge in empty talk:他这个人只知道～志向,不务实际。He talked big about his aspirations without doing a jot of practical work.

空谈主义 kōngtánzhǔyì phrase-mongering

空调 kōngtiáo ❶ (short for 空气调节) air-conditioning:～设备 air-conditioning (unit); air-conditioner /这屋里有～。This room is air-conditioned. ❷ (short for 空气调节器) air-conditioner:国产～ home-made air-conditioner

空桐树 kōngtóngshù *also* "珙桐" gǒngtóng dove tree

空头 kōngtóu ❶〈经济〉(of the stock exchange) bear; shortseller:～与多头 bears and bulls /做～ bear; shortsell /～市场 bear market (in which prices are falling) ❷ nominal; empty; phony:～计划 phony plan /～文学家 phony writer /～政治家 armchair politician /竟然有人相信他那些～允诺! How could people be so credulous as to accept his empty promises!

空头人情 kōngtóu rénqíng empty gesture of friendship or sympathy; phony or empty favour; lip-service:做～ make an empty gesture of friendship (*or* sympathy); pay lip-service; do an empty favour

空头支票 kōngtóu zhīpiào ❶ rubber or dud cheque; bounced cheque; bad cheque:开～ write a bad cheque; kite a cheque ❷ empty promise; lip-service:他只是开～而已,根本不想兑现的。That was mere lip-service. He never meant it.

空投 kōngtóu air-drop; paradrop:～救援物质 air-drop relief supplies /～人员 air-dropped personnel /～特务 air-dropped agent /～包 parapack /～鱼雷 aerial torpedo /～伞 aerial delivery parachute

空投场 kōngtóuchǎng dropping ground

空文 kōngwén ❶ empty writing; verbiage ❷ ineffective plan, rule, law, etc.:一纸～ mere scrap of paper

空吸 kōngxī 〈物理〉suction:～滤器 suction filter

空袭 kōngxí air raid; air attack:～目标 air-raid target /躲～ run for shelter during an air raid

空袭警报 kōngxí jǐngbào air-raid alarm:～器 air-raid siren

空想 kōngxiǎng ❶ indulge in daydreaming or fantasy:～成癖 be addicted to daydreaming; be given to dereism /不要尽去～,还是先调查一下情况吧。Stop daydreaming. It would be better to investigate first. ❷ idle dream; daydream; wishful thinking:离开了客观现实的想法就成为～。Any idea that departs from objective reality is mere fantasy.

空想家 kōngxiǎngjiā dreamer; visionary

空想社会主义 kōngxiǎng shèhuìzhǔyì utopian socialism:～者 utopian socialist

空心 kōngxīn ❶ (of trees, plants, etc.) become hollow inside:萝卜～了。The turnip has gone spongy. /这棵树空了心了。The tree has become hollow inside. ❷ hollow (core); air core:～变压器〈电工〉air core transformer /～线圈 air-core coil /～电缆 hollow-core cable /～导线 hollow conductor /～梁〈机械〉hollow beam /～铣刀 hollow mill /～轴 hollow shaft /～墙〈建筑〉cavity wall; hollow wall /～铸件〈冶金〉slush casting
see also kòngxīn

空心坝 kōngxīnbà hollow dam

空心病 kōngxīnbìng 〈农业〉(of plants) hollow stem or stalk; (of potatoes) hollow heart

空心菜 kōngxīncài *also* "蕹菜" wèngcài 〈植物〉water spinach (*Ipomaea aquatica*)

空心长丝 kōngxīn chángsī hollow filament

空心大老倌 kōngxīn dàlǎoguān 〈方言〉fellow of vain pretensions; stuffed shirt

空心莲子草 kōngxīn liánzǐcǎo *also* "空心苋"; "水花生" shuǐhuāshēng 〈植物〉*Alternanthera philoxeroides*

空心萝卜 kōngxīn luóbo hollow turnip — person without genuine ability or knowledge

空心面 kōngxīnmiàn macaroni

空心汤团 kōngxīn tāngtuán 〈方言〉hollow dumpling (one without filling) — empty promise or favour:你可不要给我～吃啊! I hope you're not just making me happy with an empty promise.

空心砖 kōngxīnzhuān air brick; hollow brick

空虚 kōngxū hollow; empty; void:国库～ empty national treasury /生活～ lead an aimless (*or* vacuous) life /敌人后方～。The enemy rear is weakly defended. /金钱填不满她精神上的～。Wealth cannot fill the vacuum (*or* void) in her heart.

空穴 kōngxué 〈电子〉(electronic) hole:～传导 hole conduction /～密度 hole density

空穴来风 kōngxué-láifēng an empty hole invites wind — weakness lends wings to rumours:～,理有固然。It's only natural that an empty hole invites wind. /谣言接踵而来,虽然不过是～,也不能不引起我们的警惕。Rumours are rife. Ill-founded as they may be, they should put us on our guard.

空言 kōngyán empty talk; impractical words:～无补 empty talk is of no avail /他想以～欺骗我们。He was trying to palm us off with empty promises.

空邮 kōngyóu send mail by air

空域 kōngyù airspace:搜索～ search the airspace /～划分 division of airspace

空运 kōngyùn air transport; airlift:～保险 air transport insurance /～救灾物质 airlift relief supplies /这批鲜荔枝是～来的。These fresh lichees came by air.

空运单 kōngyùndān airway bill (of lading):～条款 conditions of contract of airway bill

空运发货单 kōngyùn fāhuòdān air consignment note

空运费 kōngyùnfèi air freight:付～ pay air freight

空运公司 kōngyùn gōngsī airshipper; air transport company

空运货物 kōngyùn huòwù air freight; air cargo

空晕病 kōngyùnbìng airsickness

K

空载 kōngzài (of machinery, equipment, vehicles, etc.) operate without load:～卡车 empty truck /～设备 equipment operating without load
空战 kōngzhàn air battle; aerial combat:空中混战 (air) dogfight
空中 kōngzhōng ❶ in the air; in the sky; overhead:～警戒 air alert /～封锁 aerial blockade /～掩护 air umbrella; air cover /～侦察 aerial reconnaissance /～补给 air supply /～力量 air power /～优势 air superiority /～走廊 air corridor; air lane /～警报和控制系统 airborne warning and control system /一轮明月挂在～。A bright moon was hanging in the sky. ❷ by radio:～书场 radio story-telling programme
空中飞人 kōngzhōng fēirén 〈杂技〉trapeze show:～表演者 trapeze artist; trapezist
空中广告 kōngzhōng guǎnggào skywriting
空中花园 Kōngzhōng Huāyuán Hanging Gardens of Babylon, one of the ancient world's seven wonders
空中加油 kōngzhōng jiāyóu 〈航空〉air refueling; in-flight refueling; air-to-air refueling:～飞机 aerial refueller; in-flight refueller; tanker plane
空中交通管制 kōngzhōng jiāotōng guǎnzhì air traffic control
空中劫持 kōngzhōng jiéchí (aerial) hijacking
空中禁区 kōngzhōng jìnqū restricted airspace
空中客车 Kōngzhōng Kèchē (European passenger plane) Airbus
空中楼阁 kōngzhōng-lóugé castle in the air:这个计划听起来倒是很宏伟,实际上可能只是个～。Grand as the plan sounds, it may prove to be a castle in the air.
空中摄影 kōngzhōng shèyǐng aerial photography; aerophotography
空中体操 kōngzhōng tǐcāo aerogymnastics
空中小姐 kōngzhōng xiǎojiě *also* "空姐" air hostess; air stewardess
空重 kōngzhòng 〈交通〉empty weight; bare weight (of a vehicle without cargo or passengers)
空竹 kōngzhú *also* "空钟" diabolo:抖～ play diabolo
空转 kōngzhuàn ❶ (of a motor, etc.) operate without a load; idle:～速度 idling speed; idle speed /让马达～ idle a motor ❷ (of wheels) turn without moving forward; spin:车翻了,轮子～着。The car was overturned with its wheels spinning.

悾 kōng

悾悾 kōngkōng 〈书面〉sincere

崆 kōng

崆峒 Kōngtóng ❶ name of a mountain in Gansu Province ❷ name of an island in Shangdong Province

箜 kōng

箜篌 kōnghóu ancient plucked stringed instrument (with five to twenty-five strings)

倥 kōng

see also kǒng
倥侗 kōngtóng 〈书面〉ignorant; benighted

kǒng

K

恐 kǒng

❶ be afraid; fear; dread:惶～ fear; be filled with trepidation /惊～ be alarmed; panic /深～ be very much afraid; be in deep dread (of sth.) /惴～ be dreadfully worried /有恃无～ not fear because one has sth. up one's sleeve; feel secure in the belief that one has powerful support ❷ scare; frighten; terrify; intimidate ❸ I'm afraid:～不容易。I'm afraid it's not that easy. /～非原意。This may not be what was meant. /或～有误。There might be some mistake.
恐怖 kǒngbù terror; horror:白色～ White terror /～统治 reign of terror /～行为 terrorist action /～连环画 horror comics /～失色 be pale with panic /从这本小说里,他第一次读到现代战争的～。In this novel he read about the horrors of modern warfare for the first time. /想到这里,她觉得很～。She was gripped with a sudden fear at the thought.
恐怖分子 kǒngbùfènzǐ terrorist
恐怖症 kǒngbùzhèng 〈医学〉phobia
恐怖主义 kǒngbùzhǔyì terrorism:～行为 terrorist act (*or* action)
恐防 kǒngfáng 〈方言〉*see* "恐怕"
恐高症 kǒnggāozhèng 〈医学〉acrophobia:～患者 acrophobe
恐吓 kǒnghè intimidate; threaten; frighten; blackmail:～信 blackmailing (*or* threatening) letter /他们～她,要她在文件上签字。They tried to intimidate (*or* frighten) her into signing the paper. /面对歹徒们的～,他毫无畏惧。He betrayed not the slightest trace of fear at the thugs' intimidation.
恐慌 kǒnghuāng panic:金融～ financial panic /陷入～ fall (*or* get) into a panic; be seized with panic /制造～的人 scaremongers /村里的人听到这个消息后,一片～。Panic swept through the village at the news. *or* The news struck terror into the village people.
恐惧 kǒngjù fear; dread; terror:～不安 be frightened and worried; be filled with horror and anxiety /他突然感到～。Sudden fear came over him. *or* He was seized with fear. /这次事故以后,她对乘电梯产生了一种～心理。After the accident, she developed a lurking dread of the lift.
恐龙 kǒnglóng 〈考古〉dinosaur:～蛋 dinosaur egg /食肉～ carnivorous dinosaur
恐鸟 kǒngniǎo 〈考古〉dinornis
恐怕 kǒngpà 〈副词〉❶ *indicating doubt or anxiety about consequences*:你这样说～有些不公正。I'm afraid it was unfair of you to say so. /她踮着脚尖进了屋,～吵醒了妹妹。She tiptoed into the room for fear of waking up her sister. ❷ *indicating an estimation*:我们的会～要推迟了。It seems that (*or* looks as if) our meeting will have to be put off. *or* Perhaps our meeting will have to be postponed. /～要下雪了。It looks like snow. /～你得亲自去一趟。I think you'd better go in person.
恐慑 kǒngshè 〈书面〉fear; be frightened:～之心 frightened heart
恐兽 kǒngshòu 〈考古〉dinothere; dinotherium
恐水病 kǒngshuǐbìng hydrophobia; rabies

倥 kǒng

see also kōng
倥偬 kǒngzǒng 〈书面〉❶ pressing; urgent:戎马～ burdened with the pressing duties of a soldier ❷ poverty-stricken; destitute; impoverished

孔 kǒng

❶ hole; opening; aperture:气～ air hole /钥匙～ keyhole /照像机光～ aperture /毛～ pore /鼻～ nostril /电器插～ socket on an electrical appliance /三～桥 three-arched bridge /多～动物 porifer /在板上钻个～ bore a hole on the board /激光穿～ laser piercing ❷ 〈方言〉〈量词〉*used for caves*:一～土窑 an earthen cave-dwelling /两～砖窑 two brick-lined cave-dwellings ❸ (Kǒng) a surname
孔版印刷 kǒngbǎn yìnshuā porous printing
孔道 kǒngdào narrow passage; pass:交通～ transport (*or* traffic) junction /山洞里只有一个通往洞外的～。In this cave there is only one narrow passage leading to an opening outside.
孔洞 kǒngdòng hole; opening:金属板上钻有～。The metal board was drilled with holes.
孔方兄 kǒngfāngxiōng 〈比喻〉〈讽刺〉(derived from ancient coins with a square hole in the middle) Mr. Square Hole — money; cash
孔夫子 Kǒngfūzǐ *also* "孔子" (respectful term of address for 孔丘, Kong Qiu, 551-479 BC) Kung Fu-tzu or Confucius, Chinese philosopher, educator and founder of Confucianism in late Spring and Autumn Period:～门前卖文章 try to sell one's own work in front of the Confucius' house; show off in the presence of an expert; teach one's grandmother how to suck an egg /～搬家尽是书 when Confucius removes, there is nothing but books — you lose all the time (as 书 is a homophone for 输)
孔家店 Kǒngjiādiàn 〈贬词〉Confucius and Sons; Confucian shop:打倒～。Down with the "Confucian shop". *or* Down with Confucius and his followers. (A famous slogan during the New Culture Movement of the late 1910's and the early 1920's.)
孔径 kǒngjìng diameter of aperture; bore diameter; span (of an arch, etc.):～比 aperture ratio /～角 aperture angle /～天线 aperture antenna
孔径效应 kǒngjìng xiàoyìng 〈物理〉aperture effect
孔孟之道 Kǒng-Mèng Zhī Dào doctrines of Confucius and Men-

cius; tenets of Confucianism
孔庙 Kǒngmiào Confucian temple
孔明 Kǒngmíng another name for the famous military strategist and statesman Zhuge Liang (诸葛亮)
孔明灯 kǒngmíngdēng Kongming lantern (a kind of portable hurricane lamp said to have been invented by Zhuge Liang)
孔丘 Kǒng Qiū *see* "孔夫子"
孔雀 kǒngquè peacock: ～毛 peacock feather / ～开屏 peacock fanning out its tail in a splash of colours / ～舞 peacock dance, Chinese dance imitating the graceful movements of the peacock
孔雀绿 kǒngquèlǜ peacock green; malachite green
孔雀石 kǒngquèshí 〈矿业〉 malachite
孔蚀 kǒngshí 〈冶金〉 pitting corrosion: ～系数 pitting factor
孔武有力 kǒngwǔ-yǒulì (of one's physique) mighty and powerful
孔隙 kǒngxì small hole or opening; crevice
孔隙度 kǒngxìdù 〈地质〉 porosity
孔祥熙 Kǒng Xiángxī H. H. Kung (1881-1967), Chinese banker and KMT politician affiliated to Chiang Kai-shek (蒋介石) by marriage
孔型 kǒngxíng 〈冶金〉 pass: 初轧～ bloom pass / 精轧～ finishing pass / ～凸度 pass convexity
孔穴 kǒngxué hole; cavity
孔眼 kǒngyǎn small hole; small opening: 叶子上满是虫吃的～。The leaves were covered with holes eaten out by worms.
孔子 Kǒngzǐ *see* "孔夫子"

kòng

空 kòng ❶ leave empty or blank; leave unoccupied; vacate: ～出两个座位 leave two seats unoccupied; reserve two seats / 把房间～出来 vacate a room / 标题上下各～一行。Leave one blank line both above and below the title. / 每段开头要～两格。Indent the first line of each paragraph by two spaces. / 他退休后可以～出一个职位来。His retirement will vacate one position (*or* will leave a vacancy). ❷ vacant; unoccupied; blank: ～桌子 vacant (*or* unoccupied) table / 请往里走，车里面还～得很。Please move along, there is plenty of room inside the bus. ❸ unoccupied space; empty space; room: 衣柜里挂的都是你的衣服，也不给我留点～儿。The wardrobe is stuffed with your clothes, and there's no room for mine. / 行与行之间多留些～儿好修改。Leave enough space between the lines for corrections. / 这个～儿正好摆电视机。The TV set fits right in here. ❹ free time; spare time; leisure time: 你现在有～儿吗? Have you got a moment to spare just now? / 有～儿来玩吧。Please drop in when you're free. / 我这星期一点儿～儿都没有。I'm fully occupied this week. / 我抓住会议休息的～儿出去吃了点儿东西。I took advantage of a break in the meeting to go out and have a bite. ❺ *see* "控³" kòng
see also kōng
空白 kòngbái blank space: ～纸 blank sheet of paper / ～表格 blank form / ～支票 blank cheque / 填补了人工智能计算机技术的～ fill a gap in the technology of artificial intelligence computers / 在纸的下面留一块～。Leave a blank space in the lower part of the paper. / 这个问题的研究在我们国家目前还是一个～。This area of study is still virgin ground in our country.
空白点 kòngbáidiǎn blank spot; gap; blank: 填补一个长期以来的～ fill a long-existing gap / 仅仅几年以前，民族服饰的研究还是一个～。Only a few years ago, the study of national costumes was non-existent.
空场 kòngchǎng open ground; unused space: 这片～后面是一片小树林。Behind the open ground is a little woods.
空当 kòngdāng *also* "空当子" ❶ gap; empty space: 书架上摆满了书，没有一点～。The bookshelves are filled with books and there isn't any empty space left. / 学校的老年教师和青年教师之间有一个～。There's an unfilled gap between the senior teachers and young teachers at the school. ❷ break; interval: 在日程上留了两天的～以作机动 leave two days free (*or* blank) in the schedule for unforeseen needs / 趁这个～去喝杯茶。Let's go and have a cup of tea during the break.
空地 kòngdì ❶ unused land; open space; vacant lot: 门前那块～可以搞一个花园。We can make a garden out of the open space in front of the house. ❷ extra room; space available: 屋子的左角还有点～儿，正好放一个茶几。There's just enough space in the left corner of the room for a small tea table.
空额 kòng'é vacancy: 吃～〈旧语〉(of officers in a warlord army) pocket pay for non-existent soldiers on the payroll / 我们办公室还有一个～。你想来吗? We still have a vacancy in our office. Would you like to join us?
空格 kònggé blank; blank space (as on a form)
空格键 kònggéjiàn space key
空缺 kòngquē ❶ vacant position; vacancy: 出～ vacate a position / 系里还有一个秘书～。We still have a vacant position for a secretary in the department. ❷ gap; vacancy: 填补～ fill a gap (*or* vacancy)
空日 kòngrì undesignated date in certain calendars: 傣族历法中在除夕和次年元旦之间有一到两个～。There are one or two undesignated days between New Year's Eve and New Year's Day according to the Dai calendar.
空隙 kòngxì ❶ space; gap; interval: 生产～ intervals of production / 会议～ intervals between sessions; intervals of a meeting / 书桌不要太靠墙，留点～。Don't put the desk too close against the wall. Leave some space. / 利用停电的～擦一下机器。Clean the machine while the power is off. ❷ opening or opportunity (usu. for evil-doing)
空暇 kòngxiá free time; spare time: 我想找个～去逛书店。I want to find time to visit bookstores.
空闲 kòngxián ❶ free; leisurely: ～时间 free time; spare time / 等你～下来了，咱们去钓鱼。Let's go fishing when you are free. ❷ leisure; free time; spare time: 少有～ have little leisure / 他一有～就练习书法。He practises calligraphy whenever he has time to spare. ❸ unused; idle: ～设备 unused (*or* idle) equipment / ～房间 vacant room / 这里好几台计算机都～着。Quite a few computers here are idle.
空心 kòngxīn on an empty stomach: ～喝酒容易醉。One gets drunk easily on an empty stomach.
see also kōngxīn
空余 kòngyú free; spare; unoccupied; vacant: ～时间 free (*or* spare) time / ～病床 vacant bed (in hospital) / ～楼层 unoccupied floor / ～人手 extra hands
空子 kòngzi ❶ unoccupied space; free time; gap: 抽个～去医院看病人 find time to visit a patient in the hospital / 找个～往里面钻 find a gap and squeeze in ❷ opening; chance; opportunity (usu. for wrongdoing): 钻～ exploit an opportunity (*or* opening); avail oneself of a loophole / 找～散布流言蜚语 seize every opportunity to spread rumours

鞚 kòng 〈书面〉 headstall

控¹ kòng accuse; charge; denounce: 指～ accuse; charge / 被～犯有杀人罪 be accused of murder; be charged with murder

控² kòng control; dominate: 遥～ remote control; telecontrol / 磁～ magnetic control / 失～ out of control; unbridled / ～速行驶 drive within a speed limit

控³ kòng *also* "空" kòng ❶ keep (one's body or part of one's body) hanging in the air; keep unsupported: 腿都～麻了。My legs went numb from hanging in midair. ❷ turn (usu. a container) upside down to let the liquid trickle out: 把瓶子～干了再装油。Turn the bottle upside down for a while to empty it completely before you fill it with oil. / 把伞立在门口～一～。Put the umbrella behind the door to drain.
控扼 kòng'è control; dominate: ～南北交通 control north-south transport lines
控方 kòngfāng 〈法律〉 prosecuting party: ～证人 prosecuting witness
控告 kònggào charge; accuse; arraign: ～人 accuser; accusant; accusing party / ～某人犯了盗窃罪 charge sb. with theft; accuse sb. of theft / 向法院提出～ file a charge in court / 驳回～ rebut a charge / 撤回对某人的～ withdraw (*or* retract) a charge against sb. / 法官宣布对他的～无效。The judge quashed the charge against him.
控购 kònggòu control institutional purchases: ～指标 quota for controlled institutional purchases
控股 kònggǔ 〈金融〉 holding

控股公司 kònggǔ gōngsī holding company; proprietary company

控栅 kòngshān 〈电学〉control grid (CG)

控诉 kòngsù denounce; accuse; condemn:～旧社会 denounce the old society /～侵略者 denounce (*or* condemn) the aggressors /～书 written accusation (*or* complaint) /～会 accusation meeting; rally to denounce sb.'s atrocities, etc.

控御 kòngyù *also* "控驭" ❶ control and drive (a horse, etc.) ❷ dominate; control; rule: 善于～军队 good at keeping the armed forces under control

控制 kòngzhì control; curb; dominate:～局势 control the situation; take the situation in hand /～病情 prevent an illness from further deteriorating; curb the further deterioration of an illness /～关隘 command (*or* control) a strategic pass /自动～ autocontrol /～不住自己的感情 be unable to control (*or* restrain) one's feelings; lose control of one's feelings /他～了整个会场。He dominated the whole conference.

控制棒 kòngzhìbàng 〈核物理〉controlling rod; control rod; absorbing rod:～当量 control rod equivalent /更换～ replace control rods

控制比 kòngzhìbǐ 〈电学〉control ratio

控制电压 kòngzhì diànyā control voltage

控制阀 kòngzhìfá control valve

控制基因 kòngzhì jīyīn controlling gene

控制经济 kòngzhì jīngjì command economy

控制理论 kòngzhì lǐlùn control theory

控制联想 kòngzhì liánxiǎng 〈心理〉controlled association

控制论 kòngzhìlùn 〈数学〉cybernetics:～模型 cybernetic model /～专家 cybernetist

控制球 kòngzhìqiú 〈体育〉ball-handling; ball control:打～战术 use delaying tactics

控制数字 kòngzhì shùzì 〈经济〉control figure

控制台 kòngzhìtái 〈自控〉console; control board

控制因素 kòngzhì yīnsù governing factor

控制系统 kòngzhì xìtǒng control system

kōu

芤

kōu 〈古语〉onion; scallion

芤脉 kōumài 〈中医〉hollow pulse (usu. indicating serious haemorrhage)

抠(摳)

kōu ❶ dig (out) with a finger or sth. pointed; scratch: 从地板缝里～硬币 dig out a coin from a crevice in the floor /把粘在门上的纸条～掉 scratch a sticker off the door /～鼻孔 pick one's nose /～脸上的疱 pick a spot on one's face ❷ carve; cut: 在桌子四周～花纹 carve a pattern on the edges of a table ❸ study punctiliously; be studious or exacting to the degree of being bookish; delve into: 你需要～一下英语语法。You need to make a careful (*or* meticulous) study of English grammar. /书要读,但不要死～书本儿。It is necessary to read books, but never bury yourself in them (*or* never be a bookworm). ❹ 〈方言〉stingy; closefisted; penny-pinching: 他就给我们这点儿钱? 真是太～了。Is this all he gave us? What a stingy guy! (*or* What a miser!) /您不要对自己太～了,要多吃点有营养的东西。Don't be too hard on yourself. You should eat more nutritious food.

抠哧 kōuchi ❶ scratch: 疮口刚结痂,别～它。The wound has just formed a scab. Don't scratch it. ❷ move back and forth; fiddle with; tinker with: 你在那儿～什么? What are you fiddling with there? ❸ scrutinize; study intensively; delve or dig into: 这么难的一道算术题总算让他给～出来了。He finally solved the difficult maths problem after intensive study.

抠门儿 kōuménr 〈方言〉stingy; closefisted; penny-pinching; miserly: 我的姨妈很有钱,但特别～。I have a rich but extremely stingy aunt. /这人可～了。He is a downright miser.

抠唆 kōusuo *also* "抠挲" *see* "抠搜"

抠搜 kōusou ❶ dig (out) with one's finger or sth. pointed; scratch:～你的脸干什么? What are you scratching your face for? ❷ stingy; miserly: 这人抠抠搜搜的,真是个守财奴。The fellow is stingy enough to be called a miser. ❸ dawdle; loiter: 你这么抠抠搜搜的,什么时候才办完? When will you be done, if you keep dawdling like this?

抠字眼儿 kōu zìyǎnr be fastidious about wording; be a stickler for words; split hairs in choice of words: 这篇文章已经很不错了,就别～了。The article is good enough as it is. So don't split hairs. /起草合同,就得好好抠抠字眼儿。In drawing up a contract, we must pay close attention to the shades of meaning of each word.

眍(瞘)

kōu (of the eyes) become or be sunken: 她一连几夜没睡,眼睛都～进去了。Her eyes were sunken after several sleepless nights.

眍䁖 kōulou (of the eyes) become or be sunken

弫(彄)

kōu 〈书面〉notch on either end of a bow, used to fasten the bowstring

kǒu

口

kǒu ❶ (of a human or animal) mouth: 张～ open one's mouth /开～ open one's mouth to speak; break silence /闭～ shut up; refrain from speaking /脱～而出 say without thinking; blurt out /病从～入。The mouth is always the entrance for disease. *or* Disease always makes its entrance through the mouth. ❷ one's taste: 他吃东西～咸。He likes salty food. ❸ people; population: 家～ family members /户～ number of households in the total population ❹ (of a container, etc.)sth. resembling or functioning as a mouth: 瓶～ mouth of a bottle /盆～ rim of a basin ❺ opening; mouth; exit; entrance: 河～ mouth of a river; estuary /入～ entrance /胡同～儿 entrance of an alley /出～ exit /门～ doorway; gateway /窗～ window /枪～ muzzle of a gun /封～ seal an opening ❻ (often used in place names) gateway of the Great Wall; pass: 南～ Nankou — Southern Pass (north of Beijing) ❼ cut; hole; crack; chip: 伤～ wound; cut /箱盖上裂了个～儿。There is a crack in the lid of the box. /钉子把上衣撕了个～儿。The jacket got caught on a nail and a hole was torn in it. /花瓶缺了个～儿。The vase has a chip in the rim. ❽ general category or division grouping organs, institutions or enterprises of similar nature loosely together under an umbrella administrative body; departments of such a category or division: 工交～ departments of industry and transport /归～管理 centralized management (of enterprises, affairs, etc.) by relevant departments ❾ sharp edge of a knife, etc.; blade: 这刀～儿好。The knife has a sharp edge. /刀卷～了。The edge of the knife is turned. ❿ age of a draft animal: 两岁～的母马 two-year-old mare /这匹骡子～老。The mule is old. ⓫ 〈量词〉:一～刀 a knife /一～池塘 a pond /两～猪 two pigs /四～之家 family of four /两～子 husband and wife /吃几～饭 have a few mouthfuls of food /咬一～苹果 take a bite of an apple /吸一～烟斗 take a drag at a pipe /讲一～流利的英语 speak fluent English

口岸 kǒu'àn port: 通商～ trading port /入境～ port of entry /停靠～ port of call /～检查机关 inspection office at a port

口白 kǒubái ❶ (in an opera) words spoken; spoken parts: 她唱得不错,只是～不够清楚。She sings well but does not speak clearly enough. ❷ colourless lipstick (used to prevent the lips from being dry)

口碑 kǒubēi public praise (on people's lips, instead of praise inscribed on stone tablets):～不错 enjoy a good reputation /他为官清正,乡民皆有～。He was an honest and upright official praised by all the villagers.

口碑载道 kǒubēi-zàidào be praised everywhere; win popular praise; have a good reputation all around: 这位县长在当地～。This magistrate enjoys widespread popularity in his county.

口北 Kǒuběi *also* "口外" area north of the Great Wall, in special reference to northern Hebei and central Inner Mongolia which lie north of Zhangjiakou (张家口)

口笨舌拙 kǒubèn-shézhuō be awkward in speech

口布 kǒubù table napkin

口才 kǒucái talent for speaking; eloquence: 有～ be eloquent; have a talent for speaking; have the gift of gab /～对电视节目主持人非常重要。Eloquence is very important to a TV anchor. /她是三姐妹中～最好的。She is the most articulate of the three sisters.

口彩 kǒucǎi auspicious remarks: 讨个～ say or do sth. for luck

口沉 kǒuchén 〈方言〉❶ salty: 这菜太～。The dish is too salty. ❷

be fond of salty food:四川人往往比较～。Most Sichuan people have a taste for heavily-seasoned food.

口称 kǒuchēng say; allege:～前进,实为倒退 progress in words but retrogression in deeds /～支持, 实为拆台 help in rhetoric and hinder in practice

口吃 kǒuchī *also* "结巴" jiēba stutter; stammer:他小时候有点～。He used to stutter a little when he was a child. /老爷爷～得厉害。The old man stammers badly. *or* The old man speaks with a bad stammer.

口齿 kǒuchǐ ❶ enunciation:～清楚 have clear enunciation /～不清 speak with a mumble; have a twist in one's tongue /～便捷 have a ready tongue; have the gift of gab ❷ age of draught animals

口齿伶俐 kǒuchǐ-línglì be clever and fluent in speech; have a glib or ready tongue; be quick witted and eloquent:小姑娘～, 又会看眼色, 很讨人喜欢。She is really a little dear, quick in response and ready to take hints.

口齿留香 kǒuchǐ-liúxiāng (said of beautiful verses, etc.) leave a lingering fragrance in one's mouth

口臭 kǒuchòu 〈医学〉 halitosis; bad or foul breath

口出狂言 kǒuchū-kuángyán *also* "口出大言" talk boastfully or wildly; brag; boast

口出血 kǒuchūxuè 〈医学〉 stomatorrhagia

口传 kǒuchuán instruct orally; pass on by word of mouth:民间艺人大都用～的方法来教徒弟。Folk singers and performers generally teach their apprentices by oral instruction. /这部史诗就一直这么～了下来。This epic has been passed on by word of mouth.

口传心授 kǒuchuán-xīnshòu *also* "口传耳授" (of learning or craft handed down from a master to his disciples without any written text) oral instruction and rote memory

口疮 kǒuchuāng aphtha; canker; mouth ulcer:长了两个～ have two aphthae on the lips

口疮性溃疡 kǒuchuāngxìng kuìyáng aphthous ulcer

口袋 kǒudai ❶ bag; sack:米～ rice bag /皮～ leather bag /面～ flour sack ❷ pocket:～盖 flap (of a pocket) /～布 pocketing /这件制服上有四个～。This uniform has four pockets on it.

口淡 kǒudàn 〈方言〉 *see* "口轻 ❶❷"

口德 kǒudé restraint in one's speech; propriety of words:说话要注意～。Use proper restraint when you speak. /年轻轻的,别说话不留～! Don't hurt people with your loose tongue, young fellow!

口调 kǒudiào 〈方言〉 intonation; tone; manner of speaking:他说话的～有点儿不对头。His tone sounds queer.

口对口复苏 kǒuduìkǒu fùsū 〈医学〉 mouth-to-mouth resuscitation

口对口人工呼吸 kǒuduìkǒu réngōng hūxī *also* "口对口呼吸" 〈医学〉 mouth-to-mouth breathing; kiss-of-life respiration; kiss of life:对病人进行～抢救 apply mouth-to-mouth breathing to a patient; give a patient the kiss of life

口耳相传 kǒu-ěr xiāngchuán hand down by word of mouth; pass on orally:他的医道,得父亲～。He learned medicine directly from his father.

口耳之学 kǒu-ěrzhīxué fragmentary knowledge from hearsay

口风琴 kǒufēngqín mouth organ; harmonica

口风 kǒufeng one's intention or opinion as revealed in what one says:漏了～ betray one's intention inadvertently; give oneself away /探探某人的～ sound sb. out /我们事先给他露点～吧。Let's drop him a hint beforehand.

口锋 kǒufēng tone; manner of speaking:～凌厉 speak in a fierce, aggressive manner /～和缓 speak in a mild tone

口服 kǒufú ❶ profess to be convinced:心服～ be thoroughly convinced ❷ take orally (medicine):～药 medicine to be taken orally; oral medicine /外用药不可～。Medicine for external use must not be taken orally.

口服避孕药 kǒufú bìyùnyào oral contraceptive; the pill

口服心不服 kǒufú xīn bùfú saying one is convinced but not really so at heart:看得出来, 他是～。It is obvious that he is not really convinced.

口服液 kǒufúyè oral liquid:蜂王浆～ royal jelly liquid

口服疫苗 kǒufú yìmiáo oral vaccine:小儿麻痹症～ oral vaccine for polio

口福 kǒufú luck to enjoy delicious food; gourmet's luck:一饱～ satisfy one's appetite for delicious food; enjoy a gourmet's luck /你真有～,每次请客都被你赶上了。What a lucky gourmet you are, always getting invited when there is a dinner. /这孩子～浅,一吃海鲜就过敏。The poor child hardly has any luck when it comes to delicious food; she is allergic to seafood.

口辅 kǒufǔ lower parts of the cheeks; both sides of the mouth:～微展 have a faint smile hovering around one's lips

口赋 kǒufù *also* "口算"; "口钱"; "丁口钱" dīngkǒuqián 〈旧语〉 capitation tax; per capita tax; poll tax

口腹 kǒufù food and drinks:不贪～ not be given to food and drinks; not indulge one's appetite

口腹之欲 kǒufùzhīyù appetite or desire for food:人可不是为满足～而活着的。People do not live to eat.

口干 kǒugān dry in the mouth; thirsty

口干舌燥 kǒugān-shézào have one's mouth parched and one's tongue scorched; be extremely thirsty or dry in the mouth:我说得～,他仍是不听。Although I talked myself hoarse, he still wouldn't listen to me.

口疳 kǒugān 〈中医〉 aphthae in children's mouths; children's aphthae

口感 kǒugǎn texture of food:手擀面的～好,我最爱吃了。I adore hand-made noodles, because they feel just wonderful in the mouth (*or* because they have such a nice chewy texture).

口供 kǒugòng statement made by the accused under examination; confession; testimony:～记录 record of testimony/～证据 testimonial proof

口过 kǒuguò error resulting from an indiscreet remark; slip of the tongue

口号 kǒuhào ❶ slogan; watchword:宣传～ slogan for propaganda /呼～ shout slogans /光喊～,不见行动。All slogans, no actions. /我们的～是"永远争第一"。Our motto is "Always go for the championship". /此人～不少, 但落实不多。The man makes a lot of promises, but keeps few of them. ❷ 〈旧语〉 countersign; password

口红 kǒuhóng lipstick:珠光～ pearlescent lipstick

口惠 kǒuhuì lip-service; empty promise

口惠而实不至 kǒuhuì ér shí bù zhì make an empty promise; pay lip-service:他们许诺给该国的援助, 多半是～。Their promise to provide the country with assistance is largely lip-service. *or* Their promised aid to that country is largely empty talk.

口技 kǒujì 〈杂技〉 vocal mimicry; vocal imitation:～演员 performer of vocal mimicry /腹语～ ventriloquism

口碱 kǒujiǎn 〈方言〉 alkali produced in northwestern China (formerly marketed at Zhangjiakou 张家口)

口角 kǒujiǎo corner of the mouth:～挂笑 have a faint smile playing about the corners of one's mouth

see also kǒujué

口角垂涎 kǒujiǎo-chuíxián drip with saliva (on sight of delicious food, etc.):看到美味佳肴,一个个～。The sight of the delicious food made everybody's mouth water.

口角春风 kǒujiǎo-chūnfēng speak kindly (of sb.); sing (sb.'s) praises; put in a good word (for sb.):还望您～,多多美言。I hope you'll be kind enough to put in a good word for me.

口角生风 kǒujiǎo-shēngfēng have a smooth and agile tongue; be articulate and fluent:这种民间艺术要求演员唱得字正腔圆,说得～。This folk art requires the performer to sing the lines with accuracy and mellowness, and to enunciate the spoken parts clearly and fluently.

口角炎 kǒujiǎoyán 〈医学〉 perlèche

口紧 kǒujǐn close-mouthed; tight-lipped; secretive:她这个人～,不会随便乱说话, 你尽可放心。You can rest assured that she will not make any indiscreet remarks as she is tight-lipped.

口噤 kǒujìn 〈中医〉 lockjaw

口径 kǒujìng ❶ bore; calibre; diameter:小～步枪 small-bore rifle /大～机枪 heavy-calibre machine-gun /60 毫米～的迫击炮 60mm mortar /～130 毫米折射望远镜 refractive telescope of 130mm diameter ❷ requirements; specifications:符合～ meet the requirements (*or* specifications) /螺钉与螺母～不合。The male and female screws do not match. ❸ line of action; approach; version:对～ arrange to give the same account (*or* version) (of sth.); compare notes so as to give the same story /统一～ agree on a uniform version (*or* account) /官方～ official version (*or* account) /对外～ standard version (*or* account) for external consumption; unified statement for the public /他们说话～不一。The two of them did not speak along the same lines.

口镜 kǒujìng 〈医学〉 mouth mirror

口诀 kǒujué pithy formula or table (often in rhyme); mnemonic rhyme:乘法～ (rhyming) multiplication table /珠算～ rhymes for using the abacus; abacus rhymes

口角 kǒujué quarrel; bicker; wrangle:与某人～ quarrel (*or* bicker) with sb.; bandy words with sb. /不要为这么点小事～。Don't quarrel over such a trifle.
see also kǒujiǎo

口渴 kǒukě thirsty:～难耐 feel unbearably thirsty /～得要命 be parched; be dying for a drink (of water)

口口声声 kǒukou-shēngshēng say or claim repeatedly; keep on saying; go on prating:他～说未曾参与此事。He claimed again and again that he had not been involved in the matter.

口快 kǒukuài quick with one's tongue; thoughtless in speech; straightforward; outspoken:心直～ be frank and outspoken; wear one's heart on one's sleeve

口溃疡 kǒukuìyáng 〈医学〉canker sore

口里 Kǒulǐ area south of the Great Wall:～人 people from south of the Great Wall

口粮 kǒuliáng grain ration; grain for one's own consumption; provisions:按月发给～ issue grain rations (*or* provisions) per month /你们这个村平均每人一年吃多少～? How much grain do you consume per person per year in this village? /这次旅行要带三天的～。We must bring three days' provisions for our journey.

口令 kǒulìng ❶ word of command:新兵按班长的～操练队列。The new recruits practised formation drills according to the squad leader's word of command. ❷ password; watchword; countersign:～! Password! /这次战斗行动的～是"闪电"。The password for this operation is "lightning".

口溜子 kǒuliùzi 〈方言〉whistle:吹起～ start to whistle

口马 kǒumǎ horses bred in the area north of the Great Wall

口门 kǒumén river-mouth; estuary

口糜 kǒumí 〈中医〉aphthous stomatitis

口蜜腹剑 kǒumì-fùjiàn with honey on one's lips and murder in one's heart; honey-mouthed but dagger-hearted; hypocritical and sinister:这个人～,阴毒异常。He is a sinister and ruthless man with honey on his lips and murder in his heart. *or* He is an evil man who has a mouth that praises and a hand that kills.

口蘑 kǒumó edible mushrooms with lush white umbrellas, grown on grasslands north of the Great Wall, esp. around Zhangjiakou (张家口); *Tricholoma gambosum*

口沫 kǒumò saliva; spittle:～飞溅 with spittle spraying

口皮 kǒupí fur or pelt produced in the area north of the Great Wall, esp. the Zhangjiakou area

口器 kǒuqì mouthparts (of an arthropod)

口气 kǒuqi ❶ manner of speaking; way of speaking:～挺大 speak in a grand manner; talk big /来人表情严肃,～逼人。The visitor wore a stern expression and had an aggressive manner of speaking. ❷ what is actually meant; implication:听他的～,好像对通过考试很有把握。He sounded as if he was sure of passing the examination. /你不妨先听听他的～再说。You might as well find out his intention first. ❸ tone; note:轻松的～ easy (*or* light) tone /～不对 not sound right /～严厉的批评 harsh-toned criticism /～婉转的声明 mildly worded statement /他话里带有讽刺的～。There was a note of sarcasm in what he said.

口腔 kǒuqiāng 〈生理〉oral cavity:～卫生 oral hygiene /～保健 oral health /～疾病 mouth disease /～黏膜 mouth (*or* oral) mucosa /～材料 dental material

口腔病 kǒuqiāngbìng 〈医学〉oral disorder

口腔出血 kǒuqiāng chūxuè oral haemorrhage

口腔镜 kǒuqiāngjìng mouth mirror; stomatoscope

口腔科 kǒuqiāngkē stomatology:～医生 stomatologist

口腔外科 kǒuqiāng wàikē oral surgery:～手术 oral surgery

口腔学 kǒuqiāngxué stomatology

口腔医院 kǒuqiāng yīyuàn stomatological hospital

口琴 kǒuqín mouth organ; harmonica

口轻 kǒuqīng ❶ not too salty; lightly-seasoned:我喜欢吃～的菜。I prefer lightly-seasoned food. /这菜有些～。The dish wants a pinch of salt. ❷ be fond of food that is not too salty:南方人～。Southerners like food that is not too salty. *or* Southerners don't like heavily-seasoned food. ❸ *also* "口小" (of a horse, mule or other draught animal) young:这头毛驴～,价钱也不贵。This donkey is young and its price is reasonable.

口若悬河 kǒuruòxuánhé let loose a torrent of words; talk in a flow of eloquence; speak eloquently and volubly:刘教授～,语惊四座。Professor Liu spoke in such a flood of eloquence that people all around listened to him spell-bound. /他～,滔滔不绝,一说就是个把钟头。His talk flowed like a cataract, on and on for more than an hour.

口哨儿 kǒushàor whistle (with one's lips):吹～ whistle (with one's lips) /只听见四周都是～声、嘘声。Whistling and booing were heard all round.

口舌 kǒushé ❶ quarrel, dispute or misunderstanding caused by what one says:～是非 quarrel (*or* misunderstanding) caused by gossip /一场～ dispute; quarrel ❷ talking (round):白费～ waste one's breath; talk in vain /要说服他得费一番～。It will take a lot of talking to bring him round. /事情既已至此,我们就不必多费～了。With things as they are, we might as well save our breath.

口舌糜烂 kǒushé mílàn 〈中医〉erosion of mucous membrane in the oral cavity

口实 kǒushí 〈书面〉❶ cause for gossip; handle:不要给他留下任何～。We should not provide him with a handle against us. ❷ excuse; pretext:你以为他真的是有事? 那不过是他编的～罢了。You really believe that he was occupied? That was only his excuse.

口食 kǒushí ❶ meals; food:船上供给～。Meals are provided on board the ship. ❷ 〈方言〉grain ration; provisions:这是全营战士五天的～。Here are five days' provisions for the whole battalion.

口试 kǒushì oral examination; oral test; viva voce:上外语院校要通过～。You will need to pass an oral examination to enter a foreign languages institute.

口是心非 kǒushì-xīnfēi say yes and mean no; say one thing and mean another; be double-faced; play a double game:我们不能做～的事情。We should not say one thing and mean another. /此人向来～,极靠不住。The man was always double-faced and extremely unreliable.

口授 kǒushòu ❶ teach by oral instruction; pass on by word of mouth:～秘诀 pass on a secret knack by word of mouth /许多地方戏曲都是由艺人世代～而保存下来的。Many local operas have been preserved from one generation of performers to another through oral instruction. ❷ dictate:～遗嘱 dictate a will /经理向秘书～了一封回信。The manager dictated a reply to his secretary.

口授笔录 kǒushòu-bǐlù verbatim record of a dictation; dictation

口授打字机 kǒushòu dǎzìjī phonetic typewriter

口述 kǒushù oral account:请～文章大意。Please give an oral summary of the article.

口述历史 kǒushù lìshǐ oral history

口水 kǒushuǐ saliva:流～ slobber /这些水果看着就让人流～。The delicious fruit makes one's mouth water.

口说无凭 kǒushuō-wúpíng words alone are no proof; a verbal statement or promise is no guarantee:～,请你们拿出证据来。Words alone are no proof. Please produce your evidence. /～,还是立个字据为好。Since a verbal promise is no guarantee, we might as well write it down.

口诵 kǒusòng read out loud; read aloud:～心惟 ponder the meaning while reading sth. out loud /每日～经文 recite scripture every day

口诉 kǒusù accuse orally; denounce orally:代录～ write down an oral accusation for sb.

口算 kǒusuàn ❶ chant out the result while doing mental calculation; calculate orally:举行～比赛 hold a contest in oral calculation ❷ poll tax

口谈 kǒután talk; speak:～和平 talk about peace

口蹄疫 kǒutíyì 〈兽医〉foot-and-mouth disease; hoof-and-mouth disease; apathus fever

口条 kǒutiao pig's or ox's tongue (as food):猪～ pig's tongue /牛～ ox's tongue

口头 kǒutóu ❶ in words (as distinct from thoughts or actions):～开明派 liberal in words only /希望你的话不要光停留在～上。It is hoped that your action will match your words. ❷ oral; verbal (not written):～保证 oral (*or* verbal) guarantee /～汇报 oral report /～表扬 oral commendation /～抗议 verbal protest /～契约 verbal contract/我已～通知大家今晚开会。I have notified everyone concerned of the meeting tonight by word of mouth.

口头 kǒutou 〈方言〉taste (of fruit or melons):这个西瓜～很好。This watermelon tastes good.

口头表决 kǒutóu biǎojué voice vote; vote by "yes" and "no"
口头禅 kǒutóuchán platitude; pet phrase：有些干部常把"研究研究"这句～挂在嘴边。Some officials always say "we will study it" as a platitude for all occasions.
口头翻译 kǒutóu fānyì oral interpretation
口头福 kǒutóufú gourmet's luck; luck to get sth. nice to eat：你算有～，正赶上今天吃烤鸭。You do have a gourmet's luck; you are just in time for today's roast duck dinner.
口头交 kǒutóujiāo *also* "口头之交" relationship that appears intimate but stops at superficial conversation; mere acquaintance：我和他不过是～，算不上真正的朋友。He and I are mere acquaintances, not real friends.
口头文学 kǒutóu wénxué unwritten literature; oral literature
口头协议 kǒutóu xiéyì verbal agreement; oral agreement
口头语 kǒutóuyǔ pet phrase; habitual turn of phrase："瞧着办吧"几乎成了他的～。"Do as you think fit" has almost become his habitual turn of phrase.
口外 Kǒuwài *see* "口北"
口腕 kǒuwàn 〈动物〉oral arm
口味 kǒuwèi ❶ flavour or taste of food：～不错 be tasty／这酸奶带菠萝～。The yogurt has pineapple flavour.／这家饭店是山东～。This restaurant serves Shandong-style food. ❷ one's taste or liking：合～suit one's taste; be to one's liking (*or* taste)／流行音乐合年轻人的～。Pop music is very much to the liking of the young.
口吻 kǒuwěn ❶〈动物〉muzzle; snout ❷ tone; note：讥笑的～sneering tone／玩世不恭的～ cynical tone／命令的～ commanding tone／讽刺的～ note of sarcasm／责备的～ note of reproach
口无择言 kǒuwúzéyán speak eloquently and impeccably：他才思敏捷，～。He has an agile mind and a ready tongue.
口误 kǒuwù (make) a slip of the tongue：说话多了，难免～。One is apt to make a slip of the tongue when one talks too much.
口吸盘 kǒuxīpán oral sucker
口涎 kǒuxián saliva
口香糖 kǒuxiāngtáng chewing gum
口小 kǒuxiǎo (of a horse, mule or other draught animal) young *see also* "口轻❸"
口信 kǒuxìn oral message：给人捎～ take a message to sb.／他托人带来一个～。He sent a message through someone.
口形 kǒuxíng 〈语言〉degree of lip-rounding (when making a sound)
口型 kǒuxíng shape of the mouth when a person speaks：耳聋的人往往根据对方的～来辨别意思。Those hard of hearing often try to recognize the meaning of the words spoken by the other person by the shape of his or her mouth.
口羞 kǒuxiū 〈方言〉be too shy to speak or sing in public：这姑娘～，我替她说吧。Since the girl is very bashful, let me speak for her.
口血未干 kǒuxuè-wèigān the blood of the sacrifice is not yet dry on one's mouth (in reference to the ancient custom of smearing one's mouth when making an oath of alliance) — before the ink is dry; (breaking an oath of alliance) the moment it is made
口炎 kǒuyán 〈医学〉stomatitis：溃疡性～ stomatocace; ulcerative stomatitis／流行性～ epidemic stomatitis; epizootic stomatitis／滤疱性～ aphthous stomatitis; herpetic stomatitis; vesicular stomatitis／真菌性～ thrush／坏疽性～ gangrenous stomatitis／汞毒性～ mercurial stomatitis／寄生性～ parasitic stomatitis
口眼㖞斜 kǒu-yǎn wāixié 〈中医〉facial paralysis
口羊 kǒuyáng sheep produced in the area north of the Great Wall, esp. the Zhangjiakou area
口译 kǒuyì oral interpretation
口音 kǒuyīn 〈语言〉oral speech sounds
口音 kǒuyin ❶ voice：他还没进门，我就听出他的～了。I recognized his voice even before he entered the room. ❷ accent：说话带南方～ speak with a southern accent／讲英语时爱尔兰～很重 speak in a thick Irish brogue／他离家太久，说话已听不大出家乡～了。Having been away from his hometown for a long time, he had lost much of his native accent.
口吟 kǒuyín recite in a low voice; chant in a low voice：～唐诗一首 recite a Tang poem in a low voice
口语 kǒuyǔ ❶ spoken language：英语～ spoken English; oral English; colloquial English／～会话练习 conversation practice／～用法 spoken idiom; colloquialism ❷〈书面〉slander; calumniation：横遭～ suffer slander for no reason
口语体 kǒuyǔtǐ colloquialism; colloquial style：～的诗 poem written in the colloquial style
口育鱼 kǒuyùyú mouthbreeder
口谕 kǒuyù 〈旧语〉oral instruction or directive (by higher authorities or elders)：奉上峰～ on the oral instructions of the higher authorities
口燥唇干 kǒuzào-chúngān *also* "口干舌燥" (talk until) one's lips are dry and one's mouth is parched; talk one's tongue dry
口占 kǒuzhàn 〈书面〉❶ dictate：～电文 dictate a telegram ❷ improvise (poetry)：～一绝 improvise a quatrain
口罩 kǒuzhào gauze mask; surgical mask：戴～ wear a gauze mask
口重 kǒuzhòng ❶ salty; heavily seasoned：北方菜～，我吃不惯。I am not accustomed to salty northern food. *or* Salty northern-style food does not agree with me. ❷ be fond of salty or heavily-seasoned food：北方人～。Northerners like heavily seasoned food.
口诛笔伐 kǒuzhū-bǐfá condemn both in speech and in writing; denounce by tongue and pen; criticize in all forms：对于腐败现象，全社会都要～。Corruption in whatever form should be condemned by the whole society.
口髭 kǒuzī moustache
口子 kǒuzi ❶〈量词〉*used of people*：你们家有几～？How many are you in your family?／全村有百八十～人。The village has a hundred people or so. ❷〈口语〉my husband or wife：我们那～可固执得很呢。My wife (*or* husband) is a stubborn mule. ❸ opening; breach：山谷的～上有座选矿厂。There is an ore-dressing mill at the mouth of the valley.／这个～什么时候也开不得！We can never set such a precedent! ❹ cut; crack; hole：手被刀拉了一道～ have one's hand cut by a knife／水缸裂了道～。There is a crack in the urn.

kòu

寇 kòu ❶ bandit; invader; enemy：流～ roving bandit／海～ pirate／草～ outlaw／外～ aggressor; invader ❷ (of an enemy) invade; overrun：入～ make an incursion (*or* inroad); invade (a country) ❸ (Kòu) a surname
寇边 kòubiān 〈书面〉(of enemy troops) invade the border areas
寇仇 kòuchóu mortal enemy; foe：视若～ regard as a mortal enemy (*or* foe)／两村争水，世为～。There was a mortal feud over water resources between the two villages for generations.
寇盗 kòudào bandit; robber
寇准 Kòu Zhǔn Kou Zhun (961-1023), statesman of the northern Song Dynasty

蔻 kòu
蔻丹 kòudān (transliteration from "Cutex") nail polish
蔻蔻 kòukòu (usu. written as 可可) cocoa

彀 kòu 〈书面〉young bird; fledgling

扣(❼鈕) kòu ❶ button up; buckle; bolt：～扣子 do up the buttons／～上大衣 button up one's coat／把安全带～上 buckle up the safety belt; fasten seat belts／把门窗～好 bolt up the doors and windows／～扳机 pull the trigger ❷ place (a container, vessel, etc.) upside down; cover (with an inverted container, vessel, etc.)：把脸盆～在缸上。Place the basin upside down on the vat.／雪人的脑袋上斜～着一顶破帽。An old hat sat askew on the snowman's head. ❸ accuse unjustly; brand groundlessly; frame (up)：～上通敌的罪名 brand (*or* frame) sb. as a traitor ❹ take into custody; detain; arrest; apprehend：～了两名嫌疑人 detain two suspects／～了两名人质 take two hostages; detain two people as hostages／他因违章被交警～了驾驶执照。He had his driver's license taken away by a policeman for breaking traffic rules. ❺ deduct; discount; dock：～工资 deduct a part of one's pay; dock one's pay／～奖金 withhold sb.'s bonus／打八～ give a twenty per cent discount／不折不～ without discount or deduction; in the entirety; one-hundred-per cent; out and out ❻ knot; loop：绳～儿 knot (in a rope)／打个活～儿 tie (*or* make) a loop ❼ button; buckle：大衣～ coat button／双排～ double rows of buttons; double-breasted ❽〈体育〉smash; spike：～球 spike a ball ❾ *also* "筘" kòu〈纺织〉reed ❿ circle of thread (of a screw)：给螺丝拧了三～ give the screw three twists

K

扣除 kòuchú deduct：从稿费中～税款 deduct the income tax from the author's remuneration /～筹备时间，工期正好一年整。Not counting the time for preparations, the construction took exactly one year.

扣发 kòufā withhold；hold：～半年奖金 hold sb.'s bonus for half a year /那篇稿子被～。The article was withheld from publication.

扣关 kòuguān *see* "叩关" kòuguān

扣黑锅 kòu hēiguō make sb. a scapegoat；accuse sb. unjustly (of sb. else's crime or wrongdoing)：他被人扣上黑锅，关进大牢。He was made a scapegoat and thrown into jail. /他累了个半死，背上还给扣了个黑锅，能不生气吗？How could he not be angry when he'd worked himself to the bone only to be blamed for somebody else's mistakes?

扣减 kòujiǎn deduct；subtract；cut：由于工作质量不合要求，酌量～他的奖金。His bonus would be reduced accordingly, as his work was not up to the requirement.

扣篮 kòulán 〈体育〉dunk shot；over-the-rim shot：这个队员的～技术超人。This basketball player is exceptionally good at dunking.

扣留 kòuliú detain；arrest；hold in custody：被～者 detainee；internee /～嫌疑分子 detain a suspect /～营业执照 suspend (*or* take away) sb.'s business licence /海关～了违禁货物。The Customs have detained the contraband goods. /他被公安局～了。He is held in custody by the Public Security Bureau.

扣帽子 kòu màozi put a (usu. political) label on sb.；brand sb.：乱给人～ put labels on others indiscriminately /给人扣一大堆帽子 call sb. a host of unwarranted names /他被扣上了一顶"里通外国"的大帽子。He was wantonly branded as a "spy for a foreign country".

扣槃扪烛 kòupán-ménzhú *also* "扣盘扪烛"〈书面〉take a one-sided view of things；behave like a blindman feeling the elephant：不要信他这些～之谈。Don't believe his one-sided stories.

扣襻 kòupàn button loop：衣服袖子上好了，还没有钉～。The sleeves of the jacket have been sewed on but not the button loops.

扣人心弦 kòurénxīnxián exciting；thrilling；breathtaking；soul-stirring：～的故事 thrilling story /～的比赛 exciting game /～的悬念 breathtaking suspense /～的诗篇 soul-stirring poetry

扣杀 kòushā 〈体育〉smash or spike (the ball)：大板～ (as in table-tennis) make an overpowering smash /大力～ (as in volleyball) spike the ball powerfully /网前～ smash (*or* spike) the ball before the net

扣审 kòushěn 〈法律〉detain and interrogate：公安局～了该嫌疑人。The Public Security Bureau held and interrogated the suspect.

扣屎盆子 kòu shǐpénzi 〈俗语〉clamp a dirty name on sb.；level dirty charges against sb.：你别乱给人～，这次事故跟我们可没有一点儿关系。Don't you try to level dirty charges against us. The accident had nothing to do with us at all.

扣题 kòutí keep to the point；be relevant to the subject：作文要～。You should keep to the subject when writing an essay. /他的发言东拉西扯，不～。He made a desultory and irrelevant speech.

扣头 kòutou discount；rebate：～少，赚头不多。As the discount is too small, the transaction won't be so profitable.

扣压 kòuyā withhold；shelve；pigeonhole：～检举材料 withold written accusations (from reaching the competent authorities) /他后来才知道他的报告被～了。It was not until later that he learnt that his report had been shelved (*or* pigeonholed).

扣押 kòuyā ❶ detain；hold in custody：～刑事犯 detain criminals /因滋事被派出所～一天 be held in custody for a whole day in a police station for creating disturbances ❷〈法律〉distrain；seize：～房产以抵偿借款 distrain sb.'s house for repayment of a debt

扣眼 kòuyǎn buttonhole

扣子 kòuzi ❶ knot：在绳子上打个～ make a knot in a rope ❷ button：珍珠～ pearl button /大衣～ button for an overcoat；coat button ❸ (in traditional fiction or story-telling) abrupt break in a story to create suspense：这位说书先生善于留～。This storyteller really knows how to keep his audience in suspense.

筘(簆) kòu *also* "杼" zhù 〈纺织〉reed

叩(❶敂) kòu ❶ knock；tap；rap：～门 knock at the door /～钟 strike a bell ❷ kowtow ❸〈书面〉inquire；ask：～以文义 ask for an explication (of a text) /～其姓名 ask sb.'s name

叩拜 kòubài (as formerly required by etiquette) show one's respect by kowtowing：～双亲 prostrate oneself before one's parents (as a reverential way of greeting or bidding goodbye)

叩齿 kòuchǐ teeth-clicking (as a method of dental care)

叩打 kòudǎ knock；tap；rap：他不耐烦地用指头～着桌面。He tapped the desk impatiently with his finger.

叩关 kòuguān *also* "扣关" kòuguān ❶〈书面〉seek an audience with the monarch of a foreign state ❷〈书面〉knock at the door ❸〈书面〉launch an attack upon a fortress ❹ (of football, ice hockey, etc.) attack the goal

叩阍 kòuhūn 〈书面〉seek an imperial audience to air one's complaint；vent one's grievance in the imperial court：途穷～ go to the imperial court as a last resort to obtain justice /～无门 be denied access to the imperial court

叩击 kòujī (usu. used figuratively) knock；beat；tap：她的诉说～着我的心弦。Her narration tugged at my heartstrings. /回忆的浪花在她的心头～。Sprays of recollections were lapping her mind.

叩见 kòujiàn 〈书面〉call on (one's superior)

叩首 kòushǒu kowtow：三跪九～ (formerly as the most reverential and ceremonial ritual of greeting) kneel down three times and kowtow nine times

叩头 kòutóu kowtow：～求饶 kowtow to ask to be spared (from punishment, etc.)；beg for mercy by kowtowing /～谢罪 kowtow in apology /～如捣蒜 knock one's head against the ground as fast as one would chop onions；kowtow in fast succession

叩头虫 kòutóuchóng *also* "磕头虫" kētóuchóng click beetle；snapping beetle

叩头如仪 kòutóu-rúyí kowtow as the customs require；kowtow in accordance with etiquette

叩问 kòuwèn 〈书面〉make inquiries (reverentially)：～缘由 inquire into the causes (of sth.) /途中见一老者，他赶忙上前～。When he saw an elderly gentleman on his way, he hurriedly went up to make inquiries.

叩喜 kòuxǐ 〈旧语〉offer congratulations (to one's elder or superior) by kowtowing：老爷升官，属下纷纷～。All the subordinates congratulated their superior officer on his promotion.

叩谢 kòuxiè express thanks by kowtowing；show deep appreciation；express earnest thanks：登门～ call on sb. to express one's earnest thanks

叩询 kòuxún 〈书面〉make inquires：细加～ make careful inquires

叩谒 kòuyè 〈书面〉pay a formal visit；call to pay respects (to one's elder or superior)

叩诊 kòuzhěn 〈医学〉percussion：落锤～ drop percussion；drop stroke percussion /～锤 percussion hammer /～器 percussor；percuteur /医生～时用手指在病人的胸部轻轻击打。During the diagnosis the doctor percussed the patient's chest gently.

kū

窟 kū ❶ hole；cave；cavern；grotto：山～ mountain cave /石～ stone cave；grotto /狡兔三～。Every smart hare has three exits from his hole. ❷ den；lair：匪～ lair of bandits /赌～ gambling den /贫民～ slum；ghetto

窟窿 kūlong ❶ hole；cavity；hollow：冰～ ice-hole /路当中一个大～ big pit in the middle of the road /袜底磨破个～ wear a hole in the sole of the sock ❷ deficit；debt：他每月入不敷出，如何堵得住～？With income falling short of expenditure every month, how could he stop the deficit? ❸ loophole：堵住税收中的～ stop up loopholes in taxation

窟窿眼儿 kūlongyǎnr small hole：木板上有几个虫蛀的～。There were several worm-eaten holes in the wooden board.

窟臀 kūtún 〈方言〉buttocks

窟穴 kūxué lair；den：破获一个走私毒品的～ uncover a drug-traffickers' lair

窟宅 kūzhái den or lair (usu. of bandits, etc.)：扫荡～，肃清残匪 mop up the den to eliminate the remaining bandits

堀 kū 〈书面〉❶ hole；cavity；cave；grotto ❷ dig a hole

堀穴 kūxué cave；cavern

枯 kū ❶ (of a plant, etc.) withered：～藤 withered vine /～木 dead tree /～枝败叶 withered branches and dead leaves ❷ (of a well, river, etc.) dried up；dry：海～石烂不变心。One will remain faithful even if the seas should run dry and the rocks rot. /思源已

K

～。One's source of inspiration has dried up. ❸ thin and haggard:老人形容已～。The old man looked shrivelled. ❹ dull; uninteresting: *see* "～坐" ❺〈方言〉dregs; residue (from soybean, sesame or other oilseeds after the oil has been extracted):菜～ rapeseed residue/麻～ sesame residue

枯饼 kūbǐng oil cake (made from oilseed residue)

枯病 kūbìng 〈植物〉rot

枯草热 kūcǎorè 〈医学〉hay fever

枯肠 kūcháng 〈书面〉impoverished mind:搜索～, 一无所获 rack one's brains for ideas or expressions but to no avail

枯瘁 kūcuì withered; haggard:容颜～ look haggard/～的花朵 withered flowers

枯干 kūgān dried-up; withered; shrivelled; wizened:～的树枝 withered branch/～的脸庞 shrivelled (*or* wizened) face/河流～。The rivers dried up./禾苗因缺水而～了。The seedlings shrivelled up for lack of water.

枯槁 kūgǎo ❶ (of plants) withered; shrivelled:草木～,赤地千里。For a thousand *li* the land became barren with nothing but withered plants. ❷ haggard; wizened:形容～,骨瘦如柴 look haggard and emaciated like a bag of bones

枯骨 kūgǔ dry bones (from a decomposed dead body); skeleton:泽及～ benevolence extending even to the dead; profound kindness; overflowing bounty

枯骸 kūhái skeleton; bleached bones

枯耗 kūhào deplete; exhaust:资源日益～。The resources are being depleted daily.

枯涸 kūhé (source of water) dry up; exhaust:～的池塘 dried-up pond/财政～ drained finances; exhausted treasury

枯黄 kūhuáng withered and yellow:头发～ dry, off-colour hair/小草都～了。The grass is turning yellow.

枯瘠 kūjí emaciated; barren; infertile:～的身体 emaciated body/土地～ infertile (*or* barren) land

枯寂 kūjì dull and lonely:夜深人静,更感～ feel all the lonelier in the dead of night/他天性活泼,从不知～为何物。Jovial by nature, he never knew spells of dull solitude.

枯焦 kūjiāo dried-up; withered; shrivelled; wizened:～的尸骨 dry bones (of a person long dead)/久旱不雨,禾苗～。Seedlings became withered owing to a long drought.

枯竭 kūjié ❶ dry up:河水～。The river dried up. ❷ exhaust; deplete:自然资源～。The natural resources were exhausted (*or* depleted)./精力～。One's energy is drained.

枯井 kūjǐng dry well:心如～ one's heart is like a dry well (devoid of any desire or illusion)

枯窘 kūjiǒng 〈书面〉dried up; exhausted:文思～ have the source of inspiration dried up; be devoid of inspiration; run out of ideas to write about

枯木逢春 kūmù-féngchūn come to life again like a withered tree in spring; get a new lease of life; enjoy good fortune after a long spell of bad luck:久旱逢雨,～ like dried crops receiving rain after a long drought or a withered tree bursting into life upon the arrival of spring/病愈出院后,他如同～,身体比以前更加康健了。when he was discharged from hospital after recovery, he felt healthier than ever, as if he'd got a new lease of life.

枯木朽株 kūmù-xiǔzhū withered trees and rotten stumps — senile or sick persons; decadent and weak force:我年老久病如～,恐来日无多矣。I'm afraid my days are numbered as I'm old and have long been sick, like a withered and rotten tree.

枯荣 kū-róng (of grasses and trees) luxuriate and wither; prosper and decline; rise and fall:人生～ ups and downs in one's life; vicissitudes of life/离离原上草,一岁一～。Grasses grow tall and flourish, Then wither and die only to rise again.

枯涩 kūsè dry and puckery; dull and heavy:味道～ puckery taste/文字～ dull and heavy writing

枯瘦 kūshòu withered and skinny; emaciated:形容～ look thin and worn; look emaciated/～如柴 be all skin and bones; be a bag of bones

枯熟 kūshú 〈农业〉dead ripeness:～期 dead-ripe stage

枯水 kūshuǐ low water:～河 wadi

枯水期 kūshuǐqī dry season; low-water season:～一到,河道上只有小舟往来。In the dry season, only small boats are seen on the river.

枯索 kūsuǒ 〈书面〉❶ devoid of vitality; dried-up; shrivelled; wizened:～面孔 wizened face ❷ dull and dry; boring:蛰居山城,颇觉～。I felt rather bored living in a mountain town in seclusion.

枯萎 kūwěi wither; shrivel (up):荷叶～了。The lotus leaves have shrivelled./久旱不雨,禾苗～,村民们心急如焚。The villagers burned with anxiety as the seedlings withered because of the protracted drought.

枯萎病 kūwěibìng 〈植物〉blight; wilt

枯朽 kūxiǔ dry and decayed; rotten:初冬时节,草木都已～。It was early winter and the plants were all withered or rotten.

枯哑 kūyǎ (of voice) low and hoarse; husky:说话声音～ speak with a low, hoarse voice

枯叶蛾 kūyè'é lappet moth

枯鱼 kūyú dried fish — fish out of water; in straitened circumstances; helpless:以～自喻 compare oneself to a fish out of water

枯燥 kūzào dull and dry; uninteresting:～的工作 dull work/～的演讲 boring speech/～的生活 dreary (*or* humdrum) life

枯燥无味 kūzào-wúwèi dry as dust; dull as ditchwater:这篇文章读起来～。The article makes very dull reading.

枯痔法 kūzhìfǎ 〈中医〉necrosis therapy of haemorrhoids

枯皱 kūzhòu shrivelled; wizened; wrinkly:妈妈的脸～了,眼也花了。Mother's face was wizened and her eyesight was failing.

枯坐 kūzuò sit idly; sit with nothing to do:三十几个记者在他的办公室里～着,等待他回来。Over thirty reporters were sitting idly in his office, waiting for him to return.

骷 kū

骷髅 kūlóu ❶ human skeleton ❷ human skull; death's head

刳 kū

〈书面〉hollow out:～木为舟 hollow a (dugout) canoe out of a tree trunk

矻 kū

矻矻 kūkū 〈书面〉persevering; diligent; assiduous:孜孜～ persevere (in hard work) unflaggingly/～终日 work diligently (*or* assiduously) all day long

哭 kū

cry; weep:痛～ cry out loud; wail/～开了 burst out crying; burst into tears/～得死去活来 cry one's heart (*or* eyes) out/～着～着就睡着了 cry oneself to sleep/这孩子爱～。The child is apt to crying./《～花岗遇难同胞》(title of a poem) *Lament for Compatriots Killed in Hanaoka (Japan)*/《孟姜女～长城》(title of an opera) *The Girl Meng Jiang Bewails the Great Wall*

哭包子 kūbāozi 〈口语〉child liable to crying; crybaby; sniveller:这孩子小性儿,动不动就哭,真是个～。The peevish child cries easily; it's quite a sniveller.

哭鼻子 kū bízi 〈口语〉cry; weep; snivel:大学头一年,她经常为想家～。In her first year at college, she often wept when she was homesick./你要不听我的劝告,事情砸了可别来找我～。If you ignore my advice and fail, don't come snivelling back to me.

哭哭啼啼 kūku-títí keep crying or sobbing; weep and wail; whimper endlessly:我才不会～地叫他认母亲呢。I'm not going to fall on his neck in a flood of tears and tell him I'm his long-lost mother.

哭脸 kūliǎn 〈方言〉cry; weep; snivel

哭灵 kūlíng wail bitterly before a bier, tomb or memorial tablet (for the deceased)

哭泣 kūqì sob; weep:为死去的亲人～ weep over the death of one's beloved/为自己的悲惨命运而～ bewail one's tragic fate

哭腔 kūqiāng ❶ (in traditional opera) sobbing tune ❷ speak with sobs:她带着～说别人冤枉她了。She told in a sobbing tone how she had been wronged by others.

哭墙 Kūqiáng Wailing Wall, a historic site in Jerusalem where Jews traditionally pray and lament on Fridays

哭穷 kūqióng go about saying how hard up one is; complain of being hard up; pretend to be hard up:他天天在父母面前～,想多要几个钱。He was always telling his parents how hard up he was, in order to get more money from them./谁都知道你一个人挣的比我们俩挣的还多,在我们面前哭个什么穷! Everybody knows you make much more than the two of us together. Don't you pretend to be short of money!

哭丧 kūsāng lament sb.'s death by loud wailing; cry aloud at a funeral; keen:葬礼在一片～声中开始了。The burial service started with a loud fit of wailing.

哭丧棒 kūsāngbàng staff used by the son of the deceased in a funeral procession

哭丧着脸 kūsangzhe liǎn wear a long face; look displeased; sulk: 心里不痛快就说出来，别跟我～。Speak out if you are displeased. Don't give me that sullen look of yours. /她～，一句话也不说。She said nothing, with grief written all over her face. *or* She kept silent and sulked.

哭诉 kūsù complain tearfully; sob out; accuse while weeping: 老太太～着自己的不幸遭遇。The old woman was sobbing out her misfortunes.

哭天抹泪 kūtiān-mǒlèi 〈贬义〉wail and whine; cry piteously: 看她～的样子，好像有多大的冤屈似的。She wailed and whined as if she had been greatly wronged.

哭笑不得 kūxiào-bùdé not know whether to laugh or to cry; find sth. both funny and annoying: 这番话叫他～。These words left him wondering whether he should laugh or cry. *or* He was caught between tears and laughter at these words. /像这样让人～的事情，厂子里经常发生。Such absurdities are routine occurrences in the factory.

哭笑无常 kūxiào-wúcháng cry and laugh by turns (without any apparent reasons); cry and laugh hysterically

kǔ

苦 kǔ ❶ bitter: 生菜的味儿有些～。The lettuce has a slightly bitter taste. *or* The lettuce tastes somewhat bitter. ❷ hardship; suffering; misery: 生活很～ lead a hard life /～里生，～里长 be born and brought up in adversity and misery /怕～怕累 shrink from hardship and arduous work /同甘共～ share weal and woe ❸ cause sb. suffering; give sb. a hard time: 组织这个研讨会可～了我了。Organizing this seminar has given me a hard time. ❹ suffer from; be troubled by: ～雨 suffer from incessant rain /我们～无良策。The trouble is we have no good solution. ❺ painstakingly; assiduously; doing one's utmost: ～读诗书 study the classics assiduously /～练基本功 train hard in basic skills /～谏 do one's utmost to advise or exhort (the monarch) /我找你可找～了。I've been completely exhausted trying to get hold of you. ❻〈方言〉too much; to excess: 指甲修得太～ trim one's nails too short /树篱剪得太～ overprune (*or* overtrim) a hedge

苦艾 kǔ'ài wormwood; absinthium: ～中毒 absinthism (*Artemisia absinthium*)

苦艾酒 kǔ'àijiǔ absinthe; vermouth

苦艾油 kǔ'àiyóu wormwood oil

苦氨酸 kǔ'ānsuān 〈化学〉picramic acid: ～盐 picramate /～钠 soidum picramate

苦熬 kǔ'áo endure; go through (years of suffering, etc.): ～岁月 endure (*or* go through) years of suffering

苦不唧 kǔbujī 〈方言〉slightly bitter: 这种菜～儿的，还挺好吃。Despite a slightly bitter taste, this vegetable is quite delicious.

苦不堪言 kǔbùkānyán *also* "苦不胜言" (of a person) suffer untold misery and hardship; (of sth.) be indescribably painful (*or* miserable); the misery or hardship is beyond words: 这差事～。This is a wretched job. /这病把他折磨得～。He has suffered a great deal from (*or* has been tormented by) the illness.

苦菜 kǔcài *also* "荼" tú; "苦苣" 〈植物〉common sow thistle; sonchus (*Sonchus oleraceus*)

苦草 kǔcǎo 〈植物〉tape grass; eelgrass; *Vallisneria spiralis*

苦差 kǔchāi hard and unprofitable job; thankless job: 这是一桩谁也不愿干的～。This is a thankless job that no one wants. /这回派你一趟～，为公司去催款子。I will give you a hard nut to crack this time; go and collect debts for the company.

苦楚 kǔchǔ suffering; misery; distress: 诉说～ speak out one's misery

苦处 kǔchu suffering; hardship; difficulty: 做父母的～ what one has to suffer (*or* endure) as a parent /你可不知道我的～! If you only knew the difficulties I am in! /我俩各有各的～。Each of us has his own troubles. *or* It's no easy job for either of us.

苦大仇深 kǔdà-chóushēn have suffered bitterly and nurse deep hatred (usu. for the old society, etc.): ～的穷孩子纷纷参加了八路军。Those poor lads, who had their fill of suffering and nursed deep hatred for the old regime, joined the Eighth Route Army eagerly.

苦胆 kǔdǎn gall bladder; gall

苦迭打 kǔdiédǎ 〈旧语〉(transliteration from the French) *coup d'état*

苦丁茶 kǔdīngchá ❶ evergreen tree with oval leaves, pink pollen and oval fruit, whose slightly bitter leaves can be used as a substitute for tea ❷ beverage made from such leaves

苦斗 kǔdòu wage an arduous struggle; fight hard

苦厄 kǔ'è hardship and suffering; affliction; disaster

苦恶鸟 kǔ'èniǎo *also* "白胸秧鸟" báixiōngyāngniǎo white-breasted water rail (*Amaurornis phoenicurus chinensis*)

苦腐病 kǔfǔbìng bitter rot: 苹果～ bitter rot of apples

苦干 kǔgàn work hard; make painstaking effort: ～精神 spirit of hard work /～加巧干 combine hard work with ingenuity /～了三年，才把书写完。This book took three years' strenuous effort to finish.

苦根 kǔgēn root cause of impoverishment or suffering: 挖掉～ eradicate the root cause of poverty (*or* suffering)

苦工 kǔgōng ❶ forced hard (manual) work; hard labour: 他在矿上干了十几年～。He did hard labour at the mine for over a dozen years. ❷ person who does hard labour; coolie: 当～ work as a coolie

苦功 kǔgōng painstaking effort; hard work: 语言非下～不能学好。It requires painstaking effort to master a language. /这个芭蕾舞演员的成功是她二十年来所下～的结果。The success of this ballerina is due to her twenty years' hard work.

苦瓜 kǔguā ❶〈植物〉*also* "癞瓜" làiguā balsam pear ❷ (often used figuratively) bitter gourd: 长着一副～脸 have a miserable look /他俩是一根藤上的～。They were two bitter gourds on the same vine. *or* They had suffered the same lot.

苦果 kǔguǒ bitter fruit — evil consequence; disastrous effect; bitter pill: 自食～ eat one's own bitter fruit; swallow one's own bitter pill; reap what one has sown

苦海 kǔhǎi sea of bitterness; abyss of misery: 跳出～ get out of the abyss of misery

苦海无边，回头是岸 kǔhǎi wú biān, huítóu shì àn (formerly a Buddhist admonition) the sea of bitterness is boundless, repent and the shore is at hand — it is never too late to mend one's ways

苦害 kǔhài 〈方言〉injure; damage; harm

苦寒 kǔhán ❶ bitterly cold; frigid: 北地～，入冬四野皆白，滴水成冰。It is bitterly cold in the north. With the onset of winter the ground is covered by snow as far as the eye can see, and dripping water freezes instantly. ❷ poor; impoverished: 他家世代～。His family has been poor for generations.

苦旱 kǔhàn ❶ suffer from drought: 水多患涝，水少～ suffer from flooding in the rainy season and from drought when it's dry ❷ extremely dry; drought-stricken: 干燥～的风沙地区 extremely dry, windy and sandy area

苦瓠子 kǔhùzi ❶ bitter bottle gourd; bitter calabash ❷〈比喻〉sufferer; wretch: 我们这几个～不像你们，既不会做人，又不会看眼色，自然没有好果子吃。Unlike you, we poor wretches will naturally come to no good end, knowing neither how to please people nor how to take others' cue!

苦活儿 kǔhuór hard and unprofitable job: 干～ do a hard and low-paying job; perform a thankless task

苦尽甘来 kǔjìn-gānlái *also* "苦尽甜来" when bitterness ends, sweetness begins; after suffering comes happiness; sweet after sweat: 大家慢慢熬吧，总有～的一天。Let's hold out with patience, we'll see light at the end of the tunnel sooner or later.

苦境 kǔjìng hard and painful circumstances; miserable plight: 身陷～ be landed in a miserable plight /摆脱～ extricate oneself from hard and painful circumstances

苦酒 kǔjiǔ ❶ wine with tart flavour ❷〈方言〉vinegar ❸〈比喻〉awful result; deplorable consequence: 你自己酿的～，还得你自己喝。Since this is the bitter wine of your own brewing, you have to drink it. *or* As you have sown, so you must reap.

苦口 kǔkǒu ❶ (admonish) in earnest: ～相劝 earnestly admonish (*or* exhort) ❷ bitter to the taste: 良药～，忠言逆耳。Candid advice always sounds unpleasant, just as good medicine tastes bitter.

苦口婆心 kǔkǒu-póxīn (admonish or remonstrate) earnestly and maternally; in earnest words and with the best of intentions; with patience and sincerity: 不顾朋友～的劝告 turn a deaf ear to one's friend's earnest and well-meaning remonstrances /大家～地劝说，希望他迷途知返。Everyone exhorted (*or* admonished) him with patience and sincerity, hoping he would return to the fold.

苦苦 kǔkǔ ❶ hard; strenuously; persistently: ～思索 ponder hard;

K

rack one's brains /～追求 pursue persistently; try hard to obtain /～相逼 press sb. hard; drive sb. to the wall /～哀求 beg sorely; implore urgently; entreat piteously /他～劝我再住一两天。He did his best to persuade me to stay for a couple of days more. ❷ enduring pain or hardship; painfully: 爸爸去世后，妈妈带着我们～地熬过了十八年。After father's death, mother endured great hardship for 18 years bringing us up.

苦况 kǔkuàng difficult position; predicament; straits: 诉说自己的～ relate one's predicament; recount one's hardships (*or* difficulties)

苦喇吧唧 kǔlabājī 〈口语〉 *also* "苦喇呱唧" bittersome: 这根黄瓜～的不好吃。This cucumber doesn't taste good; it's a bit bitter.

苦劳 kǔláo credit for hard work: 勤勤恳恳地干了许多年，他没有功劳也有点～。Having worked for so many years, he should be given some credit for hard work if not for merit (*or* good work).

苦乐 kǔ-lè joy and sorrow; enjoyment and suffering; happiness and hardship: 人生～ joys and sorrows of life /～与共 share joy and sorrow; share weal and woe /～不均 unequal distribution of ease and hardship; unfair allocation of work load and reward

苦乐观 kǔlèguān view on (what constitutes) hardship and happiness

苦力 kǔlì coolie

苦恋 kǔliàn persistent unrequited love

苦楝 kǔliàn 〈植物〉 azedarach

苦楝子 kǔliànzǐ 〈中药〉 chinaberry

苦霉素 kǔméisù 〈生化〉 picromycin

苦闷 kǔmèn depressed; dejected; feeling low: 排遣～的心情 try to dispel (*or* shake off) one's depression /这汉子因失业而感到十分～。The man felt very low over the loss of his job. /那是我惟一的～。That is the only source of my unhappiness. *or* That's the only thing that bothers me.

苦命 kǔmìng bitter or sad fate; ill-fated life: ～人 person destined (*or* fated) to suffer; person born under an unlucky star /我～的孩子啊! Oh, my unfortunate (*or* poor) child!

苦难 kǔnàn suffering; misery; distress: 人生的～ misery of human life; trials of life /～的生活 hard and miserable life /内战使那个国家的人民陷入了～的深渊。The civil war plunged people of that country into the abyss of misery.

苦难深重 kǔnàn-shēnzhòng go through untold suffering; be in deep distress; be in the abyss of misery: ～的人民 people living in dire misery; deeply-distressed people

苦恼 kǔnǎo distressed; frustrated; vexed; worried: 把～和烦闷抛在一边 cast aside one's worries and annoyances /考试不及格使他很～。He was greatly distressed at his failure in the examination.

苦啤酒 kǔpíjiǔ bitters

苦荞麦 kǔqiáomài 〈植物〉 tartary buckwheat (*Fagopyrum tartaricum*)

苦情 kǔqíng ❶ sorry situation; tragic experience; misery: 吐～ relate one's miseries /这部影片记述了旧社会农民的～。The movie depicted the tragic experiences of the peasants in the old society. ❷ 〈方言〉 sad; tragic; miserable: 她死得～。She died a wretched death.

苦趣 kǔqù bitterness; vexation; worry: 四十岁以上的人，谁没尝过人生的欢乐和～? Who among people over forty has not tasted of the bitterness as well as the joy of life?

苦肉计 kǔròujì ruse of inflicting an injury on oneself to win the trust of one's enemy or critic: 巧施～ employ an artful ruse by inflicting an injury on oneself to win the confidence of one's enemy /中了敌人的～ be taken in by the enemy's ruse of self-injury

苦涩 kǔsè ❶ bitter and astringent; acrid: ～难咽 too bitter and astringent to swallow /生柿子又苦又涩。Unripe persimmons have a bitter and puckery taste. ❷ pained; agonized; anguished: ～的表情 anguished look /心中～，难对人言 find it difficult to voice one's innermost agony /他～地一笑。He forced a smile.

苦参 kǔshēn 〈中药〉 *Sophora flavescens*: ～根 *radix sophorae flavescens*

苦事 kǔshì hard job; thankless task

苦树 kǔshù *also* "黄楝树" huángliànshù 〈植物〉 chinaberry

苦水 kǔshuǐ ❶ bitter water: ～井 bitter water well ❷ gastric secretion rising to the mouth; gastroesophageal reflux ❸ suffering; misery: 吐～ pour out one's grievances (*or* sufferings) /她是在～里泡大的。She grew up in deep misery.

苦丝丝 kǔsīsī slightly bitter; bitterish: 他品着烟叶，觉得芬芳之中又有点～儿的。In sampling the tobacco leaves he found a slightly bitter flavour mixed in the fragrance.

苦思 kǔsī think hard; puzzle or ponder over sth.; cudgel or rack one's brains: ～终日 ponder over sth. all day long

苦思冥想 kǔsī-míngxiǎng ponder long and hard; cudgel or rack one's brains (to solve a problem, etc.): ～，不得其解 fail to find an answer after pondering long and hard over a question

苦痛 kǔtòng suffering; misery; pain; agony: 他经历了一段～的日子。He went through a period of mental agony. /这情景更增添了我的～。The situation added to my pain.

苦头 kǔtóu slightly bitter taste: 这种瓜带点～。This kind of melon tastes slightly bitter.

苦头 kǔtou suffering: 吃尽了不识字的～ have suffered enough from being illiterate /尝够了战争的～ endure untold sufferings in war; have had enough of the miseries of war /他不吃点～是不会回心转意的。He won't change his mind until he runs into trouble.

苦土 kǔtǔ (popular term for 氧化镁) magnesium oxide

苦味酸 kǔwèisuān picric acid; trinitrophenol: ～盐 picrate /～铵 ammonium picrate; trinitrophenolate

苦夏 kǔxià *also* "疰夏" zhùxià loss of appetite and weight in summer: 入伏～，人都打不起精神来。People usually feel dispirited during the dog days as they lose their appetite and weight.

苦想 kǔxiǎng think hard: 冥思～ rack or cudgel one's brains (about sth.)

苦笑 kǔxiào forced smile; wry smile; strained smile: 现出一丝～ force a faint smile /～一声 laugh a bitter laugh /面对此情此景，他只好～。At this he could not but give a wry smile.

苦心 kǔxīn trouble taken; pains: 煞费～ take great pains (in doing sth.); go to every trouble /～钻研 engage in painstaking research; study assiduously /不要辜负了老师们的一片～。Be worthy of all the pains your teachers have taken over you. *or* Be sure to live up to your teachers' expectations.

苦心孤诣 kǔxīn-gūyì toil or endeavour single-heartedly; make extraordinarily painstaking efforts: 李教授大半生～写成的书稿就这么被付之一炬了。The manuscript, which had taken Prof. Li's single-hearted toil for a good part of his life, was thus consumed in flames.

苦心经营 kǔxīn-jīngyíng nurse with every care (an enterprise, organization, etc.); painstakingly build up: 这家店铺亏得他～，才有了如今的局面。Thanks to his painstaking effort, the shop has become what it is today.

苦辛 kǔxīn hard work; toil; hardship: 备尝～ endure (*or* experience) untold hardship

苦行 kǔxíng 〈宗教〉 ascetic practice; asceticism

苦行僧 kǔxíngsēng ascetic (monk); person who lives a life of self-denial and mortification: 我们不是～，但我们主张先天下之忧而忧，后天下之乐而乐。Though we are no ascetics, we believe that we should be the first to endure hardship and the last to enjoy ourselves.

苦行主义 kǔxíngzhǔyì asceticism

苦刑 kǔxíng cruel torture: 受～ suffer from cruel torture /～拷打 subject sb. to savage torture

苦杏仁 kǔxìngrén bitter almond

苦言 kǔyán 〈书面〉 words unpleasant to the ear; unpalatable advice: 苦药利病，～利行。Bitter medicine cures illness; unpleasant advice benefits conduct.

苦杨 kǔyáng 〈植物〉 bitter poplar

苦野豌豆 kǔyěwāndòu 〈植物〉 bitter vetch (*Vicia ervilia*)

苦役 kǔyì 〈法律〉 hard labour; penal servitude: 服～ serve one's time in hard labour; be subjected to penal servitude; do hard labour /～犯 prisoner who is forced to do hard labour /判处～三年 sentence (sb.) to three years' penal servitude

苦于 kǔyú ❶ be troubled (over a problem); suffer (from a disadvantage): ～力不从心 be troubled that one's ability falls short of one's wishes; be sorry that one cannot do as much as one would wish to /～资金短缺 be hard pressed for funds /～不懂外语 be handicapped by not knowing a foreign language ❷ be worse (off) than; be harder up than: 贫农的生活～下中农。Life of the poor peasants was harder than that of the lower-middle peasants. *or* The poor peasants were worse off than the lower-middle peasants.

苦雨 kǔyǔ incessant rain; unbroken spell of wet weather: ～凄风 distressing rain and wind; bitterly cold rain and wind /入春以来，～

不停。There has been an unbroken spell of wet weather since the beginning of spring.

苦战 kǔzhàn ❶ bitter fighting; pitched battle:～得脱 fight one's way out through pitched battle ❷ wage an arduous struggle; work hard:村民～了一冬，终于修好了灌溉水渠。The villagers worked hard for a whole winter and finally completed the irrigation ditch. /他为赶稿通宵～。He worked throughout the night in order to finish the draft.

苦中作乐 kǔzhōng-zuòlè enjoy life in adversity; seek joy in hardship; make merry despite one's suffering

苦衷 kǔzhōng private suffering, trouble or difficulty (that one is reluctant to discuss with others or that is not easy for others to understand):难言的～ suffering, trouble or difficulty that one is reluctant to mention; sth. that is too embarrassing or painful to speak of /学会体谅别人的～ learn to make allowance for others' difficulties or problems

苦竹 kǔzhú 〈植物〉bitter bamboo (*Pleioblastus amarus*)

苦主 kǔzhǔ 〈法律〉family of the victim in a murder or manslaughter case:这桩命案，一时找不到～。It is difficult for the moment to find the family of the victim in this case of homicide.

苦子 kǔzi 〈方言〉suffering; misery; distress:吃～ endure hardship; suffer /他平生哪受过这样的～。Never had he experienced such misery in his life.

楛

kǔ 〈书面〉shoddy; of inferior quality

see also hù

kù

喾(嚳)

Kù legendary ruler of remote antiquity, father of Tang Yao (唐尧):帝～ Emperor Ku

库[1]

kù ❶ warehouse; storehouse; storage; bank:工具～ tools storehouse; tools shed /冷藏～ cold store; refrigeration storage /宝～ treasure-house /血～ blood bank /金～ treasury /国～ national (*or* state) treasury; exchequer /水～ reservoir /粮～ granary /书～ (of a library) book stacks; stackroom /军械～ armoury /汽车～ garage /思想～ brain trust; think-tank ❷〈自控〉base; library:程序～ routine library; program library /数据～ database ❸ (Kù) a surname

库[2]

kù (short for 库仑)〈电学〉coulomb

库兵 kùbīng ❶〈书面〉weaponry in the armoury or storage ❷〈旧语〉soldier guarding a warehouse

库藏 kùcáng have in storage:清点～物资 make an inventory of the equipment and materials in storage /～图书 50 万册 boast (*or* have) a book collection of 500,000 volumes

see also kùzàng

库藏股 kùcánggǔ 〈金融〉own shares; treasury stock

库车 Kùchē Kuqa or Kucha, county in western Xinjiang Uygur Autonomous Region

库存 kùcún stock; reserve; inventory:～粮食 grain in stock /～充足 plentiful stock /～产品 inventory of products; products in stock /～现金 cash on hand /盘点～ inventory one's stock; take stock /减少～ reduce one's inventory (*or* stock) /用完～ exhaust one's stock

库存控制 kùcún kòngzhì 〈经济〉stock control; inventory control

库缎 kùduàn a kind of jacquard satin (formerly collected by the imperial court of the Qing Dynasty, hence its name)

库尔德人 Kù'ěrdérén Kurd, a mainly pastoral Aryan Islamic people living in the general region known as Kurdistan

库尔德斯坦 Kù'ěrdésītǎn Kurdistan, general region inhabited by the Kurds, covering parts of Turkey, Iraq, Iran, Syria, etc.

库房 kùfáng storehouse; storeroom; stacks (of a library or archives):三间～ three-room storehouse /～重地，闲人免入。Storehouse. No admittance except on business.

库锦 kùjǐn brocade woven with gold and silver threads and coloured floss

库克群岛 Kùkè Qúndǎo Cook Islands, a group of islands in the southwest Pacific between Tonga and French Polynesia

库雷蚊 kùléiwén *see* "库蚊"

库仑 kùlún ❶ (Kùlún)Charles Augustin de Coulomb (1736-1806), French physicist ❷〈电学〉coulomb:～能 coulomb energy /～势 coulomb potential /～力 coulomb force /～场 coulomb field

库仑定律 Kùlún dìnglǜ Coulomb's law; law of electrostatic attraction

库仑计 kùlúnjì 〈电学〉coulombmeter; voltmeter

库伦 kùlún ❶ enclosed pasture (used by the Mongolian nationality) ❷ (Kùlún) former name for Ulan Bator (capital of the Republic of Mongolia)

库平 kùpíng 〈旧语〉measure adopted by the Qing Dynasty for collecting land tax and other levies, as well as for silver received or paid (one *kuping liang* was equivalent to 37.301 grams)

库券 kùquàn (short for 国库券) treasury bond

库容 kùróng storage capacity (of a reservoir, warehouse, refrigeration storage, etc.):这个水库的～为一亿立方米。This reservoir has a storage capacity of one hundred million cubic metres. *or* The reservoir can hold one hundred million cubic metres of water.

库蚊 kùwén *also* "家蚊" jiāwén; "常蚊" chángwén; "库雷蚊"〈动物〉culex

库务科 Kùwùkē (HK) Treasury Branch

库藏 kùzàng 〈书面〉warehouse; storehouse

see also kùcáng

裤

kù trousers; pants:一条长～ a pair of trousers (*or* pants) /一条短～ a pair of shorts /棉～ cotton-padded trousers /喇叭～ bell-bottomed trousers; flared pants /马～ riding breeches /便～ slacks /牛仔～ jeans /棉毛～ cotton tights; cotton underpants /毛～ woolen tights; woolen underpants /裙～ divided skirt; skirt-pants /游泳～ swimming trunks /灯笼～ knickerbockers; plus fours /三角～ panties; briefs; underpants /连～袜 panty hose; tights

裤衩 kùchǎ underpants; undershorts:三角～ panties; briefs; underpants

裤裆 kùdāng crotch (of trousers):钻～ crawl beneath someone's crotch; be humiliated

裤兜 kùdōu trouser pocket:后～ hip pocket

裤缝 kùfèng seam of a trouser leg

裤管 kùguǎn *also* "裤脚管"〈方言〉trouser leg

裤脚 kùjiǎo ❶ bottom of a trouser leg:～卷边 turnups; pants (*or* trouser) cuff /～镶边 bottom piping ❷〈方言〉trouser leg:这裤子我穿～太长了。This pair of trousers is too long for me.

裤料 kùliào panting; trousering:一块～ a piece of trousering

裤筒 kùtǒng 〈方言〉trouser leg

裤头 kùtóu 〈方言〉underpants; undershorts:游泳～ swimming (*or* bathing) trunks

裤腿 kùtuǐ trouser leg:趟过小河前把～卷起来。Roll up (*or* back) your trouser legs before you wade across the stream.

裤线 kùxiàn creases (of trousers):笔直的～ straight (*or* sharp) creases (of trousers) /熨～ crease a pair of trousers with an iron

裤腰 kùyāo waist of trousers:这条裤子的～对我太小了。This pair of trousers has too tight a waist for me.

裤腰带 kùyāodài waist belt; band; girdle

裤子 kùzi trousers; pants:条纹～ striped pants

袴

kù *see* "裤" kù

绔

kù *see* "纨绔" wánkù

酷

kù ❶ cruel; oppressive:严～ harsh; grim /冷～无情 cold and cruel ❷ very; extremely:～贫 very poor; poverty-stricken; in dire poverty

酷爱 kù'ài love ardently; be very fond of; adore:～自己的祖国 love one's motherland ardently /～滑雪 be extremely fond of skiing /～和平的人民 peace-loving people

酷毒 kùdú cruel and vicious:～的刑罚 cruel, vicious torture

酷寒 kùhán bitter cold:～的冬季 bitterly cold winter

酷寒荒原 kùhán huāngyuán 〈地理〉arctic desert

酷旱 kùhàn harsh drought; extreme aridity:～的年月 extremely dry days

酷好 kùhào be extremely fond of; be very keen on:～文艺 be extremely fond of art and literature /～古典音乐 be very keen on classical music

酷吏 kùlì 〈书面〉cruel, ruthless official:～赃官 cruel, greedy officials

酷烈 kùliè 〈书面〉❶ cruel; fierce:～的寒风 piercing cold wind /～的统治 cruel rule /当时,人民遭受的苦难极为～。In those years, the people suffered in the extreme. ❷ (of fragrance or aroma) very strong; powerful:香气～,久而不散。A powerful fragrance lingered on. ❸ extremely hot; scalding:～的阳光 scorching sun; baking sun

酷虐 kùnüè cruel; ruthless; savage; ferocious:～的暴政激起了人民的反抗。The savage tyranny roused the people's resistance.

酷评 kùpíng harsh comment; fault-finding criticism

酷热 kùrè extremely hot:～的盛夏 sweltering summer days /他不顾～,奋力写作。He wrote on despite the extreme heat.

酷暑 kùshǔ intense heat of summer:八月～ intense heat of August /～难当 suffocating (*or* oppressive) heat /～严寒 extreme heat and bitter cold; scorching summer and freezing winter

酷似 kùsì be the very image of; be exactly like:她长得～她的母亲。She is the very (*or* living) image of her mother. /兄弟俩长得～,一般人很难区分。The two brothers look so alike that few can tell them apart.

酷肖 kùxiào 〈书面〉be the very image of; be exactly like:～乃父 be the very image of his father; be a chip off the old block

酷刑 kùxíng cruel or savage torture:～拷打 torture savagely /使用～ subject sb. to torture /～之下,屈打成招 admit to false charges under savage torture

kuā

夸(誇) kuā ❶ exaggerate; overstate; boast; brag:虚～作风 boastful style of work ❷ praise; compliment:他的木工手艺人人～。He is widely praised as a good carpenter. /老～他,他就会骄傲了。Too much praise would make him big-headed. /就算你知道得多,也用不着这么自～啊。You don't have to make such a parade of your knowledge, do you?

夸大 kuādà exaggerate; overstate; magnify:～成绩 overstate (*or* exaggerate) one's achievements /～事实 stretch the facts /～敌情 overrate (*or* overestimate) the enemy /～的报道 exaggerated report /～的数字 inflated figures

夸大狂 kuādàkuáng 〈医学〉megalomania:～患者 megalomaniac

夸大其词 kuādà-qící make an overstatement; speak in superlatives; exaggerate:你总是～,别人就很难相信你了。If you always overstate your case, people will no longer believe you. /他的说法过于～。His account was full of exaggerations.

夸诞 kuādàn 〈书面〉inflated; exaggerated:其言～,多有不实之处。His statement was inflated and inaccurate in many places.

夸父追日 Kuāfù-zhuīrì *also* "夸父逐日" a legendary braggadocio conceived the vain ambition of overtaking the fleeting rays of the sun and died of thirst in his pursuit — overestimate oneself and try to do sth. beyond one's ability

夸海口 kuā hǎikǒu boast wildly; talk big; brag:不是～,我办这事是十拿九稳的。I'm not talking big; this is a sure-fire thing for me. /老伙计,这个海口你可夸不得。You'd better stop blowing your own horn, old chap.

夸奖 kuājiǎng praise; commend; compliment:老师～他学习用功。The teacher praised him for his diligence. /同事都～她穿着大方。Her colleagues complimented her on her good taste in dress.

夸克 kuākè 〈物理〉quark:～流 quark current /～模型 quark model

夸口 kuākǒu boast; brag; talk big:有什么值得～的! What's there to brag about! /他～说他马上就要被提成经理了。He boasted that he was soon to be promoted to be manager.

夸夸其谈 kuākuā-qítán indulge in verbiage; shoot one's mouth off; be full of hot air:～,不干实事 indulge in empty talk but do nothing practical; talk big and do nothing

夸示 kuāshì show off; flaunt:～于人 show off before others /～自己的成绩 flaunt one's achievements

夸饰 kuāshì give an exaggerated account; embellish:书中颇多～,难免有失真之处。With so many exaggerations in it, the book is certainly not free from inaccuracies.

夸说 kuāshuō ❶ praise; commend:村里的老人都～这姑娘孝顺。Old folks in the village all praised the girl for her filial obedience. ❷ brag about; show off; flaunt:她这个人就是喜欢到处～她的显赫门庭。She just loves bragging about her illustrious family.

夸脱 kuātuō quart (one fourth of a gallon)

夸许 kuāxǔ praise; commend:得到了老师们的～ win the praise of one's teachers

夸耀 kuāyào brag about; show off; flaunt:～财富 show off one's wealth; flaunt one's riches /～自己勇敢 brag of one's courage; boast how brave one is

夸赞 kuāzàn speak highly of; commend; praise:～他的好枪法 speak highly of his marksmanship

夸张 kuāzhāng ❶ exaggerate; overstate:～的笔调 exaggerated style /艺术～ artistic exaggeration /他的一大毛病就是爱～。His biggest failing is his love of bragging. /他说得～了,实际情况远没那么严重。He overstated the case, which is certainly not that serious. ❷ hyperbole:漫画离不开～。Hyperbole is essential in caricatures.

夸嘴 kuāzuǐ 〈口语〉boast; brag:不是我～,这事没有我办不成。It's not that I brag, but the matter cannot be done without me.

姱 kuā 〈书面〉pretty; beautiful:～容修态 beautiful look and graceful manner

姱女 kuānǚ beautiful woman; beauty

姱姿 kuāzī good looks; beautiful posture; graceful carriage

kuǎ

垮 kuǎ collapse; fall in; break down:屋顶被雪压～。The roof collapsed (*or* fell in) under the weight of the snow. /再这样干下去,你非累～了不行。If you go on working like this, you are bound to break down (*or* collapse) some day. /敌军完全被打～了。The enemy forces were thoroughly routed. /洪水冲～了堤坝。The floodwater burst the dyke. /那个公司要～了。That company is going bankrupt. /很多小商店被这个超级市场挤～了。Many small shops had to close down because of competition from the supermarket.

垮杆 kuǎgǎn 〈方言〉collapse; fail:他的买卖～了。His business failed (*or* went bust).

垮台 kuǎtái collapse; fall from power:专制独裁终究是要～的。All dictatorships will collapse sooner or later.

侉(咵) kuǎ 〈方言〉❶ (speak) with an accent (esp. a provincial one):说话～里～气的 speak with a heavy provincial accent ❷ big and clumsy; unwieldy:～大个儿 big clumsy fellow; strapping man (with unrefined manners) /这箱子太～了,携带不方便。This suitcase is too unwieldy to carry.

侉子 kuǎzi 〈方言〉one who speaks with a heavy provincial accent

kuà

挎 kuà ❶ carry on the arm:～着个包袱 with a cloth bundle on one's arm /二人～臂而行。The two of them walked arm in arm. ❷ carry over one's shoulder, or round one's neck, or at one's side:～着背包 have a bag slung over one's shoulder

挎包 kuàbāo satchel

挎兜 kuàdōu satchel

挎斗 kuàdǒu sidecar (for a motorcycle or bicycle)

跨 kuà ❶ step; stride:～上楼梯 step up the stairs /～过门槛 stride (*or* step) over the threshold /～入新世纪 stride into a new century /一步～过水沟 take a big step (*or* stride) across the ditch ❷ sit or stand astride; bestride; straddle:～在马上 sit astride a horse /～上自行车 mount a bicycle / 横～长江的大桥 gigantic bridge spanning the Yangtze /～鹤西去 (euphemistical of a deceased woman) go west astride a crane ❸ cut across; go beyond:～行业组织 multi-trade organization /～国合作 international cooperation /～太平洋电话电缆 Transpacific Telephone Cable /俄罗斯横～欧亚两洲。Russia straddles across Asia and Europe. /这位老人的一生～越清朝、民国和人民共和国三个时代。The old man has lived through the Qing Dynasty, the Republic, and the People's Republic of China. ❹ attach to the side of sth.:～间 small side room /画的旁边～着一行小字。An inscription of small characters can be seen on one side of the painting.

跨步电压 kuàbù diànyā 〈电工〉step voltage

K

跨部门 kuà bùmén transdepartmental; interdepartmental:～联合企业 transdepartmental complex /～合作 interdepartmental cooperation
跨车 kuàchē 〈机械〉straddle carrier crane
跨地区 kuà dìqū trans-regional; inter-regional:～经济联合 inter-regional economic integration /～经济实体 trans-regional economic entity
跨度 kuàdù ❶ *also* "跨径"〈建筑〉span:拱的～ span of an arch /空间～ spatial span /～净空〈交通〉clearance of span ❷ distance; span:这部小说的时间～很大,历经四个朝代。The time span of the novel is tremendous, extending over four dynasties. *or* The plot of the novel spans over four dynasties.
跨国公司 kuàguó gōngsī *also* "多国公司" duōguó gōngsī transnational corporation; multinational corporation; multinational
跨国运营 kuàguó yùnyíng 〈通信〉transborder
跨行中耕机 kuàháng zhōnggēngjī straddle-row cultivator
跨街 kuàjiē stretching over a street; across a street:～横幅上写着欢迎标语。Banners with slogans of welcome hung across the street.
跨界 kuàjiè transboundary; trans-border:～贸易 trans-border trade
跨进 kuàjìn stride or step into; enter:～大门 stride into a gate /从电气时代～原子能时代 enter into the age of nuclear energy from the electric age
跨径 kuàjìng span:主桥有五个孔,其中最大～二百二十米。The main bridge has five arches with the biggest spanning over 220 metres.
跨栏 kuàlán 〈体育〉hurdle race; the hurdles:～赛跑 hurdle race; the hurdles /百米～ hundred-metre hurdle race
跨立式输送机 kuàlìshì shūsòngjī straddle conveyor
跨年度 kuà niándù go beyond the year:～工程 project to be carried on in the next year /～预算 budget to be carried over to the next year
跨入 kuàrù enter; get into:～"百强"企业行列 enter into the ranks of the hundred biggest (*or* most advanced) enterprises
跨世纪 kuà shìjì cross-century; trans-century:～工程 project which will not be completed until the next century; trans-century project /～绿化工程 cross-century green project
跨式 kuàshì 〈机械〉straddle type:～拉刀 straddle broach /～铣刀 straddle cutter; straddle mill
跨文化研究 kuà wénhuà yánjiū cross-cultural studies
跨铣加工 kuàxǐ jiāgōng 〈机械〉straddle mill work
跨线桥 kuàxiànqiáo 〈交通〉flyover; overpass:～净空 overhead clearance
跨学科 kuà xuékē interdisciplinary:～合作 interdisciplinary cooperation /～方法 interdisciplinary method
跨业 kuàyè *also* "跨行业" (of an enterprise) concurrently engage in different trades (*or* industries):～经营 do business in different trades
跨业公司 kuàyè gōngsī conglomerate company
跨音速 kuàyīnsù transonic speed; transonic velocity (i.e. between 600-800 miles per hour):～飞机 transonic aircraft /～风洞 transonic wind tunnel /～涡轮 transonic turbine
跨音速空气动力学 kuàyīnsù kōngqì dònglìxué transonic aerodynamics; transonics
跨院儿 kuàyuànr (of a traditional Chinese compound house) house by the side of the main one; side house; side compound:小～ small adjacent house in a traditional courtyard or compound
跨越 kuàyuè stride across; step over; cut across; span:～国界 go beyond the national boundary /～界限 surpass the bounds /～九七年工程 (HK) project that went beyond 30 June, 1997; project that straddled 1997 /～两个社会发展阶段 span over (*or* cut across) two stages of social development /～障碍 surmount obstacles /～栏杆 clear a fence
跨载起重机 kuàzài qǐzhòngjī straddle carrier crane
跨灶 kuàzào 〈书面〉surpass one's father; excel one's father

胯 kuà 〈生理〉hip:～部动作 hip movement
胯裆 kuàdāng crotch (of trousers)
胯骨 kuàgǔ hipbone; innominate bone; ilium
胯下辱 kuàxiàrǔ *also* "胯下之辱";"跨下辱" kuàxiàrǔ humiliation of being forced to crawl between sb.'s legs; cup of humiliation

kuǎi

蒯 kuǎi ❶〈植物〉wool grass ❷ (Kuǎi) a surname
蒯草 kuǎicǎo 〈植物〉wool grass

㧟[1](擓) kuǎi 〈方言〉scratch:～痒痒 scratch an itch /～破了皮 have one's skin scraped

㧟[2](擓) kuǎi 〈方言〉❶ carry on the arm:～着小竹篮儿 carry a small bamboo basket on one's arm ❷ ladle out; scoop up:往这个盆儿里～点粥。Ladle some porridge into this bowl. /她从缸里～了点儿水。She scooped up some water from the vat.
㧟哧 kuǎichi 〈方言〉scratch:我脊背上老痒痒,给我～～。My back itches. Scratch it for me.

kuài

凷 kuài 〈书面〉clod

会(會) kuài grand total; total
see also huì
会计 kuàijì ❶ accounting:～学 accounting /成本～ cost accounting /工业～ industrial accounting /财务～ financial accounting /～程序 accounting procedure /～方法 accounting method /～科目 accounting item /～账簿 account book ❷ bookkeeper; accountant:担任～ be an accountant; work as an accountant /～主任 chief accountant; controller of accounts
会计报表 kuàijì bàobiǎo accounting statement
会计成本管理 kuàijì chéngběn guǎnlǐ account cost control
会计法 kuàijìfǎ accounting law
会计概念 kuàijì gàiniàn accounting concept
会计惯例 kuàijì guànlì accounting convention
会计年度 kuàijì niándù accounting year; fiscal year; financial year
会计师 kuàijìshī accountant; (UK) chartered accountant; (US) certified public accountant:～查账报告 accountant's report
会计事务所 kuàijì shìwùsuǒ accounting firm
会计收益率 kuàijì shōuyìlǜ accounting rate of return
会计责任 kuàijì zérèn accountability

浍(澮) kuài 〈书面〉field ditch

哙(噲) kuài 〈书面〉swallow down

侩(儈) kuài 〈旧语〉go-between; middleman; broker:牙～ broker; middleman /市～ philistine

脍(膾) kuài 〈书面〉❶ finely sliced meat or fish:～不厌细。The finer the slices, the more delicious the meat. ❷ cut into thin slices; slice:～鲤 slice a carp
脍炙人口 kuàizhì-rénkǒu win universal praise; enjoy great popularity; be on everybody's lips; be a household word:～的名文 oft-quoted prose

鲙(鱠) kuài
鲙鱼 kuàiyú *also* "鳓" lè;"快鱼" kuàiyú Chinese herring

狯(獪) kuài sly; cunning

郐(鄶) Kuài ❶ name of a state during the Zhou Dynasty, situated northeast of the present Mixian County (密县), Henan Province ❷ a surname

块(塊) kuài ❶ lump; piece:冰～ lump (*or* piece) of ice /糖～ lumps of sugar; fruit drops /铁～ piece of iron /砖～儿 brickbat /土～ clod /血～ clot of blood /一大～儿猪肉 a large chunk of pork /把豆腐切成～儿。Cut the bean curd into small cubes. ❷〈自控〉block:功能～ function(al) block /数据～ data block /组件～

K

building block ❸〈量词〉*used of sth. cubical or flat in shape*：一～肥皂 a cake of soap /一～水地 a piece of irrigated land /一～黑板 a blackboard /一～菜地 a vegetable plot /一～衣料 a dress length ❹〈量词〉*used as a unit of money* (such as dollar and *yuan*)：一～银元 a silver dollar /两～钱 two *yuan* /三～美金 three US dollars

块根 kuàigēn 〈植物〉root tuber：～挖掘机 root digger

块根作物 kuàigēn zuòwù tuber crop; tuber plant：～播种机 root seed drill

块规 kuàiguī *also* "量块" liángkuài 〈机械〉slip gauge; gauge block

块焊接 kuàihànjiē 〈冶金〉block welding

块结构存储器 kuàijiégòu cúnchǔqì 〈计算机〉block-organized storage

块金 kuàijīn 〈矿业〉nugget (of gold)

块茎 kuàijīng 〈植物〉stem tuber; tuber：结～ tuber setting /～嫁接 tuber grafting

块茎作物 kuàijīng zuòwù stem tuber crop; stem tuber plant

块菌 kuàijūn *also* "块菰"〈植物〉truffle

块块 kuàikuai horizontal system of leadership (e.g. the provincial government with the departments under it); relationship between localities and local units："条条"和"～"密切协调 closely coordinate the relationship between the central administrative departments and their counterparts at lower levels (e.g. Ministry of Agriculture and provincial bureaus of agriculture, etc.) and that between the local governments and units of the same level

see also "条条" tiáotiao

块垒 kuàilěi 〈书面〉frustration or resentment at heart：以酒浇我心中～ wash down sorrows in my heart with wine

块煤 kuàiméi lump coal

块儿 kuàir ❶ size; stature：把大～的煤挑出来。Pick out the big lumps of coal. ❷〈方言〉place：我在这～等了好久了！I've been waiting here for ages! /你老家在哪～？Where is your home town (*or* village)?

块儿八毛 kuàir-bāmáo *also* "块儿八角" one *yuan* or less; about one *yuan*：～的，别跟他争了。It's peanuts. Stop bargaining with him.

块然 kuàirán 〈书面〉lonely; solitary：～独处 be all on one's own; live in solitude

块石 kuàishí block of stone

块糖 kuàitáng lump sugar; loaf sugar

块头 kuàitóu 〈方言〉size：他是个大～。He is a big burly fellow. /这人～不大，却很有力气。The man is very strong though not big.

块闸 kuàizhá 〈机械〉block brake

块植法 kuàizhífǎ 〈农业〉blocking

块铸 kuàizhù 〈冶金〉block casting

快

快 kuài ❶ quick; fast; rapid; swift：行动～ act quickly; be quick in action /说话～ talk fast /～如闪电 quick as lightning /～如脱兔 swift as a fleeing hare /多～好省 more, faster, better and more economical /人口增长很～ rapid growth in population /以最～的速度奔跑 run as fast (*or* swiftly) as one can /时间过得真～呀！How time flies! ❷ speed; velocity：你能跑多～？What is your running speed? *or* How fast can you run? ❸ hurry (up); make haste：～点，不然就迟了。Hurry up, or you'll be late. ❹ soon; before long：资金～要用完了。We will soon be out of funds. *or* The funds will be exhausted before long. /我都～五十岁了。I'm almost fifty. *or* I'm going on fifty. /～要下雨了。It is about to rain. /寒假～到了。The winter vacation is drawing near. ❺ quick-witted; clever; nimble：反应～ be quick in response; have quick reaction /脑子～ have a quick (*or* nimble) mind; be quick-witted /眼疾手～ quick of eye and deft of hand ❻ sharp; keen：～刀 sharp knife; knife with a keen edge /这把剪刀不～了。The scissors are no longer sharp. ❼ straightforward; forthright; plainspoken：为人爽～ straightforward and outspoken ❽ pleased; happy; satisfied; gratified：亲痛仇～ sadden one's friends and gladden one's foes /先睹为～ consider it a pleasure to be among the first to read or see /心中不～ be displeased; feel unhappy ❾〈旧语〉sheriff; constable (in a *yamen*)

快班 kuàibān advanced class

快板 kuàibǎn ❶〈音乐〉allegro ❷〈戏曲〉quick tempo

快板儿 kuàibǎnr 〈戏曲〉*kuaiban*, rhythmic comic talk or monologue to the accompaniment of bamboo clappers; clapper talk：说～ perform a clapper talk

快板儿书 kuàibǎnrshū rhymed story recited to the rhythm of bamboo clappers; rhythmic story-telling

快报 kuàibào wall bulletin; bulletin：第一期～ first issue of a bulletin

快步 kuàibù ❶〈军事〉half step; trot：～前进！Forward march at half step! ❷ quick pace：～向前走去 walk forward at a quick pace

快步流星 kuàibù-liúxīng *also* "大步流星" dàbù-liúxīng walk with vigorous strides; stride：～地奔往会场 rush to the conference hall

快步舞 kuàibùwǔ quickstep

快餐 kuàicān quick meal; snack; fast-food：吃～ have a quick meal /～部 fast-food counter; snack counter /～店 fast-food restaurant /西式～ Western-style fast food /中式～ Chinese-style fast food /这几年～业有了很大的发展。Fast-food business has developed by leaps and bounds in recent years.

快畅 kuàichàng uninhibited and happy; carefree：欢欣～ cheerful and happy

快车 kuàichē express train or bus：直达～ through express /特别～ special express /开～ drive fast; speed

快车道 kuàichēdào 〈交通〉fast (traffic) lane：卡车不能在～上行驶。Lorries are not allowed to drive along the fast lane. /1992 年以来，该省的经济已驶上了经济发展的～。The economy of the province has got into the fast lane of development since 1992.

快当 kuàidang quick; prompt：做事～ be prompt in doing things

快刀斩乱麻 kuàidāo zhǎn luànmá cut a tangled skein of jute with a sharp knife — take resolute and effective measures to solve a complex problem; cut the Gordian knot：解决这类问题就要～。A problem of this nature requires a prompt and resolute solution. *or* You've got to cut the Gordian knot in tackling such problems.

快递 kuàidì express delivery：～邮件 express mail /～服务 express delivery service; fast mail service

快动作 kuàidòngzuò 〈影视〉fast motion;〈电工〉snap action

快帆船 kuàifānchuán clipper (ship)

快干 kuàigān quick-drying：～油漆 quick-drying paint or varnish /～水泥 quick-setting cement /～黏结剂 quick-acting binder

快感 kuàigǎn pleasant sensation; delight; pleasure：有一种～ feel a pleasant sensation /这个节目不能给人～。This performance gave the audience no pleasure at all.

快感学 kuàigǎnxué 〈心理〉hedonics

快感原则 kuàigǎn yuánzé 〈心理〉pleasure principle

快攻 kuàigōng 〈体育〉quick attack (in table tennis, volleyball, etc.); fast break (in basketball)：正手～加弧圈 forehand quick attack with loop drive /甲队一次成功的～，得了两分。A successful fast break won team A two points.

快货 kuàihuò goods that sell fast; goods in great demand; marketable commodities：这种新产品成了市场上的～。This new product sells like hot cakes.

快活 kuàihuo happy; jolly; merry; cheerful：小鸟在树林里～地唱着歌。Birds were chirping cheerfully in the woods. /他提前完成了任务，心里觉得很～。Having accomplished the task ahead of time, he felt quite happy.

快件 kuàijiàn express delivery luggage, goods or mail：寄～ send sth. by express mail; check in luggage for express delivery

快捷 kuàijié (of speed) quick; fast; nimble; agile：～的步伐 quick steps /信息传递～准确 speedy and accurate transmission of information

快进 kuàijìn (with a tape or video) fast-forward：～跳过广告 fast-forward through the commercials

快镜头 kuàijìngtóu snapshot

快克 kuàikè (transliteration) crack (purified potent cocaine)

快乐 kuàilè happy; joyful; cheerful; delightful：～的旅行 delightful journey /生日～！Happy birthday (to you)! /孩子们在沙滩上～地奔跑。The kids are running joyfully on the beach.

快乐原则 kuàilè yuánzé *also* "快感原则"〈心理〉pleasure principle

快粒子 kuàilìzǐ 〈物理〉fast particle

快利 kuàili 〈方言〉❶ quick and neat; deft; efficient：做事～ be quick and neat in everything one does ❷ sharp：刀刃～ sharp knife; sharp edge

快流量消费品 kuàiliúliàng xiāofèipǐn 〈商业〉fast-moving consumer goods

快马加鞭 kuàimǎ-jiābiān spurring on the flying horse; (ride) whip and spur; at top speed; posthaste：～赶到目的地 reach the des-

tination posthaste /在今年的最后三个月中,我们要～,按期完成任务。In the last quarter, we must work at top speed and fulfil our task in time.

快慢 kuàimàn speed:工程进度的～受天气的影响。The speed of the construction is affected by the weather. *or* The bad weather slowed down the construction.

快慢针 kuàimànzhēn (in a clock or watch) index lever; regulator

快门 kuàimén 〈摄影〉shutter:～开关 shutter release /～速度 shutter speed /～优先 shutter priority /焦点平面～ focal plane shutter /中心～ between-lens shutter /按～ press (*or* click) the shutter

快凝水泥 kuàiníng shuǐní 〈建筑〉quick-setting cement; quick-taking cement; quick cement

快枪 kuàiqiāng (in contrast with a fowling piece, etc.) fast-loading rifle or pistol

快人 kuàirén 〈书面〉straightforward, forthright or plain-spoken person:好,～一语! 就照你说的办。Good. That's very straightforward. Let's do as you say.

快人快语 kuàirén-kuàiyǔ straightforward talk from a straighforward person

快事 kuàishì happening that gives great satisfaction or pleasure; delightful event:引为生平一大～ consider (sth.) one of the most delightful (*or* pleasurable) experiences in one's life /有此～,何乐而不为? Since it is such a delight (*or* pleasure), why not do it?

快适 kuàishì pleasant and comfortable:这家餐厅的情调令人～。This restaurant has a pleasant ambience.

快手 kuàishǒu quick worker; deft hand:～快脚 be deft of hand and nimble of foot; do things very fast /他办事麻利,人称"～刘"。He is such a quick and neat worker that he is known as "deft-hand Liu".

快书 kuàishū 〈戏曲〉quick-patter (rhythmic storytelling accompanied by bamboo clappers):竹板～ bamboo clapper patter /山东～ Shandong clapper minstrelsy (*or* storytelling)

快速 kuàisù high-speed; fast; quick; rapid:～育肥〈畜牧〉fast fattening /～疲劳试验 rapid fatigue test /～染色 rapid dyeing /～烧结〈矿业〉rapid (*or* flash) sintering /～部队 mobile force (*or* troops, *or* units) /～掘进〈矿业〉high-speed (*or* speedy) drivage /～切削〈机械〉high-speed cutting /～炼钢 high-speed steelmaking /～行军 forced march

快速变换 kuàisù biànhuàn 〈机械〉quick-change:～齿轮箱 quick-change gearbox /～装置 quick-change gearing; quick-change

快速充电 kuàisù chōngdiàn quick charge or charging

快速存储 kuàisù cúnchǔ 〈计算机〉high-speed storage; rapid memory; quick-access memory

快速打印机 kuàisù dǎyìnjī 〈计算机〉quick printer; rapid printer

快速倒带 kuàisù dàodài fast-rewind

快速定影液 kuàisù dìngyǐngyè 〈摄影〉rapid-fixing solution

快速反击 kuàisù fǎnjī 〈体育〉fast counter-attack

快速反应 kuàisù fǎnyìng 〈军事〉rapid response; quick or fast reaction:～部队 rapid response force /～能力 quick reaction ability

快速活动靶 kuàisù huódòngbǎ fast-moving target

快速进带 kuàisù jìndài (of a tape or video recorder) fast-forward

快速排序 kuàisù páixù 〈信息〉quick sort

快速摄影机 kuàisù shèyǐngjī high-speed (motion-picture) camera

快速停堆 kuàisù tíngduī scram:～系统 scram system

快速显影 kuàisù xiǎnyǐng 〈摄影〉rapid development

快艇 kuàitǐng speedboat; motor boat; mosquito boat:鱼雷～ torpedo boat /巡逻～ high-speed patrolboat

快慰 kuàiwèi derive gratification and comfort (from sth.); be pleased:脸上现出～的笑容 smile with gratification /译著即将出版,她感到十分～。She felt happy because the book she had translated was going to be published.

快心 kuàixīn satisfying; gratifying; pleasant; happy:老同学聚会是件～的事。It is pleasant to meet with one's old schoolmates.

快信 kuàixìn express letter; express mail:一封～ an express letter /这一封寄～。I'll sent this letter by express mail.

快性 kuàixing 〈方言〉straightforward; outright; plain-spoken:他是个～人,想到什么就说什么。He is straightforward and always speaks his mind.

快婿 kuàixù son-in-law after one's heart:东床～ son-in-law after one's heart; ideal son-in-law /乘龙～ ideal son-in-law with a promising future (*or* of a high position)

快讯 kuàixùn news flash; flash:向各地发～ flash the news to various places

快要 kuàiyào about to; soon; before long:水～开了。The water is about to boil. /期末考试～到了。The final exams are coming soon. /新年～到了。New Years Day is approaching (*or* drawing near).

快意 kuàiyì pleased; delightful; merry; comfortable:这微风令人十分～。A gentle breeze rose, delightful and refreshing. /几杯酒下肚,他感到一阵～。He felt merry after several glasses of wine.

快鱼 kuàiyú *also* "鲙鱼" kuàiyú Chinese herring

快语 kuàiyǔ straightforward talk or words:他直言～,请别在意。Please don't take his blunt words to heart.

快悦 kuàiyuè happy; joyful; cheerful:心神～ feel happy (*or* joyful) /她看到这种情形,～的心情一下子烟消云散。When she saw this, her cheerfulness vanished instantly.

快照 kuàizhào 〈摄影〉snapshot:拍～ take a snapshot

快针 kuàizhēn 〈中医〉swift insertion

快中子 kuàizhōngzǐ 〈物理〉fast or high-speed neutron:～反应堆 fast neutron reactor /～发生器 fast neutron generator /～裂变 fast neutron fission

快装费 kuàizhuāngfèi 〈交通〉dispatch money

快子 kuàizǐ 〈物理〉tachyon

快嘴 kuàizuǐ one who readily voices his thoughts; one who has a loose tongue; one who has a big mouth; gossip:～快舌 have a loose (*or* quick) tongue; be prone to talk rashly /她真是个～。She is quite a gossip. *or* She has such a big mouth.

筷

kuài chopsticks:牙～ ivory chopsticks /碗～ bowls and chopsticks

筷子 kuàizi chopsticks:一双～ a pair of chopsticks /竹～ bamboo chopsticks /火～ fire-tongs; tongs

kuān

宽(寬)

kuān ❶ wide; broad:～边眼镜 broad-rimmed glasses /道路拓～工程 road-widening project /视野～ have a broad view /你管得太～了。Your're poking into other people's business. *or* You're taking too much into your own hands. ❷ width; breadth:长6米,～4米 six metres in length, four metres in width; six metres long, four metres wide ❸ relax; relieve:放～条件 relax the conditions; soften the terms /听说事故不大,心就～了一半。I was much relieved to learn that the accident was not serious. ❹ extend:再～几天吧。Please extend the deadline a few more days. ❺ generous; lenient:从～处理 treat with leniency /妈妈对我的要求比爸爸要～。Mother is less strict with me than father is. ❻ comfortably off; well-off:手头～ be well off; be liberal with one's money /～日子 life of comfort (*or* ease) ❼ (Kuān) a surname

宽博 kuānbó 〈书面〉❶ large-minded; magnanimous:～谨慎 be magnanimous but circumspect /～的胸怀 broad-minded and lenient ❷ (of clothes) loose:～的睡衣 loose nightgown; loose pyjamas

宽畅 kuānchàng free from worry; happy:心情～ be carefree; feel free and happy

宽敞 kuānchang spacious; roomy; commodious:～的大厅 spacious (*or* commodious) hall /～舒适 spacious and comfortable

宽弛 kuānchí flabby; slack; lax:肌肉～ flabby (*or* flaccid) muscles /政务～ lax (*or* slack) government administration

宽绰 kuānchuo ❶ spacious; commodious:院子很～。The courtyard is quite spacious. ❷ broad-minded; at ease; relaxed:把心放～些。Set your mind at ease. *or* Take things easy. ❸ comfortably off; well-off:手头～ have a lot of money at one's disposal; have no problem with cash /这几年我们的生活比以前～多了。We are much better off these years. /他的家境不～。His family is in straitened circumstances.

宽打窄用 kuāndǎ-zhǎiyòng budget liberally and spend sparingly:钱不妨多带点,出门的人嘛,～。Take some more money with you when you travel, just in case.

宽大 kuāndà ❶ spacious; roomy:～的房间 spacious room /～的睡袍 loose nightgown ❷ broad; vast:心怀～ broad-minded; generous /把眼光放～些 have a wider vision ❸ lenient; magnanimous:～处理 deal with leniently; accord lenient treatment; be clement /～无边 be excessively lenient /镇压与～相结合 combine suppression with leniency

宽大为怀 kuāndà-wéihuái be magnanimous or lenient; treat le-

K

niently or generously; be willing to let bygones be bygones

宽带 kuāndài *also* "宽频带"〈通信〉broadband; wide-band (WB): ～传输 wide-band transmission /～天线 broadband antenna; wide-band antenna /～通信 wide-band communication /～信道 broadband channel /～信号 broadband signal

宽带材 kuāndàicái 〈冶金〉wide strip: ～轧机 wide strip mill

宽贷 kuāndài pardon; forgive; treat with leniency: 首恶必办, 其余可予～。The ringleaders must be punished but the rest can be accorded lenient treatment.

宽待 kuāndài treat with leniency; be lenient in dealing with: ～俘虏 give lenient treatment to prisoners of war; treat prisoners of war leniently /感谢政府的～ be grateful for the government's leniency

宽度 kuāndù width; breadth: ～不一 vary in width; be of different widths /领海～ extent of the territorial sea /这间屋子的～只有两米多点儿。The room is only a little over two metres in width.

宽泛 kuānfàn (of meaning, definition, etc.) broad; wide; extensive: 这个词的涵义很～。The word has a broad connotation.

宽幅 kuānfú (of cloth, etc.) wide; broad: ～布 broad (*or* wide) cloth

宽广 kuānguǎng broad; extensive; vast: ～的原野 vast expanse of open country /眼界～ farsighted /道路越走越～。The further one goes, the wider the road. *or* One has an ever-brighter prospect.

宽轨 kuānguǐ broad gauge; wide gauge: ～铁路 broad-gauge railway

宽行 kuānháng 〈农业〉wide row: ～条播机 wide-row drill /～栽植 wide-row planting /～中耕机 wide-row cultivator

宽和 kuānhé generous and kind: 待人～ be generous and kind to people

宽宏 kuānhóng *also* "宽洪" large-minded; magnanimous: 气度～ be of magnanimous bearing

宽宏大量 kuānhóng-dàliàng *also* "宽宏大度"; "宽洪大量" large-minded; magnanimous: ～不等于宽大无边。Magnanimity does not mean excessive leniency.

宽洪 kuānhóng ❶ (of voice) broad and resonant: ～的歌声 broad and resonant singing ❷ *see* "宽宏"

宽厚 kuānhòu ❶ thick and broad: ～的胸膛 broad and strong chest ❷ generous and kind: ～长者 generous and kindhearted elder /～憨直 be generous and straightforward /出家人心胸～, 慈悲为怀。Monks and nuns should be generous and charitable. ❸ (of voice) deep and rich: 嗓子～嘹亮。His voice is rich and loud.

宽怀 kuānhuái set one's mind at rest; feel relieved; be at ease; rest assured: 你～吧, 你的一家老小我会替你照顾好的。Set your mind at ease. I will do my best to look after your family.

宽缓 kuānhuǎn relieved and relaxed; free of worry: 他听到洪水已退的消息以后, 紧张的心情也就～了。When he learnt that the flood had subsided his tension relaxed.

宽假 kuānjiǎ 〈书面〉pardon; forgive; treat with leniency: 这笔借款期限已到, 还请～几日。The loan is due, but please give me a few days' grace.

宽解 kuānjiě ease sb.'s anxiety; relieve sb. of his or her trouble: 心中的怨气, 一时难能～。It was difficult to ease one's resentment for the moment. /父亲生气的时候, 母亲总是设法～。When father gets angry, mother always tries to calm him down.

宽旷 kuānkuàng vast and open; extensive: 视野～ command (*or* enjoy) a vast view /～的沙滩 wide sandy beach

宽阔 kuānkuò ❶ broad; wide: ～的街道 broad (*or* wide) street /～湖面 vast lake ❷ broad-minded: 经过这些访问, 他的眼界～多了。These visits broadened his vision.

宽亮 kuānliàng 〈方言〉❶ spacious and bright: ～的展览大厅 spacious (*or* commodious) and bright exhibition hall /心里～ clear in one's mind ❷ (of voice) broad and resounding; loud and clear

宽谅 kuānliàng forgive; excuse; pardon: 请您多～。Please bear with us (for any oversight, etc.).

宽猛相济 kuānměng-xiāngjì *also* "宽猛并济"〈书面〉alternate leniency with severity; use both the stick and the carrot: ～, 政是以和。Only when leniency is combined with severity can political stability be maintained.

宽免 kuānmiǎn remit or exempt (punishment, rent, tax, etc.); pardon (an offence): 对慈善机构要～税收。Taxes should be remitted for charity organizations.

宽屏幕 kuānpíngmù wide-screen: ～电视系统 wide-screen system

宽让 kuānràng tolerant; lenient: 力主～ speak out for tolerance /不要把我们的一再～当作软弱可欺。Don't take our repeated acts of leniency as a sign of weakness to take advantage of.

宽饶 kuānráo pardon; forgive; show mercy; give quarter: 请求～ ask for mercy /暂且～你这一回! I'll forgive you this time. *or* I'll let you off this time.

宽仁 kuānrén 〈书面〉generous and kindhearted: ～豁达 kindhearted and magnanimous

宽容 kuānróng tolerant; lenient: ～大度 tolerant and generous /～不同意见 be tolerant of opinions different from one's own /这种现象决不能加以～。We must never tolerate such things.

宽蛇 kuānshé adder

宽赦 kuānshè be lenient and remit (a punishment); forgive; pardon: ～坦白认罪的犯人 accord lenient treatment to those criminals who confess their crimes and plead guilty

宽式刨床 kuānshì bàochuáng 〈机械〉widened planer; widened planing machine

宽舒 kuānshū ❶ free of worry; relaxed and happy: 心境～ feel happy and free of worry; be in a carefree mood ❷ spacious; broad: 新扩建的街道平整～。The newly-extended street looked even and broad.

宽恕 kuānshù forgive; pardon: 承认错误, 求她～。Apologize to her and ask for her forgiveness. /念其初犯, 且予～。We will show clemency to him as a first-time offender.

宽爽 kuānshuǎng free from worry; happy: 心情～ feel happy and free of worry

宽松 kuānsōng ❶ spacious; commodious; not crowded: 这间教室坐二十人比较～。This classroom allows twenty people to sit comfortably. ❷ relaxed; free from worry or restraint; happy: 政策～ relaxed policy; liberal policy /～的环境 relaxed environment (*or* circumstances) /她听了女儿劝慰的话, 心里～多了。Consolation from her daughter took the weight of her worry away. ❸ relax; loosen: ～衣带 loosen one's belt /～紧张情绪 relax one's tension ❹ ample; well-off: 手头～了 have more money to spend /他们家现在经济很～。They are comfortably off now. ❺ (of clothes) loose and comfortable: 老年人衣着要～一些才好。Elderly people should dress for comfort.

宽坦 kuāntǎn ❶ broad and level; wide and even: ～的海滩 broad and level seashore ❷ feel happy and have ease of mind: 胸怀～ feel happy and easy of mind

宽慰 kuānwèi comfort; console: 自我～ console oneself /～某人几句 say sth. to comfort sb. /他这么一说, 我心里倒～了许多。I was much relieved at his words.

宽狭 kuānxiá 〈书面〉width; breadth; size: 这套礼服～适中, 长短合度。This dress suit is of the right size.

宽限 kuānxiàn extend a time limit: ～两周 give two weeks' grace /不能再～了。The deadline can not be further extended.

宽限期 kuānxiànqī period of grace; grace period: 这笔贷款年息为百分之二, 二十年还清本息, 有五年的～。This loan is to be repaid in 20 years at an annual interest rate of 2% with a 5-year grace period.

宽乡 kuānxiāng 〈书面〉sparsely populated country or area: 塞北地处～, 土地资源丰富, 宜于发展农牧业。Sparsely populated and with rich land resources, the area north of the Great Wall is suited for developing agriculture and animal husbandry.

宽心 kuānxīn feel relieved: ～话 reassuring words (*or* remarks) /家中之事, 但请～, 不必挂念。Please set your mind at rest and don't worry about things back home.

宽心丸儿 kuānxīnwánr *also* "开心丸儿" kāixīnwánr comforting remarks; reassuring words: 儿媳妇嘴巧, 尽给她～吃。Her daughter-in-law is smooth-tongued and keeps saying comforting words to her.

宽衣 kuānyī ❶〈敬词〉take off your coat: 开会还得一会儿, 请您先～休息。It is quite a while before the meeting begins. Please take off your coat and have a rest. ❷ undress: ～解带 undress (and undo the belt)

宽银幕 kuānyínmù 〈影视〉wide screen

宽银幕电影 kuānyínmù diànyǐng wide-screen film

宽宥 kuānyòu 〈书面〉pardon; forgive: 承蒙～, 大德不忘。I shall be eternally indebted to you for your kind forgiveness.

宽余 kuānyú ❶ spacious and comfortable: 这房间～得很, 住两个人没问题。The room is big enough for two people to stay comfortably. ❷ ease of mind: 不管风吹浪打, 胜似闲庭信步, 今日得～。Let the wind blow and waves beat, Better far than idly strolling in a courtyard. Today I am at ease. ❸ *see* "宽裕"

宽裕 kuānyù well-to-do; comfortably off; ample: 手头不～ have little money to spare; be in financial straits /时间比较～，大家不要着急。No hurry. There is plenty of time. /我手头～一点，帮助别人多一些，没有什么。I don't mind giving people a helping hand, since I'm better off than they are.

宽韵 kuānyùn 〈文学〉(in contrast to 窄韵) "broad rhyme", rhyme which contains a broad range of words in a book of rhymes

宽窄 kuānzhǎi width; breadth; size: 过道～正合适。The aisle is just of the right width for its purpose.

宽展 kuānzhǎn 〈方言〉❶ free from worry; happy: 这几天病见轻，心里～多了。I feel much relieved as I've been recovering from my illness over the last few days. ❷ broad; wide: 村头的场院又平又～。The threshing ground at the entrance of the village is level and broad. ❸ *see* "宽裕"

宽中 kuānzhōng 〈中医〉eliminate swelling or pain of the chest or the upper part of the side (with medicine)

宽纵 kuānzòng indulge: 自我～ self-indulgence /你对孩子太～了! You are too indulgent to your child. *or* You're spoiling your child.

髋(髖) kuān hip

髋骨 kuāngǔ *also* "胯骨" kuàgǔ 〈生理〉hipbone; innominate bone

髋关节 kuānguānjié 〈生理〉hip joint; coxa: ～病 coxarthropathy; coxalgia /～结核 coxotuberculosis /～炎 coxarthria; coxitis /老年性～炎 senile coxitis

kuǎn

款¹(欵) kuǎn ❶ sincere: 其人愚～。The man is honest and sincere. ❷ receive with hospitality; entertain: ～客 entertain a guest

款²(欵) kuǎn ❶ section (of an article in a legal document, etc.); paragraph: 宪法第七条第二～ article 7, section 2 of the constitution ❷ sum of money for a specific purpose; fund: 现～ cash /筹～ raise funds /汇～ remit money /贷～ loan /大～ moneybags; nouveau riche /提～ get a sum of money (from a bank, fund, etc.) ❸ name of author or recipient (inscribed on a painting or a piece of calligraphy presented as a gift): 上～ recipient's name /下～ author's name /落～ signature /题～ inscribe one's name and comments (for a piece of calligraphy, painting, etc.) ❹ style; pattern (of fashion, etc.): 新～ new style /这组时装有三～。We have three styles for this fashion set. ❺ 〈量词〉kind; type; style: 两～风衣 two wind-jackets of different styles /三～点心 three kinds of pastry

款³(欵) kuǎn 〈书面〉knock; tap: ～关 knock at the gate (of a city, fortress, etc.); seek admission

款⁴(欵) kuǎn 〈书面〉leisurely; slow: 清风徐来，柳丝～摆。The willow twigs are swaying gently in the breeze.

款步 kuǎnbù leisurely steps: ～向前 walk ahead with leisurely steps /～漫游 take a leisurely stroll; roam at ease

款诚 kuǎnchéng 〈书面〉sincere; wholehearted; hearty: ～之心 sincerity /～相待 treat sb. with sincerity

款待 kuǎndài treat cordially; entertain: ～佳宾 entertain distinguished guests /设宴～ give a banquet in sb.'s honour; entertain sb. with a banquet /盛情～ entertain hospitably (*or* cordially)

款冬 kuǎndōng 〈植物〉coltsfoot

款额 kuǎn'é amount of money; sum of money: ～巨大 large amount (*or* sum) of money

款服 kuǎnfú 〈书面〉❶ pledge one's sincere allegiance; sincerely obey ❷ *also* "款伏" plead guilty; admit one's guilt

款附 kuǎnfù 〈书面〉sincerely submit (to sb.'s authority); pledge one's true allegiance

款接 kuǎnjiē treat cordially; entertain

款款 kuǎnkuǎn 〈书面〉❶ sincere; wholehearted; hearty: 情意～ with deep affection ❷ slowly; leisurely: ～而行 walk slowly /花香～飘来。The scent of flowers was wafted to us.

款留 kuǎnliú cordially urge (a guest) to stay: 主人一再～，无奈他公务在身，执意不肯。The host urged him repeatedly to stay, but he firmly declined as he had official business to attend to.

款门 kuǎnmén 〈书面〉knock on the door: ～来告 knock on the door to tell sb. sth.

款洽 kuǎnqià 〈书面〉cordial and harmonious: 多年老友，情好～。Old friends of many years cherish cordial and harmonious feelings towards each other.

款曲 kuǎnqū 〈书面〉❶ accord solicitous hospitality; treat with courtesy: 不善～ socially inept /～周至 take good care of ❷ heartfelt feelings: 互通～ express feelings of mutual affection (*or* friendship) /暗通～ convey one's heartfelt feelings (to sb.) in secret; be in secret liaison (with sb.)

款式 kuǎnshì pattern; style; design: 流行～ style in fashion /～新颖 original in design; of novel pattern /这套组合家具～很好。This set of combination furniture is elegant in style.

款闲 kuǎnxián 〈方言〉chat; chitchat: 姐妹围炉～。The sisters are chatting around the fire.

款项 kuǎnxiàng ❶ sum of money (for a specific purpose); fund: 他每天经手大笔的～。He handles huge sums of money every day. ❷ section (in a legal document, etc.); paragraph: 对条约的具体～进行修改 revise particular sections of a treaty

款爷 kuǎnyé 〈方言〉moneybags; nouveau riche

款识 kuǎnzhì ❶ inscription (on bronzes, etc.): 古鼎造型奇特，～清晰。The singularly shaped ancient tripod has clear inscriptions on it. ❷ signature (of author on a painting or calligraphy)

款子 kuǎnzi sum of money; fund: 汇一笔～ remit a sum of money /这几笔～还没有入账。These sums of money have not yet been entered into the account book.

窾 kuǎn 〈书面〉empty; hollow

kuāng

匡 kuāng ❶〈书面〉rectify; correct: 过则～之 correct an error when it occurs ❷〈书面〉assist; save: ～我不逮 assist me where I am deficient; help me to overcome my deficiency /～乏困 provide relief to the destitute ❸〈方言〉calculate roughly; estimate: ～一～ estimate ❹ (usu. used in the early vernacular) expect: 不～ did not expect ❺(Kuāng) a surname

匡扶 kuāngfú 〈书面〉rectify and assist; assist (a ruler in governing a country); uphold: ～正义 uphold justice /～社稷 assist in governing the country; help to run the state

匡复 kuāngfù 〈书面〉save (a country from perishing, etc.); restore: 平息战乱，～祖国。Restore peace and save the country.

匡计 kuāngjì roughly calculate; estimate: 以每亩增产一百公斤～ calculated on the basis of an increase of one hundred kilos per *mu*

匡济 kuāngjì 〈书面〉rescue and bring back to the right course; help to relieve: ～时艰 help to pull through existing difficulties; relieve the difficulties of the time

匡救 kuāngjiù rescue and bring back to the right course; help to save or remedy: 由于及时～，他才没有犯罪。Thanks to timely help, he did not commit the crime.

匡谬 kuāngmiù correct mistakes; rectify the erroneous: ～正俗 rectify the erroneous and help to form good customs

匡算 kuāngsuàn roughly calculate; estimate: 据初步～，今年可增产二成左右。According to preliminary estimates, the production will be increased by 20 per cent this year.

匡正 kuāngzhèng rectify; correct: ～之言 words of rectification /～之处 where corrections should be made /～时弊 rectify the ills of the times; correct current maladies /奉上诗稿，祈请～。Herewith I am presenting you the manuscript of my poems for correction.

匡助 kuāngzhù assist: 孔子周游列国，而不得可供～之贤君。In his tour of various states, Confucius failed to find a single wise monarch worthy of his assistance.

恇 kuāng 〈书面〉fear; panic: ～惧 be seized with fear

恇怯 kuāngqiè 〈书面〉fear and flinch: 临阵～ flinch from the battle

诓 kuāng deceive; cheat; hoax: 你别来～人! Don't you try to deceive me!

诓哄 kuānghǒng deceive; hoax; dupe

诓骗 kuāngpiàn deceive; cheat; hoax; dupe: ～妇女、小孩 deceive

(*or* dupe) women and children /设圈套～顾客 set traps for consumers
诓诈 kuāngzhà cheat; hoax; dupe; swindle:～行为 hoaxing; deceit

哐 kuāng 〈象声〉crash; bang:锣～地响了一声。Bang, went the gong.
哐当 kuāngdāng 〈象声〉crash; bang:～一声把书扔在桌上 bang the book down on the table
哐啷 kuānglāng 〈象声〉bang; crash:转身～一声把门关上 turn and bang the door (shut)

筐 kuāng basket:柳条～ wicker basket /粪～ manure basket /两～土 two baskets of soil /编竹～儿 weave a bamboo basket
筐菜 kuāngcài vegetables sold in whole baskets
筐柳 kuāngliǔ *also* "沙柳" shāliǔ *Salix mongolica*, a kind of willow the twigs of which can be used to weave baskets
筐子 kuāngzi small basket:菜～ vegetable basket /土～ soil basket

俇 kuāng
俇儴 kuāngráng 〈书面〉*see* "劻勷" kuāngráng

劻 kuāng
劻勷 kuāngráng *also* "俇儴" kuāngráng 〈书面〉anxious; impatient

kuáng

狂 kuáng ❶ mad; crazy; insane:发～ go mad (*or* crazy); go berserk /自大～ megalomania /偏执～ paranoia /丧心病～ frenzied; unscrupulous; perverse ❷ violent; fierce:风～浪大。The wind blew hard and the waves ran high. /物价～涨。Prices are soaring (*or* skyrocketing). ❸ unrestrained; wild:欣喜若～ be wild with joy ❹ arrogant; overbearing; presumptuous:这人也太～了! What an arrogant (*or* presumptuous) man!
狂傲 kuáng'ào wildly arrogant; presumptuous; haughty:～自大 be presumptuous and conceited
狂暴 kuángbào violent; wild; furious:脾气～ have a violent temper /～的急雨 torrential (*or* furious) rain /～不驯 wild and untrammelled; frantic and unrestrained
狂悖 kuángbèi 〈书面〉presumptuous and unreasonable; wildly arrogant and contrary to reason:凶横～ fierce and unreasonable /～无礼 presumptuous and insolent
狂奔 kuángbēn run swiftly and violently; run like mad:战马～。The war horses were gallopping like mad. /洪水～而来。The flood came swift and violent.
狂飙 kuángbiāo hurricane:国际悲歌歌一曲,～为我从天落。To the *Internationale's* stirring strains A wild whirlwind swoops from the sky.
狂飙运动 Kuángbiāo Yùndòng *Sturm und Drang*; Storm and Stress (German literary and social movement in the latter part of the 18th century, headed by Schiller, Goethe, etc.)
狂草 kuángcǎo wild cursive hand (Chinese calligraphy with unbroken and winding strokes):～是草书中最自由无拘的一种。The wild cursive is the most free and unrestrained variety of the cursive hand.
狂潮 kuángcháo (often figurative) turbulent tidewater:革命的～ turbulent revolutionary movement; unrestrained spread of the revolution
狂诞 kuángdàn presumptuous and wild (in speech or behaviour)
狂荡 kuángdàng dissolute; bohemian; unconventional:朋友们为他这种～生活担心。His friends are all worried about the bohemian life he leads.
狂放 kuángfàng unruly; unrestrained; untrammelled:～不羁 be totally unconventional and untrammelled /诗人一生性情～,酷爱饮酒。The poet was a free spirit who had an unrestrained temper and was given to drinking all his life.
狂吠 kuángfèi bark furiously; howl:猎犬对着黑影发出一阵～声。The hound gave a fit of furious barking at the black shadow. /敌对势力的～只能暴露他们的丑恶。The abominable slander by the enemies only betrayed their evil intentions.
狂奋 kuángfèn wildly excited; elated
狂风 kuángfēng ❶ fierce wind:～大作。A high wind sprang up. /～怒吼。The wind howled. ❷〈气象〉whole gale:～警报 whole-gale warning
狂风暴雨 kuángfēng-bàoyǔ violent storm:～似的反战运动 raging anti-war campaign
狂风恶浪 kuángfēng-èlàng violent winds and fierce waves; grave perils and great hazards:不管遇到什么～,都不能动摇他献身革命的初衷。No perils and dangers he encountered in his life could shake his dedication to the revolution.
狂轰滥炸 kuánghōng-lànzhà wanton and indiscriminate bombing:敌机飞来,又是一阵～。The enemy planes came and carried out another round of wanton and indiscriminate bombing.
狂欢 kuánghuān revelry; carnival:纵情～ indulge in revelry /～作乐 carouse; revel /～之夜 night of revelry; carnival night
狂欢节 kuánghuānjié carnival; festival
狂澜 kuánglán raging waves:百丈～ sky-high waves /力挽～ do one's utmost to stem a raging tide (*or* save a desperate situation)
狂烈 kuángliè extremely fierce; exceedingly violent:～的北风一连刮了三天。An extremely fierce north wind blew for three days running.
狂乱 kuángluàn ❶ extremely disorderly; utterly confused:～的人群 frantic, confused crowds /～的心情 utterly confused mood /大风中,路旁的高粱～地摇摆着。In the strong wind the sorghum at the roadside was wildly whipped back and forth. ❷〈书面〉wildly arrogant and befuddled; deranged:失魂～ be wildly presumptuous and befuddled as if totally deranged
狂怒 kuángnù wildly indignant; extremely angry:他忍不住～了。He lost control and flew into a rage. /浪涛一个接着一个,～地冲击着堤岸。The furious waves lashed at the embankment ceaselessly.
狂虐 kuángnüè furious and brutal; savage and vicious:～的风沙刮得天昏地暗。The violent and brutal wind swept by, carrying sand that darkened the sky and obscured everything else.
狂气 kuángqi arrogance; overbearing manners:一脸～ look arrogant /～不改,依然故我 remain one's old self with one's overbearing manners unchanged
狂犬病 kuángquǎnbìng *also* "恐水病" kǒngshuǐbìng hydrophobia; rabies:～病毒 rabies virus; hydrophobin /～疫苗 rabies vaccine
狂热 kuángrè fanaticism; fever:难以抑制的～情绪 uncontrollable fanaticism /～的军备竞赛 feverish arms race /宗教～ religious fever; zealotry /～性 fanaticism /小资产阶级的～ petty-bourgeois fever
狂人 kuángrén ❶ madman; maniac; lunatic:《～日记》*Diary of a Madman* (by Chinese writer Lu Xun) /战争～ war maniac ❷ person of extreme arrogance and conceit; supercilious person:目空一切的～ supercilious person who looks down upon everybody and everything
狂人呓语 kuángrén-yìyǔ ravings of a madman:他这些设想无异于～。Those ideas of his are nothing but ravings.
狂胜 kuángshèng (in sport competitions) win an overwhelming victory:甲队以八比零～乙队。Team A overwhelmed Team B by eight to nil (*or* nothing).
狂涛 kuángtāo ❶ roaring billows; great momentum or impetus:～怒浪 roaring (*or* furious) breakers ❷〈气象〉very high sea
狂妄 kuángwàng wildly arrogant; presumptuous:～无知 conceited but ignorant /在长辈面前你竟敢这样～! How can you behave so insolently before your elders?
狂妄自大 kuángwàng-zìdà arrogant and conceited:像他这样～的人,实在不多见。Very few people are so overweaning and conceited as he.
狂喜 kuángxǐ wild with joy:心中一阵～ feel a surge of wild joy /胜利之后的～ exultant joy of victory
狂想 kuángxiǎng ❶ fancy; fantasy:诗人的～ poet's fantasy /突发～ be struck with a fancy ❷ vain hope; wishful thinking; illusion:就你还想当电影明星? 简直是～! You, a movie star? What a wild dream!
狂想曲 kuángxiǎngqǔ 〈音乐〉rhapsody; fantasia
狂笑 kuángxiào laugh wildly or hysterically; laugh boisterously:～不止 burst out laughing boisterously /一阵～ a fit of hysterical laughter
狂泻 kuángxiè (of the stock market) slump; (of prices) plummet
狂言 kuángyán ravings; wild language; delirious utterances:口出

～ talk wildly; rave /大胆～ audacious wild talk

狂野 kuángyě violent and rough; wild and boorish:那帮人～的笑声使他心惊胆颤。He shuddered at the wild and hysterical laughter of that bunch.

狂躁 kuángzào rash and impatient; indiscreet and hot-headed; restless with anxiety:发出一阵阵～的叫声 send out fits of restless and anxious cries /要沉住气,不要～。Keep your head. Don't be rash and hot-headed.

狂恣 kuángzì 〈书面〉wildly arrogant and wanton; presumptuous and unbridled

诳 kuáng ❶ deceive; dupe; fool; hoodwink:你别～我。Don't you fool me. ❷〈方言〉lie; falsehood:扯了个～ tell a lie

诳诞 kuángdàn unfounded; fabricated; fantastic; absurd:～之说 unfounded theory (*or* story)

诳惑 kuánghuò deceive and confuse; deceive; dupe:用迷信来～人民 dupe people with superstitions

诳骗 kuángpiàn deceive; hoax; dupe; cheat:靠～是长久不了的。You can't go far with deception. *or* Falsehoods have but short legs.

诳语 kuángyǔ *also*"诳话" lie; falsehood:出家人不打～。Monks are not supposed to tell lies.

鵟 kuáng *also*"土豹" tǔbào buzzard

kuǎng

夼 kuǎng 〈方言〉(usually used in place names) low-lying land; depression:刘家～ *Liujiakuang*, place in Shandong Province

kuàng

圹(壙) kuàng ❶ coffin pit; open grave:打～ dig a coffin pit; dig a grave ❷〈书面〉open country; champaign

圹埌 kuànglàng 〈书面〉boundless

圹穴 kuàngxué open grave; coffin pit

矿(礦、鑛) kuàng ❶ mineral or ore deposit:采～ mining /探～ prospect for mineral deposits ❷ ore:铝土～ bauxite /选～ ore dressing; mineral separation; beneficiation ❸ mine:铜～ copper mine /厂～ factories and mines /露天～ opencast (*or* opencut) mine; strip mine; open-pit

矿藏 kuàngcáng mineral resources:～丰富 rich in mineral resources /～量 (ore) reserves /开发～ develop (*or* tap) mineral resources

矿层 kuàngcéng ore bed; ore horizon; seam:～走向 seam strike /～露头 outcropping (of a seam) /可采～ workable seam

矿产 kuàngchǎn mineral deposits; minerals:～储量 mineral reserve /～资源 mineral resources /～分布 distribution of mineral deposits (*or* resources) /～普查 general survey for mineral deposits /据勘探,这一带有十几种～。Explorations show that there are over a dozen minerals in the area.

矿产品 kuàngchǎnpǐn mineral product; mineral

矿场 kuàngchǎng mine

矿车 kuàngchē mine car; pitcar; tub

矿尘 kuàngchén mine dust:～浓度 mine dust density /～取样器 mine dust sampler /矿石倾泻而下,腾起一阵～。The ore came down in torrents, raising a cloud of mine dust.

矿床 kuàngchuáng *also*"矿体" mineral or ore deposit; deposit:金属～ metalliferous deposit /层状～ bedded deposit /海底～ submarine deposit /～评价 evaluation of deposits /～二次回采 secondary recovery (of deposits)

矿灯 kuàngdēng miner's lamp:安全～ safety lamp /～房 lamphouse

矿点 kuàngdiǎn site of a mineral deposit

矿工 kuànggōng miner; pitman

矿化 kuànghuà mineralize:～带 mineralized zone /～水 mineralized water /～剂 mineralizer; mineralizing agent

矿化度 kuànghuàdù mineralization

矿浆 kuàngjiāng ore pulp; pulp:～分析 pulp assay

矿井 kuàngjǐng mine shaft; pit; mine:～火灾 mine (*or* mineshaft) fire /～安全 mine safety /～架 headstock (of a pit) /～通风 mine ventilation /～提升机 mine hoist /～瓦斯 damp; fire-damp /废～ abandoned mine (*or* pit, *or* shaft)

矿警 kuàngjǐng mine police

矿坑 kuàngkēng pit:～水 mine-water /～下陷 mining subsidence

矿口发电厂 kuàngkǒu fādiànchǎng mine mouth power plant

矿料 kuàngliào dressed ore

矿瘤 kuàngliú nodule

矿脉 kuàngmài mineral or ore vein; (ore) lode:～交切 intersection of ore veins

矿棉 kuàngmián mineral wool:～制品 mineral wool product /～砖 mineral wool block

矿苗 kuàngmiáo *also*"露头" lùtóu outcropping; outcrop; crop

矿泥 kuàngní (in a mine) sludge; slime; slurry

矿区 kuàngqū mining area:～道路 mine road /植树造林,绿化～ plant trees to make a mining area green; afforest a mining area

矿泉 kuàngquán mineral spring; spa:～浴 mineral water bath /～疗法〈医学〉craunotherapy /～疗养地 spa /～疗养学 craunology

矿泉水 kuàngquánshuǐ mineral water

矿砂 kuàngshā ore in sand form

矿山 kuàngshān mine:～安全 mine safety /～地压 mine ground pressure; rock pressure /～灭火 mine fire-fighting /～救护队 mine rescue crew /～运输 mine haul (*or* haulage); pit haulage

矿山工程 kuàngshān gōngchéng mine engineering:～图 mine map

矿山机械 kuàngshān jīxiè mining machinery:重型～ heavy-duty mining machinery /～厂 mining machinery plant /～化 mining mechanization

矿石 kuàngshí mineral; ore:开采～ mine ore /富～ high-grade ore /贫～ low-grade ore /～品位 ore grade /～手选 ore hand sorting /～回采率 ore recovery rate /～运输船 ore carrier; ore tanker /～破碎机 ore crusher /～烧结机 ore-sintering machine /～研磨机 ore grinder

矿石收音机 kuàngshí shōuyīnjī *also*"矿石机" crystal receiver or set

矿胎 kuàngtāi protore

矿体 kuàngtǐ *also*"矿床" ore body; ore deposit

矿田 kuàngtián ore field; mine

矿物 kuàngwù mineral:稀有～ rare mineral /金属～ metallic mineral /伴生～ associated mineral /～资源 mineral resource /～标本 mineral specimen /～鞣剂 mineral tanning agent /～树脂 mineral resin /～填料 mineral filler /～膜电极 mineral membrane electrode /～探测卫星 mineralogical satellite

矿物共生 kuàngwù gòngshēng mineral association; mineral paragenesis

矿物界 kuàngwùjiè mineral kingdom

矿物棉 kuàngwùmián mineral wool

矿物燃料 kuàngwù ránliào fossil fuel; mineral fuel

矿物纤维 kuàngwù xiānwéi mineral fibre; mineral fabric

矿物学 kuàngwùxué mineralogy:～家 mineralogist

矿物油 kuàngwùyóu mineral oil

矿物质 kuàngwùzhì mineral substance:～饲料 mineral feed

矿相学 kuàngxiàngxué mineralography

矿盐 kuàngyán *also*"岩盐" yányán rock salt; halite

矿样 kuàngyàng sample ore

矿冶 kuàngyě mining and metallurgy:～学院 mining and metallurgical institute

矿业 kuàngyè mining industry:～法 law of the mining industry /～学院 mining institute /发展～ develop mining

矿用风机 kuàngyòng fēngjī mine ventilator

矿源 kuàngyuán mineral resources:勘察～ prospect for mineral resources

矿渣 kuàngzhā slag

矿渣棉 kuàngzhāmián mineral cotton

矿渣水泥 kuàngzhā shuǐní slag cement

矿渣砖 kuàngzhāzhuān slag brick

矿脂 kuàngzhī *also*"凡士林" fánshìlín mineral butter; petroleum jelly; vaseline; petrolatum:白～ petrolatum album /液体～ petrolax; petrosio

矿质肥料 kuàngzhì féiliào 〈农业〉mineral fertilizer

K

矿质营养 kuàngzhì yíngyǎng mineral nutrition

矿柱 kuàngzhù mine or pit prop; (ore) pillar; post: ～回采 pillar recovery

旷(曠)

kuàng ❶ open and empty; vast; spacious: 空～ open and uninhabited; open and spacious /地～人稀 vast territory with a sparse population ❷ free from worries and petty ideas; relaxed; expansive: 心～神怡 relaxed and content; carefree and happy ❸ neglect (duty, work, etc.); waste (time, etc.): 田园芜～。The land lay waste. ❹ loose-fitting; loose: 螺丝～了。The screw has worn loose. /这双鞋我穿着太～了。This pair of shoes is too large for me. ❺ (Kuàng) a surname

旷场 kuàngchǎng open site; open space; spacious place

旷达 kuàngdá 〈书面〉 broad-minded; big-hearted: 为人～, 不拘小节 be broad-minded and not bother about small matters

旷代 kuàngdài 〈书面〉 unrivalled by contemporaries; matchless in one's age: ～佳作 best work of an age /～奇才 unrivalled talent (for one's age)

旷荡 kuàngdàng ❶ open and broad; extensive; vast: ～的草原 open, boundless grassland; vast expanse of grassland ❷ free and unrestrained; free and open: 心怀～ be free and unrestrained (in one's thinking, etc.)

旷典 kuàngdiǎn ❶ grand ceremony that has not been held for a long time; rarest of occasions: 百年～ grandest ceremony of the century ❷ unprecedented favour or grace

旷废 kuàngfèi neglect; waste: ～学业 neglect one's studies /～青春 waste one's youth /田无～, 百姓乐业。No fields lay waste and all the people lived in peace and contentment.

旷费 kuàngfèi waste: ～钱财 waste money /～时日 neglect the passage of time; squander one's time

旷夫 kuàngfū 〈书面〉 man of marriageable age who remains unmarried for a long time: ～怨女 unmarried men and women of marriageable age

旷工 kuànggōng stay away from work without leave; be absent from work: 无故～ stay away from work without reason

旷古 kuànggǔ ❶ from time immemorial: ～奇闻 unheard-of story (*or* myth) /这样的丰功伟业, 可以说～绝伦。Such exploits are unequalled and unprecedented for all time. ❷ remote antiquity; ancient times

旷古未闻 kuànggǔ-wèiwén hitherto unknown; unheard-of; unprecedented: 此事～。Nobody has ever heard of such things.

旷课 kuàngkè be absent from school without leave; cut school; play truant: 今天有两人～。Two students are absent without leave today. *or* There are two truants today. /你这学期旷了两堂课。You cut two classes this term.

旷阔 kuàngkuò open; spacious; wild: 山脚下是一片～的田野。There is an expanse of open country at the foot of the mountain.

旷朗 kuànglǎng (of a house, etc.) spacious and bright; commodious

旷渺 kuàngmiǎo open and distant; broad and faraway

旷日持久 kuàngrì-chíjiǔ long-drawn-out; protracted; prolonged; time-consuming: ～的战争 prolonged war; protracted war /工程～。The construction has been drawn out a long time.

旷日经年 kuàngrì-jīngnián drag on endlessly; be long-drawn-out: 工程计划～, 久拖未决。The planning for the construction has been dragging on without reaching a conclusion.

旷世 kuàngshì 〈书面〉 ❶ unrivalled by one's contemporaries; matchless in one's age; unique: ～功勋 exploit unrivalled in one's time; unique deed /～无双 unmatched in one's time ❷ last a long, long time: ～难成之业 undertaking that can hardly be completed even for ages

旷芜 kuàngwú open and deserted: ～的原野 deserted open country; vast expanse of wasteland

旷野 kuàngyě wilderness; open country: ～荒郊 uninhabited open country

旷远 kuàngyuǎn ❶ open and distant; broad and faraway: 江面浩渺～。The river is a vast expanse of water stretching far into the distance. ❷ 〈书面〉 far back; ages ago; remote (antiquity): 年代～ of the remote past; of great antiquity; time-honoured

旷职 kuàngzhí be truant from one's duty; be absent from duty without leave

邝(鄺)

Kuàng a surname

纩(纊)

kuàng 〈书面〉 silk waste; silk floss: ～中引线 pull a thread from a mass of floss; bring order from chaos

框[1]

kuàng frame; case: 门～ door frame /窗～ window frame /镜～儿 picture frame /眼镜～儿 rims (of spectacles)

框[2]

kuàng (formerly pronounced kuāng) ❶ set pattern; convention; restriction ❷ draw a frame around: 排版时给这篇报道～上花边。Use fancy borders for this report (*or* Frame the report in fancy borders) while setting type. ❸ restrict; restrain; confine: ～得太死 impose (*or* make) too rigid restrictions

框架 kuàngjià ❶ 〈建筑〉 frame: ～结构 frame structure /钢筋混凝土～ reinforced concrete frame ❷ framework: ～协议 framework agreement /改革方案的～ framework of reform proposals /小说已经有了一个大致的～。A rough sketch has been worked out for the novel.

框架竖琴 kuàngjià shùqín frame harp

框框 kuàngkuang ❶ frame; circle: 他用红铅笔在照片周围画了一个～。He framed the photo in red pencil. ❷ restriction; convention; set pattern: 条条～ regulations and restrictions /打破旧～ break the set patterns (*or* conventions); break free of the old rut /我们看问题不要有～, 不能带偏见。We should not look at problems with a conventional or biased view.

框图 kuàngtú (short for 方框图) block diagram; skeleton diagram

框子 kuàngzi frame: 给这幅画配个～。Put the picture in a frame.

眶

kuàng socket of the eye: 热泪盈～ one's eyes filling (*or* welling up) with tears /眼～红了 be on the verge of tears

况[1](況)

kuàng ❶ condition; situation: 情～ state of affairs; situation /概～ general situation /盛～ grand occasion /你近～如何? How have you been recently? ❷ compare: 比～ draw an analogy /以物～人 compare things to people ❸ (Kuàng) a surname

况[2](況)

kuàng 〈书面〉 ❶ moreover; besides ❷ much less; let alone: 臣尚不能, 更～民妇? Even I as a minister cannot do it, let alone a common woman.

况兼 kuàngjiān 〈书面〉 moreover; besides; in addition: 书稿还需细细修改, ～八、九月我将外出, 出版之事似宜十月以后再议。As the manuscript needs careful revision, and since I shall be away in August and September, it seems appropriate to discuss its publication after October.

况且 kuàngqiě moreover; besides; in addition: 他工作认真, ～熟悉情况, 一定能办好。He is a conscientious worker. In addition, he knows the situation well, so I am sure he can do a good job of it.

况味 kuàngwèi 〈书面〉 ❶ situation; condition: 晚年～萧索 have a bleak old age; be desolate in one's old age ❷ flavour; appeal; charm: 园中～依旧。The garden retains its old charm (*or* appeal). /茶馆经过修饰, 别有一番～。The teahouse has acquired a distinctive air after the facelift.

贶

kuàng 〈书面〉 give as a gift; bestow; grant

絖

kuàng 〈书面〉 see "纩" kuàng

kuī

窥(闚)

kuī ❶ peep: 管中～豹 look at a leopard through a tube, seeing only one spot — a narrow view of sth.; limited knowledge /目不～园 not cast one glance at the garden — be engrossed in one's studies ❷ pry; spy: ～人阴私 pry into sb.'s secrets

窥豹一斑 kuībào-yībān see one spot on a leopard — see a (typical) segment of a whole: 这部书我只是～, 难断优劣。I am not in a position to pass any judgment on the book as I have only read bits of it.

窥测 kuīcè watch; spy out: ～真意 watch and try to figure out sb.'s true intention /躲在暗中～ watch (*or* spy on) sb. in the dark /

～方向 spy out the land; see which way the wind blows

窥察 kuīchá peep; spy upon; pry about:～敌人的动静 spy upon the enemy's movements

窥度 kuīduó surmise in secret; conjecture in private:～上司意图 guess at the intention of one's superior

窥管 kuīguǎn look at things through a bamboo tube — have a narrow view:～之见 narrow view; one-sided view

窥见 kuījiàn get or catch a glimpse of; detect:从这首诗里可以～诗人的内心世界。This poem offers an insight into the poet's inner world.

窥看 kuīkàn steal a glance at; peek or peep at; spy on:～对方的神色 steal a glance at the face of the other person /趁着夜色～敌人的防御工事 spy on enemy defences by starlight

窥器 kuīqì 〈医学〉speculum

窥觑 kuīqū steal a glance at; peek or peep at; spy on:他从统舱的窗眼中～船外的风光。From a steerage porthole, he peeped at the scenery. /这个陌生人进了屋,贼眉鼠眼,四处～。The stranger got in, his shifty eyes sweeping about the room.

窥视 kuīshì peep at; spy on; pry about:通过门上的锁孔向屋内～ peep in through a keyhole on the door

窥视镜 kuīshìjìng *also*"门镜" ménjìng;"猫眼儿" māoyǎnr peephole; spyhole:从～中看清了来人的形貌 see clearly the features of the visitor through the peephole

窥伺 kuīsì lie in wait for; be on watch for:～日久 have been on the watch for a long time /～良机 lie in wait for a good chance; bide one's time

窥探 kuītàn spy upon; pry about:～别人的隐私 nose into sb.'s privacy

窥听 kuītīng listen stealthily; eavesdrop; tap:他蹑着脚走到门边,～屋里的动静。He tiptoed to the door to eavesdrop on what was going on in the room.

窥望 kuīwàng steel a glance; peek; peep at; spy on:他舐破窗纸向里面～。He peeped in through a small hole he made in the papered window with his tongue. /老人猝然住了嘴,向窗外～。Abruptly, the old man stopped speaking and stole a glance out of the window.

亏(虧)

kuī ❶ lose (money, etc.); have a deficit:盈～ profit and loss /扭～为盈 turn from losses to profits; turn a losing enterprise into a profit-making one /～了一千元 have a deficit of 1,000 *yuan*; lose 1,000 *yuan* ❷ deficient; short:理～ be in the wrong; be at fault /功～一篑 fall short of success for lack of a final effort /月满则～。The moon begins to wane upon reaching the full. /进出相抵,我还～你一百元。On balance, I still owe you one hundred *yuan*. ❸ treat unfairly:你拿公家的东西,良心～不～? Don't you have a guilty conscience when you pinch public property? /跟我一起干吧,准～不了你。Come and work for me; you won't be sorry for it. ❹ fortunately; luckily; thanks to:～他有过一次教训,这次才没有上当。Thanks to his previous lesson, he did not get taken in this time. ❺ *used to indicate irony*:～你还有脸来见我! And you have the cheek to come and see me! /连包饺子都不会,～你还是北方人呢! Fancy a northerner like you not knowing how to make *jiaozi*!

亏本 kuīběn lose money (in business); lose one's capital:买卖～ lose money in business /～出售 sell at a loss /～生意 losing business (*or* proposition) /公司连年～,恐怕支持不了多久了。As the company has been in the red for years, it may not be able to last long.

亏舱 kuīcāng 〈航海〉broken stowage:～运费 shortfall freight

亏产 kuīchǎn fail to fulfil the production target; fall short of the production quota:变～为超产 make up the shortfall (in output) and overfulfil the production quota /上半年～原煤 500 万吨。Raw coal output for the first six months was 5 million tons short of the quota.

亏秤 kuīchèng ❶ give short measure:这人买卖公道,从不～,也不多要钱。The man is an honest tradesman. He never gives short measure nor overcharges his customers. ❷ lose weight:这菜太湿,放两天就～好几斤。As the vegetable is too moist, it will lose quite a few kilograms when stored for a couple of days.

亏待 kuīdài treat unfairly; treat shabbily:她觉得自己受了～,一脸的不高兴。She sulked, for she thought she had been unfairly treated. /好好干吧,我们不会～你的! Do a good job, and we will give you your due.

亏得 kuīde ❶ fortunately; luckily; thanks to:～我早有准备,才避免了重大损失。Fortunately, I had taken precautions beforehand. Otherwise I would have suffered a heavy loss. /～是我去了,要是你,准得给他骗了。You were lucky that I went instead of you. You would have been hooked by him. ❷ *used to indicate irony*:～你还当过运动员呢,连这么点儿路都走不了。Fancy a former (*or* one-time) athlete not being able to walk such a short distance!

亏短 kuīduǎn insufficient; deficient; short:～分量 give short measure /查一查现金有没有～。Check if the cash is short.

亏乏 kuīfá lack; be short; be deficient:原料～ be short of raw materials

亏负 kuīfù ❶ fail to measure up to; not live up to:对父母的期盼有所～ somewhat fail to live up to one's parents' expectations ❷ be unfair by; let down:我没有～你的地方。I have never done anything unfair by you. *or* I haven't let you down in any way.

亏耗 kuīhào loss by a natural process:运输中的～ losses incurred in the course of transport /减少～,降低成本 reduce losses to lower the production costs

亏空 kuīkong ❶ be in debt; have a deficit:～太大 sustain a huge loss /本月份～十余万元 have a deficit of over 100,000 *yuan* this month ❷ debt; deficit:拉了许多～ get into heavy debt /账上有～。There was a deficit in the account.

亏累 kuīlěi show repeated deficits; sustain repeated losses:截至本月份,账面已～一百多万美元。As of this month, the accounts show an aggregate (*or* cumulative) deficit of over one million US dollars.

亏欠 kuīqiàn have a deficit; be in arrears:他当了三年经理,公司一直～。He has been running the company for three years with a deficit. /从今往后,咱们谁也不～谁。We don't owe each other anything as from now. *or* We're quits as of now.

亏弱 kuīruò (of health) not strong or sturdy; weak:他病后失调,身体更～了。Lacking proper care after the illness made him all the weaker.

亏折 kuīshé lose one's capital; lose (money, etc.):～殆尽 lose almost all one's capital /市场不稳,公司～甚多。With the unstable market, the company has lost a great deal of money.

亏蚀 kuīshí ❶ eclipse of the sun or moon ❷ lose (money) in business:近来月月～ have suffered (*or* sustained) losses each month recently ❸ wear and tear; depreciation; loss:设备～严重 serious depreciation of equipment

亏数 kuīshù 〈数学〉deficiency; deficient number

亏损 kuīsǔn ❶ loss; deficit:巨额～ heavy (*or* huge) loss /～企业 losing enterprise ❷ general debility:他久病不愈,身体～太大。The long illness has greatly debilitated him.

亏心 kuīxīn have a guilty conscience:你这样对待人家,～不～? Don't you feel guilty when you treat people in such a way?

亏心事 kuīxīnshì deed that troubles one's conscience; matter for remorse:做～ do sth. with a bad conscience /为人不做～,半夜敲门心不惊。When one has a clear conscience, one does not fear midnight knocks at one's door. *or* A quiet conscience sleeps in thunder.

亏月 kuīyuè 〈天文〉waning moon

刲

kuī 〈书面〉cut; reap:～羊 kill a goat /～宰 slaughter (animals) /～麦 reap wheat

盔

kuī ❶ basin-like pottery container ❷ helmet:钢～ steel helmet ❸ any helmet-shaped hat:头～ cyclist's helmet

盔甲 kuījiǎ suit of armour:身穿～,手执利剑 wear a suit of armour and carry a sharp sword

盔头 kuītou decorative hat (worn by an actor or actress in traditional opera, varying with the role's age, sex, identity and status)

盔子 kuīzi basin-like pottery container

岿(巋)

kuī

岿然 kuīrán 〈书面〉towering; lofty:～屹立 stand towering like a giant /～独存 stand steadfast on one's own; stand alone

岿然不动 kuīrán-bùdòng steadfastly stand one's ground:这古塔,经历了千百个寒暑,仍然～,屹立在高山之巅。Exposed to the elements for a thousand years, the pagoda still stands erect on the top of the mountain.

岿巍 kuīwēi 〈书面〉tower above others:山峰～。The mountain peak towered above all.

K

kuí

逵 kuí 〈书面〉thoroughfare; road

奎 kuí ❶ one of the Chinese zodiacal constellations *see also* "二十八宿" èrshíbāxiù ❷ (Kuí) a surname

奎尼丁 kuínídīng 〈药学〉quinidine

奎宁 kuíníng *also* "金鸡纳霜" jīnjīnàshuāng 〈药学〉quinine

喹 kuí

喹啉 kuílín 〈化学〉quinoline

蝰 kuí

蝰蛇 kuíshé viper; adder

魁 kuí ❶ chief; head: 党～ party chief / 罪～ chief criminal; arch-criminal / 花～ queen of flowers; most beautiful girl (*or* courtesan) / 夺～ win the championship; come out number one ❷ tall and burly; of stalwart build: *see* "～梧" ❸ *see* "～星❶"

魁岸 kuí'àn 〈书面〉tall and burly; stalwart: ～的汉子 powerfully-built tall man

魁北克 Kuíběikè ❶ Quebec, French-speaking province of Canada ❷ Quebec, capital of Quebec Province and oldest city of Canada, on the St. Lawrence River

魁柄 kuíbǐng 〈书面〉power of government; position of prime minister: 授以～ vest sb. with the power of government / 恳辞～ ask earnestly to resign as prime minister

魁甲 kuíjiǎ *also* "状元" zhuàngyuan 〈书面〉number one successful candidate in the highest imperial examination

魁实 kuíshi 〈方言〉tall and sturdy; stalwart: 来人身材～。The visitor was of tall, sturdy physique.

魁首 kuíshǒu ❶ *also* "魁元" one who is head and shoulders above others; best and brightest; number one: 文章～ number one writer of one's day / 女中～ most outstanding woman ❷ chieftain: 群盗之～ bandit chieftain

魁伟 kuíwěi strongly-built: 体态～ be of strong build

魁梧 kuíwu big and tall; stalwart; powerfully-built: 他年纪轻轻, 却长成一副～身量。Though still young, he has grown into a giant.

魁星 kuíxīng ❶ four stars in the bowl of the Big Dipper (北斗), or the one at the tip of the bowl ❷ (Kuíxīng) god that governs literature and writing: ～楼 Pavilion of *Kuixing*

魁元 kuíyuán 〈书面〉❶ *see* "魁首" ❷ number one successful candidate: 他秋试得中～。He came out first in the autumn imperial examination.

櫆 kuí 〈书面〉Big Dipper

隗 Kuí a surname

see also Wěi

馗 kuí *also* "逵" kuí 〈书面〉thoroughfare; road

葵 kuí common name for certain herbaceous plants with big flowers: 向日～ sunflower / 蜀～ hollyhock / 锦～ high mallow

葵涌港 Kuíchōnggǎng Kwai Chung Port, container terminal of Hong Kong

葵花 kuíhuā sunflower: ～油 sunflower oil / ～向阳。Sunflowers turn to the sun.

葵花子 kuíhuāzǐ sunflower seeds

葵倾 kuíqīng 〈书面〉look up to (as sunflowers to the sun); admire

葵扇 kuíshàn palm-leaf fan

揆 kuí 〈书面〉❶ conjecture; surmise; speculate: ～之是非利害 consider the merits and demerits of a case ❷ principle; criterion; standard: 其～一也。They go by the same principles. ❸ manage; control: 总～文教 be charged with overall responsibility for culture and education ❹ premier or any official of similar rank: 阁～ premier

揆度 kuíduó 〈书面〉estimate; surmise: ～得失 estimate gain and loss / 不可～ inestimable; beyond speculation

揆情度理 kuíqíng-duólǐ consider the circumstances and judge by common sense; weigh the pros and cons: ～, 他不会不同意这样的安排。He could not but agree with such arrangements when he had considered the overall advantages and disadvantages.

揆席 kuíxí 〈旧语〉prime minister; cabinet premier

戣 kuí ancient weapon such as halberd

暌 kuí 〈书面〉(of people) separate; part

暌别 kuíbié 〈书面〉part; leave; bid farewell: ～经年 (of people) have been separated for years / ～多日。It is some time since we parted (*or* since I left this place).

暌隔 kuígé 〈书面〉separate; be away from: 故乡山川, 十年～。I have been away from the mountains and rivers of my homeland for ten years.

暌绝 kuíjué 〈书面〉separate; cut off; sever; isolate: 关山～ be separated by mountains and passes (*or* by a long distance) / 昔日好友, 一旦～, 竟成路人。Once estranged, former friends cut each other dead when they meet.

暌阔 kuíkuò 〈书面〉separate; sever; part: 两地～ be separated from each other

暌离 kuílí 〈书面〉part; leave; bid farewell: ～家人, 已有三载。It is three years since I bade farewell to my family.

暌违 kuíwéi 〈书面〉(formerly often used in correspondence) separate: ～日久。We have been separated for a long time. *or* It is a long time since we saw each other last.

睽 kuí 〈书面〉❶ *see* "暌" kuí ❷ 〈书面〉violate; go against; run contrary to: 于理无～ conform to reason

睽睽 kuíkuí stare; gaze: 众目～ in the public eye; in public

睽异 kuíyì 〈书面〉disagree; be at variance: 虽为至交, 但议论多有～。The best of friends, they often differ in opinion.

骙 kuí

骙骙 kuíkuí 〈书面〉(of horses) strong

夔[1] kuí dragonlike monopode in ancient legends

夔[2] Kuí ❶ Kuizhou, name of a prefecture in ancient China, whose seat is located in present Fengjie County (奉节县) of Chongqing Municipality ❷ a surname

kuǐ

跬 kuǐ 〈书面〉half a step

跬步 kuǐbù 〈书面〉half a step; small or short step: ～不离 not move even half a step from sb. (*or* sth.); follow closely; keep close to / ～难行 difficult even to take a small step

跬步千里 kuǐbù-qiānlǐ one can cover a thousand *li* by small steps — continued efforts may lead to great successes

硊 kuǐ

硊磊 kuǐlěi 〈书面〉❶ stones in a heap ❷ *also* "块垒" kuàilěi pent-up indignation; gloom; depression: 以酒浇心中～ drown one's pent-up indignation in alcoholic drinks / 胸中～, 不吐不快。One would not feel at ease until one has poured out all one's grievances.

傀 kuǐ

see also guī

傀儡 kuǐlěi puppet; marionette; stooge: ～政权 puppet regime / 他哪里有什么实权? 只不过是个～。He doesn't have any real power. He is nothing but a puppet.

傀儡戏 kuǐlěixì puppet show; puppet play

kuì

愧(媿) kuì ashamed; abashed; conscience-stricken: 当

之无～ fully deserve (honour, reward, praise, etc.); be worthy of / 自～弗如 feel that one's no match for sb.; consider oneself inferior to sb. /～不敢当。〈谦词〉I do not deserve such an honour (*or* gift). *or* I am flattered.

愧服 kuìfú 〈书面〉admire (sb.) while feeling ashamed of one's inferiority; consider oneself inferior (to sb.): 不禁～ cannot help admiring sb. while feeling ashamed of one's inferiority /凡是同他交过手的,无不～。No one who has played against him fails to admire him.

愧汗 kuìhàn 〈书面〉sweat from a sense of shame; feel extremely ashamed: ～无地 feel so ashamed of oneself that one does not know which way to turn

愧恨 kuìhèn ashamed and remorseful; remorseful: 深自～ feel bitterly remorseful /～不已 one's mortification knows no end

愧悔 kuìhuǐ ashamed and regretful: ～交集 be overwhelmed by remorse /～无及 be extremely ashamed and sorry when it is too late /～难言 feel too ashamed and regretful for words

愧疚 kuìjiù 〈书面〉feel ashamed and remorseful; be conscience-stricken: ～之情 sense (*or* feeling) of shame and remorse

愧领 kuìlǐng 〈谦词〉accept humbly: 你的好意,我们～啦。We accept your kindness with all humility.

愧赧 kuìnǎn blush from shame: ～汗颜 blush and sweat from shame

愧恧 kuìnǜ 〈书面〉be ashamed

愧色 kuìsè look of shame: 面带～ look ashamed /她说这话时一脸～。She looked abashed when she said this.

愧痛 kuìtòng agony from shame; pain from shame: 万分～ extreme agony from shame

愧心 kuìxīn guilty conscience; shameful feeling: 顿生～ be gripped with a feeling of shame /时间一长,遂有～。As time went by, a guilty conscience began to bother (him).

愧怍 kuìzuò 〈书面〉be ashamed: 家道日落,我又不能分忧,岂不～! How can I help feeling ashamed when I cannot do anything to stop my family fortune deteriorating daily?

溃

kuì ❶ (of floodwater, etc.) burst (a dyke or dam); break: ～堤 burst a dyke /千里之堤,～于蚁穴。One anthole may lead to the collapse of a thousand *li* long dyke. *or* One small negligence may ruin a gigantic undertaking. ❷〈书面〉break through (an encirclement, etc.): *see* "～围" ❸ be routed; fall to pieces: 崩～ collapse; crumble; fall apart /击～ rout ❹ fester; ulcerate

溃败 kuìbài be crushed; be routed: ～之师 routed army /全线～ be put to rout all along the line

溃兵 kuìbīng routed troops; defeated and dispersed soldiers

溃不成军 kuìbùchéngjūn (of an army, etc.) be utterly routed: 该部节节败退,～。The army crumbled away after a series of defeats.

溃窜 kuìcuàn be routed and flee pell-mell: 敌人纷纷～。The routed enemy troops fled helter-skelter.

溃决 kuìjué (of a dyke or dam) burst: 堤坝一旦～,千里麦田即成一片汪洋。If the dam bursts, hundreds of miles of wheat fields will be submerged.

溃军 kuìjūn routed troops or army

溃烂 kuìlàn 〈医学〉fester; ulcerate: 伤口出现大面积～。A large part of the wound festered. /脚面～,疼痛异常。The instep was ulcerating and hurting terribly.

溃乱 kuìluàn be routed and thrown into utter confusion; collapse into chaos: 他带了几个随从,于～之中连夜出逃。He fled in confusion with some of his retinue the same evening.

溃灭 kuìmiè crumble and fall: 秦王朝在农民起义的打击下迅速～。The Qin Dynasty collapsed in no time under the blows of peasant uprisings.

溃散 kuìsàn be routed and dispersed: 这群乌合之众一见敌人,就先自～了。This mob of an army crumbled away at first sight of the enemy.

溃逃 kuìtáo escape in disorder; flee pell-mell; flee helter-skelter: 败兵四处～。The defeated soldiers fled in all directions. /公路上挤满了～的敌军。The highway was crowded with fleeing enemy troops.

溃退 kuìtuì retreat in confusion; beat a disorderly retreat: 该军～时把重武器都抛下了。The routed army left all its heavy arms behind in its confused retreat.

溃围 kuìwéi 〈书面〉break through an encirclement: 乘机～ take advantage of the opportunity to break through the encirclement

溃疡 kuìyáng 〈医学〉ulcer; canker: 局部～ local ulcer /胃～ gastric ulcer /十二指肠～ duodenal ulcer /口腔～ oral ulcer; canker sore /～面 ulcerous side /～穿孔 perforated ulcer

愦

kuì muddle-headed; befuddled; senile: 昏～ befuddled; muddled-headed

愦乱 kuìluàn 〈书面〉dazed and confused; befuddled: 神志～ mentally confused

襀

kuì 〈方言〉❶ knot: 活～儿 slip-knot /死～儿 fast-knot ❷ tie; fasten; do up; button up: ～个襀儿 tie a knot /把牲口～上 tether the draught animal (to sth.)

蒉

kuì 〈书面〉straw bag for carrying earth; earth-filled straw bag: 荷～而过 pass by with a straw bag of earth on one's back; carry a straw bag of earth past

聩

kuì 〈书面〉deaf; hard of hearing: 发聋振～ rouse the deaf and awaken the unhearing; rouse even the most apathetic

匮

kuì 〈书面〉deficient; lacking

匮乏 kuìfá 〈书面〉short (of supplies, etc.); deficient: 弹药～ short of ammunition /资源～ deficient in natural resources /市场～ shortage of goods in the market; market in short supply /不虞～ not worry about supplies

匮竭 kuìjié in short supply; exhausted: 资源～。Natural resources are exhausted. /繁重的工作使他精力～。His energy was sapped by hard work.

匮缺 kuìquē short (of supplies, etc.); deficient: 器材～ lacking in equipment; short of equipment

篑

kuì 〈书面〉basket for carrying earth: 功亏一～ fail to build a mound for want of the last basketful of earth — fall short of success for want of a final effort

馈(餽)

kuì make a present of; present (a gift): ～以珠宝 make a present of jewels

馈电 kuìdiàn 〈电工〉feed: 交叉～ cross feed /～流 feed current; supply current /～点 distributing point; feeding point

馈送 kuìsòng present (a gift); make a present of (sth.): ～食物 present food

馈遗 kuìwèi 〈书面〉present (a gift); make a present of (sth.)

馈线 kuìxiàn 〈电工〉feed line; feeder

馈献 kuìxiàn present (a gift to one's seniors or superiors)

馈赠 kuìzèng present (a gift); make a present of (sth.): ～礼品 present gifts /～亲友 present gifts to relatives and friends /这种丝巾为～亲友之佳品。These silk scarves make very presentable gifts for friends and relatives.

喟

kuì 〈书面〉heave a sigh; sigh: 感～ sigh with feeling

喟然 kuìrán 〈书面〉sigh deeply: ～太息 draw a long sigh

喟然长叹 kuìrán-chángtàn sigh deeply; heave a deep sigh: 好事不成,令他～。He heaved a deep sigh over his failure to accomplish what he had desired most.

喟叹 kuìtàn 〈书面〉sigh with deep feeling: 见此情景,他不禁～不已。Seeing this, he could not but sigh with sorrow.

kūn

堃

kūn *a variant of* 坤, *mostly used in personal names*

裈(㡓、裩)

kūn 〈书面〉trousers

髡(髠)

kūn (as a punishment in ancient times) shave a man's head: ～首 shave sb.'s head as a punishment

髡钳 kūnqián 〈旧语〉shave sb.'s head and bind his neck with an iron ring as a punishment: ～为奴 work as a slave with a shaven head and an iron ring round one's neck

坤

kūn ❶ symbol for earth in the Eight Trigrams; triagram

representing earth:乾～ heaven and earth; universe ❷ female; feminine:～鞋 woman's shoes /～车 lady's (*or* woman's) bicycle

坤包 kūnbāo lady's handbag (*or* purse)

坤表 kūnbiǎo women's wristwatch

坤角儿 kūnjuér *also* "坤伶"〈旧语〉actress (in traditional opera):她是个有名的～。She was a famous actress.

坤造 kūnzào 〈旧语〉❶ woman in a marriage; bride ❷ (in fortune-telling) year, month, day and hour of a woman's birth

坤宅 kūnzhái 〈旧语〉family of the bride; family of one's wife

昆

kūn 〈书面〉❶ elder brother ❷ offspring; progeny:后～ descendents; children ❸ (short for 昆曲) *Kunqu* opera:南～ southern *Kunqu* opera (popular in southern Jiangsu Province) /北～ northern *Kunqu* opera (popular in Hebei Province and Beijing)

昆布 kūnbù 〈中药〉kelp

昆虫 kūnchóng insect:传病～ insect vector /～激素 insect hormone /～防治 insect control /制造～标本 make an insect specimen /食～的 entomophagous /～寄生真菌 entromogenous fungus

昆虫病 kūnchóngbìng entomiasis

昆虫病理学 kūnchóng bìnglǐxué insect pathology

昆虫毒理学 kūnchóng dúlǐxué insect toxicology

昆虫纲 kūnchónggāng 〈生物〉*Insecta*

昆虫生态学 kūnchóng shēngtàixué insect ecology

昆虫学 kūnchóngxué entomology; insectology:～家 entomologist

昆虫志 kūnchóngzhì entomfauna

昆弟 kūndì brother

昆季 kūnjì 〈书面〉brothers:韩氏～ the Han brothers

昆栏树 kūnlánshù 〈植物〉*Trochodendraceae*

昆仑 Kūnlún Kunlun Mountains, lying across Xinjiang, Tibet and Qinghai, and source of both the Yellow River and the Yangtze

昆仑奴 kūnlúnnú 〈旧语〉black slave during the Tang and Song dynasties

昆明 Kūnmíng Kunming, capital of Yunnan Province

昆明湖 Kūnmínghú Kunming Lake, of the Summer Palace in Beijing

昆腔 kūnqiāng *also* "昆曲";"昆山腔"〈戏曲〉melodies which originated in Kunshan (昆山), Jiangsu Province, in the Yuan Dynasty, and became popular during the ensuing Ming and Qing dynasties

昆曲 kūnqǔ ❶ *also* "昆剧" *Kunqu* opera based on *Kunqiang* melodies, popular in southern Jiangsu, Beijing, and Hepei ❷ *see* "昆腔"

昆仲 kūnzhòng (other people's) brothers:贤～〈敬词〉you and your brother(s) /周氏～三人均是文坛显赫人物。The three Zhou brothers were all celebrities in literary circles.

焜

kūn 〈书面〉bright

琨

kūn 〈书面〉a kind of jade:～玉 beautiful jade

醌

kūn 〈化学〉quinone

崑

kūn

崑崙 Kūnlún (now written as 昆仑) *Kunlun* Mountains

锟

kūn

锟铻 Kūnwú ❶ name of a mountain in ancient books, the iron from which was used to make swords ❷ sword made from *Kunwu* iron

鲲

kūn enormous legendary fish, which could change itself into a roc

鲲鹏 kūnpéng ❶ legendary fish and roc ❷ roc (an enormous legendary bird transformed from the gigantic *kun* fish):～展翅 like the roc flapping its wings — taking off with tremendous power and momentum

鹍(鵾)

kūn

鹍鸡 kūnjī crane-like bird (mentioned in ancient Chinese books)

kǔn

悃

kǔn 〈书面〉sincere:聊表谢～ as a token of my sincere gratitude

悃愊 kǔnbì 〈书面〉utter sincerity:发愤～ make a resolution from the bottom of one's heart

悃愊无华 kǔnbì-wúhuá 〈书面〉honest and simple; sincere and honest; in good earnest:～,一心为国 devote oneself sincerely and wholeheartedly to the country

悃诚 kǔnchéng 〈书面〉sincere intention; sincerity

阃

kǔn 〈书面〉❶ threshold ❷ woman's bedroom; boudoir:～闱 boudoir ❸ women:～德 women's virtue /～范 model for feminine virtue; model for all women

捆(綑)

kǔn ❶ tie; bind; bundle up:～书 tie up books /～干草 bundle up hay /把罪犯～起来 truss up a criminal ❷ bundle; bunch:菠菜～ bunch of spinach ❸〈量词〉*used of sth. bundled up*:一～稻草 a bundle of rice straw /数～行李 several bundles of luggage (*or* baggage)

捆绑 kǔnbǎng truss up (usu. people); bind; tie up:他被～,动弹不得。He was bound up and could not move. /～不成夫妻。You cannot bind a man and woman together to make them husband and wife — forced cooperation doesn't work.

捆绑销售 kǔnbǎng xiāoshòu 〈商业〉bundling

捆缚 kǔnfù truss up; bind; tie up:～送官 tie up sb. and take him to the magistrate

捆扎 kǔnzā tie up (usu. things); fasten; bundle up:把这几包东西仔细～好! Please tie up (*or* fasten) these packages carefully.

捆住手脚 kǔnzhù-shǒujiǎo bind sb. hands and feet — restrict sb.'s freedom of action:不能让那些过时的条条框框～。We must not allow those outdated conventions to restrict our freedom of action.

捆子 kǔnzi bundle:把木柴扎成～ bundle up the firewood

壸(壼)

kǔn 〈书面〉alley or path in a palace

kùn

困(❺❻睏)

kùn ❶ be stranded; be stricken; be trapped:～于孤岛 be stranded on a lone island /贫病交～ be stricken by both poverty and illness /为烦恼所～ be haunted by worries ❷ surround; hold in check:围～ besiege; hem in; pin down /把敌人～在山沟里 bottle up (*or* pin down) the enemy in a ravine ❸ difficulty; hardship:急人之～ be anxious to help those in difficulty ❹ tired; exhausted:人～马乏。Both men and horses are exhausted. ❺ sleepy; drowsy:我～极了。I feel extremely drowsy. ❻〈方言〉sleep:天不早了,快点～吧。It's getting late; why don't you go to bed!

困惫 kùnbèi 〈书面〉worn out; exhausted:～不堪 be worn out; be dog-tired /劳累终日,方感～ not feel exhausted until the day's toil is over

困补 kùnbǔ (short for 困难补助) subsidy to those in financial difficulties:申请～ apply for a grant-in-aid on account of one's straitened circumstances

困处 kùnchǔ ❶ difficult position; straits:身陷～ land in a predicament ❷ be trapped in:～一隅 be cornered; find oneself in a tight corner

困顿 kùndùn ❶ worn out; exhausted:鞍马～ travel-worn /身体～不堪 be utterly exhausted ❷ in financial straits or difficulties:～潦倒 be frustrated in life and poverty-stricken /父亲失业后,全家立即陷于～之中。When father lost his job, the whole family was plunged into financial straits.

困厄 kùn'è dire straits; distress:屡遭～ fall into adversity repeatedly /从～中奋起 pull oneself up from dire straits

困乏 kùnfá ❶ tired; fatigued:颇感～ feel quite tired /干了一天活儿,大家都～极了。Everyone felt exhausted after working the whole day. ❷〈书面〉(financial) difficulties; shortage (of supplies):生计～ lack means of livelihood /连年大旱,百姓～。Successive droughts left

the people in dire straits.

困惑 kùnhuò perplexed; puzzled:对他的无礼行为感到～不解 feel puzzled at his impudence /文化上的～ cultural confusion /对自己的前途感到～ feel uncertain about one's future /她～地看着我。She looked at me in perplexity.

困觉 kùnjiào 〈方言〉sleep:老人午饭后困了一觉,精神特别好。The old man had a nap after lunch and felt very much refreshed.

困境 kùnjìng difficult position; predicament; straits:体谅他的～ understand his difficulties /身临～ be mired in a dilemma /摆脱～ extricate oneself from a predicament /处于～的经济 beleaguered economy

困窘 kùnjiǒng ❶ be embarrassed; feel awkward:瞧着他一脸的～,她便收了话题。Seeing that he was embarrassed, she stopped pursuing the matter. /在姑娘们面前,这小伙子总感到～不自在。The young man always felt awkward with girls. ❷ in straitened circumstances; poverty-stricken:家境～ be in straitened circumstances /～的生活 poverty-stricken life

困居 kùnjū be constrained to live in a small or inhospitable place; be stranded:～异国 be constrained to live in a foreign country; be stranded in a foreign country

困倦 kùnjuàn tired and sleepy:感到～ feel tired and sleepy /耐不住～ too sleepy to keep awake

困苦 kùnkǔ hardship and privation:艰难～ difficulties and hardships /～的生活磨炼了他的意志。A difficult and hard life tempered his will-power.

困累 kùnlèi tired; fatigued; run-down:连日加班,人～得不行。Having worked overtime for the last few days, everyone feels rundown.

困难 kùnnan ❶ difficulty:条件～ difficult conditions (*or* circumstances) /进食～ (of a patient) find it hard to eat anything; eat with difficulty /尽管～重重 against heavy odds /克服～ overcome (*or* surmount) a difficulty ❷ financial difficulties; straitened circumstances; poverty:日子过得～ live in straitened circumstances; find it hard to make both ends meet /～补助 subsidy to those in straitened circumstances

困难户 kùnnanhù ❶ household in straitened circumstances; poverty-stricken family:访问～,解决实际问题 visit families who are badly off and help solve their specific difficulties ❷ family or person with difficulties of a particular kind:帮助劳力～搞好春耕、春种 help families who are short of hands to do a good job of spring ploughing and sowing /我哥哥过于怕羞,找对象可是个～。My brother is too shy and has difficulty finding a suitable wife.

困恼 kùnnǎo vex; worry:被琐事所～ be vexed by trivia /令人～的问题 worrisome problem /陷入无限的～之中 be haunted by endless anxiety

困迫 kùnpò in dire straits; hard pressed; in a tight corner:～不安 be extremely embarrassed and restless /敌人弹尽粮绝,～无奈,只得投降。Having run out of ammunition and food, the hard-pressed enemy had no alternative but to surrender.

困穷 kùnqióng poverty-stricken; impoverished; destitute

困扰 kùnrǎo ❶ besiege and harass:～敌军 besiege and harass the enemy ❷ haunt; trouble; perplex:为高通货膨胀所～的经济 economy troubled by high inflation /为一堆杂务所～ be harassed by a pile of sundry duties /这几天一种莫名的烦恼始终～着我。I have been haunted by a kind of baffling worry the last few days.

困人 kùnrén make one drowsy:～的天气 drowsy weather

困守 kùnshǒu defend against a siege; stand a siege:～待援 defend against a siege and wait for relief troops /～孤岛 defend an isolated island

困兽犹斗 kùnshòu-yóudòu a pent-up or cornered beast will turn and fight; a beast at bay will put up a desperate fight:虽然罪犯已被包围,然而～,我们不能有丝毫大意。Although the criminals have been cornered, we must be vigilant and guard against their turning to bay.

困退 kùntuì "repatriation (to one's home city) on account of family needs" (in reference to those urban school graduates sent to settle down in the countryside during the Cultural Revolution who were later granted permission to return to their home cities because of their families' difficulties)

困学 kùnxué study assiduously:求知识要有～精神。Assiduity is what we need to acquire knowledge.

kuò

廓 kuò ❶ wide; extensive; vast:寥～ vast; boundless /空～ open and spacious ❷ expand; extend:～地千里 extend the territory by a thousand *li* ❸ outer features; outline:轮～ outline; contour

廓廓 kuòkuò 〈书面〉open; spacious:～沃野,牛羊成群。Grazing on the vast expanse of fertile land are flocks of sheep and herds of cattle. /天下～无事,万民安居乐业。Peace prevailed across the land and the people lived in peace and comfort (*or* contentedness).

廓落 kuòluò 〈书面〉open and still; spacious and empty:～的夜空 vast expanse of quiet night sky

廓清 kuòqīng ❶ clean up; clarify; purify:～天下 clean up the land; bring peace and unity to the country /～异端邪说 dispel evil ideas and heresy ❷ clear away; remove:～前进道路上的一切障碍 clear away all obstacles in one's way

廓然 kuòrán vast and tranquil; open and still:四顾～。It was vast and tranquil all around. /院中～无声。The courtyard was spacious and quiet.

廓然大公 kuòrán-dàgōng broad-minded and unbiased; honest and unselfish:林公为人～,一心报国。Honest and unselfish, Mr. Lin devoted himself wholeheartedly to serving the country.

廓张 kuòzhāng 〈书面〉spread; expand; extend; stretch:名声日渐～。His reputation was growing with each passing day.

鞟(鞹) kuò 〈书面〉animal skin or hide without hair

扩(擴) kuò extend; expand; enlarge; magnify:～地 expand one's land; extend the territory /～兵 increase the number of one's troops; recruit more soldiers

扩版 kuòbǎn (of a newspaper or magazine) enlarge the format of the pages; increase or expand the number of pages:由十六开～为八开 change from 16mo to octavo pages /本刊将于明年1月起～为120页。This magazine will increase the number of its pages to 120 as from next January.

扩编 kuòbiān (of an army) enlarge the establishment; increase one's troop strength; increase the size of one's forces:～部队 enlarge an army /内战迫在眉睫,各处军阀纷纷～,招兵买马。The warlords started to increase the number of their troops (*or* increase their forces) as civil war was impending.

扩充 kuòchōng expand and strengthen; augment; enlarge:～实力 augment (*or* increase) one's (political or military) strength /～内容 add to (*or* expand *or* augment) the contents (of a book, etc.) /～设备 procure (*or* buy) more equipment; augment one's stock of equipment /～军备 engage in arms expansion /～存储器〈计算机〉enlarged storage /师资队伍需要～。The teaching staff needs to be further expanded.

扩大 kuòdà enlarge; expand; extend; broaden:～剪刀差〈经济〉enlarge a scissors' gap /～销路 expand sales /～势力范围 extend one's sphere of influence /～眼界 broaden one's horizons; widen one's vision or outlook /～知识面 extend the range of one's knowledge; broaden one's knowledge /～国有企业自主权 extend the decision-making power of state-owned enterprises; expand the autonomy of state-owned enterprises /～财源 open up new sources of revenue /充分～战果 exploit a (military) victory fully; press one's (military) advantage home /～就业面 create more jobs (*or* job opportunities); enlarge (*or* increase) employment /～瞳孔 dilate the pupil of the eye /阅读可以使词汇量逐渐～。One's vocabulary can be gradually enlarged through reading.

扩大化 kuòdàhuà magnify or extend wrongly, unrealistically, or unnecessarily:"肃反"～ mistaken (*or* erroneous) extension of the campaign for eliminating counter-revolutionaries (to cover innocent people) /不要使事态～ not let the trouble (*or* problem) get out of hand; keep an incident (*or* accident) under control /如果把咱们之间的矛盾～,只能有利于敌人。It will only play into the hands of the enemy if we aggravate the contradictions among ourselves.

扩大会议 kuòdà huìyì enlarged meeting, session or conference:～的中央全会 enlarged session of the central committee (of a party, etc.)

扩大再生产 kuòdà zàishēngchǎn extended reproduction; ex-

panded reproduction

扩建 kuòjiàn extend (a factory, mine, hospital, etc.): 图书馆～工程 library extension (*or* enlargement) project / 大力～新兴工业基地 strive to extend new industrial bases / 商场大楼的～部分正在施工。The extension to the department store is under construction.

扩军 kuòjūn arms expansion: ～备战 arms expansion and war preparations / 重新～ rearmament

扩孔 kuòkǒng 〈机械〉reaming: ～钻头 reaming bit; reamer bit

扩容 kuòróng 〈计算机〉expand the capacity

扩散 kuòsàn spread; diffuse; proliferate: 谣言的～ spread of rumours / 有害气体的～ diffusion of harmful gases / 核～ nuclear proliferation / ～常数〈物理〉diffusion constant / ～频率〈物理〉diffusion frequency / ～函数〈数学〉spread function / 癌细胞已～。The cancer cells have already proliferated.

扩销 kuòxiāo expand sales: 羽绒制品现已～到许多山区。The sales of down products have been extended to many mountainous areas.

扩写 kuòxiě expand a short article into a long one with no change of the original meaning

扩胸 kuòxiōng expand one's chest: 吸气～ expand one's chest by inhaling (so as to measure one's chest expansion in a physical exam) / ～运动 physical exercises to expand one's chest; chest-expanding exercise

扩胸器 kuòxiōngqì *also* "拉力器" lālìqì chest developer; chest expander

扩音车 kuòyīnchē vehicle equipped with a public address system

扩音器 kuòyīnqì ❶ loudspeaker; microphone ❷ audio amplifier

扩印 kuòyìn enlarge and print a photo: 本店承接冲洗、～彩色照片业务。This studio undertakes developing, enlarging and printing of coloured photos.

扩展 kuòzhǎn extend; expand; spread; develop: 这条路已～到河边。The road has been extended to the riverside. / 运动场～了一倍。The playground is twice as big as it was in the past.

扩张 kuòzhāng ❶ expand; enlarge; extend; spread: 疆域～ territorial expansion (*or* aggrandizement) / 海外～ overseas expansionism; overseas aggrandizement / ～本派势力 expand one's faction ❷ 〈医学〉dilate: 血管～ blood vessel dilatation / ～器 dilator

扩张主义 kuòzhāngzhǔyì expansionism: ～政策 expansionist policy

阔(濶)

kuò ❶ wide; broad; vast: 广～的视野 wide field of vision; broad horizons / 宽～的马路 wide (*or* broad) street / 辽～的草原 vast grassland / ～边草帽 broad-brimmed straw hat / 海～天空 boundless sea and sky; unrestrained and far-ranging / 高谈～论 indulge in oratory; declaim; mouth high-sounding words; hold forth ❷ wealthy; rich: 显～ show off one's wealth / 他家里很～。He is from a very rich family.

阔别 kuòbié have been long separated; have not seen each other for quite some time: ～多年 have not seen each other for years (*or* ages) / 这是他第一次回到～了三十多年的故乡。This is the first time he has returned to his hometown since he left it more than 30 years ago.

阔步 kuòbù take big strides; stride: ～向前 stride forward; advance in giant strides / 昂首～ stride with one's chin up; stride proudly ahead

阔绰 kuòchuò extravagant; lavish; liberal with money: 手头～ be liberal with money; throw money about / 生活～ lead an extravagent (*or* lavish) life; live in clover

阔达 kuòdá 〈书面〉open-minded: 其人～多智。He is broad-minded and resourceful.

阔幅布 kuòfúbù broadcloth

阔幅平布 kuòfú píngbù sheeting: 本色～ grey sheeting

阔朗 kuòlǎng spacious and bright: 大厅～ big and bright hall

阔老 kuòlǎo *also* "阔佬" rich man; wealthy guy; moneybags: 远近闻名的～ well-known rich man / 充～ pretend to be wealthy

阔气 kuòqi extravagant; luxurious; lavish: 摆～ show off one's wealth; flaunt an ostentatious life-style / 这屋里的摆设好～! The house is so lavishly furnished!

阔人 kuòrén rich person; the rich: 游手好闲的～们 the idle rich

阔少 kuòshào wealthy man's son; young man from a rich family

阔野 kuòyě vast expanse of open country: ～无垠 boundless open country

阔叶树 kuòyèshù broadleaf tree

栝

kuò *see* "檃栝" yǐnkuò

see also guā

括

kuò ❶ tie (up); tighten up; contract (muscles, etc.): ～发 tie up one's hair / 紧～囊口 tighten up a bag ❷ include; comprise: 概～文章要点 give (*or* summarize) the main points of an article / 总～起来 to sum up; to put it in a nutshell / 每月房租四百元, 包～水、电和煤气。The monthly rent is 400 *yuan*, including water, electricity and gas. ❸ bracket: 把这句话～起来。Bracket the sentence.

see also guā

括号 kuòhào brackets (such as (), [ ], 〈 〉): 方～ square brackets / 尖～ angle brackets / ～里的数字 bracketed figure (*or* number) / 在～内写上正确答案。Write the correct answers in the brackets. / 给这个词打～。Put this word in brackets.

括弧 kuòhú parentheses: 注意～里的话。Pay attention to the words in parentheses.

括约肌 kuòyuējī 〈生理〉sphincter

括注 kuòzhù explanatory note in brackets: 请注意这句话后面的～。Take note of the explanation in brackets at the end of the sentence.

蛞

kuò

蛞蝼 kuòlóu 〈古语〉mole cricket

蛞蝓 kuòyú *also* "鼻涕虫" bítìchóng; "蜒蚰" yányóu slug

筈

kuò 〈书面〉arrow-tail

适(适)

kuò 〈书面〉(mainly used in personal names) fast; quick

K

L

lā

垃 lā

垃圾 lājī garbage; rubbish; refuse; trash: 倒～ dump rubbish; throw away garbage /捡～ collect (*or* pick up) rubbish; scavenge /～倾倒场 garbage dump; dumping ground /～分类收集 collection of classified (*or* sorted)garbage (*or* rubbish) /清除社会～ clear society of its trash /不要随地乱扔～。Please don't litter. *or* No littering. /此处禁止倒～。No dumping here.

垃圾车 lājīchē garbage truck; dust-cart

垃圾处理 lājī chǔlǐ garbage disposal; refuse treatment: ～场 garbage disposal plant; refuse treatment plant

垃圾袋 lājīdài trash or garbage bag

垃圾堆 lājīduī rubbish heap; garbage heap; refuse dump: 扫进历史的～ sweep onto the rubbish heap (*or* dustbin) of history

垃圾发电 lājī fādiàn garbage power

垃圾翻斗箱 lājī fāndǒuxiāng dumpster

垃圾焚化炉 lājī fénhuàlú garbage incinerator; garbage furnace

垃圾食品 lājī shípǐn junk food

垃圾桶 lājītǒng garbage can; trash can

垃圾箱 lājīxiāng dustbin; garbage can; ash can; trash can: 把饮料盒扔到～里, 别乱扔。Throw the cartons into the dustbin. Don't litter.

垃圾邮件 lājī yóujiàn junk mail

垃圾债券 lājī zhàiquàn junk bond

垃圾综合处理 lājī zōnghé chǔlǐ integrated garbage treatment

拉[1] lā ❶ pull; draw; drag; tug: ～车 pull a cart (*or* carriage) /～鱼网 draw a fishing net /～窗帘 draw a curtain /把孩子～进来 pull (*or* drag) the child in /～风箱 work the bellows /～紧绳套 tighten a noose /手～手 hand in hand /～了～他的袖子 pull him by the sleeve /～起手来 join hands (with sb.) /这门～不开。The door won't open. ❷ transport by vehicle; haul: 派车去～西瓜 send a truck for the watermelons /出租车～客人去香山。The taxi took the passenger to Fragrant Hill. /这车能～五十人。This bus can carry 50 passengers. ❸ move (troops to a place): 迅速把主力～出去 move the main force out immediately /把部队～到野外操练 move troops to open country for field training ❹ play (certain musical instruments): ～二胡 play the *erhu* fiddle /手风琴～得好 play the accordion well /你～过舒伯特的曲子吗? Have you played Schubert before? ❺ drag out; draw out; space out: ～长了调子说话 speak in a drawn-out voice; drawl /战线～得太长 with one's line of defence drawn out too long (*or* over-extended) /不要把短篇～长为中篇。Don't drag (*or* draw) out a short story into a novella. ❻〈方言〉bring up: 母亲好不容易把他～大。His mother had a tough time bringing him up. ❼ give or lend a hand; help: 我处境艰难, 请～我一把! I am in difficulty; please help! ❽ drag in; implicate; involve: ～我当垫背的 make me a scapegoat /～替身儿〈迷信〉(of a ghost which would be reincarnated if it found a substitute) find a substitute for one in the netherworld; find sb. who can take over one's drudgery or who can suffer for one /好汉做事好汉当, 我绝不～别人。As a true man, I'll take sole responsibility for what I did without involving anybody else. ❾ draw or drag in; win over: ～为己用 win sb. over to work for one /～一派打一派 try to win over one faction while attacking another; draw in one faction and hit out at another ❿ organize; set up; put together: ～团伙 form a gang /～起一支游击队 organize a guerrilla force ⓫ canvass; solicit: ～广告 solicit advertisements (from companies, etc.) /～主顾 solicit customers (*or* clients) /～选票 canvass for votes; canvass /～赞助 canvass for contributions (*or* sponsors) ⓬〈方言〉chat; engage in chitchat: 今晚无事, 咱俩～～吧。Let's have a chat tonight as we're free. ⓭ press; pressgang: ～壮丁 forcibly conscript; pressgang into military service ⓮〈体育〉lift: 把球～起来 lift the ball ⓯ (Lā) *short for Latin America or Latin*: ～美 Latin America /亚、非、～ Asia, Africa and Latin America

拉[2] lā have a bowel movement; empty the bowels: ～屎 empty the bowels; shit /～痢疾 suffer from dysentery /又吐又～ throw up and have loose bowels; suffer from vomiting and diarrhoea /上午～了几次? How many times did you have a bowel movement this morning?

see also lá; lǎ; là

拉巴斯 Lābāsī La Paz, capital of Bolivia

拉巴特 Lābātè Rabat, capital of Morocco

拉巴 lāba 〈方言〉❶ take pains to bring up (a child): 她一个寡妇人家, ～几个孩子, 也真不易啊。It was hard for a widow like her to bring up several children. ❷ help and support; help (one's protégé) to advance: 刚工作时, 我什么都不懂, 多亏有师傅～我。I was lucky to have my master's help when I was a new hand and knew nothing about my job.

拉拔 lābá 〈机械〉drawing: ～机 drawbench; coil winder /～应力 drawing stress

拉帮结伙 lābāng-jiéhuǒ *also* "拉帮结派" band together; form a clique; engage in factional activities: ～, 制造分裂 engage in factional activities and create divisions

拉帮 lābang 〈方言〉❶ bring up: 我从小失去父母, 是奶奶把我～大的。I was orphaned as a child and brought up by grandma. ❷ support; help: ～穷人 help the poor

拉包月 lā bāoyuè 〈旧语〉(of rickshaw pullers or pedicab drivers) be hired (and paid) by the month; work exclusively for sb. on a monthly basis

拉鼻儿 lābír 〈口语〉sound a siren; blow a whistle

拉卜楞寺 Lābǔléngsì Labrang Monastery, well-known Lamaist temple in Xiahe County (夏河县) of Gansu Province

拉不下脸 lābuxià liǎn find oneself unable to do sth. (for fear of hurting sb.'s feelings, etc.); cannot bring oneself to do sth.: 想不借给他, 可又～来。Though I did not want to lend him the money, I just couldn't bring myself to say so.

拉铲挖土机 lāchǎn wātǔjī 〈机械〉dragline

拉长脸 lā chángliǎn pull a long face; look glum: 她一听这话, 立刻～, 满肚子不高兴。She immediately pulled a long face at the remark, not at all pleased. /他见大门关上了, 气得瘦脸拉得长长的, 像个丧门神。Seeing the gate closed, he looked like a funeral door-god, with his face stiffening with anger.

拉长线 lā chángxiàn pull a long line — adopt a long-term plan; employ long-term tactics: ～, 钓大鱼 pull a long line to catch a big fish — adopt a long-term plan to secure sth. big

拉场 lāchǎng 〈旧语〉(of supporting actors in traditional operas) intentionally prolong one's performance on stage (before the leading actor or actress, who is late, is ready)

拉场戏 lāchǎngxì song and dance opera, a variety of traditional opera derived from *errenzhuan* (二人转)

拉场子 lā chǎngzi ❶ put on an acrobatic or some other show in a street or marketplace ❷ put on a show to establish or spread one's

reputation; make a name:明晚我就给你请客～。I'll give a dinner tomorrow night so people will get to know you. /他虽新来乍到,但凭一手绝活一下子就拉开了场子。Though he was a stranger, he made a name for himself with his superb skill almost overnight.

拉扯 lāche ❶ drag; pull; tug:拉拉扯扯,打打闹闹 pull at each other and kick up a din /小姑娘～着妈妈的衣服,羞怯地站在一边。The little girl stood shyly beside her mother, pulling at her clothes. /我上前去拉架,怎么也～不开。I went up to stop them fighting but couldn't separate them at all. /别拉拉扯扯的,让别人看见多不好。Take your hands off me. What would people say if they saw us like this? ❷ take pains to bring up:这孩子是他爷爷、奶奶～大的。The child was brought up by its grandparents. ❸ help and support; promote:要不是老院长有心～你,你也不会有今天。You wouldn't be as successful as you are today but for the old president's help and support. /这小伙子很有出息。你当师傅的要特别～他一把。The young man is very promising. As his master you should give him a leg up. ❹ gang up with; rope in:吃吃喝喝、拉拉扯扯 wine and dine, and exchange flatteries and favours /同不三不四的人～在一起 gang up (*or* hang around) with dubious characters /工作中要讲原则,不要拉拉扯扯。It is essential to stick to principles in one's work and keep clear of cliques and favouritism. ❺ drag in; implicate:你的事,把我～进去干嘛? It's your business. Why should you drag me in? /放心吧,我不会～你们的。Don't worry. I won't get any of you involved. ❻ chat; chit-chat:东拉西扯 talk at random; ramble on and on /我太忙,没工夫跟你～。I'm too busy to chit-chat with you.

拉抽屉 lā chōuti 〈口语〉 go back on one's word; break one's promise:一言为定,你可不许～。That is settled, and you mustn't back out of it later.

拉床 lāchuáng 〈机械〉 broaching machine:～工 broacher

拉吹 lāchuī 〈方言〉 *see* "拉倒"

拉大片 lā dàpiān *see* "拉洋片"

拉大旗,作虎皮 lā dàqí, zuò hǔpí use a great banner as a tiger-skin — drape oneself in a tiger-skin to intimidate people; deck oneself out to cow people; use a great name as one's scarecrow:年轻人要自己奋斗,不要去～。Young people should rely on themselves and never try to use other people's names to further their own interests.

拉搭 lāda 〈方言〉 chit-chat:他俩边吃边～起来。They chatted over the meal.

拉刀 lādāo 〈机械〉 broach:～磨床 broach grinding machine

拉倒 lādǎo *also* "拉吹" forget about it; leave it at that; drop it:要就要,不要就～。Take it, or leave it. /你不借就～,我找别人借去。If you don't want to lend it to me, forget about it. I'll borrow it from somebody else.

拉道 lādào 〈方言〉 show the way; act as a guide:天黑路不好走,我给你们拉个道吧。Since it is dark and the road is rough, let me show you the way.

拉道 lādao 〈方言〉 chat; chit-chat:她们一见面就～开了。They began to chit-chat as soon as they met.

拉德 lādé 〈物理〉 (unit for measuring absorbed radiation) rad:～辐透 radphot

拉蒂迈鱼 lādìmàiyú *Latimeria chalumnae*

拉丁 lādīng ❶〈旧语〉 press-gang able-bodied men into military service ❷ force people into service ❸ (Lādīng) Latin:～民族 Latinic people (*or* nation) /～教会〈基督教〉 Latin Church /～化 Latinize

拉丁美洲 Lādīng Měizhōu Latin America:～人 Latin American; Latino /～共同市场 Latin American Common Market (LACM) /～经济委员会 Economic Commission for Latin America /～自由贸易区 Latin American Free Trade Zone

拉丁文 Lādīngwén Latin (language)

拉丁字母 Lādīng zìmǔ Latin or Roman letter: ～表 Latin alphabet; Roman alphabet

拉肚子 lā dùzi 〈口语〉 have loose bowels; have diarrhoea

拉队伍 lā duìwu raise a force; form a band:他在家乡拉起一支队伍,竖起抗日的大旗。He raised a force in his hometown and hoisted the great anti-Japanese banner. /听说县里委托他办搪瓷厂,已经拉起了百多人的队伍。I heard that in order to set up an enamel factory, as entrusted by the county authorities, he had recruited over a hundred people.

拉斐尔 Lāfěi'ěr Sanzio Raphael (1483-1520), Italian painter

拉夫 lāfū 〈旧语〉 press-gang or force people to serve as coolies (for an army, etc.):乱军四下里～,老百姓只好躲进了山里。As mutinous troops press-ganged coolies wherever they went, local people all fled to the mountains.

拉幅机 lāfújī 〈纺织〉 stenter; tenter

拉盖罐头 lāgài guàntou zip-top tin; tab-pull can

拉杆 lāgān 〈机械〉 ❶ pull rod; drag link; draw bar; tension link: ～螺母 pull-rod nut /～螺栓 stay bolt /～弹簧 pull-rod spring /～牵引力 drawbar pull /～拖车 drawbar-trailer /～式装载机 tension bar loader ❷ telescopic:～三角支架 tripod with telescopic legs; telescopic tripod

拉杆天线 lāgān tiānxiàn telescopic antenna or aerial

拉歌 lāgē invite or challenge (others) to sing:先到的两个组正在相互～儿。The two groups that came first are now challenging (*or* urging) each other to sing.

拉格朗日 Lāgélǎngrì Joseph-Louis Lagrange (1736-1813), French-Italian mathematician

拉格朗日点 Lāgélǎngrìdiǎn 〈天文〉 Lagrangian point

拉格朗日函数 Lāgélǎngrì hánshù Lagrangian function

拉各斯 Lāgèsī Lagos, capital of Nigeria

拉钩 lāgōu ❶ (of two people) hook up the little fingers of each other's right hands and give them a pull in token of good faith:你们俩～和好吧。You two had better shake hands and make up. ❷〈机械〉 drag hook; draw hook

拉呱儿 lāguǎr 〈方言〉 chat; chit-chat:歇晌时,几个老头凑在地头～。Some old men chatted at the edge of the field during the break.

拉关系 lā guānxi 〈贬义〉 try to establish a relationship (with sb. useful); cultivate; network; cotton up to:拉老乡关系 claim a special relationship (with sb.) as fellow-townsmen /拉同学关系 claim old school ties /咱们不靠～、走后门办事。We don't get things done by cultivating useful people and receiving favours from them. /这几年,他四处～,跑买卖,赚了不少钱。In recent years he's established business relations everywhere and made pots of money. /他们的推销员跟进出口公司拉上了关系。Their salesman has cottoned up to the import and export company.

拉管 lāguǎn ❶ (popular name for 长号) trombone ❷〈冶金〉 draw tubes

拉管机 lāguǎnjī tube-drawing machine

拉鼾 lāhān 〈方言〉 snore

拉合尔 Lāhé'ěr Lahore, second largest city of Pakistan

拉后腿 lā hòutuǐ *also* "扯后腿" chě hòutuǐ hold sb. back; be a drag on sb.:参军是件好事,家里人不会拉我的后腿。It is a good thing for me to join the army; my family won't hold me back. /要不是有老婆、孩子～,他早就闯了关东。He would have gone to the Northeast but for his wife and children.

拉祜族 Lāhùzú Lahu nationality, living in Yunnan Province

拉花儿 lāhuār festoons:纸～ festoons; paper garlands

拉话 lāhuà 〈方言〉 chat; chit-chat:有空就来拉拉话。Come and have a chat whenever you are free.

拉环罐 lāhuánguàn *also* "易拉罐" yìlāguàn ring-pull tin; pop-top can

拉簧 lāhuáng 〈机械〉 draw spring; tension spring; extension spring

拉魂腔 lāhúnqiāng *also* "泗州戏" sìzhōuxì Sizhou opera, popular in the Huaihe River area

拉火 lāhuǒ ❶〈方言〉 blow a fire with the help of a bellows ❷ detonate:他找了个爆破筒但不知在哪儿～。He found a bangalore torpedo but didn't know how to detonate it.

拉火绳 lāhuǒshéng 〈军事〉 lanyard

拉饥荒 lā jīhuang 〈口语〉 be in debt; get or run into debt:拉了不少饥荒 get into a mountain of debts /这个月家里开销大,怕是要～了。I'm afraid we'll run into debt this month as we've spent more than usual.

拉挤 lājǐ 〈冶金〉 pultrusion

拉家常 lā jiācháng chat about homely things; chit-chat:女县长与老大娘坐在炕头上～。The woman county magistrate was chit-chatting with the old lady sitting on the edge of the *kang*.

拉家带口 lājiā-dàikǒu have a family to provide for; be burdened with a family:李师傅～的,身体又有病,日子过得紧巴巴的。Master Li has a family to provide for and is in poor health, so he lives on a shoestring /我～的,不能和你们比,单身一人说走就走。Burdened with a family, I cannot just pull up stakes and leave any time I like, as you bachelors can.

拉架 lājià try to stop a brawl by separating the brawlers; try to

L

stop people from fighting each other:院子里～的,看热闹的,乱成了一团。The courtyard was a madhouse, with those who tried to stop the fight and those who looked on milling around the brawlers. /要不是你赶来～,他们早打得不可开交了。They would have been locked in a fierce fight if you hadn't come in time to stop them.

拉交情 lā jiāoqing 〈贬义〉claim friendship with; cultivate; cotton up to:我和他平日有些往来,为了办成这件事,只好去拉拉交情了。I have some contacts with him, and the only thing to do now is to use them to get this done.

拉脚 lājiǎo transport or carry passengers or goods by cart:他下工后又去码头～,赚几个钱补贴家用。After work he went to the dock to transport goods by cart so as to eke out a living.

拉近乎 lā jìnhu *also*"套近乎"tào jìnhu 〈贬义〉cultivate (unfamiliar people); try to get in with; cotton up to:你少跟我～,这事不行就是不行。Don't try to get in with me; if it's not right then that's all there is to it! /谁当了他的领导他就跟谁～。He cottons up to whoever is his superior.

拉锯 lājù ❶ work a two-handed saw:父子俩正在院子里～破木头。Father and son were cutting a log with a two-handed saw in the courtyard. ❷ be locked in back-and-forth warfare; fight a seesaw battle:～地带 area which frequently changes hands in a war; scene of a seesaw battle

拉锯战 lājùzhàn seesaw battle

拉开 lākāi ❶ pull open; draw back:～门 pull the door open /～抽屉 open the drawer /～窗帘 draw aside (*or* back) the curtain /～架式 get into a ready posture (for fighting) /～序幕 raise the curtains on (a performance, etc.); start (a battle or game) /～嗓门就喊 start shouting at the top of one's voice /两个孩子打起来了,快把他们～。The two children are fighting. Separate them immediately. ❷ widen; space out:～档次 widen the gaps (*or* differences) between different grades (of commodities, etc.) /～比分 widen the gap between the scores (of two competitors) /把比分～到18比8 pull away to 18-8; increase one's lead to 18-8 /～距离 increase the distance (as between marchers in a single file or competitors in a race); space out /两人之间设法～距离。The two men are trying to distance themselves from each other. /随着市场的成熟,商品的质量差价逐渐～。As a market matures, price differentials for goods of different qualities widen.

拉客 lākè ❶ (of hotels, restaurants, etc.) solicit customers or clients ❷ (of pedicab riders, taxidrivers, etc.) carry passengers ❸ (of prostitutes) solicit patrons; streetwalk

拉亏空 lā kuīkong get or run into debt; be in debt:这批货物卖不出去,眼看要～了。We'll run into debt soon, as this batch of goods doesn't sell well. /那几年,他四下里～,欠了一屁股债。In those years he borrowed right and left and was head over heels (*or* up to his ears) in debt.

拉拉队 lālāduì cheering squad; rooters:～长 cheer leader; yell leader; rooter king /～员 rooter

拉力 lālì pulling force; tension:～千斤顶 pulling jack /～试验〈机械〉pull (*or* tension) test /～表 draw-bar (*or* pull) dynamometer /～仪 tensimeter; tensometer /～弹簧 tension spring; draught spring /这套哑铃操可以锻炼双臂的～。This set of dumbbell exercises helps to increase the pulling force (*or* strength) of one's arms.

拉力器 lālìqì *also*"扩胸器"kuòxiōngqì chest-developer; chest expander

拉力赛 lālìsài 〈体育〉(cross-country) rally

拉练 lāliàn camp and field training:长途～ camp and field training including long-distance marching

拉链 lāliàn zip fastener; zipper:把～拉上 fasten a zipper; zip up/～袋 ziploc bag

拉拢 lālǒng draw over to one's side; win over; rope in:～感情 win over by appealing to people's sentiments; curry favour (with sb.) /～腐蚀干部 woo and corrupt officials /～亲信,排斥异己 rope in trusted followers and exclude those who have different views

拉马克 Lāmǎkè Jean-Baptiste de Monet Lamarck (1744-1829), French biologist:～学说 Lamarckism

拉玛古猿 Lāmǎ gǔyuán *also*"腊玛古猿"Làmǎ gǔyuán *Ramapithecus* (anthropoid ape, living some 10-14 million years ago, whose fossils were found at Lama County, Yunnan Province)

拉买卖 lā mǎimai *also*"拉生意" solicit business; canvass (business) orders; drum up trade:亏了他四处～,不然公司这个月要亏本。If it were not for his sales effectiveness, the company would have suffered a loss this month.

拉毛 lāmáo *also*"拉绒" nap; gig:～围巾 nap scarf

拉美 Lāměi (short for 拉丁美洲) Latin America:～人 Latino; Latin American /～问题专家 expert on Latin American affairs; Latin Americanist

拉美社 Lāměishè *Prensa Latina* (PL)

拉门 lāmén sliding door

拉面 lāmiàn *also*"抻面"chěnmiàn 〈方言〉hand-pulled noodles

拉磨床 lāmóchuáng 〈机械〉broach grinder

拉模 lāmú 〈机械〉drawing die:～孔 drawing pass /～板 draw plate; die plate; drawing plate

拉尼娜 Lānínà 〈气象〉La Nina (Spanish meaning "the little girl", a natural phenomenon characterized by abnormally cold ocean conditions in the Eastern Pacific)

拉皮条 lā pítiáo 〈方言〉act as a pimp; pander; procure:～的 pimp; procurer

拉偏手儿 lā piānshǒur *also*"拉偏架" show partiality to one side when apparently stopping a brawl; try to help one party while appearing to stop a quarrel

拉平 lāpíng ❶ bring to the same level; even up:把比分～ even up the scores /～收入 even up incomes ❷〈航空〉flare-out; flatten-out:～操纵 flare control

拉普拉斯 Lāpǔlāsī Pierre Simon de Laplace (1749-1827), French astronomer and mathematician:～定律 Laplace's law /～算子 Laplace operator; Laplacian

拉纤 lāqiàn ❶ tow a boat:那几年他在黄河边上～,吃够了苦。He suffered a great deal in those years when he worked as a boat tracker along the Yellow River. ❷ act as go-between or middleman:保媒～ act as go-between in arranging a marriage; make a match /为人～ serve as sb.'s broker or middleman; lobby on sb.'s behalf; canvass for sb.

拉橇狗 lāqiāogǒu sled dog

拉青丹 lāqīngdān 〈方言〉suffer from diarrhoea; have loose bowels

拉绒 lāróng *also*"拉毛"〈纺织〉nap; gig; tease:～厂 gig mill /～机 gig; napper /～毛毯 raised blanket

拉萨 Lāsà Lhasa, capital of the Tibet Autonomous Region

拉萨河 Lāsàhé Lhasa River, tributary of the Yarlung Zangbo (雅鲁藏布江) in the Tibet Autonomous Region

拉撒 lāsa *also*"拉飒"〈方言〉refuse; garbage

拉三扯四 lāsān-chěsì talk irrelevantly; wander from the subject; ramble:讲话要切题,不要～。You should speak to the point, and not wander from the subject.

拉散车 lā sǎnchē *also*"拉散座"〈旧语〉(of rickshaw pullers or pedicab drivers) carry any passengers as they come (instead of working for an employer on a regular basis)

拉山头 lā shāntóu form a faction:你这样做不是存心～,破坏团结吗? You're deliberately forming a faction and disrupting unity by doing so, aren't you?

拉伤 lāshāng injure by straining; pull:～腿部肌肉 pull a leg muscle

拉梢 lāshāo pull a cart in front or by the shaft

拉舌头 lā shétou 〈方言〉gossip; backbite; slander:不要四下～,散布流言蜚语。Don't gossip behind people's backs and spread rumours.

拉伸 lāshēn stretch; draw:～机 stretcher /～压力机 drawing press /～卷曲 crimp by stretching /～矫直〈冶金〉stretcher levelling (*or* straightening)/～试验 tensile test; elongation test /～弹性 tensile elasticity /～强度 tensile strength /～形变 tensile deformation

拉生意 lā shēngyi *also*"拉买卖" drum up trade

拉屎拉尿 lāshǐ-lāniào 〈口语〉piss and shit;〈比喻〉do whatever one pleases in a despotic manner; ride roughshod over:我可不让人在我头上～。I will never let anybody treat me like shit.

拉氏 Lāshì (short for 拉普拉斯) Laplace:～变换 Laplace transformation

拉手 lāshǒu shake hands:他上前与主人～致意。He went up to the host and shook hands with him.

拉手 lāshou handle:门～ doorknob; door handle /抽屉～ drawer-pull

拉丝 lāsī wiredrawing:～机 wiredrawing machine /～模 wiredrawing die

拉斯维加斯 Lāsīwéijiāsī Las Vegas, gambling city in Nevada,

US

拉索 lāsuǒ 〈机械〉dragline; stretching wire: ～装载机 dragline loader

拉锁 lāsuǒ *also* "拉链" zip fastener; zipper

拉谈 lātán 〈方言〉chat; chit-chat

拉套 lātào ❶ *also* "拉梢" pull a cart: ～的是匹黑马。The carriage was pulled by a black horse. ❷〈方言〉do one's best to help; slave (for sb. else): 这几年我没少替他～出力,他心里不是不清楚。He knows very well that I've slaved for him all these years.

拉条 lātiáo 〈机械〉brace; stay: ～皮带 thoroughbrace /斜～ batter brace /链～ chain stay

拉腿 lātuǐ 〈方言〉hold sb. back (from action); be a drag on sb.

拉脱维亚 Lātuōwéiyà Latvia: ～人 Latvian

拉瓦尔品第 Lāwǎ'ěrpǐndì Rawalpindi, major city and capital of Pakistan from 1959 to 1969

拉弯 lāwān 〈冶金〉stretch bending: ～机 stretch benders

拉弯子 lā wānzi 〈方言〉mediate; reconcile

拉晚儿 lāwǎnr 〈方言〉❶〈旧语〉(of ricksaw pullers) work at night ❷ indulge in night life

拉网 lāwǎng ❶ pull a fishing net out of water; draw or haul in a net: ～机 net puller ❷ tighten a ring of encirclement; close in (on the besieged)

拉稀 lāxī 〈口语〉have loose bowels; have diarrhoea

拉下脸 lāxia liǎn 〈口语〉❶ not spare sb.'s sensibilities: 我～来跟你说吧,这事我不能替你办。To be perfectly candid, I can't do it for you. /他想责备她几句,但又拉不下脸来。He wanted to scold her, but just couldn't bring himself to do it. *or* Though he wanted to reproach her, he was reluctant (*or* afraid) to hurt her feelings. ❷ look displeased; pull a long face; put on a stern expression: 被人当众抢白了几句,她一下子～来。She looked displeased at being reproved in public.

拉下马 lāxia mǎ pull off the horse; 〈比喻〉pull down from a powerful or high position; cause to fall from power: 他们经过一年多的调查,终于查清案情,把包庇罪犯的大官拉下了马。It took them over a year's investigations to get to the bottom of the case and pull down the high official who shielded the criminals. /舍得一身剐,敢把皇帝～。〈谚语〉He who is not afraid of death by a thousand cuts dares to unhorse the emperor. *or* A desperate (*or* fearless) person would go to any lengths.

拉下水 lāxia shuǐ 〈比喻〉drag into the mire or mud; make an accomplice of; corrupt: 被人用金钱、美女～ be ensnared and corrupted by money and women /他请你吃吃喝喝,我看是想把你～。I think he wants to make an accomplice of you by inviting you to wine and dine with him.

拉闲篇 lā xiánpiān 〈方言〉chat; chit-chat: 别～,快干活吧! Stop chatting. Let's get down to work.

拉线 lāxiàn act as go-between: 他俩交朋友是我拉的线。I introduced them to each other before they began dating.

拉线搭桥 lāxiàn-dāqiáo *also* "牵线搭桥" qiānxiàn-dāqiáo pull wires and build bridges — act as go-between or facilitator: 为大男大女～ act as matchmaker for single men and women over the normal matrimonial age /为人才流动～ do one's best to facilitate the circulation of talented people

拉线开关 lāxiàn kāiguān 〈电工〉pullswitch

拉线器 lāxiànqì wire grip

拉削 lāxiāo 〈机械〉broaching

拉延 lāyán *also* "拉制"〈机械〉draw (a tube, wire, etc.); stretch: ～工序 drawing operation /～模 drawing die /～压力机 drawing (*or* stretching) press

拉秧 lāyāng 〈农业〉uproot plants after their edible portions have been harvested: ～西瓜 last crop of watermelons (from a plot or field)

拉洋片 lā yángpiān *also* "拉大片" conduct peepshows with singing and commentary

拉硬弓 lā yìnggōng 〈口语〉get tough (with sb.); do (sth.) by force: 他要是跟我～,我也不怕他。I won't be afraid of him, even if he gets tough with me.

拉运 lāyùn transport by vehicle: ～钢材 transport rolled steel

拉杂 lāzá rambling, jumbled, ill-organized: 这样～的文章怎么能让读者爱看呢? How can a reader become interested in such a jumbled article? /拉拉杂杂就谈这么多,请大家批评指正。That's all I can say, such as it is. Your comments and criticisms are welcome. *or* I'm afraid I've rambled on, so please make any comments and criticisms you like.

拉闸 lāzhá switch off power or electricity

拉仗 lāzhàng 〈方言〉*see* "拉架"

拉账 lāzhàng be in debt; get or run into debt: 月月～,这日子还怎么过啊? We get further into debt with every month. How can we live on like this? /市场不景气,公司拉下了好些账。As the market remains sluggish, the company has run into heavy debt.

拉制 lāzhì *see* "拉延"

拉座儿 lāzuòr (of rickshaw pullers or pedicab riders) carry passengers; solicit clients: 在戏院门口～ solicit passengers in front of a theatre

啦 lā

see also la

啦呱儿 lāguǎr *also* "拉呱儿" lāguǎr chit-chat; chat

啦啦队 lālāduì *also* "拉拉队" lālāduì cheering squad; rooters

喇 lā *see* "哇喇" wālā; "呼喇" hūlā

see also lá; lǎ

旮 lā *see* "旮旮" kēla

邋 lā

邋里邋遢 lālilāta slovenly; sloppy; unkempt: 瞧你这一身打扮,～的! Look how slovenly you are!

邋遢 lāta slovenly; sloppy; unkempt; messy; 团长是个极其严谨的人,容不得半点～。Being a taskmaster, the regimental commander just couldn't tolerate any slovenliness. /他衣着～,可工作还挺上心。He is attentive in his work though unkempt in his dress.

lá

砬(磖) lá (mainly used in place names) big rock: 红石～ *Hongshila* (Red Crag, a place in Hebei Province)

砬子 lázi 〈方言〉(mainly used in place names) big rock: 白石～ *Baishilazi* (White Crag, a place in Heilongjiang Province)

拉(剌) lá slash; slit; cut; gash: ～玻璃 cut glass /～开皮子 slit leather /～了手 cut one's hand; get a cut on the hand /～双眼皮 have plastic surgery on one's eyelids (to make them double-fold) /把扁桃腺～掉 have one's tonsils removed

see also lā; lǎ; là

揦 lá

揦子 lázi 〈方言〉glass bottle

喇 lá *see* "哈喇子" hālázi

see also lā; lǎ

旯 lá *see* "旮旯儿" gālár

lǎ

拉 lǎ

see also lā; lá; là

拉忽 lǎhu 〈方言〉careless; negligent: 拉拉忽忽 careless; slovenly; sloppy /你怎么这么～,走时连门都忘了锁。How could you be so careless? You forgot to lock the door when you left.

喇 lǎ

see also lā; lá

喇叭 lǎba ❶ trumpet or any similar brasswind instrument (such as *suona*, a traditional wind instrument): 吹～ blow a trumpet; play the *suona* /～口 bell (of a wind instrument) ❷ loudspeaker; horn (of a vehicle): 高音～ tweeter /汽车～ horn (in a car) /～按钮 horn button /把广播～打开 turn on the loudspeaker

喇叭虫 lǎbachóng stentor

喇叭管 lǎbaguǎn 〈生理〉fallopian tube
喇叭花 lǎbahuā 〈口语〉(white-edged) morning glory
喇叭裤 lǎbakù flared trousers; bell-bottoms
喇叭鸟 lǎbaniǎo trumpeter; trumpet bird
喇叭裙 lǎbaqún flared skirt
喇叭筒 lǎbatǒng 〈口语〉❶ megaphone ❷ microphone
喇叭形天线 lǎbaxíng tiānxiàn 〈无线电〉box horn; horn antenna
喇嘛 lǎma lama:～庙 lamasery /黄帽～ yellow-hat lama
喇嘛教 Lǎmajiào Lamaism:～徒 lamaist; lamaite

là

落 là ❶ leave out; be missing:这句话～了一个字。A word is missing from this sentence. /点名时小心别～了人头。Take care not to miss any name when calling the roll. /她真有福气,什么好事都～不下她。She is such a lucky person that she never misses out on anything good. ❷ leave behind; forget to bring:糟糕,我把电影票～在家里了。It's just too bad. I left my cinema ticket at home. ❸ lag or fall behind:到拐弯处,这位选手已～下了十来米。The competitor was over a dozen metres behind when he reached the turn in the road. /他～了三天的作业。He's three days behind with his homework. /你一定要把～下的课补上。You must make up for the lessons you've missed.
see also lào; luō; luò

蜡(蠟) là ❶ wax:蜂～ beeswax /石～ paraffin wax /白～ white wax; insect wax /发～ pomade /给地板打～ wax (*or* polish) the floor ❷ candle:点上～ light a candle /～头儿 stump of a candle /瞎子点灯白费～。〈俗语〉A blind man using a candle — a sheer waste.
see also zhà
蜡白 làbái (of one's face) colourless; pale:脸色～ look ashen
蜡板 làbǎn ❶ small wax scale (on the belly of a honey bee) ❷ tool for making white wax
蜡版 làbǎn mimeograph stencil (already cut):刻～ cut a stencil
蜡版术 làbǎnshù cerography
蜡笔 làbǐ wax crayon; colour crayon:～画 crayon drawing
蜡布 làbù cerecloth
蜡虫 làchóng *also* "白蜡虫" báilàchóng wax insect
蜡床 làchuáng tool for making white wax
蜡防印花 làfáng yìnhuā 〈纺织〉batik:～布 wax print; batik /～法 batik
蜡封 làfēng wax-sealed:～文书 wax-sealed document
蜡膏 làgāo 〈药学〉cerate
蜡光纸 làguāngzhǐ glazed paper
蜡果 làguǒ 〈工美〉wax fruit
蜡花 làhuā snuff of a candle:她小心地拨去了～,屋里顿时亮了许多。As she snuffed the candle carefully, the room instantly became much brighter.
蜡画 làhuà encaustic (painting)
蜡黄 làhuáng wax-yellow; waxen; sallow:一场大病后,他脸色～,瘦了许多。After a serious illness he looked sallow and was much thinner than before.
蜡菊 làjú 〈植物〉strawflower
蜡炬 làjù 〈书面〉candle:春蚕到死丝方尽,～成灰泪始干。The spring silkworm will only end its thread when death befalls; The candle will always drip with tears until it turns to ashes.
蜡泪 làlèi dripping or guttering of a candle; drips from a burning candle
蜡疗 làliáo 〈医学〉waxtherapy
蜡料植物 làliào zhíwù wax crop
蜡梅 làméi *also* "腊梅" làméi 〈植物〉wintersweet (*Chimonanthus praecox*)
蜡模 làmó 〈冶金〉wax matrix; investment:～铸造法 investment casting
蜡泥 làní plasticine
蜡皮 làpí *also* "蜡皮子" 〈中药〉wax coating (of a pill)
蜡扦 làqiān candlestick
蜡染 làrǎn 〈纺织〉wax printing:～布 wax print; batik
蜡人 làrén waxwork; wax figure; wax doll:～馆 wax figure museum
蜡熟 làshú *also* "黄熟" huángshú 〈农业〉yellow maturity
蜡塑 làsù 〈工美〉ceroplastic; wax sculpture:～术 ceroplastics
蜡酸 làsuān 〈化工〉cerotic acid
蜡台 làtái candleholder; candlestand
蜡丸 làwán ❶ hollow waxball, containing a pill or a secret message ❷ wax-coated pill
蜡像 làxiàng wax statue; wax figure:～馆 waxworks museum; waxworks /伦敦～陈列馆 Madame Tussaud's in London
蜡缬 làxié (old term for 蜡染) wax printing
蜡印 làyìn wax seal
蜡油 làyóu dripping from a burning candle
蜡渣子 làzhāzi broken bits of candle:～黄 (of one's face) waxen-yellow; sallow /～白 (of one's face) waxen pale; pallid
蜡纸 làzhǐ ❶ waxed paper:用～包着 wrapped in waxed paper ❷ stencil paper; stencil:刻～ cut a stencil
蜡制品 làzhìpǐn waxwork
蜡珠 làzhū *see* "蜡泪"
蜡烛 làzhú candle:～芯儿 candlewick /～台 candleholder; candlestand /吹灭～ blow out a candle /把～插在生日蛋糕上 insert candles in a birthday cake /～不点不亮。〈俗语〉A candle will not burn without being lighted — some people have to be made to do things.
蜡嘴雀 làzuǐquè hawfinch

腊(臘、臈) là ❶ ancient practice of offering sacrifices to the gods in the twelfth month of the lunar year; (hence the) twelfth lunar month:～尽春回 spring returns after the 12th lunar month is over ❷ (of fish, meat, etc.) cured in winter, esp. in the twelfth lunar month:～鱼 cured fish ❸ (Là) a surname
see also xī
腊八 làbā eighth day of the twelfth lunar month (on which, as a tradition, rice porridge with nuts and dried fruit is served)
腊八醋 làbācù *laba* vinegar (vinegar with garlic soaked in it, generally made on the eighth day of the twelfth lunar month and eaten when the garlic has turned dark)
腊八豆 làbādòu beans used in *laba* porridge (such as red beans, kidney beans, peas, cow peas, etc.)
腊八米 làbāmǐ rice, glutinous rice, millet, glutinous millet, sorghum and other cereals used in *laba* porridge
腊八蒜 làbāsuàn garlic preserved in *laba* vinegar
腊八粥 làbāzhōu *laba* porridge (porridge made with cereals, beans, nuts and dried fruit, eaten on the eighth day of the twelfth lunar month)
腊肠 làcháng sausage
腊肥 làféi manure applied to wheat or other winter crops between the Winter Solstice and "Great Cold"
腊克 làkè (transliteration, same as 清喷漆) lacquer
腊玛古猿 Làmǎ gǔyuán *also* "拉玛古猿" Lāmǎ gǔyuán *Ramapithecus*
腊梅 làméi 〈植物〉wintersweet (*Chimonanthus praecox*)
腊日 làrì day of winter sacrifice, usu. the eighth day of the twelfth lunar month
腊肉 làròu cured meat; bacon
腊味 làwèi cured meat, fish, etc.
腊月 làyuè twelfth month of the lunar year; twelfth moon:寒冬～ severe winter

辣 là ❶ peppery; hot; pungent:辛～ pungent; hot /酸甜苦～ sour, sweet, bitter and hot /～婆娘〈比喻〉impetuous and overbearing woman; termagant /他胃不好,不能吃～的。Hot food is not good for his weak stomach. ❷ (of smell or taste) burn; bite; sting: 这佐料～得我舌头发麻。The hot flavouring burned my tongue. /切葱时别～了眼睛。When you chop Chinese onions, try not to get their strong sting in your eyes. /他咬了一口蒜,～得直流眼泪。No sooner had he bitten off a piece of garlic than tears started rolling down his cheeks. ❸ vicious; ruthless:手段～ vicious and ruthless means; wicked and cruel method /口甜心～ sweet-mouthed and wicked-hearted; hypocritical and malignant
辣瓣儿酱 làbànrjiàng thick chilli sauce with fermented broad beans
辣不唧 làbujī slightly hot; somewhat pungent:一碟～儿的四川泡菜 a dish of pleasantly pungent Sichuan pickles
辣根 làgēn 〈植物〉horseradish (*Armoracia lapathifolia*)

L

辣乎乎 làhūhū hot; spicy: 四川风味的菜吃起来大多～的。Most Sichuan-flavoured dishes taste rather hot. /他想到自己的错误，脸上不由得～地发烧。When he thought about his mistakes his cheeks burned with shame.
辣酱 làjiàng thick chilli sauce; chilli paste
辣酱油 làjiàngyóu pungent sauce (similar to Worcestershire sauce)
辣椒 làjiāo capsicum; chilli; hot pepper: ～粉 chilli powder /～油 chilli oil; tabasco /～酱 thick chilli sauce /灯笼～ *also*"甜～" sweet chilli /～素 capsaicin /她年轻时是个有名的"小～"。She was well-known as an impetuous, hot-tempered girl.
辣手 làshǒu ❶ ruthless method; vicious device: 他为人歹毒，～还在后头呢! As a vicious man he's bound to resort to even more ruthless devices later on. /铁肩担道义，～著文章。Shoulder a just cause with dogged courage and write without mercy (*or* fear). ❷〈方言〉vicious; ruthless: 如此～的女人真是少见! She's one of the few ruthless women I've ever seen. ❸ thorny; knotty: 再～的事情也难不倒他。No problem is too thorny for him to solve. /他感到这案子很是～。He felt the case on hand was a hard nut to crack.
辣丝丝 làsīsī *also*"辣酥酥" a bit hot or peppery: 这凉菜要～的才好吃。This cold dish tastes good only when it's a bit hot.
辣味 làwèi peppery taste; piquancy; pungency
辣子 làzi ❶ hot pepper; chilli ❷ impetuous, hot-tempered girl or woman; termagant: 她年轻时是村里有名的～。She was famous in the village as a quick-tempered girl.
辣子鸡丁 làzi jīdīng chicken dices with chilli

剌

là 〈书面〉perverse; disagreeable: 乖～ contrary to reason; perverse
剌戾 làlì 〈书面〉perverse; contrary to reason: 秉性～ perverse by nature
剌谬 làmiù 〈书面〉go against; run counter to

瘌

là
瘌痢 làli *also*"鬎鬁" làli 〈方言〉favus of the scalp
瘌痢头 làlitóu 〈方言〉❶ head affected with favus of the scalp: 他换了身衣服，～上戴了顶帽子。He changed his clothes and covered his favus-affected head with a cap. ❷ person affected with favus on the head: ～儿子自己的好。〈俗语〉The best boy in the world is one's own son even though he may be affected with favus of the scalp. *or* Every mother takes her own son as the best child in the world.

鬎

là
鬎鬁 làli see"瘌痢" làli

蝲

là
蝲蛄 làgǔ 〈动物〉crayfish
蝲蝲蛄 làlàgǔ *also*"拉拉蛄" làlàgǔ 〈动物〉mole cricket

鯻

là 〈动物〉grunt; tigerfish

癞

là
see also lài
癞痢 làli see"瘌痢" làli

拉[1]

là see"落" là

拉[2]

là
see also lā; lá; lǎ
拉拉蛄 làlàgǔ see"蝲蝲蛄" làlàgǔ

镴(鑞)

là *also*"焊锡" hànxī; "焊镴" hànlà solder

la

鞡

la see"靰鞡" wùla

啦

la 〈助词〉*combination of* 了 (le) *and* 啊 (a) *expressing exclamation, interrogation, etc.*: 上课～! Hey! It's time for class. /他们追上我们～。Look! They've caught up with us. /你亲眼看见～? You've seen it with your own eyes?
see also lā

lái

来[1](來)

lái ❶ come; arrive: ～～往往 come and go; go to and fro /跟我～! Come along. *or* Come with me. /今天报纸还没～呢。Today's newspapers haven't arrived yet. /～啦您啦。〈口语〉Hello, sir (*or* ma'am)! *or* So you're here, sir (*or* ma'am). /我去去就～。I'll be back in a minute. /他们～自世界各地。They are from all over the world. /电～啦! The electricity is on. /今天～客人啦。We have guests (*or* company) today. ❷ crop up; take place: 问题一～，他就慌了手脚。He got flustered as soon as a problem cropped up. /雷阵雨马上就要～了。A thunder shower is coming up (*or* threatening). ❸ *used as a substitute for a more specific verb*: ～一盘棋 have a game of chess /让我～～看。Let me have a try. /我累了，你～吧。I'm tired. Please take over. *or* Why don't you carry on for a while? I'm tired. /再～一杯茶吧。Would you like another cup of tea? /我自己～吧! I'll help myself (to food). *or* Let me do it myself. /我们打桥牌三缺一，你～不～? We're short of one hand for bridge. Would you like to join us? /再～一个! Encore! *or* Bring me another. /何必给我～这套。Don't give me that! ❹ *used with* 得 *or* 不 *to indicate possibility or capability, or the lack of it*: 合得～ get along well; hit it off /谈不～ find it hard to talk with sb. /这篇稿子今天出不～。This article can't be finished today. /你吃得～辣的吗? Is hot food agreeable to you? *or* Does hot food suit you? /有些人认为买房划不～。Some believe that it doesn't pay to buy housing. ❺ *used before another verb to indicate an intended or suggested action*: 我～说几句。Let me say a few words. /你～给我们谈谈国内外形势吧。Will you please tell us how things are at home and abroad? /这事怎样做才好，大家一起～出主意。Let's put our heads together and find out how best to do it. ❻ *used after another verb or verbal phrase to indicate what one has come for*: 他们给你贺喜～了。They've come to offer you their congratulations. /他回国探亲～了。He returned from abroad to see his family. ❼ *used between two verbs or verbal phrases to indicate the purpose of the former*: 这件事应写篇报道～宣传。This calls for a special feature to give it enough publicity. /你用什么办法～解决这个问题? How are you going to solve the problem? /我们决不能用这种态度～对待自己的同志。We must never treat our comrades in this way. ❽〈助词〉*used to indicate what happened in the past*: 这话你什么时候说～? When did you say it? /这件事我多会儿答应～? When did I agree to do it? ❾ future; coming; next: ～春 coming spring; next spring ❿ *used after a time phrase or its equivalent to indicate a duration that lasts from the past up to the present*: 五千年～ over the past 5,000 years /一周～ for the past week /近～ recently /别～无恙乎? How have you been since I saw you last? ⓫ *used after round numbers like* 十,百,千 *or after numerals plus measures to indicate approximation*: 十～个 about (*or* around) a dozen /七十～岁 about (*or* around) seventy /一千五百～字 about (*or* some, *or* around) fifteen hundred words /三米～深 about three metres deep ⓬ *used after numerals* 一,二,三, *to enumerate reasons or points of argument*: 退休后他开始练书法，一～培养业余爱好，二～有益于健康。He began to practise calligraphy after retirement. For one thing, it was a good hobby to develop; for another, it helped to keep fit. /他这次回国，一～是接孩子去美国，二～是探亲访友，三～是做点进出口生意。He came back to China this time to do three things: first, to take his child to the States with him; second, to visit his relatives and friends; and third, to do some import and export business. ⓭ (Lái) a surname

来[2](來)

lái *used as filler-word in a line of balladry, proverb or vendor's pitch for rhythm and euphony*: 二月里～好春光。Spring comes in the second (lunar) month with all its splendour. /不愁吃～不愁穿。We are neither worried about food nor clothing. *or* We have no lack of food and clothing. /你敲锣～我打鼓。You beat the gong while I play the drum. /磨剪子～抢菜刀! (shouted by a tradesman to solicit business) Scissors and knives sharpened!

来(來)

lai ❶ *used after a verb or verbal expression to*

L

indicate motion towards the speaker：进～ come in／出～ come out／走～ walk up／下楼～ come downstairs／你帮我拿根针～。Bring me a needle, please.／读者寄～许多宝贵意见。Readers have sent in many valuable suggestions.／消息传～，人心大振。Morale soared at the news. ❷ *used after a verb to indicate the result or estimation*：信手写～ write down one's ideas as they come to one's mind／他一觉醒～，天已大亮。When he woke up, it was broad daylight.／想～你对此已有所准备。I suppose you are prepared for this.／看～一切都已就绪。Everything seems all set.／此事说～话长。It's a long story.

来宾 láibīn guest; visitor：接待～ receive guests (*or* visitors)／～席 seats for guests／～留言簿 visitors' book／诸位朋友，诸位～！Friends and guests!／～止步。No entry. *or* Private!

来不得 láibude won't do; be impermissible：对待科学～半点虚假。Science permits no dishonesty.／这是件细活，～半点马虎。It's a delicate job that demands great care (*or* admits of no carelessness).

来不及 láibují there's not enough time (to do sth.); it's too late (to do sth.)：我当时～请示，只能自己做决定了。As there was no time for me to ask for instructions, I had to make a decision on my own.／邮汇～，还是电汇吧！It's too late to remit the money by post. Better send it by telegram.／敌人～等到增援就被打垮了。The enemy was crushed before the reinforcements arrived.

来朝 láicháo 〈旧语〉(of envoys of a tributary state or minority people) come to court; come to pay tribute
see also láizhāo

来潮 láicháo ❶ (of the tide) rise; flow：傍晚，～时分，海上刮起了大风。At dusk, as the tide was rising, it began to blow hard on the sea.／她突然心血～，把那份不错的工作辞了。Carried away by her whims, she quit her well-paid job. *or* She quit her good job on a sudden impulse. ❷ menstruate; have a period

来到 láidào arrive; come：春天～了。Spring has come (*or* arrived).／旱季～了。The dry season has set in.／经过长途跋涉，我们终于～了大西北。After a long, arduous journey we finally reached the Northwest.

来得 láide ❶ be able; be competent：家里、地里，样样活儿她都～。She's good at every chore, both in the house and in the field. ❷ emerge (from a comparison); come out as：还是用大杯子喝啤酒～痛快。It's much better to drink beer with a big glass.／打针比吃药效力～快。Injections produce quicker effects than oral medicine.／你这招儿～真绝。This move of yours is just superb.

来得及 láidejí there's still time (to do sth.); be able to do sth. in time; be able to make it：别着急，补救还～。Don't worry; there's still time for remedy.／走快点，我们还～赶头班车。Hurry up and we'll still be able to catch the first bus (*or* train).／最后的邮递时间是晚上七点，你现在骑车去还～。The last post is at seven p.m. You can still make it if you go by bike.／这个病人还～抢救吗？Is it still possible to save the patient? *or* Can the patient still be saved?

来得容易去得快 láide róngyì qùde kuài *also* "来得易，去得易" 〈谚语〉easy come, easy go; light come, light go：他手里的钱，～，全胡吃海喝了。The money he had got so easily was all squandered speedily on wining and dining.

来得早，不如来得巧 láide zǎo, bùrú láide qiǎo 〈俗语〉to come early is not as good as to come at the right time：真是～，快上桌来喝几杯吧！What beautiful timing! Sit down at the table and have your drinks!

来电 láidiàn ❶ send a telegram here：～祝贺 send telegrams of congratulations; cable congratulations／有关报告何时上报为宜，请～告知。Please inform me by telegram when it will be best to submit the relevant report. ❷ power comes on again：怎么还不～？How come power isn't on yet? ❸ incoming telegram; your telegram; your message：～收悉。Your message received.

来而不往非礼也 lái ér bù wǎng fēi lǐ yě it is impolite not to reciprocate; one should return or give as good as one gets; it is only proper to repay in kind：你们要制裁我们，我们也必然会来反制裁，这就叫～。If you want to apply sanctions, we will be sure to reply with counter-sanctions; "it is improper not to reciprocate", as the saying goes.

来犯 láifàn come to attack (us); invade one's territory：敌人胆敢～就把他们消灭光。We will resolutely wipe out any enemy that dares to attack us (*or* invade our territory).

来访 láifǎng come to visit; come to call：～者 visitors／上月群众来信～中提出的问题均已处理完毕。The problems the people raised in their letters or in person last month have all been processed.

来附 láifù 〈书面〉come to pledge allegiance; come and submit to one's authority：由于内讧，南匈奴纷纷～汉朝。Owing to internal strife, the Southern Xiongnu (*or* Hun) tribes came one after another to submit to the authority and protection of the Han Dynasty.

来复 láifù ❶ go to a place and come back; make a round trip ❷ reflex; rifling：～电路 reflex circuit／～式收音机 reflex (radio) receiver

来复枪 láifùqiāng rifle

来复线 láifùxiàn *also* "膛线" tángxiàn 〈军事〉rifling

来稿 láigǎo (used by editors and publishing houses) manuscript received; contribution：～内容不限。There are no restrictions on the content of contributions.／～概不退还。No manuscripts received will be returned (to the authors).／～截止日期四月三十日。No manuscripts will be accepted later than April 30. *or* The deadline for contributions is April 30.

来古 láigǔ since time immemorial

来归 láiguī ❶ come over and pledge allegiance; come and submit to one's authority：中原一统，四方～。The whole country was unified, with all localities pledging allegiance to the central authorities. ❷〈古语〉(of a woman by her husband's family) join the family through marriage

来函 láihán 〈书面〉incoming letter; letter received; your letter：～照登 (as a newspaper or magazine column) Letters to the Editor／请～联系。Please contact us by mail.

来翰 láihàn 〈书面〉your epistle; your letter

来亨鸡 láihēngjī leghorn

来鸿 láihóng 〈书面〉incoming letter; letter received：远方～ letter from afar

来回 láihuí ❶ go to a place and come back; make a round trip：～飞行 round-trip flight／～要多长时间？How long does it take to get there and back?／打个～也不过二、三里路。The round trip is no more than a couple of *li*.／你能游几个～？How many laps can you swim (in this pool)? ❷ to and fro; back and forth：～摆动 swing to and fro; oscillate／在走廊上～走 pace up and down the corridor; walk to and fro in the corridor／填表时不要～涂改。Please don't make changes over and over again when you fill in the form.

来回来去 láihuí-láiqù back and forth; over and over again：～两头跑 travel (*or* walk) back and forth (between two places)／～地为自己作解释 explain oneself over and over again

来回票 láihuípiào round-trip ticket; return ticket：北京到纽约的～ round-trip ticket from Beijing to New York

来火 láihuǒ get angry; flare up：他一听这事就来了火儿。He flew off the handle as soon as he heard it.

来件 láijiàn communication; document, item or parcel received：所有～均已整理分类。All the incoming documents have been sorted out.

来今 láijīn 〈书面〉from now on：往古～ from ancient times to the present; through the ages; from time immemorial

来劲 láijìn ❶ in high spirits; full of enthusiasm：他们越唱越～。The more they sang, the more enthusiastic they became.／别太～了，我们下次要打败你们。Don't be so cocky. We'll beat you next time. ❷ exciting; exhilarating; thrilling：我们赢了这场足球赛，真～。How exciting (it is) that we won the football match. ❸ be contrary, unreasonable or perverse：你怎么还不住嘴，看来我越让你越～呀！Why don't you shut up? It seems that the more I give in the more unreasonable you become.／你别跟我～。Don't you try to cross me! *or* I won't stand any nonsense from you.

来客 láikè guest; visitor：远方～ guest from afar／天外～ visitor from outer space; extraterrestrial visitor／临时～恕不接待。(sign at a hostel, fair, etc.) No accommodations for unscheduled visitors.

来历 láilì origin; source; background; antecedents; past history：～不明 (of things) of unknown origin; (of people) of dubious background (*or* questionable antecedents)／查明～ ascertain sb.'s antecedents; trace sth. to its source／我不能替你收藏这些～不明的东西。I cannot keep these suspicious articles for you.／你知道这张油画的～吗？Do you know the provenance of this oil painting?

来料加工 láiliào jiāgōng process materials supplied by clients; accept customers' materials for processing：～出口 process materials supplied by foreign customers (*or* clients) for re-export

来临 láilín come; arrive; approach：暑假即将～。The summer vacation is approaching (*or* drawing near).／每当深秋～，这里便是一片红叶。In late autumn, it is a world of red leaves all around here.

来龙去脉 láilóng-qùmài origin and evolution; beginning and end; the whence and whither: 弄清事情的～ find out the whys and wherefores of the matter /讲清事情的～ tell the whole story from beginning to end

来路 láilù ❶ incoming way; approach: 挡住～ block sb.'s approach (*or* way)/回头看看～，只见洁白的雪地上留下一长条清晰的脚印。Looking back the way he had come, he saw a long track of footprints in the white snow. ❷ source; origin: 你这不是想断我的～吗? You're going to cut off the source of my income, aren't you? *or* Do you mean to cut off my support?

来路 láilu antecedents; origin; background: ～不正的货物 goods of questionable origin /这人有点～不明。There is something fishy about his background.

来路货 láilùhuò 〈方言〉 imported goods

来年 láinián coming year; next year: 瑞雪兆丰年，～收成一定不错。As a timely snow heralds a good harvest, I'm sure we'll have a good harvest next year.

来派 láipai 〈方言〉 ❶ way or manner in which sth. comes or breaks out; symptom of a trend; oncoming force: 这病的～可不轻。The way the disease broke out was quite serious. ❷ air; manner; pose: 看他那个～，准是个大款。Judging by the way he throws his weight about, he must be a moneybags.

来去 láiqù ❶ round trip: ～共用三天时间。The round trip took three days altogether. ❷ come and go; go to and fro: 自由～ come and go freely ❸ 〈方言〉 contacts; exchanges; relations: 我们两家素无～。Our two families never had anything to do with each other.

…来…去 …lái…qù (used after two identical or synonymous words to indicate the repetition of an action) back and forth; over and over again: 跑来跑去 run back and forth /挑来挑去 pick and choose /想来想去 turn sth. over and over in one's mind /商量来商量去 discuss sth. over and over again /在床上翻来覆去 toss and turn in bed /找来找去 look for sth. all over the place /眉来眼去 flirt with each other

来去分明 láiqù-fēnmíng there is nothing secret about one's whereabouts; everything is open and aboveboard: 这件事情～，有什么值得怀疑的。We know clearly the ins and outs of the matter, so what on earth do you suspect?

来去无踪 lái-qù wúzōng come and go without leaving a trace; come and go mysteriously: 此人～，实难寻访。It is a hard job to locate this man; nobody knows when or where he comes or goes.

来去自由 lái-qù zìyóu be free to come and go: 欢迎出国留学生回国工作，并保证他们～。Chinese students who study abroad are welcome to return to China to work and are guaranteed freedom to come and go as they desire.

来人 láirén bearer; messenger: 请签收并将收条交～带回。Please sign the receipt and give it to the bearer.

来人儿 láirénr 〈方言〉〈旧语〉 middleman; go-between

来日 láirì the future; days to come: ～无多。There isn't much time left. *or* The days are numbered. /～大难。Difficult days lie ahead. *or* There will be difficulties and setbacks in the future./今天就到这里，～再继续交换意见吧。Let's call it a day now. We can continue our discussion some other time.

来日方长 láirì-fāngcháng there will be ample time; there will be time for that: ～，后会有期。There will be plenty of time yet; we are sure to meet again some day.

来神 láishén 〈口语〉 full of enthusiasm; in high spirits: 他们越谈越～儿。The longer they talked the more enthusiastic they became.

来生 láishēng *also* "来世" 〈迷信〉 next life; hereafter; sweet by-and-by: 此恩只好～再图报答。I can only repay your kindness in the next life (*or* the world to come).

来使 láishǐ emissary; envoy; messenger: 两国交恶，不辱～。No envoy should be humiliated even though two countries have become enemies.

来示 láishì 〈书面〉 your letter; incoming letter

来世 láishì *see* "来生"

来事 láishì ❶ 〈方言〉 know how to deal with people; know how to cope: 会～儿 have a way with people /不会～儿 not know how to cope ❷ 〈方言〉 (usu. used in the negative or the interrogative) be all right; will do: 这样～哦? Will that be all right? *or* Will that do? ❸ 〈书面〉 things to come; future events: 知～ know what will happen in the future

来势 láishì force with which sth. breaks out; oncoming force; gathering momentum: ～汹汹 bear down menacingly; come to look for trouble; break in (upon sb. or sth.) in full fury /一看～不好，他扭头就跑。Seeing things taking an ominous turn, he made off at once.

来书 láishū 〈书面〉 your epistle; your letter: 拜读～，暖意盈怀。Your letter warmed my heart. *or* I was heartened to read your letter.

来苏 láisū *also* "来苏儿" 〈药学〉 lysol

来岁 láisuì coming year; next year

来头 láitou ❶ background; backing; connections: 这人大有～。The guy has rather powerful backing. ❷ motive (behind sb.'s words, action, etc.); reason; cause: 他们这样做不是没有～的。They didn't do that for no reason. /你听出来没有? 他这话有～。Did you hear it? There's something more to what he said. ❸ force with which sth. breaks out; oncoming force; gathering momentum: 众人看见～不好，也有躲进里间屋里的，也有垂手侍立的。Seeing the situation turn worse, some hid in the inner room and others stood with their hands at their sides. ❹ fun; interest: 跟你下棋没～，你老悔棋。It's no fun playing chess with you; you are always retracting your moves.

来往 lái-wǎng come and go: ～旅客 incoming and outgoing travellers; arriving and departing passengers /～账目 current account /～于城乡之间 travel between town and country /上午九点至下午六点禁止车辆～。No thoroughfare from 9:00 a.m. to 6:00 p.m. /～行人，注意安全。Pedestrians, beware of the traffic.

来往 láiwang contact; intercourse; dealings: 官方～ official contacts /业务～ business dealings (*or* contacts) /通过书信～ through correspondence /我们过去常～。We used to see each other quite often. /他常和一些不三不四的人～。He often hangs around with some dubious characters.

来文 láiwén document received; incoming document

来无影去无踪 lái wú yǐng qù wú zōng come without a shadow and leave without a trace; never betray one's whereabouts

来向 láixiàng whence sth. comes; direction of sth. coming: 根据风的～施放烟幕 set a smokescreen by the way the wind blows

来项 láixiang income; revenue; receipts: 他的～可真不少。He has quite a lot of income.

来信 láixìn ❶ send a letter here: 有空请～。Please write me when you are free. /很多人～表扬他们出色的服务。Many wrote to commend them for their outstanding service. ❷ incoming letter; your letter: 人民～ letters from the people /读者～ letters to the editor /六月十日～收到。We have received your letter dated June 10. *or* Your letter of June 10 is to hand.

来样加工 láiyàng jiāgōng process materials according to samples provided by foreign businessmen or clients

来意 láiyì one's purpose in coming: 讲明～ make clear what one has come for /此人～不善，小心提防。The guy's come with an ill intent; be on your guard.

来由 láiyóu reason; cause: 她毫无～地发了一通脾气。She blew up without rhyme or reason. /这些话不是没有～的。These remarks were not without cause. *or* There must be something behind these remarks. /能谈谈你写这部小说的～吗? Could you tell us how you came to write the novel?

来源 láiyuán ❶ source; origin: 信息～ source of information /经济～ source of income /追查谣言的～ trace a rumour to its source /请你查一查这个词的～。Please look up the origin (*or* etymology) of this word. ❷ originate; stem: 艺术家的灵感～于生活。An artist's inspiration stems (*or* originates) from life. /这个剧本的情节～于民间传说。The plot of the play was based on a folk legend.

来源国 láiyuánguó sending country; country of origin

来札 láizhá 〈书面〉 your epistle; your letter

来朝 láizhāo 〈书面〉 tomorrow; the following day

see also láicháo

来哲 láizhé 〈书面〉 sage or philosopher of a later generation

来者 láizhě ❶ things to come; what is in the future; future generation: 往者不可谏，～犹可追。What is past is beyond help; what is to come may yet be saved. *or* There is still time to make amends. /前不见古人，后不见～。Behind me I do not see the ancients; before me I do not see those to come. ❷ any person or thing that comes: ～通名! (used in traditional novels, etc.) Announce your name, you who have come!

来者不拒 láizhě-bùjù all comers are welcome; nobody's request

or offer is refused; none will be turned away; favour is granted to whoever asks for it:老教授古道热肠,对登门求教的人从来是～。The old professor was so warm-hearted that he never refused anyone who came for advice or help.

来者不善,善者不来 láizhě bù shàn, shànzhě bù lái those who have come are not friendly, and those who are friendly have not come; he who has come, comes with an ill intent; he who comes is certainly strong and well prepared:他听说东家有"请",心想:～,看样子东家是想拿他开刀。When he heard that he was sent for by his master, he thought "no good will come of it", as it seemed to him that his master apparently wanted to make an example of him.

来着 láizhe 〈助词〉〈口语〉*used at the end of a sentence, usu. to indicate what happened or existed in the past*:你不要冤枉好人,她可没动你的东西～。Don't wrong an innocent person. She didn't tamper with your things. /我的球哪去了? 前两天我还玩儿～。Where is my ball? I had it only a couple of days ago. /这个字的繁体怎么写～? 我给忘了。How do you write the original complex form of this character? I cannot remember now.

来之不易 láizhī-bùyì not easily come by; hard-earned:我们要珍惜～的成绩,把它坚持下去。We should cherish our hard-earned achievement and keep it up. /这个机会～。This is a rare opportunity. /一粥一饭,当思～。We must never forget that every single grain is the result of toil.

来兹 láizī 〈书面〉next year; the future:展望～ look ahead; look into the future

来踪去迹 láizōng-qùjì clues (of sth.); traces of sb.'s movements or whereabouts; cause and effect (of sth.):为了弄清真相,一定要查明他的～。We must find out his whereabouts in order to get to the bottom of this.

莱(萊) lái

❶〈书面〉〈植物〉lamb's-quarters ❷〈古语〉fallow or waste land outside a town

莱比锡 Láibǐxī Leipzig, a city in east central Germany where an annual fair has been held since the 12th century

莱菔 láifú 〈植物〉radish:～子〈中药〉radish seed

莱诺铸排机 láinuò zhùpáijī *also*"整行铸排机" zhěngháng zhùpáijī 〈印刷〉linotype:莱诺整行铸排机 linograph

莱塞 láisè *also*"激光" jīguāng 〈物理〉laser

莱氏体 láishìtǐ 〈冶金〉ledeburite

莱索托 Láisuǒtuō Lesotho:～人 (sing.) Mosotho; (pl.) Basotho

莱茵河 Láiyīnhé Rhine, river in central and western Europe flowing from the Swiss Alps to the North Sea

莱茵石 láiyīnshí rhinestone

梾(棶) lái

梾木 láimù *also*"灯台树" dēngtáishù 〈植物〉large-leaved dogwood (*Cornus macrophylla*)

崃(崍) lái

see"邛崃" Qiónglái

铼(錸) lái

〈化学〉rhenium (Re):～合金 rhenium alloy /～同位素 rhenium isotope /～酸 rhenic acid

徕(徠、倈) lái

see"招徕" zhāolái

see also lài

鶆(鶆) lái

鶆鹋 lái'ǎo *also*"美洲鸵" měizhōutuó 〈动物〉rhea

lài

睐(睞) lài

〈书面〉❶ squint ❷ look at; glance:青～ (look upon with) favour; good graces /明眸善～ enticing glances of a bright-eyed beauty

赉(賚) lài

〈书面〉grant; bestow; confer:赏～ give a reward; bestow a favour

徕(徠) lài

〈书面〉send one's best wishes or bring gifts in recognition of services rendered:劳～ salute and encourage; bring gifts to cheer and encourage

see also lái

赖[1] lài

❶ depend; rely:依～父母 depend on one's parents /人类～以生存的环境 environment on which mankind relies (*or* depends) for existence /实验的成功有～于我们的合作。The success of the experiment hinges on our cooperation. ❷ (sometimes used as a kind of endearment) impudent; cheeky; brazen; rascally:耍～ act shamelessly or faithlessly; play the rogue; go back on one's word /这人可真～。What a brazen (*or* an impudent) guy! /瞧他那～样儿。Look how cheeky he is! *or* Isn't he quite a rascal? ❸drag out one's stay (beyond what is necessary or welcome); hang on where one does not belong:～着不走 hang on and refuse to leave /～在别国领土上 (of aggressors, etc.) hold on to the territories of other countries ❹ deny (what was previously said or done, esp. one's error or responsibility); renege; shirk:事实俱在,～是～不掉的。Such being the facts, there's no use trying to deny them. *or* You simply can't deny the facts. /你说过的话别想～。Don't you try to go back on your word. /这次一定要让他请客,前几次都让他～掉了。It must be his treat this time for he got off several times already. /赶快还钱,这回你可～不过去了。Pay back my money at once. You can't procrastinate any more. ❺ put the blame on (sb. else); shift the blame onto (sb. else):明明是你的错,你怎么能～别人呢? It's all your fault. How could you shift the blame onto others? ❻ blame:大家都～他打乱了原定的工作计划。Everybody blamed him for disrupting the original work plan. /这件事不能全～他。You can't blame the whole thing on him. *or* He's not entirely to blame for all this. ❼ (Lài) a surname

赖[2] lài

no good; poor:这幢新楼盖得真不～。The new building is not at all bad. /小伙子长得真不～。The young man is quite handsome. /不论好的～的他都照样吃,从不剩饭菜。Delicious or not, he always eats his food and leaves his plate clean.

赖氨酸 lài'ānsuān 〈生化〉lysine

赖草 làicǎo 〈植物〉*Aneurolepidium dasystachys*

赖床 làichuáng linger in bed after waking up; feel too lazy or too cozy to get out of bed:那时,屋里太冷,总要赖一会儿床才肯起来。As it was very cold in the room, we would always dawdle in our beds for quite a while before we got up reluctantly.

赖词儿 làicír 〈方言〉words meant to shirk one's responsibility or shift the blame onto sb. else; lie:他自己错了不认账,反而编出这许多～来糊弄人。Instead of owning up to his blunder, he told a pack of lies to mislead people.

赖婚 làihūn renege on a pledge to marry; repudiate a marriage contract; breach a promise of marriage

赖货 làihuò 〈口语〉rascal; villain

赖皮 làipí ❶ rascally; shameless; brazen; unreasonable:耍～ act shamelessly /这人～赖脸的真拿他没办法。What can you do about such a brazen guy? ❷ act shamelessly or brazenly:别在这儿～了,快走吧! Don't hang on brazenly; it's high time you leave.

赖学 làixué 〈方言〉cut school or classes; play truant

赖债 làizhài repudiate a debt; default:你放心,我再穷也不会赖你的债。Don't worry about the money I owe you. Poor as I am, I won't renege on my debt.

赖账 làizhàng ❶ repudiate a debt; default:这小子经常借钱不还,你要小心他～。You must be careful when you lend him money for the guy seldom pays back the money he borrows. ❷ go back on one's word:白纸黑字写得清楚,你休想～。Don't you ever try to break your promise. Everything is written clearly in black and white.

赖子 làizi faithless or shameless person; rascal

濑 lài

〈书面〉rapids

癞 lài

❶ *also*"麻风" máfēng 〈医学〉leprosy ❷〈方言〉favus of the scalp:长～ be affected with favus

see also là

癞病 làibìng leprosy

癞疮 làichuāng scabies; impetigo

癞瓜 làiguā 〈方言〉bitter gourd

癞哈蟆 làihámá *also*"癞虾蟆" toad:～想吃天鹅肉 act like a toad lusting after a swan's flesh; crave for sth. one is not worthy of

癞皮狗 làipígǒu mangy dog; loathsome creature:罪犯瘫在墙角里,

像一条断了脊梁骨的～。Crumbling into a heap in a corner, the criminal looked like a mangy dog with a broken back.

癞头 làitóu favus-infected head; scabby head：～疮 scabies on the head; favus on the head /～龟〈动物〉a kind of sea turtle

癞癣 làixuǎn scabies

癞子 làizi ❶ person affected with favus on the head ❷ favus of the scalp

籁 lài ❶ ancient musical pipe ❷ sound; noise：天～ sounds of nature /万～俱寂。All is quiet and still. *or* Silence reigns supreme.

lai

唻(唻) lai 〈方言〉〈助词〉❶ *equivalent to* 呢：你们吵吵闹闹干什么～? What are you making so much noise about? ❷ *equivalent to* 啦：我们来时车可挤～。What a crowded bus we took to get here! ❸ *equivalent to* 来着：医生怎么嘱咐你～，怎么都忘了? What did the doctor tell you? Don't you remember?

lán

阑[1] lán ❶ fence; railing *see also* "栏❶" lán ❷ bar; block *see also* "拦" lán

阑[2] lán 〈书面〉❶ drawing to an end; late：岁～ late in the year; towards the end of year /夜～人静。All is quiet late into the night. *or* Silence reigns in the dead of night. ❷ do without authorization：～出 go out (*or* leave) without permission

阑残 láncán 〈书面〉fade out：楼中歌管渐～。The songs and music in the hall faded out.

阑干 lángān ❶〈书面〉crisscross; across：星斗～(the sky is) dotted with stars /玉容寂寞泪～ tears streaming down the beautiful, lonely face ❷ *see* "栏杆" lángān

阑槛 lánjiàn 〈书面〉railing; balustrade; banister

阑人 lánrù 〈书面〉❶ enter a forbidden place without permission：～宫门 enter the imperial palace without permission ❷ interpolate; adulterate

阑珊 lánshān 〈书面〉draw to an end; wane; decline：意兴～ interest flags; enthusiasm declines /春意～。Spring is waning.

阑尾 lánwěi 〈生理〉(vermiform) appendix：切除～ have one's appendix removed; have an appendectomy /～疼痛 appendalgia /～脓肿 appendicular abscess /～穿孔 appendicular perforation

阑尾切除术 lánwěi qiēchúshù 〈医学〉appendectomy

阑尾炎 lánwěiyán 〈医学〉appendicitis

澜 lán billows; waves：波～ huge waves; billows /死水微～ ripples on stagnant waters /力挽狂～ exert one's utmost to stem a raging tide (*or* to save a desperate situation) /推波助～ make a stormy sea stormier; add fuel to the flames; aggravate an already complicated (*or* bad) situation

澜沧江 Láncāngjiāng Lancang River, major river in southwest China, called the Mekong (湄公河) when it flows through Southeast Asia

斓 lán *see* "斑斓" bānlán

谰 lán 〈书面〉❶ calumniate; slander; malign：～词 slanderous remarks; calumny ❷ deny; disavow

谰调 lándiào *see* "谰言"

谰言 lányán calumny; slander：驳斥对方的～ rebut the calumny spread by the other party

襕(幱) lán 〈古语〉dress; overall

籣(韊) lán 〈古语〉container for holding arrows; quiver

镧 lán 〈化学〉lanthanum (La)：～系 *also* "～族" lanthanide series /～系元素 lanthanide

兰(蘭) lán ❶ cymbidium; orchid：春～秋菊 orchids in spring and chrysanthemums in autumn /如～之馨 as fragrant as an orchid ❷ fragrant thoroughwort (*Eupatorium fortunei*) ❸〈古语〉lily magnolia ❹ (Lán) a surname

兰艾 lán'ài 〈书面〉orchids and mugworts; gentlemen and villains; good and bad：～难分。It is difficult to distinguish between orchids and mugworts. *or* It is hard to tell good people from bad. /～同焚。Orchids and mugworts are burnt together. *or* The noble and the mean are destroyed alike.

兰伯特投影 Lánbótè tóuyǐng 〈测绘〉Lambert projection

兰草 láncǎo ❶ fragrant thoroughwort ❷ (popular term for 兰花) orchid

兰摧玉折 láncuī-yùzhé 〈书面〉premature death of a virtuous (and gifted) person

兰闺 lánguī 〈旧语〉boudoir

兰花 lánhuā ❶ *also* "春兰" chūnlán cymbidium; orchid：～学 orchidology ❷ sword-leaved cymbidium

兰花指 lánhuāzhǐ *also* "兰花手" orchid-shaped fingers — a hand gesture with the thumb and middle finger joining in a ring and the other three fingers spreading (made in traditional Chinese operas to show delicacy and grace)

兰交 lánjiāo 〈书面〉bosom friend：二人遂为～。The two became intimate friends.

兰科 lánkē 〈植物〉orchid family; orchidaceae

兰盆 lánpén ❶ (short for 盂兰盆会) Buddhist Festival for Ghosts (15th of the 7th lunar month) ❷〈旧语〉bath tub

兰谱 lánpǔ *also* "金兰谱" jīnlánpǔ genealogical records exchanged between those who swear brotherhood：换过～的结拜兄弟 sworn brothers who have exchanged genealogical records

兰若 lánrě *also* "阿兰若" ālánrě (transliteration of Sanskrit *Aranya*) Buddhist temple

兰若 lánruò 〈书面〉fragrant thoroughwort and *Pollia japonica*

兰室 lánshì 〈旧语〉boudoir

兰因絮果 lányīn-xùguǒ a good beginning is marred by a bad conclusion; a happy marriage ends in a divorce

兰章 lánzhāng 〈书面〉〈敬词〉exquisite diction; beautiful writing：拜读～ read your beautiful writing

兰兆 lánzhào *also* "兰梦"〈旧语〉sign or omen of the birth of a male baby

兰质蕙心 lánzhì-huìxīn *also* "兰心蕙性" (of a woman) pure of heart and refined in spirit：好一个～的姑娘! What a pure-hearted girl!

兰州 Lánzhōu Lanzhou, capital of Gansu Province

栏(欄) lán ❶ fence; railing; balustrade; hurdle：栅～ fence; railing; paling; palisade /木～ wooden fence; paling /石～ stone railing; stone balustrade /铁～ iron-bar on railing; iron balustrade /凭～远望 lean on a railing and gaze into the distance / 400米跨～赛跑 400 metre hurdle race (*or* hurdles) /低～ low hurdle /高～ high hurdle /跨～运动员 hurdler ❷ pen; shed; barn：羊～ sheep pen /牛～ cowshed /用干土垫～ spread dry earth in a shed ❸ column (in a newspaper or magazine)：专～ special column /广告～ advertisement column; classified ads /体育～ sports column /金融～ financial column /读者来信～ correspondence column /社交～ society column /征聘～ "wants" column ❹ column (of a form)：姓名～ name column /备注～ "remarks" column /此～可不填。This column is optional. ❺ board (for putting up notices or newspapers)：布告～ bulletin board; notice board

栏肥 lánféi barnyard manure

栏粪 lánfèn 〈方言〉barnyard manure

栏杆 lángān *also* "阑干" lángān railing; banister; balustrade：铸铁～ cast-iron railings /请勿翻越～。Don't jump the railings.

栏柜 lánguì *also* "拦柜" lánguì shop counter

栏槛 lánjiàn railing; banister; balustrade

栏目 lánmù title of column; column (in a newspaper, magazine, etc.)：增设新～ start a new column /～繁多 have a variety of columns

栏楯 lánshǔn 〈书面〉*see* "栏杆"

栏栅 lánzhà 〈方言〉railing; paling; barrier

拦(攔) lán ❶ block; bar; hold back:～街阻路 block (*or* obstruct) traffic (in the streets) /无遮无～ with nothing to block the way; without cover or shield; completely open /～一辆出租车 stop a taxi; get a taxi /你认为对就干吧,我们不～你。Do whatever you believe is right, and we won't hold you back. /他只要下了决心,想～也～不住。It's no use trying to stop him from doing anything he's set his mind to. /无票者都被～在大门外。Those without tickets were kept outside the gate. /要不是有棵树～着,这个登山者早掉到悬崖下去了。The climber would have fallen over the cliff but for the tree. ❷ direct right at:～头一棍 give (sb.) a head-on blow

拦挡 lándǎng block; obstruct:～敌军的攻势 block (*or* stop) the enemy offensive

拦道木 lándàomù 〈交通〉 movable barrier; half-barrier (as at a level crossing)

拦柜 lánguì *also* "栏柜" lánguì shop counter

拦河坝 lánhébà dam across a river

拦洪坝 lánhóngbà flood-control dam

拦击 lánjī ❶ intercept and attack ❷〈体育〉volley

拦劫 lánjié stop and rob; waylay; mug:～行人 mug pedestrians /～过往商人 waylay passing merchants /遭到歹徒～ be stopped and robbed by some ruffians

拦截 lánjié intercept:～敌机 intercept enemy aircraft /～导弹 interceptor missile /～控制系统 interceptor control system

拦开 lánkāi separate; keep apart:用绳子把草坪从中间～ divide the lawn in the middle with a rope

拦路 lánlù block the way:～行凶 block the way and commit physical assault /～抢劫 waylay and rob; hold up; mug /～抢劫事件 highway robbery

拦路虎 lánlùhǔ stumbling block; obstacle:习惯势力是这里改革的～。The force of habit is an obstacle to carrying out reform here.

拦网 lánwǎng 〈体育〉 block (in volleyball):单人～ one-man block /双人～ two-man block /～队员 blocker /～得分 block point

拦污栅 lánwūzhà 〈水利〉 trashrack

拦蓄 lánxù retain; conserve; impound:～山洪 impound mountain torrents /这个水库可～一亿立方的洪水。This reservoir can hold one hundred million cubic metres of flood water.

拦羊 lányáng 〈方言〉 herd sheep; tend sheep

拦腰 lányāo by the waist; round the middle:～抱住 (usu. from behind) hold (*or* clasp) by the waist; seize round the middle /～截断 cut in the middle; block (a river) with a dam; dam (a river)

拦鱼栅 lányúzhà fish screen

拦阻 lánzǔ block; stop; obstruct; hold back:从中～ try to hold back; obstruct /尽力～ do everything possible to stop (sb. from doing sth.) /他一定要去冒险,我们也～不住。We can not stop him if he is bent on taking the risk.

婪 lán *see* "贪婪" tānlán

褴(襤) lán

褴褛 lánlǚ *also* "蓝缕" lánlǚ ragged; tattered:衣衫～ in rags (*or* tatters); out at elbows

褴鱼 lányú ragfish (*Icosteus aenigmaticus*)

蓝(藍) lán ❶ blue:蔚～ *also* "天～" sky blue; azure /深～ dark blue; Oxford blue /浅～ light blue; pale blue; Cambridge blue /藏～ reddish blue /孔雀～ peacock blue /宝石～ sapphire blue /普鲁士～ Prussian blue /海军～ navy blue /绿～色 turquoise blue; bluish green ❷ indigo plant:青出于～而胜于～。Blue is extracted from the indigo plant but is bluer than the latter. *or* The pupil surpasses the teacher. ❸ (Lán) a surname

蓝矮星 lán'ǎixīng 〈天文〉 blue dwarf

蓝宝石 lánbǎoshí sapphire:假～ sapphirine

蓝宝石婚 lánbǎoshíhūn sapphire or 45th wedding anniversary

蓝本 lánběn source material; original version on which later work is based:这是以《水浒》为～的同名连续剧。The TV serial *Water Margin* is based on the novel of the same title.

蓝筹股 lánchóugǔ 〈金融〉 blue chip (considered to be a safe investment)

蓝脆 láncuì 〈冶金〉 blue brittleness

蓝带 lándài 〈地质〉 blue band

蓝点鲅 lándiǎnbà 〈动物〉 Spanish mackerel

蓝点颏 lándiǎnké *also* "蓝靛颏儿"〈动物〉 bluethroat

蓝电子束 lándiànzǐshù 〈电子〉 blue beam

蓝靛 lándiàn (popular term for 靛蓝) ❶ indigo ❷ indigo blue; dark blue

蓝矾 lánfán *also* "胆矾" dǎnfán blue vitriol; blue stone; chalcanthite

蓝腹鹇 lánfùxián 〈动物〉 blue pheasant (*Lophura swinhoii*)

蓝钢 lángāng 〈冶金〉 blue steel

蓝光 lánguāng 〈物理〉 blue light:～束 blue beam

蓝黑 lánhēi blue-black:～墨水 blue-black ink

蓝蓟 lánjì 〈植物〉 blueweed

蓝晶晶 lánjīngjīng (of water, gems, etc.) blue and glittering; bright blue:～的海水 bright blue sea water

蓝晶石 lánjīngshí 〈矿业〉 cyanite; kyanite

蓝鲸 lánjīng *also* "剃刀鲸" tìdāojīng (largest animal extant) blue whale; sulphur-bottom (*Balaenoptera musculus*)

蓝孔雀石 lánkǒngquèshí 〈矿业〉 azurmalachite

蓝盔人员 lánkuī rényuán blue helmet personnel; personnel of a UN peace-keeping force

蓝岭 lánlǐng Blue Ridge Mountains, the Virginia portion of the Appalachian Mountains stretching from south Pennsylvania to north Georgia in the United States

蓝领工人 lánlǐng gōngrén blue-collar worker

蓝缕 lánlǚ *see* "褴褛" lánlǚ

蓝绿 lánlǜ bluish-green; blue-green:～闪石〈矿业〉 blue-green amphibole

蓝玛瑙 lánmǎnǎo blue agate

蓝奶酪 lánnǎilào blue cheese

蓝牛 lánniú nilgai; bluebuck (*Boselaphus tragocamelus*)

蓝皮书 lánpíshū blue paper; blue book

蓝桥路 lánqiáolù way to marriage:有情人～上喜结姻缘。Those who love each other get married happily.

蓝青 lánqīng ❶ indigo blue ❷ (of speech) imperfect; corrupt

蓝青官话 lánqīng guānhuà Mandarin Chinese spoken with a provincial accent; corrupt Mandarin:来人四十上下年纪,讲一口～。The visitor is around 40 and speaks corrupt Mandarin.

蓝闪石 lánshǎnshí 〈矿业〉 glaucophane

蓝色 lánsè blue:～标签 blue label /～痣 blue nevus /～盲 blue blindness; tritanopia

蓝舌病 lánshébìng 〈兽医〉 bluetongue

蓝田生玉 Lántián-shēngyù 〈书面〉 worthy child born of an eminent family:～,真不虚也。He is in every sense a worthy child born of an eminent family.

蓝田猿人 Lántián yuánrén *also* "蓝田人"〈考古〉 Lantian Man (*Sinanthropus lantienensis*), ape-man of about 600,000 years ago whose fossil remains were found in Lantian, Shaanxi Province in 1964

蓝铁矿 lántiěkuàng 〈矿业〉 vivianite

蓝铜矿 lántóngkuàng 〈矿业〉 azurite; chessylite

蓝图 lántú ❶ blueprint:～纸 blueprinting paper /绘制～ draw a blueprint (for sth.) ❷〈比喻〉plan; scheme:这个纲要为我们描绘了二十一世纪初的建设～。This programme is a blueprint for national development in the early 21st century.

蓝星体 lánxīngtǐ 〈天文〉 blue stellar object (BSO)

蓝盈盈 lányīngyīng *also* "蓝莹莹"〈方言〉 bright blue:～的天空 azure sky

蓝瑛 Lán Yīng Lan Ying (1585-1664), painter of the late Ming and early Qing dynasties

蓝藻 lánzǎo 〈植物〉 blue green alga

蓝湛湛 lánzhànzhàn (of the sky, the sea, etc.) deep blue:～的湖面水波不兴。Not a ripple can be seen on the dark blue lake.

篮(籃) lán ❶ basket:竹～ bamboo basket /花～ basket of flowers; bouquet /网～ basket with netting /提～ basket with a handle ❷〈体育〉goal; basket:投～ shoot (a basket) /勾手投～ hook shot /上～ lay up /塞～ dunk shot /补～ tip-in shot; follow-up shot /扣～ over-the-rim shot /擦板入～ rebound shot ❸ basketball:女～ women's basketball team /全国甲级男～联赛 men's national class A league basketball matches

篮板 lánbǎn 〈体育〉 backboard; bank

篮板球 lánbǎnqiú 〈体育〉 rebound:前场～ offensive rebound /后场

L

～ defensive rebound /控制～ control the rebounds /抢～ try to grab a rebound
篮框 lánkuàng 〈体育〉basket; ring hoop
篮球 lánqiú 〈体育〉basketball:～赛 basketball match (*or* game) / 职业～队 professional basketball team /～运动员 basketball player; cager; hoopster
篮球场 lánqiúchǎng basketball court
篮球架 lánqiújià basketball stand
篮圈 lánquān 〈体育〉ring; hoop
篮坛 lántán basketball circles:这是一支世界～劲旅。This team is one of the strongest in world basketball.
篮舆 lányú 〈书面〉bamboo sedan (-chair)
篮子 lánzi basket:菜～ basket for vegetables;〈比喻〉vegetable supply; vegetable-producing area /一～鸡蛋 a basket of eggs /挎着～ carry a basket on the arm

岚 lán 〈书面〉mountain haze or mist:山～ mountain haze /晓～ morning mist
岚烟 lányān mountain mist

lǎn

漤(灠) lǎn ❶ season or cure (raw fish, meat or fresh vegetables) in salt or other dressings:～大白菜 season (*or* dress) Chinese cabbage in salt ❷ remove the puckery taste of persimmons by steeping them in hot water or limewash:这是～过的柿子。These persimmons have been steeped in limewash.

懒(嬾) lǎn ❶ lazy; indolent; slothful:手～ lazy about writing (letters, etc.) or lifting one's hand to do any work /腿～ disinclined to move about; lazy about paying visits /偷～ loaf (*or* idle) about /犯～ feel disinclined to work; laze away one's time /好吃～做 love eating but hate working /大～使小～ the bigger lazybones make the lesser ones work /人勤地不～ where man is diligent, the soil is not idle; where the tiller is tireless the land is fertile; the land is productive when the tiller is hardworking ❷ sluggish; languid; listless:身上发～ feel sluggish (*or* languid)
懒虫 lǎnchóng 〈口语〉〈贬义〉lazybones:你这个小～,都什么时候了,还不起床! You little lazybones! It is high time you got up.
懒怠 lǎndai ❶ lazy; indolent ❷ be disinclined to; be too lazy to; not feel like doing:这几天身体不好,话也～说了。As I have not been well for the last few days, I don't feel like talking at all.
懒蛋 lǎndàn 〈口语〉〈贬义〉lazybones
懒得 lǎnde have no inclination to; not feel like; be tired of:我真～每天做饭。I'm tired of cooking every day. /天气太热,人都～出门了。It's so hot that one doesn't feel like going outdoors.
懒惰 lǎnduò lazy; indolent:～成性 be lazy by nature; be a sluggard
懒放 lǎnfàng 〈书面〉sluggish; indolent; slack:寒来弥～,数日一梳头。More sluggish with the onset of winter, I do my hair once in several days.
懒骨头 lǎngǔtou 〈口语〉〈贬义〉lazybones
懒汉 lǎnhàn lazybones; sluggard; idler:十足的～思想 sheer sluggard mentality (*or* way of thinking)
懒汉鞋 lǎnhànxié *also*"懒鞋" slip-on cloth shoes with elastic gussets for the uppers; loafers
懒猴 lǎnhóu 〈动物〉sloth monkey; slow or slender loris
懒货 lǎnhuò 〈口语〉〈贬义〉lazybones; slacker
懒几 lǎnjī *also*"懒架" bookrest
懒龙 lǎnlóng long steamed roll with layers of stuffing in it
懒驴上磨屎尿多 lǎnlǘ shàng mò shǐniào duō 〈俗语〉when a lazy donkey is hitched to the mill, he pisses and shits as often as he can — idle folks can always find excuses for not working
懒慢 lǎnmàn 〈书面〉sluggish; indolent:性情～ be indolent by temperament
懒婆娘的裹脚,又臭又长 lǎnpóniángde guǒjiǎo, yòu chòu yòu cháng 〈俗语〉foot-bindings of a slattern, long and smelly; (of a speech, lecture, essay, etc.) long and dull:这人的讲话历来是～。He always makes dull speeches, droning on and on.
懒散 lǎnsǎn sluggish; indolent; negligent; slack:工作～ sluggish and careless about one's work /想不到他会那么～。I had not the faintest notion that he could be so sluggish.
懒熊 lǎnxióng 〈动物〉sloth bear; honey bear (*Melursus ursinus*)
懒洋洋 lǎnyāngyāng languid; listless; spiritless:只见他～地走了进来。He came in listlessly.

壈(壈) lǎn *see*"坎壈" kǎnlǎn

览(覽) lǎn ❶ look at; see; view:饱～ view sth. to one's heart's content /展～ put on show; exhibit /一～无余 take in everything at a glance ❷ read:浏～ glance over; skim through (*or* over); browse through /阅～室 reading room /博～群书 widely-read
览古 lǎngǔ 〈书面〉visit places of historic interest:洛阳～ visit historic sites in Luoyang
览胜 lǎnshèng 〈书面〉tour scenic spots:到黄山～ go sightseeing on Mount Huang
览眺 lǎntiào gaze into the distance:登高～ climb a height and gaze into the distance

榄(欖) lǎn
榄香脂 lǎnxiāngzhī elemi

揽(攬) lǎn ❶ pull or take into one's arms; clasp; hold:把受惊的孩子～在怀里 clasp a frightened child to one's bosom /～镜自照 hold up a mirror to look at oneself ❷ fasten with a rope, etc.:把自行车架上的行李～上点。Put a rope round the luggage on the bicycle rack. ❸ take on; take upon oneself; canvass:把重活往自己身上～ take upon oneself all the heavy work /～买卖 canvass for business orders ❹ grasp; exercise control over; monopolize:包～ grasp everything; monopolize /总～权纲 hold the reins of government /独～大权 monopolize all power; take (*or* arrogate) all power to oneself
揽笔 lǎnbǐ 〈书面〉do the writing; take up one's pen to write; write
揽承 lǎnchéng undertake or do (sth.); take on (a job, etc.):我不想～这件事。I don't want to take it on.
揽工 lǎngōng 〈方言〉work as a (long-term) hired hand:从十几岁起,他就跟着大哥～。He began to work as a hired hand with his elder brother when he was a teenager.
揽过 lǎnguò take the blame on oneself:推功～ decline the rewards but take all the blame
揽活 lǎnhuó undertake jobs (of work); take on work:几个木工在道旁边～儿。Several carpenters stood by the roadside, soliciting work.
揽货 lǎnhuò undertake to ship or market goods
揽客 lǎnkè (of a restaurant, hotel, etc.) solicit customers
揽辔澄清 lǎnpèi-chéngqīng seize the reins and bring about peace; assume power and bring order out of chaos:临危受命,～,这位伟人对国家的功绩是不可磨灭的。Entrusted with the mandate at a critical moment, the great man successfully brought order out of chaos upon assuming power, and made an ineffaceable contribution to his country.
揽权 lǎnquán arrogate power to oneself:～怙势 grab power and use it to bully others
揽胜 lǎnshèng 〈书面〉have a panoramic view of the beauty of the landscape:西山～ enjoy the beautiful scenery of the Western Hills
揽总 lǎnzǒng take overall charge; assume overall responsibility; take on everything:这个项目人人都有明确分工并由王教授～。Everyone participating in the project had a clearcut assignment, with Professor Wang in overall charge.

缆(纜) lǎn ❶ hawser; mooring rope or cable:解～开船 cast off; set sail /砍～下水 cut the cable to launch the ship ❷ thick rope; cable:电～ power cable; cable /钢～ steel cable ❸ moor (a ship):～舟登岸 moor the ship and land
缆车 lǎnchē cable car:～铁道 cable railway /～索道 telpher; ropeway
缆道 lǎndào cableway
缆绳 lǎnshéng thick rope; cable
缆索 lǎnsuǒ thick rope; cable:～起重机 cable crane /～式输送机 telpher conveyor /～挖土机 cable scraper

缆索铁道 lǎnsuǒ tiědào funicular railway; funicular
缆桩 lǎnzhuāng bitt

罱 lǎn ❶ a kind of rectangular net used for fishing or for dredging up river sludge, collecting water weeds, etc. ❷ dredge up: ～河泥 dredge up sludge from a river
罱泥船 lǎnníchuán dredging boat used in collecting river sludge for fertilizer

làn

滥(濫) làn ❶ overflow; flood; inundate: 泛～成灾 cause a disaster by flooding ❷ excessive; indiscriminate; without restraint: ～捕～猎 fish and hunt excessively /狂轰～炸 indiscriminate bombing; wanton bombing /宁缺毋～ rather go without than have sth. shoddy; better to leave a deficiency alone than to have it covered without discretion; put quality before quantity/功不～赏，罪不～刑。Neither rewards nor penalties are meted out in excess of what is deserved. *or* Rewards should be commensurate with merit, and punishment with the crime. /这个词用得太～，已失去原意了。The word has been so abused as to lose its original meaning.
滥调 làndiào hackneyed tune; worn-out theme; trite expression; platitude: 陈词～ overused and stereotyped expression; cliché; platitude
滥发 lànfā issue excessively or indiscriminately: ～奖金 distribute bonuses indiscriminately /～钞票 issue banknotes excessively; inflate paper currency without restraint /～实物和补贴 indiscriminate handing-out of subsidies in cash and in kind
滥伐 lànfá excessive logging; indiscriminate felling (of trees): ～森林 wanton denudation of forests
滥好人 lànhǎorén 〈方言〉 one who tries to please everybody at the expense of principles
滥交 lànjiāo make friends without discrimination
滥杀无辜 lànshā-wúgū wanton slaughter or indiscriminate killing of innocent people
滥觞 lànshāng 〈书面〉 origin; beginning: 曲水～ origin of a winding river /中国古代文化大抵～于殷代。Ancient Chinese culture originated by and large from the Yin Dynasty.
滥诉 lànsù frivolous or indiscriminate lawsuit
滥套子 làntàozi (of writing) hackneyed formula or expression; platitude; cliché: 文章务求精练，杜绝～。One should try to write precisely and succinctly, and steer clear of hackneyed formulas.
滥用 lànyòng abuse; misuse; use indiscriminately: ～职权，草菅人命 abuse one's power and act with utter disregard for human lives /～成语 misuse an idiom /～补品补药 take tonics indiscriminately /～资金 squander funds
滥竽充数 lànyú-chōngshù pretend to play the *yu* (an ancient musical instrument) and retain one's position in the orchestra; (of incompetent people or inferior goods) be there just to make up the number; pass off as an expert or a brand name; fill a position without the necessary qualifications: 我算什么歌唱家啊，参加合唱不过～罢了。I'm no singer at all. I'm in the chorus just to make up the number.

烂(爛) làn ❶ sodden; pappy; mushy; soft: 一煮就～ (of food) cook quickly /煮不～ cannot be thoroughly cooked /熟而不～ well-done but not mushy /报纸给雨水一浸，都～了。The newspaper became sodden in the rainwater. /鸡烧得太～了。The chicken is overdone. ❷ rot; fester; decay: 臭鱼～虾 rotten fish and shrimps /防止～秧 prevent seedlings from rotting /这种～木头可不能用来打家具。Decayed timber such as this cannot be used for furniture. /伤口如不及时消毒会～的。The wound will fester if not sterilized immediately. /一上火就会～嘴角儿。Excessive internal heat gives rise to canker of the mouth. ❸ worn-out; tattered: 破衣～衫 worn-out (*or* tattered) clothes /破铜～铁 scrap iron and copper /他没几天就穿～一双鞋。He wore out a pair of shoes within a few days. ❹ messy; confused: *see* "～账"; "～摊子" ❺ thoroughly; very: 他是个～忠厚没用的人。He is very kind but quite incompetent. ❻〈书面〉 bright; shining: 灿～ bright; magnificent; splendid
烂肠瘟 lànchángwēn 〈方言〉 rinderpest; cattle plague
烂肠子 lànchángzi *also* "烂肚肠" 〈口语〉 have rotten bowels — be wicked or evil: 这小子烂了肠子，干下这缺德事。The guy must be thoroughly rotten to have done something like that.
烂糊 lànhu (of food) mushy; pulpy: ～面 mushy (*or* pulpy) noodles /把大米粥煮～点。Cook the rice gruel so that it becomes mushy. /老人没牙，爱吃～的东西。The toothless old man likes to have his food cooked to a pulp.
烂货 lànhuò 〈口语〉 ❶〈贬义〉 woman of easy virtue; hussy; whore ❷ goods of poor quality; shoddy stuff
烂漫 lànmàn *also* "烂熳"; "烂缦" ❶ bright-coloured; brilliant: 春光～ spring is very much in the air; spring has arrived in full splendour /待到山花～时，她在丛中笑。When the mountain flowers are in full bloom, She will smile mingling in their midst. ❷ unaffected; unpretentious: 天真～ innocent and naive /这老头儿有一颗～的童心。The old man is as unpretentious as a child.
烂熳 lànmàn *see* "烂漫"
烂泥 lànní mud; slush; mire: ～坑 muddy pond; quagmire/ 踩了一脚～ get one's feet muddied /吓得瘫成一堆～ be paralysed with fear
烂然 lànrán bright; shining: 星光～ shining stars /锦色～ riot of colours
烂舌头 làn shétou *also* "烂舌根" 〈口语〉 ❶ be fond of gossip; tell tales; backbite: 你看，她又在那儿～! Look! She is gossiping there again. ❷ gossip; scandalmonger; backbiter: 你少跟这种～交往。Stay away from the scandalmonger.
烂熟 lànshú ❶ thoroughly cooked: 羊肉炖得～了。The mutton is thoroughly cooked. ❷ know sth. thoroughly: 诗背得滚瓜～ can recite a poem backwards /他背得～的台词一上场全忘了。He forgot his lines on stage though he had learned them off pat.
烂摊子 làntānzi shambles; awful mess: 收拾～ clear up a mess /谁愿意接这个～? Who is willing to take over this messy business? /这几年他们几个为所欲为，把公司搞成个～。Their reckless management in recent years has made a shambles of the company.
烂污 lànwū 〈方言〉 ❶ watery faeces ❷ (of a woman) loose; dissolute
烂污货 lànwūhuò 〈方言〉 loose woman; hussy; harlot; whore
烂崽 lànzǎi 〈方言〉 rascal; scoundrel
烂账 lànzhàng ❶ messy accounts: 把这些～理出头绪 put these messy accounts into order ❷ bad debt; bad loan: 这几笔～怎么办? What shall we do with these bad debts?
烂醉 lànzuì dead drunk: 喝得～ be dead drunk; be as drunk as a lord
烂醉如泥 lànzuì-rúní be dead drunk; drink oneself into a stupor: 几个人把他灌得～，不省人事。He was made to drink one cup after another till he was dead drunk and unconscious.

lāng

啷 lāng
啷当 lāngdāng 〈方言〉 ❶ (of age) about; around: 他才二十～岁。He is just about twenty years old. ❷ and so on; and the works: 他作料放得挺齐全，葱、姜、蒜、花椒、糖～儿的样样不缺。He put in all kinds of seasonings, such as Chinese onion, ginger, garlic, wild pepper, sugar, and so on.

láng

郎 láng ❶〈古语〉 title for certain officials: 侍～ vice-minister /员外～ (ranking next to 侍郎) counsellor ❷ *used in forming nouns denoting a particular category of person* (*usu. male*): 少年～ youth; lad /新～ bridegroom /伴～ best man /牛～ cowherd /货～ migrant vendor /女～ girl ❸ (used by woman to address her husband or lover) darling; love: 情～ my love ❹〈旧语〉 son of another person: 令～ your son ❺ (Láng) a surname
see also làng
郎才女貌 lángcái-nǚmào (a perfect match between) a talented man and a beautiful woman: 这一对儿～，天作之合。A brilliant scholar and a beautiful lady, the couple is a heaven-made match.
郎当 lángdāng ❶ *see* "锒铛" lángdāng ❷ (of clothing) unfitting; untidy: 衣裤～，不修边幅 be poorly dressed and negligent of one's appearance ❸ dejected; dispirited: 看他走路郎当当的样子，没

L

有一点儿生气。Look at the way he shuffles along; he's so slovenly and listless. ❹ (of a person) useless; good for nothing

郎舅 lángjiù man and his wife's brother:～俩合伙做生意。He and his wife's brother run a business in partnership.

郎君 lángjūn (mainly used in the early vernacular) husband:如意～ ideal husband

郎猫 lángmāo tomcat

郎中 lángzhōng ❶〈古语〉official title (ranking next to 侍郎 and 丞) ❷〈方言〉physician trained in herbal medicine; doctor of Chinese medicine:江湖～ quack doctor

廊

láng porch; corridor; veranda:走～ corridor; passage /回～ winding corridor /游～ covered corridor; veranda /长～ Long Corridor (in the Summer Palace, Beijing) /发～ hairdressing salon (*or* parlour) /画～ art gallery; painted corridor

廊庙 lángmiào 〈书面〉royal or imperial court:～材 talented person fit to serve at court; pillar of the state; talented courtier or minister

廊檐 lángyán eaves of a veranda

廊腰 lángyāo corner of a corridor

廊子 lángzi veranda; corridor; porch

榔

láng

榔槺 lángkang bulky; cumbersome; unwieldy:无奈我这行李包着实～,不便携带。The problem is this piece of luggage of mine is too cumbersome for me to carry.

榔头 lángtou *also*"锒头"lángtou;"狼头"lángtou hammer

榔榆 lángyú 〈植物〉*Ulmus parvifolia*

螂(蜋)

láng *used in the names of certain insects, such as* 螳螂 (tángláng) *and* 蟑螂 (zhāngláng)

锒

láng

锒头 lángtou *see*"榔头"lángtou

娜

láng

娜嬛 lánghuán *see*"琅嬛"lánghuán

阆

láng *see*"闶阆"kāngláng

see also làng

琅(瑯)

láng 〈书面〉❶ a kind of jade ❷ pure white

琅玕 lánggān 〈书面〉pearl-like stone

琅嬛 lánghuán 〈书面〉*also*"娜嬛"lánghuán library of the God of Heaven (in legend)

琅琅 lángláng 〈象声〉tinkle; jingle:～的钟声 jingle of a bell /～书声 ringing sound of reading aloud /～上口 easy to read out

桹

láng

桹桹 lángláng 〈象声〉〈书面〉sound of wood striking wood:寺内木鱼～。The sound of wooden fish (a kind of wooden percussion instrument) lingered in the temple.

硠

láng 〈书面〉sound of water dashing on rocks

锒

láng

锒铛 lángdāng *also*"郎当"lángdāng ❶〈书面〉iron chains ❷ clank; clang:铁索～ clank of iron chains

锒铛入狱 lángdāng-rùyù be chained and thrown into prison

稂

láng 〈古语〉Chinese pennisetum

稂莠 lángyǒu ❶ pennisetum and green bristlegrass; weeds ❷ bad people

狼

láng 〈动物〉wolf:大灰～ timber wolf /一群～ a pack of wolves /黄鼠～ weasel /豺～当道 jackals and wolves holding sway; wicked people in power /披着羊皮的～ wolf in sheep's clothing /引～入室 bring wolves into the house; let the wolf into the fold

狼把草 lángbǎcǎo 〈植物〉beggar-ticks; beggar's-ticks

狼狈 lángbèi in a difficult position; in a tight corner:一副～相 cut a sorry figure /敌人～溃逃。The enemy fled in panic (*or* helter-skelter). /记者的问题把新闻发言人搞得很～。The reporters' questions drove the press spokesperson into a tight corner.

狼狈不堪 lángbèi-bùkān in an extremely awkward situation; in a most distressed position; in dire or sore straits:他的谎话被当面戳穿,真是～。He was most embarrassed when his lie was exposed.

狼狈为奸 lángbèi-wéijiān act in collusion or cahoots; work hand in glove; band together:他宁可饿死,也不与敌人～。He would rather starve than collaborate with the enemy.

狼狈周章 lángbèi-zhōuzhāng be scared out of one's wits; be terror-stricken:打得敌人晕头转向,～。Under our heavy blows enemy troops were scared out of their wits and thrown into utter confusion.

狼奔豕突 lángbēn-shǐtū run like a wolf and rush like a boar — tear about like mad:匪徒们在村里～,到处杀人放火。The bandits went on the rampage through the village, killing people and burning houses everywhere.

狼餐虎咽 lángcān-hǔyàn *also*"狼吞虎咽"wolf down; gobble up; devour ravenously:只见他们几个～,不一会儿,把满桌的酒菜一扫而光。Devouring ravenously, they gobbled up all the food on the table in no time.

狼疮 lángchuāng 〈医学〉lupus:红斑～ lupus erythematosus

狼毒 lángdú 〈中药〉root of *langdu* (*Euphorbia fishericana*)

狼多肉少 lángduō-ròushǎo there is too little meat for so many wolves:～,强盗们自己又火并了起来。The bandits began to fight among themselves for the limited loot.

狼狗 lánggǒu wolfhound; wolf dog

狼顾 lánggù look round worriedly or suspiciously:左右～ look right and left in a suspicious manner

狼孩 lánghái child brought up by a she-wolf; wolf-child

狼毫 lángháo writing brush made of weasel's hair

狼嗥 lángháo wolf's howl:鬼哭～ wail like ghosts and howl like wolves; cry and shriek like mad

狼獾 lánghuān 〈动物〉*also*"貂熊"diāoxióng wolverine; glutton

狼藉 lángjí 〈书面〉*also*"狼籍"in disorder; in a mess:杯盘～ with wine glasses and plates scattered about in a mess /战场上尸体～。Dead bodies were strewn all over the battlefield. /这件丑事弄得他声名～。The scandal ruined his reputation.

狼抗 lángkang *see*"躴躿"lángkang

狼山鸡 lángshānjī *Langshan* chicken (chicken with black feathers, native to Langshan, Jiangsu Province)

狼贪 lángtān greedy as a wolf

狼头 lángtou *also*"榔头"lángtou hammer

狼吞虎咽 lángtūn-hǔyàn wolf down; gobble up; devour ravenously:吃饭别～的,这对身体不好。Don't wolf your food. It's bad for your health.

狼尾草 lángwěicǎo 〈植物〉Chinese pennisetum (*Pennisetum alopecuroides*)

狼心狗肺 lángxīn-gǒufèi ❶ rapacious as a wolf and savage as a cur; cruel and unscrupulous; brutal and cold-blooded:～的匪徒,居然对老人和小孩下毒手。The brutal bandits went so far as to kill old people and children in cold blood. ❷ ungrateful:～,恩将仇报 be so ungrateful as to return evil for good

狼牙 lángyá ❶ wolf's tooth; wolf's fang:～箭 arrowhead shaped like a wolf's fang ❷〈植物〉cryptotaeneous cinquefoil (*Potentilla cryptotaeniae*)

狼牙棒 lángyábàng wolf-teeth club (ancient weapon with sharp iron spikes at the hitting end)

狼烟 lángyān (smoke from) fire built with dried wolves' dung at border posts in ancient China to signal alarm:戍卒四下里点起～报警。The frontier guards lit fires in all directions to warn of the approaching enemy forces.

狼烟四起 lángyān-sìqǐ smoke of war rising from all sides; war alarms raised everywhere:边庭～,战事不断。With alarms raised at all border posts, the country was drawn into continuous war.

狼眼 lángyǎn 〈植物〉fruit of Chinese sweetgum (*Liquidambar taiwaniana*)

狼崽子 lángzǎizi 〈口语〉wolf cub;〈贬义〉brutal or ungrateful young person

狼蛛 lángzhū wolf spider; ground spider; hunting spider

狼主 lángzhǔ 〈旧语〉tribe chieftain; monarch of a nomadic minority regime (in northern China)

狼子野心 lángzǐ-yěxīn wolf cub with a savage heart; wolfish na-

L

ture with wild ambitions:甜言蜜语掩盖不住他的～,对他我们要时时小心。Honeyed words cannot cover up his vicious and ambitious nature. We must be on our guard against him all the time.

狼走千里吃肉,狗走千里吃屎 láng zǒu qiānlǐ chī ròu, gǒu zǒu qiānlǐ chī shǐ 〈谚语〉wolves never lose their taste for meat nor dogs their taste for filth; the leopard can't change his spots

躴 láng

躴躿 lángkāng 〈书面〉tall and slender

躴躿 lángkang *also* "狼抗" lángkang 〈方言〉❶ gobble up; wolf down:他吃饭真～。He always gobbles his food. ❷ unwieldy; cumbersome:这个铁箱子真够～的。This iron box is really cumbersome. ❸ dirty; filthy

lǎng

烺 lǎng

〈书面〉(mostly used in people's names) bright and clear; bright and cheerful

朗 lǎng

❶ light; bright:明～ bright and clear /晴～ fine; sunny /豁然开～ (of space) open out abruptly; (of people) suddenly see the light ❷ loud and clear:～咏 narrate in a loud and clear voice

朗敞 lǎngchǎng bright and spacious:这间房子十分～。The room is very commodious.

朗澈 lǎngchè bright and clear; transparent:月色～。It was bright moonlight.

朗读 lǎngdú read aloud; read loudly and clearly:～课文 read a text aloud (*or* loudly) /每天做十分钟～是必要的。It's quite necessary to do reading-aloud for ten minutes every day.

朗朗 lǎnglǎng ❶〈象声〉loud and clear sound, as of reading aloud:书声～ sound of reading aloud /～闻街鼓 hear distinctly the drumming in the street ❷ bright; light:～如日月之光 bright as the sunlight or moonlight

朗姆酒 lǎngmǔjiǔ *also* "兰姆酒" lánmǔjiǔ rum (alcoholic drink made from the juice of the sugar cane)

朗目疏眉 lǎngmù-shūméi bright eyes and graceful eyebrows; with delicate features:小伙子身材修长,～,长得一表人材。He was a handsome young man, tall and slender, with delicate features.

朗然 lǎngrán ❶ bright; shining:月光～。The moon flooded the land with silvery light. ❷ (of sound) loud and clear; clear and melodious:其声～。She (*or* He) has a loud and clear voice.

朗生 lǎngshēng *also* "囊生" nángshēng 〈旧语〉Tibetan household slave

朗声 lǎngshēng loud and clear:～大笑 burst into loud laughter; burst out laughing /他把这首诗～地读了又读。He read the poem several times over in a loud and clear voice.

朗爽 lǎngshuǎng bright and clear; hearty:～的笑声 hearty laughter

朗诵 lǎngsòng read aloud with expression; recite; declaim:～诗 declaim a poem /齐声～ recite in chorus /～会 recitation /～者 reciter

朗诵比赛 lǎngsòng bǐsài recitation contest

朗悟 lǎngwù 〈书面〉agile and intelligent; quick and bright:～之士 men of agility and intelligence /性～,多口才 quick and bright by nature and with the gift of the gab

朗笑 lǎngxiào laughing heartily; hearty laughter:纵声～ burst into hearty laughter; burst out laughing

朗吟 lǎngyín 〈书面〉recite (poetry) aloud with a cadence; chant aloud:～终日,乐此不疲 chant aloud all day long and never tire of doing it /他翘足～,得意非常。Sitting with his legs crossed, he was reciting something with a cadence, looking exceedingly pleased with himself.

朗照 lǎngzhào 〈书面〉❶ shine; illuminate:月亮升起,～着山顶轮廓黝黑的松林。The moon had risen, shedding a flood of light over the dark outline of pines which crowned the mountain. ❷ observe publicly; examine publicly

làng

郎 làng

see "屎壳郎" shǐkelàng

see also láng

浪 làng

❶ wave; billow; breaker:惊涛骇～ terrifying waves /风平～静 the wind has subsided and the waves have calmed down; be calm and tranquil /乘风破～ ride the wind and cleave the waves; brave the wind and waves /冲～ surfing ❷ sth. undulating like waves:声～ sound waves /热～ heat wave; hot wave /麦～ rippling wheat ❸ unrestrained; dissolute:放～ dissolute; dissipated /孟～ rash; impetuous ❹〈方言〉ramble; roam:流～ roam about; lead a vagrant life /哥俩在街上～了一整天,天黑才回到家中。The two brothers roamed the streets for a whole day and did not return home until it was dark.

浪潮 làngcháo tide; wave:抗议的～ waves of protest /改革的～席卷全国。The wave of reform swept across the country. /革命的～汹涌澎湃。The tide of revolution was surging.

浪船 làngchuán swingboat

浪荡 làngdàng ❶ loiter about; loaf about; idle about:一春～不归家 loaf about for a whole spring without returning home ❷ dissolute; debauched; dissipated:～鬼 roué; rake; the dissipated /～娘们 debauched woman /李家大少爷生性～,常有外遇。Dissolute by nature, the eldest son of the Lis often had extramarital affairs.

浪费 làngfèi waste; squander; be extravagant:～人力 waste manpower /～钱财 squander money /～生命 loaf (*or* idle) away one's life /～时间 idle away one's time; fritter away one's time /～无度 lavish money without limit /不要～你的精力。Don't dissipate your energies.

浪高风险 lànggāo-fēngxiǎn the waves are high and the wind strong — dangerous situation:此去～,行船要小心。Watch out when you set sail as the voyage is full of risks.

浪花 lànghuā ❶ spray or foam of breaking waves; spindrift; spoondrift:～四溅 spray flying in all directions /～荡漾。The foam of breaking waves is drifting and swirling. /船头激起～。Spray flew out from the bow of the ship. ❷ special episode or phenomenon in life:生活的～ episodes in (one's) life

浪迹 làngjì drift everywhere with no fixed lodging; lead a vagrant life:～江湖 lead a wandering and vagabond life /～半生 loaf away half of one's life

浪漫 làngmàn ❶ romantic; poetic; imaginative:西湖三日～之游,大家玩得十分开心。Everybody had a very good time during the three-day romantic tour round the West Lake. ❷ abandoned; lax; loose:她为人～,常引起人们的非议。Her loose behaviour often gave rise to censure.

浪漫史 làngmànshǐ romance:总统当年的～成了反对党攻讦的材料。The president's past romance was raked up by the opposition to vilify him.

浪漫主义 làngmànzhǔyì romanticism:～者 romanticist /～派 romantic school /～运动 Romantic Movement (in Europe in the late 18th and the early 19th centuries)

浪木 làngmù *also* "浪桥" swing-bridge; swing log

浪桥 làngqiáo see "浪木"

浪人 làngrén ❶ tramp; vagrant; nomad:吾本～,一生四海为家。Vagrant as I was, I made home everywhere. ❷ (Japanese) ronin; hooligan; gangster

浪涛 làngtāo great waves; billows:～滚滚 rolling waves /～汹涌 roaring waves

浪头 làngtou ❶ wave:海风大,～高 rough sea wind and towering waves ❷ trend:办事情要实事求是,千万不要赶～。Be down-to-earth in whatever you do. Don't just try to follow the trend.

浪涌 làngyǒng 〈电学〉surge:～电流 surge current /～放电器 surge arrester (*or* suppressor) /～撞击 surging shock

浪涌电压 làngyǒng diànyā 〈电学〉surge voltage; power surge:～发生器 surge generator

浪游 làngyóu stroll about aimlessly; roam; wander; loaf:～四方 wander from place to place /终日～,无所事事 idle away one's time from one day to another

浪语 làngyǔ ❶ lewd remarks; bawdy speech:淫词～ obscene remarks ❷ groundless talk; nonsense; rubbish ❸ indulge in irresponsible remarks; be given to idle gossip:莫～。Don't make irresponsible remarks.

浪子 làngzǐ prodigal; loafer; wastrel:～回头 return of the prodigal son; reform of a loafer /昔日的～,今日已成为一名模范军人。A former loafer, he is now a model soldier.

through labour
劳改农场 láogǎi nóngchǎng reform-through-labour farm
劳工 láogōng ❶ labourer; worker: ~运动 labour movement / ~立法 labour legislation ❷〈旧语〉coolie: 当~ work as a coolie
劳绩 láojì merits and accomplishments: ~卓著 with outstanding merits and accomplishments
劳驾 láojià 〈套语〉excuse me; may I trouble you: ~! (polite expression used when one wants to get past a person, etc.) Excuse me. / ~请问去邮局怎么走? Excuse me, would you please tell me how to get to the post office? / ~请把门关上。May I trouble you to shut the door? *or* Would you please close the door? / 这件事恐怕还得多劳您大驾。I'm afraid we have to bother you with the problem.
劳教 láojiào (short for 劳动教养) reeducation (of juvenile delinquents, etc.) through labour: ~农场 reeducation-through-labour farm
劳教人员 láojiào rényuán juvenile delinquent being reeducated through labour
劳金 láojīn 〈旧语〉pay (to shop assistants or long-term hired hands by shopowners or landlords): 那些年, 父亲拿到的~不够全家糊口。During those years father didn't earn enough to support the family.
劳倦 láojuàn tired; fatigued; weary: 他连续工作了一整天也不觉得~。He worked continuously for a whole day without feeling tired.
劳军 láojūn greet and bring gifts to army units (in recognition of their services); comfort the soldiers (with entertainment, etc.): ~礼品 rewards for the soldiers / ~演出 performance for the soldiers in recognition of their services
劳苦 láokǔ toil; hard work: ~大众 toiling masses; working people / 不辞~ spare no pains / 母亲~半生, 晚年时常卧病。Having drudged for half of her life, mother was often confined to bed in her later years.
劳苦功高 láokǔ-gōnggāo have worked hard and performed meritorious service; score great achievements; make great contributions
劳困 láokùn tired; weary; run-down; overworked
劳劳 láoláo 〈书面〉distressed and disconsolate; melancholy and laden with grief: 举手长~, 二情同依依。Deep was their love for each other and lingeringly they waved a melancholy good-bye.
劳累 láolèi ❶ tired; run-down; exhausted; overworked: 才上了几天班, 就感到十分~。I felt run-down after only a few days' work. / ~了一天, 胳膊都抬不起来了。At the end of a day's tiring work I couldn't even raise my arms. / 他看上去病得很厉害, 一定是~过度了。He looked very ill. He must have overworked. ❷〈敬词〉cause sb. trouble: 又~您一趟, 真过意不去。I'm sorry to have troubled you again.
劳力 láolì ❶ labour; work: 我枉费了半天~。My half day's labour has gone to waste. *or* I've worked for the whole morning (*or* afternoon) to no avail. ❷ labour force; able-bodied person: ~市场 labour market / ~外流 brawn drain / 车间~紧张。The workshop is short of hands. ❸ use one's physical strength; do manual work: 劳心者治人, ~者治于人。(Confucian tenet) Those who work with their brains rule (*or* govern), and those who work with their brawn are ruled (*or* governed).
劳力费心 láolì-fèixīn exert one's strength and rack one's brains: 我们对这件事如此~, 但未必能如愿以偿。Hard as we have striven, we may not be able to have our wish fulfilled.
劳碌 láolù work hard; toil: 一天到晚~不堪 work extremely hard from morning till night
劳民伤财 láomín-shāngcái tire the people and drain the treasury; waste money and manpower: 干~的蠢事 do stupid things which waste both energy and money
劳模 láomó (short for 劳动模范) model worker
劳其筋骨, 苦其心志 láo qí jīngǔ, kǔ qí xīnzhì toughen one's body and harden one's will; undergo both mental trials and bodily hardships
劳伤 láoshāng 〈中医〉internal lesion caused by overexertion: 李大爷因为积久~, 吐了几次血。Uncle Li's internal lesion worsened in the course of time, and he spit blood several times.
劳神 láoshén ❶ be trying; be a tax on (one's mind): 你身体有病, 就不要为家务事~了。As you are ill, just don't bother about housework. ❷〈套语〉may I trouble you; will you please: ~帮我照看一下房子。Would you please mind the house for me?
劳神费力 láoshén-fèilì *also* "劳力费心" tax one's mind and strength
劳师 láoshī 〈书面〉take greetings and gifts to army units: 千里~ travel a thousand *li* to greet the soldiers and reward them with gifts
劳师动众 láoshī-dòngzhòng mobilize too many troops; drag in lots of people: 这点小事, 何必~的? There is no need to drag in so many people for such a trivial matter.
劳师袭远 láoshī-xíyuǎn exhaust the troops by attacking a far-away enemy: ~, 兵家所不取。Military strategists should avoid tiring out the troops by attacking an enemy in remote land.
劳师远征 láoshī-yuǎnzhēng wear down the troops on a long expedition: ~, 无功而返。The troops went on a long, tiring expedition but came back empty-handed.
劳什子 láoshízi *also* "牢什子" láoshízi 〈方言〉nuisance; plaything: 要这些~有什么用? What's the use of all these trinkets?
劳损 láosǔn 〈医学〉strain: 肌腱~ muscular strain / 腰肌~ strain of lumbar muscles; psoatic strain / 脏腑~ strain of one's internal organs
劳武结合 láo-wǔ jiéhé do both production and militia duties; engage in productive labour and perform militia duties
劳务 láowù (labour) services: ~价值 value of services / ~合同 contract for services / 购买~ purchase of services / ~输出 export of labour services / 商品和~出口 export of goods and services / ~合作 cooperation in the field of labour services
劳务费 láowùfèi service charge
劳务市场 láowù shìchǎng labour market
劳心 láoxīn ❶ rack one's brains; have on one's mind; take pains: ~苦思 cudgel (*or* rack) one's brains ❷〈书面〉work with one's brains; do mental labour: ~者 people who do mental labour ❸〈书面〉be worried: 无思远人, ~忉忉。Don't pine for people who are far away. It would fill you with anxiety if you do.
劳形苦神 láoxíng-kǔshén tire one's body and consume one's energy; exert (physical) strength and weary one's mind
劳亚古大陆 Láoyà Gǔdàlù Laurasia, supercontinent comprising North America, Europe and Asia, which is believed to have existed for millions of years before splitting up during the Cenozoic era
劳燕分飞 láoyàn-fēnfēi be like the shrike and the swallow flying in opposite directions; part; separate: 十几年中, 夫妻二人~, 难得一聚。Over the past dozen years or more, the husband and wife were mostly separate and seldom together.
劳役 láoyì ❶〈法律〉penal servitude; forced labour: 判处该犯~十五年。The criminal was sentenced to fifteen years' forced labour. ❷ corvée: 服~ do corvée labour ❸ use (as a draught animal): 家里只有一头能~的牛。There was only one ox that could be used.
劳役地租 láoyì dìzū *also* "徭役地租" yáoyì dìzū rent in the form of service; labour rent
劳逸 láo-yì work and rest: ~不均 uneven allocation of work load / 聪明人会安排时间, 有劳有逸。A wise man knows how to schedule his time, alternating work with recreation.
劳逸结合 láo-yì jiéhé strike a proper balance between work and rest; alternate work with rest and recreation: 工作中, 要注意~, 保护群众的积极性。Keep a proper balance between work and rest so as to sustain the enthusiasm of the masses.
劳资 láo-zī labour and capital: ~双方 (two parties of) labour and capital / ~关系 relations between labour and capital; labour-capital relations; employee-employer relations; labour-management relations / ~合作 collaboration between labour and capital / ~和谐 industrial harmony / ~纠纷〈法律〉industrial dispute; dispute between labour and management / ~两利 benefit both labour and capital / ~谈判 negotiations between labour and capital (*or* between employee and employer) / ~协议 collective bargaining agreement
劳资法庭 láo-zī fǎtíng industrial court
劳作 láozuò ❶〈旧语〉handiwork as a primary school course ❷ labour; work: 村民们都在地里~。The villagers were all working in the fields.

痨(癆) láo

consumptive disease; consumption; tuberculosis; TB: 肺~ pulmonary tuberculosis; phthisis / 肠~ tuberculosis of the intestines / 干血~〈中医〉type of tubercular disease found in women, usu. characterized by menostasis, recurrent low fever and general debility
痨病 láobìng 〈中医〉consumption; tuberculosis; TB; phthisis

L

塂(塂) láo see“圪塂”gēlao

唠(嘮) láo

see also lào

唠叨 láodao chatter; be talkative; be garrulous:～不休 chatter endlessly (*or* interminably); be garrulous; talk the hind leg off a donkey (*or* dog, *or* horse)/你～了半天,能不能听我说说? You have been babbling on for a good while now. Could you please listen to me? /回家来她～个不停。She goes gab, gab all the time, when she's home. /不要老是跟我唠唠叨叨,我受不了。Don't pick at me all the time. I just can't bear it.

崂(嶗) Láo

崂山 Láoshān *also*“劳山”Láoshān Laoshan mountain, in Shandong Province:～矿泉水 Laoshan mineral water

铹(鐒) láo 〈化学〉lawrencium (Lw):～化合物 lawrencium compound /～同位素 lawrencium isotope

痨(癆) láo see“簕痨竹”sīláozhú

醪 láo 〈书面〉❶ wine with dregs; undecanted wine:浊～ wine with dregs; undecanted wine ❷ mellow wine:醇～ mellow wine

醪糟 láozāo fermented glutinous rice

lǎo

潦 lǎo 〈书面〉❶ heavy rainfall:雨～ heavy rain ❷ running water or water puddles on the road

see also liáo

老 lǎo ❶ old; aged:人～志不～ old but full of youthful aspirations; old in age but young in ambition /活到～学到～ never cease to learn as long as you live; live and learn /白头偕～ remain happily married to a ripe old age ❷ (often used respectfully) elderly person; senior person; old people:邓～ revered old Deng; venerable Deng /养～院 home for the aged; senior citizens' home /敬～爱幼 respect for the old and care for the young /扶～携幼 bringing along the old and the young / ～幼咸宜 be suitable (*or* good) for people of all ages ❸〈婉词〉(mostly of old people, always accompanied by 了) go the way of all flesh; die:那位先生昨天晚上～了。The old gentleman passed away last night. ❹seasoned; experienced; veteran: *see*“～手”;“～于世故” ❺ of long standing; old:～邻居 old neighbour /～同事 long-time colleague /～革命根据地 old revolutionary base /这群干部中他的资历最～。He has the longest record of service among these cadres. ❻ outdated; old-fashioned; obsolete:～思想 old-fashioned idea /～机器 obsolete machine /～方法 outmoded method ❼ original; former; same:～地方 same place /他还是～脾气。His temperament remained unchanged. ❽ (usu. of vegetables) overgrown:黄瓜不及时摘就～了。The cucumbers will be overgrown if not picked in time. ❾ tough; overcooked:肉炖～了。The meat is overstewed. /韭菜不要炒得这么～。Don't overcook the chives. /我不喜欢太～的牛排。I don't like tough steaks. /鸡蛋炒嫩点儿还是～点儿? Do you like the eggs underdone or well-done? ❿〈化学〉change in quality; age; deteriorate:防～剂 antioxidant; antiager; antideteriorant ⓫ (of colour) dark:～绿 dark green /～红 dark red /这条裙子你穿颜色太～。This skirt is too dark for you. ⓬for a long time; long:你近来出门了吧,怎么～没见你啊? Have you been away recently? I haven't seen you for a long time. /这机器～不用,生锈了。The machine gets rusty from long disuse. ⓭always; constantly; frequently:他～是自作主张。He always likes to act on his own. /他休假期间～惦念着班里的学生。He kept thinking of the students in his class while he was on holiday. ⓮ very; extremely; terribly:～大的年纪 very old /天气～热 terribly hot /马路～宽～宽的。The boulevard is very wide. /他大～远的跑来看我。He came such a long way to see me. ⓯〈口语〉youngest:～妹子 youngest sister ⓰ *used as prefix before a person to indicate order or before some animals and plants*:～张 Lao Zhang /刘家～二 second child (*or* son) of the Lius /～鼠 mouse /～棒子儿 maize kernels ⓱ (Lǎo) a surname

老媪 lǎo'ǎo 〈书面〉old or aged woman

老八板儿 lǎobābǎnr 〈方言〉overcautious and conservative; rigid; inflexible; stick-in-the-mud:没见过你这样～的人! I've never seen such an old fogey as you!

老八辈子 lǎobābèizi ancient; age-old; hoary; stale:两家～没来往了。The two families haven't had any contacts for ages. /你说的是～的事了,如今的年轻人可不爱听。Your tales are out-of-date and boring to young people today.

老八路 lǎobālù veteran of the former Eighth Route Army

老把势 lǎobǎshi old hand

老把戏 lǎobǎxì same old stuff; same old story; old trick; outmoded method:如今你这一套～可吃不开了! Your old trick no longer works now.

老爸 lǎobà 〈口语〉(usu. used by a younger person to refer to his or her father) the old man; guvnor:～,这事可得让我自己干了。Leave this to me, guvnor.

老白干儿 lǎobáigānr 〈方言〉spirit distilled from sorghum or maize; white spirit; strong liquor

老百姓 lǎobǎixìng common people; ordinary people; civilians; men in the street:照顾～的利益 take into consideration the interest of the people /不管是～还是高级干部,在法律面前应当人人平等。Common people or high-ranking officials, all should be equal before the law.

老板 lǎobǎn ❶ shopkeeper; proprietor; boss:店里亏了本,～的脸色不好看。The shopkeeper looked sullen as the shop lost money in business. /新来的～特别喜欢她。The new boss dotes on her. ❷〈旧语〉respectful form of address for well-known opera actors or managers of theatrical troupes:梅～昨晚上那出戏真叫绝! Mr. Mei's performance last night was just superb!

老板娘 lǎobǎnniáng shopkeeper's wife; proprietress:饭馆的～ proprietress of a restaurant

老板子 lǎobǎnzi 〈方言〉cart driver; cart owner

老半天 lǎobàntiān 〈口语〉for a long time; long:怎么才来,我们等你～了。Why so late? We've been waiting for you for a long time.

老伴儿 lǎobànr 〈口语〉old spouse:我的～ my old man (*or* woman); my husband (*or* wife)

老梆子 lǎobāngzi 〈口语〉old vegetable:都～了,还卖什么俏! What a flirtatious old vegetable!

老蚌生珠 lǎobàng-shēngzhū an old clam producing a pearl — an elderly woman giving birth to a son; having a son at an old age

老保 lǎobǎo (term used derogatorily in the Cultural Revolution) conservative; die-hard conservative

老鸨 lǎobǎo *also*“老鸨子”woman running a brothel; procuress; madam

老悖晦 lǎobèihui *also*“老悖”〈方言〉old and befuddled:我都～了,说了就忘。I'm old and befuddled and always forgetting things.

老辈 lǎobèi one's elders; old folks:族里几个～坐在上方。The clan's elders sat in the seats of honour.

老本 lǎoběn principal; capital:吃～ live off one's past gains; rest on one's laurels /亏了～ lose one's capital; lose money in business /输光～ lose one's last stakes

老鼻子 lǎobízi 〈方言〉lots of; plenty of; large numbers of:你的活比他差～了。your work is far inferior to his.

老表 lǎobiǎo ❶ male cousin on mother's side ❷〈方言〉polite form of address for male strangers about one's own age:这几个～常来店里光顾。These are regular patrons of the shop.

老兵 lǎobīng old soldier; veteran

老病 lǎobìng ❶ disease that has not been fully cured and often recurs; chronic illness; chronic condition; old trouble:天一冷,～就犯了。I'm liable to have an attack of the old illness as soon as the weather gets cold. ❷ old and often ill:我虽～无能,但这点儿事还做得了。Old, sick and useless as I am, I can still manage this.

老伯 lǎobó 〈敬词〉(used to address people of father's generation) uncle:好久不见了,～近来身体安康? Haven't seen you for a long time. How is your father recently?

老伯伯 lǎobóbo 〈敬词〉(used to address elderly people) granddad; grandpa

老不死 lǎobùsǐ 〈粗话〉person who has outlived his usefulness; old devil; old scoundrel

老不正经 lǎobuzhèngjing old but still goatish; lewd old man or woman

L

老布 lǎobù 〈方言〉handwoven cloth; homespun cloth

老财 lǎocái 〈方言〉moneybags; landlord: 地主～们 landlords and moneybags; landlords

老蚕作茧 lǎocán-zuòjiǎn old silkworm spinning a silk cocoon — strive to make a living in one's old age

老苍 lǎocang old and wizened (in appearance): 他虽已六十多了，可不显得～。He doesn't look old though he's over sixty.

老巢 lǎocháo nest; den; lair: 端了土匪的～ completely destroy the bandits' den / 几个匪徒急急忙忙逃回了～。Several bandits scurried back to their lair.

老陈人儿 lǎochénrénr 〈方言〉long-time member; veteran: 他是这个药铺的～。He has been with the herbal medicine shop for many years.

老成 lǎochéng experienced; steady: 少年～ young but steady; old head on young shoulders / ～之见 prudent view

老成持重 lǎochéng-chízhòng experienced and prudent; mature; prudent and cool-headed: 经历的事情越多，他越发～了。The more experienced he is, the more mature he becomes.

老成凋谢 lǎochéng-diāoxiè a grand old man has passed away or departed this life

老成练达 lǎochéng-liàndá wise and sophisticated; experienced and worldly-wise; well acquainted with the way of the world

老成土 lǎochéngtǔ 〈地质〉ultisol

老诚 lǎochéng honest and sincere; honest: ～忠厚 sincere and tolerant / 他是一个～的孩子，从来不说一句谎话。He is an honest child and has never told a lie.

老虫 lǎochóng 〈方言〉❶ tiger ❷ mouse; rat

老处女 lǎochǔnǚ old maid; spinster

老粗 lǎocū *also* "大老粗" dàlǎocū (often used as a self-derogatory term) uneducated person; rough and ready chap: 我是个～，没上过几年学。I'm a rough man with only a few years of schooling.

老搭档 lǎodādàng old partner; old workmate: 我同他已是多年的～了。He and I have been partners for many years.

老大 lǎodà ❶〈书面〉old: 少小离家～回 leaving home when young and returning home an old man ❷ eldest child (in a family); eldest among siblings; first among equals: 他们家～参军去了。Their eldest son has joined the army. ❸〈方言〉boatman or chief boatman of a sailing vessel; captain; skipper: 船～ boatman; captain; skipper ❹ greatly; very: 心中～不忍 feel extremely reluctant / 他心里～不高兴，嘴上却什么也没说。He felt greatly annoyed but did not say anything.

老大不小 lǎodà-bùxiǎo 〈口语〉have grown up: 他～的了，也该闯练闯练了。He has already grown up and should go out to see the world. / 你也～的了，该懂事啦。You are no longer a child and should be amenable to reason.

老大哥 lǎodàgē 〈敬词〉elder brother

老大难 lǎo-dà-nán long-standing, big and difficult problem; hard nut to crack: ～单位 unit with serious and long-standing problems / ～问题 problem that has long defied solution; difficult (*or* knotty) problem of long standing / 她已经三十多了，还没有对象，都成～了。Being over thirty and finding no good match, she's really becoming a big problem (to her family, etc.) now.

老大娘 lǎodàniang 〈敬词〉(usu. of an elderly woman one doesn't know) aunty; granny: 多亏这位～指引，我才到你家。Thanks to this aunty, I've found my way to your house.

老大无成 lǎodà-wúchéng be getting old but have accomplished nothing: 他蹉跎一生，～，想起来不免悲伤。Thinking in his old age that he had idled away his life without any accomplishments, he could not help feeling sad.

老大爷 lǎodàye 〈敬词〉(usu. of an elderly man one doesn't know) uncle; grandpa

老旦 lǎodàn 〈戏曲〉*laodan*, part of an elderly woman

老当益壮 lǎodāng-yìzhuàng be aspiring despite old age; be old but vigorous; there's many a good tune played on an old fiddle: 穷当益坚，～ all the more determined in adversity and all the more aspiring in old age

老道 lǎodào 〈口语〉Taoist priest

老到 lǎodao 〈方言〉(in doing things) experienced and thoughtful: 他办事极～可靠。He is very experienced, careful and reliable in business.

老等 lǎoděng ❶ wait for a long time: 你早点动身，别让我们～。Start early and don't keep us waiting too long. ❷〈口语〉heron

老底 lǎodǐ ❶ inside story; past; unsavory background: 揭～ reveal the inside story (about sth.); dredge up some embarrassing facts about sb.'s past; drag the skeleton out of sb.'s closet (*or* cupboard) / 大伙儿都知道他的～。Everybody knows how much he is worth. *or* Everyone knows his unsavory past. ❷ family fortune; inheritance; past gains: 他家～儿厚。His family has great wealth. / 他把～儿败光了。He has squandered all he inherited.

老弟 lǎodì ❶ (familiar form of address to a man younger than oneself) young man; young fellow; buddy; my boy: 小～，别逞能了。My boy, don't try to show off. / ～，你还是听我几句劝吧。Young man, you'd better listen to my advice. ❷〈方言〉younger brother

老吊 lǎodiào 〈口语〉crane; hoisting machine

老调 lǎodiào ❶ hackneyed theme; platitude: ～子 same old story; same old tune / 少唱～，大家都不爱听! Drop your platitudes. No one is interested. ❷ *also* "直隶梆子" Zhílì bāngzi local opera popular in the Baoding (保定) area of Hebei Province

老调重弹 lǎodiào-chóngtán *also* "旧调重弹" jiùdiào-chóngtán harp on the same string; sing the same old tune

老掉牙 lǎodiàoyá out of date; obsolete; corny; ancient: ～的笑话 corny joke / ～的谎言 hoary lie / ～的故事，我都听腻了。An ancient story. I'm fed up with it.

老爹 lǎodiē 〈方言〉(respectful form of address for an old man) granddad; grandpa

老东西 lǎodōngxi useless old thing; silly old fool: 不识好歹的～。That old fogey doesn't know what's good for him.

老豆腐 lǎodòufu ❶ processed bean curd ❷ bean curd made in the northern style; firm tofu

老儿子 lǎo'érzi 〈口语〉youngest son

老而弥笃 lǎo'érmídǔ one's love grows deeper as one grows old

老而弥坚 lǎo'érmíjiān become even firmer in conviction as one grows old

老坟 lǎofén ancestral grave

老佛爷 lǎofóye ❶ Buddha ❷ popular term for empress dowager or emperor's father in the Qing Dynasty

老夫 lǎofū 〈书面〉(used by an old man to refer to himself) I; me: ～年过八十，身体尚好。I'm over eighty but still in good health.

老夫老妻 lǎofū-lǎoqī old married couple

老夫少妻 lǎofū-shàoqī old man with a young wife

老夫子 lǎofūzǐ ❶〈旧语〉tutor in an old-style private school; family tutor ❷ pedant ❸ aide; advisor (in the Qing Dynasty): 知府大人又请～重新写过奏折。His excellency the prefect asked his advisor to rewrite the memorial to the throne.

老弗大 lǎofúdà 〈方言〉〈植物〉Japanese ardisia (*Ardisia japonica*)

老赶 lǎogǎn 〈方言〉❶ have not seen the world; be inexperienced or green: 他真～，连迪斯科都不会跳。He is green and even doesn't know how to dance disco. ❷ inexperienced person; layman; greenhorn: 他拿我当～。He treats me as an amateur.

老干部 lǎogànbù veteran cadre (often used to refer to those who started working for the revolution before the establishment of the People's Republic on 1 October 1949, or to retired public servants in general)

老干部局 lǎogànbùjú bureau or department of retired cadres

老干 lǎogan 〈方言〉simple; plain: 打扮得很～ be simply dressed

老疙瘩 lǎogēda 〈方言〉youngest son or daughter; baby of the family

老庚 lǎogēng 〈方言〉(used as a form of address for people of one's own age) chap; buddy; guy

老公 lǎogōng 〈方言〉husband

老公 lǎogong 〈口语〉eunuch

老公公 lǎogōnggong ❶〈方言〉(used by children to refer to an old man) granddad; grandpa ❷〈方言〉husband's father; father-in-law (of a woman) ❸〈旧语〉eunuch

老公会 Lǎogōnghuì 〈宗教〉Old Catholic Church

老姑娘 lǎogūniang ❶ spinster; old maid; maiden lady ❷ youngest daughter

老古板 lǎogǔbǎn stick-in-the-mud; stickler for rules and regulations; fuddy-duddy

老古董 lǎogǔdǒng ❶ old-fashioned article; antique; museum piece; old idea: 他身在新社会，脑子里的～还真不少哩! Living in a new society as he does, he is full of old-fashioned ideas. ❷ old fogey; fuddy-duddy

老骨头 lǎogǔtou 〈口语〉(used irreverently or jocularly of an old

man) old bloke; old guy: 早些时候还登上泰山，可见我这把～还相当硬朗。Earlier I even climbed up Mount Tai, which shows this old bloke's still hale and hearty.

老鸹 lǎogua 〈方言〉crow: ～叫 crying of crows / ～窝里出凤凰 a phoenix grows out of a crow's nest; mediocre parents give birth to talented offspring

老关系 lǎoguānxi old-comrade network; long-standing ties or connections

老倌 lǎoguān 〈方言〉❶ *also* "老倌子" elderly man ❷ husband

老棺材 lǎoguāncai 〈贬义〉old windbag; old vegetable

老光 lǎoguāng presbyopia; presbyopy: ～眼 presbyopia / ～眼镜 presbyopic glasses / ～现象 presbyopic phenomenon

老规矩 lǎoguīju old rules and regulations; established custom or practice; convention: 按～，春节大人给孩子压岁钱。As an age-old practice adults give lucky money to children during the Spring Festival. / 都什么时候了，你那一套～吃不开了。Times have changed. Your old ways no longer hold good. / ～，国庆节放假三天。As a rule, we have a three-day holiday for National Day.

老闺女 lǎoguīnü 〈口语〉*see* "老姑娘"

老海 lǎohǎi 〈俗语〉heroin

老憨 lǎohān simpleton

老汉 lǎohàn ❶ old man: 树下有两个～在乘凉。There were two old men enjoying the cool under a tree. ❷ myself (used by an old man); old fellow like me: ～我今年八十八了。I'm eighty-eight this year.

老好人 lǎohǎorén one who tries never to offend anybody without regard to principles; one who tries to please everybody: 他是个与世无争的～。He is a man who has no quarrel with the world and tries never to antagonize anybody.

老好子 lǎohǎozi 〈方言〉*see* "老好人"

老红军 lǎohóngjūn veteran of the former Red Army (1927-1937)

老狐狸 lǎohúli old fox; crafty scoundrel; old rogue

老糊涂 lǎohútu old and confused; doting; dotard

老虎 lǎohǔ tiger: 母～ tigress; shrew

老虎车 lǎohǔchē 〈方言〉two-wheeled hand-pulled cart; hand cart

老虎窗 lǎohǔchuāng 〈方言〉roof dormer; dormer window; dormer; luthern

老虎凳 lǎohǔdèng rack (used as an instrument of torture); torture rack

老虎屁股摸不得 lǎohǔ pìgu mōbude like a tiger whose backside no one dares to touch — one who won't allow any different opinons; one who is not to be crossed: 他在机关里称王称霸，～。Lording it over everyone in his office, he simply won't tolerate any views different from his own.

老虎钳 lǎohǔqián ❶ vice ❷ pincer pliers

老虎摊儿 lǎohǔtānr 〈旧语〉sundry goods stand, where fake antiques and other articles were sold at high prices

老虎头上蹭痒 lǎohǔ tóushang cèngyǎng 〈俗语〉scratch oneself against a tiger's head — court trouble

老虎头上拍苍蝇 lǎohǔ tóushang pāi cāngying 〈俗语〉swat a fly on the head of a tiger — invite trouble; court disaster

老虎灶 lǎohǔzào 〈方言〉huge kitchen range for boiling water; place that provides hot water or boiling water

老虎嘴里拔牙 lǎohǔ zuǐli báyá 〈俗语〉pull a tooth from a tiger's mouth — dare the greatest danger; beard the lion in his den

老花 lǎohuā presbyopia

老花镜 lǎohuājìng presbyopic glasses

老花眼 lǎohuāyǎn (popular term for 老视眼) presbyopia

老花子 lǎohuāzi 〈方言〉beggar

老化 lǎohuà ❶〈化学〉ageing: 这种塑料地板砖～慢，质量不错。This plastic flooring ages slowly and is of good quality. ❷ (of people) ageing; getting older: 人口～ ageing population / 教师队伍～，后继无人现象日益严重。With the teachers growing older and older, there is an increasing shortage of successors. ❸ (of knowledge, technique, etc.) become outmoded or outdated; obsolete: 有些理论已～、过时。Some theories have become obsolete and outdated.

老话 lǎohuà ❶ old saying; saying; adage: 有句～说，"日久见人心"，时间长了你就会知道他的为人。As the saying goes, it takes time to know a person, you will learn what he is really like with the passage of time. ❷ remarks about sth. in the past: ～重提 repeat what one has said about something in the past / 他说过的一些～，我们千万别忘了。We should never forget his remarks about the past.

老皇历 lǎohuánglì calendar of the past; old history; obsolete practice: 情况变了，不能再照～办事。Things have changed. Matters can no longer be handled according to past practice.

老黄牛 lǎohuángniú willing ox — person who serves sb. wholeheartedly: 人民的～ one who serves the people with all his heart

老火 lǎohuǒ 〈方言〉❶ serious; grave; terrible; formidable ❷ (of matters) difficult to handle

老鸡头 lǎojītóu 〈方言〉〈植物〉Gorgon euryale (*Euryale ferox*)

老几 lǎojǐ ❶ order of seniority among siblings; birth order: 你排行～? Where do you come in the family? *or* Are you the eldest, the second, or what? ❷ *usu. used in rhetorical questions to indicate a negligible status*: 你算～，敢来教训我? Who do you think you are? How dare you lecture me! / 和他们比，我算～? Compared with them, I'm nobody.

老骥伏枥，志在千里 lǎojì fú lì, zhì zài qiānlǐ an old steed in the stable still aspires to gallop a thousand *li* — old people may still cherish high aspirations: 他虽然年纪大了，但是～。Although advanced in years, he still cherishes high aspirations. / ～；烈士暮年，壮心不已。A veteran thoroughbred in the stable still dreams of the wilds; a man of action, though advanced in years, aspires after great exploits.

老家 lǎojiā ❶ (as distinct from one's home away from one's native place) old home; native place: 我～还有父母和两个妹妹。Back in my native place there are my parents and two younger sisters. ❷ ancestral home: 我～是湖南。I come from Hunan.

老家儿 lǎojiār 〈方言〉parents or grandparents: 离家已十几天了，～还不知怎么惦记着我呢! I have been away from home for over ten days. My parents must be missing me a great deal.

老家贼 lǎojiāzéi 〈方言〉〈动物〉(house) sparrow

老奸巨滑 lǎojiān-jùhuá past master of machination and manoeuvre; old hand at trickery; crafty old scoundrel; wily old fox: 徐总经理一向～，很有手段。Shrewd and crafty, General Manager Xu is an old hand at trickery.

老茧 lǎojiǎn callosity; callus: 长满～的手 callused (*or* callous) hand

老趼 lǎojiǎn *see* "老茧"

老健春寒秋后热 lǎojiàn chūnhán qiūhòu rè 〈俗语〉the healthiest old people last as long or as short as a chilly spring or a hot autumn; healthy as an old man appears, it is unpredictable how long he lasts

老江湖 lǎojiānghu 〈旧语〉man of the world; well-travelled, worldly-wise person; one who has seen much of the world: 一看就知道他是见过世面的～。One look tells that he is a well-travelled, worldly-wise person, who has experienced life.

老将 lǎojiàng ❶ old general; veteran; old-timer: 体坛～ veteran sportsman ❷ commander-in-chief — chief piece in Chinese chess; king

老将出马，一个顶俩 lǎojiàng chū mǎ, yīge dǐng liǎ 〈俗语〉when a veteran goes into action, he can do the job of two

老交情 lǎojiāoqing long-standing friendship; old friend: 看在～面上，你这回一定要帮忙。For the sake of our long-standing friendship, you've got to help me this time.

老街坊 lǎojiēfang 〈口语〉old neighbour

老街旧邻 lǎojiē-jiùlín *also* "老街旧坊"〈口语〉old neighbours: ～的了，何必为这点小事红脸? We are old neighbours. Why fly off the handle for such a trivial matter?

老解放区 lǎojiěfàngqū old liberated area (revolutionary base area established in the early days of the Communist Party of China)

老景 lǎojǐng situation or circumstances in old age: ～堪怜 pitiful (*or* pitiable) circumstances in old age

老境 lǎojìng ❶ old age: 你我都渐入～，凡事都要想开些。Both you and I are getting old and should take things easy. ❷ life and circumstances in old age: ～凄凉 miserable and dreary life in old age

老九 lǎojiǔ ❶ ninth child (of a family); number nine in a group or gang ❷〈贬义〉intellectuals, stigmatized during the Cultural Revolution, as coming ninth following landlords, rich peasants, counter-revolutionaries, bad elements, rightists, etc.

老酒 lǎojiǔ 〈方言〉wine or liquor, esp. Shaoxing rice wine

老旧 lǎojiù outmoded; obsolete; old-fashioned; out-of-date: 机器～ obsolete machine / 思想～ old-fashioned idea / ～的调子 outmoded tune

老绝户 lǎojuéhu *also* "老绝户头" old people without male offspring

老客 lǎokè 〈方言〉 travelling trader
老框框 lǎokuàngkuang old ways of doing things; outmoded conventions
老辣 lǎolà ❶ seasoned and vicious; experienced and villainous:他为人～,极有心计。He is an experienced and vicious schemer. ❷ (of handwriting, etc.) smooth and vigorous:笔法～ smooth and vigorous strokes
老来俏 lǎoláiqiào 〈口语〉(usu. of a woman) old but coquettish; mutton dressed as lamb:她真是个～,六十多岁的人还打扮得花枝招展的。Although over sixty, she still likes to dress up in gaudy colours. What a coquet!
老来少 lǎoláishào ❶ old in age but young in heart; young head on old shoulders:他年过五十,是个挺爱说笑话的～。Although over fifty, he has a young heart, cracking jokes right and left. ❷ 〈方言〉〈植物〉 tricolour amaranth (*Armaranthus tricolor*)
老老少少 lǎolǎo-shàoshào old and young
老老 lǎolao also "佬佬" lǎolao ❶ maternal grandmother ❷ 〈方言〉 midwife
老老实实 lǎolao-shíshí honestly; honestly and sincerely; conscientiously; in earnest:～,勤勤恳恳 be honest and hardworking /～做人 conduct oneself honestly /～地学习别人的先进经验 learn advanced experience conscientiously from other people
老泪 lǎolèi old man's tears:洒下一把～ shed old man's tears
老泪纵横 lǎolèi-zònghéng (of an old man) have one's face covered with tears; have tears coursing down one's cheeks:面对这些遭难的文物,老人不禁～,泣不成声。Seeing the ruined cultural relics the old man could not but choke with sobs, with tears rolling down his wrinkled cheeks.
老礼 lǎolǐ old etiquette and custom:你可别按着～办新事。Never do new things according to old etiquette and practice.
老理 lǎolǐ old principle; old precept:人家是个解放军战士,不讲究这一套～儿。Being a PLA soldier he doesn't care about these old beliefs.
老吏断狱 lǎolì-duànyù seasoned magistrate deciding a legal case; wise judgment; correct decision:您是～,还能有错! Nothing will go wrong since you are experienced and able to make the right decision.
老例 lǎolì old rule, custom, habit, practice, etc.:按～,干这种活计要用三天。To go by precedent this handwork will take three days. /周三下午不接待来访,这是多年的～了。It has been an established practice for years that we do not receive visitors on Wednesday afternoons.
老脸 lǎoliǎn ❶ 〈谦词〉(of old people) reputation; prestige; face:豁出去我这张～,我再替你去求一次情。I'm going to stake my reputation and put in a good word for you again. ❷ also "老脸皮";"老面皮" thick-skinned; brazen; cheeky:这个人真是个～! What cheek!
老练 lǎoliàn seasoned; experienced; know one's way around:这两年他～多了。He has grown more mature over the last two years. /小伙子办事很～。The young man is experienced and works with a sure hand. /他很～,别以为那样愚蠢的说法能骗得了他。He wasn't born yesterday, and so don't think he can be fooled by a silly story like that.
老练通达 lǎoliàn-tōngdá seasoned and sensible; experienced and reasonable:他一向～,深谋远虑,干什么事情都有自己的一套办法。Experienced and sensible, he is a man of foresight and does everything in his own way.
老林 lǎolín virgin forest:深山～ thick forests in deep mountains; remote, thickly forested mountains
老伶工 lǎolínggōng 〈旧语〉 old skilled actor
老龄 lǎolíng old age; ageing:～保险 old-age insurance /～问题 ageing problem /当前～工作的重点之一,是致力于老有所用。One of the current focuses of work concerning senior citizens is to find ways to make them useful to society.
老龄化 lǎolínghuà ageing; ageing process:人口～ ageing population ; greying population
老龄委 lǎolíngwěi (short for 老龄问题委员会) committee for the aged
老琉璃 lǎoliúli 〈方言〉 dragonfly
老路 lǎolù ❶ old road; beaten path:走～ follow the beaten track /沿～上山 follow an old path up a mountain ❷ old rut; conventional way:穿新鞋,走～ taking the old road in new shoes — no change in substance (*or* essence) /近来,作家在题材或文体上都在追求新奇而不走传统～。Nowadays, writers aim at novelty either in subject or style, instead of following the beaten track of conventionality.
老妈妈论儿 lǎomāmalùnr also "妈妈论儿" 〈方言〉〈贬义〉 old women's views about tradition
老妈儿 lǎomār see "老妈子"
老妈子 lǎomāzi also "老妈儿" 〈旧语〉 amah; maidservant
老马恋栈 lǎomǎ-liànzhàn an old horse cannot bear to leave its stable — old but still reluctant to leave official posts:我们这些老头子怎么能～,不给年轻人让出位置来呢? How can we old fogeys cling to our official posts and block out young people?
老马识途 lǎomǎ-shítú an old horse knows the way; an old man is a good guide; an old hand knows the ropes; an old stalwart knows the twists and turns of the way
老马嘶风 lǎomǎ-sīfēng old horse whinnying for action; old man cherishing high aspirations
老迈 lǎomài aged; senile:～无力 aged and weak /老人年过七十,毫无～之态。Although over seventy, the old man (*or* woman) did not look senile in the least.
老迈昏庸 lǎomài-hūnyōng senile and fatuous; old and muddle-headed
老猫不在,耗子成精 lǎomāo bù zài, hàozi chéng jīng when the cat is away, the mouse will play
老耄 lǎomào 〈书面〉 old and feeble; decrepit; senile
老帽儿 lǎomàor 〈方言〉 foolish greenhorn; dull layman:别看他像个土～,他可是个大专家。He looks like a country bumpkin, but he is actually a great expert.
老米 lǎomǐ 〈方言〉 rice that has been stored for many years; stale rice
老米嘴 lǎomǐzuǐ 〈方言〉 ❶ toothless cricket that is unable to fight ❷ weak and incompetent:这个人不过是个～罢了。This person is nothing but a weakling.
老面 lǎomiàn 〈方言〉 leavening dough; leaven
老面孔 lǎomiànkǒng ❶ old face ❷ same old thing
老面皮 lǎomiànpí 〈方言〉 see "老脸❷"
老面子 lǎomiànzi ❶ old feelings or sensibilities ❷ elders' feelings or sensibilities:要不是买你爹的～,我早把你开除了。I would have dismissed you long since, but for your father's pleadings.
老谋深算 lǎomóu-shēnsuàn circumspect and far-sighted; experienced and astute; calculating; crafty:你的对手是个～的家伙,千万要小心从事。Your enemy is a shrewd, calculating old fox. You must think carefully before every move.
老衲 lǎonà 〈书面〉 old Buddhist monk; (used by an old Buddhist monk to refer to himself) this old monk; I; me
老奶奶 lǎonǎinai ❶ (paternal) great-grandmother ❷ (respectful form of address for old women used by children) granny; grandma
老脑筋 lǎonǎojīn old or outmoded way of thinking:你这～不中用了。Your old way of thinking is of no use (*or* good) now.
老蔫儿 lǎoniānr 〈方言〉 reticent or taciturn person
老年 lǎonián old age:～人口 elderly population
老年斑 lǎoniánbān senile plaque; old-age speckle
老年保健 lǎonián bǎojiàn also "老年摄生" geracomia
老年大学 lǎonián dàxué university for senior citizens
老年迪斯科 lǎonián dísikē disco for old folks
老年护理 lǎonián hùlǐ geriatric nursing
老年间 lǎoniánjiān formerly; in the past; during ancient times:父亲常提起～他当学徒时受过的罪。Father often mentioned the suffering he had endured in the past when he worked as an apprentice.
老年期 lǎoniánqī ❶ old age; senescence ❷ 〈地质〉 topographic age
老年人 lǎoniánrén old people; senior citizen; the aged:～公寓 old people's apartment (building); senior citizens' lodging house
老年心理学 lǎonián xīnlǐxué psychology of ageing
老年型社会 lǎoniánxíng shèhuì aged society
老年性变性 lǎoniánxìng biànxìng 〈医学〉 senile degeneration
老年性痴呆 lǎoniánxìng chīdāi 〈医学〉 senile dementia
老年性耳聋 lǎoniánxìng ěrlóng 〈医学〉 presbycusis
老年性精神病 lǎoniánxìng jīngshénbìng 〈医学〉 senile psychosis
老年性阴道炎 lǎoniánxìng yīndàoyán 〈医学〉 senile vaginitis
老年学 lǎoniánxué nostology; gerontology
老年医学 lǎonián yīxué geriatrics
老娘 lǎoniáng ❶ old mother ❷ 〈方言〉(usu. used by a middle-

L

aged or married woman to refer to herself proudly) I; me:～活了五十多岁,又不是没见过世面。I'm over fifty and have certainly seen the world.

老娘 lǎoniang ❶〈旧语〉midwife ❷〈方言〉(maternal) grandmother

老娘们儿 lǎoniángmenr 〈方言〉❶ married woman; housewife:虽然我是个～,我的见识可不比你们男人低。Although a housewife, I'm in no way inferior to you men as far as knowledge of the world is concerned. ❷〈贬义〉women:你们～,少管这些闲事。You women mind your own business. ❸ wife:他～病了。His wife is sick.

老娘婆 lǎoniangpó 〈旧语〉midwife

老牛破车 lǎoniú-pòchē *also*"老牛拉破车" old ox pulling a rickety cart — creep slowly along; drag along at a snail's pace; make slow progress

老牛舐犊 lǎoniú-shìdú old cow licking her calf — parental love:俗话说"～",谁不知道疼爱自己的孩子? As the saying goes, even an old cow licks her calf, who doesn't love his own child?

老农 lǎonóng ❶ old farmer; experienced peasant ❷ farmer:～卖的菜很新鲜。Vegetables sold by farmers are very fresh.

老牌 lǎopái ❶ old brand:～货 old brand goods ❷ old-timer; veteran:～殖民主义 old-line colonialism /～特务 old hand at espionage; experienced spy

老派 lǎopài ❶ (of bearing, manner) old-fashioned:～人 old-fashioned person; old fogey /他穿着绸子裤,裤脚系着带儿,未免太～。He looked rather old-fashioned in silk pants with both trouser legs laced up at the bottom. ❷ old-fashioned people; conservative group (school, faction, etc.); old hat; old fogey

老婆婆 lǎopópo 〈方言〉❶ (used by children, etc., for elderly women) granny ❷ husband's mother; mother-in-law (of a woman)

老婆儿 lǎopór (with a feeling of affection) old lady; granny; grandma:～,走快些,戏都开场了! Granny, make haste! The opera has already begun.

老婆子 lǎopózi ❶ old biddy:这个该死的～,一天到晚只知道搬弄是非。All day long the damned old biddy does nothing but sow discord. ❷ (used for one's wife) old woman:～,儿子明天回来,该高兴了吧! My old woman, our son will be back tomorrow. Doesn't that make you happy?

老婆 lǎopo wife

老圃 lǎopǔ 〈旧语〉expert vegetable gardener

老谱 lǎopǔ old rule, practice, or custom:袭用～ take over (*or* abide by) old rules

老气横秋 lǎoqì-héngqiū ❶ arrogant on account of one's seniority:摆出一副～的样子 give oneself the airs of a senior ❷ decrepit; lacking in youthful vigour:这人～的,一点不精神。That man looks decrepit and listless.

老气 lǎoqi ❶ mature; old-mannish:他年龄虽小,说话倒很～。He is young in age but mature in speech. ❷ (of clothes) dark and old-fashioned:打扮得～ be dressed in dark-coloured and old-fashioned clothes

老前辈 lǎoqiánbèi senior; elder; veteran:这几位革命～,都有过赫赫战功。All these revolutionary veterans have illustrious military exploits to their credit. /这位是我的～,是研究英国文学的专家。He is my senior, an expert on English literature.

老钱 lǎoqián official coins (of the Ming and Qing dynasties):～一百串 a hundred strings of coins

老枪 lǎoqiāng inveterate (esp. opium) smoker

老腔 lǎoqiāng type of shadow play popular in Tongguan (潼关) and Huayin (华阴) in Shaanxi Province

老腔老调 lǎoqiāng-lǎodiào ❶ old tunes and melodies ❷ (of a child, etc.) sound like an adult:这小孩子讲起话来～的。The young boy speaks like a grown-up.

老抢儿 lǎoqiǎngr 〈方言〉robber; bandit

老亲 lǎoqīn ❶ old relative:～旧邻 old relatives and former neighbours ❷ old parents

老秋 lǎoqiū 〈方言〉late autumn

老区 lǎoqū old liberated area:革命～ old revolutionary base areas /～的乡亲们 folks in the old liberated areas

老拳 lǎoquán fist (when used to hit people):饱以～ hit (*or* strike) with fists; fist repeatedly; give a good beating

老人 lǎorén ❶ old man or woman; the aged; the old ❷ one's aged parents or grandparents:离家后,你别忘了时时给家中的～来信。When you are away from home, don't forget to write to your old parents from time to time.

老人斑 lǎorénbān old age speckle; senile plaque

老人星 Lǎorénxīng *also*"南极老人星" Nánjí Lǎorénxīng;"寿星" Shòuxīng 〈天文〉Canopus (regarded by the ancients as symbolizing longevity)

老人政治 lǎorén zhèngzhì *also*"老人统治" gerontocracy

老人家 lǎorenjia ❶〈敬词〉venerable old person:您～ you (when addressing an old person in a respectful way) /这两位～就是烈士的父母。These two venerable elderly people are the martyr's parents. ❷ parent:你们～今年七十多了吧? Your parents must be over seventy now.

老弱 lǎo-ruò old and weak

老弱病残 lǎo-ruò-bìng-cán the old, weak, sick and disabled

老弱残兵 lǎoruò-cánbīng old, weak and wounded soldiers; remnants of a rabble army; motley troops unfit for battle; incompetents left off on account of old age or poor health:靠这么几个～怎么能拿下这一项目? How could you complete the project with these incompetents?

老弱妇幼 lǎo-ruò-fù-yòu old and weak, women and children:～专座 seats (reserved) for the old and weak, women and children

老三届 lǎosānjiè those who graduated from junior high schools and high schools in 1966, 1967 and 1968 in China (at the beginning of the Cultural Revolution, which deprived them of opportunities for further education)

老少边穷地区 lǎo-shǎo-biān-qióng dìqū old revolutionary base areas, areas inhabited by minority nationalities, frontier areas and poverty-stricken areas

老少 lǎoshào old and young; the aged and the youth:男女～ men and women, old and young

老少无欺 lǎoshào-wúqī cheat neither the old nor the young; be fair in business

老少咸宜 lǎoshào-xiányí suitable for both old and young

老少爷们 lǎoshàoyémen 〈方言〉both old and young men; all the menfolk

老身 lǎoshēn (used by an old woman in the early vernacular) I; me:～膝下无子。I have no sons.

老生 lǎoshēng *also*"须生" xūshēng *laosheng*, role of an old or middle-aged gentleman in Chinese operas

老生常谈 lǎoshēng-chángtán *also*"老生常谭" platitudes of an aged scholar; commonplace remarks; mere platitude; truism:～的报告 cut-and-dried speech

老生儿 lǎoshengr 〈口语〉youngest son or daughter born when the parents were old

老师 lǎoshī teacher:中小学～ school teacher; schoolmaster; schoolmistress /我可以提个问题吗,～? May I ask a question, Sir (*or* Ma'am)? /请刘～上台来领奖。Would Mr. Liu come to the platform for the prize, please?

老师傅 lǎoshīfu 〈敬词〉master craftsman; experienced worker

老式 lǎoshì outmoded; obsolete; old-fashioned; out-of-date; outdated:～家具 old-fashioned furniture /一只～座钟 outmoded desk clock

老视眼 lǎoshìyǎn *also*"花眼" huāyǎn;"老花眼" presbyopia

老实 lǎoshi ❶ honest; frank:忠诚～ faithful and honest /～交待 come clean; own up; make a clean breast of /这年头～人吃亏。Nowadays it is the honest people that get the worst of it. /说～话,我认为这计划不可行。To be frank, I don't think the plan is feasible. /～回答我的问题。Give me a straight answer. ❷ well-behaved; law-abiding; good:孩子们,在客人面前～点。Kids, behave yourselves before the guests. /这孩子很～,从来不同大人顶嘴。This child is well-disciplined and never talks back to adults. ❸〈婉词〉simple-minded; naive; easily taken in

老实巴交 lǎoshibājiāo 〈方言〉well-behaved; law-abiding; circumspect and timid:李老汉是个～的庄户人。Li, the old farmer, is an honest and simple soul.

老实疙瘩 lǎoshigēda 〈方言〉honest and sincere person

老实可靠 lǎoshi-kěkào honest and reliable; trustworthy; on the up-and-up:你可以信赖他,此人一向～。You can take his word for it. He's always been dependable.

老是 lǎoshi invariably; all the time:他～迟到。He is always late.

老手 lǎoshǒu old hand; old stager; veteran:个中～ old hand at sth. /丹青～ veteran painter /赌场～ old stager in gambling

老寿星 lǎoshòuxing ❶ (respectful form of address for old people)

venerable old man or lady ❷ elderly person whose birthday is being celebrated

老鼠 lǎoshǔ mouse; rat: ～药 rat poison / ～疮 scrofula / ～花〈植物〉flos genkwa

老鼠过街,人人喊打 lǎoshǔ guò jiē, rénrén hǎn dǎ when a rat runs across the street, everybody cries, "kill it!"; be chased after by all like a rat running across the street; be extremely unpopular: 我们这个时代,搞霸权主义不得人心,简直是～。Hegemonism is extremely unpopular in our time. Like a rat running across the street, it is loathed by everybody.

老帅 lǎoshuài veteran marshals, i.e. marshals who fought for the founding of the People's Republic of China

老死 lǎosǐ die a natural death

老死不相往来 lǎosǐ bù xiāng wǎnglái not visit each other all their lives; be totally separated from each other; never be in contact with each other: 鸡犬之声相闻,～。People do not visit each other all their lives, though the crowing of their cocks and the barking of their dogs are within hearing of each other.

老死牖下 lǎosǐ-yǒuxià live unknown in a small study all one's life; lead an insignificant life without any accomplishment

老宋体 lǎosòngtǐ Song typeface
see also "宋体字" sòngtǐzì

老太公 lǎotàigōng 〈方言〉venerated or revered old man

老太婆 lǎotàipó old woman

老太太 lǎotàitai 〈敬词〉❶ old lady ❷ your or his, her, etc., mother; my mother or mother-in-law

老太爷 lǎotàiyé 〈敬词〉❶ elderly gentleman ❷ your or his, her, etc., father; my father or father-in-law

老态龙钟 lǎotài-lóngzhōng senile and doddering; old and clumsy; weighed down with age: 我们谁也不敢相信,眼前这位～的老人,就是当年那个赫赫有名的将军。None of us could believe that the senile and doddering old man before us was the illustrious general of bygone days.

老汤 lǎotāng ❶ residual sauce; sauce specially reserved from previous cooking to be used as a condiment ❷ residual salt water from previous salting or pickling

老塘 lǎotáng *also* "老空"〈矿业〉mined or abandoned area

老饕 lǎotāo 〈书面〉glutton; gourmand

老套 lǎotào old stuff; old ways: 我们不需要千篇一律的～。We have no need for stereotyped old stuff.

老套子 lǎotàozi outdated custom or convention; outmoded method

老天 lǎotiān 〈口语〉God; Heaven: ～不负苦心人。Heaven helps those who help themselves. *or* Heaven rewards the faithful. *or* Keep thy shop and thy shop will keep thee.

老天爷 lǎotiānyé God; Heaven; good heavens: ～,你怎么现在才来! Good gracious, why so late?

老天有眼 lǎotiān-yǒuyǎn heaven has eyes — there is divine justice after all

老头儿 lǎotóur (often with a touch of affection) old man; old chap

老头儿鱼 lǎotóuryú (popular term for 鮟鱇) angler; angler-fish; goosefish

老头子 lǎotóuzi ❶ old fogey; old codger: 隔壁的～一天到晚骂人。The old fogey next door keeps swearing all day long. ❷ (used for one's aged husband) my old man: 你见我家～没有? Did you see my old man? ❸ chieftain of a secret society

老外 lǎowài 〈口语〉❶ layman; raw hand; nonprofessional: 一看你这架式就是个～。A look at your posture and I know you are an amateur. ❷ foreigner

老顽固 lǎowángu old stick-in-the-mud; old diehard; old fogey: 这个～,就是不信西药。The old stick-in-the-mud simply doesn't believe in Western medicine.

老王卖瓜,自卖自夸 Lǎo wáng mài guā, zì mài zì kuā Lao Wang selling melons praises his own goods; a melon pedler always says his melons are sweet; every cook praises his own broth; every potter extols his own pot: 不是我～,我们乡下人就是比你们城里人来得实在。I don't mean that everything is lovely in my garden but it's true that we country folks are more down-to-earth than you townspeople. / 有几个做广告的不是～? Every advertiser boasts of the merchandise he promotes.

老翁 lǎowēng 〈书面〉old man; greybeard: 八十～ old man of eighty

老挝 Lǎowō Laos: ～人 Laotian; Lao / ～语 Laotian (language); Lao / ～人民民主共和国 People's Democratic Republic of Laos

老倭瓜 lǎowōguā 〈方言〉pumpkin; cushaw

老窝 lǎowō lair; den: 发现了黄鼠狼的～ discover the lair of yellow weasels / 端了毒枭在边境的～ destroy the den of the drugpushers at the border

老锡儿 lǎoxīr *also* "锡嘴雀" xīzuǐquè 〈方言〉〈动物〉hawfinch

老弦 lǎoxián 〈乐器〉thick string of a Beijing opera fiddle (*erhu*, etc.)

老乡 lǎoxiāng ❶ fellow-townsman; fellow-villager: 听你的口音,咱们好像是～。Your accent suggests that we may come from the same county. ❷ form of address to a rural person whose name one doesn't know: ～,请问往县城怎么走? Hi, buddy, would you please tell me the way to the county town?

老相 lǎoxiang look older than one's actual age: 她长得～,刚刚四十,看上去有五十多。She looks older than her age. She is just forty but looks over fifty.

老小 lǎoxiǎo ❶ grown-ups and children; one's family: 一家～ whole family / 全村～ everyone in the village; whole village ❷ (mostly used in the early vernacular) wife: 他原本是外来户,年近五十,这才娶了～。Originally an outsider, he didn't get married until almost fifty.

老兄 lǎoxiōng brother; man; old chap; buddy: 此事就拜托～了。Old chap, I would leave it to you, OK?

老羞成怒 lǎoxiū-chéngnù fly into a rage out of shame; be shamed into anger; lose one's temper from embarrassment: 他从来没有受过这样的侮辱,难免～。He flew into a shameful rage, for he had never received such an insult before.

老朽 lǎoxiǔ ❶ decrepit and behind the times; old and useless: 昏庸～ dull, fatuous and decrepit / ～无能 decrepit and incompetent ❷〈谦词〉(used by old people) I; me; my decrepit self; my senile self: ～今年七十有余,膝下只有一女。I'm over seventy years of age with only one daughter.

老学究 lǎoxuéjiū old pedant: 小学原先的校长是个～。The former primary school headmaster was an old pedant.

老鸦 lǎoyā 〈方言〉crow

老腌瓜 lǎoyānguā 〈方言〉snake melon

老腌儿 lǎoyānr 〈方言〉preserved in salt for a long time: ～咸菜 long preserved vegetable; salted vegetables; pickles / ～鸡蛋 salted eggs

老眼光 lǎoyǎnguāng old way of looking at things; old view; outdated idea: 以～看人 judge people from old impressions / 你要是用～看新事物,怎么能不出错? You are bound to make mistakes if you judge new things by old standards. / 拿～看人会把人看扁了。You belittle people if you judge them by what they used to be.

老眼昏花 lǎoyǎn-hūnhuā dim-sighted from old age

老阳儿 lǎoyángr *also* "老爷儿"〈方言〉sun

老爷们儿 lǎoyémenr 〈方言〉❶ man: 谁家的～不干活,光让老娘们儿去干? Is there any man who stays idle and drives his wife to work? ❷ husband: 她～在外地做买卖。Her husband is away doing business.

老爷儿 lǎoyér *also* "老阳儿"〈方言〉sun

老爷爷 lǎoyéye ❶ great grandfather ❷〈敬词〉(used by children) grandpa

老爷子 lǎoyézi 〈方言〉❶ respectful form of address for an aged man ❷ my or your old father

老爷 lǎoye ❶ (formerly used of officials, etc., now in a derogatory sense) bureaucrat; lord: 抖～威风 give oneself the airs of an overlord / 不能用～式的态度对待群众。One must not adopt a bureaucratic attitude towards the people. / 他哪里像个人民勤务员,简直是个～! He is not behaving the way a public servant should. He is acting as a lord! ❷〈旧语〉(used by domestic servants) master; lord: ～正在客厅会客。Master is receiving visitors in the drawing room. ❸〈方言〉(maternal) grandfather; grandpa: 我～最喜欢我了。My grandpa likes me most. ❹ old; old-fashioned; old and dilapidated: ～船 old boat / ～机器 dilapidated machine

老爷兵 lǎoyebīng pampered soldier

老爷车 lǎoyechē vintage car: ～比赛 vintage car race

老一辈 lǎoyībèi older generation: 革命的～ revolutionaries of the older generation; veteran revolutionaries

老一套 lǎoyītào *also* "老套" same old stuff; same old story: 这些

～的做法，大家看得多了！People have seen too much of the same old stuff. /别来这～！Cut out the same old trick!
老衣 lǎoyī 〈婉词〉graveclothes; shroud; cerements
老鹰 lǎoyīng *also*“鸢”yuān black-eared kite; hawk; eagle
老鹰抓小鸡 lǎoyīng zhuā xiǎojī (a children's game) hawk and chicks
老营 lǎoyíng 〈旧语〉❶ old barracks：敌军直扑～。The enemy troops swooped down on the old barracks. ❷ nest; den; lair：顽匪固守～，企图垂死挣扎。Stubbornly defending their den, the hard-core bandits put up a last-ditch struggle.
老油子 lǎoyóuzi *also*“老油条”；“老油渣” wily old bird; old slicker; old campaigner：他毕竟是～，心里有鬼，脸上却显出一种和蔼的笑容。Slippery and hard-boiled, he wore an amiable smile despite the wicked scheme he had in mind.
老有所养 lǎoyǒusuǒyǎng elderly people will be properly cared for; the elderly will be provided for
老于世故 lǎoyú-shìgù versed in the ways of the world; sophisticated; worldly-wise：他走南闯北多年，自然～。Having travelled extensively for years, he was naturally well versed in the ways of the world.
老玉米 lǎoyùmǐ 〈方言〉maize; Indian corn; corn
老妪 lǎoyù 〈书面〉old woman：一位拄着拐杖的～ old woman with a walking stick
老妪能解 lǎoyù-néngjiě (of a poem or other literary work) intelligible even to an ordinary old woman; easily understandable：他力求把诗写得～。He tried to make his poems comprehensible to ordinary readers.
老丈 lǎozhàng 〈书面〉respectful form of address for an old man
老丈人 lǎozhàngren one's father-in-law
老账 lǎozhàng ❶ old debt; long-standing debt：陈年～ long-standing debt /还清～ pay off debts ❷ old scores：翻～有什么意思，我们应该向前看。It's meaningless to bring up old scores. We should look ahead. *or* We should set our sights at the future.
老者 lǎozhě old man：受人尊敬的～ respected (*or* revered) old man
老着脸皮 lǎozhe liǎnpí unabashedly; unblushingly：他～，笑嘻嘻地说："都是我不好！" Unabashedly, he said grinning, "It's all my fault." /他～又向别人借钱。He is unblushingly borrowing money from others again.
老中青三结合 lǎo-zhōng-qīng sānjiéhé three-in-one combination of the old, the middle-aged and the young：领导班子要～。Leading bodies should consist of old, middle-aged and young cadres.
老主顾 lǎozhǔgù regular customer; long-time patron
老资格 lǎozīgé old-timer; veteran; senior：～的技术员 senior technician /～的谍报人员 veteran intelligence agent /他搞土木工程是～了。He is an old-timer in civil engineering.
老子 Lǎozǐ ❶ *also*“老聃”Lǎodān Laozi (also translated as Lao-tzu), reverent term of address for Li Er (李耳), Chinese philosopher of the late Spring and Autumn Period and founder of Taoism ❷ *also*“道德经”Dàodéjīng *Classic of the Way and Virtue*, Taoist classic, attributed to Laozi
老子 lǎozi ❶ father：他～是我们厂的工人。His father is a worker in our factory. ❷ (used to show contempt for others, or said in anger, pride, or jest) I; me：～又不欠你的！I owe you nothing. /给～让路！Get out of my way!
老子天下第一 lǎozi tiānxià dì-yī regard oneself as the number one authority under heaven; think oneself the wisest person in the world：他谁也瞧不上眼，自以为～。He turns his nose up at everybody and considers himself far superior to them all.
老字辈 lǎozìbèi ❶ older generation; elders ❷ senior person with rich experience
老字号 lǎozìhào store or shop of long standing：北京有一些店铺是上百年的～。Some stores in Beijing have a history of over a century.
老总 lǎozǒng ❶ 〈旧语〉(used to address a soldier) sir：～，你行行好吧！Do have mercy please, sir. ❷ (of the PLA) marshal; general：朱～ Marshal Zhu
老祖宗 lǎozǔzong ❶ ancestor; progenitor; forefather：我一见了妹妹，心都在她身上，又是喜欢，又是伤心，竟忘记了～。I was so carried away by joy and sorrow at the sight of my little cousin, I forgot our old ancestress. ❷ grandpa (used banteringly)：别拿我开心啦，我的～，我有事要回去找老张。Don't make fun of me, grandfather; I must go back to see Lao Zhang about something.

栳 lǎo *see*“栲栳”kǎolǎo
挓 lǎo 〈方言〉take up; snatch; grab：天一亮，他就～起锄头出去了。As soon as day broke, he took a hoe and went out.
笔 lǎo *see*“笺笔”kǎolǎo
铑 lǎo 〈化学〉rhodium (Rh)
佬 lǎo 〈贬义〉man; guy; fellow：阔～ rich guy; moneybags / 美国～ Yankee /外国～ foreigner /乡巴～儿 country bumpkin
姥 lǎo
see also mǔ
姥姥 lǎolao *also*“老老”lǎolao ❶ (maternal) grandmother; (maternal) grandma ❷ 〈方言〉midwife
姥爷 lǎoye (maternal) grandfather; (maternal) grandpa

lào

涝(澇) lào ❶ waterlogging：防旱防～ prevent both drought and waterlogging /庄稼地全～了。The cropland is all waterlogged. ❷ floodwater (on low-lying land); excessive water：排～ drain off the floodwater; drain a waterlogged area
涝池 làochí cistern (usu. dug by a roadside or village for holding water on the northwestern plateau)
涝地 làodì *also*“涝田”；“涝洼地” land liable to waterlogging; waterlogged lowland
涝害 làohài crop damage or failure caused by waterlogging; waterlogging：灾区人民战胜～，迅速恢复了生产。People in the flooded area overcame the disastrous effects of the waterlogging and resumed production shortly afterwards.
涝灾 làozāi extensive damage and crop failure caused by waterlogging; natural calamity caused by waterlogging：这项水利工程建成后可以免除本地的～。When completed, the water-conservancy project will free the surrounding areas of waterlogging.
耢(耮) lào 〈农业〉❶ *also*“耱”mò；“盖”gài farm tool for levelling fields; leveller ❷ level (land)
唠(嘮) lào 〈方言〉speak; talk; say; chat：有话咱们慢慢～。If you have anything to say, let's talk it over. /他们几个正～得高兴。They were chatting happily.
see also láo
唠扯 làoche 〈方言〉chat; chitchat：两人一～就是半天。Whenever the two start to talk they will chat for a long time.
唠嗑 làokē 〈方言〉chat; chitchat：有工夫过来唠一会儿嗑。When you have time, please come over for a chat.
烙 lào ❶ brand; sear; iron：～裤线 iron or press trousers /给牲口～上印记 brand draught animals /在脑海里～下了不可磨灭的印象 sear an indelible memory on one's mind ❷ bake in a pan：～两张馅儿饼 bake a couple of meat pies /～烧饼 bake sesame pancakes；〈比喻〉rehash the same old stuff (as repeating the same motion in baking sesame pancakes)
see also luò
烙饼 làobǐng pancake：英式小～和中式～差不多，只是个儿小得多。A flapjack is similar to a Chinese pancake, only much smaller.
烙封 làofēng seal by searing; sear up
烙痕 làohén brand; mark difficult to erase：他的眼泡肿着，脸上打上了疲乏的～。His eyes were swollen and there was a clear sign of fatigue written on his face. *or* His face clearly showed signs of fatigue.
烙花 làohuā *also*“烫花”tànghuā 〈工美〉pyrograph：～图案 pyrography
烙铁 làotie ❶ flatiron; iron：老式～ old-fashioned flatiron (heated by fire before use) /电～ electric iron ❷ soldering iron; solder-iron; searing iron：用～把管子接起来 weld the pipes together with a soldering iron
烙印 làoyìn brand; stamp：打有～的牛 branded cattle /阶级的～

brand of a class /打上时代的～ stamped with the brand of the times /这一段痛苦经历，在他的心灵上留下深深的～。This period of traumatic experiences was deeply engraved upon his mind. /这种人生的苦味，～心头，终身难忘。Such bitterness of life left an indelible impression upon one's memory.

落

lào (*same as* "落❶❷❻❾❿" luò) *usu. used in the following entries*

see also là; luō; luò

落包涵 lào bāohan 〈方言〉get blamed; incur censure:帮他半天忙，还落一身包涵。I helped him a good deal only to earn his blame.

落不是 lào bùshi have blame laid at one's door; get blamed for an alleged fault; be blamed:只要你为公司尽心尽力，我做董事长的断不能让你～。So long as you do your best for our company, I as chairman certainly won't let you be treated unfairly. /跟他跑里跑外忙了半天，反落一身不是。I've been busy running errands for him all the morning, and earned nothing but blame.

落汗 làohàn have sweat (on a human body) evaporate; stop sweating:跑得满身是汗，等落了汗再干吧。I am wet with sweat from running errands. Let me dry off before I continue.

落价 làojià drop or fall in price; lower or reduce the price; mark down:录音机～了。Tape recorders have gone down in price. *or* Prices of tape recorders have been reduced. /这个专业的毕业生最近～了。Graduates of this speciality are not as highly valued as they used to be.

落架 làojià 〈方言〉〈比喻〉(of a family) decline and collapse; go to ruin:这小子吃喝嫖赌，无所不为，不几年工夫，祖业～，衣食无着。As he indulged in dining, drinking, womanizing, gambling, and what not, it took him just a few years to squander his family fortune and find himself without any means of support.

落炕 làokàng 〈方言〉sick in bed; confined to bed; laid up:他从去年冬天起～，再也没有起来过。He was laid up last winter and has not got out of bed ever since.

落儿 làor *also* "落子"〈方言〉(used only after 有 or 没有 or similar verbs) assured means of life; means of support; living; livelihood:有～ have a comfortable living; be well-off /没～ have no means of livelihood; be poverty-stricken (*or* destitute); be in straitened circumstances /找～ seek a living (*or* livelihood)

落忍 làorěn 〈方言〉(often used in the negative) not feel sorry or apologetic:老是麻烦您，心里怪不～的。I'm so sorry to be such a bother to you. *or* I feel rather sorry to have kept bothering you.

落色 làoshǎi discolour; fade:这种衣料～太厉害了。This dress material discolours too much.

落头 làotou 〈口语〉❶ surplus; profit:结账后总该有些～吧。After settling accounts, we ought to have some surplus. ❷ benefit; gain:吃到肚里才算～。Benefit in hand is benefit obtained.

落枕 làozhěn ❶ stiff neck (caused by cold or awkward sleeping posture):昨夜～，准是睡觉时招了风。I got a stiff neck last night. I must have slept in a draught. ❷ (of one's head) touch the pillow:他这个人～就着。He falls asleep as soon as he hits the sack (*or* as soon as his head hits the pillow).

落子 làozi ❶〈方言〉〈戏曲〉one type of *quyi* or folk art form with each verse beginning or ending with " lianhualao, laolianhua " (莲花落，落莲花) ❷〈戏曲〉old term for *pingju*, a local opera of north and northeast China:唐山～ Tangshan *pingju* ❸〈口语〉*see* "落儿"

酪

lào ❶ junket:奶～ cheese ❷ fruit jelly; sweet paste (made from crushed nuts):红果～ haw jelly /核桃～ walnut paste /杏仁～ apricot kernel cream

酪氨酸 lào'ānsuān 〈化学〉tyrosine:～酶 tyrosinase /～过多〈医学〉tyrosinaemia /～代谢紊乱〈医学〉tyrosinesis

酪胺 lào'àn *also* "3-对羟苯基乙胺" sān-duìqiǎngběnjīyǐ'àn 〈化学〉tyramine

酪蛋白 làodànbái 〈化学〉casein:～胶 casein glue /～酶〈生化〉casease /～原〈生化〉caseinogen /～免疫素〈生化〉caseidin

酪乳 làorǔ buttermilk

酪素 làosù *also* "酪蛋白";"干酪素" gānlàosù;"酪朊"〈化学〉casein:～胶 casein glue

酪酸 làosuān butyric acid

酪酸脂 làosuānzhī butyrate

络

lào

see also luò

络子 làozi ❶ (used to case a glass, etc.) string bag ❷ spindle:我去找她时，她正在用～绕毛线。When I went to look for her, she was winding knitting wool onto a spindle.

lē

嘞

lē

see also lei

嘞嘞 lēle 〈方言〉chatter; be garrulous:瞎～ chatter to no purpose /少～两句行不行? Cut out the garbage, will you?

肋

lē

see also lèi

肋脦 lēde *also* lēte 〈方言〉(of clothes) slovenly; sloppy; dirty and untidy:她穿一件宽松的上衣，显得那么～。She wore a loose blouse that looked very sloppy.

肋脦兵 lēdebīng untidily dressed person; sloven

lè

乐(樂)

lè ❶ happy; cheerful; joyful:欢～ be happy (*or* joyous) /其～无穷 thoroughly enjoyable /寻欢作～ seek pleasure and enjoyment /小伙子心里～开了花。The lad was overjoyed. ❷ be glad to; find pleasure in; enjoy:喜闻～见 love to hear and see; be popular /何～而不为 be only too happy to do it /～于接受 gladly accept /非我所～闻 not what I would like to hear ❸ laugh; be amused:大家都被逗～了。We were all amused. /你～什么呀? What are you laughing at? *or* What's the joke? /这有什么可～的呀? What's so funny about it? ❹ (Lè) a surname, different from 乐 (Yuè) which is also a surname

see also yuè

乐不可言 lèbùkěyán enjoy such great pleasure that it defies description; be unspeakably happy

乐不可支 lèbùkězhī be overwhelmed with joy; be beside oneself with joy; be as pleased as Punch; one's joy knows no bounds:听到这个好消息，她眉开眼笑，～。She was all smiles and overjoyed when she heard the good news.

乐不思蜀 lèbùsīshǔ indulge in pleasure and forget home and duty; abandon oneself to pleasures:泰山三日游，大家游兴十足，简直有些～了。During the three-day tour to Mount Tai we were all so enchanted by the sights that we almost forgot to return.

乐昌之镜 lèchāngzhījìng *also* "乐昌分镜" reunion of husband and wife after separation

see also "破镜重圆" pòjìng-chóngyuán

乐此不疲 lècǐ-bùpí *also* "乐此不倦" always enjoy it; never tire of it; love and indulge in it:前些时候，他迷上了写诗，大有～的劲头。Formerly he was so crazy about writing poems that he worked gladly on it and never got tired.

乐道 lèdào like or be only too glad to talk about sth; take delight in talking about sth.:津津～ take great delight in talking about; dwell upon with great relish

乐得 lèdé readily take the opportunity to; be happy to have the chance to; be only too glad to:～玩玩儿 readily take the opportunity to enjoy oneself /他不让我去，我也～在家看看书。He doesn't want me to go and I'll be only too happy to stay at home and enjoy reading.

乐颠颠 lèdiāndiān 〈口语〉bounce with joy:他打完电话～地跑回来。After making the telephone call, he ran back, bouncing with joy.

乐而不淫 lè'érbùyín joy with moderation; pleasure that does not go to excess

乐而忘返 lè'érwàngfǎn enjoy oneself so much that one doesn't want to depart; have a good time and forget all about going home:山色迷人，使人～。We were so charmed by the mountain landscape that we almost forgot to turn back.

乐观 lèguān optimistic; hopeful; sanguine:前景～ have a bright future; be sanguine (*or* optimistic) about the future /过于～ be over-optimistic /制造～气氛 make atmospherics /他的镇定和～增加了我的勇气。I was greatly encouraged by his calmness and optimism. /对会谈的前景，有大量～的报道。There are a lot of hopeful

(*or* sanguine) reports about the negotiations.

乐观主义 lèguānzhǔyì optimism:～者 optimist

乐果 lèguǒ 〈农业〉Rogor (an insecticide)

乐呵呵 lèhēhē buoyant; happy and gay:他一天到晚～的。He is cheerful and merry all the time.

乐和 lèhe 〈方言〉happy; joyful; cheerful:逢年过节,大家都愿意凑在一起～～。On New Year's Day or other festivals, people like to get together for fun (*or* a good time).

乐极生悲 lèjí-shēngbēi extreme joy begets sorrow; joy at its height engenders sorrow; drunken days all have their tomorrows; when the cup of happiness overflows, disaster follows:你不要太高兴了,小心～! Don't be too happy. Be careful lest extreme joy beget sorrow.

乐境 lèjìng comfortable circumstances

乐趣 lèqù delight; pleasure; joy:发现生活和工作中的～ discover joys of life and delight in work /生活沉闷,实在毫无～。Life was dull and there was no pleasure at all.

乐儿 lèr *see*"乐子"

乐融融 lèróngróng cheerful and harmonious; happy and amiable:今年又是大丰收,家家户户～。There is again a bumper harvest this year. Every family is happy and harmonious.

乐如枝鹊 lèrúzhīquè merry as a lark

乐山大佛 Lèshān Dàfó Giant Stone Buddha in Leshan County, Sichuan Province:中国四川的～是世界上最大的佛雕,它高达 71 米,雕刻于唐代。The 71-metre-high Giant Stone Buddha at Leshan County in China's Sichuan Province, carved in the Tang Dynasty, is the largest statue of Buddha in the world.

乐善好施 lèshàn-hàoshī be happy to do good and give alms; be glad to give to charities; love to do philanthropic work:此人～,曾经周济过许多急难之人。He is a charitable man and has helped many people in need.

乐事 lèshì pleasure; delight; bit of jam:人生～ pleasure of life /赏心～ pleasure that delights the mind /平生最大的～ biggest delight of one's life /得到那笔奖金是件～。That bonus is a bit of jam.

乐岁 lèsuì year of good harvest; good year:～终身饱。A good year ensures a life of plenty.

乐陶陶 lètáotáo cheerful; happy; joyful:幸福生活～ lead a joyful and happy life

乐天 lètiān carefree; optimistic; happy-go-lucky

乐天派 lètiānpài ❶ carefree; happy-go-lucky; easygoing ❷ optimist; free and easy person

乐天知命 lètiān-zhīmìng submit to the will of heaven and be content with one's lot; be easily contented

乐土 lètǔ land of happiness; land of promise; promised land; paradise:人间～ paradise on earth; earthly paradise; land of milk and honey

乐业 lèyè 〈书面〉work in contentment:安居～ live in peace and work in contentment /百姓～。The common people are satisfied in their employment.

乐以忘忧 lèyǐwàngyōu *also*"乐而忘忧" be so happy as to forget one's worries

乐意 lèyì ❶ be willing to; be ready to:大家都～帮助他。Everybody is ready to help him. /我～这样做。I'm quite willing to do so. ❷ pleased; happy:别说那些话让他不～。Don't say those things that will make him unhappy.

乐于 lèyú be happy to; be ready to; take delight in:～助人 be happy to help others /～挑重担 be ready to shoulder heavy responsibilities /母亲总是～操持家务,从未听她埋怨过。Mother always takes delight in housekeeping and has never complained.

乐园 lèyuán ❶ paradise:人间～ earthly paradise; paradise on earth /冒险家的～ paradise of the adventurers ❷ amusement park:儿童～ children's playground /迪斯尼～ Disneyland

乐在其中 lèzàiqízhōng find pleasure in sth.:写文章这种事,苦在其中,乐亦在其中。Writing is hard work but it is also a source of pleasure.

乐滋滋 lèzīzī contented; pleased:她嘴上不说什么,心里却～的。She was very pleased although she didn't say it.

乐子 lèzi 〈方言〉❶ pleasure; delight; fun:我养了一只鸟,不为别的,为的是找个～。I have kept a pet bird just for pleasure (*or* fun). /下雨天出不了门,下两盘棋,也是个～。As rain has kept us indoors, we may just as well enjoy ourselves playing chess. ❷ sth. laughable or causing amusement:他不小心陷进水坑里,这个～可不小。He unwittingly stepped into a puddle, and that was the cause of much merriment.

泐 lè 〈书面〉❶ (of stones) split open along its grain ❷ write:手～ (write) in one's own hand ❸ *see*"勒²" lè

玏 lè *see*"瑊玏" jiānlè

艻 lè *see*"萝艻" luólè

叻 Lè (short for 石叻 or 叻埠) Singapore, as referred to by overseas Chinese:～币 Singaporean currency

仂 lè 〈书面〉remainder; fractional amount

仂语 lèyǔ 〈语言〉word group; phrase

勒[1] lè ❶〈书面〉headstall; halter ❷ rein in:悬崖～马 rein in at the brink of the precipice — wake up to and escape disaster at the last moment ❸ force; compel; coerce:～其返乡 force sb. to return to his native place /～捐 compel sb. to make money contributions ❹〈书面〉command:亲～六军 personally take command of the army

勒[2] lè 〈书面〉carve; engrave; inscribe:～碑 inscribe on a stone tablet

勒[3] lè (short for 勒克斯)〈物理〉lux

see also lēi

勒逼 lèbī force; coerce; compel:你休要这般～! Don't you force my hand! /他多次派人前来～还债。He has time and again sent people here to press for payment of debts.

勒兵 lèbīng direct troops; command troops:～十万 command an army of a hundred thousand men /～于边 command troops in border areas

勒克斯 lèkèsī *also*"米烛光" mǐzhúguāng 〈物理〉lux; metre-candle

勒勒车 lèlechē light wooden cart used by herdsmen in the Inner Mongolia Autonomous Region

勒令 lèlìng compel (by legal authority); order:～停工 order sb. to stop work; order a plant shut down /～即日退款 order sb. to return the fund on the same day /～退学 rusticate (a student) /～服从 compel obedience

勒拿河 Lènáhé Lena River, river rising west of Lake Baikal and flowing into the Arctic Ocean

勒派 lèpài impose upon; levy on; force sb. to pay levies:无理～捐款 impose contributions without legal authority /～税款 levy a tax (on sb.)

勒石 lèshí 〈书面〉engrave on a stone:泰山～ engraved stone (*or* stone engravings) on Mount Tai

勒索 lèsuǒ extort; blackmail:敲诈～ swindle and squeeze; racketeer /～钱财 extort money (from sb.)

勒抑 lèyì ❶ compel sb. to reduce the selling price; exert pressure upon sb. to reduce the price:～市价 force the prices down ❷ extort and suppress:～侵夺,民怨入骨。Extortion and plundering incurred the bitter hatred of the population.

勒诈 lèzhà extort; racketeer

簕 lè

簕党 lèdǎng *also*"食茱萸" shízhūyú 〈植物〉ailanthus prickly ash (*Zanthoxylum ailanthoides*)

簕竹 lèzhú 〈植物〉a kind of tall bamboo

鳓 lè *also*"鲙鱼" kuàiyú;"白鳞鱼" báilínyú;"曹白鱼" cáobáiyú Chinese herring

le

饹 le *see*"饸饹" héle

see also gē

L

了 le 〈助词〉❶ *used after a verb or an adjective to indicate the completion of a real or expected action or a change* (a) *used for a real action or change*：去年村里打～两眼井。Two wells were sunk in the village last year. /这个小组的工作受到～表扬。The team has been commended for its work. /晚霞映红～半边天。Half the sky glowed as the sun went down. (b) *used for an expected or a presumed action*：等枫叶红透～的时候，我们再来游香山。We will come back to tour Fragrant Hill when the maple leaves have all turned red. /他要是知道～这个消息，一定会很高兴。He would be very pleased if he knew it. ❷ *used at the end of or in the middle of a sentence to indicate a change or new circumstances* (a) *used for new circumstances that have occurred or are about to occur*：春天～。It's already spring. /天快亮～。It will soon be dawn. (b) *used in a conditional sentence*：天一下雨，我们就不出门～。If it rains, we won't go out (*or* will stay indoors). /一开春柳树就开始吐芽～。Willow trees start sprouting when spring begins. (c) *used to indicate change in understanding, opinion, proposition, action, etc.*：他觉得贵，但还是买下～。He thought it was too expensive but he bought it in the end. /她明白～是自己的错。She realized that she had been wrong. /只见他往东走了半天，又扭头往西边去～。He was seen to be heading east for a good while and then to turn round to go to the west. (d) *used for urging or dissuasion*：走～，走～，天都大亮～。Let's go. It is already broad daylight. /别哭～！Stop crying! /好～好～，我去就是～。All right, I will go.
see also liǎo

lēi

勒 lēi ❶ tie or strap tight：～紧安全带 tighten the safety belt /中间再～根绳子，包就不会散了。The bag won't come loose if you tighten it up in the middle with a rope. /背包带太紧，～得慌。The pack straps are too tight. They cut into the flesh. /这孩子被绑票的用绳子～死了。The boy was strangled (to death) with a piece of string by the kidnappers. ❷〈方言〉force; compel; coerce：他硬～着大伙儿在地里拼命干活。He compelled us to exert ourselves in the fields.
see also lè

勒脚 lēijiǎo 〈建筑〉plinth

勒紧裤腰带 lēijǐn kùyāodài tighten one's belt — practise austerity

勒掯 lēiken 〈方言〉compel; coerce; embarrass on purpose; put sb. in an awkward position：你凭什么～我答应你们的条件？On what account do you force me to accept your terms?

léi

羸 léi 〈书面〉❶ thin; skinny; emaciated：～瘠 haggard and thin /身病体～ physical wreck /老弱～兵 old, weak and emaciated soldiers ❷ tired out; exhausted

羸惫 léibèi 〈书面〉tired out; exhausted

羸顿 léidùn 〈书面〉❶ emaciated and feeble; thin and weak ❷ exhausted; tired out

羸老 léilǎo 〈书面〉senile and thin; emaciated and decrepit

羸劣 léiliè 〈书面〉thin and weak; emaciated

羸弱 léiruò 〈书面〉thin and weak; frail：这几年，父亲常染疾病，日见～。In the last few years, father often fell ill and became thinner and weaker with each passing day.

羸瘦 léishòu 〈书面〉thin and weak; emaciated; gaunt

羸形垢面 léixíng-gòumiàn thin and filthy：虽然他只有四十左右，但～，看上去有六十多岁。Frail and filthy, he looked over sixty although he was only fortyish.

雷 léi ❶ thunder：春～ spring thunder /电闪～鸣 lightning and thundering ❷〈军事〉mine：地～ (land) mine /饵～ boobytrap; trap mine /浮～ buoyant (*or* floating) mine /石～ stone mine /水～ (submarine) mine /鱼～ torpedo /手～ antitank grenade /布～ plant (*or* lay) mines /扫～ sweep mines /探～ detect mines ❸ (Léi) a surname

雷暴 léibào 〈气象〉thunderstorm：～计 brontometer; brontograph /～日 thunderstorm day; stormy day

雷暴雨 léibàoyǔ thunderstorm

雷爆火药 léibào huǒyào fulminating powder

雷场 léichǎng area where mines have been planted; minefield

雷池 léichí 〈比喻〉limit; confinement：不可越～一步 must not go beyond the limits

雷达 léidá radar (radio detection and ranging)：全景～ panoramic radar /～测距 radar ranging /～干扰 radar jamming /～跟踪 radar tracking /～领航 radar navigation /～探测区 radar coverage /～信标 racon; radar beacon /～荧光屏 radar screen /～波束 radar beam /～测风系统 radar wind system /～测量 radar surveying /～回波 radar echo

雷达兵 léidábīng *also* "雷达员" radar operator; radarman; radar troops; ping jockey

雷达管制 léidá guǎnzhì 〈航空〉radar-based control：空中交通的～系统 radar-based air-traffic control system

雷达舰 léidájiàn 〈军事〉radarship

雷达制导 léidá zhìdǎo radar guidance; radar-homing：～导弹 radar-guided missile; radar homer

雷打不动 léidǎ-bùdòng unshakable; unyielding; (of an arrangement) not to be altered under any circumstances：～的决心 unshakable determination /他每天早晨坚持跑步，～。He jogs every morning and has never stopped for a single day.

雷电 léidiàn thunder and lightning：～交作 lightning accompanied by peals (*or* claps) of thunder

雷电计 léidiànjì ceraunograph

雷动 léidòng thunderous：欢声～ thunderous cheers /掌声～ applause that could bring the house down

雷峰塔 Léifēngtǎ Thunder Peak Pagoda in Hangzhou, Zhejiang Province

雷公 Léigōng Thunder God：～打豆腐，专拣软的欺。〈俗语〉The God of Thunder strikes bean curd — bullies always pick on the soft and weak.

雷汞 léigǒng *also* "雷酸汞"〈化学〉fulminate of mercury; mercury fulminate

雷管 léiguǎn detonator; detonating cap; blasting cap; primer：电～ electric detonator

雷害 léihài 〈农业〉damage or destruction caused by lightning strike：～、洪水对农业生产损害极大。Lightning strikes and floods cause serious damage to agricultural production.

雷轰电掣 léihōng-diànchè thunder rumbles and lightning flashes; (of momentum) be vigorous and swift：刹时间，～，风雨交加。Instantly, thunder roared and lightning flashed, accompanied by wind and rain. /刘先生极善草书，～，笔意纵横。Being extremely good at cursive hand, Mr. Liu writes with great vigour and ease.

雷击 léijī lightning strike; thunderbolt：～伤人 thunderbolts injure people /他不幸竟遭～。Unfortunately, he was struck by a thunderbolt.

雷康 léikāng *also* "雷达信标" (transliteration)〈物理〉racon (fixed radar transmitter used by ships or aircraft for navigation)

雷厉风行 léilì-fēngxíng *also* "雷动风行" with the power of a thunderbolt and the speed of lightning; (carry out orders, policies, etc.) resolutely and swiftly; (perform a task) with drive and sweep：～的工作作风 vigorous and resolute style of work /他办事一贯～，绝不拖延敷衍。He always acts swiftly and resolutely and has never been dillydallying or perfunctory in his work.

雷米封 léimǐfēng 〈药学〉rimifon

雷鸣 léimíng ❶ roaring thunder：电闪～ lightning flashes and thunder rumbles ❷ thunderous; thundery：～般的掌声经久不息 prolonged thunderous applause

雷鸟 léiniǎo 〈动物〉ptarmigan; white partridge

雷诺汽车公司 Léinuò Qìchē Gōngsī Renault, French car manufacturer

雷诺数 léinuòshù 〈物理〉Reynolds number

雷声 léishēng thunderclap; thunder：隆隆～ rumble (*or* roll) of thunder /惊天动地的～ ear-shattering thunder /～震耳。The thunderclap was deafening.

雷声大，雨点小 léishēng dà, yǔdiǎn xiǎo loud thunder but small raindrops; much said but little done; much promise but little performance; much cry and little wool：他这个人常是～，你大可不必太信他。He always says a lot but does little. You needn't take him too

seriously.
雷师 Léishī Thunder God
雷酸 léisuān 〈化学〉fulminic acid:～盐 fulminate / 雷酸银 silver fulminate
雷酸汞 léisuāngǒng *see* "雷汞"
雷霆 léitíng ❶ thunderstorm; thunderclap; thunderbolt ❷ thunder-like power or rage; great wrath:大发～ fly into a temper
雷霆万钧 léitíng-wànjūn powerful thunderbolt; devastating punch; crushing blow:万炮齐轰,～,势不可挡。Several hundred thousand cannon (*or* pieces of artillery) fired in unison with irresistible devastating force.
雷霆之怒 léitíngzhīnù thunder-like rage; violent rage
雷同 léitóng ❶ duplicate; identical:两文～。The two articles are identical. /文艺创作要有新意,不可～。Literary and artistic creation should strive for originality instead of duplication. ❷ echo what others have said
雷同剿说 léitóng-chāoshuō echo what others have said; plagiarize others' writing:此文多为～,新意无多。The essay has little more than echoing others.
雷丸 léiwán 〈中药〉stone-like omphalia (*Omphalia lapidescens*)
雷雨 léiyǔ 〈气象〉thunderstorm:～计 brontometer; brontograph / ～大作。A fierce thunderstorm broke out. /～交加。The storm was accompanied by peals of thunder.
雷雨云 léiyǔyún 〈气象〉thundercloud; thunderhead
雷阵雨 léizhènyǔ 〈气象〉thunder shower

檑 léi huge logs pushed down from a height against an attacking enemy
檑木 léimù huge logs to be pushed down from a height against the enemy

礌(礧) léi ❶ huge stones to be pushed down from a height against an attacking enemy:～击 throw stones upon the enemy from a height ❷〈书面〉beat; hit; strike:～敌 attack the enemy
礌石 léishí stone missiles:滚木～ rolling logs and stone missiles

擂 léi ❶ grind; pestle; pound:～药 pestle medicine /～豆 grind beans ❷ hit; beat:他照着那人的心窝～了一拳。He gave the guy a punch in the pit of the stomach. *or* He punched that fellow in the gut.
see also lèi
擂钵 léibō mortar
擂鼓筛锣 léigǔ-shāiluó beat the drums and sound the gongs — play up:为这点小事不值得～的。Such trifles are not worth trumpeting.

镭 léi 〈化学〉radium (Ra):～化合物 radium compound /～同位素 radium isotope
镭疗 léiliáo 〈医学〉radium therapy
镭射 léishè (transliteration) laser:～影碟 laser videodisc; video compact disc (VCD)/～唱碟 compact disc (CD)
镭射气 léishèqì 〈化学〉radium emanation
镭透照镜 léitòuzhàojìng 〈医学〉radiodiaphane

罍 léi 〈考古〉ancient urn-shaped wine-vessel

纍 léi 〈书面〉❶ rope; cord ❷ twine; bind; fasten; wind:南有樛木,葛藟～之。In the south there is a kind of tree that is crooked downwards, with kudzu vines twining around. ❸ *see* "累" léi
纍臣 léichén 〈书面〉(term used to refer to oneself) official imprisoned in a foreign country
纍囚 léiqiú 〈书面〉prisoner; convict
纍绁 léixiè *also* "缧绁" léixiè 〈书面〉rope used for binding prisoners; imprison

欙 léi 〈古语〉simple carrier for travellers in the mountains

儡 léi
儡儡 léiléi *see* "累累❶" léiléi

累(纍) léi
see also lěi; lèi
累累 léiléi ❶ *also* "儡儡" léiléi 〈书面〉haggard and dejected; gaunt and listless:～若丧家之狗 wretched as a stray cur ❷ clusters of; heaps of:果实～ fruit hanging in clusters; fruit hanging heavy / ～白骨 heaps of bleached bones /弹坑～ numerous shell-craters
see also lěilěi
累赘 léizhui *also* "累坠" ❶ (of things) superfluous; redundant; burdensome; (of writing) wordy; verbose:这段话重复～,不如删去。The paragraph is repetitive and verbose. It would be better to delete it. ❷ be a burden; be cumbersome:拖家带口的,真～人。It's a real burden to have a big family on one's hands. ❸ encumbrance; burden; nuisance:旅途遥远,行李带多了,是个～。Too much luggage on a long journey is a nuisance.
累罪 léizuì 〈法律〉cumulative offence

蔂(虆) léi 〈书面〉basket used to carry earth; earth basket

犦 léi 〈书面〉bull

嫘 léi *used in personal names*:～祖 Leizu, wife of Huangdi (黄帝), who invented sericulture according to legend

缧 léi
缧绁 léixiè *also* "纍绁" léixiè 〈书面〉rope for binding prisoners; prison:～之中 in prison /幽于～ be jailed

lěi

耒 lěi ❶ ancient fork-like farm tool ❷ wooden handle of an ancient plough
耒耜 lěisì ancient plough; farm tools in general

诔 lěi ❶〈古语〉express one's condolences and eulogize the deceased who, usu., was the speaker's subordinate or junior ❷ elegy; funeral prayer:～文 memorial speech
诔词 lěicí 〈书面〉elegy:～凄切 plaintive words of an elegy

瘤 lěi 〈中医〉pimple (on the skin)

蕾 lěi flower bud; bud:蓓～ bud
蕾铃 lěilíng 〈植物〉cotton buds and bolls

磊 lěi
磊磊 lěilěi 〈书面〉heaps of (stones):怪石～ heaps of stones of strange shapes
磊落 lěiluò ❶ open and upright:光明～ open and aboveboard /胸怀～ open-hearted and upright /为人～,极重义气 be open and upright and attach extreme importance to personal loyalty ❷〈书面〉many and jumbled:山岳～ jumbled mountain peaks
磊落不群 lěiluò-bùqún superior to or aloof from the general or common run of people
磊落奇伟 lěiluò-qíwěi open, upright and remarkable:～之才 upright person of outstanding talent

累[1](纍) lěi ❶ pile up; gather; accumulate:～数 accumulated figure /日积月～ accumulate day by day and month by month ❷ repeated; continuous; running:连篇～牍 lengthy and tedious; at great length /欢聚～日 happily gather together for days on end /～建奇功 perform daring exploits again and again ❸ *see* "垒[1]" lěi

累[2] lěi implicate; involve:牵～ implicate; involve (in trouble) /拖～ get sb. into trouble; implicate; be a burden
see also léi; lèi
累次 lěicì time and again; repeatedly:～作案 commit crimes repeatedly /～批评教育 criticize and educate time and again
累代 lěidài for many generations; generation after generation
累牍连篇 lěidú-liánpiān *also* "连篇累牍" lengthy and tedious; in

endless stream of words; at great length

累犯 lěifàn ❶ recidivist ❷ recidivism

累积 lěijī accumulate; collect; gather:～数 accumulated number /～降雨量 accumulated rainfall/～亏损 accumulated deficit /～盈余 accumulated surplus/～支出 accumulated outlay /～剂量 accumulated dose /～数据 accumulated data /～股本 cumulative capital stock /～股息 cumulative dividend /～剩余 cumulative remainder /～服刑〈法律〉accumulative sentence /～率 cumulative percentage /～量 cumulative quantity; cumulant /～概率 cumulative probability /～误差 cumulative (*or* accumulated, *or* progressive) error /～电荷 stored charge /～电路 summation circuit /他收集的邮票，～已有上千张。He has collected altogether over a thousand stamps.

累及 lěijí implicate; involve; drag in:～父母 bring sorrow to one's parents; get one's parents into trouble /～无辜，我于心何忍? How can I bear to implicate the innocent? /岂能～他人，代我受过? How could I drag in others to take the blame on my behalf?

累计 lěijì ❶ add up; total:这些数加起来～是三百零二。These figures add up to 302. /上半年全车间加班～达七百五十人次。The amount of overtime accumulated in the whole workshop during the first six months totalled seven hundred and fifty person-days. ❷ accumulative total; grand total; sum total:～金额七百万元。The sum total came to seven million *yuan*.

累计剂量计 lěijì jìliàngjì integrating dosimeter

累计曲线 lěijì qūxiàn summation curve

累加 lěijiā accumulation; cumulation; summation:～器 accumulator register; accumulator; integrator /～误差 add up error

累见不鲜 lěijiàn-bùxiān *also*"屡见不鲜" lǚjiàn-bùxiān common occurrence; nothing new

累教不改 lěijiào-bùgǎi *also*"屡教不改" lǚjiào-bùgǎi refuse to mend one's way despite repeated admonitions

累进 lěijìn progression:～税 progressive tax; progressive taxation /～增长率 progressive increase rate /～率 graduated rates

累累 lěilěi ❶ again and again; many times:此人～作案。This man has committed crimes many times. /事故～发生。Accidents happened repeatedly. /敌人～进犯，骚扰边境。The enemy kept invading and harassing the border area. ❷ innumerable; countless:罪行～ commit countless crimes; have a long criminal record /血债～ owe (*or* incur) many blood debts

see also léiléi

累卵 lěiluǎn like a stack of eggs — liable to collapse any moment; precarious:危如～ as precarious as a stack of eggs; in imminent danger /势如～ be in an extremely dangerous situation

累年 lěinián for years in succession; year after year:～欠收 have poor harvests for years running

累日 lěirì 〈书面〉for days on end; day after day:～不适 feel unwell for days on end

累时 lěishí 〈书面〉prolonged:～不衰 lasting prosperity

累世 lěishì for many generations; generation after generation:～居住此地 have lived here for generations /建～之功 have performed monumental feats

累黍不差 lěishǔ-bùchà *also*"不差累黍" not an iota of difference; completely accurate:与失物～。It's exactly the same as the lost one.

累退税 lěituìshuì 〈经济〉regressive tax

累瓦结绳 lěiwǎ-jiéshéng piled-up tiles and coiled rope knots — fancy but useless words:文贵简而精，切忌～。The soul of a piece of writing is its brevity and essence, and beware of flowery language.

累月经年 lěiyuè-jīngnián month after month and year after year; for years; year in year out:地质勘探队员～都在深山老林里跋涉着。The geological explorers trudge in remote, thickly forested mountains year in and year out.

瘰
lěi *see*"痞瘰" pēilěi

藟
lěi ❶ vine:葛～ kudzu vine ❷〈书面〉twine; bind; wind ❸〈书面〉*see*"蕾" lěi

儡
lěi *see*"傀儡" kuǐlěi

垒¹(壘)
lěi build by piling up bricks, stones, earth, etc.:～一个灶 build a stove

垒²(壘)
lěi ❶〈军事〉rampart; wall; fort; fortification:堡～ fort; fortress /壁～森严 closely guarded; strongly fortified /两军对～。The two armies were pitted against each other. ❷〈体育〉base:全～打 home run /一～，二～和三～ first, second and third bases

垒壁 lěibì 〈军事〉rampart around an ancient army barracks:～之中 within the rampart /筑～而守之 build a rampart and defend it

垒城 lěichéng 〈军事〉garrison town:大城屯兵三万，～屯兵三千。Thirty thousand troops were stationed in the big city and three thousand in the garrison town.

垒块 lěikuài *also*"块垒"〈书面〉pent-up emotions; resentment and grief:心中～难消 difficult to dispel one's pent-up emotions and resentment

垒球 lěiqiú 〈体育〉softball:打～ play softball /～棒 softball bat /～手套 mitt; mit

lèi

泪(淚)
lèi tear; teardrop:流～ shedding tears; lachrymation /挥～告别 wipe away tears and part; part in tears

泪干肠断 lèigān-chángduàn weep one's heart out; be grief-stricken

泪管 lèiguǎn tear duct; lachrymal duct

泪痕 lèihén tear stains:～满面 face bathed in tears /～斑斑 tear-stained

泪花 lèihuā tears in one's eyes:满眼～ eyes welling with tears /～滚滚 be all tears /老人眼里含着感激的～。There were tears of gratitude in the old man's eyes. /她眼里闪烁着喜悦的～。Her eyes glistened with tears of joy.

泪涟涟 lèiliánlián be tearful; be all tears:想起心上人，两眼～。The thought of one's sweetheart brings tears to one's eyes.

泪流如注 lèiliú-rúzhù tears stream down one's cheeks

泪囊 lèináng lachrymal sac; dacryocyst

泪囊炎 lèinángyán 〈医学〉dacryocystitis

泪囊肿 lèinángzhǒng 〈医学〉dacryops

泪人儿 lèirénr be bathed in tears; melt into tears; be all tears:她哭得像个～似的。She wept and melted into tears.

泪容 lèiróng tearful expression:满脸～ tearful expression on one's face

泪如泉涌 lèirúquányǒng tears well (up) like a fountain; tears gush out like a spring; tears flow plentifully:说罢，只见她～，悲痛万分。Immediately after these remarks, tears of bitter grief gushed from her eyes.

泪如雨下 lèirúyǔxià tears fall like rain; tears stream down one's cheeks; shed a flood of tears:她抓住母亲的手，顿时～。She grabbed her mother by the hand and burst into a flood of tears.

泪水 lèishuǐ tear; teardrop:流下感激的～ shed tears of gratitude /噙着幸福的～ happy tears gather in one's eyes

泪涕交流 lèi-tì jiāoliú both tears and snivel run down the face:他伤心到了极点，脸上～。He was heart-broken, with tears and snivel streaming down his face.

泪汪汪 lèiwāngwāng tearful; (eyes) brimming with tears:老乡见老乡，两眼～。When fellow-townsmen meet, their eyes are full of happy tears.

泪腺 lèixiàn lachrymal gland; tear gland

泪腺炎 lèixiànyán dacryoadenitis

泪小管 lèixiǎoguǎn lachrymal canaliculus; lachrymal canal

泪眼 lèiyǎn tearful eyes:～模糊 eyes dimmed with tears /～晶莹 tears sparkle in one's eyes; eyes glisten with tears

泪液 lèiyè tear

泪盈盈 lèiyíngyíng (eyes) brimming with tears:她两眼～的。Her eyes were brimming with tears.

泪雨 lèiyǔ shed tears profusely; shed a flood of tears; tears rain down one's cheeks

泪珠 lèizhū teardrop; tears:眼里的～簌簌地滚下来。Tears ran down her cheeks like pearls. *or* Teardrops trickled down her cheeks.

泪竹 lèizhú *also*"斑竹" bānzhú;"湘竹" xiāngzhú;"湘妃竹" xiāngfēizhú mottled bamboo

类(類) lèi ❶ kind; type; class; category: 异～ sb. or sth. of a different kind; sb. or sth. not belonging to the same category /分～ classify /物以～聚 things of one kind come together; like attracts like; birds of a feather flock together /诸如此～ things like that; and suchlike; and what not; and so on and so forth /这是两～不同的问题。They are quite different matters. ❷ resemble; be similar to: ～乎奇迹 be almost a miracle /画虎～犬 try to draw a tiger but end up with the likeness of a dog — attempt sth. overambitious and end in failure

类癌瘤 lèi'áiliú 〈医学〉carcinoid: ～综合征 carcinoid syndrome

类鼻疽 lèibíjū 〈兽医〉melioidosis

类比 lèibǐ 〈逻辑〉analogy: 把人的心脏和水泵作～ draw an analogy between the human heart and a pump /通过～论证 argue by analogy/ ～法 analogy

类别 lèibié classification; category; genre; family: 这一章讨论药品的～。This chapter discusses (*or* deals with) the classification of medicine. /请在～一栏中填写订购图书种类的名称。Please write in the category column the types of books you wish to order.

类病毒 lèibìngdú viroid: ～颗粒 virus-like particle

类丹毒 lèidāndú 〈医学〉erysipeloid

类蛋白 lèidànbái 〈生化〉albuminoid; proteoid; proteinoid

类地行星 lèidì xíngxīng 〈天文〉terrestrial planet

类毒素 lèidúsù 〈医学〉toxoid: 白喉～ diphtherial toxoid

类风湿性关节炎 lèifēngshīxìng guānjiéyán 〈医学〉atrophic arthritis; chronic infectious arthritis; proliferotive arthritis; rheumatoid arthritis

类固醇 lèigùchún *also* "甾" zāi 〈生化〉steroid; steride: ～激素 steroid hormone

类乎 lèihu seem; look like; be similar: ～神话 sound like a fairy tale

类黄酮 lèihuángtóng 〈生化〉flavonoid

类激素 lèijīsù 〈生化〉parhormone; anahormone

类金属 lèijīnshǔ 〈化学〉metalloid

类晶体 lèijīngtǐ 〈化学〉crystalloid

类聚 lèijù (short for 物以类聚) things of one kind come together; like attracts like: 物以～, 人以群分。Things of one kind come together. *or* Birds of a feather flock together.

类木行星 lèimù xíngxīng 〈天文〉Jovian planet

类牛皮癣 lèiniúpíxuǎn 〈医学〉parapsoriasis

类群 lèiqún animal or plant group with some common characteristics (mostly of a subdivision of the same kind); fauna or flora: 居住在森林中的动物～ fauna of the forest /白垩地区的植物～ flora of chalk areas

类人猿 lèirényuán 〈考古〉anthropoid (ape)

类是而非 lèishì'érfēi *also* "似是而非" sìshì'érfēi appear correct but wrong in fact: 你这番高论～, 是经不起推敲的。Your views sound plausible but they cannot stand scrutiny.

类书 lèishū reference book with material extracted from various sources and arranged according to subjects

类蜀黍 lèishǔshǔ 〈植物〉teosinte (*Zea mexicana*)

类似 lèisì similar; analogous: ～产品 similar product /～物 analogue /～事件层出不穷。There is frequent recurrence of similar incidents. /鱼类的鳃与陆上动物的肺～。The gills of fishes are analogous to the lungs in terrestrial animals.

类天花 lèitiānhuā 〈医学〉para-smallpox

类同 lèitóng resemble; be similar to: 样式～ of similar style

类推 lèituī analogize; reason by analogy: 照此～ by this analogy; by analogy to this /余可～。The rest can be deduced by analogy.

类新星 lèixīnxīng 〈天文〉nova-like star

类星体 lèixīngtǐ 〈天文〉quasi-stellar object (QSO); quasar

类星系 lèixīngxì 〈天文〉quasi-stellar galaxy

类星源 lèixīngyuán 〈天文〉quasi-stellar source

类型 lèixíng type; category; kind: 这种～的产品在国内属首创。This type of product is the first of its kind (to be made) in our country.

类型学 lèixíngxué typology

类型语言学 lèixíng yǔyánxué typological linguistics; linguistic typology

类脂 lèizhī 〈生化〉lipoid

颣 lèi 〈书面〉defect; fault; drawback; flaw: 疵～ defect; flaw /无～ flawless

酹 lèi 〈书面〉pour a libation: ～江月 pour a libation for rivers and the moon /以酒～之 make a libation to it

擂 lèi ring (for martial contests); arena
see also léi

擂台 lèitái ring or stage (for martial art contests); arena: ～赛 open contest; open challenge /摆～ give an open challenge /打～ take up the challenge; pick up the gauntlet

擂主 lèizhǔ one who gives an open challenge

累 lèi ❶ fatigue; weariness: 不怕苦, 不怕～ fear neither hardship nor fatigue /～活脏活 tiring and dirty work; heavy and filthy work ❷ tire; fatigue; weary; strain: ～坏了 tired out; worn out; exhausted /～死人的差使 fatiguing errand (*or* job) /光线太暗, 看起书来～眼睛。It'll strain your eyes to read in such dim light. /这工作～脑子。This job taxes my brains. ❸ work hard; toil: 你～了一天, 早点休息吧! You've been working hard all day. Don't sit up too late.
see also léi; lěi

累乏 lèifá tired out; worn out; exhausted: 他跑了一天, 实在～了。Having been running errands for a day, he felt dog-tired.

累活 lèihuó strenuous work; hard toil

累手 lèishǒu ❶ encumber; be a burden: 有孩子～, 她不能去。She is burdened with children and can't go. ❷ 〈方言〉get involved; have a hand (in sth.): 你干你的, 这里你就不要～了。Go ahead with your own work; you needn't get involved here.

累死累活 lèisǐ-lèihuó work one's fingers to the bone; work like a dog; toil: 他给地主～地干了一年, 什么也没有得到。He worked like a horse for the landlord for a whole year but got nothing in return.

肋 lèi rib; costal region: 两～ both sides of the chest /左～ left side of the chest /鸡～ chicken rib
see also lē

肋巴骨 lèibagǔ 〈方言〉*see* "肋骨"

肋巴扇儿 lèibashànr 〈方言〉both sides of the chest

肋叉子 lèichāzi 〈方言〉rib; part close to rib: 他笑得～生疼。He laughed so hard that his ribs ached.

肋骨 lèigǔ *also* "肋巴骨"; "肋条" 〈生理〉rib; costa (pl. costae)

肋骨切除术 lèigǔ qiēchúshù costectomy; costatectomy

肋间 lèijiān 〈生理〉intercostal: ～神经 intercostal nerve

肋间肌 lèijiānjī intercostal muscle

肋膜 lèimó 〈生理〉pleura

肋膜炎 lèimóyán pleurisy

肋木 lèimù 〈体育〉stall bars

肋软骨 lèiruǎngǔ 〈生理〉costal cartilage; costicartilage; sternate cartilage; cartilage ribs: ～炎 costal chondritis

肋条 lèitiao 〈方言〉❶ rib: 他瘦得都看得见～了。He was so skinny that his ribs showed. ❷ animal ribs: 猪～ pork ribs /牛～ beef ribs

肋痛 lèitòng 〈医学〉costalgia

肋窝 lèiwō arm pit

lei

嘞 lei 〈助词〉*similar to the usage of* 喽 *but with a lighter tone*: 好～, 我听您的! Okay, I'll do as you say. /走～, 太阳都老高了。Let's go. The sun is already high up in the sky.
see also lē

lēng

棱 lēng *see* "红不棱登" hóngbulēngdēng; "花不棱登" huābulēngdēng; "扑棱" pūlēng
see also léng

唥 lēng 〈象声〉*used to describe the sound of turning wheels, etc.*: 纺车～～转得欢。The spinning wheel creaked round.

léng

薐 léng *also*"菠薐菜"bōléngcài spinach

棱(稜) léng ❶ arris; edge:大木箱～儿 edges of a wooden trunk /有～有角 angular ❷ corrugation; ridge:瓦～ rows of tiles on a roof; corrugated tiles /搓板～儿 ridges of a washboard *see also* lēng

棱层 léngcéng *also*"崚嶒"léngcéng (ridge stones) one on top of another:自山麓至峰顶,石级～,盘旋而上。Stone steps spiralled from the foot up to the top of the mountain.

棱缝 léngfeng 〈方言〉 flaw; hole; loophole:藏严实了,别让人看出～儿来。Hide it safely. Don't leave any trace.

棱角 léngjiǎo ❶ edges and corners:山石嵯峨,～突兀。The mountain cliffs are high and steep with imposing craggy edges. ❷ edge; pointedness:他工于心计,但表面却不露～。He was crafty but hid it well. /青年人不要过早地把～磨掉。Young people should not draw (*or* pull) in their horns too soon.

棱镜 léngjìng prism; glass prism; optical prism; edge glass:三～ triangular prism /方～ quadratic prism /光谱～ spectroscopic prism /色散～ dispersion prism /～分光 prismatic decomposition /～折射 prismatic refraction

棱镜玻璃 léngjìng bōli prism glass

棱镜分光仪 léngjìng fēnguāngyí prism spectrometer

棱镜光谱 léngjìng guāngpǔ prismatic spectrum

棱镜六分仪 léngjìng liùfēnyí prismatic sextant

棱镜摄谱仪 léngjìng shèpǔyí prism spectrograph

棱镜直角器 léngjìng zhíjiǎoqì prism square

棱坎 léngkǎn bank; mound; ridge:他摸到一个～下,看见上面隐隐约约现出两个修工事的敌人。He groped his way to a ridge, where two enemy soldiers above were dimly seen building a gun position.

棱棱 léngléng ❶〈书面〉severe cold; bitter cold:～霜气 severely cold frosty weather ❷〈书面〉dignified; awe-inspiring:目光～ stern look ❸ very thin; gaunt:瘦骨～的老马 old, gaunt horse

棱棱睁睁 léngleng-zhēngzhēng rude; forbidding in manner:这人整天就是那么～的,好像对谁都有意见。He wears that cold and even rude look all day as if he has (*or* bears) grudges against everybody.

棱面 léngmiàn facet (of a cut jewel or prism)

棱台 léngtái 〈数学〉(short for 棱锥台) frustrum of a pyramid

棱线 léngxiàn 〈军事〉crest line

棱柱体 léngzhùtǐ 〈数学〉prism:斜～ oblique prism /正～ regular prism /直～ right prism /～法则 prismoidal rule

棱锥 léngzhuī 〈数学〉pyramid:～结构 pyramidal structure /～面 pyramidal surface; pyramid surface

棱锥台 léngzhuītái 〈数学〉frustrum of a pyramid

棱锥体 léngzhuītǐ 〈数学〉pyramid

棱子 léngzi 〈方言〉edge:冰～ edge of a piece of ice

崚 léng

崚嶒 léngcéng 〈书面〉(of mountains) high

塄 léng 〈方言〉sloping bank or ridge of a field:田～上长满了杂草。The ridges of the fields were overgrown with weeds.

塄坎 léngkǎn 〈方言〉sloping bank and ridge of earth between fields; ridge:她在地里劳动,让孩子在～上玩耍。She worked in the fields, leaving the children to play by themselves on the ridge.

楞 léng *see*"棱"léng

楞伽经 Léngqiéjīng 〈佛教〉Lankavatara Sutra

楞严经 Léngyánjīng 〈佛教〉Surangama Sutra

lěng

冷 lěng ❶ cold; chilly:冰～ ice cold; freezing cold /～得发抖 shiver from cold /我觉得身上发～。I'm feeling chilly. /这里真～! It's really freezing here! ❷〈方言〉(usu. of food) cool:这汤～～再喝。Let the soup cool off before you drink it. *or* Take the soup after it cools down. ❸ cold in manner; frosty; frigid; icy:～～地看了一眼 give an icy stare /～～地打了个招呼 give a frigid greeting; greet sb. in a frigid manner /对某人很～ treat sb. coldly; give sb. the cold shoulder ❹ unfrequented; deserted; forlorn; out-of-the-way: *see*"～清";"～落" ❺ strange; rare; unusual:～姓 rare surname ❻ unwelcomed; unpopular: *see*"～货";"～门" ❼ covert; underhanded; sudden:打～拳 hit sb. from behind ❽ dishearten; discourage; dampen:心灰意～ (totally) disheartened; dispirited /我的心一下子～了。I was struck cold at heart. ❾ (Lěng) a surname

冷拔 lěngbá *also*"冷拉"〈机械〉cold-drawing:～钢 cold-drawn steel /～设备 cold-draw equipment

冷板凳 lěngbǎndèng cold stool — an indifferent post or a cold reception:我特意来看他,他却让我坐了半天～。I had come all the way to see him, but he kept me cooling my heels for a long time.

冷背 lěngbèi (of goods) dull; unsalable:～货 dull goods

冷冰冰 lěngbīngbīng ❶ icy; frosty; frigid:她的脸色～的。She wore an icy expression on her face. /我受不了他那～的态度。I just can't put up with his chilly manners. *or* His coldness is unbearable. /这老头真是个～的人,我从来没有见他笑过。The old man is a real cold fish. I've never seen him laugh. ❷ ice-cold; icy:你的手怎么～的? Why, your hands are ice-cold!

冷兵器 lěngbīngqì 〈军事〉cold steel

冷布 lěngbù 〈纺织〉gauze

冷不丁 lěngbudīng 〈方言〉*see*"冷不防"

冷不防 lěngbufáng *also*"冷不丁";"冷丁";"冷孤丁" unawares; off one's guard; by surprise; unexpectedly:～挨了一拳 get a punch off one's guard /～被一个树桩绊倒 suddenly fall over the stump of a tree /我们的突然袭击把敌人打了个～,他们顿时乱作一团。Our surprise attack caught the enemy off guard (*or* unawares) and threw them into confusion.

冷菜 lěngcài cold food; cold dish; hors d'oeuvre

冷餐 lěngcān cold meal; buffet:自助～ buffet /～会 buffet reception; buffet party

冷舱 lěngcāng (on a ship) refrigerating chamber; cold storage

冷藏 lěngcáng refrigeration; cold storage:～胚胎 refrigerated embryo /～肉 chilled (*or* frozen) meat /将食物～起来。Put the food in cold storage. *or* Keep the food under refrigeration.

冷藏舱 lěngcángcāng 〈船舶〉refrigerating chamber; cold-storage room

冷藏车 lěngcángchē refrigerator car or wagon (on a train, etc.); refrigerator van, lorry, or truck; refrigerator vehicle

冷藏船 lěngcángchuán refrigeration ship; cold storage ship

冷藏罐 lěngcángguàn refrigerated container:冰激凌～ refrigerated container for ice-cream

冷藏库 lěngcángkù cold storage; freezer; ice house

冷藏设备 lěngcáng shèbèi refrigerating equipment

冷藏室 lěngcángshì refrigerating chamber; cold closet; refrigerating compartment (in a refrigerator)

冷藏条款 lěngcáng tiáokuǎn refrigeration clause

冷藏箱 lěngcángxiāng refrigerator; ice box

冷场 lěngchǎng ❶ awkward silence on the stage when an actor enters late or forgets his lines:他怎么又～了?你听观众正在起哄。How could he forget his lines again? Just listen to the boo from the audience. ❷ awkward silence at a meeting:为了打破～,他讲了个笑话。He cracked a joke in order to break the ice.

冷嘲热讽 lěngcháo-rèfěng freezing irony and burning satire; taunt and jeer; scathing sarcasm:有话就直说,何必～! Say what you like but you don't have to be so sarcastic. /鲁迅对敌人～,对人民却是满腔热忱。Lu Xun reserved the most caustic satire for the enemy, but he was all warmth towards the people.

冷冲压 lěngchòngyā 〈冶金〉cold stamping

冷处理 lěngchǔlǐ ❶〈机械〉cold treatment ❷ give sth. a cooling period before tackling it; tackle a matter after all parties concerned have cooled down

冷床 lěngchuáng 〈农业〉cold bed; coldframe:～育苗 seeding in coldframe /～催芽 coldframe forced sprouting

冷脆 lěngcuì 〈冶金〉cold short:～材料 cold short material

冷待 lěngdài treat coldly; give the cold shoulder; slight:～客人 treat guests coldly /不能～任何顾客。No clients (*or* customers) should be slighted.

冷淡 lěngdàn ❶ slack; sluggish:旅游旺季一过,这家客店的生意就～了下来。This inn's business declines when the tourist season is over. ❷ cold; indifferent; apathetic:～的表情 cold expression /语气～

L

cold tone (*or* voice) /他对这件事很~。He adopted an indifferent attitude towards the matter. /她变得对周围的事都很~。She has grown apathetic about everything around her. ❸ treat coldly; cold-shoulder; slight; estrange:我们原以为会受到热情接待,可他们对我们却非常~。We expected to be received by them with open arms, but got the cold shoulder instead. /她有意~他。She is deliberately leaving him out in the cold.

冷低压 lěngdīyā 〈气象〉cold low; cold-core cyclone; cold cyclonic depression

冷调 lěngdiào 〈美术〉cool tone; cool colour-tone

冷碟儿 lěngdiér 〈方言〉cold dish; hors d'oeuvre

冷丁 lěngdīng 〈方言〉*see*"冷不防"

冷顶锻机 lěngdǐngduànjī 〈冶金〉(cold) upsetter

冷冻 lěngdòng freezing:~食品 frozen food /~包装 frozen pack /~精液 frozen semen /~法 freezing (method) /无氟~ Freon-free refrigeration (*or* freezing)

冷冻厂 lěngdòngchǎng cold storage plant

冷冻干燥 lěngdòng gānzào freeze-drying

冷冻机 lěngdòngjī refrigerator; freezer

冷冻剂 lěngdòngjì refrigerant; cryogen; coolant:无氟~ Freon-free refrigerant

冷冻疗法 lěngdòng liáofǎ cryotherapy; cold therapy; crymotherapy

冷冻麻醉 lěngdòng mázuì crymoanesthesia

冷冻浓缩 lěngdòng nóngsuō freezing concentration

冷冻切片 lěngdòng qiēpiàn frozen section

冷冻室 lěngdòngshì chilling chamber; freezer compartment (in a refrigerator)

冷冻手术 lěngdòng shǒushù cryosurgery

冷冻探子 lěngdòng tànzi cryoprobe

冷冻压缩机 lěngdòng yāsuōjī refrigerant compressor

冷锻 lěngduàn 〈机械〉cold forging; cold hammering:~模 cold-forging die

冷镦 lěngdūn 〈冶金〉cold-heading; cold upsetting:~机 cold header; cold holder

冷风 lěngfēng ❶ cold wind; cold draught; 〈冶金〉cold air:送~ give a cold air blast /一阵~ a gust of cold wind /~机 air cooler ❷ negative remarks; unfavourable remarks:吹~ make negative remarks; spread gossip (*or* rumours)

冷锋 lěngfēng *also*"冷锋面"〈气象〉cold front

冷敷 lěngfū 〈医学〉cold compress:~法 cold application; cold compress /~布 cold compress

冷服 lěngfú (of liquid Chinese medicine) take it cold; take it when it cools down

冷高压 lěnggāoyā 〈气象〉cold high; cold anticyclone

冷宫 lěnggōng cold palace — part of the palace to which disfavoured queens or concubines were banished; limbo:被打入~ be out of favour with the emperor; be consigned to limbo; be shelved; be sent to Coventry (*or* Siberia)

冷孤丁 lěnggūdīng 〈方言〉*see*"冷不防"

冷光 lěngguāng ❶〈物理〉cold light:~灯 cold light lamp /~镜 cold mirror; diathermic mirror /~手术灯 cold light operating lamp /~源 cold light source ❷ cold eyes; cold expression:眼里闪烁着逼人的~。His eyes flashed with a cold piercing expression.

冷柜 lěngguì refrigerator (usu. of large, squat type); ice box

冷害 lěnghài 〈农业〉disaster caused by cold snaps; damage by frost; frost damage

冷汗 lěnghàn cold sweat:出~ break out in a cold sweat /吓出了一身~ be scared into a cold sweat; grow cold with fear /手里捏着一把~ with one's hands sweating coldly (with fear, anxiety, etc.)

冷焊 lěnghàn 〈机械〉cold welding

冷话 lěnghuà ironical or biting remarks; sarcastic or unfavourable comments:在背后说别人的~ make sarcartic remarks behind others' backs

L

冷荤 lěnghūn cold meat; cold meat dish

冷货 lěnghuò ❶ *also*"冷门货" unpopular or unattractive goods; dull goods; unsalable goods ❷ frozen product; chilled cargo

冷货仓位 lěnghuò cāngwèi refrigeration space

冷集装箱 lěngjízhuāngxiāng refrigerated container; reefer container

冷挤压 lěngjǐyā 〈冶金〉cold extrusion; cold-flow pressing:~力机 cold extrusion press

冷寂 lěngjì chilly and still; lonely; forlorn:~的秋夜 chilly and silent autumn night /她孤身一人,感到有些~。She was alone and felt a bit forlorn.

冷加工 lěngjiāgōng 〈机械〉cold working:~钢制品 cold-finished steel /~性 cold-workability

冷箭 lěngjiàn arrow shot from hiding; sniper's shot:放~ stab in the back; make a sneak attack /这位同事的~,实在难防。It is most difficult to guard against the sneak attacks by this colleague.

冷浇注 Lěngjiāozhù 〈冶金〉cold cast

冷浸田 lěngjìntián low-yielding paddy fields soaked in cold spring water throughout the year, esp. in hilly areas

冷噤 lěngjìn *also*"寒噤" hánjìn shiver; shudder:冻得浑身直打~ shiver all over in the cold /突然一个什么东西掉下来,她不由打了一个~。Suddenly something dropped from above, and it sent a chill down her spine.

冷静 lěngjìng ❶ deserted and quiet; still; hushed:清晨,林子里很~。In the morning, all is quiet in the woods. /天晚了,街上也~下来了。It was getting dark and the streets began to quiet down. ❷ calm; sober; unruffled; composed:他一向头脑~。He is always sober-minded. *or* He always keeps a cool (*or* level) head. /遇事要~。Play it cool when in trouble. *or* Don't panic when something unexpected happens. /请大家保持~,有话一个一个说。Please keep calm and speak in turn. /他没想到她竟十分~地同意离婚。What surprised him is that she accepted the divorce with a good grace.

冷觉 lěngjué 〈生理〉sensation of cold; sense of cold:~过敏 hypercryalgesia

冷峻 lěngjùn sober and grave; stern:~的笔触 cold and sharp style /他身材魁梧,目光~,气派不凡。A man of commanding presence, he had a powerful build and wore a stern expression on his face.

冷刻 lěngkè cold and sharp; sarcastic:~的话语 caustic remarks /待人~ be cold and sarcastic towards others

冷库 lěngkù *also*"冷藏库" cold storage; refrigerated compartment; freezer; ice house

冷酷 lěngkù cold-hearted; cold-blooded; callous; grim:~的心 cold heart /~的人 callous person /~的现实 grim reality /~的表情 stony look /对她来说,这个世界是~的。To her, the world is inhospitable.

冷酷无情 lěngkù-wúqíng unfeeling; ruthless; cold-hearted; hard as nails:~的人际关系 ruthless interpersonal relations

冷拉 lěnglā *see*"冷拔"

冷厉 lěnglì cold and stern:~的目光 cold and stern eyes; icy look

冷脸子 lěngliǎnzi 〈方言〉cold face or expression; frosty look:谁愿意一天到晚看他的~? No one wants to see his frosty expression all day.

冷冽 lěngliè ice-cold; biting:~的泉水 ice-cold spring water /~的北风 cutting (*or* biting) north wind

冷落 lěngluò ❶ unfrequented; desolate:~的小街 unfrequented narrow lane /门庭~ have few visitors /~的小山村 desolate (*or* deserted) small mountain village /战争使这个曾经十分热闹的小镇~了下来。The war deprived this little town of its past bustling life. ❷ treat coldly; cold-shoulder; slight:我可不愿让我的客人受到~。I don't want my guests to be left out in the cold. /这些年来,他连老朋友也~了。He has even slighted his old friends recently.

冷铆 lěngmǎo 〈机械〉cold riveting:~铆钉 cold-driven rivet

冷眉冷眼 lěngméi-lěngyǎn *also*"冷眉淡眼" cold eye; cold shoulder:她~地瞪了他一下。She gave him a cold eye.

冷门 lěngmén ❶ little-known profession, trade, or branch of learning:过去地质学是~儿。In the past geology was a branch of learning few people paid attention to. ❷ unexpected winner; dark horse; upset:爆~ produce an upset; upset /本届全运会~迭出。Quite a few prizes were taken by unexpected winners at this year's National Sports Meet. *or* The National Sports Meet produced quite a few dark horses (*or* upsets).

冷门货 lěngménhuò *see*"冷货"

冷面 lěngmiàn ❶ stern-looking face; cold eye; poker face:~杀手 poker-faced assassin (*or* killer) /~幽默 dry humour; telling a joke with a poker face /他们局长是个~官,很难接近。Their director is a stern-looking bureaucrat and difficult of approach. ❷ impartial and incorruptible:这个故事讲的是一个执法无私,~如铁的法官。This is a story about an impartial and incorruptible judge.

冷蔑 lěngmiè cold and scornful; stiff and disdainful:他~地看了她

一眼。He threw (*or* cast) a cold and contemptuous glance at her.

冷漠 lěngmò cold and detached; indifferent; nonchalant: 她为他的～无情深感苦恼。She was much distressed by his indifference. /他装出一副～的态度。He assumed an air of nonchalance. /这人真是一个～孤傲的人。The man was a cold fish all right.

冷凝 lěngníng 〈物理〉condensation: ～蒸气 condensed steam /～式汽轮机 condensing turbine /～温度 condensation temperature

冷凝泵 lěngníngbèng condenser pump

冷凝点 lěngníngdiǎn condensation point

冷凝管 lěngníngguǎn cold trap; drain sleeve

冷凝机 lěngníngjī freezing machine

冷凝模塑 lěngníng mósù slush moulding

冷凝器 lěngníngqì condenser

冷凝塔 lěngníngtǎ condensing tower

冷凝物 lěngníngwù condensate

冷凝箱 lěngníngxiāng cooling cylinder

冷凝液 lěngníngyè (condensate) liquid

冷凝装置 lěngníng zhuāngzhì condensing unit; condensing works

冷暖 lěngnuǎn ❶ changes in temperature: 他不管天气～，一直坚持冷水浴。He has been taking cold baths regardless of the weather. ❷ well-being: 关心群众的～ be concerned with the well-being of the masses /你一个人在外，自己要注意～。Living away from home, you must take good care of yourself.

冷暖自知 lěngnuǎn-zìzhī know what's what by one's own experience: ～，我的难处只有我自己明白。As only the wearer knows where the shoe pinches, so I know my own plight best.

冷盘 lěngpán cold dish; hors d'oeuvre: 什锦～ assorted cold dish /开胃～ cold dish starter

冷炮 lěngpào sporadic and unexpected shelling: 五点左右，敌人突然打过来几发～。At about 5 o'clock, a few enemy shells fell on our position unexpectedly. /她在会上放了个～，给领导提了一大通意见。She surprised everyone at the meeting by pouring out her complaints against the leadership.

冷僻 lěngpì ❶ deserted; desolate; out-of-the-way: ～的山村 secluded (*or* isolated) mountain village /～的去处 out-of-the-way place; unfrequented spot /性格～ be given to solitude ❷ unfamiliar; rare: ～词 rarely used word; rare word /～的典故 unfamiliar allusion /～的行业 little known profession (*or* trade)

冷凄凄 lěngqīqī cold and dreary; lonely; deserted: 这间屋子黑洞洞、～的。The room is dark and dreary.

冷起动 lěngqǐdòng 〈机械〉cold-starting

冷气 lěngqì ❶ cold air; cool air ❷ air conditioning: ～设备 air conditioning (equipment) /这家饭馆有～。This restaurant is air-conditioned.

冷气管 lěngqìguǎn cold air duct; cold air pipe

冷气机 lěngqìjī air conditioner; cooler

冷气通风舱 lěngqì tōngfēngcāng cool (ventilated) compartment (as in a ship)

冷气团 lěngqìtuán 〈气象〉cold air mass

冷气稳定系统 lěngqì wěndìng xìtǒng cold gas stablization system

冷枪 lěngqiāng sniper's shot: 打～ fire a sniper's shot; snipe at sb.

冷峭 lěngqiào ❶ bitterly cold; biting: ～的山风 biting mountain wind /春风～，天气尚寒。With a chilly wind blowing, the weather is still quite cold in early spring. ❷ sarcastic; caustic; acrimonious: ～的语言 caustic language; scathing remarks /性情～ have an acrimonious temper

冷清清 lěngqīngqīng cold and cheerless; quiet and deserted; forlorn; desolate: 街头～、黑漆漆的。The street was deserted and ink-dark. /宝塔～地耸立在月光下。The pagoda stood forlorn and solitary in the moonlight.

冷清 lěngqing cold and cheerless; deserted; lonely: ～的夜晚 cold and cheerless night /～的日子 sequestered (*or* lonely) life /院子里冷冷清清，空无一人。The courtyard looked deserted, and not a soul could be seen. /张家破产了，门前冷冷清清。The Zhang family went bankrupt and had few visitors.

冷泉 lěngquán cold spring

冷却 lěngquè make cool; cool: ～功率 cooling capacity /～热 heat of cooling /～实验 cooling test /～器 chiller; cooler /～周期 cooling-off (*or* cooling-down) period /～装置 coolant mechanism; cooling facility /～式干燥机 dehumidifier

冷却泵 lěngquèbèng cooling pump

冷却管 lěngquèguǎn cooling pipe

冷却剂 lěngquèjì coolant; cooling material; cooler

冷却介质 lěngquè jièzhì cooling medium or agent

冷却水 lěngquèshuǐ coolant water; chilled water

冷却塔 lěngquètǎ cooling tower

冷却油 lěngquèyóu coolant oil

冷然 lěngrán ❶ cold and indifferent: ～一笑 smile coldly; give a chilly smile ❷ unexpectedly; suddenly: ～一声惨叫 a sudden cry of horror

冷热病 lěngrèbìng ❶〈方言〉malaria; ague ❷ capricious changes in mood; sudden waxing and waning of enthusiasm; blowing hot and cold; mercurial: 他什么都好，就是有时犯～。He is fine except sometimes he tends to be moody. /我可从来不像你那样犯～。I never blow hot and cold as you do.

冷人 lěngrén cold or unfeeling person

冷若冰霜 lěngruòbīngshuāng (usu. of women) as cold as ice; frosty: ～的脸 frosty look; chilly manner /张教授的夫人对人总是～，叫人望而却步。Professor Zhang's wife has an icy manner that keeps people at a distance.

冷色 lěngsè 〈美术〉cold colour: 一幅～的油画 oil painting cold in tone /白、绿、兰色等～给人以凉爽的感觉。Cold colours such as white, green and blue make people feel cool and fresh.

冷涩 lěngsè ❶ (of water, air, etc.) cold; chilly: 泉水～。The spring water is ice-cold. ❷ indifferent and dull: ～的目光 indifferent and dull look (*or* gaze) ❸ (of voice) low and harsh: 那人的声音～嘶哑。The man had a low and husky voice. ❹ obscure and seldom used: ～的词语 rare and hardly intelligible words and expressions

冷森森 lěngsēnsēn (of a place) chilly and gloomy; cold and ghastly: 地下室里～的，令人悚然。The cellar is chilly and spooky.

冷杉 lěngshān *also* "枞" cōng 〈植物〉fir

冷食 lěngshí cold food; cold drinks and snacks: ～店 cold drink and snack bar /这种病忌～。People with this disease should keep away from cold drinks and food. *or* Cold drinks and food do not agree with people who have this disease.

冷室 lěngshì refrigerating room; refrigerating chamber; refrigerating compartment (in a refrigerator)

冷霜 lěngshuāng cold cream

冷水 lěngshuǐ ❶ cold water: ～浴 cold bath /～养殖 cold water culture /泼～ throw cold water on; throw a wet blanket on; dampen sb.'s enthusiasm ❷ unboiled water

冷水浇头 lěngshuǐ-jiāotóu *also* "冷水浇背" splash the head with cold water — give a great or rude shock; be a bitter disappointment; throw cold water on: 他一听这消息，犹如～，一时间没了主意。His hopes were dashed by the news. For a time, he didn't quite know what to do.

冷丝丝 lěngsīsī *also* "冷丝儿丝儿的" a bit chilly: 雨点落在脸上，～的。Chilly rain drops fell on the face.

冷飕飕 lěngsōusōu (of wind or air) chilly; chilling: 天儿～的。It's quite cold. /我衣服穿得不够，身上觉得～的。I'm not wearing enough clothes and feeling rather chilly.

冷塑 lěngsù 〈化工〉cold moulding

冷嗦嗦 lěngsuōsuō cold; chilly: 浑身～的直抖 shiver with cold

冷缩 lěngsuō shrink from cold: 热胀～ expand with heat and contract with cold

冷烫 lěngtàng (of hairdressing) cold wave: ～精 cold wave agent

冷天 lěngtiān cold day; cold weather

冷条款 lěngtiáokuǎn refrigeration clause

冷线 lěngxiàn cold line

冷笑 lěngxiào laugh grimly; sneer: 嘴角上挂着一丝～。A faint sneer hangs on the lips. /这个家伙～着，从兜里拿出一个公文信封。The man laughed scornfully and produced a sealed official letter from his pocket.

冷心肠 lěngxīncháng cold-hearted; heartless: 他是个～的人，跟他说又有什么用? What can you expect from a man with a stony heart like him?

冷星 lěngxīng 〈天文〉cool star

冷性肥料 lěngxìng féiliào manure that does not generate heat; cold manure

冷血动物 lěngxuè dòngwù ❶ cold-blooded animal; poikilothermal animal ❷ unfeeling person; cold-hearted person: 面对如此惨状而无动于衷，他真是个～。What a stony-hearted fellow he must be, to be untouched by such horrible sights.

冷血性 lěngxuèxìng coldbloodedness

冷压 lěngyā 〈冶金〉 chill pressing; cold-compacting; cold compression; cold-moulding: ～焊 cold-pressure welding /～机 cold press

冷言冷语 lěngyán-lěngyǔ sarcastic comments; ironical remarks: 她忍受不了女主人的～。She found it hard to take her mistress's sarcastic comments. /他用～把小李气走了。He sent Xiao Li away (*or* off) with a flea in his ear.

冷眼 lěngyǎn ❶ cold eye; cold detachment: 他在一旁～观察着来人的言谈举止。He stood by observing the man's behaviour with a cold eye. /～向洋看世界。Cold-eyed, I survey the world beyond the seas. ❷ cold manner; cold shoulder: ～相待 treat coldly /遭到同事们的～ be cold-shouldered by one's colleagues

冷眼旁观 lěngyǎn-pángguān look on coldly; stay aloof; watch with a critical eye: 这事确有不少人在～, 看你们怎么处理。Quite a few people are indeed watching you with a critical eye, waiting to see how you'll handle the matter. /他对世事总是抱着～的态度。He always remains aloof from what happens in the world.

冷艳 lěngyàn (usu. used with flowers in cold weather, etc.) coldly elegant; simple but elegant: ～的梅花 quietly elegant plum blossom

冷饮 lěngyǐn cold drink: ～店 cold drinks parlour (*or* bar); ice cream parlour (*or* shop) /喝点儿～ have some cold drink

冷硬 lěngyìng ❶ cold and hard: ～的烙饼 cold and hard pancake ❷ cold and harsh: ～的声音 cold and harsh voice

冷硬铸铁 lěngyìng zhùtiě 〈冶金〉 chill cast iron: ～轧辊 chill cast iron roll; chilled iron roll

冷语 lěngyǔ cold words; sarcastic remarks

冷语冰人 lěngyǔ-bīngrén sting sb. with cold or sarcastic remarks: 切莫话中有刺, ～。One's words must not carry a sting and hurt people.

冷遇 lěngyù cold reception; cold shoulder: 屡遭～, 不禁心灰意懒。His spirits sank after repeated cold receptions.

冷錾 lěngzàn 〈机械〉 cold chisel

冷轧 lěngzhá 〈冶金〉 cold rolling: ～钢 cold-rolled steel /～性 cold-rolling property /～压缩 cold-rolling reduction

冷轧机 lěngzhájī cold-rolling mill

冷战 lěngzhàn cold war: ～时期 cold war period /～心态 cold-war mentality /～思维 cold-war thinking /～后 post-cold war

冷战 lěngzhan *also* "冷颤" 〈口语〉 shiver: 吓得浑身打～ shiver all over with fear

冷炙残杯 lěngzhì-cánbēi *also* "残杯冷炙" leftover dish and wine; leftovers; handouts from the rich

冷铸 lěngzhù 〈冶金〉 chill casting: ～型 cold mould /～轮 chilled cast wheel

冷庄子 lěngzhuāngzi 〈旧语〉 restaurant which arranges banquets only; caterer's

冷字 lěngzì rarely-used word; rare word

冷子 lěngzi 〈方言〉 hail; hailstone

冷阻 lěngzǔ cold resistance

冷作 lěngzuò 〈冶金〉 cold-forming; cold-work(ing): ～硬化 cold-work hardening

lèng

愣

lèng ❶ distracted; stupefied; blank; dumbfounded: 你在那儿发什么～? Hey, what's that blank stare (of yours)? *or* Well, you're in a daze (*or* trance), aren't you? /他一听竟吓～了。He was stunned by it. *or* He was dumbfounded with fear. /别～着, 快干活儿! Don't stand gawking! Get on with your work. ❷ blunt; rash; reckless; foolhardy: 说话太～ speak very bluntly /这人办事太～。The man is a hothead. ❸ 〈方言〉 stubbornly; wilfully: 我叫他不要做, 他～是不听。I told him not to do it, but he just wouldn't listen.

愣冲冲 lèngchōngchōng rashly; recklessly: 那男孩～地从麦垛上跳下来。The little boy threw himself down from the hay stack.

愣葱 lèngcōng *also* "愣头儿葱" 〈方言〉 rash or reckless fellow; hothead: 这～有时也能干出巧活儿来。Though he's usually rash, he can do quite a smart job now and then. /别跟～似的, 什么也不在乎! Don't be a hothead and assume a devil-may-care air!

愣干 lènggàn 〈口语〉 do things recklessly or rashly; persist in going one's own way whatever the cost: 要讲究方法, 不能～。You've got to pay attention to methods. You can't do things any way you like. /你小子别～, 小心出人命! I warn you not to do anything rash. You don't want to be held responsible for the loss of somebody's life, do you?

愣乎乎 lènghūhū ❶ stupefied: 人们一见我, 都哈哈大笑, 把我笑得～的。Everyone who saw me laughed, which baffled me completely. ❷ rashly; recklessly; impetuously: 他带着一股子～的劲儿, 像是什么都不顾似的。He acts recklessly in utter disregard of any danger.

愣劲儿 lèngjìnr 〈方言〉 daring; pep; vigour: 这小伙子凭股子～, 硬是爬上了悬崖。The young man climbed to the top of the cliff by sheer daring.

愣愣 lèngleng 〈方言〉 wait for a while: 这事先～, 改天再说吧。Let's sleep on it and talk about it some other day.

愣愣瞌瞌 lènglengkēkē 〈口语〉 distracted; stupefied; in a trance: 他～地坐在那儿, 一言不发。There he sat, stupefied and speechless.

愣神儿 lèngshénr 〈方言〉 stare blankly; be in a daze; be sunk or lost in thought: 小丫头别～! 快干活儿去。Don't stare blankly, little girl. Go back to your work! /这个学生老是坐在位子上～, 不知怎么回事儿。This pupil often sits in a daze in his seat. I wonder why.

愣是 lèngshì 〈方言〉 insist wilfully (on doing sth.): 我～不信我就干不了这一行。I just don't believe that I'm no good for this line of work. /他～不接受我的礼物。He simply refused to accept the present I offered him.

愣说 lèngshuō 〈口语〉 insist; allege; assert: 你～你不会, 这不是干得很好吗? Why did you insist that you couldn't do it? You've done beautifully.

愣头愣脑 lèngtóu-lèngnǎo reckless; rash; impetuous: ～的小伙子 rash young fellow /他年轻时做事总是有些～, 现在老练多了。He used to be impetuous when he was young. Now he is quite sophisticated.

愣头儿青 lèngtóurqīng 〈方言〉 rash fellow; hothead: 这孩子～, 怕办事不牢。He is quite hotheaded and may not be reliable.

愣小子 lèngxiǎozi pig-headed or stubborn person

愣眼巴睁 lèngyǎn-bāzhēng 〈方言〉 (usu. as a result of a shock) stare blankly; stare woodenly: 他～地坐着, 呆若木鸡。He sat there staring blankly and dumb as a wooden chicken.

愣着 lèngzhe not moving; dumb: 不要～。Don't stand there doing nothing.

愣怔 lèngzheng *also* "睖睁" lèngzheng stare blankly; be in a daze

愣子眼 lèngziyǎn (look) drunken: 刘大爷一连喝了几杯, 已是～了。Grandpa Liu began to look silly after a couple of drinks. /一瓶酒下肚, 顿时把他喝的～了。He became quite tipsy (*or* had quite a buzz on) after one bottle.

睖

lèng 〈方言〉 stare in dissatisfaction: 她狠狠地～了他一眼。She threw him quite an angry, dissatisfied look.

睖睁 lèngzheng *also* "愣怔" lèngzheng ❶ stare blankly: 他～着眼睛, 一言不发。He kept staring blankly, not uttering a word. ❷ be in a daze; be stupefied: 你别老是～着发呆, 出去散散心。Don't stay in such a daze all day long. Go out and take a walk.

lī

哩

lī

see also lǐ; li

哩哩啦啦 līlilālā scattered; sporadic; on and off; here and there: 这雨～没个完。It's been raining on and off without end. /快到十二点了, 客人才～地来了。It was almost 12 o'clock when the guests arrived in dribs and drabs. /口袋没扎紧, 大米～地洒了一路。The rice bag was not properly tied up and left a spotty trace of rice all along the road.

哩哩啰啰 līliluōluō wordy and unclear in speech; rambling and indistinct: 她～地说了一大堆, 我根本没听清她在说什么。I couldn't make out what she was rambling about.

哩溜歪斜 līliu-wāixié 〈方言〉 ❶ askew; crooked; twisted: 他的字写得～的。He scrawls when he writes. /这封信一定是小李写的, 我认得他～的字体。This letter must be from Xiao Li; I recognize his scrawl. ❷ stagger; waddle; vacillate: 一个醉鬼～地走过来。A drunkard was waddling over.

administer; regulate: 允～百工 keep all the government officials functioning efficiently
厘定 lídìng 〈书面〉collate and stipulate (rules and regulations, etc.): ～规章制度 draw up rules and regulations
厘革 lígé 〈书面〉rectify and reform: ～旧制 reform the old system
厘金 líjīn *also* "厘捐"; "厘金税" (in the Qing Dynasty) tax paid at a toll-gate on the goods being transported
厘克 líkè centigram (cg)
厘米 límǐ *also* "公分" gōngfēn centimetre (cm)
厘米波 límǐbō centimetre wave: ～测高计 centimetre height finder / ～雷达 centimetre-wave radar
厘米克秒 límǐ-kè-miǎo centimetre-gram-second; cgs: ～单位 cgs unit / ～制 cgs system
厘卡 líqiǎ 〈旧语〉toll-gate where tax on transported goods was collected
厘升 líshēng centilitre (cl)
厘正 lízhèng 〈书面〉make corrections; collate; revise: ～遗文 collate texts left by a deceased author

哩

lí *see* "咖哩" gālí

狸

lí
狸猫 límāo *also* "豹猫" bàomāo leopard cat
狸藻 lízǎo 〈植物〉bladderwort (*Utricularia vulgaris*)
狸子 lízi *see* "狸猫"

罹

lí 〈书面〉suffer from: ～无妄之灾 suffer an uncalled-for misfortune; meet with an unexpected disaster / ～病 suffer from a disease; fall ill
罹患 líhuàn 〈书面〉suffer (from illness)
罹祸 líhuò 〈书面〉suffer disaster
罹难 línàn 〈书面〉die in a disaster or an accident; be murdered: 不幸～ die unfortunately in a disaster / ～身亡 have been murdered

梨(棃)

lí pear: 北京鸭～ Beijing pear / 雪花～ *xuehua* pear (large pear grown in north China, known for its sweetness)
梨膏 lígāo 〈中药〉pear syrup (for the relief of coughs)
梨花大鼓 líhuā dàgǔ 〈戏曲〉"pear-flower" *dagu*, a type of *dagu* sung to the accompaniment of a drum, a three-stringed plucked instrument (三弦), and a pair of brass castanets shaped like plough shares (犁铧), of which "pear flower" is a homophone
梨秋 líqiū season of pears; time when pears are ripe (usu. between July and October)
梨涡 líwō dimple (on a woman's face)
梨园 líyuán 〈旧语〉Pear Garden — theatre; theatrical world (from the name of a Tang Dynasty opera academy): ～世家 come from a family of Chinese opera artists
梨园戏 líyuánxì *liyuan* opera, popular in southern Fujian Province
梨园子弟 líyuán zǐdì *also* "梨园弟子" 〈旧语〉actor or actress (in Chinese local operas); theatrical performer
梨枣 lízǎo 〈旧语〉pear and date — printing plate or block (usu. made of pear or date wood): 付之～ get sth. printed; send to the press
梨子 lízi pear

蜊

lí *see* "蛤蜊" gélí

犁(犂)

lí ❶ plough: 开沟～ ditch(ing) plough / 双铧～ double-shared plough ❷ work with a plough; plough: ～地 plough fields / ～沟 furrow / 草地已经～过, 种上了小麦。The grasslands have been broken and planted with wheat.
犁壁 líbì *see* "犁镜"
犁刀 lídāo 〈农业〉plough coulter
犁底层 lídǐcéng 〈农业〉plough sole; plough pan
犁耕 lígēng 〈农业〉ploughing
犁花 líhuā wake of soil left after ploughing: 耕过的地, ～像波纹一样均匀。In the field that has just been ploughed, the up-turned soil is piled up neatly along the furrow, like waves in the ocean.
犁铧 líhuá *also* "铧" ploughshare; share
犁镜 líjìng *also* "犁壁" 〈农业〉mouldboard: ～式起垄器 mouldboard ridger
犁路机 lílùjī road rooter
犁牛 líniú 〈方言〉farm cattle
犁式挖沟机 líshì wāgōujī plough type trenching machine
犁庭扫闾 lítíng-sǎolǘ *also* "犁庭扫穴" plough the courtyard and give the residential quarters a thorough sweeping — wipe out the enemy completely
犁头 lítóu ❶ (plough) share ❷ 〈方言〉plough
犁辕 líyuán 〈农业〉beam: ～支架 beam support
犁杖 lízhàng 〈方言〉plough

蒺

lí *see* "蒺藜" jílí

黎

lí ❶ Li nationality, living in Guangdong and Hainan provinces ❷ 〈书面〉multitude; host ❸ 〈书面〉black ❹ (Lí) a surname
黎巴嫩 Líbānèn Lebanon: ～人 Lebanese
黎黑 líhēi *also* "黧黑" líhēi 〈书面〉(of complexion) dark: 面目～ have a tanned face / 肤色～ have dark skin; look tanned
黎锦 líjǐn a kind of brocade popular among the Li people; Li brocade
黎曼几何 Límàn jǐhé 〈数学〉Riemannian geometry
黎民 límín 〈书面〉common people; the multitude; the populace; the masses: ～百姓 the populace / 天下～ broad masses of the people
黎明 límíng dawn; daybreak: ～时分 at daybreak; at dawn / ～即起 rise with the sun
黎庶 líshù 〈书面〉common people; the multitude
黎元 líyuán 〈书面〉*see* "黎庶"
黎元洪 Lí Yuánhóng Li Yuanhong (formerly translated as Li Yuan-hung, 1864-1928), one of the leaders in the early Republic of China
黎族 Lízú Li nationality or the Lis, living in Guangdong and Hainan

藜

lí *also* "灰菜" huīcài 〈植物〉lamb's-quarters
藜藿 líhuò 〈书面〉plain and coarse food: ～之羹 coarse food
藜芦 lílú 〈植物〉black false hellebore

黧

lí 〈书面〉black; dark and sallow
黧黑 líhēi *also* "黎黑" líhēi 〈书面〉(of complexion) dark

鸳

lí *also* "鹂" lí oriole

蠡

lí 〈书面〉❶ calabash shell serving as a dipper; dipper; gourd ladle: 以～测海 measure the water in the sea with a calabash shell — of narrow vision; shortsighted ❷ seashell
see also lǐ
蠡测 lícè 〈书面〉measure the sea with a calabash shell; have only a skimpy understanding of sth. or sb.: 管窥～ have a narrow and superficial view
蠡帽 límào helmet (worn by soldiers in ancient times)

劙

lí 〈书面〉pierce; cut; slash

lǐ

礼(禮)

lǐ ❶ ceremony; rite; ritual: 丧～ funeral ceremony; funeral / 婚～ wedding ceremony; wedding / 毕业典～ commencement / ～不下庶人。〈旧语〉Rites do not extend to the common people. ❷ courtesy; etiquette; manners: 施～ give a salute; bow to; (of women in old times) make a curtsy / 敬～ salute / 失～ 行为 breach of etiquette; discourtesy / 顶～膜拜 pay homage to; make a fetish of / 先～后兵 use persuasion before force ❸ gift; present: 贺～ gift as a token of congratulation / 寿～ birthday present / 一份厚～ a handsome gift / 受～ accept a present (*or* gift) / 献～ present a gift; greet an occasion with (success, achievement, etc.) ❹ 〈书面〉treat with courtesy; be courteous to: ～贤远佞 be courteous to people of virtue and keep away from sycophants
礼拜 lǐbài ❶ religious service: 做～ go to church; be at church / 圣诞～ Christmas service ❷ week: 再过两个～就放寒假了。The winter

L

vacation will begin in two weeks' time. ❸ day of the week: ～一 Monday / ～二 Tuesday / ～三 Wednesday / ～四 Thursday / ～五 Friday / ～六 Saturday ❹ Sunday: 今儿过～。Today is Sunday.
礼拜日 lǐbàirì *see* "礼拜天"
礼拜寺 lǐbàisì 〈伊斯兰〉 mosque
礼拜堂 lǐbàitáng church; chapel
礼拜天 lǐbàitiān *also* "礼拜日" Sunday
礼宾 lǐbīn protocol: ～活动 protocol activities / ～事务 protocol affairs / ～规定 protocol regulations / ～要求 protocol requirements / ～服装 protocol dress / ～官员 protocol officer / ～顺序 protocol order; protocol precedence
礼宾司 lǐbīnsī department of protocol; protocol department: ～司长 director general of the protocol department; chief of protocol
礼部 Lǐbù 〈历史〉 Board of Rites; Ministry of Rites: ～尚书 Minister of Rites
礼成 lǐchéng (said by the master of ceremonies) the ceremony is over
礼单 lǐdān *also* "礼帖" list of gifts
礼多必诈 lǐduō-bìzhà full of courtesy, full of craft
礼多人不怪 lǐ duō rén bù guài you will offend no one by being courteous; no one will blame you for being too polite
礼法 lǐfǎ rules of etiquette; decorum: 不合～ be at variance with the accepted rites (*or* proprieties)
礼佛 lǐfó 〈佛教〉 pray to Buddha: 烧香～ burn incense sticks and pray to Buddha
礼服 lǐfú ceremonial robe; full dress; formal attire: 大～ full dress/ 结婚～ wedding dress or suit / 晚～(for women) evening dress (*or* gown); (for men) evening suit; dress suit; dinner suit / 军～ dress uniform / 请着～。Full dress is required.
礼服呢 lǐfúní *also* "直贡呢" zhígòngní 〈纺织〉 venetian
礼盒 lǐhé box that contains a present; gift box
礼花 lǐhuā fireworks (for ceremonies or festivals): 放～ let off fireworks / 国庆节晚上放～。There'll be a fireworks display on the evening of National Day.
礼记 Lǐjì *The Book of Rites*, one of the Confucian classics
礼教 lǐjiào Confucian or feudal ethical code: ～繁缛 unnecessary and overelaborate ethical codes / 吃人的旧～ cannibalistic feudal ethics; life-destroying feudal code of ethics
礼节 lǐjié etiquette; protocol; courtesy; ceremony: 外交～ diplomatic protocol / 社交～ social etiquette / 网上～〈信息〉 netiqette / 注重～ be strict with etiquette (*or* proprieties) / ～性拜会 courtesy call / 以隆重的～接待贵宾 receive the guest of honour with full ceremony / 根据～安排坐次 make seating arrangements according to protocol
礼金 lǐjīn cash (as a) gift; gift of money
礼路儿 lǐlur 〈方言〉 courtesy; manners: 这孩子不懂～, 请别见怪。Please forgive the child for his discourtesy.
礼帽 lǐmào hat that goes with formal dress: 大～ top hat / 常～ bowler (hat)
礼貌 lǐmào courtesy; politeness; manners: 有～ courteous; polite / 没～ lacking in manners; impolite / 讲～ mind one's manners / 文明～教育 education in courtesy and manners / 瞪眼看人是不～的。It's bad manners to stare at people.
礼炮 lǐpào salvo; (gun) salute: 鸣放～ fire a salute (*or* salvo) / 二十一响～ 21-gun salute; salvo of 21 guns
礼炮号 Lǐpàohào 〈航天〉 Salyut (name of a series of space stations launched into earth orbit by the former USSR since 1971 and operated by crews of cosmonauts who were ferried to and fro by Soyuz craft)
礼品 lǐpǐn gift; present: 生日～ birthday present / 赠送～ present a gift / 互赠～ exchange presents
礼品券 lǐpǐnquàn *also* "礼券" gift coupon or card; coupon for free goods
礼品商店 lǐpǐn shāngdiàn gift and souvenir store
礼聘 lǐpìn engage courteously; cordially enlist the service (of sb.): 重金～ engage sb. with a handsome salary / 登门～ call on sb. in order to enlist his or her service
礼器 lǐqì 〈考古〉 sacrificial vessel
礼轻情意重 lǐ qīng qíngyì zhòng the gift is trifling but the sentiment is profound; the thoughtfulness is far weightier than the gift itself: 千里送鹅毛, ～。A goose feather sent a thousand *li* as a gift means much more than its actual value. *or* It may be a small gift but, sent from afar, means a great deal.
礼让 lǐràng give precedence (to sb.) out of courtesy or thoughtfulness; comity: 国际～ comity of nations / 社交场合相互～ give each other precedence on social occasions / 行车～, 注意安全。While driving, yield right of way for safety's sake.
礼尚往来 lǐshàng-wǎnglái ❶ courtesy demands reciprocity: 国与国之间的关系应该～。Reciprocity is essential in relations between countries. ❷ deal with a man as he deals with you; give as good as one gets
礼生 lǐshēng 〈旧语〉 person who sings songs of praise at a ceremony; master of ceremonies at a Confucian ritual
礼数 lǐshù ❶〈书面〉 hierarchy of rites; rank in such hierarchy ❷ courtesy; etiquette: 不懂～ unrefined; impolite
礼俗 lǐsú etiquette and custom: 不拘～ not constrained by etiquette; without ceremony / 按我们这儿的～, 你得先拜访村里最年长的老人。By our custom here, you must first pay a visit to the eldest man in the village.
礼堂 lǐtáng assembly hall; auditorium
礼帖 lǐtiě *see* "礼单"
礼物 lǐwù gift; present
礼贤下士 lǐxián-xiàshì (of an emperor or his minister) be courteous to the wise and respectful to the learned; treat scholars and men of virtue with courtesy; go out of one's way to enlist the services of the talented and learned: ～, 广招人才 honour talented people and enlist their services
礼仪 lǐyí ceremony and propriety; etiquette; rite; protocol: ～周到 impeccable etiquette (*or* courtesy) / 外交～ diplomatic protocol
礼仪小姐 lǐyí xiǎojiě young lady serving at a ceremony
礼仪之邦 lǐyí zhī bāng land of ceremony and propriety
礼义廉耻 lǐ-yì-lián-chǐ four cardinal traditional virtues; sense of propriety, righteousness, honesty and shame; courtesy, justice, integrity and sense of shame: ～, 国之四维。Sense of propriety, righteousness, honesty and shame are the four cardinal virtues in running a country.
礼遇 lǐyù courteous reception: 受到～ be accorded a courteous reception; be received with great courtesy
礼赞 lǐzàn ❶ sing the praise of; commend: 《白杨～》 *In Praise of the Poplar* ❷〈佛教〉 pray
礼则 lǐzé rules of protocol; norms of etiquette
礼治 lǐzhì rule by rites
礼制 lǐzhì 〈旧语〉 norms of etiquette laid down by the state

李

lǐ ❶ plum: ～树 plum tree / 桃～遍天下 have one's students all over the world; have disciples everywhere ❷ (Lǐ) a surname
李白 Lǐ Bái *also* "李太白" *see* "李杜"
李冰 Lǐ Bīng Li Bing, hydraulic engineer of the State of Qin (秦国) during the later Warring States Period, who in 256-251 BC directed the building of Dujiang Weir (都江堰), still in use in present Sichuan Province
李成 Lǐ Chéng Li Cheng (919-967), painter of the early Song Dynasty
李承晚 Lǐchéngwǎn Syngman Rhee (1875-1965), first President of the Republic of Korea (1948-1961)
李春 Lǐ Chūn Li Chun, master stonemason of the Sui Dynasty who built the famous Zhaozhou Bridge (赵州桥), which remains in good shape today
李代桃僵 lǐdàitáojiāng ❶ substitute one thing or person for another; substitute this for that ❷ sacrifice oneself for another person; take the blame for other people's mistakes
李德 Lǐdé Otto Braun (1900-1974), German communist serving as military adviser to the Central Committee of the Communist Party of China in the first half of the 1930's
李杜 Lǐ-Dù Li Bai (李白, 701-762) and Du Fu (杜甫, 712-770), two most famous poets in the Tang Dynasty
李顿 Lǐdùn Victor A. G. R. Lytton (1876-1947), author of *The Report of the Commission of Enquiry into the Sino-Japanese Dispute* of the 1930's
李公麟 Lǐ Gōnglín Li Gonglin (1049-1106), painter of the Northern Song Dynasty

李光耀 Lǐ Guāngyào Lee Kuan Yew (1923-), first Prime Minister of Singapore

李广 Lǐ Guǎng Li Guang (? -119 BC), general of the Western Han Dynasty

李贺 Lǐ Hè Li He (790-816), romantic poet of the Tang Dynasty

李鸿章 Lǐ Hóngzhāng Li Hongzhang (formerly translated as Li Hung-chang, 1823-1901), chief minister of the late Qing government

李嘉图 Lǐjiātú David Ricardo (1772-1823), English economist

李逵 Lǐ Kuí one of the 108 heroes of Liangshan Mountain in the novel *Water Margin* or *Heroes of the Marshes* (水浒传), nicknamed the "Black Whirlwind" (黑旋风) and generally recognized as a typically honest, loyal but impetuous character

李隆基 Lǐ Lóngjī Li Longji (685-762), usu. referred to by his posthumous title Tang Xuanzong (唐玄宗), 6th emperor of the Tang Dynasty and known for his generally competent and flourishing reign (712-756 esp. 713-742), as well as for his later dotage on the imperial concubine Yang Yuhuan (杨玉环)
see also "开元之治" Kāiyuán Zhī Zhì

李清照 Lǐ Qīngzhào (1084-c.1151) female poet of *ci* poetry of the Southern Song Dynasty

李森科 Lǐsēnkē Trofim Denisovich Lysenko (1898-1976), biologist and geneticist of the former USSR: ～主义 Lysenkoism

李商隐 Lǐ Shāngyǐn Li Shangyin (c.813- c.858), poet of the Tang Dynasty

李时珍 Lǐ Shízhēn Li Shizhen (formerly translated as Li Shihchen, 1518-1593), Chinese pharmacologist of the Ming Dynasty

李世民 Lǐ Shìmín Li Shimin (599-649), usu. referred to by his posthumous title Tang Taizong (唐太宗), 2nd emperor of the Tang Dynasty, famous both for his ability and foresight in helping his father (Li Yuan 李渊, 566-635) to overthrow the Sui Dynasty and establish the Tang Dynasty, and for his open-minded and sagacious rule (627-649)
see also "贞观之治" Zhēnguàn Zhī Zhì

李斯 Lǐ Sī Li Si (? -208 BC), Legalist scholar and prime minister (221-208 BC) of the Qin Dynasty

李斯特 Lǐsītè Franz Liszt (1811-1886), Hungarian composer and pianist

李铁拐 Lǐ Tiěguǎi Li Tie Guai (formerly translated as Li Tiehkuai), one of the Eight Immortals in Taoist mythology

李下不整冠 lǐxià bù zhěng guān don't stop to adjust your hat under a plum tree (to avoid being suspected of stealing the fruit) — avoid suspicion

李下之嫌 lǐxiàzhīxián be under suspicion of stealing or other wrongdoing: 君子避～。A gentleman should avoid coming under suspicion.

李先念 Lǐ Xiānniàn Li Xiannian (1909-1992), President of the People's Republic of China (1983-1988)

李煜 Lǐ Yù Li Yu (937-978), king and *ci* poet of the Later Tang Dynasty (one of the Five Dynasties), known also as Li Houzhu or Li the Last Monarch (李后主)

李政道 Lǐ Zhèngdào Tsung-Dao Lee (1926-), Chinese American physicist, co-winner of Nobel Prize for 1957

李自成起义 Lǐ Zìchéng Qǐyì Li Zicheng Uprising, peasant revolt led by Li Zicheng (1606-1645) that eventually caused the downfall of the Ming Dynasty

李子 lǐzi plum

逦(邐)

lǐ *see* "迤逦" yǐlǐ

里[1](裏、裡)

lǐ ❶ lining; inside: 衬～儿 lining /大衣～儿 lining of a coat /被～儿 inside of a quilt /你怎么把夹克～儿朝外穿了? Look, you're wearing the jacket inside out! ❷ inner; inside: 圈～人 member of the inner circle; insider

里[2]

lǐ ❶ neighbourhood: 邻～ people of a neighbourhood; neighbours ❷ home town; native place: 乡～ home village; home town /故～ one's home town; one's native place /返～ return to one's home town ❸ 〈古语〉 administrative unit of twenty-five neighbouring households ❹ (Lǐ) a surname

里[3]

lǐ *also* "市里" shìlǐ *li*, Chinese unit of length (= ½ kilometre)

里(裏、裡)

li ❶ in; inside: 碗～ in one's bowl /屋～ inside the room /心～不安 feel uneasy; feel guilty /城～来的学生 students from cities /家～ in one's home; at home /到省～开会 go to the provincial capital for a meeting /他话～有话。He is hinting at something (in his speech). ❷ *used after* 这, 那, 哪 *to indicate a location*: 这～ here /那～ there /哪～ where

里昂 Lǐ'áng Lyon, second largest city in France

里边 lǐbian inside; in; within: 箱子～ in (*or* inside) a suitcase /呆在屋～ keep indoors /他一年～只回过一趟家。He went home only once during the whole year. /这事～有文章。There is something fishy about it.

里程 lǐchéng ❶ mileage: 按～付车费 pay one's fare according to the mileage /这辆车已经跑了一万五千多公里的～了。This car has a mileage of over 15, 000 kilometres. ❷ course of development; course: 科学发展的～ course of scientific development

里程碑 lǐchéngbēi milestone; marker; landmark: 每公里就有一座～。There is a stone marker every kilometre. /一九四九年十月一日是中国历史上的一个～。October 1, 1949 was a milestone in the history of China. /这是现代科学发展史上的著名～之一。It stands out as one of the notable landmarks in the progress of modern science.

里程标 lǐchéngbiāo milepost

里程表 lǐchéngbiǎo *also* "里程计" mileage meter; odometer

里出外进 lǐchū-wàijìn uneven; irregular: 牙长得～的 have irregular teeth /墙砌得～的。The wall was built with an uneven front.

里带 lǐdài inner tube (of a tyre): 钉子扎破了外胎, ～还是好的。The nail only punctured the tyre. The inner tube remained intact.

里根 Lǐgēn Ronald Reagan (1922-), 40th President of the United States (1981-1989)

里勾外联 lǐgōu-wàilián *also* "里勾外连" collusion between forces within and without; (of insiders) hand in glove with outsiders: 仓库保管员与社会上的不法分子～, 盗窃货物。The storehouse keeper worked in collusion with some gangsters in stealing the goods.

里海 Lǐhǎi Caspian Sea, land-locked salt lake between Europe and southwest Asia

里急后重 lǐjí-hòuzhòng 〈医学〉 tenesmus

里脊 lǐji tenderloin: 滑溜～ soft stir-fried tenderloin

里加 Lǐjiā Riga, capital of Latvia

里间 lǐjiān *also* "里间屋" inner room

里居 lǐjū 〈书面〉 ❶ address ❷ live in the countryside

里拉 lǐlā lira (unit of money used in Italy)

里里外外 lǐli-wàiwài inside and outside; in and out: 主妇～紧自忙活。The hostess bustled in and out. /机器～全擦了一遍。The machine has been cleaned inside and out (*or* thoroughly).

里弄 lǐlòng 〈方言〉 ❶ lanes and alleys: 城里有成千上万的～, 谁也数不清。There are thousands of lanes and alleys in the city — God knows how many. ❷ neighbourhood: ～工作 work on a neighbourhood committee /～民办工厂 factory run by a neighbourhood committee

里落 lǐluò 〈方言〉 village

里面 lǐmiàn ❶ inside; interior: 屋子～黑乎乎的。It's very dark inside the room. /我住在学校～。I live on campus. /请往～走走。Please move on. ❷ within; in: 他一年～有三个月不在家。He is away three months in a year.

里圈 lǐquān 〈体育〉 inner lane (of a running track)

里三层, 外三层 lǐ sān céng, wài sān céng 〈口语〉 in or with many layers; layer upon layer; crowded with people: 瞧你～地, 穿得真严实。How well covered you are, in so many layers of clothing. /看热闹的人围得～。Ring upon ring of onlookers were crowding round.

里手 lǐshǒu ❶ left-hand side (of a running vehicle or machine): 骑车的人都是从～上车。Cyclists always mount on the left-hand side. ❷ 〈方言〉 expert; old hand: 行家～ expert /理财的～ old hand (*or* past master) at financial matters

里首 lǐshǒu 〈方言〉 inside; interior

里斯本 Lǐsīběn Lisbon, capital of Portugal

里挑外撅 lǐtiǎo-wàijuē 〈方言〉 be double-faced; stoop to dirty tricks; stir up trouble in a clandestine way: 这个人惯于～, 跟他往来要小心。Be careful in your dealings with the bloke; he's always up

to some tricks.

里通外国 lǐtōngwàiguó have or maintain illicit relations with a foreign country; turn traitor to one's country

里头 lǐtou inside; interior: 从人群～往外挤 squeeze one's way out from inside a crowd / 屋子～坐满了人。The room is packed with people.

里外 lǐ-wài ❶ inside and outside: ～夹攻 attack from within and without; be attacked from inside and out / ～受气 be blamed (*or* bullied) both at home and outside / 他的套房分～两间。His apartment consists of an inner as well as an outer room. ❷ (used after round numbers) approximately; about; or so: 四十岁～ at forty or thereabouts; about forty

里外里 lǐwàilǐ 〈方言〉 ❶ (used when decreased income occurs along with increased expenditure or the other way round, or when unexpected income occurs in addition to expected income, or unexpected expenditure is defrayed in addition to expected expenditure) taken all together; in all: 这批货，运费节省了一千美元，又得了奖金一千美元，～有了两千美元的富余。We saved one thousand dollars in transport charges for this load of cargo and earned another thousand in bonuses, netting two thousand dollars in all. / 这个月我花了五十元钱，我弟弟又花了五十元，～花了一百元。I spent fifty *yuan* this month, and my younger brother spent another fifty, so we spent a hundred *yuan* all told. ❷ no matter how you add it up; either way: 两人干四小时和一人干八小时，～是一样。Two men working four hours or one man working eight hours, it's just the same.

里屋 lǐwū inner room: ～放东西，外屋住人。The outer room is used as a bedroom and the inner room as a storeroom.

里弦 lǐxián thicker inner string on the *huqin* (胡琴)

里厢 lǐxiāng 〈方言〉 inside (a room, etc.): 屋～ in the room / 这～是啥? What's in there?

里巷 lǐxiàng side street; alley; lane: 作品写的是～间的凡人生活。The work depicts the life of ordinary people in the city.

里谚 lǐyàn proverbs and sayings popular among urban inhabitants

里衣 lǐyī underwear

里尹 lǐyǐn *also* "里吏"; "里正"; "里君"; "里长" 〈古语〉 head of a *li* (25 neighbouring households); petty local official

里应外合 lǐyìng-wàihé act from inside in coordination with forces attacking from outside; collaborate from within with forces from without: 起义的工匠与攻城的义军～，占领了城市。The insurgent craftsmen captured the city in coordination with the attacking rebel army outside.

里语 lǐyǔ *also* "俚语" lǐyǔ slang

里约热内卢 Lǐyuērènèilú Rio de Janeiro, chief port, second-largest city and former captial of Brazil

里长 lǐzhǎng *see* "里尹"

里正 lǐzhèng *see* "里尹"

里证 lǐzhèng 〈中医〉 interior symptom-complex; disease caused by endogenous factors involving serious disorders in the internal organs

里子 lǐzi lining: 棉袄～ lining of a cotton-padded jacket / ～缎 lining satin / 这么薄的绸子做旗袍要～吧? Perhaps a lining is needed for a *qipao* (*or* cheongsam) with such fine silk?

浬

lǐ *also* hǎilǐ nautical mile; sea mile

悝

lǐ 〈书面〉 worry; sorrow

理

lǐ ❶ texture; grain (in wood, stone, skin, etc.): 木～ grain of wood; wood grain / 肌～ skin texture ❷ reason; logic; truth: 合～ logical; reasonable; conforming to reason / 伦～ ethics / 没～ be unreasonable; be in the wrong / 讲～ listen to reason; talk reasonably / 不可～喻 not listen to reason; be impervious to reason; be not amenable to reason / 他讲得有～。There is truth in what he says. ❸ natural science (esp. physics): 兼通文～ be knowledgeable both in arts and sciences / 数、～、化 mathematics, physics and chemistry / ～工科 science and engineering ❹ manage; run; administer: ～家 keep house; manage family affairs / 日～万机 attend to a thousand and one affairs of state daily / 处～ deal with; handle / 代～ act for; acting / 当家～事 be the boss in the family; wear the trousers in one's home ❺ put in order; tidy up: ～房间 tidy up a room / ～东西 put things in order / ～一～纷乱的思绪 straighten up one's muddled thinking / 她～了～被风吹乱的头发。She smoothed her hair that had been ruffled by the wind. / 剪不断，～还乱，是离愁… That which cannot be severed by scissors, Or sorted out, becomes tangled again, Is the sorrow of separation... ❻ (usu. used in the negative) pay attention to; acknowledge: 置之不～ ignore; pay no heed to; brush sth. aside / 爱答不～的 look cold and indifferent; be standoffish / 他俩谁也不～谁。They are not on speaking terms. ❼ (Lǐ) a surname

理财 lǐcái manage money matters; conduct financial transactions: ～有方 handle financial matters very well; be good at financial matters

理财家 lǐcáijiā financier

理睬 lǐcǎi (often used in the negative) pay attention to; heed; show interest in: 不加～ ignore; take no notice of; turn one's back on; pay no heed to / 谁都不～他。Nobody pays him any attention. *or* Everybody ignores him. / 这件事我们不能不～。We simply cannot remain silent about the matter.

理舱费 lǐcāngfèi stowage charges

理茬儿 lǐchár 〈方言〉 (usu. used in the negative) respond; react; pay attention: 别理他的茬儿。Don't pay any attention to what he says or does. / 人家跟你说话，你怎么不～? Why do you keep mum when you are spoken to?

理当 lǐdāng naturally; ought to; as expected; as it should be: ～如此 just as it should be; only right and proper / 小孩～尊重老人。Children should respect elders.

理短 lǐduǎn be in the wrong; have no justification: 他先动手打人，自然～了。He was in the wrong, for he hit people first.

理发 lǐfà get a haircut; go and have one's hair done; go to the barber's (*or* hairdresser's): 你该～了。You should have a haircut. *or* It's time you had your hair cut. / 班长每个月都给大家义务～。The squad leader cut our hair for free every month.

理发馆 lǐfàguǎn barbershop; barber's; hairdresser's

理发师 lǐfàshī *also* "理发员" barber; hairdresser

理藩院 Lǐfānyuàn 〈历史〉 Ministry of Tribal Affairs (handling relations with tributary and foreign states in the Ming and Qing dynasties)

理该 lǐgāi *see* "理当"

理工科大学 lǐ-gōngkē dàxué college or institute of science and engineering

理合 lǐhé 〈旧语〉 (used in official documents) naturally; ought to; should: ～及时呈文。A prompt report should be submitted.

理化 lǐ-huà physics and chemistry

理会 lǐhuì ❶ understand; comprehend; grasp: 难以～ difficult to understand / ～文章的精神 grasp the essence of an article / 不要错误地～我的用意。Don't get me wrong. / 我完全～你的意思。I see (*or* can follow) perfectly what you mean. ❷ (usu. used in the negative) take notice of; pay attention to; heed: 不～朋友的劝告 would not listen to friends' advice / 可以不～这种小事。You may ignore such trivial matters. ❸ (often used in the early vernacular) reason things out: 改日再来和你～。I'll argue it out with you some other day. ❹ (often used in the early vernacular) deal with; look after: 此事他自有～。He'll take care of this in his way.

理货 lǐhuò freight forwarding; tally

理货单 lǐhuòdān tally sheet

理货公司 lǐhuò gōngsī tally company

理货员 lǐhuòyuán tallyman; tally clerk

理解 lǐjiě understand; comprehend: 难以～ difficult to understand / 加深～ deepen one's comprehension; get (*or* acquire) a better understanding / 他这种心情是可以～的。His feelings are understandable. / 我没太～他说的意思。I didn't make much of what he said. *or* I couldn't make out what he was driving at.

理解力 lǐjiělì faculty of understanding; understanding; comprehension: ～差 have poor understanding (*or* comprehension); be slow on the uptake

理科 lǐkē science (as a field of study); science department (in a college or university): 学～ major in science / 今年报考～的学生很多。Many students chose science as their subject in this year's college entrance exam.

理亏 lǐkuī be in the wrong: 自知～ know that one is in the wrong; have a guilty conscience / ～语塞 become tongue-tied because of a bad conscience

理亏心虚 lǐkuī-xīnxū feel apprehensive for not being on solid ground; have a guilty conscience; be conscience-stricken: 他～，不敢

纠缠。Having a bad conscience, he didn't dare to argue.

理疗 lǐliáo ❶〈医学〉physiotherapy：作～ be under physiotherapy; have physiotherapy /～科 department of physiotherapy /～科医生 physiotherapist /～设备 physiotherapy equipment ❷ undergo physiotherapy：我的病经过～，很见效果。I improved appreciably after undergoing physiotherapy.

理路 lǐlù ❶ logic; train of thought; line of reasoning：这篇文章～不清。The logic of this article is confusing. *or* The article lacks coherence. ❷〈方言〉sense; reason; truth：他每句话都在～上，叫人听了心服口服。Everything he said made sense and was thoroughly convincing.

理乱 lǐluàn 〈书面〉❶ order and disorder; peace and turmoil ❷ pacify; restore to peace：～解纷 restore order and settle disputes

理论 lǐlùn ❶ theory; doctrine; principle：～知识 theoretical knowledge /～队伍 contingent of theoretical workers (*or* researchers) /在～上 in theory; on the theoretical plane; theoretically /～的抽象 theoretical abstraction /～化 theorize; raise to a theoretical plane /～联系实际 link (*or* unite) theory with practice /～脱离实际 theory divorced from practice; discrepancy between theory and practice /～与实践相结合 put theories into practice; integrate theory with practice ❷ argue; reason：不必与他～，他这种人不可理喻。There is no use arguing with him. He never listens to reason.

理论化学 lǐlùn huàxué theoretical chemistry

理论家 lǐlùnjiā theoretician; theorist

理论生物学 lǐlùn shēngwùxué theoretical biology

理论数学 lǐlùn shùxué pure mathematics

理论物理学 lǐlùn wùlǐxué theoretical physics

理念 lǐniàn 〈哲学〉idea

理赔 lǐpéi settle claims：～处 claims department; loss department /～费用 claims expense; settling fee /～代理人 (claims) settling agent /～意见 views upon examination of the claims /～理算人 claims adjuster

理气 lǐqì 〈中医〉regulate *qi* energy; regulate the flow of vital energy and remove obstruction to it：～止痛药 medicine for regulating the flow of vital energy and assuaging the pain caused by functional disorder of various organs; carminative

理气药 lǐqìyào *qi*-regulating medicine

理屈 lǐqū have a weak case; be in the wrong：他自觉～，就不再言声了。Realizing that he was wrong, he fell silent.

理屈词穷 lǐqū-cíqióng fall silent on finding oneself bested in argument; be unable to advance any further arguments to justify oneself：他～，只好求助于诡辩。As he had a weak case and could not defend himself properly, he had to resort to sophistry.

理伤 lǐshāng 〈中医〉bone-setting

理事 lǐshì ❶ handle matters; administer affairs：当家～ rule the roost /他年事已高，现在已经不～了。He no longer deals with day-to-day affairs because of old age. ❷ member of a council; director：常务～ executive member of a council; executive director

理事国 lǐshìguó member of the United Nations Security Council：安理会常任～ permanent member of the United Nations Security Council

理事会 lǐshìhuì executive council; board of directors

理事长 lǐshìzhǎng chairman of an executive council or a board of directors

理数 lǐshù 〈口语〉reason; argument：随地吐痰要罚款，这个～我也懂。I understand why those who spit on the ground should be punished with a fine.

理顺 lǐshùn straighten out; sort out; rationalize：～项目 sort out the projects /～价格和收费 rationalize prices and charges /～各方面的关系 bring into better balance the relations between the various sectors /要逐步～企业分配关系。It is necessary to straighten out income distribution in enterprises.

理所当然 lǐsuǒdāngrán (as a matter) of course; naturally：多劳者多得，这是～的事。It is only natural that those who contribute more should get more. /大家都是邻居，互相帮助是～的。As neighbours, we should of course help each other. /这些孩子认为父母给钱是～的事。These children take it for granted that their parents should give them money.

理想 lǐxiǎng ❶ ideal; aspiration：崇高～ lofty ideal; high aspiration /征服自然的宏伟～ ambitious aim of conquering nature /我的～是周游全球。What I am longing for is a trip around the world. ❷ ideal; perfect：滑冰的～天气 ideal (*or* perfect) weather for skating /～结果 optimum result /他找到了一份～的工作。He found an ideal job (*or* a job after his heart). /这样解决太～了! What a perfect solution!

理想国 lǐxiǎngguó ideal state; utopia

理想化 lǐxiǎnghuà idealize

理想气体 lǐxiǎng qìtǐ 〈物理〉perfect gas; ideal gas

理想主义 lǐxiǎngzhǔyì idealism

理性 lǐxìng ❶ rational：～知识 rational knowledge /感性和～ the perceptual and the rational ❷ rational faculty; reason：失去～ lose one's reason /恢复～ come to one's senses /听从～的召唤 answer the call of reason; succumb to reason /～时代 age of reason

理性认识 lǐxìng rènshi rational knowledge; cognition

理性主义 lǐxìngzhǔyì rationalism

理学 lǐxué ❶ *also* "道学" dàoxué; "宋学" Sòngxué 〈哲学〉Confucian school of idealist philosophy of the Song and Ming dynasties ❷ natural science：～士 Bachelor of Science (BS *or* BSc) /～硕士 Master of Science (MS *or* MSc) /～博士 Doctor of Science (DS *or* DSc)

理血 lǐxuè 〈中医〉regulate blood condition, including its generation, circulation and removal of stasis：～药 blood-regulating drug

理义 lǐyì reason and justice：出于～ for the sake of upholding justice /不辨～ have no sense of right or wrong; be unable to tell good from bad

理应 lǐyīng ought to; should：～帮助 ought to help (*or* lend a hand) /你说错了话，～道歉。I think an apology is in order for your inappropriate remarks. /他做了好事，～受到表扬。He deserves a commendation for having done something good.

理由 lǐyóu reason; ground; argument; cause：毫无～ have neither rhyme nor reason; be utterly groundless /提出的～不成立 make an untenable argument; give a lame excuse /有充分的～怀疑 have every reason to doubt (*or* suspect) /没有～自满 have no grounds for self-complacency /别想找～为自己辩解。Don't you think you can explain away your error.

理喻 lǐyù (usu. used negatively) persuade or convince with reason：不可～ be impervious to reason; would not listen to reason

理直气壮 lǐzhí-qìzhuàng feel confident with justice on one's side; be bold and assured because of the righteousness of one's cause：他说得～。He spoke in a bold and confident manner. /对这些不良现象，应该～地提出批评。We must condemn such bad practices firmly and forcefully. /理不直则气不壮。When one does not have justice on one's side, one lacks assurance.

理致 lǐzhì 〈书面〉sense and good taste：甚乏～ lacking in sense and (good) taste

理智 lǐzhì reason; intellect：丧失～ lose one's reason; take leave of one's senses /保持～ keep one's senses /有～的人 sensible person /什么也无法使他恢复～。Nothing can bring him back to his senses. /～些，别感情用事。Be reasonable, and do not act on impulse. /他若有～，不至于干出此等事情来。He should have more sense than to have done such a thing.

理中 lǐzhōng 〈中医〉regulate the functions of the stomach and spleen

哩

lǐ *also* yīnglǐ mile

see also lī; li

锂

lǐ 〈化学〉lithium (Li)

锂辉石 lǐhuīshí spodumene; triphane

锂云母 lǐyúnmǔ 〈矿业〉lepidolite; lithia mica

俚

lǐ vulgar

俚歌 lǐgē rustic song; folk song

俚曲 lǐqǔ *also* "俗曲" súqǔ 〈旧语〉popular song, tune or melody; popular ditty

俚俗 lǐsú vulgar; unrefined; uncultured：言语～ talk in vulgar language; be unrefined in one's speech

俚语 lǐyǔ slang：这部小说过多地使用了～。Too much slang is used in the novel.

鲤

lǐ carp

鲤庭之训 lǐtíngzhīxùn instructions from one's father; father's exhortation

鲤鱼 lǐyú carp：～跳龙门 carp leaping into the dragon's gate — succeed in the imperial civil service examination; (as of a commoner or an obscure person) gain fame and advancement; make a success of oneself

鲤鱼钳 lǐyúqián slip-joint pliers

娌 lǐ *see* "妯娌" zhóuli

澧 Lǐ Lishui River (澧水), in Hunan Province

醴 lǐ 〈书面〉❶ sweet wine ❷ sweet spring water

鳢 lǐ 〈动物〉murrel; snakehead

蠡 lǐ ❶ *used in personal names*：范～ Fan Li, famous minister turned merchant in the late Spring and Autumn Period ❷ Lixian (蠡县), a county in Hebei Province
see also lí

lì

立 lì ❶ stand：起～ stand up /直～ stand upright (*or* straight)/陡～ rise steeply /耸～ tower aloft /倒～ stand upside down; stand on one's hands; handstand /坐～不安 be on pins and needles; feel restless; be fidgety ❷ set or stand sth. up; erect; make sth. upright：～旗杆 set up a flagpole /～纪念碑 erect (*or* build) a monument /～标牌 put up a signboard /把箱子～着放。Place the box upright. ❸ upright; erect; vertical：～式冰柜 vertical refrigerator ❹ set up; found; establish：成～ found; establish; set up /创～ create / 到银行～个户头 open an account at the bank ❺ sign; conclude：～字据 sign a pledge /～合同 conclude a contract ❻〈书面〉ascend the throne：自～为王 make oneself king /～公子婴为王。Prince Ying was crowned king. ❼ appoint; designate; adopt：～相 appoint sb. as prime minister /～后 make sb. queen /～公子亨为太子。Prince Heng was designated crown prince. ❽ exist; live; grow：自～ be on one's own feet; be independent; be self-sustaining; be self-supporting /势不两～ absolutely antagonistic; irreconcilable ❾ immediately; instantaneously; at once; right away：～行停止 stop immediately /此事必须～办。The matter must be dealt with promptly. ❿ (Lì) a surname

立案 lì'àn ❶ register; put on record：办企业必须向主管机关～。Enterprises should register themselves with the competent authorities. ❷〈法律〉place a case on file for investigation and prosecution：～调查 start an investigation into a case /没有一定的证据是不能～的。Sufficient primary evidence is needed before a case can be put on file for investigation.

立逼 lìbī force sb. to do sth. immediately：他～我答复。He forced me to give him an immediate answer.

立标 lìbiāo standing navigation mark

立场 lìchǎng position; stand; stance; standpoint：～、观点和方法 stand, viewpoint and method /阐明～ make clear one's position (on a question) /站在被侵略国家的～说话 speak from the standpoint of the invaded state /丧失～ depart from the correct stand /～坚定 be steadfast in one's stand; take a firm stand /对此事你采取什么～? Where do you stand in this matter? *or* What's your position on the matter?

立春 Lìchūn ❶ Beginning of Spring, 1st seasonal division point, marking the sun's position at 315° on the ecliptic ❷ day marking such a seasonal division point, usu. falling on the 4th or 5th of February：～后，天气渐暖。As spring sets in, it gets warmer and warmer. ❸ period lasting from such a seasonal division point till the next one (Rain Water 雨水)
see also "节气" jiéqì; "二十四节气" èrshísì jiéqì

立此存照 lìcǐ-cúnzhào 〈套语〉a contract, an agreement, etc. is hereby concluded and to be filed for future reference

立党为公 lìdǎng-wèigōng found a party to serve the interests of the people：～还是立党为私，这是每一个党员必须面对的首要问题。It is a question of primary importance for every Party member whether he has joined the Party to serve the interests of the people or to advance his own interests.

立档 lìdàng establish a file or archives：～单位 a unit with authority to establish and maintain archives (*or* records)

立德粉 lìdéfěn 〈化学〉lithopone

立灯 lìdēng *also* "落地灯" luòdìdēng floor lamp

立等 lìděng wait for sth. to be done immediately：～可取。Instant service is provided. *or* Things can be done on the spot. /～回音。A prompt reply is required. *or* I'll wait for an immediate reply.

立地 lìdì ❶ plant one's feet on the ground：顶天～ stand on one's two legs between heaven and earth — be of gigantic stature and indomitable spirit ❷ location of a tree：这种树～不同，生长情况就不同。This kind of tree varies in the way it grows from place to place. ❸ instantly; at once：放下屠刀，～成佛。Drop your cleaver and you'll become a Buddha immediately. *or* One attains divinity the moment one lays down the butcher knife.

立定 lìdìng ❶ halt：～! Halt! ❷ stand firm：～脚跟 gain a foothold; become established ❸ resolutely determine：～主意 make up one's mind /～志向 set one's resolve

立定跳远 lìdìng tiàoyuǎn 〈体育〉standing long jump

立冬 Lìdōng ❶ Beginning of Winter, 19th seasonal division point, marking the sun's position at 225° on the ecliptic ❷ day marking such a seasonal division point, usu. falling on the 7th or 8th of November ❸ period lasting from such a seasonal division point till the next one (Slight Snow 小雪)
see also "节气" jiéqì; "二十四节气" èrshísì jiéqì

立断 lìduàn be resolute; act with resolution：事当～，切莫踌躇。An instant decision should be made without any hesitation.

立法 lìfǎ legislate; make or enact law：经济～ economic legislation /财政～ financial legislation /～意图 legislative intent /关于税收的～ legislation on taxation

立法程序 lìfǎ chéngxù legislative procedure

立法调查 lìfǎ diàochá legislative investigation

立法会 Lìfǎhuì (HK) Legislative Council; Legco

立法机关 lìfǎ jīguān *also* "立法机构" legislative body; legislature：～的权力 legislative authority

立法权 lìfǎquán legislative power

立法条款 lìfǎ tiáokuǎn law-making stipulation

立法委员会 lìfǎ wěiyuánhuì legislation council; legislative committee

立法行动 lìfǎ xíngdòng legislative action

立法院 Lìfǎyuàn Legislative *Yuan* (China before 1949)

立法者 lìfǎzhě *also* "立法人" legislator; lawmaker

立方 lìfāng ❶〈数学〉cube：5 的～ cube of 5; 5^3 ❷ (short for 立方体) cube ❸〈量词〉cubic metre; stere：一～石头 one cubic metre of stone /一～木材 one stere of wood

立方根 lìfānggēn 〈数学〉cube-foot; cubic foot

立方厘米 lìfāng límǐ cubic centimetre

立方米 lìfāngmǐ cubic metre

立方体 lìfāngtǐ *also* "正方体" zhèngfāngtǐ cube：～网络 cube network /～系数 cubicity factor

立竿见影 lìgān-jiànyǐng set up a pole and you see its shadow — do sth. to get instant results; produce an immediate effect：这种事不可能～。No instant results can be achieved in the matter.

立功 lìgōng render meritorious service; do a deed of merit; win honour; make contributions：立二等功 win a second class merit citation /立集体三等功 be awarded a class three collective commendation /～奖状 certificate for meritorious service; certificate of merit /他在侦破工作中立了大功。He has rendered outstanding service in crime investigation.

立功受奖 lìgōng-shòujiǎng those who render meritorious service are awarded

立功赎罪 lìgōng-shúzuì *also* "立功自赎" perform meritorious service to atone for one's crimes：给予罪犯～的机会 give a prisoner an opportunity to atone for his crimes by service

立柜 lìguì clothes closet; wardrobe; hanging cupboard

立柜式空调 lìguìshì kōngtiáo vertical chamber air conditioner

立国 lìguó found a state; build up a nation：工农业为～之本。Industry and agriculture are fundamental to the building of a nation. *or* Industry and agriculture are the base on which to build up a nation.

立候 lìhòu ❶ stand waiting：～多时 stand waiting for a long time ❷ wait for an immediate response：～回音 await a prompt reply

立户 lìhù ❶ register for a household residence card; set up house-

keeping ❷ open or establish an account with a bank
立即 lìjí immediately; at once; straightaway; promptly: ～照办 carry out speedily /接到命令，～出发 set out on orders without delay/ 发现情况，～报告。Any unusual situation must be reported at once./ 这个问题要～加以处理。This problem should be addressed promptly.
立交 lìjiāo (short for 立体交叉)〈建筑〉grade separation: ～工程 grade separation project
立交桥 lìjiāoqiáo (US) overpass; (UK) flyover; cloverleaf intersection: 三层～ three-level (motorway) interchange
立脚 lìjiǎo have a foothold; base oneself on: ～不稳 have not got a firm foothold /无处～ have nowhere to stand
立脚点 lìjiǎodiǎn *also* "立足点" ❶ perspective; standpoint: 为消费者服务，是产品设计的～。The designing of products must be geared to consumer needs. ❷ foothold; footing: 先巩固～，再求发展。Secure a firm footing before seeking further development.
立筋 lìjīn 〈建筑〉stud
立井 lìjǐng *also* "竖井" shùjǐng (vertical) shaft
立决 lìjué 〈书面〉execute (a criminal) immediately; carry out a summary execution: 斩～ execute immediately by beheading
立克次氏体 lìkècìshìtǐ 〈医学〉rickettsia: ～病 rickettsiosis; rickettsial disease /～痘 rickettsialpox
立刻 lìkè immediately; at once; right away: 他们～朝医院跑去。They ran towards the hospital at once. /～离开这个地方! Leave this place right now! /发现任何线索，请～向我汇报。If you find any clue to the problem, report it to me right away. /我～就听出这话并不是他自己的意思。I knew (right) off the bat that he was speaking for someone else.
立睖 lìleng 〈方言〉❶ *also* "立愣" stare: 他对我～着眼。He stared at me. ❷ stand up; erect: 他一听，头发根儿都～起来了。He bristled with anger when he heard the news.
立领 lìlǐng straight collar
立论 lìlùn set forth one's view; present one's argument; argue; reason: ～鲜明 present one's views distinctly (*or* in a clear-cut way)/ ～须言之有据。An argument should be well grounded.
立马 lìmǎ ❶〈书面〉pull up a horse; reign in a horse: ～横刀 look impressive on horseback with sword drawn ❷〈方言〉straight away; right away: 你叫他～给我个回话。Tell him to give me an immediate reply.
立眉瞪眼 lìméi-dèngyǎn *also* "立眉横眼"; "立眉竖眼" stare with raised eyebrows — look ferocious; stare angrily; be in a temper: 这些娘儿们一个个～，要跟我拼命。All the women here were looking daggers at me, as though they would fight it out with me.
立门户 lì ménhù establish or form an independent body, such as a school of thought, a party, a business, etc.: 另～ break away from the old establishment and set up one's own
立米 lìmǐ (short for 立方米) cubic metre
立面图 lìmiàntú 〈建筑〉elevation (drawing)
立苗 lìmiáo (of soil) have enough nutrient for young plants to grow; fertile: 这块地不～。This piece of land is not fertile enough for the crops.
立契 lìqì sign a contract; conclude an agreement
立秋 Lìqiū ❶ Beginning of Autumn, 13th seasonal division point, marking the sun's position at 135° on the ecliptic ❷ day marking such a seasonal division point, usu. falling on the 7th or 8th of August ❸ period lasting from such a seasonal division point till the next one (Limit of Heat 处暑)
see also "节气" jiéqi; "二十四节气" èrshísì jiéqì
立绒 lìróng cut velvet; pile cloth; raised pile
立射 lìshè 〈军事〉fire from a standing position
立身处世 lìshēn-chǔshì *also* "立身行事" the way one gets along with the world; the way one conducts oneself in society: ～，最重要的是一个"信"字。Nothing is more important than trustworthiness in human relationship.
立时 lìshí *see* "立刻"
立时三刻 lìshí-sānkè 〈方言〉right away; immediately: 这事我～就能办到。I can do it right away.
立式 lìshì 〈机械〉vertical; upright: ～车床 vertical lathe /～钻床 upright drill; vertical drill /～拉门 vertical sliding door /～犁刀 fin coulter; standing cutter
立誓 lìshì take an oath; vow; make a pledge
立嗣 lìsì 〈书面〉designate an heir; adopt a son
立陶宛 Lìtáowǎn Lithuania: ～人 Lithuanian /～语 Lithuanian (language)
立体 lìtǐ ❶ (of an object, etc.) three-dimensional; stereoscopic: ～图形 three-dimensional diagram /～平面图 stereogram /～平面法 stereography /～视觉 stereoscopic vision ❷〈数学〉solid: 正方体、长方体、球体、锥体、棱柱体、圆柱体等都是～。The cube, the quadratic prism, the sphere, the cone, the triangular prism, the cylinder, etc. are all solids. ❸ multi-level; all-round; triphibious: ～交叉桥 overpass; flyover ❹ producing a three-dimensional effect: ～动画 three-dimensional cartoon /～照片 anaglyph
立体测量学 lìtǐ cèliángxué stereology
立体电视 lìtǐ diànshì three-dimensional television
立体电影 lìtǐ diànyǐng stereoscopic film; stereo-screen; three-dimensional film; 3-D film
立体感 lìtǐgǎn three-dimensional effect
立体化学 lìtǐ huàxué stereochemistry
立体几何 lìtǐ jǐhé stereogeometry; solid geometry
立体交叉 lìtǐ jiāochā grade separation
立体角 lìtǐjiǎo *also* "多面角" duōmiànjiǎo solid angle
立体模型 lìtǐ móxíng space model
立体派 lìtǐpài cubism
立体声 lìtǐshēng stereophony; stereophonics; stereo: ～唱机 stereo recordplayer; stereo /～唱片 stereophonic record (*or* disc) /～耳机 stereophone /～音响 stereo; stereophony /～喇叭 stereo-speaker /～磁带 stereotape /～收录机 stereo radio-tape recorder; stereo taperecorder; stereo
立体图 lìtǐtú stereography; three-dimensional drawing
立体图像 lìtǐ túxiàng stereopicture
立体显微镜 lìtǐ xiǎnwēijìng stereoscopic microscope; stereomicroscope
立体战争 lìtǐ zhànzhēng three-dimensional warfare; triphibious warfare
立体照相机 lìtǐ zhàoxiàngjī stereoscopic camera; stereo camera
立夏 Lìxià ❶ Beginning of Summer, 7th seasonal division point, marking the sun's position at 45° on the ecliptic ❷ day marking such a seasonal division point, usu. falling on the 5th or 6th of May: ～以后，庄稼长势很好。When summer began, the crops were doing well. ❸ period lasting from such a seasonal division point till the next one (Grain Budding 小满)
see also "节气" jiéqi; "二十四节气" èrshísì jiéqì
立宪 lìxiàn constitutionalism: 君主～ constitutional monarchy /～政体 constitutional government; constitutionalism
立项 lìxiàng put a project under an authorized plan: 今年本市～建设的有十个工程。The city undertakes the construction of ten projects this year.
立像 lìxiàng erect statue; standing statue
立效 lìxiào ❶ produce immediate effect; be instantly effective ❷〈书面〉do a deed of merit; render meritorious service
立心 lìxīn ❶ make up one's mind; decide: 他～要当个律师。He has made up his mind to become a lawyer. ❷〈书面〉on purpose: 她～与他疏远。She deliberately kept him at arm's length.
立言 lìyán expound one's ideas in writing; gain fame by writing: 儒家学者曾把著书立说称为"代圣人～"。Confucian scholars used to regard writing as "expounding Confucius' teachings".
立业 lìyè ❶ build a career: 建功～ render meritorious service and make a career ❷ buy an estate: 成家～ get married and build up family property
立异 lìyì try to be different from others; be original; be unconventional: 标新～ do sth. unconventional or unorthodox /～鸣高 try to be unconventional and above worldly affairs
立意 lìyì ❶ be determined; make up one's mind: 这孩子～要学表演，我也只好依他了。Since my boy has made up his mind to learn acting, I suppose I have to accept the fact. ❷ conception; approach: 做诗总须～清新，不落俗套才好。The soul of a poem lies in its fresh conception and unconventional pattern.
立于不败之地 lìyú bù bài zhī dì establish oneself in an invulnerable position; be invincible; remain impregnable: 我们赢得了广大群众的支持，就能～。We will be in an unassailable position so long as we have the support of the broad masses.
立约 lìyuē conclude an agreement or a treaty; sign or draw up a contract: ～双方 contracting parties /～人 contractor
立账 lìzhàng establish or open an account of (money, goods,

sale, etc.); keep (an item) in the account; file in

立正 lìzhèng stand at attention:～! Attention! /守卫国旗的士兵始终保持着～姿势。The sentry guarding the national flag keeps a position of attention (*or* standing at attention).

立志 lìzhì be resolved; be determined:～夺魁 be bent on winning the championship /他从小就～当一名教师。When he was still a child, he made up his mind to become a teacher.

立轴 lìzhóu ❶ vertical scroll of painting or calligraphy; wall scroll ❷〈机械〉vertical shaft; upright shaft

立柱 lìzhù 〈建筑〉stud; upright column or post

立传 lìzhuàn write a biography:树碑～ glorify sb. by erecting a monument to him and writing his biography; build up sb.'s public image

立桩 lìzhuāng ❶ stake out; stake off:～标界 mark out; stake out /他们划出一块地方为孩子们作运动场，还立了桩。They staked off an area as a children's playground. ❷ stake:打～ drive a stake

立锥之地 lìzhuīzhīdì place just enough to stick an awl into — tiny bit of land:贫无～ not possess a speck of land; be penniless (*or* flat broke)

立姿 lìzī 〈军事〉standing position

立字 lìzì write and sign a pledge, receipt, IOU, contract, etc.: ～为据 sign a note as a pledge

立足 lìzú ❶ gain a foothold; establish oneself:在社会上～ establish oneself in society /～未稳之敌 enemy troops who are not yet entrenched /破产之后，他在商界已无法～。Bankruptcy deprived him of any standing in business circles. /山壁太陡，找不到～处。It was difficult to get a footing on the steep cliff. ❷ base oneself on:～于依靠本国资源发展工业。Industrial development must be based on domestic resources. /我们必须～本国，放眼世界。We must have our feet firmly planted in our own country while keeping the whole world in view.

立足点 lìzúdiǎn *also* "立脚点" ❶ standpoint; stand:把～移到人民群众这方面来。Change one's stand to that of the people. /他这样看问题，～就是错的。His view on the matter is based on a wrong approach. ❷ foothold; footing; anchor point:他只身来到国外，连个～都找不到。He went abroad alone and couldn't even find a foothold.

立足之地 lìzúzhīdì foothold; footing:天地之大，竟没有我的～! Alas! Why can't I even find a foothold in this vast world?

粒 lì ❶ grain; granule; pellet:沙～儿 grains of sand /米～儿 grains of rice /盐～儿 salt grains /豆～儿 beans /团～ granule /质～ plasmid /子～ seed; grain; kernel /微～ particle; corpuscle /脱～ thresh; shell ❷〈量词〉*used with granular objects*:一～种子 a grain of seed /几～子弹 several bullets /五～药丸 five pills

粒度 lìdù ❶ granularity ❷ grain fineness; grain size; mesh size (of flux):～分析器 particle size analyzer

粒肥 lìféi (short for 颗粒肥料) granulated fertilizer; pellet fertilizer

粒化 lìhuà 〈化学〉granulation:～金属 granulated metal /～装置 granulating device

粒食 lìshí 〈书面〉eat grain (as food):连年大旱，老百姓不～已数月之久。The area had been hit by drought for several years running, and the local people had been out of grain for quite a few months.

粒细胞 lìxìbāo 〈生物〉granulocyte:～疗法 granulotherapy

粒选 lìxuǎn 〈农业〉grain-by-grain seed selection

粒雪 lìxuě 〈地质〉granular snow; firn; névé:～化 firnification

粒状 lìzhuàng granular:～物 granules /～粉末〈冶金〉granular powder

粒子 lìzǐ 〈物理〉particle:带电～ charged particle /高能～ energetic particle

粒子发射 lìzǐ fāshè particle emission

粒子加速器 lìzǐ jiāsùqì particle accelerator

粒子束 lìzǐshù *also* "粒子流" particle beam:～聚变 particle beam fusion /～武器 particle beam weapon

粒子探测器 lìzǐ tàncèqì particle detector

粒子图像 lìzǐ túxiàng particle picture

粒子物理学 lìzǐ wùlǐxué high-energy physics; particle physics

粒子 lìzi grain:豆～ soybean grain /盐～ grain of salt

莅(蒞、涖) lì 〈书面〉arrive; be present:～场 be present on the occasion /～席 be present at a banquet

莅会 lìhuì be present at a meeting:～讲话 come and address a meeting

莅临 lìlín 〈书面〉arrive; be present:届时敬请～指导。Your presence and guidance are requested.

莅任 lìrèn 〈书面〉(of officials) assume one's office

莅止 lìzhǐ 〈书面〉arrive:嘉宾～。The guests of honour have arrived.

笠 lì large bamboo or straw hat with a conical crown and broad brim (worn by peasants or fishermen at work):斗～ large bamboo rain hat /草～ straw hat /蓑～ straw (*or* palm-bark) rain hat

戾 lì 〈书面〉❶ crime; sin:罪～ crime; evil; sin ❷ perverse; unreasonable:暴～ ruthless and tyrannical; cruel and fierce; brutally oppressive /乖～ perverse (behaviour); disagreeable (character) /拂～ go against (sb.'s wishes)

莀 lì

莀草 lìcǎo *also* "狼尾草" lángwěicǎo Chinese pennisetum (*Pennisetum alopecuroides*)

唳 lì cry (of a crane, wild goose, etc.)

缐 lì

缐木 lìmù brush or short arbor tree with white flowers

丽[1](麗) lì pretty; beautiful:美～ good-looking; beautiful /秀～ of delicate beauty; lovely /富～ sumptuous; splendid /瑰～ beautiful; magnificent /华～ magnificent; resplendent; gorgeous /壮～ majestic; glorious /风和日～。The wind is gentle and the sun radiant. *or* The weather is glorious.

丽[2](麗) lì 〈书面〉attach oneself to; rely on:附～ attach oneself to

see also lí

丽都 lìdū 〈书面〉richly ornamented and beautiful:衣饰～ gorgeously dressed

丽风 lìfēng *also* "厉风" lìfēng northwest wind

丽人 lìrén beautiful woman; beauty

丽日 lìrì 〈书面〉bright or radiant sun

丽月 lìyuè second month of the lunar calendar

丽藻 lìzǎo 〈书面〉flowery language; ornate diction; grandiloquent language

丽质 lìzhì (of a woman's looks, skin and figure) beautiful:天生～ naturally beautiful; born beautiful /天生～难自弃 graced by Heaven with a beauty that will not pass unnoticed

栭(欐) lì 〈书面〉beam

俪(儷) lì ❶ paired; parallel:骈～ art of parallelism ❷ husband and wife; married couple:伉～ married couple; husband and wife /佳～ happy couple

俪辞 lìcí antithesis; antithetic language

俪句 lìjù parallel sentences; couplet

俪影 lìyǐng photograph of a married couple; wedding picture

俪语 lìyǔ see "俪辞"

郦(酈) Lì a surname

鬲(甂、歷) lì 〈考古〉ancient cooking tripod with hollow legs

栗[1] lì ❶〈植物〉chestnut tree ❷ chestnut:板～ Chinese chestnut ❸ (Lì) a surname

栗[2](慄) lì tremble; shudder:颤～ tremble; shiver /不寒而～ shake with fear

栗暴 lìbào *also* "栗凿" knuckle on the head

栗犊 lìdú calf

栗钙土 lìgàitǔ chestnut soil

L

栗黄 lìhuáng 〈书面〉chestnut:～色的小马 chestnut colt (*or* pony)
栗栗 lìlì fearful look:战战～ with fear and trepidation; gingerly
栗然 lìrán 〈书面〉tremulous; trembling; fearful:为之～而震惊 tremble with shock; shudder
栗色 lìsè chestnut colour; maroon
栗鼠 lìshǔ 〈动物〉squirrel
栗缩 lìsuō 〈书面〉shiver and shrink; shudder and recoil
栗子 lìzi chestnut:～汁 chestnut extract /～树 chestnut tree /糖炒～ sugar-roasted chestnuts

溧

lì chilly; cold
溧冽 lìliè 〈书面〉bitterly cold:～的北风 biting (*or* cutting) north wind

篥

lì *see* "觱篥" bìlì

傈

lì
傈僳族 Lìsùzú Lisu nationality, living in Yunnan and Sichuan

吏

lì 〈旧语〉❶ petty official; government clerk:刀笔～ pettifogger /胥～ petty official /狱～ warder; prison officer ❷ official; mandarin:酷～ cruel official /官～ government official /墨～ corrupt official
吏部 Lìbù 〈历史〉Ministry of Civil Personnel; Board of Civil Office
吏胥 lìxū *also* "胥吏" 〈书面〉petty official
吏治 lìzhì administrative work of local government officials:澄清～ straighten up local administration

厉(厲)

lì ❶ strict; rigorous; rigid; stringent: *see* "～行" ❷ stern; severe; serious; fierce:严～ strict; stern; severe /攻势凌～ swift and vigorous attack /声色俱～ stern in voice and countenance ❸ (Lì) a surname
厉兵秣马 lìbīng-mòmǎ *also* "秣马厉兵" sharpen the weapons and feed the horses — get ready for battle, make preparations for war:八路军～，伺机出击。Getting ready for battle, the Eighth Route Army was waiting for the opportunity to launch an attack.
厉风 lìfēng *also* "丽风" lìfēng howling wind; northwest wind
厉鬼 lìguǐ malevolent demon; ferocious ghost; evil spirit
厉害 lìhai *also* "利害" lìhai terrible; formidable; serious:病得很～ be seriously (*or* critically) ill /这几天冷得～。It's been terribly cold these days. /这着棋十分～。That's a devastating move. /她那张嘴可真～。She's got a sharp tongue. *or* She's got a dagger of a tongue. /这种病的～我算是知道了。Now I surely know how dangerous this disease could be. /给他点～瞧瞧。Teach him a good lesson.
厉禁 lìjìn 〈书面〉❶ closely guard or watch over ❷ strict ban or prohibition
厉色 lìsè put on a stern expression; look stern; look serious:正言～ in a serious tone and with a stern look
厉声 lìshēng in a stern voice:～斥责 rebuke (*or* denounce) in a stern voice
厉行 lìxíng strictly enforce; make rigorous efforts to carry out:～节约 practise strict economy /～禁赌 strictly enforce the ban on gambling

疠(癘)

lì 〈书面〉❶ pestilence; plague:瘴～ communicable subtropical disease (such as pernicious malaria, etc.) ❷ sore; ulcer
疠疫 lìyì 〈书面〉epidemic disease; pestilence

粝(糲、糲)

lì 〈书面〉coarse grain; brown rice; unpolished rice:粗～ coarse grain
粝粱 lìliáng 〈书面〉coarse food
粝米 lìmǐ 〈书面〉unpolished rice; brown rice
粝食 lìshí coarse rice; low quality rice

砺(礪)

lì 〈书面〉❶ whetstone; grindstone ❷ whet; sharpen:淬～ temper oneself through severe trials /砥～ temper; encourage /磨～ steel (*or* harden) oneself
砺石 lìshí 〈书面〉whetstone

蛎(蠣)

lì oyster
蛎黄 lìhuáng flesh of an oyster

励(勵)

lì ❶ encourage; urge:勉～ encourage; urge /鼓～ encourage; urge; boost; inspire /督～ urge and encourage; spur on /激～ inspire; stimulate; impel /奖～ reward /惕～ be on guard ❷ (Lì) a surname
励磁 lìcí 〈电学〉field excitation:～性 excitability
励磁场 lìcíchǎng exciting field
励磁机 lìcíjī exciter; exciting dynamo
励磁器 lìcíqì magnetizing exciter
励精图治 lìjīng-túzhì (usu. of a state leader) exert oneself to make the country prosperous; make vigorous efforts to build a strong country:这个国家上下一心，～。United as one from top to bottom, the country is exerting its utmost to make itself strong and prosperous.
励行 lìxíng ❶〈书面〉try hard to be an upright man; make efforts to cultivate oneself:改过～ mend one's ways and try hard to be an upright man ❷ *also* "厉行" lìxíng strictly enforce; make rigorous efforts to carry out
励志 lìzhì 〈书面〉be bent on realizing one's aspirations; strive for success:～革新 be resolved to institute reforms; be bent on reform

詈

lì 〈书面〉rebuke; scold; berate:忿～ scold with anger
詈骂 lìmà 〈书面〉curse; swear; scold; abuse
詈言 lìyán 〈书面〉curse; abuse; rebuke

利

lì ❶ sharp; keen:锋～ sharp; keen ❷ favourable; smooth; convenient:顺～ smoothly; without a hitch /吉～ good fortune; good luck /在不～的条件下工作 work under unfavourable circumstances ❸ advantage; benefit:福～ welfare; fringe benefit /互～ mutual benefit /～多弊少。The advantages outweigh the disadvantages. /这件事～少弊多。It will do more harm than good. /这样做于你不～。It is not in your interest to do so. ❹ profit; interest:实～ actual gains; net profit /暴～ exorbitant profits /营～ seek profits /非营～ nonprofitable; non-profit-making /渔～ reap gains by unethical means; profit at others' expense /红～ dividend; bonus /名～双收 gain both fame and profit /本～两清 have paid back both principal and interest ❺ do good to; benefit:自私自～ selfish; egocentric /毫不～己，专门～人 devoted to the interest of others without any thought of self; thoroughly selfless ❻〈书面〉sharpen; perfect:工欲善其事，必先～其器。A person must first sharpen his tools if he is to do a good job. ❼ (Lì) a surname
利比里亚 Lìbǐlǐyà Liberia:～人 Liberian
利比亚 Lìbǐyà Libya:～人 Libyan
利弊 lì-bì advantages and disadvantages; pros and cons:权衡～ weigh the advantages and disadvantages; weigh the pros and cons /～各半。The advantages and disadvantages cancel each other out.
利便 lìbian 〈方言〉handy; convenient:有了这条公路，进城就～多了。With the new highway, going to the city is no longer a grind.
利病 lì-bìng 〈书面〉*see* "利弊"
利导 lìdǎo guide according to circumstances
see also "因势利导" yīnshì-lìdǎo
利钝 lì-dùn ❶ sharp or blunt:刀剑有～。There are sharp and blunt weapons. ❷ smooth or rough:成败～，在所不计 do sth. regardless of consequences; do sth. at all costs
利多卡因 lìduōkǎyīn 〈药学〉lidocaine
利福霉素 lìfúméisù 〈药学〉rifamycin
利福平 lìfúpíng 〈药学〉rifampin (RFP)
利改税 lìgǎishuì 〈经济〉policy of switching from profit deliveries to the state to tax payments; replacement of profit delivery by taxes
利滚利 lìgǔnlì *also* "利上滚利" usurious loan (in which unpaid interest due is added to the principal for more interest); compound interest
利害 lì-hài advantages and disadvantages; gains and losses:不计～ regardless of gains and losses /不知～ be unaware of the serious consequences of sth. /有～关系的人 interested party (*or* person) /你把其中的～跟他说清楚。Spell out for him the advantages and disadvantages involved. *or* Tell him plainly about the consequences involved. /作出决定之前要考虑～得失。We have to consider the pros

and cons of the matter before making a decision.

利害 lìhai *see* "厉害" lìhai

利害攸关 lìhài-yōuguān have a stake in; be closely bound up with; concern sb.'s vital interests: 国家的盛衰，和我们每个人～。Everyone is closely bound up with the prosperity or decline of the country.

利己主义 lìjǐzhǔyì egoism: ～者 egoist /民族～ national egoism

利金 lìjīn 〈方言〉 interest

利口 lìkǒu ❶ *also* "利嘴" glib tongue; sharp tongue: 她那张～，谁也敌不过。She is unmatched in sharpness of the tongue. ❷ (of fruits, vegetables, etc.) crisp, tasty and refreshing (as opposite to "greasy"): 这梨真～。This kind of pear is very tasty and refreshing.

利库德集团 Lìkùdé Jítuán Likud, a right-wing political coalition party in Israel

利亮 lìliang 〈方言〉 *see* "利落"

利令智昏 lìlìngzhìhūn be blinded by lust for gain; be blinded by greed or avarice

利隆圭 Lìlóngguī Lilongwe, capital of Malawi

利禄 lìlù 〈书面〉 (of an official) money and status; wealth and position: 功名～ fame and fortune /贪图～ hanker after wealth and position

利率 lìlǜ 〈经济〉 interest rate; rate of interest: 基本放款～ base lending rate /贴现～ discount rate /优惠～ prime rate

利率补贴 lìlǜ bǔtiē interest rate subsidy

利率差别 lìlǜ chābié interest rate differential

利率套期 lìlǜ tàoqī interest rate hedge

利落 lìluo *also* "利索" ❶ agile; nimble; dexterous: 动作～ be agile (*or* nimble) in one's movements /说话～干脆 outspoken; straightforward and articulate ❷ neat; orderly: 穿戴不～ be sloppily dressed ❸ finished; settled; completed: 屋子里收拾～了吗？Is the room tidied up? /孩子们转学的事儿还没办～。We haven't quite managed to transfer the children to another school yet.

利马 Lìmǎ Lima, capital of Peru

利马窦 Lìmǎdòu Matteo Ricci (1552-1610), Italian Catholic missionary who came to China in 1582 to preach Catholicism and died in Beijing

利麻 lìma 〈方言〉 fast and neat: 手脚～ deft; dexterous *see also* "麻利" máli

利眠灵 lìmiánlíng 〈药学〉 librium; chlordiazepoxide

利尿 lìniào 〈医学〉 diuresis: ～特性 diuretic property

利尿剂 lìniàojì 〈药学〉 diuretic

利尿素 lìniàosù 〈药学〉 diuretin

利尿酸 lìniàosuān 〈药学〉 ethacrynic (acid)

利器 lìqì ❶ sharp weapon: 身藏～ secretly armed with a sharp knife /精兵～ picked troops and sophisticated weapons ❷ good tool; efficient instrument: 工以～为用。A good tool is essential to a good craftsman.

利钱 lìqian interest

利权 lìquán economic rights and interests (of a country): ～外溢 lose economic rights to foreigners /挽回～ restore (*or* regain) economic rights

利刃 lìrèn ❶ sharp blade of a knife ❷ sharp knife or sword: 手持～ hold a sharp sword in hand

利润 lìrùn 〈经济〉 profit: 高～的买卖 high profit business /纯～ net profit /～驱动 profit-motivated /～再投资 reinvested earnings (*or* profits) / ～-成本分析 cost-benefit analysis

利润额 lìrùn'é profit margin; amount of profit

利润分配 lìrùn fēnpèi profit sharing; distribution of profits

利润挂帅 lìrùn guàshuài put profit in command; take profit as the primary motivation

利润留成 lìrùn liúchéng profit retention

利润率 lìrùnlǜ profitability; profit rate; profit margin

利润税 lìrùnshuì profit tax

利润提成 lìrùn tíchéng draw a proportionate bonus or commission from total profit

利洒 lìsa 〈方言〉 *see* "利落"

利什曼原虫 lìshímàn yuánchóng 〈医学〉 leishmania: ～病 leishmaniasis

利市 lìshì ❶ 〈书面〉 profit: ～三倍 make a huge profit; be very profitable ❷ 〈方言〉 good omen for business: 发个～ do a good business ❸ 〈方言〉 auspiciousness; good luck: 讨个～ just for luck ❹ 〈方言〉 gratuity; tip

利税 lìshuì 〈经济〉 profit and tax: 向国家上交～ turn profit and tax over to the state /～分流 separate profits from taxes

利索 lìsuo *see* "利落"

利他主义 lìtāzhǔyì altruism: ～者 altruist

利物 lìwù 〈旧语〉 prize (offered for a contest)

利息 lìxī 〈经济〉 interest: ～回扣 interest rebate /应计～ interest accrued /拖欠～ interest default /到期～ interest due /损失的～ interest foregone /应付～ interest payable /已付～ interest paid /～率 interest rate /附加～ interest surcharge

利血平 lìxuèpíng 〈药学〉 reserpine

利雅得 Lìyǎdé Riyadh, capital of Saudi Arabia

利益 lìyì interest; profit; benefit: 个人～ individual (*or* personal) interest /集体～ collective interest /国家～ national interests /既得～集团 vested interest group /～协调 harmony of interests / ～最大化 profit maximization /为人民谋～ work to benefit the people /符合群众～ be in the interests of the people /侵害他人的～ encroach upon the interests of others /充分照顾到社会各阶层的～ take into full consideration the interests of every social stratum

利用 lìyòng ❶ make use of; use; utilize: ～废物 make use of waste material; turn scrap material to good account; turn waste into useful material /～一切有利条件 benefit from every favourable condition /充分～改革开放的大好时机 make full use of the golden opportunity provided by the policy of reform and opening to the outside world /～业余时间读书 spend one's spare time reading ❷ take advantage of; exploit: ～职权 take advantage of one's position and power; exploit one's office /～别人的弱点 cash in on others' weaknesses /他叔叔～关系给他在报社谋到一个职位。His uncle pulled wires (*or* strings) to get him placed with the newspaper office. *or* His uncle got him a post with the paper through connections. /他是在～你。He is using you as his cat's paw.

利用率 lìyònglǜ utilization ratio

利用系数 lìyòng xìshù utilization coefficient; utilization factor

利诱 lìyòu lure by promise of gain: 不受～ do not succumb to the temptation of personal gain /经不起(别人的)～ yield (*or* fall) to a lure (by others) /威逼～ compel sb. to submit by threat and blandishments; use both the carrot and the stick

利于 lìyú beneficial to; of advantage to: ～团结 be helpful (*or* conducive) to unity /不～健康 be detrimental to health /凡是有～人民的事我们就应该去做。We should do anything that is in the interest of the people. /良药苦口～病。Good medicine is bitter in taste but good for the disease. *or* Bitter medicine cures sickness.

利欲熏心 lìyù-xūnxīn one's mind is clouded with avarice; be blinded by greed; be obsessed with the desire for gain; be overcome by covetousness: 此人～，明目张胆地贪污受贿。Driven by lust for money, this man has openly resorted to corruption and bribery.

利嘴 lìzuǐ glib tongue; sharp tongue: ～不饶人 sharp tongue that spares no one

痢

lì dysentery: 赤～ dysentery characterized by blood and pus in the stool /白～ dysentery characterized by white mucous stool

痢疾 lìji dysentery: 细菌性～ bacillary dysentery /阿米巴～ amoebic dysentery /～杆菌 bacillus dysenteriae /～状腹泻 dysenteric diarrhea

痢特灵 lìtèlíng 〈药学〉 furazolidone

鬁

lì *see* "鬎鬁" làli

莉

lì *see* "茉莉" mòli

俐

lì *see* "伶俐" língli

猁

lì *see* "猞猁" shēlì

例

lì ❶ example; instance: 图～ illustration; (of a map) legends /举～说明 give an example to make clear; explain by citing an instance ❷ precedent: 成～ precedent; existing model /开～ establish (*or* create) a precedent /先～ precedent /破～ break all precedents; make an exception /援～ quote (*or* follow) a precedent /史无前～ unprecedented ❸ case; instance: 这种病已发现了四～。Four cases of this disease have been reported. /这几～交通事故均由违章驾

驶造成。All these (instances of) traffic accidents were caused by violations of traffic regulations. ❹ rule; regulation:旧～ old rule /俗～ customary rules /定～ usual practice; set pattern /公～ general rules /体～ stylistic rules and layout /违～ breach (*or* violation) of rules /照～ as a rule; as usual /发凡起～ initiate a rule /均在此～。That is no exception. ❺ regular; routine:～套 regular practice; routine /～话 cliché; platitude

例规 lìguī ❶ usual practice; convention ❷〈旧语〉money gift offered according to established practice ❸ rules and regulations

例会 lìhuì regular meeting; routine meeting

例假 lìjià ❶ official holiday; legal holiday:春节～三天。The Spring Festival is a legal holiday of three days. ❷〈婉词〉menstration; period

例禁 lìjìn 〈书面〉decreed prohibitions

例句 lìjù sentence serving as an example; illustrative sentence; sample sentence:讲解～ explain the sample sentence

例如 lìrú for instance; for example (e.g.); such as:全国性的节日不少，～春节、国庆节等。There are quite a few national holidays, such as the Spring Festival, the National Day, etc.

例题 lìtí question or problem (in textbooks, etc.) to illustrate a theorem or rule

例外 lìwài exception:～情况 exceptional case /所有人都应在八时前报到，你也不能～。Everybody should report for duty before 8 a.m. and you are no exception. /所有规律都有～。There is no rule without exception. /物极必反，绝少～。Things will turn to their opposites when pushed to the extreme, and there are few deviations from this rule.

例行公事 lìxíng-gōngshì ❶ routine; routine business:到机场去取邮包是他的～。To pick up the mail pouches at the airport is his routine work. ❷ mere formality; mere routine:这是～，请别介意。This is just a formality. I hope you won't mind.

例言 lìyán introductory remarks; notes on the use of a book

例语 lìyǔ illustrative phrase; example word or phrase

例证 lìzhèng example; illustration; case in point:他列举了许多有力的～。He cited a number of compelling examples.

例子 lìzi example; instance; case

珠(瓅) lì *see*“玓珠” dìlì

栎(櫟) lì *also*“柞树” zuòshù;“麻栎” málì;“橡” xiàng 〈植物〉oak

砾(礫) lì gravel:沙～ gravel;grit /瓦～ rubble; debris /火山～ lapillus /漂～ boulder

砾漠 lìmò poor and stony land

砾石 lìshí gravel:～混凝土 gravel concrete /～路 gravel road

砾岩 lìyán 〈地质〉conglomerate

轹(轢) lì 〈书面〉❶ crush with cartwheels; run over ❷ bully; oppress:陵～ bully; oppress

跞(躒) lì 〈书面〉walk about

see also luò

隶(隸、隷) lì ❶ be subordinate to; be affiliated to or with; be under:昌平县～于北京市。Changping County is under the municipality of Beijing. ❷ person in servitude:奴～ slave /仆～ servant ❸〈旧语〉*yamen* runner:皂～ *yamen* runner ❹ *see*“～书”

隶农 lìnóng 〈书面〉slave on a farm

隶人 lìrén 〈书面〉criminal; culprit

隶书 lìshū official script, an ancient style of calligraphy current in the Han Dynasty, simplified from *xiaozhuan* (小篆)

隶属 lìshǔ be subordinate to; be under the jurisdiction or command of:～关系 relationship of administrative subordination /地方～中央。All localities are under the jurisdiction of the central government. /这几个科～于总务处。These sections are under the division of general affairs. /要搞清这两个概念的～关系。We should clarify which of the two concepts is the subordinate one.

隶字 lìzì *see*“隶书”

隶卒 lìzú *yamen* runner

力 lì ❶〈物理〉force:磁～ magnetic force /电～ electric power /向心～ centripetal force /离心～ centrifugal force /牵引～ traction force; traction; pulling force /压～ pressure ❷ power; strength; ability:听～ power of hearing /握～ power of gripping; grip /兵～ military strength; military capabilities /视～ eyesight /生命～ vitality /人～ manpower /财～ financial resources /物～ material resources /能～ ability; capability /胆～ courage; boldness; bravery /肥～ fertility (of soil, etc.) /判断～ judgment /记忆～ faculty of memory; memory /号召～ public appeal ❸ physical strength:身强～壮 man of great strength /四肢无～ feel weak all over ❹ do all one can; make every effort; exert oneself:～谏 try all one can to remontrate (esp. with a ruler or superior); strongly counsel against (doing sth.) /～劝 persuade earnestly /领导不～ poor leadership ❺ (Lì) a surname

力巴 lìba 〈方言〉❶ not adept; awkward; be all thumbs:行家莫说～话。Professionals must not talk unprofessionally. ❷ *also*“力巴头” layman:入行三日无～。Nobody remains a layman after three days in the trade. /开汽车我是个～。I know little about driving a car.

力避 lìbì do all one can to avoid:～被动 strive to avoid being on the receiving end

力臂 lìbì 〈物理〉arm of force

力不从心 lìbùcóngxīn ability falling short of one's wishes; talent not equal to one's ambition; the spirit is willing, but the flesh is weak:他想写一本自传，但人已九十，～了。Much as he wants to, it is beyond his power to write an autobiography at the age of ninety.

力不能支 lìbùnéngzhī unable to stand the strain any longer; too weak to stay on one's feet;这么重的责任，怕他～。I'm afraid that he is not equal to such a heavy responsibility.

力不胜任 lìbùshèngrèn be unequal to one's task; not have the required ability to do sth.; be incompetent:这种工作她显然有些～。It is evident that she is not quite up to the job. /我怕这是他～的。I'm afraid that's beyond his capacity.

力场 lìchǎng 〈物理〉field of force

力程 lìchéng 〈物理〉range

力持 lìchí persist; persevere; insist:～异议 insist on one's dissenting views; remain firm in one's disagreement /～正义 persevere in upholding justice

力畜 lìchù *also*“役畜” yìchù draught animal; beast of burden

力促 lìcù make every effort to get sth. done:我当～此事成功。I certainly will do my best to help make it a success.

力挫 lìcuò fight hard to defeat or frustrate:～上届网球单打冠军 play hard and defeat the defending tennis single champion

力道 lìdào 〈方言〉❶ strength; power:～大 strong; powerful ❷ role; efficacy; effect:化肥比粪肥的～来得快。Chemical fertilizers produce faster effects than barnyard manure.

力点 lìdiǎn 〈物理〉fulcrum

力度 lìdù ❶ strength; force:加强改革的～ strengthen (*or* beef up) the reforms ❷〈音乐〉dynamics ❸ intensity; depth; power:这是一部有～的好作品。This is a powerful work.

力夫 lìfū 〈旧语〉longshoreman; stevedore; docker

力耕 lìgēng work hard in the field (esp. of ploughing)

力攻 lìgōng launch a vigorous attack; fight with might and main:～顽敌 go all out to attack the stubborn enemy

力疾 lìjí 〈书面〉prop oneself up from the sickbed:～从公 work at one's public duties despite one's illness; be devoted to one's duties despite illness

力荐 lìjiàn strongly recommend:我～他接替自己的职务。I strongly recommend that he take over my job.

力竭声嘶 lìjié-shēngsī *also*“声嘶力竭” shout oneself hoarse; be hoarse and exhausted

力戒 lìjiè do everything possible to avoid; guard against:～急躁 guard against impetuosity /～自满 be vigilant against conceit /～拖沓 do everything possible to prevent delay /工作中要～形式主义。Formalism must be avoided by all means in our work.

力矩 lìjǔ 〈物理〉moment of force; moment:合～ resultant moment /俯仰～〈机械〉pitching moment /～图 moment diagram

力量 lìliang ❶ physical strength; physical power:比比谁的～大。Let's see who is stronger. /体操是一项既要求～，又要求灵巧的运动。Gymnastics is a sport that combines strength and agility. ❷ capability; power; force; strength:依靠自己的～ rely on one's own

L

strength /经济～ economic power /动员一切～ mobilize all the forces available /为建设祖国贡献自己所有的～ devote all one has to building up one's motherland /知识就是～。Knowledge is power. /团结就是～。Unity is strength. ❸ potency; efficacy; effect:这种农药～很大。This pesticide is very potent.

力谋 lìmóu try hard to get sth. done; strive:～图报 do one's utmost to show one's gratitude /～保持社会稳定 strive for social stability

力偶 lì'ǒu 〈物理〉couple (of force):～矩 moment of couple /～臂 arm of couple /～轴线 axis of couple

力排众议 lìpái-zhòngyì prevail over or override all dissenting views:他～,终于使自己的提案得以通过。He prevailed over all dissenting views and got his motion adopted. *or* He succeeded in getting his motion carried despite dissenting voices.

力气 lìqi physical strength; effort:使尽浑身～ use every ounce of one's strength /不费～是学不好外语的。You can't learn a foreign language well without making painstaking efforts. /她昨晚没睡好觉,今天浑身没～。She didn't sleep well last night and so feels very weak today.

力气活 lìqihuó manual labour; strenuous work; heavy work:我从前是干～儿的。I used to be a manual worker. /这可是个～儿。This is a job of hard manual labour.

力气头儿 lìqitóur 〈口语〉*see* "力气"

力钱 lìqian 〈旧语〉payment to a porter

力求 lìqiú make every effort to; do one's utmost to; strive to:～达成互相谅解 make every effort to achieve mutual understanding /～最佳成绩 strive for the best result /～事成 try by all means to get sth. done

力矢量 lìshǐliàng force vector

力士 lìshì person with tremendous physical power; strong man; muscleman

力所不及 lìsuǒbùjí ability falls short of the requirement; be unequal to a task; be beyond one's power:别勉强我去做这种～的事。Don't force me to do what is beyond my power.

力所能及 lìsuǒnéngjí in one's power; within one's ability:予以～的帮助 help sb. to the best of one's ability /只要～,我一定去办。I'll do everything I can. /我岁数大了,但还能做些～的工作。Old as I am, I can still do some work I'm capable of doing.

力田 lìtián *see* "力耕"

力透纸背 lìtòuzhǐbèi ❶ (of calligraphy or handwriting) the strokes are powerful enough to penetrate the paper — vigorous; forceful; powerful ❷ (of literary works) deep and powerful; penetrating

力图 lìtú ❶ try hard to; strive to:～使经济摆脱衰退 strive to get the economy out of depression /～找到新途径 make every effort (*or* attempt) to explore a new avennue /～让他信任自己 try hard to win his trust ❷〈物理〉force diagram; stress diagram

力挽狂澜 lìwǎn-kuánglán make vigorous efforts to turn the tide; strive to save a desperate situation

力线 lìxiàn 〈物理〉line of force; flux line; force line:～图 force diagram

力行 lìxíng vigorously practise:身体～ earnestly practise what one preaches

力学 lìxué ❶ mechanics:波动～ wave mechanics /断裂～ fracture mechanics /生物～ biomechanics /工程～ engineering mechanics /气体～ gas mechanics /流体～ fluid mechanics ❷〈书面〉study hard:～不倦 be tireless in one's pursuit of knowledge

力学视差 lìxué shìchā 〈物理〉dynamic parallax

力战 lìzhàn fight with might and main; fight gallantly:～群雄 fight undauntedly against a multitude of strong enemies

力争 lìzhēng ❶ work hard for; do all one can to:～主动 do one's utmost to gain the initiative /～提前完成任务 work hard to complete (*or* fulfil) a task ahead of schedule /～夺魁 spare no effort to win the championship ❷ argue strongly; contend vigorously:据理～ argue strongly on just grounds; advance (*or* put forward) a strong argument

力争上游 lìzhēng-shàngyóu aim high; strive for the best; strive to get the upper hand:在学习上～ strive for the best in one's studies /鼓足干劲,～,多快好省地建设社会主义 go all out, aim high, and achieve greater, faster, better and more economical results in building socialism

力证 lìzhèng convincing proof or evidence

力主 lìzhǔ vigorously advocate:～和平解决国际争端 strongly advocate settling international disputes by peaceful means

力租 lìzū *also* "干租" gānzū rent paid in labour; labour rent

力作 lìzuò ❶〈书面〉work hard; labour; toil:耕田～ toil in the fields ❷ masterpiece; tour de force:这个剧本是他晚年的～。This play is his masterpiece in later years.

历[1](歷)

lì ❶ go through; undergo; experience:阅～ experience /资～ qualifications and record of service; seniority /来～ origin; background /履～ personal record (of education and work experience); curriculum vitae (CV); résumé /病～ medical record; case history /～时三年的战争 war that lasted three years /他曾亲～那场灾难。He witnessed and experienced that catastrophe. ❷ all previous (years, occasions, sessions, etc.): *see* "～代"; "～次" ❸ all; one after another:～览名山大川 visit all the renowned mountains and great rivers; see the famous places one after another /～试诸方,均无成效。Prescriptions of all kinds have been tried but to no avail. ❹ (Lì) a surname

历[2](厤、曆、歴)

lì calendric system; calendar:阴～ lunar calendar /公～ Gregorian calendar /月～ monthly calendar /台～ desk calendar /挂～ wall calendar; calendar scroll /万年～ perpetual calendar /大学校～ university calendar; school calendar

历本 lìběn 〈方言〉almanac

历朝 lìcháo ❶ successive dynasties; past dynasties:～官制 officialism (*or* official systems) in successive dynasties ❷ successive reigns (within a dynasty)

历陈 lìchén expatiate or expound strongly; state point by point; explain item by item:～利弊 explain all the advantages and disadvantages item by item

历程 lìchéng course; experience:战斗的～ course of struggle /人生的～ life's journey /苦难的～ miserable experience; traumatic experience /探求真理的～ road of quest for truth /争取民族独立的～ path of struggle for national independence

历次 lìcì all previous (occassions, happenings, etc.):他～考试均名列前茅。He has always come out on top in the examinations. /本剧～公演都受到热烈的欢迎。This play was enthusiastically received by the public each time it was staged.

历代 lìdài ❶ successive dynasties; past dynasties:～君主 all previous monarchs ❷ all previous generations; successive generations:～务农 engage in farming from generation to generation ❸ all periods of time; all ages:这里的陶瓷业～不衰。The porcelain industry here has prospered through the ages.

历法 lìfǎ 〈天文〉calendric system; calendar

历阶 lìjiē 〈书面〉ascend the steps, stairs, etc.:～而上 mount the steps

历劫 lìjié experience misery and hardship one after another:～多年,他渐渐有些麻木了。He had become rather apathetic after years of miseries and hardships.

历届 lìjiè all previous (sessions, governments, etc.):～董事会 all the previous boards of directors /～毕业生 graduates of all previous years /～政府均未解决这一问题。None of the past administrations (*or* governments) has been able to solve this problem.

历尽 lìjìn experience repeatedly; suffer again and again:～千辛万苦 go through misery and hardships /～磨难 endure all kinds of trials and tribulations

历尽沧桑 lìjìn-cāngsāng experience the vicissitudes of life:这座～的古城,如今焕发了青春。Having suffered the vicissitudes of history, the ancient city has now been rejuvenated.

历经 lìjīng experience; go through:古寺数百年来～修缮。The ancient temple has been renovated time and again during past centuries.

历久 lìjiǔ for a long period of time; enduring; lasting:～不衰 lasting; abiding; longlasting /～弥坚 become even firmer as time goes by

历来 lìlái always; all along; throughout the ages:～如此 has always been the case. /我们～主张大小国家一律平等。We have all along stood for the equality among all the nations, big and small. /台湾～属于中国。Taiwan has always been part of China.

历历 lìlì distinctly; clearly:古碑字迹,～可辨。The characters on the ancient stone tablet are distinctly visible.

L

历历可数 lìlì-kěshǔ so distinct that its number can be counted：那江中来往的船只，帆樯～。The masts of the ships on the river can be seen very distinctly.

历历如画 lìlì-rúhuà *also* "历历如绘" as distinct as a picture; picturesque：两岸风景～，游人流连忘返。The picturesque scenery along the banks was a magnet for tourists.

历历在耳 lìlì-zài'ěr ring clearly in one's ears：他当年的临别赠言，犹～。His parting words still ring distinctly in my ears.

历历在目 lìlì-zàimù leap up vividly before the eyes; come clearly into view：那次水灾的情景依然～。The devastating sight of the flood is still clear before my eyes. /如今重读这本旧作，三十年前的往事～。Today when I reread this book I seem to relive what happened thirty years ago.

历练 lìliàn ❶ experience; see the world：孩子大了，应该到外面～～。As the child has grown up, he should go out and see the world for himself. ❷ experienced; seasoned：他～老成，办事稳重。He is experienced and prudent.

历乱 lìluàn 〈书面〉 chaotic; disorderly：星光～ stars gleaming in chaotic profusion /～的脚步声 flurry of footsteps

历落 lìluò 〈书面〉 ❶ uneven; irregular; scattered：天上疏星～。The stars are scattered in the sky. ❷ outstanding; unusual; uncommon

历年 lìnián ❶ over the years：这本书是他～辛劳的结晶。This book is the fruit of his hard work over the years. /类似的事～都有发生。Similar events happened every year in the past. ❷ calendar year

历任 lìrèn ❶ have successively held (posts); have served successively as：～要职 have held important positions in succession /他～科员、科长、处长、司长。He has successively served as staff member, section chief, division chief, and director of a department. ❷ successive; all previous (holders of an office, etc.)：这个部队的～指挥员现在都已是将军了。The successive commanders of this army unit are all generals now. /这个工厂的～厂长都是大学生。All the previous managers of this factory have been college graduates.

历时 lìshí last; take (a period of time)：～十年的内战 civil war that lasted ten years; decade-long civil war /这场网球比赛～三小时。The tennis match took (*or* lasted) three hours.

历史 lìshǐ ❶ history：人类的～ history of the human race; human history /歪曲～ distort history /篡改～ tamper with history /曲解～ give a biased (*or* slanted) interpretation of history; distort history /创造～ make (*or* create) history /～上 in history; historically; down the ages /～重演 history repeats itself /具有～意义 of historic significance ❷ past events：～问题 question of a political nature in sb.'s personal record /隐瞒自己的～ conceal one's past /～清白 have a clean record /这件事已成为～，知道的人不多了。It has become a thing of the past, and very few people know it. /他～上犯过错误，但仍然是一位好同志。He is a good comrade despite the mistakes he made in the past. ❸ historical record; history：从这本书里可查到一些明代～。Some records of the Ming Dynasty can be found in the book. ❹ history (as an academic discipline); historiography：他研究～。History is his field of study. /下节课是～。The next class is history.

历史比较语言学 lìshǐ bǐjiào yǔyánxué historical comparative philology or linguistics

历史博物馆 lìshǐ bówùguǎn history or historical museum：中国～ Museum of Chinese History

历史潮流 lìshǐ cháoliú tide of history; historical trend

历史地理学 lìshǐ dìlǐxué historical geography

历史地图 lìshǐ dìtú historical map or atlas

历史观 lìshǐguān view or conception of history

历史教训 lìshǐ jiàoxùn lesson of history; history lesson

历史剧 lìshǐjù historical play

历史人物 lìshǐ rénwù historical personage; historical figure

历史唯物主义 lìshǐ wéiwùzhǔyì *also* "历史唯物论"；"唯物史观" wéiwù shǐguān historical materialism

历史唯心主义 lìshǐ wéixīnzhǔyì *also* "历史唯心论"；"唯心史观" wéixīn shǐguān historical idealism

历史小说 lìshǐ xiǎoshuō historical novel or romance

历史性 lìshǐxìng historic; of historic significance：～胜利 historic victory /～的会议 meeting of historic significance; historic meeting /～的转折 historic transition; turn in history

历史学 lìshǐxué history; historiography

历史学家 lìshǐxuéjiā historian; historiographer

历史循环论 lìshǐ xúnhuánlùn idea that history occurs in cycles; cyclical view of history

历史遗产 lìshǐ yíchǎn legacy of history; historical heritage

历史语言学 lìshǐ yǔyánxué historical philology or linguistics

历世 lìshì all previous dynasties：这本书记载了～的民间传说。This book records the folklore passed down from history.

历书 lìshū almanac

历数 lìshǔ count one by one; enumerate：～对方违反协定的事实 enumerate (*or* make a list of) the violations of the agreement by the other side

历数 lìshù 〈书面〉 ❶ order of solar periods and seasons ❷ order of imperial and dynastic successions (supposedly in conformity with the movements of heavenly bodies)

历险 lìxiǎn experience danger or disaster; adventure：～记 adventures

历元 lìyuán 〈天文〉 epoch：～平极 mean pole of the epoch

历月 lìyuè 〈天文〉 calendar month

沥（瀝） lì

❶ drip; trickle：滴～ (the sound of) dripping /～干 drip-dry /披～ loyal; open and sincere ❷ drop：余～ last drops; dregs; heeltap; small share of benefit

沥陈 lìchén 〈书面〉 sincerely state (one's view, reason, etc.)：～时政得失 earnestly set forth the successes and failures of the current government

沥胆 lìdǎn ❶ with sincerity; with loyalty：～订交 become bosom friends ❷ express one's sincere feelings or loyalty

沥胆披肝 lìdǎn-pīgān *also* "披肝沥胆" open up one's heart; be all sincerity：～陈时弊 frankly expose the malpractices of the time

沥涝 lìlào waterlogging：～成灾 serious damage caused by waterlogging

沥沥 lìlì ❶〈象声〉 (of wind) whistling; rustling; (of flowing water) babbling：风声～。The wind was whistling. /溪水～而下。The stream babbles down. ❷ overflow with; drip：～拉拉弄得满地都是水。The floor is wet all over.

沥青 lìqīng pitch; asphalt; bitumen：天然～ natural asphalt; natural bitumen /～混凝土 bituminous concrete; asphalt concrete /～基原油 asphalt-base crude oil /～焦 tarcoke /～路 bituminous road; asphalt road /～煤 pitch coal /～清漆 bitumen varnish /～塑料 bituminous plastic /～油毡 asphalt felt /～油纸 asphalt paper

沥青铀矿 lìqīng yóukuàng *also* "铀沥青" yóulìqīng uraninite

沥水 lìshuǐ waterlogging caused by excessive rainfall

沥血 lìxuè shed blood; drip blood：呕心～ shed one's heart's blood; take infinite pains; work one's heart out

疬（癧） lì

see "瘰疬" luǒlì

雳（靂） lì

see "霹雳" pīlì

苈（藶） lì

see "葶苈" tínglì

枥（櫪） lì

❶〈书面〉 manger：老骥伏～ old warhorse in a manger ❷ *see* "栎" lì

呖（嚦） lì

呖呖 lìlì 〈书面〉〈象声〉 clear and melodious chirping (of a bird)：莺声～ warbling of the oriole

荔 lì

荔枝 lìzhī 〈植物〉 litchi; lichee

沴 lì

〈书面〉 ❶ ill omen：～气 bad omen (for disaster) ❷ harm; hurt

沴孽 lìniè 〈书面〉 demon; monster; evil spirit

盭 lì

〈书面〉 ferocious; ruthless; perverse

li

哩 li

〈方言〉〈助词〉 ❶ *used like* 呢 *but not in interrogative sentence*：山上的雪还没化～。The snow on the mountain has not

melted. ❷ *used like* 啦 *in enumeration*：碗～，筷子～，杯子～，都摆好了。Bowls, chopsticks, glasses — all are set out on the table.
see also lī; lǐ

liǎ

俩(倆) liǎ 〈口语〉❶ (两 and 个 combined) two：咱哥儿～ the two of us (between brothers or good male friends) /你们～ you two /爷儿～ grandpa and grandson; father and son; uncle and nephew ❷ a few; a little; some; several：给他～钱儿。Give him some money. /我一月挣那～钱儿，哪够哇！ My monthly salary? Only a pittance. Far from enough!
see also liǎng

lián

帘(❷簾) lián ❶ flag or banner used as shop sign：酒～ wineshop sign; bar sign ❷ curtain; (hanging) screen：门～儿 door curtain; portière /竹～儿 bamboo curtain; bamboo screen
帘布 liánbù *also* "帘子布" cord fabric (in tyres)
帘栊 liánlóng 〈书面〉❶ curtained window ❷ curtain
帘幔 liánmàn curtain
帘幕 liánmù (heavy) curtain：～低垂。The curtain hangs down. /拉开～，旭日当窗。Drawing back the curtains, I saw the rising sun through the window.
帘栅管 liánshānguǎn 〈电学〉screen-grid tube
帘栅极 liánshānjí 〈电学〉screen grid
帘子 liánzi (hanging) screen; curtain

廉(亷) lián ❶ honest and clean: *see* "～耻" ❷ low in price; inexpensive; cheap：价格低～。The price is low. ❸ (Lián) a surname
廉耻 liánchǐ sense of honour; sense of shame; integrity：不顾～ shameless
廉价 liánjià cheap; low-priced; inexpensive; at a bargain price：～出卖 sell off goods at reduced prices (*or* at a bargain); sell cheap /～劳动力 cheap labour /～品 cheap goods; bargain
廉价部 liánjiàbù bargain counter; bargain basement
廉洁 liánjié honest and clean：为政～ clean government /～自律 incorruptible and self-disciplined
廉洁奉公 liánjié-fènggōng be honest in performing one's official duties：～的干部 honest and incorruptible official
廉吏 liánlì honest official
廉明 liánmíng clean and honest：为官～ be a clean and honest official
廉顽立懦 liánwán-lìnuò *also* "顽廉懦立" make the corrupt honest and the cowardly brave
廉正 liánzhèng *also* "廉直" honest and upright：～无私 honest and unselfish
廉政 liánzhèng honest and clean government：～措施 measures to build an honest and clean government
廉政公署 Liánzhèng Gōngshǔ (HK) Independent Commission Against Corruption
廉政建设 liánzhèng jiànshè build or establish a clean government
廉政专员 Liánzhèng Zhuānyuán (HK) Commissioner Against Corruption
廉直 liánzhí *see* "廉正"

鬑 lián 〈书面〉long hair
鬑鬑 liánlián 〈书面〉thin or sparse hair：发～ thin hair

磏 lián 〈书面〉a kind of whetstone or grindstone

螊 lián *see* "蜚螊" fěilián

镰(鎌) lián sickle：开～ start harvesting (with sickles)
镰刀 liándāo sickle
镰鱼 liányú Moorish idol (*Zanclus canescens*)

臁 lián 〈生理〉shank
臁疮 liánchuāng 〈中医〉ulcer on the shank

怜(憐) lián ❶ sympathize with; pity：可～的小家伙！Poor little thing! /同病相～。Fellow sufferers sympathize (*or* commiserate) with each other. ❷ love tenderly; have tender affection for
怜爱 lián'ài love tenderly; have gentle affection for：～之情 tender affection /这孩子真叫人～。What a lovely child!
怜悯 liánmǐn pity; take pity on; have compassion for：～不幸的人 take pity on the unfortunate /廉价的～无异于羞辱。Cheap compassion is as bad as humiliation.
怜念 liánniàn show pity and concern; show compassion：～伤员 show pity and concern for the wounded /动人～ move people to compassion
怜贫惜老 liánpín-xīlǎo take pity on the poor and care for the aged
怜惜 liánxī show compassion and concern for; take pity on; have pity for：～倍加 have great pity for /她十分疼爱和～这个没娘的孩子。She had pity for the motherless child and loved him dearly.
怜香惜玉 liánxiāng-xīyù *also* "惜玉怜香" be tender towards women; have a tender heart for the fair sex
怜恤 liánxù take pity on; have pity for：～老弱 have pity for the aged and the weak

联(聯) lián ❶ ally oneself with; unite; combine; join：关～ be connected with; be associated with ❷ antithetical couplet：春～ Spring Festival couplets /挽～ elegiac couplet /寿～ longevity (*or* birthday) couplet
联邦 liánbāng federation; confederation; commonwealth：英～ British Commonwealth of Nations /俄罗斯～ Russian Confederation /瑞士～ Swiss Confederation /～政府 federal government /～国家 federal state
联邦储备系统 Liánbāng Chǔbèi Xìtǒng (US) Federal Reserve System (FRS)
联邦储备银行 Liánbāng Chǔbèi Yínháng (US) Federal Reserve Bank
联邦调查局 Liánbāng Diàochájú (US) Federal Bureau of Investigation (FBI)
联邦共和国 liánbāng gònghéguó federal republic; federated republic：德意志～ Federal Republic of Germany
联邦通信委员会 Liánbāng Tōngxìn Wěiyuánhuì Federal Communication Commission (FCC)
联邦院 Liánbāngyuàn (India) Rajya Sabha; Council of States
联邦制 liánbāngzhì federal system; federalism
联苯胺 liánběn'àn 〈化学〉benizidine
联苯酚 liánběnfēn 〈化学〉diphenol
联苯基 liánběnjī 〈化学〉xenyl
联苯乙烯 liánběn yǐxī 〈化学〉distyrene
联璧 liánbì (short for 珠联璧合) (of two different things) combine harmoniously; match well：兄弟～，皆有文才。The two brothers are equally matched in their literary talent.
联播 liánbō radio or TV hookup; broadcast over a radio or TV network：新闻～ network news /～节目时间 network time
联产承包责任制 liánchǎn chéngbāo zérènzhì system of contracted responsibility linking remuneration to output; contract system with remuneration linked to output
联产计酬 liánchǎn jìchóu link payment to output
联唱 liánchàng singing by more than two people in succession; singing of more than two songs by a person or a group; serial singing：民歌大～ serial singing of folk songs
联大 Liándà (short for 联合国大会) United Nations General Assembly
联单 liándān receipt or other document in duplicate：三～ receipt in triplicate
联电 liándiàn (short for 联合通电) jointly signed circular telegram：～讨逆 send a jointly signed circular telegram to denounce the traitors
联队 liánduì ❶ 〈军事〉wing (of an air force) ❷ 〈体育〉united team：曼彻斯特～ Manchester United ❸ (of some armies) regiment：

骑兵～ cavalry regiment

联防 liánfáng ❶ joint defence; joint command of defence forces: 军民～ joint defence by army and militia; army-civilian defence /治安～ joint effort to maintain public security /两军携手～，共御强敌。The two armies set up a joint defence to resist the powerful enemy. ❷〈体育〉joint defence: 甲队上半场运用～战术十分成功。Team A successfully used the tactics of joint defence during the first half.

联杆 liángǎn link rod; connecting rod

联管节 liánguǎnjié 〈机械〉pipe union; pipe coupling; union joint

联管箱 liánguǎnxiāng 〈机械〉header: 汽锅～ boiler header

联贯 liánguàn *also* "连贯" liánguàn ❶ consistent; coherent ❷ link up; piece together; join together

联合 liánhé ❶ unite; ally: 与别人～在一起 ally oneself with others /～起来，共同努力 unite and make concerted efforts /～就是力量。In union there is strength. /这种～是有条件的。This is a conditional alliance (*or* coalition). ❷ joint; combined: ～举办 jointly organize or sponsor /～声明 joint statement (*or* communique) /～诉状 combined indictment /中英～联络小组 Sino-British Joint Liaison Group /～承包商 co-contractor /～经营 coordinated management ❸〈生理〉symphysis: ～耻骨 symphysis pubis /下颌骨～ symphysis of lower jawbone; mandibular symphysis

联合兵种 liánhé bīngzhǒng combined arms: ～演习 exercise of combined arms

联合采煤机 liánhé cǎiméijī cutter-loader; combine

联合词组 liánhé cízǔ coordinative word group

联合大学 liánhé dàxué associated university

联合公报 liánhé gōngbào joint communiqué: 中美建交～ Joint Communiqué on the Establishment of Diplomatic Relations Between the United States of America and the People's Republic of China, January 1979 /中美上海～ Sino-US Joint Communiqué of February 28, 1972 (commonly known as the Shanghai Communiqué) /中美八一七～ Joint Communiqué of the United States of America and the People's Republic of China (on the reduction of US arms sale to Taiwan), August 17, 1982

联合国 Liánhéguó United Nations (UN)

联合国安全理事会 Liánhéguó Ānquán Lǐshìhuì (shortened as 安理会) United Nations Security Council

联合国大会 Liánhéguó Dàhuì United Nations General Assembly

联合国大学 Liánhéguó Dàxué United Nations University (UNU)

联合国儿童基金会 Liánhéguó Értóng Jījīnhuì United Nations Children's Fund (UNICEF)

联合国工业发展组织 Liánhéguó Gōngyè Fāzhǎn Zǔzhī (shortened as 工发组织) United Nations Industrial Development Organization (UNIDO)

联合国环境规划署 Liánhéguó Huánjìng Guīhuàshǔ United Nations Environment Programme (UNEP)

联合国教育、科学及文化组织 Liánhéguó Jiàoyù Kēxué Jí Wénhuà Zǔzhī (shortened as 教科文组织) United Nations Educational, Scientific and Cultural Organization (UNESCO)

联合国经济及社会理事会 Liánhéguó Jīngjì Jí Shèhuì Lǐshìhuì (shortened as 经社理事会) United Nations Economic and Social Council (ESC; ECOSOC)

联合国军 Liánhéguójūn United Nations Command (UNC)

联合国开发计划署 Liánhéguó Kāifā Jìhuàshǔ United Nations Development Programme (UNDP)

联合国粮食及农业组织 Liánhéguó Liángshi Jí Nóngyè Zǔzhī (shortened as 粮农组织) United Nations Food and Agriculture Organization (UNFAO)

联合国贸易和发展会议 Liánhéguó Màoyì Hé Fāzhǎn Huìyì (shortened as 贸发会议) United Nations Conference on Trade and Development (UNCTAD)

联合国秘书处 Liánhéguó Mìshūchù United Nations Secretariat

联合国难民事务高级专员办事处 Liánhéguó Nànmín Shìwù Gāojí Zhuānyuán Bànshìchù Office of the United Nations High Commissioner for Refugees (UNHCR)

联合国人口活动基金会 Liánhéguó Rénkǒu Huódòng Jījīnhuì United Nations Fund for Population Activities (UNFPA)

联合国日内瓦办事处 Liánhéguó Rìnèiwǎ Bànshìchù United Nations Office at Geneva

联合国宪章 Liánhéguó Xiànzhāng United Nations Charter

联合国宣言 Liánhéguó Xuānyán Declaration by the United Nations (1943)

联合国总部 Liánhéguó Zǒngbù headquarters of the United Nations

联合国组织 Liánhéguó Zǔzhī United Nations Organization (UNF)

联合航空公司 Liánhé Hángkōng Gōngsī China United Airlines; (US) United Airlines

联合会 liánhéhuì federation; union: 妇女～ women's federation / 学生～ students' union /工商～ association of industry and commerce

联合机 liánhéjī *also* "康拜因" kāngbàiyīn combine

联合经营 liánhé jīngyíng joint management; joint venture

联合企业 liánhé qǐyè integrated complex: 钢铁～ integrated iron and steel works; integrated steelworks

联合融资 liánhé róngzī co-financing

联合收割机 liánhé shōugējī *also* "康拜因" kāngbàiyīn combine (harvester)

联合体 liánhétǐ organic whole; association; complex

联合王国 Liánhé Wángguó United Kingdom (composed of England, Wales, Scotland and Northern Ireland); UK

联合行动 liánhé xíngdòng joint action; concerted action

联合宣言 liánhé xuānyán joint declaration

联合演习 liánhé yǎnxí 〈军事〉joint manoeuvre; joint exercise

联合战线 liánhé zhànxiàn united front

联合政府 liánhé zhèngfǔ coalition government

联合制 liánhézhì combination system

联合作战 liánhé zuòzhàn combined operation

联户 liánhù joint households: ～林场 joint-households forestry farm /～兴办的乡镇企业越来越红火。Township enterprises set up by combined households are becoming more and more prosperous.

联欢 liánhuān (have a) get-together: 兄弟院校～ intercollegiate get-together /节日～ gala celebrations

联欢会 liánhuānhuì get-together; party

联欢节 liánhuānjié festival; carnival; fiesta

联欢晚会 liánhuān wǎnhuì (evening) party (usu. for a given occasion or festival): 春节～ Spring Festival party; Chinese New Year party

联机 liánjī 〈计算机〉on-line: ～操作 on-line operation /～程序的调整 debugging on-line; on-line debugging /～磁盘文件存储器 on-line disc file /～存储器 on-line storage (*or* memory) /～计算机 on-line computer /～信息处理 on-line processing /～装置 on-line unit

联接 liánjiē *also* "连接" liánjiē ❶ join; link ❷〈航天〉mate

联结 liánjié *also* "连结" liánjié bind; tie; join; combine: 公路把山村和县城～起来了。The road connects the mountain village with the county town (*or* seat). /共同的事业把他们紧紧地～起来。A common cause bound them together.

联句 liánjù way of composing a poem in which two or more people compose one or two lines successively and put them together: 即景～ (of several people) be inspired by what they see and improvise a poem together

联军 liánjūn allied forces; united army: 东北抗日～ Anti-Japanese Amalgamated Army of Northeast China (organized and led by the Chinese Communist Party after the September 18th Incident of 1931)

联立方程 liánlì fāngchéng 〈数学〉simultaneous equation

联络 liánluò get in touch with; come into contact with: ～感情 make friendly contacts; promote friendly feelings; promote friendship /与朋友失去了～ lose contact (*or* be out of touch) with a friend /秘密～点 secret contact point /～网 liaison network /～图 contact map /对方曾派人前来～。The other side did send someone to contact us.

联络部 liánluòbù liaison department

联络处 liánluòchù liaison office

联络官 liánluòguān liaison officer

联络网 liánluòwǎng liaison network

联络员 liánluòyuán liaison person

联络站 liánluòzhàn liaison station

联袂 liánmèi 〈书面〉*also* "连袂" liánmèi join sleeves — come or go hand in hand: ～而行 walk hand in hand /～而至 come together /～登台献艺 give a joint performance

联盟 liánméng alliance; coalition; league; union: 双方结成～。The two sides formed (*or* entered into) an alliance. /苏维埃社会主义共和

L

国～ Union of Soviet Socialist Republics (1922-1990) /东南亚～ Association of Southeast Asian Nations (ASEAN)
联盟号 Liánménghào *also* "联盟号宇宙飞船"〈航天〉(former USSR) Soyuz, a series of manned spacecraft, the first of which — Soyuz 1 — was launched in April 1967
联盟院 Liánméngyuàn (former USSR) Soviet of the Union
联绵 liánmián *also* "连绵" liánmián continuous; unbroken; uninterrupted
联绵字 liánmiánzì *also* "联绵词"〈语言〉Chinese words consisting of two characters, often alliterated or rhymed (as 仿佛, 伶俐, 逍遥, 妯娌)
联名 liánmíng jointly signed; jointly: ～发出邀请 write a joint letter to invite; send a joint invitation /～致电 send a jointly-signed (*or* joint) telegram /～倡议 jointly initiate (*or* sponsor)
联翩 liánpiān *also* "连翩" liánpiān in close succession; together: 浮想～ thoughts thronging one's mind; be lost in a train of thoughts
联翩而至 liánpiān'érzhì come in close succession; come together: 各界人士～, 盛况空前。Celebrities of various circles arrived in close succession for the important occasion.
联赛 liánsài 〈体育〉league matches: 篮球～ league basketball matches /足球～ league football matches
联手 liánshǒu join hands (with a person): ～调查 joint investigation /几家电视台～摄制的电视剧 TV play produced jointly by several television networks
联锁 liánsuǒ *also* "连锁" liánsuǒ linked together
联锁店 liánsuǒdiàn *also* "连锁店" liánsuǒdiàn chain store
联锁机构 liánsuǒ jīgòu 〈机械〉interlocking mechanism
联体 liántǐ *also* "连体" liántǐ joint body: ～婴 siamese twins
联网 liánwǎng network; network access
联席会议 liánxí huìyì joint conference; joint meeting: 参谋长～主席 (US) Chairman of the Joint Chiefs of Staff /本地区的几个单位举行～, 商讨治安联防问题。Several organizations in this area met to discuss measures for maintaining public security.
联系 liánxì ❶ contact; touch; connection; relation: 建立两国之间的～ establish a link between the two countries /有广泛的～ have wide connections /兄弟多年失去～。The two brothers have been out of touch for years. ❷ integrate; relate; link; get in touch with: 被共同利益～在一起 be linked together by mutual interest /理论～实际 integrate theory with practice /密切～群众 maintain close ties (*or* links) with the people /这两个事件应～起来看。The two events should be viewed as related. ❸ arrange; regotiate: ～工作 talk business /～旅馆 arrange for hotel accommodation
联想 liánxiǎng associate; connect in the mind: 引起丰富的文学～ arouse rich literary associations /由长城～到中国 connect (*or* associate) the Great Wall with China
联想存储器 liánxiǎng cúnchǔqì 〈计算机〉catalogue memory
联想集团 Liánxiǎng Jítuán Legend Group Ltd.
联销 liánxiāo establish trade connections to sell; jointly market: 搞～业务 engage in the establishment of trade connections and sales; go in for joint marketing
联谊 liányì friendship ties; fellowship: ～会 sodality; fraternity; sorority /～活动 social activities
联姻 liányīn 〈书面〉be related by marriage: 两家世代～。The two families have been related by marriage for generations.
联营 liányíng joint management: 这个煤矿由三个县～。The coal mine is jointly managed by three counties.
联运 liányùn 〈交通〉through transport; through traffic: 国际铁路～ international railway through transport /火车汽车～ train-and-bus coordinated transport /水陆～ land-and-water coordinated transport; through transport by land and water /～业务 through service /列车晚点, 他因而误了去上海的～火车。As the train was late, he missed the connection to Shanghai.
联运票 liányùnpiào through or connection ticket
联运提单 liányùn tídān through bill of lading
联展 liánzhǎn joint exhibit: 书画和摄影作品～ (joint) exhibit of calligraphy, paintings and photographs
联轴节 liánzhóujié 〈机械〉shaft coupling; coupling: 刚性～ rigid coupling /挠性～ flexible coupling /万向～ universal coupling (*or* joint)
联珠 liánzhū 〈书面〉string of pearls; 〈比喻〉beautiful poems: 缀玉～六十年 have been composing poems for sixty years
联属 liánzhǔ *also* "连属" liánzhǔ join; link
联装炮 liánzhuāngpào 〈军事〉multiple gun
联缀 liánzhuì *also* "连缀" liánzhuì join together
联宗 liánzōng acknowledge as derived from the same lineage; treat as member of the same clan: 他们联了宗, 以兄弟相称。They have joined together as a clan and call one another brothers (*or* cousins).

奁(奩、匳、匲、籢) lián

toilet case used by women in ancient China: 妆～ dowry; trousseau
奁仪 liányí 〈书面〉gift to the bride's family
奁资 liánzī dowry; trousseau; portion

连[1] lián

❶ link; join; connect: ～成一片 join together /藕断丝～ the lotus root snaps but its fibres stay joined; apparently severed, actually still connected /书房与起居室相～。The study connects with the living room. ❷ in succession; one after another; repeatedly; continuously: ～战～北 be defeated in one battle after another /～看两场电影 see two movies in succession /～赢了三场 won the game three times running ❸ including: 这次～我一共去了十人。Ten people went there this time, including me. ❹〈军事〉company: 他率领三个～参加了战斗。He led three companies into battle. ❺ (Lián) a surname

连[2] lián

even: 你怎么～我都不认识了? How could you fail even to recognize me? /他惊讶得～话都说不出。He was too astonished even to speak.
连本带利 liánběn-dàilì both principal and interest; capital and profit: ～一共三万元。There is 30,000 *yuan* altogether, including the principal and the interest.
连比 liánbǐ 〈数学〉continued ratio
连镳并轸 liánbiāo-bìngzhěn run neck and neck; keep abreast; be on a par: 他们兄弟两人～, 在文坛上都小有名气。Both brothers enjoy some reputation in literary circles.
连鬓胡子 liánbìn húzi full beard
连播 liánbō chain or serial broadcast: 长篇～ broadcast a novel serially
连补 liánbu 〈方言〉sew and mend: 衣服破了～一下再穿。The coat is torn and needs mending before wearing.
连茬 liánchá 〈农业〉continuous cropping
连词 liáncí 〈语言〉conjunction
连乘法 liánchéngfǎ 〈数学〉continued multiplication
连带 liándài ❶ related; connected: 人的气质与教养是有～关系的。One's disposition is related to one's upbringing. ❷ involve; implicate: 他犯了案, ～我也要交代问题。As I was implicated in his case, I had to give depositions. ❸ incidentally; in passing: 洗床罩时, ～把枕套也洗一下。When you wash the bedcover, you may do the pillowcase as well. ❹〈法律〉joint: ～权利 joint right /～保证人 joint guarantor /～债务人 joint debtor /～费用 joint expense
连…带… lián…dài… ❶ *indicating the inclusion of two items*: 连筐带苹果一共九十斤。The apples weigh ninety *jin*, including the basket. /连主带客一共七个人。There are altogether seven people, counting both the host and the guests. ❷ *indicating that one action follows another or that two actions occur almost simultaneously*: 连讽刺带挖苦 taunt and mock /连说带笑 talking and laughing
连带责任 liándài zérèn 〈法律〉joint liability
连裆裤 liándāngkù ❶ child's pants with no slit in the seat ❷ (used in 穿～ only) band together; collude; gang up: 他俩向来穿～, 这里谁不知道? Everybody here knows that the two of them always band together.
连队 liánduì 〈军事〉company
连发 liánfā 〈军事〉continuous fire (as of an automatic rifle): ～手枪 repeating pistol /～枪 repeating rifle; magazine gun /～射击 burst (of fire) /～连中 fire several shots and all hit the target
连分数 liánfēnshù 〈数学〉continued fraction
连杆 liángǎn 〈机械〉connecting rod
连根拔 liángēnbá tear up by the roots; root out; eliminate; eradicate
连亘 liángèn 〈书面〉continuous: 万千大山, ～不断 continuous stretch of mountains
连拱坝 liángǒngbà 〈水利〉multiple-arch dam; multi-arch dam
连拱桥 liángǒngqiáo multiple-arch bridge; multi-arch bridge

连贯 liánguàn *also* "联贯" liánguàn ❶ link up; join together; piece together: 小桥把湖心岛和堤岸～起来了。The small bridge links the islet in the middle of the lake to the embankment. ❷ coherent; consistent: ～性 coherence; continuity /这几句话的意思上下不～。The sentences are inconsistent in meaning (*or* incoherent).

连锅端 liánguōduān remove or destroy lock, stock and barrel; get rid of the whole lot: 匪巢被～了。The bandit's lair was completely destroyed. /整个工厂～，迁到远郊区去了。The whole factory was moved to the outskirts of the city.

连环 liánhuán chain of rings: ～债 debt chain /～锁 interlock /～雷 interlinked mines /～针脚〈纺织〉loop stitch

连环保 liánhuánbǎo 〈旧语〉administrative system organized on the basis of households, holding each responsible for the action of others

连环画 liánhuánhuà book (usu. for children) with a story told in pictures; picture-story book

连环计 liánhuánjì set of interlocking stratagems; series of stratagems

连环漫画 liánhuán mànhuà comic strip; comics; strip cartoon

连环套 liánhuántào interrelated matters; series of closely-linked matters

连击 liánjī 〈体育〉double hit

连枷 liánjiā *also* "梿枷" liánjiā 〈农业〉flail

连家船 liánjiāchuán boat of those who live on the water; houseboat

连家铺 liánjiāpù *also* "连家店" store with the back serving as living quarters

连脚裤 liánjiǎokù infant's pants with stockings attached

连接 liánjiē *also* "联接" liánjiē join; link: ～(各岛屿)的水域 interconnecting waters /回廊将正房与厢房～起来。The verandas join the main house with the wings. /高楼一幢～着一幢。The buildings stand closely side by side.

连接号 liánjiēhào 〈语言〉hyphen

连接酶 liánjiēméi 〈生化〉ligase

连接线 liánjiēxiàn 〈音乐〉tie

连结 liánjié *also* "联结" liánjié join; link; connect; combine

连衿 liánjīn *see* "连襟"

连襟 liánjīn *also* "连衿"; "连袂" husbands of sisters: 他是我的～。He is my brother-in-law.

连裤袜 liánkùwà panty hose

连类 liánlèi join things of the same kind together to form a whole

连累 liánlei implicate; involve; get (sb.) into trouble: 千万不能～朋友 never get one's friends into trouble /他无缘无故地受到～。He was implicated for no reason at all.

连理 liánlǐ 〈书面〉❶ trees or plants whose branches interlock or join together: 木～ trees with joint branches /嘉禾～ fine seedlings intertwining together /在天愿为比翼鸟，在地愿为～枝。In the heavens may we be like birds that fly wing to wing; And on earth may we be like trees whose branches intertwine. ❷ marital love; loving couple: 结为～ get married

连理枝 liánlǐzhī *see* "连理"

连连 liánlián repeatedly; again and again: ～称赞 praise repeatedly /～摇头 shake one's head again and again

连忙 liánmáng promptly; quickly; at once: 老大娘一上车，他～让座。When the old woman got on the bus, he hastened to offer her his seat.

连袂 liánmèi ❶ *also* "联袂" liánmèi 〈书面〉join sleeves — come or go hand in hand ❷ *see* "连襟"

连绵 liánmián *also* "联绵" liánmián continuous; unbroken; uninterrupted: 阴雨～ succession of rainy days /～不断的思绪 unbroken train of thought

连年 liánnián in successive years; in consecutive years; for years running; for years on end: 灾荒～ successive years of famine /～丰收 reap rich (*or* bumper) harvests for many years running /农民的收入～增加。The farmers' income has increased year after year.

连皮 liánpí (weight of goods) including the packing; gross (weight): 这筐西红柿～五十三斤。The basket of tomatoes weighs 53 *jin*, including the packing.

连翩 liánpiān *also* "联翩" liánpiān in close succession; together

连篇 liánpiān ❶ one article after another; multitude of articles: ～满幅，洋洋数万言。The series of articles ran to many pages and thousands of words. ❷ throughout a piece of writing; page after page: 白字～ pages and pages of wrongly written characters /空话～ empty verbiage galore

连篇累牍 liánpiān-lěidú lengthy and tedious; at great length: ～地发表文章 publish a whole string of articles /～的空话 endless empty talk

连谱号 liánpǔhào 〈音乐〉accolade; brace

连气 liánqì coherent; consistent: 他心里一慌，话都说不～了。He was in a fit of fury and couldn't even talk coherently.

连气儿 liánqìr 〈方言〉on end; in a row; in succession: 一～干了五天夜班 work on night shift for five days at a stretch /～喝了两碗粥 have two bowls of gruel in succession

连翘 liánqiáo 〈中药〉capsule of weeping forsythia (*Forsythia suspensa*)

连任 liánrèn be reappointed or reelected consecutively; renew one's term of office: 他在竞选中～州长。He was reelected governor in the election.

连日 liánrì for days on end; day after day: 阴雨绵绵，～不晴。It has been raining for days on end.

连射 liánshè 〈军事〉continuous fire (as of an automatic rifle)

连声 liánshēng repeatedly; again and again: ～叫好 applaud repeatedly /～称赞 praise again and again

连史纸 liánshǐzhǐ fine paper made from bamboo (produced in Jiangxi Province)

连手 liánshǒu 〈方言〉❶ related; relevant: 那些～的事情都需要弄清。All related matters should be clarified. ❷ cooperator; partner; collaborator: 过去你那个老～当了主任了。Your former partner is now a director.

连书 liánshū joining of syllables in Chinese phonetic transcription, e.g. rénmín (人民), tuōlājī (拖拉机)

连锁 liánsuǒ chain; linkage: ～图 linkage map

连锁店 liánsuǒdiàn chain store: 现在北京到处都有～。Nowadays chain stores are to be seen everywhere in Beijing.

连锁反应 liánsuǒ fǎnyìng chain reaction; sequence of events: 市场扩大了就会引起生产上的～。Expansion of the market will set off a chain reaction in production.

连台本戏 liántái běnxì 〈戏曲〉drama serial

连体 liántǐ *see* "联体" liántǐ

连天 liántiān ❶ for days on end; day after day: ～连夜 for days and nights running /～赶路 hurry on with one's journey day after day ❷ incessantly: 叫苦～ incessantly complain to high heaven; make endless complaints ❸ reaching or scraping the sky: 炮火～。Gunfire licked the heavens. /远处芳草～。The grassland seems to merge with the sky in the distance.

连铁 liántiě 〈方言〉iron clappers used by a knife-sharpener to attract customers

连通 liántōng *also* "联通" liántōng connect; lead to; link up: 大桥已于昨天～。The bridge was connected yesterday. / 海底隧道即可～。The undersea tunnel is to be cut through.

连通器 liántōngqì communicating vessel; connecting vessel: ～平衡定律 law of equilibrium in connected vessels

连同 liántóng together with; along with: 鸡蛋～牛奶一起从农场运走。The eggs were delivered from the farm along with the milk.

连谓式 liánwèishì 〈语言〉sentence with consecutive predicates

连香树 liánxiāngshù katsura tree (*Cercidiphyllum japonicum*)

连宵 liánxiāo 〈方言〉*see* "连夜"

连写 liánxiě *see* "连书"

连续 liánxù continuous; successive; in a row; running: ～加班 work several extra shifts without stop /～受挫 suffer one setback after another /～性 continuity; continuance /他～两天上课迟到。Two days in a row he was late for class. /她把那曲子～弹了三遍。She played the tune three times.

连续波 liánxùbō continuous waves (CW)

连续光谱 liánxù guāngpǔ continuous spectrum

连续函数 liánxù hánshù continuous function

连续剧 liánxùjù serial: 电视～ TV serial

连续摄影机 liánxù shèyǐngjī continuous motion camera; continuous strip camera; sequence camera

连选连任 liánxuǎn liánrèn be reelected and serve another term

连夜 liányè ❶ same night; that very night: 孩子的父亲～赶进城。The boy's father rushed to town that very night. ❷ several nights running: 家家户户～打场。All families worked on the threshing ground for several nights running.

连衣裤 liányīkù catsuit; jumpsuit
连衣裙 liányīqún (women's) one-piece dress
连阴天 liányīntiān cloudy or rainy weather for several days running
连阴雨 liányīnyǔ rain for several days on end
连用 liányòng use consecutively; use together：何必～几个修饰语。It is not necessary to use several modifiers together.
连载 liánzǎi publish in instalments; serialize：报刊～ serialize in the newspaper /长篇～ serial of a novel
连轧 liánzhá 〈冶金〉tandem rolling：～机 tandem mill
连长 liánzhǎng company commander
连中三元 liánzhòng-sānyuán ❶〈旧语〉come out first in the imperial civil examinations at the provincial capital, the national capital, and the palace successively ❷ succeed in three successive examinations; win three matches in succession; win three points in a row; score three times in a row：足球赛中一人～ score a hat trick in a football match /客队～，以四比二结束比赛。The visiting team scored three goals in succession and won the game by four to two.
连种 liánzhòng *see* "连作"
连轴转 liánzhóuzhuàn work continuously day and night; work round the clock：这样白天黑夜～，谁也受不了。No one can stand working day and night like this.
连珠 liánzhū like a chain of pearls or a string of beads; in rapid succession：妙语～ pearls of wisdom; sparkling sayings /捷报～似地传来。News of victory came pouring in.
连珠箭 liánzhūjiàn volley of arrows; continuous sequence (of things)：他～似的喝了几杯酒。He gulped down several cups of wine.
连珠炮 liánzhūpào continuous firing; drumfire：说话像～似的 speak at machine-gun pace; chatter away like a machine gun /记者～似的向他提问。Reporters bombarded him with questions. *or* Reporters fired questions at him.
连属 liánzhǔ *also* "联属" liánzhǔ join; link：～成篇 join (pieces) to form a complete whole /两地～。The two areas are linked up.
连铸 liánzhù 〈冶金〉continuous casting：全～ continuous casting /～法 continuous metal cast process /～机 conticaster; continuous caster /立弯式～机 continuous casting machine with bending device
连缀 liánzhuì *also* "联缀" liánzhuì ❶ join together; put together：如把这些情节～起来就更加生动了。If these plots are threaded together, the story will be even more vivid. ❷〈语言〉cluster：辅音～ consonant cluster
连字号 liánzìhào 〈语言〉hyphen (-)
连奏 liánzòu 〈音乐〉legato
连作 liánzuò *also* "连种"；"连茬"；"重茬" chóngchá continuous cropping
连坐 liánzuò be punished for being related to or friendly with sb. who has committed an offence：实行～ put households or people (of a certain area) under joint responsibility for each other's action

涟

lián 〈书面〉❶ ripples ❷ continual flow (of tears)：泣涕～～ continual flow of tears; streaming with tears
涟虫 liánchóng hooded shrimp
涟洏 lián'ér 〈书面〉cry continuously; weep profusely：涕泪～ weep copiously
涟漪 liányī 〈书面〉ripples：水面泛起～。Ripples appeared on the water surface.

裢

lián *see* "褡裢" dālian

莲

lián ❶ *also* "荷" hé；"芙蓉" fúróng；"芙蕖" fúqú 〈植物〉lotus ❷ lotus seed：建～ lotus seeds produced in Fujian; Fujian lotus seeds
莲步 liánbù 〈书面〉graceful steps of a beauty：轻移～ take light, graceful steps
莲菜 liáncài 〈方言〉lotus root (as food)
莲房 liánfáng 〈书面〉❶ seedpod of the lotus ❷ monk's bedroom
莲花 liánhuā lotus flower; lotus：养几盆～ keep some pots of lotus
莲花白 liánhuābái 〈方言〉cabbage
莲花落 liánhuālào 〈戏曲〉popular ballad sung to the accompaniment of bamboo clappers with every stanza ending in "～，落莲花"
莲花纹 liánhuāwén lotus flower design
莲灰 liánhuī pale purplish grey
莲藕 lián'ǒu lotus and its root; lotus root：～同根 joined together like lotus and its root; with inseparable relations
莲蓬 liánpeng seedpod of the lotus
莲蓬头 liánpengtóu 〈方言〉shower nozzle
莲蓬子儿 liánpengzǐr ❶〈植物〉lotus seed ❷ lotus-seed-shaped (usu. small) things
莲肉 liánròu edible part of lotus seed
莲台 liántái *see* "莲座❷"
莲心 liánxīn ❶ plumule of lotus seed; heart of lotus seed ❷〈方言〉lotus seed
莲子 liánzǐ lotus seed
莲宗 Liánzōng *also* "净土宗" Jìngtǔzōng 〈佛教〉Pure Land Sect
莲座 liánzuò ❶ bottom of lotus flower (like an inverted cone) ❷ Buddha's seat in the form of a lotus flower; lotus throne

梿

lián
梿枷 liánjiā *also* "连枷" liánjiā flail

鲢

lián *also* "鲊" xù silver carp：～鱼 silver carp

liǎn

琏

liǎn 〈古语〉utensil for offering grain in an ancestral temple

裣(襝)

liǎn
裣衽 liǎnrèn *see* "敛衽❷" liǎnrèn

敛(斂)

liǎn ❶〈书面〉hold back; keep back; restrain：收～ restrain oneself; pull in one's horns ❷ collect：横征暴～ extort heavy taxes and levies
敛步 liǎnbù 〈书面〉hold one's step; halt; stop
敛财 liǎncái accumulate wealth by unfair or illegal means：在任数年，专事～ be bent on amassing a fortune during one's years in office
敛迹 liǎnjì 〈书面〉❶ temporarily desist from one's evil ways; go into hiding; lie low：盗匪～。The bandits went into hiding. ❷ restrain oneself：屏气～ hold one's breath and pull in one's horns ❸ go into retirement：～山林 live in deep mountains as a hermit (*or* recluse)
敛眉 liǎnméi 〈书面〉knit or contract one's brows; frown：～而立 stand with one's brows knit; stand with knit brows
敛袂 liǎnmèi 〈书面〉trim oneself up to show respect：～而往朝 trim oneself up to be presented at court
敛钱 liǎnqián collect money：挨家挨户～ collect money from door to door /敛了五十块钱 raised fifty *yuan*
敛衽 liǎnrèn 〈书面〉❶ trim or tidy oneself up to show respect：～而拜 trim oneself before bowing ❷ *also* "裣衽" liǎnrèn (of a woman) greet by holding lower corners of one's jacket
敛容 liǎnróng 〈书面〉assume a serious expression：在座之人，无不～。Everybody present looked serious.
敛声屏气 liǎnshēng-bǐngqì lower one's voice and hold one's breath：在他面前，人们无不～。In his presence, everyone was awed into silence.
敛手 liǎnshǒu 〈书面〉❶ draw back one's hand; shrink from doing sth.：诸侯～而事秦。The dukes had to wait on the State of Qin hand and foot. ❷ make an obeisance by cupping one hand in the other before one's chest
敛抑 liǎnyì restrain oneself：日后我一定深自～，再不做这等蠢事了。In the future I will restrain myself and try not to do such foolish things.
敛足 liǎnzú 〈书面〉check one's steps and not go forward; halt：屏息～ halt with bated breath

蔹(蘞)

liǎn *see* "白蔹" báiliǎn

脸(臉)

liǎn ❶ face：宽～ broad face /太阳晒黑的～ suntanned face /～上有个疤。There is a scar on the face. ❷ front：门～ outside of the gate of a courtyard house or of a city; front of a shop /鞋～儿 front of a shoe; instep ❸ face; sensibilities; credit：丢～ lose face; lose credit /争～ win credit /露～ become known; be

L

successful /没～没皮 shameless; brazen /居然有～说 have the impudence to say /撕破了～ put aside all considerations of face; not spare sb.'s sensibilities ❹ countenance; facial expression; face: 变了～ change one's countenance /笑～相迎 greet with a smiling face /做鬼～ make a face; make grimaces /他沉下～来。His face clouded (*or* darkened).

脸薄 liǎnbáo thin-skinned; shy; bashful: 这孩子～，怕见生人。The child is shy of strangers.

脸大 liǎndà ❶ thick-skinned; unashamed: 她可真～，什么话都敢说。Nothing she says embarrasses her. ❷ have pull; enjoy high prestige: 你～，他会听你的。You are widely respected, so no doubt he'll listen to you. *or* You've got the standing (*or* prestige) to make him do as you say.

脸蛋儿 liǎndànr *also* "脸蛋子" (mostly used with young people) cheeks; face: 红扑扑的～ ruddy cheeks

脸憨皮厚 liǎnhān-píhòu thick-skinned; shameless: 大家都不理睬他，但他～，根本不在乎。Nobody pays any attention to him, but he is thick-skinned and doesn't care a damn.

脸红 liǎnhóng ❶ blush with shame; blush: 你说瞎话也不～? Aren't you ashamed of telling a lie? /她一说话就～。She is sure to blush when she speaks. ❷ flush with anger; get excited; get worked up: 气得满脸通红 flush crimson with indignation /因激动而～ be flushed with excitement

脸红脖子粗 liǎn hóng bózi cū get red in the face from anger or excitement; flush with agitation: 他们俩吵得～的，谁也不让谁。The two argued so excitedly that neither would give in. /为这一点小事争得～，也值得? What's the use of getting worked up over such trifles?

脸红耳赤 liǎnhóng-ěrchì flush up to one's ears (with anger or shame); become red in the face and ears: ～地吼了一声 roar with a flushed face /臊得～ blush up to one's ears

脸厚 liǎnhòu thick-skinned; shameless; brazen: 你别以为她～，其实她是个爽快人。Don't take her for an impudent girl. In fact she has quite a frank and open personality.

脸急 liǎnjí hot-tempered; irritable: 这个人～，可别惹他。He is an irascible person, so don't rub him the wrong way (*or* don't cross him).

脸颊 liǎnjiá cheeks; face: 红润的～ rosy cheeks /汗珠子顺着～直往下淌。Beads of sweat are streaming down her face.

脸孔 liǎnkǒng face: ～红红的 flushed face /她用手掩住了～。She buried her face in her hands. *or* She covered her face with her hands.

脸面 liǎnmiàn ❶ face: 他～总是洗得干干净净的。He always keeps his face clean. ❷ self-respect; sensibilities; feelings: 看在我的～上，就饶了他这一次吧。For my sake, let him off this time. /我想不答应，可～上又过不去。I didn't want to agree to their request, but just couldn't bring myself to say no.

脸模儿 liǎnmor 〈方言〉 ❶ facial features; face: 她～长得挺俊。She's got a pretty face. *or* She is pretty. ❷ complexion; colour: 你这几天～挺好。You look very well these days.

脸嫩 liǎnnèn thin-skinned; shy; bashful: 这孩子就是～，见着生人不爱讲话。The child is shy and always keeps quiet before strangers.

脸盘儿 liǎnpánr *also* "脸盘子" cast of one's face: 她长得圆～，白白净净的，眉清目秀。She is a fair, round-faced girl with fine features.

脸庞 liǎnpáng *see* "脸盘儿"

脸盆 liǎnpén washbasin; washbowl: ～架 washstand

脸皮 liǎnpí ❶ skin of the face: 白净的～ fair skin /黑黄的～ dark and sallow complexion ❷ feelings; sensibilities: 熟人面前撕不破～。It's hard for one not to consider the sensibilities of one's friends. ❸ face; cheeks; sense of shame: ～厚 thick-skinned; shameless /羞得她没～见人。She was so ashamed that she didn't have the nerve to meet people.

脸谱 liǎnpǔ 〈戏曲〉 type of facial make-up: 京剧人物～ types of facial make-up in Beijing opera /勾～ draw facial make-up (in operas)

脸热 liǎnrè ❶ *see* "脸软" ❷ feel hot in the face; blush; be bashful; be shy: 他听了这话，觉得有点～。He blushed slightly at the remarks.

脸容 liǎnróng appearance; looks: 俊俏的～ pretty and charming looks /～严肃 stern appearance

脸软 liǎnruǎn be prone to spare others' feelings; have too much consideration for others' sensibilities: 他为人～，总不好意思拒绝别人的要求。He never has the heart to refuse other's requests.

脸腮 liǎnsāi cheek: 红润润的～ ruddy cheeks /泪水顺着他那多皱的～淌下来。Tears rolled down his wrinkled cheeks.

脸色 liǎnsè ❶ colour of the face; complexion; look: 白皙的～ fair complexion /～苍白 pale complexion /从海滨休养回来后，你～比过去好多了。Since you returned from the seaside sanatorium, you have looked much better. /他这几天～不好。He has been off colour these few days. ❷ facial expression; countenance: ～严峻 be stern-faced / 听了这个消息，她的～刷地白了。She turned pale immediately at the news. /中国奉行独立外交政策，从来不看别人～行事。China pursues an independent foreign policy and never takes cues from others.

脸上贴金 liǎnshang-tiējīn cover the face with gold leaf or foil — gild; touch up; prettify: 你别再往自己～了! Don't put feathers in your own cap! *or* Don't go blowing your own trumpet!

脸上无光 liǎnshang-wúguāng make sb. lose face; lose face: 你这种表现，做父母的也～。Your behaviour has brought discredit on your parents.

脸水 liǎnshuǐ basin of water for washing one's face

脸膛儿 liǎntángr 〈方言〉 face: 四方～ square face /晒黑的～ tanned face

脸相 liǎnxiàng facial features; looks; appearance: 他的～端正。He has regular features. /她瞪大了眼睛，显出了吃惊的～。She stared with astonishment.

脸小 liǎnxiǎo ❶ (often used of girls) thin-skinned; shy; bashful ❷ enjoy little respect; have scant prestige; have little pull: 我就知道我的～，请不动你这位大人物。I know I don't have any clout, and a VIP like you wouldn't come just for my sake.

脸形 liǎnxíng *also* "脸型" facial contour or shape: ～端正 have regular features

脸硬 liǎnyìng not easily persuaded to give in; not sparing people's feelings

脸子 liǎnzi 〈方言〉 ❶ (usu. informal) pretty face, looks, or appearance: 有一副好～ have a pretty face; have good looks ❷ unpleasant facial expression: 他不会因此给你～看的。Surely he won't chew you out for that. ❸ face; feelings; sensibilities: 要～的人 one who minds his (*or* her) own prestige; face-loving person

liàn

恋(戀) liàn ❶ love; love affair: 初～ being in love for the first time; first love /早～ calf-love; schoolgirl (*or* schoolboy) infatuation; puppy-love /失～ be disappointed in love; be love-lorn / 热～ be passionately in love /单～ unrequited love /黄昏～ love at old age /婚外～ extramarital affair ❷ long for; feel attached to: 留～ can't bear to part; recall with nostalgia /眷～ be sentimentally attached to (a person or place)

恋爱 liàn'ài love; be in love; have a courtship; have a love affair: 谈～ be in love; have a love affair /男女～ love between man and woman /自由～ freedom to arrange one's own marriage; free courtship /他俩～了三年才结婚。They had been in love for three years before they got married.

恋本 liànběn nostalgic; homesick: ～之情 nostalgia /人心～。People as a rule are nostalgic.

恋豆 liàndòu 〈书面〉 *see* "恋栈"

恋歌 liàngē love song: 缠绵的～ sentimental love song

恋家 liànjiā be reluctant to leave one's home; be deeply attached to one's home: 他们的孩子太～，不愿意到外地去上大学。Their child is too attached to his home to leave his native town for college. *or* Their boy is too much of a homebody to go to college in another town.

恋旧 liànjiù be homesick; be nostalgic: 老人常～。Old people are apt to yearn for the past.

恋恋不舍 liànliàn-bùshě reluctant to part with; hate to see sb. go: 心中～ feel reluctant to leave /他～地望着送行的人们。Looking at those who came to see him off, he found it hard to tear himself away.

恋慕 liànmù adore; admire; be sentimentally attached to (a person or place): 他话语中露出无限的～之情。His remarks betrayed his unbounded admiration.

恋念 liànniàn have a tender feeling for; think fondly of: 侨胞们～着祖国。The overseas Chinese nationals are affectionately attached to their motherland.

L

恋情 liànqíng ❶ attachment; affection:他对这工作过多年的地方至今仍怀着~。He cherishes a deep affection for the place where he worked for many years. ❷ love:动人的~ touching (*or* moving) love

恋群 liànqún ❶ be attached to one's own people:这人~,老忘不了儿时的伙伴。He had a great attachment to his childhood friends who were constantly in his mind. ❷ (of animals) be gregarious:猴子~。The monkey is a gregarious animal.

恋人 liànrén lover; sweetheart

恋头 liàntou worth missing:这个窑洞还有什么~? Is there anything worth missing about this cave dwelling?

恋土 liàntǔ 〈书面〉nostalgic; homesick; reluctant to leave one's hometown:谁无~之情? Who is free from nostalgia?

恋窝 liànwō (of birds) reluctant to leave the roost during the incubation period

恋战 liànzhàn be over-zealous in fighting:不敢~ have to disengage oneself from fighting

恋栈 liànzhàn *also* "恋豆" (originally of a horse) be attached to one's manger; 〈比喻〉cling to one's official post when one should leave:他虽然为官多年,但不存~之心。Although in office for years, he hasn't the slightest intention to hold fast to his official post.

楝 liàn

楝树 liànshù 〈植物〉chinaberry

炼(煉、鍊) liàn

❶ smelt; refine:~铜 smelt copper / 提~ extract and purify; abstract; refine ❷ burn; temper or test with fire:真金不怕火~。True gold does not fear the test of fire. ❸ polish; improve; refine: *see* "~句"; "~字"

炼丹 liàndān make pills of immortality (as a Taoist practice):~士 Taoist alchemist who tries to make such pills

炼钢 liàngāng steelmaking; steel-smelting:~设备 steelmaking equipment

炼钢厂 liàngāngchǎng steel mill; steelworks

炼钢工人 liàngāng gōngrén steelworker

炼钢炉 liàngānglú steelmaking or steelsmelting furnace

炼话 liànhuà 〈方言〉pithy expression:小说中有许多富有乡土气息的~。The novel teems with piquant expressions of local colour.

炼焦 liànjiāo coke; coking

炼焦厂 liànjiāochǎng coking plant; cokery

炼焦炉 liànjiāolú coke oven:~煤气 coke-oven gas

炼焦煤 liànjiāoméi coking coal

炼金术 liànjīnshù alchemy:~士 alchemist

炼句 liànjù work hard at improving one's diction; endeavour to find the best turn of phrase; polish and repolish a sentence:诗人在~上颇下苦功。The poet makes painstaking effort to polish up his lines.

炼气 liànqì *also* "练气" liànqì 〈书面〉do breathing exercises

炼乳 liànrǔ condensed milk

炼山 liànshān 〈林业〉burn grass, shrubs, and stumps for afforestation:秋后是~的好时机。Late autumn is the best time to burn grass, shrubs, and stumps for afforestation.

炼石补天 liànshí-bǔtiān (of legendary Chinese heroine Nüwa) melt down stones to repair the sky — display talent in remedying a situation

炼铁 liàntiě iron-smelting

炼铁厂 liàntiěchǎng ironworks; iron mill

炼铁炉 liàntiělú iron-smelting furnace; blast furnace

炼油 liànyóu ❶〈石油〉oil refining:~厂 (oil) refinery ❷ extract oil by heat ❸ heat edible oil

炼狱 liànyù ❶〈宗教〉purgatory, place where the soul of a dead person must be made pure by suffering according to Roman Catholic doctrine ❷ abyss of sufferings or misery:在~中挣扎度日 struggle for a bare subsistence in the abyss of misery

炼制 liànzhì 〈化工〉refine:石油~ petroleum refining

炼字 liànzì weigh one's words (while writing); rack one's brains for the right word; try to find *le mot juste*:大凡诗人,无不在~上刻意求工。As a rule, poets sedulously strive for perfection in the choice of words.

练(練) liàn

❶ white silk:澄江如~。The limpid river lies as smooth as silk. ❷〈书面〉boil and scour raw silk:黄缯~成素。The yellow silk is scoured white. ❸ practise; train; drill:训~ train; drill / 排~ rehearse / ~骑车 practise cycling; learn to ride a bicycle / ~气功 do breathing exercises / ~好功夫 perfect one's skill (in martial arts, etc.) / ~好身体 do exercises to keep fit; build up one's physique / 勤学苦~ study diligently and train hard ❹ experienced; skilled; seasoned:老~ experienced and assured / 干~ capable and seasoned / 熟~ skilled; practised; proficient ❺ (Liàn) a surname

练笔 liànbǐ ❶ practise writing ❷ practise calligraphy

练兵 liànbīng ❶ troop training; drill ❷ training:~项目 training courses

练兵场 liànbīngchǎng drill ground; parade ground

练操 liàncāo (of troops, etc.) drill:每天要练两个小时的操 have to drill for two hours every day

练达 liàndá 〈书面〉experienced and worldly-wise:人情~ be wise to the ways of the world / ~老成 experienced and prudent

练队 liànduì drill in formation; drill for a parade

练功 liàngōng do exercises in gymnastics, *wushu*, acrobatics, etc.; practise one's skill:~房 gym / 老人天天在公园里~。The old man practises kung fu in the park every day. / 演员正在~。The actors are practising.

练家子 liànjiāzi 〈方言〉person who is skilled in martial arts; kung fu expert

练漂 liànpiǎo 〈纺织〉scouring and bleaching

练球 liànqiú practise a ball game:赛前~ warm-up (before a match); knock-up / 这个队每天~四小时。The team practises for four hours each day.

练鹊 liànquè *also* "绶带鸟" shòudàiniǎo 〈动物〉long-tailed flycatcher

练手 liànshǒu practise one's skill; keep one's hand in

练条机 liàntiáojī 〈纺织〉reducer

练武 liànwǔ ❶ learn or practise *wushu*:~习文 practise *wushu* and writing ❷ learn or practise military skills ❸ learn or practise a skill

练习 liànxí ❶ practise; learn:~游泳 learn (how) to swim / ~武艺 practise *wushu* / ~讲英语 learn to speak English; practise speaking English ❷ exercise:做~ do exercises / ~簿 exercise-book / ~题 problems of an exercise; exercise / ~曲〈音乐〉étude / 老师布置了很多~。The teacher has assigned us a lot of exercises.

鰊 liàn

also "鲱" fēi Pacific herring

潋(瀲) liàn

潋滟 liànyàn 〈书面〉❶ flooding; overflowing:金樽~ gold cup brimful with wine ❷ rippling, wavy:湖光~ sparkling (*or* glistening) lake

殓(殮) liàn

put a body into a coffin; encoffin:入~ put a corpse in a coffin; encoffin / ~葬 put (a dead body) in a coffin and bury it

殓衣 liànyī clothes put on the dead body; grave clothes; cerements

链(鍊) liàn

❶ chain:铁~ iron chain / 锚~ anchor chain; anchor cable / 项~ necklace / 锁~ chain; shackles; fetters ❷ cable length (= $\frac{1}{10}$ of a nautical mile, or 185.2m)

链扳手 liànbānshou chain wrench

链板 liànbǎn 〈机械〉link joint:~输送机 drag conveyer; scraper chain conveyer; chain and flight conveyer

链泵 liànbèng chain pump

链传动 liànchuándòng 〈机械〉chain drive; chain transmission:~装置 chain gearing

链带 liàndài 〈机械〉link belt; chain belt:~式干燥机 continuous band dryer

链斗式提升机 liàndǒushì tíshēngjī continuous bucket elevator; endless belt conveyer

链斗式挖掘机 liàndǒushì wājuéjī ladder excavator; chain-bucket excavator

链反应 liànfǎnyìng *see* "链式反应"

链钩 liàngōu 〈机械〉chain hook; sling

链轨 liànguǐ *also*“履带”lǚdài caterpillar track (of a tractor)
链合 liànhé 〈化学〉linkage
链化合物 liànhuàhéwù 〈化学〉chain compound
链接 liànjiē 〈机械〉catenate; chaining
链节 liànjié 〈机械〉chain element; chain link
链锯 liànjù chain saw
链轮 liànlún 〈机械〉chain wheel or gear; chain pulley; sprocket; sprocket gear wheel:～绞车 sprocket winch /～铣刀 sprocket cutter
链霉素 liànméisù 〈药学〉streptomycin
链钳 liànqián chain tongs
链球 liànqiú ❶ hammer event:～冠军 champion in the hammer event /～项目的比赛正在进行。The hammer competition is going on. ❷ hammer:掷～ throw the hammer; hammer throw
链球菌 liànqiújūn 〈微生物〉streptococcus:白色～ streptococcus albus / 脓～ streptococcus pyogenes
链上取代 liànshàng qǔdài 〈化学〉chain substitution
链式反应 liànshì fǎnyìng *also*“连锁反应”liánsuǒ fǎnyìng 〈物理〉〈化学〉chain reaction
链式磨木机 liànshì mómùjī caterpillar grinder; chain grinder
链式运输机 liànshì yùnshūjī 〈机械〉chain conveyer
链套 liàntào chain case
链条 liàntiáo ❶ (transmission) chain ❷〈方言〉roller chain (of a bicycle); chain
链烃 liàntīng 〈化学〉chain hydrocarbon
链烷 liànwán 〈化学〉alkane:～醇 alkanol /～酸脂 alkanoate
链烷烃 liànwántīng 〈化学〉paraffin; paraffin hydrocarbons
链烯 liànxī 〈化学〉alkene:～基 alkenyl /～衍生物 alkeno-derivative; alkano-derivative
链罩 liànzhào chain guard; chain cover
链子 liànzi ❶ chain:铁～ iron chain ❷〈口语〉roller chain; chain: 车～生锈了。The roller chain got rusty.

liáng

粱 liáng 〈书面〉❶ fine strain of millet ❷ fine grain; choice (staple) food:膏～ fat meet and fine grain; choice food /膏～子弟 young men spoilt on rich food; good-for-nothing sons of the idle rich
粱肉 liángròu 〈书面〉fine grain and meat; good food

梁[1]**(樑)** liáng ❶ roof beam:上～ upper beam /架～ set a roof beam in place /房～ roof beam /顶～柱 pillar ❷ purlin:正～ ridge purlin /二～ second purlin ❸ bridge:桥～ bridge /津～ ferry crossing and bridge; means of transition; guide to learning ❹ ridge:山～ mountain ridge /鼻～ bridge of the nose; nose ridge

梁[2] Liáng ❶ name adopted by the State of Wei (403-225 BC) after its capital was moved to 大梁 (today's Kaifeng, Henan Province) in 361 BC during the Warring States Period ❷ Liang Dynasty (502-557), one of the Southern Dynasties ❸ Later Liang Dynasty (907-923), one of the Five Dynasties ❹ a surname
梁板结构 liángbǎn jiégòu 〈建筑〉contignation
梁地 liángdì *also*“墚地”liángdì land on a mountain ridge; ridge land
梁楷 Liáng Kǎi Liang Kai, painter of the Southern Song Dynasty
梁跨度 liángkuàdù 〈建筑〉beam span
梁龙 liánglóng 〈考古〉diplodocus
梁启超 Liáng Qǐchāo Liang Qichao (formerly translated as Liang Ch'i-ch'ao, 1873-1929), Chinese scholar and one of the leaders of the Reformist Movement of 1898
梁桥 liángqiáo beam bridge
梁上君子 liángshàng-jūnzǐ gentleman on the beam — burglar; thief:遭～光顾 be visited by a gentleman on the beam — be burgled (*or* burglarized)
梁子 liángzi ❶〈方言〉ridge (of a mountain or hill) ❷ story synopsis for an item of *quyi* or folk art performance, such as story telling, etc.

墚 liáng loess hillock in northwestern China
墚地 liángdì *see*“梁地”liángdì

凉(涼) liáng ❶ cool; cold:乘～ relax in a cool place / 受～ catch cold /阴～ shady and cool /天～了。It's getting cold. ❷ discouraged; disappointed:听说还有这么多工作要做，他心里一下就～了。His spirits sank when he heard how much work he still had to do.
see also liàng
凉白开 liángbáikāi 〈口语〉boiled water that has been chilled
凉拌 liángbàn (of food) cold and dressed with sauce:～茄泥 mashed eggplant mixed in sauce /～生菜 raw vegetable dressed in sauce; tossed salad
凉冰冰 liángbīngbīng chilly; cold:湿衣服贴在身上～的。The wet clothes felt chilly on one.
凉不丝儿 liángbusīr coolish; cool:热天喝杯～的啤酒真舒服。It's refreshing to drink a glass of cold beer in hot weather.
凉菜 liángcài cold dish
凉窗 liángchuāng 〈方言〉screen window
凉床 liángchuáng bamboo bed for summer
凉碟 liángdié cold dish (in a plate):他摆了几个～待客。He treated his guests to some cold dishes.
凉粉 liángfěn bean jelly
凉糕 liánggāo sweet cake made of glutinous rice, served cold
凉津津 liángjīnjīn somewhat chilly:微风吹得浑身～的 feel a bit chilly in the breeze
凉快 liángkuai ❶ nice and cool; pleasantly cool:一阵秋雨，天气～多了。It became pleasantly cool after a spell of autumn rain. ❷ cool oneself; cool off:在电扇下面～～ cool off under an electric fan
凉刺呱唧 liánglaguājī (unpleasantly) cold:这粥～的，我不想喝了。I don't feel like eating the gruel any more; it's already cold.
凉廊 liángláng 〈建筑〉loggia
凉了半截 liángle bànjié *also*“凉了半截子”heart chills with disappointment; be disheartened:听爸这么一说，我的心里就～。My heart sank at father's remarks.
凉帽 liángmào summer hat; sun hat
凉面 liángmiàn cold noodles dressed with sauce
凉棚 liángpéng ❶ mat-awning; mat shelter ❷〈比喻〉hand or hands spread out above one's eyes (to shelter them from strong light):手搭～往远处眺望 shelter one's eyes with one's hand and look into the distance
凉气 liángqì cool air:阵阵～ waves of cool (*or* cold) air /倒抽一口～ gasp with surprise, fear, etc.; be struck with terror, astonishment, etc.
凉伞 liángsǎn sunshade; parasol
凉森森 liángsēnsēn cold; chilly:一阵山风掠过，～的。It was rather chilly when a gust of wind from the mountain swept past.
凉薯 liángshǔ 〈方言〉yam bean
凉爽 liángshuǎng nice and cool; pleasantly cool:～的海风 pleasantly cool sea breeze
凉爽呢 liángshuǎngní 〈纺织〉a kind of dacron or terylene blended with wool
凉水 liángshuǐ ❶ cold water:用～洗澡 have a cold bath; bathe with cold water ❷ unboiled water:你喝～容易得病。You are liable to get ill if you drink unboiled water.
凉丝丝 liángsīsī coolish; rather cool; a bit cool:春风拂面，有点～的。The spring breeze feels a bit chilly on one's face.
凉飕飕 liángsōusōu (of wind) chilly; chill:初秋早晨的风～的。The early autumn wind was chilly in the morning.
凉台 liángtái balcony; veranda
凉亭 liángtíng wayside pavilion; summer house; kiosk
凉席 liángxí summer sleeping mat (of woven split bamboo, etc.)
凉鞋 liángxié sandals
凉药 liángyào 〈中药〉medicine of a cold nature (for reducing fever or inflammation); antipyretic
凉意 liángyì chill or nip in the air:初春时节，仍有～。The chill lingers in the early spring.

椋 liáng
椋鸟 liángniǎo starling

辌 liáng *see*“辒辌”wēnliáng

良 liáng ❶ good; fine:优～ fine; good; of high quality /善

L

～ good and honest; kindhearted /改～ improve; reform /消化不～ indigestion; dyspepsia ❷ good people: 除暴安～ weed out the wicked and enable the lawbiding citizens to live in peace /陷害忠～ frame up a good and loyal person /逼～为娼 force a virtuous woman (*or* girl) into prostitution; compel virtuous people to do sth. immoral ❸〈书面〉very; very much: ～深 very deep; quite profound /获益～多 benefit a great deal /用心～苦 have really given much thought to the matter ❹ (Liáng) a surname

良材 liángcái ❶ good timber ❷ talented people

良策 liángcè good plan; good idea; sound strategy: 别无～ have no other good plan /有何～? Have you got any good idea?

良辰 liángchén ❶ auspicious day; propitious time: 择～开张 choose an auspicious day for the opening of a shop ❷ fine day; pleasant time: ～难再。Pleasant times rarely repeat themselves. *or* Happy days do not last.

良辰吉日 liángchén-jírì bright and propitious day; auspicious occasion: 挑个～办喜事 choose a propitious day for a wedding

良辰美景 liángchén-měijǐng beautiful scene on a fine day; good weather coupled with beautiful scenery

良导体 liángdǎotǐ 〈物理〉good conductor

良方 liángfāng ❶ effective prescription or remedy; good recipe: ～集锦 collection of effective prescriptions ❷ good plan; sound strategy: 治国～ good plan to run a country

良港 liánggǎng fine or good harbour: 天然～ fine natural harbour

良工 liánggōng skilled worker

良工巧匠 liánggōng-qiǎojiàng *also* "能工巧匠" nénggōng-qiǎojiàng master craftsman; dab hand

良工心苦 liánggōng-xīnkǔ *also* "良工苦心" expert craftsmanship entails painstaking effort: 巧夺天工的艺术品, 无不出自～。All exquisite works of art come from the painstaking efforts of accomplished artists.

良弓 liánggōng good bow: 飞鸟尽, ～藏。〈谚语〉The good bow is put away when the birds have been shot down.

良贾深藏 liánggǔ-shēncáng a good trader keeps back valuable commodities — a man of learning does not show off his scholarship

良好 liánghǎo good; fine: ～的工作环境 good working conditions /～的结果 fine results /打下～的基础 lay a sound foundation /错过了～的时机 let slip an opportune moment (*or* good opportunity) /为双方会谈创造～的气氛 create an atmosphere favourable for bilateral talks /健康状况～ in the pink (of health) /～的开端, 意味着成功的一半。A good beginning means half the success — well begun is half done.

良机 liángjī 〈书面〉good or golden opportunity: 坐失～ lose a golden opportunity

良家 liángjiā good decent family: ～妇女 woman of good family

良家子 liángjiāzǐ child of a good family

良姜 liángjiāng 〈植物〉galangal

良将 liángjiàng fine general; capable or able general: 一代～ one of the best generals of his time

良金美玉 liángjīn-měiyù *also* "良金璞玉" pure gold and fine jade; good writing or fine painting; personal integrity

良久 liángjiǔ 〈书面〉good while; long time: 沉思～ ponder for a long time /叹息～ sigh for a good while

良吏 liánglì 〈书面〉good and honest official

良马 liángmǎ fine horse; fine steed

良民 liángmín 〈旧语〉❶ (distinct from 贱民) common people ❷ law-abiding people

良能 liángnéng 〈哲学〉intuitive ability
see also "良知良能"

良庖 liángpáo good cook: ～岁更刀。A good cook changes his knife once a year.

良朋 liángpéng good friend; true friend: ～好友 good friend

良禽择木 liángqín-zémù a good bird chooses the branch it perches on — a wise man chooses the right master to serve under: ～, 良将择主。As a good bird chooses the branch it perches upon, so a fine general chooses the liege lord he fights for.

良人 liángrén 〈古语〉❶ (used by a married woman) my good old man; my husband ❷ common people

良善 liángshàn ❶ good and honest; kindhearted: 心地～ kindhearted ❷〈书面〉good and honest people: 欺压～ bully and oppress good and honest people

良师益友 liángshī-yìyǒu good teacher and helpful friend: 广大青年读者都把他当作～。The young reading public considers him a good teacher and helpful friend.

良史之才 liángshǐ zhī cái talents of a good historian: 从问世的几部著作看, 作者有～。It is clear from his published works that the author has the makings of a good historian.

良田 liángtián good farmland; fertile farmland: 千亩～ a thousand *mu* of fertile farmland /荒地变～ turn the wilds into fertile land /～千顷, 不如薄艺随身。A thousand hectares of good farmland are less valuable than a humble craft one has learned.

良图 liángtú 〈书面〉❶ careful consideration ❷ good plan; sound strategy

良晤 liángwù 〈书面〉pleasant meeting: 望早日来京, 一图～。I am looking forward to your early arrival in the capital for a pleasant get-together.

良宵 liángxiāo 〈书面〉happy evening; pleasant night: 共度～ spend a happy evening together / 煮茗话～ enjoy a pleasant evening talking over tea

良心 liángxīn conscience: ～发现 be stung (*or* pricked) by conscience /受到～谴责 have a guilty (*or* bad) conscience; have a twinge of conscience; (of sth.) be on one's conscience /凭～说 to be fair; in all conscience /凭～办事 act according to one's conscience /昧着～说话 lie against one's conscience /丧尽～ be utterly conscienceless /有～的人 person of conscience; good-hearted person; person of gratitude /这个没～的, 早把我忘了! The ungrateful (*or* heartless) wretch! He's clean forgotten me.

良性 liángxìng ❶ good; favourable ❷ not malignant; benign: ～再发性血尿 benign recurrent hematuria

良性循环 liángxìng xúnhuán virtuous circle; beneficial cycle: 进入～ go (*or* enter) into a virtuous circle

良性肿瘤 liángxìng zhǒngliú 〈医学〉benign tumour: 切除～ remove a benign tumour

良言 liángyán good advice: ～相劝 kind admonition /金玉～ golden saying; invaluable advice

良药 liángyào good medicine; effective medicine

良药苦口 liángyào-kǔkǒu good medicine tastes bitter; bitter pills have good effects: ～利于病, 忠言逆耳利于行。〈谚语〉Just as bitter medicine cures sickness, so unpalatable advice benefits conduct.

良夜 liángyè 〈书面〉❶ lovely night ❷ late at night; in the small hours of the morning: ～静思 meditate late at night

良医 liángyī good doctor: 不为良相, 当为～。One should be a good doctor, if not a good prime minister.

良友 liángyǒu good friend; true friend

良莠不齐 liángyǒu-bùqí the good and the bad are intermingled: 人多了, 难免～, 这是不足为奇的事。It's no surprise that there are good as well as bad people in such a large crowd.

良缘 liángyuán happy fate which brings lovers together: 喜结～ be happily married

良知 liángzhī 〈哲学〉intuitive or innate knowledge

良知良能 liángzhī-liángnéng 〈哲学〉intuitive knowledge and innate ability

良种 liángzhǒng ❶〈农业〉improved variety or strain: 小麦～ improved strains of wheat /～场 seed multiplication farm ❷〈畜牧〉fine breed: ～耕畜 draught animals of fine breeds

粮(糧) liáng

❶ grain; food; provisions: 食～ foodgrain /粗～ coarse grain /细～ fine grain /口～ provisions; food ration /军～ army provisions /余～ surplus grain /五谷杂～ five cereals (rice, two kinds of millet, wheat and beans) and other food grains /干～ solid food (prepared for a journey); field rations; rations on a journey ❷ grain tax paid in kind: 公～ grain tax to the state /钱～〈旧语〉land tax

粮仓 liángcāng ❶ granary; barn: 修～ repair a barn /把粮食收进～ put grain into a granary; store grain ❷ area which abounds in grain; breadbasket: 东北是祖国的～。The Northeast is one of the granaries (*or* breadbaskets) of our country.

粮草 liángcǎo food and forage; army provisions: 兵马未动, ～先行。Food and fodder should go ahead of (*or* precede) troops and horses.

粮道 liángdào grain route: 绝其～ cut off the enemy's grain (*or* supply) route

粮店 liángdiàn grain shop

粮囤 liángdùn bulk grain store

粮行 liángháng 〈旧语〉wholesale grain shop

粮户 liánghù 〈方言〉landlord
粮荒 liánghuāng grain shortage; famine：闹～ be hit by a grain shortage; have a famine
粮库 liángkù grain depot
粮秣 liángmò grain and fodder; rations and forage; army provisions：～被服 grain, fodder, bedding and clothing /～库 ration depot; supply depot /大车上装满了军火和～。The cart is loaded with ammunitions and army provisions.
粮农 liángnóng grain farmer
粮票 liángpiào food coupon; grain coupon
粮商 liángshāng grain merchant
粮食 liángshi grain; cereals; food：～产量 grain yield /～供应 staple food supply /～水分 grain moisture content /～污染 grain contamination /～自给程度 self-sufficiency in foodgrains /～统购统销政策 policy of state monopoly for the purchase and marketing of grain
粮食储备 liángshi chǔbèi grain reserve; grain stock
粮食定量 liángshi dìngliàng grain ration; grain quota (for an individual)
粮食风险调节基金 liángshi fēngxiǎn tiáojié jījīn grain risk fund
粮食加工 liángshi jiāgōng grain processing：～业 grain-processing industry /～厂 grain-processing mill
粮食作物 liángshi zuòwù cereal crop; grain crop
粮税 liángshuì grain tax paid in kind：交纳～ pay grain tax /沉重的～负担 heavy grain tax burden
粮饷 liángxiǎng 〈旧语〉provisions and pay for troops：发～ issue provisions and pay to troops /克扣～ pocket a portion of the soldiers' provisions and pay
粮栈 liángzhàn wholesale grain store; grain depot：他原在～里当账房先生。He used to be an accountant in the wholesale grain store.
粮站 liángzhàn grain distribution station; grain supply centre
粮子 liángzi 〈方言〉〈旧语〉troop; soldier

莨 liáng
see also làng
莨绸 liángchóu *also*“黑胶绸”hēijiāochóu gambiered Guangdong silk

踉 liáng *see*“跳踉”tiàoliáng
see also liàng

俍 liáng 〈书面〉perfect; excellent

量 liáng ❶ measure; weigh：丈～土地 measure land; measure a piece of ground /～尺寸 take sb.'s measurements /～体重 weigh oneself; take sb.'s weight /～体温 take sb.'s temperature ❷ appraise; estimate; assess：打～ measure with the eye; look up and down; size up /思～ consider; turn over in one's mind
see also liàng
量杯 liángbēi measuring glass; graduate
量程 liángchéng measuring range：～开关 range switch /～电路 range circuit /～误差 range error
量度 liángdù measurement：～单位 unit of measurement
量规 liángguī gauge
量角器 liángjiǎoqì protractor
量具 liángjù measuring tool：～刃具 measuring and cutting tools
量块 liángkuài slip gauge; measuring block; gauge block
量瓶 liángpíng measuring or graduated flask
量热器 liángrèqì calorimeter
量日仪 liángrìyí 〈天文〉heliometer
量算 liángsuàn measure and calculate
量筒 liángtǒng graduated or measuring cylinder; graduate
量图仪 liángtúyí map measurer
量雪尺 liángxuěchǐ 〈气象〉snow scale
量雪器 liángxuěqì 〈气象〉snow gauge
量油尺 liángyóuchǐ 〈机械〉oil dip rod; dipstick
量雨筒 liángyǔtǒng 〈气象〉precipitation gauge

liǎng

两¹(兩) liǎng ❶ (used before a classfier or 半，千，万，亿，etc.) two：～公里 two kilometres /～岁的女孩 two-year-old girl /每隔～天 every two days /～个半小时 two and a half hours /～万元 twenty thousand *yuan* ❷ both (sides); either (side)：～侧 both sides; either flank /小路～旁 either side of the walk /敌对的～军 contending armies /～鬓斑白 grey at the temples /势不～立 irreconcilably hostile to each other; mutually exclusive ❸ a couple; a few; some：再等～天 wait for a few (*or* a couple) more days /你再拿～个走吧。Take some more with you.

两²(兩) liǎng ❶ *liang*, a unit of weight (= 50 grams) ❷ 〈旧语〉tael, a unit of weight for silver or gold (about 31 grams)：黄金千～ a thousand taels of gold
两岸 liǎng'àn ❶ both banks; both sides; either bank; either side：～垂柳 weeping willows on either bank /江～挤满了看龙舟的群众。Both sides of the river were crowded with people watching the dragon boat race. ❷ both sides of the Taiwan Strait：海峡～骨肉同胞 people of the same flesh and blood on both sides of the Strait /～政治谈判的程序性商谈 procedural talks on political negotiations between the two sides of the Taiwan Strait /经过～人民的共同努力，目前～关系有了改善。Through the joint efforts of the people on both sides, relations between the mainland and Taiwan have improved.
两岸三地 liǎng'àn sāndì China's mainland, Taiwan and Hong Kong
两把刷子 liǎngbǎ shuāzi 〈口语〉tricks of the trade; flair：他一下子就把机器修好了，真有～。He fixed the machine in no time. What a smart man! *or* He certainly has a flair for machines, since he fixed it so quickly.
两败俱伤 liǎngbài-jùshāng both sides suffer or lose; neither side wins or gains：～的前景 no-win prospect
两半儿 liǎngbànr in two halves; in half; in two：一刀切成～ cut in half /一个国家怎么能长期分成～呢？How can a country remain severed in two for long?
两倍 liǎngbèi twice; twofold：～之多 twice as much /实际大小的～ twice the actual size
两边 liǎngbiān ❶ both sides; two sides：盒子～都掉漆了。The paint has peeled off on both sides of the case. ❷ both directions; both places：敌人从～进攻。The enemy attacked from both directions. /老人～走动，看望两个儿子。The old man is going back and forth, visiting his two sons by turns. ❸ both parties; both sides：～不得罪 offend neither side /～下注 hedge one's bet /～都说妥了，明天上午八点签订合同。The two parties have agreed to sign the contract at eight o'clock tomorrow morning.
两边倒 liǎngbiāndǎo lean now to one side, now to the other; waver; vacillate：墙头草，～(behave like) a tuft of grass swaying in the wind on top of a wall /像这样风吹～的人物，政界不乏其人。Such fence-sitters are not hard to find in political circles.
两便 liǎngbiàn ❶ be convenient to both; make things easy for both：主客～。It's convenient to both the host and the guest. ❷ be advantageous or beneficial to both：～之法 mutually beneficial (*or* advantageous) solution
两波段接收机 liǎngbōduàn jiēshōujī two-band receiver
两不找 liǎngbùzhǎo goods and payments match：钱正好，～，您请拿好这双鞋。Thanks for giving me exact change. Here are the shoes.
两曹 liǎngcáo 〈书面〉*see*“两造❶”
两重 liǎngchóng double; dual; twofold：～目的 dual purpose /～天 two different worlds
两重性 liǎngchóngxìng *also*“二重性”èrchóngxìng 〈哲学〉dual nature; duality
两次三番 liǎngcì-sānfān *also*“三番两次”again and again; time and again; over and over again; repeatedly：你为何～地阻拦我？Why do you stop me again and again?
两次运球 liǎngcì yùnqiú 〈体育〉double dribble (in basketball)
两党制 liǎngdǎngzhì two-party system; bipartisan system
两抵 liǎngdǐ balance or cancel each other：收支～。Income and expenditure balance each other. *or* The accounts balance (out).
两地分居 liǎngdì fēnjū (husband and wife) live in different places：解决～问题 reunite husbands and wives who live in different places
两点论 liǎngdiǎnlùn 〈哲学〉doctrine that everything has two aspects or that "one divides into two"
两豆塞耳 liǎngdòu-sāi'ěr clog up one's ears; close or stop one's

ears; turn a deaf ear to:别人再劝说，他都～，一点儿也听不进去。Despite others' repeated exhortations, he turned a deaf ear and just wouldn't listen.

两耳不闻窗外事 liǎng ěr bù wén chuāngwài shì shut both ears to what is going on outside one's window; be oblivious of the outside world:～，一心只读圣贤书 be busy studying the classics and ignore what is going on beyond one's immediate surroundings

两分法 liǎngfēnfǎ application of the approach that "one divides into two":坚持～，避免主观唯心主义 stick to the approach of one dividing into two and avoid subjective idealism

两个文明 liǎnggè wénmíng two types of civilization, i. e. both material progress and cultural and ideological advancement; material and spiritual civilization

两公婆 liǎnggōngpó 〈方言〉 husband and wife:～成天吵架。Husband and wife quarrelled all day long. *or* The couple led a cat-and-dog life.

两广 Liǎng-Guǎng Guangdong and Guangxi:～富庶之地 rich and populous regions in Guangdong and Guangxi

两害相权取其轻 liǎng hài xiāng quán qǔ qí qīng choose the lesser of two evils

两汉 Liǎng-Hàn Western Han Dynasty and Eastern Han Dynasty:～文学 literature during the Western and Eastern Han dynasties

两合公司 liǎnghé gōngsī 〈经济〉 limited partnership

两湖 Liǎng-Hú Hubei and Hunan provinces:～之地 Hubei and Hunan regions

两虎相斗 liǎnghǔ-xiāngdòu *also* "两虎相争" fight between two tigers or powers:～，必有一伤。(usu. said of two big powers or ambitious politicians that fight an irreconcilable battle) When two tigers fight, one is sure to get injured. /～，势不两全。When two tigers fight, it is impossible for both to emerge unscathed.

两回事 liǎnghuíshì *also* "两码事" two entirely different things; different matters:批评和攻击完全是～。Criticism and attack are different matters. /这完全是～，你何必硬扯到一块呢? Why do you lump together two things of entirely different nature?

两极 liǎngjí ❶ poles of the earth; North and South Poles ❷ 〈物理〉 poles of a magnet or an electric battery; anode and cathode; positive and negative electrodes ❸ division into two opposing extremes:～相通。Extremes meet.

两极分化 liǎngjí fēnhuà polarization; division (of a group, society, etc.) into two opposing extremes:南北贫富～的现象日益严重。The disparity of wealth between the South and the North is growing ever wider.

两极化 liǎngjíhuà bipolar; polarized:～社会 polarized society /多极化世界取代了～世界。The bipolar world has been replaced by a multipolar world.

两肩担一口 liǎng jiān dān yī kǒu with nothing but the mouth on one's two shoulders — extremely poor; poor as a church mouse

两江 Liǎng-Jiāng Jiangnan (comprising present Jiangsu and Anhui) and Jiangxi provinces in early Qing Dynasty:～总督 governor-general of Jiangnan and Jiangxi provinces

两脚规 liǎngjiǎoguī ❶ compasses ❷ dividers

两脚书橱 liǎngjiǎo-shūchú 〈比喻〉 person of great learning; walking encyclopedia; erudite scholar

两晋 Liǎng-Jìn Western Jin Dynasty and Eastern Jin Dynasty

两可 liǎngkě ❶ both will do; either will do:模棱～ non-committal; equivocal; ambiguous /这种事干不干～。It does not matter one way or the other. ❷ *also* "两可之间" could go either way; maybe, maybe not:他能否当选还在～。He may or may not be elected. *or* His election still hangs in the balance.

两口子 liǎngkǒuzi *also* "两口儿" husband and wife; couple:隔壁～是新搬来的。The couple next door have just moved in.

两肋插刀 liǎnglèi-chādāo take great risks; risk one's life; put one's life on the line (for sb.):咱为朋友不怕～。I would help my friend at any cost.

两立 liǎnglì exist side by side; coexist:势不～ mutually exclusive; extremely antagonistic; irreconcilable

两利 liǎnglì be mutually beneficial; be good for both sides; benefit both:和则～。Peace will benefit both sides.

两两 liǎngliǎng in pairs:～成双 in pairs /三三～ by (*or* in) twos and threes

两路人 liǎnglùrén two kinds of people; totally different people:他们是～，很难合得来。They were people of different sorts and could not get along well.

两码事 liǎngmǎshì *see* "两回事"

两面 liǎngmiàn ❶ two sides; both sides:这块木板～都有钉子。There are nails on both sides of the board. ❷ both directions; both places:～夹攻 attack from both directions; close in from both sides; make a pincer attack /沿江而下，～都是崇山峻岭。There are high mountain ridges along either side of the river. ❸ opposite sides; dual or double character; Janus face:～手法 double-faced tactics; double-dealing; double game /～讨好 try to please two opposing sides; run with the hare and hunt with the hounds /对问题的～我们都要进行分析。We have to analyze both aspects of the problem.

两面光 liǎngmiànguāng (try to) please both parties:他为人行事向来～，谁都不得罪。He always tries to ingratiate himself with all sides and never offends anyone.

两面派 liǎngmiànpài ❶ double-dealer; double-crosser:要提防搞阴谋诡计的～。We must be on our guard against double-dealers who conspire and play tricks. ❷ double-dealing; double-crossing; Janus-faced:～手法 double-faced tactics; double-dealing gimmick /耍～ resort to double-dealing; use duplicity

两面三刀 liǎngmiàn-sāndāo double-dealing; duplicity:他惯会～，表里不一。He is given to duplicity, thinking in one way and behaving in quite another. /你大可不必这样～! You'd better stop playing a double game.

两面性 liǎngmiànxìng dual character

两难 liǎngnán face a difficult choice; be in a dilemma; be caught between the devil and the deep blue sea:～处境 predicament /这个项目上不上呢? 我们感到～。We found ourselves on the horns of a dilemma concerning the project.

两旁 liǎngpáng both sides; either side:甬道～摆满了鲜花。The paved path leading to the main hall is lined with potted flowers.

两栖 liǎngqī ❶ 〈生物〉〈军事〉 amphibious:～车辆 amphibious vehicle ❷ working or engaged in two fields or spheres:影视～明星 star in both films and TV programmes; movie-cum-TV star

两栖部队 liǎngqī bùduì amphibious force; amphibious unit or corps

两栖动物 liǎngqī dòngwù amphibious animal; amphibian

两栖舰艇 liǎngqī jiàntǐng amphibious vessel

两栖植物 liǎngqī zhíwù amphibious plant; amphibian

两栖作战 liǎngqī zuòzhàn amphibious warfare; amphibious operation:～舰艇 amphibious (warfare) vessel

两歧 liǎngqí 〈书面〉 (of views, opinions, etc.) different; at odds; at variance:双方立场各异，意见难免～。Both sides kept to their own positions and inevitably held different views.

两讫 liǎngqì 〈商业〉 goods are delivered and bill is cleared:收付～。The goods are delivered and the bill is cleared.

两千年问题 liǎngqiānnián wèntí *also* "千年虫" qiānniánchóng 〈计算机〉 millennium bug; Year 2000 problem; Y2K:这台计算机已解决了～。This computer is Year-2000-compliant.

两清 liǎngqīng square accounts between buyer and seller, or between debtor and creditor:货款～。The delivery is taken and the bill paid. /欠款已付，借贷～。With the debt paid, the accounts are squared.

两情缱绻 liǎngqíng-qiǎnquǎn be deeply attached to each other; be head over heels in love with each other

两全 liǎngquán be satisfactory to both parties; have regard for both sides; take both aspects into consideration:～之策 plan satisfactory to both sides (*or* in both respects) /势难～。It's hard to satisfy both parties.

两全其美 liǎngquánqíměi gratify both sides; satisfy rival claims; be to the satisfaction of both parties:这个问题你有没有什么～的解决办法? Have you got a solution to the problem that would satisfy both parties? /你们两厂联合，各展优势，岂不～? It would be mutually advantageous for your factories to combine and give full play to each other's strengths.

两审终审制 liǎngshěn zhōngshěnzhì 〈法律〉 system of the court of second instance being the court of last instance

两世为人 liǎngshì-wéirén barely escape with one's life; be lucky to have escaped death; have a narrow escape:我能够从战难中逃脱出来，真是～。It was most fortunate of me to make a narrow escape from the havoc of war.

两手 liǎngshǒu ❶ skill; ability; trick:有～儿 be skilful (*or* smart) /露～儿 show a trick or two /留～儿 keep sth. back (of one's skill or

tricks) ❷ both hands; both aspects; dual tactics:～空空 with both hands empty; left with nothing whatsoever; empty-handed /以革命的～对付反革命的～ counter the reactionaries' dual tactics with revolutionary dual tactics /困难很多，事先我们要做好～准备。As there are many difficulties ahead, we have to prepare ourselves for both eventualities. /物质文明、精神文明要～抓，～都要硬。We must address ourselves to the problem of material as well as cultural and ideological progress (*or* both materical and spiritual civilization) without any letup.

两条道路 liǎngtiáo dàolù two roads, i. e. the socialist road versus the capitalist road

两条路线 liǎngtiáo lùxiàn two lines:～的斗争 struggle between the two lines; two-line struggle

两条腿走路 liǎngtiáotuǐ zǒulù walking on two legs; do two interrelated things simultaneously; balance the relations between two aspects, etc.:普通教育和职业教育～ simultaneously develop both general education and vocational education

两条心 liǎngtiáoxīn fundamental disagreement; not of one mind:你我兄弟不能～。You and I are brothers and should be of one mind.

两跳 liǎngtiào 〈体育〉double bounce (in table tennis)

两头 liǎngtóu ❶ both ends; either end:一根扁担～尖。A carrying pole is pointed at both ends. /我们的政策是抓～，带中间。Our policy is to focus our work on the advanced and the backward so as to encourage the majority in between to move ahead. ❷ both parties; both sides:～讨好 curry favour with both parties /～为难 find it hard to please either side; find it difficult to satisfy two conflicting demands; find oneself on the horns of a dilemma /～受气 incur blame from both sides; be caught between the hammer and the anvil /～落空 fall between two stools ❸ two places; both places:他和父母分开住，要～照看着。He lives separately from his parents and has to go back and forth to look after both homes.

两头沉 liǎngtóuchén kneehole desk

两头小，中间大 liǎngtóu xiǎo, zhōngjiān dà small at both ends and big in the middle; a few at each extreme and many in between:凡是有人群的地方，大抵总是～。Wherever there is a group of people, it is almost always the case that those at the two poles (i. e. advanced and backward people) are few while those in the middle are many.

两下里 liǎngxiàli *also*"两下" ❶ both parties; both sides:事成之后，我们～都有好处。When this is done both of us will benefit from it. ❷ two places; both places:一家人分在～住。The family had to split up and live in two places.

两下子 liǎngxiàzi ❶ couple of times; several times:钟摆动了～，停了。The pendulum swung a few times and stopped. ❷ some tricks of the trade; flair; ability:真有～ be really good (*or* skilful) at sth. /谁不知道你有～！Everybody knows that you are smart. /我就会这～，再难一些就得找我老师问了。That's all I know (*or* am capable of). For more difficult problems you'll have to ask my teacher.

两相情愿 liǎngxiāng-qíngyuàn *also*"两厢情愿" both parties are willing:婚姻大事必得～。Marriage should be made by mutual consent.

两厢 liǎngxiāng ❶ wing-rooms on either side of a one-storey house ❷ both sides:站立～ stand on either side /～侍候 wait upon sb. on both sides

两相 liǎngxiàng 〈电学〉two-phase:～电流 two-phase current /～电动机 two-phase motor

两小无猜 liǎngxiǎowúcāi (of a young boy and a young girl) be innocent childhood playmates:青梅竹马，～。A little boy and a little girl played innocently together.

两心 liǎngxīn 〈书面〉❶ feeling for each other:～相悦，情深爱笃 give hearts to each other and be deeply in love ❷ in fundamental disagreement; not of one mind:怀有～ be of a different mind; harbour ulterior motives

两性 liǎngxìng ❶ both sexes:～比率 sex ratio /～关系 relations between the sexes; sexual relations or intercourse ❷〈化学〉amphoteric; amphiprotic:～反应 amphoteric reaction /～化合物 amphoteric compound /～胶体 amphiprotic colloid; ampholytoid

两性花 liǎngxìnghuā hermaphrodite flower

两性人 liǎngxìngrén *also*"二性子" èrxìngzi bisexual person; hermaphrodite

两性生殖 liǎngxìng shēngzhí *also*"有性生殖" yǒuxìng shēngzhí sexual reproduction; zoogamy

两性同体 liǎngxìng tóngtǐ 〈生物〉hermaphrodite

两袖清风 liǎngxiù-qīngfēng (of an official) have clean hands; be free from corruption:为官多年，～，一身正气 hold office for many years and remain honest and uncorrupted

两样 liǎngyàng not the same; different:～对待 regard as different; treat differently; make fish of one and flesh of the other /你去和我去，有什么～？What's the difference whether you go or I go?

两姨 liǎngyí maternal cousins (whose mothers are sisters):～兄妹 maternal cousins

两姨亲 liǎngyíqīn cousinship (between children of sisters)

两翼 liǎngyì ❶ both wings:鸟的～上下翻动。The bird fluttered its wings. /飞机的～被击中。The wings of the plane were hit. ❷〈军事〉both flanks; both wings:～包抄 double envelopment /～迅速推进 rapidly move forward on both flanks

两用 liǎngyòng dual purpose; dual use:～电动机 dual-purpose motor /～反应堆 dual-purpose reactor /～产品 dual-use product /～技术和设备 dual-use technologies and equipment /～雨衣 reversible raincoat /～沙发 convertible sofa

两用人材 liǎngyòng réncái qualified personnel versed in both military and civilian affairs; people qualified for both military and civilian work

两用衫 liǎngyòngshān *also*"春秋衫" chūnqiūshān jacket for spring and autumn wear

两院制 liǎngyuànzhì two-chamber system; bicameral system; bicameralism:～议会 bicameral house; two-chamber parliament

两愿离婚 liǎngyuàn líhūn divorce by mutual consent

两造 liǎngzào ❶ *also*"两曹" both parties in a lawsuit; plaintiff and defendant:～各执一辞，互不相让。Both the plaintiff and defendant stick to their own version and neither would concede. ❷〈方言〉two crops:此地气候适于～。The climate here is suited to the growth of two crops a year.

两着儿 liǎngzhāor ❶ moves in chess movements or in *wushu*:你棋下得好，教我～吧。Teach me a couple of moves at chess; you're so good at it. ❷ trick; device:他那～啊，现在吃不开啦。His tricks do not work any longer.

裲(裲) liǎng

裲裆 liǎngdāng 〈古语〉sleeveless garment; vest; waistcoat

唡(啢) liǎng *also* yīngliǎng ounce

蜽(蜽) liǎng *see*"蝄蜽" wǎngliǎng

俩(倆) liǎng *see*"伎俩" jìliǎng

see also liǎ

魉(魎) liǎng *see*"魍魉" wǎngliǎng

緉(緉) liǎng 〈书面〉(of shoes and socks) pair:一～丝履 a pair of silken shoes

liàng

凉(涼) liàng make or become cool:这粥太烫，～一～再喝。The porridge is too hot, cool it a bit before you eat.

see also liáng

谅[1] liàng forgive; excuse; understand:互～互让 mutual understanding and accommodation /体～ show consideration and sympathy for; make allowance for / 尚希见～。I sincerely hope you'll excuse me.

谅[2] liàng I think; I believe; I expect; presumably:～必不假。I believe it is true. *or* Presumably it is true. /汇款～已收到。I expect (*or* trust) you have received the remittance. /～他也不敢来！I don't think he would dare to come.

谅察 liàngchá 〈书面〉(often used in correspondence) I hope you'll understand and forgive me:因故迟复，敬希～。I hope you'll excuse me for my belated reply.

L

谅解 liàngjiě understand; appreciate; make allowance for: ~备忘录 memorandum of understanding /希望你能~他的苦衷。I hope you'll allow for (*or* appreciate) his difficulties. /双方达成~。The two parties reached an understanding.

晾 liàng ❶ dry in the air; air-dry; air: 把菜~干 dry the vegetable /~一~被子 air the quilt ❷ dry in the sun; sun: ~白薯干 sun sliced sweet potatoes ❸ ignore; slight; give the cold shoulder to: 他没完没了地打电话,把客人~在一边。He kept talking over the phone, letting his guests cool their heels. ❹ *see* "凉" liàng

晾干 liànggān dry by airing: 书湿了,要在阴处~。When books get wet, dry (*or* air) them in the shade. /你的外套已经~了。Your jacket is dry now.

晾晒 liàngshài sun; air: ~粮食 dry grain in the sun /被褥要经常~。The bedding needs frequent airing.

晾台 liàngtái ❶ *also* "亮台" liàngtái cut the ground or pull the rug from under sb.'s feet; leave in the lurch: 没等我说完,大伙都拔脚走了,晾我的台。Hardly had I stopped talking when everyone turned round and left. They were just leaving me in the lurch. ❷ terrace or veranda for sunning clothes

晾烟 liàngyān ❶ air-curing of tobacco leaves ❷ air-cured tobacco

晾衣绳 liàngyīshéng clothesline

晾纸机 liàngzhǐjī paper conditioning machine

倞 liàng 〈书面〉 request; ask for; search for
see also jìng

亮 liàng ❶ bright; light: 明~ light; bright; shining; well-lit /豁~ roomy and bright /~色调 light tone /今晚月光真~。The moon is very bright tonight. /家具擦得发~。The furniture was scrubbed clean and shiny. ❷ shine; flash: 路灯彻夜~着。Street lights shone throughout the night. /信号灯在黑暗中~了几下。The signal lamp flashed on and off for a few seconds in the dark. /天快~了。It's getting light. ❸ loud and clear; clarion: 响~ loud and clear; clarion /洪~的声音 resonant (*or* resounding) voice ❹ make loud and clear; lift (one's voice): ~起嗓子唱一支歌 lift one's voice to sing a song ❺ enlightened; clear: 心明眼~ see and think clearly; be sharp-eyed and clear-headed ❻ show; lay open; make public: ~出门证 show one's pass /把底牌~出来 lay one's cards on the table /公开~出自己的观点 make public one's view; declare one's position; air one's opinion

亮察 liàngchá 〈敬词〉 *see* "谅察" liàngchá

亮敞 liàngchang light and spacious: 这房子真~。The house is light and roomy.

亮底 liàngdǐ ❶ disclose one's true plan, stand, view, etc.; put one's cards on the table: 问了老半天,也该~啦。I have asked you about it for quite a while. It's about time you put your cards on the table. /希望你给我们亮亮底儿,我们好心中有数。Please tell us your bottom line, so we will know how things stand. ❷ show the result: 这场斗争还没~呢。The result (*or* outcome) of the struggle is yet to show.

亮度 liàngdù brightness; brilliance; luminance: ~对比 luminance (*or* brightness) contrast /~调节 luminance (*or* brightness, *or* brilliance) control /荧光屏~ screen brilliance /这种灯泡~不够。This type of bulb is not bright enough.

亮分 liàngfēn (of a judge or umpire) show or display the marks one has given: 请评委~。Will the judges (*or* umpires) please display the marks.

亮光 liàngguāng ❶ light: 深夜了,他们窗口还有~。Their window still glimmered in the dead of night. /一道~从门缝中透出。A shaft of light leaked through the door crack. ❷ shine; reflection: 瓷壶洁白而有~。The porcellain pot is white and shiny.

亮光光 liàngguāngguāng shining; gleaming; bright: 把镰刀磨得~的 grind a sickle until it shines /~的尖刀 gleaming dagger

亮光漆 liàngguāngqī polish lacquer

亮红牌 liàng hóngpái ❶ 〈体育〉 show the red card (in soccer); send off ❷ 〈比喻〉 order (a factory, etc.) to suspend production, etc.

亮话 liànghuà blunt words; naked truth: 打开窗户说~。Let's come right to the point and call a spade a spade.

亮晃晃 liànghuānghuāng dazzlingly bright; shining; gleaming: ~阳光 dazzling (*or* bright) sunlight; shining sun /~的金表 gleaming gold watch

亮黄牌 liàng huángpái ❶ 〈体育〉 show the yellow card; book ❷ give a warning

亮节高风 liàngjié-gāofēng *also* "高风亮节" exemplary conduct and noble character; outstanding moral integrity

亮晶晶 liàngjīngjīng glittering; glistening; sparkling; shining: 一串~的珠子 a string of glittering pearls /~的露珠 glistening dewdrops /星星~的 stars twinkle /窗玻璃擦得~的。The window panes were polished to a shine.

亮蓝 liànglán light blue: 星星全不见了,天变得~起来。The stars had receded and the sky turned light blue.

亮牌 liàngpái lay one's cards on the table; have a showdown: 最后~ final showdown /他后悔自己不该这么早就~。He regretted having laid his cards on the table too early.

亮牌子 liàng páizi show one's sign or identity: 他有意向对方先~。He began deliberately by revealing his identity to the other party.

亮儿 liàngr 〈口语〉 ❶ lamp; light: 照个~。Please give me a light. ❷ light; glow: 远远看见有一点~,他知道隧道快到头了。Seeing a little light (*or* glow) in the distance, he knew he was nearing the end of the tunnel. /从门缝里透出一点~来。The door crack let out a beam of light.

亮纱 liàngshā a kind of thin and transparent silk fabric; shiny gauze

亮闪闪 liàngshǎnshǎn sparkling; glistening: ~的眼睛 glistening eyes /~的启明星 sparkling Venus

亮台 liàngtái *also* "晾台" liàngtái cut the ground from under sb.; leave in the lurch

亮堂堂 liàngtāngtāng brightly lit; well lit; brilliant: 礼堂里明灯高照,~的分外耀眼。The auditorium is dazzlingly bright with lights. /他心里~。He felt as clear as clear can be.

亮堂 liàngtang ❶ light; bright: 新布置的客厅,又~又气派。The newly-decorated drawing room is both bright and splendid in style. ❷ clear; enlightened: 经过学习,大家心里就更~了。After intensive (*or* in-depth) study, we had a much better understanding of the whole problem. ❸ loud and clear; resonant: 嗓门~ rich voice /清清嗓子,唱~点 clear one's throat and sing in a sonorous voice

亮瓦 liàngwǎ *also* "明瓦" míngwǎ tile that lets through light; translucent tile

亮相 liàngxiàng ❶ (of Beijing opera, dancing, etc.) strike a pose on the stage: 她一个漂亮的~,博得了满堂喝彩。She struck a beautiful pose on the stage and won the acclaim of the audience. ❷ make one's debut: 国家奥林匹克队今晚首次~。The National Olympic Team will make its debut this evening. ❸ declare one's position; state one's views: 在弄清事情底细之前,不要急于~。Don't state your position before you get to the bottom of the matter.

亮眼 liàngyǎn ❶ visual eye; eye with sense of sight ❷ 〈方言〉 conspicuous; showy: 园里的红花,十分~。The red flowers in the garden are quite striking.

亮眼人 liàngyǎnrén (term used by the blind for) people with eyesight

亮锃锃 liàngzèngzèng shining; glittering: ~的铡刀 shiny fodder chopper /新买的钢精锅,~的。The new aluminium pan is shining.

亮铮铮 liàngzhēngzhēng shining; glittering: ~的利剑 sharp glittering sword

亮子 liàngzi vent above a door or a window; transom (window); fanlight

喨 liàng *see* "嘹喨" liáoliàng

悢 liàng 〈书面〉 sad; sorrowful: ~然 be sad

悢悢 liàngliàng 〈书面〉 ❶ sad; sorrowful; melancholy: ~不得辞 be too sad to part with each other ❷ think fondly of; feel nostalgic about: ~无已 with no end of nostalgia

踉 liàng
see also liáng

踉跄 liàngqiàng *also* "踉蹡" stagger: 行步~ stagger along /踉踉跄跄一路走来 walk up in a staggering way

靓 liàng 〈方言〉 beautiful; handsome; good-looking: ~哥

handsome brother; good-looking man /～歌 beautiful song /小姑娘长得真～。The little girl is very pretty.
see also jìng

靓女 liàngnǚ 〈方言〉beautiful girl; pretty girl

靓仔 liàngzǎi 〈方言〉handsome young man

辆(輛) liàng 〈量词〉*used with vehicles*:一～自行车 one bicycle /两～大卡车 two trucks

量 liàng ❶〈古语〉bulk measure:度～衡 length, capacity and weight; weights and measures /重～ weight ❷ capacity; capability:酒～大 have a great capacity for liquor;can hold much liquor /饭～小 not have a large appetite; not be a big eater /力～ (physical) strength; power; force /胆～ courage; guts; pluck /度～ tolerance; magnanimity; generosity ❸ quantity; amount; number; volume:质～并重 lay equal stress on both quality and quantity /降雨～ rainfall /降雪～ snowfall /音～ volume /产～ output; yield /流～ rate of flow; flow; discharge ❹ estimate; appraise; measure:～才度德 estimate (*or* appraise) sb.'s moral character and abilities; take sb.'s measure morally and intellectually /等～齐观 estimate as equal; put on a par; view in the same light /计～ calculate; estimate
see also liáng

量变 liàngbiàn 〈哲学〉quantitative change:～到质变 from quantitative to qualitative change

量才录用 liàngcái-lùyòng give sb. work suited to his or her talents; employ sb. on the basis of his or her merits; assign jobs commensurate with people's abilities:应试合格者,均可～。All those who pass the examination will be assigned jobs suited to their abilities.

量词 liàngcí 〈语言〉classifier (as 个, 只, 次, 件, 回, 条); measure word

量腹而食 liàngfù'érshí never eat more than one can digest; not indulge one's appetite to excess; be moderate:古人说～,凡事都应有节制才对。As the ancients would advise, never eat more than you can digest, so we should be moderate in everything we do.

量纲 liànggāng 〈物理〉dimension:～方程 dimension equation /～常数 dimensional constant /～分析 dimensional analysis

量化 liànghuà quantify; quantize:～噪音 quantized noise /～器 quantizer

量力 liànglì estimate one's own strength or ability (and act accordingly):不自～ overrate one's ability; overreach oneself

量力而行 liànglì'érxíng do what one's strength allows; act according to one's capability:凡事要根据情况,～。One should always act according to circumstances and never overreach oneself.

量入为出 liàngrù-wéichū keep expenditure within the limits of income; live within one's means; cut one's coat according to one's cloth:过日子应精打细算,～。One should live thriftily and keep expenses within one's income.

量体裁衣 liàngtǐ-cáiyī cut the garment according to the figure; act according to actual circumstances:俗话说"～",总要由实际情况决定解决问题的办法嘛。As the saying goes "cut the garment according to the figure", we must base ourselves on actual circumstances in finding a solution to a problem.

量小非君子 liàng xiǎo fēi jūnzǐ 〈俗语〉(as used in historical romances to describe ambitious figures) a small mind makes no gentleman; a gentleman has no petty mind:～,无毒不丈夫。As a small mind makes no gentleman, so a man of spirit lacks no venom. *or* As no gentleman has a petty mind, so no true man has qualms of conscience.

量小力微 liàngxiǎo-lìwēi small in capacity and weak in strength:这个小公司～,被一家大公司兼并了。The small and weak company was taken over by a big corporation.

量刑 liàngxíng 〈法律〉measurement of penalty:这些情况,请法庭～时予以考虑。It's my hope that the court will take these facts into consideration when meting out the penalty.

量子 liàngzǐ 〈物理〉quantum:光～ light quantum /～数 quantum number /～等离子体 quantum plasma /～定律 quantum law /～计算机 quantum computer /～波方程 quantum-wave equation

量子场 liàngzǐchǎng quantum field:～论 quantum field theory

量子光学 liàngzǐ guāngxué quantum optics

量子化 liàngzǐhuà quantize:～失真〈通信〉quantization distortion (*or* noise)

量子化学 liàngzǐ huàxué quantum chemistry

量子棘轮 liàngzǐ jílún 〈物理〉quantum ratchet

量子力学 liàngzǐ lìxué quantum mechanics:～技术 quantum-mechanics technique

量子论 liàngzǐlùn quantum theory; Planck's theory

量子生物学 liàngzǐ shēngwùxué quantum biology

量子物理学 liàngzǐ wùlǐxué quantum physics

liāo

撩 liāo ❶ hold or lift up (a curtain, skirt, etc. from the bottom):～裙子 lift up a skirt /～起窗帘 raise a curtain /～了一下头发 brush back one's hair ❷ sprinkle (with one's hand):～了一地的水 sprinkle water all over the floor
see also liáo

撩衣奋臂 liāoyī-fènbì hold up one's coat and raise one's arm; roll up one's sleeves and raise one's fists; be ready to fight:手下几个人～,只等他一声令下,就要动手。His men rolled up their sleeves, ready to fight at his order.

蹽 liāo 〈方言〉❶ walk fast; rush; run:他心里着急,一口气～了十多里地。Burning with impatience he walked over ten *li* at a stretch. ❷ sneak away; leave stealthily:他一看不妙,～起腿跑了。Sensing danger, he took to his heels at once.

liáo

膋(膋) liáo 〈古语〉fat on the intestines

聊[1] liáo ❶ barely; merely; just:～以解忧 just to assuage one's worry ❷ a little; somewhat; slightly:～表寸心 as a small token of my feelings ❸ (Liáo) a surname

聊[2] liáo 〈书面〉rely; depend:无所～生 have nothing to depend on for a living; have nothing to live on

聊[3] liáo chat; chew the fat:有时间咱们～～。Let's have a chat when you are free.

聊备一格 liáobèi-yīgé may serve as a specimen; serve as a stopgap; stand in for the time being:他的译作虽算不上什么杰作,但也可～吧。Though his translation can't be reckoned as a masterpiece, it may serve as a stopgap.

聊博一笑 liáobó-yīxiào 〈谦词〉(of one's remarks or action) just to win a smile from you; just for your amusement

聊复尔耳 liáofù'ěr'ěr *also* "聊复尔尔"〈书面〉for the sake of formality only; for show; that's all there is to it:未能免俗,～。I cannot but follow the custom (in giving or accepting presents, etc.), that's all.

聊赖 liáolài (usu. used in the negative) something to rely on (for a living); something to occupy one's mind:百无～ with nothing whatever to do; bored to death; overcome with boredom /民无～,何以为生? How can the people survive without anything to live on?

聊且 liáoqiě tentatively; merely; for the moment:奉上薄礼,～算是我的一点儿心意。The little gift is just a token of my regard.

聊生 liáoshēng 〈书面〉(often used in the negative) live on:民不～。The people have no means of livelihood. *or* The masses live in dire poverty.

聊胜于无 liáoshèngyúwú it's better than nothing; a little is better than none:我院藏书不多,但总归～,勉强还管点儿用。Although our college has only a small collection of books, it's better than nothing and may serve certain purposes.

聊天儿 liáotiānr 〈口语〉chat:我们一边喝茶,一边～。We chatted over a cup of tea.

聊以解嘲 liáoyǐjiěcháo make a feeble attempt to relieve embarrassment; try to explain things away when ridiculed:眼见下不了台,他只好开了个玩笑,～。Realizing that he couldn't back down gracefully, he cracked a joke to conceal his embarrassment.

聊以塞责 liáoyǐsèzé merely to avoid the charge of dereliction of duty; just to get by:寄上拙作两篇,只能算是～吧! I am sending you two articles of mine just to meet the minimum requirements you

L

set.

聊以自慰 liáoyǐzìwèi just to console oneself; merely to find relief in sth.:这几年无所事事,～的是我还写过几篇不太坏的文章。Although I did little work in the last several years, I comfort myself with the thought that I wrote several passable articles during the period.

聊以自娱 liáoyǐzìyú just to amuse or enjoy oneself:书不求甚解,琴～ read books without seeking thorough understanding and play the zither just to amuse oneself

聊以卒岁 liáoyǐzúsuì 〈书面〉just to tide over the year; merely to eke out a living during the year:当时,他就靠在乡下教几个小学生维持生计,～。At that time, he scraped a living by teaching a few children in the countryside.

聊斋志异 Liáozhāi Zhìyì *Strange Tales from a Lonely Studio*, a collection of about 500 stories by Pu Songling (蒲松龄, 1640-1715) of the Qing Dynasty

潦 liáo

see also lǎo

潦草 liáocǎo ❶ (of handwriting) hasty and careless; illegible:字迹～ scrawly handwriting ❷ sloppy; slipshod; slovenly:做事～ work in a slovenly (*or* slipshod) way; perform one's duty in a perfunctory manner

潦草塞责 liáocǎo-sèzé work in a careless and perfunctory manner; make a show of doing one's duty

潦倒 liáodǎo be frustrated:～不堪 be utterly frustrated /穷困～ be poverty-stricken and downtrodden; be (down) on one's uppers /～粗疏 be in straitened circumstances but unconventional /～龙钟 be senile and dispirited

寮 liáo

❶〈方言〉small house; hut:茅～ hut /茶～ teahouse ❷ (Liáo) Lao, dominent nationality of Laos:～人 Lao /巴特～ Pathet Lao (founded in 1950)

寮房 liáofáng ❶ monk's cell or hut ❷〈方言〉shed; hut

寮国 Liáoguó *also* "老挝" Lǎowō (former translation) Laos

寮棚 liáopéng shed; hut

燎 liáo

(of fire) spread; burn

see also liǎo

燎荒 liáohuāng burn the grass on wasteland

燎泡 liáopào *also* "燎浆泡" blister raised by a burn or scald

燎原 liáoyuán set the prairie ablaze:～之势 force of a prairie fire /星火～。A single spark can start a prairie fire.

燎原计划 Liáoyuán Jìhuà Prairie Fire Programme (for popularizing appropriate technologies)

燎原烈火 liáoyuán-lièhuǒ blazing prairie fire; conflagration:荒野上燃起了～,到处是滚滚浓烟。The wild is ablaze with flames and enveloped in billows of smoke.

撩 liáo

tease; provoke; stir up; excite (emotions)

see also liāo

撩拨 liáobō tease; incite; provoke:他多次～我。He teased me on many occasions.

撩动 liáodòng provoke; stir; pluck:～心弦 pluck one's heartstrings

撩逗 liáodòu provoke; tease; annoy:他生气了,别再～他。Don't provoke him any more; he is in a huff.

撩拂 liáofú pluck; stir up

撩乱 liáoluàn *see* "缭乱" liáoluàn

撩惹 liáorě provoke; tease:不要去～这号人。Don't provoke such people.

撩人 liáorén stir; excite; tease:春色～。The beautiful spring is fascinating. /花香～。The fragrance of flowers is intoxicating.

撩是生非 liáoshì-shēngfēi provoke a dispute; stir up trouble:这小子是个～的坏事包。This guy is quite a troublemaker.

L

嘹 liáo

嘹亮 liáoliàng resonant; loud and clear; clarion:歌声～。The singing is loud and clear. /吹起了～的冲锋号。The bugle sounded the charge.

嘹喨 liáoliàng *see* "嘹亮"

簝 liáo

〈古语〉sacrificial utensil made of bamboo

簝竹 liáozhú a kind of bamboo

僚 liáo

❶ official:官～ official; bureaucrat /群～ group of officials ❷ associate in office:同～ colleague

僚机 liáojī 〈军事〉❶ wing plane ❷ wingman

僚舰 liáojiàn 〈军事〉consort (ship)

僚属 liáoshǔ 〈旧语〉officials under one in authority; subordinates; staff:～无不敬服 be held in great esteem by all one's subordinates /齐集～于门下 rally together one's staff

僚婿 liáoxù 〈书面〉husband of wife's sister; brother-in-law

僚友 liáoyǒu 〈旧语〉colleague

僚佐 liáozuǒ 〈旧语〉assistant in a government office; aide:署中～,仗势欺压百姓。The aides in the government office abuse their power and bully ordinary people.

鹩 liáo

鹩哥 liáogē 〈动物〉hill myna

獠 liáo

獠牙 liáoyá long, sharp, protruding tooth; fang; bucktooth:青面～ be green-faced and long-toothed; have fiendish features; be terrifying in appearance

嫽 liáo

〈书面〉fine; lovely; charming

缭 liáo

❶ entangled ❷ sew with slanting stitches:～贴边 stitch a hem; hem /～缝儿 stitch up a seam

缭乱 liáoluàn in a tangle; confused; in a turmoil:眼花～ be dazzled /这几天心里～得很。My mind has been in a tangle in the past few days.

缭绕 liáorào curl up; wind around:夕阳西下,炊烟～。As the sun was setting in the west, smoke was curling out of kitchen chimneys. /山顶上白云～。The top of the mountain is veiled in clouds. /笛声～,韵味无穷。The sound of the flute lingered with lasting appeal.

漻 liáo

〈书面〉(of water) clear and deep

寥 liáo

❶ few; scanty ❷ silent; deserted:寂～ deserted and lonely ❸ broad and empty; vast:～无人烟 no trace of human habitation in sight

寥寂 liáojì 〈书面〉solitary; lonesome:～的夜空 solitary night sky /万籁～。All is quiet.

寥廓 liáokuò boundless; infinite; vast:～的星空 vast starlit sky /～江天万里霜 endless expanse of frosty sky and water /怅～,问苍茫大地,谁主沉浮? Brooding over this immensity, I ask, on this boundless land, Who rules over man's destiny?

寥寥 liáoliáo very few:～数语 just a few words /顾客～ just a few customers

寥寥可数 liáoliáo-kěshǔ very few:会上发言者～。Few people spoke at the meeting.

寥寥无几 liáoliáo-wújǐ very few; hardly any:他的诗作流传下来的已是～了。Few of his poems are extant today.

寥落 liáoluò ❶ few and far between; sparse; deserted:晓星～。Only a few solitary stars were twinkling in the morning sky. ❷ desolate; deserted:老屋后面的花园,～破败,非昔日可比。The garden behind the old house, desolate and ravaged, has lost all its past beauty.

寥若晨星 liáoruòchénxīng as sparse as the morning stars; few and far between:研究这个课题的人～,屈指可数。Only a few people specialize in this subject, and they can be counted on your fingers.

髎 liáo

〈中医〉space between two joints

疗(療) liáo

treat; cure:医～ medical treatment /诊～ make a diagnosis and give treatment /电～ electrotherapy /理～ physiotherapy /水～ hydropathic treatment; hydrotherapy /泥～ mud-bath treatment

疗程 liáochéng 〈医学〉course or period of treatment:口服两个～ take orally for two periods of treatment /你再看一个～,病就全好了。You will be fine after another course of treatment.

疗法 liáofǎ therapy; treatment: 化学～ chemotherapy /放射～ radio-active therapy /按摩～ massotherapy /封闭～ block therapy /针刺～ acupuncture treatment /休克～ shock therapy
疗饥 liáojī 〈书面〉allay or appease one's hunger: 食物虽少, 尚可～。Little as the food is, it's enough to allay the hunger.
疗热草 liáorècǎo feverwort
疗效 liáoxiào curative effect: ～显著 with marked curative effect; highly efficacious cure
疗养 liáoyǎng recuperate; convalesce; rest up: 去海滨～ go to the seaside to recuperate (or for a vacation)
疗养院 liáoyǎngyuàn sanatorium; convalescent hospital or home; rest home
疗治 liáozhì treat; cure: ～烧伤 treat burns

辽[1](遼) liáo distant; faraway

辽[2](遼) Liáo ❶ (at first called Khitan 契丹) Liao Dynasty (907-1125) ❷ (short for 辽宁) Liaoning Province
辽东 Liáodōng 〈地理〉region to the east of the Liaohe River, namely the eastern and southern part of Liaoning Province
辽东半岛 Liáodōng Bàndǎo Liaodong Peninsula
辽阔 liáokuò vast; extensive: ～富饶的草原 vast and fertile grasslands /土地～ vast expanse of land; vast territory /～的大海 boundless sea
辽宁 Liáoníng Liaoning (Province)
辽宁大鼓 Liáoníng dàgǔ *also* "东北大鼓" Dōngběi dàgǔ Liaoning *dagu* (versified story sung to the accompaniment of a small drum and other instruments)
辽沈战役 Liáo-Shěn Zhànyì Liaoxi-Shenyang Campaign (12 Sept.-2 Nov. 1948), first of the three decisive campaigns of the War of Liberation
辽西 Liáoxī 〈地理〉region to the west of the Liaohe River, namely the western part of Liaoning Province
辽远 liáoyuǎn distant; faraway; remote: ～的天空 distant sky /～的边疆 remote frontiers

liǎo

蓼 liǎo *also* "水蓼" shuǐliǎo 〈植物〉knotweed
see also lù
蓼花 liǎohua a kind of fried cake (made of glutinous rice flour, soybean flour, sugar, and osmanthus flowers)
蓼科 liǎokē 〈植物〉*Polygonum*
蓼蓝 liǎolán *also* "蓝"〈植物〉indigo plant

憭 liǎo 〈书面〉comprehend; understand

燎 liǎo singe: 他不小心, 把头发都～了。He accidentally singed his hair.
see also liáo
燎发摧枯 liǎofà-cuīkū 〈书面〉as easy as burning hair and crushing dry weeds; easily: 我军全歼守敌, 势如～。Our troops wiped out the defending enemy with overwhelming force.

了[1] liǎo ❶ end; finish; settle; dispose of: 不～～之 end up by doing nothing; end up with nothing definite /一～百～。All troubles end when the main trouble ends. /案子～了。The case is closed (*or* settled). /这事儿不～不行。The matter must be settled. ❷ (used in conjunction with 得, 不, after a verb) can: 做得～ can do it /跑不～ cannot escape /去得～ be able to go ❸〈书面〉(mostly used in the negative) entirely: ～无惧色 show no fear at all; look completely undaunted /～无生趣 without any joy of life /～不相涉 have nothing whatever to do with it; be totally unrelated (*or* irrelevant) /～无长进 make little progress

了[2](瞭) liǎo know clearly; understand: 明～ understand; know clearly /一目～然 be clear at a glance
see also le
了不得 liǎobude ❶ terrific; extreme; extraordinary: 兴奋得～ extremely excited /多得～ innumerable /他荣获一等奖, 这真是件～的大事。It is really terrific that he was awarded the first prize. ❷ terrible; dreadful; awful: 没有什么～的事。It's nothing serious. /可～啦, 那个女孩掉进河里去了! My God, the little girl has fallen into the river!
了不起 liǎobuqǐ ❶ amazing; remarkable; extraordinary: ～的发明 remarkable invention /自以为～ think oneself terrific; be self-important ❷ serious; grave: 对他们来说, 没什么～的困难。For them, no difficulty is insurmountable.
了当 liǎodàng ❶ frank; straightforward; outright: 他说话脆快～。He speaks frankly. *or* He does not mince his words. ❷ ready; settled; in order: 安排～ properly arranged /收拾～ put things in order ❸ (often used in the early vernacular) handle; deal with; manage: 自能～得来 can handle it by oneself
了得 liǎode ❶ *used at the end of a sentence, mostly following* 还, *to indicate seriousness*: 这么大的事, 一点招呼都不打, 这还～? We were not even notified beforehand of such an important matter. How outrageous! ❷ (often used in the early vernacular) extraordinary; outstanding: 这个人本事～。He is an extremely capable man.
了断 liǎoduàn *see* "了结"
了结 liǎojié end; finish; settle; wind up: 自作～ settle (the business) by oneself; commit suicide (as a solution) /将问题私下～ have the matter settled privately /我们之间的关系～了! Everything is finished between us.
了解 liǎojiě ❶ understand; comprehend; know: 你是～我的用意的。You know my intentions. /这样做有助于相互～。By doing so, we can better our understanding of each other. /这里的情况你又不是不～。Aren't you familiar with how things stand here? ❷ find out; acquaint oneself with: ～情况, 掌握动态 size up the situation and keep abreast of the developments /对莎士比亚的作品有透彻的～ have a thorough grasp of (*or* be well versed in) the works of Shakespeare /我只想～事实真相。I'm only interested in finding out what the facts are.
了局 liǎojú ❶ end; ending; outcome: 事情的～早在人们的意料之中。People have long anticipated the outcome of the incident. /这桩公案, 不知何日才有～。No one knows when the legal case will end. ❷ solution; settlement; way out: 像这样熬夜, 终究不是个～。Staying up late like this is after all no solution.
了了 liǎoliǎo ❶〈书面〉know clearly: 对此事不甚～ know little about the matter /心中～ be well aware of sth. ❷ clever; smart; intelligent: 小时～, 大未必佳。A smart boy may not grow up a wise man.
了却 liǎoquè finish; settle; solve: ～某人的心愿 fulfil sb.'s wish (*or* aspiration) /总算～了一桩心事 finally take a load off one's mind
了然 liǎorán understand; be clear: 不甚～ not have a thorough understanding /事情的真相, 他早已～于心。He knew the truth long ago.
了然于怀 liǎorányúhuái know well; have a pretty good idea: 您的想法我已～。I know perfectly well what is in your mind.
了如指掌 liǎorúzhǐzhǎng know like the palm or back of one's hand; have at one's fingertips; be thoroughly familiar (with sth.): 他对这个问题～。He knows the subject thoroughly (*or* backwards).
了身达命 liǎoshēn-dámìng ❶〈佛教〉see through life and world; understand this world thoroughly ❷ settle down to a quiet life; accept one's fate with resignation; find a home to return to: 世界之大, 却难找个～之处。It's really hard for me to find a home to return to in this vast world.
了事 liǎoshì dispose of a matter; get through with sth.: 含糊～ handle sth. in an ambiguous way; muddle through sth. /敷衍～ get through sth. in a careless or perfunctory way; rush through sth.
了手 liǎoshǒu 〈方言〉finish one's work on hand; dispose of a matter: 你爸爸好些事没～, 你别去打扰他。Don't disturb your father. He has his hands full right now.
了无 liǎowú not at all; not the least; not the slightest: ～睡意 not at all sleepy /～惧色 show no fear at all; look undaunted /～痕迹 without the least trace (*or* vestige); traceless
了悟 liǎowù 〈书面〉understand; comprehend; grasp: 书中的深奥学理, 尚不能～。I cannot yet grasp the profound theory discussed in the book.
了愿 liǎoyuàn fulfil a wish, promise, etc.
了账 liǎozhàng settle or square accounts; bring sth. to an end: 就此～。It's all settled.

钌 liǎo 〈化学〉ruthenium (Ru)
see also liào
钌酸 liǎosuān 〈化学〉ruthenic acid:～盐 ruthenate

liào

廖 Liào a surname
料[1] liào ❶ expect; anticipate:预～ anticipate; guess in advance /出人意～ beyond one's expectation /～不到你会来。We didn't expect you to come. /～他也无计可施。I don't suppose there's anything he can do (about this). ❷ take care of; manage:照～ take care of; look after
料[2] liào ❶ material; stuff:材～ material; data /原材～ raw and semi-finished materials /木～ timber; lumber /肥～ fertilizer /燃～ fuel /依我看,他根本不是当演员的～。I don't think he has the least makings of an actor. ❷ (grain) feed; forage; fodder:草～ forage; fodder /给牲口喂～ put more in the fodder ❸ synthetic jade; opaque coloured glass:～货 synthetic jade (*or* glassware) ❹〈量词〉〈中药〉prescription:配一～药 make up a prescription ❺〈量词〉*liao*, a former measure unit for timber (7 *chi* × 1 square *chi*):这批木材足有一百多～。This batch of timber amounts to more than a hundred *liao*.
料仓 liàocāng feed bin
料车 liàochē 〈冶金〉skip; skip car
料持 liàochí (often used in the early vernacular) arrange; attend to; take care of:～饭食 prepare meals
料到 liàodào foresee; anticipate; expect:没～事情会这么严重。I didn't expect that things could have turned out so badly.
料定 liàodìng know for sure:我～他不会食言。I'm sure he will not break his word.
料斗 liàodǒu ❶ *also*"料斗子" forage bucket, made of wicker ❷〈冶金〉(charging) hopper; skip bucket
料豆儿 liàodòur *also*"料豆子" soybeans, or black beans used as feed for livestock:给小马加了一把～ add a handful of black soybeans in the forage for the pony
料度 liàoduó estimate; assess; evaluate; size up:～敌情 take stock of the enemy's situation
料估 liàogu 〈方言〉expect; anticipate; estimate:～不到 beyond one's anticipation (*or* expectation)
料及 liàojí 〈书面〉expect; anticipate:途中大雪,我们原未～。We didn't anticipate the heavy snow on the way.
料酒 liàojiǔ cooking wine
料理 liàolǐ ❶ arrange; manage; attend to; take care of:～自己的生活 take care of oneself /～后事 make arrangements for a funeral /她把家里～得井井有条。She is an excellent household manager. ❷ cooking; cuisine:日本～ Japanese cuisine
料面 liàomiàn 〈方言〉heroin:～鬼 heroin addict
料器 liàoqì 〈工美〉glassware
料峭 liàoqiào 〈书面〉chilly:春寒～ chill of early spring in the air
料石 liàoshí processed stone used as construction material
料事如神 liàoshì-rúshén predict like a prophet; foretell with miraculous accuracy; foresee with divine precision:我又不能～,事情出点差错,也是难免的。I'm no prophet and can't help making mistakes sometimes in work.
料头 liàotóu leftover bits and pieces (of industrial material)
料想 liàoxiǎng expect; think; anticipate:事情如此复杂,谁能～得到呀! Who could have thought things would become so complicated? /事情没有我原先～的那么糟。It's not so bad as I expected.
料子 liàozi ❶ material for making clothes; dress length:买几块～ buy a few dress lengths /你这件上衣是什么～做的? What material is your jacket made of? ❷〈方言〉woollen fabric:～大衣 overcoat made of woollen fabric ❸ timber; lumber ❹ makings; stuff:教他的师傅都说他是块好～。His masters all say he has got what it takes (to do the job). ❺〈方言〉heroin:～馆 heroin house
尥 liào
尥蹶子 liào juězi ❶ *also*"撂蹶子" liào juězi;"撂蹄子" liào tízi (of mules, horses, etc.) give a backward kick:这匹马性子烈,爱～踢人。This is a vicious horse and always kicks people. ❷ lose one's temper; get angry:性情暴躁,爱～ have an irascible disposition
撂(撩) liào ❶ put down; leave behind; shelve:他～下饭碗就去工作了。Putting down his bowl, he immediately resumed his work. /她～下的活谁替她干呀? Who will take over the work she left behind? ❷ throw down; knock down; shoot down:一枪就把狼～倒了 shoot down the wolf with just one shot /一交手,我就把他～在地上了。As soon as we came to grips, I threw him down. ❸ abandon; discard; cast aside:他～下老婆孩子,当兵去了。Leaving behind his wife and children, he went to join the army.
撂地 liàodì *also*"撂地摊" give a performance in an open space:～卖艺 make a living as a street-performer
撂荒 liàohuāng 〈方言〉let the land lie idle:鼓励农民开荒,减少～面积 encourage farmers to reclaim wasteland and reduce the uncultivated area
撂荒地 liàohuāngdì idle land
撂跤 liàojiāo 〈方言〉tussle; wrestle:年轻人撂个跤、斗个嘴是常事。Tussling and quarreling are common among young people.
撂手 liàoshǒu wash one's hands of sth.; refuse to have anything more to do with the matter:这件事你哪能～不管? How could you wash your hands of this business?
撂台 liàotái refuse to do one's job; wash one's hands of the matter
撂挑子 liào tiāozi throw up one's job:他一闹气就～。He would throw up his job whenever he got angry.
撂心思 liào xīnsi 〈方言〉careful; mindful; conscientious:他对家事全不～。He is not at all mindful of housework. /个人生活是需要撂一点心思的。One needs to give some thought to problems of daily life.
瞭 liào watch from a height or a distance:爬上树去～着点儿。Climb to the top of the tree and keep watch.
瞭哨 liàoshào 〈方言〉stand sentry or sentinel; be on sentry go:战士们都睡了,只留下一个人～。With just one soldier keeping sentry all the others went to sleep.
瞭望 liàowàng ❶ look far into the distance (usu. from a height); look as far as the eye can see:极目～ look as far as the eye can see /～远方的地平线 survey the distant horizon ❷ watch from a height or a distance; keep a lookout:司令员拿起望远镜,～远处的敌阵。The commander held his field glasses and looked at the enemy's position in the distance.
瞭望哨 liàowàngshào observation post
瞭望台 liàowàngtái observation tower; lookout tower
镣 liào fetters; shackles
镣铐 liàokào fetters and handcuffs; shackles; chains; irons:他拖着沉重的～,艰难地走着。He dragged forward in heavy chains.
钌 liào
see also liǎo
钌铞儿 liàodiàor hasp and staple

liē

咧 liē
see also liě; lie
咧咧 liēliē *see*"大大咧咧" dàda-liēliē;"骂骂咧咧" màma-liēliē;"笑咧咧" xiàoliēliē
咧咧 liēlie 〈方言〉❶ speak carelessly; make irresponsible remarks; gossip:你成天到处瞎～,有什么好处? What could you possibly gain by shooting your mouth off everywhere? ❷ (of children) blubber:别在这儿～了,快找你妈去吧! Stop blubbering here. Go to your mother now!

liě

裂 liě 〈方言〉part in the middle; sever; split or break open:他的新皮鞋没穿几天就～开了嘴。The new leather shoes split open af-

ter he had worn them for only a few days. /那个疯女人～着怀，在荒野中跑着。With her coat unbuttoned, the mad woman ran about in the wild.
see also liè
裂巴 lièba 〈方言〉 bread

咧 liě ❶ grin：～着嘴笑 grin from ear to ear ❷〈方言〉〈贬义〉 talk：胡～ talk nonsense
see also liē；lie
咧扯 liěche 〈方言〉 grin：他～着嘴，做了一个鬼脸。He grinned and made a face.
咧嘴 liězuǐ grin：龇牙～ show one's teeth；look fierce /他～一笑。His face broadened into a grin. /他捂着伤口，疼得直～。He covered the wound with his hands and grinned with pain.

liè

埒 liè 〈书面〉❶ equal；on a par with：他二人才智相～，难分高下。They are on a par with each other in intelligence. ❷ low wall；ridge；dyke；embankment：河～ river embankment

列 liè ❶ arrange；line up：按字母顺序排～ arrange in alphabetical order /罗～理由 set out one's reasons (for sth.) ❷ enter in a list；list；rank：～为重点项目 be placed in the list of priority projects /～入计划 be listed in the plan /名～第一 stand (*or* rank) first on the list ❸ row；file；rank：站在最前～ stand in the front row (*or* in the forefront) /由右向左排成一～ stand in single file from the right to the left ❹〈量词〉*used of a series or row of things*：一～火车 a train ❺ kind；sort；category：不在此～ not fall into this category /此事应在考虑之～。This matter should be among the subjects to be discussed. ❻ various；each and every：*see* "～国"；"～位" ❼ (Liè) a surname
列兵 lièbīng 〈军事〉 private
列车 lièchē train：直达～ through train /国际～ international train /军用～ military train /上行～ up train /下行～ down train /特快～ express train /旅客～ passenger train /36 次～ No.36 train
列车调度员 lièchē diàodùyuán train dispatcher
列车时刻表 lièchē shíkèbiǎo train schedule；timetable
列车员 lièchēyuán attendant (on a train)；guard；train crew
列车运行图 lièchē yùnxíngtú train schedule；timetable
列车长 lièchēzhǎng head of a train crew
列当 lièdāng *also* "草苁蓉" cǎocōngróng 〈植物〉 broomrape
列岛 lièdǎo chain of islands；archipelago：长山～ Changshan Islands
列鼎而食 lièdǐng'érshí eat from tripods — hold sumptuous feasts；live an extravagant life
列队 lièduì line up：～游行 line up for a parade /～欢迎 queue up to welcome sb.
列风淫雨 lièfēng-yínyǔ fierce wind and heavy rain；be full of wrongly written characters：他途中三日，～，苦不堪言。The foul weather made his three-day journey extremely unpleasant. /这篇文章字迹潦草，～，错字连篇。The article is almost illegible and laden with wrongly written characters.
列国 lièguó various countries：周游～ tour various countries /～相争。All the states vied with each other for supremacy. /《东周～志》 *History of the Kingdoms in the Eastern Zhou Dynasty*
列举 lièjǔ enumerate；list：～事实 cite facts /法庭～了该犯的大量罪行。The court listed the many crimes committed by the culprit.
列宁 Lièníng Vladimir Ilyich Lenin (1870-1924)，leader of the Russian Revolution (7 Nov. 1917) and founder of Leninism：～墓 Lenin's Tomb (on Red Square, Moscow)
列宁格勒 Liènínggélè Leningrad, second largest city of the former USSR, now renamed St. Petersburg
列宁主义 Lièníngzhǔyì Leninism：马克思～ Marxism-Leninism
列强 lièqiáng big powers：～的炮舰政策 gunboat policy pursued by big powers
列氏温度计 Lièshì wēndùjì 〈物理〉 Reaumur thermometer
列土分疆 liètǔ-fēnjiāng divide the territory into fiefdoms and give them to royal princes
列位 lièwèi all of you；gentlemen；ladies and gentlemen：～请坐。Ladies and gentlemen, be seated, please. /～观众！Dear audience! /有事烦请～商议。I have something to discuss with you gentlemen.
列席 lièxí attend (a meeting) without voting rights：应邀～大会 be invited to the conference as a non-voting delegate
列席代表 lièxí dàibiǎo non-voting delegate
列支敦士登 Lièzhīdūnshìdēng Liechtenstein, country in central Europe located between Switzerland and Austria：～人 Liechtensteiner
列传 lièzhuàn biography (of a historical figure other than a monarch or a sage in Chinese historiography)：《廉颇蔺相如～》 *The Biographies of Lian Po and Lin Xiangru*
列子 Lièzǐ *Liezi*, Taoist classical work collected at the beginning of the Han Dynasty
列祖列宗 lièzǔ-lièzōng successive generations of ancestors

烈 liè ❶ strong；fierce；intense：激～ intense；fierce；acute /强～ strong；violent；vehement /越演越～ becoming increasingly acute (*or* aggravated)；getting worse and worse /兴高采～ in high spirits；jubilant ❷ staunch；upright；stern：刚～ fiery and forthright；upright and unyielding ❸ dying for a just cause：先～ martyr ❹〈书面〉 exploits；achievements：功～ merits and achievements；contribution
烈度 lièdù intensity：地震～ earthquake intensity
烈风 lièfēng ❶〈气象〉 force 9 wind；strong gale ❷ strong wind
烈火 lièhuǒ fierce fire；raging flames：熊熊～ blazing flames；raging fire /斗争～ fiery struggle；intense struggle
烈火见真金 lièhuǒ jiàn zhēnjīn pure gold proves its worth in a blazing fire；people of worth show their mettle during trials and tribulations
烈酒 lièjiǔ strong or stiff drink；hard liquor；spirits
烈烈轰轰 lièliè-hōnghōng *also* "轰轰烈烈" grand and spectacular；vigorous；dynamic
烈马 lièmǎ violent or untamed horse
烈女 liènǚ ❶ woman who is chaste and undefiled ❷ woman who dies in defence of her honour；woman who kills herself after her husband's death
烈日 lièrì burning sun；scorching sun：～炎炎 burning sun /～当头 with the scorching sun directly overhead
烈士 lièshì ❶ martyr：抗战死难～ martyrs who died during the anti-Japanese war ❷〈书面〉 person of high endeavour；man of heroic ambitions：宝剑赠～。A precious sword must be given to a hero.
烈士纪念碑 lièshì jìniànbēi memorial or monument to revolutionary martyrs
烈士陵园 lièshì língyuán cemetery of revolutionary martyrs
烈士墓 lièshìmù tomb or grave of a revolutionary martyr
烈士暮年，壮心不已 lièshì mùnián, zhuàngxīn bùyǐ the heart of a hero in his old age is as stout as ever；a noble-hearted man retains his high aspirations even in the evening of life
烈属 lièshǔ members of a revolutionary martyr's family：军～ soldiers' dependants and members of revolutionary martyrs' families
烈暑 lièshǔ scorching summer days；dog days
烈性 lièxìng ❶ upright and unyielding；spirited；fiery：～女子 woman of fiery character ❷ strong；intense：～酒 strong drink；hard liquor /～毒药 deadly poison /～毒品 hard drug /～感染 lytic infection /～炸药 high explosive
烈性子 lièxìngzi ❶ fierce temper or disposition ❷ person with a violent temper；spitfire
烈焰 lièyàn raging flames；roaring blaze：～腾空 soaring flames /革命的～ raging flames of revolution
烈阳 lièyáng burning sun；scorching sun；hot sun：夏季的～ scorching sun of the summer

洌 liè 〈书面〉 (of water or wine) clear；limpid：香～ fragrant and clear (*or* limpid) /清～ clear；lucid

冽 liè 〈书面〉 cold；chilly：凛～的寒风 piercingly cold wind

裂 liè ❶ split；crack；rend：破～ burst；split；rupture；crack /四分五～ fall apart；be rent by disunity；be all split up；disintegrate /那坚果～成两半。The nut cracked into two. /脚冻～了。The feet are

L

chapped by the cold. ❷〈植物〉gap
see also liě

裂变 lièbiàn ❶〈核物理〉fission:核～ nuclear fission /自发～ spontaneous fission /～材料 fissile material; fissioner ❷ split:这个大家庭～成小家庭。The extended family has split into several nuclear families.

裂变产物 lièbiàn chǎnwù fission product

裂变弹 lièbiàndàn fission bomb

裂变武器 lièbiàn wǔqì fission type of weapon

裂冰 lièbīng 〈地质〉(ice) calving

裂帛 lièbó 〈书面〉❶ tearing up silk; sound of or like tearing up silk ❷ books in ancient times

裂唇 lièchún cleft lip; harelip

裂齿 lièchǐ 〈动物〉carnassial tooth

裂地 lièdì 〈书面〉❶ cracked land:寒冻～,寸草不生。The land is cracked and barren with freezing cold. ❷ carve up land:～分封 enfeoffment

裂缝 lièfèng crack; rift; crevice; fissure:墙上的～ crevices of the wall /桌面～了。There are cracks in the table top. /水从岩石～中滴下。Water dripped from a fissure in the rock.

裂谷 liègǔ 〈地质〉rift valley

裂冠毁冕 lièguān-huǐmiǎn destroy one's official hat — quit office:自从这次打击之后,他决意～,终身不仕。After the setback, he made up his mind to quit office and remain a commoner for the rest of his life.

裂果 lièguǒ 〈植物〉dehiscent fruit

裂合酶 lièhéméi 〈生化〉lyase

裂痕 lièhén rift; crack; fissure:弥合～ span a breach; heal a rift /瓶子上有～。There is a crack in the bottle.

裂化 lièhuà 〈化工〉cracking:热～ hot cracking /加氢～ hydrogen cracking /催化～ catalytic cracking /～装置 cracking unit

裂化反应器 lièhuà fǎnyìngqì cracker

裂化炉 lièhuàlú cracking still or furnace

裂化气 lièhuàqì cracked gas

裂解 lièjiě 〈化工〉splitting decomposition; splitting:加碱～ alkaline splitting

裂解作用 lièjiě zuòyòng 〈化学〉splitting action

裂开 lièkāi split open; rend:墙上～一道缝。There is a crack in the wall. /裤子～了。The trousers split open.

裂口 lièkǒu crack; breach; split:衣服接缝处的～ split in the seam of the dress /西瓜～了。The watermelon split. /他手上有好几道～。There are several chaps in his hands.

裂口火山锥 lièkǒu huǒshānzhuī 〈地质〉breached cone

裂片 lièpiàn 〈植物〉lobe (of a leaf)

裂伤 lièshāng 〈医学〉laceration

裂纹 lièwén ❶ crack:～探测仪〈冶金〉crack detector /花瓶上有一道～。The vase has a crack in it. ❷ crackle (on pottery, porcelain, etc.)

裂璺 lièwèn ❶ crack:碗边上有道细长的～。There is a long and thin crack on the rim of the bowl. ❷ crackle (on pottery or other vessels)

裂隙 lièxì crack; crevice; fracture:弥合感情上的～ remedy (*or* overcome) estrangement (between two friends, etc.) /风从墙壁的～中灌进来。The wind blew in through the crack in the wall.

裂隙水 lièxìshuǐ crevice water

裂罅 lièxià 〈书面〉rift; crevice; rent; fissure

裂眼 lièyǎn 〈书面〉*see*"裂眦"

裂殖菌 lièzhíjūn 〈微生物〉schizomycete

裂眦 lièzì 〈书面〉stare angrily; glare (at):瞋目～ stare angrily; glare /～痛骂 scold with glaring eyes

趔 liè

趔趄 lièqie stagger; reel:他打了个～,摔倒在地。He staggered and fell onto the ground.

鴷 liè woodpecker

捩 liè twist; turn:转～点 turning point

捩转 lièzhuǎn turn round:～车身 turn round the vehicle

劣 liè ❶ bad; inferior; of low quality:恶～ abominable; mean; disgusting; despicable /低～ inferior; low-grade /拙～ clumsy; inferior ❷ minor:*see*"～弧"

劣等 lièděng of inferior quality; low-grade; poor:～品 low-grade (*or* inferior) goods /成绩～ poor academic record

劣根性 liègēnxìng deep-rooted or ingrained bad habit:国民的～ inherent weakness of a nation

劣弧 lièhú 〈数学〉minor arc

劣货 lièhuò goods of poor quality; low-grade goods

劣迹 lièjì misdeed; evildoing:～昭彰 flagrant evildoing /～被揭露,他的名声也就完了。His reputation will be ruined once the misdeed is laid bare.

劣倦 lièjuàn 〈书面〉exhausted; worn out; tired out; weary:长途跋涉之后,他已～疲极。He felt exhausted after a long, arduous journey.

劣蹶 lièjue (of animals) vicious; untamed:那匹马～,没有人敢使。As the horse is vicious, no one dares to ride it.

劣马 lièmǎ ❶ inferior horse; nag ❷ vicious horse; wild horse; fiery steed:制服～ tame a wild horse; break in a wild horse

劣弱 lièruò weak; feeble

劣绅 lièshēn evil gentry:土豪～ local tyrants and evil gentry

劣势 lièshì inferior strength or position; unfavourable or disadvantageous situation:处于～ be in an unfavourable position; be losing / 甲队迅速扭转～,把比分追了上来。Team A rapidly turned the tables on its opponent and caught up in the score.

劣质 lièzhì of poor or low quality; inferior:～烟草 inferior tobacco /～产品 product of substandard quality; substandard product

劣种 lièzhǒng inferior strain or breed:选用优种,淘汰～ select fine stocks and eliminate inferior ones

劣株 lièzhū weak plant:经过一冬的风寒雪冻,～尽死,留下的都是健壮的株苗。Only fine, strong plants survived the cold, snowy winter. The weak ones died out.

猎(獵) liè ❶ hunt:～狼 wolf hunting /以渔～为生 make a living by fishing and hunting /他们打～只是为了消遣。They hunt only for sport. ❷ hunting:～区 hunting-field

猎豹 lièbào 〈动物〉cheetah

猎捕 lièbǔ go hunting

猎场 lièchǎng hunting ground; hunting field:老猎户在～上设了几个陷阱。The old hunter set a few traps in the hunting ground.

猎刀 lièdāo hunting knife

猎狗 liègǒu *also*"猎犬"〈动物〉hunting dog; hound

猎户 lièhù ❶ household or family specialized in hunting ❷ hunter; huntsman:秋收一过,～便进山了。After the autumn harvest, the hunters went into the mountains.

猎户座 Lièhùzuò 〈天文〉Orion

猎火 lièhuǒ hunting fire:猎人在林子里燃起了～。The huntsman lit a hunting fire in the woods.

猎获 lièhuò capture or kill in hunting; bag:～一头小鹿 capture (*or* trap) a young deer /～大批野兽 bag a large number of wild animals

猎具 lièjù hunting equipment or outfit

猎猎 lièliè 〈书面〉fluttering of a flag in the wind; (of wind) whistling:朔风～。The north wind is howling. /红旗～。The red flag is fluttering in the wind.

猎奇 lièqí 〈贬义〉hunt for novelty; seek novelty:～心理 partiality for novelty

猎潜艇 lièqiántǐng *also*"猎潜舰艇"〈军事〉submarine chaser

猎枪 lièqiāng shotgun; fowling piece; hunting rifle:双筒～ double-barrel shotgun /锯短枪筒的～ sawed shotgun

猎取 lièqǔ ❶ hunt:～野兽 hunt wild animals ❷ pursue; seek; hunt for:～名利 seek (*or* hunt for) fame and wealth /～高额利润 chase big profits

猎犬 lièquǎn *see*"猎狗"

猎人 lièrén hunter; huntsman

猎杀 lièshā hunt and kill:禁止～保护区的动物。No hunting is allowed in the preserve. *or* Hunting in this area is forbidden.

猎食 lièshí 〈书面〉hunt for food:猎豹是天生的～专家。Cheetahs are born hunters.

猎手 lièshǒu hunter

猎头 liètóu headhunting

猎头公司 liètóu gōngsī (popular term for 物色人才公司) headhunting or talent search company; headhunter company; executive search company

猎围 lièwéi hunting encirclement

猎物 lièwù prey; quarry; game; bag
猎艳 lièyàn 〈书面〉❶ seek ornate phrases: ～搜奇 seek flowery and exotic phrases ❷ hunt for beauties; philander with women
猎鹰 lièyīng 〈动物〉falcon
猎逐 lièzhú hunt for: ～鸟兽 hunt for birds and animals
猎装 lièzhuāng hunting suit; hunting outfit

鬣 liè mane
鬣狗 liègǒu 〈动物〉(striped) hyena
鬣羚 lièlíng 〈动物〉serow
鬣蜥 lièxī 〈动物〉agama

躐 liè 〈书面〉❶ overstep; go beyond; skip over ❷ trample
躐等 lièděng *also* "躐级" 〈书面〉skip over the normal steps: 学不～ learn step by step /～晋升 get promoted by skipping the usual grades
躐进 lièjìn 〈书面〉get promoted over sb.'s head or by bypassing intermediate steps: 数年之间, ～而官至宰相 bypass several ranks and become prime minister within a few years

鱲 liè *also* "桃花鱼" táohuāyú 〈动物〉minnow

lie

咧 lie 〈方言〉〈助词〉*used like* 了, 啦 *or* 哩: 好～, 我这就来。Ok, I'll be with you in a moment. /来～, 小心烫着! Here it comes. Take care not to be scalded.
see also liē; liě

līn

拎 līn carry; hold; lift: ～着一桶水 carry a bucket of water
拎包 līnbāo 〈方言〉handbag; shopping bag; bag
拎勿清 līnwuqīng 〈方言〉muddle-headed; befuddled

lín

潾 lín
潾潾 línlín (of water) clear; limpid: ～的水波 clear ripples /春水～ limpid river in spring

麟(麐) lín (short for 麒麟 qílín) 〈书面〉kylin; (Chinese) unicorn: 凤毛～角 (precious and rare as) phoenix feathers and unicorn horns — rarity of rarities
麟凤龟龙 lín-fèng-guī-lóng (Chinese) unicorn, phoenix, turtle, and dragon; talented people: 科研所广揽人才, 一时间～之士济济一堂。The scientific research institute has done all it could to recruit top-notch scientists in the past few years and has now a galaxy of talents.
麟角凤距 línjiǎo-fèngjù horn of the (Chinese) unicorn and feet of the phoenix — (sth.) rare but of little use: 这些～的学问, 可暂不学。Such rare knowledge is of little use and may be put aside for the time being.
麟角凤嘴 línjiǎo-fèngzuǐ unicorn's horn and phoenix's beak — rare treasure
麟子凤雏 línzǐ-fèngchú young unicorn and phoenix — young talents: 这些年轻人都是～, 来日不可限量。These young talented people have a bright future before them.

遴 lín choose carefully; select: ～聘教师 carefully choose people to work as teachers
遴选 línxuǎn 〈书面〉❶ select for a post; recruit: ～委员会 search committee /～和起用才德兼备的青年人 select and appoint young people of both ability and integrity ❷ select; choose: ～展览样品 select exhibits

璘 lín lustre of jade
璘璘 línlín lustrous: 美玉无朋, 其色～。The beautiful and lustrous jade is of unparalleled size.

磷(燐) lín 〈化学〉phosphorus (P): 白～ white phosphorus /红～ red phosphorus /黑～ black phosphorus
磷蛋白 líndànbái 〈生化〉phosphoprotein
磷肥 línféi 〈农业〉phosphate fertilizer
磷钢 língāng 〈冶金〉phosphoretic steel
磷光 línguāng 〈物理〉phosphorescence: ～带 phosphorescence band /～涂料 phosphorescent paint
磷光体 línguāngtǐ phosphor
磷化 línhuà 〈化学〉phosphatization: ～物 phosphide
磷灰石 línhuīshí 〈矿业〉apatite
磷灰岩 línhuīyán 〈矿业〉phosphate chalk
磷火 línhuǒ *also* "鬼火" guǐhuǒ will-o'-the-wisp; phosphorescent light
磷矿粉 línkuàngfěn 〈农业〉ground phosphate rock
磷磷 línlín 〈书面〉*see* "粼粼" línlín
磷燃烧弹 línránshāodàn 〈军事〉phosphorous bomb
磷酸 línsuān 〈化学〉phosphoric acid: 亚～ phosphorous acid /～激酶〈生化〉phosphokinase /～肌醇〈生化〉phosphoinositide /～化酶〈生化〉phosphorylase /～酶 phosphatase
磷酸铵 línsuān'ǎn ammonium phosphate
磷酸钙 línsuāngài calcium phosphate
磷酸甘油 línsuān gānyóu phosphoglycerol: ～酸 phosphoglyceric acid
磷酸钠 línsuānnà sodium phosphate
磷酸盐 línsuānyán phosphate
磷糖 líntáng 〈生化〉phosphosugar: ～蛋白 phosphoglycoprotein
磷钨酸 línwūsuān 〈化学〉phosphotungstic acid: ～盐 phosphotungstate; phosphowolframate
磷细菌 línxìjūn phosphobacteria
磷虾 línxiā 〈动物〉krill
磷脂 línzhī 〈化学〉phosphatide; phospholipid: ～酸 phosphatidic acid

辚 lín
辚辚 línlín 〈象声〉rattle: 车～, 马萧萧 chariots rattling and horses neighing

瞵 lín 〈书面〉(of eagles) descry; eye: 鹰～鹗视 eye vigilantly; look fiercely (at sth.)

嶙 lín
嶙嶙 línlín 〈书面〉(of mountain rocks; cliffs, etc.) jagged; (of a person) bony; thin
嶙峋 línxún 〈书面〉❶ (of rocks, cliffs, etc.) jagged; rugged; craggy: ～的山峦 rugged hills /山石～ jagged mountain rocks ❷ (of a person) bony; thin: 瘦骨～ bag of bones; bony ❸ upright; unyielding: 气节～ be of unyielding integrity

鳞 lín ❶ scale (of fish, etc.): 鱼～ (fish) scale ❷ like the scales of a fish
鳞比 línbǐ row upon row (of houses, etc.): 两旁商店～的大街 avenue lined on both sides with shops
鳞波 línbō scale-like ripples: 轻风拂过, 湖面荡起～。A gentle breeze rippled the surface of the lake.
鳞翅目 línchìmù 〈动物〉*Lepidoptera*
鳞次栉比 líncì-zhìbǐ *also* "栉比鳞次" row upon row (of houses, etc.): 方圆数里之内, 烟囱高拔, 厂房～。Soaring chimneys and row upon row of factory buildings stretch for several *li* around.
鳞集 línjí congregate (like a school of fish); gather; assemble: 屋宇～。Houses cluster together.
鳞甲 línjiǎ scales and shell (of reptiles and arthropods)
鳞介 línjiè 〈书面〉aquatic animals
鳞茎 línjīng 〈植物〉bulb: 这种植物的～肥厚, 可食用。The bulb of this plant is thick and edible.
鳞鳞 línlín ❶〈书面〉as many as scales; in great numbers: 强敌～, 虎视眈眈。Huge in number, the formidable enemy watched menacingly like a ravening tiger. ❷ sheets of cloud; shimmering ripples: ～的白云 sheets of white cloud /湖上金光～。The lake gleams in the sunlight.

L

鳞毛蕨 línmáojué shield fern; wood fern
鳞木 línmù lepidophyte; lepidodendron
鳞片 línpiàn ❶ scale (of fish, etc.) ❷〈动物〉squama; palea ❸〈植物〉bud scale; palta
鳞伤 línshāng have as many wounds as fish scales; be covered with wounds: 遍体～ be covered with bruises (*or* injuries); be a mass of bruises; be black and blue all over
鳞屑 línxiè scale-like bits (coming off the skin)
鳞爪 línzhǎo 〈书面〉❶ scales and nails ❷ small bits; fragments; odd scraps: 事情的详细过程我不知道，我只知道一鳞半爪。I don't know the details. My knowledge of the matter is only fragmentary.

粼 lín

粼粼 línlín 〈书面〉(of water, stone, etc.) clear; limpid; crystalline: 青石～ crystalline dark stones / 微波～ tiny ripples on the water

林 lín

❶ forest; woods; grove: 雨～ rain forest / 竹～ bamboo grove / 山～ mountain forest; wooded mountain / 防沙～ sand-break (forest) / 防风～ windbreak / 用材～ timber forest; timberland / 天然～ natural forest / 造～ afforestation ❷ cluster of similar things; circles: 艺～ art circles / 碑～ forest of steles ❸ forestry: 农～牧副渔 farming, forestry, animal husbandry, sideline production and fishery / 农～口 farming and forestry sector ❹ (Lín) a surname
林表 línbiǎo 〈书面〉canopy of trees
林薄 línbó 〈书面〉overgrowth of trees, bushes and grass; heavy undergrowth
林产 línchǎn 〈林业〉forest product: 山区自有山区的优势，牧业发达，～丰富。The hilly area enjoys its own advantages, namely, flourishing animal husbandry and plentiful forest products.
林产品 línchǎnpǐn forest product: 此地的～，顺流而下，广销沿海一带。Local forest products are shipped downstream and sold in coastal areas.
林场 línchǎng ❶ forestry centre (including tree nursery, lumber camp, etc.): ～职工 staff of the forestry centre ❷ forestry farm; tree farm: 这一片～方圆数十里。This tree farm stretches for miles around.
林丛 líncóng woods; grove: 两岸的～，一望无边。The trees on both sides of the river stretch as far as the eye can see.
林带 líndài forest belt: 防风～ windbreak belt / 防沙～ sand-break belt
林地 líndì forest land; woodland; timberland
林分 línfèn 〈林业〉standing forest; stand
林副产品 línfùchǎnpǐn 〈林业〉minor or subsidiary forest product
林冠 línguān 〈林业〉crown canopy; crown cover
林海 línhǎi immense forest: ～雪原 immense forest and snowfield / ～深处 deep in the forest
林壑 línhè forest and gully
林警 línjǐng forest ranger
林卡节 Línkǎjié Lingka Festival, a traditional Tibetan festival
林可菌素 línkějūnsù *also* "洁菌素" jiéjūnsù 〈药学〉lincomycin
林肯 Línkěn Abraham Lincoln (1809-1865), 16th President of the United States (1861-1865)
林垦 línkěn forestry and land reclamation: ～战士 soldiers engaged in forestry and land reclamation
林立 línlì stand in great numbers (like trees in a forest): 高楼～。High-rise buildings stand in great numbers. / 烟囱～。There is a forest of chimneys.
林林 línlín 〈书面〉numerous; multitudinous: ～之民 large numbers of people
林林总总 línlín-zǒngzǒng in great abundance; numerous; manifold: 在～的这类故事中，七仙女和董永的故事最能打动人们的心。Among numerous stories of this type, the one about the Seventh Fairy Maiden and Dong Yong is the most touching.
林龄 línlíng 〈林业〉age of stand
林莽 línmǎng wild jungle; overgrowth of trees and bushes: ～地带 wild jungle region
林杪 línmiǎo 〈书面〉canopy of trees
林木 línmù ❶ forest; woods: ～葱郁 densely wooded ❷〈林业〉forest tree: 这一片～被山火焚烧一尽。The tract of forest was destroyed by the mountain fire.
林农 línnóng forestry farmer
林檎 línqín *also* "花红" huāhóng 〈植物〉Chinese pear-leaved crabapple
林箐 línqìng 〈方言〉large tract of bamboo forest: 山谷中～遮掩，阴森不见天日。Covered with groves of bamboo, the valley is dark and gloomy.
林区 línqū forest zone; forest region: ～建设 development of a forest region / ～学校 school in a forest area
林权 línquán ownership of a forest; forest right: 解决～之后，农民营林的积极性提高了。The solution to the problem of forest ownership has brought into play the initiative of the farmers in running forests. / 村里去年颁发了～证。Certificates of forest rights were issued last year in the village.
林泉 línquán 〈书面〉❶ woods and streams: ～幽静 quiet woods and streams ❷ quiet and secluded place: ～之士 recluse; hermit / 退隐～ withdraw from society and live in seclusion (*or* live the life of a hermit)
林薮 línsǒu 〈书面〉❶ forest and marsh; place overgrown with plants ❷ assemblage; collection: 古小说～ assemblage of ancient novels
林涛 líntāo soughing of the wind in a forest; sound as if made by billows: 一夜～之声不绝于耳。There was soughing in the trees the whole night.
林蛙 línwā 〈动物〉wood frog
林网 línwǎng forest network
林务员 línwùyuán forester
林下 línxià 〈书面〉fields; retirement from official life: 优游～ live a leisurely and carefree life after one's retirement / 退隐～ retire to some country hermitage
林下风 línxiàfēng *also* "林下风气"; "林下风致"〈书面〉(of a woman's bearing) refined; elegant; graceful
林下神仙 línxià-shénxian recluse; hermit: 罢官亦是好事，何不作个～? You're lucky to be removed from office. Why not become a recluse?
林相 línxiàng ❶ appearance or form of a forest: ～整齐 regular form of a forest ❷ (of a forest) quality: ～优良 high-quality forest
林型 línxíng type of forests
林学 línxué forestry (as a branch of learning): ～院 forestry institute
林谚 línyàn forest-related saying or proverb:《～小辑》*A Collection of Forestry Proverbs*
林业 línyè forestry (as an industry): ～生产 forest production / ～资源 forest resources / ～工人 forest worker; forester / ～专家 forestry expert / 大力发展～ devote major efforts to developing forestry
林独 línyì *also* "猞猁" shēlì 〈动物〉lynx
林阴道 línyīndào boulevard; avenue
林阴面积 línyīn miànjī forested area
林苑 línyuàn imperial hunting ground: 那几个县原是皇家～。Those counties used to be an imperial hunting ground.
林则徐 Lín Zéxú Lin Zexu (formerly translated as Lin Tse-hsu, 1785-1850), official who banned the opium trade in Guangdong
林政 línzhèng forestry administration
林芝 Línzhī Nyingchi, county in the eastern Tibet Autonomous Region
林子 línzi woods; grove; forest; thicket: 山上有一片～。There is a thicket on the mountain.

淋 lín

❶ pour; splatter; drench: 风吹雨～ wind-beaten and rain-drenched; exposed to the elements / 被雨～透 be soaked to the skin with rain ❷ sprinkle; splash; spray: 往鲜菜上～点水 sprinkle water over fresh vegetables
see also lìn
淋巴 línbā *also* "淋巴液"〈生理〉lymph
淋巴管 línbāguǎn lymphatic duct
淋巴结 línbājié *also* "淋巴腺"〈生理〉lymph node or gland: ～肿 enlargement of lymph node
淋巴结核 línbā jiéhé 〈医学〉scrofula; crewels
淋巴结炎 línbājiéyán 〈医学〉lymphnoditis
淋巴球 línbāqiú 〈生理〉lymph corpuscle
淋巴肉瘤 línbā ròuliú lymphosarcoma
淋巴系统 línbā xìtǒng lymphatic system
淋巴细胞 línbā xìbāo lymphocyte

淋巴液 línbāyè *see* "淋巴"
淋巴组织 línbā zǔzhī lymphoid tissue
淋漓 línlí ❶ dripping; streaming; pouring: 大汗～ dripping with sweat; sweating all over / 泪水～ be in tears ❷ free from inhibition; unrestrained: 痛快～ (of a piece of writing or a speech) be impassioned and forceful / 笔墨～酣畅 written (*or* painted) with ease and verve
淋漓尽致 línlí-jìnzhì incisively and vividly; thoroughly: ～的揭露 most telling exposure / 作品～地抒发了对乡土的挚爱。The work gives a full expression to the author's ardent love for his native land. / 小说～地揭露了封建愚昧的罪恶。The novel thoroughly exposes the crimes of feudal obscurantism.
淋淋 línlín dripping; drizzling; pouring: ～秋雨 drizzling autumn rain / 汗～ dripping with sweat / 血～的衣服 dress drenched in blood / 全身湿～的 be drenched all over; be soaked to the skin
淋洗 línxǐ drip washing
淋雨 línyǔ get wet in the rain; be caught in the rain
淋浴 línyù shower bath; shower

霖 lín continuous heavy rain: 秋～ continuous heavy rain in autumn / 甘～ good soaking rain; timely rain
霖雨 línyǔ continuous heavy rain: ～不晴，道路不通，受阻于半途。We were stranded halfway on our trip due to continuous downpour and blocked road.

琳 lín 〈书面〉 beautiful jade
琳琅 línláng beautiful jade; gem: 满屋～珠宝 room full of beautiful pearls and gems
琳琅满目 línláng-mǎnmù superb collection of beautiful things; feast for the eyes: 工艺品～，美不胜收。The great variety of beautiful handicraft articles in the shop are a feast for the eyes.

啉 lín *see* "喹啉" kuílín

綝 lín
see also chēn
綝缡 línlí *also* "綝纚" 〈书面〉 richly dressed

临(臨) lín ❶ face; confront; overlook; be close to: ～河 be close to a river / 濒～大海 face the sea / 居高～下 occupy a commanding position (*or* height) / 面～经济危机 face (*or* confront) an economic crisis ❷ arrive; be present: 身～其境 be personally on the scene / 敬请光～。Your presence is kindly requested. / 大祸将～。A grave danger is imminent. ❸ about to; on the point of; just before: ～分手 about to part company; at parting / ～赛之前 just before the contest ❹ copy (a model of calligraphy or painting): ～画 copy a painting ❺ (Lín) a surname
临本 línběn copy (of a painting, etc.): ～字迹工整，纸张质地亦佳。The copy (of the calligraphy) is neatly written on quality paper.
临别 línbié at parting; just before parting: ～之时 at parting; on the point of departure / ～依依 reluctant to part / ～纪念 parting souvenir; something to remember one by
临别赠言 línbié zèngyán words of advice at parting; parting advice: 我不会忘记你的～。I'll never forget what you told me at parting.
临产 línchǎn about to give birth; parturient
临产阵痛 línchǎn zhèntòng labour pains; birth pangs
临场 línchǎng ❶ take an examination; enter a competition: ～要沉着镇静 keep one's composure in the competition arena (*or* in the examination room) / ～经验不够 lack field experience ❷ be personally present (at a place): ～指导 render on-the-spot guidance
临朝 líncháo (of a sovereign) hold an audience; hold court
临池 línchí 〈书面〉 practise calligraphy; learn to write a good hand
临床 línchuáng 〈医学〉 clinical: ～经验丰富 rich in clinical experience / ～观察 clinical observation / ～检查 clinical examination / ～讲授 clinical instruction / ～诊断 clinical diagnosis
临床表现 línchuáng biǎoxiàn clinical manifestation
临床死亡 línchuáng sǐwáng clinical death
临床学 línchuángxué clinical medicine
临床医生 línchuáng yīshēng clinician
临床应用 línchuáng yìngyòng clinical practice
临到 líndào ❶ just before; about to; on the point of: 他～开车，才赶到车站。He arrived at the railway station just before the train was due to start. ❷ befall; happen to: 事情要是～他身上，他就不会这样说了。If it had happened to him, he would not have made such remarks.
临风 línfēng 〈书面〉 facing or against the wind: 城墙头上，～一杆大旗。On the top of the city wall, a huge flag was fluttering in the wind.
临高 língāo 〈书面〉 ascend a height: ～远眺 ascend a height to enjoy a distant view
临机 línjī as the occasion requires; on the spur of the moment; in an emergency: ～立断 make a quick (*or* prompt) decision at the right moment / ～处置 handle (*or* dispose of) on the spot; manage as the occasion requires
临机应变 línjī-yìngbiàn *also* "随机应变" suíjī-yìngbiàn suit one's actions to changing conditions; cope with any contingency; be resourceful: 此人善于～。He is a person of great resource.
临街 línjiē overlook or face the street; be close to the street: ～的窗口 window overlooking the street / ～三间平房 three single-storey houses facing the street / ～有三棵柳树。There are three willow trees along the street.
临界 línjiè 〈物理〉 critical: ～参数 critical parameter / ～磁场 critical magnetic field
临界点 línjièdiǎn 〈物理〉 critical point; breakthrough point; point of transition
临界角 línjièjiǎo 〈物理〉 critical angle
临界实验 línjiè shíyàn critical experiment: 高温气冷反应堆～ HTGR-CX (high-temperature gas-cooled reactor critical experiment)
临界态 línjiètài critical stage
临界体积 línjiè tǐjī critical size
临界温度 línjiè wēndù critical temperature
临近 línjìn close to; close on: 县城～铁路。The county town is close to the railway. / ～春节，到处是欢乐的气氛。As the Spring Festival is drawing near, a joyous atmosphere prevails.
临渴掘井 línkě-juéjǐng *also* "渴而掘井" kě'érjuéjǐng not dig a well until one is thirsty; make no preparation until the last moment; start acting too late: ～，不亦晚乎? Isn't it a bit too late to make this eleventh hour attempt?
临了 línliǎo *also* "临末了儿" at last; in the end: ～还是父亲说了算，全家去看电影。Father had the final say in the matter so that the whole family went to the cinema.
临门 línmén ❶ arrive at the door: 贵宾～。The distinguished guest has arrived. / 双喜～。A double blessing has descended upon the house. ❷ at the goal: ～一脚欠功夫。The shot on goal was not up to the mark.
临摹 línmó copy (a model of calligraphy or painting): ～碑帖 copy a rubbing from a stone inscription
临难 línnàn 〈书面〉 face a catastrophe or disaster: ～不屈 face up to risks; betray no fear in an hour of danger / ～毋苟免 not flinch from perils; not shrink back before dangers
临盆 línpén be giving birth to a child; be confined; be in labour
临期 línqī (of a date) draw close; arrive: 会已～。The date of the meeting is drawing near.
临氢重整 línqīngchóngzhěng 〈化学〉 hydroforming: ～汽油 hydroformer gasoline
临蓐 línrù about to deliver a child: ～之时，她正在返家的半道上。She was on her way home when labour pains started.
临深履薄 línshēn-lǚbó as if on the brink of an abyss; as if treading on thin ice; with great caution and care: 他处在这样的重要岗位上，遇事总是～。Since he holds such an important post, he exercises great caution in everything he does.
临时 línshí ❶ at the time when sth. happens: 到婚礼那天，我们～再找几个人帮忙。We'll find some people to help us on the wedding day. / 事先做好准备，省得～着急。One should be well prepared in advance so as to avoid any last-minute rush. ❷ temporary; interim; provisional; for a short time: ～贷款 interim loan; temporary loan / ～办法 temporary arrangement / ～议程 provisional agenda / ～舞台 makeshift stage / ～机构 ad hoc agency / 我～住在叔叔家里。I stayed with my uncle for the time being. / 我们在这儿～安一部电话机。We want to have a telephone temporarily installed here. / 求了半天，对方才答应～试用他。After many entreaties, they agreed to hire him on probation.

临时抱佛脚 línshí bào fójiǎo embrace Buddha's feet in one's hour of need — seek help at the eleventh hour; make a frantic last-minute effort:平时不烧香,～〈俗语〉never burn incense for Buddha, but embrace his feet in one's hour of need
临时代办 línshí dàibàn 〈外交〉*chargé d'affaires ad interim*
临时动议 línshí dòngyì extempore motion
临时法庭 línshí fǎtíng provisional court
临时费用 línshí fèiyòng interim or incidental expense
临时工 línshígōng casual labourer; temporary worker
临时户口 línshí hùkǒu temporary residence permit
临时停火 línshí tínghuǒ suspension of arms
临时信使 línshí xìnshǐ 〈外交〉*courier ad hoc*
临时证书 línshí zhèngshū 〈外交〉temporary credentials or papers
临时政府 línshí zhèngfǔ provisional government
临时主席 línshí zhǔxí interim chairman
临视 línshì 〈书面〉go personally to look into sth.; make an on-the-spot inspection
临死 línsǐ on one's deathbed:老教授～前留下遗嘱,把全部藏书捐赠给国家图书馆。The old professor made a will on his deathbed that all his books be donated to the National Library.
临眺 líntiào 〈书面〉ascend a height and look into the distance:～林海 look at the immense forest from a height
临帖 líntiè practise calligraphy after a model
临头 líntóu befall; happen:死到～ at death's door /厄运～ impending disaster
临完 línwán finally; in the end:～他又唱了一段京戏。Towards the end, he sang another piece from Beijing opera.
临危 línwēi ❶ be dying (from illness):～之时,他想到自己半世荒唐,悔恨不已。When he recalled on his deathbed that he had spent half of his life in dissipation, he was bitterly remorseful. ❷ facing death or deadly peril; in the hour of danger:～从容 remain calm (*or* composed) in the face of deadly peril
临危不惧 línwēi-bùjù face danger fearlessly; betray no fear in an hour of danger:他是一位～的好民警。He is a fine policeman not hesitating to face dangers.
临危蹈难 línwēi-dǎonàn go to one's death fearlessly
临危受命 línwēi-shòumìng be entrusted with a mission at a critical moment; take up a mission in times of danger
临危授命 línwēi-shòumìng give up one's life at a critical moment
临危制变 línwēi-zhìbiàn be able to keep the situation under control in a contingency
临尾 línwěi in the end; finally:～他又把我叫到一边,嘱咐了一阵。Finally, he took me aside, and gave me more advice.
临文 línwén write an article; write
临问 línwèn 〈书面〉go to pay one's regards or solicit opinions
临刑 línxíng at the time of execution
临行 línxíng before leaving; on departure:～之时,她才道出了事情真相。Not until she was leaving did she tell the truth.
临幸 línxìng (of an emperor) visit or arrive at some place
临渊羡鱼 línyuān-xiànyú stand on the edge of a pool and idly long for fish:与其～,不如退而结网〈谚语〉it's better to go back and make a net than to stand by the pond longing for fish; one should take practical steps to achieve one's aims
临月 línyuè month when childbirth is due
临战 línzhàn just before going into battle; on the eve of a battle; just before a game or contest:运动员投入紧张的～训练。The players took part in intense training just before the game.
临阵 línzhèn ❶ on the battlefield; on the eve of a battle; at a critical moment ❷ engage in a battle; fight a battle:～指挥 command in the battlefield /～经验丰富的军人 soldier well experienced in warfare; seasoned soldier
临阵磨枪 línzhèn-móqiāng sharpen one's spear only before going into battle; start to prepare only at the last moment; take action in great haste
临阵脱逃 línzhèn-tuōtáo desert on the eve of a battle; sneak away at a critical juncture; turn tail in the face of danger
临终 línzhōng approaching one's end; immediately before one's death; on one's deathbed:～遗言 deathbed testament; last words /他蹉跎一生,～才知悔恨。He idled away his life and began to regret it only before dying.

邻(鄰、隣) lín ❶ neighbour:四～ neighbours /睦～政策 good-neighbour policy ❷ neighbouring; near; adjacent:～村 neighbouring village /～桌 adjacent table ❸〈古语〉administrative unit covering five households
邻邦 línbāng neighbouring country:友好～ countries that are good neighbours; friendly neighbouring countries /两国接壤,互为～。The two countries are contiguous to each other.
邻比 línbǐ 〈书面〉neighbour
邻坊 línfang 〈方言〉neighbour
邻国 línguó neighbouring country
邻家 línjiā neighbour
邻角 línjiǎo 〈数学〉adjacent angle
邻接 línjiē border on; be next to; be contiguous to; adjoin:～我国西北边陲 border on China's northwest /学院～一家化工公司。The college adjoins a chemical company.
邻近 línjìn ❶ near; close to; adjacent to:保持与～国家的友好关系 maintain friendly relations with adjoining countries /我国东部与日本～。Our country is close (*or* near) to Japan in the east. ❷ in the neighbourhood; nearby:～的一座房子夜里失了火。A house in the neighbourhood caught fire at night.
邻近色 línjìnsè close colour; similar colour
邻居 línjū neighbour:左右～ close (*or* next-door) neighbours
邻里 línlǐ ❶ neighbourhood:～服务站 neighbourhood service /既然都是同乡,不能不讲～之情。Hailing from the same village, we ought to be neighbourly to each other. ❷ people of the neighbourhood; neighbours:我父母同～相处得很好。My parents get along well with our neighbours.
邻曲 línqū 〈书面〉neighbour:～时时来。My neighbours drop in from time to time.
邻人 línrén neighbour
邻舍 línshè neighbour
邻位 línwèi 〈化学〉ortho-position:～化合物 ortho-compound /～衍生物 ortho-derivative

lǐn

凛(凜) lǐn ❶ cold; frigid: *see*"～冽" ❷ strict; rigorous; stern; severe:～遵师命 strictly follow the teacher's instructions ❸〈书面〉afraid; fearful:～于夜行 dread going on a journey at night
凛冽 lǐnliè piercingly or bitingly cold:北风～。It's a freezing north wind.
凛凛 lǐnlǐn ❶ cold; frigid:朔风～ piercing north wind ❷ stern; awe-inspiring:～正气 awe-inspiring integrity /威风～ majestic-looking; with dignified bearing
凛然 lǐnrán stern; awe-inspiring:大义～ inspire awe by upholding justice /～斥敌 denounce the enemy sternly /～不可侵犯 stern and inviolable
凛若冰霜 lǐnruò-bīngshuāng *also*"冷若冰霜" lěngruò-bīngshuāng (of manners) as cold as ice; icy; forbidding

廪(廩) lǐn 〈书面〉❶ granary:仓～ granary ❷ grain
廪生 lǐnshēng *also*"廪膳生";"廪膳生员"〈旧语〉scholar of the Ming and Qing dynasties who lived on government grants
廪饩 lǐnxì 〈书面〉provisions provided by the government; grants from the government

懔(懍) lǐn *see*"凛❷❸" lǐn

檩(檁) lǐn *also*"桁" héng;"檩条"〈建筑〉purlin:上～ upper purlin
檩条 lǐntiáo 〈建筑〉purlin
檩子 lǐnzi 〈方言〉purlin

菻 lǐn *see*"拂菻" Fúlǐn

lìn

淋 lìn strain; filter:过～ filter /把咖啡～一～ strain the coffee
see also lín
淋病 lìnbìng 〈医学〉gonorrhoea

淋病性关节炎 lìnbìngxìng guānjiéyán 〈医学〉gonorrhoeal arthritis
淋病性眼炎 lìnbìngxìng yǎnyán 〈医学〉gonorrhoeal ophthalmia
淋滤 lìnlǜ *also*"淋溶" leaching
淋溶 lìnróng 〈地质〉leaching; eluviation: ～层 leached layer; eluvial horizon
淋溶土 lìnróngtǔ 〈地质〉Alfisol
淋失 lìnshī be washed away: 养分～ washing away of nutrients
淋子 lìnzi filter

吝

lìn ❶ stingy; miserly; closefisted: 悭～ stingy; miserly / 不～赐教 not stint on comments; not be grudging in giving advice ❷ (Lìn) a surname
吝色 lìnsè reluctance to give; unwillingness to spare: 倾囊相助,毫无～ give all one's money without the slightest reluctance
吝啬 lìnsè stingy; niggardly; miserly; mean: 为人十分～ very stingy person
吝啬鬼 lìnsèguǐ miser; niggard; skinflint
吝惜 lìnxī grudge; stint: 毫不～金钱 spend money without stint; be liberal with money

蔺

lìn ❶ *see*"马蔺" mǎlìn ❷ (Lìn) a surname

躏

lìn *see*"蹂躏" róulìn

赁

lìn rent; hire; lease: 租～ rent; lease; hire / 房屋出～ house to let / ～费 rent; rental / ～了一辆汽车 rent (*or* hire) a car

膦

lìn 〈化学〉phosphine
膦酸 lìnsuān phosphonic acid

líng

凌[1](淩)

líng ❶ insult; bully: 欺～ bully and humiliate / 凛然不可～ stern and forbidding ❷ approach; draw close: *see*"～晨" ❸ rise high; tower aloft: 壮志～云 with soaring aspirations ❹ (Líng) a surname

凌[2]

líng 〈方言〉ice (usu. shaped like cubes or cones): ～锥 icicle
凌逼 língbī 〈书面〉bully; humiliate; intimidate: ～良民 browbeat innocent people
凌波 língbō 〈书面〉❶ surging or rolling waves ❷ (of women) light gait: ～微步 walk with gentle and graceful steps
凌晨 língchén in the small hours; before daybreak
凌迟 língchí *also*"陵迟" língchí put to death by dismembering the body (a cruel ancient form of capital punishment): ～处死 death penalty by dismembering the body
凌泽 língduó 〈方言〉icicle
凌驾 língjià *also*"陵驾" língjià place oneself above; override: 不能把个人利益～于国家利益之上 not allow anybody to place his (*or* her) own interests above those of the state / 救孩子的念头～一切,他奋不顾身向水中跳去。Seized by the idea of saving the boy, he jumped into the water completely disregarding his own safety.
凌空 língkōng be high up in the air; soar high into the air: ～射门 make a volley shot / 雪花～飞舞。The snowflakes were whirling in the sky. / 一桥～,大江南北成通途。High up in the air a bridge flies to span the north and south of the Yangtze River.
凌厉 línglì quick and powerful; swift and fierce: 朔风～,天寒地冻。The north wind is so fierce that everything is frozen. / 客队攻势～,主队防不胜防。The host team couldn't stand up to the rapid and vigorous attacks of the visiting team.
凌轹 línglì *also*"陵轹" línglì 〈书面〉❶ bully and oppress: ～百姓 ride roughshod over the common people ❷ push out; squeeze out; exclude: ～同人 squeeze out (*or* exclude) one's colleagues
凌乱 língluàn *also*"零乱" língluàn in disorder; in confusion; in a mess: ～无序 messy; confused and disorderly
凌虐 língnüè 〈书面〉maltreat; tyrannize over: 备受～ suffer all kinds of maltreatment / 大国～小国。The big countries bully the small ones.
凌人 língrén bear down upon people; domineer: 盛气～ domineering; arrogant; overbearing
凌日 língrì 〈天文〉transit: 金星～ transit of Venus
凌辱 língrǔ insult; humiliate; treat insolently: 百般～ humiliate by every means / 他忍受不住厂主的一再～,愤而辞职。He couldn't bear the repeated insults of the factory owner any longer and quitted his job in anger.
凌替 língtì *also*"陵替" língtì 〈书面〉❶ breakdown of law and order ❷ decline
凌侮 língwǔ insult; bully; humiliate
凌霄 língxiāo ❶ reach the clouds; soar to the skies: 浩气～ lofty spirit ❷ 〈植物〉Chinese trumpet creeper (*Campsis grandiflora*)
凌霄花 língxiāohuā *also*"鬼目" guǐmù; "紫葳" zǐwēi 〈植物〉Chinese trumpet creeper (*Campsis grandiflora*)
凌虚 língxū 〈书面〉be high up in the air; soar or tower aloft: ～飞翔 soar high in the air
凌汛 língxùn ice run: 大河初开,～即至。As the frozen river thaws, the ice run is approaching.
凌压 língyā *also*"陵压" língyā bully and oppress; ride roughshod over
凌夷 língyí *also*"陵夷" língyí 〈书面〉decline; deteriorate: 国势～。The state is declining (*or* is in decline).
凌云 língyún 〈书面〉reach the clouds; soar to the skies: ～直上九重霄 soar to the skies / ～之志 high aspirations / 久有～志,重上井冈山。I have long aspired to reach the clouds, And I again ascend Jinggangshan.
凌杂 língzá in disorder; in a mess: ～不堪 in a terrible mess; in a state of utter confusion / ～的家具、衣物堆满了楼道。The corridor is jumbled up with furniture and clothes.
凌杂米盐 língzá-mǐyán messy and fragmentary; petty affairs; trifles: 这部电视剧长达四十集,情节～。This TV play has as many as forty parts and its plot is poorly constructed.
凌锥 língzhuī 〈方言〉icicle: 屋檐上挂着～。Icicles hung from the eaves of the roof.

菱

líng *also*"菱角"〈植物〉ling; water caltrop
菱花 línghuā ❶ flower of ling ❷ mirror: ～照鬓感流年。The grey hair in the mirror reminds one of the fleeting time.
菱花镜 línghuājìng *see*"菱花❷"
菱角 língjiao ling; water caltrop
菱角菜 língjiaocài 〈方言〉mustard tuber
菱镁矿 língměikuàng magnesite
菱铁矿 língtiěkuàng siderite
菱锌矿 língxīnkuàng smithsonite
菱形 língxíng rhombus; lozenge; diamond: ～六面体 rhombohedron
菱形队形 língxíng duìxíng 〈军事〉diamond formation

鲮

líng 〈动物〉dace
鲮鲤 línglǐ *also*"穿山甲" chuānshānjiǎ pangolin
鲮鱼 língyú dace

陵

líng ❶ hill; mound: 山～ hill; mound / 丘～地带 hilly land; hilly country ❷ imperial tomb; mausoleum: 中山～ Sun Yat-sen Mausoleum / 十三～ Tombs of 13 Ming Emperors; Ming Tombs / 谒～ pay homage at sb.'s mausoleum ❸ 〈书面〉bully; violate: 以强～弱。The strong bully the weak.
陵迟 língchí ❶ 〈书面〉decline ❷ 〈书面〉gentle slope or gradient ❸ *see*"凌迟" língchí
陵谷 línggǔ 〈书面〉❶ hills and valleys ❷ changes; vicissitudes
陵谷变迁 línggǔ-biànqiān *also*"陵谷易处" mountains and valleys change; cataclysmic changes occur
陵驾 língjià *see*"凌驾" língjià
陵轹 línglì *see*"凌轹" línglì
陵墓 língmù mausoleum; tomb
陵寝 língqǐn 〈书面〉emperor's or king's resting place; imperial mausoleum
陵替 língtì *also*"凌替" língtì 〈书面〉❶ breakdown of law and order: 法度～,天下大乱。The breakdown of law and order leads to social chaos (*or* upheaval). ❷ decline: 家道～ declining of a family's fortune
陵压 língyā *see*"凌压" língyā

陵夷 língyí 〈书面〉 see "凌夷" língyí
陵园 língyuán tombs surrounded by a park; cemetery: 烈士～ cemetery (or tombs) of revolutionary martyrs
陵雨 língyǔ torrential rain; rainstorm: ～终日。All day it poured in torrents.

绫

líng silk fabric resembling satin but thinner; damask silk: ～罗绸缎 silks and satins
绫子 língzi 〈纺织〉 silk fabric resembling satin but thinner; damask silk

令

líng
see also lǐng; lìng
令狐 Línghú ❶ place in Shanxi Province ❷ a surname

泠

líng ❶ 〈书面〉 cool and fresh ❷ (Líng) a surname
泠风 língfēng cool, fresh breeze
泠泠 línglíng 〈书面〉 ❶ cool; chilly: 雨霖霖, 风～。The rain is heavy and the wind chilly. ❷ clear and melodious: 泉声～ melodious gurgling of spring water
泠然 língrán 〈书面〉 clear and melodious; clear and far-reaching: 钟磬～。The bells sound loud and clear.

羚

líng ❶ antelope ❷ 〈中药〉 antelope's horn
羚牛 língniú also "扭角羚" niǔjiǎolíng; "牛羚" 〈动物〉 takin
羚羊 língyáng also "羚" 〈动物〉 antelope; gazelle: 大～ oryx / ～角 〈中药〉 antelope's horn

〇

líng (usu. used in numbers) zero sign; nought: 二～六号 No. 206 (number two-oh-six) / 一九九～年 year of nineteen ninety

零[1]

líng ❶ fractional; fragmentary; part: 合～为整 bring up the parts into a whole ❷ fraction; odd lot; extra: 老汉今年七十有～。The old man is a little more than seventy years old. / 全厂职工七百挂～儿。There are seven hundred odd staff and workers in the factory. ❸ *placed between two numbers to indicate a smaller quantity following a larger one*: 一年～五天 a year and five days / 四块～五分 four *yuan* and five *fen* ❹ zero sign (0); nought: 五～五号 No. 505 (number five-oh-five) / ～点～五 0.05 (point nought five) ❺ nought; zero; nil: 辛苦一场等于～ get nothing for one's pains / 十五比～ fifteen love (in tennis) / 比分是三比～。The score was three-nil (or three-nothing). / 五减五等于～。Five minus five leaves nought (or zero). / 这种药的效力等于～。The medicine was of no effect. ❻ zero (on a thermometer): 气温是～下二十七度。It was 27 degrees below zero. ❼ (Líng) a surname

零[2]

líng ❶ wither and fall: 凋～ wither; decline ❷ 〈书面〉 fall: 涕～ shed tears
零吃 língchī 〈口语〉 between-meal nibble: 这孩子～不断。The child has no end of between-meal nibbles.
零打碎敲 língdǎ-suìqiāo see "零敲碎打"
零担 língdàn 〈交通〉 odd cargo: 本站承办～托运。This station handles odd cargo consignment.
零蛋 língdàn zero (0); nothing: 考试得了个～ get a zero mark in an examination; lay an egg in an exam
零点 língdiǎn zero hour; midnight; twelve o'clock at night
零点方案 língdiǎn fāng'àn zero option, a disarmament proposal for the total removal of certain types of weapons on both sides
零点能 língdiǎnnéng 〈物理〉 zero-point energy
零丁 língdīng also "伶仃" língdīng lonely
零丁孤苦 língdīng-gūkǔ also "孤苦伶仃" gūkǔ-língdīng orphaned and helpless; all alone and uncared for
零度 língdù zero: 室温已降到～以下。The temperature in the room has fallen below zero. or The room temperature is below zero.
零工 línggōng ❶ odd job; short-term hired labour: 打～ do odd jobs; odd-job ❷ odd-job man; casual labourer: 雇～ hire casual labourers / 请～ hire odd-job men
零和游戏 líng hé yóuxì also "零和博弈" zero-sum game; zero game: 两市的竞争不应视为一场"～", 非赢即输, 而应创造一种双赢局面。The competition between the two cities must not be regarded as a zero game in which one must lose if the other wins; it should lead to a "win-win" situation.
零花 línghuā ❶ spend on minor items; pay incidental expenses: 这点儿钱, 你留着～吧! Keep this money for incidental expenses. ❷ pocket money: 做个小买卖挣～儿 do small business to make a little money
零活儿 línghuór odd jobs: 退休后, 他在家干点～。He did odd jobs at home after retirement.
零基预算 língjī yùsuàn 〈经济〉 zero-base budgeting
零级风 língjífēng calm
零件 língjiàn spare parts; spares: 生产汽车～的小厂 small factory which produces spare parts for cars / 组装～ spare-parts assembly
零乱 língluàn see "凌乱" língluàn
零落 língluò ❶ wither and fall: 秋风一起, 草木～。The autumn wind left behind bare trees and withered grass. / 枯枝败叶～满地。The ground is covered with withered tree branches and leaves. ❷ decline; decay: ～不堪 be far gone in decay / 战乱后的故乡已是一片凄凉～的景象。The hometown took on a desolate look after the war. ❸ scattered; sporadic: 河边响起～的枪声。From the river bank came the sound of sporadic gunfire. / 羊儿零零落落地散布在山坡上。Sheep are scattered over the hillslope.
零卖 língmài ❶ retail; sell retail ❷ sell by the piece or in small quantities: 成套餐具不～。The tea set is not sold by the piece.
零七八碎 língqībāsuì ❶ scattered and disorderly: 不要～地乱放东西。Don't leave things about. / 把你屋的这些～的东西收拾好! Tidy up your room, please! ❷ miscellaneous and trifling things; odds and ends: 一年买这些～儿就得花不少钱。Every year we spend quite some money on such odds and ends. / 这些～儿占了我不少时间。It takes me a lot of time to deal with these trivial matters.
零钱 língqián ❶ small change: 不用找～了。Keep the change. ❷ pocket money: 家里每月给我十块钱～。My family gave me ten *yuan* every month as pocket money. ❸ extra money; tip: 他在饭馆打杂, 每天可拿到块儿八毛的～。He did odd jobs at the restaurant and earned a little extra money every day.
零敲碎打 língqiāo-suìdǎ also "零打碎敲" do sth. bit by bit, off and on; adopt a piecemeal approach: 科研工作应有全盘的考虑, 不能～。Scientific research requires overall consideration instead of a piecemeal approach.
零散 língsan scattered; dispersed: 十几个学生零零散散地坐在大教室里看书。About a dozen students sat scattered in the large classroom reading.
零声母 língshēngmǔ zero initial consonant (of a Chinese syllable) begun with a vowel like a, e, and o, e.g. 爱 ài, 鹅 é, and 藕 ǒu
零时 língshí zero hour
零食 língshí between-meal nibbles; snacks: 她好吃～。She always nibbles between meals.
零售 língshòu retail; sell retail: ～总额 total volume of retail sales / 本店～兼批发。This shop sells both wholesale and retail.
零售店 língshòudiàn retail shop
零售额 língshòu'é turnover from retail sales
零售价格 língshòu jiàgé retail price
零售商 língshòushāng retail trader; retailer
零售网 língshòuwǎng retail network
零数 língshù remainder (beyond a round number); fractional amount or number
零碎 língsuì ❶ scrappy; fragmentary; trivial; trifling: 一天到晚尽干些～事儿 do nothing but odd jobs all day / 这月工厂只收到一些～活儿。The factory got only a few piecemeal orders this month. ❷ odds and ends; oddments; bits and pieces: 东西都烧光了, 只剩下这些零零碎碎。Everything was burnt except these odds and ends.
零涕 língtì 〈书面〉 tears: 感激～ be moved to tears of gratitude; shed tears of gratitude
零头 língtóu ❶ fractional amount; odd-lot piece: 她把三十块钱给了女儿, 身上只有几毛钱～了。She gave thirty *yuan* to her daughter and kept only several *jiao* for herself. ❷ remnant; oddments; bits and pieces: ～布 remnant (of cloth) / 没有整料, 都是～儿。There's not a single whole length left, only bits and pieces.
零头定价法 língtóu dìngjiàfǎ 〈商业〉 odd-even pricing
零星 língxīng ❶ fragmentary; odd; piecemeal: 谈点～的感想 express one's random thoughts / 零零星星地还钱 repay money in dribs and drabs / 冬夜, 柜台前只有几位～的顾客。There were only a few customers before the counter on the winter night. ❷ scattered; sporadic: ～小雨 occasional drizzles; scattered showers / 山冈上传来～

L

的枪声。Sporadic reports of gunfire came from the hill.
零讯 língxùn scraps of news:本报第四版新辟《市场～》。A column by the name of "Market News" was newly started on the fourth page of this newspaper.
零压 língyā ❶〈电工〉zero-voltage:～电流 zero-voltage current ❷〈机械〉zero-pressure
零用 língyòng ❶ defray incidental expenses:你把这几十块钱带上,路上～。Please take these ten *yuan* notes with you for small incidental expenses on the way. ❷ pocket money:这点钱只够做～。This is mere pocket money.
零用费 língyòngfèi petty cash
零用钱 língyòngqián pocket money
零用账 língyòngzhàng petty cash book or account
零杂 língzá ❶ odds and ends:快把这些小～儿收拾起来。Tidy up the odds and ends quickly. ❷ odd jobs:打～ do odd jobs
零增长 língzēngzhǎng 〈经济〉zero growth:人口的～ zero population growth
零指数 língzhǐshù 〈数学〉zero exponent
零族 língzú 〈化学〉zero group
零嘴 língzuǐ 〈方言〉between-meal nibbles; snacks:吃惯了～儿 be in the habit of having snacks between meals

玲 líng

玲玲 línglíng 〈书面〉〈象声〉tinkling of jade pieces
玲珑 línglóng ❶ (of things) ingeniously and delicately made; exquisite; cute:小巧～ small and exquisite; cute /～细小的首饰 dainty jewels ❷ (of people) nimble and smart:八面～ smooth and smart on all sides; sophisticated and on good terms with everybody /她身体还是那么娇小,但失去了以前的～。She is still petite, but no longer nimble.
玲珑剔透 línglóng-tītòu ❶ (of things) exquisitely made; delicately shaped:～的假山石 delicately-shaped rockeries /～的象牙球 exquisitely carved ivory ball ❷ (of people) bright and quick (in response, etc.); smart:她是多么～的一个姑娘,听了这话哪有不明白之理。How could she have missed the hint! She's such a bright and quick girl.

柃 líng

柃木 língmù *Eurya japonica*

苓 líng *see* "伏苓" fúlíng

聆 líng 〈书面〉listen; hear

聆教 língjiào 〈书面〉listen to sb.'s instruction; hear sb.'s words of wisdom; listen to sb.'s wise counsel
聆取 língqǔ 〈书面〉listen to and accept:多年～先生的教诲,身心受益匪浅。I've benefited a great deal from your instructions for years.
聆听 língtīng 〈书面〉listen (respectfully):先生之言,我们必当倾耳～。We all listen attentively to your advice.

岭 líng 〈书面〉white

瓴 líng 〈书面〉water jar

see also "高屋建瓴" gāowū-jiànlíng

龄 líng

❶ age; years:年～不大 of young age; young in age /学～前儿童 pre-school children; pre-schoolers /七十高～ advanced age of seventy ❷ length of time or service; duration:工～ length of service; number of years worked; years of service /教～ length of service as a teacher /军～ length of military service /舰～ ship's length of service /四十年党～的老干部 veteran cadre of forty years' standing in the Party ❸〈生物〉instar; stadium:幼虫～ larval instar /蛹～ pupal instar

囹 líng

囹圄 língyǔ *also* "囹圉"〈书面〉gaol; jail; prison:身在～之中 be behind prison bars /身陷～ be thrown into prison; be jailed
囹圉 língyǔ *see* "囹圄"

蛉 líng *see* "白蛉" báilíng

笭 líng

笭箵 língxīng 〈书面〉bamboo basket (used for holding fish while angling); creel

铃 líng

❶ bell:门～ door bell /电～ electric bell /车～ bicycle bell ❷ anything in the shape of a bell:哑～ dumbbell /杠～ barbell ❸ boll; bud:落～ shedding (*or* premature dropping) of cotton bolls
铃钹 língbó bell cymbals
铃铛 língdang small bell:给小马套上了一个铜～ tie a brass bell on the pony
铃鼓 línggǔ 〈乐器〉tambourine
铃兰 línglán 〈植物〉lily of the valley
铃铎 língduó bell hanging from the eaves
铃木汽车工业公司 Língmù Qìchē Gōngyè Gōngsī (Japan) Suzuki Motor Co. Ltd.
铃木善幸 Língmùshànxìng Suzuki Zenko (1911-), Japanese Prime Minister (1980-1982)
铃医 língyī itinerant doctor (ringing a bell to catch the patients' attention)

伶 líng 〈旧语〉actor or actress:名～ famous actor or actress

伶仃 língdīng *also* "零丁" língdīng ❶ left all alone; solitary; lonely:孤苦～ orphaned and helpless; friendless and wretched /自小～一人,祖母把我养大。Left alone at an early age, I was brought up by my grandmother. ❷ thin and weak:瘦骨～ mere skeleton; all skin and bones
伶俐 língli clever; bright; smart; quick-witted:口齿～ have the gift of the gab; be smart and fluent /聪明～的小孩 clever and bright child
伶俜 língpīng 〈书面〉solitary; all alone; lonely:自小～无依 be left alone and helpless from childhood
伶人 língrén actor or actress
伶牙俐齿 língyá-lìchǐ have the gift of the gab; have a glib tongue:这孩子说起话来,～,半句也不让人! The child talks glibly and never gives in to others.

舲 líng 〈书面〉❶ boat with windows ❷ small boat

鸰 líng *see* "鹡鸰" jílíng

翎 líng

❶ plume; tail or wing feather; quill:孔雀～ peacock plumes; peacock feathers /雁～ wild goose feather /鸡～儿 cock feather ❷ peacock feather worn at the back of a Qing Dynasty official's hat:顶戴花～ peacock feather and button worn on a Qing Dynasty official's hat — official position
翎毛 língmáo ❶ plume:雏鹰～未丰。The young eagle is unfledged. ❷ type of classical Chinese painting featuring birds:那位画家尤善～。That painter is particularly versed in classical Chinese paintings featuring birds.
翎扇 língshàn feather fan
翎子 língzi ❶ peacock feathers worn at the back of a Qing official's hat:一个头戴～的官员信步走过。An official wearing a feather at the back of his hat walked by at a leisurely pace. ❷〈戏曲〉long pheasant tail feathers worn on warriors' helmets in Chinese operas

灵(靈、霛) líng

❶ quick; clever; nimble; flexible:心～手巧 quick-witted and nimble-fingered; clever and deft /机～ clever; intelligent /脑子很～ have a sharp mind; be brainy /资金周转不～ have difficulty in liquidity /机器失～。The machine broke down. ❷ mind; soul; spirit; intelligence:心～ mind; soul /在天之～ sb.'s soul in heaven /从心～深处 from the heart of hearts ❸ deity; fairy; sprite; elf:神～ gods; deities; divinities ❹ efficacious; effective:办法～ effective method /这药～得很。The medicine works wonders. ❺ coffin containing a corpse; remains of the deceased; bier:辞～ bow to a coffin before it is carried to the grave /烈士～前摆满了花圈。Before the bier of the revolutionary martyr lay a lot of floral wreaths.
灵便 língbiàn ❶ nimble; agile; quick:手脚～ be nimble /大娘耳朵不～,听话费力。Grandma is hard of hearing. ❷ easy to handle;

handy:这把斧头使起来真～。The axe is quite handy.
灵车 língchē hearse
灵榇 língchèn 〈书面〉coffin containing a corpse; bier:一见父亲的～，他不禁大哭。He couldn't help bursting into tears at the sight of his father's bier.
灵床 língchuáng ❶ bed on which a corpse is laid; bier ❷ bed made ready for the dead:家人赶忙准备后事，已在屋中央安设了～。The family hurried on with the arrangements for the funeral and prepared a ritual bed in the middle of the main room.
灵丹妙药 língdān-miàoyào also "灵丹圣药" miraculous cure; panacea; cure-all
灵动 língdong nimble; agile; flexible:头脑～ be quick-witted; have a supple mind /一双～的大眼睛 a pair of large roving eyes
灵幡 língfān funeral streamer
灵泛 língfan also "灵翻" handy; agile; nimble:这小锅使着～。The small pot is very handy. /他会拳术，身体很～。He practises shadow-boxing and is quite nimble in movement.
灵符 língfú 〈迷信〉magic figures drawn by Taoist priests to invoke or exorcise spirits and bring good or ill fortune
灵府 língfǔ 〈书面〉brain
灵感 línggǎn inspiration:文学创作需要～。Literary creation needs inspiration.
灵骨 línggǔ holy ashes; Buddhist relics
灵怪 língguài ❶ legendary deity; monster; demon; goblin:～故事 stories of fairies and demons ❷〈书面〉miraculous and monstrous; bizarre:说得过于～ tell a tall story
灵光 língguāng ❶〈旧语〉miraculous luminance or light:～寺 Temple of Divine Light (in Beijing) ❷ bright light round the head of a god or Buddha in a picture; aura; halo ❸〈方言〉effective; wonderful; excellent:他的乒乓球打得真～。He is a super ping-pong player. /这个办法不～。This method doesn't work.
灵盒 línghé cinerary casket
灵慧 línghuì intelligent; bright; clever:赋性～ inherently intelligent; bright and clever
灵魂 línghún ❶〈迷信〉soul:～不死 immortal soul /她祈求～升入天界，又能和死去的孩子在一起。She prayed that her soul would ascend to heaven and reunite with her deceased child. ❷ soul; spirit:纯洁的～ pure and honest soul /他触到了她～深处的隐痛。He touched the secret anguish in the depth of her soul (or heart). ❸ conscience; soul:出卖～ sell one's soul (to the enemy, etc.) /丧失～的人 man devoid of conscience; conscienceless person ❹ decisive factor; soul:效益是企业生命的～。Efficiency is the soul of an enterprise.
灵魂论 línghúnlùn 〈宗教〉Doctrine of Soul
灵活 línghuó ❶ nimble; agile; supple; quick:动作～ dexterous and quick in action /小伙子脑筋真～。The young man is quick-witted. or The young man has a supple mind. ❷ flexible; elastic:～运用 apply (or use) sth. flexibly /～规定 elastic regulations /～的外交政策 flexible foreign policy
灵活性 línghuóxìng flexibility; elasticity; adaptability; mobility:～与原则性相结合 combine flexibility with a principled stand
灵机 língjī sudden inspiration; brainwave
灵机一动 língjī-yīdòng have a brainwave; have a sudden inspiration; strike on a bright idea
灵捷 língjié quick; nimble; agile; adroit:心思～ quick-witted; clever /他像猴子那样～，一蹿就上了房了。He was as agile as a monkey and jumped onto the roof.
灵境 língjìng 〈书面〉fairyland; wonderland; paradise:～缥缈 mysterious and intangible fairyland
灵柩 língjiù coffin containing a corpse; bier:人们随着装载～的汽车，缓缓地移动着脚步。People slowly moved their steps following the hearse.
灵快 língkuài quick; nimble; agile; deft:手脚～ be agile in movement /他的算盘打得很～，字也写得很流利。He used an abacus adroitly (or deftly) and wrote a good hand.
灵利 língli also "伶俐" língli clever; bright; quick-witted
灵猫 língmāo 〈动物〉civet (cat):大～ zibet
灵妙 língmiào wonderful; ingenious; clever:壁画中人物形象的勾勒自然～，独具一格。The sketch of the figures in the murals is natural, ingenious and unique.
灵敏 língmǐn sensitive; keen; acute; agile:感觉～ have keen senses /手脚～ be agile in one's movements /～的磅秤 sensitive pair of scales
灵敏度 língmǐndù ❶〈无线电〉sensitivity:这种三波段的收音机～很高。The three wave-band radio is known for its high sensitivity. ❷ accuracy; precision:这一批仪表质量不过关，～较差。The quality of this batch of meters is not up to standard; their accuracy is inadequate.
灵牌 língpái temporary memorial tablet (of a deceased person to receive homage, etc.)
灵棚 língpéng mourning shed or shelter
灵气 língqì ❶ intelligence; power of understanding:两眼透着～ one's eyes expressive of a native intelligence /他很有～，一定能成为出色的作家。He is a man of high intelligence and will become an outstanding writer. ❷ power or force; miraculous power or force:得天地之～ draw miraculous power from heaven and earth
灵巧 língqiǎo dexterous; agile; skilful; ingenious:这孩子心思～极了。The child has a dexterous mind. /这玩具做得真～。The toy is ingeniously made.
灵巧炸弹 língqiǎo zhàdàn 〈军事〉smart bomb
灵俏 língqiao clever; smart; bright; quick-witted
灵寝 língqǐn 〈旧语〉seat of a bier; place where a coffin is set for rituals
灵清 língqīng 〈方言〉clear:几句话说不～ can't make oneself understood in a few words /这孩子头脑特别～。The child has got an exceptionally clear mind.
灵蛇之珠 língshézhīzhū also "灵蛇珠" outstanding ability; remarkable talent; profound knowledge
灵台 língtái ❶ catafalque; seat of a bier:～左右排列着花圈。The catafalque is flanked with floral wreaths. ❷〈书面〉heart; soul; spirit
灵堂 língtáng mourning hall:告别仪式在医院的～举行。A ceremony will be held in the mourning hall of the hospital to pay last respects to the deceased.
灵猩 língtí greyhound
灵通 língtōng ❶ having quick access to information; well-informed:他消息特别～。He is very well informed. ❷〈方言〉effective; useful:别小看这玩意儿，还真～! Don't belittle the small gadget; it works well. ❸〈方言〉nimble; agile; quick:心眼儿～ be quick-witted
灵童 língtóng soul boy:十世班禅转世～ reincarnated soul boy for the 10th Panchen Lama; soul boy who is the reincarnation of the 10th Panchen Lama
灵透 língtou 〈方言〉clever; smart; bright; intelligent:这小伙子心眼儿～，学什么会什么。The young fellow is really smart and quick in learning.
灵帷 língwéi also "灵帏" funeral curtain
灵位 língwèi temporary memorial tablet (of a deceased person):兄弟几个跪在～前发誓，为父报仇。On their knees before their father's memorial tablet the brothers vowed to avenge him.
灵物 língwù ❶ magical thing; miracle ❷ ghosts and deities; spirits; supernatural beings
灵犀 língxī rhinoceros horn;〈比喻〉heart-beat in unison:心有～一点通 with hearts linked in common beat; understand each other without so many words
灵香草 língxiāngcǎo *Lysimachia foenumgraecum*
灵效 língxiào magical or miraculous effect; effect:这个药有～，服了两剂，病就好了。The medicine was highly effective, and I recovered from the illness after taking two doses.
灵醒 língxǐng 〈方言〉❶ smart and clear-headed; clever and sober:这小伙子～得很，主意也多。The young fellow is smart and resourceful. ❷ sharp; keen:耳目～ sharp ears and eyes; have keen sight and hearing ❸ be clear; understand:你怎么连这点小事都弄不～。Don't you understand such a simple thing?
灵性 língxìng ❶ intelligence; aptitude; wisdom:他具有学外语的～。He has an aptitude for foreign languages. ❷ sagacity (of animals); intelligence:那只有～的鸟，是老爷子的心爱之物。That smart bird is my father's favorite pet.
灵秀 língxiù pretty and bright; intelligent and beautiful
灵验 língyàn ❶ efficacious; effective:这个法子看来挺～。The method seemed to work well. ❷ (of a forecast, prediction, etc.) accurate; true; right:他的预测果然～。His prediction has come true.
灵药 língyào miracle drug; elixir of life:万能～ cure-all; panacea
灵异 língyì ❶ deities and spirits; fairies and elves ❷ magical; mystical; miraculous:～的岩洞 mysterious cave

灵隐寺 Língyǐnsì Lingyinsi Temple or Temple of Soul's Retreat (in Hangzhou, Zhejiang Province)
灵应 língyìng efficacious; effective
灵长目 língzhǎngmù 〈动物〉Primates:～动物 primate /人与猿猴均属～。Human beings as well as monkeys and apes belong to the order of Primates.
灵芝 língzhī glossy ganoderma (*Ganoderma lucidum*)
灵智学 língzhìxué 〈哲学〉anthroposophy
灵珠 língzhū *see* "灵蛇之珠"

棂(欞、櫺)

líng (window) lattice; latticework:窗～ window lattice

醽

líng
醽醁 línglù 〈书面〉a kind of good wine

lǐng

令

lǐng 〈量词〉ream:两～新闻纸 two reams of newsprint
see also líng; lìng

领

lǐng ❶ neck:引～而望 crane one's neck for a look; eagerly look forward to ❷ collar:衣～ collar /毛皮～ fur collar /翻～ turnover collar /蓝～工人 bluecollar worker ❸ collarband; neckband:圆～儿 round collarband /和尚～儿 neckband of a monk's robe /鸡心～ V-shaped collar ❹ outline; main point:不得要～ fail to grasp the main points (*or* essentials) /提纲挈～ concentrate on the main points; give the gist (of sth.); bring out the essence ❺〈量词〉*used of a gown, coat, mat, etc.*:穿了一～新长袍 wear a new robe /一～凉席 a summer sleeping mat ❻ lead; usher; take:～人穿过树林 lead sb. through the woods /把客人～到会客室 usher a guest into the reception room /把孩子～回家 take a child home /～大家参观图书馆 show everybody round the library ❼ have jurisdiction over; be in possession of:占～ occupy ❽ receive; draw; get:～奖 receive a prize (*or* an award) /～工资 get one's salary (*or* wages) ❾ accept:我心～了。I appreciate your kindness but cannot accept the gift (*or* invitation). ❿ understand; comprehend; grasp:心～神会 understand tacitly; know by intuition
领班 lǐngbān ❶ lead or head (a work team or group):昨天他～时出了一桩事故。An accident happened while he was supervising the production. ❷ gaffer; foreman; supervisor:车间工人没有不恨这个～的。All the workers in the workshop hated the foreman.
领唱 lǐngchàng ❶ lead a chorus:男高音～ chorus led by a tenor ❷ leading singer (of a chorus)
领带 lǐngdài necktie; tie:打～ knot a necktie /戴～ wear a tie
领带扣针 lǐngdài kòuzhēn *also* "领带别针" tiepin
领带卡 lǐngdàiqiǎ *also* "领带夹" tie clip
领导 lǐngdǎo ❶ lead; exercise leadership:～体制 system (*or* structure) of leadership /～才能 talent for leadership /～罢工 lead a strike /在总工程师的～下,我们攻克了几个技术难题。Led by the chief engineer, we overcame several technical problems. ❷ leader; leadership:担任～ assume the leadership; become a (*or* the) leader /～必须密切联系群众。The leadership must maintain close ties with the masses.
领导班子 lǐngdǎo bānzi leading group:调整～ make changes in (*or* reshuffle) the leading group (*or* line-up) /改选～ re-elect the leadership
领导地位 lǐngdǎo dìwèi position of leadership; status as a leader:确立～ establish (sb.'s) position as the leader (of a party, etc.)
领导干部 lǐngdǎo gànbù leading cadre
领导骨干 lǐngdǎo gǔgàn backbone or key members of the leadership
领导核心 lǐngdǎo héxīn leading nucleus or core
领导权 lǐngdǎoquán leadership; authority
领导水平 lǐngdǎo shuǐpíng level of leadership
领导艺术 lǐngdǎo yìshù art of leadership
领导作风 lǐngdǎo zuòfēng work style of the leadership; leadership style
领导作用 lǐngdǎo zuòyòng leading role
领道 lǐngdào lead the way:～儿的人是当地一个老乡。The man leading the way is a local peasant. /请找个人领领道儿吧。Please find a guide to show us the way.
领地 lǐngdì ❶ manor (of a feudal lord); fief:奴隶在奴隶主的～上无偿地劳动。Slaves worked without compensation in the manors of the slave-owner. ❷ territory:海外～ overseas territory; overseas possession
领读 lǐngdú lead (in) the reading:老师先～了课文。The teacher started by leading the class in reading the text aloud.
领队 lǐngduì ❶ lead a group:这次外出参观由校长～。The president of the college will lead us on this tour. ❷ leader of a group, sports team, etc.; manager:～兼教练 manager-coach; coaching manager /～是一个中年妇女。The leader of the group is a middle-aged woman.
领队机 lǐngduìjī 〈军事〉lead aircraft
领港 lǐnggǎng *also* "引港" yǐngǎng ❶ pilot a ship into or out of a harbour:他～多年,深受大家的信任。He has been piloting for many years and enjoys everybody's deep trust. ❷ (harbour) pilot
领港权 lǐnggǎngquán pilotage
领港员 lǐnggǎngyuán pilot
领工 lǐnggōng ❶ lead people in their work; supervise the work:～修路 supervise road construction ❷ foreman; supervisor
领钩 lǐnggōu hook and eye on the collar
领褂 lǐngguà 〈方言〉a kind of Chinese-style waistcoat with buttons down the front
领馆 lǐngguǎn consulate; consular office:总～ consulate-general /使～ embassies and consulates; diplomatic missions
领海 lǐnghǎi territorial waters; territorial sea:～范围 extent of territorial waters /～线 boundary line of territorial waters /～权 sovereign right over territorial waters /～及毗连区公约 Convention on the Territorial Sea and the Contiguous Zone (1958)
领航 lǐngháng ❶ navigate; pilot:～设备 navigation equipment /～图 pilot chart ❷ navigator; pilot
领航飞机 lǐngháng fēijī pathfinder aircraft
领航权 lǐnghángquán pilotage
领航员 lǐnghángyuán navigator; pilot
领花 lǐnghuā ❶ (bow) tie ❷ collar insignia
领会 lǐnghuì understand; comprehend; grasp:～事件的重大意义 grasp the significance of an event /善于～领导意图 be good at getting what is at the back of the boss' mind /她没有～你的意思。She failed to see your point. /对我的暗示,她～地点点头。She returned my hint with a knowing nod.
领家 lǐngjiā 〈旧语〉bawd:～老鸨 bawd
领江 lǐngjiāng ❶ navigate a ship on a river ❷ river pilot
领教 lǐngjiào ❶〈套语〉*used to express one's appreciation or thanks for advice, instruction, or performance*:你如此相助,～～! You have been a great help to me. I'm much obliged. /今日～张师傅武功,果然不凡。It is truly impressive to see Master Zhang's *wushu* feats today. ❷ ask advice; consult:有几个问题,特来～。I came to seek your advice on a few questions. ❸ experience; encounter:你的手段,我们早有～。We are no strangers to your tricks. /你还没～过她的倔脾气。You don't know her stubbornness yet.
领结 lǐngjié (bow) tie
领解 lǐngjiě comprehend; understand; grasp:～教义 understand religious doctrines
领巾 lǐngjīn scarf; neckerchief:红～ red scarf (as worn by a Young Pioneer)
领空 lǐngkōng territorial sky or air; territorial air space
领口 lǐngkǒu ❶ collarband; neckband:这件衣服～不合适。The neckband of the jacket doesn't fit. ❷ place where the two ends of a collar meet:她在～上别了一支别针。She pinned a brooch on her neckband.
领扣 lǐngkòu collar button; collar stud
领款 lǐngkuǎn draw money:～人 payee /～签名 signature of the payee /他到银行～去了。He went to the bank to draw money.
领陆 lǐnglù territorial land; land domain
领路 lǐnglù lead the way:～人 guide;leader /领错了路 lead astray/一位老人在前面～。An old man is leading the way ahead.
领略 lǐnglüè have a taste of; experience; appreciate:人情冷暖,世态炎凉,这几年他都一一～过。He has experienced the warmth and coldness, and the inconstancy of human relationship in the last few years. /此行要好好～一下江南风光。I'm going to fully enjoy the scenery south of the Yangtze on my trip.
领命 lǐngmìng take orders or instructions:～而去 leave with an or-

der (*or* task) /他刚领了命就行动起来。He went into action the moment he got the order.
领诺 lǐngnuò promise; agree (to do sth.); undertake to do sth.:他无法推辞，只得～。Since he could not very well decline, he had to agree.
领情 lǐngqíng feel grateful to sb.; appreciate the kindness:他从没见过这样不～的怪人! He has never met such a strange fellow who doesn't appreciate other's kindness. /我代他～了。I'm grateful to you on his behalf.
领区 lǐngqū consular district
领取 lǐngqǔ draw; receive:～护照 get one's passport /请准时前来～办公用品。Please come on time to pick up office stationery. /上月工资我尚未～。I haven't drawn last month's salary yet.
领事 lǐngshì consul:总～ consul general /副～ vice-consul /代理～ pro-consul /随习～ *consul-élève* /职业～官 career consular officer /名誉～官 honorary consular officer /～豁免 consular immunities /～特权 consular privileges /～档案 consular archives /～机关 consular post /～机关房屋 consular premises /～机关雇员 consular employee /～区域(领区) consular district /～代理 consular agent
领事裁判权 lǐngshì cáipànquán consular jurisdiction
领事处 lǐngshìchù consular section
领事馆 lǐngshìguǎn consulate:总～ consulate general
领事条例 lǐngshì tiáolì consular act
领事团 lǐngshìtuán consular corps
领事委任书 lǐngshì wěirènshū certificate of appointment of consul; consular commission
领事协定 lǐngshì xiédìng consular agreement
领事移住部 Lǐngshì Yízhùbù Consular and Emigration Affairs Department (of the Ministry of Foreign Affairs of Japan)
领事证书 lǐngshì zhèngshū exequatur
领受 lǐngshòu accept (kindness, etc.); receive:却之不恭，你带来的礼物我只好～了。It would be ungracious not to accept your gift.
领属 lǐngshǔ leader and subordinate:～关系 relationship between a superior and a subordinate; subordination
领水 lǐngshuǐ ❶ inland waters ❷ territorial waters ❸〈方言〉(harbour) pilot
领水员 lǐngshuǐyuán pilot; navigator
领条 lǐngtiáo ❶ collar strip ❷ voucher
领头 lǐngtóu take the lead; be the first (to do sth.):她～鼓起掌来。She led the applause. /我～，你们跟上。I'll take the lead and you all follow me. /狂欢节队伍由军乐队～。A military band was at the head of the carnival procession.
领头羊 lǐngtóuyáng bellwether:搞科研，我们老同志义不容辞，要做"～"。We old comrades are duty-bound to be the "bellwethers" in scientific research.
领土 lǐngtǔ territory:～割让 cession of territory /侵犯别国～ violate the territory of another country /～纠纷 territorial dispute /～管辖 territorial jurisdiction /～毗连 geographical contiguity
领土庇护 lǐngtǔ bìhù territorial asylum
领土不可侵犯性 lǐngtǔ bùkě qīnfànxìng territorial inviolabilily
领土扩张 lǐngtǔ kuòzhāng territorial expansion; territorial aggrandizement
领土收复主义 lǐngtǔ shōufùzhǔyì (esp. of Italy and Greece) irredentism
领土完整 lǐngtǔ wánzhěng territorial integrity
领土要求 lǐngtǔ yāoqiú territorial claim
领湾 lǐngwān territorial bay
领舞 lǐngwǔ ❶ lead a dance ❷ leading dancer
领悟 lǐngwù comprehend; realize; grasp:她猛然～了他话中的含义。She suddenly realized what he was driving at.
领洗 lǐngxǐ 〈宗教〉be baptised
领先 lǐngxiān be in the lead; lead:遥遥～ hold a safe lead; be far ahead of others /那个国家在石油出口方面～。That country leads in petroleum export. /他在赛跑中～。He had the lead in the race. /我队三比一～。The score was 3:1 in our favour.
领衔 lǐngxián head the list of signers (of a document); be the first on a name list:～主演 star in a film; be a featured actor (*or* actress) /刘总经理代表公司～签署了合同书。Mr. Liu, the general manager, was the first to sign the contract on behalf of the company.
领袖 lǐngxiù leader:政党～ party leader
领袖欲 lǐngxiùyù strong desire to be a leader
领养 lǐngyǎng adopt (a child):～人 adopter /她～了几个孤儿。She adopted several orphans.
领有 lǐngyǒu possess; own:寨子里的头人～大片土地和大量奴隶。The headman of the stockaded village owned a vast tract of land and a large number of slaves.
领域 lǐngyù ❶ territory; domain:河流中心线以西，属贵国的～。The territory to the west of the central line of the river falls within the jurisdiction of your country. ❷ field; sphere; domain; realm:生活～ field in life /思想～ ideological sphere /艺术～ world of art /自然科学～ domain of the natural sciences /政治～ realm of politics
领章 lǐngzhāng collar badge; collar insignia
领主 lǐngzhǔ feudal lord; suzerain
领子 lǐngzi collar
领奏 lǐngzòu ❶ lead an instrumental ensemble ❷ leading player in an instrumental ensemble
领罪 lǐngzuì plead guilty; admit one's guilt; confess a crime

岭(嶺) lǐng ❶ ridge of a mountain; mountain:崇山峻～ lofty (*or* towering) mountain ridges /翻山越～ climb mountain after mountain; cross over hill and dale ❷ mountain range:秦～ Qinling Mountains ❸ (short for 五岭) Five Ridges that separate Guangdong and Guangxi from the hinterland
岭南 Lǐngnán (area) south of the Five Ridges; area covering Guangdong and Guangxi
岭南画派 Lǐngnán Huàpài Lingnan School of Painting, one of the modern schools of Chinese brush painting

lìng

另 lìng other; another; separate:～有想法 have other (*or* different) ideas /～有所图 have other fish to fry; have ulterior motives /～一条路 another road (*or* way)/～有安排 make separate arrangements /～谋生路 find another way of earning a living /请见～页。Please see separate sheet (*or* page).
另案 lìng'àn separate case:此事将作～处理。The matter will be handled as a separate case.
另册 lìngcè "other register" (as distinct from the regular register 正册), Qing Dynasty census book for listing disreputable people:打入～ be registered as an undesirable
另当别论 lìngdāng-biélùn be viewed differently; be considered from another perspective:如果他确实不了解情况，那就～了。It'll be another matter if he knew nothing of the real situation.
另函 lìnghán ❶ separate letter:～告知 inform by a separate letter ❷ write another letter; write separately:已～主管当局。The relevant authorities have been informed by another letter.
另寄 lìngjì *also* "另邮" post separately; post under separate cover
另开 lìngkāi 〈方言〉divide up family property and live apart; (of family members) set up housekeeping separately:这兄弟俩早已～。The two brothers have long set up their own housekeeping and lived separately.
另起炉灶 lìngqǐ-lúzào ❶ set up a new kitchen; make a fresh start; start all over again:我们不打算在原书稿的基础上修改，而是～。We are not going to revise the manuscript. We'll start all over again and rewrite it. ❷ set up one's own kitchen; go one's own way:几个分公司～，生意做得不错。Several subsidiaries of the company have become independent and are quite successful in their business.
另请高明 lìngqǐng-gāomíng find someone better qualified:要是认为我不胜任，那就～吧! If you think I'm not up to the job, find someone more competent.
另外 lìngwài in addition; moreover; besides:我还要跟你谈～一个问题。There's another problem I want to talk over with you. /除了你，我们～还请了几个朋友，大家聚一聚。Besides you, we've invited some other friends for the gathering.
另行 lìngxíng separately:～通知 be notified later; wait till further notice /～规定 stipulate separately
另眼相看 lìngyǎn-xiāngkàn *also* "另眼相待" ❶ regard or look up to sb. with special respect:由于他为人诚恳，工作努力，大家都对他～。He was held in high esteem for his honesty and industry. ❷ view sb. in a new, more favourable light; see sb. in a new light:他发达以后，人们也就对他～了。He has grown prosperous, and people begin to see him in a new light.

另议 lìngyì discuss separately; negotiate as a separate case: 此事～。We'll discuss this matter separately.
另邮 lìngyóu see "另寄"

令[1]

lìng ❶ issue an order; order: ～各部队即刻执行 order all the troops to take immediate action /通～全国 issue a general order throughout the nation ❷ command; order; decree: 法～ laws and decrees /军～ military orders /口～ word of command; password ❸ make; cause: ～人生厌 make one feel disgusted /～人费解 elude understanding /利～智昏 be blinded by lust for gain ❹ drinking game: 猜拳行～ play a finger-guessing drinking game ❺ ancient official title: 县～ county magistrate /太史～ official historian

令[2]

lìng season: 时～ season /当～ in season /冬～ winter; climate in winter

令[3]

lìng 〈书面〉❶ good; excellent: *see* "～德"; "～闻" ❷〈敬词〉your: ～兄 your brother /～妹 your sister

令[4]

lìng brief song-poem; short lyric: 十六字～ short poem set to the tune of *shiliuziling*; 16-character poem
see also líng; lǐng

令爱 lìng'ài *also* "令嫒"〈敬词〉your daughter
令嫒 lìng'ài *see* "令爱"
令出法随 lìngchū-fǎsuí rigorous enforcement of the law: 这个地区之所以秩序井然, 重要的一条就是～。Strict enforcement of the laws contributes greatly to order and stability in this area.
令出如山 lìngchū-rúshān orders are like a mountain (so that they cannot be changed or shaken); every order must be obeyed: 他历来～, 雷厉风行。He is firm and resolute, always making sure that every order is executed.
令德 lìngdé excellent virtue: 此人为政多年, 不闻有～。Although an official for years, the man has little virtuous conduct to his credit.
令阁 lìnggé *see* "令阃"
令箭 lìngjiàn arrow-shaped token of authority used in the army in ancient China; arrow used as a token of authority: 拿着鸡毛当～ use (*or* take) a chicken feather as an arrow token of authority; make a mountain out of a molehill
令箭荷花 lìngjiàn héhuā 〈植物〉*Nopalxochia ackermannii*
令节 lìngjié 〈书面〉happy festive occasion; festival: 农历的八月中, 正是钱塘观潮的～。The middle of the eighth lunar month is the best time to watch tidal waves in the Qiantang River estuary.
令阃 lìngkǔn *also* "令阁"; "令室"〈旧语〉〈敬词〉your wife
令郎 lìngláng 〈敬词〉your son
令名 lìngmíng 〈书面〉good name; reputation
令旗 lìngqí order flag; flag of command
令亲 lìngqīn 〈敬词〉your relation or relative; kinsman: ～昨持书而来, 我已遵嘱安排妥当。Yesterday your relative came with your letter and I have made proper arrangements as asked.
令人齿冷 lìngrénchǐlěng arouse scorn; invite contempt: 这些颠倒黑白的言论, ～。These statements confuse right and wrong and are utterly contemptible (*or* beneath contempt).
令人发指 lìngrénfàzhǐ get one's dander up; raise one's hackles; infuriate; make one feel extremely angry: ～的罪行 atrocious (*or* horrendous) crime
令人喷饭 lìngrénpēnfàn split one's sides; be sidesplitting; be extremely funny: ～的笑话 screamingly funny joke
令人捧腹 lìngrénpěngfù set people roaring with laughter; make people burst out laughing: 这个滑稽演员的一举一动～。Every move of the comedian tickled the audience.
令人起敬 lìngrénqǐjìng command esteem; merit respect; be admirable: ～的学者 admirable scholar
令人神往 lìngrénshénwǎng cause one to crave; fire one's imagination; have a strong appeal; be enchanting: 那里的湖光山色～。The scenery there is charming indeed.
令人作呕 lìngrénzuò'ǒu sickening; nauseating; revolting: 她那种装模作样、拿腔拿调的样子, 实在～。It makes one sick to see her affected manners and mincing tones.
令室 lìngshì *see* "令阃"
令堂 lìngtáng 〈敬词〉your mother
令闻 lìngwén 〈书面〉good name; good reputation
令行禁止 lìngxíng-jìnzhǐ strict enforcement of orders and prohibitions: 纪律方面, 要做到整齐划一, ～。In matters of discipline, it is imperative to observe uniform standards and execute every order without fail.
令尹 lìngyǐn 〈古语〉❶ highest official in the State of Chu during the Spring and Autumn, and Warring States periods; prime minister ❷ county magistrate in the Ming and Qing dynasties
令誉 lìngyù 〈书面〉good reputation: 素负～ have always been well reputed
令正 lìngzhèng 〈旧语〉〈敬词〉your wife
令尊 lìngzūn 〈敬词〉your father: ～虽然年过古稀, 但看来身体还很健壮。Although your father is over seventy, he looks strong and fit.

呤

lìng *see* "嘌呤" piàolìng

liū

溜[1]

liū ❶ slide; glide: 顺着楼梯扶手～下来 slide down the banisters ❷ sneak off; slip away: ～掉 sneak off; slip away /～出房间 sneak out of the room ❸ smooth: ～圆 smooth and round ❹〈方言〉take a look; glance: ～一眼就知道是什么东西了 know what it is by a mere glance ❺ along: ～河边走 walk along the riverside ❻〈方言〉very; extremely: ～尖 very sharp /～匀 very evenly /～净 extremely clean

溜[2]

liū *see* "熘" liū
see also liù

溜边 liūbiān ❶ keep to the edge (of a road, river, etc.): 他去晚了, 只好～站在一旁。He got there late and had to stand aside. ❷ dodge; avoid: 碰着难办的事儿就～ dodge a difficulty whenever it arises
溜冰 liūbīng ❶ skating: ～鞋 skates ❷ *also* "溜旱冰"〈方言〉roller-skating
溜冰场 liūbīngchǎng skating rink
溜槽 liūcáo chute: 山路一旁是～, 运送矿石下山。The chute on one side of the path carries the ores down the mountain.
溜达 liūda *also* "蹓跶" liūda stroll; saunter; go for a walk: 晚上十点多钟, 他溜溜达达才回来。He strolled back after ten o'clock in the evening. /饭后别老坐着, 咱们～去吧! Don't always sit still after dinner. Let's go for a walk.
溜放 liūfàng slide; glide: ～货车 let the goods van slide down /原木从山上～到溪流。Logs rolled down from the hilltop to the brook.
溜干二净 liūgān-èrjìng 〈方言〉❶ very clean: 玻璃窗擦得～。The window glass is wiped spotlessly clean. ❷ have nothing left; finish; leave nothing: 钱花得～ have spent every penny /树上的梨摘个～。All the pears were picked from the tree.
溜工 liūgōng leave one's post on the sly; sneak away: 晚班有几个人～了。Several employees sneaked away during working hours on the night shift.
溜沟子 liūgōuzi 〈方言〉lick sb.'s boots; flatter; soft-soap; fawn on: 他周围全是～的人。He is surrounded by flatterers.
溜光 liūguāng 〈方言〉❶ very smooth; sleek; glossy: 她把头发梳得～, 又别上一枝花。She combed her hair smooth and then pinned a flower in it. ❷ leave nothing; finish: 山上的树砍得～, 一棵不剩了。Trees on the mountain have all been felled.
溜旱冰 liū hànbīng roller-skating
溜号 liūhào 〈方言〉sneak away; slink off: 这小子上班尽～。He often steals away in the middle of his shift. /今早上大课时你思想是不是又～了? Were you wool-gathering again when you attended the lecture this morning?
溜滑 liūhuá 〈方言〉❶ slippery; smooth: 石子儿～ smooth pebbles /～的泥鳅 slippery loaches /满街泥泞～, 要小心些! The road is muddy and slippery. Watch your steps! ❷ sly; crafty; cunning: 他为人～。He is a trickster.
溜肩膀 liūjiānbǎng ❶ sloping shoulders ❷〈方言〉devoid of any sense of responsibility; irresponsible: 他是有名的～, 让他主事可不容易。Everybody knows he likes to pass the buck to others and it won't be easy to persuade him to take charge of the work.
溜溜儿 liūliūr 〈方言〉❶ whole; full: ～等了一天 wait for a whole day ❷ burst; fit; peal: 过道里小风～的, 凉快极了。The passageway is

pleasantly cool with puffs of gentle breeze. ❸ secretly; steathily：他～地走下来。He walked down steathily.

溜溜转 liūliūzhuàn (of a round object) spin continuously; be ordered about：孩子们围着～的电动玩具，开心地笑了。The children circled round the spinning electric toy and laughed heartily. /瞧你把人支使得～，也得让人闲一会儿呀！Come on! You've ordered me about for quite a while. Give me a break.

溜门 liūmén break into (a house) to steal; burglarize; housebreak：～贼 burglar /～撬锁 burglary and lock-picking

溜平 liūpíng 〈方言〉very smooth：他把木板刨得～。He planed the board very smooth.

溜湫 liūqiu 〈方言〉❶ secretive：～着眼儿 secretive (*or* timid) look ❷ quietly and timidly：～着步儿走了过来。He walked over timidly.

溜熟 liūshú 〈方言〉very fluently：这首诗他背得～。He recited the poem effortlessly. /他算盘打得～。He is a deft hand with the abacus.

溜索 liūsuǒ suspension cable：山涧上有一条～。There is a suspension cable across the canyon.

溜须拍马 liūxū-pāimǎ 〈口语〉fawn; toady; suck up to sb.; shamelessly flatter：他靠着～，混了个一官半职。He got an official post by toadying (*or* bootlicking).

溜圆 liūyuán 〈方言〉very round：～的肩膀 round shoulders /～的皮球 round rubber ball

溜之大吉 liūzhīdàjí seek safety in flight; make oneself scarce; sneak away; slink off：他一看势头不对，就从后门～。Sensing possible danger, he slunk off through the back door.

溜之乎也 liūzhīhūyě steal away; slink off; make oneself scarce：大家干得正欢，他却～。He made himself scarce while others were working feverishly.

溜直 liūzhí 〈方言〉very straight; straight as a ramrod：～的旗杆 straight flag pole /绳子拉得～。The rope is stretched tight (*or* pulled taut).

溜桌 liūzhuō 〈口语〉slip under the table after overdrinking; get drunk：再喝我就要～了。A little more and I'll drink myself under the table (*or* be dead drunk).

溜子 liūzi chute

溜嘴 liūzuǐ make a slip of the tongue; let slip an inadvertent remark

熘(溜)

liū sauté (with thick gravy); quick-fry：～腰花 kidney *sauté* /醋～白菜 quick-fry cabbage with vinegar

瞘

liū 〈方言〉look：斜着眼～ look sideways; cast sidelong glances; eye askance

蹓

liū sneak off; slip away
see also liù

蹓跶 liūda *see* "溜达" liūda

liú

刘(劉)

Liú a surname

刘邦 Liú Bāng Liu Bang (256 *or* 247-195 BC), founder of the Western Han Dynasty, called reverently Han Gaozu (汉高祖) after death

刘备 Liú Bèi Liu Bei (formerly translated as Liu Pei, 161-223), founder of the Shu Han Kingdom of the Three Kingdoms

刘彻 Liú Chè Liu Che (156-87 BC), 5th emperor (r. 140-87 BC) of the Western Han Dynasty, called reverently Han Wudi (汉武帝) after death, who established the dominant position of Confucianism and promoted exchanges with countries of the Western Regions (西域)

刘海儿 liúhǎir ❶ (Liú Hǎir) Liu Hair, legendary child fairy ❷ bang; fringe：她留着～，显得又俊俏又活泼。She wears her hair in bangs and looks pretty and vivacious.

刘少奇 Liú Shàoqí Liu Shaoqi (formerly translated as Liu Shao-ch'i, 1898-1969), one of the top leaders of the Communist Party of China and President of the People's Republic of China (1959-1969)

刘完素 Liú Wánsù Liu Wansu (1120-1200), medical scholar of the Jin Dynasty

刘秀 Liú Xiù Liu Xiu (6 BC-57 AD), founder of the Eastern Han Dynasty, called reverently Han Guangwudi (汉光武帝) after death

刘禹锡 Liú Yǔxī Liu Yuxi (772-842), poet and philosopher of the Tang Dynasty

刘知几 Liú Zhījī Liu Zhiji (661-721), historian of the Tang Dynasty

浏(瀏)

liú 〈书面〉❶ (of water) clear; limpid ❷ (of wind) swift：～若清风 as swift as wind

浏览 liúlǎn glance over; skim through; browse：～群书 browse through books /他每天早饭时把报纸～一遍。During breakfast every day, he glances through the newspaper.

浏览器 liúlǎnqì 〈信息〉browser

浏亮 liúliàng 〈书面〉clear and bright：～的嗓音 clear and resounding voice

流[1]

liú ❶ flow：泪～ tears flow down one's cheeks /～鼻涕 have a running nose /～口水 slobber; slaver /江河～入大海。The rivers flow into the sea. ❷ moving from place to place; drifting; wandering; migrating：飘～ drift about; float /盲～ aimless migration /城乡物资交～ flow of goods between town and country ❸ spread; circulate; propagate：*see* "～言"; "～传" ❹ change for the worse; degenerate：放任自～ let things drift ❺ banish; send into exile ❻ stream of water; current; torrent：洪～ mighty torrent; powerful current /上～ upper reaches /顺～而游 swim with the current ❼ sth. resembling a stream of water; current：气～ air current /人～ stream of people /寒～ cold current; cold wave /暖～ warm current /时代潮～ trend of the times /意识～ stream of consciousness ❽ class; rate; grade：一～大学 first class university; leading university /三教九～ people in various trades; people of all sorts

流[2]

liú (short for 流明)〈物理〉lumen

流辈 liúbèi 〈书面〉same generation; one's peers

流弊 liúbì malpractice; abuse：积年～，不改不得了。The long-standing abuses will lead to ruin if not remedied. /这种做法～甚多，不妨改一改。The method has many drawbacks. We might as well change it.

流变 liúbiàn 〈书面〉evolution：语言～ language evolution

流别 liúbié ❶ branch of a river; tributary; affluent ❷ (of writing or learning) source; school; sect

流播 liúbō 〈书面〉❶ spread; circulate; hand down：英名～四方。The illustrious name is spread far and wide. ❷ wander; move; migrate：祖上遭战乱而～此地。Their forefathers were driven out of their homeland by war and settled down in this place.

流布 liúbù 〈书面〉spread; circulate; extend; disseminate

流产 liúchǎn ❶〈医学〉abortion; miscarriage：人工～ induced abortion /习惯性～ habitual abortion /先兆～ threatened abortion ❷ miscarry; abort; fall through：这套方案离实际情况太远，注定要～。Completely divorced from reality, the project is sure to fall through.

流畅 liúchàng easy and smooth; fluent：文笔～，层次清晰 write with ease, grace and coherence

流程 liúchéng ❶ flow path; distance of the flow of water：生命的～ life span /大河～七百余里。The river flows for a total distance of over seven hundred *li*. ❷ *also* "工艺流程" gōngyì liúchéng technological process; work flow：～分析 process analysis ❸〈矿业〉circuit：破碎～ crushing circuit /浮选～ flotation circuit

流程图 liúchéngtú flow chart; flow diagram

流传 liúchuán spread; circulate; hand down：广为～ spread far and wide /千古佳话，一直～至今。The much-told tale of the ancient times has been handed down to this very day.

流窜 liúcuàn flee hither and thither; scurry; be on the run：匪徒在草原四处～，为非作歹。Fleeing hither and thither on the grassland, the bandits committed crimes wherever they went.

流窜犯 liúcuànfàn criminal on the run

流弹 liúdàn stray bullet：被～击中 be hit by a stray bullet

流荡 liúdàng ❶ flow; float; move：夜半时分，街头仍有人影～。There were still people moving about in the street at midnight. /园子里～着沁人的花香。Fragrance of flowers permeated the garden. ❷ roam about; wander; rove：一年中他有大半时间在外～，以乞讨为生。He spent the better half of the year begging from place to place.

流动 liúdòng ❶ flow; move; circulate：缓缓～的人群 slow-moving

crowd /有一股寒流在城市上空～。A cold current is circulating over the city. ❷ going from place to place; on the move; mobile:剧团常在农村～演出。The troupe goes from place to place giving performances to local farmers.

流动比率 liúdòng bǐlǜ 〈经济〉current ratio

流动电影放映队 liúdòng diànyǐng fàngyìngduì travelling film projection team; mobile cinema team

流动负债 liúdòng fùzhài 〈经济〉current liabilities

流动红旗 liúdòng hóngqí mobile red banner (awarded to a team, group, etc. for outstanding performance and kept by it until another proves more deserving)

流动货车 liúdòng huòchē shop-on-wheels

流动人口 liúdòng rénkǒu floating or transient population

流动商店 liúdòng shāngdiàn mobile shop

流动哨 liúdòngshào person or soldier on patrol duty; patrol

流动图书馆 liúdòng túshūguǎn travelling library; bookmobile

流动性 liúdòngxìng mobility; fluidity

流动资本 liúdòng zīběn circulating capital; floating or working capital

流动资产 liúdòng zīchǎn liquid assets; circulating or floating assets; current assets; liquidities

流动资金 liúdòng zījīn circulating funds; circulating capital; operating fund:～分析 funds-flow analysis

流毒 liúdú ❶ spread of a pernicious or baneful influence:～四方 spread its pernicious influence far and wide /黄色淫秽书刊一时～甚烈。The pernicious influence of pornographic publications ran rampant for a while. ❷ pernicious influence; baneful influence:封建礼教的～ baneful influence of the feudal ethical code

流芳 liúfāng 〈书面〉leave a good name; leave a reputation

流芳百世 liúfāng-bǎishì leave a good name for a hundred generations; leave a lasting reputation; gain immortal fame:雷锋精神必将～。The spirit of Lei Feng will live forever.

流芳千古 liúfāng-qiāngǔ leave a good name through the ages

流放 liúfàng ❶ banish; send into exile:被～到国外 be banished from the land /～千里 be sent into exile a thousand *li* away ❷ float (logs) downstream:春汛期间，正是～木材的好季节。The spring flood season is the best time to float logs downstream.

流风 liúfēng 〈书面〉customs handed down from past generations:～尚存。Customs of the past generations still remain.

流风余韵 liúfēng-yúyùn lingering customs and life style of the past generations

流感 liúgǎn (short for 流行性感冒) flu:得～ catch the flu /～病毒 influenza virus /～疫苗 influenza vaccine

流官 liúguān magistrate in an ethnic minority region of Yunnan, Guizhou or Sichuan province during the Ming and Qing dynasties

流光 liúguāng 〈书面〉❶ time:～易逝，青春不再。Time flies and youth passes. ❷ flittering light, esp. moonlight

流滑 liúhuá ❶ (of speech, etc.) fluent and pleasant to listen to:他说的北京话地道～。His Beijing accent is perfect and pleasant to the ear. ❷ sly; cunning; tricky:为人～ be a cunning person

流会 liúhuì (of a meeting) fail to be convened for lack of a quorum

流火 liúhuǒ ❶〈方言〉filariasis ❷〈中医〉erysipelas on the leg

流箭 liújiàn see "流矢"

流金铄石 liújīn-shuòshí also "铄石流金" so hot that gold and stone will melt; extremely hot:烈日当头，～。With the scorching sun overhead, it is unbearably hot.

流浸膏 liújìngāo 〈药学〉liquid extract (from medicinal herbs)

流控 liúkòng 〈自控〉fluidic:～传感器 fluid sensor /～逻辑电路 fluid logic circuit /～学 fluidics

流寇 liúkòu also "流贼" roving bandits

流览 liúlǎn also "浏览" liúlǎn glance over; skim through; browse

流浪 liúlàng roam about; wander; lead a vagrant life:～街头 rove the streets /到处～ roam about; wander from place to place

流浪儿 liúlàng'ér waif; street urchin

流浪汉 liúlànghàn tramp; vagrant; vagabond

流离 liúlí 〈书面〉wander from place to place homeless; live the life of a vagrant:～他乡 leave home and wander about in a strange land

流离颠沛 liúlí-diānpèi also "颠沛流离" drift from place to place; be homeless and miserable; wander about in a desperate plight; lead a vagrant life

流离失所 liúlí-shīsuǒ become destitute and homeless; be forced to leave home and wander about:内战使数十万人～。The civil war made hundreds of thousands of people homeless.

流离转徙 liúlí-zhuǎnxǐ drift from place to place as refugees; wander about and scatter everywhere

流丽 liúlì (of poetry, calligraphy, etc.) smooth and beautiful; fluent and splendid:字形～而又有气势。The handwriting is smooth, beautiful, and imposing.

流利 liúlì ❶ fluent; glib:说一口～的英语 speak fluent English /文笔～ write in an easy and fluent style ❷ smooth; sleek:这种新型钢笔出水～，便于书写。The new type of fountain pen writes smoothly.

流里流气 liúliliúqì (of appearance, behaviour, etc.) flippant; not serious or proper; rascally:这个人～，品行太差。The man is a flippant rascal. /几个～的小青年常来捣乱。Some young hooligans often come here to make trouble.

流连 liúlián also "留连" liúlián linger on; bereluctant to leave; can't tear oneself away

流连忘返 liúlián-wàngfǎn enjoy oneself so much as to forget to go home; stay on with no thought of leaving; linger on, forgetting to return:桂林山水美丽如画，令游人～。The picturesque scenery of Guilin is so enchanting that travellers can't tear themselves away from it.

流量 liúliàng ❶ rate of flow; flow; discharge:油井～ oil flow of a well /水管～ discharge from a water pipe /～测定 flow measurement; discharge measurement /～指数 index of discharge ❷〈交通〉flow of traffic:交通～ flow of traffic /旅客～ flow of passengers

流量计 liúliàngjì flowmeter

流露 liúlù reveal; betray; show unintentionally:～真情 reveal one's true feelings /他脸上～出悲痛。His face betrayed his grief.

流落 liúluò wander about homeless:～街头 wander homeless in the streets

流落江湖 liúluò-jiānghú wander from place to place leading a vagrant life

流落他乡 liúluò-tāxiāng live a wretched life far from home; be stranded in a remote land:战乱中他全家～。During the war his family were forced to leave their hometown and lead a dog's life in a strange land.

流氓 liúmáng ❶ rogue; hoodlum; hooligan; gangster:小～ young rogue /～恶棍 scoundrel; rogue ❷ immoral or indecent behaviour; hooliganism; indecency:耍～ behave like a hoodlum; take liberties with women; act indecently; harass sexually /～成性 be an incorrigible rogue

流氓集团 liúmáng jítuán gang of hooligans or hoodlums

流氓无产者 liúmáng wúchǎnzhě also "游民无产者" yóumín wúchǎnzhě lumpenproletariat

流氓习气 liúmáng xíqì habit characteristic of a hooligan; hooliganism

流氓行为 liúmáng xíngwéi indecent behaviour; taking liberties (with a woman)

流眄 liúmiàn see "流盼"

流民 liúmín refugee; displaced person

流明 liúmíng 〈物理〉lumen (lm):～当量 lumen equivalent /～灵敏度 lumen sensitivity /～计 lumen meter; lumeter

流脑 liúnǎo (short for 流行性脑炎) epidemic cerebrospinal meningitis (*M. cerebrospinalis epidemica*)

流年 liúnián ❶〈书面〉fleeting time:似水～ time passing swiftly like flowing water ❷〈迷信〉prediction of a person's luck in a given year:～不利 unlucky year

流派 liúpài school; sect:哲学～ school of philosophy /书画展表现了各种～的不同风貌。The painting and calligraphy exhibition displayed the styles and features of various schools.

流盼 liúpàn also "流眄" (of a woman) sidelong glance; lingering look:左右～ cast flirtatious glances here and there

流配 liúpèi banish; send into exile; ostracize:～远方 be sent afar into exile

流痞 liúpǐ rogue; hoodlum; hooligan; gangster:满脸～气 wear a rascally look

流品 liúpǐn 〈书面〉family status; social status:不入～ people of the lowest class

流气 liúqi hooliganism; rascally behaviour:看他一身～，就知道不是好东西。Judged by his rascally appearance, he is nothing but a bad egg.

流人 liúrén 〈书面〉❶ banished person; exile ❷ one who flees;

L

fleer; refugee; exile
流洒 liúsǎ shed:为人民～热血 shed one's blood for the people
流散 liúsàn wander about and scatter:手稿～。The manuscripts got lost. /在逃荒的路上，一家人～了。The family became scattered on their way fleeing from famine.
流沙 liúshā ❶ drift sand; quicksand; shifting sand:村民们种上防沙林阻止～入侵。The villagers planted a sand-break forest to stop the encroachment of drifting sand. ❷ river silt:清理～、疏通河道的工作，正在进行之中。Work is under way to clear the silt and dredge the river course. ❸ mud and sand in between rock formations:～层 sand layer
流觞 liúshāng *also*“流杯”a kind of drinking game in ancient times:～曲水 feast at a winding canal where people picked up floating cups and drank wine with them as a game
流生 liúshēng (usu. rural) student who attends school intermittently; irregular student
流失 liúshī ❶ run off; be washed away; be eroded:防止水土～ prevent loss of water and erosion of soil ❷ loss (of resources, etc.); drain; leaching:肥效～ leaching of fertility /黄金储备～ drain on gold reserves /人才～ brain drain /国有资产～ loss of state assets ❸ (of students) drop out:防止农村学生～ prevent rural students dropping out of school
流失生 liúshīshēng school dropout
流石 liúshí 〈地质〉flow stone
流食 liúshí liquid diet:她患病期间，只能吃～，人瘦了许多。She was on a liquid diet during her illness and lost much weight.
流矢 liúshǐ *also*“流箭”flying or stray arrow:身中～ be wounded by a flying arrow /～如飞 fleeting stray arrows
流驶 liúshǐ (of time) pass; elapse:光阴～。Time elapses.
流势 liúshì (of water) speed and force:～很强 flow rapidly and vehemently /洪水经过闸门，～稳定。The flood flowed steadily through the sluice-gate.
流逝 liúshì (of time) pass; elapse:随着时间的～ with the passage of time /岁月空～ idle away one's time
流水 liúshuǐ ❶ running water:清清的～ limpid running water /车如～马如龙 incessant stream of horses and carriages; heavy traffic ❷ turnover (in business):这个月，店里做了十几万的～。The shop had a turnover of more than a hundred thousand *yuan* this month.
流水不腐，户枢不蠹 liúshuǐ bù fǔ, hùshū bù dù running water is never stale and a door-hinge never gets worm-eaten; a thing in use rots not
流水朝宗 liúshuǐ-cháozōng all rivers flow into the sea — accord with the will of the people
流水高山 liúshuǐ-gāoshān *also*“高山流水”high mountains and flowing rivers — understanding friend; bosom friend
流水号 liúshuǐhào serial number
流水落花 liúshuǐ-luòhuā flowing water and fallen flowers; fleeting time:春光易逝，使人不禁有～之叹！How fleeting spring is! One can't help feeling sad about one's bygone prime years.
流水桃花 liúshuǐ-táohuā flowing stream among peaches — lovely spring scenery; love:溪头～使人乐而忘归。The enchanting scenery at the source of the brook attracts lingering visitors. /昔年～之情，至今难以忘怀。The love of bygone years is unforgettable to this day.
流水席 liúshuǐxí continuous feast — one at which food is served separately to guests as they arrive in succession:他一连摆好了几天的～。For days on end he had been giving a continuous feast to guests who arrived successively.
流水线 liúshuǐxiàn assembly line
流水账 liúshuǐzhàng day-to-day account; current account:先父在的时候，每天要记～的。My late father used to keep a day-to-day account every day. /因为着急要走，他无心听她讲这许多～。Being in a hurry to leave he was in no mood to listen to the petty details of her account.
流水作业 liúshuǐ zuòyè flow process; assembly line method; conveyer system
流送 liúsòng float (logs) downstream:～木材 float logs downstream
流苏 liúsū tassels; fringe:饰有皮～的厚底高筒靴 top boots with thick soles and leather tassels
流苏树 liúsūshù 〈植物〉fringe tree
流俗 liúsú 〈贬义〉prevalent custom; current fashion:这种粗陋的～，在一些落后的山区还可见到。The crude custom is still prevalent in some backwater hilly areas.
流速 liúsù current velocity; velocity of flow; current speed:洪水～达每秒三点五米。The current velocity of the flood stood at 3.5 metres per second.
流速仪 liúsùyí current meter
流态 liútài 〈物理〉flow form
流淌 liútǎng (of liquids) flow; run
流体 liútǐ 〈物理〉fluid
流体动力学 liútǐ dònglìxué hydrokinetics; hydrodynamics
流体静力学 liútǐ jìnglìxué hydrostatics
流体力学 liútǐ lìxué hydromechanics; fluid mechanics
流体压力计 liútǐ yālìjì manometre
流铁槽 liútiěcáo 〈冶金〉iron runner
流通 liútōng (of air, money, commodities, etc.) flow; circulate:空气～ circulation of air /货币～ circulation of money /商品～ circulation of commodities /管理～ circulation control
流通费用 liútōng fèiyòng circulation cost
流通管 liútōngguǎn 〈机械〉runner pipe
流通货币 liútōng huòbì currency
流通基金 liútōng jījīn circulating fund
流通领域 liútōng lǐngyù field of circulation
流通渠道 liútōng qúdào circulation channel
流通券 liútōngquàn 〈旧语〉paper money issued by a provincial bank or local authority to be circulated in a given area
流通手段 liútōng shǒuduàn medium or means of circulation
流通资金 liútōng zījīn circulating fund
流亡 liúwáng be forced to leave one's native land; go into exile:～国外 go into exile abroad /～生涯 life in exile
流亡政府 liúwáng zhèngfǔ government-in-exile
流网 liúwǎng (in fishery) drift net
流纹岩 liúwényán 〈地质〉rhyolite
流徙 liúxǐ ❶ float about; drift about; wander:～他乡 leave home and drift about ❷ banish; send into exile:～边远 be sent into exile in a remote frontier region
流线型 liúxiànxíng streamline:～火车 streamliner /～汽车 streamlined car
流向 liúxiàng ❶ (of water) flow direction:地下水的～ flow direction of underground water ❷ (of people, cargo, etc.) moving direction:掌握旅客的～ find out the moving direction of passengers /重视人才的～问题 pay attention to the orientation of talents /确定商品的合理～ define the rational flow of commodities
流泻 liúxiè (of light, heat, etc.) emit; (of a liquid) discharge in a jet; pour:泉水从山上～下来。The spring water pours down from the mountain in freshets. /诗人心中的万种激情从笔端～而出。Myriads of feelings issued forth through the pen of the poet.
流星 liúxīng ❶ *also*“贼星”zéixīng 〈天文〉meteor; shooting star:一颗～从天际闪过。A meteor flashed across the sky. ❷ a kind of ancient weapon, composed of two iron balls fixed on a long iron chain ❸〈杂技〉meteors:火～ fire-meteors /水～ water-meteors
流星尘 liúxīngchén 〈天文〉meteoric dust
流星防护 liúxīng fánghù 〈航天〉meteoroid protection
流星赶月 liúxīng-gǎnyuè *also*“流星追月”like a meteor chasing the moon — at top speed; posthaste:他～般地跑回家去报信。He rushed back home to tell the news. /那一顿饭如～，顷刻而尽。The meal was eaten up in no time.
流星群 liúxīngqún 〈天文〉meteor stream; meteor swarm
流星雨 liúxīngyǔ 〈天文〉meteor or meteoric shower:狮子座～ Leonid Meteor Shower (LMS)
流刑 liúxíng penalty of banishing a convict to do forced labour in a border region:几个从犯判了～。Several accessory criminals were sentenced to doing forced labour in a remote area.
流行 liúxíng prevalent; popular; fashionable; in vogue:～一时的说法 fashionable way of saying (sth.) /～的新玩具 fad in toys /这种式样一时十分～。The fashion was all the rage at the time.
流行病 liúxíngbìng ❶ epidemic disease:克山病是这一带的～。Keshan disease is epidemic in this area. ❷ wide-spread social evil
流行病学 liúxíngbìngxué epidemiology
流行歌曲 liúxíng gēqǔ popular song; pop song; pop
流行色 liúxíngsè popular colour:海洋色是今年的～。Aquamarine is the fashionable colour this year.
流行性 liúxíngxìng 〈医学〉epidemic
流行性感冒 liúxíngxìng gǎnmào influenza; flu

流行性脑脊髓膜炎 liúxíngxìng nǎojǐsuǐmóyán epidemic cerebrospinal meningitis
流行性腮腺炎 liúxíngxìng sāixiànyán mumps
流行性乙型脑炎 liúxíngxìng yǐxíng nǎoyán epidemic encephalitis B
流行音乐 liúxíng yīnyuè popular music; pop
流血 liúxuè bleed; shed blood: ～牺牲 shed blood or lay down one's life (for a just cause) /流了一地血 cover the ground with blood /鼻子～ bleeding nose /发动一场不～的政变 stage a bloodless *coup d'état* /伤口～了。Blood was oozing from the wound.
流言 liúyán rumour; gossip: ～伤人 attack sb. with rumours
流言蜚语 liúyán-fēiyǔ *also* "流言飞语" rumours and slanders: 他悔不该误信了～。He regretted having believed the rumours and slanders.
流言止于智者 liúyán zhǐyú zhìzhě rumour stops at the wise man; rumour stands no analysis: ～，只要不轻信，流言也就起不了作用。Rumours stop at the wise man; they will get nowhere so long as we take them with a grain of salt.
流衍 liúyǎn 〈书面〉❶ spread widely: 福祚～ happiness prevails ❷ overflowing; abundant; exuberant: 仓廪～。The granary is full to the brim.
流溢 liúyì run over; flow over the brim; be overflowing: 泉水～。The spring is full to overflowing. /他眼里～着悲哀的神情。His eyes were full of sadness.
流音 liúyīn 〈语言〉liquid
流萤 liúyíng firefly; glowworm: 几点～，上下飞舞。A few glowworms were flying up and down.
流域 liúyù river basin; (river) valley; drainage area: 珠江～ Pearl River valley (*or* basin) /～面积 drainage area /～综合治理 comprehensive improvement of a river basin
流寓 liúyù 〈书面〉live away from home; live abroad: ～南方 live in the south
流贼 liúzéi roving bandit; roving rebel band
流渣槽 liúzhācáo 〈冶金〉slag trough; slag or cinder spout
流质 liúzhì 〈医学〉liquid diet: 遵医嘱，她一直吃～食物。She has been taking a liquid diet at the advice of the doctor.
流质膳食 liúzhì shànshí 〈医学〉liquid diet
流注 liúzhù ❶ pour down; stream; flow: 溪水～大江。The brook flows into the large river. /汗水～。Sweat streamed down. ❷〈中医〉deep multiple abscess
流转 liúzhuǎn ❶ wander about; roam; be on the move: 这几年，他一直～不定，没有固定的职业和住处。He has been on the move these last few years without a permanent occupation and residence. ❷ circulation (of goods or capital); turnover: 企业资金～失灵，难关重重。The circulation of funds has broken down, and the business is beset with difficulties. ❸〈书面〉(of poetry, voice, etc.) fluent and smooth; natural and mellow: 声调和谐～ harmonious and mellow tones
流转税 liúzhuǎnshuì turnover tax

鎏

liú 〈书面〉❶ fine gold ❷ *see* "镠" liú

旒

liú ❶〈书面〉flowing ribbon attached to a flag; tassels ❷〈古语〉stringed jade attached to the imperial crown

琉(瑠)

liú

琉璃 liúli coloured glaze: ～花盆 glazed flower pot
琉璃球 liúliqiú ❶ small glazed ball ❷ smart; clever: 这孩子真机灵，～儿似的。What a smart child! ❸ sleek; cunning; treacherous: 他们是一帮混账～儿。They are a group of cunning scoundrels. ❹ miser; niggard; skinflint: 他是个～，一毛不拔。He is an out-and-out penny pincher.
琉璃塔 liúlitǎ glazed pagoda
琉璃瓦 liúliwǎ glazed tile
琉球群岛 Liúqiú Qúndǎo (Japan) Ryukyu Islands, a chain of islands in the western Pacific

硫

liú 〈化学〉sulphur (S): 有机～ organic sulphur /升华～ sublimated sulphur
硫胺 liú'àn *also* "硫胺素"; "维生素 B_1" thiamine; vitamin B_1
硫醇 liúchún 〈化学〉thioalcohol; thiol: ～盐 thiolate
硫代硫酸 liúdàiliúsuān 〈化学〉thiosulfuric acid: ～钠 sodium thiosulphate
硫分 liúfèn 〈矿业〉sulphur content
硫华 liúhuá 〈化工〉sublimed sulphur
硫化 liúhuà 〈化学〉vulcanization; sulphidation
硫化汞 liúhuàgǒng mercuric sulphide
硫化机 liúhuàjī 〈化工〉vulcanizer; vulcanizing machine: 加压～ vulcanizing press
硫化剂 liúhuàjì vulcanized agent; vulcanizer
硫化氢 liúhuàqīng 〈化学〉hydrogen sulphide (H_2S)
硫化染料 liúhuà rǎnliào sulphur dye
硫化物 liúhuàwù sulphide
硫化橡胶 liúhuà xiàngjiāo vulcanized rubber; vulcanizate
硫化亚铁 liúhuàyàtiě 〈化学〉ferrous sulfide
硫化作用 liúhuà zuòyòng 〈化学〉sulphidation
硫磺 liúhuáng *also* "硫黄"〈化学〉sulphur
硫磺泉 liúhuángquán 〈地质〉sulphur spring
硫苦 liúkǔ 〈化学〉magnesium sulphate; Epsom salt *see also* "泻盐" xièyán
硫醚 liúmí 〈化学〉thioether
硫塑料 liúsùliào 〈化学〉thioplast
硫酸 liúsuān 〈化学〉sulphuric acid
硫酸铵 liúsuān'ǎn 〈化学〉ammonium sulphate
硫酸盐 liúsuānyán 〈化学〉sulphate; vitriol: ～纸 sulphate paper
硫酸酯 liúsuānzhǐ 〈生化〉sulphate: ～酶 sulphatase
硫烷 liúwán 〈化学〉sulphane
硫雾 liúwù sulphur smog
硫酯 liúzhǐ 〈化学〉thioester

镠

liú 〈书面〉fine gold

留(畱)

liú ❶ remain; stay: 独自一人～在家里 stay home alone /课后～下 remain after class ❷ study abroad: ～美 study in the United States ❸ ask sb. to stay; keep sb. where he is; detain: 挽～ persuade sb. to stay on /拘～ detain; hold in custody /不再～你了。I won't keep you any longer. /朋友～我吃晚饭。My friend asked me to stay for dinner. ❹ concentrate on sth.: *see* "～神"; "～心" ❺ reserve; keep; retain; save: ～座位 reserve a seat (for sb.) /～底稿 keep the manuscript /自～地 plot of land for personal needs; family plot; private plot /这些钱是专门为你～的。The money was set aside specifically for you. ❻ let grow; grow; wear: ～长发 wear long hair /～胡子 grow a beard (*or* moustache) /～平头 have closely cropped hair ❼ accept; take; keep: 你带来的礼物我～下了。I'll accept the gift you brought me. /书店送来的书我～下三本。I'll keep three of the books sent over by the bookshop. ❽ leave behind; leave: 给他～点地方 leave room for him /～下难以磨灭的印象 make an indelible impression /父亲给他～了一笔遗产。His father left him an inheritance. ❾ (Liú) a surname
留白 liúbái words written down at departure; message: 这儿有他的～。Here is a message he left.
留班 liúbān (of pupils, etc.) fail to go up to the next grade; stay down: 他去年考试不及格，留了一班。He failed in last year's examination and had to stay down.
留别 liúbié 〈书面〉give a souvenir at parting: ～诗 write a poem as a souvenir at parting /～赠言 parting words of advice (*or* encouragement) /我把这本书送给你，作为～纪念。I'll give you the book as a souvenir to remember me by.
留步 liúbù 〈套语〉don't bother to see me out; don't bother to come any further: 请～，别远送了。Please don't bother to come any further.
留成 liúchéng retain a portion or percentage of sth.: 利润～ retain a percentage of the profits
留传 liúchuán leave sth. to posterity; pass on to later generations; hand down: 先辈～下来的古董 antique handed down by one's ancestors; heirloom /这个美丽的故事，一直～至今。This beautiful tale has come down to this day.
留存 liúcún ❶ preserve; keep: 这些文件请～归档。Please keep these documents on file. ❷ remain; be extant: 该书只有两本～下来。There are only two extant copies of the book. /这种精神将永远～人间。This spirit will live forever.
留存利润 liúcún lìrùn retained profit

留存收益 liúcún shōuyì retained earnings
留待 liúdài leave sth. to be dealt with later; wait until later:这事~他明天回来再定。We'll set this aside until he returns tomorrow.
留党察看 liúdǎng chákàn be placed on probation within the Party (as an inner-Party disciplinary measure)
留得青山在,不怕没柴烧 liúdé qīngshān zài, bùpà méi chái shāo as long as the green mountains are there, one need not worry about firewood; while the mountain remains, we shan't lack fuel; where there is life, there is hope
留地步 liú dìbù allow for unforeseen circumstances; leave some leeway; leave room for future manoeuvre:你不要把事做绝了,要给人家留个地步! Don't go to extremes and push people too far. You'd better leave them a way out.
留点 liúdiǎn 〈天文〉stationary point
留都 liúdū old capital after a new one has been established; one-time capital
留饭 liúfàn ❶ ask sb. to stay for dinner:主人定要~,盛情难却。The host insisted on my staying for dinner and it would be ungracious (*or* impolite) not to accept it. ❷ keep or save food (for sb.):给加班的儿子~ keep dinner for one's son who is working overtime
留后路 liú hòulù keep a way open for retreat; leave a way out:凡事不要做绝了,要留点后路。One shouldn't cut off one's retreat in doing things. /你不要误会了我的意思,我这是给你留条后路。Don't misunderstand me; I'm leaving a way out for you.
留后手 liú hòushǒu leave room for manoeuvre:我们不用为他发愁,他早~了。We needn't worry for him; he has already left himself some options.
留话 liúhuà leave a message; leave word:主任~,我们谁也别走。The director has left word that none of us should leave. /他留下话叫你们晚上再来。He left a message asking you to come again tonight.
留级 liújí (of pupils, etc.) fail to go up to the next grade; repeat the year's work; stay down:~生 student (*or* pupil) who fails to go up to the next grade; repeater
留局候领 liújú hòulǐng poste restante; general delivery:把信寄至百万庄邮局~ send a letter "general delivery" to Baiwanzhuang Post Office
留空 liúkòng leave a blank; leave a space in writing:~符号 sign for leaving a space in writing /此处留三个空。Please leave three spaces here.
留扣子 liú kòuzi 〈口语〉stop at a certain point of a narration to create suspense:他讲到一半,成心~不往下说。He deliberately stopped in the middle of the story to keep his listeners in suspense.
留兰香 liúlánxiāng 〈植物〉spearmint (*Mentha spicata*):~油 spearmint oil
留连 liúlián *also*"流连" liúlián linger on; be reluctant to leave
留恋 liúliàn be reluctant to leave (a place); can't bear to part (from sb. or with sth.); recall with nostalgia:~昔日的好时光 feel nostalgic for the good old days /分手的时候,我们大家都十分~。We all felt reluctant to part from one another.
留量 liúliàng 〈机械〉allowance:机械加工~ stock allowance
留门 liúmén leave a door unlocked or unbolted:他嘱咐家人,夜里给他~。He asked his family to leave the door unlocked for him at night.
留面子 liú miànzi let sb. down gently; let sb. keep some self-respect; not completely disgrace sb.:老朋友喽,不能不给他~吧? Since we are old friends, I won't let him lose too much face.
留难 liúnàn make things difficult for sb.; put obstacles in sb.'s way:我知道他这是有意~。I know he purposely made things difficult for me.
留尼汪 Liúníwāng Réunion, island in the Indian Ocean east of Madagascar and an administrative region of France
留念 liúniàn as a souvenir; as a keepsake:赠物~ give sth. as a keepsake /合影~ have a group picture taken as a souvenir /临别~ give or accept sth. as a memento at parting /某某好友~ To my friend so-and-so
留鸟 liúniǎo 〈动物〉resident (bird):这几年,树越砍越光,~也越来越少了。With more and more trees felled over the past few years, resident birds are getting fewer in number.
留情 liúqíng show mercy or forgiveness; be lenient; relent:手下~ show some mercy; be lenient /毫不~ relentless; merciless /对这些为非作歹的人决不能~。We should show these evildoers no mercy. *or* We should give these evildoers no quarter.
留任 liúrèn retain a post; remain or continue in office:在本届内阁~财长 be retained (*or* remain) as minister of finance in the present cabinet /老主任再次~。The old director was retained in office again.
留神 liúshén be careful; take care:一不~就会把他得罪了。Be careful or you'll offend him. /~,汽车来了! Watch out! There is a car coming. /~,不要把东西丢了。Mind you don't lose it. /~,不要让牛奶煮潽了。Watch the milk doesn't boil over.
留声电话机 liúshēng diànhuàjī telegraphone; answering machine (for a telephone)
留声机 liúshēngjī *also*"话匣子" huàxiázi gramophone; phonograph
留守 liúshǒu ❶ (of ministers after the emperor has left) stay behind to take care of things:~京城 stay behind in the capital city to look after things ❷ stay behind for garrison or liaison duty (after the headquarters has moved away):部队开拔,只有一个排~。The main troops set out, leaving only a platoon behind for garrison duty.
留守处 liúshǒuchù rear office
留守人员 liúshǒu rényuán rear personnel
留宿 liúsù ❶ put up or provide lodging for a guest for the night:不得~外人。Don't put up outsiders for the night. ❷ stay overnight; put up for the night:今夜他只好在这家小店~了。He has to stay at the small inn tonight.
留题 liútí ❶ leave one's comments, impressions, etc. while visiting a place of scenic or historical interest:~簿 visitors' book ❷〈书面〉poem written while visiting a resort
留头 liútóu let the hair grow long; wear one's hair long:留平头 have closely cropped hair /夏天他从不~,总是剃得光光的。He is always shaven-headed in summer.
留尾巴 liú wěiba leave sth. unfinished:彻底平反,不~ rehabilitate sb. completely and unconditionally /工程要按期搞完,不能~。The project must be completed on schedule with nothing left unfinished.
留香久 liúxiāngjiǔ 〈方言〉*Encalyptus citriodora*
留校 liúxiào be retained or employed at a school or university as a faculty member (after graduation)
留心 liúxīn be careful; take care:稍不~,就可能出差错。Errors will crop up at the slightest carelessness. /~,别拿错了包。Mind you don't take the wrong bag.
留学 liúxué study abroad:~归来 return after studying abroad /~日本 study in Japan
留学生 liúxuéshēng student studying abroad; returned student:归国~ returned student /外国~ foreign student (studying in China) /公费~ government-funded (*or* sponsored) student (studying abroad) /自费~ self-supporting student (studying abroad) /带~ teach foreign students
留言 liúyán leave one's comments; leave a message:~牌 notice board /旅客~ messages left by passengers (usu. at a railway station or airport)
留言簿 liúyánbù visitors' book
留洋 liúyáng study abroad:他是个~的博士。He got his Ph. D. abroad.
留一手 liú yīshǒu hold back a trick or two (in teaching a trade or skill); not to lay all one's cards on the table:张师傅对这个徒弟留了一手。Master Zhang held back some tricks of the trade from this apprentice. /对他,我们可得~! We have to keep something in reserve in dealing with him.
留意 liúyì take care; look out; keep one's eyes open:~别吵醒孩子。Take care not to wake the child. /你给我~一下,有没有我要的几本书。Please look out for the books I need.
留影 liúyǐng ❶ take a photo as a memento; have a picture taken as a souvenir:在长城上留个影 have a picture taken on the Great Wall as a memento ❷ photo as a memento; picture taken as a souvenir:儿时~ photo of one's childhood /这是我在外地工作时的~。This is the photo taken when I was working away from home.
留用 liúyòng ❶ continue to employ; keep on:~察看 be kept in office on probation /降职~ be demoted in office ❷ keep for use:我们把~的东西都挑了出来。We've picked out all those articles to be used in future.
留用人员 liúyòng rényuán personnel (of the old regime) who were retained after liberation
留余地 liú yúdì *also*"留有余地" leave some elbowroom; allow for

unforeseen circumstances; provide some leeway:事情别做绝了，别一点儿不～! Don't go to extremes and leave no leeway!
留针 liúzhēn 〈中医〉 keep the needle in the acupoint for a while (for better effect)
留职 liúzhí retain one's post; remain in office; remain on the roster:～察看 remain in office on probation /～停薪 on leave without pay
留滞 liúzhì 〈书面〉 stay:～他乡 stay in a distant land
留置 liúzhì 〈书面〉 leave (sb. or sth.) in a certain place:大军南进，～少量部队戍守后方。The main troops pressed on to the south while a small number of soldiers stayed to guard the rear. /临行前，他把一束鲜花～案头。Before leaving, he placed a bunch of flowers on the desk.
留置权 liúzhìquán 〈法律〉 lien:～书 letter of lien
留种 liúzhǒng 〈农业〉 reserve seed for planting; have seed stock
留种地 liúzhǒngdì *also*"种子地" zhǒngzidì 〈农业〉 field or farmland for the cultivation of seeds; seed field
留驻 liúzhù (of troops) stay behind to garrison (a place); be stationed:部队奉命在这一带～。The troops were stationed in the area as ordered.

瘤 liú tumour:肿～ tumour /恶性～ malignant tumour /良性～ benign tumour /脑～ brain tumour /肉～ sarcoma
瘤牛 liúniú 〈动物〉 zebu (*Bos indicns*)
瘤胃 liúwèi 〈动物〉 rumen
瘤胃臌胀 liúwèi gǔzhàng 〈兽医〉 bloat
瘤子 liúzi tumour:她胃里长了个～。She has got a tumour in her stomach.

遛 liú *see*"逗遛" dòuliú
see also liù

榴 liú pomegranate
榴弹 liúdàn 〈军事〉 ❶ fragmentation shell or bomb ❷ grenade:手～ hand grenade
榴弹炮 liúdànpào 〈军事〉 howitzer
榴火 liúhuǒ garnet (colour)
榴莲 liúlián 〈植物〉 durian (*Durio zibethinus*)
榴霰弹 liúxiàndàn *also*"霰弹";"子母弹" zǐmǔdàn;"群子弹" qúnzǐdàn shrapnel; canister (shot)

镏 liú
see also liù
镏金 liújīn gold-plating; gild:～佛像 gilded Buddha statue /～戒指 gold-plated ring

鹠 liú *see*"鸺鹠" xiūliú

飗 liú *see*"飕飗" sōuliú

馏 liú distil
see also liù
馏出油 liúchūyóu 〈石油〉 distillate oil
馏分 liúfèn 〈石油〉 fraction; cut:轻～ light fraction (*or* cut) /重～ heavy fraction (*or* cut)

骝 liú 〈古语〉 red horse with black mane and tail

liǔ

柳 liǔ ❶ willow:杨～ poplar and willow; willow /垂～ weeping willow /银～ white willow ❷ 〈天文〉 one of the twenty-eight constellations in ancient Chinese astronomy *see also*"二十八宿" èrshíbāxiù ❸ (Liǔ) a surname.
柳安 liǔ'ān 〈植物〉 lauan
柳暗花明 liǔ'àn-huāmíng dense willow trees and bright flowers; enchanting sight in spring time; bright new vista:～又一村。Every cloud has a silver lining. /事情有了～的转机。Things are beginning to turn for the better.
柳编 liǔbiān wickerwork
柳笛 liǔdí willow whistle made of bark from a young willow tree
柳斗 liǔdǒu round-bottomed wicker basket
柳亸莺娇 liǔduǒ-yīngjiāo weeping willows and singing warblers; enchanting sight in spring time
柳公权 Liǔ Gōngquán Liu Gongquan (formerly translated as Liu Kung-ch'uan, 778-865), calligrapher of the Tang Dynasty
柳拐子病 liǔguǎizibìng *also*"大骨节病" dàgǔjiébìng Kaschin-Beck disease
柳罐 liǔguàn wicker pitcher
柳江人 Liǔjiāngrén 〈考古〉 Liujiang Man, a type of primitive man (late *Homo sapiens*) whose remains were found in 1958 at Liujiang (in the Guangxi Zhuang Autonomous Region)
柳栎 liǔlì 〈植物〉 willow oak
柳毛子 liǔmáozi 〈方言〉 ❶ thicket of willow trees ❷ (willow) catkins
柳眉 liǔméi *also*"柳叶眉" (of a woman) willow-leaf shaped eyebrows; arched eyebrows:～倒竖 arched eyebrows of a woman in anger
柳腔 liǔqiāng a kind of opera popular in Shandong Province
柳琴 liǔqín 〈乐器〉 a kind of plucked stringed instrument
柳杉 liǔshān 〈植物〉 cryptomeria
柳丝 liǔsī thin willow twig
柳体 Liǔtǐ calligraphy style of Liu Gongquan (柳公权) of the Tang Dynasty
柳条 liǔtiáo willow twig; osier; wicker
柳条包 liǔtiáobāo wicker suitcase or trunk
柳条筐 liǔtiáokuāng wicker basket
柳条帽 liǔtiáomào wicker cap or hat worn by workers to ensure safety
柳条箱 liǔtiáoxiāng wicker suitcase; wicker trunk
柳条椅 liǔtiáoyǐ basket chair
柳条制品 liǔtiáo zhìpǐn wicker; wickerwork
柳下借阴 liǔxià-jièyīn stay in the shade of a willow tree; shelter oneself under sb.'s influence; seek sb.'s patronage; beg for protection:他处处巴结当官的，无非是想～，找一个靠山。He missed no chance to curry favour with officeholders in order to seek their patronage.
柳巷花街 liǔxiàng-huājiē red-light district
柳絮 liǔxù (willow) catkins:～纷飞。Willow catkins are flying thick and fast.
柳絮才高 liǔxù-cáigāo (often of women) be of outstanding literary talent
柳眼 liǔyǎn slender willow leaves in early spring
柳腰 liǔyāo (of a woman) small or slender waist; narrow, soft waistline
柳叶眉 liǔyèméi ❶ *see*"柳眉" ❷ *also*"弦子戏" xiánzixì a kind of local opera in Shandong Province
柳阴 liǔyīn shade of a willow tree
柳莺 liǔyīng *also*"树串儿" shùchuànr 〈动物〉 willow warbler:黄腰～ yellow-rumped willow warbler / 花间蝴蝶飞舞，枝头～轻啭。Butterflies were dancing among the flowers while willow warblers were singing sweetly on the twigs.
柳永 Liǔ Yǒng Liu Yong, *ci* poet of the Northern Song Dynasty
柳子 liǔzi *also*"杞柳" qǐliǔ ❶ entire willow:一墩～ thicket of willow trees ❷ main tune of the *Liuzi* opera popular in parts of Shandong Province
柳子戏 liǔzixì 〈戏曲〉 *also*"弦子戏" xiánzixì a kind of local opera in Shandong Province
柳宗元 Liǔ Zōngyuán Liu Zongyuan (formerly translated as Liu Tsung-yuan, 773-819), writer and philosopher of the Tang Dynasty

罶(罜) liǔ 〈书面〉 fish hamper made of bamboo

绺 liǔ ❶ 〈量词〉 tuft; lock; skein:一～毛线 a skein of wool / 一～儿头发掉下来遮住了她的眼。A lock of hair had fallen down over her eyes. ❷ 〈方言〉 steal:钱包让人～去了。Somebody stole my purse.
绺窃 liǔqiè 〈方言〉 pick sb.'s pocket; steal; pilfer:～犯 pickpocket
绺子 liǔzi ❶ lock; tuft; skein; wisp:一～长须 a wisp (*or* lock, *or* tuft) of long beard ❷ 〈方言〉 gang of bandits

锍 liǔ sulphonium; matte

L

liù

六[1] liù six:～号房间 Room No. 6 /五～个小孩 five or six little children

六[2] liù 〈音乐〉note of the scale in *gongchipu* (工尺谱), corresponding to 5 in numbered musical notation
see also lù

六边形 liùbiānxíng hexagon

六部 liùbù six ministries of the central government beginning with the Sui and Tang dynasties, i. e. *Libu* (吏部, Ministry or Board of Civil Offices), *Hubu* (户部, Ministry or Board of Revenue), *Libu* (礼部, Ministry or Board of Rites), *Bingbu* (兵部, Ministry or Board of War), *Xingbu* (刑部, Ministry or Board of Punishments), and *Gongbu* (工部, Ministry or Board of Works)

六朝 Liùcháo ❶ Six Dynasties all with their capital located in Nanjing from 222 to 589 (with an interval of 281-316 for the Western Jin Dynasty 西晋), namely, the Kingdom of Wu (吴, 222-280), the Eastern Jin Dynasty (东晋, 317-420), the Song Dynasty (宋, 420-479), the Qi Dynasty (齐, 479-502), the Liang Dynasty (梁, 502-557) and the Chen Dynasty (陈, 557-589):南京曾为～旧都。Nanjing used to be the capital of the Six Dynasties. ❷ general term for the Northern and Southern dynasties (420-589):～书法 calligraphy of the Northern and Southern dynasties /～文 Six Dynasties prose

六朝金粉 Liùcháo-jīnfěn ❶ extravagant or wasteful life ❷ cosmetics and adornments ❸ well-known prostitutes

六尺之孤 liùchǐzhīgū young orphan:托付～ entrust one's young child to sb.'s care

六出纷飞 liùchū-fēnfēi snow falling thick and fast:春节之夜,～,天地皆白。On the night of the Spring Festival, snowflakes were falling thick and fast, and everything was dressed in silvery white.

六畜 liùchù six domestic animals (pig, ox, goat, horse, chicken, and dog); domestic livestock and fowl

六畜不安 liùchù-bù'ān even the six domestic animals are restless — very noisy:他们家姑嫂不和,闹得～。The sisters-in-law have been at odds with each other and there is no peace in their family.

六畜兴旺 liùchù-xīngwàng the domestic animals and fowls are all thriving

六分仪 liùfēnyí sextant

六氟化硫 liùfúhuàliú 〈化学〉sulphur hexafluoride

六腑 liùfǔ 〈中医〉six hollow organs (gallbladder, stomach, large intestine, small intestine, bladder, and *sanjiao* 三焦):五脏～ vital organs of the human body

六根 liùgēn 〈佛教〉six sense organs (eye, ear, nose, tongue, body, and mind):～清净 free from human perceptions, desires and passions

六谷 liùgǔ 〈方言〉maize; Indian corn; corn:～粉 corn flour; cornmeal

六合 liùhé 〈书面〉six directions: east, west, north, south, heaven (up), and earth (down); world; universe:天地～ world /横扫～ sweep across the whole country

六合拳 liùhéquán a kind of Chinese boxing

六合之内 liùhézhīnèi all within the country or universe:～,岂无王法? How could a state survive without the law?

六级风 liùjífēng 〈气象〉force 6 wind; strong breeze

六甲 liùjiǎ ❶ sixty combinations of the ten Heavenly Stems and the twelve Earthly Branches, often used for practising beginner's calligraphy:学～ learn to write ❷〈旧语〉pregnancy:身怀～ be pregnant

六角车床 liùjiǎo chēchuáng 〈机械〉turret lathe

六角形 liùjiǎoxíng hexagon

六街三市 liùjiē-sānshì busy streets; busy shopping centre; downtown area:一到节日,～张灯结彩。Whenever a festival comes, the main streets are all decorated with lanterns and coloured streamers.

六经辨证 liùjīng biànzhèng 〈中医〉analyzing and differentiating febrile diseases in accordance with the theory of six pairs of channels

六〇六 liùlíngliù 〈药学〉6-0-6; salvarsan

六六六 liùliùliù BHC (benzene hexachloride)

六路 liùlù six directions (above, below, front, back, right, and left):眼观～ have sharp alert eyes

六轮 liùlún 〈军事〉a kind of revolver which has six revolving chambers for bullets; six-shooter

六面体 liùmiàntǐ hexahedron

六气 liùqì 〈中医〉six factors in nature (wind, cold, summer heat, humidity, dryness and fire)

六亲 liùqīn six relations (father, mother, elder brothers, younger brothers, wife, children); one's kin; relations

六亲不认 liùqīn-bùrèn ❶ refuse to have anything to do with one's relations and friends; disown one's kith and kin ❷ not consider anybody's feelings; not spare anyone's sensibilities:秉公而断,～ judge impartially free from any personal considerations

六亲无靠 liùqīn-wúkào have no relatives or friends to depend on; have nobody to turn to:他初到这里时,人地生疏,～。When he first came here, he was a total stranger and had nobody to turn to.

六壬 liùrén way of fortune-telling by using the various combinations of the Heavenly Stems and the Earthly Branches:精于～ be good at fortune-telling

六神 liùshén 〈古语〉spirits governing the six vital organs (heart, lungs, liver, kidneys, spleen, and gallbladder);〈比喻〉state of mind

六神不安 liùshén-bù'ān all six vital organs are restless — be disturbed:这些天家里人来人往,闹得我～。I've been terribly disturbed these days by too many visitors.

六神无主 liùshén-wúzhǔ all six vital organs failing to function — in a state of utter stupefaction; out of one's wits:父亲走后,我们一个个～,什么事也拿不定主意。We were too distracted by father's departure to make any decisions on our own.

六十四开 liùshísìkāi 〈印刷〉sixty-four mo; 64 mo:～本 64 mo

六书 liùshū 〈语言〉six ancient categories of Chinese characters

六韬三略 liùtāo-sānlüè books on the art of war:元帅熟读～,善于用兵。Well versed in the art of war, the marshal was a skilled military commander.

六五战争 Liù-Wǔ Zhànzhēng June 5th War (Israel's third large-scale war launched on 5 June 1967 against Egypt, Syria, and Jordan)

六仙桌 liùxiānzhuō medium-sized square table (seating six people)

六弦琴 liùxiánqín *also* "吉他" jítā 〈乐器〉guitar

六言诗 liùyánshī a type of classical poem with six characters to a line

六一儿童节 Liù-Yī Értóngjié International Children's Day (June 1)

六一诗话 Liùyī Shīhuà *Comments by Retired Scholar Liuyi on Poetry* written by Ouyang Xiu (欧阳修,1007-1072) of the Northern Song Dynasty

六艺 liùyì 〈古语〉❶ six classical arts (礼 rites or propriety, 乐 music, 射 archery, 御 riding, 书 writing, and 数 arithmetic) ❷ Six Classics (诗 *The Book of Songs*, 书 *Collection of Ancient Texts*, 礼 *The Rites*, 易 *The Book of Changes*, 乐 *The Book of Music*, and 春秋 *The Spring and Autumn Annals*)

六淫 liùyín 〈中医〉six external factors which cause diseases; excessive or untimely working of the six natural factors (wind, cold, summer heat, humidity, dryness, and fire)

六欲 liùyù 〈佛教〉six sensory pleasures; various human desires:七情～ various human emotions and desires

六月 liùyuè ❶ June ❷ sixth month of the lunar year; sixth moon

六月飞霜 liùyuè-fēishuāng *also* "六月雪" snowing in June — unjust charge or verdict; miscarriage of justice; frame-up

六指儿 liùzhǐr ❶ six-finger hand ❷ one whose hand has six fingers

碌 liù
see also lù

碌碡 liùzhou *also* "石磙" shígǔn 〈农业〉stone roller (for threshing grain, levelling a threshing floor, etc.)

溜[1] (❸❹ 霤) liù ❶ swift current:河中心～很大。The river flows swiftly in the middle. ❷〈方言〉swift; rapid; deft:眼尖

L

手～ sharp-eyed and deft-handed /走得很～ walk fast ❸ rainwater from the roof：檐～ rainwater from the eaves ❹ eaves gutter：水～ eaves gutter ❺ row：一～新房子 row of new houses ❻ surroundings；neighbourhood：这～儿住着许多农户。A lot of farmers live hereabouts. ❼〈方言〉train；exercise：～嗓子 train one's voice

溜[2] liù 〈方言〉fill (a crevice, fissure, etc.)：用纸把窗户缝～上 seal the window cracks with paper /砌完砖要～缝。You have to fill the cracks with mortar after laying the bricks.
see also liū

溜颼 liùsou 〈方言〉quick；nimble；agile：动作～ be quick in movement /他跑起来很～。He runs quickly.

溜腰 liùyāo 〈方言〉waist-deep：麦子长得～深了。The wheat has grown waist-deep.

溜子 liùzi ❶〈矿业〉scraper-trough conveyer ❷〈方言〉gang of bandits ❸〈方言〉rapid flow of water；rapids；torrents

遛 liù ❶ saunter；stroll：出去～～ take a stroll outside；go for a stroll /～大街 saunter in the street ❷ walk (an animal)：～狗 walk a dog
see also liú

遛马 liùmǎ walk a horse：他顺着河边～。He is walking the horse along the river.

遛鸟 liùniǎo go for a walk in a quiet place carrying a bird (in a cage) for exercise

遛食 liùshí 〈方言〉walk after a meal (to aid digestion)

遛弯儿 liùwānr 〈方言〉take a walk；go for a stroll：晚饭后他出去遛了一个弯儿。He went for a stroll after supper.

遛早儿 liùzǎor *also* "蹓早儿" liùzǎor 〈方言〉take a walk in the morning

蹓 liù walk slowly；stroll：到公园去～一～ take a walk in the park /～大街 stroll in the street
see also liū

蹓弯儿 liùwānr *see* "遛弯儿" liùwānr

蹓早儿 liùzǎor *see* "遛早儿" liùzǎor

镏 liù
see also liú

镏子 liùzi 〈方言〉(finger) ring：金～ gold ring

馏 liù heat up (cold food in a steamer)；warm：我把饼～一下你再吃吧。Let me warm (*or* heat up) the pancake before you eat it.
see also liú

碌 liù

碌碡 liùzhou *see* "碌碡" liùzhou

鹨 liù 〈动物〉pipit：田～ paddy-field pipit /树～ tree pipit

陆(陸) liù six (used instead of the numeral 六 to avoid mistakes or alterations)
see also lù

lo

咯 lo 〈助词〉(same as "了" le but more emphatic)：那就好～！That would be much better! /走～，走～。Let's go.
see also gē；kǎ；luò

lōng

隆 lōng *see* "黑咕隆咚" hēigulōngdōng
see also lóng

lóng

龙(龍) lóng ❶ dragon：～游浅沟遭虾戏，凤入牢笼被鸟欺。〈俗语〉The dragon in a puddle is the sport of shrimps, whereas the pheonix in a cage is mocked by small birds. ❷ dragon as the symbol of the emperor；imperial：～椅 emperor's seat /～床 imperial bed ❸ anything shaped like a dragon or with the pattern of a dragon on it：～车 dragon float /～旗 dragon flag ❹〈考古〉a kind of extinct reptile：恐～ dinosaur /翼手～ pterodactyl ❺〈方言〉(of a bicycle rim) crooked；twisted：自行车前轱辘～了。The front wheel of the bike is crooked. ❻ (Lóng) a surname

龙齿 lóngchǐ 〈中医〉fossils of certain mammal teeth used as medicine

龙船 lóngchuán dragon boat：划～ paddle (*or* row) a dragon boat /赛～ hold a dragon-boat race (*or* competition)

龙胆 lóngdǎn 〈植物〉rough gentian (*Gentiana scabra*)

龙胆草 lóngdǎncǎo felwort

龙胆酸 lóngdǎnsuān gentianic acid

龙胆紫 lóngdǎnzǐ *also* "甲紫" jiǎzǐ 〈药学〉gentian violet

龙的传人 lóngde chuánrén descendants of the dragon — the Chinese nation

龙灯 lóngdēng dragon lantern：舞～ dancing with a dragon lantern；dragon lantern dance

龙洞 lóngdòng dragon's cave — stalactite cave；cavern

龙飞凤舞 lóngfēi-fèngwǔ dragons flying and phoenixes dancing；lively and vigorous flourishes in calligraphy：刘先生的书法～，令人叹服。Mr. Liu's flamboyant style of calligraphy compels admiration. /他的字写得～，让人简直无法辨认。His scribbles are hardly legible.

龙凤饼 lóngfèngbǐng 〈旧语〉ceremonial pastry sent by the bridegroom's family to that of the bride together with the betrothal gifts

龙凤呈祥 lóngfèng-chéngxiáng prosperity brought by the dragon and the phoenix；extremely good fortune

龙凤帖 lóngfèngtiě 〈旧语〉marriage certificate or lines

龙肝凤髓 lónggān-fèngsuǐ *also* "龙肝凤胆"；"龙肝豹胆" dragon's liver and phoenix's bone marrow — great or rare delicacies：他近来心情不佳，就是～，也食不甘味。He has been depressed recently and has no appetite even for great delicacies.

龙宫 lónggōng palace of the mythical Dragon King who rules over the rivers and seas, and controls the rains；Dragon King's palace：海底～ Dragon King's undersea palace /东海～ Dragon King's palace in the East Sea；East Sea Dragon King's Palace

龙骨 lónggǔ ❶ bird's sternum ❷〈中药〉dragon-bone — mammal's fossil fragments used as medicine ❸ keel：～板 keel plate /～船 keelboat /～线 keel line /～镶口〈船舶〉keel rabbet /在暴风雨的袭击下，大船的～断成两截。The rainstorm broke the keel of the big ship in two.

龙骨车 lónggǔchē dragon-bone water lift；square-pallet chain-pump

龙江剧 lóngjiāngjù local opera in Heilongjiang Province

龙睛鱼 lóngjīngyú 〈动物〉telescope goldfish；dragon-eyes

龙井 lóngjǐng *longjing*, famous green tea produced in Hangzhou, Zhejiang Province；Dragon Well tea

龙驹 lóngjū 〈书面〉spirited colt；brilliant child

龙驹凤雏 lóngjū-fèngchú dragon's colt or young phoenix — talented young man：令郎真乃～，前程不可限量。Your son is a brilliant young man and has a bright future ahead of him.

龙卷 lóngjuǎn 〈气象〉spout；funnel (of a tornado)：～日珥 tornado prominence

龙卷风 lóngjuǎnfēng tornado

龙口 lóngkǒu ❶ low-lying section of a river prone to flooding ❷ rainstorm；heavy storm ❸〈水利〉gap (in an unfinished dam across a river)：～合拢 close the gap in an unfinished dam

龙口夺粮 lóngkǒu-duóliáng *also* "龙口夺食" snatch food from the dragon's mouth — speed up the summer harvesting before the storm breaks：这几年常闹水灾，村民们～，也真不易！The place has been plagued by floods these years, and the villagers have had a tough time working hard to reap in the summer crops before the floods came.

龙裤 lóngkù black trousers worn by fishermen at sea

龙葵 lóngkuí 〈植物〉black nightshade

龙马精神 lóngmǎ jīngshén spirit of a dragon horse — (esp. of old people) healthy and vigorous in spirit；hale and hearty：这老头干起活来还是那么一股子～。The old man still works with vim and vigour.

龙眉凤目 lóngméi-fèngmù long eyebrows and slit eyes：那人～，举

止不凡。He is a man of noble appearance and dignified bearing.
龙眉皓发 lóngméi-hàofà white hair and eyebrows
龙门刨 lóngménbào *also* "龙门刨床"〈机械〉double housing planer
龙门吊 lóngméndiào 〈机械〉gantry crane; frame crane; portal crane: 固定～ fixed gantry crane / 半固定～ semi-portal bridge crane
龙门起重机 lóngmén qǐzhòngjī gantry crane: 移动式～ travelling gantry
龙门石窟 Lóngmén Shíkū Longmen Grottoes (in Luoyang, Henan Province)
龙门铣床 lóngmén xǐchuáng 〈机械〉planer-type milling machine; milling planer
龙门阵 lóngménzhèn *also* "摆龙门阵" bǎi lóngménzhèn spin a yarn; shoot the bull
龙门支柱 lóngmén zhīzhù gantry support
龙脑 lóngnǎo *also* "龙脑香"〈化学〉borneol; borneo camphor
龙脑树 lóngnǎoshù 〈植物〉*Dryobalanops aromatica*
龙脑香 lóngnǎoxiāng *see* "龙脑"
龙年 lóngnián year of the dragon
see also "十二生肖" shí'èr shēngxiào
龙盘虎踞 lóngpán-hǔjù *also* "虎踞龙盘" dragon coiling and tiger crouching — strategic stronghold (often referring to Nanjing, Jiangsu Province)
龙蟠凤逸 lóngpán-fèngyì have unrecognized talents; be talented but unknown to the world: 收罗～之士 recruit unknown talents
龙袍 lóngpáo imperial robe
龙配龙,凤配凤 lóng pèi lóng, fèng pèi fèng let like match with like and kind with kind; let beggars match with beggars
龙山文化 Lóngshān wénhuà *also* "黑陶文化" hēitáo wénhuà 〈考古〉Longshan Culture (of the late Neolithic Age characterized by a burnished black pottery, relics of which were first unearthed in Longshan, Shandong Province, in 1928)
龙舌兰 lóngshélán 〈植物〉century plant; agave (*Agave americana*)
龙舌兰酒 lóngshélánjiǔ pulque
龙蛇飞动 lóngshé-fēidòng *also* "龙蛇飞舞" (of calligraphy) vigorous style; flourishes in handwriting: 但见他提笔而书,纸上～。He lifted the brush and began to write in a flowing style.
龙蛇混杂 lóngshé-hùnzá dragons and snakes jumbled together; the good and the bad mixed up; high and low mixed together: 手下人一多,不免～。He has a lot of people working under him; as a result, it's a mixed bunch of good and bad.
龙生九子 lóngshēng-jiǔzǐ *also* "龙生九种" the dragon has nine different sons — people born of the same parents are not all alike: 俗话说"～",张家的几个大儿子都不错,惟独这小儿子也太不成器了。As the saying goes "the dragon may have nine different sons", Zhang's other sons are all quite good except the youngest, a real good-for-nothing.
龙生龙,凤生凤 lóng shēng lóng, fèng shēng fèng dragons beget dragons, phoenixes beget phoenixes — like begets like; like father, like son; each takes after its own kind
龙虱 lóngshī 〈动物〉predacious diving beetle
龙潭虎穴 lóngtán-hǔxué *also* "虎穴龙潭" dragon's pool and tiger's den; danger spot: 此去～,吉凶莫测,你们一定要小心行事。You are going to a place of great danger and nobody knows how things will turn out. You have to be very careful in every move you make.
龙套 lóngtào 〈戏曲〉❶ costume with dragon designs worn by actors playing a walk-on part in Chinese operas: 他如今岁数一大,又倒了嗓子,只能穿～混口饭吃。Since he is old and has lost his voice, he can only play a bit role to make a living. ❷ actor playing a walk-on part in traditional opera; utility man: 跑～ be a utility man; play a walk-on role / 我老了,干不了大事,给你们跑跑～还行。I am too old to play a vigorous role but can still serve as a utility man for you.
龙腾虎跃 lóngténg-hǔyuè *also* "虎跃龙腾" dragons rising and tigers leaping — scene of bustling activity: 施工工地上一派～的景象。There is a scene of bustling activity on the construction site.
龙体 lóngtǐ his or your majesty's health; emperor's health: ～无恙。His majesty feels quite well.
龙廷 lóngtíng imperial court: 端坐～ sit majestically on the imperial throne; be a powerful emperor
龙头 lóngtóu ❶ tap; faucet; cock: ～接嘴 faucet joint / 水～ (water) tap; faucet; bibcock / 把～关掉。Turn off the tap. ❷〈方言〉handlebar (of a bicycle): ～一歪,他连人带车摔倒在地。The abrupt tilt of the handlebar threw him and the bike onto the ground. ❸ leader: 大企业当～,带动中小企业 bring along medium and small enterprises with large enterprises playing the leading role / 以名牌产品为～,组织起一个跨省市的联营企业实体 organize a trans-provincial joint-management business entity with brand(-name) products at the core (*or* focused on brand-name products) ❹〈方言〉chieftain; boss; head
龙头老大 lóngtóu-lǎodà ❶ chief or chieftain (of a gang, etc.); boss; number one ❷ leader; number one: 钢铁工业的～ leading enterprise in the iron and steel industry / 该厂是集团公司的～。The factory is the flagship of the group.
龙头鱼 lóngtóuyú 〈动物〉Bombay duck
龙王 Lóngwáng Dragon King (god who rules the rivers and seas and is in charge of rain in Chinese mythology): ～庙 Temple of the Dragon King
龙舞 lóngwǔ dragon dance
龙虾 lóngxiā (bermuda) lobster: ～笼 lobster trap; lobster basket
龙涎香 lóngxiánxiāng ambergris
龙骧虎步 lóngxiāng-hǔbù full of power and grandeur; powerful; mighty: ～出皇都 leave the imperial capital with flourishes of power and grandeur
龙行虎步 lóngxíng-hǔbù majestic bearing (as of an emperor) and martial gait (as of a general); imposing and powerful bearing
龙须菜 lóngxūcài *also* "麒麟菜" qílíncài; "石刁柏" shídiāobǎi asparagus
龙须草 lóngxūcǎo 〈植物〉Chinese alpine rush (*Enlaliopsis binata*)
龙须面 lóngxūmiàn dragon whiskers noodles — very fine noodles
龙血树 lóngxuèshù 〈植物〉dragon tree (*Dracaena draco*)
龙牙草 lóngyácǎo *also* "仙鹤草" xiānhècǎo hairyvein agrimony (*Agrimonia pilosa*)
龙颜 lóngyán expression on emperor's face; imperial countenance: ～不悦。The emperor looked displeased.
龙眼 lóngyǎn *also* "桂圆" guìyuán 〈植物〉longan
龙阳癖 lóngyángpǐ 〈婉词〉male homosexuality
龙洋 lóngyáng dragon dollar, a silver dollar circulated in the late Qing Dynasty with a dragon design on the back
龙吟虎啸 lóngyín-hǔxiào roar of the dragon and the tiger; roar; howl: 夜间狂风大作,～,屋瓦齐鸣。A fierce wind howled at night, making the tiles and indeed the entire house whistle and rattle.
龙跃凤鸣 lóngyuè-fèngmíng leaping dragon and singing phoenix — prominent literary talent: ～的人物 person of outstanding talent
龙跃云津 lóngyuè-yúnjīn rapid advancement in one's career; meteoric rise: 他这几年在学术界～,除了他自己的努力外,还得力于他的导师多方提携。His meteoric rise in academic circles over the past few years was attributed not only to his own hard work but also to the patronage of his mentor.
龙章凤姿 lóngzhāng-fèngzī handsome appearance: ～之士不被重用,獐头鼠目之辈直上青云,这是什么道理? Noble and handsome people were ignored while repulsively ugly and sly-looking ones were catapulted to high positions. Why all this?
龙爪槐 lóngzhǎohuái 〈植物〉Chinese pagoda tree
龙争虎斗 lóngzhēng-hǔdòu fighting between a dragon and a tiger — fierce struggle between evenly-matched opponents; contest between giants: 双方～,十分激烈。The two (sides) were locked in a fierce struggle, fighting like Kilkenny cats.
龙钟 lóngzhōng 〈书面〉decrepit; senile: 老态～ senile; doddering / ～老者 decrepit old man / ～之年 in one's senility
龙舟 lóngzhōu dragon boat: ～赛 dragon-boat regatta; dragon-boat race

泷(瀧) lóng

〈方言〉(often used in place names) swift current; rapids: 七里～ Seven *Li* Rapids (in Zhejiang Province)

珑(瓏) lóng

珑璁 lóngcōng 〈书面〉❶ tinkling sound of jade or metal striking against each other: 玉佩～ tinkling (sound) of jade pendants ❷ *see* "龙葱" lóngcōng
珑玲 lónglíng 〈书面〉❶ tinkling sound of jade or metal striking against each other ❷ bright; brilliant: 东风吹出月～。The moon shone brightly in the east wind.

L

茏(蘢) lóng

茏葱 lóngcōng also "葱茏" verdant; luxuriantly green:垂柳依依,草木～ weeping willows and verdant grass

聋(聾) lóng

deaf; hard of hearing:耳～ deaf /～了一只耳朵 deaf in one ear /全～ as deaf as a post (*or* a door, *or* an adder) /装～作哑 pretend to be deaf and dumb; feign ignorance

聋聩 lóngkuì 〈书面〉❶ deaf ❷ ignorant

聋哑 lóngyǎ deaf and dumb; deaf-mute

聋哑人 lóngyǎrén deaf-mute:～体育 sports for deaf-mutes

聋哑人语言 lóngyǎrén yǔyán deaf-dumb language; sign language; (US) signing; dactylology

聋哑学校 lóngyǎ xuéxiào school for deaf-mutes

聋哑症 lóngyǎzhèng 〈医学〉deaf-mutism

聋子 lóngzi deaf person; the deaf:～的耳朵—摆设。A deaf man's ears are merely ornamental. *or* It is nothing but an ornament.

栊(櫳、槞) lóng

〈书面〉❶ window:帘～ curtained window ❷ cage (for keeping animals); pen:～槛 cage; pen

栊门 lóngmén door (of a room):～呀的一声开了。The door creaked open.

砻(礱) lóng

❶ rice huller (usu. made of wood) ❷ hull (rice):～了一担稻子 hull a *dan* of rice /～谷舂米 hull grain and pound rice

砻坊 lóngfáng 〈方言〉hulling mill

砻谷机 lónggǔjī 〈农业〉rice huller

砻糠 lóngkāng rice chaff

咙(嚨) lóng

see "喉咙" hóulong

昽(曨) lóng

see "曚昽" ménglóng

眬(矓) lóng

see "蒙眬" ménglóng

笼(籠) lóng

❶ cage; coop; basket:鸡～ chicken coop /竹～子 bamboo cage (*or* basket) /火～子 hand warmer ❷ 〈旧语〉wooden framework for confining prisoners; cage:牢～ cage (for prisoners) ❸ (food) steamer:蒸～ food steamer (usu. made of bamboo) /小～包子 small steamed meat dumplings /上～蒸十分钟即熟。Put it in a steamer and steam it for ten minutes and it's done. ❹ 〈方言〉put each hand in the opposite sleeve:老人～着手,慢慢向门外走去。Each hand in the opposite sleeve, the old man walked slowly out of the room.

see also lǒng

笼火 lónghuǒ light a coal fire with firewood; make a fire:趁～的工夫,她把菜洗净、切好。She washed and cut the vegetables while making the fire.

笼鸟 lóngniǎo cage bird; cageling:集市上有一处专卖～的地方。There is a section selling cage birds at the market. /老头儿退休后,爱养个～,栽盆花儿。After retirement, the old man found pleasure in keeping cage birds and growing potted flowers.

·笼式天线 lóngshì tiānxiàn cage antenna

笼屉 lóngtì (tiers of) bamboo or wooden utensil for steaming food; food steamer:她蒸了两～包子,等着丈夫、孩子回来。She steamed two steamers of stuffed buns and waited for her husband and child to return.

笼头 lóngtou headstall; halter:他在马儿的～上挂了一串响铃。He tied a string of bells on the halter of the horse.

笼养 lóngyǎng raise in a cage, coop, etc.:不少养鸡专业户实行了～,科学管理水平不断提高。Many households specializing in chicken-raising have introduced cage culture and are constantly improving their scientific management level.

笼中鸟 lóngzhōngniǎo caged bird; person deprived of freedom:她绝不会受到金钱的引诱而成为他的～。She refused to be lured by money or to become his plaything.

笼子 lóngzi cage; coop; basket:鸟～ bird cage /木～ wooden cage /关进～ cage sth. or sb. up

see also lǒngzi

笼嘴 lóngzuǐ muzzle (for a draught animal):碾场时,他给两头驴都戴上了～。He put muzzles on the two donkeys before threshing.

胧(朧) lóng

see "朦胧" ménglóng

舻(艫) lóng

〈书面〉small boat with a covering or awning

隆 lóng

❶ grand; solemn: *see* "～重" ❷ prosperous; thriving:兴～ prosperous; thriving; flourishing ❸ intense; deep:高谊～情 profound friendship ❹ swell; bulge; protrude:坟头高高地～起。The grave mound bulged high. /他头上立即～起了一个大包。He instantly got a bad bump on his head. ❺ (Lóng) a surname

see also lōng

隆背 lóngbèi humpback; hunchback

隆雕 lóngdiāo grand relief; high relief

隆冬 lóngdōng midwinter; depths of winter:～腊月 in the depths of winter; coldest time in winter; bitter winter /～季节 midwinter time

隆隆 lónglóng 〈象声〉rumble; boom:雷声～ rumble of thunder /～的炮声震撼着大地。The land was shaken by booming guns. /坦克～地驶过桥面。Tanks rumbled across the bridge.

隆起 lóngqǐ swell; bulge; protrude:～的鼻梁 high-bridged nose /她抚摸着渐渐～的肚子,心中又喜又惊。Touching her bulging belly, she felt happy and surprised. /伤口发黑～,已经化脓了。The wound swelled up and looked darkish. It was festering. /前面是一座高高～的土丘。In front of us rises a high earthen mound.

隆情 lóngqíng deep or intense feeling:～厚谊 profound sentiments of friendship; great kindness and favours

隆庆 Lóngqìng Longqing, title of the reign (1567-1572) of Zhu Zaihou (朱载垕), 13th emperor of the Ming Dynasty, called reverently Ming Muzong (明穆宗) after death

隆盛 lóngshèng ❶ prosperous; thriving; flourishing:国势～。The country is thriving. ❷ grand; splendid:～的仪式 stately ceremony

隆暑 lóngshǔ midsummer; intense heat of summer; height of summer; dog days

隆替 lóngtì 〈书面〉rise and fall (of a nation); ups and downs:国运～ rise and decline of a nation; ups and downs in the fortunes of a state

隆头鱼 lóngtóuyú 〈动物〉wrasse

隆渥 lóngwò 〈书面〉deep; profound; intense:恩情～ great kindness

隆重 lóngzhòng grand; solemn; ceremonious:～欢迎 give a ceremonious welcome; accord a grand (*or* red-carpet) reception; roll out the red carpet (for sb.) /～集会 hold a grand rally /宣布会议～开幕 solemnly declare the meeting open

隆准 lóngzhǔn 〈书面〉high nose (bridge):他宽额～,浓眉大眼,长相不俗。He has got striking features with a broad forehead, prominent nose, heavy eyebrows, and round eyes.

窿 lóng

〈方言〉gallery (in a mine):清理废～ clean an abandoned gallery

癃 lóng

❶ 〈书面〉infirm; weak; sickly:年老～病 infirmities of age ❷ 〈中医〉retention of urine; difficulty in urination

癃闭 lóngbì 〈中医〉retention of urine; difficulty in urination:久病～,苦不堪言 unspeakable sufferings from prolonged retention of urine

lǒng

垄(壟、壠) lǒng

❶ ridge (in a field):麦～ ridge in a wheat field /宽～密植 close planting on broad ridges /～地种植玉米 ridge the land for maize; sow maize on ridges ❷ raised path between fields:走在雨后的田～上,又湿又滑。The raised path in the fields was wet and slippery to walk on after the rain. ❸ ridge-like thing:瓦～ rows of tiles on a roof; tile ridge

垄播 lǒngbō bed planting; sow or dibble on ridges

垄断 lǒngduàn monopolize:国家～ state monopoly /～市场 corner the market; monopolize the market; forestall the market; engross the market

L

垄断地租 lǒngduàn dìzū monopoly rent
垄断集团 lǒngduàn jítuán monopoly group
垄断价格 lǒngduàn jiàgé monopoly price; administered price; cartel price
垄断交易 lǒngduàn jiāoyì ring trading
垄断经济学 lǒngduàn jīngjìxué monopoly economics
垄断利润 lǒngduàn lìrùn monopolist profit
垄断资本 lǒngduàn zīběn monopoly capital
垄断资本主义 lǒngduàn zīběnzhǔyì monopoly capitalism
垄断资产阶级 lǒngduàn zīchǎnjiējí monopoly capitalist class
垄断组织 lǒngduàn zǔzhī monopoly
垄沟 lǒnggōu 〈农业〉field ditch; furrow:开～ make a furrow /新开的～ newly turned furrows /～里灌满了水。The field ditch is full of water.
垄田 lǒngtián terraced fields in a valley
垄作 lǒngzuò 〈农业〉ridge culture

拢(攏) lǒng ❶ close:合～书本 close a book /他笑得嘴都～不上了。He grinned from ear to ear. ❷ draw near; approach; reach:汽船慢慢地靠～码头。The steam boat was drawing near the dock. /快～家乡时,已是黄昏时分。Dusk had descended when we approached home. ❸ add up; sum up:空时把账～一～。Add up the accounts when you're free. ❹ hold or gather together; keep close together:归～ put (*or* gather) together /你留得住他的人,～不住他的心。You can hold back the person but never his heart. ❺ comb (hair):她用梳子～了～头发。She combed her hair.
拢岸 lǒng'àn come alongside the shore:大船～时,码头上热闹极了。When the large ship was drawing alongside the shore, the dock was bustling with noise and excitement.
拢共 lǒnggòng altogether; all told; in all:小小的山村,～只有十多户人家。The mountain village is so small that there are only a dozen households or so altogether.
拢音 lǒngyīn carry sound well:这个剧场不大～。The acoustics of this theatre are not good.
拢账 lǒngzhàng 〈方言〉sum up the accounts; balance the books
拢子 lǒngzi fine-toothed comb:她长长的头发上,插了把～。She wore a fine-toothed comb in her long hair.
拢总 lǒngzǒng altogether; all told; in all:班上～十几个学生。There are a dozen or so students in the class.

笼(籠) lǒng ❶ envelop; cover; enclose:城市～在烟雾之中。The city was enveloped (*or* hidden) in mist. /暮色渐渐～住了大地。The earth is gradually shrouded in dusk. ❷ large box; chest; trunk:藤～ rattan chest /竹～ bamboo trunk
see also lóng
笼括 lǒngkuò encompass; take in:～一切 encompass everything; be all-inclusive
笼络 lǒngluò win over; draw over; rope in:她极力～每一个人,但还是没有一个人说她好。She did her utmost to ingratiate herself with everybody, but nobody spoke well of her.
笼络人心 lǒngluò-rénxīn cultivate people's good will by dispensing favours, etc.; court popularity; enlist sympathy with ulterior motives:～的手段 way to buy people's hearts; demagogic method; populist approach
笼统 lǒngtǒng general; sweeping; vague:～地说 generally (speaking); in general terms /你这样说太～了。You're rather sweeping in your statement. /对有些问题,他只是笼笼统统地作了一些解释。He just explained some problems in generalities.
笼罩 lǒngzhào envelop; encompass; shroud:月色～下的院落,竟是这样的宁静。The courtyard enveloped in the moonlight is extremely serene. /黑暗～着大地。The earth is shrouded in darkness. /整个国家都～在恐怖之中。Terror reigned over the whole country.
笼子 lǒngzi 〈方言〉large box; chest; trunk:他扛着一只装满衣物的～,吃力地向楼上走去。Straining mightily, he lugged a chest full of clothes upstairs on his shoulders.
see also lóngzi

陇(隴) Lǒng ❶ Longshan Mountain bordering on Shaanxi and Gansu provinces ❷ another name for Gansu Province:～西 Western Gansu Province /得～望蜀 cast covetous eyes on Sichuan once one controls (*or* captures) Gansu; be insatiable in one's desire; give him an inch and he will ask for a yard
陇剧 lǒngjù 〈戏曲〉local opera popular in Gansu Province

箦 lǒng ❶〈方言〉*see* "笼❷" lǒng ❷ *used in* "织箦" Zhīlǒng (a place in Guangdong Province)

lòng

弄 lòng 〈方言〉(often used in names of lanes) lane; alley; alleyway:里～ alleyway; neighbourhood /番瓜～ Fangua Lane (shanty town in old Shanghai)
see also nòng
弄堂 lòngtáng 〈方言〉lane; alley; alleyway:～口 entrance of an alley /过三条～,就到了我们家。My home is three lanes away from here.

哢 lòng 〈书面〉(of a bird) sing; chirp; tweet:百鸟～吭。Birds are twittering.

㟖 lòng (used by the Zhuang people in Guangxi) small flat ground on a mountain; benchland

lōu

搂(摟) lōu ❶ gather up; rake together:～干草 rake up hay /上山～点柴火 go up the mountain to gather some firewood ❷ hold up; tuck up; roll up:他～起袍子前摆,冲了上去。He held up the lower part of his long gown and rushed forward. /她～了～袖子,把手放在冰冷的水里。She rolled up her sleeves and put her hands into the freezing water. ❸ grab or squeeze (money); extort:～钱 grab money /这几年,你～得还少呀! What a fortune you've made over the past few years! ❹〈方言〉pull; draw:～扳机 pull a trigger ❺〈方言〉check and calculate; assess:把账～一～ check up the accounts
see also lǒu
搂草机 lōucǎojī 〈农业〉rake; hayrake
搂草耙 lōucǎopá 〈农业〉buck rake
搂火 lōuhuǒ 〈口语〉pull a trigger; fire:瞅不准就～,把狼打惊了可不好办哪。If you fire before aiming well, the wolf will be startled and it'll be hard to hit him.
搂揽 lōulǎn undertake; take on; monopolize:～生意 canvas (*or* solicit) business
搂头 lōutóu 〈方言〉right on the head; head-on:他～一棒打个正着。He clubbed him straight on the head.
搂头盖脸 lōutóu-gàiliǎn *also* "搂头盖顶" (hit) on the head and in the face; right in the face:她抄起个碗对着那个人～扔过去。She took a bowl and threw it right in that person's face.
搂子 lōuzi 〈方言〉pistol

瞜(瞜) lōu 〈方言〉(used informally) glance; look at:这是你新买的吗?让我～～。Is this what you've just bought? Let me take a look.

lóu

娄(婁) lóu ❶〈方言〉frail; feeble; infirm:他人胖,身体可～啦。He is plump but in poor health. ❷〈方言〉(used of melons) become overripe and decay; go bad:～瓜 decayed melon ❸ one of the twenty-eight constellations *see also* "二十八宿" èrshíbāxiù ❹ (Lóu) a surname
娄子 lóuzi trouble; blunder; mishap:惹～ cause trouble /出了～ make a blunder; have a mishap /捅～ make a blunder; get into trouble

耧(耬) lóu animal-drawn seed plough; drill barrow; drill:扶～下种 sow with a drill (barrow)
耧播 lóubō *also* "耩" jiǎng 〈农业〉sow with a drill (barrow); drill
耧车 lóuchē animal-drawn seed plough; drill barrow; drill

L

蒌(蔞) lóu
蒌蒿 lóuhāo 〈植物〉beach wormwood (*Artemisia stelleriana*)
蒌叶 lóuyè *also*"蒟酱" jǔjiàng 〈植物〉betel; betel pepper

楼(樓) lóu ❶ storeyed building; multi-storey house:办公～ office building /教学～ classroom building /宿舍～ dormitory building; dorm /塔～ tower building /留学生～ foreign students' building /高～大厦 high buildings and large mansions; high-rises /摩天大～ skyscraper ❷ storey; floor:一～(UK) ground floor; (US) first floor /二～(UK) first floor; (US) second floor ❸ superstructure; tower:城～ city-gate tower /望～ watchtower /箭～ (embrasured) watchtower over a city gate; city-gate watchtower ❹ (used of certain kinds of shops) house; mansion:茶～ tea house /酒～ restaurant /银～ jewelry shop /青～ brothel ❺ (Lóu) a surname
楼板 lóubǎn floor; floorslab:～隔声材料 floor filling; pugging (to deaden sound) /红松的～上铺了一张大地毯。A large carpet is laid on the Korean-pine floor.
楼板骨架 lóubǎn gǔjià floor framing
楼板架梁 lóubǎn jiàliáng floor beam
楼板铺料 lóubǎn pūliào flooring
楼板条木 lóubǎn tiáomù strip flooring
楼层 lóucéng floor; storey:～间交通 interfloor traffic /每个～都设有消火栓。Every floor is equipped with a fire hydrant.
楼船 lóuchuán ancient ship with several decks; ancient towered ship
楼道 lóudào corridor (in a storeyed building); passageway:～上空无一人。There is not a single soul in the passageway. /～两旁堆满了杂物。All kinds of stuff are heaped up on either side of the corridor.
楼顶套房 lóudǐng tàofáng penthouse
楼房 lóufáng storeyed or multi-storey building:住～比住平房方便多了。It's much more convenient to live in storeyed buildings than in single-storey houses.
楼阁 lóugé ❶ pavilion; tower ❷ multi-storey house:空中～ castle in the air
楼间架空通道 lóujiān jiàkōng tōngdào bridgeway
楼库 lóukù 〈迷信〉paper storeyed building to be burnt as a sacrifice to the dead
楼面 lóumiàn 〈建筑〉floor:～面积 floor area /～板 floor board; floor plate; flooring /～荷载 floor load
楼群 lóuqún building complex; cluster of buildings:一片～拔地而起。A cluster of buildings rose straight from the ground. /过了～,就是郊区的大片菜地。Beyond the building complex is a large stretch of suburban vegetable fields.
楼上 lóushàng upstairs:～楼下,电灯电话 storeyed house equipped with electric lighting and telephones (*or* with modern facilities) /～的房客,是一对青年夫妇。The lodgers upstairs are a young couple.
楼台 lóutái ❶〈方言〉balcony; terrace:入夜,家家户户都在～上纳凉。When night fell, people enjoyed the cool on their balconies. ❷ high building; tower:近水～先得月 a waterfront building gets the moonlight first — enjoy the benefits of a favourable position; have the advantage of being in a favoured position
楼堂馆所 lóu-táng-guǎn-suǒ office buildings, large halls and guesthouses
楼梯 lóutī stairs; staircase:上～ ascend stairs /一段十八级的～ 18-step staircase; flight of 18 stairs /多层～ multi-flight stairs /(绕柱)螺旋式～ winding staircase (with newel post) /～扶手 banisters; balustrade /～栏杆 hand-rail /～平台 landing (at the top of a staircase)/底层～ basement stairs; solid stairs /他不小心从～上滑下来。He was careless and fell down the staircase. /只听～响,不见人下来。〈俗语〉The stairs creak, but no one comes down. *or* All talk but no action.
楼下 lóuxià downstairs:～房间 downstairs room; room on the floor below; room downstairs /刚走到～,他听见有人叫他。He heard someone calling him when he just got downstairs.

喽(嘍) lóu
see also lou
喽啰 lóuluo *also*"喽罗";"偻㑩" lóuluo ❶ rank and file of a band of outlaws or bandits:山大王带着一伙～下山去了。The bandit chieftain went down the mountain with his underlings. ❷ underling; flunkey; lackey:手下的～见他倒了台,也就一哄而散了。Seeing that he fell from power, all his flunkeys broke up in babbling confusion.

蝼(螻) lóu mole cricket
蝼蛄 lóugū *also*"蝲蝲蛄" làlàgǔ;"土狗子" tǔgǒuzi mole cricket:～科 *Gryllotapidae*
蝼蚁 lóuyǐ mole crickets and ants; nobodies; nonentities:～之力 strength of nobodies; negligible strength /～尚且贪生,何况人乎? Even ants care for their lives, to say nothing of men.
蝼蝈 lóuzhì 〈古语〉*see*"蝼蛄"

髅(髏) lóu *see*"髑髅" dúlóu;"骷髅" kūlóu

偻(僂) lóu ❶ *see*"佝偻病" gōulóubìng ❷ *see*"偻㑩"
see also lǚ
偻㑩 lóuluo *see*"喽啰" lóuluo

剅(剅) lóu 〈方言〉discharge or outlet tunnel (under a dam or dyke); scour outlet; sluiceway; dyke drainage sluice:～口 sluice valve

lǒu

搂(摟) lǒu ❶ hold in one's arms; hug; embrace:她把孩子紧紧地～在怀里。She held (*or* hugged) her child closely in her arms. ❷〈量词〉circular length when one's hands meet in stretching out one's arms:两～粗的大松树 large pine tree two arm-spans round
see also lōu
搂抱 lǒubào hug; embrace; cuddle:两位好友见面时,紧紧地～在一起。The two friends hugged when they met.

嵝(嶁) lǒu 〈书面〉hilltop

篓(簍) lǒu basket:字纸～ waste paper basket; wastebasket /竹～ bamboo basket
篓子 lǒuzi basket (usu. rather deep):他一早扛着钓鱼竿,提个～,向河边走去。Fishing rod on the shoulder and basket in hand, he went to the river early in the morning.

lòu

漏 lòu ❶ trickle; ooze; leak; seep:水慢慢～下来。The water trickled. /油桶里的油～光了。The oil in the tank has all oozed (*or* seeped) out. /雨水从天花板的裂缝中～了下来。The rain leaked (*or* dripped) through a crack in the ceiling. ❷ (as of a container) leak:锅～了。The pot is leaking. ❸ water clock; hourglass:铜～ copper water clock /～尽更残。The night is waning. ❹ divulge; let out; leak:走～风声 leak (*or* let out) information /说～了嘴 divulge inadvertently; make a slip of the tongue /一个是旁敲侧击,一个是滴水不～。One tried hard to sound something out; the other was absolutely tight-lipped. ❺ miss; leave out:遗～ miss; leave out /疏～ negligence; careless omission; slip; oversight /这一行～了几个字。A few words are missing in the line. /他记～了早晨那趟火车。He forgot to include the morning train.
漏报 lòubào fail to report; fail to declare (dutiable goods); omit to report or declare (sth. taxable):～应税货品 evade declaration of dutiable goods /有一份困难补助申请～了。We failed to report an application for subsistence aid. /据查,本月份～的企业税款有数千万元。It was found out that tax evasions of enterprises this month reached dozens of millions.
漏报概率 lòubào gàilǜ miss probability
漏疮 lòuchuāng 〈医学〉anal fistula
漏窗 lòuchuāng window without glass panes or not papered over (usu. in Chinese gardens)
漏底 lòudǐ disclose a secret; let the cat out of the bag; give the bottom line:自己人嘛,漏漏底没啥。Since you're one of us, I'll let you know my secret.

漏电 lòudiàn *also* "跑电" pǎodiàn leakage (of electricity):~保护 earth leakage protection
漏电保护器 lòudiàn bǎohùqì earth leakage protective device
漏电测量器 lòudiàn cèliángqì electrical leakage tester
漏电率 lòudiànlǜ leakage rate
漏洞 lòudòng ❶ leak:房顶有~ leak in the roof /堵~ stop up (*or* plug up) a leak ❷ flaw; hole; loophole:严格检查制度,堵塞财务~。Tighten up the audit regimen and close all financial loopholes. /对方论点~很多。The other side's arguments are full of holes.
漏洞百出 lòudòng-bǎichū full of holes or contradictions, or loopholes:此文~,谬误甚多。The article is full of loopholes and errors.
漏兜 lòudōu 〈方言〉make a slip of the tongue; let slip an inadvertent remark; spill the beans:谁让你说话不小心,自己漏了兜。You could have been more careful and avoided spilling the beans.
漏斗 lòudǒu funnel; hopper:~状 funnel-shaped /~进料 hopper feed /~状细胞 funnel cell
漏斗车 lòudǒuchē hopper car; hopper wagon
漏斗口 lòudǒukǒu hopper opening
漏斗胸 lòudǒuxiōng 〈生理〉pectus excavatum
漏风 lòufēng ❶ leaking air; not airtight:窗户~,屋里冷得很。The room is terribly cold because the window leaks. /木门虽旧,但不~。The wooden door is old but airtight. ❷ speak indistinctly through having one or more front teeth missing:老人缺了两个门牙,说话~。With two front teeth missing, the old man spoke indistinctly. ❸ (of information, secrets) leak out:有人事先~,计划必须变更。Since someone had leaked out information beforehand, the plan had to be changed.
漏缝 lòufèng crack; crevice; leak:他们配合得没有一点~。Their cooperation is flawless (*or* perfect).
漏脯充饥 lòufǔ-chōngjī eat rotten or putrid meat to satisfy one's hunger; seek temporary relief regardless of the consequences
漏鼓 lòugǔ night watchman's drum or clapper
漏光 lòuguāng leak light:这卷胶片还没有冲洗,小心别~了。The film hasn't been developed, so be careful not to leak light. /这架旧相机~不~? Is the old camera leakproof?
漏壶 lòuhú *also* "漏刻" water clock; clepsydra; hourglass; sandglass
漏划 lòuhuà (used in the political movements before the 1980's) escape being classified:~富农 rich peasant who escaped being classified as such
漏检 lòujiǎn fail to check; fail to detect:~毒品 fail to detect drugs (in customs inspection, etc.) /设专人负责,以避免~事故。To avoid check failures, we must have someone in charge of the work.
漏检故障 lòujiǎn gùzhàng residual or undetected error:~率 residual (*or* undetected) error rate
漏刻 lòukè *see* "漏壶"
漏孔 lòukǒng small opening; hole
漏落 lòuluò leave out; omit; miss:文稿中~的字都已补上。The missing words of the manuscript have been supplied.
漏勺 lòusháo strainer; colander; cullender
漏失 lòushī ❶ lose as a result of leaking:水分~ lost moisture ❷ negligence; mistake:这一工作不能有半点~。No mistake is allowed in this job.
漏税 lòushuì omit to pay a tax; evade payment of a tax:偷税~ evade payment of a tax; defraud the revenue
漏天 lòutiān roof crack:这房子都~了。There are cracks in the roof. /那时候他全家都挤在一间~的破草棚里。At that time, the whole family huddled together in a leaky, dilapidated thatched shack.
漏脱 lòutuō omit; leave out; miss:无一~ with nothing left out
漏网 lòuwǎng slip through or escape from the net (of law, etc.); escape unpunished; get away scotfree:~之敌 enemy that has slipped through the net /决不让一个抢劫犯~。Don't let a single robber escape. /全歼逃敌,无一~。The fleeing enemy were all annihilated.
漏网之鱼 lòuwǎngzhīyú fish that has escaped the net; enemy who escaped unpunished; fugitive:急急如~,惶惶如丧家之犬 as hasty as a fish that has escaped the net and as panic-stricken as a stray dog /清查中,他靠着欺骗手段,居然滑了过去,成了~。In the comb-out, he cleverly managed to slip away unpunished.
漏隙 lòuxì chink; crack; crevice:他说话面面俱到,无~可挑。His remarks cover every aspect of the matter and are really unassailable.
漏泄 lòuxiè ❶ leak; seep:汽缸~。The cylinder leaks. /阳光从枝叶的缝隙中~下来。The sunlight seeped (*or* filtered) through the leaves and twigs. ❷ leak out; divulge:~试题 leak (*or* divulge) test questions
漏泄春光 lòuxiè-chūnguāng the green willow brings a message of spring; pass on information secretly; let out a secret; give away a secret
漏星堂 lòuxīngtáng dilapidated room; leaky house:一间~,五尺土炕,伴我度过了三年的知青生涯。I lived for three years as an educated youth in the countryside in a leaky house and on an adobe *kang*.
漏夜 lòuyè in the dead of night; midnight:~时分,繁星满天。Midnight saw a starry sky.
漏卮 lòuzhī 〈书面〉leaky drinking vessel — loss of economic rights to foreigners:~难满。A leaky wine cup never fills up. *or* The holes (in the economy) are hard to stop. /查堵~,严格税收,维护国家利益。Protect national interests by plugging up all leakages and tightening taxation.
漏子 lòuzi ❶ funnel:酒~ wine funnel /油~ oil funnel ❷ flaw; hole; loophole:他工作中出了不少~。He has made quite a few mistakes in work. /这出戏~很多,一看就能看出来。The play is full of loopholes, which people can detect at a glance.
漏嘴 lòuzuǐ make a slip of the tongue; let slip an inadvertent remark:他话一多就说漏了嘴。He talked too much and gave things away.

瘘(瘻、瘺) lòu

❶〈医学〉fistula:肛~ anal fistula /胆~ biliary fistula /尿~ urinary fistula /粪~ fecal fistula /内~ internal fistula ❷〈书面〉scrofula
瘘管 lòuguǎn 〈医学〉fistula:形成~ fistulization
瘘管刀 lòuguǎndāo fistulatome
瘘管切除术 lòuguǎn qiēchúshù fistulectomy; syringotomy

镂(鏤) lòu

engrave; carve
镂冰雕朽 lòubīng-diāoxiǔ engrave ice and rotten wood — work hard but to no avail; work fruitlessly:~,徒劳而已 vain attempt; futile effort
镂尘吹影 lòuchén-chuīyǐng carve the dust and blow the shadow — make futile exertions; work in vain
镂骨铭心 lòugǔ-míngxīn *also* "刻骨铭心" kègǔ-míngxīn be engraved on the bones and imprinted on the heart — be borne in mind or remembered forever with gratitude
镂花 lòuhuā 〈工美〉ornamental engraving
镂金错采 lòujīn-cuòcǎi gilt and bright colour — ornate language; flowery writing
镂刻 lòukè ❶ engrave; carve:能工巧匠们在形状、颜色迥异的玉石上~美丽的图案、花纹。Skilful craftsmen engrave rich and beautiful designs and patterns on jade of different shapes and colours. /岁月给他的额头~下一道道深深的皱纹。Time has engraved deep wrinkles on his forehead. *or* Time has furrowed his forehead. ❷ engrave (on one's mind); always remember:临别时父亲的嘱咐~在他的心中。His father's exhortation at parting was engraved in his memory.
镂空 lòukōng 〈工美〉open-work; pierced work; fretwork:~的象牙球 pierced ivory ball /~的玉石绣球 hollowed-out jade ball
镂月裁云 lòuyuè-cáiyún engraving the moon and cutting out clouds — superb craftsmanship; splendid work of art or literature:这件玉器有~之妙。This jade piece is cut with superb craftsmanship.

露 lòu

(used only in the following entries) reveal; show
see also lù
露白 lòubái (of a traveller) show one's silver, valuables, etc. unwittingly:把钱放好,别~让小偷惦记着。Put the money in a safe place and don't let it catch the eye of a pilferer.
露丑 lòuchǒu lose face; be disgraced; make a fool of oneself in public; bring shame on oneself:出乖~ make an exhibition of oneself /让我跳舞?这不成心让我~!Me? Dance? Aren't you trying to make a fool of me?
露底 lòudǐ let out a secret; reveal an inside story; disclose the ins and outs of sth.:试题要密封,千万不能~。The examination paper must be sealed up and must in no case be leaked. /你要不是成心~,谁能知道这些内幕情况? Who could have known the inside story if

L

you hadn't betrayed it on purpose? /这下子就全露了底。The whole thing thus came out.
露风 lòufēng (of information, secrets, etc.) leak out:他做这件事,对谁也没有露一丝风。He didn't leak out anything about the matter.
露富 lòufù show one's riches:刘家父子发了财,但从不在众人面前～。Although Mr. Liu and his son made a fortune, they never showed their wealth in public.
露空 lòukòng carelessness; negligence; oversight:他交代的话里有些～。There are some thoughtless (*or* inconsistent) remarks in his confession.
露脸 lòuliǎn ❶ win honour or credit; cut a figure; be successful:在人前～的是他,在底下辛苦干活的是我们。It's he that receives honour and praise in public, but it's we that do the spade work. ❷〈方言〉make an appearance; show up:他好几天没在村里～了。He hasn't shown up in the village for some time.
露两手 lòu liǎngshǒu *see* "露一手"
露马脚 lòu mǎjiǎo give oneself away; betray oneself; let the cat out of the bag:发言人言词不慎,在记者的一再追问之下露了马脚。The spokesman was careless and gave himself away under the reporters' persistent questioning.
露面 lòumiàn show one's face; make or put in an appearance; appear or reappear on public occasions:这几位政界要人已经多月未曾～。These political personages haven't made any public appearance for several months. /我这几天有事找你,总也没见你～。I've been looking for you for several days, but you didn't show up.
露苗 lòumiáo *also* "出苗" chūmiáo (of seedlings) emerge; sprout; come out:一阵春雨过后,地里～了,远看一片嫩绿。After a spring rain, seedlings sprouted in the fields and were a stretch of light green in the distance.
露怯 lòuqiè 〈方言〉display one's ignorance; make a fool of oneself:你别～了,自己不懂就说不懂得了! Don't make a fool of yourself. If you don't know, just say so!
露头 lòutóu ❶ show one's head:他从洞里爬出来,刚一～儿就被我们发现了。We discovered him as soon as he showed his head when climbing out of the hole. ❷ appear; emerge:这种迹象一～,就引起了人们的注意。Hardly had any sign of the problem emerged when it aroused people's attention.
see also lùtóu
露馅儿 lòuxiànr give the game away; let the cat out of the bag; spill the beans:他原想掩饰过去,不料说着说着就露了馅儿。At first he tried to cover it up, but gradually he gave the game away.
露相 lòuxiàng 〈方言〉show one's true colours or features:别看他说得好听,早晚他会～的! Don't believe his glib talk. Sooner or later he'll show his true colours.
露一手 lòu yīshǒu display one's abilities or skills; show off:老头子想在客人面前～,整了一桌子好菜。The old man cooked a tableful of delicious dishes to show off before his guests.

陋 lòu ❶ plain; ugly:丑～ ugly ❷ rough; coarse; crude:粗～ coarse; crude /因～就简 make do with whatever is available ❸ (of a dwelling) rude; humble; mean:～居〈谦词〉one's rude dwelling; one's humble house ❹ vulgar; corrupt; undesirable: *see* "～规";"～习" ❺(of knowledge) scanty; limited; shallow:鄙～ vulgar; not refined; mean /浅～ shallow; superficial /孤～寡闻 ignorant and ill-informed
陋规 lòuguī objectionable practice:如此～,倘不革除,岂不束缚了大家的手脚! Such stupid practices, if not abolished, will bind people hand and foot.
陋见 lòujiàn superficial or shallow view; narrow vision
陋劣 lòuliè of poor quality; shoddy; abominable; despicable:～的货色 shoddy stuff
陋识 lòushí superficial idea; shallow view
陋室 lòushì humble room; plain house
陋俗 lòusú undesirable custom:陈规～ outmoded regulations and irrational practices
陋习 lòuxí corrupt customs; bad habits:作品反映了山区的种种～对人们思想的毒害。The book reflects the pernicious influence of various corrupt customs in the mountain area on people's minds.
陋巷 lòuxiàng mean alley:穷街～ poor, narrow lanes and alleys
陋巷箪瓢 lòuxiàng-dānpiáo live in poverty:诗人晚年生活贫困,～,疾病缠身。The poet lived in straitened circumstances and was troubled by lingering diseases during his late years.

lou

喽(嘍) lou 〈助词〉❶ *used after a verb to refer to an anticipated or envisaged action*:他知道～又怎么样? What can he do about it even if he knows? ❷ *used at the end or in the middle of a sentence to attract attention*:下地～! Look, it's time to go to the fields! /走～,走～,戏快开演了! Let's go, the play is about to start.
see also lóu

lū

撸 lū 〈方言〉❶ close one's hand around (sth. long) and push; strip with the hand:他把袖子～了起来。He rolled up his sleeves. /槐树叶子都～光吃了。The Chinese scholartree was stripped of its leaves for food. ❷ remove; dismiss:他的党票、职务全给～了。He was expelled from the Party and dismissed from his post. ❸ scold; take to task; dress down:他无缘无故被上司～了一顿。His boss gave him a dressing down for no reason at all.
撸子 lūzi 〈方言〉small hand-gun; pistol
噜 lū
噜苏 lūsu 〈方言〉long-winded; wordy:少在旁边～! Stop nagging here!

lú

庐[1](廬) lú hut; hovel:茅～ thatched hut (*or* cottage)
庐[2](廬) Lú ❶ Luzhou (now Hefei in Anhui Province) ❷ a surname
庐剧 lújù *also* "倒七戏" dǎoqīxì 〈戏曲〉local opera in the Hefei area of Anhui Province
庐墓 lúmù ❶ temporary house in mourning beside the grave of one's parent or teacher ❷ farmhouse and grave
庐山真面目 Lúshān zhēnmiànmù *also* "庐山真面" true face or features of the Lushan Mountain — truth about a person or matter:不识～,只缘身在此山中。One fails to see what Lushan Mountain really looks like because one oneself is in the mountain (often quoted to mean that it is hard for those involved in a problem to be objective).
庐舍 lúshè 〈书面〉house; farmhouse:重归旧里,但见～一新,无复旧时院落。Back at home, I found a completely new house in front of me. The old courtyard was gone.
庐帐 lúzhàng tent used as a dwelling
炉(爐、鑪) lú ❶ stove; oven; furnace:煤油～ kerosene stove /电磁～ electromagnetic stove /电～ electric stove; hot plate /微波～ microwave oven /高～ blast furnace /锅～ boiler /围～而坐 sit round a fire ❷〈量词〉*used of what is made or contained in a furnace, stove or oven*:一～钢 a heat of steel /一～烧饼 a batch of baked sesame buns /一～火 a burning stove
炉箅 lúbì *also* "炉箅子" (fire) grate:～面 grate surface /～面积 grating area /～空隙 grate opening /～托架 fire grate carrier; grate bearer (*or* holder, *or* rack)
炉壁 lúbì furnace wall:～结块 wall built-up
炉侧 lúcè furnace side
炉叉 lúchā oven fork
炉产 lúchǎn furnace output
炉衬 lúchèn 〈冶金〉(furnace) lining:～寿命 lining durability; lining life /～熔蚀 lining burn-back
炉床 lúchuáng 〈冶金〉hearth; smelting hearth
炉顶 lúdǐng 〈冶金〉furnace top; furnace roof:～封闭 top closure /～加料器 top filler /～装料 top charging
炉甘石 lúgānshí 〈中药〉calamine:～洗液 calamine lotion
炉灰 lúhuī stove ashes:～混凝土 ash concrete /～坑 ashpit
炉灰槽 lúhuīcáo 〈冶金〉dust-collector; dust-catcher
炉火纯青 lúhuǒ-chúnqīng pure blue flame in the stove (when the

Taoist priests were making pills of immortality) — high degree of technical or professional proficiency; perfection:她的演技,已达到～的地步。She attained a high degree of perfection in acting.
炉具 lújù stove and its accessories
炉坑 lúkēng stove or furnace pit
炉料 lúliào 〈冶金〉furnace charge; furnace burden:～成分 charge composition /～分析 burden analysis
炉龄 lúlíng 〈冶金〉furnace life:延长～ lengthen the life of a furnace
炉门 lúmén opening or draft of a stove
炉盘 lúpán stone or metal plate for standing a stove on as a precaution against fire
炉屏 lúpíng fire screen
炉前工 lúqiángōng 〈冶金〉blast-furnace man; furnaceman
炉桥 lúqiáo 〈方言〉grate
炉身 lúshēn 〈冶金〉(furnace) shaft; furnace stack:～内衬 lining of shaft /～套壳 stack casing /～支柱 shaft supporting column
炉台 lútái stove top:把饭放在～儿上,免得凉了。Put the rice on the stove top to keep it warm.
炉膛 lútáng chamber of a stove or furnace; furnace tank; combustion chamber; hearth:～焙烧 hearth roasting /～构造 hearth construction
炉条 lútiáo fire bar; grate; grate bar
炉瓦 lúwǎ tile
炉温 lúwēn furnace temperature
炉灶 lúzào kitchen range; cooking range:不锈钢～ stainless steel cooking range /另起～ set up a new (*or* second) stove — make a fresh start
炉渣 lúzhā *also* "熔渣" róngzhā ❶〈冶金〉slag:～侵蚀 slag action /～水泥 slag cement /～砖 slag brick /～玻璃 slag glass /～石 madisonite ❷ cinder; clinker:～结块 furnace clinker
炉渣工 lúzhāgōng slagger
炉闸 lúzhá tweel
炉罩 lúzhào bonnet
炉子 lúzi stove; oven; furnace:蜂窝煤～ stove that uses honeycomb briquettes

芦(蘆) lú

❶ reed:～苇编织成的床席 (bed) mattress of woven reeds ❷ (Lú) a surname
see also lǔ
芦柴 lúchái reed stems (used as firewood)
芦荡 lúdàng reed marshes
芦丁 lúdīng 〈中药〉rutin; sophorin
芦篚 lúfèi 〈方言〉reed mat
芦根 lúgēn 〈中药〉reed rhizome
芦沟桥 Lúgōuqiáo *see* "卢沟桥" Lúgōuqiáo
芦沟桥事变 Lúgōuqiáo Shìbiàn *see* "卢沟桥事变" Lúgōuqiáo Shìbiàn
芦花 lúhuā reed catkins:～开时,淀边的芦苇荡一片雪白。When the reed catkins are in full bloom, the marshes around the lake become a vast expanse of silvery white.
芦荟 lúhuì 〈植物〉aloe
芦笙 lúshēng 〈乐器〉reed-pipe wind instrument, used by the Miao, Yao and Dong nationalities
芦笋 lúsǔn 〈植物〉asparagus
芦苇 lúwěi *also* "苇" wěi; "苇子" wěizi reed (*Phragmites communis*)
芦苇荡 lúwěidàng reed marshes
芦席 lúxí reed mat
芦竹 lúzhú *also* "荻芦竹" dílúzhú *Arudo donax*, a kind of reed

卢(盧) Lú

a surname
卢安达 Lú'āndá Ruanda, former name for "卢旺达"
卢比 lúbǐ rupee (a currency used in India and some other South Asian countries)
卢布 lúbù rouble; ruble
卢浮宫 Lúfúgōng *also* "罗浮宫" Luófúgōng Louvre (museum and art gallery in Paris that used to be the chief palace of French kings)
卢沟桥 Lúgōuqiáo *also* "芦沟桥" Lúgōuqiáo Lugou Bridge or Marco Polo Bridge, first built in 1187 to the southwest of today's Beijing
卢沟桥事变 Lúgōuqiáo Shìbiàn *also* "芦沟桥事变" Lúgōuqiáo Shìbiàn; "七七事变" Qī-Qī Shìbiàn Lugouqiao Incident, staged at Lugouqiao (*or* Lugou Bridge) near Beiping (now Beijing) on 7 July 1937 by the Japanese imperialists in their attempt to control the whole of China, which marked the beginning of China's War of Resistance Against Japanese Aggression
卢蒙巴 Lúméngbā Patrice Lumumba (1925-1961), leader of Congolese national movement and first prime minister of Congo (L)
卢萨卡 Lúsàkǎ Lusaka, capital of Zambia
卢瑟福 lúsèfú rutherford; unit of radioactive intensity (named after British physicist Ernest Rutherford)
卢森堡 Lúsēnbǎo ❶ Luxembourg:～人 Luxembourger /～大公国 Grand Duchy of Luxembourg ❷ Rosa Luxemburg (1871-1919), leader of the German Democratic Socialist Party and the Second International
卢梭 Lúsuō ❶ Jean-Jacques Rousseau (1712-1778), French philosopher and novelist born in Geneva ❷ Henri Rousseau (1844-1910), French painter
卢旺达 Lúwàngdá Rwanda:～人 Rwandese

泸(瀘) Lú

❶ Lushui River, part of the Jinsha River (金沙江) between Sichuan and Yunnan provinces ❷ Lushui River, former name for the Nujiang River (怒江)

垆[1](壚) lú

black earth:～土 black soil

垆[2](壚、鑪) lú

earthen platform where wine jars are placed; wineshop:酒～ wineshop /当～ keep a wineshop; serve in a wineshop
垆邸 lúdǐ 〈书面〉wineshop; bar:酣歌～ sing drunkenly in a wineshop
垆坶 lúmǔ (former name for 壤土)〈地质〉loam:～土 loamy soil
垆埴 lúzhí 〈书面〉black clay; dark clay

栌(櫨) lú

see "黄栌" huánglú

颅(顱) lú

〈生理〉cranium; skull:头～ head /～穿刺术 craniopuncture /～内出血 intracranial hemorrhage
颅壁 lúbì cranial wall
颅底 lúdǐ basis cranii:～蛛网膜炎 basiarachnitis
颅顶 lúdǐng calvarium
颅缝 lúfèng sutura cranii:～早闭 craniosynostosis
颅盖 lúgài skullcap; calvarium
颅骨 lúgǔ cranial bones; skull:～学 craniology
颅骨切开术 lúgǔ qiēkāishù craniotomy
颅内压 lúnèiyā 〈医学〉intracranial pressure
颅腔 lúqiāng cranial cavity
颅相学 lúxiàngxué phrenology

轳(轤) lú

see "辘轳" lùlu

舻(艫) lú

〈书面〉❶ stem (of a boat); bow; prow ❷ boat

鸬(鸕) lú

鸬鹚 lúcí *also* "墨鸦" mòyā; "鱼鹰" yúyīng 〈动物〉cormorant

胪(臚) lú

〈书面〉state; set out; display
胪陈 lúchén 〈书面〉narrate in detail; state:谨将调查之实情,～如左。I would like to state in detail what I have found out in my investigation.
胪欢 lúhuān 〈书面〉show pleasure; express joy
胪列 lúliè 〈书面〉❶ enumerate; list:～下述三种方案,谨供采择。I will enumerate the following three schemes for your choice. ❷ display:珍馐～ rare delicacies on display
胪情 lúqíng 〈书面〉state one's case

鲈(鱸) lú

〈动物〉perch

纑(纑) lú

❶〈书面〉semifinished flaxen thread ❷〈古

L

语〉ramie or similar fibrous plant

lǔ

芦(蘆) lǔ *see* "油葫芦" yóuhulǔ
see also lú

卤(鹵、滷) lǔ ❶ bittern:点～水 dribble bittern ❷〈化学〉halogen ❸ stew in salty water with spices or in soy sauce:～肉 pot-stewed meat ❹ thick gravy used as sauce for noodles, etc.:打～面 noodles served with thick gravy /鸡蛋～ thick egg gravy (usu. mixed with starch) ❺ thick infusion:茶～儿 strong tea (to be diluted before drinking)

卤簿 lǔbù guard of honour in imperial procession; bodyguard of nobility
卤菜 lǔcài pot-stewed meat dish
卤醇 lǔchún 〈化学〉halogenohydrin
卤化 lǔhuà 〈化学〉halogenate
卤化物 lǔhuàwù halogenide; halide
卤鸡 lǔjī pot-stewed chicken
卤聚物 lǔjùwù 〈化学〉halopolymer
卤莽 lǔmǎng *see* "鲁莽" lǔmǎng
卤水 lǔshuǐ ❶ bittern ❷ brine
卤素 lǔsù *also* "卤";"卤族"〈化学〉halogen
卤素灯 lǔsùdēng halogen lamp
卤烃 lǔtīng 〈化学〉halocarbons
卤味 lǔwèi pot-stewed fowl, meat, etc., served cold:～餐馆 pot-stewed food restaurant
卤钨灯 lǔwūdēng halogen tungsten lamp
卤虾 lǔxiā salted shrimp
卤虾油 lǔxiāyóu thin salty juice made from shrimps and oil; shrimp sauce
卤氧 lǔyǎng 〈化学〉oxyhalogen:～化物 oxyhalide; oxyhalogenide
卤制 lǔzhì stew in soy sauce:～品 pot-stewed food
卤质 lǔzhì 〈农业〉alkali (in the soil)
卤族 lǔzú *also* "卤素"〈化学〉halogen (family)

虏(虜) lǔ ❶ take prisoner:捕～敌酋 take the enemy chieftain prisoner ❷ captive; prisoner of war:胡～ Hu captives /俘～ war prisoner ❸〈古语〉slave ❹〈书面〉〈贬义〉enemy:～中吾矢! My arrow got the enemy!

虏获 lǔhuò ❶ capture:残匪悉数～。The remaining bandits were all captured. ❷ men and arms captured; captives and booty
虏掠 lǔlüè *see* "掳掠" lǔlüè

掳(擄) lǔ carry off; capture:～人勒赎 hold people to (*or* for) ransom

掳掠 lǔlüè *also* "虏掠" lǔlüè pillage; loot:烧杀～,无恶不作 burn, kill, loot and commit all kinds of atrocities
掳掠一空 lǔlüè-yīkōng loot everything; ransack a place:所到之处,～ (the enemy) loot everything wherever they go (*or* loot all that come their way)

鲁[1] lǔ ❶ slow-witted; stupid; dull:愚～ stupid; uncouth ❷ rash; rough; rude:粗～ rough; rude; boorish

鲁[2] Lǔ ❶ name of a state during the Eastern Zhou Dynasty ❷ another name for Shandong Province ❸ a surname

鲁班 Lǔbān legendary master carpenter of the Spring and Autumn Period
鲁班尺 lǔbānchǐ carpenter's square
鲁本斯 Lǔběnsī Peter Paul Rubens (1577-1640), Flemish painter
鲁宾逊漂流记 Lǔbīnxùn Piāoliújì *Robinson Crusoe*, a novel of adventure (1719) by Daniel Defoe
鲁菜 lǔcài Shandong cuisine; Shandong food
鲁殿灵光 lǔdiàn-língguāng sole remains (of things or people); lone survivals from the past
鲁钝 lǔdùn dull-witted; obtuse; stupid:赋性～ be born dull-witted
鲁莽 lǔmǎng *also* "卤莽" lǔmǎng crude and rash; rash; reckless:～冒失 rash and abrupt /他做事不像从前那样～了。He is much more prudent now. *or* He no longer shoots from the hip.
鲁莽灭裂 lǔmǎng-mièliè impetuous and irresponsible; rash and careless; reckless
鲁米那 lǔmǐnà 〈药学〉luminal
鲁迅 Lǔ Xùn Lu Xun (formerly translated as Lu Hsun), pen name for Zhou Shuren (周树人, 1881-1936), Chinese writer, thinker and revolutionary
鲁鱼亥豕 lǔyú-hàishǐ *also* "鲁鱼帝虎" typographic error resulting from similar stroke patterns of characters (such as that between 鲁 and 鱼, between 亥 and 豕, or between 帝 and 虎):这本书是经过多次校对的,决无～之谬。This book has been proofread many times and is free from typographic errors.
鲁直 lǔzhí rash and blunt

橹[1](樐、艪、艣) lǔ scull (at boat's stern):摇～ scull /船～ scull

橹[2] lǔ 〈书面〉big shield

镥 lǔ 〈化学〉lutetium (Lu)

lù

六 lù *used in* "六安" Lù'ān (name of a mountain or a county, both in Anhui Province) *and* "六合" Lùhé (name of a county in Jiangsu Province)
see also liù

鹿 lù ❶〈动物〉deer:驯～ reindeer /母～ doe /公～ stag; buck /幼～ fawn /梅花～ sika (deer) /马～ red deer /～脯 dried venison /指～为马 call a stag a horse — deliberately misrepresent sth. ❷ (Lù) a surname

鹿角 lùjiǎo ❶〈中药〉deerhorn; antler:～胶 deerhorn glue /～天线 deerhorn antenna ❷〈军事〉*see* "鹿砦"
鹿角菜 lùjiǎocài 〈植物〉siliquose pelvetia (*Pelvetia siliquosa*)
鹿圈 lùjuàn deer enclosure; deer pen; deer park
鹿皮 lùpí deerskin; buckskin:～装 buckskins
鹿茸 lùróng 〈中药〉pilose antler (of a young stag); pilose deerhorn:～精 pantocrine
鹿肉 lùròu venison
鹿死不择荫 lù sǐ bù zé yīn dying deer has no time to choose a shelter — a desperate person will stop at nothing
鹿死谁手 lùsǐshuíshǒu at whose hand will the deer die — who will win the prize; who will gain the upper hand:两强相遇,究竟～,尚难预料。They are evenly matched. Right now, it's still hard to tell who will emerge victorious (*or* come out on top).
鹿特丹 Lùtèdān Rotterdam, principal port of the Netherlands
鹿蹄草 lùtícǎo *also* "鹿衔草" wintergreen (*Pyrola rotundifolia*)
鹿苑 lùyuàn deer park
鹿砦 lùzhài *also* "鹿寨";"鹿角"〈军事〉abatis
鹿寨 lùzhài *see* "鹿砦"

漉 lù seep through; filter

漉漉 lùlù 〈书面〉❶ wet; dripping with sweat:天气酷热,～大汗。The sweltering hot day made people drip with sweat. ❷ sparkling and crystal-clear; glittering and translucent:月色～。The moon is crystal-clear. /玉色～。The jade is glittering and translucent.
漉网 lùwǎng vat-net (screen used in making paper)

麓 lù 〈书面〉foot of a hill or mountain:山～ foot of a hill /泰山南～ at the southern foot of Mount Tai

辘 lù

辘轳 lùlu windlass; winch; well-pulley; hoisting tackle; pulley tackle; jigger:～车 jigger /～动索 tackle-fall
辘辘 lùlù 〈象声〉*used to represent sound of wheels turning, etc.*:大车的～声 rumble of a cart /饥肠～ so hungry that one's stomach rumbles; one's stomach growling from hunger; famished /山间小路,牛车～而过。The cattle cart rumbled over the mountain path.

L

罶 lù 〈书面〉small fishnet; small fishing net

罶簌 lùsù see "簏簌" lùsù

簏 lù ❶〈书面〉woven bamboo trunk: 书～ bamboo book trunk ❷〈方言〉bamboo or wicker basket: 字纸～ wastepaper basket

簏簌 lùsù also "罶簌" lùsù 〈书面〉hang down; droop: 钗垂～ hairpin with drooping tassels

辂 lù ❶〈书面〉cross wood on a cart shaft ❷ a kind of ancient cart

赂 lù ❶ give money or goods as gifts; bribe ❷ (gift of) goods or money

赂遗 lùwèi 〈书面〉❶ give money and goods as gifts ❷ gift of money or goods as bribes: 广收～ take bribes from all quarters

路 lù ❶ road; path; way: 大～ broad road / 小～ path; trail / 公～ highway / 高速公～ superhighway; expressway; freeway / 水～ waterway; water route / 陆～ land route / 山～ mountain path / 交叉～ crossroads / 岔～ branch road / 近～ shortcut / 弯～ detour / 绝～ blind alley; impasse / 京九～ Beijing-Kowloon railway ❷ way travelled; journey; distance: 行万里～ travel ten thousand *li* / ～很远 long journey; long way / 同～人 fellow travellers ❸ way; means: 活～ means of subsistence; way out / 销～ sale; market ❹ sequence; line; logic: 理～ line of reasoning; line of argument / 思～ train of thought / 笔～ technique of calligraphy; style ❺ region; area; district: 南～货 southern products / 各～英雄 people from various places ❻ line; route: 兵分三～ divide the troops into three routes (*or* columns) / 五～电车 No. 5 trolley bus ❼ sort; grade; class: 头～产品 first-class product / 一～货色 people of the same ilk; same sort of things; birds of a feather / 我万万没有想到他竟然是他们一～人。I hadn't the faintest idea that he was one of them. ❽ (Lù) a surname

路拌 lùbàn also "路拌混合料" road mix

路拌路面 lùbàn lùmiàn road-mixed pavement

路毙 lùbì body of a person who has dropped dead by the roadside (because of hunger, cold, disease, etc.)

路边 lùbiān wayside; roadside: ～弃土 side casting / ～停车 curb parking

路边青 lùbiānqīng 〈植物〉yellow avens (*Clorodendron eyrtophyllum*)

路标 lùbiāo ❶ road sign: 司机按～所指, 飞车向南驶去。The driver raced his car southwards, following the road sign. ❷〈军事〉route marking; route sign: 先遣队一路设下～。The advance party left route markings along the road.

路不拾遗 lùbùshíyí also "道不拾遗" dàobùshíyí (as descriptive of a high moral standard in society) no one picks up and pockets anything lost on the road: ～, 夜不闭户 no one picks up and pockets anything lost on the road while no family has the need to bolt the doors at night

路程 lùchéng distance travelled; journey: 往返一百里～。It is a hundred *li* to go there and back. *or* The roundtrip is a hundred *li*. / 革命的～漫长而艰苦。The revolutionary journey is long and arduous.

路程仪 lùchéngyí viameter; vialog

路床 lùchuáng roadbed; paved road

路单 lùdān ❶ travel permit; pass ❷ waybill; original transport record of a truck

路倒儿 lùdǎor 〈方言〉see "路毙"

路道 lùdào 〈方言〉❶ way; channel; approach: 小企业～多, 经营灵活。Small enterprises are flexible and have many channels in business. ❷〈贬义〉behaviour: 此人～不正。The man's behaviour is questionable. *or* The man is a dubious character.

路德宗 Lùdézōng also "路德教"〈基督教〉Lutheranism; Lutheran Church

路灯 lùdēng street lamp; road lamp

路堤 lùdī raised roadbed; causeway; embankment

路段 lùduàn section of a highway or railway: 盘山公路有些～年久失修, 行车恐有危险。Some sections of the winding mountain road have been out of repair for years and are dangerous for vehicles.

路费 lùfèi travelling expenses; fare

路风 lùfēng style of work of railway departments; quality of railway service

路规 lùguī railway rules and regulations

路轨 lùguǐ ❶ (steel) rail ❷ track: 铺设～ lay railway tracks / 行人、车辆严禁在～上停留。Pedestrians and vehicles are strictly forbidden to stay on the tracks.

路过 lùguò pass by or through (a place): 他每天上学都要～这个小商店。He passes by the small shop every day when he goes to school. / 我去成都要～西安。I shall pass through Xi'an en route to Chengdu.

路徽 lùhuī railway logo or emblem

路基 lùjī roadbed; bed: ～很差, 交通事故连连发生。The roadbed is of poor quality and causes frequent accidents.

路祭 lùjì 〈旧语〉(of relatives or friends of the deceased) offer sacrifices on the route of a funeral procession

路加福音 Lùjiā Fúyīn *The Gospel According to Luke*

路肩 lùjiān road shoulder; shoulder; curb; berm(e)

路见不平, 拔刀相助 lù jiàn bùpíng, bá dāo xiāngzhù see injustice on the road and draw one's sword to help the victim; take up the cudgels for the injured party; be ready to come to the rescue of people in distress

路劫 lùjié commit highway robbery; hold up; mug: 遭～ be robbed (*or* held up); be mugged / 几个强人占山为王, ～行人, 为害一方。A few bandits entrenched themselves in the mountains, robbing travellers and doing great harm to local people.

路警 lùjǐng railway police

路径 lùjìng ❶ route; way: 迷失～ lose one's way / 我初到此地, 去县城的～还不熟。I'm new here and don't know how to get to the county town. ❷ method; ways and means: 试验多日, 大家总算找到了成功的～。After days of experiments, we finally found the way to success.

路局 lùjú railway administration; road bureau

路考 lùkǎo (of driving, etc.) road test

路口 lùkǒu crossing; junction; intersection: 三岔～ fork in a road / 十字～ crossroads / 丁字～ T-shaped road junction / 到了～, 车往左拐, 前面就是大桥。Turn to the left at the intersection and the bridge is right ahead.

路况 lùkuàng road condition; traffic: ～不佳 poor road conditions / ～报告 traffic report

路矿 lùkuàng railways and mines: 全国～工人总罢工 general strike of railway workers and miners

路柳墙花 lùliǔ-qiánghuā willow tree on the roadside and flower on the wall — woman of easy virtue; street girl; prostitute

路路通 lùlùtōng 〈中药〉seed of Chinese sweetgum (*Liquidambar taiwaniana*)

路面 lùmiàn road surface; pavement: 柔性～ flexible pavement / ～凹坑 pothole (in the road) / ～剥落 spalling (of pavement) / ～开裂 pavement cracking / ～移位 pavement displacement / 加宽～ widen the road surface

路碾 lùniǎn road roller

路牌 lùpái street nameplate; guideboard; street sign

路卡 lùqiǎ road checkpoint; outpost of the tax office

路签 lùqiān 〈交通〉train-staff; staff

路堑 lùqiàn 〈交通〉road cutting through high land; through cut; cutting

路人 lùrén passer-by; stranger: 兄弟俩分家后, 形同～, 很少往来了。Since the two brothers divided up the family property and lived apart, they have treated each other like strangers and have seldom visited each other. / 司马昭之心, ～皆知。Sima Zhao's ill intent is known to everyone. *or* The villain's design is only too clear.

路容 lùróng road appearance (such as road surface, greenery, etc.): 美化～ beautify road appearance

路上 lùshang ❶ on the road: 只见～车来车往, 行人不断。There is a constant stream of people and vehicles on the road. ❷ on the way; en route: ～你要多照看弟弟。Take good care of your younger brother on the journey. / 一～他俩又说又笑, 十分开心。The two of them were talking and laughing all the way. / 回家～要注意来往车辆。Mind the traffic on your way home.

路数 lùshù ❶ way; approach: 干了几个月, 我多少算摸到了一点儿～。After a few months on the job, I think I more or less know the ropes. / 他心眼活, ～多, 这工作他最合适。As he has a flexible mind and is resourceful, he is the right person for the job. ❷ movement

in martial arts：使枪的～ how to wield the spear；thrusts in spear fencing ❸ ins and outs；inside story：你去了解一下来人的～。Go and sound the visitor out. /谁也猜不出他心里的～。No one knows what's in his mind.

路条 lùtiáo travel permit；pass

路透社 Lùtòushè (UK) Reuter's News Agency；Reuters

路头 lùtou 〈口语〉❶ road；way：他对这一带～熟，不会走错。He is familiar with the roads here and won't get lost. ❷ connections；pull：这人～多，能不能托他想想办法。This man has many connections. I wonder if we can ask him for help.

路途 lùtú ❶ road；path：老人熟悉山里的～，此行非他向导不可。Since the old man knows the mountain paths like the palm of his hand, we must get him as our guide on the journey. ❷ distance travelled；way；journey：去县城～不算远，一天可以来回。The county seat isn't far away, and we can make a round trip within a day.

路网 lùwǎng road network

路线 lùxiàn ❶ route；itinerary：～图 route chart；line map /行车～ driving route /旅行～ route of a journey /参观～图 visitors' itinerary ❷ line：走群众～ follow the mass line /实事求是的思想～ ideological line of seeking truth from facts

路线斗争 lùxiàn dòuzhēng struggle between two ideological lines；two-line struggle

路向 lùxiàng road direction；way：站在路口为行人指点～ stand at the crossing to show pedestrians which way to go /看出一点～ have some idea of the way the wind blows

路遥知马力 lù yáo zhī mǎlì distance tests a horse's stamina：～，日久见人心。As distance tests a horse's strength, so time reveals a person's heart.

路椅 lùyǐ roadside bench

路易港 Lùyìgǎng Port Louis, capital of Mauritius

路易斯安那 Lùyìsī'ānnà Louisiana, a state in the southern United States

路引 lùyǐn 〈旧语〉travel permit；pass

路由器 lùyóuqì 〈信息〉router

路障 lùzhàng road barrier；barricade；roadblock：用铁丝网布下的～ set up a roadblock with wire meshes /据点周围的火力点和～已经布置停当。The fire net and wire entanglement surrounding the stronghold have been laid.

路政 lùzhèng road or railway administration

路子 lùzi ❶ connections；pull：走～ (get sth.) through pull /～硬 have very influential backers /他的～多。He has plenty of connections. ❷ way；approach：～对 adopt the right approach /～宽 have a wide range of choices (*or* options)；have many resources (to draw upon)；be a versatile performer (*or* actor, *or* writer) /这是一条成功的～。This is a way to success.

露[1]

lù ❶ dew：雨～ rain and dew /甘～ sweet dew ❷ beverage distilled from flowers, fruit or leaves；drink mixed with fruit juice；syrup：果子～ fruit syrup /玫瑰～ rose syrup /花～水 scents；Florida water

露[2]

lù ❶ in the open；outdoors：餐风宿～ be exposed to inclement weather on a journey ❷ show；reveal；betray：原形毕～ reveal one's true colours；betray oneself /～齿而笑 grin；present a toothpaste smile /～背连衣裙 backless dress

see also lòu

露板 lùbǎn *see* "露布 ❸"

露布 lùbù ❶〈书面〉official call to arms；official denunciation of the enemy；war proclamation ❷〈书面〉announcement of victory；report of a success ❸〈古语〉unsealed imperial edict or memorial to the throne ❹〈方言〉notice；bulletin；playbill

露才扬己 lùcái-yángjǐ make a display of；show off；flaunt：他最大的毛病是要小聪明，总爱～。His greatest weakness lies in his tendency to play petty tricks and show off.

露钞雪纂 lùchāo-xuězuǎn copy and compile all year round；write or compile arduously all year round：为了研究古代美学思想，他～，几经寒暑，收集了大量的资料。In order to study ancient aesthetics, he spent several years copying and compiling a whole heap of materials.

露地 lùdì ❶〈书面〉open country；champaign ❷ open vegetable field or plot：～育苗 grow (*or* raise) seedlings in the open field /春播～西红柿 spring-sown tomatoes in open plots ❸ appear above the ground；surface：～的根上也能结实。It can also bear fruit on the roots above the ground.

露地菜 lùdìcài vegetables grown in the open field

露点 lùdiǎn 〈气象〉dew point：温度～差 dew-point deficit /～温度表 dew-point thermometer

露点湿度表 lùdiǎn shīdùbiǎo dew-point hygrometer

露兜树 lùdōushù 〈植物〉aggag；pandanus；screw pine (*Pandanus odoratissimus*)

露锋芒 lù fēngmáng ❶ make a showy display of one's abilities；demonstrate one's talent ❷ (of diction) sharp；aggressive：太～ be much too aggressive

露骨 lùgǔ thinly-veiled；undisguised；barefaced：～地偏袒 show undisguised partiality /在昨晚的会议上他说得很～。He made a thinly-veiled statement at the meeting last night. /话不要说得太～。You must not be too assertive in your speech.

露光计 lùguāngjì 〈摄影〉exposure meter

露脊鲸 lùjǐjīng 〈动物〉right whale

露酒 lùjiǔ alcoholic drink mixed with fruit juice

露水 lùshui ❶〈口语〉dew：～打湿了他的衣服。Dew drops wetted his clothes. ❷ of short duration；transient；brief：～之欢 temporary joy；transient happiness

露水夫妻 lùshui-fūqī illicit lovers；one-night stand：～不久长。Illicit love affairs do not last long.

露水姻缘 lùshui-yīnyuán temporary and illegal relations between a man and a woman；one-night stand

露水珠儿 lùshuizhūr 〈口语〉dewdrop

露宿 lùsù sleep in the open：～街头 sleep in the street /野营～ go camping and sleep in the open；bivouac

露宿风餐 lùsù-fēngcān *also* "餐风宿露" sleep in the dew and eat in the wind — endure the hardships of arduous journey or fieldwork

露台 lùtái 〈方言〉flat roof (for drying clothes, etc.)

露天 lùtiān ❶ in the open (air)；outdoors：在～里堆放了一些杂物。Some odds and ends are piled up in the open air. ❷ open-air；open；uncovered；unpacked：～爆破 surface blasting /～码放 open freight storage；open-air storage

露天电影 lùtiān diànyǐng open-air cinema：看～ see a film in the open air

露天堆栈 lùtiān duīzhàn open-air repository；open-air depot

露天剧场 lùtiān jùchǎng open-air theatre；amphitheatre

露天开采 lùtiān kāicǎi opencast mining

露天看台 lùtiān kàntái bleachers

露天跨 lùtiānkuà 〈方言〉open-air workshop

露天矿 lùtiānkuàng opencut or opencast mine；open-pit mine；strip mine

露天煤矿 lùtiān méikuàng opencut coal mine

露天游泳池 lùtiān yóuyǒngchí outdoor or open-air swimming pool

露头 lùtóu *also* "矿苗" kuàngmiáo 〈矿业〉outcrop；outcropping；basset

see also lòutóu

露头角 lù tóujiǎo (of a young person) beginning to show ability or talent；budding：初～ display one's talent for the first time；begin to show one's ability (*or* talent)；cut a conspicuous figure for the first time /崭～ stand out；cut a striking figure；make oneself conspicuous /这些年，他在学术界渐渐露了头角，已是小有名气了。He is beginning to make a name for himself in the academic world these years.

露尾巴 lù wěiba show one's tail — give oneself away；show one's true colours：日子一长，他就露出狐狸尾巴了。He began to reveal his true colours as time went by.

露尾藏头 lùwěi-cángtóu *also* "藏头露尾" hide the head only to show the tail — conceal one part of sth. but reveal another；speak with obvious reservation；act stealthily

露演 lùyǎn put on the stage；perform：这个剧团每年都有几出新戏～。The opera troupe stages several new plays every year.

露营 lùyíng ❶〈军事〉camp (out)；encamp；bivouac：部队在野外～。The troops camped in the open country. ❷ go camping：学校在暑假期间组织了为期十天的～活动。The school organized a ten-day camping event during the summer vacation.

露原形 lù yuánxíng show one's true colours；give oneself away：别看他现在装得像，早晚要～的。He may disguise himself for some time,

but sooner or later he would show his cloven hoof.

露珠 lùzhū *also* "露水珠儿" dewdrop:晶莹的～ sparkling dewdrops

璐 lù 〈书面〉beautiful or fine jade

蕗 lù 〈中医〉licorice root

鹭 lù 〈动物〉egret; heron:白～ egret /苍～ heron /池～ pond heron /牛背～ cattle egret

鹭鹤 lùhè kagu

鹭鸶 lùsī *also* "白鹭" báilù egret

蓼 lù (of plants) tall and big; tall

see also liǎo

戮[1] lù kill; slay:～诛 slay

戮[2]**(勠)** lù 〈书面〉unite; join

戮力 lùlì 〈书面〉concert one's efforts; join forces:～相助 join hands to help

戮力同心 lùlì-tóngxīn 〈书面〉join forces for a common cause; unite in a concerted effort; make concerted efforts:军民～,重建家园。The army and the people worked with one mind to rebuild their homeland.

僇 lù 〈书面〉❶ insult; humiliate ❷ *see* "戮" lù

录(録) lù ❶ record; note or write down; copy:抄～ copy down /记～ take notes; keep the minutes; record /登～ record; register /誊～ copy /摘～ make extracts ❷ tape-record:～外国民歌 tape-record foreign folksongs /～一盘磁带 copy a tape ❸ use; employ; hire:收～ include (in an anthology or collection); employ; take on the staff ❹ record; register; collection:目～ catalogue; list; table of contents; contents /同学～ schoolmates' address book /通讯～ address book /语～ quotations /回忆～ memoirs; reminiscences

录波器 lùbōqì oscillograph

录播 lùbō (make a) recorded broadcast

录放 lùfàng record and play (back):～两用磁头 recording playback head

录放话机 lùfàng huàjī telediphone

录供 lùgòng 〈法律〉take down a confession or testimony during an interrogation:审讯时,有两名速记员～。At the interrogation, two stenographers took down the confession.

录取 lùqǔ enrol; recruit; admit:～标准 admission criteria /～新生 enrol new students /她已被北大～了。She has been admitted to Peking University.

录取通知书 lùqǔ tōngzhīshū admission notice; notice of acceptance

录事 lùshì 〈旧语〉copyist; office clerk

录像 lùxiàng ❶ videotape; videorecord:现场～工作正在进行。Live videotaping is under way. /报警机能自动报警并～。The warning device can give an automatic alarm and videotape. ❷ video; videotape recording:放～ play a video /看～ watch a video (show)

录像带 lùxiàngdài videotape:盒式～ videocassette

录像机 lùxiàngjī video recorder; videotape player; video

录像片 lùxiàngpiàn *also* "录像片儿" video show; video film

录写 lùxiě write down; record in writing; copy:他亲笔～了一首唐诗。He copied in his own hand a Tang Dynasty poem.

录音 lùyīn sound recording:～设备 recording equipment /同声～ simultaneous recording /转播实况～ relay the on-the-spot recording; relay live-recording

L

录音报告 lùyīn bàogào taped speech; recorded speech

录音打字 lùyīn dǎzì audiotyping

录音带 lùyīndài magnetic tape; tape

录音电话 lùyīn diànhuà answer machine; telegraphone; answer phone:～机 dictaphone

录音机 lùyīnjī tape recorder; cassette recorder; recorder

录音胶片 lùyīn jiāopiàn recording film

录音棚 lùyīnpéng sound-recording studio

录音摄像机 lùyīn shèxiàngjī sound video-camera

录音师 lùyīnshī recordist

录音室 lùyīnshì recording room

录影 lùyǐng 〈方言〉*see* "录像"

录用 lùyòng employ; recruit; take on the staff:择优～ employ on the basis of competitive selection; recruit selectively /量才～ give a person employment commensurate with his abilities /本公司拟～三名翻译人员。Our company plans to recruit three translators.

录载 lùzǎi record; account:这些传说,许多古书都有～。These legends can be found in many ancient books.

录制 lùzhì record:～唱片 make a gramophone record; cut a disc /～电视剧 record a TV play

禄 lù ❶ official's salary or stipend in feudal China; emoluments:俸～ official's salary /高官厚～ high position and handsome salary /无功不受～ must not accept undeserved emoluments /福～寿 happiness, position and longevity ❷ (Lù) a surname

禄蠹 lùdù 〈书面〉people interested only in getting fat official salaries; sinecurists

禄米 lùmǐ 〈旧语〉official's salary in the form of rice

禄位 lùwèi official salary and rank:钻营～ seek power and money /保持～ hold fast to one's office and emoluments

逯 Lù a surname

琭 lù

琭琭 lùlù 〈书面〉rare; scarce:～如玉 as rare as jade — very few

醁 lù *see* "醽醁" línglù

碌 lù ❶ commonplace; mediocre:庸～ mediocre; common and vulgar; philistine ❷ busy:忙～ be busy; bustle about

see also liù

碌碌 lùlù ❶ mediocre; commonplace:庸庸～ mediocre and unambitious ❷ busy with miscellaneous work:～半生,一无成就 be busy half of one's life and have accomplished nothing

碌碌尘寰 lùlù-chénhuán toil all the time in this earthly world; be busy with all sorts of work

碌碌无能 lùlù-wúnéng commonplace; lacking in ability; incompetent:～之辈 incompetent (*or* mediocre) people; people of low calibre

碌碌无为 lùlù-wúwéi attempt nothing and accomplish nothing; lead a plain, humdrum life:半生～,耽误的时光太多了! I've wasted too much of my time and accomplished nothing in the first half of my life.

碌碌无闻 lùlù-wúwén commonplace and little known; common and obscure:我这一辈子～,毫无建树。I have been a nobody all my life, with little to my credit.

睩 lù 〈书面〉(of eyeballs) move

崀 lù 〈方言〉tiny plot of even land between hillocks

箓(籙) lù *see* "符箓" fúlù

鲸 lù 〈动物〉*Sebastichthys elegans*

騄 lù

騄駬 lù'ěr *also* "騄耳" name of an ancient steed

绿 lù *used in such collocations as the following*

see also lǜ

绿林 lùlín the greenwood — world of brigands and outlaws:称雄～ be a hegemon in the greenwood; be a great chieftain of brigands /～间英雄辈出,豪杰无数。Among the brigands and outlaws came forth heroes and warriors in large numbers.

绿林好汉 lùlín hǎohàn hero of the greenwood; forest outlaw; bandit; brigand

绿林起义 Lùlín Qǐyì Lulin Uprising of 17 AD, a peasant rebellion towards the end of the Western Han Dynasty led by Wang Kuang

（王匡）and Wang Feng（王凤）

绿营 lùyíng green camp (Han Chinese recruited in the Qing Dynasty as local garrison troops and identified by green banners)：～兵 green banner troops

陆（陸） lù ❶ land：大～ continent /水～码头 hub of land and water transport /登～ land; disembark ❷（Lù）a surname

see also liù

陆半球 lùbànqiú 〈地理〉continental hemisphere; land hemisphere

陆边岛 lùbiāndǎo 〈地理〉continental island

陆标 lùbiāo 〈航空〉landmark：～定位 landmark fix

陆表海 lùbiǎohǎi 〈地理〉epicontinental sea; epeiric sea：～沉积 epicontinental sedimentation

陆沉 lùchén (of land) submerged in the sea;〈比喻〉(of territory) occupied by enemy troops

陆稻 lùdào *also*"旱稻"hàndào dryland rice; dry rice

陆地 lùdì dry land; land：～环境 terrestrial environment /～行舟 sail a boat on land — attempt the impossible /远洋航行，一连几天都见不到～。On an ocean voyage, one may not see land for several days on end.

陆地棉 lùdìmián upland cotton

陆地生态学 lùdì shēngtàixué terrestrial ecology

陆风 lùfēng 〈气象〉land breeze; terral

陆海分界线 lù-hǎi fēnjièxiàn landline

陆海空三军 lù-hǎi-kōng sānjūn army, navy and air force; the three armed services; armed forces

陆海潘江 lùhǎi-pānjiāng *also*"潘江陆海" Luji's (陆机) talent is like the sea and that of Pan Yue (潘岳) like the river — endowed with extraordinary talents; learned; erudite

陆基导弹 lùjī dǎodàn land-based missile：陆基巡航导弹 land-based cruise missile /陆基洲际导弹 land-based inter-continental ballistic missile

陆岬 lùjiǎ headland; cape; ness; promontory

陆架 lùjià *also*"大陆架"dàlùjià continental shelf：～外缘 shelf edge

陆九渊 Lù Jiǔyuān *also*"陆象山"Lù Xiàngshān Lu Jiuyuan (1139-1193), philosopher and educator of the Southern Song Dynasty, proponent of the theory of the mind (心学)

陆军 lùjūn ground force; land force; army：～法规 army regulations

陆军武官 lùjūn wǔguān military attaché

陆离 lùlí gaudy in colour; motley：光怪～ grotesque in shape and gaudy in colour /斑驳～ variegated

陆连岛 lùliándǎo land-tied island (as by a sand bar); tombolo

陆龙卷 lùlóngjuǎn 〈气象〉tornado

陆路 lùlù land route：～交通 overland communication; land communication /去大连，～不如水路快。It's not as fast to go to Dalian by land as by water.

陆棚 lùpéng *see*"陆架"

陆坡 lùpō continental slope

陆桥 lùqiáo land connecting two continents; land bridge：～运输 land-bridge service /欧亚大～ Eurasian landbridge

陆禽 lùqín birds that can only fly a short distance (such as quail)

陆上目标 lùshàng mùbiāo target on land; landmark

陆生动物 lùshēng dòngwù terrestrial animal

陆台 lùtái 〈地理〉table; tableland; continental block

陆相 lùxiàng 〈地理〉land facies

陆相沉积 lùxiàng chénjī 〈地理〉continental deposit or sediment

陆相地层 lùxiàng dìcéng 〈地理〉continental stratum

陆续 lùxù one after another; in succession：客人～来到，宴会即将开始。The guests arrived one after another and the banquet was to begin. /他这几年陆陆续续地发表了十篇论文。He has published ten papers over the past few years.

陆游 Lù Yóu Lu You (formerly translated as Lu Yu, 1125-1210), poet of the Southern Song Dynasty

陆缘海 lùyuánhǎi 〈地理〉epicontinental sea

陆运 lùyùn land transport

陆战队 lùzhànduì 〈军事〉marine corps; marines

lu

氇 lu *see*"氆氇"pǔlu

lǘ

闾 lǘ ❶〈书面〉gate or entrance to an alley or lane：倚～而望 wait at the entrance to the alley (for the return of one's son, etc.) ❷〈书面〉alley; lane; neighbourhood：乡～ fellow villagers ❸〈古语〉unit of twenty-five households ❹（Lǘ）a surname

闾里 lǘlǐ 〈书面〉native village; hometown

闾巷 lǘxiàng 〈书面〉❶ alley; lane; alleyway：车马盈门，～不通。The alleyway was blocked by arriving carriages. ❷ common people; ordinary people

闾阎 lǘyán 〈书面〉❶ district inhabited by the common people; neighbourhood of commoners：～繁富 affluent society of the common people ❷ common people：起于～ rise to power and position from a lowly station

闾左 lǘzuǒ 〈书面〉district inhabited by the poor; poor neighbourhood; poor people：贫居～，身无一文 live in a slum area stony broke

榈 lǘ *see*"棕榈"zōnglǘ

驴（驢） lǘ donkey; ass

驴唇不对马嘴 lǘchún bù duì mǎzuǐ *also*"牛头不对马嘴"niútóu bù duì mǎzuǐ donkeys' lips don't match horses' jaws — beside the point; far-fetched; incongruous; irrelevant：这个论点有点～。The argument is somewhat beside the point. /你们两个说的～。The two of you are talking at cross purposes.

驴打滚 lǘdǎgǔn ❶ form of usury in the old society, with the borrower having to pay double interest once the debt is overdue; snowballing usury：那年月，父亲还不起～的阎王债。In those days my father was unable to repay the snowballing usury. ❷ pastry made of steamed glutinous millet flour mixed with sugar

驴粪球 lǘfènqiú donkey droppings; person who looks impressive but has no real ability：这小子是个～，外表看着不错，其实是个草包。This young man may look impressive but is a real good-for-nothing.

驴肝肺 lǘgānfèi donkey's liver and lungs — ill intent：好心当成～ take sb.'s goodwill for ill intent

驴脸 lǘliǎn donkey's face; long face：他老拉着个～。He always pulls a long face.

驴骡 lǘluó *also*"驶骒"juétí hinny; jennet

驴鸣狗吠 lǘmíng-gǒufèi poor style of writing：这个选本，只有几个人的文章还不错，其余～，不堪卒读。Only a handful of articles in the anthology are all right; the rest are poorly written and not worth reading.

驴年马月 lǘnián-mǎyuè *also*"猴年马月"hóunián-mǎyuè;"牛年马月"niúnián-mǎyuè year of the donkey and month of the horse — impossible date; time that will never come (because there is no such year or month in the Chinese lunar calendar)：照你这么磨磨蹭蹭，～也植不成树，造不成林。If you go on dawdling like this, when on earth can we finish planting the trees and afforesting?

驴皮胶 lǘpíjiāo *also*"阿胶"ējiāo donkey-hide gelatin

驴皮影 lǘpíyǐng 〈方言〉donkey-leather silhouette show; shadow play

驴头不对马嘴 lǘtóu bù duì mǎzuǐ *see*"驴唇不对马嘴"

驴子 lǘzi 〈方言〉donkey; ass

lǚ

旅[1] lǚ ❶ travel; journey; live away from home：商～ company of travelling merchants; trade caravan /行～之人 traveller /新婚之～ honeymoon trip /～美侨胞 Chinese nationals living in the US ❷ *also*"穞"lǚ〈书面〉(of grains) naturally grown

旅[2] lǚ ❶〈军事〉brigade：加强～ reinforced brigade /混成～ mixed brigade /独立～ independent brigade ❷ troops; force：劲～ powerful army; crack force /军～生活 military life; life in the army ❸〈书面〉together; jointly：*see*"～进～退"

旅伴 lǚbàn travelling companion; fellow traveller：我们一路同行，结为～。We travelled together all the way.

旅差费 lǚchāifèi *also*"差旅费" expenses of a business trip; travel-

L

ling expenses

旅程 lǚchéng distance travelled; journey; route; itinerary:此去～千里,望你一路保重。Take good care of yourself on the thousand-*li* journey. /小册子上有我们整个～的详细情况。The brochure has the detailed information of our itinerary.

旅次 lǚcì 〈书面〉place where one stays overnight during a journey; stopover

旅店 lǚdiàn inn; hotel

旅费 lǚfèi travelling expenses; fare:国际～ international fare /～补助 travel allowance; travel grant; viaticum /报销～ reimburse travelling expenses /会期七天,～自理。The meeting will last seven days and the participants are responsible for their own travelling expenses.

旅馆 lǚguǎn hotel:住～ check in at a hotel; stay at a hotel /离开～ check out at a hotel; leave a hotel /汽车～ motel /～屋内服务 room service /～清洁工 hallgirl; hallboy /～行李员 hall porter /～管理 hotel management

旅进旅退 lǚjìn-lǚtuì 〈书面〉always follow the steps of others, forward or backward; go along with the majority; have no independent views of one's own:在这个科研项目中,我只是个～的角色,谈不到建树。I was a mere assistant and did nothing noteworthy in this research project.

旅居 lǚjū reside or live away from home; sojourn:～海外数十年,终于叶落归根,回到祖国。I have resided abroad for several decades and finally returned to my motherland, "the falling leaves eventually settling on the roots".

旅客 lǚkè hotel guest; traveller; passenger:～行李保险 passenger luggage insurance /过往～ travellers passing through; passengers

旅客登记簿 lǚkè dēngjìbù hotel register

旅鸟 lǚniǎo bird that passes a given area in its itinerary; bird of passage

旅人 lǚrén hotel guest; traveller; passenger

旅人蕉 lǚrénjiāo 〈植物〉*Strelitziaceae*

旅社 lǚshè (often used in hotel names) hotel; inn:平安～ Peace Inn

旅舍 lǚshè 〈书面〉hostel; hotel:河运一开,沿岸遍设～,甚为方便。When the river transport started, hostels sprang up on either side of the river to the convenience of the travellers.

旅途 lǚtú journey; trip:～见闻 what one hears and sees on a trip; traveller's notes /～生活,分外惬意。Life on the trip was very pleasant.

旅行 lǚxíng travel; journey; tour:长途～ long journey /徒步～ walking tour /组织去泰山～ arrange a trip (*or* tour) to Mount Tai

旅行包 lǚxíngbāo travelling bag

旅行背包 lǚxíng bēibāo packsack

旅行车 lǚxíngchē station wagon; wagon car

旅行袋 lǚxíngdài travelling bag; valise; luggage

旅行挂车 lǚxíng guàchē travel trailer

旅行剪 lǚxíngjiǎn folding scissors

旅行结婚 lǚxíng jiéhūn have an honeymoon trip

旅行闹钟 lǚxíng nàozhōng travelling alarm clock

旅行社 lǚxíngshè travel service; travel agency

旅行团 lǚxíngtuán touring party

旅行意外险 lǚxíng yìwàixiǎn travel accident insurance

旅行证 lǚxíngzhèng travel certificate; travel permit

旅行支票 lǚxíng zhīpiào traveller's cheque

旅行指南 lǚxíng zhǐnán guidebook

旅行装 lǚxíngzhuāng safari suit

旅游 lǚyóu tour; tourism:国内～ domestic tourism /～者 tourist /～观光 tourism /～胜地 tourist attraction /～景点 scenic spot; sight of interest /～旺季 peak tourist season /～收入 tourist revenue /～污染 tourist pollution

旅游热 lǚyóurè travel fever; travel bug:这里的年轻人已经传染上～。The young people here have caught the travel bug.

旅游图 lǚyóutú tourist map

旅游鞋 lǚyóuxié sneakers; trainers; walking shoes

旅游业 lǚyóuyè tourist industry; tourism

旅长 lǚzhǎng brigade commander

旅资 lǚzī travelling expenses

膂

lǚ 〈书面〉backbone

膂力 lǚlì muscular strength; physical strength; brawn:～兼人 possessing physical strength twice as much as others /～过人 possessing extraordinary physical (*or* muscular) strength

褛(褸)

lǚ *see* "褴褛" lánlǚ

偻[1](僂)

lǚ 〈书面〉crooked (back):伛～ humpback(ed); hunchback(ed)

偻[2](僂)

lǚ 〈书面〉instantly; immediately; at once:卖之不能～售 cannot sell (sth.) at once

see also lóu

屡(屢)

lǚ repeatedly; frequently; time and again:～建战功 win one victory after another in battle; have many exploits to one's credit /～劝不听 ignore (*or* turn a deaf ear to) others' repeated advice

屡次 lǚcì time and again; repeatedly:该犯～作案,不思悔改。The criminal committed crimes time and again, and has never shown any sign of repentance.

屡次三番 lǚcì-sānfān again and again; over and over again; many times:他～地邀请,我推却不过,只好来了。I couldn't possibly decline his repeated invitations, so here I am now.

屡见不鲜 lǚjiàn-bùxiān common occurrence; nothing new:像这样不应出现的错误,书中～。In the book, there are many mistakes of this kind which could have been avoided. /如今年轻人出国留学已是～了。Nowadays, there is nothing new about young people going abroad to study.

屡教不改 lǚjiào-bùgǎi *also* "累教不改" lěijiào-bùgǎi; "屡戒不悛" refuse to mend one's ways despite repeated admonition:这个～的惯犯,终于被逮捕法办了。The hardened criminal was finally arrested and brought to justice.

屡屡 lǚlǚ 〈书面〉time and again; repeatedly:写作中,他～搁笔沉思。While writing, he often put down his pen and sank into deep thought.

屡试不爽 lǚshì-bùshuǎng put to repeated tests and proved right; time-tested:他提出的建议,～,证明是行之有效的好办法。The measures he had proposed were put to repeated tests and proved right and effective each time.

屡试屡踬 lǚshì-lǚzhì fail at each trial

屡战屡败 lǚzhàn-lǚbài *also* "屡战屡北" suffer repeated defeats; fight and lose repeatedly:～,屡败屡战 lose one battle after another, but continue to fight on

屡战屡胜 lǚzhàn-lǚshèng have won every battle; have scored one victory after another

缕(縷)

lǚ ❶ thread:千丝万～ countless ties; thousand and one links /不绝如～ hanging by a thread; very precarious; almost extinct ❷ detailed; in detail:～解 explain in detail; go into particulars; elaborate ❸〈量词〉wisp; strand; lock:一～丝线 a strand of silk thread /一～炊烟 a wisp of smoke from the kitchen chimney /几～头发 several locks of hair

缕陈 lǚchén 〈书面〉state in detail (esp. when submitting a report to one's superior):～如下 state in detail as follows

缕缕 lǚlǚ continuously:暮色中,但见～炊烟,袅袅上升。In the gathering darkness, I saw wisps of smoke curling upward continuously from chimneys. /身上毛衣,丝丝～,都是母亲亲手织成。Every stitch of the sweater I wore was hand-knitted by mother herself.

缕缕行行 lǚlü-hánghang (of people, goods, etc.) in streams; in succession:街上的行人～,非常热闹。The street is thronged with people bustling with activity. /眼泪～地流了下来。Tears streamed down.

缕述 lǚshù state in detail; give all the details; go into particulars:详加～ go into particulars /～如次 state at some length (*or* in detail) as follows

缕析 lǚxī make a detailed analysis:文章条分～,思路、层次十分清晰。The article is clear in analysis, arrangement of ideas, and train of thought.

捋

lǚ smooth out with the fingers; stroke:～绳子 smooth out a rope /老人～了～胡子,微笑着摇摇头。The old man stroked his beard and shook his head with a smile.

see also luō

吕 lǚ ❶〈音乐〉temperament *see also*"律吕" lǜlǚ ❷（Lǚ）a surname

吕洞宾 Lǚ Dòngbīn Lü Dongbin (formerly translated as Lü Tung-pin), one of the Eight Immortals in Taoist mythology who is a scholar

吕剧 lǚjù 〈戏曲〉Lü opera (of Shandong Province)

吕氏春秋 Lǚshì Chūnqiū *Lü's Spring and Autumn Annals*, compiled under the sponsorship of Lü Buwei（吕不韦，? -235 BC), prime minister of the State of Qin in the late Warring States Period

吕宋 Lǚsòng Luzon, biggest of the Philippine islands

吕宋烟 lǚsòngyān Luzon cigar; cigar

铝 lǚ 〈化学〉aluminium (Al)：～铸造〈冶金〉aluminium casting / ～铸造合金 ceralumin / ～导线〈电工〉aluminium conductor

铝板 lǚbǎn 〈冶金〉aluminium sheet：～轧机 aluminium sheet mill

铝版 lǚbǎn 〈印刷〉aluminium plate：～印刷术 aluminography

铝箔 lǚbó aluminium foil

铝锭 lǚdìng aluminium ingot; aluminium pig

铝材 lǚcái 〈冶金〉aluminium product：～冷轧机 aluminium cold mill

铝矾土 lǚfántǔ bauxite

铝合金 lǚhéjīn aluminium alloy

铝化 lǚhuà 〈冶金〉aluminium impregnation; aluminization：～低碳钢 aluminized mild steel / ～物 aluminide / ～荧光屏〈电子〉aluminized screen

铝胶 lǚjiāo alumina gel

铝矿 lǚkuàng aluminium ore

铝热剂 lǚrèjì 〈化学〉thermite：～燃烧弹 thermite bomb

铝酸 lǚsuān 〈化学〉alumine acid; aluminic acid：～盐 aluminate / ～钾 potassium aluminate

铝土矿 lǚtǔkuàng *see*"铝矾土"

铝线 lǚxiàn 〈电工〉aluminium wire

铝芯电缆 lǚxīn diànlǎn 〈电工〉aluminium cable

稆(穭) lǚ (of grains) naturally grown：～生 naturally-grown; self-sown

侣 lǚ companion; associate：游～ fellow traveller; fellow tourist; playmate / 情～ lover; sweetheart / 旧～ former companion

侣伴 lǚbàn companion; partner; associate

履 lǚ ❶ shoe：西服革～ Western-style clothes and leather shoes / 削足适～ cut the feet to fit the shoes; act in a Procrustean manner ❷ tread on; walk on：如～薄冰 as if treading on thin ice; gingerly / 如～平地 as if walking on flat ground ❸ footstep：步～艰难 walk (*or* move) with difficulty; hobble along ❹ carry out; implement; honour; fulfil：*see*"～约"

履穿踵决 lǚchuān-zhǒngjué with shoes worn out and heels chapped; dressed shabbily; living in abject poverty：穷困潦倒，～ live in complete destitution

履带 lǚdài *also*"链轨" liànguǐ 〈机械〉caterpillar tread; track; apron wheel; crawler belt：～式拖拉机 caterpillar (*or* crawler) tractor / ～车 creeper truck; tracked vehicle / ～自行火炮 tracked howitzer / ～牵引装置 caterpillar; crawler track; crawler / ～坦克 caterpillar tank / ～拖车 crawler trailer

履端 lǚduān 〈书面〉❶ first day on the Chinese lunar calendar ❷ beginning of an imperial reign ❸ start; beginning

履历 lǚlì ❶ personal record (of education and work experience); antecedents：～书 form of personal record / 他的～很简单。His personal record is quite simple. ❷ curriculum vitae (CV); résumé：申请人必须交一份英文～。Applicants are required to submit (*or* hand in) their CV in English.

履历表 lǚlìbiǎo biographic sketch; curriculum vitae (CV); résumé

履霜坚冰 lǚshuāng-jiānbīng *also*"履霜知冰" tread on frost and you know solid ice is not far off; from the first small beginnings one can see how things will develop; from one small clue one can see what is coming：君子～，推微知著。An intelligent person can see how things will develop from a small clue.

履舄交错 lǚxì-jiāocuò jumble of shoes — a multitude of guests (esp. a festive gathering of both male and female guests)

履险蹈难 lǚxiǎn-dǎonàn tread on a dangerous path and go through a crisis; press forward arduously：～的任务多由他承担。He was assigned most of the dangerous tasks.

履险如夷 lǚxiǎn-rúyí cross a dangerous pass as easily as walking on level ground; handle a crisis without difficulty; weather a storm unscathed

履新 lǚxīn 〈书面〉❶ celebrate the New Year：～之庆 celebration of the New Year ❷ take up or assume one's new office

履行 lǚxíng perform; execute; fulfil; carry out：～诺言 keep one's word; honour one's word; fulfil (*or* carry out) one's promise / ～职责 do one's duty / ～手续 go through the procedures (*or* formalities) / ～合同 enforce a contract; execute (*or* fulfil) a contract / ～义务 discharge one's obligations; perform one's duty

履约 lǚyuē 〈书面〉fulfil one's promises; keep an agreement, appointment, etc.：如一方不能～，须按协定赔偿对方损失。If one party fails to abide by his promises, he is obliged to compensate for the other party's losses arising therefrom in accordance with the agreement.

lǜ

率 lǜ rate; ratio; proportion：圆周～ ratio of the circumference of a circle to its diameter / 利～ interest rate / 汇～ exchange rate / 回流～〈物理〉reflux ratio / 出勤～ rate of attendance; attendance / 税～ tax rate; rate of taxation; tariff rate / 效～ efficiency

see also shuài

虑(慮) lǜ ❶ consider; ponder; mull (over)：深谋远～ think deeply and plan carefully; be circumspect and far-sighted / ～无不周 leave nothing unconsidered; think thoroughly / 考～ think over; mull; consider ❷ concern; anxiety; worry：忧～ worry; be anxious / 疑～ misgivings; doubt / 无忧无～ carefree / 顾～ worry; be concerned

虑恋 lǜlian 〈方言〉❶ worry; be concerned about or with ❷ think over; consider

虑周藻密 lǜzhōu-zǎomì (of an article) coherent and refined; excellent：拜读大作，～，气势恢弘，不胜佩服。I can't help admiring you after reading your article which is coherent, refined and powerful.

滤(濾) lǜ strain; filter：过～器 filter / 把蔬菜～干 strain the water from the vegetables

滤波 lǜbō 〈无线电〉filtering; filtration; smoothing

滤波器 lǜbōqì 〈电子〉electric filter; wave filter：带通～ band-pass filter / 高通～ high-pass filter / ～电路 filter circuit / ～容量 filter capacity

滤光器 lǜguāngqì 〈物理〉light filter; optical filter：红外线～ infrared filter

滤过性病毒 lǜguòxìng bìngdú 〈医学〉filterable virus; filter passer *see also*"病毒" bìngdú

滤浆 lǜjiāng filter pulp

滤泡 lǜpào 〈生理〉follicle：～炎〈医学〉folliculitis / ～性淋巴瘤 follicular lymphoma

滤器 lǜqì filter：粗～ strainer

滤色镜 lǜsèjìng 〈摄影〉(colour) filter

滤网 lǜwǎng filter screen; filter gauze

滤液 lǜyè 〈化学〉filtrate

滤渣 lǜzhā filter residue; residue

滤纸 lǜzhǐ filter paper：定量～ quantitative filter paper / 定性～ qualitative filter paper

镳(鑢) lǜ 〈书面〉file; rasp; polish

律 lǜ ❶ law; statute; rule; regulation：规～ law; regular pattern / 纪～ discipline / 定～ law / 法～ law; statute / 刑～ criminal law / 同一～ law of identity ❷〈音乐〉ancient Chinese standard of pitch; tone：六～ six-tone / 十二～ twelve-tone / 音～ music; temperament ❸ name of a classical Chinese poetic form：五～ eight-line poem with five characters to each line and a strict tonal pattern and

L

rhyme scheme /七～ eight-line poem with seven characters to each line and a strict tonal pattern and rhyme scheme /排～ long *lüshi*, usu. with each line containing five characters ❹〈书面〉restrain; keep under control ❺ (Lǜ) a surname

律动 lǜdòng rhythm:心脏的～ rhythm of the heart

律己 lǜjǐ discipline oneself; exercise self-discipline; be strict with oneself:律人先～。Be strict with yourself if you want to be strict with others. *or* To command your men you must first discipline yourself. /王教授～甚严。Professor Wang observes stringent self-discipline.

律例 lǜlì laws; statutes and precedents

律令 lǜlìng laws and decrees

律吕 lǜlǚ 〈音乐〉❶ bamboo pitch-pipes used as standards of pitch in ancient China ❷ temperament; music:老先生对～声韵之学颇有研究。The old gentleman is versed in temperament and phonology.

律师 lǜshī (US) attorney:～费 attorney fee; lawyer's fee /女～ woman lawyer /出庭～ (UK) barrister /诉状～ (UK) solicitor /～业 lawyering /请～ retain counsel; engage (*or* hire) a lawyer /～协会 law society

律师楼 lǜshīlóu 〈方言〉law firm; lawyer's office

律师事务所 lǜshī shìwùsuǒ lawyer's office; law firm

律诗 lǜshī *lüshi*, a classical poem of eight lines, each containing five or seven characters, with a strict tonal pattern and rhyme scheme:五言～ poem with five characters to each of the eight lines / 七言～ poem with seven characters to each of the eight lines

律条 lǜtiáo ❶ legal articles or clauses; legal provisions; law:触犯～ violate (*or* break) the law ❷ norm; standard:做人的～ code of conduct

律政司 Lǜzhèngsī ❶ (HK before 1 July 1997) Attorney General:～署 Attorney General's Chambers ❷ (HK since 1 July 1997) Department of Justice:～长 Attorney General

律宗 Lǜzōng *Lü* sect of Buddhism, founded in the Tang Dynasty, and famous for its enforcement of commandments

葎 lǜ

葎草 lǜcǎo scandent hop (*Humulus scandens*):～属 Humulus /～霉菌 hop mildew

律 lǜ

see "猰律" hūlǜ

菉 lǜ

菉豆 lǜdòu *also* "绿豆" lǜdòu mung bean; green gram

氯 lǜ

〈化学〉chlorine (Cl)

氯胺 lǜ'àn chloramine

氯苯 lǜběn 〈化学〉chlorobenzene; chlorobenzol:～胺 chloraniline /～甲醛 chlorobenzaldehyde

氯丙嗪 lǜbǐngqín 〈药学〉chlorpromazine; wintermine

氯醇 lǜchún 〈化学〉chlorohydrin

氯丁橡胶 lǜdīng xiàngjiāo 〈化学〉chloroprene rubber; neoprene

氯度 lǜdù 〈化学〉chlorinity

氯仿 lǜfǎng 〈化学〉*also* "哥罗仿" gēluófǎng chloroform

氯仿中毒 lǜfǎng zhòngdú chloroformism

氯氟化 lǜfúhuà 〈化学〉chlorofluorination:～物 chlorofluoride

氯氟烃 lǜfútīng *also* "氯化氟" chlorofluorocarbons (CFCs) *see also* "氟利昂" fúlì'áng

氯化铵 lǜhuà'ǎn 〈化学〉ammonium chloride; salmiac

氯化钾 lǜhuàjiǎ 〈化学〉potassium chloride

氯化钠 lǜhuànà 〈化学〉sodium chloride

氯化物 lǜhuàwù 〈化学〉chloride

氯洁霉素 lǜjiéméisù 〈药学〉clindamycin

氯喹 lǜkuí 〈药学〉chloroquine

氯林可霉素 lǜlínkěméisù *also* "氯洁霉素"〈药学〉clindamycin

氯磷定 lǜlíndìng 〈药学〉pyraloxime methylchloride (PAMCL)

氯纶 lǜlún 〈纺织〉polyvinyl chloride fibre

氯霉素 lǜméisù 〈药学〉chloramphenicol; chloromycetin

氯气 lǜqì 〈化学〉chlorine:～灭菌 chlorination /～消毒室 chlorine contact chamber

氯醛 lǜquán 〈化学〉chloral:～酶〈生化〉chloralase /～糖 chloralose

氯噻酮 lǜsāitóng 〈药学〉chlorthalidone

氯杀螨 lǜshāmǎn 〈农业〉chlorbenside

氯四环素 lǜsìhuánsù 〈药学〉*also* "金霉素" jīnméisù chlortetracycline; aureomycin

氯酸 lǜsuān 〈化学〉chloric acid:～钾 potassium chlorate /～钠 sodium chlorate /～盐 chlorate /～盐炸药 chlorate explosive; chlorate powder

氯烃 lǜtīng chlorocarbon

氯氧化物 lǜyǎnghuàwù oxychloride

氯乙烯 lǜyǐxī 〈化学〉vinyl chloride:聚～ polyvinyl chloride /～树脂 vinyl chloride resin; Koroseal /～塑料 Koroseal

绿 lǜ

green:碧～ dark green /巴黎～ Paris green /油～ glossy dark green /青山～水 green hills and rivers /红花还须～叶扶。Red flowers need to be set off by green leaves.

see also lù

绿宝石 lǜbǎoshí emerald

绿草如茵 lǜcǎo-rúyīn *also* "芳草如茵" fāngcǎo-rúyīn lush grass looking like a green carpet; carpet of lush green grass

绿茶 lǜchá green tea

绿葱葱 lǜcōngcōng verdant; luxuriant and green:～的山林 verdant wooded mountain

绿党 Lǜdǎng Green Party

绿灯 lǜdēng green light; permission to go ahead (with sth.):开～ give the green light

绿地 lǜdì afforested land:具有江南园林风光的～工程,座落在市中心。The greening project, featuring garden scenery popular south of the Yangtze River, is sited in the heart of the city.

绿豆 lǜdòu *also* "菉豆" lǜdòu mung bean; green gram:～粥 mung bean porridge

绿豆糕 lǜdòugāo sweet cakes made with mung bean flour; mung-bean cake

绿豆象 lǜdòuxiàng *also* "小豆象" xiǎodòuxiàng *Callosobruchus chinensis*, a kind of pest for mung beans

绿豆芽 lǜdòuyá mung bean sprouts

绿豆蝇 lǜdòuyíng a kind of yellowish-green fly, larger than the housefly

绿矾 lǜfán 〈化学〉green vitriol; copperas

绿肥 lǜféi green manure:施～ spread (*or* apply) green manure

绿肥红瘦 lǜféi-hóngshòu lush green leaves and withered red flowers — transient scene of beauty:暮春时节,～,怎不使人顿生感叹! How can one help but sigh with emotion at the sight of lush green leaves and withered red flowers in late spring? /知否? 知否? 应是～。Can't you see? Can't you see? The green leaves are fresh but the red flowers are fading.

绿肥作物 lǜféi zuòwù green manure crop

绿猴 lǜhóu grivet (*Cercopithecus aethiops*)

绿化 lǜhuà make (a place) green by planting trees, flowers, etc.; afforest:～城市 plant trees in and around the city /～山区 afforest mountain district /～工程 landscape engineering /这里已经开始～了。This area is greening up.

绿化地带 lǜhuà dìdài green belt

绿僵菌 lǜjiāngjūn green muscardine fungus

绿卡 lǜkǎ green card — permanent residence permit

绿蓝色 lǜlánsè turquoise (blue)

绿篱 lǜlí hedgerow; hedge:一道又高又长的～,把院子和公路隔开。The courtyard and the road are separated by a high, long hedge.

绿帘石 lǜliánshí 〈矿业〉epidote

绿毛龟 lǜmáoguī mossback

绿帽子 lǜmàozi *see* "绿头巾"

绿霉 lǜméi green mould:～病 green mould

绿内障 lǜnèizhàng *also* "青光眼" qīngguāngyǎn 〈医学〉glaucoma

绿泥石 lǜníshí 〈矿业〉chlorite

绿茸茸 lǜrōngrōng luxuriant and bluish green:～的草地 lush, bluish green lawn /～的稻田 luxuriant, green paddy field

绿色贝雷帽 lǜsè bèiléimào Green Beret, an informal name for a British or US commando:～部队 Green Berets; Special Forces

绿色长城 lǜsè chángchéng green great wall, referring to the proposed green belt from Xinjiang to Heilongjiang

绿色革命 lǜsè gémìng green revolution (introduction of high-yielding seeds and modern agricultural techniques in developing countries in the sixties)

绿色和平组织 Lǜsè Hépíng Zǔzhī Greenpeace, an international

environmental organization
绿色激光器 lǜsè jīguāngqì green-light laser
绿色盲 lǜsèmáng 〈医学〉deuteranopia:～者 deuteranope
绿色贫血 lǜsè pínxuè 〈医学〉*also*"萎黄病" wěihuángbìng chlorosis
绿色食品 lǜsè shípǐn green food
绿色植物 lǜsè zhíwù green plant
绿生生 lǜshēngshēng green and tender:～的菠菜 green and tender spinach /田野披上了～的春装。The fields have turned green in spring.
绿视症 lǜshìzhèng 〈医学〉chloropsia
绿水青山 lǜshuǐ-qīngshān *also*"青山绿水" green mountains and blue waters — beautiful scenery:～枉自多,华佗无奈小虫何! So many green streams and blue hills, but to what avail? This tiny creature left even Hua Tuo powerless!
绿松石 lǜsōngshí 〈矿业〉turquoise
绿酸 lǜsuān 〈化学〉green acid
绿头巾 lǜtóujīn *also*"绿帽子" ❶ green scarf worn by panders or procurers as decreed in the Yuan and Ming dynasties ❷ cuckold:给她男人戴～ cuckold one's husband
绿头鸭 lǜtóuyā *also*"野鸭" yěyā mallard
绿岩 lǜyán 〈矿业〉greenstone; greenrock
绿盐 lǜyán 〈化学〉green salt; uranium tetrafluoride
绿叶成阴 lǜyè-chéngyīn green leaves make a shade; 〈比喻〉a girl has become a mother of many children
绿衣使者 lǜyī shǐzhě postman; mailman:这个年轻的～,天天送报上门,风雨无阻。The young postman delivers newspapers to the door every day rain or shine.
绿阴 lǜyīn shade (of a tree):～如盖 canopy of leaves /～蔽日 with the sun screened off by the shade of the tree
绿茵 lǜyīn green meadow:～场 (green meadow) football field
绿茵茵 lǜyīnyīn *also*"绿阴阴" verdant; dark green:～的草原 green grassland /～的秧苗 verdant seedlings; carpet of seedlings
绿莹莹 lǜyīngyīng glittering and green:禾苗在蒙蒙细雨中更显得～的。The seedlings appear strikingly green in the fine drizzle.
绿油油 lǜyōuyōu green and sleek; green and lush:～的蔬菜 green and lush vegetables /～的麦苗随风起伏。Shiny green wheat seedlings are undulating in the wind. /小鸟一身～的羽毛,真让人喜欢。What a lovely bird with bright green feathers all over!
绿铀矿 lǜyóukuàng 〈矿业〉uranolepidite
绿藻 lǜzǎo 〈植物〉green alga
绿洲 lǜzhōu oasis:千里荒漠中有一片～。There is an oasis in the boundless desert.
绿柱石 lǜzhùshí 〈矿业〉beryl

luán

栾(欒) luán ❶〈植物〉goldenrain tree ❷ (Luán) a surname
滦(灤) Luán Luanhe River (in Hebei Province)
圞(圝、圞) luán 〈方言〉❶ round:皮球溜～ round leather ball ❷ whole:清蒸～鸡 steamed whole chicken
脔(臠) luán 〈书面〉small slice of meat:尝鼎一～ conjure up the whole thing through seeing a part of it
脔割 luángē 〈书面〉slice up; cut up; carve up:国土被列强～。The country was carved up among the big powers.
峦(巒) luán 〈书面〉hills or mountains in a range:山～ chain of mountains /峰～ ridges and peaks /重～叠嶂 peaks rising one upon the other
峦嶂 luánzhàng low but steep and pointed hills; screen-shaped mountain peaks
銮(鑾) luán ❶ small tinkling bell ❷ tinkling bells on the emperor's carriage; imperial carriage:迎～ greet (*or* welcome) the imperial carriage
銮架 luánjià emperor's carriage
銮铃 luánlíng small tinkling bell on a cart
銮舆 luányú emperor's carriage
挛(攣) luán contraction:拘～ contraction /痉～ spasm; convulsion
挛缩 luánsuō contracture:局部软组织～ local contracture of soft tissue /他吓得～成一团。He huddled himself up with fright.
鸾(鸞) luán legendary bird like a phoenix
鸾俦 luánchóu 〈书面〉husband and wife:永结～ forge ties of abiding matrimony
鸾凤 luánfèng husband and wife:～之情 conjugal love /情同～ as affectionate as husband and wife
鸾凤分飞 luánfèng-fēnfēi separation of husband and wife
鸾凤和鸣 luánfèng-hèmíng be blessed with conjugal felicity; be a happy couple:"～"四个大红剪字非常醒目,给新房增添了几分喜庆的色彩。Four eye-catching scissored red characters meaning conjugal felicity adds joy to the bridal chamber.
鸾孤凤只 luángū-fèngzhī (of lovers or husband and wife) separated; left alone:十几年～,他日夜怀念远隔重洋的妻子。He missed his wife day and night as she had been overseas for over a decade.
鸾胶 luánjiāo *also*"鸾胶再续" remarry after the death of one's wife
see also"续弦" xùxián
鸾交凤友 luánjiāo-fèngyǒu couple deeply in love:但愿你我～,白头偕老。I hope you and I will remain a devoted couple to the end of our lives.
鸾飘凤泊 luánpiāo-fèngbó ❶ natural and unrestrained style of calligraphy:老先生晚年的楷书、行草,更显～,俊秀非凡。The old gentleman's regular script and cursive and running hand are all the more natural, unrestrained, and beautiful in his late years. ❷ (of husband and wife) be separated; be frustrated and lead a vagrant life:战乱中夫妻二人～,天各一方。The husband and wife were separated in the war and lost contact.
鸾翔凤集 luánxiáng-fèngjí galaxy of talent:不要小瞧这所小小的学院,倒是～,人才济济啊! Don't belittle this small college, it actually boasts a galaxy of talent.
鸾翔凤翥 luánxiáng-fèngzhù easy and free strokes of calligraphy:怀素的狂草,～,气势恢宏,是书法中的一绝。The cursive hand of Huai Su, one of the best in all calligraphy, is powerful and free.
鸾枭并栖 luán-xiāo bìngqī phoenix and owl stay together — good and bad people mixed up
娈(孌) luán 〈书面〉beautiful
娈童 luántóng handsome boy; male prostitute; gigolo
孪(孿) luán 〈书面〉twin:～子 twin sons
孪晶 luánjīng 〈物理〉twin crystal:～位错 twinning dislocation /～面 twin plane
孪生 luánshēng twin:～兄弟 twin brothers /～姐妹 twin sisters /～子 twin children

luǎn

卵 luǎn ❶ ovum; egg; spawn:产～ lay eggs; spawn /排～ ovulate /受精～ zygote; oosperm ❷〈生物〉zygote ❸〈方言〉testicles; penis
卵白 luǎnbái white of an egg; albumen
see also"蛋白❶" dànbái
卵巢 luǎncháo 〈生理〉ovary; oophoron:～囊肿 cystic ovary /～病〈医学〉oophoropathy; ovariopathy /～功能不全 ovarian insufficiency /～瘤 oophoroma /～破裂 ovariorrhexis /～炎 oophoritis; ovaritis /～切除术 ovariectomy (*or* ovariotomy) /～妊娠 ovariocyesis; oocyesis /～制剂疗法 ootherapy; ovariotherapy (*or* ovarotherapy); ovotherapy
卵黄 luǎnhuáng *also*"蛋黄" dànhuáng yolk; vitellus; vitelline:～核 yolk nucleus /～素 vitellin
卵镜 luǎnjìng ooscope
卵块 luǎnkuài egg cluster
卵磷脂 luǎnlínzhī 〈生化〉lecithin:～白蛋白 lecithalbumin /～酶

L

lecithinase
卵囊 luǎnnáng 〈生物〉oogonium; ootheca; ovisac; egg capsule
卵泡 luǎnpāo follicle:～瘤 folliculoma
卵生 luǎnshēng 〈动物〉oviparity:大多数鱼类是～的。Most fish are oviparous
卵生动物 luǎnshēng dòngwù oviparous animal; ovipara
卵石 luǎnshí cobble; pebble; shingle:鹅～ cobblestone; cobble
卵胎生 luǎntāishēng 〈动物〉ovoviviparity
卵胎生动物 luǎntāishēng dòngwù ovoviviparous animal; ovo-vivipara
卵细胞 luǎnxìbāo egg cell; ovum
卵星体 luǎnxīngtǐ 〈天文〉egg aster
卵形 luǎnxíng oviform; oval; ovoid
卵学 luǎnxué oology:～家 oologist
卵翼 luǎnyì cover with wings as in brooding; shield:在社会黑暗势力的～之下,这里的毒品交易发展很快。Under the aegis of the Mafia, drug-trafficking grows rapidly here.
卵用鸡 luǎnyòngjī laying fowl; layer
卵与石斗 luǎnyǔshídòu throw an egg against a rock; court certain defeat by fighting against overwhelming odds:～,你这岂不是自找倒霉? Aren't you courting trouble by throwing an egg against a rock?
卵子 luǎnzǐ 〈生物〉ovum; egg
卵子 luǎnzi 〈方言〉testicles; penis:大～ hernia

luàn

乱(亂) luàn ❶ in disorder or chaos; in disarray; in a mess; in confusion:～作一团 in great confusion /快刀斩～麻 cut a tangled skein of jute with a sharp knife; cut the Gordian knot /手忙脚～ be so confused as not to know what to do /工作杂～无章 make a mess of one's work /敌人慌～逃窜。The enemy fled helter-skelter. *or* The enemy scurried away in disarray. ❷ upheaval; rebellion; unrest; turmoil:叛～ armed rebellion; mutiny /动～ unrest; disturbance /战～ chaos caused by war /兵～ turmoil (*or* havoc) brought about by war ❸ confuse; mix up; jumble:扰～ create confusion; disturb; harass ❹ confused or unsettled (state of mind); in a turmoil:心烦意～ be terribly upset /这几天心～如麻。My mind has been in a turmoil these past few days. ❺ indiscriminate; random; arbitrary:～加批评 criticize indiscriminately /～来一气 act recklessly; take arbitrary action /～扣大帽子 slap political labels right and left /～穿马路 jaywalk /～出主意 advise offhand /～搞男女关系 carry on (*or* have) an affair with sb.; be promiscuous ❻ promiscuous sexual behaviour; promiscuity:淫～ (sexually) promiscuous; licentious
乱兵 luànbīng mutinous soldiers; totally undisciplined troops:～一路抢劫,弄得人心惶惶。The undisciplined soldiers plundered all the way creating great anxiety among the people.
乱臣 luànchén rebellious minister or subject
乱臣贼子 luànchén-zéizǐ traitors and usurpers:～,人人得而诛之。Everybody has the right to punish traitors and usurpers.
乱点鸳鸯 luàndiǎn-yuānyang ❶ mistakenly cause an exchange of partners between two couples engaged to marry:你不问明白就要给人家配对儿,真是～! You are pairing them off without knowing who's who. What a blunder! ❷ allocate personnel and jobs at random
乱放炮 luànfàngpào *also*"乱放枪" speak carelessly; make irresponsible remarks:你可不要到处～,说话注意着点! You shouldn't shoot your mouth off and must take care what you say.
乱纷纷 luànfēnfēn disorderly; confused; chaotic; tumultuous:这几天心里～的,一刻也不平静。My mind has been in a turmoil these days without a moment of peace.
乱坟岗 luànféngǎng unmarked common graves; unmarked burial-mound:村东不远,有一片～。To the east of the village lies a stretch of unmarked burial-mound.
乱哄哄 luànhōnghōng in noisy disorder; in a hubbub; tumultuous; in an uproar:～的人群 noisy disorderly crowd; tumultuous crowd /台下～地嚷成一片。There came an uproar from off-stage.
乱乎 luànhu *also*"乱糊"〈方言〉confusion; disorder; chaos:这里本来够～的了,你别再裹乱了。It's confused enough here, don't make it even worse!
乱阶 luànjiē 〈书面〉cause of upheaval or trouble
乱经 luànjīng 〈医学〉irregular menstrual period
乱砍滥伐 luànkǎn-lànfá indiscriminate felling of trees; cutting trees at random
乱了营 luànleyíng 〈方言〉be thrown into confusion; be in disarray:村里～,大人哭小孩叫。The village was plunged into chaos with grown-ups howling and children yelling.
乱离 luànlí be rendered homeless by war:内战使那个国家的人民饱尝～之苦。The civil war made the people of that country destitute and displaced.
乱流 luànliú ❶ irregular flow of air ❷〈书面〉cross (a river, etc.):乘舟～而南 cross a river by boat to the southern bank ❸〈书面〉irregular flow of water
乱伦 luànlún commit incest:～受害者 incest victim
乱麻麻 luànmāmā disorderly; messy; vexed; annoyed:这些天,她心上～的,夜里总做恶梦。She is upset these days and often has nightmares.
乱民 luànmín 〈旧语〉rebellious people; rebels
乱蓬蓬 luànpēngpēng dishevelled; tangled; jumbled; ragged:～的头发 dishevelled hair; tangled hair /院墙角是一堆～的柴草。A heap of firewood is jumbled in the corner of the courtyard.
乱七八糟 luànqībāzāo at sixes and sevens; in a mess; in a muddle:屋里～。The room is in a mess. /脑子里～的。One's mind is in a whirl. /房间被搞得～的。Everything is topsy-turvy in the room.
乱儿 luànr disturbance; trouble; disorder
乱世 luànshì troubled times; period of turmoil; turbulent days:苟安于～ try to keep body and soul together in troubled times /～出英雄。Heroes emerge in turbulent times.
乱世鬼 luànshìguǐ troublemaker:这小子是有名的～,什么事做不出来? The fellow is an infamous troublemaker. He's capable of anything.
乱世英雄 luànshì yīngxióng hero in turbulent times
乱视 luànshì *also*"散光" sǎnguāng astigmatism
乱说 luànshuō speak carelessly; make irresponsible remarks; gossip:当面不说,背后～ gossip behind people's backs but say nothing to their faces /～一通 shoot one's mouth off /对这些事,不要随便～。Don't make any irresponsible comments on these matters.
乱说乱动 luànshuō-luàndòng speak and act irresponsibly; be unruly in word and deed:你我初来乍到,不宜～。We'd better be careful in what we say or do, as we're new here.
乱弹 luàntán 〈戏曲〉general term used in mid-Qing period for Chinese opera melodies other than Kunshan and Yiyang melodies:以皮黄为主的京戏是由～发展而来的。Beijing opera composed mainly of *xipi* and *erhuang* melodies is derived from *luantan*.
乱弹琴 luàntánqín act or talk like a fool; talk nonsense:不懂收音机还要瞎捣鼓,简直是～。You're behaving like a fool to tamper with the radio without elementary knowledge. /他这话牛头不对马嘴,真是～。His remarks are wide of the mark. They're sheer nonsense!
乱套 luàntào mess up things; turn things upside down:要像你们这样干,没有不～的! It will be a muddle if things are done in your way.
乱腾腾 luànténgtēng confused; tumultuous; upset; disturbed:心里～的 be much disturbed; feel upset and confused /屋子里满是人,～的。Crowded with people, the room was like a beehive.
乱腾 luànteng confusion; disorder; unrest:没见过这样～的地方,让人一分钟也呆不下去。I've never seen such a hullabaloo before. I can hardly stay here for a minute.
乱杂 luànzá mixed and disorderly; in a jumble; in a muddle:库房里～不堪。The storehouse is in a complete jumble.
乱葬岗子 luànzàng gǎngzi *see*"乱坟岗"
乱糟糟 luànzāozāo chaotic; in a mess; in a pickle; confused:丈夫住院后,她心里一直～的。She felt greatly distressed after her husband was hospitalized. /他看不惯工地上那种～的样子。He was fed up with the mess the construction site was in.
乱真 luànzhēn ❶ (of fakes) look genuine; pass off as genuine:以假～ pass off a fake as the genuine stuff; substitute the spurious for the genuine /这种～的字画如今太多了! Nowadays, there are lots of fake paintings which are passed off as genuine! /这些走私的赝品几乎可以达到～的地步。These smuggled fakes almost look genuine. ❷〈物理〉spurious:～放电 spurious discharge /～脉冲 spurious pulse
乱子 luànzi disturbance; trouble; disorder:你们小心别出～。Be careful not to get into trouble.

lüě

掠 lüě 〈方言〉grab; take up:他不由分说,～起一根棍子就打。He picked up a stick to hit me, allowing no explanation.
see also lüè

lüè

掠 lüè ❶ rob; plunder; pillage; sack:奸淫掳～ rape and loot /抢～ rob; sack; plunder ❷ sweep past; brush past; graze; skim over:凉风～面,心里爽快极了。I was greatly refreshed to feel the cool breeze on my face. /一颗流星～过夜空。A shooting star flashed across the night sky. /小燕～檐而过。Some young swallows brushed past the eaves. /她～了一下额前的头发。She brushed aside her hair on the forehead. ❸〈书面〉hit with a club or a whip; flog:拷～ flog; beat; torture
see also lüě

掠地飞行 lüèdì fēixíng minimum-altitude flight; treetop flight; hedge-hopping:侦察机～,机智地避过了雷达。The reconnaissance (*or* scout) plane hedge-hopped and cleverly avoided the radar search.

掠夺 lüèduó plunder; loot; pillage:～成性 be predatory by nature /～式开采 indiscriminate mining /地主残酷的～和压榨,激起了农民的反抗。The landlord's ruthless plunder and exploitation aroused strong opposition from the peasants.

掠夺采伐 lüèduó cǎifá 〈林业〉cut out and get out

掠夺婚 lüèduóhūn *also* "抢婚" qiǎnghūn marriage by capture

掠卖 lüèmài kidnap and sell:～人口 engage in kidnapping and trafficking of human beings

掠美 lüèměi grab the credit; claim credit due to sb. else:不敢～ cannot claim credit (for sth.) /此人有～之嫌。The man came under suspicion of claiming credit for something he did not do.

掠目 lüèmù flash past before one's eyes:他坐在急驶的汽车里,路旁的景物～而过。The scene on the roadside flashed past as his car speeded along.

掠取 lüèqǔ seize; grab; plunder:帝国主义疯狂地～殖民地的丰富资源。The imperialists wantonly plundered the rich resources of the colonies.

掠人之美 lüèrénzhīměi claim credit due to sb. else
see also "掠美"

掠视 lüèshì look or glance around; sweep one's eyes over:他在房间里～一周。He cast a quick glance round the room.

掠水飞行 lüèshuǐ fēixíng wave-hopping

掠影 lüèyǐng bird's-eye view; panorama:自然博物馆～ bird's-eye view of the natural museum

略[1](畧) lüè ❶ brief; sketchy; rough:粗～ rough; sketchy /～述一二 give a brief account /～有所知 have an inkling of the matter /英雄所见～同。Great minds think alike. ❷ brief account; summary; outline; sketch:事～ biographical sketch /要～ outline; summary /史～ outline history ❸ omit; delete; leave out:从～ be omitted /省～ omit; leave out; make no mention of /修改稿把这一段话都～去了。This paragraph was deleted in the revised version.

略[2](畧) lüè plan; strategy; scheme:胆～ boldness; daring /谋～ astuteness and resourcefulness; stratagem /策～ tactics /韬～ military strategy /智～过人 be superbly wise and resourceful

略[3](畧) lüè capture (city or land); seize:侵～ aggression; invasion /攻城～地 attack cities and seize territories

略称 lüèchēng abbreviated name; abbreviation

略迹原情 lüèjì-yuánqíng ignore what is superficial and forgive sb. for doing what is reasonable:他是位宽厚长者,对人往往能～。Being a magnanimous elder, he often forgives and forgets.

略见一斑 lüèjiàn-yībān catch a glimpse of; get a rough idea of:书中讹误甚多,仅举一、二,由此可以～。The book is full of errors. You can get a rough idea of this from the examples listed here.

略略 lüèlüè a little; slightly; briefly:一场小雨只～打湿了地皮。The light rain merely wetted the ground surface.

略胜一筹 lüèshèng-yīchóu a notch or cut above; slightly better:甲队～,终以微弱的比分获胜。Team A was slightly better; it finally won by a narrow margin.

略识之无 lüèshí-zhīwú only slightly or marginally literate; semiliterate

略图 lüètú sketch map; sketch:文中附有～,可资佐证。Included in the article are some sketches which can serve as evidence.

略微 lüèwēi slightly; a little; somewhat:他心里～有点不快。He felt somewhat unhappy (*or* displeased). /他手上～蹭破了一点儿皮。He had a little skin rubbed off his hand.

略为 lüèwéi a little; a bit; slightly; a trifle:～增加 slightly increase /他～定了定神。He collected himself a bit.

略逊一筹 lüèxùn-yīchóu a notch below; be slightly inferior:青年队在耐力、技巧和经验等方面,比国家队还是～。The youth team is slightly inferior to the national team in terms of stamina, skill and experience.

略语 lüèyǔ 〈语言〉abbreviation; shortening:沧海桑田,～作"沧桑"。"Cang Sang" is short for "Cang Hai Sang Tian" (Time brings great changes to the world).

略知皮毛 lüèzhī-pímáo have a shallow understanding or superficial knowledge:我不过～,不敢在行家面前乱说。I do not dare to make comments in the presence of experts, for I have only a smattering of knowledge of the subject.

略知一二 lüèzhī-yī'èr have a smattering of; know just a little; have a rough idea:此事我只是～,怕说不清楚。Little as I know, I'm afraid I can't explain it clearly.

锊 lüè *lüe*, an ancient unit of weight (about 0.6 *jin* or 300 grams)

lūn

抡(掄) lūn ❶ swing; brandish:～锤 swing a hammer /～刀 brandish a sword /～拳 shake one's fist ❷ fling; throw; scatter:把菜～了一地。Vegetables were thrown all over the floor.
see also lún

lún

仑(崙) lún 〈书面〉logical sequence; coherence

沦(淪) lún ❶ sink; subside:沉～ sink into depravity, etc. /～于深渊 plunge into an abyss ❷ fall; degenerate; be reduced to:～陷 be occupied by the enemy; fall into enemy hands /～为奴隶 be reduced to slavery

沦废 lúnfèi be neglected and abandoned:由于政府重视保护古迹,这座古刹才免于～。The ancient Buddhist temple did not fall into ruins thanks to the government's efforts to preserve places of historic interest.

沦肌浃髓 lúnjī-jiāsuǐ go right to the marrow; be greatly influenced:这些年先生的学问、人品对我的影响,可以说～,刻骨铭心。Over the years, the learning and moral integrity of my teacher have greatly influenced me, for which I'll always be grateful.

沦浃 lúnjiā 〈书面〉greatly influence; be deeply ingrained:深仁厚泽,～寰宇。Great benevolence and bounty spread far and wide in the universe.

沦落 lúnluò ❶ become a vagabond; be homeless:～海外 become a vagrant in a foreign land /同是天涯～人,相逢何必曾相识。Both losers in this wide world running into each other, It mattered not whether we had met before or not. ❷〈书面〉decline; fall low; come down in the world:家境～ destitute family circumstances /道德～ moral depravity ❸ sink; fall; degenerate:江山～。The land fell into the hands of the enemy.

沦落风尘 lúnluò-fēngchén be driven to prostitution; become a prostitute

沦落街头 lúnluò-jiētóu be driven into the street — become a tramp or beggar:～,终日乞讨 be driven onto the streets and go beg-

L

ging

沦灭 lúnmiè wither away; die out

沦没 lúnmò 〈书面〉❶ sink; sink into oblivion; become extinct:有关此事的史料早已～。Historical records about the event have sunk into oblivion. ❷ die; pass away:挚友～。A bosom friend passed away.

沦丧 lúnsàng wither away; be forfeited; be lost or ruined:国土～loss of territory /国家主权日渐～,几乎成了附庸国。The country forfeited its sovereignty gradually and was almost reduced to a vassal.

沦亡 lúnwáng ❶ (of a country) be annexed or subjugated; perish:三省～,国难当头 (of a state) have lost three provinces and be plunged into a national crisis ❷ fall low; be lost; be depraved:道德～ moral depravity

沦陷 lúnxiàn ❶ (of territory, etc.) be occupied by the enemy; fall into enemy hands:国土～敌手,人民流离失所。The territory fell into enemy hands and the people became destitute and homeless. ❷〈书面〉submerge; flood; inundate

沦陷区 lúnxiànqū enemy-occupied area (i.e. an area occupied by the Japanese during the War of Resistance Against Japanese Aggression, 1937-1945)

论(論)

Lún *The Analects of Confucius*:上～ Volume One of the *Analects* /下～ Volume Two of the *Analects*

see also lùn

论语 Lúnyǔ *The Analects of Confucius*; *The Analects*:半部《～》治天下 rule the country by resorting to half of *the Analects*; (be able to) rule the country well if one knows half of the *Analects* and follows its teachings

see also "四书" Sìshū

抡(掄)

lún 〈书面〉choose; select:～材 select (suitable) material

see also lūn

轮(輪)

lún ❶ wheel:车～ wheel (of a vehicle) /齿～ gear wheel; gear /独～车 wheelbarrow /三～车 pedicab; tricycle ❷ sth. resembling a wheel; disc; ring:日～ sun's disc; sun /月～ moon /年～〈植物〉annual ring; growth ring /耳～ helix /滑～ pulley ❸ steamboat; steamer:江～ river steamer /远洋～ oceanliner /渔～ fishing vessel /渡～ ferry; ferry boat ❹ take turns; do by turns:下一次～到我开车了。It's my turn to drive next. /许多人都想看这本书,每人～一天吧。As so many people want to read the book, each can only have it for one day by turns. ❺〈量词〉(a) *used of the sun, moon, etc.*:一～红日冉冉升起。A red sun slowly rose. /一～明月高挂半空。A bright moon was hanging in the sky. (b) *used of things or actions that rotate*:赛罢首～ after the first round (of matches) /第二～会谈 second round of talks /他岁数比我大一～。He is twelve years older than me. (each cycle of symbolic animals 生肖 taking 12 years)

轮班 lúnbān in shifts; in relays; by turns; in rotation:下半夜我们分几拨～看场。We divided ourselves into groups and guarded the threshing ground in shifts after midnight. /工厂开工不足,车间只好～歇工。Since the factory is operating under capacity, the workshops have to stop work in rotation.

轮拨儿 lúnbōr 〈方言〉in shifts; in relays; by turns; in rotation:～守夜 keep vigil by turns (*or* in rotation)

轮埠 lúnbù port; harbour; wharf

轮唱 lúnchàng 〈音乐〉round

轮齿 lúnchǐ 〈机械〉tooth of a cogwheel; cog

轮虫 lúnchóng 〈动物〉wheel animalcule; rotifer

轮船 lúnchuán steamer; steamship; steamboat

轮次 lúncì ❶ in turn; by turns:～入内 enter in turn /～上场 enter the field one after another ❷ number of turns; times:每日由一人值班,十个人轮流,一个月也就三个～。One person is on duty each day. If ten people take turns, it's only three times for one person every month.

轮带 lúndài tyre:汽车～放炮了。The car's tyre had a blowout.

轮刀 lúndāo 〈机械〉flywheel knife:～式切碎机 flywheel chopper; flywheel cutter; flywheel-type cutter head

轮渡 lúndù (steam) ferry:火车～ train ferry /大桥修通之前,来往行人和货物都靠～过河。Before the bridge was built, people and goods crossed the river by ferryboat.

轮番 lúnfān take turns:～干活 take turns at a job /～轰炸 bomb in waves /核军备～升级 spiralling escalation of the nuclear arms race

轮辐 lúnfú spoke

轮箍 lúngū tyre; rim; strake:～术 tyring

轮毂 lúngǔ (wheel) hub; (wheel) boss; nave

轮换 lúnhuàn rotate; take turns:大家～着帮老李伺候生病的老母亲。Everybody took turns to help Lao Li look after his sick old mother. /一个月一～,谁也没意见了。Nobody objected to taking turns once a month.

轮回 lúnhuí ❶〈宗教〉samsara; transmigration:生死～ transmigration of life and death ❷ turn; rotate:四季～。The four seasons succeed each other.

轮机 lúnjī ❶ (short for 涡轮机) turbine:燃气～ combustion gas turbine /冲压空气～ ram-air turbine ❷ motorship engine; engine

轮机室 lúnjīshì engine room

轮机员 lúnjīyuán engineer; engineman

轮机长 lúnjīzhǎng chief engineer

轮奸 lúnjiān gang rape

轮距 lúnjù track; tread; gauge

轮空 lúnkōng 〈体育〉bye:第一轮比赛抽签～ draw a first-round bye

轮廓 lúnkuò ❶ outline; profile; contour; rough sketch:他三、两笔就把画面的～勾好了。He outlined the picture in a couple of strokes. /在朦胧的夜色中,学校只能看见一个～。The school was reduced to a contour in (*or* stood in silhouette against) the dim moonlight. ❷ general or rough idea:他对单位的情况只知道一个大致的～。He has got only a rough idea of how things stand in the unit.

轮流 lúnliú take turns; do sth. in turn:车间活紧,只好～休礼拜天。Because of pressure of work in the workshop, everybody had to take turns to rest on Sundays.

轮牧 lúnmù 〈畜牧〉rotation grazing

轮盘赌 lúnpándǔ roulette:俄罗斯～ Russian roulette

轮批 lúnpī in batches; by turns; in turn:场地较小,大家要～参观。Since the space is limited, we have to visit it in groups.

轮生 lúnshēng 〈植物〉verticillate:～叶 verticillate leaves

轮式 lúnshì wheeled:～拖拉机 wheeled tractor /～推土机 wheel dozer

轮胎 lúntāi tyre:实心～ solid tyre /充气～ pneumatic tyre /防滑～ antiskid tyre; nonskid tyre /双层～ two-ply tyre /翻制～ retreaded tyre /～花纹 tyre tread /～气压 tyre pressure /～行驶里程 tread life

轮胎工 lúntāigōng tyreman

轮胎帘子线 lúntāi liánzixiàn tyre cord

轮胎压力计 lúntāi yālìjì tyre pressure gauge

轮替 lúntì take turns; do sth. in turn:他们～着休息。They take turns to have a day off.

轮辋 lúnwǎng rim (of a wheel)

轮系 lúnxì wheel train; gear train

轮休 lúnxiū ❶〈农业〉rotation farming:在宽乡广土,可以采用～的办法,恢复地力,提高单位产量。In country with extensive land, rotation farming can be introduced to restore soil fertility and increase per unit yield. ❷ have holidays by turns; rotate days off; stagger holidays:由于任务重,工程队实行～。The construction brigade has staggered holidays because of the heavy load of work.

轮训 lúnxùn training in rotation:在职～ in-service training by rotation /～之后,青年职工的知识、技能有了较大提高。After the rotation training, the knowledge and skill of the young workers and staff have been considerably improved.

轮训班 lúnxùnbān rotational training course

轮养 lúnyǎng raise various species of fish in rotation in the same fishpond

轮椅 lúnyǐ wheelchair

轮栽 lúnzāi *see* "轮作"

轮闸 lúnzhá hub brake

轮值 lúnzhí be on duty in turns:制定了～制度之后,单位的日常工作更有条理了。The establishment of the on-duty-in-turn system helped streamline the routine work of the unit.

轮种 lúnzhòng *see* "轮作"

轮轴 lúnzhóu 〈物理〉axletree; axle; wheel shaft

轮转 lúnzhuàn ❶ rotate:四时～ rotating seasons ❷〈方言〉take turns:～着值夜班 work night shifts by turns

轮转印刷机 lúnzhuàn yìnshuājī rotary press

轮子 lúnzi wheel

轮作 lúnzuò *also* "轮栽"; "轮种"; "倒茬" dǎochá; "调茬" diàochá 〈农业〉crop rotation:粮棉～ rotation of cereal crops and cotton /～栽培 rotation cropping; alternate culture

囵(圇) lún *see* "囫囵" húlún

崘(崙) lún *see* "昆仑" Kūnlún

伦(倫) lún ❶ human relations, esp. as conceived in terms of ethics:五～ (in feudal China) five cardinal relationships between ruler and subject, father and son, husband and wife, between brothers and between friends /天～ natural bonds and ethical relationships between members of a family /天～之乐 family happiness /人～ human relations in terms of ethics ❷ logic; order:先后有～ order of priority; sequential order ❸ peer; match:不～不类 neither fish nor fowl; nondescript /荒谬绝～ absolutely preposterous; utterly absurd ❹ (Lún) a surname

伦巴 lúnbā rumba (a dance)

伦比 lúnbǐ 〈书面〉rival; equal:无与～ unrivalled; unequalled; peerless /史无～ unequalled (*or* unparalleled) in history

伦常 lúncháng order of importance or seniority in human relationships, conceived as constant and unchangeable in terms of feudal ethics:整饬纲纪～ strengthen the order and moral obligations

伦次 lúncì coherence; logical sequence:语无～ speak incoherently; ramble on; babble like an idiot

伦敦 Lúndūn London:～警察厅 Scotland Yard

伦敦股票交易所 Lúndūn Gǔpiào Jiāoyìsuǒ London Stock Exchange (LSE)

伦敦国际金融期货交易所 Lúndūn Guójì Jīnróng Qīhuò Jiāoyìsuǒ London International Financial Futures Exchange (LIFFE)

伦敦银行同业拆借率 Lúndūn yínháng tóngyè chāijièlǜ 〈金融〉London interbank offered rate (LIBOR)

伦纪 lúnjì (short for 伦常纲纪)〈书面〉feudal moral principles and order of importance or seniority

伦类 lúnlèi 〈书面〉❶ proper or logical arrangement of things; orderliness ❷ (of the) same kind, class or species

伦理 lúnlǐ ethics; moral principles:封建的～道德 feudal moral principles and ethics

伦理学 lúnlǐxué ethics

伦琴 lúnqín 〈物理〉rontgen; roentgen:～仪 roentgenometer

伦琴射线 lúnqín shèxiàn 〈物理〉rontgen or roentgen rays *see also* "爱克斯射线" àikèsī shèxiàn

纶(綸) lún ❶〈书面〉black silk ribbon:青～ black silk ribbon ❷〈书面〉fishing line:垂～ go fishing; go angling ❸〈纺织〉synthetic fibre:锦～ polyamide fibre /丙～ polypropylene fibre /涤～ polyester fibre; Terylene /维尼～ polyvinyl alcohol fibre; Vinylon *see also* guān

纶音 lúnyīn 〈书面〉imperial edict

lǔn

埨(埨) lǔn 〈方言〉earth ridge in a field:～上青草 green grass on the earth ridge

lùn

论(論) lùn ❶ comment; discuss; talk about:谈～ talk about /议～ comment /讨～ discuss /辩～ argue; debate /《～当前形势》*Concerning the Current Situation* ❷ view; opinion; statement; essay:社～ editorial /评～ comment; commentary; review /短～ short commentary /舆～ public opinion /空～ empty talk /长篇大～ lengthy statement (*or* remarks) ❸ theory; doctrine:相对～ theory of relativity /认识～ theory of knowledge; epistemology /唯物～ materialism /无神～ atheism /有神～ theism / 方法～ methodology /宿命～ fatalism ❹ speak of; mention; treat; consider:相提并～ mention in the same breath /存而不～ leave the question open /此事不能一概而～。This shouldn't be lumped together with other things. ❺ measure; appraise; decide on; determine:按质～价 determine the price according to the quality /以挪用公款～ be treated as a case of embezzlement of public funds ❻ by; in terms of:～天计酬 be paid by day /豆腐是～斤卖,还是～块儿卖? Is the bean curd sold by the *jin* or by piece? /～人品,她是数一数二的。She ranks very high in terms of personality. /～能力,他比别人都强些。He is above others as far as ability is concerned. ❼ (Lùn) a surname *see also* Lún

论辩 lùnbiàn argue; debate:～有力 cogent argument

论辩文 lùnbiànwén argumentation; apology

论处 lùnchǔ decide on sb.'s punishment; punish:依法～ punish according to law; deal with in accordance with the law; bring to justice /以玩忽职守～ impose a penalty on sb. for negligence of duty

论敌 lùndí opponent in a debate:文笔犀利,常能一击而制～于死命。With his caustic pen he can often down his debate opponent at a stroke.

论点 lùndiǎn argument; thesis; point of view:中心～ essential argument; principal thesis /～新颖 original concept (*or* notion)

论调 lùndiào 〈贬义〉view; argument:这种蛊惑人心的～非常有害。Such demagogic views are very harmful.

论断 lùnduàn inference; judgment; thesis:生物进化的著名～,是由让·拉马克于1801年首先提出的。The famous theory of biological evolution was first set forth (*or* put forward) by Jean Lamark in 1801. /文章对国际新格局的～,引起了广泛的注意。The article's thesis on the new international structure has drawn wide attention.

论锋 lùnfēng edge or force of an argument; edge or force of one's remarks

论功行赏 lùngōng-xíngshǎng dispense rewards or honours according to merit; award people according to their contributions:我的成绩有限,～也不会轮到我的头上。I've done very little, and so if awards are given according to merit, I can't lay claim to any.

论衡 Lùnhéng *Discourses Weighed in the Balance* written by Wang Chong (王充, 27-c.97) of the Eastern Han Dynasty

论黄数黑 lùnhuáng-shǔhēi *also* "数黑论黄" make irresponsible remarks; indulge in idle gossip:此人惯于舞文弄墨,～。The man is given to phrase-mongering and idle gossip.

论据 lùnjù ❶〈逻辑〉reasoning ❷ grounds of argument; argument:充足的～ adequate argument; ample reasons

论客 lùnkè critic; commentator

论理 lùnlǐ ❶ reason with sb.; argue:你把他叫来,我同他论论理。Go and bring him here. I'll argue it out with him. /他找她～,问她答应的事为什么不算数了。He went to ask her why she failed to keep her promise. ❷ normally; as things should be:～他今天应该来,可他因病不能来了。Normally he should come today, but he can't because of illness. ❸ logic; reason:合乎～ be reasonable (*or* logical); stand to reason /这种违背～的话是站不住脚的。Such illogical views are untenable.

论理学 lùnlǐxué 〈旧语〉logic

论列 lùnliè expound one by one:凡此种种,无须笔者～,读者自有看法。It's not necessary for this author to explain them one by one; the readers will form their own judgment.

论难 lùnnàn debate; challenge (in debate); argue against the opponent's viewpoint:两个学派互相～,难分高下。The two schools of thought argue against each other's views, and it's hard to tell which side has got the upper hand.

论儿 lùnr 〈口语〉principle; idea; taboo:早先有个～,破五才能出门,商店才开始营业。In the past, there was a taboo that people shouldn't go out and shops shouldn't start business until after the fifth day of the first lunar month.

论述 lùnshù discuss; explicate; expound:文中精辟的～,给读者以深刻的印象。The brilliant exposition (*or* explication) in the article made a deep impression on the readers.

论说 lùnshuō ❶ exposition and argumentation:～体 argumentation (as a category of writing) ❷〈口语〉normally; as things should be:～他应该知道这件事。Ordinarily, he should have known about it.

论说文 lùnshuōwén (a piece of) argumentation; argumentative essay

论坛 lùntán forum; tribune:读者～ readers' forum /《～报》*The Tribune* /史学～ forum on historical science /时事～ current affairs symposium (*or* forum)

论题 lùntí 〈逻辑〉proposition:文章提出的这一～,还须进一步分析和讨论。The proposition conceived in the article needs further analysis and discussion.

论文 lùnwén thesis; dissertation; treatise; paper:毕业～ graduation thesis (*or* dissertation) /～讨论会 thesis symposium /(文学)硕士～ MA thesis /他在权威性刊物上发表过多篇学术～。He has published a number of scholarly (*or* academic) papers in authoritative journals.
论文答辩 lùnwén dábiàn thesis defence:明天我进行～。I'll defend my thesis tomorrow.
论议 lùnyì comment; talk; discuss:～政事 discuss government affairs
论战 lùnzhàn polemic; debate:这一场大～,引起广泛的关注。The polemic has drawn wide attention.
论争 lùnzhēng argument; debate; controversy:关于人权问题的～ controversy over human rights
论证 lùnzhèng ❶〈逻辑〉demonstration; proof ❷ expound and prove; appraise; evaluate:～会 meeting to appraise a project (*or* sb.'s work) /作者有力地～了非洲沙漠化日益严重的历史和现实的原因。The author expounded in a convincing way the historical and immediate causes of the desertification in Africa. ❸ grounds of argument; argument:无懈可击的～ unassailable arguments
论旨 lùnzhǐ purport or object of an argument:阐明～ clarify the purport
论著 lùnzhù treatise; work; book:一本关于国际法的最新～ latest work on international law
论资排辈 lùnzī-páibèi go by seniority; stress seniority in promotion:在用人上,要打破～的旧观点。It's necessary to part with the outdated practice of promotion by seniority.
论罪 lùnzuì punish as guilty of a crime; decide on the nature of the guilt:依法～ punish according to law; bring to justice /法庭按叛国通敌～,判之以终生监禁。The court found him guilty of treason and sentenced him to life imprisonment.

luō

落 luō *see*"大大落落" dàda-luōluō
see also là; lào; luò

捋 luō rub one's palm along (sth. long); strip sth. by closing the palm around it and running one's hand along the length; hand-strip:～起袖子 roll up one's sleeve /～榆钱儿 strip an elm branch of its seeds
see also lǚ
捋胳膊,挽袖子 luō gēbo, wǎn xiùzi push up one's sleeve:你动不动就～,太缺乏教养了。How boorish of you to roll up your sleeves at the slightest provocation!
捋虎须 luō hǔxū stroke a tiger's whiskers — do sth. very daring; run great risks:谅你有何本事,敢来～? Who are you to come and provoke me?

啰(囉) luō
see also luó; luo
啰唆 luōsuo *also*"啰嗦" ❶ long-winded; verbose; wordy:说话～ be long-winded /她啰啰唆唆地说了半天,还是没说明白。She kept talking for a long time but failed to get her ideas across. /我再～几句,把心里想说的说完。Bear with me a little longer and let me finish what I want to say. ❷ overelaborate; fussy; troublesome:～事 troublesome business; fussy job /这些手续真～,办了一天还没办完。All these formalities are so elaborate that I haven't got through them after spending a whole day.
啰嗦 luōsuo *see*"啰唆"

luó

螺 luó ❶〈动物〉spiral shell; snail:田～ river snail /海～ conch /钉～ oncomelania; snail ❷ whorl (in fingerprint):他右手有三个～。He has got three whorls in the right hand. /他大拇指是个破～。He's got a broken whorl on the thumb.
螺钿 luódiàn *also*"螺甸"〈工美〉mother-of-pearl inlay:～漆盘 lacquer tray inlaid with mother-of-pearl
螺钉 luódīng *also*"螺丝钉";"螺丝" screw:木～ wood screw; screwnail /圆头～ button-head cap screw /扁头～ brazier-head screw /十字槽～ Philips screw /有环～ collar screw /～头 screwhead
螺杆 luógǎn screw bolt; screw:～泵 screw pump
螺杆传动 luógǎn chuándòng 〈机械〉screw drive:～刨床 screw-driven planer (*or* planing machine) /～牛头刨 screw-driven shaper (*or* shaping machine) /～插床 screw-driven slotter (*or* slotting machine)
螺管 luóguǎn 〈机械〉screwed pipe:～接头 screwed joint /～套管 screwed sleeve
螺号 luóhào conch; shell trumpet:渔家女吹起了～。The fishing girl blew a shell trumpet.
螺髻 luójì hair-style done in a shell-shaped bun or coil
螺桨 luójiǎng 〈机械〉propeller:～风机 propeller fan /～透平 propeller turbine
螺距 luójù 〈机械〉(screw) pitch; thread pitch:～测量仪 pitchometer /～规 pitch gauge
螺菌 luójūn 〈微生物〉spirillum
螺孔 luókǒng screwhole
螺口 luókǒu screw
螺口灯泡 luókǒu dēngpào screw bulb
螺口灯头 luókǒu dēngtóu screw socket
螺帽 luómào *see*"螺母"
螺母 luómǔ *also*"螺帽";"螺丝母";"螺丝帽"〈机械〉(screw) nut; jam nut:～垫圈 nut collar; nut lock washer
螺圈 luóquān eyebolt
螺栓 luóshuān 〈机械〉(screw) bolt:连接～ binder bolt; connecting bolt /地脚～ foundation bolt /～垫圈 bolt washer /～紧固器 bolt tightener /～帽 bolt cap /带眼～ eyebolt /～直径 diameter of bolt
螺丝 luósī 〈口语〉screw:～圈 eyebolt
see also"螺钉"
螺丝板牙 luósī bǎnyá screw die; threading die
螺丝刀 luósīdāo screw driver
see also"改锥" gǎizhuī
螺丝垫 luósīdiàn screw washer
螺丝钉 luósīdīng 〈口语〉*see*"螺钉"
螺丝攻 luósīgōng *also*"丝锥" sīzhuī screw tap:～扳手 tap wrench
螺丝扣 luósīkòu 〈口语〉*see*"螺纹❷"
螺丝帽 luósīmào *see*"螺母"
螺丝母 luósīmǔ 〈口语〉*see*"螺母"
螺丝起子 luósī qǐzi *see*"螺丝刀"
螺丝钻 luósīzuàn *see*"螺旋钻"
螺蛳 luósi spiral shell; snail
螺蛳转儿 luósizhuànr (baked) snail-shaped bun or cake
螺纹 luówén ❶ whorl (in fingerprint):他手上的～特别,全是破螺。He's got strange whorls on his hands; all of them are broken ones. *see also*"罗纹" luówén ❷ *also*"螺丝扣"〈机械〉thread (of a screw):公制～ metric thread /惠氏～ Whitworth thread /左～ left-hand screw thread; minus screw /右～ right-hand screw thread
螺纹刀具 luówén dāojù threading tool; screw tool
螺线 luóxiàn spiral; spire:～轨道 spiral orbit /～形 scroll
螺线管 luóxiànguǎn 〈物理〉solenoid (coil):～线圈 solenoid coil
螺旋 luóxuán ❶ spiral; helix:～式上升 spiral escalation; spiralling ❷〈机械〉screw:～管 spiral vessel; spiral duct /～线 helix; helical line; spiral /～钻 spiral drill; (screw) auger
螺旋桨 luóxuánjiǎng *also*"螺旋推进器"〈机械〉(screw) propeller; screw:飞机～ airscrew; aircraft propeller
螺旋桨调速器 luóxuánjiǎng tiáosùqì propeller governor
螺旋桨叶 luóxuánjiǎngyè propeller blade
螺旋霉素 luóxuánméisù 〈药学〉spiramycin; rovamycin
螺旋式 luóxuánshì spiral:～楼梯 spiral staircase /～通货膨胀 spiralling inflation
螺旋体 luóxuántǐ 〈微生物〉spirochaeta:～感染 spirochaeta infection
螺旋推进器 luóxuán tuījìnqì *see*"螺旋桨"
螺旋线 luóxuánxiàn helix; helical line; spiral
螺旋型 luóxuánxíng screw-type:～定向天线 helical beam antenna /～环形天线 spiral loop
螺旋藻 luóxuánzǎo 〈生物〉spirulina
螺旋钻 luóxuánzuàn spiral drill; (screw) auger
螺原子 luóyuánzǐ spiro-atom

L

骡(驘) luó mule:驴~ hinny /马~ mule /赶~人 muleteer
骡马店 luómǎdiàn inn with sheds for carts and animals
骡鹿 luólù mule deer (*Odocileus hemionus*)
骡子 luózi mule

罗[1](羅) luó ❶ net for catching birds:~网 net; trap /天~地网 nets above and snares below; tight encirclement ❷ catch (birds) with a net:门可~雀 you could catch sparrows on the doorstep — visitors are so few and far between ❸ collect; recruit; gather together:网~人才 enlist able men /搜~ collect; gather; recruit ❹ display; set out; spread out:星~棋布 spread out like stars in the sky or chessmen on the chessboard ❺ sieve; sifter; screen:铜丝~ copper wire sieve /绢~ silk sieve ❻ sieve; sift:把这袋子面再~一遍。Sift the sack of flour again. ❼ silk gauze:绫~绸缎 silks and satins ❽ (Luó) a surname

罗[2](羅) luó 〈量词〉(transliteration) gross; twelve dozen
罗安达 Luó'āndá Luanda, capital of Angola
罗拜 luóbài 〈书面〉bow or salute (round sb.) in a circle
罗宾汉 Luóbīnhàn Robin Hood, a semi-legendary, medieval English popular hero
罗布 luóbù set out; scatter; spread out:山旁帐篷~。Camps spread out along the hillside.
罗布麻 luóbùmá *also* "茶叶花" cháyèhuā 〈植物〉bluish dogbane (*Apocynum venetum*)
罗布泊 Luóbùpō Lop Nor, a vast salt lake now dried up (in Xinjiang)
罗刹 luóchà 〈佛教〉*Rakshasa*, a general name for evil spirits and devils:~女 female devil; monster of a girl
罗城 luóchéng additional wall (built for defence) outside a city wall
罗丹 Luódān Augustin Rodin (1840-1917), French sculptor
罗得西亚 Luódéxīyà (former name for 津巴布韦) Rhodesia (now known as Zimbabwe):北~ Northern Rhodesia (now known as Zambia)
罗尔斯-罗伊斯公司 Luó'ěrsī-Luóyīsī Gōngsī Rolls Royce Ltd., British car and engine manufacturer
罗非鱼 luófēiyú *Tilapia mossambica*, an African carp
罗浮宫 Luófúgōng *also* "卢浮宫" Lúfúgōng Louvre Museum (in Paris)
罗贯中 Luó Guànzhōng Luo Guanzhong (c.1330-c.1400), novelist and author of *The Romance of the Three Kingdoms* (三国演义)
罗锅 luóguō ❶ hunchbacked; humpbacked:他有点~儿。He is a bit hunchbacked. ❷ *also* "罗锅子" humpback:老汉是个~儿。The old man is a humpback. ❸ arched:~桥 arch bridge
罗锅 luóguo bend; arch; flex:老爷子~着腰坐在炕上。The old man bent over while sitting on the *kang*.
罗汉 luóhàn 〈佛教〉*arhat*:十八~斗悟空。The eighteen *arhats* fought in a pitched battle against the Monkey King.
罗汉病 luóhànbìng 〈方言〉snail fever; schistosomiasis
罗汉豆 luóhàndòu 〈方言〉broad bean
罗汉果 luóhànguǒ 〈植物〉(fruit of) *Momordica grosvenori*
罗汉松 luóhànsōng *also* "土杉" tǔshān 〈植物〉podocarpus (*Podocarpus macrophyllus*)
罗汉须 luóhànxū a kind of chrysanthemum with slender, bent petals
罗汉竹 luóhànzhú 〈植物〉❶ *Phillostachys aurea*, a kind of slender bamboo used to make walking sticks ❷ *also* "龟甲竹" guījiǎzhú *Phyllostachys pubescens* var. *heterocycla* (a variety of 毛竹)
罗经 luójīng 〈航海〉compass:电~ gyrocompass /磁~ magnetic compass /航海~ mariner's compass
罗掘 luójué try by all means to raise money:四处~ run about to raise money /~俱穷 exhaust all means of getting money; fail to raise any money
罗掘一空 luójué-yīkōng nothing left after being ransacked:官窃匪盗,全城早已被~,百姓叫苦连天。People of the city grieved bitterly at being bled white by the corrupt officials and bandits.
罗口 luókǒu 〈纺织〉rib cuff; rib collar; rib top (of socks):~短袜 socks with rib tops
罗口灯泡 luókǒu dēngpào screw bulb
罗口灯头 luókǒu dēngtóu screw socket
罗拉 luólā ❶ *also* "辊" gǔn 〈机械〉roller ❷ 〈纺织〉roller:~座 roller stand
罗兰之歌 Luólán Zhī Gē *Chanson de Rolland*, French epic completed at the end of the 11th century or the beginning of the 12th century
罗勒 luólè *also* "矮糠" ǎikāng; "萝艻" luólè 〈植物〉sweet basil:~油 basil oil
罗列 luóliè ❶ spread out; set out:亭台楼阁,~湖畔。The pavilions and kiosks spread out round the lake. *or* The lake was ringed by pavilions and kiosks. ❷ enumerate; list:文章~了大量事实,但分析略感不足。The article presented a lot of facts but lacked analysis.
罗马 Luómǎ Rome:~帝国 Roman Empire (27 BC-476 AD) /~军团 Roman legion /~大写字体 Roman capital /条条大路通~。All roads lead to Rome.
罗马法 Luómǎfǎ 〈法律〉Roman law
罗马公教 Luómǎ Gōngjiào *also* "天主教" tiānzhǔjiào 〈宗教〉Roman Catholicism
罗马教廷 Luómǎ Jiàotíng Roman Curia; the Holy See; papacy:~代表 representative of the Holy See; nuncio
罗马尼亚 Luómǎníyà Romania:~人 Romanian /~语 Romanian (language)
罗马式建筑 Luómǎshì jiànzhù Romanesque architecture; Romanesque building
罗马数字 Luómǎ shùzì Roman numerals
罗马天主教 Luómǎ Tiānzhǔjiào Roman Catholicism; Church of Rome
罗马天主教会 Luómǎ Tiānzhǔ Jiàohuì Roman Catholic Church
罗马字母 Luómǎ zìmǔ Roman alphabet
罗曼蒂克 luómàndìkè romantic:这个女子有些~。The woman is somewhat romantic.
罗曼·罗兰 Luómàn Luólán Romain Rolland (1866-1944), French writer, winner of the Nobel Prize for Literature (1915)
罗曼诺夫 Luómànnuòfū Romanov, name of Russian dynasty (1613-1917):~王朝 Romanov dynasty
罗曼司 luómànsī *also* "罗曼史" romance
罗曼语 Luómànyǔ 〈语言〉Romance language:~族 Romance group of languages; Romance languages /法语是一种~。French is a Romance language.
罗盘 luópán compass:~方位 compass bearing; quadrantal bearing /~偏差 compass deviation /~星座 Malus /~仪 compass; box compass
罗圈 luóquān round frame of a sieve:这只筛子的~松了。The frame of the sieve is loose.
罗圈儿揖 luóquānryī bow to people around:他进到茶馆,先是一个~,连声向众人问好。Entering the tea house, he bowed to everybody around and said hello to them.
罗圈腿 luóquāntuǐ ❶ bow-legs; bandy legs ❷ bow-legged; bandy-legged
罗圈椅 luóquānyǐ chair with round armrests
罗雀掘鼠 luóquè-juéshǔ spread nets for sparrows and dig holes for rats as food in times of starvation; exhaust all means of getting food:城池被困,弹尽粮绝,百姓~。Running out of ammunition and food supplies in the besieged city, people had to use every possible means to stave off starvation.
罗裙 luóqún skirt of thin silk
罗扇 luóshàn silk gauze fan
罗斯福 Luósīfú ❶ Franklin D. Roosevelt (1882-1945), 32nd President of the United States from 1933 to 1945:~夫人 (Anna) Eleanor Roosevelt (1884-1962), wife of F.D.R. /~新政 The New Deal ❷ Theodore Roosevelt (1858-1919), 26th President of the United States from 1901 to 1909
罗宋汤 luósòngtāng borscht or borsch, Russian beet soup
罗素 Luósù Bertrand Arthur William Russell (1873-1970), British philosopher and mathematician, winner of Nobel Prize for Literature (1950)
罗网 luówǎng net; trap:布下~ lay (*or* set) a trap
罗望子 luówàngzǐ 〈植物〉(fruit of) tamarind
罗帷 luówéi gauze curtain

罗纹 luówén whorl
see also“螺纹❶” luówén
罗纹机 luówénjī rib knitting machine; ribber
罗纹鸭 luówényā falcated teal; falcated duck
罗衣 luóyī garment of thin silk
罗印 luóyìn 〈方言〉fingerprint; fingermark
罗唣 luózào *also*“啰唣” luózào (often used in the early vernacular) make trouble:休得～! Don't make trouble!
罗织 luózhī 〈书面〉frame up:～诬陷 frame sb. up /～成狱 convict sb. by trumped-up charges /为了达到打击别人的目的,他～构陷,无所不用其极。He resorted to every conceivable way to cook up charges against others.
罗织罪名 luózhī-zuìmíng cook up charges; frame a case against sb.:～,屈打成招 cook up charges and extort a confession by torture
罗致 luózhì enlist the services of; secure in one's employment; recruit; gather together:～天下英才于门下 enlist the services of many people of outstanding ability far and wide
罗致人才 luózhì-réncái recruit talents:多方～ recruit talented people from all quarters

逻(邏) luó patrol:巡～ patrol

逻辑 luóji ❶ reason; sense; logic:不合～ contrary to reason (*or* sense); illogical /～上的错误 error in reasoning (*or* logic) /我不懂这算什么～! I just can't follow such logic! ❷ objective law; logic:生活的～ logic of life /既要前进,就可能有挫折和失败,这就是事物发展的～。No progress can be attained without setbacks and failures; such is the law of development. ❸ logic as a science of reasoning, proof, thinking or inference:～代数 logic algebra /～方法 logical method /～分析 logic analysis /～符号 logic symbol /～规律 logical law /～经验论 logical empiricism /～实证主义 logical positivism /～哲学 philosophy of logic /～主义 logicism /形式～ formal logic /辩证～ dialectical logic /数理～ mathematical logic
逻辑电路 luóji diànlù logical circuit
逻辑思维 luóji sīwéi logical thinking
逻辑性 luójixìng logicality; logic:缺乏～ lack logic (*or* coherence) /她说起话来颠三倒四,没有一点儿～。Her remarks are incoherent and illogical.
逻辑学 luójixué logic:～家 logician
逻辑主语 luóji zhǔyǔ 〈语言〉logical subject
逻骑 luóqí patrolling mounted police
逻卒 luózú patrolling soldier; patrolman

椤(欏) luó *see*“珂椤版” kēluóbǎn

萝(蘿) luó 〈植物〉trailing plant; vine:藤～ Chinese wistaria /茑～ cypress vine /松～ usnea /女～ usnea

萝卜 luóbo *also*“莱菔” láifú 〈植物〉radish; turnip:～青菜,各有所爱 no dish suits all tastes; one man's meat is another man's poison; every Jack has his Jill
萝卜花 luóbohuā ❶〈医学〉white dots left on the cornea after keratitis ❷ flower carved out of radish or turnip decorating the dinner table
萝芙木 luófúmù *also*“蛇根草” shégēncǎo 〈植物〉devilpepper
萝艻 luólè *also*“罗勒” luólè 〈植物〉sweet basil; basil
萝藦 luómó 〈植物〉asclepiad

椤(欏) luó *see*“桫椤” suōluó

啰(囉) luó

see also luō; luo
啰唣 luózào (usu. used in the early vernacular) make a row; incite strife

箩(籮) luó square-bottomed bamboo basket

箩筐 luókuāng large bamboo or wicker basket

锣(鑼) luó 〈乐器〉gong:敲～打鼓 beat drums and gongs /破～嗓子 voice as poor as a broken gong; broken (*or* hoarse) voice /鸣～开道 strike gongs to clear the way

锣槌 luóchuí 〈乐器〉(gong) hammer
锣鼓 luógǔ ❶ gong and drum:～喧天,鞭炮齐鸣,到处是一派节日的气象。There was a festival atmosphere everywhere with a deafening sound of gongs, drums and firecrackers. ❷〈乐器〉traditional percussion instruments:小院的右边是剧团,终日可以听到～之声。To the right of the courtyard house is an opera troupe which sends out the sound of musical instruments all day long. /～听音,听话听声。Listen to the sound when a gong or drum is beaten and get the underlying meaning when someone is talking.

偻(儸) luó *see*“偻啰” lóuluo

猡(玀) luó *see*“猪猡” zhūluó

锣(鑼) luó *see*“饽锣” bìluó

脶(腡) luó fingerprint; fingermark

觌(覼) luó

觌缕 luólǚ 〈书面〉tell or narrate in detail:不烦～ no need to go into details

luǒ

瘰 luǒ

瘰疬 luǒlì 〈中医〉scrofula

蠃 luǒ *see*“蜾蠃” guǒluǒ

蓏 luǒ 〈古语〉different kinds of melon

裸(躶、羸) luǒ bare; naked; nude; exposed:赤～～ stark-naked; barefaced; undisguised /～女 nude (*or* naked) woman /～电线 bare (electric) wire

裸鲤 luǒlǐ 〈动物〉naked carp:～属 *Gymnocypris*
裸露 luǒlù bare; uncovered; exposed:岩石～ exposed rock /～土壤 bare soil /～地 open ground
裸露癖 luǒlùpǐ 〈心理〉exhibitionism
裸麦 luǒmài *also*“青稞” qīngkē 〈植物〉naked barley; highland barley
裸视 luǒshì ❶ see with one's naked eyes:～所及 as far as the naked eye can see /～视力 naked eyesight ❷ naked eyesight; unaided eyesight
裸体 luǒtǐ nakedness; nude; nudity:～相 nude photo /～模特 nude model /～狂 nudism /～主义 naturalism; nudism /～浴场 naturalist beach /～者俱乐部 naturalist club /～营 naturalist camp; nudist colony /～飞跑 streaking
裸体画 luǒtǐhuà painting of a nude; nude painting; nude
裸体色情影片 luǒtǐ sèqíng yǐngpiàn skin flick
裸体像 luǒtǐxiàng nude figure or statue; nude
裸线 luǒxiàn 〈电工〉bare wire; naked wire; open wire
裸芽 luǒyá 〈植物〉naked bud
裸眼 luǒyǎn naked eye
裸泳 luǒyǒng skinny-dipping
裸装 luǒzhuāng nude loading:木材可以～。Timber can be loaded nude.
裸装货 luǒzhuānghuò nude cargo:这几辆大卡车是专门拉～的。These trucks are used solely to carry nude cargoes.
裸子植物 luǒzǐ zhíwù gymnosperm

倮 luǒ 〈书面〉*see*“裸” luǒ

luò

荦(犖) luò 〈书面〉prominent; extraordinary; outstanding:卓～ pre-eminent; remarkable

荦荦 luòluò 〈书面〉conspicuous; obvious; evident; manifest
荦荦大端 luòluò-dàduān *also*“荦荦大者” major items; salient points:此其～,若至委曲小变,不可胜道。These are the salient points. Minor details are too numerous to list.

L

漯 luò

漯河 Luòhé Luohe, city in Henan Province

摞 luò

❶ pile up; heap up; stack up: 把蜂窝煤块～起来 stack up the honeycomb briquettes /把这几包书靠墙～好 pile up these packages of books against the wall ❷〈量词〉pile; stack: 一～碗 a stack of bowls /一～竹筐 a pile of bamboo baskets

洛 Luò

❶ Luohe (洛河), river in Shaanxi Province ❷ Luohe (洛河), river which rises in Shaanxi Province and flows into Henan Province ❸ a surname

洛克菲勒基金会 Luòkèfēilè Jījīnhuì (US) Rockefeller Foundation

洛克希德飞机公司 Luòkèxīdé Fēijī Gōngsī (US) Lockheed Aircraft Corporation, now called Lockheed-Martin Aircraft Corporation

洛美 Luòměi Lomé, capital and chief port of Togo

洛美协定 Luòměi Xiédìng Lomé Convention, trade and assistance agreement first concluded in Lomé in 1975 between the EEC and 46 African, Caribbean and Pacific states and renewed at regular intervals with a larger group of participants

洛桑 Luòsāng Lausanne, Swiss town on the north shore of Lake Geneva

洛杉矶 Luòshānjī Los Angeles, 2nd largest US city, on the coast of California

洛氏硬度 Luòshì yìngdù 〈物理〉Rockwell hardness: ～计 Rockwell apparatus; Rockwell hardness tester /～值 Rockwell hardness number

洛阳 Luòyáng Luoyang, ancient city on the south bank of the Yellow River in Henan and capital of many dynasties beginning with Eastern Zhou

洛阳纸贵 Luòyáng-zhǐguì paper has become very expensive in Luoyang (said of the wide circulation of Zuo Si's 左思 poem *San Du Fu* 三都赋 in the Jin Dynasty, which caused a paper shortage in Luoyang); become a best seller: 这本小说一版再版，大受欢迎，颇有～的势头。The novel has become all the rage and has had to be printed and reprinted.

烙 luò

see "炮烙" páoluò

see also lào

珞 luò

see "赛璐珞" sàilùluò

珞巴族 Luòbāzú Lhoba nationality, living in the Tibet Autonomous Region

落 luò

❶ fall; drop: 花开花～ flowers bloom and fall (*or* wither) /脱～ drop; fall; come off ❷ go down; descend; land; set: 降～ descend; land /溅～ splash down /潮涨潮～ rising tide and falling tide; ebb and flow /陨石自天而～。An acrolite fell from the sky. ❸ lower; let down: ～下旗子 lower the flag /响铃～幕 ring the curtain down ❹ decline; come down; deteriorate: 破～户 family that has gone down in the world /败～ decline /冷～ cold-shoulder /堕～ degenerate ❺ lag behind; fall behind; fail: 名～孙山 fail an examination ❻ stay behind; remain: 不～痕迹 leave no trace ❼ whereabouts: 下～ whereabouts /着～ whereabouts; assured source ❽ settlement: 村～ small village; hamlet /千村万～ myriads of villages /聚～ village (*or* hamlet); settlement /屯～ village ❾ fall onto; belong to; rest with: 任务～到我们肩上。The task fell onto us. /证据～到我们手中。The evidence fell into our hands. ❿ get; gain; receive: ～埋怨 be blamed /～了这个结果 come to such an end ⓫ write; put down: *see* "～账"; "～款"

see also là; lào; luō

落案 luò'àn wind up a case: 他受贿一事，已经～。The trial of his case of accepting bribery has concluded.

落榜 luòbǎng flunk a competitive examination for a job or school admission; fail an examination: 高考～ fail the college entrance examination

落褒贬 luò bāobian be criticized; lay oneself open to censure: 我想为大伙儿办件好事，不料反而～。I had meant to do something good for all of us, only to let myself in for criticism.

落笔 luòbǐ start to write or draw; put pen to paper: 他写文章，善于从大处～，很有深度。In writing, he is always good at highlighting the key points and making an in-depth analysis.

落标 luòbiāo fail to win a bid; fail in an election or competition: 这次～的建筑公司可不少。This time, quite a few construction firms failed to win a bid. /这位候选人～了。The candidate failed in the election.

落膘 luòbiāo (of livestock) lose weight; become thin: 天太热，牲畜都～了。The livestock have become thin due to hot weather.

落泊 luòbó *also* "落魄"〈书面〉❶ be in dire straits; be down and out: 父亲～半生，事事皆不遂意。Father had been going downhill half of his life and felt frustrated in whatever he did. ❷ bold and generous; unconstrained: 为人～，不拘小节 be unconstrained and not be punctilious

落魄 luòbó 〈书面〉*see* "落泊"

see also luòpò

落槽 luòcáo ❶ (of water) go down ❷〈方言〉(of family fortune) decline ❸ fit a tenon into a mortise ❹〈方言〉feel at ease: 这件事不办好，心里总是不～。I won't feel at ease until the matter is properly settled.

落草 luòcǎo ❶ (often used in the early vernacular) take to the greenwood; take to the heather; become an outlaw: ～的几个弟兄，都是出于不得已。The pals here took to the greenwood as they had no choice. ❷〈方言〉(of a baby) be born

落草为寇 luòcǎo-wéikòu take to the greenwood; take to the heather; become an outlaw

落差 luòchā ❶〈水利〉drop (in elevation); fall: 利用河水～发电 utilize the fall (*or* drop) of a river for power generation ❷ gap: 心理上的～ psychological gap /两种工资之间的～较大。The differential between the two salaries is quite big.

落产 luòchǎn 〈方言〉be born: 小牛犊～ birth of a calf /孩子已经～了。The child had been born.

落场 luòchǎng 〈方言〉wind up; end up; stop: 麻烦闹大了，可就难～了。Once the trouble is aggravated, you will find it difficult to wind up.

落潮 luòcháo falling tide; ebb tide: ～流 ebb current

落尘 luòchén dust fall; falling dust

落成 luòchéng completion (of a building, etc.): 大楼半月之内即可～。The building will be completed in half a month.

落成典礼 luòchéng diǎnlǐ inauguration ceremony

落锤 luòchuí 〈机械〉drop hammer; drop stamp; drop weight: ～试验 drop test /～试验机 drop hammer tester /～捣矿机〈矿业〉gravity stamp /～锻造〈冶金〉drop forging; drop stamping

落袋台球 luòdài táiqiú pocket billiards

落胆 luòdǎn panic-stricken; struck with horror; scared out of one's wits: 吓得他落了胆。He was scared out of his wits.

落得 luòde get; end up in: ～个身败名裂 end up bringing shame and ruin upon oneself /他闹了半天也没～什么好结果。He came to no good end for all his clamours.

落底 luòdǐ ❶〈方言〉end of a year or a month: 三月～，邻里例行检查环境卫生。As a rule, an inspection of general sanitation is carried out in the neighbourhood at the end of March. ❷ feel at ease: 这件事办好，咱们的心就～了。We will feel relieved when the matter is properly handled.

落地 luòdì ❶ fall to the ground: 花轿～ (when) the bridal sedan-chair was set down on the ground /红旗～ the red flag (representing revolution) falls to the ground ❷〈比喻〉feel relieved: 他心里一块石头落了地。A heavy burden is off his mind. ❸ (of babies) be born: 呱呱～ come into the world with a cry; be born

落地车床 luòdì chēchuáng 〈机械〉face lathe; face-plate lathe; T lathe

落地窗 luòdìchuāng French window: 房间右侧是一排～，隔窗可以望见大海。To the right of the room is a row of French windows through which one can see the sea.

落地灯 luòdìdēng floor lamp; standard lamp

落地户 luòdìhù native: 他是本乡本土的～。He is a native here.

落地镜 luòdìjìng floor mirror

落地生根 luòdì shēnggēn ❶〈植物〉air plant; life plant ❷ take root; strike root: ～，开花结果 strike root, blossom and bear fruit /他在山区工作了半辈子，～，已经深深爱上了这方土地。After working in the mountain area for half of his life, he has put down roots here and deeply loves the land.

落地式电扇 luòdìshì diànshàn standard fan; foot-mounted electric fan
落地式收音机 luòdìshì shōuyīnjī console (radio) set
落地税 luòdìshuì 〈旧语〉 tax levied on goods taken to and sold in a place (such as a fair or town)
落地罩 luòdìzhào wooden partition screen (in a room)
落第 luòdì fail in an imperial examination: ～秀才 scholar who failed in the imperial examination above the county level
落点 luòdiǎn ❶〈体育〉placement (of a ball): 10号球员脚功好,～准。The No.10 player has good footwork and is accurate in placement. ❷ point of fall: 炮弹的～ shell's point of fall ❸〈方言〉(of remarks) end; stop: 他的话音还没～,大家就纷纷议论开了。Hardly had he finished his words when everybody started talking.
落顶 luòdǐng 〈矿业〉caving: ～开采法 caving
落发 luòfà shave one's head; become a Buddhist monk or nun: ～为僧 shave one's head and become a monk
落谷 luògǔ 〈方言〉sow rice seeds in a paddy field
落果 luòguǒ ❶ abscission of fruits; premature drop: 看到成片的果树开始～,老人又心疼又着急。Seeing so many fruit trees suffer from premature drop the old farmer felt distressed and worried. ❷ fruit of premature drops
落黑 luòhēi 〈方言〉get dark: 天还没～,他就到了。He arrived before dusk. /讨论直到～才散会。The discussion didn't break up till it got dark.
落后 luòhòu ❶ fall behind; lag behind: 走在半山腰,几个女孩子明显～了。Midway up the mountain, the girls lagged far behind. /她在这场女子单打中,比分一直～。She was trailing (behind) throughout the women's singles. ❷ behind schedule: 桥面施工进度～,拖了整个工程的后腿。The work on the bridge surface is behind schedule and has become a drag on the whole project. ❸ backward; underdeveloped: 改变穷困～的面貌 lift oneself from poverty and backwardness /～地区 backward region; underdeveloped area /谦虚使人进步,骄傲使人～。Modesty helps one make progress as conceit makes one fall behind.
落后分子 luòhòufènzǐ laggard; backward element
落户 luòhù ❶ settle: 那几年,我们全家在农村～。My whole family settled down in the countryside during those years. ❷ register for residence: 新生儿应及时～。The newly born must be registered in good time.
落花流水 luòhuā-liúshuǐ (like) fallen flowers carried away by the flowing water; scene of late spring; crushing defeat: ～春去也,天上人间。The blossoms fall, the water flows. The glory of the spring is done, In nature's world as in human one. /敌人被打得～。The enemy was soundly defeated (*or* utterly routed).
落花生 luòhuāshēng *also* "花生"; "仁果" rénguǒ; "长生果" chángshēngguǒ 〈植物〉peanut; groundnut
落花有意,流水无情 luòhuā yǒu yì, liúshuǐ wú qíng shedding petals, the waterside flower pines for love, while the heartless brook babbles on — one's love is unrequited: 他一片痴情,然而～,她对他毫不理睬。His ardent love for her was completely ignored. What unrequited love!
落荒 luòhuāng (often used in the early vernacular) take to the wilds
落荒而逃 luòhuāng'értáo *also* "落荒而走" take to the wilds; be defeated and flee the battlefield; take to one's heels; take to flight: 败兵一路丢盔卸甲,～。The routed troops took to headlong flight, throwing away their helmets and coats of mail as they fled.
落黄 luòhuáng (of rice seedlings, etc.) have leaves turning yellow after transplant
落基山脉 Luòjī Shānmài Rocky Mountains, great mountain system of western North America
落籍 luòjí ❶ settle: 他家在祖父一辈迁到吉林～为农。During his grandfather's generation his family migrated to Jilin and settled there as farmers. ❷〈书面〉cross out sb.'s name from a namelist; strike sb.'s name off a register
落角 luòjiǎo 〈军事〉angle of fall
落脚 luòjiǎo ❶ stay (for a time); stop over; put up: 就近找个旅馆～ look for a nearby hotel to stay the night /临街一间破房子,这就是我们的～处。The shabby house along the street was our temporary lodging. ❷ inferior and unsalable
落脚菜 luòjiǎocài unsalable inferior vegetable
落脚点 luòjiǎodiǎn foothold; footing; standpoint; stand: 改革的出发点和～就是要把企业搞活。The point of departure as well as the goal of the reform is to revitalize the enterprises.
落脚货 luòjiǎohuò unsalable inferior goods
落井下石 luòjǐng-xiàshí *also* "投井下石" tóujǐng-xiàshí drop stones on someone who has fallen into a well — hit a person when he's down: 没想到他竟是个～的小人。I have never thought that he would be so mean as to hit those who are already down and out.
落空 luòkōng come to nothing; fail; fall through: 这项计划又～了。The plan came to naught again. /他乘兴而来,谁知希望～,只得扫兴而归。He came in high spirits but returned disappointed, as his hopes were dashed.
落款 luòkuǎn names of the sender and the recipient written on a painting, letter or gift; inscription (on a gift, etc.): 由于年代久远,这部珍贵的手抄本的～已难以辨认。The inscription on the rare handwritten copy is hard to make out due to its age.
落雷 luòléi thunderbolt; thunderclap
see also "霹雳" pīlì
落泪 luòlèi shed tears; weep: 伤心～ weep in sorrow /人不伤心不～。One will not shed tears unless his heart aches.
落力 luòlì 〈方言〉make great efforts; try hard; exert oneself: ～大搞生产 step up the effort to expand production
落铃 luòlíng 〈农业〉premature shedding or dropping of cotton bolls
落令 luòlìng not in season; out of season: ～商品 goods out of season
落落 luòluò ❶ (of demeanour) natural and unrestrained: 此人心怀坦荡,举止～。He is broad-minded and conducts himself naturally and with ease. ❷ unsociable: ～穷士 poor withdrawn scholar
落落大方 luòluò-dàfang natural and graceful; unrestrained and at ease: 姑娘长得清秀俊俏,举止～,不少小伙子为之倾倒。The girl is good-looking and graceful, an object of admiration for many young men.
落落寡合 luòluò-guǎhé *also* "落落难合" stand-offish; uncommunicative; square peg in a round hole; unsociable: 他从来～,不爱凑热闹。He is always unsociable and keeps others at a distance.
落马 luòmǎ ❶ fall off a horse: 中弹～ fall from the horseback after being shot /～而逃 fall off the horse and flee ❷〈比喻〉be defeated: 半决赛中,上届冠亚军双双～。In the semi-finals both the champion and the runner-up in the last tournament were eliminated.
落寞 luòmò *also* "落漠"; "落莫" lonely; desolate: 她老年孤独,生活十分～。She felt extremely lonely in the evening of her life.
落墨 luòmò start to write or draw; put pen to paper: 他多次提笔,但却难以～。He picked up his pen many times but was hesitant to set it to paper.
落幕 luòmù curtain falls; lower the curtain; close; conclude: 代表大会于昨日～。The congress ended yesterday.
落难 luònàn meet with misfortune; be in straits; be in distress: ～之时 in times of distress /人家是一时～,我们怎能袖手不管? How can we stand by with folded arms when they are having a hard time?
落聘 luòpìn be turned down in one's job application
落魄 luòpò *also* luòtuò 〈书面〉❶ be in dire straits; be down on one's luck: ～江湖 roam about the rivers and lakes — lead the life of a vagrant ❷ bold and generous; unconstrained: 他～大度,深得友人称赞。He won his friends' admiration for his broad-mindedness and generosity.
see also luòbó
落气 luòqì 〈方言〉breathe one's last; die: 病人快～了。The sick man is dying. /老人不一会儿就落了气。The old man soon breathed his last.
落取 luòqǔ fail (in) a competitive examination for admission
落日 luòrì setting sun: ～余辉 lingering light of the setting sun
落腮胡子 luòsāi húzi whiskers; full beard
see also "络腮胡子" luòsāi húzi
落纱 luòshā 〈纺织〉doff: ～工 doffer
落纱机 luòshājī 〈纺织〉doffer
落砂 luòshā 〈冶金〉shakeout; knockout: ～机 shakeout; shakeout machine; knockout machine /～设备 shakeout equipment
落神 luòshén 〈方言〉feel at ease; feel relieved; set one's mind at rest: 他在屋里兜了一个圈子,觉得两手空空,心里不～。Walking around the room with empty hands, he was in an agitated state.
落生 luòshēng 〈方言〉(of babies) be born
落实 luòshí ❶ practicable; workable: 工作计划要订得明确～。The work programme must be clear and practicable. ❷ fix or

determine; ascertain; make sure; carry out: ～措施 decide on the measures (to be taken) /～责任 ascertain the responsibilities (each is to shoulder) /明天出发时间要～一下。Make sure when we are supposed to set out tomorrow. /这几项数字还要最后～一下。The figures are to be verified. /项目的资金已全部～。The funding for the project has been finalized (*or* guaranteed). ❸〈方言〉feel at ease: 火车票买好了, 他心里就～了。He felt at ease once he had bought the train ticket.

落市 luòshì ❶ (of fruits, vegetables, etc.) be out of season ❷ (of market) close

落水 luòshuǐ ❶ fall into water; go astray; degenerate ❷〈方言〉rain

落水狗 luòshuǐgǒu dog in the water — bad guy in straits: 打～ flog the cur that's fallen into the water; be merciless with bad people even if they're down /～上了岸还要咬人。Once ashore, the drowning dog will bite just as before.

落水管 luòshuǐguǎn downspout; downpipe

落苏 luòsū〈方言〉eggplant; aubergine

落俗 luòsú vulgar; philistine: 谈吐诙谐而不～ talk with humour without being vulgar /帮助别人而希望得到回报就太～了。It is bad taste to expect repayment for one's help.

落速 luòsù〈物理〉terminal velocity

落宿 luòsù〈方言〉stay; put up; get accomodation: 今晚在旅店～ put up in a hotel for the night

落锁 luòsuǒ be locked: 大门已～。The door is locked.

落汤鸡 luòtāngjī like a drenched chicken; soaked through; drenched and bedraggled: 一场暴雨, 把我们都浇成～了。We were soaked to the skin after being caught in the rainstorm.

落汤螃蟹 luòtāng-pángxiè like a crab in hot water — be at a loss what to do in time of danger

落套 luòtào conform to conventional patterns: 创作一定要有新意, 不要～。Artistic creation must be original and not fall into a rut.

落体 luòtǐ ❶〈物理〉falling body: 自由～ freely falling body /～的加速度与物体自身的质量无关。The acceleration of a falling body has nothing to do with its mass. ❷〈方言〉rest assured: 那人很老练, 他去我就落了体了。That man is experienced and I'll be more assured (of success) if he goes.

落托 luòtuō *see* "落拓"

落拓 luòtuò〈书面〉❶ in dire straits; down and out: 一生～不得志 be left out in the cold all life long ❷ untrammelled by conventions; casual; unconventional

落拓不羁 luòtuò-bùjī unconventional and uninhibited; not fettered by formalities and conventions: 这位画家, 向来是不修边幅, ～。The painter is quite unconventional, not paying the least attention to his appearance or manners.

落晚 luòwǎn〈方言〉at dusk: 他们最近很忙, 就是破晓～有点空儿。They have been terribly busy recently; they're free only at dawn or dusk.

落网 luòwǎng (of a criminal) fall into the net — be caught; be captured: 巧设机关, 专等罪犯～ lay a trap for the criminal to fall into

落屋 luòwū〈方言〉enter a room (to rest): 回到村上还没～, 就看他的试验田去了。Hardly had he arrived back in the village when he went to see his experimental plot before going home.

落伍 luòwǔ ❶ drop out or off; fall behind: 队伍行进很快, 眼看有几个就要～了。The troops moved forward so fast that some of them were about to fall behind. ❷ lag behind; become outdated or old-fashioned: 思想～ behind the times in thinking /产品设计～ out-of-fashion product designing /有了电灯, 煤油灯就～了。After the electric lamp came into being, the kerosene lamp became outdated.

落霞 luòxiá sunset clouds: ～映红了山村。The sunset clouds crimsoned the mountain village.

落线 luòxiàn〈军事〉line of fall

落乡 luòxiāng〈方言〉(of a place) away from a city or town; outlying

落心 luòxīn〈方言〉❶ feel at ease; rest assured: 睡个～觉 sleep without any worry ❷ to one's liking: 他仔细地听着, 句句入耳, 字字～。He listened carefully, and every word or sentence was pleasant to his ear.

落选 luòxuǎn fail to be chosen or elected; lose an election: 委员会改选时, 他～了。He was defeated in the re-election of the committee.

落扬 luòyáng〈方言〉(of crops) finish last threshing: 麦子～后, 天已经大黑了。After the last threshing of the wheat was done, it had turned completely dark.

落叶 luòyè ❶ (of leaves) fall down: 秋风一起, 树木开始～了。Leaves began to fall in the autumn wind. ❷ fallen leaves: 秋风卷起地上的～。The autumn wind swirled up the fallen leaves on the ground. ❸〈植物〉deciduous leaf: ～林 deciduous wood

落叶归根 luòyè-guīgēn falling leaves return to their roots — person residing elsewhere goes back to his or her ancestral home towards the end of his or her life: 王先生在海外闯荡了几十年, 年老时～, 回到了故乡。Having seen much of the world in foreign lands for decades, Mr. Wang returned to his country of birth in the evening of his life.

落叶树 luòyèshù〈植物〉deciduous tree

落叶松 luòyèsōng〈植物〉larch

落叶知秋 luòyè-zhīqiū the falling leaves portend the approach of autumn; events foretell things to come; be a straw in the wind: 高明的政治家应该善于把握局势的变化, 见落叶而知秋。A brilliant statesman should be able to predict possible changes in the situation from a few revealing signs.

落音 luòyīn (of speaking, singing, etc.) stop; end; come to a pause: 演唱刚一～, 大厅里就立刻响起了如雷的掌声。Scarcely had the singing ended when the hall burst into thunderous applause.

落英 luòyīng〈书面〉❶ fallen petals ❷ flower in fresh blossom

落英缤纷 luòyīng-bīnfēn petals fall in riotous profusion; fallen petals lie in tumultuous abundance

落羽杉 luòyǔshān *also* "落羽松"〈植物〉sabino; swamp cypress; bald cypress (*Taxodium distichum*)

落葬 luòzàng〈方言〉bury; inter

落账 luòzhàng enter in an account; keep accounts: 这笔款还没～。The sum of money hasn't been entered.

落照 luòzhào glow of the setting sun: ～辉映下的草原竟是这样的迷人! The grassland in the glow of the setting sun was so enchanting.

落职 luòzhí dismiss sb. from his post; remove sb. from office; be demoted

落纸如飞 luòzhǐ-rúfēi write quickly: 他边听边记, 真是～。Taking notes while listening, he wrote unbelievably fast. /诗人豪兴大发, ～, 一挥而就。The poet, in high spirits, finished writing at one go.

落纸云烟 luòzhǐ-yúnyān excellent calligraphy; superb writing

落座 luòzuò take one's seat; be seated: 客人～之后, 主人举杯敬酒。After the guests were seated, the host raised his glass to propose a toast.

硌

luò〈书面〉big rock or boulder on a mountain

see also gè

咯

luò *see* "吡咯" bǐluò

see also gē; kǎ; lo

雒

Luò ❶ *see* "洛❷" luò ❷ a surname

骆

luò ❶〈古语〉white horse with a black mane ❷ (Luò) a surname

骆驼 luòtuo〈动物〉camel: 单峰～ dromedary; one-humped camel /双峰～ Bactrian camel; two-humped camel /无峰～ llama

骆驼刺 luòtuocì〈植物〉camel thorn; alhagi

骆驼队 luòtuoduì camel train; caravan: 沙漠的尽头, 有一支～在暮色中行进。On the distant horizon of the desert, there was a caravan moving forward in the dusk.

骆驼绒 luòtuoróng *also* "驼绒" camel hair cloth

络

luò ❶ sth. resembling a net: 橘～ tangerine pith /丝瓜～ loofah ❷〈中医〉collateral channels in the human body through which vital energy and blood circulate: 经～ main and collateral channels (regarded as a network of passages, through which vital energy circulates and along which the acupuncture points are distributed) ❸ hold sth. in place with a net: 棉花套子上～着一层线网。The cotton padding is held together by a thread net. ❹ twine; coil; wind: ～丝 winding silk

see also lào

络合 luòhé〈化学〉complexing: ～物 complex compound /～剂 complexing agent /～作用 complexing action

络离子 luòlízǐ〈化学〉complex ion

络脉 luòmài 〈中医〉collaterals which connect channels; branches of channels

络腮胡子 luòsāi húzi *also*"落腮胡子" luòsāi húzi whiskers; full beard：新来的头儿是个～，看起来很精明。The new boss is a full-bearded man and looks smart.

络纱 luòshā *also*"落纱" luòshā winding yarn; spooling：～机 winder; spooler

络筒机 luòtǒngjī 〈纺织〉(high speed) cone winder; winding machine; winder

络续 luòxù one after another; in succession：～退场 leave (*or* exit) one after another / 夏初～开花。Flowers bloom in succession at the threshold of summer.

络盐 luòyán 〈化学〉complex salt

络绎 luòyì 〈书面〉in an endless stream：人马往来，前后～。People and carts are coming and going in an endless stream.

络绎不绝 luòyì-bùjué in an endless stream：前来招工办公室应聘者～。Respondents to the job advertisement streamed to the recruiting office.

跞(躒)

luò *see*"卓跞" zhuōluò

see also lì

luo

啰(囉)

luo 〈助词〉*used at the end of a sentence to indicate affirmation*：这件事不成问题～。Surely, that's no problem. / 你放心好～。You may just as well set your mind at rest.

see also luō; luó

L

M

m̄

姆 m̄
see also mǔ

姆妈 m̄mā 〈方言〉❶ mum; mom; mother ❷ wife of father's elder brother; aunt ❸ aunt, a respectful form of address for an elderly married woman:张家～ Aunt Zhang

ḿ

呒(嘸) ḿ 〈方言〉no; nothing; none

呒没 ḿméi 〈方言〉not have; there is not; be without:～办法 can't be done; no way

呒啥 ḿshá 〈方言〉nothing:他身体很好,～毛病。He is as fit as a fiddle and there is nothing wrong with him. /"你怎么啦?""～。""What is the matter with you?" "Nothing."

呣 ḿ 〈叹词〉*used in an interrogative sentence*:～,什么? Eh? What did you say? *or* Pardon? /～,真有这回事吗? What? Is it true? *or* Oh, really?
see also m̀

m̀

呣 m̀ 〈叹词〉*used by way of response*:～,我明白了。Um (*or* Uh-huh), I see. *or* Yeah, now I see. /～,别着急。Hum, there is no hurry. *or* Hum, take it easy. /～,就这么办吧。Hum, that settles it.
see also ḿ

mā

麻 mā
see also má

麻麻黑 māmahēi 〈方言〉gathering dusk:天～了,远处的村庄逐渐模糊起来。Dusk was gathering, and the village in the distance gradually became indistinct. /天～的时候,我们终于到达了一个称作狮子林的地方。By dusk, we had reached a place called Lion Forest.

麻麻亮 māmaliàng 〈方言〉before dawn; at daybreak:去上海的那一天,天～我就起床了。I got up at dawn on the day of my departure for Shanghai.

摩 mā
see also mó

摩挲 māsa ❶ smooth out with one's hand or palm; stroke gently; caress:～桌布 smooth out a tablecloth /她对着镜子～头发。Looking into the mirror, she patted her hair into place. ❷〈方言〉wash perfunctorily; do a quick and careless job of washing:他把碗筷好歹～了一下,就走了。He went through the motions of washing the bowls and chopsticks before he left. ❸〈方言〉coax; sweet-talk:别来～我,早干吗啦? Don't you try to sweet-talk me now. What were you doing earlier? /她真的生气了,你得去～她一把。She's really in a huff. You'd better go and calm her down.
see also mósuō

嬷 mā *see* "嬷" mó

嬷嬷 māma *see* "嬷嬷" mómo

抹(❷摲) mā ❶ wipe; mop:～桌子 wipe a table clean /～地板 mop the floor /～眼泪 wipe away one's tears ❷ put sth. down; slip sth. off:～下手表 take one's watch off the wrist
see also mǒ; mò

抹布 mābù rag (to wipe things with)

抹搭 māda 〈方言〉have one's eyelids half-open:～着眼皮 with one's eyes half-closed

抹脸 māliǎn 〈口语〉put on a stern expression; throw sentiment or shame to the winds:他从来就抹不下脸来给别人提意见。He has never been able to muster enough courage to criticize others. /他真抹得下脸来,向别人借钱,一张口就是好几百。He didn't bother about the face problem, and started to borrow from others several hundred *yuan* at a time. *or* He had the cheek to ask for a loan of several hundred *yuan* at every turn.

抹澡 māzǎo 〈方言〉rub oneself down with a wet towel; take a sponge bath

蚂 mā
see also mǎ; mà

蚂螂 mālang 〈方言〉dragonfly

妈 mā 〈口语〉❶ ma; mom; mum; mother:干～ adoptive mother; godmother ❷ form of address for an elderly married woman or a married woman of the elder generation:姑～ aunt (paternal) /姨～ aunt (maternal) /大～ aunt (form of address for the wife of one's father's elder brother or for any elderly married woman) /舅～ aunt (form of address for the wife of one's mother's brother) ❸ form of address for a housemaid or maidservant:老～子 maidservant /奶～ wet nurse /阿～ amah

妈妈 māma ❶〈口语〉mum; mom; mummy; mommy ❷〈方言〉aunt (a respectful form of address for an elderly woman):这位～,您能告诉我到动物园怎么走吗? Ma'am, could you show me the way to the zoo?

妈妈论儿 māmalùnr *also* "老妈妈论儿" lǎomāmalùnr〈方言〉〈贬义〉old women's exhortations concerning conventions

妈咪 māmī mummy; mommy

妈祖 Māzǔ Mazu (legendary goddess of the sea mainly worshipped in the coastal areas in southeast China):～庙 Mazu temple

孖 mā 〈方言〉twins; a pair

孖仔 māzǎi 〈方言〉boy twins

má

麻[1](蔴) má ❶ general term for fibrous crops:大～ hemp /亚～ flax /黄～ jute /洋～ ambary hemp /苎～ ramie; ramee /剑～ sisal-hemp /罗布～ bluish dogbane /蓖～ castor-oil plant /～籽 castor bean ❷ fibre of fibrous crops:快刀斩乱～ cut a tangled skein of jute with a sharp knife; cut the Gordian knot /心乱如～ with one's mind confused like entangled hemp; with one's

heart in a turmoil; perplexed in mind ❸ sesame: ～糖 sesame candy

麻[2] má ❶ rough; rugged; coarse: ～玻璃 frosted glass; ground glass / 这种布背面～。The reverse side of the cloth is rough. ❷ pockmarks: see "～脸" ❸ speckled; dotted; spotted: see "～蝇"; "～雀" ❹ (Má) a surname

麻[3] má ❶ numb; dead: 腿发～ have a tingling feeling in the legs / 我的手冻～了。My hands are numb with cold. ❷ anaesthesia: 针～ acupuncture anaesthesia

see also mā

麻包 mábāo gunny-bag; gunnysack; sack

麻痹 mábì *also* "麻痺" mábì ❶〈医学〉paralysis; palsy: 面部神经～ facial paralysis; Bell's palsy / 小儿～ infantile paralysis; poliomyelitis; polio / 局部～ paresis / ～病人 paralytic / 有些杀虫药能～昆虫的神经系统。Some insecticides can paralyze the nervous system of an insect. ❷ benumb; lull; blunt: ～意志 lull one's will to fight ❸ slacken one's vigilance; drop one's guard: ～大意 be off guard; be careless / 看管仓库要注意防火防盗, 不能～。If you are in charge of a warehouse, you must take precautions against fire and burglary, and should never be caught off guard.

麻痹性痴呆 mábìxìng chīdāi paresis

麻痹性失禁 mábìxìng shījìn 〈医学〉paralytic incontinence (of feces or urine)

麻布 mábù ❶ gunny (cloth); sackcloth; burlap; hessian ❷ linen: ～女衬衫 linen blouse

麻缠 máchán 〈方言〉❶ nag; worry; pester: 孩子抓住妈妈的衣袖, 一个劲儿的～。Grabbing at the mother's sleeves, the child kept pestering her. ❷ trouble; bother; put to trouble: 厂里的经理们都很忙, 别为个人的小事～他们了。As the managers of the factory are all very busy, we had better not bother them with such trifling personal matters.

麻袋 mádài gunny-bag; gunnysack; sack: 两～玉米 two sacks of corn

麻捣 mádǎo 〈书面〉*see* "麻刀"

麻刀 mádao 〈建筑〉hemp bits mixed with plaster for coating walls; hemp; hair: ～灰泥 hemp-fibred plaster

麻豆腐 mádòufu cooking starch residue

麻烦 máfan ❶ troublesome; bothersome; inconvenient: 遇到～ be in something of a pickle / 真对不起, 给你添了～。Sorry to have given you so much trouble. / 你这样干下去就是自找～。If you go on like this, you are asking for (*or* inviting) trouble. / 这是件～事, 要有耐心。This is a real headache, and you must have patience. / 这病很～, 但没有危险。The illness is a nuisance, but no danger. / 这位售货员接待顾客从不怕～。This salesperson spares no pains in serving customers. ❷ put to trouble or inconvenience: ～你把盐递给我。Could you pass me the salt? *or* May I trouble you for the salt? / 自己能做的事决不～别人。I would never trouble others to do whatever I could do myself.

麻纺 máfǎng flax yarn; yarn of bast-fibre plant

麻沸散 máfèisǎn 〈中药〉Chinese anaesthesia drugs

麻风 máfēng *also* "痳风" máfēng 〈医学〉leprosy: ～病人 leper / ～医院 leprosarium

麻风反应 máfēng fǎnyìng lepra reaction

麻风菌素 máfēngjūnsù lepromin

麻风恐怖 máfēng kǒngbù 〈心理〉lepraphobia

麻风溃疡 máfēng kuìyáng 〈医学〉leprelcosis

麻风学 máfēngxué 〈医学〉leprology

麻风学家 máfēngxuéjiā leprologist

麻风肿 máfēngzhǒng leproma

麻花 máhuā ❶ fried dough twist ❷〈口语〉(of dress) threadbare: 球衫的两只袖子都～了。This sweater has worn thin at the sleeves.

麻花钻 máhuāzuàn 〈机械〉fluted twist drill

麻黄 máhuáng 〈植物〉Chinese ephedra (*Ephedra sinica*); *mahuang*: ～片〈药学〉ephedrine tablet

麻黄素 máhuángsù *also* "麻黄硷"〈化学〉ephedrine

麻将 májiàng *also* "麻雀" mah-jong: ～牌 mah-jong pieces; mah-jong tiles / 打～ play mah-jong

麻酱 májiàng sesame butter

麻秸 májie stalk of skinned bast-fibre plant

麻经儿 májīngr string of raw flax (to tie small things with): 你找点～, 把这两个纸盒子捆上。Try to get some flax strings to tie up the two cardboard boxes.

麻口铁 mákǒutiě 〈冶金〉mottled cast iron; mottled (pig) iron

麻辣辣 málālā have pins and needles; tingle: 一阵阵的刺痛, ～地很难受 suffer from fits of piercing (*or* searing) pain

麻雷子 máléizi a kind of firecracker which explodes very loudly

麻利 máli ❶ nimble; dexterous; deft; neat: 手脚～ nimble of limbs / 干活～ work deftly; be efficient (in work) ❷〈方言〉quickly; immediately: 听见叫声, 她～往屋外跑。She ran outside on hearing the cry.

麻利脆 málicuì 〈口语〉deft; dexterous; nimble; neat: 他干起活来可真～。How skilful he is when he gets to work!

麻脸 máliǎn pock-marked face

麻溜 máliu 〈方言〉fast; quickly; at once: 你～回家去! You go home right away! / 有了他们的消息, ～递个话给我。Let me know as soon as you hear from them.

麻乱 máluàn numerous and disorderly; helter-skelter; chaotic: ～的情绪 be agitated / 他一时拿不定主意, 心里～极了。Unable to make up his mind, he felt as if in a turmoil. *or* He was at sixes and sevens about what to do.

麻密 mámì dense; close and numerous; thickly dotted: ～的枪炮声 intensive gunfire / 他脸上皱纹～。There are wrinkles all over his face.

麻面 mámiàn 〈方言〉pock-marked face

麻木 mámù ❶ numb; dead: 双腿冻得～了。My legs are numb with cold. / 我左手～得抬不起来。I can hardly lift my left hand, which has gone dead. ❷ apathetic; lethargic: 他脸上露出～的神情。He looked apathetic. / 他思想迟钝得近乎～。His mind is so dull that it verges on insensitivity.

麻木不仁 mámù-bùrén apathetic; insensitive; indifferent; unfeeling: 他好像～, 其实心里却是一团火。His apparent apathy belied his warm-heartedness. *or* He looked cold but was warm at heart.

麻婆豆腐 mápó dòufu pock-marked grandma's bean curd; stir-fried bean curd in hot sauce

麻钱 máqián 〈方言〉coin; copper: 他把一个～看得磨盘大。In his eyes, a copper is as big as a millstone. *or* He is a penny-pinching miser.

麻雀 máquè ❶ (house) sparrow ❷ *see* "麻将"

麻雀导弹 máquè dǎodàn 〈军事〉Sparrow (an air-to-air guided missile)

麻雀虽小, 五脏俱全 máquè suī xiǎo, wǔzàng jù quán small as a sparrow is, it has all the vital organs — small but complete

麻雀战 máquèzhàn sparrow warfare (as a form of guerrilla warfare)

麻仁 márén kernels of hempseeds

麻纱 máshā ❶ yarn of bast-fibre plants like ramie, flax, etc. ❷ cambric

麻绳 máshéng rope made of bast-fibre plants like hemp, flax, jute, etc.

麻绳偏从细处断 máshéng piān cóng xìchu duàn 〈俗语〉a rope breaks where it's worn thin — a weak link is most vulnerable: ～, 我们要特别注意工作的薄弱环节。As the saying goes, a rope breaks where it's worn thin. We should pay close attention to the weak spots in our work.

麻省理工学院 Máshěng Lǐgōng Xuéyuàn (US) Massachusetts Institute of Technology (MIT), a private university chartered in 1861

麻石 máshí chiselled stone (for building houses or paving roads)

麻梳 máshū 〈纺织〉hackle

麻酥酥 másūsū tingling: 针扎入身体某些部位时, 患者有一种～的感觉。The patient has a tingling sensation when acupuncture needles are inserted into certain parts of the body.

麻线 máxiàn flaxen thread; linen thread

麻芯钢丝绳 máxìn gāngsīshéng hemp-core wire

麻药 máyào anaesthetic

麻衣 máyī 〈旧语〉mourning garment made of hemp

麻蝇 máyíng flesh fly

麻油 máyóu sesame oil

麻扎塔格 Mázhātǎgé Mazartag Mountains, in Xinjiang Uygur Autonomous Region

麻渣 mázhā sesame residue (after extracting oil)

麻渣渣 mázhāzhā 〈方言〉in a mess; at sixes and sevens; chaotic: 这次会真开得～的。The session was a scene of noisy disorder.

麻疹 mázhěn *also*"痳疹" mázhěn 〈医学〉measles; rubeola: ～免疫球蛋白 measles immune globulin
麻疹病毒 mázhěn bìngdú 〈医学〉measles virus
麻疹脑炎 mázhěn nǎoyán 〈医学〉measles encephalitis
麻疹疫苗 mázhěn yìmiáo 〈医学〉measles virus vaccine
麻织品 mázhīpǐn linen fabric; fabric of bast-fibre plant
麻爪 mázhuǎ 〈方言〉be so terrified as to be at a loss what to do; be scared stiff: 他吓～了。He was scared out of his wits.
麻子 mázi ❶ pockmarks: 要不是脸上有几点～, 他可真是个英俊的少年。He would be a handsome young man but for a few pockmarks on his face. ❷ person with a pock-marked face
麻醉 mázuì ❶〈医学〉anaesthesia; narcosis: 全身～ general anaesthesia / 局部～ local anaesthesia / 脊髓～ spinal anaesthesia / 针刺～ acupuncture anaesthesia / 药物～ drug anaesthesia ❷ poison; enervate: 用淫秽书刊～青少年 contaminate teenagers with pornographic publications / 鸦片～吸食者的身心。Opium poisons the user's body and mind.
麻醉剂 mázuìjì *also*"麻药"; "蒙药" méngyào anaesthetic; narcotic
麻醉疗法 mázuì liáofǎ narcosis therapy; narcotherapy
麻醉品 mázuìpǐn narcotic; drug
麻醉师 mázuìshī anaesthetist
麻醉学 mázuìxué 〈医学〉anesthesiology: ～家 anesthesiologist

痳 má

痳痹 mábì *see* "麻痹" mábì
痳风 máfēng *see* "麻风" máfēng
痳疹 mázhěn *see* "麻疹" mázhěn

蟆(蟇) má *see* "蛤蟆" háma

吗 má

〈方言〉what: 干～? What for? / ～事? What's cooking? / 你说～? What did you say? *or* I beg your pardon? / 要～有～。You'll have everything you need here.
see also mǎ; ma

mǎ

马(馬) mǎ

❶ horse: 战～ battle steed; warhorse / 种～ stud; stallion / 骏～ fine horse; steed / 野～ wild horse / 头～ lead horse / 母～ mare / 小～ pony; colt / 千里～ horse that can cover a thousand *li* a day; winged steed / 特洛伊木～ Trojan Horse / 赛～ (have a) horse race / 喂～ feed a horse / 骑～ ride a horse / 套～ harness a horse / 下～ dismount (from) a horse; discontinue a project / 中途换～ swap (*or* change) horses in midstream ❷ horse, one of the pieces in Chinese chess ❸ big; great: *see* "～勺" ❹ (Mǎ) a surname
马鞍 mǎ'ān ❶ *also* "马鞍子" saddle: ～革 saddle leather ❷ *see* "马鞍形"
马鞍剪床 mǎ'ān jiǎnchuáng 〈机械〉gap shear
马鞍形 mǎ'ānxíng shape of a saddle — a falling-off between two peak periods; trough: 厂里今年的生产出现了～。There has been a trough in production at the factory this year.
马鞍形车床 mǎ'ānxíng chēchuáng 〈机械〉gap lathe; gap-bed lathe
马鞍压床 mǎ'ān yāchuáng 〈机械〉gap hydraulic press; gap press
马帮 mǎbāng a train of horses laden with merchandise travelling through difficult or dangerous terrains; caravan
马瓟儿 mǎbáor 〈植物〉*Melothria indica*
马宝 mǎbǎo 〈药学〉bezoar of a horse
马鼻疽 mǎbíjū 〈兽医〉glanders; equinia
马鼻胃蝇 mǎbí wèiyíng throat botfly
马鞭 mǎbiān *also* "马鞭子" horsewhip
马鞭草 mǎbiāncǎo vervain (*Verbena officinalis*)
马弁 mǎbiàn 〈旧语〉(officer's) bodyguard
马表 mǎbiǎo *also* "停表" tíngbiǎo; "跑表" pǎobiǎo stopwatch
马鳖 mǎbiē 〈方言〉leech
马兵 mǎbīng 〈旧语〉cavalry; cavalryman
马伯六 mǎbóliù *also* "马泊六" (often used in the early vernacular) person who arranges rendezvous for illicit lovers
马勃 mǎbó 〈植物〉puffball (*Lasiosphaera fenzlii*)
马不停蹄 mǎbùtíngtí continue one's journey non-stop; go on without a stop: 他们攻克了这个技术难关后, 又～地去解决新问题。After solving the key technical problem, they went on to tackle new issues without any delay. / 我们人不歇脚, ～, 直奔目的地。We rushed direct to our destination without calling a halt.
马槽 mǎcáo manger; horse feed: 狗卧～ dog in the manger
马车 mǎchē ❶ (horse-drawn) carriage; wagon: 两匹马拉的载人～ carriage and pair / 大篷～ wagon ❷ cart: 昔日运菜进城的～如今已被机动车代替了。Those horse-drawn carts used in the old days to deliver vegetables for urban consumption have now been replaced by motor vehicles.
马齿徒增 mǎchǐ-túzēng grow older just like the teeth of a horse growing in length — while away one's youthful years without anything to one's credit: 我这十年一事无成, ～而已。Ten years have passed and I have accomplished nothing.
马齿苋 mǎchǐxiàn 〈植物〉purslane
马刺 mǎcì spur
马褡子 mǎdāzi long, rectangular bag sewn up at both ends with an opening in the middle worn across a horseback
马达 mǎdá (transliteration) motor: ～效应 motor effect / ～性能 motor performance / ～转速 motor speed / ～润滑油 motor-oil / ～起动机 motor starter
马达泵 mǎdábèng 〈机械〉motor pump
马达加斯加 Mǎdájiāsījiā Madagascar: ～人 Madagascan / ～语 Malagasy (language)
马大哈 mǎdàhā ❶ careless; negligent; absent-minded; forgetful: 这人真够～的, 去图书馆借书经常不带借书证。He is so forgetful that he often goes to the loan desk of the library without bringing a library card. ❷ careless person; scatterbrain: 这本书不知是哪位～丢的。We don't know which scatterbrain left the book here.
马当毒气 mǎdāng dúqì 〈化学〉martonite
马刀 mǎdāo sabre: 挥舞～ sabre-rattling (to frighten or intimidate people)
马到成功 mǎdào-chénggōng win instant success; achieve immediate victory: 旗开得胜, ～ win speedy victory in the first battle / 这次出使非洲, 祝您～。I wish you instant success in your mission to Africa.
马德拉斯 Mǎdélāsī Madras, a seaport on the east coast of India
马德里 Mǎdélǐ Madrid, capital of Spain
马德望 Mǎdéwàng Battambang, second largest city in Cambodia to the west of Phnom Penh
马灯 mǎdēng barn lantern; lantern
马镫 mǎdèng stirrup: ～皮带 stirrup strap; stirrup leather
马蒂斯 Mǎdìsī Henri Emile Benoît Matisse (1869-1954), French painter who also made prints and sculpture
马店 mǎdiàn inn for drivers of carts and caravans; caravansary
马丁炉 mǎdīnglú Martin furnace; open hearth furnace
马丁·路德·金 Mǎdīng Lùdé Jīn Martin Luther King, Jr. (1929-1968), American Black Baptist minister and civil rights leader
马丁水泥 Mǎdīng shuǐní 〈建筑〉Martin's cement
马丁体 mǎdīngtǐ 〈冶金〉martensite
马兜铃 mǎdōulíng 〈植物〉birthwort
马痘 mǎdòu 〈兽医〉horsepox
马肚带 mǎdùdài bellyband
马队 mǎduì ❶ train of horses laden with merchandise; caravan ❷ cavalry; contingent of mounted troops
马尔代夫 Mǎ'ěrdàifū Maldives: ～人 Maldivian
马尔加什语 Mǎ'ěrjiāshíyǔ Malagasy (language)
马尔萨斯 Mǎ'ěrsàsī Thomas Robert Malthus (1766-1834), English economist, known for his *Essay on the Principle of Population*: ～人口论 Malthusian Theory of Population
马尔萨斯主义 Mǎ'ěrsàsīzhǔyì Malthusianism: 新～ Neo-Malthusianism
马耳他 Mǎ'ěrtā Malta: ～人 Maltese / ～语 Maltese (language)
马尔维纳斯群岛 Mǎ'ěrwéinàsī Qúndǎo Malvinas Islands, a group of islands in the south Atlantic referred to as Falkland Islands in the United Kingdom
马贩子 mǎfànzi horse dealer; coper
马粪纸 mǎfènzhǐ strawboard
马蜂 mǎfēng *also* "蚂蜂" mǎfēng hornet; wasp
马蜂窝 mǎfēngwō hornet's nest: 捅～ stir up a hornet's nest
马夫 mǎfū 〈旧语〉groom

马弗炉 mǎfúlú 〈冶金〉 muffle furnace
马佛生 mǎfúshēng 〈药学〉 mephenesin
马竿 mǎgān blindman's staff
马革裹尸 mǎgé-guǒshī be wrapped in a horse's hide — die in battle; be killed in action:青山处处埋忠骨,何必~还? The green hills all over the world are fitting burial grounds for loyal bones. Why bring the body back in horse hide?
马格里布 Mǎgélǐbù Maghrib or Maghreb, a region of north and northwest Africa between the Atlantic and Egypt
马更些河 Mǎgēngxiēhé Mackenzie River, longest river in Canada
马褂 mǎguà mandarin jacket:长袍~ mandarin jacket and long gown — formal dress in old days
马关条约 Mǎguān Tiáoyuē Treaty of Shimonoseki (1895), unequal treaty imposed on the Qing government by Japan after the Sino-Japanese war of 1894-1895
马倌 mǎguān groom; stableman; stableboy
马锅头 mǎguōtóu leader of a caravan
马海毛 mǎhǎimáo mohair
马号 mǎhào ❶ stable ❷ cavalry bugle
马赫 mǎhè 〈物理〉 Mach:~波 Mach wave
马赫数 mǎhèshù Mach number; Mach
马赫原理 Mǎhè yuánlǐ Mach principle
马赫主义 Mǎhèzhǔyì 〈哲学〉 Machism:~者 Machist
马后炮 mǎhòupào belated action or advice; belated effort:事情都办过了才出点子,真是~。To give advice after the event — that is too late to be useful. /这个点子不错,但已经是~了。That is sound but belated advice. /我为什么一点预见性也没有呢? 我为什么老走~呢? How is it that I had no foresight and always took belated action?
马虎 mǎhu *also* "马糊" careless; casual; slipshod; slapdash:~大意 careless and negligent /工作~ slapdash with one's work /这事挺要紧,千万~不得。This business is too important to be handled casually. /这样~,要坏事的。You would get into trouble for such carelessness. *or* Such carelessness would get you into trouble.
马鸡 mǎjī 〈动物〉 eared pheasant
马甲 mǎjiǎ ❶ armour on horse ❷ 〈方言〉 vest; waistcoat
马架 mǎjià *also* "马架子" ❶ small shack or shed ❷ triangular wooden rack for carrying things on one's back
马鲛鱼 mǎjiāoyú Spanish mackerel
马脚 mǎjiǎo clue; trace; sth. that gives the game away:露出~ betray; let slip; give away /这个骗子一说话就露了~。The swindler showed his forked tongue as soon as he opened his mouth.
马颈圈 mǎjǐngquān horse collar
马厩 mǎjiù stable
马驹子 mǎjūzi 〈口语〉 colt; foal; pony
马具 mǎjù horse harness; horse gear
马钧 Mǎ Jūn Ma Jun, engineer of the Period of the Three Kingdoms, who invented the water wheels
马卡林星系 Mǎkǎlín xīngxì 〈天文〉 Markarian galaxy
马可·波罗 Mǎkěbōluó *also* "马哥·孛罗" Marco Polo (1254-1324), Italian traveller who stayed in China from 1275 to 1292:《~游记》 *The Travels of Marco Polo*
马可福音 Mǎkě Fúyīn 〈基督教〉 *The Gospel According to Mark*
马克 mǎkè ❶ mark:德国~ Deutsche Mark; Deutschmark ❷ markka:芬兰~ Finnish markka
马克思 Mǎkèsī Karl Marx (1818-1883)
马克思列宁主义 Mǎkèsī-Lièníngzhǔyì Marxism-Leninism:~者 Marxist-Leninist
马克思主义 Mǎkèsīzhǔyì Marxism:~者 Marxist /~哲学 Marxist philosophy /~政治经济学 Marxist political economy /~认识论 Marxist epistemology
马克·吐温 Mǎkè Tǔwēn Mark Twain, pseudonym of Samuel Langhorne Clemens (1835-1910), Amercian writer whose works include *The Adventures of Tom Sawyer* (1876) and *The Adventures of Huckleberry Finn* (1884)
马口铁 mǎkǒutiě tinplate; galvanized iron
马裤 mǎkù riding breeches
马裤呢 mǎkùní whipcord
马拉博 Mǎlābó Malabo, capital of Equatorial Guinea
马拉开波湖 Mǎlākāibōhú Lake Maracaibo, largest lake in South America
马拉犁 mǎlālí 〈农业〉 horse-drawn plough
马拉松 mǎlāsōng ❶ marathon:~赛跑 marathon; marathon race /~战役 Battle of Marathon (490 BC) ❷ tedious; lengthy; long-winded:~演说 marathon speech; lengthy speech /~谈判 marathon talks; long, drawn-out negotiation
马拉维 Mǎlāwéi Malawi:~人 Malawian
马拉维湖 Mǎlāwéihú Lake Malawi, third largest lake in Africa
马来半岛 Mǎlái Bàndǎo Malay Peninsula
马来獾 mǎláihuān 〈动物〉 teledu; Malayan stink badger
马来群岛 Mǎlái Qúndǎo Malay Archipelago, lying southeast of Asia and northeast of Australia
马来人 Mǎláirén Malay
马来西亚 Mǎláixīyà Malaysia:~人 Malaysian
马来语 Mǎláiyǔ Malay (language)
马兰 mǎlán ❶ 〈植物〉 *Kalimeris indica*, herb used as medicine ❷ *see* "马蔺"
马蓝 mǎlán 〈植物〉 acanthaceous indigo (*Strobilanthes cusia*)
马累 Mǎléi Malé, capital of the Maldives
马里 Mǎlǐ Mali:~人 Malian
马里亚纳海沟 Mǎlǐyànà Hǎigōu Mariana Trench, greatest known ocean depth, to the southeast of the Mariana Islands in the Pacific
马里亚纳群岛 Mǎlǐyànà Qúndǎo Mariana Islands, a group of islands in the northwest Pacific
马力 mǎlì 〈物理〉 horsepower (hp):~小时 horsepower hour (hp-hr) /开足~ at full (*or* top) speed; full steam ahead
马立克派 Mǎlìkèpài 〈伊斯兰〉 Malikite school
马利亚 Mǎlìyà *also* "玛利亚" Mǎlìyà Virgin Mary:圣母~ Holy Mary
马栗 mǎlì 〈植物〉 horse-chestnut
马列主义 Mǎ-Lièzhǔyì (short for 马克思列宁主义) Marxism-Leninism:~政党 Marxist-Leninist party /~学说 theory of Marxism-Leninism
马林科夫 Mǎlínkēfū Georgiy Maximilianovich Malenkov (1902-1988), First Secretary of the Central Committee of the CPSU (March-September 1953) and Chairman of the Council of Ministers of the USSR (1953-1955)
马蔺 mǎlìn *also* "马莲";"马兰" 〈植物〉 Chinese small iris (*Iris pallasii* var. *chinensis*)
马铃薯 mǎlíngshǔ potato (*Solanum tuberosum*); white potato:~种植机 potato setter /~中耕机 potato cultivator /~挖掘机 potato lifter; potato raiser /~联合种植机 combine potato planter /~泥 mashed potato /~晚疫病 late blight of potato
马铃薯淀粉 mǎlíngshǔ diànfěn farina
马六甲海峡 Mǎliùjiǎ Hǎixiá Strait of Malacca
马陆 mǎlù *also* "百足" bǎizú 〈动物〉 julid (*Orthomorpha Pekuensis*), a millipede of the family *Julidae*
马鹿 mǎlù 〈动物〉 red deer
马路 mǎlù road; street; avenue:他住在~的那头。He lives down the road. /~两旁绿树成荫。Green trees cast shade on both sides of the street.
马路消息 mǎlù xiāoxi *see* "马路新闻"
马路新闻 mǎlù xīnwén grapevine telegraph; hearsay; rumour; gossip
马锣 mǎluó small brass gong
马骡 mǎluó 〈动物〉 mule
马马虎虎 mǎma-hūhū ❶ careless; casual; slipshod; slapdash:干活~ be slack in one's work /质量检查就是企业的生命,~是不行的。Quality control is the lifeline of an enterprise and must not be taken lightly. /我~地读了这篇报告文学,觉得很有意思。I glanced through this reportage and found it of great interest. ❷ fair to middling; just passable; just so-so:"这本书的译文怎么样?" "~。" "How about the translation of the book?" "Just middling." /"生意怎么样?" "~,不如去年。" "How's business?" "So-so. Not as good as last year's." /~算是北京烤鸭吧。This is an apology for roast Beijing duck.
马毛 mǎmáo horsehair:~疫 horsehair blight
马面鲀 mǎmiàntún 〈动物〉 black scraper
马那瓜 Mǎnàguā Managua, capital of Nicaragua
马奶 mǎnǎi mare's milk
马尼拉 Mǎnílā Manila, capital of the Philippines
马尼拉麻 mǎnílāmá manila hemp
马趴 mǎpā fall on one's face:摔了个大~ fall flat on one's face
马匹 mǎpǐ (general term for 马) horses
马屁 mǎpì 〈比喻〉 sycophancy; flattery; toadyism:~拍得不是地方

rub up (*or* soft-soap) sb. the wrong way
马屁精 mǎpìjīng 〈贬义〉ass-kisser; lick-spittle: 他精于阿谀逢迎,被人骂为"~"。He is nicknamed ass-licker for his consummate art of flattery.
马普托 Mǎpǔtuō Maputo, capital and chief port of Mozambique
马其顿 Mǎqídùn Macedon; Macedonia: ~共和国 Republic of Macedonia
马其诺防线 Mǎqínuò Fángxiàn Maginot Line, a line of defensive fortifications built along France's northeast frontier in 1936
马前卒 mǎqiánzú 〈贬义〉pawn; catspaw: 反动派的~ catspaw of reaction / 他这人真没骨气,就会当别人的~。He is so spineless that he is willing and ready to serve as a pawn for others.
马钱子 mǎqiánzi 〈植物〉vomiting nut; nuxvomica
马枪 mǎqiāng *also* "骑枪" qíqiāng carbine
马球 mǎqiú 〈体育〉polo
马日事变 Mǎrì Shìbiàn May 21st Incident — the counter-revolutionary rebellion masterminded by reactionary army officer Xu Kexiang (许克祥) and others in Changsha, Hunan Province, on 21 May 1927, for which the telegram code was "马日" (day of the horse). Hence the name of the incident.
马赛 Mǎsài Marseille, France's second largest city, and a seaport on the Mediterranean coast
马赛克 mǎsàikè 〈建筑〉mosaic: ~铺面 mosaic pavement / ~地板 mosaic floor
马赛卢 Mǎsàilú Maseru, capital of Lesotho
马赛曲 Mǎsàiqǔ *La Marseillaise*, national anthem of France
马上 mǎshàng at once; immediately; straight away; right away: 我~就去。I'll be right there. / 我~就与他联系。I'll get in touch with him at once. / 他笑了笑,没有~回答我的话。He gave a smile without replying directly to my queries. / 戏~就要开演了。The play will be on in a minute. / 他一进门,我~就认出他了。I recognized him the moment he entered the room. / 我们~出发去颐和园。We are leaving for the Summer Palace right now. / 他总说~办,~办,可就是拖着不解决。He would always say, "I'll see to it right away", but never get down to it.
马勺 mǎsháo (so called because bigger than 勺) ladle
马绍尔群岛 Mǎshào'ěr Qúndǎo Marshall Islands, a group of islands in the northwest Pacific which became a republic in 1986
马失前蹄 mǎshīqiántí make a mistake by accident; have an accidental setback: 谁没有个~的时候? Who can always be free from setbacks and mistakes? *or* To err is human.
马氏体 mǎshìtǐ 〈冶金〉martensite: ~不锈钢 martensitic stainless steel / ~等温淬火 martemper / ~时效钢 maraging steel
马首是瞻 mǎshǒu-shìzhān In ancient battles, the rank-and-file soldiers always watched the head of the general's horse as a signal to advance or retreat — follow sb.'s lead: 此人足智多谋,部下惟其~。As he is intelligent and resourceful, his men all follow his lead.
马术 mǎshù horsemanship; equestrian skill
马斯卡林群岛 Mǎsīkǎlín Qúndǎo Mascarene Islands, a group of islands in the Indian Ocean
马斯喀特 Mǎsīkātè Muscat, capital of Oman
马太福音 Mǎtài Fúyīn 〈基督教〉*The Gospel According to Matthew*
马唐 mǎtáng 〈植物〉*Digitaria sanguinalis*
马蹄 mǎtí ❶ horse's hoof: ~声 hoofbeat; clip-clop / ~得得 clatter of a horse's hoofs ❷ 〈方言〉water chestnut
马蹄表 mǎtíbiǎo alarm clock; round or hoof-shaped desk clock
马蹄规 mǎtíguī horseshoe gauge
马蹄金 mǎtíjīn U-shaped gold ingot
马蹄莲 mǎtílián calla lily
马蹄螺 mǎtíluó top shell
马蹄铁 mǎtítiě ❶ horseshoe ❷ U-shaped magnet; horseshoe magnet
马蹄蟹 mǎtíxiè horse crab
马蹄形 mǎtíxíng U-shaped; of the shape of a hoof / ~电磁铁 horseshoe electromagnet
马蹄袖 mǎtíxiù horse-hoof-shaped cuff (of a Manchu jacket or gown)
马蹄银 mǎtíyín U-shaped silver ingot
马铁 mǎtiě malleable cast iron
马童 mǎtóng 〈戏曲〉stable boy
马桶 mǎtǒng nightstool; closestool; commode; chamberpot
马桶包 mǎtǒngbāo a kind of cylindrical backpack
马头 mǎtóu ❶ horse's head ❷ 〈书面〉wharf; dock; quay; pier
马头琴 mǎtóuqín bowed stringed instrument with a scroll carved like a horse's head, used by the Mongol nationality
马头鱼 mǎtóuyú tilefish (*Branchiostegidae*)
马王堆汉墓 Mǎwángduī Hànmù tombs of the Western Han Dynasty at Mawangdui, excavated in 1972-1974 in Hunan Province
马尾 mǎwěi ❶ horsetail ❷(Mǎwěi) harbour in Fujian Province
马尾草 mǎwěicǎo 〈植物〉gulfweed
马尾衬 mǎwěichèn 〈纺织〉haircloth
马尾松 mǎwěisōng 〈植物〉masson pine
马尾藻 mǎwěizǎo sargasso; gulfweed
马胃蝇 mǎwèiyíng horse botfly; equine gasterophilosis
马瘟病 mǎwēnbìng 〈兽医〉equine distemper
马西型球磨机 mǎxīxíng qiúmójī 〈矿业〉Marcy mill
马戏 mǎxì circus: ~团 circus troupe / 流动~团 travelling circus
马歇尔 Mǎxiē'ěr George Catlett Marshall (1880-1959), special US Presidential envoy to China from 1945 to 1947 and US Secretary of State from 1947 to 1949
马歇尔计划 Mǎxiē'ěr Jìhuà Marshall Plan (officially referred to as European Recovery Programme initiated in 1947 and ended in 1952)
马熊 mǎxióng 〈动物〉brown bear
马靴 mǎxuē riding boots
马雅可夫斯基 Mǎyǎkěfūsījī Vladimir Vladimirovich Mayakovsky (1893-1930), Russian poet
马仰人翻 mǎyǎng-rénfān *also* "人仰马翻"; "马翻人仰" men and horses thrown off their feet — be routed; be plunged into chaos
马缨丹 mǎyīngdān 〈植物〉lantana
马缨花 mǎyīnghuā 〈植物〉silk tree
马蝇 mǎyíng (horse) botfly
马有失蹄,人有失言 mǎ yǒu shī tí, rén yǒu shī yán 〈俗语〉just as a horse may stumble, a man may have a slip of the tongue — to err is only human
马贼 mǎzéi 〈旧语〉mounted bandit: 这是过去~经常出没的地方。This was the haunt of mounted bandits in the old days.
马扎 mǎzhá *also* "马劄" campstool; folding stool
马长犄角牛打滚 mǎ zhǎng jījiao niú dǎgǔn 〈俗语〉it's like a horse growing a pair of horns or a bull turning a somersault — something impossible; a cock-and-bull story: 谁见过~,尽是些没影的事儿。This is sheer nonsense. No one would believe it any more than he would believe the story of a horse growing two horns or a bull turning a somersault.
马掌 mǎzhǎng ❶ cutin skin of a horse's hoof ❷ horseshoe
马志尼 Mǎzhìní Giuseppe Mazzini (1805-1872), Italian revolutionary
马致远 Mǎ Zhìyuǎn Ma Zhiyuan (formerly translated as Ma Chihyuan, c. 1250-c. 1324), playwright of the Yuan Dynasty
马注 Mǎ Zhù Ma Zhu (1640-1711), Islamic scholar of the early Qing Dynasty, of the Hui nationality
马桩 mǎzhuāng hitching post
马子 mǎzi 〈方言〉❶ *see* "马桶" ❷ bandit; brigand
马鬃 mǎzōng horse's mane
马祖岛 Mǎzǔdǎo Mazu Island, off the east coast of Fujian Province
马醉木 mǎzuìmù *also* "梫木" qǐnmù *Pieris japonica*

玛 mǎ

玛钢 mǎgāng malleable (cast) iron
玛瑙 mǎnǎo agate: ~念珠 agate beads / ~蛋白石 agate opal / ~轴承 agate bearing
玛雅人 Mǎyǎrén *also* "马亚人" Mǎyǎrén Maya, an Indian people in Central America who developed a high level of culture in c. 1st to 16th centuries and still maintain some aspects of their ancient culture
玛雅文化 Mǎyǎ wénhuà *also* "马亚文化" Mǎyǎ wénhuà Mayan Civilization (c. 1st-16th centuries), in Central America
玛祖卡 mǎzǔkǎ 〈音乐〉mazurka

码[1] mǎ

❶ sign or thing indicating number: 号~ number / 页~ page number / 价~ marked price; price / 尺~ size / 加~ raise the

price of commodities; raise the quota /暗～ secret code /密～ cipher code /明～标价 with the price clearly marked ❷ instrument or device used to indicate number:筹～ counter; chip /砝～ weight (used on a balance) ❸ same thing; thing of the same category:你跟他说的是一～事。You and he talk about the same thing. /那是另一～事。That is another cup of tea.

码[2] mǎ 〈口语〉pile up; stack:～砖头 stack bricks /把木板沿墙～齐 stack planks of wood neatly against the wall

码[3] mǎ yard (yd):三～布 three yards of cloth

码布机 mǎbùjī 〈纺织〉cloth plaiting machine

码尺 mǎchǐ yard measure; yardstick:～圆规 yardstick compass

码垛 mǎduò pile up; lump; stack:粮食包～不齐容易倒。The grain sacks often collapse if they are not stacked in good order.

码放 mǎfàng place or pile up in good order:各种器材～得井井有条。All appliances and materials are kept in perfect order (*or* in apple-pie order).

码分多址 mǎfēn duōzhǐ 〈通信〉code division multiple access (CDMA)

码群 mǎqún 〈通信〉code group

码头 mǎtou ❶ wharf; dock; quay; pier:客运～ passenger dock /货运～ freight dock ❷ port city; commercial and transportation centre:跑～ travel from port to port as a trader; be a travelling salesman /水陆～ port city easy of access by both road and waterways /大～ great metropolitan centre; business metropolis

码头费 mǎtoufèi dockage; wharfage

码头工人 mǎtou gōngrén dock workers; docker; stevedore; longshoreman

码头交货 mǎtou jiāohuò ex wharf; ex pier; ex quay

码头延误费 mǎtou yánwùfèi wharf demurrage

码头栈单 mǎtou zhàndān dock warrant

码洋 mǎyáng total price (of books):这部词典第一版印刷一万册，～为一百万元。The first edition of this dictionary has an impression of 10,000 copies and the total price is 1,000,000 *yuan*.

码元 mǎyuán 〈通信〉code element

码子 mǎzi ❶ numeral:苏州～ Suzhou numerals (traditionally used by shopkeepers to mark prices) ❷ counter; chip ❸ 〈旧语〉ready money; cash

吗 mǎ

see also má; ma

吗啡 mǎfēi morphine:～瘾 morphinism; morphinomania /～中毒 morphinism /～脱瘾法 demorphinization /～含量检定法 morphinometry; morphiometry /为了止痛，他打了一针～。To stop pain, he had an injection of morphine.

吗啡酚 mǎfēifēn morphol

蚂 mǎ

see also mā; mà

蚂蜂 mǎfēng *see* "马蜂" mǎfēng

蚂蟥 mǎhuáng 〈动物〉leech

蚂蟥见血 mǎhuáng-jiànxiě 〈俗语〉It's like a leech scenting blood — would never give up:像"～"一样，一看见这些古玩儿，他们哪里还肯走开! Like "a leech scenting blood", they could hardly tear themselves away from those antiques and curios.

蚂蚁 mǎyǐ ant:白～ termite /～山 ant-hill

蚂蚁搬泰山 mǎyǐ bān Tàishān ants removing Mount Tai — the concerted efforts of the masses can help accomplish giant projects

蚂蚁顶不翻锅 mǎyǐ dǐngbufān guō 〈俗语〉It's impossible for ants to turn over a pan — a handful of evildoers cannot change the overall situation:～，这几个人成不了气候。Just as ants could not turn over a pan, these people would get nowhere.

蚂蚁啃骨头 mǎyǐ kěn gǔtou ants gnawing at a bone — plod away at a big job bit by bit:这个小厂用～的办法完成了万吨水压机的加工任务。Like ants gnawing at a bone, this small plant eventually completed a 10,000-ton hydraulic press by plodding away at it bit by bit.

蚂蚁缘槐 mǎyǐ-yuánhuái ants on the locust tree — little people puffed up with arrogance:～夸大国，蚍蜉撼树谈何易。Ants on the locust tree assume a great-nation swagger And mayflies lightly plot to topple the giant tree.

犸 mǎ *see* "猛犸" měngmǎ

mà

蚂 mà

see also mā; mǎ

蚂蚱 màzha 〈方言〉locust:像秋后的～，他们长不了。Like locusts in late fall, they won't last much longer. *or* Their days are numbered.

骂(罵) mà ❶ abuse; curse; swear; call names:～脏话 shout curses (*or* abuse) /破口大～ let loose a stream of abuse /痛～ curse sb. roundly /对～ call each other names; trade insults /笑～ deride and taunt /～得狗血喷头 bite one's head off; blow sb. up /～不还口 do not return a curse with a curse /她是要～他一顿的。She would definitely chew him out. ❷ chide; reproach; reprove; scold:～我笨 scold me for being clumsy /～他傻 chide him for being so silly /～了她一顿 give her a good dressing down /大家都～他太大手大脚。Everybody criticized him for his extravagance.

骂大街 mà dàjiē shout abuse in the street:他喝得醉醺醺地～。Terribly drunk, he was shouting abuses in public.

骂挡子 màdǎngzi 〈方言〉butt or target of scolding:他简直成了老婆的～。He simply has become a target of curses for his wife.

骂架 màjià quarrel; kick up a row:两口子经常～，最后还是离婚了。The couple quarreled constantly and got divorced in the end.

骂街 màjiē shout abuse in the street; swear in public:他一有不顺心的事就～。If something went wrong, he would swear like crazy. /有话好说，谁也不许～。Say what you will, but no one is allowed to use coarse language.

骂詈 màlì 〈书面〉scold; abuse; curse

骂骂咧咧 màma-liēliē be foul-mouthed:近来他情绪不好，一张口就～的。He is in a bad mood lately, so he is rather foul-mouthed.

骂名 màmíng bad name; infamy; bad reputation:留下了千古～ earn oneself eternal infamy in history /你得好处，我背～。You have got all the credit while I have got a bad reputation.

骂娘 màniáng abuse; curse; swear

骂山门 mà shānmén 〈方言〉curse roundly; abuse; call names

骂阵 màzhèn ❶ (often used in traditional novels) let loose a stream of abuse at the enemy in order to provoke him into accepting a battle ❷ 〈方言〉*see* "骂街"

骂座 màzuò 〈书面〉curse other guests at the same table

唛 mà *also* mài 〈方言〉trade mark:～头 trade mark

唛瑶 màyáo 〈方言〉〈植物〉*Amesiodendron chinensis*

ma

嘛(么) ma 〈助词〉❶ *indicating that the reason is obvious*:有意见就提～。Air your complaints if you have any. /别责怪孩子，他才六岁～。Don't blame the boy. He is only six years old. /干起来再说～。Let's get started first. /你是科长，带个头～! You are a section chief, so you have to take the lead. ❷ *used to indicate an expectation or an attempt at dissuasion*:不让你去，就别去～! Since they don't want you to go, why don't you do as they say? ❸ *used within a sentence to mark a pause drawing attention to what is coming*:其实～，这也并不神秘。As a matter of fact, this is nothing mysterious. /情况变了～，我们的对策也得变。As the situation has changed, we have to modify our countermeasures accordingly.

吗(么) ma 〈助词〉❶ *used at the end of a question*:你去邮局～? Are you going to the post office? /你听明白了～? Did you get what I said? /这个研讨会有意思～? Did you find the seminar interesting? ❷ *used before a pause in the middle of a sentence to indicate the subject in question*:这件事情～，其实也不能怪他。As regards the matter in question, he is not to blame indeed. ❸ *used at the end of a rhetorical question to indicate dissatisfaction or disagreement*:这样做公平～? Is this fair? /你这些话不是自相矛盾～? Aren't you being self-contradictory by saying all that? /难道就没有

M

一点希望了～? Is there really no hope at all?
see also má; mǎ

mái

埋 mái ❶ cover up (with earth, sand, snow, etc.); bury: 掩～ bury /活～ bury alive /～地雷 lay a landmine /这件文物在地下～了三千多年才出土。This historical relic that was recently unearthed had lain buried for more than three thousand years. ❷ conceal; hide: ～忧 hide one's sorrow
see also mán

埋殡 máibìn 〈方言〉 bury

埋藏 máicáng ❶ lie hidden in the earth; bury: 他把珍宝～在这棵大树下。He buried his treasure under the tree. /我国近海地区～着丰富的石油资源。There are rich oil resources in the offshore regions of China. ❷ keep secret; hide; conceal: 母亲总是装作很高兴的样子，其实她心里～着多少悲痛和忧愁啊! Mother pretended to be cheerful, but deep down in her heart lay hidden a tremendous load of grief and sorrow. ❸ implant; embed: ～电极 implanted electrode

埋地天线 máidì tiānxiàn 〈无线电〉 buried antenna

埋伏 máifu ❶ ambush: 设～ lay an ambush /中～ fall (*or* walk) into an ambush /遭到～ be attacked from (an) ambush; be ambushed /我们发现敌军在两山之间～有重兵。We discovered large contingents of enemy troops lying in ambush between two mountain ridges. ❷ hide; lie low; lie in wait: 为了躲避警察的追捕，他～起来了。To escape arrest by the police, he went into hiding. /成功的后面～着不稳定因素。Some destabilizing factors lay hidden behind apparent success.

埋弧焊 máihúhàn 〈冶金〉 submerged-arc welding

埋弧炉 máihúlú 〈冶金〉 submerged-arc furnace

埋名 máimíng conceal one's name; live incognito: 隐姓～ conceal one's identity; live in anonymity; live incognito

埋没 máimò ❶ bury; cover up (with earth, snow, rocks, etc.): 流沙～了大片良田。Vast tracts of good farm land were engulfed by drifting sands. ❷ neglect; stifle; hide: ～人材 stifle real talents; stunt the growth of talent /～了一篇好稿子 neglect (*or* suppress) a good article /我不相信造谣毁谤可以～真相。I don't believe that rumour and slander can hide the truth.

埋青 máiqīng bury green manure in the fields as base fertilizer

埋人锚 máirùmáo 〈船舶〉 embedment anchor

埋设 máishè lay and bury underground: ～管道 lay pipelines

埋首 máishǒu immerse oneself in; be engrossed in: ～写作 devote all one's time and energy to writing

埋汰 máitai 〈方言〉 ❶ unclean; dirty: 这么～的衣服，怎么能穿呀? How can I wear such dirty colthes? ❷ ridicule; make fun of: 你这不是～我吗? You're trying to make a fool of me, aren't you?

埋头 máitóu concentrate on; devote all one's time to: ～读书 be absorbed (*or* engrossed) in one's studies /～苦干 concentrate on one's work; work hard with concentrated attention /～研究 dedicate oneself to research work /～业务 devote oneself entirely to professional work

埋头铆钉 máitóu mǎodīng countersunk rivet; blind rivet; sunk rivet

埋头钻 máitóuzuàn countersink drill

埋线疗法 máixiàn liáofǎ 〈中医〉 thread burial therapy; catgut embedding therapy (embedding a piece of catgut in a selected location of the body to produce protracted stimulation)

埋药疗法 máiyào liáofǎ drug embedding therapy

埋葬 máizàng ❶ bury: 这个陵墓里～着明代的最后一个皇帝。This is the tomb of the last emperor of the Ming Dynasty. /老人的遗体，就～在他晚年日夜思念的故乡。The remains of the old man lie buried in his hometown, a place that he always recalled with nostalgia in old age. /公元前 79 年，意大利古城庞贝在一次火山爆发中被～了。Pompeii, an ancient city in Italy, was buried by a volcanic eruption in 79 BC. ❷ destroy; wipe out: ～旧世界 smash the old world /他的家庭、理想和事业全让毒品～了! Drugs ruined him, his family, ideals and career.

埋针疗法 máizhēn liáofǎ needle embedding therapy

埋置电缆 máizhì diànlǎn 〈电工〉 buried cable

霾 mái thick haze: 阴～ thick dark haze

霾层 máicéng 〈气象〉 haze layer: ～顶 haze horizon

霾滴 máidī 〈气象〉 haze droplet

霾线 máixiàn 〈气象〉 haze line or level

mǎi

买(買) mǎi ❶ buy; purchase: 采～ purchase; procure /～东西 go shopping /收～ buy over; bribe /收～人心 buy popularity /～齐了吗? Have you finished with your shopping list? /电冰箱，农民～得起。Farmers can afford refrigerators now. /五元钱可～不下来。You can't get it for 5 *yuan*. /这本词典好～吗? Is this dictionary available now in the bookshops? /有钱难～老来瘦。Money cannot buy slimness in old age. ❷ (Mǎi) a surname

买办 mǎibàn comprador: ～资本家 comprador capitalist /～阶级 comprador class /～资本主义 comprador capitalism

买办资本 mǎibàn zīběn capital of comprador bourgeoisie (in colonial and semi-colonial countries); comprador capital

买办资产阶级 mǎibàn zīchǎnjiējí comprador bourgeoisie

买春 mǎichūn 〈书面〉 buy alcoholic drinks (春 "spring" was often used in ancient times in the names of alcoholic drinks, such as 竹叶春 "spring bamboo leaves" and 梨花春 "spring pear blossom" and thus became another name for liquor)

买单 mǎidān (used when asking to pay for a meal at a restaurant) bill; check: 小姐，～。Bill please, waitress.

买椟还珠 mǎidú-huánzhū buy the case but refuse the pearls (a pearl seller from the State of Chu 楚 had his pearls placed in a lavishly adorned case for sale in the State of Zheng 郑, where a buyer kept the glittering case but returned the pearls to the seller); lack acumen or sense of discrimination: 读书忽略了书中的精华，岂不是～? If one fails to catch the essence of a book while reading it, he is merely buying a case and discarding the pearls in it.

买多市场 mǎiduō shìchǎng 〈经济〉 long market

买方 mǎifāng buying party (of a contract, etc.); buyer: ～贷款 buyer's credit /～期货 buyer's hedging /～专利 buyer's monopoly /一切费用由～负责。All costs involved will be borne by the buyer.

买方市场 mǎifāng shìchǎng 〈经济〉 buyer's market

买方信贷 mǎifāng xìndài buyer's credit

买关节 mǎi guānjié 〈旧语〉 bribe or buy off sb.; grease sb.'s palm: 在封建时代，告状也要先买通关节。In feudal times, it was necessary to offer bribes to start a lawsuit.

买官 mǎiguān 〈旧语〉 buy a public post; pay a bribe to obtain an official post

买好 mǎihǎo go out of one's way to please; curry favour with; ingratiate oneself with: 他凭本事吃饭，不想对人～。He earns his bread by ability and has no inclination to win anybody's favour.

买价 mǎijià buying price; purchasing price

买进 mǎijìn buy in

买空卖空 mǎikōng-màikōng ❶ buy long and sell short; speculate (in stocks, etc.): 他搞了一段股票的～生意，结果赔了不少钱。He speculated in the stock market for some time, only to lose a lot of money. ❷ swindle or engage in profiteering activities: 这家公司因为投机倒把、～，而被关闭了。This firm was closed down because of its profiteering activities.

买邻 mǎilín 〈书面〉 find good neighbours before moving into a new house; find a good neighbourhood before settling down

买路钱 mǎilùqián ❶ 〈旧语〉 paper money thrown over the road during a funeral procession ❷ money extorted by highwaymen ❸ 〈戏谑〉 toll money

买麻藤 mǎimáténg 〈植物〉 sweetberry jointfir (*Gentum montanum*)

买卖 mǎimài buying and selling: ～法 law on sales

买卖公平 mǎimài gōngpíng buy and sell at reasonable prices; be fair in business transactions

买卖婚姻 mǎimài hūnyīn mercenary marriage; wife-buying: 在一些落后的地方，还有～。There are still cases of mercenary marriage in some backward villages.

买卖 mǎimai ❶ purchase and sale; business; transaction; deal: 做笔～ make a deal /做～ go into business /～兴隆。Business is booming. /～不成情义在。Friendly relations should exist between buyer and seller even if they fail to clinch a deal. ❷ (private) shop; store: 他在闹市开了家～。He opened a shop in the downtown area.

买卖人 mǎimairén private businessman or trader; merchant: 他是个～，当然对价钱斤斤计较。He is a private businessman, and will naturally haggle over prices.

买面子 mǎi miànzi adopt an accommodating attitude or stretch rules out of respect for sb.'s feelings: 不是我不买你的面子，实在这件事不好办。Not that I wouldn't make an exception in your case, but I am not in a position to do so.

买青卖青 mǎiqīng-màiqīng 〈旧语〉buy and sell green crops still growing in the fields — a way of exploiting impoverished peasants

买权 mǎiquán 〈金融〉call option

买通 mǎitōng bribe; buy over; buy off; grease sb.'s palm: ～官府 bribe court officials

买账 mǎizhàng (often used in the negative) show admiration or respect for: 谁也不买他的账。Nobody has any respect for him. *or* No one gives a damn what he says. /他如此霸道，我绝不～！ How bossy he is! But I won't buy it. /对于他的指示，没人～。Nobody seems to care about his instructions.

买主 mǎizhǔ buyer; purchaser; customer: 有支付能力的～ effective purchaser /有偿付能力的～ solvent purchaser

买主当心 mǎizhǔ dāngxīn *caveat emptor* (let the buyer beware)

买嘱 mǎizhǔ 〈书面〉bribe somebody to enlist his service

买醉 mǎizuì buy liquor and drink one's fill (for pleasure or to drown sorrow)

荬(蕒) mǎi *see* "苣荬菜" qǔmaicài

mài

麦[1](麥) mài ❶ general term for wheat, barley, oats, rye, etc.: 大～ barley /小～ wheat /燕～ oats rye /荞～ Indian wheat /元～ highland barley (grown in Tibet and Qinghai) ❷ wheat ❸ (Mài) a surname

麦[2](麥) mài (short for 麦克斯韦)〈电学〉maxwell

麦草 màicǎo 〈方言〉wheat straw

麦茬 màichá 〈农业〉❶ wheat stubble ❷ land that has been sown to a new crop after the wheat harvest; crop grown or to be grown after the wheat harvest: ～白薯 sweet potatoes grown after the wheat harvest /～地 field sown to a new crop after the wheat harvest

麦当劳 Màidāngláo (trade name for 麦克唐纳公司) (US) McDonald's Corporation, a fast-food restaurant chain: 吃～ have a meal at McDonald's; have a hamburger snack

麦道公司 Màidào Gōngsī (short for 麦克唐纳－道格拉斯公司) (US) McDonnell-Douglass Corporation, now merged with Boeing under the name of Boeing-McDonnell-Douglass (波音－麦道)

麦迪逊 Màidíxùn James Madison (1751-1836), 4th President of the United States (1809-1817), who had a leading part in drawing up the US constitution (1787)

麦地霉素 màidìméisù 〈药学〉mydecamycin

麦地那 Màidìnà Medina, city in Saudi Arabia, which ranks after Mecca as a holy city

麦冬 màidōng 〈中药〉tuber of dwarf lilyturf (*Ophiopogon japonicus*)

麦蛾 mài'é gelechiid (moth): ～科 *Gelechiidae*

麦尔登呢 mài'ěrdēngní 〈纺织〉melton

麦粉 màifěn wheat flour

麦麸 màifū wheat bran

麦秆 màigǎn 〈农业〉wheat straw

麦秆虫 màigǎnchóng skeleton shrimp

麦秆画 màigǎnhuà straw patchwork

麦谷蛋白 màigǔ dànbái 〈生化〉glutenin

麦红吸浆虫 màihóngxījiāngchóng wheat midge

麦积山石窟 Màijīshān Shíkū Maijishan Grottoes, ancient grottoes in Gansu Province, whose construction started in the early 5th century and continued until the 17th century

麦季 màijì season for wheat harvest

麦加 Màijiā Mecca, No. 1 sacred Moslem city in Saudi Arabia known as the birthplace of Mohammed

麦角 màijiǎo 〈药学〉ergot: ～胺 ergotamine / ～精 ergotin /～酸 ergotic acid /～新碱 ergometrine /～甾醇 ergosterol /～中毒 ergotism

麦秸 màijiē wheat straw: ～画 straw patchwork

麦金利山 Màijīnlìshān Mount McKinley in Alaska, highest in North Amercia, named after William McKinley (1843-1901, 25th President of the United States, 1897-1901)

麦精 màijīng malt extract: ～鱼肝油 cod-liver oil with malt extract

麦酒 màijiǔ beer

麦卡锡 Màikǎxī Joseph Raymond McCarthy (1908-1957), US Senator: ～主义 McCarthyism (anti-Communist persecution led by J.R. McCarthy, prevalent in the United States in the decade following the Second World War)

麦糠 màikāng wheat bran

麦克阿瑟 Màikè'āsè Douglas MacArthur (1880-1964), American general who commanded allied forces in southwest Pacific during the Second World War and was commander of American troops in Japan and South Korea (1945-1951)

麦克风 màikèfēng microphone; mike: 她对着～，带着她独有的那种热情讲话。She spoke into the microphone with her characteristic fervour.

麦克马洪线 Màikèmǎhóngxiàn McMahon line, a line of demarcation drawn illegally by British colonialist Henry McMahon and the local representatives of China's Tibet in 1914, never recognized by any central government of China

麦克米伦 Màikèmǐlún Maurice Harold MacMillan (1894-1987), British conservative statesman and prime minister (1957-1963)

麦克斯韦 màikèsīwéi (simplified as 麦)〈电学〉maxwell (after British physicist James Clerk Maxwell, 1831-1879)

麦客 màikè 〈方言〉hand hired for harvesting wheat

麦口 màikǒu *also* "麦口期"; "麦口上"〈方言〉ripening stage of wheat

麦浪 màilàng field of billowing wheat: 一眼望不到头的～令人欣喜。It is gratifying to look at the fields of billowing wheat stretching to the horizon.

麦粒肿 màilìzhǒng 〈医学〉sty; hordeolum

麦芒 màimáng awn of wheat

麦门冬 màiméndōng *see* "麦冬"

麦苗 màimiáo 〈农业〉wheat seedling

麦纳麦 Màinàmài Manama, captial of Bahrain

麦片 màipiàn oatmeal: ～粥 oatmeal; oatmeal porridge

麦淇淋 màiqílín (transliteration) margarine

麦清蛋白 màiqīng dànbái 〈生化〉leucosin

麦秋 màiqiū season for harvesting wheat; wheat harvest season: ～假 wheat harvest vacation (for village schools)

麦乳精 màirǔjīng extract of malt and milk

麦收 màishōu wheat harvest

麦斯林纱 màisīlínshā 〈纺织〉muslin

麦穗 màisuì wheat head; ear of wheat

麦莛 màitíng wheat stalk

麦芽 màiyá malt: ～酶 maltose /～威士忌 malt whisky

麦芽醇 màiyáchún maltol

麦芽浆 màiyájiāng mash

麦芽糖 màiyátáng malt sugar; maltose

麦芽汁 màiyázhī wort

麦蚜 màiyá *also* "麦蚜虫"〈动物〉wheat aphid

麦鱼子 màiyúzi wheat chaff, ears, blighted grains, etc., left after threshing

麦哲伦 Màizhélún Ferdinand Magellan (1480-1521), Portuguese navigator

麦哲伦海峡 Màizhélún Hǎixiá Straits of Magellan, at the southern tip of South America, separating it from Tierra del Fuego island

麦哲伦云 màizhélúnyún Magellanic cloud

麦蜘蛛 màizhīzhū wheat mite

麦子 màizi wheat

唛 mài 〈方言〉(trade) mark
see also mà

唛头 màitóu 〈方言〉(trade) mark

卖(賣) mài ❶ sell: ～得快 sell like hot cakes /～不动 not sell well; be unsalable /～高价 sell at an exorbitant price /变～ sell off (one's property) /标～ sell at marked prices /倒～ profiteer; re-

sell at a profit / 义～ charity sale / 票～光了。Tickets are all sold out. ❷ betray; sell down the river:出～朋友 doublecross a friend / 他把自己良心都～了。He betrayed his own conscience. *or* He sold his soul to the devil. ❸ do one's utmost; spare or stint no effort: *see* "～命";"～力" ❹ show off; vaunt: ～巧 show off one's petty cleverness ❺〈量词〉dish (a term used in old-time restaurants):一～炒腰花 a dish of fried kidney

卖卜 màibǔ 〈旧语〉live as a fortune-teller:～为生 make a living as a fortune-teller

卖唱 màichàng sing for a living:沿街～ make a living by singing from door to door

卖春 màichūn prostitution

卖大号 mài dàhào *also* "卖大户" sell large quantities of goods in short supply to one person or unit at high prices; sell retail goods as wholesale; sell retail goods in large quantity

卖呆儿 màidāir 〈方言〉❶ (usu. of a woman) stand idly at the gate and gaze vacantly ❷ stare blankly; be in a trance ❸ watch the excitement; watch the fun

卖底 màidǐ 〈方言〉deliberately let out a secret

卖恩 mài'ēn do a favour with an ulterior motive

卖儿鬻女 mài'ér-yùnǚ (be forced to) sell one's children — consequence of dire straits

卖方 màifāng selling party (of a contract, etc.); seller: ～信贷 seller's credit

卖方市场 màifāng shìchǎng seller's market

卖风流 mài fēngliú play the coquette; flirt

卖富 màifù show off one's wealth; vaunt riches: ～斗阔 vie for wealth and extravagance / 吹牛～ boast about one's wealth / 先富裕起来的人万万不可～。Those who have got better-off earlier than others should never become ostentatious.

卖工夫 mài gōngfu 〈旧语〉work as a hired hand

卖功 màigōng brag about one's own merit: 在众人面前～ talk unashamedly in public about one's own contribution

卖狗皮膏药 mài gǒupí gāoyao sell quack remedies; fob sth. off on sb.:你这种～的话，我可听得够多的了。I am fed up with your self-advertising nonsense.

卖乖 màiguāi flaunt one's petty cleverness; pretend to behave graciously:得便宜～ pretend to behave graciously after obtaining some petty gains / 他总爱在人前～。He is prone to flaunt his petty cleverness in public.

卖关节 mài guānjié take bribes from sb. and do him a favour:他那场官司能打赢，据说是有人～。It is said he won the lawsuit by bribing someone.

卖关子 mài guānzi pause at a climax in storytelling to keep the listeners in suspense; keep people guessing; be deliberately mystifying:快往下说，别～了。Come on! Don't keep us guessing any longer. / 他故意～，不往下说。He deliberately stopped short in the middle of his story to keep us in suspense.

卖官鬻爵 màiguān-yùjué sell official posts and titles — a gross form of corruption

卖国 màiguó betray one's country; commit treason; become traitor to one's country: ～政策 traitorous policy / ～条约 traitorous treaty / ～行为 act of treason / ～政府 traitorous government

卖国求荣 màiguó-qiúróng betray one's country in pursuit of money and position; turn traitor for personal gain

卖国贼 màiguózéi traitor to one's country

卖好 màihǎo curry favour with; ingratiate oneself with:他挖空心思在经理面前～。He went out of his way to fawn on (*or* suck up to) the manager.

卖价 màijià selling price

卖交情 mài jiāoqing 〈方言〉do sb. a favour because he is a good friend

卖劲儿 màijìnr exert one's utmost; spare no effort:大伙儿干活可～了。Everyone is working like a horse.

卖空 màikōng sell short

卖老 màilǎo behave with exaggerated self-importance as a senior person; put on the airs of a senior:倚老～ flaunt one's seniority; put on the airs of a veteran; take advantage of one's seniority in age to ignore manners, regulations, etc. / 我那点技术很有限，不敢在你跟前～。I know far too little to parade my expertise before you. *or* I have no intention to parade my limited skill in your presence.

卖力 màilì do all one can; do one's best; spare no effort:大家卖卖力，天黑前把活干完。Beef up your effort to get the work finished before dark.

卖力气 mài lìqi ❶ exert one's utmost; spare no effort; do one's very best: 这是个要～的活儿。This work requires great physical strength. / 他干什么活儿都很～。He always works hard in whatever he does. ❷ live by the sweat of one's brow; make a living by doing manual labour:他的祖辈都靠～餬口。His ancestors lived by the sweat of their brow.

卖命 màimìng ❶ exert one's utmost: 悠着点，不要太～了。Don't overwork yourself; you've got to take things easy. ❷ work like a galley-slave:不要再为他～了。Don't slave for him any longer.

卖弄 màinong make a show of; show off; parade: ～小聪明 show off one's petty cleverness / ～才华 parade one's talent / ～风骚的女人 coquettish woman / 他不喜欢在人前～。He does not like to flaunt himself in public.

卖破绽 mài pòzhan 〈旧语〉feign an opening (as in a fight) to deceive the opponent (into doing sth. rash)

卖气力 mài qìlì 〈方言〉*see* "卖力气"

卖俏 màiqiào play the coquette; coquette; flirt:她那种～丑态，实在叫人恶心。I am disgusted with her flirtations.

卖青 màiqīng 〈旧语〉sell a standing crop before harvest at low prices

卖嚷嚷 mài rāngrang 〈方言〉make a good deal of noise; make an uproar: 就这点小事，他天天出来进去地～。 He complained loudly about this trivial matter every day wherever he was.

卖人情 mài rénqíng do sb. a favour

卖身 màishēn ❶ sell oneself or a member of one's family: ～契 indenture by which one sells oneself or a member of one's family / ～求荣 sell one's soul for material gains ❷〈口语〉sell one's body; be a prostitute

卖身投靠 màishēn-tóukào sell one's soul (to the devil); seek the patronage of influential people by serving them abjectly:他是一个～反动军阀的无耻文人。He was a shameless literary hack who threw himself prostrate under the feet of a reactionary warlord.

卖头卖脚 màitóu-màijiǎo 〈俗语〉be in the limelight; show off:在众人面前～的 make frequent public appearances

卖文 màiwén make a living by writing: ～所得 payment for one's article or book; author's remuneration / ～生涯 write for a living; make a living by the pen

卖相 màixiàng 〈方言〉❶ appearance; looks; exterior: 她～漂亮。She has good looks. *or* She looks pretty. / 这书橱～蛮好。This bookcase looks fine. ❷ demeanour; bearing; manner; style: ～十足 look very smart or stylish / 他大衣一穿还真有～。With the overcoat on, he does look smart.

卖笑 màixiào make a living as a prostitute or singing girl: ～生涯耗尽了她的青春。She spent her youth making a living as a singing girl.

卖解 màixiè 〈旧语〉make a living by performing acrobatic tricks: ～班子 acrobatic troupe / 跑马～ trick horse riding / 踩绳～ tight-rope dancing or walking

卖艺 màiyì be an acrobatic performer:他是街头～出身的。He started life as an acrobatic performer on the streets.

卖淫 màiyín prostitution:严禁赌博、～等社会公害。Gambling, prostitution and other social evils are strictly banned.

卖友 màiyǒu betray one's friend: ～投敌 betray one's comrades and defect to the enemy

卖主 màizhǔ seller

卖壮丁 mài zhuàngdīng 〈旧语〉sell oneself out as a conscript in another's name

卖嘴 màizuǐ show off one's ability or good nature by trying to talk cleverly:别～了，有本事练两下让我们开开眼。Don't go on chatting about your skill but do a few stunts to entertain us.

卖座 màizuò (of a theatre, cinema, etc.) draw large audiences; (of a movie, etc.) be a box-office success; (of a restaurant, club, etc.) attract many customers:这个电影不～。This film attracts only small audiences.

迈[1]（邁） mài walk; step; stride: *see* "～步";"～进"

迈[2]（邁） mài advanced in age; old: 年～ old; aged / 朽～〈书面〉old and weak; senile / 高～〈书面〉advanced in years

迈[3]**（邁）** mài (usu. used to indicate the speed of a vehicle, often confused in popular usage for 公里) mile:车速为一小时六十～。The car is driving at a speed of 60 miles per hour.
迈阿密 Mài'āmì Miami, a city and port on the east coast of Florida of the United States:～滩 Miami Beach
迈步 màibù take a step; step forward; make a step:向前～ make a step forward /迈开大步往前走 march forward with big strides /迈出了可喜的一步 make a significant step forward; make gratifying progress / 迈出了决定性的一步 make a decisive move; take a decisive step
迈步式挖煤机 màibùshì wāméijī 〈矿业〉 walking excavator
迈方步 mài fāngbù *also* "迈四方步" stage-walk in Chinese traditional opera; walk slowly and steadily:他迈着方步在那里沉思。Deep in thought, he moved around in slow and measured steps. /快走，别～了! Hurry up! Don't walk in such a leisurely manner.
迈进 màijìn forge ahead; make rapid headway; advance with big strides; stride forward:向前～ advance forward with big strides /向更高的目标～ strive to scale new heights

劢（勱） mài 〈书面〉 make an effort; exert oneself

脉（脈、衇） mài ❶〈生理〉 arteries and veins:动～ artery / 大动～ main artery; aorta /主动～ aorta /肺动～ pulmonary artery /尺动～ ulnar artery /静～ vein /大静～ vena cava /肺静～ pulmonary vein /门静～ portal vein ❷ (short for 脉搏) pulse:号～ feel sb.'s pulse /按～ take sb.'s pulse /病～ abnormal pulse /沉～ deep pulse (which can be felt only by pressing hard) /洪～ full pulse; pulse beating like waves /涩～ weak, thready, uneven pulse /波状～ undulating pulse /促～ quick pulse; short pulse; abrupt pulse /稀～ infrequent pulse /弦～ wiry pulse ❸ vein (of leaves or insects' wings):翅～ vein (of the wings of an insect) /叶～ vein (in a leaf) /网状～ netted veins; reticulate veins ❹ range; row; line:山～ mountain range; mountain chain /矿～ mineral ore; mineral vein; lode /支～ offshoot (*or* spur) (of a mountain range) /命～ lifeline; lifeblood /地～ layout of strata in the land; geographical position
see also mò
脉案 mài'àn 〈中医〉 diagnosis (usu. written on the prescription)
脉搏 màibó *also* "脉息" pulse; 〈生理〉 sphygmus:量～ count one's pulse /～波图〈医学〉 sphygmogram /～消失〈医学〉 asthyxia /思想的～ pulse of one's thought /感情的～ ups and downs of one's emotion /～每分钟六十五次。Pulse is 65 per minute.
脉搏计 màibójì 〈医学〉 sphygmometer
脉冲 màichōng 〈物理〉 pulse; impulse:～功率 impulse power /～技术 pulse technique /～讯号 pulsing signal /～传输 impulse transmission /～电流 impulse current
脉冲变压器 màichōng biànyāqì pulse transformer
脉冲传感器 màichōng chuángǎnqì impulser
脉冲电码 màichōng diànmǎ pulse code
脉冲发射器 màichōng fāshèqì impulse sender
脉冲发生器 màichōng fāshēngqì pulser
脉冲计 màichōngjì pulsimeter
脉冲计量 màichōng jìliàng pulse measurement
脉冲计时 màichōng jìshí pulse timing
脉冲计数 màichōng jìshù step-by-step counting
脉冲雷达 màichōng léidá pulse radar
脉冲马达 màichōng mǎdá impulse motor
脉冲式喷气发动机 màichōngshì pēnqì fādòngjī 〈航空〉 aeropulse engine; pulse-jet engine
脉冲塔 màichōngtǎ 〈化工〉 pulse-column
脉冲星 màichōngxīng 〈天文〉 pulsar
脉冲周期 màichōng zhōuqī impulse period; recurrence interval
脉动 màidòng 〈物理〉〈天文〉 pulsation; pulse ripple:～频率 ripple frequency /～焊接 pulsating welding
脉动波 màidòngbō pulsating wave
脉动电流 màidòng diànliú pulsating current
脉动力 màidònglì pulsating force
脉动能 màidòngnéng pulsating energy
脉动器 màidòngqì 〈农业〉 pulsator
脉动式燃气轮机 màidòngshì ránqì lúnjī 〈机械〉 pulsating flow gas-turbine
脉动星 màidòngxīng 〈天文〉 pulsating star
脉动周期 màidòng zhōuqī pulsation cycle
脉峰 màifēng 〈物理〉 pulse peak
脉幅调制调频 màifú tiáozhì tiáopín pulse-amplitude modulation frequency modulation
脉管炎 màiguǎnyán 〈医学〉 vasculitis; angiitis
脉金 màijīn ❶ *also* "脉钱" 〈中医〉 consultation fee ❷ *also* "山金" grain of gold in quartzite
脉口 màikǒu 〈中医〉 location on the wrist for feeling the pulse
脉礼 màilǐ *see* "脉金❶"
脉理 màilǐ ❶〈书面〉 run; alignment; coherence or sequence (of ideas):山川～ run of mountains and rivers ❷〈中医〉 principles of traditional Chinese medicine:精通～ be expert in traditional Chinese medicine
脉络 màiluò ❶〈中医〉 general term for arteries and veins ❷ vein (of a leaf, etc.) ❸ thread of thought; sequence of ideas:～清楚 ideas presented in a clear and logical way; clear line of thought
脉络膜 màiluòmó 〈医学〉 choroid:～炎 choroiditis /～视网膜炎 choroidoretinitis /～病 choroidopathy
脉络球 màiluòqiú 〈生理〉 glomus
脉码调制 màimǎ tiáozhì pulse-code modulation (PCM)
脉门 màimén location on the wrist where the throbbing of the pulse is visible
脉石 màishí 〈矿业〉 gangue; veinstone:～矿物 gangue mineral
脉窝 màiwō 〈方言〉 ❶ *see* "脉口" ❷ *also* "脉窝子" 〈比喻〉 key; crux:抓住工作的～ grasp the key link of the work
脉息 màixī pulse:～微弱 weak pulse
脉象 màixiàng 〈中医〉 pulse condition; type of pulse
脉压 màiyā pulse pressure
脉泽 màizé *also* "脉塞" 〈物理〉 maser (microwave amplification by stimulated emission or radiation):～振荡器 maser oscillator
脉诊 màizhěn 〈中医〉 diagnosis by feeling the pulse
脉枕 màizhěn 〈中医〉 wrist-cushion (used when the doctor feels the patient's pulse)

霡（霢） mài
霡霂 màimù 〈书面〉 drizzle

mān

颟（顢） mān
颟顸 mānhan muddle-headed; scatterbrained:那人太～，什么事都做不了。The chap is so muddle-headed that he is capable of nothing (*or* he is good for nothing).

嫚 mān 〈方言〉 *also* "嫚子" girl
see also màn

mán

蛮（蠻） mán ❶ savage; fierce; unreasonable; boorish:野～ savage; barbarous; cruel /横～ arrogant and unreasonable ❷ reckless; rash; brute: *see* "～干"; "～劲" ❸ ancient derogatory name for China's southern nationalities ❹〈方言〉 jolly; pretty:～好 jolly good /～有趣 pretty interesting
蛮不讲理 mánbùjiǎnglǐ not amenable to reason; unreasonable; perverse:这个人常干些～的事。He is often intractably unreasonable (*or* pig-headed) in whatever he does.
蛮缠 mánchán nag sb. with unreasonable demands; pester sb. endlessly:胡搅～ harass sb. by making unreasonable demands
蛮干 mángàn act rashly or recklessly; be headstrong; be foolhardy:这个人一味～。The man has been acting rashly (*or* tactlessly) all the time. /他只会～一通。He has only foolhardiness to his credit.
蛮悍 mánhàn savage and fierce; reckless and ferocious
蛮横 mánhèng rude and unreasonable; arbitrary; peremptory:～无理的要求 peremptory demand /～地干涉别国内政 wilfully interfere in another country's internal affairs /态度～ truculent and unreasonable /举止～ behave rudely
蛮荒 mánhuāng ❶ barbarous and remote:～时代 barbarous age of

remote antiquity ❷〈书面〉out-of-the-way and culturally backward place：历险阻，入～ experience formidable hardship and danger and go deep into the barbarous wilderness

蛮劲 mánjìn sheer animal strength；mere brute force

蛮性 mánxìng savage nature；truculent character；rude behaviour：～不改 one's savage nature remains unchanged

蛮子 mánzi〈旧语〉barbarian（contemptuous term that northerners applied to southerners who spoke with a different accent）：南～ barbarian from the south

瞒（瞞） mán hide the truth from；cover up；conceal：隐～ conceal；cover up／欺～ dupe；kid；hoodwink／不～你说 to tell you the truth；to be quite frank／想～是～不住的。It's difficult to keep the matter secret．／什么事能～得过他？You can not keep anything from him，can you?

瞒报 mánbào fail to report the true state of affairs；conceal facts from the relevant authorities：为了偷税而～营业额 conceal the volume of business to evade taxation

瞒产私分 mánchǎn-sīfēn （as of peasants in the days of the people's communes）share out in private the portion of harvests concealed

瞒哄 mánhǒng deceive；hoodwink：这件事你骗得了我，可～不了大家。You could fool me on this matter，but you can't possibly hoodwink everybody.

瞒上不瞒下 mán shàng bù mán xià 〈俗语〉keep those above in ignorance but not those below；work in collusion to deceive those above

瞒上欺下 mánshàng-qīxià deceive those above and browbeat those below：我们要对上级和群众负责，千万不可～。We are responsible to the higher organization and the public，and should never keep our superiors in the dark and ride roughshod over the people below.

瞒天大谎 mántiān-dàhuǎng monstrous lie；outrageous lie：他扯了个～，说家里要他马上回去。He lied brazenly that his family wanted him to go back right away.

瞒天过海 mántiān-guòhǎi cross the sea by keeping heaven in ignorance — practise colossal deception：众目睽睽之下，想～是做不到的。Nobody could practise such huge deception in the public eye.

瞒天昧地 mántiān-mèidì keep heaven and earth in the dark — sheer fraudulence；utter deception：～的勾当 gigantic deceit

瞒心昧己 mánxīn-mèijǐ act against one's conscience；delude oneself：千万千不得这种～的事。You must never act against your own conscience（*or* in self-delusion）.

埋 mán

see also mái

埋三怨四 mánsān-yuànsì 〈方言〉grumble about everything：他总是～，叨叨个没完。He is always grumbling about something.

埋怨 mányuàn complain；blame；grouse；grumble：有～情绪 be resentful／不要相互～。Don't try to shift the blame on to each other．*or* Stop blaming each other．／她～等的时间太长了。She complained she had been kept waiting too long.

谩 mán cheat；deceive；hoodwink：～语 deceitful words／～天～地 try to deceive everybody

see also màn

蔓 mán

see also màn；wàn

蔓菁 mánjing *also*“芜菁”wújīng〈植物〉turnip

鬘 mán 〈书面〉(of hair) beautiful

鳗 mán eel：～鱼苗 eel fry／电～ electric eel／盲～ hagfish／鳃～ lamprey／河～ river eel

鳗草 háncǎo eelgrass

鳗鲡 mánlí eel

馒 mán

馒首 mánshǒu〈方言〉steamed bun

馒头 mántou steamed bun or bread

馒头柳 mántouliǔ a variety of *Salix matsudana*

鞔 mán ❶ fasten skin onto a drum：～鼓 fasten a piece of skin on a drum ❷ fix the vamp on a shoe last：～鞋 shoe making

mǎn

满¹（滿） mǎn ❶ full；filled；brimful；packed：客～ full house／～屋的人 room packed with people；crowded room／粮食～仓。The granary is bursting with grain．／他给自己倒了一～杯茶。He poured himself a full cup of tea．／～地是绿油油的庄稼。Stretching all around was a vast expanse of green crops. ❷ fill；replenish：～上一杯吧！Let me fill your glass. ❸ expire；complete；reach a deadline，quota，or limit：修业期～ have completed one's term of study／年～十八 reach the age of 18／试用期已～。The probation is over．／条约有效期未～。The validity of the agreement has not yet expired．／他参加工作还不～两年。It's not yet two years since he took on the job. ❹ fully；completely；entirely；very：～高兴 very pleased；quite happy／年过得～不错。We had a very enjoyable Spring Festival．／～不是那么回事。That's not at all true．*or* That's a completely different story．／我～以为他可以考上。I took it for granted that he would pass the entrance exam．／访问圆～成功。This visit was crowned with（complete）success. ❺ satisfied；gratified；contented：不～ dissatisfied；discontented／心怀不～ nurse a grievance；feel discontented；be hostile／心～意足 be perfectly satisfied；be in perfect contentment ❻ proud；complacent；smug；conceited：自～ conceited；self-satisfied／自～到了令人不可容忍的地步 unbearably smug

满²（滿） Mǎn ❶ Man or Manchu nationality ❷ a surname

满不在乎 mǎnbùzàihu not worry at all；not care a damn；be insouciant about；be completely indifferent：～的样子 air of insouciance／这人不修边幅，～。He was entirely indifferent to his personal appearance．／"那有什么关系！"他～地说。"What does that matter?" he said casually．／民警指出他骑车违章，他却一副～的样子。The policeman told the cyclist that he had violated the traffic regulations，but the chap didn't seem to care in the least．／他心里挺着急，但脸上依然保持着～的样子。He was very worried，but he looked as if he couldn't care less．／她故意露出～的微笑，点着头。Deliberately assuming a nonchalant smile，she nodded.

满城风雨 mǎnchéng-fēngyǔ send rumours flying all over（the town）；be the talk of the town；cause a great sensation；cause a furore：这件事已闹得～了。This has become the talk of the town．*or* The scandal has caused quite a furore．／警察到处搜寻他，弄得～。The police were searching for him high and low，creating a great commotion throughout the city.

满城桃李 mǎnchéng-táolǐ have disciples everywhere

满打 mǎndǎ〈方言〉even if；even though：～你浑身是铁，也架不住昼夜劳神。You couldn't stand the fatigue of working day and night even if you were a man of steel.

满打满算 mǎndǎ-mǎnsuàn counting in every item；taking everything into account；at the utmost：这个项目～有五百万投资足够了。Taking everything into account，the project requires an investment of five million *yuan*．／这部小说～再有五天就可译完。It will take five more days at most to finish translating the novel.

满当当 mǎndāngdāng full；packed：会议室里坐得～的。The conference room is packed with people.

满登登 mǎndēngdēng full；packed：～一车货 full truckload of goods／这粮食袋子装得～的。The sack is bulging with grain.

满点 mǎndiǎn reach working hours：出满勤，干～ guarantee full attendance and full working hours／～营业是一种商业规范。Adherence to full working hours is general commercial practice.

满额 mǎn'é fulfil the quota：去年招生未～。Last year's quota for enrolment was not fulfilled.

满分 mǎnfēn full marks；full credit：她考试得了～。She passed the exam with full marks.

满服 mǎnfú〈旧语〉have fully observed the period of mourning for a deceased person of the elder generation；reach the end of the mourning period for a deceased elder

满负荷工作法 mǎnfùhè gōngzuòfǎ full-load working system

满腹 mǎnfù have one's mind filled with；be full of：～牢骚 nurse

M

grievances; be full of complaints /～心事 be eaten up with anxiety; be extremely worried /～文章 be talented and versed in writing
满腹狐疑 mǎnfù-húyí also "满腹疑团" be filled with misgivings; feel extremely suspicious
满腹经纶 mǎnfù-jīnglún full of learning and wisdom: 他～，有问必答。Being a man of great learning and wisdom, he has a ready answer for every question.
满腹珠玑 mǎnfù-zhūjī of great talent
满共 mǎngòng 〈方言〉 in all; all told; altogether: 三个班级～是九十八个学生。Altogether there are 98 students in the three classes. *or* The three classes have 98 students all told.
满贯 mǎnguàn ❶ reach the limit ❷ (in mah-jong, card games, etc.) perfect score; slam: 小～ little slam / 大～ grand slam
满怀 mǎnhuái ❶ be filled with; be imbued with: ～信心 be full of confidence; be fully confident /豪情～ be inspired by a sense of pride /～壮志 be imbued with lofty ideals ❷ bosom: 跟他撞了个～ (literally) bump into him ❸ (of sheep, cattle, etc.) bear a full litter of young; be all pregnant
满江红 mǎnjiānghóng also "红萍" hóngpíng; "紫藻" zǐzǎo 〈植物〉 *Azolla imbricata*; *Azolla japonica*
满浆穗 mǎnjiāngsuì laden earhead; full grain
满坑满谷 mǎnkēng-mǎngǔ to be seen everywhere; in profusion; in abundance; in plenty: 屋里的书～的。The room is stacked with books.
满口 mǎnkǒu ❶ whole of one's mouth: ～假牙 whole set of artificial teeth ❷ (of accent) pure; standard; (of speech) completely; glibly: ～北京话 speak with standard Beijing dialect /～乡音 talk with a heavy native accent /～谎言 say sth. tongue in cheek; tell barefaced lies /～之乎者也 talk like a village pedant (*or* like a book) /～胡言乱语 talk nonsense (*or* rubbish); rave /～仁义道德〈贬义〉 talk glibly about virtue; mouth sanctimonious platitudes ❸ unreservedly; profusely: ～答应 readily agree
满口胡柴 mǎnkǒu-húchái talk nonsense; rave: ～，谁信你说的! You are talking nonsense and nobody will believe you.
满礼 mǎnlǐ also "满理"〈方言〉 very reasonable; in the right: ～的事情，还怕什么! We have nothing to fear, for we are in the right. /～也要让人。You'll have to be accommodating even if you have a strong case.
满脸 mǎnliǎn one's whole face: ～皱纹 have wrinkles all over one's face /～笑容 grin from ear to ear; be all smiles /～雀斑 have a freckled face /～晦气 look depressed (*or* glum) /～横肉 cross-grained features; ugly ferocious features /她羞得～通红。She flushed with embarrassment.
满脸花 mǎnliǎnhuā (get) a swollen face and a bleeding nose (as the result of a fall or a fist fight): 他被打得～。He was beaten black and blue.
满满当当 mǎnman-dāngdāng also "满满堂堂" full to the brim; packed: ～的一卡车蔬菜 full truckload of vegetables /会议大厅里挤得～的。The assembly hall was filled to capacity. /仓库装得～。The warehouse is stacked full.
满满登登 mǎnman-dēngdēng full; filled: 他的日程排得～。He has a full schedule.
满满实实 mǎnman-shíshí full to the brim: 箩筐里的花生装得～的。The basket was packed with peanuts.
满满堂堂 mǎnman-tángtáng see "满满当当"
满门 mǎnmén whole family: ～抄斩 (punishment in feudal China) search out and execute the entire family; confiscate sb.'s property and execute every member of his family /春满乾坤福～。As spring pervades the earth, luck comes to the family.
满面 mǎnmiàn one's whole face: ～泪痕 one's face covered with traces of tears /愁容～ look deeply worried /红光～ glow with health /泪流～ tears streaming down one's cheeks
满面春风 mǎnmiàn-chūnfēng be radiant with joy; be radiant with pleasure; beam with happiness: 他～地走进门来。He came in, wearing a broad smile.
满目 mǎnmù come into view; meet the eye on every side: 琳琅～ superb array of beautiful things; feast for the eyes /～凄凉。There is a scene of desolation all around (as far as the eye can see). /～青山，一派生机。Before our eyes is a range of green mountains full of life and vitality.
满目疮痍 mǎnmù-chuāngyí also "疮痍满目" a spectacle of devastation meets the eye on every side; see ruins everywhere
满脑子 mǎnnǎozi one's whole mind: ～的偏见 be steeped in prejudice /～糊涂思想 be shot through with muddle-headed ideas
满拧 mǎnnǐng 〈方言〉 entirely contrary; diametrically opposite: 你说的和我想的～。What you said is the very opposite of what I thought.
满七 mǎnqī 49 days (7×7 days) after the passing away of a person
满期 mǎnqī expire; come to an end; run out: 合同还有两个月～。The contract expires in two months. /协议～后将自动延长一年。The agreement shall be extended automatically for another year upon its expiration.
满腔 mǎnqiāng (with one's heart) filled with; full of: ～热情 full of enthusiasm; warm-heartedly /～怒火 be filled with indignation; boil with rage /～悲愤 be filled with grief and indignation /青年们～热情沸腾了。The young people are burning with great zeal.
满腔热忱 mǎnqiāng-rèchén be filled with ardour and zest; be full of enthusiasm
满勤 mǎnqín have full attendance; attend regularly: 出～ turn out in full force for work /出～纪录 full attendance record /他每月都是～。He attends regularly every month.
满人 Mǎnrén Manchu
满山遍野 mǎnshān-biànyě also "漫山遍野" mànshān-biànyě all over the mountains and plains; numerous: 这里～都是果树。There are fruit trees all over the hills. /我多么想去看看那～的万树红花呀! How I wish to see the endless stretch of trees in full flower on the slopes and in the fields!
满山红 mǎnshānhóng 〈植物〉 a variety of *Rhododendron*
满身 mǎnshēn all over one's body; from head to toe; covered with: ～泥土 splashed all over with mud stains; covered with mud /～是汗 be soaked with sweat
满师 mǎnshī (of an apprentice) complete one's term of service; serve out one's apprenticeship: 学徒一般三年～。It usually takes an apprentice three years to complete his term of service. *or* An apprenticeship usually takes three years.
满世界 mǎnshìjie 〈方言〉 everywhere: 你这孩子在家干点什么不好，～瞎跑什么? Why run around everywhere, you naughty boy! Can't you find something useful to do at home?
满堂 mǎntáng ❶ whole house; entire audience; all those present: 博得～笑声 make the audience roar with laughter ❷ 〈方言〉 be all booked up; have a full house: 这个剧场天天～。The theatre is full every day. ❸ (of a house, room, etc.) filled; packed: 宾朋～ have a great gathering of guests and friends in one's house
满堂彩 mǎntángcǎi (of performance) bring the house down; win universal applause: 他唱头一句就得了个～。He brought the house down by singing the very first line. /她的歌声赢得了～。Her excellent singing won deafening applause.
满堂灌 mǎntángguàn full-class instillation; saturation lecturing — cramming or force-feeding the students
满堂红 mǎntánghóng ❶ success in every field; all-round victory: 企业全面完成了全年的指标，实现了～。The enterprise achieved complete success in fulfilling the annual targets. /这个厂的生产搞得～。The factory is thriving in every branch of production. ❷ also "紫薇" zǐwēi 〈植物〉 crape myrtle (*Lagerstroemia indica*)
满天 mǎntiān all over the sky: ～星斗 star-lit sky; sky studded with stars /～乌云 sky covered with dark clouds; overcast sky /雪花～飞。Snow flakes are dancing all around.
满天飞 mǎntiānfēi 〈比喻〉 go everywhere; be found everywhere: 钦差大臣～。Imperial envoys are sent everywhere. /他这人～，让我到哪儿去找? The chap is running about all day. Where can I find him?
满天星 mǎntiānxīng 〈植物〉 baby's breath (*Gypsophila*)
满-通古斯语族 Mǎn-Tōnggǔsī yǔzú 〈语言〉 Manchu-Tungusic group
满头 mǎntóu all over the head: ～大汗 sweat dripping from the head /～银发 grey-headed; hoary-headed; silver-haired
满徒 mǎntú see "满师"
满孝 mǎnxiào 〈旧语〉 complete the prescribed period of mourning for a deceased elder
满心 mǎnxīn feel from the bottom of one's heart; genuinely feel: ～欢喜 be genuinely overjoyed or elated; be filled with real joy
满眼 mǎnyǎn ❶ fill one's eyes: ～泪花 one's eyes filled with tears /～倦意 look visibly tired; feel sleepy ❷ come into view: ～繁华 picture of prosperity /山谷里～桃花。Peach blossoms came into full view in

the valley.

满意 mǎnyì satisfied; gratified; contented; pleased: 大家对他的做法很～。We are all pleased with the way he handled the matter. /老师～地点点头。The teacher smiled approvingly. /她露出～的微笑。She gave a gratified smile. /双方对会谈结果表示～。Both sides expressed satisfaction with the results of the talks.

满应满许 mǎnyīng-mǎnxǔ promise everything; promise readily: 他～，恐怕靠不住。He promised too readily to sound sincere.

满语 Mǎnyǔ Manchu (language); language used by China's Manchu nationality

满员 mǎnyuán ❶ full staffed; at full strength: 我们的编制已经～。We are already fully staffed. /部队经常保持～。The armed forces are always maintained at full strength. ❷ fully booked up: 列车已经～。The passenger coaches of the train are all booked up.

满园春色 mǎnyuán-chūnsè *also* "春色满园" the garden is permeated with the air of spring — a picture of growing prosperity

满月 mǎnyuè ❶ full moon: 一轮～像玉盘一样嵌在蓝色天幕里。The full moon is like a jade disc set in the blue sky. ❷ one full month after birth: 小家伙今天～。The baby is exactly one month old today.

满载 mǎnzài ❶ loaded to capacity; fully loaded: ～试验 full-load test /～吃水线 full-load waterline; deep waterline /这列货车已经～。This cargo train is already loaded to capacity. /卡车～着救济物资前往灾区。Trucks fully loaded with relief supplies were heading for disaster-stricken areas. /～着各国人民的友好情谊回到北京。They returned to Beijing bringing back the good will of the people of different countries. ❷ full load (FL): ～超轴〈交通〉full load and over haulage

满载而归 mǎnzài'érguī come back very much enlightened; have a rewarding experience: 这次实习收获很大，人人～。All the trainees benefited greatly from this fieldwork, each achieving in his own way the best possible results.

满招损,谦受益 mǎn zhāo sǔn, qiān shòu yì one loses by complacency and gains by modesty; complacency spells loss, while modesty brings benefit: 牢记"～"的古训。For ever keep in mind the time-honoured dictum that "pride goes before a fall".

满洲 Mǎnzhōu ❶ old name for the Manchu nationality ❷〈旧语〉Manchuria — northeastern China

满洲国 Mǎnzhōuguó Manchukuo (a puppet regime created in China's northeastern provinces by the Japanese imperialists, 1931-1945)

满足 mǎnzú ❶ satisfied; gratified; contented: ～现状 be content with things as they are (*or* the status quo) /～于已有的成就 rest on one's laurels / 刚成功就感到～了 feel contented in the first flush of success /脸上露出～的神情 wear a complacent look on one's face ❷ meet; satisfy; gratify: ～市场需要 meet the market demand /～群众的愿望 live up to the expectations of the public /～心愿 fulfil one's wish; gratify sb.'s wish /无法～付款条件 cannot comply with the terms of payment /你永远也～不了他贪得无厌的欲望。You can never satisfy (*or* gratify) his insatiable desire.

满族 Mǎnzú Man or Manchu nationality, mainly distributed over the provinces of Liaoning, Heilongjiang, Jilin, and Hebei, the municipality of Beijing, and Inner Mongolia

满嘴 mǎnzuǐ one's entire mouth: ～起疱 one's lips are infected all over with boils /～喷粪〈粗话〉talk nonsense; shit

满座 mǎnzuò all booked up; attended by capacity audiences: 演出场场～。The show was fully booked up (*or* was attended by capacity audiences) at every performance.

螨(蟎) mǎn

〈动物〉mite; acarid: 杀～剂 acaricide; miticide

螨病 mǎnbìng 〈医学〉acariasis

螨感染 mǎngǎnrǎn mite infestation

螨性皮炎 mǎnxìng píyán 〈医学〉acarodermatitis

màn

曼 màn

❶ gracefully; gently; exquisitely: 轻歌～舞 sing softly and dance gracefully ❷ prolonged; long-drawn-out

曼彻斯特 Mànchèsītè Manchester, an industrial city in northwest England

曼辞 màncí 〈书面〉ornate language; fine-sounding words (intended to gloss over the unpleasant truth): ～自饰 praise oneself in glowing germs

曼德琳 màndélín 〈乐器〉(transliteration) mandolin

曼丁哥人 Màndīnggērén Mandingo (of West Africa)

曼丁哥语 Màndīnggēyǔ Mande; Mandingo (language)

曼多林琴 mànduōlínqín *see* "曼德琳"

曼谷 Màngǔ Bangkok, capital of Thailand

曼哈顿 Mànhādùn Manhattan, island at the mouth of the Hudson River and now a borough containing the commercial and cultural centre of New York city

曼靡 mànmǐ 〈书面〉(of voice) prolonged and soft: ～之声 prolonged soft voice

曼妙 mànmiào 〈书面〉(of dancing) lithe and graceful: ～的舞姿 graceful dancing

曼声 mànshēng (of singing or recitation) prolonged or lengthened sounds: ～低语 speak in a low continuous voice; speak softly and unhurriedly /～吟诵 recite rhythmically and unhurriedly

曼荼罗 màntúluó *also* "坛场" tánchǎng 〈宗教〉mandala

曼陀铃 màntuólíng *see* "曼德琳"

曼陀罗 màntuóluó 〈植物〉datura; jimsonweed; *datura stramonium*

曼延 mànyán stretch; draw out (in length); lengthen: ～曲折的小道 meandering footpath

漫 màn

❶ overflow; run over; brim over; flood; inundate: 河水～出来了。The river overflowed its banks. /风暴来时,江水～过农田,毁了庄稼。With the raging wind storm, the river inundated the farmland destroying all the crops. /溪水只～过膝盖。The stream is only knee-deep. ❷ all over the place; in all places; everywhere: 弥～ spread all over the place; permeate /～山果树。There are fruit trees all over the mountain. ❸ broad; extensive; long: 长夜～～ very long night ❹ without restraint or purpose; casual; random: ～无目的 aimless /～无标准 without standard or principle to go by /～无限制 without any restriction /散～ careless and sloppy; undisciplined ❺ no; not: *see* "～道"; "～说"

漫笔 mànbǐ random thoughts or notes; literary notes; sketch: 灯下～ sketches by lamplight /书林～ rambling notes on books

漫不经心 mànbùjīngxīn careless; totally unconcerned; absent-minded: ～的样子 offhand (*or* casual) manner /他对事总有些～，真叫人担心。He tends to be absent-minded in what he does, and that is what is worrying us.

漫步 mànbù stroll; saunter; ramble; roam: 在乡村小道上～ take a stroll along a country footpath /～江边，欣赏夜景。I strolled on the riverside, enjoying the wonderful views at night.

漫长 màncháng very long; prolonged; protracted: ～的岁月 prolonged period of time /～的海岸 extended coastline /～而痛苦的日子 long-drawn-out days of gruelling misery /～的演化过程 protracted process of evolution /～而曲折的道路 long and tortuous course

漫道 màndào let alone; to say nothing of: 有经验的人都干不了这工作，～新手了。Even the experienced ones cannot cope with the job, let alone the greenhorns.

漫反射 mànfǎnshè 〈物理〉diffuse reflection: ～率 diffuse reflection factor /～体 diffuse reflector /～系数 diffuse reflectance

漫灌 mànguàn ❶ flood irrigation ❷ be flooded: 大片棉花地被洪水～。Large tracts of cotton fields were flooded.

漫瀚调 mànhàndiào popular folk song in western Inner Mongolia

漫画 mànhuà caricature; cartoon: ～大师 master of caricature /政治～ political cartoon /～家 cartoonist

漫话 mànhuà informal talk; rambling talk: ～家常 engage in small talk (*or* chitchat)

漫漶 mànhuàn (of script or painting) become blurred or indistinct: 字迹～。The handwriting is blurred.

漫卷 mànjuǎn (of banners or flags) flutter: 红旗～西风。Red banners fluttered in the west wind.

漫流 mànliú ❶ rainwater flowing in small streams; run-off (in patches of streams) ❷ overflow; brim over: 沿湖筑堤，不让湖水～。A dyke has been built round the lake to prevent it from brimming over.

漫骂 mànmà fling abuses; hurl invectives; rail: 一篇充满～的发言 speech filled with personal abuse /肆意～某人 rail at sb.

漫漫 mànmàn very long; without end; endless: 黄沙～ huge clouds of dust /春水～ (of a river) overflowing with spring tide /路～。The

road is without end.

漫灭 mànmiè (of written words, drawings, etc.) be obliterated little by little; be worn away; become blurred:碑上字迹～。The inscription on the tablet has become blurred beyond recognition.

漫坡 mànpō gentle slope

漫儿 mànr side of a copper coin without words on it

漫然 mànrán at random; casually; unconcernedly:他～应了一句。He replied with obvious unconcern.

漫散 mànsàn disperse; scatter:天边黑云正向四处～。Dark clouds are drifting in all directions.

漫山遍野 mànshān-biànyě all over the mountains and plains; all across the countryside; over hill and dale:这一带～都是茶树。Tea bushes are planted here, over the hills and dales.

漫射 mànshè 〈物理〉diffusion:～光 diffused light /～线 diffused rays /～照明 diffuse illumination /～体 diffuser

漫说 mànshuō see "慢说" mànshuō

漫滩 màntān flood land

漫滩沼泽 màntān zhǎozé backswamp

漫谈 màntán informal discussion; random talk:我们一边散步,一边～。While we were taking a walk, we talked about almost anything under the sun. /大家～一下实习体会。Let's have an exchange of views about our fieldwork experience.

漫天 màntiān ❶ all over the sky; whole sky:～风雪。There is strong wind and drifting snow across the sky. /梅花欢喜～雪。Plum blossoms welcome the whirling snow. /风一吹,柳絮～盖地。A gust of wind set the catkins flying in the air, blurring our view. ❷ sky-high; boundless; limitless:他撒了个～大谎。He told an outrageous lie.

漫天要价 màntiān-yàojià ask a sky-high or exorbitant price:～,就地还钱。The seller can ask a maximum price; the buyer can make a minimum offer.

漫无边际 mànwúbiānjì ❶ boundless; without limit:～的大草原 boundless grassland ❷ disconnected; rambling; discursive:他～地谈了两个小时,不知要说明什么。He kept talking at random for two hours, and no one knows what he was driving at. /他们～地谈些趣闻轶事。They were talking among themselves, going from one amusing anecdote to another.

漫无止境 mànwúzhǐjìng know no bounds; be without limit:科学的探索是～的。There is no limit to the exploration of science.

漫延 mànyán stretch; extend:沙漠一直～到遥远的天边。The desert extends (*or* stretches) to the distant horizon.

漫野 mànyě extend all over the fields:～的青纱帐 green curtain of tall crops in the fields

漫溢 mànyì flow over; overflow; flood; brim over:洪流～。The mighty torrent is brimming over.

漫游 mànyóu ❶ go on a pleasure trip; ramble; roam; wander:～田野 roam across the fields /～北京城 have a sightseeing trip around Beijing /～长江三峡 have a boat cruise through the Three Gorges of the Yangtze River ❷ 〈通信〉roaming:～因特网 roam the Internet

漫语 mànyǔ ❶ random remarks; casual comments ❷ informal talk (often used in titles of books, articles, etc.):《青春～》*Remarks on Youth*

慢[1]

màn ❶ slow; sluggish; tardy:反应太～ be too slow in response; respond too slowly /～得令人发急 irritatingly slow /这钟～了三分钟。The clock is three minutes slow. /路很滑,最好～一点。As the road is slippery, you'd better slow down. /我的表每天～三秒。My watch loses three seconds a day. /她会～～把他忘掉的。She will forget him by and by. ❷ take one's time; postpone; defer:且～! Hold on a moment. *or* Just a moment. /别急,这事～两天再说。There is no hurry and we may put the matter off for a couple of days. ❸ no; not: see "～道";"～说"

慢[2]

màn cold and indifferent; supercilious; rude:傲～ arrogant; haughty; overbearing /简～ give sb. short shrift

慢班 mànbān slow class — class composed of slower students

慢步 mànbù (of equestrianism) walk; (of a dancer or pedestrian) slow pace or speed

慢藏海盗 màncáng-huìdào to expose valuables to the public eye is to invite robbery:～,冶容诲淫。To be careless of one's jewels is to invite theft; to dress provocatively is to court sexual assault.

慢超新星 mànchāoxīnxīng 〈天文〉slow supernova

慢车 mànchē slow train

慢车道 mànchēdào slow (traffic) lane; inside lane

慢词 màncí (in classical *ci* poetry) long poem of slow rhythm

慢辞 màncí 〈书面〉disparaging remarks; abusive language:满口～ full of abusive language; foul-mouthed /信中多有～。The letter teems with disparaging expressions.

慢待 màndài ❶ treat coldly; cold-shoulder:不能～了朋友。We should not give short shrift to our friends. ❷ 〈套语〉treat (a guest) inadequately:今天太～了,请多包涵。Forgive us for our inadequate hospitality.

慢道 màndào *also* "漫道" màndào don't say; to say nothing of; let alone:～别人有意见,连我们自己也不满。Don't say others are complaining; we ourselves are not happy for that matter. *or* We ourselves are dissatisfied, let alone other people. /～显赫,还有萧条。Don't say that they enjoy power and wealth, or they will have unhappy days ahead.

慢动作 màndòngzuò 〈影视〉slow motion

慢工出巧匠 màngōng chū qiǎojiàng 〈俗语〉slow work helps to cultivate a skilful craftsman

慢工出细活 màngōng chū xìhuó 〈俗语〉a slow artisan produces skilled work; slow work brings forth fine skill; meticulous work makes (for) exquisite craftsmanship

慢化 mànhuà 〈核物理〉slowing-down; moderation:～比 moderation ratio /～密度 slowing-down density

慢化剂 mànhuàjì moderator

慢化效应 mànhuà xiàoyìng moderating effect

慢火 mànhuǒ slow fire; low fire:炖牛肉要用～。Braised beef needs slow fire.

慢件 mànjiàn regular, non-express delivery; ordinary service (as opposed to express service):彩色扩印的～三天可取。Ordinary service for colour prints takes three days.

慢惊风 mànjīngfēng 〈中医〉recurrent convulsion (of children) due to vomiting and diarrhoea

慢镜头 mànjìngtóu 〈影视〉slow motion

慢慢腾腾 mànman-tēngtēng *also* "慢慢吞吞" unhurriedly; at a leisurely pace; sluggishly:在公园里～地散步 take a leisurely stroll in the park /她～地走了出来。She walked out at an unhurried pace. /她胃口不好,吃东西～的。She had no good appetite and ate slowly.

慢慢悠悠 mànman-yōuyōu slowly; unhurriedly; at a leisurely pace:～地吸着烟斗 smoke one's pipe leisurely

慢凝水泥 mànníng shuǐní 〈建筑〉slow-setting cement; slow cement

慢跑 mànpǎo jogging:～步 (of horses) canter /～的人 jogger

慢坡 mànpō gentle slope

慢世 mànshì 〈书面〉be cynical:～之人 cynic /～之辞 cynical remark /素来恃才～ be proud of one's talent and scornful of everybody else

慢说 mànshuō let alone; to say nothing of:～是你,谁来也不能进去。Nobody is allowed to enter, let alone you. /在公司里干活,～工资高,其他福利待遇也好。One enjoys better bonuses and fringe benefits working in a firm, to say nothing of a higher salary.

慢速 mànsù 〈机械〉idling:～调节 idling adjustment

慢速存储器 mànsù cúnchǔqì slow storage

慢速摄影 mànsù shèyǐng low-speed cinematography

慢速摄影机 mànsù shèyǐngjī slow-motion camera

慢腾腾 màntēngtēng *also* "慢吞吞" unhurriedly; without haste; at a leisurely pace:这么～地干,能出活吗? How can we accomplish anything if we go on at this snail's pace?

慢条斯理 màntiáosīlǐ leisurely; slowly; unhurriedly:他言谈举止总是～的。He always speaks and acts methodically.

慢物 mànwù 〈书面〉arrogant; haughty:他向来～倨傲。He always treats people with disrespect and arrogance. /才高者不应～。A talented person should in no case be haughty.

慢新星 mànxīnxīng 〈天文〉slow nova

慢性 mànxìng ❶ chronic:～静脉炎 chronic phlebitis /～间质性肝炎 chronic interstitial hepatitis ❷ slow (in taking effect):～中毒 slow poisoning /～病毒 slow virus /～氧化〈化学〉eremacausis ❸ see "慢性子"

慢性白血病 mànxìng báixuèbìng 〈医学〉chronic leukemia

慢性鼻炎 mànxìng bíyán 〈医学〉chronic rhinitis

慢性病 mànxìngbìng chronic disease:～患者 chronic

慢性阑尾炎 mànxìng lánwěiyán 〈医学〉chronic appendicitis
慢性脓肿 mànxìng nóngzhǒng 〈医学〉cold abscess; chronic abscess
慢性子 mànxìngzi ❶ phlegmatic in character ❷ slowcoach; slowpoke: 他是个～，什么事也不着急。He is a slowcoach and rarely gets flurried.
慢悠悠 mànyōuyōu *also* "慢慢悠悠" unhurriedly; without haste; leisurely: 我们～地边走边谈。We talked as we walked leisurely along.
慢中子 mànzhōngzǐ 〈物理〉slow neutron; slow-speed neutron: ～反应堆〈核物理〉slow reactor
慢转唱片 mànzhuàn chàngpiàn *also* "密纹唱片" mìwén chàngpiàn long-playing (LP) record: ～唱机 long-player
慢走 mànzǒu ❶ wait a minute; just a minute: ～，我还没说完。Wait a minute please. I haven't finished yet. ❷ (at parting) good-bye; take care: 请～，有空再来坐坐。Good-bye; drop in again when you are free.

熳

màn *see* "烂熳" lànmàn

谩

màn disrespectful; uncivil; rude
see also mán
谩骂 mànmà hurl or fling abuses; vilify: ～性的语言 abusive language / 遭到包工头的～ be vilified by the labour contractor

墁

màn ❶ pave; surface; macadamize: 花砖～地 pave the floor with coloured tiles ❷〈方言〉plaster a wall: 他把墙壁～得很平。He applied plaster on the wall and made its surface very smooth.

蔓

màn tendrilled vine: 滋～〈书面〉grow and spread; grow vigorously
see also mán; wàn
蔓草 màncǎo creeping weed
蔓生植物 mànshēng zhíwù trailing plant
蔓延 mànyán spread; stretch; extend: 制止不良风气的～ curb unhealthy social trends / 经济萧条使罢工浪潮很快向全国～。Thanks to the economic depression the strike soon spread nationwide. / 流行性感冒的～使一些学校都停课了。Widespread influenza compelled some schools to suspend their classes.

幔

màn curtain; screen: 帷～ heavy curtain / 孝～ curtain hung before a coffin / 纱～ gauze curtain / 窗～ window curtain
幔帷 mànwéi *also* "帷幔" heavy curtain
幔帐 mànzhàng curtain; screen; canopy
幔子 mànzi 〈方言〉curtain; screen

镘(槾)

màn ❶〈书面〉trowel ❷〈旧语〉back of a coin
镘刀 màndāo 〈建筑〉trowel
镘工 màngōng 〈建筑〉floater

嫚

màn 〈书面〉scorn; despise; humiliate
see also mān
嫚骂 mànmà *see* "谩骂" mànmà

缦

màn 〈书面〉plain silk fabric
缦立 mànlì 〈书面〉stand a long time: ～远视 stand looking into the distance for a long time

māng

牤(牻)

māng
牤牛 māngniú 〈方言〉bull
牤子 māngzi 〈方言〉bull

máng

忙

máng ❶ busy; fully occupied: 瞎～ busy about nothing; much ado about nothing / ～死了 be terribly busy / ～得团团转 as busy as a bee / ～不过来 have more work than one can cope with; bite off more than one can chew / ～得不可开交 be completely snowed under with work; be swamped (*or* heavily pressed) with work; be bogged down with work / ～人闲不住。A busy man enjoys no leisure. / 我们都～得要死。We're all up to our eyes in work. ❷ hurry; rush; hasten; make haste: ～着烧水做饭 hurriedly get down to boiling water and cooking rice / ～着往外走，看发生了什么事 rush out to see what's happening / 这一整天把人～得脚丫子朝天。I've been rushed off my feet all day. / 别～于下结论。Don't jump to conclusions. *or* Don't draw hasty conclusions.
忙不迭 mángbùdié hastily; hurriedly; in a hurry: ～地赔不是 apologize in haste / 他正在～地拨电话。He is dialing a phone in a hurry.
忙不及履 mángbùjílǚ be too busy to put on one's shoes; be terribly busy
忙不急 mángbùjí 〈方言〉in a hurry; in haste: 姑娘～地打扮起来。The young woman dressed up hastily.
忙不择价 mángbùzéjià cannot wait for the best offer when one is anxious to sell something off
忙叨 mángdao *also* "忙叨叨" 〈方言〉busy: 啥事儿这样～? What keeps you so busy?
忙工 mánggōng seasonal labourer
忙合 mánghe 〈口语〉be busy; bustle about: 整天～ be busy all day long / ～了两天，终于把文章写完了。I finished my essay after two solid days of hard work. *or* It took me two busy days to write this essay.
忙乎 mánghu busy: 他～了一天，但一点儿也不觉得累。He has been busy all day but does not feel tired in the least.
忙活 mánghuó ❶ be busy doing sth.; be engaged in feverish activity: 你忙着什么活? What are you busy about? ❷ urgent work; pressing job: 这是件～，要先做。This is an urgent job and must be tackled first. *or* As it is an urgent piece of work, it must be given top priority.
忙活 mánghuo be hard at work; be busy; bustle about: 他们已～了一上午了。They have been bustling about the whole morning. / 你这几天～什么呢? What has been keeping you so busy these days?
忙里忙外 mánglǐ-mángwài bustle around; be busy both inside and outside the house: 他～折腾了两天，才搬进了新居。He moved into a new apartment after spending two hectic days running in and out to fix things up.
忙里偷闲 mánglǐ-tōuxián have a bit of time off on the quiet; snatch a little leisure from a busy schedule; take a breather: 他～地读了不少书。He managed to do a good deal of reading despite a busy schedule.
忙碌 mánglù be busy; bustle about: 这是一天中最～的时刻。This is the busiest moment of the day. / 建筑工人们在脚手架上～地施工。The construction workers are busy working on the scaffolding. / 这人一辈子忙忙碌碌，一事无成。He was as busy as a bee all his life but accomplished nothing.
忙乱 mángluàn confused bustle; muddled rush or haste: 克服工作中的～现象 overcome chaos in work / 他心里越急就越～。The more excited he was, the more confused he became. / 最近会议多，太～了。There have been too many meetings lately, and everything seems to be in a muddled rush. / 干什么这样忙忙乱乱? Why all this bustle? *or* Why this tearing hurry?
忙忙叨叨 mángmang-dāodāo hustle and bustle; bustle about: 一天到晚～ bustle about from morning till night / 我这一阵子总～的。I have been rushed off my feet lately.
忙迫 mángpò hastily; in a hurry
忙人 mángrén busy person
忙三迭四 mángsān-diésì *also* "忙三颠四" in great haste; in a big hurry: 他～地吃了几口饭，就扛着锄下地了。After taking a few bites hastily, he left for the fields with a hoe. / 他二话不说，～地走出门去。Without another word, he hurried away.
忙音 mángyīn 〈通信〉busy tone or signal
忙于 mángyú be busy with: ～工作 be busy with one's work / ～整理行装 be busy packing up
忙月 mángyuè ❶ busy farming season: 一到～，全家都搞农活儿。The whole family go to work on the farm when the busy season sets in. ❷〈方言〉〈旧语〉casual labourer hired during the busy season or festivals such as the New Year
忙中有错 mángzhōng-yǒucuò haste engenders error; haste makes waste

芒 máng ❶〈植物〉Chinese silvergrass ❷ awn; beard; arista:麦～ awn of wheat

芒草 mángcǎo Chinese silvergrass

芒车前 mángchēqián 〈植物〉plantain

芒茨合金 mángcí héjīn 〈冶金〉Muntz metal

芒刺在背 mángcì-zàibèi feel prickles down one's back; be ill at ease; feel nervous and uneasy:他一想到过去的错,犹如～。He felt nervous and uncomfortable when he thought of his past error.

芒果 mángguǒ *also*"杧果" mángguǒ 〈植物〉mango

芒果蝇 mángguǒyíng athericera

芒硝 mángxiāo *also*"硭硝" mángxiāo 〈化学〉mirabilite; Glauber's salt

芒鞋 mángxié straw sandals:～竹杖 straw sandals and bamboo stick

芒种 Mángzhòng ❶ Grain in Ear, 9th seasonal division point, marking the sun's position at 75° on the ecliptic ❷ day marking such a seasonal division point, usu. falling on the 6th or 7th of June ❸ period lasting from such a seasonal division point till the next one (Summer Solstice 夏至)

see also"节气" jiéqì;"二十四节气" èrshísì jiéqì

芒状细胞 mángzhuàng xìbāo collencyte

茫 máng ❶ (of water, etc.) vast; boundless; hazy:渺～ distant and indistinct; bleak; uncertain / 淼～ (of an expanse of water) stretch as far as the eye can see / 微～〈书面〉blurred; hazy ❷ unaware; ignorant; in the dark:迷～ confused; perplexed

茫茫 mángmáng boundless; vast:～大海 vast sea; boundless sea / ～烟水 vast expanse of mist and water / ～暮色 growing dusk / 前途～ have an uncertain future; face a bleak prospect / 人世～,坎坷殊多。Life is full of uncertainties and frustrations.

茫昧 mángmèi 〈书面〉❶ dim; blurred:往事多已～。Past events have mostly become blurred. ❷ ignorant; untutored

茫漠 mángmò 〈书面〉open; spacious:～的草原 boundless grassland

茫然 mángrán ❶ ignorant; in the dark; at a loss:～不知 be completely in the dark / ～不解 be quite at a loss / ～无措 be helpless; be all at sea / 我不禁感到前途～。I shuddered to think of what the future held in store for me. ❷〈书面〉vast expanse; limitless expanses (of water, desert, etc.) ❸ frustrated; thwarted; disappointed:～若失 be lost in thought / 显出～的神情 have a blank look; have a vacant expression on one's face

茫无边际 mángwúbiānjì boundless; limitless; vast:～的大草原 boundless grassland

茫无所知 mángwúsuǒzhī be utterly ignorant; be totally at sea:如果对下情～,就容易出差错。Those who are ignorant of conditions at the grass roots are prone to error.

茫无头绪 mángwútóuxù not know what to do; have no clue whatever:这件事情他们已研究了一个多月,至今还～。They have studied the matter for over a month, but still do not know what to do about it.

杧 máng

杧果 mángguǒ *also*"芒果" mángguǒ 〈植物〉mango:～属 *Mangifera*

硭 máng

硭硝 mángxiāo *also*"芒硝" mángxiāo 〈化学〉mirabilite; Glauber's salt

铓 máng

铓锣 mángluó percussion instrument of the various nationalities living in Yunnan Province, usu. a set of three or more gongs hung on a frame

盲 máng ❶ blind:色～ colour blindness; achromatopia / 全色～ panchromatic blindness / 雪～ snow blindness / 夜～ night blindness; nyctalopia / ～如蝙蝠 as blind as a bat (*or* as a mole) / 问道于～ ask the way from the blind; take the blind as the guide; seek advice from the ignorant ❷ one who lacks knowledge; illiterate:文～ illiterate person; illiterate / 扫～ eliminate illiteracy / 脱～ be able to read and write after a period of learning / 音～ one who has no ear for music / 法～ one who is ignorant of law

盲边 mángbiān 〈体育〉blind side

盲肠 mángcháng blind gut; caecum; (popularly for 阑尾) appendix:～造口术 cecostomy / ～固定术 cecopexy

盲肠炎 mángchángyán *also*"阑尾炎" lánwěiyán appendicitis; cecitis; typhlitis

盲椿象 mángchūnxiàng 〈动物〉plant bug

盲从 mángcóng obey blindly:他吃了不少～的苦头。He suffered a lot from blind obedience.

盲打 mángdǎ touch system:～式打字 touch-type

盲道 mángdào blind track — grooved track for the blind (along the middle of a sidewalk)

盲点 mángdiǎn 〈生理〉blind spot; scotoma

盲动 mángdòng act blindly; act rashly:纠正～行为。Rectify (*or* Overcome) rashness in action. / 工作中切不可～。Never make a risky move in one's work.

盲动主义 mángdòngzhǔyì putschism:～者 putschist

盲干 mánggàn act rashly; go it blind:一味～,非碰壁不可。If you act blindly, you will run into a stone wall (*or* you'll run your head against a brick wall).

盲谷 mánggǔ 〈地质〉blind valley

盲角 mángjiǎo 〈军事〉blind angle

盲井 mángjǐng blind shaft; winze

盲流 mángliú ❶ blind influx (mainly referring to labourers aimlessly flowing from rural areas or small towns into large cities):～人口 people who have blindly drifted from rural to urban areas; floating population ❷ person who has blindly migrated to urban areas; migrant

盲螺 mángluó 〈动物〉blind shell:～科 *Caecidae*

盲鳗 mángmán 〈动物〉hagfish:～科 *Myxinees*

盲目 mángmù blind; unseeing; ignorant:～崇拜 worship blindly / ～行动 blind move / ～生产 blind production / 政治上～无知 be politically ignorant / ～乐观 be unrealistically optimistic; entertain purblind optimism / ～的优越感 unwarranted sense of superiority / ～竞争 unbridled competition / ～扩大建设规模 indiscriminately increase the scale of construction / ～上项目 launch new projects rashly

盲目发送 mángmù fāsòng 〈无线电〉blind transmission

盲目飞行 mángmù fēixíng blind flight; instrument flying

盲目轰炸 mángmù hōngzhà 〈军事〉blind bombing

盲目探测器 mángmù tàncèqì 〈军事〉miss-fire detector

盲目性 mángmùxìng blindness (in action):加强计划和市场预测,避免生产～。Do a better job in planning and marketing so as to avoid blindness in production.

盲目着陆 mángmù zhuólù 〈航空〉blind landing; instrument landing:～系统 air track blind landing system

盲目钻探 mángmù zuāntàn 〈矿业〉wildcat drilling; wildcatting

盲棋 mángqí blindfold chess:这位大师擅长下～。This master is good at playing blindfold chess.

盲区 mángqū 〈通信〉blind zone

盲人 mángrén blind person; the blind:～读物 publication in braille / ～手表 blindman's watch; touch watch

盲人光声阅读器 mángrén guāngshēng yuèdúqì optophone

盲人摸象 mángrén-mōxiàng like the blind men trying to size up the elephant — taking a part for the whole

盲人瞎马 mángrén-xiāmǎ blind man on a blind horse — galloping headlong into disaster:我不能让你～地去乱闯。I simply cannot allow you to go and act blindly.

盲人阅读器 mángrén yuèdúqì optacon

盲蛇 mángshé 〈动物〉blind snake:～科 *Typhlopidac*

盲鼠 mángshǔ zokor

盲树 mángshù 〈林业〉blind tree

盲文 mángwén ❶ braille:用～读写 read and write in braille / ～打字机 braillewriter; Brailler ❷ publication in braille

盲文读物 mángwén dúwù book in braille

盲校 mángxiào school for the blind

盲信 mángxìn undelivered letter

盲学 mángxué typhlology

盲哑教育 máng-yǎ jiàoyù education for the blind and the deaf-mute

盲鱼 mángyú blindfish

盲障 mángzhàng 〈军事〉blindage

盲字 mángzì braille

氓 máng see "流氓" liúmáng
see also méng

龙 máng 〈书面〉❶ a kind of long-haired dog ❷ mixed colours:～服 mixed coloured dress
see also méng

牻 máng 〈书面〉black-and-white cattle

mǎng

莽[1] mǎng ❶ rank grass; thick undergrowth:草～ rank growth of grass; wilderness; wild jungle /榛～〈书面〉luxuriant vegetation /丛～ a wildness of bushes ❷〈书面〉vast; colossal; boundless:苍～ vast; boundless ❸ (Mǎng) a surname

莽[2] mǎng rude; crude; rash; reckless:鲁～ crude and rash

莽苍 mǎngcāng wide, wild country; (of scenery) blurred; misty:烟雨～ blurred with mist and rain

莽草 mǎngcǎo poisonous bushy plant (*Illicium anisatum shikimmi*):～毒 shikimmi toxin

莽动 mǎngdòng 〈方言〉act rashly; start a fight:有话好讲嘛,何必这样～干什么? Come on, we could surely talk things out. There is no need of coming to blows.

莽夫 mǎngfū see "莽汉"

莽汉 mǎnghàn rude fellow; boor

莽莽 mǎngmǎng ❶ overgrown (with grass); luxuriant; rank:草木～ luxuriant vegetation; lush grass and trees ❷ (of fields, plains, etc.) vast; endless; boundless:～万重山 endless chain of mountain ranges /望长城内外,惟余～;大河上下,顿失滔滔。Both sides of the Great Wall, One single white immensity; The Yellow River's swift current, Is stilled from end to end.

莽原 mǎngyuán wilderness overgrown with grass:千里～ vast expanse of grassland stretching to infinity

莽撞 mǎngzhuàng rash; reckless; impetuous:性格～ impetuous temperament /～的小伙子 rash young man; young harum-scarum /他开车～,执照被扣了。His driving license was suspended (*or* withheld) for reckless driving. /我懊悔自己的～。I regret my own foolhardiness. /你怎么这样～,也不想想后果。How can you act so impulsively, never giving a thought to the consequences?

漭 mǎng

漭漭 mǎngmǎng 〈书面〉boundless; vast:水～ vast expanse of water

蟒 mǎng boa; python

蟒袍 mǎngpáo also"蟒衣" ceremonial robe for princes and court ministers during the Ming and Qing dynasties embroidered with boa design; boa-design robe

蟒蛇 mǎngshé also "蚺蛇" ránshé python; boa:～科 *Pythonidae*

māo

猫(貓) māo ❶ cat; feline:豹～ leopard cat /雄～ tomcat /小～ kitten /灵～ civet cat /野～ wildcat; stray cat /波斯～ Persian cat /大熊～ giant panda; panda /小熊～ lesser panda /长尾麝香～ paradoxure /～叫 mewing; purring /照～画虎 draw a tiger with a cat as a model — imitate sth. without catching the spirit /～儿一跑,耗子就闹。When the cat's away, the mice will play. ❷〈方言〉hide:藏～儿〈口语〉play hide-and-seek
see also máo

猫豹 māobào clouded leopard (*Neofelis nebulosa*)

猫貂 māodiāo 〈动物〉cat squirrel; *Bassaria astuta*

猫耳洞 māo'ěrdòng cat's-ear-shaped cave — cave dug on both sides of an entrenchment for soldiers to shelter themselves in

猫肺炎 māofèiyán cat's flu; feline influenza; feline pneumonitis

猫睛石 māojīngshí 〈矿业〉cat's eye (stone); cymophane

猫科 māokē 〈动物〉Felidae:～动物 feline; felid

猫哭老鼠 māokūlǎoshǔ cat weeping over the dead mouse — shedding crocodile tears:～假慈悲 cat crying over the mouse's death — hypocritical show of sorrow or sympathy

猫儿腻 māornì also "猫腻儿"〈口语〉cunning plot; underhand act; trick:正派人不玩～。An honest person never plays tricks. /这事儿准有～。There is something fishy behind this.

猫儿食 māorshí 〈比喻〉small appetite

猫儿眼 māoryǎn 〈矿业〉cat's eye (stone); cymophane

猫儿眼睛草 māoryǎnjingcǎo *Euphorbia helioscopia*

猫鼠同眠 māoshǔ-tóngmián the cat and the rat sleep together — big officials countenance their subordinates doing evil; corrupt officials big and small act in cahoots

猫头鹰 māotóuyīng also "鸱鸺" chīxiū owl

猫熊 māoxióng also "熊猫" panda; giant panda

猫眼 māoyǎn ❶ peephole (fixed in a door); spyhole ❷ see "猫眼道钉"

猫眼道钉 māoyǎn dàodīng (popular term for 道钉❷) cat's eye; reflector stud

猫眼石 māoyǎnshí 〈矿业〉cat's eye (stone); cymophane

猫鱼 māoyú small fish as cat's food

猫仔 māozǎi kitten

猫抓病 māozhuābìng 〈医学〉cat scratch disease; benign lymphoreticulosis

猫爪相思树 māozhuǎ xiāngsīshù catclaw acacia

máo

毛[1] máo ❶ hair; feather; down:眉～ eyebrow; brow /鹅～ goose feather /汗～ fine hair on the human body /毫～ soft hair on the body /睫～ eyelash; lash /卷～ curly hair /绒～ fine hair; down; nap /茸～〈植物〉down; nap /胎～ foetal hair; lanugo /纤～ cilium /鬃～ bristle /羊～ sheep's wool; fleece /鞭～ flagellum /羽～ feather; plume /棕～ palm fibre /多如牛～ as many as the hairs on an ox — innumerable; too many to count /不～之地 land without vegetation; barren land /一～不拔 unwilling to give away even a hair — penny-pinching; too stingy to part with a farthing /这猫有一身好～。The cat has a fine coat of hair. ❷ wool: see"～纺";"～料" ❸ mildew; mould:长～ become mildewed; be covered with mildew ❹ coarse; semifinished:～铁 pig iron ❺ gross:～保险费 gross premium /～贸易条件 gross trade terms ❻ very young; raw:～贼 petty thief; pilferer /小～头 little baby ❼ (of currency) devalue; depreciate:这钱又～了。The money (*or* currency) has been devalued again. ❽ (Máo) a surname

毛[2] máo ❶ careless; unthinking; crude; rash: see "～头～脑";"～手～脚" ❷ flurried; nervous; scared:心里发～ feel scared /吓得发～ be frightened out of one's wits /他一听到这消息就～。He panicked at the news. ❸〈方言〉get angry; flare up:老汉～了。The old man lost his temper.

毛[3] máo 〈口语〉*mao*, fractional money unit in China (= *jiao* 角, = $\frac{1}{10}$ *yuan or* 10 *fen*): 三块五～ three *yuan* and five *mao*

毛白杨 máobáiyáng 〈植物〉Chinese white poplar

毛百合 máobǎihé 〈植物〉solol

毛背心 máobèixīn woollen vest

毛笔 máobǐ writing brush

毛边 máobiān ❶ (of books, clothes, etc.) selvage; raw edge:～书 uncut books ❷ see "毛边纸"

毛边纸 máobiānzhǐ (shortened as 毛边) *maobian* paper, a kind of pale-yellow writing paper made from bamboo pulp

毛冰 máobīng (of aircraft) rime

毛病 máobing ❶ trouble; failure; blunder; mistake:她的工作出了什么～,她自己心里有数。She is fully aware what went wrong with her work. /这汽车出～了。The car has broken down. /这炉子有～。There's something wrong with the cooking range. ❷ bad habit; defect; shortcoming; weakness:他有个偷懒的～。His fault is his laziness. *or* He is lazy — that's the trouble with him. /他的工作方法有

～。Something is wrong with the way he goes about his business. /我们的工作还有不少～，欢迎大家指正。As we still have shortcomings in our work, please feel free to point them out. ❸〈方言〉illness; ailment; trouble: 他的心脏有点～，但不厉害。He has heart trouble, but it is not serious. /她的～就那么重，需要住院吗? Is she so seriously ill that she should be hospitalized? /我的肠胃有～。I suffer from stomach disorder.

毛玻璃 máobōli *also*"磨砂玻璃" móshā bōli frosted glass; ground glass

毛布 máobù coarse cotton cloth; coarse calico

毛糙 máocao crude; rough; careless: 这活儿做得太～。This is a bit (*or* piece) of slipshod work.

毛茶 máochá *also*"毛条" unprocessed tea leaves

毛虫 máochóng *also*"毛毛虫" caterpillar

毛刺 máocì 〈机械〉burr

毛掸虫 máodǎnchóng feather-duster worm

毛滴虫 máodīchóng trichomonad: ～病 trichomoniasis

毛地黄 máodìhuáng 〈药学〉digitalis

毛豆 máodòu green or young soya beans

毛发 máofà hair (on the human body and head): 他不觉肌肤战栗，～倒竖。He trembled and his hair stood on end in spite of himself.

毛发病 máofàbìng trichopathy; trichosis

毛发学 máofàxué trichology: ～家 trichologist

毛发之功 máofàzhīgōng negligible contribution; petty achievement

毛纺 máofǎng wool spinning: 粗梳～ woollen spinning /精梳～ worsted spinning /～厂 woollen mill /～工艺 wool spinning

毛感 máogǎn feel of wool: 温暖的～ warm woolly feel

毛葛 máogé 〈纺织〉poplin: 织花～ poplin broché

毛茛 máogèn 〈植物〉buttercup: ～科 *Ranunculaceal*

毛估 máogū make a rough estimate: ～一下，这片早稻亩产不低于八百斤。The per-*mu* yield of early rice in this area is roughly estimated to be not less than 800 *jin*.

毛骨悚然 máogǔ-sǒngrán have one's hair stand on end — be absolutely horrified; shudder or shiver with fear; make one's flesh creep: 令人～ send cold shivers down one's spine; be bloodcurdling /～，周身寒栗 have gooseflesh and shudder with fear /他讲的可怖的故事使我们～。His terrible stories made our blood freeze (*or* run cold).

毛咕 máogu 〈方言〉filled with apprehension and fear: 他瞪着眼看我，看得我心里直～。I was filled with apprehension as he was staring at me wide-eyed.

毛管 máoguǎn 〈农业〉capillary; capillary tube: ～水 capillary moisture; capillary water

毛孩 máohái 〈生理〉hairy child

毛孩子 máoháizi 〈口语〉little child; ignorant kid: 十年前我还是一个不懂事的～呢! I was a mere child ten years ago.

毛海芋 máohǎiyù 〈植物〉hairy arum

毛蚶 máohān 〈动物〉〈方言〉blood clam

毛烘烘 máohōnghōng hairy; hirsute; woolly; furry: ～的手臂 hairy arms /～的小猫 furry cat

毛乎乎 máohūhū hairy; furry: ～的小狗 furry small dog /这东西～的，是个什么动物? What sort of animal is this hairy thing?

毛活 máohuó 〈口语〉wool knitting: 织～儿 make woollen knitwear; knit a woollen sweater

毛火虫 máohuǒchóng 〈方言〉pine moth

毛髻 máojì *also*"刘海儿" liúhǎir 〈方言〉bang; fringe

毛价 máojià gross price

毛尖 máojiān a kind of high-quality Chinese green tea

毛姜 máojiāng *also*"菊芋" júyù 〈方言〉Jerusalem artichoke

毛焦火辣 máojiāo-huǒlà *also*"毛焦火燎" very anxious or worried; fidgety; on pins and needles: 他心里～，坐立不安。Deeply worried, he kept fidgeting.

毛脚鸡 máojiǎojī 〈方言〉clumsy oaf

毛脚女婿 máojiǎo nǚxù 〈方言〉son-in-law to be; daughter's fiancé

毛校样 máojiàoyàng 〈印刷〉foul proof

毛巾 máojīn towel: ～布 towelling

毛巾被 máojīnbèi *also*"毛巾毯" towelling coverlet

毛巾衫 máojīnshān terrycloth shirt

毛举 máojǔ 〈书面〉❶ cite at random: ～其目 cite some items at random ❷ list or cite lots of trifles: ～缕析 list minute details and make elaborate analysis

毛举细故 máojǔ-xìgù *also*"毛举细务" enumerate all the details; talk about trifling matters

毛孔 máokǒng 〈生理〉pore

毛孔透药疗法 máokǒng tòuyào liáofǎ poropathy

毛口 máokǒu 〈机械〉burr: 去～ burring

毛口虫 máokǒuchóng trichostome

毛裤 máokù long woollen underwear; woollen pants

毛拉 máolā ❶〈伊斯兰〉maula; mullah ❷ (among some Muslim communities in the Xinjiang Uygur Autonomous Region) ahung; imam

毛辣火热 máolà-huǒrè *also*"毛热火辣" worried; anxious; on tenterhooks

毛梾 máolái 〈植物〉long-petioled dogwood (*Cornus walteri*)

毛蓝 máolán darkish blue: ～土布 dyed or blue mankeen

毛里求斯 Máolǐqiúsī Mauritius: ～人 Mauritian

毛里塔尼亚 Máolǐtǎníyà Mauritania: ～人 Mauritanian

毛利 máolì gross profit; markup; gross earnings: ～比率 gross profit ratio /～分析 gross profit analysis

毛利率 máolìlǜ gross profit rate

毛利人 Máolìrén Maori, an ethnic minority and indigenous people of New Zealand

毛粒 máolì 〈纺织〉neps

毛料 máoliào woollen fabrics; woollens: 一套～的西服 Western-style woollen suit

毛柳 máoliǔ almond-leaved willow

毛驴 máolǘ donkey: 小～使不出黄牛劲。A little donkey cannot be expected to have the strength of an ox.

毛毛 máomao 〈方言〉pet name for a baby

毛毛虫 máomaochóng caterpillar

毛毛腾腾 máomao-tēngtēng 〈方言〉flustered; nervous; uncontrolled: 说完，他～地站起来就走。After finishing speaking, he stood up nervously and bustled away.

毛毛雨 máomaoyǔ ❶ drizzle: 毛毛细雨 fine drizzling rain /断断续续地下着～。It drizzled intermittently. ❷ let sb. in on sth. in advance; tip off: 在正式文件下达之前，你要先给他下点～。You need to tip him off before the official document arrives.

毛蠓 máoměng 〈动物〉moth fly: ～科 *Psychodidae*

毛面 máomiàn frosted; ground; matte: ～浮雕 bas-relief

毛面纸 máomiànzhǐ flock-paper

毛姆 Máomǔ William Somerset Maugham (1874-1965), English novelist and dramatist

毛南族 Máonánzú Maonan nationality, living in the Guangxi Zhuang Autonomous Region

毛囊 máonáng hair follicle: ～蠕形螨 follicle mite /～炎 dolliculitis /～癣 favus

毛囊角化病 máonáng jiǎohuàbìng keratosis; follicularis

毛呢 máoní woollen cloth (for heavy clothing); heavy woollen cloth; wool coating or suiting: ～大衣 woollen overcoat

毛蓬蓬 máopēngpēng (of grass, hair, etc.) thick and messy: ～的络腮胡子 stubby and messy whiskers

毛坯 máopī *also*"坯料" pīliào ❶ semifinished product such as unbaked earthenware ❷〈机械〉blank

毛皮 máopí fur; pelt: ～兽 fur-bearing animal; furbearer /～兽饲养 fur farming

毛片 máopiàn ❶ unprocessed film after shooting ❷ pornographic film or telefilm

毛票 máopiào 〈口语〉banknotes of one, two or five *jiao* denominations

毛渠 máoqú sublateral canal; sublateral

毛人 máorén person with hair growing on his face or over his entire body (a sign of atavism)

毛茸茸 máorōngrōng hairy; downy: ～的小猫 downy kitten

毛茸 máoróng fine hair; down; villus

毛绒 máoróng wistiti: ～卷曲工艺 friezing

毛毵毵 máosānsān (of hair, down, branch, twig, etc.) thick, fine and long: 他几天没有刮胡子，满脸～的。He has not shaven for several days and has a stubby chin.

毛瑟枪 máosèqiāng Mauser rifle

毛纱 máoshā 〈纺织〉wool yarn: 粗纺～ woollen yarn /精纺～ worsted yarn

毛衫儿 máoshanr swaddling clothes

毛石 máoshí 〈建筑〉rubble: ～混凝土 rubble concrete; cyclopean

concrete /～工程 rubble masonry /～排水沟 French drain
毛收入 máoshōurù gross income:～税 gross income tax; turnover tax
毛手毛脚 máoshǒu-máojiǎo careless (in handling things); slipshod; brash and clumsy:他干活～只图快。He has always had his work done hastily and, of course, carelessly.
毛刷 máoshuā brush
毛丝 máosī 〈纺织〉broken filament
毛遂自荐 máosuì-zìjiàn recommend oneself for a position as Mao Sui (of the Warring States Period in ancient China) did; volunteer one's services; volunteer for a task or job:这苦差事只好由我来～了。I will have to recommend myself for this thankless job. /她～到边远地区去当了一名教师。She volunteered to become a teacher in a remote mountainous area.
毛损 máosǔn gross loss
毛笋 máosǔn shoot of *mao* bamboo
毛太纸 máotàizhǐ *maotai* paper, writing paper thinner and darker than *maobian* paper, usu. produced in Fujian
毛毯 máotǎn ❶ woollen blanket ❷ carpet
毛桃 máotáo wild peach
毛体积 máotǐjī bulk volume
毛条 máotiáo ❶ semi-processed tea leaves used for making either green or black tea ❷〈纺织〉woollen sliver
毛条校样 máotiáo jiàoyàng 〈印刷〉galley proof; galley
毛头毛脑 máotóu-máonǎo ❶ blunt and rash:他就是这样～地瞎说一气。He is always talking foolishly like this. ❷ anxious; worried; on pins and needles:三个战士正～没有办法，见他回来了很高兴。The three soldiers were at their wit's end (*or* at the end of their tether) when, to their delight, they saw him coming back.
毛头纸 máotóuzhǐ *also*"东昌纸" dōngchāngzhǐ a kind of soft white paper used over a window lattice in traditional Chinese architecture or used as a wrapper
毛团 máotuán hair ball
毛蛙 máowā 〈动物〉hairy frog
毛猬 máowèi 〈动物〉moon rat; gymnure; hairy hedgehog
毛蚊 máowén 〈动物〉March fly:～科 *Bibionidae*
毛窝 máowō 〈方言〉cotton padded shoes
毛乌素沙地 Máowūsù Shādì Mu Us Desert, in the Inner Mongolia Autonomous Region
毛细斥力 máoxì chìlì 〈物理〉capillary repulsion
毛细管 máoxìguǎn ❶ capillary; capillary tube:～瘤〈生理〉telangioma /～充血〈生理〉capillary congestion /～扩张 telangiectasica /～显微镜检查 capillaroscopy ❷ very thin pipe
毛细渗透 máoxì shèntòu capillary percolation
毛细现象 máoxì xiànxiàng 〈物理〉capillary phenomenon; capillarity
毛细血管 máoxì xuèguǎn 〈生理〉blood capillary:～瘤 capillary hemangioma /～襻 capillary loops
毛细引力 máoxì yǐnlì 〈物理〉capillary attraction
毛细蒸发 máoxì zhēngfā capillary evaporation
毛细作用 máoxì zuòyòng 〈物理〉capillary action; capillarity
毛虾 máoxiā shrimp
毛纤维 máoxiānwéi 〈纺织〉wool
毛线 máoxiàn knitting wool:～针 knitting needle
毛腺 máoxiàn 〈生理〉hair gland
毛象 máoxiàng *also*"猛犸" měngmǎ mammoth
毛心 máoxīn 〈方言〉evil intention; ill will:见利忘义，遂起～。Gain makes one forget all about honour and act against his conscience.
毛选 Máoxuǎn (short for 毛泽东选集) *Selected Works of Mao Zedong* (of five volumes, published in 1951-1960 and 1977 respectively)
毛丫头 máoyātou 〈口语〉little girl; slip of a girl
毛样 máoyàng 〈印刷〉galley proof
毛腰 máoyāo *also*"猫腰" máoyāo 〈方言〉arch one's back; stoop:他毛下腰从地下拾起一块石头。He stooped down and picked up a stone from the ground.
毛衣 máoyī woollen sweater; sweater; woolly coat; woolly
毛蚴 máoyòu 〈动物〉miracidium
毛羽 máoyǔ feathers:～未丰 unfledged; young and immature
毛崽子 máozǎizi 〈粗话〉little dirty brat
毛躁 máozao ❶ short-tempered; irritable:他这个人脾气～。He has a quick temper. ❷ rash and careless:办事～ act rashly
毛泽东 Máo Zédōng Mao Zedong (formerly translated as Mao Tse-tung, 1893-1976):～故居 Mao Zedong's birthplace (in Shaoshan, Hunan Province)
毛泽东思想 Máo Zédōng Sīxiǎng Mao Zedong Thought
毛毡 máozhān felt:～纸 felt paper
毛织品 máozhīpǐn ❶ woollens; wool fabric ❷ woollen knitwear
毛痣 máozhì 〈生理〉hairy mole; hairy nevus
毛重 máozhòng gross weight
毛猪 máozhū 〈商业〉live pig
毛竹 máozhú *also*"南竹" nánzhú *mao* bamboo
毛主席纪念堂 Máozhǔxí Jìniàntáng Mao Zedong Memorial Hall (in Tian'anmen Square) in Beijing
毛著 Máozhù (short for 毛泽东著作) works of Mao Zedong
毛装 máozhuāng binding books without trimming
毛锥 máozhuī another name for the writing brush
毛子 máozi ❶〈旧语〉〈贬义〉hairy fellow; westerner ❷〈旧语〉〈方言〉bandit; robber ❸〈方言〉broken bits of hair or thread

旄 máo

ancient flag decorated with yak's tail
旄倪 máoní the old and the young
旄牛 máoniú *also*"牦牛" máoniú yak

髦 máo

❶ horse's mane ❷〈古语〉children's bangs ❸ handsome and talented:～俊之士 handsome, outstanding scholar
髦儿戏 máorxì 〈旧语〉drama played by women

酕 máo

drunk
酕醄 máotáo 〈书面〉as drunk as a fiddler

牦(氂) máo

牦牛 máoniú *also*"旄牛" máoniú yak (*Bos grunniens*)

锚 máo

anchor:抛～ drop anchor; cast anchor; (of vehicles) break down /起～ weigh anchor; set sail /起～装置 anchor gear /小～ kedge anchor /备用大～ sheet anchor
锚标 máobiāo 〈航海〉anchor buoy
锚泊 máobó lie at anchor:～地 berthage; anchor ground; anchorage /～装置 ground tackle
锚泊灯 máobódēng 〈船舶〉anchor light
锚泊球 máobóqiú anchor ball
锚地 máodì ❶ anchorage; anchor station ❷〈航海〉holding ground
锚定板 máodìngbǎn 〈建筑〉anchor plate
锚定式悬桥 máodìngshì xuánqiáo anchored suspension bridge
锚杆 máogān 〈矿业〉roof bolt:～支护法 pin timbering
锚更 máogēng anchor watch
锚固 máogù 〈建筑〉anchor; anchorage
锚固吊桥 máogù diàoqiáo anchored suspension bridge
锚固法施工 máogùfǎ shīgōng anchoring construction
锚固式起重机 máogùshì qǐzhòngjī grapple equipped crane
锚雷 máoléi 〈军事〉mooring mine; moored buoyant mine
锚链 máoliàn 〈船舶〉hawser; anchor line
锚索 máosuǒ cable
锚塔 máotǎ anchor tower
锚位 máowèi location where a ship casts anchor; anchorage
锚爪 máozhuǎ fluke (of an anchor)

猫(貓) máo

see also māo
猫腰 máoyāo stoop down
see also"毛腰" máoyāo

茆 máo

❶〈植物〉cogongrass (*Imperata cylindrica*) ❷ (Máo) a surname

矛 máo

spear; lance; pike:长～兵 pikeman /持～者 spearman /～和盾 spear and shield
矛盾 máodùn ❶ contradictory; conflicting; opposing:自相～的推论 self-contradictory reasoning /两位专家对这一问题的看法是相互～的。The two experts had conflicting views on the matter. *or* The views of the two experts on this matter are contradictory. /他们的行为与他们所宣扬的原则是～的。What they do contradicts their pro-

fessed principle. *or* They do not perform what they preach. ❷〈哲学〉〈逻辑〉contradiction: ～的普遍性 universality of contradiction / ～的特殊性 particularity of contradiction / 主要～ principal contradiction / 非主要～ nonprincipal contradiction / ～的主要方面 principal aspect of a contradiction / ～的次要方面 secondary aspect of a contradiction / ～规律 law of contradiction / ～的对立面 opposites in contradiction / 对抗性～ antagonistic contradiction / 非对抗性～ nonantagonistic contradiction / ～的统一 unity of opposites / ～的转化 transformation of a contradiction / ～诸方面的同一性和斗争性 identity and struggle of the aspects of a contradiction ❸ problem; contradiction; difficulty: ～百出 riddled with contradictions; a bundle of inconsistencies / ～上交 pass on difficulties to the leadership; pass on the buck to a higher level

矛盾律 máodùnlǜ 〈逻辑〉law of contradiction

矛盾论 Máodùnlùn *On Contradiction* (1937), by Mao Zedong

矛头 máotóu spearhead: ～所向 target of attack / ～向下 direct the spearhead of attack at the masses / ～向上 level the attack against the higher authorities / 把打击的～指向贪污腐败 spearhead the attack on corruption

矛尾鱼 máowěiyú *also* "拉蒂迈鱼" lādìmàiyú *Latimeria chalumae*

矛蚁 máoyǐ driver ant

矛鱼 máoyú spearfish

茅 máo ❶〈植物〉cogongrass: 白～ cogongrass (*Imperata cylindrica*) / 香～ lemon-grass / 草～下士〈谦词〉humble scholar / 名列前～ come out on top; be among the best of the successful candidates / 拔～连茹 pull up the rushes with their roots — promote virtuous and capable men along with their worthy associates ❷ (Máo) a surname

茅庵 máo'ān thatched hut

茅草 máocǎo 〈植物〉cogongrass: ～棚 thatched shed; thatched shack / ～屋 thatched hut / ～蜡〈化工〉esparto wax

茅柴 máochái dry weeds (for use as fuel)

茅茨土阶 máocí-tǔjiē *also* "茅室土阶" grass roof and earthen steps — simple or humble abode

茅道 máodào trail: 他们顺着～上山。They followed the trail (*or* beaten path) uphill.

茅房 máofáng 〈口语〉latrine; water closet

茅膏菜 máogāocài 〈植物〉sundew

茅坑 máokēng ❶〈口语〉latrine pit: ～里的石头 — 又臭又硬 like a stone in a latrine pit, hard and stinking (usu. used to describe a person who is unreasonable and obstinate) ❷〈方言〉latrine

茅楼 máolóu 〈方言〉latrine

茅庐 máolú thatched cottage: 初出～ step into society for the first time; be at the beginning of one's career; be young and inexperienced; be fledgling

茅茅运动 Máomáo Yùndòng Mau Mau (patriotic armed organization in Kenya, with members mostly from the Kikuyu people, which organized uprisings between 1952 and 1956 against British colonial rule)

茅棚 máopéng thatched shed

茅塞顿开 máosè-dùnkāi suddenly see the light; become enlightened all of a sudden: 听他一说，～。I was suddenly enlightened by his remarks.

茅舍 máoshè 〈书面〉thatched cottage

茅厕 máosi 〈口语〉latrine

茅台酒 máotáijiǔ *Maotai* (spirit)

茅亭 máotíng pavilion with a thatched roof

茅屋 máowū thatched cottage

蟊 máo insect that destroys the roots of seedlings

蟊贼 máozéi person harmful to society; vermin: 人类的～ vermin of mankind

蝥 máo *see* "斑蝥" bānmáo

mǎo

有 mǎo 〈方言〉none; nothing

卯[1] mǎo fourth of the twelve Earthly Branches: 点～〈旧语〉call the roll in the morning / 应～〈旧语〉answer roll call or sign in upon arrival in one's office; put in a routine appearance / 误～ be late at roll call / 死～ time of death

卯[2] mǎo mortise

卯劲儿 mǎojìnr *also* "铆劲儿" mǎojìnr 〈口语〉with a spurt of energy: 我们一～把木箱抬起来了。With an effort, we lifted the wooden case.

卯酒 mǎojiǔ morning drink; wine taken in the morning

卯年卯月 mǎonián-mǎoyuè ages ago; far back: 这可是～的事了。This was an event of the remote past.

卯期 mǎoqī 〈旧语〉deadline; time limit: 误了～ late for the deadline; behind schedule

卯时 mǎoshí 〈旧语〉period of the day from 5 a.m. to 7 a.m.

卯睡 mǎoshuì sleep in the morning

卯榫 mǎosǔn mortise and tenon

卯眼 mǎoyǎn mortise

卯酉圈 mǎoyǒuquān 〈天文〉prime vertical circle

卯月 mǎoyuè second lunar month

卯子工 mǎozigōng work paid by the day

卯子活 mǎozihuó work paid by the day

泖 mǎo small calm lake: 三～ San Mao, name of a no longer existing lake in today's Shanghai

昴 mǎo one of the twenty-eight constellations: ～星 Pleiades

峁 mǎo tableland of the loess plateau in China's northwestern region

铆 mǎo fasten with a rivet; rivet: 冷～ cold-riveting / 风动～ pneumatic riveting / 对接～ butt riveting / 搭接～ lap riveting

铆锤 mǎochuí riveting hammer

铆钉 mǎodīng rivet: ～夹 rivet clamps / ～钢 rivet steel / ～锤 riveting hammer / ～距 rivet pitch / ～用具 rivet set

铆钉枪 mǎodīngqiāng riveting gun

铆工 mǎogōng ❶ riveting (job) ❷ riveter; rivet worker

铆机 mǎojī 〈机械〉riveter: 风动～ pneumatic riveter / 水力～ hydraulic riveter

铆接 mǎojiē rivet; rivet-joint: ～机 riveter; riveting machine / ～工具 riveting set (*or* tool)

铆劲儿 mǎojìnr *also* "卯劲儿" mǎojìnr ❶ with a spurt of energy: 铆着劲儿干 work with an outburst of energy / 我这次没成功，明年再铆把劲儿。I didn't succeed this time, but I'll work with redoubled effort next year. ❷〈方言〉match strength; vie; compete: 他跟我铆上劲了。He's trying to outdo me.

铆距 mǎojù rivet pitch

mào

茂[1] mào ❶ luxuriant; exuberant; lush; flourishing: 蕃～ luxuriant; lush / 繁～ flourishing; luxuriant / 丰～ lush; profuse / 根深叶～ have deep roots and thick foliage; be well established ❷ rich and exquisite; splendid; excellent: 图文并～ be well written and beautifully illustrated / 朴～ sincere and honest

茂[2] mào 〈化学〉cyclopentadiene

茂才 màocái ❶ (another name for 秀才) one who passed the imperial examination at the county level during the Ming and Qing dynasties ❷ scholar; skilful writer

茂齿 màochǐ 〈书面〉in the prime of life: 君已～。You are now in the prime of life.

茂林修竹 màolín-xiūzhú thick forest and tall bamboos

茂密 màomì (of grass or trees) dense; thick; lush: ～的森林 dense forest / 枝叶～的大树 big tree thick with foliage

茂年 màonián in one's vigorous years; in the prime of life

茂盛 màoshèng ❶ luxuriant; exuberant; vigorous; flourishing: 草

木～ luxuriant vegetation /园中花木～ garden flourishing with flowers and plants /枝叶～的植物 plants with exuberant foliage /庄稼长得很～。The crops are growing well. ❷ (of economy, etc.) prosperous; thriving:财源～ rich in financial resources
茂士 màoshì 〈旧语〉 scholar of integrity and talent
茂物 Màowù Bogor, a city in Java Barat of Indonesia
茂郁 màoyù exuberant; luxuriant; flourishing: ～的林带 lush forests

冒

mào ❶ emit; issue; give off; send out, up, or forth: 水壶在～热气。Water in the kettle is boiling. /伤口还在～血。Blood was still oozing from the wound. /从墙后～出一个人头来。Someone peeped out from behind the wall. /他火～三丈。He flew into a towering rage. ❷ run the risk of; risk; brave: ～雪 brave the snow /～风险 run risks; brave danger /～着生命危险救人 rescue people at the risk of one's life /～着枪林弹雨往前冲 charge ahead in the midst of flying bullets ❸ imprudently; recklessly; boldly; rashly: ～言天下大事 venture to comment on world events ❹ falsely; dishonestly: ～称 falsely claim /以假～真 pass off the false as genuine /谨防假～。Beware of imitations! *or* Beware of fakes. ❺ (Mào) a surname
冒场 màochǎng (of actors, actresses, etc.) enter stage early before one's cue
冒充 màochōng feign; pretend to be; pass oneself off as: ～名牌货 pass goods off as famous-brand (*or* name-brand) products /～新闻记者 pretend to be a reporter; pose as a reporter
冒顶 màodǐng 〈矿业〉 roof fall; roof caving: 工作面～ face fall /大～ bulk caving
冒渎 màodú 〈书面〉 bother or annoy (a superior, an elder, etc.): ～清神 sorry to bother you /他言语粗鲁，～了总经理。The general manager took offence at his rude remarks.
冒犯 màofàn wound; offend; affront: ～尊严 wound (*or* affront) sb.'s dignity /如有～之处，请原谅。Please forgive me if I have offended you. *or* Excuse me for any offence that I might have given.
冒富 màofù become better off; become richer than the average: ～大叔 Uncle Maofu (in reference to village folks who have prospered through honest labour)
冒功 màogōng claim another's credit for oneself: ～请赏 ask for reward by claiming sb. else's meritorious deed for oneself
冒汗 màohàn sweat; perspire: 全身～ sweat all over; drip with sweat
冒号 màohào colon (:)
冒红 màohóng ❶ (of the rising sun) emerge (in its crimson hue); emit crimson rays: 他们来到这个村子时，太阳已经～了。The sun was rising when they reached the village. ❷ 〈旧语〉 (of an actor or actress) become popular; become a star
冒坏 màohuài *also* "冒坏水儿" 〈方言〉 be up to mischief; play a dirty trick: 心里～ be given to mischief /大家都知道是他冒的坏。Everybody knew that it was he who played the dirty trick.
冒火 màohuǒ get angry; fly into a temper; flare up; burn with anger: 她心里直～。She was burning with anger. /他一听批评就～。He invariably flared up at criticisms. /这种背后不负责任的议论真使我～。I was infuriated at the irresponsible comments behind my back.
冒尖 màojiān ❶ piled high above the brim; brimful: 筐里的水果装得～了。The basket was fully laden with fruit. ❷ a little over; a little more than: 二十岁刚～的年纪 just over twenty years old ❸ outstanding; conspicuous: ～的人物 conspicuous figure /他在班里算～的。He was top notch in his class. /她干什么都想～儿。She has a desire to excel in whatever she does. ❹ begin to crop up; emerge; appear: 问题一～，就要及时解决。Timely measures must be taken to cope with problems as soon as they emerge.
冒尖户 màojiānhù families or individuals conspicuous for their success either in production or in business, especially those who have become better off quickly
冒金星 mào jīnxīng stars dance before one's eyes (as when one feels dizzy); see stars: 他打得我直～。He hit me so hard on the head that I saw stars. /他跌在台底下，头发晕，两眼～。As he fell down to the foot of the stage, his head began to swim and stars danced before his eyes.
冒进 màojìn premature advance; rash development: 发展经济不能搞～。Premature advance is not the way to develop the economy.
冒口 màokǒu 〈机械〉 rising head; riser: ～浇注 riser gating /～切割 arm sprue cut /～模棒 riser pin /～压力 riser pressure
冒领 màolǐng claim what belongs to others as one's own: 虚报～ fraudulent applications and claims /～失物 falsely claim lost articles
冒昧 màomèi (often used in a self-deprecating manner) venture; take the liberty of; make bold; be presumptuous: ～行事 act presumptuously /～陈辞 venture an opinion /不揣～ I venture to (say sth., ask a question, etc.) /恕我～提出一个问题。Forgive me for taking the liberty to ask a question.
冒名 màomíng go under sb. else's name; assume another's name; pretend to be sb. else: ～货 fake article; fake
冒名顶替 màomíng-dǐngtì pretend to be sb. by assuming his or her name: 从考场上查出一名～者。We identified an imposter among the examinees.
冒牌 màopái counterfeit of well-known trade mark; imitation; fake: ～货 imitation goods; counterfeit goods /～医生 quack doctor; charlatan
冒炮 màopào 〈方言〉 talk nonsense; make irresponsible remarks
冒儿咕咚 màorgūdōng 〈方言〉 rash; hasty; abrupt: ～进来一个人。All of a sudden, a person pushed in.
冒然 màorán rashly; hastily; without careful consideration: 他不听别人的劝告，～做了决定。Rejecting all advice, he made a hasty decision. /对于了解不多的人，当然不能～置信。You should not put your trust lightly in a man about whom you know very little.
冒傻气 mào shǎqì speak or act like a fool: 你看他那样子，浑身～。He looks like a perfect fool.
冒失 màoshi rash; thoughtless; imprudent; reckless: 冒冒失失 recklessly and abruptly /行动～ take rash action; act rashly /说话～ speak without due consideration; talk imprudently /不要～地作出决定。Don't make any decisions off-handedly. /这样去找她未免太～了。It would be indiscreet to drop in on her so casually.
冒失鬼 màoshiguǐ harum-scarum; madcap: 这个～差点儿把我撞倒。The madcap very nearly knocked me over.
冒暑憋寒 màoshǔ-biēhán put up with cold and heat
冒死 màosǐ risk one's life (to do sth.): ～救人 risk one's life to help sb. out of danger; rescue sb. at the risk of one's life
冒天下之大不韪 mào tiānxià zhī dà bùwěi defy world opinion; act against the will of the people; fly in the face of universal condemnation
冒头 màotóu ❶ begin to crop up; emerge; appear: 不良倾向一～我们就要立即设法制止。Whenever an unhealthy trend appears, we must immediately try to stop it. /这个间谍隐藏十年后终于～了。The spy who was in hiding for ten years finally surfaced. ❷ more than: 年纪有三十～ over thirty years old
冒险 màoxiǎn venture; take a risk; take chances; have an adventure: ～航海 venture the seas / 军事～ military adventure /～政策 adventurist policy /～犯难 brave danger and difficulty; take the bull by the horns /～抢救落水儿童 rescue a drowning child despite the risk /投资时不要～。Don't take chances with your investments. /他从不在结了冰的路上～骑车。He never risked cycling on icy roads.
冒险家 màoxiǎnjiā adventurer: 上海解放前是～的乐园。Before liberation, Shanghai was an adventurers' paradise.
冒险主义 màoxiǎnzhǔyì adventurism: ～者 adventurist
冒烟 màoyān ❶ (of smoke) rise; (of a chimney, etc.) belch smoke: 烟囱～。Smoke is rising from the chimney. *or* The chimney is belching smoke. ❷ 〈方言〉 fly into a rage; flare up: 他一听这话就～，追问是谁说的。He flared up at these words and insisted on knowing who said them.
冒雨 màoyǔ brave rains: ～抢修 make hasty (*or* rushed) repairs in the teeth of a rainstorm /他们～回家。They returned home in spite of the rain.
冒支 màozhī withdraw money under an assumed name: ～赈款 withdraw relief funds for other purposes
冒撞 màozhuàng rash; crude and rash: 办事～ act rashly
冒嘴 màozuǐ 〈口语〉 (of the sun) rise just above the horizon: 太阳都～了，该赶路了。The sun is up already. It's time we started on our journey.

瑁

mào *see* "玳瑁" dàimào

帽

mào ❶ headgear; cap; hat: 便～ cap /草～ straw hat /风～ cowl-like hat worn in winter /八角～ octagonal cap /军～ army cap; service cap /礼～ hat worn on formal occasions /瓜皮～ skullcap /安全～ safety helmet /箬～ broad-rimmed hat made of indo-

calamus splints and leaves /纱~ gauze cap (worn by feudal officials) /乌纱~ black gauze cap for court officials /鸭舌~ peaked cap /潜水~ diving helmet /睡~ nightcap /柳条~ wicker cap /太阳~ sun hat; topee; pith helmet /缨~ hat or cap with tassels /雨~ rain cap; hood /飞行~ aviator's helmet /棉~ cotton-padded cap /贝雷~ beret /喜欢戴高~ fond of flattery ❷ cap-like cover:笔~儿 cap of a pen, pencil or writing brush /钉~ head of a nail /螺~ (screw) nut /螺丝~ (screw) nut /子宫~ cervical cap

帽边 màobiān flat; brim (of a hat)

帽翅 màochì two wing-like parts stretching from the back of a gauze cap worn by court officials in old times

帽带 màodài hatband

帽耳 mào'ěr flaps of a cap (for the protection of ears)

帽钩 màogōu hatpin

帽盒 màohé hat box

帽花 màohuā 〈口语〉 insignia or badge on a cap

帽徽 màohuī insignia or badge on a cap; cap insignia:红星~ red star insignia on a cap

帽盔儿 màokuīr skullcap; helmet

帽料 màoliào hatting

帽舌 màoshé peak of a cap; visor

帽头 màotóu old-style cap:毡~ felt cap /小~ skullcap

帽檐 màoyán brim of a hat

帽章 màozhāng *see* "帽徽"

帽子 màozi ❶ headgear; hat; cap: 毛皮~ fur-lined hat ❷ label; tag; brand:乱扣~ indiscriminately stick political labels (on people); engage in indiscriminate name-calling /摘~ rid (sb.) of a label; remove a label (from sb.) /开~工厂〈贬义〉 specialize in sticking vicious labels on others /甩掉落后的~ be lifted out of backwardness

耄

mào ❶ octogenarian ❷ advanced in years; aged:~耋之年 advanced in age

耄期 màoqī octogenarians and centenarians

耄思 màosī confused thoughts

芼

mào 〈书面〉 pick; pull up (grass, vegetables, etc.)

芼羹 màogēng vegetable soup

眊

mào 〈书面〉 dim-sighted; blurred in eyesight

眊聩 màokuì weak in eyesight and hard of hearing

眊眊 màomào dim in vision

皃

mào *see* "貌"

貌

mào looks; look; appearance:美~ good looks /新~ new look /其~不扬 ugly (*or* awkward) in one's appearance; unpleasant look /风~ style and features; graceful bearing and handsome appearance; scenery /地~ general configuration of the earth's surface; topography /概~ general picture /面~ appearance; features /品~ character and looks /全~ complete picture; full view /容~ facial appearance; looks /体~ (of a person) posture and facial features /外~ look; appearance /相~ looks; facial features /笑~ smiling expression /才~双全 be both talented and good-looking; be both beautiful and gifted /~慧心毒 bear the semblance of an angel but have the heart of a devil /以~取人 judge people by outward appearance /花容月~ (of a woman) fair as a flower and beautiful as the moon

貌不惊人 màobùjīngrén one's looks are not attractive — quite ordinary in appearance; plain

貌合神离 màohé-shénlí (of two persons or parties) look united but differ at heart; be apparently in harmony but essentially at variance:这些国家的所谓团结合作从来就是~，明争暗斗。Despite the apparent unity and cooperation, these countries have actually been at loggerheads with each other.

貌似 màosì in appearance; seemingly: ~公正 seem to be impartial /~强大 seem strong; appear to be powerful /~鲜花，心如蛇蝎 have a serpent's heart hidden under the guise of an angel's face

貌相 màoxiàng ❶ facial features; looks; appearance ❷ judge by appearance:人不可~，海水不可斗量。Never judge people by their appearance; never measure sea water with a *dou* (a small grain-measure).

贸

mào trade; commerce; exchange of goods:外~ foreign trade /财~ finance and trade (*or* commerce) /抱布~丝 carry (cloth-)money to buy silk (in ancient times)

贸促会 màocùhuì ❶ (short for 贸易促进会) trade promotion council; committee or board for promoting trade ❷ (Màocùhuì) China Council for the Promotion of International Trade

贸发会议 Màofā Huìyì (short for 联合国贸易发展会议) United Nations Conference on Trade and Development (UNCTAD)

贸迁 màoqiān 〈书面〉 trade: ~有无 supply each other's needs through trade /~致富 get rich through trade

贸然 màorán rashly; hastily; without careful thought: ~决定 make a hasty decision /~行动 act rashly /不敢~下笔 dare not begin writing or painting without careful consideration

贸易 màoyì trade; commerce; exchange of goods: 对外~ foreign trade /国内~ domestic trade /国际~ international trade /边境~ border trade /民间~ non-governmental trade /有形~ visible trade /无形~ invisible trade /转口~ transit trade; entrepôt /记账~ trade under clearing agreement /补偿~ compensatory trade /直接~ direct trade /易货~ barter trade /三角~ triangular trade /~中心 trade centre /~政策 trade policy /自由~区 free trade zone /关税及~总协定 General Agreement on Tariffs and Trade (GATT) /~顺差 favourable balance of trade /~逆差 unfavourable balance of trade /~外汇 foreign exchange earnings through trade /~自由化 trade liberalization /~年度 trade year /~往来 commercial interflow

贸易保护主义 màoyì bǎohùzhǔyì (trade) protectionism

贸易壁垒 màoyì bìlěi trade barrier

贸易差额 màoyì chā'é balance of trade

贸易赤字 màoyì chìzì trade deficit

贸易风 màoyìfēng 〈气象〉 trade wind

贸易界 màoyìjiè trading or business community

贸易平衡 màoyì pínghéng trade balance

贸易融资 màoyì róngzī trade financing

贸易条件 màoyì tiáojiàn terms of trade

贸易限制 màoyì xiànzhì trade restrictions

贸易协定 màoyì xiédìng trade agreement

贸易协定书 màoyì xiédìngshū trade protocol

贸易战 màoyìzhàn trade war

贸易总额 màoyì zǒng'é total volume of trade

袤

mào 〈书面〉 lengthwise (from north to south):广~ vast expanse

菽

mào

菽蕿 màosǎo 〈植物〉 *Butomus umbellatus*

懋

mào ❶ 〈书面〉 urge; encourage: ~穑 encourage hard work in farming ❷ grand; majestic; splendid: ~绩 splendid achievements /~典 grand ceremony ❸ *see* "茂[1]" mào

懋迁 màoqiān *also* "贸迁" màoqiān 〈书面〉 trade; commerce

懋赏 màoshǎng 〈书面〉 reward with money, promotion, etc. in order to encourage:破格~ break a rule to promote sb. in rank (*or* offer sb. a rich reward)

瞀

mào 〈书面〉 ❶ indistinct vision; dizzy ❷ confused; bewildered ❸ ignorant; benighted; purblind: ~儒 stupid or ignorant scholar

瞀瘛 màochì 〈中医〉 symptoms of indistinct vision and spasms

瞀乱 màoluàn 〈书面〉 ❶ confused; delirious; muddled ❷ chaotic; in disorder: 纲纪~。Law and order have broken down. /是非~。Right and wrong are confounded.

瞀瞀 màomào not daring to look someone in the eye

me

嚜

me *see* "嘛" ma

么(麽、[1]末)

me ❶ *used as suffix*:那~，我们呆在家里好了。In that case we may as well stay at home. /那~，他是无辜的了。If so, he is innocent. /多~美! How beautiful! /多~好的天气!

What a fine (*or* beautiful) day! /怎～不自己去? Why not go yourself? /怎～办? What is to be done? /多～可怕! How terrible it is! /不那～现实。It's not so realistic (*or* not very practical). /我们要办的事这～多。We've got so much to do. /要～他去,要～我去。Either he or I must go. ❷ *used in a line of verse for balance or euphony*: 金秋的北京美呀～美如花。Beautiful as a garden of flowers is the city of Beijing in this golden season of autumn.

méi

没 méi *see* "没有" méiyǒu

see also mò

没边儿 méibiānr 〈方言〉 ❶ groundless; baseless; unfounded: 别说这～的话。Don't make such groundless remarks. *or* Don't say things which you know are not true. ❷ without limit; excessively; over: 吹牛吹得～了 bragging most unashamedly and wildly; unabashed bragging /这孩子淘气淘得～了。This child is hopelessly naughty.

没出息 méi chūxi unworthy; good-for-nothing: 这人终日游手好闲,是个～的人。He loiters about all day long, and is really a good-for-nothing.

没词儿 méicír 〈口语〉 be at a loss for words; get stuck; be speechless: 他说了半截就～了。He was at a loss for words and stopped short in the middle of a sentence.

没错儿 méicuòr ❶ to be sure; surely; certainly: ～,就是这么回事。I'm quite sure that this is what happened. /～,准是她把书放错了地方。That's it! She must have mislaid the book somewhere. ❷ can't go wrong; be a sure success: 照我说的办法去做,准保～。Do as I say and you won't go wrong.

没大没小 méidà-méixiǎo be impolite to one's superiors or elders; have no manners

没胆气 méi dǎnqì lacking in courage; wimpy: 他怎么这样～,没果断! How could he be so wimpy, so wishy-washy!

没得 méide 〈方言〉 not have; there is not; be without: 这个厂长～一点架子。The director of the factory is very modest and unassuming. /光急也是～用的。It's no use getting so worried about it.

没得说 méideshuō 〈方言〉 ❶ be on intimate terms; be cronies: 老弟,咱哥俩儿～。My boy, we are buddies, aren't we? ❷ really good; incomparably fine; perfect: 这东西的质量～。This product is of very high quality. /这里的服务态度～。The service here is excellent. *or* You couldn't find a place with better service.

没法儿 méifǎr ❶ *also* "没法子" cannot help it; can do nothing about it: 他～,只好答应。He has no alternative (*or* choice) but to comply. /他这件事我真～去说。I'm really in no position to bring up the matter on his behalf. /她如果真的不来,我也～。I can do nothing about it if she should choose not to come. /他拿他那个宝贝女儿～。He could do nothing with that spoiled daughter of his. ❷ 〈方言〉 incomparably fine; extremely good: 今天这场戏,～那么好的了。You couldn't find a better play than the one we had today. *or* Today's theatrical performance is simply perfect by any standard. ❸ be impossible; can't possibly: 这事儿你～不知道。You can't possibly be unaware of the matter. *or* It is impossible that you don't know anything about the matter.

没分晓 méi fēnxiǎo (mostly used in the early vernacular) lack common sense; be muddled; be confused: 这人好～。The chap simply has no sense! *or* What a muddle-headed guy!

没稿子 méi gǎozi 〈方言〉 have no plan; have no idea: 这件事该怎么办,我还～呢。I don't know yet how to handle this. /明天到哪儿去,我也没准稿子。I have no definite idea where to go tomorrow.

没骨头 méi gǔtou 〈口语〉 have no backbone; be spineless: 他这人怎么这样～! How is it that he is so spineless!

没关系 méi guānxi it doesn't matter; it's nothing; that's all right; never mind: 如果大家都觉得～,我可得开窗了。If nobody minds, I'll open the window. /"真对不起,我把汤洒在桌布上了。""～,能洗掉。""I'm sorry I've spilt some soup on the tablecloth." "Never mind (*or* That's all right). It'll wash out." /听不懂～,我再讲解一遍。It doesn't matter if you find it difficult to follow me. I'll explain it once again.

没规矩 méi guīju have bad manners: 这孩子真～。This boy has no manners.

没好气 méi hǎoqì be ill-humoured; be cross; sulk: 他在外边碰了钉子,回到家里就～。Every time he ran into trouble somewhere, he would come back and take it out on his family.

没结没完 méijié-méiwán 〈方言〉 without end; endless: 这事儿你不解决好,我可跟你～! If you don't handle this well, I'll never let you off.

没斤两 méi jīnliǎng 〈口语〉 (of persons) commonplace; ordinary; mediocre: 他们尽是些～的人,成不了什么气候。They are a bunch of mediocrities, capable of nothing.

没劲 méijìn ❶ weak: 浑身～ feel very weak ❷ uninteresting: 这电影真～。This film is dull as ditchwater.

没精打采 méijīng-dǎcǎi *also* "无精打采" wújīng-dǎcǎi listless; in low spirits; languid; lackadaisical: 他升学考试没考好,近来总是～的。He has been listless lately as he failed the entrance examination. /她一夜没睡,脸上～的。She looked lackadaisical after a sleepless night.

没救 méijiù beyond cure; incurable; hopeless: 他伤势严重,恐怕是～了。He is probably beyond cure, as he is so seriously wounded. /这人屡教不改,真～。The man is simply hopeless, for he has refused to mend his ways despite repeated admonition.

没空儿 méikòngr have no time (for sth. or sb.): 我这两天很忙,～看电影。I have been too busy for the past few days to go to the movies.

没来头 méi láitou ❶ without rhyme or reason; uncalled for; unprovoked ❷ 〈方言〉 it doesn't matter; it's nothing; that's all right; never mind: ～,这件事就包在我身上。Never mind. Just leave the matter to me.

没来由 méi láiyóu (mostly used in the early vernacular) without rhyme or reason; uncalled for; unprovoked: 我好～地挨了一顿骂。I got a scolding for no reason at all.

没落儿 méilàor *also* "没落子" 〈方言〉 poor; without the means of livelihood: 他穷得～,吃尽了苦头。He suffered untold hardships in dire poverty.

没脸 méiliǎn be too ashamed (to do sth.): ～见人 too ashamed to show one's face /～出门 too ashamed to appear in public

没良心 méi liángxīn have no conscience; be ungrateful; be heartless: 他是个～的人,我不愿同他打交道。I don't want to have anything to do with him, he is so ungrateful. /以恶报善,此人真～。Returning evil for good, this fellow has no conscience at all.

没…没… méi…méi… ❶ *used before two synonyms to emphasize negation*: 没完没了 interminable; endless; ceaseless /没羞没臊 shameless; have no sense of shame /没亲没故 without any relatives or friends — having no intimate relationship whatsoever /没规没矩 have no manners ❷ *used before two antonyms to indicate failure to distinguish things*: 没轻没重 with no sense of propriety; tactless /没早没晚 have no sense of time /没日没夜 day and night; days on end /这简直是没上没下了! This was gross disrespect (for one's elders and superiors).

没门儿 méiménr 〈方言〉 ❶ have no means of doing sth.: 奔走好几天,还是～。I've been rushed off my feet for days but still cannot find a way out. /要办这件事儿,我可～。I haven't got the knack of handling matters like this. ❷ impossible: 今年要完成这项工作,我看～。I think it is out of the question to complete the project by the end of the year. ❸ no way; nothing doing: 他想得头等奖,～。He hasn't got the ghost of a chance of getting the first prize. /他想骗我,～。If he wants to fool me, he has got the wrong man. /你想不干了?～! You want to back out? No way!

没命 méimìng ❶ die: 他要不是及时被送到医院,早就～了。If he had not been rushed to hospital in time, he would have given up the ghost. ❷ desperately; for all one is worth; like mad: ～地工作 work with all one's might; exert all one's strength; put one's shoulder to the wheel /溃败的敌军～地逃跑。The routed enemy troops fled for dear life. /我推着大车～地向前奔。I pushed the cart, rushing forward for all I was worth. ❸ not born under a lucky star; having no luck: 看来我没有这个命。It seems as if I was not predestined to enjoy such good luck.

没跑儿 méipǎor certainly; undoubtedly: 这次你输定了,～! Without a doubt, you are bound to lose this time.

没皮没脸 méipí-méiliǎn *also* "没脸没皮" have no sense of shame; be shameless: 你好意思干出这种～的事! How could you have done such a shameful (*or* disgraceful) thing!

没谱儿 méipǔr 〈方言〉 not be certain; be unsure; have no idea: 今晚吃什么,我还～呢。I have no idea what we are going to have for

dinner. /事情下一步该怎么进行,她心里一点谱也没有。So far she has no inkling for the next move. /这人尽干些~的事。He is always doing something unimaginable.

没趣 méiqù feel neglected; get snubbed; feel unwanted:自讨~ ask for a snub; court a rebuff /没人理她,她觉得~,只好走了。Feeling left out in the cold, she slunk off.

没商量儿 méi shāngliangr not be open to discussion or negotiation; no room for mediation or compromise:你一点儿不让步,这事儿~了。There's nothing more to discuss since you wouldn't make any concessions.

没深没浅 méishēn-méiqiǎn with no sense of propriety; tactless; improper:对老人家怎能那样~地说话! How could you speak so tactlessly to an elder!

没什么 méi shénme ❶ it doesn't matter; it's nothing; that's all right; never mind:一点小病,~。Well, a bit under the weather, nothing serious. ❷ don't mention it; it's a pleasure; you're welcome:"谢谢你的帮助。""~。""Thank you for your kindness." "Don't mention it."

没事 méishì ❶ have nothing to do; be free:今晚~,咱俩去喝一杯,好吗? Shall we go for a drink this evening as we have nothing to do? /~咱俩下盘棋。Let's have a game of chess since we are free now. ❷ unemployed; out of work:他近来~,在家闲着。Recently he has been out of work, staying idle at home. ❸ it doesn't matter; it's nothing; never mind:"对不起踩了你一脚。""~。""Sorry to have stepped on your foot." "That's all right." ❹ out of danger; nothing serious:经过医生抢救,他~了。After the emergency treatment, he was out of danger. /只磕破皮,~。Just a scratch. Nothing serious. ❺ have no responsibility; not get involved or implicated:你把问题交代清楚就~了。You won't get implicated if you make a clean breast of all the problems.

没事人 méishìrén person not involved in a matter; person who does not care (about a matter, situation, etc.):他捅了那么大的娄子,却像个~儿似的。He has caused such serious trouble and yet looks as if he had nothing to do with it.

没事找事 méishì-zhǎoshì ❶ not let the sleeping dog lie; ask for trouble:你去瞎掺和什么,真是~。Why chip in? Aren't you asking for trouble? *or* Why don't you leave the sleeping dog lie? ❷ kick up a fuss; nit-pick:别跟我过不去,~。Don't nit-pick. That's deliberately kicking up a fuss.

没说的 méishuōde *also*"没有说的";"没的说" ❶ faultless; perfect; impeccable:这活儿干得很好,~。The job is really well done. It's perfect. /他的文笔是~。He writes in an impeccable style. /他的发音是~。His pronunciation is faultless. ❷ without question; undoubtedly:~,他是最适合干这活的人。Without question, he is the right man for the job. /~,他肯定会同意这个建议。Undoubtedly, he will agree to the proposal. ❸ naturally; of course:这点小事我能帮助,~。Of course, I can do something to help in such small matters.

没挑儿 méitiāor flawless; impeccable; perfect:这些橘子真~。You couldn't find better tangerines anywhere. /她的服务态度那是~了。Her service attitude couldn't be more friendly.

没头没脑 méitóu-méinǎo ❶ (say or do sth.) lacking in coherence or logic; abrupt:他听了这句~的话愣住了。He was struck dumb by this abrupt remark. ❷ for no reason; uncalled-for; unwarranted; unprovoked:我被他~地训了一顿。He gave me a talking-to for no conceivable reason. ❸ regardless of consequences:举起皮鞭~地打 whip relentlessly

没完 méiwán not over; not through:雨下个~。It rained interminably. /他欺负人,我跟他~。He is such a bully that I won't let him off by any means.

没味道 méi wèidao ❶ tasteless; not tasty; bland:这个菜太~。The dish is too bland for me. ❷ dull; insipid; uninteresting:这部影片太长,没有味道。The film is too long to be interesting.

没味儿 méiwèir ❶ tasteless:嘴里~ have a jaded appetite ❷ uninteresting:下棋~,咱还是打乒乓球去。It is no fun playing chess. Let's go and play table tennis.

没戏 méixì 〈方言〉 beyond hope; hopeless:这件事~了。This matter is hopeless. /他~了。There is no longer any hope for him.

没下梢 méi xiàshāo (mostly used in the early vernacular) come to no good end; end up badly:怎么做这~的事! Why should you do this sort of thing? It will end up badly for you.

没想儿 méixiǎngr no likelihood; no chance:今天晚上停电,文艺演出~了。As there is no electricity tonight, we cannot expect the performance to take place as scheduled.

没心肝 méi xīngān heartless; unconscionable:无所不用其极的~的坏人 heartless wretch who would go to any length

没心拉肠 méixīn-lācháng 〈方言〉 in no mood:她连烧火做饭都~的,不是忘了刷锅,就是忘了添柴。She is not even in a mood to feed the fire or cook a meal, forgetting either to clean the pot or add firewood to the fire.

没心没肺 méixīn-méifèi unthinking:他是个炮筒子,说话做事~。He always shoots off his mouth, saying or doing something without thinking.

没心眼儿 méi xīnyǎnr not calculating; simple and direct:他这个人~。He is not the calculating type. *or* He is simple and direct.

没行止 méi xíngzhǐ (mostly used in the early vernacular) guilty of a misdemeanour or of immoral conduct

没兴 méixìng (mostly used in the early vernacular) be down on one's luck; be out of luck

没羞 méixiū unabashed; without shame; shameless:你嘴真馋,~。You are such a glutton, shame on you. /她不答理他,他还追着说,真~! He really degraded himself by following her and talking to her when she gave him the cold shoulder.

没眼色 méi yǎnsè be slow in taking hints; not know how to do the right thing at the right time

没样儿 méiyàngr have no manners; be unruly:这孩子成天价乱打乱闹,真~。This child has no manners, unruly and rowdy all day.

没意思 méi yìsi ❶ bored:她一个人待在家里实在~。Staying at home all day, she is bored stiff. ❷ uninteresting; dull; flat:这个电影平淡无奇,真~! The story of the film is insipid. It is truly dull. *or* What a boring film!

没影儿 méiyǐngr ❶ without a trace; out of sight:等我追出门,他早跑得~了。When I rushed out of the gate, he had already vanished without a trace. ❷ groundless; baseless; unfounded; not true:你说他去过,这是~的事。You say he has been there, but it is not true.

没有 méiyǒu ❶ not have; be without:他~票。He has no ticket. /她~理由不去。She has no excuse for not going. /那谣言是~根据的。The rumour was baseless. /鱼~水就活不了。Fish cannot live without water. /~火药的爆竹 — 中看不中用 fire-cracker without powder — good only for show /~见过世面 green and inexperienced ❷ there is not:那里~人。There is nobody there. /柜子里什么也~。There is nothing whatsoever in the cabinet. /草坪上~人了,只是铁栏杆旁边还有个黑影。The lawn was deserted except for one lone dark figure beside the iron railing. ❸ *used before* 谁 *or* 哪个 *to mean* "*nobody*":~谁会这样做。Nobody would care to act like that. /~哪个说过这样的话。No one seems to have said such words (*or* made such remarks). ❹ not as...as...; not...than...:问题~那么严重。The problem is not that serious. /事情~你想的那么容易。Things are not as simple as you think. /谁都~他跑得快。Nobody runs as fast as he does. ❺ scarcely; less than:他跑了~几步就站住了。Scarcely had he run a few steps when he stopped. /这间房子~十平方米。The floor space of the room is less than ten square metres. ❻ not yet:我~收到他的来信。I haven't heard from him yet. ❼ did not:银行昨天~开门。The bank did not open yesterday.

没有的话 méiyǒudehuà it's not true; there's nothing of the sort

没有的事儿 méiyǒudeshìr there's nothing of the sort; it's out of the question

没有种 méiyǒuzhǒng *also* "没种" gutless; chicken-hearted; faint-hearted; timid; cowardly

没缘 méiyuán have not had the good fortune (to do sth.)

没辙 méizhé can find no way out; be at one's wits' end; be helpless:我也~,你看怎么办好? I have reached the end of my tether. What do you think we should do?

没治 méizhì 〈方言〉❶ incurable; beyond cure, hopeless:他病到这个程度,已经~了。He is so ill that he is beyond cure. ❷ not know how to deal (with sb. or sth.); be helpless:这孩子忒淘气,大人拿他~。The child is so naughty that even grown-ups cannot do anything with him. ❸ first-class; perfect:全聚德的烤鸭,~啦。The roast duck served in Quanjude Restaurant is simply superb.

没准儿 méizhǔnr maybe; perhaps; probably:他~病了。Maybe he has fallen ill. /他~四十出头了。He is probably over 40. /他在那儿要待上一个星期还是一个月,都~。There is no telling whether he will stay there for a week or even a month.

糜（穈、穈） méi

see also mí

糜子 méizi 〈植物〉broom corn millet

煤 méi coal：褐～ brown coal; lignite /焦～ coking coal /块～ lump coal /气～ gas coal /沥青～ pitch coal /石～ bone coal /瘦～ lean coal /肥～ fat coal; rich coal /多灰分～ ashcoal /烟～ bituminous coal; soft coal /无烟～ anthracite; hard coal /原～ raw coal /粉～ fine coal /泥～ peat /蜂窝～ honey-comb briquet /采～ coal mining /洗～ coal washing /碎～机 coal cracker /装～站 coal station /采～工作面 coal face

煤刨 méibào coal plough

煤仓 méicāng coal bunker; bunker

煤藏 méicáng coal deposits; coal reserves

煤层 méicéng coal seam; coal bed：～巷道 heading /～密度 density of seam /～厚度 coal seam thickness

煤铲 méichǎn coal shovel

煤场 méichǎng coal yard

煤车 méichē coaler; coal scuttle; coal car

煤尘 méichén coal dust：～爆炸 coal dust explosion

煤尘肺 méichénfèi 〈医学〉anthracosis; black lung

煤斗 méidǒu coal scuttle; scuttle

煤毒 méidú gas poisoning; carbon monoxide poisoning

煤房 méifáng bordroom：～杂工 bordroom man

煤肺 méifèi coal pneumoconiosis

煤肺病 méifèibìng anthrocosis; black lung

煤肺症 méifèizhèng soot lung

煤酚皂溶液 méifēnzào róngyè 〈药学〉creosol and soup solution; saponated creosol solution; lysol

煤粉 méifěn barings; dust from cutting coal seams

煤粉发动机 méifěn fādòngjī 〈机械〉coal dust engine

煤粉清除器 méifěn qīngchúqì fine coal cleaner

煤矸石 méigānshí coal gangue

煤港 méigǎng coal harbour

煤柜 méiguì bunker

煤耗 méihào coal consumption

煤黑油 méihēiyóu *also*"煤焦油" coal tar

煤黑子 méihēizi 〈旧语〉〈贬义〉coal miner

煤核儿 méihúr partly-burnt briquet; coal cinder

煤化作用 méihuà zuòyòng coalification; carbonification

煤灰 méihuī coal ash; coom

煤火盆 méihuǒpén brazier; brasier

煤焦油 méijiāoyóu coal tar

煤精 méijīng *also*"煤玉" jet; black amber

煤矿 méikuàng coal mine; coalpit; colliery：～工人 coal miner; collier /～业 coal mining

煤老虎 méilǎohǔ enterprise which consumes huge amounts of coal

煤面 méimiàn *also*"煤面子" coal dust

煤末 méimò *also*"煤末子" culm：～沉着病 bituminosis

煤泥 méiní slush; slurry

煤气 méiqì gas; coal gas：～设备 gas fitting /～中毒 carbon monoxide poisoning; gas poisoning /～工 gasman /～装修工 gas fitter

煤气爆炸 méiqì bàozhà explosion of coal gas

煤气表 méiqìbiǎo gas meter

煤气厂 méiqìchǎng gasworks; gashouse

煤气灯 méiqìdēng gas lamp：～光 gaslight

煤气发生炉 méiqì fāshēnglú gas producer

煤气管道 méiqì guǎndào gas conduit; gas pipe

煤气罐 méiqìguàn gas tank; gas container

煤气机 méiqìjī gas engine

煤气井 méiqìjǐng 〈石油〉gasser

煤气警报器 méiqì jǐngbàoqì gas alarm

煤气炉 méiqìlú gas stove; gas cooker

煤气热水器 méiqì rèshuǐqì gas water-heater

煤气灶 méiqìzào gas burner; gas range

煤气灶具 méiqì zàojù gas appliance

煤气总管 méiqì zǒngguǎn gas main

煤球 méiqiú (egg-shaped) briquet

煤山 Méishān Coal Hill (in Beijing), known today as Jingshan (景山)

煤山雀 méishānquè 〈动物〉coalmouse; coal tit

煤溚 méitǎ *see*"煤焦油"

煤炱 méitái soot

煤炭 méitàn coal：～工业 coal industry

煤炭基地 méitàn jīdì coal base

煤田 méitián coalfield：～地质学 coal geology

煤烃 méitīng 〈化工〉coaleum

煤矽肺 méixīfèi anthracosilicosis; miner's phthisis

煤相 méixiàng 〈矿业〉coaly facies

煤烟 méiyān ❶ smoke from burning coal：～污染 smoke pollution ❷ coal soot; soot

煤烟子 méiyānzi soot

煤窑 méiyáo coalpit

煤油 méiyóu kerosene; paraffin：～灯 kerosene lamp /～炉 kerosene stove

煤玉 méiyù jet; black amber：～页岩 jet shale

煤渣 méizhā coal cinder：～路 cinder road /～跑道 cinder track /～砖 cinder block

煤砟子 méizhǎzi small piece of coal

煤站 méizhàn coaling station; coaling base

煤柱 méizhù 〈矿业〉pillar：～采煤法 pillar working

煤砖 méizhuān briquet

煤钻 méizuàn 〈矿业〉coal borer

媒 méi ❶ matchmaker; go-between：保～ act as matchmaker /做～ play cupid; be a go-between ❷ intermediary; vehicle; medium：触～ catalyst; catalytic agent /传～ (mass) media /虫～ antomophily; insect pollination /风～ wind pollination /酒为色之～。Intemperance often leads to sexual indulgence.

媒介 méijiè medium; vehicle; vector：～过程 vection /～昆虫 insect vector /传染疾病的～ vehicle of disease; vector /蜜蜂是传播花粉的～。Bees are a medium of pollination. /他在两公司之间起拉线搭桥的～作用。He played an intermediary role between the two firms by helping them establish contacts.

媒介物 méijièwù vector; intermedium

媒鸟 méiniǎo decoy

媒婆 méipó 〈旧语〉(professional) woman matchmaker

媒染 méirǎn mordant dyeing：～染料 mordant dye

媒染剂 méirǎnjì 〈化学〉mordant

媒人 méiren matchmaker; go-between

媒妁 méishuò 〈书面〉matchmaker; go-between：父母之命，～之言 (of old-fashioned marriage) will of the parents and words of a matchmaker

媒体 méitǐ medium; media; mass media：多～ multimedia

媒体经纪人 méitǐ jīngjìrén media broker

媒体转换 méitǐ zhuǎnhuàn media conversion

媒怨 méiyuàn 〈书面〉cause ill will; be invidious：此人过于刚直，是以～。He is upright to a fault and is apt to offend people.

媒质 méizhì 〈物理〉medium：吸收～ absorbing medium

媒子 méizi decoy：鸟～ decoy bird /他是个诱顾客买假货的～。He is a decoy for tricking customers into buying fake goods.

玫 méi 〈书面〉a kind of jade

玫瑰 méigui 〈植物〉rugosa rose; rose：～花 rose /～树 rose bush /～色 rosiness

玫瑰醇 méiguichún 〈化工〉rhodinol

玫瑰红 méiguihóng rose-coloured; rose-red; rosy

玫瑰精 méiguijīng rhodamine toner

玫瑰糠疹 méigui kāngzhěn 〈医学〉pityriasis rosea

玫瑰露酒 méigui lùjiǔ rosolio; rosoglio

玫瑰蜜 méiguimì honey of rose

玫瑰油 méiguiyóu rose oil; attar

玫瑰疹 méiguizhěn 〈医学〉roseola; rose-rash

玫瑰紫 méiguizǐ *also*"玫瑰红" (of colour) rosy; rose-red

枚 méi ❶〈量词〉*used of small objects*：一～纪念章 a badge /两～古币 two ancient coins ❷(Méi) a surname

霉（❶黴） méi ❶ mould; mildew：黑～ mould; mildew /曲～ aspergillus ❷ go mouldy; become mildew：发～ go mouldy

霉斑 méibān mildew

M

霉变 méibiàn go mouldy; become mildewed: ~了的粮食当然不能出售。Sale of mouldy grain is of course forbidden.
霉病 méibìng 〈农业〉mildew
霉草 méicǎo 〈植物〉triurid: ~科 triuris
霉臭味 méichòuwèi frowsty; musty
霉大豆 méidàdòu fermented soybeans; tempeh
霉蠹 méidù mildewed and moth-eaten: 这本书保藏了数百年, 仍未~。Though the book has been preserved for several hundred years, it is not mildewed or moth-eaten.
霉腐 méifǔ mildew and rot
霉菌 méijūn mould
霉菌病 méijūnbìng mycosis
霉菌毒素 méijūn dúsù mycotoxin
霉菌素 méijūnsù mycin; mycomycin
霉菌学 méijūnxué mycology: ~家 mycologist
霉烂 méilàn mildewed and rotten; rotten
霉脑 méinǎo (short for 霉菌性脑膜炎)〈医学〉mycomeningitis
霉气 méiqi ❶ damp; musty: 箱笼里只剩些破烂的衣裳, 散发着~。In the suitcase there were some worn-out clothes smelling of mildew. *or* The ragged clothes in the suitcase gave off a mouldy smell. ❷〈方言〉bad luck: 刚出门就下雨, 真~! What bad luck! We had just gone out when it started to rain.
霉乳酒 méirǔjiǔ koumiss; kumiss; kumys; kumyssce
霉天 méitiān *also* "黄梅天" huángméitiān rainy season (usu. in April and May, in the middle and lower reaches of the Yangtze River)
霉头 méitóu bad luck: 触~ have a stroke of bad luck
霉雨 méiyǔ *also* "梅雨" méiyǔ; "黄梅雨" huángméiyǔ intermittent drizzles (in the rainy season in the middle and lower reaches of the Yangtze River)
霉玉米中毒 méiyùmǐ zhòngdú mouldy corn poisoning

莓(苺)

méi certain kinds of berries: 草~ strawberry / 黑~ blackberry / 蛇~ mock-strawberry

梅(楳、槑)

méi ❶ Chinese *mei* flower or its tree (*Prunus mume*); Chinese plum: 话~ preserved plum / 青~ green plum / 酸~ smoked plum; dark plum / 乌~ smoked plum; dark plum / 腊~ wintersweet / 陈皮~ preserved prune / 杨~ red bayberry (*Myrica rubra*) / 榆叶~ flowering plum / 珍珠~ false spiraea ❷ (Méi) a surname

梅毒 méidú 〈医学〉syphilis: ~血清沉淀反应 *also* "康氏试验" Kahn test / ~疗法 syphilotherapy / ~患者 syphilitic / ~专科医师 syphilologist
梅毒瘤 méidúliú gumma
梅毒性溃烂 méidúxìng kuìlàn syphilelcosis
梅毒性眼炎 méidúxìng yǎnyán syphilidophthalmia
梅毒学 méidúxué syphilology
梅毒疹 méidúzhěn syphilide
梅果 méiguǒ 〈植物〉ciruela
梅红色 méihóngsè plum (colour); plum purple
梅红紫色 méihóng zǐsè plum violet
梅花 méihuā ❶ Chinese *mei* blossom; Chinese plum flower ❷〈方言〉wintersweet
梅花扳手 méihuā bānshou double offset ring spanner
梅花草 méihuācǎo bog star; grass-of-parnassus: ~科 *Parnassiaceae*
梅花鹿 méihuālù sika deer; sika; spotted deer
梅花雀 méihuāquè astrild; waxbill
梅花针 méihuāzhēn 〈中医〉cutaneous acupuncture
梅花桩 méihuāzhuāng ❶ pointed bamboo or wooden stakes set in the ground in front of positions or barracks to impede enemy movement ❷ *also* "梅花拳" a kind of Chinese shadow boxing (which requires training to be carried out on wooden piles)
梅尼埃尔氏综合征 Méiní'āi'ěrshì zōnghézhēng *also* "内耳性眩晕综合征" nèi'ěrxìng xuànyùn zōnghézhēng 〈医学〉Ménière's syndrome; Ménière's disease
梅瓶 méipíng prunus vase, a kind of celadon vase popular in the Song Dynasty
梅天 méitiān *see* "霉天" méitiān
梅童鱼 méitóngyú baby croaker
梅文鼎 Méi Wéndǐng Mei Wending (formerly translated as Mei Wen-ting, 1633-1721), mathematician and astronomer of the Qing Dynasty
梅香 méixiāng (mostly used in the early vernacular) servant-girl
梅雨 méiyǔ *also* "黄梅雨" huángméiyǔ *see* "霉雨" méiyǔ
梅子 méizi Chinese plum tree or its fruit

酶

méi 〈生化〉enzyme; ferment: 诱导~ induced enzyme / 蛋白~ protease; proteinase / 胃蛋白~ pepsin / 胰蛋白~ trypsin / 合成~ synzyme / 脂肪~ lipase / 淀粉~ amylase / 同功~ isoenzyme / 消化~ digestive ferment / 赖氨基~ transaminase / 肠激~ enterokinase / 肽~ peptase / 多肽~ polypeptidae / 糖~ carbohydrase / 多糖~ polysaccharase; polyase / 乳糖~ lactase / 蔗糖~ thrombin / 胰~ pancreatin / 还原~ reductase / 胰脂~ pancreatic lipase; steapsin

酶变化 méibiànhuà enzymic change
酶病 méibìng enzymopathy
酶催化 méicuīhuà enzymatic
酶催化合成 méicuīhuà héchéng enzymatic synthesis
酶蛋白 méidànbái 〈生化〉zymoprotein
酶化学 méihuàxué 〈生化〉zymochemistry
酶解 méijiě 〈生化〉zymolysis: ~作用 zymolysis; enzymolysis
酶谱 méipǔ 〈生化〉zymogram
酶水解 méishuǐjiě enzyme hydrolysis
酶学 méixué 〈生化〉enzymology
酶血症 méixuèzhèng fermentemia
酶原 méiyuán zymogen; fermentogen
酶制剂 méizhìjì enzymic preparation

脢(脥)

méi loin; tenderloin

脢子肉 méizìròu tenderloin

眉

méi ❶ eyebrow; brow: 柳叶~ arch eyebrows / 浓~ heavy (*or* thick) eyebrows; bushy eyebrows / 剑~ straight eyebrows slanting upwards and outwards; dashing eyebrows / 蛾~ pretty eyebrows; pretty woman / 愁~ knitted brows; worried look / 横~ frowning / 慈~善目 benevolent and kind countenance / 挤~弄眼 wink at sb. (*or* make eyes at sb.) / 柳~倒竖 (of a woman) raise her eyebrows in anger / 扬~吐气 hold one's head high; feel happy and proud / 举案齐~。A wife lifts the tray to a level with her eyebrows to show respect for her husband. *or* A married couple love and respect each other for life. / 须~皆白。Both one's beard and eyebrows have turned hoary. ❷ top margin of a page: 书~ top of a page; top margin

眉笔 méibǐ eyebrow pencil
眉黛 méidài 〈书面〉eyebrows (in ancient times women used 黛, a black pigment, to paint their eyebrows)
眉豆 méidòu 〈方言〉red bean
眉端 méiduān ❶ glabella; space between the eyebrows: 愁上~ grief clouds one's eyebrows ❷ top margin of a page in a book
眉飞色舞 méifēi-sèwǔ (of one's face) brighten up; beam with joy: 小苏考了个好成绩, 不禁~。Xiao Su couldn't help feeling elated for her good exam results. / 周围的人都惊异地望着她那副~的神情。People around her gazed in surprise at her animated expression.
眉峰 méifēng eyebrows: ~紧皱 with knitted eyebrows
眉高眼低 méigāo-yǎndī facial expression; look: 他就是不愿看人~来行事。He would never watch another's expression and act accordingly. *or* He would never be a yesman.
眉欢眼笑 méihuān-yǎnxiào *also* "眉花眼笑" be all smiles; beam with joy; be very happy
眉急 méijí (short for 燃眉之急) extremely urgent; in urgent or imminent need: 解救~ relieve an urgent need
眉脊 méijǐ superciliary arch; bulge of the forehead
眉尖 méijiān eyebrows: 她把~微微一皱。She knitted her eyebrows slightly.
眉睫 méijié (as close to the eye as) the eyebrow and eyelash: 迫在~ urgent; imminent / 危在~ be in imminent danger / 祸在~。Disaster is impending (*or* close at hand).
眉开眼笑 méikāi-yǎnxiào be all smiles; beam with joy; be wreathed in smiles: 喜得~ be so happy that one's face melts in smiles / 他听到这个消息后, 不禁~。His face lit up after he heard the news.
眉来眼去 méilái-yǎnqù make eyes at each other; flirt with each

other：两人～，似乎彼此有情。It seems that they are in love, for they are making eyes at each other.

眉棱 méiléng brow

眉棱骨 méiléngɡǔ superciliary ridge or arch

眉脸 méiliǎn 〈方言〉face：她～红一阵，白一阵。Her face flushed and turned pale by turns.

眉毛 méimao eyebrow; brow

眉毛胡子一把抓 méimao húzi yībǎzhuā try to grasp the eyebrows and the beard all at the same time — try to attend to everything at once irrespective of priority

眉目 méimù ❶ one's eyebrows and eyes — one's features; looks ❷ essentials; logic; sequence of ideas：文章的～不清楚。The essay is not well organized.

眉目 méimu sign of a possible solution; clue of an outcome：我们的计划已经有了点～了。We are getting somewhere with our plan. /你把事情弄出点～再走。Don't leave here before things begin to take shape. /调动的事情总算有了点～。There is some likelihood (*or* There are signs) that my application for a transfer will be approved.

眉目传情 méimù-chuánqínɡ make sheep's eyes; cast amorous glances：两人～。The two made goo-goo eyes at each other.

眉批 méipī notes made at the top of a page; marginal notes; notes and comments in the (top) margin

眉清目秀 méiqīnɡ-mùxiù fine brows and clear eyes; delicate features; fair complexion：那孩子生得～，十分俊俏。The boy was remarkably handsome.

眉梢 méishāo tip of the brow：喜上～ look very happy /愁锁～ eyebrows furrowed with sorrow /～间露出忧愁的神色 look worried and dejected

眉舒目展 méishū-mùzhǎn look unusually happy; one's face beams with joy

眉题 méití (of newspapers and magazines) bold-faced indicative title above the formal title of an article

眉头 méitóu brows：皱～ knit the brows; frown /～紧锁 with knitted eyebrows

眉头一皱，计上心来 méitóu yī zhòu, jì shànɡ xīn lái knit the brows and a stratagem comes to mind

眉心 méixīn space between the eyebrows

眉眼 méiyǎn eyebrows and eyes; features (of one's face); appearance：～长得很俊 look highly attractive; be very lovely

眉眼高低 méiyǎn-ɡāodī one's real thought and feelings：你这人真不识～，谁都看得出他正发愁呢。You should learn to read a person's thoughts from the look on his face. It's evident that he's worrying about something.

眉宇 méiyǔ 〈书面〉forehead：这人～间显出一股豪气。You can tell from his face that he is a man of valour.

眉月 méiyuè ❶ crescent：一钩～ crescent moon /初三的～ crescent on the 3rd day of the lunar month ❷〈书面〉(of women) crescent-shaped eyebrows

湄

méi 〈书面〉river bank; waterside：在水之～ by the river side

湄公河 Méiɡōnɡhé Mekong River, major river in Southeast Asia, rising in China's Tibet (called Lancang River 澜沧江), flowing out of China's Yunnan Province through Burma, Laos, Thailand, Cambodia and Vietnam into the South China Sea：～三角洲 Mekong Delta

湄南河 Méinánhé Chao Phraya, major waterway of central Thailand

楣

méi lintel (over a door); house：有辱门～ be a disgrace to the family

楣窗 méichuānɡ fanlight; transom; transom window

楣式构造 méishì ɡòuzào 〈建筑〉trabeated construction

嵋

méi *see*“峨嵋”Éméi

镅

méi 〈化学〉americium (Am)

鹛

méi 〈动物〉babbler：钩嘴～ scimitar babbler /噪～ laughing thrush

猸

méi

猸子 méizi 〈动物〉crab-eating mongoose

郿

méi

郿鄠 méihù one of the folk operas in Shaanxi Province originating in the Mei and Hu (now written as 眉 and 户) counties of the province, later quite popular in Shaanxi, Shanxi and Gansu

měi

美[1]

měi ❶ beautiful; pretty; handsome; attractive：健～ healthy and attractive; vigorous and graceful /真、善、～ the true, the good, and the beautiful /风景优～。The landscape is beautiful. ❷ beautify：*see*“～容” ❸ satisfactory; good; gratifying：价廉物～ of reasonable price but high quality; good but inexpensive /完～无缺 perfect in every way (*or* respect) /小两口的日子过得挺～。The young couple lived a life of idyllic happiness. /你想得太～了。I'm afraid you have painted too rosy a picture. ❹ good deed; satisfaction：成人之～ help sb. achieve success /天公不作～。The weather is disappointing. *or* The weather is not cooperative. /何不两全其～? Why not satisfy both sides (*or* parties)? *or* Why not meet both claims? ❺〈方言〉be pleased with oneself; feel smug：瞧他那个样儿，可～得不得了了。Look how pleased he is with himself.

美[2]

Měi ❶ (short for 美洲)：南～ South America ❷ United States of America; America; US：《中～上海公报》*Sino-US Joint Communiqué of 1972* (also known as *Shanghai Communiqué*)

美不胜收 měibùshènɡshōu there are more beautiful things than the eye can take in; be of dazzling splendour：本届菊展，～。This year's chrysanthemum show is a scene of dazzling beauty.

美不胜言 měibùshènɡyán (of landscape) be too beautiful for words; beggar description

美不滋 měibuzī 〈方言〉very pleased with oneself; very proud of oneself：他数学考试得了第一名，心里～的。He was very proud of himself for winning first place in the maths exam.

美餐 měicān ❶ delicious food：～佳肴 delicious food; gourmet food ❷ eat one's fill; have a nice meal：～一顿 have a wonderful meal; eat a square meal

美差 měichāi enviable mission; cushy job; junket：出差桂林可是件～。A business trip to the scenic town of Guilin is a cushy job.

美钞 měichāo American dollar; US paper money; US banknotes; greenback

美称 měichēnɡ laudatory title; good name：苏南素有鱼米之乡的～。The southern part of Jiangsu Province has always enjoyed the reputation of being a land of plenty.

美传 měichuán legendary story (about sb. or sth.)：他早年参加革命，在当地群众中曾有许多～。He joined the revolution at an early age and many a legendary story about him circulated among the local people.

美大司 Měidàsī Department of Affairs of North America and Oceania (of China's Ministry of Foreign Affairs)

美德 měidé virtue; moral excellence：敬老爱幼是中国人民的传统～。Respect for the old and care for the young are traditional virtues of the Chinese people.

美吨 měidūn *also*“短吨” duǎndūn short ton (＝2000 pounds, or 907.18 kilos)

美发 měifà ❶ beautiful hair ❷ (of men) get a haircut; (of women) go to the hairdresser's

美发厅 měifàtīnɡ barber's; hairdresser's

美孚石油公司和托拉斯 Měifú Shíyóu Gōnɡsī hé Tuōlāsī Standard Oil Company and Trust; Standard Oil Company; Standard Oil

美感 měiɡǎn aesthetic feeling; aesthetic perception; sense of beauty：房间的布置给人以～。The interior decorations of the room inspire an aesthetic feeling (*or* are highly aesthetic).

美工 měiɡōnɡ ❶ art designing ❷ art designer

美观 měiɡuān beautiful; artistic; pleasing to the eye：～大方 simple and artistic; elegant and in good taste /室内的布置很～。The room is artistically appointed (*or* decorated).

美国 Měiɡuó United States of America (USA); America：～人

American / ～梦 American dream / ～生活方式 American way of life / ～国会 US Congress / ～海外领地 United States Outlying Territories / ～邮区编码制 ZIP code
美国白蜡树 Měiguó báilàshù American ash; white ash
美国百科全书 Měiguó Bǎikē Quánshū *Encyclopedia Americana*
美国第七舰队 Měiguó Dì-qī Jiànduì US 7th Fleet
美国电话电报公司 Měiguó Diànhuà Diànbào Gōngsī American Telephone and Telegraph Company (AT&T)
美国独立宣言 Měiguó Dúlì Xuānyán Declaration of (American) Independence (July 4, 1776)
美国独立战争 Měiguó Dúlì Zhànzhēng American War of Independence; American Revolution (1775-1783)
美国毒漆树 Měiguó dúqīshù poison sumac
美国革命 Měiguó Gémìng *see* "美国独立战争"
美国公开赛 Měiguó Gōngkāisài 〈体育〉US Open (as in golf)
美国广播公司 Měiguó Guǎngbō Gōngsī American Broadcasting Corporation (ABC)
美国国家标准协会 Měiguó Guójiā Biāozhǔn Xiéhuì American National Standards Institute (ANSI)
美国航空公司 Měiguó Hángkōng Gōngsī American Airlines
美国黑人 Měiguó Hēirén African-American; Black American; Afro-American
美国化 Měiguóhuà Americanization
美国军团 Měiguó Jūntuán American Legion (national veterans organization chartered in 1919)
美国劳工联合会 Měiguó Láogōng Liánhéhuì American Federation of Labor (AFL, established in 1886), now called American Federation of Labor-Congress of Industrial Organizations (AFL-CIO, 劳联-产联)
美国佬 Měiguólǎo 〈贬义〉Yankee
美国南北战争 Měiguó Nán-Běi Zhànzhēng American Civil War (between the northern Union and the Confederate South, 1861-1865)
美国全国商会 Měiguó Quánguó Shānghuì United States Chamber of Commerce
美国石竹 Měiguó shízhú sweet william; bunch pink; *Dianthus barbatus*
美国西部铁杉 Měiguó Xībù tiěshān west coast hemlock
美国新闻署 Měiguó Xīnwénshǔ United States Information Agency (USIA)
美国新闻与世界报导 Měiguó Xīnwén Yǔ Shìjiè Bàodǎo *US News & World Report*, a news weekly first published in 1933 in the United States
美国英语 Měiguó Yīngyǔ *also* "美式英语" American English
美国运通公司 Měiguó Yùntōng Gōngsī American Express Company, established in New York in 1850
美国运通信用卡 Měiguó Yùntōng Xìnyòngkǎ American Express (credit) card
美国在线 Měiguó Zàixiàn America Online (AOL), largest company in the on-line world, founded in 1985, and acquiring Time-Warner in Jan. 2000
美国正教会 Měiguó Zhèngjiàohuì 〈宗教〉American Orthodox Church
美国证券交易所 Měiguó Zhèngquàn Jiāoyìsuǒ American Stock Exchange (ASE *or* AMEX)
美国之音 Měiguó Zhī Yīn Voice of America (VOA)
美国志愿航空队 Měiguó Zhìyuàn Hángkōngduì American Volunteer Group (US air force volunteers under the command of Claire Lee Chennault during China's War of Resistance Against Japanese Aggression), nicknamed the Flying Tigers (飞虎队)
美国仲裁协会 Měiguó Zhòngcái Xiéhuì American Arbitration Association
美好 měihǎo happy; bright; pleasant: ～的未来 bright future / ～的前途 bright (*or* excellent) prospects / ～的形象 beautiful image / ～的回忆 pleasant memories (*or* reminiscences) / ～的希望 high hopes / ～的祝愿 one's best wishes
美化 měihuà beautify; prettify; embellish: ～环境 beautify the surroundings; enhance the beauty of the environment / ～祖国山河 turn the country into a land of beauty / 他不但不认错，反而处处～自己。Instead of admitting his mistake, he tried in every way to make himself look good.
美金 měijīn *see* "美圆"
美劲儿 měijìnr 〈口语〉❶ air of self-satisfaction: 瞧你的～! Look how you are pleased with yourself! ❷ feeling of being relaxed and comfortable: 饭后散散步，那个～就别提啦! Take a walk after dinner, and you'll feel wonderfully relaxed.
美景 měijǐng beautiful scenery or landscape: 良辰～ fine scenery on a bright day
美酒 měijiǔ good wine: ～佳肴 vintage wine and choice food; mellow wine and delicious food
美拉尼西亚 Měilāníxīyà Melanesia (island groups in the southwestern Pacific)
美利坚合众国 Měilìjiān Hézhòngguó *see* "美国"
美利奴羊 měilìnúyáng merino (sheep) (*Ovis aries*)
美丽 měilì beautiful; pretty; fair: ～的鲜花 lovely flower / 洁白～的雪花 white, beautiful flakes of snow / ～动人的故事 beautiful, moving story / ～的姑娘 pretty (*or* charming, *or* attractive) girl
美联社 Měiliánshè (short for 美国联合通讯社) US Associated Press (AP)
美轮美奂 měilún-měihuàn (of a new house, mansion, etc.) tall and splendid; magnificent: ～的北京西客站 magnificent Beijing West Railway Station
美满 měimǎn happy; very satisfactory: ～的婚姻 felicitous marriage / ～的结果 very satisfactory result / ～的结局 happy ending
美貌 měimào ❶ good looks: 此人徒有一副～。The man has nothing but a handsome face. ❷ beautiful; pretty: 年轻～的女子 attractive young woman
美美 měiměi to one's heart's content; to one's great satisfaction: ～地吃一顿 eat one's fill; enjoy a nice square meal / ～地睡上一觉 have a sound sleep
美梦 měimèng fond or pipe dream: ～破灭了 come to the end of a beautiful dream; one's fond dream is shattered
美妙 měimiào exquisite; splendid; wonderful; beautiful: ～的音乐 splendid music; exquisite melody / ～的歌喉 sweet (*or* lovely) voice / ～的诗句 beautiful verse / 生动～的文笔 graphic and graceful style of writing / 发展趋势很不～。The trend of development is rather discouraging (*or* by no means encouraging).
美名 měimíng good name; good reputation: 博得～ win a good reputation / ～传四海。A good name spreads far and wide. / 英雄～传千古。The hero's name shall resound throughout the ages.
美男子 měinánzǐ handsome man; Adonis
美尼尔氏症 měiní'ěrshìzhèng *see* "梅尼埃尔氏综合征" Méiní'āi'ěrshì zōnghézhēng
美女 měinǚ beautiful woman; beauty
美女簪花 měinǚ-zānhuā graceful strokes of calligraphic works
美其名曰 měiqímíngyuē call it by the fine-sounding name of; describe euphemistically as: ～"有利共享" be described euphemistically as "profit-sharing"
美气 měiqì 〈方言〉comfortable; happy; pleasant: 一家人和和睦睦地过日子，该有多～。Isn't it a pleasure and comfort when there is perfect harmony among family members?
美缺 měiquē ideal position or assignment; fat job
美人 měirén beautiful woman; beauty: 她可是我们学校的大～。She is really the queen of the school.
美人斑 měirénbān *also* "美人痣" beauty spot
美人迟暮 měirén-chímù a beauty in her old age — regret over the passing of one's prime
美人计 měirénjì use of a woman to ensnare a man; sex-trap: 外国的某些情报机关常使用～。Some foreign spy rings often employ sex-traps for intelligence purposes.
美人蕉 měirénjiāo 〈植物〉canna; indian shot
美人拳 měirénquán a kind of instrument for massaging an elderly person's back and thigh
美人虾 měirénxiā ghost shrimp
美人香草 měirén-xiāngcǎo beautiful woman and fragrant grass — loyalty to one's sovereign and country
美人鱼 měirényú mermaid
美容 měiróng beauty treatment: ～院 beauty parlour; beauty saloon / ～术 cosmetology / ～专家 cosmetologist / ～手术 plastic surgery / ～师 beauty specialist; beautician
美如冠玉 měirúguānyù (of a man) as beautiful as the jade ornament of a hat — handsome
美色 měisè attractive woman; beauty
美声唱法 měishēng chàngfǎ bel canto: ～歌唱家 bel canto singer /

她擅长～。Her forte is bel canto.
美食 měishí delicious food; delicacies; choice food: ～餐厅 gourmet restaurant
美食家 měishíjiā gourmet; gastronome: 他不是真正的～,只是贪吃而已。He is more the gourmand than the gourmet.
美事 měishì ❶ laudable act; worthy deed ❷ good fortune; stroke of luck: 没想到这样的～会轮到我! Little did I imagine that I should be blessed with such a good fortune.
美术 měishù ❶ fine arts: 工艺～ arts and crafts / ～学院 school of fine arts / ～爱好者 lovers of arts / ～工作者 artist; art workers / ～玻璃器皿 art glass ❷ painting
美术革 měishùgé fancy leather
美术馆 měishùguǎn art gallery
美术家 měishùjiā artist
美术明信片 měishù míngxìnpiàn picture or pictorial postcard
美术片 měishùpiàn 〈影视〉 cartoons, puppet films, etc.
美术品 měishùpǐn work of art; art product
美术设计 měishù shèjì artistic design: 舞台～ stage design
美术字 měishùzì artistic calligraphy; art lettering
美索不达米亚 Měisuǒbùdámǐyà Mesopotamia (a region of southwest Asia between the Tigris and Euphrates rivers)
美谈 měitán salutary tale; anecdote: 传为～ be circulated as an anecdote worthy of emulation
美味 měiwèi ❶ delicious food; delicacy; dainty: 珍馐～ delicacies and dainties / ～佳肴 slap-up meal ❷ delicious; tasty; savoury: ～小吃 dainty (*or* delicious) snacks
美西战争 Měi-Xī Zhànzhēng Spanish-American War (1898)
美秀 měixiù 〈书面〉 ❶ handsome; delicate: 容颜～ be beautiful; be handsome looking; have delicate features ❷ man of outstanding talent: 所交皆一时～。He made friends with those who were the elite of his time (*or* the best and brightest of his time).
美学 měixué aesthetics: ～理论 aesthetic theory / 芭蕾舞～ aesthetics of ballet
美学家 měixuéjiā aesthetician
美言 měiyán ❶ put in a good word (for sb.): 有劳您代为～几句。Please be kind enough to put in a few good words for me. ❷ 〈书面〉 nice or fine works: ～不善,善言不美。Fine words may not be well-intentioned, while words from one's heart may not be pleasant to the ear.
美言不信 měiyán-bùxìn high-sounding words may not necessarily be true
美艳 měiyàn beautiful and glamourous
美以美会 Měiyǐměihuì 〈基督教〉 Methodist Episcopal Church
美意 měiyì kindness; goodwill: 谢谢你的一番～。Thank you very much for your hospitality and kindness. / ～延年。A carefree life insures longevity.
美玉 měiyù fine jade
美育 měiyù aesthetic education; art education
美誉 měiyù good reputation; fame; glory
美元 měiyuán *see* "美圆"
美圆 měiyuán *also* "美元"; "美金" US dollar; American dollar; buck: 欧洲～ Eurodollar / ～区 dollar area / ～外交 dollar diplomacy / ～储备 dollar reserve / ～黄金本位 dollar-gold standard / ～集团 dollar bloc / ～挤兑黄金风潮 rush on gold against US dollars / ～实际价格 real dollar value / ～外汇 exchanges in dollar; dollar exchanges / ～危机 dollar crisis / ～信用 dollar credibility / ～国家 dollar country / ～荒 dollar shortage / ～购买力 dollar's buying power
美院 měiyuàn (short for 美术学院) school of fine arts
美展 měizhǎn (short for 美术作品展览) art exhibition: 工艺～ exhibition of arts and crafts
美制 měizhì American system of weights and measures (with the foot as the unit of length, the pound as the unit of mass and the second as the unit of time)
美中不足 měizhōng-bùzú flaw in something which might otherwise be perfect; fly in the ointment: 他们到了北京而未去长城,不免有点～之感。It was a trip short of perfection when they failed to climb up the Great Wall during their stay in Beijing.
美中关系全国委员会 Měi-Zhōng Guānxì Quánguó Wěiyuánhuì (US) National Committee on US-China Relations
美中贸易委员会 Měi-Zhōng Màoyì Wěiyuánhuì (US) National Council for US-China Trade
美中人民友协 Měi-Zhōng Rénmín Yǒuxié (US) US-China People's Friendship Association (USCPFA)
美中协会 Měi-Zhōng Xiéhuì (US) America-China Society
美中学术交流委员会 Měi-Zhōng Xuéshù Jiāoliú Wěiyuánhuì (US) Committee on Scholarly Communications with the People's Republic of China
美洲 Měizhōu America: 北～ North America / 南～ South America / 拉丁～ Latin America / ～印地安人 American Indian; Amerindian / ～文化研究者 Americanist
美洲豹 měizhōubào panther
美洲貂 měizhōudiāo American marten
美洲国家组织 Měizhōu Guójiā Zǔzhī Organization of American States (OAS)
美洲河鸟 Měizhōu héniǎo American dipper
美洲虎 měizhōuhǔ American tiger; jaguar
美洲开发银行 Měizhōu Kāifā Yínháng Inter-American Development Bank
美洲人权公约 Měizhōu Rénquán Gōngyuē American Convention on Human Rights
美洲狮 měizhōushī cougar; puma; mountain lion
美洲驼 měizhōutuó *also* "羁鹅" lái'ǎo llama
美洲野牛 Měizhōu yěniú American buffalo; bison
美洲银行 Měizhōu Yínháng Bank of America
美洲榆 měizhōuyú American elm
美滋滋 měizīzī extremely pleased with oneself: 他听到老师的赞扬,心里～的。He felt very pleased with himself when the teacher praised him. / 他看着茂盛的庄稼,～地咧着嘴笑了。Looking at the luxuriant crops, he grinned with satisfaction.

渼 měi 〈书面〉 ripples

镁 měi 〈化学〉 magnesium (Mg): 硫酸～ magnesium sulphate / 氧化～ magnesia / 含～石灰岩 magnesium limestone / 菱～矿 magnesite
镁弹 měidàn 〈军事〉 magnesium bomb
镁粉 měifěn 〈冶金〉 magnesium dust
镁铬合金 měigè héjīn 〈冶金〉 magnesia-chrome; magnesite-chrome
镁光 měiguāng magnesium light: ～照明弹 magnesium flare
镁光灯 měiguāngdēng magnesium lamp
镁合金 měihéjīn 〈冶金〉 magnesium alloy
镁基合金 měijī héjīn 〈冶金〉 magnesium-base alloy
镁铝合金 měilǚ héjīn 〈冶金〉 magnalium
镁燃烧弹 měiránshāodàn 〈军事〉 magnesium bomb
镁乳 měirǔ milk of magnesia; magnesia magma
镁砂 měishā 〈冶金〉 magnesia; magnesite
镁铁矿 měitiěkuàng 〈矿业〉 magnesioferrite; magnoferrite
镁氧 měiyǎng 〈矿业〉 magnesia: ～水泥 magnesia cement
镁砖 měizhuān 〈冶金〉 magnesia brick

每 měi ❶ every; each: 给他们～人一册 give a copy to each of them / ～两周集会一次 meet once every two weeks / ～人的性格都不一样。People differ from each other in character. / ～个疗程十天。Each therapy takes ten days. / 车速～小时九十公里。The car is running at a speed of 90 km per hour. / ～演出三天,休息一天。We had one day off after giving three days' performances. ❷ every time; whenever; per: ～隔五米种一棵树 plant trees at intervals of five metres (*or* five metres apart) / ～百元投入的新增国民收入 sum of newly gained national income provided by input of every 100 *yuan* / 她～隔一天回家一次。She goes back home every other day (*or* on alternate days) ❸ often: ～有忧虑 often have a lot of worries
每常 měicháng ❶ habitually in the past: 学校～都是下午四时放学。The school usually closes at 4 p.m. ❷ often; frequently
每当 měidāng whenever; every time: ～下雨,他的腰疼就犯。His back aches whenever it rains. / ～我看到她时就想起她的父亲。She reminds me of her father every time I see her. / ～情况紧急的时刻,他总能保持冷静。He always remained cool-headed in times of urgency.
每逢 měiféng whenever; every time: ～佳节倍思亲。On festive occasions more than ever one thinks of one's dear ones far away. / 这本月刊～十五日出版。This monthly is published on the fifteenth day of each month. / 这个小组～星期日开会。This group meets on Sundays.

每况愈下 měikuàngyùxià *also* "每下愈况" steadily deteriorate; get even worse than before; go from bad to worse: 他的体质～。His health was steadily deteriorating. /他的家境～。Things got steadily worse for his family.

每每 měiměi often; frequently; usually: ～如此。That's usually the case. /两人见面，～争论不休。The two of them would get into an endless argument whenever they met.

每年 měinián ❶ every year: 我们～暑假都组织一次夏令营。We always organize camping activities during summer vacations. ❷〈方言〉in the past; (in) former years: ～是这么安排，今年不一样了。It had been so arranged in the past, but things are different this year.

每日电讯报 Měirì Diànxùnbào *Daily Telegraph*, British newspaper started in 1855

每日镜报 Měirì Jìngbào *Daily Mirror*, British newspaper started in 1903

每日快报 Měirì Kuàibào *Daily Express*, popular newspaper in Britain first published in 1900

每日新闻 Měirì Xīnwén *Mainichi Shimbun*, one of the major newspapers in Japan

每日邮报 Měirì Yóubào *Daily Mail*, British newspaper first published in 1896

每时每刻 měishí-měikè at all times; all the time: ～都要防止骄傲自满。We must always guard against arrogance and complacency.

每时每日 měishí-měirì daily and hourly: ～都不能忘记今天的幸福生活是怎么来的。One should never forget how today's happy life was brought about.

浼

měi 〈书面〉❶ pollute; contaminate ❷ ask and commit sth. to sb.'s care: 央～ go and ask sb. a favour

浼渎 měidú 〈谦词〉bother: ～清听 bother sb. with a request

浼浼 měiměi (of water) flow smoothly: 河水～river with smooth-flowing water

浼托 měituō 〈谦词〉entrust sb. to do sth.; ask sb. for a favour

浼污 měiwū ruin one's reputation

mèi

谜

mèi

see also mí

谜儿 mèir 〈方言〉riddle: 猜～ guess a riddle /破～ solve a riddle

痗

mèi 〈书面〉illness caused by anxiety: 令人心～。It makes one's heart ache.

寐

mèi 〈书面〉sleep: 假～ catnap; doze; drowse /梦～ sleep; dream /梦～以求 long (*or* yearn) for sth. day and night /夜不能～ cannot go to sleep at night

昧

mèi ❶ ignorant; bewildered; confused: 愚～无知 ignorant and stupid /素～平生 had not the pleasure of making sb.'s acquaintance before /暧～ in ambiguous or equivocal terms / 茫～〈书面〉indistinct; vague; uncertain /蒙～ uncultured; uncivilized; ignorant ❷ hide; conceal: 拾金不～ not pocket the money one happens to pick up ❸〈书面〉dim; dark; gloomy: 幽～的书房 dim study ❹〈书面〉offend; venture; risk: *see* "～死"

昧旦 mèidàn 〈书面〉dawn; daybreak

昧良心 mèi liángxīn (do evil) against one's conscience: 他昧着良心作伪证。He perjured himself against his conscience.

昧爽 mèishuǎng 〈书面〉early dawn; daybreak

昧死 mèisǐ 〈书面〉risk one's life: ～陈言〈旧语〉state one's views at the risk of one's life; risk one's life to candidly state one's views (before the emperor)

昧心 mèixīn (do evil) against one's conscience: 不说～话。Never say anything against one's conscience.

昧心钱 mèixīnqián filthy money; ill-gotten money: 搞歪门邪道赚～ make money by dishonest means

昧信 mèixìn break one's promise; go back on one's word: ～于人 fail to keep one's promise to sb. /你莫非～不成? Do you mean to go back on your word?

昧于 mèiyú be ignorant of (sth.): ～世故 be ignorant of the ways of the world /～形势的变化 be unaware of the changed situation

魅

mèi 〈书面〉evil spirit; demons; monster: 魑～ evil spirits; demons and monsters /鬼～ ghosts and goblins; forces of evil

魅惑 mèihuò bedevil; bewitch; captivate: ～力 attractiveness; charm

魅力 mèilì glamour; charm; fascination; charisma: 艺术～ artistic charm /青少年常被侦探小说的某种～所吸引。Detective stories have some special appeal for teenagers.

魅人 mèirén attractive; intoxicating; charming; enchanting: 春天的果园越发增添了～的力量。Springtime adds to the enchanting beauty of the orchard.

妹

mèi ❶ younger sister: 胞～ full (*or* blood) younger sister /兄～ brother and sister /姐～ sisters ❷ junior female relative of the same generation: 表～ younger female cousin (bearing a different surname) /堂～ younger female cousin (bearing the same surname) /弟～ younger brother and sister; younger brother's wife; sister-in-law ❸〈方言〉young girl: 外来～ non-local girl /农家～ country girl

妹夫 mèifu younger sister's husband; brother-in-law

妹妹 mèimei younger sister

妹婿 mèixù 〈书面〉younger sister's husband; brother-in-law

妹丈 mèizhàng husband of a younger sister

妹子 mèizi 〈方言〉❶ younger sister ❷ young girl: 细～ little girl

袂

mèi 〈书面〉sleeve: 分～ part; say goodbye to each other / 奋～ roll up one's sleeves to get ready for a fight or struggle /联～〈比喻〉(come or go) hand in hand; together

媚

mèi ❶ fawn on; curry favour with; be servile to; toady to: 谄～ flatter; fawn on; curry favour with /狐～ charm by cajolery; entice by flattery /献～ try to ingratiate oneself with; curry favour with; flatter ❷ charming; attractive; fascinating; lovely: 春光明～ scene of enchanting beauty in spring /娇～ coquettish; charming /柔～ gentle and lovely; graceful and charming /妩～ lovely; charming; graceful /秀～ elegant and graceful /妖～ (of women) seductively charming; bewitching

媚敌 mèidí curry favour with or toady to the enemy

媚骨 mèigǔ sycophancy; mentality of a sycophant; obsequiousness

媚惑 mèihuò seduce; bewitch

媚脸 mèiliǎn charming looks

媚气 mèiqi ❶ charming; attractive: 她的脸蛋胖乎乎的，脖子上围着条雪白的丝巾，衬得她怪～的。With chubby cheeks and a snow-white silk kerchief round her neck, she looks exceedingly charming. ❷ *see* "媚态❷"

媚上骄下 mèishàng-jiāoxià obsequious to one's superiors and arrogant to one's subordinates

媚上欺下 mèishàng-qīxià fawn upon one's superior and bully one's subordinates

媚世 mèishì *also* "媚俗"〈书面〉cater to the vulgar tastes of society; fish for cheap popularity: ～之作 works that play to the gallery

媚态 mèitài ❶ fawning expression; obsequiousness: 种种～，一副奴才相。All these expressions of fawning are nothing but the servile features of a flunkey. ❷ attractive appearance or gestures (of a woman)

媚态娇容 mèitài-jiāoróng seductive in appearance and attractive in manner; coquettish

媚外 mèiwài fawn on or toady to foreign powers: 崇洋～ worship things foreign and fawn on foreigners /～政策 policy of toadying to foreigners

媚妩 mèiwǔ 〈书面〉charming; lovely; attractive

媚笑 mèixiào coquettish smile; bewitching smile: 一脸～ wear a coquettish smile on one's face

媚眼 mèiyǎn charming eyes; bewitching eyes

媚悦 mèiyuè toady to; curry favour with; please: ～流俗 cater to the current fashion

mēn

闷

mēn ❶ stuffy; stifling: 屋子里人太多，空气太～。It's really

stuffy with so many people in the room. /房间里很～。It's stifling in the room. *or* The air is oppressive in the room. ❷ cover tightly:茶还要～一～。Let the tea brew a bit longer. ❸ silent; speechless:你有话就说出来，别～在心里。Speak out. Don't have a fit of the sulks. ❹〈方言〉(of a sound) muffled; subdued:～声～气地说话 speak in a muffled (*or* subdued) voice ❺ shut oneself indoors:整天～在家里可不好呀。It will do you nothing but harm to shut yourself up at home all day long.
see also mèn

闷沉沉 mēnchénchén ❶ stuffy; close:～的房间 stuffy room ❷ (of noise, voice, sound, etc.) low; muffled:雷在远处～地响。From far away came muffled thunder.
see also mènchénchén

闷锄 mēnchú 〈农业〉loosen the top soil and do weeding to let the seeds germinate

闷气 mēnqì stuffy; close:屋里怎么这么～? Why is the room so stuffy?
see also mènqì

闷热 mēnrè hot and stuffy; oppressively hot; sultry; sweltering:～的天气 sultry (*or* muggy) weather /～得很,开开窗吧。Open the window please, it's hot and stuffy in here.

闷声 mēnshēng remain silent;be mute:～对坐 sitting face to face without a word

闷声不响 mēnshēng-bùxiǎng be silent; not say a word:～地听她发牢骚 listening to her grumble without saying anything /他～地坐在那里,像有满腹心事。He sat silent over there as if laden with misgivings.

闷声闷气 mēnshēng-mēnqì (of voice, sound, etc.) low; muffled; throaty:他感冒了,说话的声音～的。He has a cold and sounds throaty.

闷头儿 mēntóur quietly; doggedly; with a quiet resolve:～干活 plod away quietly; work with dogged perseverance

mén

门(門) mén ❶ (of a building, vehicle, or vessel) entrance:前～ entrance; front door /正～ main entrance /便～ side door; wicket door /送货上～ home delivery service; delivery of goods to the doorstep of a customer ❷ door; gate:铁～ iron door; grille /旋转～ revolving door /单扇～ univalve door /双扇～ bivalve door /拉～ sliding door /朱～ vermilion gate; red-lacquered gate of a mansion /拱～ arch /凯旋～ triumphal arch ❸ any opening:炉～ opening of a stove (*or* furnace) ❹ valve; switch:气～ air valve; spiracle /电～ switch /油～ throttle;〈口语〉accelerator / 球～ goal;〈口语〉goalkeeper /阀～ valve /闸～ floodgate /快～ (of camera) shutter ❺ way to do sth.; knack:窍～ key to a problem; knack /摸～儿〈口语〉learn the ropes; get the hang of sth. /没～儿 have not the ghost of a chance of doing sth.; can get no access to sth. /入～ cross the threshold; know the rudiments of sth.; elementary course; ABC (of sth.) /有～儿 be hopeful; have access ❻ branch of a family or clan; family:长～ eldest (*or* major) branch /豪～ wealthy family with powerful connections; wealthy and influential family /寒～〈书面〉my humble family; my humble abode /将～ family of a distinguished warrior /双喜临～ blessed with double luck ❼ sect; school of thought:孔～ Confucianism /会道～ superstitious sects and secret societies /佛～子弟 Buddhist follower (believer); Buddhist ❽ derived from the same master or teacher:同～ taught by the same master or teacher; followers of the same master or teacher /拜～ acknowledge (a person) as one's master in a ceremony /桃李盈～ have large numbers of disciples ❾ class; category; branch:分～别类 divide into different categories /部～ department; branch /热～ popular; in great demand /缺～ gap; vacuum /冷～ discipline or trade or a branch of learning that few people are enthusiastic about ❿〈生物〉phylum:亚～ subphylum /脊椎动物～ Vertebrata /原生动物～ protozoa ⓫ position in a gambling game (relative to where one sits or where one lays a stake):天～ position opposite to one ⓬〈量词〉(a) *of artillery*:一～大炮 a cannon; a piece of artillery (b) *of field of study or technical training*:一～学科 a discipline; a branch of learning /两～科学 two branches of science /三～功课 three courses of study (c) *of marriage*:一～亲事 a marriage (d) *of relatives*:一～亲戚 a group of relatives (usu. from the same family or clan) ⓭ (Mén) a surname

门巴 ménbā doctor (in Tibetan language)

门巴族 Ménbāzú Monba nationality, living in the Tibet Autonomous Region

门把 ménbà door knob; door handle

门板 ménbǎn ❶ door plank ❷ shutter:上～儿 put up the shutters

门包 ménbāo 〈旧语〉gift of money given to the gatekeeper of an official (when one sought an audience with the latter):门子接过～,这才进去禀报。Only after the gatekeeper received the gift of money did he go in to report to his master.

门杯 ménbēi cup of wine in front of everyone at table:干了～。Drink up the cup of wine before you, everybody.

门鼻儿 ménbír staple (of a door)

门匾 ménbiǎn horizontal inscribed board placed above a gate or door

门钹 ménbó cymbal-shaped metal plate on a door (with a ringlike knocker)

门插关儿 ménchāguanr short door bolt or bar

门齿 ménchǐ *also* "板牙" bǎnyá front tooth; incisor

门窗钩 ménchuānggōu cabin hook

门刺 méncì 〈书面〉visiting card; calling card

门当户对 méndāng-hùduì be well-matched in social status:这一对夫妇虽说是～,但是性情不合。The couple were well-matched in social status, but were temperamentally incompatible.

门道 méndào gateway; doorway

门道 méndao 〈口语〉way to do sth.; knack:这是劳动致富的～。This is the way to get rich through honest labour. /增产节约的～很多。There is no lack of ways and means to boost production and practise economy. /外行看热闹,内行看～。While the laymen watch only the fanfare, the professionals are keen to see the tricks of the trade. /学习没有什么特别的～,关键是要刻苦。There is no short cut in study. What is important is hard work.

门德尔松 Méndé'ěrsōng Felix Mendelssohn (1809-1847), German composer

门第 méndì 〈旧语〉family status:有～ well-connected /书香～ an intellectual background /～寒微。The family is of humble origin.

门吊 méndiào 〈机械〉gantry crane

门吊儿 méndiàor hasp and staple

门丁 méndīng gatekeeper (of an official or a rich family)

门钉 méndīng round-headed decoration on the gate (of a palace, temple, etc.)

门洞儿 méndòngr gateway; doorway

门斗 méndǒu ❶ top of the lintel of a door ❷ small vestibule outside the door of a house to keep off the cold, wind, etc.

门对 ménduì gatepost couplet

门墩 méndūn wooden or stone block supporting the pivot of a door

门额 mén'é upper part of the lintel of a door

门阀 ménfá 〈旧语〉distinguished family of hereditary power and influence

门房 ménfáng ❶ gate house; janitor's room; porter's lodge ❷ gatekeeper; doorman; janitor; porter

门扉 ménfēi door leaf:～半掩。The door is left half open.

门风 ménfēng family's established moral standards and way of life:严守～strictly abide by the family's moral standards

门缝 ménfèng crack between a door and its frame (*or* between a pair of doors); chink:～里瞧人 look at sb. through the crack of a door — belittle sb.

门岗 méngǎng gate sentry

门钩 méngōu door stop

门馆 ménguǎn ❶ old-style private family school:～先生 resident private tutor (in a family school) ❷ resident private tutor ❸ living quarters for hangers-on (of aristocrats, bureaucrats, etc.)

门轨 ménguǐ door track

门户 ménhù ❶ door; gate:～紧闭 with the doors tightly shut (*or* bolted) /～洞开。The door is wide open. /小心～。Beware of the door. /～不关紧,圣贤起盗心。〈俗语〉An open door may tempt a saint. *or* A door not locked invites robbery. ❷ gateway; important passageway:三峡是水路入川的～。The Three Gorges is the important passageway to Sichuan. /上海是我国东海岸的～之一。Shanghai is one of China's gateways on the eastern coast. ❸ family; home:兄弟分居,各立～。The brothers have set up their own homes. ❹ fac-

tion; sect: ～之争 sectarian disputes /他在学术上自立～。He established a school of his own in his academic studies. ❺ family status: ～相当 be on a par in family status

门户开放政策 ménhù kāifàng zhèngcè "Open Door" policy (which the United States foisted on China in the late 19th century to secure the same privileges as the other imperialist powers)

门户之见 ménhùzhījiàn parochial prejudice; sectarian bias: 两位先生在笔墨官司中都有些～。The two gentlemen are both prone to sectarian bias in their written polemics.

门环子 ménhuánzi knocker

门将 ménjiàng 〈体育〉goal-keeper: 主力～ top goal-keeper

门捷列夫 Ménjiélièfū Dmitry Ivanovich Mendeleyev (1834-1907), Russian chemist who developed the periodic table for classifying chemical elements according to their atomic weights

门捷列夫周期率 Ménjiélièfū zhōuqīlǜ Mendeleyev's Law

门禁 ménjìn guarding of an entrance: ～森严。The gate (*or* entrance) is heavily guarded.

门警 ménjǐng police on guard at the gate or entrance

门径 ménjìng access; key; way; path: 解决问题的～ key to the problem /通向权力的～ path to power

门静脉 ménjìngmài 〈生理〉portal vein: ～系统 portal system

门静脉高血压 ménjìngmài gāoxuèyā portal hypertension

门静脉吻合术 ménjìngmài wěnhéshù portacaval anastomosis

门静脉炎 ménjìngmàiyán pylephlebitis

门静脉造影术 ménjìngmài zàoyǐngshù portal venography; portography

门镜 ménjìng (popularly called 猫眼) peephole (in a door)

门臼 ménjiù ❶ socket for gate or door post on gate or door pier ❷〈方言〉gate or door pier

门槛 ménkǎn *also* "门坎" ❶ threshold; doorsill: 迈过～ step over the threshold /在～上绊了一下 stumble over the doorsill ❷〈方言〉knack; trick; know-how: ～精 be shrewd (in business dealings); be calculating /他～精, 不会上当。He is too smart to be taken in. /你不懂～。You don't know the ropes.

门可罗雀 ménkěluóquè (of a building) you can catch sparrows on the doorstep (usually said of a place which attracts few visitors); the place is practically deserted: 生意清淡, ～。Business is sluggish and there are few customers.

门客 ménkè hanger-on of an aristocrat; follower of a powerful or wealthy person

门口 ménkǒu entrance; doorway: 送客到～ walk (*or* see) the guest to the door /他站在～似乎等候什么人。He stood at the entrance as if waiting for somebody. /～围了一堆人。There is a big crowd at the gate.

门框 ménkuàng doorframe; door case

门廊 ménláng 〈建筑〉porch; portico

门类 ménlèi class; department; category: ～齐全的工业体系 industrial system complete with all necessary departments

门里出身 ménli-chūshēn 〈方言〉be born into a professional's family; have a professional background: 说到变戏法, 他是～。Talking of conjurers, he is one from a real professional's family.

门帘 ménlián *also* "门帘子" door curtain; portière

门联 ménlián gatepost couplet

门脸儿 ménliǎnr 〈方言〉❶ vicinity of an ancient city gate: 北京前门～两侧是个热闹的地方。The vicinity of Beijing's Qianmen Gate (*or* Front Gate) is a bustling downtown area. ❷ shop facade; shop front: 这商店的～很时髦。This shop has a fashionable facade.

门铃 ménlíng doorbell: 音乐～ musical doorbell /叮咚～ jingle bell

门楼 ménlóu arch over a gateway

门路 ménlu ❶ knack; way; channel: 广开～ tap all the potential channels /经商自有经商的～。In doing business one must know the ropes. ❷ social connections; pull: 找～ solicit social connections /在旧社会, 没有一点～就很难找到职业。In the old society, it was very difficult for anybody to get a job without help from the right places.

门罗 Ménluó James Monroe (1758-1831), 5th President of the United States (1816-1824)

门罗主义 Ménluózhǔyì Monroe Doctrine (1823)

门脉 ménmài (short for 门静脉) portal vein (*vena portal*): ～循环 circulation of portal vein

门脉性肝硬化 ménmàixìng gānyìnghuà 〈医学〉portal cirrhosis; Laennec's cirrhosis

门脉循环 ménmài xúnhuán 〈生理〉portal circulation

门楣 ménméi ❶ lintel (of a door): 对联的横批贴在～上。The horizontal scroll bearing an inscribed couplet is pasted on the door lintel. ❷ *see* "门第"

门面 ménmiàn ❶ facade of a shop; shop front: 三间～的铺子 shop with a three-bay front ❷ appearance; facade: 为了装～ to keep up appearances /最近宣传钢铁厂工人的劳动热情不是为了装点～, 而是实事求是的报道。The recent publicity campaign to highlight the labour enthusiasm of the workers at the steel plant is not window dressing, but a realistic assessment of fact.

门面话 ménmianhuà banal remarks; lip service: 大家客客气气, 说一些无关痛痒的～。Everyone behaved politely and exchanged some remarks that were neither here nor there.

门钮 ménniǔ door knob

门牌 ménpái plate number; house number: 能不能告诉我贵公司的～号码? Can you tell me the street number of your company?

门碰 ménpèng door knob: ～球 ball catch

门票 ménpiào entrance ticket; admission ticket: 凡重大节日, 北京的公园不收～, 免费开放。On major holidays, visiting the public parks in Beijing is free of charge. *or* On major holidays, admission to Beijing's public parks is free.

门前三包 ménqián sānbāo undertake three responsibilities for the area in front of one's workplace (cleanliness, care of trees and lawn, and public order)

门墙 ménqiáng ❶ garden wall ❷〈书面〉master-disciple relationship: 忝列～ have the honour to be counted among sb.'s disciples ❸〈书面〉〈旧语〉advisers, etc., employed by an influential official

门桥 ménqiáo 〈军事〉raft of pontoons; boat raft

门窍 ménqiào key (to a problem); knack: 看出了～ find the key to a problem; get the knack of doing sth. /看不出～ fail to find a solution; not know the ropes

门球 ménqiú 〈体育〉croquet

门券 ménquàn entrance ticket; admission ticket: 买一张～ buy an entrance ticket

门儿清 ménrqīng 〈方言〉know very well; know everything inside out: 他干了多年的会计, ～, 一准错不了。There can't be any mistakes, since he has been an accountant for years and knows everything well.

门人 ménrén ❶ disciple; follower ❷ retainer

门扇 ménshàn door leaf

门上 ménshang ❶ on the door: ～有个字帖儿。Somebody has left a note on the door. ❷ residence: 到～请罪 come to sb.'s home to apologize in person /～准出了事。Something must have happened to the family. ❸ doorman; janitor

门神 ménshen 〈迷信〉(picture of) door-god (posted on the front door of a house to ward off evil spirits)

门生 ménshēng ❶ pupil; disciple: 得意～ one's brilliant student /天子～ emperor's disciple — successful candidate of the palace examination (highest civil service examination) /他是清朝一位有名的宰相, ～遍天下。He was a renowned Qing chief minister whose disciples could be found all over the country. ❷ me; I; your student (a term used by a successful candidate in an imperial examination to refer to himself before the chief examiner)

门市 ménshì retail sales: ～价格 retail price /～部 retail department; sales department

门式搬运起重机 ménshì bānyùn qǐzhòngjī gantry transfer crane

门式起重机 ménshì qǐzhòngjī 〈机械〉portal crane; gantry

门首 ménshǒu entrance; doorway

门枢 ménshū door hinge

门闩 ménshuān door bolt; door bar

门帖 méntiě ❶ scrolls pasted on either side of the door forming a couplet; gatepost couplet ❷〈旧语〉poster on a door (for rent or sale)

门厅 méntīng 〈建筑〉entrance hall; portico; vestibule

门庭 méntíng ❶ doorway and courtyard: 洒扫～ clean the courtyard ❷ family or family status: 光耀～ bring honour to one's family

门庭若市 méntíng-ruòshì the courtyard is alive with activity; the courtyard is as crowded as a marketplace; have visitors at all times: 原先～, 现在却冷落了。His courtyard which used to be crowded with visitors is now a deserted place. /家中～, 亲戚朋友, 川流不息。His house was thronged with a constant stream of friends and relatives.

门头 méntou 〈方言〉❶ door: 大～儿 large door; gate ❷ way to at-

tain one's goal：你找着～儿，可别忘了我。When you have learned the ropes, don't forget to let me know.
门徒 méntú disciple; pupil; follower; adherent
门外汉 ménwàihàn layman; greenhorn; novice; outsider：他在这个领域里还是个～。He is still a greenhorn in this field. /在这些问题上，～的判断可能胜过专家。A layman may prove a better judge than a professional in these matters.
门卫 ménwèi entrance guard
门下 ménxià ❶ hanger-on of an aristocrat：当年宰相～众多、人才济济。There was a galaxy of talent among the many followers of the chief minister. ❷ I; me; your student：～多蒙先生指教，受益非浅。I have benefited a great deal from your instructions. ❸ study under (sb. who has a special skill)：这位画家出自徐悲鸿大师～。This artist studied under Master Xu Beihong.
门限 ménxiàn 〈书面〉threshold
门婿 ménxù son-in-law
门牙 ményá front tooth; incisor
门役 ményì 〈旧语〉gatekeeper; concierge
门诊 ménzhěn outpatient service (in a hospital)：～病人 outpatient; clinic patient /～时间 consulting hours
门诊部 ménzhěnbù outpatient department (OPD); clinic; polyclinic
门枕 ménzhěn block of stone used as base of door shaft
门轴 ménzhóu door shaft
门柱 ménzhù 〈建筑〉goalpost; gate post
门子 ménzi ❶ gatekeeper or doorman at a *yamen* or at the house of a senior official ❷ social connections：钻～ jockey for advantage (*or* favours) /他有～。He has the backing of powerful connections. ❸〈方言〉〈量词〉piece; item：他娘早年给他订下了这～亲事。His mother concluded this marriage contract for him in his early years. /你生的是哪～气! What are you angry about?

扪

mén 〈书面〉touch; feel; stroke
扪心 ménxīn 〈书面〉search one's heart：～无愧 feel that one has not done anything wrong; have a good (*or* clear) conscience
扪心自问 ménxīn-zìwèn examine one's own conscience; search one's heart
扪诊 ménzhěn 〈医学〉palpation

钔

mén 〈化学〉mendelevium (Md)

璊(瑞)

mén 〈书面〉red jade

mèn

闷

mèn ❶ bored; dejected; depressed; in low spirits：烦～ unhappy; vexed /下棋解～ divert oneself from boredom by playing a chess game; play a game of chess to relieve oneself of boredom /愁～ feel gloomy; be in low spirits; be depressed /苦～ depressed; dejected /～得发慌 be bored stiff; be bored to death ❷ tightly closed; shut up; sealed
see also mēn
闷沉沉 mènchénchén (of mood) depressed：她整天呆在家里，无处可去，心里～的。She felt depressed, staying at home all day long with nowhere to go.
see also mēnchénchén
闷罐车 mènguànchē 〈方言〉boxcar
闷光玻璃 mènguāng bōli 〈化工〉devitrified glass; obscured glass
闷棍 mèngùn staggering blow (with a cudgel); unexpected blow：歹徒从后面给他一～。A thug struck him a blow from behind. /他没想到一进门就吃了她一～。He had not expected to be greeted with the sharp end of her tongue the moment he stepped inside the door.
闷葫芦 mènhúlu ❶ enigma; puzzle：有话直说，谁有那么多心思来猜～。Get it off your chest. I am in no mood to be kept guessing. /大家都知道了，只有他还装在～里。Everyone else knows about it, but he is still in the dark. ❷ man of few words; taciturn person：他本来就是个～，这时一句话也说不出来了。Reticent by nature, he is now unable to utter a word.
闷葫芦罐儿 mènhúluguànr 〈口语〉earthenware money box; piggy bank
闷酒 mènjiǔ wine drunk in moments of loneliness：他喝了两杯～。He drank a couple of glasses by himself.
闷倦 mènjuàn feeling bored and listless; ennui
闷雷 mènléi ❶ muffled thunder ❷ shock：挨～ receive a shock; be shocked
闷闷不乐 mènmèn-bùlè depressed; dejected; in low spirits：他这几天～，不知出了什么事儿。He is in low spirits these days and no one knows why.
闷气 mènqì the sulks：生～ have a fit of the sulks /憋～ feel injured and resentful
see also mēnqì
闷痛 mèntòng (of chest, etc.) feel tight and painful：一般冠心病患者老是感到胸部～。As a rule, people who suffer from coronary heart disease often feel oppressed and painful in the chest.
闷香 mènxiāng narcotic incense burned to make victims lose consciousness
闷郁 mènyù gloomy; depressed：心情～ feel disheartened
闷子车 mènzichē boxcar

焖

mèn boil in a covered pot over a slow fire; braise：～饭 cook rice over a slow fire /油～笋 braised bamboo shoots with vegetable oil /～了一锅肉 stew a pot of pork /红～牛肉 braised beef in soy sauce

懑(懣)

mèn 〈书面〉❶ feel vexed ❷ angry; indignant：愤～ feel indignant

men

们

men ❶ *suffix used to form a plural number when added to a personal pronoun or a noun referring to a person* (not used when the pronoun or noun is preceded by a numeral or an intensifier, e.g. 三个老师 three teachers /许多人 many people)：他～ they /人～ people /孩子～ children /女士～、先生～ ladies and gentlemen ❷ (in personification) *when added to a noun referring to an animal or thing*：小兔子～在树林里唱歌、跳舞。The rabbits were singing and dancing in the wood. /春天一到，鸟、树、鱼、虫～都活跃起来。With the coming of spring, the birds, trees, fish and insects all became active again. ❸ *when added to the name of a person to indicate people of the same kind or those who associate with him or her*：爱迪生～ the Edisons ❹〈贬义〉*when added to a noun referring to a despised person*：大小霸权主义者～ hegemonists big or small /希特勒的徒子徒孙～ Hitler's latter-day followers

mēng

蒙[1](矇)

mēng ❶ cheat; deceive; fool; kid：别～人! Stop kidding! /他编了个故事就把许多人～住了。Many people have been fooled by the story he invented. ❷ take a random guess; make a wild guess：这回让他～对了。He made a random answer and was lucky enough to guess right. *or* He made a lucky guess this time. /别瞎～! No wild guesses!

蒙[2]

mēng 〈口语〉unconscious; senseless：头发～ feel one's head spinning (*or* swimming) /吓～了 be scared stiff /我简直被他闹～了。I was simply confused by the rumpus he kicked up.
see also méng; Měng
蒙哄 mēnghǒng *see*"蒙骗"
蒙蒙黑 mēngmēnghēi before dark; at dusk
蒙蒙亮 mēngmēngliàng first glimmers of dawn; daybreak：天刚～ at daybreak
蒙骗 mēngpiàn deceive; hoodwink; fool; cheat：以假药～病人 cheat patients with fake medicine /他提出假证，企图～群众。He gave false evidence in an attempt to hoodwink the public.
蒙事 mēngshì 〈方言〉deceive; hoodwink; sham：到处～ go about telling lies everywhere /纯粹～ sheer fabrication
蒙松雨 mēngsongyǔ 〈方言〉fine drizzle
蒙头转向 mēngtóu-zhuànxiàng lose one's bearings; be completely at sea; be utterly confused：他被人哄得～。He was roundly swindled.

méng

虻(蝱) méng horsefly; gadfly:牛～ gadfly

氓(甿) méng *also*“萌”méng common people:群～〈书面〉common herd /愚～ fool
see also máng

蒙 méng ❶ cover:～上眼睛 cover sb.'s eyes; blindfold /给两国关系～上一层阴影 cloud the relations between the two countries ❷ suffer; incur; encounter:～受不白之冤 suffer a gross injustice /～你夸奖。Thank you for your compliment. /承～招待,感谢之至。Thank you very much for your kind hospitality. ❸ ignorance:启～ enlighten /发～〈旧语〉teach a child to read and write ❹ (Méng) a surname
see also mēng; Měng

蒙巴萨 Méngbāsà Mombasa, seaport and industrial city of southeast Kenya on the Indian Ocean

蒙蔽 méngbì deceive; fool; mislead; pull the wool over sb.'s eyes:～群众 mislead the public /一时受了～ be fooled for the moment /有些人很容易受～。There are people who can be easily taken in.

蒙尘 méngchén 〈书面〉(of the emperor) be exposed to wind and dust — flee the capital because of the turmoil of war:天子～。The emperor fled the capital.

蒙冲 méngchōng *see*“艨艟”méngchōng

蒙导法 méngdǎofǎ 〈生理〉mentor method

蒙德 Méngdé Ludwig Mond (1839-1909), German chemist

蒙德煤气 Méngdé méiqì Mond gas

蒙德维的亚 Méngdéwéidìyà Montevideo, capital and chief port of Uruguay

蒙哥马利 Ménggēmǎlì Bernard Law Montgomery (1887-1976), British field marshal during World War II

蒙垢 ménggòu 〈书面〉be disgraced; be humiliated

蒙馆 méngguǎn 〈旧语〉old-style private primary school

蒙汗药 ménghànyào knock-out or sleeping drug

蒙哄 ménghǒng deceive; hoodwink; fool; cheat:你别甜言蜜语地～我。Don't try to deceive me (*or* take me in) by your fine-sounding words.

蒙混 ménghùn fool or mislead people

蒙混过关 ménghùn-guòguān muddle through; get by under false pretenses:他企图～,却成了笑柄。He attempted to muddle through only to make a laughing stock of himself.

蒙茏 ménglóng 〈书面〉luxuriant; exuberant; flourishing:草木～ luxuriant vegetation

蒙眬 ménglóng *also*“曚眬”ménglóng drowsy; half asleep; hazy:睡眼～ drowsy eyes; eyes heavy with sleep /我刚刚～入睡,便听到大门口传来的停车声。I was just drifting off to sleep when I heard the sound of a car pulling up at our gate.

蒙罗维亚 Méngluówéiyà Monrovia, capital of Liberia

蒙昧 méngmèi ❶ uncivilized; uncultured; illiterate:～时代 age of barbarism; uncivilized age /～状态 uncivilized state ❷ ignorant; unenlightened:～无知 unenlightened; stupid and ignorant

蒙昧主义 méngmèizhǔyì obscurantism

蒙蒙 méngméng ❶ *also*“濛濛”méngméng drizzly:～细雨,越下越密。A misty drizzle fell thicker and thicker. ❷ misty; hazy:雾气～ misty; boggy /烟雾～ misty

蒙面大盗 méngmiàn dàdào masked bandit; masked burglar

蒙面人 méngmiànrén masked man

蒙面袜 méngmiànwà stocking mask

蒙娜·丽莎 Méngnà Lìshā Mona Lisa, a painting (now in the Louvre) executed 1503-1506 by Leonardo da Vinci and known also as La Gioconda, the sitter generally regarded as the wife of Francesco del Giocondo, a Florentine merchant

蒙难 méngnàn (of a celebrity, etc.) encounter danger; fall into imminent danger; fall into the hands of the enemy

蒙皮 méngpí 〈航空〉envelope; covering; skin

蒙求 méngqiú 〈书面〉(often used in the title of a textbook) elementary course:《文字～》*Introduction to Written Chinese*

蒙茸 méngróng hairy; furry; (of plants) growing profusely:草木～ overgrown with vegetation /～的长发 dishevelled long hair

蒙师 méngshī ❶〈旧语〉old-style private school teacher; teacher who teaches pupils to read and write ❷ teacher who introduces one into a certain field of study

蒙受 méngshòu suffer; sustain; incur:～沉重的打击 suffer a heavy blow/～耻辱 be subjected to humiliation; be humiliated /～恩惠 receive a favour /这些争端使双方都～了重大损失。The disputes inflicted heavy losses on both parties.

蒙塾 méngshú old-style private school for boy beginners

蒙太奇 méngtàiqí 〈影视〉montage

蒙特卡洛 Méngtè-Kǎluò Monte Carlo, one of the three communes of the principality of Monaco, famous as a gambling resort and as the terminus of a car rally

蒙特利尔 Méngtèlì'ěr Montreal, port and largest city in Canada

蒙童 méngtóng 〈旧语〉child who has just started to learn to read and write

蒙头红 méngtóuhóng 〈旧语〉head cover or veil for the bride at a wedding

蒙脱石 méngtuōshí 〈矿业〉montmorillonite

蒙学 méngxué 〈旧语〉old-style private school

蒙药 méngyào narcotic; anaesthetic

蒙冤 méngyuān suffer wrong; be wronged; suffer an injustice:他～十载,终于洗雪。The injustice he suffered for ten years was finally redressed.

蒙在鼓里 méngzàigǔlǐ be kept in the dark; be all at sea:这个丑闻很多人都知道了,就你还～。This scandal is known to many people; only you are in the dark.

蒙罩 méngzhào envelop; shroud:湖上～着一层烟雾。The lake was shrouded in mist.

蒙子 méngzi ❶ watch glass; crystal ❷〈方言〉dial; dial plate:表～上面画着个火车头。There is a picture of a locomotive on the dial plate.

濛 méng 〈书面〉drizzle:细雨其～ drizzling rain

濛濛 méngméng *also*“蒙蒙”méngméng drizzly; misty

檬 méng *see*“柠檬”níngméng

曚 méng

曚昽 ménglóng 〈书面〉(of daylight) dim

矇 méng 〈书面〉go blind

矇眬 ménglóng *see*“蒙眬”ménglóng

幪 méng *see*“帡幪”píngméng

艨 méng

艨艟 méngchōng *also*“蒙冲”méngchōng warship in ancient times

鹲 méng 〈动物〉Phaethon, a sort of pelagic fishing bird of the tropics

朦 méng

朦胧 ménglóng ❶ dim; hazy:～的月色 dim moonlight ❷ obscure; misty; hazy:暮色～ evening haze /～的念头在他脑际盘旋着。Some vague ideas kept coming up in his mind.

朦胧诗 ménglóngshī 〈文学〉obscure avant-garde poetry

甍 méng 〈书面〉ridge (of a roof)

瞢 méng 〈书面〉(of eyes) blurred; dim:目光～然 have dim eyesight

萌[1] méng sprout; bud; germinate:故态复～ relapse into one's old bad habits; revert to type /明者远见于未～。The discerning can foresee the future course of events (*or* what is going to happen).

萌[2] méng *see*“氓”méng

萌动 méngdòng ❶ bud; sprout; germinate:春意渐浓,草木～。

Spring is very much in the air and the plants are coming into leaf. ❷ put forth; spring up; start up:春意～。Spring awakens. /他心里～起了一个念头。An idea came to his mind.

萌发 méngfā ❶ bud; sprout; shoot:开始～ begin to bud /玫瑰～了新芽。The rose sprouted new buds. /春天使万树～出新枝。The trees begin to shoot new branches with the coming of spring. ❷ emerge; come forth:～一种强烈的求知欲 be seized with a thirst for knowledge

萌蘖 méngniè 〈书面〉❶ (of plant) new sprouts which come out after a plant is cut down ❷〈比喻〉in the bud; at the outset:～之谋 conspiracy being newly hatched

萌生 méngshēng germinate; sprout: 野草～。Weeds began to sprout. /我心底～出一种强烈的求知愿望。A keen desire to seek knowledge came over me.

萌生林 méngshēnglín coppice forest; copse forest

萌条 méngtiáo young twigs

萌芽 méngyá ❶ sprout; germinate; originate:芭蕾舞～于意大利。Ballet originated in Italy. ❷ rudiment; shoot; seed; germ:～阶段 rudimentary (*or* early) stage /处于～状态 in the embryonic stage; in the bud /把事故消灭在～状态 remove the causes of accidents; nip the accidents in the bud /中国封建社会的后期已经孕育着资本主义的～。Rudiments of capitalism began to take shape during the late stage of China's feudal society.

萌芽林 méngyálín sprout forest

萌兆 méngzhào 〈书面〉omen; foreboding

萌茁 méngzhuó 〈书面〉sprout; germinate; bud; shoot:百草～。All kinds of plants are budding forth.

盟[1]

méng ❶ alliance; coalition:结～ form an alliance; enter into an alliance; become allies /联～ alliance; coalition; league /工农联～ worker-peasant alliance /军事同～ military alliance; military league ❷ sworn: *see*“～兄弟” ❸ league (an administrative division of the Inner Mongolian Autonomous Region, corresponding to a prefecture)

盟[2]

méng take one's oath; swear

盟邦 méngbāng *also*“盟国” ally; allied country

盟国 méngguó allied country; ally:～对德管制委员会 Allied Control Council for Germany (1945-1948) /～对日管制委员会 Allied Control Council for Japan (1945-1952)

盟军 méngjūn allied forces

盟军登陆日 Méngjūn Dēnglùrì D-Day (6 June 1944)

盟旗制度 méngqí zhìdù league-banner administrative system, applied by China's Qing government in Mongolia (league corresponds to a prefecture and banner to a county)

盟誓 méngshì ❶〈书面〉treaty of alliance; oath of alliance ❷ swear; vow; pledge:当众～ vow in public /咱们盟个誓。Let's swear an oath.

盟委 méngwěi league committee of the Communist Party of China

盟兄弟 méngxiōngdì sworn brothers

盟友 méngyǒu ally; sworn friend

盟员 méngyuán member of an alliance or league

盟约 méngyuē oath of alliance; treaty of alliance:单方面撕毁～ unilaterally terminate a treaty of alliance

盟主 méngzhǔ leader or chief of an alliance

尨

méng

see also máng

尨茸 méngróng 〈书面〉fluffy; puffy

měng

蒙

Měng Mongol or Mongolian nationality

see also mēng; méng

蒙戈 měnggē mungo; mongo (Mongolian fractional money)

蒙古 Měnggǔ Mongolia:～人 Mongolian; Mongol /～语 Mongol (*or* Mongolian) language /内～ Inner Mongolia (of China) /外～ Outer Mongolia (old name for the Republic of Mongolia)

蒙古包 měnggǔbāo (Mongolian) yurt

蒙古高原 Měnggǔ Gāoyuán Mongolian Plateau

蒙古人种 Měnggǔ rénzhǒng Mongoloid race

蒙古通讯社 Měnggǔ Tōngxùnshè Montsame (of the Republic of Mongolia)

蒙古族 Měnggǔzú ❶ Mongol or Mongolian nationality (distributed over the Inner Mongolian Autonomous Region, Jilin, Liaoning, Heilongjiang, the Xinjiang Uygur Autonomous Region, Gansu, Qinghai, the Ningxia Hui Autonomous Region, Hebei and Henan) ❷ Mongols (majority ethnic group of Mongolia)

蒙栎 měnglì 〈植物〉Mongolian oak (*Quercus mongolica*)

蒙医 měngyī traditional Mongolian medicine

蒙族 Měngzú (short for 蒙古族) Mongolian nationality

蠓

měng 〈动物〉midge; biting midge

蠓虫儿 měngchóngr 〈动物〉midge; biting midge

獴

měng 〈动物〉mongoose:蟹～ crab-eating mongoose

懵(懞)

měng muddled; ignorant:～然无知 stupid and ignorant; utterly ignorant

懵懂 měngdǒng muddled; ignorant:我说了半天，他仍然～。He was still unclear despite my repeated explanation. /我懵懵懂懂地又睡着了。Being drowsy I dozed (*or* nodded) off again.

懵腾 měngténg half asleep, half awake; muddle-headed; confused

蜢

měng *see*“蚱蜢” zhàměng

锰

měng 〈化学〉manganese (Mn):～合金 manganese alloy /～细菌 manganese bacteria

锰矾 měngfán szmikite

锰钢 měnggāng manganese steel

锰结核 měngjiéhé 〈矿业〉manganese nodule; halobolite

锰矿床 měngkuàngchuáng manganese ore deposit

锰矿球 měngkuàngqiú *see*“锰结核”

锰铝矾 měnglǚfán apjohnite

锰青铜 měngqīngtóng 〈冶金〉manganese bronze

锰酸盐 měngsuānyán manganate

锰铁 měngtiě ferromanganese:～橄榄石 knebelite /～锌矾 dietrichite

锰铜 měngtóng 〈冶金〉manganin:～线〈电工〉manganin wire

锰铜矿 měngtóngkuàng crednerite

锰土 měngtǔ 〈矿业〉wad, a sort of manganese oxide mineral

锰系元素 měngxì yuánsù 〈化学〉manganides

锰柱石 měngzhùshí orientite

艋

měng *see*“舴艋” zéměng

猛

měng ❶ fierce; violent; strong; vigorous:凶～ violent; ferocious /勇～ intrepid; valiant /～攻 attack with violence; storm /～打～冲 go at full blast ahead /酒力很～。The liquor is very strong. /苛政～于虎。Tyranny is more dreaded than tigers. /他用力过～。He overexerted himself. ❷ suddenly; abruptly:～一转身 turn around abruptly /～一刹车 apply (put on) the brake suddenly; pull the emergency brake /从梦中～地惊醒 wake up from a dream with a start ❸ with a spurt of force:～着劲儿干 work with all one's strength

猛不丁 měngbudīng 〈方言〉suddenly; abruptly; unexpectedly:他～大喊了起来。Suddenly he gave out a yell.

猛不防 měngbufáng by surprise; unexpectedly; unawares:～被一辆自行车撞倒 be knocked down unexpectedly by a bicycle

猛跌 měngdiē plummet; drop sharply; come down with a run

猛丁 měngdīng 〈方言〉*see*“猛不丁”

猛孤丁 měnggūdīng 〈方言〉suddenly; abruptly:～地坐起来 sit up all of a sudden /～停住车 stop the car abruptly /～转了弯 make a sharp turn /～他站定不走了。He stopped short and remained planted there.

猛拐 měngguǎi make a sudden turn; turn a corner suddenly:骑自行车不能猛冲、～。No cyclist should dash around and make abrupt turns.

猛悍 měnghàn bold and powerful; full of valour and vigour; fero-

cious；fierce：在战场上，他简直就像一只～异常的老虎。On the battlefield he fought like a fierce tiger.

猛虎 měnghǔ fierce tiger：如～下山 like a fierce tiger running down a mountain — a fresh powerful force

猛火 měnghuǒ blazing fire

猛火油 měnghuǒyóu 〈旧语〉petroleum；oil

猛将 měngjiàng valiant general：技术攻关的～ path-breaker in technical innovation /～如云。A great many valiant warriors came to the fore.

猛捷 měngjié fierce and nimble：～如虎 fierce and nimble like a tiger

猛进 měngjìn push ahead vigorously：突飞～ advance by leaps and bounds /高歌～ stride forward singing songs of triumph

猛劲儿 měngjìnr 〈口语〉❶ spurt of force；dash：他一～就把杠铃举起来。Putting on a spurt (*or* with a jerk), he lifted the barbell up. ❷ great force；concentrated force：搬重家具要用～。You have to make a very strenuous effort to move heavy furniture around. ❸ great vigour：他干起活来有股子～。He works with a will, his every movement overflowing with energy.

猛可 měngkě (mostly used in the earlier vernacular) suddenly；all of a sudden：经刘大妈这么一提，他才～想起这件事的经过。Aunt Liu's words suddenly reminded him of what had happened.

猛力 měnglì vigorously；with great force：～扣杀〈体育〉smash vigorously /～冲刺 sprint with all one's strength

猛厉 měnglì fierce；violent：朔风～。The north wind was fierce and violent. /太阳～地放射光芒。The sun was beating down relentlessly with its scorching brilliance.

猛烈 měngliè strong；powerful；fierce；violent：～的海风 strong wind from the sea /～的风暴 violent storm /发动～的进攻 launch a powerful offensive /他的心脏～地跳动。His heart was beating furiously. /小树在狂风中～地晃动。The small tree swayed vigorously in the wind storm.

猛犸 měngmǎ *also*“猛犸象”；“毛象” máoxiàng〈考古〉mammoth

猛禽 měngqín bird of prey

猛然 měngrán all of a sudden；suddenly；abruptly：精神～一振 pull oneself together determinedly /～想起 remember in a flash /～回头 turn back all of a sudden /车子～停住。The car jerked to a halt.

猛锐 měngruì brave and vigorous：～长驱 push on vigorously

猛士 měngshì brave warrior

猛兽 měngshòu beast of prey

猛省 měngxǐng *see*“猛醒”

猛醒 měngxǐng *also*“猛省” suddenly realize or wake up：从错误中～ suddenly realize one's mistakes

猛药 měngyào potent drug；potent medicine

猛饮暴食 měngyǐn-bàoshí immoderate or inordinate eating and drinking

猛乍 měngzhà 〈方言〉suddenly：～地一阵子机枪声。Suddenly there came a barrage of machine-gun fire.

猛涨 měngzhǎng skyrocket；jump；soar：零售价格～。Retail prices skyrocketed. /开支～，超出预算六十亿元。The expenditure careered 6 billion *yuan* over budget.

猛鸷 měngzhì hawk；eagle

猛子 měngzi dive into the water：扎～ do a dive /这人在水中一个～就无影无踪了。The man dived into the water and disappeared.

勐[1] měng 〈书面〉brave；courageous

勐[2] měng former administrative district in Xishuangbanna, Yunnan Province

mèng

梦（夢） mèng ❶ dream：黄粱～〈比喻〉pipe dream /噩～ frightening dream；nightmare /托～〈迷信〉sb.'s ghost appears in one's dream and makes a request /圆～ interpret dreams /白日～ daydream /事情变化这么快，她做～也没想到。Things developed so fast that it was beyond her wildest dream. /夜长～多。A long night is fraught with dreams. *or* There is many a slip between the cup and the lip. ❷ illusion：幻～ illusion；fancy；dream

梦笔生花 mèngbǐ-shēnghuā dream about the blooming of one's writing brush — inspired display of literary talents

梦话 mènghuà ❶ *also*“梦呓”；“呓语” yìyǔ talking in one's sleep；somniloquy：说～ talk in one's sleep ❷ nonsense；raving：他的来信真是～连篇，全是办不到的事。His letter is full of idle dreams incapable of fulfilment.

梦幻 mènghuàn dream；chimera；illusion：他离奇的遭遇犹如～。His strange experience was exactly like a fantastic dream.

梦幻泡影 mènghuàn-pàoyǐng pipe dream；illusion；hallucination；bubble：多年的希望如今都成了～。His long-cherished hopes have all burst like soap bubbles.

梦幻曲 mènghuànqǔ 〈音乐〉reverie

梦见 mèngjiàn see in a dream；dream about：他～自己乘船回家了。He dreamt that he was going back home on board a steamer. /她～母亲来看她了。She dreamt about her mother visiting her.

梦境 mèngjìng dreamland；dreamlike world：他在～中遇到了亲人。He met his dear ones in his dream. /在冰雕世界里，就像置身于～之中。Walking among ice carvings, one may feel as if one were in a dreamland.

梦露 Mènglù Marilyn Monroe (1926-1962), American film actress

梦寐 mèngmèi dream；sleep：～难忘 cannot forget it even in one's dream；be unforgettable

梦寐以求 mèngmèiyǐqiú long for sth. day and night：为家乡办几件好事是他～的愿望。To do some solid work for his hometown has been his lifelong wish.

梦溪笔谈 Mèngxī Bǐtán *Sketchbook of Dream Brook*, major work on science and technology by Shen Kuo (沈括) of the Northern Song Dynasty

梦乡 mèngxiāng dream；dreamland：这人一躺下就进入～。No sooner had he touched his pillow than he fell asleep.

梦想 mèngxiǎng ❶ dream；hope in vain；have a fond dream of：你别～了，那是根本办不到的。Stop dreaming. That's absolutely impossible. /他从未有过那种不切实际的～。Never has he harboured (*or* entertained) such unrealistic notions. ❷ earnest wish；cherished desire；dream：他的～实现了。His dream has come true. /根治黄河，自古以来就是中国人民的～。To harness the Yellow River has been a long-cherished desire of the Chinese people since ancient times.

梦魇 mèngyǎn 〈医学〉nightmare

梦遗 mèngyí 〈医学〉nocturnal emission

梦呓 mèngyì ❶ somniloquence；somniloquy；sleep-talking ❷ rigmarole：他的那些设想只不过是～。Those proposals of his are nothing but rigmarole.

梦游症 mèngyóuzhèng *also*“梦行症” sleep-walk；somnambulism

梦之队 mèngzhīduì 〈体育〉dream team

孟 mèng ❶ first month of a season (of the Chinese lunar calendar) ❷ eldest (brother) ❸ (Mèng) a surname

孟春 mèngchūn first month of spring, i.e. first lunar month

孟德尔 Mèngdé'ěr Gregor Johann Mendel (1822-1884), Austrian scientist and "father of genetics"：～学说 Mendelism

孟德尔定律 Mèngdé'ěr dìnglǜ 〈生物〉Mendelism；Mendel's law

孟德尔学派 Mèngdé'ěr Xuépài 〈生物〉Mendelian School

孟德尔主义 Mèngdé'ěrzhǔyì 〈生物〉Mendelism

孟冬 mèngdōng first month of winter, i.e. tenth lunar month

孟府 Mèngfǔ Family Mansion of Mencius in Zouxian County(邹县), Shandong Province

孟浩然 Mèng Hàorán Meng Haoran (formerly translated as Meng Hao-jan, 689-740), poet of the Tang Dynasty

孟加拉 Mèngjiālā Bengal；Bangladesh：～湾 Bay of Bengal /～语 Bengali (language) /～人 Bengali；Bengalese

孟加拉国 Mèngjiālāguó Bangladesh

孟轲 Mèng Kē *see*“孟子”

孟浪 mènglàng rash；reckless；impetuous；impulsive：千万不要～从事。Never act on the spur of the moment. *or* Don't act rashly.

孟买 Mèngmǎi Bombay, port city of India

孟庙 Mèngmiào Mencius Temple, in Zouxian County(邹县) of Shandong Province

孟秋 mèngqiū first month of autumn, i.e. seventh lunar month

孟什维克 Mèngshíwéikè Menshevik

孟什维克主义 Mèngshíwéikèzhǔyì Menshevism

孟夏 mèngxià first month of summer, i.e. fourth lunar month

孟子 Mèngzǐ ❶ (reverent term of address for 孟轲) Mencius (c. 372-289 BC), Chinese philosopher and one of the greatest Confucian

M

scholars ❷ *Mengzi* (*The Book of Mencius*), one of the four great texts of Confucianism *see also* "四书" Sìshū

mī

咪 mī

咪咪 mīmī 〈象声〉mew; miaow: 小猫饿得～叫。The kitten is mewing for food.

眯(瞇) mī ❶ narrow (one's eyes): ～着眼笑 smile with half-closed eyes /她～起眼睛看了半天。She narrowed her eyes and gazed for a long while. ❷ 〈方言〉take a short sleep; nap; doze off: ～一会儿 take a nap; have forty winks

see also mí

眯搭 mīda 〈方言〉slit one's eyes; squint: 那个老头～着眼睛坐在椅子上。The old man sat on the chair with half-closed eyes.

眯瞪 mīdeng 〈方言〉❶ blink (eyes): 他说话时老爱～眼睛。He keeps blinking when he speaks. ❷ take a nap: 他太乏了, 让他先～一会儿。Let him take a short nap; he is so dog-tired.

眯盹儿 mīdǔnr 〈方言〉take a nap; doze off: 他每天中午眯个盹儿。He has a nap after lunch every day.

眯缝 mīfeng narrow (one's eyes): 他～着眼睛笑。His face is wreathed in smiles, his eyes narrowed into slits.

眯糊 mīhu 〈方言〉❶ narrow or close (eyes): 他躺在炕上, ～上眼睛, 怎么也睡不着。Lying on the *kang*, he closed his eyes, but just could not get a wink of sleep. ❷ take a nap: 他躺下～了一会儿。He lay down and had a short nap.

眯� mīxi *also* "眯细" 〈方言〉narrow (eyes); close (eyes): 他～着眼, 有些发困。His eyes half-closed, he felt drowsy.

mí

靡 mí waste; extravagance: 奢～ wasteful; extravagant

see also mǐ

靡费 míféi waste; squander; dissipate; spend extravagantly: 他科研毫无成果, ～甚多。He achieved nothing in his scientific research though he had spent large sums of money on it. *or* He wasted a good deal of money on his fruitless research.

醾(醿、醚) mí *see* "酴醾" túmí

縻 mí 〈书面〉fasten; tie; do up: 羁～ win sb. over by hook or by crook; draw over

蘼 mí *see* "荼蘼" túmí

糜 mí ❶ gruel: 肉～ gruel with mincemeat ❷ rot: ～灭 rot away ❸ wasteful; extravagant: 侈～ 〈书面〉wasteful; extravagant ❹ (Mí) a surname

see also méi

糜费 míféi *also* "靡费" míféi waste; squander; dissipate: ～钱财 waste (*or* squander) money /防止～人力 avoid any waste of manpower /～精力 dissipate (*or* dissipation of) energy

糜烂 mílàn ❶ rotten; dissipated; debauched: ～不堪 rotten to the core /他生活～。He led a thoroughly depraved life. *or* He led a life of dissipation. ❷ 〈医学〉erosion

糜烂性毒剂 mílànxìng dújì 〈医学〉vesicant agent; blister agent

糜烂性毒气 mílànxìng dúqì blister gas; lewisite

糜棱岩 míléngyán 〈矿业〉mylonite

麋 mí elk

麋羚 mílíng hartebeest

麋鹿 mílù *also* "四不象" sìbùxiàng *milu*; David's deer

迷 mí ❶ be confused; be lost: ～了方向 lose one's way; lose one's bearings ❷ fascinated by; engrossed in; crazy about: 对数学入了～ be fascinated by mathematics /看电影着了～ be absolutely addicted to movies /她看小说入～了。She was absorbed (*or* engrossed) in reading novels. /他～上了一位护士。He was infatuated with a hospital nurse. /孩子们被橱窗里的玩具～住了。The children were spellbound by the toys in the show windows. ❸ fan; enthusiast; buff: 财～ money-grubber; miser /棋～ chess fiend (*or* enthusiast) /足球～ football fan ❹ bewitch; fascinate; enchant; perplex: 景色～人 fascinating scenery (*or* landscape) /财～心窍 be obsessed by lust for wealth; have an uncontrollable passion for wealth

迷彩 mícǎi 〈军事〉camouflage (coat): ～伪装 camouflage

迷彩服 mícǎifú battle fatigues: 沙漠～ desert fatigues

迷瞪 mídeng 〈方言〉confused; puzzled; perplexed; dazed: 他干什么都心神不定, 老那么～。He was absent-minded in whatever he did; he always seemed to be in a trance.

迷地裙 mídìqún midiskirt

迷地装 mídìzhuāng midi; midiskirt

迷迭香 mídiéxiāng 〈植物〉rosemary: ～油 rosemary oil

迷宫 mígōng ❶ maze; labyrinth: 这个游乐园里有座大型～。There is a large maze in the amusement park. /我们在闹市区大街小巷的～里走不出来了。We lost our way in the labyrinth of avenues and lanes crisscrossing the downtown area. ❷ unknown area: 探索科学～ explore the unknown areas of science

迷航 míháng (of a plane, ship, etc.) drift off course; lose one's course; get lost: 一艘轮船在大海中～了。A ship lost its course in a boundless ocean.

迷糊 míhu ❶ (of vision) dim: 雨水淋得眼睛都～了。My eyes were blurred by drifting rain. ❷ dazed; muddled: 气～了 foam with rage /他这个人有点～。He's somewhat muddle-headed (*or* scatter-brained). /我心里有些～。I felt I was in a daze. /他态度忽然变化, 真把我搞～了。I was perplexed by his sudden change of attitude.

迷幻迪斯科 míhuàn dísīkē acid house

迷幻药 míhuànyào *also* "迷幻剂" hallucinogen; psychedelic; dimethyltryptamine (DMT); mind-blower

迷魂汤 míhúntāng *also* "迷魂药" 〈迷信〉magic potion which deprives a human soul in hell of its essential character; 〈比喻〉bewitching words or action: 灌～ flatter sb. profusely, usually with evil intentions /喝了～ be taken in by sb.'s flattery

迷魂阵 míhúnzhèn scheme laid out to confuse the enemy; trap; maze; decoy: 摆～ set a trap to lure sb. /落入～ fall (*or* walk) into a trap; be caught in a trap /山道七弯八拐像个～。The path zigzags its way in the mountains like a maze pattern. /他们在这个问题上摆下了～。They are deliberately throwing dust in everyone's eyes in this matter.

迷昏 míhun ❶ unconscious; delirious; dazed: 他时常觉着头脑～。He often feels dazed. /他的伤势沉重, 夜间～了几次。Seriously wounded, he fell unconscious several times during the night. ❷ confuse; puzzle; tempt; mislead: 功名利禄不知～了多少人。So many people have fallen victim to the temptations of power and wealth.

迷惑 míhuo ❶ confused; puzzled; baffled: ～不解 feel baffled (*or* perplexed) /这到底是怎么回事? 他感到十分～。He was very much at a loss what it was all about. ❷ puzzle; confuse; perplex; baffle: ～敌人 confuse the enemy; purposely mislead the enemy /～人心 delude the public; throw dust in the eyes of the people /花言巧语～不了明眼人。Discerning people will not be misled by honeyed words.

迷惑性干扰 míhuoxìng gānrǎo 〈军事〉confusion jamming

迷津 míjīn 〈书面〉wrong path one is often tempted to take: 误入～ follow the wrong track by mistake /指点～ point out to sb. that he has been on the wrong track; show sb. how to get onto the right path

迷离 mílí indistinct; blurred: ～恍惚 be completely bewildered /泪眼～。One's eyes misted over with tears. *or* Tears blurred one's eyes.

迷离惝恍 mílí-chǎnghuǎng indistinct; dim; vague

迷离扑朔 mílí-pūshuò *also* "扑朔迷离" disorderly and confusing; labyrinthine

迷恋 míliàn indulge in; be addicted to: ～奢侈的生活方式 indulge in an extravagant life-style /他年轻时～京剧。When he was a young man, he took a passionate interest in Beijing opera.

迷路 mílù ❶ lose one's way; get lost: 林中～ lose one's way in a forest ❷ lose one's proper orientation; go astray: 她一度在生活的旅途上迷了路。She once went astray on her life's journey. ❸ 〈生理〉inner ear; labyrinth: ～积水 〈医学〉hydrolabyrinth /～炎 labyrinthitis /～反射 labyrinthian reflex

迷乱 míluàn confused; bewildered: 神志～ be delirious

M

迷漫 mímàn fill the air; spread all over the place; permeate; pervade:烟雾～ be shrouded in mist; be thick with smoke; be permeated with fog and smoke /大雪～ be filled with drifting heavy snow
迷茫 mímáng ❶ vast and hazy:远处一片～。A vast hazy expanse stretches into the distance. /原野一片混沌～,不见一个人影。The vast plain was covered with mist, and completely deserted. ❷ confused; baffled; dazed:神情～ look confused /目光～而呆滞 with glazed, glassy eyes /对未来感到～ feel perplexed by the uncertainties of the future
迷蒙 míméng ❶ dim; hazy:烟雨～ enveloped in rain and mist /夜雾～ covered in blurring night haze /暮色～ shrouded in gathering dusk ❷ (of the mind) in a trance; in a state of delirium:他从～中醒了过来。He regained consciousness from a state of delirium. ❸〈书面〉be deceived; be confused
迷梦 mímèng illusion; delusive or fond dream
迷迷怔怔 mími-zhēngzhēng dazed; in a trance; absent-minded:他睡得～的。He was dazed with sleep.
迷你 mínǐ mini:～裙 *also*"超短裙" miniskirt /～计算机 *also*"微型计算机" minicomputer
迷人 mírén ❶ enchanting; fascinating; bewitching:～的景色 scenery of enchanting beauty /桂林是个～的地方。Guilin is a dream of a place. ❷ confuse; perplex; puzzle; mislead:～眼目 mislead (*or* misguide) the public; puzzle ordinary people
迷失 míshī lose (one's way, etc.):～方向 lose one's bearings; get lost /～归路 unable to find one's way back
迷汤 mítāng *see*"迷魂汤"
迷头 mítóu〈方言〉confused; muddled; perplexed:一遇到问题他就迷了头。Whenever a problem crops up, he is at a loss.
迷途 mítú ❶ lose one's way:～羔羊 errant sheep; stray lamb /他在黑夜中～了。He lost his way in the dark night. ❷ wrong path:误入～ go astray
迷途知返 mítú-zhīfǎn turn back from the wrong path; realize one's errors and mend one's ways; recover one's bearings and return to the fold:我们都希望他～。We all hope that he will mend his ways.
迷惘 míwǎng perplexed; at a loss:～的一代 lost generation /眼睛里显露出～的神情 wear a puzzled look in one's eyes; look perplexed /他的发言似乎都有道理,但我仍然感到～。I was still rather confused though what he said sounded plausible.
迷误 míwù mistake; error
迷雾 míwù ❶ dense fog ❷ miasma; unhealthy or evil influence:妖风～ evil wind and miasma
迷信 míxìn ❶ superstition; superstitious belief:～思想 superstitious idea /～鬼神 have a superstitious belief in ghosts and spirits ❷ blind faith; blind worship:破除～,解放思想 do away with fetishes and superstitions and liberate (*or* emancipate) the mind /～权威 have blind faith in authority /～书本 book worship /个人～ personality cult; worship of the individual
迷眩 míxuàn confuse; mislead; perplex:这种理论容易～人。This theory is apt to mislead people.
迷阵 mízhèn *see*"迷魂阵"
迷走神经 mízǒu shénjīng〈生理〉vagus (nerve)
迷走神经过敏 mízǒu shénjīng guòmǐn〈医学〉vagotonia
迷走神经切断术 mízǒu shénjīng qiēduànshù〈医学〉vagatomy
迷走神经兴奋过度 mízǒu shénjīng xīngfèn guòdù〈医学〉hypervagotonia
迷走神经性心律失常 mízǒu shénjīngxìng xīnlǜ shīcháng〈医学〉vagal arrhythmia
迷走神经炎 mízǒu shénjīngyán〈医学〉vagitis
迷醉 mízuì intoxicate; enchant:山上采茶姑娘的歌声此起彼落,令人～。The hill resounded with the enchanting modulating songs of girls picking tea. /～于过去,就会妨碍更好地前进。Resting on one's laurels will hamper further progress.

谜 mí ❶ riddle; conundrum:灯～ riddles written on lanterns; lantern riddles /哑～ puzzling remark; riddle /字～ riddle about a Chinese character ❷ enigma; mystery; puzzle:那个问题是个猜不透的～。The question was an enigma to which no one knew the answer.
see also mèi
谜底 mídǐ ❶ answer or solution to a riddle ❷ truth:揭穿～ reveal the true story /～败露。The truth was finally brought to light.
谜面 mímiàn clue to a riddle; riddle
谜团 mítuán enigma; mystery; doubts and suspicions:他们终于揭开这个～。They finally unveiled the mystery.
谜语 míyǔ riddle; conundrum
谜子 mízi〈方言〉riddle; conundrum:猜～ guess a riddle

醚 mí〈化学〉ether
醚化 míhuà etherification
醚化物 míhuàwù etherate
醚麻醉 mímázuì〈医学〉etherize

蒾 mí *see*"荚蒾" jiámí

眯(瞇) mí (of dust, etc.) get into one's eye:沙子～了眼。Some dust got into my eyes.
see also mī

祢(禰) Mí a surname

弥(彌) mí ❶ full of; overflowing:～山遍野 all over the mountains and plains; over hill and dale ❷ fill; cover: *see*"～补" ❸ even more; still more:欲盖～彰 try to cover up a fault only to make it more glaring /欲简～繁 try to simplify matters only to make them more complicated ❹ (Mí) a surname
弥补 míbǔ make up; remedy; rectify; make good:不可～的损失 irreparable (*or* irretrievable) loss /～不利局势 remedy an unfavourable situation /～漏洞 plug (*or* fill up) a leak /～学识之不足 make up for one's inadequate knowledge /～赤字 meet a deficit
弥尔顿 Mí'ěrdùn John Milton (1608-1674), English poet and author of *Paradise Lost* (1667) and *Paradise Regained* (1671)
弥封 mífēng fold or seal the corner of an examination paper where the examinee's name or number is entered (to guard against fraudulent practice)
弥缝 míféng gloss over; cover up:事已败露,不可～。The whole thing has been brought to light, and it is no longer possible to cover it up.
弥合 míhé heal; close; bridge:～伤口 heal the wound /～裂痕 close a rift
弥勒 Mílè〈佛教〉*Maitreya*:～下生经 *Maitreyavyakarana*
弥勒佛 Mílèfó Laughing Buddha
弥留 míliú〈书面〉on the verge of death; dying:～之际 on one's deathbed
弥满 mímǎn *also*"瀰满" mímǎn ❶ vigorous; full:精力～ vigorous; full of vim and vigour ❷ fill; permeate:烟味～了小屋。The hut was permeated with (*or* full of) smoke.
弥漫 mímàn *also*"瀰漫" mímàn permeate; fill; diffuse; spread all over the place:～星云 diffuse nebula /阵地上硝烟～。The fumes of gunpowder filled the battlefield. /果园里～着苹果的芳香。The orchard is permeated with the delicate fragrance of apples.
弥漫性动脉瘤 mímànxìng dòngmàiliú〈医学〉diffuse aneurysm
弥漫性腹膜炎 mímànxìng fùmóyán〈医学〉general peritonitis; diffuse peritonitis
弥蒙 míméng *also*"瀰濛" míméng (of mists, smoke, etc.) vast and vague; boundless and indistinct:云雾～ vast expanse of drifting cloud and mist /硝烟～ filled with the smoke of gunpowder
弥撒 mísa〈宗教〉mass; *missa*:听～ hear mass; attend (*or* go to) mass /做～ say (*or* read) mass /大～ high mass /小～ low mass
弥撒曲 mísaqǔ *also*"吟唱弥撒" *missa cantata*
弥撒书 mísashū missal; *missa*
弥赛亚 Mísàiyà Messiah
弥散 mísàn〈物理〉dispersion:～度 degree of dispersion; dispersity /～力 dispersion force /～硬化 dispersion hardening
弥散剂 mísànjì〈物理〉disperser; dispersive medium
弥散系 mísànxì〈物理〉dispersed system
弥天 mítiān all over the universe; vast:～大祸 most dreadful disaster /～漫野 all over the land; everywhere
弥天大谎 mítiān-dàhuǎng monstrous or outrageous lie; barefaced lie
弥天大罪 mítiān-dàzuì monstrous or heinous crime; towering crime
弥天盖地 mítiān-gàidì with tremendous force; with great momen-

tum：大雪纷纷扬扬，～。Snow was falling thick and fast with increasing intensity. /雨～地下着。Down poured the rain obliterating the sky.
弥陀 Mítuó *also*"弥陀佛"(short for 阿弥陀佛)*Amitabha*
弥望 míwàng 〈书面〉meet the eye on every side：春色～。It is spring everywhere.
弥月 míyuè 〈书面〉❶ baby's completion of its first month of life ❷ full month：开业～，生意一直红火。The business has been running well since its start a month ago.

瀰 mí
瀰满 mímǎn *see*"弥满" mímǎn
瀰漫 mímàn *also*"弥漫" mímàn spread over；permeate：战云～。War clouds hang low over the horizon.
瀰濛 míméng *see*"弥蒙" míméng

弥(籋) mí *also*"篾子" thin bamboo strips；rind of reeds：席～儿 bamboo mattress

猕(獼) mí
猕猴 míhóu macaque；rhesus monkey；monkey
猕猴桃 míhóutáo *also*"羊桃" yángtáo；"杨桃" yángtáo 〈植物〉*Actinidia chinensis*；Chinese gooseberry；kiwi fruit

mǐ

靡[1] mǐ ❶〈书面〉bend with the wind：风～一时 be (all) the rage；be all the vogue；be fashionable for a time；be popular for a time /披～ (of grass, etc.) be bent by the wind；be routed ❷ fine；wonderful；excellent：～衣 gorgeous dress

靡[2] mǐ 〈书面〉no；not：～事不为 like to try one's hand at anything /～不有初。Everything has a beginning.
see also mí
靡丽 mǐlì 〈书面〉splendid；extravagant；luxurious
靡靡 mǐmǐ decadent；demoralizing
靡靡之音 mǐmǐzhīyīn decadent music；music or song which appeals to depraved tastes
靡然 mǐrán universally：～成风 carry the day；carry all before one /天下～从之 enjoy universal support

米[1] mǐ ❶ rice：精白～ polished rice /糙～ brown rice /陈～ rice stocked for years /大～ (husked) rice /红～ red rice /机～ machine-processed rice；polished long-grained nonglutinous rice /粳～ polished round-grained nonglutinous rice /糯～ *also*"江～" polished glutinous rice ❷ shelled or husked seed (usu. edible)：花生～ peanut seed /秫～ husked sorghum /燕麦～ grains of oats /小～ husked millet /高粱～ husked *gaoliang* (*or* sorghum) ❸ anything like a grain of rice：海～ dried shelled shrimps ❹ (Mǐ) a surname

米[2] mǐ 〈量词〉metre：立方～ cubic metre /平方～ square metre /分～ decimetre /厘～ centimetre /毫～ milimetre /忽～ centimilimetre /千～ kilometre /克～ gram-centimetre /秒立方～ cubic metre per second
米波 mǐbō 〈无线电〉metric wave
米醋 mǐcù rice vinegar
米豆腐 mǐdòufu 〈方言〉rice curd, a kind of food made from thick liquid of rice
米饭 mǐfàn cooked rice
米粉 mǐfěn ❶ ground rice；rice flour ❷ rice-flour noodles：炒～ fried rice-noodles
米粉肉 mǐfěnròu *also*"粉蒸肉" fěnzhēngròu pork steamed with rice flour
米麸 mǐfū rice bran
米芾 Mǐ Fú Mi Fu (1051-1107), calligrapher and painter of the Northern Song Dynasty
米泔水 mǐgānshuǐ water in which rice has been washed
米高梅影片公司 Mǐgāomé Yǐngpiàn Gōngsī (US) Metro-Goldwyn-Mayer Inc., a Hollywood film studio
米糕 mǐgāo rice cake；rice pudding
米格 mǐgé MIG；Mig：～战斗机 Mig fighter
米黄 mǐhuáng cream-coloured
米酒 mǐjiǔ rice wine；(Japan) sake
米糠 mǐkāng rice bran
米糠油 mǐkāngyóu rice bran oil
米兰 Mǐlán Milan；Milano — industrial centre of northwest Italy
米老鼠 mǐlǎoshǔ Mickey Mouse；mickey mouse
米粒 mǐlì grain of rice
米粮川 mǐliángchuān rich rice-producing area：荒滩变成～。The barren land has now been turned into a granary.
米面 mǐmiàn ❶ rice and wheat flour ❷ rice flour；ground rice ❸ 〈方言〉rice-flour noodles
米铺 mǐpù rice store；grain store
米·千克·秒制 mǐ-qiānkè-miǎozhì M.K.S. system
米丘林 Mǐqiūlín Ivan Vladimirovich Michurin (1855-1935), Russian horticulturist：～学说 Michurinism
米色 mǐsè cream-coloured：～陶器 creamware
米汤 mǐtang ❶ water in which rice has been cooked ❷ thin rice or millet gruel
米突 mǐtū *see*"米[2]"
米虾 mǐxiā *also*"草虾" cǎoxiā a kind of shrimp (*Caridina*)
米线 mǐxiàn 〈方言〉rice noodle：过桥～ rice noodles steeped in piping hot sauce
米象 mǐxiàng 〈动物〉rice weevil
米制 mǐzhì metric system
米珠薪桂 mǐzhū-xīnguì Every grain of rice is worth a pearl and firewood is as precious as cassia — exorbitant prices of commodities：此地～，居家大不易。It's hard to make ends meet here because of the very high cost of living.
米猪 mǐzhū pig infected with cysticercus
米烛光 mǐzhúguāng 〈物理〉metre-candle；lux
米蛀虫 mǐzhùchóng ❶ rice worm ❷ profiteer hoarding rice

敉 mǐ 〈书面〉placate；pacify；appease
敉平 mǐpíng suppress；quell；put down：～叛乱 put down (*or* quell) a rebellion

脒 mǐ 〈化学〉amidine：磺胺～ sulphaguanidine (SG)

芈 mǐ ❶〈象声〉(of a sheep) baa；bleat ❷ (Mǐ) a surname

弭 mǐ ❶〈书面〉put down；quell；remove：消～ put an end to；prevent (future trouble) ❷ (Mǐ) a surname
弭谤 mǐbàng 〈书面〉stop slander
弭兵 mǐbīng 〈书面〉put an end to war；cease hostilities
弭除 mǐchú 〈书面〉remove；get rid of；do away with：～成见 do away with bias
弭患 mǐhuàn 〈书面〉remove a source of trouble；pacify a disturbance
弭乱 mǐluàn 〈书面〉suppress a revolt；put an end to war

洣(瀰) mǐ 〈书面〉full of water
洣迤 mǐyǐ 〈书面〉(of land, etc.) level；flat；even：～平原 stretch of flat land；plain

mì

泌 mì secrete：分～ secrete /内分～ endocrine；internal secretion /外分～ exocrine；external secretion
泌尿道感染 mìniàodào gǎnrǎn 〈医学〉urethral infection
泌尿科 mìniàokē 〈医学〉urological department
泌尿器官 mìniào qìguān 〈生理〉urinary organ
泌尿生殖系统 mìniào shēngzhí xìtǒng 〈生理〉urogenital system
泌尿系统 mìniào xìtǒng 〈生理〉urinary system
泌尿学 mìniàoxué 〈医学〉urology；urinology：～家 urologist
泌乳 mìrǔ lactation：～过多 polygalactia /～停止 galactostasis
泌丝腺 mìsīxiàn serictery；sericterium
泌脂腺 mìzhīxiàn oil gland

宓 mì ❶〈书面〉peaceful; tranquil; quiet ❷ (Mì) a surname

蜜 mì ❶ honey: 蜂～ honey /割～ cut off a honey comb in order to get honey /酿～ make honey ❷ honey-like thing: 花～ nectar /糖～ molasses /蔗糖～ cane molasses ❸ sweet; honeyed; luscious: 甜～ sweet; happy /甜言～语 sugared (*or* honeyed) words; sweet words and honeyed phrases; honeymouthed; honeylipped /甜情～意 sweet feeling and honeyed sentiment — being in love

蜜胺 mì'àn melamine: ～树脂 melamine resin

蜜草 mìcǎo honeywort

蜜虫 mìchóng *also* "蚜虫" yáchóng 〈方言〉aphid; aphis

蜜滴 mìdī honey drop

蜜蜂 mìfēng honeybee; bee: ～巢 honeycomb /～舞蹈 bee dance

蜜蜂学 mìfēngxué apiology

蜜柑 mìgān mandarin orange; tangerine orange

蜜供 mìgòng fried and honeyed noodles (formerly used in sacrifices)

蜜管 mìguǎn honey tube

蜜果 mìguǒ Spanish lime (*Melicoccus bijugus*)

蜜花 mìhuā honey flower

蜜环菌 mìhuánjūn hallimasch; halimasch

蜜黄色 mìhuángsè honey gold; honey yellow

蜜饯 mìjiàn candied (fruit); preserved (fruit): ～糖果 sweetmeats made of fruit and sugar

蜜酒 mìjiǔ mead; mulse

蜜橘 mìjú tangerine

蜜蜡 mìlà beeswax

蜜里调油 mìlǐ-tiáoyóu on very intimate terms: 小两口的感情真是好得～似的。The young couple are deeply attached to each other.

蜜露 mìlù honeydew: ～甜瓜 honeydew melon

蜜木 mìmù honeywood

蜜鸟 mìniǎo honeycreeper

蜜色 mìsè colour of honey; light yellow

蜜树 mìshù honey tree

蜜桃 mìtáo 〈植物〉nectarine (*Prunus persica* var. *nectarina*)

蜜甜 mìtián honey-sweet; very sweet: ～的西瓜 honey-sweet water melon

蜜丸子 mìwánzi 〈中医〉bolus made of powdered Chinese medicine and honey

蜜胃 mìwèi honey stomach

蜜腺 mìxiàn 〈植物〉nectary; nectarium; honey gland

蜜香草 mìxiāngcǎo honey balm

蜜熊 mìxióng honey bear; kinkajou; sloth bear

蜜叶 mìyè honey-leaf

蜜蚁 mìyǐ honey ant

蜜语 mìyǔ honeyed-words; sweet words

蜜源 mìyuán nectar source: ～植物 nectariferous (*or* bee, *or* honey) plant; nectar plant

蜜源区 mìyuánqū (bee) pasture

蜜月 mìyuè honeymoon: ～旅行 honeymoon trip; travel in honeymoon /～桥牌 honeymoon bridge

蜜枣 mìzǎo candied date or jujube

蜜钟花 mìzhōnghuā honeybells

蜜渍 mìzì preserved in sugar; candied

密 mì ❶ dense; heavy; close; thick: 头发很～ have thick hair /枪声很～ intensive gunfire; heavy shooting (*or* fire) /人口稠～地区 densely populated area /经～〈纺织〉warp density /纬～〈纺织〉weft density / ～不透风 airtight /树种得太～。The trees are too closely planted. /山坡上长着一片茂～的树林。On the mountain slope there was a thick (*or* dense) wood. /梳子的齿儿过～。The teeth of the comb are too close. ❷ intimate; familiar; close: 与某人往来甚～ be on intimate terms with someone; be thick with sb. /亲～ close; intimate /他俩关系很～。They are as thick as thieves. ❸ fine; precise; meticulous: 精～ precise; accurate /周～ carefully considered; meticulous ❹ secret; confidential: 绝～ top secret; strictly confidential; circumspect; eyes only /泄～ leak a secret /告～ inform on (*or* against) sb. /机～ secret; classified; confidential /～通声息 pass on (*or* exchange) secret information; keep each other imformed (*or* posted) in secret /失～问题很严重 grave situation arising from leakage of secrets ❺ (Mì) a surname

密斑油 mìbānyóu 〈化学〉mirbane oil

密报 mìbào ❶ inform secretly; tip off: 是谁～了这件事? Who was the tattler? ❷ secret message; confidential report: 他得到了前方战斗的～。He received confidential information about the war situation at the front.

密闭 mìbì ❶ tightly closed: 门窗～ tightly shut doors and windows ❷ airtight; hermetic: ～容器 airtight container

密闭式叶片搅拌机 mìbìshì yèpiàn jiǎobànjī 〈建筑〉close blade pug mill

密播 mìbō 〈农业〉dense sowing

密布 mìbù be densely distributed or spread; be densely covered: 彤云～。Dark clouds covered the sky. /繁星～。Twinkling stars dotted the sky. /入口处岗哨～。The entrance was heavily guarded. /山头上云雾～。The mountain top is shrouded in mist.

密丛丛 mìcóngcóng very dense; very thick: 他腮边长着～的胡子。He wears very thick whiskers. /遍野葱绿的庄稼和草木～地遮蔽着附近的村庄。Nearby villages are hidden in the lush crops and woods.

密德兰银行 Mìdélán Yínháng (UK) Midland Bank Ltd.

密电 mìdiàn ❶ coded telegram; cipher telegram ❷ send a coded telegram (to sb.); secretly telegraph or wire

密电码 mìdiànmǎ cipher; code

密电码回译 mìdiànmǎ huíyì decipher; decrypt

密度 mìdù density; thickness: 人口～ population density /电流～ current density /作物种植～ density of crops /～分布〈物理〉density distribution

密度计 mìdùjì 〈物理〉densimeter; densitometer; density indicator

密度计量学 mìdù jìliàngxué 〈摄影〉densitometry

密度镜 mìdùjìng 〈纺织〉pick glass

密耳 mì'ěr mil (a measure of length equal to 0.001 of an inch)

密耳圆 mì'ěryuán circular mil

密封 mìfēng seal up; seal airtight; seal hermetically: ～文件 seal a document /～药瓶 seal up a medicine bottle; make a medicine bottle airtight

密封舱 mìfēngcāng 〈航天〉capsule; 〈航空〉〈船舶〉sealed cabin; airtight cabin or compartment

密封层 mìfēngcéng sealant

密封窗 mìfēngchuāng hermetic window

密封带 mìfēngdài seal tape

密封垫 mìfēngdiàn gasket

密封焊接 mìfēng hànjiē seal welding

密封机身 mìfēng jīshēn closed fuselage

密封剂 mìfēngjì sealant; sealing compound

密封胶 mìfēngjiāo fluid sealant

密封孔 mìfēngkǒng closed hole

密封圈 mìfēngquān seal ring

密封条 mìfēngtiáo sealing strips

密封性 mìfēngxìng tightness: ～试验 encapsulation test; leakage test

密封压盖 mìfēng yāgài sealing gland

密封轴承 mìfēng zhóuchéng sealed bearing

密告 mìgào secretly report; inform: 有人～了他们的走私活动。Somebody secretly reported their smuggling activities.

密会 mìhuì ❶ meet in secret ❷ closed session; secret meeting

密级 mìjí classification (of government confidential documents): 标明文件的～ mark the classification of a document /一封～为"机密"的文件 document classified as "confidential"

密集 mìjí dense; concentrated; crowded together: ～的人群 dense crowd /人口～地区 densely populated area /～轰炸 heavy (*or* mass) bombing /劳动～型企业 labour-intensive enterprise /资本～型项目 capital-intensive project /技术～型 technology-intensive /～队形〈军事〉close (*or* tight) formation /高楼大厦～的闹市区 downtown area where tall buildings are concentrated

密件 mìjiàn confidential paper or letter; classified matter or material

密接 mìjiē joined closely; close

密径 mìjìng secret path: 羊肠～ secret narrow path

密聚花 mìjùhuā aggregate flower

密克罗尼西亚 Mìkèluóníxīyà Micronesia (island chain in the western Pacific): ～联邦 Federated States of Micronesia

密款 mìkuǎn ❶〈书面〉sincerity: 上陈～ state one's view in all sincerity ❷ (of treaty, agreement, etc.) secret clause; secret term

M

密勒氏评论报 Mìlèshì Pínglùnbào *The China Weekly Review*, English language newspaper started by Thomas F. Millard and published in Shanghai between 1917 and 1953

密理根辐射线 Mìlǐgēn fúshèxiàn 〈物理〉Millikan rays

密林 mìlín dense wood: ～深处 in the heart of the dense wood; deep in the forest

密令 mìlìng secret order; secret missive

密锣紧鼓 mìluó-jǐngǔ *also* "紧锣密鼓" loud beating of gongs and drums — big publicity campaign

密麻麻 mìmámá close and numerous: ～的下着鹅毛大雪。Snow was falling thick and fast in big flakes.

密码 mìmǎ ❶ cipher; cipher code: ～电报 cipher telegram / ～电话机 ciphony equipment; ciphertelephone; ciphone ❷〈生物〉code: 遗传～ genetic code

密码传真 mìmǎ chuánzhēn cifax

密码电话学 mìmǎ diànhuàxué cipher telephony; ciphony

密码电文 mìmǎ diànwén cryptogram; cryptotext; encrypted text (of a telegram)

密码机 mìmǎjī cipher machine; cryptograph

密码酶 mìmǎméi 〈生化〉codase

密码破译 mìmǎ pòyì decryptography

密码锁 mìmǎsuǒ trick lock

密码学 mìmǎxué cryptology

密码员 mìmǎyuán cryptographer; cipher clerk

密码子 mìmǎzi 〈生理〉codon: ～识别 codon recognition

密铆 mìmǎo close riveting

密密 mìmì ❶ dense; thick: 两边都是～的树林。On either side there are dense woods. ❷ close; tight: 室内有窗帷的地方都～地拉严。All the window curtains in the room are tightly drawn.

密密层层 mìmi-céngcéng ring upon ring; layer after layer: ～的灌木丛 clump of thick bushes / ～的警戒网 rings of security sentries / 被敌军～地包围了 be surrounded ring upon ring by the enemy

密密丛丛 mìmi-cóngcóng luxuriant; exuberant: ～的杨树林 luxuriant wood of poplars

密密麻麻 mìmi-mámá 〈口语〉close and numerous; thickly dotted: 广场上的人～的。The square is packed with people. / 他～地在本子上写了一大篇。He filled his notebook with small and closely-written characters. / 天上的星星～。The sky is thickly studded with stars. / 荧光屏幕上航班起飞和抵达时刻表～的, 绿光闪烁。Fluorescent screens were bristling with flight arrival and departure times, the green figures gleaming.

密密匝匝 mìmi-zāzā *also* "密匝匝" thick; dense: 两腿～地缠满绷带。His legs were dressed with several thick layers of bandage.

密谋 mìmóu conspire; intrigue; plot; scheme: ～推翻现政权 plot (*or* conspire) to overthrow the present regime; make a plot for the overthrow of the present regime

密切 mìqiè ❶ close; bosom; intimate: 保持～关系 maintain close contacts with each other / 理论与实践～结合 closely integrate theory with practice / 他俩关系很～。The two of them are on intimate terms (*or* are very pally). ❷ make close; become intimate: 进一步～两国关系 forge stronger ties between the two countries / 我们今后应～往来, 加强合作。We should keep in close touch and strengthen our cooperation in the days ahead. ❸ carefully; closely: ～注视形势的发展 closely watch (*or* follow) the development of the situation (*or* events) / ～配合 act in concert / 目前情况须～注意。The current situation calls for our full attention. ❹〈数学〉osculation: ～点 point of osculation / ～轨道 osculating orbit / ～坐标 osculating coordinates

密商 mìshāng hold private counsel; hold secret sessions; negotiate in secret: ～对策 hold private talks to devise countermeasures (*or* decide on countermoves)

密使 mìshǐ secret emissary; secret envoy

密室 mìshì secret room: 策划于～之中 plot behind closed doors

密实 mìshi closely knit; tight; dense; thick: 麦子种得太～了。The wheat is too densely planted. / 这幅布织得挺～。The cloth is tightly woven.

密司脱 mìsītuō (transliteration) mister; Mr.

密斯 mìsī (transliteration) miss

密苏里号 Mìsūlǐhào USS Missouri, flagship of the US Pacific Fleet in the Second World War, on which Japan signed its surrender

密苏里河 Mìsūlǐhé Missouri River, one of the main tributaries of the Mississippi

密谈 mìtán secret or confidential or private talks; talk behind closed doors: 附耳～ talk in whispers

密探 mìtàn secret agent; spy

密贴 mìtiē stuck together; close-knit; seamless: ～无缝 close-knit and seamless / 大雪把山峦覆盖得密密贴贴的。The mountains are entirely covered by heavy snow. / 瓶口封闭得严实～。The battle is very firmly sealed.

密陀僧 mìtuósēng 〈化学〉litharge; lead monoxide

密陀僧中毒 mìtuósēng zhòngdú lithargysmus

密位 mìwèi 〈军事〉mil

密纹 mìwén microgroove: ～录音 microgroove recording

密纹唱片 mìwén chàngpiàn long-playing record; micro-groove record

密西西比河 Mìxīxībǐhé Mississippi River, the longest river of North America

密歇根湖 Mìxiēgēnhú Lake Michigan, one of the five Great Lakes of North America and wholly within the United States

密写 mìxiě secret writing: ～情报 intelligence written in invisible ink / ～药水 invisible (*or* sympathetic) ink

密信 mìxìn confidential letter; secret letter

密旋霉素 mìxuánméisù 〈药学〉pactamycin

密讯 mìxùn secret classified information; confidential message

密议 mìyì hold a secret conference; discuss behind closed doors; discuss in closed session

密友 mìyǒu close or fast friend; bosom friend; close and trusted friend; alter ego

密语 mìyǔ ❶ *also* "暗语" ànyǔ code; code word; coded language: ～通信 communication in coded language; crypto-communication ❷ talk in private; secret talks: 二人低声～。The two of them whispered to each other in private.

密约 mìyuē secret agreement or treaty

密钥 mìyuè key secret code

密云不雨 mìyún-bùyǔ dense clouds but no rain — trouble is brewing: 西线战场～, 一场大战就要展开了。The storm was gathering over the west front and a major battle was imminent. / 运动～, 令人莫测高深。The campaign was still an unknown quantity, like gathering clouds before the storm.

密匝匝 mìzāzā *also* "密密匝匝" 〈口语〉thick; dense: 稻子熟了, ～地垂着穗子。The rice was ripe with heavy drooping ears.

密召 mìzhào serve secret summons on; summon secretly: ～回京。He was secretly summoned back to the capital.

密诏 mìzhào secret or confidential imperial edict

密植 mìzhí 〈农业〉close planting: 合理～ rational close planting

密旨 mìzhǐ secret edict

密致 mìzhì compact

嘧 mì

嘧啶 mìdìng 〈化学〉pyrimidine: ～二聚体 pyrimidine dimer / ～核苷 pyrimidine nucleoside / ～碱基 pyrimidine bases

谧 mì

〈书面〉tranquil; peaceful: 安～ quiet; tranquil

谧静 mìjìng quiet; serene; tranquil: ～的田野 tranquil fields

秘(祕) mì

❶ secret; confidential: 奥～ profoundly mysterious; abstruse; enigmatic / 神～ mysterious; mystical / 诡～ surreptitious; occult; secretive ❷ make a secret of; keep sth. secret; hold sth. back: ～而不露 conceal; hide ❸ seldom seen; rare: *see* "～籍"

see also bì

秘奥 mì'ào profound mystery: 生命的～ mystery of life

秘宝 mìbǎo rare treasure

秘本 mìběn treasured private copy or edition of a rare book or text

秘藏 mìcáng store up; hide: ～古画 closely guarded ancient paintings / 他真想说出多年来～在心底的话。How he wanted to pour out what he had kept to himself all these years!

秘传 mìchuán hand down (sth. such as a recipe) from generation to generation as a close family secret

秘而不宣 mì'érbùxuān not let anyone in on a secret; keep mum about sth. regarded as a secret; keep sth. confidential: 此药方历时百年, ～。This recipe has been kept secret for almost a hundred years.

秘方 mìfāng esoteric recipe：祖传～ esoteric recipe handed down from one's ancestors
秘府 mìfǔ palace repository of classics where books, particularly rare and valuable books, were kept
秘籍 mìjí rare and valuable book
秘计 mìjì ❶ secret plot：阴谋～ conspiracy ❷ remarkable ploy; brilliant stratagem：奇谋～ wonderful stratagem
秘结 mìjié constipation
秘诀 mìjué recipe; secret：成功的～ recipe for success
秘密 mìmì ❶ secret; private; confidential; clandestine：～会议 secret meeting; closed-door session; private session /～文件 secret papers; confidential (*or* classified) document /～条约 secret treaty /～投票 secret ballot; Australian ballot /～活动 undercover (*or* covert) activities /～工作 underground work /～电台 clandestine radio station /～佣金 undeclared commission /～卫星 unannounced satellite ❷ sth. secret; secret：保守～ keep a secret /泄露～ disclose (*or* reveal) a secret; let the cat out of the bag /这已是公开的～。It's already an open secret.
秘密警察 mìmì jǐngchá secret police; secret policeman
秘史 mìshǐ secret history (of a feudal dynasty); inside story：清宫～ inside story of the Qing court /明星～ private life of a film star
秘事 mìshì private affair; confidential information
秘书 mìshū secretary：机要～ confidential secretary /私人～ private secretary /行政～ administrative secretary /一等～〈外交〉 first secretary /警卫～ security secretary /～长 secretary-general /他担任部长的～。He works (*or* serves) as secretary to the minister.
秘书处 mìshūchù secretariat：总理府～ secretariat of the prime minister's office
秘闻 mìwén unknown information, esp. secrets of sb.'s private life：披露～ disclose hitherto unknown information (about sb.'s private life)

幂(冪) mì

❶〈书面〉 cloth cover ❷〈书面〉 cover; hood ❸〈数学〉 power：～乘积 power product /～函数 power function
幂等 mìděng 〈数学〉 idempotent：～矩阵 idempotent matrix /～性 idempotence; idempotent property /～因子 idemfactor
幂级数 mìjíshù 〈数学〉 power series
幂零 mìlíng 〈数学〉 nilpotent：～代数 nilpotent algebra /～积 nilpotent product /～性 nilpotency
幂律 mìlǜ *also* "幂定律"〈数学〉 power law

幎 mì

〈书面〉 *see* "幂" mì

汨 mì

汨罗 Mìluó river that originates in Jiangxi Province and ends in Hunan Province, emptying into the Dongting Lake：～江 Miluo River

蓂 mì

see "菥蓂" xīmì

觅(覓) mì

look for; seek：寻踪～迹 look for the traces of sb. or sth.; trace out
觅汉 mìhàn 〈方言〉 farm labourer hired by the year; long-term hired hand
觅句 mìjù seek after the most appropriate line (for a poem)
觅求 mìqiú seek; look for：四处～ search high and low; seek everywhere /～知音 look for an understanding friend
觅取 mìqǔ search; seek; hunt for; look for：我们来到深山老林～珍贵的木材。We've come to the remote mountains and primitive forest to search for valuable wood.
觅食 mìshí (of birds, beasts, etc.) hunt for food

mián

棉 mián

❶ general term for cotton and kapok：草～ cotton/ 木～ kapok ❷ cotton：～纺织品 cotton textiles /纯～ pure cotton /皮～ ginned cotton; lint (cotton) /原～ raw cotton / 长绒～ longstaple cotton / 陆地～ upland cotton /药～ absorbent cotton; surgical cotton; cotton wool ❸ cotton-like material：腈纶～ acrylic fibres /石～ asbestos /矿物～ mineral wool /人造～ rayon ❹ cotton-padded：～大衣 cotton-padded overcoat
棉袄 mián'ǎo cotton-padded jacket
棉白杨 miánbáiyáng 〈植物〉 cottonwood
棉包 miánbāo bale of cotton
棉包电缆 miánbāo diànlǎn 〈电工〉 cotton insulation cable
棉被 miánbèi quilt with cotton wadding; cotton-padded quilt
棉哔叽衬料 miánbìjī chènliào finette
棉饼 miánbǐng *also* "棉子饼" cottonseed cake
棉布 miánbù cotton cloth; cotton：纯～ pure cotton cloth /漂白～ bleached cotton cloth
棉柴 miánchái 〈方言〉 cotton plant used as firewood (after the bolls have been picked)
棉尘肺 miánchénfèi 〈医学〉 byssinosis
棉的确良 miándíquèliáng synthetic material of cotton and dacron
棉垫料 miándiànliào cotton padding
棉纺 miánfǎng cotton spinning; cotton textile
棉纺厂 miánfǎngchǎng cotton mill
棉纺业 miánfǎngyè cotton textile industry
棉凫 miánfú 〈动物〉 cotton teal
棉根腐病 miángēnfǔbìng 〈农业〉 cotton root rot
棉红铃虫 miánhónglíngchóng pink bollworm
棉红蜘蛛 miánhóngzhīzhū two-spotted spider mite
棉猴儿 miánhóur hooded cotton-padded coat; cotton-padded parka or anorak
棉花 miánhua cotton：摘～ pick cotton /弹～ fluff cotton / ～大王 cotton king / ～加工 cotton ginning or processing
棉花打包机 miánhua dǎbāojī cotton press
棉花耳朵 miánhua ěrduo 〈口语〉 soft-eared — easily persuaded; credulous：有名的～ person known for his credulity; notorious soft-touch
棉花间苗机 miánhua jiànmiáojī 〈农业〉 cotton chopper
棉花签 miánhuaqiān cotton swab
棉花蛆 miánhuaqū 〈方言〉 pink bollworm
棉花绒 miánhuaróng ❶ cotton fluff ❷〈纺织〉 a kind of cotton fabric made of coarse yarn, usu. as the lining of a garment; cotton velvet
棉花胎 miánhuatāi 〈方言〉 cotton wadding (for a quilt)
棉花糖 miánhuatáng cotton candy
棉花套子 miánhua tàozi 〈方言〉 cotton wadding (for a quilt)
棉花嘴儿 miánhuazuǐr 〈口语〉 be full of honeyed words; be honey-mouthed：耍～ use sweet words; use sweet-talk /谁信你那～! Your honeyed words (*or* sweet-talk) won't fool anyone.
棉卷 miánjuǎn 〈纺织〉 lap
棉枯萎病 miánkūwěibìng fusarium wilt of cotton
棉裤 miánkù cotton-padded trousers
棉兰 Miánlán Medan, city in Indonesia, on the Deli River in northeast Sumatra
棉兰老 Miánlánlǎo Mindanao, second largest island of the Philippines
棉铃 miánlíng cotton boll
棉铃虫 miánlíngchóng bollworm
棉铃梳摘器 miánlíng shūzhāiqì 〈农业〉 stripping comb
棉铃象虫 miánlíng xiàngchóng cotton boll weevil
棉毛 miánmáo cotton and wool：～织物 fabrics made of cotton and wool
棉毛机 miánmáojī interlock (knitting) machine
棉毛裤 miánmáokù (interlock) long cotton underwear
棉毛衫 miánmáoshān (interlock) cotton jersey：～布 interlock cotton fabric
棉农 miánnóng cotton grower; cotton farmer
棉袍子 miánpáozi *also* "棉袍儿" cotton-padded gown
棉皮鞋 miánpíxié lined leather shoe; winter leather shoe
棉签 miánqiān *see* "棉花签"
棉绒 miánróng cotton velvet
棉绒布 miánróngbù 〈纺织〉 winsey
棉纱 miánshā cotton yarn
棉纱头 miánshātóu cotton waste
棉毯 miántǎn cotton blanket
棉桃 miántáo cotton boll
棉套 miántào cotton-padded covering for keeping sth. warm
棉田 miántián cotton field
棉条 miántiáo 〈纺织〉 sliver：～桶 sliver can

棉尾兔 miánwěitù cottontail; cottontail rabbit
棉线 miánxiàn cotton thread; cotton
棉鞋 miánxié cotton-padded shoes
棉锈病 miánxiùbìng 〈农业〉cotton rust
棉絮 miánxù ❶ cotton fibre ❷ cotton wadding (for a quilt)
棉絮状沉淀物 miánxùzhuàng chéndiànwù flocculent precipitation
棉蚜虫 miányáchóng cotton aphid
棉衣 miányī cotton-padded clothes
棉油 miányóu *see* "棉子油"
棉织品 miánzhīpǐn cotton goods; cotton fabrics; cotton textiles
棉子 miánzǐ *also* "棉籽" cottonseed
棉子饼 miánzǐbǐng cottonseed cake
棉子分离机 miánzǐ fēnlíjī 〈纺织〉gin saw
棉子绒 miánzǐróng cotton linters
棉子油 miánzǐyóu *also* "棉油"; "卫生油" wèishēngyóu cottonseed oil
棉籽 miánzǐ *see* "棉子"

绵(緜)

mián ❶ silk floss ❷ continuous; consecutive: ～亘 continuous; unending /连～ unbroken; uninterrupted; interminable ❸ thin; weak; soft: 力～ not powerful /软～～ soft; feathery ❹ (of a person's temper) gentle; meek: 你别瞧他不声不响, 性子挺～, 心可大了。He may be quiet and as meek as a lamb, but he has great ambitions.
绵白糖 miánbáitáng *also* "绵糖" powdered sugar; fine white sugar
绵薄 miánbó 〈谦词〉meagre strength; humble effort: 略尽～ do what little one can; do one's bit /为人民竭尽～ do all one can for the people; do one's level best for the people
绵长 miáncháng last a long time: 福寿～ (used on the occasion of an elderly person's birthday) happy long life; happiness and longevity
绵绸 miánchóu 〈纺织〉fabric made from waste silk
绵惙 miánchuò 〈书面〉be critically ill: 沉病～ be critically ill; be dying
绵笃 miándǔ 〈书面〉be critically ill: 病情～, 难以久保。The patient is in critical condition and will not last long.
绵顿 miándùn 〈书面〉be (critically) ill for a long time: ～在床 be bedridden with prolonged illness /病已～, 恐难医治。He has been seriously ill for a long time and stands little chance of recovery. *or* He is terminally ill.
绵亘 miángèn (as of mountain ranges, etc.) extend continuously; stretch in an unbroken chain: 长城逶迤～在中国北部的崇山峻岭之上。The Great Wall zigzags along the lofty mountains in northern China.
绵和 miánhe 〈方言〉(of a person's temper) gentle; soft; mild: 他脾气挺～的。He has a gentle disposition.
绵里藏针 miánlǐ-cángzhēn ❶ needle hidden in silk floss — tough despite superficial softness; gentle but firm ❷ ruthless character behind a gentle appearance; iron hand in a velvet glove
绵力 miánlì humble effort; what little one can do: 我虽已年迈, 也要为家乡的发展竭尽～。Though advanced in years, I would still like to do my level best for the development of my hometown.
绵历 miánlì 〈书面〉last; continue; go on; extend: ～岁时 go on for years /～千年 last a thousand years /山路～七十里。The mountain path extends a full 70 *li*.
绵连 miánlián *also* "绵联" continuous; unbroken: ～不绝的山岭 unbroken chain of mountains
绵马 miánmǎ *also* "羊齿" yángchǐ fern
绵蔓 miánmàn 〈书面〉stretching; straggling: 藤叶～ stretching vines /满墙～纷披的枝叶 wall overgrown with creepers
绵密 miánmì (of words and deeds, etc.) well-considered; meticulously planned: 用意～ have well considered plans (for doing sth.)
绵绵 miánmián continuous; uninterrupted: 思绪～ all kinds of thoughts welling up in one's mind; be lost in thought /情意～ full of affection; affectionate /～大雪 snow heavily /此恨～无绝期。But sorrow such as theirs will never end.
绵邈 miánmiǎo 〈书面〉long ago; far away: 年代～ go back to years of remote antiquity; from time immemorial /道路～ far away; long way off
绵软 miánruǎn ❶ soft: ～的声音 soft (*or* gentle) voice /～的手 soft tender hand ❷ weak: 只觉得浑身～ feel weak all over
绵善 miánshàn soft-hearted; meek and gentle: 再～不过的性格 extremely soft-hearted; as meek as a lamb /为人～, 少言少语 be tender-hearted and quiet
绵糖 miántáng *see* "绵白糖"
绵甜 miántián mild and sweet: 清泉～ clear and sweet spring water /～甘洌的好酒 mellow wine (*or* liquor)
绵延 miányán (as of mountain ranges, etc.) be continuous; stretch long and unbroken: ～不断的原始森林 primeval forests stretching endlessly /秋雨～, 一连下了许多天。Autumn rains fell for days on end.
绵羊 miányáng sheep
绵羊病毒性流产 miányáng bìngdúxìng liúchǎn 〈兽医〉enzootic ovine abortion
绵羊疥癣 miányáng jièxuǎn 〈兽医〉scab rubbers
绵远 miányuǎn far away; long ago
绵纸 miánzhǐ tissue paper
绵子 miánzi 〈方言〉silk floss; silk wadding: 她做了一件背心, 里面薄薄地絮着一层～。She carefully padded a new waistcoat with silk floss.

眠

mián ❶ sleep: 安～ sleep peacefully /失～ (suffer from) insomnia; sleeplessness /夜不成～ be unable to go to sleep all night; be wide awake all night /不～之夜 sleepless night; white night ❷ dormancy: 冬～ hibernate /蚕～ inactive state of the silkworm before it sheds its skin
眠尔通 mián'ěrtōng 〈药学〉miltown; meprobamate

miǎn

丏

miǎn 〈书面〉covered; out of sight

湎

miǎn *see* "沉湎" chénmiǎn

愐

miǎn 〈书面〉❶ think; ponder; consider ❷ diligent

靦

miǎn
see also tiǎn
靦覥 miǎntian *see* "腼腆" miǎntian

偭

miǎn 〈书面〉❶ face; turn towards ❷ violate: ～规越矩 violate the rules and regulations

腼

miǎn
腼腆 miǎntian *also* "靦覥" miǎntian shy; bashful; diffident: ～温柔的少女 meek and gentle girl /小伙子～地微笑着。The young man smiled bashfully. /他在女孩子面前很～。He is shy with girls.

勔

miǎn 〈书面〉diligent; industrious

缅[1]

miǎn remote; far back

缅[2]

miǎn 〈方言〉roll up: ～袖子 roll up the sleeves
缅甸 Miǎndiàn Myanmar; Burma: ～人 Myanmese; Burmese /～语 Myanmese (language); Burmese
缅怀 miǎnhuái cherish the memory of; recall; reminisce: ～先辈 cherish the memory of one's forefathers /～往事 reminisce about past events /～之情 sentiments of nostalgia
缅邈 miǎnmiǎo 〈书面〉remote; far away: 两兄弟骨肉分离, ～两绝。Separated by a great distance, the two brothers have not even heard from each other.
缅茄 miǎnqié 〈植物〉Shan pahudia (*Pahudia xylocarpa*)
缅想 miǎnxiǎng recall; cherish the memory of: 这些令人～不已。The recollections have inspired a feeling of nostalgia.

免

miǎn ❶ excuse or free (sb. from sth.); exempt; dispense with: ～于体检 be excused from a physical examination /～予罚款 be exempt from a fine /减～所得税 reduce or remit income tax /～签证协议 agreement on mutual exemption of visas /大家都是熟人, 礼节就～了吧。As friends, we may as well dispense with formalities.

or As friends we need not stand on ceremony. ❷ remove from office; dismiss; sack; relieve: 任～名单 list of appointments and removals /他被～去主任的职务。He has been removed from his position as director. /他身体不好,应～掉点工作。As he is in poor health, he should be relieved of part of his work. ❸ avoid; avert; evade; escape: ～受嫌疑 avert suspicion; be free from suspicion /在所难～ hard to avoid; unavoidable /事先做好准备,以～临时抓瞎。Get things ready in advance so as not to be in a rush at the last moment. /临难毋苟～。〈书面〉Do not compromise honour to escape danger. or Do not flinch in face of danger. ❹ do not (do): 在今天的聚会上,大家叙叙旧,工作～谈。Today we meet to renew our friendship. No business at the party. /闲人～进。Do not enter except on business. or No admittance except on business.

免不得 miǎnbude hard to avoid; unavoidable: ～又有一场争吵。There is bound to be another squabble (or dispute).

免不了 miǎnbuliǎo unavoidable; sure to happen: ～受周围环境的影响 be susceptible to the influence of one's environment /老朋友相会,～多谈几句。When old friends meet, it's natural that they have much to talk about. /刚会走的孩子～要摔跤。Babies who have just learned to walk are liable to trip and fall. /人都～犯错误。No one is free from error. or To err is human.

免除 miǎnchú ❶ avoid; avert; prevent: ～误会 avoid misunderstanding /～水旱灾害 prevent floods and droughts ❷ exempt; excuse; relieve: ～烦恼 relieve sb. of worries /～债务 remit a debt

免得 miǎnde so as to avoid; so as not to: 你要经常来信,～大家挂念。Please write regularly so we won't worry about you. /他踮着脚尖走进屋子,～吵醒他人。He tiptoed into the room so as not to wake up the others. /我们最好公事公办,～别人讲闲话。To avoid gossip, we'd better be business-like.

免罚 miǎnfá 〈法律〉impunity; indemnity

免费 miǎnfèi free (of charge); gratis: ～咨询 free consultation /～午餐 free lunch /～赠送 give (be given) as a gift /～入场 free admission; be admitted gratis /～入学 be enrolled with tuition waived /～教育 free education; compulsory education /展览会～参观。Admission to the exhibition is free (of charge). /照顾你们～乘车。You'll get a free ride as a courtesy.

免耕法 miǎngēngfǎ 〈农业〉no-till or no-tillage — method of cultivation suited to arid or hilly land by which sowing is done directly after harvesting without ploughing the land

免官 miǎnguān dismiss from office

免冠 miǎnguān ❶ take off one's hat: ～三鞠躬 take off one's hat and bow three times ❷ without a hat on; bareheaded: 身份证上要贴一张本人半身～正面照片。You'll need a half-length, bareheaded, full-faced photo for your ID card.

免检 miǎnjiǎn exempt from inspection or examination: ～物品 articles exempt from inspection or examination

免开尊口 miǎnkāizūnkǒu keep quiet; not broach (the subject); keep one's mouth shut: 这件事由他出面,你就～了。You'd better keep your mouth shut and leave the matter to him.

免考 miǎnkǎo *see* "免试❶"

免礼 miǎnlǐ (as spoken by an officer to his subordinates) forego or dispense with formalities (esp. salute, etc.); be at ease

免票 miǎnpiào ❶ free pass; free ticket: 铁路职工每人发一张～。Each railway worker is given a free pass. ❷ without having to buy a ticket; free of charge: 一米以下儿童～乘车。(sign on buses, etc.) Free of charge: children under a metre in height.

免勤 miǎnqín be exempt from duty; be excused from service

免试 miǎnshì ❶ *also* "免考" be exempted from an examination (for admission to college or for promotion): ～入学 be exempted from the entrance examination (to a school or college) /～外语 be exempted from the foreign language examination ❷ be exempted from a test

免税 miǎnshuì exempt from taxation or tariff: 准许～ grant exemption from taxation

免税单 miǎnshuìdān bill of sufferance; exemption certificate; duty free certificate

免税期 miǎnshuìqī tax holiday

免税商店 miǎnshuì shāngdiàn duty-free shop

免税债券 miǎnshuì zhàiquàn tax exempt bond

免俗 miǎnsú (often used in the negative) act contrary to common practice: 未能～ unable to break away from convention

免烫 miǎntàng 〈纺织〉easy-care

免息 miǎnxī free of interest

免刑 miǎnxíng 〈法律〉exempt from punishment

免修 miǎnxiū be exempt from a required course: ～外语 be exempt from required foreign language courses

免验 miǎnyàn exempt from customs examination: ～物品 goods exempt from customs examination /～证 laissez-passer (for exemption from customs examination) /～放行 (allow to) pass without examination (PWE)

免役 miǎnyì exempt from service

免疫 miǎnyì immunity (from disease): ～性 immunity /自动～ active immunity /先天性～ congenital (or natural) immunity /获得性～ acquired immunity

免疫避孕 miǎnyì bìyùn immunological contraception

免疫病理学 miǎnyì bìnglǐxué immunopathology

免疫测定 miǎnyì cèdìng immunoassays

免疫法 miǎnyìfǎ immunification; immunization

免疫反应 miǎnyì fǎnyìng 〈医学〉immunologic reaction

免疫接种 miǎnyì jiēzhòng immunization

免疫力 miǎnyìlì immunity: 对白喉有～ have immunity against diphtheria; be immune to diphtheria /获得对麻疹的终生～ acquire lifetime immunity against measles; be immunized from measles for life /增强政治上的～ improve one's political immunity

免疫球蛋白 miǎnyì qiúdànbái immune globulin; immunoglobulin

免疫缺损 miǎnyì quēsǔn immunodeficiency: ～患者 immunologic cripple

免疫细胞 miǎnyì xìbāo immunocyte

免疫学 miǎnyìxué 〈植物〉immunology

免疫血清 miǎnyì xuèqīng immune serum

免疫遗传学 miǎnyì yíchuánxué 〈医学〉immunogenetics

免疫障碍 miǎnyì zhàng'ài dysimmunity

免疫诊断 miǎnyì zhěnduàn immunodiagnosis

免疫组织学 miǎnyì zǔzhīxué immunohistology

免于起诉 miǎnyú qǐsù be exempted from prosecution

免战牌 miǎnzhànpái 〈旧语〉sign indicating refusal to fight: 挂～ refuse battle

免征 miǎnzhēng exempt from (taxes, grain delivered to the state, etc.): 受灾地区～一年农业税。The stricken area was exempted from agricultural tax for a year.

免职 miǎnzhí remove from office; dismiss: 受到～处分 be dismissed from office as a disciplinary measure; get disciplinary dismissal /他因工作不力被～了。He has been removed from office for incompetence.

免罪 miǎnzuì exempt from punishment

冕 miǎn crown; coronet: 加～ coronation /无～之王 crownless king; uncrowned king

冕洞 miǎndòng 〈天文〉coronal hole (area of the solar corona which generates high speed solar wind)

冕旒 miǎnliú 〈古语〉crown with jade ornaments hanging both at front and back

俛 miǎn *see* "僶俛" mǐnmiǎn
see also fǔ

鮸 miǎn 〈动物〉slate cod croaker

勉 miǎn ❶ make an effort; exert oneself; strive: 奋～ exert oneself; make a great effort ❷ encourage; spur; urge: ～人为善 urge people to do good /互～ encourage one another /自～ spur oneself on /以此共～ for the sake of mutual encouragement ❸ try to do what is almost beyond one's power or act against one's will: *see* "～强"; "～为其难"

勉力 miǎnlì exert oneself; make an effort; take pains (to do sth.); strive: ～支撑 strain one's utmost (to keep sth. going) /望君～为之。It is hoped that you will do your best.

勉励 miǎnlì encourage; urge: ～他继续努力 encourage him to continue his efforts

勉强 miǎnqiǎng ❶ manage with an effort; do with difficulty: ～坚持到了终点 manage to reach the finishing-line with an effort /弄不了就别～了。Leave off if you can't manage it. or Don't overstrain yourself if it's too much for you. ❷ reluctantly; grudgingly; unwill-

ingly：～答应 agree grudgingly /笑得很～ force a smile; give a strained smile /他很～地把我让到屋里。He reluctantly showed me into his room. ❸ force sb. to do sth：她不想多吃就算了，不要～。Don't oblige her to eat more if she doesn't want to. /～他做不愿做的事只能把事情搞得更糟。It will only make matters worse to force him to act against his will. ❹ unconvincing; far-fetched; strained：这种说法听起来有些～。The argument sounds a bit far-fetched. /这个理由太～。This is a lame (*or* poor) excuse. ❺ barely (enough)：～够用 be just about enough /～及格 barely pass the examination /～度日 eke out a living; scrape along /"他的英语怎么样?" "勉勉强强。" "What about his English?" "Just so-so." /我每月寄回二百元，家里～可以维持。I sent back two hundred *yuan* every month, and that was barely enough for my family to live on.

勉为其难 miǎnwéiqínán try to do what is beyond one's power; be obliged to undertake a difficult task：我们不会跳舞，无奈主人一再邀请，只好～了。We do not know how to dance. However, we had to because the host had invited us repeatedly.

娩（挽） miǎn *see* "分娩" fēnmiǎn

see also wǎn

娩出 miǎnchū 〈医学〉 be delivered of a baby with its placenta and foetal membrane

miàn

面[1]（面） miàn

❶ face; visage：～带笑容 have (*or* wear) a smile on one's face /～无惧色 one's face shows no fear ❷ face (a certain direction)：～壁而立 stand facing the wall /背山～水 with hills behind and a river (*or* lake) in front ❸ surface; top; face：江～ surface of a river /桌～ top of a table; tabletop /钟～ clock face; dial ❹ face-to-face; personally; directly：*see* "～议"；"～交"；"～授"；"～试" ❺ right side; cover; outside：被～儿 top covering of a quilt /鞋～儿 outside of a shoe; upper of a shoe ❻〈数学〉surface：平～ plane /六～体 hexahedron ❼ side; aspect：正～ front /侧～ side /全～ overall; all-round; comprehensive /多～手 versatile person; all-rounder /这只是问题的一～。This is only one aspect of the question. ❽ *used as a suffix to form a noun of locality*：前～ in front /左～ on the left /外～ outside /上～ above /下～ under /后～ at the back /南～ south ❾ extent; range; scale; scope：扩大知识～ enlarge one's range of knowledge /接触～很窄 have a limited circle of acquaintance; have limited knowledge of a subject ❿ entire range or area (as distinct from particular points); overall situation：你去调查那个案子吧，～上的事我来应付。Go and investigate that case and I'll take care of our day-to-day work. /点和～都要考虑到。Take into consideration both the overall situation and the conditions of specific localities (*or* units). ⓫〈量词〉(a) *used for flat and smooth objects*：一～锣 a gong /两～镜子 two mirrors (b) *used to indicate the times people meet one another*：见过一次～ have met once

面[2]（麵、麪） miàn

❶ wheat flour; flour; meal：白～ wheat flour /玉米～ corn flour; maizemeal /豆～ bean flour /江米～ glutinous rice flour /揉～ knead dough /发～ leaven dough ❷ powder：辣椒～ chilli powder /胡椒～ ground pepper /药～儿 medicinal powder ❸ noodles：方便～ instant noodles /切～ machine-made noodles /抻～ hand-pulled noodles /刀削～ hand-sliced noodles /挂～ fine dried noodles /汤～ noodle soup /炸酱～ noodles served with fried soya paste /打卤～ noodles served with sauce ❹〈方言〉(of food) soft and mealy：～倭瓜 mealy pumpkin /这苹果吃起来有点儿～。This apple tastes soft and mealy.

面案 miàn'àn *also* "白案" bái'àn (of cooking) such work as cooking rice, baking pancakes, making steamed bread, etc.

面板 miànbǎn ❶ board for kneading dough ❷〈机械〉〈电子〉face plate; front board; front panel：～开关 panel-switch /～调谐装置 front-panel tuning controls

面包 miànbāo bread：一个～ a loaf of bread /一片～ a slice of bread /黄油～ bread and butter /奶油～ bread stuffed with cream /果料～ dried fruit bread /烤～ bake bread; toast

面包车 miànbāochē mini-bus; van

面包房 miànbāofáng bakery

面包干 miànbāogān rusk

面包果 miànbāoguǒ *also* "面包树"〈植物〉breadfruit (tree)

面包圈 miànbāoquān doughnut; fried bread ring

面包师 miànbāoshī baker

面包渣儿 miànbāozhār breadcrumbs; crumbs

面壁 miànbì ❶ face the wall — not care about anything; not give serious thought to anything ❷〈佛教〉face the wall and meditate;〈比喻〉study with undivided attention ❸ (a kind of punishment in old times) stand facing the wall

面禀 miànbǐng report (to an elder or to one's superior) in person

面不改色 miànbùgǎisè not change colour — remain calm; keep composure; show no sign of fear or surprise; without turning a hair; without batting an eyelid：～心不跳 remain absolutely calm

面部对瘫 miànbù duìtān 〈医学〉prosopodiplegia

面部模型 miànbù móxíng mask

面茶 miànchá seasoned flour (formerly millet, now usu. wheat or corn) mush (made by stirring flour with boiling water and served with pepper, salt and sesame butter)：沏碗～ make a bowl of seasoned flour mush

面陈 miànchén state (one's views) or expound (one's position) in person：～时政得失 state in person one's views on the advantages and disadvantages of the current policies

面呈 miànchéng hand in or deliver (a letter, etc.) in person

面斥 miànchì reprimand in person; denounce face-to-face

面辞 miàncí take leave (of sb.); say goodbye (to sb.)

面从 miàncóng 〈书面〉feign obedience (in sb.'s presence)

面从后言 miàncóng-hòuyán feign compliance to sb. (in sb.'s presence) while complaining behind his back

面的 miàndí small yellow van (a kind of cheap taxi in Beijing); minibus taxi

面点 miàndiǎn snacks made from wheat or rice flour

面对 miànduì face; encounter; confront：～无边的大海 face the boundless sea /～现实 face reality; be realistic /～强敌，毫不畏惧 confront a formidable foe fearlessly; stand in no fear of a formidable enemy /～这种局面，我们要有应变的准备。Confronted with such circumstances, we must be fully prepared for any emergency.

面对面 miànduìmiàn face-to-face; vis-a-vis：～站着 stand face-to-face /～地提意见 make comments and criticisms to sb.'s (*or* to each other's) face

面额 miàn'é ❶ (of banknotes, etc.) denomination：大～的纸币 notes of large denomination /～为五十元的人民币 *renminbi* in 50-*yuan* notes; 50-*yuan renminbi* notes ❷ forehead：他～上有一颗痣。There is a mole on his forehead.

面坊 miànfáng old fashioned flour mill (without modern machinery)

面肥 miànféi ❶ *also* "老面" lǎomiàn; "面头" leavening dough：留一块面当～使。Save a small piece of dough to be used as leavening (dough) next time. ❷〈农业〉fertilizer sprinkled on topsoil (usually chemical fertilizer); topdressing：地里施了一层～。A layer of fertilizer was applied to the topsoil in the field.

面粉 miànfěn wheat flour; flour：～厂 flour mill

面缚 miànfù 〈书面〉truss up; bind sb.'s hands behind his back：～归降 surrender with hands tied behind one's back

面疙瘩 miàngēda balls of dough：～汤 dough ball soup /炒～ fried dough balls

面革 miàngé upper leather

面馆 miànguǎn eatery selling cooked wheaten food such as noodles, dumplings, etc.

面和心不和 miàn hé xīn bùhé be friendly in appearance but estranged at heart

面红耳赤 miànhóng-ěrchì be red in the face; be flushed：急得～ be flushed with anxiety /她听了不觉～。This made her blush from ear to ear. /即使我们老朋友之间有时争得～，但是还是和过去一样无话不谈。Even though we sometimes argued with each other until we were red in the face, we still talked openly and frankly as old friends do.

面糊 miànhú ❶ cooked flour paste (as food)：小时候家里穷，早上能喝一碗～就不错了。When I was a small boy, I would be quite happy if I had a bowlful of cooked flour paste for breakfast, for my family was very poor. ❷〈方言〉flour paste

面糊 miànhu 〈方言〉soft and mealy：白薯蒸熟了，很～。The steamed sweet potato tastes soft and mealy.

面黄肌瘦 miànhuáng-jīshòu sallow and emaciated; lean and haggard：这人～，形如病夫。The man looks lean and haggard like a sick

man. /他们一个个~。They all looked pale and thin.

面积 miànjī area; space: 受灾~ stricken (*or* afflicted, *or* affected) area /耕地~ cultivated area /棉花种植~ acreage under cotton; area planted to cotton /单位~产量 yield per unit area /建筑~ floor space /使用~ usable floor space /住房~ housing space; living space /占地~为 160 平方米 occupy a ground space of 160 square metres /阅览室的~很有限。The reading room is very limited in space. /展览会~为 4000 平方米。The exhibition covers a floor space of 4,000 square metres.

面肌 miànjī facial muscle (*musculus facialis*)

面肌抽搐 miànjī chōuchù 〈医学〉mimetic convulsion; mimic convulsion

面肌麻痹 miànjī mábì 〈医学〉facial paralysis

面颊 miànjiá cheek

面交 miànjiāo deliver (sth. to recipient) in person; hand-deliver: 这封信请~校长。Please hand-deliver this letter to the president in person.

面巾 miànjīn 〈方言〉face towel

面巾纸 miànjīnzhǐ face tissue

面筋 miànjin gluten

面痉挛 miànjìngluán 〈医学〉prosopospasm

面具 miànjù ❶ mask: 防毒~ gas mask; gas helmet /防尘~ dust mask ❷ mask; false facade: 假~ mask /剥去假~ unmask; expose; see through sb.'s false facade

面孔 miànkǒng face: 饱经风霜的~ weather-beaten face /喜气洋洋的~ beaming face /拉长了~ pull a long face /板起~ put on a stern expression (*or* countenance) /装出一副悲天悯人的~ assume a compassionate face; put on a compassionate look

面宽 miànkuan ❶ width of the broad side of a room or house: 这房子~不小。This house is quite wide. ❷ width of cloth: 这种布~三尺三寸。This cloth is 3.3 *chi* wide.

面料 miànliào ❶ (as opposed to lining or wadding of a garment) surface cloth or material ❷ veneer

面临 miànlín face; confront; be faced with; be confronted with: ~考验 face a test (*or* trial) /~挑战 be confronted with challenges /我们正~一场新的斗争。A new struggle lies ahead of us.

面聆 miànlíng hear or listen in person: ~教导 listen to sb.'s instructions in person

面码儿 miànmǎr vegetable served with noodles; vegetable trimmings for noodles

面貌 miànmào ❶ face; features: 他~清秀, 五官端正。He has delicate, regular features. ❷ appearance; look; aspect: 精神~ mental outlook; moral attitude /政治~ political outlook (*or* background, *or* affiliation)

面门 miànmén face; visage

面面观 miànmiànguān comprehensive observation and analysis; multi-dimensional view: 《婚恋~》*Multi-Dimensional View of Love and Marriage*

面面俱到 miànmiàn-jùdào attend to each and every aspect of a matter; be well considered in every aspect: 写文章切忌~。The greatest danger in writing is to try to cover everything about the topic. /他办事总是~。Whatever he does, he gives thought to every aspect of the matter. *or* He is punctilious in everything he does. /工作要分主次, 抓重点, 不可~。One must get one's priorities right. It's not possible to give equal attention to every aspect of one's work.

面面相觑 miànmiàn-xiāngqù gaze at each other in blank dismay; exchange uneasy glances; exchange glances in bewilderment: 他们~, 束手无策。They looked at each other in helpless despair. /这两位卫士惊得~。The two guards looked at each other blankly in astonishment.

面膜 miànmó face pack; mask

面模 miànmú 〈方言〉features; looks: 他那微长的~还是那样英俊。His longish face is still very handsome.

面目 miànmù ❶ face; features; countenance; visage: ~狰狞 ferocious features; vile visage /举动粗鲁, ~可憎 boorish in manner and revolting in appearance ❷ appearance; look; aspect: 还其本来~ show sb.'s (or its) true colours /恢复历史的本来~ restore the historical truth ❸ self-respect; sense of shame; face: 有何~去见父母 feel too ashamed to face one's parents; have no face to see one's parents

面目可憎 miànmù-kězēng repulsive appearance; disgusting look: 语言无味, ~ drab in language and repulsive in appearance

面目全非 miànmù-quánfēi be changed or distorted beyond recognition: 这座古墓已被毁得~了。This ancient tomb was damaged beyond recognition.

面目一新 miànmù-yīxīn take on an entirely new look; present a completely new appearance; have a face-lift

面幕 miànmù (women's) veil

面嫩 miànnèn ❶ look younger than one's age: 您~, 不像五十来岁的样子。You look younger than your age, not at all like a man in his fifties. ❷ shy: 少年~ young and shy /~心软 shy and soft-hearted

面盘 miànpán 〈方言〉cast of one's face

面庞 miànpáng contours of the face; face: 孩子们圆圆的~ round, chubby faces of children

面盆 miànpén ❶〈方言〉washbasin; washbowl ❷ mixing bowl (for making dough)

面坯儿 miànpīr cooked noodles before being served with sauces and dressings

面皮 miànpí ❶ face; cheek: ~薄 shy; sensitive /~厚 brazen; impudent; cheeky ❷〈方言〉wrapper (of dumpling): 擀~儿 make dumpling wrappers

面片儿 miànpiànr dough strips: ~汤 dough strip soup

面洽 miànqià discuss face to face; take up (with sb.) personally: 详情请和来人~。Please talk it over with the bearer of the note. *or* Please discuss the details with the bearer of the note. /有关事宜可与李先生~。For particulars you can go and see Mr. Li.

面前 miànqián in front of; in (the) face of; ahead of; before: 几个人从他~走过。Several people passed by in front of him (*or* before him). /一大堆问题摆在我们~。We are confronted with a lot of problems. *or* Many problems lie before us.

面罄 miànqìng 〈书面〉state in detail in person: 略叙一二, 余容~。Here I will confine myself to a few points and, with your permission, I will personally report to you in more detail later.

面人儿 miànrénr dough figurine: 捏~ mould dough figurines

面容 miànróng facial features; facial expression; look; face: ~憔悴 wear a haggard look; look careworn

面如死灰 miànrúsǐhuī look like dying embers; look ashen; look deathly pale

面如土色 miànrútǔsè *also* "面色如土" look ashen; look pale: 吓得~ turn pale in terror

面软 miànruǎn soft-hearted; soft: 心慈~ soft-hearted /他这人面太软, 总不愿面对面地给人提意见。He is too soft to criticize anyone to his face.

面色 miànsè complexion: ~红润 rosy (*or* ruddy) complexion /~黑黝黝的游泳运动员 swimmer with a swarthy complexion

面纱 miànshā veil: 她戴着黑色的~。She was wearing a black veil. /他们的可耻用心蒙上了一层美丽的~。Their evil intention is thus beautifully veiled.

面善 miànshàn ❶ look familiar: 刚才走过去的人好~。The man who just passed by looked familiar. ❷ look benevolent or kindly: ~心慈 be benevolent and kind-hearted

面商 miànshāng consult face to face; discuss personally: ~大计 discuss (with sb.) matters of vital importance

面神经 miànshénjīng 〈生理〉facial nerves: ~麻痹 facial paralysis

面生 miànshēng look unfamiliar

面食 miànshí pasta; wheaten food: 北方人爱吃~。People from the north are keen on (*or* partial to) wheaten food.

面市 miànshì go into the market; be put on sale: 这家工厂每个月都有新产品~。This factory puts new products into the market every month.

面世 miànshì (of art or literary works, products, etc.) be published; come out: 这两部小说不久~。These two novels will soon be published.

面试 miànshì oral quiz; audition; interview; viva

面饰 miànshì ❶ (women's) ornaments on face ❷〈建筑〉exterior or face decoration

面首 miànshǒu 〈书面〉male concubine (for a woman); gigolo

面授 miànshòu personally instruct or brief: ~机宜 personally instruct (sb.) on the line of action to pursue; give confidential briefing on guidelines

面熟 miànshú look familiar: 他看着挺~, 就是想不起他的名字了。He looks familiar, but I just can't recall his name.

面诉 miànsù recount or relate in person: ~冤情 personally recount

the wrongs one has suffered
面塑 miànsù 〈工美〉dough modelling
面瘫 miàntān 〈医学〉facial paralysis
面谈 miàntán have a face-to-face talk; speak (to sb.) face to face; take up a matter (with sb.) personally:请你来我这里一趟,有事～。Please come to my office. I've something to talk over with you.
面汤 miàntāng ❶〈方言〉warm water prepared for washing one's face ❷ water in which noodles have been boiled
面汤 miàntang 〈方言〉noodle soup:晚上咱们吃～就烧饼。This evening, we are going to have noodle soup with sesame seed cakes.
面膛 miàntáng 〈方言〉face:紫色～ dark complexion
面条儿 miàntiáor noodles:擀～ make noodles /下～ put noodles into a boiling pan;cook noodles /烂～ overcooked noodles
面头 miàntóu *see* "面肥❶"
面团 miàntuán dough
面团团 miàntuántuán round, fleshy face; moon face:只缘心混混,所以～。As he is dim-witted so he is fleshy-faced.
面纹 miànwén wrinkle:老人家白发稀疏,～深密。The old man has thin white hair and a wrinkled face.
面无人色 miànwúrénsè look ghastly pale:吓得～ be so frightened that one's face turns deathly pale; turn ghastly pale with fright
面晤 miànwù 〈书面〉meet or confer in person:～在即 will soon meet (in person)
面线 miànxiàn upper thread (of sewing)
面向 miànxiàng ❶ turn one's face to; turn towards; face:～观众挥手致意 stand facing the audience and wave greetings ❷ be geared to the needs of; be oriented towards; cater to:～群众 be geared to the needs of the people /～青少年 be oriented towards children and adolescents /立足国内,～世界 have one's feet firmly planted in the country yet keep the whole world in view
面向低收入阶层的市场 miànxiàng dīshōurù jiēcéng de shìchǎng 〈经济〉downmarket
面相 miànxiàng 〈方言〉facial features; looks; appearance; physiognomy:因为天黑,没有看清他是什么～。It was so dark that I didn't see clearly what he looked like.
面谢 miànxiè thank sb. in person
面形 miànxíng *also* "面型" shape of face
面叙 miànxù talk face to face:余俟～。I'll acquaint you with the rest when we meet.
面颜 miànyán look; appearance:慈祥的～ kind look /清瘦的～ thin face
面议 miànyì discuss or negotiate personally; hold personal negotiations
面影 miànyǐng facial contour (as remembered):他脑子里浮现出母亲的～。He seemed to see the face of his mother in his mind's eye.
面有菜色 miànyǒu-càisè look famished; be unhealthily pale because of hunger
面有愧色 miànyǒu-kuìsè look guilty or ashamed
面有难色 miànyǒu-nánsè show signs of discomfiture or reluctance
面谀 miànyú 〈书面〉flatter sb. to his face:～之辞 flattery
面谕 miànyù give orders personally:奉上司～ on the personal orders of the authorities
面誉背毁 miànyù-bèihuǐ praise sb. to his face and abuse him behind his back; double-deal
面罩 miànzhào face guard; face shield; mask; visor
面罩送话器 miànzhào sònghuàqì mask microphone
面针 miànzhēn facio-acupuncture:～疗法 facio-acupuncture therapy
面值 miànzhí ❶ par value; face value; nominal value ❷ denomination
面砖 miànzhuān 〈建筑〉face brick
面子 miànzi ❶ outer part; outside:这件羽绒衣的～挺好的,就是里子旧了点。The outside of this down coat is quite good, and only its lining is a bit worn. ❷ reputation; prestige; face:爱～ anxious to save face; concerned about face-saving; vain /有～ enjoy due respect /保全～ save face /丢～ lose face /这几年他虽万分拮据,～上还遮得过去。Although he has been having a hard time over the past few years, he has been able to keep up appearances. ❸ feelings; sensibilities:给～ show due respect for sb.'s feelings; do sb. a favour /留～ spare sb.'s susceptibilities /撕破～ cast aside all considerations of face; not spare sb.'s feelings /不讲～ show no consideration for others' sensibilities; not spare sb.'s feelings /不顾～ disregard one's dignity ❹〈口语〉powder:药～ powdered medicine

眄 miàn *also* miǎn 〈书面〉cast sidelong glances at sb.; look sideways at sb.:按剑相～。With hands on swords, they looked at each other sideways.
眄视 miànshì 〈书面〉look askance at sb.; look at sb. with suspicion

miāo

喵 miāo 〈象声〉mew; miaow

miáo

苗 miáo ❶ shoot; sprout; seedling; young plant:树～ tree seedling /麦～ wheat seedling /蒜～ garlic shoots /育～ grow seedlings /保～ keep a full stand of seedlings /蹲～ restrain the growth of seedlings (for root development) /间～〈农业〉thin out the sprouts or seedlings /补～〈农业〉fill the gaps with seedlings ❷ offspring; male child; son:好～～ promising child; promising youngster /他是陈家的独～。He is the only son of the Chens. /这一大家子就留下这一根～儿。He is the only boy who carries on the family name. ❸ young of some animals:鱼～ fry /猪～ piglets ❹ vaccine:卡介～ BCG (Bacille Calmette-Guerin) vaccine /牛痘～ (bovine) vaccine ❺ sth. resembling a young plant:火～儿 flames /扫帚～儿 broom spikes or straws (as made of broomcorn spikes, bamboo twigs, etc.) ❻ Miao nationality:～人 member of the Miao nationality; Miao /～瑶语族 Miao-Yao language family ❼ (Miáo) a surname
苗床 miáochuáng seedbed
苗而不秀 miáo'érbùxiù sprout well but grow no ears (of grain) — show early promise that is not borne out by achievement (usu. of a talented youth dying a premature death, or of a seemingly talented person not living up to expectations)
苗肥 miáoféi fertilizer applied during seedling stage
苗剧 miáojù Miao opera
苗龄 miáolíng (of young plants) period in the nursery before transplantation or from the time of sowing to that of transplantation:这些稻秧～不够。These rice seedlings are not old enough for transplanting.
苗木 miáomù 〈林业〉nursery stock
苗圃 miáopǔ nursery (of young plants)
苗期 miáoqī 〈农业〉seedling stage
苗禽 miáoqín young of poultry; poults:优种～ poults of an excellent breed /～产地 breeding area for young poultry /计划生产～二十万只 plan to breed 200,000 poults /～市场供应充足。The young poultry market has an ample supply.
苗情 miáoqíng way the seedlings are growing; growth of seedlings:今年小麦～很好。This year the wheat is growing very well during the seedling stage.
苗儿 miáor 〈方言〉symptom of a trend; early developments:事情有点～了。Things are getting into shape.
苗条 miáotiao (of a woman) slender; slim:身材～ look slim; have a slender figure
苗头 miáotou symptom of a trend; straw in the wind; suggestion of a new development:看～ watch out for what is going to happen; see how the wind is blowing /～不对。Things are not going the right way. /要注意事故的～。Watch out for symptoms of accidents.
苗细 miáoxì 〈方言〉thin; slender:～的辫子 very thin braids
苗绣 miáoxiù Miao embroidery; embroidery done by Miao women
苗眼 miáoyǎn 〈方言〉width of a row of planted seeds
苗裔 miáoyì 〈书面〉progeny; offspring; descendant:炎黄～ descendants of Yandi and Huangdi (legendary founders of the Chinese nation); members of the Han nationality
苗猪 miáozhū *also* "仔猪" zǐzhū piglet; pigling
苗子 miáozi ❶〈方言〉seedling; young plant ❷ young successor:这个年轻人是个好～。He is a very promising young man. ❷〈方言〉symptom of a trend

苗族 Miáozú Miao nationality, distributed mainly over Guizhou, Hunan, Yunnan, the Guangxi Zhuang Autonomous Region, Sichuan, and Guangdong

描

miáo ❶ trace; copy:～图样 trace or copy a design /～张花样子 trace or copy a flower pattern ❷ touch up; retouch:～眉 pencil one's eyebrows /练中国书法,下笔成形,不能～。In practising Chinese calligraphy, one is supposed to write with a sure hand, and not to retouch.

描笔式示波器 miáobǐshì shìbōqì pen oscillograph

描红 miáohóng ❶ (children) trace in black ink over the strokes of model Chinese characters printed in red (in learning to write characters with a brush):先～,后临帖 trace model characters before emulating a copybook for calligraphy ❷ sheet of paper with red characters printed on it, to be traced over by children learning calligraphy

描红纸 miáohóngzhǐ *also* "描红格" *see* "描红❷"

描画 miáohuà draw; paint; depict; describe:把湖光山色～下来 paint a picture of beautiful lakes and hills /～蓝图 draw a blueprint /难以～ be hard to paint; defy description

描绘 miáohuì depict; describe; portray:～得有声有色 give a graphic account (of sth.) /～了许多国家的风土人情 depict the scenery and customs of many countries /把自己～成一位自由斗士 portray oneself as a champion for freedom (*or* as a freedom fighter)

描记 miáojì (in monitoring) record of electrical or light curves on a screen

描金 miáojīn 〈工美〉trace (a design) in gold; paint in gold lines

描摹 miáomó ❶ trace:～花样 trace a flower pattern ❷ depict; portray; delineate:作品生动地～了社会生活的各个侧面。The work gives a vivid description of various aspects of social life.

描述 miáoshù describe:详细～战斗经过 describe the battle in full detail /难以～ beggar (*or* defy) description

描图 miáotú tracing:～员 tracer /～纸 tracing paper

描写 miáoxiě describe; delineate; depict; portray:～人物 portray (*or* delineate) characters /～都市生活的书 book about metropolitan life

描写语言学 miáoxiě yǔyánxué descriptive linguistics

描叙 miáoxù describe;depict:诗里～了农村欣欣向荣的景象。The poem depicts a thriving village scene.

描状 miáozhuàng depict; portray; delineate:不可～ be beyond description; beggar description

瞄

miáo aim; take aim:～得准 take good aim (at the target) /我不知道怎么就给他～上了。I have no idea how I became his target.

瞄准 miáozhǔn ❶ take aim; aim; train on; sight:练习～ practise aiming /把枪口～敌人 train one's gun on the enemy ❷ (in a general sense) aim at;cater to;be oriented towards:这个工厂～城乡的需求,生产多种规格的暖气炉,畅销各地。To satisfy (*or* To cater to) the needs of both rural and urban areas, this factory produces a variety of heat stoves which sell well round the country.

瞄准环 miáozhǔnhuán ring sight

瞄准具 miáozhǔnjù *also* "瞄准器"〈军事〉gunsighting device; gunsight /～计算机 gunsight computer

瞄准式干扰 miáozhǔnshì gānrǎo spot jamming

瞄准式火箭 miáozhǔnshì huǒjiàn aimed rocket

瞄准手 miáozhǔnshǒu one who aims or trains a canon or artillery piece on a target; (gun) layer; pointer

鹋

miáo *see* "鸸鹋" érmiáo

miǎo

杪

miǎo 〈书面〉❶ tip of a twig;top of a tree:木～ tree top ❷ end (of a year, month or season):岁～ end of the year; year-end /月～ end of the month; close of the month

秒

miǎo second ($=\frac{1}{60}$ of a minute)

秒表 miǎobiǎo stopwatch

秒差距 miǎochājù 〈天文〉parsec, equal to about 3.25 light years

秒立方米 miǎolìfāngmǐ 〈水利〉cubic metre per second

秒寿命放射性同位素 miǎoshòumìng fàngshèxìng tóngwèisù seconds living radioisotope; radioisotope that lives only for a few seconds

秒针 miǎozhēn second hand (of a clock or watch)

眇

miǎo 〈书面〉❶ blind:生而～者不识日。Those who are born blind do not know the sun. ❷ tiny; minute:形貌～小 be of tiny stature; look tiny

渺

miǎo ❶ distant and indistinct; nebulous; vague:～若烟云 as obscure as mist /～无声息 devoid of noise — still; quiet /～无人迹 remote and uninhabited /音信～然 (of sb. or sth.) be never heard of again /烟波浩～ vast and misty (of lake, etc.) ❷ tiny; insignificant; trivial:～不足道 not worth mentioning; insignificant; negligible

渺茫 miǎománg ❶ remote and vague;distant and indistinct:烟雾～ misty and vague /音信～ have no news (of sb. or sth.) /往事～,只有星星点点的记忆留在他的脑海中。He has but scattered memories of the dim past. *or* He has only a misty recollection of remote past events. ❷ uncertain; indefinite:前途～ be uncertain of one's future; have an uncertain future /希望～ hold out little hope (for success) /这个计划～得很。This plan is hardly practicable. *or* It's a plan in the air.

渺瀰 miǎomí 〈书面〉(of a vast expanse of water) boundless:大江～ boundless Yangtze

渺渺 miǎomiǎo 〈书面〉stretching far; boundless:云海～无际 boundless sea of clouds /～海岸 never-ending seacoast

渺然 miǎorán distant and indistinct; vague; elusive; without a trace:踪迹～ disappear (*or* vanish) without a trace

渺无人烟 miǎowúrényān bleak and desolate; uninhabited

渺无音信 miǎowúyīnxìn not hear a word (from sb.); have no news (about sb.):他这一去从此～。Nothing has been heard of him since he left.

渺小 miǎoxiǎo tiny; insignificant; paltry:～的利己主义者 paltry egoist /在这个品德高尚的老人面前,他显得多么～啊! What a dwarf (*or* How petty) he appears before that old man of lofty morality.

渺远 miǎoyuǎn remote; distant; far off or away:乡关～。One's native place is far off.

缈

miǎo *see* "缥缈" piāomiǎo

眇

miǎo 〈中医〉flanks — the two sides of the abdomen

邈

miǎo 〈书面〉remote; far away:～不可见 too distant to be seen

邈邈 miǎomiǎo 〈书面〉far away; remote; distant

邈远 miǎoyuǎn *also* "渺远" miǎoyuǎn distant; remote:～的古代 remotest ancient times; age of remote antiquity /～的蓝天 distant blue skies

藐

miǎo ❶ small; petty: *see* "～小" ❷ despise; slight; belittle:言者谆谆,听者～～。The speaker is earnest, but his words fall on deaf ears.

藐视 miǎoshì despise; scorn; look down upon; belittle:～困难 scorn difficulty /～法庭 contempt of court /在战略上我们要～一切敌人,在战术上我们要重视一切敌人。Strategically we should despise all our enemies, but tactically we should take them all seriously. /你不要～这个年轻人。Don't you underestimate this young man.

藐小 miǎoxiǎo tiny; negligible; insignificant; paltry:与集体的力量相比,个人的力量是～的。The strength of an individual is insignificant compared to that of the collective.

淼

miǎo 〈书面〉(of an expanse of water) vast:烟波浩～ vast and misty

淼茫 miǎománg remote; vague

miào

庙(廟)

miào ❶ temple; shrine:宗～ ancestral temple

(*or* hall) /家～ family shrine /土地～ temple of the village god /城隍～ temple of the city god /龙王～ temple of the Dragon King (the God of Rain and Waters) /孔～ Confucian temple ❷〈书面〉imperial court:廊～ imperial court /～议 deliberations in the imperial court; court conference ❸〈书面〉late emperor:～讳 name of a late emperor ❹ temple fair:赶～ go to a (temple) fair

庙产 miàochǎn buildings, land, etc., belonging to a temple; temple property

庙号 miàohào posthumous title of honour given to a deceased emperor (for worship in the Imperial Ancestral Temple, etc.)

庙会 miàohuì temple fair; fair:赶～ go to the fair /逛～ stroll around a fair

庙算 miàosuàn *also* "庙略"〈书面〉war plan made in the imperial court

庙堂 miàotáng ❶ temple; monastery ❷〈书面〉imperial court:～伟器 pillar of the court /～文学 court literature (as contrasted with literature for the common people)

庙田 miàotián 〈旧语〉fields belonging to a temple, monastery, nunnery, etc.

庙宇 miàoyǔ temple building; temple

庙主 miàozhǔ abbot; Buddhist monk or Taoist priest in charge of a temple

庙祝 miàozhù person in charge of incense and religious service in a temple

庙子 miàozi 〈方言〉temple

玅 miào 〈书面〉*see* "妙" miào

妙 miào ❶ wonderful; superb; excellent; marvellous:绝～ marvellous; excellent; most wonderful /精～ exquisite; superb /处境不～ be in a disagreeable situation /～极了! Wonderful! *or* Terrific! /你去则更～。If you go, all the better. /此计甚～。That is a superb stratagem. *or* That is a brilliant idea. ❷ ingenious; clever; abstruse; subtle:深得其中之～ have got the trick of it; fully appreciate its subtlety /～在不言中。The best thing is what is left unsaid. *or* The subtlety lies in the implication.

妙笔 miàobǐ ingenious or exquisite writing:～生花 ingenious writing with exquisite description

妙不可言 miàobùkěyán too wonderful for words; most intriguing; ingenious beyond description

妙策 miàocè excellent scheme; wonderful plan; brilliant idea:别无～ there's no better plan; cannot think of a better solution

妙处 miàochù ❶ ideal place; suitable location:西山是休养的～。The Western Hills is an ideal place for rest and recuperation. ❷ merit; advantage; fine point:这种方法也有它的～。This method has its merit (*or* advantage), too. /这首诗的～在什么地方? What is so wonderful about this poem?

妙法 miàofǎ ❶ ingenious method; clever way ❷〈佛教〉profound ideas (contained in a sutra or sermon)

妙法莲华经 Miàofǎ Liánhuájīng *also* "法华经" Fǎhuájīng *Saddharmapundarika Sutra*, one of the early Buddhist classics of Mahayana doctrine

妙峰山 Miàofēngshān Divine Peak Mountain (in Beijing):《～进香图》*Pilgrimage to the Divine Peak Mountain*, a painting of the Qing Dynasty

妙计 miàojì clever ruse; brilliant idea:想了个～ think up (*or* hit upon) a peachy idea; have a brainwave

妙境 miàojìng wonderland; dreamland:交响乐的演奏把人们带入了～。The performance of the symphony held the audience spellbound. *or* The audience was completely enthralled by the performance of the symphony.

妙句 miàojù excellent sentence; happy turn of phrase

妙诀 miàojué clever way (of doing sth.); secret formula; knack:作文别无～,只能多读多写。The only knack in composition, if there is any, is to read more and write more.

妙绝 miàojué perfect; supreme; superb:～时人 (usu. of a master of art) have no contemporary peer; be unrivalled in one's time

妙丽 miàolì 〈书面〉beautiful; graceful; exquisite:～善舞 beautiful and good at dancing; charming and graceful dancer

妙龄 miàolíng (of girls) lovely age; early youth:～女郎 sweet young girl

妙论 miàolùn (often satirical) brilliant comment; profound remark

妙年 miàonián *also* "妙龄" young; of tender age:～玉貌 young and beautiful; (a maiden) of tender age and delicate features /～的女儿 blooming daughter

妙品 miàopǐn ❶ fine quality goods:调味～ best-quality condiment ❷ fine work of art; exquisite work; work of exquisite craftsmanship

妙趣 miàoqù wit and interest:～无穷 full of wit and interest /～天成 natural wit and humour

妙趣横生 miàoqù-héngshēng be full of wit and humour; brim with interest:他画的花鸟虫鱼无不～。Whatever he paints — flowers, birds, insects or fish — it is always full of wit and interest.

妙手 miàoshǒu skilled or deft hand; person with superb skills:～丹青 superb skill at painting; master of painting

妙手回春 miàoshǒu-huíchūn (of a doctor) effect a miraculous cure and bring the dying back to life; restore (a patient) to health:全仗大夫～。It all depends on the doctor to cure the patient. /这个快要垮台的厂让他救活了,真是～。What a miracle he worked bringing the dying factory back to life.

妙手空空 miàoshǒu-kōngkōng ❶〈戏谑〉out of cash; penniless; not owning a thing in the world ❷ (of a crafty but impecunious financier, etc.) wheeling-dealing ❸ clever or good at stealing (esp. pocket-picking)

妙算 miàosuàn excellent scheme; wonderful plan or stratagem:神机～ superb strategy; miracle of foresight; wonderful foresight in military operations

妙药 miàoyào magic medicine; wonder drug; panacea; elixir:灵丹～ panacea

妙用 miàoyòng magical effect:～无穷 work infinite wonders

妙语 miàoyǔ witty remark; witticism:～惊人 astonishingly witty remarks /～如珠 full of witty remarks; sparkling discourse

妙语解颐 miàoyǔ-jiěyí 〈书面〉wisecrack that tickles; witty remarks that make people smile or laugh

妙语双关 miàoyǔ-shuāngguān clever pun

妙招 miàozhāo *also* "妙着" clever trick; ingenious device:他在中盘连出～。He made one clever move after another in the middle of the chess game. /想不到你会有此～。I never expected that you could think of such an ingenious device.

妙着 miàozhāo *see* "妙招"

缪 Miào a surname

see also miù; móu

缪斯 Miàosī *also* Miùsī Muse, any of the nine sister goddesses in Greek mythology, each of whom was regarded as the protectress of a different art or science

miē

咩(哶) miē 〈象声〉baa; bleat

乜 miē 〈方言〉*see* "乜斜❶"

see also Niè

乜斜 miēxie ❶ squint:醉眼～ squint drunkenly /眼～着,脸上挂着讥诮的微笑。He squinted with a scornful smile on his face. ❷ (of eyes) half-closed:～的睡眼 half-closed eyes heavy with sleep

miè

灭(滅) miè ❶ (of a light, fire, etc.) go out:灯～了。The light has gone out. ❷ extinguish; put out; turn off:烟消火～。The smoke dispersed as the fire was extinguished. /你走时把灯～了。Turn off the lights when you leave. /请把烟～了。Please put out your cigarette. ❸ submerge; drown: *see* "～顶" ❹ perish; die out; wither away; become extinct:自生自～ emerge and perish of itself /物质不～ (the law of) conservation of matter ❺ destroy; exterminate; annihilate:～蚊 kill mosquitoes /长自己的志气,～敌人的威风 boost one's own morale and deflate the arrogance of the enemy /他的功绩不可磨～。His contribution can never be obliterated. *or* His

M

merits are indelible.
灭茬 mièchá 〈农业〉clean the stubble:～机 stubble cleaner
灭虫宁 mièchóngníng 〈药学〉bephenium
灭此朝食 miècǐ-zhāoshí will not have breakfast until the enemy is wiped out — be determined to finish off the enemy as soon as possible
灭滴灵 mièdīlíng 〈药学〉metronidazole; flagyl
灭谛 Mièdì 〈佛教〉*Nirodhasatya*, one of the *Catursatya* (Buddhist truth)
灭顶 mièdǐng be drowned; be swamped:遭受～之灾 get drowned; be swamped; go bankrupt
灭弧 mièhú 〈物理〉blowout; magnetic blowout; quench
灭活 mièhuó ❶ blanching ❷〈医学〉inactivate
灭活疫苗 mièhuó yìmiáo 〈医学〉inactivated vaccine
灭火 mièhuǒ ❶ put out a fire; extinguish a fire:～沙 sand for extinguishing a fire ❷ (of an engine) be cut; cut or turn off the engine
灭火弹 mièhuǒdàn fire-extinguishing bomb; fire extinguisher
灭火剂 mièhuǒjì fire-extinguishing chemical or agent
灭火器 mièhuǒqì fire extinguisher
灭迹 mièjì destroy the evidence (of one's evildoing):销赃～ destroy the evidence (of one's evildoing) by disposing of the spoils /焚尸～ burn up the corpse so as to leave no evidence behind
灭绝 mièjué ❶ become extinct:早已～的物种 species long extinct /面临～的危险 be in danger of extinction /～种族罪行 crime of genocide ❷ lose sth. completely:良心～ have no conscience whatsoever; be totally heartless
灭绝人性 mièjué-rénxìng inhuman; savage:～的大屠杀 massacre of inhuman savagery; ferocious massacre /匪徒～,杀了许多妇女和儿童。The bandits killed large numbers of women and children in cold blood.
灭菌 mièjūn 〈医学〉sterilize:这套器械是经过～处理的。This set of instruments has been sterilized.
灭菌检验 mièjūn jiǎnyàn sterilizing test
灭菌器 mièjūnqì sterilizer
灭口 mièkǒu (of a criminal) do away with a witness or accomplice to prevent leakage of information:杀人～ kill off a witness to one's crime
灭裂 mièliè 〈书面〉❶ careless; scatter-brained; perfunctory:鲁莽～ rash and careless; blunt and scatter-brained ❷ wreck; break; destroy:支离～ be torn asunder; be broken to pieces
灭伦 mièlún 〈旧语〉violate the accepted code of family and human relationship
灭门 mièmén (as punishment in ancient times) kill off the entire family:～绝户 put a whole family to death /～之灾 (in feudal times) disaster of execution for the whole family
灭却 mièquè ❶ lose; be devoid:～良心 lose one's conscience ❷ put out; quell; extinguish; wipe out:～心头之火 quell one's anger; repress one's anger
灭鼠剂 mièshǔjì rat-bane
灭绦灵 miètāoling 〈药学〉niclosamide
灭亡 mièwáng be destroyed; become extinct; perish:宋朝的～ downfall of the Song Dynasty /自取～ bring ruin upon oneself; court destruction /濒于～ on the verge (*or* brink) of extinction
灭音器 mièyīnqì 〈方言〉muffler
灭种 mièzhǒng ❶ extermination of an entire race or people; genocide:亡国～ national subjugation and racial extinction ❷ become extinct
灭族 mièzú extermination of an entire extended family or clan

蔑[1] miè 〈书面〉❶ small; slight; petty; paltry:视日月而知众星之～也。How small the stars look when compared with the sun and the moon. ❷ not; no; none; nothing:～以复加 could not be surpassed; reach the limit; in the extreme

蔑[2](衊) miè see "诬蔑" wūmiè
蔑称 mièchēng ❶ call in contempt:我常被她～为傻瓜蛋。I'm often scornfully referred to as a fool by her. ❷ contemptuous name
蔑弃 mièqì despise and discard; cast away; throw overboard:～古训 cast aside a time-honoured motto
蔑视 mièshì despise; scorn; look down on; show contempt for:～困难 despise difficulties /～同行 hold one's colleagues in contempt /～妇女 look down upon women /这是一种公然～人道和别国利益的政策。It is a policy in flagrant disregard of humanity and other countries' interests.

蠛 miè
蠛蠓 mièměng 〈古语〉midge

篾 miè ❶ thin bamboo strip ❷ husk or outer layer of reed or sorghum stalks
篾白 mièbái 〈方言〉see "篾黄"
篾刀 mièdāo bamboo splitter
篾工 miègōng ❶ bamboo work; bamboo-weavers' craft ❷ craftsman who makes articles from bamboo strips; bamboo craftsman
篾黄 mièhuáng also "篾白" inner skin of a bamboo stem
篾货 mièhuò article made from bamboo strips; woven bamboo article
篾匠 mièjiàng craftsman who makes articles from bamboo strips
篾片 mièpiàn ❶ thin bamboo strip ❷〈旧语〉hanger-on; sycophant
篾青 mièqīng outer skin of a bamboo stem
蔑条 miètiáo bamboo strip (for weaving bamboo wares)
篾席 mièxí mat made of thin bamboo strips
篾子 mièzi thin bamboo strip:竹～ bamboo strips

mín

忞 mín 〈书面〉exert oneself; strive

旻 mín ❶ autumn ❷ sky:苍～ blue sky
旻天 míntiān ❶autumn ❷ heaven;sky

民 mín ❶ the people:人～ the people /公～ citizen /国～ national /黎～ common people; the masses /选～ voter; elector /臣～ subjects (of a feudal ruler) /为～除害 rid the people of a scourge ❷ member of a nationality:汉～ a Han /回～ a Hui /藏～ a Tibetan ❸ person of a certain occupation:农～ peasant; farmer /盐～ salter /牧～ herdsman /渔～ fisherman ❹ of the people; popular; folk: see "～歌"; "～谣" ❺ civilian; civil:军转～ convert from military to civil production /军～联欢 get-together of soldiers and civilians /军爱～,～拥军。The army cherish the people and the people support the army. ❻〈旧语〉(used by commoners before officials) my:～妻 my wife /～母 my mother
民办 mínbàn run by the community; privately-run:～企业 privately-run business /～小学 primary school run by the local people; community primary school /～教师 teacher in a community school (paid by the community)
民办公助 mínbàn gōngzhù run by the community or private citizens, and supported by the government
民办机构 mínbàn jīgòu community-run institution
民变 mínbiàn popular revolt; mass uprising:～蜂起 popular revolts breaking out all over the country; widespread popular revolt /激起～ drive the people into rebellion
民兵 mínbīng militia:女～ militiawoman /～师 contingent of the militia /～小分队 detachment of the militia
民兵式洲际弹道导弹 mínbīngshì zhōujì dàndào dǎodàn (US) Minuteman intercontinental ballistic missile
民不堪命 mínbùkānmìng the people can hardly bear their load (of taxation, etc.):苛捐杂税,～。The people groaned under heavy burdens of exorbitant taxes and levies.
民不聊生 mínbùliáoshēng the people have no means of livelihood; the people live in dire poverty; the people can hardly survive:闹得当地～ reduce the local people to destitution /连年征战,～。The people were driven into dire poverty by successive years of war. *or* Successive years of war made life impossible for the people.
民不畏死,奈何以死惧之 mín bù wèi sǐ, nàihé yǐ sǐ jù zhī the people fear not death, why threaten them with it?
民船 mínchuán boat or ship for civilian use
民粹派 Míncuìpài (in 19th century Russia) Populists
民粹主义 míncuìzhǔyì (in 19th century Russia) Populism

M

民法 mínfǎ civil law; civil code: ~通则 civil code

民法典 mínfǎdiǎn civil code

民法学 mínfǎxué 〈法律〉 science of civil law: ~家 civil jurist / ~效力 validity of civil law

民防 mínfáng civil defence

民房 mínfáng house owned by a private citizen: 侵占~ seize a private house; squat (in a private house)

民愤 mínfèn popular indignation; public grievances; people's wrath: 平~ pacify (*or* assuage) public indignation / ~极大 have aroused (*or* incurred) the greatest public indignation; have excited the wrath of the public; have earned the bitter hatred of the people

民风 mínfēng customs and morals of the people; popular customs and morals; folkways; local traits: 此地~淳朴。The people here are simple and honest. / ~强悍。The people are fierce and doughty.

民夫 mínfū *also* "民伕" 〈旧语〉 civilian labourer (working for the military or an official project as corvée); conscripted labourer

民负 mínfù (of taxation, etc.) burden on the people

民富国强 mínfù-guóqiáng the people are affluent and the country is strong

民歌 míngē folk song: ~手 folk song singer

民革 Míngé (short for 中国国民党革命委员会) Revolutionary Committee of the Chinese Kuomintang, one of China's patriotic democratic parties

民工 míngōng ❶ labourer working on a public project ❷ peasants who do manual work in the city

民国 mínguó ❶ (Mínguó) Republic of China (1912-1949) ❷ republic: 大韩~ Republic of Korea

民航 mínháng (short for 民用航空) civil aviation: ~班机 civil airliner / 中国~总局 CAAC (Civil Aviation Administration of China)

民航处 Mínhángchù (HK) Civil Aviation Department

民家 mínjiā ❶ 〈旧语〉 civilian household; home of a civilian ❷ (Mínjiā) former name of the Bai or Pai nationality (白族)

民间 mínjiān ❶ among or of the people; popular; folk: ~故事 folktale; folk story / ~传说 folk legend; folklore / ~疾苦 hardships of the people / ~验方 folk recipe; folk remedy / 在~广为流传 spread far and wide among the people ❷ unofficial; non-governmental; people-to-people: ~组织 non-governmental organization (NGO)/促进两国之间的~往来 promote unofficial (*or* people-to-people) exchanges between the two countries

民间贸易 mínjiān màoyì non-governmental trade

民间兽医 mínjiān shòuyī colt's cutter

民间团体 mínjiān tuántǐ non-governmental organization

民间外交 mínjiān wàijiāo people-to-people diplomacy

民间文学 mínjiān wénxué folk literature

民间舞蹈 mínjiān wǔdǎo folk dance

民间协定 mínjiān xiédìng non-governmental agreement

民间医药 mínjiān yīyào folk medicine

民间艺人 mínjiān yìrén folk artisan; folk artist

民间艺术 mínjiān yìshù folk art

民间音乐 mínjiān yīnyuè folk music

民柬 Mín-Jiǎn (short for 民主柬埔寨) Democratic Kampuchea (between 1976 and 1989)

民建 Mínjiàn (short for 中国民主建国会) China Democratic National Construction Association, one of China's patriotic democratic parties

民进 Mínjìn (short for 中国民主促进会) China Association for Promoting Democracy, one of China's patriotic democratic parties

民进党 Mínjìndǎng Democratic Progressive Party (DPP), a registered party in China's Taiwan

民警 mínjǐng people's police; police: 女~ people's policewoman; policewoman / 交通~ traffic police

民居 mínjū civilian residential housing

民康物阜 mínkāng-wùfù the people live in peace and products abound; society is prosperous and stable

民力 mínlì financial resources of the people: ~凋尽 have exhausted the financial resources of the people / 减省赋徭，以宽~。Taxes and corvée must be reduced in order to foster the financial resources of the people.

民萌 mínméng *also* "民氓" 〈书面〉 the people; common people; the populace

民盟 Mínméng (short for 中国民主同盟) China Democratic League (one of China's patriotic democratic parties, founded in March 1941 as League of Democratic Parties and Organizations of China and changed to the present name in September, 1944)

民命 mínmìng lives of the people

民瘼 mínmò 〈书面〉 hardships or miseries of the people: 广求~ inquire far and wide about the hardships and sufferings of the people

民女 mínnǚ girls from ordinary families: 强抢~ forcibly take away daughters of ordinary people

民品 mínpǐn products for civil use, esp. those produced by military enterprises: 转为生产~ (of military factories) transfer (*or* shift) to the production of goods for civilian use

民气 mínqì morale of the people; popular morale; public morale: ~旺盛。The people's morale is high.

民情 mínqíng ❶ condition of the people: 熟悉~ be familiar with the condition of the people ❷ feelings of the people; public feelings: 体贴~ care for feelings of the people

民穷财尽 mínqióng-cáijìn the people are destitute, deprived of all their money and possessions

民权 mínquán civil rights; civil liberties; democratic rights: 保障~ safeguard civil rights / 侵犯~ infringe upon democratic rights (*or* civil liberties) / ~运动 civil rights movement

民权主义 mínquánzhǔyì Principle of Democracy (as one of the Three People's Principles formulated by Dr. Sun Yat-sen in 1905)

民社党 Mínshèdǎng Democratic Socialist Party

民生 mínshēng the people's livelihood: 国计~ national economy and the people's livelihood / 连绵内战，~涂炭。Continuous civil war has plunged the people into an abyss of misery.

民生凋敝 mínshēng-diāobì the people live in destitution

民生主义 mínshēngzhǔyì Principle of the People's Livelihood (one of the Three People's Principles formulated by Dr. Sun Yat-sen in 1905)

民时 mínshí farming season: 不误~ not miss the farming season; do farm work at the right time / 无夺~ do not take up the peasants' time during the farming season / ~多艰。Times were hard for the people.

民食 mínshí food for the people; provisions for the people

民事 mínshì 〈法律〉 relating to civil law; civil: ~案件 civil case / ~纠纷 civil dispute

民事法庭 mínshì fǎtíng *also* "民庭" civil court

民事法院 mínshì fǎyuàn *also* "普通诉讼法院" pǔtōng sùsòng fǎyuàn civil court; (UK) Court of Common Pleas

民事犯 mínshìfàn 〈法律〉 civil prisoner

民事管辖权 mínshì guǎnxiáquán civil jurisdiction

民事检查专员 Mínshì Jiǎnchá Zhuānyuán (HK before July 1997) Crown Solicitor

民事权利 mínshì quánlì rights under the civil code; civil rights

民事审判庭 mínshì shěnpàntíng civil division of a people's court; civil court

民事诉讼 mínshì sùsòng civil lawsuit or action

民事诉讼法 mínshì sùsòngfǎ 〈法律〉 law of civil procedure; civil procedure act

民事责任 mínshì zérèn 〈法律〉 civil liability; obligation relating to civil law

民俗 mínsú folk custom; folkways: 尊重当地~ respect local customs

民俗学 mínsúxué folklore

民庭 míntíng (short for 民事法庭) civil court

民团 míntuán 〈旧语〉 civil corps or militia (organized by local landlords)

民望 mínwàng 〈书面〉 ❶ popular expectation; public confidence: ~所归 enjoy popular confidence (*or* trust) ❷ model for the people

民为邦本 mínwéibāngběn the people are the foundation of the state: ~，本固邦宁。The people are the foundation of a country; when the foundation is solid, the country is stable.

民委 Mínwěi (short for 民族事务委员会) Ethnic Affairs Commission

民物 mínwù possessions of the people: ~繁富。The people are comfortably well-off.

民校 mínxiào ❶ spare-time school for adults ❷ school run by the local people; community school

民心 mínxīn popular feelings; common aspirations of the people; will of the people: ~所向 what conforms to the common aspirations of the people; trend of public feeling / ~向背 will of the people;

whether the people are for or against sb. or sth. /违背～ go against the will of the people /深得～ enjoy the ardent support of the people
民信 mínxìn ❶ popular trust:恢复～ regain people's trust ❷ civilian correspondence
民信局 mínxìnjú 〈旧语〉 private organization handling personal letters, parcels, remittances, etc.
民选 mínxuǎn elected by the people:～政府 democratically elected government
民谚 mínyàn popular proverb
民谣 mínyáo folk rhyme (esp. of the topical and political type); folk song or ballad:搜集～ collect folk rhymes
民以食为天 mín yǐ shí wéi tiān people regard food as their prime want; food is the first necessity of man; people cannot survive without food
民意 mínyì opinion or will of the people; public opinion:～代表 people's representative (e.g. member of parliament) /～机关 people's representative body (e.g. parliament) /顺民心,合～ accord with the aspirations and opinions of the people; act in conformity with popular feeling and will
民意测验 mínyì cèyàn public opinion poll; poll
民隐 mínyǐn 〈书面〉 distress of the people; sufferings of the people
民营 mínyíng run by private citizens:转为～ turn over to private management
民营企业 mínyíng qǐyè enterprise run by private citizens
民用 mínyòng for civil use; civil:～航空 civil aviation /～机场 civil airport /～建筑 civil architecture /～五金器材 hardware for civil use
民用产品 mínyòng chǎnpǐn product for civilian use
民用航空总局 Mínyòng Hángkōng Zǒngjú Civil Aviation Administration:中国～ Civil Aviation Administration of China (CAAC)
民有、民治、民享 mínyǒu mínzhì mínxiǎng of the people, by the people, and for the people (mentioned in the Gettysburg Address delivered by US President Abraham Lincoln on 9 Nov. 1863)
民院 mínyuàn (short for 民族学院) institute or college for minority nationalities
民怨 mínyuàn people's resentment; mass or popular discontent; public grievances
民怨沸腾 mínyuàn-fèiténg popular grievances run high:贪污腐化闹得～。The people are seething with resentment at corruption.
民乐 mínyuè music, esp. folk music, for traditional instruments:～队 traditional instruments orchestra /～合奏 ensemble of traditional instruments
民运 mínyùn ❶ civil transport ❷ 〈旧语〉 privately run transport ❸ people's movement; movement for democracy; civil rights movement:～领袖 leader of the civil rights movement /～干部 cadre for work among the civilian people /～工作 mass work /～干事 person in charge of mass work
民贼 mínzéi traitor to the people: 独夫～ autocrat and traitor to the people
民宅 mínzhái private residence
民政 mínzhèng civil administration:～机关 civil administration organ
民政部 Mínzhèngbù Ministry of Civil Affairs
民政科 Mínzhèngkē (HK) Home Affairs Branch
民政司 Mínzhèngsī (HK before July 1997) Secretary for Home Affairs
民脂民膏 mínzhī-míngāo flesh and blood of the people:搜刮～ amass great wealth by fleecing the people
民智 mínzhì educational level of the people:～不开。The people are not educated (*or* enlightened).
民众 mínzhòng masses; the common people; the populace:唤起～ arouse the masses /～团体 people's organization; mass organization
民主 mínzhǔ democracy:党内～ inner-party democracy /实行～ practise democracy /充分发扬～ give full play to democracy /～评定 democratic evaluation /～作风 democratic work-style /～气氛 democratic atmosphere
民主党 Mínzhǔdǎng (US) Democratic Party
民主党派 mínzhǔ dǎngpài democratic parties (political parties that acknowledge the leadership of the Chinese Communist Party and work in cooperation with it)
民主德国 Mínzhǔ Déguó (short for 德意志民主共和国) German Democratic Republic (GDR), also known as East Germany, founded in 1949 and reunified with the Federal Republic of Germany in 1990
民主改革 mínzhǔ gǎigé democratic reform
民主革命 mínzhǔ gémìng democratic revolution
民主共和国 mínzhǔ gònghéguó democratic republic
民主国家 mínzhǔ guójiā democratic country; democracy
民主集中制 mínzhǔ jízhōngzhì democratic centralism (organizational principle of the Communist Party, namely, centralism on the basis of democracy and democracy under centralized guidance):实行～ practise (*or* carry out) democratic centralism /依照～的原则办 act according to the principles of democratic centralism
民主监督 mínzhǔ jiāndū democratic supervision
民主柬埔寨 Mínzhǔ Jiǎnpǔzhài Democratic Kampuchea (between 1976 and 1989)
民主决策 mínzhǔ juécè democratic decision-making
民主派 mínzhǔpài democrat
民主人士 mínzhǔ rénshì democratic personage
民主生活 mínzhǔ shēnghuó democratic life (as within the Communist Party):～会 democratic life meeting /坚持正常的～ maintain the normal practice of democracy / ～不健全。Democratic life is upset.
民主协商 mínzhǔ xiéshāng democratic consultation
民族 mínzú people; nation; nationality; ethnic community:游牧～ nomadic people /古代～ ancient people /犹太～ Jewish people /中华～ Chinese nation /被压迫～ oppressed nations /少数～ ethnic group; minority nationality; national minority /国内各～的团结 unity of the various nationalities of the country /～败类 scum of a nation /～大家庭 great family of nationalities /多～国家 multinational country /～大义 cardinal principle of national interest /～动乱 ethnic unrest /～复兴 national rejuvenation /～独立 national independence /～服装 national costume /～歧视 ethnic discrimination /～杂居地区 multinational area /～政策 policy towards nationalities /～自信心 national self-confidence /～自尊心 national pride; national self-respect /～尊严 national dignity /～学院 institute or college for minority nationalities
民族工业 mínzú gōngyè national industry
民族共同语 mínzú gòngtóngyǔ common national language
民族国家 mínzú guójiā nation-state
民族魂 mínzúhún noble spirit of a nation:中华～的赞歌 paean to the noble spirit of the Chinese nation
民族解放运动 mínzú jiěfàng yùndòng national liberation movement
民族经济 mínzú jīngjì national economy
民族利己主义 mínzú lìjǐzhǔyì national egoism
民族民主革命 mínzú mínzhǔ gémìng national democratic revolution
民族气节 mínzú qìjié integrity or moral courage of a patriot
民族区域自治 mínzú qūyù zìzhì regional autonomy of ethnic groups; regional national autonomy
民族融合 mínzú rónghé merging of nationalities
民族沙文主义 mínzú shāwénzhǔyì national chauvinism
民族实体 mínzú shítǐ national entity
民族同化 mínzú tónghuà national assimilation
民族统一战线 mínzú tǒngyī zhànxiàn national united front
民族文化 mínzú wénhuà national culture
民族文化宫 Mínzú Wénhuàgōng Culture Palace of the Nationalities (in Beijing)
民族乡 mínzúxiāng local administrative unit (corresponding to a township) of an ethnic group
民族形式 mínzú xíngshì national style; national form
民族虚无主义 mínzú xūwúzhǔyì national nihilism
民族学 mínzúxué ethnology
民族意识 mínzú yìshi national consciousness
民族英雄 mínzú yīngxióng national hero:～主义 national heroism
民族语义学 mínzú yǔyìxué ethnosemantics
民族运动 mínzú yùndòng movement against national oppression and for independence and equality among nations
民族志 mínzúzhì ethnography
民族主义 mínzúzhǔyì ❶ nationalism:狭隘的～ narrow nationalism ❷ Principle of Nationalism (one of the three People's Principles formulated by Dr. Sun Yat-sen in 1905)
民族资本 mínzú zīběn capital of the national bourgeoisie (in colonial, semi-colonial or independent nationalist countries); national

capital
民族资本家 mínzú zīběnjiā national capitalist
民族资产阶级 mínzú zīchǎnjiējí national bourgeoisie
民族自决 mínzú zìjué national self-determination
民族自治 mínzú zìzhì national autonomy

珉(瑉、碈) mín 〈书面〉 jade-like stone

苠 mín crop that grows longer and ripens later: ～高粱 late sorghum

缗(緍) mín 〈书面〉❶ string used in ancient times to hold copper cash ❷〈量词〉monetary unit of ancient China, equal to 1,000 *wen*: 铜钱三百～ three hundred *min* of copper cash

mǐn

闵 mǐn ❶ *see* "悯" mǐn ❷ (Mǐn) a surname

悯 mǐn ❶ pity; commiserate; sympathize: ～弱摧强 sympathize with the weak and overthrow the strong /其情可～。This is a case which evokes commiseration (*or* deserves sympathy). ❷〈书面〉sorrow; grief: ～然涕下 weep sadly
悯恻 mǐncè 〈书面〉pity; take pity on (a person)
悯惜 mǐnxī have compassion for; take pity on; pity
悯恤 mǐnxù pity and help; feel compassion for: ～孤儿 pity and help orphans

闽 Mǐn ❶ name of a river in Fujian Province: ～江 Min River ❷ another name for Fujian Province: ～南 Southern Fujian
闽菜 mǐncài dishes of Fujian style; Fujian cooking; Fujian cuisine
闽剧 mǐnjù *also* "福州戏" fúzhōuxì local opera popular in northeastern Fujian Province

黾(黽) mǐn
黾勉 mǐnmiǎn 〈书面〉make efforts; strive: ～从事 exert oneself (in doing sth.)

僶(僶) mǐn
僶俛 mǐnmiǎn *see* "黾勉" mǐnmiǎn

皿 mǐn *see* "器皿" qìmǐn

敏 mǐn ❶ quick; lithe; nimble; agile: 灵～ keen; agile; acute /锐～ sensitive; keen; sharp-witted ❷ quick-witted; acute; keen; smart: 聪～ clever; smart ❸ (Mǐn) a surname
敏感 mǐngǎn sensitive; responsive; delicate; susceptible: 对新鲜事物～ be responsive to new things /艺术家的～ sensibility of an artist /对某些花粉很～ be allergic to certain kinds of pollen /对批评过于～ be oversensitive to criticism /这是个很～的问题。It's a very sensitive issue (*or* delicate subject). /有些动物对天气变化十分～。Some animals are highly susceptible to changes in weather.
敏感度 mǐngǎndù sensibility; sensitivity; susceptibility
敏感元件 mǐngǎn yuánjiàn 〈无线电〉sensitive element; sensor
敏化 mǐnhuà 〈物理〉sensitization: ～剂 sensitizer /～纸 sensitized paper
敏化光电管 mǐnhuà guāngdiànguǎn 〈无线电〉sensitized photocell
敏慧 mǐnhuì clever; quick-witted; intelligent: ～的姑娘 smart girl
敏捷 mǐnjié quick; alert; nimble; agile: 动作～ be quick (*or* agile) in movement /传球～ pass a ball nimbly /思维～ have an agile (*or* alert, *or* nimble) mind /办事～ be efficient; get things done quickly
敏快 mǐnkuài quick; agile: 刚听到门铃响, 他就～地站起来。He stood up quickly the moment he heard the doorbell ring.
敏求 mǐnqiú 〈书面〉exert oneself to the utmost to seek or study: ～古道 exert oneself to seek ancient truths /君子～。A gentleman seeks knowledge eagerly and assiduously. *or* A gentleman devotes himself to the pursuit of knowledge.
敏锐 mǐnruì sharp; acute; keen; discerning: 思想～ have a penetrating (*or* acute) mind /听觉～ be keen of hearing; have good ears /嗅觉～ have an acute sense of smell /视觉～ be keen of sight; have a keen eyesight /～的眼光 have a discerning eye; be sharp-eyed /具有～观察力的人 man of shrewd observation
敏行 mǐnxíng 〈书面〉strive hard to cultivate one's mind: ～不怠 make unremitting efforts at self-cultivation

慜 mǐn 〈书面〉smart and quick

鳘 mǐn 〈动物〉(popular name for 鮸鱼) slate cod croaker

泯 mǐn get rid of; lose; vanish; die out: 永存不～ be everlasting /良心未～ have not totally lost one's conscience
泯除 mǐnchú eradicate; get rid of; cast aside; cast away: ～成见 banish (*or* get rid of) prejudices; root out biases
泯灭 mǐnmiè get rid of; vanish; die out: 难以～的印象 indelible impression /不能～的影响 influences impossible to efface /幻想～ be disillusioned /～人性 devoid of humanity; inhuman
泯没 mǐnmò vanish; disappear; become lost; sink into oblivion: 他搞文学创作的宿愿至今也未曾～。He has never abandoned his desire to be a writer. /他的功绩永远不可～。His merits shall never be forgotten.

抿[1] mǐn smooth (hair, etc.) with a wet brush: ～了～头发 give one's hair a brush

抿[2] mǐn ❶ (of mouth, ear, wing, etc.) close lightly; tuck; furl: ～着嘴笑 smile with closed lips /鸟～起双翼。The bird tucked its wings. ❷ sip: ～了一口酒 take a sip of the wine /一口一口地～咖啡 sip at coffee
抿子 mǐnzi *also* "笢子" mǐnzi small hair brush

笢 mǐn thin bamboo strip
笢子 mǐnzi *see* "抿子" mǐnzi

愍(惽) mǐn 〈书面〉*see* "悯" mǐn

暋(敃) mǐn 〈书面〉rude and unreasonable; arrogant

míng

冥 míng ❶ dark; dim; obscure: 晦～ dark and gloomy /幽～ dark; obscure ❷ deep; abstruse; profound: ～思 be deep in thought; be immersed in meditation ❸ dull; stupid; foolish: *see* "～顽" ❹ underworld; nether world: ～间 nether world
冥暗 míng'àn dark; dim; dusky: 日落西山, 天渐～。With the sun setting in the west, it is getting dark.
冥币 míngbì *see* "冥钞"
冥钞 míngchāo 〈迷信〉paper made to resemble money and burned as an offering to the dead
冥福 míngfú 〈迷信〉good fortune for people after death in the nether world; happiness in the after life
冥府 míngfǔ 〈迷信〉underworld; nether world; land of the dead; Hades
冥茫 míngmáng *also* "溟茫" míngmáng 〈书面〉indistinct; vast and hazy; dusky: 夜色～。The dusk is deepening.
冥蒙 míngméng *also* "溟濛" míngméng hazy; misty: 暮雾渐起, 夜色～。It grew hazy with the fall of evening mists.
冥冥 míngmíng 〈书面〉❶ dark; dim: ～之中 in the unseen world /暮色～。It is dusk. ❷ ignorant; benighted; thickheaded: 何其～。How ignorant! ❸ high in the sky and far away: 鸿飞～。Wild geese fly high and far.
冥器 míngqì funeral object; burial furnishings
冥寿 míngshòu birth anniversary of a person already dead
冥思苦想 míngsī-kǔxiǎng *also* "冥思苦索" think long and hard; rack or cudgel one's brains: 关在屋子里～ shut oneself in a small room and cudgel one's brains
冥顽 míngwán 〈书面〉dull and stubborn; thickheaded: ～不灵 impenetrably thickheaded
冥王星 Míngwángxīng 〈天文〉Pluto

冥卫一 Míngwèi Yī Charon, the only satellite of Pluto, discovered in 1978

冥想 míngxiǎng deep thought; reverie; daydreaming: 窗外的秋色, 引起了他的无限~。The autumn scene outside the window plunged him in reverie.

冥衣 míngyī grave clothes; burial clothes

溟 míng 〈书面〉 sea: 东~ east sea

溟茫 míngmáng see "冥茫" míngmáng

溟濛 míngméng also "冥蒙" míngméng 〈书面〉 misty; drizzly: ~细雨 fine drizzle

溟溟 míngmíng 〈书面〉 ❶ dark; dim; dusky: 云雾~ dim misty clouds ❷ wet; drizzling

暝 míng 〈书面〉 ❶ (of the sun) set; (of the sky) grow dark: 日将~。The sun is going down. /天已~。Dusk has descended. ❷ dusk; evening twilight

暝色 míngsè dusk; evening twilight: ~四合。Dusk is gathering. /窗外已经一片~。Outside it is already dark.

瞑 míng ❶ shut one's eyes: 通夜不~ remain awake all night ❷ be dim-sighted; have blurred vision: 耳聋目~ be hard of hearing and dim-sighted

瞑目 míngmù die with one's eyes closed — die contented: 死不~ be unable to rest in one's grave; die with everlasting regret /死而~ be able to close one's eyes peacefully when one dies; die contented

瞑眩 míngxuàn 〈中医〉 dizziness, nausea, etc. as a side effect of drugs

螟 míng snout moth's larva

螟虫 míngchóng snout moth's larva

螟蛾 míng'é snout moth

螟害 mínghài snout moth attack

螟蛉 mínglíng ❶ corn earworm ❷ adopted son

榠 míng

榠楂 míngzhā also "榅桲" wēnbo 〈植物〉 quince (*Cydonia oblonga*)

明[1] míng ❶ bright; brilliant; light: 灯火通~ be brightly lit; be brilliantly illuminated /月是故乡~。The moon is brighter in one's hometown (than anywhere else). /天已微~。It is getting light. *or* Day is breaking. ❷ obvious; clear; distinct: 心~眼亮 be sharp-eyed and clear-headed /~若观火 as obvious as a glowing fire /不~不白地被撤了职 be dismissed from one's post for unspecified reasons /真相不~。The facts are not clear. *or* The truth is not out yet. ❸ open; plain; overt; explicit: ~弃暗取 take back secretly what one has openly discarded /~升暗降 promote in appearance but demote in reality; kick upstairs ❹ sharp-eyed; clear-sighted: 耳聪目~ have sharp ears and eyes /眼~手快 be quick of eye and deft of hand ❺ brightness; light; honesty: 光~磊落 open and above-board /弃暗投~ discard darkness for light — renounce an evil cause and cross over to the side of justice ❻ sight: 复~ regain one's sight /双目失~ go blind in both eyes ❼ understand; realize; know: 深~大义 be deeply conscious of the cardinal principles of right and wrong; have a strong sense of justice /不~利害 not know on which side one's bread is buttered ❽ 〈书面〉 make known; make clear; demonstrate: 开宗~义 make clear the purpose and theme of an undertaking from the very beginning ❾ 〈副词〉 obviously; plainly: see "~~"; "~知故问"

明[2] míng immediately following in time; next: ~春 next spring /~晨 tomorrow morning

明[3] Míng ❶ Ming Dynasty (1368-1644): see "~史" ❷ a surname

明安图 Míng Āntú Ming Antu (?-1765), mathematician and astronomer of the Qing Dynasty

明暗 míng'àn light and shade: ~扫描 brightness scanning

明暗灯 míng'àndēng occulting light

明暗对照法 míng'àn duìzhàofǎ 〈美术〉 chiaroscuro

明暗界线 míng'àn jièxiàn 〈天文〉 terminator (the line separating illuminated and dark portions of a nonluminous body as the moon)

明摆着 míngbǎizhe obvious; evident; clear; plain: 事情只能这样办, 这是~的。It's obvious that this has got to be done the way we did. /这道理不是~吗? Isn't the reason as clear as daylight?

明白 míngbai ❶ clear; explicit; obvious; plain: 说得~ explain clearly (*or* in explicit terms) /他的意思是十分~的。What he means is quite obvious. *or* His intention is very clear. ❷ frank; explicit; unequivocal: 有意见就~地提出来。State your views unequivocally. /他们的关系有些不明不白的。Their relationship is somewhat dubious (*or* shady). /你把事情讲~就不会有什么误会了。There would be no misunderstanding if you told everything. ❸ sensible; reasonable: 你要放~点。Be sensible. ❹ know; comprehend; understand; realize: ~事理 know what's what; show good sense /我~你这句话的用意。I know what you mean by this. *or* I see your point. /他忽然~了。The truth suddenly dawned on him.

明白人 míngbairén person with common sense; sensible person

明报 Míngbào *Ming Bao Daily News*, Chinese-language newspaper in Hong Kong

明辨是非 míngbiàn-shìfēi make a clear distinction between right and wrong; tell right from wrong

明补 míngbǔ open allowance; direct subsidy: 把暗补改为~ change indirect into direct subsidy

明灿灿 míngcàncàn very bright: ~的阳光 dazzling sun /~的街灯 bright street lights /一双~的大眼睛 a pair of bright eyes

明查暗访 míngchá-ànfǎng observe publicly and investigate privately — conduct an investigation: 案件正处于~阶段。The case is now under investigation.

明查秋毫 míngchá-qiūháo be sharp-eyed enough to perceive the minutest detail; have an extremely discerning eye

明察 míngchá observe or see clearly; judge judiciously: ~秋毫之末而不见舆薪 be sharp-sighted enough to perceive the tip of an animal's autumn hair but unable to see a cartload of firewood — see the minute detail but miss the major issue; miss the wood for the trees /所言属实, 敬希~。What I have said is true, and I respectfully await your judicious judgement.

明畅 míngchàng lucid and fluent: 文笔~ lucid and fluent style of writing

明澈 míngchè bright and limpid; clear and transparent: 一双~的眼睛 a pair of bright, limpid eyes /溪水~见底。The brook is so clear that you can see its bottom.

明澄 míngchéng bright and limpid; transparent: ~的晴空 bright and sunny skies

明出大卖 míngchū-dàmài sell openly in large quantities — engage in overt activities

明处 míngchù ❶ where there is light: 把地图拿到~看。Bring the map to the light to study. ❷ openly; in public: 有话说在~, 不要背后议论。Say what is on your mind. Don't gossip behind anybody's back. /占领军在~, 游击队在暗处。The guerrillas were under cover while the occupation army was in the open.

明窗净几 míngchuāng-jìngjī also "窗明几净" neat desk before a bright window — the room is spotless

明达 míngdá be sensible and understanding: ~公正 fair and sensible

明打明 míngdǎmíng 〈方言〉 clearly; obviously; plainly: 这一切都是~地在那儿摆着的。All this is there for everybody to see. *or* All this is clear and obvious. /你干脆就~地告诉他。You had better frankly tell him everything.

明打威群岛 Míngdǎwēi Qúndǎo Mentawai Islands, west of Sumatra, Indonesia

明德 míngdé highest virtue; virtue

明灯 míngdēng bright light; beacon: 心中有一盏~ hold a bright light inside oneself; be guided by a bright inner light

明断 míngduàn 〈书面〉 pass or render fair judgement: 此事须请上级~。The matter will have to be referred to the higher authorities for decision.

明矾 míngfán also "白矾" báifán alum: ~石 alumstone; alumite

明公正道 mínggōng-zhèngdào also "明公正气" open and above-board; just and honourable

明沟 mínggōu open drain; open sewer

明故宫 Míng Gùgōng Imperial Palace of the (early) Ming Dy-

nasty (in Nanjing)

明光 míngguāng ❶ bright light: ~耀眼 dazzling light ❷ bright; light; well-lit: ~大道 well-lit road /~的月亮 bright moon

明光光 míngguāngguāng bright; shiny; luminous: 桌面擦得~的。The table was wiped till it shone.

明光瓦亮 míngguāng-wǎliàng 〈口语〉very bright; very shiny: 玻璃窗擦得~。The glass windows were wiped clean and shiny.

明河 Mínghé 〈书面〉Milky Way: ~在天 the Milky Way in the sky

明后天 míng-hòutiān 〈口语〉tomorrow or the day after; in a couple of days: 眼下无货，您~不妨来看看。We are out of stock right now. Please come again in a couple of days.

明晃晃 mínghuānghuāng shining; gleaming: 一把~的钢刀 a gleaming knife

明黄 mínghuáng pure and bright yellow

明慧 mínghuì 〈书面〉bright; intelligent; sagacious; perceptive

明火 mínghuǒ ❶〈古语〉fire made by turning a bronze mirror to reflect the sun ❷ (as distinguished from 暗火) burning fire ❸ carry torches (in a robbery): ~抢劫 carry torches in a robbery; carry out a robbery in broad daylight

明火执仗 mínghuǒ-zhízhàng carry torches and weapons (in a robbery) — do evil things in broad daylight; operate openly: ~地拦路抢劫 waylay sb. in broad daylight

明间儿 míngjiānr 〈口语〉room (in a house) whose door opens directly onto a courtyard or street

明鉴 míngjiàn ❶ clear mirror ❷ clear precedent to be cited for reference; example to be followed ❸〈敬词〉your penetrating judgement; your brilliant views: 望君~。I crave your sagacious understanding.

明胶 míngjiāo gelatin

明教 míngjiào ❶〈书面〉〈敬词〉wise advice: 仁候~ await your wise instructions /敢闻~ hope to get the benefit of your advice ❷ (Míngjiào) a Chinese version of Manichaeism with an admixture of Taoist and Buddhist doctrines popular among peasants and artisans as a secret religion from 10th-14th centuries

明接管 míngjiēguǎn open-jointed pipe

明洁 míngjié bright and pure; clear and bright: ~的月光 bright moonlight

明净 míngjìng bright and clean: 湖面~如镜。The lake is as clear as a mirror.

明静 míngjìng clear and tranquil: 温和~的春天 mild, bright and quiet spring

明镜 míngjìng clear mirror; bright mirror

明镜高悬 míngjìng-gāoxuán *also* "秦镜高悬" qínjìng-gāoxuán with a clear mirror hung on high — perspicacious and impartial in judgement

明镜周刊 Míngjìng Zhōukān *Der Spiegel*, German weekly started in 1946

明据 míngjù clear evidence; irrefutable proof or evidence: 请问有何~? Is there any clear evidence?

明决 míngjué sensible and resolute: 少有~。He was sensible and decisive even when a boy.

明快 míngkuài ❶ lucid and lively; vivacious; sprightly: ~的节奏 sprightly rhythm /他的散文犀利~。His prose is trenchant, lucid and lively. ❷ straightforward; frank; forthright: 一看就知道他是个~人。Anyone will find at first meeting that he is frank and straightforward. ❸〈方言〉bright: 月亮照得院子里挺~。The moon shone bright on the courtyard.

明来暗往 mínglái-ànwǎng have overt and covert contacts with sb.: 他与那几个不三不四的人仍然~。He still keeps in touch with those dubious characters either openly or on the sly.

明朗 mínglǎng ❶ bright and clear: ~辽阔的天空 clear and boundless sky /月色格外~。The moonlight is especially bright. ❷ clear; obvious; unambiguous: 他们的态度还不~。Their attitude is still equivocal (*or* ambiguous). /局势已经~。The situation has already become clear. ❸ forthright; straightforward; bright and cheerful: 他的性格不像他弟弟那么~、活泼。He is not as forthright and lively as his brother. /这幅画色调~。This picture is painted in bright, warm hues.

明理 mínglǐ ❶ sensible; understanding; reasonable: 读书~ be educated and reasonable ❷ plain truth: ~不用细讲。Plain truth needs no elaboration. *or* The reason is too obvious to require exposition.

明丽 mínglì bright and beautiful: 阳光灿烂，山川~。The mountains and rivers are resplendent with sunshine.

明里 míngli on a public occasion; publicly; openly; in the open: ~同意，暗里反对 agree in public but disagree in secret; agree to one's face but disagree behind one's back; agree in public but oppose in private

明亮 míngliàng ❶ bright; well-lit: 灯光~ be brilliantly lit /室内光线~。The room is well-lit. /黑夜里，星星显得特别~。Stars appear especially bright on a moonless night. ❷ bright; dazzling; shining: 一双清澈~的眼睛 a pair of clear and bright eyes ❸ become clear: 听了解释后，他心里~了。Hearing the explanation, he felt enlightened. ❹ loud and clear; clarion: 嗓音~ loud and clear voice /歌声~ loud and distinct singing

明了 míngliǎo ❶ understand; be aware; be clear about: 不~交通规则，怎么能开车? How can you drive without knowing the traffic regulations? ❷ clear; obvious; plain: 文章的主旨简单~。The theme of the article is simple and clear.

明令 mínglìng explicit order; formal decree; public proclamation: ~嘉奖 issue a commendation; mention in a citation /~禁止 ban by decree

明楼 mínglóu ❶ watchtower ❷ tallest building above ground in an emperor's mausoleum

明码 míngmǎ ❶ plain code: ~发报 send a telegram in plain code ❷ with the prices clearly marked: ~标价 mark the prices clearly /~售货 sell goods at (clearly) marked prices

明媒正娶 míngméi-zhèngqǔ 〈旧语〉be legitimately and properly married; be legally married

明媚 míngmèi ❶ (of scenery) bright and beautiful; radiant and enchanting: ~的阳光 bright sunshine /春光~ radiant and enchanting spring scene ❷ (of eyes) bright and lovely: 她的眼睛~动人。Her eyes are bright and attractive.

明面 míngmiàn on the surface; apparently: 他~上是说儿子，其实是说给别人听的。Apparently reproaching his son, he actually meant those remarks for others. *or* While reproaching his son, he was actually blaming others by insinuation. /把问题摆到~上倒好解决些。These questions, if put on the table, could be solved more easily.

明灭 míngmiè bright one minute and faint the next; now clearly visible and now hidden from view; twinkling: 星光~。The stars twinkle.

明敏 míngmǐn clear and quick: 头脑~ keen mind

明明 míngmíng evidently; obviously; undoubtedly; plainly: ~不懂，为什么装懂? Why pretend to know what you plainly don't? /这不~是给我出难题吗? Isn't it obvious that you are making things difficult for me? /他~醒了，却装睡不吭声。Although he was awake, he pretended to be asleep and kept silent.

明眸 míngmóu bright eyes: ~皓齿 (of a pretty woman) have bright eyes and white teeth

明目 míngmù ❶〈书面〉eyes that see clearly; good eyesight ❷ brighten the eye; improve eyesight: 石决明、蝉蜕可以解热~。Abalone and cicada slough can allay a fever and improve eyesight.

明目张胆 míngmù-zhāngdǎn brazenly; flagrantly: ~地行凶 commit violence flagrantly

明年 míngnián next year

明盘 míngpán (openly) negotiated price

明铺暗盖 míngpū-àngài *also* "明铺夜盖"〈方言〉have illicit relations (with sb.); have an affair (with sb.)

明器 míngqì *also* "冥器" míngqì funeral object; burial furnishings

明前 míngqián green tea made from tea leaves picked before Pure Brightness (清明)

明枪暗箭 míngqiāng-ànjiàn open spear thrusts plus arrows shot in the dark — both open and secret attacks: 他没想到成了~的目标。He never expected that he would become a target for overt and covert attacks.

明枪易躲，暗箭难防 míngqiāng yì duǒ, ànjiàn nán fáng 〈俗语〉it is easy to dodge an open spear thrust but difficult to guard against an arrow shot from behind; better an open enemy than a false friend

明抢 míngqiǎng daylight robbery: ~暗偷 rob in broad daylight and steal in dark corners

明情 míngqíng ❶ sensible; understanding: ~察理 reasonable and understanding ❷〈方言〉obviously; evidently; plainly: 这不~糊弄我嘛，我怎么能信以为真呢? As this was evidently meant to fool me, how could I possibly believe it?

明情理儿 míngqínglǐr 〈方言〉obvious and self-evident reason
明渠 míngqú open ditch or canal:输水～ open irrigation canal
明确 míngquè ❶ clear and definite; unequivocal; explicit; clear-cut:目的～ have a clear aim / 要求～ make an explicit demand / ～分工 have a specific division of work; have a clearly defined share of work / ～的答复 clear-cut (*or* unequivocal) answer ❷ make clear; clarify; make definite:这次会议～了我们的任务。The meeting clarified our tasks.
明儿 míngr *also* "明儿个"〈口语〉❶ tomorrow:～见。See you tomorrow. ❷ one of these days; some day:赶～我也买台录像机。I'll buy a VCR (*or* video cassette recorder) some day.
明人 míngrén ❶ seeing person (as contrasted with the blind) ❷ honest, forthright or sensible person:～不用细提 a sensible man or a wise man needs no elaborate explanation; a word to the wise
明人不说暗话 míngrén bù shuō ànhuà 〈俗语〉a forthright man has no use for insinuation
明人不做暗事 míngrén bù zuò ànshì 〈俗语〉an honest man will never do anything underhand
明仁天皇 Míngrén Tiānhuáng Akihito (1933-), 123rd Japanese emperor who ascended the throne in Jan. 1989
明日 míngrì tomorrow:～复～,～何其多! Tomorrow and tomorrow — there are so many tomorrows! *or* Do not put off till tomorrow what you have to do today.
明日黄花 míngrì-huánghuā chrysanthemums after the Double Ninth Festival (time for enjoying chrysanthemums and autumn scenery) — things that are stale and no longer of interest; yesterday's newspaper
明锐 míngruì ❶ clear and sharp; bright and keen:目光～ bright and keen eyes / ～的刀锋 shiny and sharp blade (*or* edge) of a sword ❷〈书面〉clear and quick:性～,有决断。He is quick and resolute.
明睿 míngruì 〈书面〉sensible; sagacious; wise
明闪闪 míngshǎnshǎn sparkling; glittering; glistening:～的灯光 glittering lights / 一双～的大眼睛 a pair of large bright eyes
明十三陵 Míng Shísānlíng Tombs of Thirteen Emperors of the Ming Dynasty to the north of Beijing
明石 míngshí alum
明史 Míngshǐ *History of Ming*, compiled by Zhang Tingyu (张廷玉) et al. and published in 1739, one of the Twenty-Four Histories (二十四史)
明示 míngshì ❶〈法律〉clear and definite; express:～引渡 express extradition / ～同意 express consent / ～担保 express guaranteeship; express warranty / ～条款 express terms ❷〈谦词〉clear instructions; clear indication:～后学。As a junior scholar, I await your enlightening instructions. / 伫候～。I look forward to hearing your instructions.
明是一盆火,暗是一把刀 míng shì yī pén huǒ, àn shì yī bǎ dāo 〈俗语〉make a show of great warmth while stabbing sb. in the back; have honey on one's lips but murder at heart:这个人～,我们都要提防点儿。He is a double-dealer, and we have to be on our guard.
明誓 míngshì take an oath; make a pledge
明爽 míngshuǎng ❶ bright and clear:～的厅堂 bright halls / ～天气 bright and clear day ❷ cheerful; happy:这几年她不愁吃,不愁穿,不受气,心里自然～得多啦。In the past few years she has had no worries about food or clothing and no unpleasant experience. Naturally she is far more cheerful than ever.
明说 míngshuō speak frankly; say openly:有话～ speak one's mind plainly; lay the cards on the table / 他虽未～,但意思是清楚的。Though he did not say it openly, what he meant was quite obvious.
明斯克 Míngsīkè Minsk, capital of the Republic of Belarus
明太鱼 míngtàiyú walleye pollack
明堂堂 míngtāngtāng brightly lit; well lit; brilliant; clear:月亮～地从花格窗子洒进来。Bright moonlight came in through the lattice window. / 他心里～的。He had a clear picture of the situation. *or* He was clear about what was what.
明堂 míngtáng *also* "明唐"❶ hall where imperial edicts concerning punishment and reward or education were announced ❷〈方言〉grain threshing and sunning ground ❸〈方言〉courtyard
明天 míngtiān ❶ tomorrow:～我休息。I'll have a day off tomorrow. ❷ near future:展望～ look forward to the future / 美好的～ bright future
明贴 míngtiē *see* "明补"
明挖隧道 míngwā suìdào opencut tunnel
明瓦 míngwǎ thin semi-transparent piece made from shells to be fixed in a window or skylight in place of glass; transparent tile
明文 míngwén (of laws, regulations, etc.) (proclaim) in writing; (print) in black and white:～公布 announce in written form / ～规定 stipulate in explicit terms
明晰 míngxī clear; distinct:～的印象 distinct impression
明细 míngxì clear and detailed:分工～ clear and minute division of work / ～账簿 subsidiary (account) book
明细账 míngxìzhàng minute account book (with customers' names entered under minute categories); itemized account; itemized bill
明虾 míngxiā prawn
明显 míngxiǎn clear; obvious; apparent; evident:界限～ clear line of demarcation / ～的错误 glaring mistake / ～改善 noticeable (*or* significant) improvement / ～的进步 marked progress / 十分～,什么力量也动摇不了他的决心。Obviously nothing will change his mind. / 他～是在说谎。He was evidently telling a lie.
明线 míngxiàn ❶〈电工〉open-wire; open-wire line ❷〈电子〉open-wire line; open wire:～载波设备 open-wire carrier equipment ❸ (of literary works) apparent sequence of events or of actions of characters
明线光谱 míngxiàn guāngpǔ bright light spectrum
明晓 míngxiǎo understand; be versed in; be familiar with:～音律 be well versed in music
明孝陵 Míng Xiàolíng Xiaoling Mausoleum of the Ming Dynasty in Nanjing, tomb of its first emperor Zhu Yuanzhang (朱元璋)
明效大验 míngxiào-dàyàn clinching proof of effectiveness; outstanding effect:长期服用这种药,定有～。Taking this medicine for an uninterrupted period of time would prove its sure effectiveness.
明心 míngxīn ❶ tell what is on one's mind; get (purpose, intention, etc.) off one's chest:敢对日月～ can bare one's innermost thoughts to heaven and earth — be open and aboveboard; have nothing to hide ❷ (of *Chan* or Zen Buddhism) introspection; self-questioning; self-examination:～见性 engage in introspection and perceive the true nature of one's being
明信片 míngxìnpiàn postcard:美术～ picture postcard / 风景～ scenic postcard
明星 míngxīng ❶ planet Venus (mentioned in ancient Chinese books) ❷ bright star; star:电影～ film star; movie star
明修栈道,暗渡陈仓 míng xiū zhàndào, àn dù Chéncāng pretend to prepare to advance along one path while secretly going along another; make a feint in one direction while attacking in another; do one thing under cover of another
明秀 míngxiù bright and beautiful:～的江南景色 beautiful scenery south of the lower reaches of the Yangtze River
明言 míngyán state one's views frankly; speak frankly; speak up:敢于～。Be bold enough to speak up.
明眼人 míngyǎnrén person with a discerning eye; person of good sense:～不难看出其中的奥妙。It's not difficult for a discerning person to see what is behind it.
明艳 míngyàn bright-coloured and beautiful; gorgeous:风光～ beautiful landscape / 服饰～ gorgeous dress / ～的石榴花 bright-coloured pomegranate blossoms
明耀 míngyào dazzling; glaring:电光～ glaring lightning / 秋阳～的海边 beach dazzling under the autumn sun
明一套,暗一套 míng yī tào, àn yī tào act one way in the open and another way in secret; play a double game; double-deal:此人惯于～,很不光明磊落。A past master at deception, he is never open and above-board.
明莹 míngyíng sparkling and crystal-clear; glittering and translucent:～的珍珠 sparkling pearl / 溪流～ glittering brook
明油 míngyóu oil poured on a cooked dish:这鱼出锅装盘后要淋点～。Some oil should be poured on the fish when it is cooked.
明喻 míngyù 〈修辞〉simile
明月 míngyuè ❶ bright moon:～入怀 (of a person) open and broad-minded ❷ *also* "夜明珠" yèmíngzhū 〈书面〉legendary luminous pearl
明早 míngzǎo ❶ tomorrow morning ❷〈方言〉tomorrow
明杖 míngzhàng stick used by a blind person in walking; blindman's staff
明朝 míngzhāo tomorrow
明哲保身 míngzhé-bǎoshēn use one's wits to ensure one's own

survival (and shirk moral responsibilities); be worldly wise and play safe:他一向信奉~的处事哲学。He has always believed in the philosophy of self-preservation.

明争暗斗 míngzhēng-àndòu both open strife and veiled rivalry:双方~,矛盾重重。The two sides were at loggerheads, locked in open and smouldering strife. /他俩没有一天不在~。Never a day goes by without open quarrels and secret wrangles between the two.

明正典刑 míngzhèng-diǎnxíng execute in accordance with the law:杀人犯经过审判,已经~。After the trial and sentence the murderer was executed.

明证 míngzhèng clear proof or evidence

明知 míngzhī know very well; be fully aware:~不可为而为之 attempt what one knows is impossible; try the impossible /~山有虎,偏向虎山行 go deep into the mountains, fully aware that they are haunted by tigers — go on undeterred by the dangers (*or* difficulties) ahead /你~他们的行为不对,为何不制止? Why didn't you stop them when you knew perfectly well that they were doing wrong?

明知故犯 míngzhī-gùfàn knowingly break (a rule, etc.); deliberately violate (discipline, etc.); commit an offence with full knowledge of its implications:~者要加重处罚。Those who knowingly break the law deserve heavier punishment.

明知故问 míngzhī-gùwèn ask while knowing the answer:事情的经过你是清楚的,何必~。You know the story from beginning to end. Why bother to ask?

明志 míngzhì state one's views, attitude, ambition, etc.:淡泊~ show high ideals by simple living /这首诗借菊花以~。In this poem, the poet gives expression to his lofty aspirations by writing about chrysanthemums.

明治天皇 Míngzhì Tiānhuáng Meiji Tenno (1852-1912), Emperor of Japan (1867-1912)

明治维新 Míngzhì Wéixīn (Japan) Meiji Reform (also translated as Meiji Restoration, 1868-1912)

明智 míngzhì sensible; wise; judicious; sagacious:~的态度 sensible attitude /~的措施 wise (*or* intelligent) measures /~的选择 judicious choice

明珠 míngzhū bright pearl; jewel:掌上~ pearl in the palm — beloved daughter; apple of one's eye

明珠暗投 míngzhū-àntóu ❶ cast pearls before swine; find one's ability unrecognized:这张名画落入他手,岂不是~! Isn't it just like casting pearls before swine that the famous painting should have fallen into his hands! ❷ good person fallen among bad company

明珠弹雀 míngzhū-tánquè hit a sparrow with a pearl — the gain is outweighed by the loss; pay (dear) for one's whistle

明主 míngzhǔ enlightened ruler

明柱 míngzhù 〈建筑〉 pilaster

明子 míngzi pine torch

鸣

míng ❶ cry of birds; chirping of insects or small animals:鸟~ singing (*or* chirping) of a bird /蝉~ singing of a cicada /鸡~狗叫。Cocks crow and dogs bark. ❷ ring; sound:~鼓 beat a drum /~笛 blow a whistle /~礼炮二十一响 fire a 21-gun salute /耳~ ring in the ears /雷~ roll of thunder ❸ express; air; voice:自~得意 be very pleased with oneself; preen oneself

鸣鞭 míngbiān ❶ crack a whip:~走马 crack the whip to spur the horse on; whip a horse on ❷ *also* "静鞭" jìngbiān a special kind of whip carried by an imperial guard of honour which made a cracking sound when waved as a signal for silence

鸣不平 míng bùpíng complain about wrongdoing; cry out against an injustice:人们为他的遭遇~。People cried out against the injustice done to him.

鸣唱 míngchàng (of birds, insects, etc.) warble; chirp; cry; sing:秋蝉~。Autumn cicadas are singing.

鸣镝 míngdí whistling arrow (used in ancient times)

鸣放 míngfàng ❶ (of guns, cannons, etc.) fire; shoot:拔出手枪,冲天~ pull out one's pistol and shoot into the air ❷ give voice to; express:~会 mass meeting for airing views

鸣鼓而攻之 míng gǔ ér gōng zhī beat the drum and condemn sb. — denounce sb. with furore:小子~可也。You may publicly denounce him. /对这种丑恶行为,必须~。It is imperative to denounce such evil practices in public.

鸣叫 míngjiào (of birds, insects, etc.) chirp; twitter; sound:汽笛~。The whistle is sounding.

鸣金 míngjīn sound the signal (such as a copper gong in ancient times) for retreat (in battle) or closing (of game, etc.):国际象棋冠军赛已于昨日~收兵。The chess tournament came to a close yesterday.

鸣锣开道 míngluó-kāidào beat gongs to clear the way (for feudal officials) — pave the way for:这种论调是为他们干涉别国内政~的。This argument was an attempt to open a gate for interference in other countries' internal affairs.

鸣禽 míngqín ❶ *also* "鸣禽类"〈动物〉 *Passeriformes* ❷ songbird; singing bird

鸣响 míngxiǎng (of bells, guns, etc.) sound; sing:钟声~。The bells were singing. /礼炮在~。The guns are firing in salute.

鸣谢 míngxiè formally express one's thanks:~启事 public notice of thanks; thank-you notice (in public) /登报~ print a notice of thanks in the newspaper

鸣冤 míngyuān voice grievances:击鼓~ beat the drum to ask the magistrate to redress a wrong

鸣冤叫屈 míngyuān-jiàoqū complain and call for redress:他不该为贪污分子~。He should not have voiced grievances for the grafters.

鸣噪 míngzào (of birds and insects) twitter; chatter:秋虫~ Autumn insects chirp

鸣啭 míngzhuàn (of songbirds, etc.) sing; warble

鸣奏 míngzòu sound; ring; resound:大厅里~着嘹亮的钢琴声。The hall resounded with piano music.

名

míng ❶ name; appellation:人~ person's name /专~ proper name /笔~ pen name; nom-de-plume; pseudonym /假~ assumed name; alias /书~ title of a book /~、字、号 (of a person) official given name (used when referring to oneself formally) and substitute names (usu. derived from official name and often used by friends on informal occasions) ❷ given name:这位女演员姓孟~晓英。The actress's surname is Meng and her given name, Xiaoying. ❸ name; excuse; pretext:以援助为~而行侵略之实 carry out aggression in the name of assistance (*or* under the pretext of offering assistance) /以派她出去办事为~把她支开 shake her off by sending her on an errand /我可不担这个~。I'm not going to bear responsibility for this. *or* I wouldn't have anything to do with it. ❹ fame; reputation; renown:不为~,不为利 seek neither fame nor wealth /慕~而来 come to see sb. on account of his established reputation /~闻中外 well-known both at home and abroad ❺ famous; well-known; renowned; celebrated; noted:~茶 famous tea /~厨 well-known chef /~工巧匠 noted artisans and skilled craftsmen ❻〈书面〉 express; describe:无以~之 not know by what name it is to be called; not know what to call it; cannot describe it properly /感激莫~ one's gratitude knows no bounds; be very grateful ❼〈书面〉 possess; have:一文不~ not have a single penny in one's pocket; be penniless ❽〈量词〉 *used of persons*:这个班有三十~学生。There are 30 students in this class. ❾ (Míng) a surname

名不副实 míngbùfùshí *also* "名不符实" the name falls short of the reality; be in name but not in fact; be unworthy of the name:~的专家 expert not worthy of the name; not an expert in the real sense of the word; not a really qualified expert /这家商店的服务态度~。The service in this shop is not as good as it is reputed to be (*or* does not live up to its reputation).

名不虚传 míngbùxūchuán be true to one's name; enjoy a well-deserved reputation; live up to one's name:~的神枪手 crack shot worthy of the name (*or* who enjoys no empty reputation) /他的医道果然~。His medical skills prove that his reputation is well deserved. /这茶叶叶绿、清香、味醇,可真是~。The tea certainly measures up to its fame; its leaves are a tender green, and its flavour is fragrant and pure.

名不正,言不顺 míng bù zhèng, yán bù shùn if names are not right, arguments will not be tenable:名不正则言不顺,言不顺则事不成。When things are not called by their proper names, one's argument cannot stand to reason, and when one's argument does not stand to reason, nothing can be done.

名菜 míngcài famous dish; speciality dish:~谱 menu of speciality dishes

名册 míngcè register; roll:职工~ staff register; staff roll /部队~ muster roll

名茶 míngchá famous brand of tea:龙井是我国的~。Longjing (*or* Dragon Well) is a famous brand of tea in China.

名刹 míngchà celebrated temple or monastery
名产 míngchǎn famous product:板鸭是南京的～。Pressed salted duck is a renowned product of Nanjing.
名场 míngchǎng ❶〈旧语〉site of the imperial examination ❷ place where people seek fame and position; vanity fair
名臣 míngchén official (in dynastic China) noted for wisdom and ability; renowned court official:一代～ renowned official (*or* one of the most celebrated officials) of his time /～逸事 anecdotes of celebrated officials
名称 míngchēng name (of a thing or organization); appellation
名称服务器 míngchēng fúwùqì 〈信息〉name server
名城 míngchéng famous city:洛阳是历史～。Luoyang is a well-known historical city.
名垂千古 míngchuíqiāngǔ *also* "名垂千秋" one's name will go down to posterity:为人民做了这么多好事的人，怎能不～? Having done so many good deeds for the people, he would surely be remembered for centuries to come.
名垂青史 míngchuíqīngshǐ one's name will go down in the annals of history; be forever remembered and revered by posterity
名词 míngcí ❶〈语言〉noun; substantive ❷ term; word; phrase:技术～ technical term; technical terminology /新～儿 new expression; vogue word ❸〈逻辑〉name
名次 míngcì position in a name list; place in a competition:取得～ win a place in a competition /争～ compete for prizes (as in a game); fight over matters of precedence /按成绩排～ arrange (the names of the contestants, etc.) in the order of final results /本次测验不计～。Participants in this test will not be graded according to their scores.
名刺 míngcì 〈书面〉visiting card; calling card:投～ send in a visiting card (when calling at sb.'s office or residence)
名存实亡 míngcún-shíwáng cease to exist but in name:这种风味食品早就～了。This kind of speciality food has long since lost its distinctive flavour.
名单 míngdān name list:开列求职者～ make a list of the applicants for the job /将某人列入～ put (*or* place) sb.'s name on a list /从～上去掉某人 take (*or* strike) sb.'s name off a list
名都 míngdū renowned city; famous metropolis
名额 míng'é number enrolled; quota (of people):本年我校招生的～为三百人。Our college has an enrolment of 300 students for this academic year. /今年征兵～略低于去年。The enlistment figure for this year is slightly lower than last year's. /由于～有限,不能满足所有申请者的要求。As the quota is limited, we cannot satisfy all the applicants. /去年招工,给了我们街道五个～。Last year our neighbourhood had a quota of 5 recruits for labour.
名分 míngfèn person's social status:古代贵族的～是世袭的。In ancient times the social status of the aristocracy was hereditary.
名副其实 míngfùqíshí *also* "名符其实" the name matches the reality; be worthy of the name:他们是一支～的生力军。They are a vital force true to its name. /他们是～的国家主人。They are masters of the country not only in name but in reality as well. /他是一位～的优秀科学家。He really lives up to his reputation as an outstanding scientist. /现在我是一名～的工人了。Now I am a bona fide worker.
名公 mínggōng ❶ prestigious official:～巨卿 prestigious officials and ranking ministers ❷ celebrity
名古屋 Mínggǔwū Nagoya, industrial and port city on Honshu Island of Japan
名贯 míngguàn 〈书面〉(of a person) name and place of origin
名贵 míngguì famous; precious; rare:展览会展出的有～的字画。On show at the exhibition are priceless scrolls of painting and calligraphy. /这种～的药材不易得到。Rare medicinal herbs of this kind are not easy to come by.
名过其实 míngguòqíshí the reputation exceeds the reality; the reality falls short of the name; not live up to one's reputation
名号 mínghào person's official and courtesy names; person's name
名讳 mínghuì 〈旧语〉(used in regard to one's elders and betters) respected name
名籍 míngjí 〈书面〉register; roll
名迹 míngjì ❶ famous historical site or relic ❷ original calligraphy or painting of a famous master ❸〈书面〉fame and deed:一生～ one's reputation and achievements in life
名家 míngjiā ❶ (Míngjiā) School of Logicians (flourishing in the periods of the Spring and Autumn Annals and of the Warring States) ❷ person of academic or artistic distinction; famous expert; accomplished master:书法～ accomplished master of calligraphy /翻译～ famous translator /经～指点 have had the benefit of guidance by a master
名缰利锁 míngjiāng-lìsuǒ shackles of fame and wealth:摆脱～的束缚,获得精神的解放。There will be emancipation of the mind when the shackles (*or* chains) of fame and wealth are broken.
名将 míngjiàng famous general; great soldier; master:当代～ great soldier of our time /体育～ master of sports; famous sportsman /体操～ gymnastics star (*or* hero); famous gymnast
名教 míngjiào Confucian moral concepts and values; Confucian canon
名节 míngjié good name and moral integrity:保全～ preserve one's good name and integrity
名句 míngjù well-known phrase; famous quotation
名剧 míngjù well-known play or opera
名角儿 míngjuér famous actor or actress (in traditional Chinese operas)
名款 míngkuǎn signature of a painter or calligrapher on his work
名利 mínglì fame and wealth:～双收 gain both fame and fortune /不求～ seek neither prestige nor riches /～思想 desire for personal fame and wealth
名利场 mínglìchǎng vanity fair; arena where people jockey for position and wealth:他不愿涉足～。He fights shy of pursuing fame and wealth.
名列前茅 mínglièqiánmáo be among the best of the successful candidates (competitors, etc.); come out on top:他在全国网球赛中～。He came out on top in the national tennis tournament.
名伶 mínglíng 〈旧语〉famous actor or actress in Chinese operas
名流 míngliú distinguished personage; eminent person; celebrity:社会～ celebrities from all walks of life /学术界～ renowned figures of academic circles
名录 mínglù roster; roll:本校历届毕业生～ roster of graduates of all previous years of this college
名录服务 mínglù fúwù 〈信息〉directory service
名落孙山 míngluòsūnshān fall behind Sun Shan (who was last on the list of successful candidates) — fail in an examination or competition:这次高考他又～。He failed again in the college entrance examination.
名门 míngmén eminent family; illustrious family:～贵族 eminent families and the nobility /～闺秀 daughter of an illustrious family
名模 míngmó famous model; first-class model
名目 míngmù name of a thing; name; item:～繁多 multitude of items; names (*or* items) of every description /巧立～ invent all kinds of names; make various pretexts /以何～? In what capacity?
名牌 míngpái ❶ famous brand; brand name:～货 goods of a famous brand; brand name commodity; branded product /～大学 prestigious university /创～ create a brand name (product) ❷ nameplate; name tag
名片 míngpiàn visiting card; calling card:递上～ present one's card
名票 míngpiào 〈旧语〉popular amateur performing artist (of Beijing opera, etc.)
名品 míngpǐn valuable object; famous artifact; treasure:馆内珍藏的～很多。There are quite a number of rare treasures in the museum. *or* The museum has a large collection of rare treasures.
名器 míngqì 〈书面〉❶ precious article ❷ paraphernalia of rank (such as title, carriage and costume)
名气 míngqi 〈口语〉fame; reputation; distinction; name:有～的学者 distinguished scholar /大有～ enjoy a great reputation /有点～ enjoy some reputation; be quite well known
名人 míngrén famous person; eminent person:～墨迹 calligraphy of a celebrity
名人录 míngrénlù who's who; list of celebrities
名色 míngsè ❶ name; item; variety:展出的品种极多,我也叫不出～来。There were so many varieties on show that I could not name them. ❷〈方言〉nominal; in name:他以祝寿的～为我备了丰盛的酒席。He gave a sumptuous banquet to celebrate my birthday. ❸〈旧语〉famous beauty or courtesan
名山大川 míngshān-dàchuān famous mountains and great rivers:他的足迹遍布～。He travelled across many famous mountains and

rivers.
名山事业 míngshān-shìyè 〈书面〉(take up) writing as one's life-long career
名声 míngshēng repute; reputation; name; renown: 好~ good name (*or* reputation) /~很坏 have an unsavoury reputation; be held in ill repute /~大振 win great renown; make a big name /他在官场上的~扶摇直上。He achieved a meteoric rise to fame in officialdom. /这份假报告, 败坏了他作为科学家的~。By making a false report, he actually tarnished his own reputation as a scientist.
名胜 míngshèng place famous for its scenery or historic relics; well-known scenic spot; point of tourist interest
名胜古迹 míngshèng-gǔjì places of historic interest and scenic beauty; scenic spots and historical sites
名师 míngshī great teacher or master: ~出高徒〈俗语〉a great master brings up brilliant disciples
名实 míngshí ❶ name and reality (used usu. in certain phrases): ~不符。The name does not accord with the reality. ❷〈书面〉reputation and accomplishments; fame and wealth ❸〈哲学〉concept and reality
名士 míngshì 〈旧语〉❶ person of literary talent or with a literary reputation ❷ celebrity without any official post
名士风流 míngshì-fēngliú unconventional and unrestrained behaviour of talented scholars
名士派 míngshìpài scholar of the unconventional or romantic type; Bohemian
名士气 míngshìqì behaviour of unconventional and self-indulgent old-style intellectuals
名氏 míngshì person's name
名世 míngshì 〈书面〉become famous in one's time; be well-known among one's contemporaries: 他有多部著作~。Many of his works are well known to his contemporaries.
名手 míngshǒu famous artist, player, etc.: 丹青~ famous painter /围棋~ *weiqi* master
名数 míngshù 〈数学〉concrete number
名宿 míngsù well-known veteran (esp. in sports); renowned scholar of the elder generation: 教育界的~ renowned senior scholar in educational circles /棋坛~ well-known master chess-player
名堂 míngtang ❶ variety; item; trick: 联欢会的~真多, 让人眼花缭乱! There was such a great variety of items at the get-together that you couldn't take all of them in. /他又在搞什么~呢! He must be up to some mischief! /就数她~多。She is just full of tricks. ❷ achievement; result: 她在语言学上已经搞出了点~。She already has some achievement in linguistics to her credit. / 他这个人很迟钝, 问不出个~来。He is so dull-witted that you cannot get anything out of him. ❸ reason; what lies behind sth.: 他为什么要这样做, 连自己也说不出个~来。He couldn't even account for what he did himself. /事情不会这么简单, 里面一定还有什么~。Things can't be that simple. There must be some reason there.
名特优新 míng-tè-yōu-xīn (collective appellation for) famous, special, superior and new products
名帖 míngtiě calling card; visiting card: 客人递上~。The visitor presented his card.
名头 míngtou 〈方言〉reputation; renown
名望 míngwàng prestige; renown: 很有~ enjoy a high reputation (*or* prestige) /颇有~的学者 prestigious scholar
名位 míngwèi official rank; fame and position: ~未定 (one's) official rank has not been set /贪图~ covet fame and position /~思想 desire for personal fame and position
名物 míngwù things and their names: 辨其~ distinguish things and their names
名下 míngxià under sb.'s name; belonging or related to sb.: 不能把成绩都记在个人~ should not claim all the credit for oneself /这事怎么搞到我~来了? How come all this is blamed on me? /把账记在我的~吧。Please charge the expenses to my account.
名下无虚 míngxià-wúxū *also* "名下无虚士" be worthy of one's reputation; have a well-deserved reputation; live up to one's reputation: 这位画家作画挥笔而就, 果然是~。The painter deserves his fame, for he finished the painting at a stroke.
名衔 míngxián title
名姓 míngxìng name
名学 míngxué 〈旧语〉logic
名言 míngyán well-known saying; famous dictum: 至理~ wise dictum; golden saying
名扬四海 míngyángsìhǎi become famous all over the world; be world-renowned: 这项重大发明使他~。This important invention has made him world-famous.
名医 míngyī well-known doctor; celebrated physician
名义 míngyì ❶ name: 我代表全系教师并以个人的~讲几句话。I wish to say a few words on behalf of the department faculty as well as in my own name. /秘书以总经理的~向大会发出贺电。The secretary sent a telegram of congratulations to the conference in the name of the company president. ❷ (as opposed to reality) nominal; titular; in name: ~汇价〈经济〉nominal rate (of exchange) /他~上是顾问, 实际上不过问业务。He is a titular consultant, and actually pays very little attention to the work. /假借困难补助的~, 变相发放年终奖。Year-end bonuses were distributed under the guise of relief funds.
名义工资 míngyì gōngzī nominal wages
名义价值 míngyì jiàzhí nominal value
名义主权 míngyì zhǔquán nominal sovereignty
名优 míngyōu ❶〈旧语〉famous actor or actress: 一代~ one of the most famous actors (*or* actresses) of his (*or* her) time ❷ famous and of excellent quality: ~产品 famous quality product
名誉 míngyù ❶ fame; reputation; name: 追求个人的~地位 run after (*or* seek) personal fame and position /使某人~扫地 discredit sb. thoroughly; drag sb.'s reputation through mud /爱惜~ cherish one's good name /恢复~ rehabilitate sb.'s reputation; rehabilitate sb. ❷ honorary: ~会员 honorary member
名誉公民 míngyù gōngmín honorary citizen
名誉教授 míngyù jiàoshòu professor emeritus
名誉领事 míngyù lǐngshì honorary consul
名誉校长 míngyù xiàozhǎng honorary president
名誉主席 míngyù zhǔxí honorary chairman or president
名媛 míngyuàn young lady of note; daughter of a well-known family: ~闺秀 daughter of an eminent family /~淑女 fair young lady of note
名噪一时 míngzào-yīshí gain fame for a time; be all the rage or vogue: ~的歌星 very popular singer of one's time
名章 míngzhāng seal inscribed with a person's name
名正言顺 míngzhèng-yánshùn fit and proper; within one's jurisdiction: 这事由系主任来做才~。If the department head were to do it, it would be perfectly justifiable. /他既说得~, 那也不妨一试。As his argument is sound, he may as well go ahead with it.
名著 míngzhù famous work; masterpiece; classic: 文学~ literary masterpiece; literary classic /科学~ science classic
名状 míngzhuàng (usu. used after words of negation) describe: 莫可~ beyond description /难以~的奇花异卉 exotic flowers that defy description /兴奋之情, 不可~。One's excitement was beyond words.
名子 míngzi name
名字 míngzi *also* "名子" name; given or personal name: 他的~是爷爷取的。His name was given by his grandpa.
名作 míngzuò famous work; masterpiece

茗 míng 〈书面〉tea: 香~ scented tea /品~ drink tea; sip tea for judgement of its quality; sample tea

铭 míng ❶ inscription: 砚~ inscription on an inkslab ❷ engrave: ~功 inscribe one's exploits /金石之音, 定当~诸肺腑。Your sound advice will be borne firmly in mind.
铭感 mínggǎn 〈书面〉engrave in one's memory with deep gratitude; bear firmly in mind: 终身~ remain deeply grateful for the rest of one's life; remain forever indebted (to sb.) /他那种舍生忘死的精神, 不能不使人~。His spirit of selfless devotion cannot be lost to memory.
铭记 míngjì ❶ engrave on one's mind; remember for ever: 永远~ always remember; will never forget /您的恩德定当永远~于心。Your great kindness will always be treasured in my memory. ❷ epigraph; inscription
铭刻 míngkè ❶ inscription: 古代~ ancient inscription ❷ inscribe in one's memory; engrave on one's mind: 他的光辉业绩永远~在人们心中。His glorious achievements are indelibly engraved in the memory of the people.
铭牌 míngpái 〈机械〉data plate; nameplate
铭佩 míngpèi 〈书面〉bear in mind; cherish; be engraved on one's mind; always remember: 恩师之情, 弟子寸心~。As your disciple I

shall forever remain grateful to you for your kind guidance.

铭石 míngshí stone tablet with inscription

铭文 míngwén inscription; epigraph:铜器～ inscription on bronze or copper wares

铭心 míngxīn be engraved on one's heart:足下之言,鄙人敢不～。I shall never forget for a single moment your advice, which is already engraved on my heart.

铭心刻骨 míngxīn-kègǔ *also*"铭心镂骨";"刻骨铭心"be engraved on one's bones and heart — be indelibly engraved on one's mind; be remembered with great gratitude

mǐng

酩 mǐng

酩酊 mǐngdǐng be drunk:～大醉 be dead drunk; be drunk as a fiddler; drink oneself blotto

mìng

命[1] mìng ❶ life:救～ save sb.'s life /～在旦夕 be on one's last legs; one's life hangs in the balance /死于非～ die an unnatural death; die a violent death /丧～ get killed; meet one's death /逃～ run for one's life ❷ life; life span:短～ die young; be short-lived /长～百岁 may you live to be a hundred (an expression of congratulations) ❸ fate; destiny; lot:～薄 doomed to a hapless life /～好 born under a lucky star /～苦 be doomed to a life of misfortunes; have a hard lot; be born under an unlucky star /～里注定 it is one's lot; be predestined /听天由～ be resigned to fate /不信天,不信～ believe neither in heaven nor fate

命[2] mìng ❶ order; command; instruct:～其返航 order a ship or plane to return to port (*or* base) /奉～出发 receive orders to set out /待～ await instructions ❷ assign (a name, title, etc.); name: *see*"～名";"～题"

命案 mìng'àn case involving the killing of a person; homicide or murder case:这人有几条～。The man is involved in several murder cases.

命笔 mìngbǐ 〈书面〉set pen to paper; take up one's pen:欣然～ gladly set pen to paper; be delighted to start writing /～直书 write (what one has in mind, etc.) without hesitation /～抒怀 set pen to paper to express one's sentiments

命大 mìngdà of extremely good fortune; very lucky:他空难余生,真是～。He was extremely lucky to survive the air crash.

命定 mìngdìng 〈迷信〉determined by fate; predestined

命妇 mìngfù 〈旧语〉woman with a title or rank conferred by the emperor, usu. wife or mother of a senior official

命根 mìnggēn *also*"命根子"one's very life; lifeblood:这小孩是她奶奶的～。This child is her grandma's very life. /土地是农民的～。Land is the lifeline of the farmers.

命官 mìngguān 〈旧语〉ranking official

命驾 mìngjià 〈书面〉order one's carriage (and set out); set out:～西行 order one's carriage and set out westward /书到之日,即请～。When the letter arrives, be sure to set off immediately.

命蹇 mìngjiǎn 〈书面〉have a life beset with trouble; have an unhappy lot; born under an unlucky star

命理学 mìnglǐxué numerology

命令 mìnglìng ❶ command; order; instruct:连长～一班守仓库。The company commander ordered the first squad to guard the warehouse. /他讲话好像给人下～。He spoke as if he were giving orders. /师部接到～,部队进入临战状态。Following an instruction received by the division headquarters, the troops became combat-ready. ❷〈电子〉command:～方式 command mode /～控制程序 command control program

命令处理 mìnglìng chǔlǐ 〈计算机〉command processing

命令句 mìnglìngjù 〈语言〉imperative sentence

命令系统 mìnglìng xìtǒng 〈计算机〉command system

命令主义 mìnglìngzhǔyì commandism

命脉 mìngmài lifeline; lifeblood:经济～ economic lifelines /交通～ lifelines of transportation /水利是农业的～。Water is the lifeblood of agriculture.

命门 mìngmén 〈中医〉gate of vitality, area between the kidneys, generally regarded as the source of vitality, the function of which is to promote respiration, digestion, reproduction and the metabolism of body fluid

命名 mìngmíng give a name to; name:以孙中山～的公园 park named after Dr. Sun Yat-sen /这个医院被～为友谊医院。The hospital was named Friendship Hospital.

命名典礼 mìngmíng diǎnlǐ naming ceremony

命名法 mìngmíngfǎ nomenclature

命世 mìngshì 〈书面〉renowned:～之才 person renowned for his or her talents; well-known person of great talent

命数 mìngshù luck; fortune; fate

命数法 mìngshùfǎ 〈数学〉numeration

命题 mìngtí ❶ set a question or assign a topic:～作文 give a topic for composition (*or* essay-writing) /这次考试由他～。He will set the examination paper. ❷〈数学〉〈逻辑〉proposition:～演算 propositional calculus

命途 mìngtú one's life or experience:～多舛 suffer many setbacks in one's life

命相 mìngxiàng person's birthday in eight characters (indicating the year, month, day and hour of his birth) and the animal symbol of the year he was born in, on the basis of which a fortune-teller could foretell what would happen in the course of that person's life, including marriage, etc.

命意 mìngyì ❶ (of composition, painting, etc.) set a theme; fix a motif:写文章要在～布局上多下功夫。In learning to write, one should lay emphasis on the choice of theme and structural development. ❷ meaning; implication:这首诗～深刻。This poem has significant implications. *or* This poem is pregnant with meaning.

命运 mìngyùn ❶ fate; predestination:她相信～,常常烧香拜佛。She believed in fate and often worshipped Buddha by burning joss sticks. ❷〈比喻〉destiny; fate; lot:决定某人的～ decide (*or* determine) sb.'s fate /左右国家～的力量 forces that shape (*or* sway) the destiny of a nation /掌握自己的～ hold one's destiny in one's own hands; be master of one's own fate /个人的～与国家的前途密切相关。The destiny of the individual is closely associated with the prospects of his country.

命中 mìngzhòng score a hit; hit the target:～率 percentage of hits/～偏差 deviation of impact /他这一枪没有～靶心。That shot of his missed the bull's-eye.

miù

谬 miù false; wrong; erroneous; mistaken:大～不然 be entirely wrong; be grossly mistaken

谬爱 miù'ài 〈谦词〉undeserved kindness:多蒙～,感激莫名。I am extremely grateful to you for the kindness you have lavished on me.

谬传 miùchuán falsely circulated:此间～他已去世。It was falsely circulated here that he had passed away.

谬错 miùcuò falsehood; error; mistake

谬见 miùjiàn fallacious opinion; erroneous view:勇于服从真理,不固执～。One must accept the truth with courage and not stubbornly cling to one's own erroneous views.

谬奖 miùjiǎng 〈谦词〉misplaced compliment:承蒙～,不胜惶恐。I feel overwhelmed by the lavish compliments you have showered on me.

谬论 miùlùn wrong view; absurd theory; falsehood; fallacy:对这种～必须驳斥。Such a fallacy must be refuted.

谬说 miùshuō fallacy; absurdity

谬托 miùtuō pretend; dissemble:～知己 pretend to be sb.'s bosom friend

谬误 miùwù falsehood; error; mistake:真理与～的斗争 struggle between truth and falsehood /勘正书中的～ correct errors in the book

谬议 miùyì fallacy; false or absurd theory; falsehood:大发～ sport fallacies (*or* fallacious arguments) /狂妄的～ presumptuous fallacy /用事实驳斥～ refute fallacies with facts

谬悠 miùyōu 〈书面〉absurd; preposterous:～之说 absurd assertion; preposterous statement

谬种 miùzhǒng ❶ error; fallacy:～流传 dissemination of an error;

spread of a fallacy; circulation of absurdities ❷〈粗话〉bastard; son of a bitch

缪

miù see "纰缪" pīmiù

see also Miào; móu

缪斯 Miùsī also Miàosī Muse, any of the nine sister goddesses who presided over the arts and sciences in Greek mythology

mō

摸

mō ❶ feel; stroke; caress; touch: ～～刀刃 feel the edge of a knife /～～小孩的手 stroke a child's hand /勿～展品。Do not touch the exhibits. /这衣料～着很软。The material feels soft. ❷ grope; fumble: ～鱼 catch fish (as in a shallow pond) with one's hands /在口袋里～钱 grope for some money in one's pocket /从书包里～出钢笔 fish out a pen from one's satchel /你在那儿瞎～什么呢? What are you fumbling there for? ❸ try to find out; feel out; sound out: 下厂去～情况 go to a factory to find out how things stand /～不透他是个什么样的人 cannot make out what sort of person he is /你去～～他对这个问题有什么看法。Go and sound him out on this matter. ❹ grope in the dark: ～敌人岗哨 steal up to an enemy sentinel (usu. under cover of night) to catch him alive or kill him /洞里太黑,我们得～着走。The cave was so dark that we had to grope our way about. ❺ see "摹" mó

摸不着头脑 mōbuzháo tóunǎo also "摸不清头脑"; "摸不着门儿" be unable to make head or tail of sth.; be totally at a loss; be unable to understand what it is all about; be bewildered: ～的事儿 puzzling matter /越听越～。The longer you listen, the more confused you feel. /我听了半天也～。I have been listening for some time but still cannot make out what he is driving at. /我初来乍到,好多事情还～。As a newcomer, I found that there was a lot I did not understand.

摸底 mōdǐ know or get to know the actual situation: 这里的情况他都～。He has a clear picture of what the situation is like here. /我只问了几句就摸清了他的底。After asking him a couple of questions, I found out where he stood. /我亲自拜访他,想摸摸他的底。I paid a personal visit to him with the intention of sounding him out. /战斗中我们摸了一下敌军的底。In the fighting we took measure of the enemy forces. /他摸了对方在这个问题上的底。He managed to flush out the position of the other side on the issue. /我们和他们打了多年的交道,把他们的底摸熟了。We have had dealings with them for a long time and got to know what they are worth.

摸黑儿 mōhēir 〈口语〉grope in the dark: ～下楼 grope one's way downstairs in the dark /～赶路 hurry on in the dark night /起早～ from early in the morning till late at night

摸老虎屁股 mō lǎohǔ pìgu touch the backsides of a tiger; beard the lion in his den: 听说他批评不得,今天我可要～。I hear that no one dares to criticize him, but I am ready to beard the lion in his den today.

摸棱 mōléng see "模棱" móléng

摸量 mōliáng 〈口语〉reckon; think over: ～着办 handle matters by a rule of thumb /再三～ turn over in one's mind /我～事情不好办。I reckon it's a thorny problem.

摸门儿 mōménr 〈口语〉get the hang of sth., learn the ropes: 不～ have no idea (how to go about sth.) /我刚摸着一点门儿。I've learned only a bit of the knack.

摸明儿 mōmíngr also "摸亮儿"〈方言〉daybreak; dawn: 天～～就动身。We'll set off at dawn.

摸弄 mōnòng ❶ stroke (sb.'s hair, etc.): 他～着孩子的头发。He stroked the child's hair. ❷ tend; look after: 他从十几岁起就～牲口。He began to tend draught animals when he was in his teens. /他～拖拉机很在行。He is quite an expert with tractors.

摸哨 mōshào attack enemy sentinels under cover of darkness

摸索 mōsuo ❶ grope; feel about; fumble: 夜里～着前进 grope one's way forward at night ❷ try to find out (direction, method, experience, etc.): ～经验 try to gather experience; learn the ropes bit by bit

摸头 mōtóu 〈口语〉(usu. used in the negative) make out: 事情摸着了点头。We have got some inkling of the matter. /我摸不着头。I cannot make head or tail of the matter. /到现在我还不～。I'm still at a loss (or in the dark).

摸透 mōtòu get to know (sb. or sth.) well; have sth. at one's fingertips

摸瞎 mōxiā 〈口语〉grope one's way in the dark

摸营 mōyíng raid the enemy camp under cover of night; launch a surprise attack on the enemy camp at night

摸着石头过河 mōzhe shítou guò hé 〈俗语〉wade across the river by feeling out for stones — try to gain experience while actually doing the job: ～,走一步看一步。Cross the river by feeling for the stones — take one step and look around before taking another.

mó

磨

mó ❶ rub; wear: 脚～起了泡 get blisters on one's feet (from too much walking or by wearing tight shoes) /～出老茧的手 callused hands /鞋有点儿～脚。The shoe rubs a bit. /鞋底～薄了。The soles (of shoes) have worn thin. /绳子～断了。The rope snapped from the scraping. ❷ sharpen; whet; grind; polish: ～刀 sharpen a knife; grind a knife /～玻璃 polish glass /～墨 rub an ink stick against an inkstone; make ink for a writing brush ❸ torment; wear down: 病把他～得不成样子了。The illness wore him down to a mere shadow. /好事多～。Success is a triumph over continual difficulties. *or* The road to happiness is strewn with setbacks. *or* Love's course seldom runs smooth. ❹ keep nagging; plague; pester: 这孩子真～人! What a trying child! /他终于从妈妈那儿把东西～到了手。He kept on at Mom and finally got what he wanted. /他同他们～了半天,结果人家只是含糊地答应帮忙。He plagued them for hours, but all he could get was a vague promise to help. ❺ sink into oblivion; die out; erase; obliterate: 丰功伟绩,百世不～。His great contributions will be remembered by all successive generations. ❻ dawdle; waste (time); while away: 孩子们上学时间都～在路上了。The children dawdled all the way to school. /我们可～不起时间。We haven't got so much time to waste. *or* We can't afford the time.

see also mò

磨版 móbǎn 〈印刷〉(plate) grinding

磨版工人 móbǎn gōngrén 〈印刷〉grainer

磨版机 móbǎnjī 〈印刷〉graining machine

磨擦 mócā see "摩擦" mócā

磨蹭 móceng ❶ rub slightly; scrape: 他有点紧张,右脚在地上～着。He was a little nervous, his right foot rubbing gently against the ground. ❷ dawdle; loiter: 快点儿,别像老太太似的穷～啦! Hurry up. Don't loiter like an old lady. /你们磨磨蹭蹭的,连我都替你们着急。You are moving like a snail and making me impatient. ❸ nag; pester; plague: 一点事儿她总跟你～起来没完。She will never cease to nag at you even if it's just for something trivial.

磨缠 móchan nag; plague; pester: 这孩子老是～人。This child is always pestering people. /我还有急事,没工夫跟你～! I have urgent business to attend to and have no time to argue endlessly with you.

磨杵成针 móchǔ-chéngzhēn grind a pestle into a needle — work persistently to achieve a seemingly impossible task; perseverance means success: 要想得到真正的学问,必须有～的精神。A pestle can be ground into a needle and true knowledge comes from perseverance. see also "只要功夫深,铁杵磨成针" zhǐyào gōngfu shēn, tiěchǔ móchéng zhēn

磨穿铁砚 móchuān-tiěyàn grind a hole in an iron inkstone with an inkstick — study hard for years on end

磨床 móchuáng 〈机械〉grinding machine; grinder: 内圆～ internal grinder /外圆～ cylindrical grinder

磨刀不误砍柴工 módāo bù wù kǎnchái gōng sharpening the axe does not delay the work of a woodcutter — making preparations is not wasting time: ～嘛! 看起来是慢,实际是快。Deliberating is not delaying. It seems slower, but it is really faster.

磨刀霍霍 módāo-huòhuò sharpening one's sword; rattling one's sabre: 那个坏蛋～,正在寻找机会报复。Sabre-rattling, that thug is looking for an opportunity for revenge.

磨刀石 módāoshí grindstone; whetstone

磨电灯 módiàndēng see "摩电灯" módiàndēng

磨对 móduì 〈书面〉compare; contrast

磨对 módui also "磨兑"〈方言〉negotiate (prices, etc.); bargain: 这筐鲜鱼的价儿双方总～不下来。They failed to strike a bargain over the basket of fish.

磨革 mógé buffing: ～机 buffing machine

磨工 mógōng 〈机械〉❶ grinding work ❷ one who works a grinding machine; grinder:～车间 grindery

磨工夫 mó gōngfu take time; be time-consuming:跟他商量事真～。It always takes a lot of time to discuss anything with him.

磨光 móguāng ❶ polish:～玻璃 polished glass /～机 polishing machine; glazing machine ❷ wear off:外套的绒毛都～了。The nap of the overcoat is worn off.

磨耗 móhào wear and tear

磨合 móhé *also*"走合" zǒuhé (of machines) grind in; wear in:新汽车正式启用前必须有一段～时间。 A new car must go through a period of breaking in before use.

磨滑 móhuá 〈方言〉go slow; go through the motions; work perfunctorily; muddle through:他干活不叫苦,不～。He never complains of hardship, nor does he loaf on the job.

磨剂 mójì 〈机械〉grinding composition; grinding compound

磨具 mójù 〈机械〉grinding apparatus

磨勘 mókān ❶ (in the Tang and Song dynasties) review the records of officials to determine promotion or demotion ❷ (under the imperial examination system) review examination papers

磨口机 mókǒujī socket grinder

磨砺 mólì go through the mill; harden oneself; steel oneself; discipline oneself:艰苦的生活可以～心志。You can steel your will (*or* temper yourself) in hardship.

磨粒 mólì 〈机械〉abrasive particle

磨炼 móliàn *also*"磨练" put oneself through the mill; steel oneself; temper oneself:经过艰苦工作的～,他越发显得成熟、果断。Tempered under difficult circumstances, he became even more mature and resolute than before.

磨料 móliào abrasive; abradant

磨轮 mólún 〈机械〉abrasive wheel

磨面革 mómiàngé 〈皮革〉buffed leather

磨灭 mómiè wear away; rub out; efface; obliterate:不可～的功绩 ineffaceable feat (*or* achievement) /不可～的印象 indelible impression /年深月久,碑文已经～。The inscription was worn away in the course of centuries.

磨木机 mómùjī (wood) grinder:链式～ caterpillar grinder /袋式～ pocket grinder

磨难 mónàn *also*"魔难" mónàn tribulation; hardship; misery; suffering:久历～ go through prolonged trials and tribulations

磨漆画 móqīhuà 〈工美〉polished lacquer painting

磨砂玻璃 móshā bōli ground glass; frosted glass

磨砂灯泡 móshā dēngpào frosted bulb

磨舌头 mó shétou 〈方言〉waste one's breath; argue pointlessly:早知他这么不开窍,我何必去磨这半天舌头。Had I known he was such an idiot, I would not have wasted my breath.

磨石 móshí 〈机械〉grindstone

磨石子 móshízǐ 〈建筑〉terrazzo

磨蚀 móshí ❶ abrasion:～剂〈机械〉abrasive; abradant /岩石的～〈地质〉abrasion of rocks ❷ erode; blunt; wear off:岁月～了他当年的锐气。His dashing spirit has been blunted with the passage of time.

磨碎机 mósuìjī 〈机械〉grinding mill

磨损 mósǔn wear and tear; wear; abrasion:检查机器的～情况 check a machine for signs of wear /～程度 degree of wear (*or* abrasion) /～率 wear rate /～系数〈机械〉coefficient of wear /～留量〈机械〉wear allowance /这个齿轮已经～了。The gear is worn out.

磨头 mótóu 〈机械〉grinding head; grinding unit

磨洗 móxǐ (usu. used figuratively) rub and wash:古迹经受了岁月的～,仍异彩夺目。The ancient relics, though (they have been) subjected to the ravages of time, still impress people with a dazzling hue.

磨削 móxiāo 〈机械〉grinding:～裕量 grinding tolerance

磨屑 móxiè 〈机械〉abrasive dust

磨牙 móyá ❶ grind one's teeth (in sleep) ❷ 〈方言〉indulge in idle talk; argue pointlessly:没功夫和你们～。I've no time to thrash it out with you. /你俩别～了,干点正经事去。Stop quibbling, the pair of you, and get down to business. *or* You two, stop bickering and get to work. ❸ 〈生理〉molar

磨洋工 mó yánggōng loaf on the job; dawdle along; spin out one's work:快点! 别～了。Hurry up. No more waste of time.

磨折 mózhé cause physical or mental suffering; torment

磨砖对缝 mózhuān-duìfèng ground bricks and superb masonry:这堵山墙～,十分讲究。This gable is built with ground bricks and the masonry is superb.

磨钻 mózuàn 〈机械〉abrasive drilling

磨嘴 mózuǐ *also*"磨嘴皮子"〈方言〉talk a lot (often unnecessarily); argue pointlessly; jabber:他成天～,不干正事。He goes about everywhere, babbling all day but never caring to attend to serious business. /和经理磨了半天嘴,结果还是等于零。I did a hell of a lot of talking with the manager but it got me nowhere. /这事交给我去办,我不怕磨嘴皮子。Leave it to me. I'm not afraid of doing a bit of talking.

蘑 mó mushroom:鲜～ fresh mushroom /口～ a kind of dried mushroom (from Zhangjiakou 张家口)

蘑菇 mógu ❶ mushroom:采～ pick mushrooms; gather mushrooms ❷ pester; badger:她想去动物园,这两天老跟她妈～。She has been pestering her mother for a couple of days to take her to the zoo. ❸ dawdle; loiter; dillydally:再～车就开了。You'll miss the train if you are so slow going about your business.

蘑菇形天线 móguxíng tiānxiàn mushroom antenna

蘑菇云 móguyún mushroom cloud (produced by the explosion of an atomic or hydrogen bomb)

蘑菇战术 mógu zhànshù tactics of "wear and tear" (wearing the enemy down and then wiping them out)

蘑菇中毒 mógu zhòngdú mushroom poisoning; toadstool poisoning

劘 mó 〈书面〉cut; hack

摩[1] mó ❶ rub; scrape; touch:那马在树上～痒。The horse is scratching its back against the tree. /峻岭～天。The high mountains soar into the clouds. ❷ caress; stroke:按～ massage /轻轻～着孩子的脸 caress lovingly the child's face ❸ mull over; study; fathom:心～意揣 try to fathom; try to work out

摩[2] mó (short for 摩尔)〈物理〉mole

see also mā

摩擦 mócā *also*"磨擦" mócā ❶ rub:猫在她的腿上轻轻地～。The kitten is rubbing gently against her leg. ❷〈物理〉friction:滚动～ rolling friction /滑动～ sliding friction /～系数 frictional factor /～阻力 frictional resistance /～生电。Friction generates electricity. ❸ friction; clash:与人发生～ have a brush with sb. /这两派在闹～。The two factions are in for a clash. /在这个问题上他们之间有～。They have some friction over this problem.

摩擦电 mócādiàn 〈物理〉franklinic electricity; frictional electricity

摩擦鼓 mócāgǔ friction drum

摩擦离合器 mócā líhéqì friction clutch

摩擦力 mócālì 〈物理〉friction

摩擦抛光 mócā pāoguāng 〈机械〉burnishing

摩擦起爆器 mócā qǐbàoqì friction primer

摩擦音 mócāyīn 〈语言〉fricative

摩擦桩 mócāzhuāng 〈建筑〉friction pile

摩登 módēng modern; modish; fashionable:～女郎 fashionable girl /打扮得很～ dress in a fashionable way; be modishly dressed

摩电灯 módiàndēng *also*"磨电灯" módiàndēng dynamo-powered lamp (on a bicycle, etc.)

摩顶放踵 módǐng-fàngzhǒng wear oneself out from head to foot (to help others) — defy all hardships and be ready to lay down one's life to save the world:墨子兼爱,～利天下为之。The philosopher Mozi loved all equally. He would brave all difficulties for the benefit of the country.

摩尔 mó'ěr 〈化学〉mole, molecular weight of a substance expressed in grams:～数 mole number /～百分数 mole percent

摩尔多瓦 Mó'ěrduōwǎ (formerly Moldavia) Moldova

摩尔根 Mó'ěrgēn Thomas Hunt Morgan (1866-1945), American geneticist and winner of the Nobel Prize for 1933:～主义 Morganism

摩尔浓度 Mó'ěr nóngdù 〈化学〉M (concentration of one litre of solution); molar or mol concentration; molarity

摩菲定律 Mófēi dìnglǜ 〈经济〉Murphy's Law

摩抚 mófǔ *also*"抚摩" stroke

摩根 Mógēn John Pierpont Morgan (1837-1913), American fi-

nancier, industrialist and one of the leading art collectors
摩加迪沙 Mójiādíshā Mogadishu, capital of Somalia
摩肩击毂 mójiān-jīgǔ *also* "肩摩毂击" people jostling and carriages bumping into each other — bustling activity
摩肩接踵 mójiān-jiēzhǒng jostle each other in a crowd; rub elbows: 看热闹的人～。There was a jostling crowd of onlookers. *or* There were crowds of people watching the fun.
摩羯 mójié 〈书面〉 male goat
摩羯座 Mójiézuò 〈天文〉 Capricorn; Capricornus
see also "黄道十二宫" huángdào shí'èrgōng
摩厉以须 mólìyǐxū grind one's weapon sharp in preparation for combat — be ready for action
摩洛哥 Móluògē Morocco: ～人 Moroccan
摩门教 Móménjiào Mormonism, a millenary religion founded in New York (1830) by Joseph Smith (1805-1844)
摩门经 Móménjīng 〈宗教〉 Book of Mormon
摩纳哥 Mónàgē Monaco: ～人 Monacan
摩尼教 Móníjiào Manichaeism, a religious system with Christian, gnostic and pagan elements, founded in Persia in the 3rd century by Manes and spread widely in Europe and Asia
see also "明教" Míngjiào
摩弄 mónòng ❶ stroke ❷ handle
摩拳擦掌 móquán-cāzhǎng rub one's hands and clench one's fists; rub one's fists and palms — be ready for a fight: 他卷起袖子～,好像要和谁打架似的。He rolled up his sleeves and clenched his fists as if itching for a fight.
摩氏硬度表 Móshì yìngdùbiǎo 〈冶金〉 Mohs' scale (after Frederich Mohs)
摩丝 mósī styling mousse; mousse
摩挲 mósuō stroke; caress: 他爱不释手地～着我们送给他的一件玉器。With great fondness, he caressed one of the jade pieces we gave him.
see also māsa
摩天 mótiān skyscraping: ～岭 towering mountain ridge / ～大楼 skyscraper; highrise (building)
摩托 mótuō (transliteration) motor
摩托车 mótuōchē motorcycle; motorbike; motor bicycle
摩托船 mótuōchuán motorboat
摩托化 mótuōhuà 〈机械〉 motorization
摩托化部队 mótuōhuà bùduì motorized troops
摩托艇 mótuōtǐng 〈船舶〉 motor dory; motorboat
摩西 Móxī Moses, Hebrew patriarch who was born in Egypt and led the Jews across the desert away from their bondage
摩崖 móyá engravings on a cliff

麿 mó *see* "萝藦" luómó

魔 mó ❶ evil spirit; demon; fiend; devil: 恶～ demon; devil / 病～ serious illness / 走火入～ be possessed by the Devil / 打扑克着了～ be addicted to playing cards; be crazy about playing cards ❷ magic; occult; mystic: ～毯 magic carpet
魔道 módào ❶〈宗教〉 domain of the devil ❷ black magic; witchcraft; sorcery ❸ evil ways; vice
魔法 mófǎ black magic; witchcraft; sorcery
魔方 mófāng Rubic's cube
魔怪 móguài demons and monsters; fiends; 〈比喻〉 evildoers or evil force: 百年～舞翩跹。For a century, demons and monsters whirled in a wild dance.
魔鬼 móguǐ devil; demon; monster: 他们是一伙杀人不眨眼的～。They are trigger-happy (*or* blood-thirsty) monsters.
魔棍 mógùn magic wand; magic stick
魔君 mójūn 〈比喻〉 fierce and brutal villain
魔窟 mókū den of monsters; sink of iniquity
魔力 mólì magic power; magic; charm: 这幅画具有巨大的艺术～。This painting has great artistic charm for us.
魔魔道道 mómo-dāodāo 〈方言〉 act as if one were mentally deranged; behave like a lunatic: 他整天～地自言自语。All day long he keeps talking to himself like a lunatic.
魔难 mónàn *see* "磨难" mónàn
魔手 móshǒu *see* "魔掌"
魔术 móshù *also* "幻术" huànshù; "戏法" xìfǎ magic; conjury; sleight of hand: 变～ do magic tricks / 表演～ perform magic / ～师 magician
魔头 mótóu ❶ devil; demon; evil spirit ❷ 〈方言〉 wizard; sorcerer
魔王 mówáng ❶ prince of the demons; Devil ❷ tyrant; despot; fiend
魔影 móyǐng shadow of a demon or monster; spectre of evil force: 战争的～时时威胁着那个国家。The spectre of war is constantly haunting that country.
魔芋 móyù *also* "蒟蒻" jǔruò 〈植物〉 *Amorphophallus rivieri*
魔掌 mózhǎng devil's clutches; evil hands: 他们终于逃出了恐怖分子的～。They finally succeeded in escaping from the clutches of the terrorists.
魔杖 mózhàng magic wand
魔障 mózhàng (originally a Buddhist term, from Sanskrit *Mara*) obstacles or temptations set by devils
魔爪 mózhǎo devil's claws; talons; tentacles; clutches: 斩断敌人的～ cut off the claws of the enemy / 伸出～ extend one's tentacles
魔怔 mózheng 〈口语〉 "devil's craze" — being out of one's mind or obsessed: 她像是得了～,一天到晚总是絮叨她失去的孩子。She was jabbering about her lost son all day as if possessed by a demon. / 他这些日子不知犯了什么～,一天到晚精神恍惚。God knows what has come over him these days. He moves about as if in a trance.

麽 mó *see* "幺麽" yāomó

嬷 mó (formally pronounced as mā)
see also mā
嬷嬷 mómo 〈方言〉 ❶ form of address for an elderly woman ❷ wet nurse: 他是由～带大的。He was brought up by his wet nurse.

无(無) mó *see* "南无" nāmó
see also wú

谟 mó 〈书面〉 plan: 宏～ grand plan; great project

模 mó ❶ pattern; standard: 楷～ model; paragon ❷ imitate: *see* "～仿"; "～拟" ❸ model: 劳～ model worker ❹ 〈数学〉 modulo; module
see also mú
模本 móběn model of calligraphy or painting
模范 mófàn model; example: ～学校 model school / ～事迹 exemplary deeds / 劳动～ model worker / 服务行业的～ advanced worker in the service trades / 起～作用 set an example; play an exemplary role / ～地执行自己的职责 carry out one's duties in an exemplary way
模仿 mófǎng *also* "摹仿" mófǎng imitate; model on; mimic; copy: ～小孩的声音 mimic a child's voice / 写字、画画,都是从～开始的。Writing and painting begin with imitation. / 机器人能～人的动作。Robots can imitate man's actions. / 这种电视机是～一种新产品制造的。The TV set is modelled on a new brand.
模光纤 móguāngxiān 〈通信〉 mode fibre
模胡 móhu *see* "模糊"
模糊 móhu *also* "模胡" ❶ blurred; indistinct; hazy; vague; fuzzy: ～的远山 hazy mountains in the distance / 图像～ blurred (*or* fuzzy) picture / 字迹～ blurred (*or* faded) writing / 血肉～ badly mauled / 意思～ vague (*or* ambiguous) meaning / 认识～ have confused ideas / 模模糊糊地记得 remember dimly; have a vague memory ❷ blur; film: 决不能～是非界限。Never should we obscure (*or* blur) the distinction between right and wrong. / 屋里的热气～了他的镜片。His glasses became misty with the steam in the room. / 泪水～了她的眼睛。Her eyes filmed over (*or* became blurred) with tears.
模糊理论 móhu lǐlùn 〈数学〉 fuzzy theory
模糊逻辑 móhu luóji fuzzy logic
模糊数学 móhu shùxué 〈数学〉 fuzzy mathematics
模楷 mókǎi *also* "楷模" model; pattern: 天下～ model for everybody
模块 mókuài 〈电子〉 module: ～电路 modular circuit / ～化 modularity / ～结构 modular structure
模棱 móléng (of attitude, opinion, etc.) vague; indistinct
模棱两可 móléng-liǎngkě equivocal; ambivalent; ambiguous: 对待原则问题,决不能～。One should never prevaricate on matters of principle.

M

模拟 mónǐ also"摹拟"mónǐ ❶ imitate; simulate:～之作 imitation /～考试 simulated examination; mock examination ❷ virtual reality:～技术 virtual reality technology
模拟飞行 mónǐ fēixíng 〈军事〉simulated flight
模拟火箭 mónǐ huǒjiàn simulated rocket
模拟计算机 mónǐ jìsuànjī analogue computer
模拟加法器 mónǐ jiāfǎqì analogue adder
模拟器 mónǐqì 〈电子〉simulator
模拟试验 mónǐ shìyàn simulated test
模拟数据 mónǐ shùjù analogue data
模拟数据转换器 mónǐ shùjù zhuǎnhuànqì analogue-digital converter
模拟通信 mónǐ tōngxìn analogue communication
模拟像 mónǐxiàng effigy:烧毁某人的～ burn sb. in effigy
模拟原子爆炸 mónǐ yuánzǐ bàozhà atomic blast simulation
模拟装置 mónǐ zhuāngzhì analogue device
模式 móshì pattern; model:～化 patterning /要解放思想,必须打破各种陈旧的～。To liberate our thinking, it is necessary to break down antiquated patterns. /要从实际出发,不能盲目照搬别国的～。One should proceed from the actual circumstances instead of copying any foreign pattern blindly.
模式识别 móshì shíbié 〈自控〉pattern recognition
模式图 móshìtú ideograph
模数 móshù also"模量"〈物理〉modulus:弹性～ modulus of elasticity
模态 mótài 〈逻辑〉modality:～逻辑 modal logic
模特儿 mótèr ❶〈美术〉model ❷ model; dummy:时装～ dress model; fashion model /时装表演现在有中老年～。Nowadays we find elderly models in fashion shows.
模效 móxiào see"摹效"móxiào
模写 móxiě see"摹写"móxiě
模型 móxíng ❶ model:飞机～ model aircraft /结构～ model structure /～展品 scale model; replica ❷ mould; matrix; pattern:～板 mould plate
模压 móyā die stamping; moulding; mould pressing:～机 moulding press; mould press; block press /～底皮鞋 leather shoes with moulded-on rubber soles

摹

mó copy; trace:描～ depict; portray; delineate /临～ copy (a model of calligraphy or painting)
摹本 móběn album of artistic or calligraphic reproduction:许多名画都有～。Many famous drawings are produced in facsimile.
摹仿 mófǎng see"模仿"mófǎng
摹绘 móhuì 〈书面〉imitate or copy a model of painting; reproduce; portray:这幅画～了海上日出的奇景。The painting portrays the spectacle of sunrise on the sea.
摹刻 mókè ❶ carve a reproduction of an inscription or painting ❷ carved reproduction of an inscription or painting
摹拟 mónǐ also"模拟"mónǐ imitate; simulate
摹效 móxiào also"模效"móxiào imitate; copy; model oneself on
摹写 móxiě also"模写"móxiě ❶ copy; imitate:照着字帖～ imitate a copybook of calligraphy; learn calligraphy by imitating a copybook ❷ depict; describe; portray:～人物的特征和性格 describe the features and temperament of a character
摹印 móyìn ❶ copy and print ❷ style of characters or lettering used on (imperial) seals in ancient times
摹状 mózhuàng depict; describe; portray

膜

mó ❶ membrane:耳～ tympanic membrane /横膈～ diaphragm ❷ film; thin coating:笛～ film for *dizi*, Chinese bamboo flute /塑料薄～ plastic film /牛奶的表面结了一层～。A thin cream formed on the surface of the milk.
膜拜 móbài prostrate oneself in worship; worship:低首～ lower one's head in worship /顶礼～ prostrate oneself in worship; pay homage to /～金钱 worship money
膜翅目 móchìmù 〈动物〉*Hymenoptera*
膜电极 módiànjí membrane electrode
膜电流 módiànliú membrane current
膜电势 módiànshì membrane potential
膜电阻 módiànzǔ film resistance
膜法 mófǎ 〈环保〉membrane method
膜集成电路 mójíchéng diànlù 〈电子〉film integrated circuit
膜滤器 mólǜqì 〈化工〉membrane filter
膜鸣乐器 mómíng yuèqì membranophone
膜片 mópiàn (as in a telephone or microphone) diaphragm

馍(饝、䭔)

mó 〈方言〉steamed bun; steamed bread:蒸～ steamed bun /白面～ steamed wheat flour bread

mǒ

抹

mǒ ❶ smear; apply; put on:～肥皂 smear with soap /～红药水 apply mercurochrome /～点防晒霜 put on some sunscreen cream /薄薄地～上一层黄油 spread a thin layer of butter ❷ wipe; clean off:～汗 wipe off sweat /别用手～嘴,用纸巾。Don't wipe your mouth with your hand. Use a paper napkin. /说着说着她就～开眼泪了。As she went on she began to weep. ❸ cross out; delete; erase:用铅笔在原稿上～去一段 cross out a paragraph from the original writing with a pencil /～去零头 delete the fractional amount /～掉磁带上的歌曲 erase songs from a tape /这段不光彩的历史,他想～也～不掉。He could not erase this shameful experience of his, no matter how he wished to. ❹〈量词〉*used of cloud, etc.*:一～浮云 a floating cloud
see also mā; mò
抹鼻子 mǒ bízi 〈方言〉weep; snivel:她动不动就～。She is a cry-baby.
抹脖子 mǒ bózi 〈口语〉cut one's own throat; commit suicide:她实在想不开,就抹了脖子。She took things so hard that she cut her own throat.
抹彩 mǒcǎi (of Beijing opera) do facial make-up
抹刀 mǒdāo also"抹子"trowel (for plastering)
抹粉 mǒfěn apply face powder — prettify; whitewash:他不但不承认错误,反而替自己～。He not only refused to admit his mistake but even tried to whitewash himself.
抹黑 mǒhēi blacken (sb.'s name); throw mud at; bring disgrace on; discredit:往别人脸上～ sling mud at other people; try to discredit (*or* smear) others /他这样做给祖国抹了黑。What he did brought disgrace on the motherland.
抹灰 mǒhuī ❶〈建筑〉rendering; plastering:～工 plasterer ❷〈比喻〉smear; defame; vilify:决不能给咱们工厂～。We mustn't do anything to discredit our factory.
抹零 mǒlíng not count the small change (in a payment); delete the fractional amount
抹杀 mǒshā also"抹煞"blot out; obliterate; cancel; write off:一笔～ write off at one stroke /这个事实谁也～不了。There is no gainsaying this fact. /其历史功绩,不容～。His past merits cannot be blotted out.
抹身 mǒshēn 〈方言〉rub oneself down with a wet towel; take a sponge bath
see also mòshēn
抹拭 mǒshì wipe; clean; cleanse
抹稀泥 mǒ xīní also"和稀泥"huò xīní 〈方言〉try to mediate differences at the sacrifice of principle; try to paper over the cracks; try to smooth things over; blur the line between right and wrong:他这个人生性就爱～。He has a natural inclination to gloss things over.
抹香鲸 mǒxiāngjīng sperm whale
抹消 mǒxiāo eliminate; remove; strike out; write off:这点儿疑惑从他心里～了。These misgivings were removed from his mind.
抹一鼻子灰 mǒ yī bízi huī also"碰一鼻子灰"pèng yī bízi huī have one's nose rubbed in the dust; suffer a snub; meet with a rebuff; be sent off with a flea in one's ear:他自告奋勇要去采买,却～。He volunteered his service to do the shopping, but he got a snub. /他怕～,话到了嘴边又吞了下去。For fear of a rebuff, he held back when he was about to speak out.
抹音 mǒyīn 〈电子〉erasure:～头 erase head; erasing head; eraser
抹子 mǒzi 〈建筑〉trowel

mò

磨

mò ❶ mill; millstones:一盘～ a pair of millstones; a

handmill /电～ electric mill /石～ millstone /推～ work a handmill (*or* a pair of millstones) ❷ grind; mill:把麦子～成面粉 grind wheat into flour /～粮食 mill grain ❸ turn round:这小胡同里不能～车。The alley is too narrow for a car to turn round.

see also mó

磨不开 mòbukāi *also* "抹不开" mòbukāi ❶ feel embarrassed; hesitate (for fear of losing face, impairing personal relations or hurting feelings):我本不愿把这本书借给他,可面子上又～。I did not want to lend him the book, but I felt embarrassed to tell him so. /她想认错又～脸。She felt too ashamed to admit her mistake, though she wanted to. /公事公办,有什么～的? Business is business, and face saving isn't a consideration, is it? ❷〈方言〉be unable to straighten out one's thinking; not know what to do:我有了～的事,就找他去商量。Whenever I've something I can't straighten out, I turn to him for help.

磨不住 mòbuzhù feel ashamed or embarrassed; be ill at ease:这事你得跟他当面谈,没什么～的。You'll have to talk this over with him personally. There's no reason why you should feel put out.

磨道 mòdào path round the nether millstone:～的驴,听喝 allow oneself to be ordered about like a donkey working at the mill

磨叨 mòdao ❶〈口语〉talk on and on; chatter away; babble on:妈妈～起来,没完没结。Whenever Mom started (*or* began) to talk, she would drag on for God knows how long. ❷〈方言〉talk;gossip:你们在～谁? Who are you folks talking about?

磨得开 mòdekāi *also* "抹得开" mòdekāi ❶ be at ease; not feel embarrassed or ashamed:你当面挖苦人,人家脸上～吗? Wouldn't he be terribly embarrassed if you speak sarcastically to his face? ❷ have the nerve:她请客你不去,你～吗? Do you really have the nerve to turn down her invitation? ❸〈方言〉be convinced; come round; understand; work out:这个理我～,您就放心吧! Don't worry. I can well see the reason.

磨豆腐 mò dòufu ❶ grind soya beans to make bean curd ❷〈方言〉say sth. repeatedly:别紧跟这儿～。Stop talking about it over and over again.

磨烦 mòfan ❶ nag;plague;pester:这孩子常常～他姐姐给他讲故事。The child often pestered his sister to tell him stories. ❷ dawdle; loiter; delay:不必～了,说办就办吧。Let's delay no more and get the work done straight away.

磨坊 mòfáng *also* "磨房" mill

磨粉机 mòfěnjī 〈机械〉pulverizer

磨倌 mòguān 〈旧语〉miller

磨面机 mòmiànjī flour-milling machine

磨盘 mòpán millstones, particularly the nether millstone

磨棚 mòpéng grinding shed; mill shed

磨扇 mòshàn millstone(s)

磨子 mòzi 〈方言〉mill; flour-milling machine:～雷 rolling (*or* rumbling) thunder; rumble of thunder

糖

mò a kind of farm tool used to level land

末[1]

mò ❶ point; tip; end:刀锥之～ point of a knife or an awl /秋毫之～ tip of an animal's autumn hair — minutest tittle ❷ nonessentials; trifles; minor details:舍本逐～ attend to trifles to the neglect of essentials; fail to see the wood for the trees /本～倒置 put trifles before essentials; put the cart before the horse ❸ end; last; bottom:月～ end of a month /周～ weekend /～着儿〈口语〉last measure; last trick; last resort /他现在在全班可数老～了。He is now at the very bottom of the class. ❹ powder; dust:粉～ powder /药～ (medicinal) powder /胡椒～ pepper powder /茶叶～ tea dust /锯～ sawdust ❺ (often used in a self-derogatory way) humble; petty; worthless:～将愿往。I (a humble general) would like to go and carry out this task.

末[2]

mò 〈戏曲〉role of middle-aged man

末班车 mòbānchē ❶ *also* "末车" last bus or train ❷〈口语〉last chance or turn:他退休前搭上了那次调资的～。He was lucky enough to get a pay rise before retirement.

末代 mòdài last reign (of a dynasty); last generation:～子孙 last generation of a dynasty or an aristocratic family; remnants of an ancient regime /～皇帝 last emperor (of a dynasty)

末端 mòduān end; bottom:那篇文章登在报纸的～。That article was carried at the end of the newspaper.

末端基因 mòduān jīyīn terminal gene

末端效应 mòduān xiàoyìng end or tip effect

末伏 mòfú *also* "终伏" zhōngfú;"三伏" sānfú ❶ last of the three ten-day periods of the hot season ❷ first day of the last period of the hot season

末官 mòguān ❶ petty official; low official ❷〈谦词〉this official; I

末后 mòhòu 〈口语〉finally; last:现在你满不在乎,～你会后悔的。You seem to be indifferent, but later you'll be sorry.

末技 mòjì petty skill; insignificant skill; skill of no high order

末减 mòjiǎn 〈书面〉leniently convict sb.; lighten a penalty

末节 mòjié minor details; trifles; nonessentials:那些细枝～的事可先不去管它。We can leave the minor details till later.

末了 mòliǎo *also* "末末了儿"〈口语〉last; finally; eventually; in the end:最初,他不愿意管这些事,但～他还是同意为双方调解。At first, he did not want to have anything to do with the matter, but finally he agreed to mediate between the two sides.

末流 mòliú ❶ (of art and literature) school of thought that has lost its original colouring ❷ inferior; of the lowest quality; shoddy; poor:～演员 poor actor

末路 mòlù blind alley; dead end; impasse:看来,他们已日薄西山,穷途～了。It seems that they have reached a dead end like the sun setting in the west.

末民 mòmín 〈旧语〉lower orders — labourers and traders

末年 mònián (as of a dynasty or reign) last years:明朝～ last years of the Ming Dynasty

末期 mòqī last phase; final period; last stage:第二次世界大战～ final phase of World War II /70年代～ late seventies

末日 mòrì ❶〈宗教〉Doomsday; Day of Judgement; Judgement Day:～审判 Last Judgement ❷ end; doom:王朝～ end of a dynasty

末日机 mòrìjī *also* "末日武器" doomsday machine; D-machine (an assumed starter to set off nuclear weapons)

末梢 mòshāo tip; end:树枝的～ tip of a twig /五月～ end of May

末梢神经 mòshāo shénjīng nerve end

末世 mòshì last phase (of an age); *fin de siècle*

末俗 mòsú 〈旧语〉bad moral influence or corrupt morals(shaped in troubled times)

末尾 mòwěi end:书的～ end of the book /故事的～ end of the story; ending of the story /来信～有一句话,叫人心里很不安。There is a disquieting remark at the end of the letter.

末席 mòxí end seat

末屑 mòxiè dust; fine pieces; crumb:面包～ breadcrumbs

末学 mòxué 〈书面〉❶ (have) superficial knowledge; limited learning; poor scholarship:～肤受 have meagre knowledge ❷〈谦词〉your humble student:～小生 your humble student

末药 mòyào *also* "没药" mòyào myrrh

末叶 mòyè last years (of a century or dynasty):清朝～ last years of the Qing Dynasty /18 世纪～ end of the 18th century

末业 mòyè 〈旧语〉lower trades — business, handicraft, industry and commerce

末艺 mòyì petty skill; insignificant skill; skill of no high order

末议 mòyì 〈书面〉〈谦词〉my one man's view; personally, I think (feel, see, etc.); to my mind

末造 mòzào 〈书面〉declining dynasty; dynasty on the decline; last phase of an age; *fin de siècle*

末子 mòzi powder; dust:煤～ coal dust

末座 mòzuò seat the end of a table or row — seat for an inferior:敬陪～。I would be happy to take my seat at the end of the table. *or* I would accept the pleasure of your invitation.

沫

mò ❶ foam; froth:肥皂～儿 soap suds; lather /啤酒～ froth on beer; head on a glass of beer /口流白～ foam at the mouth; froth at the mouth /这种洗衣粉不太起～。This kind of washing powder doesn't produce much foam. ❷〈书面〉saliva; spittle:相濡以～ help each other in adversity

沫子 mòzi foam; froth; scum:把汤上面的～撇掉 skim off the scum on a soup

茉

mò

茉莉 mòli 〈植物〉jasmine:～花茶 jasmine tea

靺 mò

靺鞨 Mòhé ethnic group living in northeast China in ancient times

抹 mò

❶ daub; plaster: ～墙 plaster a wall ❷ skirt; bypass: 拐弯～角 talk in a roundabout way; beat about the bush
see also mā; mǒ

抹不开 mòbukāi *see* "磨不开" mòbukāi
抹得开 mòdekāi *see* "磨得开" mòdekāi
抹额 mò'é *also* "抹头" 〈旧语〉 tiara
抹面 mòmiàn 〈建筑〉 face (a wall, etc.) with plaster or cement
抹身 mòshēn turn; turn round: ～往回走。He turned round and walked back.
see also mǒshēn
抹头 mòtóu ❶ turn; turn round: ～就走。He turned and left. ❷ *see* "抹额"
抹弯 mòwān 〈方言〉 turn a corner; turn round; beat about the bush: 说话可不要～，有啥困难只管说。Don't beat about the bush. Let me know if you have any difficulty. /经他一说，我脑子里就抹过弯儿来了。After listening to what he said, I straightened out my ideas.
抹胸 mòxiōng undergarment covering the chest and abdomen; 〈旧语〉 woman's tight vest for pressing down and concealing breasts

眜 mò

〈书面〉 ❶ poor eye sight; squint eyes ❷ disregard dangers, unfriendly environment, etc.; take risks: ～险登崖 climb a cliff in total disregard of the risks involved

秣 mò

❶ fodder; forage: 粮～ grain and fodder; (army) rations and forage ❷ feed (animals)

秣马厉兵 mòmǎ-lìbīng *also* "厉兵秣马" feed the horses and sharpen the weapons — prepare for battle: ～以待时机 get everything ready and bide one's time

莫 mò

❶ 〈书面〉 no one; none; nothing: ～要于此。There is nothing more important than this. ❷ not; no: 望尘～及 fall far behind; be unequal to /一筹～展 be at one's wit's end; be at the end of one's tether /爱～能助 be desirous but unable to help; be willing but powerless to help /概～能外 admit of no exception ❸ don't: 请～见怪。I hope you'll not mind (take no offence). /～哭。Don't cry. /闲人～入。No admittance except on business. ❹ *indicating speculation or questioning*: *see* "～非" ❺ (Mò) a surname

莫比尔公司 Mòbǐ'ěr Gōngsī *also* "飞马石油公司" Fēimǎ Shíyóu Gōngsī (US) Mobil Corporation
莫不 mòbù there is no one who doesn't or isn't; everybody does or is: ～喜笑颜开。All faces lit up with pleasure. /～拍手称快。Everybody was clapping and cheering.
莫不是 mòbùshì *see* "莫非"
莫测高深 mòcè-gāoshēn unable to fathom; unfathomable: 刘先生的演说有点玄妙，叫我～。Mr. Liu's esoteric speech rather baffled me.
莫愁湖 Mòchóuhú Sorrow-Free Lake (in Nanjing)
莫此为甚 mòcǐwéishèn it couldn't be worse; a more flagrant instance has yet to be found: 残暴狠毒，～。They were brutal and vicious to the extreme.
莫大 mòdà greatest; extreme; utmost: ～的幸福 greatest happiness /～的侮辱 gross insult /～的损失 colossal loss
莫尔斯 Mò'ěrsī Samuel Finley Breese Morse (1791-1872), American painter and pioneer in the use of electric telegraph
莫尔斯电码 Mò'ěrsī diànmǎ Morse code
莫尔兹比港 Mò'ěrzībǐgǎng Port Moresby, capital of Papua New Guinea
莫非 mòfēi is it possible that...; can it be possible that...: 今天她没来，～又病了? She is absent today. Is she ill again? /你自己不干，～要我替你干不成? You are sitting on the sidelines. Is it that you expect me to attend to it? /～他生我的气了? Is it possible that he is angry with me?
莫过于 mòguòyú nothing is more... than: 他最大的兴趣～工作。His greatest interest is in work, and nothing else.
莫霍界面 Mòhuò jièmiàn *also* "莫霍面" 〈地质〉 Moho discontinuity; Moho
莫可名状 mòkě-míngzhuàng indescribable; beyond description: 胜利的喜悦，～。The joy over the victory was beyond words.
莫可指数 mòkě-zhǐshǔ countless; innumerable: 来往车辆～。There is an endless stream of traffic.
莫里哀 Mòlǐ'āi Jean Baptiste Poquelin Molière (1622-1673), French dramatist
莫罗尼 Mòluóní Moroni, capital of the Comoros Islands
莫洛托夫 Mòluòtuōfū Vyacheslav Mikhaylovich Molotov (1890-1986), Russian statesman and diplomat: ～汽油弹 Molotov cocktail
莫名 mòmíng indescribable; inexpressible: ～所以 find it difficult to explain /突然感到一种～的紧张。He suddenly felt inexplicably nervous (*or* edgy). /感谢～。I'm deeply grateful.
莫名其妙 mòmíng-qímiào *also* "莫明其妙" ❶ be unable to make head or tail (of sth.); be puzzled: 他匆匆离开上海也不跟朋友打个招呼，真弄得我～。I was baffled at his sudden departure from Shanghai without even letting his friends know. /大家搞不清他这话是什么意思，都～地望着他。Nobody could make out what he meant, so they all looked at him in perplexity. ❷ without rhyme or reason; for no apparent reason; unaccountable; inexplicable: 他～地发起脾气。Quite unaccountably he flew into a rage. /我常常～地受到呵斥和挑剔。I was often berated and picked on for no apparent reason.
莫逆 mònì intimate; very friendly
莫逆之交 mònìzhījiāo bosom or sworn friends
莫泊桑 Mòpōsāng Guy de Maupassant (1850-1893), French short-story writer and novelist
莫如 mòrú *also* "莫若" would be better; might as well: 这件事与其让他做，～我自己做。It would be better for me to attend to the matter myself than to entrust it to him. /在这儿闲着没事，～到湖边去散散步。For want of anything to do, we might as well take a walk by the lake.
莫桑比克 Mòsāngbǐkè Mozambique: ～人 Mozambican
莫氏黏度计 Mòshì niándùjì 〈化工〉 Mooney viscosimeter
莫氏硬度 Mòshì yìngdù Mohs hardness
莫氏硬度表 Mòshì yìngdùbiǎo Mohs' scale (invented by Friedrich Mohs, 1773-1839)
莫斯科 Mòsīkē Moscow, capital of the Russian Federation
莫斯科运河 Mòsīkē Yùnhé Moscow Canal
莫卧尔帝国 Mòwò'ěr Dìguó Mogul Empire (1526-1857), Moslem kingdom on the Indian peninsula
莫信直中直，须防人不仁 mò xìn zhí zhōng zhí, xū fáng rén bù rén Believe not that in straightforwardness there is only honesty. Beware, rather, that evil lurks behind the guise of virtue.
莫须有 mòxūyǒu groundless; unwarranted; imaginary; trumped-up; fabricated: 以～的罪名把他们囚禁起来。They were put in prison on trumped-up charges.
莫邪 mòyé *see* "镆铘" mòyé
莫余毒也 mòyúdúyě nobody can harm me — be arrogant
莫扎特 Mòzātè Wolfgang Amadeus Mozart (1756-1791), Austrian composer
莫衷一是 mòzhōngyīshì unable to agree or decide which is right; without unanimous conclusion; not know whom to follow: 这本古典名著的作者，众说纷纭，～。No conclusion could be drawn about the differing views as to who was the author of this classical writing.

漠 mò

❶ desert: 大～ vast expanse of desert /～北 〈古语〉 north of the Gobi desert (what is now the Republic of Mongolia) ❷ indifferent; unconcerned: 淡～ indifferent; apathetic

漠不关心 mòbùguānxīn indifferent; unconcerned: 对人民的福祉岂能～! How can we remain indifferent to the welfare (*or* well-being) of the people?
漠漠 mòmò ❶ misty; foggy: 远处烟雾～。There were smoky mists in the distance. ❷ vast and silent: 平湖～ wide and still lake /黄沙～ boundless stretch of yellow sand /～荒原 vast expanse of wasteland
漠然 mòrán indifferent; apathetic: 处之～ remain indifferent (towards sth.) /神情～ look apathetic
漠视 mòshì treat with indifference; overlook; ignore: ～一切 treat everything with unconcern /不能～群众的利益。The interests of the people cannot be ignored.

寞 mò

lonely; solitary; deserted: 落～ lonely; desolate

瘼 mò

〈书面〉 disease; hardship: 民～ sufferings of the peo-

M

ple

貘(獏) mò 〈动物〉tapir

镆 mò

镆铘 mòyé also "莫邪" mòyé name of a famous ancient double-edged sword

蓦 mò suddenly

蓦地 mòdì all of a sudden; suddenly; abruptly; unexpectedly:傍晚～刮起了漫天风沙。Towards evening, suddenly a strong wind blew, raising clouds of dust. /他～站起来。He stood up abruptly. /汽车～来了个急刹车,几个乘客差点儿摔倒。Several passengers almost fell when the driver put on the emergency brake.

蓦然 mòrán suddenly;abruptly:～回首 abruptly turn round /～泪下 burst into tears /我～想起我曾答应去看他的。It suddenly occurred to me that I had promised to go and see him.

万 mò

see also wàn

万俟 Mòqí a surname

貊(貉) Mò Mo, an ethnic group living in northeast China in ancient times

陌 mò ❶ footpath between fields (running east and west):阡～ paths in the fields ❷ road:～头杨柳 roadside willows

陌路 mòlù also "陌路人"〈书面〉stranger:视同～ treat like a stranger

陌生 mòshēng strange; foreign; unfamiliar:～人 stranger /～的城市 unfamiliar city /感到～ feel like a stranger /这活对我来说并不～。This job is nothing new for me. /我对这种事很～。I know little about such things.

陌头 mòtóu 〈书面〉roadside:忽见～杨柳色,悔教夫婿觅封侯。Suddenly she sees the colour of willows along the road, And regrets urging her husband to go far away and seek renown.

墨[1] mò ❶ Chinese ink; ink stick:文房四宝:笔～纸砚 writing brush, inkstick, paper and inkstone — the four treasures of Chinese stationery /一锭～ an ingot-shaped tablet of Chinese ink /研～ rub an inkstick on an inkstone ❷ pigment;ink:油～ printing ink ❸ calligraphy or painting:遗～ calligraphy or painting left by a deceased artist /笔～ words; writing; article /翰～〈书面〉ink and writing brush — writings and paintings /舞文弄～ show off one's literary skill; play with the pen ❹〈比喻〉learning; literacy:文～ learning; literary skill /胸无点～ without a jot of learning; illiterate ❺ line in a carpenter's ink marker — rules and regulations:绳～ carpenter's ink marker; rules and regulations ❻ black; pitch-dark:朱～套印 be printed in red and black /～兰 orchids painted in black and white ❼〈书面〉corruption; graft; embezzlement:贪～ embezzlement ❽ tattooing the face or forehead in ink (as punishment in ancient China) ❾ (Mò) Mohist school; Mohism ❿ (Mò) a surname

墨[2] Mò (short for 墨西哥) Mexico:～洋 Mexican silver dollar

墨宝 mòbǎo treasured calligraphy or painting:敬求～ request a sample of your beautiful calligraphy (*or* painting)

墨笔 mòbǐ also "毛笔" máobǐ writing brush

墨翟 Mò Dí see "墨子"

墨斗 mòdǒu carpenter's ink marker

墨斗鱼 mòdǒuyú also "墨鱼" inkfish; cuttlefish

墨尔本 Mò'ěrběn Melbourne, second largest city in Australia

墨辊 mògǔn 〈印刷〉ink roller

墨海 mòhǎi big basin-shaped inkstone

墨旱莲 mòhànlián also "鳢肠" lǐcháng 〈植物〉*Eclipta prostrata*

墨盒 mòhé also "墨盒子" ink box (for Chinese calligraphy or painting)

墨黑 mòhēi black as ink; inky black; inky; pitch-dark:～的夜晚 pitch-dark evening /两眼～ be in the dark /天阴得～,恐怕要下大雨了。It's inky black. I'm afraid a downpour is imminent.

墨迹 mòjì ❶ ink marks:～未干 before the ink is dry ❷ sb.'s handwriting or painting:收集名人～ collect calligraphy and paintings of celebrated people

墨家 Mòjiā Mohist School (school of thought founded by Mozi):～学说 Mohism

墨经 Mòjīng *Technological Volumes of Mozi*, completed c. 5th to 4th century BC

墨晶 mòjīng smoky quartz

墨镜 mòjìng dark glasses; sunglasses

墨菊 mòjú dark chrysanthemum (with dark purple petals)

墨卷 mòjuàn (under the imperial examination system) examination paper written in ink by the examinee (as distinguished from 朱卷, examination paper copied in red by the clerk to be read by the examiner)

墨客 mòkè 〈书面〉man of letters; literary person; poet or writer:骚人～ literary men; men of letters

墨累河 Mòlèihé Murray River, principal river of Australia

墨吏 mòlì 〈书面〉corrupt official

墨绿 mòlǜ dark green

墨面 mòmiàn ❶ (of complexion) dark; (of looks) wan and sallow; thin and pale; dark and emaciated:万家～ the poor masses look wan and sallow ❷ tattooing on the face as punishment in ancient times; tattooing of the face

墨囊 mònáng 〈动物〉ink sac (of a cuttlefish)

墨试 mòshì 〈旧语〉written examination

墨守 mòshǒu good defender of cities (after Mo Di or Mozi who was expert at the defence of cities); conservative person opposed to change:～旧法 get (*or* fall) into a rut /不必～那些过时的形式。There's no need to stick to those outmoded forms.

墨守成规 mòshǒu-chéngguī stick to convention; stay in a rut; be a stick in the mud; go round like a horse in a mill:～的人 stickler for conventions; stick-in-the-mud /一味～而从不知变通 go by the book without a moment's flexibility

墨水 mòshuǐ ❶ prepared Chinese ink ❷ ink:～瓶 ink bottle ❸ book learning:他喝了一点～就自以为是。He became conceited after he had got a smattering of knowledge. /他肚子里的～还不少。He is fairly learned.

墨水池 mòshuǐchí inkwell

墨水台 mòshuǐtái ink stand

墨索里尼 Mòsuǒlǐní Benito Mussolini (1883-1945), Italian Fascist dictator (1922-1945)

墨西哥 Mòxīgē Mexico:～人 Mexican /～城 Mexico City /～湾 Gulf of Mexico /～湾流 Gulf Stream

墨线 mòxiàn ❶ line in a carpenter's ink marker ❷ straight line made by a carpenter's ink marker

墨刑 mòxíng tattoo and paint a convict's face black as punishment in ancient times

墨鸦 mòyā ❶〈书面〉scribbling; poor handwriting ❷〈方言〉cormorant

墨鱼 mòyú inkfish; cuttlefish

墨汁 mòzhī prepared Chinese ink

墨竹 mòzhú ❶ black bamboo (a variety of bamboo) ❷〈美术〉painting of bamboo done in ink

墨子 Mòzǐ ❶ Mozi, reverent name for Mo Di (墨翟, c. 468-376 BC), a thinker of the pre-Qin period and founder of Mohism ❷ *Mozi* (*The Book of Mozi*), complete works of the Mohist school of thought

墨渍 mòzì ink stain:～未干 before the ink is dry

缧 mò 〈书面〉rope

默 mò ❶ silent; quiet; tacit:～坐 sit quietly /沉～ silent ❷ write from memory:～生字 write new words from memory ❸(Mò) a surname

默哀 mò'āi pay silent tribute;observe silence:～三分钟 observe three minutes' silence /我站在亡友遗像前～。I stood in silent tribute before the portrait of my deceased friend.

默察 mòchá watch quietly:静观～ watch quietly /～近况 follow the latest developments

默祷 mòdǎo pray in silence; say a silent prayer:我～他们旅途平安。I prayed in silence that they have a smooth and safe journey.

默悼 mòdào pay silent tribute; observe silence in memory of (sb.):向烈士遗像～致哀 stand in silent tribute to the martyr before

his portrait
默读 mòdú read silently
默化潜移 mòhuà-qiányí *also*“潜移默化” exert a subtle formative effect on sb.'s character, thinking, etc.; imperceptibly influence
默记 mòjì learn by heart; commit to memory; remember:～经文 silently memorize the classics
默剧 mòjù pantomime; mime
默默 mòmò silent; quiet:～无言 remain silent (*or* speechless) /～地出神 be lost in thought
默默无闻 mòmò-wúwén *also*“没没无闻” mòmò-wúwén unknown to the public; obscure:一生～ remain obscure all one's life /她由一个～的中学教师一跃而成为名闻遐迩的作家。She rose from an unknown middle-school teacher to a famous writer. /他只求～地多做些工作,以弥补自己所犯下的过失。All he wanted was to do more work in obscurity to atone for his past mistakes.
默念 mòniàn ❶ read silently:～古诗 read classical poetry silently ❷ ponder or reflect; meditate:～童年情景,如在昨日。As he reminisced about his childhood, he felt as if it were only yesterday.
默片 mòpiàn silent film
默契 mòqì ❶ be mutually and tacitly understood or agreed; be well coordinated:配合～ be well coordinated /不够～ (of a team, etc.) lack co-ordination (among the players) ❷ secretly agree:互相～,共同行动。They secretly agreed to take joint action. ❸ secret (oral or written) agreement; tacit understanding:达成～ reach tacit understanding /双方在行动之前已有～。The two sides had reached a secret agreement before taking action.
默然 mòrán silent; speechless:相对～ look at each other without saying a word
默认 mòrèn give tacit consent or approval to; acquiesce in:～既成事实 accept a fait accompli tacitly /他既不说话,就是～了。His silence meant tacit consent.
默示 mòshì 〈法律〉implied:～同意 implied consent /～放弃 implied waiver /～承认 implied recognition /～担保 implied warrant
默书 mòshū write from memory books one has read or texts one has studied
默诵 mòsòng ❶ recite silently (a passage, etc.) ❷ read silently
默算 mòsuàn ❶ calculate or plan in mind ❷ mental arithmetic; do sums in one's head
默想 mòxiǎng contemplate; ponder; reflect; meditate:沉思～ meditate /他坐在那里～着各种计划。He sat there pondering over various plans.
默写 mòxiě write from memory:～课文 write the text from memory
默许 mòxǔ tacitly consent to; acquiesce in:女儿不吭声,母亲估计她是～了。The girl kept silent so her mother reckoned that she had tacitly consented.
默志 mòzhì remember silently; commit to memory silently; make a mental note of:～不忘 silently commit sth. to memory
默字 mòzì write from memory words one has learned
默坐 mòzuò sit in silence; sit still:整日～ sit still all day

嘿

mò *see*“默”mò
see also hēi

脈

mò
脈脈 mòmò *see*“脉脉”mòmò

脉(脈)

mò
see also mài
脉脉 mòmò *also*“脈脈”mòmò affectionately; lovingly; tenderly:～含情 full of tenderness and love; amorously; with goo-goo eyes /～不语 remain affectionately speechless /～传情 look (at sb.) lovingly

冒

mò
see also mào
冒顿 Mòdú name of a chieftain of Xiongnu or the Huns in the early Han Dynasty

殁

mò 〈书面〉die:病～ die of illness /～而不朽 be immortal though dead

没[1]

mò ❶ sink; submerge:日～西山。The sun sank below the western hills. /那个小岛已～入水中。The islet has submerged. ❷ overflow; rise higher than:洪水～堤 floodwater overflowing the dyke /～膝的积雪 knee-deep snow /庄稼长得～人了。The crops stand higher than a man. ❸ hide; conceal; disappear:隐～ hide; go into hiding /出～无常 appear irregularly ❹ confiscate; impound; seize:抄～ search and confiscate /吞～ engulf; embezzle ❺ till the end; to the last:～齿 all one's life; life long ❻ die:不幸早～ unfortunately die young

没[2]

mò *see*“没奈何”
see also méi
没齿不忘 mòchǐ-bùwàng *also*“没世不忘” will never forget to the end of one's days; remember for the rest of one's life:奇耻大辱,～。Such humiliation will never be forgotten. /恩师教导～。I will always bear in mind my beloved teacher's advice.
没顶 mòdǐng *also*“灭顶” mièdǐng be drowned
没骨画 mògǔhuà school of Chinese painting resembling present-day water colour, characterized by using the colours directly without first making sketches
没落 mòluò decline; decay; wane:～文化 dying culture /～的帝国 empire in decline /日趋～ be increasingly on the wane
没没无闻 mòmò-wúwén *see*“默默无闻”mòmò-wúwén
没奈何 mònàihé have no (other) way out; could do nothing (but...); be helpless:末班车已过,～只得步行回家。As I missed the last bus, I could do nothing but walk home.
没人 mòrù 〈旧语〉confiscate as punishment
没食子酸 mòshízǐsuān *also*“五倍子酸” wǔbèizǐsuān gallic acid
没世 mòshì all one's life:～不忘 never forget throughout one's life
没收 mòshōu seize; confiscate; expropriate:～财产 confiscate or expropriate sb.'s property /～一切禁运物品 seize all contraband
没药 mòyào *also*“末药” mòyào myrrh
没药树 mòyàoshù myrrh tree (*Commiphora myrrha*)

mōu

哞

mōu 〈象声〉(of a cow) moo; low; bellow

móu

谋

móu ❶ design; plan; scheme; stratagem:阴～ plot; conspiracy; scheme /阳～ (in contrast to 阴谋) open plan /有勇有～ brave and resourceful /多～善断 resourceful and resolute ❷ work for; seek; strive:为人民～幸福 work for the happiness of the people /～章布局 plan the structure ❸ consult; deliberate:不～而合 agree without prior consultation
谋财害命 móucái-hàimìng murder sb. for his or her money
谋臣 móuchén resourceful court official; (emperor's) counsellor:猛将如云,～如雨 have a multitude of brave generals as well as resourceful court officials
谋刺 móucì plot an assassination
谋反 móufǎn scheme for a rebellion; conspire (against the state, etc.)
谋国 móuguó 〈书面〉work hard in the interest of one's country:忠诚～ work for the interest of one's nation with single-hearted loyalty
谋害 móuhài ❶ plot to murder; murder:～亲夫 (of a woman) murder one's own husband ❷ plot a frame-up against:有意～ frame sb. deliberately
谋和 móuhé seek peace or reconciliation:交战双方通过第三者～。The belligerents tried to seek peace through a third party.
谋划 móuhuà plan; contrive:精心～ plan carefully /～一个妥善的解决办法 try to find a proper solution /帮他～一下 help him work out a plan
谋利 móulì make a profit; seek gain
谋虑 móulǜ consider; think over; deliberate; ponder carefully:他很精明,～事情很少有差错。He is very astute and seldom miscalculates. *or* He is very shrewd and hardly makes any wrong calcula-

tions.

谋略 móulüè astuteness and ingenuity; strategy:此人颇有～。He is a man of great resource.

谋面 móumiàn 〈书面〉meet each other; make the acquaintance of: 素未～ have never made sb.'s acquaintance; have never met before

谋叛 móupàn plot a rebellion; conspire against the state

谋篇 móupiān 〈书面〉(of writing) design the structure: 布局～ design the structure and organize the paragraphs

谋求 móuqiú seek; strive for; pursue: ～公众福利 work for the public well-being /～改善两国关系 seek better (*or* improved) relations between the two countries /～职业 be in search of a job; hunt for a job; seek employment

谋取 móuqǔ try to gain; seek; be after: ～私利 seek personal gain

谋杀 móushā (premeditated) murder

谋杀案 móushā'àn 〈法律〉case of murder

谋杀罪 móushāzuì 〈法律〉offence of murder

谋生 móushēng seek a livelihood; make a living: 无以～ cannot even scrape a living; cannot earn one's livelihood /～手段 means of subsistence; livelihood /外出～ leave home to earn a living

谋食 móushí make a living; seek a livelihood: ～异乡 seek a livelihood in a strange land

谋士 móushì adviser; counsellor

谋事 móushì ❶ plan matters; scheme: ～在人, 成事在天 man makes plans but heaven decides their outcome; man proposes, God disposes ❷ seek employment; look for a job: 去一家公司～ try to find a job with a firm

谋私 móusī pursue selfish interests; seek private gain: 以权～ seek personal gains by abusing one's power; jobbery

谋算 móusuàn ❶ plan; try to find a solution: 村长正在～着春季的生产安排。The village head is making arrangements for production in the spring. ❷ scheme or plot (against sb.): 他存心～我。He is scheming against me. ❸ calculate; reckon; weigh up: 这人很会～。He is very calculating.

谋陷 móuxiàn frame; set up: 遭人～ be framed

谋寻 móuxún seek; try to find: ～生路 seek a livelihood

谋议 móuyì 〈书面〉plan and discuss; meet and plan; confer: 参与～ participate in planning and deliberation /这件事, 大家几经～, 总算定下来了。We finally arrived at a decision after several rounds of discussion.

谋猷 móuyóu 〈书面〉strategy; scheme; plot

谋职 móuzhí seek employment; try to find a job: 外出～ go out to find a job

谋主 móuzhǔ mastermind; arch-plotter

牟 móu ❶ seek; try to gain ❷ (Móu) a surname

牟利 móulì seek profit; seek personal gain: 走私～ seek huge profits by smuggling

牟取 móuqǔ try to gain (fame or wealth); seek: ～暴利 seek exorbitant profits; profiteer

粦 móu 〈古语〉barley

眸 móu pupil (of the eye); eye: 明～皓齿 (of girls) bright eyes and white teeth /凝～远望 gaze into the distance

眸子 móuzǐ pupil of the eye; eye

蛑 móu *see* "蝤蛑" yóumóu

侔 móu 〈书面〉equal; match: 相～ be equal

鍪 móu *see* "兜鍪" dōumóu

缪 móu *see* "绸缪" chóumóu; "未雨绸缪" wèiyǔ-chóumóu

see also Miào; miù

mǒu

某 mǒu ❶ certain; some: ～年 in a certain year /～日 at a certain date /邻居刘～ a certain neighbour called Liu /江苏～地 somewhere in Jiangsu /据说有了～种线索。It is said that certain clues have been found. /从～种意义上说, 这次试验是成功的。The experiment was successful in a sense. ❷ (usu. used with one's surname to refer to oneself) yours truly: 我张～从不说谎。Yours truly has never told a lie. /赴汤蹈火, 杨～在所不辞。You can count on me. I'll never balk at going through fire and water. ❸ *often used instead of sb.'s given name in an impolite way*: 他李～实在太吝啬了。That fellow Li is a real skinflint.

某某 mǒumǒu so-and-so: ～先生 Mr. so-and-so /～学校 a certain school

某人 mǒurén ❶ somebody; a certain person: 信中要点明某月某日、某地、～干了某事。You must state clearly in the letter when, where, and what somebody did. ❷ *used after one's surname to refer to oneself*: 我李～不吃这一套。Don't expect me to take this lying down.

某些 mǒuxiē certain; some; a few: ～村子被水淹了。Some villages were flooded.

mú

模 mú mould; die; matrix; pattern: 字～ (type) matrix /锭～ ingot mould /锻～ forging die /拉～ drawing die /陷型～ swage /印～ moulage /铸～ mould; casting form /压～ moulding-die; compression moulding

see also mó

模板 múbǎn ❶〈建筑〉shuttering; formwork ❷〈机械〉pattern plate

模版 múbǎn masterplate

模锻 múduàn 〈机械〉die-forging

模具 mújù mould; matrix; die; pattern

模具钢 mújùgāng die steel

模样 múyàng ❶ appearance; countenance; look: 这孩子的～儿讨人喜欢。The child looks cute. /看～, 她在四十岁上下。Judging from her appearance, she is around 40. /那人长得什么～? What does the man look like? /这男孩的～儿像他的父亲。The boy takes after his father. ❷ (of time and age only) about; approximately: 过了半小时～ about (*or* approximately) half an hour later /来人三十岁～。The visitor was about 30. ❸ trend; inclination: 都夜里十二点了, 他还没有起身告辞的～。It's almost midnight now. But he shows no intention of leaving.

模子 múzi mould; pattern; matrix; die: 铜～ copper mould /一个～里铸出来的 cast from the same mould; as like as two peas

氁 mú

氁子 múzi woollen fabric made in Tibet

mǔ

亩(畝) mǔ *also* "市亩" shìmǔ *mu*, a Chinese unit of area equal to $\frac{1}{15}$ of a hectare or $\frac{1}{6}$ of an acre: ～产量 per *mu* yield

牡 mǔ male: ～牛 bull

牡丹 mǔdan tree peony; peony: ～虽好, 全仗绿叶扶持。〈俗语〉Lovely as the peony is, it needs the support of green leaves. *or* With all its beauty, the peony needs green leaves to set it off.

牡丹亭 Mǔdantíng *The Peony Pavilion*, a romantic drama written by Tang Xianzu (汤显祖) of the Ming Dynasty

牡蛎 mǔlì *also* "蚝" háo; "海蛎子" hǎilìzi 〈动物〉oyster

牡鹿 mǔlù buck; stag

牡马 mǔmǎ stallion

姥 mǔ 〈书面〉old lady

see also lǎo

母 mǔ ❶ mother: 继～ stepmother /养～ foster mother /寡～ widowed mother /慈～ loving mother /乳～〈书面〉one's wet nurse ❷ one's female elder: 祖～ grandmother /姑～ father's sister; aunt ❸ female (animal): ～鸡 hen /～鸭 duck /～鹅 goose /～牛 cow /～马 mare /～驴 jenny /～羊 ewe /～猪 sow /～狗 bitch /～鹿 doe /～兔 doe /～山羊 nanny /～狼 she-wolf /～狮 lioness /～虎 ti-

gress ❹ nut (so called because of the female screw thread): 螺～ nut /子～扣 snap fastener ❺ origin; parent; mother: 失败是成功之～。Failure is the mother of success. ❻ (Mǔ) a surname
母爱 mǔ'ài mother love; motherly love; maternal love
母版 mǔbǎn master matrix
母本 mǔběn *also* "母株"〈植物〉female parent: ～植株 maternal plant
母本遗传 mǔběn yíchuán 〈植物〉maternal inheritance
母畜 mǔchù female animal; dam
母带 mǔdài master tape
母党 mǔdǎng clan on the mother's side; maternal relatives
母丁香 mǔdīngxiāng 〈中药〉fruit of lilac (*Syzygium aromaticum*)
母法 mǔfǎ ❶ constitution ❷ foreign laws on which domestic laws are modelled
母蜂 mǔfēng *also* "蜂王" fēngwáng queen bee
母羔 mǔgāo ewe lamb
母公司 mǔgōngsī parent company
母国 mǔguó mother country; motherland
母函数 mǔhánshù generating function
母合金 mǔhéjīn 〈冶金〉mother alloy
母后 mǔhòu ❶ term of respect used by a prince or a princess in addressing or referring to his or her mother who is also queen or empress ❷ (term used by a king or emperor in addressing or referring to his widowed mother) queen mother; empress dowager
母化合物 mǔhuàhéwù 〈化学〉parent compound
母机 mǔjī machine tool
母家 mǔjiā 〈方言〉married woman's parents' home
母舰 mǔjiàn 〈旧语〉mother ship: 航空～ aircraft carrier
母金 mǔjīn capital; principal
母舅 mǔjiù maternal uncle
母驹 mǔjū 〈畜牧〉filly
母老虎 mǔlǎohǔ ❶ tigress ❷ shrew; termagant; virago; vixen
母脉 mǔmài 〈矿业〉mother lode
母模 mǔmú 〈冶金〉mother plate
母片集成电路 mǔpiàn jíchéng diànlù 〈电子〉master-chip integrated circuit
母亲 mǔqin mother: 人们常把祖国比作～。People often compare their homeland to their mother.
母权制 mǔquánzhì matriarchy
母乳 mǔrǔ mother's milk: ～喂养 breast feeding
母树 mǔshù 〈林业〉maternal tree; mother tree; seed tree: ～林 maternal wood
母体 mǔtǐ mother's body; (female) parent; 〈比喻〉matrix
母体免疫 mǔtǐ miǎnyì maternal immunity
母系 mǔxì ❶ maternal (side): ～亲属 maternal relatives ❷ matrilineal; matriarchal: ～氏族 matrilineal clan /～氏族公社 matrilineal commune /～社会 matriarchal society
母系血统 mǔxì xuètǒng matrilineage
母系遗传 mǔxì yíchuán 〈生物〉matrilinear inheritance
母线 mǔxiàn ❶〈电学〉bus; bus bar ❷〈数学〉generatrix; generator
母校 mǔxiào one's old school; alma mater
母性 mǔxìng maternal instinct
母性本能 mǔxìng běnnéng maternal instinct
母姓制 mǔxìngzhì metronymy
母液 mǔyè 〈化学〉mother liquor; mother solution
母夜叉 mǔyècha ❶ female devil ❷ fierce and ugly woman; vixen
母音 mǔyīn 〈语言〉vowel
母忧 mǔyōu 〈书面〉death of mother: 遭～ suffer the loss of one's mother
母语 mǔyǔ ❶ mother tongue ❷ parent language; linguistic parent
母韵 mǔyùn 〈语言〉assonance
母钟 mǔzhōng master clock (in a synchronized clock system)
see also "子母钟" zǐmǔzhōng
母质 mǔzhì 〈地质〉parent material
母株 mǔzhū *see* "母本"
母子 mǔ-zǐ mother and child; mother and her baby: ～都平安。Both the mother and her baby are safe and sound.

坶 mǔ *see* "垆坶" lúmǔ

拇 mǔ
拇战 mǔzhàn finger-guessing game: 两人～半日，喝得酩酊大醉。The two played finger-guessing games for hours, drunk as lords.
拇指 mǔzhǐ *also* "大拇指" dàmǔzhǐ ❶ thumb: 竖起大～ hold up one's thumb in approval; thumbs up ❷ big toe

铒 mǔ *see* "钴铒" gǔmǔ

姆 mǔ ❶ *see* "保姆" bǎomǔ ❷ (short for 姆欧)〈电学〉mho
see also m
姆欧 mǔ'ōu 〈电学〉mho: ～计 mhometer

mù

墓 mù grave; tomb: 公～ cemetery /陵～ mausoleum; tomb /扫～ sweep a grave — pay respects to a dead person at his or her grave /掘～人 gravedigger /盗～ rob a grave; commit grave (*or* tomb) robbery
墓碑 mùbēi tombstone; gravestone
墓表 mùbiǎo ❶ gravestone; tombstone ❷ epitaph inscribed on a gravestone
墓场 mùchǎng graveyard; burial ground; cemetery
墓道 mùdào ❶ path leading to a grave or tomb ❷ passage in an ancient tomb leading to the coffin chamber
墓地 mùdì graveyard; burial ground; cemetery
墓椁室 mùguǒshì coffin chamber; funeral chamber
墓祭 mùjì pay respects to a deceased person at his or her grave
墓碣 mùjié tombstone; gravestone
墓门 mùmén door of a coffin chamber
墓木 mùmù trees in a graveyard: ～已拱 (of a person) have been dead for many years
墓室 mùshì coffin chamber (in a tomb)
墓头回 mùtóuhuí 〈中药〉root of certain varieties of *Patrinia scabiosaefolia*
墓穴 mùxué pit for coffin or ashes of the dead; open grave
墓茔 mùyíng ❶ grave; tomb ❷ graveyard; cemetery
墓园 mùyuán cemetery: 烈士～ cemetery (*or* tombs) of revolutionary martyrs
墓葬 mùzàng 〈考古〉grave: ～群 group of graves
墓志 mùzhì inscription on the memorial tablet within a tomb
墓志铭 mùzhìmíng epitaph
墓子 mùzi 〈方言〉grave; tomb

暮 mù ❶ dusk; sunset; evening: 日～ sunset /朝思～想 yearn day and night ❷ (of time) towards the end; late: 垂～之年 in old age /天寒岁～。It gets cold as the year draws to an end.
暮霭 mù'ǎi evening mist; evening haze: ～低垂。The evening mist hangs low.
暮齿 mùchǐ 〈书面〉old age; one's later years
暮春 mùchūn late spring; third month of the lunar calendar: ～三月，江南草长。In late spring, the land south of the Yangtze River is a carpet of lush vegetation.
暮鼓晨钟 mùgǔ-chénzhōng *also* "晨钟暮鼓" evening drum and morning bell (in a monastery) — timely exhortations to virtue and purity
暮景 mùjǐng ❶ dusk; twilight; gloaming ❷ old age; one's remaining years; evening of life
暮龄 mùlíng old age; one's later years
暮年 mùnián evening of one's life; old age; declining years: 烈士～，壮心不已。A heroic man, though declining in years, still has lofty aspirations.
暮气 mùqì lethargy; apathy; languor: ～沉沉 lethargic; apathetic; lifeless /～十足 very lethargic; very picture of lethargy /一扫往日的～ throw off one's previous apathy; shake oneself out of one's former listlessness (*or* languor) /在旧家庭里他是一个～十足的少爷。In the midst of his old-fashioned family, he was a spiritless, supine young master.
暮秋 mùqiū late autumn; ninth lunar month
暮色 mùsè dusk; twilight; gloaming: ～苍茫 gathering dusk;

widening shades of dusk / ～渐浓 (gradually) deepening dusk
暮生儿 mùshengr 〈方言〉posthumous child
暮世 mùshì recent years; modern times
暮岁 mùsuì ❶ end of the year ❷ closing years of one's life; twilight of one's life; evening of one's life
暮云春树 mùyún-chūnshù evening clouds and spring trees — longing for a faraway friend

幕 mù ❶ canopy; tent: 帐～ tent / 夜～ veil of night ❷ curtain; screen: 银～ screen / 开～ rise of curtain; opening / 闭～ fall of curtain; closing ❸ 〈旧语〉office or headquarters of a general: *see* "～府"; "～僚" ❹ act: 序～ prologue; prelude / 独～剧 one-act play / 一出三～七场的话剧 a play in three acts and seven scenes / 儿时的情景一～～地重现在我的眼前。Scene after scene of my childhood reappeared before my eyes.
幕宾 mùbīn 〈旧语〉❶ *also* "幕僚" aide to a ranking official or general ❷ *also* "幕友" private assistant attending to legal, fiscal or secretarial duties in a local *yamen*; private adviser
幕布 mùbù (theatre) curtain; (cinema) screen
幕府 mùfǔ ❶ 〈旧语〉office of a commander-in-chief or general ❷ shogun, warlord who ruled Japan before the Meiji Reform; shogunate: 德川～ Tokugawa shogunate
幕府制度 mùfǔ zhìdù shogunate, a kind of military dictatorship in Japan from 1192 to 1867
幕后 mùhòu backstage; behind the scenes: ～策划 backstage manoeuvring
幕后操纵 mùhòu cāozòng pull strings from behind the scenes
幕后交易 mùhòu jiāoyì behind-the-scenes deal; backstage deal
幕后人物 mùhòu rénwù wirepuller; backstage manipulator
幕间休息 mùjiān xiūxi interval; intermission
幕客 mùkè *see* "幕宾"
幕帘 mùlián curtains (for windows, etc.)
幕僚 mùliáo aide to a ranking official or general
幕天席地 mùtiān-xídì ❶ have the sky for canopy and earth for mat — be broad-minded ❷ outdoor life: 在野游中，大家～，举杯叙旧。We went camping, staying in the open, drinking and talking about the good old days.
幕友 mùyǒu *also* "师爷" shīye private assistant attending to legal, fiscal, or secretarial duties in a local *yamen* in the Ming and Qing dynasties

慕 mù ❶ admire; envy: 仰～ look up to; admire ❷ long for; yearn for: 爱～ adore; admire / 思～ miss ❸ (Mù) a surname
慕光性 mùguāngxìng *also* "趋光性" qūguāngxìng phototaxis
慕名 mùmíng admiration for a famous name: 我～前来参观古刹。I was attracted to the ancient temple by its reputation.
慕尼黑 Mùníhēi Munich (capital of Bavaria, Germany): ～协定 Munich Agreement (1938) / ～阴谋 Munich conspiracy
慕容 Mùróng a surname
慕士塔格山 Mùshìtǎgéshān Muztagata Mountains, in China's Xinjiang Uygur Autonomous Region
慕田峪长城 Mùtiányù Chángchéng Mutianyu section of the Great Wall in Beijing
慕悦 mùyuè love; adore: 互相～ love (*or* adore) each other

募 mù raise; collect; enlist; recruit: 招～ recruit; enlist
募兵 mùbīng recruit soldiers: ～三千 recruit 3,000 soldiers
募兵制 mùbīngzhì mercenary system (for recruiting soldiers)
募股 mùgǔ raise capital by floating shares
募化 mùhuà (of Buddhist monks or Taoist priests) collect alms
募集 mùjí raise; collect: ～资金 raise funds
募捐 mùjuān make or take up a collection; solicit donations: 为修复古迹而～ take up collection for renovating historic sites / ～资助失学儿童 solicit donations to help children who can not afford to go to school
募款 mùkuǎn raise funds; raise money

木[1] mù ❶ tree: 乔～ arbor; tree / 果～ fruit tree ❷ timber; lumber; wood: 原～ log / 松～ pinewood / 枕～ 〈铁路〉sleeper; tie / ～理 grain of wood; wood grain / ～屑 wood chips; sawdust ❸ made of wood; wooden: ～椅 wooden chair / ～栅栏 wooden fence; palings; pales / ～船 wooden boat ❹ coffin: 寿～ coffin (esp. one prepared during one's lifetime against one's death) / 行将就～ have one foot in the grave ❺ (Mù) a surname

木[2] mù ❶ simple; unsophisticated; dense: 这人有点发～。The man is a bit dense. / 他不是～脑壳。He was no numskull. ❷ numb; wooden: 她吓得手脚麻～。She was so frightened that her limbs went numb.
木板 mùbǎn plank; board: ～床 plank bed / ～房 plank house
木版 mùbǎn printing block
木版画 mùbǎnhuà woodcut; wood engraving
木版印花 mùbǎn yìnhuā 〈纺织〉block printing
木版印刷 mùbǎn yìnshuā block printing
木柈 mùbàn 〈方言〉large piece of firewood
木本 mùběn 〈植物〉xylophytic; woody
木本棉 mùběnmián bombax cotton
see also "木棉"
木本水源 mùběn-shuǐyuán root of a tree and source of a river — origin of a matter; root of a matter
木本植物 mùběn zhíwù 〈植物〉xylophyte; woody plant
木笔 mùbǐ *see* "木兰"
木变石 mùbiànshí *see* "木化石"
木菠萝 mùbōluó *also* "菠萝蜜" bōluómì 〈植物〉jackfruit
木材 mùcái wood; timber; lumber: ～厂 timber mill / ～防腐 wood preservation
木材复合塑料板 mùcái fùhé sùliàobǎn wood plastics composite
木材滑道 mùcái huádào log slip; skid
木材学 mùcáixué wood science
木柴 mùchái firewood
木船 mùchuán wooden boat
木醇 mùchún *also* "甲醇" jiǎchún 〈化学〉methyl alcohol; methanol; wood spirit
木醋酸 mùcùsuān 〈化学〉pyroligneous acid
木呆呆 mùdāidāi be in a daze; be in a trance: 他像失去了知觉似的，～地站在窗前。He stood before the window staring blankly, as if he had lost consciousness.
木雕 mùdiāo wood carving; wood sculpture
木雕泥塑 mùdiāo-nísù *also* "泥塑木雕" like an idol carved in wood or moulded in clay — as wooden as a dummy: 他坐在那里像～一般，一声不吭。He sat there silent, like a wooden figure.
木豆 mùdòu *also* "豆蓉" dòuróng 〈植物〉wood vetch
木牍 mùdú 〈考古〉inscribed wooden tablet
木蠹蛾 mùdù'é 〈动物〉wood moth; carpenter moth
木耳 mù'ěr edible black fungus (*Auricularia auricula*)
木筏 mùfá *also* "木筏子" raft
木芙蓉 mùfúróng *also* "芙蓉" fúróng; "木莲" 〈植物〉cotton rose (*Hibiscus mutabilis*)
木工 mùgōng ❶ woodwork; carpentry: 做～活儿 do woodwork (or carpentry) / ～机械 woodworking machinery ❷ carpenter; woodworker: 细～ cabinetmaker; joiner
木工刨床 mùgōng bàochuáng wood planing machine; wood planer
木工车床 mùgōng chēchuáng woodworking lathe; wood processing lathe
木工工具 mùgōng gōngjù woodworking instrument; woodworking tool
木工机床 mùgōng jīchuáng woodworking machine tool
木构件 mùgòujiàn wooden component
木瓜 mùguā 〈植物〉❶ Chinese flowering quince ❷ 〈口语〉papaya; pawpaw
木管乐器 mùguǎn yuèqì woodwind instrument; woodwind
木胡蜂 mùhúfēng 〈动物〉wood wasp
木蝴蝶 mùhúdié 〈植物〉*Oroxylon indicum*
木花 mùhuā 〈方言〉wood shavings
木化石 mùhuàshí *also* "木变石" petrified wood; woodstone
木婚 mùhūn wooden wedding anniversary — the 5th wedding anniversary
木活 mùhuó ❶ wooden part or object ❷ *also* "木工活" woodwork; carpentry
木屐 mùjī wooden sandal; clog
木简 mùjiǎn 〈考古〉inscribed wooden slip
木浆 mùjiāng wood pulp; 化学～ chemical wood pulp

木僵 mùjiāng numb and stiff：手指～ numb and stiff fingers
木强 mùjiàng 〈书面〉honest and staunch：为人～敦厚 be upright and unyielding
木匠 mùjiang carpenter
木焦油 mùjiāoyóu 〈化工〉wood tar
木结构 mùjiégòu 〈建筑〉timber structure; wood construction
木槿 mùjǐn 〈植物〉hibiscus (*Hibiscus syriacus*); rose of sharon
木精 mùjīng *see*"木醇"
木绝缘 mùjuéyuán 〈电工〉wooden insulation
木刻 mùkè *also*"木版画" woodcut; wood engraving：～术 xylography /～艺术 art of woodcut
木刻水印 mùkè shuǐyìn 〈美术〉watercolour block printing
木兰 mùlán *also*"辛夷"xīnyí;"木笔"〈植物〉lily magnolia
木兰辞 Mùláncí *Song of the Heroine Mulan* or *The Ballad of Mulan*, a popular folk ballad composed during the Northern Dynasties
木蓝 mùlán 〈植物〉indigo
木理学 mùlǐxué xylography
木立 mùlì stand like a post; stand motionless：他～岸边，凝望着远航的亲人。He stood motionless on the shore, staring at his dear ones sailing away.
木莲 mùlián 〈植物〉❶ *Manglietia fordiana* ❷ *see*"木芙蓉"
木料 mùliào timber; lumber
木瘤 mùliú (of timber or tree) gnarl; knaur
木螺钻 mùluózuàn auger
木麻黄 mùmáhuáng *also*"驳骨松" bógǔsōng 〈植物〉*Casuarina equisetifolia*
木马 mùmǎ ❶ wooden horse ❷〈体育〉vaulting or pommelled horse ❸ (children's) hobby horse; rocking horse
木马计 mùmǎjì stratagem of the Trojan Horse; Trojan Horse：他们巧设～，潜入敌人的心脏打击敌人。By using the stratagem of the Trojan Horse, they sneaked deep into the enemy area and launched attacks.
木煤 mùméi 〈地质〉bituminous wood; board coal; wood coal
木煤气 mùméiqì wood gas
木棉 mùmián ❶〈植物〉bombax：～科 *Bombacaceae* ❷ silk cotton; kapok
木模 mùmú wooden mould
木乃伊 mùnǎiyī ❶ mummy ❷ sth. rigid or ossified
木讷 mùnè 〈书面〉simple and slow of speech; inarticulate：为人～ man of simple manners and few words /～寡言 inarticulate and taciturn
木牛流马 mùniú-liúmǎ wooden oxen and gliding horses — transport vehicle allegedly invented by Zhuge Liang (诸葛亮) for carrying military supplies over difficult terrain
木偶 mù'ǒu ❶ wooden figure; carved image：他坐在台上一动不动，活像一尊～。Sitting motionless on the stage, he looked exactly like a carved figure. ❷ puppet; marionette：～剧团 puppet show company
木偶片儿 mù'ǒupiānr *see*"木偶片"
木偶片 mù'ǒupiàn puppet film
木偶戏 mù'ǒuxì *also*"傀儡戏" kuǐlěixì puppet show; puppet play
木排 mùpái raft
木片 mùpiàn wood chip
木器 mùqì wooden furniture; wooden article; treen; treenware
木琴 mùqín 〈乐器〉xylophone
木然 mùrán stupefied：他～地望着我。He looked at me, stupefied.
木人石心 mùrén-shíxīn ❶ person of strong will and determination who is immune from the temptation of power and wealth ❷ pitiless; unfeeling; heartless
木石 mùshí wood and stone — lifeless thing; senseless being：～心肠 hard-hearted; unfeeling /人非～，孰能无情？We are neither wood nor stone. How can we have no feeling?
木薯 mùshǔ 〈植物〉cassava：～淀粉 tapioca
木梳 mùshu wooden comb
木栓 mùshuān 〈植物〉cork; phellem：～形成层〈植物〉cork cambium; phellogen
木栓层 mùshuāncéng 〈植物〉phellem
木丝 mùsī wood wool：～板〈建筑〉wood wool board
木素 mùsù *see*"木质素"
木炭 mùtàn charcoal：烧～ make charcoal /～火 charcoal fire
木炭画 mùtànhuà charcoal drawing
木糖 mùtáng 〈生化〉xylose; wood sugar
木通 mùtōng 〈植物〉akebi
木头木脑 mùtóu-mùnǎo block-headed; slow-witted：他～坐在那里，一言不发。He sat there motionless and speechless.
木头 mùtou 〈口语〉wood; log; timber：一根～ a piece of wood
木头人儿 mùtourénr 〈口语〉wooden figure; blockhead：他戳在那儿跟～似的。He stood riveted to the spot like a wooden figure.
木卫三 Mùwèi Sān 〈天文〉Ganymede, the largest satellite of Jupiter
木卫四 Mùwèi Sì 〈天文〉Callisto, the most distant of the four largest of the twelve satellites of Jupiter
木屋 mùwū log cabin; wood house
木犀 mùxi *also*"木樨" ❶ *also*"桂花" guìhuā 〈植物〉sweet-scented osmanthus：～属 *Osmanthus fragrans* ❷ cooked beaten egg：～汤 eggdrop soup /～饭 fried rice with scrambled eggs
木樨 mùxi *see*"木犀"
木锨 mùxiān wooden spade (usu. used for winnowing grain)
木香 mùxiāng 〈植物〉❶ *also*"木香花" banksia rose ❷ *Aueklandia lappa*; *Saussurea lappa*
木星 Mùxīng 〈天文〉Jupiter
木须肉 mùxūròu fried shredded port and beaten eggs with black fungus
木曜日 mùyàorì 〈旧语〉Friday
木叶蝶 mùyèdié 〈动物〉*Kallima chinensis*
木已成舟 mùyǐchéngzhōu the wood is already made into a boat — what is done cannot be undone; water under the bridge; water over the dam：～，后悔也没有用了。It is too late for regret. *or* It is no use crying over spilt milk.
木俑 mùyǒng 〈考古〉wooden figurine (used as a burial object)
木油 mùyóu 〈化学〉wood oil
木鱼 mùyú wooden fish (hollow wooden block used by Buddhist monks to beat rhythm when chanting scriptures, also used as percussion instrument)：和尚身披袈裟，敲着～，正在念经。The robed monks beating their wooden blocks chanted Buddhist sutra.
木贼 mùzéi 〈植物〉horsetail; scouring rush
木枕 mùzhěn *also*"枕木"〈铁路〉sleeper; tie
木质 mùzhì *see*"木质素"
木质部 mùzhìbù 〈植物〉xylem
木质化 mùzhìhuà lignification
木质茎 mùzhìjīng 〈植物〉ligneous stem
木质酶 mùzhìméi 〈生化〉ligninase
木质素 mùzhìsù *also*"木质";"木素"〈植物〉lignin
木主 mùzhǔ *also*"神主" shénzhǔ ancestral tablet; sacred wooden tablet (at a temple, etc.)
木蛀虫 mùzhùchóng wood borer
木砖 mùzhuān wooden block (of the size of a brick)
木作 mùzuō ❶ carpenter's shop ❷ carpenter

沐 mù ❶ wash one's hair; wash; bathe：*see*"～浴";"～雨栉风" ❷〈书面〉receive; be given：*see*"～恩" ❸ (Mù) a surname
沐恩 mù'ēn 〈书面〉bask in sb.'s kindness (as of the emperor); receive a favour or kindness：～图报 try to requite sb.'s kindness or favour
沐猴而冠 mùhóu'érguàn monkey with a hat on — a worthless person dressed up as an important figure：此人～，不足与谋。He is not the sort of person to be associated with. Though looking imposing, he is no more than an oaf.
沐雨栉风 mùyǔ-zhìfēng *also*"栉风沐雨" bathed by the rain and combed by the wind — be exposed to all kinds of risks and hardships
沐浴 mùyù ❶ take or have a bath：～更衣 take a bath and change one's clothes /～斋戒 take a bath and go fasting ❷ bathe; immerse：树木花草都～在灿烂的阳光里。Trees, flowers and grass — all were bathed in brilliant sunshine. /人们～在节日的欢乐之中。People were immersed in joyful festivities.
沐浴节 Mùyùjié Bathing Festival (for seven days during the first half of the 7th month of the Tibetan calendar, with Tibetan people taking baths in rivers or lakes to wash away evils)

霂 mù *see*"霢霂" màimù

目 mù ❶ eye：～疾 eye trouble /～眶 eye socket /历历在～ appear vividly before one's eyes; come readily to one's mind /耳濡～

染 be influenced by what one hears and sees constantly ❷ mesh; eye; hole:八十～筛 eighty-hole sieve ❸〈书面〉look; see:～为奇迹 look on (or regard) as a miracle /一～十行 read ten lines at a glance; skim over quickly ❹ item; number:细～ detailed items; inventory ❺〈生物〉order:银杏～ *Ginkgoales* /亚～ suborder ❻ list; catalogue:书～ catalogue; booklist /剧～ list of plays or operas; repertoire /总～ comprehensive table of contents ❼ name; title:题～ title; topic /巧立名～ invent all sorts of names; make various pretexts ❽ (in *weiqi* or go) eye

目标 mùbiāo ❶ target; objective:命中～ hit the target /军事～ military objective or target /攻击～ target for attack /暴露～ give away one's position /转移～ distract attention (or divert) from sth. or sb. ❷ goal; aim; objective:共同～ common objective; common purpose /～一致,步调一致 have a common goal and keep in step /～不能定得过高 must not aim too high; must not set one's sights too high

目标跟踪雷达 mùbiāo gēnzōng léidá *also*"目标自动跟踪雷达" target-tracking radar (TTR)

目标观众 mùbiāo guānzhòng 〈商业〉target audience

目标管理 mùbiāo guǎnlǐ management by objectives

目标价 mùbiāojià 〈商业〉target price

目标市场 mùbiāo shìchǎng 〈商业〉target market

目标搜索 mùbiāo sōusuǒ target search

目标位置指示器 mùbiāo wèizhì zhǐshìqì target position indicator (TPI)

目不见睫 mùbùjiànjié the eye cannot see its lashes — be unable to see one's own limitations; lack self-knowledge

目不交睫 mùbùjiāojié not sleep a wink; stay up:为了思考对策,他通夜～。He stayed up the whole night, racking his brains for a countermeasure.

目不窥园 mùbùkuīyuán never take a peep into a garden — bury oneself in one's studies; immerse oneself in books; not take time to smell the roses:数年间他闭门读书,～。For years he's been engrossed in his studies.

目不忍睹 mùbùrěndǔ *also*"目不忍视" cannot stand the sight; be too sad or tragic to look at:战场的惨象令人～。The terrible scene at the battlefield was too tragic to watch.

目不识丁 mùbùshídīng not know one's ABCs; be totally illiterate

目不暇接 mùbùxiájiē *also*"目不暇给" the eye cannot take it all in; there are too many things for one's eyes to feast on:春节期间电视节目丰富多彩,真令人～! There is such a great variety of TV programmes during the Spring Festival that one cannot take them all in with one's eyes.

目不邪视 mùbùxiéshì not cast sidelong glances — be honest and proper; be indifferent or unconcerned

目不斜视 mùbùxiéshì not look sideways:～,耳不旁听 be deaf and blind to everything around; concentrate on sth.

目不转睛 mùbùzhuǎnjīng rivet one's eyes upon; gaze intently:雷达兵～地注视荧光屏。The radarman watched the screen intently. *or* The radarman fixed his eyes on the screen.

目测 mùcè 〈军事〉visual range estimation

目次 mùcì table of contents

目瞪口呆 mùdèng-kǒudāi gape goggle-eyed and dumbstruck; be flabbergasted; be stupefied; be stunned:惊得～ be struck dumb with fear /这位魔术师的表演,使大家看得～。The audience gazed spellbound as the conjurer performed. /霎时间他吓得～。For a moment he was so stunned that he did not know what to think.

目的 mùdì purpose; intention; goal; objective:根本～ fundamental objective /生活～ one's goal in life; what one pursues in one's life /怀有不可告人的～ harbour ulterior motives; have evil intentions /不达～誓不罢休 never give up until one's purpose (or goal) is achieved /采用不正当的手段来实现个人的～ use inappropriate means to achieve one's selfish ends

目的地 mùdìdì destination

目的港 mùdìgǎng port of destination

目的论 mùdìlùn 〈哲学〉teleology

目的性 mùdìxìng purpose; aim; objective

目睹 mùdǔ see with one's own eyes; witness:耳闻～ what one sees and hears /～事故的经过 witness an incident

目光 mùguāng ❶ look; gaze:避开某人的～ avoid sb.'s eyes ❷ expression in one's eyes:～炯炯 penetrating eyes /投以仇视的～ throw (or cast) a hostile look at sb. /他流露出询问的～。An inquiring look comes into his eyes. /她露出了绝望的～。Despair crept into her eyes. ❸ sight; vision:～远大 farsighted; farseeing /～敏锐 keen-eyed; sharp-sighted

目光短浅 mùguāng-duǎnqiǎn shortsighted:这个计划未免显得～了。That seems to be a rather shortsighted plan.

目光如豆 mùguāng-rúdòu see no further than the end of one's nose; be myopic

目光如炬 mùguāng-rújù ❶ eyes blazing like torches — glare with anger ❷ have wide vision; farsighted:这位政治家～。He is a statesman of great foresight.

目击 mùjī see with one's own eyes; witness:～其事 saw sth. with one's own eyes /此乃我身经～。It was what I witnessed.

目见 mùjiàn see for oneself:耳闻～ what one hears and sees /耳闻不如～。Seeing for oneself is better than hearing from others. *or* Seeing is believing.

目睫之论 mùjiézhīlùn shortsighted view; superficial idea

目今 mùjīn nowadays; these days

目镜 mùjìng *also*"接目镜" jiēmùjìng 〈物理〉eyepiece; ocular

目空一切 mùkōngyīqiè look down upon everyone else; be extremely supercilious or arrogant:自以为知识渊博而～ consider oneself a man of vast learning and behave in a most supercilious manner

目力 mùlì *also*"视力" shìlì vision; sight

目力表 mùlìbiǎo *also*"视力表" shìlìbiǎo visual chart; eye chart

目录 mùlù ❶ list; catalogue; inventory:图书～ library catalogue /出口产品～ export list (or catalogue) /财产～ inventory of one's property /编～ compile a catalogue /查～ look up a catalogue ❷ table of contents; contents

目录文件 mùlù wénjiàn directory file

目录学 mùlùxué bibliography

目论 mùlùn 〈书面〉superficial or parochial view that reveals lack of self-knowledge:此言实属～。That is really a shallow idea.

目迷五色 mùmíwǔsè dazzled by a riot of colours; bewildered by a complicated situation

目前 mùqián present; current:～形势 present (or current) situation /在～条件下 under the existing circumstances /到～为止 up to the present moment; up till now; so far; to date

目视飞行 mùshì fēixíng 〈航空〉visual flight

目送 mùsòng follow (sb.) with one's eyes; watch (sb.) go (when seeing him or her off); gaze after:～亲人离去 watch one's dear one leaving

目无法纪 mùwúfǎjì disregard or defy law and discipline:此人～,公然索贿受贿。He brazenly exacted and accepted bribes in utter disregard of law and discipline.

目无全牛 mùwúquánniú (of an experienced butcher) see an ox not as a whole (but only as parts to be cut) — be supremely skilled

目无余子 mùwúyúzǐ behave as if nobody else existed; be inordinately conceited and arrogant

目无组织 mùwú-zǔzhī defy the authority of one's organization

目下 mùxià at present; at the moment:～腾不出人手。We have no hands to spare at the moment.

目眩 mùxuàn dizzy; giddy; dazzled:头晕～ feel dizzy and faint /使人～的灯光 dazzling lights

目语 mùyǔ communicate with one's eyes

目指气使 mùzhǐ-qìshǐ give orders by a glance or glare; be intolerably arrogant or overweening:他官大权重,对手下不免～。Holding a high position with great power, he is sometimes insufferably arrogant to his subordinates.

目中无人 mùzhōng-wúrén consider nobody worth one's notice; look down upon everyone else:看她神气的,简直是～。Look at her haughty airs, as if no one was fit to hold a candle to her!

苜 mù

苜蓿 mùxu 〈植物〉lucerne; alfalfa

钼 mù 〈化学〉molybdenum (Mo)

钼钢 mùgāng molybdenum steel

钼酸 mùsuān molybdic acid:～铵 ammonium molybdate

钼酸盐 mùsuānyán 〈化学〉molybdate

睦 mù ❶ peaceful; harmonious:婆媳不～。The old lady and her daughter-in-law do not get along. ❷ (Mù) a surname

睦剧 mùjù 〈戏曲〉one of the local operas of Zhejiang Province
睦邻 mùlín good-neighbourliness: ～关系 friendly relations between neighbouring countries; good-neighbourly relations /～政策 good-neighbour policy
睦南关 Mùnánguān (old name for today's 友谊关) Friendship Pass (on China's border with Viet Nam)

牧

mù ❶ herd; tend: ～羊 tend sheep /畜～ livestock breeding; animal husbandry ❷ animal husbandry; livestock-raising: 农～结合 combine farming with animal husbandry
牧草 mùcǎo forage grass; herbage
牧草收获机 mùcǎo shōuhuòjī 〈畜牧〉hay machine; hay-making machine
牧场 mùchǎng ❶ *also* "牧地" grazing land; pasture ❷ livestock farm or ranch
牧放 mùfàng *also* "放牧" herd; tend; put out to pasture: ～能力 (of a pasture) carrying capacity
牧夫星座 Mùfū Xīngzuò 〈天文〉Bear Driver
牧歌 mùgē pastoral song; pastoral; madrigal
牧工 mùgōng hired herdsman
牧工商联合企业 mù-gōng-shāng liánhé qǐyè enterprise integrating stock-raising, processing and marketing
牧马 mùmǎ pasture horses: ～人 herdsman (of horses)
牧马中原 mùmǎ-zhōngyuán pasture horses in the central plains — become master of the country
牧民 mùmín herdsman
牧区 mùqū ❶ pastureland: 我们把村南的一大片草原划分为十几块～, 分给牧民放牧、管理。We divided up a large tract of grassland south of the village into a dozen pastures for stock-raising and management by the herdsmen. ❷ region of animal husbandry; pastoral area: 近年来, ～各方面发展很快。These years, pastoral regions of animal husbandry have seen a fast all-round development.
牧犬 mùquǎn shepherd dog; collie
牧群 mùqún herd
牧人 mùrén herdsman
牧师 mùshi 〈基督教〉pastor; minister; clergyman: 副～ assistant pastor /随军～ chaplain /教区～ rector; vicar
牧竖 mùshù 〈书面〉shepherd boy; buffalo boy
牧童 mùtóng shepherd boy; buffalo boy
牧畜 mùxù livestock breeding; animal husbandry
牧羊犬 mùyángquǎn collie; shepherd dog
牧羊人 mùyángrén shepherd
牧野之战 Mùyě Zhī Zhàn Battle of Muye (in present Henan) in which King Wu of Zhou (周武王) routed the Shang army, thus replacing the Shang Dynasty with Zhou
牧业 mùyè animal husbandry; stock raising; livestock farming
牧主 mùzhǔ herd owner (one who owns livestock and pastures and hires herdsmen)

穆

mù ❶ reverent; solemn: 静～ quiet and solemn ❷ (Mù) a surname
穆夫提 mùfūtí mufti, a Muslim legal expert empowered to give rulings on religious matters
穆罕默德 Mùhǎnmòdé Muhammad (c. 570 - 632), founder of the Islamic faith and community
穆勒 Mùlè John Stuart Mill (1806-1873), English philosopher and economist
穆民 mùmín believer in Islam
穆斯林 mùsīlín Moslem; Muslim

仫

mù
仫佬族 Mùlǎozú Mulao or Mulam nationality, living in the Guangxi Zhuang Autonomous Region

M

N

ń

嗯(唔) ń see“嗯”ńg

ň

嗯(吪) ň see“嗯”ňg

ǹ

嗯(叽) ǹ see“嗯”ǹg

nā

南 nā
see also nán

南无 nāmó 〈佛教〉transliteration of the Sanskrit *Namo*, which means “salute”

南无阿弥陀佛 Nāmó Ēmítuófó 〈佛教〉Namo Amita Buddha (homage to the Buddha Amita)

那 Nā a surname
see also nà; nè; nèi

ná

拿(挐) ná ❶ hold; take; bring; fetch:给我～本词典来。Bring me a dictionary. /把杯子～走。Take the glass away. /他去～钥匙了。He has gone to fetch the keys. /她手里～着一只花瓶。She held a vase in her hand. /这么重,我～不动。It's too heavy for me to carry. /要下雨了,你还是～把雨伞去吧。It looks like rain. You'd better take your umbrella with you. /要～身分证才能进去。You can't go in without showing your ID card. ❷ seize; capture; catch; take over:猫～老鼠。Cats catch mice. /首犯终于被～住了。The chief criminal was captured finally. /这个集团发展很快,去年又～下了两家公司。The fast-expanding group took over another two companies last year. ❸ have a firm grasp of; control; manage:大权～在手里 with power firmly held in one's hand /～他的短处 find out his Achilles' heel (in order to keep him under control) /把柄让人家～住了,有什么办法呢! Now that they have got us on the raw spot, what can we do? /这项工作他～得起来。He is equal to this job. *or* He is competent for the job. /这事儿你～得稳吗? Are you sure about it? ❹ put sb. in a difficult position; make things difficult for sb.:他在这个问题上～了我一把,逼我接受他的条件。He deliberately created difficulties for me on this question, so as to force me to accept his terms. /这样的事～不住人。You can't bluff me in such matters. ❺ pretend; put on:～派头 put on a show; strike a pose ❻ get; receive; gain; win:～工资 get one's pay; receive wages /～冠军 win the championship ❼ (as of a chemical agent) cause some change to; affect:碱搁得太多,把馒头～黄了。Too much soda has browned the steamed bread. /便池得用硝酸～一～。The urinal needs to be cleaned with nitric acid. ❽〈介词〉(used in the same sense as 用)with; by means of; by; in:～水冲 flush out with water /～凉水洗 wash in cold water /～油漆把墙刷一遍 daub the wall with paint /～原则作交易 barter away principles; trade in principles /～事实来证明 prove with facts; cite facts to prove ❾〈介词〉*introducing the object of a following verbal phrase*:～他开刀 first make an example of him /我真～这孩子没办法。I simply can't take the child in hand. /你心里不痛快,也不能～孩子出气啊。I know you're feeling upset, but you shouldn't take it out on the child. /不能～工作当儿戏。Work is not something to be trifled with. /她～我当亲生女儿看。She treats me as if I were her own daughter. ❿〈中医〉massage:推～ massage

拿把 nábǎ 〈方言〉pretend to be embarrassed; strike a pose:叫你唱你就唱,别故意～。Come on and sing us a song. None of your silly excuses.

拿班 nábān (often used in the early vernacular) put on airs; put on an act:～作势 assume airs; strike a pose

拿办 nábàn arrest and deal with (according to law); bring to justice:立刻～ make the arrest and start the prosecution at once

拿不出手 nábuchūshǒu *also*“拿不出去”not presentable; not good enough:这点钱～。The money is too little as a gift. /我这笔字怎么也～哇! My handwriting cannot serve as an acceptable piece of calligraphy in any circumstances.

拿不稳 nábuwěn be not sure of (sth.); be uncertain about (sth.):这事儿我也～。I'm not certain about it either. /我一听就知道他～,躲躲闪闪的。The moment he opened his mouth humming and hawing, I knew that he was on slippery ground.

拿粗挟细 nácū-xiéxì *also*“挟细拿粗”(often used in the early vernacular); stir up trouble; create difficulties:这种人～,我们得离他们远一点。As these people are likely to stir up trouble, we had better give them a wide berth.

拿大 nádà give oneself airs; be haughty; be supercilious:别看是个名角儿,他一点也不～。He is a famous actor but never puts on airs.

拿大头 ná dàtóu *also*“抓大头”zhuā dàtóu ❶ draw lots, etc. to decide who is to play the host ❷ cheat (sb.) out of his money; fleece (sb.); sucker (sb.):给人～了 be had (*or* fleeced)

拿刀动杖 nádāo-dòngzhàng take up swords and cudgels; fight with weapons

拿得起,放得下 nádeqǐ, fàngdexià take something up or put it down with equal ease — one can settle down to any work and easily transfer to sth. else when it is called for; be flexible; be adaptable

拿顶 nádǐng *also*“拿大顶”〈体育〉handstand:几个孩子正在～。Several children are doing handstands.

拿讹头 ná étou extort; blackmail:～收昧心钱 extort money with threats /他想拿我的讹头。He wanted to blackmail me.

拿放 náfang *also*“拿伏”〈方言〉threaten to do sth. or not to do it; say or do sth. as a threat:你别～人,没有你别人也会做。Stop bluffing; we can easily ask somebody else to do it.

拿获 náhuò apprehend (a criminal); catch; capture:当场～ catch (a criminal) red-handed

拿架子 ná jiàzi put on airs; be haughty:我最讨厌别人～。I detest people giving themselves airs. /他那架子可是拿足了。He surely was on his high horse.

拿款 nákuǎn 〈口语〉put on airs

拿老 nálǎo flaunt one's seniority; put on the airs of a veteran; show off or parade one's expertise:他就喜欢在年轻人面前～。He enjoys flaunting his seniority before young people. /他不过比我早来两年,有什么可～的! After all, he is only two years my senior in terms of work experience here. What's there to brag about?

拿摩温 námówēn *see* "那摩温" nàmówēn

拿捏 nánie 〈方言〉❶ affectedly; with a show of hesitation:有话快说,～什么劲儿? Don't shilly-shally. Say it straight out. ❷ make it hot for sb.; threaten:故意～她 deliberately make things difficult for her /我才不受人家～呢! I won't bow to any blackmail.

拿破仑 Nápòlún Napoleon Bonaparte I (1769-1821), Emperor of the First French Empire(1804-1814):～法典 Napoleonic Code /～战争 Napoleonic Wars (1799-1815) /～帝国 Empire of Napoleon (1804-1815)

拿腔拿调 náqiāng-nádiào *also* "拿腔捏调";"拿腔作调" assume a peculiar voice or tone:这样～,真受不了。We cannot stand him talking to us in such an affected tone.

拿腔作势 náqiāng-zuòshì behave affectedly; be pretentious; strike a pose:今天的晚会上她怎么～的? How is it she appeared so affected at the party tonight? /自然些,别～就好。Don't get stagy. Be natural. /大家都是老熟人了,他拿什么腔作什么势! As we are all old acquaintances, there is really no need for him to be so pretentious.

拿乔 náqiáo strike a pose to impress people; assume airs:你求他他也会答应,但总要～。He will agree if you ask him (for help), but he will do it with such a condescending air. /我这不是～,实在是不能胜任。Not that I disdain to do it, but I am unequal to the job.

拿权 náquán wield power; be in the saddle; be in power:这里谁～? Who is in charge here? *or* Who is the boss here? /这是个危险人物,他一旦拿了权,我们都会遭殃的。He is a dangerous man. Once he is in power, we are bound to suffer. /他家里妻子～。His wife wears the trousers in the house.

拿人 nárén ❶ raise difficulties; make things difficult:就凭你这两下子拿得住人吗? Do you really think that a man of your calibre can browbeat us? ❷ attract; fascinate:他讲起故事来很能～。He can make his story very fascinating.

拿三搬四 násān-bānsì assume great airs; put on airs:你别～的。Don't put on such airs.

拿骚 Násāo Nassau, capital of the Bahamas

拿痧 náshā 〈中医〉pinching (the front of one's neck to cure sunstroke or heatstroke)

拿事 náshì be in control; have the final say; have the power to make the final decision:这人可从来没有拿过事。He has never assumed responsibililty for major decisions.

拿手 náshǒu ❶ skilled; adept; deft; expert:她织毛衣最～。She is a deft hand at knitting sweaters. ❷ confidence; certainty:干这个工作他有～。He is sure he can do the job well.

拿手好戏 náshǒu-hǎoxì *also* "拿手戏" ❶ part (in an opera) an actor or actress plays best:演曹操是这位演员的～。He is at his best when he plays the part of Cao Cao. ❷ one's speciality:修个电器什么的,是他的～。He is very good at fixing electrical appliances.

拿糖 nátáng 〈方言〉put on airs:～作醋 assume airs; be pretentious

拿问 náwèn 〈旧语〉be brought to trial:革职～ be dismissed from one's post and brought to book

拿下马 náxiàmǎ 〈俗语〉subdue; tame; vanquish:有人要千方百计把他～。Some people are trying every means possible to unseat him.

拿印把儿 ná yìnbàr *also* "拿印把子" be in control; have authority; be in power

拿贼拿赃 názéi-názāng you can't arrest sb. for theft without the loot as evidence — one cannot bring a charge against sb. without evidence

拿着鸡毛当令箭 názhe jīmáo dàng lìngjiàn 〈俗语〉regard a chicken feather as a warrant to issue orders — treat any casual remarks from higher-up as a command and make much ado about nothing

拿主意 ná zhǔyi make up one's mind; make a decision:你得拿个准主意。You must make up your mind. *or* You must make a definite decision, one way or the other. /去不去我还拿不定主意。I am in two minds whether to go or not. /主意你要自己拿。You should decide for yourself.

拿住刀把儿 názhu dāobàr 〈俗语〉hold the handle of a knife — be in an advantageous position; seize on sb.'s fault:咱们～,不怕他不承认。He simply cannot deny the charge for we have strong evidence against him. /现在我～了,看他怎么办! Now that I've caught him in the wrong, I'd like to see what he has to say.

拿总儿 názǒngr 〈口语〉have overall control:大伙儿出了这么多主意,最后还得队长～。We have put forward our suggestions, but still it's up to the team leader to make the final decision.

镎 ná 〈化学〉neptunium (Np)

镎酸 násuān neptunic acid

镎酸盐 násuānyán neptunate

nǎ

哪[1](**那**) nǎ ❶ which; what:这儿有三种颜色,你最喜欢～种? Here are three colours. Which do you like best? /你～天走? What day are you leaving? *or* When are you leaving? /你讲的是～国话? What language are you speaking? ❷ any:这些颜色我～个都不喜欢。I like none of these colours. /这话对～个人都不许说。Don't breathe a word to anyone. /～种样子都行,只要她喜欢。Any style will do, so long as she likes it.

哪[2](**那**) nǎ (used in rhetorical questions) how can; how could; how is it possible:～有你这样说话的? How could you talk like this? /她是我最好的朋友,她的生日我～能不去? How can I miss my best friend's birthday party? /～有这样的好事? This is too good to be true, isn't it?

see also na; né; něi

哪个 nǎge ❶ which:你的孩子上的是～学校? Which school do your children go to? /你在～单位工作? Where do you work? ❷〈方言〉who:～在敲门? Who is it? /～到这儿来过? Who has been here?

哪会儿 nǎhuìr *also* "哪会子" ❶ when:你是～来的? When did you come? /屋子里这么冷,～才能来暖气啊! It's freezing in the room. When will the heating be on? ❷ any time:不忙,你～办都行。There's no hurry. You can do it anytime. /我现在不急需,你～还我都没关系。As I don't need it right now, it doesn't matter when you bring it back.

哪家子 nǎjiāzi 〈口语〉*usually used in a rhetorical question to denote the speaker's displeasure and surprise*:你干吗这么大火儿,生～的气呀? Why are you getting so worked up? Who with?

哪里 nǎli ❶ where:这是～? Where are we? /你是～人? Where are you from? *or* What part of the country (*or* province) are you from? /身上～不舒服? What's wrong with you? *or* What's the problem? ❷ somewhere; anywhere:我好像在～见过这个人。It seems that I have met the person somewhere before. /干工作～都一样。It makes no difference where you work. /～困难就到～去。Go and work where the challenge is greatest. ❸ *used to form a rhetorical question of negation*:我～知道你心里想什么? How do I know what's in your mind? /她～知道公司已经亏空了五十万元! She hasn't the faintest idea that the company is in the red with a deficit of 500,000 *yuan*. ❹〈谦词〉not at all:"这事真麻烦你了。""～～!" "Thank you very much for the trouble (*or* help)". "Not at all." *or* "That's nothing." /～,你过奖了。You are flattering me.

哪门子 nǎménzi 〈方言〉*used to add force to a rhetorical question*:你这生的是～的气啊? What on earth has made you so angry? /我跟他是～亲戚? How could I be related to him?

哪能 nǎnéng (used in rhetorical question to express negation) how is it possible; how could:我～这样傻。How could I be so foolish?

哪怕 nǎpà 〈连词〉even if; even though; no matter how:～豁上命,我也要去救他。I'll go to his rescue even at the cost of my life. /我们已经决定了,～天气不好也要去。We have decided to go, rain or shine.

哪儿 nǎr where; anywhere:你从～来? Where have you been? /我好像～要出问题了。It seems that I'm coming down with something. /这样能干的秘书～找啊? Where else can you find a better secretary? /我～知道他今天会来? How was I to know he would come today?

哪儿的话 nǎrdehuà 〈谦词〉not at all; don't mention it; it's all right:"太麻烦你了。""～。" "Sorry to have troubled you." "Don't mention it."

哪些 nǎxiē which; who; what:明天～人来? Who will be coming tomorrow? /今晚有～节目? What's on the programme tonight? /你说说计算机都有～好处。Please tell me what advantages a computer has?

哪样 nǎyàng ❶ what kind of:这些削笔器,你觉得～的好? What kind of pencil-sharpener do you prefer? /～颜色最适合我? What

colour suits me best? ❷ any kind:我觉得～都可以。Any kind will do for me. /这两种,我～都不喜欢。I like neither of the two.

哪知 nǎzhī who would have known or thought:～会出这种事。Who would have thought such a thing could happen?

娿 nǎ 〈书面〉female:鸡～ hen

nà

捺 nà ❶ press; push; put:～手印 put one's figner-print (to a document) ❷ hold back; press down; restrain:按～不住激动的心情 unable to conceal one's excitement /在这种情况下,～着性子是不易做到的。It is difficult to control one's temper under such circumstances. ❸ right-falling stroke (in Chinese characters)

衲 nà ❶ patch up (esp. with close stitches):千补百～ (a jacket) with many patches ❷ vestment worn by a Buddhist monk (a term which may also be used by a monk to refer to himself):老～ I (the monk)

呐 nà

see also nè

呐喊 nàhǎn cry out; shout loudly; cheer:摇旗～ wave flags and shout loudly — beat the drum for sb. /～助威 shout encouragement; cheer /～着冲上去 charge while shouting battle cries

钠 nà 〈化学〉sodium (Na):～平衡 sodium balance

钠玻璃 nàbōli 〈化工〉soda glass

钠长石 nàchángshí 〈矿业〉albite

钠灯 nàdēng sodium lamp (usually used for illumination in mines and streets)

钠钙玻璃 nàgài bōli 〈化工〉soda-lime glass

钠光 nàguāng sodium light

钠冷堆 nàlěngduī 〈核物理〉sodium-cooled reactor

钠冷重水反应堆 nàlěng zhòngshuǐ fǎnyìngduī 〈核物理〉Sodium-D_2O Reactor (SDR)

钠离子 nàlízǐ sodium ion

钠气灯 nàqìdēng sodium discharge lamp

钠橡胶 nàxiàngjiāo 〈化工〉sodium rubber

钠硝石 nàxiāoshí 〈矿业〉chilisaltpeter; nitratine; soda niter

钠盐 nàyán sodium salt

钠云母 nàyúnmǔ 〈矿业〉paragonite; soda-mica

钠皂润滑脂 nàzào rùnhuázhī 〈化工〉sodium-soap grease

肭 nà *see* "腽肭" wànà

纳[1] nà ❶ receive; let in; admit:收～ receive /闭门不～ refuse to admit; deny sb. entrance ❷ accept; take:采～ adopt (a proposal, a plan, etc.) /请笑～。(of a gift) Hope you'll graciously accept this gift from me. *or* This is presented to you with compliments. ❸ enjoy: *see* "～凉" ❹ bring into (a plan, a project, etc.): *see* "～入" ❺ pay; give (as a duty required by the authorities):缴～所得税 pay income tax ❻ (Nà) a surname

纳[2] nà sew close stitches (over sth. rather thick):～鞋底儿 stitch soles (of cloth shoes) /这鞋垫儿～得真精细。The stitches on the insoles are so fine.

纳[3] nà 〈物理〉noy

纳彩 nàcǎi 〈古语〉(of a prospective bridegroom's family) present gifts to the girls' family at the time of betrothal

纳粹 Nàcuì Nazi (the German National Socialist Party led by Adolf Hitler):～分子 Nazi (a member of the Nazi) /～党 Nazi Party /～主义 Nazism /～军官 Nazi officer

纳呆 nàdāi *also* "胃呆" wèidāi 〈中医〉indigestion or loss of appetite

纳福 nàfú (of elderly people) live a life of ease

纳贡 nàgòng pay tribute (to a suzerain or emperor)

纳罕 nàhǎn be surprised; wonder:他见家中空无一人,心里很～。He was surprised that no one was at home.

纳贿 nàhuì ❶ take or accept bribes:他为政清廉,从不～。He is an honest official and never accepts bribes. ❷ offer or give bribes:～是严重的犯罪行为。Bribery is a serious crime.

纳谏 nàjiàn 〈书面〉(of an emperor or a ruler) accept advice from a court official

纳交 nàjiāo 〈书面〉associate with; make friends with:～文人学士 associate with men of letters

纳款 nàkuǎn 〈书面〉(of enemy troops, rebels or bandits) swear allegiance ; surrender; cross over

纳凉 nàliáng enjoy the cool (in the open air or in the shade):晚上一家人坐在院子里～。The whole family sat around in the yard, enjoying the cool of the evening.

纳粮 nàliáng 〈旧语〉pay or hand in grain tax (to the state or to landlords)

纳闷 nàmèn ❶〈口语〉feel puzzled or perplexed, be bewildered; wonder:我也～他为什么要亲自去一趟。I was wondering, too, why he wanted to go there in person. /她突然改变了主意,我心里有些～。I was somewhat puzzled at her sudden change of mind. ❷ (often used in the early vernacular) moody; unhappy:他坐在房中～。He brooded in his room.

纳米 nàmǐ *also* "毫微米" háowēimǐ nanometre (nm = 10^{-9} metre)

纳米比亚 Nàmǐbǐyà Namibia:～人 Namibian

纳米科学 nàmǐkēxué nanoscience

纳秒 nàmiǎo *also* "毫微秒" háowēimiǎo nanosecond

纳木湖 Nàmùhú Nam Co, largest inland lake in Tibet Autonomous Region

纳聘 nàpìn 〈旧语〉(of a prospective bridegroom's family) send betrothal gifts to the girl's family at the time of engagement

纳妾 nàqiè take a concubine

纳入 nàrù bring into; channel into; incorporate into:～国家计划 bring sth. into the state plan /～健康发展的轨道 put sth. on the basis of healthy development /～高科技发展的轨道 bring sth. into the orbit of high-technology development

纳赛尔 Nàsài'ěr Gamal Abdel Nasser (1918-1970), President of Egypt (1956-1970)

纳赛尔水库 Nàsài'ěr Shuǐkù Lake Nasser, a huge reservoir in southern Egypt created by the building of the two dams at Aswan

纳纱 nàshā 〈工美〉a kind of handicraft (made by using coloured silk-threads to embroider pictures on handbags, etc.)

纳纱制品 nàshā zhìpǐn 〈工美〉petit-point article

纳税 nàshuì pay taxes:～人 taxpayer /～优惠条件 tax advantages /～责任 tax liability /～准备金 tax reserve /～年度 tax year /这类收入是应该～的。Income of this sort is subject to taxation. *or* This kind of income is taxable.

纳头 nàtóu (often used in the early vernacular) lower one's head (as a form of salutation):～便拜 kneel down with one's head lowered and make salutations

纳维方程 Nàwéi fāngchéng 〈物理〉Navier's equation

纳西族 Nàxīzú Naxi (formerly translated as Nahsi) nationality living in Yunnan Province

纳降 nàxiáng accept the enemy's surrender

纳小 nàxiǎo *see* "纳妾"

纳新 nàxīn take in the fresh:吐故～ exhale the old and inhale the new; discard what is old and embrace what is new /政党应经常～。A political party should regularly take in new members.

那[1] nà *used to indicate sb. or sth. away from the speaker*:看～儿棵树长得多好哇! Look at those trees! So sturdy and luxuriant! /～不是我的。That isn't mine. /～天我没去。I didn't go that day. /～是谁? Who is it? *or* Who is he (*or* she)? /～就是你迟到的原因啊! So that's why you are late!

那[2] nà then; in that case:你既然不同意,～这事就算了吧。Since you don't agree, then let's drop the matter . /～你怎么回答他的呢? What did you say to him then? /～我们下一步怎么办? Well, what are we going to do next? /要干,～就好好干吧。If you are set to do it, do it well.

see also Nā; nè; nèi

那不勒斯 Nàbùlèsī Naples, city and port on the west coast of Italy, south of Rome

N

那程子 nàchéngzi 〈方言〉at that time;(in) those days:～我正忙，没有功夫来看你。I was very busy those days and couldn't find time to visit you.
那达慕 nàdámù Nadam Fair, a Mongolian traditional sports fair
那当儿 nàdāngr 〈口语〉at that time;(in)those days:～我常到河里游泳。In those days I used to go swimming in the river.
那个 nàge ❶ that:～重要的问题还得研究。That important issue has yet to be examined. /你还是三年前～样。You haven't changed a bit since we met three years ago. *or* You look very much the same as three years ago. ❷ that thing; that matter:～你不用担心，我去想办法。You needn't worry about that. Leave it to me. /别提～了。Don't bring the matter up. /他这个～的买了一大堆礼物。He bought a large assortment of gifts. ❸ *used before a verb or an adjective to indicate a certain degree of exaggeration*:大伙儿～高兴啊! Everybody was so happy! /瞧你～嚷嚷，谁听得清你说的什么! You were shouting yourself hoarse, but no one could make out what you were saying. ❹ *used instead of a certain word or statement to avoid bluntness or with a touch of humour*:他人不错，就是脾气～了一点。He is a good man except for his temper. /这样做不是有点～了吗? Don't you think it's not quite the thing to do?
那鸿书 Nàhóngshū *The Book of Nahum*, a book of the *Old Testament* containing Nahum's prophecy of the fall of Nineveh (early 7th century BC)
那会儿 nàhuìr *indicating a time in the past or in the future*:～我还小，不懂事。I was then too young to be sensible. /到工作～，我就可以独立了。I will be on my own once I have a job. /～的情形跟现在不一样。Things were different in those days.
那里 nàli that place; there:从这里到～ from here to there; from this place to that / ～热，不用带这么多衣服。It's quite warm there; you needn't take so many clothes with you.
那么 nàme *also*"那末" ❶ like that; in that way; in that manner; to that extent:他头～一扬就出去了。With a toss of his head he went out. /明年你就有他～高了。You'll be as tall as he next year. /情况～复杂，要认真研究。Things are so complicated that we will have to study them seriously. ❷ (used before a number to indicate estimation or approximation) about; some; or so:到火车站还得走～十来分钟。We have to walk some ten more minutes before we can get to the railway station. /有～两、三个人帮忙就行了。It will do if we can get two or three people to help. /再来～二十份就差不多了。Get another 20 copies or so, and that will probably be enough. ❸ then; in that case:～，我们干什么呢? 游泳还是骑车? What shall we do, then? Shall we go swimming or cycling? /这也不对，那也不对，～你打算怎么样? This isn't right and that isn't right either. Then, what are you planning to do?
那么点儿 nàmediǎnr so little:～年纪就懂这么多事，真不简单。It is remarkable that such a little child should know so much of the world. /～活儿，半天足够了。Half a day would be more than enough for this bit of work.
那么些 nàmexiē so much; so many:～天不照面，你上哪儿去了? Haven't seen you for so long (*or* ages). Where have you been? /～书你两三天内看得完吗? Can you manage to read so many books in a couple of days?
那么着 nàmezhe (do sth.) that way; like that:你～想就错了。If you think like that, you are wrong. /～怕要出错儿。Things will probably go wrong if you do it that way. /要～，一切都好办了。If that is the case, there'll be no problem at all.
那末 nàme *see*"那么"
那摩温 nàmówēn *also*"拿摩温" námówēn 〈旧语〉(transliteration of "number one", used in pre-1949 Shanghai) foreman; forewoman; overseer
那曲 Nàqū Nagqu, county in the north of Tibet Autonomous Region
那儿 nàr ❶ there;that place:～谁也没去过。No one has ever been there. /请～坐。Take a seat over there, please. ❷ (used after 打，从，由) that time; then: 打～起，他就戒了烟。He stopped smoking after that. *or* He has given up smoking since then./ 由～开始，他常常在晚上注意观察星球的运动。He has since often gone out in the evening to observe the stars in the sky.
那时 nàshí at that time; in those days; then:说时迟～快 quicker than words can tell; in the twinkling of an eye; instantly /～他还只是个孩子。He was only a child at the time. /～人们的价值观念不一样。In those days, the moral values were different.
那些 nàxiē those:把～箱子搬开。Move those boxes away. /我永远忘不了在那个小村庄度过的～日子。I'll never forget the days I spent in that small village. /事情早过去了，别再提～了。Let bygones be bygones. Don't ever mention it again.
那样 nàyàng like that; of that kind; such; so:～的机会可不多。Such chances are rare. /你不该～胡说。You shouldn't have talked irresponsibly like that. /他的语气是～坚决，～自信。He sounds so resolute, so confident! /只有～，才能学好外语。Only thus can you master a foreign language.
那咱 nàzan *also*"那早晚" at that time:想起～受的苦，现在心里还难受。Recalling the misery I suffered at that time, I still feel very bad.
那阵儿 nàzhènr *indicating a period of time in the past*:昨天吃晚饭～，你上哪儿去了? Where were you at supper time yesterday? /刚才～，好大的雨呀! What a big shower we had a moment ago!

娜 nà used in feminine names
see also nuó

na

哪(呐) na 〈助词〉*used after a word ending in* n *to tone up what is being said*:多谢您～。Thank you very much, sir. /咱们什么时候一块儿吃顿饭～? Shall we have dinner together sometime? *see also* nǎ; né; něi

nǎi

倷 nǎi 〈方言〉you

乃(迺、廼) nǎi 〈书面〉❶ be:北京～中国之首都。Beijing is the capital of China. ❷ so; therefore:因时间仓促，～作罢。The matter had to be dropped for I was hard pressed for time. ❸ only then;only thus:惟努力～能成功。You cannot succeed unless you work hard. *or* Only when you work hard can you expect to succeed. ❹ you; your:～翁 your father /～兄 your brother
乃尔 nǎi'ěr 〈书面〉like this; to such an extent:何其相似～! What striking similarity! /何为～! Why should it be so? /此地风俗敦直～! How simple and honest the people here are!
乃是 nǎishì be:锻炼～健身之道。Physical exercise is the way to keep fit. *or* Exercises are essential in body-building.
乃至 nǎizhì *also*"乃至于" and even:这次会议对本地区～全国的纺织业都是很大的促进。This conference will give great impetus to the textile industry in this region and even in the country as a whole.

艿 nǎi *see*"芋艿" yùnǎi

氖 nǎi 〈化学〉neon (Ne)
氖灯 nǎidēng neon lamp;neon light; neon
氖管 nǎiguǎn neon tube
氖辉光灯管 nǎihuīguāng dēngguǎn neon glow lamp
氖气 nǎiqì neon

奶(嬭) nǎi ❶ breast:*see*"～头";"～房" ❷ milk:牛～(cow) milk /羊～ goat's milk /人～ human milk; milk /脱脂～ skimmed milk /低脂～ low-fat milk /巧克力～ chocolate milk /全脂～ whole milk /喂～ nurse (feed) a baby /吃～的孩子 suckling baby; suckling ❸ breastfeed; nurse; suckle:～孩子 breastfeed (*or* suckle, *or* nurse) a baby
奶媪 nǎi'ǎo 〈方言〉wet nurse
奶茶 nǎichá tea with milk; milk tea
奶畜 nǎichù newborn animal; sucking animal; suckling
奶疮 nǎichuāng 〈医学〉mastitis
奶爹 nǎidiē 〈方言〉husband of one's wet nurse
奶房 nǎifáng 〈方言〉breast; mamma
奶粉 nǎifěn milk powder; powdered milk; dried milk:全脂～ whole milk powder
奶糕 nǎigāo baby food made of rice-flour, sugar, and sometimes powdered milk

奶公 nǎigōng 〈方言〉husband of one's wet nurse
奶积 nǎijī 〈中医〉indigestion of a suckling baby
奶酒 nǎijiǔ *also* "奶子酒" fermented (cow's or mare's) milk, a kind of alcoholic drink of the Mongolians
奶酪 nǎilào cheese
奶妈 nǎimā wet nurse
奶毛 nǎimáo first hairs of a newborn baby
奶名 nǎimíng child's pet name; infant name
奶母 nǎimǔ wet nurse
奶奶 nǎinai ❶ (paternal) grandmother; grandma ❷ respectful form of address for an elderly woman ❸〈方言〉(form of address formerly used by servants of the house) young mistress
奶娘 nǎiniáng *see* "奶妈"
奶牛 nǎiniú milk cow; milch cow; cow: ～场 cow farm
奶农 nǎinóng dairy farmer
奶膀子 nǎipāngzi 〈方言〉breast; mamma
奶皮 nǎipí milk skin
奶品 nǎipǐn milk product; dairy product
奶瓶 nǎipíng feeding bottle; nursing bottle; baby's bottle: 一次性～ disposable bottle /塑料～ plastic feeding bottle
奶声奶气 nǎishēng-nǎiqì speak in a baby or child-like voice; lisp: 那么大人, 说起话来～的, 真讨厌。It gets on my nerves to hear such a grown-up speak in a child-like voice. /孩子们～地说: "爷爷新年好。" The children piped in their sweet baby voices: "Happy New Year, Grandpa!"
奶水 nǎishuǐ 〈口语〉milk: ～不足 not have enough milk for breast-feeding
奶糖 nǎitáng toffee
奶头 nǎitóu 〈口语〉❶ nipple; teat; tit ❷ nipple (of a feeding bottle)
奶娃 nǎiwá *also* "奶娃娃"〈方言〉breast-fed baby; sucking baby
奶牙 nǎiyá milk tooth
奶羊 nǎiyáng milch goat
奶油 nǎiyóu cream: ～糖 toffee /～色 creamy colour /～蛋糕 cake with cream on top; birthday cake /～分离器 cream separator
奶油冻 nǎiyóudòng mousse
奶油瓜子 nǎiyóu guāzǐ cream-coated melon seeds
奶油小生 nǎiyóu xiǎoshēng handsome but effeminate young man or actor
奶罩 nǎizhào *also* "胸罩" xiōngzhào; "文胸" wénxiōng; "乳罩" rǔzhào brassiere; bra
奶汁 nǎizhī milk
奶粥节 Nǎizhōujié Pongal, the Tamil New Year festival in December on which new rice is cooked
奶子 nǎizi ❶〈口语〉milk ❷〈方言〉breast ❸〈方言〉wet nurse
奶子酒 nǎizijiǔ *see* "奶酒"
奶嘴 nǎizuǐ nipple (of a feeding bottle)

迺

nǎi ❶ *see* "乃" nǎi ❷ (Nǎi) a surname

nài

柰

nài a kind of apple
柰子 nàizi a kind of apple

奈

nài ❶ how; however: 无～ not know how (to solve a problem, etc.); be helpless; cannot but /她日日思念老母, 怎～关山阻隔, 难得一见。She missed her mother every day; however, the long distance separating them made it difficult for them to meet. ❷〈书面〉*short for* 怎奈 *or* 无奈: 待要回去, ～事未毕。He wanted to return home, only his business had not been finished. ❸ (same as 耐) bear: 我丑便丑, ～看。Plain as I am, I bear scrutinizing. /罗衾不～秋风力。The thin silk quilt was not warm enough to resist the piercing autumnal draught.
奈耳 nài'ěr ❶〈核物理〉nile ❷ (Nài'ěr) Louis Eugène Felix Néel (1904-), French physicist, Nobel prizewinner for 1970: ～理论 Néel's theory / ～温度 Néel's temperature
奈何 nàihé ❶ *used in a rhetorical question to express helplessness*: 无可～ utterly helpless; powerless /～不得 can do nothing about sth. (*or* to sb.) / 无可～花落去, 似曾相识燕归来。Deeply I sigh for the fallen flowers in rain, Vaguely I remember the swallows come again. ❷〈书面〉*used in a rhetorical question to express futility*: 民不畏死, ～以死惧之? The people fear not death. Why threaten them with it? ❸ *used rhetorically with a pronoun in between to express futility in an attempt to influence sb.*: 他就是不肯, 你又奈他何? He simply wouldn't agree. What can you do with him? /其奈我何? What can they do to me?
奈基 Nàijī Nike, goddess of victory in Greek mythology
奈基导弹 Nàijī dǎodàn 〈军事〉Nike
奈基-X 反弹道导弹系统 Nàijī-àikèsī fǎndàndào dǎodàn xìtǒng 〈军事〉Nike-X
奈基-宙斯导弹 Nàijī-Zhòusī dǎodàn 〈军事〉Nike-Zeus
奈克鞋 nàikèxié Nike, an American trademark for sports shoes
奈良 Nàiliáng Nara, a city and ancient capital on Honshu Island, Japan

萘

nài 〈化学〉naphthalene: ～球 *also* "樟脑丸"; "卫生球" naphthalene ball; moth ball
萘胺 nài'àn 〈化学〉naphthylamine
萘酚 nàifēn 〈化学〉naphthol
萘乙酸 nàiyǐsuān 〈农业〉naphthaleneacetic acid (used to prevent premature dropping of fruit or seed)
萘油 nàiyóu 〈化学〉fraction of coal tar, the boiling point of which is between 210-218℃.

耐

nài be able to bear or endure: ～穿 (of clothing) stand wear and tear; stand hard wear; be durable; can last long /～用 (of things) be durable; can last long /忍～ bear; endure; put up with; stand /～着性子听 listen patiently /这种材料～高温。This material is heat-resistant. *or* This material can stand very high temperature. /牛仔裤很～洗。Blue jeans wash well (*or* bear washing). /他早～不住了。He could no longer hold back his anger (*or* excitement).
耐病性 nàibìngxìng disease tolerance
耐波力 nàibōlì 〈航海〉seaworthy qualities (of a vessel); seaworthiness
耐低温橡胶 nàidīwēn xiàngjiāo cold resistant rubber
耐烦 nàifán patient: 他等得不～了。He is waiting impatiently. /她教学生十分～。She is very patient with her students.
耐辐照度 nàifúzhàodù radioresistance
耐腐蚀性 nàifǔshíxìng corrosion resistance
耐高温陶瓷 nàigāowēn táocí pyroceram; refractory ceramics
耐高温纤维 nàigāowēn xiānwéi high temperature fibre
耐寒 nàihán endure cold weather; be cold-resistant: ～性 resistance to cold /～作物 cold-resistant crop
耐旱植物 nàihàn zhíwù drought-enduring plant
耐火 nàihuǒ fire-resistant; refractory: ～水泥 refractory cement /～衬砌 refractory lining
耐火玻璃 nàihuǒ bōli 〈化工〉hard borosilicate glass
耐火材料 nàihuǒ cáiliào refractory material; fire-proof material
耐火层 nàihuǒcéng flame retardant coating
耐火泥 nàihuǒní 〈冶金〉fire clay; refractory clay
耐火黏土 nàihuǒ niántǔ refractory clay
耐火漆 nàihuǒqī 〈化工〉fire-retardant paint; flame-proof paint
耐火涂料 nàihuǒ túliào fireproof coating; refractory dressing; fireproof or fire-resistant dope
耐火砖 nàihuǒzhuān refractory brick; firebrick
耐碱漆 nàijiǎnqī 〈化工〉alkali-resisting paint
耐久 nàijiǔ lasting long; durable: 坚固～ strong and durable/～性 durability; viability
耐看 nàikàn (of a work of art or scenery) stand scrutiny; be of lasting interest: 这幅画不～。The painting does not stand close examination. /这部小说中的木刻插图精美～。The woodcut plates in this novel are extremely elegant and of durable interest.
耐苦 nàikǔ (of a person) be able to stand hardship: 他种地为生, 很是勤快～。Doing farming for a living, he is diligent and capable of enduring much hardship.
耐劳 nàiláo work tirelessly: 吃苦～ be of great endurance
耐力 nàilì endurance; stamina; staying power: 跑马拉松需要很大的～。You need great stamina to run a marathon. *or* The marathon demands great stamina.
耐磨 nàimó wear-resisting; wearproof: 布袜子不～。Cotton socks don't wear. /这地毯极其～。This carpet will stand hard wear. /这种

材料薄是薄,可很～。This material looks thin but it wears amazingly well.
耐磨钢 nàimógāng abrasion-resistant steel
耐磨合金钢 nàimó héjīngāng wear-resisting alloy steel
耐磨性 nàimóxìng wearability; resistance to wear
耐磨硬度 nàimó yìngdù abrasion hardness
耐疲劳 nàipíláo 〈冶金〉 anti-fatigue
耐气 nàiqì 〈方言〉 endurance; patience
耐热 nàirè heat-resistant; heat-resisting; heatproof; thermotolerant:一种～的玻璃盘 a kind of glass dish that resists heat /～性 heat resistance
耐热合金 nàirè héjīn heat-resisting alloy
耐热塑料 nàirè sùliào 〈化工〉 heat resistance plastic (HRP)
耐热涂料 nàirè túliào 〈化工〉 heat resistant paint (HRP)
耐人寻味 nàirénxúnwèi give one plenty of food for thought; be intriguing:这篇短文读起来句句～。Almost every sentence of this short essay is thought-provoking. /她这一举动真～。This act of hers is certainly worth a closer look.
耐蚀钢 nàishígāng 〈冶金〉 corrosion-resisting steel
耐蚀合金 nàishí héjīn 〈冶金〉 stain-resistant alloy; anticorrosion alloy; chlorimet
耐受 nàishòu endure; be able to stand or bear:经过长期锻炼,人能够在短时间内～快速的心跳。Man can bear speedy heart-beats for a short time after a protracted work-out.
耐受性 nàishòuxìng 〈军事〉 survivability; tolerance
耐水作物 nàishuǐ zuòwù water-tolerant crop
耐酸 nàisuān acid-proof; acid-resisting:～混凝土 acid-resisting concrete /～缸器 acid-proof stoneware /～涂料 acid-proof coating
耐洗涤性 nàixǐdíxìng launderability
耐心 nàixīn patience:有～ be patient /缺乏～ lack patience /～等待 wait patiently /～说服 persuade with patience; use patient persuasion
耐心烦 nàixīnfán 〈口语〉 patience; forbearance:伺候病人没有～儿不行。You have to have great patience to look after an invalid.
耐性 nàixìng patience; endurance:～到了限度 be stretched to the limit of one's patience; have reached the limit of one's endurance / 跟他这种人打交道得耐着性子。It taxes one's patience to deal with people like him.
耐锈 nàixiù 〈冶金〉 antirust
耐压 nàiyā 〈物理〉 pressure proof:～壳体 pressure hull /～试验 pressure-tight test
耐用 nàiyòng durable:～物品 durable goods; durables /～消费品 durable consumer goods /搪瓷器皿比玻璃器皿～。Enamel ware is more durable than glassware.
耐战 nàizhàn well-trained for battle:这支部队十分～。The troops are all remarkably seasoned warriors.
耐震 nàizhèn shock resistant:～设备 shock proof apparatus
耐重力 nàizhònglì 〈物理〉 antigravity:～装置 antigravity device

褦 nài

褦襶 nàidài 〈书面〉 not sensible:～子 unreasonable person

鼐 nài 〈书面〉 big tripod

nān

囡(囝) nān 〈方言〉 ❶child:小～ little child /男小～ little boy /女小～ little girl ❷ daughter:她有一个儿子一个～。She has a son and a daughter.

囡囡 nānnān 〈方言〉 little darling (used as a term of endearment for a baby or a child)

nán

南 nán ❶ south:山～ south of the mountain /江～ south of the lower reaches of the Yangtze River /～风 south wind /坐～朝北 face north; have a northern exposure ❷ southern region; Yangtze River valley and areas south of the river:～席 banquet of southern cuisine ❸ (Nán) a surname

see also nā

南半球 nánbànqiú southern hemisphere
南梆子 nánbāngzi one of the singing styles of Beijing Opera
南北 nán-běi ❶ north and south:～风味 both south and north cuisines /京广线是沟通～的大动脉。The Beijing-Guangzhou line is a main artery in the railway system connecting the north and south of China. ❷ from north to south:大江～ south and north of the Yangtze River; across China /市区～有八公里。The city proper has a length of 8 kilometres from south to north.
南北朝 Nán-Běicháo Northern and Southern dynasties (420-589)
南北对话 Nán-Běi duìhuà North-South dialogue (dialogue between developed and developing countries)
南北战争 Nán-Běi Zhànzhēng *also* "美国内战" Měiguó Nèizhàn American Civil War (1861-1865), a war between the northern states (known as the Union) and the Confederate States of the South
南边 nánbian ❶ south:房子～ south of the house ❷ 〈口语〉 areas south of the Yangtze River:这些青菜是从～来的。These greens are from the South.
南部 nánbù southern part; south:～非洲 southern Africa /中国～的雨水很充足。There is plenty of rainfall in the south of China.
南昌 Nánchāng Nanchang (capital of Jiangxi Province)
南昌起义 Nánchāng Qǐyì *also* "八一南昌起义" Bā-Yī Nánchāng Qǐyì The August 1 Nanchang Uprising (1927) against the Kuomintang reactionaries, which marked the beginning of the Chinese Communist Party's independent leadership of China's revolutionary war
南朝 Náncháo Southern dynasties (420-589)
南朝鲜 Náncháoxiān informal name for the Republic of Korea (ROK)
南磁极 náncíjí geo-magnetic south pole
南岛 Nándǎo South Island, one of two major islands of New Zealand
南地理极 nándìlǐjí 〈地理〉 south geographical pole
南丁格尔 Nándīnggé'ěr Florence Nightingale (1820-1910), English nurse and medical reformer
南斗 Nándǒu 〈天文〉 Southern Dipper
南豆腐 nándòufu tender southern-style bean curd
南方 nánfāng ❶ south:村子在城市的～。The village lies to the south of the city. ❷ areas south of the Yangtze River; southern China:～话 southern dialect /～人 southerner /～风味 southern flavour /在～工作 work in the south
南方古猿 nánfāng gǔyuán *also* "南猿" 〈考古〉 *Australopithecus*, also called Southern Ape, a kind of animal between man and ancient ape, the fossil of which was first discovered in south Africa
南非 Nánfēi South Africa:～人 South African
南风 nánfēng south wind
南宫 Nángōng Nangong, a surname
南瓜 nánguā pumpkin; cushaw; Chinese squash
南瓜子 nánguāzǐ pumpkin seed; squash seed
南管 nánguǎn *see* "南音❷"
南国 nánguó 〈书面〉 the south; southern part of the country:～风光 southern scenery /～春来早。Spring comes early in the south.
南海 Nánhǎi Nanhai Sea; South China Sea:～舰队 South China Sea Fleet
南海诸岛 Nánhǎi Zhūdǎo South China Sea Islands, which consists of China's Dongsha (东沙), Xisha (西沙), Zhongsha (中沙) and Nansha (南沙) Islands and their adjacent islands
南寒带 nánhándài south frigid zone
南胡 nánhú another name for *erhu* (二胡), a two-stringed bowed instrument
南华早报 Nánhuá Zǎobào *South China Morning Post*, an English language newspaper in Hong Kong
南回归线 nánhuíguīxiàn 〈地理〉 Tropic of Capricorn
南货 nánhuò specialities or delicacies from south China
南极 nánjí ❶ South Pole; the Antarctic:～地带 Antarctic area /～考察站 research station in the Antarctic ❷ south magnetic pole(s)
南极光 nánjíguāng 〈天文〉 *aurora australis*; southern lights
南极海 Nánjíhǎi Antarctic Ocean
南极圈 nánjíquān Antarctic Circle
南极条约 Nánjí Tiáoyuē Antarctic Treaty, concluded in 1959 by 12 countries for governing the exploitation of Antarctica

南极虾 nánjíxiā *also* "磷虾" línxiā 〈动物〉 euphausiid shrimp; krill

南极洲 Nánjízhōu Antarctic Continent; Antarctica: ～半岛 Antarctic Peninsula

南伽山 Nánjiāshān *Nanga Parbat*, 8126m above sea level in the west Himalayas

南京 Nánjīng Nanjing, capital of Jiangsu Province

南京大屠杀 Nánjīng Dàtúshā Nanjing Massacre, atrocities committed by Japanese aggressors against the civilians in Nanjing in December 1937, leaving a death toll of over 300,000

南京条约 Nánjīng Tiáoyuē Treaty of Nanjing (1842), an unequal treaty imposed on the Qing government by the British government after the Opium War

南柯一梦 nánkē-yīmèng Nanke dream (from the story of a man who dreamed that he became governor of Nanke in the Kingdom of Ants); fond dream; pipe dream; illusory joy: 他的各种打算一夜之间化为～。All his plans turned out to be but a pipe dream overnight. *or* All his dreams vanished overnight like soap bubbles.

南来北往 nánlái-běiwǎng go north and south; come and go in all directions: 街上满是～的车辆。There is heavy traffic in the street.

南美洲 Nánměizhōu South America

南面 nánmiàn ❶ facing the south: ～称王 proclaim oneself emperor ❷ south

南南合作 Nán-Nán hézuò South-South cooperation (cooperation among developing countries)

南南会议 Nán-Nán huìyì South-South conference (attended by delegations from developing countries)

南泥湾精神 Nánníwān Jīngshén Nanniwan Spirit (the spirit of hard work of the 359th Brigade of the Eighth Route Army, stationed at Nanniwan, Yan'an, in its struggle for self sufficiency in food and clothing amid great hardship in the years of 1941-1944)

南宁 Nánníng Nanning, capital of the Guangxi Zhuang Autonomous Region

南欧 Nán Ōu Southern Europe

南浦 Nánpǔ Nampo, city and sea port in South Pyongan of the Democratic People's Republic of Korea

南齐 Nán Qí Southern Qi Dynasty (479-502), one of the Southern dynasties

南腔北调 nánqiāng-běidiào medley of north and south accents; mixed accent: 他来北方多年，可说起话来仍是～。After all these years in the north, he still speaks with a mixed accent.

南曲 nánqǔ ❶ southern tunes (soft and sweet melodies popular in the south during the Song, Yuan and Ming dynasties) ❷ opera in southern tunes

南人 nánrén southerner

南沙群岛 Nánshā Qúndǎo Nansha Islands (known in the West as the Spratlys)

南沙参 nánshāshēn 〈植物〉 root of straight ladybell (*Adenophora stricta*)

南式 nánshì southern style: ～糕点 cakes and pastries of southern style

南水北调 nánshuǐ-běidiào divert water from the south to the north: ～工程 projects to divert water from the south to the north

南斯拉夫 Nánsīlāfū Yugoslavia: ～人 Yugoslav

南宋 Nán Sòng Southern Song Dynasty (1127-1279)

南太平洋论坛 Nántàipíngyáng Lùntán South Pacific Forum, an organization set up in 1971 and composed of countries in the South Pacific region with its head office in Fiji

南糖 nántáng southern sweets

南天 nántiān southern skies: 遥望～ gaze from afar at the southern skies

南天极 nántiānjí celestial pole in the Southern Hemisphere

南天竹 nántiānzhú 〈植物〉 nandina

南纬 nánwěi south or southern latitude

南味 nánwèi southern flavour: ～小吃 snacks of southern flavour

南温带 nánwēndài south temperate zone

南戏 nánxì *also* "戏文" xìwén southern drama (which made its first appearance in the Wenzhou 温州 area in southern China during the early Southern Song Dynasty)

南下 nánxià go down south: 他近日将动身～。He is going down south shortly.

南亚 Nán Yà South Asia: ～次大陆 South Asian subcontinent

南洋 Nányáng ❶ (used in the late Qing Dynasty) general name for the coastal provinces of Jiangsu, Zhejiang, Fujian and Guangdong ❷ old name for areas lying further south beyond the South China Sea (including Malay Archipelago, the Malay Peninsula and Indonesia)

南音 nányīn ❶ a kind of ballad singing popular in the Pearl River Delta ❷ *also* "南管"; "南乐" classical music popular in China's Fujian Province

南猿 nányuán *see* "南方古猿"

南辕北辙 nányuán-běizhé try to go south by driving the chariot northward — act in a way that defeats one's purpose; be poles apart: 如果这样下去，那将是～，一事无成。If you go on like this, it will be self-defeating and you will end up achieving nothing.

南乐 nányuè *see* "南音❷"

南岳 Nányuè Southern Sacred Mountain, also known as Mount Heng (衡山)

see also "五岳" Wǔyuè

南诏 Nánzhào Nanzhao, local regime in Yunnan Province in the 8-10th centuries

南针 nánzhēn ❶ compass ❷ guide (to action)

南征北战 nánzhēng-běizhàn fight north and south; fight battles across the country: 他是一位老战士，一辈子～，为革命事业立下了汗马功劳。He is a veteran warrior who has fought battles throughout the length and breadth of the country and rendered meritorious services to the cause of the revolution.

南竹 nánzhú *see* "楠竹" nánzhú

楠（枏） nán

楠木 nánmù 〈植物〉 *nanmu* (*Phoebe nanmu*)

楠竹 nánzhú *also* "毛竹" máozhú 〈植物〉 *mao* bamboo (*Phyllostachys edulis*)

喃 nán

喃喃 nánnán 〈象声〉 mutter; murmur: ～絮语 murmuring (as of babies) / ～自语 mutter (*or* mumble) to oneself / 他～地絮叨了一路，抱怨不停。He was muttering complaints all the way.

男[1] nán

❶ man; male: ～青年 young man / ～学生 male student; boy student / ～职工 male staff / ～演员 actor / ～主人公 hero (in a novel or play) / ～病房 men's ward / ～排 men's volleyball team / ～耕女织。(division of labour between men and women in a family in ancient China) The man works in the fields while the woman sits at the loom. ❷ son; boy: 长～ eldest son / 生有两～两女 have two sons and two daughters

男[2] nán

lowest of the five ranks of nobility in feudal times; baron

男阿飞 nán'āfēi Teddy boy

男扮女装 nánbàn-nǚzhuāng man disguised as a woman; man in drag

男傧相 nánbīnxiàng best man

男不男，女不女 nán bù nán, nǚ bù nǚ neither fish, flesh nor fowl: 你看他打扮得～的，成什么样子! Look, he is half dressed like a woman. How revolting! *or* Look at the revolting way he's dressed. As the saying goes, neither fish, flesh nor fowl!

男厕所 náncèsuǒ ❶ men's lavatory; men's room ❷ (sign on men's lavatory) Men; Gentlemen; Gents

男单 nándān (short for 男子单打)〈体育〉 men's singles (of tennis, table tennis, etc.)

男盗女娼 nándào-nǚchāng behave like thieves and whores — be full of greed and lust: 满口仁义道德，一肚子～。One's mouth overflows with pious rhetoric while one's heart contains nothing but greed and lust. / 这些人，看似文明，其实是～，无恶不作。Despite their genteel appearance these people have nasty minds and stop at no evil.

男低音 nándīyīn 〈音乐〉 bass

男丁 nándīng able-bodied man; grown-up man

男儿 nán'ér man: ～当自强。A man should seek self-improvement. / ～志在四方。A real man goes wherever his ambition takes him. / ～有泪不轻弹。A man does not easily shed tears (until his heart is broken).

男方 nánfāng (usu. of a marriage) bridegroom's or husband's side:～父母 bridegroom's parents
男风 nánfēng sodomy
男高音 nángāoyīn 〈音乐〉 tenor
男孩儿 nánháir *also* "男孩子" boy; son
男化女子 nánhuà nǚzǐ 〈生理〉 gynandroid
男妓 nánjì male prostitute; gigolo
男家 nánjiā bridegroom's or husband's family
男角 nánjué male role (in a play)
男爵 nánjué baron:～夫人 baroness /女～ baroness
男科 nánkē ❶ andrologic department (of a hospital):～大夫 andrologic doctor ❷ andrology
男科学 nánkēxué 〈医学〉 andrology
男篮 nánlán men's basketball:～队 men's basketball team
男男女女 nánnán-nǚnǚ men and women:村内～,老老少少,都兴高采烈。All villagers, men and women, old and young, were overjoyed.
男女 ná-nǚ ❶ man and woman:一对～ a couple; a man and a woman /～青年 young men and women /～老少 men and women, old and young /不分～ regardless of sex /～关系 sexual relations; liaison; affair /～平等 equality between men and women; gender equality /～同工同酬。Both men and women get equal pay for equal work. ❷〈方言〉 sons and daughters ❸ (often used in the early vernacular) *term of abuse*:一对狗～ a bitch and a bastard
男女混合双打 nán-nǚ hùnhé shuāngdǎ (shortened as 混双)〈体育〉 mixed doubles
男排 nánpái men's volleyball:～队 men's volleyball team
男胚瘤 nánpēiliú 〈医学〉 arrhenoblastoma
男朋友 nánpéngyou boyfriend; gentleman friend
男人 nánrén ❶ man ❷ menfolk
男人 nánren 〈口语〉 husband; hubby:她～是个钢铁工厂的工人。Her husband is a worker in a steel plant.
男生 nánshēng ❶ boy student; man student:你们班有个叫王强的～吗? Do you have a boy student named Wang Qiang in your class? ❷〈方言〉man; boy
男声 nánshēng 〈音乐〉 male voice:～合唱 men's chorus; male chorus /～四重唱 male quartet
男士 nánshì man; gentleman
男双 nánshuāng (short for 男子双打)〈体育〉 men's doubles (of table tennis, tennis, etc.)
男相 nánxiàng woman whose manner, expression and features are like those of a man:她的脸有些～,浓眉大眼,说话粗声粗气。With big eyes and bushy eyebrows, she looks sowewhat like a man and speaks in a loud voice.
男性 nánxìng male sex:～公民 male citizen /～特征 male features /未婚～ single man
男性病 nánxìngbìng 〈医学〉 andropathy
男性不育症 nánxìng bùyùzhèng 〈医学〉 male sterility
男性更年期 nánxìng gēngniánqī 〈医学〉 male climacteric
男性化 nánxìnghuà 〈生理〉 virilism; virilization
男性科 nánxìngkē andriatry; andriatrics
男性淋病 nánxìng lìnbìng 〈医学〉 phallorrhea
男性细胞瘤 nánxìng xìbāoliú 〈医学〉 andreioma; andreoblastoma; androma; masculinoma
男中音 nánzhōngyīn 〈音乐〉 baritone
男装 nánzhuāng men's clothing:这里专卖～。This shop sells men's garments only. /她常常穿～。She is often dressed like a man. /你得扮～,别人才认不出来。You must disguise yourself as a man so that nobody will recognize you.
男子 nánzǐ man:～气概 manly qualities; masculinity
男子单打 nánzǐ dāndǎ 〈体育〉 men's singles
男子个人项目 nánzǐ gèrén xiàngmù 〈体育〉 men's individual event
男子汉 nánzǐhàn man; man of honour:～大丈夫 true man; real man; he-man /真不像个～! He is not manly.
男子女化 nánzǐ nǚhuà 〈生理〉 androgyneity; androgynism
男子双打 nánzǐ shuāngdǎ 〈体育〉 men's doubles
男子团体赛 nánzǐ tuántǐsài 〈体育〉 men's team event
男尊女卑 nánzūn-nǚbēi concept that men are superior to women; men enjoying higher status than women; male superiority

难(難) nán

❶ hard; difficult:卖粮～ difficult to sell the grain /买菜～ not easy to get fresh vegetables in the market /凡事开头～。Nothing is easy at the beginning. /他讲得太快,很～听清楚。He spoke so fast that we could hardly follow him. /他同我关系一般,这件事很～向他启齿。I am not on very familiar terms with him, so I would find it difficult to bring up the matter with him. /这有什么～的! What's so difficult about it! *or* This is child's play! /他可是个～对付的人。He is a hard nut to crack. ❷ put sb. in a difficult position:这可真～住了他。That really put him on the spot (*or* in a fix). *or* You've got him there. /你这是故意～我吧? You are not trying to make things hard for me, are you? *or* Are you trying to embarrass me? ❸ uncertain; hardly possible; unlikely:这个会什么时候开,现在还～定。It's still uncertain when the meeting will be held. /目前,地震仍然很～准确预测。To this day, it is hardly possible to predict earthquakes accurately. ❹ unpleasant; not good; bad:这药太～吃。The medicine tastes nasty. /这支歌～听。The song is unpleasant to the ear. /臭味～闻。The smell is foul. *or* It is stinking.
see also nàn

难熬 nán'áo find it difficult to bear (pain, hardship, etc.):饥饿～ can hardly bear the pain of hunger
难办 nánbàn hard to do; difficult:我感到事情越来越～。I have a feeling that things are getting more difficult.
难保 nánbǎo cannot say for sure:～他不说出去。No one can say for sure that he will keep his mouth shut.
难不倒 nánbudǎo cannot beat (sb.):不管你提多难的问题,也～我们。You can ask questions as difficult as you like, and you still won't outwit us. *or* You cannot beat us no matter what difficult questions you raise.
难缠 nánchán unreasonable; hard to deal with:这个人强词夺理,节外生枝,真～。The chap is simply impossible, absolutely refusing to see reason and often raising irrelevant issues.
难产 nánchǎn ❶〈医学〉 difficult labour or delivery; dystocia ❷ (of literary work, plan, etc.) be difficult of fulfilment; be slow in coming:他的电影剧本长期～。His film script is long overdue. /这个计划可能要～。The plan seems to have hit some snags. *or* This plan seems to be petering out.
难处 nánchǔ difficult to deal with; not easy to get along with:这个人并不～。This man is actually not difficult to get along with.
难处 nánchu trouble; difficulty; problem:家家都有～。Every family has its own problems. /你不理解他的～。You don't appreciate his difficulties. *or* You don't know where the shoe pinches him.
难当 nándāng ❶ hard to undertake or assume:～重任 not equal to a position of heavy responsibility ❷ hard to bear:羞愧～ feel unbearably ashamed; feel ashamed beyond words
难倒 nándǎo beat; daunt:这件事把我们～了。The matter has put us in a hole. /没有什么东西能～他。Nothing can beat him.
难道 nándào *used in a rhetorical question for emphasis*:～这是偶然的吗? How can this be accidental? /这～还不明白吗? Isn't this perfectly clear? /这种事情～见得还少吗? We have seen enough of such things, haven't we?
难得 nándé ❶ hard to come by; rare:机会～呀! This is a rare opportunity indeed! /这样的人材确实～。Such talents (*or* People of such talent) are hard to come by. /～他如此尽心。It's really great of him to go into the matter with such devotion. ❷ hardly; rarely; seldom:我家～有人来。We seldom have visitors. /这种树～开一次花。This kind of plant rarely flowers. /我们～见面,再聊一会儿吧。Let's chat a bit more for we do not meet very often.
难得糊涂 nándé hútu where ignorance is bliss; 'tis folly to be wise
难点 nándiǎn difficult point; difficulty:攻克～overcome the difficulty /本文有几处～,不易剖析。There are several difficult points in the text which defy analysis.
难度 nándù degree of difficulty:这个体操动作的～很大。This gymnastic movements is very difficult. /要在五月底完成这项任务是有一定～的。It is not easy to finish the job by the end of May.
难分难解 nánfēn-nánjiě *see* "难解难分"
难割难舍 nángē-nánshě loath to part from each other; too sentimentally attached to part from each other:两口子乍一离别,真是～。The parting was so sudden that the couple found it almost unbearable.
难怪 nánguài ❶ no wonder:冷空气南下,～这么冷。Well, a chill front is coming south. No wonder it's so cold. ❷ understandable; pardonable:这也～,她刚来车间工作,没有经验。You can hardly blame her for it, as she is new in the workshop and has no experience to

speak of.

难关 nánguān barrier; difficulty; crisis: 攻克～ break through a barrier; overcome an obstacle / 技术～ technical problem; technical barrier / 渡过～ tide over a crisis

难过 nánguò ❶ have a hard time: 产品销路不畅, 工厂的日子～。The factory is having a hard time as a result of its poor sales. ❷ feel sorry; feel bad; be distressed: 为你感到～ feel sorry for you / ～极了 be deeply grieved or distressed

难乎为继 nánhūwéijì *also* "难以为继" difficult to follow up (the example set by a predecessor); hard to keep up: 生活～ find it difficult to make ends meet / 工厂的原料已经到了～的程度。The factory is almost running out of raw materials.

难活 nánhuó 〈方言〉❶ illness; sickness; disease: 这个方子治不了我的～。This recipe cannot cure my illness. ❷ be ill; fall ill: 他身体不好, 总是～。He is delicate in health and is always ailing. / 你～了? 穿了棉衣, 手还是冰冷的! Your hands are icy cold and you are in cotton-padded clothes. Are you ill?

难解难分 nánjiě-nánfēn *also* "难分难解" ❶ be inextricably linked; be locked together (as in struggle): 这场棋杀得～。The chess game reached the stage where the players were locked in a stalemate. ❷ be sentimentally attached: 他俩柔情缱绻, ～。They were so sentimentally attached to each other that they could not bear to part.

难堪 nánkān ❶ unbearable; intolerable; unendurable: 她说了许多～的话, 把他气走了。Her remarks became so unbearable that he went off in a huff. / 会议室里一片令人～的静默。The conference room was reduced to a state of uncomfortable silence. ❷ embarrassed; embarrassing; ill at ease: 他说这话, 明明叫人～。What he said was obviously meant to embarrass me. / 她客气得令人～。She was so polite that it made people feel ill at ease. / 她处于十分～的境地。She found herself caught in a very awkward situation.

难看 nánkàn ❶ ugly; homely; unsightly; grotesque: 她长得不～。She is not at all homely. ❷ shameful; disgraceful; embarrassing: 当着这么多人耍脾气, 也不觉得～?! Aren't you ashamed of yourself flying into a temper in front of so many people? / 比赛要是输了, 那多～啊! It would be just too embarrassing if we should lose the game. / 他们这样粗暴对待顾客也不觉得～。They didn't seem to realize that they had brought discredit on their shop by behaving so outrageously to their customers. ❸ (of look or expression) unpleasant; not quite normal: 他时常给人一点～的脸色。He often gave people a sour look. / 他的脸色突然变得～起来。His face suddenly darkened. / 你的脸色这么～, 该不是病了吧? You look so pale. Are you ill?

难免 nánmiǎn be hard to avoid; cannot help: 同志之间, 看法有时～不一致。Disagreements do sometimes occur among comrades. / 一个人～不犯错误, 重要的是知过能改。Nobody is free from error. The important thing is to correct it as soon as one realizes it. / 看来他这场灾难是～的了。It seems that he's booked for the disaster. / 要是不准时回来, 你就～受罚。You will be in for it if you don't get back on time.

难耐 nánnài be hard to put up with; be unable to bear: ～的不眠之夜 miserable sleepless night / ～的病痛 unbearable ailment

难能可贵 nánnéng-kěguì deserve credit for doing sth. difficult of attainment; be commendable; be praiseworthy: 他见义勇为的精神是～的。His readiness to take up the cudgels for a just cause is commendable. / 他一生当会计没有出差错, 实在～。The fact that he has never made a single mistake in his lifelong service as a book-keeper is worthy of praise indeed.

难人 nánrén ❶ difficult; delicate; thorny: 这种～的事, 多亏你办成了。We owe it all to you to solve such thorny issues. ❷ person left alone to handle a delicate matter or face a difficult situation: 有麻烦我们会尽量帮助你, 决不会叫你做～。We'll help you to the best of our ability if you're in trouble; we won't leave you in the lurch.

难忍 nánrěn *also* "难耐" hard to endure: 饥寒～ hard to endure hunger and cold

难容 nánróng cannot put up with; cannot tolerate: 情理～ contrary to reason / 法纪～ not be tolerated by law or discipline

难熔合金 nánróng héjīn 〈冶金〉refractory alloy (metal)

难熔矿石 nánróng kuàngshí 〈矿业〉refractory ore

难色 nánsè appear to be reluctant; look hesitant: 面有～ show signs of reluctance or hesitation

难上难 nánshàngnán *also* "难上加难" extremely difficult; next to impossible: 要一个偏见很深的人顷刻改变自己的看法, 真是～。It would be exceedingly difficult to bring round overnight a man with such biased views.

难舍难分 nánshě-nánfēn cannot bear to part; loathe to part: 飞机就要起飞了, 他俩还是～。The plane was to take off in a minute, and yet the two of them could hardly bear to part from each other.

难事 nánshì difficult endeavour; difficulty: 天下无～, 只怕有心人。Where there is a will, there is a way.

难受 nánshòu ❶ feel unwell; suffer pain; feel uncomfortable: 肚子～ have stomach trouble; suffer a pain in the abdomen / 热得～ unbearably hot / 渴得～ be dying of thirst; be parched / 头疼得～ have a splitting headache / 我今天有点～。I feel a bit under the weather today. ❷ feel bad (about sth.); feel unhappy; feel sorry: 听到这个不幸的消息, 大家都很～。Everybody felt sad at the bad news. / 做错了事, 你也不～? Don't you feel sorry about the mistake you've made?

难说 nánshuō ❶ it's hard to say; you never can tell: 这场比赛谁胜谁负还很～。It's still hard to say which side will win the game. *or* The outcome of the game still remains to be seen. ❷ cannot bring oneself to say it: 事到如今, 再～也得如实说了。When things come to such a pass, you have to tell the truth, however difficult it may be.

难说话儿 nánshuōhuàr not accommodating; not flexible: 这个人～, 你去求他也没有用。It's no use begging him. He never stretches a point.

难题 nántí thorny problem; hard nut to crack; poser: 出～ pose a difficult question; put sb. in an awkward situation / 这是一个十分棘手的～。This is a real hard nut to crack. *or* This is indeed a thorny problem. / 我知道他是想让我来处理这个～。I know he wants me to handle this hot potato for him.

难听 nántīng ❶ unpleasant to the ear: 这支歌怎么这么～! What an awful song this is! / 那曲子嗲声嗲气的, 真～! That purring song is just revolting. ❷ vulgar; coarse; offensive: 他骂的话～极了! The way he swears is simply shocking! / 别说～的话! Don't use strong language! *or* Don't swear! ❸ scandalous; disreputable: 这种事情说出去多～。This sort of thing will become most scandalous once it gets out. *or* If the story gets out, it is bound to be a scandal.

难忘 nánwàng unforgettable; memorable: 那段生活令人～。Those years are indelibly printed on my memory. / 你的恩情我终生～。I will never forget your kindness for the rest of my life.

难为情 nánwéiqíng shy; embarrassed; ashamed: 她有一副好嗓子, 只是在大庭广众前唱歌总是～。She has a good voice, but she is too shy to sing before a large audience. / 最好先找人跟他们通通气, 免得到时候大家觉得～。To avoid discomfiture, we should get somebody to pass on a message to them first. / 这事很难, 答应了办不到, 不答应又～。The matter is indeed difficult to handle. It's not practicable to comply, but embarrassing to decline.

难为 nánwei ❶ make it hard or difficult for sb.; embarrass: 故意～人 deliberately make it difficult for sb. / 他不会唱歌, 就别～他了。He can't sing, so don't press him to. ❷ be a tough job for (sb.): 我工作太忙, 爱人把家务、孩子都包了, 也真～她。As I am very busy at work, my wife takes care of everything at home — housework and children, and that is not easy. ❸〈套语〉(used to express gratitude to sb. for his assistance) it is generous of (sb.); it is kind of (sb.): 连晚饭也为我准备好了, 真～你呀。So you've even got the dinner ready for me. It's really very kind of you.

难闻 nánwén smell bad; have an unpleasant smell; stink: 什么味儿这么～? What smells so bad? / 他身上有一股～的汗臭。He has a bad odour of perspiration.

难心 nánxīn 〈方言〉be worried; feel embarrassed: 想到孩子的病, 他不由得～起来。When he thinks of his child's illness, he can't help feeling worried.

难兄难弟 nánxiōng-nándì 〈讽刺〉well-matched pair of brothers; birds of a feather; two of a kind: 这对～可没少干坏事啊! The two of them are a perfect pair of double-dyed evil-doers.

see also nànxiōng-nàndì

难言之隐 nányánzhīyǐn sth. difficult to express or awkward to disclose; unmentionable secret: 看他说话吞吞吐吐的, 好像有什么～。He spoke with hesitation as if there was something embarrassing to mention.

难以 nányǐ difficult to; hard to: 心情～平静 not easy to keep one's excitement down; unable to calm oneself down / ～下笔 hard to start (a piece of writing) / ～忘怀 hard to forget; unforgettable / ～理解 hard to understand; incomprehensible / ～置信 incredible; unbelievable; beyond belief / ～捉摸 elusive; unfathomable; difficult to pin down (the meaning of sth.) / ～形容 indescribable; beyond description / ～启齿 embarrassing to mention (sth.) / 悲痛的心情～用言

N

语来表达。The grief cannot be conveyed in speech. /这种局面如不立即改变则会变得～收拾。This situation must be changed at once, or it will get out of hand.

难于 nányú difficult to; hard to; not likely to: ～见效 not likely to produce (satisfactory) results; hardly effective /～登天 as difficult as climbing to heaven; well-nigh impossible /这个计划～实行。This plan is not really feasible. /学生们对他的理论感到～理解。The students were out of their depth at his theory.

难字 nánzì hard word; rare word

nǎn

赧(赧) nǎn blushing

赧红 nǎnhóng blush with embarrassment or shame; crimson with shame: ～的脸庞 flushed cheeks

赧愧 nǎnkuì 〈书面〉 ashamed; embarrassed: 言念及此，不胜～。He felt very much ashamed of himself when he thought of this.

赧赧 nǎnnǎn bashful; blushing; shy: 其色～ look shamefaced

赧然 nǎnrán 〈书面〉 blushing: 她～一笑。She blushed and smiled.

赧颜 nǎnyán 〈书面〉 blush; be shamefaced: 他～汗下。He was sweating with shame.

蝻 nǎn 〈动物〉 nymph of a locust

蝻子 nǎnzi nymph of a locust

腩 nǎn *see* "牛腩" niúnǎn

nàn

难(難) nàn ❶ trouble; disaster; calamity; catastrophe: 遭～ get into trouble; suffer a disaster /国～ national disaster /避～ escape danger; avert disaster; ward off a calamity; lie low /大～不死 survive a catastrophe /五十人遇～。Fifty people were killed in the disaster (*or* accident). ❷ blame; censure; take to task: 责～ blame; reproach /非～ censure

see also nán

难胞 nànbāo compatriots who are victims of persecution or of a calamity

难船 nànchuán ship in distress; sinking ship

难经 Nànjīng *Classic on Ailments*, a book of medicine mainly in explication of *Classic of Internal Medicine* (内经), written probably between the Qin and Han dynasties or in early Han, and considered one of the classics on traditional Chinese medicine

难民 nànmín refugee: ～营 refugee camp /～问题 refugee issue

难侨 nànqiáo nationals of a country residing abroad, who have become refugees in a disaster or as a result of persecution; overseas countrymen in distress

难属 nànshǔ victim's family

难兄难弟 nànxiōng-nàndì fellow sufferers; people in the same boat: 这是一群流落异国他乡的～。These are people of the same fate, wandering destitute in an alien land.

see also nánxiōng-nándì

难友 nànyǒu fellow sufferer: 老张和我是当年狱中的～。Lao Zhang and I were inmates of the same prison.

nāng

囊 nāng

see also náng

囊揣 nāngchuài ❶ (often used in the early vernacular) weak; feeble; cowardly: 身体～ be in poor health ❷ *see* "囊膪"

囊膪 nāngchuài (of pigs) loose, fat meat from the breast and abdomen

囔 nāng

囔囔 nāngnang murmur; mutter

náng

囊 náng ❶ bag; sack; pocket: 布～ cloth bag /行～ travel bag /药～ medicine bag /皮～ leather bag; 〈贬义〉 body /背～ knapsack; backpack ❷ anything shaped like a bag; bladder: 胆～ gallbladder /智～ brain trust(er); think tank /小～ 〈生理〉 saccule /液～ 〈生理〉 sac /滑～ 〈生理〉 bursa ❸ 〈书面〉 put into a bag; bag: ～米 bag (up) rice

see also nāng

囊虫 nángchóng cysticercus: ～病 〈医学〉 cysticercosis

囊果 nángguǒ 〈植物〉 cystocarp

囊空如洗 nángkōng-rúxǐ with empty pockets; penniless; broke: 他失业了，～。He lost his job and had not a single penny to his name.

囊括 nángkuò embrace (all): ～四海 (of the founder of a new dynasty) bring the whole country under one's rule /～全部六项冠军 sweep all the six championships into one's net; make a clean sweep of all six championships

囊瘤 nángliú 〈医学〉 cystoma

囊玛 nángmǎ a kind of Tibetan folk song and dance deeply influenced by the classic music of the Han nationality, and divided into two parts: one for the song and the other for the dance

囊胚 nángpēi 〈生物〉 blastula

囊切除术 nángqiēchúshù 〈医学〉 cystectomy

囊切开术 nángqiēkāishù 〈医学〉 capsulotomy

囊生 nángshēng *also* "朗生" lǎngshēng (before 1959) Tibetan household slave

囊尾蚴 nángwěiyòu cysticercus

囊腺癌 nángxiàn'ái 〈医学〉 cystadenocarcinoma; cystocarcinoma

囊性瘤 nángxìngliú 〈医学〉 cystadenoma

囊性肉瘤 nángxìng ròuliú 〈医学〉 cystosarcoma

囊性肾 nángxìngshèn cystic kidney

囊中物 nángzhōngwù that which is already in the bag — sth. certain of attainment: 看来全国象棋冠军是他的～。It seems that he is certain to be the champion in the national chess contest.

囊中羞涩 nángzhōng-xiūsè 〈书面〉 be short of money; be hard up: 他很想买下这部词典，怎奈～，只得作罢。He wanted this dictionary very much, but could ill afford it.

囊肿 nángzhǒng 〈医学〉 cyst; cystis: ～生成 cystogenia; cystogenesis

囊肿性纤维化 nángzhǒngxìng xiānwéihuà 〈医学〉 cystic fibrosis

囊状矿脉 nángzhuàng kuàngmài 〈矿业〉 chambered vein

馕 náng a kind of crusty pancake (staple food of the Uygur and Kazak nationalities)

see also nǎng

nǎng

攮 nǎng stab: 他一刀子～死了劫机者，救了飞机上的乘客。He stabbed the hijacker to death and saved the passengers on the plane.

攮子 nǎngzi dagger

馕 nǎng cram food into one's mouth: ～食包 big eater

see also náng

曩 nǎng 〈书面〉 former; past: ～日 *also* "～时" in olden days; of yore /～者 in the past; formerly

曩昔 nǎngxī 〈书面〉 in olden days; of yore

nàng

齉 nàng snuffling: 受了凉，鼻子发～ snuffle with a cold

齉鼻儿 nàngbír ❶ snuffle; speak through the nose: 他感冒了，说话有点～。He had a cold and spoke with a slight snuffle. ❷ person who speaks in a nasal voice; person who speaks with a twang

N

nāo

孬 nāo 〈方言〉❶ bad：把好桃留在筐里，～的挑出来。Keep the good peaches in the basket, and pick out the bad ones. ❷ chicken-hearted; cowardly：那人太～，许多朋友都笑话他。He is so lily-livered that many of his friends laugh at him.

孬种 nāozhǒng 〈口语〉chicken-hearted person; coward; cowardly and incompetent person：他可不是～，别把他惹毛了。He is no coward. Don't rub him up the wrong way.

náo

侬（憹） náo see “懊侬” àonáo

硇（硇、碙） náo

硇砂 náoshā 〈化学〉sal ammoniac

诶（譊） náo

诶诶 náonáo 〈书面〉sound of argument or debate; wrangle

挠（撓） náo ❶ scratch：～痒痒 scratch an itch /把脸～破了 scratch and abrade the face ❷ obstruct; hinder; block：阻～ obstruct ❸ yield; flinch; give in：百折不～ unflinching /不屈不～ unbending; unyielding; indomitable

挠度 náodù ❶〈建筑〉deflection：～计 deflectometer ❷〈物理〉flexibility：～计 fleximeter /～试验 flexibility test

挠钩 náogōu long-handled hook

挠曲 náoqū ❶ winding; curved; bent; twisted ❷〈机械〉flexion; flexure; flex：～试验机 flexometer; flexer; flexing machine /～系数 flexibility factor

挠弹性 náotánxìng 〈物理〉flexiblility; resilience

挠头 náotóu ❶ scratch one's head ❷ hard to tackle; thorny：这真是件～的事。This is indeed a thorny issue (*or* a headache). /公司里现在最～的问题就是人手不齐。The biggest problem confronting the firm is that it is understaffed.

挠性 náoxìng 〈物理〉flexibility：～螺旋 flexible auger /～轴承 flexible bearing

挠性管 náoxìngguǎn flexible pipe

挠性连轴节 náoxìng liánzhóujié 〈机械〉flexible coupling; flexible connection

挠秧 náoyāng 〈农业〉loosen the soil around the seedlings in the paddy fields

挠应力 náoyìnglì 〈物理〉flexure stress

蛲（蟯） náo

蛲虫 náochóng pinworm (*Enterobius vermicularis*)：～病 enterobiasis; oxyurisasis

铙（鐃） náo ❶ a kind of cymbal ❷ ancient musical instrument used in the army, resembling an inverted tongueless bell ❸ (Náo) a surname

铙钹 náobó big cymbals

呶 náo 〈书面〉clamour; talk noisily

呶呶 náonáo 〈书面〉talk tediously; prattle：一点小事她却常～，叫人心烦。It is so annoying that she often babbles on and on about trifles.

呶呶不休 náonáo-bùxiū gab; patter; babble on：不论大事小事，他总是～。He chatters away on every issue, big or small.

猱 náo 〈古语〉a kind of monkey

猱犬 náoquǎn 〈动物〉dhole; red dog

猱升 náoshēng 〈书面〉climb as nimbly as a monkey

nǎo

恼（惱） nǎo ❶ angry; upset; irritated; annoyed：别把他惹～了。Don't provoke him. *or* Don't make him angry. ❷ unhappy; vexed; worried：苦～ distressed; miserable /烦～ vexed; worried /懊～ unhappy; filled with regret /困～ puzzled and worried

恼恨 nǎohèn resent; hate：他～儿子不争气。He deeply regrets the fact that his son is so unworthy of him. /我是好意，你可别～我。I did it with the best of intentions. Please don't bear any grudge against me.

恼火 nǎohuǒ annoyed; irritated; riled; vexed：动不动就～ get irritated easily; be irascible /他打乱了我的整个计划，弄得我十分～。He messed up (*or* upset) the whole plan so that I was very annoyed. /一跟他说话我就～。It nettles me to speak to him.

恼怒 nǎonù angry; irritated; exasperated; furious：感到十分～ get furious at sth. /这种事真让人～。Such things do infuriate people.

恼人 nǎorén irritating; annoying; vexing：怎么什么东西都坏了，真～！Nothing is working properly. How annoying! /她成天缠着我买这买那，你说～不～？It's really irritating, isn't it, that she should pester me for money to buy this and that all day long. /这些苍蝇实在是～！What a nuisance these flies are!

恼丧 nǎosàng dejected; upset; depressed; despondent：她～浪费了那么多时间。She was upset that she had wasted so much time . /这事使她感到十分～。This put her in deep dejection.

恼羞成怒 nǎoxiū-chéngnù be shamed into anger; fly into a rage out of wounded pride; be piqued：他～，从地上爬起来，向对手扑过去。Shamed and angered, he scrambled up and threw himself at his opponent. /局长～，当即叫秘书通知取消这次会议。The director, in a fit of pique, told the secretary to put up a notice saying that the meeting was cancelled.

瑙 nǎo see “玛瑙” mǎnǎo

瑙鲁 Nǎolǔ Nauru, island country in the West Pacific：～人 Nauruan

脑（腦） nǎo ❶ brain; encephalon：大～ cerebrum /小～ cerebellum /～学 cerebrology; encephalology /～损伤 cerebral injury ❷ head：探头探～ pop one's head out or in; act stealthily ❸ brain; mind：很有头～ have plenty of brains; be smart /用～过度 overtax one's brain /洗～ brainwash /电～ computer /他既动～，又动手。He works with his head as well as his hands. ❹ best part (of sth.); cream：樟～ camphor /薄荷～ peppermint camphor; methol ❺ bits; residue; odds and ends：针头线～ odds and ends/田头地～ little bits of land

脑癌 nǎo'ái 〈医学〉cancer of the brain; cerebral cancer

脑包虫病 nǎobāochóngbìng 〈医学〉cenuriasis; coenurosis

脑病 nǎobìng 〈医学〉encephalopathia; encephalopathy; cerebropathia; cerebrosis

脑充血 nǎochōngxuè 〈医学〉encephalemia

脑出血 nǎochūxuè 〈医学〉encephalorrhagia; cerebral hemorrhage

脑穿刺术 nǎochuāncìshù 〈医学〉encephalopuncture

脑创伤 nǎochuāngshāng cerebral trauma

脑垂体 nǎochuítǐ 〈生理〉hypophysis cerebri; pituitary body or gland

脑袋 nǎodai ❶〈口语〉head：冬瓜～ head shaped like a wax-gourd; elliptically shaped head /你有几个～，敢跟这种有权有势的人作对？How many heads do you think you have, to confront a man with so much power? ❷ mind; brains：她～里充满了各种新奇的想法。Her mind is full of fancy ideas. /你的～怎么不开窍？Don't be so dumb! *or* How can you be so stupid?

脑袋搬家 nǎodai-bānjiā get killed：不出三日，我一定得叫他～！I swear I'll get him bumped off within three days!

脑袋瓜 nǎodaiguā *also* “脑袋瓜子”〈方言〉see “脑袋”

脑电波 nǎodiànbō 〈生理〉brain wave

脑电图 nǎodiàntú 〈医学〉electroencephalogram (EEG)

脑动脉 nǎodòngmài 〈生理〉cerebral artery

脑动脉硬化 nǎodòngmài yìnghuà 〈医学〉cerebral arteriosclerosis

脑干 nǎogàn 〈生理〉brainstem

脑瓜儿 nǎoguār *also* “脑瓜子”〈方言〉head; mind：～特灵 be sharp-minded; be quick-witted

脑海 nǎohǎi mind; mind's eye：往事又浮上他的～。Memories of the past flashed across his mind. /他～中又浮现出那个小村。He saw that little village again in his mind's eye. /她在他的～里留下了不可磨灭的印象。She left an indelible impression on him.

N

脑黄金 nǎohuángjīn (popular term for 多烯不饱和脂肪酸 or 22碳6烯酸) DHA (docosahexaenoic acid)
脑灰质炎 nǎohuīzhìyán 〈医学〉 polioencephalitis
脑积水 nǎojīshuǐ 〈医学〉 hydrocephalus
脑激素 nǎojīsù 〈生理〉 brain hormone (BH)
脑脊髓炎 nǎojǐsuǐyán 〈医学〉 encephalomyelitis
脑脊液 nǎojǐyè *also* "脑脊髓液" 〈生理〉 cerebrospinal fluid (CSF)
脑际 nǎojì mind:一个念头闪过他的～。An idea flashed across his mind. /往事萦绕在他的～。Memories of the past haunt his mind.
脑寄生虫病 nǎojìshēngchóngbìng cerebral parasitic disease
脑浆 nǎojiāng brains:他从山顶跌落下来摔在岩石上,～四迸。He fell from the mountain-top and dashed his brains out on the rocks.
脑筋 nǎojīn ❶ brains; mind:开动～ use one's brains or head /伤～ bothersome; vexatious; troublesome /费～ tax one's brains /洗～ brainwash /还是你们年轻人～好,记得快。After all, you young people have a keener mind and a better memory. ❷ way of thinking; ideas:老～ person who moves in a rut; old fogey /死～ inflexible person
脑壳 nǎoké 〈方言〉 head; cranium; brain case
脑力 nǎolì brain; mind; mental power:消耗～ wear out one's brain /～工作 mental work
脑力劳动 nǎolì láodòng mental work:从事～ be engaged in mental work /～者 mental worker; brainworker /～和体力劳动只是分工的不同,并无高低贵贱之分。The division of labour into mental and manual work does not mean that one is superior to the other.
脑磷脂 nǎolínzhī 〈生化〉 cephalin; kephalin
脑瘤 nǎoliú 〈医学〉 cerebroma; encephaloma
脑漏 nǎolòu (a common saying for 鼻渊) nasosinusitis
脑颅 nǎolú skull
脑满肠肥 nǎomǎn-chángféi heavy-jowled and potbellied — the idle rich
脑门子 nǎoménzi *also* "脑门儿" 〈口语〉 forehead; brow:惹一～气 get very upset or angry /满～心事 be filled with worries; be vexed
脑膜 nǎomó 〈生理〉 meninx
脑膜炎 nǎomóyán 〈医学〉 meningitis
脑囊肿 nǎonángzhǒng 〈医学〉 perencephaly
脑脓肿 nǎonóngzhǒng 〈医学〉 encephalopyosis; brain abscess
脑瓢儿 nǎopiáor 〈方言〉 top of head:开～ break one's head
脑贫血 nǎopínxuè 〈医学〉 cerebral anaemia; anencephalohemia
脑桥 nǎoqiáo 〈生理〉 pons varolii; pons
脑切开术 nǎoqiēkāishù 〈医学〉 encephalotomy; cerebrotomy
脑儿 nǎor ❶ brains of certain animals (as food):猪～ brains of pigs ❷ anything edible that looks like the brains of animals:豆腐～ jelly bean curd
脑仁儿 nǎorénr 〈方言〉 brain:～疼 headache
脑软化症 nǎoruǎnhuàzhèng 〈医学〉 encephalomalacia
脑疝 nǎoshàn 〈医学〉 cerebral hernia
脑上体 nǎoshàngtǐ *also* "松果腺" sōngguǒxiàn; "松果体" sōngguǒtǐ 〈生理〉 pineal body
脑勺 nǎosháo *also* "脑勺子" 〈方言〉 back of the head:后～ back of the head
脑神经 nǎoshénjīng 〈生理〉 cranial nerve
脑室 nǎoshì 〈生理〉 ventricle of the brain:～穿刺术 ventriculocentesis /～镜 ventriculoscope /～造影 ventriculography
脑衰竭 nǎoshuāijié 〈医学〉 brain fag
脑水肿 nǎoshuǐzhǒng 〈医学〉 encephaledema
脑死亡 nǎosǐwáng 〈医学〉 brain death:～者 the braindead
脑髓 nǎosuǐ 〈生理〉 brains
脑外科 nǎowàikē 〈医学〉 cerebral surgery
脑萎缩 nǎowěisuō 〈医学〉 encephalatrophy
脑体倒挂 nǎo-tǐ dàoguà income of mental workers falling short of that of manual workers; irrational income differential between white and blue collar workers in favour of the latter
脑下垂体 nǎoxià chuítǐ 〈医学〉 pituitary gland
脑心肌炎 nǎoxīnjīyán 〈医学〉 encephalomyocarditis
脑血管 nǎoxuèguǎn 〈生理〉 cerebral vessel:～疾病 cerebrovascular disease /～畸形 cerebrovascular malformation /～造影 cerebral angiography
脑血管系统 nǎoxuèguǎn xìtǒng 〈生理〉 cerebrovascular system
脑血栓 nǎoxuèshuān *also* "脑栓塞" 〈医学〉 cerebral thrombus
脑血栓形成 nǎoxuèshuān xíngchéng cerebral thrombosis
脑炎 nǎoyán *also* "大脑炎" dànǎoyán 〈医学〉 cerebritis:流行性乙型～ epidemic encephalitis B
脑溢血 nǎoyìxuè 〈医学〉 cerebral haemorrhage
脑震荡 nǎozhèndàng 〈医学〉 cerebral concussion; concussion of the brain
脑汁 nǎozhī brains:绞尽～ rack (*or* beat, *or* cudgel) one's brains (for sth.)
脑肿瘤 nǎozhǒngliú 〈医学〉 cerebral tumour
脑子 nǎozi 〈口语〉 ❶ brain:人～ human brain ❷ brain; mind; head:～好 have a good brain /这工作太费～。This job taxes one's brains. /这些事都把我～搞糊涂了。I am bewildered by these things. /他现在～不太清醒。He is not in his right mind at this moment.

nào

淖 nào 〈书面〉 mire:泥～ mire; deep mud
淖尔 nào'ěr nur (Mongolian word for "lake")
闹(鬧) nào ❶ noisy:～中取静 seek or enjoy peace and quiet from noisy surroundings /隔壁在～什么? What's all that din about next door? /孩子们太～了,我思想简直没法集中。The children are so rowdy that I can't concentrate. /别～! 好好站着听。Stop mucking around! Stand properly and listen carefully. ❷ clamour; make a scene;stir up trouble:大～一场 make a (big)scene/ 又哭又～ make a tearful scene / ～会场 stir up trouble at a meeting / ～名誉, ～地位 clamour for fame and position /这事要是处理得不好,他家长会～的。If the matter is not properly settled, his parents will no doubt make a big issue of it. ❸ give vent to (one's anger, resentment, etc.);vent: ～脾气 vent one's anger; get into a huff; throw a tantrum ❹ suffer from; be troubled by:～水灾 suffer from floods / ～矛盾 be at odds with one another; clash with one another; fall out with one another ❺ do; make; engage oneself in; go in for:～生产 go in for production; be engaged in production /把问题～清楚 find out the truth about sth.; get to the bottom of a matter ❻ crack jokes; tease:打～ horseplay /我只不过是～着玩儿的。I was only joking.
闹别扭 nào bièniu be at odds (with sb.); fall out (with sb.):他们两口子又～了。The couple fell out again.
闹病 nàobìng fall ill; be unwell:老母亲三天两头地～。My old mother is often ill.
闹场 nàochǎng *also* "开台锣鼓" kāitái luógǔ 〈旧语〉 beating of gongs and drums that usually served as a prologue in Beijing opera and some other local operas to attract the audience, or sometimes as a send-off after a performance
闹地震 nào dìzhèn ❶ have an earthquake ❷ 〈比喻〉 cause disturbance or unrest
闹洞房 nào dòngfáng old custom esp. in rural China whereby guests and relatives crowd in the bridal chamber to tease the new couple on their wedding night and play practical jokes on them
闹独立性 nào dúlìxìng assert one's independence — refuse to obey the leadership (of the central authorities)
闹肚子 nào dùzi 〈口语〉 have loose bowels; have a running stool; suffer from diarrhoea:我最近一直～。I have had loose bowels recently. /闹了两天肚子,人一点精神都没有了。Two days of diarrhoea sapped all the vim from me.
闹翻 nàofān fall out (with sb.):他跟女朋友～了。He has fallen out with his girlfriend.
闹翻身 nào fānshēn (of oppressed people) fight for emancipation:～,求解放 fight for liberation
闹翻天 nàofāntiān raise hell; raise a rumpus; kick up a racket:我才离开几天,这里就～啦! I've been away for only a few days, and everything is turned upside down here.
闹房 nàofáng *see* "闹洞房"
闹风潮 nào fēngcháo 〈旧语〉 go on strike or stage a demonstration (to vent popular grievances);stir up unrest
闹革命 nào gémìng carry out revolution; make revolution
闹鬼 nàoguǐ ❶ be haunted:有些老人仍相信这座房子以往闹过鬼。Some old people still believe that this house was once haunted by ghosts or apparitions. ❷ *also* "捣鬼" play tricks (behind people's backs); resort to underhand devices:你背地里闹什么鬼? What trick are you up to behind my back?

闹哄哄 nàohōnghōng noisy; uproarious; clamorous: 前厅～的不知出了什么事? What's happening in the lobby with all that din (*or* noise)? /大街上车来车往～的, 我实在是受不了。The clamour of the traffic is getting on my nerves.

闹哄 nàohong 〈口语〉❶ make a row; wrangle: 大家不要～, 有话坐下来好好说。Stop shouting! We can sit down and talk the matter over. /这个问题已有明文规定, 你在这儿瞎～什么? We have written regulations about this. What on earth are you clamouring for? /谁要不按她的意思办, 她就会跟谁～。If you don't go along with her, she would keep on pestering you. ❷ (a group of people) do sth. together; hustle and bustle: 大家～了半天, 才把屋子腾出来。It took them a good half day to finally empty the room. *or* They hustled and bustled for quite a long time to empty the room.

闹荒 nàohuāng 〈旧语〉(of hungry peasants) surge into a landlord's home to seize grain during a famine; start a famine riot

闹慌 nàohuang 〈方言〉toss about; sicken; feel restless: 他觉得心里～, 但竭尽全力稳住自己。He felt dizzy and sick, but he tried his best to pull himself together.

闹饥荒 nào jīhuang ❶ suffer from famine: 过去我们那里三年两头～。In the old days famine occurred in our area almost every other year. ❷ 〈方言〉be hard up; be broke: 小张用钱从不计划, 每到月底就要～。Xiao Zhang was careless with his money and would invariably be broke at the end of every month.

闹架 nàojià 〈方言〉quarrel and come to blows: 两口子常～。The couple often fall out with each other and exchange blows.

闹监 nàojiān (prisoners) create disturbances in prison cells

闹将 nàojiàng 〈口语〉trouble-maker; mischief-maker: 他是个有名的～, 谁也管不了。He is a notorious trouble-maker, and no one is able to take him in hand.

闹剧 nàojù farce: 可笑的～ ludicrous farce /那里的民主选举变成了一场～。The democratic election there turned into a farce.

闹客套 nào kètào stand on ceremony: 这可是自己家里, 不要～啊! This is your own home, so let's not get caught up in polite ceremony here.

闹了归齐 nàoleguīqí 〈方言〉after all; in the end; at last: 我找你半天, ～, 你在这儿。So, you are here at long last. I've been looking for you everywhere.

闹乱子 nào luànzi create a disturbance; cause trouble; get into trouble: 这次他可闹下了大乱子了。This time he has got into dreadful trouble.

闹猛 nàoměng *also* "闹忙" 〈方言〉lively; bustling with noise and excitement: 街上人山人海, 十分～。There are huge crowds in the street, bustling with noise and excitement.

闹脾气 nào píqi get into a huff; be in a tantrum: 你的宝贝女儿又在～呢! That darling daughter of yours is throwing one of her tantrums (*or* has got into a huff) again!

闹气 nàoqì 〈方言〉be in a huff (with sb.): 他爱人跟他～, 不理他。His wife is in a fit of pique, pretending to ignore him altogether.

闹情绪 nào qíngxù be in a fit of pique; be disgruntled: 他没被提拔, 正～呢。He is in low spirits because he didn't get the promotion he had expected. /今天早晨我批评他厉害一点, 他就～。He is disgruntled because I spoke sharply to him this morning.

闹嚷嚷 nàorāngrāng noisy; clamorous: 人们～的, 她说什么我都听不见。I can't hear her above the din of the crowd.

闹嚷 nàorǎng kick up a row; hubbub: 谁在那里～? Who's making a terrific racket there?

闹热 nàorè 〈方言〉full of activity; bustling with noise and excitement

闹嗓子 nào sǎngzi 〈口语〉have a sore throat: 他这两天～, 吃不下饭。He can't eat much for he has had a sore throat for a couple of days.

闹社 nàoshè 〈旧语〉❶ cause trouble within an agricultural cooperative (which was first formed in the 1950's) ❷ withdraw from a cooperative

闹市 nàoshì busy street; downtown area: 从～搬到郊区 moving from a busy street to the suburbs /我们在～区租了一间办公室。We have rented an office in the downtown area of the city.

闹事 nàoshì make trouble; create disturbances; stir up trouble: 寻衅～ pick a quarrel with sb. and stir up trouble /聚众～ gather a crowd to create disturbances

闹腾 nàoteng 〈口语〉❶ wrangle; create a disturbance; kick up a rumpus: 她要一～起来, 我们谁也甭想定下心来。When she starts to wrangle, none of us can expect to have a moment's ease. /她～了半天, 谁也没理她。She made a big scene, but no one paid any attention to her. /每次犯病, 他总要这么～两天。At each attack of the illness, he would lie in agony like this for a couple of days. ❷ have fun; amuse oneself: 咱们谈咱们的, 让孩子们～去。Let the kids have fun by themselves so that we can talk. ❸ knock together; set up; establish: 这个厂子是几个退休老工人～起来的。This factory was knocked together by a few retired old workers.

闹天儿 nàotiānr 〈方言〉when the weather gets bad: 一～, 伤口就发痒。The wound gets itchy in bad weather.

闹戏 nàoxì old-style comic opera, in which the leading role is played by a comedian

闹笑话 nào xiàohua make a fool of oneself; make a laughing stock of oneself; make a stupid mistake; open oneself to ridicule: 我刚去不懂那里的规矩, 闹了许多笑话。I cut a sorry figure when I first got there as I didn't know the rules of the department. /还是仔细一些, 弄不好要～的。We can't be too careful. We don't want to lay ourselves open to ridicule, do we?

闹心 nàoxīn 〈方言〉❶ be worried or disturbed; be vexed: 他体弱多病, 不能～, 应该在家休养。As he is weak physically and often falls ill, he should rest at home and not allow himself to be disturbed. ❷ feel bad in the stomach: 我吃凉饭要～。I would feel upset in my stomach if I had a cold meal.

闹新房 nào xīnfáng *see* "闹洞房"

闹性子 nào xìngzi be at odds (with sb.); lose one's temper; get angry: 她在家里时常与人闹点儿小性子。She often gets a bit difficult with others at home. *or* She is apt to lose her temper at home now and then.

闹虚 nàoxū 〈方言〉pretend to be courteous: 我不跟您～, 真的吃不下。I am not pretending. I am really full.

闹玄虚 nào xuánxū purposefully make simple things complicated; be deliberately mystifying things: 你把事情说明白, 别跟我～。Please be frank with me. Don't beat about the bush.

闹檐 nàoyán eaves of a palace or temple that are hung with small bells and tinkling pieces of metal

闹羊花 nàoyánghuā *also* "羊踯躅" yángzhízhú 〈植物〉Chinese azalea

闹意见 nào yìjiàn be divided in opinion and engage in bickerings: 同志之间要讲团结, 不要～。We must stress unity and refrain from bickering among comrades. /我们内部不要～。We mustn't fall out among ourselves.

闹意气 nào yìqì feel sulky because sth. is not to one's liking; let one's personal feelings get the better of one's reason; allow oneself to be swayed by personal feeling: 批评可不是～, 泄私愤。One must not give vent to one's personal grievance or anger in making criticism.

闹盈盈 nàoyīngyīng bustling with activity; noisy: 张家娶亲, 门前～。There is a wedding ceremony going on in Zhang's house, and the courtyard is bustling with noise and excitement.

闹杂 nàozá 〈方言〉noise and excitement; bustle: ～的声音 hubbub of noises

闹灾 nàozāi suffer from a natural disaster; be disaster-stricken

闹贼 nàozéi 〈口语〉burglary: 昨天晚上他家～了。Burglars broke into his house last night.

闹仗 nàozhàng 〈方言〉come to blows; scuffle

闹着玩儿 nàozhe wánr ❶ play; have fun; amuse oneself: 门口儿个孩子在～。Some kids were playing by the door. /工作时间是～的吗? Stop horsing around! It's work time. ❷ joke; tease: 我跟你～的, 别当真。I was teasing you. Don't take it to heart. *or* I was only joking. Don't take it seriously. ❸ treat a serious matter lightly; slight: 这可不是～的事儿。This is no joke. *or* This is no trifling matter.

闹着玩儿似的 nàozhe wánr shìde 〈方言〉as easy as playing; easy as pie: 这点事儿, 我们俩～就干了。We two can do it hands down. /搬这东西, 我跟～。Moving this is easy meat for me.

闹钟 nàozhōng alarm clock

闹嘴 nàozuǐ 〈方言〉quarrel; wrangle; bicker: 她又跟你～了? Did she quarrel with you again?

né

哪 né

哪吒 Nézha *Nezha*, divine warrior portrayed as a boy walking on

two firing wheels in the novel *Pilgrimage to the West*
see also nǎ; na; něi

nè

讷 nè 〈书面〉slow (of speech):口～少言 slow and clumsy of speech /～于言而敏于行 deliberate in speech but swift in action

讷讷 nènè 〈书面〉speak clumsily:～不出于口 speak under one's breath; mutter; mumble

呐 nè *see* "讷" nè
see also nà

那 nè 〈口语〉that
see also Nā; nà; nèi

ne

呢(呐) ne 〈助词〉❶ *used at the end of an interrogative sentence*:她怎么一点儿也不知道～? How come she didn't know anything about it? /你说是谁错了～? Who do you think is wrong? /那你怎么不说出来～? Then why didn't you say it? /我不去，你～? I'm not going. What about you? (*or* And you?) /我的钱包～? Where is my wallet? /你喜欢红色的～，还是蓝色的～? Which do you like, the red one or the blue one? ❷ *used at the end of a statement to give emphasis*:昨晚的灯会可热闹～。The lantern show last night was such great fun! /还得干九个月～。It will take us nine more months to complete the job. /他还会写诗～。He writes good poems too! /我才不会告诉你～! I am the last person to tell you that! *or* Catch me telling you that! ❸ *used at the end of a statement to indicate continuation of action*:外边正在下雪～。It's snowing outside. /别吵! 他在睡觉～。Be quiet. He's sleeping. /这些天我忙着～。I'm pretty busy these days. ❹ *used to make a pause within a sentence usu. to show a contrast*:伤是治好了，可是身体～，还有些虚弱。His wound is healed, but he is still rather weak. /小孩子～，算了，就别去了。As for the children, well, they'd better not go. /东西～，就先放在我这里吧。You may leave your things here with me for the time being.
see also ní

něi

哪(那) něi 〈口语〉(colloquial pronunciation for 哪 nǎ) which; what:～个学校? Which school? /～个人? Who? /～种材料? What kind of material?
see also nǎ; na; né

馁 něi ❶〈书面〉hungry; famished:冻～ cold and hungry ❷ lose heart; be disheartened:气～ be disheartened (*or* discouraged); lose heart /胜不骄，败不～。Do not be dizzy with success, nor be discouraged by failure. /不要自～。Keep your chin up. *or* Don't lose confidence. ❸〈书面〉(of fish) putrid; rotten:鱼～肉败。Both fish and meat have gone bad.

馁怯 něiqiè become dejected and timid:～的心情 feeling frustrated and subdued; losing one's nerve

nèi

内 nèi ❶ inner; inside; interior; within:～圈 inner circle /～港 inner harbour /室～ inside the room; indoors /市～交通 municipal transport /国～外 at home and abroad /校～ within (*or* inside) the school; on campus /～衣～裤 underclothes /一年～ within a year /党～斗争 inner-party struggle /请勿入～。No admittance. ❷ one's wife or her relatives:贱～〈谦词〉my wife /～嫂 wife of wife's elder brother /～妹 wife's younger sister /惧～ be henpecked ❸ internal organs; heart:五～俱焚 feel one's five internal organs are burning — one's heart is torn by grief or anxiety /色厉～荏 outwardly fierce but inwardly shaky; fierce of mien but faint of heart ❹ of the imperial palace:～廷 imperial palace /～库 imperial treasury /～苑 palace grounds /～侍 *also* "～监" eunuch /～嬖 favourite imperial concubine /大～ imperial residential palace ❺ female:～眷 female members of a family

内白 nèibái 〈戏剧〉words spoken by an actor or actress from offstage

内包装 nèibāozhuāng inner packing; internal packing

内宾 nèibīn ❶ guest or visitor from within the country ❷ female guests

内部 nèibù inside; interior; internal:国家～事务 internal affairs of a country /～联系 internal relations /～消息 confidential news /～矛盾 internal contradictions /～文件 restricted document /～通报 internal circular /～团结 unity among the members of a group /～刊物 publication for internal circulation; restricted publication /～纠纷 internal dispute /～收益率 internal rate of return /从～攻破 capture from within

内部发行 nèibù fāxíng (of newspapers, magazines, books, etc.) for restricted circulation

内部机制 nèibù jīzhì internal mechanism

内部价 nèibùjià internal discounted price; bargain price offered internally

内部审计 nèibù shěnjì internal audit

内部装饰 nèibù zhuāngshì 〈建筑〉interior decoration

内参 nèicān reference material for restricted circulation; internal reference:这条消息登在～上。This piece of information is carried in the internal reference news.

内查外调 nèichá-wàidiào carry out investigations both inside and outside an organization:经过多年的～，事情终于搞清楚了。The problems have been clarified after years of extensive investigations.

内场 nèichǎng ❶〈戏曲〉area behind the table on the stage:～椅 chair behind the table on the stage ❷〈体育〉(of baseball) infield:～手 infielder

内臣 nèichén ❶ close court official; chamberlain ❷ eunuch

内城 nèichéng inner city

内齿轮 nèichǐlún 〈机械〉internal gear

内宠 nèichǒng 〈旧语〉favourite imperial concubine; court favourite (such as a eunuch)

内出血 nèichūxuè 〈医学〉internal haemorrhage or bleeding

内存 nèicún *also* "随机存取存储器" suíjī cúnqǔ cúnchǔqì 〈计算机〉random access memory (RAM)

内存储器 nèicúnchǔqì 〈计算机〉inner memory; internal storage or memory; built-in storage

内错角 nèicuòjiǎo 〈数学〉alternate interior angle

内当家 nèidāngjiā *also* "内当家的"〈方言〉❶ wife ❷ wife of one's boss or master

内盗 nèidào theft committed by people from within; internal theft :这家商场发生了几起重大～案件。Several cases of serious internal thefts in the department store were reported.

内地 nèidì ❶ inland; interior; hinterland:～建设 construction in the hinterland /～工业 industry in the interior; industry in the hinterland /～城市 inland city /到祖国的～去 go to the interior of our motherland ❷ (as used by residents in Hong Kong or Macao) mainland:他去～谈一笔生意。He's gone to the mainland to negotiate a business deal.

内地会 Nèidìhuì 〈基督教〉China Inland Mission

内弟 nèidì wife's younger brother; brother-in-law

内典 nèidiǎn Buddhist canon (as called by Buddhists)

内电路 nèidiànlù internal circuit

内电阻 nèidiànzǔ 〈电子〉internal resistance

内定 nèidìng (usu. of personnel appointment) decided (at the higher level, etc.) prior to official announcement:他已经～为副院长了。It has been decided at the top level that he is to be the vice president.

内毒素 nèidúsù 〈医学〉endotoxin

内耳 nèi'ěr 〈生理〉inner ear; internal ear:～道 internal auditory meatus; internal acoustic meatus; *meatus acusticus internus*

内耳性眩晕综合征 nèi'ěrxìng xuànyùn zōnghézhēng *also* "梅尼埃尔氏综合征" Méiní'āi'ěr shì zōnghézhēng 〈医学〉Ménière's syndrome; Ménière's disease

内耳炎 nèi'ěryán 〈医学〉otitis interna

内犯 nèifàn 〈书面〉(of a nomadic people) invasion; inroad: 是年,

匈奴～。In that year, the Xiongnu made an inroad (into China).
内分泌 nèifēnmì 〈生理〉 endocrine; internal secretion: ～巢 endocrinology / ～腺 endocrine gland / ～系统 endocrine system; endocriniam / ～物 endocrine; endocritic
内分泌病 nèifēnmìbìng 〈医学〉 endocrinopathy; endocrinosis
内分泌疗法 nèifēnmì liáofǎ 〈医学〉 endocrinotherapy
内分泌失调 nèifēnmì shītiáo 〈医学〉 endocrinopathy
内分泌紊乱 nèifēnmì wěnluàn 〈医学〉endocrine disorder
内分泌障碍 nèifēnmì zhàng'ài 〈医学〉 dysendocrinism; dysendocrisiasis
内风 nèifēng 〈中医〉 disease caused by pathological changes of internal organs, with dizziness, fever, twitch, etc. as symptoms
内封 nèifēng 〈印刷〉 title page
内锋 nèifēng 〈体育〉 (of football) inside forward: 他踢右～。He plays right inside forward. *or* He plays inside right.
内稃 nèifū 〈植物〉 palea; palet
内服 nèifú (of medicine) to be taken orally: ～药 oral medicine; medicine for oral administration
内府 nèifǔ imperial or royal storehouse
内阁 nèigé ❶ cabinet: ～部长 cabinet minister / 影子～ shadow cabinet / ～制政府 cabinet system of government / ～改组 cabinet reshuffle / ～危机 cabinet crisis ❷ Grand Secretariat (of the Ming and Qing dynasties): ～大学士 senior secretary of the Grand Secretariat
内阁总理大臣 nèigé zǒnglǐ dàchén (Japan) Prime Minister
内公切线 nèigōngqiēxiàn 〈数学〉 internal common tangent
内功 nèigōng (of *qigong* or *wushu*) ❶ exercises to benefit the internal organs ❷ internal energy or power
内骨骼 nèigǔgé 〈生理〉 endoskeleton
内顾 nèigù 〈书面〉 ❶ look back ❷ worry about domestic problems when one is away from home
内顾之忧 nèigùzhīyōu family or domestic troubles: 我在国外可以呆上三四年, 我没有～。I can stay abroad for three or four years, for I have no domestic problems to worry about. / 国会与内阁闹矛盾, 这位总理出访期间颇有～。The prime minister was troubled by domestic problems while on an official visit abroad because the parliament and the cabinet were at daggers drawn.
内果皮 nèiguǒpí 〈植物〉 endocarp
内海 nèihǎi ❶ *also* "内陆海" inland sea ❷ continental sea
内涵 nèihán ❶ 〈逻辑〉 intension; connotation ❷ ability of exercising self-control; self-restraint: 这年轻人很有～。The young man knows well how to control himself.
内行 nèiháng expert; virtuoso; professional: ～话 comment or advice from a professional / 冒充～ pose as an expert / 变外行为～ turn a layman into a professional / 这方面我不～。I'm no expert in this field. / 他对金融很～。He is well versed in finance. / 养殖珍珠她是～。She is a dab at culturing pearls.
内耗 nèihào ❶ dissipation of energy through the internal friction of a machine ❷ losses caused by internal strife: 他把许多精力都花在解决本单位的～上了。He has expended a lot of time and energy on settling the internal strife of his working unit.
内河 nèihé inland river or water, or waterway: ～航行 inland navigation / ～运输 inland water transport
内核 nèihé core; essence
内讧 nèihòng *also* "内哄" internal conflict or strife: 敌军发生～。Internal strife arose among the enemy forces.
内华达 Nèihuádá Nevada, a state of the western United States
内画 nèihuà inside-bottle painting
内画壶 nèihuàhú glassware bottle whose interior is painted with landscape, figures or flowers, etc.
内踝 nèihuái 〈生理〉 internal malleolus; medial malleolus
内婚制 nèihūnzhì *also* "族内婚" zúnèihūn a form of marriage in primitive society, which allows intermarriage between clans within a tribe
内急 nèijí be dying to go to the toilet; be dying for a leak
内寄生 nèijìshēng 〈生理〉 endoparasitism
内寄生虫 nèijìshēngchóng 〈生理〉 endoparasite
内奸 nèijiān enemy agent hidden within one's ranks; hidden spy; fifth columnist; mole
内间 nèijiān 〈方言〉 inner room
内艰 nèijiān 〈书面〉 mother's funeral
内监 nèijiàn eunuch
内角 nèijiǎo 〈数学〉 interior angle
内接多边形 nèijiē duōbiānxíng 〈数学〉 inscribed polygon
内接形 nèijiēxíng 〈数学〉 inscribed figure
内紧外松 nèijǐn-wàisōng be relaxed outwardly but vigilant or alert inwardly: 他～, 做出一副没事儿的样子。Though tense and nervous, he put up a facade of composure and indifference. *or* He felt nervous but looked calm as if nothing had happened.
内经 Nèijīng *also* "黄帝内经" Huángdì Nèijīng *Classic of Internal Medicine*, most ancient traditional medical work of China providing both comprehensive diagnoses and theoretical basis for Chinese medicine, compiled in the Eastern Zhou Dynasty
内景 nèijǐng indoor scene; indoor setting; interior
内径 nèijìng 〈机械〉 internal diameter; inside or inner diameter (ID): ～千分尺 inside micrometer / ～规 internal gauge
内疚 nèijiù guilty conscience; qualms (of conscience); compunction: 觉得～ feel guilty; have qualms of conscience / 我一直感到很～。I have been tormented by a guilty conscience. / 他没有同我说实话, 也不觉得～。He didn't have the slightest compunction about not telling me the truth.
内举 nèijǔ 〈旧语〉 recommend one's relative (for an official position): ～不避亲, 外举不避仇 shun neither one's relatives nor one's personal foes when making recommendations for official posts; recommend people regardless of their relationships with oneself
内聚力 nèijùlì 〈物理〉 cohesive force; cohesion
内眷 nèijuàn females in one's family
内卡钳 nèikǎqián 〈机械〉 inside callipers
内科 nèikē 〈医学〉 (department of) internal medicine: ～病房 medical ward / ～医生 physician
内裤 nèikù underpants; briefs (for men); knickers; panties (for women)
内窥镜 nèikuījìng 〈医学〉 endoscope: ～检查 endoscopy
内愧 nèikuì compunction; guilty conscience: 深感～ have deep compunction; have a guilty conscience
内涝 nèilào waterlogging
内里 nèilǐ 〈方言〉 inside: 这事儿～还有些曲折。There are still some complications about the matter.
内力 nèilì 〈物理〉 internal force
内联企业 nèilián qǐyè domestically-associated enterprise (i.e. an enterprise linked to another in the country, usu. one in the eastern part to another in the middle or western part of the country)
内联网 nèiliánwǎng 〈信息〉 intranet
内流河 nèiliúhé inland river
内六角螺钉 nèiliùjiǎo luódīng 〈机械〉 socket head cap screw
内陆 nèilù inland; continental; landlocked: ～城市 inland city / ～平原 inland plain
内陆国 nèilùguó landlocked country
内陆海 nèilùhǎi continental sea; inland sea
内陆河 nèilùhé continental river
内陆湖 nèilùhú inland lake
内陆盆地 nèilù péndì inland or interior basin
内陆水域 nèilù shuǐyù inland waters
内陆性气候 nèilùxìng qìhòu inland climate
内乱 nèiluàn internal disorder or turmoil; civil strife: 平定～ put down (*or* quell) an internal rebellion / ～时起 be frequently plunged into internal turmoil; be frequently afflicted by internal disturbances
内罗毕 Nèiluóbì Nairobi, capital of Kenya: ～国家公园 Nairobi National Park
内螺纹 nèiluówén 〈机械〉 female screw; female (screw) thread; internal screw; internal (screw) thread: ～车削 internal threading / ～磨床 internal thread grinder; internal thread grinding machine
内螺旋 nèiluóxuán internal spin
内贸 nèimào domestic trade; domestic commerce
内酶 nèiméi 〈生化〉 endoenzyme; endoferment
内蒙古 Nèiměnggǔ Inner Mongolia: ～草原 Inner Mongolian grasslands
内蒙古高原 Nèiměnggǔ Gāoyuán Inner Mongolian Plateau
内蒙古自治区 Nèiměnggǔ Zìzhìqū Inner Mongolian Autonomous Region
内膜 nèimó 〈生理〉 endomembrane; inner membrane
内磨擦 nèimócā 〈物理〉 internal friction
内幕 nèimù what goes on behind the scenes; inside story: 了解～

get the inside story; know sth. from the inside /泄露～ reveal the inside story; let the cat out of the bag /揭开～ unveil the inside story /他知道这些交易的全部～。He is on the inside in all those deals.
内幕交易 nèimù jiāoyì insider dealing
内难 nèinàn internal disturbance; civil commotion
内能 nèinéng 〈物理〉internal energy; intrinsic energy
内啮合 nèinièhé 〈机械〉internal toothing
内胚层 nèipēicéng *also* "内胚叶"〈生物〉entoblast; entoderm
内皮 nèipí 〈生理〉endothelium:～系统 endothetial system /～瘤〈医学〉endothelioma /～炎 endotheliitis
内壳 nèiqiào endoconch
内壳层 nèiqiàocéng inner shell
内切圆 nèiqiēyuán 〈数学〉inscribed circle; incircle
内亲 nèiqīn relative on one's wife's side; in-law
内侵 nèiqīn (as of a nomadic people) invasion;inroad:强敌大举～。A formidable enemy is invading our country.
内勤 nèiqín ❶ office work; (in contrast to 外勤); clerical work in the office:～人员 office staff /手术后，我就转干～了。I switched to office (*or* clerical) work after recovering from the operation. ❷ office staff; clerk
内倾 nèiqīng 〈心理〉introvert
内情 nèiqíng inside information; inside story:熟悉～ be in the know; be an insider /这个案子的～复杂。The case is literally a labyrinth of intricate clues. *or* This is a complicated case.
内燃锅炉 nèirán guōlú internally fired boiler
内燃机 nèiránjī internal combustion engine
内燃机车 nèirán jīchē diesel locomotive
内燃机船 nèirán jīchuán motorship
内燃水泵 nèirán shuǐbèng Humphrey gas pump
内瓤 nèiráng ❶ pulp; interior part of certain things:这手表的～还不错。The interior part of the watch is not bad. ❷ what goes on behind the scenes; inside:这个药房外表看是做生意的，～里它是个特务组织。By appearance it is a drugstore but in fact it is a spy ring.
内热 nèirè ❶〈书面〉anxiety ❷〈中医〉pathological phenomenon caused by deficiency of *yin*, with thirst, irritability, constipation, etc. as symptoms
内人 nèirén my wife
内容 nèiróng content; substance:主要～ main or essential points (of a plan or a project); gist (of a story or a report); main content (of a book etc.) /实质～ substance /毫无～ be devoid of any content; have no substance at all /～单薄 thin in terms of content /发言的一个重要～ important element in one's speech /谈话涉及的～很广。The talk covered a lot of ground. *or* The talk covered a wide range of topics. /～比形式更重要。The substance is more important than the form.
内容产业 nèiróng chǎnyè 〈信息〉content industry
内容矿物 nèiróng kuàngwù 〈矿业〉endomorph
内容提要 nèiróng tíyào extract; synopsis; summary
内疝 nèishàn 〈医学〉internal hernia
内伤 nèishāng ❶ internal injury ❷〈中医〉disorder of internal organs (as caused by improper diet, fatigue, emotional strain, sexual excess, etc.)
内生殖器 nèishēngzhíqì internal genitalia
内室 nèishì inner room; inner chamber (usually refering to bedroom)
内视反听 nèishì-fǎntīng make self-examination or self-criticism and accept criticism from others:一个人能时时～,实在难能可贵。Whoever welcomes criticisms and often makes self-examinations is worthy of esteem.
内视图 nèishìtú inside view
内收肌 nèishōujī adductor muscles
内水 nèishuǐ inland waters of a country including rivers, lakes, continental seas, ports, bays, etc.
内斯湖 Nèisīhú Loch Ness, in the Highlands of Scotlands:～水怪 Loch Ness monster
内胎 nèitāi inner tube of a tyre
内廷 nèitíng inner court, residential quarters of an emperor or king
内外 nèi-wài ❶ inside and outside; domestic and foreign:长城～ on both sides of the Great Wall /～宾客 visitors from home and abroad; Chinese and foreign guests ❷ (used to indicate approximation) around; about:估计这项工程一年～就可以完成。The general estimate is that the project will be completed in a year or so.
内外夹攻 nèi-wài jiāgōng attack from both within and without:对敌人采取～的战术 adopt the tactics of attacking the enemy from inside and outside
内外交困 nèi-wài jiāokùn beset with difficulties both at home and abroad; plagued by both internal and external troubles:陷于～的境地 be on the horns of a dilemma in both internal and external affairs
内外有别 nèi-wài yǒubié distinguish between what is for internal information and what is for external publicity;distinguish between one's own people and outsiders
内外自动电话系统 nèi-wài zìdòng diànhuà xìtǒng 〈通信〉inward-outward dialing system
内务 nèiwù ❶ domestic affairs; internal affairs; family affairs:我们要花几天时间处理～。We'll have to devote a few days to sorting out certain outstanding internal problems. ❷ routine tasks to maintain cleanliness and orderliness in dormitories or barracks:整理～ tidy up the barracks (*or* dormitories) /～条例〈军事〉interior service regulations
内务部 nèiwùbù Ministry of Internal Affairs; (ROK) Ministry of Home Affairs
内务府 Nèiwùfǔ Office of the Imperial Household (of the Qing Dynasty)
内吸剂 nèixījì *also* "内吸杀虫剂"〈农业〉systemic insecticide
内吸磷 nèixīlín 〈农业〉demeton
内线 nèixiàn ❶ planted agent; informer;mole:敌人可能在我们组织里安插了～。The enemy has probably planted agents in our organization. ❷〈军事〉interior lines:～作战 fight on interior lines ❸ inside telephone connections:我的电话是～，不是直通的。Mine is an extension number, not for direct dialing. ❹ (of politics) inside:～人物 insider /～联系 inside connections /～关系 inside network /走～ (wangle sth.) through personal channels
内线自动电话机 nèixiàn zìdòng diànhuàjī 〈通信〉interphone; talk-back circuit
内详 nèixiáng name and address of sender not written on the envelope as required but mentioned in the letter;"see inside"
内向 nèixiàng ❶ inward:枪口～ fire on one's own people ❷〈心理〉introversion:～型 introverted type /他是一个性格～的人。He is an introvert (*or* is introverted). ❸〈书面〉pledge allegiance to the central authorities:翻然～ transfer one's allegiance to the central government
内向型经济 nèixiàngxíng jīngjì domestically-oriented economy
内项 nèixiàng 〈数学〉mean term
内销 nèixiāo (goods) for domestic market:～产品 products for the domestic market /某些出口商品已转～。Some goods earmarked for export have been relegated to the domestic market.
内斜视 nèixiéshì 〈医学〉esotropia; cross-eye
内心 nèixīn ❶ innermost being; heart:～深处 at the bottom of one's heart; in one's heart of hearts /发自～ from the bottom of one's heart /～世界 inner world /一个～纯洁的姑娘 a pure-hearted girl /～像一团火 have a fervent heart /～受到谴责 be conscience-stricken /～处在一种感情的矛盾之中 feel as if one's heart is rent by conflicting emotions /压抑不住～的激动 can not hold back (*or* suppress) one's excitement /～独白 internal monologue ❷〈数学〉incentre (of a triangle)
内行星 nèixíngxīng 〈天文〉inferior planet (planet whose orbit is inside that of the earth's orbit)
内省 nèixǐng introspection:～无疚 not have qualms of conscience upon introspection /忧郁而性喜～的人 moody introspective person /～主义者 introspectionist /～心理学 introspective psychology
内兄 nèixiōng wife's elder brother; brother-in-law
内秀 nèixiù intelligent and circumspect though seemingly unrefined; with inward grace
内压力 nèiyālì 〈物理〉intrinsic pressure; internal pressure
内焰 nèiyàn 〈化学〉inner flame
内衣 nèiyī underwear; underclothes; undergarment
内因 nèiyīn 〈哲学〉internal cause; internal factor:外因通过～起作用。External causes become operative through internal causes. /～是起主导作用的。It is the internal factors that play the main role.
内营力 nèiyínglì force that comes from within the earth and changes its exterior
内应 nèiyìng ❶ act in coordination with forces from outside:起事时有人在城中～。When we attack the city, someone inside the city

will help us. ❷ planted agent; plant

内应力 nèiyìnglì 〈机械〉internal stress

内忧 nèiyōu ❶ domestic trouble:这位总统执政以来,～频仍。The president has been plagued by domestic troubles since he came to office. ❷〈书面〉anxiety:国难当头,他～如焚。Overwhelmed by the national crisis he was torn by anxiety. ❸〈书面〉the passing away of one's mother

内忧外患 nèiyōu-wàihuàn domestic trouble and foreign invasion; disturbance within and attack from without:这个小国正处在～的严重时刻。This small country is at a critical moment, threatened as it is by both domestic trouble and foreign invasion.

内圆珩磨 nèiyuán héngmó 〈机械〉internal honing

内圆磨床 nèiyuán móchuáng 〈机械〉internal grinder

内蕴 nèiyùn ❶ lie hidden inside; be latent:～雄图 have grand plans in one's mind ❷ inherent spirit:这部话剧有深刻的时代～。The play fully embodies the spirit of our age.

内在 nèizài ❶ inherent; intrinsic; internal; inner:～规律 inherent law /～矛盾 inherent or inner contradiction /～力量 inner strength (*or* power) /～联系 inner link; internal relations /～的特点 intrinsic characteristics ❷ withdrawn; concealed; introvert:感情～ be introverted

内在论 nèizàilùn 〈哲学〉immanentism

内脏 nèizàng 〈生理〉internal organs; viscera

内宅 nèizhái 〈旧语〉inner chambers for female members of a family

内债 nèizhài internal debt (usu. in the form of government bonds)

内战 nèizhàn civil war:～连年 (a country) be ripped apart by protracted civil war /～内行,外战外行 in one's element when fighting an internal war, but out of one's element when it comes to fighting an external war

内掌柜 nèizhǎngguì *also*“内掌柜的”〈口语〉shop owner's wife; wife

内障 nèizhàng *also*“白内障” báinèizhàng 〈医学〉cataract

内争 nèizhēng internal strife; internal dispute

内政 nèizhèng internal affairs; domestic or home affairs:互不干涉～ non-interference in each other's internal affairs /这纯属～问题。This is purely an internal matter.

内政部 nèizhèngbù Ministry of the Interior; Ministry of Home Affairs; (US) Department of the Interior; (UK) Home Office

内政部长 nèizhèng bùzhǎng Minister of Home Affairs; Minister of Internal Affairs; (US) Secretary of the Interior

内政大臣 nèizhèng dàchén Minister of Home Affairs; (UK) Home Secretary; Secretary of State for the Home Department

内侄 nèizhí son of wife's brother; wife's nephew

内侄女 nèizhínǚ daughter of wife's brother; wife's niece

内痔 nèizhì 〈医学〉internal piles or haemorrhoids

内中 nèizhōng inside:秀在～ have inward grace /～奥妙鲜为人知。Few people are aware of the subtleties of the matter.

内衷 nèizhōng heart; inmost being:发自～的欢乐 joy coming from the inmost recesses of one's heart; heartfelt joy

内助 nèizhù 〈书面〉wife:贤～ virtuous and capable wife; one's better half

内传 nèizhuàn ❶ anecdotal biography; life and anecdotes (of a person); private life (of a person) ❷〈古语〉book on exegesis of classics

内资 nèizī domestic financing; investment from domestic sources

内子 nèizǐ *also*“内人”〈书面〉my wife:～酷爱书画。My wife is very fond of calligraphy and painting.

内阻 nèizǔ 〈电工〉internal resistance

那 nèi colloquial pronunciation for“那” nà

see also Nā; nà; nè

nèn

恁 nèn 〈方言〉❶ so; such:～有劲儿 so strong; so powerful /要不了～些 not need that much /～大胆! How dare you! *or* What audacity! ❷ that; those:～时节 at that time; those days ❸ this; this much:没料到等～久 not expect to wait this long

see also nín

恁般 nènbān 〈方言〉like that

恁地 nèndì 〈方言〉❶ in this or that way; thus:不要～说。Don't say this. /你要～做,我就再不理你了。If you persist, I'll never have anything to do with you again. ❷ how; why:这东西放在哪里了,～想不起来? Where did I put the thing? Why can't I recall it?

嫩 nèn ❶ tender; delicate; sensitive:～叶 tender leaf /～芽 bud /脸皮～ shy; bashful; thin-skinned ❷ (of food) under-done; soft; tender:煮得～点儿的鸡蛋 soft-boiled egg /牛排要～的还是老的? Do you want your steak rare or well-done? ❸ (of colour) light: *see*“～黄”;“～绿” ❹ inexperienced; immature; unskilled:～手 new hand; green hand; raw hand /处理这种复杂的事,他是太～了点儿。He is too inexperienced (*or* immature) to cope with such a complicated matter.

嫩豆腐 nèndòufu tender bean curd

嫩寒 nènhán ❶ first days of cold weather ❷〈书面〉slightly cold

嫩红 nènhóng pale-red; pink

嫩黄 nènhuáng light yellow

嫩绿 nènlǜ light green

嫩气 nènqi ❶ state of being tender and lovely; daintiness:丰润的脸上透着粉红的～。There is a glow of pink tenderness on her chubby face. ❷ tender; dainty-looking:她已是五十多岁的人了,穿水红色褂子是不是～了点儿? As a woman of over fifty, isn't it a bit garish for her to wear a pink blouse?

嫩晴 nènqíng 〈书面〉clear up; the sun has just started shining:～天气 it's clearing up

嫩弱 nènruò tender; frail; delicate:～的花蕊 tender stamen

嫩色 nènsè soft or light colour

嫩生生 nènshēngshēng very tender

嫩生 nènsheng 〈方言〉❶ tender:这韭菜真～,包饺子最好。The chives are very tender and best for making dumpling stuffing. ❷ immature; unsophisticated:我弟弟还～,您多照顾点。I hope you will be kind enough to take care of my brother, who is still inexperienced.

嫩鲜鲜 nènxiānxiān tender and fresh:主人拿出～的莲藕请我们吃。The host treated us to fresh tender lotus roots.

néng

能 néng ❶ ability; capability; competence:才～ talent /技～ technical skill /逞～ show off one's ability or skill /无～之辈 people lacking in ability; incompetent people ❷〈物理〉energy:热～ thermal energy /原子～ atomic energy /太阳～ solar energy /核～ nuclear energy /电～ electric energy ❸ able; capable:贤～ virtuous and capable person /～攻～守 be good at both attack and defence /～书不择笔。People good at calligraphy are not particular about the brush. *or* A good workman does not complain about the tools. ❹ (indicating possibility or permission) can; may:一小时～完成 can be done within an hour /我～去吗? Can (*or* May) I go? /这本书什么时候～出版? When will this book be published? /你说他干这活儿～行吗? Do you think he is fit for the job? /他什么事都～干得出来。He is capable of anything.

能臣 néngchén 〈旧语〉competent official; capable minister:任用～ appoint competent officials /～干吏 competent ministers and efficient officials

能动 néngdòng active; dynamic:人的～作用 man's initiative; man's dynamic role /～力量 dynamic force /认识上～的飞跃 active leap in cognition

能动武器 néngdòng wǔqì kinetic energy weapon

能动性 néngdòngxìng initiative; active or dynamic role; activity:主观～ subjective activity; initiative

能干 nénggàn able; capable; competent:精明～ capable and shrewd; able and astute /他有一名～的助手。He has an able assistant. /这孩子真～! What a capable boy!

能歌善舞 nénggē-shànwǔ good at (both) singing and dancing

能个儿 nénggèr 〈方言〉❶ ability; skill:有～ be able or capable/没～ be not able; be inept ❷ versatile; smart; deft:这孩子真～,学什么一学就会。The child is so smart and deft that he knows whatever he learns.

能工巧匠 nénggōng-qiǎojiàng skilful craftsman; master artisan:这座雄伟的建筑,是许多～智慧和汗水的结晶。The magnificent building is

N

the crystallization of the wisdom and labour of many a master craftsman.

能够 nénggòu ❶ can; be able to; be capable of:～独立工作 be able to work on one's own /这个工厂～生产多种产品。This factory can make a variety of products. ❷ (indicating possibility, permission, etc.) can; may:儿童不～去舞厅。Children must not go to dance halls. /在大坝修建之前，这条河的中、上游都不～行船。Before the dam was constructed, the upper and middle reaches of the river were not navigable. /今天的晚会家属也～参加。Family members are also welcome to the party tonight.

能谷 nénggǔ 〈物理〉energy-valley

能官能民 néngguān-néngmín be ready to accept an official post or live as an ordinary citizen; take or leave office with equanimity

能耗 nénghào energy consumption; energy cost

能级 néngjí 〈物理〉energy level; energy state:费密～ Fermi level /基态～ ground state level /～图 energy level diagram; level scheme /～参数 level parameter /～密度 level density

能见半径 néngjiàn bànjìng 〈航空〉〈航海〉radius of visibility

能见度 néngjiàndù 〈气象〉visibility:地面～ ground visibility /～计 visibility meter /～差 poor visibility /～极好 ceiling and visibility unlimited /～为零。The visibility is nil.

能剧 néngjù *No* or *Nogaku*, classic Japanese dance-drama

能力 nénglì ability; capability; capacity; competence:～不够 lacking in ability /～强 have great ability; be very capable /学术～ scholarly competence /业务～ professional competence /语言～ linguistic ability /阅读～ reading ability /培养分析问题的～ develop one's analytical capacity /他是一个很有～的律师。He is a highly competent lawyer.

能量 néngliàng ❶〈物理〉energy:～密度 energy density /～梯度 energy gradient /～耗散 energy dissipation /～吸收 energy absorption /～均分〈化学〉equipartition of energy /～代谢〈生物〉energy metabolism /～单位 energy unit ❷ capabilities; capacity:你别小看他，他的～不可轻视。Don't underestimate him. He has ample capacity for winning people round.

能量守恒 néngliàng shǒuhéng 〈物理〉conservation of energy; energy conservation:～定律 law of conservation of energy

能量转换 néngliàng zhuǎnhuàn 〈物理〉energy conversion; energy transformation:～装置 energy conversion device

能耐 néngnai 〈口语〉ability; capability:这人还真有～，不到三天就完成了一百个订单。He is really capable; he secured 100 orders in less than three days. /这些没～的东西，真叫我失望！I am really disappointed with these incompetents.

能…能… néng…néng… be able to do both...and...; be capable in ...and...:能文能武 be equally capable in civilian and military affairs; be able to do both mental and manual labour /能写能算 be literate; be good at the three R.'s (*r*eading, w*r*iting and a*r*ithmetic) /能吃能喝 eat heartily and sleep soundly — be in normal or good health; show no sign of ailment

能谱 néngpǔ 〈物理〉energy spectrum; energy distribution

能掐会算 néngqiā-huìsuàn tell fortunes; be able to predict the future course of events

能屈能伸 néngqū-néngshēn be ready to stoop or stand erect — submit or assert oneself as the occasion requires; be adaptable to circumstances:大丈夫～。He is a real man who knows when to eat humble pie and when to hold his head high. *or* A real man should learn to be flexible.

能人 néngrén able person; talent:行行有～。There are able people in every walk of life. /谈判桌上的女～ talented woman negotiator

能人背后有能人 néngrén bèihòu yǒu néngrén however able a person may be, there is always someone still abler

能人统治 néngrén tǒngzhì meritocracy

能上能下 néngshàng-néngxià be ready to accept a higher or lower post; take promotion or demotion with equal composure

能士 néngshì 〈书面〉talented people; talents:广收天下～ recruit talented people all over the country

能事 néngshì (often used with 尽) what one is particularly good at:竭尽歪曲篡改之～ stop at nothing to distort facts /以推诿责任为～ be particularly good at shifting responsibilities onto others (*or* passing the buck)

能手 néngshǒu dab hand; expert; crackajack:生产～ good hand (at one's work); good worker /技术～ technical expert /养蚕～ dab hand at silkworm breeding

能说会道 néngshuō-huìdào have the gift of the gab; have a glib tongue; be articulate; have a facile tongue:张三的老婆～，无人不晓。Zhangsan's wife is well known for her glib tongue. /谁又有你那么～呢？Who is more eloquent than you?

能斯脱灯 néngsītuōdēng 〈电工〉Nernst glower; Nernst lamp

能态 néngtài 〈物理〉energy state

能为 néngwéi 〈方言〉ability; capability; skill:他心里想，就你这样一个初出茅庐的作家，有多大～？A fledgling writer like you, what skills do you have? He thought to himself.

能行 néngxíng 〈方言〉able; skilful; competent:这些人真～，一个月的任务半个月就干完了。They really know their job. They have completed one month's work in half a month. *or* These people are really efficient; they have fulfilled one month's quota in half a month.

能言善辩 néngyán-shànbiàn be eloquent; have the gift of the gab:～之士 eloquent speaker /搞外事的总要～才好。One who works in the foreign service should have a ready tongue.

能以 néngyǐ capable; able:他在这样艰苦环境中～坚持工作，真是难得。It is truly commendable that he was able to carry on under such difficult circumstances.

能源 néngyuán sources of energy; energy resource; energy:节约～ energy conservation /再生～ renewable sources of energy /～密集型工业 energy-intensive industry /节约～计划 energy conservation programme /消耗～项目 energy intensive project /合理开发和使用～ rational development and utilization of energy resources

能源经济学 néngyuán jīngjìxué energy economics

能源危机 néngyuán wēijī energy crisis

能愿动词 néngyuàn dòngcí 〈语言〉modal verb

能者多劳 néngzhě-duōláo (often used to persuade people to take on heavier tasks or do extra work) able people should do more work; an able person has numerous calls upon his or her time; the abler one is, the more one should do:～，这些事情还是请你多费心吧。An able man gets little leisure. I hope you will look after these matters.

能者为师 néngzhě-wéishī let those who know teach

能征惯战 néngzhēng-guànzhàn be a seasoned warrior:～的骁将 seasoned valiant general

ńg

嗯(唔) ńg *or* ń 〈叹词〉*used in questioning*:～，这是什么？Eh? What is this? /～，你说什么？What? What did you say?

ňg

嗯(𠮾) ňg *or* ň 〈叹词〉*used to indicate surprise*:～，你怎么还在这儿？Why, you are still here! /～，怎么有煤气味儿？Hey, I can smell gas! /～，你把那幅画送人了？What! You have given that painting away?

ǹg

嗯(叿) ǹg *or* ǹ 〈叹词〉*used to indicate positive response*:～，你就这么办！Ok, it's settled. /～，让我考虑考虑。All right. Let me think it over. /他～了一声，二话不说就走了。He merely mumbled "Hm", and went away without a word.

nī

妮 nī

妮子 nīzi *also* "妮儿"〈方言〉girl; lass

ní

麑 ní 〈古语〉young deer

霓(蜺) ní *also* "副虹" fùhóng 〈气象〉secondary rain-

bow
霓虹灯 níhóngdēng neon light; neon lamp; neon
霓石 níshí 〈矿业〉aegirine

輗 ní 〈古语〉joints of the axle with the ends of carriage poles

齯 ní 〈书面〉small new tooth of a toothless old person (considered as a sign of longevity)

蜺 ní 〈书面〉❶cicada in cold weather ❷ *see*"霓"ní

倪 ní ❶ *see*"端倪" duānní ❷ (Ní) a surname

鲵 ní 〈动物〉salamander:大~ giant salamander (*Megalobatrachus davidianus*)

猊 ní *see*"狻猊" suānní

婗 ní *see*"婴婗" yīní

尼 ní nun:僧~ Buddhist monks and nuns
尼安德特人 Ní'āndétèrén 〈考古〉Neanderthal Man, an extinct type of early man living during the Old Stone Age, whose fossil remains were first found in the caves in Neanderthal, Germany, in 1856
尼庵 ní'ān Buddhist nunnery; convent
尼泊尔 Níbó'ěr Nepal:~人 Nepalese /~语 Nepali
尼布楚条约 Níbùchǔ Tiáoyuē *also* "中俄尼布楚议界条约" Zhōng-É Níbùchǔ Yìjiè Tiáoyuē Sino-Russian Treaty of Nerchinsk (1689), the first border agreement between the Qing government and the imperial Russian government
尼采 Nícǎi Friedrich Wilhelm Nietzsche (1844-1900), German philosopher and writer of Polish descent
尼格罗-澳大利亚人种 Nígéluó-Àodàlìyà rénzhǒng *also* "黑种" hēizhǒng Negroid-Australian race; black race
尼格罗人 Nígéluórén *also* "黑人" hēirén Negro, a member of the black- or dark-skinned group of human population that originated south of the Sahara in Africa; black
尼姑 nígū Buddhist nun
尼古丁 nígǔdīng nicotine:~含量 nicotine content
尼赫鲁 Níhèlǔ Pandit Jawaharlal Nehru (1889-1964), first Prime Minister of independent India from 1947 until his death in 1964
尼加拉瓜 Níjiālāguā Nicaragua:~人 Nicaraguan
尼加拉瓜湖 Níjiālāguāhú Lake Nicaragua, largest lake in Central America, near the west coast of Nicaragua
尼克松 Níkèsōng Richard Milhous Nixon (1913-1994), 37th President of the US (1969-1974), who visited the People's Republic of China in Feb. 1972 to start the normalization of Sino-US relations:~主义 Nixon Doctrine
尼雷尔 Níléi'ěr Julius Kambarage Nyerere (1922-1999), President of Tanzania(1964-1985)
尼龙 nílóng 〈纺织〉nylon:~长袜 nylon hose (*or* stockings)/~丝 nylon yarn
尼龙钉 nílóngdīng nylon staple
尼龙绳 nílóngshéng nylon cord
尼龙线 nílóngxiàn nylon wire
尼罗河 Níluóhé Nile; Nile River (longest river of Africa):~三角洲 Nile delta
尼日尔 Nírì'ěr Niger:~人 Nigerois
尼日尔河 Nírì'ěrhé Niger River in west Africa, third longest river of Africa
尼日利亚 Nírìlìyà Nigeria:~人 Nigerian
尼亚加拉瀑布 Níyàjiālā Pùbù Niagara Falls (waterfall on the Niagara River of North America)
尼亚美 Níyàměi Niamey, capital of Niger

泥 ní ❶ mud; silt; mire:淤~ silt; sludge; ooze /污~ mire; sludge; slush; slosh /塘~ pond sludge; pond silt; pond slush ❷ mashed things, esp. vegetables and fruit; soft, pulpy mixture:土豆~ mashed potato /枣~ date paste /苹果~ apple sauce /印~ red ink paste used for seals; ink wax /封~ lute
see also nì
泥巴 níbā 〈方言〉mud, mire
泥笆墙 níbāqiáng wattle and daub
泥饭碗 nífànwǎn clay rice bowl — insecure job
泥肥 níféi 〈农业〉sludge; slush
泥封 nífēng lute
泥佛劝土佛 nífó quàn tǔfó the mud idol soothes the clay idol— those who have the same complaints sympathize with each other:~,同洒伤心泪。Fellow sufferers sympathize with each other, shedding sad tears in each other's company.
泥工 nígōng 〈方言〉plasterer; tiler; bricklayer
泥垢 nígòu dirt; grime; soot; filth:满身~。His body is covered with dirt.
泥龟 níguī 〈动物〉mud turtle (*Kinosternidae*)
泥滑 níhuá muddy and slippery:一遇下雨,这路面~,无法行车。In rainy days, the road became muddy and slippery, impassable for cars.
泥灰岩 níhuīyán 〈地质〉marl
泥火山 níhuǒshān mud volcano
泥浆 níjiāng slop; slurry; mud:挡~板 mud apron; mud guard
泥浆泵 níjiāngbèng mud pump
泥浆搅拌器 níjiāng jiǎobànqì slurry mixer
泥脚 níjiǎo 〈方言〉bottom mud of a paddy field or pond:这一块稻田~深。The bottom mud of this plot of rice field is deep.
泥金 níjīn golden paint; mixture of glue, powdered gold or other metals for coating
泥坑 níkēng mud pit; morass; bog; mire:陷入~ get stuck in the mud; be bogged down in a morass /和那些人纠缠在一起,总有一天要堕入~。You will be dragged into the mire one day if you associate with those people.
泥疗 níliáo 〈医学〉mud therapy
泥流 níliú 〈地质〉mud flow; soilflow; soil fluction; sludging
泥煤 níméi peat
泥淖 nínào mire; bog; morass:身陷~而不能自拔 be inextricably bogged down in the mud; fall into a mire from which one could not extricate oneself /雨后遍地~。Muddy puddles can be found everywhere after the rain.
泥泞 nínìng muddy; miry:小巷雨后~不堪。The lane became very muddy after the rain.
泥牛入海 níniú-rùhǎi like a clay buffalo going into the sea — not to be heard of again; gone for good:他一去如~,永无消息。Like a clay ox disappearing into the sea, he was heard of no more.
泥盆纪 Nípénjì 〈地质〉Devonian Period
泥盆系 Nípénxì fourth period of the Paleozoic era; Devonian
泥菩萨 nípúsà clay idol:~洗脸,越洗越难看。Like the clay idol washing its face, the more one tries to whitewash oneself the uglier one looks.
泥菩萨过河,自身难保 nípúsà guò hé, zìshēn nán bǎo like a clay idol crossing a river, one is hardly able to save oneself, let alone assist others
泥丘 níqiū 〈地质〉mudlump
泥鳅 níqiu 〈动物〉loach
泥人 nírén 〈工美〉clay figurine; clay statuette:~张 Zhang the clay-figurine master
泥熔岩 níróngyán 〈地质〉argillaceous rock; pelite; pelyte
泥沙 níshā 〈地质〉silt:~淤积 sedimentation
泥沙俱下 níshā-jùxià mud and sand are carried along — there is a mingling of good and bad:时局不清,~,鱼龙混杂。When the political firmament is murky, the bad mix with the good, and you can't easily tell them apart .
泥石流 níshíliú 〈地质〉mud-rock flow
泥水匠 níshuǐjiàng plasterer; tiler; bricklayer
泥塑 nísù clay sculpture; clay figure modelling
泥塑木雕 nísù-mùdiāo *also* "木雕泥塑" like an idol carved in wood or moulded in clay — as dead as a door-nail:一个个吓得像~一般,动弹不得。Dumbstruck, they all stood there immobile, as if their feet were planted in earth.
泥胎 nítāi clay idol not yet painted
泥胎儿 nítāir unbaked and unfired pottery; virgin pottery
泥滩 nítān 〈地质〉(mud) flat
泥潭 nítán mire; morass; quagmire; marsh:深陷~ sunk deep in a

N

mire
泥炭 nítàn *also*"泥煤"peat:～肥料 peat fertilizer
泥炭沼泽 nítàn zhǎozé peat bog
泥塘 nítáng bog; mire; morass
泥土 nítǔ ❶ earth; soil; dirt:春天的原野散发着～的芳香。In spring, the fields send forth an aroma of earth. /他抓起一把家乡的～。He held up a handful of soil of his native place. ❷ clay
泥腿 nítuǐ *also* "泥腿子"〈旧语〉〈贬义〉bumpkin; clodhopper; yokel; country lout
泥洼 níwā *also* "泥洼子" low-lying land where mud is silted up
泥瓦匠 níwǎjiàng *also* "泥水匠" bricklayer; tiler; plasterer
泥丸 níwán mud ball:五岭逶迤腾细浪,乌蒙磅礴走～。The Five Ridges wind like gentle ripples And the majestic Wumeng (mountains) roll by, globules of clay.
泥汪 níwāng 〈方言〉pond of mud
泥污 níwū mud stain; grime:浑身～ have mud stains all over one's body; be covered with mud stains
泥芯 níxìn 〈冶金〉(loam) core:～干燥炉 core-baking oven /～落砂机 core jarring machine /～磨光机 core grinder
泥岩 níyán mudstone
泥俑 níyǒng 〈考古〉clay figure buried with the dead; funerary clay figure; earthen figurine
泥雨 níyǔ rain that carries a large quantity of dust; fallout in the raindrops
泥浴 níyù mud bath; bog bath
泥浴疗法 níyù liáofǎ 〈医学〉mud-bath treatment
泥沼 nízhǎo swamp; morass; marsh; slough
泥质岩 nízhìyán 〈地质〉argillaceous rocks; pelite; pelyte
泥足巨人 nízú-jùrén colossus with feet of clay — strong in appearance but weak in nature:这个政府貌似强大,其实是～,不久就要崩溃。Powerful in appearance, the regime was a colossus with feet of clay, and it would not be long before it collapsed.
泥醉 nízuì dead drunk:喝得～ be as drunk as a lord; be dead drunk

怩 ní *see*"忸怩"niǔní

坭 ní *see*"红毛坭"hóngmáoní

呢 ní cloth made of wool; (heavy) woollen cloth:毛～ woollens; woollen cloth /格子～ woollen check /花～ fancy suiting; wool coating /～大衣 woollen overcoat
see also ne
呢喃 nínán ❶ (of swallows) twitter; chirrup ❷〈书面〉speak in a low voice; murmur; mutter:他忘不了花前月下的～细语。He cannot forget the tender words whispered amidst flowers in the moonlight.
呢绒 níróng woolen goods; woollen fabric
呢子 nízi woollen cloth; heavy woollen cloth; wool coating or suiting

铌 ní 〈化学〉niobium (Nb)
铌酸锂集成光路 nísuānlǐ jíchéng guānglù lithium niobate integrated circuit
铌酸盐 nísuānyán 〈化学〉niobate:～集成光路 niobate integrated circuit /～陶瓷 niobate ceramics
铌铁矿 nítiěkuàng 〈冶金〉columbite

nǐ

你 nǐ ❶ you (second person singular, sometimes also plural):～厂 your factory /～在哪里工作? Where do you work? ❷ you; one; anyone:～推给他,他推给～,谁也不愿接受这个活儿。Nobody was willing to take on the job, each trying to pass it on to the other. /这个人不爱说话,～问他十句,他才答～一句。He is a man of few words. If you ask him ten questions, he will probably answer only one. /～也说,他也说,我究竟听谁的? Everybody speaks (*or* All of you speak) at the same time. Who should I listen to?
你好 nǐhǎo hi; hello; how do you do; how are you
你们 nǐmen ❶ you (second person plural):～都是专家,我可是个外行。You are all experts while I am only a layman. /～教师是受人尊敬的。You teachers are respected by people. ❷ your:～学校什么时候放寒假? When does your school start winter vacation?
你死我活 nǐsǐ-wǒhuó life-and-death; mortal:拼个～ fight to the bitter end /为这点小事争得～不值得。It's not worth it, fighting tooth and nail over a trivial matter like this.
你追我赶 nǐzhuī-wǒgǎn strive to catch up and overtake one another; try to outstrip each other; vie with each other:四个班～,互不相让。The four classes carried out friendly emulation, each trying to outpace the other.

旎 nǐ *see*"旖旎"yǐnǐ

拟(擬) nǐ ❶ draw up; draft:～个初稿 make a draft; draw up a draft /～计划 devise a plan; draft a plan ❷ plan; intend:暑期～往东北一游 intend to make a trip to northeast China during the summer holidays /本部～于九月开办经理培训班。The department plans to start a training class for managers in September. ❸ imitate; mimic; simulate:模～考试 mock exams /模～战 simulation battle ❹ comparison:比～ compare; draw a parallel ❺ conjecture; suppose; guess:这只是一个虚～的故事。This is only a fiction.
拟订 nǐdìng draw up; draft; map out:～计划 draft a plan; map out a programme /～调查的详细规划 draw up (*or* work out) a detailed plan for investigation into the problem
拟定 nǐdìng ❶ work out; devise; contrive; formulate:～解决争端的方案 formulate a plan for solution to the problem ❷ suppose; assume; surmise
拟稿 nǐgǎo make a draft; draft (a letter or document):我们给部里的报告,请你先拟个稿。Would you make a draft of our report to the ministry? /每次讲话,他都是亲自～。He always writes his own speech each time he speaks to an audience.
拟古 nǐgǔ model one's work after the style or artistic form of the ancients:文章古奥,盖系～之作。The essay is a little quaint and abstruse; it is modelled on the style of the ancients.
拟话本 nǐhuàběn 〈文学〉(text of) fiction written in imitation of scripts for storytelling in the Song and Yuan dynasties
拟染色体 nǐrǎnsètǐ chromosomoid
拟人 nǐrén 〈语言〉personification
拟色 nǐsè mimic colouring (of birds, insects, etc.)
拟胎 nǐtāi simulation; mimicry; imitation
拟态 nǐtài simulation; mimicry:～为枯叶的蝴蝶 butterfly simulating a withered leaf /昆虫中～最多。Simulation is found most among insects.
拟议 nǐyì ❶ counsel; proposal; recommendation; advice:上次会议的～已得到采纳。The proposal made at the last meeting is adopted. ❷ draw up; draft:这事恐怕要先～出一个方案来。It's probably best to draw up a plan first.
拟音 nǐyīn (produce a) sound effect
拟于不伦 nǐyú-bùlún draw an inapt parallel; give an inapt analogy:～,非愚即妄。If a man makes an inapt analogy, he is either stupid or absurd.
拟作 nǐzuò work modelled after a certain author:这虽是部～,但也值得认真研究。The work itself is written in imitation of a certain writer, but it is nonetheless worth serious study.

薿 nǐ
薿薿 nǐnǐ 〈书面〉luxuriant; flourishing:黍稷～ crops growing luxuriantly

儗 nǐ 〈书面〉*see*"拟"nǐ

nì

逆 nì ❶ counter; contrary; inverse:横～ perversion /～时针方向转动 move counterclockwise (*or* anticlockwise, *or* contraclockwise) ❷ go against; disobey; resist; defy:悖～ run counter /一个人～世界潮流而动是注定要失败的。A person is doomed to fail if he goes against the current of the world. ❸ adverse: *see*"～境" ❹ traitor:叛～ turn traitor; commit treason; be a rebel /附～ defect to the rebels ❺〈书面〉salute; greet; meet; welcome:～客 greet guests ❻ beforehand; in advance:～知 have knowledge of sth. in advance

逆变换 nìbiànhuàn reverse transformation
逆变器 nìbiànqì 〈电工〉inverter; DC-AC converter; DC-AC inverter
逆差 nìchā 〈商业〉unfavourable or adverse balance of trade; trade deficit
逆产 nìchǎn ❶ traitor's property ❷ *also* "倒产" dàochǎn (of a baby) breech birth; breech delivery
逆颤音 nìchànyīn 〈音乐〉inverted trill
逆地址解析协议 nìdìzhǐ jiěxī xiéyì 〈信息〉reverse address resolution protocol (RARP)
逆电流 nìdiànliú 〈电工〉counter current
逆定理 nìdìnglǐ 〈数学〉converse theorem
逆耳 nì'ěr scrape, grate or jar on the ear; be unpleasant to the ear: ~之言 words jarring on the ear /忠言~。Good advice often falls on deaf ears. *or* Good advice often jars on the ear.
逆反 nìfǎn rebellious; adverse
逆反心理 nìfǎn xīnlǐ psychology of aversion; rebellious psychology: 产生厌恶学习的~ develop an aversion for study /青年人的~并不可怕,关键在于引导。It is not alarming that some young people are developing a psychology of aversion. The important thing is to give them proper guidance.
逆反应 nìfǎnyìng 〈化学〉counter-reaction
逆风 nìfēng ❶ against the wind; in the teeth of the wind: ~行船 sail against the wind /飞机正在~飞行。The aircraft is flying into a head-wind. ❷ contrary winds; adverse winds: 今天是~,不能扬帆。With contrary winds, we can't set sail.
逆光 nìguāng 〈摄影〉backlighting; counterlight
逆汇 nìhuì 〈金融〉adverse exchange; reverse remittance
逆弧 nìhú 〈物理〉backfire; arc-back
逆回旋加速器 nìhuíxuán jiāsùqì 〈物理〉reverse cyclotron
逆火 nìhuǒ backfire; flashback: ~式超音速轰炸机 Backfire supersonic bomber
逆经 nìjīng *also* "倒经" dàojīng retrograde menstruation; regurgitant menstruation
逆境 nìjìng unfavourable circumstances; adverse circumstances: 面临~ in the face of adversity /身处~而不气馁 not feel discouraged in time of distress /他已不是第一次身陷~。He is no stranger to adversity. /有时~更能磨练人的意志。Sometimes misfortune can better toughen man's will than anything else.
逆来顺受 nìlái-shùnshòu accept humiliation and adversity meekly; be submissive and patient in adversity; take insults lying down; turn the other cheek: 在父亲的暴力面前,母亲忍气吞声,~。Mother has had to choke back her anger and put up with father's violence.
逆利率 nìlìlǜ 〈金融〉negative interest (rate)
逆料 nìliào foresee; foretell; predict; prophesy; anticipate: 是福是祸,尚难~。It's still hard to say whether this is an omen of good fortune or misfortune. /滥伐森林带来了无法~的灾难。Deforestation brings unpredictable disaster. /情况复杂,难以~。The situation is so complicated that one cannot foretell what is going to happen.
逆流 nìliú ❶ go against the current: ~而上 sail against the current; go upstream ❷ counter-current; countertrend; 〈比喻〉reactionary trend or current: 顶住~ resist the adverse current ❸ 〈物理〉counter-stream; reverse-flow; countertide: ~式热交换器〈机械〉counterflow heat changer
逆流继电器 nìliú jìdiànqì 〈电工〉reverse-current relay
逆旅 nìlǚ 〈书面〉hotel; inn: ~主人 landlord of an inn /天地者乃万物之~。Heaven and earth are the temporary abode of all living things.
逆伦 nìlún 〈书面〉violate the ethical code of human relationship (such as fratricide)
逆命题 nìmìngtí 〈数学〉converse
逆平行 nìpíngxíng 〈物理〉antiparallel: ~磁化 antiparallel magetization
逆倾销 nìqīngxiāo 〈商业〉reverse dumping
逆事 nìshì ❶ something that does not go smoothly; mishap ❷ rebellion against authority
逆水 nìshuǐ counter-current; adverse current: ~而行 sail against the current
逆水行舟 nìshuǐ-xíngzhōu sailing against the current: 学习如~,不进则退。Study is like sailing against the stream: you either forge ahead or fall behind.
逆贴水 nìtiēshuǐ 〈金融〉disagio
逆温 nìwēn 〈气象〉temperature inversion
逆温层 nìwēncéng 〈气象〉inversion layer
逆铣 nìxǐ 〈机械〉up milling; up-cutting
逆向 nìxiàng opposite direction: ~行驶 drive in a direction not allowed by traffic regulations /~收购〈经济〉reverse takeover
逆心 nìxīn go wrong; act against one's desire: 她遇着~的事,总要抹儿滴眼泪。She is apt to shed tears when things go wrong.
逆行 nìxíng ❶ go in opposition to the right course; (of vehicles) go in a direction not allowed by traffic regulations ❷ 〈天文〉retrograde motion
逆行传导 nìxíng chuándǎo *also* "逆向传导" 〈生理〉antidromic conduction
逆序 nìxù *also* "倒序" dàoxù backward sequence
逆引词典 nìyǐn cídiǎn 〈语言〉reverse dictionary
逆运 nìyùn misfortune; adversity; bad luck: 他正在跟人诉说他的~。He is telling a tale of woe to somebody. *or* He is recounting the run of bad luck he has had.
逆运算 nìyùnsuàn 〈数学〉inversion operation; inverse, reciprocal operation
逆证 nìzhèng 〈医学〉severe case, with untoward condition and unfavourable prognosis
逆转 nìzhuǎn develop in a reverse direction; deteriorate; degenerate: 局势不可~。The situation is irreversible. /形势~。The situation is taking a turn for the worse. /战局~。The war situation has deteriorated (*or* worsened).
逆子 nìzǐ 〈旧语〉unfilial son (referring to one's son who has done wrong)

匿

nì hide; conceal; cache; bury: 隐~ conceal oneself; lie low; go into hiding /土匪~于深山老林之中。The bandits had their hideout in the remote, thickly forested mountains.
匿报 nìbào not declare; conceal; withhold information: ~收费金额 conceal the amount of money one has collected
匿藏 nìcáng go into hiding; conceal; hide
匿伏 nìfú lurk; lie in hiding: 警察到处搜捕~中的逃犯。Police searched everywhere for the escaped convict who was lying in hiding.
匿迹 nìjì go into hiding: 销声~ lie low; disappear from the scene /~海外 go into hiding abroad
匿名 nìmíng anonymous: ~诽谤 spread slander under an assumed name /~FTP服务器〈信息〉anonymous FTP server; anonymous file transfer protocol server
匿名信 nìmíngxìn anonymous letter: 他接到一封对他进行恫吓的~。He received an anonymous letter of intimidation.
匿笑 nìxiào laugh stealthily; laugh in one's sleeve
匿影藏形 nìyǐng-cángxíng *also* "匿影潜形" conceal one's identity; disguise oneself; lie low: 他~,在暗中活动。He concealed his identity and carried on clandestine activities.

暨(䘌)

nì 〈中医〉disease caused by an insect's bite

榧

nì
榧木 nìmù *also* "八角枫" bājiǎofēng 〈植物〉alangium

腻

nì ❶ greasy; oily: 油~ oily; greasy /这肥肉太~人。The fat meat is too greasy for my palate. ❷ be bored with; be tired of; be fed up with: 他的演讲我越听越~。I became increasingly bored with his speeches. /这种自我吹嘘我听~了。I am fed up with such self-advertisements. ❸ meticulous; scrupulous: 细~ delicate; exquisite; subtle; intricate ❹ viscous; sticky; gummy; glutinous: 炉台太~了。The cooking range has become so filthy. ❺ close; intimate: *see* "~友" ❻ dirt; filth; grime; soil; soot: 尘~ soot; dirt; grime
腻虫 nìchóng aphid; plant louse
腻烦 nìfan 〈口语〉❶ be tired of; be bored with; be fed up with; be weary of: 雨下个不停,他心里~透了。He was vexed by the continuous rain. /你老是哼那个小曲儿,不觉得~吗? Aren't you weary of constantly humming that tune? /那终日不断的汽车喇叭声,真叫人~。The unceasing honking of vehicles gets on my nerves. ❷ loathe; abhor; hate: 他从心里~这班人。He found these people disgusting. /

我对那些说大话的～极了。I cannot suffer those fools who talk big.

腻糊 nìhu *also*“腻糊糊”〈方言〉sticky; glutinous:这桌上是什么东西,这么～? What's so sticky on the table? /屋子漆黑一片,脚下腻腻糊糊的,但不知是什么东西。He felt something sticky on the floor but he couldn't tell what, as it was pitch-dark in the room.

腻人 nìrén ❶ be too oily or greasy:肥肉这么做就不～。Fat meat cooked this way is not too greasy. /这种蛋糕太～。This kind of cake is too sweet. ❷ boring; tiring:他老重复那几句话,真～。It gets on one's nerves to hear him harp on the same string. ❸ (as of a child, etc.)cling to people; bother people; pester:这孩子又有点发烧,老～。The child is a little feverish again, and hangs on to me all the time.

腻歪 nìwai 〈方言〉be bored; be weary:真～人! It's really boring!

腻味 nìwei 〈方言〉be sick of; be fed up with:一听见她那婆婆妈妈的事,我就～。I'm sick of her nagging about trivialities.

腻友 nìyǒu 〈书面〉intimate friend; close friend:假日总有～一二来访。On holidays I usually have a couple of close friends visiting .

腻子 nìzi *also*“泥子”nìzi 〈建筑〉(lacquer) putty

惄

nì 〈书面〉be worried; be anxious

埦

nì *see*“埤埦”pìnì

睨

nì 〈书面〉look askance; cast an oblique look

睨视 nìshì look askance:他不怀好意地～着她。He threw a greedy oblique look at her.

溺

nì ❶ be submerged; be drowned:～死 drowned ❷ be addicted to:～于名利 be addicted to fame and gain; lust for fame and fortune

see also niào

溺爱 nì'ài spoil; pamper; dote on:对孩子不应该～。One shouldn't pamper one's children. /她尝到了～与放任独生子的苦果。She is taking the bitter consequences of indulging and spoiling her only child.

溺谷 nìgǔ 〈地质〉drowned valley

溺水 nìshuǐ sink in water; drown:抢救～儿童 rescue a drowning child

溺婴 nìyīng drown an infant; infanticide by drowning

溺婴罪 nìyīngzuì 〈法律〉infanticide by drowning

溺职 nìzhí 〈书面〉be derelict in one's duty; be remiss in one's duty; neglect one's duty:他因～而罢官。He was removed from office for dereliction of duty. /狱吏因囚犯逃脱而被定为～。The warden was found derelict in letting the prisoner escape.

泥

nì ❶ cover, daub, smear or coat with plaster, putty etc.; plaster:～墙 daub a wall with mud; cover the crevices in a wall with mud or plaster /把窗玻璃用油灰～上 fix a windowpane in frame with putty (*or* slush) /把炉子～一～ smear a stove with plaster ❷ stubborn; obstinate; rigid; obdurate:拘～ punctilious; scrupulous; inflexible

see also ní

泥缝儿 nìfèngr cover the crevices in a wall with plaster; cover the seams in wooden articles with putty

泥古 nìgǔ have bigoted belief in the ancients; obstinately follow ancient ways; stick to the ancient ways blindly

泥古不化 nìgǔ-bùhuà have adamant belief in the ancients; worship the ancients and reject the moderns

泥守 nìshǒu be bigoted; be stubborn:～旧规 stick to the old way; strictly follow the convention

泥子 nìzi *also*“腻子”nìzi putty; daub; plaster

昵(暱)

nì close; intimate; confidential:亲～ close; confidential /～交 get along intimately; be on close terms

昵爱 nì'ài love dearly; cherish; be very fond of

昵称 nìchēng intimate address; term of endearment; pet name

伲

nì 〈方言〉I; we

嶷

nì 〈书面〉high and steep

see also yí

niān

拈

niān pick up (with the thumb and one or two other fingers); pinch:从罐子里～出一块糖 take a piece of candy out of (*or* from) a jar /信手～来 pick up at random

拈过拿错 niānguò-nácuò seize on other people's faults

拈花惹草 niānhuā-rěcǎo *also*“沾花惹草”zhānhuā-rěcǎo toy with flowers and grass — have affairs with women with no serious intentions; dally with women; philander

拈阄儿 niānjiūr draw lots:最后大家只得～。Finally, we decided to draw lots.

拈轻怕重 niānqīng-pàzhòng prefer the light to the heavy — pick easy jobs and shirk hard ones:如果人人都～,那什么事都干不了。If everybody is choosy about their jobs, it would be impossible to get anything done.

拈香 niānxiāng (of Buddhist believers) burn joss sticks (before an image of Buddha) in a temple

蔫

niān ❶ (of flower, tree, fruit, etc.) wither; sag; shrivel up; droop:芹菜搁～了。The celery is shrivelled up. /新移栽的苗让太阳给晒～了。The newly transplanted seedlings drooped in the heat of the sun. ❷ listless; spiritless; lethargic; languid:这几天他～巴巴的,少言少语。He looks dispirited these days and is very quiet: /这么又热又湿的天气,人还能不～? How can people be other than lethargic in such hot and humid weather? ❸〈方言〉(of temperament)slow; not open or direct:这人做事太～。This man is slow in doing things. /他表面上很～,心里可有主意呢。He may look quiet and resigned, but he really has very strong views.

蔫巴 niānba *also*“蔫巴巴”〈口语〉shrivel up; droop; wither:叶子都～了。The leaves are shrivelled up. /听到落榜的消息,他耷拉下脑袋,～了。Hearing that his name was not on the list of successful candidates, he drooped his head and looked depressed.

蔫不出溜 niānbuchūliū 〈方言〉quietly; on the quiet:谁也没有听见,他～地就进来了。He came in so quietly that nobody heard him.

蔫不唧 niānbujī 〈方言〉❶ listless; sluggish; languid; lethargic:他老是～儿的,也许由于童年不幸的缘故吧。He always appears languid. Maybe this is because he had an unhappy childhood. ❷ noiseless; quiet; on the sly:好哇,他跟我～儿地较上劲了! Well, He has been trying to outdo me on the quiet(*or* sly)! /他～的就走了。He sneaked away.

蔫不溜 niānbuliū 〈方言〉*see*“蔫不出溜”

蔫不悄儿 niānbuqiāor 〈方言〉quietly; on the quiet:临出门,姑姑～地给我兜里塞了十元钱。Before I set off, my aunt tucked 10 *yuan* in my pocket quietly.

蔫不声 niānbushēng silent; quiet; noiseless

蔫耷耷 niāndādā listless and droopy:他们疲倦极了,～的头都抬不起来。They were so tired that they could hardly lift their heads.

蔫甘 niāngan 〈方言〉quiet and good-natured:她姐姐脾气～,说不出那种粗话。Her sister is good-natured and incapable of such crude remarks.

蔫呼呼 niānhūhū (of a person with a weak character) be slow and indecisive:这一位～的,不像个大小伙子。Slow and indecisive, he doesn't behave like a virile young man.

蔫溜儿 niānliūr 〈方言〉leave (a trouble spot) stealthily

蔫蔫 niānniān 〈方言〉❶ quietly:他什么话都没说,～地走了。He went away quietly without saying a word. ❷ listless; depressed:他感到没脸见人,成天～儿的。Feeling too ashamed to see anybody, he looked dejected all day.

蔫儿拱 niānrgǒng 〈方言〉sow dissent behind one's back; make trouble in secret:他当面装好人,背后老是～,让人讨厌。He is the sort of man you loathe, for he always pretends to be nice to you while making trouble behind your back.

蔫儿坏 niānrhuài apt to do harm or work mischief in secret:这个人～,你要留神。The man is wicked though quiet and you have to be on your guard.

蔫儿淘 niānrtáo 〈方言〉(of a child) naughty or mischievous in a quiet way

蔫头耷脑 niāntóu-dānǎo 〈口语〉droopy; shrivelled up; listless; dejected:他干了一天的活,累得～的,连句话也不愿意说。He was pretty exhausted after the day's work and did not even want to utter a

single word. /今天怎么～的? Why look so crestfallen today?

nián

粘 nián ❶ *see* "黏" nián ❷ (Nián) a surname *see also* zhān
粘孢子虫病 niánbāozǐchóngbìng myxosporidiasis
粘稠 niánchóu thick and sticky; viscous:～的泥浆 sticky mud
粘皮带骨 niánpí-dàigǔ ❶punctilious; rigid; stubborn:世间许多事都不可～去看。One must not try to fit everything into a cut-and-dried pattern in this world. ❷ slowly and indecisively:你怎么办事如此～，真让人着急! Do you realize you are irritatingly slow on the job? /办事痛快点，别～的! Get things done promptly and stop dallying.
粘砂 niánshā adhering sand
黏 nián sticky; glutinous:这米很～。The rice is very glutinous. /胶水很～。The glue is quite sticky.
黏巴 niánba *also* "黏巴巴的" sticky; glutinous; gluey:～的物质 gummy substance
黏缠 niánchan 〈方言〉❶ adhere to; cling to:湿手捏了干面粉，～极了。The flour became very sticky in my wet hands. ❷ (of a disease) difficult to cure; lingering:这病太～，一年怕不能好。This is a lingering disease which can't be shaken off in a year.
黏虫 niánchóng *also* "行军虫" xíngjūnchóng; "剃枝虫" tìzhīchóng armyworm
黏蛋白 niándànbái 〈生化〉mucoprotein; mucin
黏度 niándù 〈化学〉viscosity:恩氏～ Engler viscosity /～计 viscosimeter /～指数 viscosity index
黏附 niánfù 〈化学〉adhesive:～层 adhesive coating /～力 adhesive power; adhesion /～体 adherend
黏糕 niángāo New Year cake (made of glutinous rice flour)
黏合 niánhé bind; bond; adhere
黏合剂 niánhéjì binder; adhesive; bonding agent
黏糊 niánhu *also* "黏糊糊的" ❶ sticky; glutinous:孩子的手上黏黏糊糊的粘满了果酱。The child's fingers are sticky with jam. /这粥是～的。The gruel is pretty glutinous. ❷ languid; slow-moving:他就这么个～性子。He is just the slow-moving type.
黏胶 niánjiāo 〈化工〉viscose
黏胶长丝 niánjiāo chángsī 〈纺织〉viscose filament yarn
黏胶短纤维 niánjiāo duǎnxiānwéi 〈纺织〉viscose staple fibre
黏胶纱 niánjiāoshā 〈纺织〉spun rayon
黏胶丝 niánjiāosī 〈纺织〉viscose rayon
黏胶纤维 niánjiāo xiānwéi 〈纺织〉viscose fibre
黏结 niánjié cohere:～力 cohesion; cohesive force /～性 cohesiveness
黏菌 niánjūn 〈微生物〉slime mould or fungus
黏米 niánmǐ ❶ glutinous rice ❷〈方言〉broomcorn millet
黏膜 niánmó 〈生理〉mucous membrane; mucosa:～炎 mucositis
黏儿 niánr 〈方言〉thick, sticky liquid; gluey substance:松树流～了。Pine glue was oozing out from the tree.
黏酸 niánsuān 〈化学〉mucic acid; glactaric acid; saccharolactic acid
黏土 niántǔ clay:耐火～ refractory clay
黏土矿物 niántǔ kuàngwù clay mineral
黏土岩 niántǔyán clay rock
黏涎子 niánxiánzi 〈方言〉salivate; slobber; slaver:看把你馋的，口里都流～了。So your mouth is watering, eh?
黏涎 niánxian 〈方言〉(of speech, movement, etc.) sloppy and boring:瞧你这个～样! 麻利点儿行不行? Stop being so sloppy about it. Can't you be quicker?
黏性 niánxìng stickiness; viscidity; viscosity:～油 viscous oil
黏液 niányè 〈生理〉mucus:～组织 mucous connective tissue
黏液肌瘤 niányè jīliú 〈医学〉myxomyoma
黏液瘤 niányèliú 〈医学〉myxoma
黏液囊肿 niányè nángzhǒng 〈医学〉mucocele
黏液性水肿 niányèxìng shuǐzhǒng 〈医学〉myxoedema
黏着 niánzhuó stick together; adhere:～剂 adhesion agent /～性 adhesivity
黏着力 niánzhuólì *also* "附着力" fùzhuólì adhesive force; adhesion
黏着语 niánzhuóyǔ 〈语言〉agglutinative language
鲇(鯰) nián catfish
鲇鱼 niányú catfish
年(秊) nián ❶ year:今～ this year /去～ last year /学～ school year /一～半载 in less than a year /～复一～ year after year; year in year out ❷ annual; yearly:～收入 annual income ❸ age:～满五十 50 years old /～过六旬 over sixty (years old); in one's sixties /～迫桑榆 advanced in age; late in life ❹ period in one's life:童～ childhood /少～ early youth (from ten to sixteen); early teens; juvenile /青～ youth; young people /祥和的晚～ happy and peaceful old age/人到中～，应该更现实些。When a person reaches middle age, he should be more realistic. ❺ period (in history); time:近～ recent years /汉朝初～ at the beginning of the Han Dynasty; in the early Han Dynasty /明朝末～ towards the end of the Ming Dynasty; in the late Ming Dynasty ❻ harvest:丰～ rich harvest /荒～ famine (*or* lean) year /歉～ lean year /大～ (of fruit trees) on-year /小～ off-year ❼ New Year:拜～ pay a New Year visit; send New Year's greetings (to sb.) /过～ celebrate the New Year; spend the New Year /团～ family get-together (*or* reunion) on lunar New Year's Eve /旧历～ lunar New Year; Spring Festival /阳历～ New Year ❽ (of articles for use) related to the New Year ❾〈旧语〉friendship between those who passed the imperial examinations in the same year: *see* "～兄"; "～谊" ❿ (Nián) a surname
年把 niánbǎ year or so:离开老家，转眼有～了。A year or so has passed since I left my hometown.
年报 niánbào ❶ annuals (of a learned society):法学～ legal studies annuals ❷ annual report
年辈 niánbèi seniority in the family or clan:～高 be a senior (in the family or clan)
年表 niánbiǎo chronological table
年菜 niáncài dishes for the dinner on lunar New Year's Eve:丰盛的～ dishes for a sumptuous Chinese New Year's Eve dinner
年产 niánchǎn annual production
年辰 niánchen 〈方言〉years; days:这是好些～以前的事了。This happened many years ago.
年成 niáncheng year's harvest:好～ good harvest /丰收的～ abundant year; bumper harvest /～不好 lean year /～不错 fairly good year
年齿 niánchǐ 〈书面〉age:～日增 grow older with each passing day
年初 niánchū beginning of the year:～预算 budget prepared at the beginning of the year
年楚河 Niánchǔhé Nyang Qu, river in south Tibet
年代 niándài ❶ age; years; time:远古～ in remote antiquity /战争～ during the war years /～久远 of the remote past; age-old; time-honoured; from time immemorial /鉴定一件古董的～ judge the age of an antique /展出的古代文物都标明了～。The antiques on display are all marked with dates. ❷ decade of a century:20 世纪 90～是个瞬息万变的～。The 1990's is a fast-changing decade.
年代学 niándàixué chronology
年底 niándǐ end of the year; year-end
年度 niándù year:财政～ financial year; fiscal year /～计划 annual plan /～报告 annual report
年饭 niánfàn dinner on lunar New Year's Eve to celebrate the family reunion
年份 niánfèn ❶ particular year:这件事的～我记不清了。I don't remember the particular year when it happened. ❷ age; time:这瓶酒的～比那瓶久。This bottle of wine is older than that one. /我在单位的～不够，还不能申请一套三室住房。I haven't served long enough in my institution to apply for a three-room flat.
年丰物阜 niánfēng-wùfù good year and abundance of produce
年俸 niánfèng 〈旧语〉annual salary for an official, etc.
年富力强 niánfù-lìqiáng in the prime of life; in one's prime:这后生～，大有作为。The man is in the flower of life and certainly has bright prospects. *or* The man is young and promising. /你何不趁～，多写几本书呢? Why don't you try to write more books while you are still young and energetic?
年高 niángāo of venerable age; aged:～望重 of venerable age and high prestige /他虽～，但精力充沛。Though advanced in years, he is full of vim and vigour.
年高德劭 niángāo-déshào of venerable age and eminent virtue;

venerable:这位老先生～,爱国至诚。This venerable man is a true patriot.

年糕 niángāo New Year cake (made of glutinous rice flour)

年根 niángēn end of the year:到了～儿了。The end of the year is drawing near.

年庚 niángēng time (year, month, day and hour) of a person's birth; date of birth

年关 niánguān end of the year (i.e. end of the lunar year, when accounts had to be settled in former times):旧社会许多穷人都怕过～。In the old society many poor people always dreaded the approaching end of the lunar year.

年光 niánguāng ❶ time; years:～易逝。How time flies. ❷ year's harvest:今年又是个好～。Again it's a good harvest this year. ❸〈方言〉days; times:那～,穷人简直没法儿活。In those days the poor could hardly scrape a living.

年号 niánhào title of an emperor's reign

年华 niánhuá time; years:虚度～ idle away one's time; waste one's life /～未暮,容貌先衰 get old before one's time; look prematurely aged; look older for one's years

年画 niánhuà New Year picture (esp. popular in rural China)

年会 niánhuì annual meeting (of a learned society, etc.)

年货 niánhuò special purchases for the Spring Festival:置办～ do Spring Festival shopping

年级 niánjí grade; year:小学一～学生 first grade pupil /中学二～学生 high school student, second grade /大学三～学生 third-year college student; junior

年集 niánjí country fair held at the end of the lunar year:赶～ go to the year-end country fair

年纪 niánjì age:～轻 young /～相仿 be of similar age; be about the same age /～有了一大把 be old or advanced in years

年假 niánjià ❶ winter vacation ❷ New Year holidays

年间 niánjiān during a certain period of time:乾隆～ during (*or* in) the reign of Emperor Qianlong

年检 niánjiǎn annual inspection:汽车～ annual inspection of motor vehicles

年鉴 niánjiàn yearbook; almanac:天文～ astronomical almanac /《中国法律～》*Law Yearbook of China*

年节 niánjié Spring Festival (holidays)

年金 niánjīn money paid annually to pensioners;annuity

年馑 niánjǐn 〈方言〉famine or lean year

年景 niánjǐng ❶ year's harvest:好～ good harvest /正常～ normal harvest year /今年的～不好。It's a lean year this year. ❷ holiday atmosphere of the Spring Festival; scene of the Spring Festival celebrations:眼前是一片繁荣～。Before our eyes is a prosperous scene of the Spring Festival.

年久月深 niánjiǔ-yuèshēn *see* "年深月久"

年均 niánjūn annual average:～产量 annual average output /这个县每人～收入为六千元。The average annual per capita income in this county is 6,000 *yuan*.

年来 niánlái for the past year; in recent years:～身体稍好。My health has somewhat improved in recent years.

年礼 niánlǐ 〈旧语〉gift given at the end of a year

年历 niánlì calendar with the whole year printed on one sheet; single page calendar

年利 niánlì annual interest:～率 annual interest rate

年例 niánlì as a rule annually;every year:山区的深秋,～都要来场大风。In this hilly region, there is a strong wind in late autumn every year.

年龄 niánlíng age:他还不到上学～。He hasn't reached school age yet. /她已过了生育～。She is past child-bearing age. /～不饶人。Age tells. *or* Age will show itself.

年龄结构 niánlíng jiégòu age distribution

年率 niánlǜ annual rate

年轮 niánlún 〈植物〉annual ring; growth ring

年迈 niánmài old; aged:～力衰 old and infirm; senile /他虽然～,但精神矍铄。He is aged but hale and hearty.

年貌 niánmào age and appearance:这个人的～和装束,我记得很清楚。I remember very clearly the person's age, appearance and attire.

年命 niánmìng 〈书面〉❶ life span ❷ fate; destiny:～蹇滞 be out of luck all one's life; be ill-fated; be born under an unlucky star

年末 niánmò end of a year

年年 niánnián every year; year after year:～丰收 bumper harvest year after year

年年防俭,夜夜防贼 niánnián fáng jiǎn, yèyè fáng zéi 〈俗语〉guard against famines every year and thieves every night;be careful or cautious all the time; be always on your guard

年盘 niánpán 〈方言〉*see* "年礼"

年迫日索 niánpò-rìsuǒ one's years and days are running out; be advanced in age

年谱 niánpǔ chronicle of sb.'s life

年青 niánqīng young:他觉得自己仍然～,并未意识到老之将至。He is not conscious of age creeping on him; he still feels young.

年轻 niánqīng young:～人 young people; youth /～力壮 young and vigorous /～有为 young and promising /～一代 younger generation /他～的时候是有过放荡行为,不过现在持重多了。It's true that he sowed his wild oats while he was young. But he is now a wiser and better man. /领导班子应该～化。The leading body should be younger.

年三十儿 niánsānshír last day of the lunar year; lunar New Year's Eve

年上 niánshang 〈方言〉last year

年少 niánshào 〈书面〉❶ young:～有为 be young and promising ❷ teenager (male); young man:翩翩～ elegant young man

年深日久 niánshēn-rìjiǔ *also* "年深月久";"年久月深" with the passage of time; as the years go by:～,知道这件事的人已经很少了。With the years gone by there are very few people who know about it. /这已经是～的事情了。This is something that occurred many years ago.

年时 niánshí ❶〈方言〉years; long time:他干这一行有～了。It's years since he took on the job (*or* started pursuing the profession). ❷〈书面〉former years; previous year

年时 niánshi 〈方言〉last year:他们是～才毕业的。They graduated only last year.

年事 niánshì 〈书面〉age:～已高 advanced in age

年寿 niánshòu lifespan; life expectancy

年岁 niánsuì ❶ age:上了～的人 person who is getting on in years /～不饶人。Nobody can escape the ravages of time. *or* Time tells on everybody. /她～可不小啦。She is for sure not young. ❷ years; time:因为～久远,大家把这件事情忘了。People have all forgotten about the matter as it happened so many years ago. ❸〈方言〉harvest:老家今年～如何? How was the harvest this year in our home village?

年头儿 niántóur ❶ year:我到北京已经三十个～了。It's thirty years since I came to Beijing. ❷ years; long time:熬～ go through years of suffering;accumulate seniority as the years go by /他晋级还不到～。He is not eligible for promotion according to the order of seniority. /他是个老会计,干这行有～了。He is an old accountant with many years' experience in the job. ❸ days; times:那～谁的日子都不好过。Nobody had an easy time in those days. ❹ harvest:今年～不错。This year's harvest is quite good.

年尾 niánwěi end of a year:1980 年～,他回到了故乡北京。He returned to his hometown, Beijing, at the end of 1980.

年息 niánxī annual interest

年下 niánxia 〈口语〉days around the lunar New Year, usu. referring to the first half of the first lunar month

年限 niánxiàn number of years required:学习～ required years of study /精心保养,可以延长机器的使用～。The service life of a machine can be extended by careful maintenance.

年宵 niánxiāo lunar New Year's Eve

年薪 niánxīn annual salary; yearly pay

年兄 niánxiōng 〈旧语〉form of address among those who succeeded in the imperial examination in the same year

年夜 niányè lunar New Year's Eve:吃～饭 have dinner on lunar New Year's Eve; eat New Year's Eve dinner

年谊 niányì 〈旧语〉friendship between those who came out as successful candidates of the imperial examination in the same year

年幼 niányòu young; juvenile:～无知 young and inexperienced

年月 niányue ❶ days; years:过去的～ past years ❷〈口语〉times; age; era; epoch:解放前那～ in pre-liberation days /太平～ peaceful times

年载 niánzǎi 〈方言〉year; times:这房子虽然大有～,却一点不显得老旧。Although an ancient building, it doesn't show signs of disrepair.

年长 niánzhǎng older; senior in age: 他比我～五岁。He is older than I am by five years. *or* He is five years my senior. /他比我～，我应该向他请教。He is my senior, so I ought to ask his advice.
年终 niánzhōng end of the year; year-end: ～鉴定 year-end appraisal
年终奖 niánzhōngjiǎng year-end bonus
年资 niánzī age and qualifications: 她是～较高的医生。She is a senior doctor with good qualifications.
年子 niánzi 〈方言〉year; times: 这是解放那～的事了，你还记得么？This is what happened in the year of liberation. Do you still remember it?
年租 niánzū annual rent
年尊 niánzūn advanced in years: ～辈长 advanced in years and senior in generation

niǎn

辇 niǎn ❶〈古语〉man-drawn carriage ❷ imperial carriage: 龙车凤～ dragon- and phoenix-design carriages; imperial carriages

撵 niǎn ❶ drive out; oust; expel; banish: 把侵略者～出国境。Drive the aggressors out of the land. /～他出去! Get him out of here! /你要～我啊? 那我走。So you want me to go? Well, I'll go then. /要是他再到这里来，我立刻就用讥诮话把他～走。If he calls here again, I'll soon send him off with a flea in his ear. /他在这里尽惹祸，我只好～他走了。As he has done nothing but cause trouble here, I have to send him packing. ❷〈方言〉catch up; run after; pursue: 努力～上 try one's best to catch up /这孩子走路总爱～人。This child is such a tail, wherever I go.

捻(撚) niǎn ❶ twist with the fingers: ～麻绳 make cord by twisting hemp fibres /把油灯～大些 turn up the wick (of a lamp) ❷ sth. made by twisting: 纸～儿 paper spill /灯～儿 lampwick ❸〈方言〉dredge up: ～河泥 dredge up silt (*or* sludge) from a river
捻度 niǎndù 〈纺织〉number of turns or twists; twist
捻烦 niǎnfán 〈谦词〉disturb; trouble; bother: 有事相求，今日特来～。Today I've come to ask a favour of you. /无事不敢～。I wouldn't come to bother you if there were nothing amiss.
捻军 Niǎnjūn Nian Army or the Torch Bearers, a peasant army that rose against the Qing Dynasty in the middle of the 19th century: ～起义 Nian Uprising (1852-1868)
捻捻转儿 niǎnnianzhuànr wooden or plastic top set in motion by hand
捻神捻鬼 niǎnshén-niǎnguǐ be even afraid of one's own shadow; look frightened and flustered: 他～的，扭头就跑。He was so frightened that he immediately turned around and took to his heels. /别整天～的，根本就没有这种事。Stop imagining things. There is no fear of that happening.
捻手捻脚 niǎnshǒu-niǎnjiǎo be almost too timid to move forward: 每次经过这个地方，我都～的，别提多害怕了。Every time I passed by the place, I had to walk stealthily, and it is difficult to describe how scared I was.
捻线机 niǎnxiànjī 〈纺织〉twisting frame
捻着鼻子 niǎnzhe bízi pocket one's pride; endure without complaining: ～受人欺负 pocket an insult; stomach humiliation /看看事情办不成了，他只好～走了。Seeing that there was no sign of hope or success, he went away crestfallen.
捻针 niǎnzhēn 〈中医〉twirling or rotating of the acupuncture needle
捻子 niǎnzi ❶ spill: 纸～ spill of rolled paper used to light a pipe, lamp, etc.; spill /药～〈中医〉slender roll of medicated paper or gauze (to be inserted into wounds, boils, etc.) ❷ wick: 灯～ lampwick

碾 niǎn ❶ roller: 石～ stone roller /水～ water-powered roller (for grinding grain) ❷ grind or husk with a roller; crush: ～米 husk rice /～烂 crush to pieces; crush to powder /～平 flatten or level (with a roller); roll out ～碎 pulverize; crush to pieces ❸〈书面〉cut and polish: ～玉 cut and polish jade
碾场 niǎncháng threshing ground
碾槌 niǎnchuí pestle
碾坊 niǎnfáng *also* "碾房" grain mill
碾磙子 niǎngǔnzi *also* "碾砣" stone roller
碾米厂 niǎnmǐchǎng rice-husking mill
碾米机 niǎnmǐjī rice mill; rice-husking machine
碾盘 niǎnpán millstone
碾砣 niǎntuó *see* "碾磙子"
碾压 niǎnyā (of wheel, etc.) roll over (the ground): 车轮在松软的地面上～出两道辙印。The wheels rolled over the soft surface of the road, leaving two tracks behind.
碾子 niǎnzi ❶ stone roller (for threshing); millstone ❷ roller

蹍 niǎn 〈方言〉stepon; tread

涊 niǎn 〈书面〉sweating; perspiring

niàn

廿 niàn twenty

念[1] niàn ❶ think of; long for; miss: 思～故人 think about one's old friends /怀～故乡 reminisce about one's hometown /大家老～着他。We all miss him very much. ❷ thought; idea: 信～ faith; belief; conviction /闪～ idea that flashes through one's mind; momentary desire /私～ selfish motive /邪～ evil thought; wicked idea /杂～ distracting thought /一～之差 wrong decision made in a moment of weakness (with serious consequences); moment's slip ❸ (Niàn) a surname

念[2](唸) niàn ❶ read aloud: 给大家～报 read out a newspaper to everyone present /你给我～一～好吗? Would you read it to me, please? ❷ study; attend school: ～大学 study in college /他～过初中。He has been to junior secondary school.

念[3] niàn capital form of 廿 (twenty)
念白 niànbái spoken parts of a Chinese opera
念叨 niàndao *also* "念道" ❶ talk about again and again in recollection or anticipation; harp on: 打那以后，她没有一天不～小儿子。Ever since then, she has always been talking about her youngest son. ❷〈方言〉talk over; tell about; discuss: 请他把参观首都的情况给大家～～吧。Let's ask him to tell us about his recent visit to the capital.
念佛 niànfó chant sutra; pray to Buddha: 吃斋～ practise abstinence (from meat) and chant sutra; be a pious Buddhist /老太太跪在一个小佛龛前～。The old lady knelt before a small Buddhist shrine, muttering her prayers.
念记 niànjì be very much concerned about; keep thinking about; miss: 她～着在国外的儿子，心中很不安。She kept thinking about her son who was abroad, with anxiety.
念经 niànjīng recite or chant Buddhist scripture: 念了经打和尚〈俗语〉hit the monks after having them chant scripture — drop one's benefactor as soon as his help is not required; drop sb. as soon as one has no further use for him/her
念旧 niànjiù keep alive memories of old friendships; remember old friends; treasure old friendships: 他这人很～，你去找他，他肯定会帮你的。As he cherishes old friendships, he will be sure to help you out if you call on him.
念念不忘 niànniàn-bùwàng constantly bear in mind; always remember: ～至理名言 always bear in mind profound truths and celebrated sayings
念念有词 niànniàn-yǒucí ❶ mutter incantations ❷ mutter; mumble: 不知他心中在想什么，但见他口中～。He kept muttering to himself, and nobody knew what was on his mind.
念青唐古拉山 Niànqīngtánggǔlāshān Nyainqentanglha Mountains, in the east of the Tibet Autonomous Region
念书 niànshū ❶ read; study: 他的毛病是不好好～。The trouble with him is that he puts too little stock in study. ❷ attend school: 你在哪个学校～? Which school do you go to? /初中毕业我就不想～了。I didn't want to continue schooling when I'd finished junior high.

念诵 niànsòng read aloud; chant (poems, essays, etc.): ～经文 chant a scripture

念诵 niànsong talk about in recollection or anticipation: 刚才我们还～呢，可巧你就来了。We were talking about you when you came in.

念酸 niànsuān *also* "拈酸" niānsuān; "捻酸" niǎnsuān 〈方言〉 be jealous of; envy: ～吃醋的性儿 be jealous by temperament

念头 niàntou thought; idea; motive; intention: 转～ think better of; change one's mind /起了一个～ an idea occurs to sb. (*or* comes to mind) /你不该有这种～。You shouldn't entertain such an idea.

念物 niànwù souvenir; keepsake: 这本画册送给你做个～吧! Keep this album as a memento.

念心儿 niànxinr 〈方言〉 souvenir; memento

念央儿 niànyāngr *also* "念央子" 〈方言〉 say something by implication; hint: 他没有催我还钱，而是当着我的面～，说最近手头怎么紧。He did not ask me to pay off my debt but hinted that he was running out of money.

念秧 niànyāng 〈旧语〉 lay a trap to extort money, etc.

念咒 niànzhòu chant incantations

念珠 niànzhū beads; rosary; *subhah*

念珠菌病 niànzhūjūnbìng candidiasis; moniliasis

念兹在兹 niànzī-zàizī 〈书面〉 bear sth. in mind constantly; keep sth. fresh in one's memory

埝

niàn low bank between fields or shallow waters: 打～ build banks between fields

niáng

娘(孃)

niáng ❶ ma; mum; mom; mother: 老～ one's aged mother /亲～ one's own mother /后～ step mother ❷ form of address for an elderly married woman: 大～ aunt /婶～ wife of one's father's younger brother; aunt /姨～ (married) maternal aunt; aunt /师～ wife of one's teacher or master ❸ young woman: 姑～ girl /新～ bride

娘家 niángjia home or family of a married woman's parents: 回～ (of a woman) return to one's parents' home for a visit after marriage

娘舅 niángjiù 〈方言〉 brother of one's mother; uncle

娘老子 niánglǎozi ❶ 〈方言〉 mother ❷ 〈口语〉 your granny (often used by a middle-aged woman to refer to herself while joking or in anger)

娘娘 niángniang ❶ empress or imperial concubine of the first rank: 正宫～ emperor's wife; empress ❷ goddess: ～庙 temple of a goddess

娘亲 niángqīn mother

娘儿 niángr 〈口语〉 woman along with her juniors, e. g. mother and her children, aunt and her nephews or nieces: ～俩 mother and her child /她们～三个 three of them, mother and children

娘儿们 niángrmen ❶ 〈口语〉 *see* "娘儿" ❷ 〈方言〉 women; womenfolk: 这些～真厉害，比我们大老爷们儿干得还快。How incredible these dames are! They work even faster than we men. ❸ 〈方言〉 wife: 我那狠心的～把我甩了。My heartless wife has deserted me.

娘胎 niángtāi mother's womb: 他打～里出来就不知道什么叫害怕。He has stood in fear of nothing since he was born. *or* He is intrepid by nature.

娘姨 niángyí 〈方言〉 maidservant

娘子 niángzǐ ❶ 〈方言〉 form of address for one's wife ❷ (often used in the early vernacular) polite form of address for a young or middle-aged woman

娘子军 niángzǐjūn detachment of women; women soldiers; women

niàng

酿(釀)

niàng ❶ make (wine); brew (beer); ferment: ～了一坛黄酒 brew a jar of rice (*or* millet) wine /一种新～的红葡萄酒 new brew of port ❷ make (honey): 蜜蜂～蜜。Bees make honey. ❸ lead to; result in: *see* "～成" ❹ (method of cooking) fill (hollowed bell peppers, etc. with minced meat, etc.) and fry or steam (them): ～甜椒 fried stuffed sweet peppers ❺ wine: 佳～ vintage wine; good wine

酿成 niàngchéng lead to; breed; result in: ～水灾 cause floods /～巨变 lead to a great upheaval /正在～一场悲剧。A tragedy is brewing.

酿酒 niàngjiǔ make wine; distil alcoholic drinks; brew beer: ～厂 winery; distillery; brewery /～业 wine-making industry; brewing industry

酿酶 niàngméi 〈化学〉 zymase

酿母菌 niàngmǔjūn *also* "酵母" jiàomǔ yeast

酿热物 niàngrèwù 〈农业〉 ferment material

酿造 niàngzào make (wine, vinegar, etc.); brew (beer, etc.); distil (alcoholic drink): 我们～干白葡萄酒的经验不足。We lack experience in brewing dry white wine. /酒的～是很复杂的。Brewage requires complicated procedures.

niǎo

袅

niǎo *see* "袅" niǎo

袅(嬝、嫋)

niǎo slender and delicate

袅袅 niǎoniǎo ❶ (of smoke, etc.) curl upwards: ～炊烟。Smoke was curling upwards from kitchen chimneys. /烟雾～腾腾。Billows of smoke were coiling up. ❷ (of slender and delicate objects) wave in the wind: 垂杨～。Weeping willows were swaying in the wind. ❸ (of sound) linger: ～的歌声 lingering song /余音～。The music lingered in the air long (after the performance ended).

袅袅婷婷 niǎoniǎo-tíngtíng 〈书面〉 (of a woman's manner of walking) lithe and graceful: 一位时髦女郎～地走了进来。A girl in a fashionable dress walked in gracefully.

袅娜 niǎonuó 〈书面〉 ❶ (of grass, tree, etc.) lithe and slender: 春风吹着～的柳丝。The spring wind is caressing the lithe and slender willows. ❷ (of a woman) graceful: 舞姿～ dance gracefully

袅绕 niǎorào 〈书面〉 linger; curl up; wind around: 歌声～。The song lingered in the air.

鸟(鳥)

niǎo bird: ～鸣 singing of birds /～巢 nest /飞～ flying bird /海～ sea bird /水～ water (*or* aquatic) bird /候～ migratory bird; migrant /留～ resident (bird) /笼～ cage bird

see also diǎo

鸟氨酸 niǎo'ānsuān 〈生化〉 ornithine; ornithuric acid: ～脱羧酶 ornithine decarboxylase

鸟岛 Niǎodǎo Bird Islet, in Lake Qinghai (青海湖), Qinghai Province

鸟道 niǎodào 〈书面〉 path or trail which only birds can fly over — a dangerous pass or an extremely rugged and narrow mountain trail

鸟粪 niǎofèn ❶ bird's droppings: ～石 struvite ❷ guano

鸟粪层 niǎofèncéng guano

鸟害 niǎohài damage to crops or farm produce by birds; bird pest

鸟喙 niǎohuì bill; beak

鸟尽弓藏 niǎojìn-gōngcáng put aside the bow once the birds are killed — cast sb. aside when he has served his purpose; kick out sb. when his service is no longer needed; when people have outlived their usefulness, they are put in cold storage: ～，兔死狗烹。Trusted aides are eliminated once they have served their purpose.

鸟瞰 niǎokàn ❶ get a bird's-eye view: ～全城 get a bird's-eye view of the city /～图 bird's-eye view; bird's-eye perspective ❷ general survey of a subject; bird's-eye view: 世界大势～ general survey of the world situation

鸟类 niǎolèi birds

鸟类学 niǎolèixué ornithology: ～家 ornithologist

鸟笼 niǎolóng bird cage; aviary

鸟媒 niǎoméi 〈植物〉 ornithophily: ～花 ornithophilous flower /～植物 ornithophilous plant

鸟枪 niǎoqiāng fowling piece; air gun

鸟枪换炮 niǎoqiāng-huànpào change from fowling pieces into guns — become much better equipped; have much better conditions; improve greatly: 老兄如今～了，从头到脚一色新，全是高档的。You've really changed greatly for the better, wearing the latest

fashions from head to foot.
鸟儿 niǎor 〈口语〉little bird that can fly：养～ keep birds
鸟兽 niǎoshòu birds and beasts；fur and feather
鸟兽散 niǎoshòusàn (of birds and beasts) scatter；stampede；flee in all directions：作～ scatter like frightened birds and beasts；flee helter-skelter／这群新兵一接火就各～。The recruits took to their heels the moment fire was exchanged.
鸟为食亡 niǎowèishíwáng 〈俗语〉birds die in pursuit of food：人为财死，～。Men die in seeking wealth，as birds die in seeking food.
鸟眼 niǎoyǎn 〈林业〉bird's eye：～纹理 bird's eye grain
鸟疫 niǎoyì 〈兽医〉ornithosis
鸟语花香 niǎoyǔ-huāxiāng *also*"花香鸟语" birds are singing and flowers are giving forth their fragrance — a fine spring day：春和日丽，～。It's a warm，bright，sunny spring day. Birds are singing and the air is permeated with the fragrance of flowers.
鸟葬 niǎozàng celestial burial (by which bodies are exposed to birds of prey)
鸟篆 niǎozhuàn bird script，an ancient form of Chinese written characters，resembling bird's footprints
鸟之将死，其鸣也哀 niǎo zhī jiāng sǐ，qí míng yě āi when a bird is dying，its cry is pathetic：～，人之将死，其言也善。When a bird is dying，its cry is sad；when a man is dying，he speaks from his heart.
鸟嘴 niǎozuǐ beak；bill

茑

niǎo

茑萝 niǎoluó 〈植物〉cypress vine (*Quamoclit pennata*)

嬲

niǎo 〈书面〉❶ tease；flirt with ❷ pester；annoy

niào

尿

niào ❶ urine：排～ urinate；micturate／撒～ piss；pee；make water ❷ urinate；make water；pass water：～尿 urinate；make water；pass water
see also suī
尿崩症 niàobēngzhèng 〈医学〉diabetes insipidus
尿闭 niàobì 〈医学〉anuria
尿不湿 niàobùshī paper nappy；disposable diaper
尿布 niàobù *also*"褯子" jièzi diaper；napkin；nappy
尿床 niàochuáng wet the bed；bed-wetting
尿胆素 niàodǎnsù 〈生化〉urobilin
尿胆素血 niàodǎnsùxuè 〈医学〉urobilinemia
尿胆素原 niàodǎnsùyuán urobilinogen
尿蛋白 niàodànbái 〈生化〉urinary albumin
尿氮过多 niàodàn guòduō 〈医学〉hyperazoturia
尿氮过少 niàodàn guòshǎo 〈医学〉hypazoturia
尿道 niàodào 〈生理〉urethra：～腺 urethral glands
尿道闭锁 niàodào bìsuǒ urethratresia
尿道管 niàodàoguǎn *also*"尿管"〈医学〉catheter
尿道球腺 niàodào qiúxiàn 〈生理〉bulbourethral glands；Cowper's glands
尿道渗血 niàodào shènxuè 〈医学〉urethrostaxis
尿道炎 niàodàoyán 〈医学〉urethritis
尿道造影 niàodào zàoyǐng 〈医学〉urethrography
尿毒症 niàodúzhèng 〈医学〉uraemia
尿肥 niàoféi 〈农业〉urine (used as manure)
尿分析 niàofēnxī 〈医学〉urinalysis
尿壶 niàohú ❶ night pot ❷ urinal；urodochium
尿急 niàojí urgency of micturition
尿检 niàojiǎn 〈医学〉urinalysis：～法 urinoscopy
尿结石 niàojiéshí 〈医学〉urinary calculus
尿炕 niàokàng wet the *kang* or bed；*kang* wetting；bed-wetting
尿瘘 niàolòu 〈医学〉urinary fistula
尿路病 niàolùbìng 〈医学〉urosis
尿路梗阻 niàolù gěngzǔ 〈医学〉urinary tract obstruction
尿路结石 niàolù jiéshí 〈医学〉lithangiuria
尿路溃疡 niàolù kuìyáng 〈医学〉urelcosis
尿路造影术 niàolù zàoyǐngshù urography
尿囊 niàonáng 〈生理〉allantois
尿脓毒病 niàonóngdúbìng 〈医学〉urosepsis
尿盆 niàopén chamber pot；urinal
尿频 niàopín 〈医学〉micturition
尿少症 niàoshǎozhèng 〈医学〉oliguria
尿失禁 niàoshījìn 〈医学〉urinary incontinence
尿石 niàoshí 〈医学〉urolith；urinary calculus：～病 urolithiasis
尿素 niàosù 〈化学〉*also*"脲" niào urea；carbamide
尿素氮 niàosùdàn urea nitrogen
尿素酶 niàosùméi urease；urase
尿素脱蜡 niàosù tuōlà 〈石油〉urea dewaxing
尿酸 niàosuān 〈化学〉uric acid：～盐结石 uratoma／～石 uric-acid calculus／～酶 uricase
尿烷 niàowán 〈化工〉urethane：～人造橡胶 urethane elastomer
尿血 niàoxiě 〈医学〉hacmaturia
尿脂石 niàozhīshí 〈医学〉urostealith
尿潴留 niàozhūliú 〈医学〉retention of urine

脲

niào *see*"尿素" niàosù

脲酶 niàoméi 〈生化〉urease；urase
脲醛类树脂黏合剂 niàoquánlèi shùzhī niánhéjì 〈化工〉urac
脲醛树脂 niàoquán shùzhī 〈化工〉Pollopas；urea-formaldehyde resin
脲醛塑料 niàoquán sùliào 〈化工〉urea-formaldehyde plastics
脲羰基 niàotāngjī 〈化工〉allophanyl

溺

niào *see*"尿" niào
see also nì

niē

捏(揑)

niē ❶ hold between the thumb and other fingers；pinch：～着一根火柴 hold a match in one's fingers／～住笔 keep hold of a pen／命～在人家手里 have one's life at sb.'s mercy；be under sb.'s thumb ❷ knead with the fingers；mould：～饺子 knead the wrappers when making dumplings／～橡皮泥 knead plasticine／～面人儿 mould clay figurines ❸ bind or put together；link：这是两码事儿，何必往一块～？These are two different things. Why should you try to lump them together？❹ fabricate；make up；frame up：*see*"～造"
捏咕 niēgu 〈口语〉❶ toy with；fiddle with：你在～什么呢？What are you fiddling with？❷ make a match；act as a go-between；play Cupid：你把他们俩～到一块儿，合适吗？Is it right for you to play Cupid for the two of them？❸ discuss a matter in private；give secret counsel：他们凑到一块又～什么呢？What are they talking about in secret？
捏合 niēhé ❶ bind or put together：没有感情何必还～在一块儿？Why should the couple stay together when they no longer love each other？／不管他们有多大分歧，到头来总要被共同的利害关系～在一块的。No matter what differences they may have，they will eventually find themselves tied together by the bond of common interests. ❷ (often used in the early vernacular) fabricate；concoct；fake；trump up
捏合机 niēhéjī 〈化工〉kneading machine
捏积 niējī 〈中医〉treating children's digestive disorders by kneading or massaging the muscles along the spine；chiropractic
捏弄 niēnong ❶ toy with；play with；fiddle with：说话时，她下意识地～着衣服上的钮扣。She subconsciously toyed with a button on her blouse while talking. ❷ order about；manipulate：我们得自己拿主意，不能由他们～。We should decide for ourselves and not allow them to order us about. ❸ consult in private：这事他俩一～，就那么办了。The matter was settled straight away after the two of them had a private consultation. ❹ fabricate；make up：根本没那回事，全是他们～的。There was no such a thing at all. They simply fabricated the story.
捏腔拿调 niēqiāng-nádiào *also*"拿腔拿调" náqiāng-nádiào assume a peculiar voice or tone；speak in an affected tone
捏一把汗 niē yībǎhàn be breathless with anxiety or nervous tension；hold one's breath in suspense：杂技演员表演空中飞人，真叫观众～。The spectators held their breath watching the acrobats performing on the flying trapeze.／总算过了关，我可捏了一把汗。We may

have come out of it all right, but it gave me such a turn. /同事们都为他捏着一把冷汗。His colleagues' hearts were in their mouths for him. *or* They were in a sweat for him.
捏造 niēzào fabricate; concoct; trump up; make up: ～事实 invent a story; make up a story /～证据 fake (*or* fabricate) evidence /～罪名 trump up charges /～数字 conjure up (*or* concoct) figures /这事纯属～。It's sheer fabrication.
捏闸 niēzhá apply the handbrake

nié

苶 nié tired; listless; lethargic; languid: 他今天有点～。He is a bit listless today.

niè

聂(聶) Niè a surname
聂耳 Niè Ěr Nie Er (1912-1935), Chinese composer who wrote the music of *March of the Volunteers* (《义勇军进行曲》, 1935), now China's national anthem
颞(顳) niè
颞骨 niègǔ 〈生理〉 temporal bone
颞颥 nièrú 〈生理〉 temple
嗫(囁) niè
嗫嚅 nièrú 〈书面〉 speak haltingly; hesitate in speech; hem and haw: 口将言而～ hold words back from the tip of one's tongue and hem and haw
蹑(躡) niè ❶ lighten (one's step); walk on tiptoe: 他轻轻地站起来, ～着脚走进里屋。He stood up quietly and tiptoed into the room. ❷ follow; dog; track: ～迹 follow the trace; track ❸ 〈书面〉 tread; step on; walk with: *see* "～足"
蹑悄悄 nièqiāoqiāo gently; softly: 为了不惊醒母亲, 她～地把门打开。She opened the door gently so as not to wake up her mother.
蹑手蹑脚 nièshǒu-nièjiǎo walk gingerly; walk on tiptoe: 从门外～地走进一个人来。A man stole in through the door.
蹑踪 nièzōng follow along (behind sb.); track
蹑足 nièzú ❶ walk softly; walk gingerly: 他～走到门口。He walked on tiptoe to the door. ❷ 〈书面〉 participate (in some activity); take part in; join: ～其间 join (a profession); follow (a trade); associate with (a certain type of people) /～行伍之间 join the ranks of the army
蹑足潜踪 nièzú-qiánzōng walk on tiptoe so as not to be discovered: 他～, 前去探个究竟。He walked over gingerly to see what was happening there.
镊(鑷) niè ❶ tweezers: *see* "～子" ❷ pick up sth. with tweezers: ～出了一个酒精棉球 pick up an alcohol cotton ball with tweezers
镊子 nièzi tweezers: 一把～ a pain of tweezers
槷 niè 〈书面〉 ❶ centre of a target (for arrows); bull's-eye ❷ pole that measures the height of the sun (in order to show the time)
糵(糱) niè 〈书面〉 leaven (for making wine); yeast
蘖 niè 〈植物〉 tiller: 萌～ begin to tiller
蘖枝 nièzhī tillering branch
孽(孼) niè ❶ evil or wicked creature; monster: 余～ remnant diehards /妖～ evildoer; monster ❷ evil; crime; sin: 作～ do evil; commit a sin /罪～ wrongdoing that is bound to bring retribution; sin /冤～ wrongdoings; sinful injustice ❸ 〈书面〉 unfaithful; treacherous; unfilial: ～臣 traitorous vassal /～子 unfilial son
孽报 nièbào retribution for evils done
孽根 niègēn root of sins; root of evil: ～未除。The roots of evil have not been eliminated.
孽海 nièhǎi sea of iniquity
孽障 nièzhàng ❶〈佛教〉 sin that will lead to retribution ❷ 〈旧语〉 (used by elders of a clan cursing their juniors) evil creature; vile spawn
孽种 nièzhǒng ❶ root of trouble ❷ (a term of abuse formerly applied by elders to their juniors) unworthy offspring; worthless creature
涅 niè 〈书面〉 ❶ alunite ❷ dye black
涅白 nièbái opaque white
涅而不缁 niè'érbùzī not become black even when dyed with alunite; (of a man of noble character) remain uncontaminated in an unhealthy environment: 这个人～, 清白一生。Though brought up in an unhealthy environment, he has been a man of noble and impeccable character all his life.
涅槃 nièpán 〈佛教〉 nirvana — extinction of all desire and pain; absolute blessedness; death
陧(隉) niè *see* "杌陧" wùniè
啮(齧、囓) niè 〈书面〉 gnaw: 虫咬鼠～ biting of pests and gnawing of mice
啮齿动物 nièchǐ dòngwù rodent
啮齿目 nièchǐmù rodent order
啮合 nièhé clench the teeth; (of gears) mesh; engage: 两个齿轮～在一起。The two cogwheels interlock.
啮噬 nièshì gnaw; torture: 失子的悲痛, ～着母亲的心。The loss of her son broke the heart of the mother.
敜(籋) niè 〈书面〉 *see* "镊" niè
臬 niè 〈书面〉 ❶ target (for arrows) ❷ sunshadow-surveying pole used in ancient times; gnomon ❸ standard; criterion
臬台 nièdái *see* "臬司"
臬司 nièsī *also* "臬台" 〈旧语〉 official title in imperial days for the public procurator of a province
臬兀 nièwù *also* "鹝鹝" nièwù 〈书面〉 unstable
嵲 niè *see* "嵽嵲" diéniè
镍 niè 〈化学〉 nickel (Ni): 镀～ nickel-plating; nickeling
镍币 nièbì coin made of nickel; nickel coin; nickel
镍箔 nièbó nickel foil
镍钢 niègāng 〈冶金〉 nickel steel
镍镉电池 niègé diànchí nickel-cadmium cell
镍铬钢 niègègāng 〈冶金〉 nickel-chromium steel
镍铬合金 niègè héjīn 〈冶金〉 nickel-chrome; nichrome; Chromel
镍合金 nièhéjīn 〈冶金〉 nickel alloy
镍黄铁矿 nièhuángtiěkuàng 〈矿业〉 pentlandite; nicopyrite
镍基合金 nièjī héjīn 〈冶金〉 nickel base alloy
镍锰钢 nièměnggāng 〈冶金〉 nickel manganese steel
镍钼钢 nièmùgāng 〈冶金〉 nickel-molybdenum steel
镍铸铁 nièzhùtiě 〈冶金〉 nickel castiron; Ni-tensilorin
鹝 niè
鹝鹝 nièwù *also* "臬兀" nièwù 〈书面〉 unstable
乜 Niè a surname
see also miē

nín

恁 nín *see* "您"
see also nèn
您 nín 〈敬词〉 you: ～好! How are you? *or* How do you do? /～请留步。Please don't bother to come any further.

níng

宁(寧、甯) níng ❶ peaceful; serene; tranquil: 康～ peace and tranquillity ❷〈书面〉pacify; appease: 息事～人 give way to be on friendly terms; patch up a quarrel ❸〈书面〉pay a visit to (one's parents or elders): 归～ return to one's hometown to visit one's parents ❹ (Níng) another name for Nanjing: 沪～线 Shanghai-Nanjing Railway
see also nìng

宁靖 níngjìng 〈书面〉(of local public order) stable; quiet; settled: 这个地区一直是很～的。Law and order prevail in this region.

宁静 níngjìng (of surroundings or feelings) peaceful; tranquil; quiet; calm: 黎明前的～ tranquility before daybreak / 山区的生活是～的。Life in the mountain area is quiet and peaceful. / 这几天我心里很不～。I do not feel very easy lately.

宁谧 níngmì 〈书面〉quiet; serene; tranquil: ～的墓园 tranquil cemetery / 这里游人甚少，委实～。It's really quiet here with so few visitors.

宁耐 níngnài 〈书面〉exercise patience; exercise restraint; restrain oneself: ～几日，便有何妨？You should have the patience to wait for a couple of days, shouldn't you? / 凡事～，不可造次。Be patient in whatever you do and never act rashly.

宁亲 níngqīn 〈书面〉pay a visit to one's parents or elders

宁日 níngrì peaceful, tranquil or quiet days: 国无～。The nation was thrown into turmoil.

宁帖 níngtiē (of mental state) peaceful; tranquil; quiet; calm: 他近来心境不如以往～。His frame of mind is not as calm as it used to be. *or* He is not as calm as he used to be.

宁夏回族自治区 Níngxià Huízú Zìzhìqū Ningxia Hui Autonomous Region, in northwest China

宁馨儿 níngxīn'ér 〈书面〉lovely child

擰(鬡) níng *see* "鬇擰" zhēngníng

苧(薴) níng 〈化学〉limonene

聹(聹) níng *see* "耵聍" dīngníng

柠(檸) níng

柠檬 níngméng lemon: ～糖 lemon drops / ～色 lemon yellow

柠檬桉 níngméng'ān *also* "留香久" liúxiāngjiǔ lemon gum (*Eucalyptus citriodora*)

柠檬茶 níngméngchá lemon tea

柠檬黄 níngménghuáng citrine; lemon-coloured

柠檬醛 níngméngquán citral

柠檬水 níngméngshuǐ lemonade

柠檬苏打水 níngméng sūdáshuǐ lemonade; lemon squash

柠檬素 níngméngsù citrin; vitamin P

柠檬酸 níngméngsuān *also* "枸橼酸" jǔyuánsuān 〈化学〉citric acid

柠檬汁 níngméngzhī lemon-juice

拧(擰) níng ❶ twist; wring: ～毛巾 wring a towel / 把衣服～干 wring out wet clothes / 将几根线～成绳子 twist several pieces of string into a rope ❷ pinch; tweak: ～他一把 give him a pinch / ～耳朵 pinch sb.'s ears / 在孩子脸颊上～了一下 give the child a pinch on the cheek
see also nǐng; nìng

拧成一股绳 níngchéng yī gǔ shéng twist into a rope — pull together; make joint efforts: 几家科研单位～，要把这个项目拿下来。The research institutes have joined their forces to make a success of this programme.

咛(嚀) níng *see* "叮咛" dīngníng

狞(獰) níng ferocious; hideous: 狰～ ferocious; savage; hideous; vile

狞恶 níng'è ferocious; savage: ～的嘴脸 ferocious (*or* ugly) features

狞视 níngshì glare rapaciously: 他恶魔似的～着我。He stared at me fiercely like a demon.

狞笑 níngxiào grin hideously; give a grim laugh: 歹徒有恃无恐地～着。Sure of his own strength, the ruffian was grinning sinisterly.

凝 níng ❶ congeal; curdle; coagulate: 大油已经～住了。The lard has already congealed. / 水已～成冰。The water has frozen to ice. / 我们的战斗友谊是用鲜血～成的。Our militant friendship was cemented with blood. ❷ with fixed attention; attentively: 独坐～思 sit alone, lost in thought

凝碧 níngbì dark green: 湖水～。The lake is dark green.

凝睇 níngdì 〈书面〉gaze intently: 含情～ gaze affectionately (*or* lovingly)

凝点 níngdiǎn 〈物理〉condensation point

凝定 níngdìng fixed; glassy; glazed: ～的眼神 glazed eyes

凝冻 níngdòng stiffen; freeze: 凉爽清新的空气，使他因疲劳而～的思路又开始活动了。The cool fresh air restored his thinking process which had been impeded by a feeling of fatigue.

凝固 nínggù ❶ solidify; curdle; congeal; coagulate: 铁水～了。The molten iron solidified. / 血液～了。One's blood curdled. / 蜡油～了。The wax oil congealed. / 混凝土～了。The concrete has coagulated. / 不要把发展变化的事物看作僵死、～的东西。Don't regard the things that develop and change as dead or fossilized objects. ❷ inflexible; rigid: 思想～，行为保守 stereotyped in thinking and conservative in action / 行动迟缓，目光～ move slowly and look dull

凝固点 nínggùdiǎn 〈物理〉solidifying point; freezing point; condensation point

凝固剂 nínggùjì coagulant

凝固酶 nínggùméi coagulase

凝固汽油 nínggù qìyóu 〈化工〉gelatinized gasoline; incinderjell; jellied gasoline

凝固汽油弹 nínggù qìyóudàn 〈军事〉napalm (bomb)

凝固热 nínggùrè heat released on solidification; heat of solidification

凝固素 nínggùsù coagulin

凝固浴 nínggùyù 〈纺织〉coagulating bath

凝含 nínghán contain in condensed form: ～着深情 embody a profound feeling of friendship

凝寒 nínghán severe cold; bitter cold: 天气～ very cold weather; freezing weather / 松柏不畏～。Pine and cypress do not fear bitter cold.

凝合 nínghé coagulate; congeal; form: 共同利益把他俩～在一起。Common interests bound the two of them together. / 长期共同的学习生活使他们～深厚的友谊。Having been schoolmates for years, they became close friends.

凝华 nínghuá 〈气象〉sublimate: ～核 sublimation nucleus

凝灰岩 nínghuīyán 〈地质〉tuff

凝积 níngjī clot; coagulate: 伤口～着血。The wound was clotted with blood.

凝集 níngjí agglomerate; agglutinate: ～反应〈生化〉agglomeration / ～素〈生化〉agglutinin; agglutinator / ～原〈生化〉agglutinogen / 这项发明～了许多科学家的智慧。The invention is an embodiment of the wisdom of many scientists.

凝寂 níngjì quiet and still; extremely tranquil: ～的夜晚 very peaceful night

凝胶 níngjiāo 〈化学〉gel: ～水泥〈建筑〉gel cement / ～层〈化工〉gel coat

凝结 níngjié coagulate; congeal; condense; curdle: 池塘里～了一层薄冰。A thin layer of ice formed over the pool. / 我们不能浪费这些用心血和汗水～成的国家财富。We must (should) not squander the wealth of the nation acquired by the sweat and blood of the people.

凝结核 níngjiéhé nucleus of condensation

凝结剂 níngjiéjì 〈化学〉coagulant; coagulator

凝结力 níngjiélì coagulating power; coagulability

凝结酶 níngjiéméi 〈生化〉coagulase

凝结尾迹 níngjié wěijì *also* "飞行云" fēixíngyún; "航空云" hángkōngyún (of a missile, plane, etc.) contrail; condensation trail

凝结物 níngjiéwù coagulum

凝聚 níngjù ❶ (of vapour) condense; cohere: ～层〈化学〉coacervate / 荷叶上～着晶莹的露珠 lotus leaves glistening with dewdrops / 大雨快到了，黑云正在～。A heavy rain is imminent, for dark clouds

N

are gathering. ❷ gather; accumulate:这项工程～着许多人的辛勤劳动。The project is a crystallization of many people's hard work.

凝聚力 níngjùlì cohesion; cohesive force:我对中华民族的自信和～深信不疑。I firmly believe in the self-confidence and cohesiveness of the Chinese nation.

凝练 níngliàn *also*"凝炼" concise; condensed; compact:文笔～concise writing /语言～ terse and succinct language

凝眸 níngmóu 〈书面〉(look) with fixed eyes; (watch) with the utmost concentration:～远望 gaze afar into the distance

凝目 níngmù look steadily; gaze

凝汽器 níngqìqì (steam) condenser

凝然 níngrán in a resolute manner:～不动 remain unperturbed

凝乳酶 níngrǔméi 〈生化〉rennin

凝神 níngshén with fixed or rapt attention:～思索 be deep in thought /～观察 observe with concentrated attention /～静听 listen with rapt attention; listen attentively /听众屏息～。The audience were all attention. *or* The audience held their breath listening.

凝视 níngshì gaze; stare:她～林海，似在回忆，又似在遐想。Gazing at the immense forest, she was apparently lost in recollection and reverie.

凝思 níngsī think deeply;be lost in thought:他陷入～之中。He was lost in thought. /他望着窗外的夜色，深沉地～着。Looking at the night scene outside the window, he was plunged into meditation.

凝听 níngtīng listen with rapt attention:他～着远方的声音。He listened intently to the sound that came from afar.

凝望 níngwàng look with fixed eyes;gaze:～远山 gaze at the distant mountains /久久地～着夜空 watch the night sky intently for a long time

凝析气井 níngxī qìjǐng 〈石油〉gas-condensate well

凝析油 níngxīyóu 〈石油〉condensate

凝想 níngxiǎng be lost in thought; meditate:他时而奋笔疾书，时而又搁笔～。At one moment he would take up his pen and write rapidly and at another he would put it down, lost in thought.

凝血酶 níngxuèméi 〈生化〉thrombin

凝血细胞 níngxuè xìbāo blood platelet; thrombocyte

凝血药 níngxuèyào coagulant

凝脂 níngzhī 〈书面〉coagulated grease — fair and delicate skin:肤如～ have fair and delicate skin (*or* complexion) /温泉水滑洗～。The water from the hot spring (*or* spa) laved and smoothed her creamy skin.

凝滞 níngzhì ❶ stagnate; move sluggishly:神色～呆板 with a dull look /沟水～污臭 stagnant and foul ditch-water /我的思想似乎～了。It seemed that my mind was a blank. ❷ condense; congeal:这本著作～着他毕生的心血。This book is the fruit of his lifework.

凝重 níngzhòng ❶ dignified; grave; imposing:举止～ grave manner /神态～ imposing look /雍容～ dignified and poised ❷ (of sound or voice) solemn and vigorous:声音～有力 deep resonant voice /～深沉的乐曲 solemn music ❸ dense; thick; strong:～的乌云 thick dark clouds /天色～漆黑。The sky was completely dark with dense clouds.

凝瞩 níngzhǔ gaze; stare:她抬起头来，～着窗外的天空。Raising her head, she gazed out of the window at the sky.

凝注 níngzhù gaze fixedly; stare:她～着墙上的画像，不禁泪如雨下。She gazed at the portrait on the wall, tears streaming down her face.

凝铸 níngzhù ❶〈冶金〉coagulated casting ❷ express; embody:～着作者的心血 embody the painstaking effort of the author

凝妆 níngzhuāng splendid attire; rich dress and heavy makeup:春日～上翠楼 be dressed in splendid attire and mount a tower on a spring day

nǐng

拧(擰) nǐng ❶ twist; screw; turn:～门把 twist the door knob /把灯泡～上 screw the bulb on /螺丝～紧了。The screw is tightened up. ❷ wrong; erroneous; mistaken:他把话听～了。He got it the wrong way. /你把问题弄～了。You completely misunderstand the problem (*or* have hold of the wrong end of the stick). ❸ differ; disagree; be at cross-purposes; be at odds:两个人～着劲儿。The two of them were at odds.

see also níng; nìng

拧葱 nǐngcōng 〈方言〉come amiss; blunder:就怕人多心不齐，那就越来越～了。I am afraid the more people there are, the more talk there will be, and then things will go astray.

拧咕 nǐnggu 〈口语〉❶ *also*"拧股" unfit; askew; wry:这双袜子穿着正合适，一点也不～着。The socks fit perfectly, nothing wrong at all. ❷ *also*"拧股" disagree; be at loggerheads:他俩老～，整天吵嘴。The couple are at odds, bickering all the time. ❸ twist; turn round:这台收音机让孩子给～坏了。The radio has been damaged by the child turning the knob round and round.

拧劲儿 nǐngjìnr 〈方言〉be at cross-purposes; differ; disagree:同学们都说去游泳，他偏要去爬山，老跟大伙儿拧着劲儿。All our fellow students wanted to go swimming, but he insisted on climbing the mountain, just trying to be contrary.

see also nìngjìnr

nìng

宁[1](寧、甯) nìng ❶ would rather; better:我～输这盘棋也不悔棋。I'd rather lose the game than retract a move. /不自由，毋～死。Give me liberty, or give me death. ❷〈书面〉could there be;could it be:水流之湍急，～有逾此? Could there be a river more torrential than this? / 王侯将相，～有种乎! Birth cannot make a great general or minister.

宁[2](甯) Nìng a surname

see also níng

宁可 nìngkě would rather; better:～少睡点儿觉，也要把这篇文章写完。I would rather sleep less and finish the article. /工作中～把困难想得多一点。You'd better think of more difficulties in your work. /～我负天下人，不可天下人负我。(proverbially attributed to Cao Cao 曹操) Better I betray the people than let the people betray me.

宁肯 nìngkěn would rather:～少些，但要好些。We would rather have fewer but better. *or* Fewer, but better.

宁缺毋滥 nìngquē-wúlàn rather go without than have something shoddy — place quality above quantity:评选优质产品要严格掌握标准，～。The criterion should be strictly adhered to in the appraisal of high-quality products, and it's better to go without than make do with anything not up to standard.

宁死不屈 nìngsǐ-bùqū rather die than submit; prefer death to surrender:表现了～的崇高品质 display the lofty spirit of unswerving loyalty in the face of death

宁为鸡口，无为牛后 nìng wéi jīkǒu, wú wéi niúhòu better be the head of an ass than the tail of a horse; better reign in hell than serve in heaven

宁为玉碎，不为瓦全 nìng wéi yù suì, bù wéi wǎ quán rather be a shattered vessel of jade than an unbroken piece of pottery; rather fall to pieces like broken jade than remain intact as a worthless tile; rather die like a hero than live in dishonour:大丈夫～。A real man would prefer death to dishonour. /当年，他抱定了～的决心奔赴抗日前线。Resolving that he would rather die in glory than live in disgrace, he set out for the anti-Japanese front.

宁愿 nìngyuàn would rather; better:～立着死，不愿跪着生 would rather die on one's feet than live on one's knees /为了集体，他～牺牲个人利益。He's willing to sacrifice his own interest for the sake of the collective.

宁"左"勿右 nìngzuǒ-wùyòu mentality of those who always prefer being on the "left" to being on the right politically

泞(濘) nìng 〈书面〉mud; slush:雨后路～。The road was muddy after the rain.

泞滑 nìnghuá muddy and slippery:山路～，很不好走。It would be difficult to take the mountain path which is muddy and slippery.

泞泥 nìngní muddy; miry

拧(擰) nìng 〈方言〉pigheaded; stubborn; obstinate; unbending:他脾气真～。He is always surly.

see also níng; nǐng

拧劲儿 nìngjìnr stubborn; bigoted; obstinate:他又上了～，思想一下子转不过弯儿来。He is getting pigheaded again, and it is difficult to bring him round for the time being. *or* He is again in a fit of

N

mulish obstinacy and nothing could make him change his mind at present.
see also nǐngjìnr
拧种 nìngzhǒng obstinate person; stubborn person：他是个～。He is as obstinate as a mule.

佞 nìng ❶ given to flattery; sycophantic：～人 sycophant; toady; toad-eater ❷〈书面〉able and wise; gifted：不～〈旧语〉〈谦词〉your unintelligent servant — I; me
佞臣 nìngchén sycophantic courtier; treacherous court official
佞笑 nìngxiào ingratiating smile; sinister smile
佞幸 nìngxìng 〈书面〉❶ win favour by flattery ❷ person who wins favour from the sovereign by sycophantic behaviour：任用～ appoint sycophants to official posts

niū

妞 niū 〈口语〉girl：小～ little girl／大～ big girl／他家有两个～儿。There are two girls in his family.
妞妞 niūniu 〈方言〉little girl
妞子 niūzi 〈方言〉little girl

niú

牛[1] niú ❶ ox; cattle：水～(water) buffalo／黄～ ox; cattle／母～ cow／公～ bull／小～ calf／菜～ beef cattle ❷ stubborn; proud：这人是～性子。The man is rather stubborn. ❸ one of the 28 star constellations in ancient astronomy *see also* "二十八宿" èrshíbāxiù ❹ (Niú) a surname
牛[2] niú (short for 牛顿) newton (used as a unit of force)
牛百叶 niúbǎiyè *also* "牛千张" stomach of cow or ox (eaten as food)
牛蒡 niúbàng 〈植物〉great burdock：～子〈中药〉achene of great burdock
牛鼻子 niúbízi ❶ nose or muzzle of an ox：牵着～走 lead an ox by the halter ❷〈贬义〉Taoist priest ❸〈比喻〉key to sth.; essence：弄清市场供求关系，就抓住了销售的～。The essence of marketing lies in a clear understanding of the relationship between supply and demand.
牛病毒性瘫痪 niúbìngdúxìng tānhuàn 〈兽医〉derriengue
牛脖子 niúbózi 〈方言〉stubbornness; obstinacy; pigheadedness：我知道那个小胖子有些～。I know that little fatty is a bit stubborn.
牛不喝水强按头 niú bù hēshuǐ qiáng àn tóu 〈俗语〉try to make an ox drink by forcing its head into the water — try vainly to dictate to others：他不愿意就算了，何必～呢？Forget it if he is not willing; why should we force him against his will?
牛车 niúchē ox cart; bullock cart
牛传染性脑膜肺炎 niúchuánrǎnxìng nǎomó fèiyán 〈兽医〉contagious bovine pleuropneumonia
牛刀 niúdāo knife used to kill an ox — sth. too big or sb. overqualified for a given purpose：杀鸡焉用～？You don't have to kill a chicken with an ox-slaughtering knife. *or* You don't have to break a butterfly on the wheel. *or* Why use a sledge hammer to swat a fly?
牛刀小试 niúdāo-xiǎoshì display only a small part of one's talent
牛鼎烹鸡 niúdǐng-pēngjī cook chicken in a huge ox-cooking vessel — use talented people for trivial tasks; waste one's talent on a petty job
牛痘 niúdòu ❶ cowpox ❷ smallpox pustule; vaccine：种～ be vaccinated
牛痘苗 niúdòumiáo *also* "痘苗" (bovine) vaccine
牛犊 niúdú *also* "牛犊子" calf
牛肚 niúdǔ tripe：烧～ stewed tripe
牛顿 Niúdùn ❶ Sir Isaac Newton (1642-1727), English mathematician and physicist：～望远镜 Newtonian telescope ❷〈物理〉newton, the SI unit of force
牛顿力学 Niúdùn lìxué 〈物理〉Newtonian mechanics
牛顿万有引力定律 Niúdùn wànyǒu yǐnlì dìnglǜ Newton's law of universal gravitation
牛顿运动定律 Niúdùn yùndòng dìnglǜ 〈物理〉Newton's law of motion
牛轭湖 niú'èhú 〈地理〉oxbow (lake)
牛耳 niú'ěr leading role; dominant position
see also "执牛耳" zhí niú'ěr
牛肺疫 niúfèiyì 〈兽医〉pleuropneumonia (of cattle)
牛粪 niúfèn cow dung
牛肝菌 niúgānjūn bolete
牛感冒 niúgǎnmào ox influenza
牛牯 niúgǔ 〈方言〉bull
牛倌 niúguān oxherd; cowherd
牛鬼蛇神 niúguǐ-shéshén monsters and demons — forces of evil; wicked people of all descriptions
牛黄 niúhuáng 〈中药〉bezoar
牛骥同皂 niújì-tóngzào *also* "牛骥同牢" keep oxen and thoroughbred horses in the same stable — the good and the bad, the wise and the stupid, are intermingled; make no distinction between the wise and the foolish
牛角 niújiǎo ❶ ox horn：～画 horn mosaic／～制品 hornware ❷ wind instrument made of a hollowed-out ox horn; horn
牛角挂书 niújiǎo-guàshū hang the *History of the Han Dynasty* on an ox horn — be assiduous in one's studies
牛角尖 niújiǎojiān tip of a horn — insignificant or insoluble problem：钻～ take unnecessary pains to study an insignificant or insoluble problem; split hairs
牛津英文词典 Niújīn Yīngwén Cídiǎn *Oxford English Dictionary* (OED) (1884-1928), originally entitled *A New English Dictionary on Historical Principles* with Sir James Augustus Henry Murray (1837-1915) as chief editor
牛劲 niújìn ❶ great strength; tremendous efforts：费了～才把他说通。It took tremendous efforts to bring him round. ❷ stubbornness; obstinacy; tenacity：年纪轻轻的，不要犯～。Don't be so stubborn, young man.
牛栏 niúlán cattle pen; ox fence
牛郎 niúláng cowherd in the legend "the Cowherd and the Girl Weaver"
牛郎星 Niúlángxīng 〈天文〉Altair
牛郎织女 niúláng-zhīnǚ ❶〈天文〉Altair and Vega ❷ "the Cowherd and the Girl Weaver", two figures in an ancient Chinese fairy tale; husband and wife who live far apart：我们应该尽可能地为～搭桥。We should spare no efforts to reunite husbands and wives who live far apart from each other.
牛羚 niúlíng 〈动物〉takin
牛马 niúmǎ oxen and horses — beasts of burden：在封建社会，贫苦农民生活不如～。In feudal society the poor peasants lived worse than beasts of burden.
牛马走 niúmǎzǒu 〈书面〉one who serves the king like a beast of burden — self-depreciatory expression referring to oneself
牛毛 niúmáo ox hair：多如～ as many as the hairs on an ox; countless; innumerable／～细雨 drizzle
牛毛雨 niúmáoyǔ drizzle：灰蒙蒙的～ greyish drizzle
牛毛毡 niúmáozhān *see* "牛毛草"
牛虻 niúméng 〈动物〉ox gadfly (*Tabanus bovinus*)
牛奶 niúnǎi milk：～场 dairy／～糖 toffee
牛腩 niúnǎn 〈方言〉loose, chewy beef (from the belly, close to the ribs)：烧～ braised chewy beef
牛年马月 niúnián-mǎyuè *also* "驴年马月" lǘnián-mǎyuè year of the donkey and month of the horse — a time that will never come (because no such year or month ever exists in the lunar calendar)：研究研究，研究到～！They say they'll study the question. Why, they'll study till doom's day!
牛排 niúpái beefsteak; steak
牛棚 niúpéng ❶ cowshed ❷ detention house set up by "Red Guards" in the Cultural Revolution for those regarded as "monsters and demons"(牛鬼蛇神)：蹲～ be kept in a "cowshed" — be kept in a detention house (as a punishment during the Cultural Revolution, 1966-1976)
牛皮 niúpí ❶ cattle hide ❷ pliable and tough：～糖 sticky kind of candy ❸ brag; boast：吹～ talk big; talk grand; brag／～大王 person given to gross exaggerations; braggart

牛皮癣 niúpíxuǎn 〈医学〉psoriasis
牛皮蝇 niúpíyíng 〈动物〉ox warble; cattle grub (*Hypoderma bovis*)
牛皮纸 niúpízhǐ kraft paper; brown paper
牛脾气 niúpíqi stubbornness; obstinacy; pigheadedness：发～ fly into a mulish temper /他～一上来，什么也不顾了。When he was in a fit of pique, he was capable of anything.
牛气 niúqi 〈方言〉self-important; conceited; arrogant：他比以前越发骄傲，越发～了。He has become more haughty than ever. /你有什么可～的？What makes you so conceited?
牛肉 niúròu beef：～面 noodles with beef
牛肉绦虫 niúròu tāochóng beef tapeworm (*Taenia saginata*)
牛舌草 niúshécǎo 〈植物〉oxtongue (*Anchusa*)
牛舌鱼 niúshéyú tonguefish; tongue sole
牛虱 niúshī ox louse
牛市 niúshì bull market(referring to a generally rising market)
牛溲马勃 niúsōu-mǎbó something cheap but useful
牛头刨床 niútóu bàochuáng 〈机械〉shaping machine; shaper
牛头不对马嘴 niútóu bù duì mǎzuǐ horses' jaws don't match cows' heads — incongruous; irrelevant：只要是恭维的话，就是～，他也高兴。He is fond of flattery, even of the most fantastic kind.
牛头马面 niútóu-mǎmiàn two armed runners under the king of the underworld, one with an ox head and the other a horse face — hideous lackeys; wicked people of all descriptions：他们也不过是人家手下的～而已。They are nothing but somebody's hideous cat's paws.
牛腿琴 niútuǐqín a kind of stringed instrument popular among the Tong and Miao national minorities
牛蛙 niúwā bullfrog (*Rana catesbeiana*)
牛尾 niúwěi oxtail：～汤 oxtail soup
牛尾鱼 niúwěiyú 〈动物〉flathead
牛瘟 niúwēn rinderpest; cattle plague; steppe murrain; contagious bovine typhus
牛屋 niúwū cattle pen; ox fence
牛膝 niúxī 〈中药〉root of bidentate achyranthes (*Achyranthes bidentata*)
牛心 niúxīn stubborn; obstinate：他～，不听劝说。He is mulish, listening to no advice.
牛心左性 niúxīn-zuǒxìng *also* "牛心古怪" (of temperament) stubborn; obstinate; unbending：这个人～的，不易处。He is stubborn by nature and very difficult to get along with.
牛性 niúxìng stubbornness; obstinacy; pigheadedness：他这个人容易使～。He is prone to pigheaded petulance.
牛眼菊 niúyǎnjú 〈植物〉oxeye (*Baphthalmum*)
牛鞅 niúyāng *also* "牛鞅子" a kind of wooden yoke for a draught ox
牛医 niúyī veterinarian who specializes in ox diseases
牛饮 niúyǐn drink like a fish
牛蝇 niúyíng gadfly
牛油 niúyóu butter
牛仔 niúzǎi cowboy
牛仔布 niúzǎibù denim
牛仔裤 niúzǎikù close-fitting pants; jeans; levis
牛轧糖 niúzhátáng nougat
牛脂 niúzhī tallow
牛至 niúzhì 〈植物〉oregano; origanum (*Origanum vulgare*)

niǔ

忸 niǔ
忸怩 niǔní bashful; coy：他今天这么～，怎么回事？He is so coy today. What's the matter with him?
忸怩作态 niǔní-zuòtài behave coyly; be affectedly shy

杻 niǔ 〈古语〉a kind of tree

扭 niǔ ❶ turn：她～过脸去，不让别人看见她掉泪。She turned aside to hide her tears. /他气得～身就走。He turned round and left in anger. /把上面那个旋钮向左～一下。Turn that upper knob to the left. ❷ twist; contort; wrench：他痛得脸都～歪了。His face was contorted with pain. /把两根铁丝～在一起。Twist the two wires together. /他"叭"的一声把门把～断了。He wrenched off the knob with a snap. /几个字，东～西歪，好像是摸着黑写的。There were a few words written in a twisted manner, as if scrawled out in the dark. ❸ sprain; wrench; strain：～了脚 sprain one's ankle /他踢球时～伤了大腿。He wrenched his thigh while playing football. ❹ (usu. used to describe the manner of walking) swing; sway：～着腰走路 walk with a rolling gait/走路不要～屁股，太难看。Don't swing your hips when you walk. It looks repulsive. ❺ seize; grapple：两人～在一起。The two were grappling with each other. ❻ twisted; slanted：歪歪～～ twisted
扭摆 niǔbǎi (of body) sway; swing：她～着腰肢走进房间。She came into the room swaying her hips.
扭摆舞 niǔbǎiwǔ twist
扭缠 niǔchán get in a tangle; keep bothering; pester：她费了好大劲，才摆脱了他的～。It was with a great effort that she managed to shake him off.
扭扯 niǔchě ❶ twitch; wriggle：他～着嘴角。His mouth twitched. ❷ get entangled; grapple (with each other); be in a tangle：几个孩子～成一团。The children got entangled together. ❸ keep bothering; pester; get into a tangle：他跟老王～了半天。He pestered Lao Wang for quite a while.
扭秤 niǔchèng torsion balance; torsion scale
扭打 niǔdǎ be locked in a fist-fight; grapple; wrestle：他俩～在一起，拉也拉不开。The two were locked in a fist-fight and it was hard to separate them.
扭搭 niǔda 〈口语〉walk with a swing of the body; have a rolling gait：他～～走来了。He walked over with a rolling gait.
扭动 niǔdòng sway or twist from side to side：她走起路来总爱～腰肢。She swayed her body while walking. *or* She walked down the road, swaying from side to side./ 鱼儿在鱼叉上～着。A fish was struggling on top of the fish fork.
扭杆 niǔgǎn 〈机械〉torsion bar
扭股儿糖 niǔgǔrtáng twisted roll of sticky candy (made of malt dust)：她～似的缠着妈妈要买玩具。She nagged her mother for the toy without letup.
扭角羚 niǔjiǎolíng 〈动物〉takin (*Buaorcas taxicolor*)
扭结 niǔjié twist together; tangle up：线都～在一起了。The skein is all tangled up.
扭矩 niǔjǔ 〈物理〉torque; twisting moment; twisting couple
扭亏为盈 niǔkuī-wéiyíng 〈经济〉wipe out deficits to go into the black; turn loss into gain：改进了管理方法，使这家企业～。Improved management put the losing enterprise in the black.
扭亏增盈 niǔkuī-zēngyíng make up losses and increase profits
扭力 niǔlì 〈物理〉twisting force; torque; torsion
扭力计 niǔlìjì 〈物理〉torsionmeter; torsional dynamometer
扭力天平 niǔlì tiānpíng torque balance; torsion balance
扭捏 niǔnie be affectedly bashful; be coy; hum and haw：她～了老半天，才说出一句话来。After a show of coy reluctance, she finally uttered a short sentence. /说话别扭扭捏捏的。Stop humming and hawing. Say what's in your mind.
扭曲 niǔqū ❶ twist; contort：～波〈物理〉twisted wave /铁轨～。The rail was twisted. ❷ warp; distort：～的心态 warped mentality /他的原意被～了。His original intention was misrepresented.
扭曲应力 niǔqū yìnglì 〈物理〉torsional stress; twisting stress
扭伤 niǔshāng sprain; wrench：他昨天打羽毛球～了手腕。He sprained his wrist yesterday when playing badminton.
扭伤性骨折 niǔshāngxìng gǔzhé 〈医学〉sprain fracture
扭送 niǔsòng (citizens) seize sb. and hand him over to the public security authorities：殴打服务员的醉汉被～派出所。The drunkard who had assaulted the attendant was seized and handed over to the police substation.
扭头 niǔtóu ❶ turn one's head away：他扭过头去，一句话也不说。He turned away, refusing to answer. ❷ turn round：她二话没说，～就走。She turned round on her heel without saying a word.
扭秧歌 niǔ yāngge do a *yangge* dance
扭应变 niǔyìngbiàn 〈物理〉torsional shear strain; torsional strain
扭应力 niǔyìnglì 〈物理〉distorting stress
扭转 niǔzhuǎn ❶ turn round：他～身子朝我走来。He turned round and walked towards me. ❷ (of direction, situation, tendency, etc.) turn back; change radically：～局势 reverse a trend; turn the tide; turn the tables /～不良倾向 check (*or* put an end to) an un-

healthy trend /～亏损的局面 put an end to deficits /～历史的车轮 turn back the wheel of history

扭转乾坤 niǔzhuǎn-qiánkūn bring about a radical transformation; reverse the course of events

扭转弹性 niǔzhuǎn tánxìng 〈物理〉elasticity of torsion

扭转形变 niǔzhuǎn xíngbiàn 〈物理〉torsion deformation

钮 niǔ ❶ *see* "纽" niǔ ❷ *also* "电钮" diànniǔ button; push button ❸ (Niǔ) a surname

狃 niǔ be bound by; be constrained by:～于成见 bound by prejudice; prejudiced or biased

纽 niǔ ❶ handle; knob:印～ handle of a seal /秤～ lifting cord of a steelyard ❷ button:衣～ button (as on a jacket) ❸ pivot; hub: *see* "～带" ❹ newly grown fruit or melon on a vine, etc.:南瓜～ new fruit of pumpkin

纽带 niǔdài pivot;link; tie; bond:团结的～ ties of unity /精神～ spiritual bond /干部联系群众的～ link between the cadres and the masses

纽结 niǔjié ❶〈方言〉knot; button:系上袍子上的～ tie up the knots on a traditional gown ❷ crucial point of a contradiction; crux of a matter:他们终于把多年来的矛盾～解开了。They finally succeeded in resolving their contradictions of many years' standing. /问题的～不在这里。This is not where the crux of the matter lies. *or* This is not where things go wrong.

纽扣 niǔkòu button

纽伦堡 Niǔlúnbǎo Nuremberg:～审判 Nuremberg Trials (Nov. 1945-Oct. 1946)

纽襻 niǔpàn button loop

纽眼 niǔyǎn 〈方言〉button hole

纽约 Niǔyuē New York, most populous city and largest port of the United States, as well as locus of the headquarters of the United Nations:～市 New York City; "Big Apple" /～州 New York State;Empire State

纽约票据交换所 Niǔyuē Piàojù Jiāohuànsuǒ New York Clearing House

纽约时报 Niǔyuē Shíbào *The New York Times*, major US newspaper published in New York City since 1851

纽约证券交易所 Niǔyuē Zhèngquàn Jiāoyìsuǒ New York Stock Exchange (NYSE):～指数 New York Stock Exchange Index; NYSE index

纽子 niǔzi 〈口语〉button

niù

拗(抝) niù stubborn; bigoted; obstinate; stiff-necked:执～ stubborn; obstinate /脾气很～ stubborn by nature; bullheaded; mulish

see also ǎo; ào

拗不过 niùbuguò unable to dissuade or bring (sb.) round:她～儿子,最后只好同意了他们的婚事。She could not make her son change his mind and finally had to give her consent to the marriage. /他这个人呀,谁也～他。He is such an obstinate character that no one is able to bring him round.

拗劲 niùjìn stubborn spirit; obstinacy; stiff neck:他有股～,别人不干的活他干。There is a peculiar stubbornness in his character which often leads him to volunteer his service where others would stay away.

nóng

农(農、辳) nóng ❶ agriculture; farming:务～ go in for farming /以工补～ subsidize agriculture with income from industry /弃～经商 give up farming to go into business ❷ farmer; peasant:贫～ poor-peasant /中～ middle-peasant /富～ rich-peasant; (in Russia) *kulak* /贫下中～ poor- and lower-middle peasants /菜～ vegetable grower (*or* farmer) /棉～ cotton grower (*or* farmer) /小～意识 small peasant mentality /老～ old farm hand; old farmer ❸ (Nóng) a surname

农本 nóngběn cost of farming:旱地育秧便于管理,省～。It is easier and cheaper to raise rice seedlings on dry land.

农产 nóngchǎn ❶ agricultural production:～区 farming district ❷ farm produce;agricultural product:这里有丰富的～。There are ample farm products in this district. *or* The district is rich in farm produce.

农产品 nóngchǎnpǐn agricultural product; farm produce:～比价 relative pricing of agricultural products /～商品率 commodity rate of agricultural produce

农产品加工学 nóngchǎnpǐn jiāgōngxué 〈农业〉agrotechny

农场 nóngchǎng farm:国营～ state farm /试验～ experimental farm

农场主 nóngchǎngzhǔ farm owner; farmer

农村 nóngcūn rural area; countryside; country; village:～人口 rural population /～经济 rural economy /我家住在～。My home is in the countryside. /我家的保姆是个～妇女。Our baby-sitter is a country woman. *or* Our maid is from the country.

农村户 nóngcūnhù rural household (registration):他想把～的侄子调到城里来。He is trying to arrange a transfer for his nephew from rural to urban household registration.

农村人民公社 nóngcūn rénmín gōngshè rural people's commune (prevalent from 1958 to the 1980's)

农贷 nóngdài agricultural loan or credit

农夫 nóngfū 〈旧语〉peasant; farmer

农妇 nóngfù peasant woman; country woman

农副产品 nóng-fù chǎnpǐn agricultural and side-line products

农副业 nóng-fùyè agriculture and side-line occupations

农耕 nónggēng farm; cultivate:不事～ not attend to farming /在多年的～劳作中,他学会了地里的全部活计。He learnt all the farm work during his stay on the farm over the years.

农工 nónggōng ❶ peasants and workers ❷ (short for 农业工人) agricultural worker; farm worker or labourer

农工党 Nónggōngdǎng (short for 中国农工民主党) Chinese Peasants' and Workers' Democratic Party

农工联合体 nónggōng liánhétǐ agro-industrial complex

农功 nónggōng 〈书面〉farming; farm work

农行 Nóngháng (short for 中国农业银行) Agricultural Bank of China

农户 nónghù peasant or farm household

农会 nónghuì *see* "农协"

农活 nónghuó farm work:等～儿不忙的时候,我到北京来看你。I'll come to Beijing to visit you in the slack season.

农机 nóngjī agricultural machinery; farm machinery:～作业 farm machine operation /～修配站 farm machinery repairing centre

农机具 nóngjījù agricultural machinery and tools

农家 nóngjiā ❶ peasant family; rural household:～肥 farmyard manure /～乐 scene of happy rural life ❷ (Nóngjiā) school of agriculturalists;physiocratic school — a school of thought in the period of Eastern Zhou

农家肥料 nóngjiā féiliào farmyard manure such as green manure and muck (as distinguished from chemical fertilizer)

农具 nóngjù farm tool; farm implement

农垦 nóngkěn reclaim and cultivate wasteland for agriculture

农垦部 Nóngkěnbù Ministry of State Farms and Land Reclamation, which functioned for some decades before the 1980's and is now incorporated into the Ministry of Agriculture

农垦企业 nóngkěn qǐyè state-owned land reclamation enterprise

农历 nónglì ❶ Chinese lunar calendar ❷ farmer's almanac

农林 nóng-lín farming and forestry

农林轮作 nóng-lín lúnzuò 〈农业〉alternation of agricutural and forest crops

农林牧副渔 nóng-lín-mù-fù-yú agriculture, forestry, animal husbandry, sideline production, and fishery(formerly regarded as the main industries of the rural areas)

农忙 nóngmáng busy season in farming:～季节 busy farming season

农贸市场 nóngmào shìchǎng market for farm produce (in cities); free market (primarily for agricultural products)

农民 nóngmín peasant; farmer:～出身 of peasant background /～意识 peasant mentality /～阶级 peasantry

农民工 nóngmíngōng peasant labourer

农民起义 nóngmín qǐyì peasant uprising; peasant revolt
农民协会 nóngmín xiéhuì peasant association
农民运动讲习所 Nóngmín Yùndòng Jiǎngxísuǒ Peasant Movement Institute, an institute to train cadres for the peasant movement in the First Revolutionary Civil War, 1924-1927
农民战争 nóngmín zhànzhēng peasant war; peasant uprising
农膜 nóngmó agricultural plastic sheeting
农牧经济 nóngmù jīngjì agropastoral economy
农牧民 nóngmùmín ❶ farmers and herdsmen ❷ farmer-cum-herdsman
农牧区 nóngmùqū agricultural and pastoral areas; farming and stock breeding areas
农奴 nóngnú serf:～制度 serfdom
农奴主 nóngnúzhǔ serfowner
农女 nóngnǚ peasant woman
农轻重 nóng-qīng-zhòng agriculture, light industry, and heavy industry (advocated as the order of priority under planned economy before the 1990's)
农情 nóngqíng situation or condition of agricultural production
农渠 nóngqú field ditch
农人 nóngrén peasant; farmer
农桑 nóngsāng farming and sericulture
农舍 nóngshè farm house
农神时代 nóngshén shídài 〈历史〉(in Roman civilization) Saturnian age; golden age
农时 nóngshí farming season:不误～ farming in the right season
农事 nóngshì farm work; farming:忙于～ busy with farm work
农田 nóngtián farmland; cropland; cultivated land:～管理 field management /～基本建设 farmland capital construction
农田水利 nóngtián shuǐlì irrigation and water conservancy
农隙 nóngxì 〈书面〉slack season (in farming)
农闲 nóngxián (of farming) slack season
农协 nóngxié *also* "农会"(short for 农民协会) peasant association
农械 nóngxiè implement or machinery for applying farm chemicals, such as sprayers, etc.
农学 nóngxué agriculture; agronomy:～家 agronomist
农谚 nóngyàn farmer's proverb; farmer's saying
农药 nóngyào agricultural chemical; farm chemical; pesticide:～中毒 pesticide poisoning /～残留 pesticide residue /～污染 pesticide pollution
农业 nóngyè agriculture; farming:～人口 agricultural population; people engaged in farm work /～机械 agricultural machinery /～社 agricultural cooperative /～生产责任制 agricultural production responsibility system /～区划 agricultural zoning
农业八字宪法 nóngyè bāzì xiànfǎ Eight-Point Charter for Agriculture (drawn up under Mao Zedong's guidance in 1958, namely, 土 soil improvement, 肥 rational application of fertilizer, 水 water conservancy, 种 improved seed strains, 密 rational close planting, 保 plant protection, 管 field management, 工 improvement of farm implements)
农业部 Nóngyèbù Ministry of Agriculture
农业地质学 nóngyè dìzhìxué agricultural geology; agrogeology
农业工程学 nóngyè gōngchéngxué agricultural engineering
农业工人 nóngyè gōngrén agricultural worker
农业国 nóngyèguó agricultural country
农业合作化 nóngyè hézuòhuà *also* "农业集体化" agricultural cooperation:～运动 agricultural cooperative movement
农业化学 nóngyè huàxué agricultural chemistry
农业集体化 nóngyè jítǐhuà agricultural collectivization
农业集约化 nóngyè jíyuēhuà intensification of agriculture; technology-intensive farming
农业技术 nóngyè jìshù agricultural technology; agrotechnique:～改造 technical transformation of agriculture /～员 agrotechnician /～站 agrotechnical station
农业经济 nóngyè jīngjì agricultural economy; agrarian economy
农业旅游 nóngyè lǚyóu agricultural tourism
农业气象学 nóngyè qìxiàngxué agrometeorology
农业气象站 nóngyè qìxiàngzhàn 〈农业〉agrometeorological station
农业生产合作社 nóngyè shēngchǎn hézuòshè agricultural producers' cooperative
农业生态学 nóngyè shēngtàixué 〈农业〉agroecology
农业生物环境工程 nóngyè shēngwù huánjìng gōngchéng agrobiological environment engineering
农业生物学 nóngyè shēngwùxué agrobiology
农业水文学 nóngyè shuǐwénxué 〈农业〉agrohydrology
农业税 nóngyèshuì agricultural tax
农业土壤学 nóngyè tǔrǎngxué 〈农业〉agrology
农业中学 nóngyè zhōngxué secondary school of agriculture; agricultural secondary school
农业资本家 nóngyè zīběnjiā agricultural capitalist
农业综合经营 nóngyè zōnghé jīngyíng *also* "农业商业化经营" agri-business
农艺 nóngyì agronomy
农艺师 nóngyìshī agronomist
农艺学 nóngyìxué agronomy
农用 nóngyòng for use in agricultural production:～物资 farming materials
农用喷雾机 nóngyòng pēnwùjī 〈农业〉agrisprayer
农用拖拉机 nóngyòng tuōlājī 〈农业〉agricultural tractor; agrimotor
农用直升飞机 nóngyòng zhíshēng fēijī 〈农业〉agricopter
农友 nóngyǒu (a term often used during the 1920's and 1930's) peasant comrade; fellow peasant
农运会 nóngyùnhuì (short for 农民运动会) sports meet of farmers; rural sports meet
农政全书 Nóngzhèng Quánshū *Complete Treatise on Agriculture* compiled by Xu Guangqi (徐光启, 1562-1633) of the Ming Dynasty and published in 1639
农转非 nóngzhuǎnfēi change from rural residence registration to non-rural residence registration; change from rural to non-rural registration
农庄 nóngzhuāng farm:集体～ collective farm; (Soviet) kolkhoz
农作 nóngzuò farming:他过去当吹鼓手,有时也兼点～。He was a bugler and occasionally did some farming too.
农作物 nóngzuòwù crops:～病虫害 plant diseases and insect pests

浓(濃) nóng ❶ concentrated; thick; dense; heavy:～墨 thick ink /～烟 dense smoke /～雾 heavy fog /～茶 strong tea /～云密布 be overcast /淡妆～抹总相宜 (as of a woman) always look beautiful with either light or heavy make-up ❷ (of degree or extent) strong; great; deep:兴趣很～ take a great (*or* deep) interest (in sth.) /这幅画的色彩过～。The colours of this painting are too strong (*or* heavy). /汤味不太～。The soup is a little bland.
浓春 nóngchūn late spring:田里新秧出水,一派～景象。Rice seedlings have emerged out of the paddy fields and a scene of late spring meets the eye.
浓淡 nóngdàn degree of density:～适宜 of proper density; just right (in colour, flavour, smell, etc.)
浓度 nóngdù concentration; density:高～的维他命C饮料 drink with high concentration of vitamin C; vitamin C-rich drink /达到一定的～ reach a certain level of concentration /牛奶的～不够。The milk is watery.
浓馥 nóngfù (of flower, perfume, etc.) fragrance; strong scent:北京街道两旁已是满树～的槐花。The blossoms of the scholartrees began to cast their fragrance over the sidewalks of Beijing.
浓厚 nónghòu ❶ thick; dense:～的大雾 dense (*or* thick, *or* heavy) fog /轮船被～的黑烟笼罩着。The steamer is enveloped in a pall of black smoke. ❷ (of colour, smell, atmosphere, interest, etc.) strong; rich:～的肉香味儿 strong (*or* rich) smell of cooked meat /～的宗教色彩 of rich religious colouring /～的封建意识 strong feudal mentality /～的民主空气 prevalent atmosphere of democracy /生活气息～ full of life /～的地方色彩 pronounced local colour ❸ (of interest) great; deep:我对国际象棋产生了～的兴趣。I began to take a deep interest in chess. /他读书的兴趣越来越～。He grew more and more interested in reading.
浓积云 nóngjīyún 〈气象〉cumulus congestus
浓集 nóngjí condense; compress
浓丽 nónglì (of colour) bright and beautiful:鲜红～的花朵 brilliantly red flowers
浓烈 nóngliè rich; strong:香气～ rich perfume /～的乡土气息 strong flavour of rural life
浓硫酸分解炉 nóngliúsuān fēnjiělú 〈化工〉sulphator
浓眉 nóngméi heavy or thick eyebrows; bushy; shaggy:～大眼

have big eyes and bushy brows; have prominent features

浓密 nóngmì dense; thick:树木～ be densely (*or* thickly) wooded /～的枝叶 thick foliage /一头～的黑发 a head of rich black hair

浓墨重彩 nóngmò-zhòngcǎi describe in a rich and colourful manner:这位作者善于以～突出重要细节。The author is good at bringing important details into bold relief through rich and colourful portrayal.

浓缩 nóngsuō ❶ concentrate; condense:～物 concentrate /～果汁 fruit juice concentrate; condensed fruit juice /～稀释实验 concentration-dilution test /把糖液～成糖浆 concentrate sugar solution into syrup ❷ enrich:～铀 enriched uranium

浓香 nóngxiāng ❶ of rich flavour; of strong fragrance or aroma:茅台酒味～。*Maotai* has a rich aroma. ❷ strong fragrance; rich aroma:～袭人。A strong fragrance assails one's nose. *or* One is intoxicated by the sweet aroma.

浓艳 nóngyàn rich and gaudy:色调～ gaudy colours /服饰～ gaudily dressed /这条裙子的色彩是不是太～了? Is this skirt too loud?

浓荫 nóngyīn dark shadow:～蔽日。The trees blocking the sun cast dark shadows on the ground.

浓郁 nóngyù ❶ (of smell, flavour, etc.) strong; rich:～的花香阵阵袭来。The sweet fragrance of flowers assailed my nostrils. ❷ dense; thick:山南是一片～的松林。The mountain is covered with a dense pine grove on the southern slope. ❸ heavy; rich:色调～ rich colour /～的乡土气息 strong flavour of rural life ❹ (of interest) great; deep:兴致～地看着 watch with great interest

浓挚 nóngzhì deep and sincere:怀着～的感情 cherish a deep and sincere feeling

浓重 nóngzhòng thick; dense; heavy; strong:～的土腥味 strong smell of earth /～的口音 strong (*or* thick) accent /着色～ painted in rich colours /山雾～。The mountains are shrouded in heavy fog.

浓妆 nóngzhuāng heavy make-up

浓妆艳抹 nóngzhuāng-yànmǒ (of a woman) richly attired and heavily made-up

浓浊 nóngzhuó ❶ (of air, fog, etc.) thick and foul:～的雾气里带着稀疏的雨滴。There are scattering raindrops in the dense, smoky mists. ❷ (of voice) deep and gruff:隔壁响起了一个男人的～的声音。From the next door came a man's deep and gruff voice.

酴(醲) nóng
〈书面〉(of wine flavour) rich

哝(噥) nóng

哝哝 nóngnong murmur; mutter:两个姑娘在那儿唧唧～。The two girls are whispering to each other.

秾(穠) nóng
〈书面〉(of plants, trees, etc.) luxuriant:夭桃～李 peach and plum trees in luxuriant growth

秾艳 nóngyàn bright coloured:～的红梅 brilliantly red plum blossoms

侬(儂) nóng
❶〈方言〉you ❷ (used in classical poetry) I ❸ (Nóng) a surname

侬人 Nóngrén Zhuang people living in an area bordering Guangxi and Yunnan

脓(膿) nóng
pus:～袋 pus-pocket /化～ suppuration /化～性感染 pyogenic infection

脓包 nóngbāo ❶ *also* "脓疱"〈医学〉pustule ❷ good-for-nothing; wastrel; worthless fellow:我怎么嫁给了你这个～! How come I married you, such a good-for-nothing!

脓疮 nóngchuāng running sore

脓毒病 nóngdúbìng 〈医学〉sepsis

脓毒症 nóngdúzhèng 〈医学〉pyaemia; pyohemia; sepsis

脓囊肿 nóngnángzhǒng 〈医学〉pyocyst

脓尿 nóngniào 〈医学〉pyuria

脓疱病 nóngpàobìng 〈医学〉pustulosis; impetigo

脓皮病 nóngpíbìng 〈医学〉pyodermia; pyoderma

脓球菌 nóngqiújūn 〈微生物〉pyococcus

脓斜症 nóngxiézhèng 〈医学〉pyohemia

脓性肾炎 nóngxìng shènyán 〈医学〉pyonephritis

脓性心包炎 nóngxìng xīnbāoyán 〈医学〉empyema of pericardium

脓胸 nóngxiōng 〈医学〉pyothorax

脓溢 nóngyì 〈医学〉pyorrhea

脓肿 nóngzhǒng 〈医学〉abscess:肺～ pulmonary abscess /肝～ liver abscess /盆腔～ pelvic abscess

nòng

弄 nòng
❶ play with; fiddle with; fumble about or with:男孩子从小就喜舞刀～枪。Boys often like to play with toy knives and guns from childhood. /他一天到晚就知道～他那收音机。He spends all his time fiddling with that radio of his. /你在那儿瞎～什么? What are you fumbling with there? /他退休后喜欢～点花草。He took up flower growing after retirement. ❷ do; make; fix; handle:～了不少菜 prepare quite a feast /这么些书,你们几个～得了吗? Can you people handle all those books? /这事把我～得很苦。This made me quite miserable. /我怎么也～不明白。I just couldn't get it straight. /厕所坏了,你能来～一下吗? The toilet doesn't flush. Could you come and fix it? /屋子～得很干净。The room is kept clean. ❸ get; fetch; wangle:去～点米来。Go and fetch some rice. /帮我～张机票。Please get me an airplane ticket. ❹ play (tricks):舞文～墨 play with words

see also lòng

弄潮 nòngcháo 〈书面〉paddle in the sea; ride the tide

弄潮儿 nòngcháo'ér ❶ young man who paddles on the beach at the incoming tide ❷ one who rides the tide in times of political and economic changes

弄臣 nòngchén 〈旧语〉official who was on terms of improper intimacy with the emperor; favourite courtier

弄鬼 nòngguǐ 〈方言〉play tricks:装神～ act like a man possessed; make much ado in order to mystify /别在我背后～! Don't play tricks behind my back!

弄鬼掉猴 nòngguǐ-diàohóu play the fool; play pranks; be mischievous:叫那些孩子别～的! Tell the children to keep out of mischief!

弄好 nònghǎo ❶ pretend to be nice or innocent:你别在我面前～。Don't try to pretend innocence before me. ❷ do well:不要搞得太累了,你首先要把身体～。Don't work too hard. You've got to get well first. /这个收音机弄不好了。This radio cannot be fixed. *or* This radio is beyond repair. ❸ finish doing:总结报告～了没有? Is the summary report ready?

弄坏 nònghuài ❶ be up to mischief; play a dirty trick:他老在别人面前给我～。He always tries to make a fool of me in front of others. ❷ damage; ruin; make a mess of:把事情～了 mess up things; make a mess of things /电脑给～了。The computer is damaged. *or* The computer has broken down. /别把身体～了。Don't ruin your health.

弄假 nòngjiǎ practise fraud; resort to deception:暗中～,骗取信任 win trust by fraud and deception

弄假成真 nòngjiǎ-chéngzhēn what was make-believe has become reality; what began in fun ends in dead earnest:他俩本是闹着玩儿的,谁知后来～,真的打起来了。They were sparring at first but somehow became serious and fell to a real fight.

弄僵 nòngjiāng bring to a deadlock:事情让你～了。You have brought the matter to a deadlock. /他俩在会上发生争执,结果把关系～了。After they clashed at the meeting their relations became strained.

弄巧成拙 nòngqiǎo-chéngzhuō try to be clever only to end up with a blunder; outsmart oneself:他原本想在众人面前露一手,结果～,当场出丑。Trying to impress others, he only managed to make a fool of himself in public.

弄权 nòngquán manipulate power (for selfish ends); resort to Machiavellian manoeuvers

弄手脚 nòng shǒujiǎo *also* "做手脚" zuò shǒujiǎo play tricks; play foul:小心别人～。Watch out for any foul play. /看样子,八成弄了手脚了。Most likely this has been rigged.

弄瓦 nòngwǎ 〈书面〉〈旧语〉birth of a girl:～之喜 good news of the birth of a baby girl

弄性 nòngxìng vent one's spleen:这个人脾气暴躁,喝了酒更～。The fellow has a fiery temper and is even more liable to vent his spleen when he has had a drop too much.

弄虚作假 nòngxū-zuòjiǎ practise fraud; resort to deception; falsify:～,骗取信任 gain trust (of sb.) through deception

弄璋 nòngzhāng 〈书面〉birth of a boy:～之喜 good news of the

N

birth of a baby boy

nòu

耨(鎒) nòu 〈书面〉❶ weeding hoe ❷ weeding:深耕细～ deep ploughing and careful weeding; intensive cultivation

nú

奴 nú ❶ slave; bondservant:家～ bondservant of a family /女～ slave woman; serf woman; bondswoman /农～ serf /亡国～ persons without a country; conquered people /守财～ miser /洋～ person servile to foreigners; flunkey of foreigners /卖身为～ sell oneself as a slave or bondservant ❷ (used by a girl to refer to herself in the early vernacular) I; me ❸ enslave; treat as a slave: *see* "～役";"～使"

奴婢 núbì ❶ (man- or woman-) servant; (man- or woman-) slave ❷ (used by a eunuch to refer to himself while addressing royalty) your humble slave

奴才 núcai ❶ bondservant ❷ (formerly used to refer to oneself while addressing royalty or one's master) your humble slave ❸ lackey; flunkey:供人驱使的～ lackey at sb.'s beck and call /～相 very picture of servility; shameless fawning /～哲学 slavish mentality

奴化 núhuà enslave:～教育 education of enslavement /～政策 policy of enslavement

奴家 nújiā (often used in the early vernacular) *girl's or young woman's self-depreciating way of referring to herself*

奴隶 núlì slave:～制度 slave-owning system; slavery /～起义 slave uprising /任人宰割的～ downtrodden slaves

奴隶海岸 Núlì Hǎi'àn Slave Coast, that part of West African coast from the Volta river to the Niger river where slave trade was rampant in the 15th-19th centuries

奴隶贸易 núlì màoyì slave trade (the procuring, transporting and selling of human beings, esp. African blacks, as slaves, by Western colonialists from the 15th to 19th centuries)

奴隶社会 núlì shèhuì slave society

奴隶主 núlìzhǔ slaveowner; slaveholder

奴隶主义 núlìzhǔyì slavishness; slavish mentality

奴仆 núpú servant; lackey: 帝国主义的～ lackey of the imperialists; henchman of imperialism

奴使 núshǐ 〈书面〉enslave:落到了供人～的地步 be reduced to slavery; sink so low as to be at sb.'s beck and call

奴性 núxìng servility; slavishness:～十足 abject slavishness; utter servility; sheer subservience

奴颜婢膝 núyán-bìxī servile; subservient: 在上司面前～ behave servilely before one's superiors /就是死,也不能在敌人面前～。I'd rather die than bend the knee to the enemy. /他们对外～,甘心卖国求荣。To betray their own country in pursuit of personal gains, they bowed and scraped like slaves to foreign aggressors.

奴颜媚骨 núyán-mèigǔ sycophancy and obsequiousness:他在敌人面前没有丝毫的～。He was free from all sycophancy and obsequiousness before the enemy. /她讨厌他那副～的样子。She detested him for his servile obedience.

奴役 núyì enslave: 被～的人民 enslaved peoples/不堪～ cannot stand the misery of slavery

奴子 núzǐ 〈书面〉servant; lackey

孥 nú 〈书面〉❶ sons and daughters; children ❷ wife and children

驽 nú 〈书面〉❶ inferior horse; jade ❷ incompetent; dull:～才 incompetent *or* slow-witted person; dullard

驽钝 núdùn 〈书面〉dull; slow-witted; stupid

驽马 númǎ 〈书面〉inferior horse; jade; nag

驽马铅刀 númǎ-qiāndāo inferior horse and blunt knife — incompetence; incompetent person

驽马十驾 númǎ-shíjià ten days' journey of an inferior horse:～,功在不舍。If a jade travels a thousand *li*, it is perseverance that does it.

驽骀 nútái 〈书面〉inferior horse; mediocre person:～之才,不足大用。As a person of petty talent, he should not be appointed to a post of responsibility.

nǔ

砮 nǔ 〈书面〉stone that can be made into an arrowhead

胬 nǔ

胬肉 nǔròu pterygium:～攀睛〈中医〉pterygium of the eye extending over (a part of) the cornea

弩 nǔ crossbow:万～齐发。Ten thousand arrows were shot all at once.

弩弓 nǔgōng crossbow

弩机 nǔjī mechanical device on a crossbow

弩箭 nǔjiàn arrow discharged by a crossbow

弩炮 nǔpào catapult

努(❷拗、呶、㖔) nǔ ❶ exert; strive: *see* "～力";"～劲儿" ❷ pout; bulge:～目 stare with bulging eyes ❸〈方言〉injure oneself through overexertion;strain oneself:～伤 sustain an injury through overexertion /别用力过猛,小心～着! Don't overexert yourself, or you'll get a bad sprain.

努尔哈赤 Nǔ'ěrhāchì Nurhachi (1559-1626), founder of Great Jin (大金), or Later Jin (1616), predecessor of the Qing Dynasty.

努劲儿 nǔjìnr make more effort; exert oneself:再努把劲儿就行了。Just a bit more effort and the work will be done. /现在要再不～就晚了。It'll be too late if you don't exert yourself now.

努库阿洛法 Nǔkù'āluòfǎ Nuku'alofa, capital of Tonga

努力 nǔlì make efforts; strive; exert oneself:～工作 work hard /～不懈 make unremitting efforts /～克服困难 exert oneself to overcome difficulties /尽最大的～ try one's utmost; do one's best /为祖国的四化建设而～ strive for the modernization of the country

努美阿 Nǔměi'ā Nouméa, capital of New Caledonia

努瓦克肖特 Nǔwǎkèxiāotè Nouakchott, capital of Mauritania

努嘴 nǔzuǐ pout one's lips as a signal:奶奶向我～,让我别说了。Grandma pouted her lips, hinting that I should shut up.

nù

怒 nù ❶ anger; rage; fury; wrath:发～ get angry; fly into a rage /愤～ angry; indignant; wrathful /盛～ in a rage; furious /息～ cease to be angry; calm down (from anger) /老羞成～ fly into a rage out of shame or embarrassment ❷ vigorous; flourishing:草木～生 plants growing in profusion; (of a place) be overgrown with vegetation.

怒不可遏 nùbùkě'è cannot restrain one's fury; boil with anger; foam with rage:她几句话说得他～。He quivered with rage at her words. /他～地大声咒骂敌人。He thundered his wrathful condemnation at the enemy.

怒潮 nùcháo ❶ (usu. figurative) angry tide; raging tide:反战的～汹涌澎湃。The anti-war tide was surging up. ❷ surging tide; tidal bore:钱塘江前观～ watch the surging tide in the Qiantang River

怒斥 nùchì rebuke angrily; denounce indignantly or wrathfully:～这种不道德的行为 denounce this immoral behaviour indignantly

怒叱 nùchì angrily rebuke or reproach:老爷子～儿子不长进。The old man angrily took his son to task for his failure to make any progress.

怒冲冲 nùchōngchōng angrily; furiously; in a rage

怒发冲冠 nùfà-chōngguān bristle with anger; swell with rage; be in a towering passion or rage:想到此处,他不觉～。When he thought of this, he boiled with anger.

怒放 nùfàng (of trees, flowers, etc.) be in full bloom or blossom:春天,桃花、李花争相～。In spring, peach trees and plum trees are all in full blossom, vying for glamour. /喜讯传来,他不禁心花～。He was wild with joy at the good news.

怒号 nùháo howl; roar:北风～,大雪纷飞。A north wind was howl-

ing; snow flakes were dancing wildly.
怒喝 nùhè shout angrily:～一声 give an angry shout
怒吼 nùhǒu roar with anger; thunder:他仍可听到远处狮子的～。He could still hear the angry roar of the lion in the distance. /示威的群众在～。The demonstrators were shouting angrily. /"你们都给我滚出去!"他对手下人～道。"Get out of here! All of you!" he thundered at his men.
怒火 nùhuǒ flames of fury; fury:仇恨的～ flames of hatred /满腔～ be filled with wrath /压住心头的～ restrain one's anger
怒火中烧 nùhuǒ-zhōngshāo be burning with rage
怒骂 nùmà shout angry abuse; swear angrily; lash out:嬉笑～ merry laugh or angry curse /她站在窗户下面冲着屋里～。She stood under the window and poured forth a stream of angry invective into the room. /没想到迎接他的却是她劈头盖脸的一阵～。He was greeted, beyond his expectation, with a sudden lash of her angry tongue.
怒目 nùmù ❶ angry or fierce stare:～圆睁 glare; glower ❷ glaring eyes
怒目而视 nùmù'érshì stare angrily; look daggers (at sb.)
怒目横眉 nùmù-héngméi *also* "横眉怒目" with frowning brows:他在敌人面前,～,忠贞不屈。He remained loyal and unyielding, glaring angrily and frowning scornfully at the enemy.
怒目切齿 nùmù-qièchǐ stare fiercely and gnash one's teeth
怒气 nùqì anger; rage; fume; fury:～不息 be in an unabated rage /他满脸～地闯进来。He rushed into the room with fury written all over his face.
怒气冲冲 nùqì-chōngchōng be in a towering rage
怒气冲天 nùqì-chōngtiān boiling with rage; mad with fury
怒气填胸 nùqì-tiánxiōng be filled with anger or wrath
怒容 nùróng angry look; scowl:面带～ look angry /满脸～ have one's face contorted with anger; look as black as thunder; scowl /不露～ not show one's anger; keep one's anger under control
怒色 nùsè angry look:面有～ look angry /满脸～ look as black as thunder
怒视 nùshì glare angrily; glower; scowl:孩子在父亲的～下不敢抬头。The boy bowed his head under his father's angry glare.
怒涛 nùtāo raging billows; torrents:～汹涌 billows raging furiously /黄河～ torrents of the Yellow River
怒形于色 nùxíngyúsè go black in the face; be ablaze with anger:他～,激动异常。He blazed with anger, getting extremely agitated.
怒族 Nùzú Nu nationality, living in Yunnan Province

nǚ

女 nǚ ❶ woman; female:男～平等 equality between men and women; equality of the sexes; gender equality /男耕～织 the man works in the fields while the woman sits at the loom (division of labour between men and women in a family in ancient China) /少～ young (unmarried) girl; maiden /处～ virgin /～教师 woman teacher /～英雄 heroine /～运动员 sportswoman /～工 woman worker, female worker /～医生 woman doctor /～发言人 spokeswoman /～作家 woman writer; authoress /～演员 actress /～民兵 militia woman /～甥〈书面〉sister's daughter; niece /～孙〈书面〉granddaughter /～式上衣 women's jacket /～中尧舜 wise and virtuous woman ❷ daughter:儿～ sons and daughters; children /生儿育～ bear and raise children /长～ eldest daughter /养～ adopted or foster daughter /侄～ one's brother's daughter; niece /外甥～ one's sister's daughter; niece /孙～ one's son's daughter; granddaughter /外孙～ one's daughter's daughter; granddaughter ❸ one of the twenty-eight constellations in ancient astronomy *see also* "二十八宿" èrshíbāxiù
女阿飞 nǚ'āfēi Teddy girl
女扮男装 nǚbàn-nánzhuāng girl or woman disguised as boy or man
女伴儿 nǚbànr female companion
女傧相 nǚbīnxiàng bride's maid
女厕所 nǚcèsuǒ ❶ women's lavatory; women's toilet ❷ (used on signs for public lavatories) Ladies; Women
女车 nǚchē woman's bicycle; lady's bicycle
女大十八变 nǚ dà shíbā biàn〈俗语〉a girl changes eighteen times before reaching womanhood:～,越变越好看。A girl changes eighteen times before coming of age, each time looking prettier than before.
女单 nǚdān (short for 女子单打)〈体育〉women's singles
女道士 nǚdàoshi〈道教〉Taoist nun
女低音 nǚdīyīn〈音乐〉alto
女弟 nǚdì〈书面〉younger sister
女丁 nǚdīng grown-up woman
女儿 nǚ'ér daughter; girl
女儿寡 nǚ'érguǎ *also* "望门寡" wàngménguǎ〈旧语〉woman who remained unmarried all life long after the death of her betrothed
女儿酒 nǚ'érjiǔ〈方言〉〈旧语〉wine brewed after a daughter is born, buried underground and taken out to entertain guests when the daughter gets married
女儿墙 nǚ'érqiáng *also* "女墙"〈建筑〉parapet (of wall)
女方 nǚfāng bride's side; wife's side
女服务员 nǚfúwùyuán waitress; woman attendant; stewardess
女高音 nǚgāoyīn〈音乐〉soprano
女工 nǚgōng ❶ female worker ❷〈旧语〉maid servant ❸ *also* "女红"〈旧语〉needlework (by women)
女公子 nǚgōngzǐ〈敬词〉your (distinguished) daughter; daughter (of a distinguished family)
女红 nǚgōng *also* "女工"〈书面〉needlework
女冠 nǚguān〈书面〉female Taoist priest
女孩儿 nǚháir *also* "女孩";"女孩子" ❶ girl ❷ daughter
女皇 nǚhuáng empress
女家 nǚjiā bride's family; wife's family
女监 nǚjiān *also* "女牢" jail for female prisoners
女将 nǚjiàng ❶ woman general ❷ outstanding woman in a certain field of activity:棋坛～ outstanding woman chessplayer
女界 nǚjiè womenfolk in society; feminine world
女眷 nǚjuàn womenfolk of a family
女角 nǚjué female part or role; female character
女篮 nǚlán〈体育〉❶ (short for 女子篮球队) women's basketball team ❷ (short for 女子篮球) women's basketball game
女郎 nǚláng young woman; girl:金发～ blonde
女里女气 nǚlinǚqì (of a man) look or act like a woman; be effeminate; be sissy;我不喜欢那个人,～的! I don't like the chap. He is a sissy!
女伶 nǚlíng〈旧语〉actress
女流 nǚliú〈贬义〉weaker sex; women:～之辈 weaker sex
女萝 nǚluó *also* "松萝" sōngluó〈植物〉usnea
女猫 nǚmāo〈方言〉female cat
女能人 nǚnéngrén woman of exceptional ability; capable career woman
女排 nǚpái〈体育〉❶ (short for 女子排球队) women's volleyball team ❷ (short for 女子排球) women's volleyball
女朋友 nǚpéngyou girl friend; lady friend
女气 nǚqì womanish; womanly:这个男的说话嗲声嗲气的,太～了。The man is really womanish; he is so soft-spoken.
女强人 nǚqiángrén capable career woman; woman of strong character
女墙 nǚqiáng *see* "女儿墙"
女青年会 Nǚqīngniánhuì (short for 基督教女青年会) Young Women's Christian Association (YWCA)
女权 nǚquán woman's right:～运动 women's movement; women's lib; feminist movement /～主义 feminism /～主义者 feminist; women's lib activist
女人 nǚrén *also* "女人家" woman; womenfolk
女人 nǚren〈口语〉wife; missus
女色 nǚsè woman; woman's beauty; woman's sexual attraction:沉湎～ womanize; be obsessed with women /不近～ be sexually continent
女神 nǚshén goddess:自由～像 Statue of Liberty
女生 nǚshēng ❶ girl student; woman student ❷〈方言〉girl; woman
女声 nǚshēng〈音乐〉female voice:～独唱 female solo /～合唱 female chorus
女史 nǚshǐ〈旧语〉❶ female official ❷ female intellectual
女士 nǚshì (a polite form of address for a woman) lady; madam:～们,先生们 ladies and gentlemen
女式 nǚshì of women's style; style that suits women:～手表 women's watch /～大衣 women's coat /～自行车 women's bicycle
女侍 nǚshì ❶〈旧语〉waitress ❷ maid servant

N

女双 nǚshuāng (short for 女子双打)〈体育〉women's doubles
女同胞 nǚtóngbāo female compatriot; woman; womenfolk
女童子军 nǚtóngzǐjūn girl scout or girl guide, member of an organization for girls established in 1910
女娲 Nǚwā Nüwa or Nü Wa, Chinese goddess who, according to legend, created human beings and patched up the sky
女王 nǚwáng queen
女巫 nǚwū *also* "巫婆" wūpó witch; sorceress
女兮兮的 nǚxīxīde 〈方言〉(of a man) effeminate; sissy
女相 nǚxiàng (of a man) features of a woman: 他长得有点～，说话还有点腼腆。He looks like a woman and is even bashful while speaking.
女性 nǚxìng ❶ female sex: 这种疾病多见于～。This disease is often found among the female sex. *or* Women are susceptible to this disease. ❷ woman: 职业～ career woman /新～ modern woman; emancipated woman /已婚～ married woman
女性不育症 nǚxìng bùyùzhèng 〈医学〉atocia
女性化 nǚxìnghuà feminization
女性色情狂 nǚxìng sèqíngkuáng 〈医学〉nymphomania; nymphomaniac
女性性别检测 nǚxìng xìngbié jiǎncè femininity test
女兄 nǚxiōng 〈书面〉elder sister
女修道院 nǚxiūdàoyuàn convent; nunnery: ～院长 abbess
女秀 nǚxiù outstanding woman: 佼佼～ outstanding woman /文坛～ outstanding woman writer
女秀才 nǚxiùcai fine woman scholar; woman who writes well; knowledgable woman
女婿 nǚxu ❶ son-in-law ❷〈口语〉husband; hubby
女阴 nǚyīn 〈生理〉vulva
女优 nǚyōu 〈旧语〉(of traditional opera) actress
女乐 nǚyuè 〈古语〉female singer, musician or dancer; female entertainment troupe
女招待 nǚzhāodài waitress; barmaid
女贞 nǚzhēn 〈植物〉glossy privet (*Ligustrum lucidum*): ～子〈中药〉fruit of glossy privet
女真 Nǚzhēn Nüzhen, ancient nationality in northeast China, later called the Manchu
女中豪杰 nǚzhōng-háojié outstanding woman
女中音 nǚzhōngyīn 〈音乐〉mezzo-soprano
女主角 nǚzhǔjué feminine lead (in a film, play, opera, etc.); heroine (of a novel, story, etc.)
女主人 nǚzhǔren hostess; mistress
女装 nǚzhuāng ❶ woman's dress; woman's clothing ❷ dressed like a woman: 男扮～ man disguised as woman; man in drag
女子 nǚzǐ woman; female: 俊俏～ pretty girl; beautiful woman /～体操运动冠军 women's gymnastics champion /～单打 women's singles /～双打 women's doubles /～团体赛 women's team event/～排球队 women's volleyball team /～无挡板篮球 netball /～无才便是德。〈旧语〉A woman without talent is thereby virtuous.
女足 nǚzú (short for 女子足球队)〈体育〉women's football

钕 nǚ 〈化学〉neodymium (Nd)
钕玻璃 nǚbōli 〈化工〉neodymium glass; neophane glass: ～激光器 neodymium glass laser
钕激光器 nǚjīguāngqì neodymium laser
钕镨 nǚpǔ 〈化学〉didymium

nǜ

恧 nǜ 〈书面〉be ashamed: 自～ feel ashamed /～缩 flinch from shame
衄(衂、鼽) nǜ 〈书面〉❶ nosebleed; bleed: 鼻～ nosebleed /齿～ gumbleed ❷ be defeated in battle: 败～ be defeated
朒 nǜ 〈书面〉❶ crescent moon that appears in the east at the beginning of each lunar month; moonlight at that time ❷ be deficient in; lack

nuǎn

暖(煖、煗、暝) nuǎn ❶ warm; genial: 冬～夏凉 cool in summer and warm in winter /去年冬天很～。We had a very warm winter last year. ❷ warm up; heat: ～～手脚 warm up one's hands and feet /～酒 warm (*or* heat) wine /～人心 warm the heart
暖低压 nuǎndīyā 〈气象〉warm cyclone; warm low pressure system
暖调 nuǎndiào 〈美术〉(of colour) warm tone
暖洞子 nuǎndòngzi 〈方言〉greenhouse
暖耳 nuǎn'ěr ear-flap
暖房 nuǎnfáng ❶〈旧语〉go to the bridal chamber to extend one's congratulations on the eve of a wedding ❷ pay a house-warming visit; have a house-warming party ❸〈方言〉greenhouse; hothouse
暖锋 nuǎnfēng 〈气象〉warm front
暖高压 nuǎngāoyā 〈气象〉warm anticyclone; warm high pressure system
暖阁 nuǎngé 〈旧语〉enclosed heated space within a larger room
暖锅 nuǎnguō 〈方言〉chafing dish
暖烘烘 nuǎnhōnghōng nice and warm; warm and cosy: 春天里太阳～的。The spring sun feels warm and nice. /外面冰天雪地，可室内却是～。It is a world of ice and snow outside, but here inside it's cosy and warm.
暖呼呼 nuǎnhūhū warm: ～的南风轻轻地吹着。A warm south wind is blowing gently. /听了老师这番话，孩子们心里～的。On hearing what the teacher said, the children felt warm at heart.
暖壶 nuǎnhú ❶ thermos flask; thermos bottle ❷ teapot with a cosy ❸ hotwater bottle (made of metal or clay)
暖和 nuǎnhuo ❶ warm; nice and warm: 这件皮大衣真～。This fur coat is very warm. /这儿～，到这儿来坐吧。Come and sit over here, where it's nice and warm. ❷ warm up: 你先烤烤火，～～。Warm yourself up by the fire first.
暖帘 nuǎnlián cotton-padded door curtain
暖流 nuǎnliú ❶〈气象〉warm current ❷ sudden surge of warmth: 他觉得一股～涌上心头。He felt a sudden surge of warmth.
暖炉 nuǎnlú 〈旧语〉stove for heating
暖瓶 nuǎnpíng thermos bottle, thermos flask
暖气 nuǎnqì ❶ heating; central heating: ～管道 heating pipe /～设施 heating system /水～ hot water heating /气～ steam heating /电～ electric heater /屋里有～。The room is centrally-heated. ❷ central heating equipment ❸ warm air or current
暖气片 nuǎnqìpiàn (popular term for 散热器) (heating) radiator
暖气团 nuǎnqìtuán 〈气象〉warm air mass
暖热 nuǎnrè 〈方言〉warm: 今天天气比昨天～。It's warmer today than yesterday.
暖融融 nuǎnróngróng nice and warm: 炭火驱走了寒气，整个房间～的。The entire room became nice and warm as the charcoal fire warded off the cold.
暖色 nuǎnsè 〈美术〉warm colour
暖室 nuǎnshì greenhouse; hothouse
暖寿 nuǎnshòu 〈旧语〉celebrations on the eve of one's birthday
暖水瓶 nuǎnshuǐpíng *also* "暖水壶" thermos flask; thermos bottle
暖袖 nuǎnxiù lengthened section of the sleeves of a padded coat to ward off cold in winter
暖洋洋 nuǎnyángyáng nice and warm: 外面风雪交加，屋里炉火正旺，～的。The room was warm with a coal fire burning briskly, while there was raging wind and snow outside. /太阳晒得他浑身～的。He was enjoying the genial warmth of the sun.

nüè

疟(瘧) nüè malaria
see also yào
疟涤平 nüèdípíng *also* "阿的平" ādìpíng 〈药学〉atabrine
疟疾 nüèji 〈医学〉malaria; ague: 恶性～ pernicious malaria
疟疾性心脏病 nüèjixìng xīnzàngbìng 〈医学〉cardipaludis; cardiopaludism
疟蚊 nüèwén malarial mosquito
疟原虫 nüèyuánchóng plasmodium; malarial parasite

N

虐 nüè ❶ cruel; ferocious; tyrannical:暴～ violence and cruelty /肆～ indulge in wanton massacre; wreak havoc ❷〈书面〉disaster; calamity:乱～并生 outbreak of disorder and calamities

虐待 nüèdài ill-treat; maltreat; tyrannize; abuse:受到～ be maltreated /～老人 ill-treat old people /～儿童 abuse children /性～ sexual abuse /～狂 sadism /被～狂 masochism

虐杀 nüèshā kill through maltreatment:～无辜 maltreat and kill the innocent

虐政 nüèzhèng tyrannical government; tyranny

nún

磨 nún 〈书面〉fragrance; aroma:温～ warm and fragrant

nuó

挪 nuó move; shift; change:把椅子～一～。Move the chair a little. /这个商店～地方了。The shop has moved away. /我在这儿工作十多年了,也该～～地儿了。I've been working here for over 10 years. It's time I changed my job.

挪蹭 nuóceng 〈口语〉walk slowly:他累得腿都抬不起来了,一步步地往家～。He was so exhausted that he could hardly move his legs on his way home.

挪动 nuódong move; shift:把床朝窗户那边～一下。Move the bed a little towards the window. /他谨慎地沿着墙根～。He moved cautiously along the wall. /他拖着伤腿,艰难地往前～着。Dragging his injured leg, he inched his way forward with great difficulty.

挪借 nuójiè get a short-term loan:他向亲友～一笔钱给儿子办喜事。He borrowed money from his relatives and friends for his son's wedding.

挪威 Nuówēi Norway:～语 Norwegian (language) /～人 Norwegian

挪窝儿 nuówōr 〈方言〉move (to another place):我一直站在这儿没～呀。I have been standing pat on this very spot. /有适合的住房我想挪挪窝儿。I'll move away if I can find proper housing. /他工作不安心,老想～。He is not happy with his job and keeps thinking about getting a transfer.

挪亚 Nuóyà *also* "诺亚" Nuòyà Noah, Hebrew patriarch who saved himself, his family, etc. from the deluge by following God's command and building a ship (i. e. Noah's Ark)

挪亚方舟 Nuóyà fāngzhōu Noah's Ark

挪移 nuóyí 〈方言〉❶ borrow money for a short time ❷ move; shift:老人艰难地～了几步。The old man moved a few steps with great difficulty.

挪用 nuóyòng ❶ divert (funds):教育经费不得～。Funds earmarked for education are not to be diverted to any other purpose. ❷ embezzle:～公款 embezzle or misappropriate public funds

娜 nuó *see* "婀娜" ēnuó;"袅娜" niǎonuó
see also nà

傩(儺) nuó exorcise

傩神 nuóshén god which drives away pestilence

傩舞 nuówǔ exorcising dance

傩戏 nuóxì ❶ one of the Chinese local operas popular at Guizhi and Qinyang in Anhui Province ❷ one of the Chinese local operas popular in the western hilly regions of Hubei Province

nuò

懦 nuò cowardly; faint-hearted:怯～ timid and chicken-hearted

懦夫 nuòfū coward; weakling; craven; weak-willed person:克服～懒汉思想 overcome the coward's and sluggard's way of thinking

懦弱 nuòruò cowardly; weak-kneed:～无能 weak-minded and incompetent /生性～ weak by nature

糯(稬、穤) nuò glutinous (cereal)

糯稻 nuòdào glutinous rice (in the husk)

糯米 nuòmǐ *also* "江米" jiāngmǐ (threshed and polished) glutinousrice

糯米糍粑 nuòmǐ cíbā cooked glutinous rice wrapped in lotus leaves

糯米酒 nuòmǐjiǔ glutinous rice wine

糯米汤团 nuòmǐ tāngtuán glutinous rice *tangtuan* (a kind of sweet dumpling made of glutinous rice flour)

糯米纸 nuòmǐzhǐ edible membrane made of starch, used to wrap candies

糯米粥 nuòmǐzhōu glutinous rice congee

诺 nuò ❶ promise; assent:一～千金 promise worth a thousand ounces of gold—a promise that can be counted on /慨～ promise generously ❷ yes; yeah:～～连声 keep on saying "yes"; eagerly agree /唯唯～～ always ready to agree with others without showing one's own judgement

诺贝尔 Nuòbèi'ěr Alfred Bernhard Nobel (1833-1896), Swedish chemist and inventor of dynamite

诺贝尔奖 Nuòbèi'ěrjiǎng Nobel Prize (established by the will of Alfred B. Nobel):诺贝尔文学奖 Nobel Prize for Literature

诺尔 nuò'ěr *also* "淖尔" nào'ěr Mongolian word for "lake"

诺曼底登陆 Nuòmàndǐ Dēnglù invasion of Normandy (June 1944)

诺苏 Nuòsū name used by the Yi people living in some parts of Sichuan, Guizhou, and Yunnan provinces to refer to themselves

诺亚 Nuòyà *see* "挪亚" Nuóyà

诺言 nuòyán promise; word:恪守～ fulfil one's promise; keep one's word /违背～ go back on one's word; break one's promise /他曾许下～要带我回老家。He promised to take me back to our home village.

喏[1] nuò 〈叹词〉〈方言〉*used to call attention to the matter or object one is mentioning*:～,你说的那本书不就在这儿吗? There! Isn't that the book you mentioned? /～,这样做才对。Look, this is the right way to do it.

喏[2] nuò 〈书面〉*see* "诺" nuò
see also rě

锘 nuò 〈化学〉nobelium (No)

搦 nuò 〈书面〉❶ hold in the hand; hold; grasp:～笔疾书 hold the brush and write swiftly ❷ provoke; challenge: *see* "～战"

搦管 nuòguǎn 〈书面〉take up the brush; wield the pen:老来多病,久不～。Being old and in bad health, I haven't taken up the brush for a long time.

搦战 nuòzhàn (often used in the early vernacular) challenge (sb.) to battle

O

O

ō

噢 ō 〈叹词〉*used to indicate understanding*：～，原来是你干的。So it was you (who did it).

ó

哦 ó 〈叹词〉*used to indicate doubt*：～，这件事我怎么没听说？Really? I haven't heard anything about it.
see also é；ò

ǒ

嚄 ǒ 〈叹词〉*used to indicate surprise*：～，他有两米高！What? He's two metres tall?
see also huō；huò

ò

哦 ò 〈叹词〉*used to indicate realization or understanding*：～，护照忘在家里了。Now, I've left my passport at home. *or* Ah, my passport has been left at home.
see also é；ó

ōu

区（區） Ōu a surname
see also qū

沤（漚） ōu water bubble：浮～ bubbles gathering on the surface of water
see also òu

讴（謳） ōu ❶ sing：*see* "～歌" ❷ folk songs；ballads：吴～ folk songs from the former State of Wu (covering the present Jiangsu Province and parts of Anhui and Zhejiang)

讴歌 ōugē 〈书面〉sing the praises of；eulogize：这些最平凡的清洁工人，难道不值得我们～吗？Don't you think these ordinary street cleaners deserve our praises?

讴颂 ōusòng 〈书面〉extol；sing the praises of；eulogize

讴吟 ōuyín 〈书面〉sing；chant：他们时而低声细语，时而高声～。They sometimes spoke softly and sometimes sang at the top of their voices. *or* Sometimes they talked in whispers and sometimes they sang lustily.

瓯[1]（甌） ōu 〈方言〉cup；bowl：茶～ tea cup /酒～ wine cup；drinking vessel

瓯[2]（甌） Ōu another name for Wenzhou（温州），a city in Zhejiang Province

瓯剧 ōujù Wenzhou opera, local opera popular in Wenzhou and northeastern Fujian Province

瓯绣 ōuxiù Wenzhou embroidery

瓯子 ōuzi 〈方言〉cup；bowl

鸥（鷗） ōu gull：海～ sea gull

欧[1]（歐） Ōu a surname

欧[2]（歐） Ōu (short for 欧洲) Europe：北～ northern Europe

欧[3] ōu (short for 欧姆)〈电学〉ohm

欧安会 Ōu'ānhuì (short for 欧洲安全和合作会议) Conference on Security and Cooperation in Europe (CSCE)

欧鲌 ōubó 〈动物〉bleak (*Alburnus alburnus*)

欧共体 Ōugòngtǐ (short for 欧洲共同体) European Community

欧化 ōuhuà Europeanize；Westernize：这篇文章用了不少～句式。This article is full of Europeanized sentence structures.

欧几里得 Ōujǐlǐdé Euclid (c.300 BC), Greek mathematician

欧几里得几何 Ōujǐlǐdé jǐhé 〈数学〉Euclidean geometry

欧拉定理 Ōulā dìnglǐ 〈数学〉Euler's theorem (after Leonhard Euler, 1707-1783, Swiss-born mathematician)

欧椋鸟 ōuliángniǎo starling

欧罗巴人种 Ōuluóbā Rénzhǒng Caucasoid race；white race

欧罗巴洲 Ōuluóbāzhōu continent of Europe；Europe

欧盟 Ōuméng European Union (EU)：～理事会 European Union Council /～外长会议 conference (*or* meeting) of EU foreign ministers

欧姆 Ōumǔ ❶ Georg Simon Ohm (1787-1854), German physicist：～定律 Ohm's law ❷〈电学〉ohm

欧姆表 ōumǔbiǎo ohmmeter

欧佩克 Ōupèikè OPEC (Organization of Petroleum Exporting Countries)

欧芹 ōuqín 〈植物〉parsley (*Petroselinum crispum*)

欧鸲 ōuqú 〈动物〉robin；redbreast

欧氏管 ōushìguǎn *also* "耳咽管" ěryānguǎn 〈生理〉Eustachian tube (after Bartolomeo Eustachio, 1520-1574, Italian anatomist)

欧体 Ōutǐ style of calligraphy represented by Ouyang Xun (557-641) of the Tang Dynasty

欧文 Ōuwén Washington Irving (1783-1859), Amerian writer

欧西 Ōuxī 〈旧语〉Europe：～各国 European countries

欧亚大陆 Ō-Yà dàlù Eurasia；Eurasian land mass

欧阳 Ōuyáng a surname

欧阳修 Ōuyáng Xiū Ouyang Xiu (1007-1072), writer and historian of the Northern Song Dynasty

欧阳询 Ōuyáng Xún Ouyang Xun (557-641), calligrapher of the early Tang Dynasty

欧元 ōuyuán euro, legal tender of the integrated European Community, beginning on 1 Jan.1999 with 11 countries：～区 euro area

欧洲 Ōuzhōu (short for 欧罗巴洲) Europe：～共同市场 European Common Market (Euromart) /～议会 European Parliament

欧洲电信标准化协会 Ōuzhōu Diànxìn Biāozhǔnhuà xiéhuì European Telecoms Standards Institute (ETSI)

欧洲共同体 Ōuzhōu Gòngtóngtǐ European Community (EC)

欧洲货币单位 Ōuzhōu huòbì dānwèi *also* "埃居" āijū European Currency Unit (ECU), accounting unit based on the average of several European currencies, replaced by euro

欧洲货币市场 Ōuzhōu huòbì shìchǎng Euromarket
欧洲经济共同体 Ōuzhōu Jīngjì Gòngtóngtǐ European Economic Community (EEC)
欧洲经济区 Ōuzhōu jīngjìqū European Economic Area (EEA)
欧洲美元 Ōuzhōu měiyuán Eurodollars, US dollars held by Europeans
欧洲市场 Ōuzhōu Shìchǎng Euromarket
欧洲通信卫星组织 Ōuzhōu Tōngxìn Wèixīng Zǔzhī European Telecommunications Satellite Organization (EUTELSAT)
欧洲投资银行 Ōuzhōu Tóuzī Yínháng European Investment Bank (EIB)
欧洲学 Ōuzhōuxué European studies
欧洲一体化 Ōuzhōu yītǐhuà integration of Europe
欧洲英镑 Ōuzhōu yīngbàng Eurosterling
欧洲债券 Ōuzhōu zhàiquàn Eurobond
欧洲自由贸易联盟 Ōuzhōu Zìyóu Màoyì Liánméng European Free Trade Association (EFTA)

嗽(嘔) ōu ❶〈叹词〉*used to indicate understanding or surprise*:～,我想起来了。Oh, yes, I've got it. /～,你们俩倒挺对脾气。Oh, you two are very much alike in temperament. ❷〈象声〉sound of crying:他急得～～地哭。He was so worried that he started blubbering.

殴(毆) ōu beat up; hit; strike:斗～ get into a fist fight (with sb.) /～伤 beat and injure; sustain an injury through a fist fight
殴打 ōudǎ beat up; assault:互相～ come to blows; exchange blows /遭人～ be beaten up
殴打罪 ōudǎzuì 〈法律〉offence of assault and battery
殴斗 ōudòu come to blows; have a fist fight
殴辱 ōurǔ insult and beat:他痛遭～。He was humiliated and beaten up.
殴杀 ōushā beat to death

ǒu

耦 ǒu ❶〈书面〉two people plough side by side ❷ *see* "偶²"
耦合 ǒuhé 〈物理〉coupling:～系数 coupling coefficient /机械～ mechanical coupling
耦合变压器 ǒuhé biànyāqì 〈电工〉coupling transformer
耦合电容器 ǒuhé diànróngqì 〈电工〉coupling capacitor; blacking capacitor; stopping capacitor
耦合器 ǒuhéqì 〈机械〉coupler
耦联晶体管 ǒulián jīngtǐguǎn 〈电子〉coupled transistor

藕(蕅) ǒu lotus root
藕断丝连 ǒuduàn-sīlián (usu. of separated lovers who cherish lingering affection for each other) the lotus root snaps but its fibres stay joined — still in each other's thoughts though apparently separated:虽说是离了婚,可他跟她还是～,不时地去看她。They are divorced but not entirely severed, and he calls on her from time to time.
藕粉 ǒufěn lotus root starch
藕荷 ǒuhé *also* "藕合" pale pinkish purple
藕灰 ǒuhuī pale pinkish grey
藕节儿 ǒujiér joints or sections of a lotus root, often used in traditional Chinese medicine
藕煤 ǒuméi 〈方言〉honeycomb briquette
藕色 ǒusè pale pinkish grey

偶¹ ǒu figure; image; idol (made of wood, clay or stone):木～ wooden figure; puppet /玩～ doll; puppet

偶² ǒu ❶ even (number); in pairs:无独有～。It is not a unique instance, but has its counterpart. ❷ mate; spouse:佳～ good spouse /丧～ lose one's wife (or husband)

偶³ ǒu by chance; by accident; occasionally:～见 see by accident; happen to witness /～闻 learn (*or* hear) by chance; happen to hear
偶氮基 ǒudànjī 〈化学〉azo group or radical:～胆红素〈生化〉azobilirubin /～磷〈农业〉azothoate
偶氮染料 ǒudàn rǎnliào 〈化学〉azo-dyes
偶电荷 ǒudiànhè 〈物理〉even-charge
偶尔 ǒu'ěr ❶ once in a while; occasionally:我～也去自由市场买东西。Occasionally I go shopping in the free market. /星期日他～出去看看电影。Once in a while he went to see a film on Sunday. ❷ accidental:一个～的机会使我们相识。We met each other by chance. /～之事,并非预谋。It was only accidental, not premeditated.
偶发 ǒufā accidental; fortuitous:～事件 accident
偶犯 ǒufàn ❶ casual offence ❷ casual offender
偶方 ǒufāng 〈中医〉prescription with ingredients even in number
偶感 ǒugǎn ❶ random thoughts (usually used as the title of an article) ❷ suddenly feel:～不适 feel out of sorts quite accidentally
偶函数 ǒuhánshù 〈数学〉even function
偶合 ǒuhé coincidence:见解～ coincidental agreement
偶合反应 ǒuhé fǎnyìng 〈化学〉coupled reaction
偶或 ǒuhuò occasionally; once in a while:～迟到一次,他就感到内心不安。He felt uneasy even if he was a little late by accident. /星期天我常在家,～也会到公园走走。I usually stay at home on Sundays, but occasionally I also take a walk in the park.
偶极天线 ǒují tiānxiàn dipole antenna
偶然 ǒurán ❶ accidental; fortuitous; chance:～事件 accidental occurrence /～相遇 chance meeting (*or* encounter)/事出～。It happened only accidentally. *or* It's a pure coincidence. /他犯这样的错误绝不是～的。It's by no means fortuitous that he made such a mistake. ❷ sometimes; ocassionally:他～也哼几句京戏。He would ocassionally hum a tune from some Beijing opera.
偶然论 ǒuránlùn 〈哲学〉fortuitism
偶然性 ǒuránxìng 〈哲学〉contingency; fortuity
偶人 ǒurén clay or wooden figure
偶数 ǒushù 〈数学〉even number:～齿数 even number of teeth
偶数页 ǒushùyè 〈印刷〉even page
偶蹄动物 ǒutí dòngwù artiodactyl; even-toed mammal:猪是～。The pig is an artiodactyl.
偶蹄目 ǒutímù (the order) *Artiodactyla*
偶像 ǒuxiàng idol; image:～崇拜 worship of idols; idolatry /～化 idolization /打倒～ iconoclasm
偶一 ǒuyī once in a long while; occasionally; by chance:～不慎,就会犯错误。You are liable to err if you happen to be less careful than you should.
偶一为之 ǒuyīwéizhī do sth. occasionally:这种杂文,我只是～,不能多写。I write this type of essay only by way of exception.
偶影 ǒuyǐng 〈书面〉seek company with one's own shadow (used to describe loneliness):终日～无伴 live an extremely lonely life
偶语 ǒuyǔ 〈书面〉(of two persons) talk in private
偶遇 ǒuyù meet by chance; bump into (sb.); run into (sb.) by accident
偶整数 ǒuzhěngshù 〈数学〉even-integral number

炬(熰) ǒu ❶ give off heavy smoke when not burning firewood efficiently:～了一屋子的烟 fill the entire room with smoke ❷ smoke and burn without flame:把这堆柴火～了。Burn off this pile of firewood. ❸ burn mugwort to produce smoke so as to keep flies and mosquitoes away:～蚊子 keep mosquitoes away by burning mugwort

呕(嘔) ǒu vomit; throw up; retch:作～ feel sick; feel like vomiting /干～ retch /令人作～ make one sick; bring on a feeling of nausea; revolting; nauseating
呕吐 ǒutù vomit; throw up:～物 vomit; vomitus
呕吐性毒气 ǒutùxìng dúqì 〈化工〉vomiting gas
呕心 ǒuxīn exert one's utmost:～之作 works embodying the author's utmost exertion /～教诲 teach sb. with all one's heart
呕心沥血 ǒuxīn-lìxuè take infinite pains; work one's heart out:我们的老师为培养下一代而～。Our teachers take great pains in nurturing the younger generation.
呕血 ǒuxuè 〈医学〉hematemesis; spitting blood

O

òu

沤(漚) òu soak; steep; macerate: ~粪 make compost

see also ōu

沤肥 òuféi ❶ make compost ❷ *also* "窖肥" jiàoféi wet compost; waterlogged compost

沤麻 òumá 〈纺织〉ret flax or hemp; retting; rotting

沤田 òutián low-lying land covered with water all the year round; water-logged land

沤子 òuzi 〈方言〉a kind of cosmetic in former times used to moisten the skin

怄(慪) òu 〈方言〉annoy; upset; irritate: 别~了,不要为这点小事~病了! Don't be annoyed and make yourself ill over a trifle like this! /我也没说什么,怎么就~她了? I don't know why she is annoyed. I didn't say anything. /你别拿这话来~他。Don't you say this to rub him the wrong way.

怄气 òuqì be sulky and difficult; be in a fit of the sulks: 这种事儿司空见惯,怄什么气呀! Such things are not unusual. Why are you so annoyed? /光~能解决问题吗? Would it help just being upset and sulky?

P

pā

啪 pā 〈象声〉*indicating the sound of clapping, striking, or shooting*：台下～～地鼓掌。The audience clapped loudly. /整夜都听到～～的枪声。The crack-crack of rifle fire was heard throughout the night.

啪嚓 pāchā 〈象声〉*indicating the sound of a clash or crash*：一摞碗掉在地上，～一声全碎了。The whole stack of bowls fell to the ground and broke with a crash.

啪嗒 pādā 〈象声〉*indicating the sound of something dropping or knocking against hard objects*：夜雨敲窗，～～响个不停。The rain beat pit-a-pat against the windows all night. /豆大的雨点～～落在地上。Large heavy drops of rain began pitter-pattering on the ground. /办公室里十几架打字机～～地响着。In the office a dozen or so typewriters were clattering away.

啪唧 pājī 〈象声〉*indicating the sound of an object dashing against or striking sth.*：小孩光着脚在路上～～地跑。Bare-footed, the little child ran pitter-patter on the road. /他说完话，～一声放下电话听筒。He banged the receiver on the hook when he finished.

啪啦 pāla 〈象声〉*indicating the dull sound of a cracked utensil*：这个砂锅敲起来～～的。This earthen pot sounds dull when you tap it.

葩 pā 〈书面〉flower：奇～异草 exotic flowers and rare plants / 艺术新～ new work of art; new genre of art

派 pā
see also pài

派司 pāsi (transliteration) ❶ pass; ID card：把～给门卫看了才能进去。You must show your pass to the guard before you can get in. ❷ get through; pass：他的英语考试已经～了。He has passed the exam in English.

趴 pā ❶ lie on one's stomach; lie prone：～在床上 lie prone on the bed /决不在困难面前～下。Never take a difficulty lying down. ❷ lean on; bend over：～在桌子上写字 bend over the desk writing

趴蛋 pādàn 〈方言〉break down; collapse; be unable to move：十辆卡车，只能开动四辆，其余的全～了。Only four trucks out of ten are still in good condition. The rest have all broken down. /幸亏他身子骨结实，不然早就累～了。He would have burned himself out long ago had he not been in excellent health.

趴伏 pāfú lie on one's stomach; crouch：那畜生～在地上，两眼直愣愣瞪着羊群。The beast crouched and glared at the flock of sheep.

趴虎 pāhǔ 〈方言〉fall flat on one's stomach

趴架 pājià collapse; fall apart：凉棚趴了架。The awning has collapsed.

趴窝 pāwō 〈方言〉❶ (of a hen) brood; hatch chickens; be sitting ❷ (of a female domestic animal) lie prone on the ground before giving birth to a young animal：那匹母马已经～了，呼呼地喘着粗气，快下驹了。The mare is lying on its side and panting. It is giving birth to a foal. ❸ be worn out：他累～了。He is exhausted from overwork. ❹ (of a machine or motor-vehicle) out of order; grounded：公司班车趴了窝，我们只好坐公共汽车回家了。The company's shuttle-bus is out of order, and we have to go back home by public bus. /经过抢修，～的卡车又开动起来了。After a rush-repair job, the broken-down truck got started again.

炬 pā 〈方言〉❶ (of food) mashed; pulpy：～红薯 baked sweet potato / 饭煮～了。The rice is overcooked (*or* cooked too soft). ❷ become soft：经你一说，他的态度～下来了。His attitude has softened after your persuasion.

炬耳朵 pā'ěrduo 〈方言〉❶ credulous person (especially referring to a man ready to believe his wife's words) ❷ henpecked husband

pá

扒 pá ❶ gather up or spread out as with a rake：～枯叶 rake up dead leaves /～土 rake the soil smooth ❷〈方言〉scratch：～痒 scratch an itch ❸ steal：我的钱包被小偷～走了。My wallet was stolen. *or* Someone pinched my wallet. ❹ stew; braise：～肉 stewed meat /～鸡 braised chicken /～鲍鱼龙须 braised abalone with asparagus /～鱼肚菜心 braised fish maw with cabbage heart
see also bā

扒带 pádài 〈口语〉reproduce an audiotape or videotape without permission

扒糕 págāo buckwheat pudding served cold with sweet sauce

扒灰 páhuī *also* "爬灰" páhuī 〈俗语〉scratch in the ashes — commit incest with one's daughter-in-law, etc.

扒拉 pála 〈方言〉rake rice into one's mouth with chopsticks (usu. in a hurried manner)：一碗饭他几口就～完了。He wolfed down a bowl of rice in just a few mouthfuls.
see also bāla

扒犁 páli *also* "爬犁" páli 〈方言〉sledge; sleigh

扒搂 pálou 〈方言〉gather up as with a rake：把玻璃碎片～在一块儿。Rake up the broken pieces of glass.

扒窃 páqiè pick people's pockets：他在车上～，一下子被人抓住了。He was caught red-handed when picking someone's pocket on a bus.

扒手 páshǒu *also* "搿手" páshǒu pickpocket：政治～ political swindler

搿 pá

搿手 páshǒu *see* "扒手" páshǒu

耙（钯） pá ❶ rake：九齿钉～ nine-toothed iron rake /粪～ manure rake ❷ make smooth with a rake; rake：把沙～平 rake the sand smooth /地已～好。The soil has been raked over. /把谷子～开晒晒。Rake (*or* Spread) out the grain for sunning.
see also bà

耙子 pázi rake

琶 pá *see* "琵琶" pípa

琶音 páyīn 〈音乐〉*arpeggio*

杷 pá *see* "枇杷" pípa

筢 pá bamboo rake

筢子 pázi bamboo rake

爬 pá ❶ crawl; creep：小孩会～了。The baby can crawl

about now. /那条蛇沿着墙～走了。The snake crept away along the wall. ❷ climb; clamber: ～树 climb a tree /～上山坡 climb up a slope /墙上～满藤蔓。The wall was covered with vines. ❸ sit up; stand up; get up: 他每天六点钟～起来去晨练。He gets up at 6:00 every morning to do some physical exercises. /在哪里跌倒,就在哪里～起来。Get up from where you slip and fall. *or* Correct your mistake where you make it.

爬虫 páchóng 〈动物〉(old name for 爬行动物) reptile: ～学 herpetology

爬得高,跌得重 pádegāo, diēdezhòng the higher the climb, the harder the fall

爬竿 págān 〈体育〉❶ pole-climbing ❷ climbing pole

爬高 págāo ❶ climb up: 蹬梯子～ climb up a ladder ❷ (of a plane) rise; climb; soar

爬高枝儿 pá gāozhīr 〈俗语〉climb a tall tree — climb high up in society: 他想通过结识权贵～。He tried to climb up the social ladder by associating with bigwigs.

爬格子 pá gézi 〈口语〉write on ruled paper; make a living by one's pen (often as a hack writer): 他拼命～,为的是养家糊口。He sweated blood at hack work to support his family.

爬灰 páhuī *also* "扒灰" páhuī scratching in the ashes — have illicit relations with one's daughter-in-law, etc.

爬景天 pájǐngtiān *also* "垂盆草" chuípéncǎo 〈植物〉stringy stonecrop (*Sedum sarmentosum*)

爬犁 páli *also* "扒犁" páli 〈方言〉sledge; sleigh

爬罗剔抉 páluó-tījué dig what is useful and reject what is useless; collect and select: 从这里可以看出来他～的功夫。This is an example showing how skilful he is at making the best selection from a wealth of materials.

爬坡 pápō 〈交通〉grade climbing: ～能力 gradeability

爬墙虎 páqiánghǔ *see* "爬山虎❶"

爬搔 pásāo scratch (with fingernails): 两手不停地在身上～ keep scratching one's body with both hands

爬山虎 páshānhǔ ❶〈植物〉Boston ivy ❷〈方言〉sedan chair or litter to carry a person up a mountain

爬升 páshēng ❶〈航空〉climb; soar; ascend; gain altitude: ～角 angle of climb ❷ rise; improve: 商品销售量～。Sales of the commodity are picking up.

爬升式起重机 páshēngshì qǐzhòngjī 〈建筑〉climbing crane

爬梳 páshū 〈书面〉arrange (hair) with a comb; tidy up: 情况复杂,一时难以～。The situation is complicated, and it is impossible to straighten it out right now.

爬水蝽 páshuǐchūn 〈动物〉creeping water bug

爬藤榕 páténgróng *also* "爬墙虎"〈植物〉Boston ivy

爬梯 pátī ❶ staircase ❷ vertical ladder

爬行 páxíng ❶ crawl; creep: 在一块布满苔藓的岩石上,成群的蚂蚁～着。Groups of ants are crawling on a piece of mossy rock. ❷ work or go slowly by following the convention or imitating others slavishly: ～思想 mentality of trailing behind others / 在一个充满竞争的社会里我们不能跟在人家后面～。In a competitive society we cannot trail behind others at a snail's pace.

爬行动物 páxíng dòngwù reptile

爬行通货膨胀 páxíng tōnghuò péngzhàng 〈经济〉creeping inflation

爬行主义 páxíngzhǔyì crawler's mentality

爬泳 páyǒng 〈体育〉crawl stroke; crawl

pà

怕

pà ❶ be afraid; fear; dread: ～挨骂 be afraid of getting a scolding /不～吃苦 fear no hardship /～热 be susceptible to heat; dread hot weather /～辣 shy away from spicy food (for fear of upsetting one's digestion, etc.) /～麻烦 hate to put oneself to any trouble /病人～着凉。The patient must not catch cold. /不～慢,就～站。Slow progress is better than a standstill. ❷ worried; anxious; concerned: 他们～我太累,所以让李大夫来帮助我。They are worried that I may be overworked and so have asked Dr. Li to help me. /我～他会出事。I fear he will get into trouble. ❸ I'm afraid (that); I suppose; probably: 下这么大的雨,我～他来不了了。I'm afraid he won't be able to come; it's raining so hard. /他这样说,～别有用意吧。By saying so he probably had something else in his mind.

怕敢 pàgǎn ❶〈方言〉I dare not: 我～向他再提此事。I dare not bring up the matter to him again. ❷ *also* "敢怕" (often used in the early vernacular) maybe; perhaps

怕惧 pàjù 〈方言〉fear; dread; be scared of: 他对这班流氓没有一点～。He did not have the slightest fear of these thugs.

怕老婆 pà lǎopo under the thumb of one's wife; henpecked: 村儿里数他最～。He is the most pitiable henpecked man in the village.

怕莫 pàmò 〈方言〉〈副词〉probably; perhaps: 这头猪～有两百斤重了。The pig probably weighs about 200 *jin*. /这个姑娘～是来找李先生的。The girl is perhaps looking for Mr. Li.

怕人 pàrén ❶ be afraid of people; be shy: 小猫～。The kitten is shy of people. ❷ terrible; dreadful; frightening: 天上黑云真～。The dark clouds are frightening. /夜里林子里阴森得～。The wood is dreadfully eerie at night. /山峰险得～。The cliff is terribly precipitous.

怕三怕四 pàsān-pàsì be full of misgivings; be apprehensive: 叫你去你就去,～干什么? Do as you are told. What's the use of worrying?

怕生 pàshēng (of a child) be afraid of strangers; be shy with strangers: 这孩子～,离不得他妈。This child is always clinging to his mother; he is very shy with strangers.

怕事 pàshì shy away from responsibility; be fearful of trouble; be overcautious: 此人胆小～,成不了大事。He is chicken-hearted and overcautious, and can get nowhere.

怕是 pàshì 〈方言〉probably; perhaps: 她头上包着一条白毛巾,～用来遮土的。She had a white towel tied round her head, probably to keep off dust. /我～哪个呢! 原来是你。I was wondering who it was; and so it's you!

怕死 pàsǐ fear death; be afraid to die: 贪生～ cling to life and be afraid of death

怕死鬼 pàsǐguǐ coward; poltroon

怕头 pàtou 〈方言〉something dreadful: 有啥～? What's there to be afraid of?

怕羞 pàxiū coy; shy; bashful: 都要上大学了,见了人还～! You are about to enter college and you are still so shy of strangers!

怕字当头 pàzì-dāngtóu put fear before everything else: 他是～,别叫他当代表了。Don't ask him to act as a representative for us, for he dreads to make a single move.

帕[1]

pà kerchief; handkerchief: 手～ handkerchief / 头～ kerchief

帕[2]

pà (short for 帕斯卡)〈物理〉pascal

帕金森定律 Pàjīnsēn dìnglǜ 〈经济〉Parkinson's law

帕金森氏病 pàjīnsēnshìbìng Parkinson's disease; shaking palsy; paralysis agitans

帕拉马里博 Pàlāmǎlǐbó Paramaribo, capital of Suriname

帕劳 Pàláo Palau, a group of islands in the western Pacific Ocean, part of a US trust territory from 1947 and internally self-governing since 1980: ～语 Palauan language

帕里 Pàlǐ Pagri, highest town in the world situated in the south of China's Tibet Autonomous Region

帕米尔高原 Pàmǐ'ěr Gāoyuán The Pamirs

帕皮提 Pàpítí Papeete, capital of French Polynesia, situated on the northwest coast of Tahiti

帕斯卡 pàsīkǎ ❶ (Pàsīkǎ) Blaise Pascal (1623-1662), French mathematician, physicist and religious philosopher: ～原理 Pascal's principle ❷〈物理〉pascal, a unit of intensity of pressure

帕台农神庙 Pàtáinóng Shénmiào Parthenon, the temple of Athene Parthenos built in the Acropolis of Athens in 447-432 BC by Pericles

帕瓦罗蒂 Pàwǎluódì Luciano Pavarotti (1935-), Italian operatic tenor

帕子 pàzi handkerchief; kerchief

杷

pà 〈书面〉*see* "帕[1]" pà

pāi

拍

pāi ❶ pound; pat; clap; beat: ～手 clap one's hands /～球 bounce a ball /～翅膀 flap wings /～～某人肩膀 pat sb. on the

shoulder /～掉身上的雪 beat the snow off one's coat /～案大怒 pound the table in great anger /一个巴掌～不响。One palm can't clap — it takes two to make a deal, quarrel, etc. ❷ (of waves) lash; strike; beat:惊涛～岸 mighty waves beating (*or* lashing at) the shore ❸ bat; racket:乒乓球～儿 table-tennis bat (*or* paddle) /网球～儿 tennis racket /苍蝇～儿 flyswatter ❹〈音乐〉beat; time:合～ in time; in step; in harmony /二分之一～ one-half time /四分之三～ three-quarter time /四分之四～ four-four time ❺ take (a photo); shoot (a film):～照 take a picture /～记录片 shoot (*or* make) a documentary /《红楼梦》已经被～成电影和电视系列片。*A Dream of Red Mansions* has been made into a film and a TV series. ❻ send (a telegram, etc.):～电报 send a telegram ❼〈口语〉flatter; fawn on:他就会吹吹～～,一心想向上爬。He is a regular social climber and certainly knows how to boast about himself and flatter others.

拍案 pāi'àn strike the table (in anger, surprise, admiration, wonder, etc.):～称快 strike the table and shout "bravo!"; slap the table in delight / ～称奇 (in reading) pound the table and exclaim with admiration

拍案而起 pāi'àn'érqǐ smite the table and rise to one's feet in indignation: ～,投入抗争 rise in indignation and plunge into the struggle

拍案叫绝 pāi'àn-jiàojué thump the table and cry out with admiration:这个办法亏他想得出,真叫人～! What a clever idea he has come up with! Everybody is struck with admiration.

拍巴掌 pāi bāzhang clap; applause

拍板 pāibǎn ❶ beat time with clappers:你唱,我来～。You sing, and I'll beat time for you. ❷ rap the gavel to clinch a business deal ❸〈比喻〉call the shots; make a final decision:～定案 give the final verdict; make a final decision /这事他拍不了板。He doesn't have the final say in the matter. ❹ *also* "鼓板" gǔbǎn clappers

拍板成交 pāibǎn-chéngjiāo conclude a deal; clinch a deal

拍打 pāida ❶ pat; beat:他脱掉上衣,～衣上的尘土。He took off his coat to pat off the dust. /浪花～着船舷。The waves were lapping against the sides of the boat. ❷ flap:鸟儿～着翅膀向远方飞去。The bird flapped its wings and flew away.

拍档 pāidàng 〈方言〉❶ cooperate; collaborate:这两位演员在剧中～主演。The two actors play the two leading characters in the drama. ❷ partner; collaborator; cooperator:最佳～ best partner

拍发 pāifā send (a telegram, etc.); dispatch: ～电报 send a telegram /这条消息要立即向总社～。This news must be dispatched to the head office at once.

拍抚 pāifǔ pat and stroke lightly:母亲～着小孩,哄他入睡。The mother patted and caressed her child, trying to lull him to sleep.

拍号 pāihào 〈音乐〉time signature

拍花 pāihuā 〈旧语〉kidnap children by using narcotics:～子 *also* "～的" person who kidnaps children by using knockout drops

拍击 pāijī (of waves) dash against; lash; lap:河水～着船舷。The water gently lapped against the sides of the boat. /巨浪～着礁石。Big waves lashed (*or* dashed, *or* crashed) against the reef.

拍节器 pāijiéqì 〈音乐〉metronome

拍马 pāimǎ flatter; fawn; soft-soap: 逢迎～ toady to sb.

拍马屁 pāi mǎpì 〈口语〉lick (sb.'s) boots; soft-soap; toady to; fawn on: 他最瞧不起～的人。He has great contempt for sycophants. /你拍他的马屁有什么用! It's no use trying to soft-soap him.

拍卖 pāimài ❶ auction: ～家具 furniture auction /交付～ be on the auction block; come under the hammer ❷ selling off goods at reduced prices; sale:大～ bargain sale /积压商品全部～了。The overstocked goods were all sold (off) at reduced prices.

拍卖行 pāimàiháng auction house

拍卖人 pāimàirén *also* "拍卖商" auctioneer

拍卖市场 pāimài shìchǎng auction market

拍摄 pāishè take (a photo); shoot (a film): ～一部电视片 shoot a telefilm /～全景 shoot a full view /～外景〈影视〉go on location

拍手 pāishǒu clap one's hands; applaud: ～叫好 clap one's hands and shout "bravo!"

拍手称快 pāishǒu-chēngkuài clap and cheer (with great satisfaction)

拍拖 pāituō 〈方言〉courting:公园里有几对～的青年男女。There were several courting young couples in the park.

拍戏 pāixì film a play; shoot a scene: 拍宴会这场戏 shoot the banquet scene /～可是个苦差事。Filming is a hard job. /他～的时候拒绝会客。He refused to see visitors when shooting a scene. /我一定尽全力拍好戏。I'll do my best to make a success of the filming project.

拍胸脯 pāi xiōngpú 〈口语〉slap one's chest as a gesture of promise or guarantee:这件事你拍过胸脯,一定要负责到底。Since you have promised to take care of this matter, you must see it through. /老板～了,你的计划准能成功。Now that the boss has given his blessing to the plan, you are sure to succeed.

拍掌 pāizhǎng *see* "拍巴掌"

拍照 pāizhào take a picture; have a picture taken: ～之前,她着意地打扮了一番。She carefully made herself up before posing for a photograph.

拍纸簿 pāizhǐbù writing pad; memo pad

拍子 pāizi ❶ bat; racket:乒乓球～ ping-pong bat (*or* paddle) /羽毛球～ badminton racket /网球～ tennis racket ❷〈音乐〉beat; time:打～ beat time

P

pái

棑 pái *see* "排[2]" pái

排[1] pái ❶ arrange in order; line up: ～名单 arrange the order of names on a list /～坐次 arrange the seating order; make seating arrangements (as at a meeting or dinner) /～名次 list the names in proper order (according to examination results, etc.) /稿子已付～。The manuscript has been sent to the press. /目录正在编～。A catalogue (of books, etc.) is being made. ❷ line; row:前～ front row /后～ back row /前～议员 (UK) front bencher /他坐在第二～。He sat in the second row. /游行队伍五人一列并～前进。The procession marched five abreast. ❸〈军事〉platoon:一个连通常有三个～。A company usually consists of three platoons. ❹〈量词〉row; line:一～树 a row of trees /两～牙齿 two rows of teeth /一～子弹 a clip of cartridges ❺ rehearse: ～节目 rehearse a performance programme /彩～ dress rehearsal /剧团正在～一个新剧目。The company is rehearsing a new play.

排[2] pái raft; floating bridge:竹～ bamboo raft /木～ log (*or* timber) raft /大桥正在改建,河上临时搭起木～供行人往来。As the old bridge was being reconstructed, a makeshift wooden bridge was set up for pedestrians.

排[3] pái ❶ exclude; expel; reject; drain: ～出一股废气 let out (*or* emit) a puff of exhaust /把水～尽 drain up the water /～犹运动 anti-Semitic campaign /力～众议 reject all prevailing opinions; override all objections ❷ push: ～门而出 throw open the door and walk out

排[4] pái (transliteration) pie:苹果～ apple pie
see also pǎi

排奡 pái'ào 〈书面〉(of writing) vigorous and powerful:其文纵横～。He writes in a free and vigorous style.

排班 páibān ❶ arrange the order of shifts, runs, or classes and grades ❷ queue up

排版 páibǎn set type; compose: 程控～ programmed composition /机器～ machine composition /照相～ photo composition; phototypesetting /计算机～ computer typesetting /自动～ automatic typesetting (*or* composition) /今天的晚报正在～。Today's evening paper is being typeset (*or* composed).

排刨 páibào 〈机械〉gang planing

排比 páibǐ 〈修辞〉parallelism: ～句 parallel sentences

排笔 páibǐ broad brush made of a row of pen-shaped brushes (used for whitewashing, picture colouring or house-painting)

排便困难 páibiàn kùnnan 〈医学〉dyschesia

排便习惯 páibiàn xíguàn bowel evacuation habit

排便异常 páibiàn yìcháng 〈医学〉abnormal defecation

排摈 páibìn 〈书面〉exclude; squeeze out; push out:相与～ be mutually exclusive; each tries to push the other out

排布 páibù arrangement; distribution:原子的核外电子的～是有规律的。The distribution of electrons outside the atomic nucleus is regular.

排叉儿 páichàr deep-fried and crisp flat piece of wheat flour dough

排杈儿 páichàr ❶ *also* "排岔儿" a kind of low and narrow partition of a room ❷ *see* "排叉儿"

排场 páichang ❶ extravagance; ostentation; grand style: ～大 do things in a grand style / 讲～ have a penchant for ostentation; go in for the grandiose ❷ extravagant; ostentatious: 他的喜事办得过于～了。His wedding was too much a show of extravagance. ❸ 〈方言〉 honourable; respectable; dignified: 集体婚礼又～、又省钱。A collective wedding is both dignified and economical.

排斥 páichì repel; exclude; reject; shut out: ～不同的艺术风格流派 reject those styles and schools of art different from one's own / 不能把他～在入选者名单之外。We should not exclude him from the list of successful candidates. / 同种电荷互相～。Two like electric charges repel each other. / 我们不～艺术上的夸张。We do not oppose artistic exaggeration.

排斥异己 páichì-yìjǐ discriminate against anybody who does not belong to one's coterie; push aside people of different views; reject those who disagree; tolerate no dissenting voices

排除 páichú ❶ get rid of; remove; exclude; eliminate: ～障碍 remove obstacles / ～故障 fix a breakdown / ～干扰 eliminate interference / ～了病情恶化的可能性 rule out the possibility of the worsening of the patient's condition ❷ excrete; discharge; clean out: ～体内毒素 discharge toxins from the body; purge the body of toxins / 把不良分子从这个组织中～出去。Rid the organization of undesirable elements.

排除万难 páichú-wànnán overcome all obstacles; surmount every difficulty: 我们一定能够～,到达胜利的彼岸。We can certainly ride out all difficulties and emerge victorious.

排挡 páidǎng gear (of a car, tractor, etc.): 自动～ automatic gear / 手动～ manual gear

排档 páidàng 〈方言〉 street or market stalls: 服装～ clothing stalls / 吃大～ eat in a street restaurant

排灯节 Páidēngjié Diwali, a Hindu festival with illumination, held between September and November in honour of the goddess of wealth

排队 páiduì form a line; line up; queue up: 你去～,给我占个位置。Queue up and save a space for me, won't you? / 必须在售票处前～购票。One should line up for tickets at the booking office. / 问题成堆,我们得先排排队,然后逐个解决。There are so many problems that we'll have to sort them out in order of importance and urgency and then tackle them one by one.

排筏 páifá timber or bamboo raft

排放 páifàng ❶ arrange in order: 供桌上～着香炉、蜡烛和供品。Laid on the altar are an incense burner, some candlesticks, and offerings. ❷ discharge; release (waste gas, waste water and residue, etc.): ～污水 discharge waste water / 含强放射性物质的废水是禁止向海域～的。It is forbidden to discharge liquid wastes with intensely radioactive substance into the sea. ❸ (of animal) ovulate; discharge semen

排粪 páifèn defecation; bowel movement

排风扇 páifēngshàn ventilating fan; ventilator

排骨 páigǔ spareribs: 红烧～ pork ribs braised in soy sauce / ～汤 pork rib soup / ～面 noodles with spareribs

排鼓 páigǔ percussion instrument composed of five or six drums of different sizes

排灌 páiguàn irrigation and drainage: 机械～ irrigation and drainage by machinery

排灌网 páiguànwǎng irrigation and drainage network

排灌站 páiguànzhàn irrigation and drainage pumping station

排行 páiháng seniority among siblings: ～大 seniority among siblings of an extended family (derived from the same grandfather or great-grandfather) / 他～老二。He is the second child of the family.

排行榜 páihángbǎng ranking; (best-seller) list: 流行歌曲～ best pop song list / 登上畅销书～ appear on the best-seller list / ～上第五名 be the fifth on the list

排号 páihào ❶ 〈口语〉 get a number according to one's place in a queue ❷ 〈方言〉 stand in a queue; form a line; queue or line up

排洪 páihóng discharge floodwater; drain off floodwater; drain the flooded area

排华 pái-Huá discriminate against or persecute overseas Chinese or ethnic Chinese: ～骚乱 anti-Chinese riot

排击 páijī push out and attack: 屡遭～ suffer repeated blows / 大肆～ single people out and make unbridled attacks on them

排挤 páijǐ push out; exclude; discriminate against: 受～ be discriminated against / 拉拢一些人, ～一些人 try to win over some and push out others

排检 páijiǎn arrange and refer to: ～法 method of arrangement and retrieval

排解 páijiě ❶ mediate; reconcile: ～纠纷 mediate disputes; reconcile quarrels ❷ dispel; assuage; relieve (sorrow, loneliness, boredom, worry, etc.): 难以～的忧愁 sorrow that is hard to get rid of / 找老朋友聊聊, ～心中的烦闷。Go and have a good chat with some of your old friends and you'll feel much relieved. *or* Get everything off your chest with some old friends and you'll feel better.

排锯 páijù 〈机械〉 gang saw

排空 páikōng ❶ shoot up into the air; soar aloft: 我军炮火～而过。Volleys of gunfire of our troops flew overhead. ❷ discharge waste gas into the air ❸ empty a space of sth.: 把锅炉中的水～,再进行修理。Empty the boiler before fixing it.

排涝 páilào drain waterlogged fields

排雷 páiléi 〈军事〉 removal of mines; mine clearance

排立 páilì stand in row: 群众～在马路的两旁。Crowds lined the streets.

排练 páiliàn rehearse: 那部舞剧还须多次～。That dance drama still needs a lot of rehearsal.

排列 páiliè ❶ put in order; rank: 按次序～ line up in proper order / 按姓氏笔画～ be listed according to the number of strokes in one's surname / 按音序～ be arranged in phonetic order / 商店里货物～得整整齐齐。All the goods in the store are neatly arranged. ❷ 〈数学〉 permutation: ～表 permutation table / ～符号 permutation symbol / ～数 number of permutations

排律 páilǜ long poem in regulated verse, usu. pentasyllabic

排卵 páiluǎn 〈生理〉 ovulate: ～期 period of ovulation

排门 páimén 〈方言〉 door planks of a store, to be removed when business starts and put up when business is over

排名 páimíng sequence of names; ranking: 他在初赛中～暂列第三。He came third in the preliminary.

排难解纷 páinàn-jiěfēn clear up misunderstandings and mediate disputes: 宋大妈是个热心肠的人,总为邻居们～。Grandma Song is such a kind soul that she always tries to pour oil on troubled waters whenever disputes arise among her neighbours.

排泥泵 páiníbèng sludge pump

排尿 páiniào urinate; micturate

排尿反射 páiniào fǎnshè 〈医学〉 urinary reflex

排尿困难 páiniào kùnnan 〈医学〉 dysuria

排尿频繁 páiniào pínfán frequent urination

排尿疼痛 páiniào téngtòng 〈医学〉 urodynia

排脓 páinóng 〈医学〉 apocenosis

排偶 pái'ǒu 〈语言〉 antithetic parallelism: ～句 antithetic couplet

排炮 páipào ❶ remove a dead shell; remove a dud ❷ (artillery) salvo; volley of guns ❸ (in construction) chain explosion

排气 páiqì 〈机械〉 exhaust

排气泵 páiqìbèng 〈机械〉 air pump; off-gas pump

排气管 páiqìguǎn exhaust pipe

排气扇 páiqìshàn discharge fan

排遣 páiqiǎn dispel; divert; relieve: 无法～的悲哀沉重地压在他心里。He was weighed down with unrelieved grief.

排枪 páiqiāng volley of rifle fire

排球 páiqiú volleyball: 沙滩～ beach volleyball

排沙简金 páishā-jiǎnjīn *also* "披沙拣金" pīshā-jiǎnjīn sort out the fine gold from the sand — extract the essentials from a mass of material

排山倒海 páishān-dǎohǎi topple the mountains and overturn the seas — great in momentum and irresistible: 以～之势 with the force of a landslide and the power of a tidal wave; with the momentum of an avalanche / 改革浪潮～,任何人也阻挡不了。With its sweeping momentum, the reform is irresistible.

排射 páishè fire a volley of guns or cannons; cannonade

排笙 páishēng 〈乐器〉 reed pipe wind instrument with a key board

排式冲床 páishì chòngchuáng 〈机械〉 gang punch

排式压床 páishì yāchuáng 〈机械〉 gang press

排水 páishuǐ drain off water: ～工程 drainage works

排水泵 páishuǐbèng drainage pump

排水沟 páishuǐgōu drainage ditch; gutter

排水干渠 páishuǐ gànqú 〈水利〉main drain
排水管 páishuǐguǎn drain pipe; escape pipe
排水量 páishuǐliàng ❶ displacement:～二万吨的轮船 ship with a displacement of 20,000 tons ❷ discharge capacity (of a canal, spillway, etc.):这条运河建成后的～约为500秒立方公尺。When completed, the canal will be able to discharge 500 cubic metres of water per second.
排他性 páitāxìng exclusiveness:～集团 exclusive bloc /～条约 exclusive treaty /～区域合作 closed regional cooperation /有人说爱情具有～。Some people say that love is exclusive.
排闼 páità 〈书面〉push the door open:登楼远眺,秀丽的景色～而来。A stretch of enchanting scenery came into full view when I ascended the tower and looked far into the distance.
排闼直入 páità-zhírù enter by pushing the door open; force one's way into a room
排坛 páitán volleyball circles:～健将 ace volleyball player
排调 páitiáo 〈书面〉mock; deride
排头 páitóu person at the head of a procession or line; file leader:向～看齐 dress to (*or* keep level with) the file leader /在经济改革中要做～ take the lead (*or* be a pace-setter) in carrying out economic reforms
排头兵 páitóubīng ❶ file leader ❷〈比喻〉one who takes the lead; pace-setter:群众夸他是生产上的～。People speak of him as pacemaker (*or* pace-setter) in production.
排外 páiwài antiforeign; xenophobic:盲目～ be blindly xenophobic; blindly oppose everything foreign /～风潮 antiforeign agitation /某些国家的～情绪很强烈。Antiforeign sentiment is strong in some countries.
排外心理 páiwài xīnlǐ xenophobia
排外主义 páiwàizhǔyì exclusivism; antiforeignism
排湾族 Páiwānzú Paiwan nationality, one of the minor ethnic communities in Taiwan Province
排尾 páiwěi last person in a row; (person at the) end of a procession or line:站在～ stand at the end of a file
排污管 páiwūguǎn cesspipe; sewer pipe; drain
排铣 páixǐ 〈机械〉gang milling:～机 gang mill
排戏 páixì rehearse a play:今晚要～。We'll have a rehearsal of the play this evening.
排险 páixiǎn remove a danger; defuse a dangerous situation
排陷 páixiàn reject and frame sb.; push sb. aside and make false charges against him:～忠良的奸臣 treacherous courtier who brings false charges against loyal officials in an attempt to eliminate them
排箫 páixiāo panpipe
排协 páixié (short for 排球协会) Volleyball Association (of the People's Republic of China)
排泄 páixiè ❶ drain:把雨水尽快～出去 drain out rain water as soon as possible /～不畅 drainage difficulty ❷ excrete; void:皮肤的重要功能之一是～汗液。One of the important functions of the skin is to excrete sweat.
排泄器官 páixiè qìguān excretory organ
排泄失禁 páixiè shījìn 〈医学〉acathexia
排泄物 páixièwù 〈生理〉excrement; excreta; excretion
排序 páixù (arrange a) sequence; order
排揎 páixuan 〈方言〉scold; dress down:她当着一群人的面～起她妹妹来。She started to scold her sister in the presence of a group of people.
排衙 páiyá 〈旧语〉ceremony for all the officials of a government agency to line up and salute a superior
排烟 páiyān exhaust fume:～设备 fume tractor
排演 páiyǎn rehearse:～小品 rehearse a skit /团长认为这个戏很好,决定立即～。The manager of the troupe thought that the play was very good and decided on its immediate rehearsal.
排椅 páiyǐ chairs fixed in rows (as in cinemas, theatres and auditoriums)
排印 páiyìn typesetting and printing:准备～ ready for the press
排忧解难 páiyōu-jiěnàn mediate disputes; pour oil on troubled waters:想尽办法为群众～。Try every means possible to solve problems for the people and alleviate their sufferings.
排运 páiyùn rafting timber down the river; rafting
排长 páizhǎng 〈军事〉platoon leader
排针 páizhēn needle extraction
排中律 páizhōnglǜ 〈逻辑〉law of excluded middle
排钟 páizhōng 〈音乐〉chimes; tubular bells
排种 páizhǒng 〈农业〉feed:～孔 feed outlet
排置 páizhì arrange in order:过廊里～着二十多盆菊花。More than twenty pots of chrysanthemums were put in a row along the corridor.
排字 páizì composing; typesetting:～车间 composing room /～工人 typesetter; compositor /～机 composing machine; typesetter /～架 composing frame /～手托 composing stick /～印刷机 gang printer

俳

pái ❶〈旧语〉variety show or farce ❷〈书面〉humorous; funny; comical: see "～谐"
俳句 páijù 〈文学〉haiku, a form of Japanese poetry with each verse consisting of seventeen syllables i.e. five in both the first and third lines and seven in the middle one
俳谐 páixié 〈书面〉humorous:～文〈旧语〉metaphorical, humorous, or satirical writing
俳优 páiyōu 〈旧语〉comedian in a variety show

徘

pái
徘徊 páihuái ❶ pace up and down; walk to and fro:她在小径上独自～。She paced up and down the path alone. /生产～不前。Production has remained stagnant. ❷ hesitate; waver; oscillate:持～观望态度 adopt a wait-and-see attitude /在两种意见之间～ waver between two views /他碰到一点小问题也会犹豫～。He will hesitate even over petty problems. ❸ move up and down; fluctuate:彩电销量在百万台上下～。The sales volume of colour TVs fluctuated around 1million sets.

牌

pái ❶ board:广告～ billboard /标语～ placard ❷ plate; sign; tablet:门～儿 house number plate; door plate /车～儿 number plate; license plate /招～ shop sign; signboard /存车～ parking check (for bicycle etc.) /指路～ signpost ❸ brand; make; trademark:名～ well-known brand; brand name /老～货 goods of an old brand /冒～ fake /杂～ unknown brand /这表是什么～的? What make is this watch? ❹ cards, dominoes, etc.:打～ play cards, mah-jong, or any such game /麻将～ mah-jong pieces /扑克～ playing cards /王～ trump card /打完一盘～ finish a hand ❺ title (of a *ci* or *qu* tune):词～ title of a *ci* tune /曲～ title of a *qu* tune
牌匾 páibiǎn board (fixed to a wall or the lintel of a door) with characters carved or written on it; plaque
牌赌 páidǔ gamble with playing cards, mah-jong, etc.
牌额 pái'é horizontal inscribed board
牌坊 páifāng memorial arch:贞节～ chastity arch (built as a memorial to a chaste woman in feudal times) /功德～ achievement arch (as memorial to a magistrate, etc.)
牌号 páihào ❶ name of a shop; shop sign ❷ trademark
牌价 páijià ❶ list price; posted price:按～打九折出售 (goods) sold at a discount of 10% off the posted ❷ market quotation:开盘～ opening price; opening rate /收盘～ closing price; closing rate /外汇～ foreign exchange quotations
牌九 páijiǔ *paijiu*, a game of Chinese dominoes:推～ play *paijiu*
牌局 páijú gambling game at dominoes, cards or mah-jong; bridge party or mah-jong party
牌楼 páilou ❶ decorated archway:西四～ *Xisi Pailou* (a former ceremonial gate in Beijing) ❷ temporary ceremonial gateway:鲜花扎的～ gateway decorated with flowers (put up for a welcoming ceremony)
牌示 páishì 〈旧语〉official bulletin or notice (put up on a notice-board)
牌头 páitóu 〈方言〉powerful connection that one relies on for support:他自以为～很硬。He thinks that he can count on powerful backing. /他靠着谁的～? Whose patronage is he relying on?
牌位 páiwèi memorial tablet (for the deceased, deities, or other objects of worship)
牌照 páizhào licence; licence plate; licence tag; licence certificate:汽车～ automobile licence plate /自行车～ bicycle licence tag /个体经营要亮出～。A self-employed businessman must show his or her licence in the market.
牌照税 páizhàoshuì licence tax
牌子 páizi ❶ board:这里广告～随处可见。You can see ad boards

everywhere around here. ❷ plate; sign; tablet:存车～ parking check (for a bicycle, etc.) ❸ brand; make; trademark:这种～的毛线很受欢迎。Knitting wool of this brand is very popular. ❹ title of a *ci* or *qu* tune:京剧有许多曲～。Beijing opera boasts many tune titles.

牌子曲 páiziqǔ a kind of *quyi*, consisting in the singing of stories to the tune of various ballads (each of which has a title)

箄(簰) pái raft; floating bridge

箪 pái see "箄" pái

see also bēi

pǎi

排 pǎi 〈方言〉stretch with a (shoe) last:把这双鞋～一～。Stretch this pair of shoes with lasts.

see also pái

排子车 pǎizichē *also* "大板车" dàbǎnchē large handcart

排子门 pǎizimén 〈方言〉makeshift door or gate made of sorghum stalks or twigs

迫(廹) pǎi

see also pò

迫击炮 pǎijīpào (trench) mortar:～弹 mortar shell

pài

湃 pài see "滂湃" pāngpài;"澎湃" pēngpài

派 pài ❶ group of people sharing identical views, style or tastes; sect; faction:党～ political parties and groups /宗～ faction /教～ sect /宁马～ *or* "红教" Ningmapa (Red Sect, of Tibetan Buddhism) /噶举～ *or* "白教" Kargyupa (White Sect) /萨迦～ *or* "花教" Sagyapa (Flower Sect) /格鲁～ *or* "黄教" Gelugpa (Yellow Sect) /流～ school (of theories, art, etc.) /正统～ traditionalist; orthodox /少壮～ young turks /乐观～ optimists /老～人 old-fashioned person; conservative type ❷ style; bearing; manner and air:气～不凡 of elegant bearing ❸〈方言〉stylish; graceful; handsome:这人的长相够～的。He is quite handsome. /他要的就是这份儿～。Great style is what he is after. ❹〈量词〉(a) *used for parties, schools, factions, etc.*:这个问题两～学者之间有争论。This issue is controversial among scholars of the two schools. (b) *used with words indicating scenery, atmosphere, sound, voice, language, etc., and preceded by the word* 一:一～欣欣向荣的气象 a thriving atmosphere/一～胡言 a pack of nonsense /好一～春光! What beautiful spring scenery! ❺〈书面〉branch of a river:这河流至此处分为两～。The river bifurcates (*or* divides, *or* branches) at this place. ❻ send; dispatch; assign; appoint:～活 assign jobs /～留学生 send students to study abroad /～老周担任组长。Lao Zhou was appointed group leader. /把小陈～给你当助手。We'll assign Xiao Chen to be your assistant. ❼ apportion; assign:～粮～款 levy grain and money ❽ find fault; censure:～别人不是 shift the blame onto sb. else

see also pā

派别 pàibié group; school; clique; faction:政治～ political groups (*or* factions) /学术上的不同～ different academic schools /～斗争 factional strife /这种宗教很早就分成两个～。This religion split into two sects at an early stage of its development.

派不是 pài bùshi put the blame on (sb.); take to task:现在又来派我的不是了。So it's my turn to take the blame, isn't it?

派差 pàichāi send (sb.) on public errands

派出机构 pàichū jīgòu agency; representative office

派出所 pàichūsuǒ local police station; police substation; precinct station

派定 pàidìng ❶ appoint; designate; assign:～谈判代表 appoint a representative for negotiation ❷ feel certain; believe:不少读者～作者就是这本小说的主人公原型。Many readers feel certain that the author himself is the prototype of the novel's hero.

派对 pàiduì 〈方言〉(transliteration) party:生日～ birthday party

派饭 pàifàn arranged meal — meal prepared by a farmer's family for an official, student, etc., who has been assigned to eat in his home:吃～ eat with a designated farmer's family

派赴 pàifù send; dispatch:他被～国外进行科学研究。He was sent abroad to do scientific research.

派购 pàigòu (of the state) prescribe purchases (of farm produce); set quotas for state purchase at a fixed price; procure by quota

派活 pàihuó assign work (usu. of a manual nature):组长已经给我～了。The group leader has assigned me a job. /师傅,今天派我什么活? Master, what's my work for today?

派款 pàikuǎn 〈旧语〉impose levies of money; fix the amount of money contribution

派拉蒙影片公司 Pàilāméng Yǐngpiàn Gōngsī (US) Paramount Pictures Corporation

派力司 pàilìsī 〈纺织〉palace

派令 pàilìng order of appointment

派遣 pàiqiǎn send; dispatch:～大使 accredit an ambassador (to a foreign country) /～代表团出国访问 send a delegation on a visit to foreign countries

派遣国 pàiqiǎnguó sending state; accrediting state

派儿 pàir 〈方言〉airs; hauteur:多大的～! What airs he puts on!

派生 pàishēng derive:意识是从物质～出来的。Consciousness is derived from matter. /从一门科学～出许多分支学科。One discipline may evolve into many branches of learning.

派生部门 pàishēng bùmén derivative department

派生词 pàishēngcí *also* "合成词" héchéngcí 〈语言〉derivative

派生物 pàishēngwù derivative; derivation; outgrowth

派生语言 pàishēng yǔyán derivative language:法语是拉丁语的～。French is a derivative of Latin.

派生元素 pàishēng yuánsù 〈化学〉daughter element

派生中子 pàishēng zhōngzǐ 〈物理〉daughter neutron

派势 pàishi manner; bearing

派头 pàitóu bearing; manner:有～ have an impressive (*or* elegant) air /讲～ have a penchant for impressive manners /首长～ carriage of a senior official /军人～ soldierly bearing /官儿不大,～不小。He is not an important official, but he puts on such an air of importance.

派系 pàixì faction (within a political party, etc.); clique:～之争 factional strife /自成～ form one's own clique

派销 pàixiāo promote the sale of goods or bonds by mandatory or compulsory means

派性 pàixìng factionalism:闹～ engage in factionalist activities /消除～ eliminate factionalism

派用场 pài yòngchǎng put to use; turn to account:这些材料终于派上了用场。These materials have at last been put to good use.

派仗 pàizhàng factional fight:打～ be locked in factional fight

派住地 pàizhùdì place of one's appointment

派驻 pàizhù ❶ post; station:在沿海地区～重兵 station large numbers of troops (*or* mass huge forces) along the coast /～该国首都的外国记者 foreign journalists resident in the capital of that country /他已被～美国工作。He has been given an overseas posting to the United States. /各省、直辖市、自治区在北京都设有～机构。All the provinces, municipalities under the central government, and autonomous regions have their representative offices in Beijing. ❷〈外交〉accredit:～外国 be accredited to a foreign country

蒎 pài 〈化学〉pinane

哌 pài

哌嗪 pàiqín 〈化学〉piperazine

pān

攀 pān ❶ climb; clamber:～大树 climb up a big tree /～山越岭 trek over mountains and ridges ❷ cling; hold; grasp:他～住我的肩膀不放。He held fast to my shoulder. ❸ seek connections in high places:～亲戚 claim kinship (with people in high places) /～关系 seek powerful connections /我们实在高～不上您啊! We certainly do not aspire to associate with a person of your importance. ❹ in-

volve; implicate:乱咬胡～ make wild charges to implicate others

攀比 pānbǐ compete (with each other socially):互相～ keep up with the Joneses; beggar thy neighbour

攀缠 pānchán get entangled; be in a tangle:满山坡～着各种各样的热带植物。The whole hillside was covered with all kinds of intertwining tropical plants.

攀扯 pānchě involve; implicate:这个案件～了许多人,要格外慎重处理。This case has involved many people and has to be handled with extreme caution. /你怕他把与你有关的事～出来吗? Are you afraid he would give away things that might get you into trouble?

攀登 pāndēng climb; clamber; scale:～顶峰 climb up to the summit /在陡峭的山路上～ climb up a steep mountain path /～科学高峰 scale the heights of science

攀登架 pāndēngjià jungle gym (a playground apparatus for children to climb on)

攀附 pānfù ❶ (of a plant) climb; cling to:藤蔓～树木。Vines climb up trees. ❷ attach oneself to or seek connection with (sb. powerful):～权贵 attach oneself to powerful people

攀钢 Pāngāng (short for 攀枝花钢铁公司) Panzhihua Iron and Steel Company (in southwest China)

攀高 pāngāo ❶ climb up; scale a height ❷〈方言〉try to forge relationships with people of higher social status:不敢～。I dare not aspire to this honour.

攀高枝儿 pān gāozhīr make friends or forge kinship with people of higher social status

攀供 pāngòng groundlessly implicate others in one's confession

攀话 pānhuà 〈方言〉accost; engage in small talk:他很随和,谁都喜欢跟他～儿。He was so amiable that everyone would like to hobnob with him.

攀交 pānjiāo associate with people of higher social status:他想～的都是些专家和名人。It is scholars and public figures that he would like to associate with.

攀龙附凤 pānlóng-fùfèng *also*"附凤攀龙" attach oneself to dragons and phoenixes — play up to people of power and influence

攀鲈 pānlú 〈动物〉climbing perch; walking fish (*Anabas testudineus*)

攀爬 pānpá hold on to sth. and climb up; clamber; scale:战士们抠着石缝,艰难地向上～。The soldiers inched upward, hanging on to the crevices of the rocks.

攀配 pānpèi try to establish ties with some prominent family through marriage:他家是大干部,我家是大老粗,怎么～得起? He is from a senior cadre's family while I come from a peasant background. How can I aspire to such a match?

攀亲 pānqīn ❶ claim kinship ❷〈方言〉arrange a match; be betrothed to

攀亲道故 pānqīn-dàogù claim ties of blood or friendship

攀禽 pānqín bird with sharp claws and beak (such as a woodpecker), good at hanging on a tree; scansorial bird

攀雀 pānquè 〈动物〉penduline tit

攀绕 pānrào twine upwards; spiral

攀谈 pāntán *also*"扳谈" pāntán chat; chitchat:我和他天南海北地～起来。We started to chat about everything under the sun.

攀诬 pānwū implicate and frame:～好人 implicate the innocent

攀岩 pānyán 〈体育〉rock-climbing

攀缘 pānyuán *also*"攀援" ❶ climb; clamber:～峭壁,登上山顶 climb up a cliff and reach the mountaintop ❷ seek the patronage of influential people or the powers that be:他想当公司的经理,便～董事长。He tried to get the job of manager of the firm by grovelling to the chairman of the board.

攀缘草本 pānyuán cǎoběn scandent herb; climbing herb

攀缘灌木 pānyuán guànmù scandent shrub; climbing shrub

攀缘茎 pānyuánjīng 〈植物〉climbing stem

攀缘式起重机 pānyuánshì qǐzhòngjī 〈机械〉climbing crane

攀缘藤本 pānyuán téngběn climbing vine

攀缘植物 pānyuán zhíwù climbing plant; scandent plant

攀辕卧辙 pānyuán-wòzhé 〈旧语〉people gather to urge an honest official to stay on at the end of his tenure

攀越 pānyuè climb up and cross over:～险峰 scale a perilous peak

攀摘 pānzhāi pick sth. from a high place:～果实 pick fruit /他一心要～数学皇冠上的明珠。He made a determined effort to pluck the pearl off the crown of mathematics. *or* He was determined to win a particularly high honour in the study of mathematics.

攀折 pānzhé pull down and break off (twigs, etc.):请勿～花木。Please don't pluck the flowers or break off the branches.

攀枝花 pānzhīhuā ❶ *also*"木棉" mùmián silk cotton; kapok ❷ (Pānzhīhuā) city and industrial centre in southwest China

扳

pān *see*"攀" pān

see also bān

扳谈 pāntán *see*"攀谈" pāntán

番

pān *used in*"番禺" Pānyú (place in Guangdong)

see also fān

潘

Pān a surname

潘多拉 Pānduōlā Pandora, the first woman created for mankind in Greek mythology:～的盒子 Pandora's box, a process that once activated will generate many unmanageable problems

潘生丁 pānshēngdīng 〈药学〉persantine

潘天寿 Pān Tiānshòu Pan Tianshou (formerly translated as P'an T'ien-shou, 1897-1971), Chinese brush painter and calligrapher

潘兴导弹 pānxīng dǎodàn 〈军事〉(US) Pershing missile

pán

胖

pán 〈书面〉easy and carefree; fit and happy:心广体～。A carefree mind engenders health and happiness.

see also pàng

蹒(蹣)

pán

蹒跚 pánshān *also*"盘跚" pánshān stagger; falter; limp:步履～ hobble along /从室内～地走出一个人来。Somebody staggered out of the room.

蟠

pán coil; curl:～伏 lie curled up; coil

蟠结 pánjié coil; twine

蟠踞 pánjù *also*"蟠据" be entrenched; illegally or forcibly occupy

蟠曲 pánqū *also*"盘曲" pánqū wind; twist:～的山径 winding mountain path

蟠桃 pántáo ❶ flat peach ❷ legendary peach grown in the land of immortals; peach of longevity:～会 meeting of immortals at which peaches of longevity are offered /～宫 Hall of Immortal Peach (in Beijing)

盘(盤)

pán ❶〈古语〉a kind of basin (for washing one's face, etc.) ❷ tray; plate; dish:托～ tray /茶～儿 tea tray /青花～ blue and white plate ❸ sth. shaped like or used as a tray, plate, etc.:磨～ grindstone /算～ abacus /棋～ chessboard /轮～ wheel /罗～ compass ❹ market quotation; current price:开～ open quotations /收～ close quotations ❺ coil; wind; twist:～山公路 winding mountain highway /把头发～上 coil one's hair (on the top of one's head) /上山十八～ eighteen hairpin bends on the way up a mountain ❻ build with bricks:～炕 build a *kang* /～灶 build a brick cooking range ❼ check; examine; investigate; interrogate:一月～一次账 check accounts once a month /～根究底 ask about something in great detail; try to get to the bottom of a matter ❽ transfer; sell:招～ put up (one's shop or company, etc.) for sale /受～ take over; buy over /～店 sell a shop along with its stock, furniture and equipment ❾ move; transfer:把这些家具～到二楼去。Move the furniture to the first floor. ❿〈体育〉game; match:一～棋 a game of chess /乒乓球比赛有的一～三局,有的一～为五局。In a table-tennis tournament, one match may consist of three or five sets. ⓫〈量词〉:一～菜 a dish of food; a course; a dish /一～磁带 a tape ⓬ (Pán) a surname

盘剥 pánbō practise usury; exploit:重利～ lend money at a usurious rate of interest; exploit by usury /贪得无厌地～穷人 exploit the poor with an insatiable greed

盘驳 pánbó interrogate and refute

盘查 pánchá interrogate and check; question and examine:仔细～ closely interrogate and carefully examine /～可疑的过路行人 question all suspicious passers-by /十字路口处处设卡,～严密。Checkpoints are set up at every crossing to make a rigorous search.

盘察 pánchá interrogate and examine

盘缠 pánchán wind; coil:把缆绳～在树桩上。Wind the cable round the tree stump.
盘缠 pánchan 〈口语〉money needed for a journey; travel money; travelling expenses:缺少～ can hardly afford the travelling expenses /出门要多带～。Be sure to take enough money with you when you are going on a journey.
盘秤 pánchèng steelyard with a pan
盘川 pánchuān 〈方言〉money for travel expenses:借～ borrow some money to pay (*or* meet) the travel expenses
盘存 páncún take inventory; take stock:年底～ take inventory at the end of a year
盘存成本 páncún chéngběn cost of inventory
盘存管理 páncún guǎnlǐ inventory control; inventory management
盘错 páncuò 〈书面〉intertwining; intricate; complicated and difficult:～古树 ancient tree that has twisted roots and gnarled branches /此案头绪～。This is an intricate case.
盘道 pándào winding path; bends in a road
盘底 pándǐ interrogate closely; cross-examine
盘点 pándiǎn check; make an inventory of:～存货 take stock /本店今日～,暂停营业。Business is suspended today for stock-taking.
盘店 pándiàn sell one's bankrupt business (usu. a shop):买卖连续亏本,他只好把店盘给了别人。After repeated losses in business for several years running, he had to sell off his shop.
盘费 pánfei 〈口语〉money needed for a journey; travelling expenses
盘杠子 pán gàngzi 〈口语〉exercise on the horizontal-bar (and sometimes also the parallel bars):他～身手矫健。He stays nimble and agile when exercising on the bar.
盘根 pángēn get to the root of sth.
盘根错节 pángēn-cuòjié with twisted roots and gnarled branches — complicated and difficult to deal with; deep-rooted and hard to get rid of:～的老榕树 old banyan with twisted roots and gnarled branches /在这个偏僻的山村,宗法势力仍然～。Patriachal clan forces are deep-rooted in this out-of-the-way mountain village.
盘根问底 pángēn-wèndǐ *also* "盘根究底" get to the bottom of a matter:他遇事总爱～。He likes to find out the whys and wherefores of everything.
盘亘 pángèn 〈书面〉(of mountains) interlocked with each other:山岭～交错 interlocking mountain ranges
盘庚 Pángēng Pangeng, 18th ruler of the Shang Dynasty who reformed the court politics and moved the capital from Yan (奄 in present western Shandong) to Yin (殷 in present northern Henan), beginning a new dynastic period when the dynasty is known as Yin-Shang (殷商)
盘古 Pángǔ Pan Gu, creator of the universe in Chinese mythology:自从～开天辟地以来 since Pan Gu separated heaven and earth; since the beginning of the world; from time immemorial
盘管 pánguǎn 〈机械〉coil (pipe)
盘管锅炉 pánguǎn guōlú coil boiler
盘管机 pánguǎnjī coiler
盘管冷凝器 pánguǎn lěngníngqì coil condenser
盘桓 pánhuán ❶〈书面〉pace up and down; linger:他在童年时住过的老宅前～多时,不忍离去。Lingering in front of the house of his childhood, he just could not tear himself away. /我想在这里～几天,与老朋友聚一聚。I would like to stay here for a couple of days and see my old friends. ❷ twist; coil; wind:曲折～的枝条 twisted and coiling branches /她爱梳～髻。She likes to wear her hair coiled up. /缕缕炊烟～在村子上空。Wisps of smoke curled up from the village chimneys. ❸ wind round and round:这个想法一直～脑际。The idea has been lingering in my mind.
盘簧 pánhuáng 〈机械〉coil spring
盘货 pánhuò take an inventory of stock on hand; take stock
盘获 pánhuò seize (booty) or capture (bandits) as a result of what is learnt from interrogation
盘缴 pánjiǎo 〈方言〉❶ running or operating expenditure:他家里人口多,～大。He has a big family and incurs large running expenses. ❷ travelling expenses
盘诘 pánjié 〈书面〉cross-examine; question:宫廷门卫对来访者仔细～了一番。The palace guard questioned the visitors closely.
盘结 pánjié coil around:寺庙里古木参天,粗藤～。In the temple ancient trees soared towards the skies, with thick vines coiling round them.
盘究 pánjiū persistent inquiry; repeated questioning
盘踞 pánjù *also* "盘据" illegally or forcibly occupy; be entrenched:过去,有一股土匪～在这深山老林里。A gang of bandits used to entrench themselves in these densely wooded mountains. /一种悲观情绪～在她的脑海。She fell into a pessimistic mood. *or* Her mind was filled with pessimism.
盘考 pánkǎo conduct interrogation and inquiry
盘空 pánkōng circle or whirl in the air
盘口瓶 pánkǒupíng vase with a dish-shaped mouth
盘库 pánkù make an inventory of goods in a warehouse:这家商店是星期日～。The shop regularly makes an inventory of the goods on Sundays.
盘量 pánliang calculate; figure
盘络 pánluò intertwine; coil:杂木丛生,古藤～ be overgrown with shrubs and coiling old vines
盘马弯弓 pánmǎ-wāngōng ride round and bend one's bow as if ready to shoot — assume an imposing posture but take no action
盘磨机 pánmójī 〈机械〉disc grinder or mill
盘尼西林 pánníxīlín *also* "青霉素" qīngméisù penicillin
盘弄 pánnòng play with; fiddle with:孩子拿着个玩具来回～。The little kid kept playing with the toy.
盘盘 pánpán 〈书面〉zigzag; meander:沿着～的山路寻找山中寺庙 zigzag up a mountain path in search of a temple
盘曲 pánqū *also* "蟠曲" pánqū 〈书面〉wind; twist:山路～ meandering mountain path
盘儿菜 pánrcài ready-to-cook dish of meat, vegetables, etc. (sold at the food market)
盘绕 pánrào twine; coil; wind:枯藤～的峭岩 rock cliff covered with withered vines /大串问题在他心上～。A number of questions kept cropping up in his mind.
盘山 pánshān wind up a mountain:～公路 winding mountain road
盘跚 pánshān *also* "蹒跚" pánshān hobble; limp; stagger
盘石 pánshí *also* "磐石" pánshí huge rock:坚如～ firm as a monolith
盘式压碎机 pánshì yāsuìjī 〈矿业〉disc crusher
盘算 pánsuan consider; calculate; figure; plan:～下一步怎么办 ponder over what to do next; think over what is to be done /他有他的～,你就不要勉强他了。He has his own considerations, so don't ask him to do anything against his will. /盖房子之前,老人想好好儿～～。The old man wanted to make a careful calculation before building the house.
盘梯 pántī winding or spiral staircase
盘条 pántiáo 〈冶金〉wire rod
盘头 pántóu ❶ a kind of woman's hair-style or hairdo (with hair coiled in various styles either on the top or at the back of the head) ❷〈旧语〉turban
盘腿 pántuǐ cross one's legs:～坐在床上 sit on the bed with crossed legs
盘陀 pántuó *also* "盘陁"〈书面〉❶ (of rocks or boulders) rugged:谷底乱石～。The bottom of the valley was covered with rocks and boulders. ❷ winding; twisting; circular:庄前有一段～路。There is a winding path in front of the village.
盘陁 pántuó *see* "盘陀"
盘问 pánwèn question; interrogate; cross-examine:再三～ question repeatedly /～些情况 get some information through interrogation /～事情的经过 make careful inquiries about how the incident happened
盘膝 pánxī 〈书面〉cross one's legs:～而坐 sit with one's legs crossed; sit crosslegged
盘香 pánxiāng coil incense
盘旋 pánxuán ❶ spiral; circle; wheel:飞机在机场上空～。The plane circled above the airport. /苍鹰在云中～出没。The hawks wheeled in and out of the clouds. /山路曲折,游人～而上。Tourists made their way up the hill along a zigzag path. ❷ pace up and down; linger:他在幽静的小路上～。He strolled leisurely along the quiet path. /他在公园里～了许久。He lingered in the park for quite some time. ❸ think over; turn over; ponder:这件事在他脑子里～了很久。It's something he has been mulling over for a long time.
盘牙 pányá 〈方言〉molar
盘羊 pányáng 〈动物〉argali:加拿大～ bighorn sheep
盘运 pányùn move; carry; transport

盘账 pánzhàng check accounts
盘折 pánzhé (of a mountain path) meandering; zigzagging; winding:上山的路～难行。The path up the mountain is as treacherous as it is tortuous.
盘子 pánzi ❶ tray; plate; dish ❷ price; market quotation
盘坐 pánzuò sit cross-legged:老大娘～在炕上,又唠叨开了。Sitting cross-legged on the *kang*, granny started babbling again.

般 pán 〈书面〉joy; delight:～乐 pleasure; enjoyment
see also bān; bō

鞶(❷鞶) pán 〈书面〉❶ belt; band; ribbon ❷ small bag

槃 pán *see* "盘❶❷❺" pán
槃根错节 pángēn-cuòjié *see* "盘根错节" pángēn-cuòjié

磐 pán 〈书面〉huge rock
磐石 pánshí *also* "盘石" pánshí huge rock; monolith
磐石之安 pánshízhī'ān *also* "磐石之固" solid as a rock; of great stability

爿 pán 〈方言〉❶ thin broad piece of split bamboo or wood:竹～ split bamboo /柴～ chopped firewood ❷〈量词〉*used of land*:一～田 a plot; a piece of land ❸〈量词〉*used of shops, factories, etc.*:一～店 a shop /一～厂 a factory

pàn

泮 pàn ❶〈书面〉thaw; melt; dissolve:湖冰未～。The ice on the lake has not started to melt yet. ❷ official school in ancient times:入～ (in the Qing Dynasty) pass the civil service examination at the county level (for *xiucai*) ❸ (Pàn) a surname
泮宫 pàngōng school in ancient times

判 pàn ❶ distinguish; differentiate; separate: *see* "～别"; "～明" ❷ obviously (different): *see* "～然"; "～若两人" ❸ judge; decide; grade:评～ pass judgement (on sth. or sb.) /裁～ judge; referee; umpire /～作业 grade students' homework /～卷 mark (examination) papers ❹ sentence; condemn:～了三年徒刑 be sentenced to 3 years' imprisonment /被～为无罪 be declared not guilty
判案 pàn'àn 〈法律〉decide a case; make a judgement
判辨 pànbiàn distinguish; differentiate; tell apart
判别 pànbié distinguish; differentiate; tell apart:～是非 distinguish between right and wrong
判别式 pànbiéshì 〈数学〉discriminant
判处 pànchǔ sentence; condemn:～徒刑 sentence sb. to penal servitude
判词 pàncí ❶〈法律〉written court decision; court verdict ❷ judgement; conclusion:导师对他的论文下了颇有创见的～。The supervisor's comment on his dissertation is that it contains some original ideas.
判定 pàndìng ❶ judge; decide; determine:不能根据一两件小事就～一个人品质。One cannot judge a person by a couple of trifles. ❷〈机械〉decision:～机构 decision mechanism /～元件 decision element; decision gate
判读 pàndú 〈信息〉interpretation; reading:卫星照片～ interpretation of satellite photos /～仪 interpretoscope
判牍 pàndú 〈书面〉document relating to the decision of a law case
判断 pànduàn ❶〈逻辑〉judgement ❷ judge; decide; determine:～出土文物的年代 determine the age of an unearthed relic /～方位 take (*or* get) one's bearings /～风向 find out in which direction the wind is blowing /～错了 bet on the wrong horse /你下这样的～,恐怕为时太早。I am afraid it is still too early for you to draw such a conclusion. ❸〈书面〉〈法律〉pass judgement
判断词 pànduàncí 〈语言〉defining word, i.e. 是, used to form a compound predicate with a noun or an adjective, which defines the identity or quality of the subject (e.g. 他是大哥。He is my eldest brother. 雪是白的。Snow is white.), or the group it belongs to (e.g. 他是中国人。He is a Chinese.)
判断力 pànduànlì ability to make correct judgement; judgement:我完全相信你的～。I have every confidence in your judgement.
判断性抽样 pànduànxìng chōuyàng judgement sampling
判罚 pànfá (in a football or basketball match) decision by a referee to penalize an offender; penalize:违反本规定者将予～。Violaters of the regulations will be penalized accordingly.
判分 pànfēn give a mark; mark; score:由评委～。Judges will give them marks.
判官 pànguān ❶ (in the Tang and Song dynasties) official assisting a local magistrate, esp., in trying cases ❷ judge in the nether world who keeps an account of living people's merits and wrongdoings and who decides how long they should live
判据 pànjù ❶ evidence ❷〈物理〉criterion
判决 pànjué ❶ court decision; judgment:～无罪 pronounce sb. not guilty /法院依法～如下… The court decides according to law that... ❷ decision; judgement:运动员要服从裁判的～。Sportsmen should respect the decisions of the umpire.
判决书 pànjuéshū court decision; written judgement; court verdict
判例 pànlì legal or judicial precedent:国际法～ cases in international law
判例法 pànlìfǎ 〈法律〉case law
判袂 pànmèi 〈书面〉bid farewell; part:金陵～,瞬已数月。Since we parted at Nanjing, several months have passed in the twinkling of an eye.
判明 pànmíng distinguish; ascertain:～真伪 ascertain whether sth. is genuine /～情况 find out the facts /～责任 decide who should be held responsible
判然 pànrán be obviously or clearly different:两人性格～不同。The two of them are markedly different in character.
判若鸿沟 pànruòhónggōu as different as if separated by a yawning gulf; completely different; poles apart
判若两人 pànruòliǎngrén be no longer one's old self; become a totally different person:何以如今～? How come he is not at all his former self?
判若云泥 pànruòyúnní *also* "判若天渊" as far removed as heaven is from earth; poles apart:两种精神境界之高下可谓～。The two moral (*or* mental) outlooks are literally poles apart.
判事 pànshì justice of the Japanese judicial system
判刑 pànxíng pass or impose a sentence; sentence:这批罪犯已经～。Sentences were already handed down on these criminals.
判罪 pànzuì declare guilty; convict:量刑～ pass judgement and mete out punishment

袢 pàn ❶ *see* "襻" pàn ❷ *see* "袷袢" qiāpàn

畔 pàn ❶ side; bank:河～ river bank; riverside /湖～ shore of a lake; lakeside /桥～ beside a bridge ❷ border (of a field); edge:田～小憩 take a short break at the edge of the field

叛 pàn betray; revolt; rebel:反～ revolt; rebel /众～亲离 be spurned by the people and deserted by one's followers; be totally isolated
叛变 pànbiàn betray (one's country, party, etc.); turn traitor or renegade; defect:他宁死也不～。He would rather die than turn traitor. /从掌握的证据来看,这个人一定是～了。Judging by the evidence we have, the man must have defected to the enemy.
叛兵 pànbīng mutinous soldiers; insurgent troops; rebels
叛党 pàndǎng betray one's party (esp. the Communist Party); turn traitor to one's party; become a turncoat or renegade
叛匪 pànfěi rebel:一股流窜的～ band of roving rebels
叛国 pànguó betray one's country; commit treason:～外逃 flee the country after committing treason /～案 case of treason
叛国罪 pànguózuì high treason; treason
叛军 pànjūn rebel army; insurgent or mutinous troops
叛离 pànlí desert; defect from:部下～之后,他处境十分孤立。He was totally isolated after his followers had deserted him.
叛乱 pànluàn rebellion; insurrection; revolt:武装～ armed rebellion /平息～ suppress (*or* quell, *or* put down) a rebellion /～分子 rebel; insurgent; insurrectionist
叛卖 pànmài betray; be treacherous; sell out:～民族利益 sell out

P

national interests

叛逆 pànnì ❶ rebel against; revolt against: ～行为 act of rebellion /～活动 rebellious activities ❷ rebel: 塑造了一个封建礼教的～形象 portray (*or* characterize) a rebel against feudal ethics

叛逃 pàntáo defect; desert: ～者 defector; deserter

叛徒 pàntú traitor; renegade; turncoat

叛亡 pànwáng 〈书面〉 *see* "叛逃"

叛嫌 pànxián suspected renegade; renegade suspect; suspected traitor; traitor suspect

襻 pàn ❶ loop for fastening a button: 纽～儿 button loop ❷ sth. shaped like a button loop or used for a similar purpose: 鞋～儿 shoe strap /提篮～儿 handle of a basket ❸ fasten (as with a rope, string, etc.); tie: ～上几针 darn (*or* mend) with a few stitches

鋬 pàn handle of a utensil

拚 pàn

拚命 pànmìng 〈方言〉 go all out in total disregard of danger to one's life; defy death

拚弃 pànqì 〈书面〉 discard; throw overboard; abandon

盼 pàn ❶ hope for; yearn for; long for; expect: ～亲人 long for one's dear ones /～新年 look forward to the New Year /这些年来左～右～，终于把你给～回来了。So you've finally come back after all these years of our painful waiting. /～复。〈套语〉 I await your reply eagerly. /～君果断行事，切勿迟延。I hope you will act decisively and brook no delay. /亟～大驾光临。〈套语〉 It is earnestly hoped that you will honour us with your gracious presence. ❷ look: 左顾右～ look (*or* glance) right and left; look round

盼顾 pàngù look around: 引领～ stretch out (*or* crane) one's neck and look left and right

盼念 pànniàn long for; look forward to; miss: 我们日夜在～着你! You are constantly in our thoughts. *or* We miss you day and night.

盼头 pàntou sth. to hope for; sth. to look forward to; good prospects: 没有什么～了。There is practically nothing to look forward to. /祥林嫂失去了儿子，生活就没有了～。Life no longer held out any hope for Sister Xianglin after she lost her son.

盼望 pànwàng eagerly await; hope for; long for; look forward to: ～早日与某人见面 hope to meet sb. as soon as possible /我们～你能回来过年。We are all expecting you to come back and spend the Spring Festival with us.

pāng

滂 pāng 〈书面〉 ❶ (of water) overflowing ❷ gushing; rushing

滂湃 pāngpài (of water) roaring and rushing: ～的浪涛 roaring waves

滂沛 pāngpèi 〈书面〉 ❶ (of water) roaring and rushing: 江涛～ surging waves ❷ (of rain) pouring; torrential; pelting: 大雨～。The rain is pouring down. ❸ with great momentum; powerful: 文辞～。The language is forceful.

滂田 pāngtián 〈方言〉 paddy field with a thick layer of mud

滂沱 pāngtuó torrential: 涕泣～ tears streaming down one's cheeks /～大雨铺天盖地而来。The torrential rain poured down blotting out the sky and the land.

膀(胮) pāng swell: ～肿 swollen; bloated /腿～了 have got swollen legs

see also bǎng; bàng; páng

雱(雰、霶) pāng 〈书面〉 ❶ snow thick and fast: 雨雪其～。It snowed heavily. ❷ *see* "滂" pāng

乓 pāng 〈象声〉 bang: 暖水瓶～地一声摔碎了。The thermos smashed with a bang. /门～地一声关上了。The door slammed shut. /窗没关，被风刮得～～响。The unshut window was banging in the wind.

páng

旁 páng ❶ side: 目不～视 look straight ahead /两～都是高楼。There are tall buildings on both sides. ❷ else; other: 今天我还有～的事。I have other things to attend to today. ❸ lateral radical of a Chinese character (e.g. 亻, 讠, etc.) ❹ extensive; wide-ranging: ～求俊彦 look for talents far and near

旁白 pángbái (in a play) aside

旁边 pángbiān side: 马路～停着许多小汽车。Many cars were packed by the road side. /邮局～有一家小餐馆。Near the post office is a small restaurant.

旁薄 pángbó *also* "旁礴" *see* "磅礴" pángbó

旁侧 pángcè side

旁岔儿 pángchàr 〈方言〉 digression (from the subject): 你扯到～上去了。You're straying from the point.

旁出 pángchū branch out from the side: 有条～小道可通湖边。There is a side path leading to the lake.

旁顾 pánggù attend to other matters: 无暇～ have no time to attend to other affairs

旁观 pángguān look on; be an onlooker: 袖手～ look on with folded arms /冷眼～ look on with a critical eye; stand aloof /这场斗争不容我们～。We simply cannot afford to stand on the sidelines in this trial of strength.

旁观者 pángguānzhě onlooker; bystander; spectator

旁观者清 pángguānzhěqīng the spectator is often a better judge of the game than the player; the onlooker sees the game best: ～，当局者迷。The spectator sees most of the game while the player sees no further than his nose.

旁皇 pánghuáng *also* "彷徨" pánghuáng hesitate; vacillate

旁及 pángjí take up or be keen on (other things apart from one's main interest): 他的兴趣很广泛，除研究音乐外，还～文学和哲学。He has a wide range of interests. Apart from majoring in music he has an interest in literature and philosophy.

旁路 pánglù ❶ *also* "旁道" side road: 大街上在游行，咱们走～去吧。The main street is crowded with people holding a demonstration. We'd better take the side road. ❷ *also* "分流" fēnliú 〈电学〉 bypass: ～电容 bypass capacitor (*or* condenser)

旁落 pángluò (of power) slip into other people's hands: 大权～。Power has passed into others' hands.

旁门 pángmén side door (gate); side entrance

旁门左道 pángmén-zuǒdào *also* "左道旁门" ❶ heretical sect; heterodox school ❷ heresy; heterodoxy

旁敲侧击 pángqiāo-cèjī beat about the bush; attack by innuendo; make oblique references or thrusts: 他总爱～地说些讽刺话。He often makes ironical remarks in a roundabout way. *or* He often speaks ironically with oblique insinuations.

旁切圆 pángqiēyuán 〈数学〉 escribed circle (of a triangle)

旁人 pángrén other people; sb. else: 这件事～不知道。Nobody else knows anything about it. /是你自己搞错了，与～无关。It is you who made the mistake and it had nothing to do with anybody else. *or* You alone, and nobody else, are responsible for the mistake.

旁若无人 pángruòwúrén act as if there were no one else present — be self-assured or overweening: 他态度傲慢，～。He behaved arrogantly as if nobody could compare with him.

旁听 pángtīng attend as a visitor or auditor: ～法院的审判 attend a trial as a visitor /～过他的课。I've sat in on his classes.

旁听生 pángtīngshēng auditor

旁听席 pángtīngxí visitors' seat; public gallery

旁通道 pángtōngdào 〈机械〉 bypass (pipe)

旁通阀 pángtōngfá 〈机械〉 bypass valve

旁通管 pángtōngguǎn 〈机械〉 bypass pipe

旁通隧洞 pángtōng suìdòng 〈建筑〉 bypass tunnel

旁骛 pángwù 〈书面〉 pursue sth. that is outside one's regular occupation or duties; fail to concentrate: 驰心～ be obsessed with unwarranted pursuits /心不～ complete concentration; single-mindedness

旁系 pángxì collateral line: ～继承人 collateral heir

旁系亲属 pángxì qīnshǔ collateral relative

旁系血亲 pángxì xuèqīn collateral relative by blood

旁心 pángxīn 〈数学〉 centre of an escribed circle

旁压力 pángyālì *also* "侧压力" cèyālì 〈物理〉lateral pressure
旁遮普 Pángzhēpǔ ❶ Punjab, a province of Pakistan ❷ Punjab, a state in northwest India
旁征博引 pángzhēng-bóyǐn quote copiously from a great variety of sources (to support one's argument, etc.); be well documented (with copious quotations, etc.):这本书～,资料丰富,对我很有参考价值。This book is of great help to me, as it is both informative and well documented.
旁证 pángzhèng circumstantial evidence; collateral evidence:提供～ provide collateral (*or* corroborative) evidence /他不是作案的目击者,他所说的至多只能算作～。He was not an eyewitness. What he said may at best provide circumstantial evidence.
旁支 pángzhī collateral branch (of a family)
旁坐 pángzuò 〈书面〉be punished for being related to sb. who has committed an offence

磅 páng
see also bàng
磅礴 pángbó *also* "旁薄" pángbó; "磅磚" pángbó ❶ boundless; majestic:气势～ of great momentum; powerful and majestic ❷ fill; permeate:我感到一股热情～于心头。I feel my heart is permeated with enthusiasm. *or* I am full of enthusiasm.
磅逊 Pángxùn Kompong Som, chief deep-water port of Cambodia on the Gulf of Thailand

螃 páng
螃蟹 pángxiè crab

膀 páng
see also bǎng; bàng; pāng
膀胱 pángguāng (urinary) bladder
膀胱结核 pángguāng jiéhé 〈医学〉cystophthisis
膀胱镜 pángguāngjìng 〈医学〉cystoscope
膀胱石 pángguāngshí 〈医学〉cystolith:～病 cystolithiasis
膀胱炎 pángguāngyán 〈医学〉cystitis
膀胱造影 pángguāng zàoyǐng 〈医学〉cystography

鳑 páng
鳑鲏 pángpí 〈动物〉bitterling

彷(徬) páng
see also fǎng
彷徨 pánghuáng *also* "旁皇" pánghuáng walk to and fro, not knowing which way to turn; hesitate; waver:～歧途 waver at the crossroads /～观望 hesitate and choose to wait and see /他陷于～苦恼的境地。He was plunged into a state of indecision and agony.
彷徉 pángyáng 〈书面〉wander; hang around; linger

庞[1](龐、❶❷厖) páng
❶ huge: *see* "～大" ❷ numerous and disordered: *see* "～杂" ❸ (Páng) a surname

庞[2](龐) páng
face:面～ face
庞贝 Pángbèi Pompeii, ancient town southeast of Naples in Italy, buried by the Vesuvius eruption of AD 79
庞大 pángdà huge; immense; enormous; colossal:机构～ unwieldy organization /开支～ enormous expenditure /～的军事集结 massive military build-up /在郑州发现了一个规模～的商代城址。The site of an extensive town of the Shang Dynasty was discovered at Zhengzhou.
庞然大物 pángrán-dàwù huge monster; colossus; formidable giant:那个公司看起来是个～,其实已经债台高筑,摇摇欲坠了。Outwardly, the firm is a giant organization but it has in fact run heavily into debt and is teetering on the brink of collapse.
庞杂 pángzá numerous and jumbled:内容～ numerous and jumbled in content /～的事务性工作 cumbersome routine work /一个组织成员～,工作效率往往不高。An organization with a heterogeneous composition often lacks efficiency.

逄 Páng
a surname

pǎng

耪 pǎng
loosen soil with a hoe:～地 hoe the soil /～草 weed a field (with a hoe)

嗙 pǎng
〈方言〉sing one's own praises; blow one's own trumpet; brag:开～ start crowing about oneself /胡吹乱～ shoot one's mouth off

髈 pǎng
〈方言〉thigh
see alse bǎng

pàng

胖(肨) pàng
fat; stout; plump:发～ put on weight /～娃娃 chubby child; cherub /他长得很～。He is quite plump. /她似乎比从前～了点。She seems a little more filled-out than before.
see also pán
胖大海 pàngdàhǎi *also* "膨大海" péngdàhǎi 〈中药〉seed of sterculia with boat-like fruit (*Sterculia lychnophora*); sterculia seed
胖嘟嘟 pàngdūdū plump; chubby:迎面走来一个～的小伙子。A plump young chap walked towards me.
胖墩墩 pàngdūndūn short and sturdy; dumpy; thickset:～的男孩 dumpy little boy /那人有四十多岁,长得～的。The man was in his forties, short and thickset.
胖墩儿 pàngdūnr 〈口语〉chubby child:这小～,长得多可爱呀! What a cute chubby child!
胖鼓鼓 pànggǔgǔ (of a person) fat; plump; (of fruit or grain) full:～的脸蛋儿 chubby cheeks /～的麦粒 plump (*or* full) ears of wheat
胖乎乎 pànghūhū plump; fleshy; chubby; pudgy:～的小脸儿 fleshy (*or* chubby) cheeks /～的小手 pudgy fingers /这人长得～的。The fellow is on the fat (*or* fleshy) side.
胖头鱼 pàngtóuyú *also* "鳙" yōng variegated carp; bighead
胖子 pàngzi fat person; fatty

pāo

泡[1] pāo
❶ sth. puffy and soft:豆～儿 beancurd puff /眼～ upper eyelid ❷ 〈方言〉spongy; puffy and soft:～枣 spongy dates /哎,这面发得真～。My, the dough has risen high.

泡[2] pāo
〈方言〉small lake, usu. used in the name of a place:月亮～ Moon Lake (in Jilin Province)

泡[3] pāo
〈口语〉〈量词〉*used of excrement and urine*:撒一～尿 have a piss /拉一～屎 take a shit
see also pào
泡货 pāohuò 〈方言〉goods that are bulky but not heavy
泡桐 pāotóng *also* "桐" 〈植物〉paulownia
泡子 pāozi 〈方言〉small lake usu. used in the name of a place:干～ Dry Lake (in Inner Mongolia)
see also pàozi

抛(拋) pāo
❶ throw; hurl; toss; fling:～石头 throw (*or* toss) a stone /～出一项提案 (usu. derogatory) dish out (*or* trot out) a proposal ❷ leave behind; cast aside:～开私心杂念 cast aside selfish ideas and personal considerations /他第一个游到终点,把第二名～下了三米。He was the first to swim to the finish, leaving the runner-up more than 3 metres behind. /把果皮～进垃圾箱。Throw the litter into the dustbin. ❸ expose; reveal; lay bare: *see* "～头露面" ❹ *see* "抛售"
抛费 pāofèi 〈方言〉waste:你这样～东西,可真不该。You really shouldn't waste things like this. /我真不愿看到～东西。I don't like to see anything going to waste.
抛光 pāoguāng 〈机械〉burnishing; polishing; buffing:摩擦～ bur-

P

nishing
抛光车床 pāoguāng chēchuáng 〈机械〉polishing lathe
抛光机 pāoguāngjī 〈机械〉polishing, burnishing or buffing machine
抛光剂 pāoguāngjì polishing compound; polish
抛光轮 pāoguānglún polishing wheel; buff
抛海 pāohai 〈方言〉plentiful; abundant:今天接待客人,酒饭要～些。We should prepare a big dinner today, as we are going to entertain guests.
抛荒 pāohuāng ❶ allow (land) to go out of cultivation; leave (land) uncultivated:～地 land that has gone to waste; uncultivated land ❷ (of studies or skills) allow to go out of practice; neglect:～学业 neglect one's studies
抛货 pāohuò sell (goods, etc.) in large quantities; dump goods onto the market
抛离 pāolí forsake; abandon:～骨肉 forsake one's own flesh and blood /～家乡 leave one's native place for good
抛脸 pāoliǎn 〈方言〉lose face; be disgraced:这不是什么～的事。This is nothing to be ashamed of.
抛锚 pāomáo ❶ (of ships) drop anchor; cast anchor; (of vehicles) break down:这辆车～了。The car has broken down. ❷〈方言〉(of ongoing projects, etc.) discontinue; be suspended:由于某种原因,厂房的设计工作中途～了。For some reasons, the designing of the factory buildings stopped half way.
抛锚地 pāomáodì anchorage
抛撇 pāopiē leave; abandon:你怎能背井离乡,～妻子呢? How could you desert your native place, leaving behind your wife and children?
抛弃 pāoqì abandon; forsake; discard; cast aside:～旧观念 discard old concepts /一个被～了的女人 a deserted woman /我们不会在困难的时候～自己的朋友。We will never leave our friends in the lurch. /看来她已～了她的男朋友。It seems that she has jilted her boyfriend.
抛却 pāoquè give up; abandon; forsake:～不切实际的想法 discard all illusions (*or* unrealistic notions)
抛洒 pāosǎ *also* "抛撒" throw; scatter:～热血 shed one's blood /人们欢呼着,向空中～着鲜花。People cheered and threw flowers into the air. /他以为上帝会向他抛金洒玉。He thought God would favour him with wealth.
抛砂机 pāoshājī 〈冶金〉sand slinging machine; sandslinger; slinger; sand projection machine; sand thrower
抛闪 pāoshǎn (often used in the early vernacular) abandon; throw away
抛舍 pāoshě abandon; give up; throw away:她怎么忍心～亲生骨肉! How could she be so heartless as to have abandoned her own child!
抛射 pāoshè project
抛射式卫星 pāoshèshì wèixīng dropping satellite
抛射体 pāoshètǐ 〈物理〉projectile
抛售 pāoshòu sell (goods, shares, etc.) in big quantities (usu. in anticipation of or in order to bring about a fall in price); dump; unload:黑色星期五那天,他～了十万股,引起证券市场的波动。He dumped 100,000 shares on Black Friday and caused serious fluctuations in the stock exchange.
抛头颅,洒热血 pāo tóulú, sǎ rèxuè shed one's blood and sacrifice one's life (for a just cause)
抛头露面 pāotóu-lùmiàn 〈贬义〉(esp. of a woman in feudal society) show one's face in public; appear in public:她近来不大～。She has scarcely appeared in public of late. /他这个人就喜欢在大庭广众之中～。He is just too fond of the limelight.
抛物面 pāowùmiàn paraboloid:～天线 parabolic antenna (*or* aerial)
抛物面镜 pāowùmiànjìng *also* "抛物镜" parabolic mirror or reflector
抛物线 pāowùxiàn 〈数学〉parabola; para-curve:～轨迹 parabolic trajectory; parabolic path /～速度 parabolic velocity
抛物线方程 pāowùxiàn fāngchéng parabolic equation
抛物型天线 pāowùxíng tiānxiàn paraboloid antenna
抛掷 pāozhì 〈书面〉throw; cast; abandon
抛砖引玉 pāozhuān-yǐnyù 〈谦词〉cast a brick to attract jade — offer a few commonplace remarks by way of introduction so that others may come up with valuable opinions:我这些话只算是～而已。My remarks may only serve as a modest spur to induce you to come forward with better ideas. /既然无人发言,我就～,先说几句吧。Since no one is ready to speak yet, let me say a few words to set the ball rolling.

脬 pāo ❶ *see* "尿脬" suīpao ❷〈量词〉*see* "泡³" pāo

páo

庖 páo 〈书面〉❶ kitchen:*see* "～厨❶" ❷ cook:良～岁更刀。A good cook changes his knife each year.
庖厨 páochú 〈书面〉❶ kitchen ❷ chef; cook
庖代 páodài *also* "代庖"〈书面〉act in sb.'s place; do what is sb. else's job
see also "越俎代庖" yuèzǔ-dàipáo
庖丁 páodīng 〈书面〉cook; chef; butcher
庖丁解牛 páodīng-jiěniú work methodically and expertly like a skilled butcher cutting up an ox carcass; do sth. with great expertise
庖人 páorén 〈书面〉chef; cook

炮 páo ❶〈中医〉prepare (Chinese medicine) by roasting it in a hot iron pan:～姜 roasted ginger ❷〈书面〉bake; roast; toast:烹龙～凤 (prepare) luxurious food
see also bāo; pào
炮格 páogé *see* "炮烙"
炮炼 páoliàn 〈中医〉refine and dehydrate (Chinese medicine) by heating
炮烙 páoluò *also* "炮格" hot pillar, a kind of cruel torture applied in ancient times
炮制 páozhì ❶〈中医〉(the process of) preparing Chinese medicine, as by roasting, baking, simmering, etc. ❷〈贬义〉concoct; cook up:如法～ act in the same fashion; do sth. according to a set pattern; follow suit /～反华提案 cook up an anti-China proposal
炮炙 páozhì prepare (herbal medicine)

袍 páo *also* "袍子" robe; gown:皮～ fur gown /长～ long gown; robe /睡～ sleeping gown /官～ official gown /旗～ close-fitting woman's dress with high neck and slit skirt; cheongsam
袍哥 páogē 〈旧语〉old-time underworld organization in southwestern China with massive following; member of such a gang
袍笏登场 páohù-dēngchǎng 〈讽刺〉dress up and go on stage — (said of a politician, esp. a puppet) assume an official post
袍泽 páozé 〈书面〉fellow officer:～之谊 camaraderie (*or* friendship) of fellow officers /～故旧 friends who used to be one's fellow officers
袍罩 páozhào dust-robe; dust-gown; duster; overall
袍子 páozi robe; gown:棉～ cotton-padded gown

匏 páo
匏瓜 páoguā 〈植物〉a kind of gourd (*Lagenaria siceraria* var. *depressa*)

咆 páo 〈书面〉(of beasts) howl
咆哮 páoxiào ❶ roar; howl:老虎在森林里～。Tigers are roaring in the woods. ❷ (of a human being) roar with fury:～如雷 roar with rage; be in a thundering rage ❸ (of torrents) thunder away; roar on:大海在～。The sea is thundering away.

跑 páo (of a beast) dig (the ground) with hoofs or paws:～槽 (of draft animals, etc.) dig a trough (while feeding) /虎～泉 Tiger-dug Spring (in Hangzhou)
see also pǎo

刨 páo ❶ dig; excavate:～花生 dig (up) peanuts /～地 dig the ground; hoe a field ❷〈口语〉excluding; not counting; minus:～去他还有两个人。There are two people, not counting him. /这趟买卖,～去本和税,所赚甚少。Minus the cost and taxes, I earned little from this deal. /这事～去他还有谁会干呢! Nobody would do it except him.

see also bào
刨除 páochú deduct; minus; exclude
刨分儿 páofēnr (in exam) subtract marks:他第一道题刨了五分儿。Five points were deducted for his answer to the first question. *or* He lost five marks on the first question.
刨根儿 páogēnr 〈口语〉get to the root or bottom of a matter:这孩子好奇心强,什么事都爱~,问个为什么。The boy is of an inquiring mind and will never be satisfied until he gets the truth.
刨根问底儿 páogēn-wèndǐr get to the bottom of things:不可能事事都~。It's impossible to get to the root of everything.
刨煤机 páoméijī coal plough; coal planer
刨闹 páonào 〈方言〉❶ till; cultivate:他家那几亩地,全凭儿子~。He had to rely entirely on his son to till the few *mu* of land owned by his family. ❷ make; do:生活上的美好东西都是人~的。All good things in life are created by man.

狍(麅) páo 〈动物〉roe (deer)

狍子 páozi 〈动物〉roe (deer)

pǎo

跑 pǎo ❶ run; race; gallop:飞~ race along; (of a horse) gallop /~马拉松 run the marathon race /~百米 run the 100-metre dash /长~ long-distance running /短~ short-distance running; sprint /慢~ jog ❷ run away; escape; flee:那些小流氓~了。Those hooligans managed to escape. ❸ 〈方言〉walk; stroll:~了许多冤枉路 do a lot of legwork for nothing ❹ run about (doing sth.); go about (for sth.); busy oneself (with sth.) /~材料 go about getting the needed materials; run hither and thither collecting evidence (as in an investigation) ❺ go away or off; leak:皮球~气了。The ball is leaky (*or* flat). /水管~水了。The pipe is leaking water. /他帽子给风刮~了。His hat was blown away by the wind. ❻ (of a liquid) evaporate:酒精~了。The ethyl alcohol has evaporated. /酒有点~味了。The wine has lost some of its flavour. ❼ (used as a complement to a verb) off; away:你把他气~了。You sent him away with a flea in his ear.

see also páo
跑表 pǎobiǎo *also* "马表" mǎbiǎo 〈体育〉stopwatch
跑步 pǎobù run; jog; march at the double:~走! At the double, quick march! /~前进! Double time! /我天天早晨~。I go jogging every morning.
跑车 pǎochē ❶ 〈矿业〉(of a cable-car) slide down (e.g. after the steel cable snaps) ❷ (of train attendants) work on a train ❸ racing bike; racing car ❹ 〈林业〉timber carriage
跑驰 pǎochi *also* "跑哧" 〈口语〉run about (doing sth.); hurry here and there:白~了半天,什么也没弄到。I ran around the whole day for nothing.
跑跶 pǎoda 〈方言〉run about; rush about; be busy running about:他~了多半天,又累又饿。He was tired and hungry after rushing about the whole day on business.
跑单帮 pǎo dānbāng travel around trading on one's own: ~的 travelling trader
跑刀 pǎodāo 〈体育〉racing skate
跑道 pǎodào ❶ 〈航空〉runway; tarmac ❷ 〈体育〉track:煤渣~ cinder track /塑胶~ plastic track /第四~ lane 4
跑道儿 pǎodàor 〈口语〉run errands; do legwork:别的他干不了,~还可以。He can run errands if he can't do anything else.
跑电 pǎodiàn *also* "漏电" lòudiàn leakage of electricity
跑调 pǎodiào out of tune:我唱歌老~。I often sing out of tune.
跑动 pǎodòng ❶ (person or thing) start moving:他~没多远就摔倒了。He had moved only a few steps before he fell down. ❷ run round (doing sth.); rush about (for sth.):一大家子全靠他一个人~着养活。Busy all day long, he is the only breadwinner for the family.
跑肚 pǎodù have loose bowels; have diarrhoea
跑反 pǎofǎn *also* "逃反" táofǎn 〈方言〉flee from war or banditry
跑光 pǎoguāng (of sensitive paper or film) be exposed to light (usu. by accident):胶卷~了。The film was exposed accidentally.
跑旱船 pǎo hànchuán *also* "采莲船" cǎiliánchuán (do a) folk dance with one dancer playing the woman passenger carrying the prop boat around her and another playing the boatman with an oar
跑合儿 pǎohér 〈旧语〉act as a middleman in a business transaction; bring parties together for a deal
跑江湖 pǎo jiānghú wander about making a living as an acrobat, fortune-teller, physiognomist, etc.: ~的 itinerant acrobat, etc.; quack
跑交通 pǎo jiāotōng (during the Anti-Japanese and Liberation Wars) act as an underground messenger
跑脚 pǎojiǎo 〈方言〉lead a donkey or mule for hire
跑街 pǎojiē 〈方言〉❶ act as a salesman ❷ salesman; travelling agent
跑警报 pǎo jǐngbào run for shelter during an air raid
跑了和尚跑不了庙 pǎole héshang pǎobuliǎo miào 〈俗语〉the monk may run away, but not the temple — a fugitive must belong to some place that can provide clues (to his whereabouts)
跑垒 pǎolěi 〈体育〉baserunning:~员 base runner
跑龙套 pǎo lóngtào 〈戏曲〉carry a spear and play a walk-on role; play a bit part; be a utility man:我在这位主任手下~。I just play a "walk-on role" under the director.
跑马 pǎomǎ ❶ go for a ride (on a horse) ❷ racing horse ❸ 〈方言〉seminal emission
跑马场 pǎomǎchǎng *also* "跑马所" horse-racing course; racecourse
跑马卖解 pǎomǎ-màixiè *also* "跑马解";"跑解马" 〈旧语〉make a living by performing acrobatics on horseback
跑码头 pǎo mǎtou 〈旧语〉travel from port to port as a trader; be a travelling merchant
跑买卖 pǎo mǎimai *also* "跑生意" travel around doing business; go from place to place buying or selling goods; work as a commercial traveller
跑面 pǎomiàn (of government official, etc.) take charge of the overall situation by going round at the grass roots
跑跑颠颠 pǎopǎo-diāndiān bustle about; be always on the move:他都五十多岁的人了,成天~的,一点不嫌累。Though in his fifties, he is always on the go and never feels tired.
跑跑跳跳 pǎopǎo-tiàotiào run and jump; run about:这孩子屋里屋外~的,闹得人不能安生。The child keeps running in and out and never gives you a moment of peace.
跑片儿 pǎopiānr *also* "跑片子" rush the copy of a film from one cinema to another
跑坡 pǎopō 〈方言〉slip down from a hillside:他上山砍柴,跑了坡,受伤啦。He went up a hill to cut firewood but slipped down the slope and got injured.
跑青 pǎoqīng 〈方言〉put cattle out to graze
跑情况 pǎo qíngkuàng ❶ 〈旧语〉(as in a war) go into hiding on learning about the enemy's approach ❷ 〈口语〉run about gathering information or intelligence
跑墒 pǎoshāng *also* "走墒" zǒushāng 〈农业〉evaporation of moisture in soil; loss of soil moisture
跑生意 pǎo shēngyi *see* "跑买卖"
跑滩 pǎotān 〈方言〉wander about everywhere; tramp all round; lead a wandering life
跑堂儿 pǎotángr be a waiter or waitress in a restaurant
跑堂儿的 pǎotángrde 〈旧语〉waiter in a restaurant; boy
跑腾 pǎoteng 〈方言〉rush about; run about:你~了一天,也该歇歇啦。You deserve a rest as you have been busy running around the whole day.
跑题 pǎotí stray from the subject; digress from the point:你怎么又~了? Here you go again, straying from the point!
跑腿儿 pǎotuǐr 〈口语〉fetch and carry; run errands; do legwork:他整个上午都在~。His whole morning was spent in fetching and carrying. /为这桩生意我可没少~。I've done quite a bit of legwork for this deal. /他们那里缺个~的。They need someone to run errands for them.
跑腿子 pǎotuǐzi 〈方言〉bachelor
跑外 pǎowài (of staff in a shop or plant) travel around handling business for a shop; act as a travelling agent
跑鞋 pǎoxié running shoes; track shoes
跑圆场 pǎo yuánchǎng 〈戏曲〉walk in circles on the stage at a heel-and-toe pace to signify travelling a long distance in haste
跑账 pǎozhàng (of a salesclerk) go out collecting money owed to the shop by customers

P

跑辙 pǎozhé 〈方言〉get or go off the track; digress from the subject; stray from the point:他不说正题,老～。He keeps straying from the subject.
跑猪 pǎozhū release pigs from the pen to look for food in the day time
跑猪靶 pǎozhūbǎ 〈体育〉running boar target (a target pasted with a picture of a boar)

pào

奅 pào 〈书面〉large

泡 pào ❶ bubble:水～ bubbles /气～ air bubbles ❷ sth. shaped like a bubble:灯～ electric light bulb /走了三十里路,他脚上起了～。Having walked for 30 *li*, he got blisters on his feet. ❸ steep; soak:衬衣～在水里。The shirts are steeping. /他两手在水里～得发白。His hands turned pale after being soaked in water. ❹ dawdle; loiter:～时间 dawdle away time /孩子们整天～在电子游戏机里怎么行! It won't do for children to play computer games all day. /你做点正事好不好? 别老～在酒馆里。Can't you do anything decent? Don't just hang about in that bar.
see also pāo
泡病号 pào bìnghào use illness (often imaginary) as an excuse for not going to work; sham ill; malinger:老钱～儿泡了两个月。Lao Qian stayed away from work for two months by malingering.
泡菜 pàocài pickled vegetables; pickles:四川～ Sichuan pickles / 朝鲜～ *Kimchi* (a kind of spiced sauerkraut done in the Korean style)
泡茶 pàochá make tea
泡饭 pàofàn ❶ soak cooked rice in soup or water:他喜欢吃汤～。He likes to eat rice soaked in soup. ❷ cooked rice reheated in boiling water
泡沸石 pàofèishí 〈矿业〉zeolite
泡服 pàofú 〈中医〉to be taken after being infused in hot water
泡螺 pàoluó 〈动物〉bubble shell
泡蘑菇 pào mógu ❶ use delaying tactics; go slow; dawdle:别～了,快干正经事吧! Stop dawdling and get down to work at once. ❷ importune; plague; pester:你要不答应他,他且跟你～呢。If you don't comply with his request, he will keep pestering you.
泡沫 pàomò foam; froth; bubble:啤酒～ head on a glass of beer / ～发生塔 〈化工〉foam column
泡沫玻璃 pàomò bōli cellularglass; foamglass
泡沫浮选 pàomò fúxuǎn froth flotation
泡沫混凝土 pàomò hùnníngtǔ foam or cellular concrete
泡沫剂 pàomòjì foaming agent
泡沫经济 pàomò jīngjì bubble economy; foamy economy
泡沫灭火剂 pàomò mièhuǒjì foamite
泡沫灭火器 pàomò mièhuǒqì foamite extinguisher
泡沫水泥 pàomò shuǐní *see* "泡沫混凝土"
泡沫塑料 pàomò sùliào foam plastic
泡沫陶瓷 pàomò táocí foamed ceramics
泡沫橡胶 pàomò xiàngjiāo foam rubber; cellular rubber
泡沫浴 pàomòyù bubble bath
泡泡纱 pàopaoshā 〈纺织〉crimp cloth; seersucker
泡泡糖 pàopaotáng bubblegum: ～摇滚乐 bubblegum music
泡汤 pàotāng ❶ stall; dawdle; play for time:实行责任制后,～的吃不开了。With the introduction of the responsibility system nobody can afford to loiter on the job. ❷〈方言〉come to nothing; fall through:听说春游的事儿要～。It's said that the spring outing will be cancelled.
泡漩 pàoxuán whirling current
泡影 pàoyǐng (as of hope, plan, scheme, etc.) bubble; illusion:变为～ fizzle out completely; dissipate like a bubble /计划成为～。The scheme went up in smoke. *or* The project has melted into thin air. /一切希望都化为～。All his hopes vanished (*or* burst) like soap bubbles.
泡澡 pàozǎo soak one's body in bath water; take a soaking bath
泡罩 pàozhào 〈化工〉bubble cap: ～塔 bubble cap tower (*or* column)
泡子 pàozi 〈方言〉light bulb; bulb
see also pāozi

疱(皰) pào blister; bleb
疱疹 pàozhěn 〈医学〉❶ bleb ❷ herpes:～病毒 herpes virus /带状～ herpes zoster; zoster /单纯～ herps simplex
疱疹净 pàozhěnjìng 〈药学〉idoxuridine
疱疹性脑炎 pàozhěnxìng nǎoyán 〈医学〉herpetic encephalitis
疱疹性咽峡炎 pàozhěnxìng yānxiáyán 〈医学〉herpangina
疱疹样皮炎 pàozhěnyàng píyán 〈医学〉dermatitis herpetiformis

炮(砲、礮) pào ❶ (big) gun; cannon; artillery (piece):大～ cannon /高射～ anti-aircraft gun (*or* artillery) /榴弹～ howitzer /迫击～ trench mortar /火箭～ bazooka /自行火～ self-propelled cannon ❷ firecracker:花～ firecrackers /鞭～ firecrackers ❸ load of explosive (as for demolition of rocks, etc.):点～ set off an explosion (*or* a blast) ❹ "cannon", one of the pieces in Chinese chess
see also bāo; páo
炮兵 pàobīng artillery; artilleryman: ～部队 artillery (troops) /～连 battery /～阵地 artillery position; gun emplacement /～学校 artillery school
炮车 pàochē gun carriage
炮铳 pàochong 〈方言〉firecracker:放～ let off firecrackers
炮打灯儿 pàodǎdēngr 〈方言〉illuminant firecracker
炮弹 pàodàn shell
炮弹树 pàodànshù 〈植物〉cannonball tree (*Couroupita guianensis*)
炮轰 pàohōng bombard; shell
炮灰 pàohuī cannon fodder:他叔叔给旧军阀当～送了命。His uncle served as cannon fodder for the old warlords and bit the dust.
炮火 pàohuǒ artillery fire; gunfire:掩护～ (artillery) fire cover / ～支援 artillery support /～连天。Gunfire licked the heavens.
炮击 pàojī bombard; shell:停止～ stop the bombardment
炮架 pàojià gun mount
炮舰 pàojiàn gunboat
炮舰外交 pàojiàn wàijiāo gunboat diplomacy
炮舰政策 pàojiàn zhèngcè gunboat policy
炮口 pàokǒu gun muzzle
炮楼 pàolóu blockhouse
炮捻 pàoniǎn (blasting) fuse
炮钎 pàoqiān *also* "钎子" qiānzi rock drill
炮声 pàoshēng report (of a gun); boom (of guns):隔江～隆隆。Guns boomed across the river. /～震天。The cannon fire reached the sky. /黄洋界上～隆,报道敌军宵遁。From Huangyangjie roars the thunder of guns, Word comes the enemy has fled into the night.
炮手 pàoshǒu cannoneer; gunner; artilleryman
炮栓 pàoshuān breechblock
炮塔 pàotǎ gun turret; turret: 旋转～ revolving turret
炮台 pàotái fort; battery
炮膛 pàotáng bore (of a big gun)
炮艇 pàotǐng gunboat
炮铜 pàotóng 〈军事〉gun metal
炮筒 pàotǒng barrel (of a big gun)
炮筒子 pàotǒngzi ❶ barrel (of a big gun) ❷ person who shoots off his mouth; blunt guy:他们有意让那个～先发言。They deliberately got the hot head to take the floor first. /他是个～,有嘴没心的,别理他就是了。Don't take what he says too seriously. He's blunt and doesn't mince his words, but he means no harm.
炮尾 pàowěi gun breech
炮位 pàowèi emplacement
炮校 pàoxiào (short for 炮兵学校) artillery school
炮眼 pàoyǎn ❶ porthole (for a gun); embrasure ❷ blasthole; dynamite hole; borehole:现在都用风钻打～了。Pneumatic drills are now used to bore blastholes.
炮衣 pàoyī gun cover
炮战 pàozhàn artillery duel or engagement: ～之后步兵开始冲锋。The infantry started the charge after an exchange of artillery fire.
炮仗 pàozhang firecracker
炮竹 pàozhú firecracker
炮子儿 pàozǐr 〈口语〉❶ small shell ❷ cartridge; bullet
炮座 pàozuò gun platform

pēi

瘖 pēi *also* pèi 〈中医〉sore

瘖瘟 pēilěi 〈中医〉nettle rash; urticaria

醅 pēi 〈书面〉unfiltered wine

呸 pēi 〈叹词〉(indicating contempt or censure) pah; bah; pooh; pfui:～！你想骗谁呀！Bah! You can fool nobody!

衃 pēi 〈书面〉coagulated, congealed, or curdled blood

胚(肧) pēi 〈生物〉embryo

胚层 pēicéng *also*“胚叶”〈生物〉germinal layer:内～ endoderm (*or* entoderm) /外～ ectoderm /中～ mesoderm

胚根 pēigēn 〈植物〉radicle

胚孔 pēikǒng 〈生物〉blastopore

胚瘤 pēiliú *also*“胚组织瘤”〈医学〉embryoma

胚膜 pēimó 〈生物〉embryonic membrane; blastoderm

胚囊 pēináng 〈生物〉embryo sac

胚盘 pēipán 〈生物〉blastodisc; blastoderm; germinal disc

胚泡 pēipào blastocyst; germinal vesicle

胚乳 pēirǔ 〈生物〉endosperm

胚胎 pēitāi ❶〈生物〉embryo:～移植 embryo transfer; embryo implantation /～发生 embryogeny; embryogenesis ❷ embryonic form; embryo

胚胎学 pēitāixué embryology

胚细胞瘤 pēixìbāoliú 〈医学〉blastoma

胚芽 pēiyá ❶〈植物〉plumule:～生殖 germiparity ❷ bud; sprout:她觉得跟他似乎有了些爱情的～。She felt the first stirrings of love between him and herself.

胚叶 pēiyè *see*“胚层”

胚轴 pēizhóu 〈植物〉plumular axis

胚珠 pēizhū 〈植物〉ovule

胚状体 pēizhuàngtǐ 〈生物〉embryoid

胚子 pēizi ❶〈俗语〉embryo of a silkworm's egg ❷〈比喻〉breed; strain:坏～ bad egg; bastard /这姑娘是练体操的好～。The girl has the making of a good gymnast.

péi

培 péi ❶ bank up (with earth); earth up:把河堤加高～厚 build up an earth dyke ❷ cultivate; foster; train:栽～ foster; train; educate

培根 Péigēn Francis Bacon (1561-1626), English philosopher and essayist

培护 péihù foster and protect:～草地 cultivate and protect the lawn

培土 péitǔ *also*“壅土”yōngtǔ 〈农业〉bank up with earth; hill up; earth up:给树根培上土 bank up the roots of a tree

培修 péixiū repair (earthwork):～大堤 repair a dyke /～宅基 strengthen the foundations of a house

培训 péixùn cultivate; train:岗前～ training before posting /在职～ in-service training; on-the-job training /～技术骨干 train technical backbones

培训班 péixùnbān training class

培训中心 péixùn zhōngxīn training centre

培养 péiyǎng ❶〈生物〉culture:～细菌 culture of bacteria /液体～ liquid culture /固体～ solid culture ❷ foster; train; develop:在实际工作中～人 train people on the job /～学生团结友爱的精神 foster the spirit of unity and friendship among the students /～有理想、有道德、有文化、有纪律的社会主义公民 develop (*or* cultivate) a socialist citizenry who have high ideals and moral integrity and who are well educated and have a strong sense of discipline

培养基 péiyǎngjī culture medium

培养瓶 péiyǎngpíng culture bottle

培壅 péiyōng 〈书面〉❶ put more earth around the plants ❷ foster; train; cultivate

培育 péiyù cultivate; foster; breed:利用杂交方式～水稻新品种 breed new varieties of rice by hybridization /～一代新人 rear a new generation /两国的友谊是由两国人民共同～的。The friendship between the two countries was jointly forged by their people.

培植 péizhí ❶ plant; grow; cultivate:～防护林带 plant a shelter belt /人工～ artificial cultivation ❷ foster; build up:～个人势力 build up one's personal influence /～亲信 foster one's trusted followers; build up one's coterie

培殖 péizhí breed; reproduce:在淡水里～海虾 breed sea-prawns in fresh water

培种 péizhòng grow; plant:～中草药 cultivate medicinal herbs

赔 péi ❶ compensate; pay for; refund:退～ refund sb. his money; pay back what one has appropriated; refund the price of a defective article /损坏了东西你得～。You have got to pay for any goods damaged. ❷ apologize: *see*“～礼”;“～罪” ❸ stand or incur a loss; lose:这笔生意～了 lose money in the business transaction

赔本 péiběn sustain losses in business:～的买卖 bad deal; unprofitable business /～出售 sell sth. at a loss

赔本出口 péiběn chūkǒu bleeding export

赔补 péibǔ compensate and make up a deficiency:所差数额由经手人～。The deficiency will be made up by the person handling the transaction.

赔不是 péi bùshi apologize; offer one's apologies:给他赔个不是。You'd better apologize to him. *or* Tell him you are sorry.

赔偿 péicháng ❶ compensate; indemnify; pay for:～转运过程中的损失 pay for the loss incurred in transit /照价～ refund the cost; compensate according to the price /如数～ pay back the exact amount /加倍～ compensate at double the amount (*or* value) /心灵上的创伤无法～。It is impossible to compensate for one's emotional trauma. ❷ reparation; damages; indemnity:战争～ war reparations (*or* indemnity) /精神～ moral reparation /～协定 reparations agreement /保留要求～的权利 reserve the right to demand compensation (*or* damages)

赔偿费 péichángfèi *also*“赔偿金”〈法律〉(compensatory) damages

赔偿人 péichángrén compensator

赔偿物 péichángwù indemnity; compensation

赔错 péicuò apologize; admit one's mistake:我向您～来啦。I have come to offer you an apology.

赔垫 péidiàn pay a sum of money for any possible loss:钱数太大，我可～不起。I just can't afford to advance such a large sum of money for the possible initial loss.

赔话 péihuà apologize:再三～ apologize again and again /登门～ call on sb. specifically to make one's apologies

赔还 péihuán repay; pay back:～欠款 repay a debt

赔款 péikuǎn ❶ pay money as compensation; make compensatory payment:原物买不到了，只好折价～。We can only refund you the cost as the article is not available in the market. ❷ indemnity; reparations:割地～ cede territory and pay indemnities /甲午战争后中国给日本的～高达二万万两白银。After the Sino-Japanese war of 1894-1895, China was forced to pay Japan as much as 200 million taels of silver in war reparations.

赔了夫人又折兵 péile fūren yòu zhé bīng present (one's enemy) with a wife and lose one's men into the bargain; suffer a double loss instead of making a gain; pay a double penalty

赔累 péilěi not only lose one's capital but incur debts:这趟买卖～大啦。I sustained great losses in this business transaction.

赔礼 péilǐ offer or make a formal apology; apologize formally:～道歉 make a humble apology; offer formal apologies

赔钱 péiqián ❶ sustain losses in business ❷ compensate for the loss or damage of property

赔青 péiqīng compensate for the still unripe crops when land is requisitioned

赔情 péiqíng 〈方言〉apologize:你既然错怪了他，那就赶快给他赔个情吧！Since you have wrongly blamed him, you'd better go and apologize to him.

赔贴 péitiē offer compensation and subsidy:如果只提高收购价，而不提高销售价格，政府就要～很多钱。The government would have to spend a lot of money on compensation and subsidy if only the purchase price alone is raised while the sale price remains the same.

赔小心 péi xiǎoxin try hard to placate or appease; apologize in a

P

humble way：他自知说错了话，一个劲儿向我～。He looked subdued and apologized to me again and again, as he realized he had said something he should not have said.

赔笑 péixiào *also* "赔笑脸" smile placatingly or apologetically：店家赔着笑，把客人让进另一间房间。Smiling apologetically, the innkeeper helped the customer into another room.

赔账 péizhàng ❶ pay back the shortfall or loss of the cash or goods entrusted to one：她初当出纳时赔了好几次账。When she was new as a cashier, she had to pay back the shortfalls in her account quite a few times. ❷〈方言〉sustain losses in business：这一阵子生意清淡，尽～了。We incurred heavy losses, for business has been slack lately.

赔罪 péizuì apologize (usu. for having offended sb.)：是我不对，我向你～。It is all my fault. Please accept my apology.

P

锫 péi 〈化学〉berkelium (Bk), an artificial radioactive element

陪 péi ❶ accompany; keep sb. company：～外宾参观 show foreign visitors around / ～住 stay in the ward to look after a bedridden patient / ～总理访问加拿大 accompany the premier on his visit to Canada / 你～我去一趟，行吗？Will you please go with me? ❷ assist; help: *see* "～祭"

陪伴 péibàn accompany; keep sb. company：她所以不寂寞，是因为有你～她。It is because you kept her company that she didn't feel lonely. / 母亲病了，这几天我一直在家～她。Mother is ill and I've been looking after her at home these days.

陪绑 péibǎng ❶〈旧语〉(of criminals) be taken to the execution ground along with those to be executed (to watch the horrible scene as a warning) ❷ (of an innocent person) be an unwilling party to sth. unpleasant (as criticism, punishment, or any gruelling experience)：难题你自己去解决，别拉我去～。You had better solve the thorny problem yourself. Don't drag me into it.

陪餐 péicān accompany the host to entertain guests at a dinner party：宴请的客人只有三位，～的领导多达十人。There were only three guests at the dinner party, but as many as ten officials were accompanying them.

陪衬 péichèn ❶ serve as a contrast or foil; set off：红花还得绿叶～。Red flowers stand out only when they are set off by green leaves. *or* It is the green leaves that set off the beauty of the red flowers. ❷ foil; set-off：在这个场合里，他只是个～而已。On this occasion, he was merely acting as a foil.

陪吃 péichī *see* "陪餐"

陪床 péichuáng person, usually a patient's relative, allowed to stay in a hospital ward to look after him or her

陪吊 péidiào 〈旧语〉person invited by the bereaved to help with reception when relatives and friends of the family come to offer condolences

陪都 péidū *also* "陪京" auxiliary or secondary capital of a country

陪读 péidú be a companion to sb. in study

陪房 péifang 〈旧语〉maid servant brought by the bride from her parents' home

陪护 péihù accompany and look after：请人～老人 hire sb. to keep old people company and look after them

陪祭 péijì assist in presiding over a sacrificial rite or memorial ceremony; one who does this

陪嫁 péijià dowry

陪酒 péijiǔ be a drinking partner

陪酒女郎 péijiǔ nǚláng girl who accompanies patrons in drinking for a fee; bar girl

陪考 péikǎo ❶ assist the chief examiner in presiding over an examination ❷ assistant examiner

陪客 péike those invited to a dinner party to help entertain the guest of honour; guests other than the guest of honour

陪奁 péilián 〈方言〉dowry

陪练 péiliàn (be a) training partner; sparring partner (in boxing)

陪审 péishěn ❶ act or serve as an assessor (in a court trial) / 人民～员 people's assessor ❷ serve on a jury

陪审团 péishěntuán jury：大～ grand jury

陪审员 péishěnyuán ❶ juror; juryman ❷ assessor

陪审制 péishěnzhì jury system

陪侍 péishì wait upon one's seniors：老人病重期间一直有儿女～。When the old man was seriously ill, his sons and daughters looked after him all the time.

陪送 péisòng accompany (sb.) on a trip：他亲自～我回上海。He personally accompanied me (on my journey back) to Shanghai.

陪送 péisong ❶ give (dowry) to the bride ❷ dowry

陪同 péitóng accompany：总统在外长的～下出访欧洲。The President was accompanied by the Foreign Minister on his visit to Europe. / 外国元首一般由一位中国部长～离开北京前往外地访问。The visiting head of state of a foreign country is usually escorted by a Chinese minister when he leaves Beijing for other cities.

陪同人员 péitóng rényuán entourage; party：总统的主要～ main (*or* chief) members of the presidential entourage

陪同团 péitóngtuán hosting team; reception committee：～团长 leader of a hosting team; chairman of the reception committee

陪舞 péiwǔ be a dancing partner (esp. for a fee)：有些舞厅搞所谓～女郎，变相卖淫，必须取缔。Some ballrooms provide girls as dancing partners. This practice must be banned because these girls are clandestine prostitutes.

陪夜 péiyè stay up throughout the night to look after a patient

陪音 péiyīn *also* "泛音" fànyīn 〈音乐〉harmonic; overtone

陪葬 péizàng 〈旧语〉❶ be buried alive with the dead ❷ (of figurines and objects) be buried with the dead ❸ be buried close to the grave of one's husband or overlord

陪葬品 péizàngpǐn funerary object; burial article (figurines, etc.)

陪住 péizhù stay with a patient in the ward and look after him or her

裴 Péi a surname

裴多菲 Péiduōfēi Sandor Petofi (1823-1849), Hungarian poet：～俱乐部 Petofi club (usu. in reference to a group of dissidents)

pèi

沛 pèi 〈书面〉copious; abundant：丰～ plentiful; abundant / 精力充～ full of energy; vigorous

霈 pèi 〈书面〉❶ heavy rain：甘～ auspicious rain; timely rain ❷ (of rain) heavy; plentiful：雨～ copious rainfall

旆(斾) pèi ❶ ancient swallow-tail pennant ❷〈书面〉flag; banner; pennant

配 pèi ❶ join or match in marriage：匹～ marry; match / 许～ (as of a girl in an arranged match) betroth; be betrothed / 才子～佳人。(theme of traditional romance) A fine scholar and a beautiful girl make a good match. ❷ spouse (usu. wife)：原～ first wife ❸ (of animals) mate：～猪 mate pigs ❹ blend; mix：～酒 mix drinks / ～佐料 mix condiments / ～药 make up a prescription / ～拼盘 put together an assorted cold dish ❺ distribute according to plan; apportion; assign; allot：分～任务 assign tasks; give out assignments / 我给你～一个助手。I'll assign someone to assist you. / 这是国家～给你们的煤。This is your quota of coal apportioned (*or* allotted) by the state. ❻ find sth. to fit or replace sth. else; replace：～一只手套 replace a missing glove / ～钥匙 have a key made to fit a lock / 为商店～货 replenish the stocks (*or* supplies) of a store / ～眼镜 have a pair of glasses made / 这只花瓶不成对，再～一只吧。Let's find a match for this vase so as to make a pair. ❼ foil; set off：红花～绿叶 red flowers set off by green leaves ❽ match; go well together; harmonize with：蓝色裙子～有白色腰带 a blue skirt with a matching white belt / 裤子与上衣不～。The trousers and the jacket don't match. / 这个舞蹈要～一首好歌。The dance has to have a good song to match it. / 这地毯和窗帘的颜色～得很协调。The carpet and curtain are well matched in colour. ❾ deserve; be worthy of; be qualified：他～当先进工作者。He is qualified to be an advanced worker. / 我～演主角吗？Am I good enough to play the hero (*or* heroine)? / 这姑娘～得上他。The girl makes a good match for him. / 我不～做你的妻子。I am not your worthy wife. *or* I don't deserve to be your wife. ❿ exile for penal servitude; banish：发～ banish; exile / 管～所 place of exile

配备 pèibèi ❶ allocate; provide; equip; fit out：～了必要的技术力

量 be provided with necessary technical personnel /工厂～了新式机器。The factory is equipped with sophisticated machinery. /公司给推销部～了两部汽车。The company has allocated two cars to its sales department. ❷ dispose (troops, etc.); deploy: ～火力 dispose firepower ❸ outfit; equipment: 带有自动控制系统的～ equipment with an auto-control system

配比 pèibǐ proportion of different elements in the composition of sth.

配菜 pèicài garnish; trim: 这豆腐用蘑菇做～。The beancurd is garnished with mushrooms.

配餐 pèicān ❶ prepare mixed food according to given standards: 为病人～ prepare an assortment of food for a patient ❷ assortment of various kinds of food such as bread, sausage, ham, etc. put together in a dish or a box: 方便～ convenient assorted food

配餐室 pèicānshì pantry

配称 pèichèn well matched: 各种家具的色调都很淡雅, 很～。The articles of furniture are all light and elegant in colour and well-matched.

配搭 pèidā ❶ supplement; accompany: 他的几个助手～得很好。He is ably supported by a few assistants. ❷ match: 这几道菜, 不仅味道鲜美, 颜色也～得好。These dishes are not only delicious, but perfectly matched in colour.

配搭儿 pèidar assistant; foil; setoff: 搞这项科研, 他是主角, 我不过是一个～。He plays the major role in this scientific research project. I am just an assistant.

配电 pèidiàn 〈电工〉 power distribution: ～线路 distribution line

配电盘 pèidiànpán distributor

配电网 pèidiànwǎng distribution network

配电站 pèidiànzhàn distributing substation; distributing station

配电装置 pèidiàn zhuāngzhì power distribution unit

配殿 pèidiàn side hall (in a palace or temple)

配对 pèiduì ❶ pair; match: 这两只鞋不～儿。These two shoes don't match (*or* aren't a pair). ❷ (of animals) mate

配额 pèi'é quota: 进口～ quota on imports /移民～ immigration quota /给本市的纺织品出口～一年只有五万米。The quota of textile export for this city amounts only to fifty thousand metres annually.

配额分配 pèi'é fēnpèi quota allocation

配额管理 pèi'é guǎnlǐ quota administration

配额制 pèi'ézhì quota system

配发 pèifā ❶ distribute; issue: 车间每个工人～一套工作服。Every worker in the shop is issued a working outfit. ❷ publish (photos, commentary, etc. relating to certain news): 各大报在报道这条新闻的同时, 还～了评论。The major newspapers published commentaries together with the news report.

配方 pèifāng ❶〈数学〉change an incomplete square form into a complete one ❷make up or fill a prescription ❸ directions for producing chemicals or metallurgical products; (dispensation) formula; recèpé

配房 pèifáng wing (usu. of a one-storeyed house); side house or room: 东～ east wing

配购 pèigòu purchase rationed good: ～汽油 buy rationed petrol

配股 pèigǔ 〈金融〉 scrip issue

配合 pèihé ❶ coordinate; cooperate; concert: 海陆空～作战 coordinated operations of the army, navy and air-force /整顿市容要各方面～行动。It takes concerted action from all sides to keep city clean and tidy. /共青团起了很好的～作用。The Youth League has played a good supporting role. /在工作中他一点儿也不～。He refused to be cooperative in work. ❷〈机械〉fit: 压～ interference fit /轻压～ light-press fit /～公差 fit tolerance /～等级 fit quality

配合 pèihe match; go well together: 这小两口～得太理想了。The young couple are perfectly matched.

配合饲料 pèihé sìliào 〈牧业〉 mixed feed; compound feed

配婚 pèihūn get married (usu. of an arranged marriage); marry: 给儿子～ arrange a marriage for one's son

配火 pèihuǒ tempering (of metal): ～炉 tempering furnace

配给 pèijǐ ration: ～证 ration card (*or* book)

配给制 pèijǐzhì ration system; rationing

配件 pèijiàn ❶ fitting (of a machine, etc.); accessory part; accessory: 窗～ window fittings /管子～ pipe fittings ❷ replacement; spare part: 零～ spare parts /汽车～ car spare parts

配筋 pèijīn 〈建筑〉 reinforcing bar

配角 pèijué ❶ appear with another leading player; co-star: 他们俩经常在演出中～儿。The two of them have often appeared together in performances. *or* They have co-starred in many plays. ❷ supporting role; minor role: 最佳男～奖 award for the best supporting actor /他在这出戏里演～。He played a supporting role in the play. /在这项工作中, 我搞对外联络, 是个～。I play a minor role in this project; I handle liaison work.

配军 pèijūn (often used in the early vernacular) convict sentenced to banishment; exile

配克 pèikè peck, measure of capacity for dry goods equal to 8 quarts or $\frac{1}{4}$ bushel

配料 pèiliào ❶ preparation or assortment of various materials for making sth. ❷〈冶金〉burden: 高炉～ blast-furnace burden /～表 burden sheet /～计算 burden calculation

配流 pèiliú banish; exile

配偶 pèi'ǒu spouse

配平 pèipíng ❶〈化学〉balancing: ～方程式 balancing equation ❷〈航空〉trim: ～补翼 trimming tab; trim tab; / ～失误 mistrim

配器 pèiqì 〈音乐〉 orchestration: ～法〈音乐〉orchestration

配曲 pèiqǔ set (the words of a song) to music; compose music (for the words of a song)

配色 pèisè mix colours in the right proportion

配售 pèishòu ration; placing

配属 pèishǔ 〈军事〉 attach (troops to a subordinate unit): 连长命令机枪班～在二排。The company commander ordered that the machine-gun squad be attached to the second platoon.

配水 pèishuǐ ❶〈水利〉distribution of water (in irrigation): ～管网 water distribution network /～池 distribution reservoir /～闸 distribution structure ❷〈建筑〉distribution: ～总管 distribution main

配所 pèisuǒ 〈书面〉 place where a convict is exiled; place of exile

配糖物 pèitángwù *also* "甙" dài 〈化学〉 glucoside

配套 pèitào form a complete set: ～产品 complete set of products; accessory product /～器材 necessary accessories

配套成龙 pèitào-chénglóng *also* "成龙配套" fill in the gaps to complete a chain (of equipment, construction projects, etc.); facilitate so as to make a complete system; link up the parts to form a whole

配套改革 pèitào gǎigé coordinated reforms

配套工程 pèitào gōngchéng accessory or subsidiary project; 〈水利〉 conveyance system

配位场理论 pèiwèichǎng lǐlùn 〈化学〉 ligand field theory

配位化合物 pèiwèi huàhéwù 〈化学〉 coordination compounds

配位数 pèiwèishù 〈化学〉 coordination number

配位体 pèiwèitǐ 〈化学〉 ligand

配伍 pèiwǔ 〈医药〉 compatibility of medicines: ～禁忌 incompatibility (of medicines)

配戏 pèixì support a leading actor; play a supporting role: 他常跟几位名角～。He often plays a supporting role for famous actors.

配系 pèixì system of military dispositions: 工事～ disposition of fortifications

配线 pèixiàn 〈电工〉 conductor arrangement; conductor configuration: ～电缆 distribution cable /～架 distributing frame

配享 pèixiǎng (of a deceased minister) be offered sacrifices together with the deceased emperor; (of Confucius' disciples or other learned scholars) be worshiped together with Confucius

配烟 pèiyān tobacco blending

配演 pèiyǎn ❶ appear in a supporting role: 在这部电影里, 她～主要人物夫人。In this film, she plays a secondary role as wife of the leading charactor. ❷ (in drama, film, etc.) supporting role; minor role

配药 pèiyào ❶ make up or dispense a prescription ❷ go about seeking medicinal herbs: 跑了许多中药店才配上这两味药。Only after going to several Chinese pharmacies did I manage to get the two medicinal herbs.

配页 pèiyè 〈印刷〉 assembling (leaves of a book)

配页机 pèiyèjī 〈印刷〉 assembling machine

配音 pèiyīn dub (a film, etc.): 给外国影片～ dub a foreign film in Chinese /由…～ dubbed by... /这部电影没有～, 只有字幕。This film is not dubbed. It's only captioned.

配音机 pèiyīnjī dubbing machine

配音棚 pèiyīnpéng dubbing studio or room

配音演员 pèiyīn yǎnyuán dubbing actor or actress

配乐 pèiyuè provide background music: ～诗朗诵 poetry recital

P

with background music /给电影～ compose background music for a film
配载 pèizài optimum arrangement of cargo on a ship
配制 pèizhì ❶ compound; make up:～药丸 compound medicinal pills ❷ supplement; accompany:书内～了多幅精美插图。There are quite a few beautiful plates in the book.
配制酒 pèizhìjiǔ *also* "鸡尾酒" jīwěijiǔ cocktail; mixed drink (as opposed to taking one's liquor neat or straight)
配置 pèizhì dispose (troops, etc.); deploy:～兵力 dispose forces /纵深～ disposition in depth /资源～ allocation of resources
配种 pèizhǒng 〈畜牧〉breeding:～率 breeding rate /这匹马是上星期配的种。The horse was bred last week.
配种站 pèizhǒngzhàn breeding station
配子 pèizǐ 〈生物〉gamete
配子囊 pèizǐnáng gametan
配子体 pèizǐtǐ gametophyte

帔

pèi short embroidered cape (worn over a woman's shoulders):凤冠霞～ phoenix coronet and colourful embroidered cape

佩(❷珮)

pèi ❶ wear (at the waist, etc.):胸～校徽 wear a school badge on one's chest ❷ pendant worn at the waist:玉～ jade pendant ❸ admire:他的忘我牺牲精神令人钦～。His selfless spirit is very admirable.
佩带 pèidài ❶ carry at the waist:～手枪 carry a pistol at one's waist ❷ *see* "佩戴"
佩戴 pèidài *also* "佩带" wear:～纪念章 wear a badge
佩刀 pèidāo sword or sabre worn at the waist
佩服 pèifu admire:～他的辩才 admire him for his eloquence /他讲得真棒,我算是～了。His lecture was brilliant and I've got to hand it to him.
佩剑 pèijiàn ❶〈体育〉(fencing with) sabre:～运动员 sabre fencer; sabreur /～护手盘 sabre guard ❷ sabre
佩兰 pèilán *also* "兰草" láncǎo fragrant thoroughwort (*Eupatorium fortunei*)

辔

pèi bridle:鞍～ saddle and bridle /按～徐行 keep a grip on the bridle and amble along
辔头 pèitóu bridle

pēn

喷

pēn spurt; gush; spray; sprinkle:～水 spurt water /往身上～点香水 sprinkle some perfume on oneself /往木器上～漆 spray paint on wooden utensils /火山岩浆往外～。Lava kept gushing from the volcano. /水从壁孔里～了出来。Water spouted out from a hole in the wall.
see also pèn
喷薄 pēnbó gush; spurt; spout:岩石罅隙之间清泉～。Water gushes out from the crevices in the rocks.
喷薄欲出 pēnbó-yùchū (of water) gush out in full force; (of the sun) emerge with brilliant magnificence:一轮朝日～。The sun is emerging in all its splendour.
喷出岩 pēnchūyán 〈地质〉extrusive rock
喷灯 pēndēng blowtorch; blowlamp
喷镀 pēndù 〈冶金〉spraying:～枪 spray torch /～金属 metallize
喷发 pēnfā erupt; explode:沉睡的火山重新～了。The dormant volcano erupted. /大家都愕然了,接着是～的笑声。An astonished silence was followed by an outburst of laughter.
喷发胶 pēnfàjiāo hair spray; conditioner
喷饭 pēnfàn be seized with such a violent fit of laughter that one even spews out one's food (at dinner):这些话出自一位所谓学者之口,令人～。These remarks coming from a so-called scholar make one split one's sides with laughter.
喷纺法 pēnfǎngfǎ 〈化工〉jet spinning
喷放 pēnfàng spray; jet:节日的烟火在夜空中～出五颜六色的火花。The festive fireworks displayed multicoloured sparks in the evening sky.
喷粉器 pēnfěnqì 〈农业〉duster
喷粪 pēnfèn 〈粗话〉make groundless or senseless remarks; talk shit:你满嘴喷的啥粪! What bullshit!
喷瓜 pēnguā 〈植物〉squirting cucumber (*Ecballium elaterium*)
喷管 pēnguǎn 〈航天〉(exhaust) nozzle (external part of a rocket engine which directs the exhaust gases to maximize propulsion):～旋转 nozzle swivelling
喷灌 pēnguàn sprinkling irrigation; spray irrigation
喷灌器 pēnguànqì sprinkler
喷壶 pēnhú *also* "喷桶" water can; sprinkling can
喷花 pēnhuā spray paint or colour with a stencil (as on a wall to have the patterns printed)
喷火器 pēnhuǒqì *also* "火焰喷射器" huǒyàn pēnshèqì 〈军事〉flamethrower
喷溅 pēnjiàn send forth; shoot up; jet:海浪扑向礁石,～着雪白的泡沫。The waves dashed against the rocks, shooting up snow-white foam.
喷浆 pēnjiāng 〈建筑〉❶ whitewashing ❷ guniting
喷口 pēnkǒu 〈戏曲〉articulate suddenly and vigorouly
喷磨 pēnmó 〈机械〉abrasive blasting
喷墨打印机 pēnmò dǎyìnjī 〈计算机〉ink-jet printer
喷墨法 pēnmòfǎ 〈印刷〉ink-jet method
喷漆 pēnqī spray paint; spray lacquer:～枪 paint (spraying) gun
喷气发动机 pēnqì fādòngjī jet engine:～推力 engine jet thrust
喷气燃料 pēnqì ránliào jet fuel
喷气式 pēnqìshì (short for 喷气式飞机) jet plane; jet
喷气式飞机 pēnqìshì fēijī jet plane; jet aircraft; jet
喷气式客机 pēnqìshì kèjī jet airliner
喷气速度 pēnqì sùdù exhaust velocity
喷气织机 pēnqì zhījī 〈纺织〉air-jet loom
喷枪 pēnqiāng spray gun
喷泉 pēnquán fountain:间歇～ geyser
喷染 pēnrǎn spray dyeing
喷洒 pēnsǎ spray; sprinkle:～除草剂 spray herbicide
喷洒灌溉法 pēnsǎ guàngàifǎ 〈农业〉spray irrigation
喷散 pēnsàn send forth; spread; diffuse:稻田里～出的香气,沁人心脾。We were elated at the redolent aroma of the rice paddies.
喷杀 pēnshā kill (pests) by spraying insecticide
喷砂 pēnshā sand-blast; sand-jet:～机 sand-blasting machine; sand-blast machine; sand ejector
喷射 pēnshè ❶ spray; spurt; dart:远处鲸鱼～出高高的水柱。The whale is shooting up tall columns of water in the distance. /黑乎乎的石油从井口～出来。Black crude oil spurted from the well. ❷〈机械〉inject:～泵 injection pump /～器 injector; jet eductor /～钻 jet drilling; wash boring
喷射剂 pēnshèjì *also* "推进剂" tuījìnjì propellant
喷施 pēnshī spray (fertilizer, insecticide, etc.)
喷水池 pēnshuǐchí fountain
喷水淬火 pēnshuǐ cuìhuǒ 〈冶金〉stream hardening
喷水灭火系统 pēnshuǐ mièhuǒ xìtǒng sprinkler system
喷水器 pēnshuǐqì 〈农业〉sprinkling machine
喷水艇 pēnshuǐtǐng jet boat
喷丝头 pēnsītóu 〈纺织〉spinning jet; spinning nozzle:～牵伸 spinneret draft /～组件 spinneret assembly
喷腾 pēnténg (of water, fire, smoke, etc.) gush; spout:火车头上～着白烟。A puff of white smoke spurted from the locomotive.
喷嚏 pēntì *also* "嚏喷" sneeze:打～ sneeze
喷桶 pēntǒng 〈方言〉*see* "喷壶"
喷头 pēntóu *also* "莲蓬头" liánpengtóu ❶ shower nozzle ❷ sprinkler head
喷涂 pēntú 〈化工〉spray coating:～金属 metalling; metallizing /～装置 spraying plant
喷吐 pēntǔ shoot out; spurt; send forth:炉口～着红色的火苗。Red flames were spurting from the furnace. /树上的槐花～浓香。The flowers of the locust tree are sending forth a heavy fragrance.
喷丸 pēnwán 〈冶金〉shot blast(ing); shot-peening:～硬化 shot ball peening; peening
喷雾 pēnwù spraying:～塔〈化工〉spray tower /～淬火〈冶金〉fog quenching
喷雾器 pēnwùqì sprayer; atomiser; inhaler
喷泻 pēnxiè (of liquid) gush out:火山～出滚滚的岩浆。Tremendous columns of lava gushed out from the volcano.
喷液 pēnyè hydrojet:～淬火〈冶金〉spray quenching
喷溢 pēnyì (of gas, liquid) spurt; gush; overflow:院中的鲜花～出

清淡的馨香。The garden overflows with the delicate fragrance of flowers.
喷涌 pēnyǒng (of liquid) gush; spout:黑色的原油从井口～而出。Dark crude oil gushed from the wells.
喷油 pēnyóu oil gush
喷油泵 pēnyóubèng 〈机械〉injection pump
喷云吐雾 pēnyún-tǔwù ❶ puff cigarette or opium smoke:他坐在长凳上,叼着烟卷,～。Sitting on a bench with a cigarette dangling from his lips, he was puffing wisps of smoke into the air. ❷ (chimneys) belch forth smoke:他望着～的大烟囱,皱了皱眉头。He frowned at the huge columns of smoke belching forth from a tall chimney.
喷子 pēnzi sprayer; spraying apparatus
喷嘴 pēnzuǐ spray nozzle; spray head

pén

盆 pén ❶ basin; tub; pot:脸～ washbasin /澡～ bathtub /火～ firepan; brazier /花～ flower pot /汤～ soup plate ❷ sth. like a basin:骨～ pelvis ❸〈量词〉*for things held in a basin or pot*:两～花 two pots of flowers
盆钵移栽 pénbō yízāi pot transplanting
盆菜 péncài *also* "盘儿菜" pánrcài 〈方言〉ready-to-cook dish of meat, vegetables, etc. sold at a food market
盆地 péndì 〈地理〉basin:塔里木～ Tarim Basin /四川～ Sichuan Basin
盆花 pénhuā potted flower
盆景 pénjǐng 〈工美〉potted landscape; miniature trees and rockery; bonsai
盆盆罐罐 pénpén-guànguàn all the household utensils; pots and pans:搬家时,家里的那些～他一点儿也舍不得扔掉。He hated to part with any of his pots and pans when moving house.
盆腔 pénqiāng 〈生理〉pelvic cavity
盆腔炎 pénqiāngyán pelvic infection
盆汤 péntāng *also* "盆塘" bathtub cubicle:洗～ bath in a bathtub cubicle of a public bath
盆浴 pényù take a bath in a bathtub
盆栽 pénzāi ❶ plant or grow in a flowerpot:～葡萄 grapes grown from a flowerpot ❷ flowers and plants grown in flowerpots; bonsai:案头罗列着常绿的～。On the desk are some flowerpots with evergreen plants. ❸〈农业〉potting; pot culture:～棚 potting shed /～试验 pot experiment /～植物 pot plant
盆子 pénzi 〈口语〉basin; tub; pot

湓 pén 〈书面〉gush; well; surge:～涌 gush /～溢 overflow

pèn

喷 pèn 〈方言〉❶ in season:西瓜～儿 watermelon season /对虾正在～儿上。Prawns are in season. ❷〈量词〉*used of flowering, fruitbearing, or harvesting*:麦子开头～花儿了。The wheat is flowering for the first time. /豆子结二～角了。The string beans are bearing their second crop of pods.
see also pēn
喷红 pènhóng very red:她羞得满脸～。She blushed with embarrassment, colouring to the ears. *or* She blushed profusely.
喷香 pènxiāng *also* "喷喷香" richly fragrant; very delicious:～的红烧肉 delicious braised pork in brown sauce /阳台上的盆花开得～。The flowers on the balcony are in full blossom and give out a rich fragrance.

pēng

烹 pēng ❶ cook; boil:～煮鱼肉 cook fish and pork ❷ quick-fry in hot oil and stir in sauce:～豆芽菜 quick-fried bean sprouts
烹茶 pēngchá make tea
烹饪 pēngrèn cuisine; culinary art:这位厨师～手艺很高。The chef is completely at home with the culinary art.
烹饪法 pēngrènfǎ cookery; cuisine; recipe
烹调 pēngtiáo cook (dishes):～技术 cooking skills; culinary art /～佳肴 cook delicacies /粤式～ Guangdong cooking; Guangdong cuisine /菜的滋味主要取决于～手艺。The taste of a dish largely depends on the skill of the cook.

怦 pēng 〈象声〉pound; thump:他的心老是～～地跳。His heart kept thumping. *or* His heart pounded violently.

砰 pēng 〈象声〉thump; bang:地板被锤子砸得～～响。The floor was thumping under the hammer. /～的一声,广告牌被大风刮倒下来了。The ads board was brought down by the wind on the ground with a thump.
砰訇 pēnghōng *also* "砰轰"〈书面〉bang or thump:雷声～ rumblings of thunder
砰然 pēngrán loud bang:～一声,关上了车门。The car door was banged shut.

抨 pēng 〈书面〉impeach; censure; denounce
抨击 pēngjī attack or assail by words; lash out at; criticize:～时弊 denounce current evil practices
抨弹 pēngtán 〈书面〉❶ attack (often in writing); assail; lash out at:～社会不正风气 launch a fervent attack on (*or* lash out at) the unhealthy social trends ❷ impeach; censure:～不避亲疏 impeach an unqualified official regardless of one's relationship with him or her

澎 pēng 〈方言〉splash; spatter:～了一身水 be splashed all over with water
see also péng

嘭 pēng 〈象声〉:我听到一阵子～～的敲门声。I heard somebody banging the door repeatedly.

péng

彭 Péng a surname
彭斯 Péngsī Robert Burns (1759-1796), Scottish poet
彭塔阿雷纳斯 Péngtǎ'āléinàsī Punta Arenas, city in southern Chile and southernmost city in the world

澎 péng (short for 澎湖列岛) Penghu Islands:台、～、金、马 Taiwan, Penghu, Jinmen and Matsu
see also pēng
澎湖列岛 Pēnghú Lièdǎo (once called the Pescadores by the Portuguese) Penghu Islands, a group of islands to the southeast of Taiwan Province and administratively part of it
澎湃 péngpài ❶ surge:汹涌～ surging; turbulent; tempestuous /激流～ surging torrents ❷ very great; vast and mighty:热情～ surge of enthusiasm /心潮～ feel an upsurge of emotion

蟛 péng
蟛蜞 péngqí 〈动物〉amphibious crab; brackish-water crab

膨 péng expand; swell
膨大 péngdà expand; inflate:机构有些～,人浮于事。The department is inflated and overstuffed.
膨大海 péngdàhǎi *also* "胖大海" pàngdàhǎi 〈中药〉seed of boat-fruited sterculia
膨脝 pénghēng ❶〈书面〉potbellied:～大腹 a big potbelly ❷〈方言〉bulky; unwieldy; cumbersome
膨化 pénghuà dilatation; dilation:～食品 dilated food; inflated food /～玉米 popcorn
膨润土 péngrùntǔ 〈化工〉bentonite:～润滑脂 bentone grease; thickened grease; bentonite thickened grease
膨松度 péngsōngdù 〈纺织〉bulkiness; bulking intensity
膨松剂 péngsōngjì leavening agent
膨体纱 péngtǐshā 〈纺织〉bulk yarn
膨胀 péngzhàng ❶ expand; swell; dilate:金属受热～。Metals expand when heated. ❷ inflate:通货～ inflation (of the currency) /人

口～ expansion of population / 它的帝国主义野心日益～。Its imperialist ambition was growing with each passing day.
膨胀计 péngzhàngjì 〈物理〉 dilatometer
膨胀系数 péngzhàng xìshù coefficient of expansion or dilation
膨胀性 péngzhàngxìng expansibility; dilatancy

搒(榜) péng 〈书面〉 beat with a rod
see also bàng

芃 péng
芃芃 péngpéng 〈书面〉(of plants) luxuriant; exuberant

塳 péng 〈方言〉 ❶ dust: ～尘 dust ❷ whirling dust

蓬 péng ❶ 〈植物〉 bitter flea bane (*Erigeron acris*) ❷ fluffy; dishevelled: ～头散发 shock-headed; with dishevelled hair ❸ 〈量词〉(of luxuriant flowers or grass) clump; tangle: 一～凤尾竹 a clump of fernleaf hedge bamboo
蓬荜增辉 péngbì-zēnghuī *also* "蓬荜生辉" 〈谦词〉 lustre is lent to my humble abode (said as an expression of thanks for sb.'s visit or his gift such as a scroll of calligraphy or painting); my humble house is honoured by your presence
蓬勃 péngbó prosperous; vigorous; flourishing: ～兴起 flourish; forge ahead vigorously / 朝气～ full of youthful vitality / ～发展的商业和服务行业 vigorous growth (*or* rapid development) of commerce and services trades / 楼前的青草长得蓬蓬勃勃。There is lush grass in front of the building.
蓬蒿 pénghāo ❶ 〈方言〉〈植物〉 crowndaisy chrysanthemum ❷ bitter fleabane and wormwood; weeds; 〈比喻〉 commoner: ～之人 ordinary person; uncouth rustic / ～满径。The path was overgrown with weeds.
蓬户 pénghù 〈书面〉 weed-grown door — hut; shack; humble abode
蓬户瓮牖 pénghù-wèngyǒu dwelling for the poor; ramshackle shack; shanty
蓬莱 Pénglái Penglai Island, fabled abode of the immortals: ～仙境 fabled fairyland of immortals
蓬乱 péngluàn (of hair and grass) growing in disorder; untidy; unkempt
蓬门荜户 péngmén-bìhù (shortened as 蓬荜) house with a wicker door; humble abode
蓬蓬 péngpéng (of grass, trees, hair and beard) thick and disorderly; untidy; unkempt: 母亲的坟墓已是这样乱草～了。Mother's grave is overgrown with weeds.
蓬茸 péngróng 〈书面〉(of trees and grass) luxuriant; exuberant; profuse: 绿草～。The grass is lush and luxuriant.
蓬散 péngsan (of hair or grass) fluffy and dishevelled: 长发像堆乱草似的～着 long dishevelled hair tangled like a jumbled mass of weeds
蓬松 péngsōng fluffy; puffy: 这种香波能使你的头发光亮～。This kind of shampoo leaves your hair fluffy and glossy.
蓬头垢面 péngtóu-gòumiàn with dishevelled hair and a grimy face; untidy; unkempt: 一群～的囚徒 a group of unkempt prisoners

篷 péng ❶ covering or awning on a car, boat, etc.: 船～ mat (*or* wooden) roofing of a boat / 敞～车 open car / 帐～ tent / 斗～ cape; cloak ❷ sail (of a boat): 扯～ hoist the sails
篷布 péngbù awning; tarpaulin: 卡车上的货物都用～盖好了。A tarpaulin was strapped over the load of the truck.
篷车 péngchē *also* "棚车" péngchē ❶ 〈铁路〉 box wagon; boxcar ❷ 〈旧语〉 horse-drawn carriage with a covering: 大～ covered wagon
篷帐 péngzhàng tent
篷子 péngzi shed made of bamboo, wood, straw matting or canvas to shelter people from wind and rain: 茅草～ thatched hut

朋 péng ❶ friend: 亲～ relatives and friends / 有～自远方来 have friends coming from afar / 高～满座。There was a gathering of distinguished guests. *or* Distinguished guests and friends filled the room. ❷ 〈书面〉 form a clique; gang up for evil purposes ❸ match; equal: 硕大无～ incomparably huge; colossal
朋辈 péngbèi 〈书面〉 friends; acquaintances
朋比为奸 péngbǐ-wéijiān gang up to do evil; act in collusion with each other; scratch my back and I'll scratch yours
朋侪 péngchái 〈书面〉 friends; acquaintances
朋俦 péngchóu 〈书面〉 *see* "朋辈"
朋党 péngdǎng clique; faction; cabal: 结为～ form a clique; gang up / ～之争 factional strife
朋分 péngfēn 〈书面〉 share; partake: ～利益 share gains
朋僚 péngliáo 〈书面〉 ❶ colleague ❷ friend
朋友 péngyou ❶ friend: 好～ good (*or* bosom) friend / 多年老～ old friend of long standing / 酒肉～ fair-weather friend / 交～ make friends ❷ boy friend or girl friend: 他俩正在交～。They have begun courting. *or* They are going steady.

堋 péng 〈水利〉 a kind of bifurcation dyke which reduces the flow of water

鬅 péng (of hair) fluffy and loose
鬅克 péngkè *also* "朋克" péngkè; "篷克" péngkè; "碰克" pèngkè; "崩克" bēngkè (transliteration) punk
鬅克摇滚乐 péngkè yáogǔnyuè punk-rock
鬅鬙 péngsēng 〈书面〉(of hair) fluffy and dishevelled
鬅松 péngsōng *also* "蓬松" péngsōng fluffy; puffy
鬅头 péngtóu ❶ dishevelled; in disarray: ～散发 dishevelled hair ❷ (of hair) loose hair-style high on top: 梳着～ have a high-top hairdo

棚 péng ❶ awning of straw mats propped up with wooden or bamboo poles to keep off wind and rain: 凉～ awning providing shelter from wind, rain and sunlight / 在园子里搭了个～子 rig up an awning in the garden ❷ shed; shack: 工～ work shed / 窝～ shack; shed; shanty / 牛～ cow shed / 自行车～ bicycle shed / 瓜～ awning in a melon field ❸ room ceiling: 糊～ paper the ceiling ❹ trelis: 丝瓜～ towel gourd trelis
棚车 péngchē *see* "篷车" péngchē
棚户 pénghù slum dwellers; shanty dwellers: ～区 slum area; shanty town
棚圈 péngjuàn shed or covered pen; shed fold
棚寮 péngliáo 〈方言〉 tiny and ramshackle house; shanty
棚子 péngzi 〈口语〉 shed; shack: 草～ straw mat shed / 牛～ cow shed

硼 péng 〈化学〉 boron (B)
硼玻璃 péngbōli borax glass
硼钢 pénggāng steel boride; boron steel
硼化 pénghuà 〈冶金〉 boronize
硼化物 pénghuàwù 〈化学〉 boride
硼化塑料 pénghuà sùliào boron plastic
硼氢化物 péngqīnghuàwù hydroboron
硼砂 péngshā borax; sodium borate
硼酸 péngsuān boric acid
硼酸普鲁卡因 péngsuān pǔlǔkǎyīn 〈药学〉 borocaine
硼酸盐 péngsuānyán borate
硼铁 péngtiě 〈冶金〉 ferroboron
硼中毒 péngzhòngdú 〈医学〉 borism

鹏 péng roc, a huge legendary bird
鹏程万里 péngchéng-wànlǐ embark on a roc's journey of 10,000 *li* — have a brilliant career: 青年人～，应好自为之。Young people must give a good account of themselves, for they have a great future ahead of them.

弸 péng 〈书面〉 fill; be full

pěng

捧 pěng ❶ hold or carry in both hands: 手～奖杯 hold the trophy in both hands / ～一束鲜花 carry a bunch of flowers / ～着一盒糕点 hold a box of pastry / ～起一把泥土 scoop up a handful of earth ❷ 〈量词〉 *used of what can be held in both hands*: 一～花生 a

double handful of groundnuts ❸ flatter; promote; boost:吹～ laud; trumpet; flatter

捧杯 pěngbēi (of sports competition) win the cup; be a champion:上海队在公开赛中～。The Shanghai team won the cup in the open championship.

捧场 pěngchǎng ❶ be a member of a claque (for an actor or actress) ❷ give patronage to; boost; support an activity by being present:他走红那阵子，～的可多啦。Lots of people came in person to boost his performance when he was at the height of his glory.

捧臭脚 pěng chòujiǎo 〈口语〉〈贬义〉lick sb.'s boots; toady to sb.:一帮～的人把他的几篇小说吹得天花乱坠。A group of lickspittles lauded some of his novels to the sky.

捧读 pěngdú 〈书面〉read with respect:～来书，倍感亲切。I was extremely happy to read your letter.

捧腹 pěngfù split or burst one's sides with laughter:令人～ set people roaring with laughter /～大笑 be convulsed with laughter

捧哏 pěnggén (of the supporting actor in a cross talk) help the leading actor in amusing the audience by funny words and gestures

捧角 pěngjué give support to a particular actor or actress by clapping; lavish a lot of praise on an actor or actress; boost an actor or actress

捧杀 pěngshā destroy sb. by extolling him to the skies:"～"与"棒杀"均可以置人于死地。Excessive praise and excessive criticism are equally destructive.

捧胜 pěngshèng 〈方言〉lavish fulsome expressions on an important official; speak of a person in power in most flattering terms:溜须～ suck up to sb.; butter sb. up

捧托 pěngtuō hold sth. with both hands:她～着汤盘走进来。She came in carrying a plate of soup with both hands.

pèng

椪 pèng

椪柑 pènggān a kind of mandarin orange

碰(掽、踫) pèng

❶ touch; knock; bump:自行车～到电线杆子上了。The bike ran into a lamppost. /他头～到了门上。He bumped his head against the door. /花瓶～碎了。The vase is broken. /这个瓷碗给～掉了一块。This china bowl has a chip. ❷ meet; come across; run into:在百货商场～到了一位朋友 run into a friend in the department store /幸亏～到他，问题才得到解决。Fortunately I ran across him and the problem was solved. ❸ have a try; take a chance; try one's luck:事情很难说，～～机会吧。It is very difficult to predict, but we can take a chance. /我想自己去～一下，看他是否会答应。I'll contact him personally and see if he will agree to it.

碰杯 pèngbēi clink glasses

碰壁 pèngbì run into a brick wall; run up against a stone wall; meet with a major setback; be rebuffed:四处～ run into snags and be foiled everywhere /经过几次～之后，他变得聪明起来。He has become wiser after suffering several setbacks.

碰瓷儿 pèngcír 〈方言〉use sth. as a pretext to make trouble; pick a quarrel; find fault:你别～，没有人怕你。Don't try to kick up a row. Nobody is scared of you.

碰钉子 pèng dīngzi meet with a rebuff; be up against a brick wall:他到处～。Everywhere he turned, he ran into a brick wall. /他在她面前碰了个大钉子。He met with a bad rebuff from her.

碰顶 pèngdǐng 〈方言〉at the maximum; at most:今天来开会的～超不过五十人。The number of people attending today's meeting did not exceed fifty at the maximum. /今年能收入七、八十斤蜜已经～啦。The honey to be collected this year will be 70 or 80 *jin* at most.

碰焊 pènghàn 〈冶金〉butt-weld

碰簧锁 pènghuángsuǒ spring lock

碰击 pèngjī strike; ram; dash against:工地上发出锤子～石头的声音。From the construction site came the sound of hammers hitting stones.

碰见 pèngjian meet unexpectedly; run or bump into:这位朋友现在很少～了。Lately I have seldom met this friend of mine. /我～他正在买梨。I happened to see him buying peaches.

碰劲儿 pèngjìnr *also* "碰巧劲儿"〈方言〉accidentally; by chance:～打中了靶子 hit the target by chance

碰铃 pènglíng pair of hand-held bells played by striking one against the other — a percussion instrument used in traditional operas

碰面 pèngmiàn meet; meet with:我们约定今天在这里～。We have agreed to meet here.

碰碰车 pèngpengchē bumper car; dodgem (car)

碰碰船 pèngpengchuán bumper boat

碰巧 pèngqiǎo by chance; by coincidence; accidentally:这东西很难买到，昨天～在一家小店里发现了。I chanced on this article in a small shop yesterday. Normally, it is very hard to come by. /我正想去找他，～他来了。I was going out to see him when he turned up.

碰锁 pèngsuǒ *also* "碰簧锁" spring lock

碰头 pèngtóu ❶ meet and discuss; put one's heads together:我们约好在老伊家～。We have agreed to meet at Lao Yi's. /他们决定～解决余留下来的问题。They decided to solve the remaining problem by putting their heads together. ❷〈方言〉kowtow:～求饶 kowtow for mercy

碰头会 pèngtóuhuì brief meeting:今天下午开个～，交流一下情况。Let's have a brief meeting this afternoon to exchange information.

碰心 pèngxīn 〈方言〉find each other congenial; hit it off:他们俩谈得挺～。The two of them found each other very congenial as they talked.

碰一鼻子灰 pèng yī bízi huī get the cold shoulder; be snubbed; meet with a rebuff:他热切地去求援，谁料竟碰了一鼻子灰。He went earnestly to solicit help, but met with a totally unexpected rebuff.

碰硬 pèngyìng resolutely face up to a formidable opponent (e.g. a powerful official who has violated the law):敢于～ have the courage to stand up against powerful adversaries; dare to take a thorny issue head-on

碰运气 pèng yùnqi try one's luck; take a chance:我想去报考，碰碰运气。I would like to sit for the examination, just to try my luck.

碰撞 pèngzhuàng ❶ collide; run into; strike:搬运瓷器要避免～。Avoid bumping into anything when transporting porcelain. *or* Avoid rough handling in transporting porcelain. ❷ offend; provoke:不要拿话语去～他。Don't provoke him with any uncalled-for remarks. ❸〈物理〉collision; impact:核～ nuclear collision /～负载 impact load

pī

丕 pī

〈书面〉big; great:～业 great cause /～变 immense change

坯(坏) pī

❶ base; blank:铜～ copper base ❷ unburnt brick; earthen brick; adobe:脱～ mould adobe blocks ❸〈方言〉semifinished product:钢～ steel billet

坯布 pībù 〈纺织〉grey (cloth); unbleached, undyed cloth

坯革 pīgé 〈皮革〉crust leather

坯件 pījiàn 〈机械〉blank:螺栓～ bolt blank

坯料 pīliào *also* "毛坯" máopī ❶ semi-finished product ❷〈机械〉blank

坯胎 pītāi base; blank; semi-finished product:搪瓷的金属～ metal base for enamel

坯子 pīzi ❶ base; blank ❷ semi-finished product ❸ makings; material:这小家伙是个踢足球的～。This boy will make a good football player.

伾 pī

伾伾 pīpī 〈书面〉strong; muscular:～武士 mighty warrior

狉 pī

狉狉 pīpī 〈书面〉(of beasts) roam about:鹿豕～。Deer and boars were roaming in herds.

狉獉 pīzhēn *also* "獉狉"〈书面〉overgrown with trees and shrubs and haunted by wild animals

怌 pī

〈书面〉fallacy; falsehood

砒 pī

❶ (old name for 砷) arsenic (As) ❷ (white) arsenic

砒霜 pīshuāng *also* "白砒" báipī; "红砒" hóngpī; "信石" xìnshí; "红矾" hóngfán (white) arsenic

批[1] pī ❶〈书面〉slap:～其颊 slap sb.'s face; box sb.'s ear ❷〈书面〉scrape; pare ❸ write instructions or comments on (a report from a subordinate, etc.):～请示 write comments on a request for instructions /眉～ notes and commentary at the top of a page ❹ officially approve:审～ examine and approve /领导～了我三天假。The leadership allowed me three days' leave. ❺ criticize; refute:～他的错误 criticize him for his mistakes /揭～ expose and criticize

批[2] pī ❶ wholesale:整～购进 buy goods wholesale ❷〈量词〉batch; lot; group:刚到的一～货 a new lot of goods /大～旅游者 large numbers of tourists /参观者分三～入场。Visitors are to enter the hall in three batches.

P

批[3] pī fibres of cotton, flax, etc., ready to be drawn and twisted:线～儿 cotton fibre (for making thread or yarn)

批办 pībàn approve the investigation of a case:那是中央纪律检查委员会～的大案。That was a case of major importance handed down by the Central Disciplinary Committee for investigation.

批驳 pībó ❶ reject (an opinion or a request from a subordinate body):～请求 reject a request (by a subordinate) ❷ criticize; refute:～各种偏见 criticize all kinds of biased views /逐一～ refute point by point

批捕 pībǔ approve an arrest:～要犯 approve the arrest of important criminals

批处理 pīchǔlǐ 〈信息〉batch processing:～文件 bat

批次 pīcì batch (of aircraft, etc.);group (of people, etc.)

批答 pīdá 〈书面〉reply in writing to a memo from below:那个报告昨已～。A written reply was made to the submitted report yesterday.

批点 pīdiǎn ❶write notes and commentary or mark phrases and sentences with small circles or dots on the right-side for emphasis:他读书十分认真,而且常有～。He is a very serious reader; he often makes marginal notes on a text and underlines what he considers important. ❷〈方言〉criticize; censure:你要把这件事做好,不要让人～。You must do it well and let nobody find fault with you.

批斗 pīdòu criticize and denounce sb. at a public meeting for his errors (often imaginary ones) during the Cultural Revolution

批发 pīfā ❶ wholesale:～价格 wholesale price/本店～零售各种灯具。This shop deals in lamps and illuminators by wholesale or at retail. ❷ (of dispatch of an official document) be authorized:这是部长亲自～的文件。The dispatch of the document was authorized by the minister himself.

批发部 pīfābù wholesale department

批发店 pīfādiàn jobbing house; wholesale house

批发合作社 pīfā hézuòshè cooperative wholesale society

批发价格指数 pīfā jiàgé zhǐshù wholesale price index

批发贸易 pīfā màoyì wholesale trade

批发商 pīfāshāng wholesale dealer; wholesaler; jobber

批发市场 pīfā shìchǎng wholesale market; terminal market

批发业 pīfāyè wholesale business; wholesale establishment

批复 pīfù comment on a memo, or give a reply to a request, submitted by a subordinate body:上级已有～。The higher-up has commented on the memo. *or* A written reply has been made by the superiors.

批改 pīgǎi correct; revise; go over:～作业 correct students' papers /～总结初稿 go over the first draft of a summary

批购 pīgòu large-scale purchase; buying wholesale

批亢捣虚 pīháng-dǎoxū go for an enemy's jugular and break through its defences:～者,兵家之长策也。Attacking an enemy at its soft spot is the best military strategy.

批号 pīhào (of a product) batch number

批汇 pīhuì approve an application for foreign exchange

批活 pīhuó goods in batches; products in large quantities

批假 pījià approve a request for leave:他家里有病人需要他照料,为什么不～? Why don't you approve his leave of absence since he has a sick person to look after at home?

批件 pījiàn lower-level report with a reply or comments by a higher-up

批量 pīliàng ❶ (produce) in batches:这种仪器已经定型,开始～生产。The apparatus is being batch-produced since its design has been finalized. ❷ size of batch (of products):大～ mass quantities / 小～ small quantities

批零 pī-líng wholesale and retail:本店兼营～。This shop is for both wholesale and retail.

批零差价 pī-líng chājià price difference between the wholesale and the retail; wholesale-retail price differential

批判 pīpàn criticize; critique:～错误思想 criticize erroneous ideas /～地吸收一切有益的东西 critically assimilate what is beneficial /空洞的～是没有说服力的。Criticisms not backed up by facts are unconvincing. *or* A criticism couched in vague terms convinces nobody. / 要用～的眼光去分析这些问题。We must take a critical approach to these issues.

批判现实主义 pīpàn xiànshízhǔyì critical realism

批评 pīpíng ❶ criticism (involving both positive and negative aspects):文学～ literary criticism /开展文艺～,繁荣文艺事业。Unfold the criticism of art and literature to foster them. ❷ criticize; censure:～官僚主义作风 criticize the bureaucratic style of work /正确对待群众～ take a correct attitude towards public criticism

批示 pīshì ❶ write comments to show approval or disapproval (on a memo submitted by a subordinate):写个报告请领导～ draw up a memo asking for instructions from above ❷ such written comments:对上级的～要认真执行 strictly carry out the instructions of the leadership given on the memo

批条 pītiáo note with instructions or comments by the leadership

批条子 pī tiáozi write out a note with instructions on it:执行规定,最怕领导～,开口子。In the implementation of rules and regulations the worst fear is that some leaders may send a note with their personal instructions, trying to make an exception.

批文 pīwén lower-level report or document sent back with comments by the higher-ups concerned; document with written reply or instructions by the competent authorities

批郤导窾 pīxì-dǎokuǎn cut up an ox according to its anatomy — be good at grasping the key to an issue

批销 pīxiāo wholesale:经营报刊零售和～业务 deal in newspapers and magazines both retail and wholesale

批语 pīyǔ ❶ comments on a piece of writing:在学生的作文上写了许多～ write many comments on students' essays /函中附有局领导的～。Included herewith is a note with instructions from the head of the bureau. ❷ *see* "批示"

批阅 pīyuè read over (official papers), giving comments or making corrections:这份报告经部长～过的。This is the memo that the minister has read over and commented on.

批注 pīzhù ❶ annotate and comment on; put notes and commentary to (a book, etc.):边读边～ make annotations while reading ❷ annotations and commentaries; marginalia

批转 pīzhuǎn write comments or instructions on a report from below and transmit it to units or departments concerned

批准 pīzhǔn ratify; approve; sanction:～条约 ratify a treaty /～他们的科研计划 approve their plan of scientific research /～该单位要求资助的请求 grant the department's request for financial assistance

批准书 pīzhǔnshū (of treaties, conventions, agreements, etc.) instrument of ratification:递交～ deliver an instrument of ratification /本条约自互换～之日起生效。The present treaty shall come into force on the date of exchange of instruments.

纰 pī (of cloth, silk thread, etc.) become unwoven or untwisted; be spoilt:这只袜子有根线～了。There is an untwisted thread in the sock.

纰漏 pīlòu careless mistake; small error; slip:他再三叮咛,生怕出～。He told us over and over again to avoid any slip.

纰缪 pīmiù 〈书面〉error; mistake:此书实多～。The book is full of mistakes.

披 pī ❶ drape over one's shoulders; wrap around:把大衣～在身上 drape an overcoat over one's shoulders /～戴红花 wear a red silk flower on the breast /～上节日的盛装 be brilliantly decorated for a festival /～着合法的外衣在进行破坏活动 commit sabotage under the cloak of legality /～着保护人权的外衣 deck oneself out as a defender of human rights ❷ open; unroll; unfold; spread out:～襟 loosen one's jacket ❸ split open; crack:指甲～了。There was a crack in the finger nail. /椅子腿～开了。The chair's leg has split.

披猖 pīchāng 〈书面〉❶ rampant; ferocious; arrogant:走私活动～

rampant smuggling ❷ scatter; wildly disperse
披读 pīdú open a book and start to read; read
披发 pīfà ❶〈书面〉with hair dishevelled; with hair in disarray: ～入山 go into the mountains with dishevelled hair (as a protest against society) ❷ dishevelled hair: 蓬松的～ long and dishevelled hair
披发左衽 pīfà-zuǒrèn grow long hair hanging down over one's neck and wear a jacket buttoned on the left — characteristic of certain ethnic tribes in ancient times
披风 pīfēng cape; cloak; mantle
披拂 pīfú 〈书面〉flutter; flap; sway: 枝叶～ the branches were swaying and the leaves fluttering
披肝沥胆 pīgān-lìdǎn ❶ bare one's heart; unbosom oneself: ～以相告 speak with the utmost candour ❷ be loyal and faithful: 朋友间应该～, 以诚相见。There should be absolute sincerity and staunch loyalty among friends.
披挂 pīguà ❶ put on a suit of armour: ～上阵 buckle on one's armour and go into battle; be ready to fight in the thick of a battle ❷ put on dress; wear: 大家～整齐, 准备登山。Everybody is in climbing gear and ready for the mountaineering. ❸ (often used in the early vernacular) suit of armour
披红 pīhóng drape a band of red silk across sb.'s shoulders (on a festive occasion or as a mark of recognition for meritorious services)
披红戴花 pīhóng-dàihuā have red silk draped over one's shoulders and flowers pinned on one's breast (as a token of honour)
披怀 pīhuái 〈书面〉treat sb. with sincerity: ～畅谈 engage sb. in a heart-to-heart talk
披枷带锁 pījiā-dàisuǒ be fettered and shackled
披甲 pījiǎ put on a suit of armour: ～持矛 put on a suit of armour and grasp a spear
披坚执锐 pījiān-zhíruì buckle on one's armour and take up a weapon; don one's armour and grip one's weapon — be fully armed and ready for combat
披肩 pījiān ❶ cape ❷ shawl
披肩发 pījiānfà shoulder length hair: 留～的女郎 girl wearing her hair long
披巾 pījīn shawl
披荆斩棘 pījīng-zhǎnjí break through brambles and thorns; blaze a new trail through brambles; hew one's way through difficulties: 为了开发油田, 他们～, 历尽艰辛。To open up oilfields, they endured untold difficulties and hardships. /我们一定要～, 开拓我国科学发展的道路。We must blaze new trails and open up our own road of scientific development.
披卷 pījuàn leaf through books
披览 pīlǎn also "披阅"〈书面〉open and read (a book); peruse: ～群书 read numerous volumes voraciously
披离 pīlí irregular; entangled: 大树上挂满了～的藤萝。The big tree is overhung with entangled wisteria.
披沥 pīlì 〈书面〉be open and sincere: ～陈辞 state one's views without the slightest reservation
披露 pīlù ❶ publish; announce: 录取名单已经～。The list of successful candidates has been made public. ❷ reveal; show; disclose: ～心迹 reveal one's true feelings
披麻带孝 pīmá-dàixiào also "披麻戴孝"〈旧语〉be dressed in white and with burlap draped over one's shoulders in mourning for one's parent; be dressed in deep mourning
披麻救火 pīmá-jiùhuǒ go in a flaxen cape to put out a fire — draw the fire upon oneself; the means defeat the end
披毛犀 pīmáoxī also "毛犀"〈动物〉woolly rhinoceros
披靡 pīmǐ ❶ (of trees and grass, etc.) cannot stand the force of wind: 百花凋零, 草木～。The flowers withered and the branches bent in the wind. ❷〈军事〉collapse before a formidable enemy: 望风～ turn tail (*or* collapse) at the mere rustle of a leaf /我军所向～。Enemy troops fled at the advance of our troops.
披散 pīsan (of hair, etc.) hang down loosely: 她～着头发, 冲出门外。She dashed out of the gate, her hair hanging loosely on her shoulders.
披沙拣金 pīshā-jiǎnjīn sift out fine gold from sand — extract the essentials from a large mass of material
披厦 pīshà also "披屋" outhouse
披剃 pītì 〈佛教〉tonsure
披头 pītóu fringe: 这个女子前额有像"～"一样的短发覆盖着。The girl's forehead was covered by a fringe.
披头散发 pītóu-sànfà dishevelled hair; with hair hanging loose: 梦中一女子～, 满面哀容地站在他面前。He dreamed of a woman standing before him, with dishevelled hair and an expression of grief.
披头士 pītóushì Beatle: ～乐队 the Beatles (in the 1950's and 1960's) /～发型 Beatle cut /～狂 Beatlemania
披玩 pīwán 〈书面〉enjoy or read sth.: ～古字画 enjoy ancient calligraphic works and paintings
披屋 pīwū see "披厦"
披星戴月 pīxīng-dàiyuè under the moon and stars; work from before dawn till after dark: 大忙季节, 他～地在田间劳作。During the busy farming season he worked from dawn to dusk in the field.
披阅 pīyuè see "披览"
披针形 pīzhēnxíng 〈植物〉lanceolar; lanceolate
披针叶南洋杉 pīzhēnyè nányángshān 〈植物〉bunya-bunya; bunya pine (*Araucaria bidwillii*)

铍

pī 〈书面〉❶ long needle for acupuncture ❷ long spear; lance
see also pí

铌

pī 〈书面〉metal arrowhead
see also bī

辟(闢)

pī
see also bì; pì
辟头 pītóu see "劈头❷" pītóu

霹

pī
霹雷 pīléi 〈口语〉thunderbolt; thunderclap
霹雳 pīlì also "落雷" luòléi thunderbolt; thunderclap: 晴天～ bolt from the blue /一声震耳欲聋的～ deafening thunderbolt
霹雳舞 pīlìwǔ break dance; break dancing

噼

pī
噼里啪啦 pīlipālā see "劈里啪啦" pīlipālā
噼啪 pīpā see "劈啪" pīpā

劈

pī ❶ split; chop; cleave: ～柴火 chop wood /把竹子～成两半 split a bamboo in two /在丛林中～开一条路来 cleave a path through a jungle ❷ split; cracked; broken: 钢笔尖～了。The pen nib is broken. / 板子压～了。The plank cracked under the weight. ❸〈方言〉hoarse: 嗓子嚷～了 shout oneself hoarse ❹ right against (one's face, etc.): see "～头"; "～脸" ❺ (of thunder) strike: 一根大树杈让雷给～断了。A big branch was struck down by lightning. ❻ also "尖劈" jiānpī wedge
see also pǐ
劈波斩浪 pībō-zhǎnlàng also "劈风斩浪" (of a ship) cleave through the waves; 〈比喻〉surmount difficulties and forge ahead: 江轮～, 向前驶去。The steamer moved on fast, cleaving through the waves.
劈刺 pīcì 〈军事〉sabre or bayonet fighting: ～训练 bayonet drill
劈刀 pīdāo ❶ chopper ❷〈军事〉sabre fighting
劈角儿 pījiǎor 〈口语〉right overhead; right on sb.'s head; head on: ～一掌击去 head-on strike
劈空 pīkōng without foundation; groundless: ～诬人清白 make groundless accusations against sb.; smear sb.'s reputation without foundation; spread unfounded rumours about sb.
劈口 pīkǒu 〈方言〉say sth. right away (indicating urgency): 小刘气喘喘地跑进来, ～便对团长说: "有敌情…" Xiao Liu ran in panting, saying to the regimental commander: "Signs of enemy movement…"
劈理 pīlǐ 〈矿业〉cleavage
劈里啪啦 pīlipālā also "噼里啪啦" pīlipālā 〈象声〉pitter-patter: 掌声～地响起来。There was a burst of applause. /小院里响起了～的鞭炮声。Firecrackers spluttered in the courtyard. /我们听到屋顶～的雨点声。We heard the pitter-patter of raindrops on the roof.
劈脸 pīliǎn right in the face; head-on: ～一拳 punch sb. on the nose /他～就向我提出一连串的问题。He confronted me with a barrage of questions.
劈面 pīmiàn right in the face; head-on: ～撞见 bump right into

sb.

劈啪 pīpā *also*“噼啪”pīpā〈象声〉pit-a-pat：竹子烧得～响。The bamboo cracked in the fire. /我还没有走进大厅，就听到听众劈劈啪啪的掌声。I heard the audience clapping enthusiastically before I entered the hall.

劈杀 pīshā (of cavalrymen) fight or attack with sabres

劈山 pīshān level off hilltops; blast cliffs：～引水 cut through mountains to bring in water /为了便利运输，我们不得不～筑路。We had to level off hilltops to build a road to facilitate transportation.

劈手 pīshǒu too quickly for response; swiftly：她～夺过他的球拍。She snatched the bat from him before he was aware of it.

劈天盖地 pītiān-gàidì come down like an avalanche：大雨倾盆泻下，雷声闪电～掠过。The rain came pelting down with thunder roaring and lightning flashing across the sky.

P

劈头 pītóu ❶ straight on the head; right in the face; head-on：～就打 hit sb. right on the head /他黑暗中～撞到了电线杆上。He bumped straight into a lamppost in the dark. ❷ *also*“辟头”pītóu at the very outset：他见到我，～一句就是："我不干了！" The moment he saw me, he said, "I've washed my hands of the business." /你～就这么一句，让我摸不着头脑。You blurted out such an abrupt remark that I had no idea what you were driving at.

劈头盖脸 pītóu-gàiliǎn *also*“劈头盖脑”；“劈头盖顶” right in the face; suddenly and fiercely：～给他一巴掌 slap him right across the face /瓢泼似的大雨～地浇下来。The rain is pouring down. /爸爸总爱～地教训我。Father often gave me a dressing-down without a word of warning.

劈胸 pīxiōng right on the chest：他想逃，我～一把抓住他。He attempted to escape, but I grabbed him by the front of his jacket.

pí

琵 pí

琵鹭 pílù〈动物〉spoonbill (*Plataleinae*)

琵琶 pípa *pipa*, a plucked string instrument with a fretted fingerboard

琵琶歌 pípagē a kind of folk song of the Dong nationality, sung to the accompaniment of the Dong *pipa*

琵琶骨 pípagǔ〈方言〉scapula; shoulder blade

琵琶记 Pípajì *Tale of the Pipa*, play by Gao Zecheng (高则诚) in the late Yuan Dynasty

琵琶襟 pípajīn a kind of dress for ladies, the front of which is buttoned up to the right just a little distance away from the armpit

琵琶桶 pípatǒng barrel

琵嘴鸭 pízuǐyā〈动物〉shoveler

枇 pí

枇杷 pípa loquat

芘 pí

芘芣 pífú〈古语〉〈植物〉high mallow

毗(毘) pí

〈书面〉❶ adjoin; be contiguous; be adjacent：*see*“～连”；“～邻” ❷ supplementary; auxiliary; subsidiary

毗连 pílián adjoin; border on; be contiguous with; be adjacent to：中国北部与俄罗斯和蒙古～。Northern China borders on Russia and Mongolia.

毗连岛屿 pílián dǎoyǔ contiguous island

毗连国 píliánguó contiguous state

毗连海区 pílián hǎiqū contiguous sea area

毗连区 píliánqū adjacent area; contiguous zone

毗连性 píliánxìng contiguity

毗邻 pílín adjoin; border on; be adjacent to：我国和朝鲜～。China borders on Korea. *or* China and Korea are neighbours.

蚍 pí

蚍蜉 pífú〈书面〉big ant

蚍蜉撼大树 pífú hàn dàshù an ant trying to topple a giant tree — ridiculously overrating one's own strength

貔 pí

〈书面〉mythical bearlike animal

貔虎 píhǔ tigers' brigade; (crack troops of a) mighty army

貔貅 píxiū ❶ mythical fierce animal ❷ crack troops：～之士 brave fighters

貔子 pízi〈方言〉yellow weasel

膍 pí

〈古语〉stomach of an ox (as food)

膍胵 píchī〈方言〉stomach of birds; crop：鸡～ stomach of a chicken; gizzard

罴(羆) pí

〈动物〉brown bear

裨 pí

〈书面〉assistant; secondary：偏～ adjutant

see also bì

裨将 píjiàng adjutant general (in ancient China)

埤 pí

〈书面〉increase; augment

see also pì

鼙 pí

鼙鼓 pígǔ〈古语〉small drum used in the army：～喧天。Army drums sent up a noise up to heaven.

椑 pí

〈古语〉elliptic wine bessel

啤 pí

啤酒 píjiǔ *also*“麦酒”màijiǔ beer：生～ draught beer /黑～ porter; brown ale; stout /～厂 brewery

啤酒花 píjiǔhuā *also*“忽布”hūbù；“蛇麻”shémá；“酒花”〈植物〉hops

蜱 pí

also“壁虱”bìshī〈动物〉tick

脾 pí

also“脾脏”spleen

脾出血 píchūxuè〈医学〉splenorrhagia

脾溃疡 píkuìyáng〈医学〉splenelcosis

脾瘤 píliú〈医学〉splenoma; splenoncus

脾气 píqi ❶ temperament; disposition; temper：～好 be good-tempered; have a good (*or* gentle) disposition /他俩～很合得来。They are temperamentally compatible. /久病使他～变得很坏。His prolonged illness made him as cross as two sticks. ❷ bad temper：发～ lose one's temper; flare up; get into a huff /～大 be hot-tempered /～暴烈 have a violent (*or* fiery) temper

脾切除 píqiēchú〈医学〉splenectomy

脾胃 píwèi temperament; taste：他与我～相投。He and I are kindred spirits. /这事不合他的～。The work does not fit (*or* suit) his temperament.

脾性 píxìng〈方言〉temperament; disposition：一个人有一个人的～。Everyone has his own temperamental peculiarity. /养花要懂得各种花的～。If you grow flowers, you'll have to know, as it were, their idiosyncrasies.

脾性贫血 píxìng pínxuè〈医学〉splenic anemia

脾炎 píyán〈医学〉lienitis; splenitis

脾硬化 píyìnghuà〈医学〉splenceratosis; splenkeratosis

脾脏 pízàng spleen

脾肿大 pízhǒngdà〈医学〉splenomegaly

陴 pí

〈书面〉parapet wall; parapet

皮 pí

❶ skin; cutis：羊～ sheepskin /真～ cutis vera/牛～ cowhide /～试 skin test /擦破一层～ scrape a bit of skin off ❷ leather; fur：～大衣 fur coat ❸ peel; rind：橘子～ orange peel /西瓜～ watermelon rind /柠檬～ lemon rind /香蕉～ banana skin /麦～ (wheat) bran ❹ cover; wrapper：包袱～儿 (cloth) wrapper for a parcel / 封～ (book) dust jacket /书～ book cover; jacket ❺ surface：水～儿 surface of water /地～ ground ❻ broad, flat piece (of some thin material); sheet：铁～ iron sheet /草～ sod; turf /豆腐～ bean curd skin /海蜇～ jellyfish skin /粉～ sheet jelly made from bean or sweet potato starch ❼ pliable; tough：牛～糖 sticky candy ❽ no longer crisp; soggy：饼干～了。The biscuits have become soggy. ❾ naughty; mischievous：这孩子～得很。The child is too

naughty. ⑩ case-hardened; apathetic: 你老是批评他, 他有点～了。You have criticized him much too often, and now he doesn't seem to care. ⑪ rubber: 橡～ rubber eraser /胶～ (vulcanized) rubber ⑫ (Pí) a surname
皮袄 pí'ǎo fur-lined jacket
皮板儿 píbǎnr skin of the fur lining
皮包 píbāo leather handbag; briefcase; portfolio
皮包公司 píbāo gōngsī briefcase company — bubble company; fly-by-night company
皮包骨 píbāogǔ *also* "皮包骨头" skin and bones; bag of bones: 他大病之后, 已经是～了。After a serious illness, he was reduced to skin and bones (*or* a mere skeleton).
皮包商 píbāoshāng briefcase businessman — wildcat merchant; fly-by-nighter: 我们不是～, 我们来这里是有长期打算的。We're no fly-by-nighters. We're in here for the long haul.
皮鞭 píbiān *also* "皮鞭子" leather-thonged whip
皮层 pícéng ❶〈生物〉cortex ❷〈生理〉cerebral cortex
皮缠 píchán (often used in the early vernacular) endless haggling
皮尺 píchǐ tape measure; tape
皮带 pídài ❶ leather belt: 鳄鱼～ crocodile skin belt ❷〈机械〉(driving) belt: 交叉～ cross belt /三角～ triangle belt /～车床 belt-driven lathe /～传动 belt transmission /～运输机 belt conveyer
皮带轮 pídàilún〈机械〉belt pulley
皮蛋 pídàn *also* "松花" sōnghuā preserved duck egg
皮垫圈 pídiànquān *also* "皮钱儿"〈机械〉leather washer; leather packing collar
皮尔·卡丹 Pí'ěr Kǎdān Pierre Cardin, a trade name of garments after Pierre Cardin (1922-), French couturier
皮耳 pí'ěr a kind of edible black fungus, grown on live trees
皮筏 pífá skin raft: 羊～ goat skin raft
皮肤 pífū ❶ skin; dermis: ～白 fair (*or* pale) skin ❷〈书面〉skin-deep; superficial; shallow: ～之见 superficial view (*or* opinion)
皮肤病 pífūbìng skin disease; dermatosis
皮肤坏死霉素 pífū huàisǐ méisù dermotoxin
皮肤角化病 pífū jiǎohuàbìng〈医学〉keratoderma; keratoma; keratosis
皮肤结核 pífū jiéhé〈医学〉tuberculous gumma; scrofulous gumma; scrofuloderma
皮肤科 pífūkē〈医学〉dermatological department; dermatology: ～医生 dermatologist
皮肤瘤 pífūliú dermatoma
皮肤色素沉着 pífū sèsù chénzhuó〈医学〉cutaneous pigmentation
皮肤松垂 pífū sōngchuí〈医学〉demotolysis
皮肤移植 pífū yízhí skin graft
皮肤针 pífūzhēn〈中医〉cutaneous acupuncture (using a stick with five or seven needles tied vertically to its end to tap lightly at the skin surface of the affected area)
皮肤真菌病 pífū zhēnjūnbìng〈医学〉dermatomycosis
皮傅 pífù〈书面〉draw far-fetched conclusions from superficial understanding of a problem: 后来学者对本书的解释多有～。Subsequent scholars mostly interpreted the book on the basis of their superficial understanding.
皮革 pígé leather; tanned hide
皮辊花 pígǔnhuā *also* "白花" báihuā〈纺织〉lap waste
皮猴儿 píhóur fur-lined hooded overcoat; fur parka; fur anorak
皮胡 píhú *huqin*, a two-stringed bowed instrument with snake-skin covering one end of its bamboo tube
皮花 píhuā ginned cotton; lint (cotton)
皮划艇 píhuátǐng〈体育〉kayak: 单人～ single kayak /双人～ double kayak; kayak pair; two-seater kayak; K-2 /四人～ kayak four; K-4
皮划艇运动 píhuátǐng yùndòng canoeing: ～员 canoeist
皮黄 píhuáng *also* "皮簧" ❶ (short for 西皮 and 二黄) two chief tunes in Beijing opera ❷ Beijing opera
皮货 píhuò fur goods: ～商 furrier; fur trader
皮肌炎 píjīyán〈医学〉dermatomyositis
皮夹克 píjiākè leather jacket
皮夹子 píjiāzi *also* "皮夹儿" wallet; pocketbook; purse
皮匠 píjiang ❶ cobbler ❷ tanner
皮胶 píjiāo hide glue
皮接 píjiē〈林业〉bark graft
皮金龟 píjīnguī〈动物〉skin beetle (Trogidae)
皮筋儿 píjīnr *also* "猴皮筋儿" hóupíjīnr〈口语〉rubber band
皮具 píjù leatherware
皮开肉绽 píkāi-ròuzhàn with the skin torn and the flesh gaping open: 他被打得～。He was beaten until his skin burst (*or* split) open and his flesh hung in shreds. *or* He was badly beaten up, with blood flowing from his lacerated flesh.
皮科儿 píkēr *also* "皮磕儿"〈方言〉funny remarks: 他这个人很随便, 说话离不开～笑话。He is the casual sort and never ceases to mingle his remarks with jokes.
皮库 píkù〈医学〉skin bank
皮拉 píla *also* "皮辣"〈方言〉❶ not care a pin for what people say about oneself; be indifferent or apathetic: 他挺～的, 谁说他两句他都不在乎。He doesn't seem to care at all, even if you take him to task. ❷ tough; sturdy: 他～着呢, 腿上划了个大口子跟没事一样。He is a tough guy. He felt as if nothing had happened when he got a big cut in his leg.
皮里抽肉 pílǐ-chōuròu grow thin: 如今缺草少料, 我们只好眼看着牲口～。We could only watch the livestock getting thinner for lack of fodder.
皮里阳秋 pílǐ-yángqiū *also* "皮里春秋" veiled criticism: ～的笔法 style of veiled criticism; art of making veiled criticism
皮脸 píliǎn〈方言〉❶ naughty ❷ shameless: 他可真够～的。He has virtually lost all sense of shame.
皮脸儿 píliǎnr old-style cloth shoes whose vamp has two slips of leather sewn up in the shape of a stem
皮箩 píluó basket woven with thin bamboo strips; bamboo basket
皮毛 pímáo ❶ fur: 貂皮是一种极贵重的～, 买得起的人不多。Mink is a very expensive fur, which few people can afford. ❷ smattering; inkling; superficial knowledge: 仅知～ have only a rudimentary knowledge (of a subject) /有些人学了点～就充内行了。Some people with a smattering of knowledge pose as experts. /这篇文章仅仅涉及到这个问题的～。This article only skims the surface of the subject.
皮帽子 pímàozi *also* "皮帽儿" fur cap; fur hat
皮棉 pímián *also* "皮花" ginned cotton; lint (cotton)
皮面 pímiàn epidermis; surface
皮囊 pínáng ❶ leather bag ❷〈贬义〉person's body: 臭～ vile skin-bag; this mortal flesh
皮内 pínèi intradermal: ～注射 intradermal injection /～试验 intradermal test
皮内针 pínèizhēn intradermal needling (acupuncture by embedding the needle subcutaneously for one or several days)
皮袍 pípáo fur gown
皮钱儿 píqiánr *see* "皮垫圈"
皮球 píqiú rubber ball; ball
皮肉 píròu skin and flesh: ～之苦 physical suffering; physical pain /我不过伤了点～, 没什么。It's nothing serious — just a scratch (*or* bruise).
皮肉生涯 píròu-shēngyá livelihood based on one's body — life of a prostitute
皮褥子 pírùzi *also* "皮褥" fur-lined mattress
皮软 píruǎn〈方言〉pliable; limp: 晒干的小麦受了潮, 又变得～了。The dried wheat got damp again and became soggy.
皮氏卧式转炉 Píshì wòshì zhuànlú〈冶金〉Pierce-Smith converter
皮实 píshi ❶ (of people) sturdy; tough: 学生们练得～点才好。The students should have more physical training and make themselves tougher. ❷ (of things) durable; stout
皮糖 pítáng a kind of sticky candy
皮条 pítiáo leather strap
皮条纤 pítiáoqiàn middleman who runs errands for illicit sexual relations; pimp; procurer
皮艇 pítǐng ❶ canoe racing ❷ kayak
皮桶子 pítǒngzi *also* "皮桶儿"〈方言〉fur lining (for a jacket or an overcoat)
皮纹 píwén〈生理〉dermatoglyphics
皮下 píxià〈医学〉subcutaneous; hypodermic
皮下投药法 píxià tóuyàofǎ hypodermic medication
皮下心脏起搏器 píxià xīnzàng qǐbóqì hypodermic cardiac pacemaker
皮下注射 píxià zhùshè subcutaneous or hypodermic injection: ～器 hypodermic syringe
皮下组织 píxià zǔzhī〈生理〉subcutaneous tissue; hypodermis; subcutis

P

皮线 píxiàn 〈电工〉rubber-insulated wire; rubber-covered wire
皮箱 píxiāng leather suitcase; leather trunk
皮相 píxiàng shallow; superficial: ～之士 indifferent scholar
皮相之见 píxiàngzhījiàn *also* "皮相之谈" superficial perception; shallow idea: 这种看法乃～。This viewpoint was merely superficial.
皮硝 píxiāo (common term for 朴硝) mirabilite; Glauber's salt
皮笑肉不笑 pí xiào ròu bù xiào put on a false smile: 他说起话来总是～的，一脸奸相。He often gives a hypocritical smile when he starts to speak, the very picture of villainy.
皮鞋 píxié leather shoes: ～油 shoe polish / 擦～ polish shoes; shoeshine
皮屑 píxiè 〈生理〉scurf: 头～ dandruff
皮癣病 píxuǎnbìng 〈医学〉dermatophytosis
皮靴 píxuē leather boots
皮炎 píyán 〈医学〉dermatitis; cutitis: 神经性～ neurodermatitis / 接触性～ contact dermatitis / 湿疹性～ eczematous dermatitis
皮衣 píyī ❶ leather jacket ❷ fur coat
皮影戏 píyǐngxì *also* "驴皮影" lǘpíyǐng leather-silhouette show; shadow play
皮张 pízhāng pelt; hide
皮掌儿 pízhǎngr outsole
皮疹 pízhěn 〈医学〉rash; eruption
皮之不存，毛将焉附 pí zhī bù cún, máo jiāng yān fù 〈谚语〉with the skin gone, what can the hair adhere to — a thing cannot exist without its basis
皮脂 pízhī 〈生理〉sebum: ～溢 seborrh(o)ea; steatorrhea / ～溢性脱发 seborrheic alopecia / ～溢性皮炎 seborrheic dermatitis
皮脂瘤 pízhīliú 〈医学〉dermolipoma
皮脂囊肿 pízhī nángzhǒng 〈医学〉sebaceous cyst
皮脂腺 pízhīxiàn 〈生理〉sebaceous gland
皮纸 pízhǐ tough paper made from bast fibre of mulberry trees, etc., formerly used for making umbrellas
皮质 pízhì 〈生理〉❶ surperficial cells (of certain internal organs) ❷ cortex: 大脑～ cerebral cortex
皮质激素 pízhì jīsù 〈生化〉cortical hormene: ～类 corticoid
皮重 pízhòng tare (weight): 扣除～计算 tare and tret
皮子 pízi ❶ leather; hide ❷ fur

疲

pí ❶ tired; weary; exhausted: 精～力尽 completely exhausted; tired out ❷ weaken; slump: 乐此不～ have unflagging interest in sth.; always enjoy (doing) sth. / 这种空调畅销不～。This brand of air conditioners sells well on the market.
疲惫 píbèi ❶ tired out; exhausted: 他回来时已～不堪了。He returned exhausted. ❷ tire out; wear out: 采取拖延战术，以～对手。Delaying tactics were employed to wear out the opponent.
疲敝 píbì (of manpower, resources, etc.) become inadequate: 师出历年，百姓～。With the war going on for years, the people were drained of their resources.
疲病 píbìng tired and ill: ～之卒 exhausted and sick soldiers
疲怠 pídài tired; weary: ～的身体 be physically exhausted
疲顿 pídùn 〈书面〉tired out; exhausted: 长途跋涉，人人～。They were all overcome with fatigue after the long journey.
疲乏 pífá weary; tired: 显露出～的神情 have a weary look; look tired / ～得睁不开眼 too tired to keep one's eyes open
疲竭 píjié 〈书面〉(of energy) completely exhausted: 侵略军被拖得～不堪。The aggressor troops were completely worn out.
疲倦 píjuàn tired; weary: ～已极 be tired out; be dog-tired / 不知～ be tireless / 我的头昏了，身体也很～。I felt dizzy and fatigued.
疲困 píkùn ❶ tire; weary: ～不堪 be dog-tired; be exhausted / 诱敌深入，频频出击，以～敌人。Lure the enemy in deep and tire them by launching frequent attacks. ❷ (of economic situation, etc.) weak; slumping: 该公司近来日显～。This company has been lagging in business recently.
疲劳 píláo ❶ tired; fatigued; weary: 过分～ be extremely tired / 身心～ be weary both in body and mind / 不顾～连续工作 continue to work despite fatigue ❷ 〈生理〉〈物理〉fatigue: 肌肉～ muscular fatigue / 听觉～ auditory fatigue / 音响～ sonic fatigue / 金属～ metal fatigue / 弹性～ elastic fatigue / 磁性～ magnetic fatigue / ～部位 seat of fatigue
疲劳感觉阈 píláo gǎnjuéyù sensitivity threshold of fatigue
疲劳强度 píláo qiángdù 〈物理〉fatigue strength
疲劳审讯 píláo shěnxùn gruelling trial
疲劳试验 píláo shìyàn 〈物理〉fatigue test
疲劳战术 píláo zhànshù gruelling tactic (used in an interrogation): 他们是在对我搞～。They were trying to tire me out.
疲劳综合征 píláo zōnghézhēng 〈医学〉exhaustion syndrome
疲累 pílèi worn out; weary: 走了一天的路，着实有些～。After walking the whole day, I am really exhausted.
疲癃 pílóng 〈书面〉ageing and ailing
疲苶 píníe 〈书面〉completely exhausted
疲软 píruǎn ❶ fatigued and weak; weak and frail: 病后浑身～ feel weak all over after illness ❷ 〈金融〉weak; slumping; sluggish: 市场～ sluggish market / 价格～ slumping prices / 股市～ bearish stock market
疲弱 píruò feeble; weak: 身体～ be worn out / 他拖着～的双腿继续前进。He staggered onward with feeble legs.
疲塌 píta *also* "疲沓" slack; negligent: 工作拖拉～ dilatory and lackadaisical / 他工作～被辞退了。He was sacked for slackness.
疲于奔命 píyú-bēnmìng be kept constantly on the run: 我一天到晚～，真有点支不住了。I am always on the go and feel pretty worn out.

铍

pí 〈化学〉beryllium (Be)
see also pī
铍合金 píhéjīn 〈冶金〉beryllium alloy
铍铜合金 pítóng héjīn 〈冶金〉beallon
铍中毒 pízhòngdú 〈医学〉berylliosis

鲏

pí *see* "鳑鲏" pángpí

狓

pí *see* "獾狮狓" huòjiāpí

pǐ

否

pǐ ❶ bad; evil: ～泰 bad and good luck ❷ censure; condemn: 臧～人物 〈书面〉pass judgement on people
see also fǒu
否极泰来 pǐjí-tàilái extreme adversity marks the beginning of fortune; out of the depth of misfortune comes bliss: 乐极生悲，～。Extreme joy begets sorrow, while calamity engenders good fortune.

痞

pǐ ❶ lump in the abdomen ❷ ruffian; hooligan; riffraff: 地～流氓 local ruffians and hooligans / 文～ hack writer; hack / 兵～ army riffraff; soldier of fortune
痞棍 pǐgùn ruffian; riffraff
痞话 pǐhuà *also* "痞子话" 〈方言〉vulgar or coarse language; four-letter words
痞块 pǐkuài *also* "痞积" 〈中医〉lump in the abdomen
痞里痞气 pǐlipǐqì be casual and happy-go-lucky; fool around
痞子 pǐzi 〈口语〉ruffian; rascal; riffraff: 这个人是个小～。This guy is a bit of a rascal.

嚭(噽)

pǐ 〈书面〉big; large; huge

庀

pǐ 〈书面〉❶ possess; be provided with ❷ administer; manage

吡

pǐ 〈书面〉❶ slander; defame; calumniate ❷ reprimand; rebuke
see also bǐ

仳

pǐ
仳离 pǐlí 〈书面〉❶ (of husband and wife) be separated ❷ divorce one's spouse, esp. one's wife: 有女～，慨其叹矣。A woman abandoned by her husband sighed sadly.

圮

pǐ 〈书面〉collapse; fall apart; be in ruin: 朝堂倾～。The imperial court collapsed in total ruin.

匹[1]

pǐ ❶ be equal to; be a match for; rival: 无有其～ (there is) no match for him / 难与为～ matchless; peerless ❷ alone; single: *see* "～夫"

匹[2]（❷疋） pǐ 〈量词〉❶ *used of horses, mules, etc.*: 一～马 a horse / 两～骡子 two mules ❷ *used of bolts of silk or cloth*: 一～布 a bolt of cloth ❸〈方言〉*used of a mountain*: 一～山 a mountain

匹俦 pǐchóu 〈书面〉match; equal: 二人堪称～。The two of them could be described as equals.

匹敌 pǐdí be equal (to); match; rival: 无可～ matchless; peerless / 双方实力～。The two sides are well matched.

匹夫 pǐfū ❶ ordinary man; common man: ～不可夺志。Every man is entitled to his ambition. ❷ (usu. used in the early vernacular) ignorant person: ～之辈 ignoramuses

匹夫匹妇 pǐfū-pǐfù ordinary man and woman; common people

匹夫有责 pǐfū-yǒuzé every one has the duty: 天下兴亡，～。Every individual must hold himself responsible for the prosperity or decline of his country.

匹夫之勇 pǐfūzhīyǒng reckless physical courage; fool-hardiness: 不可逞～。One should not allow oneself to display reckless physical courage.

匹克威克外传 Pǐkèwēikè Wàizhuàn *The Pickwick Papers* (1837) by Charles Dickens (1812-1870), English novelist

匹拉米洞 pǐlāmǐdòng 〈药学〉pyramidon

匹练 pǐliàn bolt of white silk (used to describe a water fall or a pillar of light): 从山崖倾泻而下的～极为壮观。The fall rushing down the cliff like a bolt of white silk is a magnificent spectacle.

匹马单枪 pǐmǎ-dānqiāng *also* "单枪匹马" single-handed; all by oneself; alone

匹鸟 pǐniǎo *also* "匹禽" pair of birds, esp. of mandarin ducks

匹配 pǐpèi ❶〈书面〉mate; marry: ～良缘 be united in wedlock; be happily married ❷〈电工〉matching: 阻抗～ impedance matching

匹配变压器 pǐpèi biànyāqì matching transformer

匹配滤波器 pǐpèi lǜbōqì matched filter

匹染 pǐrǎn 〈纺织〉piece dyeing: ～色布 piece-dyed cloth

匹庶 pǐshù common people; populace

匹头 pǐtou 〈方言〉❶ piece goods or fabrics ❷ bolt of cloth

匹亚 pǐyà 〈书面〉equally matched; about the same: 此文甚佳，可与名篇～。The essay is very well written and compares favourably with some masterpieces.

癖 pǐ addiction: 烟～ be addicted to smoking / 怪～ be eccentric / 爱洁成～ make a fetish of tidiness

癖好 pǐhào favourite hobby; fondness: 她有逛市场的～。She is fond of window-shopping. / 他有收集古币的～。His favourite hobby is collecting ancient coins.

癖气 pǐqì innate liking; natural inclination: 他好酒贪杯的～老是改不了。He has never been able to give up drinking.

癖习 pǐxí idiosyncrasy; peculiar habit

癖性 pǐxìng natural inclination; proclivity; propensity

擗 pǐ ❶ break off: ～棒子 pick corn ❷〈书面〉beat one's breast

擗踊 pǐyǒng 〈书面〉beat one's breast and stamp one's feet in deep sorrow

劈 pǐ ❶ cut; split; divide: 把冻肉～成两半 cut the frozen meat into two portions / 我～一半甘蔗给你。I'll cut the sugar cane and give you half of it. ❷ break off; strip off: 把干树枝～掉 break off dry twigs ❸ open one's legs or fingers too wide: ～了腿了 sprain one's legs

see also pī

劈叉 pǐchà 〈体育〉do the splits

劈柴 pǐchai kindling; firewood: 劈～ chop firewood

劈成 pǐchéng deduct a percentage (from a sum of money, etc.)

劈账 pǐzhàng divide a sum of money: 三七～ divide a sum by a seventy-thirty (*or* seven-to-three) ratio

pì

釽（鈚） pì 〈书面〉cut apart

埤 pì

see also pí

埤堄 pìnì 〈书面〉battlements

睥 pì

睥睨 pìnì 〈书面〉consider every one and everything beneath one's notice; look scornfully at: ～一切 look superciliously at the whole world

屁 pì ❶ wind (from bowels); fart; flatulence: 放～ break wind; fart ❷〈粗话〉damned; worthless and trivial thing: ～点大的事，你也来问我! Do you have to bother me about such damned trifles? / 放～!〈比喻〉Crap! *or* Shit! / 这有什么～用? Does this serve any damned purpose? / 你说话管个～。What you say is not worth a farthing. ❸ (often used in a negative sense or as a rebuke) what; anything: 你懂个～! What an idiot you are! / 家里穷得～也没有。The family was desperately poor.

屁股 pìgu ❶ buttocks; bottom; ass: 讲话很长，他～有点坐不住了。The speech was lengthy and he shuffled uneasily on his seat. / 出了事，就要打你的～了。If anything goes wrong, you'll get a spanking. / 难道我得给他擦～? Must I clean up the mess he left behind? ❷ (of animals) rump; haunch; hindquarters: 牛～ rump of an ox / 老虎～摸不得 like a tiger whose backside no one dares to touch — not to be provoked ❸ protruding part on the back of an object; end of a slender object; butt: 烟～ cigarette butt / 汽车～ rear of a car

屁股沉 pìguchén (of a guest) be apt to overstay one's visit

屁股蛋儿 pìgudànr *also* "屁股蛋子"〈方言〉buttocks; behind; bottom

屁股蹲儿 pìgudūnr 〈方言〉buttocks; bottom: 摔了个～ fall on one's bottom

屁股帘儿 pìguliánr *also* "屁股帘子"; "屁帘儿" piece of cloth tied to the waist of a child with slit pants to cover his or her behind: 他打系～的时候淘得邪乎。He was quite a mischief when he was a little child.

屁滚尿流 pìgǔn-niàoliú piss in one's pants (in terror); wet one's pants; be frightened out of one's wits: 吓得他们～ get them wetting their pants with fright; scare the shit out of them / 打得侵略者～ send the aggressor troops fleeing helter-skelter

屁话 pìhuà shit; nonsense; rubbish: 尽说些～! It's all shit!

屁事 pìshì trivial matter; useless thing; rubbish: 他～也不管。He doesn't bother about a damned thing in his charge. / 你爱上哪儿就上哪儿，关我～! Go wherever you like for all I care.

媲 pì be equal to; match

媲美 pìměi compare well with; rival: 这种产品可与世界名牌～。This kind of product compares well with world-famous brand names.

辟[1]（闢） pì ❶ open up (territory, land, etc.); reclaim: 另～文学专栏 start a literary column (in a newspaper, etc.) / 这一带将～为新的旅游区。This area will be opened up as a new tourist attraction. ❷ penetrating; incisive: 精～ profound; in-depth / 透～ penetrating; deep-going ❸ refute; repudiate: 力～邪说 energetically refute heresies

辟[2] pì 〈书面〉law: 大～〈旧语〉capital punishment

see also bì; pī

辟设 pìshè open up; set up; establish: ～公关部 set up a PR department

辟谣 pìyáo refute a rumour: 在报纸上～ publish a statement in the newspaper refuting a rumour / 当众～ repudiate a rumour in public

辟易 pìyì 〈书面〉retreat out of terror: ～再三 retreat repeatedly out of fear

澼 pì *see* "洴澼" píngpì

譬 pì example; analogy: 设～ draw an analogy

譬方 pìfāng analogy; instance: ～说 for example; for instance

譬解 pìjiě 〈书面〉❶ convince or persuade by patient explanation;

P

explain to sb. so as to bring him around：用各种办法去～他 try to convince him by all available means ❷ explain：走了三十里路就很累，我自己～，这是缺乏训练之故。I felt very tired after I walked only for 30 *li*. I explained to myself that this was due to lack of training.

譬如 pìrú for example; for instance; such as：我们要设想最坏的情况，～头一场就输了球。We must be prepared for the worst, such as losing the first game of the match.

譬若 pìruò for example; for instance

譬说 pìshuō demonstrate or illustrate a viewpoint：百般～ illustrate a point repeatedly

譬语 pìyǔ words said by way of analogy

譬喻 pìyù metaphor; simile; analogy：一个好的～往往胜过冗长的解释。A good analogy is often more illuminating than a lengthy explanation.

P

甓 pì 〈书面〉brick

僻 pì ❶ out-of-the-way; secluded：荒～ desolate and out-of-the-way /偏～的山乡 remote mountain village ❷ eccentric; odd：怪～ eccentric /孤～ unsociable and whimsical ❸ rare; uncommon：生～字 rarely used word

僻地 pìdì out-of-the-way place：山村～ faraway mountainous village

僻典 pìdiǎn unfamiliar allusion

僻见 pìjiàn bias; prejudice

僻径 pìjìng out-of-the-way path

僻静 pìjìng secluded; out-of-the-way：找个～的角落坐坐。Let's find a secluded corner to sit in for a while.

僻陋 pìlòu (of a place or an area) backward and out-of-the-way：过去这里是一个～的小村子。This used to be a backward and out-of-the-way village.

僻壤 pìrǎng out-of-the-way place：穷乡～ remote, backward place

僻性 pìxìng eccentric disposition; eccentricity

僻野 pìyě desolate open country; wilderness

僻远 pìyuǎn remote; out-of-the-way：现在～的山区也能看到电影。Nowadays movies are shown even in remote mountainous areas.

䴙 pì

䴙䴘 pìtī 〈动物〉grebe

piǎ

𠺗 piǎ 〈方言〉❶ talk; gossip; chat：可别听他胡～。Don't believe him. He is talking nonsense. /这人真能～。The guy certainly has a glib tongue. ❷ speak sarcastically and scornfully：你别～人！Don't be so sarcastic!

𠺗子 piǎzi 〈方言〉glib talker

piān

扁 piān

see also biǎn

扁舟 piānzhōu 〈书面〉small boat; skiff：驾一叶之～ row a small boat

篇 piān ❶ piece of writing：通～ throughout the piece (poem, article, book, etc.) /长～小说 novel ❷ printed sheet (of paper, etc.)：歌～儿 song sheet /单～儿讲义 sheets of teaching materials ❸ 〈量词〉*used of writing, paper, or publication*：一～论文 a thesis /一～文章 a piece of writing; an essay (*or* article) /两～儿纸 two sheets of paper /文本残缺不全，缺了好几～。The text is fragmentary with quite a few leaves missing.

篇幅 piānfu ❶ length (of a piece of writing)：这篇社论～不长，只有一千多字。This editorial is not very long; it is about 1,000-odd words. ❷ space (as of printed matter)：整版～ whole page (of a newspaper, etc.) / ～有限，希望写短文。Short essays are preferred because of limited space. /晚报用较大～报道了这场足球赛。The evening paper gave the football match considerable coverage.

篇籍 piānjí 〈书面〉books; ancient books and records

篇目 piānmù ❶ titles of chapters or articles in a book：这句话出自《论语》，但～记不清了。The sentence is from *The Analects*, but I cannot quote chapter and verse. ❷ table of such titles：这本古书可惜只流传下来一个～。Unfortunately, all that is extant is the table of contents of this ancient work.

篇什 piānshí group of 10 poems (as in *The Book of Songs*); poems

篇页 piānyè chapters and pages; writing

篇章 piānzhāng sections and chapters; writing：这一部分是书中最精彩的～。This is the best-written part of the book. /唐诗是中国文学史上的光辉～。The poetry of the Tang Dynasty constitutes a glorious chapter in the history of Chinese literature.

篇子 piānzi 〈口语〉❶ printed sheet (of paper, etc.) ❷ essay; piece of writing：这部选集共收了五十个作家的～。This anthology contains selections from fifty authors.

犏 piān

犏牛 piānniú *pien niu* (offspring of a bull and a female yak)

偏[1] piān ❶ inclined or leaning to one side; slanting; diverging：～过身去 turn sideways /正南～东 south by east /中间～右 right of centre /这一处理～宽。The verdict erred on the lenient side. /太阳～西了。The sun slanted to the west. /他打～了。He overshot the mark. ❷ partial; prejudiced：不可～于一方 must not be partial to either party /不～不倚 even-handed; impartial /纠～ correct a deviation/这本书～于叙事而略于分析。The book is rich in description but scanty in analysis. ❸ supplementary; supporting; auxiliary: *see* "～师"；"～将" ❹ different (e.g. higher or lower) from a certain standard：工资～低。The wage is somewhat low. *or* The wage is on the low side. ❺ 〈套语〉*used to mean having had sth.* (*tea or a meal*) *earlier*："吃过了吗？""～过了您啦。""Have you had your meal?" "I ate earlier than you."

偏[2] piān 〈副词〉*showing perversity, stubbornness or ill luck*：我～不去。I just won't go. /老天～不下雨。The weather simply does not cooperate; it doesn't rain at all.

偏爱 piān'ài have partiality for; show favour to：孩子中他～小儿子。Of all his children, he dotes on the youngest son. /她对你有点～。She has a tender spot for you. /这些小说我都喜欢，并无～。I like all these novels without any preference.

偏安 piān'ān (of a regime) be content to retain control over part of the country (after losing the major portion of the territory, esp. the central plains of northern China)

偏安一隅 piān'ān-yīyú be content to exercise control over part of the country

偏才 piāncái ❶ skill or cleverness in handling trifling matters; smartness on petty things ❷ talent for a particular field of human endeavour

偏差 piānchā deviation; error：修正～ correct a deviation or error /～逐渐减少。The deviation is reduced by degrees. /瞄准有～。The aiming was inaccurate. /工作中出了～，要及时纠正。When errors occur in the work, we should remedy them as soon as possible.

偏差均衡器 piānchā jūnhéngqì deviation equalizer

偏宠 piānchǒng show particular favour (to sb.)

偏处 piānchǔ (of a place) remote; out-of-the-way：这座古城～于大西北。The ancient city is located in the deep recesses of the great Northwest.

偏待 piāndài give particularly generous treatment (to one of the parties concerned)

偏殿 piāndiàn auxiliary palace; side hall in a palace or temple

偏饭 piānfàn preferential treatment

see also "吃偏饭" chī piānfàn

偏方 piānfāng 〈中医〉folk prescription (for some diseases)

偏房 piānfáng ❶ wing of a house, especially the east or west wing of a quadrangular courtyard house ❷ concubine：要～ take a concubine

偏废 piānfèi do one thing to the neglect of another; emphasize one thing at the expense of another：二者不可～。Neither should be overemphasized at the expense of the other. /在教育中，德、智、体三者不可～。Moral, intellectual and physical education should receive equal emphasis in education.

偏锋 piānfēng ❶ (Chinese calligraphy) oblique force of the writing brush：他的书法常用～，别具一格。The uniqueness of his calligraphy is due to his frequent use of the oblique force of the brush. ❷ talk or write with oblique references (rather than tackle issues directly)：这人说话爱使～。He prefers to talk by innuendo.
偏光 piānguāng *see* "偏振光"
偏光镜 piānguāngjìng polariscope
偏航 piānháng go or veer off-course; yaw
偏航指示器 piānháng zhǐshìqì 〈航空〉yaw indicator; yaw meter
偏好 piānhǎo 〈方言〉it so happens; by mere accident：我正去他家叫他，～在街上碰着了。I was going to call for him at his home when we bumped into each other in the street.
偏好 piānhào have a great liking (for sth.)：他对于京剧有特别的～。He is passionately fond of Beijing opera.
偏护 piānhù be partial to and shield：我们对谁也不～。We shall show partiality to nobody. /对子女的过错不可～。It is unwise to shield the faults of one's children.
偏畸 piānjī 〈书面〉unfair; biased
偏激 piānjī go to extremes; be extreme：他很冷静，从不～。He is level-headed and never goes to extremes. /这种观点有些～。Such views are rather extreme.
偏见 piānjiàn prejudice; bias; one-sided attitude：我认为他不是完全没有～的。I don't think he is entirely free from prejudice. /在重大问题上有～是最危险不过的。It is dangerous to hold biased views on important issues.
偏将 piānjiàng adjutant general (in ancient times)
偏介 piānjiè 〈书面〉stubborn and aloof：性情～ obstinate and aloof in temperament
偏襟 piānjīn (of traditional Chinese garment) with the front part slanted to one side
偏晶 piānjīng 〈物理〉monotectic
偏举 piānjǔ 〈书面〉practise favouritism in personnel appointments
偏口鱼 piānkǒuyú 〈动物〉flatfish
偏枯 piānkū ❶〈中医〉hemiplegia ❷ lopsided (development, etc.)
偏狂 piānkuáng 〈医学〉monomania
偏劳 piānláo 〈套语〉*used either to ask for help or thank people for it*：请你～吧，眼下我实在脱不开身。Could I trouble you to act on my behalf? I could hardly tear myself away from my work for the moment.
偏离 piānlí deviate (from the right course); veer：～航线 veer away from the charted course /他已经～了文学创作的正道。He has deviated from the correct path of literary creation.
偏磷酸 piānlínsuān 〈化学〉metaphosphoric acid：～盐 metaphosphate
偏流 piānliú 〈物理〉bias current; bias battery; bias cell
偏盲 piānmáng blind in one eye
偏门 piānmén ❶ side door ❷ improper channel
偏旁 piānpáng 〈语言〉basic structural part of a Chinese character (as 亻 in 住，囗 in 固，匚 in 匾，令 in 拎，etc.)；radical
偏裨 piānpí (in ancient China) deputy military commander; senior army officer
偏僻 piānpì secluded; out-of-the-way：～小村 out-of-the-way small village /那儿是～山区，交通不便。It's a remote mountainous area difficult of access. /这是个～的火车小站。It was a tiny backwater of a train station.
偏偏 piānpiān 〈副词〉❶ *showing wilful action contrary to objective conditions or requirement*：你为什么～要钻牛角尖？Why should you deliberately try to split hairs and get into a dead end? ❷ *showing that reality is contrary to one's hopes or expectations*：麦子正在抽穗，老天～不下雨！The wheat is earing but it just would not rain. /～不凑巧，他出门了。Unfortunately, he was out. ❸ *showing limit of range or scope*：这么多的花，为什么～这一盆花开得不好？Of all these pots of flowers, why should this one not bloom as well as the rest? /为什么～不提取得的成绩呢？Why should you avoid mentioning what has been accomplished?
偏颇 piānpō 〈书面〉unfair; biased：～之见 prejudiced view /这篇文章立论失之～。The argument of the essay is biased.
偏栖 piānqī 〈书面〉❶ live alone ❷ live in widowhood
偏巧 piānqiǎo ❶ it so happens; as luck would have it：地里缺水的时候，老天～就下起雨来了。Luckily it began to rain when the fields were in dire need of water. ❷ against one's expectation：他需要清静，～有人来打扰他。Unluckily, somebody came to bother him when he wanted very much to be let alone.
偏厦 piānshà small room built along the side wall of a house
偏衫 piānshān a kind of Buddhist cassock, draped over the left shoulder
偏晌儿 piānshǎngr 〈方言〉afternoon
偏生 piānshēng 〈方言〉*see* "偏偏 ❶❷"
偏师 piānshī 〈书面〉auxiliary force
偏食 piānshí ❶〈天文〉partial eclipse：日～ partial solar eclipse /月～ partial lunar eclipse ❷ (have a) partiality for a particular kind of food (often resulting in unbalanced nutrition)
偏手儿 piānshǒur help one side when apparently trying to separate two persons in a fist fight
偏私 piānsī allow personal relationship to affect one's judgement; be partial：处理问题不能～。One should not show favouritism to one's friends and relatives in anything one does.
偏酸 piānsuān 〈化学〉meta-acid
偏瘫 piāntān *also* "半身不遂" bànshēn-bùsuí 〈医学〉paralysis of one side of the body; hemiplegia
偏袒 piāntǎn be partial (to one side)：我觉得裁判有～之嫌。I have a hunch that the referee was not particularly impartial.
偏疼 piānténg 〈口语〉show favouritism (to one or some of one's juniors)：爷爷～小孙女。The youngest granddaughter is the old man's favourite (*or* darling).
偏题 piāntí catch or tricky question (in an examination)：考官是不应该出～、怪题的。The examiners are not supposed to set catch questions.
偏听偏信 piāntīng-piānxìn heed and trust only one side; listen only to one side：要了解真实情况，不能～。It is imperative to know what the situation is really like instead of lending an ear to one side.
偏头痛 piāntóutòng 〈医学〉migraine
偏微分 piānwēifēn 〈数学〉partial differential：～法 partial differentiation /～方程 partial differential equation
偏西 piānxī the sun has just moved to the western side (indicating it's already past midday)：他一个午觉睡到日头大～。He took a nap and did not wake up till it was late in the afternoon.
偏析 piānxī 〈冶金〉segregate
偏狭 piānxiá biased and narrow-minded：他对于这部作品的理解过于～。His view of this literary work is too biased.
偏向 piānxiàng ❶ erroneous tendency; deviation：学校要纠正忽视德育的～。It is essential to rectify the tendency to neglect moral education in schools and colleges. ❷ favour; prefer：这两种建议我～于前者。I am in favour of the first of the two proposals. ❸ shield; be on the side of：做家长的，不管有理无理总是～自己的子女，这其实是害了他们。Parents who are always behind their children, right or wrong, are only doing them harm.
偏斜 piānxié crooked; askew：他～着眼一瞅，囤里约莫有一石粮。Casting a sidelong glance at the grain bin, he found that there was about one *dan* of grain left.
偏心 piānxīn ❶ partiality; bias：毫无～ be absolutely impartial (*or* unbiased) /她没有任何～。She is entirely free from bias. ❷〈机械〉eccentric：～凸轮 eccentric cam /～轮 eccentric wheel
偏心率 piānxīnlǜ 〈航天〉eccentricity (measure of the non-circularity of an orbit)
偏心轮 piānxīnlún 〈机械〉eccentric (wheel)
偏心眼儿 piānxīnyǎnr *also* "偏心眼子"〈口语〉prejudiced; partial：我看爷爷对弟弟是有～的。I believe that grandpa is partial to my younger brother.
偏压 piānyā 〈电学〉bias (voltage)：～电压器 biasing transformer /～电池 bias battery
偏倚 piānyǐ be partial to：不管我们做什么事，都必须保证没有～。We must make sure that we are even-handed in whatever we do.
偏远 piānyuǎn remote and out-of-the-way：～边区 remote border area
偏灾 piānzāi flood or drought disaster：一连三年这里赶上了水旱～。This locality has been hit by flood or drought for three years running.
偏振 piānzhèn 〈物理〉polarization：光的～ polarization of light
偏振光 piānzhènguāng *also* "偏光"〈物理〉polarized light
偏振光镜 piānzhènguāngjìng polariscope
偏振光显微镜 piānzhènguāng xiǎnwēijìng polarizing microscope
偏振计 piānzhènjì 〈物理〉polarimeter (device for measuring the

P

amount of polarization in a light beam)
偏正词组 piānzhèng cízǔ 〈语言〉word group consisting of a substantive word and its modifier
偏执 piānzhí extreme; stubborn
偏执狂 piānzhíkuáng 〈医学〉paranoia:～患者 paranoiac; paranoid
偏重 piānzhòng lay particular stress on:他们～于课文的分析与理解,忽视了写作技巧的训练。They stress text analysis and comprehension and neglect the training of writing technique.
偏注 piānzhù lopsidedness; one-sided emphasis:～形式,忽视实质 overemphasize the form to the neglect of the substance
偏转 piānzhuǎn 〈物理〉deflection:～系统 deflection system
偏坠 piānzhuì 〈中医〉swelling and hanging down of one of the testes due to hernia, orchitis, etc.

P

翩

piān 〈书面〉fly swiftly
翩翩 piānpiān ❶ (dance, flutter, etc.) lightly:～起舞 dance gracefully ❷〈书面〉graceful; elegant:～少年 elegant young man /风度～ have an elegant manner; behave with grace and ease
翩然 piānrán 〈书面〉lightly; trippingly:～而至 come tripping down /～飞舞 flutter (*or* fly about) lightly
翩若惊鸿 piānruòjīnghóng fly as swiftly as a startled wild goose — (of a woman) walk briskly and gracefully
翩跹 piānxiān 〈书面〉lightly; trippingly:～起舞 dance with light steps

片

piān
see also piàn
片儿 piānr (of photo, picture, record, etc.) flat, thin piece:相～儿 photo /画～儿 picture /唱～儿 record
片子 piānzi ❶ roll of film; film; movie ❷ negative of a roentgenogram ❸ gramophone record; disc
see also piànzi

pián

跰

pián
跰胝 piánzhī *see* "胼胝" piánzhī

胼

pián
胼手胝足 piánshǒu-zhīzú callosity forming on palms or feet because of hard labour:世界上没有～的劳动者,就不会有人类的一切文明。There would be no human civilization of any kind were there no hard-working labourers.
胼胝 piánzhī *also* "跰胝" piánzhī callosity; callus:手足～,以养其亲。He worked so hard to support his parents that he got calluses on his feet and hands.
胼胝体 piánzhītǐ 〈生理〉corpus callosum
胼胝性溃疡 piánzhīxìng kuìyáng 〈医学〉callous ulcer

骈

pián ❶ pair of horses ❷ parallel; antithetical: *see* "～句" ❸ stand, lie, or go side by side: *see* "～肩"
骈比 piánbǐ 〈书面〉close to each other; side by side:屋宇～。Houses stand close to one another.
骈肩 piánjiān 〈书面〉(of many people) shoulder to shoulder; packed like sardines; crowded:参观者相与～。There was a jostling crowd of visitors.
骈俪 piánlì art of parallelism; ornate style of writing consisting of antithetical or parallel constructions of characters
骈列 piánliè 〈书面〉stand side by side; spread out:群山～ mountains stand in a connected line; chain of mountains; mountain range
骈拇枝指 piánmǔ-zhīzhǐ extra toe or finger — sth. superfluous or unnecessary
骈四俪六 piánsì-lìliù (of writing) parallel style with pairs of sentences of four and six Chinese characters
骈体 piántǐ ornate style of writing characterized by parallelism and rhythmical arrangement
骈阗 piántián *also* "骈填";"骈田"〈书面〉gather; assemble; spread out in a row or stretch:奇花异草,～阶砌。The stone steps are lined with exotic flowers and grass.
骈文 piánwén rhythmical prose characterized by parallelism and ornateness; parallel prose
骈枝 piánzhī 〈书面〉❶ extra toe or finger ❷ superfluous:～机构 superfluous organization

蹁

pián 〈书面〉walk on the side of one's foot
蹁跹 piánxiān 〈书面〉whirl about (in dancing):舞池中几对青年男女～起舞。A few pairs of young people were spinning around on the dance floor. /百年魔怪舞～,人民五亿不团圆。For a century demons and monsters whirled in a wild dance, And the five hundred million people were disunited.

便

pián
see also biàn
便嬖 piánbì 〈书面〉emperor's or king's favourite
便佞 piánnìng 〈书面〉flatterer who seeks to ingratiate himself with others
便便 piánpián bulging; exceedingly fat:那位大腹～的商人态度异常傲慢。The pot-bellied businessman looked extremely arrogant.
便宜 piányi ❶ cheap:价钱很～。The price is quite reasonable. *or* It's a bargain. /仔细算来,并不～。It is not at all worth the money when you take everything into consideration. /～没好货,好货不～。Good goods are not cheap, and cheap goods are not good. ❷ undeserved gain; petty advantage:光看到鼻子底下的小～ look merely for small advantages under one's nose/贪小～吃大亏。The greed for petty gains may bring heavy losses in its train. ❸ let sb. off lightly:这回决不能～了他。We mustn't let him off lightly this time. *or* He won't get off too easily this time.
see also biànyí

缏

pián 〈方言〉stitch; sew
see also biàn

piǎn

谝

piǎn 〈方言〉show off:～能 show off one's abilities, skills, etc.

piàn

片

piàn ❶ flat, thin piece; slice; flake:面包～ slices of bread/皂～ soap flakes /布～ (small) pieces of cloth /药～ tablet /叶～ leaf /相～ photo /胶～ film /图～ picture; illustration /瓦～ tile /名～ visiting card /明信～ postcard /碎纸～儿 pieces (*or* scraps) of paper /电报如雪～飞来。Telegrams poured in thick and fast like snowflakes. ❷ motion picture; TV film:制～人 (film) producer ❸ subarea; section of a place:分～传达 divide a unit into different groups for the relay of the higher-ups' instructions ❹ cut into slices; slice:～羊肉片儿 slice mutton /把豆腐干～一～ slice bean curds ❺ incomplete; fragmentary; partial; brief: *see* "～言只语";"～断" ❻〈量词〉(a) *of things that are in the form of flat, thin pieces*:两～药 two tablets /几～雪花 some snowflakes /一～黄瓜 a slice of cucumber /天边飘着几～白云。Patches of fluffy white clouds are floating high in the sky. (b) *of land, waters, etc.*:一～树林 a stretch of woods /一大～水 a vast expanse of water /一～菜地 a vegetable plot /一大～新楼房 a long row of new buildings /一大～庄稼 a vast stretch of crops (c) *of scenery, atmosphere, sound, feeling, etc.*:一～新气象 a new atmosphere /一～欢腾 a scene of great rejoicing /我是一～真心。I am all sincerity. /四周一～沉寂。All was quiet and still.
see also piān
片酬 piànchóu payment for making a film or TV play
片段 piànduàn part; passage; snatch; extract; fragment:这是那部长篇小说的一个～。This is only a passage of the novel. /《回忆录》记述了他文学生涯中的几个～。*The Reminiscences* records several episodes of his literary career. /学生们演出了《雷雨》的几个～。The students put on a performance of parts of the play *Thunderstorm*.
片断 piànduàn ❶ *see* "片段" ❷ scrappy; fragmentary; scattered; incomplete:～经验 scattered experiences /隔壁传来～的谈话声。Snatches of conversation could sometimes be heard from the next

room.
片盒 piànhé 〈影视〉film magazine
片簧 piànhuáng 〈机械〉leaf spring：多～ multiple leaf spring
片剂 piànjì 〈药物〉tablet
片甲不存 piànjiǎ-bùcún *also*"片甲不留" not a fragment of armour remains; not a single armed man is left — the army is completely wiped out：如敌人敢于侵犯，将杀得他们～。If the enemy dare invade our land, we will see that they are thoroughly wiped out.
片假名 piànjiǎmíng katakana, Japanese regular script
片警 piànjǐng *also*"片儿警" neighbourhood police (responsible for the registration of residents, security, etc. of a designated neighbourhood in a city)
片刻 piànkè short while; instant; moment：～之间 in an instant /思索了～ think for a short while /整天忙得没有～休息时间 too busy to enjoy a moment of leisure all day long
片孔 piànkǒng film perforation; perforation
片理 piànlǐ 〈地质〉schistosity
片流 piànliú 〈物理〉laminar flow
片麻岩 piànmáyán 〈地质〉gneiss
片面 piànmiàn ❶ unilateral：～作出决定 make a unilateral decision /～之词 one person's (*or* party's) version of an incident /他错在～推测。His fault lies in putting too much stock in unfounded conjecture. ❷ one-sided：～观点 biased view /～强调数量 stress quantity at the expense of quality; go after quantity alone /叙述有些～。The account of the incident was somewhat one-sided.
片面性 piànmiànxìng one-sidedness：认识上的～ one-sidedness in understanding
片盘 piànpán 〈影视〉film reel
片儿会 piànrhuì meeting held for each group or subarea
片儿警 piànrjǐng *see*"片警"
片儿汤 piànrtāng flat pieces of dough served with soup; soup of flat noodles
片山氏疾病 Piànshānshì jíbìng 〈医学〉Katayama disease
片山哲 Piànshānzhé Katayama Tetsu (1887-1978), Prime Minister of Japan from 1947 to 1948
片晌 piànshǎng 〈方言〉short while; moment：他在廊子上徘徊了～。He walked up and down the corridor for a little while.
片石 piànshí slabstone; slate
片时 piànshí short while; moment：请略坐～。Please wait for a little while.
片梭织机 piànsuō zhījī 〈纺织〉gripper loom
片头 piàntóu preamble of a film or TV film where the title of the film, name of the studio, etc., are given; title and credits at the beginning of a film
片瓦无存 piànwǎ-wúcún not a single tile remains — be razed to the ground; be a heap of rubble：一场火把那些老房子烧得～。Those old buildings were razed to the ground in the fire.
片选 piànxuǎn (of farming) select a plot of fine crops for seeds (from which to plant next year's crop)
片言 piànyán a few words; brief note：临别之际，有～相赠。I have a few words of parting advice for you.
片言只字 piànyán-zhīzì *also*"片言只语" a few isolated words：～，不足为凭。A phrase or two cannot serve as conclusive evidence. /自她去沪后，我从未收到她～。I have not received even a scribble from her since she went to Shanghai.
片岩 piànyán 〈地质〉schist
片艳纸 piànyànzhǐ machine-glazed paper (glossy on one side)
片约 piànyuē contract with an actor or actress to shoot a film or TV film
片纸只字 piànzhǐ-zhīzì just a short piece of writing; brief note or letter：只有～的旁证材料，这个问题恐难落实。It's difficult to give a verdict with this scrawl as circumstantial evidence. /文稿散失，只剩下一些～。The bulk of the manuscript is lost, leaving behind only a few scattered pages.
片状石墨 piànzhuàng shímò 〈冶金〉graphite flake
片状树脂 piànzhuàng shùzhī 〈化工〉flaky resin
片子 piànzi ❶ flat, thin piece; slice; flake; scrap：铁～ small pieces of sheet iron ❷ visiting card; name card
see also piānzi
片子地 piànzidì 〈方言〉uncultivated wasteland; virgin land

骗[1] piàn ❶ deceive; cheat; dupe; fool：欺～ deceive; cheat; dupe /拐～ abduct /行～ practise deception; swindle; cheat /受～上当 be taken in; be fooled /我不～你。I'm not diddling. *or* I'm not kidding you. /这种玩艺很～人。People are easily taken in by such tricks. /他们编出这一套鬼话来～人的。They told us that story to throw dust in our eyes. ❷ gain by swindle：～钱 cheat sb. of his money; swindle sb. out of his money; get money by swindle

骗[2]（騗） piàn mount; bestride; jump onto
骗供 piàngòng make sb. confess by fraud or deception
骗局 piànjú fraud; hoax; deception; swindle：政治～ political fraud /纯属～ nothing but a swindle; deception pure and simple /政治～的牺牲品 victim of political chicanery /这不过是个～。This is nothing but a hoax. /他在这场～中扮演什么角色？What role did he play in this trickery?
骗口张舌 piànkǒu-zhāngshé sow discord; tell tales; make mischief
骗马 piànmǎ swing or leap into the saddle; mount or jump onto a horse
骗买骗卖 piànmǎi-piànmài make fraudulent business deals; do business by crooked means：利用假合同～ strike business deals by using fake contracts
骗取 piànqǔ obtain by cheating; trick, or swindle sb. out of sth.; defraud：～钱财 swindle sb. out of his money; obtain money under false pretenses /～领导的信任 worm one's way into the confidence of the leadership; gain the confidence of one's superior by sham loyalty /～群众的支持 gain popular support by foul means /～选票 wangle votes /假装忏悔以～人们的怜悯 beg for mercy by pretending repentance /编造事实，～荣誉 fabricate facts to gain honour
骗人 piànrén hoodwink people; practise deception or fraudulence：～的鬼话 deceitful damned nonsense /～的把戏 hoax /尽干些～的勾当 be given to fraudulent practice /他们的宣传都是～的。All their propaganda was sheer humbug. /你认为这一套就能～？Do you think you can take people in by such tricks of yours?
骗术 piànshù deceitful trick; fraud; ruse：玩弄～ resort to fraud /不高明的～ clumsy tricks
骗腿儿 piàntuǐr raise one leg sideways
骗子 piànzi fraud; swindler; impostor：政治～ political swindler
骗子手 piànzishǒu 〈方言〉swindler; trickster; master at deception
骗嘴 piànzuǐ boast; brag; talk big：你以为～可以糊弄人？Do you think you can fool people by talking big?

piāo

漂 piāo ❶ float; stay afloat：水上～着一层油 a sheet of oil floating on the water ❷ drift：大海上～着一艘小帆船。A small sailing boat was drifting on the vast sea.
see also piǎo; piào
漂泊 piāobó *also*"飘泊" piāobó ❶ float; berth：游艇～在附近的海面上。The yacht was lying at anchor off the coast. ❷ lead a wandering life; drift aimlessly：多年～海外 wander overseas for many years /～流浪 drift along from place to place /他这几年～在外，受了不少的苦。He has suffered a good deal during his wanderings over the past few years.
漂冰 piāobīng floating ice; drift ice; flow berg
漂泛 piāofàn *also*"飘泛" piāofàn float
漂浮 piāofú *also*"飘浮" piāofú ❶ float：朝雾在群山间～。Morning mists floated about over the hills. ❷ float or hover before the eyes or in the mind：他的亲切笑容常～在我的脑海里。His face beaming with a kindly smile often flashes across my mind. ❸ (of style of work) superficial; impractical：他作风～，从不坐下来做点实际工作。His work style is superficial, and he never thinks of getting down to work.
漂浮生物 piāofú shēngwù neuston
漂浮植物 piāofú zhíwù pleuston
漂海 piāohǎi *also*"飘海" piāohǎi go on a sea voyage：他～出洋，三年无音讯。We have heard nothing of him since he went on a sea voyage three years ago.
漂砾 piāolì 〈地质〉erratic (boulder)
漂流 piāoliú *also*"飘流" piāoliú ❶ be driven by the current;

drift about:河上～着一条独木船。A canoe was drifting about on the water. ❷ *see*"漂泊"

漂没 piāomò 〈书面〉carried away by the flood:大水～,庐舍无存。The flood washed away everything on its path, leaving no house standing.

漂木 piāomù driftwood

漂萍 piāopíng 〈书面〉float about like duckweed; lead a vigrant life:此身有如～,常无定所。Like floating duckweed, I used to wander about with no permanent abode.

漂儿 piāor 〈方言〉cork on a fishing line; float

漂网 piāowǎng drift net:～渔船 drifter

漂洋 piāoyáng *also*"飘洋"piāoyáng cross the ocean

漂洋过海 piāoyáng-guòhǎi *also* "飘洋过海" piāoyáng-guòhǎi cross the seven seas:他～去了北美。He arrived in North America after crossing the vast ocean.

P

漂移 piāoyí ❶ drift about:冰山～ drift of an iceberg ❷〈电子〉drift:频率～ frequency drift /零点～ zero drift /～晶体管 drift transistor

漂游 piāoyóu ❶ float slowly;drift:一条小船顺水～过来。A small boat is drifting along with the current. ❷ wander about:从前,他四处～谋生。In the past, he used to wander from place to place trying to earn a living.

慓

piāo 〈书面〉*see*"剽❷"piāo

慓悍 piāohàn *see*"剽悍"piāohàn

螵

piāo

螵蛸 piāoxiāo cluster of mantis eggs (used as medicine when dried)

剽

piāo ❶ rob;loot;plunder:*see*"～掠";"～窃" ❷ nimble; swift:～疾 fierce and nimble

剽悍 piāohàn intrepid; quick and fierce:～善战 be intrepid and adept at fighting

剽掠 piāolüè loot; plunder:敌兵～附近的村落。The enemy soldiers looted the neighbouring villages.

剽窃 piāoqiè plagiarize; lift:～行为 act of plagiarism /～他人成果 plagiarize other people's achievements /文章某些段落都是从别处～来的。Certain parts of the article are entirely lifted from other works.

剽窃物 piāoqièwù plagiarism; plagiary

剽窃者 piāoqièzhě plagiarist

剽取 piāoqǔ plagiarize; lift

剽袭 piāoxí plagiarize; lift;copy

飘(飃)

piāo ❶ flutter; float (in the air); waft:红旗～～ fluttering red flags /雪花～～ swirling snowflakes /《～》*Gone with the Wind* (1936, novel by American author Margaret Mitchell)/乐曲～过水面。The music wafted across the water. /空中～着柳絮。Willow catkins are floating in the air. /野花～香。The air is thick with the fragrance of wild flowers. ❷ weak; wobbly; feeble:他两腿发～。His legs felt weak. ❸ superficial;frivolous; flippant:行为有点～ behave frivolously

飘摆 piāobǎi flutter or sway with wind:红灯笼下面的金穗子被风吹得轻轻～。The golden tassels under the red lantern are swinging slightly in the wind. /彩旗随风～。Coloured banners were fluttering in the wind.

飘泊 piāobó *see*"漂泊"piāobó

飘布 piāobù *also*"票布"piàobù〈旧语〉cloth identity issued by secret societies in old China to their members

飘尘 piāochén small particles of dust floating in the air:这个城市～污染严重。This city is seriously polluted by small airborne dust.

飘带 piāodài streamer; ribbon

飘荡 piāodàng ❶ drift; wave; flutter:国旗迎风～。The national flag flapped in the wind. /幼儿园里～着孩子们的欢笑声。The kindergarten rang with the joyous laughter of the children. /他在椅子上打盹,脑子飘飘荡荡的似乎是做梦,可又不是梦。He was dozing in a chair, his mind drifting off, almost dreaming but not quite. ❷ wander about; drift aimlessly:四处～,无家可归 wander about homeless

飘动 piāodòng sway (with wind); flutter (in the air); float (with waves):鲜艳的红旗迎风～。Bright red flags were fluttering in the wind. /几只白鹅在水面上安祥地浮着,随着水波～。A few white geese were floating quietly on the water, moving with the waves.

飘泛 piāofàn *see*"漂泛"piāofàn

飘飞 piāofēi drift; flutter:秋天是落叶～的季节。Autumn is the season when fallen leaves begin to drift in the air. /彩蝶在花丛中～。Butterflies are flying about among the flowers.

飘风 piāofēng 〈书面〉whirlwind; storm wind

飘拂 piāofú drift; wave:空中白云～。White clouds are drifting in the sky. /柳条在水面上轻轻地～着。The willow branches are swaying lightly over the water.

飘浮 piāofú *see*"漂浮"piāofú

飘高 piāogāo 〈方言〉(of a person) fall from tall buildings or scaffoldings

飘海 piāohǎi *see*"漂海"piāohǎi

飘忽 piāohū ❶ (of wind, clouds, etc.) float in the air; move quickly:一片树叶被吹向空中,又轻捷地～下来。A small leaf was blown aloft in the air, but it lightly fluttered to the ground. ❷ capricious; uncertain:他的行踪～不定。Nobody is sure where he is. *or* His whereabouts are uncertain.

飘疾 piāojí 〈书面〉speedy; quick; swift

飘降 piāojiàng float down;swirl down:雪花～。Big snowflakes are swirling down.

飘卷 piāojuǎn flap; toss to and fro:火焰随风～。The tongues of flames are leaping in the wind. /晨风吹拂,红旗上下～。The red flag was fluttering in the morning wind.

飘零 piāolíng ❶ (of flowers, leaves, etc.) withered and fallen:黄叶～。The withered leaves were scattered about. ❷ wandering; drifting alone; homeless and friendless; forsaken:孤苦～ wander alone from place to place; be wretched and friendless /半生～ drift along homeless for half of his lifetime

飘流 piāoliú *see*"漂流"piāoliú

飘落 piāoluò fall down; descend slowly in the air:伞兵徐徐～着地。Dropping from the sky, the parachutists (*or* paratroopers) landed lightly.

飘渺 piāomiǎo *see*"缥缈"piāomiǎo

飘蓬 piāopéng drifting straw — a person drifting homeless from place to place:母子茕茕,～南北。Lonely and helpless, mother and son wandered about in north and south.

飘飘然 piāopiāorán ❶ feeling as if treading on air or as if one were tipsy:他喝了几杯酒,脚下不禁有些～。After a couple of drinks, he walked as if he were treading on air. ❷ smug; self-satisfied; complacent:刚取得了一点成绩,他就～忘乎所以了。After some initial success he became swollen-headed.

飘飘欲仙 piāopiāo-yùxiān float up towards heaven like an angel; feel as if one were in paradise:有～之感 feeling very much at ease

飘然 piāorán ❶ floating in the air:树叶～而下。The leaves fluttering to the ground. ❷ lightly; speedily:少女～而至。The young lady sailed in gracefully. ❸ relaxed and happy:～自在 happy and carefree

飘洒 piāosǎ swirl down:天空～着微微的雨丝。A fine rain is falling lightly (from the sky).

飘洒 piāosa (of a person) elegant; (of calligraphy) graceful:态度～ have elegant manners; act with grace and ease /他的字很～。His calligraphy is graceful.

飘散 piāosàn (of smoke and air) float and scatter:微风里～着一股清香。A faint scent was wafted on the breeze.

飘闪 piāoshǎn drift and glisten:萤火虫在小树林中～。Fireflies were blinking among the bush.

飘逝 piāoshì ❶ float and scatter; drift away:白云～。White clouds are beginning to clear away. ❷ die away; vanish:岁月～。Time slips by.

飘舞 piāowǔ flutter or wave in the air:雪花随风～。The snowflakes danced in the wind.

飘扬 piāoyáng *also*"飘飏" wave; flutter; fly:国旗在楼顶～。The national flag is fluttering at the top of the building.

飘洋 piāoyáng *see*"漂洋"piāoyáng

飘漾 piāoyàng float; undulate:公园里～着浓郁的桂花香。The air was heavy with the aroma of the osmanthus in the park.

飘摇 piāoyáo *also*"飘飖" sway; totter; toss about in the wind:～欲坠 teeter on the brink of collapse; tottering /炊烟缭绕,～上升。Wisps of kitchen smoke are curling up into the air.

飘飖 piāoyáo *see*"飘摇"

飘曳 piāoyè sway in the wind; flicker:柔软的柳枝在晨风中～。The

soft willow branches swayed gently in the morning breeze.
飘移 piāoyí drift; drift about: 降落伞向着目标方向～。The parachute drifted in the direction of the target.
飘移轨道 piāoyí guǐdào 〈航天〉 drift orbit
飘逸 piāoyì ❶〈书面〉graceful; elegant: 神采～ have an elegant bearing /才气～ overflow with talent ❷ float and scatter; drift; disperse: 白云～。White clouds were dispersing.
飘溢 piāoyì float in the air; be permeated with: 公园里～着花香。The park was permeated with the scent of flowers.
飘游 piāoyóu roam about; wander: 四处～ rove from place to place
飘悠 piāoyou float in the air; drift on the water: 小船在水面～。A small boat was drifting about on the water.
飘展 piāozhǎn (of flag) flutter; fly: 彩旗迎风～。Multicoloured flags are fluttering in the wind.

缥 piāo

see also piǎo
缥缈 piāomiǎo *also* "飘渺" piāomiǎo dimly discernible; misty; elusive: 虚无～的海市幻景 elusive mirage /云雾中群峰～。The peaks are dimly discernible in the mist.

piáo

朴 Piáo a surname

see also pō; pò; pǔ

薸 piáo 〈方言〉duckweed

瓢 piáo gourd ladle; wooden dipper

瓢虫 piáochóng ladybug; ladybird (beetle)
瓢泼 piáopō (of rain) pouring; very heavy: ～大雨 pouring rain; torrential rain; downpour; raining cats and dogs
瓢泼瓦灌 piáopō-wǎguàn rain cats and dogs; rain heavily: 下了一天～的大雨，把公路淹没了。The rain bucketed down all day and the roads were all under water.
瓢儿菜 piáorcài gourd-ladle-shaped vegetable
瓢子 piáozi 〈方言〉❶ gourd ladle ❷ spoon

嫖(闞) piáo frequent brothels; go whoring: ～妓 visit prostitutes; go whoring

嫖客 piáokè brothel or whorehouse frequenter; (prostitute's) client
嫖宿 piáosù sleep with a prostitute

piǎo

漂 piǎo ❶ bleach: ～布 bleach cloth ❷ rinse: 洗衣粉洗过的衣服，要用清水多～～。Powder-washed clothes should be thoroughly rinsed in water.

see also piāo; piào
漂白 piǎobái bleach: ～棉布 bleached cotton cloth /～剂 bleach /～机 bleaching machine; bleacher /～率 bleachability
漂白粉 piǎobáifěn bleaching powder
漂白土 piǎobáitǔ fuller's earth
漂染 piǎorǎn bleach and dye
漂洗 piǎoxǐ rinse
漂洗槽 piǎoxǐcáo 〈化工〉potcher

瞟 piǎo look sidelong or askance at; glance sideways at: 用眼～了他 give him a sidelong glance

缥 piǎo 〈书面〉❶ light blue ❷ light-blue silk fabric

see also piāo
缥瓷 piǎocí 〈考古〉light-blue-glazed chinaware, produced in today's Zhejiang Province in 265-589

莩 piǎo *see* "殍" piǎo

see also fú

殍 piǎo *see* "饿殍" èpiǎo

piào

票 piào ❶ printed slip as certificate; ticket: 船～ boat ticket /半～ half fare /站台～ platform ticket /门～ ticket for admission /选～ ballot; vote /唱～ announce ballots (*or* votes) /邮～ postage stamp /印花～ tax stamp /股～ stock; share /支～ bank cheque /拘～ arrest warrant ❷ bank note; bill: 大～儿 notes of large denominations /零～儿 notes of small denominations; small change ❸ person held for ransom by brigands; hostage: 绑～儿 kidnap (for ransom) /肉～儿 hostage /撕～ kill the hostage /赎～ pay the ransom ❹〈方言〉〈量词〉: 一～货 a batch of goods /一～生意 a deal; a transaction ❺ amateur performance (of Beijing opera, etc.): 玩儿～ be an amateur performer; play a role in a performance as amateur

票霸 piàobà ticket monopolizer (one who monopolizes the sale of tickets of train, ship, etc., for profits)
票布 piàobù *see* "飘布" piāobù
票车 piàochē 〈方言〉passenger train
票额 piào'é sum stated on a cheque or bill; denomination: ～壹佰圆的人民币 one-hundred *yuan* RMB note
票贩子 piàofànzi tout; scalper
票房 piàofáng ❶ booking office (of a railway station, etc.); box office (of a theatre, stadium, etc.) ❷〈旧语〉club for amateur performers (of Beijing opera, etc.)
票房价值 piàofáng jiàzhí box-office value; box-office receipts: ～很高 be a box-office success
票匪 piàofěi kidnapper
票根 piàogēn counterfoil; stub
票匦 piàoguǐ ballot box
票号 piàohào *also* "票庄"〈旧语〉firm for exchange and transfer of money; exchange shop
票汇 piàohuì remit by a postal money order or a bank draft; send a money order or bank draft
票活 piàohuó unpaid job
票价 piàojià price of a ticket; price of admission (to a theatre, etc.); admission fee; fee: 首映电影～每张三十元。Admission to the premiere of the film is 30 *yuan* per person.
票据 piàojù ❶ bill; note: 应收～ bill receivable /即期～ demand note /定期～ time note /流通～ negotiable instruments; negotiable papers /到期未付～ overdue bill ❷ voucher; receipt: 凭～提货 delivery of cargo against voucher /凭～报销 reimburse expenses on producing receipts
票据背书 piàojù bèishū endorsement (of a bill)
票据法 piàojùfǎ 〈法律〉negotiable instruments law
票据交换 piàojù jiāohuàn clearance
票据交换所 piàojù jiāohuànsuǒ clearing house
票据交换业务 piàojù jiāohuàn yèwù clearing service
票据经纪人 piàojù jīngjìrén bill broker; note broker
票据贴现市场 piàojù tiēxiàn shìchǎng bill discounting market
票据托收 piàojù tuōshōu collection of instruments; bill collection
票面 piàomiàn face, par, or nominal value: ～数额 nominal amount /～壹佰圆的钞票 bill in 100 *yuan* denomination
票面价值 piàomiàn jiàzhí face value; par value; nominal value
票箱 piàoxiāng ballot box
票选 piàoxuǎn elect by ballot; vote (for sb.)
票姚 piàoyáo 〈书面〉swift and vigorous
票友 piàoyǒu 〈旧语〉amateur performer (of Beijing opera, etc.): ～下海 (of a former amateur performer) become a professional performer
票证 piàozhèng coupons (for buying ration oil, food, etc.)
票庄 piàozhuāng *see* "票号"
票子 piàozi bank note; paper money; bill

漂 piào 〈方言〉come to nothing; fail; peter out: 这个计划恐怕要～了。I'm afraid the plan is petering out.

see also piāo; piǎo
漂亮 piàoliang ❶ handsome; beautiful; good-looking; smart: 容貌～ good-looking /她很～。She is an attractive girl. /他个子高，皮肤黝

黑，长得英俊～。He is tall, dark and handsome. /家具够～的。The furniture is pretty stylish. ❷ remarkable; brilliant; wonderful: 她说一口～的英语。She speaks flawless English. /这篇文章写得～。The article is very well written. /我不会讲～的大道理。I am not good at high-flown rhetoric.

漂亮话 piàolianghuà fine words; high-sounding words: 单是说～没有用，做出来才算。It's no use mouthing fine words. What counts is getting things done. *or* Fine words butter no parsnips.

漂账 piàozhàng 〈方言〉 refuse to repay debts

嘌 piào 〈书面〉 swift; quick

嘌呤 piàolìng 〈化学〉 purine

僄 piào 〈书面〉 ❶ quick and nimble ❷ frivolous; flippant

骠 piào 〈书面〉 ❶ (of horses) gallop fast ❷ brave; valiant; intrepid: ～悍 intrepid

see also biāo

骠骑 piàoqí title of a high-ranking general of cavalry in ancient times: ～将军 cavalry general

piē

撇[1] piē put aside; discard; leave behind: 我们把小事暂且～在一边。Let's put aside such trifling matters for the time being. /妈妈死了，～下了一儿一女。The mother died, leaving behind a boy and a girl.

撇[2] piē skim: ～沫子 skim off the scum /～去汤面上的油 skim the fat from the soup

see also piě

撇开 piēkāi leave aside; bypass: 我们不能～这个问题，而去谈其它次要问题。We cannot bypass this issue to discuss other questions of minor importance. /～他健康情况不谈，从业务上看也不是最理想的人选。Leaving aside the problem of his health, he is professionally not the best eligible candidate.

撇弃 piēqì abandon; give up; desert: 他不该～本职工作去跑买卖。He shouldn't have thrown up his job to go into business.

撇清 piēqīng claim to be innocent; whitewash oneself: 人家还没有开口问，你怎么倒先～，不是露出了马脚吗? Aren't you giving yourself away by protesting your innocence before they ask you about it?

撇闪 piēshǎn abandon; desert: 想不到他居然会～下妻儿不管。No one would expect that he could have abandoned his wife and children.

撇脱 piētuō 〈方言〉 ❶ simple and plain; easy: 他讲话很～。He always speaks simply and plainly. ❷ frank; candid; straightforward: 他是一个～人。He is a man of candour.

撇漾 piēyàng (usu. used in the early vernacular) forsake; abandon

撇油 piēyóu gain petty advantages; cash in on

瞥 piē shoot a glance at; catch a glimpse of: 她～我一眼，流露出明显的不满。She darted a glance at me, obviously displeased.

瞥见 piējiàn get a glimpse of; catch sight of: 昨天在天安门～了一位多年不见的老友。In Tian'anmen Square yesterday, I caught sight of an old friend whom I had not seen for years.

瞥然 piērán 〈书面〉 appear in a flash

瞥视 piēshì shoot a glance at: 他会心地～了我们一眼。He shot a knowing glance at us.

瞥眼 piēyǎn 〈书面〉 in an instant; in the twinkling of an eye

氕 piē 〈化学〉 protium ($^1_1$H)

piě

撇 piě ❶ throw; fling; cast: 这事儿早让他～到脑后去了。He has already cast the matter out of his mind. ❷ pout one's lips in disdain or displeasure: 她嘴一～，什么也没说，走开了。She curled her lips and left without a word. ❸ left-falling stroke (in Chinese characters) ❹ 〈量词〉: 两～胡子 two strokes of moustache; moustache resembling the Chinese character for 八 (eight) with two opposing down-sweeping parts

see also piē

撇耻 piěchi *also* "撇哧"; "撇嗤" 〈方言〉 look down upon; despise: 不要～人，你也不怎么高明。Don't look down upon others when you are not particularly brilliant yourself.

撇京腔 piě jīngqiāng (of people in places other than Beijing) speak with an affected Beijing accent

撇口碗 piěkǒuwǎn cymbal-shaped bowl

撇嘴 piězuǐ purse one's lips (in disdain, disbelief or disappointment): ～摇头 purse one's lips and shake one's head /小孩一～，母亲就知道她要哭了。Once the child's mouth twitched, the mother would know that it was going to cry. /她很失望地一～。She pouted her lips with great disappointment.

苤 piě

苤蓝 piělan *also* "球茎甘蓝" qiújīng gānlán 〈植物〉 kohlrabi

piè

嫳 piè

嫳屑 pièxiè 〈书面〉 (of clothes) flutter

pīn

拼[1]**(拚)** pīn put together; piece together: 用几块板子～成桌面 nail a few boards together to make a table top

拼[2]**(拚)** pīn risk all (in doing sth.); exert one's utmost in work; fight tooth and nail: ～体力 risk exhausting all one's physical strength /～时间 race against time /～到底 fight to the finish /硬～ fight with sheer physical courage; put up a foolhardy fight

拼版 pīnbǎn 〈印刷〉 makeup

拼板玩具 pīnbǎn wánjù jigsaw puzzle

拼搏 pīnbó take (a challenge) head-on; go all out in one's struggle; stand up to hardship: 勇于～ dare to struggle against heavy odds /～精神 spirit of going all out to win success

拼刺 pīncì ❶ bayonet drill; bayonet practice ❷ bayonet charge: 和敌人～ engage in a bayonet fight with the enemy

拼刺刀 pīn cìdāo bayonet charge

拼凑 pīncòu piece together; knock together; throw together: ～一笔钱 scrape together a sum of money /如果把这些零散的信息～起来，就可以看清局势的严重性。If you piece together the bits of information, you will get a clear picture of the serious situation. /那是一支临时～的队伍，不堪一击。Hurriedly thrown together, the troops would collapse at the first blow.

拼攒 pīncuán piece together different spare parts; assemble (a car, watch, etc.): ～汽车 assemble cars (with spare-parts)

拼合 pīnhé piece together

拼火 pīnhuǒ open fire at each other; exchange fire

拼接 pīnjiē join; piece together: 把几块布～在一起 join pieces of cloth with a few stitches

拼劲儿 pīnjìnr resolution and perseverance; drive; dogged determination: 在完成这项技术革新中，他的～发挥了很大作用。His boundless enthusiasm contributed greatly to the successful completion of the technological innovation.

拼力 pīnlì exert oneself to the utmost; spare no efforts: ～奋战 fight with might and main

拼拢 pīnlǒng piece together; put together: 这笔款子是大家给他～来的。We raised a sum of money for him by pooling our own resources.

拼命 pīnmìng ❶ risk one's life; act desperately regardless of consequences: 事情到了这个地步，和人家～也无用了。As things have come to such a pass, it would be of no use even if you want a showdown with them. /他会跟你～的。He will fight you tooth and nail. /别人遇难，他会～相救的。When he sees someone in distress, he'll try to save him at his own risk. ❷ exerting one's utmost; straining every

nerve; for all one is worth; desperately:～奔跑 run like crazy /～地干 work like a house on fire /～捞钱 do all one can to make money /～挣扎 struggle desperately /他们～喝酒。They drank for all they were worth.
拼盘 pīnpán assorted cold dishes; hors d'oeuvres
拼配 pīnpèi piece together and assemble
拼抢 pīnqiǎng wrest or struggle (for a ball) with all one's might: 队员们在球场上～凶猛,却很少犯规。The players fought for the ball fiercely but had very few fouls.
拼杀 pīnshā fight desperately
拼死 pīnsǐ risk one's life; fight desperately:～挣扎 wage a desperate struggle; put up a last-ditch fight /～抵抗 put up a stubborn resistance
拼死拼活 pīnsǐ-pīnhuó ❶ wage a life-and-death struggle:义军～地杀出了敌人的重重包围。The rebel army broke through the enemy encirclement after a desperate fight. ❷ do one's utmost; sweat one's guts out; work one's fingers to the bone:他不肯为这点微薄收入而～地干。He refused to sweat his guts out for such meagre earnings.
拼图游戏 pīntú yóuxì jigsaw puzzle
拼箱货 pīnxiānghuò less-than-container-load cargo; LCL cargo
拼箱货运服务 pīnxiāng huòyùn fúwù LCL service
拼箱站 pīnxiāngzhàn consolidation depot; consolidation station
拼箱作业 pīnxiāng zuòyè consolidation service
拼写 pīnxiě spell; transliterate:～游戏 spelling bee /～练习 spelling exercise /用拼音～汉字 transliterate Chinese characters into Pinyin
拼写法 pīnxiěfǎ spelling; orthography
拼音 pīnyīn ❶ combine sounds into syllables ❷ spell; phoneticize:英美～差别并不如有些人想像的那么大。The difference between British and American spellings is not as great as some people tend to think. ❸ Pinyin, phonetic system for transcribing Chinese characters
拼音文字 pīnyīn wénzì alphabetic language; phonetic language
拼音字母 pīnyīn zìmǔ phonetic alphabet; phonetic symbol
拼争 pīnzhēng compete with all one's might; contend with one's utmost strength:与世界强队～ compete most courageously with the world's strong teams /主队顽强～,才与客队打成平局。Only by making an all-out effort was the home team able to fight the visiting team to a draw.
拼装 pīnzhuāng assemble:这台～的收音机只能凑合着用。We could only make do with this self-assembled radio.
拼缀 pīnzhuì combine; stitch together:这件用碎布～而成的背心倒也别致。The vest made of pieces of cloth stitched together seems to be in good taste.
拼字游戏 pīnzì yóuxì scrabble

姘 pīn have illicit relations with
姘度 pīndù (of a man and his kept mistress) live together illicitly
姘夫 pīnfū illicit male lover of a woman
姘妇 pīnfù mistress; paramour
姘居 pīnjū cohabit (usually between a married person and someone who is not his or her spouse)
姘识 pīnshí 〈书面〉 have illicit sexual relations after getting acquainted with each other
姘头 pīntou mistress or lover:轧～〈方言〉 have a mistress (*or* lover); have an affair

pín

玭(蠙) pín 〈书面〉 pearl

嫔(嬪) pín 〈书面〉 ❶ concubine of an emperor:妃～ imperial concubines ❷ woman attendant at court; lady-in-waiting

频 pín ❶ frequently; repeatedly:尿～ frequent micturition (*or* urination) /差错～出。Errors kept occurring. ❷〈物理〉 frequency:音～ audio frequency /视～ video frequency /声～ acoustic frequency /高～ high frequency /中～ intermediate frequency /低～ low frequency/调～ frequency modulation (FM)
频传 pínchuán (good news) keep pouring in:喜讯～。Good news poured in thick and fast.
频次 píncì frequency
频带 píndài 〈物理〉 frequency range:～宽度 band width
频道 píndào 〈影视〉 frequency channel:二～ Channel 2 /现在有二十个～。There are at present twenty television channels.
频段 pínduàn frequency band
频繁 pínfán frequently; incessant:交往～ have frequent contacts /～地交换意见 repeated exchanges of views /交通事故日益～。Traffic accidents are on the rise. /此处车辆往来～。Traffic is rather heavy here. /自然灾害～,庄稼连年歉收。The recurrent natural disasters have caused successive crop failures.
频率 pínlǜ ❶ *also* "周率" zhōulǜ 〈物理〉 frequency:～范围 frequency range /～调制 FM (frequency modulation) /高～ high frequency /～分辨率 frequency resolution /～跟踪〈航天〉 frequency tracking ❷ frequency:事故发生的～ incidence of accidents
频率词典 pínlǜ cídiǎn dictionary of word frequency
频率分布 pínlǜ fēnbù 〈商业〉 frequency distribution
频率计 pínlǜjì frequency meter
频率曲线 pínlǜ qūxiàn frequency curve
频年 pínnián for successive years; for several years running:～荒歉 successive famines /～累月 for months and years
频偏 pínpiān 〈物理〉 frequency deviation; frequency shift
频频 pínpín time and again; repeatedly:～点头 nod repeatedly /～举杯 propose toasts again and again /她～拭泪,依依难舍。Wiping away her tears, she was reluctant to leave.
频谱 pínpǔ 〈物理〉 frequency spectrum:～分析 frequency analysis /～仪 frequency spectrograph
频谱分配 pínpǔ fēnpèi 〈电信〉 spectrum allocation
频谱管理 pínpǔ guǎnlǐ 〈电信〉 spectrum management
频谱拍卖 pínpǔ pāimài 〈电信〉 spectrum auction
频仍 pínréng 〈书面〉 frequent; repeated:内乱～ be torn by frequent internal disorder (*or* warfare) /外患～ suffer from repeated foreign invasion
频数 pínshuò 〈书面〉 frequent and continuous:病人腹泻～。The patient suffered from diarrhoea.
频域 pínyù frequency domain

蘋 pín *also* "田字草" tiánzìcǎo 〈植物〉 clover fern

嚬 pín 〈书面〉 *see* "颦" pín

颦 pín 〈书面〉 frown; knit one's brows:～眉凝望 gaze with knitted brows /效～ knit one's brow by imitating the beauty Xi Shi (西施) only to make oneself uglier
颦蹙 píncù 〈书面〉 knit one's brows:双眉～ look sad with knitted brows

贫[1] pín ❶ poor; needy; impoverished:赤～ live in penury; be utterly destitute /清～ (usu. of scholars in old days) live in genteel poverty /脱～ shake off poverty; become better off /扶～ help the poor to become better off; assist an area shake off poverty /一～如洗 penniless; as poor as a church mouse /～富鸿沟日益扩大 widening gap between the rich and the poor ❷ inadequate; deficient; poor:～油 poor (*or* deficient) in oil deposits; oil-poor ❸〈旧语〉 *used by a Buddhist monk or Taoist priest to refer to himself*: *see* "～道"; "～僧"

贫[2] pín 〈方言〉 garrulous; loquacious:你说过几十遍了,不嫌～吗? Don't you think you are too garrulous? You've talked about it dozens of times.
贫病交迫 pín-bìng jiāopò be worn down by poverty and illness; be poor and ill
贫薄 pínbó 〈书面〉 poor; impoverished:～的山区 poor hilly region
贫齿动物 pínchǐ dòngwù edentate (animal)
贫代会 píndàihuì (short for 贫下中农代表大会) conference of representatives of the poor and lower-middle peasants (organized during the Cultural Revolution)
贫道 píndào 〈谦词〉 (self-depreciatory expression used by a Taoist priest) my humble self; I
贫乏 pínfá ❶ poor; destitute:家境～ poor family; family of destitute circumstances /～而封闭的山区 impoverished and inaccessible mountainous region ❷ deficient; scanty; poor:知识～ deficient in

knowledge /词汇～ meagre vocabulary /石油资源～ poor in oil deposits /思想～ lacking in new ideas

贫富悬殊 pín-fù xuánshū extremes of poverty and wealth; wide gap between the rich and the poor

贫骨头 píngǔtou 〈方言〉❶ person who is out for small advantages; miser; stingy person: 他越来越～，一分钱也不肯花。He has become increasingly stingy, loathing to part with even a penny. ❷ garrulous or loquacious person; chatterbox: 此人真是个～，说起来没结没完。The man really is a chatterbox, babbling on without end.

贫雇农 pín-gùnóng poor peasants and hired farmhands

贫寒 pínhán poor; poverty-stricken: 出身～ be born into an impoverished family

贫化 pínhuà 〈矿业〉dilution: 矿石～ ore dilution

贫瘠 pínjí poor; barren; infertile: ～的土地 infertile land /～的山区 barren mountain areas

贫贱 pínjiàn poor and lowly; in straitened and humble circumstances: 出身～ be born into an impoverished family of humble origin

贫贱不能移 pínjiàn bùnéng yí remain firm in one's principle despite poverty; poverty cannot alter one's resolve

贫贱之交 pínjiànzhījiāo friends made in days when one was poor and in humble station; friends in times of poverty: ～不可忘，糟糠之妻不下堂。One must not forget those who befriended one when one was poor or unknown, nor should one forsake the wife who accompanied one in times of difficulty and hardship.

贫窭 pínjù 〈书面〉poor; impoverished; needy

贫苦 pínkǔ poor; destitute: 生活～ live in poverty and misery

贫矿 pínkuàng *also* "贫矿石" lean ore (deposit); low-grade ore (deposit)

贫困 pínkùn poor; impoverished; in straitened circumstances: ～地区 poverty-stricken area /摆脱～ get rid of poverty; shake off poverty /～户 impoverished family /～化 pauperization

贫困线 pínkùnxiàn poverty line; poverty level; subsistence level

贫民 pínmín poor people; pauper: 城市～ urban poor; city pauper /救济～ provide relief to the poor

贫民窟 pínmínkū slum; ghetto

贫民区 pínmínqū slum area; slum district

贫尼 pínní 〈谦词〉(self-depreciating reference used by a nun) my humble self; I

贫农 pínnóng poor peasant: ～团 poor peasant league

贫气 pínqi ❶ affected; stingy; niggardly; mean: 他钱来得容易，总嫌人～。He would often call a person tight-fisted (*or* stingy), probably because he made money easily. ❷ long-winded; garrulous; loquacious: 一句话说好几遍，真～。He said the same thing several times over again. Really long-winded, wasn't he?

贫穷 pínqióng poor; needy; impoverished: ～的国家 poor country /过着～的生活 live in poverty /～落后的村落 impoverished, backward village

贫弱 pínruò (of a country or nation) poor and weak

贫僧 pínsēng 〈谦词〉(self-depreciatory expression used by a Buddhist monk) my humble self; I

贫无立锥之地 pín wú lì zhuī zhī dì *also* "贫无立锥" so poor as not to even have room to swing a cat in; extremely impoverished

贫相 pínxiàng have a niggardly appearance; have a mean look: 此人虽已发迹，在社交场合仍然不时露出一副～。Though he had become rich and influential, the man betrayed his original niggardliness on social occasions now and then.

贫下中牧 pín-xiàzhōngmù poor and lower-middle herdsmen

贫下中农 pín-xiàzhōngnóng poor and lower-middle peasants

贫协 pínxié (short for 贫下中农协会) association of poor and lower-middle peasants

贫血 pínxuè 〈医学〉anaemia: 脑～ cerebral anaemia /再生障碍性～ aplastic anaemia

贫油 pínyóu poor in oil deposits; oil-poor

贫油国 pínyóuguó oil-poor country

贫铀 pínyóu 〈物理〉depleted uranium: ～炸弹〈军事〉depleted uranium bomb

贫嘴 pínzuǐ speak garrulously or flippantly; be frivolous or garrulous; be loquacious: 耍～ play the garrulous idiot

贫嘴薄舌 pínzuǐ-bóshé *also* "贫嘴贱舌" garrulous and sharp-tongued; flippant and cynical: 此人～，我真厌烦。I am fed up with him, he is so flippant and cynical. /他不愿学那些人的～。He did not try to imitate those people's spiteful talk.

pǐn

品 pǐn ❶ article; product; goods: 食～ food; foodstuff /礼～ gift; present /展～ exhibit /非卖～ goods not for sale /商～ commodity; merchandise /农产～ farm produce /工业～ industrial products ❷ grade; class; rank: 上～ highest grade; top grade /三～〈语言〉three ranks /精～瓷器 choice porcelain; fine-quality china ❸ official ranks in dynastic times: 七～芝麻官 a mere grade-seven offical ❹ kind; type; variety: ～种繁多 great variety of goods; rich assortment of commodities ❺ character; quality: 人～ moral quality; character ❻ taste sth. with discrimination; sample; savour: ～～味儿 savour sth. /这人究竟怎么样，你慢慢就～出来了。You will gradually find out what sort of person he is. ❼ play (wind instrument, esp. *xiao*, a vertical bamboo flute): ～箫 play the flageolet /～竹弹丝 play musical instruments ❽ (Pǐn) a surname

品茶 pǐnchá sip tea and taste its flavour

品尝 pǐncháng taste; savour; sample: 请外宾～北京烤鸭 treat foreign guests to roast Beijing duck

品德 pǐndé moral character: ～高尚的人 man of moral integrity

品第 pǐndì 〈书面〉❶ appraise; judge; comment on: ～高下 assess quality ❷ grade; rank; status; position: 这种菊花～甚高。This kind of chrysanthemum is of high grade.

品服 pǐnfú 〈旧语〉official dress indicating the rank of the wearer

品格 pǐngé ❶ one's character and morals ❷ quality and style (of artistic or literary works): 这位书法家的作品～不凡。The works of the calligrapher have an outstanding quality.

品红 pǐnhóng ❶ pinkish red ❷〈化工〉fuchsin

品级 pǐnjí ❶ official rank in dynastic times ❷ grade (of products, commodities, etc.)

品鉴 pǐnjiàn assess and judge: ～古画 assess an ancient painting

品节 pǐnjié one's character and moral integrity: ～高尚 have noble character and moral integrity

品酒 pǐnjiǔ savour the flavour of a wine

品蓝 pǐnlán reddish blue

品类 pǐnlèi category; class: ～齐全 have a complete assortment

品绿 pǐnlǜ light green; malachite green; bamboo green

品貌 pǐnmào ❶ looks; appearance: ～俊俏 be handsome and attractive ❷ character and looks: ～兼优 be handsome and of fine character

品名 pǐnmíng name of an article; description of a commodity

品茗 pǐnmíng *see* "品茶"

品目 pǐnmù name of an article: ～繁多 multitude of names (*or* items); names of every description

品排 pǐnpái 〈方言〉side by side; abreast: 他们～走进了教室。They filed abreast into the classroom.

品牌 pǐnpái brand (name); make: ～策划 branding /～估价 brand valuation /～管理 brand management /～形象 brand image /～忠诚度 brand loyalty /著名～(famous) brand name /建立自己的～ establish one's own brand names

品评 pǐnpíng judge; appraise; assess; comment on: ～电冰箱的优劣 assess the quality of the refrigerators /经过再三～，确定这两种手表为第一名。After repeated appraisals, it was decided that these two types of wrist watches should be awarded first prize.

品色 pǐnsè ❶ variety; breed: 这个茶店的茶叶～多样。There is a great variety of tea in this tea shop. ❷ colours in general such as pinkish red, reddish blue, light green, etc.

品题 pǐntí 〈书面〉appraise (a person or a work of art)

品头论足 pǐntóu-lùnzú *also* "评头论足" píngtóu-lùnzú ❶ make frivolous remarks about a woman's appearance ❷ find fault; nit-pick: 此人最爱～，说得别人一无是处。He is fond of nit-picking, speaking ill of anyone he knows.

品脱 pǐntuō pint (= $\frac{1}{2}$ quart)

品位 pǐnwèi ❶〈书面〉official rank ❷〈矿业〉grade: 边际～ marginal grade ❸ quality (of products, literary works, etc.): 高～的茶叶 tea of high quality/～不高的作品 work of rather low quality; vulgar (*or* indifferent) work

品味 pǐnwèi ❶ taste; savour; sample: ～陈酒 savour an old wine /细细～诗中的含义 ponder on the meaning of a poem ❷ quality; flavour: 新茶的～ flavour of new tea leaves

品系 pǐnxì strain; line
品行 pǐnxíng conduct; behaviour: ～端庄 of good conduct; known for one's impeccable moral behaviour /～不端 notorious in moral conduct; of loose morals
品性 pǐnxìng moral character: 这部小说描写了一个乡村教师美好的～。The novel depicts the virtuous character of a village teacher.
品学 pǐnxué moral quality and scholarship: ～兼优 good both in character and in scholarship
品议 pǐnyì *see* "品评"
品月 pǐnyuè pale blue
品藻 pǐnzǎo 〈书面〉judge, evaluate: ～古今 pass judgement on people of the past and the present
品择 pǐnzé carefully select; choose with care
品质 pǐnzhì ❶ character; quality: 诚实是他的一种可贵～。Honesty is one of his virtues. ❷ quality (of commodities, etc.): ～证明书 certificate of quality /～与订单不符 variation from quality offered /～与样品不符 quality variation from sample
品质因数 pǐnzhì yīnshù 〈电学〉quality factor
品秩 pǐnzhì 〈书面〉official rank and remuneration
品种 pǐnzhǒng ❶〈生物〉breed; strain; variety: 优良～ improved breeds /一种高产的水稻新～ new strain of high-yielding rice ❷ variety; assortment: 花色～ variety of colours and designs /～单调 lacking in variety
品族 pǐnzú cattle born of the same dam

榀 pǐn 〈量词〉*used of roof trusses*: 一～ a roof truss

pìn

聘 pìn ❶ engage; employ; appoint: 招～ advertise for; solicit applications for a job; recruit /～请顾问 engage sb. as a consultant /被～为兼职教授 be appointed a part-time professor /解～ terminate a contract of employment; dismiss ❷〈书面〉visit a friendly country on behalf of one's government: 报～ return an official visit /～使往来 exchange of envoys (*or* official visits) ❸ betroth: *see* "～礼" ❹ (of a girl) get married or be married off: 出～ get married
聘金 pìnjīn ❶ betrothal money (from the bridegroom's to the bride's family) ❷ money paid when employing sb.
聘礼 pìnlǐ ❶ gifts given when engaging sb.: 给家庭教师送～ give presents to a private tutor ❷ betrothal gifts (from the bridegroom's to the bride's family): 下～ deliver betrothal gifts
聘期 pìnqī term of engagement or appointment: ～二年 two-year engagement
聘请 pìnqǐng engage; employ; hire: ～律师 engage a lawyer
聘任 pìnrèn engage; appoint to a position: 这个系～了几名教授。The department has engaged several professors.
聘任制 pìnrènzhì system of appointment
聘书 pìnshū letter of appointment; contract of employment: 下～ offer a letter of appointment
聘问 pìnwèn 〈古语〉visit a friendly nation on behalf of one's government: 两国互通～。The two countries exchanged official visits.
聘用 pìnyòng engage; recruit; appoint sb. to a position: 他被～为公司会计。He was appointed accountant of the company.
聘用制 pìnyòngzhì *see* "聘任制"
聘约 pìnyuē engagement; contract of employment

牝 pìn (of some birds and animals) female: ～马 mare /～鸡 hen /～牛 cow
牝鸡司晨 pìnjī-sīchén 〈旧语〉a hen cackles in the morning — it is the wife who wears the trousers in the family; a woman usurps man's power /～，惟家之索。A hen that crows at dawn invites disaster. *or* It is the misfortune of a family (*or* a country, etc.) to be ruled by a woman.
牝牡骊黄 pìnmǔ-líhuáng yellow mare and black stallion — a matter of outward appearance, not substance (from a story with the moral that horses should be selected in the light of their true worth instead of their colour or sex)

pīng

俜 pīng *see* "伶俜" língpīng

娉 pīng
娉婷 pīngtíng 〈书面〉(of a woman) graceful in demeanour: 人影～ graceful shadows of human figures /池中荷花～而立。The lotus flowers in the pond have, as it were, a peculiar natural grace.

乒 pīng ❶〈象声〉ping, a short high-ringing sound: ～的一声枪响 crack of a gun shot /～的一声暖水瓶爆炸了。The thermos bottle burst with a bang. ❷ table tennis; ping-pong: ～赛 table tennis game /～坛老将 veteran table tennis player
乒乓 pīngpāng ❶〈象声〉rattling or clattering sound: 门被他敲得～作响。The door was banging away under his knocking. /石头～、～砸在铁板上。Stones fell rattling on the steel plate. ❷ table tennis; ping-pong: 打～ play table tennis (*or* ping-pong) /～外交 "ping-pong" diplomacy
乒乓球 pīngpāngqiú ❶ table tennis; ping-pong: ～运动员 table tennis player ❷ table tennis ball; ping-pong ball: 红双喜牌～ table tennis balls of the Double Red Happiness brand
乒乓球拍 pīngpāngqiúpāi table tennis paddle or bat
乒乓球台 pīngpāngqiútái table tennis table
乒乓球网 pīngpāngqiúwǎng table tennis net
乒乒乓乓 pīngpīng-pāngpāng 〈象声〉with a great rattle or clatter: ～地洗碗 wash dishes and bowls with a great rattle
乒坛 pīngtán table tennis circles: ～新星 rising star in table tennis circles
乒协 pīngxié (short for 乒乓球协会) table tennis association: 中国～ Table Tennis Association of the People's Republic of China

píng

洴 píng
洴澼 píngpì 〈书面〉rinse (silk waste, etc.)

瓶(缾) píng bottle; jar; flask: 药～ medicine bottle /果酱～ jam jar /暖～ thermos (flask) /花～ (flower) vase
瓶胆 píngdǎn glass liner (of a thermos flask)
瓶颈 píngjǐng ❶ neck of a bottle; bottleneck ❷〈比喻〉bottleneck: 这个问题成了制约经济发展的～。This problem has become a bottleneck in economic development.
瓶式千斤顶 píngshì qiānjīndǐng 〈机械〉bottle jack
瓶式通货膨胀 píngshì tōnghuò péngzhàng bottleneck inflation
瓶装 píngzhuāng bottled: ～啤酒 bottled beer
瓶装液化石油气 píngzhuāng yèhuà shíyóuqì 〈石油〉bottled LP-gas (liquefield petroleum gas)
瓶子 píngzi bottle
瓶子草 píngzicǎo 〈植物〉*Sarracenia purpurea*

帡 píng
帡幪 píngméng ❶〈古语〉canopy, tent or suchlike cover ❷〈书面〉protective shelter: 幸托～ (a polite epistolary formula) have the good fortune to count upon your protection

屏 píng ❶ screen: 彩～ colourful screen ❷ set of scrolls of painting or calligraphy: 四扇～儿 four-sheet scroll ❸ shield sb. or sth.; screen: *see* "～蔽"
see also bīng; bǐng
屏蔽 píngbì ❶ shield; screen: ～一方 provide a protective screen for the area /东海岛是广州湾的～。East Sea Island provides a natural defence for Guangzhou Bay. ❷〈无线电〉shielded; screened
屏蔽电缆 píngbì diànlǎn shielded or screened cable; H-cable; H type cable
屏蔽极电动机 píngbìjí diàndòngjī 〈电工〉shaded-pole motor
屏蔽天线 píngbì tiānxiàn screened or shielded antenna
屏蔽装甲 píngbì zhuāngjiǎ 〈军事〉spaced armour
屏藩 píngfān *also* "藩屏"〈书面〉❶ screen and fence; shield (referring to border areas) ❷ shield; defend
屏风 píngfēng screen: 迎门一道～，上绘花鸟鱼虫。Behind the door was a screen painted with flowers, birds, fish, and insects.
屏极 píngjí 〈电子〉plate: ～电路 plate circuit
屏门 píngmén screen door (between the outer and inner court-

yards of a traditional Chinese residence)

屏幕 píngmù 〈电子〉screen:电视～ telescreen; screen /大～big-screen /在～上出现 appear on the screen

屏条 píngtiáo set of hanging scrolls (usu. four)

屏障 píngzhàng ❶ protective screen:南面苍翠的群山是我们村天然的～。The green hills in the south provide a natural protective screen for our village. ❷ form a protective screen; shield: ～华北 constitute a protective screen for northern China

帡 píng see "屏" píng

平 píng ❶ flat; level; smooth: 马路很～。The road is smooth. /他们在沙上～躺着。They lay flat on the sand. ❷ make even; level: ～一～路面 level a road /～沟 fill in a ditch /把地图铺～ spread out a map ❸ be on the same level; be on a par; equal; 〈体育〉draw: 洪水～了堤岸。The flood water was level with the embankment. /今年粮食产量与去年持～。This year's grain output equals that of last year. /这盘棋下～了。The chess game ended in a draw. ❹ equal; just; fair; impartial: 公～合理 fair and reasonable /持～之论 fair argument; unbiased view /不～则鸣。Complaint comes when there is injustice. *or* Injustice will cry out. ❺ calm; tranquil; peaceful; quiet: 愤愤不～ feel resentful (*or* indignant) /世界并不太～。The world is by no means tranquil. ❻ put down; quell; suppress: 治国～天下 manage state affairs and put the country in order /～定内乱 quell (*or* put down) domestic rebellion ❼ pacify; calm; soothe: 使她～下来 calm (*or* soothe) her down /～民愤 assuage popular indignation /竭力把怒气～下去 try one's level best to suppress one's anger ❽ common; ordinary; usual: *see* "～淡"; "～时" ❾ 〈语言〉*see* "平声" píngshēng ❿ (short for 北平) Beiping or Peiping, erstwhile name for Beijing ⓫ (Píng) a surname

平安 píng'ān safe and sound; without mishap; well: 写一封报～的家信 write home to say that all is well /～抵达上海 arrive in Shanghai safe and sound /平平安安过日子 live in quiet and peace /～无事。All is well. /祝你一路～。Wish you a pleasant journey! *or* Bon voyage!

平安险 píng'ānxiǎn (in insurance) free of particular average (f. p. a.)

平白 píngbái ❶ for no reason whatever; gratuitously: 他家～遭火灾, 房屋被烧毁了。His house was unfortunately destroyed in a fire. /这不是～拿人消遣吗? Isn't this deliberately pulling one's leg? *or* Are you amusing yourself at my expense by this? ❷ plain; easy to understand: 他的诗～易懂。His poem is simple and easily intelligible.

平白无故 píngbái-wúgù for no apparent reason; for no reason whatever; without rhyme or reason: 不容你～地攻击他人! You are not supposed to attack others for no reason at all!

平板 píngbǎn ❶ dull and stereotyped; insipid; flat: 故事情节太～。The plot of the story is too insipid. ❷ flat scraper ❸ flat-plate; flat sheet

平板玻璃 píngbǎn bōli plate glass

平板车 píngbǎnchē flat-bed tricycle; flat-bed pedicart

平板大卡车 píngbǎn dàkǎchē platform truck

平板货车 píngbǎn huòchē platform truck

平板仪 píngbǎnyí 〈测绘〉surveyor's table

平版 píngbǎn 〈印刷〉lithographic plate: ～印刷 lithographic printing; planographic printing

平辈 píngbèi people of the same generation: 不必多礼, 我们是～。Don't stand on ceremony. We are of one and the same generation.

平布 píngbù 〈纺织〉plain cloth

平步青云 píngbù-qīngyún suddenly rise to fame; have a meteoric rise: 他～, 许多人都惊讶不已。Many people are more than surprised at his rapid rise to fame.

平舱费 píngcāngfèi trimming charges

平槽 píngcáo (of water in a river) be level with the banks: 大雨下得平了槽。The downpour caused the river to be level with its banks.

平产 píngchǎn level output; no increase or decrease in output; be equal in output: 由于水灾严重, 本省大多数县粮食减产, 只有少数地区～。Owing to serious floods, grain yields decreased in most counties of the province and only in a few areas remained at the same level as before.

平常 píngcháng ❶ ordinary; usual; common: ～人 ordinary people; man in the street /手艺～ of average craftsmanship /1991年是不～的一年。1991 was an eventful year. ❷ generally; ordinarily; as a rule: 她～星期天总去图书馆看书。As a rule, she goes to the library to read on Sundays. /他～很少请假。Generally, he seldom asks for leave of absence. /今天她和～一样, 六点钟就起了床。Today she got up at six as usual.

平车 píngchē ❶ 〈铁路〉flatcar; platform wagon ❷ flatbed tricycle; flatbed cart drawn by animal

平成 Píngchéng (Japan) Heisei Era, reign title of Emperor Akihito who succeeded to the throne in 1989

平畴 píngchóu 〈书面〉level, smooth land: ～千里 vast expanse of cultivated land

平楚 píngchǔ 〈书面〉flat top of a thicket as seen from a distance

平川 píngchuān level land; flat, open country; plain: ～广野 vast plains /眼前是一马～。Before our eyes lies a large stretch of flatland.

平旦 píngdàn 〈书面〉daybreak; dawn: ～即起 get up soon after daybreak

平淡 píngdàn dull; insipid; prosaic; pedestrian: 这场戏实在～无味。The play is indeed very dull.

平淡无奇 píngdàn-wúqí commonplace; trite; prosaic: 这些～的评论当然不值得考虑。These comments, which are trite and insignificant, of course do not deserve serious consideration. /他的话～, 却很实在。His words are prosaic yet sound and practical.

平等 píngděng equal: 建立～互利的经济关系 establish equal and mutually beneficial economic and trade relations /男女～ gender equality; equality between the sexes /不～条约 unequal treaty /国家不分大小, 一律～。All nations, big or small, are equal. /法律面前, 人人～。We are all equals in the eyes of the law.

平粜 píngdí 〈旧语〉government purchase of grain at a normal price in times of good harvest (to sell it in lean years at the same price)

平底 píngdǐ flat-bottomed (boat, etc.); low-heeled (shoe, etc.): ～船 flat-bottomed boat; flatboat; punt /～鞋 low-heeled shoes /～炒锅 frying-pan

平地 píngdì ❶ level the land or ground; rake the soil smooth ❷ level ground; flat ground: 万丈高楼～起。High buildings rise from the ground.

平地风波 píngdì-fēngbō sudden storm on a calm sea; unexpected turn of events; unforeseen trouble or dispute

平地机 píngdìjī ❶ 〈农业〉land leveller ❷ 〈交通〉road grader; bulldozer

平地楼台 píngdì-lóutái (like) a high building rising from the level ground — start from scratch: 这个厂就像～, 转眼就建立起来了。As if conjured up from the ground, the factory building was completed in an amazingly short time.

平地木 píngdìmù *also* "紫金牛" zǐjīnniú 〈植物〉Japanese ardisia (*Ardisia japonica*)

平地一声雷 píngdì yī shēng léi a sudden peal of thunder roars over the horizon — sudden big change; meteoric rise to fame or fortune; unexpected joyous occasion: ～, 默默无闻的演员顿时成了全城新闻人物。Most unexpectedly, an unknown actor suddenly became a household word in the city.

平电 píngdiàn 〈电信〉ordinary telegram

平调 píngdiào ❶ transfer and use the means of production or capital of individuals or subordinate units without compensation; requisition: 严禁以任何名义～农民的车辆和船只。It is strictly forbidden to requisition vehicles or boats of the farmers in any name. ❷ local opera mainly popular in the Handan (邯郸) region of Hebei Province

平顶 píngdǐng flat-roofed; flat-topped: ～房 flat-roofed house

平定 píngdìng ❶ calm down; pacify; stabilize: ～局势 stabilize the situation /他的心情过了好几天才～下来。It took him quite a few days to calm down. ❷ suppress; quell; put down: 动乱业已～。The riot has already been put down.

平动 píngdòng *also* "平移" 〈物理〉translation: ～光谱 translation spectrum /～速度 translatory velocity /～阻力 translatory resistance

平垌 píngdòng 〈矿业〉adit; tunnel

平凡 píngfán ordinary; common: ～的人 common man /～的岗位 ordinary post /不～的业绩 extraordinary achievements

平反 píngfǎn redress (a mishandled case); reverse an unjust verdict; rehabilitate: ～昭雪 redress fabricated cases and rehabilitate those who have been wronged /"四人帮"垮台后他就～了。He was rehabilitated after the downfall of the "Gang of Four".

平泛 píngfàn (of writings or novels) flat; insipid: 写剧本切忌～, 要

有起伏。There must be climaxes and denouements in drama, and pedestrianism should be avoided by all means.
平畈田 píngfàntián big tract of farmland
平方 píngfāng ❶〈数学〉square:三的～是九。The square of 3 is 9. ❷ square metre:占地面积一百～ take up 100 square metres
平方根 píngfānggēn square root
平方公里 píngfāng gōnglǐ square kilometre
平方米 píngfāngmǐ square metre
平方数 píngfāngshù square number
平房 píngfáng ❶ single-storey house; one-storey building:不少老人觉得住～方便些。Many elderly people find it more convenient to live in a one-storey house. ❷〈方言〉house with a mortared flat roof
平分 píngfēn divide equally; share and share alike; go halves:家庭财产由子女三人～。The family property was equally divided among the three children. /工作将由参与者～。The work will be shared by all participants.
平分秋色 píngfēn-qiūsè (of two parties) share (honour, power, glory, etc.) on a fifty-fifty basis;share equally
平分线 píngfēnxiàn 〈数学〉bisector
平伏 píngfú ❶ calm down; subside:他的心情久久不能～下来。For a long time he could not quiet down. ❷ lie on one's stomach:那人～在那里,穿着臃肿的脏衣服。The man lay flat on his stomach in soggy dirty clothes.
平服 píngfú ❶ calm;go back to normal:心情难以～ can not calm down ❷ be convinced:虽经过对方解释,但我们谁也没有～。None of us were convinced despite the other party's explanation.
平复 píngfu ❶ calm down; subside; be pacified:劝了半天,她的气才逐渐～了。It took much persuading to calm her down. /海面～如初。The sea regained its calm after the storm. /局势现已～。The situation is now back to normal. ❷ be cured; be healed;recover:他的腿伤～如故。His leg injury is completely healed. /这病经他治疗,你在一个月之内便可～了。With his medical attention, you will be well again within a month.
平肝止血 pínggān-zhǐxuè 〈中医〉calming the liver to stop bleeding
平沟机 pínggōujī 〈建筑〉trench filler
平光 píngguāng zero dioptre; plain glass:～眼镜 plain glass spectacles
平焊 pínghàn 〈冶金〉flat welding
平巷 pínghàng 〈矿业〉drift; level; gallery:主运输～gangway /～掘进机 header /～输送机 gate conveyor /～运输机 gangway conveyor /～装载机 gangway loader
平和 pínghé ❶ gentle; mild; moderate:语气～(speak) in a mild tone /尽量把话说得～些 try to put it as gently as possible; try so far as possible to speak in mild terms ❷ (of medicine) mild:这种药药性～,服用安全。This medicine is quite mild and safe to take. ❸ calm; serene;tranquil:心境渐渐～下来 gradually recover one's composure; soon calm down ❹〈方言〉(of struggle, dispute, etc.) stop; ease:双方的争斗日趋～。The contention between the two parties is beginning to ease off.
平衡 pínghéng balance; equilibrium:产销～ balance between production and marketing /收支～ balance between income and expenditure /保持收支～ balance the accounts /失去～ lose one's balance /保持心理～ maintain one's mental equilibrium /发展不～ uneven development /财政上不～ financial imbalance /保持供求关系的～ keep a balanced relationship between supply and demand /稳定～ stable equilibrium
平衡表 pínghéngbiǎo balance sheet
平衡常数 pínghéng chángshù 〈化学〉equilibrium constant
平衡价位 pínghéng jiàwèi equilibrium price
平衡觉 pínghéngjué 〈生理〉sense of equilibrium
平衡力 pínghénglì equilibrant
平衡木 pínghéngmù 〈体育〉balance beam
平衡器 pínghéngqì balancer
平衡曲线 pínghéng qūxiàn profile of equilibrium
平衡图 pínghéngtú 〈物理〉equilibrium diagram:铁碳～〈冶金〉iron-carbon diagram
平衡预算 pínghéng yùsuàn balanced budget
平滑 pínghuá level and smooth; smooth:冰场～如镜。The skating rink was as smooth as a mirror.
平滑肌 pínghuájī *also*"不随意肌" bùsuíyìjī 〈生理〉smooth muscle; involuntary muscle:～瘤〈医学〉leiomyoma /～肉瘤 leiomyosarcoma
平话 pínghuà *also*"评话" pínghuà ❶ style of storytelling (sometimes mixed with singing) popular esp. in the Song Dynasty ❷ such popular stories
平缓 pínghuǎn ❶ (of terrain) level; (of slopes, etc.) gentle:这一带地势～。The terrain in this area is quite level. /坡度极不～。The slope is very rugged and steep. ❷ slow and steady;gentle:水流～。The water flows gently. ❸ (of feeling, voice, etc.) mild; placid; gentle:他讲话时语气～。He spoke unhurriedly.
平毁 pínghuǐ destroy; demolish; raze:～旧碉堡 demolish old fortifications /那里的破房子已全部～。All the ramshackle houses there have been razed.
平假名 píngjiǎmíng hiragana, letters in Japanese executed swiftly and with strokes flowing together (such as あ,ひ etc.)
平价 píngjià ❶ curb rising prices; stabilize prices:～米 rice sold at government-controlled price; low-price rice ❷ reasonable price:～交易 fair deal ❸ par; parity:汇兑～ par of exchange /铸币～ specie par /固定～ fixed parity
平价商店 píngjià shāngdiàn low-price shop; fair-price shop; bargain shop
平交 píngjiāo 〈书面〉❶ deal with each other on an equal footing ❷ everyday friendly contact
平角 píngjiǎo 〈数学〉straight angle; 180-degree angle
平金 píngjīn a kind of golden and silvery-thread embroidery
平津战役 Píng-Jīn Zhànyì Beiping-Tianjin Campaign, one of three decisive battles launched by the People's Liberation Army against the KMT troops in the Beiping (now Beijing), Tianjin, and Zhangjiakou region from 5 Dec. 1948 to 31 Jan. 1949, ending in the peaceful liberation of Beiping
平靖 píngjìng ❶ suppress; put down (a rebellion, etc.); pacify (a region, country etc.) ❷ (of society) stable and peaceful
平静 píngjìng calm; quiet; peaceful; tranquil:心情～ be in a calm frame of mind /～的环境 peaceful environment /过着～的生活 lead (*or* live) a quiet life /这突发事件打破了他内心的～。The sudden turn of events upset his mental composure. /院子里恢复了往日的～。The compound regained its usual peace and tranquillity. *or* Peace and tranquillity eventually returned to the compound.
平居 píngjū 〈书面〉ordinarily:～多病 be invalid for most of the time
平局 píngjú draw; tie:打成～ end in a draw (*or* tie); tie (with one's competitor) /扳成～ equalize the score /在十六次比赛中,他取得四胜、二负和九次～的成绩。In 16 games he had a record of 4 wins, 2 losses and 9 draws.
平均 píngjūn ❶ average; mean:～速度 mean velocity; average speed /～尺寸 mean size /～积分点〈教育〉grade-point average (GPA) /～寿命 average life span; life expectancy;〈物理〉mean life /～海平面 mean sea level /～偏差〈统计〉mean deviation /按人口～的国民生产总值 per capita GNP /～每年增长百分之七 increase by an annual average of 7% /这次捐款,～每人五十元。This time the donation is 50 *yuan* per person on the average. ❷ equally; share and share alike:～分配 share out (*or* distribute) equally /～发展 equal (*or* even) development ❸〈天文〉mean:～历表日 ephemeris mean day /～太阳日 mean solar day
平均潮升 píngjūn cháoshēng mean rise of tide
平均出厂质量 píngjūn chūchǎng zhìliàng average outgoing quality (AOQ)
平均地权 píngjūn dìquán equal distribution of land ownership
平均海水面 píngjūn hǎishuǐmiàn average sea level
平均汇率 píngjūn huìlǜ 〈金融〉midpoint rate of exchange; equilibrium rate; average rate
平均利润 píngjūn lìrùn 〈经济〉average profit
平均律 píngjūnlǜ 〈音乐〉equal temperament:十二～ twelve-tone equal temperament
平均数 píngjūnshù 〈数学〉average; mean value
平均值 píngjūnzhí average value; mean value
平均主义 píngjūnzhǔyì equalitarianism; egalitarianism:～的社会主义 equal-shares-for-all socialism; egalitarian socialism /～毕竟有弊病。Share and share alike has its drawbacks after all.
平康 píngkāng ❶ safe and sound ❷〈书面〉brothel (from the name of a district called "Pingkangfang" 平康坊 in Chang'an, in the Tang Dynasty, which was inhabited mostly by prostitutes); red-

light district:流落~ become a prostitute
平空 píngkōng *also* "凭空" píngkōng out of the void; without foundation; baseless
平口钳 píngkǒuqián flat-nose pliers
平旷 píngkuàng 〈书面〉(of land) level and broad:~的原野 level and broad plains
平阔 píngkuò (of terrain) level and extensive:~的大地 vast expanse of level land
平列 píngliè place side by side; place on a par with each other:这些因素轻重有别,不能~。These factors which vary in degree of significance should not be mentioned in the same breath.
平流 píngliú 〈气象〉advection
平流层 píngliúcéng 〈气象〉stratosphere:~顶 stratopause /~探测装置 stratosphere sounding unit /~空悬微尘测量仪 stratospheric aerosol measurement /~和中间层探测器 stratospheric and mesospheric sounder
平窿 pínglóng level or slightly sloping gallery in a mine with one end on the horizontal
平炉 pínglú *also* "马丁炉" mǎdīnglú 〈冶金〉open-hearth furnace; open hearth
平炉钢 pínglúgāng open-hearth steel
平炉利用系数 pínglú lìyòng xìshù capacity factor of an open-hearth furnace
平炉炼钢法 pínglú liàngāngfǎ open-hearth process
平路机 pínglùjī 〈建筑〉blader; bulldozer
平乱 píngluàn quell a revolt; suppress a rebellion
平轮压路机 pínglún yālùjī 〈建筑〉flat-wheel roller
平落 píngluò (of prices) drop to normal
平脉 píngmài 〈中医〉normal pulse
平米 píngmǐ square metre
平面 píngmiàn plane
平面波 píngmiànbō 〈物理〉plane wave
平面海图 píngmiàn hǎitú plane chart
平面几何 píngmiàn jǐhé 〈数学〉plane geometry
平面交叉 píngmiàn jiāochā level crossing; grade crossing
平面角 píngmiànjiǎo 〈数学〉plane angle
平面镜 píngmiànjìng 〈物理〉plane mirror
平面磨床 píngmiàn móchuáng surface grinding machine
平面图 píngmiàntú ❶ plan ❷ plane figure
平民 píngmín common people; populace:所谓"民情"就是~情绪的反映。The so-called public mood is nothing but a reflection of the feelings of the man in the street. /政府领导人应经常关心~百姓的疾苦。Government leaders should always keep in mind the well-being of the common people.
平明 píngmíng 〈书面〉dawn
平年 píngnián ❶〈天文〉non-leap year; common year ❷〈农业〉average year (in crop yield, etc.)
平叛 píngpàn *see* "平乱"
平平 píngpíng average; middling; mediocre; indifferent:技术~ of middling skill /所言~。There is nothing worth special attention in what he said. /她的表演~,名不符实。Her performance was just so-so, falling far short of her reputation.
平平当当 píngpíng-dāngdāng smoothly; without a hitch:这件事~地完成了。The task was fulfilled (*or* accomplished) without mishap.
平铺直叙 píngpū-zhíxù tell in a simple, straightforward way; speak or write in a flat or monotonous style:文学作品,一定要避免~。As a rule, one should try to avoid (using) a dull and flat style in literary writing.
平起平坐 píngqǐ-píngzuò sit as equals at the same table; be on an equal footing:夫妻俩在厂里是~的一对儿车间主任。The couple were both floor managers of equal status in the factory.
平钳 píngqián 〈机械〉flat pliers
平权 píngquán (enjoy) equal rights:男女~ equal rights for men and women
平壤 Píngrǎng Pyongyang, capital of the Democratic People's Republic of Korea (DPRK)
平人 píngrén 〈书面〉the populace; the common people
平日 píngrì ordinary days (in contrast to special occasions):~他们家的饭菜很简单。They have simple dishes (*or* homely meals) on ordinary days. /她~很少注意这些事。Ordinarily, she pays very little attention to these things.
平绒 píngróng 〈纺织〉velveteen
平沙 píngshā level sands; sand beach
平射 píngshè 〈军事〉flat (trajectory) fire
平射炮 píngshèpào 〈军事〉flat fire gun; flat trajectory gun
平伸 píngshēn level stretch:两腿直立,两臂~。Stand straight and stretch both arms level.
平身 píngshēn 〈旧语〉(of a court official) rise to one's feet after kneeling and kowtowing to the throne
平生 píngshēng ❶ all one's life; one's whole life:为科学而献身是他~的志愿。His lifelong aspiration was to dedicate himself to science. ❷ ever:他~从不抽烟。He never smoked in his life.
平生不做亏心事,夜半敲门心不惊 píngshēng bù zuò kuīxīn shì, yè bàn qiāomén xīn bù jīng a man with a good conscience will not be startled if he hears knocks on his door at midnight; a clear conscience laughs at false accusations; a clean conscience is a soft pillow
平声 píngshēng 〈语言〉level tone — first of the four tones in classical Chinese, which has evolved into 阴平 (the high and level tone, marked with "ˉ") and 阳平 (the rising tone, marked with "ˊ") in *putonghua* (modern standard pronunciation)
see also "四声" sìshēng
平时 píngshí ❶ ordinarily; usually:他们~很少来往。They seldom call on each other. *or* Usually they have very little contact. ❷ peacetime:~编制 peacetime establishment (*or* organization) /~兵力 peacetime strength
平时不烧香,急来抱佛脚 píngshí bù shāoxiāng, jí lái bào fójiǎo 〈俗语〉never burn incense when all is well but clasp Buddha's feet when in distress; do nothing till the situation is getting desperate
平实 píngshí 〈方言〉unadorned; natural:文章~无华,堪称上乘之作。The essay which is terse and unadorned is a work of the first order.
平实 píngshi (of ground) level; flat; smooth; even
平世 píngshì 〈书面〉peacetime; times of peace and stability
平式提花针织机 píngshì tíhuā zhēnzhījī 〈纺织〉flat jacquard knitter
平视 píngshì look straight forward:立正时两眼要~。One should look straight forward when standing at attention.
平手 píngshǒu draw; tie:这盘棋两人下了个~。The chess game ended in a draw.
平水期 píngshuǐqī *also* "中水期" zhōngshuǐqī time when the river water is at normal level
平顺 píngshùn smooth-going; uneventful:工作~。The work was just plain sailing.
平素 píngsù usually; customarily; habitually:他~对子女要求很严。He is usually very strict with his children. /她~就爱整洁。She habitually likes to be clean and tidy.
平台 píngtái ❶ terrace (of a house) ❷ flat-roofed house ❸ platform:~甲板 platform deck /装货~ loading platform
平台网球 píngtái wǎngqiú platform tennis
平台印刷机 píngtái yìnshuājī flatbed press
平坦 píngtǎn (of land, etc.) level; even; smooth:广场宽广~。The square is level and spacious. /通向成功的道路从来不是~的。The road to success has never been smooth.
平添 píngtiān increase naturally; add to:这个街心公园给周围居民~了许多乐趣。The street park has greatly added to the joys of the residents in the neighbourhood.
平粜 píngtiào 〈旧语〉government-sponsored sale of grain at normal price in years of famine
平帖 píngtiē *also* "平贴" fitting and proper; appropriate:窗户纸糊得很~。The sheets of paper are pasted neatly and smoothly over lattices of the window.
平头 píngtóu ❶ closely cropped hair; crew cut:理个~ have a crew cut /留着~ have closely cropped hair ❷ common; ordinary (people):~百姓 common people ❸〈方言〉(used before a figure) whole; just; exactly:~二十岁 exactly twenty years old
平头钉 píngtóudīng tack
平头数 píngtóushù 〈方言〉round number
平头鱼 píngtóuyú slickhead; smoothhead (*Alepocephalidae*)
平头正脸 píngtóu-zhèngliǎn have regular features
平凸弹头 píngtū dàntóu 〈军事〉flat nose
平土机 píngtǔjī 〈机械〉grader
平妥 píngtuǒ smooth and proper:措词~ appropriately worded
平瓦 píngwǎ 〈建筑〉plain tile
平温 píngwēn moderate temperature (usually at 28°C for agricul-

ture)

平纹 píngwén 〈纺织〉 plain weave:～布 plain cloth

平稳 píngwěn ❶ steady; normal; stable:生产～。Production is steady./飞行～。It was a smooth flight./他的血压一向～。His blood pressure has always been stable. ❷ (of an object) steady; firm:把桌子放～了。Make the table steady.

平屋 píngwū single-storey house; one-storey house

平芜 píngwú 〈书面〉 open weedy country; wilderness

平西 píngxī (of the sun) be setting:太阳～的时候,我们收工了。We knocked off at sunset.

平昔 píngxī in the past:他～就不大注意锻炼身体,所以抵抗力很弱。He neglected physical training in the past and so had low resistance to diseases.

平息 píngxī ❶ calm down; quiet down; die down; subside:～争端 settle a dispute/～怒火 appease sb.'s anger/一场风波～了。The storm has blown over./晚上,风渐渐～。The wind subsided (*or* died down) during the night. ❷ put down (a rebellion, etc.); quell; suppress:那次叛乱很快就～了。The rebellion was quelled (*or* put down) quickly.

平铣刀 píngxǐdāo *also* "平面铣刀" 〈机械〉 plain milling cutter; slab cutter

平晓 píngxiǎo 〈书面〉 time of daybreak; dawn

平心 píngxīn calmly; fairly; unemotionally:～想来,他的话是很有道理的。Reflecting on it without any bias, I think he really has a point there.

平心而论 píngxīn'érlùn in all fairness; to be fair; to do (sb.) justice:～,我自己也有错。In all fairness, I am also to blame./～,他的用意还是好的。To give him his due, he meant well.

平心静气 píngxīn-jìngqì calmly; dispassionately:我们～地谈一谈。Let's calmly go over the problem together./我～地想过。I've thought about it quite dispassionately.

平信 píngxìn ❶ ordinary mail ❷ surface mail

平行 píngxíng ❶ of equal rank; on an equal footing; parallel:～机关 departments of equal rank; parallel departments ❷ 〈数学〉 parallel ❸ simultaneous; parallel:就各种问题举行～的会谈 hold parallel talks on separate issues/～研究 parallel study/～不悖的利益 parallel interests

平行六面体 píngxíng liùmiàntǐ 〈数学〉 parallelepiped

平行脉 píngxíngmài 〈植物〉 parallel veins

平行四边形 píngxíng sìbiānxíng 〈数学〉 parallelogram

平行线 píngxíngxiàn parallel lines

平行职权 píngxíng zhíquán concurrent competence

平行主权 píngxíng zhǔquán concurrent sovereignty

平行作业 píngxíng zuòyè parallel operations; simultaneous operations

平型关战斗 Píngxíngguān Zhàndòu Battle at Pingxingguan Pass (where the first victory was won by the Chinese in their War of Resistance against Japanese Aggression on 25 Sept. 1937)

平衍 píngyǎn 〈书面〉 (of land, etc.) level; smooth:原野～ a stretch of level open country

平阳 píngyáng flat land; level ground:虎落～被犬欺 a tiger may be bullied by dogs when it finds itself on level ground — even a talented person is helpless in adverse circumstances

平野 píngyě open country fields:一望无际的～ boundless expanse of flat cultivated land

平一 píngyī 〈书面〉 unify:～宇内 unify all land on earth; bring peace to the land

平移 píngyí *see* "平动"

平议 píngyì ❶ judge fairly; make a fair assessment ❷ *see* "评议" píngyì

平抑 píngyì stabilize; restrain; pacify:～物价 stabilize the prices/他静静地坐在地上,尽力使自己的怒火～下来。Sitting silent on the ground, he tried his best to restrain his anger.

平易 píngyì ❶ unassuming; amiable:～可亲 amiable; affable ❷ (of a piece of writing) easy; plain:语言～ in simple plain language

平易近人 píngyì-jìnrén ❶ modest and easy of access; modest and unassuming:这位校长～。The president is modest and easy of approach. ❷ (of literature) simple and plain; easy to understand:他的文章写得～。His essay is written in a simple, plain style.

平英团 Píngyīngtuán League of Resistance Against the British Invaders, armed force organized spontaneously by the people of Guangzhou and Xiamen during the Opium War, 1839-1842

平庸 píngyōng mediocre; commonplace:～之辈 mediocre people; mediocrities/～之作 mediocre work/小聪明就是～的标志。Petty smartness is a token of mediocrity.

平鱼 píngyú *also* "鲳" chāng silvery pomfret; butterfish

平原 píngyuán plain; flatland:华北～ North China Plain/冲积～ alluvial plain/侵蚀～ eroded plain/海岸～ coastal plain

平月 píngyuè February of a non-leap year (with 28 days)

平匀 píngyún even; well-distributed:速度～ even speed/天气正好不冷不热,昼夜的长短也分得～。The weather is neither cold nor hot and the day and night are also evenly divided in length.

平允 píngyǔn 〈书面〉 fair and just; equitable:分配～ equitable distribution/他言语～,令人心服。His words were fair and just, and we were all convinced.

平仄 píngzè ❶ level and oblique tones ❷ tonal patterns in classical Chinese poetry:这首律诗～不调。This *lü* poem is unsatisfactory in tonal patterns.

平展 píngzhǎn ❶ (of land, etc.) open and flat:山坡下是一片平展的庄稼地。At the foot of the hills lies a great stretch of open, flat cropland. ❷ even and smooth:他显得年轻了许多,脸上的皱纹～了不少。With many wrinkles on his face smoothed away, he looked much younger for his age.

平展展 píngzhǎnzhǎn very smooth and even:～的高速公路伸向远方。The broad and even motorway (*or* freeway) stretches away into the distance.

平战转换 píngzhàn zhuǎnhuàn convert from wartime to peacetime production and vice versa

平章 píngzhāng 〈书面〉 ❶ discuss and handle; plan and prepare:～国事 deal with state affairs ❷ judge; comment on:～西湖风景 make comments on the scenic beauty of West Lake

平针 píngzhēn plain stitch

平整 píngzhěng ❶ level:～土地 level land ❷ neat; smooth:这片土地很～。The land is level and smooth.

平整机 píngzhěngjī 〈冶金〉 planisher

平正 píngzheng ❶ smooth; even:这张纸很～。This sheet of paper is very smooth. ❷ straight; upright; neat:被子叠得很～。The quilt was neatly folded on the bed.

平直 píngzhí ❶ level and straight:尽可能把管道布置得～些。Try to lay the pipes as level and straight as possible. ❷ tell in a simple and straightforward way:～浅露 simple and shallow ❸ 〈书面〉 upright; honest:为人～ be an honest man by nature

平治 píngzhì 〈书面〉 ❶ put in order; bring under control:水土～ harnessing of rivers and conservation of soil; water and soil conservation ❷ reign of peace:天下～。Peace prevails in the country.

平转塔六角车床 píngzhuǎntǎ liùjiǎo chēchuáng 〈机械〉 flat turret lathe

平装 píngzhuāng paperback; paper-cover; paperbound:～本 paperback (book); paperbound edition

平装开关 píngzhuāng kāiguān 〈电工〉 flush switch

平足 píngzú 〈医学〉 flatfoot

平作 píngzuò (of farming) sowing seeds in the extensive level fields

评

píng ❶ make comments; comment; criticize; review:短～ brief comments/时～ commentary on current affairs/影～ film review/获得好～ be well (*or* favourably) received/已有定～。There is a general verdict on it. *or* There is a consensus of opinion about it. ❷ judge; assess; appraise:～其优劣 appraise the merits and demerits of sb. (*or* sth.)/～满分 award (*or* give) full marks/你来～一～谁是谁非。Now you may judge and say who is right and who is wrong./大家一致～他为先进工作者。We unanimously elected him advanced worker.

评比 píngbǐ appraise through comparison; compare and evaluate:年终～ year-end appraisal of work/～教学效果 compare and appraise the results of teaching; make a public appraisal of the results of teaching

评产 píngchǎn assess the quantity of products; evaluate the output

评点 píngdiǎn appraise and mark words and phrases (in a poem or book) with small circles or points on the right side; edit with comments; annotate

评定 píngdìng pass judgement on; evaluate; assess:～名次 decide on the relative places or ranks (of competing performers, products,

etc.) /～分数 give marks; grade /～职称 determine academic titles

评断 píngduàn judge; arbitrate:～得失 weigh the pros and cons /～价值 judge the value of; evaluate

评分 píngfēn give a mark; mark (students' papers, etc.):这次测验不～。The papers for this test won't be graded. /他的自由体操评了 9.95 分。He was given a score of 9.95 in the floor exercise.

评改 pínggǎi correct and grade (sb.'s homework):～作文 correct and grade compositions by students

评工 pínggōng evaluate work (esp. of a commune member):～定级 evaluate sb.'s work performance and determine his grade on the wage scale

评功 pínggōng appraise sb.'s merits:～授奖 give awards on the basis of assessed merits

评功摆好 pínggōng-bǎihǎo enumerate sb.'s merits in flattering terms; evaluate and praise (sb.'s) merits:不能光给他～,还要指出他的不足。We are not supposed to be all praises for his work. We should point out his shortcomings as well.

评估 pínggū evaluate and estimate:资产～ evaluation of assets /对入股资金的经济效益进行～ assess and estimate the economic returns of the investment

评话 pínghuà ❶ see "平话" pínghuà ❷ professional storytelling in a local dialect:苏州～ storytelling in Suzhou dialect

评级 píngjí ❶ grade cadres, workers, etc. according to qualifications and performance ❷ grade products, etc. according to quality

评价 píngjià pass judgement on; appraise; evaluate:实事求是地～历史人物 pass equitable judgement on historical figures /我们高度～他的学术成就。We have a very high opinion of his academic achievement. /这个～对他来说是当之无愧的。He fully deserves the tribute paid to him. /这部电影由于当时的种种原因～过高了。For various reasons the film was somewhat overrated.

评奖 píngjiǎng give awards after panel discussion:对儿童文学定期～。Prizes for children's literature are regularly awarded.

评介 píngjiè review (a new book, etc.):电影～ film review /对这篇小说已经发表了几篇～文章。There have been several reviews of the novel. *or* The novel has been reviewed several times in the press.

评剧 píngjù *also* "蹦蹦儿戏" bèngbèngrxì; "落子" làozi 〈戏曲〉 *pingju*, a local opera of north and northeast China

评卷 píngjuàn mark exam or test papers

评理 pínglǐ ❶ give a verdict on a dispute; pass judgement on a matter:两口子吵架,这个理很难评。It is very difficult to pass judgement on a quarrel between man and wife. ❷ reason things out; have it out:经过～之后,他们认识了自己的过错。He came to acknowledge his fault when things were reasoned out.

评论 pínglùn ❶ discuss; comment:～好坏 comment on sb.'s merits and demerits ❷ review; commentary:时事～ commentary on current affairs /发表～ publish a review

评论家 pínglùnjiā critic; reviewer

评论员 pínglùnyuán commentator

评脉 píngmài 〈方言〉〈中医〉 feel the pulse

评模 píngmó choose or elect model workers:开～会议 hold a meeting to elect model workers

评判 píngpàn pass judgement on; judge; decide:～得失 judge the advantages and disadvantages /～好坏 decide who (*or* which) is better /～公允 make a fair and just verdict /他的工作,我无从～。I'm not in a position to judge his work. /名次由评委们～。The placements of winners are to be determined by the judges.

评判员 píngpànyuán (of sports and speech contests) judge; (of musical contests, etc.) adjudicator

评品 píngpǐn 〈书面〉 judge; pass judgement on; evaluate

评审 píngshěn comment on and examine:～文艺作品 assess (*or* evaluate) art and literary works

评书 píngshū storytelling (by a professional storyteller):～艺人 professional storyteller

评述 píngshù appraise sth. through comments

评说 píngshuō comment on; appraise; evaluate:他的是非功过,自有后人～。Posterity will give verdict on his rights and wrongs, merits and demerits. /千秋功罪,谁人曾与～? Who has passed judgement on the good and ill You have wrought these thousand autumns?

评弹 píngtán ❶ storytelling combined with ballad singing in Suzhou (苏州) dialect ❷ style of storytelling combined with ballad singing popular in the Song Dynasty

评头论足 píngtóu-lùnzú ❶ make frivolous remarks about a woman's looks ❷ carp at; nit-pick

see also "品头论足" pǐntóu-lùnzú

评委 píngwěi (short for 评审委员会委员) member of a review committee

评委会 píngwěihuì (short for 评审委员会) review committee

评析 píngxī comment on and analyse:当前经济状况～ analytical review of the current economic situation

评戏 píngxì see "评剧"

评薪 píngxīn fix a person's grade on the wage scale according to his qualifications (usually through democratic appraisal)

评叙 píngxù see "评述"

评选 píngxuǎn choose through public appraisal:被～为优秀干部 be chosen as a model cadre /～1992 年优秀文学作品 select fine literary works for 1992 through extensive consultation

评议 píngyì appraise through discussion:群众～ popular appraisal /这项工作的好坏,应由大家～。The merits or otherwise of the project should be a matter for public discussion.

评语 píngyǔ comment; remark

评阅 píngyuè read and appraise (sb.'s writing, etc.):～试卷 read and grade the examination; go over the papers

评赞 píngzàn comment on and praise:人们都在～她的种种美德。People are all speaking of her virtues in glowing terms.

评职 píngzhí assess and ascertain the title of one's official, academic or technical post or job title

评骘 píngzhì 〈书面〉 judge; evaluate; assess:～书画 pass judgement on paintings and works of calligraphy

评注 píngzhù ❶ annotate often with textual comments:～《史记》 annotate the *Historical Records* ❷ notes and commentary

评传 píngzhuàn critical biography:李白～ critical biography of Li Bai

坪

píng ❶ level ground (in hilly or loess regions, often used in place names):王家～ Wangjiaping village (in Shaanxi Province) /草～ lawn; grass plot /停机～ aircraft park; apron; tarmac ❷ 〈方言〉 unit of area (=3.3 square metres)

坪坝 píngbà 〈方言〉 level ground

苹(蘋) píng

苹果 píngguǒ apple:黄香蕉～ yellow apple with a banana-like odour /红富士～ red Fuji apple

苹果脯 píngguǒfǔ preserved apple

苹果干 píngguǒgān dried apple slices

苹果公司 Píngguǒ Gōngsī (US) Apple Computer, Inc.

苹果酱 píngguǒjiàng apple jam; apple butter

苹果酒 píngguǒjiǔ applejack; cider

苹果绿 píngguǒlǜ apple green

苹果园 píngguǒyuán apple orchard

萍(蓱) píng duckweed

萍泊 píngbó *also* "萍泛"; "萍漂" 〈书面〉 lead a wandering life:～他乡 wander in an alien land

萍梗 pínggěng 〈书面〉 live a wandering life

萍寄 píngjì 〈书面〉 live everywhere away from home

萍蓬 píngpéng 〈书面〉 go adrift; lead a vagrant's life

萍蓬草 píngpéngcǎo 〈植物〉 spatterdock

萍水相逢 píngshuǐ-xiāngféng (of strangers) meet by chance like patches of drifting duckweed:他们二人～,一见如故。The two of them felt like old friends though they met by chance for the first time. /～,尽是他乡之客。Drifting together like duckweeds, we were strangers from different towns.

萍踪 píngzōng 〈书面〉 whereabouts (of a wanderer):～无定 drift about with great uncertainty; wander from place to place

萍踪浪迹 píngzōng-làngjì *also* "萍踪浪影" (of wanderers) leave no traces like duckweed and waves:他～,不知所止。He drifted from one place to another, and nobody knew his whereabouts.

枰

píng 〈书面〉 chessboard; checkerboard:棋～ chessboard; checkerboard

鲆

píng 〈动物〉 left-eyed flounder

凭[1]（**憑、凴**） píng ❶ lean on; lean against:～窗远眺 stand at a window gazing into the distance ❷ rely on; depend on: ～手艺吃饭 make a living by one's craftsmanship /工作能搞好，全～大家的努力。The success of the work was due to our concerted efforts. /海阔～鱼跃。The sea is so vast that any fish can frolic freely in it — there is scope for everyone to exercise his talents freely. ❸ evidence; proof; guarantee:文～ diploma /真～实据 iron-clad or conclusive evidence /空口无～。Verbal assurances are no bond. *or* Words spoken casually are no guarantee. /以此为～。This will serve as proof. ❹ go by; base on; act according to:～常识判断 judge by common sense /～经验办事 act by rule of thumb /～良心说 in all conscience; to be fair /～单据报销 refund by invoices /～身分证入内。Admission by identity card (*or* ID card) only. /你～什么不让我去? What is the ground for your decision not to let me go there?

凭[2]（**憑、凴**） píng 〈连词〉 no matter (what, how, etc.):～大家怎样劝，她还是不听。She just refused to listen, no matter how hard we tried to talk her round. /～他是谁，迟到了也不能入场。No one who is late will be admitted, no matter who he is.

凭单 píngdān certificate for drawing money, goods, etc.; voucher; certificate

凭吊 píngdiào visit (a historical site, etc.) and meditate on the past:去先人坟墓～ pay a visit to the site of one's ancestral tomb / 每次到南京，他都必去中山陵～一番。Whenever he went to Nanjing, he would pay his respects at Dr. Sun Yat-sen's mausoleum.

凭借 píngjiè take advantage of; rely on; depend on:～我厂的优势 rely on the strengths of our factory /～有利的地形顽抗 put up a stubborn resistance by taking advantage of favourable terrain /～权势胡作非为 commit outrages by abusing one's power

凭据 píngjù evidence; proof:没有足够的～，不能定案。No verdict shall be given without sufficient evidence. /你有何～? Have you any proof?

凭靠 píngkào rely on; depend on:农民～肩挑背扛，向前线运送弹药。The peasants had to rely on their shoulders and backs to transport ammunition to the front.

凭空 píngkōng *also* "平空" píngkōng out of thin air; without foundation; groundless:～想像 pure imagination; figment of one's imagination

凭空捏造 píngkōng-niēzào make something out of nothing; concoct; fabricate:这些罪名都是～的。These charges were all fabrications.

凭栏 pínglán *also* "凭阑" lean on a railing:～沉思 lean on a railing lost in thought /～处，潇潇雨歇。Leaning on the railings, I see the pouring rain has ceased.

凭陵 pínglíng 〈书面〉 ❶ use one's power to bully:～弱国 bully (*or* encroach on) a weaker country ❷ rely on; depend on:～权势 on the strength of one's power and influence

凭恃 píngshì count on; rely on:～天险 rely on natural barriers

凭眺 píngtiào gaze (from a high place) into the distance; enjoy a distant view:～大海 gaze into the distant sea /山上有个亭子，可供～。At the top of the hill is a pavilion where one can view the surrounding scenery.

凭险 píngxiǎn make use of a strategic vantage point:～抵抗 offer resistance by taking advantage of favourable terrain

凭信 píngxìn trust; believe:不足～ not trustworthy, unreliable /此话可以～。These words can be trusted.

凭依 píngyī base oneself on; rely on:无所～ have nothing to go by; have nobody to fall back upon /年轻人要有独立生活的能力，哪能一辈子～父母。Young people ought to be able to fend for themselves, how can they depend on their parents for support all their lives?

凭倚 píngyǐ lean on or against; rest on or against:她～在池塘的扶栏上观鱼。She leant against the railing round the pond watching fish.

凭仗 píngzhàng rely on; depend on:他们全～着勇气和毅力克服了难以想像的困难。They overcame incredible difficulties by dint of sheer courage and fortitude.

凭照 píngzhào certificate; permit; licence:领取～ receive one's licence

凭证 píngzhèng evidence; certificate; voucher:结算～ voucher of clearing /纳税～ tax payment receipt /取货～ bill of lading

凭准 píngzhǔn reliable evidence or criterion:真理的～ criterion of truth

冯 píng *see* "暴虎冯河" bàohǔ-pínghé
see also Féng

pō

朴 pō
see also Piáo; pò; pǔ

朴刀 pōdāo sword with a long narrow blade and a relatively short hilt wielded with both hands

钋 pō 〈化学〉 polonium (Po)

泊（**泺**） pō lake (often used in place names):梁山～ Liangshan Lake (in Shandong Province) /罗布～ Lop Nor (in Xinjiang) /他倒在血～中。He lay in a pool of blood.
see also bó

泊地 pōdì lake-bank; land beside a lake

坡 pō ❶ slope:斜～ slope /山～ mountain slope; hillside /陡～ steep slope /上～ go up a slope; go uphill ❷ sloping; slanting:把扁担～着靠在墙上。Lean the shoulder pole against the wall at a slant. /井台的两侧再～一点。The raised platforms of the well should be sloped a bit more.

坡岸 pō'àn sloping bank

坡道 pōdào sloping path or road:顺～而下 go down a sloping path

坡地 pōdì hillside fields; land on the slopes:～梯田化 terracing the slopes

坡度 pōdù slope; gradient; degree of incline:这段山路～不大。The slope of this section of the mountain path is not very steep.

坡跟鞋 pōgēnxié wedge heel

坡降 pōjiàng ❶ slope:水顺着～向东流去。The water flows eastwards along the slope. ❷ gradient; slope:～大，水流急。The water flows swiftly because the slope is steep.

坡垒 pōlěi 〈植物〉 *Hopea hainanensis*

坡鹿 pōlù *also* "泽鹿" zélù 〈动物〉 slope deer (*Cervus eldi*)

坡莫合金 pōmò héjīn permalloy

坡田 pōtián hillside fields; sloping fields

颇[1] pō 〈书面〉 inclined to one side; oblique; partial:这些意见似嫌偏～，宜再讨论。The views seem biased and should be further deliberated.

颇[2] pō quite; rather; considerably:～有研究 have done considerable research on sth. /此文～佳。The article is quite good. /顾客对他的服务态度～为满意。Customers are quite satisfied with his service attitude. /我对绘画～感兴趣。I was rather interested in painting.

颇为 pōwéi 〈副词〉 to a considerable extent:～感动 quite moved / ～重要 rather important

陂 pō
see also bēi

陂陀 pōtuó 〈书面〉 uneven; not smooth:山道～ rugged mountain path

泼[1]（**潑**） pō sprinkle; splash; spill:把脏水～掉 throw away the slops /～水难收。Spilt water can't be scooped up. /天太热，在地上～点儿凉水。Sprinkle some cold water on the ground, since it is so hot.

泼[2]（**潑**） pō ❶ rude and unreasonable; shrewish:撒～ act hysterically and refuse to see reason; make a scene ❷〈方言〉 daring and resolute; bold:他干事很～。He is bold and resolute (*or* decisive) in action.

泼烦 pōfán 〈方言〉 unhappy; worried; fed up with:解放前，穷人吃

不饱，穿不暖，日子越过越～。In pre-liberation days the poor had not enough to eat and wear, and life became increasingly intolerable.
泼妇 pōfù shrew; virago; vixen; termagant：得治治这个～。This shrew must be properly taken in hand.
泼妇骂街 pōfù-màjiē like a shrew letting loose a stream of abuse in the street：写论战文章，不要染上～的恶习气。A polemical article must not be tainted by a stream of abuse. *or* We must not use abusive language in polemic.
泼悍 pōhàn fierce and tough; ferocious
泼剌 pōlà *also*"泼剌剌" ❶〈象声〉sound as of fish splashing in the water：湖里时有鱼儿～跃水。You can hear fish splashing in the lake every now and then. ❷ *see*"泼辣"
泼辣 pōla ❶ rude and unreasonable; shrewish：～货 shrew; termagant /那姑娘被娇养得很是～。The spoiled girl behaved like a shrew. /你为什么学得这样～? What makes you so caustic? ❷ pungent and forceful; bold and vigorous：文风～ write a pungent style / 工作～ bold and decisive in one's work
泼辣旦 pōladàn shrewish role in traditional Chinese opera
泼赖 pōlài be unreasonable and quarrelsome：那孩子～，一个劲儿地大哭大闹。The kid kept wailing and made a terrible scene.
泼冷水 pō lěngshuǐ pour or throw cold water on; discourage：对他的积极性要鼓励而不要～。We should encourage his enthusiasm instead of putting a wet blanket over it. /我一听他这话，就像头上泼了一瓢冷水。I was thoroughly discouraged at his remarks.
泼墨 pōmò ❶〈美术〉splash-ink, a technique of Chinese ink-painting：～山水 splashed-ink landscape ❷ do a traditional Chinese painting：新年伊始，请诸位画家相聚并为展览会～。To celebrate the New Year, we have arranged for painters to get together and draw a few pictures for the exhibition.
泼醅 pōpēi *see*"酦醅" pōpēi
泼皮 pōpí hooligan; hoodlum; ruffian：～无赖 rascals and scoundrels
泼洒 pōsǎ sprinkle; splash：牛奶～了一地。The milk has spilled all over the place. /月光如水，～在静谧的原野上。The tranquil fields were bathed in silvery moonlight.
泼洒 pōsa〈方言〉easy and unconventional in manner：这姑娘～爽快，招人喜爱。This girl is liked for her easy and natural manner.
泼实 pōshi〈方言〉strong and able to stand hardship：这些小伙子真～，到东北很快就适应了冰天雪地的生活。Those were indeed sturdy hard-working lads, and soon got used to a world of ice and snow in the Northeast.
泼水节 Pōshuǐjié Water-Sprinkling Festival of the Dai（傣）and some other minority nationalities（mostly living in Yunnan Province), occuring usu. in mid-April
泼天 pōtiān (often used in the early vernacular) extremely big; excessive：～大祸 catastrophe
泼野 pōyě uncivilized in behaviour and fiery in temper：由于父母的娇纵，这孩子自幼养成了～粗鲁的性格。Pampered by his parents, the child has got accustomed to rude behaviour.
泼脏水 pō zāngshuǐ sling mud at; slander：有人为了诋毁他，一个劲儿地往他身上～。Someone has kept throwing mud at him in order to smear his reputation.

酦(醱)

pō〈书面〉make (wine); brew (beer)
see also fā
酦醅 pōpēi *also*"泼醅" pōpēi〈书面〉make wine

钹(鏺)

pō〈方言〉❶ cut or reap (grass, crop, etc.) with a sickle ❷ a kind of sickle

pó

婆

pó ❶ old woman：老太～ old woman ❷ woman in a certain occupation：媒～儿 professional woman matchmaker /产～儿 midwife /巫～ witch; sorceress ❸ husband's mother; mother-in-law：公～ husband's parents; parents-in-law
婆家 pójia *also*"婆婆家" husband's family (in contrast to 娘家, woman's own family)：给她找个～(in traditional arranged marriage) find a husband for her /姑娘多大了? 有了～没有? How old is the girl? Is she betrothed yet?
婆罗门 Póluómén Brahman, (member of the) highest rank in the Hindu caste system, traditionally eligible for the priesthood
婆罗门教 Póluóménjiào Brahmanism, the sacrificial religion that emerged in post-Vedic India (c. 900 BC) under the influence of the dominant priesthood (Brahmans)
婆罗洲 Póluózhōu Borneo, a large island of the Malay Archipelago, comprising Kalimantan, Sabah and Sarawak, and Brunei
婆母 pómǔ husband's mother; mother-in-law
婆娘 póniáng〈方言〉❶ married woman ❷ wife
婆婆 pópo ❶ husband's mother; mother-in-law：～太多，难以办事。It's hard to get anything done when you have too many bosses. ❷〈方言〉grandmother：老～ old lady; old woman; granny
婆婆家 pópojiā husband's family
婆婆妈妈 pópo-māmā ❶ act slowly like an old woman：你快一点吧，别这么～的了。Hurry up! Don't dawdle any more. ❷ sentimental; mawkish; maudlin：她就是这么～的，动不动就掉眼泪。She is so sentimental that she would shed tears over the slightest provocation.
婆婆嘴 pópozuǐ ❶ toothless mouth of an old woman ❷ long-tongued person：她是个～，说起来就没完没了。She is a chatterbox; she babbles on interminably once she gets started.
婆娑 pósuō whirling; dancing：～多姿的柳树 willows swaying gracefully in a breeze /月光下花影～。Shadows of flowers dance about in the moonlight.
婆娑起舞 pósuō-qǐwǔ start dancing：一对彩蝶在花间～。A pair of butterflies were fluttering among the flowers.
婆媳 pó-xí mother-in-law and daughter-in-law
婆心 póxīn kind heart：苦口～ admonish earnestly /一片～ exhort kind-heartedly
婆姨 póyí〈方言〉❶ married woman ❷ wife
婆子 pózi ❶〈贬义〉woman ❷ wife ❸ elderly maid-servant：粗使～ old woman servant doing household chores

皤

pó〈书面〉❶ white：白发～然 white-haired ❷ big (belly)：～其腹 pot bellied; big-bellied /～腹瓶 big-belly bottle

鄱

pó (used in place names)：～阳湖 Poyang Lake (in Jiangxi Province)

pǒ

叵

pǒ〈书面〉❶ not; impossible：*see*"～测"；"～耐" ❷ at once; right away：～欲讨之 plan to launch an immediate punitive expedition
叵测 pǒcè (derogatory) unfathomable; unpredictable：心怀～ harbour dark designs; nurse evil intentions /他这些甜言蜜语，居心～。He must have an ulterior motive in mouthing these sweet words.
叵罗 pǒluó〈古语〉shallow wine vessel
叵耐 pǒnài *also*"叵奈"(usu. used in the early vernacular) ❶ hard to bear; intolerable：～薄情夫，一行书也无。How insupportable is the heartless husband, not writing a single line since he left! ❷ have no choice

笸

pǒ
笸篮 pǒlán basket made of wicker or bamboo strips
笸箩 pǒluo shallow (usually round) basket made of wicker or bamboo strips

钷

pǒ〈化学〉promethium (Pm)

pò

朴

pò〈植物〉Chinese hackberry (*Celtis sinensis*)
see also Piáo; pō; pǔ
朴硝 pòxiāo *also*"皮硝" píxiāo；"芒硝" mángxiāo mirabilite; Glauber's salt

破

pò ❶ broken; cracked; torn; worn-out：牢不可～ unbreakable; indestructible /杯子打～了。The glass is broken. /鞋子～

了。The shoes are worn out. /我手指~了。I've cut my finger. /袜子~了一个洞。There is a hole in the sock. ❷ destroy; damage:爆~ blow up; demolish /只种不管,打~金碗。If you should overlook field management after sowing the seeds, you would break your rice bowl. ❸ split; break; cleave; cut:把板子~开 break (*or* cut) a plank in two /乘风~浪 brave the wind and waves /势如~竹 like splitting a bamboo; like a hot knife cutting through butter; with increasing momentum ❹ break a banknote into small change:我跟您~点儿零钱。May I trouble you to break this note for me? ❺ break; break with; get rid of:~迷信,树新风 do away with superstition and establish new customs / 他~了铁饼的世界记录。He broke the world record in the discus throw. ❻ defeat (enemy); capture (a city, etc.):连~三处要塞 capture three strongholds one after another /攻~敌军 rout the enemy ❼ spend; expend:你索性~点时间亲自跑一趟吧。You might as well spare some time to make a trip yourself. ❽ 〈口语〉not spare; risk:~着性命去救人 go to sb.'s rescue at the risk of one's life /~着脸皮去求助 swallow one's pride to solicit help ❾ reveal the truth of; lay bare; show up:看~其中奥秘 see through the mystery /一语道~真相 reveal the truth with one remark /识~某人真面目 see sb. in his true colours ❿ poor; wretched; lousy:我这~嗓子请大家包涵。Excuse me for my poor voice./ 这个~自行车挡路。This lousy bike stands in the way. /这种~地方谁都不愿去。Nobody would care to visit such a god-forsaken place.

破案 pò'àn solve a case; crack a (criminal) case:尚未~。The case remains unsolved. /限期~。The case must be cleared up within the specified time.

破败 pòbài ❶ ruined; dilapidated; decrepit:一间~不堪的草房 dilapidated (*or* tumbledown) thatched cottage ❷ deteriorate; decline:~的家庭 family on the decline

破敝 pòbì worn out; threadbare; run-down:衣服~ worn-out clothes /~的门楼 dilapidated gateway arch

破壁 pòbì ❶ damaged wall:~残垣 dilapidated walls ❷ break down the wall:面壁十年图~ sit facing a wall for 10 years in order to break it down — work hard and long to better oneself

破壁飞去 pòbì-fēiqù break the wall and fly away — rise from obscurity to renown; make a meteoric rise to fame (an allusion to the four dragons said to be painted on a wall of the Anle Temple in Nanjing by Zhang Sengyou 张僧繇 of the Liang Dynasty, two of which broke away from the wall and flew off into the sky the moment the pupils of their eyes were put in)

破冰船 pòbīngchuán icebreaker:原子~ atomic icebreaker

破擦音 pòcāyīn 〈语言〉affricate

破财 pòcái suffer unexpected loss of money:~免灾。An unexpected loss of money might be a fortune in disguise.

破产 pòchǎn ❶ bankruptcy:宣告~ (of a company, etc.) declare bankruptcy; go into bankruptcy /~申请 bankruptcy petition /工厂~ bankruptcy of a factory /银行~ bank failure ❷ go bankrupt; become insolvent; become impoverished:~农民 impoverished peasants ❸ 〈贬义〉come to naught; fall through:谣言~了。The rumour was exploded. /阴谋~了。The plot fell through.

破产程序 pòchǎn chéngxù bankruptcy proceedings; insolvency proceedings

破产法 pòchǎnfǎ 〈法律〉insolvency law; law of bankruptcy

破钞 pòchāo (often used in expressing one's thanks) spend money (on entertainment, gifts, donations, etc.); go to some expense:真不好意思再让你~了。It wouldn't be right to put you to any more expense.

破除 pòchú do away with; get rid of; eradicate:~迷信,解放思想 do away with blind faith and emancipate the mind /~旧风俗 abolish old customs /~情面,秉公而断 make an impartial judgment without sparing anybody's susceptibilities

破的 pòdì hit the target; speak to the point:一语~ hit the mark with a single comment; hit the nail on the head with one remark

破读 pòdú variant pronunciation (of a Chinese character) with a different meaning:"好"通常念 hǎo,但在"好学"中~为 hào。好,which is generally pronounced "hǎo" (good), sometimes reads as "hào", as in 好学 (fond of learning).

破读字 pòdúzì Chinese character which is not pronounced in the usual way because of a different meaning

破费 pòfèi spend money or time:父亲责备儿子不应该为他这样~。The father took his son to task for going to this expense for his sake. /我得~点儿时间织完这件毛衣。I have to spend some time finishing knitting this sweater.

破釜沉舟 pòfǔ-chénzhōu break the cauldrons and sink the boats (after crossing a river) — cut off all means of retreat to show one's determination to press ahead; burn one's boats; burn one's bridges:事已至此,非~干到底不可了。At this stage we have to burn our bridges and stick it out. *or* As it is, we have to go ahead at all cost.

破腹 pòfù ❶ caesarean operation:~产 caesarean birth ❷ (often used in the early vernacular) diarrhoea

破格 pògé break a rule or convention; make an exception:~提拔 promote sb. ahead of time for exceptional ability; break a rule to promote sb. /~优待 go out of one's way to grant preferential treatment /要大胆地~选拔人才。It is essential to make a bold effort to recruit able people by breaking conventions.

破工夫 pò gōngfu take pains; require plenty of efforts:这项工作要~才能完成。It will take a tremendous effort to bring this project to completion.

破骨细胞 pògǔ xìbāo 〈生理〉osteoclast

破骨细胞瘤 pògǔ xìbāoliú 〈医学〉osteoclastoma; giant cell tumour of the bone

破故纸 pògùzhǐ (popular term for 补骨脂)〈植物〉*Psoralea corylifolia*

破瓜 pòguā ❶ (of a girl) be 16 years old ❷ (usu. of a man) be 64 years old ❸ (of a girl) lose virginity

破关斩将 pòguān-zhǎnjiàng force the passes and slay enemy captains — surmount numerous difficulties and defeat many adversaries

破罐破摔 pòguàn-pòshuāi smash a jar to pieces just because it's already cracked — act recklessly and irresponsibly when in adversity or despair:出狱以后,他并没有~,而是通过自己的奋斗,成了一名能干的企业家。He did not write himself off as hopeless after serving his time; through great exertion, he eventually became a capable entrepreneur.

破耗 pòhào spend; cost

破坏 pòhuài ❶ destroy; demolish; wreck:~城市建筑 destroy city buildings ❷ do great damage to; undermine; sabotage:~生产 sabotage production /~活动 disruptive activities /~团结 harm unity /~了他的计划 wreck his plan /~了他的威信 undermine his prestige /~国家和平统一 jeopardize the peaceful reunification of the country ❸ change (a social system, tradition, custom, etc.) completely or violently:~旧的国家机器 smash the old state apparatus ❹ violate (an agreement, a regulation, etc.); break; go against:~纪律 break the discipline /~经济政策 go against the economic policy ❺ destroy (the composition of a substance); decompose:高温会~某些食品的营养。High temperature destroys the nutrients of some food items.

破坏分子 pòhuàifènzǐ saboteur

破坏力 pòhuàilì destructive power

破坏性 pòhuàixìng destructiveness

破毁 pòhuǐ dilapidated; old and wrecked:~的房屋 old dilapidated house

破货 pòhuò 〈粗话〉woman of loose morals; loose woman; fast woman

破获 pòhuò ❶ unearth; uncover; crack:~盗窃集团 unearth (*or* uncover) a gang of burglars /~一起走私案 crack a case of smuggling ❷ identify and capture:~敌台密码 decipher an enemy secret code

破击 pòjī attack and destroy; demolish; sabotage:~敌人的指挥所 destroy an enemy command post /~残匪暗堡 demolish bunkers of remnant bandits

破击战 pòjīzhàn *also* "破袭"〈军事〉sabotage operation

破家 pòjiā ❶ ruin one's family fortune:~荡产 spend (*or* squander) all one's family fortune /~为国 dispose of one's family property in the service of one's country ❷ property of a house in decline:~值万贯。The assets of a declining house may be worth ten thousand strings of cash.

破甲弹 pòjiǎdàn 〈军事〉metal patch bullet

破解 pòjiě analyze and solve:经他这么一~,老大娘明白了。The granny saw the light after he explained the problem.

破戒 pòjiè ❶ break a religious precept ❷ break one's vow of abstinence (as from smoking or drinking):他多次戒烟,多次~。He tried to give up smoking many times, but broke his vow each time.

破镜重圆 pòjìng-chóngyuán join together a broken mirror; put together the wreckage of a married life; retie a marriage knot after a separation (of a couple); achieve reunion and reconciliation after a

P

rupture:王老师的帮助使他俩～。Thanks to Mr. Wang's help, the estranged couple were reunited.

破旧 pòjiù old and shabby; worn-out; rickety; dilapidated:～衣服 worn-out clothes /～的草帽 shabby straw hat /房屋～ dilapidated building /～的家具 old, rickety furniture

破旧立新 pòjiù-lìxīn abolish the old and build up the new:真正做到～是需要胆略的。It takes great daring to create something new in place of the old.

破句 pòjù pause at the wrong place in a sentence; make a wrong pause

破口 pòkǒu ❶ have a cut:手上破了个口儿。He's got a cut on his hand. ❷ hole;crack; breach:粮食袋上有个～。There was a hole in the grain bag. ❸ let loose a stream of abuse; abuse:不管怎么发火,他也不会～骂人。No matter how angry he was, he would not call anybody names.

破口大骂 pòkǒu-dàmà let loose a torrent of filthy abuse:一言不合,他便～。He would let loose torrents of four-letter words the moment he was contradicted.

破烂 pòlàn ❶ tattered; ragged; shabby; worn-out:～的手工作坊 ramshackle workshop /他穿了一件～不堪的上衣。He wore a tattered coat. ❷〈口语〉junk; scrap; waste:收～ collect waste /收～的 rag-and-bone man /把贮藏室里的～都搬走。Remove all the junk from the storeroom.

破烂货 pòlànhuò worthless stuff; rubbish; refuse; trash

破浪 pòlàng cleave the waves:乘风～ ride the winds and plough the waves /在急流中～前进 ride the waves in a swift current

破例 pòlì break a rule; make an exception:制度必须严格遵守,任何人也不能～。Regulations should be strictly observed without exception. /那天,妈妈非常高兴,～喝了一杯酒。Mother was so happy that day that she drank a glass of wine against her own rule.

破脸 pòliǎn (as of acquaintances or associates) fall out; quarrel openly:一对好朋友,因为一点小事破了脸。The two of them used to be good friends but fell out over a mere trifle.

破裂 pòliè burst; split; rupture; break:水管～ rupture of a water pipe /这楼房墙面～了。There are cracks in the walls of the building. /谈判中途～。The negotiation broke down halfway. /两国关系的～,导致这个地区的局势紧张。The rupture of the friendly relationship between the two countries led to tension in the region. /这对夫妻感情已经～。This couple have become estranged.

破裂摩擦音 pòliè mócāyīn *also* "塞擦音" sècāyīn 〈语言〉affricate

破裂音 pòlièyīn *also* "塞音" sèyīn 〈语言〉plosive; stop

破陋 pòlòu old and shabby:房屋～ old shabby house

破露 pòlù fall through and stand exposed; uncover:他知道事情已经～,惊慌失措。He was seized with fear when he became aware that things had been uncovered.

破落 pòluò ❶ decline (in wealth and position):家景～ live in straitened circumstances ❷ dilapidated; tumbledown:～的草屋 dilapidated thatched cottage

破落户 pòluòhù family that has become impoverished and declined in social status; family that has gone down in the world; family that has seen better days

破马张飞 pòmǎ Zhāng Fēi 〈方言〉rough and boorish:这个人～,蛮不讲理。The man was very rough and impervious to reason.

破谜儿 pòmèir ❶〈口语〉solve or guess a riddle:灯谜大约有一百个,破一个谜儿就领一份奖。There are about 100 lantern riddles altogether. Anyone who solves a riddle will get a prize. ❷〈方言〉ask a riddle

破门 pòmén ❶ burst or force the door open:几个歹徒～而入。Several thugs pushed the door open and burst into the house. ❷ (of football, handball, ice hockey, etc.) score a goal:上半时双方均未～。Neither team scored a goal in the first half of the match. ❸〈宗教〉excommunicate

破门而出 pòmén'érchū storm out of the room or house; break out of one's accustomed field of study:作为史学家,他～,写起了经济论文。A historian by profession, he broke out of his own field and wrote essays on economics. /他～,竟然以身试法,走私毒品。He went so far as to fly in the face of the law by trafficking in narcotic drugs.

破闷 pòmèn 〈方言〉kill time; divert oneself (from boredom):他在那里看小说～儿。He is reading a novel to kill time.

破灭 pòmiè be shattered; melt into thin air; evaporate:他的希望～了。His hopes were dashed. /他的美梦～了。His fond dream was shattered. /幻想如同肥皂泡一样～了。Illusions vanished like soap bubbles.

破命 pòmìng 〈方言〉work hard for all one's worth; work flat out:他只顾～干活,连饭都忘了吃了。He was so concentrated on his work that he even forgot his meal.

破墨 pòmò technique of traditional Chinese painting using dark ink to seep into thin ink, or vice versa

破伤风 pòshāngfēng 〈医学〉tetanus

破身 pòshēn (of a girl) have sex with a man for the first time; lose virginity

破声 pòshēng speak with a loud voice:～大叫 shout at the top of one's voice

破水 pòshuǐ flowing out of amniotic fluid at the time of delivery

破说 pòshuō 〈方言〉explain in great detail; elaborate:～事理 elaborate on the whys and wherefores

破私立公 pòsī-lìgōng overcome selfishness and foster public spirit (a slogan in the Cultural Revolution)

破四旧 pò sìjiù cast away the four olds — old ideas, old culture, old customs, and old habits (a slogan used at the beginning of the Cultural Revolution in China in the mid-1960's)

破碎 pòsuì ❶ broken; in pieces;in tatters:支离～ torn to pieces; fragmented /～的镜片 pieces of broken glasses /山河～。The country has gone to rack and ruin. ❷ smash or break sth. to pieces; shatter; crush:这机器每小时可以～百吨矿石。This machine can crush 100 tons of ore in an hour.

破碎机 pòsuìjī crusher; breaker

破碎险 pòsuìxiǎn 〈商业〉risk of breakage

破损 pòsǔn damaged; broken:如有～,可以退换。The goods can be returned if damaged. /这座房子多年失修,已严重～。This building, which has been in bad disrepair for years, is practically ruined. /这些货物转运中未受到任何～。These goods have suffered no damage in transit. /风暴后,门窗都未～。The doors and windows remained intact after the storm.

破损险 pòsǔnxiǎn insurance against breakage; breakage risks

破题 pòtí ❶ first two sentences of an essay giving the theme (originaly said of a stereotyped essay) ❷ give the theme in a sentence or two

破题儿第一遭 pòtír dì-yī zāo for the very first time; without precedent; first time ever:她同我讲话如此严厉还是～。It was the first time that she had ever spoken to me in such harsh terms.

破体字 pòtǐzì 〈旧语〉corrupted form of a Chinese character

破涕 pòtì stop crying:她不得不～强笑。She could not but force a smile through her tears.

破涕为笑 pòtì-wéixiào smile through tears; smile away one's tears:逗得小孩～。The child was so amused by the joke that he laughed in spite of his tears.

破天荒 pòtiānhuāng occur for the first time; be unheard-of; be unprecedented:中国的青年农民现在也去跳舞,参加运动竞赛,这是～的事。Young Chinese farmers now go to dances and take part in sports competition. This is something unheard-of before.

破土 pòtǔ ❶ break ground (in starting a building project, etc.); start a construction project by digging for the foundation:～动工 break ground on a construction project /～仪式 ground-breaking ceremony ❷ start spring ploughing ❸ (of a seedling) break through the soil

破瓦寒窑 pòwǎ-hányáo shabby and dilapidated dwelling

破网 pòwǎng *also* "破门"〈体育〉(in football) score a goal:一记劲射～ score a goal with a powerful kick

破五 pòwǔ 5th day of the first lunar month (after which most shops in the old days would resume business)

破袭战 pòxízhàn 〈军事〉sabotage operation

破相 pòxiàng (of facial features) be marred by a scar, etc.; be disfigured:战争中面部受伤,他端正的五官～了。The wound he received in war left a permanent scar on his cheek, marring his otherwise regular features.

破晓 pòxiǎo dawn; daybreak:～就起程 set out at daybreak /一觉醒来,天已～。It was dawn when we woke up.

破鞋 pòxié 〈口语〉promiscuous woman; loose woman; slut

破鞋筒 pòxiétǒng 〈方言〉hooligan; rascal; rogue

破颜 pòyán break into a smile:强为～ force a smile on one's face; give a forced smile /～一笑。A smile crept over his face.

破衣烂衫 pòyī-lànshān old and worn-out clothes; rags:他穿着～,

简直认不出来了。As he was in rags, he was almost beyond recognition.
破译 pòyì decode (an intercepted message); decipher
破约 pòyuē break one's promise; break an agreement:我写信批评他～。I wrote him a letter criticizing him for his failure to keep a promise.
破绽 pòzhàn ❶ burst seam:衣服上的～都缝好了。All the burst seams have been stitched. ❷ flaw; weak point; loophole:不小心露出～ unwittingly give away the show; let the cat out of the bag /看出～ discover sb.'s Achilles' heel; see through the game
破绽百出 pòzhàn-bǎichū full of flaws or holes; riddled with errors:～的发言 speech riddled with holes
破折号 pòzhéhào dash (—)
破竹之势 pòzhúzhīshì advance like splitting a bamboo — advance victoriously; carry all before one:我军以～直捣敌穴。Our troops overwhelmed all resistance and advanced triumphantly to the enemy's headquarters.

粕

pò 〈书面〉dregs of rice:糟～waste matter; dross; dregs

迫(廹)

pò ❶ compel; force; drive; press:胁～ coerce; force /～其投降 compel sb. to surrender /贫病交～ suffer from both poverty and illness /～于形势不得不采取预防措施。The exigencies of the situation demanded precautionary measures. /他们为饥饿所～,铤而走险。Hunger drove them to take desperate action. ❷ urgent; critical; pressing:紧～ pressing; urgent; critical /从容不～ be calm and unhurried /窘～ be caught in a dilemma ❸ approach; go towards or near: *see* "～近"
see also pǎi
迫不得已 pòbùdéyǐ have no choice (but to do sth.); be compelled (to do sth.); (do sth.) against one's will:我这样做,实在是～。I had no alternative but to do what I did. /早年他～闯关东。In his early years, he had no option but to go and try his fortune in northeastern China.
迫不及待 pòbùjídài unable to hold oneself back; too impatient to wait; itching to do sth.:～地制造种种谣言 lose no time in spreading rumours /～地抢先发言 be among the first to take the floor /一走出来,她就～地问我。As soon as we were out of the house, her questions tumbled out.
迫促 pòcù ❶ rapid; hurried:呼吸～ be short of breath /由于时间～,来不及通知他了。We were too hurried to notify him in time. ❷ urge; press; hasten:经过许多人的～,他才答应做这件事。It took a lot of persuading by many people to get him to consent to take on the job.
迫害 pòhài persecute:受到～ come under persecution; be subjected to persecution /～者 persecutor /受～者 victim of persecution /文革中,许多无辜者被～致死。During the Cultural Revolution many innocent people were harassed to death.
迫降 pòjiàng 〈航空〉forced landing; distress landing; crash landing:飞机迷失航向,在沙漠～。机组人员与乘客都安然无恙。The plane lost its bearings and made a forced landing on the desert. The crew and passengers were all unhurt.
see also pòxiáng
迫近 pòjìn approach; get close to; draw near; near:～衰老 approaching senility /敌人正从各方面～我军阵地。The enemy are closing in on the position of our troops from all sides. /考期～。The day of the examination is drawing near. /～年关。The year is drawing to a close.
迫临 pòlín *see* "迫近"
迫令 pòlìng order; force; compel:几家商店被～停业。Several shops were ordered to close down.
迫切 pòqiè urgent; pressing; compelling; imperative:～的要求 urgent request /～的需要 crying need /～愿望 fervent wish /～的任务 an urgent task /～性 urgency /我们～期待你们成功的喜讯。We are eagerly looking forward to the happy news of your success.
迫使 pòshǐ force; compel; regard at close range:～对方作出让步 force the other side to make concessions /落后的形势～他们急起直追。Lagging far behind others, they were compelled to try their best to catch up quickly.
迫视 pòshì watch intently; look at from close-up:他带着疑惑的神情～着这个陌生人。He looked at the stranger from head to foot with suspicion.
迫降 pòxiáng force the enemy to surrender
see also pòjiàng
迫胁 pòxié coerce; force
迫拶 pòzā 〈书面〉press; coerce:强敌～。A formidable enemy is bearing down on us.
迫在眉睫 pòzàiméijié extremely urgent; imminent:双方剑拔弩张,战争～。With both sides at daggers drawn, war was imminent.

珀

pò
珀耳帖 Pò'ěrtiē Jean-Charles-Athanase Peltier (1785-1845), French physicist:～效应 Peltier effect

魄

pò ❶ soul:魂～ soul /失魂落～ driven to distraction; distracted ❷ vigour; energy; spirit:气～ broadness of one's mental horizon /体～ physique; constitution
see also bó; tuò
魄力 pòli daring and resolution; boldness; sweep:做事有～ show daring and determination in whatever one does /人们无不为他那惊人的～所折服。People are most impressed by his amazing courage and resolution. /他手面不小,也有一些商业经营方面的～。He wanted to make big deals and had some drive in business management.
魄散魂飞 pòsàn-húnfēi *also* "魂飞魄散" be frightened out of one's wits; be scared to death

po

栲

po *see* "榅栲" wēnpo

pōu

剖

pōu ❶ cut open; rip open:把瓜～成两半 cut a melon in two /解～ dissect ❷ analyse; examine: *see* "～析";"～明"
剖白 pōubái explain oneself; vindicate oneself:利用机会～自己的心迹。I took the opportunity to explain my true intentions. /我自堂堂正正,不必向他人～。Since I am always open and above-board, I owe nobody any explanation.
剖辨 pōubiàn analyse; distinguish:～详明 give a detailed analysis
剖断 pōuduàn 〈书面〉analyse and decide the rights and wrongs of a case:～如流 (formerly of a magistrate) be highly competent in judging lawsuits
剖分 pōufēn cut sth. open in the middle
剖腹 pōufù cut open one's belly
剖腹藏珠 pōufù-cángzhū rip open one's belly to store pearls — put the incidental before the fundamental; place the trivial above the essential
剖腹产 pōufùchǎn 〈医学〉Caesarean (birth):～术 Caesarean section (*or* operation) /为了避免难产,大夫作了～。The doctor did a Caesarean to avoid a difficult birth.
剖腹取儿切宫术 pōufù qǔ'ér qiēgōngshù 〈医学〉Caesarean hysterectomy
剖腹术 pōufùshù 〈医学〉laparotomy
剖腹探查术 pōufù tànchάshù 〈医学〉exploratory laparotomy
剖腹自杀 pōufù zìshā (commit) hara-kiri
剖解 pōujiě analyse; examine:～细密 make a minute and in-depth analysis
剖决 pōujué 〈书面〉analyse and decide; examine and judge:～如流 decide and solve a problem expeditiously
剖里革 pōulǐgé 〈皮革〉split
剖露 pōulù cut open and expose; lay bare:作者在这个剧本里深刻地～了一个电影明星的性格。The playwright makes a penetrating analysis of a film-star's psychology.
剖面 pōumiàn *also* "截面" jiémiàn;"切面" qiēmiàn;"断面" duànmiàn section; profile:横～ cross section /纵～ longitudinal section /～测量 profile survey /～符号 section symbol
剖面图 pōumiàntú sectional drawing; section:人脑～ section of a human brain
剖明 pōumíng analyse clearly:～事理 analyse the whys and wherefores of a matter /～利弊 state the advantages and disadvantages in explicit terms

剖尸 pōushī dissect a dead body; autopsy: ～验看 autopsy; postmortem

剖视 pōushì dissect and observe

剖视图 pōushìtú cutaway view

剖释 pōushì dissect and explain; analyse: 作者详细地～了剧中人物的思想感情。The author gives a detailed analysis of the thoughts and feelings of the characters in the play.

剖析 pōuxī analyse; dissect: ～当前形势 analyse the current situation / 经他一～,问题的实质我就清楚了。After listening to his analysis, I can now grasp the essence of the problem.

剖心 pōuxīn 〈书面〉unbosom oneself; open one's heart: ～以待 treat people with sincerity and candour

剖胸探查术 pōuxiōng tànchάshù 〈医学〉exploratory thoracotomy

póu

裒 póu 〈书面〉❶ gather; get together: ～然成集 gather into a collection ❷ take out: *see* "～多益寡"

裒多益寡 póuduō-yìguǎ take from the fat to pad the lean; take from those who have too much and give to those who have too little

裒辑 póují 〈书面〉compile; collect; gather: 本书系从类书中～而成。This book is compiled on the basis of materials taken from various sources.

裒敛 póuliǎn 〈书面〉amass wealth by force or trickery: ～无厌 insatiably rapacious

掊 póu 〈书面〉❶ amass; extort ❷ dig; excavate
see also pǒu

抔 póu 〈书面〉hold sth. with cupped hands: 一～黄土 a handful of earth — a grave

pǒu

掊 pǒu 〈书面〉❶ strike; hit: *see* "～击" ❷ split; cut; cleave
see also póu

掊击 pǒujī attack (in speech or writing); blast; lash out at

pū

潽 pū (as of water) boil over: 牛奶～了。The milk boiled over. / 饭～了。The rice pot boiled over.

铺 pū ❶ spread; lay; pave: ～管道 lay pipes / ～被褥 spread a quilt / ～草皮 turf; lay turf (*or* sod) / 屋里～着地毯。The room was carpeted. / 工程已经全面～开。The project is in full swing. ❷ 〈方言〉〈量词〉*used of kang*: 房间里除了一～炕之外,只有一张小桌和两张椅子。Aside from a *kang* there are only a small table and two chairs.
see also pù

铺摆 pūbai ❶ put things on display or for sale: 广场上不准～小摊。Nobody is allowed to set up a stall on the square. ❷ 〈方言〉arrange; put in order: ～伙计 assign jobs to the shop attendants ❸ 〈方言〉narrate; elaborate: 您等一下,我再跟您～～这个理吧。Wait a minute and I'll further elaborate on this matter.

铺陈 pūchén ❶ 〈方言〉spread out; decorate: 客厅～了地毯和沙发。The living-room is furnished with carpet and easy chairs. ❷narrate in detail; describe at length; elaborate: ～经过 give a detailed account of what happened ❸ 〈方言〉bedclothes: 床上的～很讲究。The bed was lavishly covered.

铺衬 pūchen small pieces of cloth used for patches or padding

铺床 pūchuáng make the bed; spread bedding on a bed

铺地植物 pūdì zhíwù mattae; paving plant

铺地砖 pūdìzhuān ❶ cover a floor with tiles; tile a floor ❷ floor tile; paving tile

铺垫 pūdiàn ❶ spread; lay: 床上～了褥子。A quilt has been laid over the bed. / 给猪圈～一层干草。Spread some hay in the pigsty. ❷ bedding ❸ foil; set off: 用写景为故事作～ use the description of nature as the background of a story / 这一情节为戏的高潮作了～。This episode sets off the climax of the play.

铺盖 pūgài cover; spread: 老农小心地把草木灰～在苗床上。The old farmer carefully spread the seedbed with plant ash.

铺盖 pūgai bedding; bedclothes: 再不好好干,就让他卷～走人。If he doesn't work harder, I'll send him packing.

铺盖卷儿 pūgaijuǎnr *also* "行李卷儿" xínglijuǎnr bedding roll; bedroll; luggage roll

铺管机 pūguǎnjī 〈机械〉pipelayer

铺轨 pūguǐ lay a railway track

铺轨机 pūguǐjī track-laying machine; tracklayer

铺炕 pūkàng spread bedding on a *kang*

铺路 pūlù ❶ pave a road: 前面正在～。The road ahead is being paved. ❷ 〈比喻〉pave the way; make necessary preparations

铺路搭桥 pūlù-dāqiáo *also* "铺路架桥" ❶ build bridges and pave roads ❷ pave the way for: 为科学研究～pave the way for scientific research; create necessary conditions for scientific research / 利用别人成果为自己～是不道德的。It is unethical to appropriate the results of other people's labour and use them as a stepping-stone to fame (*or* honour).

铺路机 pūlùjī paver

铺路石 pūlùshí stones used to pave a road — people who sacrifice themselves for the benefit of others

铺墁 pūmàn pave the ground (with bricks or stones): 院子里都用青砖～。The courtyard is paved with grey bricks.

铺排 pūpái ❶ arrange; map out; plan: 单位里许多事情必须事先～。We have to plan many things of the department in advance. / 我们不需要为自己的孩子～未来。We do not need to map out a future career for our children. ❷ extravagant: 婚事不要～。There is no need to go to great expense for the wedding.

铺平 pūpíng ❶ spread out sth. and make it smooth: 把弄皱的床单～ smooth out a creased bed-sheet ❷ pave: 为进一步改革开放～道路 pave the way for further reform and opening

铺砌 pūqì pave: 大厅地面用大理石～而成。The floor of the hall is paved with marble.

铺设 pūshè ❶ lay; build: ～水下电缆 lay an under-water cable / ～铁路 build railways ❷ furnish; arrange: 卧室～得很素雅。The bedroom is simply but elegantly furnished.

铺摊 pūtan 〈方言〉spread out: 我们把地图～开,看看县城离这里多远。Let's spread out the map and see how far the county is from here.

铺天盖地 pūtiān-gàidì blanket the earth and eclipse the sky: 那一年大旱,蝗虫又～而来。We had a drought that year and the locusts came in such swarms that they seemed to block out the sky.

铺叙 pūxù narrate at length; describe in detail; elaborate: 小说对这一情节～得很细致。There is an elaborate description of the incident in the novel.

铺展 pūzhǎn spread out; sprawl: 蔚蓝的天空～着一片片白云。White fluffy clouds spread over the azure sky.

铺张 pūzhāng ❶ extravagant; ostentatious: 商店开业,何必如此～? Why such extravagance in celebrating the opening of a new shop? ❷ exaggerate; overstate: 老王这个人就喜欢～,芝麻也要说成是西瓜。Lao Wang is fond of exaggerating things. What is as small as a sesame seed would be the size of a watermelon in his description (*or* He could make a mountain out of a molehill).

铺张浪费 pūzhāng-làngfèi extravagance and waste

铺张扬厉 pūzhāng-yánglì be extremely extravagant; indulge in extravagance and ostentation

铺植 pūzhí plant; grow; lay out: 院内～了草坪。A lawn was laid out in the courtyard.

扑(撲) pū ❶ throw oneself on; pounce on; dash at; attack: 鱼跃～球〈体育〉dive for the ball / 侧身～〈体育〉cartwheel block / ～杀 beat to death; kill / ～蝇 swat flies / 她～向刚断气的丈夫,放声痛哭。She threw herself on her husband who had just died, and cried bitterly. / 这是飞蛾～火,自取灭亡。This is simply courting destruction like a moth dashing at a fire. / 这班歹徒还没有离开作案现场,公安人员就向他们～去。The gang had scarcely left the scene of the crime when the police swooped in. / 守门员～出了好几个球。The goalkeeper pulled off quite a few saves. ❷ throw oneself (heart and soul) into; devote oneself to: 一心～在工作上 throw oneself heart and soul into one's work; bend one's mind to one's job ❸ pat; flap; plop: ～去衣服上的尘土 brush the dirt off one's clothes; dust off one's clothes / 孩子身上～了痱子粉 dab the child with prickly-heat

powder /老鹰～着翅膀在天空飞翔。The eagle soared in the sky, flapping its wings. /他心头～～地跳。His heart thumped with excitement. ❹〈方言〉bend over:他～在机器上查看毛病。He bent over the machine looking for defects.

扑奔 pūben ❶ head straight for the destination:一下火车我就～你这儿来了。As soon as I got off the train I headed straight for your place here. ❷ devote oneself whole-heartedly to (a job or cause):他的心一盆火似地～在改良小麦品种上。He is passionately devoted to improvement of the wheat strain.

扑鼻 pūbí assail the nostrils:她一进花园,就感觉芳香～。She was greeted by a fragrant odour of the flowers when she strolled into the garden.

扑哧 pūchī *also* "噗嗤" pūchī 〈象声〉sound of laughter, gushing water or air:她～一声笑出来了。She tittered. *or* She gave a snigger. /～一声,皮球撒气了。The rubber ball went soft with a hiss.

扑打 pūdǎ swat:～苍蝇 swat flies

扑打 pūda beat; pat:～身上的雪花 beat the snow off one's clothes

扑灯蛾子 pūdēng ézi 〈口语〉grain moth

扑跌 pūdiē ❶ wrestling (in *wushu*) ❷ fall forward:他脚下一绊,～在地上。He tripped and fell on the ground.

扑冬 pūdōng *also* "噗咚" pūdōng 〈象声〉thump; flop; splash:～一声摔倒在地 fall on the ground with a thump

扑尔敏 pū'ěrmǐn 〈药学〉chlorpheniramine

扑粉 pūfěn ❶ face powder ❷ talcum powder ❸ apply powder:这个丑角脸上扑着厚厚的粉。The clown had his face covered with a thick layer of powder.

扑虎儿 pūhǔr 〈方言〉fall forward with two hands touching the ground

扑击 pūjī ❶ rush at; throw oneself on:老鹰自空而降,～小鸡。Descending from the sky, the hawk swooped on the chickens. ❷ slap; beat:浪涛～着岸边的礁石 waves beating (*or* dashing) against the reefs along the shore

扑救 pūjiù ❶ put out a fire:家中失火,邻居们赶来～。Our neighbours rushed to our house and helped put out the fire. ❷ (in football, volleyball, etc.) throw oneself forward to retrieve a ball:鱼跃～ make a diving save

扑克 pūkè ❶ playing cards:玩～ play cards ❷ poker:打～ play poker

扑空 pūkōng fail to find what one looks for (at a designated place); come away empty-handed:几次去他家都扑了空。He was out each time I went to see him. /公安人员冲进匪巢,却扑了个空。The police found the bandit's den empty when they swooped down on it.

扑拉 pūla ❶ (of duck, chicken) flap or spread (its wings):老鹰～着翅膀掠过天空。The eagle flapped across the sky. ❷ beat lightly; pat:用手～身上的尘土 get off the dust by patting one's clothes ❸ (of tears, etc.) trickle down:眼泪～～往下掉 tears trickling (*or* streaming) down ❹〈方言〉manage; attend to; take care of:村上的事太多,我实在有些～不开。There are so many things to attend to in the village that I can hardly manage. ❺〈方言〉seek; look for:我得～点事儿干。I have to look for some work to do.

扑棱 pūlēng 〈象声〉flapping sound of wings:～一声,芦苇中飞出一只野鸡。With a flap a pheasant flew out of the reeds.

扑棱 pūleng flap; flutter:鸽子受了伤,～着翅膀飞不起来。The wounded pigeon fluttered its wings up and down but could not fly.

扑脸儿 pūliǎnr 〈口语〉blow on or brush ones' face:热气～。The hot air was brushing our faces.

扑亮 pūliàng 〈方言〉(of day) break:天一～,队长就带人出发了。As soon as day broke, the team-leader set out with his men.

扑笼 pūlong 〈方言〉cluster; bundle; heap:山坡上长着一～一～的野葡萄秧子。On the slope are clusters of wild grape vines.

扑噜 pūlū 〈象声〉flapping sound of wings or flags

扑落 pūluò ❶ shake off; shake out:他～身上的尘土。He shook off the dust from his clothes. ❷〈书面〉spread widely in all directions; scattered ❸〈方言〉〈电工〉plug

扑满 pūmǎn earthenware money box; piggy bank

扑面 pūmiàn touch one's face:和风～。A gentle breeze caressed our faces. /柳絮～。The floating willow catkins lightly touched our cheeks.

扑灭 pūmiè stamp or put out; eradicate; extinguish; exterminate:～森林火灾 put out a forest fire /～蚊蝇 wipe out mosquitoes and flies /任何～革命烈火的企图是注定要失败的。Any attempt to quell the flames of revolution is doomed to fail.

扑热息痛 pūrèxītòng 〈药学〉paracetamol

扑闪 pūshan blink; wink:一双明亮的大眼睛好奇地～着。A pair of big bright eyes are twinkling with curiosity.

扑扇 pūshan 〈方言〉*see* "扑棱" pūleng

扑朔迷离 pūshuò-mílí bewildering; confusing; complicated:～的情景 bewildering scene /～的侦探故事 intricate detective story

扑簌 pūsù *also* "扑簌簌" (of tears) trickle down; course down:她的眼泪～而下。Her tears coursed down her cheeks.

扑腾 pūtēng 〈象声〉thump; thud:小王～一声从墙上跳下来。Xiao Wang jumped down from the wall with a thud. /我看见他～～踏着雪地往前走。I saw him trudging along on the snow.

扑腾 pūteng ❶ beat the water with one's feet when swimming:他两脚一～,就游出去了好远。By one kick of his legs, he was quite a distance away on the water. /我游得不好,只会在水里瞎～。I am not a good swimmer. All I can do is paddle in the water. ❷ move up and down; throb; palpitate:他吓得心里直～。His heart thumped with fear. /鱼卡在冰窟窿口直～。The fish caught in the ice hole flopped helplessly. ❸〈方言〉wangle; wheel and deal:这人挺能～。The man is adept at wangling. *or* He's quite a wheeler-dealer. ❹ spend lavishly; waste; squander:他把钱全～光了。He has played ducks and drakes with all his money.

扑通 pūtōng *also* "噗通" pūtōng 〈象声〉flop; splash; pit-a-pat:～一声他掉进水里。He fell with a flop into the water. /她紧张得心里～直跳。Her heart throbbed with excitement. /他～一声跳入水里。He dived into the water with a splash.

扑翼 pūyì (as of a bird) flap or flutter its wings:～飞机 flapping-wing aircraft; ornithopter /海鸥在帆船左右～飞翔。The seagulls are flying around the sails, fluttering their wings.

仆

pū fall forward; fall prostrate:前～后继 as one falls, others step into the breach; advance wave upon wave

see also pú

噗

pū 〈象声〉puff:她轻轻地走进房间,～的一声,把桌上的蜡烛吹灭了。She tiptoed into the room and with one puff blew out the candle on the table.

噗咘噔儿 pūbudēngr a kind of toy made of thin glass in the form of a small trumpet

噗嗤 pūchī *also* "扑哧" pūchī 〈象声〉hiss; fizz; snigger

噗咚 pūdōng *also* "扑冬" pūdōng 〈象声〉thud; thump

噗噜噜 pūlūlū *also* "噗碌碌"〈象声〉(of tears) trickle or stream down:她眼泪～地往下掉。Tears fell down her cheeks unrestrainedly.

噗通 pūtōng *also* "扑通" pūtōng 〈象声〉thud; flap:～一声,他跳入水里。Flap! He jumped into the water.

pú

菩

pú

菩萨 púsà ❶ Bodhisattva ❷ Buddha; Buddhist idol ❸ Buddha-like person; kind-hearted person

菩萨心肠 púsà xīncháng with the heart of a Buddha; kind-hearted:他是个～的人。He is a kind-hearted person.

菩提 pútí 〈佛教〉(transliteration from Sanskrit) *bodhi*; state of enlightenment attained by a Buddhist who has achieved salvation

菩提树 pútíshù pipal; *bo* tree; *bodhi* tree (under which Sakyamuni sat meditating and attained the state of enlightenment)

莆

Pú ❶ (short for 莆田) county in Fujian Province ❷ a surname

莆仙戏 púxiānxì *also* "兴化戏" xīnghuàxì local opera popular in Putian (莆田) and Xianyou (仙游) counties in Fujian Province

蒲[1]

pú 〈植物〉cattail; reed mace; club grass:菖～ calamus /香～ cattail

蒲[2]

Pú ❶ former place name (in Shanxi Province) ❷ a surname

蒲棒 púbàng 〈口语〉clublike flower spike of cattail

蒲包 púbāo ❶ cattail bag; rush bag ❷〈旧语〉gift of fruit or pas-

try (wrapped in a cattail bag)
蒲草 púcǎo ❶ stem or leaf of cattail ❷〈方言〉dwarf lily turf
蒲垫 púdiàn rush cushion; rush mat
蒲墩 púdūn cattail hassock; rush cushion
蒲福风级 Púfú fēngjí Beaufort scale, a scale of wind speed ranging from 0 (calm) to 12 (hurricane) named after the English admiral Sir Francis Beaufort (1774-1857)
蒲公英 púgōngyīng *also*"黄花地丁" huánghuā dìdīng 〈植物〉 dandelion (*Taraxacum mongolicum*)
蒲瓜 púguā 〈方言〉white flowered gourd
蒲黄 púhuáng 〈中药〉cattail pollen
蒲剑 pújiàn calamus leaf
蒲节 Pújié another name for Dragon Boat Festival (the 5th day of the 5th lunar month) when calamus leaves were hung over the door in former days to repel evil spirits
蒲剧 pújù *also*"蒲州梆子" *Pu* opera (indigenous to Shanxi Province, and popular in southern Shanxi, and parts of Henan, Shaanxi, Gansu, Ningxia, and Qinghai)
蒲葵 púkuí 〈植物〉Chinese fan palm (*Livistona chinensis*)
蒲柳 púliǔ *also*"水杨" shuǐyáng 〈植物〉big catkin willow (*Salix gracilistyla*)
蒲柳之姿 púliǔzhīzī 〈谦词〉feel like a willow withering in autumn — be not in good health: 鄙人以～，怎能当此大任? Being frail in health, how can I shoulder this responsibility?
蒲鲁东 Púlǔdōng Pierre-Joseph Proudhon (1809-1865), French social reformer
蒲绒 púróng *also*"蒲茸" cattail wool, used for stuffing pillows
蒲扇 púshàn cattail leaf fan
蒲式耳 púshì'ěr bushel, a dry measure (=8 gallons)
蒲松龄 Pú Sōnglíng Pu Songling (formerly translated as Pu Sung-Ling, 1640-1715), writer of the Qing Dynasty
蒲桃 pútao *see*"葡萄" pútao
蒲团 pútuán cattail hassock; rush cushion
蒲苇 púwěi 〈植物〉pampas grass (*Cortaderia selloana*)
蒲席 púxí cattail mat; rush mat

蒱

pú *see*"摴蒱" chūpú

葡

pú

葡糖 pútáng (short for 葡萄糖) glucose; grape sugar; dextrose
葡萄 pútao *also*"蒲桃" pútao; "蒲陶" pútao; "蒲萄" pútao grape: 晶莹的～ sparkling grapes /～架 grape trellis /～藤 grapevine /～园 vineyard; grapery /酸～ sour grapes
葡萄弹 pútaodàn 〈军事〉grapeshot; grape
葡萄干 pútaogān raisin
葡萄灰 pútaohuī (of colour) light greyish pink
葡萄酒 pútaojiǔ (grape) wine; port
葡萄球菌 pútao qiújūn 〈微生物〉staphylococcus
葡萄胎 pútaotāi 〈医学〉hydatidiform mole; vesicular mole
葡萄糖 pútaotáng glucose; grape sugar; dextrose
葡萄牙 Pútaoyá Portugal: ～人 Portuguese /～语 Portuguese (language)
葡萄柚 pútaoyòu 〈植物〉grapefruit (*Cirus paradisi*)
葡萄肿 pútaozhǒng 〈医学〉staphyloma
葡萄紫 pútaozǐ (of colour) dark greyish purple

酺

pú 〈书面〉meet and drink together

匍

pú

匍匐 púfú ❶ crawl; creep: ～而行 crawl on all fours; inch one's way forward /～奔丧 hurry back for the funeral of one's parent; attend the funeral of a close relative /～哀求 beg piteously ❷ lie prostrate; (of a plant) trail: ～在地主脚下 lie prostrate before the landowner
匍匐茎 púfújīng 〈植物〉stolon
匍匐植物 púfú zhíwù creeper

脯

pú chest; breast
see also fǔ
脯氨酸 pú'ānsuān 〈生化〉proline
脯子 púzi breast meat (of chicken, duck, etc.): 鸡～ chicken breast /鸭～ duck breast

璞

pú uncut jade
璞玉浑金 púyù-húnjīn *also*"浑金璞玉" uncut jade and unrefined gold — unadorned beauty; natural beauty: 李白这几首诗不假雕琢，真乃～。Like uncut jade or unrefined gold, these lines by Li Bai have a distinctive natural grace of their own.

镤

pú 〈化学〉protactinium (Pa)

仆(僕)

pú ❶ servant: 奴～ slave; lackey /公～ public servant ❷〈旧语〉〈谦词〉(referring to oneself when addressing sb. in writing) your humble servant
see also pū
仆从 púcóng footman; flunkey: ～如云 with numerous attendants /～国 vassal country
仆妇 púfù 〈旧语〉elderly maidservant
仆仆风尘 púpú-fēngchén *also*"风尘仆仆" be travel-stained and travel-worn; be travel-worn and weary; endure the fatigue of a long journey
仆人 púrén (domestic) servant
仆役 púyì servant

pǔ

普

pǔ ❶ general; common; universal: ～天之下 all over the world; in every part of the world; in this wide world ❷ (Pǔ) a surname
普奥战争 Pǔ-Ào Zhànzhēng Austro-Prussian War (1866)
普遍 pǔbiàn universal; general; widespread; common: ～性 universality /～应用 universal application /～流行 very popular in society /～现象 common phenomenon /～感兴趣的问题 matter of common interest /～真理 universal truth /～规律 universal law /这种事相当～。Such things are by no means rare. *or* These are common occurrences. /人们～赞成这种做法。People are all in favour of this practice. /全省～降大雨。It rained heavily throughout the province.
普遍优惠税 pǔbiàn yōuhuìshuì general preferential duties
普遍优惠制 pǔbiàn yōuhuìzhì generalized system of preferences (GSP)
普测 pǔcè general survey
普查 pǔchá general investigation or survey: 地质～ geological survey; reconnaissance survey /健康状况～ general health survey /人口～ census
普查区 pǔcháqū census area
普查员 pǔcháyuán census worker; enumerator
普度 pǔdù 〈佛教〉liberate all: ～众生 liberate all living beings from this mortal world; deliver all living creatures from worldly sufferings
普洱茶 pǔ'ěrchá Pu'er tea (produced in Pu'er of southwestern Yunnan)
普法 pǔfǎ (short for 普及法律常识) spread or disseminate general knowledge of law among the people: ～教育 education in the general knowledge of law /～领导机构 leading body for the dissemination of general knowledge of law
普泛 pǔfàn universal; widespread: 定期的集市贸易～地出现于各乡镇。Regular fairs have mushroomed in all small towns.
普惠制 pǔhuìzhì (short for 普遍优惠制) generalized system of preference (GSP); general preferential scheme
普及 pǔjí ❶ extend far and wide; be popular: 这书已～全国。This book is used throughout the country. ❷ popularize; disseminate; spread: ～教育 make education universal /～与提高 popularization and raising of standards /～文化科学知识 disseminate cultural and scientific knowledge /～读物 popular books
普及本 pǔjíběn popular edition
普济方 Pǔjìfāng *Universal Prescriptions*, a collection containing over 60,000 prescriptions, compiled by Zhu Su (朱橚) et al. in 1406
普济寺 Pǔjìsì Temple of Universal Relief, in Puto (普陀) County, Zhejiang Province
普降 pǔjiàng (of rain, or snow) fall extensively: ～喜雨 (there is) widespread timely rain

普教 pǔjiào *see* "普通教育"
普救寺 Pǔjiùsì Temple of Universal Salvation, in Yongji(永济) County, Shanxi Province
普利策 Pǔlìcè Joseph Pulitzer (1847-1911), American newspaper-owner and editor, of Hungarian origin
普利策奖 Pǔlìcèjiǎng Pulitzer Prize, any of a group of money prizes established under the will of Joseph Pulitzer and offered annually to American citizens for work in music, journalism, American history and biography, poetry, drama, etc.
普列汉诺夫 Pǔlièhànnuòfū Georgy Valentinovich Plekhanov (1856-1918), Russian philosopher and Marxist theoretician
普鲁本辛 pǔlǔběnxīn *also* "溴化丙胺太林" xiùhuàbǐng'àntàilín 〈药学〉propantheline (bromide); probanthine (bromide)
普鲁卡因 pǔlǔkǎyīn 〈药学〉procaine
普鲁士 Pǔlǔshì Prussia, a former German kingdom centred along the south coast of the Baltic: ～人 Prussian /～蓝〈化工〉Prussian blue
普罗 pǔluó (short for 普罗列塔利亚) proletariat: ～作家 proletarian writer /～文学 proletarian literature
普罗米修斯 Pǔluómǐxiūsī Prometheus, demigod of Greek mythology who brought fire to mankind
普米族 Pǔmǐzú Pumi or Primi nationality (living in Yunnan Province)
普什图语 Pǔshítúyǔ Pushtu; Pashto
普特 pǔtè pood, a Russian measure of weight (=16.38 kilos)
普天同庆 pǔtiān-tóngqìng the whole world or nation joining in the jubilation; universal rejoicing: 战争结束,～。There was world-wide jubilation when the war ended.
普通 pǔtōng ordinary; common; average: ～市民 ordinary citizen; man in the street /～党员 rank-and-file party member /～穿着 everyday clothes /～税率 *also* "一般税率" general tariff /这个道理很～。The reason is not far to seek. *or* The reason is very plain (*or* obvious).
普通车床 pǔtōng chēchuáng 〈机械〉engine lathe; power lathe
普通法 pǔtōngfǎ common law: ～适用地区 common law jurisdiction
普通钢 pǔtōnggāng 〈冶金〉simple steel; ordinary steel
普通工具钢 pǔtōng gōngjùgāng 〈冶金〉ordinary tool steel
普通股 pǔtōnggǔ 〈经济〉common stock; equity shares; ordinary shares
普通话 pǔtōnghuà *putonghua*; common speech (of the Chinese language); standard Chinese pronunciation
普通建筑 pǔtōng jiànzhù ordinary construction
普通教育 pǔtōng jiàoyù general education; elementary and secondary education
普通水泥 pǔtōng shuǐní 〈建筑〉Portland cement
普通税则 pǔtōng shuìzé general tax regulations
普通物理学 pǔtōng wùlǐxué general physics
普通心理学 pǔtōng xīnlǐxué general psychology
普通邮票 pǔtōng yóupiào postage stamp
普通语言学 pǔtōng yǔyánxué general linguistics
普通债务 pǔtōng zhàiwù general debt
普通照会 pǔtōng zhàohuì 〈外交〉verbal note; *note verbale*
普希金 Pǔxījīn Aleksander Pushkin (1799-1837), Russian poet
普选 pǔxuǎn general election
普选权 pǔxuǎnquán universal suffrage
普照 pǔzhào shine all over; illuminate all things: 阳光～大地。The sun shines all over the land. *or* The land is bathed in sunshine.
普照寺 Pǔzhàosì Monastery of Omnipresent Light, on Mount Tai, Shandong Province

谱

pǔ ❶ chronology; record; register: 家～ family tree; genealogy /族～ *also* "宗～" genealogy of a clan /菜～ cookbook; menu /光～ spectrum /年～ chronicle (of sb.'s life) ❷ manual; guide: 棋～ chess manual /画～ book of model paintings (*or* drawings) /脸～ types of facial make-up in Chinese operas /印～ collection of impressions of seals by famous seal-engravers; book of ancient seals ❸ music score; music: 乐～ music score; music /曲～ music score of a song /简～ numbered musical notation /五线～ staff; stave ❹ set to music; compose: 把这首诗～成歌曲 set the poem to music ❺ sth. to count on; fair amount of confidence: 干这事心里没个～儿。I have no idea how to go about the business. /经过调查研究,你对新的工作就会有～儿了。After some investigation and study, you will know what is what about your new job. ❻ airs; pretentions: 摆～ put on airs; strike a pose /他的～儿够大的。What airs he has given himself!
谱斑 pǔbān 〈天文〉flocculus
谱表 pǔbiǎo 〈音乐〉stave; staff: 大～ great stave
谱牒 pǔdié 〈书面〉family tree; genealogy
谱函数 pǔhánshù 〈数学〉spectral function
谱号 pǔhào 〈音乐〉clef: 高音～ treble clef; G clef /中音～ tenor clef; alto clef; C clef /低音～ bass clef; F clef
谱架 pǔjià music stand
谱曲 pǔqǔ set to music; compose tunes; compose a song
谱系 pǔxì ❶ genealogical system; system of a family tree ❷ system of change or development of a thing ❸〈生物〉pedigree
谱线系 pǔxiànxì 〈物理〉series of lines
谱写 pǔxiě compose (music): 这首歌曲是他～的。He was the composer of the song. /这首挽歌是为悼念一位战死的英雄而～的。This elegy was written in memory of a hero who had fallen in battle.
谱制 pǔzhì compose a musical score
谱子 pǔzi 〈口语〉music score; music

镨

pǔ 〈化学〉praseodymium (Pr), a rare earth metal

氆

pǔ

氆氇 pǔlu woollen fabric made in Tibet

浦

pǔ ❶ (used in place names) water's edge; river mouth: ～口 Pukou (a place in Jiangsu Province) ❷ (Pǔ) a surname
浦东开发区 Pǔdōng Kāifāqū Pudong Development Zone

溥

pǔ ❶〈书面〉broad; wide; vast: ～原 vast plains ❷〈书面〉common; universal: ～天同庆 *see* "普天同庆" ❸ (Pǔ) a surname
溥仪 Pǔyí Aisin Gioro Puyi (known in the West as Henry Pu-I, 1906-1967), the last emperor (with the reign title of Xuantong 宣统, 1909-1911) of China's Qing Dynasty

埔

pǔ *used in place names*: 黄～ Huangpu (*or* Whampoa) (in Guangdong Province)

圃

pǔ plot of land for growing plants; garden: 园～ garden (for growing vegetables, flowers or fruit) /花～ flower garden (*or* bed) /苗～ sapling (*or* seedling) nursery /菜～ vegetable plot (*or* garden)
圃地 pǔdì nursery (of young plants); nursery garden

朴(樸)

pǔ simple; plain; honest: 俭～ thrifty; frugal /诚～ simple and honest
see also Piáo; pō; pò
朴钝 pǔdùn 〈书面〉❶ (of knives) blunt ❷ unintelligent; not clever
朴厚 pǔhòu simple and honest: 心地～ simple and guileless /民风～。The people have a simple down-to-earth tradition.
朴陋 pǔlòu simple and crude: ～而实用的家具 crude but serviceable furniture
朴茂 pǔmào 〈书面〉simple and honest
朴讷 pǔnè 〈书面〉simple and slow of speech
朴实 pǔshí ❶ simple and plain: 穿着～ be dressed plainly /陈设～ be simply furnished ❷ sincere; honest: 性格～ be sincere and honest ❸ solid and unpretentious; matter-of-fact: 话讲得既简短又～。He spoke simply and in a matter-of-fact way. /他给我们留下了～敦厚的好印象。He impressed us as a sincere and honest man.
朴实无华 pǔshí-wúhuá simple and unaffected: 他们的表演都～,但又各具风格。Their performances are simple and unsophisticated, but display their distinctive styles.
朴素 pǔsù ❶ (of colour, design, etc.) simple; plain: 穿戴～大方 dressed simply and in good taste /室内布置得整洁～。The room was arranged in a neat, simple style. ❷ (of life) thrifty; economical; frugal: 艰苦～ hard work and plain living ❸ plain and unadorned: ～的语言 plain language ❹ undeveloped; in the embryonic stage
朴素唯物主义 pǔsù wéiwùzhǔyì naive materialism: 古代～哲学 naive ancient philosophy of materialism

朴学 pǔxué plain learning, esp. with reference to the textual criticism or research of the Qing Dynasty

朴雅 pǔyǎ simple and elegant: 这所房子不但是质量好，而且～可爱。The house is not only solidly built but elegant, unadorned and in good taste.

朴直 pǔzhí honest and straightforward: 性格～ be honest and straightforward / 语言～ be plain in language

朴质 pǔzhì simple and unaffected; natural; unsophisticated: 举止～simple and unaffected behaviour

朴拙 pǔzhuō 〈书面〉simple and unadorned: 风格～simple and unadorned style

蹼 pǔ web (of the feet of ducks, frogs, etc.)

蹼趾 pǔzhǐ webbed toe

蹼足 pǔzú webfoot; palmate foot

pù

铺[1]（舖） pù shop; store: 肉～ butcher's shop; butchery / 饭～ small restaurant; eating house / 杂货～ grocery store

铺[2]（舖） pù plank bed: 床～ bed

铺[3]（舖） pù ❶〈旧语〉post (where couriers changed horses or rested); courier station ❷ now used in place names: 三十里～ Thirty-*li* Pu

see also pū

铺板 pùbǎn bed board; bed plank

铺保 pùbǎo 〈旧语〉guarantee for a person, usually given by a shopkeeper

铺底 pùdǐ 〈旧语〉❶ shop furniture and miscellany ❷ key money for the right to rent shop premises, paid to renter

铺底资金 pùdǐ zījīn minimum capital

铺底滚动资金 pùdǐ gǔndòng zījīn start-up capital

铺户 pùhù shop; store

铺伙 pùhuǒ 〈旧语〉shop assistant

铺家 pùjia 〈方言〉shop; store

铺捐 pùjuān 〈旧语〉taxes paid by a shop in accordance with its grade

铺面 pùmiàn ❶ shop front: ～装潢一新 boast a newly-decorated shop front; put up a brand-new facade ❷ sales area: 鞋帽部设在二楼～。The shoes and hats counter is on the first floor.

铺面房 pùmiànfáng house that has a front facing the street and can be used as a shop; shop building

铺位 pùwèi bunk; berth; bed: 这个旅社有二百多个～。The hotel has over 200 beds.

铺子 pùzi shop; store

瀑 pù waterfall

瀑布 pùbù waterfall; cataract; cascade: 黄果树～ Huangguoshu Falls (in Guizhou Province)

曝（暴） pù 〈书面〉expose to the sun: 一～十寒 one day's sun and ten day's cold — by fits and starts; inconstant; lacking in perseverance

see also bào

曝露 pùlù 〈书面〉exposed to the open air: 这座多年～于原野之中的古庙已经破落了。The ancient temple which has been exposed to the wind and rain in open country for years is dilapidated.

曝气池 pùqìchí 〈环保〉aeration tank

曝晒 pùshài (of the sun) shine upon: 经过夏季烈日的～，他的脸变得黑红黑红的。His face was tanned by exposure to the scorching summer sun.

堡 pù *used in place names in lieu of* 铺: 十里～ Ten-*li* Pu

see also bǎo; bǔ

Q

qī

蛣 qī
蛣蜣 qīqiāng 〈古语〉dung beetle
颠(魌) qī ❶〈古语〉ugly mask worn by the impersonator of a god in rituals to drive away pestilence ❷〈书面〉ugly
期 qī ❶ scheduled time; appointed day or date: 婚～ wedding day /行～ date of departure /到～ fall due /过～ exceed the time limit; be overdue /定～ fix (*or* set) a time limit (*or* deadline) /延～ postpone; put off /如～完成 complete on time; finish on schedule /遥遥无～ not (achievable, etc.) within the foreseeable future ❷ period of time; term; stage; phase: 工～ time limit for a project /学～ school term /刑～ term of imprisonment; prison term /假～ vacation; holiday /汛～ flood season /周～ cycle /长～贷款 long-term loan /短～培训 short-term training /任～ term of office /无霜～ frost-free period ❸〈量词〉*referring to things done periodically*: 这个刊物每月出一～。This magazine is published monthly. /我们办了两～培训班。We have run the training course for two terms. ❹ appoint (a time); schedule: 不～而遇 meet by chance; run into ❺ await(sb. by appointment); expect; anticipate; hope: 预～ expect; anticipate /以～有所建树 in the hope that I may be able to make some contribution /甚～鼎力相助。I earnestly hope that you will kindly lend me a hand.
see also jī
期待 qīdài expect; await; anticipate; look forward to: 他们～他今天到达。They are looking forward to his arrival today. *or* They expect him to arrive today. /来的正是他们所～的人。He is exactly the man they are waiting for. /我相信他们决不会辜负老一辈人的～。I believe they will never disappoint the hopes of the older generation.
期度 qīdù 〈书面〉restrictions: 毫无～ without any restrictions /机要重地，进出应有～。Restrictions must be placed on access to areas where confidential documents are kept.
期汇 qīhuì forward exchange
期货 qīhuò 〈经济〉futures: ～价格 futures price; forward price /～汇率 forward exchange rate /～保值 hedging
期货合同 qīhuò hétong forward contract; futures contract
期货交易 qīhuò jiāoyì 〈经济〉futures; futures transaction
期货市场 qīhuò shìchǎng futures market
期冀 qījì 〈书面〉expect; hope: 我不想表白什么，也不～得到报偿。I don't want to defend myself for what I did, nor do I expect to be paid for it.
期间 qījiān time; period; course: 春节～ in the course of the Spring Festival /病休～ on one's sick leave /监禁～ while in confinement /二次大战～ during World War II
期刊 qīkān periodical: 文艺～ art and literary periodicals /～发行量 circulation of periodicals
期刊阅览室 qīkān yuèlǎnshì periodicals reading-room; periodicals room
期考 qīkǎo end-of-term exam; term examination
期满 qīmǎn expire; come to an end; end: 学徒～ at the end of one's apprenticeship /合同～ at the expiration of the contract /学习～ at the end of the term of study; when one has completed one's term of studies
期盼 qīpàn expect; await: 他～着久别的友人早日归来。He looked forward to the early return of his friends who had been away for so long.
期票 qīpiào promissory note
期期艾艾 qīqī-ài'ài stammer; stutter: 别看他说话～，文章却写得很好。He may sometimes stutter, but he writes beautifully.
期求 qīqiú hope to get; want; desire; hanker after: 他只～一个安静的环境，好认真读点儿书。All he asks for is a quiet place where he can concentrate on his studies. /许多封建皇帝曾经～长生不老之术。Many feudal emperors vainly attempted to achieve immortality.
期权 qīquán 〈金融〉option
期日 qīrì date set; appointed or designated time: ～必至 must come on the designated date /～归来 return at the designated time
期望 qīwàng hope; expect; look forward to: 人们～着足球队胜利归来。People wish to see the national football team return with flying colours. /我们衷心～试验成功。We sincerely hope that the experiment will be crowned with success.
期望值 qīwàngzhí expectations: ～过高 expectations that run too high
期限 qīxiàn allotted time; set time; deadline: 上级规定的～是星期五，现在只剩下三天了。The deadline set by the higher authorities is Friday, that is, only three days from now. /交货的～快到了。The target date for the delivery of the goods was fast approaching. /任务很紧，只给了五天的～。Only five days were allowed for the completion of the urgent task.
期许 qīxǔ place high hopes; expect: 老教授对他的学生～甚高。The old professor placed high hopes on his students.
期颐 qīyí 〈书面〉one hundred years of age: 寿登～ live to be a hundred years old (*or* a centenarian)
期于 qīyú hope to realize; aim at: 他们潜心科技，～他日学有所成，为国增光。They devote themselves to science and technology in the hope that they may shine in their studies and bring credit to the country.
欺 qī ❶ cheat; dupe; deceive: 童叟无～ cheat neither old folk nor children /因无知而受～于人 be duped (*or* taken in) owing to ignorance ❷ bully; intimidate; take advantage of: 仗势～人 act as a bully under the protection of powerful connections; use one's power to intimidate people /以大～小，以强凌弱。The big bully the small; the strong bully the weak. /他可不是软弱可～之辈。He is not the type to be pushed around. /请你不要把我的忍让看成软弱可～。Don't mistake my forbearance for weakness.
欺负 qīfu ❶ act like a bully towards weaker people; bully: 受人～ be bullied /你这不是～人吗? What a bully you are! ❷ take advantage of (sb.'s ignorance, weaknesses, etc.); cheat: 别～人家忠厚老实。Don't take advantage of his honesty. / 过去城里人往往～乡下人。In the past, the city dwellers often cheated the simple countryfolk.
欺行霸市 qīháng-bàshì bully others in the same trade and monopolize the market: 严禁～。It is strictly forbidden for anybody to bully others for control of the market.
欺哄 qīhǒng deceive by lying; hoodwink: 孩子们也许会相信这种谎言，但他这种年岁的人是不会受～的。Children might believe such lies, but people of his age will not be taken in. /如果你认为可以编造故事～同僚，你就大错特错了。You are sadly mistaken if you think you can invent a story to deceive your colleagues.
欺凌 qīlíng bully; insult; humiliate: 任人～ be subject to insult and humiliation /尽管这个国家十分弱小，也决不会受别国～。The country, though small and weak, will never allow itself to be trodden underfoot by any other country.

欺瞒 qīmán dupe; defraud; hoodwink; pull the wool over sb.'s eyes: ～上级 hoodwink the higher-ups
欺瞒夹账 qīmán-jiāzhàng engage in fraud; falsify accounts; practise graft: 那些行贿受贿或～的人迟早会受到法办。Those who give or take bribes and those who falsify accounts will be brought to justice sooner or later.
欺蒙 qīméng deceive by concealing the truth; dupe; befuddle: 他们企图隐瞒事实真相，～群众。They tried to deceive the masses by concealing the truth of the matter. /伪造事实～公众是某些政客的惯技。It is an old trick of some politicians to try to misguide the public with falsified facts.
欺弄 qīnòng bully and make a fool of sb.: 常受人～ be often bullied and made a fool of
欺骗 qīpiàn deceive; cheat; dupe; hoodwink: 这是一种彻头彻尾的～。This is sheer fraud. /他善于～人。He is an old hand at befuddling people. /想到我一直受人～，心里就不免有不舒服的感觉。It often evokes in me an uncomfortable feeling that I have been duped all along.
欺骗性 qīpiànxìng duplicity: ～大 very deceptive
欺人太甚 qīrén-tàishèn the insult is too hard to endure; that's going too far: 你不要～! Don't you dare push me too hard! /他这番话～，激起了在场所有人的公愤。His insulting remarks aroused indignation among all those present.
欺人之谈 qīrénzhītán deceitful words; deceptive talk; lie: 纯属～。It's a pack of lies. /如此露骨的～，骗得了孩子，却骗不了成年人。Such a cock-and-bull story can only deceive children; it can never fool adults. /这不过是～罢了。This is nothing but a smokescreen.
欺辱 qīrǔ bully; humiliate: 文革期间，他受尽了～。During the Cultural Revolution he was humiliated and insulted in every possible way.
欺软怕硬 qīruǎn-pàyìng bully the weak and fear the strong: 他们原来是一群～的家伙。They are just a horde of cowardly bullies. /～是懦夫的特征。To overbear (*or* bully) the weak while cringing before the strong is the characteristic of a coward.
欺善怕恶 qīshàn-pà'è bully good people and fear evil ones: ～是可耻的、不道德的。It is contemptible and immoral to bully good, honest people while standing in fear of evildoers.
欺上瞒下 qīshàng-mánxià hoodwink those above and delude those below: 此人～，无所不为。He stopped at nothing in committing evil, withholding facts from his superiors and keeping his subordinates in the dark about what was actually going on.
欺生 qīshēng ❶ be inhospitable to strangers; bully or cheat strangers: 那地方～，对外地口音的人常常不爱答理。That is an inhospitable place where people who speak with a non-local accent are likely to get short shrift. ❷ (of horses, mules, etc.) be refractory to strangers: 怎么这里的黄牛水牛都～? How is it that the oxen and buffaloes in this locality turn so intractable with strangers?
欺世盗名 qīshì-dàomíng gain fame by dishonest means; win popularity by deception: 此等人不学无术，～，为知识界所不齿。These ignoramuses gained fame by dishonest means and thus earned themselves the contempt of the intellectuals.
欺世惑众 qīshì-huòzhòng mislead the public under false pretences; practise demagoguery: 他们以革命的假象～。They deceived and confused the public with pseudo-revolutionary rhetoric.
欺罔 qīwǎng 〈书面〉 deceive; hoodwink: ～世人 hoodwink the public; pull the wool over the eyes of the public /～视听 confuse the minds of the people
欺侮 qīwǔ behave rudely or coarsely; bully; insult: 他可不是好～的! He is not a person to be trifled with! /不要～她，她快要掉眼泪了。Don't act the bully! She is on the verge of tears. /他～其他孩子，硬叫他们逃课。He bullied the other children into playing truant.
欺压 qīyā bully and oppress; ride roughshod over; tyrannize: 当时土豪劣绅任意～良民。In those days the evil gentry and local bullies rode roughshod over honest common people. /那些都是没有脊梁骨的人，甘心忍受别人的～。Those were spineless people, who were resigned to being bullied and oppressed.
欺诈 qīzhà deceive; cheat; swindle: 贩卖伪劣商品～顾客 cheat customers by selling fake and inferior goods /他是个～钱财的恶棍。He is a scoundrel who goes about swindling people. /他用～手段骗取别人的信任。He wormed himself into the confidence of other people by resorting to falsehood.
欺嘴 qīzuǐ 〈方言〉 tell lies; lie: ～蒙人 mislead people by telling lies /行家面前，不敢～ dare not say anything tongue in cheek in the presence of an expert

桤(榿) qī 〈植物〉 alder
桤木 qīmù alder

桼 qī 〈书面〉 *see* "漆" qī

漆 qī ❶ lacquer; paint: 生～ raw lacquer /油～ paint /清～ varnish /朱～ red paint /油～未干 wet paint ❷ paint; cover with paint: ～家具 paint furniture /～两遍 give two coats of paint /我把门～成红色。I painted the door red. ❸ (Qī) a surname
漆包线 qībāoxiàn 〈电工〉 enamel-insulated wire
漆布 qībù varnished cloth
漆雕 qīdiāo ❶ carved lacquer ❷ (Qīdiāo) a surname
漆革 qīgé patent leather
漆工 qīgōng ❶ lacquering; painting ❷ lacquerer; lacquer man; painter
漆黑 qīhēi pitch-dark; pitch-black: ～的头发 jet-black hair/～中看不见路。We could not see our way in the pitch-dark.
漆黑一团 qīhēi-yītuán *also* "一团漆黑" ❶ pitch-dark: 眼前～，伸手不见五指。It was pitch-dark and nothing could be seen ahead. /我们不应该把世界形势描绘成一片光明，也不应该把它说成～。We should not paint too rosy a picture of the world situation, nor should we describe it as shrouded in total darkness. ❷ be ignorant of; be blind to; be in the dark about: 我们应该怎样应付这个局面，至今心中仍然是～。We are still at a loss how to cope with the situation.
漆画 qīhuà 〈美术〉 lacquer painting
漆匠 qījiang ❶ lacquerware worker ❷ lacquerer; lacquer man; painter
漆皮 qīpí ❶ coat of paint ❷ shellac
漆片 qīpiàn a kind of highly volatile paint
漆器 qīqì lacquerware; lacquerwork: 脱胎～ bodiless lacquerware
漆树 qīshù lacquer tree; varnish tree; wood oil tree

敧 qī 〈书面〉 slant
敧侧 qīcè 〈书面〉 lean to one side; lean over; slant
敧斜 qīxié slant: 岸边柳树～。The willow trees are hanging low on a slant.

欹 qī 〈书面〉 *see* "敧" qī
see also yī

戚[1] qī ❶ relative; kin: ～属 kinsfolk; relatives /外～ relatives of the mother or wife of the emperor ❷ (Qī) a surname

戚[2]**(慼)** qī sorrow; grief: 不胜哀～ be in deep sorrow; be overcome with sorrow /我们休～相关，甘苦与共。We are bound by a common cause and go through thick and thin together.

戚[3]**(鏚)** qī a kind of ancient weapon, like an axe: 干～ axe and shield
戚串 qīguàn 〈书面〉 relative by marriage
戚继光 Qī Jìguāng Qi Jiguang (1528-1587), general and poet of the Ming Dynasty, famous for his feats in suppressing the Wokou (倭寇, Japanese pirates in alliance with Chinese bandits) in Zhejiang, Fujian and Guangdong
戚家军 Qījiājūn General Qi's army, made up mainly of peasants and miners from eastern Zhejiang and personally led and trained by Qi Jiguang
戚旧 qījiù relatives and old acquaintances
戚戚 qīqī 〈书面〉 ❶ mutual affection or love: ～兄弟，莫远具尔。Brothers born of the same parents should remain close to each other and avoid being estranged. ❷ sad; distressed; anxious: 不～于贫贱，不汲汲于富贵。Never worry about poverty and lowly station; never hanker after wealth and position. ❸ be touched or moved; be inspired: 夫子言之，于我心有～焉。Sir, what you've said inspires me greatly.
戚然 qīrán 〈书面〉 look worried; be sorrowful: ～不语 look worried and say nothing; remain silent with knitted brows /神态～

wear a woeful expression

戚畹 qīwǎn 〈书面〉imperial relatives; relatives of the royal family

戚谊 qīyì ties of kinship; feeling of kinship

戚友 qīyǒu relatives and friends:父亲生日那天,家里来的~很多。On my father's birthday, many of our relatives and friends came to our home.

戚族 qīzú family members; members of the clan

嘁 qī low sibilant sound such as whispering or hissing

嘁哩喀嚓 qīlikāchā (of speech) directly and succinctly; (of action) decisively and effectively:他~几句话就把问题解决了。With a few words, concise and to the point, he solved the question right away.

嘁嘁喳喳 qīqi-chāchā 〈象声〉chatter away; jabber away; rattle on; babble on:一群妇女在院子里~地谈论东家长,西家短。A group of women chattered away in the courtyard, gossiping about their neighbours.

蜮 qī general name for mollusc

七 qī ❶ seven ❷ *see* "七七"

七…八… qī…bā… *used in conjunction with verbs or nouns to indicate multiplicity or disorder*:七碟八碗 with a lot of bowls and dishes; plenty of dishes /七病八痛 (suffer from) ailments and diseases of all kinds

七倍体 qībèitǐ heptaploid

七边形 qībiānxíng 〈数学〉heptagon

七步之才 qībùzhīcái ability of quick, spontaneous literary creation; facile imagination:在吟诗做对方面,他可真是出口成章,有~。He does have a ready wit in composing poems and couplets.

七尺之躯 qīchǐzhīqū 〈旧语〉true man; real man; manly man

七出 qīchū 〈旧语〉seven reasons for which a husband can send off his wife

七搭八搭 qīdā-bādā 〈方言〉argue endlessly; chatter

七打八 qīdǎbā 〈方言〉little remains:一场大火,烧了个~。Very little was left after the big fire.

七大八小 qīdà-bāxiǎo of different sizes:这里有~的一大堆毛线衣,你自己挑吧! There are a lot of different sized woolen sweaters here. You can pick and choose.

七颠八倒 qīdiān-bādǎo at sixes and sevens; upside down; topsy-turvy:他几天不在,屋里便闹得~。His room is a complete mess after he has been absent for a few days. /这单相思害得他~,失魂落魄。Unrequited love befuddled him as if he had taken leave of his senses.

七姑八姨儿 qīgū-bāyír 〈口语〉female relations, distant or close; distant relatives

七古 qīgǔ form of pre-Tang poetry with seven characters to each line but with no strict tonal pattern or rhyming scheme

七国集团 Qīguó Jítuán Group of Seven, the seven major industrial nations of the West, i.e., the United States, Japan, Germany, France, the United Kingdom, Italy, and Canada

七级风 qījífēng 〈气象〉force 7 wind; moderate gale

七极管 qījíguǎn 〈电子〉heptode

七价 qījià 〈化学〉heptavalent; septavalent

七件事 qījiànshì seven necessities of life:开门~:柴米油盐酱醋茶。Every day one is faced with the seven necessities of life: firewood, rice, cooking oil, salt, soy-sauce, vinegar, and tea.

七绝 qījué (of classical poetry) four-line poem with seven characters to a line and a strict tonal pattern and rhyming scheme

七孔 qīkǒng *also* "七窍" seven apertures of one's head (nostrils, eyes, ears, and mouth):~出血 bleed from the seven apertures

七老八十 qīlǎo-bāshí in one's seventies or eighties; very old:别看他~的,身子骨还硬朗着呢。Though an old man in his seventies or eighties, he is still as fit as a fiddle. *or* Though advanced in age, he is still hale and hearty.

七了八当 qīliǎo-bādàng 〈口语〉have properly handled most of the problems:忙了半天,~的差不多了。We have been busy working the whole morning and have now nearly finished.

七零八落 qīlíng-bāluò scattered here and there; in great confusion; in disarray:把敌军打了个~,抱头鼠窜而逃。The enemy troops were thoroughly trounced and sent fleeing helter-skelter. /文章被他删得~。His deletions left the essay fragmented and incoherent.

七律 qīlǜ (of classical poetry) eight-line poem with seven characters to a line and a strict tonal pattern and rhyming scheme

七略 Qīlüè *Qi Lüe* or *Compendium of Books in Seven Categories*, said to be China's first compendium of books, compiled by Liu Xin (刘歆, ? - 23AD) of the Western Han Dynasty

七拼八凑 qīpīn-bācòu put together; knock together:这是本~的书,不值一读。The book is not worth reading; it is a scissors-and-paste affair. /这套家具的木料是~的。This set of furniture is made of odd pieces of wood.

七品芝麻官 qīpǐn zhīmaguān lowly official, usually referring to a county magistrate

七七 qīqī *also* "尽七" jìnqī; "满七" mǎnqī; "断七" duànqī "double seven" (According to old Chinese custom, a memorial ceremony was to be held for the deceased every seven days after his death until the 49th day when the seventh ceremony of the seven-day periods was finally held.)

七七事变 Qī-Qī Shìbiàn *also* "卢沟桥事变" Lúgōuqiáo Shìbiàn July 7 Incident of 1937, an incident staged at Lugouqiao(卢沟桥), Beiping (now Beijing) on July 7, 1937 by Japanese imperialists, which marked the beginning of an all-out war of aggression against China by Japan

七七八八 qīqi-bābā 〈口语〉off and on; sundry:他每天挑水扫地,刷锅洗碗,做些~的事。He does all the odd jobs: fetching water, sweeping the floor, cleaning, washing dishes, and so on. /他~加起来,才念过三年书。He had, off and on, three years of formal schooling.

七巧板 qīqiǎobǎn seven-piece puzzle; tangram

七窍 qīqiào seven apertures in the human head, i.e. eyes, ears, nostrils and mouth:他~流血。He was bleeding from every orifice.

七窍生烟 qīqiào-shēngyān infuriated; mad with rage:气得他~,说不出话来。He was so infuriated that he could hardly utter a word.

七擒七纵 qīqín-qīzòng capture and release seven times — referring to a story in *The Romance of the Three Kingdoms* (三国演义), in which Zhuge Liang (诸葛亮), the prime minister of Shu (蜀) and famous military strategist, is described as having captured and released the chief of an ethnic tribe seven times to win him over finally; win confidence and support by tact

七青八黄 qīqīng-bāhuáng money and property; wealth

七情 qīqíng ❶ seven human emotions, namely, joy, anger, sorrow, fear, love, hate and desire:~六欲 seven emotions and six sensual pleasures; various human emotions and desires ❷ 〈中医〉seven emotional factors (joy, anger, melancholy, brooding, sorrow, fear and shock) which are considered to be the internal factors of disease

七日风 qīrìfēng 〈医学〉trismus nascentium; trismus neonatorum

七鳃鳗 qīsāimán 〈动物〉lamprey

七色板 qīsèbǎn Newton's disk

七上八下 qīshàng-bāxià be in a nervous state of mind; be on tenterhooks; be on pins and needles:他心里~,不知道该怎么办。He was seriously perturbed, not knowing what to do with himself.

七声 qīshēng 〈音乐〉seven notes of the ancient Chinese musical scale: *gong*, *shang*, *jue*, *bianzhi*, *zhi*, *yu*, *biangong* (宫,商,角,变徵,徵,羽,变宫), which are basically the same as *do*, *re*, *me*, *fa*, *so*, *la*, *te*

七十二变 qīshí'èrbiàn seventy-two metamorphoses (said of the Monkey King in the *Pilgrimage to the West*《西游记》, who could transform himself into anything); countless changes in tactics:他纵有~,也逃不出我们的掌心。Even if he had the 72 metamorphoses like the Monkey King, we would still hold him in the palm of our hand. *or* He could not escape from our grasp despite his countless changes in tactics.

七十二行 qīshí'èrháng all sorts of trades; in every conceivable line of work:~,行行出状元。One can chalk up outstanding achievements in every profession or trade.

七十七国集团 Qīshíqīguó Jítuán Group of 77; G-77 (a group formed by the majority of the developing countries for protecting their own interest in international relations)

七手八脚 qīshǒu-bājiǎo with many people taking part or pitching in; with everybody lending a hand:大家~一忽儿便把房间收拾得干干净净。With everybody joining in, the room was tidied up in no time.

七损八伤 qīsǔn-bāshāng (suffer) injuries of all sorts

七夕 qīxī seventh evening of the seventh moon of the lunar calendar (according to legend the Cowherd 牛郎 and the Weaver Maid 织女 meet on that evening every year in Heaven)
七弦琴 qīxiánqín seven-stringed musical instrument
七星针 qīxīngzhēn *also*"皮肤针" pífūzhēn 〈中医〉cutaneous acupuncture
七言诗 qīyánshī (of classical poetry) poem with seven characters to a line
七叶树 qīyèshù buckeye (*Aesculus chinensis*)
七一 Qī-Yī July 1, anniversary of the founding of the Communist Party of China (1921)
七月 qīyuè ❶ July ❷ seventh month of the lunar year; seventh moon
七折八扣 qīzhé-bākòu (with) various deductions or cuts: 拨款本来就不多,再~,剩下的连维持门面都不够。The appropriation was not plentiful to start with, and after various deductions and cuts, was hardly enough to keep the show going.
七政仪 qīzhèngyí 〈天文〉orrery
七嘴八舌 qīzuǐ-bāshé with many people speaking all at once: 一群人围着他~,闹得他也没了主意。He was surrounded by a group of people all trying to speak to him, so that he was unable to make up his mind.

Q

柒

qī ❶ seven, used for the numeral 七 on cheques, etc. to avoid mistakes or alterations ❷ (Qī) a surname

沏

qī infuse: ~一杯花茶 infuse (*or* make) a cup of jasmine tea / 用热水~点洗衣粉 put some washing powder (*or* detergent) in hot water and stir it

栖(棲)

qī ❶ (of birds) perch; rest ❷ dwell; live; stay: 两~动物 amphibious animals / 吾将安~? Where shall I find a place to stay? / 他觉得天地虽大,而自己却无地可~。He felt that he had nowhere to dwell in this wide world.
see also xī
栖遁 qīdùn 〈书面〉live as a recluse or hermit; live alone
栖遑 qīhuáng *also*"栖皇"〈书面〉uneasy and anxious; embarrassed: 神情~ look uneasy and worried
栖集 qījí dwell; rest: 在这个荒岛上~了各种野生动物。The desert island swarms with wild life of various kinds.
栖居 qījū (of animals) dwell: 这个森林是野兽~之地。Wild animals dwell in this forest. *or* This forest is the haunt of wild animals.
栖身 qīshēn stay; sojourn; reside: ~异邦,心怀祖国。Residing in a strange land, he misses his native country. / 偌大一个城市,哪里不能~? Surely one can find a place to stay here in this big city.
栖宿 qīsù *see*"栖息"
栖息 qīxī (of birds) perch; rest: ~环境 natural living environment / 水鸟成群地~在芦苇深处。Flocks of water fowls dwell in the depths of the reeds. / 这个自然保护区~着许多珍贵鸟类。Many rare birds have made their homes on this wildlife preserve (*or* in this nature protection zone).
栖息地 qīxīdì habitat
栖止 qīzhǐ reside; live; dwell; take up abode

妻

qī wife: 夫~ husband (*or* man) and wife / 未婚~ fiancée
see also qì
妻党 qīdǎng relatives of one's wife
妻弟 qīdì younger brother of one's wife; (younger) brother-in-law
妻儿老小 qī'ér-lǎoxiǎo one's parents, wife and children: 他家里有~,却无隔宿之粮。He is a married man with his parents, wife and children all relying on him for support, yet they have to live from hand to mouth.
妻舅 qījiù wife's brother
妻离子散 qīlí-zǐsàn breaking up of a family, with the wife and children drifting apart: 内战使许多普通老百姓~,家破人亡。The civil war caused countless broken families and took a heavy toll of civilians.
妻孥 qīnú 〈书面〉wife and children
妻室 qīshì 〈书面〉wife: 未有~ (of a man) not get married
妻小 qīxiǎo wife and children; wife
妻子 qīzǐ wife and children
妻子 qīzi wife

凄(❶❷淒、❸悽)

qī ❶ chilly; freezing; cold: 风~,雨淋淋 chilly wind and incessant rain ❷ bleak and desolate; dreary: *see*"~清";"~凉" ❸ sad; wretched; dejected; melancholy: *see*"~惨";"~切"
凄哀 qī'āi dreary and sad; plaintive: 远处传来~的笛声。A plaintive note of the flute was heard from afar.
凄暗 qī'àn gloomy: ~的灯光 gloomy light
凄惨 qīcǎn wretched; horrible; dreadful: ~的景象 dreadful scene; horrible sight / ~的气氛 melancholy atmosphere / ~的哭叫声 heart-rending cries / ~的生活 wretched life
凄恻 qīcè 〈书面〉(of sounds, feelings) mournful; sorrowful; sad: ~的曲调 mournful tunes / 状甚~ look extremely sad
凄楚 qīchǔ 〈书面〉grieved; sad; sorrowful: 他长叹一声,声极~。He heaved a long sigh, which sounded dreadfully sad.
凄怆 qīchuàng 〈书面〉tragic; sorrowful; sad: 内心有一种不可名状的~。An indescribable feeling of sadness welled up in his heart. / 她满面~,热泪纵横。She looked absolutely heartbroken, and hot tears streamed down her cheeks.
凄风苦雨 qīfēng-kǔyǔ *also*"凄风冷雨" chilly wind and unremitting rain — foul weather; wretched circumstances; sad plight: ~难眠夜 sleepless night with the wind wailing and the rain pattering
凄寒 qīhán desolate and cold: 这里并不像想象中的那样荒凉~。The place is not so bleak and desolate as one might imagine.
凄惶 qīhuáng sad and anxious; miserable and nervous: 神色~ look nervous and miserable
凄寂 qījì ❶ desolate and still: 眼前是一片~的原野。Before our eyes was a vast expanse of desolate land. ❷ dreary and lonely: 生活~ dreary and lonely life
凄紧 qījǐn ❶ (of wind) cold and strong: 秋风~。The autumn wind is cold and intense. ❷ (of sound) sad and hurried: 呼唤声惨烈而~。The shouting carried a violent note of tragedy, sad and hurried.
凄苦 qīkǔ sad and miserable: 多年来,他过着孤独的生活,怪~的。It's indeed saddening that he has all these years led such a lonely and friendless life.
凄冷 qīlěng ❶ desolate; dreary: 天黑了,周围显得格外~。With night falling, the place appeared peculiarly desolate all around. ❷ chilly; cold: 雨下个不停,江边异常~。The rain kept falling, and it chilled one to the bone standing on the riverbank.
凄厉 qīlì mournful and shrill: ~的哭声 shrill cry / 北风~。The north wind is howling (*or* wailing).
凄凉 qīliáng ❶ bleak; desolate: 晚景~ spend the evening of one's life in great misery / 前景~ bleak prospects / 战后农村是一派~景象。After the war the countryside was a scene of desolation. / 天上的黑云,地上的石碑和零散的花圈,都显得~惨淡。The dark clouds above and the tombstone and broken wreaths below made for a desolate ambiance. ❷ dismal; miserable; wretched: ~的生活 wretched life / 音调~ distressing melody
凄迷 qīmí 〈书面〉❶ (of scenery) desolate and hazy; bleak: 夜色~。The scene is dreary at night. / 烟雨~。The enveloping mist and rain shrouded a scene of unrelieved gloom. ❷ grieved; unhappy: 予心~。My heart is filled with grief.
凄切 qīqiè sad and plaintive; melancholy: 哭声~ weep sadly / 旷野寒风~。A shrill cold wind was sweeping across the fields. / 歌声~动人。There was a sad, plaintive note in the singing that moved us all.
凄清 qīqīng ❶ chill; chilly: 月色~。There was a chilly touch about the rays of moonlight. ❷ bleak; gloomy: 琴声~。There are melancholy notes in the tone of the piano. / 雪后四处一片~。All around was a dreary, monotonous expanse of snow.
凄然 qīrán 〈书面〉sorrowful; sad; mournful: ~泪下 shed tears sadly / ~一笑 give a forlorn smile / 神态~ wear a sorrowful look / 听者无不为之~。All those who heard the story felt dejected.
凄伤 qīshāng mournful; melancholy: 这首诗过于~。This poem is too melancholy.
凄酸 qīsuān gloomy and melancholy: 想起亡友,他心中一阵~,哭出声来。When he thought of his departed friend, a feeling of unspeakable sadness came over him and he cried.
凄婉 qīwǎn ❶ sad; mournful; doleful: 神情~ doleful expression on the face ❷ (of sound) sad and moving; plaintive: ~的笛声 plain-

tive sound of the flute

凄惘 qīwǎng sad and frustrated：强烈的～之情，骤然涌上心头。A strong feeling of sadness and frustration welled up in the mind.

凄咽 qīyè (of sound) sad and mournful; sobbing：笛声～，令人心碎。The wailing notes of the flute were heartrending.

凄怨 qīyuàn (of sound) sad and plaintive：～的曲调 sad and plaintive melody

凄壮 qīzhuàng melancholy and moving：～的乐曲 sad and moving melody of the music

萋 qī

萋萋 qīqī lush and luxuriant：芳草～ lush green grass /绿叶～ lush green leaves

缉 qī

hem clothing, etc. in close and joint stitches：～边儿 hem the edges

see also jī

暚 qī

❶ drying; almost dry：雨过了，道路渐渐～了。After the rain (*or* the passing shower), the road soon became dry. ❷ soak up water with sand or earth：地上有水，铺点沙子～一～。Spread some sand over the puddles in the road to soak up the rain water.

蹊 qī

see also xī

蹊跷 qīqiāo odd; mysterious; suspicious：事情有些～。The whole business smells fishy. /他今天神态反常，内中定有～。He is not his usual self today. There must be something wrong with him. /他突然从政坛上消失，令人感到十分～。His sudden disappearance from the political stage struck many people as rather mysterious. /我也感觉着有点～。I also feel there is mischief brewing. *or* I smell a rat, too.

qí

齐[1]（齊） qí

❶ neat; even; in order：树篱剪得很～。The hedge is evenly trimmed. /队伍走得很～。The procession marched in step. /十个指头不一般～。The ten fingers are not even in length. /把这些书摆～放在书架上。Arrange these books in order and put them on the shelves. ❷ reach the same level; be of the same level：他们的水平参差不～。Their level is rather uneven. /向日葵都～了房檐了。The sunflowers have reached the eaves. /河水～腰深。The river is waist deep. ❸ equal; identical：人心不～则不能办大事。When people do not work for the same goal they cannot achieve any real success. ❹ together; in unison：并驾～驱 run neck and neck; keep abreast of sb. /百花～放。A hundred flowers blossom at the same time. ❺ all ready; in order：材料预备～了。All the materials are now ready. /文件都办～了。The papers are all in order. /客人还没有到～。Some guests have not arrived. ❻ even out; cut close to：～线裁 even out along the line /～根儿剪断 cut off close to the roots ❼ (formerly jì) alloy：锰镍铜～ alloy of manganese, nickel and copper

齐[2]（齊） Qí

❶ name of a kingdom of the Zhou Dynasty (mid-11th century BC-221 BC) ❷ Southern Qi Dynasty (479-502 AD) ❸ Northern Qi Dynasty (550-577 AD) ❹ name of a kingdom set up by the rebel peasant leader Huang Chao(黄巢) towards the end of the Tang Dynasty (618-907 AD) ❺ a surname

see also jì

齐白石 Qí Báishí Qi Baishi (formerly translated as Chi Pai-shih, 1863-1957), Chinese painter

齐备 qíbèi all ready：行装～，马上出发。Let's set out right away since we have got everything ready for the journey.

齐步走 qíbùzǒu 〈军事〉quick march; Quick-time, march!

齐唱 qíchàng 〈音乐〉group singing in which everyone sings the same note; singing in unison; unison

齐齿呼 qíchǐhū 〈语言〉syllables with i as the final (韵母) or a final beginning with i

see also "四呼" sìhū

齐楚 qíchǔ neat and smart：衣冠～ be immaculately dressed

齐次积分方程 qícì jīfēn fāngchéng 〈数学〉homogeneous integral equation

齐打伙儿 qídǎhuǒr *also* "齐打呼"〈方言〉together; in a group：明儿咱们～去摘豆角儿。Let's all go together and pick fresh kidney beans tomorrow.

齐东野语 Qídōng-yěyǔ 〈书面〉hearsay; rumour

齐墩果 qídūnguǒ *also* "油橄榄" yóugǎnlǎn olive

齐桓公 Qíhuángōng Duke Huan of Qi State (? -643 BC), born Xiao Bai (小白), succeeded to the dukedom in 685 BC, made Qi strong and became the first hegemon in the Spring and Autumn Period

齐集 qíjí assemble; gather：全校师生～礼堂，举行开学典礼。All faculty members and students assembled in the auditorium for the school-opening ceremony.

齐家文化 Qíjiā wénhuà 〈考古〉Qijia culture, a culture of the Chalcolithic period at the time of the disintegration of primitive society, relics of which were first unearthed at Qijiaping (齐家坪), Gansu Province, in 1924

齐截 qíjie 〈方言〉❶ neat; even：他穿着～。He is neatly dressed. /这些松树长得挺～。These pine trees are of even height. ❷complete; all ready：所需资金～了。All the necessary funds were made available.

齐理 qíli 〈口语〉put in order; arrange; tidy up：把桌上的东西～～。Tidy away the things on the table.

齐眉穗儿 qíméisuìr (of short hair of a woman or a child) hang down to the eyebrows：小姑娘留着个～。The little girl wears her hair in bangs.

齐民 qímín 〈书面〉populace; common people

齐民要术 Qímín Yàoshù *Qi Min Yao Shu* or *Important Arts for the People's Welfare*, agricultural encyclopaedia of the 6th century compiled by Jia Sixie (贾思勰)

齐名 qímíng enjoy equal renown; be equally famous：在中国文学史上李白与杜甫～。In the literary history of China Li Bai and Du Fu enjoy equal fame.

齐明 qímíng 〈物理〉aplanatic：～成像 aplanatic image formation /～点 aplanatic foci /～镜 aplanat /～条件 aplanatic condition /～望远镜 aplanatic telescope

齐齐哈尔 Qíqíhā'ěr Qiqihar, second largest city in Heilongjiang Province

齐巧 qíqiǎo 〈方言〉by chance; as luck would have it：我正要去找他，～他来了。I was going to look for him when he turned up.

齐全 qíquán complete; ready：百货公司已经把冬令商品准备～。The department store has in stock a whole array of winter commodities. /阅读书单远不～。The reading list is far from complete (*or* exhaustive). /新建住宅设备～。The new apartment houses have all necessary modern facilities.

齐射 qíshè 〈军事〉salvo; volley

齐声 qíshēng (of many people) speak, sing or laugh all at once; be in chorus; be in unison：人们～叫好。People applauded in chorus. /他们～歌唱。They are singing in unison. /他说得大家～大笑。He set us all laughing.

齐刷刷 qíshuāshuā neat; uniform：队伍～地前进。The troops marched in step.

齐头 qítóu simultaneously; at the same time：火势～爆发，一霎时满城都是火。Fire broke out at several places almost at the same time, and in a minute the whole city was a sea of flames.

齐头并进 qítóu-bìngjìn advance in parallel; undertake two or more tasks at the same time：小分队分三路～，直捣匪穴。The detachment advanced in three parallel lines, converging on the bandits' den. /这几项工作是相辅相成的，应该～。As these tasks are complementary, they should be undertaken simultaneously. /～，步步为营，稳扎稳打。Advance abreast, consolidate at every step, and strike sure blows.

齐头儿齐脑儿 qítóur-qínǎor 〈口语〉uniform; tidy：树苗长得～的，真好看。The saplings are almost the same height. What a fine sight!

齐心 qíxīn be of one mind; have a common goal; act in concert; pull together：这个组的工人～，月月都提前完成定额。The workers of this team are so devoted in their joint effort that they have overfulfilled their production quota every month. /如果中国人民～朝着一个共同目标奋斗，那么在本世纪末一定可以达到小康水平。If everyone in China pulls together and aims for the same goal, the country should be fairly well-off by the end of the century.

齐心协力 qíxīn-xiélì work as one; act in concert：只要我们～，这件事准能办成。The task can certainly be accomplished with our con-

certed effort.
齐一 qíyī in unison; uniform: 他们的动作迅速而～。Their movements were swift and uniform.
齐崭崭 qízhǎnzhǎn *also* "齐展展" uniform; even: ～的堤岸是卵石砌成的。The embankment is evenly paved with pebbles.
齐账 qízhàng 〈方言〉settle accounts: 你还没有～呢。You haven't settled your account yet.
齐臻臻 qízhēnzhēn neat; in good order: 广场上～地排列着欢迎贵宾的队伍。On the square stood rows of people greeting the guests of honour.
齐整 qízhěng neat; well arranged: 现在农村妇女穿戴都很～。Nowadays women in rural areas are always neatly dressed. /城里人烟不多，街市～。The town is not densely populated and the streets are clean and tidy. /餐厅里的椅子摆得不够～。The chairs in the dining room are not as properly arranged as they should be.
齐奏 qízòu 〈音乐〉playing (musical instruments) in unison; unison

荠(薺) qí *see* "荸荠" bíqi
see also jì

蛴(蠐) qí
蛴螬 qícáo 〈动物〉grub

脐(臍) qí ❶〈生理〉navel; umbilicus ❷ abdomen of a crab: 尖～ pointed belly flap in a male crab /团～ round belly flap in a female crab
脐出血 qíchūxuè 〈医学〉omphalorrhagia
脐带 qídài 〈生理〉umbilical cord
脐带式连接器 qídàishì liánjiēqì umbilical connector
脐风 qífēng 〈中医〉umbilical tetanus
脐溃疡 qíkuìyáng 〈医学〉omphalelcosis
脐瘤 qíliú 〈医学〉omphaloma
脐瘘 qílòu 〈医学〉umbilical fistula
脐炎 qíyán 〈医学〉omphalitis

祁 Qí a surname
祁红 qíhóng *keemun* (black tea produced at Qimen 祁门 of Anhui Province)
祁剧 qíjù a kind of local opera popular in Hunan Province
祁曼塔格山 Qímàntǎgéshān Qimantage Mountains, in Xinjiang and Qinghai

其[1] qí ❶ his; her; its; their: 自食～力 support oneself by the sweat of one's brow; earn one's own living (*or* bread) /人尽～才，物尽～用 make the best possible use of men and material /自圆～说 justify one's argument; justify oneself ❷ he; she; it; they: 令～即日报到 tell him to report for duty immediately /促～回心转意 make an effort to bring him around /听～自然 let matters take their own course ❸ that; such: 不堪～苦 cannot endure such hardship /有～父，必有～子。Like father, like son. /以～人之道，还治～人之身。Do onto others as they do to you. ❹ *used as a functional word*: 夸夸～谈 talk big; indulge in verbiage /大上～当 walk straight into the trap; play into sb.'s hands /大发～脾气 blow one's top; give vent to one's temper; fly into a rage

其[2] qí 〈书面〉〈助词〉❶ *expressing conjecture or retort*: 欲加之罪，～无辞乎? He who is bent on condemning sb. can always trump up a charge. ❷ *expressing an order or instruction*: 尔～无忘乃父之志! Always bear your father's wish in mind!

其[3] qí *used as a suffix*: 极～ extremely /尤～ particularly; especially /大概～ generally; presumably; probably
其次 qícì ❶ next; then: 他第一个发言，～就轮到我了。He was the first to take the floor, and I was the next. ❷ second; secondary: 这部影片最大的毛病是缺乏艺术感染力，摄影技术差还在～。The most serious drawback of this film is its lack of artistic appeal while poor photography is only secondary.
其后 qíhòu later on; thereafter; afterwards: ～，两国开始谋求关系正常化。Later on, the two countries began to work for the normalization of relations.
其间 qíjiān ❶ inside; implicit: 他有点鬼鬼祟祟，～定有不可告人的秘密。He seems to be engaged in some furtive activity, and there must be something behind it. ❷ during; in the course of; in the interval: 我出国进修两年，这～国家的面貌发生了很大变化。In the two years when I pursued advanced studies abroad, the country underwent a facelift.
其乐无穷 qílè-wúqióng infinite delight or joy: 能与棋友们拼杀几盘，他觉得～。It was an immense pleasure for him to lock horns with his fellow players in a few games of chess.
其貌不扬 qímào-bùyáng unprepossessing to look at; of undistinguished appearance: 想不到本省的这位大诗人，竟是这般的～。Little did I imagine that the great poet of this province was so homely in appearance.
其内 qínèi inclusive of: 给你的那笔钱，车钱饭钱都在～。Fares and food are included in the sum of money I gave you.
其实 qíshí in fact; in reality; actually; as a matter of fact: 说是花园，～是果园。A garden in name, it is really an orchard. /她以为我很了解情况，～不然。She thought that I was well acquainted with the situation, but this is certainly not the case.
其他 qítā *also* "其它" other (than); else: 先办完这件事，再办～的事。Let's first finish this before we take up anything else. /这件事儿够麻烦的了，我没有心思再考虑～。I am in no mood to consider other matters; the problem in hand has already given me a lot of headache.
其外 qíwài besides; in addition: 今天来这儿的，有他的父母、亲戚，～就是一些同事、同学。Present here today are his parents and relatives as well as some old colleagues and schoolmates.
其味无穷 qíwèi-wúqióng have a fine flavour that endures; be highly rewarding or enjoyable: 这首诗，具有我这种经历的人读起来会觉得～。The poem is a source of infinite pleasure to people with experiences similar to mine.
其先 qíxiān at first; initially: 他家～很富，后来才败落下来。At first his family was wealthy, but it declined later.
其余 qíyú the rest; the others; the remainder: 攻其一点，不及～ pounce on one point and ignore all others — attack sb. for a single fault without considering the overall picture /小张一马当先，～的人也不落后。Xiao Zhang took the lead, and all the others were trying to keep up with him. /来客当中我只认识两位，～的没见过。I knew only two of the guests and had never met the rest before.
其中 qízhōng among (which, them, etc.); in (which, it, etc.): 他新买了近百本书，～经典著作占多数。Recently, he has bought nearly a hundred books, most (*or* the greater part) of which are classics. /我有好几个朋友得了演说比赛奖，～有小刘和老张。Several of my friends won prizes at the speech contest; among them were Xiao Liu and Lao Zhang.

淇 qí *see* "冰淇淋" bīngqílín

麒 qí ❶ *see* "麒麟" ❷ (Qí) a surname
麒麟 qílín *also* "麟" kylin, an auspicious legendary animal with a horn and scales all over; (Chinese) unicorn
麒麟菜 qílíncài 〈植物〉Chinese alpine rush (*Eulaliopais binata*)
麒麟竭 qílínjié 〈中药〉dragon's blood (*Daemonorops draco*)
麒麟座 Qílínzuò 〈天文〉Monoceros

旗(❶旂) qí ❶ flag; banner; pennant; standard: 国～ national flag /彩～ colour flags /信号～ bunting /队～ team pennant /锦～ brocade banner /升～ hoist the flag /降半～ fly the flag at half mast ❷ "Eight Banners" (八旗), military-administrative organizations of the Manchu nationality before and during the Qing Dynasty: 在～ be of one of the "Eight Banners" ❸ of the "Eight Banners", esp. of the Manchu nationality: *see* "～人"; "～袍" ❹ name of place where the troops of the "Eight Banners" used to be stationed: 正蓝～ Zhenglan (Xunlun Hoh) Qi /镶黄～ Xianghuang (Hobot Xar) Qi /正镶白～ Zhengxiangbai (Xulun Hobot Qagan) Qi ❺ banner, an administrative division of county level in the Inner Mongolia Autonomous Region: 敖汉～ Aohan Banner /鄂伦春自治～ Oroqen Autonomous Banner
旗兵 qíbīng *also* "八旗兵" bāqíbīng bannerman, soldier of one of the military-administrative organizations of the Manchu national-

ity

旗杆 qígān flagpole; flag post

旗鼓相当 qígǔ-xiāngdāng be equal in strength; be well matched: 这是些～的选手。These contestants are well matched. /两位棋手～, 很难预料谁会胜。As the two chess players are about equal, it is very difficult to predict which of them will win.

旗号 qíhào 〈贬义〉banner; flag; pretext: 他们打着为集体的～营私舞弊。They engaged in corrupt practices under the banner of "For the benefit of the collective".

旗籍 qíjí household registered in the "Eight Banners"

旗舰 qíjiàn 〈军事〉flagship

旗开得胜 qíkāi-déshèng win a battle soon after the standard is raised; triumph in the first battle; succeed from the very start; achieve speedy success: 篮球赛一开始, 客队就～, 连得八分。As soon as the basketball match started, the visiting team took the lead, scoring eight points in quick succession.

旗袍 qípáo close-fitting woman's dress with high neck and slit skirt as worn by women of the Manchu nationality; cheongsam

旗枪 qíqiāng ❶ flagpole with a sharp metal end ❷ a kind of green tea produced in Hangzhou, Zhejiang Province

旗人 Qírén Manchu

旗纱 qíshā a kind of woollen fabric, mainly used for making flags

旗绳 qíshéng halyard

旗手 qíshǒu standard-bearer; pioneer: 孙中山是中国民主革命的伟大～。Dr. Sun Yat-sen was the great standard-bearer of the democratic revolution in China.

旗鱼 qíyú sailfish (*Istiopphorus*)

旗语 qíyǔ flag signal; semaphore

旗云 qíyún banner-shaped cloud floating above a mountain top

旗帜 qízhì ❶ banner; flag; colours: 会场上～很多。There are a lot of flags at the rally. /各运动队的前头, 都有醒目的～。Every sports team was preceded by eye-catching banners. /决议号召全体人民高举邓小平理论的～, 坚持改革开放。The resolution called on all the people to hold high the banner of Deng Xiaoping Theory and carry forward the policy of reform and opening to the world. ❷ example; model: 他是我们学习的一面～。He is an example for us to learn from.

旗帜鲜明 qízhì xiānmíng be clear-cut in one's stand: 一个人应该光明磊落, ～。One should be honest and aboveboard and take a clear stand.

旗装 qízhuāng Manchu attire

旗子 qízi flag; banner; pennant: 火车头上插着一面小～。There is a pennant on the front of the locomotive. /每人手中都摇晃着一面～。Everybody was waving a small flag.

祺

qí 〈书面〉good luck; blessing: 敬颂近～。(used at the end of a letter) Wishing you the best of luck.

琪

qí 〈书面〉fine jade: ～树 jade tree /～花瑶草 jade flowers of a fairy land

萁

qí 〈方言〉stalk: 豆～ beanstalk

棋(棊、碁)

qí ❶ chess or any board game: 跳～ chequers; draughts /围～ *weiqi*; go /象～ Chinese chess /军～ military chess /国际象～ (international) chess /下～ play chess /举～不定 hesitate about what move to make; be unable to make up one's mind; vacillate; shilly-shally ❷ piece; chessman: 落～无悔。(in chess) No retracting any move once you've made it.

棋布 qíbù as many as pieces on a chessboard; scattered all over the place: 这里群山环抱, 村落～。The place is surrounded by hills and dotted with villages.

棋错一着, 满盘皆输 qí cuò yī zhāo, mǎnpán jiē shū a false move (in chess) may mean the loss of the whole game — a wrong step may cause overall defeat

棋锋 qífēng outstanding ability as demonstrated in playing chess: ～犀利 be capable of making fast, devastating moves in chess

棋逢对手 qíféng-duìshǒu *also* "棋逢敌手" meet one's match in a game of chess; diamond cut diamond: ～, 必然有一场恶战。When Greek meets Greek, then comes the tug of war!

棋高一着, 缚手缚脚 qí gāo yī zhāo, fù shǒu fù jiǎo you play as if with your hands tied when meeting a chess opponent who is a notch above you — one is always on the receiving end when confronted with a superior opponent

棋局 qíjú ❶ situation confronting the players in a chess game ❷ 〈旧语〉chessboard

棋路 qílù tactics in chess playing: 他的～很高明。He has superior tactics in chess.

棋迷 qímí chess fan; chess enthusiast

棋盘 qípán chessboard; chequerboard; draughtboard

棋枰 qípíng 〈书面〉*see* "棋盘"

棋谱 qípǔ chess manual: 打～ play chess games as explained in a chess manual (so as to improve one's skill)

棋圣 qíshèng chess or *weiqi* player of the highest level; grand master of chess or *weiqi*

棋手 qíshǒu *also* "棋师" skilful chess or *weiqi* player

棋坛 qítán chess or *weiqi* circles: ～老将 veteran in chess (*or weiqi*) circles

棋艺 qíyì technique of playing chess: ～精湛 have superb skill in chess (*or weiqi*)

棋友 qíyǒu (one of the) people who play chess with one; chess pal

棋苑 qíyuàn world of chess; chess circles

棋峙 qízhì confrontation as in playing chess: 群雄～ situation of powerful adversaries confronting each other

棋子 qízǐ chessman; piece

蜞

qí *see* "蟛蜞" péngqí

䱻

qí

䱻鳅 qíqiū 〈动物〉dorado; dolphinfish

綦

qí 〈书面〉very; exceedingly; extremely: 言之～详 describe (explain, etc.) sth. down to every detail

綦切 qíqiè 〈书面〉urgent; ardent; earnest: 希望～ very sincere hope

骐

qí 〈书面〉black horse

骐骥 qíjì 〈书面〉thoroughbred horse

歧

qí ❶ fork; branch: *see* "～途"; "～路" ❷ divergent; varied; different: 此事意见分～。There are divergent views about the matter. /我们应该消除分～, 处理实际问题。We should sink our differences and get down to brass tacks.

歧出 qíchū fork out; be inconsistent: 文章里术语～, 引起不少混乱。The technical terms used in the article are not consistent and cause considerable confusion.

歧管 qíguǎn 〈机械〉manifold

歧化 qíhuà 〈化学〉disproportionate: ～反应 disproportionated reaction

歧路 qílù branch; forked road: 徘徊～ hesitate at a crossroads

歧路亡羊 qílù-wángyáng lose one's sheep on forked roads — lose one's bearings when the situation is too complicated or changeable

歧视 qíshì discriminate against: 种族～ racial discrimination / 妇女在许多国家里仍然受到～。Women are still discriminated against in many countries. /不要～犯过错误的青年。We must not be biased against young people who have once committed mistakes.

歧途 qítú wrong path: 引入～ lead (sb.) astray / 他自幼孤苦伶仃, 无家可归, 以致误入～。He went astray as he was homeless and alone since childhood.

歧义 qíyì different meanings; polysemy; ambiguity: 这个词有～。The word has several meanings. *or* The word is capable of various interpretations.

歧异 qíyì distinction; difference: 专家们对这个问题的见解～。Experts differ in their views on this question.

跂

qí ❶ extra toe ❷ (of insects) crawl

see also qì

岐

qí ❶ used in "岐山" (Qishan, a county in Shaanxi Province) ❷ *see* "歧" qí ❸ (Qí) a surname

岐黄 qíhuáng (As *Classic of Internal Medicine*《黄帝内经》or

Q

Medical Canon, a famous ancient book of traditional Chinese medicine, was written in the form of a dialogue between Huangdi, the legendary ruler, and Qibo 岐伯, the term "Qi Huang" came to represent traditional Chinese medicine in general) traditional Chinese medicine (TCM): 精通～ be an expert of TCM

奇 qí ❶ strange; unusual; extraordinary: 海外～谈 strange tale from overseas; traveller's tale /千古～闻 unheard-of fantastic tale /～花异草 exotic flowers and strange grasses ❷ unexpected; surprising: 出～制胜 overwhelm the enemy by a surprise attack ❸ surprise; wonder; astonish: 引以为～ consider sth. to be quite astonishing /不足为～ nothing wonderful; not at all surprising ❹ very; singularly: ～痒 awfully itchy ❺(Qí) a surname

see also jī

奇昂 qí'áng (of prices) very costly; terribly expensive; exorbitant

奇拔 qíbá towering in an unusual way; unique and outstanding: 山峰～。The peaks rise magnificently into the clouds. /他才藻～。He is an outstanding literary talent.

奇兵 qíbīng troops moving swiftly and unexpectedly (to spring a surprise attack on the enemy): 出～制胜 win victory by staging a surprise attack

Q

奇才 qícái ❶ outstanding talent; genius ❷ person of genius

奇彩 qícǎi brilliant splendour; dazzling brilliance

奇策 qícè extraordinary stratagem; superb strategy

奇耻大辱 qíchǐ-dàrǔ great shame and humiliation; deep disgrace: 我们不能忘记那些～。We will never forget those outrageous insults. /这种做法对我来说简直是～，无法忍受。Such an act is simply too monstrous and humiliating for me to tolerate. /他们怎能容忍这种～? How could they have stomached this terrible insult?

奇峰 qífēng fantastic peak: ～突起 grotesque peaks towering into the sky

奇功 qígōng outstanding service; extraordinary exploits: 屡建～ perform many daring exploits; win a series of signal successes /～殊勋 outstanding achievement and extraordinary feat

奇怪 qíguài ❶ strange; odd; eccentric: ～的性格 eccentric temperament /～的举止 odd behaviour /他的话说得有点～。What he said sounded strange. ❷ unexpected and hard to understand; incomprehensible: 他拒绝参加这样一次重要会议真叫人～。His refusal to attend this important meeting is simply incomprehensible. /这没有什么好～的。There is nothing to be surprised at. /大家都～你干吗为一点小事发脾气。All of us wondered why you lost your temper over such a trifle.

奇观 qíguān marvellous spectacle; marvel; wonder: 钱塘潮汐，天下～。The tidal waves of the Qiantang River are one of the wonders of the world. /海上日出，蔚为～。The sunrise on the sea is a spectacular sight.

奇瑰 qíguī unusual und beautiful; magnificent: ～的景象 scene of unusual beauty

奇诡 qíguǐ odd; eccentric; eerie; bizarre: 言行～ odd remarks and eccentric behaviour

奇花异卉 qíhuā-yìhuì exotic flowers and rare herbs

奇幻 qíhuàn ❶ strange and illusory: ～的遐想 fantastic reverie ❷ kaleidoscopic: 景色～ landscape of magical charm

奇货可居 qíhuò-kějū rare commodity worth hoarding (for a better price)

奇祸 qíhuò unexpected misfortune or disaster: 险遭～ escape a sudden disaster by inches

奇计 qíjì usually clever stratagem; ingenious ploy

奇技 qíjì special skill; remarkable feat

奇迹 qíjì miracle; wonder; marvel: 我们并不指望你创造～，只希望你更为勤奋些。We do not expect you to work wonders, but we do expect you to work harder. /他得了这样重的病而能迅速恢复健康，真是～! He is recovering fast from such serious illness. It's really a miracle.

奇景 qíjǐng wonderful view: 一幅无比壮丽的～ a splendid view of incomparable grandeur

奇绝 qíjué 〈书面〉wonderful; marvellous; magnificent: 怪石嶙峋，山势～。With jagged rocks of grotesque shapes, the mountain is unsurpassed in its magnificence.

奇崛 qíjué 〈书面〉distinctly peculiar: 他文笔～，不落前人窠臼。His style is markedly peculiar, untrammeled by convention.

奇谲 qíjué 〈书面〉amazing and crafty: 用兵～ use amazingly guileful tactics in directing military operations

奇丽 qílì unique and beautiful: ～的边疆风光 frontier scene of peculiar charm

奇门 qímén *also* "奇门遁甲" magic skill by which to tell what is going to happen in the future; a variety of fortune-telling

奇妙 qímiào wonderful; marvellous: ～的魔术表演 wonderful juggling performance /这座冰雕太～了。The ice carving is really superb. /他的作品表现了一种～的异国情调。His works give expression to a singular exotic sentiment.

奇谋 qímóu *see* "奇计"

奇男子 qínánzǐ man of unusual talents; remarkable man

奇南香 qínánxiāng 〈植物〉agalloch; eaglewood

奇女子 qínǚzǐ remarkable woman

奇葩 qípā exotic, enchanting flower: ～异草 exotic flowers and rare grasses /这篇小说是近来文坛上出现的一朵～。The novel is an outstanding work in the literary world in recent years.

奇癖 qípǐ rare hobby; strange addiction (to sth.)

奇僻 qípì ❶ (of language) uncommon; rare: ～的字眼儿 rarely used words ❷ exceedingly unusual; very singular: ～之服 bizarre dress

奇篇 qípiān remarkable essay; valuable text: ～秘籍 valuable rare books

奇巧 qíqiǎo (of art or handicraft) of unusual ingenuity: ～的象牙雕刻 exquisitely executed ivory carving

奇趣 qíqù wit and humour: ～横生 full of wit and humour

奇缺 qíquē be extremely short of: 这是市场上～的商品。This commodity is in great demand in the market.

奇人 qírén ❶ odd person; eccentric ❷ person of rare talent

奇事 qíshì strange affair; uncommon phenomenon

奇书 qíshū unique or remarkable book

奇谈 qítán bizarre tale; absurd argument: 真乃天下～! It is indeed the height of absurdity!

奇谈怪论 qítán-guàilùn strange theory and absurd argument; bizarre tale

奇特 qítè unusual; singular: 这把茶壶的样子很～。This teapot has a rather uncommon shape. /这幅山水画构思～，布局精妙。The composition of this landscape painting strikes one as ingenious and unusual. /草原风光具有一种说不出的～魅力。The scenery of the grasslands has an indefinable, peculiar charm.

奇突 qítū ❶ all of a sudden: 这件事来得太～了，我简直不知所措。I simply didn't know what to do with myself; the affair was so sudden. ❷ extraordinary; peculiar: 此文～之处，时足惊人。We are often struck by the stylistic peculiarities of the essay. ❸ protruding: 他用两只骨节～的手指轻轻地敲着桌子。He was beating a tattoo on the table with the protruding knuckles of two fingers.

奇伟 qíwěi extraordinary and magnificent; unusually grand: ～的北国风光 singularly magnificent landscape of northern land

奇文 qíwén ❶ singular piece of writing ❷ ludicrous writing

奇文共赏 qíwén-gòngshǎng the pleasure of reading a remarkable piece of writing should be shared

奇闻 qíwén sth. unheard-of; fantastic story: ～逸事 strange stories and anecdotes

奇袭 qíxí surprise attack; raid: ～敌营 launch a surprise attack on the enemy camp /飞兵～ make a forced march and catch the enemy unawares

奇效 qíxiào (of medicine) extraordinary efficacy: 这种药对医治肝炎有～。The medicine has a miraculous cure for hepatitis.

奇形怪状 qíxíng-guàizhuàng of grotesque shapes and appearances; fantastic in form: 满山都是～的老松。The mountain is covered with ancient pine trees of grotesque shapes and appearances.

奇秀 qíxiù extraordinary and beautiful: 峰峦～。The ridges and peaks are a scene of enchanting beauty.

奇勋 qíxūn 〈书面〉outstanding service; phenomenal contribution: 他为革命事业建立过～。He has made outstanding contributions to the revolutionary cause.

奇验 qíyàn ❶ (of medicine) miraculous efficacy ❷ (of fortune-telling) extraordinary accuracy

奇异 qíyì ❶ queer; strange; bizzare: ～的花草 exotic flowers and grasses /～的幻想 fantasies /海底是一个～的世界。The seabed is a world of wonders. ❷ curious; astounded: 看到她这身打扮，人们无不显露出～的神色。People could not help casting curious glances at her when they saw the way she was dressed.

奇遇 qíyù happy or lucky encounter; fortuitous meeting; adventure: 海外～ adventures overseas / 我与朋友阔别多年昨日重逢,真乃～。It was indeed a happy encounter that I ran into a friend of mine whom I had not seen for many years.
奇缘 qíyuán strange affair of the heart; romance
奇珍 qízhēn rarity; curio: ～异宝 rare treasures; treasures that are hard to come by
奇志 qízhì high aspirations; great ambition; lofty ideal: 他在少年时代即有～。He already had lofty ambitions when a child. / 中华儿女多～,不爱红装爱武装。China's daughters have high-aspiring minds, They love their battle array, not silks and satins.
奇装异服 qízhuāng-yìfú exotic costume; bizarre dress; outlandish attire or outfit: 那些穿～的年轻人大都是嬉皮士。Those youngsters in bizarre clothes are mostly hippies.

琦

qí 〈书面〉❶ fine jade ❷ out of the ordinary run; uncommon: ～行 fine virtues; noble character

埼(碕)

qí 〈书面〉meandering coast or bank

崎

qí 〈书面〉sloping; uneven; rugged: ～径 rugged path
崎岖 qíqū rugged; rough: ～不平 rough and uneven / 人生的道路是～的。Life is full of twists and turns. *or* Life's journey is not plain sailing.

锜

qí 〈古语〉❶ tripod cooker ❷ chisel

骑

qí ❶ ride; sit (on a horse, etc.): ～自行车 ride a bicycle; cycle / ～在某人背上 ride on sb.'s back / ～驴觅驴 look for a donkey while riding one — be absent-minded ❷ straddle: *see* "～楼" ❸ horse or other animal one rides: 坐～ one's mount ❹ cavalryman; cavalry; horseman or rider: 轻～(兵) light cavalry(man); hussar / 铁～ cavalry; good war horse / 车～ horse and carriage
骑兵 qíbīng horse soldier; cavalryman; cavalry: ～部队 mounted troops; cavalry unit
骑缝 qífèng junction of the edges of two sheets of paper: ～印 (put a) seal across (two sheets of) a voucher
骑虎难下 qíhǔ-nánxià ride a tiger and find it hard to dismount; get a tiger by the tail and be unable to let go; have no way to back down: 事到如今,已经是～了。As things stand, it is already impossible to back down.
骑虎之势 qíhǔzhīshì like one who rides a tiger — difficult situation; awkward predicament; dilemma: 已成～ be caught on the horns of a dilemma; find oneself in an impasse
骑楼 qílóu 〈方言〉arcade-house
骑马订 qímǎdìng 〈印刷〉saddle stitching
骑马找马 qímǎ-zhǎomǎ look for a horse on horseback — try to find sth. which one already has; hold on to one's job while seeking a new one
骑枪 qíqiāng carbine
骑墙 qíqiáng sit on or straddle the fence: ～派 fencesitter; weathercock
骑射 qíshè horsemanship and archery: 善～ excel in horsemanship and archery / 蒙古族士兵精于～。Soldiers of Mongolian nationality are excellent horsemen and archers.
骑士 qíshì knight; cavalier
骑手 qíshǒu rider; jockey
骑术 qíshù horsemanship; equestrian skill
骑月雨 qíyuèyǔ rain which keeps falling from the end of one month to the beginning of the next

畦

qí rectangular pieces of land in a field surrounded by ridges: 菜～ vegetable bed / 两～白菜 two beds growing cabbages
畦灌 qíguàn 〈农业〉method of irrigation by which the land to be irrigated is divided into small plots bordered with ridges; plot-by-plot irrigation
畦田 qítián 〈农业〉plot of land bordered by earth ridges for the purpose of irrigation and water storage; embanked field
畦作 qízuò 〈农业〉plant crop seedlings in small plots of land bordered by earth ridges

俟

qí *see* "万俟" Mòqí
see also sì

旂

qí ❶〈古语〉dragon flag with bells on tassels ❷ *see* "旗❶"

祈

qí ❶ pray: ～雨 pray for rain / ～福 pray for good fortune ❷ request; entreat: 不当之处,敬～赐教。I hope you will not spare your advice if there is anything inappropriate. ❸ (Qí) a surname
祈祷 qídǎo pray; say one's prayers: 举行～仪式 hold a prayer session
祈年 qínián pray for a bumper harvest
祈年殿 Qíniándiàn Hall of Prayer for Good Harvests (in the Temple of Heaven, Beijing)
祈请 qíqǐng earnestly request; beseech
祈求 qíqiú plead for; earnestly hope: ～谅解 beseech sb.'s understanding / ～饶恕 plead for pardon
祈使句 qíshǐjù 〈语言〉imperative sentence
祈望 qíwàng hope; wish: 春节将临,～早归。As the Spring Festival is drawing near, it is our hope that you will return at an early date. / ～鼎力支持。We hope to have your full support.
祈愿 qíyuàn ❶ hope; wish: 他～与亲人早日团聚。He hoped for an early reunion with his family. ❷ desire: 使国家富强是我们的～。It is our aspiration to make our country prosperous and strong.

圻

qí 〈书面〉boundary
see also yín

颀

qí 〈书面〉tall
颀长 qícháng 〈书面〉tall; of high stature
颀伟 qíwěi (of human stature) tall and strong; big

蕲[1](蘄)

qí 〈书面〉beg

蕲[2](蘄)

Qí ❶ Qizhou (蕲州, former prefecture which had its capital city south of the present Qichun 蕲春 County, Hubei Province) ❷ a surname
蕲艾 qí'ài Chinese mugwort (*Aztemisia argyi*)
蕲求 qíqiú 〈书面〉beg; implore
蕲蛇 qíshé 〈动物〉long-nosed pit viper

疧

qí 〈书面〉disease; malady

祇

qí 〈书面〉god of the earth: 天神地～ all the gods of heaven and earth

芪

qí *see* "黄芪" huángqí

耆

qí over sixty years of age: ～年 old age
耆艾 qí'ài 〈书面〉old people
耆旧 qíjiù 〈书面〉old acquaintances of advanced age; esteemed old people
耆老 qílǎo 〈书面〉man of advanced age; old man
耆年硕德 qínián-shuòdé of venerable age and great virtue; of advanced years and moral integrity: 评审委员由几位～的一流专家担任。The evaluation committee was composed of several elderly and prestigious experts who were all leading authorities in their respective fields of study.
耆绅 qíshēn 〈书面〉old gentleman
耆宿 qísù esteemed old people (of a community): ～大贤 venerable sage

鬐

qí 〈书面〉horse mane

鳍

qí 〈动物〉fin: 胸～ pectoral fin / 腹～ ventral fin / 背～ dorsal fin / 臀～ anal fin / 尾～ caudal fin
鳍鲸 qíjīng *also* "长须鲸" chángxūjīng fin whale; finback whale; razobrack whale; *Balaenoptera physalus*
鳍足 qízú 〈动物〉clasper
鳍足动物 qízú dòngwù Pinnipedia; pinniped

Q

qǐ

启(啟、啓) qǐ ❶ open:亲~ open personally (set expression written after the name of the person to whom the letter is delivered); private ❷ enlighten; inspire; awaken: *see* "~发"❸ start; begin; initiate:承上~下 form a connecting link between the preceding and the following (as in a piece of writing) ❹〈书面〉state; declare; inform:敬~者 I beg to state (set expression used at the beginning of a letter) /谨~ respectfully yours (set expression formally written after one's signature in a letter to one's parents, elders, superiors, etc.) ❺〈书面〉letter; note:书~ letter /谢~ note of thanks; thank-you note /小~ brief note ❻ (Qǐ) a surname

启禀 qǐbǐng report (to one's superior, elder, etc.)

启程 qǐchéng set out; set off; start on a journey:从西安~ set out from Xi'an /明早七点~ leave at seven tomorrow morning /他已~去中东进行正式访问。He has left for the Middle East on an official visit.

启齿 qǐchǐ open one's mouth; mention:不便~ find it difficult to mention /他狠下一条心,把难以~的话说了出来。He made a painful decision to unburden himself of what he had found very difficult to broach to anybody.

启唇 qǐchún open one's mouth; speak

启德机场 Qǐdé Jīchǎng (HK) Kai Tak Airport (no longer in use)

启迪 qǐdí 〈书面〉enlighten; inspire; shed light on:受到~ be enlightened /好书可以增长知识,~智慧。Good books can augment people's knowledge and sharpen their intellect. /我在他的~下提高了政治认识。Under his guidance, I increased my political awareness.

启碇 qǐdìng weigh anchor:~出航 weigh anchor and set sail

启动 qǐdòng start (a machine, etc.); turn on; switch on;〈经济〉start up:~电机 switch on the motor /项目~ start-up of a project /水泵~了。The water pump has been started.

启动电压 qǐdòng diànyā starting voltage; trigger voltage

启动继电器 qǐdòng jìdiànqì starting relay

启动期 qǐdòngqī start-up phase:联合国维和行动~ start-up phase of a UN peace-keeping operation

启动系统 qǐdòng xìtǒng start-up system

启动资金 qǐdòng zījīn start-up fund; seed money

启发 qǐfā arouse; stimulate; inspire; enlighten:受到很大~ be greatly inspired /~性 instructive; enlightening; thought-provoking /~诱导 enlighten and persuade /老师应善于~学生的思维。Teachers ought to be good at setting the students thinking.

启发式 qǐfāshì elicitation method (of teaching); heuristic method

启封 qǐfēng unseal; break or remove the seal; open an envelope:当众~ remove the seal in public / 这个酒坛子尚未~。The wine jug is still sealed.

启航 qǐháng set sail; weigh anchor:鸣笛~ sound the siren and weigh anchor /解缆~ unmoor and set sail

启口 qǐkǒu open one's mouth; start to talk:我尚未~,他就来了个先发制人的批评。He made a preemptive criticism of me before I opened my mouth.

启蒙 qǐméng ❶ impart elementary knowledge to beginners; initiate:~教师 teacher who initiates his students into a specific field of study /~书籍 children's primers ❷ enlighten:祛蔽~ free from ignorance /人类的~时代 age of enlightenment of mankind

启蒙运动 qǐméng yùndòng Enlightenment:欧洲~ European Enlightenment Movement (of the 18th century)

启明星 Qǐmíngxīng 〈天文〉Venus

启瓶器 qǐpíngqì bottle opener

启示 qǐshì enlightenment; inspiration; revelation:他这话给了我很大的~。I was greatly enlightened by what he said. /这个笑话颇能~人思索一些问题。This joke provides much food for thought (*or* sets people thinking).

启示录 Qǐshìlù 〈基督教〉*The Revelation* or *The Apocalypse* (the last book of the *New Testament*)

启示神学 qǐshì shénxué 〈基督教〉revealed theology

启事 qǐshì notice; announcement:招领~ announcement for claiming lost property; lost-and-found notice /寻人~ notice of looking for a missing person

启衅 qǐxìn start a quarrel; provoke a dispute; kick up a row:对方是这场边界冲突的~者。The other side was responsible for provoking this border clash.

启行 qǐxíng set out; start on a journey:~赴沪 set off for Shanghai; go on a trip to Shanghai

启颜 qǐyán (of a face) light up:~一笑 beam with joy; light up with joy

启用 qǐyòng start using; employ:经上级批准,本局自即日起~新公章。With the approval of the superior authorities, the bureau starts using its new official seal as from today. / 新楼的电梯明晨六时~。The lift in the new building will start operation at 6 o'clock tomorrow morning. /要大胆~年轻人。We must boldly employ young people.

启用前检查 qǐyòngqián jiǎnchá 〈计算机〉readiness review

启运 qǐyùn start shipment (of goods); ship:发往灾区的救济物资已经~。Relief goods are being shipped to the disaster-stricken area. *or* The shipment of relief goods for the disaster-stricken area is on the way.

启运地船边交货价 qǐyùndì chuánbiān jiāohuòjià free alongside ship

启运点交货价 qǐyùndiǎn jiāohuòjià FOB (free on board) shipping point

启运港 qǐyùngǎng port of departure

启运国 qǐyùnguó country of departure; country of shipment

启运机场交货价 qǐyùn jīchǎng jiāohuòjià FOB airport

启运价格 qǐyùn jiàgé shipment price

启运日期 qǐyùn rìqī date of departure; date of shipment

启运重量 qǐyùn zhòngliàng shipping weight

启蛰 qǐzhé (of insects) wake up in spring after hibernation

启奏 qǐzòu (of officials) present one's views on state affairs or clarify certain issues to the emperor

棨 qǐ 〈古语〉object used to certify an official's identity when he was on an inspection tour

棨戟 qǐjǐ 〈古语〉guard of honour preceding the carriage of a senior official on his inspection tour

綮 qǐ 〈古语〉calf (of the leg)

綮 qǐ *see* "棨" qǐ
see also qìng

企 qǐ stand on tiptoe; look forward to; expect:延颈~踵 crane forward and stand on tiptoe in anticipation /~候回音 eagerly look forward to hearing from you

企待 qǐdài look forward to; expect:妈妈~着儿子的音讯。The mother is looking forward to hearing from her son.

企祷 qǐdǎo eagerly expect; earnestly hope:~迅作决定,刻日南旋。We earnestly hope that you will make a prompt decision and return to the south instantly.

企鹅 qǐ'é 〈动物〉penguin

企及 qǐjí aspire to reach; try to catch up with:难以~ can hardly expect to attain

企口 qǐkǒu 〈建筑〉tongue-and-groove:~接合 tongue-and-groove joint; match joint

企口板 qǐkǒubǎn 〈建筑〉board with a tongue on one end and a groove on the other; matched board

企慕 qǐmù admire; esteem:我~这位教授的为人。I hold the professor in high esteem for his noble character.

企盼 qǐpàn expect; hope for:~未来,不胜雀跃。We jumped for joy at the bright prospects ahead.

企求 qǐqiú seek for; yearn for; hanker after:~和平 crave for peace /~名利 hanker after fame and profit /~出国深造 desire to go abroad for advanced studies

企图 qǐtú attempt; try; strive; seek:~暗中操纵大会 seek to manipulate the conference behind the scenes /不要~推卸自己应该承担的责任。Don't try to shirk your responsibility.

企望 qǐwàng look forward to; hope for; aspire; expect:父母总~孩子在学习上出人头地。Parents always expect their children to distinguish themselves in their studies.

企羡 qǐxiàn admire; envy

企业 qǐyè enterprise; business:中小~ small and medium-sized enterprises /乡镇~ rural enterprise; township enterprise /~法 law of

enterprises /～核算 business accounting /～管理 business management /～承包经营责任制 contract managerial responsibility system in enterprises; enterprise-contract responsibility system /～自我约束的机制 self-regulating mechanism of enterprises

企业化 qǐyèhuà ❶ (of business, transport and other departments) calculate profits and losses on principles of economic accounting ❷ reorganize a non-profit-making unit along the lines of an enterprise to ensure a steady income

企业集团 qǐyè jítuán enterprise group; association of enterprises

企业家 qǐyèjiā entrepreneur; enterpriser

企业结构 qǐyè jiégòu enterprise structure

企业精神 qǐyè jīngshén entrepreneurship

企业群体 qǐyè qúntǐ group or association of enterprises

企业升级 qǐyè shēngjí enterprise upgrading

企业文化 qǐyè wénhuà corporate culture

企业自主权 qǐyè zìzhǔquán decision-making power or autonomy of enterprises

企足而待 qǐzú'érdài wait on tiptoe; expect with eagerness: 随着科学的发展，实现人们的许多梦想，可以～了。With the advancement of science, we can now look forward to the realization of many of man's dreams.

稽

qǐ

see also jī

稽首 qǐshǒu kowtow

乞

qǐ ❶ beg (for alms, etc.); seek charity; supplicate: 行～ go begging /～恕 beg sb.'s pardon; ask sb. for forgiveness ❷ (Qǐ) a surname

乞哀告怜 qǐ'āi-gàolián beg for mercy; beg piteously: 荒时暴月，向亲友～，借得几斗几升，敷衍三日五日。In hard times they piteously begged for help from relatives and friends, borrowing a few *dou* or *sheng* of grain which would last them a few days.

乞贷 qǐdài 〈书面〉ask for a loan; beg for a loan: 他近来手头很紧，只好向友人～。He is so hard up nowadays that he has to ask for a loan from his friends.

乞儿 qǐ'ér beggar

乞丐 qǐgài beggar

乞力马扎罗. Qǐlìmǎzhāluó Kilimanjaro, a volcanic massif in northern Tanzania, the highest peak in Africa (5898m.)

乞怜 qǐlián beg for pity or mercy; 摇尾～ be like a dog wagging its tail to seek pity; abjectly beg for mercy; fawn obsequiously /谁也不会料到那个自命为英雄的人竟然跪倒在敌人面前～。Nobody would have imagined that the self-styled hero would go down on his knees before the enemy to beg for mercy.

乞灵 qǐlíng 〈书面〉invoke help from deities; have recourse to; resort to; seek help from: ～鬼神 seek help from supernatural beings /这班人不肯与我们公开辩论，只有～于谣言和诽谤。They refused to argue with us and the only thing they could do was to resort to rumour-mongering and slander.

乞盟 qǐméng sue for peace

乞免 qǐmiǎn ❶beg for forgiveness; beg off: ～受罚 beg for exemption from punishment ❷ request to be relieved of office

乞巧 qǐqiǎo 〈旧语〉on the evening of the seventh day of the seventh moon, young women offer melons and other fruit to the Weaving Maid and pray to her that she may teach them the skill of sewing and embroidering (in Chinese mythology the Cowherd and the Weaving Maid are lovers allowed to meet in heaven only once a year on that day)

乞求 qǐqiú beg for; entreat; implore: ～施舍 beg for alms (*or* handouts) /受害者～地方当局对此事立即进行调查。The victims besought the local authorities to conduct an immediate investigation into the matter. /他～友人的谅解。He entreated his friends for understanding.

乞师 qǐshī 〈书面〉ask for reinforcements: 兵败被围，向朝廷～。Defeated and under seige, they had to ask the royal court for reinforcements.

乞食 qǐshí beg for food: ～街头 beg for food on the street

乞讨 qǐtǎo beg; go begging: 向行人～ beg (for) money from passers-by

乞降 qǐxiáng beg to surrender; wave the white flag: 他们兵败～。When they were defeated in battle, they hoisted the white flag.

乞援 qǐyuán ask for assistance; beg for aid; beg for reinforcements: 他们多方～。They asked for assistance from many quarters.

起[1]

qǐ ❶ get up; rise; arise; stand up: ～五更，睡半夜 rise at daybreak and retire at midnight /拍案而～ stand up pounding the desk; smite the table and rise to one's feet ❷ move; leave: ～重 lift and move heavy objects ❸ rise; go up: 气球从地面～来了。The balloon is rising from the ground. /皮球不～了。This rubber ball won't bounce. ❹ get; appear: ～痱子 get prickly heat /头上～了一个包。He got a lump on the forehead. /一见风，他身上就～疙瘩。He breaks into goose pimples when he is exposed to the wind. ❺ remove; draw; extract; pull: ～螺丝钉 draw out a screw /到栈房～货 get the goods from a warehouse ❻ crop up; rise; grow: ～风。The wind rose. /～浪。The waves are rising up. /他～了坏心。An evil idea occurred to him. *or* He conceived an evil design. /这病是怎么～的? What is the cause of the illness? ❼ initiate; launch: 发～ initiate /～师 launch an expedition; start an armed revolt /掀～高潮 bring sth. to a climax ❽ draft; make; work out: ～草稿 make (*or* work out) a draft /这孩子的名儿是他爷爷～的。The baby's name was given by its grandpa. ❾ set up; put up; build: ～道墙 build a wall /～伙 set up a mess /～了三间新房 put up a three-room house ❿ obtain; secure; buy: ～执照 secure a licence /～行李票 get a luggage check /～护照 obtain a passport ⓫ start; begin: ～止 beginning and end /从今天～实行新规定。New regulations go into effect as from today. /本条例自公布之日～实行。This regulation takes effect on the day of its publication. ⓬ *used after verbs to indicate the beginning or starting point*: 从头做～ start from the very beginning; start all over again from the beginning /一部二十四史不知从何说～。The situation is so complicated that I really don't know where to start. ⓭〈方言〉*used before nouns of time and place to indicate the point of departure*: 您～哪儿来? Where did you come from? ⓮〈方言〉*used before nouns of place to indicate movement*: 我看见一个人～窗户外走过去。I saw a man passing by the window.

起[2]

qǐ ❶〈量词〉case; instance: 前天发生一～火灾。A fire broke out the day before yesterday. /昨天发生两～交通事故。Two traffic accidents ocurred yesterday. ❷〈量词〉batch; group; party: 他们分三～上车。They boarded the train in three batches. /闯进来一～来历不明的人。In rushed a group of people of dubious background.

起

qi ❶ *used after verbs to indicate upward movement*: 抬～头来 raise one's head /鸟儿飞～又落下。The bird took to its wings and then alighted. ❷ *used after verbs and often preceded by* 不 *or* 得 *to indicate whether it is within or beyond one's power to do sth.*: 惹不～ cannot afford to offend sb. /经得～考验 be able to stand the test /太贵了买不～。This is so expensive that I can't afford it. ❸ *used after verbs to indicate sth. happening right after the action*: 奏～国歌 play the national anthem /点～篝火 light a bonfire ❹ *used after verbs to indicate the person or thing involved in the action*: 他提～了这件事。He mentioned the event.

起岸 qǐ'àn unload a ship: ～时间 unloading time

起霸 qǐbà 〈戏曲〉(of warriors) adjust helmet and armour upon entrance on stage

起爆 qǐbào detonate: ～帽 detonating cap /～剂 detonating agent; primer /～药 detonating powder

起笔 qǐbǐ ❶ first stroke of a Chinese character ❷ start of each stroke in writing a Chinese character

起兵 qǐbīng ❶ bring one's soldiers into battle; despatch troops: ～抗敌 despatch troops to resist enemy invasion ❷launch an armed revolt

起驳 qǐbó begin shipping goods by barge or lighter

起搏器 qǐbóqì 〈医学〉pacemaker: 埋入～ implanted pacemaker /体外～ external pacemaker

起步 qǐbù ❶〈方言〉leave; start to move: 车子～了。The car is starting. ❷ start doing sth.: 我们的事业刚刚～。We have just made a start in our undertaking. /这个乡镇在经济改革方面～较晚，落后于本地很多别的乡镇。The township started later than it should in the race for economic reform, and so it is falling behind many others.

起草 qǐcǎo draft; draw up: ～文稿 draft a document /～一个计划 draw up a plan /～人 draftsman

起草委员会 qǐcǎo wěiyuánhuì drafting committee

起场 qǐcháng gather the unhusked grains from the thrashing ground
起承转合 qǐ-chéng-zhuǎn-hé introduction, elucidation of the theme, change of approach and summing up — the four steps in the composition of an essay; opening, developing, changing and concluding — the four steps of Chinese classic writing; composition of an essay
起程 qǐchéng set out; start a journey:车队明早七点～。The convoy is to set out at 7 tomorrow morning. /我一早～，中午就可到达北京。I could get to Beijing at noon if I start the journey early in the morning.
起初 qǐchū originally; initially; at first; at the beginning:这篇文章～我读不懂，后来才慢慢悟出点道理。At first, I couldn't quite make out this essay, but then I gradually came to grasp what it was all about. /他的意见我～是不同意的。I did not agree with his view originally. *or* At the beginning I was not buying his idea.
起床 qǐchuáng get up; get out of bed: 他还没有～。He is not up yet.
起床号 qǐchuánghào reveille: 司号兵正在吹～。The bugler was blowing (*or* sounding) the reveille.
起打 qǐdǎ 〈戏曲〉 start of martial acrobatics
起道机 qǐdàojī 〈铁路〉 track jack
起点 qǐdiǎn ❶ starting point: ～站 starting station /大规模建设的～ starting point for large-scale construction ❷ starting line or mark of a race:百米跑～ starting line for the 100-metre dash
起点运费 qǐdiǎn yùnfèi minimum freight; minimum charge per bill of lading
起电 qǐdiàn 〈物理〉 electrification; charge: ～机 electrizer / ～盘 electrophorus
起吊 qǐdiào lift heavy objects with a crane
起钉锤 qǐdīngchuí claw hammer
起钉杆 qǐdīnggǎn wrenching bar
起钉钳 qǐdīngqián nail nippers
起碇 qǐdìng weigh anchor:航船～。The ship weighed anchor.
起动 qǐdòng start (a machine, etc.): ～电动机 starting motor
起动机 qǐdòngjī starter
起端 qǐduān (of an event, etc.) origin; beginning:事情的～在一年以前。The matter had its beginning a year ago.
起发 qǐfa 〈方言〉 gain by cheating: 要～他的钱可不那么容易。It's not that easy to swindle him out of his money.
起反 qǐfǎn 〈方言〉 rebel; revolt:这里是晚清捻军～的地方。This is where the Nian Army rose in the late Qing Dynasty.
起飞 qǐfēi ❶ (of aircraft) take off: ～全重 all-up weight / 982 航班十点～。Flight 982 takes off at 10 o'clock. ❷ (of an enterprise or economy) take off; be off to a flying start:经济～ economic takeoff/这个厂所以能～，主要靠科学管理。It is mainly because of its scientific method of management that the factory has started to develop speedily. *or* The economic takeoff of the factory largely depends on the scientific way it is managed.
起伏 qǐfú ❶ rise and fall; undulate:连绵～的群山 meandering mountain ranges /波浪汹涌～。The roaring waves rise and fall (*or* roll on). ❷(of emotions, relationship, etc.) rise and fall; surge and subside:心潮～。One's thoughts surged and subsided alternately like the waves. *or* One feels in one's heart a sudden onrush of undulating emotion. /他俩的关系有些～。There have been ups and downs in their relations.
起复 qǐfù ❶ 〈旧语〉 be called upon to assume duties before the mourning period for one's parents is over; (in the Ming and Qing dynasties) resume office after the period of mourning for one's parents ends ❷ (of officials) be reappointed after removal from office
起稿 qǐgǎo make a draft; draft:决议草案由谁～? Who will undertake to draft the resolution?
起根 qǐgēn 〈方言〉 all along; from the very beginning:这件事我～儿就不同意。I did not agree to it from the very beginning. *or* I've disapproved of it all along.
起根由头 qǐgēn-yóutóu (state) from the very beginning; from start to finish:他～把事情的经过详细地说了一遍。He recounted the whole story from start to finish. *or* He gave an account of the ins and outs of the whole matter.
起更 qǐgēng 〈旧语〉 sound the first night watch
起轨机 qǐguǐjī track winch; track lifter
起旱 qǐhàn take an overland route; trek:从远方城镇～去长沙 trek to Changsha from a distant town
起航 qǐháng begin a voyage or flight; take off; set sail
起哄 qǐhòng ❶ gather together to create a disturbance:大伙儿别跟着～。You gentlemen should stay away from the brawl. /你是真不懂这儿的规矩还是～? Do you really not know the rules here, or are you out to pick a quarrel? ❷ (of a crowd of people) make fun of; play a joke on:你们别跟我～，好不好? Please stop making fun of me, will you?
起花 qǐhua *see* "起火" qǐhuo
起火 qǐhuǒ ❶ cook meals:儿媳单独过，自己～。My daughter-in-law lives apart from us and cooks her own meals. ❷ (of fire) break out:楼上～了。A fire has broken out upstairs. ❸ get worked up; become angry; flare up:有话慢慢说，你先别～儿。Tell us calmly what you've got to say. Don't fly off the handle.
起火 qǐhuo a kind of firecracker
起获 qǐhuò recover stolen goods or contraband from hoarding places:这次发还的被窃财物是最近破获三个盗窃集团时～的。The stolen goods and money being returned to the owners were recovered when three gangs of thieves were captured.
起急 qǐjí 〈方言〉 get anxious; be worried:他就是这么个慢性人儿，你越～，他越沉得住气。He is such a slow coach that the more anxious you get the more unhurried he becomes. /这是个细活儿，不能～。This piece of work requires care and must not be rushed.
起家 qǐjiā build up; grow and thrive; become prosperous; make one's fortune, name, etc.:白手～ build up from nothing; start from scratch /这家公司靠一台复印机～。This firm has grown and prospered starting with a photocopier.
起价 qǐjià 〈方言〉 raise prices; jack up prices
起驾 qǐjià (of emperors or kings) set out (now often used humorously):阁下何时～? When is Your Excellency leaving?
起见 qǐjiàn (used together with 为 wèi) for the purpose of; in order to:为醒目～ to attract attention /为慎重～，我们再来征求一下你的意见。To make doubly sure, we have come again to solicit your advice.
起讲 qǐjiǎng third "leg" of the "eight-legged" essay (a kind of stereotyped writing composed of eight parts and prescribed for the imperial examinations), where a general statement is made marking the beginning of the main theme
起降 qǐjiàng (of airplanes) take off and land:我们要修建供喷气飞机～的大型机场。We'll build a large airfield for jet planes to take off and land.
起脚 qǐjiǎo 〈方言〉 start walking:从～到城里，要步行二十多里地。We'll have to walk over 20 *li* to get to town from here.
起解 qǐjiè 〈旧语〉 send (prisoners) away under escort; be taken (to one's place of exile, etc.) under escort
起劲 qǐjìn vigorously; energetically; zealously; enthusiastically:活儿干得很～ work vigorously /谈得十分～ talk enthusiastically /他工作似乎不很～。He seems to be showing little zeal in his work. /组织课外活动他特别～。He was particularly keen on organizing extra-curricular activities.
起敬 qǐjìng call forth a feeling of respect; inspire respect:令人肃然～ call forth a feeling of profound respect
起居 qǐjū daily life:孩子在托儿所，饮食～都有规律。Children in the nursery observe a regular schedule of daily life.
起居室 qǐjūshì living-room; sitting-room
起居注 qǐjūzhù ❶ record of the emperor's everyday remarks and actions ❷ official historian who records the emperor's remarks and deeds
起句 qǐjù first line of a poem:这首诗的～就不同凡响。The very first line of the poem is out of the common run.
起圈 qǐjuàn remove manure from a cattle pen, pigsty, sheepfold, etc.
起开 qǐkai 〈方言〉 step aside; stand aside:劳驾，～一点儿，让我过去。Excuse me, will you please step aside and let me pass.
起课 qǐkè resort to divination (by tossing coins, or counting the Heavenly Stems and Earthly Branches on one's fingers)
起来 qǐlai ❶ rise; stand up; sit up:从前座儿上～一个中年人，慷慨激昂地驳斥这个新建议。From the front row rose a middle-aged man, who started to argue vehemently against the new proposal. /他坐时间长了，有时还得～伸伸懒腰。He had to stand up for a good stretch after having sat long. ❷ get out of bed; get up:快叫他～，有急事商量。Tell him to get up quickly, I have something urgent to discuss

with him. ❸ rise; arise; arouse: ～反抗迫害 rise against persecution / 群众的劲头～了。The enthusiasm of the masses has been aroused. / 从青年中～一大批人才。A large number of talented people are coming to the fore from among the youth.

起来 qǐlai ❶ *used after verbs to indicate upward movement*: 太阳升～了。The sun has risen. /请把头抬～。Raise your head, please. / 中国人民站～了。The Chinese people have stood up. ❷ *used after verbs or adjectives to indicate the commencement and continuation of action or state*: 欢呼～ start to cheer /紧张～ key up /一句话引得人们笑了～。The remark set people laughing. /讨论不～。The discussion failed to get going. /天冷～了。It is getting cold. ❸ *used after verbs to indicate the completion of action or the achievement of goals*: 把大家意见集中～。Let's pool our ideas. /我想不～了。I can't recall it. *or* It has slipped my memory. /这项工作开展～了。The work is under way. ❹ *used after verbs to indicate an impression, estimate or idea*: 听～不错。It sounds all right. /说～话长。It's a long story. /算～,他已去了一个月了。I calculate that he has been away for a month. /说～容易, 做～难。It's easier said than done. / 看～如果要把这件事办好还得做很多工作。It seems that much remains to be done if we want to make a success of the work.

起雷 qǐléi remove or clear mines

起立 qǐlì stand up; rise to one's feet: ～表决 vote by sitting and standing /～欢呼 standing ovation /全体～。Stand up, everybody. *or* All stand up. /人们纷纷～致敬。All rose to their feet as a mark of respect for him.

起灵 qǐlíng carry a coffin to the burial ground

起垄 qǐlǒng 〈农业〉 ridging: ～犁 furrower; ridging plough; ridger/ ～器 tie ridger

起落 qǐluò go up and come down; rise and fall: 我看见直升飞机频繁～。I saw helicopters land and take off in quick succession.

起落架 qǐluòjià 〈航空〉 landing gear; alighting gear; undercarriage: ～放下 gear down; landing gear lowering /～收上 gear up; landing gear raising / ～支柱 undercarriage leg; landing gear leg /～轮胎 gear tyre

起落架舱 qǐluòjiàcāng landing gear compartment

起码 qǐmǎ ❶ minimum; rudimentary; basic; elementary: 经济学的～知识 ABC of economics /对当前形势缺乏～的了解 lack a minimum understanding of the present-day situation /这些是研究生～的条件。These are basic requirements for graduate students. /任何国家都不能违反国际关系中～的准则。No country can go against the most rudimentary principles governing international relations. ❷ at least: 这座大楼～可住一百户。This tall apartment building can accommodate at least 100 families. /这篇文章最～也要到明天才能写好。This essay won't be finished until tomorrow at the earliest.

起毛 qǐmáo ❶ be scared; get gooseflesh: 一听说他舅舅明天来,他心里直～。He felt disconcerted upon learning that his uncle would be coming the next day. ❷(of woollen cloth) pill: 这种特殊加工的毛料不会～。This specially processed woollen material does not pill. ❸ 〈纺织〉 teasel: ～机 teaseller

起锚 qǐmáo weigh anchor; set sail

起苗 qǐmiáo move seedlings from the nursery for transplantation

起名儿 qǐmíngr give a name; name: 给孩子起个名儿 give the baby a name /他～叫约翰。He was named (*or* christened) John.

起腻 qǐnì 〈口语〉 ❶ call forth a feeling of boredom; be bored: 一看见油炸的东西就～。I'm sick at the sight of fried stuff. ❷ pester: 这孩子老爱跟人～。The child is always pestering people for something.

起跑 qǐpǎo 〈体育〉 start of a race: 这个运动员由于～犯规被取消比赛资格。The athlete was disqualified for making false starts.

起跑线 qǐpǎoxiàn starting line (for a race); scratch line (for a relay race): 在同一～上展开公平竞争 engage in fair competition by setting off from the same starting line

起泡 qǐpào ❶ blister; bubble: 手臂上～ raise a blister on one's arm ❷ foam: ～剂 blowing (*or* foaming) agent

起疱 qǐpào vesiculate

起讫 qǐ-qì beginning and end

起球 qǐqiú (of woollen or dacron materials) pill: 这种人造纤维爱～。This synthetic material pills easily.

起绒机 qǐróngjī 〈纺织〉 cloth raising machine; teasel

起色 qǐsè signs of improvement: 病势未见～。The patient shows no signs of improvement. /生产大有～。Production is evidently picking up.

起晌 qǐshǎng 〈方言〉 get up after a nap: 刚～, 就下地干活儿。He went to work in the field right after a noontime nap.

起身 qǐshēn ❶ go off; set out; depart; leave: 明日他～去厦门。He is leaving for Xiamen tomorrow. ❷ get up; get out of bed: 他每天六点就得～去上班。He has to get up at six every morning to go to work. ❸ stand up; rise: 她～去开门。She rose to open the door.

起始 qǐshǐ 〈口语〉 from the outset; at first: ～他有点吃惊, 过一会儿才镇定下来。At first he was somewhat shocked, but he calmed down after a little while.

起事 qǐshì start an armed rising: 这支农民军是在 1540 年 7 月 9 日～的。The peasant army staged an uprising on 9 July 1540.

起誓 qǐshì take an oath; swear; vow: 对天～ swear by God /他～不把这件事情说出去。He vowed to keep the matter secret. *or* He swore that he would never let out the secret.

起手 qǐshǒu get sth. started; set about doing sth.: 这件事一～就碰到麻烦。We ran into trouble over this right from the beginning.

起手回春 qǐshǒu-huíchūn *also* "妙手回春" miàoshǒu-huíchūn; "着手成春" zhuóshǒu-chéngchūn effect a miraculous cure; save a patient who is critically ill

起首 qǐshǒu at first; initially; originally: ～事情便不顺当。The matter was far from plain sailing at the outset.

起水 qǐshuǐ ❶〈方言〉 get rich ❷ catch fish from a fish farm

起死回生 qǐsǐ-huíshēng (of a doctor's skill) bring life to the dying; raise from the dead: ～之术 skill to save a patient from the brink of death /～的灵丹妙药 elixir for deadly diseases /求一个～之法 find a formula for bringing the dead back to life

起死人,肉白骨 qǐ sǐrén, ròu báigǔ revive the dead and flesh up the bones — do sb. a great kindness

起酥油 qǐsūyóu shortening

起诉 qǐsù 〈法律〉 bring a suit or an action against sb.; take legal proceedings; sue; prosecute: 如果他们不肯协商解决, 我们要～。If they refuse to settle the matter through consultation, we will sue.

起诉权 qǐsùquán 〈法律〉 right of action; right to bring an action; legal capacity to sue

起诉人 qǐsùrén suitor; prosecutor

起诉书 qǐsùshū 〈法律〉 indictment; bill of complaint

起粟 qǐsù 〈方言〉 skin rashes

起算 qǐsuàn start counting (from a specific point): 从教小学时～, 她已经在各类学校执教三十多年了。Starting from the days when she taught in a primary school, she has been teaching in various types of schools for over thirty years.

起跳 qǐtiào 〈体育〉 take off: ～板 take-off board /～线 take-off line (*or* mark) /～高度 trial height /他从一米八十～。He started to jump at 1.8 metres.

起头 qǐtóu ❶ start; commence: 先从我这儿～。Start from me first. /你先给大家起个头儿吧。Please give us a lead. /万事～难。All things are difficult at the start. ❷ at first; at the outset; in the beginning: ～谁也不知道事情会这么难办。At first, nobody knew that things would turn out to be so difficult. ❸ beginning; start: 这事儿你从～儿给他说一遍。Please explain the matter to him again from the very beginning.

起网 qǐwǎng (net) hauling: ～机 hauling machine; net hauler /～速度 hauling speed; hauling velocity

起卧 qǐ-wò get up and go to bed; rise and retire: ～有定时 get up and go to bed at regular hours

起席 qǐxí leave one's seat at a banquet: ～离去 get up from one's seat and leave; leave a banquet table

起先 qǐxiān at the outset; in the beginning: ～我还以为出了什么事。At the beginning I thought that something had gone wrong. /这样做我～有些想不通, 后来才通了。The way the matter had been handled was a bit of a puzzle to me and I didn't get over it till some time afterwards.

起小儿 qǐxiǎor 〈方言〉 from childhood: 他～在英国长大的。He was brought up in England.

起心 qǐxīn 〈贬义〉 have designs on: ～不良 cherish evil intentions; harbour ulterior motives

起心里 qǐ xīnli from the bottom of one's heart: 我～佩服他。I admire him from the bottom of my heart.

起薪 qǐxīn starting salary: ～每月五百六十元, 以后视工作成绩再定增加与否。Your starting salary is 560 *yuan* per month, and whether it will be raised or not will depend on your work performance.

起衅 qǐxìn *also* "启衅" qǐxìn kick up a rumpus

起行 qǐxíng embark on a journey; set out: 他们次日清晨～。They

set out early the next morning.

起兴 qǐxìng be interested in; be keen on:我看书正看得～，外面忽然传来一阵笑声。I was engrossed in reading when there came a burst of laughter from outside.

起眼儿 qǐyǎnr (usu. used in the negative) attractive; eye-catching:收了个不～的徒弟 take on a run-of-the-mill apprentice /这人从哪方面说都不～。This chap is not outstanding in any way.

起夜 qǐyè get up in the night to urinate:昨晚由于啤酒喝多了只好～。I had to get up to urinate last night for I had drunk too much beer.

起疑 qǐyí begin to suspect; become suspicious:他对我殷勤得令人～。He is so eager to please me that I can't but suspect his true intentions.

起义 qǐyì ❶ revolt; insurrection; uprising:武装～ armed revolt /农民～ peasant uprising /～军 insurrectionary army ❷ stage a rebellion and cross over to the righteous side:～投诚 revolt and cross over /～将领 general who crossed over to the side of the people

起意 qǐyì 〈贬义〉harbour a vicious design; entertain an evil intention:见财～ fall to evil designs at the sight of money

起因 qǐyīn cause; source; origin:必须认真研究这种歪风的～。It is necessary to make a careful study of the origin of such an unhealthy trend.

起用 qǐyòng ❶ reinstate (an official who has been relieved of his duties) ❷ employ or promote:～一批新人 promote a group of new people to leading posts /必须～年轻有为的人去代替那些效率低、能力差的干部。It is necessary to recruit young and talented people to replace those cadres who are inefficient and incompetent.

起源 qǐyuán originate; begin:知识～于生产劳动。Knowledge stems from productive labour. /生命的～至今还是个谜。The origin of life is still a mystery.

起运 qǐyùn start shipment:～点 starting place for shipment; place of dispatch /一批出口冰箱正待～。A consignment of refrigerators for export is awaiting shipment.

起赃 qǐzāng search for and recover stolen goods

起早贪黑 qǐzǎo-tānhēi *also*“起早搭黑”；“起早摸黑” start work early and knock off late; work from dawn to dusk; early to rise and late to rest:他这个人只知道～地苦干。He slogs away all day at his work, and never bothers about anything else.

起止 qǐ-zhǐ beginning and end:～日期 dates of beginning and end

起重车 qǐzhòngchē derrick car

起重船 qǐzhòngchuán crane ship

起重机 qǐzhòngjī hoist; crane; derrick:～的起重能力 the lifting (*or* hoisting) capacity of a crane /龙门～ gantry crane /塔式～ tower crane /门式～ portal crane /～桥 crane bridge /～司机 hoister /～载运车 crane carrier

起绉 qǐzhòu crumple; get wrinkled:这衣料不易～。This suiting does not wrinkle easily.

起绉工艺 qǐzhòu gōngyì 〈纺织〉creping

起子 qǐzi ❶ bottle opener ❷〈方言〉screwdriver ❸〈方言〉baking powder:你瞧我这记性，要蒸馒头还没～呢! Look how forgetful I am! I haven't got any baking powder yet and I am starting to make steamed bread! ❹〈量词〉group; batch:来了一～学生。There come a group of students.

起坐间 qǐzuòjiān 〈方言〉sitting room; living room

玘

qǐ 〈书面〉a kind of jade

杞

Qǐ ❶ name of an ancient kingdom during the Zhou Dynasty ❷ a surname

杞柳 qǐliǔ purple willow (*Salix sino-purpurea*)

杞人忧天 Qǐrén-yōutiān like the man of Qi who feared that the sky might fall — haunted by imaginary fears:但愿我这种担心只不过是～而已。If only my worries prove entirely unnecessary.

杞忧 qǐyōu *also*“杞人忧天” unnecessary worry

岂(豈)

qǐ 〈书面〉*used to introduce a rhetorical question*:孩子落水，～能见死不救? How could we stand by with folded arms when a child is drowning? /中国内政～容他国干涉! China's internal affairs admit of no external interference. /如此而已，～有他哉? That's all there is to it!

岂不 qǐbù isn't it; wouldn't it be:这样做～更好? Isn't it better to do things this way? /那～更稳妥多了? Wouldn't that be much safer?

岂但 qǐdàn not only:～你我不知道，恐怕连他自己也不清楚。Not only are you and I in the dark, he himself may not be at all clear about it.

岂非 qǐfēi should it not be; would it not be; isn't it:～咄咄怪事? Wouldn't it be the height of absurdity? /把稗草当秧苗，～笑话? Isn't it ridiculous to mistake weeds for rice seedlings?

岂敢 qǐgǎn ❶ how dare:我～单独行动? How dare I go it alone? /为了一点小事，我～打扰你。I would not dare to bother you for such a trifling matter. ❷〈套语〉you flatter me; I don't deserve such praise or honour:～～，一点小事，何足挂齿。I wish I deserved your compliment. This is only a modest effort on my part, which is not worth mentioning.

岂堪 qǐkān would it not be:后果～设想! The consequences would be disastrous (*or* dreadful).

岂可 qǐkě how could:～言而无信! How could you go back on your word?

岂肯 qǐkěn how would; how could:既然是你先动了手，他～与你善罢干休? How could he let the matter drop since you struck the first blow?

岂能 qǐnéng how could; how is it possible:～无动于衷? How could one remain aloof and indifferent? /他～保持沉默? How could he possibly keep quiet?

岂是 qǐshì how is it possible:这～他所能忍受的? How could he possibly put up with it?

岂有此理 qǐyǒucǐlǐ outrageous; shameless:真是～! What nonsense! /如此胡搅蛮缠，真是～! It's outrageous that you should plague him with such unreasonable demands.

岂止 qǐzhǐ not only:为难的事还多呢，～这一件? There are many hard nuts to crack, not to mention the present one.

屺

qǐ 〈书面〉barren hill

绮

qǐ ❶ figured woven silk material; damask:罗～ thin silk gauze /纨～ white stiff silk ❷ beautiful; exquisite:～情 tender feeling; sweet love; (of writing) beautiful thoughts /～札 letter written in flowery language (*or* ornate style)

绮丽 qǐlì exquisite; beautiful; gorgeous:风景～ beautiful scenery /文词～ ornate style /沿湖一带，景色～。The scenery by the lake is simply gorgeous.

绮罗 qǐluó ❶ gorgeous silk fabrics ❷ woman:～丛中数她最引人注目。Of all the ladies present she was the most conspicuous (*or* eye-catching).

绮靡 qǐmǐ 〈书面〉(of poetry or prose) showy; ornate:文辞～。The style is ornate.

绮年 qǐnián 〈书面〉adolescence; youth

绮思 qǐsī (of writing) beautiful thoughts

绮霞 qǐxiá rosy clouds:灿烂的～ gorgeous evening glow

绮语 qǐyǔ ❶ poetic diction ❷ intimate speech in the boudoir

qì

泣

qì ❶ weep; sob:暗～ shed tears secretly (*or* in private) /相对而～ weep in each other's presence /终日悲～ sob all day long ❷ tears:饮～ swallow one's tears /～涕涟涟 weep copious tears

泣不成声 qìbùchéngshēng choke with sobs:丈夫的噩耗传来，她～，当场昏倒在地。On hearing the sad news of her husband's death, she choked with sobs and fell down to the ground unconscious. /她抚抱着儿子，～。She embraced her son and cried silently.

泣诉 qìsù accuse while weeping; tearfully recount:～自己受害的经过 tearfully tell the story of how one was persecuted

泣下如雨 qìxià-rúyǔ shed tears like rain; tears stream down one's cheeks:说到伤心处，她～。Tears coursed down her cheeks as she told us her sad story.

弃(棄)

qì throw away; abandon; forsake; discard:抛～ throw away; cast off /遗～ abandon; forsake /他～文就武。He put down the pen and took up the sword.

弃暗投明 qì'àn-tóumíng forsake darkness for light — break away from reaction and side with the people:何不改邪归正，～? Why

don't you give up the unjust cause and come over to the side of progress?

弃儿 qì'ér abandoned child; foundling; waifs and strays

弃妇 qìfù 〈书面〉abandoned wife

弃官 qìguān give up one's office; resign one's official post: ～归里 give up one's official position and return to one's native place

弃甲曳兵 qìjiǎ-yèbīng (of troops) throw away one's arms; be routed; flee helter-skelter: 杀得敌军～，逃命不迭。The enemy troops were routed, running for their lives.

弃旧图新 qìjiù-túxīn reject the old for the new; turn over a new leaf: 翻然改悔，～ make a determined effort to atone for one's misdeeds and turn over a new leaf / 他决心～。He is determined to mend his ways and start afresh.

弃捐 qìjuān 〈书面〉discard; abandon: ～不顾 abandon; throw away without hesitation

弃绝 qìjué abandon; renounce; desert: ～亲友 desert one's relatives and friends / 他要～一切生活享受，去过隐士生活。He wants to renounce all comforts of life and live the life of a recluse.

弃取 qì-qǔ refuse or accept; reject or adopt

弃权 qìquán ❶ abstain from voting: 你们表决吧，我～。You go ahead with the voting. I abstain. / 这次表决有一人～。There was one abstention in the voting. ❷〈体育〉waive the right (to play); default; forfeit: 甲队～，乙队顺利进入第二轮比赛。With Team A defaulting, Team B walked over into the second round.

弃若敝屣 qìruòbìxǐ cast away like a pair of worn-out shoes: 不义之财，～。Ill-gotten wealth should be spurned like trash.

弃舍 qìshě throw away; give up: ～了一次极好的机会 squander a golden opportunity

弃市 qìshì 〈旧语〉execution carried out in public (with the body of the executed left in the street)

弃世 qìshì die; pass away: ～过早 die prematurely

弃瑕录用 qìxiá-lùyòng recruit people despite the mistakes they made in the past; use a capable man despite his defects: 人无完人，不肯～是毫无理由的。No one is perfect. There is absolutely no reason why we shouldn't recruit a person who has committed mistakes.

弃嫌 qìxián regard as beneath one's notice; look down upon: 如不～，请在这儿暂时委屈一夜。You might as well put up here for one night if you don't regard this as beneath your dignity.

弃邪归正 qìxié-guīzhèng *also* "改邪归正" gǎixié-guīzhèng give up evil and return to virtue; turn over a new leaf

弃学 qìxué drop out of school: 成百万的儿童曾一度因为家庭困难而～。Millions of children were once forced to drop out of school because of family difficulties.

弃养 qìyǎng 〈书面〉〈婉词〉death (of one's parents): 双亲～后，我只有自己谋生。After the death of my parents, I had to fend (*or* shift) for myself.

弃婴 qìyīng abandoned baby; foundling

弃之可惜 qìzhī-kěxī loath to discard; unwilling to throw away: 食之无味，～ hardly worth eating but not bad enough to throw away

弃掷 qìzhì throw away; discard

弃置 qìzhì throw aside; cast away: ～不问 be consigned to oblivion; be put into storage

契(栔)

qì ❶〈书面〉carve; engrave; chisel: ～舟求剑 mark the moving boat to locate the place where the sword has dropped into the river — take measures without regard to changed circumstances ❷〈书面〉carved inscriptions: 书～ carved characters / 殷～ bone inscriptions of the Yin (*or* late Shang) Dynasty ❸ agreement; contract; deed: 地～ title deed for land / 卖身～ indenture by which one sells oneself or a member of one's family ❹ agree; match together: 默～ tacit agreement (*or* understanding)

see also Xiè

契丹 Qìdān Qidan, or Khitan, an ancient nationality in northern China

契诃夫 Qìhēfū Anton Chekhov (1860-1904), Russian dramatist and short-story writer

契合 qìhé ❶ agree with; accord with; tally with; correspond to: 我们俩的见解不期然而～。Unexpectedly, our views coincided. ❷ get along well with sb.; share the same interest: 他俩一向～。The two of them hit it off well.

契机 qìjī 〈哲学〉moment; turning point; pivot: 近代中国以鸦片战争为～，迅速沦为半殖民地。With the Opium War of 1840-1842 as the turning point, modern China was rapidly reduced to a semi-colony. / 以抗日战争为～，中国人民赢得全国的解放。With the War of Resistance Against Japan as a pivot, the Chinese people won nationwide liberation.

契据 qìjù contract; written agreement; deed; receipt

契卡 Qìkǎ (transliteration from a Russian abbreviation) Cheka, an organization set up in 1917 under the Soviet government for the investigation of counter-revolutionary activities

契刻 qìkè carve; engrave

契券 qìquàn contract; title deed

契税 qìshuì tax paid by the buyer according to a stipulation as provided in a real estate contract signed by both parties

契文 qìwén oracle bone writing

契爷 qìyé 〈方言〉godfather

契友 qìyǒu close friend; bosom friend

契约 qìyuē contract; deed; charter: 租船～ contract of affreightment; charter party / 签订～ sign a contract / ～俱在。All contractual evidence is available.

契约法 qìyuēfǎ 〈法律〉contract law; law of contract

契纸 qìzhǐ title deed

碶

qì 〈方言〉stone-built dam: ～闸 build a dam with stones

槭

qì maple

槭树 qìshù maple

葺

qì 〈书面〉❶ cover a roof with straw; thatch ❷ repair; fix; mend: ～篱笆 mend a fence / 修～ repair (a house); make repairs

蟿

qì

蟿螽 qìzhōng 〈古语〉grasshopper

碛

qì ❶ moraine: ～砾 gravel ❷ desert: 沙～ sand and gravel / ～北 north of the Gobi Desert

砌

qì ❶ lay bricks or stones to build: ～砖 lay bricks / 铺～ pave / ～灶 build a stove / ～烟囱 put up (*or* construct) a chimney ❷ step: 石～ stone steps / 雕栏玉～ carved balustrades and marble steps

see also qiè

砌块 qìkuài building material made of light concrete and industrial waste used as a substitute for bricks

妻

qì 〈书面〉marry a girl to (a man): 以女～之 marry one's daughter to sb.

see also qī

跂

qì 〈书面〉stand on tiptoe: ～望 anxiously look forward to sth.

see also qí

器(噐)

qì ❶ instrument; implement; utensil; tool; ware: 木～ wooden implement / 铁～ iron tools / 电～ electric appliances / 漆～ lacquerware / 瓷～ china; chinaware; porcelain / 乐～ musical instrument / 拾音～ pickup; adapter / 玉～ jade article / 仪～ instrument / 容～ container; vessel ❷ organ: 呼吸～ respiratory organs / 消化～ digestive organs / 生殖～ reproductive organs; generative organs; genitals ❸ tolerance; forbearance: *see* "～量" ❹ talent; ability: 成～ make one's mark / 理财之～ talent for financial management ❺〈方言〉value; think highly of

器材 qìcái equipment; gear; material: 建筑～ construction equipment / 铁路～ railway gear / 五金～ hardware materials

器度 qìdù ability and broad-mindedness

器官 qìguān organ; apparatus: 视觉～ optical organs / 泌尿～ urinary organs / 发音～ organs of speech / ～移植 organ transplant / ～捐赠 organ donation / ～捐赠者 organ donor

器件 qìjiàn parts of an apparatus or appliance; component: 电子～ electronic components

器局 qìjú 〈书面〉capability and broad-mindedness

器具 qìjù utensil; tool; inplement; appliance: 灭火～ fire extinguisher; fire-fighting implement / 救生～ life-saving appliance / 办公

～ office appliances／日用～ household utensils; articles of daily use
器量 qìliàng magnanimity; tolerance:～广大 large-minded; generous／～狭小 narrow-minded; petty
器皿 qìmǐn containers esp. for use in the house; household utensils; household ware:玻璃～ glass ware／搪瓷～ enamel ware
器任 qìrèn 〈书面〉think highly of and have trust in sb.:他德才兼备，甚见～。A man of integrity and ability, he enjoys everybody's respect and confidence.
器识 qìshí 〈书面〉large-mindedness as well as knowledge and experience:～非凡 be extremely broad-minded and knowledgeable
器使 qìshǐ 〈书面〉appoint sb. according to his merit
器物 qìwù implement; utensil; article
器械 qìxiè ❶ apparatus; appliance; instrument:理疗～ appliances for physiotherapy／体育～ sports apparatus／手术～ surgical instruments ❷ weapon
器械体操 qìxiè tǐcāo gymnastics on or with apparatus
器用 qìyòng ❶ household utensils:～什物 household articles of daily use ❷〈书面〉person who is both talented and trustworthy
器宇 qìyǔ 〈书面〉bearing; carriage; deportment:～不凡 extraordinary carriage
器宇轩昂 qìyǔ xuān'áng of dignified bearing:但见来人～，一表人才。The newcomer was a person of dignified carriage and striking appearance.
器乐 qìyuè 〈音乐〉instrumental music:～曲 composition for an instrument
器质病 qìzhìbìng 〈医学〉structural disease
器质性心脏病 qìzhìxìng xīnzàngbìng 〈医学〉vitium cordis
器重 qìzhòng think highly of (one's subordinates); set great store by:甚见～ regard sb. highly／领导很～他的办事能力。The leadership sets great store by his ability to get things done (*or* by his abilities).

炁

qì *see*"气"qì

气(氣)

qì ❶ gas:煤～ coal gas; gas／蒸～ steam／氧～ oxygen／沼～ marsh gas; methane ❷ air:给自行车打～ blow up (*or* inflate) a bike tyre／开窗透～ open the window to let in some fresh air ❸ breath:喘～ breathe hard; gasp for breath／吐～ exhale／歇口～ stop to get one's breath back／没～了 stop breathing; cease to breathe ❹ weather:天～ weather／节～ seasonal changes in the weather／秋高～爽 fine autumn weather ❺ smell; odour:香～扑鼻 sweet smell assailing the nostrils; inviting smell／油～呛人 suffocating oil smell／臭～熏天 disgusting foul odour／腥～ smell of fish, seafood, etc.; stinking; fishy ❻ mental state; spirit; morale:志～ resolve; determination; will／骨～ strength of character; moral integrity; backbone／火～ anger; temper／怨～ grievance; complaint; resentment／朝～ vigorous; full of vigour／和～ gentle; kind; amiable／英～勃勃 dashing and spirited ❼ momentum; drive; daring:力拔山兮～盖世。My strength can uproot a mountain and my valour is second to none. ❽airs; manners:秀～ elegance; grace／义～ chivalry; honour／阔～ extravagant style／书呆子～ bookishness; pedantry／孩子～ childishness／市侩～ air of a vulgar businessman; philistinism／怪里怪～ eccentric; odd; queer ❾ anger; rage:动～ fly into a rage; get worked up／一～之下转身就走了 leave abruptly in a huff／他的漠不关心使我很生～。I was very annoyed about his indifference.／老人～得脸都紫了。The old man's face turned purple with rage. ❿ enrage; make angry; provoke:他就是想～～你。He was deliberately trying to provoke you.／别～我了！Stop annoying me. ⓫ insult; ridicule; bully:他老受别人的～。He is a ready target of other people's spleen. ⓬〈中医〉*qi* or vital energy; life force:补中益～ essential to the building up of man's vital energy／～血两亏 malfunction of vital energy complicated by anaemia; malfunction of vital energy and deficiency of blood ⓭〈中医〉certain symptoms:湿～ eczema; fungus infection of hand or foot／肝～ diseases with such symptoms as costal pain, vomiting, diarrhoea, etc.
气昂昂 qì'áng'áng full of beans; full of dash:雄赳赳，～ valiantly and spiritedly
气疤 qìbā 〈冶金〉body scab
气包子 qìbāozi 〈口语〉bundle of petulance:怎么老生气，跟～似的。You are always taking umbrage as if you were a bundle of petulance.
气刨 qìbào 〈机械〉air gouging
气爆 qìbào gas explosion
气泵 qìbèng 〈机械〉air pump
气不打一处来 qì bù dǎ yīchù lái full of anger; seized by uncontrollable fury:看见儿子那身打扮，他就～。He was overcome with anger at the sight of his son's bizarre attire.
气不忿儿 qìbùfènr 〈方言〉feel unhappy about what is unjust or unfair:他受到处罚是理所应当的，你不必那样～。He deserves his punishment, and you don't have to feel unhappy about it.
气不公 qìbùgōng *see*"气不平"
气不过 qìbùguò beyond endurance:我实在～，狠狠地说了他一顿。I could not take it any more and gave him a good dressing down.
气不平 qìbùpíng be indignant at an injustice; refuse to be reconciled:他这样偏袒一方，真叫人～。It really makes me mad that he should be so partial to one side. *or* The partiality he shows to one side is simply maddening.
气层 qìcéng *also*"～藏"〈石油〉gas pool
气冲冲 qìchōngchōng be furious; fume with rage:～地走进屋来 sail into the room angrily／他～的好像要跟人打架。He has got a chip on his shoulder.
气冲牛斗 qìchōng-niúdǒu beside oneself with fury; fly into a towering rage
气冲霄汉 qìchōng-xiāohàn showing a lofty and dauntless spirit
气喘 qìchuǎn ❶ *also*"哮喘"xiàochuǎn 〈医学〉asthma:阵发性～ spasmodic asthma ❷ be out of breath; breathe hard; pant:他～吁吁地爬上楼梯。He went huffing and puffing up the stairs.／接近山顶的时侯，他～起来。He began to breathe hard when getting near the top of the hill.
气窗 qìchuāng transom (window); fanlight
气锤 qìchuí 〈机械〉pneumatic hammer; air hammer
气粗 qìcū ❶ have a fiery temper; be hot-tempered:我这个人～，大家多担待点。I hope you will bear with my temper. ❷ overbearing; overweening:财大～〈俗语〉a millionaire can afford to be high and mighty; be purse-proud／他一看自己在理上占了上风，说话也～了。Sensing that he had an edge over others in his argument, he began to speak in a peremptory voice.
气促 qìcù breathe with difficulty; be short of breath; pant for breath:他从外面跑进来，～得说不出话来。When he came hurriedly into the room, he was so short of breath that he couldn't even utter a word.
气袋 qìdài air pocket; air-bag (for a car driver, etc.)
气垫 qìdiàn 〈交通〉❶ air cushion; pneumatic cushion:～汽车 aeromobile ❷ high-pressure air from the bottom of a hovercraft
气垫爆破 qìdiàn bàopò 〈矿业〉air shooting; cushion shooting
气垫车 qìdiànchē hovercar
气垫船 qìdiànchuán hovercraft; hydroskimmer
气垫渡船 qìdiàn dùchuán hoverferry
气垫火车 qìdiàn huǒchē hovertrain
气垫输送机 qìdiàn shūsòngjī 〈机械〉air cushion conveyor
气垫鞋 qìdiànxié air-cushioned shoe
气顶 qìdǐng 〈石油〉gas cap
气动 qìdòng pneumatic:～开关 pneumatic switch; air pressure switch
气动激光器 qìdòng jīguāngqì gas dynamic laser;〈军事〉pneumatic laser
气动力 qìdònglì aerodynamic force:～干扰 aerodynamic interference
气度 qìdù ❶ magnanimity; forbearance; tolerance ❷ appearance; bearing:～不凡 impressive-looking／表现大家～ have the proud bearing of a family of social distinction
气短 qìduǎn ❶ breathe hard; be short of breath; pant:上年岁了，他上楼就感到～。As he was getting on in years, he often panted for breath when going up stairs. ❷ depressed; in low spirits:屡受挫折而不～ be undaunted though one has suffered repeated setbacks／英雄～，儿女情长。(said of a man who turns away from duty for the sake of love) The spirit of a hero is short, but the love between a man and woman is long.
气氛 qìfēn atmosphere; air:紧张的～ tense atmosphere; tension／静谧的～ air of tranquillity／欢乐的～ joyous mood／政治～ political climate／比赛在友好热烈的～中进行。The contest was conducted in a cordial and friendly atmosphere.
气忿忿 qìfènfèn be in a huff; pant with rage:他～地站起来走了。He got up from his seat and left in a huff.

气愤 qìfèn indignant; enraged; furious: ～极了 be overcome with indignation / 焦虑和～，使她病了。She was ill from worry and anger. / 一说到"四人帮"的横行不法，他总是～异常。Whenever we talked about the tyranny and lawlessness of the "gang of four", he would get all worked up.

气浮式摇床 qìfúshì yáochuáng 〈矿业〉 air-float table; air table

气腹 qìfù 〈医学〉 (artificial) pneumoperitoneum

气概 qìgài noble quality; mettle; drive; spirit: 英雄～ heroic spirit / 革命～ revolutionary valour / 大无畏的～ dauntless (*or* gallant) mettle / 藐视一切的～ daring spirit of defying all difficulties / 作为一个男人，他缺少一种～。He lacked the strength of character one hoped to find in a man. / 虽属小吏，但～凛然。Though a minor official, he had a stern and upright demeanour.

气缸 qìgāng 〈机械〉 air cylinder; cylinder

气割 qìgē 〈机械〉 gas cutting

气根 qìgēn *also* "气生根" 〈植物〉 aerial root

气功 qìgōng *qigong*, a system of deep breathing exercises

气功疗法 qìgōng liáofǎ *qigong* therapy; breathing technique therapy

气鼓鼓 qìgūgū highly displeased; angry: 她～地瞪了那人一眼。She gave him an angry stare.

气臌 qìgǔ 〈中医〉 distension of the abdomen caused by accumulation of gas resulting from dysfunction of the spleen or from emotional factors; tympanites

气管 qìguǎn 〈生理〉 windpipe; trachea

气管瘘 qìguǎnlòu 〈医学〉 tracheal fistula

气管切开术 qìguǎn qiēkāishù 〈医学〉 tracheotomy

气管炎 qìguǎnyán ❶〈医学〉 tracheitis: 慢性～ chronic tracheitis ❷〈戏谑〉 (a near homophone of 妻管严) be afraid of one's wife; be hen-pecked: 这年头，男的都是"～"。These days men all live under "petticoat government".

气贯长虹 qìguàn-chánghóng lofty as the rainbow spanning the sky; full of noble aspirations: 他在战争年代写下的诗篇真是～。The poems he wrote in war years are indeed shot through with noble aspirations.

气锅 qìguō Yunnan-style steampot; casserole

气锅鸡 qìguōjī chicken cooked with medicinal herbs in a steampot; casserole chicken

气焊 qìhàn 〈机械〉 gas welding

气恨 qìhèn ❶ angry; indignant: 听了这话，他～得半天说不出话来。When he heard the remark, he got so furious that it took him quite some time before he could gasp out a few words. ❷ feel jealous: 别人干得好，你不应该～，要向人家学习。If people do well in their jobs, you should learn from them and not be jealous of them.

气哼哼 qìhēnghēng *also* "气哄哄" in a huff; in anger: 老头子～地顶了他一句。The old man rebutted him angrily.

气候 qìhòu ❶ climate: 热带～ tropical climate / ～变化 climatic change / 我国北方～干燥寒冷。The climate in the northern part of our country is dry and cold. ❷ climate; situation: 当前的政治～ present political climate ❸ progress; achievement: 这个人成不了大～。The chap won't be able to play any significant role. *or* This fellow will get nowhere.

气候带 qìhòudài climate zone

气候控制室 qìhòu kòngzhìshì biotron

气候实验室 qìhòu shíyànshì climalizer

气候图 qìhòutú climatic chart

气候学 qìhòuxué climatology

气候志 qìhòuzhì climatography

气呼呼 qìhūhū panting with rage; gasping with fury: 他～地冲进屋来，说他给人家出卖了。Panting with rage, he rushed into the room saying that he had been let down.

气化 qìhuà ❶〈化工〉 gasification; 〈地质〉 pneumatolysis: 油～ oil gasification / ～期〈地质〉 pneumatolytic stage ❷〈中医〉 movement and change of *qi* in the human body or of the *sanjiao* (三焦, i. e. from below the tongue to the abdomen)

气话 qìhuà unguarded remark made in a fit of fury: 刚才我说的都是～，千万不要介意。I said that in a fit of temper. Please don't take it to heart. *or* I hope you will not mind the ill-considered words I have just made.

气辉 qìhuī airglow

气火 qìhuǒ ❶ fury: 他说着说着，就～上来，憋红了脸。He was overcome with anger as he went on talking, and his cheeks flushed crimson. ❷ become furious; get into a rage: 他～得如同泼了一瓢油。He flew into a fury as if he were on fire.

气火山 qìhuǒshān 〈地质〉 air volcano

气机 qìjī 〈中医〉 performance and movement of *qi*

气急 qìjí panting and exasperated; incoherent with rage

气急败坏 qìjí-bàihuài flustered and exasperated; flurried and furious: ～地从椅子上跳起来 jump up from the chair in uncontrollable anger / 孩子闯了祸，老张～地大骂了他一顿。As his child got into dreadful trouble, the exasperated Lao Zhang gave him a good telling-off.

气节 qìjié moral integrity; moral courage: 面临敌人的威胁和利诱，一定要保持～。Moral integrity must be maintained when one is faced with the enemy's threat and blandishments. / 在动乱时期，一个人的～很重要。During troubled times, character is of paramount importance.

气结 qìjié ❶〈书面〉 pent-up: ～不能言 choke with pent-up grievances ❷〈中医〉 stagnation of vital energy

气井 qìjǐng 〈石油〉 gas well

气阱 qìjǐng 〈气象〉 air pocket

气撅撅 qìjuējuē sulky; sullen: 这孩子～地蹲在地上，不说话了。The child squatted on the ground, sulky and silent.

气绝 qìjué stop breathing; die: ～身亡 breathe one's last

气厥 qìjué faint; become unconscious: 听到丈夫去世的消息，她一下子就～了。She fainted the moment she learned of her husband's death.

气可鼓而不可泄 qì kě gǔ ér bùkě xiè morale should be boosted, not dampened; spirit must be braced up, not bowed down

气孔 qìkǒng ❶〈植物〉 stoma ❷〈动物〉 spiracle ❸〈冶金〉 gas hole ❹〈建筑〉 air hole

气口 qìkǒu 〈戏曲〉 the way one manages to take a breath while singing

气浪 qìlàng blast (of an explosion)

气类 qìlèi ❶ things of the same category: ～相同 be of the same group ❷〈书面〉 birds of a feather

气累脖儿 qìleibór inflated neck, popular name for goitre

气冷 qìlěng 〈机械〉 air cooling

气冷堆 qìlěngduī *also* "气冷式反应堆" 〈原子能〉 gas-cooled reactor (GCR)

气冷式变压器 qìlěngshì biànyāqì 〈电工〉 air blast transformer

气冷式发动机 qìlěngshì fādòngjī air-cooled engine

气力 qìlì strength; energy; effort; exertion: 用尽～ exert oneself to the utmost; with all one's strength / 他的～远不如从前。He is far less strong than he used to be. / 完成这项工作，需要花费很大～。You will have to make a tremendous effort to accomplish this task.

气力输送机 qìlì shūsòngjī 〈机械〉 pneumatic conveyer

气量 qìliàng ❶ talent; moral character ❷ tolerance; magnanimity: 这人没有～，你提意见要小心。You must be careful offering your advice to him, as he is not so broad-minded.

气量表 qìliàngbiǎo gas meter

气流 qìliú ❶ air current; airflow; air stream ❷〈语言〉 breath

气流纺纱 qìliú fǎngshā open-end spinning

气流干扰 qìliú gānrǎo interference in airflow

气流畸变 qìliú jībiàn flow distortion

气流速度 qìliú sùdù air velocity

气瘤 qìliú 〈医学〉 pneumatocele

气楼 qìlóu small tower for ventilation on the top of a roof

气轮机 qìlúnjī (short for 燃气轮机) steam turbine; air-turbine

气脉 qìmài ❶ vigour and pulse: ～调和。The sap and pulse are in perfect condition. ❷ (of literary composition) line of thought; sequence of ideas

气脉儿 qìmair physical vigour or energy: 我父亲病已愈，～也还不错。Fully recovered from his ailment, my father is in quite good form.

气煤 qìméi gas coal

气门 qìmén ❶ *also* "气孔" 〈动物〉 spiracle; stigma ❷ (air) valve of a tyre ❸ air drain (in some machines)

气门心 qìménxīn 〈口语〉 ❶ valve inside ❷ valve rubber tube (of a tyre)

气闷 qìmèn ❶ upset; vexed: 心中～ feel vexed / 满腹～ full of worries; be badly upset ❷ stuffy; close: 屋里真～，快打开窗户。Open the windows, please; it's so close (*or* stuffy) in the room.

气密 qìmì airtight; gastight; gasproof: ～结合 〈机械〉 airtight joint /

～试验〈航空〉air seal test; leakage test /～座舱 pressure cabin /～室 sealed chamber; hermetic cabin

气囔囔 qìnāngnāng highly displeased:他～地走进屋来。He came into the room, looking highly displeased.

气囊 qìnáng ❶ (of birds) air sac ❷ (of an aerostat) gas-bag

气恼 qìnǎo offended; angry:她心情很不好,一切可能～她的话都不要说。She is very much upset, so you had better say nothing that might offend her.

气馁 qìněi be disheartened; lose heart:失败了不～ keep one's chin up despite failure; refuse to take one's defeat lying down /怎能受点挫折就～? How can you lose heart over such small setbacks?

气逆 qìnì 〈中医〉 circulation of vital energy in the wrong direction:气顺则平,～则病。One feels calm when the circulation of vital energy is in the right direction, and poorly when it is in the wrong direction. *or* Good circulation of vital energy keeps one fit while poor circulation indicates some ailment.

气派 qìpài ❶ manner; style:他有一个大学者的～。He has the impressive manner of a great scholar. /这个庭院很有点与众不同的～。This garden is unique in style and layout. ❷ impressive; imposing; spirited:他穿军装特别～。He looks quite spirited in an army uniform.

Q

气泡 qìpào air bubble; bubble

气喷 qìpēn 〈石油〉gas blowout

气魄 qìpò ❶ courage; daring; boldness of vision:我缺乏他的经验和～。I cannot compare with him either in experience or boldness of vision. /这个规划纲要充分显示了领导的～。The outline programme fully demonstrates the leadership's sweep and determination. ❷ momentum; impressive manner:江河入海,～浩瀚。As a river rushes into the sea, its rapid currents gather tremendous momentum. /壶口瀑布,～非凡。The Hukou Falls present a scene of amazing grandeur.

气枪 qìqiāng air gun; pneumatic gun:玩具～ popgun

气壳星 qìqiàoxīng 〈天文〉shell star

气球 qìqiú balloon:测风～ pilot balloon /定高～ constant-level balloon /～驾驶员 balloonist /～探测 balloon sounding /～卫星 balloon satellite /～跳伞 balloon parachuting /探空～ air-sounding balloon

气驱油田 qìqū yóutián 〈石油〉gas controlled field

气圈 qìquān ❶〈纺织〉balloon ❷〈气象〉aerosphere

气泉 qìquán 〈地质〉hot air jetted from deep underground through a rock crevice

气嗓 qìsǎng 〈方言〉windpipe; trachea

气色 qìsè colour; complexion:他～不大好。He is a bit off colour. *or* He looks a little pale. /他～很好。He is the very picture of health. *or* He is in the pink.

气盛 qìshèng ❶ apt to flare up; quick-tempered:他少年～,说话不客气,容易伤人。Young and impetuous, he often offends people by his rude remarks. ❷ (of writing) mighty; forceful:～言宜。When the style of an essay is forceful, the language naturally falls into place.

气蚀 qìshí 〈物理〉cavitation; cavitation erosion

气势 qìshì momentum; impetus; imposing manner:人民大会堂～雄伟。The Great Hall of the People is imposing and magnificent.

气势磅礴 qìshì-pángbó full of power and grandeur:长城以～闻名于世,为世界奇观之一。The Great Wall, known for its incomparable grandeur, is one of the wonders of the world. /这是一部～的史诗。This is an epic of great power.

气势汹汹 qìshì-xiōngxiōng truculent; overbearing; aggressive:他～地对我说:"如果你不同意,我就辞职不干了!" He shouted at me in an aggressive manner:"If you don't agree, I'll quit!" /这三个人突然～地走了进来。These three stalked defiantly into the room.

气数 qìshu fate; destiny (as reckoned in divination):中日甲午战败后,清朝的～已尽。The Qing Dynasty was doomed to fall after its defeat in the Sino-Japanese War of 1894-1895. /从他目前健康情况看,似乎～已尽。Judging from his present state of health, his days seem to be numbered.

气水胸 qìshuǐxiōng 〈医学〉pneumohydrothorax

气死人 qìsǐrén infuriating; exasperating; outrageous:售货员的态度～。The demeanour of the shop assistant was driving people mad. /事情这样不公平,真是～。It was really exasperating to see the matter handled so unfairly.

气态 qìtài ❶〈物理〉gaseous state ❷〈书面〉deportment; bearing:风雅～ refined deportment /～雍容华贵。One's bearing is dignified and noble.

气体 qìtǐ gas:～发生器 gas generator /～分离器 gas separator

气体保护焊 qìtǐ bǎohùhàn 〈冶金〉(gas) shielded welding

气体动力学 qìtǐ dònglìxué aerodynamics

气体分子运动论 qìtǐ fēnzǐ yùndònglùn 〈化学〉gas-kinetic theory

气体激光器 qìtǐ jīguāngqì gas laser

气体力学 qìtǐ lìxué pneumatics

气体燃料 qìtǐ ránliào gaseous fuel

气体渗碳 qìtǐ shèntàn 〈冶金〉gas-carburization

气体压缩机 qìtǐ yāsuōjī 〈机械〉gas compressor

气田 qìtián 〈石油〉gas field

气筒 qìtǒng inflator; bicycle pump

气头上 qìtóushang in a fit of anger; in an ugly mood; in a foul temper:他在～,别碰他。He is boiling with rage, better stay away from him!

气团 qìtuán 〈气象〉air mass:冷～ cold air mass /～变性 air-mass modification /～源地 air-mass source region /～气候学 air-mass climatology

气吞山河 qìtūn-shānhé filled with the heroic spirit that conquers mountains and rivers; full of daring:他在战场上横刀跃马,～。He fought with incredible valour on the battlefield.

气味 qìwèi ❶ smell; scent; odour; flavour:玉兰花的～幽雅清香。Magnolia gives off a sweet and pleasant smell. ❷〈贬义〉smack; taste; reek:有强权政治的～ smack of power politics /这部书宣传～太浓。This book savours too much of propaganda.

气味相投 qìwèi-xiāngtóu be two of a kind; be congenial to each other; be like-minded:他们～,互相勾结。They are birds of a feather, acting in cahoots with each other. /在这方面我们可以说多少是～。In this respect, we were somewhat like-minded.

气温 qìwēn 〈气象〉air temperature; atmospheric temperature

气息 qìxī ❶ breath:屏住～ hold one's breath /～均匀 breathe evenly ❷ scent; smell; tang:春天的～ scent of spring /晚会充满青春的～。The evening party was permeated with an atmosphere of youthful exuberance. /空气里充溢着湿润泥土的芬芳～。The air was filled with the tang of moist earth.

气息奄奄 qìxī-yǎnyǎn be at one's last gasp; breathe one's last:病人已是～,处于昏迷状态。The patient is sinking fast; he is in a coma. /前次在医院见到他时,他已～了。He was dying when I last saw him in the hospital. /这种腐朽思想已经～。This decadent ideology is actually moribund.

气相色谱法 qìxiàng sèpǔfǎ gas chromatography

气象 qìxiàng ❶〈气象〉meteorological phenomenon:～气球 meteorological balloon ❷ meteorology ❸ atmosphere; scene; spectacle:一派新～ completely new atmosphere /这几年,大草原已是～一新。In recent years, the vast grassland has taken on an entirely new look. /市面上已有了些过年的～。There is already an atmosphere of New Year festivity in town. ❹ airs; appearance:宏伟～ imposing appearance

气象潮 qìxiàngcháo sea surge

气象观测 qìxiàng guāncè meteorological observation

气象火箭 qìxiàng huǒjiàn meteorological rocket

气象雷达 qìxiàng léidá weather radar; weather observation radar; meteorological radar

气象台 qìxiàngtái meteorological observatory

气象图 qìxiàngtú meteorological map

气象万千 qìxiàng-wànqiān spectacular; majestic:洞庭湖朝晖夕阴,～。Dazzling in the morning sun and fading into the gray evening mist, the Dong Ting is a magnificent lake of a myriad scenes.

气象卫星 qìxiàng wèixīng meteorological satellite; meteosat; weather satellite

气象学 qìxiàngxué meteorology:～家 meteorologist

气象预报 qìxiàng yùbào meteorological report; weather forecast:～今夜有小雨。According to weather forecast there will be light rain tonight.

气象员 qìxiàngyuán weatherman

气象站 qìxiàngzhàn meteorological station

气性 qìxing ❶ temperament; disposition:我很了解他的～。I know his temperament very well. ❷ temper:这姑娘～大。The girl has a fiery temper.

气汹汹 qìxiōngxiōng in a rush of anger; in a threatening manner:他～的,啪的一声关上门。He angrily slammed the door.

气胸 qìxiōng 〈医学〉❶ pneumothorax:自发性～ spontaneous

pneumothorax ❷ artificial pneumothorax
气咻咻 qìxiūxiū gasp; be out of breath:他急急忙忙跑进屋来,~地报告了这个消息。He rushed into the room, gasping out the message.
气吁吁 qìxūxū pant; gasp for breath:我看见他~地爬上楼梯。I saw him go huffing and puffing up the stairs.
气虚 qìxū 〈中医〉deficiency of vital energy
气旋 qìxuán 〈气象〉cyclone:反~ anticyclone
气血 qì-xuè 〈中医〉vital energy and the state of blood in the human body
气血辨证 qì-xuè biànzhèng 〈中医〉analyzing and differentiating the pathological condition according to the function of vital energy and the state of the blood
气血两虚 qì-xuè liǎngxū 〈中医〉deficiency of vital energy and blood; *qi*-blood deficiency
气压 qìyā 〈气象〉atmospheric pressure; barometric pressure:高~ high pressure / 低~ low pressure
气压表 qìyābiǎo barometer
气压沉箱 qìyā chénxiāng 〈建筑〉pneumatic caisson
气压千斤顶 qìyā qiānjīndǐng 〈机械〉pneumatic jack
气压输物管 qìyā shūwùguǎn 〈机械〉pneumatic tube
气压性鼻窦炎 qìyāxìng bídòuyán 〈医学〉barosinusitis; aerosinusitis
气压性耳炎 qìyāxìng ěryán 〈医学〉barotitis; aerotitis
气眼 qìyǎn ❶〈建筑〉air hole ❷〈冶金〉gas hole
气焰 qìyàn 〈贬义〉arrogance; bluster:此人~嚣张,得治他一下。The chap is puffed with pride; we have got to take him down a peg or two. / 我们必须采取坚决措施打击敌人的嚣张~。We must take resolute measures to deflate the arrogance of the enemy.
气焰熏天 qìyàn-xūntiān be swollen with arrogance; be puffed up with overbearing pride:此人~,普通群众哪在他眼里。The chap is so arrogant that the common people are beneath his notice.
气硬钢 qìyìnggāng 〈冶金〉air-cooled steel
气宇 qìyǔ bearing; demeanour
气宇轩昂 qìyǔ-xuān'áng impressive bearing; dignified appearance:这位知名学者~,缓步进入会议厅。The well-known scholar, who looked very dignified, walked into the conference hall with measured steps.
气郁 qìyù 〈中医〉obstruction of the circulation of vital energy
气运 qìyùn fate; luck; fortune:他~不佳,买卖连连失败。He is down on his luck and has sustained repeated losses in business.
气韵 qìyùn flavour and tone:有人认为文章以~为主。Some think that the essence of writing lies in its flavour and tone.
气栽法 qìzāifǎ 〈农业〉aeroponics
气闸 qìzhá 〈机械〉air-brake
气闸室 qìzháshì air lock
气胀病 qìzhàngbìng bloat; hoven; tympanites
气质 qìzhì ❶ spirit; temperament; disposition:这孩子的~很好,总是那么活泼可爱。The child has a very nice temperament, and is lovely and vivacious. ❷ qualities; attributes; makings:他有优秀教师的~。He has the makings of a good teacher.
气滞 qìzhì 〈中医〉stagnation of the circulation of vital energy
气肿疽 qìzhǒngjū 〈兽医〉blackleg; black quarter
气壮如牛 qìzhuàng-rúniú sturdy as a bull; strong as an ox:这个人表面上~,实际上胆小如鼠。The man appears as fierce as a bull but is actually chicken-hearted.
气壮山河 qìzhuàngshānhé majestic as high mountains and mighty rivers; full of power and grandeur; imbued with sublime heroism:他就义前的那番话真是~。The words he said before he went to his death stamped him as a hero of extraordinary courage.

汽

qì ❶ gas; vapour ❷ water steam; steam
汽车 qìchē automobile; motor vehicle; motor car; car:小~ car / 豪华小~ limousine / 公共~ bus / 小公共~ minibus / 出租~ taxi; taxicab / ~俱乐部 automobile club / ~拉力赛 car rally / ~赛 automobile racing / 国际~大奖赛 Grand Prix / ~三层玻璃 triplex
汽车吊 qìchēdiào truck crane; autolift
汽车队 qìchēduì motor transport corps; fleet of cars or trucks
汽车蜂鸣器 qìchē fēngmíngqì fuzzbuster
汽车工业 qìchē gōngyè auto industry; car industry
汽车驾驶赛 qìchē jiàshǐsài gymkhana
汽车驾驶执照 qìchē jiàshǐ zhízhào driver's license
汽车库 qìchēkù garage
汽车旅馆 qìchē lǚguǎn motor hotel; motel
汽车起重机 qìchē qǐzhòngjī *see* "汽车吊"
汽车式混凝土搅拌机 qìchēshì hùnníngtǔ jiǎobànjī 〈建筑〉mixer-lorry; truck mixer
汽车式装载机 qìchēshì zhuāngzàijī 〈机械〉lorry loader
汽车修配厂 qìchē xiūpèichǎng motor repair shop; auto repair garage
汽车运输 qìchē yùnshū 〈交通〉motoring
汽车制造厂 qìchē zhìzàochǎng automobile factory; motor works
汽船 qìchuán steamship; steamer
汽锤 qìchuí 〈机械〉steam hammer:龙门~ arch-type steam hammer / ~打桩机 ram steam pile driver
汽灯 qìdēng gas lamp:~罩 gas mantle
汽笛 qìdí steam whistle; siren; hooter:~长鸣。The siren wailed loud and long.
汽缸 qìgāng 〈机械〉cylinder:~盖 cylinder head / ~组 cylinder block
汽锅 qìguō steam boiler; boiler
汽化 qìhuà 〈物理〉vaporization; carburation:~冷却 evaporative cooling
汽化器 qìhuàqì ❶〈机械〉carburettor:~回火制止器 carburettor backfire arrester / ~主射口 carburettor main jet ❷〈化学〉vaporizer
汽化热 qìhuàrè heat of vaporization
汽机 qìjī ❶ (short for 蒸汽机) steam engine ❷ (short for 汽轮机) steam turbine
汽酒 qìjiǔ light sparkling wine
汽冷式发动机 qìlěngshì fādòngjī steam-cooled engine
汽轮发电机 qìlún fādiànjī turbogenerator:双水内冷~ turbogenerator with inner water-cooled stator and rotor / ~组 turbo-unit
汽轮机 qìlúnjī *also* "汽机" steam turbine:~组 turbo-set
汽碾 qìniǎn *also* "汽碾子"〈机械〉steamroller
汽暖 qìnuǎn steam heating (system)
汽密 qìmì 〈机械〉steam tight
汽热 qìrè 〈机械〉steam heat:~机 steam heater
汽水 qìshuǐ aerated water; soda water:柠檬~ lemonade / 桔子~ orangeade
汽水制造机 qìshuǐ zhìzàojī 〈机械〉gasogene
汽锁 qìsuǒ vapour lock
汽提 qìtí 〈石油〉strip:~油 stripped oil / ~法 vaporizing extract process / ~塔 stripping tower; stripper
汽艇 qìtǐng motorboat
汽艇旅馆 qìtǐng lǚguǎn boatel
汽相 qìxiàng 〈物理〉vapour phase:~反应〈化工〉vapour reaction / ~反应器 vapour-phase reactor / ~精炼 vapour-phase refining
汽油 qìyóu petrol; gasoline; gas:航空~ aviation gasoline / 合成~ synthetic gasoline / ~添加剂 gasoline additive / 加氧~ oxygenated gasoline / 抗爆~ anti-knock gasoline / 无铅~ unleaded gasoline / 凝固~ napalm / 凝固~弹 napalm bomb / ~发动机 gasoline engine; gasoline motor
汽油机 qìyóujī 〈机械〉gasoline engine; petrol engine
汽蒸 qìzhēng steaming

汔

qì 〈书面〉so that; so as to

讫

qì ❶ settled; accomplished; completed:付~ paid / 查~ checked; examined / 现金收~ cash received / 事~即买舟东渡日本。When he was through with the business, he went to Japan by ship. ❷ end:这项工程起~共二十年。It took 20 years to complete the project from beginning to end.

迄

qì ❶ up to; till; until:长城东起山海关,西~嘉峪关。The Great Wall runs all the way from Shanhaiguan in the east to Jiayuguan in the west. ❷ (used before 未 or 无) so far; yet:此种疗法~无成效。So far this treatment has not produced any effect. / 冲突~未停止。Hostilities have not ceased yet.
迄今 qìjīn up to now; to this day; so far:自古~ from ancient times to the present / 他离家~已二年。It is two years since he left home. / 事情~尚无头绪。Things have not taken shape yet.

憩(憇)

qì 〈书面〉rest:小~ take a short rest / 同作同~ work and rest together / 休~ take a rest

憩室 qìshì 〈医学〉diverticulum
憩息 qìxī 〈书面〉rest; relax:我看见好几个人在大树阴下乘凉～。I saw several people relaxing in the cool shade of a tree.

愒 qì 〈书面〉see "憩" qì
see also hè; kài

亟 qì 〈书面〉repeatedly; time and again:～经洽商 after repeated consultation /～来搅扰 come again and again to disturb sb.
see also jí

qiā

袷 qiā
袷袢 qiāpàn Uygur or Tajik robe buttoning down the front

葜 qiā see "菝葜" báqiā

掐 qiā ❶ pinch; nip; pick:～胳膊 pinch sb.'s arm /～豆角儿 pick tender kidney beans /～花 nip off flowers /公共汽车上不能吸烟,请把香烟～了。Smoking is not allowed on the bus. Please put (*or* stub) out your cigarette. ❷ clutch; grip:一把～住他的手臂 grip his arm /双手～腰 with arms akimbo /～死在摇篮里 stifle in the cradle; nip in the bud ❸ 〈方言〉〈量词〉a pinch, bunch, handful, etc. of:一～小葱 a handful of spring onions /一大～子韭菜 a big bunch of leeks
掐巴 qiāba 〈方言〉grasp tightly; clamp down on; control:别让人～。Don't let anybody get you under his thumb.
掐菜 qiācài bean sprouts with their fibrous roots nipped off
掐断 qiāduàn nip off; cut off; sever:～水电 cut off water and power supply
掐架 qiājià 〈口语〉(of cocks, dogs, etc.) fight; scramble; tussle:这两只公鸡掐了半天架。The two roosters fought long and hard. /你又跟谁～了? Who are you quarrelling with this time?
掐尖儿 qiājiānr ❶ pinch off young shoots, etc.; top:地里的棉花该～了。It's time to trim the cotton plants in the field. ❷ dismiss; throw out:你太突出了,小心别掐了你的尖儿。You have made yourself too conspicuous. Watch out or you might get the axe.
掐诀 qiājué (of a Buddhist monk or Taoist priest) pinch the knuckles of the fingers with the thumb while chanting incantations
掐丝 qiāsī 〈工美〉wire inlay; filigree:景泰蓝的～技艺最为复杂细致。The wire inlay technique in cloisonné is most complex and meticulous.
掐算 qiāsuàn count on one's fingers:～下来,这次住院花了一万多。I've figured out that my hospitalization expenses totalled more than 10,000 *yuan*. /掐指算来,他已走了二十五天了。I reckon that it is already 25 days since he left.
掐头去尾 qiātóu-qùwěi break off both ends:她吃鱼要～。She eats fish cooked without head or tail. /这段话一～,意思就变了。Quoted out of context, the passage would have a different meaning.
掐子 qiāzi 〈方言〉〈量词〉a handful, bunch, pinch, etc. of:一大～草 a big bunch of grass

齣 qiā bite; hold sth. between the teeth

qiá

拤 qiá clutch or grip with both hands

qiǎ

卡 qiǎ ❶ 〈口语〉wedge; stick; get stuck:他嗓子被枣核～住了。The date stone stuck in his throat. /东西～在抽屉里了。Something got stuck in (*or* wedged inside) the drawer. ❷ withhold; hold back:～住敌军后路 cut off the enemy's retreat /目前银行对贷款～得很紧。At present, the banks are keeping tight control over credit and loans. ❸ strangle: see "～脖子" ❹ clip; clasp; fastener:发～ hair clip; hairpin ❺ checkpost; post:哨～ patrol post /税～ tax checkpost
see also kǎ
卡脖子 qiǎ bózi ❶ seize sb. by the throat; have sb. by the throat:一个蒙面歹徒卡住他的脖子,抢走了他的公文包。A masked ruffian gripped his throat and snatched his briefcase. ❷ have a stranglehold on:～旱 strangler drought — drought occurring when crops are earring /～逼债 press hard for debt repayment /用停电来卡用户的脖子 intimidate clients by withholding power supply /～地段 bottleneck
卡具 qiǎjù 〈机械〉clamping apparatus; fixture
卡壳 qiǎké ❶ 〈军事〉jamming of cartridge or shell case:子弹～了。The cartridge got jammed in the magazine. ❷ get stuck; be held up; be unable to proceed:谈判一开始就～了,双方互不相让,争吵得很厉害。The negotiation ran into a deadlock soon after it began, with each party refusing to make any concessions and arguing back and forth heatedly. /桩子怎么也打不下去,工程卡了壳儿。The construction was brought to a halt as there was no way to drive the piles down. /一个小时的发言,他一口气说了下来,当中都不带～儿的。He finished his hour-long speech in one breath without a hitch.
卡口插座 qiǎkǒu chāzuò aligning plug
卡口灯泡 qiǎkǒu dēngpào bayonet socket bulb
卡口灯头 qiǎkǒu dēngtóu bayonet socket; bayonet cap
卡盘 qiǎpán 〈机械〉chuck
卡子 qiǎzi ❶ clip; clasp; fastener:报～ newspaper clips ❷ checkpost:桥头有～收养路费。There is a checkpost collecting toll at the bridgehead.
卡钻 qiǎzuàn 〈石油〉jamming of a drilling tool

qià

髂 qià
髂骨 qiàgǔ 〈生理〉ilium
髂肌 qiàjī 〈生理〉iliacus

洽 qià ❶ in harmony; in agreement:感情融～ on very good terms; in perfect harmony /这次讨论气氛不佳,意见不～。The atmosphere of the discussion was less than congenial, and the parties did not see eye to eye on the issue. ❷ consult; discuss; arrange:面～ talk things over personally; discuss in person /～办 arrange with sb. to get sth. done /～借 explore the possibility of borrowing sth. (*or* of a loan) ❸ wide; broad; extensive:博识～闻 experienced and knowledgeable; erudite
洽购 qiàgòu arrange or negotiate a purchase:函电～ arrange the purchase of sth. by mail or cable /～进口商品 negotiate the purchase of imported goods /这部电视系列片正在～之中。The purchase of this TV series is under discussion.
洽平 qiàpíng 〈书面〉peace and stability; universal peace and tranquillity:天下～。Peace and tranquillity prevail everywhere. /万方～。Peace reigns in every corner of the land.
洽商 qiàshāng consult with; talk over with:当面～ personal consultation /贸易～ trade talks /经过多次～,双方签署了长期合作协定。After several rounds of consultation, the two sides concluded an agreement for long-term co-operation.
洽谈 qiàtán hold talks; negotiate:～生意 hold trade talks
洽妥 qiàtuǒ reach an agreement
洽闻 qiàwén 〈书面〉highly knowledgeable; well informed; well read

落 qià
落草 qiàcǎo a kind of perennial grass good as fodder

恰 qià ❶ suitable; fitting; appropriate:用词不～ inappropriate wording ❷ precisely; exactly:左边锋疾射入网,～在此时鸣笛终场。The left forward had just shot the ball into the net when the referee whistled and the game ended. /我到南昌时～逢春节。It was the Spring Festival when I arrived in Nanchang.
恰当 qiàdàng suitable; appropriate; apt; proper:措辞～ fitting remarks /比喻不～ inapt analogy /作出～的分析 make a proper analysis /我要找个～的机会同他交换意见。I am looking for an appropriate opportunity to exchange views with him.
恰到好处 qiàdào-hǎochù just right (for the purpose, occasion,

etc.):菜的火候～。The dish was done to a turn. /这个词用得～。This word is well chosen. *or* It's *le mot juste*. /我们这番富有成果的谈话结束得～。We concluded this fruitful discussion at exactly the right time.

恰好 qiàhǎo exactly; just right:大小～合适 just the right size /～及时赶到 arrive in the nick of time /距此～五十米。It is exactly 50 metres away from here. /你要的书我～有。I happen to have the book you need. /我正要出去,～老陈来找我。I was just leaving home when Mr. Chen came to see me.

恰恰 qiàqià just; precisely; exactly:他们的意见～相反。Their views are diametrically opposed.

恰恰舞 qiàqiàwǔ cha-cha (dance)

恰巧 qiàqiǎo by chance; as chance would have it:他说这些话的时候,～我也在场。I happened to be present when he made these remarks.

恰切 qiàqiè apt and accurate:～的译文 apt and accurate translation

恰如 qiàrú just like:晚霞～一幅图画。The sunset glow is as beautiful as a painting.

恰如其分 qiàrú-qífèn just right; proper; appropriate:给以～的接待 give sb. a proper reception (*or* a reception befitting his or her status) /他不知怎样才能把自己的心事～地表达出来。He did not know how best to express his feelings./ 这个评价实事求是,～。This assessment is based on facts and most appropriate.

恰似 qiàsì be just like:光阴～东流水,一去不复回。Time is just like the water of a river flowing east, never to return.

qiān

褰 qiān 〈书面〉lift up (one's coat, etc.):～裳 lift up one's coat /～帷 raise the curtain

搴 qiān 〈书面〉❶ uproot;capture:斩将～旗 (in ancient warfare) kill the enemy generals and capture their standards ❷ *see* "褰" qiān

骞 qiān 〈书面〉❶ hold high; hold aloft:王虺～只。A big snake reared its head. ❷ *see* "搴"qiān

骞驴 qiānlǘ kiang, popular name in the Tibet Autonomous Region for the wild Asiatic ass

谦 qiān modest; unassuming:自～ self-depreciating /他说自己拉丁文懂得极少,有点过～了。He says he has only a meagre knowledge of Latin; he is modest to a fault.

谦卑 qiānbēi humble; modest; meek:在他的上司面前,他～之至。In the presence of his superiors he was all humility.

谦诚 qiānchéng modest and sincere:～待人 treat people with modesty and sincerity

谦辞 qiāncí ❶ self-depreciatory expression ❷ modestly decline:大会主席一职非你莫属,不必～了。You are the most suitable person for the chairmanship of the meeting. Please don't decline it any more.

谦恭 qiāngōng modest and polite:言行～ be modest in speech and courteous in behaviour /～下士 treat scholars with respect /他是一个～不过的人。He is a man of extreme modesty and courtesy.

谦和 qiānhé modest and friendly; modest and gentle:态度～ be modest and amiable /神情～ have a polite and friendly demeanour /他秉性～。He has a modest, amiable nature.

谦谦君子 qiānqiān-jūnzǐ ❶〈旧语〉modest and self-disciplined gentleman ❷ hypocrite who pretends to be modest:在大原则问题上,要立场鲜明,不能做个～! On major issues of principle, one must show clearly where one stands and not play the hypocritical gentleman.

谦让 qiānràng decline an offer out of modesty; decline politely:他们两人在荣誉面前总是彼此～。The two of them often modestly decline honours which are their due, each insisting that the other is more worthy of them. /二人～了一番才落了座。Each had politely asked the other to take precedence before they finally took their seats. /这事儿非你不行,你就不要～了。You're the very person for the job. So don't refuse any more.

谦慎 qiānshèn modest and prudent; unassuming and circumspect

谦顺 qiānshùn modest and submissive

谦退 qiāntuì modest and conciliatory or accommodating

谦虚 qiānxū ❶ modest; open-minded:他为人热情、～。He is by nature warm-hearted and open-minded. /他对自己学术上的成就很～。He is very modest about his own academic achievement. ❷ speak modestly:别看他嘴上～,心里可瞧不起人。He may be mouthing a self-effacing platitude, but deep down in his heart he thinks poorly of others. /他～了一番,才在主席台上就座。After a show of polite reluctance, he took his seat on the rostrum.

谦虚谨慎 qiānxū-jǐnshèn modest and circumspect:～,戒骄戒躁。Be modest and prudent; guard against conceit and impetuosity.

谦逊 qiānxùn modest and unassuming; unpretentious:～的长者 modest and unassuming old gentleman /我向他打招呼,他站起来～地微笑点头。When I greeted him, he stood up smiling and politely nodding recognition.

谦抑 qiānyì 〈书面〉unpretentious; modest and conciliatory

韆 qiān *see* "鞦韆" qiūqiān

牵(牽) qiān ❶ lead along; lead; pull:～马 lead a horse along /他是～儿带女的,负担沉重。The burden of a big family with children to look after weighed heavily on him. ❷ involve; entangle:她不想被～在这场纠纷里。She didn't want to get entangled (*or* involved) in this dispute.

牵绊 qiānbàn interfere with each other; be entangled:看来这两种体系互相～,需要进一步调整。It seems that these two systems are interfering with each other, and some sort of readjustment will have to be made.

牵鼻子 qiān bízi lead by the nose:他觉得自己被人牵着鼻子走,心里总不是滋味。He felt he was being led by the nose, and he was not at all happy about it.

牵缠 qiānchán get bogged down; be involved:这场丑闻也许会～到他。He may get involved in this scandal.

牵肠挂肚 qiāncháng-guàdù be full of anxiety and worry; be beside oneself with anxiety; worry one's head off:儿女远行,做父母的怎能不～? Won't parents feel deeply worried when their children are going far away from home? /我想他们接到信将会更加～。I was afraid my letters might cause them even more worry and anxiety.

牵扯 qiānchě involve; embroil; drag in; implicate:那个案子已经～到他。He is implicated in the case, as it is. /不要把个人关系～到工作关系上去。Never allow personal relationships to get in the way of our work.

牵掣 qiānchè ❶ hinder; impede; be an obstacle to:互相～ restrict each other /那时候,她想参加工作,然而小孩总在～她。In those days, she wanted very much to find employment, but her children were a drag on her. ❷ contain; keep in check; pin down; hold back:这个问题受各方面的～太大,甚为棘手。This is a most thorny question as there is pressure from various quarters.

牵动 qiāndòng ❶ influence; affect; set sb. astir:一伸手臂,就会～背部的创伤。To stretch the arm would make the wound in the back hurt again. /这件事要～全局。The event will affect the situation as a whole. ❷ move; touch:这位小姑娘的病,～了多少单位,～了多少人! The illness of the little girl has struck a sympathetic chord in many institutions and individuals.

牵挂 qiānguà worry; care; think about:～儿女 be concerned about one's children /他在国外,心里总是～着老祖母。When he was abroad, he was always thinking about his aging grandmother. /现在我已经没有什么～了。I have nothing to worry about now.

牵合 qiānhé link together; bring together:我想为他们～一下,让他们有机会互相了解。I'll try to bring them together so that they may have a chance to get to know each other.

牵记 qiānjì worry about; think about:他回到家里,还老～着工厂。He would not take his mind off the problems at the factory even when he was at home.

牵就 qiānjiù give in to; humour:～错误思想是不对的。It is wrong to give in to erroneous thinking.

牵拉机构 qiānlā jīgòu 〈机械〉draw-off mechanism

牵累 qiānlěi ❶ tie down; burden:她有家务～。She is tied down with household work. /孩子太小,～她不能上夜大。The burden of having to look after a small child made it impossible for her to attend evening school. ❷ be implicated; be involved:他觉得这事追究起来自己也会受～。He realized that he might get implicated in the

matter if the investigation went further. /她自己闯了祸还～别人。She got into trouble and dragged everybody along with her.

牵连 qiānlián ❶ involve (in trouble); incriminate; implicate: 受此案～的人数达一百以上。Upwards of 100 people are implicated in this case. ❷ tie up with; be related to: 周围的许多人～着他的心。His heart goes out towards many people around him.

牵连犯 qiānliánfàn 〈法律〉implicated offender

牵念 qiānniàn worry about; be concerned about: 父母年老多病,还时刻～远适异邦的儿女。The aging and ailing parents are constantly concerned about their sons and daughters now residing abroad.

牵牛花 qiānniúhuā 〈植物〉(white-edged) morning-glory

牵牛星 Qiānniúxīng 〈天文〉Altair

牵强 qiānqiǎng forced (interpretation, etc.); strained; far-fetched: 你的理由未免～。The reasons you give are a bit farfetched.

牵强附会 qiānqiǎng-fùhuì stretch the meaning; draw a farfetched conclusion; give a strained interpretation: 这样的论证显然有些～。Such an argument is obviously stretching it a little bit.

牵切纺 qiānqiēfǎng 〈纺织〉tow-to-yarn direct spinning

牵惹 qiānrě involve: 据说这个案子～许多人。They say many people are involved in this case.

牵涉 qiānshè involve; concern; drag in: 这是一个非常复杂的问题,～到很多方面。It was an extremely complicated problem which involved quite a lot of factors. /这个案子～到了几个干部。This case implicated several officials.

牵伸 qiānshēn 〈纺织〉draft; drawing

牵伸术 qiānshēnshù 〈医学〉extension

牵索 qiānsuǒ 〈机械〉traction cable; pull rope

牵头 qiāntóu ❶ take the lead; take the responsibility (of convening a meeting, etc.): 最近由研究所～,十来个科研单位参加,召开了有关人才交流的讨论会。Under the auspices of the research institute and with the participation of about a dozen other research units, a symposium was recently held to discuss the exchange of qualified personnel. ❷ act as go-between: 他俩是去年由张婶～,订下了亲事的。They were engaged last year with Aunt Zhang acting as go-between. ❸ go-between; intermediary

牵系 qiānxì tie up; link together: 深厚的友情,把我们远隔千里的心～在一起。Though we are separated by a thousand *li*, the ties of profound friendship have linked our hearts together.

牵线 qiānxiàn ❶ pull strings; pull wires; manipulate from behind the scenes: 这些活动显然有人在背后～。There must be someone pulling the strings behind these activities. ❷ act as go-between; serve as intermediary: 他们俩谈恋爱是工会主席牵的线。They met through the good offices of the chairman of the trade union and fell in love.

牵线搭桥 qiānxiàn-dāqiáo *also* "搭桥牵线" act as go-between; bring one person into contact with another: 她力图为两家企业～。She is trying to bring the two enterprises into contact with each other.

牵线人 qiānxiànrén wire-puller; go-between

牵心 qiānxīn worry; care; be concerned about: 机关里的一些重要事情不能不让他～。He cannot but concern himself with some important matters in the office.

牵曳 qiānyè pull; lead along (by holding the hand, the halter, etc.): ～牲口 lead the draught animal

牵一发而动全身 qiān yī fà ér dòng quánshēn pull one hair and you move the whole body — a slight move in one part may affect the whole situation; a minor step may lead to major consequences: 此等事所在多有,处理时要谨慎,以免～。As cases like this abound, we should handle them with caution so that the situation as a whole may not be adversely affected.

牵引 qiānyǐn ❶ drag; draw; tow: 机车～列车前进。The locomotive is drawing the train forward. ❷〈医学〉traction: 他背部受伤,正在作～治疗。He has injured his back and is now in traction.

牵引车 qiānyǐnchē tractor; tractor truck

牵引飞机 qiānyǐn fēijī towing aircraft

牵引犁 qiānyǐnlí trailed plough

牵引力 qiānyǐnlì 〈物理〉traction force; pulling force; traction

牵引能量 qiānyǐn néngliàng 〈交通〉haulage capacity

牵引炮 qiānyǐnpào towed artillery

牵引器 qiānyǐnqì 〈医学〉tractor

牵引式 qiānyǐnshì 〈机械〉trail-behind; pull-type: ～播种机 trail-behind planter /～中耕机 trailed cultivator /～割草机 trail-behind mower; drawn mower; traction mower /～滑翔机 towed glider

牵引索 qiānyǐnsuǒ traction rope; trail rope

牵引装置 qiānyǐn zhuāngzhì trailer gear

牵萦 qiānyíng keep thinking about: 他的话一直～着我。I kept thinking about his words.

牵运机 qiānyùnjī 〈机械〉hauling engine

牵制 qiānzhì 〈军事〉contain; check; pin down: ～敌军的主力 pin down the enemy's main forces /～行动 containing action /～性攻击 diversionary (*or* holding) attack /各路敌军互相猜疑,互相～,行动迟缓。The movement of the enemy forces, held up by mutual distrust, was very slow.

悭(慳) qiān

❶ miserly; parsimonious; stingy: *see* "～吝" ❷ lack: 缘～一面 not have had the luck of ever meeting sb.; be denied the chance of making sb.'s acquaintance /仲冬雪犹～。There was still very little snow by mid-winter.

悭吝 qiānlìn stingy; parsimonious: ～成性 be stingy by nature; be a born miser /～鬼 skinflint; penny pincher

佥[1](僉) qiān

〈书面〉whole; total

佥[2](僉) qiān

see "签" qiān

佥事 qiānshì ❶〈旧语〉title of an official ❷ (in government offices under the reign of the Northern Warlords, 1912-1927) low-ranking official appointed upon recommendation by a minister

佥同 qiāntóng 〈书面〉unanimously agree; reach consensus: 众意～。They have identical views.

签[1](簽) qiān

❶ write one's signature; sign; autograph: 请把名字～到来宾签名簿上。Please sign your name in the visitors' book. /这个文件需要会～。This document requires countersigning. ❷ make brief comments: ～个意见 write a brief comment on a document /他在备注栏里～了几点看法。He wrote down a few ideas in the remarks column.

签[2](簽、籤) qiān

❶ bamboo slip used for divination, gambling, etc.: 求～ ask for divination by drawing bamboo slips /中～ draw the right lot /转世灵童最后要经金瓶掣～确定。(As in Tibetan Buddhism) The soulboy is to be chosen finally by having the candidates draw lots from a gold vase. ❷ label; sticker; tag: 标～ label; sticker /题～ label with the name of a book on it /浮～ note glued on the margin of a book /航空邮～ air mail sticker ❸ slender pointed chip of bamboo or wood: 竹～ bamboo chip or stick /牙～ tooth pick ❹ tack: ～被里 tack a lining on a quilt /～花边 tack on a piece of lace

签呈 qiānchéng 〈旧语〉submit a document (to one's superiors)

签到 qiāndào register one's attendance (at a meeting or at an office); sign in: 来宾请～。Visitors please sign in here. /～处 sign-in desk / ～簿 attendance book

签订 qiāndìng conclude and sign: ～贸易协定 sign a trade agreement /～公约的各方 parties signatory to the pact /两国正式～友好条约。The two countries formally concluded a treaty of friendship.

签发 qiānfā sign and issue (a document, certificate, etc.): ～文件 endorse the dispatch of a document /～护照 issue a passport /这篇稿子总编辑已经～。The editor-in-chief has approved the publication of this article.

签名 qiānmíng put one's signature to; sign one's name; autograph: 请作者在书上～ ask the author to autograph his book /～盖章 sign one's name and affix one's seal; set one's hand and seal to /在意见书上～ sign one's name in a comment book /～簿 visitors' book /～运动 signature drive

签收 qiānshōu sign upon receiving sth.: 这份文件很重要,要由收件人本人～。This document is very important and it is necessary for the recipient to sign for it in person.

签署 qiānshǔ sign: ～命令 sign an order /～证书 sign a certificate /两国总理～了联合公报。The prime ministers of the two countries signed a joint communique.

签署人 qiānshǔrén undersigned

签条 qiāntiáo ❶ short note ❷ bookmark

签筒 qiāntǒng ❶ container for lots or chips (for divination, gambling, etc.) ❷ *also* "扦子" qiānzi sharp pointed metal tube or prod used to extract samples from sacks of grain, etc.

签押 qiānyā 〈旧语〉sign one's name or make any other personal mark on a document
签押房 qiānyāfáng 〈旧语〉government office for registration of all incoming and outgoing documents; correspondence registry (office)
签约 qiānyuē sign a contract or agreement: ～仪式 signing ceremony
签证 qiānzhèng (grant a) visa: ～处 visa office (*or* section) /互免～ mutual exemption of visas /～费 visa fee / ～申请表 visa application form / 入境～ entry visa / 出境～ exit visa /过境～ transit visa / 申请～ apply for a visa /办理～手续 go through the formalities for obtaining a visa /批发或拒发～ issue or refuse a visa /一次有效出入境～ entry-exit visa valid for a single journey /多次有效出入境～ multiple entry-exit visa
签注 qiānzhù ❶ attach a slip of paper (to a document) or insert one (in a book) with relevant reference on it; write comments and proposed solutions on a document to be submitted to one's superiors for approval: 他读书每有～。He never reads but he writes down comments or relevant references. /送到厂长手中的这份报告,已由办公室主任～。The director of the administrative office has written comments on this report to be submitted to the factory manager for approval. ❷ write comments or note about relevant matters (on papers, documents, forms, etc.): 这份证明信上有人事部门～的意见。This testimonial bears the written remarks of the personnel department.
签字 qiānzì sign; affix one's signature: ～画押 set one's hand and seal to sth. /中转～ sign a transfer (as for a train passenger) /～仪式 signing ceremony /～国 signatory state (*or* power); signatory /～后立即生效 come into force (*or* effect) upon signature /该国没有在这个条约上～。That country did not sign the treaty. /报销单据上应有主管领导人的～。Bills submitted for reimbursement must bear the signatures of the leading cadre in charge.
签子 qiānzi 〈口语〉❶ bamboo slip used for divination, gambling, etc. ❷ slender pointed chip of bamboo or wood

铅

qiān ❶ lead (Pb) ❷ lead (in a pencil); black lead
铅白 qiānbái 〈化学〉white lead
铅板 qiānbǎn lead plate
铅版 qiānbǎn 〈印刷〉stereotype
铅版工 qiānbǎngōng stereotyper
铅版浇注机 qiānbǎn jiāozhùjī stereotype casting machine
铅笔 qiānbǐ pencil: 蓝～ blue pencil /自动～ propelling pencil
铅笔刀 qiānbǐdāo pen-knife; pencil sharpener
铅笔盒 qiānbǐhé pencil case; pencil box
铅笔画 qiānbǐhuà pencil drawing
铅笔心 qiānbǐxīn lead (in a pencil); black lead
铅玻璃 qiānbōli 〈化学〉lead glass; flint glass
铅垂线 qiānchuíxiàn 〈建筑〉plumb line; 〈航海〉lead line; sounding line
铅锤 qiānchuí 〈建筑〉plummet; plumb (bob)
铅丹 qiāndān 〈化学〉red lead (Pb_3O_4); minium
铅弹 qiāndàn plumb
铅弹头 qiāndàntóu lead bullet
铅刀一割 qiāndāo-yīgē 〈谦词〉a blunt knife can still cut; a person without talent, if put to proper use, has also a role to play: 发挥～之用 do one's humble part; do one's bit /我虽平庸,也许还能～吧。Inspite of my limited ability, I may still be of some use.
铅锭 qiāndìng lead pig
铅粉 qiānfěn 〈化学〉lead powder
铅封 qiānfēng lead sealing
铅焊 qiānhàn 〈冶金〉lead burning: ～料 lead solder
铅华 qiānhuá face-powder; white lead
铅黄 qiānhuáng 〈书面〉lead used in editing for making corrections or crossing out lines; collation (because lead and yellow ochre were used to collate manuscripts in former times)
铅灰 qiānhuī leaden; lead gray: ～色的云 leaden clouds
铅基合金 qiānjīhéjīn 〈冶金〉lead base alloy
铅皮 qiānpí 〈冶金〉lead sheath; lead sheet
铅皮电缆 qiānpí diànlǎn lead-covered cable; lead-sheathed cable
铅椠 qiānqiàn 〈书面〉lead used in writing and wood blocks — writing: 久不事～。It has been a long time since I last laid down my pen.
铅球 qiānqiú 〈体育〉shot: 推～ putting the shot; shot put /～运动员 shot-putter
铅熔炼炉 qiānrónglìànlú 〈冶金〉lead smelter
铅丝 qiānsī ❶ galvanized wire ❷ 〈电力〉lead wire
铅酸性蓄电池 qiānsuānxìng xùdiànchí 〈化工〉lead-acid battery
铅条 qiāntiáo ❶ 〈印刷〉slug; lead ❷ lead (for a propelling pencil)
铅铁 qiāntiě zinc-plated iron; galvanized iron
铅锌合金 qiānxīn héjīn 〈冶金〉hard lead
铅蓄电池 qiānxùdiànchí lead storage battery; lead accumulator
铅印 qiānyìn letterpress printing; relief printing; typographic printing; stereotype
铅浴 qiānyù 〈冶金〉lead bath: ～淬火 lead bath quenching; lead hardening /～回火 lead tempering /～炉 lead bath furnace; lead-pot furnace /～退火 lead annealing
铅直 qiānzhí perpendicular; vertical; plumb
铅制品 qiānzhìpǐn leadwork
铅中毒 qiānzhòngdú 〈医学〉lead poisoning; saturnism
铅坠 qiānzhuì plummet
铅子 qiānzǐ 〈口语〉bullet
铅字 qiānzì 〈印刷〉type; letter: 大号～ large type /小号～ small type /黑体～ boldface /～面 typeface /～盘 type case; letter board /～凸模 standard
铅字合金 qiānzì héjīn type metal

千

qiān ❶ thousand: 数以～计 count by the thousand /拥有良田～顷 boast a thousand of hectares of fertile land ❷ large numbers of; innumerable: 成～上万的人 thousands and tens of thousands of people; large numbers of people /社会主义建设事业一日～里。Our socialist construction is forging ahead with giant strides. /～言万语,万语～言,并作一句话:途中珍重。Numerous words are concentrated in one sentence: take good care of yourself on the journey. /看～帆竞过。I watched a thousand sails pass by. ❸ (Qiān) a surname
千安 qiān'ān 〈电学〉kiloampere(ka): ～束流 kiloampere beam current
千巴 qiānbā 〈物理〉kilobar (kb)
千磅 qiānbàng 〈物理〉kilo pounds
千比特 qiānbǐtè 〈信息〉kilobit
千变万化 qiānbiàn-wànhuà be constantly changing; be subject to a myriad changes: 局势～,尚不可逆料。The situation is unpredictable for it is subject to many and often unexpected changes. *or* The situation is volatile.
千部一腔,千人一面 qiānbù yī qiāng, qiānrén yī miàn all in the same tune, all with the same features — (of literary works or theatrical performance) stereotyped; formulistic; stylized
千层饼 qiāncéngbǐng pancake with numerous thin layers; layered pancake
千层底 qiāncéngdǐ shoe sole made of many layers of cloth stitched together: ～鞋 cloth shoes with such soles
千差万别 qiānchā-wànbié vary greatly; differ in a thousand and one ways: 各国国情,～。Conditions vary greatly from country to country. /这些事物表面上虽然相似,但实质上～。These things are similar on the surface, but essentially they are vastly different.
千疮百孔 qiānchuāng-bǎikǒng *also* "百孔千疮" riddled with gaping wounds; afflicted with all kinds of ills
千愁万绪 qiānchóu-wànxù be sad and worried
千锤百炼 qiānchuí-bǎiliàn ❶ steeled and tempered: 他是一位经过～的老战士。He is a tempered (*or* seasoned) veteran fighter. ❷ be polished again and again; be highly finished: ～出佳作。A fine piece of writing is the product of repeated polishing.
千刀万剐 qiāndāo-wànguǎ punishment of "ten thousand cuts"; hack sb. to a thousand pieces; punishment by dismemberment: 将这个卖国贼～,人们也不解恨。Hacking the traitor to a thousand pieces would not slake people's hatred for him. /他们至少该～。They deserve nothing less than dismemberment.
千岛群岛 Qiāndǎo Qúndǎo Kurile Islands or Chishima Islands now under Russian jurisdiction with some islands claimed by Japan
千电子伏 qiāndiànzǐfú 〈物理〉kiloelectron-volt (kev)
千叮万嘱 qiāndīng-wànzhǔ repeated exhortations
千吨 qiāndūn 〈物理〉kiloton (kt)
千恩万谢 qiān'ēn-wànxiè express a thousand thanks; be extremely grateful
千乏 qiānfá 〈电力〉kilovar (kvar)

千方百计 qiānfāng-bǎijì in a thousand and one ways; by every possible means; by fair means or foul; by hook or by crook:～地增产节约 do one's best to increase production and practise economy / 庸医们总是～地骗钱。Quack doctors always try in a hundred and one ways to cheat people out of their money.

千分表 qiānfēnbiǎo dial gauge; dial indicator

千分尺 qiānfēnchǐ micrometer:圆径～ annular micrometer /外径～ outside micrometer / 内径～ inside micrometer /游标～ vernier micrometer

千分点 qiānfēndiǎn one-tenth of a percentage point; permillage point:人口出生率比去年下降了两个～。The current birthrate is two permillage points lower than that of last year.

千分号 qiānfēnhào per mill or mil

千分数 qiānfēnshù *see* "千分号"

千分之一 qiānfēnzhīyī one thousandth; milli:～克 milligram

千佛殿 Qiānfódiàn Thousand-Buddha Hall, on Mount Tai(泰山), Shandong Province

千夫 qiānfū 〈书面〉numerous people:十夫所守,～不过。Guarded by ten soldiers, the pass is impregnable to a thousand attackers.

千夫所指 qiānfūsuǒzhǐ face a thousand accusing fingers; be universally condemned:～,无病而死 when a man is condemned by all, his days are numbered even though he is not ill — it is perilous to incur public wrath

千伏 qiānfú *also* "千伏特"〈电力〉kilovolt (kv):～安 kilovolt-ampere (kva)

千古 qiāngǔ ❶ through the ages; eternal:～奇冤 (suffer) a wrong as great as history has ever known /～流传 be handed down from generation to generation /～名言 celebrated saying known through the ages /～卓绝 be unmatched (*or* peerless) past and present ❷ (used in elegiac inscription or elegiac couplets for the deceased):某某先生～。Eternal glory to Mr. So-and-so!

千古奇闻 qiāngǔ-qíwén fantastic story; unheard-of strange tale

千古一人 qiāngǔ-yīrén an outstanding person appears only once in a thousand years — talented people are hard to come by

千古罪人 qiāngǔ-zuìrén man of eternal guilt; person held up to infamy through the ages; one who goes down in history as a man of infamy; villain of all time; eternal villain

千赫 qiānhè kilohertz

千呼万唤 qiānhū-wànhuàn be called again and again; be called and called:～始出来,犹抱琵琶半遮面。She appeared after being called and called, Holding a *pipa* that half hid her face.

千户 qiānhù 〈旧语〉officer commanding one thousand soldiers; official governing one thousand households

千回百转 qiānhuí-bǎizhuǎn revolve continuously; be full of twists and turns:崎岖的山路～。The rugged mountain path is full of twists and turns.

千家诗 Qiānjiāshī *Poetry from a Thousand Poets*, collection of ancient poetry originally compiled by Liu Kezhuang (刘克庄, 1187-1269), whose condensed version later became a popular primer in poetry for children

千家万户 qiānjiā-wànhù millions of households; countless people:对于价格改革我们特别小心,那是影响～的事。We have been particularly cautious about price reform which affects all households.

千娇百媚 qiānjiāo-bǎimèi *also* "千娇百态" (of a woman) ravishingly beautiful

千斤 qiānjīn thousand *jin* — very heavy; extremely weighty:我觉得有～重担压在我的肩膀上。I felt as if a load of tremendous weight were resting on my shoulders.

千斤 qiānjin 〈机械〉❶ (short for 千斤顶) hoisting jack; jack ❷ pawl

千斤顶 qiānjīndǐng 〈机械〉hoisting jack; jack:油压～ hydraulic jack

千金 qiānjīn ❶ thousand pieces of gold; large amount of money:～一笑。A single smile is worth a thousand pieces of gold. /这幅画～难买。The painting is not to be had for a thousand pieces of gold. *or* The painting is priceless. ❷ 〈敬词〉daughter (other than one's own):～小姐 daughter of a noble family /恭喜你家添了一位～。Congratulations to you on the birth of your baby girl.

千金买骨 qiānjīn-mǎigǔ thirst for talent; be eager to recruit talentd people

千金要方 Qiānjīn Yàofāng *also* "备急千金要方" Bèijí Qiānjīn Yàofāng *Priceless Vital Prescriptions*, medical compendium of diagnoses and prescriptions (over 5,000) compiled in 652 by Sun Simiao (孙思邈, 581-682), physician of the Tang Dynasty

千金一诺 qiānjīn-yīnuò *also* "一诺千金" a promise is worth a thousand pieces of gold — a man's promise can always be counted on

千金一掷 qiānjīn-yīzhì *also* "一掷千金" bet a thousand pieces of gold on a single throw; gamble at high stakes; spend money lavishly:他是都中一位～的阔少爷。He is the son of a wealthy family in the capital who spends money like water.

千军万马 qiānjūn-wànmǎ thousands upon thousands of horses and soldiers; thousands upon thousands of troops:～捣敌巢。A mighty force was closing in on the enemy stronghold. /潮水像～一般,直涌了过来。With the force of thousands of charging troops, the tide was surging and roaring.

千军易得,一将难求 qiānjūn yì dé, yī jiàng nán qiú It is much easier to recruit a thousand troops than find a general to command them — there are not many outstanding leaders

千钧一发 qiānjūn-yīfà *also* "一发千钧" hang by a hair; be in an extremely precarious situation:当时国运危如～。At that time the fate of the state seemed to be hanging by a thread.

千钧重负 qiānjūn-zhòngfù very heavy burden; grave responsibility:这个任务对我来说真是～。For me this task involves tremendous responsibility.

千卡 qiānkǎ 〈物理〉kilocalorie (kcal; Cal)

千克 qiānkè kilogram (kg)

千里 qiānlǐ thousand *li* — long distance:～客 guest from afar /不积跬步,无以至～。One cannot expect to cover a thousand *li* without moving ahead step by step. *or* Great achievements are founded on small, sustained efforts. /欲穷～目,更上一层楼。To look farther afield, One needs to ascend another storey.

千里鹅毛 qiānlǐ-émáo goose feather sent from a thousand *li* away — a small gift sent from afar conveys deep feeling (from the proverb:"千里送鹅毛,礼轻情意重。" The gift itself may be light as a goose feather, but sent from a thousand *li* away, it conveys deep feeling. *or* The gift itself may be insignificant, but coming from afar, it conveys the sender's deep feeling.) ～意不轻。A gift sent from afar, a token of warm friendship.

千里光 qiānlǐguāng 〈植物〉climbing groundsel (*Senecio scandens*)

千里驹 qiānlǐjū thousand-*li* colt; fine racing pony — promising young man

千里马 qiānlǐmǎ winged steed; person of great talent:有伯乐而后得～。Only a Bo Le can discover a winged steed. *or* Only an experienced talent scout can discover really talented people. / 给那些德才兼备的"～"充分施展才能的机会。People of talent and integrity should be provided with opportunities to fully display their potential.

千里马运动 Qiānlǐmǎ Yùndòng Chollima Movement, a movement to speed up the socialist construction in the Democratic People's Republic of Korea

千里挑一 qiānlǐ-tiāoyī one (picked) out of a thousand — person not easily found; outstanding person

千里迢迢 qiānlǐ-tiáotiáo thousands of *li* away; from afar:对那些～从世界遥远的地区来参加这次会议的代表,我们表示热烈欢迎。We wish to extend a warm welcome to those delegates who came to this conference all the way from distant places on the globe.

千里眼 qiānlǐyǎn ❶ 〈旧语〉telescope; field glass ❷ clairvoyant (person); farsighted person

千里姻缘一线牵 qiānlǐ yīnyuán yī xiàn qiān a thousand *li* can not keep apart a couple cut out for each other; a thread can draw together a fated match across a thousand *li*; matrimony is a predestined bond

千里之堤,溃于蚁穴 qiānlǐ zhī dī, kuì yú yǐxué one ant-hole may cause the collapse of a thousand-*li* dyke; a small leak will sink a great ship; slight negligence may lead to great disaster

千里之行,始于足下 qiānlǐ zhī xíng, shǐ yú zú xià a thousand-*li* journey begins with the first step; the highest eminence is to be gained step by step

千立方米 qiānlìfāngmǐ kilostere

千粒重 qiānlìzhòng 〈农业〉thousand-grain weight

千了百当 qiānliǎo-bǎidàng be perfect in every respect:他不是～的人。His character is not impeccable. *or* He is far from perfect.

千伶百俐 qiānlíng-bǎilì very clever and lively:他的儿媳妇心地好,而且～。His daughter-in-law is kind-hearted and very bright.

千虑一得 qiānlǜ-yīdé ❶ (condensed from 愚者千虑，必有一得) even the slow-witted occasionally hit upon a good idea ❷〈谦词〉my humble opinion; my observation: 愚陈～之见。I'd like to offer my humble opinion.

千虑一失 qiānlǜ-yīshī (condensed from 智者千虑，必有一失) even the wise are not always free from error: 这些不足之处，仅是作者的～。These inadequacies are the results of the author's occasional laxity. / 有关事项他们都作了安排，但也难免～，请大家多提意见。Although they have made arrangements for everything concerned, oversight is hardly avoidable and your comments and suggestions for improvement are welcome.

千枚岩 qiānméiyán 〈地质〉phyllite

千米 qiānmǐ kilometre (km)

千磨百折 qiānmó-bǎizhé repeated trials and tribulations: ～不动摇 never waver despite hardships and trials

千难万险 qiānnán-wànxiǎn innumerable dangers and hardships

千年虫 qiānniánchóng *also* "两千年问题" liǎngqiānnián wèntí 〈计算机〉millennium bug; Y2K (problem)

千篇一律 qiānpiān-yīlǜ harp on the same old subject; follow the same pattern; be stereotyped; be monotonous: 文章要有新意，不能～。Freshness is the essence of good writing; one should not harp on the same old tune all the time. / 衬衫料子是好的，可惜样式～，没有吸引力。The shirting is good but the pattern is common and unattractive.

千奇百怪 qiānqí-bǎiguài all kinds of strange things; infinite variety of fantastic phenomena; most bizzare; grotesque: 山峰形状各异，真是～。The cliffs on the mountain are indeed grotesque in size and have shapes of infinite variety.

千千万万 qiānqiān-wànwàn millions upon millions; innumerable: 我们的文艺应当为～劳动人民服务。Our art and literature should serve millions upon millions of working people.

千切 qiānqiè be sure; make sure: ～早日回来。Be sure to return at an early date.

千秋 qiānqiū ❶ thousand years; ages: ～功罪，谁人曾与评说？Who has passed judgement on the good and ill, You have wrought these thousand autumns? ❷〈敬词〉birthday: 儿孙欢聚一堂，为老人作～之祝。The old man's children and grandchildren gathered together joyously to mark his birthday.

千秋万代 qiānqiū-wàndài (for) thousands of years: ～的大事业 great undertaking of lasting importance / 这种光荣传统将～地传下去。This glorious tradition will be handed down from generation to generation.

千屈菜 qiānqūcài 〈植物〉purple lythrum (*Lythrum salicaria*)

千儿八百 qiānrbābǎi 〈口语〉about a thousand: 这套家具少说也值～。This set of furniture is worth a thousand *yuan* or so at least.

千日红 qiānrìhóng 〈植物〉globe amaranth (*Gomphrena globosa*)

千山万水 qiānshān-wànshuǐ *also* "万水千山" a thousand mountains and ten thousand rivers — a long and arduous journey: 唐玄奘去印度取经，经过了～。In the Tang Dynasty when Xuan Zhuang travelled to India in search of Buddhist scriptures, he had to cross numerous mountains and rivers. / 此去～，望君多多保重。You have a long and arduous journey ahead. Please take good care of yourself.

千升 qiānshēng kilolitre (kl)

千手观音 Qiānshǒu Guānyīn *Avalokitesvara*, Goddess of Mercy with a Thousand Arms

千丝万缕 qiānsī-wànlǚ innumerable links; countless ties: 这两个国家仍然保持～的联系，虽然它们的外交关系已经中断。The two countries maintain innumerable ties with each other although they have severed diplomatic relations.

千岁 qiānsuì thousand years — a deferential allusion to a prince, used especially in traditional operas: ～爷 His (*or* Her, *or* Your) Royal Highness

千穗谷 qiānsuìgǔ 〈植物〉*Amaranthus hybridus* var. *hypochondriacus*

千头万绪 qiāntóu-wànxù have thousands of strands and loose ends; have a multitude of things to cope with; be faced with an extremely complicated situation: 案情～，一时不知从何着手。The case was so complicated that we simply didn't know where to start. / 脑子里～，现在总算理清楚了。I have at long last sorted out the many ideas in my mind.

千瓦 qiānwǎ kilowatt (kw): ～小时 kilowatt-hour (kwh)

千万 qiānwàn ❶ ten million; millions; countless: 这种普通农家，在中国何止～。There are millions upon millions of ordinary farmer families like this in China. ❷ (used in earnest entreatment, exhortation, etc.) must; be sure to: 为人处事，～小心谨慎。Be sure to act with caution. / ～不能麻痹大意。In no case must we relax our vigilance. / 这个教训～要记取。We must always bear this lesson in mind. / ～注意防火。Do take the greatest care to prevent fire. / 托你办的事～别忘了。Please don't forget what I have asked you to do for me.

千…万… qiān…wàn… ❶ many; countless; numerous: 千村万落 thousands upon thousands of villages / 千山万壑 countless mountains and valleys / 千年万载 millions of years / 千仇万恨 undying hatred; deadly animosity ❷ *used for emphasis*: 千不该万不该 regret a thousand times over — regret deeply; have no excuse whatsoever / 千叮咛万嘱咐 exhort sb. repeatedly

千万买邻 qiānwàn-mǎilín it's difficult to find a good neighbour *see also* "百万买宅，千万买邻" bǎiwàn mǎi zhái, qiānwàn mǎi lín

千辛万苦 qiānxīn-wànkǔ all kinds of hardships; untold hardships: 历尽～，他们才到达白雪覆盖着的高山顶峰。After experiencing untold hardships, they reached the highest peak of the snow-capped mountain.

千言万语 qiānyán-wànyǔ innumerable words (of solicitude); a multitude of tender words: ～，不知从何处说起。She was tongue-tied though she had a thousand tender words to say to him. / ～，难表深情。No words can express what I feel deeply in my heart.

千叶 Qiānyè Chiba, an industrial city on Honshu Island(本州岛), Japan

千依百顺 qiānyī-bǎishùn *also* "千随百顺" be obedient and docile: 她对丈夫～。She was all obedience to her husband.

千载难逢 qiānzǎi-nánféng not likely to occur once in a thousand years; once in a blue moon: 这种事是～的。Such an event is very rare indeed. / 这种～的好机遇，谁也不肯放过的。This is a chance of a lifetime which no one would let slip through his fingers.

千载一时 qiānzǎi-yīshí *also* "千载一遇" (of an opportunity) once in a thousand years: 这种～的机遇，我们有幸碰到了！We were lucky to come across such a golden opportunity which presents itself only once in a blue moon.

千张 qiānzhang sheets of dried cream of bean curd

千兆 qiānzhào kilomega: ～位〈数学〉kilomegabit / ～周〈物理〉kilomegacycle

千真万确 qiānzhēn-wànquè absolutely true: 此事系我亲眼所见，～。This is undoubtedly true for I actually saw with my own eyes what was happening.

千周 qiānzhōu kilocycle (kc)

千姿百态 qiānzī-bǎitài of all kinds of shapes and postures: 碧云寺的罗汉～，绝不雷同。The sculptures of *arhats* in the Blue Cloud Temple are of such a great variety of shapes and postures that none resembles another.

千字文 Qiānzìwén *Thousand Character Reader*, ancient primer for children written in the sixth century by Zhou Xinsi (周兴嗣) in rhymed sentences of four characters each

迁(遷) qiān

❶ move; remove: ～厂 move a factory to another site / 乔～ move house / ～户口 change one's residence registration ❷ change: 变～ changes / 见异思～ change one's mind the moment one sees something new; be inconstant / 情随事～ man's feelings change with changing circumstances / 事过境～。This is a thing of the past and the circumstances have changed. *or* A lot of water has run (*or* flowed) under the bridge. ❸〈书面〉change one's official post: 左～ be demoted

迁变 qiānbiàn changes; vicissitudes: 古今风俗，～甚多。There have been numerous changes in customs from ancient times to the present.

迁并 qiānbìng move and merge with: 这个学校将～到第二中学去。This school will move and merge with No.2 Secondary School.

迁除 qiānchú 〈书面〉be appointed to (a post)

迁调 qiāndiào 〈书面〉be transferred (to another post)

迁鼎 qiāndǐng 〈书面〉removal of the tripods (the nine tripods symbolizing state power) — fall of an empire (kingdom, etc.); collapse or subversion of a state; dynastic change

迁都 qiāndū move the capital (to another place)

迁飞 qiānfēi (of birds or insects) migrate in flocks or swarms

迁化 qiānhuà 〈书面〉❶ change ❷ (of persons) pass away; die

迁建 qiānjiàn move and reconstruct the original building

迁就 qiānjiù readily change one's ideas to suit; accommodate (oneself to); give in to; humour:不应该～不合理的要求。We should never give in to unreasonable demands. /不能～错误倾向。We must not yield to any erroneous tendency. /他对手下的工作人员作了不少～。He made quite a few accommodations to his subordinates. /她是个从来不肯～别人的姑娘。She is a girl who must always have her own way.

迁居 qiānjū change one's dwelling place; take up residence in another place; move (house):一年来我们几次～。We have removed several times within the past year. /山林被毁，鸟兽～。When the forest was destroyed, the birds and beasts left the mountain.

迁客 qiānkè 〈书面〉〈旧语〉official demoted and banished to a remote place

迁兰变鲍 qiānlán-biànbào exert a subtle influence (on sb.)

迁离 qiānlí move or migrate to another place; leave:～故土 leave one's native land

迁流 qiānliú 〈书面〉passage of time:岁月～，瞬已五十。Time goes like flowing water, and I am already 50.

迁怒 qiānnù vent one's anger (on an innocent person); take it out (on sb.):应责怪自己，不能～于人。You have only yourself to blame, and should not take it out on anybody. /挨了上级的批评，他～于左右的人。After being criticized by his superior, he vented his anger on those around him.

迁善改过 qiānshàn-gǎiguò correct one's mistakes; mend one's ways

迁徙 qiānxǐ move; migrate; change one's abode:人口～ human migration; population movement /游牧部落逐水草而～。Nomadic tribes migrate in search of pasture.

迁徙自由 qiānxǐ zìyóu freedom of migration; freedom of movement; freedom of changing one's abode

迁延 qiānyán delay; postpone; defer; procrastinate:此系急务，不可～时日。This is an urgent matter which brooks no delay. /这个问题甚为重要，但～至今尚未解决。The problem is very important, but no solution has been suggested up to now.

迁移 qiānyí move; remove; migrate; change:～户口 transfer one's household registration /～驻地 (of soldiers, local government or geological teams) move to another place /大～ exodus; diaspora /会址已经～，请通知与会人员。The venue of the conference has been changed. Please notify the participants.

迁移性 qiānyíxìng 〈动物〉migratory nature

迁葬 qiānzàng remove a coffin from one grave to another

迁谪 qiānzhé also "迁贬"〈书面〉(of officials in feudal times) be exiled; be banished to a remote place:这位朝廷大臣因得罪宦官而～云南。The minister was banished to Yunnan as he had incurred the displeasure of the eunuchs.

芊 qiān

芊绵 qiānmián also "芊眠"〈书面〉(of trees or grass) thick; dense; lush; profuse:绿草～。The grass is luxuriant and lush green.

芊芊 qiānqiān 〈书面〉luxuriant; lush green:～芳草 lush green grass /野花野草，～莽莽。Exuberant wild flowers and grasses stretch into the distance.

扦 qiān

❶ poker; pick:火～ fire poker /牙～ toothpick /蜡～儿 candlestick ❷ sharp-pointed implement or prod used to extract samples from sacks of grain, etc. ❸〈方言〉fasten; insert:～门 bolt the door /用针～住 fasten with a pin /把花～在瓶子里。Put the flowers in the vase. ❹〈方言〉pedicure; peel:～苹果 peel an apple

扦插 qiānchā 〈农业〉cuttage

扦担 qiāndàn 〈方言〉❶ wooden pole, pointed at both ends (usually for carrying firewood) ❷ instigator; one who sows dissension

扦脚 qiānjiǎo 〈方言〉pedicure:～师傅 pedicure; pedicurist

扦手 qiānshǒu also "扦子手"〈旧语〉customs inspector

扦子 qiānzi ❶ slender pointed stick made of metal, bamboo, etc.:铁～ iron poker /竹～ bamboo spike ❷ sharp pointed metal tube or prod used to extract samples from sacks of grain, etc.

钎 qiān

drill rod; drill steel; borer:钢～ drill steel /打～ drill holes in rock for blasting with a hammer and a drill rod

钎焊 qiānhàn 〈冶金〉brizing; braze welding; brass solder:～合金 brazing alloy /～剂 soldering flux /～炉 brazier

钎子 qiānzi also "炮钎" pàoqiān rock drill; hammer drill

仟 qiān

(capital form for the numeral 千) thousand

阡 qiān

〈书面〉❶ footpath between fields, running north and south ❷ narrow path leading to a grave

阡陌 qiānmò crisscross footpaths between fields:～纵横 footpaths crisscrossing the fields /～纵横的稻田 paddy fields crisscrossed with dykes

僉 qiān

〈书面〉see "愆" qiān

愆 qiān

〈书面〉❶ transgression; mistake:罪～ sins of transgression /以赎前～ atone for a past fault ❷ miss the deadline; pass the time limit

愆期 qiānqī 〈书面〉exceed the time limit; delay (payment, etc.)

愆忒 qiāntè 〈书面〉fault; error; sin

愆尤 qiānyóu 〈书面〉error; fault; sin:他为官一任，～甚多。He made many mistakes during his term of office.

鸽 qiān

(of birds with sharp beaks) peck

瓩 qiānwǎ

(now written as 千瓦) kilowatt

qián

前 qián

❶ front; in front:～庭后院 front and back yards /床～ before the bed /屋～有两棵大树。There are two trees in front of the house. ❷ forward; ahead:勇往直～ forge ahead; advance bravely /畏缩不～ hang back in fear; hesitate to press forward /停滞不～ be at a standstill ❸ first; front:～三名 first three places /我坐在最～面。I was sitting in the front row. ❹ before; ago:解放～ before Liberation /奥运会～一段时间 during the run-up to the Olympic Games /～几天我还看见过他。I saw him only a few days ago. /临出发～才通知他。He was notified of it shortly before his departure. ❺ former; formerly:～苏联 former Soviet Union /他是公司的～顾问。He was formerly adviser to the firm. /新乡是～平原省省会。Xinxiang used to be the capital city of the former Pingyuan Province. ❻ earlier than; prior to; pre-:～资本主义 pre-capitalism /～寒武纪 pre-Cambrian Period ❼ prospect; future: see "～程";"～景" ❽ battlefront; front:支～物资 materials for supporting the battlefront

前半场 qiánbànchǎng also "上半场" shàngbànchǎng first half (of a game, concert, play, etc.)

前半晌 qiánbànshǎng 〈方言〉forenoon; morning:明天～我一点空也没有。I'll be fully occupied tomorrow morning.

前半生 qiánbànshēng first half of one's life or lifetime:他～为国家做了许多有益的事。He did a lot for the country during the first half of his life.

前半天 qiánbàntiān before noon; morning:～干点工作，下午休息。Get some work done in the morning and have a rest in the afternoon.

前半夜 qiánbànyè first half of the night (before midnight):～他睡得很好，后半夜就差了。He was sound asleep for the first half of the night, but he didn't sleep so well after midnight.

前辈 qiánbèi senior (person); elder; veteran; older generation:学术界～ senior scholars /文艺界老～ veteran writers and artists /现在我们要把事情做得更好，不辜负～对我们的教导。We must do a better job today, so as to live up to the teachings of the older generation.

前臂 qiánbì 〈生理〉forearm

前边 qiánbian ❶ in front; ahead; before:走在队伍最～ walk at the head of the procession /后边没路，我们得从～绕过去。We have to make a detour ahead for there is no way out behind. ❷ above; preceding:～一段详细地分析了社会主义市场经济问题。The preceding paragraph gives an in-depth analysis of the socialist market economy.

前不巴村，后不着店 qián bù bā cūn, hòu bù zháo diàn with no village ahead and no tavern behind — get stranded in an uninhabited area; be suspended in midair:这件事弄得我～，不知如何是好。This development has left me at a loss what to do next.

前不见古人,后不见来者 qián bù jiàn gǔrén, hòu bù jiàn láizhě I can't see the ancients when looking back; nor can I see the future generations when looking ahead — feel all alone in this wide world
前舱 qiáncāng forecabin; nose cabin
前舱口 qiáncāngkǒu forehatch
前叉 qiánchā front fork (of a bicycle)
前朝 qiáncháo preceding dynasty; previous dynasties
前车之覆,后车之鉴 qiánchē zhī fù, hòuchē zhī jiàn the overturning of the cart ahead is a warning to the cart behind; we should take warning from the mistakes of those before us
前车之鉴 qiánchēzhījiàn warning taken from the overturned cart ahead; lessons drawn from others' mistakes:"骄兵必败"的例子很多,无不是我们的~。"Pride goes before a fall." Such instances are numerous and they should all serve as a lesson for us.
前尘 qiánchén 〈书面〉the past:回首~,感慨万端。Looking back on the past, I felt a thousand feelings rushing upon me.
前沉 qiánchén front part of a cart being more heavily loaded than the rear
前程 qiánchéng ❶ prospect; future: ~似锦 glorious future; bright prospects ❷〈旧语〉career; official position:为自己的~,他竟不惜投靠宦官。To secure an official position, he didn't hesitate to throw in his lot with the eunuchs.
前程万里 qiánchéng-wànlǐ have a brilliant future; have very fine prospects:年轻人~,还要靠自己去努力。Young people have a bright future, but they should work hard for it.
前池 qiánchí 〈水利〉forebay
前仇 qiánchóu old score; old enmity:不记~ forget about old enmity; forgive and forget
前此 qiáncǐ prior to this
前导 qiándǎo ❶ lead the way; march in front; head (a procession, etc.); precede:队伍由仪仗队~。The guard of honour marched at the head of the procession. ❷ one who leads the way; guide
前敌 qiándí front line:军长亲临~指挥作战。The army commander himself rushed to the front line to direct the operations.
前敌委员会 qiándí wěiyuánhuì front committee
前殿 qiándiàn antechamber; front hall
前度刘郎 qiándù-Liúláng young Master Liu of those days (from Liu Yuxi's 刘禹锡 lines "种桃道士归何处? ~今又来"。Whither has the Taoist who planted the peach-trees gone? The young Master Liu of those days has come again!) — person who returns to a place where he once lived or worked:多年前他本是这里的县长,此次回归可谓~。Years ago he was a county magistrate here and now he has come to visit the place again.
前额 qián'é forehead
前方 qiánfāng ❶ ahead; in front: 正~ right ahead; straight ahead /她凝视~,恍然若失。Gazing into the distance, she was lost in thought. /~是一片开阔地。There is a stretch of open country ahead. ❷ the front: ~将士 officers and men at the front /~医院 field hospital /~指战员 frontline commanders and fighters /~吃紧。The front has come under heavy pressure.
前房 qiánfáng ❶ one's late wife ❷〈生理〉atrium: 心室~ atrium of ventricle /听泡~ atrium of otocyst
前锋 qiánfēng ❶ vanguard:此时我军~已渡过大河。By this time the vanguard of our army had crossed the big river. ❷〈体育〉forward:这个队有两名优秀的~。This team has two ace forwards. ❸〈气象〉front:冷空气的~已经进入新疆北部。The cold front has moved into northern Xinjiang.
前夫 qiánfū former husband; ex-husband:她的~留下两个孩子。She had two children by her ex-husband.
前赴后继 qiánfù-hòujì advance wave upon wave:为了祖国的繁荣富强,多少代人~,英勇斗争。Generations of the people have advanced wave upon wave fighting valiantly against heavy odds for the prosperity of the country.
前功尽弃 qiángōng-jìnqì have forfeited all that one has achieved; all one's previous efforts are wasted:一举不当,~。One wrong move, and our effort will go down the drain. /成功的把握不大,还可能~。The chances of success are not great; moreover, it is highly probable that all our previous efforts will come to naught.
前滚翻 qiángǔnfān 〈体育〉forward roll
前汉 Qián Hàn *also* "西汉" Xī Hàn Former Han or Western Han (Dynasty), 206 BC-24 AD
前后 qiánhòu ❶ shortly before and after; around (a certain time); about:五一~ around May First /国庆节~ round about National Day ❷ *also* "前前后后" from beginning to end; altogether:~来了好几次电话。There have been several phone calls so far. /今年~有五批北京的学生访问了西安。Five batches of Beijing students have visited Xi'an this year. ❸ in front and behind:~一贯 consistent /~左右 on all sides; all around /~有高层建筑。There are highrise buildings both in front and behind. /房屋~都是草地。There are lawns both in front and at the back of the house. ❹ following one after another; successive:~两任村长 two successive village heads /这本书~五种版本我都买了。I've bought all the five consecutive editions of the book.
前…后… qián…hòu… ❶ *used to indicate the sequential connection between two actions or two things either in space or in time*:前店后厂 store at the front and workshop at the back /前松后紧 be slack at the start and have to work extra hard towards the end ❷ *used to indicate forward or backward movements of a body*:前俯后仰 bend forwards and backwards
前后夹攻 qián-hòu jiāgōng make a frontal and rear attack at the same time; be caught between two fires:对敌取~的态势 assume the posture for making a simultaneous frontal and rear attack on the enemy
前后脚儿 qiánhòujiǎor (of two or more people) leave or arrive nearly at the same time or in close sequence:他们俩~到的。They arrived one on the heels of the other.
前后文 qiánhòuwén beginning and ending of an article, novel, etc.:~互相矛盾。The beginning and the ending of the article are contradictory. *or* The statement at the end of the article contradicts that at the beginning.
前呼后拥 qiánhū-hòuyōng *also* "前遮后拥" be accompanied by numerous retainers; have attendants both in front and behind:~的高官 high official escorted by an imposing retinue /~地进了村 come into the village with a host of retainers
前胡 qiánhú 〈中药〉root of purple-flowered peucedanum (*Peucedanum decursivum*)
前级泵 qiánjíbèng prepump; forepump
前记 qiánjì *also* "前言" introduction; preface; foreward
前脚 qiánjiǎo ❶ forward foot in a step:~一滑,就站不稳了。The body could not remain steady when the forward foot slipped. ❷ (used in conjunction with 后脚) no sooner... than; as soon as; the moment (when):我~进了院子,他后脚就赶到了。He arrived the moment I got into the courtyard.
前襟 qiánjīn front part of a Chinese robe or jacket
前进 qiánjìn march on; advance; go forward; forge ahead:徒步~ walk on foot /匍匐~ crawl forward /急速地~ press ahead /顶着风~ advance in the teeth of the wind /大踏步~ stride ahead /奋勇~ forge ahead courageously
前景 qiánjǐng ❶ foreground:这幅画的~是茅舍和杨树。The picture has a cottage and some poplar trees in the foreground. ❷ prospect; future; vista; perspective:无限光明的~ boundless bright prospects (*or* future) /~暗淡 bleak future; gloomy perspective /两国扩大经济文化交流的~非常广阔。There is great promise for further economic and cultural exchanges between the two countries.
前臼齿 qiánjiùchǐ 〈生理〉premolar teeth
前倨后恭 qiánjù-hòugōng be first haughty and then excessively polite; change from arrogance to humility:我们禁不住笑那些~的人。We cannot help laughing at those who first behave with arrogance but suddenly switch to slavish humility.
前科 qiánkē previous criminal record: ~记录 record of previous crime /这个被拘留的小伙子据说有~。This young detainee was said to have a previous criminal record.
前科犯 qiánkēfàn 〈法律〉criminal with a previous conviction; ex-convict; ex-prisoner
前科学 qiánkēxué pre-science
前科罪 qiánkēzuì 〈法律〉previous crime
前空翻 qiánkōngfān 〈体育〉forward somersault in the air
前劳 qiánláo 〈书面〉past meritorious deeds; past laurels:毋废~ do not forfeit your previous meritorious record
前例 qiánlì precedent:无~可援 have no precedent to go by/ 史无~ unprecedented in history; without any parallel in history
前脸儿 qiánliǎnr 〈方言〉front part of a person, building, etc.; frontage:这个人~特别像他哥哥。He resembles his brother very much in facial appearance. /房子~是三间书店。In the front part of

Q

the building are three bookshops.

前梁 qiánliáng (of a bicycle, etc.) front-axle beam

前列 qiánliè front row or rank; forefront; van:雄踞世界排坛的～ be in the front rank of world volley ball teams /站在谋求妇女解放斗争的最～ be in the forefront of the struggle for the emancipation of women

前列腺 qiánlièxiàn 〈生理〉prostate (gland):～素〈药学〉prostaglandin

前列腺肥大 qiánlièxiàn féidà 〈医学〉hypertrophy of the prostate; prostatauxe; prostatomegaly

前列腺切除术 qiánlièxiàn qiēchúshù 〈医学〉prostatectomy

前列腺石 qiánlièxiànshí 〈医学〉prostatolith:～切除术 prostatolithotomy

前列腺炎 qiánlièxiànyán prostatitis

前烈 qiánliè 〈书面〉❶ achievements of our forefathers ❷ ancient sages

前路 qiánlù journey ahead; road ahead

前掠翼 qiánlüèyì 〈航空〉buzzard-type wing

前轮 qiánlún 〈汽车〉front wheel;〈航空〉nosewheel

前茅 qiánmáo be among the vanguard; rank among the best:名列～ one's name heads the list; come out at the top; be among the best (of the successful candidates)

前门 qiánmén ❶ front door ❷〈比喻〉(as opposite to 后门) open and fair way of doing things; proper channels:这些铺子不肯搞后门交易,一切商业往来都经～。These shops refuse to have any back-door (*or* underhand) dealings, and all business transactions are carried out through proper channels. ❸ (Qiánmén) Front Gate (of the former city wall), Beijing

前门拒虎,后门进狼 qiánmén jù hǔ, hòumén jìn láng drive a tiger out of the front door while letting a wolf in at the back — ward off one danger only to fall prey to another:～,未得其益,先受其害。One can only expect more harm than good by trying to drive the tiger from the front door while letting a wolf sneak in at the back.

前面 qiánmian ❶ in front; forward; ahead:走在我们～的是个抱小孩的老太婆。Walking ahead of us is an old woman carrying a baby. /办公楼～是个大操场。Opposite the office building is a huge sportsground. ❷ above; afore-mentioned; preceding:这个道理～已经讲得很清楚了。The reason has already been clearly stated above. /以后我还会再谈～提出的问题。I'll come back to the above-mentioned problem later. /结论似乎与～几段的意思相矛盾。The conclusion seems contradictory to the ideas in the preceding paragraphs.

前脑 qiánnǎo 〈生理〉forebrain

前年 qiánnián year before last

前怕狼,后怕虎 qián pà láng, hòu pà hǔ fear wolves ahead and tigers behind — be plagued by all sorts of fears; be overcautious:我们不要"～",否则将一事无成。We must banish all unnecessary fears, otherwise we will achieve nothing.

前排 qiánpái front row:他不想在～就坐,以免太显眼。He didn't want to sit in a front row lest he should be too conspicuous.

前炮 qiánpào 〈军事〉forward gun (on a ship); bow-piece

前仆后继 qiánpū-hòujì as one falls, others step into the breach; advance fearlessly:他们在民族解放的道路上～,英勇前进。They fought courageously in the course of national liberation, one stepping into the breach the moment others fell.

前妻 qiánqī former wife; ex-wife

前期 qiánqī early stage; early days:20世纪～ in the early phase of the 20th century /二次大战～ in the early stage of World War II

前期仔鱼 qiánqī zǐyú 〈动物〉prelarva

前愆 qiánqiān 〈书面〉past wrongdoings:这些被释放的罪犯决心重新作人,以赎～。The ex-convicts vowed to make a fresh start to atone for their past misdeeds.

前前后后 qiánqián-hòuhòu ❶ whole story; ins and outs:事情的～他都清楚。He knows the story from beginning to end. ❷ *see* "前后❷"

前桥 qiánqiáo (of a car) front axle:～壳 front axle housing /～梁 front axle beam

前倾翻斗车 qiánqīng fāndǒuchē front tipper

前清 Qián Qīng Qing Dynasty (1644-1911)

前情 qiánqíng ❶ condition leading to the event; what happened before the incident; cause:～后尾 cause and effect ❷ old friendship:回忆～,惘然若失。Recalling the old friendship, he felt dreadfully depressed.

前鞧 qiánqiū headstall (headpiece and halter, etc. for a horse)

前驱 qiánqū forerunner; harbinger; pioneer; precursor:革命～ revolutionary forerunner (*or* predecessor) /他是作为近代医学的～闻名于世的。He is well known as a pioneer of modern medical science. /这些书是代表新趋向的～作品。These works are a trailblazer.

前驱期 qiánqūqī 〈医学〉prodromal stage

前儿 qiánr *also* "前儿个"〈口语〉day before yesterday:他是～来的。He came here the day before yesterday.

前人 qiánrén forefathers; forebears; predecessors:这些都是～几百年来英勇捍卫过的理想。These are the ideals our forefathers bravely defended for centuries. /我们现在进行的伟大事业是～不能想像的。The great undertaking in which we are engaged today was beyond our forefathers' imagination.

前人栽树,后人乘凉 qiánrén zāi shù, hòurén chéng liáng while earlier generations plant trees, posterity will enjoy the cool under the shade — profit by the labour of one's forefathers; toil for the benefit of one's descendants

前任 qiánrèn predecessor:～部长 former minister /他是我的～。He was my predecessor.

前日 qiánrì day before yesterday

前晌 qiánshǎng 〈方言〉forenoon; morning:我昨儿～见过他。I saw him yesterday morning.

前哨 qiánshào group of soldiers some distance ahead of the main army; advance guard; outpost:双方～已经接火。The advance guards of the two sides have had skirmishes already.

前哨战 qiánshàozhàn 〈军事〉skirmish

前身 qiánshēn ❶ predecessor:这个钢铁公司的～是个小铁厂。The predecessor of this iron and steel complex was a small iron foundry. ❷ front part of a Chinese robe, jacket, etc.:这件衣服的～长,后身短。The front of this jacket is longer than its back.

前生 qiánshēng 〈迷信〉previous existence:～缘分 predestined bond

前失 qiánshī ❶ (of horses, mules, etc.) fall down because of unsteady front legs ❷〈书面〉previous error:痛悔～ be deeply regretful for one's past misdeeds

前时 qiánshí lately; recently

前世 qiánshì 〈迷信〉previous existence:～无冤,今世无仇。We had no hatred for each other in the past, nor are we enemies at present. /这是～姻缘。This was a predestined matrimonial bond.

前市 qiánshì 〈旧语〉stock exchange transaction done before noon

前事 qiánshì past experiences; past happenings; past events

前事不忘,后事之师 qiánshì bù wàng, hòushì zhī shī past experience, if not forgotten, is a guide for the future; lessons learned from the past can serve as a guide for the future; bear past experience in mind and you will profit by it

前视红外仪 qiánshì hóngwàiyí 〈无线电〉forward looking infrared

前视图 qiánshìtú 〈机械〉front view

前室 qiánshì former wife; ex-wife

前束 qiánshù toe-in (of a car)

前思后想 qiánsī-hòuxiǎng think over again and again; ponder over:他～,总觉得这件事办得不妥。He was mulling over the matter and felt he had not handled it properly.

前所未闻 qiánsuǒwèiwén never heard of before:此事～。This sort of thing was practically unheard of in the past.

前所未有 qiánsuǒwèiyǒu hitherto unknown; unprecedented:表现出～的热情 display unprecedented enthusiasm /感到一种～的喜悦 experience a peculiar joy rarely felt in the past /这是～的伟大事业。This is a great cause unparalleled in history.

前台 qiántái ❶ proscenium;〈比喻〉routine work concerning a performance:他在剧团里专打～。He engages in routine work for the troupe. ❷ stage; downstage ❸〈贬义〉on stage; in public:从幕后跳到～ jump on to the stage from behind the scenes

前提 qiántí ❶ premise:大～ major premise /小～ minor premise /～是推出结论的根据。A premise provides the basis on which to work out a conclusion. ❷ prerequisite; presupposition; predicate:纪律以服从为～。Discipline presupposes compliance. /生活改善要以发展经济为～。The improvement of our living standard is predicated on the development of our economy.

前天 qiántiān day before yesterday:～晚上 night before last /～上午我见到过他。I saw him in the morning the day before yesterday.

前厅 qiántīng 〈建筑〉antechamber; vestibule

前庭 qiántíng 〈生理〉vestibule

前庭炎 qiántíngyán 〈医学〉vestibulitis
前头 qiántou *also* "前面" ❶ in front; at the head; ahead: 他在～跑,其他的人在后头紧追。He was running ahead while the others followed him closely. ❷ above; preceding: 这个问题～已经谈到了。This question has been mentioned above.
前途 qiántú future; prospect: ～光明 bright future /～渺茫 bleak future; gloomy prospects /送别时,他祝我～无量。At parting, he wished me the best of luck. /我不禁感到～茫然。I shuddered to think of what the future held in store for me.
前途茫茫 qiántú-mángmáng blurred, bleak future; unclear, gloomy prospects: 连年军阀混战,青年学生们感到～。In the face of the incessant fighting among the warlords young students felt that their future was very bleak indeed.
前腿 qiántuǐ foreleg
前往 qiánwǎng make for; go to; proceed to: 明日启程～东京 leave for Tokyo tomorrow /在～机场途中遇到了雨 be caught in the rain on one's way to the airport /～农村作实地调查研究 go to the countryside to make on-the-spot investigations /应邀～访问 go on a visit upon invitation
前委 qiánwěi (short for 前敌委员会) front committee
前卫 qiánwèi ❶〈军事〉advance guard; vanguard: ～部队 vanguard troops /以二营为～ with the second battalion as advance guards ❷〈体育〉halfback: 足球～技术要全面。The halfback must have all-round technique in a football game.
前无古人 qiánwúgǔrén have no parallel in history; unprecedented in history: ～,后无来者 not to be found either in the past or in the future; unique /这样规模的改革～。The fact that the reform was carried out on such a scale was without parallel in history.
前夕 qiánxī eve: 全国解放～ on the eve of the nationwide liberation
前吸盘 qiánxīpán anterior sucker
前贤 qiánxián 〈书面〉wise and virtuous elders; sages: 德高望重的～ venerable sages
前嫌 qiánxián past grievances; previous feeling of animosity: 捐弃～,共商国是。We should discard past enmity and discuss affairs of national interest.
前线 qiánxiàn front; battlefront; frontline: 奔赴～ rush to the front /～阵地 frontline positions /厂领导身临生产～指挥工作。The leadership of the factory went to the workshops in person to give on-the-spot instructions.
前项 qiánxiàng 〈数学〉antecedent
前修 qiánxiū 〈书面〉persons of virtue and integrity in ancient times; ancient sages
前悬挂式播种机 qiánxuánguàshì bōzhǒngjī forward planter
前言 qiányán ❶ preface; foreword; introduction: 这本书的～很精彩。The preface of this book is very well written. ❷ words said earlier; previous statements: 书中的～与后语多有抵牾。There are many contradictory remarks in the book. ❸〈书面〉earlier promise: 自食～ go back on one's word; break one's promise ❹〈书面〉sayings of our forefathers
前言不搭后语 qiányán bù dā hòuyǔ talk disjointedly; babble disconnected phrases: 此公说话往往～。The chap is often incoherent (*or* often speaks incoherently).
前沿 qiányán 〈军事〉forward position: ～指挥所 forward command post
前沿科学 qiányán kēxué frontier science
前仰后合 qiányǎng-hòuhé *also* "前俯后合";"前俯后仰" sway to and fro; rock backwards and forwards: 笑得～ shake (*or* rock) with laughter; double up with mirth; split one's sides laughing /那人醉得东倒西歪,～。Dead drunk, the man swayed from side to side, unable even to sit up straight.
前夜 qiányè eve: 五四运动的～,知识分子已经明白了中国需要科学与民主。On the eve of the May 4th Movement in 1919, the intellectuals were well aware of China's need for science and democracy.
前因 qiányīn cause
前因后果 qiányīn-hòuguǒ cause and effect; entire process: 我们还得进一步调查,才可能了解这个事件的～。We have to make further investigations to understand the cause and effect of the incident.
前缘 qiányuán 〈佛教〉predestined relationship or bond: 他们有些～。They had some predestined bond.
前院 qiányuàn front courtyard
前站 qiánzhàn point at which a travelling party is to stop; next stop on a march, etc.: 打～ go in advance to make arrangements for food and lodgings of the whole party /那里是这次行军的～。That place will be our next stop on the march.
前兆 qiánzhào omen; augury; premonition: 台风将临的～ indications of an impending typhoon /他在心脏病发生之前已有～。He had a premonition of a heart attack before it actually happened.
前哲 qiánzhé ancient sages
前者 qiánzhě the former: ～后者是相互关联的名词。The former and the latter are correlative nouns.
前震 qiánzhèn 〈地质〉pre-earthquake; foreshock; tremor before the earthquake
前肢 qiánzhī 〈动物〉forelimb; foreleg
前置 qiánzhì prepose; pre-: ～放大器 preamplifier; head amplifier
前置词 qiánzhìcí 〈语言〉preposition
前轴 qiánzhóu 〈机械〉fore axle; forward shaft
前装炮 qiánzhuāngpào 〈军事〉muzzle-loading gun; muzzle-loader
前装载机 qiánzhuāngzàijī frontloader
前缀 qiánzhuì 〈语言〉prefix
前奏 qiánzòu ❶ *see* "前奏曲" ❷ prelude; preliminary preparations: 攻占敌人的桥头堡,是整个战役的～。Capturing the enemy's bridgehead fortification was the prelude to the entire campaign.
前奏曲 qiánzòuqǔ ❶〈音乐〉prelude ❷〈比喻〉prelude — initial action
前座议员 qiánzuò yìyuán (UK) front bencher (leading member of Parliament of both the government and the opposition)

掮

qián 〈方言〉carry on the shoulder: ～一袋米 carry a bag of rice on the shoulder /～行李 carry luggage (*or* traveller's bags)
掮客 qiánkè broker: 政治～ political broker

潜(潛)

qián ❶ hide under water; submerge: ～入河底 dive to the bottom of a river /鱼～水底。Fish stay hidden in the depths of the river. ❷ hide; be latent; lurk: *see* "～伏" ❸ secretly; stealthily; on the sly: ～师 move troops in secret /～以舟载兵入渭。Troops were transported stealthily to River Wei by boat. ❹ potential: 从内部挖～ tap the potential from within ❺(Qián) a surname
潜步 qiánbù walk stealthily or on tiptoe: ～而行 walk on tiptoe
潜藏 qiáncáng be latent; be hidden; hide: 小鱼～在芦苇根底下。Small fish hide at the roots of the reeds. /他身上～着一种还没有充分表现出来的才能。He has latent talents which have yet to be fully exercised. /人民的意志里～着巨大的力量。Implicit in the will of the people is a force of tremendous magnitude.
潜存 qiáncún lie hidden; be inherent; be latent: ～于人们头脑中的旧观念不易去掉。Old concepts ingrained in people's minds die hard. /～的封建意识危害极大。Latent survivals of feudal ideology are most harmful.
潜邸 qiándǐ 〈旧语〉residence of a crown prince
潜对潜导弹 qiánduìqián dǎodàn 〈军事〉underwater-to-underwater missile (UUM)
潜遁 qiándùn stealthily run away
潜伏 qiánfú hide; be latent; lie low; lurk: ～的疾病 latent disease /这种昆虫～在土层里过冬。This insect hibernates in the soil during the winter. /各种细菌在人体内～着。All kinds of bacteria incubate in the human body. /平静之中往往～着危险。Danger often lies hidden in an atmosphere of peace and tranquillity.
潜伏期 qiánfúqī 〈医学〉incubation period: 病毒～ incubation (*or* latency) period of a virus
潜伏哨 qiánfúshào 〈军事〉undercover secret sentry posted beyond an outpost
潜航 qiánháng (of a submarine) submerge: ～速度 submerged speed /～深度 submerged depth
潜弧焊 qiánhúhàn 〈冶金〉submerged arc welding
潜居 qiánjū live in seclusion; live in solitude; be a hermit: ～乡间 live in seclusion in the countryside
潜科学 qiánkēxué latent science; potential science; embryonic science
潜力 qiánlì potential; potentiality; latent capacity: 还有很大的～没有发挥出来 have a great potential yet to be tapped
潜流 qiánliú ❶〈地质〉undercurrent; underflow ❷ (of public opinion, emotion, etc.) undercurrent; hidden opinion or feeling: 正在得意之时,他心头却又泛起了一股失落的～。An undercurrent of emptiness was welling up in his heart even though he felt elated

with success.
潜没油罐 qiánmò yóuguàn 〈石油〉submerged tank
潜能 qiánnéng 〈物理〉latent energy
潜匿 qiánnì keep out of sight; go into hiding; hide
潜鸟 qiánniǎo 〈动物〉loon
潜热 qiánrè 〈物理〉latent heat
潜入 qiánrù ❶ infiltrate; sneak; steal:～敌后 sneak in behind enemy lines /昨天,两个毒品走私犯～国境。Two drug traffickers slipped into the country yesterday. ❷ dive down; submerge:潜水艇迅速～水中。The submarine quickly submerged.
潜射导弹 qiánshè dǎodàn submarine-launched missile
潜水 qiánshuǐ ❶ go under water; dive:～作业 underwater operations /水兵大都会～。Most seamen can dive. ❷〈地质〉phreatic water
潜水泵 qiánshuǐbèng 〈机械〉sinking pump; submerged pump; submersible pump
潜水反应堆 qiánshuǐ fǎnyìngduī 〈原子能〉submarine reactor
潜水服 qiánshuǐfú diving suit
潜水器 qiánshuǐqì scuba
潜水式电动机 qiánshuǐshì diàndòngjī 〈电工〉submersible motor
潜水艇 qiánshuǐtǐng *also* "潜艇" submarine; U boat
潜水鸭 qiánshuǐyā diving duck
潜水衣 qiánshuǐyī diving suit
潜水员 qiánshuǐyuán diver; frogman:～病 caisson disease; decompression sickness
潜水运动 qiánshuǐ yùndòng 〈体育〉underwater swimming
潜水钟 qiánshuǐzhōng diving bell
潜台词 qiántáicí ❶〈戏剧〉unspoken words in a play left to the understanding of the audience:导演要帮助演员琢磨好～。It is for the director to help his cast to fully understand what is implicit in the lines. ❷〈比喻〉implied meaning; implication:他这番话的～不难猜测。It is not difficult to get at the implications of his observation.
潜逃 qiántáo abscond:携赃物～ abscond with stolen goods /畏罪～ flee after committing a crime; be a fugitive from justice
潜艇 qiántǐng submarine; U boat:～探测器 submarine detector /～跟踪 submarine tracking /～发射的弹道导弹 submarine-launched ballistic missile (SLBM)
潜艇部队 qiántǐng bùduì (US) silent service
潜艇母舰 qiántǐng mǔjiàn 〈军事〉submarine depot board
潜艇声纳 qiántǐng shēngnà submarine sonar
潜望镜 qiánwàngjìng periscope
潜望雷达 qiánwàng léidá 〈军事〉periscope radar
潜心 qiánxīn devote oneself ; work with great concentration:～典籍,孜孜不倦 apply oneself to the study of historical records /～写作 devote oneself to writing /他正在找一个他可以潜下心来搞学问的工作。He is looking for some research work he can get his teeth into.
潜行 qiánxíng ❶ move under water:潜水员在海底～。The frogman moved about under the sea. ❷ move stealthily; slink:夜间～ move about stealthily at night
潜血 qiánxuè 〈医学〉occult blood:～试验 occult blood test
潜移默化 qiányí-mòhuà exert a subtle influence (on sb.'s character, thinking, etc.); act on subtlely; influence imperceptibly:家长的一言一行都对孩子产生～的影响。The parents exert a gradual and imperceptible influence on their children in everything they say and do.
潜意识 qiányìshí the subconscious; subconsciousness: ～的自我 subconscious self
潜因子 qiányīnzǐ 〈物理〉potential factor
潜隐 qiányǐn ❶ hide; conceal; remain under cover:他淡淡地一笑,笑里～着悲哀。He gave a faint smile that betokened sorrow. *or* He gave a faint smile, which had a trace of sadness. ❷〈书面〉live in seclusion
潜泳 qiányǒng underwater swimming:他的～技术很高。He is very skilful in underwater swimming.
潜鱼 qiányú 〈动物〉pearlfish
潜在 qiánzài hidden; latent; potential: ～意识 the subconscious; subconsciousness /～力量 latent force /～对手 potential adversary /～的威胁 hidden threat
潜在市场 qiánzài shìchǎng potential market
潜滋暗长 qiánzī-ànzhǎng grow imperceptibly; develop unconsciously:警惕不良的思想作风～。Guard against the imperceptible growth of evil (*or* unhealthy) social trends.
潜踪 qiánzōng 〈贬义〉go into hiding; conceal one's whereabouts:我们要把～的匪徒们引出来消灭。We must draw out the hidden bandits and eliminate them.

乾

qián ❶ first of the Eight Trigrams (八卦), denoting the principle of heaven, the sovereign, the male, and strength ❷〈旧语〉male: *see* "～宅"
乾坤 qiánkūn heaven and earth; universe:扭转～ effect a radical change in the existing state of affairs; reverse the course of events /～再造 remake the world; rearrange the mountains and rivers
乾陵 Qiánlíng Qianling Mausoleum, tomb of Tang Emperor Gaozong(高宗) and Empress Wu Zetian(武则天) in Qianxian County(乾县), Shaanxi Province
乾隆 Qiánlóng Qianlong (formerly translated as Ch'ien Lung), title of the reign (1736-1795) of Aisin Gioro Hongli (爱新觉罗·弘历, 1711-1799), 4th emperor of the Qing Dynasty, called reverently Qing Gaozong (清高宗) after death:～元年 first year of (the reign of) Qianlong (1736) / ～皇帝 Emperor Qianlong
乾乾 qiánqián work ceaselessly; strive relentlessly:君子终日～。A superior man must always strive to improve himself.
乾清宫 Qiánqīnggōng Palace of Heavenly Purity in the Palace Museum, Beijing
乾图 qiántú astronomical phenomena; celestial phenomena; heavenly bodies
乾象 qiánxiàng celestial phenomena; heavenly bodies:夜观～ observing the heavenly bodies at night; nocturnal observation of astronomical phenomena
乾曜 qiányào sun; sun rays
乾造 qiánzào 〈旧语〉❶ bridegroom ❷(fortune-telling) man's horoscope
乾宅 qiánzhái 〈旧语〉bridegroom's family

虔

qián ❶ pious; devout; sincere: *see* "～诚";"～心"❷ plunder; slaughter: *see* "～刘"
虔诚 qiánchéng devout; reverent; pious; sincere:～的基督教徒 pious Christian /他在遗像前～地鞠了一躬。He bowed before the portrait of the deceased with devout reverence. /我～地希望母亲将来能够现实地看待这个问题。It is my sincere hope that mother would eventually look at the problem in a realistic way.
虔敬 qiánjìng reverent; highly respectful:他在老师面前,态度非常～。He was all reverence before his teachers.
虔刘 qiánliú 〈书面〉plunder; kill:～边陲百姓 plunder the border inhabitants
虔婆 qiánpó 〈旧语〉vixen; old hag; procuress
虔心 qiánxīn sincere; pious; devout:～祈祷 pray devoutly /～忏悔 repent sincerely /我～虔意地希望他事业一帆风顺。I sincerely hope that his career will be plain sailing.
虔信 qiánxìn piety; devoutness

黔[1]

qián 〈书面〉black

黔[2]

Qián another name for Guizhou Province
黔剧 qiánjù *Qian* opera, local opera of Guizhou Province
黔黎 qiánlí 〈书面〉ordinary people; man in the street
黔驴技穷 qiánlǘ-jìqióng the Guizhou donkey has used up all its tricks; the lion's skin falls off, and beneath it is only a donkey — be at the end of one's resources
黔驴之技 qiánlǘzhījì tricks of the Guizhou donkey; cheap tricks
黔首 qiánshǒu 〈古语〉common people

钤

qián ❶ seal ❷ affix a seal to ❸〈书面〉lock; control; restrict:～束 keep under control; restrict
钤记 qiánjì 〈旧语〉seal of a government office
钤键 qiánjiàn 〈书面〉❶ key; crux ❷ scheme; stratagem
钤印 qiányìn affix a seal to (a document, etc.)
钤章 qiánzhāng official stamp

钱[1](錢)

qián ❶ coin; cash:铜～ copper coins /大～ big coins /小～ small coins ❷ money:纸～ paper money; banknotes /洋～ silver dollar /赚大～ make pots of money/ 身边有小～吗? Got any small change? ❸ fund; sum:工～ wage /饭～ money for a restau-

rant bill; money for food ❹ wealth: 有～有势 enjoy both wealth and position; be both wealthy and influential ❺ anything that resembles a coin in shape: 榆～儿 elm tree seeds ❻ (Qián) a surname

钱[2](錢) qián *qian*, a unit of weight (=5 grams): 十分为一～, 十～为一两。Ten *fen* makes up one *qian*, whereas ten *qian* constitutes one *liang*.

钱板儿 qiánbǎnr ❶ wooden board with grooves for keeping coins ❷〈方言〉washboard

钱包 qiánbāo wallet; purse

钱币 qiánbì coin

钱币学 qiánbìxué numismatics

钱财 qiáncái riches; wealth; money: 广有～ roll in money/ 聚敛～ amass wealth /这不仅浪费～, 而且浪费时间。This is not only a waste of money, but also a waste of time.

钱钞 qiánchāo 〈旧语〉money in general

钱串子 qiánchuànzi ❶ string running through the square holes of copper coins — be money-minded; miserly: 那个人可是个～脑袋。That fellow is really money-minded. ❷ *also* "钱龙"〈动物〉arthropod; millipede

钱褡 qiándā *also* "钱褡裢"; "钱褡子" big cloth bag for keeping money

钱刀 qiándāo knife-shaped coin

钱谷 qiángǔ ❶ money and grain; levies in kind and cash ❷ *also* "钱谷师爷" (in the Qing Dynasty) magistrate's assistant charged with the collection of taxes; revenue clerk

钱柜 qiánguì money-locker; money-box; till

钱狠子 qiánhěnzi 〈方言〉miser; skinflint

钱可通神 qiánkětōngshén money can bedevil the devil himself; money makes the mare go: ～, 此言差矣! The saying "Money talks" is not quite true!

钱粮 qiánliáng 〈旧语〉❶ land tax: 完～ pay land tax ❷ revenue: ～师爷 revenue clerk

钱龙 qiánlóng *see* "钱串子❷"

钱癖 qiánpǐ parsimony; love of money: 此人有～。This fellow has a peculiar fondness for money. *or* He is a pinchpenny.

钱票 qiánpiào 〈口语〉❶ paper money or currency; banknotes ❷ vouchers used in canteens in place of cash

钱儿癣 qiánrxuǎn 〈口语〉ringworm

钱塘潮 Qiántángcháo Qiantang tide or bore

钱塘江 Qiántángjiāng Qiantang River in Zhejiang Province

钱眼 qiányǎn hole in the center of a copper coin: 你钻～儿里了。You are a real money grabber.

钱纸 qiánzhǐ 〈方言〉paper money burned as an offering to the dead: 烧～ burn paper money

钱庄 qiánzhuāng old-style banking house

钱租 qiánzū money rent

钳(箝、[2]拑) qián ❶ pincers; pliers; tongs: 火～ fire (*or* coal) tongs /尖口～ pointed-nose pliers /老虎～ pincer pliers /台～ bench clamp /克丝～ combination pliers/ 圆头～ round-nose pliers /平口～ flat-nose pliers /焊～ welding pliers /台～ *also* "虎～" vice /手～ hand vice ❷ hold with pincers: 把铁丝～住 grip an iron wire with pincers ❸ clamp; restrain: ～天下人之口 gag public criticism; suppress public opinion

钳床 qiánchuáng plier lathe

钳工 qiángōng ❶ benchwork ❷ fitter

钳击 qiánjī (short for 钳形突击) two-pronged surprise attack or offensive; pincer movement

钳口 qiánkǒu ❶ seal sb.'s lips by threat or manipulation ❷ keep one's mouth shut: 这些人个个～无言, 其中定有缘故。There must be a reason why they all kept mum.

钳口结舌 qiánkǒu-jiéshé keep one's mouth shut; keep mum: ～, 非国家之福也。It is against the interest of the state when the public refuse to speak up on all occasions. *or* It is not in the best interest of the country for the public to keep silent at all times.

钳形 qiánxíng pincerlike: ～包围 pincer-like encirclement / ～攻击 (make a) pincers attack

钳制 qiánzhì pin down; clamp down on; suppress: 游击队对敌军起了～作用。The guerrillas played the role of pinning down the enemy troops. /她那张嘴确实被～住了, 老实了好几天。There is no doubt that she has been muzzled, as she is rather quiet these days. /新闻界受到～。The press is gagged.

钳爪 qiánzhuǎ chela (of a crab, lobster, etc.)

钳子 qiánzi ❶ pliers; pincers; forceps ❷〈方言〉earrings

荨(蕁、蕣) qián

see also xún

荨麻 qiánmá 〈植物〉nettle

qiǎn

浅(淺) qiǎn ❶ shallow; of little depth: ～水 shallow water /～碟子 saucer / 湖水太～, 不好游泳! The lake is too shallow for swimming. / 屋子的进深～。There is little depth from the entrance of the room to its rear. ❷ simple; easy; not difficult: 深入～出 explain the profound in simple terms /课文很～。The text is simple and easy. ❸ superficial: 功夫～ not well trained /阅历～ have scanty experience; have not seen much of the world /才疏学～ have little talent and less learning ❹ not familiar; not chummy: 交情～ not on familiar terms; of nodding acquaintance ❺ (of colour) light: ～红 light red ❻ not long in time; for a short while: 这件事年代～, 大家都记得。This is a matter of the recent past and everybody can still remember it. /他们相处日子～, 还谈不到什么交情。They are probably not on intimate terms as they have only been together for a short period.

see also jiān

浅白 qiǎnbái clear and plain: 这道理很～。The reason is very simple.

浅薄 qiǎnbó ❶ shallow; superficial; scanty; meagre: 学识～ meagre knowledge; superficial scholarship /根底～ be of shallow roots / 他～而自以为是。Though empty-headed, he thinks very highly of himself. ❷ (of feelings) lacking depth; shallow: 她对我的情谊～。She has little affection for me. ❸ frivolous; flighty: 我觉得她太～。I feel that she is too frivolous.

浅尝 qiǎncháng stop after scratching the surface of a subject

浅尝辄止 qiǎncháng-zhézhǐ put away the cup after taking a sip — make a superficial study only; stop striving after obtaining a little knowledge about something; be satisfied with a smattering of knowledge: ～的人学不到真本事。He who stops after dabbling at a subject will never be able to master it.

浅成岩 qiǎnchéngyán 〈地质〉hypabyssal rock

浅刺 qiǎncì 〈中医〉shallow puncture; shallow needling

浅催眠状态 qiǎncuīmián zhuàngtài 〈心理〉minor hypnotism

浅淬硬钢 qiǎncuì yìnggāng 〈冶金〉shallow-hardening steel

浅淡 qiǎndàn (of colours) light; (of feelings) shallow; not deep: ～的红色 light red /他的脸上流露出一～的哀愁。A tinge of sadness appeared on his face.

浅短 qiǎnduǎn meagre; narrow and shallow: 目光～ be short-sighted /智力～ have meagre intelligence

浅耕 qiǎngēng shallow ploughing

浅海 qiǎnhǎi 〈地质〉sea less than 200 metres deep; shallow sea; epeiric sea; epicontinental sea: ～水域 shallow waters along the coast

浅海电缆 qiǎnhǎi diànlǎn shallow water cable

浅海养殖 qiǎnhǎi yǎngzhí fish farming in shallow marine water

浅豁 qiǎnhuò clear and plain: 文章要写得～, 使人容易懂。An essay should be written clearly and plainly so that it is readily comprehensible.

浅见 qiǎnjiàn 〈谦词〉superficial view; humble opinion: 这是我个人的～, 仅供参考。This is merely my humble opinion. It is for your reference only.

浅见寡闻 qiǎnjiàn-guǎwén superficial in views and meagre in knowledge: 以我的～, 对这些情况是万万估计不到的。With my limited knowledge and information I could never have anticipated these developments.

浅近 qiǎnjìn simple; plain; clear; easy to understand: ～易懂 plain and easily comprehensible /用～的事例打比方 use simple and explicit analogies

浅口鞋 qiǎnkǒuxié shoes with low-cut uppers

浅矿床开采 qiǎnkuàngchuáng kāicǎi 〈矿业〉drift mining

浅陋 qiǎnlòu meagre; mean; narrow-minded: 文意～ threadbare article /～无知 mean and ignorant

Q

浅露 qiǎnlù (of wording) blunt; explicit:词意～ explicit phrase
浅明 qiǎnmíng simple and clear:～的道理 simple reason
浅末 qiǎnmò shallow; superficial:词旨～ simple word; elementary word
浅切削 qiǎnqiēxiāo 〈机械〉shallow cut
浅儿 qiǎnr *also*"浅子" shallow round container open at the top
浅人 qiǎnrén 〈书面〉shallow person
浅色 qiǎnsè light colour:～夏装 light-coloured summer garment
浅山 qiǎnshān small hill
浅生矿床 qiǎnshēng kuàngchuáng 〈矿业〉supergene; hypergene
浅室型自由沉降分级机 qiǎnshìxíng zìyóu chénjiàng fēnjījī 〈矿业〉shallow-pocket free settling classifier
浅释 qiǎnshì simple explanation; concise account; explicit interpretation
浅水池 qiǎnshuǐchí shallow end of a swimming pool; shallow pool
浅水船 qiǎnshuǐchuán shallow-draft vessel
浅说 qiǎnshuō elementary introduction:《病理学～》*An Elementary Introduction to Pathology*
浅滩 qiǎntān shoal; shallow
浅谈 qiǎntán (usu. used in titles of books and articles) brief talk:《～市场管理》*A Brief Talk on Market Management*
浅显 qiǎnxiǎn plain; obvious; easy to read and understand:～的儿童读物 children's elementary reading materials / 语言～明白 in simple and easy language / 他讲的都是最～最实际的道理。What he said was the most plain (*or* obvious) and practical truth.
浅鲜 qiǎnxiǎn 〈书面〉(of reception) lukewarm; (of knowledge) little; flimsy:相待～ be cold-shouldered
浅笑 qiǎnxiào smile:嘴角挂着～。A faint smile came to the corners of one's mouth.
浅学 qiǎnxué superficial knowledge; shallow learning:～之人 superficial scholar; person of meagre knowledge / ～寡闻 little learning and meagre knowledge (*or* information)
浅易 qiǎnyì simple; easy:英汉对照～读物 easy English readings with Chinese translation / 这篇文章的语言生动活泼，～近人。Written in a vivid and lively style, the essay is simple and caters to popular tastes.
浅源地震 qiǎnyuán dìzhèn 〈地质〉shallow-focus earthquake
浅斟低唱 qiǎnzhēn-dīchàng sip wine slowly and hum a tune — easy life of the leisured literati
浅种 qiǎnzhòng shallow sowing
浅子 qiǎnzi *also*"浅儿" shallow round container open at the top

嗛

qiǎn ape's jaws

肷(膁)

qiǎn (usu. of animal) fur on the belly and breast:狐～ fox's fur between the breast and the legs

遣

qiǎn ❶ send; transmit; dispatch:差～ send sb. on a mission / 调～ deploy; dispatch / 调兵～将守住第二道防线 move troops (*or* deploy forces) to hold the second line of defence ❷ drive away; dispel; expel:消～ diversion; pastime / 自～ find something to amuse oneself
遣词 qiǎncí *also*"遣辞" wording:～颇见功力。The wording shows the hand of a master.
遣词造句 qiǎncí-zàojù choice of words and construction of sentences; wording and phrasing; diction
遣返 qiǎnfǎn repatriate:～非法移民 repatriate illegal immigrants / ～原籍 send sb. back to his native place / 自愿或强制～ voluntary or compulsory repatriation
遣怀 qiǎnhuái 〈书面〉give expression to one's feelings:赋诗～ write (*or* compose) poems to express one's thoughts and feelings
遣闷 qiǎnmèn relieve boredom; seek relief from boredom; have a diversion
遣派 qiǎnpài dispatch; send
遣散 qiǎnsàn ❶ disband; dismiss; send away:当年老父的机关撤销后，人员全部被～。Father's unit was disbanded in those days and the entire staff were sent away. ❷ disband and repatriate captured enemy troops, staff members of enemy government organizations, etc.:全部伪军立即缴械～。All the puppet troops were disarmed and repatriated.
遣散费 qiǎnsànfèi severance pay; release pay; compensation for disbandment
遣戍 qiǎnshù 〈书面〉banish; exile
遣送 qiǎnsòng send back; repatriate:～出境 deport / ～到边远地区 be sent off to a remote area / ～家眷回乡 send one's dependents back to one's hometown
遣唐使 qiǎntángshǐ 〈历史〉Japanese envoys sent to China in the 7th-9th centuries during the Tang Dynasty to learn its system and culture
遣兴 qiǎnxìng *also*"遣怀" give vent to one's feelings:～之作 sth. (such as poem, essay, etc.) written to express one's thoughts and feelings

谴

qiǎn ❶ censure; reprimand; reproach:自～ self-reproach ❷〈书面〉(of officials) be demoted on account of wrongdoing
谴责 qiǎnzé denounce; condemn; reproach; censure:～种族隔离政策 denounce apartheid policies / 受到良心的～ feel guilty for having done something wrong; have a guilty conscience; be conscience-stricken (*or* smitten) / 侵略行径遭到世界舆论的强烈～。The act of aggression was strongly condemned by world public opinion.
谴谪 qiǎnzhé 〈书面〉(of officals) be demoted (because of offenses, mistakes, etc.):因直谏而遭～ be demoted for straight-forward remonstrances with the emperor

缱

qiǎn
缱绻 qiǎnquǎn 〈书面〉(of love between man and woman) deeply attached to each other:情意～ deep attachment; sentimental attachment

qiàn

慊

qiàn 〈书面〉regret; sorrow; hate:何～之有? What regret is there?
see also qiè
慊慊 qiànqiàn discontented; dissatisfied:～常苦不足 often feel discontented about the deficiency

歉

qiàn ❶ crop failure:荒～ crop failure; famine / 以丰补～ store up in fat years to make up for lean ones ❷ apology; regret:写信致～ write to apologize / 抱～ be sorry; apologize
歉忱 qiànchén 〈书面〉apology; expression of regret:致书以表～ write a letter to offer one's apologies
歉疚 qiànjiù feel guilty; be remorseful:迟迟作答，殊为～。I wish to apologize for my tardy reply.
歉年 qiànnián lean year; year of poor harvest
歉然 qiànrán regret; feel apologetic:～不语 feel apologetic and remain silent
歉收 qiànshōu crop failure; bad harvest:粮食～ poor grain harvest / 油菜子～ bad harvest of rapeseed / ～地区 areas of crop failure
歉岁 qiànsuì lean year; year of poor harvest:遇丰年而思～ think of lean years when you enjoy a bumper harvest
歉意 qiànyì regret; apology:深致～ extend sincere apologies; express profound regrets
歉仄 qiànzè be sorry; regret; feel upset:适才说话过于冒失，殊觉～。I feel very sorry that I should have spoken to you so abruptly just now.

倩[1]

qiàn 〈书面〉beautiful; attractive

倩[2]

qiàn ask sb. to do sth. for one:～人相助 ask sb. to give a helping hand
倩男倩女 qiànnán-qiànnǚ handsome men and beautiful women; men and women dressed in the latest fashion
倩盼 qiànpàn 〈书面〉(of appearance) beautiful; attractive; pleasing
倩影 qiànyǐng photo (of a beautiful woman)
倩妆 qiànzhuāng 〈书面〉beautiful make-up
倩装 qiànzhuāng handsome dress; beautiful attire

绛

qiàn 〈书面〉dark red silk, now only used in people's names

茜（蒨） qiàn ❶ *see*“茜草” ❷ alizarin crimson：～纱 red gauze
see also xī
茜草 qiàncǎo 〈植物〉madder
茜素染料 qiànsù rǎnliào 〈化工〉alizarin dye

堑 qiàn moat；chasm；ditch：长江天～ with the Yangtze River providing a natural barrier against attack／高垒深～ high walls and deep moats／吃一～，长一智。A fall into the pit, a gain in your wit.
堑壕 qiànháo 〈军事〉trench；entrenchment：～工事 entrenchment
堑壕战 qiànháozhàn trench warfare

椠 qiàn 〈书面〉❶ wood block used in ancient China to record events on ❷ engraved edition of books：宋～ Song Dynasty wood-block edition
椠本 qiànběn 〈书面〉block-printed edition

欠[1] qiàn ❶ yawn：打呵～ yawn ❷ raise slightly (part of one's body)；stretch：车厢太挤，～不了身子。The compartment was too crowded for the passengers to stretch.／他～着脚看了半天热闹。He stood on tiptoe watching the fun for quite a while.

欠[2] qiàn ❶ owe；be behind with；be in debt：赊～ buy or sell on credit；give or get credit／拖～ be behind with repayment of a loan；delay the repayment of debts；be in arrears／～债累累 burdened with debts／～人情 be indebted to sb. for a favour done；owe sb. a debt of gratitude／～一顿饭 owe sb. a dinner／我们谁也不～谁的钱。We are quits. ❷ not enough；insufficient；wanting：～说服力 not be persuasive；not be convincing enough／～火候 be underdone；be undercooked／馒头～碱 not enough soda in the steamed bread／办事～周到 fail to take all major aspects into account in handling a problem；lack careful consideration in handling the matter ❸〈方言〉fidgety；troublesome：手～ be prone to fiddle with things／嘴～ have a loose tongue；have a big mouth；say sth. out of place／这人特～，一天到晚招惹是非。This man is very meddlesome, stirring up troubles all day long. ❹〈方言〉deserve to be punished；want；need：～抽 need a good thrashing／～批 should be taken to task
欠安 qiàn'ān (referring to others) not feel well；be slightly indisposed：父亲身体～。Father was a bit under the weather.／闻令堂日来～，特驰书问候。I am writing to ask after your mother as I have just learned that she is slightly indisposed.
欠补偿 qiànbǔcháng undercompensation：～光纤 undercompensated optical fibre
欠产 qiànchǎn shortfall in production：秋粮～。The autumn crops had a shortfall in output.
欠单 qiàndān accommodation bill or note；IOU
欠发达国家 qiànfādá guójiā less developed country (LDC)
欠付工资 qiànfù gōngzī back pay；back wages
欠负 qiànfù 〈方言〉be unfair (to others)：她觉得～他一些什么。She felt that she had treated him somewhat unfairly.
欠户 qiànhù debtor
欠火 qiànhuǒ be undercooked
欠据 qiànjù *see*“欠条”
欠款 qiànkuǎn ❶ owe a debt：我共～五百元。I altogether owe a debt of 500 *yuan*. ❷ money that is owed from the past；arrears；outstanding debts；balance due：收回～ recover arrears；claim the balance due／及时归还～ pay the debts in time
欠情 qiànqíng have yet to return the favour done to one by somebody；owe sb. a favour；owe sb. a debt of gratitude：咱俩谁也不欠谁的情。Now neither of us owes the other a favour；we are even.
欠缺 qiànquē ❶ be deficient in；be inadequate；be short of：经验～ be deficient (*or* lacking) in experience；not be experienced enough／劳力十分～ be seriously short of labour；have a severe shortage of labour ❷ shortcoming；inadequacy；deficiency：没有什么～ almost flawless／手续上有～ not quite proper in procedure；still some formalities to go through
欠少 qiànshǎo be short of；lack
欠伸 qiànshēn stretch oneself and yawn：孩子～着醒了过来。The child woke up, stretching himself and yawning.／他～了一下身子又伏案写书。He stretched his limbs and bent down at his desk to write again.
欠身 qiànshēn rise slightly；half rise from one's seat：老人微微～，示意那年轻人坐下。The old gentleman half rose from his seat, beckoning the young man to sit down.／他急忙～答话。He hastened to raise himself slightly to answer.
欠条 qiàntiáo written pledge for borrowing sth. or money；receipt for a loan；piece of paper signed in acknowledgement of debt；IOU：我可以给他打张～。I'll give him an IOU.
欠妥 qiàntuǒ not proper；far from correct or appropriate：措词～。The wording is not quite appropriate.／坐次安排～。The seating arrangement is somewhat faulty.
欠息 qiànxī debit interest；interest owed
欠项 qiànxiàng liabilities
欠薪 qiànxīn ❶ not pay a salary on time ❷ back pay；overdue salaries
欠债 qiànzhài be in debt；owe a debt；run into debt：他欠了一屁股的债。He is up to his neck in debt.
欠债人 qiànzhàirén debtor
欠账 qiànzhàng bills due；outstanding accounts：～甚多 numerous outstanding accounts；backlog of unreturned favours／还清～ pay up all the debts；settle all the outstanding accounts
欠资 qiànzī 〈通信〉postage due：～信 postage-due letter
欠揍 qiànzòu 〈口语〉need a spanking：好说不听，我看你～。If persuasion doesn't work, what you need is a sound thrashing.
欠租 qiànzū back rent

芡 qiàn ❶ *also*“鸡头” jītóu；“老鸡头” lǎojītóu〈植物〉Gorgon euryale (*Euryale ferox*) ❷ starch used in cooking：汤里勾点～。Add some starch to the soup to make it thicker.
芡粉 qiànfěn seed powder of Gorgon euryale
芡实 qiànshí *also*“鸡头米” jītóumǐ Gorgon fruit

嵌 qiàn inlay；embed；set：镶～ inlay pieces as decoration／～石 inlaid stone pieces／～银 be set with silver pieces／匣子上～着象牙雕的花。The box is inlaid with flowers carved out of ivory.
see also kàn
嵌镶 qiànxiāng *also*“镶嵌” inlay；embed；set

纤（縴） qiàn rope for towing a boat；tow-rope：背～ pull the tow line on the shoulder／拉～ track (a boat)
see also xiān
纤夫 qiànfū boat tracker
纤歌 qiàngē song sung by boat trackers while towing a boat
纤路 qiànlù towpath；towing path；track road
纤绳 qiànshéng rope for towing a boat；tow-rope
纤手 qiànshǒu *also*“拉纤的” lāqiànde 〈旧语〉estate agent；real estate broker

qiāng

羌 Qiāng ❶ Qiang, an ancient ethnic group in China ❷ *see*“羌族”
羌笛 qiāngdí Qiang flute
羌活 qiānghuó 〈植物〉notopterygium (*Notopterygium incisium*)
羌无故实 qiāngwúgùshí without basis in fact：此皆纸上空文，～。It is pure fiction without any substance or basis.
羌语 Qiāngyǔ Qiang language
羌族 Qiāngzú Qiang or Ch'iang nationality living in Sichuan Province

蜣 qiāng
蜣螂 qiāngláng *also*“屎壳郎” shǐkelàng 〈动物〉dung beetle

腔 qiāng ❶ cavity：鼻～ nasal cavity／口～ oral cavity／颅～ cranal cavity／腹～ abdominal cavity／胸～ thoracic cavity／盆～ pelvic cavity／满～热情 brim with enthusiasm ❷ speech；talk：开～ start talking／不开～ keep mum／答～ respond (to a question)；answer／帮～ side with sb. in a quarrel ❸ tune：唱～ singing tunes／花～ coloratura／高～ high pitched tune／字正～圆 meticulously exe-

cuted singing or reading /离～走板 sing out of tune and go off key / 梆子～ general term for local operas in Shanxi, Shaanxi, Henan, Hebei, Shandong, etc. performed to the accompaniment of *bangzi* (梆子) ❹ tone; accent: 打官～ talk like a bureaucrat; stall with official jargon /洋～怪调 talk with a mixture of accents /一口京～ pure Beijing dialect /装～作势 be affected or pretentious; strike a pose; put on airs ❺〈量词〉〈旧语〉carcass (of slaughtered sheep): 一～羊 a mutton carcass

腔肠动物 qiāngcháng dòngwù coelenterate

腔调 qiāngdiào ❶ tune: 越剧的～常是低沉而带伤感的。The tunes of Shaoxing Opera are often low and sentimental. /地方戏曲各有独特的～。Each local opera has its own peculiar tunes. ❷ tone: 这些话尽是征服者的～。These remarks are shot through with the arrogance of a conqueror. ❸ accent; intonation: 讥讽的～ talk sarcastically /学着大人的～说话 imitate an adult's tone of speech /一副十足的流氓～ talk exactly like a hooligan /满口广东～ speak with a typical Guangdong accent

腔骨 qiānggǔ spine of pork

腔棘鱼 qiāngjíyú coelacanth

腔静脉 qiāngjìngmài 〈生理〉caval vein

腔口 qiāngkou 〈方言〉one's particular way of speaking; accent: 虽天黑看不清脸，可听说话的～，知道是小王。I could not see Xiao Wang's face distinctly as it was dark, but I knew it was him by his accent.

腔子 qiāngzi ❶ chest; bosom: 一～热血 be filled with patriotic enthusiasm; be inspired by a noble cause ❷ headless carcasses of animals

将(將) qiāng

〈书面〉please; wish: ～子毋怒。Pray refrain from anger.

see also jiāng; jiàng

将伯之助 qiāngbózhīzhù *also* "将伯助"〈敬词〉(in asking or thanking an elder for help) your guidance is deeply appreciated

蹡(蹌) qiāng

see also qiàng

蹡蹡 qiāngqiāng *also* "跄跄" qiāngqiāng 〈书面〉walk properly

锵(鏘) qiāng

〈象声〉clang; gong: 锣声～～ continuous clanging of gongs

玱(瑲) qiāng

〈书面〉〈象声〉jingling sound of jade

枪[1](槍、鎗) qiāng

❶ spear: 红缨～ red tasselled spear /长～ long spear /标～ javelin ❷ rifle; gun; firearm: 手～ pistol; revolver /自动手～ automatic /步～ rifle /机～ machine gun /猎～ hunting gun /卡宾～ carbine /冲锋～ sub-machine gun; tommy-gun /鸟～ fowling piece; shotgun /打～ shoot; fire a shot /冷～ sniper's shot ❸ any appliance which functions like a gun or resembles it in shape: 焊～ welding torch; (welding) blowpipe /烟～ opium pipe /水～ giant; (hydraulic) monitor

枪[2](槍) qiāng

serve as a substitute for sb. at an examination

枪靶 qiāngbǎ (shooting) target

枪把 qiāngbà small of the stock; pistol grip

枪崩 qiāngbēng 〈口语〉execute by shooting; shoot (dead)

枪毙 qiāngbì ❶ execute by shooting: 那个罪行累累的抢劫犯已被～。That robber with a long criminal record has already been executed. ❷ turn down; overrule; reject: 他的意见被会议主席～了。His proposal was dismissed by the chairman.

枪刺 qiāngcì bayonet

枪打出头鸟 qiāng dǎ chūtóuniǎo one who sticks his neck out gets hit first; the outstanding usually bear the brunt of attack: 凡事不可太过招摇，俗话说得好："～。" One should not pull too much ahead of the pack, for, as the old saying goes, the outstanding are usually most exposed to attack.

枪带 qiāngdài sling

枪弹 qiāngdàn *also* "子弹" zǐdàn ❶ cartridge ❷ bullet

枪法 qiāngfǎ ❶ marksmanship: 他～高明，百发百中。He is an excellent marksman, a crack shot. ❷ skill to wield the spear: 白袍小将～纯熟。The white-robed young general was a skilful spearman.

枪放下 qiāngfàngxià (word of command) Order arms!

枪杆 qiānggǎn *also* "枪杆子" gun; stock of a gun: ～子里面出政权。Political power grows out of the barrel of a gun. /他掌握～。He had the armed forces under his control.

枪管 qiāngguǎn barrel (of a gun)

枪花 qiānghuā movements of a spear in *wushu* (武术): 掉～ play tricks

枪击 qiāngjī shoot with gun: 遭～身亡 be shot dead

枪机 qiāngjī rifle bolt; bolt

枪架 qiāngjià rifle rack; arm rack

枪决 qiāngjué execute by shooting: 犯人被绑赴刑场，执行～。The criminal was trussed up and escorted to the execution ground for immediate execution.

枪口 qiāngkǒu muzzle: ～对外 direct the muzzle of a gun outwards; point the gun at external enemies

枪林弹雨 qiānglín-dànyǔ hail of bullets: ～的战争年代 in those war years characterized by roaring guns and flying bullets /战士们在～里浴血奋战。Bathed in blood, the soldiers fought under heavy fire.

枪榴弹 qiāngliúdàn rifle grenade; grenade

枪炮 qiāngpào arms; guns

枪杀 qiāngshā shoot dead; kill by firearm

枪伤 qiāngshāng bullet wound; gunshot wound

枪上肩 qiāngshàngjiān (word of command) Shoulder arms!

枪声 qiāngshēng report of a gun; shot; crack: ～大作 thunderous discharge of guns; fierce fusillade

枪手 qiāngshǒu ❶〈旧语〉spearman ❷ marksman; gunner; gunman: 神～ expert marksman; crack shot

枪手 qiāngshou substitute for another at examinations: 雇请～ hire a substitute for oneself at examinations

枪栓 qiāngshuān rifle bolt; bolt

枪探子 qiāngtànzi iron stick used for cleaning the bore (of a gun)

枪膛 qiāngtáng bore (of a gun)

枪替 qiāngtì *also* "打枪" dǎqiāng serve or act as a substitute for sb. at an examination

枪托 qiāngtuō *also* "枪托子" (rifle) butt; shoulder stock; butt-stock: 用～打人 hit sb. with the rifle butt

枪乌贼 qiāngwūzéi 〈动物〉(Loligo) squid; calamary

枪械 qiāngxiè firearms; armaments: ～库 arsenal

枪眼 qiāngyǎn ❶ embrasure; loophole ❷ bullet hole; post

枪衣 qiāngyī cloth cover of a machine-gun

枪用瞄准镜 qiāngyòng miáozhǔnjìng rifle scope

枪鱼 qiāngyú 〈动物〉marlin

枪战 qiāngzhàn gun battle: 双方在城里发生～。The two sides exchanged fire in the town.

枪支 qiāngzhī firearms; gun: ～弹药 arms and ammunition

枪子儿 qiāngzǐr 〈口语〉❶ cartridge ❷ bullet; shot: 飞过一粒～。A bullet flew past. /你这个挨～的! A plague on you!

戗(戧) qiāng

Tibetan liquor made from highland barley

抢(搶) qiāng

❶〈书面〉knock; touch: 呼天～地 cry out to heaven and knock one's head on earth — utter cries of anguish ❷ be in the opposite direction; go against: ～风 go against the wind; brave the wind

see also qiǎng

抢呼 qiānghū 〈方言〉utter cries of anguish: 她悲痛地大声～。She cried bitterly and loudly.

抢眼 qiāngyǎn conspicuous; striking to the eye: 十分～ rather showy /衣服衬里的颜色更为～。The colour of the lining is even more glaring.

戗(戧) qiāng

❶ be in the opposite direction: ～水行船 sail against the current ❷ verbal clash: 他们俩说～了。Their argument ended in a row.

see also qiàng

戗茬 qiāngchá 〈口语〉be at loggerheads with sb.; be at odds with sb.: 有话好好说，别老是戗着茬。Talk the matter over with us calmly. Don't always try to be contrary.

戗风 qiāngfēng against the wind: 回来的路上～，车骑得很慢。On

our way back we were cycling slowly against the wind./烟筒～。The chimney draws the wind in.

戗顺不吃 qiāng-shùn bùchī yield neither to coercion nor to persuasion:别跟他废话了,他就是那种～的人。Don't waste your breath on him. He would neither listen to reason nor bow to force.

呛(嗆) qiāng be unable to breathe because one's windpipe is blocked by sth.; choke:吃～着了 choke over one's food / 烟雾几乎把我～死了。The fumes almost choked me./喝水喝～了。The water went down the wrong way.

see also qiàng

呛咕 qiānggu 〈方言〉gather together and discuss

呛呛 qiāngqiang kick up a terrible din:大家乱～地闹了一阵,还是没谱儿。They talked confusedly and made a terrible noise, but no solution was found.

跄(蹌) qiāng walk

see also qiàng

跄跄 qiāngqiāng *also* "跻跻" qiāngqiāng 〈书面〉walk in a correct, formal manner

锖 qiāng

锖色 qiāngsè tarnish

戕 qiāng 〈书面〉kill:自～ take one's own life; kill oneself; commit suicide

戕害 qiānghài injure; damage; ruin:封建家庭～了他的进取心。His feudal family background stifled his enterprising spirit./饮酒无度,～了他的身体。Excessive drinking ruined his health.

戕虐 qiāngnüè barbarous; despotic:为人～ be despotic in character

戕忍 qiāngrěn cruel; ruthless:生性～ be ruthless by nature

戕杀 qiāngshā kill ruthlessly:～无辜 slaughter the innocent

戕贼 qiāngzéi harm; injure; undermine:～自身 do harm to one's own health; undermine one's own constitution

斨 qiāng 〈古语〉a kind of axe

镪 qiāng

see also qiǎng

镪水 qiāngshuǐ (popular term for 强酸) strong acid:盐～ saline acid /硝～ nitric acid

qiáng

墙(墻、牆) qiáng ❶ wall:砖～ brick wall /土～ earthen wall; wall made of earth /灰～ plaster wall /围～ enclosure; enclosing wall /城～ city walls /砌～ build a wall (with bricks, stones, etc.) /抹～ plaster a wall /垒～ build a wall by piling up bricks, stones and earth, etc. /狗急跳～ a dog jumps over the wall once it finds itself cornered — be driven to desperate action ❷ anything that looks like a wall or serves the purpose of partitioning

墙板 qiángbǎn wallboard

墙报 qiángbào wall newspaper

墙壁 qiángbì wall

墙倒众人推 qiáng dǎo zhòngrén tuī if a wall starts tottering, everybody gives it a shove — everybody kicks somebody who is down:～的事情咱不干。I will never join others in kicking a fellow when he is down.

墙根 qiánggēn foot of a wall

墙角 qiángjiǎo corner formed by two walls; wall corner:衣柜靠～放 place the wardrobe in the corner

墙脚 qiángjiǎo ❶ foot of a wall:～下杂草丛生。The foot of the wall is overgrown with weeds. ❷ foundation:挖～ cut the ground from under sb.'s feet; undermine sb.'s foundation

墙里开花墙外香 qiángli kāihuā qiángwài xiāng the fragrance of the flowers growing in the garden smells sweeter to people outside the wall than to those inside — one's achievements are often unrecognized in one's own community

墙面磁砖 qiángmiàn cízhuān 〈建筑〉furring tile

墙面涂料 qiángmiàn túliào wall covering

墙裙 qiángqún 〈建筑〉dado

墙上插座 qiángshàng chāzuò *also* "墙装插座" wall socket

墙上起重机 qiángshàng qǐzhòngjī 〈建筑〉wall crane

墙式电话机 qiángshì diànhuàjī wall (telephone) set

墙头 qiángtóu ❶ top of a wall:攀上～往外瞧 climb to the top of the wall to look outside ❷ low and short enclosure ❸ 〈方言〉wall

墙头草 qiángtóucǎo grass atop a wall — person who bends with the wind; time server

墙头草,随风倒 qiángtóucǎo, suí fēng dǎo grass atop a wall bends with the wind — a fence-sitter goes with the crowd

墙头马上 qiángtóu-mǎshàng a young girl leans over a wall and a young man comes by on horseback — love at first sight

墙头诗 qiángtóushī *also* "街头诗" jiētóushī poem written on a wall along a street:他的创作生涯,是从抗战时写～开始的。His literary career began with the poems he wrote on the walls along the streets during the Anti-Japanese War.

墙外汉 qiángwàihàn outsider

墙网球 qiángwǎngqiú 〈体育〉rackets; squash rackets

墙垣 qiángyuán 〈书面〉wall

墙纸 qiángzhǐ *also* "壁纸" bìzhǐ 〈建筑〉wallpaper

墙装钻床 qiángzhuāng zuànchuáng 〈机械〉wall drilling machine

蔷(薔) qiáng

蔷薇 qiángwēi *also* "野蔷薇" yěqiángwēi 〈植物〉rose:～科 rose family

樯(檣、艢) qiáng 〈书面〉mast:～折舟覆。The mast broke and the ship capsized.

嫱(嬙) qiáng 〈古语〉lady-in-waiting

强(強、彊) qiáng ❶ strong; mighty; powerful:富～ rich and powerful /战斗力～ high combat effectiveness /年富力～ in the prime of life; in one's prime /～国不该欺负弱国。Strong countries should not bully weak ones. ❷ excel; be demanding; be resolute:要～ be eager to excel; be anxious to outdo others /好～ be keen to excel in any work one undertakes /争～ strive to move ahead of others; try to outshine others /责任心～ have a strong sense of responsibility ❸ forcibly; by force:～夺民财 take possession of other people's property by forcible means ❹ strengthen; enhance:富国～兵 enrich the country and strengthen national defence ❺ better; stronger:身体～过往年 be in better health than in previous years /他们的技术比我们～。They were more skilled than we were. ❻ a little over; plus:五分之二～ a little over two fifths ❼ (Qiáng) a surname

see also jiàng; qiǎng

强半 qiángbàn 〈书面〉more than half; most:～选民未参加选举。The greater part of the electorate did not go to the polls.

强暴 qiángbào ❶ violent; ferocious; brutal:～的敌人 ruthless enemy /他们～的行径激起了民愤。Their acts of violence incurred the wrath of the people. ❷ brute force; despotic strength:铲除～ root out tyrannies /不畏～ defy brute force ❸ violate (a girl, etc.); ravish; rape:遭人～ be raped

强本节用 qiángběn-jiéyòng (as a Confucian economic policy) step up agricultural development and cut back on expenses; develop agriculture and practise economy

强辩 qiángbiàn 〈书面〉forceful argument; eloquence:服其～ be convinced by sb.'s forceful argument

see also qiǎngbiàn

强兵劲旅 qiángbīng-jìnglǚ formidable force; strong army to be reckoned with

强大 qiángdà big and strong; powerful; mighty; formidable:～的祖国 our powerful motherland /～的攻势 formidable offensive /～的科技队伍 strong contingent of scientific and technical personnel /比过去任何时候都～有力 be more vigorous than ever before /这种植物有～的生命力。This kind of plant has great vitality.

强盗 qiángdào robber; bandit:～行径 banditry; robbery /～头子 bandit chieftain; gang boss /～窝 den of bandits

强盗逻辑 qiángdào luóji gangster logic

强敌 qiángdí formidable foe; strong opponent:面对～不示弱 re-

Q

main calm in the face of a formidable enemy
强的松 qiángdìsōng 〈药学〉prednisone
强点 qiángdiǎn strong point; strength; forte: 发球不是他的～。Serving (the ball) is not his strong point (*or* forte).
强电流 qiángdiànliú 〈电工〉heavy current; strong current; high current
强调 qiángdiào stress; emphasize; underline; underscore: 在会上～了我们的原则立场。At the meeting, we stressed our stand on matters of principle. /不要～客观原因。Don't overstress the objective factors. /特别要～勤俭建国。Special emphasis should be placed on building up the country through frugality.
强度 qiángdù ❶ intensity: 音响～ sound (*or* acoustic) intensity /磁场～ intensity of a magnetic field /辐射～ radiation intensity /劳动～ labour intensity; intensity of labour ❷ strength: 抗拉～ tensile strength /抗张～ tensile strength /抗震～ shock strength; anti-seismic strength /抗压～ compressive strength
强渡 qiángdù 〈军事〉force or fight one's way across a river; force a river: 我军～黄河。Our army forced the Yellow River.
强队 qiángduì strong team
强风 qiángfēng 〈气象〉strong breeze; force 6 wind
强干 qiánggàn capable: 精明～ bright and capable
强干弱枝 qiánggàn-ruòzhī strengthen the trunk and weaken the branches — strengthen the central administration at the expense of the local authorities
强告化 qiánggàohuà 〈方言〉beggar who forces people to give him money or food
强攻 qiánggōng attack violently and force one's way into; storm: 这座敌堡只能智取，不可～。It is more advisable to capture the enemy stronghold by strategem than by sheer force.
强固 qiánggù strong; impregnable; solid: 为国防现代化打下一个～的基础 lay a solid foundation for the modernization of national defence /敌人～的工事被我军炮火全部摧毁。The enemy's strong bulwarks were razed to the ground by the gunfire of our army.
强光眼炎 qiángguāng yǎnyán 〈医学〉photophthalmia
强国 qiángguó ❶ strong country; powerful nation; power: 经济～ economic power /军事～ military power /建设现代化～ build a powerful modern state ❷ make a nation powerful: ～富民 build up the strength of a nation and enrich its people
强悍 qiánghàn valiant; intrepid; doughty: ～精明 intrepid and intelligent /～善战 valiant and good at fighting /勇猛～ full of vigour and valour
强横 qiánghèng brutal and unreasonable; despotic: 态度～ despotic attitude /说话～ speak imperiously /～无理 overbearing and unreasonable; unruly /～霸道 brutal and domineering /他～狡猾，不守法纪。Arrogant and cunning, he has no regard at all for law and discipline. /那些国家曾遭受～残暴的压迫。Those countries were once subjected to brutal and ruthless oppression.
强化 qiánghuà strengthen; enhance; intensify; step up: ～预算概念 heighten one's budget awareness /～指标管理 tighten management by quotas /竞争意识应该进一步～。The sense of competition should be further enhanced. /急需稳住情绪和～信念。It is imperative to reassure people and fortify their confidence.
强化基因 qiánghuà jīyīn enhancer gene
强化开采 qiánghuà kāicǎi intensified mining
强化食品 qiánghuà shípǐn condensed food
强化因子 qiánghuà yīnzǐ enhancer; intensifier
强击机 qiángjījī 〈军事〉attack plane
强记 qiángjì 〈书面〉retentive memory: 博闻～ be erudite and have a retentive memory
see also qiǎngjì
强加 qiángjiā impose; force people to accept: 我并非想～于你，但是我希望你重新考虑自己的立场。I don't want to force anything on you, but I do hope you'll reconsider your position. /我不能同意你～的这些不实之词。I can't accept these groundless accusations you level against me.
强加于人 qiángjiāyúrén impose (one's views, will, etc.) on others: 要互相尊重，不要～。We must respect each other and refrain from dictating to others.
强奸 qiángjiān rape; defile; violate
强奸犯 qiángjiānfàn 〈法律〉raper; rapist
强奸民意 qiángjiān-mínyì outrage public opinion: 这不过是一种～的惯用伎俩罢了。It was nothing but the usual trick to defile public opinion.
强奸罪 qiángjiānzuì 〈法律〉offence of rape; rape: 法定～ statutory rape (i.e. sex with an underage girl)
强碱 qiángjiǎn 〈化学〉alkali; strong base
强健 qiángjiàn strong and healthy; sturdy: ～的体魄 be physically strong; have a strong constitution; be of sturdy build /脚力～ have strong legs /～的小伙子 young men of strong build
强将 qiángjiàng brilliant general; outstanding commander: 精兵～ crack troops and able generals
强将手下无弱兵 qiángjiàng shǒuxià wú ruòbīng 〈俗语〉there are no weak troops under an able general
强劲 qiángjìng powerful; vigorous; forceful: ～的北风袭来，卷起漫天黄沙。A strong north wind raised a cloud of sand. /改革正以～的势头向前推进。The reform is pushing ahead with gathering momentum.
强劳 qiángláo (short for 强制劳动) forced labour (as a means of reforming criminals)
强劳力 qiángláolì able-bodied labourer
强力 qiánglì ❶ great force: 他用～压下自己的感情。He suppressed his own feelings with a strong will. ❷ power of resistance; strength: 纱的～ strength of yarn
强力钢 qiánglìgāng 〈冶金〉strong steel
强力霉素 qiánglìméisù 〈药学〉doxycycline
强力起重机 qiánglì qǐzhòngjī 〈机械〉goliath crane
强梁 qiángliáng brutal (force); ferocious (bully): 不畏～ stand in no fear of bullies
强烈 qiángliè ❶ strong; powerful; violent: ～的探照灯光 strong searchlights /～的求知欲 yearning for knowledge /～的冷空气 cold air that chills one to the bones /～的爆炸声 violent reports of explosion /茶花散出～的香味。The camellias gave off a rich fragrance. ❷ keen; sharp; striking; intense: ～的民族自尊心 keen sense of national pride /～的义愤 intense righteous indignation /～的印象 forceful impression /～的爱国感情 fervent patriotic sentiments /两者形成了～的对比。There is a sharp (*or* striking) contrast between the two. ❸ strong and vehement: ～反对 fiercely oppose
强令 qiánglìng by arbitrary order: 原计划已被～取消。The original plan was cancelled peremptorily.
强龙不压地头蛇 qiánglóng bù yā dìtóushé a mighty dragon can't overpower a snake in its lair — a local villain is hard to subdue
强蛮 qiángmán arbitrary and arrogant; brutal and unreasoning: ～不讲理 arrogant and impervious to reason /他～得不让你开口说话。He was so arbitrary and overbearing that he did not allow you to open your mouth. /鹞鹰个子虽小，却异常凶猛～。The harrier may be small in size, yet it is most ferocious among the birds.
强弩之末 qiángnǔzhīmò arrow at the end of its flight — a spent force: 几场硬仗之后，敌军已是～。After a few fierce battles, the enemy troops' morale was at a low ebb. /这里冬无严寒，东亚大陆寒潮至此已成～。It is quite mild here in winter, for the East Asian continental cold front has lost much of its severity when it reaches this place.
强拍 qiángpāi 〈音乐〉strong beat; accented beat: 次～ subsidiary strong beat
强取豪夺 qiángqǔ-háoduó secure (sb.'s property, etc.) by force or power; grab and keep
强权 qiángquán power; might: 不畏～ be unafraid of might /～即公理是霸权主义逻辑。It is the logic of the hegemonists to say that might is right.
强权外交 qiángquán wàijiāo power diplomacy
强权政治 qiángquán zhèngzhì power politics: 在国际事务中推行～ pursue power politics in international affairs
强人 qiángrén ❶ strong man: 女～ woman of strong character capable of exercising efficient leadership; iron lady / 企业界的女～之一 one of the strong women in the business world ❷ (often used in the early vernacular) bandit; robber: ～出没之处 haunt of robbers
强韧 qiángrèn tough but pliable; strong and tenacious; durable: ～的生命力 enduring vitality /这种料子质地～，略有弹性。This woollen material is rather strong but somewhat tensile. /他有～无畏的品格。He is a man of tough and fearless character.
强溶剂 qiángróngjì 〈化学〉strong solvent
强身 qiángshēn keep fit by physical exercise or by taking tonics: 经常跑步可以～。You can keep fit by jogging regularly.
强盛 qiángshèng (of a country) powerful and prosperous: 国力～

powerful and prosperous country /～时期 period of great strength and prosperity /我们祖国一天比一天～。Our country is growing from strength to strength.
强仕之年 qiángshìzhīnián age of forty, when men are considered sufficiently experienced and qualified to hold important offices
强手 qiángshǒu person of ability and talent:～如林 plenty of capable people
强似 qiángsì *also* "强如" better than; superior to:身体～去年 be much stronger than last year; be in better health than last year /我们的生活～往昔。We are leading a much better life than before.
强酸 qiángsuān (popularly known as 镪水) strong acid
强徒 qiángtú (usu. used in the early vernacular) robber; bandit
强袭 qiángxí raid with overwhelming force; storm
强项 qiángxiàng ❶〈体育〉game or event in which one is strong; forte:乒乓球是中国的～。China is strong in table tennis. ❷〈书面〉unyielding; resolute; inflexible:～令 upright magistrate
强心剂 qiángxīnjì 〈医学〉cardiac stimulant; cardiotonic
强信号 qiángxìnhào 〈无线电〉strong signal
强行 qiángxíng force:～拆除 demolishing a structure without the consent of the owner; forced demolition /～阻止 stop sth. by force /～决定 force a decision /有人想～闯入赛场。Some people are trying to force their way into the sportsground.
强行法 qiángxíngfǎ 〈法律〉*jus cogens*; binding law
强行军 qiángxíngjūn 〈军事〉forced march
强行送电 qiángxíng sòngdiàn 〈电工〉forced power transmission
强压 qiángyā hold down; suppress:～怒火 hold back one's anger /不屈服于～ not to succumb to high-handed pressure/ 在～下讲的违心话 something admitted against one's will under duress
强毅 qiángyì resolute and steadfast:～果敢 firm and bold
强硬 qiángyìng tough; strong; hard-line; unyielding:～的对手 tough opponent /使用～的办法 adopt hard-line tactics / 态度～ unyielding attitude; hard-nosed approach /语气十分～ in a forceful tone
强硬派 qiángyìngpài hardliner; hawk
强有力 qiángyǒulì strong; powerful; vigorous; forceful:采取～的措施 adopt resolute measures; take vigorous action
强于 qiángyú better than; superior to
强占 qiángzhàn ❶ forcibly take; seize:～民房 forcibly take a civilian's house /收回被～的田产 recover the land property seized by others ❷ occupy by force of arms:～邻国的土地 occupy (*or* grab) the territory of a neighbouring country /以优势兵力～前方的高地 occupy the height by superior force
强震 qiángzhèn 〈地质〉strong shock
强直 qiángzhí ❶〈医学〉rigidity; tetany:膝关节～ rigidity in the knee joints ❷〈书面〉strong-willed and upright:其人～不阿。He is an upright man and never curries favour with the powerful and influential.
强直性 qiángzhíxìng 〈医学〉tetanic:～麻痹 tetanic paralysis
强制 qiángzhì force; compel; impel; coerce:～冷却 forced cooling /～停机〈机械〉forced stoppage /～通风 forced ventilation /～施行 compulsory implementation /～性制裁 compulsory (*or* mandatory) sanctions /采取～方法 adopt coercive methods /发布～性行政命令 promulgate mandatory administrative orders /不能～人们不信教 cannot compel people not to believe in religion /观众的取舍是没法～的。No one can force the audience to like or dislike anything.
强制保险 qiángzhì bǎoxiǎn 〈商业〉forced insurance; mandatory insurance
强制法 qiángzhìfǎ 〈法律〉mandatory law
强制改造 qiángzhì gǎizào 〈法律〉coercive or forced remoulding
强制劳动 qiángzhì láodòng 〈法律〉forced labour
强中自有强中手 qiángzhōng zìyǒu qiángzhōng shǒu however strong one may be, there is always someone stronger; however good you are at something, there's always someone better; diamond cuts diamond:～,莫向人前夸海口。Never brag about your prowess in public, as there is always someone stronger than you in the crowd.
强壮 qiángzhuàng ❶ strong; powerful; sturdy; robust:体格～ of strong build; of robust constitution /他年轻英俊,健康～。He is young, handsome, and in the pink of health. /～的战马喘着粗气。The sturdy battle steed was breathing hard. ❷ strengthen; build up:坚持体育锻炼可以～你的身体。Regular physical exercises will keep you fit.
强壮剂 qiángzhuàngjì 〈医学〉roborant; tonic
强子 qiángzǐ 〈物理〉hadron:～动力学 hadrodynamics
强宗 qiángzōng wealthy and powerful family or clan

qiǎng

抢[1](搶) qiǎng ❶ rob; loot; snatch; grab:～球 snatch the ball from someone's hands /几个人～一张电影票。Several people scrambled for a film ticket. /匪徒～银行。Bandits robbed a bank. ❷ vie for; compete for: *see* "～镜头" ❸ hurry; rush:～着把活儿干完 rush to get a job done /～在雨季前修好房顶 hurry to repair the roof before the rainy season sets in

抢[2](搶) qiǎng scrape; scratch; sharpen:～～墙皮 scrape the coat off the wall /～破了皮 scratch the skin; be bruised /～菜刀 sharpen kitchen knives
see also qiāng

抢白 qiǎngbái reproach; tell off; ridicule:他无缘无故地被～了几句。He was reproached for no reason at all.
抢背 qiǎngbèi 〈戏曲〉gesture of falling down in an acrobatic performance
抢答 qiǎngdá hurry to answer a question before others
抢点 qiǎngdiǎn ❶(of a train, plane or ship which is delayed during the journey) pick up speed in order to arrive on schedule:～运行 try to arrive on time by picking up speed ❷ (of a football striker, etc.) race to a favourable position (to shoot at the goal)
抢渡 qiǎngdù swiftly cross (a river):先头部队在作～准备。The vanguards were getting ready to cross the river speedily.
抢夺 qiǎngduó snatch; grab; wrest; seize:～劳动果实 seize the fruits of labour /互相～ scuffle with each other for sth. /～地盘 turf grabbing
抢饭碗 qiǎng fànwǎn fight for a job; compete for a position; snatch sb. else's job
抢工 qiǎnggōng rush-produce goods or speed up construction in order to complete a project on time or ahead of schedule
抢攻 qiǎnggōng race to attack:～桥头堡 race to attack a bridgehead
抢购 qiǎnggòu rushing to purchase; run on the shops:～紧俏物品 rush to buy goods in short supply /～粮食 panic purchasing of food grains
抢购风 qiǎnggòufēng panic buying
抢话 qiǎnghuà snatch the chance to speak right before somebody is going to start:我刚一张嘴,他就～。I was just going to speak when he butted in.
抢荒粮 qiǎnghuāngliáng 〈旧语〉rush to gather sb. else's crops which can not be harvested upon ripening for some reason
抢婚 qiǎnghūn marriage by capture
抢火 qiǎnghuǒ 〈方言〉rush to move out things from a burning house
抢建 qiǎngjiàn do a rush job of construction in order to fulfil one's task in time or ahead of schedule:我们～了一个供全国游泳比赛用的标准游泳池。We did a rush job of building a standard swimming-pool for the national swimming contest.
抢劫 qiǎngjié rob; loot; plunder:拦路～ waylay and rob; mug
抢劫案 qiǎngjié'àn 〈法律〉robbery case
抢劫犯 qiǎngjiéfàn one who commits robbery; robber
抢劫罪 qiǎngjiézuì 〈法律〉crime of pillage; offence of robbery
抢截 qiǎngjié (of football etc.) intercept
抢镜头 qiǎng jìngtóu ❶ seek the spotlight or limelight; steal the show:～,出风头 seek the limelight so as to cut a figure ❷ (of a cameraman, etc.) take a snapshot at the right moment:善于～ good at taking snapshots
抢救 qiǎngjiù rescue; save; salvage:～文物古籍 salvage archaeological relics and rare ancient books /～公共财产 save public property /～工作 rescue work /～组 rescue party /张医生正在～病人。Doctor Zhang is giving emergency treatment to a patient. /～无效。All rescue measures failed. *or* All rescue efforts came to naught.
抢脸 qiǎngliǎn ❶ bruise one's face through falling down ❷ be disgraced; lose face:丢人～的事我不干。I would not do anything I would be ashamed of.

抢掠 qiǎnglüè loot; grab; sack:烧杀～ burn down houses, kill innocent people and plunder their property; burning, killing and looting /珍宝财物被侵略者～一空。All the treasures had been looted by the aggressors.
抢拍 qiǎngpāi rush to film; take a snap-shot of:～镜头 rush to shoot the scenes /～外景 take snapshots of the outdoor scene
抢亲 qiǎngqīn ❶ traditional wedding custom according to which the bridegroom pretends to kidnap the bride ❷ grab a woman from her home for forced marriage
抢青 qiǎngqīng get in the crops before they are ripe
抢墒 qiǎngshāng plant while the soil is still moist
抢时间 qiǎng shíjiān race against time; lose no time:～把稿子写出来 lose no time in finishing the article
抢市 qiǎngshì rush farm produce to the market before it is in season (in anticipation of a good price)
抢收 qiǎngshōu rush in the harvest; get in the crops quickly
抢手 qiǎngshǒu (of goods, etc.) sell like hot cakes:世界杯足球赛的门票很快售完，十分～。Tickets for World Cup Football Championships were going so quickly that they were very soon sold out.
抢手货 qiǎngshǒuhuò goods in short supply; commodities that customers rush to buy
抢滩 qiǎngtān try to make a sinking ship run aground in order to avert its going under
抢先 qiǎngxiān try to be the first to do sth.; act before others; forestall:～发言 try to be the first on the floor; rush to speak before anyone else /～干活 manage to be the first to get started when there is work to be done /他凡事都爱～。He hates to fall behind others in whatever he does.
抢险 qiǎngxiǎn rush to meet an emergency (e.g. a breach in an embankment, a cave-in, etc.):上河堤～ rush to the river embankment to strengthen a dike (*or* to fill a breach)
抢修 qiǎngxiū rush to repair; do rush repairs; rush-repair:～下水道 rush to repair a sewerage-pipe /～危房 do rush repairs to crumbling houses
抢眼 qiǎngyǎn eye-catching; conspicuous
抢运 qiǎngyùn rush to transport:～粮食 rush-transport foodgrains
抢占 qiǎngzhàn ❶ race to seize or occupy:～对岸的河滩 race to take the opposite river bank ❷ take illegal possession of sth.; occupy illegally; squat:～公房 illegally occupy government-built houses /～公共财产者应依法惩处。Those who illegally take possession of public property shall be prosecuted according to law.
抢种 qiǎngzhòng rush-planting:～玉米 rush-plant maize
抢嘴 qiǎngzuǐ ❶〈方言〉try to get the first chance to speak:大家挨着说，谁也别～。Let's speak one by one and not try to talk all at once. ❷ scramble for food:几个孩子在饭桌上～。Several children all tried to get a taste of the food at the same time.

羟(羥) qiǎng 〈化学〉hydroxyl (group)

羟氨基 qiǎng'ānjī 〈化学〉hydroxamino
羟化酶 qiǎnghuàméi 〈生化〉hydroxylase
羟基 qiǎngjī 〈化学〉hydroxyl (group):～氨基酸 hydroxy-amino-acid /～化 hydroxylation /～化物 hydroxylate /～氯化物 hydroxychloride /～卤化物 hydroxyhalide
羟基酸 qiǎngjīsuān 〈化学〉oxyacid; hydroxy acid
羟离子 qiǎnglízǐ 〈化学〉hydroxidion; hydroxide ion
羟酸 qiǎngsuān 〈化学〉hydroxy-acid

强(強、彊) qiǎng make an effort; try hard; force:～打精神 try hard to appear unperturbed; pull oneself together

see also jiàng; qiáng
强逼 qiǎngbī force; compel; coerce:～就范 force sb. to toe the line (*or* submit)
强辩 qiǎngbiàn try to make out a case by false arguments:矢口～ attempt to defend oneself by sophistry /事实昭著，不容～。The facts are so obvious that they admit of no quibble.
see also qiángbiàn
强不知以为知 qiǎng bùzhī yǐwéi zhī pretend to know what one does not know:此人一味大话欺人，～。This fellow is always bragging and pretending to know what he is entirely ignorant of.
强词夺理 qiǎngcí-duólǐ use lame arguments; resort to sophistry; be unreasonable:他只是在澄清事实，并非～。He was merely stating the facts, and was by no means trying to be unreasonable.
强聒不舍 qiǎngguō-bùshě talk endlessly and not care whether the audience is bored or not; talk one's head off
强记 qiǎngjì mechanically memorize; learn by rote; make an effort to remember:为考试而～的东西不易巩固。It is difficult to remember what you have crammed up for an examination.
see also qiángjì
强留 qiǎngliú press a reluctant person to stay; make sb. stay against his will:愿意退出的决不～。We'll never ask those who want to withdraw to stay on against their will.
强买强卖 qiǎngmǎi-qiǎngmài force people to buy or sell
强扭的瓜不甜 qiǎngniǔdeguā bù tián a forcibly picked melon is not sweet — no arrangement is sound without the consent of the parties concerned
强迫 qiǎngpò force; compel; coerce:～手段 coercive measures /谁也没～他这样干。Nobody has forced him to do so./ 他们用大炮～清政府签订卖国条约。They compelled the Qing government to sign traitorous treaties under threat of artillery bombardment.
强迫命令 qiǎngpò mìnglìng coercion and commandism:～的做法不得人心。Recourse to coercion and commandism never wins popular support.
强求 qiǎngqiú insist on; impose; force:～一律 impose uniformity; insist on uniformity /每个人都可以有自己的看法，我不想～你。I don't intend to impose my own views on you, as everybody is entitled to his own opinion. /人生有许多事都是不能～的。There are quite a number of things in our life which cannot be sought after.
强人所难 qiǎngrénsuǒnán make sb. do what is beyond his power or against his will; try to make sb. do what he won't or can't:各人有各人的爱好，不要～。Don't try to make anybody do anything against his will, for everyone has his own preferences.
强使 qiǎngshǐ force; compel; drive:你不能～孩子放弃自己的选择。You cannot force your children to give up their own choice.
强笑 qiǎngxiào give a forced smile; force a smile:面对这尴尬场面，他也只好摇头～。Caught in the embarrassing situation, he could only shake his head and force a smile.
强颜 qiǎngyán put on an air of cheerfulness
强颜为笑 qiǎngyán-wéixiào *also*"强颜欢笑" force a smile to one's face when one is not in a good mood; try to look cheerful
强作解人 qiǎngzuò-jiěrén pretend to be in the know; feign understanding

襁(繦) qiǎng 〈书面〉belt to carry a baby on the back

with:～负其子而立 come with a child sitting on one's back
襁褓 qiǎngbǎo swaddling clothes:尚在～之中 be still in one's infancy

镪 qiǎng string of copper coins:藏～巨万 accumulate huge sums of money

see also qiāng

qiàng

跄(蹌) qiàng

see also qiāng
跄踉 qiàngliàng *also*"跄踉" qiàngliàng walk improperly; stagger

炝(熗) qiàng ❶ boil sth. in water for a while, and then dress it with soy sauce, vinegar, etc.:～黄瓜 boiled cucumber chips with soy source dressing /～腰花 boiled and dressed pork kidney ❷ fry sth. quickly in hot oil, then cook it with sauce and water:用葱花～～锅 fry chopped spring onions in hot oil (to flavour a dish)

戗(戧) qiàng ❶〈建筑〉prop ❷ wooden support:这堵危墙要支根～木。This unsafe wall must be propped up with a log. ❸ buttress; shore up:用木头～住 buttress up with a piece of timber

see also qiāng
戗堤 qiàngdī side dyke for reinforcement
戗金 qiàngjīn inlay sth. with gold; be inlaid with gold
戗面 qiàngmiàn ❶ add dry flour while kneading the dough ❷

leavened dough so mixed with flour：～馒头 steamed bread made of leavened dough mixed with flour

呛(嗆) qiàng irritate (respiratory organs)：油烟～嗓子。The oil smoke irritated my throat. /辣椒味儿～得人喘不过气来。The smell of red pepper being fried is so irritating that it often makes you choke.
see also qiāng

跄(蹌) qiàng
see also qiāng

跄踉 qiàngliàng *also* "踉跄" qiàngliàng；"踉跄" stagger；walk improperly：老妇人跄跄踉踉退下几步。The old lady hobbled a few steps backward.

qiāo

敲 qiāo ❶ knock；rap；beat；strike：～门 knock at the gate /～桌子 rap on the table /十二点钟刚～过。Twelve (o'clock) has just struck. /他们～起锣跳起舞来。They began to beat gongs and started to dance. /大夫用小槌儿～着病人的膝盖。The doctor tapped the patient's knees with a little hammer. ❷〈口语〉swindle money out of sb.；force sb. to pay through the nose；fleece：～了这女人一千元 sting the woman for a thousand *yuan* /昨天他让骗子～了不少钱。Yesterday, a crook swindled him out of a considerble sum of money.

敲边鼓 qiāo biāngǔ try to assist from the sidelines；speak or act to back sb. up：我极力劝她回心转意，老郭也不断地～。I tried hard to bring her around, while Lao Guo threw in a few words from time to time.

敲剥 qiāobō blackmail and exploit：～农民 blackmail and exploit peasants (*or* farmers)

敲打 qiāoda ❶ beat；knock；strike；rap：锣鼓～得震天响。Loud beating of drums and gongs reverberated in the air. ❷〈方言〉say sth. to irritate sb.；utter a few words to make sb. wake up to his own faults；keep sb. in his place with criticisms：干吗借着这件事没完没了地～我？Why on earth are you annoying me endlessly with sarcastic remarks over this matter? /他这个人老要～着点，不要让他翘尾巴。We should knock some sense into him from time to time before he gets too cocky.

敲定 qiāodìng decide finally；make a final decision：事先～ decide beforehand /正式～ formally decide；officially decide /这是会上～的决议草案。This is the draft resolution thrashed out at the meeting. /这件事是双方当面～的。The final decision was reached at a meeting between the two parties.

敲骨吸髓 qiāogǔ-xīsuǐ break the bones and suck the marrow — cruel, bloodsucking exploitation：此人为官多年，～以肥私囊。He has been an official for years, doing nothing but sucking the life-blood of the public and amassing wealth for himself.

敲击 qiāojī beat；strike；tap：用锤子轻轻～琴键，声音清亮悠扬。If you strike the keyboard lightly with a hammer, it'll produce a clear and melodious sound.

敲击乐器 qiāojī yuèqì percussion instrument

敲金击石 qiāojīn-jīshí *also* "敲金戛玉" make metallic sounds；(of sonorous composition) ring in the ears：此诗有～之声。This poem has a metallic ring to it.

敲警钟 qiāo jǐngzhōng sound the alarm bell；forewarn：这起事故虽小，但向我们敲起了警钟。Although this is a minor accident, it has served as a warning to us all.

敲锣边儿 qiāo luóbiānr 〈方言〉make ironical remarks；make sarcastic comments：他只顾～，可把老王气坏了。He made nothing but sarcastic remarks, thus driving Lao Wang mad.

敲锣打鼓 qiāoluó-dǎgǔ beat drums and gongs (in celebration of sth.)：～庆丰收 beat drums and gongs in celebration of a bumper harvest /台上～，大戏开始了。The theatrical performance began amid the boisterous sound of drums and gongs.

敲门砖 qiāoménzhuān brick picked up to knock on the door and thrown away when it has served its purpose — a mere tool to achieve one's aim；a stepping stone to success：旧时读书人把八股文当作～。In the dynastic days, scholars used to regard the eight-part (*or* eight-legged) essay writing as a stepping stone to officialdom.

敲棋 qiāoqí play go

敲丧钟 qiāo sāngzhōng ring the funeral bell；sound the death knell：这次起义敲响了封建王朝的丧钟。This uprising sounded the death knell of the feudal dynasty.

敲山震虎 qiāoshān-zhènhǔ strike at the mountain to frighten the tiger (living in it)—make a move to give a warning to the other side：他们这样做是～，好让对方收敛点。They did so to warn and restrain the other party.

敲石 qiāoshí flint

敲小鼓 qiāo xiǎogǔ feel as if beating a little drum in one's heart — be pricked by conscience；feel nervous；be fidgety or uneasy：干完那件坑害顾客的缺德事，他心里一直敲着小鼓。He has had no peace of mind since he played the mean trick on his customers.

敲诈 qiāozhà extort；blackmail；shake down：倚仗官势，～百姓 extort money from ordinary folks by dint of one's official position

敲诈勒索 qiāozhà-lèsuǒ swindle and squeeze：当年那几个土豪劣绅～，无恶不作。In those days, the local bullies and evil gentry bled the villagers white, committing all kinds of atrocities.

敲竹杠 qiāo zhúgàng make sb. pay through the nose；put the lug on；fleece：不可以服务为名，敲用户的竹杠。It is impermissible to overcharge customers by allegedly providing more service. /这帮人～是出了名的。These people are notorious blackmailers.

硗(磽、墝) qiāo

硗薄 qiāobó (of soil) hard and infertile；unproductive；barren：～的土地 barren land

硗瘠 qiāojí (of land) barren；infertile：～的山区 infertile mountainous area

硗确 qiāoquè (of land) barren；unproductive：土壤～ unproductive soil

跷(蹺) qiāo ❶ lift up (a leg)；hold up (a finger)：他～起大拇指，连声叫好。He shouted "Bravo", holding up his thumb. /他～起二郎腿，斜靠在沙发上。He was sitting with his ankle on his knee, leaning aslant against the sofa. ❷ on tiptoe：～起脚来看布告 stand on tiptoe to read a bulletin ❸ stilts：踩高～ walk on stilts ❹〈方言〉limp；hobble：他一～一拐地走进来。He limped in.

跷蹊 qiāoqi fishy；dubious；suspicious：他说话有些～。There is something fishy in what he said.

跷跷板 qiāoqiāobǎn seesaw：玩～ play on a seesaw

雀 qiāo
see also qiǎo；què

雀子 qiāozi *also* "雀斑" quèbān freckles

悄 qiāo
see also qiǎo

悄悄 qiāoqiāo quietly；secretly；on the quiet：他～地溜出宿舍。He sneaked out of the dormitory. /深夜静～。Night was deepening, and all was quiet. /她～地把家里的活儿都干了才走。She had quietly done all the chores before she left home.

悄悄话 qiāoqiaohuà whisper in private；words for one's private ear；confidential talk：两个姑娘躲在一旁说～。The two girls were talking in whispers in the corner of the room.

幧 qiāo

幧头 qiāotóu *also* "帩头" qiàotóu narrow strip of cloth used by men in ancient China to tie up their hair

缲(帬) qiāo hem with invisible stitches：～边儿 hem the edges /～带子 hem a belt

橇 qiāo sledge；sled；sleigh：雪～ snow sledge

锹(鍫) qiāo spade；shovel：铁～ spade；shovel /挖一～土 dig a spadeful of earth

跻(蹻) qiāo *see* "跷" qiāo

劁 qiāo geld；castrate：～牛 castrate a bull /～羊 geld a goat

qiáo

翘(翹) qiáo ❶ raise (one's head); lift up:～望四周 raise one's head to look around ❷ become warped or bent:这尺子有点儿～,不能用了。We have no use for the ruler; it's a little warped. *see also* qiào

翘楚 qiáochǔ 〈书面〉person of outstanding ability:他们都是商界～。They are all eminent figures in the business world.

翘棱 qiáoleng 〈方言〉become warped or bent:板子日晒雨淋的,全～了。The planks have been exposed to the sun and rain and are totally warped.

翘盼 qiáopàn eagerly look forward to; earnestly expect

翘企 qiáoqǐ 〈书面〉raise one's head and stand on tiptoe — eagerly await:欣闻阁下不日驾临北京,不胜～之至。We hear that your excellency will be visiting Beijing, and we are eagerly looking forward to your arrival.

翘首 qiáoshǒu 〈书面〉lift up or raise one's head and look; crane one's neck:～瞻仰 look up at sth. reverentially /～四望 raise one's head and look around /～南天,神驰左右。When I looked up at the southern sky, my thoughts went to you. /足下马到成功,我等～以待。We are in eager expectation of your instant success.

Q

翘首企足 qiáoshǒu-qǐzú crane one's neck and stand on tiptoe — eagerly await

翘望 qiáowàng ❶ raise one's head to look at sth.:～着丈夫远去的身影。Raising her head, she gazed at her husband's receding figure. ❷ look forward to; expect:观众～已久的电影周下月初在北京开幕。The film week, which audiences have long been anticipating, will start in Beijing at the beginning of next month.

翘足 qiáozú 〈书面〉stand on tiptoe — eagerly look or wait for:百姓～切盼和平。The people longed eagerly for peace.

翘足而待 qiáozú'érdài wait on tiptoe — expect sth. to happen in no time:丧失民心,灭亡可～。When a regime has lost popular support, its days are numbered.

翘足引领 qiáozú-yǐnlǐng stand on tiptoe and crane one's neck — eagerly wait for somebody to come or something to happen

乔¹(喬) qiáo ❶ tall:～松 tall pine trees ❷ (Qiáo) a surname

乔²(喬) qiáo pretend to be; disguise: *see* "～装"

乔林 qiáolín 〈林业〉timber-forest; high forest

乔模乔样 qiáomú-qiáoyàng ❶ insincere; hypocritical; in an affected manner ❷ coquettish; seductive

乔木 qiáomù 〈植物〉arbor; tree:故园～,应似当年。The trees in our hometown should be much the same as in old days.

乔木果树 qiáomù guǒshù 〈林业〉standard fruit-tree

乔其绒 qiáoqíróng 〈纺织〉georgette velvet

乔其纱 qiáoqíshā 〈纺织〉crêpe georgette

乔迁 qiáoqiān move to a better place; be transferred to a higher post:举行宴会庆祝～ throw a house-warming party /祝贺老兄～。Congratulations on your promotion, old pal.

乔迁之喜 qiáoqiānzhīxǐ happy occasion of moving into a new residence:祝贺～ congratulate sb. on moving into a new residence

乔松之寿 qiáosōngzhīshòu life as long as that of a tall pine — great longevity

乔叟 Qiáosǒu Geoffrey Chaucer (c. 1340-1400), English writer and poet

乔治敦 Qiáozhìdūn Georgetown, capital and chief port of Guyana

乔装 qiáozhuāng disguise; simulate:他～税收干部在集市上进行敲诈。He disguised himself as a tax collector and extorted money at the fair.

乔装打扮 qiáozhuāng-dǎbàn deck oneself out as sb.; masquerade; disguise

乔梓 qiáozǐ *also* "桥梓" qiáozǐ 〈书面〉(used of others) father and son:贤～ esteemed father and son

荞(蕎) qiáo

荞麦 qiáomài buckwheat

鞒(鞽) qiáo pommel and cantle of a saddle

桥(橋) qiáo ❶ bridge:木～ wooden (*or* plank) bridge /石～ stone bridge /铁～ iron bridge /过街～ foot bridge; pedestrian bridge /立交～ flyover (bridge); overpass /天～ platform bridge /引～ approach to a bridge; approach span /便～ temporary (*or* make-shift) bridge /吊～ drawbridge /独木～ single-plank bridge /双曲拱～ two-way curved arch bridge /索～ rope bridge; cable bridge /铁索～ chain bridge /索拉钢～ cable-braced steel bridge /钢结构铁路～ steel lattice railway bridge /钢筋混凝土公路～ reinforced concrete highway bridge /预应力混凝土～ prestressed concrete bridge /开合～ bascule bridge /旋转～ swing bridge; revolving bridge /升降～ lift bridge /悬臂～ cantilever bridge /桁架～ truss bridge /高架～ trestle bridge /预制～ prefabricated bridge /浮～ pontoon bridge / 双线、双层铁路公路两用～ double-track, double-deck rail and road bridge /连拱～ multiple-arch bridge /多跨～ multiple-span bridge /悬索～ suspension bridge ❷ (Qiáo) a surname

桥本龙太郎 Qiáoběnlóngtàiláng Ryutaro Hashimoto (1937-), Japanese Prime Minister (1996-1998)

桥洞 qiáodòng bridge opening; bridge arch

桥墩 qiáodūn (bridge) pier:水下～ underwater foundation / ～破冰构造 ice guard

桥拱 qiáogǒng bridge arch

桥涵 qiáohán bridge and its culvert

桥脚舟 qiáojiǎozhōu pontoon

桥接 qiáojiē 〈电工〉bridging; bridge connection:～电路 bridge circuit /～线 bridge connector

桥孔 qiáokǒng bridge opening; arch under the bridge

桥跨 qiáokuà bridge span

桥栏杆 qiáolángān bridge railing

桥梁 qiáoliáng bridge:～建筑 bridge building (*or* construction) /～建筑工程 bridge construction project / 起纽带和～作用 play the role of a bridge; serve as a link /你们是增进两国人民友谊的～。You can be a bridge in enhancing the friendship between our two peoples.

桥梁工程 qiáoliáng gōngchéng 〈建筑〉bridgework

桥楼室 qiáolóushì 〈造船〉bridge house

桥面 qiáomiàn 〈建筑〉deck; bridge floor

桥牌 qiáopái bridge:～搭档 bridge partner /我们打了几个晚上的～。We had a few bridge evenings.

桥式起重机 qiáoshì qǐzhòngjī bridge crane; overhead travelling crane

桥式整流器 qiáoshì zhěngliúqì 〈电工〉bridge rectifier

桥塔 qiáotǎ 〈建筑〉bridge tower

桥台 qiáotái 〈建筑〉abutment

桥头 qiáotóu either end of a bridge

桥头堡 qiáotóubǎo ❶〈军事〉bridgehead ❷〈建筑〉bridge tower

桥堍 qiáotù either end of a bridge

桥支座 qiáozhīzuò bridge seat

桥桩 qiáozhuāng bridge pier

桥梓 qiáozǐ *see* "乔梓" qiáozǐ

峤(嶠) qiáo 〈书面〉pointed high mountain *see also* jiào

盉(盉) qiáo 〈古语〉container similar to a bowl

侨(僑) qiáo ❶ live abroad; reside in a foreign country: *see* "～居";"～胞"❷ person living abroad; resident in a foreign country:外～ foreign residents; aliens /华～ Chinese nationals living (*or* residing) abroad; overseas Chinese nationals /归国华～ returned overseas Chinese

侨办 Qiáobàn (short for 华侨事务办公室) Office of Overseas Chinese Affairs (under the State Council)

侨胞 qiáobāo countrymen or nationals living abroad:海外～ overseas nationals; nationals residing abroad /爱国～ patriotic overseas nationals

侨汇 qiáohuì overseas remittance

侨汇券 qiáohuìquàn overseas remittance coupon (now out of use)

侨居 qiáojū live abroad:～异国 reside in an alien land; live in a

foreign country
侨居国 qiáojūguó country of residence
侨眷 qiáojuàn relatives of nationals living abroad; relatives of overseas Chinese
侨联 Qiáolián (short for 归国华侨联合会) Returned Overseas Chinese Federation
侨民 qiáomín national of a particular country residing abroad: 外国～ foreign resident; alien; expatriate
侨民法 qiáomínfǎ 〈法律〉 alien act
侨商 qiáoshāng overseas Chinese businessman
侨生 qiáoshēng ❶ children born abroad of overseas Chinese parents ❷ overseas Chinese studying in China
侨属 qiáoshǔ relatives of Chinese nationals residing abroad; relatives of overseas Chinese
侨团 qiáotuán overseas Chinese community: 墨尔本～ Chinese community in Melbourne
侨委 Qiáowěi (short for 华侨事务委员会) Committee for Overseas Chinese Affairs
侨务 qiáowù affairs concerning Chinese nationals residing abroad; overseas Chinese affairs
侨乡 qiáoxiāng area inhabited by returned overseas Chinese and the relatives of overseas Chinese
侨寓 qiáoyù 〈书面〉 live abroad; live in a place away from one's hometown
侨资 qiáozī capital invested by Chinese nationals residing abroad; investment by overseas Chinese: ～企业 enterprise funded by overseas Chinese

憔 qiáo

憔悴 qiáocuì *also* "颤顇" qiáocuì ill and emaciated; haggard; (of plants) withered: 最后一次见到她时，她异常～。She was extremely haggard when I last saw her. /刮了一夜的秋风，草木都显得～。All the trees and grass withered after the autumn wind had blown hard for the whole night.

谯 qiáo ❶ *see* "谯楼" ❷ (Qiáo) a surname

谯楼 qiáolóu 〈书面〉 ❶ watchtower ❷ drum tower

蕉 qiáo

see also jiāo
蕉萃 qiáocuì *see* "憔悴" qiáocuì

樵 qiáo ❶ firewood: 采～ gather firewood ❷ 〈书面〉 gather firewood: 当年这一带许多人靠渔～为生。In the old days many people in this area lived by fishing and cutting wood in the mountains.

樵夫 qiáofū woodcutter; woodman

颤 qiáo

颤顇 qiáocuì *see* "憔悴" qiáocuì

瞧 qiáo 〈口语〉 look; watch; see: ～书 read a book /～戏 go to the theatre /～一～ take a look /往外～ look outside /让他～着办吧。Let him do as he sees fit. /～我的。Now it's my turn. *or* Now let me show you how to do it. /她去晚了，没～上电影。She was late and missed the film.

瞧病 qiáobìng 〈口语〉 ❶ (of a patient) see or consult a doctor: 你脸色不好，得赶快去～。You don't look well and must see a doctor at once. ❷ (of a doctor) see or visit a patient
瞧不起 qiáobuqǐ 〈口语〉 look down upon; despise: 他太～人，不可能不招致别人的不满。He is much too cocky and is bound to offend people.
瞧不上眼 qiáobushàngyǎn *also* "瞧不上" 〈口语〉 look down one's nose (at sth. or sb.); think little of; be cocky: 虽然他自己本事不大，却对同事们～。He didn't think much of his colleagues although he was not much good himself.
瞧得起 qiáodeqǐ *also* "瞧得上" 〈口语〉 think much or highly of: 承你～，我必定好好干。Thank you for your high opinion, I'll definitely do my very best.
瞧哈哈 qiáo hāha 〈口语〉 gloat (over other people's misfortune); have a good laugh: 我们遭难，他却站在一边～。While we had a mishap, he was standing by and having a good laugh over it.
瞧好儿 qiáohǎor 〈口语〉 see a good show; see good results: 到时候自然让你们～。I'll certainly show you what I can achieve in due course. /谁叫他逞能耐，不用多久你就～吧！He tries to show off, but will soon be making a fool of himself.
瞧见 qiáojian 〈口语〉 see; notice; catch sight of: 一～妈妈，孩子就哭了起来。The child began to cry at the sight of his mother.
瞧热闹 qiáo rènao 〈口语〉 ❶ watch the fun: 假日到街上去～ go and watch the fun in the streets on holidays ❷ look on with folded arms; be an onlooker in a dispute, quarrel, fight, etc.: 别人打架，他在旁边～。While the others got into a brawl, he looked on gleefully.
瞧香的 qiáoxiāngde 〈方言〉 witch; wizard; sorcerer; sorceress

荍 qiáo ❶ 〈古语〉 high mallow ❷ buckwheat

qiǎo

悄 qiǎo ❶ quiet; silent: 低声～语 speak in a low voice; whisper ❷ 〈书面〉 sad; worried; grieved: 忧心～～ feel sad; be worried

see also qiāo
悄不言声 qiǎobuyánshēng 〈方言〉 ❶ be silent: 她愁容满面，～地坐了很久。She sat there for a long time, sad and silent. ❷ speak in a very low voice
悄寂 qiǎojì silent; quiet; noiseless: 山野～ tranquil mountain scene
悄静 qiǎojìng quiet and still; tranquil; hushed: 树林～。All is hushed in the woods. /～无声。It's quiet and still.
悄没声儿 qiǎomoshēngr 〈方言〉 quietly; without making any noise: 她～地进了屋。She entered the room quietly.
悄然 qiǎorán ❶ sadly; sorrowfully: ～落泪 shed tears sadly ❷ quietly; softly: 庭院寂寥，～无声。The courtyard was deserted and silence reigned supreme.
悄声 qiǎoshēng quietly; softly: ～出屋 leave the house quietly /她趴在妈妈的耳边～地说了几句。She whispered softly in her mother's ear.

愀 qiǎo

愀怆 qiǎochuàng sorrowful; sad-looking: ～伤心 grieve
愀然 qiǎorán 〈书面〉 ❶ look grave or stern: ～作色 turn stern /～改容 change one's countenance ❷ look unhappy or displeased: ～不乐 look displeased

巧 qiǎo ❶ skilful; adept; ingenious; clever: 能工～匠 skilful worker and ingenious artisan /手艺～ excellent workmanship /熟能生～ skill comes from practice; practice makes perfect /轻～ light to carry and easy to handle /灵～ dexterous; ingenious ❷ (of hand and tongue) deft; glib; clever: 手～ with skilful hands; clever with one's hands /嘴～ have a glib tongue ❸ opportunely; luckily; accidentally: 我赶～买了这本书。I got this book by mere chance. /真不凑～，暖瓶刚刚卖完。Unluckily, the thermos flasks have just been sold out. /那球正～砸在他头上。That ball happened to hit him right on the head. /他恰～买到最后一张车票。As luck would have it, he got the last train ticket. ❹ (of words) fine-sounding; sly; artful: 花言～语 fine words; fine-sounding words

巧辩 qiǎobiàn argue cleverly or smartly: 你错了，再～也没有用。You are wrong, and there's no use trying to argue.
巧不可阶 qiǎobùkějiē extraordinarily skilful; unexcelled: 这篇文章文思俱佳，～。This article is matchless in either structure or ideas. /展出的工艺品～。The handicraft articles on display were exquisite.
巧夺天工 qiǎoduó-tiāngōng so wonderful in workmanship as to excel nature: 这件湘绣精品真可谓～。This piece of choice Hunan embroidery is superb indeed.
巧发奇中 qiǎofā-qízhòng shoot an arrow most skilfully and hit the bull's eye — say the most appropriate words at the most opportune moment to the liking of the right audience: 善为～ be good at saying the right thing to the right person
巧方儿 qiǎofāngr 〈口语〉 tricks; humbug; bluff: 别拿～蒙人。Don't bluff. /别以为人家看不透你的～！Don't think others will not be able to see through your humbug.
巧妇难为无米之炊 qiǎofù nán wéi wú mǐ zhī chuī even a clever

housewife can't cook without rice — one can't make bricks without straw：并不是儿媳不把老太太的生日当回事儿，而是她手头太紧，叫她～。It was not that the daughter-in-law didn't take the old lady's birthday celebration seriously, but being hard-pressed for money, she couldn't possibly have done anything better.

巧妇鸟 qiǎofùniǎo 〈动物〉wren

巧干 qiǎogàn do sth. cleverly; work ingeniously：实干加～ work in earnest and with ingenuity

巧合 qiǎohé coincidence; pure chance：这位作家善于在情节～上作文章。This writer is adept at weaving plausible coincidences into the plot. /小两口同年同月同日生，真是～。It was a sheer coincidence that the couple were born on the same day of the same month in the same year.

巧计 qiǎojì clever device; artful scheme; smart trick：施～ resort to a stratagem

巧匠 qiǎojiàng fine craftsman：他是制作竹笛的～。He is good at making bamboo flutes.

巧劲儿 qiǎojìnr 〈方言〉❶ clever method; trick：光蛮干不行，要掌握～。It won't do to work blindly without trying to find a clever way to do it. ❷ coincidence：我正找他，他就来了，真是～。What a coincidence! He showed up just when I was looking for him.

Q

巧克力 qiǎokèlì (transliteration) chocolate

巧立名目 qiǎolì-míngmù invent all sorts of names; concoct various excuses：这帮人～，欺骗人民。These people are trying to hoodwink the public under all sorts of pretexts.

巧妙 qiǎomiào ingenious; smart; clever：～的计策 smart scheme; crafty strategem /小说的结构～。The plot of the novel is cleverly constructed. /影片的剪接很～。The montage of the film was done with ingenuity. /他～地处理了这个问题。He handled the problem with great finesse./戏法人人会变，各有～不同。Everybody can do some tricks, but each does so in his own way.

巧取豪夺 qiǎoqǔ-háoduó get by cheating or by force; grab and keep：这些～的行为令人发指。These "grab and keep" practices make people bristle with anger.

巧舌如簧 qiǎoshé-rúhuáng *see* "巧言如簧"

巧事 qiǎoshì coincidence：天底下哪有这种～？How could there possibly be such a coincidence?

巧手 qiǎoshǒu ❶ clever with one's hands：她有双～，能织各种毛衣。Clever with her hands, she can do all sorts of knitwear. ❷ dab hand; dexterous person：姑娘是个～，什么家务活儿都能干。The girl is a dab hand, able to do any kind of household chores.

巧思 qiǎosī (of art or literary work) ingenious conception：庭园中布置的山石花木，各具～。The rocks and plants in the garden are all ingeniously conceived and designed.

巧黠 qiǎoxiá 〈书面〉cunning; sly; wily

巧笑 qiǎoxiào winsome smile：她面露～，迎了过来。She greeted us with the most winsome smile.

巧言令色 qiǎoyán-lìngsè have a glib tongue and ingratiating manner; be hypocritical：～以惑众 mislead people with clever talk and an ingratiating manner

巧言如簧 qiǎoyán-rúhuáng *also* "巧舌如簧" talk glibly; sweet-talk：～，乱人听闻 talk glibly to mislead public opinion; speak eloquently only to misinform the public /尽管他～，但在场的人谁也不信他。Despite his smooth talk, none of those present were convinced.

巧遇 qiǎoyù encounter by chance; run into sb. by accident：昨天我～多年不见的老友。Yesterday I ran across an old friend I hadn't seen for years.

巧诈 qiǎozhà cunning and hypocritical：～百出 full of cunning and wiles

巧诈不如拙诚 qiǎozhà bùrú zhuōchéng better clumsy and honest than clever but cunning; honesty is the best policy：～，为人还是老实点儿好！Honesty pays. *or* He is wise who is honest.

巧致 qiǎozhì fine; lovely：～的书架 nice bookshelf

巧主儿 qiǎozhǔr 〈口语〉clever or smart person：他是有名的～，办事从不吃亏。He's known for his cleverness, for he always comes off well in everything he does. /这事难办，另找～去吧！This is really a knotty problem. You'd better go and find a wiser man to handle it!

巧宗儿 qiǎozōngr rare opportunity：他听说有这～，高兴得跳起来了。He jumped for joy when he learned of such a rare opportunity.

雀 qiǎo sparrow

see also qiāo; què

雀盲眼 qiǎomangyǎn 〈方言〉night blindness; nyctalopia

qiào

窍(竅) qiào

❶ aperture; orifice：七～ seven orifices (of the head, i. e. the eyes, ears, nostrils, and mouth)/ 鬼迷心～ be possessed; be obsessed ❷ key to sth.; knack：干这个你算通～了。Now you've got the knack of the trade (*or* the hang of it)! /我如今也开～了。I've come to see the light.

窍诀 qiàojué *also* "诀窍" knack; trick

窍门 qiàomén key (to a problem); trick; knack：找～ try to find the key to a problem; try to get the knack of doing sth. /做这件事有个～儿。There is a clever way to do this. /～四两拨千斤。A brilliant idea can solve very difficult problems.

壳(殼) qiào

hard outer covering of sth.; shell; crust：地～ earth's crust /甲～ crust /花生去～ shelling of peanuts /金蝉脱～ a cicada sloughs off its skin — escape by cunning manoeuvres

see also ké

壳菜 qiàocài 〈动物〉(as food) mussel

壳斗 qiàodǒu 〈植物〉cupule

壳牌石油公司 Qiàopái Shíyóu Gōngsī Shell Oil Company

壳质 qiàozhì shell material or substance; chitin

翘(翹、㯯) qiào

stick up; hold up; turn upwards：把椅子腿～起来 lift the legs of a chair from the floor (while sitting in it) /气得胡子都～起来 so angry that one's beard stands on end — foam with rage

see also qiáo

翘板 qiàobǎn *also* "翘翘板"；"压板" yàbǎn seesaw

翘辫子 qiào biànzi kick the bucket：那个家伙早～了。That fellow kicked the bucket a long time ago. /去年我生了一场大病，差点儿～。Last year I was seriously ill, and very nearly popped off.

翘尾巴 qiào wěiba stick one's tail up — be cocky; be haughty and snooty：即使有成绩也没有理由～。There is no reason for you to be cocky even if you have done very well in your work.

诮(譙) qiào

〈书面〉❶ blame; censure; reproach; upbraid：*see* "～呵" ❷ sneer at; deride：讥～ jeer at sb.; criticize sarcastically

诮呵 qiàohē 〈书面〉reproach; rebuke; reprove：～之词 reproachful remarks

诮让 qiàoràng 〈书面〉condemn; censure

鞘 qiào

sheath; scabbard：剑～ sword sheath /刀出～ unsheathe a knife

see also shāo

鞘翅 qiàochì 〈动物〉elytrum

鞘翅目 qiàochìmù 〈动物〉*Coleopteron*

鞘子 qiàozi scabbard; sheath

鞘嘴鸥 qiàozuǐ'ōu 〈动物〉sheathbill

帩 qiào

帩头 qiàotóu *also* "幧头" qiāotóu narrow strip of cloth used by men to tie up their hair in ancient China

峭(陗) qiào

❶ high and steep; abrupt; precipitous：山势陡～。The mountain rises high and sheer. ❷ stern; harsh; severe：冷～ cold and stern

峭拔 qiàobá ❶ high and steep; perilous：山峰～ towering peaks ❷ vigorous; robust：文笔～ write a vigorous style

峭壁 qiàobì cliff; precipice; steep：万丈～ towering cliff /两岸～耸立。There are towering crags rising from either side of the river.

峭寒 qiàohán cold; chilly; frigid：海风～ chilly wind from the sea

峭急 qiàojí 〈书面〉(of temperament) stern and impetuous：父亲～，孩子们都怕他。Father was stern and all the children were afraid of him.

峭劲 qiàojìng strong; forceful; powerful：～的山风 strong mountain wind

峭峻 qiàojùn ❶ (of mountains) high and steep：山势～。The

mountain stands high and steep. ❷ stern; severe:此人正直～，多谋善断。The man is just and stern, resourceful and decisive.
峭立 qiàolì rise steeply:险岩～。Perilous cliffs shoot up steeply.
峭厉 qiàolì 〈书面〉❶ (of wind, cold air, etc.) chilly; bitter:春风～。There is a nip in the spring wind. ❷ stern; frosty:～的表情 stern expression
峭丽 qiàolì ❶ (of mountains) steep and picturesque ❷〈书面〉(of diction) forceful and elegant:辞章～。The style of the writing is vigorous and graceful.
峭直 qiàozhí 〈书面〉stern; strict:为人～。He is stern and straightforward.

俏 qiào ❶ stylish; handsome; good-looking:模样儿～ pretty; good-looking /～也不争春。Sweet and fair, she craves not spring for herself. /她的发型做得很～。Her hair is stylishly done. ❷ sell well; be salable:眼下地毯走～。Nowadays, carpets are in great demand. ❸〈方言〉seasoning:～点儿韭菜 season the food with leeks
俏货 qiàohuò goods that sell well; commodities in great demand; highly salable goods
俏丽 qiàolì charming; attractive; handsome:雨后桃花，更添几分～。The peach blossoms took on an added charm after the rain.
俏美 qiàoměi cute and pretty
俏媚 qiàomèi handsome and charming; attractive:姿容～ good-looking; charming
俏皮 qiàopi ❶ handsome; stylish; smart:她模样儿～。She looks quite smart. ❷ lively; witty:她的话说得很～。Her remarks are full of wit and humour.
俏皮话 qiàopihuà ❶ sarcastic or ironical remarks:他的那点儿聪明都用在说～上了。All his cleverness has been directed, as it were, to the spouting of wilful expressions of sarcasm. ❷ witty remarks; witticisms:我们非常欣赏他在宴会上讲的～。We very much appreciated his witty remarks at the banquet. ❸ two-part allegorical saying, with the first part describing the situation and the second part (often understood) carrying the message
俏生生 qiàoshēngshēng good-looking; handsome; pretty:～的瓜子脸 nice-looking oval face
俏事 qiàoshì advantage gained by unfair means; profit gained at other people's expense:他尽想～。He is out to gain advantages through unfair means.
俏式 qiàoshi 〈方言〉handsome; charming:～利落的女子 attractive, vivacious woman
俏爽 qiàoshuǎng handsome and valiant:这个青年军官精悍～，声音洪亮。The young officer is capable and handsome, and has a sonorous voice.
俏头 qiàotou 〈方言〉❶ seasoning:他炒菜很会配～儿。He knows pretty well how to season the dishes he prepares. ❷〈戏曲〉tidbits (such as gestures, remarks or episodes) used to make the performance more intriguing:有经验的评书演员会安排～儿。A practised story-teller knows how to lace his stories with intriguing episodes.
俏销 qiàoxiāo sell well; be in great demand:金银首饰～。Gold and silver jewellery sells well. /校园歌曲磁带～不衰。There has been a sustained market for tapes of campus songs.
俏冤家 qiàoyuānjia affectionate reference to one's sweetheart

撬 qiào prize; pry; jimmy:把门～开 prize a door open /～窗户 pry a window open
撬棒 qiàobàng 〈方言〉crowbar
撬杠 qiàogàng crowbar
撬棍 qiàogùn crowbar
撬锁 qiàosuǒ pick a lock:～工具 picklock /溜门～ burglary
撬锁贼 qiàosuǒzéi picklock

撽 qiào 〈书面〉beat from the sides

躈 qiào 〈书面〉anus of an animal

俅 qiào 〈方言〉foolish; stupid

qiē

切 qiē ❶ cut; chop; slice:～瓜 slice up a melon/～面包片 cut slices of bread /～白菜丝 shred cabbage /把肉～一～。Chop the pork. ❷〈数学〉tangency:两圆相～ two circles tangent to each other

see also qiè

切边机 qiēbiānjī edge cutter
切变 qiēbiàn 〈物理〉shear:风～〈气象〉wind shear
切布机 qiēbùjī rag cutter or chopper
切菜机 qiēcàijī vegetable-chopper; vegetable-cutter
切槽 qiēcáo 〈机械〉grooving
切草机 qiēcǎojī 〈畜牧〉hay cutter
切齿刀 qiēchǐdāo 〈机械〉gear cutter
切齿机 qiēchǐjī 〈机械〉gear cutting machine
切除 qiēchú 〈医学〉remove; excise; resect:胃～ removal of part or all of the stomach; gastrectomy /做阑尾～手术 have one's appendix removed; have an appendectomy /部分～ partial excision /全部～ total excision
切磋 qiēcuō learn from each other by exchanging views; compare notes:与同行互相～ exchange views (*or* compare notes) with one's colleagues
切磋琢磨 qiēcuō-zhuómó carve and polish — learn from each other by comparing notes; swap pointers:春秋佳日，二三同好，～，其乐融融。It is most delightful to exchange ideas with a couple of friends on bright days of spring or autumn.
切点 qiēdiǎn 〈数学〉point of tangency; point of contact
切断 qiēduàn cut off:～水源 cut off water supply /～敌军逃路 cut off the enemy's retreat /～车床 cutting-off lathe /～锯 cut-off saw/～电源 cut off the electricity (supply)
切断继电器 qiēduàn jìdiànqì 〈电工〉trip relay
切断术 qiēduànshù 〈医学〉amputation:穿骨～ diaclastic amputation /关节～ amputation in contiguity
切分音 qiēfēnyīn 〈音乐〉syncopation
切腹 qiēfù seppuku or hara-kiri, a ritual suicide by disembowelment with a sword by Japanese samurai:～自杀 commit seppuku (*or* hara-kiri)
切糕 qiēgāo cake made of sticky rice with a layer of sweetened bean paste (eaten by slices)
切割 qiēgē cut; carve up:把肉～开 cut up the meat /金属～ cut through metal /～机 cutting machine; cutter /电弧～〈冶金〉arc cutting /～吹管 cutting torch; cutting blowpipe /～器 cutting apparatus; cutting mechanism
切根虫 qiēgēnchóng 〈方言〉cutworm
切管机 qiēguǎnjī pipe cutter
切花 qiēhuā cut flowers (for decoration, etc.):鲜～ freshly cut flowers
切换 qiēhuàn 〈通信〉cut; change over:节目～器 cut key /视频～台 (video-frequency) cut bank
切开 qiēkāi ❶〈医学〉incision:～引流 incision and drainage ❷ cut open; cut apart:～土豆 cut up a potato
切口 qiēkǒu ❶〈印刷〉margin (on a book page) ❷〈医学〉incision ❸〈冶金〉notching:～试验 notch test

see also qièkǒu

切块 qiēkuài (of food) stripping and slicing:～牛排 cube steak
切力 qiēlì 〈物理〉shearing force; shear:横～ transverse shear /～效应 shear effect
切面 qiēmiàn ❶ cut noodles; machine-made noodles:买二斤～。Buy me a kilo of cut noodles. ❷ section:横～ cross section /纵～ vertical section ❸〈数学〉tangent plane
切片 qiēpiàn ❶ cut into slices; slice:把猪肉切成片 slice the pork ❷〈医学〉section:～检查 cut sections (of organic tissues) for microscopic examination
切片法 qiēpiànfǎ 〈医学〉microtomy
切片机 qiēpiànjī ❶ slicer ❷〈纺织〉chipper ❸〈医学〉microtome
切入 qiērù 〈体育〉(of football) penetrate
切矢量 qiēshǐliàng 〈物理〉tangent vector
切书边机 qiēshūbiānjī plow press
切条 qiētiáo 〈机械〉slitting:～机 slitter; slitting shear machine
切线 qiēxiàn 〈数学〉tangent (line)
切削 qiēxiāo 〈机械〉cut; cutting:金属～ metal cutting /粗～ rough cutting; rough(ing) cut; lower cut /细～ fine cut; upper cut /高速～ high speed cutting /机械～ machine cut /～工具 cutting tool /～机床 cutting machine tool /～液 cutting fluid; cutting compound
切屑 qiēxiè cutting scrap; smear metal; swarf

切牙 qiēyá incisor teeth; front teeth
切造车间 qiēzào chējiān 〈机械〉 cut-up mill
切纸机 qiēzhǐjī paper cutting machine; paper cutter

qié

茄 qié eggplant; aubergine: 拌～泥 mashed eggplant (a cold dish) / 炸～盒 fried stuffed eggplant slices
see also jiā
茄碱 qiéjiǎn 〈生化〉 solanine base
茄皮紫 qiépízǐ eggplant purple; aubergine
茄汁牛肉 qiézhī niúròu braised beef with tomato source
茄子 qiézi eggplant; aubergine

伽 qié word used in transliteration of *Sanskrit*
see also gā; jiā
伽蓝 qiélán Buddhist temple; *samgharama*
伽蓝鸟 qiélánniǎo white pelican
伽罗 qiéluó 〈植物〉 Cambodian wood prized for its scent
伽南香 qiénánxiāng *also* "沉香" chénxiāng 〈植物〉 agalloch eaglewood

Q

qiě

且[1] qiě ❶ just; for the time being; for a while: 你～坐下来歇歇吧! Just sit down and take a rest! / 他们的事情你～别管。Let them mind their own business. / 话还没说完，你～慢走。Stay a while longer. I haven't finished (what I have to say) yet. / 我们～先听听群众的意见，然后订计划。We may as well consult the public before we draw up a plan. ❷ 〈方言〉 for a long time; for quite some time: 买支圆珠笔～使呢。Get a ball-point pen, it will last you quite some time. / 他才出去，～回不来呢。He has just gone out, so it will be quite a while before he comes back. ❸ (Qiě) a surname

且[2] qiě 〈书面〉 ❶ even: 君～如此，况他人乎? If you are in this frame of mind, how could I expect others to think differently? ❷ also; and: 这个故事既有趣～有教育意义。The story is both entertaining and instructive. / 方案已定，～经上级批准，即可动工。Construction is to get under way immediately now that the plan has been decided on and approved by the higher authorities.
see also jū
且慢 qiěmàn wait a minute; hold it; not go or do just yet: ～发火。Control your anger for the moment. / ～，让他把话讲完。Wait a minute. Let's hear him out. / ～下结论。Don't rush to a conclusion yet. *or* Don't jump to conclusions.
且…且… qiě…qiě… while; as: 且歌且舞 sing and dance at the same time / 且看且记 take notes while reading
且说 qiěshuō (usually used in old Chinese novels) let's begin with...

qiè

妾 qiè ❶ concubine ❷ 〈旧语〉 *used by women in humble reference to themselves*: 夫是田中郎，～是田中女。My husband is a peasant and I am a peasant woman.

慊 qiè 〈书面〉 contented; satisfied; gratified; pleased
see also qiàn

锲 qiè 〈书面〉 chisel; carve; engrave
锲而不舍 qiè'érbùshě keep on chiseling or chipping away—stick to sth. with persistence; work with perseverance; make unflagging efforts: 他一直～地研究古生物学。He has been studying palaeontology with great tenacity. / 你如能～，必定学有所成。If you peg away at it, you'll succeed in your studies.

挈 qiè ❶ lift; hoist; take up; raise: 现在只有几分钟了，这个问题我只能提纲～领地讲一讲。As there are only a few minutes left, I'll just have to hit the high spots on this issue. ❷ take along: ～妻女入川 take one's wife and daughter along with one to Sichuan Province
挈带 qièdài ❶ take along: ～家眷 take one's family along ❷ promote; foster: ～门生 promote one's disciples

怯 qiè ❶ timid; cowardly; chicken-hearted; nervous: 胆～ timid; cowardly ❷ 〈贬义〉 *used by people in Beijing to refer to all other northern dialects*: 他的口音带点～。He speaks with a northern accent. ❸ 〈方言〉 inelegant; outmoded; vulgar: 穿得～ be inelegantly dressed / 这颜色配得多～! What a gaudy mix of colours! ❹ 〈方言〉 lacking in knowledge; superficial; shallow: 露～ reveal one's inadequacies; cut a poor figure
怯步 qièbù be afraid to go forward: 殿堂幽黑阴森，令人～。The hall is dark and gloomy, and has a forbidding air.
怯场 qièchǎng stage fright: 她第一次登台就不～。She was not nervous even at her first appearance on the stage.
怯防勇战 qièfáng-yǒngzhàn be cautious in defence and brave in attack
怯惧 qièjù feel timid; fear: 他脸上毫无～之色。His face betrays no trace of fear.
怯口 qièkǒu 〈方言〉 non-native accent: 他说话有点儿～。He speaks with a non-native local accent.
怯懦 qiènuò timid and afraid; weak and cowardly: ～往往带来耻辱。Cowardice is often accompanied by humiliation.
怯弱 qièruò chicken-hearted; timid and weak-willed: 他不～，但也不恃勇蛮干。He is neither faint-hearted, nor foolhardy.
怯生 qièshēng 〈方言〉 timid and diffident in the presence of strangers: 小孩有点～。The child was a bit shy with strangers.
怯生生 qièshēngshēng shy and timid; nervous: 你不是个孩子了，见了人大方一点儿，别那么～的。You are no longer a child, so you should feel at ease with people and not be so shy.
怯声怯气 qièshēng-qièqì (talk) timidly or nervously: 他说话～的。He speaks nervously.
怯头怯脑 qiètóu-qiènǎo boorish; uncouth; old-fashioned: 我不大喜欢这个人，他总是那样～。I don't like the chap. He is always so boorish.
怯阵 qièzhèn ❶ feel nervous right before going into battle; be battle-shy ❷ have stage fright: 别看她爱唱，真要她上台表演，却又～了。She likes singing. Nevertheless, she will feel very nervous when you ask her to perform on the stage.
怯子 qièzi 〈方言〉 person with a non-native local accent

朅 qiè 〈书面〉 ❶ go; leave ❷ brave; courageous

惬(愜、悘) qiè 〈书面〉 gratify; satisfy: 未～人意 unsatisfactory
惬当 qièdàng 〈书面〉 proper; appropriate: 词理～ appropriate in both language and reasoning
惬怀 qièhuái 〈书面〉 pleased; satisfied: 甚为～ feel very pleased
惬心 qièxīn 〈书面〉 satisfied; heartened: 天下莫不～。No one was not heartened.
惬意 qièyì satisfied; pleased: ～的微笑 give a happy smile

箧(篋) qiè 〈书面〉 small suitcase; small box: 书～ small rattan box for books / 行～ travelling box

趄 qiè slanting; inclined: 趔～ walk unsteadily; stagger / 病人～着身子想站起来。The patient leaned sideways, trying to stand up.
see also jū

切 qiè ❶ correspond to; accord with; conform to or with: 不～实际的要求 unrealistic request ❷ close to; warm: 亲～ warm; kind ❸ eager; keen; anxious: 回家心～ eager to be home / 言词恳～ sincere and earnest words ❹ be sure to; make sure that...: ～不可当耳旁风。Be sure not to treat it as of no consequence. / ～勿存任何幻想。Never cherish any illusions. / 在下直言，～勿见怪! If I speak frankly, don't hold it against me. ❺ *see* "反切" fǎnqiè
see also qiē
切齿 qièchǐ gnash one's teeth; grind one's teeth (in hatred, re-

gret, etc.)：咬牙～ gnash one's teeth /～痛恨 grind one's teeth in hatred; cherish a bitter hatred /～咒骂 curse with clenched teeth

切齿腐心 qièchǐ-fǔxīn *also* "切齿拊心" gnash one's teeth in a surge of hatred; hate with all one's soul：这是我日夜～的事情。That's what I have an implacable hatred for day and night.

切当 qièdàng proper; appropriate; to the point：用词～ be properly worded; use the right word in the right place /对情况要作～的分析 make a proper analysis of the situation /不～地夸大了困难 improperly exaggerate the difficulties; blow up the difficulties out of all proportion

切尔诺贝利事件 Qiè'ěrnuòbèilì shìjiàn Chernobyl Accident (explosion of a nuclear power station in Chernobyl in April 1986, a city near Kiev, Ukraine, in the then USSR)

切肤之痛 qièfūzhītòng keenly felt pain; agony：落后就要挨打，对这一点，老一代人是有～的。To lag behind is to get beaten — that's a painful lesson people of the older generation have learned.

切骨 qiègǔ to the bone：～之寒 bitter cold; icy cold

切骨之仇 qiègǔzhīchóu *also* "切骨之恨" strongly felt hatred; bitter enmity; profound animosity：～，三世未了。It is a vendetta which has existed for three generations.

切合 qièhé correspond to; accord with; fit in with：～实际 fit in with the reality; be practical /这些话并不～他自己的真实感受。These words did not reflect his true feelings.

切激 qièjī vehement; impassioned：词甚～。The speech is impassioned.

切己 qièjǐ of immediate concern to oneself; of great interest to oneself

切记 qièjì keep firmly in mind; must always remember：此事至关重要，望你～勿忘。This is a matter of crucial importance which you must engrave on your mind. /～以往的教训。Do not forget past lessons.

切忌 qièjì must not do in any circumstances; avoid by all means; must guard against：写文章～人云亦云。It is essential that in your writing you should guard against repeating other people's views without thinking. /你病体尚未复原，～生冷。You should refrain from cold and raw food as you are hardly recovered yet.

切谏 qièjiàn 〈书面〉admonish sb. to desist from certain action; earnestly entreat sb. not to do sth.

切近 qièjìn ❶ near; nearby：远大的事业要从～处做起。A grand undertaking always has a humble beginning. *or* A great cause must begin with what is ordinary and close to reality. ❷ similar; close to：他的小说大都～生活。Most of his novels are close to life.

切口 qièkǒu secret language of underground gangs; password; cant; jargon

see also qiēkǒu

切脉 qièmài 〈中医〉feel the pulse

切末 qièmo 〈戏曲〉simple stage property

切盼 qièpàn eagerly look forward to; eagerly expect; sincerely hope：～你们做出更好的成绩。We sincerely hope that you will make even better contributions.

切迫 qièpò urgent; pressing; imperative

切切 qièqiè ❶ (used mostly in letters) be sure to; must do：～牢记 must always remember; be sure not to forget ❷ *used in public notices, orders, decrees, etc. to express exhortation or warning*：～此布。This is hereby solemnly proclaimed. /～此令。This order is to be regarded with all seriousness. ❸ earnest; eager：～请求 request earnestly ❹ *also* "窃窃" qièqiè murmuring sound：～私语 whisper under one's breath

切身 qièshēn ❶ of immediate concern or interest to oneself：～利害 of immediate or vital interest to one /这是他们的～大事。This is a matter of utmost importance to them. ❷ personal：～体验 learn through one's personal experience /我在这方面可有一些～体会。I have acquired some intimate knowledge of this.

切实 qièshí practical; feasible; realistic; earnest：～的步骤 effective steps /～的措施 feasible measures /～的保证 firm guarantee; earnest assurance /～加强消防工作 step up fire control in earnest /作点～的调查研究 conduct investigations and studies in a down-to-earth manner /切切实实地总结经验教训 sum up one's experience and lessons conscientiously /方案不～。The plan is not realistic(*or* practical).

切题 qiètí keep to the point; be relevant to the subject; be related to the topic under discussion：这段文章不～。This part of the article is irrelevant to the subject. /发言要～。When speaking at a meeting, one must try to keep to the point.

切贴 qiètiē apt; appropriate; suitable

切望 qièwàng *see* "切盼"

切勿 qièwù (of a request or warning) must not do; never try to do：～倒置 keep upright /～靠近 keep off /～受潮 keep dry; caution against wet /～颠倒。No turning over. /～吸烟。No smoking.

切要 qièyào vital; essential; indispensable：措施～。These measures are indispensable. /此乃～之举。This is a step of vital importance.

切音 qièyīn use two Chinese characters to represent the pronunciation of a third character

切愿 qièyuàn earnestly hope：～跟他一见。I earnestly hope that I'll be able to meet him.

切责 qièzé 〈书面〉denounce in harsh terms; sternly condemn

切诊 qièzhěn 〈中医〉pulse feeling and palpation, one of the four methods of diagnosis

切中 qièzhòng hit (the mark)：～要害 hit the nail on the head; strike home

切中时弊 qièzhòng-shíbì criticize the ills of the society sharply; strike hard at current social evils

切嘱 qièzhǔ 〈书面〉advise sb. time and again; exhort sb. again and again

窃(竊) qiè

❶ steal; pilfer; pinch：偷～ steal /盗～ practise theft; steal; burglarize /～书 steal books /失～ be stolen (*or* pinched) /此文所论，大都～人之说。This article is little more than plagiarism. ❷ secretly; furtively; stealthily; surreptitiously：～窥 peep ❸〈书面〉〈谦词〉*used to refer to oneself*：～以为不可。In my humble opinion, this won't work.

窃案 qiè'àn 〈法律〉case of theft; burglary

窃夺 qièduó usurp; seize by illegal means：～国柄 usurp state power

窃鈇之疑 qièfūzhīyí unfounded suspicion; bias

窃钩窃国 qiègōu-qièguó *also* "窃钩者诛，窃国者侯" he who steals a hook is killed as a crook; he who steals a kingdom is made a duke — little thieves are hanged, but great ones honoured

窃国 qièguó usurp state power; seize supreme power by force or wile：～大盗 arch-usurper of state power

窃据 qièjù usurp; illegally occupy：～高位 occupy a high position by foul means

窃据要津 qièjù-yàojīn occupy an important post unjustly

窃密 qièmì steal secret information

窃窃 qièqiè ❶ *also* "切切" qièqiè in a low voice; whispering ❷ in secret; stealthily

窃窃私议 qièqiè-sīyì exchange whispered remarks or comments：这件事已引起人们的～。This matter has given rise to whispered discussion among many people.

窃窃私语 qièqiè-sīyǔ talk privately or secretly; whisper：两个人在～。Two people are whispering to each other. /她们正在～，不知议论什么呢。They are discussing something in a subdued voice(*or* in hushed tones). Who knows what they are talking about?

窃取 qièqǔ usurp; steal; seize; grab：～职位 usurp an official position /～情报 steal secret information /～他人的劳动成果 grab the fruits of other people's labour

窃听 qiètīng eavesdrop; wiretap; bug：～某人办公室的电话 bug (*or* tap) sb.'s office phone /对他们的谈话进行～ eavesdrop on their conversation

窃听电话机 qiètīng diànhuàjī detectaphone

窃听器 qiètīngqì tapping device; listening-in device; bug; tap

窃笑 qièxiào laugh up one's sleeve：有人～他不自量力。Some people are laughing up their sleeve at him for overrating himself.

窃衣 qièyī 〈植物〉hemlock chervil

窃玉偷香 qièyù-tōuxiāng *also* "偷香窃玉" (of a man) have illicit sexual relations with a woman

窃贼 qièzéi thief; burglar; pilferer

砌 qiè

see also qì

砌末 qièmo *see* "切末" qièmo

qīn

亲(親) qīn ❶ parent:父~ father /母~ mother /双~ parents ❷ one's own flesh and blood:~女儿 one's own daughter ❸ blood relations; next of kin:~姊妹 blood sister/~叔叔 one's first uncle (younger than one's father) ❹ kin; relative:远~ distant relative /探~ visit one's family or relatives at another town /沾~带故 be related somehow or other; have ties of kinship or friendship ❺ marriage; match:定~ engagement; betrothal/结~ marry; get married ❻ bride:娶~ (of a man) get married ❼ close; intimate; near and dear:众叛~离 be spurned by the people and deserted by one's followers; be utterly isolated /不分~疏 make no distinction between close associates and mere acquaintances ❽ in person; personally:~赴现场 personally rush to the scene ❾ in favour of; supporting:~美派 pro-American elements ❿ kiss:妈妈~了~孩子。The mother kissed the baby.
see also qìng

Q

亲爱 qīn'ài dear; beloved; cherished:~的妈妈 dear mother /~的祖国 one's beloved country (*or* homeland)

亲本 qīnběn 〈生物〉parent:~染色体组 parental set of chromosomes / 轮回~ recurrent parent

亲笔 qīnbǐ ❶ write in one's own hand; autograph:~签名的照片 autographed photograph/这封信是他~写的。This letter is in his own writing. ❷ one's own handwriting; autograph:这几个字确系他的~。These words are indeed his handwriting.

亲笔信 qīnbǐxìn letter in longhand; personal letter:特使带来了总统的~。The special envoy has brought a personal letter from the president.

亲兵 qīnbīng 〈旧语〉bodyguard of an officer

亲不间疏,先不僭后 qīn bù jiàn shū, xiān bù jiàn hòu close relations come before distant ones, and old friendships before new ones

亲传 qīnchuán impart(knowlege) or teach personally:~弟子 disciple whom one has taught personally; one's own disciple

亲代 qīndài 〈生物〉parental generation

亲等 qīnděng degree of kinship

亲丁 qīndīng 〈旧语〉kith and kin; blood kin

亲睹 qīndǔ see with one's own eyes; personally witness

亲房 qīnfáng persons of close blood lineage in the same clan:本家~ blood relations of one's clan

亲骨肉 qīngǔròu one's own flesh and blood; one's own offspring:儿是娘的~。The son is the mother's own flesh and blood. /她对待孤儿像~一样。She treats the orphans like her own children.

亲故 qīngù relatives and old acquaintances:多年来,~久疏。I have had virtually no contact with many of my relations and friends all these years.

亲串 qīnguàn 〈书面〉❶ relation; relative:远房~ distant relation ❷ close associate

亲贵 qīnguì 〈书面〉emperor's trusted relatives and courtiers:~当权 royal kin in positions of power

亲和 qīnhé ❶ be on intimate terms ❷〈生物〉fertilization

亲和力 qīnhélì 〈化学〉affinity

亲和数 qīnhéshù 〈数学〉amicable numbers

亲近 qīnjìn be close to; be friendly with; be on intimate terms with:~的朋友 close associates; bosom friends /两家一向是很~的。The two families have always been on intimate terms. /他过于严肃,令人不敢~。He is so grave in manner that he appears rather standoffish. /两个人不知不觉地~起来了。The two of them felt gradually drawn towards each other.

亲旧 qīnjiù relatives and old acquaintances

亲眷 qīnjuàn ❶ one's relatives:进城去看一位~ visit a relative in town ❷ one's family members, especially one's wife and children:内室住着他的~。His wife and children live in the inner room.

亲口 qīnkǒu (say or speak) personally:这是他~对人说的。This is what he said to others himself.

亲历 qīnlì 〈书面〉experience personally; be involved directly:未尝~其事 have never had any such experience before; have had no personal experience about such matters

亲邻 qīnlín relatives and neighbours

亲临 qīnlín make personal appearance (at a place):希~指导。We hope that you will be present to give guidance.

亲聆 qīnlíng hear with one's own ears:年轻时候,我曾~他的教诲。When I was a young man, I had the opportunity of personally attending his lectures (*or* of receiving his instruction).

亲密 qīnmì close; intimate; near and dear:关系~ be on intimate terms /~合作 close cooperation

亲密无间 qīnmì-wújiàn be on very intimate terms with each other:他俩志同道合,~。They both share identical aspirations and are on the best of terms.

亲睦 qīnmù 〈书面〉close and harmonious

亲昵 qīnnì intimate; attached; affectionate:他们手拉手说个没完,~极了。Holding each other by the hand, they kept talking affectionately.

亲朋 qīnpéng relatives and acquaintances:~戚友 relatives and friends

亲启 qīnqǐ (written immediately after the addressee's name on a letter, etc.) to be opened personally by the addressee; personal; private:琼斯先生~ To Mr. Jones (private)

亲戚 qīnqi relative:到~家串门 pay a call on a relative /攀~ claim kinship (as with a bigwig)

亲切 qīnqiè ❶ warm; close; affectionate:~握手 shake hands warmly /回到阔别多年的故乡,倍感~。I felt a surge of warm feeling when revisiting my hometown after years of absence. ❷ kind; hearty; cordial:~的问候 cordial greetings/~的关怀 kind attention/~友好的谈话 warm and friendly conversation

亲切感 qīnqiègǎn warm feeling; feeling of cordiality:他们的答复给人一种~。They gave us a hearty reply.

亲情 qīnqíng emotional attachment among family members:父子~ affection beween father and son

亲热 qīnrè warmhearted; loving; affectionate; intimate:老朋友久别重逢,分外~。When the two old friends met again after a long separation, their faces beamed with joy and warmheartedness. /姨妈一见我,便~地把我抱住了。My aunt embraced me most affectionately the moment she saw me.

亲人 qīnrén ❶ one's parents, spouse, children, etc.; one's family members; one's kith and kin:病人动手术时,必须有~在场。When a patient has an operation, a family member should be present. /女儿去了美国,他们身边再也没有~了。With their daughter away in the United States, they no longer had any close relative living near them. ❷ beloved ones; those dear to one:服务员照顾旅客像对待自己的~一样。The attendants cared for the passengers as though they were their dear ones.

亲如手足 qīnrúshǒuzú *also* "亲如兄弟" dear to each other as brothers:我国各族人民~。The various nationalities of our country live happily together like brothers.

亲如一家 qīnrúyījiā dear to each other as members of the same family:他待我~。He treated me as if I were a member of his family.

亲善 qīnshàn (as between countries) friendship; goodwill:两国世代~。The two countries have maintained friendly relations for generations.

亲上加亲 qīnshàngjiāqīn cement old ties by marriage; be doubly related

亲身 qīnshēn done or made by oneself; personal; firsthand:将军~视察了地形。The general made a personal survey of the terrain. /他想把自己的~经历写下来。He is thinking of writing a book describing his firsthand experiences.

亲生 qīnshēng one's own (as distinct from foster children or parents):~子女 one's own children/~父母 one's own parents /~骨肉 one's own flesh and blood /这女孩是她~的。The girl is her own child.

亲事 qīnshi marriage:这对年轻人的~快成了。The young man and woman are about to get married.

亲手 qīnshǒu with one's own hands; in person; oneself:东西是他~交给我的。He gave it to me himself.

亲疏 qīn-shū close and distant:不分~,一律按原则办事。We make no distinction between those who are our relatives or friends and those who are not, but act strictly according to principle.

亲疏贵贱 qīn-shū-guì-jiàn close and distant relatives, the highly placed and the lowly:~,应一视同仁。They should all be treated equally, regardless of their status or their relationship to you.

亲属 qīnshǔ kinsfolk; relatives:直系~ lineal relatives /旁系~ collateral relatives

亲水性 qīnshuǐxìng hydrophily: ~粉末 hydrophilic powder
亲随 qīnsuí 〈旧语〉personal attendant
亲体 qīntǐ 〈生物〉parent
亲痛仇快 qīntòng-chóukuài sadden one's own people and gladden the enemy: 希望你们不要做~的事。We hope that you will not do anything to grieve your friends and delight your enemies (*or* to bring sorrow to your friends and joy to your enemies).
亲王 qīnwáng prince
亲吻 qīnwěn kiss
亲系 qīnxì kinship system
亲狎 qīnxiá be improperly intimate with; build up intimacies with
亲信 qīnxìn ❶ close and trusted: 他是我所~的人。He is a person that I could trust. ❷〈贬义〉trusted follower; confidant: 他只听几个~的话。He listens only to a few trusted followers.
亲兄弟,明账目 qīnxiōngdì, míngzhàngmù *also* "亲兄弟,明算账" money matters should be accounted for even among brothers; business is business
亲眼 qīnyǎn (see) with one's own eyes; personally (witness): ~所见 see with one's own eyes /我们~看见了贵国的建设成就。We have seen for ourselves the achievements your great country has scored in national construction.
亲谊 qīnyì feeling of kinship: 骨肉~ feeling of flesh-and-blood kinship
亲迎 qīnyíng 〈旧语〉(of a bridegroom) go to the bride's home in person to bring back the bride (in a sedan chair) for the marriage ceremony
亲友 qīnyǒu relatives and friends; kith and kin: 他动身的时候没有一个~来送行。None of his relatives and friends came to see him off when he was leaving.
亲鱼 qīnyú *also* "种鱼" zhǒngyú parent fish
亲缘 qīnyuán blood relations; consanguinity
亲缘交配 qīnyuán jiāopèi consanguineous mating
亲征 qīnzhēng (of a monarch) personally lead an expedition
亲政 qīnzhèng (of a young sovereign) assume the reins of government upon coming of age
亲知 qīnzhī ❶ know at first hand: 真正~的是天下实践着的人。Those who are in possession of real knowledge have always acquired it through practice. ❷〈书面〉relatives and friends
亲炙 qīnzhì 〈书面〉be directly under sb.'s tutorship: 久仰大名, 无由~。I've long heard of your great name, but I've not had the benefit of your personal guidance.
亲子 qīnzǐ parents and children — two immediate generations: ~关系 generational relations
亲自 qīnzì in person; personally; oneself: ~过问 intervene personally /~去处理 attend to sth. oneself /~主持会议 preside over (*or* chair) a meeting in person
亲族 qīnzú members of the same clan
亲嘴 qīnzuǐ kiss

衾

qīn 〈书面〉❶ quilt: 布~ cloth quilt ❷ pall: 衣~棺椁 pall and coffin
衾冷枕寒 qīnlěng-zhěnhán *also* "衾寒枕冷" one's quilt and pillow are cold— feel lonely when one's beloved is far away
衾衽 qīnrèn in the privacy of bedroom
衾影无愧 qīnyǐng-wúkuì *also* "衾影无惭" be open and aboveboard and have done nothing to be ashamed of; have a clear conscience

钦

qīn ❶ admire; adore; respect: 可~可佩 worthy of admiration and respect ❷ by the emperor himself: ~赐 granted or bestowed by the emperor ❸ (Qīn) a surname
钦差 qīnchāi imperial envoy; imperial commissioner
钦差大臣 qīnchāi dàchén ❶ imperial envoy; imperial commissioner ❷ people sent by the higher authorities with full powers: ~满天飞 imperial envoys all over the place
钦迟 qīnchí 〈旧语〉(used in letters) admire: 不胜~ admire immensely
钦定 qīndìng (of writings) authorized by the sovereign himself
钦服 qīnfú hold (sb.) in high esteem and great reverence
钦敬 qīnjìng admire and respect: 他的品德使我~。I admire and respect him for his moral integrity.
钦命 qīnmìng ❶ imperial edict or decree ❷ (of an emperor) issue an imperial decree; decree
钦慕 qīnmù respect and admire; hold in esteem: ~之情 feeling of reverence mixed with admiration
钦佩 qīnpèi hold in high regard; admire; esteem: 令人~的高尚品质 noble quality worthy of esteem /他的治学精神受到同行们的~。He was held in respect by his colleagues for his meticulous scholarship. /我十分~他的为人。I have great admiration for his integrity.
钦羡 qīnxiàn respect and admire: 他用异常~的眼光望着这位杰出的科学家。He looked at the outstanding scientist with admiration and reverence.
钦仰 qīnyǎng 〈书面〉revere; respect; venerate; esteem: 不胜~ revere sb. highly
钦挹 qīnyì 〈书面〉hold in high esteem
钦赞 qīnzàn admire and appreciate: 他渊博的学识, 严肃的工作态度, 一直受到人们的~。He was always held in high regard for his erudition and conscientious work style.
钦伫 qīnzhù 〈书面〉respect; adoration: 载怀~ be filled with respect and admiration

嵚

qīn
嵚崟 qīnyín 〈书面〉(of a mountain) high; towering

侵

qīn ❶ invade; intrude into; encroach on; infringe upon: 入~ invade; make inroads into ❷ approaching: *see* "~早"; "~晨"
侵晨 qīnchén towards daybreak; at the approach of dawn: ~发动进攻 launch an attack at the break of dawn /柳树的枝子在~的寒冷微风中轻轻飘荡。The willow trees are gently swaying in the light chilly breeze that comes with approaching dawn.
侵夺 qīnduó encroach upon; violate; take away: 公家的财产不能任人~。Public property must not be encroached upon.
侵犯 qīnfàn ❶ encroach upon; infringe on; violate: ~人权 infringe on human rights /神圣不可~ sacred and inviolable; sacrosanct /公民的权利不得~。The citizens' rights must not be violated. /个人财产不受~。Personal property is protected against infringement. ❷ invade (the territory of another country); make an inroad; encroach or infringe on: ~别国主权 infringe on another country's sovereignty /~边境 encroach upon the boundary /国土不容别人~。A country's territory brooks no encroachment.
侵害 qīnhài ❶ invade; encroach on; make inroads on: 防止害虫~农作物 prevent pests from harming farm crops/那些文艺垃圾~了他的身心。The literary trash has corrupted his mind. ❷ damage or harm by force or by unlawful means: 群众的利益受到了~。The interests of the people came under attack.
侵凌 qīnlíng bully and humiliate; browbeat and insult: 豪强~孤弱。The despots bullied and humiliated the weak and orphaned.
侵掠 qīnlüè 〈书面〉seize by force; plunder
侵略 qīnlüè aggression; invasion: 发动~战争 launch an aggressive war /反抗~ resist (*or* combat) aggression /谴责~和扩张行径 condemn acts of aggression and expansion /跟着武装~而来的是经济~和文化~。Economic and cultural invasion follows armed invasion.
侵略国 qīnlüèguó aggressor country
侵略军 qīnlüèjūn aggressor troops; invading army
侵略者 qīnlüèzhě aggressor; invader
侵略罪 qīnlüèzuì 〈法律〉crime of aggression
侵权 qīnquán violate others' lawful rights; infringe on sb.'s rights: 被控~ be accused of infringing on sb.'s rights
侵权人 qīnquánrén 〈法律〉tortfeasor; infringer
侵权行为 qīnquán xíngwéi 〈法律〉act of tort; infringement act
侵染 qīnrǎn be infected (with disease)
侵扰 qīnrǎo invade and harass: 防止敌人~我国领土 prevent enemy invasions into our territory /他不想~别人, 但也不想别人~他。He doesn't want to harass others, nor does he like to be harassed.
侵人犯规 qīnrén fànguī 〈体育〉(of basketball) personal foul
侵入 qīnrù invade; intrude into; make inroads on: 敌机~我领空。Enemy planes intruded into our air space./病毒~他的体内。The virus has invaded his body./由于寒潮~, 气温下降。The temperature dropped owing to the intrusion of a cold current.
侵入岩 qīnrùyán 〈地质〉intrusive rock; irruptive rock
侵蚀 qīnshí ❶ corrode; erode; eat into: 抵制各种腐朽没落思想的~ resist the corrosive influence of all kinds of corrupt and decadent ideas /经过几百年的风雨~, 石碑上的字迹已经模糊了。Exposed to the elements for hundreds of years, the inscriptions on the stone tablet have been eroded beyond recognition. ❷ misappropriate or embez-

zle (public funds) bit by bit
侵蚀土 qīnshítǔ eroded soil
侵蚀性溃疡 qīnshíxìng kuìyáng 〈医学〉rodent ulcer
侵吞 qīntūn ❶ misappropriate; embezzle; defalcate: ～公款 embezzle public funds / ～钱粮 misappropriate money and provisions / ～人民的劳动果实 gobble up the fruit of the people's labour ❷ swallow up; forcibly seize; annex: 派兵～别国领土 send troops to annex another country's territory
侵袭 qīnxí make incursions into; invade and attack; assault: 东南沿海常遭台风～。The coastal areas in southeast China are often hit by typhoons. / 一阵恐怖～了他的内心。He was seized with fear.
侵晓 qīnxiǎo before daybreak: 狂风～即起, 入夜始息。A strong wind rose before daybreak and did not subside until nightfall.
侵渔 qīnyú 〈书面〉harass and loot; grab sb.'s property: ～百姓 live off the ordinary people
侵越 qīnyuè go beyond one's brief; exceed or overstep one's power or authority; *ultra vires*
侵早 qīnzǎo at the crack of dawn; at dawn; approaching daybreak
侵占 qīnzhàn ❶ occupy by force; take illegal possession of sth.: 他～了弟妹的房产。He occupied his sister-in-law's house illegally. / 这件事不得不～你一点时间。I'm afraid this matter will have to take up a little of your time. ❷ invade and occupy; seize: ～别国领土 seize another country's territory

Q

骎 qīn

骎骎 qīnqīn 〈书面〉(of horses) gallop; advance rapidly: 祖国建设～日上。Our motherland is advancing speedily in its economic development.

qín

秦 Qín

❶ State of Qin (897-221 BC) ❷ Qin Dynasty (221-206 BC) ❸ another name for Shaanxi and Gansu provinces (especially Shaanxi) ❹ a surname
秦兵马俑博物馆 Qín-Bīngmǎyǒng Bówùguǎn Museum of the Qin Terracotta Warriors and Horses, Xi'an
秦川 Qínchuān ❶ another name for the Shaanxi plain: 八百里～ the 800-*li*-wide Shaanxi plain ❷ another name for the Shaanxi and Gansu plains
秦桧 Qín Huì Qin Hui (formerly translated as Ch'in Hui, 1090-1155), Prime Minister of the Southern Song Dynasty detested as a traitor in Chinese history
秦吉了 qínjíliǎo 〈动物〉a kind of bird like the parrot, often mentioned in literary works
秦艽 qínjiāo 〈植物〉large-leaved gentian (*Gentiana macrophylla*)
秦椒 qínjiāo 〈方言〉〈植物〉red pepper; capsicum
秦晋 Qín-Jìn (During the Spring and Autumn Period the princes of the states Qin and Jin forged a good relationship by marriage for several generations) matrimonial ties between two families: 结为～ (of two families, etc.) be allied through marriage
秦晋之好 Qín-Jìn zhī hǎo amity between Qin and Jin (sealed by a marriage alliance between the two royal houses) — a marriage alliance between two families
秦镜高悬 qínjìng-gāoxuán *also* "明镜高悬" míngjìng-gāoxuán (of judges, officials, etc.) have discerning eyes and dispense justice impartially
秦岭 Qínlǐng Qinling Mountains, a mountain range running east-west in central China and a watershed between the Yellow River and the Yangtze River valleys
秦楼楚馆 qínlóu-chǔguǎn 〈旧语〉quarters of pleasure; brothels
秦皮 qínpí 〈中药〉bark of ash (*Fraxinus bungeana*)
秦腔 qínqiāng Shaanxi opera, popular in China's northwestern provinces
秦始皇 Qínshǐhuáng First Emperor of the Qin Dynasty, named Ying Zheng (嬴政, 259-210 BC), who unified China for the first time in history
秦始皇陵 Qínshǐhuánglíng Qinshihuang Mausoleum (tomb of the first Emperor of the Qin Dynasty) in Xi'an
秦庭之哭 Qíntíng zhī kū tearful imploration for help
秦越 Qín-Yuè (Qin and Yue were two states in the Spring and Autumn Period situated far apart and having very little contact with each other) distant cold relations between two parties
秦越肥瘠 Qín-Yuè féijí 〈书面〉like the people of Qin and Yue who were totally indifferent to each other's welfare or misery — utter lack of interest or concern; perfect nonchalance
秦篆 qínzhuàn form of script of the Qin Dynasty (often used on seals)

嗪 qín

see "哌嗪" pàiqín

螓 qín

〈古语〉a kind of cicada
螓首蛾眉 qínshǒu-éméi cicada hairdo and moth feeler eyebrows — beautiful woman

廑 qín

〈书面〉*see* "勤" qín
see also jǐn

勤 qín

❶ diligent; assiduous; industrious; hardworking: 手～ diligent hands / 四体不～ not toil with one's limbs — be extremely lazy / 书山有路～为径。Diligence is the only path to success in one's studies. ❷ frequently; often: ～洗澡 take baths regularly / 他来得～。He often comes here. *or* He is a frequent visitor here. ❸ work; duty: 内～ office work / 外～ field work / 后～ logistics ❹ (office, school, etc.) attendance: 出～ attend class; be at the work place / 考～ check on attendance / 值～ be on duty / 缺～ absent from school or the work place ❺ (Qín) a surname
勤奋 qínfèn diligent; assiduous; industrious; untiring: ～好学 diligent and eager to learn / ～工作 work assiduously / 成功在于～。Success comes with industry.
勤工俭学 qíngōng-jiǎnxué part-work and part-study system; work-study programme
勤俭 qínjiǎn hardworking and frugal; industrious and thrifty: ～持家 be industrious and thrifty in managing a household / ～建国 build up the country through hard work and frugality / ～节约 work hard and practise economy / 她的～为人称道。She is highly commended for her diligence and thrift.
勤谨 qínjin 〈方言〉hardworking; industrious: 你怎么今日～起来了? How come you are working so hard today?
勤恳 qínkěn diligent and earnest: ～笔耕 diligently apply oneself to writing / 几十年来, 她总是勤勤恳恳地工作。For several decades she has worked industriously and conscientiously.
勤苦 qínkǔ hard work and plain living: 一生～ live a life of hard work and frugality / 山里人过去终年～, 但不得温饱。The hill-dwellers could not afford decent food and clothes even though they toiled all the year round.
勤快 qínkuai 〈口语〉diligent; industrious; hardworking: 她真～, 一会儿也不闲着。She works very hard, without taking a moment's rest. / 他性情好, 人也～。He is good-natured and diligent.
勤劳 qínláo diligent; assiduous; industrious; hardworking: 中国人民一向以～勇敢著称。The Chinese people are renowned for their diligence and courage. / 他从小就养成了～的习惯。He has formed the habit of working industriously since childhood.
勤劳致富 qínláo-zhìfù get rich through honest labour
勤力 qínlì 〈方言〉diligent; industrious
勤密 qínmì frequent; constant: 两家来往很～。The two families maintained close social contact.
勤勉 qínmiǎn hardworking; assiduous; diligent: ～的学生 diligent student / 他十分～, 将资料全部抄录下来。He took great pains to record all the data.
勤敏 qínmǐn diligent and intelligent: 他很～, 在科研方面取得较大成绩。Hardworking and intelligent, he scored no small success in scientific research.
勤能补拙 qínnéngbǔzhuō diligence can make up for one's slowness in learning
勤娘子 qínniángzǐ 〈植物〉(popular name for 牵牛花) morning glory
勤朴 qínpǔ industrious and simple: 他们是一些～的乡下人。They are hardworking and simple country folks.
勤勤 qínqín attentive; considerate; solicitous
勤劬 qínqú 〈书面〉diligent; assiduous: 一生～ work hard all one's life
勤王 qínwáng 〈书面〉❶ (of subjects) send troops to support the

emperor when he is in trouble：诏天下～ issue an edict calling on all the troops to rescue the emperor from peril／～之师 armies coming to the rescue of the throne ❷ serve the royal house

勤务 qínwù ❶ duty；service ❷〈军事〉odd-jobman

勤务兵 qínwùbīng 〈军事〉orderly

勤务员 qínwùyuán ❶ orderly；odd-jobman ❷ servant：各级干部都是人民的～。All the cadres，whatever their rank，are servants of the people.

勤学苦练 qínxué-kǔliàn study diligently and train hard：他那一笔好字全靠～而成。As a result of diligent study and painstaking training，he now writes a beautiful hand.

勤杂 qínzá ❶ odd job ❷ odd-jobman

勤杂工 qínzágōng odd-jobman；handyman

勤杂人员 qínzá rényuán odd-jobmen；subsidiary staff doing odd jobs

勤政 qínzhèng diligent government

勤政廉政 qínzhèng-liánzhèng be diligent and honest in attending to state affairs

懃 qín see "慇懃" yīnqín

芹 qín celery：药～ medicinal celery

芹菜 qíncài 〈植物〉celery

芹曝 qínpù also "曝芹"〈书面〉humble gift

芹献 qínxiàn also "献芹"〈书面〉humble gift：聊充～ just a humble gift

芹藻 qínzǎo 〈书面〉my flimsy worth

覃 Qín a surname

see also tán

捡 qín 〈书面〉see "擒" qín

禽 qín ❶ birds；fowl：飞～ flying birds／家～ domestic fowl；poultry／珍～ rare species of birds ❷〈书面〉fowls and animals：五～戏 ancient gymnastics modelled on the movements of fowls and animals

禽流感 qínliúgǎn bird flu：～病毒 bird flu virus

禽龙 qínlóng 〈考古〉iguanodon

禽舍 qínshè artificial bird's nest；poultry housing

禽兽 qínshòu birds and beasts：～行为 brutish acts；bestial acts／～不如 more beastly than beasts／事实证明，这个所谓的正人君子，原来是个衣冠～！Facts show that this so-called man of honour is nothing but a beast in human shape.

檎 qín see "林檎" línqín

擒 qín capture；catch；take；seize：生～活捉 catch alive／束手就～ be captured without resistance

擒获 qínhuò catch；arrest；capture：～毒品贩子 take drug pushers into custody

擒拿 qínná ❶ martial skills for overpowering an opponent ❷ capture；arrest：～归案 be tracked down to face criminal charges

擒贼先擒王 qín zéi xiān qín wáng to catch a gang of bandits，first catch their chieftain：射人先射马，～。To shoot the rider，first shoot his horse；to catch bandits，first catch their ringleader.

擒纵轮 qínzònglún 〈机械〉escape wheel

噙 qín hold in the mouth or the eyes：～着糖 hold a piece of candy in one's mouth／～一口水 have a gulp of water in one's mouth／她两眼～着泪水。Her eyes were brimming with tears.

噙化 qínhuà 〈中医〉dissolve a pill in the mouth

溹 qín 〈书面〉see "琴" qín

琴 qín ❶ *qin*，a seven-stringed plucked instrument in some ways similar to the zither：抚～ play the zither／对牛弹～ play the lute to a cow — address the wrong audience；talk over sb.'s head ❷ general name for certain musical instruments：小提～ violin／中提～ viola／大提～ cello；violoncello／低音提～ double-bass；contrabass／竖～ harp／六弦～ also "吉他" guitar／班卓～ banjo／三角～ balaika／口～ mouth-organ；harmonica／木～ xylophone／钢～ piano／管风～ pipe organ；organ／簧风～ reed organ；harmonium／手风～ accordion／电子～ electronic organ (or keyboard)／胡～ *huqin*，Chinese violin／洋～ dulcimer ❸（Qín）a surname

琴拨 qínbō plectrum

琴凳 qíndèng music stool

琴断朱弦 qínduàn-zhūxián one of the two strings of a *huqin* is snapped — lose one's spouse

琴弓 qíngōng bow

琴剑飘零 qínjiàn-piāolíng be a homeless man of letters

琴键 qínjiàn key (on a musical instrument)

琴马 qínmǎ 〈音乐〉bridge (of a stringed instrument)

琴鸟 qínniǎo lyrebird

琴棋书画 qín-qí-shū-huà (talent for) music，chess，calligraphy，and painting — all artistic accomplishments：～，他无所不通。He excels in painting，calligraphy，music and chess.

琴瑟 qínsè *qin* and *se*，two stringed musical instruments which play in great harmony — harmony between husband and wife

琴瑟不调 qínsè-bùtiáo conjugal disharmony；marital discord

琴瑟和谐 qínsè-héxié also "琴瑟和好" matrimonial harmony；conjugal bliss

琴瑟之好 qínsèzhīhǎo accord of *qin* and *se* — matrimonial harmony；conjugal happiness

琴师 qínshī *jinghu*（京胡）performer who plays the stringed instrument as an accompanist in traditional Chinese opera

琴书 qínshū storytelling，mainly in songs，with musical accompaniment

琴弦 qínxián string (of a musical instrument)

琴心剑胆 qínxīn-jiàndǎn have the sentiments of a musician and the spirit of a knight；have both a tender heart and a bold vision

琴心相挑 qínxīn-xiāngtiāo play the *qin* to express one's profound feelings of love

芩 qín 〈古语〉reeds：黄～ skullcap (*Scuttelaria biacalensis*)

矜（穜） qín 〈古语〉handle of a spear

see also guān；jīn

qǐn

寝（寢） qǐn ❶ sleep：废～忘食 (so engrossed or absorbed as to) forget food and rest／食肉～皮 (want to) eat sb.'s flesh and sleep on his hide — (want to) see the person one hates destroyed ❷ bedroom：内～ inner bedroom／就～ go to bed；turn in／入～ go to sleep／寿终正～ pass away ❸ coffin chamber；tomb：陵～ imperial burial place；mausoleum ❹〈书面〉stop；cease；end：事遂～。The affair then came to an end. *or* The matter was then dropped.

寝不安席 qǐnbù'ānxí cannot sleep soundly at night；feel uneasy even when sleeping：受命之后，～，食不甘味。In the days after his appointment to the post he could neither sleep in peace nor eat with relish.

寝车 qǐnchē sleeping car；sleeper

寝宫 qǐngōng ❶ palace where the royal couple sleep ❷ chamber containing the coffins of a royal couple in a mausoleum

寝具 qǐnjù bed-clothes；bedding

寝馈 qǐnkuì sleeping and eating：～不宁 feel uneasy even when eating or sleeping；be deeply worried

寝食 qǐnshí sleeping and eating；food and rest

寝食不安 qǐnshí-bù'ān feel worried waking or sleeping；unable to sleep and eat peacefully：焦虑万分，～ be so worried that one has no peace of mind day and night

寝食俱废 qǐnshí-jùfèi forget to sleep and eat：这项试验忙得他～。He was so occupied with this experiment that he even forgot about eating and sleeping.

寝室 qǐnshì bedroom；dormitory

梫 qǐn ❶〈古语〉cinnamon tree；Chinese cinnamon tree；cassia-bark tree ❷ see "梫木"

梫木 qǐnmù Japanese andromeda

锓 qǐn 〈书面〉carve; engrave; etch: ～版 carved block (for printing)

qìn

沁 qìn ❶ (of fragrance, liquid, etc.) ooze; seep; exude: 鼻上～着汗珠。Beads of sweat stood on his nose. /寒气～骨。The cold air chills one to the bone. /香气～鼻。A sweet smell assailed my nostrils. ❷〈方言〉lower one's head: ～着头 bend one's head ❸〈方言〉soak in liquid

沁凉 qìnliáng 〈方言〉very cool; cold: ～的风 icy wind

沁人心脾 qìnrén-xīnpí *also* "沁人肺腑" seep into the heart; be refreshing; be invigorating: 这首小诗，读来～。This is a short, refreshing poem. /桌上放着一个小花瓶，插着一束水红色的康乃馨，散发着淡淡的～的香味。On the table stood a small vase containing a spray of pale-red carnations which emanated a faint, sweet fragrance.

沁润 qìnrùn (of fragrance, liquid, etc.) permeate; seep into: 绵绵春雨～着土地。The continuous spring drizzle seeped into the earth.

吣(唚、嚊) qìn ❶ (of animals such as dogs and cats) vomit: ～食 (of a cat or a dog) vomit ❷〈口语〉rail; yelp; spit out hogwash: 满嘴胡～ be foul-mouthed; let out a stream of abuse; spout invectives /别上这儿瞎～来! Don't talk hogwash here!

揿(搇) qìn 〈方言〉press; push: ～电铃 ring a bell /～电钮 press a button

揿钉 qìndīng 〈方言〉drawing pin; thumbtack

揿纽 qìnniǔ 〈方言〉snap fastener

qīng

青 qīng ❶ blue; green: 返～〈农业〉(of winter crops, transplanted seedlings, etc.) turn green /雪～ pale mauve colour /铁～ ashen; livid /万古长～ remain fresh forever ❷ black: 玄～ deep black /～线 black thread ❸ green grass; young crop: 踏～ walk on green meadows — go for an outing in early spring /放～ turn (cattle, etc.) out to graze ❹ young in age: *see* "～年" ❺ youth; young people: 老中～ old, middle-aged, and young people ❻ (Qīng) (short for 青海) Qinghai Province ❼ (Qīng) a surname

青白 qīngbái (of face) be off colour; pale: 脸色～ be off colour; (of one's face) look ashen

青白瓷 qīngbáicí *also* "影青" yǐngqīng shadowy blue porcelain, well-known porcelain made first in Jingdezhen (景德镇) since the Song Dynasty

青白晦气 qīngbái-huìqì 〈方言〉run into unexpected bad luck: 平白无故赖到我头上来，真是～。It was my bad luck to be blamed for no reason at all. /今天真倒霉，遭了这～! It is very unfortunate that everything has gone wrong today.

青帮 Qīngbāng *Qingbang* or Green Gang (a secret society founded towards the last years of the Qing Dynasty)

青碧 qīngbì ❶ dark green: 远峰～ dark green distant mountains ❷ azure; sky blue: 天空～万里。The blue sky is boundless.

青布 qīngbù black cloth

青菜 qīngcài ❶ *also* "小白菜" xiǎobáicài a variety of Chinese cabbage ❷ green vegetables; greens: 常吃～对身体有好处。It is good to eat green vegetables regularly.

青苍 qīngcāng ❶ dark blue; dark green: 林木～ dark green foliage ❷〈书面〉sky

青草 qīngcǎo green grass: ～池塘处处蛙。The frogs are croaking all over the green banks of the pond.

青出于蓝 qīngchūyúlán (short for 青出于蓝，而胜于蓝) indigo blue is extracted from the indigo plant (but is bluer); blue comes from the indigo plant but is bluer than the plant itself — the disciple surpasses the master

青春 qīngchūn ❶ youth; youthfulness: 莫让～虚度。Don't waste your youthful years. /她告别伦敦时，她也告别了自己的～。When she bid farewell to London, she was bidding farewell to her youth. /这座古庙又恢复了～。The ancient temple has regained its former splendour. /祖国处处都充满～的活力。The motherland is brimming with youthful vitality everywhere. ❷ (often used in the early vernacular) age of young people: 这姑娘～几何? How old is the young girl?

青春痘 qīngchūndòu (common name for 痤疮) acne: 她脸上长了几颗～。There are some acnes on her face.

青春饭 qīngchūnfàn jobs for young persons only: 吃～ hold a job that lasts only as long as one's youth

青春期 qīngchūnqī puberty; adolescence

青春型精神分裂症 qīngchūnxíng jīngshén fēnlièzhèng 〈医学〉hebephrenia: 单纯型～ heboid /～患者 hebephreniac

青词 qīngcí prayers of the Taoists written in red on black paper

青瓷 qīngcí celadon (ware)

青葱 qīngcōng ❶ verdant; fresh green; lush: 林木～ lush woods /这座美丽的城镇，到处是～的树木和碧波荡漾的湖泊。The beauty of the town is everywhere set off by green woods and rippling lakes. ❷ *also* "火葱" huǒcōng shallot (*Allium ascalonicum*)

青翠 qīngcuì fresh green; luxuriant green; verdant: 丛丛村树，～欲滴。Rows upon rows of trees around the village are covered with lush foliage. /庄稼给雨水洗得～水绿。The rains have made the fields a carpet of fresh green. /春天的郊野，满目～。The fields are a vast green expanse in spring.

青黛 qīngdài dark blue

青灯 qīngdēng 〈书面〉oil lamp

青灯黄卷 qīngdēng-huángjuàn *also* "黄卷青灯" read ancient classics by oil lamp: ～，苦读不倦 (of ancient scholars) burn the midnight oil

青帝司权 Qīngdì-sīquán 〈书面〉spring is here; spring awakens

青豆 qīngdòu green soya bean

青娥 qīng'é 〈书面〉young girl

青肥 qīngféi green manure

青蚨 qīngfú 〈书面〉money; cash: 囊中缺少～ have little money in one's pocket; be broke

青冈 qīnggāng *also* "青枫"〈植物〉big leaf oak (*Quercus dentata*)

青工 qīnggōng young worker

青宫 qīnggōng 〈旧语〉crown prince's residential palace

青钩栲 qīnggōukǎo 〈植物〉*Castanopsis kawakamii*

青光眼 qīngguāngyǎn 〈医学〉glaucoma: ～晕轮 glaucomatous halo

青果 qīngguǒ 〈方言〉Chinese olive

青海 Qīnghǎi Qinghai (Province)

青海湖 Qīnghǎihú Qinghai Lake; Kokonor

青函隧道 Qīnghán Suìdào SeiKan Tunnel, a 53.8-km long seabed tunnel between Honsu and Hokkaido of Japan completed in 1988

青蒿 qīnghāo *also* 香蒿 xiānghāo〈植物〉*Artemisia apiacea*

青红皂白 qīnghóng-zàobái black and white; right and wrong; good and bad: 不分～ make no distinction between right and wrong /不问～ be undiscriminating; do sth. rashly without first asking what the matter is about /他不分～，训我一顿。He blamed me without really knowing who was guilty.

青花瓷 qīnghuācí blue and white porcelain

青黄不接 qīnghuáng-bùjiē when the new crop is still in the blade and the old one is all consumed; the granary is nearly empty but the new crop is not yet ripe — food shortage between two harvests; temporary shortage: 旧日～之际，粮价往往暴涨。Food prices tended to soar between two harvests in the old days. /老专家陆续退休，训练有素的人才又不足，我们面临～的问题。The problem is that we are short of trained professionals to take over as older experts retire one after another.

青灰 qīnghuī greenish lime

青简 qīngjiǎn 〈旧语〉bamboo strips — books

青椒 qīngjiāo green pepper

青椒鸡丁 qīngjiāo jīdīng fried diced chicken with green pepper

青衿 qīngjīn 〈书面〉❶ scholars' garment in old days ❷ scholars; young intellectuals

青筋 qīngjīn blue veins: 手上～外露。The veins on one's hands are clearly visible.

青稞 qīngkē highland barley (grown in Tibet and Qinghai); *qingke* barley

青稞酒 qīngkējiǔ *qingke* barley beer

青空 qīngkōng blue sky

青睐 qīnglài 〈书面〉favour; good graces: 受到上级的～ win his superior's favour /他颇受权贵～，得以爬上高位。Having won the

good graces of the powerful, he was able to worm his way to this high post.
青帘 qīnglián 〈旧语〉sign hung in front of a wine shop
青莲色 qīngliánsè pale purple; heliotrope
青联 qīnglián (short for 青年联合会) youth federation
青龙 qīnglóng ❶ collective name of the seven eastern constellations of the twenty-eight constellations *see also* "二十八宿" èrshíbāxiù ❷ oriental god worshipped in Taoism
青楼 qīnglóu 〈书面〉brothel: ~女子 courtesan; prostitute
青庐 qīnglú (in ancient northern China) a kind of blue cloth tent set up for a wedding
青绿 qīnglǜ dark green: ~的松林 dark green pine forest
青绿山水 qīnglǜ-shānshuǐ blue-and-green landscape (a kind of Chinese traditional painting done in blues and greens)
青麻 qīngmá (common term for 苘麻)〈植物〉piemarker
青盲 qīngmáng 〈中医〉glaucoma
青梅 qīngméi green plum
青梅竹马 qīngméi-zhúmǎ green plums and a bamboo horse — a girl and a boy playing innocently together; childhood playmates: ~, 两小无猜 (of a girl and a boy) be innocent playmates in childhood
青霉素 qīngméisù *also* "盘尼西林" pánníxīlín 〈药学〉penicillin
青面獠牙 qīngmiàn-liáoyá green-faced and long-toothed; blue face and protruding fangs — frightening in appearance: 一群~的妖怪 a group of ogres with horrifying features / 那~的一伙人, 便都哄笑起来。Those creatures with ferocious features began to hoot and roar.
青苗 qīngmiáo young crop; green shoots of grains
青尼罗河 Qīngníluóhé Blue Nile River, one of the two source rivers of the Nile with its origin in Ethiopia
青年 qīngnián ❶ youthful; young: ~学生 young student; student youth/~企业家 young entrepreneur or businessman /应当珍惜~时代。One should cherish one's youthful years. ❷ youth; young people: 知识~ educated youth /爱国~ patriotic youth /~之家 Home for Young People /~组织 youth organization /他是个有为的~。He is a young man of promise.
青年会 Qīngniánhuì (short for 基督教青年会) Young Men's Christian Association (YMCA)
青年节 Qīngniánjié Youth Day (May 4)
青鸟 qīngniǎo (of ancient mythology) blue bird (a messenger-bird for *Xiwangmu*, the mother-goddess); messenger
青盼 qīngpàn 〈书面〉favour; goodwill; good graces
青皮 qīngpí ❶〈中药〉green peels of unripe orange ❷〈方言〉ne'er-do-well; scoundrel: ~流氓 impertinent rascal /~光棍 roguish chap
青纱帐 qīngshāzhàng *also* "青纱障" green curtain of tall crops: ~常为游击队提供掩蔽。The green curtain of tall crops often provided cover for guerrillas.
青山 qīngshān green hill: 留得~在, 不怕没柴烧。As long as the green hills are there, one need not worry about firewood. /~依旧, 人事全非。The green hills remain the same, but people have all changed.
青山不老 qīngshān-bùlǎo green hills never grow old — eternity: ~, 绿水长存。Green hills never turn bare, and blue waters never run dry.
青山绿水 qīngshān-lǜshuǐ *also* "绿水青山" green hills and blue waters — beautiful country scene; beautiful scenery; scenic spot
青衫 qīngshān black dress; black gown
青少年 qīng-shàonián juvenile persons; youngsters; teenagers: ~犯罪 juvenile delinquency /~感化院 borstal; youth custody center
青史 qīngshǐ annals of history; history: 名留~ leave a name in history; have a niche in history; be crowned with eternal glory; go down in the annals of history
青史传名 qīngshǐ-chuánmíng *also* "青史流芳"; "青史留名" have one's good name recorded in history: 这位英雄将~, 流芳百世。The name of the hero will go down in the annals of history and be remembered by posterity. /久后纵无功赏, 也得~。I may not receive any rewards eventually, but I'll leave behind a clean name.
青丝 qīngsī ❶〈书面〉black hair (of a woman or girl): 一缕~ a lock of black hair /三尺~ flowing long hair ❷ finely cut green plums, etc. used as fillings of cakes or cake decoration
青饲料 qīngsìliào greenfeed; green fodder
青松 qīngsōng pine
青蒜 qīngsuàn garlic shoots
青苔 qīngtái moss
青檀 qīngtán 〈植物〉wingceltis (*Pteroceltis tatarinowii*)
青堂瓦舍 qīngtáng-wǎshè brick house with a tiled roof
青天 qīngtiān ❶ blue sky: 那山峰似乎和~连起来了。That mountain peak seems to merge into the blue sky. ❷〈旧语〉just-minded judge; upright magistrate: 包~ Bao, the Just-minded Magistrate (referring to Bao Zheng of the Song Dynasty) /~大老爷 my lord (term of address to judge or magistrate) ❸ blue sky as a symbol of justice: 重见~ regain freedom; be freed from prison
青天白日 qīngtiān-báirì bright daylight: ~的, 竟敢拦路抢劫。They even dared mug people in broad daylight.
青天霹雳 qīngtiān-pīlì *also* "晴天霹雳" qíngtiān-pīlì bolt from the blue
青田石 qīngtiánshí seal stone quarried in Qingtian County, Zhejiang Province
青铜 qīngtóng bronze
青铜器 qīngtóngqì bronze ware
青铜器时代 qīngtóngqì shídài *also* "青铜时代" Bronze Age
青铜峡水利枢纽工程 Qīngtóngxiá Shuǐlì Shūniǔ Gōngchéng Qingtongxia Key Water Control Project (in the middle reaches of the Yellow River, completed in 1967)
青蛙 qīngwā frog
青瓦 qīngwǎ grey tile
青虾 qīngxiā freshwater shrimp
青香薷 qīngxiāngrú 〈中药〉Chinese mosla (*Mosla chinensis*)
青葙 qīngxiāng 〈植物〉feather cockscomb (*Celosia argentea*): ~子〈中药〉seed of cockscomb
青鞋布袜 qīngxié-bùwà life of a recluse in a faraway place
青魆魆 qīngxūxū *also* "青虚虚" (of colour) darkish; blackish: 布满嘴巴的~胡茬子 blackish unshaven chin /~的山峰直插云霄。Darkish peaks tower to the skies.
青眼 qīngyǎn favour; good graces: ~相待 treat sb. with favour / 以~看某人 look upon sb. with good graces
青杨 qīngyáng 〈植物〉Cathay poplar (*Populus cathayana*)
青猺 qīngyáo *also* "花面狸" huāmiànlí 〈动物〉masked civet
青衣 qīngyī ❶ black clothes: ~小帽 casual clothes; plain informal dress ❷〈古语〉housemaid ❸〈戏曲〉role of an actress in Beijing opera: 工~ excel in playing the role of *qingyi* in Beijing opera
青蝇 qīngyíng greenbottle (fly)
青蝇吊客 qīngyíng-diàokè be only visited by green bottle flies after death — a person who has no friends in his lifetime will have no mourners after death
青油油 qīngyōuyōu ❶ dark green: 稻子长得~的。The rice field is a stretch of dark green. ❷ shining black: ~的头发 lustrous black hair
青鼬 qīngyòu *also* "黄猺" huángyáo 〈动物〉yellow-throated marten (*Charronia flavigula*)
青鱼 qīngyú black carp
青郁 qīngyù lush and verdant: ~的竹林 luxuriant grove of bamboo
青云 qīngyún high official position: 平步~ rise rapidly in the (official) world; have a meteoric rise
青云直上 qīngyún-zhíshàng be promoted rapidly in one's political career; rise rapidly from obscurity to dominance or fame: 他近几年节节高升, ~。In recent years, he has kept moving up, winning one promotion after another.
青云志 qīngyúnzhì high aspirations; lofty ideals
青运会 qīngyùnhuì (short for 青年运动会) youth sports meet
青藏高原 Qīng-Zàng Gāoyuán Qinghai-Tibet Plateau, in southwest China
青冢 qīngzhǒng tomb of Wang Zhaojun, a famed beauty of the Han Dynasty
see also "王昭君" Wáng Zhāojūn
青州从事 Qīngzhōu-cóngshì implicit reference to good wine: ~难再得。Good wine is no longer easily available.
青贮 qīngzhù 〈畜牧〉store in silo; ensile: ~饲料 ensilage; silage
青贮塔 qīngzhùtǎ 〈畜牧〉tower silo
青砖 qīngzhuān grey brick; blue brick
青紫 qīngzǐ ❶〈书面〉official of high rank (dressed in purple and green): ~被体 be in purple and green ❷ *also* "发绀" fāgàn 〈医学〉cyanosis

清[1] qīng ❶ (of liquids and gases) pure; clear:天朗气~ blue skies and clear air / 水~见底。The water is so limpid that the bottom can be seen. ❷ quiet; silent; still:~夜 quiet night /冷~ cold and cheerless; lonely; deserted ❸ honest and upright:为官~正 be an honest and upright official ❹ clear; lucid:讲~道理 clearly explain the reason; reason things out /两种颜色分不~。The two colours are indistinguishable. ❺ clear; plain: *see* "~汤" ❻ completely; entirely; thoroughly:把债还~ pay up what one owes ❼ clear up; purify; clean up: *see* "~党" ❽ settle accounts:账已经结~了。The accounts have all been settled. ❾ count; check:~一~出席人数 check the number of people attending; check people's attendance

清[2] Qīng ❶ Qing Dynasty (1644-1911) ❷ a surname

清拔 qīngbá 〈书面〉(of an essay) graceful and refined:文体~。The literary style is elegant and refined.

清白 qīngbái ❶ pure; clean; immaculate:~人家 family of stainless reputation /凭空污人~ smear sb.'s good name with groundless charges /~无瑕的美玉 pure flawless piece of jade /他是~的。He was innocent. *or* He had a clean record. ❷〈方言〉clear; lucid:你要把事情说~。You must give a full account of the matter.

清碧 qīngbì (of water and sky, etc.) limpid and blue:~的湖水 limpid and blue lake /天空~无云。The sky is azure and cloudless.

清仓 qīngcāng make an inventory of the storage:~查库 make an inventory of (*or* check up on) warehouses /~摸底 check up on the warehouse and have an idea of the goods in stock

清操 qīngcāo 〈书面〉untarnished reputation; perfect integrity:以~知名 be known for one's moral integrity

清册 qīngcè detailed list; all-inclusive inventory:材料~ detailed list of materials /固定资产~ inventory of fixed assets

清茶 qīngchá ❶ green tea ❷ tea served without refreshments

清茶淡饭 qīngchá-dànfàn *also* "粗茶淡饭" cūchá-dànfàn weak tea and simple food; homely fare:他吃的是~。He lives simply and thriftily.

清查 qīngchá ❶ check; examine:~遗失图书 check the library's missing books /~公司账目 examine the accounts of the firm ❷ ferret out; winkle out:~不法分子 ferret out unlawful elements

清产核资 qīngchǎn-hézī make an inventory of one's assests and liabilities

清偿 qīngcháng pay back; pay off; clear off:~旧欠 pay off old debts /必须先~债务才可以向银行贷款。You must clear your debts before you can have another loan from the bank.

清偿能力 qīngcháng nénglì 〈经济〉liquidity; solvency

清场 qīngchǎng clear a public place of visitors, etc.:这个戏园子每晚十一点~。This opera house clears and closes at eleven o'clock every night.

清唱 qīngchàng sing opera arias (to an audience) without make-up

清唱剧 qīngchàngjù 〈音乐〉oratorio

清炒虾仁 qīngchǎo xiārén stir-fried shelled shrimps

清澈 qīngchè *also* "清彻" crystal-clear; limpid; transparent:潭水~,游鱼历历可见。The pond water is crystal-clear and you can see the fish swimming at the bottom. /~的湖水,佛塔的倒影,增添了湖区的媚丽。The limpid lake water and the reflection of the pagoda on it added to the beauty and charm of the lake district./远处传来的~钟声。The resonant bell can be heard distinctly from the distance.

清尘 qīngchén ❶ sweep off dust; dust ❷〈书面〉〈敬词〉your noble self:有犯~ give offence to you; give you bother

清尘浊水 qīngchén-zhuóshuǐ be cut off from each other and unable to meet again

清晨 qīngchén early morning:~,公园里到处是锻炼身体的人群。In the early morning, you find people all over the park, doing exercises. /~,阳光洒满了江畔。The river bank is bathed in the first rays of the sun.

清澄 qīngchéng (of water and sky) clear; limpid:~的溪流 limpid stream /~的蓝天 clear blue sky

清除 qīngchú clear away; get rid of; clean up; remove:~路障 remove obstruction (*or* an obstacle) on the road /~堆积如山的垃圾 clear away mountains of garbage /~出党 expel from a political party /~放射性污染物 clean up radioactivity /~操作〈计算机〉clear operation

清楚 qīngchu ❶ clear; explicit; distinct:他的意图是~的。His intention is quite obvious. /大厅里静得连人们呼吸的声音也听得十分~。It was so quiet in the hall that you could even hear the sound of breathing distinctly. /我们已经跟他讲~了。We have explained the matter to him in explicit terms. /文章条理~。The essay is well-organized. /他这个人口齿不~。He doesn't have a clear articulation. ❷ be clear about; grasp; understand:这件事他比谁都~。He understands this better than anybody else. /你对这个问题的认识很~。You have a thorough grasp of the question. /我们完全~他在耍什么花招。We are perfectly clear what trick he's playing. ❸ be aware; know:我的处境他非常~。He is fully aware of the situation I am in. /这件事的经过你~不~? Do you know how it happened?

清创术 qīngchuāngshù 〈医学〉debridement

清纯 qīngchún ❶ pretty and pure:~少女 pretty and innocent girl; ingénue ❷ fresh and pure:~的矿泉水 fresh and clear mineral water

清醇 qīngchún mellow and pure:酒味~可口。The wine tastes mellow and savoury.

清词 qīngcí elegant phrases:~丽句 elegant phrases and refined sentences

清脆 qīngcuì ❶ clear and pleasant to the ear:~的笑声 ringing laughter /~的枪声 crisp reports of gun shots /她的歌声~嘹亮,曲调又极为美妙动听。She possessed a rich and clear voice, and the tune sounded unusually melodious. ❷ (of food) crisp and delicious:~的藕片 crisp and tasty lotus root slices

清单 qīngdān complete list; catalogue; inventory:支付~ complete list of payments /开列资财~ make an inventory of the assets

清淡 qīngdàn ❶ light; plain; weak; delicate:绿茶~可口。Green tea is not strong but refreshing. /这块布料花色过于~。The pattern of the material is plain and simple to a fault. /我特别喜欢~的荷花香味。I'm particularly fond of the delicate fragrance of lotus flowers. ❷ (of food) light; not greasy or rich:我这几天感冒了,要吃点~的菜。I've had a cold for several days and would prefer some light food. ❸ fresh and delicate:她装束~。She was elegantly and tastefully dressed. ❹ (of business) dull; slack:销路~ be slow in sales /生意~。Business is stagnant.

清党 qīngdǎng purge (a political party); carry out a purge

清道 qīngdào ❶ sweep the street clean; clear the road of barricades ❷〈旧语〉clear the way for the carriage of the emperor or a high official (with runners walking ahead and calling pedestrians to shove off and make room for it)

清道夫 qīngdàofū 〈旧语〉scavenger; street cleaner

清德 qīngdé 〈书面〉unyielding integrity; pure virtue:仰其~ revere sb. for his unyielding integrity

清点 qīngdiǎn sort and count; make an inventory of; check:~一天的营业额 make an inventory of the day's volume of business /~到场人数 check attendance /~仓库 stock-taking

清东陵 Qīng-Dōnglíng Eastern Tombs of the Qing emperors in Zunhua (遵化) County of Hebei Province

清队 qīngduì purify one's ranks of alien elements

清炖 qīngdùn boil in clear soup (without any soy sauce):~牛肉 stewed beef without soya sauce

清芬 qīngfēn 〈书面〉❶ delicate fragrance:茉莉花~宜人。The faint scent of jasmine is refreshing. ❷〈比喻〉noble virtue; moral integrity:先世~ noble virtue of one's ancestors

清风 qīngfēng cool breeze; soothing or refreshing breeze:~徐来,水波不兴。A cool breeze is blowing gently over the calm water. /~习习,凉爽宜人。Slowly blows the cool soothing breeze.

清风两袖 qīngfēng-liǎngxiù *also* "两袖清风" (of an official) remain uncorrupted; have clean hands

清风明月 qīngfēng-míngyuè cool breeze and bright moon — beautiful natural scenery, alluding to men of profound learning and noble character or to hermits and recluses

清福 qīngfú life of ease and good fortune:享~ enjoy a leisured life and good fortune

清高 qīnggāo (of intellectuals) aloof from petty politics and material pursuits:自视~ consider oneself to be above politics and all worldly considerations; imagine oneself to be morally superior to other people /人多慕其~。People admire him for his moral integrity and disdain for material pursuits. /他一向装得那样的~。That purity of his is just a pose.

清稿 qīnggǎo fair copy; clean copy

清歌 qīnggē ❶〈书面〉unaccompanied singing ❷ clear singing voice

清歌妙舞 qīnggē-miàowǔ sweet singing and exquisite dancing

清供 qīnggòng ❶ vegetarian offerings, such as flowers, bamboos and vegetarian food ❷ ornaments such as curios, potted landscapes, etc.:案头～ desk ornaments

清官 qīngguān honest and upright official

清官难断家务事 qīngguān nán duàn jiāwùshì〈俗语〉even an upright magistrate finds it difficult to settle a family quarrel; an honest official reserves judgement in family quarrels

清光 qīngguāng ❶〈书面〉graceful demeanour ❷ (of sun, moon, metal, etc.) bright radiance:星月交辉，～四溢。The sky is lit up with the bright radiance of the moon and the stars.

清酤 qīnggū good wine

清规 qīngguī〈佛教〉monastic commandments for Buddhists

清规戒律 qīngguī-jièlǜ ❶ regulations, taboos and commandments for Buddhists and Taoists ❷(rigid) rules and conventions; do's and don'ts; taboos:文艺批评的这种～是非常多的。There are numerous such taboos in literary criticism. /我们反对束缚人们积极性的各种～。We are opposed to rules and regulations which fetter people's initiative.

清贵 qīngguì ❶ distinguished and aloof from worldly considerations; eminent but indifferent to worldly success ❷ one who holds a high post but without actual power

清锅冷灶 qīngguō-lěngzào (of home, restaurant, etc.) deserted; desolate:他回到家里一看，～的，一个人也没有。When he returned home, not a single soul was to be found and the place seemed deserted.

清寒 qīnghán ❶ poor; impoverished; in reduced circumstances:他自幼失怙，家境～。Losing his father in early childhood, he came of an impoverished family. ❷ clear and cold:月色～，庭院冷落。The moon was clear and cold and the courtyard deserted.

清和 qīnghé ❶ bright and warm:天气～，不冷不热。The day is bright and warm, neither cold nor hot. ❷〈书面〉(of a country) tranquil and peaceful

清华 qīnghuá〈书面〉❶ (of an essay or scenery) graceful; elegant:词藻～ refined and elegant diction ❷ distinguished family; high office post

清华大学 Qīnghuá Dàxué Qinghua or Tsinghua University (established in 1911), Beijing

清还 qīnghuán pay off; pay back:历年的拖欠已经～。All the debts contracted over the past years have been paid off.

清辉 qīnghuī *also*"清晖" brilliant light (especially sunlight or moonlight):月亮的～从窗口泻进来。Moonlight poured in through the window. /淡淡的晨光穿过玻璃窗，给满屋洒上了一层～。The faint rays of the morning sun piercing through the window illuminated the whole room.

清火 qīnghuǒ〈中医〉relieve inflammation or internal heat

清基 qīngjī clear away rocks for the foundation:他们组织民工参加水坝的～工程。They organized labourers to clear away earth and stones for the foundation of the dam.

清寂 qīngjì cold and silent:～的月夜 chilly and quiet moonlit night

清检 qīngjiǎn clear up; check up; sort out:～什物 clear up odds and ends

清减 qīngjiǎn〈书面〉〈婉词〉thin; slender:你越发～了。You are much slimmer than before.

清健 qīngjiàn (usually of old people) hale and hearty:他老人家倒很～，每天还打太极拳呢。The old man is spry as a kitten and still does *taiji* boxing every day.

清剿 qīngjiǎo clean up; mope up; suppress; eliminate:～残匪 clean up remnant bandits /～叛军 suppress rebel troops

清缴 qīngjiǎo ❶ clear accounts and pay:～税款 duly pay all the taxes ❷ clear and confiscate:～非法出版物和音像制品 check up and confiscate illegal publications and audio-visual products

清教 Qīngjiào〈基督教〉Puritanism:～徒 Puritan

清节 qīngjié〈书面〉noble integrity; high morality:～之士 man of moral integrity

清洁 qīngjié clean:～幽美的城市 clean and beautiful city /有～癖 make a fetish of tidiness and hygiene /保持房间～整齐 keep the room clean and tidy /注意～卫生 pay attention to environmental sanitation and personal hygiene

清洁工 qīngjiégōng (street) cleaner; garbage collector; nightsoil collector

清洁提单 qīngjié tídān〈运输〉clean bill of lading

清结 qīngjié (of accounts, etc.) clear or settle:～旧账 clear old accounts /这事早该～。The matter should have been settled long ago.

清介 qīngjiè〈书面〉upright and above worldly considerations:～自持 keep upright and aloof from petty politics and material pursuits

清津 Qīngjīn Chongjin, industrial city and port in northeast DPRK

清劲风 qīngjìngfēng〈气象〉fresh breeze; force 5 wind

清净 qīngjìng ❶ peace and quiet:耳根～ attain peace of mind by keeping away from unpleasant noise of any kind /图个～ seek peace and quiet ❷clear; limpid:池水～ clear pond

清静 qīngjìng quiet; tranquil; serene:四周非常～ very peaceful surroundings /小花园～幽雅。The small garden is quiet and arranged in good taste.

清酒 qīngjiǔ ❶〈古语〉old wine used as sacrificial offering ❷ pure mellow wine ❸ (Japan) *sake*

清君侧 qīng jūncè (often used as an excuse for staging a *coup d'état* or an armed rebellion) rid the emperor of his favorite but "evil" court officials in an attempt to uphold justice and restore security and stability to the nation; purge the emperor's court

清俊 qīngjùn delicate and handsome:面目～ of fine and delicate features

清峻 qīngjùn〈书面〉❶ (of an essay) concise and thorough:他的散文以～通脱著称。His prose is known for its simplicity and depth of thought. ❷ show no interest in politics or material pursuits:节操～。He is above worldly considerations or material pursuits.

清客 qīngkè hangers-on of high-ranking officials or men of wealth:豪门～ hangers-on of influential families

清口 qīngkǒu tasty and refreshing:泡菜～。Pickles are tasty and refreshing.

清苦 qīngkǔ simple and often devoid of the ordinary comforts of life; spartan:生活～ spartan living conditions /教书生涯比较～。The teaching profession offers relatively few comforts.

清旷 qīngkuàng〈书面〉❶ quiet and spacious:田野～ quiet and open country ❷ clear:耳目～ see and hear clearly

清蜡 qīnglà〈石油〉parafin removal

清栏 qīnglán〈方言〉clear the stable

清览 qīnglǎn〈书面〉〈敬词〉(often used in letters) for your reading

清朗 qīnglǎng ❶ cool and clear; crisp and bright:～的月夜 serene moonlit night /晚秋天气～。The weather is crisp and bright in late autumn. ❷ clear and bright:眉目～ shapely eyebrows and bright eyes /～有神 bright and lively ❸ clear and resounding:～的笑声 ringing laughter; peals of laughter ❹ (of writings) refreshingly clear and lively:笔调～ write in a refreshingly lucid and lively style

清冷 qīnglěng ❶ chilly; rather cold:秋月当空，把～的光洒向大地。A bright autumn moon is hanging in the sky, flooding the earth with chilly beams. ❷ deserted; desolate; empty:旅客们都离开了，站台上十分～。The passengers were all gone and the platform was completely deserted.

清理 qīnglǐ sort out; clear up; tidy up; straighten up;〈经济〉wind up:～房间 tidy up (*or* clean up) the room /～垃圾 clear away the rubbish /～欠税 clear up cases of arrear tax /把报纸杂志～一下 put the newspapers and magazines in order /～文件 sort out documents /～一下自己的思想 straighten out one's thinking/～三角债 break up debt chains /～破产企业 wind up bankrupt businesses /我～书时，又发现了这张照片。I spotted the photo again when I was arranging the books.

清丽 qīnglì ❶(of writing) lucid and graceful:字迹～ (write a) clear and graceful hand ❷(of a scene) fresh and charming:～的景色 poetic charming scenery

清利 qīngli〈方言〉❶ quiet; tranquil:孩子们一上学去，家里就～了。It is all quiet at home the moment the children are off to school. ❷ clear:口齿～ clear articulation /这事的原委要说～。It is necessary to give a clear account of all the details. ❸ settled; finished; solved completely:去年那场大病，早就好～了。I've long since recovered from the serious illness I had last year.

清涟 qīnglián〈书面〉limpid and rippling:溪水～。The stream is crystal-clear and is flowing in faint ripples.

Q

清廉 qīnglián honest and upright; fair and square: 他为官～。He is an incorruptible official.

清凉 qīngliáng pleasantly cool; cool and pleasant: 这里白天热，夜里却很～。It is hot here in the daytime, but at night it is pleasantly cool. /夏天，体力活动之后喝冰镇啤酒特别～。Iced beer is particularly cool and refreshing when you drink it after some physical exertion in summer. /公众对他的批评将是一服～剂。Public criticism will eventually sober him up.

清凉饮料 qīngliáng yǐnliào cold drinks

清凉油 qīngliángyóu *also* "万金油" wànjīnyóu cooling ointment; essential balm; Tiger balm

清亮 qīngliàng clear and resonant; ringing: 广播员的嗓子～动听。The announcer has a clear, charming voice.

清亮 qīngliang ❶ crystal-clear; limpid: 阳光下，河水显得格外～。The water appeared particularly limpid in the sun. ❷ understand; be clear about: 经他一讲，我～了许多。I understood it much better after his explanation. ❸〈方言〉clear; sharp: 这台电视图像特别～。This TV set shows sharp images.

清冽 qīngliè 〈书面〉chilly; rather cold: 时值寒秋，湖水～。It's late autumn now and the water in the lake feels chilly.

Q

清凌凌 qīnglínglíng *also* "清泠泠" limpid and rippling: 微风吹拂，湖水～的。The pond is crystal-clear and ripples gently when a light breeze blows.

清流 qīngliú ❶ clear flowing water: 一溪～ stream of clear flowing water ❷〈书面〉renowned scholars who refuse to associate with officials of doubtful reputation

清虑 qīnglǜ 〈书面〉〈敬词〉your kind consideration: 有劳～。Please kindly give it your consideration.

清迈 Qīngmài Chiengmai, second largest city of Thailand

清美 qīngměi ❶ mellow and pure: 味道～。It tastes mellow and savoury. ❷ delicate and pretty; charming: ～的景物 charming scenery /山川～ beautiful landscape ❸ (of voice or sound) clear and melodious: ～的调子 sweet and melodious tune

清门 qīngmén 〈旧语〉impoverished family

清棉 qīngmián 〈纺织〉scutching: ～机 scutcher; picker /～尘笼 clearer cage /～间 blowing room

清名 qīngmíng reputation of being honest and upright; good name: 他为官素有～。He has been well known for his rectitude as an official.

清明 qīngmíng ❶ (of politics) characterized by good government and prevalence of justice: 政治～，国泰民安。With good government, the country is prosperous and the people happy. ❷ sober and calm: 神志～ be as cool as a cucumber ❸ clear and bright: 月色～。The moonlight is bright. /天气～。It's a fine day. ❹ (Qīngmíng) Pure Brightness, 5th seasonal division point, marking the sun's position at 15° on the ecliptic ❺ (Qīngmíng) day marking such a seasonal division point, usu. falling on the 5th or 6th of April: ～扫墓 pay respects to a dead person at his tomb on Qingming ❻ (Qīngmíng) period lasting from such a seasonal division point till the next one (Grain Rain 谷雨) *see also* "节气" jiéqì; "二十四节气" èrshísì jiéqì

清明菜 qīngmíngcài 〈植物〉*Salvia japonica*

清明上河图 Qīngmíng Shànghétú scroll of painting entitled *The Festival of Pure Brightness on the River*

清盘 qīngpán 〈商业〉liquidation

清喷漆 qīngpēnqī 〈化工〉clear lacquer

清贫 qīngpín (usu. of scholars in old days) be poor; be impoverished: 家道～ come of an impoverished family /父子两代～自守。The father and son maintained their personal integrity despite reduced circumstances.

清平 qīngpíng peaceful and tranquil: 海内～ tranquility within the four seas

清平世界 qīngpíng-shìjiè all is peaceful and tranquil throughout the world; peace reigns over the world: ～，光天化日，谁敢在这里劫路? Who dare commit highway robbery in broad daylight here in this peaceful country?

清漆 qīngqī varnish: 透明～ clear varnish /皱纹～ shrivel varnish /～树脂 varnish gum

清奇 qīngqí graceful and refined: 相貌～ have elegant features

清绮 qīngqǐ refined and elegant: 文辞～绝世。The language is uniquely refined and elegant.

清气 qīngqì ❶ fresh air ❷ refreshing smell: 这酒香味里带着股～，很有点鲜荔枝的味儿。The wine is fragrant with a flavour of litchi.

清讫 qīngqì (of accounts) paid off

清浅 qīngqiǎn ❶ (of water) clear and shallow: 河水～。The river is clear and shallow. ❷ plain and easy to understand: 大道理用～的话说出来才容易懂。Abstract truth is easier to understand if explained in plain words.

清欠 qīngqiàn pay off arrears: 年底必须～。All debts must be paid off by the end of the year.

清切 qīngqiè ❶ clear and distinct: 她说话声音太低了，我怎么也听不～。She spoke in such a low voice that I simply couldn't catch what she was saying. ❷ plaintive; mournful; sad: 不时传来孤雁～的哀鸣。We could hear from time to time the sad cry of a lone wild goose.

清穹 qīngqióng heaven; sky

清秋 qīngqiū autumn, especially late autumn: ～天气，校园还是一片浓绿。It was late autumn, but the campus was still a scene of deep green.

清癯 qīngqú 〈书面〉thin; lean: 跟他说话的是一位～的老者。The person talking with him was a thin old man.

清曲 qīngqǔ ❶ sing without accompaniment ❷ *also* "散曲" sǎnqǔ non-dramatic songs

清趣 qīngqù elegant taste: 他工作之余，练字养花，颇富～。He is a person of refined tastes with hobbies for calligraphy and growing flowers in his spare time.

清泉 qīngquán water; limpid spring

清热 qīngrè 〈中医〉relieve inflammation or internal heat: ～解毒 relieve internal heat or fever /～化痰 relieve internal heat and reduce phlegm

清热法 qīngrèfǎ 〈中医〉antipyretic method (using medicines of a cold nature to treat acute febrile diseases)

清热药 qīngrèyào antipyretic

清润 qīngrùn ❶ clear and mellow: ～的歌喉 clear and mellow singing voice ❷ fresh and humid: 春雨初晴，空气十分～。The air is fresh and moist with the sun coming out after the spring rain. ❸ bright and smooth: 石料光泽～。The stone is smooth and glossy.

清扫 qīngsǎo sweep; clean up: 把房间整理～一番 sweep and tidy up the room

清赏 qīngshǎng *see* "清玩"

清神 qīngshén 〈书面〉〈敬词〉(often used in letters) your attention or notice: 有渎～ unduly claim your attention; intrude upon your time

清识 qīngshí 〈书面〉brilliant idea

清士 qīngshì 〈书面〉man of superb moral principles

清世 qīngshì *also* "清时" piping times of peace; peaceful times

清室 Qīngshì royal family of the Qing Dynasty

清瘦 qīngshòu 〈婉词〉thin; lean; slender; spare: 她比病前～了好些。She looks much thinner than before her illness.

清刷 qīngshuā wash and brush; clean; scrub: 把桶～干净 scrub the pail clean

清爽 qīngshuǎng ❶ clean and fresh: 雨后空气～。The air is clean and fresh after the rain. ❷ relieved; relaxed; at ease: 他终于完成了任务，心里异常～。He felt greatly relieved when he had finally fulfilled his mission. ❸〈方言〉neat; tidy: 她换上了一身～的衣裳回娘家了。Putting on a neat dress, she went to her parents' home. /母亲把客厅收拾得清清爽爽。Mother has carefully tidied up the sitting room. ❹〈方言〉clearly: 三言两语说不～。It cannot be explained clearly in just a few words. ❺〈方言〉light and tasty: 这道菜口味～。The dish was light and tasty.

清水货 qīngshuǐhuò goods of sterling qualities

清水脸儿 qīngshuǐliǎnr 〈旧语〉woman's face without make-up

清水墙 qīngshuǐqiáng 〈建筑〉dry wall

清水衙门 qīngshuǐ-yámen government office which does not handle money matters and therefore does not lend itself easily to corruption; organization with inadequate funds and scanty benefits: 文教部门一向被视为～。Cultural and educational institutions in China are traditionally regarded as wanting in funds and benefits.

清顺 qīngshùn well-organized and fluent

清肃 qīngsù 〈书面〉❶ tranquil; peaceful: 地方～。There is peace and tranquility in the district. ❷ cold: ～的冬晨 cold winter morning

清算 qīngsuàn ❶ carefully calculate and check; settle; clear: ～账目 settle accounts /对厂里的财产进行全盘～ carefully check all the assets of the factory ❷ expose and condemn; liquidate: 彻底～这股土匪的罪行 thoroughly expose and punish the crimes of this gang of bandits

清算协定 qīngsuàn xiédìng clearing agreement

清算银行 qīngsuàn yínháng clearing bank; settlement bank: 欧洲～ European Settlement Bank

清算账户 qīngsuàn zhànghù clearing account

清谈 qīngtán ❶ philosophical disputes among the literati during the Wei-Jin period, which were completely divorced from reality ❷ idle talk; empty talk: ～误国。Idle talk led the nation astray. /～之风甚盛。The tendency to indulge in empty talk was on the upsurge.

清汤 qīngtāng clear soup; light soup; consommé

清汤八珍 qīngtāng bāzhēn consommé with eight delicacies

清汤寡水 qīngtāng-guǎshuǐ (of a dish, etc.) watery and tasteless: 这种～他可不爱喝。He wouldn't like this tasteless soup. /这种～的文章,实在不值一读。This kind of insipid and pointless essay is not worth reading at all.

清甜 qīngtián (of taste and flavour) clear and sweet: ～的矿泉水 clear and sweet mineral water

清听 qīngtīng 〈旧语〉〈敬词〉(in epistolary writing) your kind attention: 冒昧陈辞, 有辱～。I beg to state my views which might require your kind attention.

清通 qīngtōng well-organized and fluent; smooth: 此文～简要。This essay is fluent and concise.

清退 qīngtuì check up and return: ～"文革"时被占用的私房 check up and return to the owners private housing unlawfully occupied during the Cultural Revolution

清玩 qīngwán ❶ elegant objects for refined enjoyment: 此公颇富～。This gentleman has a sizable collection of objets d'art. ❷ refined pastimes

清婉 qīngwǎn (of voice) clear and sweet: 她的歌声～。Her singing is clear and agreeable.

清望 qīngwàng 〈书面〉 honourable reputation

清问 qīngwèn 〈书面〉〈敬词〉 your question: 既承～, 敢不敬复。I am honoured to answer your question.

清西陵 Qīng-Xīlíng Western Tombs of the Qing emperors in Yixian County (易县), Hebei Province

清晰 qīngxī clear; distinct; well-defined: 口齿～ have a clear articulation /条理～ methodical; be well arranged /两道～的脚印 two distinct lines of footprints /电话里她的声音～悦耳。Her voice sounded distinct and pleasant over the telephone. /外面脚步声越来越～。Footsteps could be heard approaching steadily.

清晰度 qīngxīdù (of TV) clarity; definition; (of telecommunications) articulation; (of images) resolution: 图像～ resolution of images/高～电视 high definition TV

清洗 qīngxǐ ❶ rinse; wash; clean: 用抗菌剂～口腔 rinse the mouth with an antiseptic /我们还得～一下厨房用具。We have yet to wash the kitchen utensils. ❷ purge; eliminate; get rid of: ～殖民主义的遗毒 eradicate the remnants of colonialism /他是那次大～的受害者。He was a victim of the big purge.

清鲜 qīngxiān (of air and water) clean and fresh: 打开窗户, 放进～的空气。Open the windows to let in fresh air.

清闲 qīngxián quiet; at leisure: ～自在 feel very much at ease; be carefree; be peaceful and comfortable /我不曾有一刻～。I have not had a single moment's leisure.

清显 qīngxiǎn ❶ obvious; evident: 花瓶上裂痕～。There is an obvious crack in the vase. ❷〈书面〉(of one's official post or family status) high and influential: 历职～ held successive important posts

清乡 qīngxiāng 〈旧语〉(of a ruling regime, etc.) search for and ferret out rebels in the rural area; pacify the countryside

清香 qīngxiāng delicate fragrance; faint scent: 荷花飘着～。The lotus flowers give off a faint scent. /这些松子有一股～味儿。These pine nuts have a delicate flavour.

清晓 qīngxiǎo early morning: ～的微风, 略带凉意。The breeze is a little chilly in the early morning.

清心 qīngxīn ❶ tranquil and unperturbed: 摆脱家务就可以～了。One can be carefree without family matters to attend to. ❷ free one's mind of worries; set one's mind at ease: ～是治好你这病的首要条件。The prerequisite to curing your disease is to free your mind of all worries. ❸〈中医〉 allay or relieve internal heat

清心寡欲 qīngxīn-guǎyù have a pure heart and few worldly desires: 他一向～, 埋头于学术研究。He has few worldly desires; all he wants to do is to bury himself in academic researches.

清新 qīngxīn ❶ fresh; refreshing: 清晨游客少, 公园里空气～。There were few visitors in the park in the early morning, and the air was very fresh. /他的写作风格～淡雅。He wrote in a fresh, chaste style. ❷ original; tasteful: 客厅布置得～别致。The sitting room is tastefully furnished.

清馨 qīngxīn 〈书面〉 delicate fragrance: 微风过处, 送来阵阵～。A gentle breeze carried with it whiffs of delicate fragrance. /松林间空气～, 令人心旷神怡。The air in the wood, permeated with the scent of pine trees, is very refreshing.

清醒 qīngxǐng ❶ fresh; clear-headed; sober-minded: 早晨起来, 头脑特别～。Your mind is particularly fresh after you get up in the morning. /你对自己的缺点应有～的认识。You should be fully aware of your own weaknesses. /这次挫折使他变得～起来。The setback he received this time has sobered him up. ❷ regain consciousness; come to: 他已从昏迷中～过来。He fell into a coma, but he has come to. *or* He has regained his consciousness.

清兴 qīngxìng aesthetic mood; mood for refined enjoyment: 您真难得有此～。It's indeed rare to see you in such an agreeable mood.

清秀 qīngxiù pretty and graceful; fine and delicate: 小伙子面目～。The young man has fine and delicate features. /桂林山水～无比。Guilin boasts unparalleled natural grace and beauty.

清虚 qīngxū 〈书面〉 live a simple life and have few worries: ～淡泊。Rid yourself of worries and never seek fame and wealth.

清选机 qīngxuǎnjī 〈农机〉 cleaner

清雅 qīngyǎ ❶ elegant; refined; graceful: 这位小姐的居室～绝尘。The young lady's room is elegantly furnished and spotlessly clean. /他的文风～。He has a refined style of writing. ❷ delicate; cultured: ～的仪容 graceful appearance

清言 qīngyán idle talk; empty talk

清扬 qīngyáng 〈书面〉❶ have delicate features ❷ distinct and melodious: 钟声～。The sound of the bell is clear and melodious.

清样 qīngyàng final proof; foundry proof

清恙 qīngyàng 〈书面〉〈敬词〉 your illness: ～想已痊愈。I hope you are fully recovered by now.

清野 qīngyě ❶〈书面〉 quiet open country ❷ clear away houses and trees near the battlefield and evacuate people and their belongings so that the invading enemy can get nothing: 坚壁～ strengthen the defences, evacuate all non-combatants, and hide provisions

清夜 qīngyè in the still of night: ～自思 fall into a pensive mood in the depths of night

清夜扪心 qīngyè-ménxīn examine one's conscience in the depths of night: ～, 不胜汗颜。I felt ashamed of myself when I examined my conscience in the middle of night.

清一色 qīngyīsè ❶ (of mah-jong) all of one suit ❷ uniform; homogeneous; undiversified: 一队小学生, ～地戴着小黄帽。Every pupil on the team wore a small yellow cap. /他们～地都是职业外交家。They are all career diplomats.

清议 qīngyì 〈旧语〉 political criticism by well-known scholars, esp. in the later Han Dynasty; public opinion: 纲维不摄, 天下无复～。With law and order in total disarray, public opinion was silenced.

清逸 qīngyì fresh and delicate: 笔锋～ write in a fresh and elegant style

清音 qīngyīn ❶ type of ballad-singing popular in Sichuan Province ❷〈旧语〉wind music played during wedding and funeral ceremonies ❸〈语言〉 voiceless sound

清莹 qīngyíng limpid and bright: ～的湖水 limpid and shimmering lake /～的泪珠 sparkling tears

清幽 qīngyōu (of a landscape) enchanting and secluded: 山谷～。The valley is secluded and has a charm of its own. /她平生就爱～的去处。She has always liked places of peace and quiet.

清油 qīngyóu 〈方言〉❶ rapeseed oil; rape oil ❷ tea oil ❸ edible vegetable oil: ～大饼 pancake baked with vegetable oil

清游 qīngyóu go on a trip and have a good time: 我们准备去西山作一天的～。We plan to go on a one-day excursion to the Western Hills.

清越 qīngyuè clear and melodious: 歌声～。The singing is clear and melodious.

清运 qīngyùn (of garbage, etc.) clean up and carry away: ～垃圾 clear and remove the garbage

清早 qīngzǎo 〈口语〉 early in the morning: 他～起来的第一件事就是跑步。The first thing he does after getting up in the early morning is jogging.

清湛 qīngzhàn 〈书面〉 limpid; crystal clear: ～如水的月光 clear and bright moonlight /池水～。The pond is crystal clear.

清丈 qīngzhàng (of land) survey; measure land:这个村的土地都~完了。All the land in this village has been covered in the survey.

清账 qīngzhàng ❶ close or wind up an account; settle accounts:逐月~ settle monthly accounts ❷ cleared accounts

清真 qīngzhēn ❶〈书面〉simple and unadorned; plain:此人~寡欲。The person is unsophisticated and has few worldly desires. ❷Islamic; Muslim:~食品 Muslim food /~饭店 Muslim restaurant

清真教 Qīngzhēnjiào Islam; Islamism

清真寺 qīngzhēnsì *also* "礼拜寺" lǐbàisì mosque

清真言 qīngzhēnyán 〈伊斯兰〉name used by Chinese-speaking Muslims for *shahadah*, the basic Islamic profession of faith that "There is no god but Allah, and Muhammad is his messenger"

清蒸 qīngzhēng steam in clear soup (usu. without soy sauce):~螃蟹 steamed crabs

清正 qīngzhèng honest and upright:~廉明 clean, honest and just / 为官~ be an honest and upright official

清浊 qīng-zhuó ❶ pure and impure; good and evil ❷〈语言〉voiceless and voiced sounds

清浊同流 qīng-zhuó tóngliú clean and dirty water flow together — the good and the evil are mixed:~,以植其私。He deliberately mixed up the good and the evil for personal gains.

Q

圊

qīng 〈书面〉latrine:~土 human excrement; night soil / ~粪 manure from latrines

圊肥 qīngféi 〈方言〉barnyard manure

蜻

qīng

蜻蜓 qīngtíng 〈动物〉dragonfly

蜻蜓点水 qīngtíng-diǎnshuǐ like a dragonfly skimming the surface of the water — not even scratch the surface of a problem:我对这些问题只是~,谈不上深入研究。I have only a superficial understanding of these problems. I don't claim to have made any in-depth study.

鲭

qīng 〈动物〉mackerel

see also zhēng

倾

qīng ❶ slant; incline; bend:身体稍向前~ bend slightly forward /日已西~。The sun is setting in the west. ❷ tendency; deviation:左~ left deviation /右~ right deviation /右~机会主义 Right opportunism ❸ collapse; topple:国家将~。The state is about to fall. ❹ overturn and pour out; dump; empty: *see* "~箱倒箧";"~倒" ❺ use up (all one's energy); exhaust:我们一定~全力支持你。We will stand foursquare behind you. ❻〈书面〉overwhelm; overbear:权~天下。His power dominated the entire country.

倾背 qīngbèi 〈书面〉die; pass away; breathe one's last:父母~,终日戚戚。His parents passed away, and he was in deep sorrow all day long.

倾侧 qīngcè tilt; lean or incline to one side; bend sideways:船身向左~。The boat tilted to the left.

倾巢 qīngcháo (of the enemy or bandits) sally forth in full force

倾巢而出 qīng cháo'érchū *also* "倾巢出动"(of hordes of bandits, etc.) turn out in full strength:敌军~,受到我军迎头痛击。The enemy troops sallied forth in full force only to be dealt a head-on blow by our army.

倾城 qīngchéng ❶ whole city:~而出,迎接贵宾。The whole city turned out to welcome the distinguished guests. ❷ (of a woman) exceedingly beautiful

倾城倾国 qīngchéng-qīngguó *also* "倾国倾城"(of a woman) lovely enough to cause the fall of a city or a state; ravishingly beautiful:有~之貌 be of unmatched beauty

倾倒 qīngdǎo ❶ topple over; fall over:这所楼房年久失修,随时有~的危险。This building which has been in disrepair for years is in imminent danger of collapse. ❷ greatly admire; adore; prostrate oneself before:他的雄辩真令人~。We do admire him for his eloquence.

倾倒 qīngdào dump; empty; pour out:把脏物~到垃圾筒里 dump trash into a refuse bin /把一肚子委屈~出来 pour out all one's grievances

倾点 qīngdiǎn 〈化学〉pour point; flow point

倾跌 qīngdiē lean to one side and fall down

倾动 qīngdòng win popular admiration and sympathy:~一时 be all the rage

倾动装置 qīngdòng zhuāngzhì 〈机械〉tilting equipment; tilting machinery

倾耳 qīng'ěr listen carefully; be all ears:~细听 listen with great attention

倾耳注目 qīng'ěr-zhùmù listen and watch carefully; pay full attention:令人~的权威 man of authority who attracts public attention

倾服 qīngfú admire whole-heartedly; have a great admiration for

倾覆 qīngfù ❶ overturn; collapse:前车~,后车之诫。The cart overturned in front can be taken as a warning to the cart behind. /飓风来时,不少舟车房屋~。Many ships, cars and buildings were destroyed by the typhoon. ❷ overthrow; topple:一群下级军官企图~那个国家的现政权。A group of junior army officers attempted to topple the regime of that country.

倾盖 qīnggài 〈书面〉new acquaintance:~如故 treat each other like old friends at first acquaintance

倾国倾城 qīngguó-qīngchéng *see* "倾城倾国"

倾家荡产 qīngjiā-dàngchǎn lose all one's property; be reduced to poverty and ruin; become homeless and bankrupt:赌博使他~。He squandered all his family fortune in gambling.

倾架 qīngjià 〈机械〉tilter

倾角 qīngjiǎo ❶〈物理〉dip ❷〈数学〉inclination ❸〈地质〉dip angle

倾角测量仪 qīngjiǎo cèliángyí dipmeter

倾筐倒箧 qīngkuāng-dǎoqiè *see* "倾箱倒箧"

倾慕 qīngmù hold in high esteem; greatly admire; adore:她暗暗地~这位诗人。She secretly adored the poet. /他知识渊博,令人~不已。He is held in great esteem by everybody for his erudition.

倾囊 qīngnáng empty one's purse (to help)

倾囊相助 qīngnáng-xiāngzhù give to sb. all the money in one's purse; give generously to help

倾佩 qīngpèi *see* "倾服"

倾盆大雨 qīngpén-dàyǔ downpour; torrential rain:下了~。The rain poured down in sheets. /四边黑云陡合,预示着一场~。Dark clouds banked, heralding a downpour. /他们冒着~赶往工地。They hurried to the construction site despite a torrential rain.

倾圮 qīngpǐ 〈书面〉collapse; downfall:古塔已经~。The ancient pagoda has collapsed.

倾攲 qīngqī 〈书面〉tilt; slant

倾弃 qīngqì dumping:~核废料 dumping of nuclear waste

倾洒 qīngsǎ (of snow, sweat, tear, etc.) fall down in great quantity; pour down:他把一腔心血都~在牧区里。He threw himself into his work in the pastoral area. /天空~着鹅毛大雪。Snow is falling in big feather-like flakes.

倾诉 qīngsù pour out (one's worries, grievances, etc.):她能够向谁~自己的哀怨与痛苦呢? To whom could she pour out her grievances and sufferings? /他们促膝谈心,~衷情。They had a heart-to-heart talk, sharing their innermost feelings.

倾塌 qīngtā collapse; crumble:大风雨中不少村舍~。Many huts collapsed in the storm.

倾谈 qīngtán have a good, heart-to-heart talk; talk heartily:他们常在一起~世界大事。They often talked long and with deep interest about world events. /他是我的一位可以与之~的朋友。He is a friend I can confide in.

倾听 qīngtīng listen attentively or carefully to:~各种意见 listen attentively to different views /我们应该~群众呼声。We must heed public opinion. /我当然要~你的高见。Of course I would like to have the benefit of your advice.

倾吐 qīngtǔ say freely what is on one's mind; vent:~内心的苦闷 vent one's pent-up grievances /~衷情 unbosom oneself; open one's heart to sb.

倾颓 qīngtuí 〈书面〉❶ collapse; break down:墙壁~。The walls are falling apart. ❷ downfall of a regime:汉室~ decline and fall of the Han Dynasty

倾陷 qīngxiàn plot to frame sb.:~忠良 frame good and loyal officials

倾羡 qīngxiàn admire with all one's heart

倾箱倒箧 qīngxiāng-dǎoqiè turn out all one's boxes and suitcases; empty everything from one's trunks; rummage through chests and cupboards; give all one has:他~也没找到那本书。He couldn't find the book even though he had searched high and low for it.

倾向 qīngxiàng ❶ be inclined to; be in favour of; prefer:他~于我们的观点。He is in favour of our point of view. /这种办法,他~于接受。He was inclined to accept this approach. ❷ tendency; trend; inclination; deviation:政治~ political inclination /进步~ progressive tendency /危险~ dangerous trend /文艺作品要防止公式化概念化~。The tendency towards formalism and abstraction in literary and artistic works should be guarded against. /要反对右的和"左"的两种错误,尤其是"左"的错误~。It is imperative to oppose both Right and "Left" deviations, particularly the latter. /他的身体略微有些浮肿的~。He is showing signs of edema.

倾向性 qīngxiàngxìng ❶ tendentiousness; bias; prejudice:这些作品的~是十分明显的。There is an obvious tendentiousness in these works. ❷ preference:他的话虽委婉,但~仍然比较明显。Though he didn't say it in exactly so many words, his implicit preference was quite apparent.

倾销 qīngxiāo dump:廉价~ dump at a low price /两国签订合同,禁止~农产品。The two countries signed an agreement banning the dumping of agricultural products.

倾销价格 qīngxiāo jiàgé dumping price

倾斜 qīngxié ❶ tilt; slant; slope; gravitate towards:身子向前~ lean forward /船向左边~。The boat tilted to the left (*or* to port). ❷〈比喻〉lean to one side; give preferential treatment:政策向中西部~。The policy tilts in favour of (the development of) the middle and western provinces and regions.

倾斜度 qīngxiédù gradient

倾斜角 qīngxiéjiǎo angle of inclination;〈航空〉bank angle

倾斜面 qīngxiémiàn inclined plane

倾斜政策 qīngxié zhèngcè preferential policy; affirmative policy:采取对农业的~ adopt a policy favourable to agriculture; pursue a policy of giving more incentive to the development of agriculture

倾泄 qīngxiè pour down; gush out:水从水管裂口~而出,我们费了一个小时左右才把它堵住。It took us an hour to stop the flow of the water which gushed out of a broken pipe. /暴雨之后,大量的泥土从山坡上~下去,造成巨大损失。After torrential rains, tons of mud poured down the denuded mountainside, causing tremendous damage.

倾泻 qīngxiè rush down in torrents; pour down:冰川的雪水,从山豁口~下来,形成瀑布。The melted snow of the glacier rushes through the breach in the mountain and forms a waterfall. /月光静静地~在树林和山谷里。Moonlight pours down silently over the woods and valley.

倾卸 qīngxiè dump out; tip:轮船向海洋里~了大量废物,造成严重污染。Ships dumped large quantities of garbage into the sea, causing serious pollution.

倾卸车 qīngxièchē 〈机械〉tip-cart; dump truck; tilting wagon; tipping vehicle:~厢 tilter

倾卸汽车 qīngxiè qìchē dump truck; tipper

倾心 qīngxīn ❶ greatly admire; adore; fall in love with:一见~ fall in love at first sight /他脸上流露出~爱慕的表情。He wore on his face an expression of adoration. ❷ wholehearted; cordial; sincere:他们作了一次~的长谈。They had a long, intimate talk. /必须~听取意见。It's necessary to solicit others' advice wholeheartedly.

倾心吐胆 qīngxīn-tǔdǎn pour one's heart out; air one's innermost feelings; unburden oneself of everything that is on one's mind:她把自己的心事~地告诉了姐姐。She confided her secret to her sister without reservation. /这里没有外人,你尽可~。You are among friends here and may just pour out everything that's on your mind.

倾轧 qīngyà engage in factional strife (in a political party or in the political world in general):各派勾心斗角,互相~。The factions scheme and plot against each other, jockeying for position.

倾注 qīngzhù ❶ pour into or down:天像漏了似的,往下~着大雨。A torrential rain was pouring down as though the sky were opening. ❷ concentrate (one's energy, etc.) on:全神~ be engrossed in; concentrate one's attention on; be absorbed in /~全力 dedicate oneself to; be devoted heart and soul to /这位青年教师,向山村的孩子们~了真挚深厚的感情。The young teacher has devoted himself heart and soul to the children in this mountain village.

卿

qīng ❶ minister or senior official in ancient times:~相 high court official and chief minister /客~ guest minister(non-native politician appointed to high position) ❷ (emperor's form of address for a court official) you:吹皱一池春水,干~底事? If the spring breeze ruffles the surface of the water, what's it to do with you, dear? ❸ term of endearment used between husband and wife or among close friends in ancient times ❹ (Qīng) a surname

卿卿 qīngqīng term of endearment formerly used between husband and wife, later also used to refer to somebody dear to one, sometimes sarcastically:机关算尽太聪明,反误了~性命。He is too clever by half and will bring about his own ruin for all his wiles.

卿卿我我 qīngqīng-wǒwǒ (term descriptive of intimacy between man and woman) bill and coo

轻(輕)

qīng ❶ of little weight; light:纸箱比木箱~。A paper box is lighter than a wooden one. /他的体重比我~。He weighs less than I do. ❷ easy to carry; light; simple: *see* "~武器"; "~装" ❸ small in number, degree, etc.:年纪~ be young /病得不~ fall seriously ill /处分很~ be let off lightly /口~ prefer food or soup less salty than usual ❹ relaxed; light: *see* "~音乐" ❺ not important; be of no significance:工作~ light load of work /这件事关系可不~。This matter is quite important. ❻ gently; softly:~~推一下 give a gentle push; push gently /~抬~放 handle gently; handle with care ❼ rashly; impetuously: *see* "~信"; "~举妄动" ❽ flighty; frivolous: *see* "~薄"; "~浮" ❾ regard sb. or sth. as of no importance; make light of; belittle:重男~女 regard men as superior to women /文人相~。Scholars disparage one another.

轻磅纸 qīngbàngzhǐ lightweight paper

轻便 qīngbiàn ❶ light; portable:~的行装 light luggage /~物品 portable goods /~自行车 light-bodied bicycle /这种机械~灵巧。This kind of machine is light in weight and easy to operate. ❷ convenient; easy:这种工作需一定体力,青年人干起来~些。As this kind of work requires a certain amount of physical strength, it will be easier for young people.

轻便机车 qīngbiàn jīchē 〈交通〉light locomotive

轻便货车 qīngbiàn huòchē light-duty truck

轻便型激光器 qīngbiànxíng jīguāngqì lightweight laser

轻薄 qīngbó frivolous; flirtatious:态度~ frivolous attitude /~无知 frivolous and ignorant /~少年 young man given to philandering

轻擦音 qīngcāyīn 〈语言〉spirant

轻财 qīngcái despise wealth; belittle money

轻财重义 qīngcái-zhòngyì treasure friendship more than wealth; be big-hearted

轻车简从 qīngchē-jiǎncóng travel light and with a small entourage:领导人出行应~。Leaders should travel light and with a small entourage when they are on inspection tours.

轻车熟路 qīngchē-shúlù (drive in) a light carriage on a familiar road — (do) sth. one knows well enough to manage with ease; as easy as travelling along a familiar road in a light carriage:他办这事~,准保成功。I am certain that his experience will enable him to handle the job with success.

轻淡 qīngdàn ❶ thin; faint:~的炊烟 thin smoke curling up from kitchen chimneys /他~地笑了笑。He gave a faint smile. ❷ casual; indifferent:有人只是~地谈起这件事。Someone casually mentioned the matter.

轻敌 qīngdí underestimate the strength of the enemy; take the enemy lightly:你如果有~思想,就会招来大祸。You'll come to grief if you underestimate the enemy.

轻而易举 qīng'éryìjǔ be easy to do; come easy (to sb.):你把什么事都看得太~啦! You think, don't you, nothing is difficult under the sun! /学好外语决非~。It is definitely no easy job mastering a foreign language.

轻纺工业 qīng-fǎng gōngyè light textile industry

轻粉 qīngfěn 〈口语〉light powder — calomel; mercurous chloride

轻粉壤土 qīngfěn rǎngtǔ 〈农业〉light silty loam

轻风 qīngfēng 〈气象〉light breeze; force 2 wind

轻浮 qīngfú frivolous; flighty; light-headed:举动~ be frivolous in behaviour /为人~ be rather casual and light-headed /好些人都批评他的工作作风~。Quite a few people criticized him for his careless style of work.

轻歌剧 qīnggējù 〈音乐〉operetta

轻歌曼舞 qīnggē-mànwǔ light music and graceful dance:节日之夜,人们在广场上~。On the night of the festival, people gathered on the square, singing softly and dancing with grace and ease.

轻工业 qīnggōngyè light industry

轻工业部 qīnggōngyèbù ministry of light industry

轻工业局 qīnggōngyèjú bureau of light industry:国家~ State Bu-

reau of Light Industry
轻骨头 qīnggǔtou 〈方言〉❶ frivolous; flighty ❷ contemptible wretch
轻轨 qīngguǐ 〈交通〉light rail: ~火车 light rail train
轻轨铁路 qīngguǐ tiělù 〈交通〉light railway
轻寒 qīnghán slightly cold; chilly
轻合金 qīnghéjīn 〈冶金〉light alloy: ~结构 light-alloy structure
轻核 qīnghé 〈物理〉light nucleus
轻忽 qīnghū attach no importance to; pay little attention to; act rashly: 事关重大, 不容~。The matter is of such great importance that we can't afford to make light of it.
轻缓 qīnghuǎn light and slow: 他迈着~的步子走进屋来。He came into the room with light leisurely steps.
轻混凝土 qīnghùnníngtǔ 〈建筑〉lightweight concrete
轻活 qīnghuó light work; easy job: 让她干点~儿吧, 她的伤还未痊愈。Let her have some soft jobs since her wound has not fully healed.
轻货 qīnghuò ❶ goods of big volume but light weight (such as cotton, foam rubber, etc.) ❷〈书面〉petty property
轻机关枪 qīngjīguānqiāng light machine gun
轻减 qīngjiǎn lighten; alleviate; mitigate: 病势已见~。The patient has got better. /卸去一包大米, 重量~了许多。With one bag of rice off, the load is much lighter.
轻贱 qīngjiàn ❶ inferior; lowly; worthless: 戏曲演员在旧社会被视为~的人。In old days, the performing artists of Chinese opera were regarded as lowly. /社会上任何工作都不能说是~的。There is nothing in society which you can call inferior work. ❷ belittle; despise: 任何~体力劳动的倾向都是错误的。Any tendency to belittle manual labour is erroneous.
轻健 qīngjiàn brisk; nimble: 步履~ walk in brisk (*or* springy) steps
轻捷 qīngjié light; springy; agile: ~地走上楼梯 walk briskly up the stairs
轻金属 qīngjīnshǔ light metal
轻举妄动 qīngjǔ-wàngdòng act impetuously; make some rash move; take reckless action: 他对有些年轻人的~看不顺眼。Some of the young people annoyed him by their impetuous and hare-brained behaviour. /在这种微妙的情况下, 你决不可~。In the present delicate situation, you should never make a rash move.
轻看 qīngkàn belittle; underestimate: 你不要~这个组织在国际政治舞台上所起的作用。You shouldn't underestimate the role this organization is playing in international politics.
轻口薄舌 qīngkǒu-bóshé *also* "轻嘴薄舌" say nasty things about: 此人常常~奚落人。He often makes derisive (*or* caustic) remarks about others.
轻快 qīngkuài ❶ brisk; light; spry: 她步履~。She is light on her feet. /小车~地奔驰。The car is running smoothly at a rapid speed. ❷ light; relaxed; lively: 乐队奏起~的乐曲。The band struck up a lively tune. /游泳后他觉得特别~。He felt especially relaxed after swimming.
轻狂 qīngkuáng excessively frivolous: 她那股~劲儿谁都看不惯。Her frivolities made everyone frown.
轻量级 qīngliàngjí 〈体育〉lightweight
轻灵 qīnglíng ❶ light and nimble: 舞姿~ dance gracefully ❷ (of essay) elegant and vivid: 文笔~ write in a graceful and lively style
轻虑浅谋 qīnglǜ-qiǎnmóu think casually and plan carelessly; be imprudent and short-sighted
轻慢 qīngmàn treat sb. rudely; slight: 作为主人, 他是不应该~客人的。As a host, he shouldn't have slighted any guest.
轻描淡写 qīngmiáo-dànxiě mention casually; slur over; play down: 他在讲话时对这件事的重要性只~地提了一下。He played down the importance of the matter in his speech. /次要的情节, 报告人就~了。The speaker only made casual mention of things of lesser importance.
轻藐 qīngmiǎo despise; scorn; look down upon: ~的口气 contemptuous tone
轻妙 qīngmiào light and graceful; sweet and lively: ~的歌声 sweet and lively singing
轻蔑 qīngmiè scornful; disdainful; contemptuous: 她~地瞥了发言人一眼。She cast a contemptuous glance at the speaker. /这个人发出~的冷笑。The man gave a disdainful laugh. /他被她讲话时的那种~态度激怒了。He was enraged by the supercilious manner in which she spoke.
轻暖 qīngnuǎn ❶ slightly warm: 春风~ warm spring breeze ❷ light and warm: ~的狐裘 light and warm fur coat
轻诺寡信 qīngnuò-guǎxìn be ready to make promises but seldom keep them; be liberal with promises that one does not mean to keep: 他非~之辈。He is not the kind of person to easily go back upon his word.
轻泡货 qīngpàohuò 〈交通〉light cargo
轻炮兵 qīngpàobīng 〈军事〉light artillery
轻飘 qīngpiāo ❶ light; fluffy: ~的柳絮在空中飞扬。The fluffy willow catkins floated in the air. ❷ flighty and impractical: 他做事~, 靠不住。He is unsteady by nature and not to be trusted.
轻飘飘 qīngpiāopiāo ❶ light: 小船~地在水面上浮动。A small boat was gliding on the water. ❷ (of human movement) nimble; agile; (of a mood) buoyant: 她很神气地一扭头, ~地走进了房间。She sailed into the room with a proud toss of her head.
轻骑 qīngqí ❶ light cavalry ❷ moped
轻骑兵 qīngqíbīng 〈军事〉light cavalry
轻倩 qīngqiàn gentle and charming: ~的身影 gentle and charming figure /~的纱帷 light pretty veil
轻悄悄 qīngqiāoqiāo (of action) gently and noiselessly: 他~地走了出去。He tiptoed out of the room.
轻俏 qīngqiào ❶ lively and elegant: 文笔~ wield a lively pen ❷ frivolous; flighty: 举止~ behave frivolously
轻巧 qīngqiao ❶ light and ingenious: 这摩托车很~。This motorcycle is light and handy. ❷ agile; nimble: 她动作很~。She is nimble in movement. ❸ simple and easy: 你说得倒~, 你也给我捧个奖杯回来。You talk as if it were just a walkover. Why not try yourself and see if you can bring back a trophy, too? /这问题可不太~。The problem is not as simple as it appears to be.
轻裘肥马 qīngqiú-féimǎ *also* "肥马轻裘"; "轻肥" soft furs and well-fed horses — wealthy; luxurious
轻裘缓带 qīngqiú-huǎndài soft fur and loose girdles — live a life of comfort and ease; live in clover: 食则山珍海味, 衣则~ dress in most expensive clothes and eat the most delicious food
轻取 qīngqǔ win without difficulty; win hands down; just walk over: 主队以三比〇~客队。The home team easily beat the guest team by 3 to zero.
轻柔 qīngróu soft; gentle; pliable: 柳枝~ pliable willow twigs /语调~ with a soft voice; soft-spoken /~地抚摸 caress gently /屋顶上飘着~的炊烟。Pale whiffs of kitchen smoke curled gently up over the roof of the house. /小河在月光下泛着~的银光。Flooded with moonlight, the stream shimmered like silver.
轻软 qīngruǎn light and soft: 质地~ light and soft in texture
轻锐 qīngruì 〈书面〉(of troops) lightly-equipped and with high combat effectiveness
轻润滑油 qīngrùnhuáyóu 〈化工〉light lubricant
轻纱 qīngshā fine gauze
轻伤 qīngshāng ❶ slight injury; minor wound: 负~ be slightly wounded; sustain a minor injury ❷ person slightly wounded or injured: ~送包扎所 send those slightly wounded to the first-aid station
轻伤员 qīngshāngyuán one who has received a minor injury or wound; ambulant patient
轻身 qīngshēn ❶ make one feel relaxed: 广告里说, 久服此药可~延年。If you keep taking this medicine for a long period of time, you will, as the ad says, feel relaxed all over and live long. ❷〈书面〉humble oneself: ~下气 be humble and submissive ❸ (often used in the early vernacular) single; unmarried: ~逃窜 flee by oneself
轻生 qīngshēng take one's own life; kill oneself; commit suicide: 惨重的挫折使她起过~的念头。The grave setbacks made her toy with the idea of suicide.
轻声 qīngshēng ❶ in a soft voice; softly: ~! 隔墙有耳。Speak softly! Walls have ears. /我开门时, 他们正在~交谈。They were talking in whispers when I opened the door. ❷〈语言〉(in Chinese pronunciation) light tone—unstressed syllable pronounced without its original pitch as in particles like 了, 着, 的 and in suffixes like 子, 头
轻省 qīngsheng 〈方言〉❶ easy; relaxed: 如今添个助手, 你可以稍为~点。Now you have an assistant, you'll find your job easier. ❷ light: 这个箱子挺~。This suitcase is very easy to carry.
轻世傲物 qīngshì-àowù be extremely conceited and scornful of the world

轻视 qīngshì despise; belittle; scorn; look down on:绝不能~敌人。In no case should we take the enemy lightly. /他对他们的建议十分~。He pours scorn on their suggestions. /在这个节骨眼上,谁也不能~他的作用。Nobody can belittle the importance of his role at this juncture.

轻手轻脚 qīngshǒu-qīngjiǎo gently; quietly; softly:她~地走了出去。She tiptoed out of the room.

轻率 qīngshuài thoughtless; rash; hasty:这种~的行动不足取。Such rash action is inadvisable. /证据不足,我们不能~地下结论。We cannot jump to conclusions when there is insufficient evidence. /这问题如果~处理,必然导致严重的后果。Any indiscreet handling of the matter would necessarily lead to disastrous consequences.

轻爽 qīngshuǎng relaxed:凉风一吹, 顿觉浑身~。A whiff of cool breeze refreshed him.

轻水 qīngshuǐ 〈物理〉light water

轻水反应堆 qīngshuǐ fǎnyìngduī 〈核物理〉light-water reactor (LWR)

轻松 qīngsōng carefree; light-hearted; relaxed:~的神气 light-hearted air /会见以后, 他感到~了。When the interview was over, he felt light and easy. /他接到女儿脱离危险的消息后, 心里~了许多。He felt very much relaxed when he received the information that his daughter was out of danger. /他穿着浅蓝的衬衫,看起来很~潇洒。His light blue shirt gave him a carefree, debonair look.

轻瘫 qīngtān 〈医学〉paresis

轻佻 qīngtiāo frivolous; skittish; flirtatious:~的眼神 flirtatious twinkle /他迷恋这样一个~的女子,真令人惊讶不已。It's surprising that he should be infatuated with such a skittish girl.

轻脱 qīngtuō frivolous; skittish; flippant

轻婉 qīngwǎn soft and sweet:~的笛声 soft enchanting strains of the flute

轻微 qīngwēi light; slight; negligible:~劳动 light work /~感冒 touch of flu /听到响声, 她的脸~地抽动了一下。Her face twitched slightly at the noise. /这次的损失是很~的。The loss involved is negligible.

轻武器 qīngwǔqì light armament; light weapon; small arms

轻侮 qīngwǔ trifle with; treat with disrespect:这些事实表明中国人民是不可~的。The facts have shown that the Chinese people are not to be bullied.

轻喜剧 qīngxǐjù light comedy

轻闲 qīngxián relaxed; light:~自在 enjoy leisure and comfort /我年岁大了, 只能干点~活儿。As I'm getting on in years, I'm only fit for light jobs.

轻泻 qīngxiè have loose bowels; have slight diarrhoea

轻泻剂 qīngxièjì 〈药学〉laxative

轻心 qīngxīn careless; negligent; casual:掉以~ be careless about sth.; take sth. lightly

轻信 qīngxìn gullible; credulous:不要~流言。Don't give ready credence to rumours. /他过于~, 常常不知不觉地上了人家的当。He was so gullible (that) he was often taken in before he was aware of it.

轻型 qīngxíng light-duty; light:~机械 light-duty machinery /~载重汽车 light truck; light-duty truck

轻型车床 qīngxíng chēchuáng 〈机械〉light-duty lathe; light lathe

轻型防空导弹 qīngxíng fángkōng dǎodàn 〈军事〉light anti-air missile (LAAM)

轻型飞机 qīngxíng fēijī light aircraft

轻型机车 qīngxíng jīchē 〈交通〉light rail locomotive

轻型轮式拖拉机 qīngxíng lúnshì tuōlājī 〈农业〉light wheel tractor

轻型坦克 qīngxíng tǎnkè 〈军事〉light tank

轻型原子武器 qīngxíng yuánzǐ wǔqì 〈军事〉light atomic ordnance

轻型装甲车 qīngxíng zhuāngjiǎchē 〈军事〉light armoured car; combat car

轻言细语 qīngyán-xìyǔ (of voice) soft-spoken:老两口儿在~地说家常。The old couple were chatting softly about their family affairs.

轻飏 qīngyáng *also* "轻扬" float; sway:柳枝随风~。The willow twigs are swaying softly in the breeze./杨柳~直上重霄九。Poplar and Willow soar to the Ninth Heaven.

轻易 qīngyì ❶ easy; simple:把这几门功课学好,不是那么~的事。It is no easy job to master these courses. ❷ rashly; off-handed:情况尚不明朗,不能~作出决定。As the situation is still murky, we should refrain from any rash decision. /你怎能~地加以否定? How could you negate it so off-handedly?

轻音乐 qīngyīnyuè light music

轻盈 qīngyíng ❶ (as of a woman) slender and graceful; nimble; lithe:她体态~,舞姿优美。She has a slender figure and dances gracefully. /海鸥~地在浪花上飞翔。The seagulls were flying lithely above the waves. ❷ lighthearted; melodious:~的笑声 lighthearted laughter /~的音乐 melodious music

轻悠悠 qīngyōuyōu ❶ gently; quietly:蝴蝶在花间~地飞舞着。The butterflies are fluttering quietly among flowers. ❷ (of voice or music) gentle and pleasant:远处传来~的乐曲。Gentle and melodious music could be heard in the distance.

轻油 qīngyóu light oil; naphtha

轻于鸿毛 qīngyú-hóngmáo lighter than a goose feather — said of one whose death is of no consequence:人固有一死, 或重于泰山, 或~。Though death befalls all men alike, it may be weightier than Mount Tai, or lighter than a feather.

轻元素 qīngyuánsù 〈化学〉light elements

轻载 qīngzài light load:~运转〈机械〉light running

轻质耐火砖 qīngzhì nàihuǒzhuān 〈建筑〉light fire brick

轻质石油产品 qīngzhì shíyóu chǎnpǐn clean oils

轻制 qīngzhì 〈化工〉cutback:~柏油 cutback tar /~沥青 cutback asphalt /~焦油沥青 cutback tar /~产品 cutback product

轻重 qīngzhòng ❶ weight:不过秤怎能知道~? How could we know its weight without weighing it? ❷ (degree of) intensity; relative importance:病情的~一时还拿不准。At the moment, we are still not sure how serious the illness is. ❸ proper limits; propriety:说话不分~ not know the proper way to talk; fail to say the right thing at the right moment; talk improperly /不知~ have no sense of propriety /此人讲话常常没个~。The chap often speaks bluntly without regard to occasion (*or* without a sense of proportion).

轻重倒置 qīngzhòng-dàozhì put the trivial before the important; reverse the order of importance:这种~的做法必然导致工作的混乱。To reverse the order of importance in our work will definitely lead to chaos. /工作要分主次, 不能~。We should distinguish between major and minor work and get our priorities right.

轻重缓急 qīngzhòng-huǎnjí order of importance and urgency; priorities:工作要分~,不能齐头并进。These jobs should be arranged in order of priority and are not to be undertaken all at once.

轻重两用机枪 qīng-zhòng liǎngyòng jīqiāng 〈军事〉general purpose machine gun

轻重量级 qīngzhòngliàngjí 〈体育〉light heavyweight

轻舟 qīngzhōu 〈书面〉small boat; skiff

轻装 qīngzhuāng ❶ light; with light packs:~出行 travel light ❷ light military equipment:~部队 troops with light equipment

轻装简从 qīngzhuāng-jiǎncóng travel with little luggage and a small entourage; travel light

轻装上阵 qīngzhuāng-shàngzhèn go into battle with a light pack — take part in a political movement or get down to work without any mental burdens:他把家事处理完毕,决心~,大干一番。After he attended to his family matters, he decided to throw himself into his work whole-heartedly.

轻子 qīngzǐ 〈物理〉lepton:~数 lepton number

轻嘴薄舌 qīngzuǐ-bóshé *also* "轻口薄舌" like to say nasty things about others; be acerbic; be sharp-tongued

轻罪 qīngzuì 〈法律〉misdemeanour; minor offence; minor crime:这是~,不可重判。This is a minor offence and should not be dealt with too severely.

氢(氫)

qīng 〈化学〉hydrogen (H):~同位素 hydrogen isotope

氢脆 qīngcuì 〈冶金〉hydrogen embrittlement; hydrogen brittleness

氢弹 qīngdàn 〈军事〉hydrogen bomb:~头 hydrogen warhead; H-warhead

氢弹头导弹 qīngdàntóu dǎodàn 〈军事〉missile with a hydrogen warhead

氢当量 qīngdāngliàng 〈化学〉hydrogen equivalent

氢碘化物 qīngdiǎnhuàwù 〈化学〉hydriodide

氢碘酸 qīngdiǎnsuān 〈化学〉hydriodic acid

氢氟酸 qīngfúsuān 〈化学〉hydrofluoric acid

氢化 qīnghuà 〈化工〉hydrogenate:~处理 hydrotreating /~精制 hydrofining /~聚合物 hydropolymer /~裂解 hydrocracking /~润滑油 hydrolube /~橡胶 hydrocaoutchouc; hydrorubber /~装置 hydrogenation apparatus

Q

氢化钾 qīnghuàjiǎ potassium hydride
氢化可的松 qīnghuà kědìsōng 〈生化〉hydrocortisone; cortisol
氢化酶 qīnghuàméi 〈生化〉hydrogenase
氢化物 qīnghuàwù 〈化学〉hydride; hydrogenate; hydrogenide
氢激光器 qīngjīguāngqì 〈军事〉hydrogen laser
氢解 qīngjiě 〈化学〉hydrogenolysis: ～作用 hydrogenesis /～酶 hydrogenlyase
氢醌 qīngkūn 〈化学〉hydroquinone
氢冷式电机 qīnglěngshì diànjī 〈机械〉hydrogen-cooled machine
氢离子 qīnglízǐ 〈化学〉hydrogen ion: ～浓度 hydrogen ion concentration /～指数 hydrogen ion exponent
氢硫化物 qīngliúhuàwù 〈化学〉hydrosulfide; hydrosulphide
氢卤化物 qīnglǔhuàwù hydrohalide
氢氯化物 qīnglǜhuàwù hydrochloride
氢气 qīngqì hydrogen
氢气球 qīngqìqiú hydrogen balloon
氢氰酸 qīngqíngsuān 〈化学〉hydrocyanic acid
氢燃料 qīngránliào hydrogen fuel: ～电池汽车 hydrogen fuel-cell vehicle (*or* car)
氢酸 qīngsuān *also* "无氧酸" wúyǎngsuān hydracid
氢武器 qīngwǔqì hydrogen weapon
氢溴酸 qīngxiùsuān 〈化学〉hydrobromic acid
氢氧 qīngyǎng 〈化学〉oxyhydrogen: ～焰 oxyhydrogen flame
氢氧吹管 qīngyǎng chuīguǎn oxyhydrogen blowpipe
氢氧化铵 qīngyǎnghuà'ǎn ammonium hydroxide
氢氧化钙 qīngyǎnghuàgài calcium hydroxide
氢氧化钾 qīngyǎnghuàjiǎ potassium hydroxide
氢氧化镁 qīngyǎnghuàměi magnesium hydroxide
氢氧化钠 qīngyǎnghuànà sodium hydroxide
氢氧化物 qīngyǎnghuàwù 〈化学〉hydroxide
氢氧基 qīngyǎngjī *also* "氢氧根"; "羟基" qiǎngjī hydroxyl (group)
氢原子钟 qīngyuánzǐzhōng hydrogen clock

qíng

黥(剠) qíng 〈书面〉❶ (as punishment for a criminal in ancient times) brand the face ❷ tattoo

勍 qíng 〈书面〉powerful; strong: ～敌 powerful foe

情 qíng ❶ feeling; emotion; affection; sentiment: 豪～ noble sentiment /多～ of romantic temperament; sentimental /热～ warm; enthusiastic /无～ heartless; faithless; ruthless /鱼水～ close bonds of mutual dependence as between fish and water /柔～ tender feelings ❷ kindness; favour: 讨～ ask for a favour; plead with sb. /说～ intercede and ask for leniency or special consideration (for sb. or sth.) /手下留～ hold your hand and show mercy; be lenient ❸ love; passion: 恋～ love affair; love /痴～ infatuation /殉～ die for love /谈～说爱 court; date/他俩已经有～了。They are falling in love. ❹ intense sexual desire; lust: 发～期 heat period; oestrus ❺ situation; circumstance; state; condition: 国～ actual conditions of a country /民～ public feeling; popular mood /军～ military situation /案～ case /灾～ condition of a disaster /剧～ plot of a play ❻reason; sense: 合～合理 reasonable

情爱 qíng'ài ❶ (esp. beween man and woman) love; affection: 他们～甚笃。They are very much in love with each other. ❷love and care: 我们这个集体充满～。We all care for each other in this community.
情报 qíngbào information; intelligence: 军事～ military intelligence /科学～ scientific information /技术～ technological intelligence /刺探～ pry for information /搜集～ collect intelligence /～人员 intelligence personnel; intellignece agent /中央～局 (US) Central Intelligence Agency (CIA) /共产党～局 Cominform(Communist Information Bureau, 1947-1956)
情报检索 qíngbào jiǎnsuǒ information retrieval: ～系统 information retrieval system
情报网 qíngbàowǎng intelligence network
情报学 qíngbàoxué informatics; information science
情不可却 qíngbùkěquè cannot refuse for the sake of friendship: 他非常诚恳地邀我与会，我～。As he was most sincere in inviting me to the party, I couldn't very well decline.
情不自禁 qíngbùzìjìn cannot refrain from; cannot contain one's feelings; be seized with a sudden desire to; let oneself go: ～地哭出声来 cannot help sobbing /他们阔别多年，一旦重逢，都～地追忆起往事来。They could not refrain from recalling the past when they met for the first time after a long separation. /他深为这一场面所感动，～地欢呼起来。Moved by the spectacle, he let himself go and cheered wildly.
情不自胜 qíngbùzìshèng succumb under the pressure of sorrow: 他捧书哀咽，～。Overwhelmed by sorrow, he broke down as he read the letter.
情操 qíngcāo sentiment; character: 高尚的～ noble sentiment /一个人的～往往从行为中表现出来。A person's character is often revealed in his behaviour.
情场 qíngchǎng man-woman relationship in love; arena of love: ～失意 disappointment in love /据说他在～中是胜利者，而在商场上老是失败。It is said that he was a victor in romance, but a failure in business.
情痴 qíngchī one who is infatuated in love; love maniac
情辞 qíngcí *also* "情词" sentiment and words: ～恳切 sincere both in sentiment and words; speak earnestly and with feeling
情敌 qíngdí rival in a love triangle
情调 qíngdiào emotional appeal; taste; atmosphere; mood: 东方～ oriental taste /异国～ exotic atmosphere /颓废～ decadent mood /感伤～ mawkish vein /哀怜～ pathos
情窦初开 qíngdòu-chūkāi (esp. of a young girl) first awakening or stirrings of love
情分 qíngfen mutual affection: 手足～ brotherly love; fraternity /夫妻～ love and friendship between husband and wife; conjugal affection /同窗～ fellowship /碍着朋友～，我不能不帮他一把。For friendship's sake I had to lend him a helping hand.
情夫 qíngfū lover
情妇 qíngfù mistress; amour
情甘 qínggān 〈方言〉willingly and gladly
情感 qínggǎn ❶ emotion; feeling: 思旧的～ nostalgia; nostalgic feeling /思念的～ longing /复杂的～ mixed feelings /强烈的～ strong emotion /有一种火辣辣的～ burning passion ❷ affection; attachment: 他们的～很深。They are strongly attached to each other.
情感性精神病 qínggǎnxìng jīngshénbìng 〈医学〉affective psychosis
情歌 qínggē love song: 著名的康定～ famous love songs in the Kangding area of southwest China
情海 qínghǎi deep love: 坠入～ fall into love head over heels
情话 qínghuà ❶ lovers' prattle: 喁喁～ whispered lovers' prattle ❷〈书面〉heart-to-heart talk
情怀 qínghuái sentiments; feelings: 抒发～ express one's thoughts and feelings
情急 qíngjí moment of desperation: 这只是～时的权宜措施。This was only an expedient adopted in a moment of desperation.
情急智生 qíngjí-zhìshēng have a brainwave on the spur of the moment; hit on a good idea in a moment of desperation; have quick wits in emergency: 绝望中，他～，忽然有了一个好主意。In a moment of despair, he struck on a brilliant idea.
情节 qíngjié ❶ plot: 故事～ plot /～离奇 fantastic plot ❷ case; circumstances: 这件事的～很复杂，要彻底调查。The circumstances surrounding this incident are very complicated and require thorough investigation.
情结 qíngjié complex: 恋母～ Oedipus complex /思乡～ nostalgia for one's native place
情景 qíngjǐng scene; spectacle; sight; circumstances: 这种恐怖的～我头一回看到。This was the very first time I had ever seen such a terrifying scene. /往日的～又浮现在眼前。Past events flashed across my mind.
情景交融 qíng-jǐng jiāoróng (of literary work) fusion of the feelings with the natural setting; feeling and setting happily blended
情景教学法 qíngjǐng jiàoxuéfǎ situational teaching method
情境 qíngjìng circumstances; condition; situation: 这～使我很尴尬。This situation was very embarrassing to me. /影片开头，音乐和画面渲染出一种凄凉的～。At the beginning of the movie, the music and the frame combined to set off a scene of desolation.
情况 qíngkuàng ❶ situation; condition; case; state of affairs: 思想

～ state of mind; thinking /工作～ how one works; work experience /健康～ state of health; health; physical condition /在正常～下 under (*or* in) normal cricumstances /准备应付各种～ be prepared to deal with all kinds of eventualities /～并非如此。This is by no means the case. /病人～正在恶化。The patient's condition is worsening. /～就是这样。This is how matters stand. /我不了解她的～。I don't know how she is getting on. /沉住气等着～的变化。Wait patiently and see how things will work out. ❷ military situation or developments:这两天前线没有新～。There has been no change in the situation at the front these past two days. /一有～, 部队立刻行动。The troops should take immediate action if there is any enemy movement.

情郎 qíngláng (girl's) lover

情理 qínglǐ reason; sense:在这次纠纷中,她采取中立态度是完全合乎～的。It stands to reason that she took a neutral stand in the dispute. /你这样对待她～难容。The way you treat her is beyond all reason. /事情的变化虽在意料之外, 却也在～之中。What happened was beyond expectations but within the bounds of reason.

情侣 qínglǚ lovers; sweethearts:一对很般配的～ a pair of well-matched lovers

情侣鹦鹉 qínglǚ yīngwǔ lovebird

情面 qíngmiàn feelings; sensibilities:讲～ spare sb.'s sensibilities /我不能不考虑他的～问题。I have to take into account the problem of his sensibilities /宁可和他撕破～也不牺牲原则。I would rather offend his feelings than barter away principle.

情趣 qíngqù ❶ temperament and taste:他们～相投。They have similar temperaments and tastes. /父子二人的～不尽相同。Father and son are not at all alike in temperament or interests. ❷ emotional appeal; interest:这篇散文写得颇有～。This essay appeals to your emotion and shows good taste. /他们的对话～横生。Their conversation sparkles with wit and humour.

情人 qíngrén sweetheart

情人眼里出西施 qíngrén yǎnli chū Xīshī in the eyes of a lover, his girl is a rare beauty; beauty is in the eye of the beholder

情杀 qíngshā murder for love

情商 qíngshāng EQ (emotion quotient)

情诗 qíngshī love poem

情实 qíngshí 〈书面〉❶ actual situation; true state of affairs; truth:经过审讯,得其～。The truth was revealed through interrogation. ❷ sincerity; truth:与朋友交,不可无～。Sincerity is the first requisite for friendship. ❸ charges in an indictment established

情势 qíngshì trend of events; situation:～险恶。The situation is pregnant with danger. /～好转。Things are changing for the better.

情势不变 qíngshì bùbiàn 〈外交〉 *rebus sic stantibus*

情事 qíngshì case; phenomenon:此等～虽属罕见, 但必须予以严重关注。These cases, though rare, deserve serious attention.

情书 qíngshū love letter; billet-doux

情丝 qíngsī tender feelings of love; tender affection:～万缕 multitude of tender feelings of love

情思 qíngsī ❶ emotion; sentiment:故乡～ sentiments for one's native place ❷ thoughts and feelings:勾起心头一缕依恋的～arouse a tender feelings for sb. /除夕赋诗,以表～。I wrote a poem on New Year's Eve to express my thoughts and sentiments.

情死 qíngsǐ (of lovers) commit suicide for failing to marry the person one loves; die for love

情愫 qíngsù *also* "情素"〈书面〉❶ friendly feelings; attachment:朝夕相处, 增加了他们之间的～。They have been together for quite some time, and that adds to the friendly feelings between them. ❷ true feelings; original intentions:他们的～我是知道的。I am fully aware of their true feelings.

情随事迁 qíngsuíshìqiān people's feelings change with the circumstances:大抵～, 昔日的许多追求, 如今也淡然了。Generally, one's feeling changes with changed circumstances and one often becomes indifferent to the things one once passionately sought after.

情态 qíngtài mood; spirit:画家画像, 必须得其～。In painting a portrait, the painter must try to catch the spirit of his object.

情态动词 qíngtài dòngcí 〈语言〉modal verb

情同骨肉 qíngtóng-gǔròu as dear to one as one's own flesh and blood

情同手足 qíngtóng-shǒuzú be as intimate or affectionate as brothers; regard each other as brothers:他们两个人从小就是好朋友, ～。The two of them who have been good friends since childhood cherish brotherly affection for each other.

情同一家 qíngtóng-yījiā be close to each other as members of the same family:两家人同甘共苦, ～。The two families share weal and woe as if they were one and the same family.

情投意合 qíngtóu-yìhé be in complete agreement; be well suited to each other temperamentally:他们～,是事业上的挚友。Seeing eye to eye with each other in everything they undertake, they have become bosom friends devoted to a common cause. /小两口～。The young couple suit each other perfectly.

情网 qíngwǎng meshes of love:坠入～ fall into the meshes of love; fall in love

情味 qíngwèi sentiment; mood; taste; overtone:田园～ pastoral sentiments; pastoral overtones / 这首小诗很合我的～。The little poem appeals to my taste.

情文并茂 qíng-wén bìngmào be excellent in both content and language; be superior in both content and style of writing:他的随笔～, 很耐读。Superior in both content and style, his essays are very readable.

情见乎辞 qíngxiànhūcí one's true feelings find expression in one's words:作者～,感人至深。The author expresses his real emotion in his writing and exercises a profound influence on us.

情兴 qíngxìng 〈书面〉mood; interest:赏玩多时,～颇佳。I have enjoyed myself for quite some time and I am in a very good mood.

情性 qíngxìng disposition; temperament; temper: 他俩虽是兄弟, ～各不相同。Brothers as they are, they're poles apart in disposition.

情形 qíngxing situation; condition; state; state of affairs:这以后的～就不得而知了。Nobody knows what happened afterwards. /实际的～不如想像的好。In actual fact, things are not as good as we expected. /看～, 这场球是要输了。It appears that we are going to lose the game.

情绪 qíngxù ❶ morale; feeling; state; mood:工作～ work enthusiasm /乐观～ optimism; optimistic mood /稳定一下～ steady one's jangled nerves /任何情况下都要防止急躁～。Guard against impetuosity under any circumstances. /首战前夕, ～高昂。Their morale was high on the eve of the first battle. /骄傲自满～只能阻碍你的进步。Complacency and conceit can only serve to hinder your progress. ❷ moodiness; dejection; depression:她好像有点儿～。She seemed to be rather moody. /他正在闹～。He is in a fit of depression. *or* He is in the sulks.

情义 qíngyì mutual affection between friends, relatives and comrades; emotional attachment; ties of friendship; comradeship:她是个最重～的人。She is a person who values friendship above anything else. /你姐姐待他很有～。Your sister is warmly and sincerely attached to him.

情谊 qíngyì friendly feelings or sentiments:两国人民的长期交往, 增进了相互的了解和～。The people of the two countries have increased their mutual understanding and friendly sentiments through long years of exchange. /他们有共患难的～。They have forged bonds of comradeship in their common suffering.

情意 qíngyì friendly regard; affection:我将永远怀念你的～。I will forever remember your kindness with gratitude. /他对她有着深厚的～。He cherishes a profound attachment for her. /你这番～我心领了。I appreciate your kind regards for me.

情由 qíngyóu hows and whys; ins and outs:你得把～原原本本地说出来。You have to tell me in detail how this happened and why. *or* You have to make a clean breast of everything. /他不问～就发火。He flared up without asking about the circumstances.

情有可原 qíngyǒukěyuán excusable; forgivable; pardonable:看来他是不得已才这样做的,～。We should make allowances for him, for it seems that he was compelled to take this course.

情欲 qíngyù sexual urge; lust; carnal desire

情缘 qíngyuán lot of being in love; (predestined) sentimental bond:他们的～未了。Their love has not yet run its course.

情愿 qíngyuàn ❶ willingly; of one's own accord; of one's free will:甘心～ willingly; of one's own volition /～为正义事业牺牲自己的生命 be ready (*or* willing) to lay down one's life for a just cause ❷ would rather; prefer:他～自己承担全部责任,也不肯把别人攀扯进来。He would rather take the blame entirely on himself than have other people involved.

情韵 qíngyùn mood; taste; interest; charm: 别有一番～ have a charm of one's own; offer unique interest

Q

情知 qíngzhī know full well; be in full knowledge of:你～我做不了,为何非要我做? Why do you insist on my doing it when you know well that I am not up to it?
情致 qíngzhì interest; taste; wit and humour:这位作家的散文甚有～。This writer's prose is full of wit and humour.
情种 qíngzhǒng person of the sentimental type, especially one who easily falls in love
情状 qíngzhuàng circumstances; condition; situation:对～不甚了了 be in the dark about the circumstances /～不明。The situation is murky.

晴

qíng sunny; fine; clear:多云转～。It will clear up after a cloudy spell. *or* (as a weather forecast) cloudy to clear. /雨过天～。The sun shines again after the rain. *or* After a shower the sky cleared.
晴霭 qíng'ǎi 〈书面〉thin patches of cloud on a fine day
晴碧 qíngbì ❶ (of sky) bright and blue:～的天空 bright and blue skies ❷ azure skies on a sunny day
晴光 qíngguāng sunlight on a fine day
晴好 qínghǎo fine and beautiful:天气～。It is a fine and beautiful day.
晴和 qínghé bright and sunny:一个～的日子 bright sunny day
晴霁 qíngjì 〈书面〉fine; sunny
晴空 qíngkōng clear sky; cloudless sky:蔚蓝的～ bright and azure sky
晴空万里 qíngkōng-wànlǐ clear and boundless sky; stretch of cloudless blue skies; not a speck of cloud in the sky:从山顶上远眺,但见～,江流如带。Looking afar from the hilltop, you could see the river stretching away like a ribbon under a clear and boundless sky.
晴朗 qínglǎng fine; sunny:～的天空 blue and clear sky /～的月夜 clear moonlit night
晴丽 qínglì sunny and bright
晴美 qíngměi fine and beautiful:～的阳光 bright sunlight /根据风向,明天是个～的日子。The wind direction means a splendid day tomorrow.
晴明 qíngmíng sunny; fine:天气～, 万里无云。It's a fine day and the sky is cloudless.
晴爽 qíngshuǎng cloudless and crystal clear:天气～ bright sunny day
晴丝 qíngsī *also* "游丝" yóusī floating threads of a spider's web one sometimes finds on a sunny day; gossamer
晴天 qíngtiān fine day; sunny day
晴天霹雳 qíngtiān-pīlì *also* "青天霹雳" qīngtiān-pīlì thunderbolt from a clear sky; bolt from the blue:这消息真如～! The news hit us like a thunderbolt. /犹如～。It was as if hailstones dropped out of a clear sky. /噩耗传来,犹如～,把大家都惊呆了。Like a bolt from the blue, the bad news left everybody transfixed.
晴雨表 qíngyǔbiǎo weatherglass; barometer; 〈比喻〉sth. that shows change or signs of change:政治风云的～ political barometer
晴雨伞 qíngyǔsǎn a kind of umbrella used for protecting one against rain or giving shade from the sun

赗

qíng inherit; take over; bear; be responsible for:～受财产 inherit property /有什么后果我都～着。I will hold myself responsible for all the consequences.
赗等 qíngděng 〈方言〉❶ wait passively for (censure, etc.):～挨罚吧。You'll wait your turn for the punishment to be meted out to you. ❷ enjoy what other people have made:别人动手,他～现成儿。While everybody was busy working, he was sitting back ready to enjoy the fruit of their labour.
赗受 qíngshòu inherit; accept:～遗产 come into a heritage

氰

qíng 〈化学〉cyanogen; dicyanogen
氰醇 qíngchún 〈化学〉cyanohydrin; cyanoalcohol
氰氮化物 qíngdànhuàwù 〈化学〉cyanonitride
氰钴胺 qínggǔ'àn 〈药学〉cyanocobalamin; vitamin B_{12}
氰化 qínghuà 〈冶金〉carbonitriding; cyanide carburizing; cyaniding:～淬硬 cyanide (case) hardening /～法 cyanation /～热处理 cyanide carburizing; cyanide case hardening
氰化钾 qínghuàjiǎ potassium cyanide
氰化氢激光器 qínghuàqīng jīguāngqì hydrogen cyanide laser
氰化物 qínghuàwù 〈化学〉cyanogen compound; cyanide
氰基 qíngjī 〈化工〉cyan:～传感器 cyanosensor /～树脂 cyanaloc /～衍生物 cyano derivative
氰酸 qíngsuān 〈化学〉cyanic acid:～盐 cyanate / ～钠 sodium cyanate

檠(檠)

qíng 〈书面〉❶ lamp stand; candle stand:灯～ lamp stand ❷ device for holding the crossbow in position

擎

qíng raise; hold up; lift up:～起一块巨石 lift up a big rock /众～易举。With everybody lending a hand, it is easy to lift a load. *or* Many hands make light work.
擎天柱 qíngtiānzhù 〈比喻〉one who shoulders heavy responsibility; pillar of state or society:就算你是～,没有群众,也是独木难支。Even if you are a pillar of society, you cannot possibly prop it up without the help of the people.

qǐng

请

qǐng ❶ request; ask; entreat:～人出点主意 ask (someone) for advice /报～批示 submit a written request for instructions /恳～鼎力协助 entreat sb. for assistance /不情之～,敬祈鉴谅。Forgive my presumptuous request. ❷ invite; engage; send for:～助手 engage (*or* hire, *or* employ) an assistant /～人担任顾问 ask (*or* invite) sb. to be a consultant; offer sb. a position as adviser /～医生 send for a doctor /他～我到他家去玩。He invited me to his home. /我～你吃冰淇淋。Let me treat you to some ice-cream. /这回吃饭由我～。The meal is on me. *or* The meal is my treat. ❸〈敬词〉please:～入席。Please be seated (at the table). /～别客气。Please make yourself at home. *or* Please don't stand on ceremony. /～,～。(urging others to eat or drink) Please help yourselves. /～留步。Please don't bother to see me out. *or* Please don't bother to come any further. /务～出席。〈套语〉I hereby request the pleasure of your company. ❹〈旧语〉buy (incense, joss sticks, and various other accessories for religious worship); set out (image, statue, etc.) for worship:～香蜡 buy joss sticks and candles (for a religious service, etc.) /～神主 set out the ancestral tablet (for worship)
请安 qǐng'ān ❶ pay respects (usu. to elders); wish good health:那时候,做媳妇的每天早上都要给公公、婆婆～。In those days, the daughter-in-law had to pay respects to her parents-in-law every morning. ❷ *also* "打千"〈方言〉〈旧语〉salute by bending one's left knee and drooping one's right hand:小的给您老人家～啦。Your excellency, here's your humble servant's salute.
请便 qǐngbiàn please or suit yourself; do as you wish:你实在要这样做,那就～吧。If you insist, you may do as you please.
请不动 qǐngbudòng be unable to make sb. comply with a request:我可～他,还是你自己去吧。I tried in vain to invite him over; you'd better go and ask him yourself.
请不起 qǐngbuqǐ cannot afford to (give a dinner, or hire a person for a certain purpose):他说这样的盛筵他是～的。He said he could hardly afford such a sumptuous dinner. /他们家境还不算富裕,～住家保姆。They are not well-off and cannot afford a live-in maid.
请春客 qǐng chūnkè 〈旧语〉spring entertaining — custom of asking relatives, friends or neighbours to dinner shortly after the Spring Festival
请调 qǐngdiào ask for a transfer (to another job):～报告 application for a transfer
请功 qǐnggōng recommend that somebody or some people be awarded for their meritorious deeds:团长为这个班～。The regimental commander recommended the squad for an honourable citation.
请假 qǐngjià ask for leave of absence; ask for leave:请两天病假 ask for two days' sick leave
请假条 qǐngjiàtiáo written request for leave (of absence)
请柬 qǐngjiǎn 〈书面〉invitation card:持～入场 admission by invitation card only /展览会送来了三张～。The organizers of the exhibition sent us three invitation cards.
请见 qǐngjiàn 〈书面〉ask to see (sb.); request an interview; seek an audience with:有人～部长。Somebody wants to see the minister.
请教 qǐngjiào consult; seek advice:虚心～ ask modestly for advice; solicit counsel from others /向你～一个问题。May I ask you for your advice on this matter? /要多向专家～。You must make it

your business to consult the experts.

请君入瓮 qǐngjūnrùwèng kindly step into the vat yourself — hoist sb. with his own petard; pay sb. in his own coin (During the Tang Dynasty, Lai Junchen 来俊臣 was ordered to investigate a cruel and cunning colleague, Zhou Xing 周兴. Without warning Zhou of his intention, Lai asked Zhou what he should do if a criminal should refuse to confess. Zhou suggested bringing in a big vat surrounded by burning coals and throwing the criminal into it. When a vat was brought and coals were set ablaze round it, Lai told him: "I am under the empress's orders to investigate your case. Please step into the vat.")

请客 qǐngkè play the host; stand treat; give a dinner for the guests; entertain guests: ～送礼 give lavish dinners and gifts (in order to curry sb.'s favour) /今天我来～。Let me foot the bill. /这几样菜是饭馆～。These few dishes are on the house. /用公款～,大吃大喝,已成为一种严重的社会问题。Wining and dining out of public funds has become a bane to society.

请命 qǐngmìng ❶ plead on sb.'s behalf: 为民～ plead (*or* speak) for the people ❷〈旧语〉ask (higher authorities) for instructions

请求 qǐngqiú ask; entreat; request: ～发言 ask for (*or* request) the floor /～特赦 ask (*or* plead) for a special pardon /他～上级再给他一个机会。He entreated the higher-ups to give him another chance. /市政府已批准我们的～。The municipal government has approved our request.

请赏 qǐngshǎng petition the leadership to bestow a reward on sb. for his merit

请示 qǐngshì ask for or request instructions: ～工作 ask for instructions on one's work or assignment /及时～汇报是我们的职责。It is our duty to request instructions and submit reports in time.

请受 qǐngshòu (often used in the early vernacular) official's salary; government salary

请帖 qǐngtiě invitation card; written invitation: 我们已给他下了～。We have sent him an invitation.

请托 qǐngtuō request sb. to act on one's behalf; ask sb. to intervene on one's behalf; solicit sb. for help: 他上任的第一件事,就是把～的人统统打发回去。The first thing he did upon taking office was to send away all those who had come to ask for favours.

请问 qǐngwèn ❶〈敬词〉excuse me; please: ～尊姓大名? May I know your name, please? /～去王府井百货大楼坐几路车? Excuse me, but could you tell me which bus goes to the Wang Fujing Department Store? ❷ one may ask; I should like to ask: 你老说以后解决,～,以后是什么时候? You've time and again promised to solve this problem later, but may I ask just when "later" will be?

请勿 qǐngwù please don't: ～喧哗。Please keep quiet. /正在开会,～打扰。The meeting is in session. Please don't disturb. /～触摸展品。Please do not touch the exhibits. /～随地吐痰。No spitting.

请降 qǐngxiáng offer to surrender or capitulate

请谒 qǐngyè〈书面〉request a reception or audience

请益 qǐngyì〈书面〉❶ ask for instructions or advice: ～于师友。ask for advice from one's teachers and friends ❷ ask for an increase (in pay, etc.)

请缨 qǐngyīng〈书面〉request a long cord from the emperor with which to bind the dragon — submit a request or application for a military assignment: ～杀敌 ask for a battle assignment; volunteer for battle

请援 qǐngyuán send for reinforcements; ask for assistance: 向上级～ ask the high command for reinforcements; ask the higher authorities for help

请愿 qǐngyuàn present a petition; petition: 向政府～ present a petition to the government /他们～,要求准予还乡参加乡镇企业工作。They petitioned to be allowed to return to rural areas for employment in township enterprises.

请愿书 qǐngyuànshū petiton: 在～上签字 sign the petition

请战 qǐngzhàn ask for permission to go into battle; ask for a battle assignment

请战书 qǐngzhànshū written request for a battle assignment

请罪 qǐngzuì ask for punishment because one has committed an unpardonable error; apologize: 负荆～ bring a rod upon one's back and ask for punishment — be contrite and ask for pardon; offer a humble apology

謦 qǐng

謦欬 qǐngkài〈书面〉❶ cough ❷ talk and laugh: 亲承～ listen with reverence to sb. (often an elderly scholar) talk

苘(檾、苘) qǐng

苘麻 qǐngmá〈植物〉(usu. called 青麻) Indian mallow; piemarker; *Abutilon theophrasti*

顷[1] qǐng

qing, unit of area equal to one hundred *mu* or 6.66 hectares, or 16.47 acres: 良田百～ one hundred *qing* of fertile land / 万～碧涛 billows; boundless expanse of surging waves

顷[2] qǐng

〈书面〉❶ short while; moment; instant: 有～ for a while /俄～即去 soon disappear ❷ just; just now: ～闻噩耗,不胜悲痛。I am very much grieved to hear the sad news just now. ❸ (of time) about: 光绪二十年～ about the 20th year of Emperor Guangxu's reign (1895)

顷刻 qǐngkè in a twinkling; in an instant; instantly: 西北风一刮,天气～变冷。As soon as the northwest wind began to blow, the weather turned cold. /～之间,风云突变,双方谈判破裂,战争迫在眉睫。The situation took a sudden turn as the negotiation between the two sides broke down, and war seemed imminent.

庼(廎) qǐng

〈书面〉small hall or chamber

qìng

亲(親) qìng

see also qīn

亲家 qìngjia ❶ relatives by marriage: 儿女～ relatives by the marriage of their children ❷ parent-in-law of one's child: ～,我女儿很任性,您要多包涵。My esteemed in-law, I hope you will bear with my daughter, for she has often behaved like a spoiled child.

亲家公 qìngjiagōng〈口语〉father-in-law of one's daughter or son

亲家母 qìngjiamǔ〈口语〉mother-in-law of one's daughter or son

庆(慶) qìng

❶ celebrate: 欢～大桥通车 celebrate the opening to traffic of the bridge /普天同～的节日 festival for nationwide celebration /喜～的日子 auspicious day of joy; happy day or occasion ❷ occasion for celebration: 国～ National Day /校～ celebrations on the anniversary of the founding of a school ❸ (Qìng) a surname

庆大霉素 qìngdàméisù〈医学〉gentamicin

庆典 qìngdiǎn celebration; ceremony: 建军节～在人民大会堂举行。The Army Day celebration will be held in the Great Hall of the People.

庆父不死,鲁难未已 Qìngfǔ bù sǐ, Lǔ nàn wèi yǐ the crisis in the State of Lu will not end until Qing Fu is dead — there will always be trouble in the state until the trouble-maker is removed (Qing Fu, an ambitious noble in the State of Lu in the Spring and Autumn Period, repeatedly stirred up internal strife.)

庆功会 qìnggōnghuì meeting to celebrate a victory

庆贺 qìnghè celebrate; congratulate: ～卫星发射成功 celebrate the successful launching of a satellite /～某人顺利通过答辩 congratulate sb. on passing his oral defence /他们聚在一起共同～新年。They gathered together to wish each other a happy new year.

庆赏 qìngshǎng〈书面〉❶ award; reward: 刑罚～ mete out punishment and bestow rewards ❷ congratulate; celebrate: ～团圆 celebrate a reunion

庆幸 qìngxìng congratulate oneself; rejoice: 我～自己没有上当。I considered myself lucky enough not to have been taken in. /值得～的是,那种动荡的年代终于结束了。It is a matter for rejoicing that those turbulent years came to an end at long last.

庆祝 qìngzhù celebrate; mark: 参加～辛亥革命八十周年大会 attend a meeting to mark the 80th anniversary of the 1911 Revolution /我们全家聚会～祖母九十寿诞。We held a family reunion to celebrate grandmother's ninetieth birthday.

綮 qìng

see "肯綮" kěnqìng

see also qǐ

清 qìng 〈书面〉 cool

箐 qìng 〈方言〉 (often used in place names) big bamboo groves in mountain valleys; wooded mountain valleys

磬 qìng ❶ ancient percussion instrument made of jade or stone, shaped like a carpenter's square ❷ Buddhist percussion instrument made of bronze and shaped like an alms bowl

罄 qìng 〈书面〉 use up; consume; exhaust: 售～ be all sold out /粮食告～。Food is running out. /他将～其所有以资助"希望"工程。He will offer all he has to help raise funds for the "Hope" project.

罄尽 qìngjìn with nothing left; exhausted: 数年前募集的基金即将～。The fund raised several years ago will soon be exhausted.

罄竹难书 qìngzhú-nánshū (竹 here refers to "bamboo slips" used for writing on in ancient times.) one would find it difficult to record all the facts, esp. crimes, even if one used up all the bamboo slips — be too numerous to enumerate: 纳粹党徒，罪行累累，～。The crimes of the Nazis were far too numerous to record. /罄南山之竹，难书封建王朝之淫污。Even if we used up all our writing material, it would still be difficult to give a complete list of the acts of debauchery and depravity of the feudal rulers.

qióng

琼(瓊) qióng ❶〈书面〉fine jade; exquisite thing: 仙山～阁 magnificent palaces on celestial hills ❷ (Qióng) (short for 琼崖) Qiongya or Hainan Island: ～岛 Hainan Island

琼浆 qióngjiāng top-quality wine; nectar

琼剧 qióngjù *also* "海南戏" hǎinánxì Hainan opera

琼楼玉宇 qiónglóu-yùyǔ marble towers and jade halls; beautiful jade palace: 月宫上的～ jade palace in the moon

琼瑶 qióngyáo 〈书面〉❶ fine jade ❷〈比喻〉gift, poem or letter sent by a friend as a reply

琼脂 qióngzhī agar-agar; agar: ～培养基 agar medium

琼脂酸 qióngzhīsuān agar acid

琼脂糖 qióngzhītáng agarose

琼州海峡 Qióngzhōu Hǎixiá Qiongzhou Strait, separating Hainan Island from the mainland

蛩 qióng 〈古语〉cricket: 飞～〈古语〉locust

跫 qióng

跫然 qióngrán 〈书面〉sound of footsteps; footfall: 闻足音～而喜 feel rejoiced at the approaching sound of footsteps

銎 qióng 〈书面〉hole in an ax (for the handle)

邛 qióng

邛崃 Qiónglái mountain in Sichuan Province

筇 qióng a kind of bamboo recorded in ancient literature (usu. used to make walking sticks)

穹 qióng 〈书面〉❶ vault; dome ❷ sky: 苍～ blue dome of the sky

穹苍 qióngcāng 〈书面〉vault of heaven; the firmament; sky

穹地 qióngdì *also* "穹丘"〈地质〉dome

穹顶 qióngdǐng 〈建筑〉dome; crown

穹隆 qiónglóng 〈书面〉vault; dome: ～构造的天文馆屋顶 arched roof of the planetarium

穹庐 qiónglú 〈书面〉tent with a vaulted roof inhabited by nomandic tribes

穹形 qióngxíng vaulted; arched; curved: ～的园门 arched gate /大厅的顶是～的。The ceiling of the hall is vaulted.

穷(窮) qióng ❶ with little money; poor: ～亲戚 poor relation /摆脱贫～ shake off poverty/～不夺志 remain firm in one's faith despite straitened circumstances ❷ end; limit: 无～无尽的麻烦 endless trouble; sea of troubles /诗虽短，其意无～。Though the poem is short, its meaning is inexhaustible. ❸ exhaust; use up: 黔驴技～ run out of tricks; be at one's wits' end /欲～千里目，更上一层楼。Ascend another storey to see a thousand *li* farther. ❹ thoroughly (investigate); through to the end: 未能～究其事 unable to carry the investigation through to the end ❺ utterly; extremely: *see* "～极无聊"

穷棒子 qióngbàngzi ❶〈旧语〉〈贬义〉poor peasant; pauper ❷ person who is poor but has high aspirations: ～精神 spirit of the self-reliant, hard-working poor peasants; spirit of self-reliance and hard struggle

穷兵黩武 qióngbīng-dúwǔ wantonly engage in military ventures; indulge in wars of aggression and crave military exploits

穷愁 qióngchóu poverty-stricken and full of worries: ～潦倒 impoverished and dejected

穷蹙 qióngcù 〈书面〉in extremely straitened circumstances; in dire straits

穷措大 qióngcuòdà *also* "穷醋大"〈贬义〉impoverished intellectual: 他是个～，但骄傲得要命。He is an indifferent scholar, poor as a church mouse, but proud as a peacock.

穷达有命 qióngdá-yǒumìng obscurity or eminence is predestined

穷当益坚 qióngdāngyìjiān *also* "穷且益坚" the more difficult the circumstances, the firmer the will; one should become more resolate in poverty: 大丈夫～，老而益壮。A true man should become firmer in adversity and remain aspiring in old age.

穷得丁当响 qióngde dīngdāngxiǎng extremely poor: 过去，这个村家家～。In those days, every family in the village lived in abject poverty.

穷冬 qióngdōng 〈书面〉midwinter; depths of winter: 时值～，寒风刺骨。It was midwinter, and the cold wind cut one to the bone.

穷对付 qióngduìfu 〈口语〉shift for oneself as best one can: 他只好这么着～。He had to shift for himself as best he could.

穷乏 qióngfá live in reduced circumstances; not have a single penny to bless himself with: ～之家，哪有能力供子弟上学。How could these poor families afford to send their children to school?

穷根 qiónggēn ❶ root of poverty: 挖掉～ dig out the root of poverty; shake off poverty ❷〈方言〉the penniless; pauper

穷根究底 qiónggēn-jiūdǐ get to the bottom of the matter; make a thorough inquiry into sth.: 他～地问个没完。He asked one question after another, trying to get to the bottom of the matter.

穷骨头 qiónggǔtou 〈贬义〉pauper; poor wretch

穷光蛋 qióngguāngdàn 〈口语〉〈贬义〉pauper; poor wretch: 他的祖父是个货真价实的～，过去给人家当长工。His grandfather was literally a pauper who had to hire himself out as a farmhand.

穷极无聊 qióngjí-wúliáo ❶ destitute and helpless ❷ bored stiff: 他～拿起书来看。He picked up a book to read in utter boredom. ❸ absolutely silly or absurd; disgusting: 开这种玩笑，简直是～！It's abominably silly playing such a joke!

穷家富路 qióngjiā-fùlù be thrifty at home but be well-provided while travelling (so as not to get into difficulties): 俗话说"～"，再穷，盘缠却宜多备。As the saying goes, one should be frugal at home but well-equipped for a journey. However hard up one may be, one should have enough money on hand when travelling.

穷讲究 qióngjiǎngjiu 〈口语〉be fastidious or fussy despite difficult (financial) conditions; be overly choosy or picky: 咱们今晚将就着在地板上睡吧，别～了。We'll have to shake down (*or* bed down) on the floor for the night. Don't you fuss any more.

穷嚼 qióngjiáo 〈方言〉argue over insignificant matters or matters of little practical value

穷竭 qióngjié 〈书面〉exhaust; consume; use up: ～心计，妄图卷土重来 rack one's brains vainly scheming to stage a come-back

穷尽 qióngjìn limit; finish; end: 人的智慧是没有～的。Human wisdom is inexhaustible.

穷窘 qióngjiǒng in straitened circumstances; poverty-stricken: 那年头，你我都～已极。In those days you and I both lived in penury.

穷究 qióngjiū make a thorough study of sth.; probe deeply into sth.: ～其理 probe deeply into the matter to find the cause

穷开心 qióngkāixīn try to enjoy oneself amid misery: 你别拿我～好不好! Don't try to make merry at my expense!

穷寇 qióngkòu hard-pressed enemy; fleeing routed enemy: 宜将剩勇追～。With power and to spare we must pursue the tottering foe.

穷寇勿追 qióngkòu-wùzhuī never corner a defeated enemy; do

not pursue an enemy who is desperate

穷苦 qióngkǔ poor and miserable; impoverished:他们都是～人家出身，生活十分俭朴。As they all come from poor families, they lead a very frugal life.

穷匮 qióngkuì 〈书面〉poverty and deprivations:国库～。The state coffers are almost empty.

穷困 qióngkùn poverty-stricken; impoverished; destitute:～无告 poor and helpless /陷入～的境地 be reduced to penury /他幼时家境～。When he was a child, his family lived in straitened circumstances.

穷困潦倒 qióngkùn-liáodǎo be hard pressed and down on one's luck:那位画家晚年的生活～。Penniless and frustrated, the artist spent his remaining years in misery.

穷忙 qióngmáng ❶〈旧语〉busy trying to make both ends meet ❷〈口语〉awfully busy:只顾了～，连客人进来都没看见。I was so busy that I didn't even notice the guests coming in.

穷目 qióngmù look as far as the eye can see:～远望 gaze far afield

穷年累月 qióngnián-lěiyuè for many years; year after year:过去，他们～地辛勤劳动，仅足糊口。In the old days they toiled year after year and were barely able to keep body and soul together.

穷僻 qióngpì poor and remote:往日的～山村已有了明显变化。Marked changes have taken place in the formerly impoverished, out-of-the-way mountain villages.

穷期 qióngqī 〈书面〉termination; limit; end:治学当无～。There is no end to one's pursuit of learning.

穷人 qióngrén those living below the poverty line; poor people; the destitute

穷日子 qióngrìzi days passed in poverty; life of poverty:以前我过的是～。I used to live in reduced circumstances.

穷山恶水 qióngshān-èshuǐ rugged hills and turbulent waters:要改变贫困地区的面貌，我们就要向～宣战。We have to battle against barren mountains and untamed rivers if we want to transform the poor areas.

穷烧 qióngshāo ❶ burn down (houses, etc.):敌寇所至，～极杀。The enemy troops burnt all and killed all wherever they went. ❷〈方言〉〈讽刺〉go out of the way to parade wealth; be extravagant and ostentatious

穷奢极侈 qióngshē-jíchǐ *also* "穷奢极欲" live in extreme extravagance; wallow in luxury:那个时候，穷人忍饥挨饿，富人～。In those days, the poor were on the verge of starvation, while millionaires were lapped in luxury.

穷酸 qióngsuān (of an old-time scholar) impoverished and pedantic:一副～相 the very image of an impoverished pedant /过去那种～的教书先生现在已经见不到了。Those destitute teachers of the past are no longer to be seen nowadays.

穷酸饿醋 qióngsuān-ècù ❶ (of a person) shabby and pedantic ❷ impoverished scholar

穷通 qióngtōng 〈书面〉adversity or prosperity; failure or success:～寿夭 poverty or prosperity, longevity or premature death

穷途 qióngtú dead end; extreme poverty:～落魄 be in dire straits; be down and out

穷途潦倒 qióngtú-liáodǎo penniless and frustrated; overwhelmed by misfortune and misery; at the end of one's tether

穷途末路 qióngtú-mòlù impasse; dead end:他们已是～，还企图作垂死挣扎。They have come to a dead end, but they are still trying to put up a desperate fight.

穷乡僻壤 qióngxiāng-pìrǎng district shut off from the outside world; remote, out-of-the-way place:以前的～，现在也因改革开放而沸腾起来了。This formerly impoverished and backward village is now bubbling with activity as a result of the policy of reform and opening to the outside world.

穷巷 qióngxiàng out-of-the-way lane or alley:小街～ small streets and out-of-the-way alleys

穷相 qióngxiàng look or appearance of a poverty-stricken person

穷形尽相 qióngxíng-jìnxiàng ❶ describe in minute, graphic details:这篇故事写得～，引人入胜。The story told in minute, vivid details is simply fascinating. ❷ behave in a revolting manner; appear in all one's ugliness:他巴结上级～，令人恶心! The way he toadies to his boss is obvious and revolting.

穷凶极恶 qióngxiōng-jí'è extremely brutal and vicious; incredibly ferocious and wicked; most barbarous:他露出一副～的样子。He revealed his true colours as a fiendish brute.

穷原竟委 qióngyuán-jìngwěi investigate thoroughly the origin and development of an event; get to the bottom of sth.:问题实际上已解决了，我们不必再～了。The problem is as good as settled, and there is no need to make any further inquiries.

穷源溯流 qióngyuán-sùliú explore sth. from beginning to end; trace sth. to its very source:不～，怎能对问题有深入了解? How can you expect to have a good grasp of the question if you fail to make an in-depth investigation?

穷则思变 qióngzésībiàn poverty gives rise to a desire for change; when all means are exhausted, changes become necessary:～，人之常情也。It is common to human nature that when a person is in poverty, he will start thinking about changes.

穷追 qióngzhuī ❶ pursue rigorously; go in hot pursuit:～不舍 pursue relentlessly ❷ search thoroughly:广搜史料，～原委 extensively collect historical data and thoroughly investigate the origin and development of an event

穷追猛打 qióngzhuī-měngdǎ go in hot pursuit and make a fierce attack; rigorously pursue and fiercely maul:对溃退敌军～ give hot pursuit to the routed enemy troops

䓖(藭) qióng *see* "芎䓖" xiōngqióng

茕(煢、惸) qióng 〈书面〉❶ solitary; all alone ❷ worried; sad

茕独 qióngdú 〈书面〉all alone; lonely:无虐～。Inflict no harm on anybody who lives all alone.

茕茕 qióngqióng all alone; lonely:～孑立 stand all by oneself, quiet and solitary

qiū

鞧(鞦) qiū ❶ *see* "后鞧" hòuqiū ❷〈方言〉contract; shrink:～着眉毛 knit one's brows; frown

秋(烁) qiū ❶ autumn; fall:初～ early autumn /～雨 autumn rain /一叶知～ the falling of one leaf heralds the autumn—a small sign can indicate a great trend ❷ harvest time:大～ autumn harvest /麦～ wheat harvest /收～ reap the harvest; get in the crops ❸ year:千～万代 for thousands of years; for ever /一日不见，如隔三～。One day away from you is like three years — How I miss you. ❹ (troubled) period of time; juncture:国家存亡危急之～ critical time for national survival ❺ (Qiū) a surname

秋波 qiūbō bright eyes (of a beautiful woman):暗送～ give the glad eye (to sb.); cast coquettish glances (at sb.); exchange tender glances /那个国家这样做是向其邻邦送～。By so doing, that country meant to make secret overtures to its neighbours.

秋播 qiūbō autumn sowing

秋菜 qiūcài vegetables harvested in autumn, such as turnip, Chinese cabbage, etc.

秋地 qiūdì land prepared (after the summer harvest) for autumn sowing

秋分 Qiūfēn ❶ Autumnal Equinox, 16th seasonal division point, marking the sun's position at 180° on the ecliptic ❷ day marking such a seasonal division point, usu. falling on the 23rd or 24th of September ❸ period lasting from such a seasonal division point till the next one (Cold Dew 寒露)

see also "节气" jiéqi；"二十四节气" èrshísì jiéqi

秋分点 qiūfēndiǎn autumnal equinoctial point; autumnal equinox

秋风 qiūfēng ❶ autumn wind:～秋雨愁煞人。How the autumn winds and rains sadden one's heart! ❷ *see* "打秋风" dǎ qiūfēng

秋风过耳 qiūfēng-guò'ěr a puff of autumn wind passes the ear — going in one ear and out the other; (of advice) be totally unheeded

秋风扫落叶 qiūfēng sǎo luòyè the autumn wind blows away dead leaves — a powerful force makes a clean sweep of things rotten or decayed:我军以～之势向前推进。Our army pushed forward with the momentum of a tremendous force, carrying everything before it.

秋高气爽 qiūgāo-qìshuǎng clear sky and crisp air in autumn; high autumn and bracing weather; fine autumn weather

秋耕 qiūgēng autumn ploughing

秋灌 qiūguàn irrigating the fields in autumn; autumn irrigation

秋海棠 qiūhǎitáng 〈植物〉 begonia (*Begonia evansiana*)
秋毫 qiūháo (of an animal or bird) autumn hair; minute detail: 明察～ have eyes sharp enough to see an animal's autumn hair — be very discerning
秋毫无犯 qiūháo-wúfàn (of troops) there's not the slightest violation of discipline; not encroach on people's interests in the least: 部队所到之处，～。Wherever the troops went, they maintained the strictest of discipline.
秋毫之末 qiūháozhīmò tip of an animal's or bird's autumn hair — sth. so small that one can hardly see
秋后蚂蚱 qiūhòu-màzha grasshopper at the end of autumn, nearing its end: ～，敌人蹦跶不了几天了。Like a grasshopper in late autumn, the enemy's days are numbered.
秋后算账 qiūhòu-suànzhàng square accounts after the autumn harvest — wait until the dust settles to reckon with sb.; bide one's time to clear the scores with sb.
秋季 qiūjì autumn: ～班 class that begins the academic year in autumn; autumn course
see also "四季" sìjì
秋交会 Qiūjiāohuì (short for 中国出口商品秋季交易会) Autumn Fair of Chinese Export Commodities
秋瑾 Qiū Jǐn born Gui Jin (闺瑾) in 1877, became a resolute fighter for women's rights and a republic under the present name (Qiu Jin), and was killed by the Qing court in 1907
秋景 qiūjǐng ❶ autumn scenery; bright autumn scene: ～宜人 charming autumn scenery ❷ prospect for autumn harvest: 今年是个好～。In all likelihood, we'll have a good autumn harvest.
秋景天 qiūjingtiān 〈方言〉 autumn; fall season
秋空 qiūkōng autumn sky: 明净的～ clear autumn sky
秋葵 qiūkuí 〈植物〉 gumbo; okra (*Hibiscus esculentus*)
秋老虎 qiūlǎohǔ spell of hot weather after the "Beginning of Autumn" (the 13th seasonal point, occurring around August 7): 这几天正赶上～，天热得要命。Vicious heat seems to have staged a comeback in autumn; it is unbearably hot these days.
秋凉 qiūliáng cool autumn days: 等～后再动工吧。We'd better wait for the cool autumn days to start the construction. /～了，要注意添加衣服。Be sure to put on warmer clothes as the early cold spell of autumn has set in.
秋粮 qiūliáng crops harvested in autumn; autumn crops
秋令 qiūlìng ❶ autumn ❷ autumn weather: 冬行～。Though it is winter, the weather is as mild as in autumn. *or* We have a very mild winter.
秋娘 qiūniáng 〈书面〉 ❶ female entertainer ❷ aged woman (whose beauty has faded with age)
秋气 qiūqì ❶ cool autumn weather ❷ melancholy; gloom; dejection; sadness
秋千 qiūqiān swing: 打～ play on the swing
秋日 qiūrì ❶ autumn ❷ 〈书面〉 autumn sun
秋色 qiūsè autumn scenery: 绚丽灿烂的～ bright, colourful autumn scenery
秋扇 qiūshàn 〈书面〉 fan in autumn; woman losing her beauty with age: ～见捐 woman abandoned or ignored by her man because of her faded beauty
秋审 qiūshěn practice in the Ming and Qing dynasties according to which all death sentences were to be reviewed in autumn by the central justice department and submitted to the emperor for approval
秋试 qiūshì *also* "秋闱"; "乡试" xiāngshì (in the Ming and Qing dynasties) imperial civil examinations held at the provincial capital in the autumn when successful examinees were awarded the title of *Juren* (举人)
秋收 qiūshōu ❶ autumn harvest: ～冬藏 autumn harvest and winter storage (of crops) /农民忙着～。The farmers are busy getting in the autumn harvest. ❷ autumn crops
秋收起义 Qiūshōu Qǐyì Autumn Harvest Uprising — armed uprising led by Mao Zedong in September, 1927 in the rural areas bordering Hunan and Jiangxi provinces, resulting in the organization of the First Division of the First Army of the Workers' and Peasants' Revolutionary Army of China and the establishment of the first rural revolutionary base area in the Jinggang Mountains (井冈山)
秋熟 qiūshú (crops) become ripe in autumn: ～作物 autumn crops
秋霜 qiūshuāng ❶ autumn frost: 嫩芽经不起～。The tender sprouts will not survive an autumn frost. ❷ grey hair: 染上～ get a touch of grey in one's hair
秋水 qiūshuǐ autumn waters — bright eyes (of a woman): 望穿～ keep gazing until one's eyes are strained; wait with anxious (*or* eager) expectations /一双瞳人剪～。Her eyes are limpid as autumn water.
秋水仙 qiūshuǐxiān 〈植物〉 meadow saffron; autumn crocus
秋水仙素 qiūshuǐxiānsù 〈药物〉 colchicine
秋水伊人 qiūshuǐ-yīrén think of an old acquaintance when one sees a familiar scene
秋天 qiūtiān autumn season; autumn: 北京的～最美。Autumn is the most beautiful season in Beijing.
秋闱 qiūwéi *see* "秋试"
秋汛 qiūxùn autumn flood
秋游 qiūyóu (go on) an outing in autumn; autumn outing
秋征 qiūzhēng collection of agricultural tax in kind after the autumn harvest
秋庄稼 qiūzhuāngjia autumn crop

湫
qiū pond; pool
see also jiǎo

萩
qiū 〈古语〉 wormwood

鞦
qiū ❶ *see* "鞧" qiū ❷ *see* "鞦韆"
鞦韆 qiūqiān *also* "秋千" qiūqiān swing

楸
qiū 〈植物〉 Chinese catalpa

鹙
qiū 〈古语〉 bald crane

鳅(鰌)
qiū *see* "泥鳅" níqiu; "鳈鳅" qíqiū

丘(❸坵)
qiū ❶ mound; hillock: 土～ heap of earth; mound /荒～ barren hillock /沙～ sand dune /蚁～ ant hill ❷ cover with earth or bricks and stones prior to burial: 把棺材～起来 cover the coffin with earth (*or* bricks and stones) ❸ 〈量词〉 plot (of paddy field bordered by ridges): 一～水田 a plot of paddy field ❹ (Qiū) a surname
丘八 qiūbā 〈旧语〉〈贬义〉 soldier: 过去在军阀统治下，～无恶不作而可逍遥法外。Under the rule of warlords the soldiers could commit all sorts of evil with impunity.
丘比特 Qiūbǐtè Cupid, Roman god of love
丘吉尔 Qiūjí'ěr Sir Winston Leonard Spencer Churchill (1874-1965), British Prime Minister in 1940-1945 and 1951-1955
丘井 qiūjǐng dried-up well; old useless person
丘陵 qiūlíng hills: ～地 hill land /～地带 hilly area; hilly country /这一带～起伏，荆棘遍野。This area is a range of undulating hills overgrown with brambles.
丘墓 qiūmù 〈书面〉 grave; tomb
丘脑 qiūnǎo 〈生理〉 thalamencephalon; thalamus: ～底部 subthalamus /～上部 epithalamus /～下部 hypothalamus /～后部 metathalamus
丘脑切开术 qiūnǎo qiēkāishù 〈医学〉 thalamotomy
丘脑综合征 qiūnǎo zōnghézhēng 〈医学〉 thalamic syndrome
丘鹬 qiūyù 〈动物〉 woodcock (*Scolopax rusticola*)
丘疹 qiūzhěn papule; pimple

蚯
qiū
蚯蚓 qiūyǐn earthworm: ～粪 wormcast

邱
qiū ❶ *see* "丘" qiū ❷ (Qiū) a surname

龟(龜)
qiū
see also guī, jūn
龟兹 Qiūcí ancient state in the Western Regions (in present Kuche 库车 County, Xinjiang)

穐(龝)
qiū 〈书面〉 *see* "秋" qiū

qiú

酋 qiú ❶ chief (of a tribe) ❷ chieftain (of bandits, aggressors, etc.): 匪～ bandit chief / 贼～ ringleader of a gang of thieves / 敌～ enemy chieftain

酋长 qiúzhǎng tribal chief; emir; sheik(h)

酋长国 qiúzhǎngguó sheikhdom; emirate: 阿拉伯联合～ The United Arab Emirates (UAE)

遒 qiú 〈书面〉 powerful; vigorous; forceful: 猎猎晚风～。Powerfully the evening wind whistles.

遒健 qiújiàn 〈书面〉 strong; vigorous: 笔势～ bold strokes of the brush

遒劲 qiújìng powerful; vigorous; sturdy: 笔锋～ powerful strokes (in calligraphy)

遒炼 qiúliàn 〈书面〉 (of poems, paintings, calligraphy, etc.) powerful and succinct: 文笔～ write in a terse and forceful style

遒媚 qiúmèi 〈书面〉 (usually of calligraphy) powerful and elegant; vigorous and graceful

蝤 qiú
see also yóu

蝤蛴 qiúqí 〈古语〉 longicorn's larva

求 qiú ❶ ask; beg; request; entreat: 我想～你帮个忙。I'd like to ask you for a favour. / 我～你别这样干了。I beg you to stop it. ❷ strive for: ～团结 strive for unity / 精益～精 keep improving (one's work, etc.) / 训练～严 go in for rigorous training ❸ try; seek; search: 不～名, 不～利 seek neither fame nor gain / ～才 search for talent; scout for talent / ～共识 seek common understanding / 力～控制局势 make a vigorous effort to get the situation in hand ❹ demand: 供～关系 relation between supply and demand / 供过于～ supply exceeds demand / 市场需～结构 pattern of market demand ❺ (Qiú) a surname

求爱 qiú'ài pay suit to; woo; court: 现在儿童不喜欢读那些王子向公主～的故事。Children are no longer interested in reading stories about a prince courting a princess.

求备 qiúbèi ask for perfection: 不能事事～。We shouldn't ask for excellence in everything. / 毋～于一人。Don't demand perfection in any man.

求成 qiúchéng hope for success: 做学问不可急于～。In doing research, we should not be anxious for quick results.

求大同, 存小异 qiú dàtóng, cún xiǎoyì seek common ground on major issues while reserving differences on minor ones

求告 qiúgào implore; beseech; entreat: 苦苦～ entreat piteously

求告无门 qiúgào-wúmén have no one or nowhere to turn to for assistance

求根 qiúgēn 〈数学〉 extract a root

求根仪 qiúgēnyí isograph

求和 qiúhé ❶ sue for peace: 忍辱～ sue for peace under humiliating circumstances ❷ (in ball games or chess) try to draw a match; strive for a draw: 他这一局～看来也做不到了。It would seem hardly possible for him even to obtain a drawn game.

求婚 qiúhūn ask for a lady's hand; make an offer of marriage; propose: 向她～了吗? Did you propose to her?

求婚者 qiúhūnzhě suitor

求积仪 qiújīyí 〈数学〉 planimeter

求见 qiújiàn ask to see; request an interview; seek an audience: 登门～ pay a personal call on sb.; call at sb.'s house and seek an audience with him

求教 qiújiào ask for advice; seek counsel: 虚心～ listen to advice with an open mind / 写信向老师～ write to a teacher for advice

求解 qiújiě (of mathematics) seek solution of a question (by working on given postulates according to laws and theorems)

求借 qiújiè ask sb. to lend sth.: 除了向他～外别无他法。I had no alternative but to ask him for a loan.

求救 qiújiù send (signals, etc.) for help; ask sb. to come to the rescue: ～信号 GMDSS (formerly SOS) signal; distress call; distress signal / 被围部队向司令部～。The besieged troops asked the headquarters for reinforcements.

求靠 qiúkào 〈方言〉 ask for support; seek refuge with sb.: 向亲友～ seek refuge with relatives or friends

求马唐肆 qiúmǎ-tángsì attempt to purchase a horse from where there is none — bark up the wrong tree

求偶 qiú'ǒu seeking a spouse; courtship: 登报～ advertise for a lifelong partner (*or* a spouse) / ～行为〈生物〉 courtship behaviour

求乞 qiúqǐ beg: ～于亲友 beg from relatives and friends / 沿街～ go begging in the street

求签 qiúqiān 〈迷信〉 draw a lot at a temple for an oracle

求亲 qiúqīn (of a family or its head) seek a marriage alliance (with another family); make an offer of marriage (on behalf of the son, etc.)

求亲靠友 qiúqīn-kàoyǒu *also* "求亲告友" ask for favours (usu. loans) from relatives and friends: 两口子～地借了一笔钱, 让儿子出国留学。By obtaining a loan from relatives and friends, the couple sent their son to study abroad.

求情 qiúqíng plead or beg for leniency; intercede (in sb.'s behalf); put in a good word (for sb.): ～告饶 plead for forgiveness or mercy / 代人～ plead on sb.'s behalf; intercede for sb. / 你去向他求个情就没事了。Go and plead with him and everything will be all right. / 我决不会要你为我～的。You'd be the last person I'd ask to put in a good word for me.

求全 qiúquán ❶ 〈贬义〉 ask for perfection: ～思想 perfectionist ideas ❷ try to round sth. off; try to achieve sth. through compromise: 委曲～ make compromises or concessions to achieve one's purpose; stoop to compromise

求全责备 qiúquán-zébèi criticize a person for failing to be perfect; nitpick: 对人不可～。We shouldn't expect perfection of anybody.

求饶 qiúráo beg for mercy; ask for forgiveness: 屈膝～ beg for mercy on one's knees

求人 qiúrén ask for help: 这些事情自己能做就不必～。Don't solicit help when you can manage on your own.

求人不如求己 qiúrén bùrú qiú jǐ better depend on oneself than ask for help from others; better seek help from oneself than from others; better turn to one's own folk than to outsiders; God helps those that help themselves: ～, 还是自己咬牙干吧! We would rather grit our teeth and depend on our own efforts than seek help from others.

求仁得仁 qiúrén-dérén seek virtue and have it; achieve what one seeks; have one's wish fulfilled: ～, 又何怨焉? What are you sorry for when you have achieved what you sought?

求荣 qiúróng seek personal glory or high position: 这无异于卖国～。This was tantamount to seeking personal glory by betraying one's own country.

求神 qiúshén ask for blessings from God; seek God's protection: ～问卜 ask God's favour and practise divination

求生 qiúshēng seek survival; keep oneself alive: ～的愿望 will to live; desire to live / ～不得, 求死不能 can neither live nor die — be in utter misery

求胜 qiúshèng seek victory: ～心切 have an eager desire for victory; be too eager for success

求实 qiúshí be realistic; be practical-minded: 提倡～精神 promote a down-to-earth approach

求售 qiúshòu have sth. for sale: 低价～ have sth. for sale at a reduced price

求索 qiúsuǒ ❶ seek; explore: ～新的路子 explore a new path ❷ demand; extort: ～无厌 be driven by insatiable avarice

求田问舍 qiútián-wènshè try to buy land and houses — (a man) have no lofty aspirations

求同存异 qiútóng-cúnyì seek common ground while reserving differences: 在国际交往中, 我们主张～。In international contacts we advocate seeking common ground while reserving differences.

求仙 qiúxiān ❶ be in quest of immortality: ～学道 seek instruction from immortals and learn to practise Taoist principle ❷ *see* "求神"

求贤若渴 qiúxián-ruòkě look for virtuous talent as if to quench one's thirst; be eager to enlist the help of the virtuous and talented; seek talent eagerly

求降 qiúxiáng beg to surrender or capitulate

求学 qiúxué ❶ go to school; attend school; pursue one's studies: 来北京～ come to Beijing to pursue one's studies ❷ seek knowledge;

孜孜不倦的～、求真理的精神 tireless in the pursuit of knowledge and truth
求爷爷告奶奶 qiú yéye gào nǎinai 〈口语〉piteously beg everybody everywhere; kowtow to the powers that be:为这点儿事，也要到处～? Do you have to go begging on all fours just for such a trifle? /办事人员经常要～。People trying to get things done often had to kowtow to the powers that be.
求医 qiúyī seek for medical treatment; see a doctor:登门～ call on a doctor for medical attention
求雨 qiúyǔ pray for rainfall
求援 qiúyuán ask for help or assistance; request reinforcements:向当地政府～ request assistance from the local government
求战 qiúzhàn ❶ seek battle:敌军～不成，只得回兵。Having sought battle in vain, the enemy had to withdraw. ❷ ask to go into battle:战士们纷纷～。One after another, the men asked to go into action.
求证 qiúzhèng seek proof or confirmation:科学上可以大胆假设，但必须切实地去～。In scientific study you can put forward a bold hypothesis, but you must seek proof conscientiously.
求之不得 qiúzhī-bùdé more than one could wish for:～的机会 rare, golden opportunity; most welcome opportunity /对我来说，这所大学提供的奖学金真是～，因为我自己没有钱到国外去上大学。The scholarship offered by the university was a godsend, for I couldn't afford to pursue my studies abroad at my own expense. /能到他手下去工作，是～的事。I'm only too glad to work under him.
求知 qiúzhī seek knowledge:～欲 thirst for knowledge /～精神 desire to seek knowledge
求值 qiúzhí 〈数学〉evaluation
求职 qiúzhí seek a position; apply for a job:向这家公司～ apply for a job with the company /托人～ ask sb. to find one a job /～书 application for employment
求治 qiúzhì seek medical treatment:他曾多方～，但疗效不佳。Although he has been looking for a cure in all possible quarters, the result so far is unsatisfactory.
求助 qiúzhù call for assistance; turn to sb. for help:多方～ seek help from various quarters /向同事～ turn to one's colleagues for help /～于编造谣言 resort to fabrications or rumour-mongering
求最小值 qiú zuìxiǎozhí 〈数学〉minimization

裘 qiú ❶〈书面〉fur coat:貂～ mink coat /轻～肥马 wear a light fur coat riding a well-fed horse — live in luxury ❷ (Qiú) a surname
裘弊金尽 qiúbì-jīnjìn *also* "裘敝金尽" with one's fur coat in tatters and gold gone — be reduced to poverty
裘皮 qiúpí fur:～大衣 fur coat

逑 qiú 〈书面〉spouse; consort; life mate

球(❸毬) qiú ❶ sphere; globe: *see* "～体"; "～心" ❷ anything shaped like a sphere; ball:眼～ eyeball /雪～ snowball ❸ ball, etc. (used in games):篮～ basketball /网～ tennis-ball /棒～ baseball /冰～ ice hockey /马～polo /羽毛～ badminton /乒乓～ table tennis; ping-pong /垒～ softball /接～ catch the ball /发～ serve the ball /换发～ change of service /传～ pass the ball ❹ ball game:看～ watch a ball game ❺ globe; world:南半～ Southern Hemisphere /全～战略 global strategy /环～ round the world /月～ moon /星～ celestial body; heavenly body
球操 qiúcāo 〈体育〉ball gymnastics
球场 qiúchǎng ground or court for ball games:篮～ basketball court /网～ tennis court /排～ volleyball court /棒～ baseball diamond; baseball field /足～ football field
球潮虫 qiúcháochóng pill bug; wood louse
球胆 qiúdǎn bladder (of a ball)
球蛋白 qiúdànbái 〈生化〉globulin; fibralbumin
球刀 qiúdāo ice-hockey skate blade
球队 qiúduì (ball game) team
球阀 qiúfá 〈机械〉ball check; globe valve
球风 qiúfēng spirit of competition as shown in a ball game; sportsmanship as demonstrated in a ball game:～不正 lack of sportsmanship
球杆 qiúgān (golf) club
球关节 qiúguānjié 〈自控〉globe joint
球冠 qiúguān 〈数学〉spherical crown
球罐 qiúguàn 〈石油〉sphere
球果 qiúguǒ 〈植物〉cone
球焊 qiúhàn 〈冶金〉ball bonding
球化 qiúhuà 〈冶金〉globuling:～处理 spheroidization /～退火 globurizing; spheroidal annealing
球技 qiújì skill in a ball game
球接头 qiújiētóu 〈机械〉spherojoint
球茎 qiújīng 〈植物〉corm
球茎甘蓝 qiújīng gānlán *also* "苤蓝" piělan 〈植物〉kohlrabi
球菌 qiújūn coccus
球壳式水轮机 qiúkéshì shuǐlúnjī 〈机械〉globe cased turbine
球类运动 qiúlèi yùndòng ball games
球粒 qiúlì 〈地质〉spherulite
球粒结构 qiúlì jiégòu chondrules
球龄 qiúlíng years one has spent on playing a ball game; ball-game seniority
球路 qiúlù tactics in a ball game:不摸对方的～，拦网连连失误。They made repeated errors in their blocking, because they were not familiar with the tactics of their opponents.
球门 qiúmén goal:～柱 goalpost /射进～ score a goal; net a goal
球迷 qiúmí (ball game) fan; buff; aficionado:篮～ basketball fan /足～ football fan /网球～ tennis buff /～协会 association of sports fans /～闹事 disturbance caused by fans
球面 qiúmiàn spherical surface
球面车床 qiúmiàn chēchuáng 〈机械〉spherical turning lathe
球面度 qiúmiàndù spherical degree; steradian; sterad
球面几何学 qiúmiàn jǐhéxué 〈数学〉spherical geometry; geometry of spheres
球面角 qiúmiànjiǎo spherical angle
球面镜 qiúmiànjìng spherical mirror
球面三角形 qiúmiàn sānjiǎoxíng spherical triangle
球面三角学 qiúmiàn sānjiǎoxué spherical trigonometry
球面天文学 qiúmiàn tiānwénxué spherical astronomy
球面投影 qiúmiàn tóuyǐng stereographic projection
球面像差 qiúmiàn xiàngchā spherical aberration
球面应力 qiúmiàn yìnglì spherical stress
球面坐标 qiúmiàn zuòbiāo spherical coordinate
球磨床 qiúmóchuáng ball grinder
球磨机 qiúmójī ball mill
球墨铸铁 qiúmò zhùtiě 〈冶金〉nodular cast iron
球拍 qiúpāi *also* "球拍子" (tennis, badminton, etc.) racket; (ping-pong) bat or paddle:正或反面贴海绵～ outward or inward pimpled rubber bat
球曲率 qiúqūlǜ spherical curvature:～中心 centre of spherical curvature
球儿 qiúr ❶ (small) ball ❷ glass ball (children play with); marble:玩弹～ play marbles
球赛 qiúsài ball game; match
球社 qiúshè 〈旧语〉place where one plays billiards or bowls
球台 qiútái billiard or ping-pong table
球坛 qiútán ball-playing world or circles; ball-players:～老将 veteran ball-player /～新秀 new ace player /～盛会 grand gathering of ball-players; grand occasion for ball-players
球体 qiútǐ sphere; spheroid
球团矿 qiútuánkuàng 〈冶金〉pellet
球网 qiúwǎng net (for a ball game)
球窝关节 qiúwō guānjié 〈生理〉spheroidal joint; ball-and-socket joint; enarthrodial joint; multiaxial joint
球鞋 qiúxié gym shoes; tennis shoes; sneakers
球心 qiúxīn centre of a sphere or ball:～投影 gnomonic projection /～投影图 gnomonic chart
球星 qiúxīng ace at ball game; ball-game star; star player; ace player
球形 qiúxíng spherical; globular
球形阀 qiúxíngfá globe valve
球形反射面天线 qiúxíng fǎnshèmiàn tiānxiàn spherical-reflector antenna
球形门把手 qiúxíng ménbǎshou door-knob
球艺 qiúyì skill in a ball game; ball-game skill:～高超 superb skill in a ball game /交流～ exchange ball-game techniques
球银幕电影 qiúyínmù diànyǐng *also* "球幕电影" spherical screen

film
球郁金香 qiúyùjīnxiāng globe tulip
球轴承 qiúzhóuchéng ball bearing
球柱镜 qiúzhùjìng 〈物理〉spherocylinder
球状瘤 qiúzhuàngliú 〈医学〉spheroma
球状容器 qiúzhuàng róngqì spheroid
球状星团 qiúzhuàng xīngtuán globular cluster
球座 qiúzuò (golf) tee

赇 qiú 〈书面〉bribe:受～ accept bribes

銶 qiú 〈古语〉a kind of chisel

俅[1] qiú see "俅人"

俅[2] qiú see "俅俅"

俅人 Qiúrén (old name for 独龙族) Qiuren, one of China's minority nationalities
俅俅 qiúqiú 〈书面〉in a respectful and submissive manner

尿 qiú 〈方言〉cock; penis

璆 qiú 〈书面〉beautiful jade

虬(虯) qiú ❶ see "虬龙" ❷ 〈书面〉coiled; curled:其髯密而～。His whiskers are dense and curled.
虬龙 qiúlóng (legendary) small dragon with horns
虬髯 qiúrán 〈书面〉curly whiskers:～大汉 hefty fellow with curly sideburns
虬须 qiúxū 〈书面〉curly beard or moustache

囚 qiú ❶ imprison; jail:幽～ imprison; keep in captivity /～于密室 be imprisoned in a secret cell ❷ prisoner; convict:罪～ convict /阶下～ prisoner; captive
囚车 qiúchē prison van; prisoners' van
囚犯 qiúfàn prisoner; convict:重要～ important prisoner /越狱潜逃～ escaped prisoner (*or* convict) /改造～ reform prisoners
囚房 qiúfáng prison cell; prison; jail
囚禁 qiújìn imprison; put in jail; hold in captivity
囚困 qiúkùn imprison; put in jail; put behind bars
囚牢 qiúláo prison; jail
囚笼 qiúlóng (wooden) prisoner's cage (used in ancient China)
囚室 qiúshì prison cell; prison
囚首垢面 qiúshǒu-gòumiàn with unkempt hair and dirty face (like those of a convict in former times)
囚徒 qiútú convict; prisoner
囚系 qiúxì 〈书面〉imprison; put in jail; place in prison; put behind bars
囚衣 qiúyī prison clothes

泅 qiú float on water; swim
泅渡 qiúdù swim across:武装～ swim across with one's weapons; swim across in battle gear
泅水 qiúshuǐ float on water; swim:～而过 float across the water; swim across the water
泅泳 qiúyǒng swim
泅游 qiúyóu swim

巭 qiú 〈书面〉force; compel

仇 Qiú a surname
see also chóu
仇英 Qiú Yīng Qiu Ying (c. 1509-c. 1552), painter of the Ming Dynasty

鼽 qiú have a stuffy nose
鼽鼻 qiúbí have a stuffy nose

犰 qiú
犰狳 qiúyú 〈动物〉armadillo

巯(巰) qiú 〈化学〉sulphydryl; mercapto
巯基 qiújī sulphydryl:～化合物 mercapto compound /～乙醇 mercaptoethanol

qiǔ

糗 qiǔ ❶ 〈古语〉solid food ❷ 〈方言〉(of rice or noodles) be clotted or caked:这碗面条放～了。The bowl of noodles got clotted.

qū

祛 qū dispel; prevent; remove; ward off:～病延年 prevent disease and prolong life /～蠹除奸 get rid of harmful elements and evil-doers
祛除 qūchú dispel; get rid of; drive away:～疾病 prevent or cure disease /～紧张心情 relieve tension
祛风 qūfēng 〈中医〉dispel or disperse the wind; remove rheumatic pain, cold, etc.:～去湿 disperse the wind and damp vapours
祛风湿药 qūfēngshīyào medicine for rheumatism
祛暑 qūshǔ drive away or ward off summer heat
祛痰 qūtán promote or facilitate expectoration
祛痰剂 qūtánjì expectorant; solvent; solventia
祛疑 qūyí 〈书面〉remove suspicion or doubt
祛瘀 qūyū 〈中医〉remove blood stasis
祛瘀活血 qūyū-huóxuè 〈中医〉remove blood stasis and promote blood circulation

袪 qū ❶ sleeve cuff ❷ see "祛" qū

佉 qū 〈书面〉expel; drive out

胠 qū 〈书面〉❶ (of human body) part between armpit and waist; flank ❷ pry open:～箧 prize open a trunk to steal

区(區) qū ❶ distinguish; differentiate; classify; subdivide: see "～别";"～分" ❷ area; zone; district; region:市～ city proper; urban district /郊～ suburban district; suburb /住宅小～ residential sub-area /使馆～ embassy quarter /牧～ pastoral area /工业～ industrial area /工业园～ industrial park/经济特～ special economic zone ❸ (as an administrative division) district; region; division:自治～ autonomous region /市辖～ district under municipal jurisdiction
see also Ōu
区别 qūbié ❶ distinguish; differentiate; discriminate; make a distinction between:～善恶 distinguish between good and evil; differentiate good from evil /～利用 use different things or people in different ways /这两者是不难～开的。It's not difficult to make a distinction between the two. ❷ difference; distinction:有很大～ there is a world of difference /学英语的学生必须了解这种～。Students of English must learn this distinction.
区处 qūchǔ 〈书面〉arrange; handle; manage
区队 qūduì military unit equivalent to that of a platoon
区分 qūfēn differentiate; distinguish; delineate:～事物的性质 differentiate the nature of things /～两个历史时期 mark off (*or* delineate, *or* demarcate) two historical periods /这对孪生兄弟很难～开。The twins are hardly distinguishable from each other.
区划 qūhuà divide into districts:行政～ administrative divisions
区寰 qūhuán 〈书面〉human world; world
区徽 qūhuī regional emblem:香港特别行政区的～ emblem of the Hong Kong Special Administrative Region
区间 qūjiān part of the normal route of a bus or trolley-bus
区间车 qūjiānchē bus that travels only part of its normal route; shuttle bus; suburban bus
区间贸易 qūjiān màoyì inter-regional trade
区块 qūkuài region; area; district:两个～之间的公共关系 public relations between the two districts /两个～之间的横向联系 horizontal association of the two regions /对中国南海珠江口的两个～合作勘探 cooperative exploration of the two areas at the mouth of the Pearl

River on the South China Sea
区旗 qūqí regional flag
区区 qūqū ❶ petty; trivial; trifling: ~之数 petty sum; peanuts / ~小事, 何足挂齿? Such a trifling thing is hardly worth mentioning. ❷〈旧语〉〈谦词〉me; my humble self: 此非别人, 正是~。It's none other than my humble self.
区时 qūshí 〈天文〉zone time
区夏 Qūxià 〈书面〉China
区议会 qūyìhuì (HK) urban district board; district council
区域 qūyù region; area; district: ~自治 regional autonomy / ~经济 regional economy / ~会议 regional (*or* local) conference / ~合作 inter-regional cooperation / 边远~ remote frontier area
区域地理学 qūyù dìlǐxué regional geography
区域防御导弹 qūyù fángyù dǎodàn area defence missile
区域供暖 qūyù gōngnuǎn district heating
区域经济学 qūyù jīngjìxué regional economics
区域时间 qūyù shíjiān zone time
区域市政局 qūyù shìzhèngjú (HK) regional council
区域性 qūyùxìng regional: ~同盟 regional alliance / ~而非全国性问题 matter of regional, not national significance / ~公约 regional convention
区长 qūzhǎng head of a district (as in a city)

Q

岖(嶇)

qū *see* "崎岖" qíqū

躯(軀)

qū human body: 身~ body; stature / 七尺之~ body of seven *chi* — a fully grown man / 为国捐~ lay down one's life for one's country
躯干 qūgàn 〈生理〉trunk; torso
躯壳 qūqiào body (as opposed to soul); outer form: 失去精神, 就成了没有灵魂的~。Once the spirit is lost, what is left is only the body without the soul.
躯体 qūtǐ body; soma: 思维与~的关系 relationship between the psyche and the soma (*or* the mind and the body)

驱(驅、敺)

qū ❶ drive (a horse, etc.); spur: ~马前进 spur a horse on / 扬鞭~马 whip up a horse; whip a horse forward; whip a horse on ❷ run quickly; drive: 长~直入 drive deep into an area or a country; drive straight in / 并驾齐~ run neck and neck; keep pace with sb.; be on a par with sb. ❸ expel; drive away; exorcise: 为渊~鱼 drive the fish into deep waters — drive friends over to the side of the enemy / 作法~鬼 (of a wizard, etc.) use magic to exorcise spirits
驱策 qūcè ❶ drive; whip on; spur: 迅猛发展的形势~我们在经济改革上加快步伐。The rapidly unfolding situation urges us to quicken our pace in economic reform. ❷ order people about
驱肠虫剂 qūchángchóngjì 〈药学〉anthelmintic
驱车 qūchē drive; drive a car: ~前往 go in a car; drive to a place / ~越过荒原 drive across the wilderness
驱驰 qūchí 〈书面〉❶ spur on a horse; run ❷ exert one's effort on behalf of others; render service: 由是感激, 遂许先帝以~。Filled with gratitude, I pledged my humble service to the late emperor.
驱虫剂 qūchóngjì insectifuge; anthelmintic
驱虫净 qūchóngjìng tetramisole; tetramizole
驱虫药 qūchóngyào insect repellent; anthelmintic; vermifuge; insectifuge
驱除 qūchú drive out; eliminate; get rid of: ~害虫 get rid of (*or* kill) injurious insects
驱动 qūdòng ❶urge; impel; drive: 在暴利的~下, 他们制造大量假酒。Driven by the lust for excessive profits, they made large quantities of fake liquor. ❷〈机械〉drive: 前轮~ front-wheel drive / 四轮~ four-wheel drive / ~轮 drive-wheel / ~轴 drive shaft / ~齿轮 driving gear / 核动力~的潜艇 nuclear-powered submarine
驱动器 qūdòngqì 〈计算机〉disc driver: 硬盘~ hard (disc) driver / 软盘~ soft driver
驱风剂 qūfēngjì 〈药学〉carminative
驱赶 qūgǎn ❶ drive: ~马车 drive a horse-cart ❷ drive away; expel: ~苍蝇 shoo (*or* whisk away) flies
驱寒 qūhán dispel cold: 喝点酒~。Drink a little wine to keep warm. / 这药是~的。This medicine is to dispel internal coldness.
驱蛔灵 qūhuílíng 〈药学〉piperazine citrate
驱傩 qūnuó 〈旧语〉folk performance held at the end of a year or at the beginning of spring to greet celestial beings and repel plague spirits; exorcism
驱迫 qūpò drive; impel; force; compel: 在旧社会, 饥寒~他去行窃。Driven by hunger and cold, he once committed theft in the old society.
驱遣 qūqiǎn ❶ force; compel; drive: 他们~她去做粗活。She was forced to do heavy manual labour. / 军阀~老百姓给他们当炮灰。The warlords drove ordinary people to serve as their cannon-fodder. ❷〈书面〉expel; banish; deport: ~非法入境者 expel (*or* deport) illegal immigrants ❸ eliminate; dispel; remove: ~寂寞和忧郁 relieve one's loneliness and melancholy / ~隐患 remove a hidden danger / ~一切忧虑 banish all cares from one's mind
驱蠕虫药 qūrúchóngyào vermifuge
驱散 qūsàn ❶ break up; scatter; disperse: 警察~了围观的人群。The police dispersed the crowd of onlookers. ❷ dispel; drive away: 晚风~了一天的闷热。The evening breeze drove away the heat of the day. / 太阳升起的时候, 浓雾渐渐地被~了。As the sun rose, the dense fog gradually dispersed.
驱使 qūshǐ ❶ order about; push around: 受人~ be ordered about / 有许多仆役供他~。A crowd of servants are at his beck and call. ❷ impel; prompt; spur on: 为习惯势力所~ prompted by force of habit / 良心的~ promptings of conscience / 受一种说不出的心情~ spurred on by an indescribable feeling
驱绦虫药 qūtāochóngyào taeniafuge; taeniacide; taenicide
驱蚊剂 qūwénjì culicifuge; anophelifuge
驱雾系统 qūwù xìtǒng fog dispersion system
驱邪 qūxié ward off evils; exorcize evil spirits; drive away demons
驱逐 qūzhú throw out; expel; oust: 他们将一一受审, 分别~出境。They will all be tried and deported in batches.
驱逐机 qūzhújī 〈军事〉pursuit plane
驱逐舰 qūzhújiàn 〈军事〉destroyer
驱逐令 qūzhúlìng 〈法律〉order for ejectment; order of expulsion; expulsion order
驱走 qūzǒu drive out; get rid of; expel: 通红的炭火, ~了寒气, 整个房间暖融融的。The burning charcoal fire kept away the cold and made the room pleasantly warm.

觑(覰、覻)

qū 〈口语〉screw up one's eyes; squint: 在强烈的阳光下~起双眼 screw up one's eyes in the bright sunlight *see also* qù
觑觑眼 qūqūyǎn 〈方言〉short-sighted; near-sighted

蛆

qū 〈动物〉maggot
蛆病 qūbìng myiasis
蛆虫 qūchóng ❶ maggot ❷ scoundrel; shameless wretch
蛆治疗法 qūzhìliáofǎ 〈医学〉maggot therapy

曲[1]

qū ❶ bent; crooked: 弯~ winding; curved; zigzag / 山道盘~ winding path in the mountains ❷ bend; flex; curve; crook: ~肱而枕 sleep with one's head resting on a bent arm ❸ bend: 河~ bend of a river ❹ wrong; false; unjustifiable: 理~ be in the wrong; justice is not on one's side ❺ (Qū) a surname

曲[2](麯、粬)

qū leaven; yeast *see also* qǔ
曲笔 qūbǐ ❶ (of an official historian) distort facts to hide the truth ❷ deliberate digression in writing: 他写文章喜欢用~。It is his style to digress deliberately in writing.
曲臂 qūbì 〈机械〉crank arm; crank radius
曲别针 qūbiézhēn paper clip
曲柄 qūbǐng 〈机械〉crank
曲柄销 qūbǐngxiāo wrist pin; crank pin
曲柄压床 qūbǐng yāchuáng 〈机械〉crank press
曲柄轴 qūbǐngzhóu crank axle
曲柄钻 qūbǐngzuàn brace drill
曲尺 qūchǐ carpenter's square; zigzag rule
曲阜 Qūfù Qufu, hometown of Confucius (551-479 BC) in Shandong Province
曲躬 qūgōng bow in respect and submission: ~事人 serve others

humbly; be subservient to others /不为斗米～ never humble oneself for petty gains
曲拱 qūgǒng arched:～石桥 arched stone bridge
曲古霉素 qūgǔméisù 〈药学〉trichomycin
曲光度 qūguāngdù 〈物理〉diopter
曲棍球 qūgùnqiú ❶ field hockey ❷ hockey ball
曲解 qūjiě (deliberately) misinterpret; distort; twist:有意无意地～了原意 wittingly or unwittingly distort the original meaning /你的发言～了我的意思。Your statement misinterpreted what I meant.
曲尽其妙 qūjìn-qímiào (describe, portray, express, etc.) with subtle and superb skill:此书描写世态人情，无不～。This book depicts with superb art the various aspects of human nature and social life.
曲颈甑 qūjǐngzèng 〈化学〉retort
曲径 qūjìng winding path; devious trail:沿山后～而行，可达湖边。Go along the winding path behind the hill and you'll reach the lake.
曲径通幽 qūjìng-tōngyōu winding path leading to a secluded spot
曲里拐弯 qūliguǎiwān 〈口语〉winding; tortuous; zigzag:～的小溪 winding stream; meandering brook /～的小径 zigzag path
曲率 qūlǜ 〈数学〉curvature
曲率计 qūlǜjì 〈数学〉flexometer
曲霉 qūméi aspergillus:黑～ *Aspergillus niger* /黄～ *Aspergillus flavus* /～中毒 aspergillustoxicosis
曲霉病 qūméibìng aspergillosis
曲霉素 qūméisù aspergillin
曲面 qūmiàn curved surface; camber:内～ negative camber /外～ positive camber /～图 surface chart or diagram
曲奇 qūqí *also*“曲奇饼”(transliteration) cookie; cooky:丹麦～ Denmark cookies
曲曲弯弯 qūqū-wānwān full of twists and turns:山麓有一条～的羊肠小道。There is a narrow tortuous trail at the foot of the mountain. /这条河～地流过富饶的农田。The river meanders through rich farmlands.
曲蟮 qūshan *also*“蛐蟮”qūshan 〈口语〉earthworm
曲射 qūshè 〈军事〉curved fire:～弹道 curved trajectory
曲射炮 qūshèpào curved-fire gun
曲室 qūshì 〈书面〉inmost recesses of a house; secret room
曲说 qūshuō one-sided statement; biased remark:不要被～所蒙蔽。Don't allow yourself to be hoodwinked by biased remarks.
曲酸 qūsuān 〈化学〉Kojic acid
曲突徙薪 qūtū-xǐxīn bend the chimney and remove the fuel — take measures to prevent a possible fire; be guarded against a possible danger:宜早为～之计。You'd better make provisions before troubles occur.
曲席 qūxí sit close together:～而坐 sit close together
曲线 qūxiàn ❶ curve ❷ sth., esp. a female body, having the shape of a curve:她喜欢穿紧身服以显示她身体的～。She likes to wear a close-fitting dress in order to show her graceful figure.
曲线板 qūxiànbǎn French curve; irregular curve; curve board
曲线救国 qūxiàn jiùguó saving the nation in a devious way — a theory propounded by Chinese collaborators during the anti-Japanese war (1937-1945) to justify their capitulation
曲线美 qūxiànměi graceful curve
曲线球 qūxiànqiú (of baseball, softball, etc.) curve ball
曲线图 qūxiàntú diagram of curves
曲线运动 qūxiàn yùndòng 〈物理〉curvilinear motion
曲意逢迎 qūyì-féngyíng go out of one's way to ingratiate oneself (with one's superiors):他对上司每每～，以讨欢心。In order to curry favour with his superiors, he did everything possible to cater to their wishes.
曲折 qūzhé ❶ tortuous; circuitous; winding:航道狭窄～。The channel is narrow and winding. /小路～向南。The path zigzags southward. ❷ complications; intricacies:我们还不完全清楚此事的～。We are not fully aware of the intricacies of the matter yet. /不管还要经过多少～，我们的事业都总是要前进的。No matter how many twists and turns still lie ahead of us, our cause is bound to advance.
曲知 qūzhī have scanty knowledge; have a smattering of knowledge:～之人 person with half-baked knowledge /不为～所惑 not be misled (*or* led astray) by a mere pittance of learning
曲直 qūzhí crooked and straight — right and wrong:分清是非～ make a distinction between right and wrong; tell right from wrong
曲衷 qūzhōng 〈书面〉inner feelings:畅谈～ have a heart-to-heart chat
曲轴 qūzhóu 〈机械〉crankshaft; bent axle:～箱 crankcase
曲轴磨床 qūzhóu móchuáng crankshaft grinding machine
曲子 qūzi 〈生化〉leaven; yeast

蛐 qū

蛐蛐儿 qūqur 〈方言〉〈动物〉cricket
蛐蟮 qūshan earthworm

嚯 qū 〈象声〉❶ sound of whistling ❷ chirping of a cricket

麹 qū ❶ leaven; yeast ❷ (Qū) a surname

趋(趨) qū ❶ hasten; rush; hurry along:～迎 hasten forward to meet sb. /亦步亦～ ape sb. at every step; imitate sb.'s every move ❷ tend towards; head for; tend to become:日～繁荣 get more prosperous with each passing day /局势～于稳定。The situation is heading for stability (*or* seems to be stabilizing). ❸ (of a goose or snake) pop its head to bite at people; snap at

趋避 qūbì hasten to keep clear of sth. or sb.:遥见奔马，～路旁。Seeing a galloping horse from a distance, he quickly dodged to the roadside.
趋承 qūchéng 〈书面〉toady to; fawn on:奔走～ busy trying to toady to sb.
趋奉 qūfèng toady to; be obsequious:他对上级百般～。He fawned on his superior in every possible way.
趋附 qūfù ingratiate oneself with; curry favour with; pander to:看到他这样地～权贵，真叫我发呕。It is disgusting to see him currying favour with the powers that be.
趋光性 qūguāngxìng *also*“慕光性”mùguāngxìng 〈生物〉phototaxis; phototropism:正～ positive phototaxis / 负～ negative phototaxis /～植物 phototactic plant
趋候 qūhòu (usu. in letters) pay respects to sb.:久未～。It is a long time since I last paid a call on you.
趋坏死性 qūhuàisǐxìng 〈医学〉necrotaxis
趋利 qūlì seek profit; go after gain:～避害 seek advantages and avoid disadvantages
趋热性 qūrèxìng 〈生物〉thermotaxis
趋湿性 qūshīxìng 〈生物〉hygrotaxis
趋时 qūshí 〈书面〉follow the fashion; be trendy; try to be in the swim or swing:足下此举颇有～之嫌。This act of yours will make people suspect that you, of all people, are following the fashion.
趋势 qūshì trend; tendency; inclination:必然～ inexorable trend /这种用金钱衡量一切的～值得注意。This tendency of evaluating everything in terms of money calls for attention. /世界总的～是和解而不是对抗。Reconciliation instead of confrontation is the overall world trend.
趋水性 qūshuǐxìng 〈生物〉hydrotaxis
趋挺 qūtǐng (of prices, stock shares, etc.) be on an upward trend
趋同 qūtóng tend to converge; tend to be the same:二者存在着一些～现象。There is a tendency towards convergence between the two.
趋同论 qūtónglùn 〈经济〉convergency theory
趋温性 qūwēnxìng 〈生物〉thermotaxis
趋向 qūxiàng ❶ lean towards; tend to; incline to:条例在实践中已～完善。The regulations are being perfected daily in practice. ❷ trend; inclination; bent; direction:这种～是不可逆转的。This trend is irreversible.
趋向动词 qūxiàng dòngcí 〈语言〉directional verb
趋向性 qūxiàngxìng 〈生物〉taxis
趋炎附势 qūyán-fùshì curry favour with the powerful; play up to those in power:堂堂七尺，岂能～！How could a true man cater to those in power?
趋氧性 qūyǎngxìng 〈生物〉aerotaxis; oxygenotaxis
趋药性 qūyàoxìng 〈生物〉chemotaxis
趋之若鹜 qūzhī-ruòwù go after sth. like a flock of ducks; fall over each other to get sth.; scramble for sth.:有些人看见蝇头小利，就～。There are people who scramble for every petty gain in sight.
趋走 qūzǒu hurry; walk quickly

焌 qū 〈口语〉❶ put sth. burning in water; douse sth. burning in water to extinguish the fire:把香火儿～了。Put the burn-

ing joss sticks in water. ❷ (of cooking method) stir-fry vegetables as soon as the condiments are mixed with the boiling oil: ～豆芽 sauted green bean sprouts

see also jùn

焌油 qūyóu 〈方言〉(in cooking) pour heated oil over cooked dishes

黢 qū black; dark: 黑～～ pitch-black; pitch-dark

黢黑 qūhēi pitch-black; pitch-dark: 夜～, 伸手不见五指。The night was pitch-dark, and one couldn't see one's fingers in front of one.

诎 qū ❶〈书面〉shorten; curtail ❷〈书面〉slow of speech ❸ *see* "屈" qū ❹ (Qū) a surname

屈 qū ❶ bend; bow; crouch; crook: ～腿 bend one's legs ❷ subdue; yield; submit: 威武不～ not to be subdued by force; unyielding in the face of force ❸ in the wrong: 理～ have a weak case ❹ wrong; injustice; wrongful treatment: 冤～ wrong; injustice /负～含冤 suffer a gross injustice ❺ (Qū) a surname

屈才 qūcái put sb. on a job unworthy of his talents; waste one's talents: 让他干这种工作可是大大地～。It is a waste of talent to put him on such a petty job.

屈从 qūcóng submit to; knuckle under to: ～于外界压力 yield (*or* bow) to outside pressure /当时, 他们不能不～于他的淫威。At that time, they had no alternative but to submit to his tyranny.

屈打成招 qūdǎ-chéngzhāo confess to false charges under torture; torture a person in order to extort a confession: 这是一桩～的冤案。This is a case of injustice where confession was extorted under torture. /他是～。He made a spurious confession under coercion.

屈服 qūfú succumb; yield; knuckle under: 迫使敌人～ bring the enemy to its knees /我们决不～于困难。We'll never bow before difficulties.

屈服强度 qūfú qiángdù 〈物理〉yield strength

屈光 qūguāng 〈物理〉dioptric: ～玻璃 dioptric glass / ～影像 dioptric image

屈光不正 qūguāng bùzhèng 〈医学〉ametropia

屈光度 qūguāngdù dioptre

屈光检查器 qūguāng jiǎncháqì striascope

屈光透镜 qūguāng tòujìng diopter lens

屈光学 qūguāngxué dioptrics

屈肌 qūjī 〈生理〉flexor

屈己 qūjǐ deny or inconvenience oneself; get down from one's high horse: ～待人 accommodate others by denying oneself / ～以求存 have to swallow humiliation for one's survival

屈驾 qūjià 〈敬词〉condescend to make the journey; be kind enough to honour us with your presence: 研讨会明日上午九时开幕, 敬请～光临。We wish you would honour us with your gracious presence at the opening ceremony of the seminar at nine tomorrow morning.

屈节 qūjié 〈书面〉❶ forfeit one's honour; humble oneself: ～辱命 lose one's honour and fail in one's mission /～事人 forfeit one's honour and serve as sb.'s underling; humble oneself in serving sb. ❷ stoop; act servilely: 卑躬～ bow and scrape; act obsequiously

屈就 qūjiù 〈套语〉condescend to take a post offered: 这主任一职就请你暂时～, 好吗? Would you care to take over the job as director for the time being?

屈居 qūjū be reconciled to a lower position than one deserves: ～亚军 have to be content with the position of a runner-up; have to settle for the second place

屈赖 qūlài wrong; falsely incriminate: ～好人 incriminate innocent people

屈理 qūlǐ in the wrong; unfair; unreasonable: 不做～的事情。We must not do anything unreasonable.

屈量 qūliàng 〈口语〉have not done justice to one's drinking capacity; have not drunk enough: 您有点儿～吧? You can't have drunk your fill, I suppose.

屈挠 qūnáo 〈书面〉surrender; yield; knuckle under

屈曲 qūqū (of arms, etc.) bend

屈戌儿 qūqur metal fastening for window, door, box, case, etc.

屈辱 qūrǔ humiliation; dishonour; mortification: 打败了, 国家难逃～的命运。Defeated, the nation could not escape deep humiliation. /清政府被迫签订了许多～的不平等条约。The Qing government was forced to sign many humiliating unequal treaties. /以往的～压在心头, 使她透不过气来。She often feels deeply oppressed with past mortification.

屈伸起重机 qūshēn qǐzhòngjī 〈机械〉lazy-jack

屈氏体 qūshìtǐ 〈冶金〉troostite: 原生～ primary troostite

屈死 qūsǐ be persecuted and driven to death: 我的父亲～在狱中。My father was persecuted to death in prison.

屈枉 qūwang wrong; maltreat; treat unjustly: ～好人是良心所不容的。Conscience will rebel against any wrong you may inflict on the innocent.

屈膝 qūxī go down on one's knees; submit: ～投降 abjectly surrender; knuckle under /不向恶势力～ refuse to yield to evil forces

屈心 qūxīn 〈口语〉do sth. against one's conscience; have a guilty conscience; be conscience-stricken: 你说这话不～? Don't you feel guilty (*or* ashamed) about making such remarks?

屈戌 qūxū 〈书面〉*see* "屈戌儿"

屈原 Qū Yuán Qu Yuan (formerly translated as Ch'u Yuan, c.340-277 BC), minister of the State of Chu and one of China's earliest poets

屈折语 qūzhéyǔ 〈语言〉inflexional language

屈肢葬 qūzhīzàng 〈考古〉flexed burial

屈指 qūzhǐ count on one's fingers: 离开家～已有三年。Exactly three years have passed since I left home.

屈指可数 qūzhǐ-kěshǔ can be counted on one's fingers; be rare: 像他那样的作家真是～。Writers like him can be counted on one's fingers. *or* Scholars like him are indeed very rare.

屈尊 qūzūn 〈套语〉condescend; stoop: 务请您～俯就。We do hope you would care to accept the offer. /您亲临这个小会, 大大～了。You have greatly honoured us by attending this small conference.

qú

渠[1] qú ❶ canal; conduit; ditch; channel: 沟～ ditches; irrigation canals and ditches /干～ main canal; trunk canal /支～ branch canal /漕～ canal; channel /河～ channel /引水～ inlet channel; aqueduct /灌溉～ irrigation canal ❷〈书面〉great: ～首 leader ❸ (Qú) a surname

渠[2]**(佢)** qú 〈方言〉he; him: ～辈 they; those people/不知～为何人? I don't know who he is.

渠道 qúdào ❶ canal; channel; irrigation ditch ❷ medium of communication; channel; means: 沟通联系群众的～ open up avenues of communication with the masses /通过正常的外交～谋求问题的解决 seek solution to the problem through normal diplomatic channels / 要通过种种～, 把工业品送到农村去。It is imperative to use every means to supply the countryside with industrial products (*or* provide the countryside with industrial products through all channels).

渠灌 qúguàn canal irrigation

渠魁 qúkuí 〈旧语〉chieftain of an armed rebel group; enemy chief

渠们 qúmen 〈方言〉they; them

渠首工程 qúshǒu gōngchéng 〈水利〉headwork

渠帅 qúshuài rebel leader; tribe chief

渠水 qúshuǐ canal

蕖 qú *see* "芙蕖" fúqú

磲 qú *see* "砗磲" chēqú

璩 qú ❶〈书面〉jade bracelet or earrings ❷ (Qú) a surname

蘧 qú ❶ pleasantly surprised ❷ (Qú) a surname

蘧庐 qúlú 〈书面〉dwelling place; humble home

蘧然 qúrán 〈书面〉pleasantly surprised

籧 qú

籧篨 qúchú 〈旧语〉coarse mat of bamboo or straw

瞿 Qú a surname

see also jù

瞿麦 qúmài 〈植物〉fringed pink

癯 qú 〈书面〉thin; emaciated:面容清～ look quite thin

蠼 qú

蠼螋 qúsōu *also*“蠷螋”〈动物〉earwig

蠷 qú

蠷螋 qúsōu *see*“蠼螋” qúsōu

氍(毹) qú

氍毹 qúshū ❶ wool carpet ❷〈旧语〉stage

衢 qú 〈书面〉thoroughfare; main road:通～ thoroughfare; broad avenue /～肆 business area; shopping centre /街～ street in downtown area

鸜 qú

鸜鹆 qúyù *see*“鸲鹆” qúyù

臞 qú 〈书面〉*see*“癯” qú

鼩 qú

鼩鼱 qújīng 〈动物〉shrew

鸲 qú

鸲鹆 qúyù myna

劬 qú 〈书面〉❶ very tired; fatigued ❷ diligent; industrious; hardworking

劬劳 qúláo 〈书面〉overworked; exhausted

qǔ

取 qǔ ❶ get; draw; collect; fetch:～报 fetch the newspapers /～款 draw money /～行李 get one's luggage /～邮包 collect a postal parcel /～回自己的提包 retrieve one's bag ❷ aim at; gain; seek:钻木～火 drill a piece of wood to make fire /咎由自～ have only oneself to blame ❸ adopt; assume; select; choose:两害相权～其轻 choose the lesser of two evils /一所体校～了他。He was admitted to a physical culture institute. /这种做法不可～。Such practice is inadvisable. /我们采～折中方案。We'll adopt a compromise proposal.

取保 qǔbǎo 〈法律〉get sb. to go bail for one; ask sb. to bail one out:～释放 be released on bail; be out on bail; be bailed out /～就医 bail sb. out for medical treatment /～候审 be out on bail

取便 qǔbiàn ❶ (often used in the early vernacular) do as one pleases:大家都～坐下。Be at home and sit down. *or* Make yourself at home and be seated. ❷ suit one's convenience

取材 qǔcái draw materials:就地～ put local materials to use /这出戏～于农民生活。This play has drawn material from the life of peasants.

取长补短 qǔcháng-bǔduǎn learn from each other's strong points to offset one's weaknesses; overcome one's own shortcomings by learning from others' strong points; draw on the strong points of others to make up for one's own weak points:互相学习，～ learn from and help each other to make up each other's deficiencies

取偿 qǔcháng get or obtain compensation; reimburse:我弟弟欠了他的账，他想从我这里～。He wanted me to reimburse him for the debt that my brother owed him.

取代 qǔdài ❶ replace; take over; substitute; supersede:激光照排～了手工排字。Laser phototypesetting has replaced hand composition. /有好几个人想在他退休后～他的职务。Quite a few people want to take over his post after his retirement. ❷〈化学〉displacement; substitution:～衍生物 substitution derivate

取道 qǔdào by way of; through; via:他～巴黎前往开罗。He went to Cairo via Paris.

取得 qǔdé get; gain; obtain; achieve:～联系 get in touch with /～经验 gain experience /～主动 take the initiative /～成绩 achieve good results /～丰收 have (*or* reap) a bumper harvest /～独立 win independence /～政权 take hold of (*or* seize) political power /会谈双方～广泛的一致。The two sides reached wide-ranging agreement in the talks. /会议～圆满成功。The meeting was completely successful. *or* The meeting was crowned with success. /我们设法～对方的谅解。We tried to reach an understanding with the other side.

取灯儿 qǔdēngr 〈方言〉match (to light a cigarette, etc. with)

取缔 qǔdì outlaw; prohibit; ban; suppress:～赌博 ban gambling /～无照经营 outlaw unlicensed business

取而代之 qǔ'érdàizhī replace sb.; supersede sb.; facilitate a takeover:文人政府已由军人统治～。The civilian government has been replaced by military rule.

取法 qǔfǎ follow the example of; take as one's model; draw on:～前人 draw on the experience of one's predecessors

取法乎上，仅得其中 qǔ fǎ hū shàng, jǐn dé qí zhōng even if you take the best as your model, you may only achieve the average

取给 qǔjǐ draw (supplies, etc.):粮食供应主要～于当地人民。The grain supply was mainly drawn from the local people.

取经 qǔjīng ❶ go on a pilgrimage to India for Buddhist scriptures ❷ learn from the experience of advanced persons, enterprises or localities:我们远去广东，向一些成功的企业～。We went on a long journey to Guangdong Province to learn from the experience of some successful enterprises.

取精用弘 qǔjīng-yònghóng *also*“取精用宏” select the essence from an abundance of materials:书读得多，自然能～。If you read extensively, you will be able to draw the essence from a vast amount of works.

取景 qǔjǐng find a view or scene (to paint, photograph, etc.):他的摄影多从大自然～。Most of his photographs are of natural landscapes.

取景器 qǔjǐngqì 〈摄影〉viewfinder

取径 qǔjìng selected route; chosen path

取决 qǔjué be decided by; be determined by; depend on; hinge on:工资的增长应～于生产的增长。The increase in wage should be geared to the increase in production. /谈判的成功与否～于双方的诚意。Whether the negotiations will end in success or not depends on the sincerity of both sides.

取乐 qǔlè enjoy or amuse oneself; make merry:讲笑话～ make merry by cracking jokes

取力器 qǔlìqì 〈汽车〉power takeoff

取凉 qǔliáng 〈方言〉enjoy the cool (in the open air)

取录 qǔlù enrol; admit; recruit

取媚 qǔmèi try to please sb.; curry favour with sb.; try to ingratiate oneself with sb.

取名 qǔmíng give a name; name:她生在隆冬，故～盼春。She was born in the depths of winter, and she was therefore given the name Panchun (Expecting Spring).

取闹 qǔnào ❶ make a row; wrangle:无理～ kick up a row ❷ make fun of sb.; play pranks on:不该拿残疾人～。You should not make fun of a disabled person.

取暖 qǔnuǎn warm oneself (by a fire, etc.); keep warm:围炉～ sit round a fire to keep warm /～设备 heating facilities

取暖器 qǔnuǎnqì heater:红外线～ infrared heater

取譬 qǔpì cite as an example:善于～ good at analogy

取平 qǔpíng make level; make even

取齐 qǔqí ❶ make even; even up; level:这些纸张大小不一，无法～。These sheets are of different sizes, and it is impossible to even them up. /那个班以前水平低些，现在跟我们～了。That class used to be on a lower level, but they are on a par with us now. ❷ assemble; gather; meet each other:大家在博物馆门前～后入场。The whole group will assemble at the front gate before entering the museum.

取枪 qǔqiāng 〈军事〉take arms:～！(word of command) To arms!

取巧 qǔqiǎo resort to wiles or trickery (for personal gain):投机～ cash in on every chance to advance one's interests /这人专会挖空心思～。The man always racks his brains to feather his own nest by trickery.

取容 qǔróng try to please; be ingratiating

取舍 qǔshě decide which to accept and which not; make one's choice:写作时对材料必须有所～。While writing an essay, we must determine which material to use and which to reject.

取胜 qǔshèng win victory; achieve success; triumph:轻易～ win

Q

an easy victory; have a walk-over /产品要靠质量～。All goods have to rely on their quality for success. *or* The competitiveness of a product is determined by its quality.

取士 qǔshì 〈旧语〉select scholars to be government officials; recruit government officials from among scholars

取水口 qǔshuǐkǒu 〈水利〉water intake

取向 qǔxiàng ❶〈物理〉orientation:～角 angle of orientation /～力 orientation force; dipole-dipole force ❷ sense of direction; orientation:人生～ orientation of life /价值观～ orientation of value

取消 qǔxiāo *also* "取销" cancel; call off; rescind; countermand: ～比赛资格 be disqualified from the contest /～谈判条件 withdraw the conditions for negotiations /～禁令和限制 lift the ban and restrictions /这个权利被～了。The right has been revoked. /因为资金不足，这个项目只好～。The project had to be abandoned because of shortage of funds. /会议延期了而不是～了。The meeting is postponed but not cancelled.

取消主义 qǔxiāozhǔyì liquidationism

取笑 qǔxiào laugh at; poke fun at; ridicule:招人～ invite ridicule /不要～他。Don't make fun of him. /他讲得不一定对，请不要～。What he has just said may not hold water, but I hope you will not sneer at him. /他成了人们～的对象。He has become something of a laughing stock.

取芯钻探法 qǔxìn zuàntànfǎ 〈矿业〉core-drill method; core-drilling

取芯作业 qǔxìn zuòyè 〈石油〉coring

取信 qǔxìn win confidence or trust:保证质量，～用户。Guarantee quality so as to earn customers' trust.

取信于民 qǔxìnyúmín gain the confidence of the people; win public trust:政策兑现，～ honour one's commitment so as to gain public trust (*or* confidence)

取样 qǔyàng sampling:～办法 sampling method /～检查 take a sample to check /混成～ composite sampling /～管 probe tube

取予 qǔ-yǔ give and take:～有节 be moderate in giving and taking

取悦 qǔyuè try to please; curry favour with:～读者 cater to the taste of readers /～领导 play up to the boss

取证 qǔzhèng gather or collect evidence:广泛～ gather evidence on a broad basis

取之不尽，用之不竭 qǔ zhī bù jìn, yòng zhī bù jié inexhaustible; unlimited:不要以为地下水是～的。Don't think ground water can be tapped without limit. /人民生活是一切文学艺术～的源泉。The life of the people is an inexhaustible source for all art and literature.

取之于民，用之于民 qǔ zhī yú mín, yòng zhī yú mín what is taken from the people is to be used in the interests of the people

娶 qǔ marry (a woman); take to wife:婚～ marriage /～妻 take a wife

娶亲 qǔqīn (of a man) get married

苣 qǔ

see also jù

苣荬菜 qǔmaicài 〈植物〉endive (*Cichorium endivia*)

龋 qǔ

龋齿 qǔchǐ ❶ tooth decay; dental caries ❷ decayed tooth

曲 qǔ ❶ *qu*, a type of verse for singing originated in folk ballads, which emerged in the Southern Song and Jin dynasties and became popular in the Yuan Dynasty:元～ *Yuanqu* or Yuan verse /散～ a type of verse popular in the Yuan, Ming, and Qing dynasties, with tonal patterns modelled on tunes drawn from folk music /南～ southern forms of drama ❷ song; tune; melody:戏～ traditional opera /小～儿 ditty; ballad/圆舞～ waltz /序～ overture /组～ suite /前奏～ prelude /协奏～ concerto /奏鸣～ sonata /练习～ étude/进行～ march /流行歌～ popular song ❸ music (of a song):作～ compose music /谱～ compose; set to music

see also qū

曲笛 qǔdí a kind of flute often used to accompany the singing of *kunqu* (昆曲), hence the name

曲调 qǔdiào tune (of a song); melody

曲高和寡 qǔgāo-hèguǎ highbrow songs find few singers; (of artistic and intellectual matters) so highbrow that few people can enjoy or understand:这个歌剧虽几经改写，仍然有～之嫌。Though the opera has been revised several times, it is still hard for ordinary folk to follow.

曲话 qǔhuà books on Chinese operas and their development as well as ballads and musical instruments

曲剧 qǔjù *quju*, opera derived from ballad singing

曲目 qǔmù names of songs, melodies, arias, or operas; repertoire

曲牌 qǔpái names of the tunes to which *qu* (曲) is composed

曲谱 qǔpǔ ❶ collection of tunes of *qu* (曲) ❷ music score of Chinese opera

曲式 qǔshì 〈音乐〉musical form

曲坛 qǔtán circle of *quyi* performers

曲协 qǔxié (short for 曲艺工作者协会) association of folk art workers

曲艺 qǔyì folk art forms rich in local flavour which include ballad singing, storytelling, comic dialogues, clapper talks, etc.

曲终奏雅 qǔzhōng-zòuyǎ brilliant conclusion of an essay or a performance; grand finale

曲子 qǔzi song; tune; melody

qù

阒 qù 〈书面〉quiet; still; silent:～无一人。It was dead still, and not a soul was around.

阒寂 qùjì 〈书面〉quiet; tranquil:原野～。All is quiet and still in the open country.

阒然 qùrán 〈书面〉very quiet; absolutely still:四野～。Silence reigns supreme over the vast stretch of open country.

趣 qù ❶ interest; amuse; delight:没～ boring; uninteresting; dull /逗～儿 set people laughing (by funny remarks, etc.); amuse people /相映成～ form a delightful contrast; contrast well with each other ❷ interesting; amusing; diverting; pleasant: *see* "～话"; "～闻" ❸ bent; purport; inclination:异～ of different purpose or nature

趣话 qùhuà funny remarks:大家都被他的～逗笑了。His funny remarks made everybody laugh.

趣剧 qùjù farce; burlesque

趣事 qùshì amusing episode:他常常说起少年时代的～。He often talked about his amusing childhood episodes.

趣谈 qùtán funny remarks; amusing talk

趣味 qùwèi interest; delight; taste:～性 interest; popular appeal /低级～ in bad taste; boorish; vulgar /爷爷觉得养花～无穷。Grandpa believes that flower-growing is of infinite interest.

趣闻 qùwén interesting gossip; amusing anecdote:～逸事 interesting hearsay and anecdotes

趣旨 qùzhǐ 〈书面〉purport; aim; principle

去[1] qù ❶ go (from here to another place); travel:他～火车站接人了。He has gone to the railway station to meet somebody. /他天津～过好几趟了。He has been to Tianjin many times. /立刻给他～个电报。Telegraph him immediately. *or* Cable him right now. /昨天我～过电话。I called him yesterday. ❷ depart; leave; go (away):一怒而～ leave in anger; storm out /一～不返 gone for ever; gone never to return /来～匆匆 come and go in a hurry ❸ lose; forfeit:大势已～。The game is as good as lost. *or* The situation is beyond salvation. ❹ remove; get rid of; shake off:这句话很关键，～不得。This is a key sentence not to be crossed out. /凉水洗碗～不了油。You cannot remove the grease from the bowls if you wash them in cold water. ❺ be away from; be apart from:我们学校～此不远。Our school is not far from here. /此事发生在清末，～今已逾百年。This incident occurred in the late Qing Dynasty, over 100 years ago. ❻ past; of last year:～冬 last winter /～岁末 at the end of last year ❼〈婉词〉pass away; depart; die:老人昨天晚上～了。The old man was gone last night. ❽ *used before another verb to indicate an action*: 这件事让他～办。We may as well leave the matter to him. /他～看电影了。He has gone to the cinema. ❾ *used after a verb-object structure to indicate an intention of doing sth.*: 打篮球～。Let's go and play basketball. /我要浇花～。I'm going to water the flowers. /他上街买东西～了。He has gone out shopping. ❿ *used between a verbial*

or a propositional structure, and a verb or a verbial structure to indicate the latter is the purpose of the former：拿着鱼竿～钓鱼 take along one's fishing rod for angling／要从不同角度～考虑这些新措施。It is necessary to consider these new measures from different angles. ⓫〈方言〉(used after adjectives like 大，多，远，etc.) very; extremely：他的话可多了～了。He is very loquacious. ／他们劲头可大了～了。They are overflowing with enthusiasm. ／走这条道儿近，走那条道儿可远了～了。This way is a shortcut. If you take that road, you'll have to travel much farther. ⓬〈语言〉*see*"去声"

去[2] qù play the part or role of; act (the part of)：适合～正面人物 be fit for the part of a hero／他在戏里～反派人物。He played the villain in the play.

去 qu ❶ *used after a verb to indicate movement away from the speaker*：拍～身上的尘土 flick the dust off one's clothes／队伍向远方开～。The troops are marching off to a distant place. ／他从我这儿借了几本书～。He borrowed a few books from me. ／把多余的枝叶剪～。Trim off the superflous leaves and branches. ／他的父母已相继死～。His parents died one after the other. ❷ *used after a verb to indicate continuation of an action*：一眼看～ look far ahead／他太累了，由他睡～。Let him sleep. He is too tired. ／让孩子们尽情地玩～。Let the children play to their hearts' content.

去病 qùbìng cure or prevent disease：常吃青菜水果能～。Frequent eating of vegetables and fruit can prevent disease.

去病毒 qù bìngdú 〈计算机〉debug：请把这个软盘先～再用。Please debug the floppy before using it.

去草胺 qùcǎo'àn 〈农业〉butachlor

去臭 qùchòu 〈化工〉deodorizing

去处 qùchù ❶ whereabouts：我不知道他的～。I don't know his whereabouts. ❷ place; spot; site：风景优美的～ place of beautiful scenery; scenic spot／那是个避暑的好～。It's a nice summer resort.

去磁 qùcí 〈物理〉deperm; demagnetise; degauss：～器 degausser; demagnetiser／～装置 demagnetiser

去粗取精 qùcū-qǔjīng discard the dross and keep the essence; get rid of the coarse to obtain the refined：广泛收集材料，之后要进行整理，～。Gather materials extensively and sort them out carefully to discard the dross and assimilate the essential.

去妇 qùfù abandoned wife：～之哀，甚难笔述。It is very hard to describe the sorrows of an abandoned wife.

去垢剂 qùgòujì detergent

去骨 qùgǔ boning：～肉 boned meat; boneless meat／～肋条肉 clear belly

去官 qùguān resign or relinquish one's official post：～归故里 resign one's official post and retire to one's hometown

去国 qùguó depart one's motherland or its capital：～三千里 far far away from one's native land

去火 qùhuǒ 〈中医〉reduce internal heat; relieve inflammation or fever：消痰～ reduce phlegm and relieve internal heat

去旧更新 qùjiù-gēngxīn do away with the old and usher in the new

去就 qù-jiù accept or reject (a job)：工作我已经替你找好了，～你自己考虑。I have got a job for you. It's up to you to take it or leave it.

去壳 qùké hull; shell; dehull：～蚕豆 hulled (*or* shelled) broad beans／～机 scourer

去留 qù-liú quit or stay put; leave or remain：～悉听尊便。You are free (*or* at liberty) to go or stay.

去路 qùlù way of progress; passage; outlet：敌人发现他们的～已被堵死。The enemy found their road of advance had been blocked. ／我们用分洪办法使横溢的流水有个～。We provided the overflowing water with an outlet by means of diversion.

去敏灵 qùmǐnlíng 〈药学〉tripelennamine

去末归本 qùmò-guīběn 〈旧语〉(末 refers to trade in ancient China while 本 refers to farming) give up all commercial activities in favour of farming

去年 qùnián last year：～今日 today last year

去皮 qùpí ❶ remove the peel or skin：～猪肉 skinless pork／～机 decorticator; sheller ❷ net weight：～五十公斤 fifty kilos in net weight

去取 qù-qǔ discard or retain; give up or hold back：决定～ decide whether to discard or retain sth.

去任 qùrèn no longer hold an official post; relinquish an official post

去日 qùrì 〈书面〉bygone days：～苦多。Many are the days that have gone by. *or* How much water has flowed under the bridge!

去声 qùshēng 〈语言〉falling tone, one of the four tones in classical Chinese and the fourth tone in modern standard Chinese pronunciation

see also"四声" sìshēng

去湿 qùshī 〈物理〉dehydrate

去世 qùshì (of grown-ups) die; expire; pass away：他～多年了。He has been dead for many years. ／他的父母早年～。His parents died when he was young.

去势 qùshì ❶ (of animals) castrate; emasculate ❷ momentum at the end of an action or event：来头大，～小 a magnificent start but a dismal ending

去暑 qùshǔ get rid of summer heat：冰镇西瓜真能～生凉。Iced watermelons relieve heat and are very refreshing.

去岁 qùsuì last year

去梯之言 qùtīzhīyán *also*"去梯言" talk upstairs with the ladder removed — confidential talk

去痛定 qùtòngdìng 〈药学〉piminodine esylate

去伪存真 qùwěi-cúnzhēn discard the fake and retain the genuine; eliminate the false and retain the true：对材料要反复鉴别，～。Check the materials repeatedly and sift the true from the false.

去污 qùwū decontamination

去污粉 qùwūfěn household cleanser; cleanser

去芜存菁 qùwú-cúnjīng get rid of the dross and keep the essence; eliminate impurities and retain the pure

去向 qùxiàng direction in which sb. or sth. has gone; whereabouts：～不明 whereabouts unknown／至今不知他的～。We don't know even now where he has gone.

去雄 qùxióng 〈植物〉emasculate; castrate

去油 qùyóu 〈化工〉remove the oil from; deoil

去杂去劣 qùzá-qùliè 〈农业〉roguing

去职 qùzhí no longer hold the post; quit the job：校长上月～。The principal (*or* president) was relieved of his post last month.

觑(覰、覻) qù 〈书面〉look; stare; gaze：偷～ steel a glance at sb. ／面面相～ look at each other in speechless despair (*or* in blank dismay); gaze at each other helplessly

see also qū

觑视 qùshì 〈书面〉look; gaze

qu

戌 qu *see*"屈戌儿" qūqur

see also xū

quān

悛 quān 〈书面〉be penitent; repent; make amends：过而不～ refuse to mend one's ways／怙恶不～ be steeped in evil and refuse to change／改～ reform; change; rectify

弮 quān 〈书面〉crossbow

棬 quān 〈书面〉drinking vessel made of wood

圈 quān ❶ circle; ring; hoop：圆～ circle／花～ wreath／橡皮～ rubber band／救生～ life belt／吐烟～ blow smoke rings／我在城里转了一～。I had a stroll round the town. ／请大家围个～坐下。Let's be seated in a circle. ❷ circle; set; coterie：他们搞小～子，以维护既得利益。They formed an inner circle to protect their vested interests. ／只有他信任的几个人才算～里的人。Only those he trusted were regarded as insiders. ❸ enclose; surround; encircle：房子四周～着栅栏。The house is enclosed by a fence. ❹ mark with a circle：把正确的答案～出来。Circle the correct answers.

see also juān; juàn

圈闭 quānbì 〈石油〉trap：地层～ stratigraphic trap／背斜～ anticli-

nal trap /～油藏 closed reservoir

圈操 quāncāo 〈体育〉hoop exercise

圈地运动 Quāndì Yùndòng enclosure movement, or enclosing of common field, carried out at various periods in England, esp. between the 12th and 14th centuries and finally in the 18th and 19th centuries

圈点 quāndiǎn ❶ punctuate (with periods or small circles) ❷ mark words and phrases for special attention with dots or small circles on the right side

圈定 quāndìng approve (the scope of work or the selection of personnel) by drawing a circle on the relevant document

圈口儿 quānkǒur calibre or size of a bracelet, a ring or any ring-like article

圈梁 quānliáng 〈建筑〉girth

圈拢 quānlong 〈方言〉❶ unite; hold together:当前最主要的是把人～起来。The most important thing at present is to hold people together. ❷ draw people over to one's side; rope in; win round:他很会～人。He is adept in winning people over.

圈弄 quānnong lay a snare; snare:这是他出的鬼点子，想～我。This is one of his tricks designed to trap me.

圈套 quāntào snare; trap; ploy:落入～ fall into a trap; play into sb.'s hands /识破～ see through a trick /做好～ 让人上钩 lay a snare for sb.; set a trap for sb.

圈椅 quānyǐ round-backed armchair

圈阅 quānyuè circle one's name on a document submitted for approval to show that one has read it; tick off one's name listed (and sometimes make comments) on a circular, notice, etc. after reading it:～文件 tick off one's name listed on a document after reading it; write down comments on a document after reading it /这个请示已经主任～。The director has read and commented on the request for instructions.

圈占 quānzhàn forcibly occupy (land, fields, etc.) by enclosing it:～大片良田 seize vast tracts of fertile farmland by enclosing them

圈子 quānzi ❶ ring; circle:孩子们围成一个～做游戏。The children formed a circle to play a game. /我到外面去兜个～就回来。I am going out for a stroll and will soon be back. /他说话爱绕～。He tends to speak in a roundabout way. ❷ circle; clique; coterie; set:不要搞小～。Don't band together to form a clique. /他与外界很少接触，生活～狭小。He has few contacts outside the small circle in which he moves.

quán

拳 quán ❶ fist:握～ clench one's fists /猜～ *mora*; finger-guessing game /赤手空～ bare-handed; unarmed /抱～ cup one hand in the other as a form of salute ❷ boxing; pugilism:打～ practise Chinese boxing /太极～ *taijiquan* (*or* t'ai chi ch'uan); shadow boxing ❸ curl; twist; warp; bend:～起腿来 bend one's legs

拳棒 quánbàng *wushu*, martial arts such as shadow boxing, club-play, etc., formerly cultivated for self-defence, now a form of physical culture:精于～ very good (*or* excellent) performer of martial arts

拳不离手，曲不离口 quán bù lí shǒu, qǔ bù lí kǒu a boxer never spends a day without practising boxing, and a singer never passes a day without practising singing — always keep in practice; practice makes perfect

拳打脚踢 quándǎ-jiǎotī cuff and kick; strike and kick; beat up:挨了别人一顿～ be beaten up; get a beating

拳匪 Quánfěi 〈旧语〉"boxer bandit", an insulting reference to people who rose against foreign aggressors before and in 1900 *see also* 义和团 Yìhétuán

拳击 quánjī boxing; pugilism:～台 boxing ring /～运动 boxing /～运动员 boxer; pugilist /～冠军 boxing champion; champion boxer

拳脚 quánjiǎo ❶ fists and feet; beat and kick:～相加 come to blows ❷ Chinese boxing:会几套～ can perform a few sets of Chinese boxing

拳捷 quánjié valiant and quick:～非凡 of outstanding valiance and nimbleness

拳派 quánpài school of boxing

拳谱 quánpǔ illustrative chart of boxing

拳曲 quánqū curl; coil; twist; bend:头发～ curly hair /树干～ twisted trunk

拳拳 quánquán *also* "惓惓" quánquán 〈书面〉earnest; sincere:情意～ sincere affection /～之意，谅蒙明察。It is my belief that you will understand my sincere intentions.

拳拳服膺 quánquán-fúyīng always bear in mind; have sincere belief in; place implicit faith in

拳师 quánshī boxing coach; pugilist

拳手 quánshǒu boxer:他是世界著名～。He is a world-famous boxer.

拳术 quánshù Chinese boxing; boxing

拳坛 quántán boxing world; *wushu* circles

拳套 quántào fixed series of skills and tricks in Chinese boxing:意拳强调以意念诱导动作，无固定招法和～。*Yi* boxing emphasizes the induced reaction of one's mind; it has no fixed skills and tricks.

拳头 quántou fist:怒气冲冲地挥动～ shake one's fist at sb. in anger

拳头产品 quántou chǎnpǐn product of good quality and competitiveness; highly competitive product; knockout product

拳头上立得人，臂膊上走得马 quántoushang lìde rén, bìbóshang zǒude mǎ *also* "拳头上走得马，臂膊上立得人"〈俗语〉decent, open, and aboveboard

拳王 quánwáng ace boxer; boxing champion

惓 quán

惓惓 quánquán *see* "拳拳" quánquán

鬈 quán ❶ curly; wavy:满头～发 one's head covered with crimps ❷ (of hair) lovely

鬈曲 quánqū 〈纺织〉crimp; crinkle; curl:～羊毛 crinkled wool

蜷(踡) quán coil (as a snake); curl up; huddle up:他胃疼得厉害，身体～作一团。He curled up, trying to mollify his terrible stomachache.

蜷伏 quánfú lie with the arms and legs drawn close to the body; curl up; huddle up:一只狗～在火炉前面。A dog lay curled up in front of the fire. /夜间，那些工人都～在草席棚子里睡觉。At night the workers slept all huddled up in a straw shed.

蜷局 quánjú 〈书面〉curl; coil; wind; twist

蜷曲 quánqū curl; coil; wind; twist:～着的毒蛇 coiled poisonous snake

蜷缩 quánsuō huddle up; roll up; curl up:小女孩儿冷得～成一团。The little girl was so cold that she huddled herself up.

蜷卧 quánwò lie with the knees drawn up

颧 quán

颧骨 quángǔ cheekbone:她～高。She has high cheekbones.

权(權) quán ❶〈书面〉counterpoise; sliding weight of a steelyard:铜～ copper sliding weight (of a steelyard) ❷〈书面〉weigh; consider:～其轻重 weigh up one thing against another; weigh the pros and cons ❸ power; authority:军～ military power /职～ powers of office; authority of office /立法～ legislative power /检察～ procuratorial power /司法～ judicial power /终审～ power of final adjudication /掌～ be in power; wield power; exercise control /越～ overstep one's authority /受～ be authorized (to do sth.) /受～有限 have limited authority /他无～作出这个决定。He is not entitled to make such a decision. ❹ right:人～ human rights /民～ people's rights; civic rights /选举～ right to vote; franchise /公民～ civil rights /居留～ right of abode; right of residence /继承～ right to inherit private property /隐私～ right to privacy /生存～ right to survival; right to life /知识产～ intellectual property right /版～ copyright /特～ privilege; prerogative ❺ advantageous or favourable position:主动～ initiative /制空～ mastery of the air; air supremacy ❻ expediency; adaptability:通～达变 adapt oneself to circumstances; be flexible ❼ tentatively; provisionally; for the time being:～代办理 act on sb.'s behalf for the time being /我岂有表演才能，～充龙套而已。I have no talent for acting. I am just standing in as a utility man. ❽ (Quán) a surname

权变 quánbiàn adaptability or flexibility in tactics; tact:长于～ be good at varying one's tactics; adopt varied tactics in varied circumstances

权便 quánbiàn expedient
权标 quánbiāo symbol of authority; sceptre; fasces
权柄 quánbǐng power; authority: 掌握～ wield power; be in the saddle / 此人掌握～后就立即排除异己。As soon as he came to power, he got rid of all those who disagreed with him.
权臣 quánchén senior court official wielding influence with the emperor
权宠 quánchǒng powerful court official in high favour with the emperor
权贵 quánguì influential officials; powers that be: 奔走于～之间 court the favour of the bigwigs
权豪 quánháo 〈旧语〉 influential and powerful officials: 不畏～ have no fear of the big shots
权衡 quánhéng weigh; balance: ～得失 weigh the gains and losses; weigh the costs and benefits / 这件事值不值得一做，行动前要慎重～。We must weigh the odds carefully before we act on this.
权衡轻重 quánhéng-qīngzhòng weigh up one thing against another; weigh the relative importance of things: 他善于从各种矛盾中～。He is good at weighing the relative importance of things in the face of all sorts of contradictions.
权奸 quánjiān wicked and powerful official who rides roughshod over the people; treacherous high official: ～柄政 evil high officials wielding state power
权力 quánlì ❶ power; authority: 国家～机关 organ of state power / 他握有很大的～。He wields tremendous power. ❷ jurisdiction: 这不是他～范围内的事。This matter does not come within his jurisdiction.
权力斗争 quánlì dòuzhēng power struggle
权力机构 quánlì jīgòu organ of power
权力结构 quánlì jiégòu power structure
权力下放 quánlì xiàfàng delegate or devolve power to the lower levels
权利 quánlì right: 公民的～ citizens' (*or* civic) rights / 基本～ basic right / 合法～ legitimate right / ～与义务 rights and obligations / 劳动者有休息的～。Labourers have the right to rest.
权利能力 quánlì nénglì ability to exercise one's rights and honour one's obligations
权略 quánlüè astuteness and resourcefulness; tactics: 有～ astute and resourceful
权门 quánmén 〈旧语〉 influential family; noble family: 依托～ attach oneself to influential people
权迷心窍 quánmíxīnqiào obsessed with lust for power
权谋 quánmóu political trickery; plotting and scheming: 此人一生好弄～。All his life he never tired of plotting and scheming.
权能 quánnéng powers and functions: 司法部有这样的～。The Ministry of Justice is invested with such powers and functions.
权钱交易 quán-qián jiāoyì deal between power and money; corruption
权且 quánqiě for the time being; as a stopgap measure: ～避避雨 take shelter from rain for a while / 死马～当作活马医。We had no choice but to treat a dead horse as if it were still alive. *or* We had no option but to do what was humanly possible to save an apparently hopeless case.
权时 quánshí ❶ temporary; expedient: 此系～措施，未能尽如人意。This is an expedient measure and cannot possibly live up to everybody's expectations. ❷ 〈书面〉 size up the situation: ～度势 take stock of the current situation
权势 quánshì power and position: 贪图～ hanker after power and position / 靠～发财 make money through influence and power
权势集团 quánshì jítuán the establishment
权术 quánshù art of political manoeuvring; political trickery; Machiavellian politics: 这个人靠耍～起家。This chap started his career by playing politics.
权数 quánshù 〈书面〉 ability to cope with difficult situations; resourcefulness: 闻此人有～，遂向其求教。They asked him for enlightenment as he was well known for his resourcefulness in all difficult situations.
权威 quánwēi ❶ authority; authoritativeness: ～著作 authoritative works / 从这里人们可以感到他的话是有～的。From this we can feel that his words carry a good deal of authority. ❷ person or thing of authority: 他是医学界的～。He is an authority in medicine.
权威人士 quánwēi rénshì authoritative person; authoritative sources; authority: 据～称 according to authoritative sources
权位 quánwèi power and position: 贪恋～ cling greedily to one's power and position
权限 quánxiàn jurisdiction; competence; terms of reference; extent of authority: 超越～ overstep or exceed one's authority; go beyond one's brief / 只要在公司法规定的经理～之内，你做什么都可以。You can do whatever you like within the limits of your managerial authority as prescribed by the corporation law. / 确定理事会的～为时尚早。It is too early to define the competence (*or* terms of reference) of the council.
权要 quányào influential officials; bigwigs: ～之臣 influential minister of the imperial court / 阿谀～ toady to high officials
权阉 quányān 〈贬义〉 powerful and influential eunuch
权宜 quányí expedient: 此系～，非永久之策。This is an expedient and by no means a permanent measure. / 这是我们的基本国策，不是一时的～。This is our basic state policy, not an act of expediency.
权宜之计 quányízhījì expedient; makeshift device; stopgap measure
权益 quányì rights and interests: 维护中国海外侨民的合法～是我们不可推卸的责任。It is our bounden duty to safeguard the legitimate rights and interests of the Chinese nationals residing abroad.
权舆 quányú 〈书面〉 ❶ sprout; germinate; shoot; bud: 百草～。All plants are beginning to sprout. ❷ inception
权欲 quányù lust for power: ～熏心 be blinded by power; be obsessed with political power / ～重是这个人的最大弱点。His greatest weakness lies in his obsession with power.
权责 quánzé rights and duties; power and responsibility: 各部门应有明确的～。The powers and responsibilities of each department should be clearly defined.
权诈 quánzhà trickery; chicanery; duplicity; craftiness: 此人很是～。This fellow is full of cunning. *or* He is very sly.
权杖 quánzhàng staff held as a symbol of power: 主教～ crosier / 国王～ sceptre

全

quán ❶ all ready; complete: 手稿残缺不～。The manuscript is fragmentary. / 资料收集得比较～。The data collected are fairly complete. ❷ keep from harm or damage; keep intact: 苟～性命于乱世 manage to survive in troubled times / 此事实难两～。It is hard to satisfy both sides in this case. ❸ whole; entire; all; full: ～世界 all over the world; the whole world / 这条铁路～长五百多公里。The railway line is more than five hundred kilometres long. ❹ wholly; entirely; completely: ～忘记了 clean forget (sth.) / ～新的设备 brand-new equipment / 孩子们～都很健康。Every child enjoys good health. / 这些诗歌我～爱读。I like to read all these poems. ❺ (Quán) a surname
全般 quánbān whole; complete; total; entire
全豹 quánbào whole picture; overall situation; thing in its entirety: 未窥～ fail to see the whole picture; be unable to grasp the overall situation; only have a limited view of sth. / 窥一斑而知～。Look at a spot on a leopard and you can visualize the whole animal. *or* One can conjure up the whole thing through seeing a part of it.
全备 quánbèi complete; perfect: 武器～ armed to the teeth; fully armed
全本 quánběn ❶ complete version of a long traditional opera ❷ unabridged copy or version (of a book, etc.)
全波段 quánbōduàn 〈无线电〉 all band; all-wave band; full range: ～接收机 all-wave receiver
全部 quánbù whole; entire; complete; full: ～力量 every ounce of one's strength / ～免税 blanket tax exemption / ～毁坏 destroy lock, stock and barrel / 赔偿～损失 fully compensate for the loss incurred / 问题已经～解决。All the problems have been resolved. / 那批产品～报废。The whole batch of products became rejects. / 他的手稿～在大火中烧毁。His manuscripts were completely destroyed in the conflagration.
全才 quáncái versatile mind; all-rounder: 文武～ be versatile in the art of war as well as government / 搞文体活动他可是个～。He is an all-rounder in organising sports and recreational activities.
全场 quánchǎng ❶ whole audience; entire house; all those present: ～起立。The entire audience rose to their feet. / ～掌声雷动。The whole house broke into thunderous applause. ❷ 〈体育〉 full-court; all-court: ～紧逼 all-court press; full-court press
全称 quánchēng full name; unabbreviated form: 英国的～是大不列

颠及北爱尔兰联合王国。The full name of Britain is the United Kingdom of Great Britain and Northern Ireland.
全程 quánchéng entire journey; whole course: 铁路～约一万公里。The whole course of the railway is about 10,000 kilometres long.
全虫 quánchóng 〈中医〉dried whole scorpion
全磁化 quáncíhuà 〈物理〉holomagnetization
全大规模集成小型计算机 quándàguīmó jíchéng xiǎoxíng jìsuànjī all-LSI minicomputer
全等 quánděng 〈数学〉congruent
全等形 quánděngxíng 〈数学〉congruent figure
全丁 quándīng male adult
全动机翼 quándòng jīyì 〈航空〉all-moving wing
全都 quándōu all; every; without exception: 你想看的书～在这儿。Here are the whole lot of books you want to read. /这些衣服～给虫咬了。These clothes are all moth-eaten.
全斗焕 Quándǒuhuàn Chon Du Hwan (1931-), army general and President of the Republic of Korea (1980-1988)
全对称 quánduìchèn 〈数学〉pantomorphia
全额 quán'é full amount: ～分期付款 instalment in full /～利润分成 share the entire profit
全额保险 quán'é bǎoxiǎn full insurance
全反射 quánfǎnshè 〈物理〉total reflection
全方位 quánfāngwèi omnidirectional; all-dimensional; all-round: ～外交 all-round diplomacy /～出击 all-round attack /～开放 open in all domains; open to all countries
全份 quánfèn complete set: ～资料 complete set of data
全封闭式电动机 quánfēngbìshì diàndòngjī 〈电工〉totally enclosed motor; fully enclosed motor
全负载 quánfùzài *also* "全负荷" full load
全副 quánfù complete; full; all: ～武装 fully armed; in full battle array; armed to the teeth /他把～精力都倾注在工作上。He channelled all his energies into his work.
全福人儿 quánfurénr *see* "全科人儿"
全个 quángè whole: 喜讯传开，～县城都沸腾起来了。When the good news spread, the whole county town was seething with excitement.
全攻全守 quángōng-quánshǒu 〈体育〉total play
全光通信 quánguāng tōngxìn all optical communication
全国 quánguó of the whole nation or country; all over the country; nation-wide; national: ～税收、财务、物价大检查 general review of taxation, finance and prices throughout the country /～哗然。The whole nation was in uproar. /～人民团结一致。The people of the country are united as one. /这种倾向波及～。This trend is spreading nationwide.
全国导弹防御系统 quánguó dǎodàn fángyù xìtǒng *also* "国家导弹防御系统"〈军事〉(US) NMD (National Missile Defense)
全国地理杂志 Quánguó Dìlǐ Zázhì (US) *National Geographic*
全国广播公司 Quánguó Guǎngbō Gōngsī (US) National Broadcasting Co. Inc. (NBC)
全国粮票 quánguó liángpiào national grain coupons, used in China in nearly four decades before abolished in the early 1990's
全国农业发展纲要 Quánguó Nóngyè Fāzhǎn Gāngyào National Programme for Agricultural Development (1956-1967)
全国人大 Quánguó Réndà (short for 全国人民代表大会) National People's Congress (NPC): ～代表 deputy to the National People's Congress; NPC deputy
全国人民代表大会 Quánguó Rénmín Dàibiǎo Dàhuì National People's Congress (NPC)
全国性 quánguóxìng nationwide; countrywide; on a national scale: ～报纸 national newspaper /～刊物 nationwide publication
全国一盘棋 quánguó yīpánqí coordinate all the activities of the nation like moves in a chess game; take the overall situation in the country into account: ～，全省也应该一盘棋。Like the whole nation, the province must coordinate its moves as in a game of chess.
全国证券交易商协会自动报价系统 Quánguó Zhèngquàn Jiāoyìshāng Xiéhuì Zìdòng Bàojià Xìtǒng (US) National Association of Security Dealers Active Quotations (NASDAQ)
全国政协 Quánguó Zhèngxié (short for 中国人民政治协商会议全国委员会) National Committee of the Chinese People's Political Consultative Conference (CPPCC): ～委员 member of the national committee of CPPCC
全国知事会 Quánguó Zhīshìhuì (Japan) National Governors' Council
全乎 quánhu 〈口语〉complete; all in readiness: 这商店虽小，货物倒是～的。The shop is small but it has a full array of goods in stock.
全会 quánhuì plenary meeting; plenary session; plenum: 十四届一中～ First Plenary Session of the Fourteenth Central Committee of the Party
全活 quánhuó ❶〈书面〉rescue or save lives: 赈济灾民，～无数 relieve the people in stricken areas and save many lives ❷ whole process of a job in certain service trades: 她很快掌握理发的～。She soon mastered all the skills of hairdressing.
全集 quánjí complete works; collected works: 《孙中山～》*Collected Works of Dr. Sun Yat-sen* /《莎士比亚～》*Complete Works of Shakespeare*
全家福 quánjiāfú ❶ photograph of the whole family ❷ hotchpotch (an assortment of delicacies as a dish in a Chinese dinner)
全歼 quánjiān destroy completely; annihilate: ～残敌 wipe out the enemy remnants
全金元词 Quán Jīn-Yuán Cí *Quan Jin Yuan Ci* or *Complete Collection of Jin and Yuan Ci Poetry*, published in 1979
全景 quánjǐng panorama; complete view; whole scene: 颐和园～ full view of the Summer Palace /～小说 panoramic novel
全景宽银幕电影 quánjǐng kuānyínmù diànyǐng cinepanoramic
全景雷达 quánjǐng léidá 〈电信〉panoramic radar
全景摄影机 quánjǐng shèyǐngjī panoramic camera
全局 quánjú general or overall situation; situation as a whole: 关系～ concern the overall situation /地区的利益应该服从国家的～利益。Local interests should be subordinate to the overall interests of the nation. /战争的～不乐观。The war situation as a whole is not at all encouraging. /这个地区的经济发展关乎～。The economic development of the locality is a matter of nationwide significance.
全军 quánjūn ❶ of the whole or entire army; throughout the army: ～处于战备状态。The whole army was in a state of combat readiness. /他的英勇事迹是～指战员的光辉典范。His heroic deed is a shining example for all the officers and men of the army. /他的讲话在～引起巨大的反响。His speech evoked great repercussions throughout the army. ❷〈书面〉preserve military strength: 用兵之法，～为上。In the art of war nothing is more important than the preservation of military strength.
全军覆没 quánjūn-fùmò ❶ total destruction of an army; complete annihilation: 前锋的错误行动几乎导致～。The wrong move of the vanguard all but led to the débâcle of the army. ❷ be thoroughly trounced: 本队在全国足球联赛中场场都输，～。Having lost every game, our team was thoroughly trounced in the national league football matches.
全开 quánkāi 〈印刷〉standard-sized sheet: 一张～的挂历 full-size wall calender
全科医生 quánkē yīshēng general practitioner
全科 quánke 〈方言〉complete: 这里又卖针线，又卖副食，东西真叫～。The store sells not only needles and threads, but also groceries. They do have a complete inventory here.
全科人儿 quánkerénr *also* "全福人儿"; "全乎人儿" one (usually a woman) whose parents, spouse and children are all living
全口托牙 quánkǒu tuōyá complete denture; full mouth (denture)
全劳动力 quánláodònglì *also* "全劳力" able-bodied worker (esp. on the farm)
全力 quánlì exert all one's strength; go all out; spare no effort: 我们将～推销这个新产品。We will go all out to boost the new product. /我们将竭尽～防止病人情况进一步恶化。We will do all we can to prevent the patient's condition from further deterioration.
全力爬升 quánlì páshēng 〈航空〉full climb
全力以赴 quánlìyǐfù go all out; spare no effort; do one's utmost: 为了提前完工，我们将～。We'll exert ourselves to the full to complete the project ahead of time.
全麻 quánmá 〈医学〉general anaesthesia
全麦 quánmài whole wheat: ～面包 whole wheat bread
全毛虫 quánmáochóng 〈生物〉holotrich
全貌 quánmào complete picture; full view: 了解事情的～ get a complete picture of the matter /站在山顶上可以看到城市的～。Standing on the top of the hill, you can get a panoramic view of the whole city.
全酶 quánméi 〈生化〉holoenzyme
全美橄榄球联合会 Quán Měi Gǎnlǎnqiú Liánhéhuì (US) All

America Football Conference (AAFC)

全面 quánmiàn overall; all-round; general; comprehensive: ~安排 overall arrangement / ~裁军 general disarmament / ~战争 full-scale war / ~发展 all-round development; develop in an all-round way / ~质量管理〈经济〉total quality control (TQC); total quality management (TQM) / ~落实知识分子政策 fully implement the policy towards the intellectuals / 他的发言很~。His speech covered all the points. / 我们向来主张~禁止和彻底销毁核武器。We have always stood for complete prohibition and thorough destruction of nuclear weapons. / 我们将提出一个~建议供你考虑。We'll put forward a comprehensive proposal for your consideration. / 这两座城市间修建一条高速公路的工程正在~展开。The construction of an expressway between the two cities is in full swing.

全苗 quánmiáo full-stand: 保证棉花~ ensure a full stand of cotton shoots

全民 quánmín whole people; entire people; all the people: ~健身运动 nationwide body-building campaign / ~动员 mobilization of the whole nation; general mobilization / ~皆兵 entire nation in arms; every citizen a soldier / 法律常识要普及到~。The elementary knowledge of law should be made a must to every citizen.

全民党 quánmíndǎng party of the entire people

全民国家 quánmín guójiā state of the whole people

全民所有制 quánmín suǒyǒuzhì ownership by the whole people

全名 quánmíng full name: 请写下~。Please give your full name.

全能 quánnéng all-round; universal: ~冠军 all-round champion / ~体操比赛 combined exercises / ~输血者 universal blood donor

全能加速器 quánnéng jiāsùqì 〈物理〉omnitron

全能炉 quánnénglú 〈冶金〉all-case furnace

全能运动 quánnéng yùndòng 〈体育〉all-round athletic event: 五项~ pentathlon / 十项~ decathlon

全年 quánnián for the whole year; annual; yearly: ~收入 annual income or earnings / ~支出 annual expenditure / ~雨量 yearly rainfall; annual precipitation / ~平均气温 mean annual temperature / 那个国家1968年~财政赤字达到惊人的数字。That country's financial deficit for 1968 reached staggering figures.

全盘 quánpán overall; comprehensive; wholesale: ~计划 overall plan / ~肯定 wholesale approval / ~否定 total negation / ~否认 catagorical denial / ~西化 wholesale Westernization; all-out Westernization / ~考虑 give comprehensive consideration / ~接受 full and uncritical acceptance / 叫他掌握~。Put him in overall charge.

全票 quánpiào ❶ full-price ticket ❷ all the votes in an election: 他以~当选为代表。He was unanimously elected a representative.

全频道 quánpíndào all-channel: ~电视机 all-channel TV set

全勤 quánqín regular or full attendance during a certain period: 他在冬训中出~受到表扬。He was praised for his regular attendance in the winter training period.

全勤奖 quánqínjiǎng reward for full attendance; full attendence bonus

全球 quánqiú whole world; entire globe: 誉满~ be of world renown / 名震~ be famous all over the world / ~战略 global strategy / ~气候变暖 global warming / ~投影地图 globular chart / ~主义 globalism / ~环境 global environment / ~环境监测系统 global environmental monitoring system / ~大气研究 global atmospheric research / ~数据处理系统 global data-processing system / 粮食和农业~资料和预警系统 global information and early warning system on food and agriculture / ~观测系统 global observing system / 海洋环境污染~调查 global investigation of pollution in the marine environment / ~电讯系统 global telecommunication system / ~天气实验 global weather experiment

全球定位系统 quánqiú dìngwèi xìtǒng GPS (global positioning system)

全球化 quánqiúhuà globalization

全球通信系统 quánqiú tōngxìn xìtǒng Globecom (Global Communication System)

全球移动通信系统 quánqiú yídòng tōngxìn xìtǒng global system for mobile communication (GSM)

全权 quánquán full powers; full authority; plenary powers: 授以~ vest sb. with full authority / 特命~大使 ambassador plenipotentiary and extraordinary / 特命~公使 envoy extraordinary and minister plenipotentiary / 由你~处理。You have full authority to act as you think fit. *or* You may act entirely on your own. *or* You have a carte blanche to act.

全权代表 quánquán dàibiǎo plenipotentiary

全权证书 quánquán zhèngshū full powers

全然 quánrán wholly; completely; entirely: 他这话并非~没有根据。What he said is not entirely without foundation. / 我~不了解情况，怎么发表意见? As I am completely in the dark about the matter, how can I hazard an opinion? / 他~不考虑个人得失。He gives no thought at all to his personal gain or loss.

全人 quánrén 〈书面〉❶ sage; perfect man ❷ able-bodied person

全日本航空公司 Quán Rìběn Hángkōng Gōngsī (Japan) All Nippon Airway (ANA)

全日制 quánrìzhì full-time: ~学校 full-time school / ~教育 full-time schooling

全色盲 quánsèmáng 〈医学〉total colour blindness; achromatopsia

全色片 quánsèpiàn *also* "全色胶片"〈摄影〉panchromatic film

全色乳剂 quánsè rǔjì 〈摄影〉panchromatic emulsion

全色摄影 quánsè shèyǐng holography

全色素 quánsèsù holochrome

全身 quánshēn ❶ of the whole body; all over the body: ~像 full-length picture / 吓得~发抖 tremble with fear / ~是汗 sweat all over / 使出~的力气 use all one's energy / 我路上碰到阵雨，~湿透。I was caught in a shower and got soaked to the skin. ❷〈书面〉protect one's body; preserve oneself: ~远祸 stay away from danger to protect oneself

全身麻醉 quánshēn mázuì 〈医学〉general anaesthesia

全身水肿 quánshēn shuǐzhǒng 〈医学〉anasarca

全身萎缩 quánshēn wěisuō 〈医学〉pantatrophia

全神贯注 quánshén-guànzhù absorbed or engrossed in; wrapped up in; with great concentration: ~地听讲 listen to a lecture attentively (*or* with rapt attention) / ~地进行实验 immersed in one's experiment / ~地下棋 absorbed in playing chess / 她~地思考烦扰她的许多问题。She was preoccupied with the problems that had been plaguing her.

全胜 quánshèng win all-round victory; be completely triumphant: 不获~，决不收兵。We'll never stop fighting until total victory is assured. / 这次女子排球赛，我们七场~，荣获冠军。Our team won all seven games in the women's volley-ball tournament and chalked up the championship.

全盛 quánshèng flourishing; in full bloom; in the prime; at the zenith: 唐代~时期在开元年间。The Tang Dynasty was at its zenith during the reign of Emperor Li Longji (李隆基, r. 713-741).

全食 quánshí total eclipse: 日~ total solar eclipse / 月~ total lunar eclipse / ~带 path of total eclipse; belt (*or* zone) of totality

全始全终 quánshǐ-quánzhōng see sth. through; stick it out; not stop until sth. is completed: 办事情务要~。Be sure to keep at it from start to finish no matter what you do. / 这个工作不容易，但是既然你已经开始，就应当~。The job is not easy, but since you have started, you will have to see it through.

全视图 quánshìtú full view; general view; panorama

全数 quánshù total amount; whole sum: 付款~收到。The payment was received in full. / 实到人数不足会员~的三分之一。Less than one-third of the membership was present.

全数字 quánshùzì all-digital: ~电视广播 all-digital TV broadcast / ~时代 all-digital age

全宋词 Quán Sòng Cí *Quan Song Ci* or *Complete Collection of Song Ci Poetry*, first published in 1940 with an enlarged edition issued in 1965

全速 quánsù full or maximum speed; top gear: ~后退 (of a ship) full speed astern

全损 quánsǔn total loss: ~险〈经济〉total loss only (TLO)

全瘫 quántān 〈医学〉pamplegia; panplegia

全唐诗 Quán Táng Shī *Quan Tang Shi* or *Complete Collection of Tang Poetry*, compiled by the order of Emperor Kangxi of the Qing Dynasty and completed in 1706

全唐文 Quán Táng Wén *Quan Tang Wen* or *Complete Collection of Tang Prose*, compiled by the order of Emperor Jiaqing of the Qing Dynasty and completed in 1814

全套 quántào complete set: 引进~设备 import whole sets of equipment

全体 quántǐ ❶ all; entire; total; whole: ~教职员工 entire teaching, administrative and supporting staff / ~代表 all the representatives / ~会议 plenary session / ~辞职 resign en bloc (*or* en masse) / ~起立默哀。All stood in silent tribute. / ~起立，向演讲人长

时间鼓掌欢呼。The speaker was given a long standing ovation. /要避免片面性，要看到事物的～。We should take every aspect of the matter into consideration and avoid one-sided views. ❷ all over the body: ～透湿 wet all over; soaked to the skin

全天候 quántiānhòu all-weather: ～公路 all-weather highway/～飞机 all-weather aircraft /～导弹 all-weather missile /～导航 all-weather navigation /～朋友 all-weather friend; friend, (come) rain or shine

全通网络 quántōng wǎngluò 〈计算机〉all-pass network

全托 quántuō *also* "整托" zhěngtuō boarding nursery; total child-care: ～托儿所 boarding nursery /这所幼儿园可以～。Children can board in this nursery. *or* This is a boarding nursery. /我的孩子进日托而不是～，每晚都要接他回来。My child goes to a day-nursery, not a boarding one; I have to collect him every evening.

全脱氧钢 quántuōyǎnggāng 〈冶金〉fully killed steel; fully deoxidized steel

全微分 quánwēifēn 〈数学〉complete differential; total differential

全文 quánwén full text: ～转载 be reprinted in full /～发表 publish in full /～记录 verbatim record /这是个节录，我要看一看～。This is only an excerpt; I would like to read the full text.

全无心肝 quánwúxīngān heartless: 这些人～，什么都做得出。These people are heartless, capable of anything.

全武行 quánwǔháng ❶ (in Beijing opera) big-scale acrobatic fighting ❷ gang fight; free-for-all: 堂堂的董事会上竟然演出了～。There was a free-for-all at the august board meeting.

全息 quánxī holographic: ～激光器 hololaser /～录音机 holophone /～透镜 hololens /～信息存储 holographical information accumulation (*or* storage)

全息电影 quánxī diànyǐng holographic movie

全息摄影 quánxī shèyǐng holography

全息术 quánxīshù holography

全息图 quánxītú holograph; hologram

全息医疗 quánxī yīliáo 〈医学〉holotherapy (application of holographic technology to the diagnosis and treatment of diseases)

全息照相 quánxī zhàoxiàng hologram: ～机 holoscope; holocamera /～存储器 holographic memory

全线 quánxiàn ❶ on all fronts; all along the line: ～展开猛烈战斗。Fierce battle is going on all along the line. /我军～反攻。Our troops are launching a counter-attack (*or* counter-offensive) on all fronts. ❷ whole line; entire length: 这条地铁已～通车。The entire underground railway line has been opened to traffic. /地道～超过五千米。The whole length of the tunnel exceeds 5,000 metres.

全向弹头 quánxiàng dàntóu 〈军事〉omnidirectional warhead

全向导航 quánxiàng dǎoháng 〈航海〉omnirange; omnidirectional range

全向天线 quánxiàng tiānxiàn 〈无线电〉omnidirectional antenna; nondirectional antenna

全蝎 quánxiē whole scorpion (as medicine or food): 炸～ deep-fried whole scorpions

全心全意 quánxīn-quányì wholeheartedly; with all one's heart; heart and soul: ～为人民服务首先要有无私奉献的精神。Wholehearted service to the people presupposes a spirit of selfless dedication. /半个世纪以来，他～地研究中国医学。For half a century, he has engaged, heart and soul, into the study of Chinese medicine.

全心炎 quánxīnyán 〈医学〉pancarditis

全新 quánxīn entirely new; brand-new: ～的面貌 entirely new look

全新世 Quánxīnshì 〈地质〉Recent Epoch; Holocene Epoch

全休 quánxiū complete rest: 医嘱～一个月。The doctor prescribes a month's good rest.

全音 quányīn 〈音乐〉whole tone

全音符 quányīnfú 〈音乐〉whole note; semibreve

全印刷电路 quányìnshuā diànlù 〈电子〉all print circuit

全英锦标赛 Quán Yīng Jǐnbiāosài All-England Championships, or Wimbledon Championships, the oldest lawn tennis tournament since 1877 in Wimbledon, a suburb of London

全优 quányōu excellent in all aspects; of all-round excellence: ～工程 all-excellent project /他功课成绩～。He got "excellent" in all subjects. *or* He got straight aces in his studies.

全元散曲 Quán Yuán Sǎnqǔ *Quan Yuan Sanqu* or *Complete Collection of Yuan Sanqu Songs*, published in 1964

全员 quányuán entire staff; all members: 各企业～培训取得了很好成绩。Good results have been reaped in the training of the entire staff in various enterprises.

全员劳动生产率 quányuán láodòng shēngchǎnlǜ overall labour productivity

全运会 quányùnhuì (short for 全国运动会) national games

全知全能 quánzhī-quánnéng *also* "全智全能" all knowing and all powerful; omniscient and omnipotent: 只有上帝才能～。Only God can be omniscient and omnipotent.

全脂奶粉 quánzhī nǎifěn whole milk powder

全自动 quánzìdòng fully automatic: ～电镀〈冶金〉fully automatic plating /～焊接〈冶金〉fully automatic arc welding

痊

quán fully recover from an illness

痊愈 quányù be fully recovered: 祝你早日～。I hope you'll be well again soon.

诠

quán 〈书面〉❶ expound; annotate; provide a gloss; interpret: ～明辞义 clarify semantic implications ❷ reason; logic; truth: 真～ truth

诠次 quáncì 〈书面〉❶ arrange the order; put in order: 以优劣为～ arrange the order in terms of quality /～不精 inaccurate order arrangement ❷ organize ideas properly in a speech or a piece of writing: 辞无～ incoherent writing or speech

诠度 quánduó weigh; balance: ～众寡 consider a problem or situation in terms of numerical superiority or inferiority

诠释 quánshì annotation; explanatory notes; glossary: 唐诗～ Tang poems edited with annotations; annotated edition of Tang poems

诠注 quánzhù edit with notes and commentary

荃

quán aromatic or fragrant plant

荃察 quánchá 〈套语〉your esteemed approval or understanding

醛

quán 〈化学〉aldehyde

醛聚合物 quánjùhéwù aldehyde polymer

醛酸 quánsuān aldehydic acid

醛糖 quántáng aldose

醛脂 quánzhī aldehydo-ester

辁

quán 〈书面〉❶ wheel without spokes ❷ shallow; superficial; limited: ～才 limited ability; superficial knowledge

筌

quán 〈书面〉bamboo trap for fish: 得鱼而忘～ forget the trap after catching fish — forget the means by which the end is attained; forget the things or conditions which bring one success

铨

quán 〈书面〉❶ choose; select: *see* "～叙" ❷ estimate the quality or quantity of sth.; weigh; balance: ～度利弊 weigh the advantages and disadvantages; weigh the pros and cons

铨衡 quánhéng 〈书面〉❶ weighing apparatus; weighing machine ❷ judge; gauge: ～人才 judge a person

铨叙 quánxù 〈旧语〉check sb.'s qualifications when making an official appointment; examine officials' credentials so as to fix their grades and ranks

铨叙司 Quánxùsī (HK) (prior to 1 July 1997) Secretary of Civil Service

铨选 quánxuǎn 〈旧语〉select and appoint officials according to rules and regulations

泉

quán ❶ spring: 清～ crystal-clear spring /甘～ sweet spring water /喷～ fountain /温～ hot spring ❷ mouth of a spring ❸ ancient term for coin: ～币 ancient coin ❹ (Quán) a surname

泉华 quánhuá 〈地质〉sinter: ～丘 sinter cone /～沉积 sinter deposit

泉流 quánliú stream formed by spring; spring-fed stream

泉路 quánlù nether world

泉瀑 quánpù fall formed by a spring flowing down from a height

泉壤 quánrǎng *also* "泉下"〈书面〉place where one is buried after death; grave

泉石膏肓 quánshí-gāohuāng be intoxicated with springs and rocks — have passionate love for beautiful scenery

泉世 quánshì *also* "黄泉" huángquán 〈书面〉 nether world; Hades
泉水 quánshuǐ spring water; spring: 矿～ mineral water
泉台 quántái *see* "泉世"
泉下 quánxià in the nether world: 死者有知，～亦不瞑目。If he knew all this, he would turn in his grave.
泉眼 quányǎn mouth of a spring; spring
泉涌 quányǒng gush out like a fountain: 泪如～ tears well up like a fountain; weep copiously
泉源 quányuán ❶ fountainhead; springhead; wellspring ❷ source: 力量的～ source of strength / 生命的～ source of life / 生活是作家创作的～。Life is the wellspring of literary creation for writers.

鳈

quán 〈动物〉 *quan*, a small fish of the carp family, indigenous in eastern China

quǎn

犬

quǎn dog: 猎～ hunting dog; hound / 牧～ shepherd dog; sheep dog / 警～ police dog / 军～ police dog for military use / 家～ domestic dog / 鹰～ falcons and hounds; lackeys; hired thugs
犬齿 quǎnchǐ canine tooth
犬科动物 quǎnkē dòngwù canine
犬马 quǎnmǎ dog or horse — used by courtiers to refer to themselves before the sovereign
犬马之劳 quǎnmǎzhīláo serve faithfully like a dog or horse: 敢不效～。I'm perfectly willing to offer my humble service.
犬儒 quǎnrú cynic: ～主义 cynicism
犬牙 quǎnyá ❶ canine tooth ❷ fang (of a dog)
犬牙交错 quǎnyá-jiāocuò jigsaw-like; jagged; interlocking: 敌我～。Our troops and the enemy formed a jagged, interlocking pattern. / 两国疆界～。The border-line between the two countries zigzags. / ～的战争，在历史上是不少的。There have been many wars of a jig-saw pattern in history. / 路两边是～的石块。The path is flanked on either side by jagged rocks.
犬牙式砌合法 quǎnyáshì qìhéfǎ 〈建筑〉 dog's tooth
犬子 quǎnzǐ 〈谦词〉 my son

畎

quǎn 〈书面〉 ditch on a farm or in the field
畎亩 quǎnmǔ 〈书面〉 field; farmland

绻

quǎn *see* "缱绻" qiǎnquǎn

quàn

券

quàn certificate; ticket; voucher: 奖～ lottery ticket / 礼～ gift voucher / 债～ bond; debenture / 入场～ admission ticket
see also xuàn

劝(勸)

quàn ❶ talk (sb.) round by reasoning; try to persuade; advise; urge: 良言相～ try to talk sb. round by reasoning / 我～他不要酗酒。I advised him to refrain from immoderate drinking. *or* I urged him not to drink so much. / 我怎么～他也不听。He turned a deaf ear to whatever I had to say. / 你去～～他，不要太伤心了。Please go and talk to (*or* console) him. He must not be over-grieved. ❷ encourage; foster: *see* "～善"
劝导 quàndǎo persuade; advise; exhort: 经过再三～，他终于改邪归正了。After repeated exhortations, we succeeded in making him turn over a new leaf. / ～得法，人家才听得进去。If you want anybody to listen to you, you have to go about it in the right way.
劝告 quàngào advise; urge; exhort: 我多次～他不要轻信谣言。I have advised him many times not to give any credence to rumours. / 他从不听别人的～。He never cares to take anybody's advice. / 听我的～，赶快戒烟，作个胸透。Take my tip; stop smoking and have your chest X-rayed.
劝和 quànhé mediate; make peace: 向交战双方耐心～ mediate patiently between the two warring parties
劝化 quànhuà ❶〈佛教〉 urge people to do good ❷ solicit donations for a temple; collect alms
劝驾 quànjià urge or try to persuade (sb. to accept a post or an invitation): 虽然～的人不少，但他执意不肯就职。He flatly refused to accept the position despite many attempts to persuade him to do so.
劝架 quànjià try to reconcile quarrelling parties; try to stop a fist fight; mediate: 两个醉汉动起手来，许多人都来～。Many people tried to separate the two drunkards who had come to blows.
劝谏 quànjiàn (usually of officials in relation to the emperor) exhort; advise
劝教 quànjiào admonish and give guidance: 接受老人的～ accept the exhortation and guidance of the elders
劝解 quànjiě ❶ mollify; allay: 经过大家～，他想通了。He came round after listening to our words of solace. ❷ mediate (as in a fight or quarrel); bring people together: 她闹得太凶了，我只得上去～。She made such a scene that I had to step over and try to calm her down.
劝戒 quànjiè admonish; exhort; expostulate: 我们都～他不要鲁莽从事。We all admonished him against any rash action.
劝进 quànjìn 〈旧语〉 make a formal appeal to a powerful minister or general coveting the throne to declare himself king or emperor: ～表 letter of appeal to a powerful minister to ascend the throne
劝酒 quànjiǔ urge sb. (usu. a guest) to drink more (at a banquet)
劝捐 quànjuān urge sb. to donate
劝勉 quànmiǎn admonish and encourage: 望着她那郁郁的脸色，我总想说两句～的话。Looking at her joyless face, I felt like saying a few words to encourage her.
劝募 quànmù solicit contributions
劝善 quànshàn encourage people to do good deeds: 惩恶～ punish evils and encourage virtue / ～规过 promote good and criticize wrong
劝说 quànshuō exhort; admonish; advise: 我只得耐着性子反复～。I had to patiently repeat my exhortations to him. *or* I had to make repeated patient efforts to bring him back to his senses.
劝慰 quànwèi comfort; console; solace: 大家千方百计地～她。They comforted her in every possible way.
劝降 quànxiáng try to induce (the enemy) to capitulate: 他们向敌军～。They tried to induce the enemy to lay down their arms.
劝学 quànxué exhort people to study; encourage learning
劝业场 quànyèchǎng *also* "劝工场" 〈旧语〉 bazaar where general merchandise is sold
劝诱 quànyòu induce; bring round; prevail upon: 老师～他走上了正道。His teacher guided him on to the right course.
劝谕 quànyù gently try to persuade; plead tactfully: ～他们改邪归正。Urge them tactfully to give up vice and return to virtue.
劝止 quànzhǐ *see* "劝阻"
劝阻 quànzǔ advise sb. to refrain from; dissuade: 极力～孩子不要吸烟 make every effort to dissuade one's child from smoking; exert oneself to talk one's child out of smoking / 他们不听～，一意孤行。They were bent on acting wilfully despite repeated exhortations.

quē

阙

quē 〈书面〉 ❶ fault; error; mistake: ～失 mistake; fault ❷ *see* "缺" quē ❸ (Quē) a surname
see also què
阙如 quērú 〈书面〉 deficient; yet to be provided: 语言实验室内许多必要仪器尚付～。Much of the necessary equipment has yet to be provided for the language laboratory.
阙文 quēwén omissions or missing parts (in a book); hiatus (in a text)
阙疑 quēyí leave a question open; reserve judgment for the time being: 多闻～ be well-read and always ready to leave a question open

炔

quē 〈化学〉 alkyne: 乙～ acetylene
see also Guì
炔雌醇 quēcíchún 〈药物〉 ethinyloestradiol
炔烃 quētīng 〈化学〉 alkyne

缺

quē ❶ be short; be deficient; lack: ～钱 be short of money; lack money / ～肥 fertilizer deficiency / 这个年头好诗比较～。Good poetry is comparatively rare nowadays. / 我们～他不行。We cannot dispense with him. / ～医少药的现象在某些边远地区仍是很普

遍的。A dearth of doctors and medicine is still common in some remote areas. ❷ with parts missing; incomplete; imperfect: 完美无～ flawless; without blemish; perfect / 抱残守～ cherish the outmoded and stick to the outworn — cling to bygone values / 这本书～两页。Two pages are missing from this book. / 稿子残～不全，没有多少价值。The manuscript is too fragmentary to be of any value. ❸ not present; absent: 他～了半天工。He was absent from work for half a day. ❹ unfilled position; vacancy; opening: 还有一个空～。There is still one vacancy.

缺编 quēbiān understaffed: 这所学校教职员工严重～。The school is badly understaffed.

缺蟾 quēchán 〈书面〉 waning moon: ～西坠。The waning moon is setting in the west.

缺档 quēdàng (of goods) be out of stock; be in short supply; be understocked

缺德 quēdé wicked; mean; vicious; mischievous: ～话 vicious words / ～事 sth. mean; mean trick / ～鬼 rascal; mischief / 他真～，背后使绊子。It was wicked of him to hit people below the belt (*or* stab people in the back). / 你不觉得这事办得～? Don't you feel it was mean to do that?

缺德少才 quēdé-shǎocái have neither ability nor virtue: 这种～的人不可重用。People with neither ability nor virtue are not to be given positions of responsibility.

缺点 quēdiǎn shortcoming; defect; weakness; failing: 正视～ take one's shortcomings seriously / 掩饰～ gloss over one's defect / 你这个人的～是有时太固执。One weakness of yours is that you are sometimes too stubborn. / 没有没～的人。No person is entirely impeccable. *or* Nobody is perfect.

缺短 quēduǎn shortage; lack; deficiency

缺额 quē'é vacancy: 这个公司的公关人员还有～。There are still some vacancies for public relations in the company.

缺乏 quēfá be deficient; be short of; be wanting in; lack: ～营养 lack nutrition; be deficient in nutrition / ～经验 have little experience; be inexperienced / ～了解 lack understanding / ～积极性 be wanting in initiative / ～感情 indifferent; cold; unsympathetic; unfeeling / ～说服力 not convincing enough; not persuasive enough / ～生命力 lack vitality; be lifeless / ～语言基本功 show an inadequate grasp of the fundamentals of the language / ～有经验的人手 be in want of experienced personnel

缺分 quēfen 〈旧语〉 vacancy (of official position)

缺钙 quēgài 〈医学〉 acalcerosis; calcium deficiency: ～症 calcifames; acalcerosis / 这小孩～。The child is deficient in calcium. *or* The child suffers from acalcerosis.

缺憾 quēhàn imperfection; disappointment; regret: 这篇文章有新意，但文字稍嫌粗糙，这也是一种～。The essay has a fresh approach, but is not refined enough in language, which is a pity.

缺货 quēhuò be in short supply; be understocked: 您要买的这种鞋目前～。The kind of shoes you want are out of stock. / 新鲜西红柿冬天～。Fresh tomatoes are in short supply in winter.

缺斤短两 quējīn-duǎnliǎng *also* "缺斤少两" give short measure or weight: 这家商店～，欺骗顾客。Customers are cheated by the shop giving short measure.

缺刻 quēkè (of leaves) incision: ～叶 incised leaf / ～翅 notch wing

缺课 quēkè be absent from class; miss a class: ～不少 miss many lessons / 很少～ seldom miss a class

缺口 quēkǒu ❶ breach; gap; crack: 杯子边上的～ broken edge of a cup / 大浪在海堤上冲出一个～。The huge waves made a breach in the sea wall. / 闸门有个～。There is a gap in the floodgate. ❷ (of funds, materials, etc.) gap; shortfall: 科研经费还有～。There is still a shortfall in the funding for scientific research. ❸ 〈机械〉 notch

缺口分析 quēkǒu fēnxī 〈经济〉 gap analysis

缺粮户 quēliánghù grain-deficient household

缺漏 quēlòu gaps and omissions: 这份名单有若干～。The list of names has a few omissions.

缺略 quēlüè incomplete; imperfect; deficient: 此书所载史实，时有～。The historical facts stated in the book are more often than not incomplete.

缺门 quēmén gap (in a branch of learning, etc.): 我们在高科技方面的～尚多。We still have many gaps in the field of high technology.

缺欠 quēqiàn ❶ shortcoming; defect; weakness; drawback: 计划虽然大体上可行，仍不无～。The plan is on the whole feasible, but there is still room for improvement. ❷ lack; be deficient in: 由于经验～，他没有完成任务。He failed in his mission for lack of experience.

缺勤 quēqín absence from duty or work: 因病～ be absent on grounds of ill health

缺勤率 quēqínlǜ absence or absentee rate: ～高达百分之三十五。Absenteeism was as high as 35%.

缺如 quērú be wanting; have yet to be provided: 规章制度尚付～。Rules and regulations are wanting.

缺三短四 quēsān-duǎnsì incomplete; fragmentary: ～的桌椅 desks and chairs with missing parts

缺少 quēshǎo lack; be short of: ～技术干部 be short of technical personnel / ～必要的条件 lack necessary conditions / ～雨水 have low rainfall / 不可～的支持 indispensable support

缺失 quēshī defect; flaw; drawback; shortcoming

缺市 quēshì (of certain goods) in short supply in the market: 改变鸡蛋供应的～情况 remedy the short supply of eggs in the market

缺损 quēsǔn ❶ damaged; torn ❷ 〈医学〉 lack or underdevelopment of a certain part or organ of the human body; physiological defect: 先天～ congenital defect; birth defect / 后天～ acquired defect

缺铁性贫血 quētiěxìng pínxuè 〈医学〉 iron-deficiency anemia; nutritional hypochromic anemia

缺位 quēwèi ❶ (of a high post) fall vacant: 总统～的时候，由副总统接任总统的职位。When the presidency of the Republic becomes vacant, the Vice-President shall assume the post. ❷ vacant post: 他毛遂自荐，补上了小学教师的～。He offered himself for the job as a primary school teacher to fill the vacancy.

缺席 quēxí absent; not present: 借故～ be absent with an excuse; beg off / 受～裁判 〈法律〉 suffer a default / 今天会议有三人～。Three people are absent from today's meeting.

缺席判决 quēxí pànjué judgement by default

缺席审判 quēxí shěnpàn 〈法律〉 trial by default

缺席投票 quēxí tóupiào absentee vote or ballot

缺陷 quēxiàn defect; shortcoming; fault; blemish: 这花瓶有个～。The vase has a blemish. / 很难补救生理上的～。It is very difficult to remedy a physical defect. / 不必掩饰工作上的～。There is no need to cover up the shortcomings in your work. / 耳聋是一种严重的～。Deafness is a serious handicap.

缺陷心理学 quēxiàn xīnlǐxué defect psychology

缺心少肺 quēxīn-shǎofèi lack ingenuity and imagination: 他～的，往后您得多给出点儿主意。He is not very resourceful. I hope you will give him advice from time to time.

缺心眼儿 quēxīnyǎnr ❶ lack intelligence; be scatterbrained: 他这个人～，您多指教他。You should give him the benefit of your guidance; he is so simple-minded. ❷ retarded; mentally deficient

缺血性坏死 quēxuèxìng huàisǐ 〈医学〉 ischemic necrosis

缺氧 quēyǎng 〈医学〉 oxygen deficiency; oxygen deficit

缺氧病 quēyǎngbìng 〈医学〉 anoxia

缺氧性脑病 quēyǎngxìng nǎobìng 〈医学〉 hypoxic encephalopathy

缺氧血 quēyǎngxuè 〈医学〉 anoxaemia

缺嘴 quēzuǐ 〈方言〉 ❶ harelip ❷ with one's appetite for food unsatisfied; greedy: 这孩子～，看见什么都要吃。The child was so greedy that he would eat anything in sight. / 干重活儿，别缺着嘴。Don't let yourself go hungry while you are doing heavy work.

qué

瘸 qué 〈口语〉 lame; (walk) with a limp: 摔～了腿 go lame in the leg after sustaining a fall or injury / 一～一拐 walk with a limp; limp; hobble

瘸腿 quétuǐ lame: 他那条～拖累了他。He suffered a great deal from being lame.

瘸子 quézi 〈口语〉 lame person; cripple

què

阙 què ❶ watchtower on either side of a palace gate: 城～ watchtower on either side of a city gate ❷ imperial palace: 宫～ imperial palace ❸ stone carvings erected in front of a temple or tomb

see also quē

阕 què ❶〈书面〉end：乐～。The music ended. ❷〈量词〉(a) *used in a song or ci poem*：一～新词 a new *ci* poem (b) stanza of a *ci* poem：这首词分为上～和下～。This *ci* poem is divided into an upper stanza and a lower stanza.

悫（慤、愨） què 〈书面〉honest；sincere：诚～ sincere

却[1]（卻） què ❶ fall back；retreat：敌军连夜退～。The enemy fell back in retreat under the cover of night. ❷ drive back；beat back；repulse：～敌数百里 drive the enemy back for several hundred *li* ❸ refuse；decline；reject，turn down：情不可～ can hardly decline sb.'s kind offer ❹ lose；get rid of：冷～ cool off /忘～ forget /失～信心 lose confidence

却[2]（卻） què 〈副词〉*used to indicate a transition，but somewhat weaker than* 倒 *or* 可：今天下雪，～不冷。It's snowy，but not cold. /文章虽短，～很有内容。The essay is short，and yet it is full of meat.

却病 quèbìng 〈书面〉ward off or cure a disease：～延年 ward off disease and prolong life /这种补酒～强身。This tonic helps prevent disease and build up health.

却步 quèbù step back（in fear or disgust）；hang back；shrink：望而～ shrink from（danger，difficulty，a scene of horror，etc.）；step back in fear（before danger，etc.）

却说 quèshuō *used in storytelling to begin a new section*（often by recalling what has been told before）：～那日王小二正在街上行走。The story goes（*or* It just so happened）that Wang Xiao'er was walking along the street that day.

却之不恭 quèzhī-bùgōng it would be impolite to decline：如此厚赠，～，受之有愧。It would be embarrassing to accept such an expensive present but disrespectful to decline it.

鹊 què magpie：喜～ magpie

鹊报 quèbào magpie's cry — good omen

鹊巢鸠占 quècháo-jiūzhàn *also*“鸠占鹊巢”the magpie's nest is occupied by the turtledove — occupy some place belonging to another：他的行动实有～之意。His action smacks of cynically seizing another person's place for himself.

鹊起 quèqǐ 〈书面〉❶ seize an opportunity that rises；take advantage of circumstances ❷ gain quick fame：声誉～ gain resounding fame

鹊桥 quèqiáo "Magpie Bridge" — on the 7th day of the 7th lunar month，the magpies spread their wings to form a bridge，thus enabling the lovers in heaven（Cowherd and Weaving Girl）to meet that night：～相会 meet on the magpie bridge；reunion of lovers or parted husband and wife

鹊鸲 quèqú 〈动物〉magpie robin

鹊雁 quèyàn 〈动物〉magpie goose；pied goose；semi-palmated goose；*Anseranas semipalmata*

榷[1] què 〈书面〉monopoly：～盐 monopoly of salt /～税 tax on monopoly

榷[2]（搉） què discuss：有要事和你商～。I have something important to discuss with you.

雀 què sparrow

see also qiāo；qiǎo

雀稗 quèbài ditch millet

雀斑 quèbān freckle

雀巢食品公司 Quècháo Shípǐn Gōngsī （Switzerland）Nestle Alimentana SA

雀鲷 quèdiāo 〈动物〉damselfish

雀麦 quèmài 〈植物〉bromegrass；brome

雀鹰 quèyīng 〈动物〉sparrow hawk

雀跃 quèyuè jump for joy：捷报频传，人们欢欣～。People jumped for joy at the repeated messages of success. /会场欢呼～，掌声雷动。The conference hall reverberated with cheers and thunderous applause.

雀躁 quèzào 〈贬义〉gain some kind of fame：声名～一时 enjoy fleeting（*or* transient）fame

埆 què 〈书面〉infertile soil

确[1]（確、塙、碻） què ❶ true；reliable；authentic：正～ correct；right；proper /千真万～ absolutely true；very real /～有其人。There is indeed such a person. ❷ rock-solid；firm：*see*“～立”；“～信”

确[2] què 〈书面〉*see*“埆”què

确保 quèbǎo see to it；ensure；guarantee：～丰收 ensure a good harvest /～化肥供应 guarantee the supply of chemical fertilizer /～边境安全 safeguard the security of the borders /～打响头一炮。Make sure that we succeed in the first battle（*or* we start off on the right track）.

确当 quèdàng proper；suitable；appropriate：用词～。The wording is appropriate. /他们不知道如何～地处理这个问题。They don't know how to deal with the problem properly.

确定 quèdìng ❶ definite；certain；for sure：～的答复 definite reply /～的胜利 certain victory/主队的失败已经～无疑。The defeat of the host team is a foregone conclusion. ❷ determine；decide；fix；ascertain：～大计 decide on matters of cardinal importance /～比赛日期和地点 fix the time and place of the contest /～成书的年代 ascertain the year when the book was finished /～适当人选 choose suitable candidates /～任务 set the tasks /本书的作者尚不能～。It is still uncertain who the author of the book is. *or* The authorship of the book has yet to be established. /他已经被～为候选人。He was affirmed as a candidate.

确乎 quèhū really；positively；indeed：这办法～不行。This method really won't do. /这样美妙的音乐，我过去～未曾听到过。Indeed，I've never heard such beautiful music.

确乎不拔 quèhū-bùbá firm in one's stand or decision；unflinching；adamant

确据 quèjù reliable evidence；ironclad proof；conclusive evidence

确立 quèlì set up；establish：他在80年代以前就～自己音乐家的地位了。He had established himself as a musician by the 1980's. /有些重要的规章制度还得～起来。Some important rules and regulations have yet to be set up.

确论 quèlùn sound argument；justified assertion

确评 quèpíng proper appraisal；appropriate comment

确切 quèqiè ❶ definite；appropriate；exact；precise：～的含义 exact meaning /～的评价 appropriate appraisal /更～地说 to put it more precisely；to be more precise；to be exact /他用词～。His wording is unequivocal. ❷ true；reliable；dependable：完成这项任务是有～保证的。There are reliable guarantees for the accomplishment of the task. /有～的消息，我就告诉你。I'll let you know as soon as I learn anything definite.

确情 quèqíng actual situation；true state of affairs

确认 quèrèn confirm；authenticate；affirm；acknowledge：～为鲁迅手迹 authenticate the writing as Lu Xun's /这些是为国际社会～的原则。These principles are affirmed by the international community. /政府发言人既不～也不否认内阁即将改组的传言。The government spokesperson neither confirmed nor denied the rumour that the cabinet would soon be reshuffled.

确认书 quèrènshū 〈法律〉letter of confirmation

确实 quèshí ❶ reliable；exact；true：我们尚不知道他的～下落。We don't know yet his exact whereabouts. /我得到了有关大选的～消息。I have received reliable information about the elections. ❷ truly；really；indeed：效果～显著。The effect was indeed very marked. /我们～可以说这是个奇迹。We could really call it a miracle.

确守 quèshǒu faithfully abide by；uphold firmly：许多国家都宣布过要～和平共处的五项原则。Many nations have declared that they will strictly abide by the five principles of peaceful coexistence.

确数 quèshù precise figure；exact number

确息 quèxī reliable or dependable information

确信 quèxìn ❶ be certain；be sure；be convinced：我们～最后胜利是属于我们的。We firmly believe that final victory will be ours. ❷ reliable information：这件事至今尚无～。There is no reliable information about the matter even now.

Q

确凿 quèzáo conclusive; authentic; undeniable; irrefutable: 证据～ conclusive (*or* verified) evidence: ～的事实 indisputable facts /证据～无疑，不容狡辩。The evidence is ironclad and there is no quibbling about it.
确凿不移 quèzáo-bùyí absolutely true and irrefutable
确诊 quèzhěn make or give a diagnosis of; diagnose: 他的病已～为肝炎。His illness has been diagnosed as hepatitis. /我的病至今尚未～。No diagnosis has been made of my disease.
确证 quèzhèng ❶ conclusively prove; bear out convincingly: 我们可以～他的论断是错误的。We can prove without the shadow of a doubt that his judgement is incorrect. ❷ conclusive evidence: 在～面前他不得不承认自己的罪行。He could not but admit his crimes in the face of the ironclad evidence.

qūn

囷 qūn 〈古语〉circular granary or barn
逡 qūn 〈书面〉yield; give in; shrink from
逡巡 qūnxún 〈书面〉not be bold enough to step ahead; hang back; hesitate: ～不前 hesitate to move ahead

qún

麇(麏) qún 〈书面〉in groups; in large numbers
see also jūn
麇集 qúnjí swarm; assemble; flock together: 成千上万的农民～庙市。Thousands of farmers flocked to the temple fair.
宭 qún 〈书面〉living in groups; gregarious
群(羣) qún ❶ crowd; group: 人～ crowd /马～ drove of horses /鱼～ shoals of fish /机～ airplanes flying in formation/ 流星～ meteor stream /蜂～ bee colony /害～之马 evil member of the herd; one who brings disgrace on his group; black sheep; rotten apple in the barrel ❷ large numbers of people: 超～ outshine the others; be outstanding ❸ in groups; in large numbers: ～邦 various countries /～贤 numerous persons of virtue and ability /～斗 gang fight ❹〈量词〉group; herd; swarm; flock: 一～流浪者 a group of bums /一～鹿 a herd of deer /一～狼 a pack of wolves /一～蚂蚁 a swarm of ants /一～蜜蜂 a swarm of bees /一～鸽子 a flock of doves /一～小岛 a cluster of islets /一～石油工人 a crowd of oil workers
群采 qúncǎi ❶ mining by groups of people; group mining ❷ gathered or collected by a group of people: 黄金～量 output of gold by group mining /暑假中～植物标本十六件。During the summer vacation sixteen specimens of plants were gathered by groups of students.
群策群力 qúncè-qúnlì pool the wisdom and efforts of the masses; make joint efforts; join hands to take concerted action: 这样大的事情能够办成，靠的是～。The fulfilment of such a gigantic project relied on collective wisdom and concerted efforts.
群唱 qúnchàng *see* "群口"
群岛 qúndǎo group of islands; archipelago: 夏威夷～ Hawaiian Islands
群岛国 qúndǎoguó archipelagic state
群雕 qúndiāo sculpture consisting of a number of statues
群芳 qúnfāng all kinds of flowers; beautiful women: ～谱 catalogue of all flowers /～争艳 flowers vying with each other for glamour /技压～ outstanding skill /～之冠 queen of flowers; beauty queen
群峰 qúnfēng chain of mountain peaks: ～耸立 a chain of peaks tower aloft
群婚 qúnhūn group marriage; communal marriage
群集 qúnjí crowd together; assemble together: 人们～在议会大厦前。People gathered in front of the parliament building.
群籍 qúnjí *see* "群书"
群架 qúnjià gang fight; scuffle: 打～ engage in a gang fight
群居 qúnjū ❶ living in groups; gregarious; social: ～动物 gregarious (*or* social) animal /～昆虫 social insect /～穴处 live in groups in caves ❷〈书面〉live together; collect; gather: ～终日，言不及义 be (*or* live) together all day long but never talk about anything serious
群聚 qúnjù *see* "群集"
群口 qúnkǒu 〈曲艺〉form of performance in which three or more people sing or talk alternately
群口词 qúnkǒucí group crosstalk
群黎 qúnlí 〈书面〉common people; the multitude
群龙无首 qúnlóng-wúshǒu a host of dragons without a head — a group without a leader; an army without a general: ～，成不了大气候。These people can get nowhere now that they are without a leader.
群论 qúnlùn 〈数学〉group theory
群落 qúnluò ❶〈生物〉community; colony ❷ group; collection: 古建筑～ group of ancient buildings
群氓 qúnméng 〈书面〉〈贬义〉common herd
群魔乱舞 qúnmó-luànwǔ demons and monsters dancing in riotous revelry — rogues of all kinds running amok
群殴 qún'ōu gang fight
群配 qúnpèi (of domestic animals) group breeding
群起 qúnqǐ all rise up: ～响应 all rise up to respond (to a call)
群起而攻之 qúnqǐ ér gōng zhī all rise against sb.; rally together to attack sb.; all turn against sb.; all rally together and come down strongly on sb.
群青 qúnqīng 〈化学〉ultramarine
群轻折轴 qúnqīng-zhézhóu many a light load piled up on a cart may break its axle — a minor error, if not corrected in time, may lead to serious consequences
群情 qúnqíng public sentiment; popular feelings: ～鼎沸。Public sentiment was seething. *or* Popular feeling ran high. /～激奋。Everyone was roused to action. /～欢洽。Joy and harmony prevailed.
群山 qúnshān continuous unbroken mountain range
群生 qúnshēng ❶ all living things: 万物不伤，～不夭。Nature will take good care of human beings if they take good care of nature. ❷ Confucian scholars; group of scholars
群生植物 qúnshēng zhíwù social plant
群书 qúnshū all categories of books: 博览～ be well read; read extensively; be erudite
群塑 qúnsù group of sculptures
群体 qúntǐ ❶〈生物〉colony ❷ collective; group: 英雄～ group of heroes
群体取向 qúntǐ qǔxiàng group orientation: ～的文化 group-oriented culture
群体认同 qúntǐ rèntóng group identification
群体行为 qúntǐ xíngwéi group behaviour
群体选择 qúntǐ xuǎnzé group selection
群体遗传学 qúntǐ yíchuánxué population genetics
群威群胆 qúnwēi-qúndǎn mass heroism and spirit of daring
群舞 qúnwǔ collective dance
群像 qúnxiàng 〈文学〉image of a group of people: 小说塑造了30年代小市民的～。The group image of the urban petty bourgeoisie in the 1930's was reproduced in the novel.
群小 qúnxiǎo 〈书面〉group of villains or mean persons: 为～所误 ruined by a group of scoundrels
群雄 qúnxióng 〈旧语〉group of separatist warlords: ～割据 carving up of a country by rival warlord regimes /～逐鹿 fight among separatist warlords for the throne
群言堂 qúnyántáng let everyone have his say; allow everybody to air his views; rule by the voice of the many: 我们这里是～，不搞一言堂，有意见尽管提。We're not a one-man band; we let everyone have his say, so if you have an idea, please speak up.
群蚁附膻 qúnyǐ-fùshān a myriad of ants swarm about a piece of meat that smells — people of the same tastes gang together and curry favour with the powerful
群英 qúnyīng galaxy of talents: 今天来的都是卓有成就的专家，可谓～聚会。Present here today are all accomplished experts, a galaxy of talents.
群英会 qúnyīnghuì gathering of heroes
群阵 qúnzhèn 〈数学〉group-matrix
群众 qúnzhòng ❶ the masses; the people: ～大会 mass rally /～监督 supervision by the masses /工人～ workers; worker masses /密切联系～ form intimate ties with the masses; maintain close links with the people /～是真正的英雄。The people are the real heroes. ❷ peo-

ple who are not members of the Chinese Communist Party or the Chinese Communist Youth League:非党～ non-Party people ❸ the rank and file; grass roots:要倾听～意见 listen to what people at the grass roots have to say

群众工作 qúnzhòng gōngzuò mass work

群众观点 qúnzhòng guāndiǎn mass viewpoint

群众关系 qúnzhòng guānxi relationship or ties with the popular masses:他的～很好。He is on good terms with grassroots people.

群众路线 qúnzhòng lùxiàn mass line:走～ follow the mass line

群众团体 qúnzhòng tuántǐ mass or non-governmental organization

群众性 qúnzhòngxìng of a mass character:要积极开展～的文体活动。It is necessary to initiate mass sports and recreational activities. /要注意这项工作的～。Pay attention to mass participation in the work.

群众运动 qúnzhòng yùndòng mass movement; mass campaign:～的原始意图是要充分发挥广大人民的主动性与热情。The original idea of a mass campaign is to give full play to popular initiative and enthusiasm.

群众组织 qúnzhòng zǔzhī mass organization; non-government organization

群子弹 qúnzǐdàn 〈军事〉case shot; canister (shot)

裙(帬) qún

❶ skirt:布～ cloth skirt /短～ short skirt /衬～ slip; petticoat /连衣～ woman's dress /百折～ pleated skirt /超短～ miniskirt /苏格兰褶裥短～ kilt ❷ sth. like a skirt:围～ apron /墙～ dado /鳖～ calipash

裙钗 qúnchāi 〈旧语〉womenfolk:～政治 petticoat government (either in domestic life or political activities)

裙撑 qúnchēng bustle (for an old-fashioned European lady's skirt or dress)

裙带 qúndài ❶ skirt belt or sash; skirt girdle ❷ connection through one's female relatives; nepotism

裙带菜 qúndàicài 〈植物〉a kind of seaweed (*Undaria pinnatifida*)

裙带风 qúndàifēng nepotism; petticoat influence

裙带关系 qúndài guānxi networking through petticoat influence

裙带官 qúndàiguān one who owes his official position to petticoat influence; one who gets a desirable appointment through nepotism

裙礁 qúnjiāo coral reef along the coast; fringing reef

裙裤 qúnkù pantskirt; culottes

裙子 qúnzi skirt

Q

R

rán

髯(髥) rán whiskers; beard:虬～ curly whiskers /长～ long beard /美～公 man wearing a well-trimmed beard and moustache /白发苍～ hoary-headed

髯口 ránkou 〈戏曲〉false beard and whiskers: 挂～ wear a false beard and whiskers

蚺(蚦) rán

蚺蛇 ránshé *also* "蟒蛇" mǎngshé python

然 rán ❶ right; correct; accurate:我一再指出困难在哪里,他都不以为～。I repeatedly pointed out where the difficulty lay, but he disagreed with me. ❷ so; like that:知其～而不知其所以～ know the hows but not the whys /他今天也许病了,不～他会来的。He may be ill today; otherwise, he is bound to turn up. /他把局面描绘得很暗淡,但情况并不尽～。He painted a very gloomy picture of the situation, but it was not exactly like that. ❸〈书面〉〈连词〉but; yet; nevertheless; however:其人虽逝,～精神长存。He has died, but his spirit will live on. /此事关系重大,～未引起人们的严重关注。This is a matter of great consequence. However, it has not attracted serious attention. ❹ *used as an adjectival or adverbial suffix*:公～ openly; undisguisedly; brazenly /突～ suddenly; all of a sudden /显～ obviously; clearly /全～ completely; entirely; utterly /欣～ joyfully; readily; happily /飘飘～ smug; complacent /巍～屹立 stand rock-firm /勃～大怒 flare up; fly into a rage /悄～无声 be quiet and still /举座哗～。The whole room burst into an uproar.

然而 rán'ér yet; but; however; nonetheless:他说的也许有点道理,～我难以接受。There may be some truth in what he says but I find it hard to reconcile myself to it.

然后 ránhòu then; after that; afterwards:学～知不足。The more you learn, the more you will find out how much you don't know. /岁寒～知松柏之后凋。Only when winter comes are we fully aware that the pine and cypress can survive the cold. /先是猛刮了几天风,～又下了几天雨。It blew hard for several days and then kept raining for a few more days.

然诺 ránnuò 〈书面〉word of honour; promise; pledge:不负～ never break a promise; never go back on one's word /君子重～。A gentleman always stands by his promise. *or* A gentleman is as good as his word.

然则 ránzé 〈书面〉in that case; then:～怨我乎? In that case do you think I'm to blame (*or* it is my fault)?

燃 rán ❶ burn:～为灰烬 be burned to ashes /内～机 internal-combustion engine ❷ ignite; light; set fire to:～火 light (*or* kindle) a fire /点～仇恨的火焰 kindle the flames of hatred

燃点 rándiǎn ❶ ignite; kindle; set fire to:厅里～着许多蜡烛。Many candles are burning in the hall. ❷ *also* "着火点" zháohuǒdiǎn 〈化学〉ignition or burning point

燃放 ránfàng 〈书面〉set off; let off (fireworks, etc.):～花炮 set off fireworks and firecrackers

燃料 ránliào fuel:气体～ gaseous (*or* gas) fuel /固体～ solid fuel /液体～ liquid fuel /核～ nuclear fuel /标准～ ideal fuels /低热值～ low-calorie fuel /代用～ alternative fuel

燃料比 ránliàobǐ 〈冶金〉fuel ratio

燃料电池 ránliào diànchí fuel cell:～发电 fuel cell power generation

燃料动力工业 ránliào dònglì gōngyè fuel and power industry

燃料库 ránliàokù fuel depot; fuel reservoir; fuel warehouse

燃料油 ránliàoyóu fuel oil

燃眉之急 ránméizhījí as pressing as a fire singeing one's eyebrows — a matter of great urgency; pressing or desperate need:能否惠借百金以济～。Could you lend me a hundred *yuan* to help me tide over a most pressing need?

燃煤电厂 ránméi diànchǎng coal-fired power plant; coal-fired power station

燃煤燃气轮机 ránméi ránqìlúnjī 〈机械〉coal-fired gas turbine

燃气轮机 ránqìlúnjī gas turbine:～发电厂 gas turbine power station

燃烧 ránshāo ❶ burn; kindle:这种煤不易～。This type of coal does not burn easily. /大火还在～。The conflagration is raging. ❷ (of strong feeling, such as love, anger, desire, etc.) burn; rage: 怒火在胸中～ burn with anger ❸〈化学〉combustion; inflammation: ～性能 combustibility

燃烧弹 ránshāodàn *also* "烧夷弹" shāoyídàn fire bomb; incendiary bomb

燃烧点 ránshāodiǎn point of ignition; ignition point; burning point

燃烧剂 ránshāojì incendiary agent

燃烧瓶 ránshāopíng 〈军事〉incendiary bottle; Molotov cocktail

燃烧热 ránshāorè combustion heat

燃烧室 ránshāoshì 〈机械〉combustion chamber; blast chamber; combustor

燃烧手榴弹 ránshāo shǒuliúdàn 〈军事〉incendiary grenade

燃烧值 ránshāozhí combustion value

燃油泵 rányóubèng fuel pump

rǎn

染 rǎn ❶ dye:～毛线 dye knitting wool /洗～店 cleaners and dyers; laundry /把头发～黑 dye (*or* tint) one's hair black /～指甲 paint fingernails /夕阳～红了半个天空。The setting sun dyed half the sky red. ❷ catch (a disease); acquire or contract (a bad habit, etc.); be stained or contaminated (by sth.):～上流感 catch influenza (*or* the flu) /～上恶习 contract a bad habit; fall into evil ways /耳濡目～ be imperceptibly influenced by what one constantly hears and sees /环境污～ environmental pollution /出污泥而不～ emerge unstained from the filth

染病 rǎnbìng catch or contract an illness; be infected with a disease; fall ill:身染重病 fall gravely ill

染毒 rǎndú 〈军事〉(toxic) contamination:～区域 contaminated area

染发 rǎnfà dye or tint one's hair

染坊 rǎnfang dyehouse; dye-works

染缸 rǎngāng dye vat; dyejigger:社会如同一个大～。The society is just like a big dye vat.

染患 rǎnhuàn catch or contract a disease; be infected with a disease

染剂 rǎnjì 〈化工〉dye:活体～ vital dye /碱性～ basic dye; cationic dye /酸性～ acid dye

染料 rǎnliào 〈化工〉dye; dyestuff; dyeware:异染～ metachromatic dye /正染～ orthochromatic dye /活性～ reactive dye /～浓度 dye

strength /～制造 dyemaking /～敏化 dye sensitization
染料激光器 rǎnliào jīguāngqì dye laser
染色 rǎnsè ❶ dyeing; colouring:～性 dyeability /～法 staining ❷ colour bacteria for easy observation under the microscope
染色剂 rǎnsèjì colouring agent
染色体 rǎnsètǐ 〈生物〉chromosome:～畸变 chromosome aberration /～组 chromosome complement
染色体遗传学 rǎnsètǐ yíchuánxué chromosome genetics
染色质 rǎnsèzhì 〈生化〉chromatin
染业 rǎnyè 〈化工〉dyeing
染液 rǎnyè dye liquor
染印法 rǎnyìnfǎ 〈影视〉dye transfer process:～彩色电影 colour film made by the dye transfer process; technicolour
染指 rǎnzhǐ reap undeserved profit from; encroach upon:不容他人～ allow nobody to meddle for selfish purposes /～别国领土 encroach upon another country's territory /他绝无～之心。He hasn't the least intention of profiting from it personally. *or* He has no axe to grind.

冉(冄) rǎn a surname
冉冉 rǎnrǎn 〈书面〉❶ (of tree branches, etc.) hanging down loosely:柳枝～,随风摆动。The weeping willow is swaying in the wind. ❷ slowly; gradually:～而来的春天的足音 slowly approaching footsteps of spring /月亮～上升。The moon rose slowly./夕阳的余辉～消逝。The sunset glow gradually faded away.

苒(苒) rǎn *see* "荏苒" rěnrǎn

rāng

嚷 rāng
see also rǎng
嚷嚷 rāngrang ❶ shout; yell; make an uproar:你们～什么! Don't yell! *or* Shut up! /外头乱～的,不知出了什么事。There is a lot of shouting and yelling outside. I don't know what's up. ❷ make known; make public:这件事要保密,不能～。This is strictly confidential. Don't breathe a word about it. *or* This is only between you and me. /这事～出去可不好。It will be bad if the cat is let out of the bag. /他这人沉不住气,就爱～。He is not the steady sort and easily blurts things out.

ráng

瀼 ráng
瀼瀼 rángráng 〈书面〉dewy:零露～ wet with dew

禳 ráng 〈书面〉keep off evil; exorcise (spirits):～灾 avert a disaster by prayers, etc. /把艾蒿挂在门上,以～瘴气。Hang moxa on the door to keep off miasma.
禳解 rángjiě 〈书面〉〈迷信〉keep off evil spirits or disasters by saying prayers; exorcise (spirits):老太太要请个尼僧来～。The old woman wanted to send for a Buddhist nun to ward off evil spirits.

穰 ráng 〈旧语〉dirty:衣服～了。The clothes have become dirty.

蘘 ráng
蘘荷 ránghé mioga ginger (*Zingiber mioga*)

穣 ráng ❶ 〈方言〉rice or wheat stalk:～草 rice (*or* wheat) straw ❷ *see* "瓤" ráng
穣穣 rángráng 〈书面〉abundant grain:～满家 enjoy a good harvest and a full granary

儴 ráng *see* "劻儴" kuāngráng

瓤 ráng ❶ pulp; flesh; pith:红～的西瓜 watermelon with red flesh /橘子～儿 orange pulp ❷ interior part of certain things:秫秸～ inside of a corn stalk /光有信皮,没有信～儿。There's only an empty envelope, with nothing inside. ❸ 〈方言〉weak; bad:他修车的技术真不～。He is a really good car mechanic. /他身体很～。He has a weak constitution.
瓤口 rángkou 〈口语〉taste or flavour (of watermelon, etc.):这西瓜～好,特甜。This watermelon tastes very sweet.
瓤子 rángzi ❶ pulp; flesh; pith ❷ inside; filling:表～ inner works of a watch /点心～ cake's filling

勷 ráng *see* "劻勷" kuāngráng

rǎng

壤 rǎng ❶ soil; earth:红～ red earth (*or* soil) /土～ soil; earth ❷ earth; ground:天～之别 as different as earth is from heaven — a world of difference ❸ area; land; territory:过去这里是穷乡僻～。This place used to be a remote poverty-stricken village. /印度缅甸接～。India and Burma share a common border.
壤地 rǎngdì 〈书面〉land; territory
壤界 rǎngjiè 〈书面〉boundary; border
壤土 rǎngtǔ ❶ 〈农业〉loam ❷ 〈书面〉land; territory:夺我～,戮我人民。They seized our territories and slaughtered our people.

攘(❸纕) rǎng 〈书面〉❶ reject; resist expel:～敌 resist the enemy ❷ seize; snatch; grab ❸ roll or turn up (one's sleeves):～袖 roll up one's sleeves ❹ trouble; disturb:干戈扰～ war-torn
攘臂 rǎngbì 〈书面〉roll up one's sleeves and raise one's arms (in excitement or agitation):～高呼 raise one's arms and shout at the top of one's voice /～瞋目 raise one's arms and glare in indignation
攘除 rǎngchú 〈书面〉get rid of; weed out; eliminate; reject:～邪恶 root out all evils
攘夺 rǎngduó 〈书面〉seize; snatch; grab:～国柄 seize state power
攘窃 rǎngqiè 〈书面〉steal; pilfer; swipe
攘攘 rǎngrǎng 〈书面〉chaotic; disorderly:天下～ big upheaval across the land; great disorder throughout the world
攘善 rǎngshàn 〈书面〉appropriate to oneself credit (honour, etc.) one does not deserve; claim all the credit for oneself
攘往熙来 rǎngwǎng-xīlái *also* "熙来攘往" with people bustling about:广场上人群～。There was a bustling crowd on the square.
攘外 rǎngwài resist or expel foreign aggression:"安内必先～" (there must be) internal pacification before resistance to foreign aggression (a slogan put forward by Kuomintang reactionaries to justify its policy of suppression of the Chinese Communists before the Anti-Japanese War, 1937-1945)

嚷 rǎng ❶ shout; yell:高声～叫 shout in a loud voice /他使劲～了一嗓子。He yelled at the top of his voice. ❷ argue heatedly or noisily (with):他们～了半天,互不相让。They've been arguing heatedly for quite some time, and neither side is ready to give in. ❸ 〈方言〉scold; reprimand; reproach:他动不动就～人。He is prone to yell at people. /爸爸～了我一顿。Father gave me a good scolding.
see also rāng
嚷叫 rǎngjiào shout; yell:楼下为何～声不断? Why is such a din downstairs?
嚷嘴 rǎngzuǐ 〈方言〉quarrel; row; squabble

ràng

让(讓) ràng ❶ give way; give in; give up; yield:～权 give up power /不肯相～ neither is willing to yield; neither is prepared to make concessions /寸步不～ refuse to yield an inch; not budge an inch /～着妹妹一点。You ought to give in a little more with your younger sister. /他们之间应当～着点。They ought to be more accommodating. /请～一下。Excuse me. ❷ offer; invite; treat:～茶 offer sb. tea /～宾客就坐 show the guests to their seats; offer sb. a seat /把大家～进屋里 invite everybody in ❸ let sb. have sth. at a price; sell; transfer:出～ sell (off) articles /转～ transfer the possession of; make over /我们可按原价的75%把这台机器～给你们。We can let you have this machine at 75 per cent of its original

R

price. ❹ allow; let; give sb. a free hand:～我试试。Let me have a try. /对不起，～你费心了。Sorry to have put you to so much trouble. /他不～弟弟拨弄他的打字机。He doesn't allow his younger brother to meddle with his typewriter. /谁～你这么干了? Who told you to do it the way you did? /我～他坐下，把事情的经过说一遍。I asked him to sit down and give an account of the incident. /别理他，～他说去。Don't mind him. Let him say what he will. ❺ make way; make room: 他赶忙把车～到一旁。He moved his cart out of the way promptly. ❻ *used in the passive voice to introduce the agent*: 这杯子～我给打碎了。I am the one who broke the cup. /他～雨给淋了。He got wet through in the rain.

让步 ràngbù give in; give way; yield; make a concession:两人谁也不肯作出～。Neither was willing to make concessions. /双方都有些～。Both sides have somewhat retreated from their original positions. /绝不作无原则的～。Never make an unprincipled concession. *or* Never yield on matters of principle. /只要别人～，他自己却寸步不让。He wanted others to concede, but refused to yield any ground himself.

让车线 ràngchēxiàn 〈交通〉passing track or lane

让渡 ràngdù 〈法律〉alienate (property); transfer the ownership or possession of sth.:～证书 transfer certificate / ～主权 transfer sovereign power / ～条款 devolution clause / ～占有权 yield possession

让价 ràngjià reduce the price (in haggling): 不～。No bargaining.

让开 ràngkāi get out of the way; step aside; make way: 请把路～。Make way, please. /～! 否则我可叫警察了。Get out of the way (*or* Be off with you), or I'll call the police.

让利 rànglì cut profit for the benefit of the customers: ～促销 promote (*or* boost) sales by cutting profits

让利销售 rànglì xiāoshòu cut-price sale

让路 rànglù make way (for sb. or sth.); give way; yield the right of way:给急救车～ make way for an ambulance /给救灾工作～ give top priority to disaster relief

让手 ràngshǒu sell:这批货要尽快～。These goods must be disposed of as soon as possible.

让位 ràngwèi ❶ resign sovereign authority; abdicate; resign:他决心～，请更合适的人来当厂长。He has decided to resign as factory manager in favour of a better qualified person. ❷ give up or offer one's seat (to sb.):请你们让让位，这儿有一位孕妇。Will someone kindly offer his seat to the expectant mother, please? ❸ yield to; give way to; change into:时下旧式长裤已～于牛仔裤了。Old-fashioned trousers have now given way to blue jeans.

让贤 ràngxián yield one's position to a person of virtue and talent; give up one's position in favour of a better qualified person: 他没有理由留恋权位而不～。There is no reason why he should hang on to his post and refuse to step down for a more competent person.

让枣推梨 ràngzǎo-tuīlí show fraternal love among brothers (from the story of Wang Tai 王泰 of the Liang Dynasty, who yielded the dates to other children, and that of Kong Rong 孔融 of the Eastern Han Dynasty, who let his elder brother have the bigger pear)

让账 ràngzhàng vie with each other to pay the bill (in restaurants, bars, etc.):中国人有～的习惯。The Chinese always try to outdo others in paying the bill at a restaurant.

让座 ràngzuò ❶ give up or offer one's seat (to sb.):他在公共汽车上给一位老人～。He offered his seat to an old man on the bus. ❷ ask guests to be seated:他赶忙起身给来人～。He promptly stood up and asked the visitor to be seated.

ráo

荛(蕘) ráo 〈书面〉firewood; faggot:刍～ collect firewood and mow grass /行牧且～ collect firewood while herding

荛花 ráohuā 〈植物〉canescent wikstroemia (*Wikstroemia canescens*)

桡(橈) ráo 〈书面〉oar

桡动脉 ráodòngmài 〈生理〉radial artery (*arteria radialis*)

桡骨 ráogǔ 〈生理〉radius

桡神经 ráoshénjīng 〈生理〉radial nerve (*nervus radialis*)

饶(饒) ráo ❶ rich; abundant; plentiful:他们谈话颇～风趣。Their conversation sparkled with wit and humour. ❷ throw in; give or get sth. extra for nothing:水果店老板给我把两斤梨装好，还～了我两个。The fruiterer wrapped up a kilogram of pears for me and threw in two extra. /老太太买菜总想多～上点儿。Old ladies always try to get more than is due from the greengrocer. /他去就行了，别把我给～进去。It will do for him to go alone and don't drag me in (*or* and I do wish to be excused). ❸ have mercy on; let sb. off; forgive:讨～ beg for mercy; ask for quarter /～他这一回。Let him off this time. /已经认错了，就～了他吧。Since he's admitted his mistake, you may as well forgive him. /他心挺好，就是嘴巴不～人。He is kind-hearted though he has a sharp tongue. ❹〈口语〉although; despite: ～这么着，还有人说闲话。As it is, there's still a lot of gossip going on. /～这么检查还有漏洞呢。For all our efforts in the check up, there are still loopholes. ❺ (Ráo) a surname

饶富 ráofù *also* "富饶" abundant; richly endowed:～之地 land of plenty

饶命 ráomìng spare sb.'s life:一再哀求～ repeatedly beg to be spared /"～!" "Have mercy, please." *or* "Please spare me."

饶人 ráorén forgive sb.:说两句得了，别得理不～。One or two words of criticism will suffice. Don't pick on him endlessly when you're in the right. /得～处且～。Forgive where you may. *or* Be merciful whenever you can.

饶舌 ráoshé ❶ loquacious; garrulous:她的一大缺点就是～。One serious failing of hers is loquacity. ❷ say more than is proper; shoot off one's mouth; babble out (a secret):就怪你～，弄得他们两口子不和睦。Your gossip is the cause of their strained relationship.

饶恕 ráoshù forgive; pardon:犯下不可～的罪行 commit an unpardonable crime

饶头 ráotou 〈口语〉give gratis; throw in sth.:这两个苹果算是～。I'll give you two extra apples, free of charge.

饶沃 ráowò 〈书面〉(of soil) fertile; rich

饶裕 ráoyù 〈书面〉well-to-do; richly-endowed

娆(嬈) ráo *see* "娇娆" jiāoráo; "妖娆" yāoráo

see also rǎo

rǎo

扰(擾) rǎo ❶ harass; trouble; harry; molest:官匪并～ be harassed by both officials and bandits /视察工作时千万不可～民。Don't bring extra trouble to the people in your supervisory tour. /天下本无事，庸人自～之。In truth, all is well; it is the ignorant who make so much ado. *or* There's nothing wrong with the world. Only the dull make a fuss over nothing. ❷〈书面〉disorder; chaos; confusion:纷～ confusion; chaos ❸〈套语〉give sb. a good deal of bother:我～了他的喜酒。I was kindly entertained at his wedding feast. /多～了。Thank you very much for your warm hospitality.

扰动 rǎodòng ❶ turmoil; turbulence:那次叛乱，～及于全国。That armed rebellion caused a nationwide disturbance. ❷ excite; disturb :～速度 disturbance velocity /～中心 centre of disturbance / ～高层大气 disturbed upper atmosphere

扰聒 rǎoguō (often used in the earlier vernacular)〈套语〉thank you for your hospitality

扰害 rǎohài disturb; be harmful to:～公共秩序 disturb public order

扰流器 rǎoliúqì spoiler; vortex generator

扰乱 rǎoluàn harass; disturb; confuse; disrupt:～视听 confuse the public; mislead public opinion /～会场秩序 disrupt order in a conference hall; throw a meeting place into disorder /～市场 rig the market /～民心 sap public confidence /～思路 interrupt one's train of thought /～了内心的平静 disturb one's peace of mind /这严重地～了我们的工作。Our work has been thrown into chaos. /他们聚众闹事，～乡曲。They incited people to break the peace in the village.

扰攘 rǎorǎng 〈书面〉hustle and bustle; tumult; confusion; hurly-burly:天下～。The whole world (*or* country) is in turmoil./值此～之时，人心惶惶。People were eaten up with anxiety in those turbulent years.

扰扰 rǎorǎo 〈书面〉tumult; uproar; disturbance:心绪～ in a dis-

turbed state of mind

扰袭 rǎoxí harass and attack:～敌人 harass and attack the enemy

扰杂 rǎozá in disorder; in a jumble; in a muddle:良莠～。The good and the bad are all mixed up.

娆(嬈) rǎo 〈书面〉tumult; perturbation:他一向心神平和,不躁不～。He is always calm and composed, acting neither rashly nor on impulse.
see also ráo

rào

绕(繞、❷❸遶) rào ❶ wind; coil:～线圈 coil the thread/把绳子～起来 coil the rope; wind the rope into coils/把头发～在头顶 coil one's hair in a bunch at the top of the head ❷ move or go round; circle; revolve:～场一周(of athletes) go round the arena/月亮～着地球转。The moon revolves round the earth./我～着操场跑了两圈儿。I ran round the sportsground twice./这两个孩子～着桌子追,一边笑,一边嚷着。The two kids chased each other round the table, laughing and shouting./他心中烦闷,在房中～圈子。He was bored stiff, walking round and round the room (*or* pacing up and down the room). ❸ make a detour; bypass; circumvent; go round:道路施工,车辆～行。Detour: Road under repair./这段路坑洼不平,咱们～着走吧。Let's make a detour to avoid the bumpy road ahead./前面是陡壁悬崖,无处可～。It's a sheer precipice ahead and we cannot skirt around it. ❹ confuse; baffle; confound:百事～心,不得清闲。With all sorts of worries gnawing at me, I had scarcely a moment of peace./他一时给～住了,愣了半天。He was perplexed, feeling at a loss for a good while.

绕脖子 rào bózi 〈方言〉❶ beat about the bush; make oblique references; speak or act in a roundabout way:有话直说,别跟我～。Speak straight to the point and don't beat about the bush. ❷ involved; stiff; complicated; intricate:这道数学题还真有点～。This maths problem is really complicated./这种解释太～了。The explanation is much too involved.

绕搭 ràoda 〈方言〉❶ wind; coil:把这绺线～上。Wind round this skein of thread. ❷ confuse; baffle; befuddle:这个难题可把我～住了。This problem really baffles me. ❸ cheat; hoodwink:他变着法儿把我的钱～去了。By hook or (by) crook he cheated me ou tof my money.

绕道 ràodào make a detour; take a devious route; go by a roundabout route:这里正在施工,我们得～走。Construction is in progress here. We've got to make a detour./工作中遇到难题不能～走。We must not try to bypass difficulties (*or* skirt round difficulties, *or* steer clear of difficulties) in our work.

绕地球飞行 ràodìqiú fēixíng 〈航天〉circumterrestrial flight

绕杆式天线 ràogānshì tiānxiàn 〈无线电〉turnstile antenna

绕焊 ràohàn 〈冶金〉boxing; end turning

绕接 ràojiē 〈电工〉wire-wrap connection; wrapped connection; solderless wrapped connection

绕口令 ràokǒulìng *also* "拗口令" àokǒulìng; "急口令" jíkǒulìng tongue twister:～是相声演员的基本功。Doing the tongue twister is a basic technique of a crosstalker.

绕梁三日 ràoliáng-sānrì (of beautiful music, etc.) reverberate and linger long in the air

绕路 ràolù *see* "绕道"

绕圈子 rào quānzi ❶ circle; go round and round:一路～走了许多冤枉路。We walked round and round and wasted a lot of time on the way. ❷ speak in a roundabout way; beat about the bush:他们绕了好几个圈子才说到正题。They'd beaten about the bush one way or another before they finally came to the subject./你怎么老是在～?Why do you keep skirting the issue?

绕射 ràoshè *also* "衍射" yǎnshè 〈物理〉diffraction

绕手 ràoshǒu 〈方言〉(of matter, etc.) difficult to handle:这件事真有点儿～。This is a rather delicate matter. *or* This is truly a hot potato.

绕丝机 ràosījī wire-coiling machine

绕腾 ràoteng (of speech, behaviour, etc.) be indirect; not be straightforward; beat about the bush; talk in a roundabout way:他～了半天,原来是不想干这件事。He kept beating about the bush before intimating that he would decline the job.

绕弯儿 ràowānr ❶〈方言〉go for a walk; take a stroll:他吃完饭就～去了。He went out for a stroll right after dinner. ❷ *see* "绕弯子"

绕弯子 rào wānzi *also* "绕弯儿" talk in a roundabout way; beat about the bush:他说话老爱～。He always talks in a roundabout way. *or* He never comes straight to the point.

绕线筒 ràoxiàntǒng reel; bobbin

绕行 ràoxíng ❶ make a detour; go by a roundabout route:前方施工,车辆～。Construction is under way and all vehicles must make a detour. *or* Construction under way. No thoroughfare. ❷ go round:～湖边一周 walk all the way round the lake

绕远儿 ràoyuǎnr ❶ (of a route) be longer:那样走就～了。That'll be taking a longer route. ❷ go the long way round:我宁可～,也不翻山。I'd rather go the long way round than climb over the hill.

绕越 ràoyuè cross or pass by a detour:～暗礁 steer clear of a submerged rock

绕组 ràozǔ 〈电工〉winding:双线～ bifilar winding/～线 winding wire

绕嘴 ràozuǐ (of a sentence, etc.) tongue-twisting; difficult to articulate:这话真～。It's really a bit of a mouthful.

rě

若 rě *see* "般若" bōrě
see also ruò

惹 rě ❶ bring upon oneself (sth. unpleasant); incur:招～是非 bring trouble on (*or* to) oneself; invite trouble/招～不快 incur displeasure/他在工作单位～了许多麻烦。He got himself into a lot of trouble in his work unit. ❷ offend; provoke; annoy; tease:他从不～别人。He never gives offence to anybody./此人是个烈性子,～不得。The chap has a fiery temper and is not to be provoked (*or* trifled with)./他这个人～不起。You can't afford to displease him. ❸ attract; draw; cause:尽量不要～人注意。Try as best as you can not to attract (*or* draw) attention./他很～人讨厌。He is making a nuisance of himself. *or* He is a damned nuisance./这件工艺品真～人爱。It's such a fine piece of craftsmanship./羊肉不曾吃,空～一身膻。〈俗语〉Go for wool and come home shorn.

惹草拈花 rěcǎo-niānhuā *also* "拈花惹草" (of men) go whoring; visit brothels; sow one's wild oats; have illicit relations with women:此人薄幸,最喜～。Inconstant in love, this fellow was sowing a large crop of wild oats.

惹火烧身 rěhuǒshāoshēn he who plays with fire will get his fingers burnt — court disaster; ask for trouble:惟恐～ lest (*or* for fear that) one should burn one's fingers/这样做势必～。By so doing you will most likely get your fingers burnt. *or* This is simply courting disaster./警告他不要～。Let's warn him not to play with fire.

惹祸 rěhuò invite disaster; ask for trouble:这孩子经常～。The boy is always causing trouble./他惹了大祸了。He has got into dreadful trouble.

惹乱子 rě luànzi cause trouble; court disaster; commit a misdemeanour or crime:一路上他尽给我们～。He caused us a lot of headaches on our way here.

惹目 rěmù attractive; showy; conspicuous; eye-catching:她站在人堆中十分～。She stood most conspicuous in the crowd.

惹恼 rěnǎo *also* "惹怒" make angry; offend; annoy; provoke:我就为这件小事～了他。It was exactly over this trifling matter that I put his back up.

惹气 rěqì become angry; be offended or upset:为这点小事～不值得。It makes no sense getting upset over such a trifle.

惹事 rěshì cause trouble:你千万小心,别～。Be sure not to kick up a fuss./他在村里惹出一场事来。He stirred up a disturbance in the village.

惹是非 rě shìfei provoke a dispute; kick up a fuss; kick up a row:他生性稳重,不爱～。He has too mild a nature to cause any trouble.

惹是生非 rěshì-shēngfēi stir up trouble; create a disturbance; make mischief:他是个安分守己的人,从不～。He is a law-abiding person and never kicks up a row./你这样大了,还一天到晚～。You are old enough to refrain from making mischief all the time.

惹眼 rěyǎn 〈方言〉eye-catching; conspicuous; showy:你穿得这么花里胡哨太～。You look too conspicuous in such a showy dress.

R

惹怨 rěyuàn incur displeasure or resentment：你做这种工作很难不～。You can hardly avoid offending people in this sort of job.

喏 rě *see* "唱喏" chàngrě
see also nuò

rè

热(熱) rè ❶ heat：传～ conduct heat；transmit heat；transfer heat／导～性 heat conductivity／汽化～ heat of vaporization／物质燃烧产生～能。Heat is produced by burning matter. ❷ hot：一杯～茶 a hot cup of tea／天渐渐～了。It's getting warmer.／南方人不怕～。People from the south are accustomed to hot weather.／天～得叫人喘不过气来。It's stifling hot. *or* I'm suffocating in here. ❸ make hot；heat up；warm up：把剩菜剩饭～一下。Heat up the left-overs.／饭凉了，先～～再吃。The meal is cold；heat it before you eat it. ❹ fever；temperature：发～头疼 have a fever and a headache／他患感冒，发了一天～。He caught cold and ran a high fever the whole day.／给她打过针后，～还是不退。Her temperature didn't come down after the injection. ❺ ardent；chummy；deep；thick：他们对我们还是那么～。They are still chummy with us. *or* They are still on very friendly terms with us. ❻ envious；keen；eager：看到他们一个个发了财，他不觉眼～。When he saw everyone was getting rich he couldn't help feeling envious of them. ❼ in great demand；popular：*see* "～货"；"～销" ❽ (used after a noun, a noun phrase or a verb) craze；fever；fad：网球～ tennis craze；intense popular interest in tennis／中国～ China fever／八十年代初北京出现过一股超短裙～。The mini-skirt was a fad (*or* all the rage) in the early 80's in Beijing. ❾〈物理〉strongly radioactive；thermal；thermo-：～原子 thermal atom

热爱 rè'ài deep affection；ardent love；devotion：～祖国 have ardent love for one's country／～工作 devote oneself wholeheartedly to one's work；have one's heart in one's work／深受群众～ enjoy the deep affection of the public／他的报告激发了我们对边疆生活的～。His talk inspired us with ardent love for life at the frontier.

热巴 rèbā ❶ *reba*, a type of Tibetan performing art which combines singing, dancing, story-telling and acrobatics ❷ *reba* performer

热拔 rèbá〈机械〉hot drawing

热泵 rèbèng〈机械〉heat pump

热币 rèbì *also* "游资" yóuzī〈经济〉hot money

热病 rèbìng〈医学〉pyreticosis；febris；fever

热病学 rèbìngxué pyretology

热补 rèbǔ vulcanize (tire, etc.)

热层 rècéng〈气象〉thermosphere

热肠 rècháng warm-heartedness；enthusiasm：古道～ considerate and warm-hearted；sympathetic

热潮 rècháo mass enthusiasm；campaign；upsurge：掀起植树～ unfold a tree-planting campaign／练气功已形成一股～。*Qigong* has become a craze nowadays.

热忱 rèchén zeal；zest；warm-heartedness；enthusiasm：爱国～ patriotic sentiment／劳动～ labour enthusiasm／满腔～ full of enthusiasm；zealous；very enthusiastic／待人～ treat people warm-heartedly／他极大的工作～使我深受感动。His utter devotion to work impressed me greatly.

热成风 rèchéngfēng〈气象〉shamal

热成形 rèchéngxíng〈机械〉hot-forming

热诚 rèchéng sincere and warm-hearted；cordial：缺乏～ lack warmth／～接待 cordially receive／为人～ be sincere and warm-hearted／他的～感人肺腑。His sincerity and warm nature touched me to the depths of my soul.

热赤道 rèchìdào〈气象〉heat equator；thermal equator

热处理 rèchǔlǐ〈机械〉heat treatment；thermal treatment：～钢 heat-treated steel

热处理炉 rèchǔlǐlú heat-treating or heat-treatment furnace

热传导 rèchuándǎo *also* "导热" dǎorè heat conduction

热传递 rèchuándì〈物理〉heat transfer；heat transmission

热磁 rècí〈物理〉thermomagnetic：～化 thermomagnetization／～效应 thermomagnetic effect；pyromagnetic effect

热磁发电机 rècí fādiànjī pyromagnetic generator；thermomagnetic generator

热脆 rècuì〈冶金〉hotshort；red-short；short brittle：～钢 red-short steel／～性 hot-shortness；red-shortness

热大气层 rèdàqìcéng〈气象〉thermosphere (atmospheric layer of increasing temperature from about 80km to roughly 400km above the earth)

热带 rèdài *also* "回归带" huíguīdài tropical or torrid zone；the tropics：～病 tropical disease／～风暴 tropical storm／～植物 tropical plant

热带草原 rèdài cǎoyuán savanna

热带兰 rèdàilán *also* "附生兰" fùshēnglán tropical orchid

热带鱼 rèdàiyú tropical fish

热带雨林 rèdài yǔlín〈林业〉selva；tropical rain forest：～气候 tropical rainforest climate；tropical wet climate

热当量 rèdāngliàng〈物理〉heat-equivalent

热导率 rèdǎolǜ〈物理〉thermal conductivity

热导体 rèdǎotǐ〈物理〉heat conductor

热得快 rèdekuài immersion heater

热点 rèdiǎn ❶ hot spot；flash point：这个领域是两大集团争夺的～。This area is a hot spot of contention between the two rival groups. ❷ attraction；centre of attention：北京的故宫是旅游～之一。The Palace Museum in Beijing is one of the tourist attractions.／这个问题已成为公众关注的～。The problem has become the focus of public attention. ❸〈物理〉hot-spot：～因子 hot-spot factor

热电 rèdiàn〈物理〉pyroelectricity；thermoelectricity

热电厂 rèdiànchǎng thermal-power plant

热电堆 rèdiànduī thermopile；thermogenerator

热电离层 rèdiànlícéng thermosphere

热电偶 rèdiàn'ǒu thermocouple

热电式发电机 rèdiànshì fādiànjī thermoelectric generator (TEG)

热电体 rèdiàntǐ pyroelectrics

热电效应 rèdiàn xiàoyìng pyroelectric effect

热电学 rèdiànxué pyroelectricity

热电子 rèdiànzǐ thermoelectron；thermion

热电阻 rèdiànzǔ thermal resistance

热定型 rèdìngxíng〈化工〉heat setting；thermosetting

热度 rèdù ❶ degree of heat；heat：物体燃烧需要一定的～。Objects need to reach a certain degree of heat before they burn. *or* Objects burn only when they are heated up to a certain point. ❷〈口语〉fever；temperature：她吃了药后～就退了。Her temperature dropped (*or* came down) after she had taken the medicine. ❸ zeal；fervour：他呀，干什么都只有五分钟的～。His enthusiasm will not last long for whatever he does.

热锻 rèduàn〈冶金〉hot-forging

热对流 rèduìliú〈物理〉thermal-convection

热法 rèfǎ hot method or process：～磨木浆 hot-ground pulp

热风 rèfēng hot wind；hot air；hot-blast air

热风干燥机 rèfēng gānzàojī hot-air drier

热风烤炉 rèfēng kǎolú hot-air roaster

热风炉 rèfēnglú ❶〈冶金〉hot blast stove ❷ (for food) hot-air oven

热敷 rèfū *also* "热罨"〈医学〉hot compress

热服 rèfú〈中医〉(of decoction of herbal medicine) to be taken (when it is) hot

热辐射 rèfúshè〈物理〉heat or thermal radiation

热工学 règōngxué〈物理〉thermal engineering

热功当量 règōng dāngliàng〈物理〉mechanical equivalent of heat

热狗 règǒu hotdog

热固 règù〈化工〉hot-set；heat-set：～化 thermofixation／～性 thermofixability／～树脂 resinoid；heat convertible resin

热固塑料 règù sùliào〈化工〉thermoset plastic

热管 règuǎn heat pipe；heating pipe；radiator

热光度 règuāngdù〈物理〉bolometric luminosity

热锅上的蚂蚁 règuōshangde mǎyǐ ants crawling frantically on a hot pan；be on pins and needles：他犹如～，急得团团转。He was at his wit's end, as desperate as an ant on a hot pan (*or* like a cat on a hot tin roof).

热函 rèhán〈物理〉enthalpy；total heat

热耗 rèhào heat consumption

热合 rèhé〈化工〉thermofixation；heatseal

热核 rèhé thermonuclear：～爆炸 thermonuclear explosion／～变化 thermonuclear transformation

热核弹 rèhédàn〈军事〉fusion or thermonuclear bomb：～头 nuclear warhead

热核反应 rèhé fǎnyìng *also* "聚变" jùbiàn〈物理〉thermonuclear reaction:受控～ controlled thermonuclear reaction
热核反应堆 rèhé fǎnyìngduī thermonuclear reactor
热核技术 rèhé jìshù thermonucleonics
热核武器 rèhé wǔqì thermonuclear weapon
热核子学 rèhézǐxué thermonucleonics
热烘烘 rèhōnghōng very warm:今天不算冷,我穿了一件毛衣,浑身～的。It's not really cold today, and I feel quite warm in a woollen sweater. /我答不上那个问题,不觉脸上～的。I felt my cheeks burning when I was not able to answer the question.
热红外线 rèhóngwàixiàn〈物理〉thermal infra-red rays:～光谱 thermal infra-red spectrum
热虹吸管 rèhóngxīguǎn thermosiphon
热乎乎 rèhūhū *also* "热呼呼" warm:～的茶点 hot tea and pastry / 被窝里～的。It was warm under the quilt.
热乎 rèhu *also* "热呼" ❶ warm; nice and warm:食堂保证大家全天吃上～的饭菜。The canteen guaranteed to serve hot meals round the clock. /他喝了两杯酒,身上开始～起来。After drinking two glasses of wine, he began to feel warm all over. ❷ warm-natured and friendly; pally; chummy; thick:他们俩挺～的。They are quite chummy.
热化 rèhuà ❶ thermalization ❷ melt with heat
热化学 rèhuàxué thermochemistry
热回收 rèhuíshōu heat recovery
热昏 rèhūn〈方言〉❶ dizzy; giddy ❷ (of degree, extent) very; much:大得～ very big
热火朝天 rèhuǒ-cháotiān reach the peak of enthusiasm; be in full swing; be bustling or buzzing with activity:掀起～的生产高潮 arouse (*or* inspire) tremendous labour enthusiasm in production /工地上～。Work on the construction site was in full swing.
热火 rèhuo ❶ at the peak of excitement; in full swing; exciting:比赛进行得正～。The match is most exciting just at the moment. /今年春节闹得可～啦。There was a lot of merrymaking and excitement during the Spring Festival. ❷ *see* "热和"
热货 rèhuò *also* "热门货" popular commodities; goods in great demand; goods that sell well; hot cakes:这些商品本来是～,由于市场疲软,反而不易销售了。These goods used to be in great demand, but owing to the sluggish market, they don't sell easily now.
热和 rèhuo〈口语〉❶ warm; nice and warm:刚出笼的馒头,真～。The buns just out of the steamer are deliciously warm. ❷ warm and friendly; pally; chummy:孩子们一见面就这么～。The children chummed up with one another the moment they met (*or* took to each other immediately).
热机 rèjī〈机械〉heat engine
热剂焊 rèjìhàn〈冶金〉thermite welding
热寂 rèjì〈物理〉heat death
热加工 rèjiāgōng〈冶金〉hot working; hot work
热交换 rèjiāohuàn heat interchange; heat exchange:～器 heat interchanger; heat exchanger
热劲 rèjìn warm feeling; enthusiasm; ardour:他看着这些亲手移栽成活的小树,心里有说不出来的一股～。He was filled with a warm feeling as he looked at the thriving young saplings that he had transplanted himself.
热静电学 rèjìngdiànxué〈物理〉thermoelectrostatics
热静力学 rèjìnglìxué thermostatics
热锯机 rèjùjī〈冶金〉hot-metal sawing machine
热聚合 rèjùhé〈化工〉thermal polymerization:～橡胶 hot rubber
热聚物 rèjùwù〈化工〉thermopolymer
热客 rèkè ❶〈方言〉frequent caller ❷〈旧语〉man infatuated with a prostitute
热狂 rèkuáng fanatic; fanaticism
热扩散 rèkuòsàn〈物理〉thermal diffusion
热拉伸 rèlāshēn〈冶金〉hot-stretch
热辣辣 rèlālā burning hot; scorching:～的太阳 scorching sun /脸上～的 feel one's cheeks burning
热浪 rèlàng ❶ strong current of warm air:～袭来,使人头晕目眩。I felt my head swim when a strong current of warm air brushed past. ❷〈比喻〉fervour; enthusiasm; craze:这阵子涌起了一股学电脑的～。There rose a surge of fervour for computers. ❸〈气象〉heat wave
热泪 rèlèi hot tears; tears:他眼含～接过银牌。His eyes filled with tears as he was handed the silver medal.
热泪盈眶 rèlèi-yíngkuàng one's eyes brimming with tears; tears coming to one's eyes:感动得～ be moved to tears; be so touched that one's eyes brim with tears
热离子 rèlízǐ〈物理〉thermion; thermoion:～管 thermionic tube
热离子学 rèlízǐxué thermionics
热力 rèlì〈机械〉heating power
热力学 rèlìxué thermodynamics
热力学温标 rèlìxué wēnbiāo thermodynamic scale; thermodynamic scale of temperature
热力学温度 rèlìxué wēndù thermodynamic temperature
热恋 rèliàn be infatuated with; be head over heels in love:他～一个邻家少女。He is captivated by a girl next door. /他俩处在～之中。They were head over heels in love.
热量 rèliàng〈物理〉quantity of heat:～单位 heat unit; thermal unit
热量分析 rèliàng fēnxī calorimetric analysis
热量计 rèliàngjì calorimeter
热疗 rèliáo thermal therapy
热烈 rèliè warm; enthusiastic; ardent:～的掌声 warm applause / ～的气氛 lively atmosphere /～欢呼 warmly hail /～响应 respond enthusiastically /～握手 shake hands cordially / 对真理的～追求 in ardent pursuit of truth
热裂化 rèlièhuà〈石油〉thermal cracking
热流 rèliú ❶〈气象〉thermal current ❷ warm current:一股～涌上心头。A warm current of emotion welled up in me. ❸ upsurge:改革的～ high tide of reform
热络 rèluò *also* "热落"〈方言〉very intimate; very warm
热门 rèmén in great demand; popular:现在外贸专业很～。Foreign trade is a popular speciality nowadays. /咱们不赶那个～。We'll not follow the craze.
热门货 rèménhuò goods which are in great demand or sell well:我们进了一批～。We replenished our stock with goods that sell like hot cakes.
热敏电阻 rèmǐn diànzǔ〈电学〉thermal resistor; thermister hub
热敏性 rèmǐnxìng thermosensitivity
热模压 rèmóyā hot moulding
热那亚 Rènàyà Genoa, major seaport of northwestern Italy
热闹 rènao ❶ busy; bustling:～的街道 busy street /～的庙会 bustling temple fair /星期天这里向来是～的。This district is a hub of activity on Sundays. /家中一下来了四位客人,立刻打破了原来的寂静,显得～起来。The arrival of four guests immediately set our home buzzing with activity. ❷ have a jolly good time; enjoy oneself:每个人都即兴表演,～了一番。They each gave an impromptu performance and had a jolly good time. /今天过节,大家～～吧。Let's enjoy ourselves to the full on this festive occasion. ❸ scene of bustling activity; fun:我们到外面看～去。Let's go out to watch the fun.
热能 rènéng〈物理〉heat or thermal energy
热喷喷 rèpēnpēn steaming hot; piping hot:一碗～的米饭 a bowl of piping hot rice
热膨胀 rèpéngzhàng〈物理〉thermal expansion; heat expansion
热平衡 rèpínghéng〈物理〉thermal equilibrium
热屏蔽 rèpíngbì〈物理〉thermo-shield
热启动 rèqǐdòng〈信息〉vulcan nerve pinch
热气 rèqì steam; heat:～扑面 be greeted by a warm current of air /开水冒着～。The boiling water is giving off steam. /大家～高,干劲大。Everybody was full of enthusiasm and drive.
热气灭菌器 rèqì mièjūnqì hot-air oven
热气球 rèqìqiú hot-air balloon:目前,世界上～升空最高已达一万六千多米。Up to now, the world-record altitude for hot-air balloons is more than 16,000 metres.
热气腾腾 rèqì-téngténg ❶ steaming hot:四人分吃了那一屉～的馒头。The four of them wolfed down a tray of steaming buns. ❷ go on at a vigorous pace:工地上～。The construction site is seething with activity. /该校课外活动搞得～。Extracurricular activities at this school are in full swing.
热气田 rèqìtián hot-gas field
热强度 rèqiángdù〈物理〉calorific intensity
热切 rèqiè ardent; earnest; fervent:～的话语 ardent words; fervent remarks /我～地期待他们在未来的日子里取得更大的成绩。I earnestly expect them to make even better progress. /～希望各位再次光临我厂。It's our earnest wish that you will visit our plant again.
热情 rèqíng enthusiasm; zeal; ardour; warmth:爱国～ patriotic ardour; passionate love for one's country /革命～ revolutionary fer-

R

vour (*or* zeal) /～洋溢的讲话 heart-warming speech /～奔放 overflow with enthusiasm (*or* emotion) /～支持 warm-hearted support /我佩服他的学习～。I admire his devotion to study. /他为人～。He has a warm heart. /他～地接待了我们。He gave us a cordial reception.

热容量 rèróngliàng 〈物理〉 thermal capacity; heat capacity; calorific capacity

热丧 rèsāng be newly bereaved of a parent: ～期间 period of mourning for the death of one's parent

热身 rèshēn warm up; limber up: ～训练 warm-up training /这次比赛属～性质。This game was held as warm-up.

热身赛 rèshēnsài warm-up match; warm-up exercise; warming-up competition: 全国运动会之前将进行一次～。A warm-up match will be held before the National Games.

热声学 rèshēngxué 〈物理〉 thermoacoustics

热释光 rèshìguāng *also* "热发光" 〈考古〉 thermoluminescence (TL): 运用～等新技术来测定陶器的年代。New techniques such as thermoluminescence are employed in the dating of pottery.

热水袋 rèshuǐdài hot water bottle

热水瓶 rèshuǐpíng 〈口语〉 thermos (bottle); thermos flask; vacuum bottle or flask

热水器 rèshuǐqì water heater

热水田 rèshuǐtián geothermal field with hot springs

热塑塑料 rèsù sùliào thermoplastic

热塑性 rèsùxìng 〈化工〉 thermoplasticity

热损耗 rèsǔnhào 〈物理〉 thermosteresis

热缩包装 rèsuō bāozhuāng shrink wrap

热弹性 rètánxìng 〈物理〉 thermoelasticity

热汤面 rètāngmiàn hot noodle soup

热腾腾 rètēngtēng (of food or water) steaming hot: 饭菜～的，我想等它稍微凉一些再吃。The food is steaming hot. I prefer to wait for it to cool a little before eating it.

热天 rètiān hot weather; sweltering heat: ～吃不下饭 can't eat much in the sweltering heat

热田 rètián *also* "地热田" dìrètián geothermal field

热图像 rètúxiàng 〈物理〉 thermal image (image acquired by thermal infrared or microwave radiation, representing the surface temperature)

热土 rètǔ homeland; native place: 穷家难舍，～难离。It is hard to take leave of one's native place (*or* one's home) however humble it may be.

热瓦普 rèwǎpǔ five-stringed musical instrument (of the Uighurs, Tajiks and Uzbeks)

热望 rèwàng ❶ earnestly hope; ardently wish: 他～当一名称职的教师。It's his ardent wish to become a qualified teacher. /她～儿子早日归来。She is fervently expecting her son to return soon. /他从～的顶峰跌到失望的深渊里。He was cast from the height of enthusiasm to the depths of despair. ❷ strong desire; sincere hope: 心中的～终于如愿以偿。His aspirations were fulfilled.

热污染 rèwūrǎn thermal pollution

热物理学 rèwùlǐxué thermophysics

热线 rèxiàn ❶ *also* "红外线" hóngwàixiàn infrared ray ❷ 〈通信〉 hot-line: 卫星～ satellite hot-line /电话～ hot-line telephone /～服务 hot-line service ❸ busy route: 旅游～ busy tourist route

热像仪 rèxiàngyí 〈电子〉 thermal imaging system

热销 rèxiāo (of goods) in great demand: ～商品 goods in great demand; goods that sell like hot cakes /今年夏季，人造棉将～。Staple rayon will have a ready market this summer. /上海西装领带～。Western-style suits and ties made in Shanghai have a huge market.

热孝 rèxiào (of women) in mourning over the recent death of grandparents, parents or husband: ～在身 be in mourning

热效率 rèxiàolǜ heat efficiency; thermal efficiency; calorific efficiency

热效应 rèxiàoyìng 〈物理〉 calorific effect; fuel factor

热心 rèxīn enthusiastic; ardent; sincere; earnest; warm-hearted: ～街道事务 be enthusiastic about neighbourhood affairs /～照顾旅客 look carefully after the comfort of passengers /～于公益事业 be devoted to public good /对这些他一点也不～。He showed little interest in such matters.

热心肠 rèxīncháng 〈口语〉 warm-heartedness; warm heart: 他有副～，肯帮别人的忙。He is warm-hearted and always ready to help others.

热性肥料 rèxìng féiliào 〈农业〉 hot manure

热学 rèxué 〈物理〉 heat; calorifics; thermology; thermotics

热血 rèxuè warm blood; indignation: 抛头颅，洒～ shed one's blood /～男儿 red-blooded youth /甘洒～ be ready to lay down one's life (for a cause)

热血动物 rèxuè dòngwù warm-blooded animal; warm blood

热血沸腾 rèxuè-fèiténg one's blood boils; seethe with righteous indignation: 这电影看得人～。The film filled me with great indignation.

热循环 rèxúnhuán 〈物理〉 heat cycle

热压 rèyā 〈化工〉 hot pressing; thermocompression: ～成形 hot forming /～机 thermocompressor; hot-press

热罨 rèyǎn *see* "热敷"

热药 rèyào 〈中医〉 medicine of a hot or warm nature; tonics and stimulants

热饮 rèyǐn hot drinks

热郁 rèyù 〈中医〉 hot and suffocating; muggy

热源 rèyuán 〈物理〉 heat source

热轧 rèzhá 〈冶金〉 hot-rolling: ～机 hot-rolling mill /～带钢 hot-strip /～钢 hot rolled steel (HRS)

热战 rèzhàn hot war; shooting war

热障 rèzhàng 〈物理〉 heat barrier

热振寺 Rèzhènsì Redreng monastery (in Tibet)

热症 rèzhèng 〈中医〉 heat symptom-complex; febrile symptoms

热值 rèzhí 〈物理〉 calorific value; thermal value

热挚 rèzhì fervent and sincere: 这些文字都是作者～情感的真实流露。The writing truly reflects the fervent and sincere feelings of the author.

热中 rèzhōng *also* "热衷" ❶ develop an intense desire for; hanker after; hanker for; crave: ～名利 crave fame and gain ❷ be deeply interested in; develop an intense interest in; be mad about: ～于数学 develop an intense interest in (*or* be deeply interested in) mathematics /～于教育事业 devote oneself, heart and soul, to the cause of education /他们现在～的是流行音乐。What they are mad about is pop music.

热中子 rèzhōngzǐ 〈物理〉 thermal neutron

热灼伤 rèzhuóshāng thermal burn

热阻 rèzǔ 〈物理〉 heat resistance

rén

人 rén ❶ human being; man; person; people: 妇～ (married) woman /老～ old man or woman; the aged; one's aged parents or grandparents /白～ white man; white people (*or* population) /黑～ black man; black people /中国～ Chinese (people) /欧洲～ European /城里～ townsman; townswoman; townspeople; city dwellers /乡下～ country folk; countryman; country cousin; bumpkin /湖南～ native of Hunan; Hunanese /汉～ Hans; Han people /～的需要 human needs; man's needs /～喊马嘶 people shouting and horses neighing /没有别～知道这件事。Nobody else knows about this. /你一个～行吗? Can you manage on your own? /他的主张是"天地间，～为贵"。Of all that is in heaven and earth, he holds man most precious. ❷ everybody; each; all: 令～景仰 command universal respect; be held in high esteem /胆略过～ possess peerless courage and resourcefulness; be exceedingly brave and resourceful /出～头地 rise head and shoulders above others; stand out among one's fellows; outshine others /～手一册。Each has a copy. /这是～所共知的事情。This is known to all. *or* This is general knowledge. /保护环境，～～有责。It's everyone's responsibility to protect the environment. *or* Environmental protection is the responsibility of every individual. ❸ adult; grown-up: 长大成～ grow to manhood; come of age /她生过六个孩子，但五个都没成～。She gave birth to six children, but five of them died before they grew up. ❹ person engaged in a particular activity: 客～ guest /证～ witness /文化～ man of letters; intellectual /国家领导～ state (*or* government) leaders; leadership of the state /说这种话的～太没有修养。Those who make such remarks can scarcely be considered educated. /支持他的～日益减少。The number of his supporters dwindled day by day. ❺ other people; people: 待～宽，律己严 be lenient towards others but strict with oneself /助～为乐 derive joy from rendering services to others; regard service to people as a source of joy ❻ personality; character:

文如其～。The style is the man. /他～怎么样? How do you like him? *or* What do you think of him? /他为～直爽。He is frank and straightforward. /这里～好, 自然条件也好。The people here are friendly and the natural environment is excellent. ❼ one's state of health or mind: 我看见他时, ～已经昏过去了。When I saw him, he was in a coma (*or* he had lost consciousness). /他～在这里, 心不在这里。He is with us here physically, but his heart is elsewhere. ❽ hand; manpower: 他们那里缺～。They are short of hands. *or* They are understaffed. /我们这里藏龙卧虎, 谁说没～? We have a galaxy of talents here. Who can say we are lacking in gifted people?

人保 rénbǎo 〈旧语〉personal guarantee

人本主义 rénběnzhǔyì 〈哲学〉humanism

人比人,气死人 rén bǐ rén, qì sǐ rén 〈俗语〉it would make you hopping mad if you compare yourself with luckier people

人不犯我,我不犯人 rén bù fàn wǒ, wǒ bù fàn rén we will not attack unless we are attacked: ～, 人若犯我, 我必犯人。We will not attack unless we are attacked; if we are attacked, we will certainly counterattack.

人不可以貌相 rén bù kěyǐ mào xiàng never judge a person by his appearence: ～, 海水不可斗量。A man can not be known by his looks, nor can the sea be measured with a dipper.

人不为己,天诛地灭 rén bù wèi jǐ, tiān zhū dì miè 〈旧语〉heaven and earth will destroy those who are not self-centred; every man for himself and the devil take the hindmost

人不知,鬼不觉 rén bù zhī, guǐ bù jué without anybody's knowledge; in absolute secrecy: 他～就把事情办好了。He had done his job before anybody was aware of it. /他～地溜走了。He simply vanished without a trace.

人才 réncái *also* "人材" ❶ qualified personnel; person of ability; talented person; talent: ～浪费 waste of talent /科技～ scientists and technicians ❷ 〈口语〉handsome appearance: 一表～ man of remarkable (*or* striking) appearance

人才辈出 réncái-bèichū people of talent emerge in succession; large numbers of outstanding people are coming forward: 这个学科～。Brilliant scholars have emerged in this field of study wave upon wave.

人才出众 réncái-chūzhòng person of exceptional ability or beauty; outstanding talent; strikingly beautiful woman

人才断层 réncái duàncéng fault or break in the continuity of talented people; shortage of a whole generation of qualified personnel: 这批中年教师退休后, 就会出现～。By the time these middle-aged teachers have retired, there will be a fault in the teaching staff.

人才荟萃 réncái- huìcuì gathering of distinquished people or scholar: 这所大学是～之所。There is a galaxy of talent in this university.

人才济济 réncái-jǐjǐ abundance of talented people; galaxy of talent: 这个研究所～, 科研取得了丰硕成果。This research institute, staffed by distinguished scientists, has registered many impressive results.

人才交流 réncái jiāoliú exchange of talent; flow of trained personnel

人才交流中心 réncái jiāoliú zhōngxīn personnel exchange centre; job centre

人才库 réncáikù brain trust; talent bank

人才流动 réncái liúdòng flow or mobility of trained people

人才难得 réncái-nándé ❶ real talent is hard to come by ❷ rare talent: 领导称他～, 应该予以重用。Regarding him as a rare talent, his leader promised to give him an important position.

人才市场 réncái shìchǎng employment market; job centre

人才外流 réncái wàiliú brain drain

人材 réncái see "人才"

人财两空 rén-cái liǎngkōng sustain both human and material loss (as when a man's mistress absconds with his money and valuables); lose both people and money

人潮 rénchāo huge crowd of people; stream of people; flow of people; sea of faces: 足球赛场上鼓乐喧天, ～涌动。Huge crowds of people milled about in the stadium amidst crescendos of music and drumbeats while the football match was going on. /展览会自开幕以来, 每天～川流不息。There has been a continual stream of visitors to the exhibition every day since its opening.

人臣 rénchén official in a royal court; vassal

人称 rénchēng 〈语言〉person: 第三～单数 third person singular /不定～ indefinite person

人称代词 rénchēng dàicí 〈语言〉personal pronoun

人次 réncì person-time; man-time: 来本医院挂专家门诊的每周达五百～。Consultations with specialists in this hospital have reached 500 person-times per week. /一周就有一万～参观了画展。Admissions to the art exhibition totalled over ten thousand in a week.

人丛 réncóng crowd of people: 他从～中挤了出来。He elbowed his way out through the crowd.

人存政举 réncún-zhèngjǔ when the man is in power, his policy remains in force: ～, 人亡政息。A policy rises and falls with the man — rule by personality, not by law.

人大 Réndà ❶ (short for 人民代表大会) (National) People's Congress: 全国～ NPC (the National People's Congress)/市～ Municipal People's Congress ❷ (short for 中国人民大学) People's University of China

人大常委会 Réndà Chángwěihuì Standing Committee of the (National) People's Congress

人大代表 Réndà dàibiǎo Deputy to the (National) People's Congress: 省～ deputy to the Provincial People's Congress

人道 réndào ❶ humanity; human sympathy: 这种作法极不～。Such practice is most inhuman. ❷〈旧语〉human relations based upon feudal ethics ❸〈书面〉moral standards; moral principles: 欺凌弱者是违反～的。It goes against moral principles to bully the weak. ❹ (often used negatively) have sex: 不能～ impotent; incapable of sexual intercourse

人道报 Réndàobào *L'Humanité*, French daily newspaper published by the Communist Party of France since 1904

人道主义 réndàozhǔyì humanitarianism: ～的援助 humanitarian aid

人地生疏 rén-dì shēngshū be a complete or total stranger: 他新来乍到, ～。Being a newcomer, he is a total stranger to the place.

人丁 réndīng ❶〈旧语〉adult ❷ population; number of family members: ～不旺 have a small population; have a small family /～兴旺 have a large (*or* growing) family; have a flourishing population

人定胜天réndìngshèngtiān man is bound to conquer nature; man's will, not heaven, decides: 这个故事表现了～的思想。This story tells of man's eventual triumph over nature. /他们坚信～, 誓与洪水展开搏斗。Convinced that man will conquer nature, they are determined to fight the floods.

人堆儿 rénduīr 〈口语〉crowd: 他就喜欢往～里扎。He enjoys mixing with the crowd.

人多势众 rénduō-shìzhòng enjoy numerical superiority and consequently great strength; overwhelm by numerical superiority; dominate by sheer force of numbers: ～, 不用怕。There is strength in numbers; we've nothing to be afraid of.

人多智广 rénduō-zhìguǎng two heads are better than one; more people, greater wisdom: 我们相信～, 没有解决不了的难题。We believe in collective wisdom, and there is no difficulty the people cannot surmount.

人多嘴杂 rénduō-zuǐzá ❶ a babel of voices spells divided counsel; consensus is difficult when there is a big crowd; many people, many voices ❷ it is difficult to keep a secret when it is shared by many people; the more people, the more talk

人而无信,不知其可 rén ér wú xìn, bù zhī qí kě if a man does not keep his word, what is he good for; a faithless man is not worth a farthing

人犯 rénfàn 〈旧语〉the accused or his accessory: 逮捕所有～ round up all offenders

人贩子 rénfànzi trafficker in human beings: 拐卖妇女儿童的～ man who abducts and sells women and children

人防 rénfáng (short for 人民防空) civil defence; people's air defence

人非草木 rénfēicǎomù neither wood nor grass but man; normal human being: ～, 孰能无情? Human beings are not inanimate things; how can they be free from emotions?

人非圣贤,孰能无过 rén fēi shèngxián, shú néng wú guò as all men are not sages, how can they be free from faults; to err is human: ～, 过而能改, 善莫大焉。There is no virtue greater than to mend one's way, as to err is only human.

人份 rénfèn person-portion; portion: 麻疹疫苗三万～ thirty thousand measles inoculations

人粪尿 rénfènniào 〈农业〉night soil; human waste; excrement

人逢喜事精神爽 rén féng xǐshì jīngshen shuǎng happiness braces the spirit; joy gives heart to man:～,闷上心头瞌睡多。While happy events boost a person's spirit, depression induces drowsiness.

人夫 rénfū *also* "人伕"〈旧语〉servant; corvée labourer

人浮于事 rénfúyúshì have more workers than are needed; be overstaffed:有的单位机构臃肿,～。Some institutions are unwieldy in structure and have more workers than are needed.

人格 réngé ❶ personality:双重～ split personality /法律～ legal personality ❷human dignity; person's moral quality:～高尚 have a noble character; have moral integrity /尊重～ respect one's dignity / 污辱～ be an insult to human dignity /降低～ sink to a lower level in human dignity; stoop beneath one's dignity; cheapen oneself /以～担保 upon my honour /做人总得讲点～。People should have a sense of moral integrity. /人有～,国有国格。Just as a man has his dignity, a country has her dignity, too. ❸ person:～不可侵犯 inviolability of person ❹ attributing human characteristics to things; personification:童话往往赋予动植物以～。Animals and plants are often represented as having human characteristics in fairy tales.

人格层 réngécéng stratum of personality

人格化 réngéhuà personify:在这段描写中,动物都～了。In the description, the animals are personified.

人格权 réngéquán right to human dignity

人格障碍 réngé zhàng'ài personality disorder

人格主义 réngézhǔyì personalism

人各有志 réngèyǒuzhì everyone has his own will or aspiration:～,不可勉强。As everyone has his aspirations, you must not force anyone to do things against his will.

人工 réngōng ❶ artificial; man-made:～自然 artificial nature /～生态系统 artificial ecosystem ❷ manual labour or work; work done by hand:～制造 made (*or* produced) by hand /～打井 dig (*or* drill) a well by human power ❸ manpower; man-day:估计一下,这项工程需要多少～。Let's make a rough estimate of the number of man-days needed for the project.

人工岛 réngōngdǎo man-made island; port island

人工繁殖 réngōng fánzhí 〈农业〉artificial propagation

人工放顶 réngōng fàngdǐng 〈矿业〉artificial caving

人工孵化 réngōng fūhuà artificial incubation

人工更新 réngōng gēngxīn 〈林业〉artificial regeneration

人工合成蛋白质 réngōng héchéng dànbáizhì synthetic protein

人工合成结晶胰岛素 réngōng héchéng jiéjīng yídǎosù synthetic crystaline insulin

人工合成胰岛素 réngōng héchéng yídǎosù synthetic insulin

人工喉 réngōnghóu artificial larynx

人工呼吸 réngōng hūxī artificial respiration:～器 artificial respirator; spirophore; pulmotor

人工湖 réngōnghú man-made lake

人工降水 réngōng jiàngshuǐ artificial precipitation

人工降雨 réngōng jiàngyǔ artificial rainfall; rain making; design rain:～器 raingun /～设备 rainmaker /～装置 rainer; artificial rain device; sprinkler

人工流产 réngōng liúchǎn induced abortion; abortion

人工免疫 réngōng miǎnyì artificial immunization

人工脑 réngōngnǎo mechanical brains

人工皮 réngōngpí artificial skin

人工气腹 réngōng qìfù artificial pneumoperitoneum (APP)

人工气候实验室 réngōng qìhòu shíyànshì artificial climate laboratory

人工气胸 réngōng qìxiōng artificial pneumothorax

人工器官 réngōng qìguān artificial organ

人工肾 réngōngshèn artificial kidney

人工生态系统 réngōng shēngtài xìtǒng artificial ecosystem

人工授粉 réngōng shòufěn 〈农业〉artificial pollination

人工授精 réngōng shòujīng 〈畜牧〉artificial insemination; artificial fertilization; artificial service:～器 impregnator

人工授胎 réngōng shòutāi artificial impregnation

人工心肺机 réngōng xīnfèijī heart-lung machine; extra-corporal circulation apparatus

人工选择 réngōng xuǎnzé 〈生物〉artificial selection

人工智能 réngōng zhìnéng artificial intelligence:～电子学 intellectronics /～的研究进展很快。Research in artificial intelligence has been developing rapidly.

人公里 réngōnglǐ 〈交通〉passenger-kilometre

人海 rénhǎi ❶ sea of faces; huge crowd (of people):～战术 human sea tactics /我一直目送他消失在～里。I watched him disappearing into the crowd. /茫茫～,哪里能找到他啊! In this vast human sea he is nowhere to be found. ❷〈书面〉human world:～沧桑 human vicissitudes /～沉浮 ups and downs of human life

人豪 rénháo giant of a man; ablest and bravest of men; man of outstanding personality

人和 rénhé harmony of people; popular support:得～ enjoy popular support /天时、地利、～ favourable climatic, geographical and human conditions /政通～。Wise leadership enjoys the people's support.

人和生物圈 rén hé shēngwùquān man and biosphere (MAB)

人户 rénhù *also* "人家"〈方言〉household; family; fiancé's family:走～ call on friends; pay visits to friends /媒人给她介绍了一个～。The matchmaker has found her a prospective husband.

人花花儿 rénhuāhuār 〈方言〉shadow of any person:四周空荡荡的,不见～。The place was deserted, and not a single soul could be seen.

人话 rénhuà (usually ironical) talk befitting a rational being; sensible or reasonable words:你怎么不说～? How come you don't talk sense? /这还算～。Now you're talking (sense).

人欢马叫 rénhuān-mǎjiào people bustling and horses neighing — a busy thriving village scene or worksite

人寰 rénhuán 〈书面〉human world; world; the earth:惨绝～ tragic beyond compare in this human world; extremely tragic /誉满～ be widely known all over the world; be world-famous

人祸 rénhuò man-made calamity; artificially created disaster:天灾～,接踵而来。Natural and man-made calamities came one after another.

人机工程 rén-jī gōngchéng man-machine engineering; human engineering

人机联系 rén-jī liánxì man-machine interface or interaction

人机模拟 rén-jī mónǐ man-machine simulation

人机通信 rén-jī tōngxìn man-machine communication

人机系统 rén-jī xìtǒng 〈计算机〉man-machine system

人急造反,狗急跳墙 rén jí zàofǎn, gǒu jí tiàoqiáng 〈俗语〉as the desperate dog will jump a wall, so the desperate man will hazard all

人给家足 rénjǐ-jiāzú every household is well-fed and well-clothed

人际 rénjì between persons; interpersonal:～交往 human communication /～交往技巧 interpersonal skill

人际法 rénjìfǎ interpersonal law

人际关系 rénjì guānxì interpersonal relationship; human relationship:～学 study of interpersonal relations

人迹 rénjì human footprints or footmarks; human traces; traces of human presence or habitation:渺无～ wild and uninhabited; without a trace of human presence

人迹罕至 rénjì-hǎnzhì (of place) rarely visited by human beings; seldom trodden by people; untraversed:城南深山中有一古寺,～。Deep in the mountain recess south of the city was an ancient temple rarely visited by people.

人祭 rénjì human sacrifice

人家 rénjiā ❶ household:村子里只有十几户～。There are only a dozen households or so in the village. ❷ family:勤俭～ hardworking and frugal family /殷实～ well-off (*or* well-to-do) family ❸ fiancé's family:这姑娘有了～了。The girl is betrothed.

人家 rénjia ❶ other people; others:～都出发了,就你迟迟不动,却是为何? Why are you still hesitating to move while the others have all left? ❷ certain person; certain persons:～一气,就决定把我们辞了。He got furious and decided to sack us. /你把礼物给～送去吧。Take the gifts to them, will you? ❸ I; me:～想要这件衣服嘛! But that dress is what I really want. /～情绪不好,最好别啰唆了。I'm in a bad mood. You'd better stop nagging.

人尖子 rénjiānzi *also* "人尖儿" outstanding personality; topnotch person:要论庄稼活,在村里他是个～。He is the village's top farmer.

人间 rénjiān human world; world; the earth:～乐园 earthly paradise /饱尝～的苦难 taste life's hardships to the full /～悲剧 human tragedy /～奇迹 man-made miracle /～自有真情在。Genuine feelings do exist on earth.

人间词话 Rénjiān Cíhuà *Renjian Cihua*, or *Prosody of Ci Poetry*, by Wang Guowei (王国维,1877-1927), published in 1908

人间地狱 rénjiān-dìyù hell on earth

人间天堂 rénjiān-tiāntáng heaven on earth; paradise on earth

人杰 rénjié 〈书面〉outstanding character; remarkable personality:

生为～，死为鬼雄 live and die like a hero
人杰地灵 rénjié-dìlíng ❶ an outstanding man gives an air of sanctity to his birthplace; a fair place tends to produce outstanding people：此处山青水秀，～。The outstanding personalities who have lived here lend miraculous lustre to the landscape of the locality.
人尽其才 rénjìnqícái let every individual give full play to his talent
人精 rénjīng 〈方言〉❶ worldly-wise person ❷ exceedingly clever child
人居学 rénjūxué ekistics
人均 rénjūn per person; per capita; per head：～分配 distribution per person /～收入 income per person; per capita income /全村栽了四万多株树，～一百株。More than 40 thousand trees were planted in the whole village, an average of 100 trees per head.
人均国民生产总值 rénjūn guómín shēngchǎn zǒngzhí per capita GNP (gross national product)
人均国民收入 rénjūn guómín shōurù per capita national income
人均国内生产总值 rénjūn guónèi shēngchǎn zǒngzhí per capita GDP (gross domestic product)
人君 rénjūn 〈书面〉monarch; king; sovereign
人科 rénkē 〈动物〉*Hominidae*; the family of man
人客 rénkè 〈方言〉guest; visitor
人孔 rénkǒng 〈建筑〉manhole
人控 rénkòng manned; man-operated; by manual operation：～实验〈航天〉manned experiment (space experiment requiring direct human intervention) /～推进系统 man-operated propulsion system /～机器人〈自控〉robot
人口 rénkǒu ❶ population：这个村有多少～？What is the population of the village? /～稠密 densely populated /城市～ urban population /流动～ transient population /在业～ working population /待业～ population waiting for employment /盲流～ drifting population; drifter /～不足 underpopulation /～减少 population decline /～结构 population structure /马尔萨斯～论 Malthusianism (doctrine of Thomas Robert Malthus, 1766-1834, British economist) ❷ family size：家庭～ number of family members /我们家～多。Ours is a large family. ❸ man; person：贩卖～ human trafficking /家里又添了～。The family has a new-born baby. ❹ mouth(of a person)：脍炙～ much praised
人口爆炸 rénkǒu bàozhà population explosion
人口出生率 rénkǒu chūshēnglǜ birth rate; human fertility
人口动态统计 rénkǒu dòngtài tǒngjì vital statistics
人口动态学 rénkǒu dòngtàixué population dynamics
人口分布 rénkǒu fēnbù population distribution
人口负增长 rénkǒu fùzēngzhǎng negative population growth (NPG)
人口过剩 rénkǒu guòshèng overpopulation
人口基数 rénkǒu jīshù population base
人口金字塔 rénkǒu jīnzìtǎ population pyramid
人口老化 rénkǒu lǎohuà aging of population：中国～ greying of China
人口密度 rénkǒu mìdù population density
人口年轻化 rénkǒu niánqīnghuà rejuvenation of population
人口普查 rénkǒu pǔchá (population) census
人口税 rénkǒushuì poll tax
人口死亡率 rénkǒu sǐwánglǜ human mortality
人口统计 rénkǒu tǒngjì population statistics
人口统计学 rénkǒu tǒngjìxué demography
人口学 rénkǒuxué demography：～家 demographer
人口意识 rénkǒu yìshi awareness of the population problem
人口预测 rénkǒu yùcè population projection
人口质量 rénkǒu zhìliàng population quality
人口转化期 rénkǒu zhuǎnhuàqī period of demographic transition
人口自然增长率 rénkǒu zìrán zēngzhǎnglǜ natural growth rate of population
人口组成 rénkǒu zǔchéng population composition
人困马乏 rénkùn-mǎfá both men and their horses are worn out：他们走得～。They were overcome with fatigue after the long hike.
人来疯 rénláifēng *also* "人来风"〈方言〉(of children) behave like a spoiled child before guests; play childish pranks in the presence of guests
人老珠黄 rénlǎo-zhūhuáng (originally of women) one's looks fade like pearls yellowing; people grow old like pearls turning yellow：～不值钱。In old age, one is like a pearl which has lost its lustre and no longer held in esteem.
人类 rénlèi Homo sapiens; mankind; humanity; human race：～社会 human society /～的命运 destiny of mankind /～的生存 human existence /～的古代和现代文明 ancient and modern civilization of the human race /长城属于全～。The Great Wall belongs to humanity.
人类工程学 rénlèi gōngchéngxué ergonomics
人类环境学 rénlèi huánjìngxué proxemics
人类起源 rénlèi qǐyuán origin of the human species; origin of mankind
人类圈 rénlèiquān anthroposphere
人类生态学 rénlèi shēngtàixué human ecology
人类学 rénlèixué anthropology
人类遗传学 rénlèi yíchuánxué human genetics
人类语言学 rénlèi yǔyánxué anthropological linguistics
人力 rénlì manpower; labour power：爱护～物力 treasure manpower and material resources /用机械代替～ employ machinery to replace labour power /非～所及 beyond human control /我们的～资源很丰富。We have rich human resources.
人力车 rénlìchē ❶ vehicle drawn or driven by man ❷ rickshaw
人流 rénliú ❶ stream or flow of people：～如潮 sea of faces; huge crowds of people ❷ (short for 人工流产) induced abortion：她刚做完～。She has just had her baby aborted. *or* She's just had an abortion.
人龙 rénlóng long lines of people; constant flow of people
人伦 rénlún human relations (according to feudal ethics)：封建～ feudal human relations
人马 rénmǎ ❶ troops; forces：全部～已开到平原地区。All the troops have been dispatched to the plains. ❷ staff; set-up：原班～ original team; old set-up (*or* cast) /科研所～整齐。The institute is well staffed.
人马座 Rénmǎzuò 〈天文〉Sagittarius
人满为患 rénmǎnwéihuàn (trouble of) having too many people; overcrowded; overstaffed：夏日的游泳池～。In summer, the swimming pool was overcrowded with people.
人们 rénmen people; the public：～都说她不错。People all speak well of her. /如今～看这个问题的角度变了。The problem is viewed from a different perspective (*or* seen in a different light) today.
人面 rénmiàn social contacts：他外头～广，办事有路子。Having plenty of social connections, he can always get things done.
人面兽心 rénmiàn-shòuxīn have a human face but a wolfish heart; beast in human shape
人面桃花 rénmiàn-táohuā woman's face and peach-blossoms — the pinings of a lover
人面竹 rénmiànzhú *also* "佛肚竹" fódùzhú a variety of bamboo, which is stumpy between joints
人民 rénmín the people：～群众 the masses; the mass of people /我国～ people of our country /世界～ people of the world /～资本主义 people's capitalism /～是历史的创造者。It is the people who create history. *or* History is created by the mass of people.
人民币 rénmínbì renminbi; RMB：外汇～(no longer in use) foreign exchange certificate (FEC) /～汇价平稳。The exchange rate of RMB is stable.
人民大会堂 Rénmín Dàhuìtáng Great Hall of the People (venue of the National People's Congress, in Beijing)
人民代表大会 rénmín dàibiǎo dàhuì people's congress
人民党 Rénmíndǎng Janata Party (in India, 1977-)：印度～ Bhatatiya Janata Party (of India)
人民法院 rénmín fǎyuàn people's court：～院长 president of the people's court
人民公社 rénmín gōngshè people's commune
人民画报 Rénmín Huàbào *China Pictorial*
人民检察院 rénmín jiǎncháyuàn people's procuratorate：～检察长 chief procurator of the people's procuratorate
人民解放军 Rénmín Jiěfàngjūn People's Liberation Army (PLA)
人民警察 rénmín jǐngchá people's police
人民来信 rénmín láixìn letters from the masses
人民民主专政 rénmín mínzhǔ zhuānzhèng people's democratic dictatorship
人民内部矛盾 rénmín nèibù máodùn contradictions among the people
人民陪审员 rénmín péishěnyuán 〈法律〉people's assessor

R

人民勤务员 rénmín qínwùyuán servant of the people
人民日报 Rénmín Rìbào *Renmin Ribao* or *People's Daily*, organ of the Communist Party of China published since 1949
人民入境事务处 Rénmín Rùjìng Shìwùchù (HK) Immigration Department
人民团体 rénmín tuántǐ people's organization; mass organization
人民委员会 rénmín wěiyuánhuì people's committee
人民武装 rénmín wǔzhuāng people's armed forces, including the People's Liberation Army and people's militia; militia
人民武装部 rénmín wǔzhuāngbù people's armed forces department
人民性 rénmínxìng affinity to the people
人民英雄纪念碑 Rénmín Yīngxióng Jìniànbēi Monument to the People's Heroes (on Tian'anmen Square, Beijing)
人民院 Rénmínyuàn (India) Lok Sabha, or House of the People
人民战争 rénmín zhànzhēng people's war
人民阵线 rénmín zhènxiàn popular front
人民政府 rénmín zhèngfǔ people's government
人名 rénmíng name (of a person): ～索引 index of names; *index nominum*
人命 rénmìng human life: ～案子 case of homicide (*or* manslaughter) /此案关系到两条～。This is a case involving two deaths (*or* the life or death of two people).
人命关天 rénmìng-guāntiān a case involving human life is a matter of great consequence: 此事～, 非同儿戏。It's a case involving human life, and no joking matter.
人命危浅 rénmìng-wēiqiǎn be dying; be on one's last legs; have one foot in the grave: ～, 朝不虑夕 be sinking fast
人莫予毒 rénmòyúdú no one dares to harm me — an arrogant boast
人脑 rénnǎo human brain: ～模拟 brain simulation /～系统功能 function of the human brain system
人年 rénnián man-year
人怕出名猪怕壮 rén pà chūmíng zhū pà zhuàng 〈俗语〉 fame is fatal to men as fatness is to pigs; it's bad for a man to become famous and for a pig to grow fat; fame portends trouble for men just as fattening does for pigs
人品 rénpǐn ❶ moral quality; moral strength; character: ～甚高 be (a person) of very good character (*or* high moral stature) /～不佳 be (a person) of disreputable character ❷ 〈口语〉 looks; bearing: 这孩子～好。The boy is quite handsome.
人气 rénqì 〈方言〉 ❶ fine qualities and style: 这人好～。What a fine chap he is! /村里谁不知道他的～! His fine qualities are known to everyone in the village. /他连一点～也没有。There is not even an iota of human decency in him. ❷ mood; frame of mind; popular feeling; public feeling: 行情浮动, 市场～看低, 估计还要跌呢。Right now, prices are fluctuating and the public's confidence in the market is waning. The prices will probably drop even further.
人弃我取 rénqì-wǒqǔ take what other people discard; buy in while others sell off (so as to make big profits later); 〈比喻〉 have interests or views different from other people; have ideas of one's own: ～, 人取我与。I take what others discard, and I give up what others desire.
人强马壮 rénqiáng-mǎzhuàng both men and horses are in fine fettle; be adequately staffed; have great effective strength
人墙 rénqiáng wall of people (as in football games during a free kick); wall: 筑～ set a wall
人琴俱亡 rén-qín jùwáng the man and his lute are both dead (a lament over the death of a bosom friend, attributed to Wang Huizhi 王徽之 of the Jin Dynasty)
人勤地不懒 rén qín dì bù lǎn where the tiller is diligent, the land is productive
人情 rénqíng ❶ human nature; human feelings; sympathy: 不近～ unsympathetic; unreasonable /不知～世故 unacquainted with the ways of the world; not worldly-wise; unsociable /违背～ unnatural and abnormal /～之所不能忍者, 圣人不能禁。What human nature cannot control, a sage cannot prevent. ❷ sensibilities; feelings: 托～ seek sb.'s good offices /不讲～ spare no sensibilities /可是～不能不讲啊。One can't lose sight of the human side of things. ❸ favour: 做个～ do sb. a favour /空头～ (pay) lip service /收到的钱不多, 但使他感到一种～, 一种温暖。It was not a big sum of money that he received, but it brought him a warm feeling of being cared for. ❹ etiquette; custom; convention: 随～ follow the customary practice /此属～往来。This is a matter of social behaviour. ❺ gift; present: 送～ give presents
人情冷暖 rénqíng-lěngnuǎn fickleness of human relationship; social snobbery: 节物后先南北异, ～古今同。Although the north and the south vary in products and seasons, social snobbery remains unchanged throughout the ages.
人情礼 rénqínglǐ gift presented to strenghten interpersonal relations
人情练达 rénqíng-liàndá experienced in the ways of the world; worldly-wise: 世事洞明皆学问, ～即文章。A grasp of mundane affairs is genuine knowledge; worldly wisdom is sure learning.
人情世故 rénqíng-shìgù worldly wisdom; ways of the world: 她人小, 却很懂得～。Young as she is, she is worldly-wise.
人情味 rénqíngwèi empathy; human kindness; human interest: 他没一点～。He is apathetic by nature. *or* He has no empathy for others. /这部电影很有～。This film has much human appeal.
人情债 rénqíngzhài debt of gratitude
人情纸薄 rénqíng-zhǐbáo human feelings are as thin as a sheet of paper — flimsy human relationship
人穷志不穷 rén qióng zhì bù qióng though one is poor, one has high aspiration; cherish great ambition despite one's lowly position
人穷志短 rénqióng-zhìduǎn poverty stifles ambition: 他～, 近来做了好些丢脸的事。He has lost all sense of dignity because of poverty and has recently stooped to disgraceful practices.
人去楼空 rénqù-lóukōng the dear one is gone and the room is empty — old sights recall to mind fond memories of the past
人权 rénquán human rights; rights of man: 违反～ violate human rights /维护～ protect human rights /尊重～ respect the rights of man /侵犯～ encroach upon human rights
人权法案 Rénquán Fǎ'àn (US) Bill of Rights (comprising the first ten amendments to the US Constitution, adopted at the first Congress, 1791)
人权宣言 Rénquán Xuānyán ❶ *see* "人权与公民权宣言" ❷ Universal Declaration of Human Rights (of the United Nations, 1948)
人权与公民权宣言 Rénquán Yǔ Gōngmínquán Xuānyán Declaration of the Rights of Man and of the Citizen (of France, 1789)
人群 rénqún crowd; throng; multitude: 他在～中挤着向前走。He is squeezing his way through the crowd. /正在这时, 一位高级官员出现在～中。Just at that moment, a senior official appeared among the masses.
人儿 rénr ❶ small figure; figurine: 捏个泥～ mould a clay figurine ❷ 〈方言〉 behaviour and manners, etc.: 他～还不错。He is a decent chap.
人人 rénrén everybody; everyone: ～皆知 be known to all; it is public knowledge /～都要遵守交通规则。Everybody should observe the traffic regulations. /爱护公物, ～有责。It's everyone's responsibility to take care of public property.
人人自危 rénrén-zìwēi everyone feels endangered; nobody feels secure: 时疫流行, 居民～。In the face of the spreading epidemic every inhabitant felt endangered.
人日 rénrì ❶ 〈旧语〉 7th day of the 1st lunar month of the Chinese calendar ❷ man-day
人山人海 rénshān-rénhǎi multitude of people; sea of people: 他站在三层楼上, 只见～, 像流水般涌来涌去。He stood on the second floor watching the milling crowd jostling to and fro.
人身 rénshēn person: ～不可侵犯 inviolability of the person /～侵犯 personal abuse /～伤害 personal injury /～侮辱 personal insult
人身安全 rénshēn ānquán personal safety or security: 保证～ guarantee personal safety
人身保护令 rénshēn bǎohùlìng writ of habeas corpus
人身保险 rénshēn bǎoxiǎn life insurance and accident insurance
人身攻击 rénshēn gōngjī personal attack or abuse
人身权 rénshēnquán right of person
人身事故 rénshēn shìgù accident involving casualties
人身自由 rénshēn zìyóu personal freedom; freedom of person
人参 rénshēn ginseng: ～酒 ginseng liquor
人参芦 rénshēnlú 〈中医〉 root-shaped stem of ginseng
人神共愤 rén-shén gòngfèn incur the wrath of both man and god: 此种暴行, ～, 法令不容。No law will tolerate such atrocities which have aroused the indignation of both man and god.
人生 rénshēng human experience; life: ～如朝露。Life is as transi-

tory as morning dew. /～自古谁无死，留取丹心照汗青。No one can live forever; let me die with a loyal heart shining in the pages of history.

人生地不熟 rén shēng dì bù shú total stranger to the place and its people：他来到此地～。He arrived a total stranger to the place.

人生观 rénshēngguān outlook on life

人生七十古来稀 rénshēng qīshí gǔlái xī men seldom lived up to the age of seventy (in the past)：～，八十老翁何所求。It was unusual enough to reach seventy; what more can I want at eighty?

人生如梦 rénshēng-rúmèng life is but a dream; life is like a dream

人生如寄 rénshēng-rújì man's life is like a traveller's sojourn：～，多虑何为！Life is but a short span. What need is there to worry!

人生一世，草木一春 rénshēng-yīshì, cǎomù-yīchūn man has only one life to live and grass one spring to prosper; life is but a short span

人生长激素 rénshēngzhǎng jīsù 〈生化〉human growth hormone (HGH)

人生朝露 rénshēng-zhāolù man's life is like the morning dew; life is nothing but a bubble

人生哲学 rénshēng zhéxué philosophy of life

人声 rénshēng voice：室内～嘈杂。There are confused voices in the room.

人声鼎沸 rénshēng-dǐngfèi babel of voices; terrible din：消息传来，～。There was an uproar when the news was announced.

人时 rénshí man-hour

人士 rénshì personage; person; public figure; personality：知名～ well-known figures; celebrities; eminent persons /民主～ democratic personages /各界～ personalities of various circles /官方～ government officials; official sources /卫生界～ people of medical circles /知识界～ intellectuals; members of the intelligentsia /知情～ informed sources (*or* quarters) /他是著名的爱国～。He is a well-known patriot.

人氏 rénshì native：本地～ local /河南～ native of Henan /何方～？Where is he from?

人世 rénshì human world; world; this world：他将不久于～。He has one foot in the grave already.

人世沧桑 rénshì-cāngsāng man's world has witnessed many vicissitudes; there have been tremendous changes in this world

人世间 rénshìjiān human world; this world：～的事物往往难以预料。Affairs in this world are often unpredictable.

人市 rénshì ❶ gathering place ❷〈旧语〉labour or slave traffic market

人是衣裳马是鞍 rén shì yīshang mǎ shì ān 〈俗语〉clothes make the man as the saddle makes the horse — a man is what he wears

人事 rénshì ❶ human affairs; vicissitudes in life：离开这里几年，～变化很大。Since I left here a few years ago, enormous changes have taken place. ❷ personnel matters：～调动和调整 transfer and reshuffle of personnel /～安排 personnel arrangement /～权 control over personnel affairs /管～ be in charge of personnel affairs /～更迭 change of personnel ❸ interpersonal relationship：～纠纷 interpersonal strife; personal dispute ❹ ways of the world：他年幼无知，不懂～。He is young and raw, unaware of the ways of society. ❺ what is humanly possible：眼看他已没救了，医生们还在竭尽～。His chances for survival are slim, but the doctors are still doing what they regard as their last duty. ❻ consciousness of the outside world：他已昏迷不知～。He has lost consciousness. ❼〈方言〉gift; present：拿些～送他吧。Give him some gifts. ❽〈婉词〉facts of sexual life：渐省～ begin to be sexually aware

人事部 Rénshìbù Ministry of Personnel

人事处 rénshìchù personnel division

人事代谢 rénshì-dàixiè supersession of the old by the new：人事有代谢，往事成古今。As the new replaces the old, what has transpired becomes a thing of the past.

人事档案 rénshì dàng'àn personnel archives; personal file; dossier

人事工程 rénshì gōngchéng personnel engineering

人事关系 rénshì guānxì organizational affiliation

人事院 Rénshìyuàn (Japan) National Personnel Authority

人事制度 rénshì zhìdù personnel system

人手 rénshǒu manpower; hand; staff：～不足 short of hands; shorthanded; understaffed /～过剩 overstaffed

人寿保险 rénshòu bǎoxiǎn life insurance

人寿年丰 rénshòu-niánfēng land yielding good harvests and people enjoying good health; long life and good harvests：祝你们～。I wish you an abundant year and good health.

人丝斜纹绸 rénsī xiéwénchóu 〈纺织〉rayon twill

人死如灯灭 rén sǐ rú dēng miè a man dies the way a lamp goes out — everything is gone after death

人梯 réntī ❶ human pyramid or ladder：搭～ stand (*or* climb) one upon the other's shoulders ❷〈比喻〉(serve as) a human ladder to scientific or academic success; people who willingly make sacrifices for others' progress or success：老科学家甘为后辈当～。The older generation of scientists are ready to serve as a human ladder to scientific success for the younger generation. /他甘当～，言传身教，培养青年一代。Teaching by example as well as precept, he is devoted to the education of the younger generation.

人体 réntǐ human body：～模型 manikin

人体工程学 réntǐ gōngchéngxué ergonomics

人体节律 réntǐ jiélǜ biorhythm

人体解剖学 réntǐ jiěpōuxué anthropotomy

人体冷冻学 réntǐ lěngdòngxué cryonics

人体生理学 réntǐ shēnglǐxué human physiology

人体生物钟 réntǐ shēngwùzhōng biological clock (of the human body)

人体特异功能 réntǐ tèyì gōngnéng extrasensory perception or function

人同此心，心同此理 rén tóng cǐ xīn, xīn tóng cǐ lǐ everybody shares the same feeling and comes to the same conclusion; we all feel and think the same

人头 réntóu ❶ human head; man's head ❷ number of people：按～派活 assign jobs according to the number of people ❸ relations with people：她初来乍到，～不熟。As a newcomer, she doesn't know many people. ❹〈方言〉moral quality or character：这个人～真次！What a mean person he is!

人头税 réntóushuì poll tax; capitation (tax)

人亡政息 rénwáng-zhèngxī when a person (in power) dies, his political measures die with him：～，这是人治制度的致命缺点。The fatal drawback of rule by man (as opposed to rule by law) is that the death of the leader means the end of his policies.

人望 rénwàng 〈书面〉popular expectations; public confidence; prestige：不负～ live up to people's expectations; not fall short of people's expectations; prove worthy of people's trust

人微言轻 rénwēi-yánqīng the words of a person in humble position carry little weight：我～，意见自然不被重视。As I'm but a nobody, my suggestions was not taken seriously.

人为 rénwéi ❶〈书面〉human effort：事在～。Human effort is the decisive factor. *or* Where there is a will, there is a way. ❷ man-made; artificial：～的矛盾 artificially created contradictions

人为刀俎，我为鱼肉 rén wéi dāozǔ, wǒ wéi yúròu be meat on sb.'s chopping block — be at sb.'s mercy

人为地貌 rénwéi dìmào 〈军事〉man-made alterations to the terrain; man-made obstructions

人为干扰 rénwéi gānrǎo 〈电子〉jamming; active jamming; electronic jamming

人为嬗变 rénwéi shànbiàn 〈物理〉artificial transmutation

人为万物之灵 rén wéi wànwù zhī líng of all living creatures the human being is the one endowed with most intelligence

人为财死，鸟为食亡 rén wèi cái sǐ, niǎo wèi shí wáng as birds die for food, so men die for wealth

人味 rénwèi ❶ basic qualities of a man：谁想他竟连一点～都没有。Who would have imagined that he had not the least bit of human decency! ❷ joy of life; joy of human relationship：享受一下～。Let's taste the joys of life.

人文 rénwén all cultural activities in human society

人文景观 rénwén jǐngguān place of cultural interest

人文科学 rénwén kēxué humanities; humane studies

人文主义 rénwénzhǔyì humanism

人无完人，金无足赤 rén wú wánrén, jīn wú zúchì no man is perfect just as no gold is one hundred per cent pure：～，何苦对人求全责备？As no man is perfect, why do you nitpick at others?

人无远虑，必有近忧 rén wú yuǎn lǜ, bì yǒu jìn yōu one who fails to see far ahead will face danger close at hand; he who doesn't plan for the future will find trouble at his doorstep

人五人六 rénwǔ-rénliù strike poses; be affected; put on an act

R

人物 rénwù ❶ personage; figure:伟大～ great man /先进～ advanced element (*or* individual) /优秀～ outstanding personality (*or* person) /神秘～ mysterious person /头面～ prominent figure; bigwig; big shot; leading figure /大～ very important person (VIP); dignitary /小～ nobody; small potato /他可真算得上个～。He is quite a character. ❷ character; person who acts a part in a literary work:正面～ hero (*or* heroine); positive character /反面～ villain; negative character /～的内心世界 character's inner world ❸ figure painting (as a branch of traditional Chinese painting):老画家擅长～和山水。The old painter is good at character sketching and landscape drawing.

人物表 rénwùbiǎo cast or list of characters (in a play or novel); characters

人物画 rénwùhuà figure painting

人物头 rénwùtóu 〈方言〉person standing out among his fellows; leading public figure:混充～ pass oneself off as a dignitary /他一心要当～。He is bent on becoming an outstanding person. *or* He is set to be a leader. /他真是个办事的～。What a man of rare practical sense he is!

人像 rénxiàng portrait; figure; bust

人像靶 rénxiàngbǎ silhouette target

人心 rénxīn ❶ popular or public feeling; public will; popularity; support of the people:得～ gain popular support /～大快 most satisfying to the public mood; most gratifying to the public /鼓舞～ encouraging; inspiring /深入～ strike (*or* take) root in the hearts of the people /笼络～ curry favour with the public; try to win popular support by demagoguery /安定～ set the minds of people at ease; reassure the public /～叵测。Man's heart is unpredictable. /～涣散。People are demoralized. ❷ (good) heart; sense; reason:他并不是没有～的人。He is not a heartless man.

人心不古 rénxīn-bùgǔ public morality is no longer what it used to be — moral degeneration:看到社会上的一些不良现象,有些人发出了～的感叹。Witnessing some unhealthy social practices, certain people lamented over the debasement of public morality.

人心不足蛇吞象 rénxīn bù zú shé tūn xiàng there are people who are as greedy as a snake trying to swallow an elephant

人心隔肚皮 rénxīn gé dùpí different hearts in different breasts — it is hard to tell what is going on in the minds of other people:～,你在外人面前,可不要这么说呀! As you never can tell people's real intention, you must not say this in the presence of strangers!

人心果 rénxīnguǒ 〈植物〉sapodilla (*Achras zapota*)

人心惶惶 rénxīn-huánghuáng popular disquiet; popular anxiety:一时镇上～。The whole town was on tenterhooks.

人心齐,泰山移 rénxīn qí, Tàishān yí working with one will, people can move Mount Tai; a united people can achieve great things

人心如面 rénxīn-rúmiàn people's hearts are just as different as their faces

人心所向 rénxīn-suǒxiàng direction of popular sentiment; will of the people:和平与发展,乃当今世界～。Peace and development are the aspirations of the people all over the world.

人心惟危 rénxīn-wéiwēi the heart of the evildoer is unpredictable

人心向背 rénxīn-xiàngbèi whether the people are for or against; trend of public feeling

人行道 rénxíngdào pavement; sidewalk

人行横道 rénxíng héngdào pedestrian crossing; crosswalk; zebra crossing

人性 rénxìng human nature (as shaped by social and historical conditions); humanity:丧失～ utterly inhuman; most barbarous /这帮没有～的家伙。They are a bunch of brutes. /那不是真正把诗里的～都丢失干净了吗? Isn't that divesting poetry of all human feelings?

人性 rénxing attributes of human beings; human characteristic: 灭绝～ inhuman /不通～ have no human conscience; unfeeling and unreasonable

人性论 rénxìnglùn theory of human nature

人熊 rénxióng 〈口语〉〈动物〉brown bear

人选 rénxuǎn candidate:我们先酝酿一下小组长～。Let's have a brief discussion about the candidate(s) for group (*or* panel) leadership. /下届委员会的～已经确定。The membership of the next committee has been decided on.

人学 rénxué human science; human studies:～辩证法 dialectics of human study

人牙子 rényázi 〈旧语〉one who engages in slave traffic; trafficker in human beings

人烟 rényān signs of human presence or habitation:这里～稀少,很难找到住宿的地方。It is difficult to find accommodation in this sparsely populated area. /他们在沙漠里走了许多天仍不见～。They trudged for days in the desert without finding any trace of a human being.

人烟稠密 rényān-chóumì densely populated; populous:这个城市～。The city is densely populated.

人言籍籍 rényán-jíjí *also* "人言啧啧" plenty of unfavourable comment:这件事～,持批评意见者居多。The matter has set tongues wagging with a lot of negative comments.

人言可畏 rényán-kěwèi gossip is a fearful thing; one has to be very wary of gossip:～,还是及早澄清事实为好。It would be better to clarify the facts as soon as possible to set the malicious gossip at rest.

人仰马翻 rényǎng-mǎfān *also* "马仰人翻" both men and their horses are fallen — locked in fierce fight; utterly routed:双方直杀到～。Bitterly did they fight till they had both fallen from their steeds. /我们要杀他个～。We'll slaughter their men and down their horses. *or* We'll crush them like mincemeat.

人样 rényàng ❶ human shape; decent personal appearance or conduct:脏的不像个～。He was so dirty that he was beyond recognition. *or* He was filthy beyond description. /他们把孩子惯得一点～都没有。They so spoiled the child that he does not know how to behave properly. ❷ person with a future; somebody:不混出个～来,决不回来见你。I'll never come back and see you if I fail to make the grade.

人以群分 rényǐqúnfēn like attracts like; birds of a feather flock together

see also "物以类聚" wùyǐlèijù

人意 rényì one's wish or expectation:不尽～ not quite up to one's expectations; not quite satisfactory

人影儿 rényǐngr ❶ shadow of a human figure:拐弯处好像有个～闪动。There seemed to be a human shadow flickering at the corner. ❷ human figure; trace of a person's presence:天黑得对面看不见～。It was so dark that he couldn't see anything ahead of him. /旷野里不见一个～。There was not a single soul in sight in the wilderness. /一转身他就不见～了。When I turned round, he had disappeared.

人有脸,树有皮 rén yǒu liǎn, shù yǒu pí a man has his face just as a tree has its bark — a man has a sense of shame:～,人必须谨言慎行。People must be prudent in both words and deeds so as not to lose face.

人鱼 rényú *also* "儒艮" rúgèn 〈口语〉〈动物〉dugong; sea cow; manatee

人欲 rényù 〈书面〉carnal desires or pleasures

人欲横流 rényù-hénglíu unbridled indulgence of human lust; univeral decadence; moral degeneration:～实堪忧。It is deeply disturbing (*or* upsetting) to see such widespread debauchery and disspation.

人员 rényuán personnel; staff; employee:勤杂～ odd-job man; orderly; servant /行政～ administrative staff (*or* personnel) /技术～ technical personnel /教学～ teaching staff; the faculty /教辅～ auxiliary staff (for teaching) /业务～ specialized staff; professionals /政府机关～ government functionaries /值班～ man on duty /外交～ members of the diplomatic staff; diplomatic personnel /随行～ entourage; party

人猿 rényuán anthropoid

人缘儿 rényuánr relationship with people; popularity:～好 on good terms with everyone; popular /没～ not get along with people; be unpopular /他有～,好办事。He has good relations with everybody and can get things done easily.

人云亦云 rényún-yìyún echo the views of others without thinking; parrot:～有时是很危险的。To repeat the words of others without thinking can be very dangerous sometimes.

人造 rénzào artificial; man-made; imitation

人造宝石 rénzào bǎoshí imitation jewel; man-made precious stone

人造冰 rénzàobīng artificial ice

人造磁铁 rénzào cítiě artificial magnet

人造地球卫星 rénzào dìqiú wèixīng man-made earth satellite; sputnik

人造革 rénzàogé imitation leather; leatherette

人造黄油 rénzào huángyóu margarine
人造金刚钻 rénzào jīngāngzuàn 〈化工〉synthetic corundum
人造景观 rénzào jǐngguān man-made scenery; man-made scenic spot
人造毛 rénzàomáo artificial wool; man-made feather
人造棉 rénzàomián 〈纺织〉staple rayon; artificial cotton
人造奶油 rénzào nǎiyóu margarine; oleomargarine
人造肉 rénzàoròu textured vegetable protein (TVP)
人造石油 rénzào shíyóu artificial petroleum
人造树脂 rénzào shùzhī artificial or synthetic resin
人造丝 rénzàosī artificial silk; rayon
人造卫星 rénzào wèixīng man-made satellite
人造纤维 rénzào xiānwéi man-made fibre; synthetic fibre
人造橡胶 rénzào xiàngjiāo artificial or synthetic rubber; chloroprene
人造心脏 rénzào xīnzàng 〈医学〉artificial heart
人造羊毛 rénzào yángmáo artificial wool
人渣 rénzhā social trash; dregs:他是个专干坏事的～。He was a social scum doing all sorts of evil things.
人证 rénzhèng 〈法律〉(testimony of) an eyewitness:～物证俱在 availability of eyewitnesses and material evidence
人之常情 rénzhīchángqíng human nature; normal practice (in human relationships); ways of society:初次见面,说话不多,也是～。It's natural for people to be a little reserved at their first meeting.
人之将死,其言也善 rén zhī jiāng sǐ, qí yán yě shàn the words of a dying man are sincere:鸟之将死,其鸣也哀;～。Mournful are the cries of a dying bird; sincere are the words of a dying man.
人质 rénzhì hostage:当～ be kept as a hostage; be held hostage / 劫持～ take (sb.) a hostage /释放～ free hostages
人治 rénzhì rule by man (as distinct from rule by law) — (the monarch) rule the country by relying on a few able and virtuous persons (political thought of the Confucianists)
人中 rénzhōng 〈生理〉philtrum
人中之龙 rénzhōngzhīlóng dragon in the midst of men — the best and the brightest:他乃～,不可慢待。He is an outstanding man and should be offered great hospitality.
人种 rénzhǒng ethnic group; race
人种学 rénzhǒngxué ethnology:～家 ethnologist
人众 rénzhòng crowds of people; everyone:～稍稍聚拢,立刻又散开了。The crowd closed up a little, then quickly dispersed. /他从～中挤了出来。He pushed his way out of the crowd.
人主 rénzhǔ 〈书面〉monarch; sovereign
人字齿轮 rénzì chǐlún 〈机械〉chevron gear; chevron wheel; double helical (spur) gear; herring-bone gear
人字呢 rénzìní 〈纺织〉herringbone
人字形 rénzìxíng 〈建筑〉herringbone
人字形排水系统 rénzìxíng páishuǐ xìtǒng 〈农业〉herringbone drainage system
人自为战 rénzìwéizhàn each man fighting by himself; one putting up a stubborn resistance

仁[1] rén ❶ benevolence; kindheartedness; humanity:～心 kindheartedness /为富不～ be wealthy and heartless ❷〈敬词〉you; your:～伯 your honorable father ❸(Rén) a surname

仁[2] rén kernel; stone (of a peach, plum, etc.):杏～儿 apricot stone /花生～ shelled peanuts /松～ pine nut kernel (*or* meat) / 果～ nut meat; meat of nuts /虾～儿 small shrimp or bits of shrimp; popcorn shrimp /五～月饼 five-nut moon cake (cake with filling of assorted nut meat)

仁爱 rén'ài benevolence; kindheartedness:中国古代君主常讲～,但却骑在人民头上作威作福。Sovereigns in ancient China often prated about benevolence, while they rode roughshod over the people.
仁川 Rénchuān Inchon, port of the Republic of Korea on the Yellow Sea, west of Seoul
仁慈 réncí benevolence; mercy; kindness:～的老人 kind old man
仁丹 réndān throat lozenge
仁德 réndé benevolence; magnanimity; kindness:儒家重～。Confucian scholars set great store by benevolence.
仁弟 réndì 〈书面〉(used to address one's juniors) brother; my dear friend
仁果 rénguǒ ❶ pulp fruits (such as apple and pear) ❷〈方言〉peanut
仁厚 rénhòu kind and generous:～待人 treat people with kindness and generosity
仁惠 rénhuì 〈书面〉kindness; tender mercy; benevolence
仁人君子 rénrén-jūnzǐ benevolent gentleman; kindly folk
仁人志士 rénrén-zhìshì people with lofty ideals; public-spirited people:在旧社会,大批～想有所为而不能为。In the old society, large numbers of public-spirited people wished to do something for their country, but were not able to.
仁兄 rénxiōng 〈书面〉(used to address one's senior friends) elder brother; my dear friend
仁学 Rénxué *Ren Xue* or *Study on Benevolence*, a philosophical work written in 1896-1897 by Chinese thinker Tan Sitong (谭嗣同, 1865-1898)
仁义 rényì humanity and justice; benovolence and virtue
仁义 rényi 〈方言〉amiable and reasonable; gentle and sensible:他是个～的孩子。He is a gentle and sensible child.
仁义道德 rényì-dàodé benevolence and righteouness; virtue and morality:他满嘴的～,一肚子男盗女娼。He has virtue and morality on his lips but lust and cupidity in his heart.
仁者见仁,智者见智 rénzhě jiàn rén, zhìzhě jiàn zhì the benevolent see benevolence and the wise see wisdom; opinions differ from person to person; there are as many men as opinions; everyone has his own views:这种事情很难有个统一的标准,往往是～。As it is hardly possible to set uniform standards on such a matter, different persons often render different judgments.
仁政 rénzhèng policy of benevolence; benevolent government:孟子主张施～。Mencius was for benevolent government.
仁至义尽 rénzhì-yìjìn treat sb. with the utmost decency and kindness; do everything possible to help; be extremely tolerant:我们对他已是～了。We've done what's humanly possible for him. /我刚才的话已经是～了。I have shown the utmost tolerance and patience in what I've just said.

壬 rén ❶ ninth of the ten Heavenly Stem ❷ (Rén) a surname

任 Rén a surname
see also rèn

任颐 Rén Yí *also* "任伯年", Ren Bonian (formerly translate as Jen I, 1840-1895), traditional Chinese painter of the late Qing Dynasty

rěn

荏[1] rěn 〈植物〉common perilla

荏[2] rěn 〈书面〉weak; cowardly:他色厉而内～,骨子里是软弱的。He is fierce of mien but faint of heart.

荏苒 rěnrǎn 〈书面〉(of time) elapse imperceptibly; slip by:光阴～,转瞬十年。Time flies and ten years have elapsed in the twinkling of an eye.
荏弱 rěnruò 〈书面〉weak:～难持 too weak to behave with dignity

稔 rěn 〈书面〉❶ (of grain) ripe:丰～ bumper harvest ❷ year:此地水稻一～三熟。They have three crops of rice a year here. ❸ familiar; acquainted (usu. with people):相～ be on familiar terms /素～此君 have long been acquainted with the gentleman

稔年 rěnnián 〈书面〉bumper harvest year; good or abundant year
稔熟 rěnshú 〈书面〉familiar:～的声音 familiar voice /～的朋友 close friends
稔知 rěnzhī 〈书面〉know well; be familiar with:～其为人 know him intimately; know very well what he is like

忍 rěn ❶ bear; endure; stand; tolerate:～泪告别 hold back one's tears to say good-bye /她说她什么苦都能～。She said she could endure whatever suffering she might come across. /是可～,孰不可～? If this can be tolerated, what cannot? /她～住悲伤,强颜欢笑。She forced a smile despite her sorrow. ❷ have the heart to:惨不～闻 dreadful to hear /惨不～睹 too tragic to witness /这样做于心不～

haven't the heart to do so /我不～拒绝他。I can't find it in my heart to refuse him.

忍不住 rěnbuzhù cannot help (doing sth.); be unable to bear: ～流泪 cannot help shedding tears /疼得～了。The pain was unbearable.

忍耻 rěnchǐ bear humiliation; swallow insults: 含垢～，以图再起 have to suffer indignity and live in disgrace in an attempt to stage a comeback

忍冬 rěndōng *also* "金银花" jīnyínhuā 〈植物〉 honeysuckle

忍饥挨饿 rěnjī-ái'è endure the torments of hunger; suffer starvation

忍俊不禁 rěnjùn-bùjīn cannot help laughing; be unable to keep a straight face: 听他说到滑稽处，人们都～。When he came to the funny part of the story, people couldn't refrain from laughter.

忍耐 rěnnài exercise patience or restraint; restrain oneself: 我使劲～，才没有发火。I tried hard to restrain myself, or I would have flared up. /人的～是有限的。There's a limit to everybody's patience. /我有点～不住了。My patience has reached breaking point. *or* My patience is wearing thin.

忍气吞声 rěnqì-tūnshēng swallow rude remarks; submit to humiliation; eat dirt: 她一辈子都是～过来的。She was submissive and had to suffer humiliation in silence all her life.

忍让 rěnràng show or exercise forbearance; be conciliatory: 他比我小两岁，所以我常要～几分。He is two years my junior, so I have to bear with him now and then.

忍辱负重 rěnrǔ-fùzhòng endure humiliation in order to discharge important duties: 为了顾全大局，他只有～。For the sake of overall interests, he showed great fortitude under humiliating circumstances.

忍辱含垢 rěnrǔ-hángòu swallow insults and suffer indignity; eat humble pie

忍辱偷生 rěnrǔ-tōushēng endure humiliation in order to survive

忍受 rěnshòu stand; endure; bear; put up with: ～苦难 endure hardships /～屈辱 swallow one's humiliation /我们绝不能～这种侮辱。We will never tolerate such an insult.

忍痛 rěntòng bear or suffer pain: ～离去 leave with a heavy heart; depart reluctantly /～割爱 reluctantly part with sth. one loves

忍无可忍 rěnwúkěrěn be pushed beyond the limit of endurance; be provoked beyond endurance: 他对我如此无礼，我实在～。His impudence drove me beyond the limit of my patience. /我们已经到了～的地步了。Our patience has worn out.

忍心 rěnxīn have the heart to; be hardhearted enough to: 他～抛下亲人，远走他乡，永不回来。He had the heart to leave his dear ones behind and be off to a distant land, never to return. /我只好～同他告别了。I had to take leave of him, though most reluctantly.

忍心害理 rěnxīn-hàilǐ be wicked and cruel; treat people heartlessly

rèn

认(認) rèn ❶ recognize; identify; distinguish; tell: *see* "～出"; "～清"; "～得" ❷ enter into a certain kind of relationship with; acknowledge; adopt: ～了一位名医为师傅 acknowledge a famous doctor as one's master /～干儿子 adopt sb. as one's son ❸ admit; accept; recognize: 公～事实 established facts; universally accepted facts /否～ deny ❹(followed by 了) resign oneself to a loss, etc.; accept as unavoidable: 就是吃亏，我也～了。Even if I suffer a loss, I will swallow it.

认辨 rènbiàn identify; recognize: 仔细～ identify with care; examine / 字迹难以～。The handwriting is hardly legible.

认不是 rèn bùshi admit a fault; make an apology: 他不愿当着许多人～。He did not want to say he was sorry before so many people. /你就不能认个不是? Couldn't you offer an apology?

认出 rènchū recognize; identify; determine; make out: 我拿起话筒就～了她的声音。I recognized her voice the moment I picked up the receiver. /他认不出是谁的笔迹。He failed to identify the handwriting.

认错 rèncuò admit a fault; acknowledge a mistake; make an apology: 他做得不对，还不肯～。Though he is wrong, he won't admit it. /他既然～了，就原谅他吧。Let him off now that he has apologized.

认得 rènde know; recognize; tell: 这个人我～。I know this person. /这些花我全～。I know all these flowers by name. /他想到市里逛逛，却又怕不～路。He'd like to go sight-seeing in town but he was afraid that he might get lost.

认定 rèndìng ❶ firmly believe; aver; hold; maintain: 他～这辆自行车是他的失物。He maintained that this bicycle was his lost property. ❷ confirm; affirm; set one's mind on; decide on: 我已～了我毕生要走的路。I've already decided on the course I'm going to take for the rest of my life. /该合同业经双方审核～。The two sides have checked and confirmed the contract. /法院已～他的犯罪事实。The court affirmed his crimes.

认罚 rènfá admit that one deserves punishment; submit to punishment: 情愿～ ready to take any punishment /干错了，我～。I am ready to take the blame if I have done anything wrong.

认负 rènfù acknowledge defeat; own up to failure: 棋赛中他沉着应付，迫使对手中盘～。During the chess tournament, he played with calm and composure and forced his opponent to acknowledge defeat half way through the game.

认购 rèngòu offer to buy; subscribe: ～国库券 subscribe for (*or* offer to buy) treasury bonds /踊跃～ vie with one another to buy

认股权证 rèngǔquánzhèng 〈金融〉 warrant

认脚 rènjiǎo 〈方言〉 (of footwear) fit only for one or the other foot: 袜子一般不～。Generally, socks fit both feet.

认捐 rènjuān agree or signal one's desire to donate (a certain sum of money); offer a donation

认可 rènkě accept; approve; confirm: 点头～ nod (in) approval / 议程已经得到与会各方～。The agenda has been approved by all parties to the conference.

认领 rènlǐng ❶ claim: 到失物招领处去～你丢失的钱包。Go and claim your lost purse at the lost property office. /这把雨伞无人～。Nobody came to claim the umbrella. ❷ adopt: 他～了一个孩子。He adopted a child.

认命 rènmìng 〈迷信〉 resign oneself to fate: 事已至此，只好～吧。Since things have come to such a pass, we'll have to bow to the inevitable.

认赔 rènpéi admit an obligation to pay (for damage done, etc.); agree to pay compensation

认亲 rènqīn ❶〈旧语〉 reciprocal visits made by members of the families of the bridegroom and the bride after the wedding (to acknowledge the relationship) ❷ (in a general sense) acknowledge one's relationship with a relative: 我跟他是本家，假如要～，他还比我晚两辈呢。He and I are of the same clan, and if our relation has to be acknowledged, he would be my junior by two generations.

认清 rènqīng see clearly; clearly recognize: ～形势 understand the situation clearly; see things as they are / ～是非 distinguish between right and wrong; tell right from wrong / ～自己的优势与不足 have a sober assessment of one's own strengths and weaknesses / ～其人真面目 see sb.'s true colours

认人 rènrén ❶ (usually said of babies) recognize people by their looks, voices, etc.: 这孩子才三个多月，就开始～了。This baby is barely over three months old, yet he has already begun to recognize different faces. ❷〈方言〉(of a child) be shy with strangers

认生 rènshēng (of a child) be shy with strangers

认识 rènshi ❶ recognize; realize; understand; know: 我～他。I know (of) him. /我对他有了新的～。I've come to see him in a new light. /～真理要有个过程。The realization of truth is a gradual process. /艰难的生活让他～了自己。Life's trials have made him discover who he really is. ❷ understanding; knowledge; cognition: 感性～ perceptual knowledge /理性～ rational knowledge /～的理性阶段 stage of rational knowledge /～源于实践。Knowledge originates in practice. /对这个问题要有正确～。We should have a correct understanding of the problem.

认识过程 rènshi guòchéng process of cognition

认识论 rènshilùn theory of knowledge; epistemology

认识能力 rènshi nénglì cognitive ability

认识水平 rènshi shuǐpíng level of understanding

认输 rènshū admit defeat; give in; give up; throw in the sponge: 死不肯～ obstinately refuse to throw in the sponge (*or* to be reconciled to defeat)

认死理 rèn sǐlǐ *also* "认死扣儿" be stubborn or obstinate; be inflexible; have a one-track mind: 这个人就是有点～，心还是好的。He has his heart in the right place, only he is a bit too stubborn.

认同 rèntóng ❶ identify: 民族～感 sense of national identity ❷ ap-

prove; acknowledge:这一成果得到学术界的广泛～。This result was widely acknowledged in the academic circles.

认同作用 rèntóng zuòyòng identification

认头 rèntóu resign oneself to; acknowledge reluctantly:违心地～accept reluctantly /明知吃亏也只好～ resign oneself to a loss with one's eyes wide open

认为 rènwéi consider; think; believe; hold:我～他可以胜任这项工作。I believe that he is equal to the task. /一致～必须立即行动。It was unanimously agreed that action (should) be taken immediately. /我～可以照常进行,他～不可以。In my opinion, we can go on as usual, but he thinks otherwise. /人们～他是当代最有成就的作家之一。He is considered to be one of the most accomplished writers of our time. /我们～和平与发展是当前世界的两大主题。We hold (*or* maintain) that peace and development are the two main themes facing the world today.

认贼作父 rènzéizuòfù take one's enemy for one's father; regard one's foe as kith and kin; go over to the enemy and serve him abjectly:此人～,为虎作伥。The man kowtowed to the enemy and acted as his cat's-paw.

认账 rènzhàng acknowledge a debt; admit what one has said or done; bear responsibility:这就是你干的,不～不行。You can't deny this is what you did. /他干的事情,我们不能～。We are not responsible for what he did.

认真 rènzhēn ❶ serious; earnest; conscientious: 学习～ study earnestly /办事～ handle matters seriously /～工作 work conscientiously /～研究 study carefully; make a careful study (of) /～严谨的治学态度 rigorous scholarship /你办事～得过头了。You are being conscientious to a fault in the conduct of business. ❷ take seriously; take to heart:开个玩笑,何必过于～。You shouldn't take it too much to heart, I was only joking. /对她的话,你不必～。You should not take her words seriously.

认证 rènzhèng 〈法律〉attestation; authentication:～费 certification fee /签字～ attest a signature /～文件 authenticated document /～者 authenticator

认知 rènzhī 〈心理〉cognition

认知法 rènzhīfǎ 〈心理〉cognitive approach

认知失调 rènzhī shītiáo cognitive dissonance

认准 rènzhǔn firmly believe; maintain; hold: 他～了的理儿一下子扭不过来。It is not easy for him to give up all at once what he has firmly believed in.

认字 rènzì be able to read; be literate:这村里的许多老人都几乎不～。Many old people in this village are practically illiterate.

认罪 rènzuì admit one's guilt; plead guilty; admit that one is guilty:低头～ hang one's head and plead guilty /他～态度好。He admitted his crimes honestly.

刃(刄)

rèn ❶ edge of a knife, scissors, etc.; blade:刀～ knife blade /这把刀卷了～了。The blade is blunted. ❷ sword; knife:白～ naked sword /白～战 bayonet charge (*or* fighting); hand-to-hand combat /手持利～ with a sharp knife (*or* dagger) in hand ❸〈书面〉kill with a sword or knife:手～寇仇 stab an enemy to death; knife an enemy with one's own hand

刃创 rènchuāng 〈书面〉wound from a knife or sword; stab wound

刃具 rènjù 〈机械〉cutting tool; cutlery:～钢 cutlery steel

刃口 rènkǒu blade or edge of a knife or scissors, etc.: ～锋利 sharp edge of a knife

讱

rèn 〈书面〉inarticulate; slow of speech

韧(靭、韌)

rèn pliable but strong; likely to bend but not to crack; tough:坚～ tenacious; tensile

韧带 rèndài 〈生理〉ligament:～病 desmopathy /～破裂 desmorrhexis /～炎 desmitis; syndesmitis

韧度 rèndù ❶〈纺织〉tenacity ❷〈冶金〉temper; toughness

韧钢 rèngāng annealed steel; malleable steel

韧化 rènhuà 〈冶金〉malleablize; toughen

韧劲 rènjìn tenacity; stead fastness; pesseverance: 他有股～儿。He has a tenacious streak in his character.

韧力 rènlì dauntless will; perseverance:百折不回的～ indomitable will

韧皮部 rènpíbù 〈植物〉bast; phloem

韧皮纤维 rènpí xiānwéi bast fibre

韧铁 rèntiě 〈冶金〉tough iron

韧铜 rèntóng 〈冶金〉tough copper; annealed copper

韧性 rènxìng ❶〈物理〉toughness;〈冶金〉malleability:～铁 malleable iron /～铸件 malleable casting /～铸铁 malleable hard iron; malleable pig ❷ toughness; tenacity: ～的反抗 unyielding resistance /～的战斗 tenacious (*or* stubborn) fight

轫

rèn 〈书面〉log used to stop wheels:发～ lift the log to set the carriage going; commence an undertaking; start (*or* set) the ball rolling

牣

rèn 〈书面〉full of; brimming with; imbued with:充～其中 be filled with sth.

仞

rèn ancient measure of length equal to seven or eight *chi*:万～高山 immeasurably high mountains

纫

rèn ❶ thread (a needle):～针 thread a needle ❷ sew; stitch:缝～ sewing; tailoring ❸〈书面〉be very grateful; be very much obliged:感～盛情 be deeply grateful for sb.'s hospitality /至～高谊 be extremely grateful to sb. for his noble feeling of friendship

纫佩 rènpèi 〈书面〉thankful and appreciative:～教益 be grateful for (*or* appreciative of) sb.'s advice

葚

rèn *see* "桑葚儿" sāngrènr

see also shèn

衽(袵)

rèn 〈书面〉❶ one or two pieces making up the front of a Chinese gown ❷ sleeping mat:～席 sleeping mat; place for sleeping

R

任[1]

rèn ❶ appoint; engage:举贤～能 give positions to those with virtue and ability /他被委～为厂长。He was appointed factory manager. ❷ assume; undertake; hold; take up:担～要职 hold an important post (*or* a position of great responsibility) /他曾～系主任。He was once dean (*or* chairman) of a department. ❸ bear; face:众怒难～。It is hard to face public wrath. ❹ office; official post:就～ assume office /离～ leave office /～满 at the expiration (*or* expiry) of one's term of office /到～ take office; arrive at one's post; assume office /调～ be transferred to another post /继～ be a successor; succeed sb. as ❺〈量词〉term of office:当过两～委员会主席 have been chairman of the committee for two terms

任[2]

rèn ❶ let; allow; permit; give rein to:～人摆布 allow oneself to be ordered about /～人宰割 submit to oppression without offering any resistance; allow oneself to be trampled upon /听之～之 let things go unchecked; let things drift; adopt a laissez-faire attitude /～你挑选。You are free to choose. ❷ no matter (how, what, etc.):～你怎么说,他也不听。No matter what you say, he won't listen. /后来我昏迷了,～什么也不知道了。Then I fainted (*or* fell unconscious) and everything went black.

see also rén

任便 rènbiàn as you like; as you see fit; as you please:去不去～。You may or may not go, as you see fit. *or* It is up to you whether you go or not.

任从 rèncóng allow; let (sb. do as he pleases); no matter (how, what, etc.)

任达 rèndá 〈书面〉(of disposition) unrestrained:～不拘 have a free and indulgent disposition

任诞 rèndàn 〈书面〉wild in speech and behaviour; unconventional; dissipated; dissolute:～不羁 unconventional and unrestrained

任管 rènguǎn 〈方言〉in spite of; no matter (how, what, etc.):～他说什么,我的主意是不会变的。Whatever he may say, I will never change my mind.

任何 rènhé any; whatever; whichever; whoever:～困难也吓不倒我们。We are not to be cowed by any difficulty. /没有～例外。There is no exception. /～解释都无济于事。No explanation whatsoever will be of any use.

任教 rènjiào teach; be a teacher; take a teaching job:他在大学～。

He teaches at a university.
任咎 rènjiù 〈书面〉take all the blame upon oneself
任课 rènkè give lessons; teach at a school:～教师 teaching teacher
任劳任怨 rènláo-rènyuàn work hard and never feel upset by criticism; stand the strain of labour and injustice:他历来～。He works hard and never complains.
任吗 rènmá 〈方言〉no matter (what, how, etc.); anything:～也看不见。Nothing was to be seen. /那时候他还是～不懂的小孩子。Then he was only a child who knew nothing whatsoever.
任免 rènmiǎn appoint and remove:～名单 list of appointments and removals /～公务人员 appoint and remove public servants
任命 rènmìng appoint:～某人为研究所所长 appoint sb. director of a research institute
任命状 rènmìngzhuàng commission; credential; letter of appointment
任凭 rènpíng ❶ at one's convenience, disposal, or discretion:去与不去,～你决定。It is up to you to decide whether to go or not. /～狂风怒吼,海涛汹涌,海燕却坚定地飞翔着。In defiance of the howling winds and turbulent seas, the petrel was flying steadily. /你如果～自己的主观愿望去办事,那就非碰壁不可。You are running your head against a stone wall if you always allow yourself to be carried away by your subjective desire. ❷ no matter (who, how, what, which, etc.):～谁都要遵守法律。No matter who you are, you must abide by the law. /～我怎么苦思苦想,也想不出个究竟来。However hard I racked my brain, I still couldn't make out what it was all about.
任凭风浪起,稳坐钓鱼船 rènpíng fēnglàng qǐ, wěn zuò diàoyúchuán sit tight in one's fishing boat despite the rising wind and waves — remain unruffled and steady under adverse circumstances; face danger with calm confidence
任期 rènqī term of office; tenure of office:他的～是三年。His term of office is three years.
任期制 rènqīzhì system of fixed tenures (for government officials); (fixed) tenure system
任其自然 rènqízìrán let things run their own course; let nature take its course
任情 rènqíng ❶ to one's heart's content; as much as one likes:～欢乐 make merry to one's heart's content ❷〈书面〉wilful; headstrong:～不拘 self-willed /～胡为 wayward and unbridled
任人 rènrén ❶ appoint people (to positions); use people ❷ let people (do what they please):商品～挑选 commodities displayed for all to choose from /公共场所,～出入。Public places are open to one and all.
任人唯亲 rènrén-wéiqīn appoint people by favouritism; practise cronyism:～,结党营私 appoint people by favouritism and gang up to pursue selfish interests
任人唯贤 rènrén-wéixián appoint people on their merits:只有～才能使国家走上健康发展的道路。Only by offering official positions to people of virtue and ability can we lead the state onto the road of healthy development.
任啥 rènshá 〈方言〉no matter what:他光顾走路,～也没看见。He walked along taking no notice of things around him.
任事 rènshì ❶ assume certain duties; undertake a task:勇于～ be bold in shouldering responsibility ❷〈方言〉anything whatever:～也不在乎 care about nothing /他在家里～不用管,清闲得很。At home he has nothing to attend to and is completely carefree.
任率 rènshuài 〈书面〉frank and unaffected; simple and natural
任谁 rènshuí 〈方言〉no matter who; anyone:这是历史事实,～也不能否认。This is an undeniable historical fact.
任随 rènsuí give free rein to; let; allow:我没打断他的话,～他说下去。I let him hold forth without interrupting him.
任所 rènsuǒ place of office; location of post; duty station
任听 rèntīng allow; let (sb. do as he pleases)
任务 rènwu assignment; mission; task; job:执行～ carry out a task; perform a mission /完成～ complete one's mission; accomplish a task; discharge one's duty /首要～ task of primary (*or* cardinal) importance /艰巨～ arduous undertaking (*or* task) /历史～ historical mission /他的～是跟先行人员去上海安排住宿。His assignment is to go to Shanghai with the advance party to make arrangements for our accommodation. /我们的～是清理仓库。Our job is to make an inventory of warehouse stocks. /你的～是看管这些孩子。Your duty is keeping an eye on (*or* looking after) the children. /～紧,时间不多了。The matter is pressing and time is running out.
任务观点 rènwu guāndiǎn get-it-over-and-done-with attitude; half-hearted attitude; perfunctory approach
任侠 rènxiá 〈书面〉be loyal (to one's friend), sacrifice one's own interests for the sake of others, and support the weak against the strong; be upright and chivalrous
任性 rènxìng wilful; self-willed; headstrong; capricious:他很～,想干什么就干什么。He is rather impulsive and ready to do what he wants. /由于～不听劝告,她碰到不少麻烦。She has run into a great deal of trouble for her wilful disregard of advice.
任意 rènyì ❶ wilfully; arbitrarily; wantonly:～行动 act wantonly /～歪曲事实 wilful distortion of facts /～挥霍 spend freely; squander money without batting an eye /～卸货港交货 optional delivery /～条款 optional clause; permissive provision /～砍伐必然毁坏森林。Indiscriminate felling will lead to the destruction of forests. ❷ unconditional; unqualified:～三角形 unconditional triangle
任意常数 rènyì chángshù 〈数学〉arbitrary constant
任意球 rènyìqiú (of football) free kick; (of handball) free throw
任用 rènyòng appoint; assign sb. to a post:他免除现职,另有～。He will be relieved of his present post and get a new appointment.
任择 rènzé optional:～条款 optional clause /～议定书 optional protocol
任职 rènzhí hold a post; be in office:在外贸部门～多年 hold a post in a department of foreign trade for many years /他自～以来,非常辛苦。He has worked extremely hard since he took office.
任重道远 rènzhòng-dàoyuǎn the task is arduous and the road ahead is long — shoulder heavy responsibilities in years to come:你还年轻,～,切勿骄傲。You must guard against conceit as you are still young and will have to shoulder heavy responsibilities in the future.
任纵 rènzòng 〈书面〉unrestrained; undisciplined; self-indulgent

饪(飪) rèn cook:烹～ cooking; culinary art

妊(姙) rèn pregnancy
妊妇 rènfù pregnant woman
妊娠 rènshēn pregnancy; gestation
妊娠期 rènshēnqī gestation; gestation period; term of pregnancy
妊娠试验 rènshēn shìyàn 〈医学〉pregnancy test
妊娠中毒 rènshēn zhòngdú 〈医学〉gestosis

纴(紝) rèn 〈书面〉weave

rēng

扔 rēng ❶ throw; cast; toss; fling:把球～给我。Toss (*or* Throw) me the ball. ❷ throw away; cast aside:～掉这些无用的东西。Throw away the junk. /他～下笔就匆匆忙忙地走了。Putting down his pen, he left hurriedly. /这件事被他～在一边,不闻不问了。He has dismissed the matter, never mentioning it again.
扔崩 rēngbēng 〈方言〉throw away; discard; abandon; give up:～一走就完事了。Throw up the job and quit, and that will be the end of it.
扔掉 rēngdiào throw away; shake off:～包袱 shake off the burdon
扔弃 rēngqì discard; abandon; give up
扔下 rēngxia abandon; cast aside; leave behind:贼～赃物跑了。The thief dropped the loot and showed a clean pair of heels. /她身后～个三岁男孩儿。She left behind a little boy of three when she died.

réng

礽 réng 〈书面〉good fortune; blessing

仍 réng ❶ remain:一～旧贯 remain the same as before; continue as before; follow the beaten track ❷〈书面〉frequently; often:兵祸频～ ravaged by successive wars; war-torn; war-ridden ❸〈书面〉still; yet:问题～待解决。The problem remains unsolved. /病人～未脱离危险。The patient is not yet out of danger. /我调动未成,～在工厂上班。I'm still with the plant as I have yet to arrange a job

transfer.

仍旧 réngjiù ❶ remain the same：修订版体例～。The revised edition will follow the same printing conventions as before. *or* The printing conventions for the revised version will remain unchanged. ❷ still; yet; as ever：等了三天，～无消息。Three days passed, and still nothing happened. /他虽然体弱多病，～坚持努力工作。He is working as hard as ever in spite of his poor health. /邀请～有效。Our invitation still stands.

仍然 réngrán still; yet：他在床上躺了好几天了，伤风～没有好。He has been laid up in bed for several days, but he has not been able to shake off his cold. /水电浪费目前～十分严重。The waste of water and electricity remains a serious problem today.

rì

日 rì ❶ sun：旭～ rising sun /烈～ scorching sun /～晒雨淋 be exposed to the sun and rain; be weather-beaten ❷ (Rì) (short for 日本) Japan：中～关系 Sino-Japanese relations ❸ daytime; day：*see* "～班"；"～夜"；"～以继夜" ❹ day：～复一～ day after day; day in and day out /几～未曾上班 have not been to work for a few days /改～再来 come some other day ❺ every day; daily; with each passing day：体力～衰 be declining in health /声誉～增 enjoy a growing reputation (*or* prestige) /这个工程旷～持久，所费不赀。The project which has been going on for a long time is proving to be terribly expensive. ❻ time; period：来～ days to come; the future /往～ days that have gone by; the past ❼ specified day：假～ holiday /生～ birthday /冬至～ winter solstice

日班 rìbān day shift：上～ be on the day shift /我刚由夜班倒～。I've just changed from night shift to day shift.

日斑 rìbān *also* "太阳黑子" tàiyáng hēizǐ 〈天文〉sunspot

日报 rìbào daily paper; daily：《中国～》*China Daily*

日本 Rìběn Japan; Nippon：～人 Japanese /～海 Sea of Japan /～脑炎 encephalitis B; Japanese encephalitis

日本电气公司 Rìběn Diànqì Gōngsī Nippon Electric Co. Ltd.

日本电视广播网公司 Rìběn Diànshì Guǎngbōwǎng Gōngsī Nippon Television Network Corporation (NTV)

日本共产党 Rìběn Gòngchǎndǎng Communist Party of Japan

日本广播协会 Rìběn Guǎngbō Xiéhuì *Nippon Hoso Kyokai* (NHK)

日本航空公司 Rìběn Hángkōng Gōngsī Japan Air Lines Co. Ltd. (JAL)

日本经济新闻 Rìběn Jīngjì Xīnwén *Nihon Keizai Shimbun*, Japanese newspaper published since 1876

日本社会党 Rìběn Shèhuìdǎng Social Democratic Party of Japan

日本投降日 Rìběn Tóuxiángrì V-J Day (Victory over Japan Day), referring to 14 Aug. 1945, day of Japanese surrender or 2 Sept. 1945, day of signature of Japanese surrender

日本兴业银行 Rìběn Xīngyè Yínháng Industrial Bank of Japan

日本最高裁判所 Rìběn Zuìgāo Cáipànsuǒ Supreme Court of Japan

日薄西山 rìbóxīshān the sun is setting beyond the western hills — be on the decline or wane; be drawing near one's end or doom：他已～，一无所求。He is sinking fast and has nothing to look forward to.

日不暇给 rìbùxiájǐ be fully occupied; have no time to spare：他自从当部长以来，公务繁忙，～。Since he was appointed minister, he has not been able to take any time off from his busy schedule.

日产汽车公司 Rìchǎn Qìchē Gōngsī Nissan Motor Co. Ltd.

日长石 rìchángshí 〈矿业〉sunstone

日常 rìcháng day-to-day; everyday; daily：处理～工作 handle day-to-day work; discharge routine duties /～事务 day-to-day business /～用品 articles for everyday use; daily necessities /他的～生活需人照料。He needs somebody to look after him in his daily life. /我们～往来甚多。We have frequent friendly contact with each other.

日场 rìchǎng day show; daytime performance; matinée

日程 rìchéng schedule; programme：制订旅行～ draw up an itinerary of a journey /比赛～ programme of matches /这个问题已提到议事～上来了。The question has been put on the agenda.

日程表 rìchéngbiǎo schedule

日出 rìchū sunrise

日戳 rìchuō ❶ datemark ❷ date stamp; dater

日耳曼人 Rì'ěrmànrén Germanic people

日珥 rì'ěr 〈天文〉(solar) prominence

日工 rìgōng ❶ day work; day labour ❷ day labourer

日光 rìguāng ❶ sunlight; sunbeam; daylight ❷ (often used in the early vernacular) time; hour：～尚早。It's still early.

日光灯 rìguāngdēng fluorescent lamp; daylight lamp：～镇流器 fluorescent lamp ballast; current stabilizer /～起动器 fluorescent lamp starter

日光疗法 rìguāng liáofǎ 〈医学〉heliotherapy

日光皮炎 rìguāng píyán 〈医学〉solar dermatitis

日光摄谱仪 rìguāng shèpǔyí spectropheliograph

日光时 rìguāngshí *also* "日光节约时" DT (daylight time); daylight-saving time
see also "夏令时" xiàlìngshí

日光效应 rìguāng xiàoyìng sun effect; sunlight effect

日光浴 rìguāngyù sunbath：～室 solarium /～衣 sunsuit

日晷 rìguǐ *also* "日规" sundial; gnomon

日后 rìhòu in the days to come; in the future：他的观点是否正确，～便会得到验证。Whether his views are correct will be verified in the days to come. /说这些话～他会后悔的。Someday, he will regret what he has said.

日华 rìhuá 〈气象〉solar halo

日环食 rìhuánshí *also* "环食"〈天文〉annular eclipse of the sun

日积月累 rìjī-yuèlěi by piecemeal accumulation; gradually：他勤奋工作，～，已经有了丰富的经验。He has worked very hard and gradually accumulated a wealth of experience.

日记 rìjì diary; journal：记～ keep a diary /生产～ production journal /翻阅～ glance through the diary

日记本 rìjìběn diary (book)

日记账 rìjìzhàng *also* "序时账" xùshízhàng journal; daybook

日间 rìjiān during the day; in the daytime

日间不做亏心事，半夜敲门不吃惊 rìjiān bù zuò kuīxīnshì, bànyè qiāomén bù chījīng 〈俗语〉he who has done nothing against his conscience by day is not alarmed by a knock on the door at night

日见 rìjiàn with each passing day; day by day：经过整治，河水污染～减轻。After the dredging of the river, the water has become less polluted day by day.

日渐 rìjiàn day by day; gradually：产品质量～提高。The quality of products is getting better and better.

日脚 rìjiǎo ❶〈书面〉sunlight coming through clouds：～已偏西。The sun is already setting. ❷〈方言〉life; livelihood：现在～好过了。Life is easier now.

日较差 rìjiàochā daily range

日界线 rìjièxiàn international date line; date line

日经-道琼斯平均指数 Rìjīng-Dàoqióngsī Píngjūn Zhǐshù 〈金融〉Nikkei-Dow Jones Average

日景 rìjǐng day scene

日久 rìjiǔ with the passage of time：～岁深 after a considerable length of time

日久见人心 rìjiǔ jiàn rénxīn time reveals a person's character; one will gradually come to know a person with the passage of time; it takes time to know a person：路遥知马力，～。Distance is the test of a horse's stamina and time a person's character.

日久天长 rìjiǔ-tiāncháng as the years go by; in (the) course of time：如果继续不断实践，～，你也会掌握这门技术的。If you keep up the practice, you will master the skill eventually. /～，他总会认识到自己是错的。I believe he will one day realize his error.

日就月将 rìjiù-yuèjiāng continue to make progress every day and every month; many a little makes a mickle：他刻苦学习，～，终于取得优异成绩。He studied hard and eventually distinguished himself in his own field.

日居月诸 rìjū-yuèzhū time flies

日均 rìjūn daily average; average per day

日喀则 Rìkāzé Xigaze or Shigatse, second largest city in the Tibet Autonomous Region

日课 rìkè 〈书面〉daily assignment; lesson for the day

日来 rìlái recently; lately; of late; in the past few days：她～心情不佳。She has been very unhappy recently.

日里 rìlǐ 〈方言〉daytime; day：这东西～还在，怎么晚上就不见了。Why, it was here during the day! How come it's gone by night!

日理万机 rìlǐ-wànjī be busy or occupied with a myriad of state affairs; have numerous problems to attend to every day：周总理～，常

年少有休息。The late Premier Zhou had numerous state affairs to attend to every day and hardly had a real break throughout the years.
日历 rìlì calendar:～年度 calendar year
日历手表 rìlì shǒubiǎo calendar watch
日立制作所 Rìlì Zhìzuòsuǒ Hitachi Ltd.
日利 rìlì daily interest; interest per diem
日轮 rìlún sun disk; sun
日落 rìluò sunset
日冕 rìmiǎn 〈天文〉(solar) corona:～仪 coronagraph
日暮 rìmù dusk; evening:～归来 come back at dusk
日暮途穷 rìmù-túqióng the sun is waning and the road is at an end — approach the end of one's days; be on one's last legs; be on the decline and draw near one's end; head for doom:匪徒们已是～,但要防备他们作垂死挣扎。The bandits are on their last legs, but we must take precautions against their deathbed kicks.
日内 rìnèi one of these days; in a day or two; in a few days:会议将于～举行。The meeting will be held in a few days' time.
日内瓦 Rìnèiwǎ Geneva (Switzerland):～湖 Lake Geneva
日期 rìqī date:比赛～还未定下来。The date for the match hasn't been fixed. /文件上的～是一月四日。The document was dated January the fourth.
日期变更线 rìqī biàngēngxiàn date line
日前 rìqián a few days ago; the other day:代表团～访问过桂林。The delegation visited Guilin a few days ago.
日趋 rìqū day by day; with each passing day; step by step; gradually:这个地区局势～紧张。Tension is building up in the region. /战争发生前这个封建王朝已～没落。Before the outbreak of the war, the feudal dynasty had been on the decline.
日惹 Rìrě Togyakarta, ancient city and cultural centre on Java, Indonesia
日日 rìrì every day; day after day; daily; day in, day out:～如此。It goes on like this day in, day out.
日日夜夜 rìrì-yèyè day and night; night and day:防洪的～ days and nights spent on preventing flood
日色 rìsè light of the sun — time of the day:～不早了,我们歇工吧! It's getting late. Let's call it a day.
日上三竿 rìshàng-sāngān the sun is three poles high — it is very late in the morning:他一觉醒来,已是～。It was late morning when he woke up.
日射 rìshè 〈气象〉insolation
日射表 rìshèbiǎo actinometer
日射病 rìshèbìng 〈医学〉insolation; sunstroke; heliosis
日升月恒 rìshēng-yuègèng the sun is rising and the moon is waxing — growing prosperity
日食 rìshí 〈天文〉solar eclipse:日偏食 partial solar eclipse /日全食 total solar eclipse /～限 solar eclipse limit /～界限图 eclipse map
日食万钱 rìshíwànqián lead a life of extravagance
日塌 rìtā 〈方言〉exhausted; fatigued:把身体累～了 be exhausted from overwork
日坛 Rìtán Altar of the Sun, Beijing:～公园 Altar-of-the-Sun Park; Ritan Park
日头 rìtóu (often used in the early vernacular) ❶ date ❷ day time; day:半个～ half a day
日头 rìtou 〈方言〉sun:～老高了。The sun is high up in the sky.
日托 rìtuō day care
日托托儿所 rìtuō tuō'érsuǒ day nursery
日夕 rìxī 〈书面〉day and night; night and day:～揣摩 keep thinking about sth. day and night
日息 rìxī also "日利" interest per diem; daily rate of interest
日下 rìxià ❶〈书面〉at present; present time:～天气已凉。It is already getting cold now. ❷〈旧语〉national capital (the city where the emperor resides)
日下无双 rìxià-wúshuāng no one can match him in talent in the capital — of outstanding talent
日心说 rìxīnshuō heliocentric theory
日新月异 rìxīn-yuèyì change with each passing day; undergo changes day by day:家乡面貌～。My hometown has been undergoing great changes with each passing day. /科学技术的发展～。Science and technology have been developing at an amazing speed.
日薪 rìxīn day wages
日阳 rìyáng ❶〈书面〉sun ❷〈方言〉sunlight:爷俩坐在～底下唠扯着。Father and son sat chatting in the sunlight.
日野汽车工业公司 Rìyě Qìchē Gōngyè Gōngsī Hino Motors Ltd.
日夜 rìyè day and night; round the clock:大河奔流,～不息。The river flows on night and day.
日夜商店 rìyè shāngdiàn shop which opens day and night; round-the-clock shop
日以继夜 rìyǐjìyè also "夜以继日" day and night; round the clock; night and day:几个月来他～地写作,很少出门。He kept writing for several months on end and seldom went out.
日益 rìyì day by day; more and more; increasingly:农村生活～改善。Life in rural areas is getting better and better. /空气污染对人类威胁～严重。Air pollution poses an increasingly serious threat to mankind. /这是政府威信～提高的证明。This is a clear manifestation of the government's growing prestige.
日影 rìyǐng shadow cast by the sun
日用 rìyòng ❶ of everyday use:～百货 articles of daily use /～工业品 manufactured goods for everyday use ❷ daily expenses:～开支 running (*or* daily) expenses /这笔钱一部分做～,一部分储蓄。Of this sum, part will be used to cover daily expenses while the rest can be put in the bank.
日用品 rìyòngpǐn articles of everyday use; house wares:～供应十分充足。There's an abundant supply of articles of everyday use.
日语 Rìyǔ Japanese (language)
日元 rìyuán *see* "日圆"
日圆 rìyuán *also* "日元" (Japanese) yen
日月 rìyuè ❶ livelihood; life:那些～真难过啊! Life in those days was very hard indeed! ❷ time; days:母女俩苦度～。The mother and daughter spent their days in misery.
日月重光 rìyuè-chóngguāng the sun and the moon are shining again — back to peace and prosperity after a period of turmoil:可喜的是战乱过后,山河依旧,～。What is gratifying is that things are back to normal, and peace and prosperity once again prevail throughout the country after the war.
日月经天,江河行地 rìyuè jīng tiān, jiānghé xíng dì the sun and the moon move across the sky, while the rivers flow on the earth — be of lasting glory or splendour
日月如梭 rìyuè-rúsuō the sun and the moon move back and forth like a shuttle — time flies:光阴似箭,～,转眼就要到国庆节了。How time flies! National Day will be here before you know it.
日月潭 Rìyuètán Sun Moon Lake, or Riyuetan Lake, biggest lake in Taiwan Province
日月星辰 rì-yuè-xīngchén sun, moon and stars; heavenly bodies
日晕 rìyùn 〈气象〉solar halo:～知风。A solar halo means wind.
日照 rìzhào sunshine:～时间 sunshine time /长～植物 long-day plant /短～植物 short-day plant /～计 sunshine recorder /～能量 illumination capacity
日臻 rìzhēn day by day:时机～成熟。The time is getting ripe.
日之丸 Rìzhīwán *also* "太阳旗" Tàiyángqí *Hinomaru*, or the "Rising Sun", representing a red disc in the centre of a white field — de facto Japanese national flag legalized in 1999
日知录 Rìzhīlù *Ri Zhi Lu* or *Notes on Knowledge Accumulated from Day to Day*, in 32 volumes, by Gu Yanwu (顾炎武) of the late Ming and early Qing dynasties
日至 rìzhì 〈书面〉solstice (winter or summer)
日志 rìzhì journal; daily record:航海～ logbook; log
日中 rìzhōng 〈书面〉❶ noon; midday:大雨～方止。The downpour did not stop until midday. ❷ equinox
日中则昃 rìzhōng-zézè the sun begins to decline when it reaches its apex:～,月满则亏。The sun rises to the meridian and then declines; the moon waxes to the full and then wanes. *or* The sun declines after reaching the zenith; the moon wanes after waxing to the full.
日子 rìzi ❶ date; day:今天国庆节,是个喜庆的～。Today is National Day, a day of jubilation. /定个～郊游。Let's fix a date for an outing. ❷ days; time:我有些～没见到他了。I have not seen him for a long time. ❸ life; livelihood:他们过着简朴的～。They live a simple life. /这些年～好过多了。Life is much easier these years. /我们家的～过得还不错。We are moderately well-off.
日子口儿 rìzikǒur 〈方言〉important day:在这大喜的～,你干吗愁眉苦脸的? Why pull such a long face in these days of great rejoicing?

驲 rì 〈古语〉carriage for a post station; post-chaise

róng

容[1] róng ❶ hold; contain:这座体育馆可～五万人。This gymnasium has a seating capacity of 50,000. *or* This gymnasium can hold 50,000 people. /这是一只可～五公斤油的桶。This is a 5-kilo oil bucket. ❷ tolerate; excuse; forgive:宽～ be tolerant /情理难～ totally unacceptable by standards of reason and common sense; totally unreasonable /工作中～不得一点马虎 cannot tolerate (*or* forgive) any negligence of duty ❸ permit; allow; let:～我考虑一下。Let me think it over. /别着急,～我慢慢说来。Be patient. I'll explain it in detail (*or* in time). /事情很急,不～拖延。This is a matter of urgency which allows of (*or* brooks) no delay. /他不～分说就破口大骂。He started to curse without waiting for any explanation. ❹〈书面〉perhaps; maybe; probably: *see* "～或" ❺ (Róng) a surname

容[2] róng ❶ facial expression; look:她笑～可掬。She is all smiles. /他面有怒～。He looks angry. /他满脸愁～。He wears a worried look. /无不为之动～。Everyone was moved. ❷ facial features; looks; appearance:整～术 face lifting; cosmetic operation; plastic surgery; cosmetology ❸ appearance; look:军～ soldiers' appearance and bearing; army discipline / 市～整洁。The city is clean and tidy. /这部电影演员阵～强大。The film has a first-rate cast.

容长脸儿 róngchángliǎnr 〈方言〉longish face

容电器 róngdiànqì *also* "电容器" condenser; capacitor

容光 róngguāng glow of the face

容光焕发 róngguāng-huànfā with one's face glowing with health; in buoyant spirit; in a buoyant mood; radiant with health:小伙子～,必有喜事。The young man is in a buoyant mood. There must be some happy event.

容华 rónghuá 〈书面〉features and bearing; looks:～绝世 of unrivalled beauty

容或 rónghuò 〈书面〉perhaps; probably:～有之,但不常见。Probably, there are such instances, but they are rare. /他所说的～与事实有出入。What he says may not accord strictly with facts.

容积 róngjī volume:～流量 volume flow

容积吨 róngjīdūn measurement ton

容积式泵 róngjīshìbèng 〈机械〉positive-displacement pump

容抗 róngkàng 〈电学〉capacitive reactance; condensance; condensine reactance

容量 róngliàng capacity:电～ electric capacity; capacitance /通讯～ communications capacity

容留 róngliú allow to stay; take in; shelter:他这样的人,我们无法～。We can't afford to keep (*or* shelter) such a person.

容貌 róngmào features; looks; appearance:～端正 have regular features /～端庄 look serene and dignified /兄妹俩～相似。The brother and sister look much alike. *or* The brother and sister resemble each other.

容纳 róngnà hold; accommodate; have a capacity of:这个宾馆可～五百名客人。This guest house can accommodate 500 people. /这么多顾客,小店～不下。There were too many customers for the small shop. /要有～不同意见的气度。One must have an open mind and tolerate views different from one's own.

容器 róngqì container; receptacle; vessel

容情 róngqíng (used usu. in the negative) show mercy; put up with:对自己的错误不应～。One should not easily let one's own mistakes pass. /对贪污腐化分子决不～。We'll never show mercy to grafters and degenerates.

容让 róngràng tolerant; lenient; yielding:过于～ excessively tolerant /夫妻之间应当～。Both husband and wife should learn to be accommodating to each other.

容人 róngrén tolerant towards others; broad-minded; magnanimous:此人不能～,很难与人合作。He is too intolerant to cooperate with others.

容忍 róngrěn put up with; tolerate; stand; condone:我们不能～这种粗暴的语言。We can't put up with such rude remarks. /他们竟能～这种奇耻大辱! They were actually able to stomach such terrible humiliation!

容色 róngsè look; facial expression; appearance:～安然自若 look calm and composed

容身 róngshēn find shelter; take shelter; shelter oneself:无处～ find no shelter for oneself

容身之地 róngshēnzhīdì place to stay; shelter; refuge:天地虽大,却无我等～。Big as the world is, there is nowhere for us to rest.

容受 róngshòu endure; tolerate; put up with:他那种傲慢的态度令人无法～。His arrogance is intolerable.

容恕 róngshù tolerate and forgive; pardon:对出卖国家民族利益的人,断难～。Those who betray the interests of the nation can never be forgiven. *or* We give no quarter to traitors.

容态 róngtài 〈书面〉appearance; looks

容物 róngwù tolerant; forebearing

容限 róngxiàn 〈物理〉tolerance; allowance:光学～ optical tolerance /～分析 tolerance analysis /～频率 tolerance frequency

容心 róngxīn (used usu. in the negative) be concerned about; care for:无所～ care for nothing; be carefree /全不～ not at all concerned (about sth.); be totally indifferent

容许 róngxǔ ❶ permit; allow; let:如时间～ if time permits /如果条件～ if circumstances allow /不～考试作弊 not tolerate cheating at exams /我们要～人家改正错误。We should allow them a chance to correct their mistakes (*or* to mend their ways). /请～我说几句话。Please let me (*or* allow me to) say a few words. /当时的情况不～我讲真话。Under those circumstances then, I couldn't afford to tell the truth. ❷ perhaps; possibly:他～说过这件事。He may have mentioned this in passing.

容许负荷 róngxǔ fùhè *also* "容许负载" allowable load

容许收缩量 róngxǔ shōusuōliàng shrinkage allowance

容许误差 róngxǔ wùchā admissible error

容许压力 róngxǔ yālì allowable pressure

容颜 róngyán looks; appearance:～娇美 look delicate and charming /～憔悴 look haggard /她的～渐衰。She is a woman of fading charms.

容仪 róngyí *also* "仪容" looks and manners; bearing:一表～ handsome; good-looking

容易 róngyì ❶ easy:数学考题很～。The maths exam is easy. /说比做～。It's easier said than done. /这些建设资金来得并不～。Those funds for construction were hard to come by. ❷ easily; likely; liable; apt:这两个字形体相似,～混淆。These two words are similar in form and easily get mixed up. /这种机器零件～损坏。These machine parts wear out quickly. /她～晕飞机。She is liable to become airsick. /酒后驾车～出事。Drivers are prone to accidents when they drive under the influence of alcohol.

容与 róngyǔ 〈书面〉❶ move slowly:船～而不进。The boat moved slowly, as if making no headway. ❷ carefree; at ease ❸ hesitant

容止 róngzhǐ 〈书面〉bearing; demeanour; mien; manner:～优雅 carry (*or* bear, *or* deport) oneself with grace; have a graceful manner; be of graceful mien

容重 róngzhòng 〈水利〉unit weight

容姿 róngzī *also* "姿容"〈书面〉looks; features:～秀美 pretty; nice-looking; beautiful

溶 róng dissolve; thaw; meet:遇热即～ meet when exposed to heat /糖～于水。Sugar dissolves in water.

溶洞 róngdòng (limestone) cave; cavern

溶化 rónghuà ❶ dissolve:将樟脑～于酒精之中。Dissolve camphor in alcohol. ❷ melt; thaw:天一暖和,湖面上的冰就要～了。When it gets warm, the ice on the lake will start to thaw.

溶汇 rónghuì ❶ thaw and converge:山上的冰雪～成浩荡的河流。The ice and snow on the mountains thawed and converged into a vast and mighty river. ❷ blend harmoniously:把捕鱼劳动中常见的动作经过艺术加工,～在舞蹈中。The common rhythmic movements in fishing are artistically blended into the dance.

溶剂 róngjì 〈化学〉solvent; dissolvent; menstruum

溶胶 róngjiāo *also* "胶体溶液" jiāotǐ róngyè 〈化学〉sol

溶解 róngjiě dissolve; thaw; meet:盐～于水。Salt dissolves in water.

溶解度 róngjiědù solubility

溶解热 róngjiěrè heat of solution

溶解物 róngjiěwù dissolved matter

溶解型 róngjiěxíng lysotype

溶菌剂 róngjūnjì bacteriolysant

溶菌酶 róngjūnméi lysozyme
溶菌素 róngjūnsù 〈医学〉bacteriolysin
溶媒 róngméi 〈化学〉solvent; menstruum
溶溶 róngróng 〈书面〉broad; vast: ～的江水 vast expanse of waters / 月色～。The ground is flooded with moonlight.
溶蚀 róngshí 〈地质〉corrosion
溶体 róngtǐ 〈化学〉solution; fluid
溶田 róngtián 〈农业〉soak paddy fields with water (to get ready for transplanting the seedlings)
溶性油 róngxìngyóu 〈化学〉soluble oil
溶血 róngxuè 〈医学〉haemolysis: ～现象 haemolysis
溶漾 róngyàng 〈书面〉ripple; undulate
溶液 róngyè *also* "溶体"〈化学〉solution: 实在～ real solution / 当量～ normal solution / ～处理 solution treatment / ～电解 electrolysis of solutions / ～压力 solution pressure
溶液栽培 róngyè zāipéi hydroponics; soil-less culture; tank farming
溶胀 róngzhàng swelling: ～值 swelling value
溶质 róngzhì 〈化学〉solute

熔

róng melt; fuse; smelt: ～滴 molten drop
熔池 róngchí 〈冶金〉(molten) bath
熔点 róngdiǎn 〈物理〉melting point; fusing or fusion point
熔度 róngdù meltability
熔断 róngduàn 〈电学〉fusing
熔断器 róngduànqì fuse (box)
熔焊 rónghàn 〈冶金〉burning-in; fusion welding; fusion soldering; melting welding
熔合 rónghé (of two or more metals) melt into one; alloy; merge: 铜与锡或其它金属～为青铜。Copper and tin or some other metal are alloyed into bronze.
熔化 rónghuà *also* "熔解"; "熔融" fuse; melt: ～废钢铁 melt scrap iron and steel / 铅～的温度比其他一些金属低。Lead will fuse (*or* melt) at a lower temperature than some other metals.
熔化炉 rónghuàlú melting furnace
熔化期 rónghuàqī 〈冶金〉melting stage
熔化速率 rónghuà sùlǜ 〈冶金〉melting rate
熔剂 róngjì 〈冶金〉flux
熔接 róngjiē butt fusion
熔解 róngjiě 〈物理〉fuse; fusion
熔解热 róngjiěrè heat of fusion
熔解温度 róngjiě wēndù melting temperature
熔矿炉 róngkuànglú 〈冶金〉arc furnace
熔炼 róngliàn ❶ smelt: 闪速～ flash smelting ❷〈比喻〉temper: 艰苦的生活～了他的意志力。Hardships tempered his will.
熔炼炉 róngliànlú smelting furnace
熔炉 rónglú ❶ smelting furnace; melting pot ❷ crucible; furnace; melting pot: 在苦难的～中经受锻炼 be tried in the furnace of adversity / 在战争的～中得到锻炼 be tempered in the crucible of war / 过去人们称美国是座民族大～。The United States used to be called a melting pot of many races.
熔模铸造 róngmó zhùzào 〈冶金〉investing: ～法 investment casting
熔融 róngróng melt; fuse
熔融纺丝 róngróng fǎngsī 〈纺织〉melting spinning
熔融挤压法 róngróng jǐyāfǎ 〈化工〉extrusion by melting
熔丝 róngsī 〈电工〉fuse-element: ～断路器 fusible circuit breaker
熔丝管 róngsīguǎn cartridge fuse
熔岩 róngyán 〈地质〉lava
熔盐 róngyán 〈化学〉fused-salt: ～电解 fused-salt electrolysis
熔冶 róngyě smelt
熔渣 róngzhā 〈冶金〉dross; scoria; molten slag; sullage
熔铸 róngzhù founding; casting: ～生铁 casting of iron
熔铸工 róngzhùgōng smelter

瑢

róng *see* "玐瑢" cōngróng

蓉

róng ❶ mashed fruit or seeds: 豆～ fine bean mash (as stuffing) / 椰～ mashed coconut kernal stuffing ❷ *also* "芙蓉" fúróng; "苁蓉" cōngróng cottonrose hibiscus ❸ (Róng) another name for Chengdu (成都), Sichuan Province
蓉城 Róngchéng another name for the city of Chengdu

榕

róng ❶〈植物〉small-fruited fig tree; banyan ❷ (Róng) another name for Fuzhou (福州), Fujian Province
榕城 Róngchéng another name for the city of Fuzhou
榕树 róngshù banyan (*Ficus benghalensis*; *Ficus indica*)

镕

róng *see* "熔" róng

戎[1]

róng 〈书面〉❶ arms; weaponry: 兵～相见 resort to arms (to settle a dispute) ❷ army; military affairs: 投笔从～ cast aside the pen and take up the sword; give up the career of a scholar for that of a soldier

戎[2]

Róng ❶ ancient name for ethnic groups inhabiting west China ❷ a surname
戎服 róngfú 〈书面〉martial attire; military uniform
戎行 rónghάng 〈书面〉army: 久历～ have long served in the army; be a seasoned soldier / ～出身 rise from the ranks
戎机 róngjī 〈书面〉❶ war; military operations ❷ opportunity for combat: 贻误～ let slip a good opportunity in a military operation; forfeit the chance of a successful battle
戎马 róngmǎ 〈书面〉war-horse; army horse; steed: ～半生 spend half of one's life in the army
戎马倥偬 róngmǎ-kǒngzǒng be busy with military duties: ～，略无暇晷 have little time to spare beyond the discharge of military duties
戎马生涯 róngmǎ-shēngyá armylife; military life: 他在革命队伍里度过了三十年～。He spent thirty years in the army during the revolutionary wars.
戎首 róngshǒu 〈书面〉one who starts a war; warmonger
戎装 róngzhuāng 〈书面〉army uniform; martial attire; battle dress: 全副～ in full military attire

绒(羢、毧)

róng ❶ fine soft hair; down: 羊～ wool / 鸭～ eiderdown / 羽～ down / 呢～ wool fabric ❷ nap or pile of cloth: 棉～ cotton velvet / 丝～ velvet / 长毛～ plush / 灯芯～ corduroy / 法兰～ flannel ❸ fine floss for embroidery: 红绿～儿 red and green floss
绒布 róngbù lint; flannelette; cotton flannel
绒花 rónghuā 〈工美〉velvet flowers, birds, etc.: ～绸〈纺织〉velveteen rayon
绒裤 róngkù sweat pants
绒毛 róngmáo ❶ fine hair; down; villi; villus ❷〈纺织〉nap; pile
绒毛瘤 róngmáoliú 〈医学〉villoma
绒毛膜 róngmáomó 〈生理〉chorion: ～上皮瘤 chorio-epithelioma
绒毛状腺瘤 róngmáozhuàng xiànliú villous adenoma
绒面革 róngmiàngé suede (leather)
绒膜 róngmó *also* "绒毛膜" chorion: ～癌 choriocarcinoma; chorioepithelioma / ～瘤 chorioma; choriomata / ～腺瘤 chorio-adenoma
绒绳 róngshéng 〈方言〉knitting wool
绒毯 róngtǎn flannelette blanket
绒头绳 róngtóushéng ❶ wool (for tying pigtails) ❷〈方言〉knitting wool
绒线 róngxiàn ❶ floss for embroidery: 双股细～ crewel (yarn) ❷〈方言〉knitting wool
绒线编织 róngxiàn biānzhī chenille
绒线刺绣 róngxiàn cìxiù crewel work
绒线衫 róngxiànshān woollen sweater; sweater
绒绣 róngxiù 〈工美〉woollen embroidery; woollen needlepoint tapestry: ～地毯 finished needlepoint carpet
绒鸭 róngyā 〈动物〉eider: ～绒 eider; eiderdown
绒叶 róngyè velvetleaf: ～荷麻 *Abutilon theophrasti*
绒衣 róngyī sweat shirt

荣(榮)

róng ❶ grow exuberantly or luxuriantly: 春天草木欣欣向～。The trees and grass grow luxuriantly when spring comes. ❷ prosper; flourish; succeed; thrive: 一～俱～ (of closed related families, or of crongism) when one flourishes, all the others flourish also; thrive together / 卖友求～ betray one's friends for one's own advancement / 一国的繁～富强,有赖人民。The prosperity, wealth and strength of a nation depend on its people. ❸ honour; glory: 孩子得了奖,母亲引以为～。The mother felt greatly honoured

that her child had won a prize. /在旧社会，惟一～宗耀祖的事就是做官。In the old society the only way to bring glory on one's ancestors was to become a government official. ❹ (Róng) a surname

荣宝斋 Róngbǎozhāi Rongbaozhai, or Studio of Glorious Treasures, an arts and relics shop of long standing in Beijing

荣宠 róngchǒng 〈书面〉imperial favour; honours：备受～ enjoy (*or* bask in) high imperial favour

荣悴 róngcuì 〈书面〉*see*“荣枯”

荣达 róngdá 〈书面〉(of high officials) illustrious and influential

荣光 róngguāng honour; glory

荣归 róngguī return in glory; return in triumph：～故里 make a triumphal return to one's native place (*or* hometown)

荣华 rónghuá flowering; glory and splendour：他家世代光耀～。His family has basked in splendour and wealth for generations.

荣华富贵 rónghuá-fùguì glory, splendour, wealth and rank; high position and great wealth：享尽～ enjoy all the benifits of wealth and power; enjoy all the comforts of luxury and pomp

荣获 rónghuò have the honour to obtain; win; be awarded：～银牌 be awarded a silver medal /～劳动模范的称号 win the honourable title of model worker

荣军 róngjūn (short for 荣誉军人) disabled soldier (wounded in battle)

荣枯 róngkū ❶ (of vegetation) flourishing and withering ❷〈比喻〉vicissitudes; rise and fall; ups and downs

荣利 rónglì riches and influence; position and wealth：不慕～ not care for position and gain /热中～ hanker after wealth and high office

荣民 róngmín (Taiwan Province) retired army personnel; demobilized soldier; veteran

荣名 róngmíng honour; fame; good reputation

荣任 róngrèn have the honour of being appointed (to a public office)

荣辱 róngrǔ honour or disgrace：盛衰～ prosperity or decline, honour or disgrace

荣辱与共 róngrǔ-yǔgòng share weal and woe

荣升 róngshēng have the honour of being promoted (to a public office)

荣退 róngtuì resign from office with honour

荣衔 róngxián honourable title

荣幸 róngxìng be honoured; be privileged：三年前，我～地访问过贵国。Three years ago, I had the honour of visiting your country. /我能见到您，感到～。It's my honour to meet you. /蒙您首肯，不胜～。We feel highly flattered by your gracious approval.

荣耀 róngyào honour; glory：对我们来说，这是极不寻常的～。This is a special honour to all of us.

荣膺 róngyīng 〈书面〉have the honour to receive or accept：～勋章 be awarded a medal

荣誉 róngyù honour; glory; credit：有强烈的～感 have a strong sense of honour /～称号 honourary title /～学位 honourary degree /维护祖国的～ safeguard (*or* protect) the honour (*or* dignity) of one's country /他骗取了～。He gained credit under false pretences.

荣誉军人 róngyù jūnrén disabled soldier (wounded in battle)

蝾(蠑) róng

蝾螺 róngluó 〈动物〉turban shell (*Turbinidae*)

蝾螈 róngyuán 〈动物〉salamander; newt

嵘(嶸) róng *see*“峥嵘” zhēngróng

茸 róng

❶ (of grass) newly-grown, soft and fine; downy ❷ young pilose antler

茸毛 róngmáo (of man and animal) fine hair

茸茸 róngróng (of grass, hair, etc.) soft, smooth and thick：绿～的秧苗 carpet of green rice shoots /这孩子长着一头～的头发。This child has thick hair.

融 róng

❶ melt; thaw：冰消雪～。The ice melted and the snow thawed. ❷ fuse; merge; blend; be in harmony：水乳交～ blend as well as milk and water; be in perfect harmony /情景交～ (of literary works) with feeling and setting happily blended ❸ circulation：金～ finance

融合 rónghé *also*“融和” fuse; merge; mix together：这张画～了中西绘画的某些特点。This painting has (*or* displays) certain characteristics of both Chinese and Western art.

融合遗传学说 rónghé yíchuán xuéshuō 〈生物〉theory of blending inheritance

融和 rónghé ❶ warm and genial：天气～。It was warm and genial. ❷ harmonious; friendly; genial：气氛～ genial (*or* harmonious) atmosphere /关系～ be on friendly terms ❸ *see*“融合”

融化 rónghuà *also*“溶化” rónghuà melt; thaw; dissolve：春天到了，冰雪开始～。As spring is setting in, the snow and ice begin to thaw. /食盐～于水。Salt melts (*or* dissolves) in water. /～了的雪水顺着山沟流下来。The melted snow is running down the gully.

融会 rónghuì mix together; fuse; merge：远处的灯光与星光～成一片。Lights in the distance merged into the starlit sky.

融会贯通 rónghuì-guàntōng achieve thorough understanding of a subject through mastery of all relevant material：他阅读广泛，善于～。He reads extensively and knows how to digest what he has read.

融解 róngjiě melt; thaw：山顶的积雪～了。The snow which covered the mountaintop melted away.

融洽 róngqià harmonious; getting along well; on friendly terms：气氛～。The atmosphere is harmonious. /他们相处～。They hit it off well.

融然 róngrán 〈书面〉❶ happy and harmonious：情趣～ be temperamentally compatible (with each other) ❷ mix together; blend：～一体 blend into one

融融 róngróng ❶ happy and chummy：大家欢聚一堂，其乐～。We are happily gathered together and feel particularly chummy. ❷ warm：屋子里暖～的。It was warm in the room. *or* The room was warm and cosy.

融通 róngtōng ❶ circulate：建立资金横向～联络网 establish a horizantal network for the circulation of funds ❷ achieve a comprehensive and thorough understanding：～古今，自成一家之说。He formulated a theory of his own on the basis of a thorough understanding of the past and the present. ❸ harmonize; communicate：～感情 have a communion of feelings

融通票据 róngtōng piàojù accommodation bill or note; accommodation paper

融资 róngzī ❶ financing：～项目 financing project /～五百万元 raise five million *yuan* through financing ❷ money raised through financing

融资方针 róngzī fāngzhēn credit policy

融资租赁 róngzī zūlìn financial lease

肜 róng

ancient sacrificial offerings

rǒng

冗(宂) rǒng

〈书面〉❶ redundant; superfluous：*see*“～员”；“～笔” ❷ loaded with trivial details：繁～ lengthy and tedious ❸ busy schedule：拨～ put aside the various claims upon one's time (and do sth.); find time from a busy schedule

冗笔 rǒngbǐ redundancy or superfluity in writing or painting：文中多有～，必须删节。The article is verbose and has to be tightened up. *or* The essay has to be pruned of its numerous redundancies.

冗长 rǒngcháng lengthy; long-winded; prolix; verbose：他作了一次～的演讲。He made a long-winded (*or* lengthy) speech. *or* He held forth at great length.

冗词 rǒngcí superfluous word

冗词赘句 rǒngcí-zhuìjù superfluous or redundant words and sentences; verbosity：～是这篇文章的缺点。The use of superfluous words and expressions is a shortcoming of this essay.

冗繁 rǒngfán miscellaneous; full of trivial details：他被～的琐事拖住了腿。He was tied down by trivial matters.

冗官 rǒngguān official who holds a sinecure

冗弱 rǒngruò 〈书面〉(of writing) lengthy and pedestrian：文笔～ write in a redundant and pedestrian style

冗散 rǒngsǎn 〈书面〉leisurely; relaxed

冗务 rǒngwù multifarious routines; all sorts of daily chores：～缠身 be tied up with daily chores of all sorts

冗余测试 rǒngyú cèshì redundancy testing

冗员 rǒngyuán redundant personnel：裁减～ trimming (of an orga-

nization, etc.); cut redundant staff
冗杂 rǒngzá miscellaneous; numerous and complicated:事情～。Things are diverse and complex.
冗赘 rǒngzhuì diffuse; prolix; verbose:讲话～ give a marathon lecture; drone on and on
氄(毹、毳) rǒng (of hair or feather) fine and soft:羽毛发～。The feathers are fine and soft.
氄毛 rǒngmáo fine and soft hair or feathers; down:刚孵出来的小鸡长着一身～。The newly hatched chickens have fine and soft down all over their bodies.

róu

柔 róu ❶ soft; supple; pliant; flexible:～桑 supple mulberry leaves ❷ soften: *see* "～麻" ❸ gentle; tender; yielding; mild:刚中有～ have tender feelings hidden under a stern appearance /以～克刚 combat hard tactics with soft tactics; overcome roughness with tenderness /优～寡断 indecisive ❹ (Róu) a surname
柔板 róubǎn 〈音乐〉adagio
柔布机 róubùjī 〈纺织〉cloth breaking machine
柔肠 róucháng tender heart; affectionate sentiment; tender feelings:～百折 broken-hearted; laden with sorrow; deeply grieved
柔肠寸断 róucháng-cùnduàn lovelorn; heartbroken:丈夫英年早逝,使她～。She was heartbroken because of her husband's premature death.
柔道 róudào 〈体育〉(Japan) judo
柔和 róuhé mild; gentle; soft; tender:～的微风 balmy breeze /～的歌声 soft singing /她性格～。She is gentle by nature. *or* She has a gentle disposition. /这幅画线条～。The picture is drawn in graceful lines. /秋天的阳光显得格外～可爱。The autumn sunshine is particularly mild and lovely. /这料子手感～。The material feels soft.
柔滑 róuhuá soft and smooth:～如脂 soft and smooth like wax
柔静 róujìng tender and quiet; gentle and peaceful:～的气氛 gentle and peaceful atmosphere /她说话总是那么～。She always speaks softly. *or* She is always soft-spoken.
柔量 róuliàng 〈物理〉compliance
柔麻 róumá soak jute (hemp, etc.) to soften it
柔曼 róumàn ❶ gentle; soft:～的旋律 soft and beautiful melody /～的唱腔 soft and gentle music for voices in Chinese operas ❷〈书面〉(of skin) soft and smooth; (of looks, appearance) gentle and beautiful
柔毛 róumáo soft, short hair; down; pubescence; pubes
柔美 róuměi gentle and lovely; graceful:～的舞姿 graceful dance /～的黑发 downy dark hair /音色～ soft and exquisite tone colour /～的晚霞像彩绸似的。The soft sunset glow looked like a long strip of coloured silk.
柔媚 róumèi ❶soft and delicate; gentle and lovely:桃花鲜艳～。The peach blossoms are a picture of fresh splendour and pure delicacy. ❷ tender and charming:她的目光透着几分～。Her eyes sparkle with tenderness and charm.
柔嫩 róunèn tender; delicate:～的小草 tender grass /皮肤～ delicate skin
柔能制刚 róunéngzhìgāng *also* "柔能克刚" soft tactics can disarm the hardest; gentleness is the antidote to roughness
柔腻 róunì soft and smooth:婴儿举起～的双手。The baby lifted its soft hands.
柔懦 róunuò soft; weak; cowardly:～的性格 meek and docile by nature
柔情 róuqíng tender feelings; tenderness:～似水 deep affection; boundless tender feelings /～侠骨 compassionate and gallant /她满怀～地说了这一番话。This is how she made these affectionate remarks.
柔情蜜意 róuqíng-mìyì tender affectionate love
柔荏 róurěn 〈书面〉weak; feeble
柔韧 róurèn pliable; supple:～的枝蔓 supple twigs and tendrils
柔茹刚吐 róurú-gāngtǔ bully the weak and dread the strong
柔软 róuruǎn soft; supple; lithe:动作～ lithe movements /～的头发 soft hair /丝绸～滑爽。Silk is soft and smooth.
柔软体操 róuruǎn tǐcāo callisthenics
柔润 róurùn soft and smooth; supple:皮肤～ soft-skinned /～的嗓音 soft and mellow voice
柔弱 róuruò weak; delicate; tender:～的嫩芽 tender sprouts /体质～ frail; fragile; in delicate health /性格～ submissive; meek; weak-willed
柔术 róushù 〈体育〉(Japan) ju-jitsu
柔顺 róushùn gentle and meek:性情～ have a meek disposition; be obedient and docile
柔荑 róutí 〈书面〉(of plants) tender buds — woman's white, slender and soft-skinned hands; hands of a woman
柔荑花序 róutí huāxù 〈植物〉catkin; ament
柔婉 róuwǎn gentle and agreeable; soft and sweet; meek:性格～ soft-tempered /～的语调 speak in a soft and sweet voice
柔细 róuxì soft and thin:～的声音 soft and thin voice /～的柳条 soft and thin willow twigs
柔心弱骨 róuxīn-ruògǔ soft heart and weak bone — meek; submissive
柔性 róuxìng 〈物理〉flexibility:～连接〈机械〉flexible joint /～制造 flexible manufacture /～制造系统 flexible manufacturing system (FMS)
柔性塑料 róuxìng sùliào 〈化工〉flexiplast
柔鱼 róuyú 〈书面〉(popularly known as 鱿鱼) squid
柔中有刚 róuzhōng-yǒugāng iron fist in a velvet glove; gentle but firm
糅 róu mingle; mix:杂～ mix; mingle
糅合 róuhé mix; form a mixture:这本书系由许多材料～而成,质量不高。The book is a hotchpotch; it is not highly rated.
糅杂 róuzá mixture; hotchpotch
煣 róu 〈书面〉bend (a piece of wood) on fire
鞣 róu tan:～皮子 tan hides
鞣革 róugé tannage:～厂 tannery
鞣料 róuliào tanning material
鞣料浸膏 róuliào jìngāo tanning extract
鞣皮栎 róupílì 〈植物〉tanbark oak; tanoak (*Lithocrpus densiforus*)
鞣酸 róusuān 〈化学〉tannin; tannic acid; digallic acid
鞣制 róuzhì tan (hide, etc.):他把～皮张的手艺传给徒弟。He passed on tanning techniques to the apprentices.
揉 róu ❶ rub:～眼 rub one's eyes /～胸口 rub the pit of one's stomach /～后背 knead one's back ❷ knead; crumple into a ball:～面 knead dough /把纸～成一团 crumple a piece of paper into a ball ❸〈书面〉bend; reform:～木为耒 make a farm tool out of a log
揉搓 róucuo ❶ rub:这本书传来传去,都～烂了。The book which has passed through different hands is now in tatters. ❷〈方言〉torture; torment; cause severe suffering to:你分明是想～人。You are obviously trying to torment me. /我的心都给～碎了。My heart is broken.
揉磨 róumo 〈方言〉torture; torment:自个儿玩儿去,别～人。Go and play by yourself. Don't harass me.
輮 róu 〈书面〉❶ rim of a wheel ❷ *see* "揉 ❸"
蹂 róu 〈书面〉stamp; trample:～踏 trample
蹂躏 róulìn trample underfoot; trample on; ravage; ravish:匪徒杀人放火,～妇女,无所不为。The bandits committed murder, arson, and rape, and stopped at nothing. /入侵者正在～这个国家的领土主权。The invaders are trampling upon the territorial integrity and sovereignty of the land.
鰇 róu 〈古语〉squid

ròu

肉 ròu ❶ flesh; meat:猪～ pork /牛～ beef /小牛～ veal /羊～ mutton /鸭～ duck /鸡～ chicken /鱼～ fish /腊～ cured meat; bacon /熏～ smoked meat /熟～ cooked meat;delicatessens /肥～ fat meat; fat /瘦～ lean meat /肌～ muscle /里肌～ tenderloin meat /骨～ flesh and blood /净～ dressed carcass; dressed meat /～心馒头

R

steamed meat-stuffed roll /那些猪已经～膘肥满。The pigs have fattened. ❷ pulp; flesh (of fruits):桂圆～ longan pulp /椰子～ coconut meat ❸〈方言〉not crisp; mushy:～瓤西瓜 watermelon of mushy flesh (*or* pulp) ❹〈方言〉phlegmatic:～性子 phlegmatic temperament /～脾气 habitually slow

肉案 ròu'àn *also*"肉案子"〈方言〉butcher's (shop)

肉包 ròubāo *also*"肉包子" steamed bun with minced meat stuffing

肉包子打狗 ròubāozi dǎ gǒu throw a meat-stuffed bun at a dog — sth. gone, never to return

肉饼 ròubǐng meat pie; mince pie

肉饼蒸蛋 ròubǐng zhēngdàn steamed minced pork with egg

肉搏 ròubó fight hand-to-hand; fight at close quarters

肉搏战 ròubózhàn hand-to-hand fight or combat; bayonet charge:跟敌人展开～ engage the enemy in a hand-to-hand (*or* bayonet) fight

肉畜 ròuchù meat livestock; beef cattle

肉垂 ròuchuí〈动物〉wattle

肉苁蓉 ròucōngróng〈中药〉saline cistanche (*Cistanche salsa*)

肉弹 ròudàn ❶ *nikudan*, suicidal operation by Japanese war planes in WWII ❷ "flesh bomb" — use of woman as bait; woman so used

肉店 ròudiàn butcher's (shop)

肉丁 ròudīng diced meat:酱爆～ stir-fried diced pork in soya sauce

肉冻 ròudòng meat jelly; aspic:鱼～ fish in aspic

肉豆蔻 ròudòukòu *also*"肉果"〈中药〉nutmeg

肉嘟嘟 ròudūdū plump; fat:～的小手 plump little hands /小孩儿长得～的,非常可爱。The child is chubby and very lovely.

肉毒杆菌 ròudú gǎnjūn〈医学〉*Clostridium botulinum*

肉毒菌 ròudújūn botulinum

肉毒素 ròudúsù creotoxin

肉墩墩 ròudūndūn *also*"肉敦敦" fleshy and sturdy:他那黑红的脊背,～的。His dark-skinned back is fleshy and sturdy.

肉感 ròugǎn (usually of women) voluptuousness; sexiness; sensual attraction; sex appeal

肉杠 ròugàng〈方言〉〈旧语〉counter or shop selling pork (hanging on bars)

肉鸽 ròugē squab

肉冠 ròuguān〈动物〉comb

肉桂 ròuguì *also*"桂"〈植物〉Chinese cassia tree; cinnamon

肉果 ròuguǒ〈植物〉❶ sarcocarp:桃、李都属～类。Peaches and plums are both sarcocarps. ❷ *see*"肉豆蔻"

肉红 ròuhóng pink; pinkish red

肉乎乎 ròuhūhū *also*"肉呼呼" fat;fleshy:～的脑袋 fleshy head /～的一头小猪娃 very fat piglet

肉鸡 ròujī *also*"肉用鸡" chicken; table hen; broiler

肉碱 ròujiǎn〈生化〉carnitine

肉酱 ròujiàng meat pulp; minced meat:剁成～ chop into meat pulp; make mincemeat of

肉茎植物 ròujīng zhíwù〈植物〉sarcocaul

肉类 ròulèi meats

肉类加工厂 ròulèi jiāgōngchǎng meat-processing plant

肉林酒池 ròulín-jiǔchí *also*"酒池肉林" woods of meat and ponds of wine — wining, dining and womanizing; life of extreme extravagance and debauchery

肉瘤 ròuliú〈医学〉sarcoma

肉瘤霉素 ròuliú méisù〈微生物〉sarkomycin

肉麻 ròumá sickening; nauseating; fulsome; disgusting:多～。It's enough to turn my stomach. /这些赞美的话真～。These words of adulation were fulsome. /他在大会上的讲话把这班人捧上了天,太～了。His speech at the rally, which lauded these people to the skies, was really sickening.

肉糜 ròumí〈方言〉fine minced meat; meat paste

肉末 ròumò minced meat; ground meat

肉囊囊 ròunāngnāng fat; fleshy; puffy:～的脸 puffy face /～的大腿 fleshy thighs

肉牛 ròuniú beef cattle

肉排 ròupái steak:牛～ steak /猪～ pork chop

肉泡眼 ròupāoyǎn eyes with fleshy eyelids; pouchy eyes

肉皮 ròupí pork skin:～冻 pork skin jelly

肉皮儿 ròupír〈方言〉(human) skin

肉片 ròupiàn sliced meat; meat slice:熘～ meat slices sauté

肉票 ròupiào person kidnapped by bandits; hostage:撕～ (bandits) kill a hostage

肉鳍 ròuqí (of a squid, etc.) (boneless) tail; fin

肉禽 ròuqín fowl

肉色 ròusè flesh-coloured; yellowish pink:～连裤袜 flesh-tinted (*or* -coloured) pantyhose

肉身 ròushēn〈宗教〉flesh; human body

肉食 ròushí carnivorous; meat-eating:～动物 carnivorous animal; carnivore

肉食者 ròushízhě〈旧语〉"meateater" — high official:～鄙。High officials are short-sighted.

肉食 ròushi meat:每天都有点～。There is some meat in the diet every day.

肉丝 ròusī shredded meat:辣椒～ shredded meat with hot pepper /～炒面 fried noodles with shredded pork

肉松 ròusōng dried mince meat; dried meat floss

肉穗花序 ròusuì huāxù〈植物〉spadix

肉袒 ròutǎn〈书面〉strip off the upper garment as a token of sincere apology or reverence:～负荆 strip off the upper garment and proffer a birch — ready to submit to any punishment the other party may want to give; asking (for) forgiveness

肉汤 ròutāng broth;meat gravy

肉体 ròutǐ flesh; human body:出卖～ sell one's body; practise prostitution /～和精神都受到摧残 be made to suffer both physically and mentally

肉痛 ròutòng〈方言〉feel sorry or reluctant (to partwith money or thing); be distressed or grieved (at waste)

肉头 ròutóu〈方言〉❶ dull-witted; weak-willed:他真～到家了,怎么说他也没用。He is so dull-witted that whatever you say will serve no purpose (*or* that no amount of persuasion can bring him around). ❷ foolish; silly:他净办这种～事! He is always doing such silly things! ❸ mean; stingy; miserly; niggardly

肉头 ròutou〈方言〉round and soft; fleshy; chubby:这个孩子的脸多～! What chubby cheeks the child has got!

肉丸子 ròuwánzi meatball

肉馅 ròuxiàn chopped or minced meat; meat stuffing

肉星儿 ròuxīngr tiny bits of meat:菜里不见～。There is not even the slightest bit of meat in this dish.

肉刑 ròuxíng corporal punishment

肉芽 ròuyá〈医学〉granulation:～肿 granuloma

肉眼 ròuyǎn ❶ naked eye:～难以看到 hardly invisible to the naked eye ❷ layman's eyes; common or vulgar views:～不识泰山 cannot see Mount Tai with a layman's eyes — entertain an angel unawares

肉眼凡胎 ròuyǎn-fántāi common mortal; mediocrity; ordinary man

肉眼泡儿 ròuyǎnpāor *also*"肉眼泡子" eyes with fleshy eyelids

肉叶植物 ròuyè zhíwù leaf succulent

肉用家禽 ròuyòng jiāqín〈农业〉table poultry

肉欲 ròuyù carnal desire; sensual desire:放纵～ unbridled sensual indulgence; indulging in sensual pleasures

肉圆 ròuyuán meatball:～粉丝汤 soup with meatballs and starch noodles

肉汁 ròuzhī gravy; meat extract

肉质 ròuzhì fleshy:～根 fleshy root /～果 fleshy fruit /～种子 fleshy seed

肉制品 ròuzhìpǐn meat product

肉中刺 ròuzhōngcì thorn in one's flesh:他把小李看成眼中钉,～,想着法儿整人家。He regards Xiao Li as a thorn in the flesh and is always trying to make trouble for him.

肉猪 ròuzhū porker; hog suitable for slaughter

肉赘 ròuzhuì wart

肉孜节 Ròuzījié *also*"开斋节" Kāizhāijié〈伊斯兰〉Lesser Bairam; Festival of Fast-breaking; *Rozah*

肉足纲 ròuzúgāng〈动物〉*Sarcodina*

rú

濡 rú〈书面〉❶ immerse; dip in; moisten; catch:相～以沫 (people in adverse circumstances) help each other; be friends in need /耳～目染 be imperceptibly influenced by what one constantly

sees and hears ❷ stay; linger: ～迹(break off a journey to) stay; linger /～缓 slow-moving

濡笔 rúbǐ *also* "濡毫"〈书面〉dip a writing brush in Chinese ink — write: 凭案一～, 万言俱落纸。Sit at the desk wielding the brush and ten thousand words appear on paper.

濡染 rúrǎn ❶ be influenced by; catch: 受父亲～, 他也喜爱诗画。Influenced by his father, he is fond of poetry and painting. ❷ immerse; dip in: 大笔～, 一挥而就。He dipped the writing brush in ink and finished his calligraphy with a flourish.

濡润 rúrùn wet; moist

濡湿 rúshī soak; become or make wet: 晓来大雾, 草木～。There was a dense fog at dawn, which moistened all plants.

濡泄 rúxiè 〈中医〉diarrhoea

濡滞 rúzhì 〈书面〉procrastinate; tarry; be sluggish: 行动有意～ be deliberately slow in action

襦

rú 〈书面〉blouse; short jacket: 上着绣～, 下穿长裙 wear an embroidered blouse and a long skirt

薷

rú *see* "香薷" xiāngrú

颥

rú *see* "颞颥" nièrú

嚅

rú

嚅动 rúdòng (of lips) open and close: 她～着嘴唇, 好像有话要说。Her lips parted, as if she had something to say.

嚅嗫 rúniè 〈书面〉speak haltingly

嚅嚅 rúrú hesitate in speech; hem and haw

蠕(蝡)

rú wriggle; squirm

蠕变 rúbiàn ❶ change slowly ❷〈物理〉creep; deformation; creep strain: ～试验 creep test

蠕虫 rúchóng worm; helminth: ～学 helminthology

蠕动 rúdòng ❶ peristalsis: 胃肠～ peristalsis of stomach and intestines ❷ wriggle; squirm: 蚯蚓在泥土上～着。The earthworms are wriggling on the earth. /一支队伍在山路上～。A contingent of troops zigzagged along the mountain path.

蠕螺 rúluó worm shell

蠕蠕 rúrú wriggling; squirming: ～而行 wriggle along; crawl along

蠕形动物 rúxíng dòngwù any creature belonging to the general class of worms; worm (*Vermes*)

儒

rú ❶ (Rú) Confucianism; Confucianist: *see* "～家"; "～教" ❷〈旧语〉scholar; learned man: 名～ well-known scholar /腐～ pedantic scholar; pedant

儒道 Rúdào Confucianism and Taoism

儒艮 rúgèn *also* "人鱼" rényú 〈动物〉dugong (*Halicore dugong*); sea cow

儒家 Rújiā Confucian school; Confucianists: ～经典 Confucian canon /～学说 Confucian doctrine /～思想 Confucianism /新～ neo-Confucianists /～代表人物 representative of the Confucian school

儒将 rújiàng scholar-general

儒教 Rújiào (used from the 5th century on when compared to Buddhism and Taoism) Confucianism

儒林 rúlín 〈旧语〉scholars; academic circles

儒林外史 Rúlín Wàishǐ *The Scholars*, novel by Wu Jingzi (吴敬梓, 1701-1754) of the Qing Dynasty

儒略历 Rúlüèlì Julian calendar, predecessor of the current Gregorian calendar, adopted by Julius Caesar in 46 BC

儒门 rúmén Confucian school of thought

儒生 rúshēng 〈旧语〉Confucian scholar

儒士 rúshì *see* "儒生"

儒术 rúshù Confucian teachings

儒学 rúxué ❶ Confucian studies; Confucian teachings ❷ government-run Confucian schools at county and prefectural levels in the Yuan, Ming and Qing dynasties

儒雅 rúyǎ 〈书面〉❶ well-educated; erudite ❷ courteous and dignified: 风流～ elegant in manners

儒医 rúyī doctor of traditional Chinese medicine who began his career as a scholar; scholar-doctor

儒宗 rúzōng 〈书面〉Confucian scholar whom others look up to for guidance; one who is held in great esteem by other Confucian scholars

孺

rú child: 妇～ women and children

孺慕 rúmù 〈书面〉adore as a child does its parents; love and admire profoundly

孺人 rúrén 〈旧语〉mother or wife of a seventh rank official in the Ming and Qing dynasties

孺子 rúzǐ 〈书面〉child: 黄口～ mere child

孺子可教 rúzǐ-kějiào the kid is teachable; the young man is worth teaching

孺子牛 rúzǐniú ox led by the child (alluding to the story of the Prince of Qi who played "ox" in a children's game with his son leading him by the nose with a rope held in his mouth); ox led by the nose; 〈比喻〉person willingly serving the interests of the people: 横眉冷对千夫指, 俯首甘为～。Fierce-browed, I coolly defy a thousand pointing fingers. Head bowed, like a willing ox I serve the children.

如[1]

rú ❶ according to; in comformity with: ～约 keep one's appointment appropriate /恰～其分 appropriate; just right ❷ like; as; as if: 亲～一家 as intimate as members of the same family /整旧～新 restore sth. to its original shape and appearance /吓得面～土色 turn pale with fright /泪～雨下 tears streaming down one's cheeks /～上所述 as is mentioned above ❸ (used in the negative) be as good as; can compare with: 你不～他。You are not as good as he is. /与其闭门造车, 不～向下级请教。It is better to consult those below rather than try to devise plans behind closed doors. ❹ be more than; suspass: 粮食产量一年强～一年。The grain yield increases every year. ❺ for example; for instance; such as; as: 我厂生产多种纤维, ～腈纶、维纶、涤纶等。Our factory produces various synthetic fibres, such as acrylic, polyvinyl and polyester fibres. ❻〈书面〉go to; arrive at: ～厕 go to the bathroom (*or* toilet, *or* WC) ❼ (Rú) a surname

如[2]

rú if: ～不能按期离京, 务请尽早告知。If you are not able to leave Beijing as scheduled, do let us know as soon as possible. /～无意外, 我将于下月来沪。I'll come to Shanghai next month, barring accidents.

如[3]

rú *used as a suffix of certain adjectives or adverbs in classical Chinese to indicate a state or manner*: 突～其来 unexpectedly; suddenly; to one's surprise /空空～也 be empty; be penniless

如臂使指 rúbìshǐzhǐ have everything under perfect control; be at home with: 他操作计算机, ～, 从心所欲。He is a past master at the computer, operating it just as he likes.

如常 rúcháng as usual: 平静～ calm as usual /起居～ be in as good health as before

如出一口 rúchūyīkǒu with one voice; in unison; unanimously

如出一辙 rúchūyīzhé run in the same groove; be cut from the same cloth; follow the same pattern; as like as two peas: 他们的做法～。Their ways of doing things are identical. /两人的观点～。The views of the two practically coincide.

如初 rúchū as before; as always; as of old: 和好～ be good friends again as they used to

如此 rúcǐ such; so; like that; in this way: 理当～ rightly so /原文～ (usu. in brackets) sic /但愿～。I wish it were so. /天天～。Each day is no different from the other. /他竟然～狂妄。How could he be so arrogant! /～好机会, 你决不能错过。You mustn't let slip such a good opportunity. /既然～, 我们必须重新考虑这个问题。Such being the case, we must reconsider the problem.

如此等等 rúcǐ děngděng and so on and so forth

如此而已 rúcǐ éryǐ that is what it all adds up to; that is all there is to it: 说到底也不过～。In the final analysis, this is what it all amounts to. /～, 岂有他哉! That's all there is to it! /他的业务水平也就～。Professionally, he is just so-so.

如此这般 rúcǐ zhèbān and so on and so forth; in this way; thus: ～地说了一通 hold forth in this way /你只要～, 老太太准会答应。If you do this and that, the old lady will certainly agree.

如次 rúcì as follows: 调查情况～。The findings of the investigation are stated below. /原文～。The text is (*or* reads) as follows.

如弟 rúdì 〈书面〉〈旧语〉younger sworn brother

如堕五里雾中 rú duò wǔlǐwù zhōng as if lost in a dense fog; losing one's bearings; utterly perplexed: 搞得我昏头昏脑，~。I was completely puzzled as if I had lost my bearings in a dense fog.

如堕烟海 rúduòyānhǎi as if lost on a foggy sea; completely at sea; totally at a loss: 面对如此复杂的情况，我~，一时不知如何是好。Facing such a complex situation, I was totally at a loss as to what to do.

如法炮制 rúfǎ-páozhì concoct herbal medicine by a prescribed method — follow sb.'s example; follow suit: 他们~，也搞了个花展。They followed suit and put on a flower show of their own.

如夫人 rúfūren 〈旧语〉concubine

如故 rúgù ❶ as before: 年已古稀，性格依然~。Though he is over seventy years of age, his temperament remains unaltered. ❷ like old friends: 一见~ feel like old friends at the first meeting; be like old friends from the very start; become friends at first sight

如果 rúguǒ if; in case; in the event of: ~他想这样做的话 were he so inclined / ~你现在有事，我明天再来。If you are busy, I'll come again tomorrow. / ~时间来得及，我想行前拜访他。If time permits, I'd like to pay him a visit before I leave. / ~下雨，运动会将延期举行。In the event of rain the sports meet will be postponed (*or* put off).

如何 rúhé how; what: 你意~？What do you think (of it)? *or* How do you like it? / 群众反映~？How did the public react (*or* respond) to it? / 将来情况~，殊难预料。What is going to happen is hardly predictable. / 不管她说得~好听，都不要轻易相信。However fine-sounding her words may be, you mustn't believe them too readily.

如虎添翼 rúhǔtiānyì like a tiger that has grown wings — with added strength; further strengthened: 有了科学管理，厂里生产就~。With scientific management, the factory's production increased even further.

如花美眷 rúhuā-měijuàn wife as beautiful as a flower; happy matrimony; conjugal felicity

如花似锦 rúhuā-sìjǐn (of scenery, landscape, one's future, etc.) splendid; wonderful: 他有一个~的前程。He has a splendid future. *or* He has very bright prospects.

如花似玉 rúhuā-sìyù like flowers and jade — ravishingly beautiful (woman)

如火燎原 rúhuǒ-liáoyuán like a prairie fire — sth. that develops rapidly with irresistible force or momentum

如火如荼 rúhuǒ-rútú like a raging fire; fiery: ~的爱国运动正在展开。A vigorous patriotic movement was under way. *or* A patriotic movement spread like wildfire.

如获至宝 rúhuòzhìbǎo as if one had found a treasure: 他得到这个消息，~，立即奔走传告。When he received the information, he felt as if he had obtained a rare treasure and lost no time in telling his friends about it.

如饥似渴 rújī-sìkě as if thirsting or hungering for sth.; eagerly; avidly: 他~地阅读这部小说。He devoured the novel avidly.

如箭在弦 rújiànzàixián like an arrow fitted to the bowstring — cannot but go ahead; reach the point of no return: 双方加紧调兵遣将，一场更大的冲突~。An even larger conflict seemed imminent, as the two sides were busy mustering their forces.

如胶似漆 rújiāo-sìqī cling to each other like glue or lacquer; be deeply attached to each other; be deeply in love with each other: 他们亲密得~。They were deeply attached to each other. / 这一对新婚夫妇真是~。The newlyweds are almost inseparable.

如今 rújīn nowadays; now; today: ~他已长大成人。He has grown into manhood. / 事到~，也只好这么办了。As it is, we have no other way out.

如旧 rújiù as before; as of old; as usual: 安堵~ secure as before

如来 Rúlái 〈佛教〉*Tathagata*; Buddha

如狼牧羊 rúlángmùyáng like a wolf shepherding sheep — trample underfoot: 这个军阀对老百姓的统治，~。This warlord rode roughshod over the ordinary folk.

如狼似虎 rúláng-sìhǔ as savage as wolves or tigers; brutal: 一伙强盗~般闯了进来。A gang of bandits, savage as wolves and tigers, forced their way in.

如雷贯耳 rúléiguàn'ěr resound like thunder: 久闻大名，~。I have long heard of your great name. *or* Your exalted name is known to all.

如临大敌 rúlíndàdí as if faced with a formidable foe — be heavily guarded: 沿街岗哨林立，巡逻士兵荷枪实弹，~。With sentries posted everywhere and heavily armed soldiers patrolling the street, the authorities behaved as if they were faced with a formidable enemy.

如临深渊，如履薄冰 rú lín shēnyuān, rú lǚ bóbīng as if standing on the brink of an abyss or treading on thin ice — exercise great caution

如芒在背 rúmángzàibèi *also* "芒刺在背" mángcì-zàibèi feel prickled down one's back — (feel) nervous and uneasy; be on pins and needles; have a thorn in one's flesh or side: 他这几句话使我坐立不安，~。I was on pins and needles at hearing his remarks.

如梦初醒 rúmèngchūxǐng feel as if one were waking from a dream; wake up all of a sudden; be startled into attentiveness: 听了你这番议论，我~。After listening to your words, I woke up with a start. / 我终于~，明白了真相。As if waking up from a dream, I was fully aware of the truth.

如命 rúmìng in compliance with your order; in conformity with the instructions

如鸟兽散 rúniǎoshòusàn flee helter-skelter; be in full rout: 警察到来时，那些流氓~。The hooligans fled helter-skelter when the police arrived.

如牛负重 rúniúfùzhòng like an ox carrying a heavy load — weighed down by heavy burdens: 债务堆积如山，~。Their debts pile up like loads on the backs of oxen.

如期 rúqī as scheduled; on schedule; in time: ~到达 arrive in time / ~交付 delivered at a specified date / 会议~举行。The conference was convened as scheduled.

如其 rúqí if; in case (of): ~不然 if not / 你最好明天去一趟，~天气不好，下星期再去。You'd better go tomorrow, if the weather is not good, you may postpone your trip till next week.

如泣如诉 rúqì-rúsù (of sound) like weeping; like pouring out one's grievances — very pathetic and touching: 有人吹着洞箫，其声哀婉，~。We heard somebody playing the bamboo flute, and its strains were sad and plaintive.

如日方升 rúrìfāngshēng rising like the morning sun — having a bright future; with boundless prospects: 这位青年在事业上~，前途无量。Like the rising sun, the young fellow has a bright future ahead of him.

如日中天 rúrìzhōngtiān like the sun at high noon; at the height of one's power, career, etc.: 这里的乡镇企业兴旺发达，~。Township enterprises in this area are flourishing like the sun at high noon. / 阁下不惑之年，~，正可大展鸿图。At forty you are in the prime of life and have plenty of scope to display your talent.

如人无人之境 rú rù wú rén zhī jìng feel as if entering empty land — encountering no resistance at all; smash all resistance; carry all before one: 我军渡江之后，一路前进，~。Having crossed the river, our troops pressed ahead like a hot knife through butter.

如若 rúruò if; in case: ~有时间，请你来一趟。Please come over if you have time. / 情况~有变，请随时告知。In case there is any change in the situation, please let me know at once. / ~不然，即请自便。Otherwise, do as you think fit.

如丧考妣 rúsàngkǎobǐ as if one had lost one's parents — very sad or sorrowful: 听说自己的财产被没收，这个贪官号啕大哭，~。On hearing that his property had been confiscated, the corrupt official burst into tears, as if he had lost his parents.

如上 rúshàng as above: 详情~。The details are stated (*or* mentioned) above. / 处理意见报告~，急盼批复。The above are my recommendations and I anxiously await your instructions.

如实 rúshí strictly according to the facts: ~汇报 report exactly how things stand / ~招来 own up; make a clean breast of everything

如是 rúshì so; such; in this way; like that: 手都冻僵了，想不到阳历三月还~之冷。My fingers are numb with cold. Who would have imagined that it would be so cold in March?

如适 rúshì 〈方言〉❶ suitable; proper ❷ (usu. in the negative) comfortable; at ease: 近来身体不~。I haven't been very well lately.

如释重负 rúshìzhòngfù as if relieved of a heavy burden: 交代清楚后，我才~。I felt greatly relieved after I made a clean breast of everything. / 她~地松了口气。She heaved a sigh of relief.

如数家珍 rúshǔjiāzhēn as if enumerating one's family treasures; having sth. at one's fingertips: 他向我们介绍公司情况，~。He briefed us on the company, rattling on as if enumerating his family valuables. / 这个题目他讲起来~。He has got the subject at his fingertips.

如数 rúshù exactly the number or amount; in full: ~缴纳税款 pay

taxes in full /～补齐 make up in full; bring to the full number (*or* amount)

如斯 rúsī 〈书面〉so; in this way; therefore; like that:此人愚腐～，无可救药。He is hopelessly pedantic. /逝者～夫。Thus do things flow (*or* pass) away.

如汤沃雪 rútāngwòxuě like pouring hot water on snow — easily and speedily done:若有炮兵配合，拿下此城～。Given artillery support, it's a walkover to capture the city.

如天之福 rútiānzhīfú godsend; blessing:双方如能和解，这才是我们百姓的～。It would be a blessing for ordinary people if the two parties to the civil strife could come to terms with each other.

如同 rútóng like; as:灯火通明，～白昼。It was brilliantly lit as if it were daytime.

如闻其声，如见其人 rú wén qí shēng, rú jiàn qí rén (the description is so vivid) you seem to see and hear the person:读罢《阿Q正传》，对阿Q这个人物真有～的感觉。After reading *The True Story of Ah Q*, one feels as if one could almost see what he was doing and hear what he was saying.

如下 rúxià as follows; following:作～说明 make the following explanations /列举～ be listed below /发起者有～几个单位。The following is a list of the sponsoring organizations. /发表～声明。The statement is as follows. /全文～。The full text follows.

如像 rúxiàng *see* "如同"

如心 rúxīn pleased; gratified; satisfied; contented:事事～。Everything went as one had wished.

如兄 rúxiōng 〈书面〉〈旧语〉sworn elder brother

如许 rúxǔ 〈书面〉❶ so; such; like that:问渠那得清～，为有源头活水来。Why is the pond so limpid? Because fresh water pours in from its source. ❷ so much; so many:枉费～钱财 squander so much money

如一 rúyī identical; consistent; without change:始终～ be consistent throughout (*or* all along)/表里～ think and behave in one and the same way

如仪 rúyí in accordance with the rules of etiquette:行礼～ perform the ceremony in accordance with the rules of etiquette

如蚁附膻 rúyǐfùshān behave like ants clinging to sth. rank — swarm after unwholesome things; toady to influential people:此等人一见低级下流刊物就～。These people are attracted to publications of vulgar taste like ants swarming to filthy, rank-smelling objects.

如意 rúyì ❶ comply with one's wishes:遂心～ be perfectly satisfied /祝您万事～。I wish you success in everything you undertake. /事情往往不能～。Things do not often turn out as one wishes. ❷ *ruyi*, an S-shaped wand or sceptre, usu. made of jade, symbolizing good fortune

如意算盘 rúyì-suànpan wishful thinking:他们的想法只是～而已。Their hopes are but wishful thinking. /这种～与实际情况正好相反。This kind of smug calculation runs counter to actual practice.

如蝇逐臭 rúyíngzhúchòu *also* "如蝇逐膻" behave like flies going after a foul smell — go after illicit gain or vulgar attractions

如影随形 rúyǐngsuíxíng like the shadow following the body; always in each other's company:他俩～，总在一起。They are practically inseparable just like the shadow following the body.

如鱼得水 rúyúdéshuǐ feel just like fish in water; be in congenial company; be happy and satisfied:他到艺术研究院后，～，干得十分顺心。He was in his element at the arts research institute and all went well with him.

如愿 rúyuàn do as one wishes:他想去黄山旅游，但总不能～。His wish to tour Huang Shan Mountain has never been fulfilled.

如愿以偿 rúyuàn-yǐcháng have one's wish fulfilled:他终于～，成了艺术家。He eventually became an artist, his long-cherished wish fulfilled. *or* His heart's desire to become an artist was eventually fulfilled.

如云 rúyún cloudlike; abundant:仕女～ large groups of ladies

如之奈何 rúzhīnàihé not know what to do; what's to be done:此事若让对方发觉，～? What is to be done if the other side got to know about it?

如字 rúzì pronounce a Chinese character as it is commonly enunciated (even if it has a number of pronunciations)

如醉方醒 rúzuìfāngxǐng sober up:众人闻言，～。These words sobered them up.

如醉如痴 rúzuì-rúchī as if intoxicated and enthralled:这些少男少女对流行音乐迷恋得～。These teenagers were infatuated with (*or* mad about) pop music.

如坐针毡 rúzuòzhēnzhān feel as though sitting on a rug full of needles; be on pins and needles; be on tenterhooks:在接到母亲病重的消息后，她终日心慌意乱，～。She's been on tenterhooks all day ever since she learned that her mother was seriously ill. /他出了一身冷汗，心神不定，～。He broke into a cold sweat and felt deeply perturbed as if sitting on a bed of nails.

茹 rú 〈书面〉❶ eat:～素 eat grain and vegetables only; be on a vegetarian diet ❷ (Rú) a surname

茹苦含辛 rúkǔ-hánxīn *also* "含辛茹苦" endure hardships

茹毛饮血 rúmáo-yǐnxuè (of primitive man) eat the raw flesh of birds and animals:人类是从～的蛮荒时代进化到文明时代的。Human civilization has evolved from primitive barbarism when people ate things raw.

茹素吃斋 rúsù-chīzhāi go vegetarian; be a vegetarian as a religious believer:我祖母长年～。My grandma lives on vegetables all year long.

铷 rú 〈化学〉rubidium (Rb)

rǔ

汝 rǔ ❶〈书面〉you:～等 you people ❷ (Rǔ) a surname

汝辈 rǔbèi 〈书面〉(used by a senior to a junior) you people; you:～何敢如此粗鲁? Why are you people so rude?

汝曹 rǔcáo 〈书面〉(used by a senior to a junior or subordinate) you people; you:愿～效之。I hope you people will follow his example.

汝窑 Rǔyáo Ruzhou Kiln, in today's Linru County (临汝) of Henan Province, producing quality porcelain wares in the Song Dynasty

擩 rǔ 〈方言〉thrust; tuck; put in:两手往口袋里一～ thrust one's hands into one's pockets /别把书往枕头下～。Don't tuck the book under the pillow. /他～到烂泥里，把脚弄脏了。He stepped in the mud and got his foot dirty.

辱 rǔ ❶ disgrace; dishonour:羞～ humiliation; insult; disgrace ❷humiliate; insult:丧权～国 humiliate the nation and forfeit its sovereignty /宁死不～ would rather die than suffer humiliation ❸ bring disgrace or humiliation; be unworthy of:惟恐力薄才疏而～尊命。I'm afraid that being deficient in virtue and ability I should fail to carry out your instructions. ❹〈书面〉〈谦词〉be honoured; be grateful:～承指教 be honoured by your advice; thank you for giving me the benefit of your wise counsel

辱骂 rǔmà abuse; curse; call (sb.) names; hurl insults (upon sb.):～和恐吓决不是战斗。Hurling insults and making threats is certainly not fighting.

辱命 rǔmìng fail to accomplish a mission:不辱使命 fulfil one's mission; accomplish an assignment /幸未～。I am fortunate enough not to have failed in my mission.

辱没 rǔmò bring discredit to; sully; tarnish:我们决不～这个集体的荣誉。We shall never do anything to sully the reputation of the collective.

乳 rǔ ❶ reproduce:孳～ reproduction (of animals, etc.) ❷ breast:*see* "～罩" ❸ milk:人～ human milk /代～粉 ersatz milk powder /炼～ condensed milk /脱脂～ skimmed milk /低脂～ low-fat milk /全脂～ whole milk /正在哺～的婴孩 baby sucking at its mother's breast ❹ any milk-like liquid:胶～ latex /石灰～ milk of lime /豆～ soybean milk ❺ newborn (animal); suckling:*see* "～燕"

乳癌 rǔ'ái 〈医学〉breast cancer; mastoscirrhus

乳媪 rǔ'ǎo wet nurse

乳白 rǔbái milky white; creamy:～色的玻璃 milk glass; opal glass; opalescent glass /～灯泡 opal bulb /～色的云朵 milky white cloud

乳钵 rǔbō mortar (hollow vessel for grinding powders)

乳齿 rǔchǐ milk tooth; deciduous tooth

乳畜 rǔchù dairy cattle (such as milch cow, milch goat, etc.)

乳蛾 rǔ'é 〈中医〉acute tonsillitis
乳儿 rǔ'ér nursing infant; suckling; sucking babe
乳房 rǔfáng ❶ breast; mamma:～癌 mastocarcinoma /～切除术 mammectomy; mastectomy /～成形术 mammilliplasty /～切开术 mammotomy /～溃疡 masthelcosis ❷ (of an animal) udder
乳峰 rǔfēng rounded breasts (of a woman)
乳腐 rǔfǔ 〈方言〉fermented bean curd
乳虎 rǔhǔ ❶ suckling tigress ❷ young tiger; cub
乳化 rǔhuà 〈化学〉emulsification; emulsifying
乳化剂 rǔhuàjì emulsifying agent; emulsifier; emulsor
乳化漆 rǔhuàqī emulsion paint
乳化液 rǔhuàyè 〈化学〉emulsion:水包油～ oil-in-water emulsion / 油包水～ water-in-oil emulsion
乳化油 rǔhuàyóu emulsible or emulsified oil
乳化原油 rǔhuà yuányóu emulsified crude oil
乳黄 rǔhuáng pale yellow; creamy:～色的墙壁 creamy wall
乳剂 rǔjì 〈化学〉emulsion:全色～〈摄影〉panchromatic emulsion
乳浆 rǔjiāng milk
乳胶 rǔjiāo 〈化学〉emulsion:～漆 emulsion paint; latex paint
乳胶激光存储器 rǔjiāo jīguāng cúnchǔqì emulsion-laser storage
乳疽 rǔjū 〈中医〉intramammary abscess; mastoscirrhus
乳酪 rǔlào cheese
乳酪塑料 rǔlào sùliào lactolite
乳酶 rǔméi galaclenzyme
乳酶生 rǔméishēng 〈医学〉biofermin; lactasin
乳糜 rǔmí 〈生理〉chyle:～尿 chyluria
乳名 rǔmíng infant name; child's pet name
乳母 rǔmǔ wet nurse
乳娘 rǔniáng 〈方言〉wet nurse
乳牛 rǔniú dairy cattle; milch cow; milker
乳牛场 rǔniúchǎng dairy farm
乳清蛋白 rǔqīng dànbái 〈生化〉lactalbumin
乳球蛋白 rǔqiú dànbái 〈生化〉lactoglobulin
乳熟 rǔshú (of grain) be in the milk
乳酸 rǔsuān 〈生化〉lactic acid:副～ paralactic acid
乳酸钙 rǔsuāngài calcium lactate
乳酸菌酶 rǔsuān jūnméi lactacidase; lactalase
乳酸酶 rǔsuānméi lactolase
乳酸盐 rǔsuānyán lactate
乳糖 rǔtáng lactose; milk sugar:～酶 lactase /～尿 lactosuria
乳头 rǔtóu ❶ nipple; teat; mammilla ❷ papilla:舌～ papilla lingualis /视神经～ optic papilla
乳头炎 rǔtóuyán 〈医学〉mammilitis
乳头状癌 rǔtóuzhuàng'ái 〈医学〉papillary carcinoma; papillocarcinoma
乳头状瘤 rǔtóuzhuàngliú 〈医学〉papilloma
乳突炎 rǔtūyán 〈医学〉mastoiditis; papillitis
乳细 rǔxì 〈中医〉grind ingredients of herbal medicine into fine powder
乳腺 rǔxiàn 〈生理〉mammary gland; lactiferous gland:～病 mastopathy
乳腺癌 rǔxiàn'ái 〈医学〉breast cancer; mastoscirrhus
乳腺出血 rǔxiàn chūxuè 〈医学〉mastorrhagia
乳腺瘤 rǔxiànliú 〈医学〉mastadenoma
乳腺囊肿 rǔxiàn nángzhǒng 〈医学〉galactoma; galactocele
乳腺炎 rǔxiànyán 〈医学〉mastitis
乳腺硬化 rǔxiàn yìnghuà 〈医学〉mastoscirrhus
乳腺增生 rǔxiàn zēngshēng 〈医学〉cyclomastopathy
乳香 rǔxiāng frankincense
乳香黄连木 rǔxiāng huángliánmù 〈植物〉lentiscus (*Pistacia lentiscus*)
乳臭 rǔxiù smelling of milk; childish; green:～小儿 mere suckling; greenhorn
乳臭未干 rǔxiù-wèigān wet behind the ears; unfledged; greenhorn; fledgling:一个～的毛孩子,不必理他。Take no notice of him. He hasn't lost his milk teeth yet.
乳牙 rǔyá milk tooth; deciduous tooth; primary tooth
乳燕 rǔyàn newly hatched swallow; young swallow
乳液 rǔyè emulsion
乳溢 rǔyì 〈医学〉galactorrhea
乳油 rǔyóu ❶ cream ❷ emulsion
乳罩 rǔzhào brassiere; bra
乳汁 rǔzhī milk
乳脂 rǔzhī *also* "乳脂肪" butterfat; cream:～奶酪 cream cheese
乳脂糖 rǔzhītáng toffee; taffy
乳制品 rǔzhìpǐn dairy product:～工业 dairy industry
乳猪 rǔzhū sucking pig; suckling pig
乳状洗涤剂 rǔzhuàng xǐdíjì 〈化工〉emulsion cleaner
乳浊液 rǔzhuóyè 〈化学〉emulsion

rù

溽 rù 〈书面〉humid; damp
溽热 rùrè damp and close; hot and suffocating; humid and sultry; muggy:天气～。It's suffocatingly hot.
溽暑 rùshǔ sweltering summer weather

褥 rù padded mattress:被～ bedding; bedclothes /棉～ cotton-padded mattress /皮～ fur mattress /狗皮～ dog skin mattress
褥疮 rùchuāng 〈医学〉bedsore; decubitus ulcer; pressure sore
褥单 rùdān (bed) sheet
褥套 rùtào ❶ bedding sack (to be carried over the shoulder, or over the back of a pack animal) ❷ bedtick ❸ mattress cover
褥子 rùzi (cotton, kapok, etc.) padded mattress:皮～ (animal) hide mattress

蓐 rù 〈书面〉straw mat or mattress:坐～ chair mat

缛 rù elaborate; intricate; cumbersome:～礼 elaborate rules of etiquette /繁文～节 red tape; unnecessary and overelaborate formalities

洳 rù *see* "沮洳" jùrù

入 rù ❶ enter; go in; come in:～内 enter; go (*or* come) in /由浅～深 go from simple to complex /纳～正规 form a regular feature of the routine /纳～计划 incorporate in the plan /这个问题已纳～议程。This question has been put on the agenda. ❷ join; become a member of: *see* "～党";"～伙";"～学" ❸ income:年收～ annual income /月～万元 earn ten thousand *yuan* a month ❹ agree with; conform to:他说得～理。His words are perfectly reasonable. ❺〈语言〉*see* "入声"
入不敷出 rùbùfūchū income falling short of expenditure; living beyond one's means:他挥霍无度,～。A spendthrift, he could not make both ends meet.
入仓 rùcāng ❶ be stored in a barn; be put in storage ❷〈经济〉warehousing
入场 rùchǎng enter; be admitted:运动员～ march-in (*or* parade) of athletes /请大家依次凭票～。Please enter by ticket in proper order. /儿童谢绝～。Adults only. *or* No children allowed.
入场券 rùchǎngquàn (admission) ticket
入超 rùchāo unfavourable balance of trade; import surplus; trade deficit:～国 country of import surplus
入党 rùdǎng join the Party; become a Party member
入定 rùdìng 〈宗教〉achieve a state of absolute mental tranquillity in meditation; meditate:犹如老僧～ like an old monk sitting in meditation
入肚 rùdù swallow; consume; eat:转眼间一盘饺子就～了。He ate up a plateful of dumplings in no time. /三大杯热水～,身上才觉得有了点暖意。Having downed three large glasses of hot water, he began to feel a little bit warmer.
入耳 rù'ěr pleasant to the ear; palatable:口吐秽言,不堪～。He let out a lot of filth that was most offensive to the ear. /这句话十分～。This remark sounds quite acceptable.
入犯 rùfàn invade:坚决消灭～之敌。Resolutely wipe out the invading enemy troops.
入伏 rùfú beginning of the hottest part of the summer:已经～了,天气热得很。It is getting very hot as the dog days have set in.
入港 rùgǎng ❶〈交通〉come into port ❷ find (conversation, etc.) particularly congenial:他们正谈得～,忽听有人敲门。They were deep in conversation when they heard a knock at the door.
入港税 rùgǎngshuì port duties; inward charges; keelage

入彀 rùgòu ❶〈书面〉come within arrow's range ❷〈比喻〉fall under sb.'s control: 天下英雄尽～矣! All talented men have come under one's thumb. ❸〈比喻〉conform to general formalities and requirements ❹ concentrated; absorbed: 他们谈得～,不觉已过了半天。They were so absorbed in the conversation that they did not realize half a day had passed.

入股 rùgǔ buy a share; become a shareholder

入骨 rùgǔ to the marrow: 他对仇人恨之～。He nurses a deadly hatred for his enemy.

入官 rùguān ❶〈旧语〉confiscate: 财产～。His property was confiscated. ❷〈书面〉become an official

入国问禁 rùguó-wènjìn ask about the taboos upon arrival in a foreign country

入海口 rùhǎikǒu 〈地理〉estuary

入黑 rùhēi get dark: 他们俩一直谈到～。They talked until dark.

入户 rùhù ❶ go to sb.'s home ❷ register residence in a certain place: 申报～ apply for permanent residence in a certain place

入画 rùhuà can be made into a picture; be picturesque: 此等湖光山色,处处皆可～。Every bit of such beautiful landscape is worthy of a painter's brush.

入话 rùhuà *also* "得胜头回" déshèng tóuhuí; "得胜利市头回" déshèng lìshì tóuhuí (of script for storytelling or professional storyteller in the Song and Yuan dynasties) introductory story or verse before the main tale

入潢 rùhuáng dye paper with the juice of a cork tree (*Phellodendron*) to keep bookworms away

入会 rùhuì enrol as a member; be a member of an association, a club, etc.

入伙 rùhuǒ ❶ join a gang; go into partnership: 拉人～ induce sb. to join a gang (*or* to become a partner) ❷ join a mess; eat regularly at the school (factory, etc.) canteen: 在食堂～,省去了许多麻烦。It saves a lot of trouble to eat at the mess.

入籍 rùjí naturalize; be naturalized; acquire citizenship (of a country)

入籍人 rùjírén naturalized person

入籍证书 rùjí zhèngshū naturalization certificate

入寂 rùjì 〈宗教〉(of monks and nuns) death; nirvana

入教 rùjiào become a follower or believer of a religion; be converted to a religion

入静 rùjìng 〈宗教〉sit in meditation

入境 rùjìng enter a country: ～签证 entry visa /～证书 entry certificate /～登记 entrance registration /～申报单 customs declaration (form) /办理～手续 go through entry formalities /～许可证 entry permit /从北京～ enter at Beijing

入境口岸 rùjìng kǒu'àn port of entry

入境问俗 rùjìng-wènsú inquire about the habits and customs on entering a foreign country: 出国旅游,应该～。When arriving in a foreign country, tourists should familiarize themselves with its habits and customs.

入口 rùkǒu ❶ enter the mouth: 不可～! Not to be taken orally! ❷ import: ～税 import tax /～商品 imported goods /～货 imported items ❸ entrance: 礼堂～ entrance of the auditorium /机场～ entrance to the airport /～界灯 threshold lights ❹ entrance; 〈自控〉point of entry: ～指令 entry instructions /～数据 entry data /～程序 entry programme

入寇 rùkòu 〈书面〉invade: 强敌～ be invaded by a formidable enemy

入库 rùkù put in storage; lay up: 图书～ put books in the stacks / 刀枪～ put the weapons back in the arsenal

入款 rùkuǎn income; receipt

入理 rùlǐ reasonable; sensible: 他的话很～。He is quite right.

入殓 rùliàn encoffin

入列 rùliè 〈军事〉join the ranks; take one's place (in the ranks); fall in

入流 rùliú ❶〈旧语〉(of the feudal official hierarchy) belong to any one of the nine grades of officialdom ❷ (in a general sense) qualified: 他是个不～的电影演员。He is not a qualified film (*or* movie) actor.

入垄 rùlǒng 〈方言〉(of conversation) congenial; agreeable: 二人谈得～。The two of them found each other congenial in their talk.

入马 rùmǎ (often used in the early vernacular) get along smoothly in an affair; have an affair

入梅 rùméi the rainy season begins
see also "黄梅季" huángméijì

入寐 rùmèi fall asleep; go to sleep: 辗转不能～ toss and turn in bed, unable to fall asleep

入门 rùmén ❶ learn the rudiments of a subject: ～师傅 master who initiates someone into a craft /～不难,学好不易。Rudimentary knowledge is easy to obtain but mastery is difficult to achieve. *or* It is easy to learn the rudiments of a subject but difficult to master it. /我学了半年中国画,还没有～。I've spent half a year studying Chinese painting, but I've scarcely mastered the basic skills. ❷ elementary course: 《中医～》*The ABC of Traditional Chinese Medicine* /《语音～》*Introduction to Phonetics* /《英语语法～》*The Elements of English Grammar*

入梦 rùmèng ❶ start dreaming; go to sleep: 久久不能～ be a long time falling asleep ❷ appear in one's dream

入迷 rùmí be fascinated; be enthralled: 看电视看得～ be addicted to television /听故事听得～ be enthralled by a story /杂技的精彩表演使观众～了。The audience watched spellbound the superb performances of the acrobats.

入眠 rùmián ❶ fall asleep; go to sleep: 他由于过度兴奋,深夜不能～。Owing to nervous tension, he remained wide awake even at midnight. ❷ (of silkworms) neither move nor eat (when casting off a skin)

入灭 rùmiè 〈宗教〉*see* "入寂"

入魔 rùmó absolutely addicted; mad about; infatuated with; enthralled: 玩电子游戏机都～了 be absolutely addicted to the electronic game machine

入木三分 rùmù-sānfēn sinking deep into wood — written in vigorous strokes; penetrating; piercing; incisive: 分析得～ give a penetrating analysis /将人物刻画得～ make a vivid description of a character /真是一句精辟的话,一针见血,～。This is incisive language that goes to the heart of the matter.

入暮 rùmù at dusk; towards evening: ～时分,村内炊烟四起。At dusk, smoke rises from kitchen chimneys all over the village.

入其彀中 rùqígòuzhōng fall into a snare; walk into a trap

入侵 rùqīn invade; intrude; make an incursion; make inroads: 围歼～之敌 surround and annihilate the intruding enemy troops

入情入理 rùqíng-rùlǐ fair and just; perfectly logical and reasonable: 你所拟的处分～。The disciplinary action you propose to take is both fair and reasonable.

入射波 rùshèbō 〈物理〉incident wave

入射点 rùshèdiǎn 〈物理〉point of incidence

入射角 rùshèjiǎo 〈物理〉angle of incidence; incident angle

入射线 rùshèxiàn 〈物理〉incident ray

入神 rùshén ❶ be entranced or spellbound: 听得入了神 listen spellbound /看小说～了 be enthralled by a novel ❷ superb; wonderful: 这小说的主人公写得真～。The portrayal of the hero of the novel was simply marvellous.

入声 rùshēng 〈语言〉entering tone, one of the four tones in classical Chinese pronunciation, now extinct in *putonghua*

入胜 rùshèng fascinated; enthralled: 他看书正看得～时,听到有人敲门。He was reading a most fascinating passage when he heard somebody knocking at the door. /这部小说他看得非常～。He was very much engrossed in the novel.

入时 rùshí fashionable; à la mode: 穿着～的姑娘 fashionably dressed girl /文章容易～难。Writing may not be difficult, but it is certainly not easy to cater to the tastes of the times.

入世 rùshì enter society: ～不深 be inexperienced in life and the way of society; haven't seen much of the world

入市壁垒 rùshì bìlěi 〈经济〉barrier of entry

入室 rùshì 〈书面〉attain profundity in scholastic pursuits: 登堂～ pass through the hall into the chamber — gain the mastery of a branch of learning; become proficient in one's profession

入室操戈 rùshì-cāogē 〈比喻〉refute sb. with his own writings or statements; turn sb.'s argument against him

入室弟子 rùshì dìzǐ disciple who has inherited the mantle from his master; initiated pupil

入手 rùshǒu start with; take as the point of departure: 从抓质量检查～ start with quality control /足球腾飞要从儿童～。If the Chinese football team is to take a big leap, we will have to begin with the training of child players.

入睡 rùshuì go to sleep; fall asleep: 他很快就～了。He soon fell

asleep. /躺在床上辗转反侧，难以～。I lay wide awake in bed, tossing from side to side.

入头 rùtóu (often used in the early vernacular) cross the threshold; learn the rudiments of a subject; get started

入土 rùtǔ be buried; be interred：我已经是快～的人啦。I have one foot in the grave already. *or* I am living on borrowed time.

入团 rùtuán join or be admitted to the Chinese Communist Youth League; become a member of the Youth League

入托 rùtuō be sent to a nursery：小孩～难的问题已经解决。It was once difficult to have kids admitted to nurseries, but now the problem has been solved. /我女儿～了。My daughter is in the nursery.

入微 rùwēi in every possible way; in every detail：体贴～ look after sb. in every possible way; be extremely thoughtful to sb.; attend to sb.'s comfort with loving care /剖析～ make (*or* give) a penetrating, in-depth analysis (of sth.) /细腻～的表演 exquisite performance

入闱 rùwéi ❶〈旧语〉(of examinees and invigilators) enter the imperial examination hall ❷ be selected; be recruited (out of many candidates)：全国女排决赛，四川队败于上海队，未能～。During the finals of the National Women's Volleyball Tournament, the Sichuan team lost to the Shanghai team and failed to make the grade. /这次招考国家工作人员，他～了。He was recruited as a public functionary after passing the state personnel examination.

入味 rùwèi ❶ tasty：这个餐馆的川菜很～。The Sichuan dishes offered in the restaurant are quite delicious. ❷ interesting：这戏演得真～。The performance of the play is superb.

入伍 rùwǔ enlist; join the services：热烈欢迎新兵～。Give a warm welcome to the new recruits. /他～多年了，深知纪律的重要性。As a veteran, he is fully aware of the importance of discipline.

入坞 rùwù dock：～检查修理 dockyard overhaul /～设备 docking accommodation / 该船下午二时～。The ship docked at 2 p.m.

入席 rùxí take one's seat at a banquet, ceremony, etc.：请大家～。Please be seated, everyone.

入乡随俗 rùxiāng-suísú *also* "入乡随乡"；"随乡入乡" suíxiāng-rùxiāng; follow local customs wherever you are; when in Rome, do as the Romans do

入邪 rùxié lead a depraved life; abandon oneself to evil ways

入绪 rùxù begin to take shape：工作刚刚～。Things are just beginning to take shape.

入选 rùxuǎn be chosen, selected, etc.：他的小说已经～为今年最佳作品之一。His novel has been chosen as one of the best literary works of the year.

入学 rùxué ❶ go to school：～考试 entrance examination / 我们孩子现在都～了。Our children are all going to school now. ❷ start school：～年龄 school age /我国城市儿童～年龄为六岁。In China children in the cities start school at the age of six.

入眼 rùyǎn pleasant to the eye：看得～ look attractive; be to one's liking /她这身打扮真不～。She doesn't look at all becoming in her dress.

入眼货 rùyǎnhuò sth. (especially goods) people like：这台彩电外形美观，真是～。The colour TV set is really attractive with its elegant exterior.

入药 rùyào be used as medicine

入夜 rùyè at nightfall：～，俱乐部就热闹起来了。The club livens up when night falls. /～后，雪越下越大。It snowed more and more heavily after night came.

入瘾 rùyǐn be addicted (to sth.); get into the habit (of doing sth.)

入狱 rùyù be put behind bars; be thrown into jail

入院 rùyuàn be hospitalized; be put into a hospital：办～手续 make arrangements for hospitalization /大夫让我～治疗。The doctor told me to stay in hospital for treatment.

入账 rùzhàng enter an item in an account; enter into the account book：这笔货款还未～。This payment has not been entered into the account book.

入蛰 rùzhé〈生物〉dormancy; hibernation

入主出奴 rùzhǔ-chūnú〈比喻〉take sectarian views (academically)：～，谣诼繁兴。Sectarianism was rampant and rumours rife.

入赘 rùzhuì marry into and live with one's bride's family：～女婿 man who comes to live with the family of his parents-in-law

入坐 rùzuò *also* "入座" take one's seat; be properly seated：请他～ show him to his seat /对号～ take one's seat according to the number on the ticket; sit in the right seat

ruá

挼 ruá〈方言〉❶ (of cloth or paper) crumple; crease：这张纸～了。This sheet of paper is crumpled. ❷ wear thin; be threadbare：这条裤子穿～了。The trousers are quite worn out.

see also ruó

ruán

堧(壖) ruán〈书面〉open space outside a city wall, palace, temple, etc.; open river bank：河～ riparian land

ruǎn

朊 ruǎn protein

see also "蛋白质" dànbáizhì

阮 ruǎn ❶ (short for 阮咸)〈音乐〉plucked stringed instrument ❷ (Ruǎn) a surname

阮朝 Ruǎncháo Nguyen Dynasty (1802-1945), the last dynasty in Viet Nam

阮籍 Ruǎn Jí Ruan Ji (formerly translated as Juan Chi, 210-263), Chinese poet of the Kingdom of Wei during the Three Kingdoms

阮囊羞涩 ruǎnnáng-xiūsè be embarrassingly short of money; run out of money; have not a single cent to bless oneself with：本拟去京访友，无奈～，未能成行。I was short of money, and had to abandon the plan to visit my friends in the capital.

阮咸 ruǎnxián〈音乐〉plucked stringed instrument

耎 ruǎn〈书面〉*see* "软" ruǎn

软(輭) ruǎn ❶ soft; supple; pliable：面和～了。The dough is too soft. /她体态婀～。She is supple and graceful. ❷ gentle; mild; soft：你对他太～。You are too soft with him. ❸ weak; shaky; feeble：欺～怕硬 bully the weak and fear the strong; be scared of the strong but brave with the weak /吓得他两腿发～。This gave him such a fright that his legs felt like jelly. ❹ poor in quality, ability, etc.：他为人诚实，就是业务上～点。He is an honest man but he is not well-trained professionally. /他扮主角功夫还～点儿。He is a bit weak as a leading actor. /货色太～。The goods are of poor quality. ❺ easily moved; apt to be influenced：耳根子～ credulous; gullible /心慈手～ be too kind-hearted to act resolutely / 一席话把他说～了。He was completely disarmed by these words. ❻ (Ruǎn) a surname

软包装 ruǎnbāozhuāng ❶ soft package：～饮料 soft-packaged drinks ❷ soft packing：食品用～ soft packing for food

软鼻涕 ruǎnbítì〈方言〉〈比喻〉weakling; coward：他是个～，不中用。He is chicken-hearted, absolutely spineless.

软币 ruǎnbì *also* "软通货"；"软货币" ❶ paper money ❷ soft money; soft currency

软玻璃 ruǎnbōli〈化工〉soft glass

软磁盘 ruǎncípán〈电子〉diskette; floppy disk (FD)

软贷款 ruǎndàikuǎn soft loan; low-interest loan

软蛋 ruǎndàn ❶ soft-shelled egg ❷〈方言〉〈比喻〉timid and over-cautious person; weakling：看你吓成这个样子，真是个～。You are really chicken-hearted, looking scared like this.

软刀子 ruǎndāozi soft knife — means of harming people imperceptibly：～割头不觉死。A soft knife kills a person imperceptibly.

软底鞋 ruǎndǐxié soft-soled shoes

软雕塑 ruǎndiāosù soft sculpture：～作品已经进入了寻常百姓家。Soft sculpture has become very popular.

软钉子 ruǎndīngzi〈比喻〉polite refusal; snub：我找他谈话，没想到竟碰了个～。I talked to him only to be snubbed! /我想请他主持会议，而他却让我碰了个～。I asked him to chair the meeting, but he declined politely.

软缎 ruǎnduàn soft silk fabric in satin weave

软腭 ruǎn'è〈生理〉soft palate

软耳朵 ruǎn'ěrduo credulous or gullible person; person who is easily influenced by other people's opinions
软肥皂 ruǎnféizào soft soap
软风 ruǎnfēng ❶ gentle wind; breeze:～拂面。A gentle breeze brushed his face. ❷〈气象〉force 1 wind; light air
软腐病 ruǎnfǔbìng 〈农业〉soft rot
软腹部 ruǎnfùbù soft underbelly; vulnerable area
软钢 ruǎngāng 〈冶金〉mild steel; soft steel:～管 flexible metallic hose
软膏 ruǎngāo ointment; paste
软骨 ruǎngǔ 〈生理〉cartilage
软骨癌 ruǎngǔ'ái 〈医学〉chondrocarcinoma
软骨病 ruǎngǔbìng 〈医学〉osteomalacia
软骨发育不全 ruǎngǔ fāyù bùquán 〈医学〉achondroplasia
软骨截除术 ruǎngǔ jiéchúshù 〈医学〉chondrectomy
软骨瘤 ruǎngǔliú 〈医学〉chondroma
软骨痛 ruǎngǔtòng 〈医学〉chondralgia
软骨头 ruǎngǔtou spineless person; coward:屈服于外来压力,露出一副～的丑恶嘴脸 bow to outside pressure and reveal the ugly features of a coward / 他听了把桌子一拍,狠狠地骂了一声"～"。On hearing this, he struck the table and cursed fiercely, "The softie!"
软骨炎 ruǎngǔyán 〈医学〉chondritis:肋～ costal chondritis
软骨鱼 ruǎngǔyú cartilaginous fish
软管 ruǎnguǎn flexible pipe or tube; hose:铠装～ armoured hose / ～接头 hose coupler
软罐头 ruǎnguàntou soft package; food in sealed plastic bags
软焊 ruǎnhàn soft soldering; soldering:～料 soft solder
软乎乎 ruǎnhūhū soft:～的泥土 oozy soil
软化 ruǎnhuà ❶ change from hard to soft:硬水～ soften hard water / 髌骨～ patella softening ❷ change from steadfast to wavering; change from stiff to compliant:他们的态度逐渐～。Their attitude has softened. ❸ soften up; weaken:目的在于～他,使他屈服。The purpose was to soften him up and bring him to his knees. ❹ bate (leather)
软化栽培 ruǎnhuà zāipéi blanching culture
软话 ruǎnhuà *also* "软和话儿"(usu. in making an apology, begging for pardon, soothing sb., etc.) conciliatory or complaisant remarks; gentle and kind words:你就说几句～,让老爷子消消气吧。Why don't you say a few conciliatory words to pacify the old man?
软货币 ruǎnhuòbì *see* "软币"
软和 ruǎnhuo 〈口语〉❶ soft:～的棉袄 soft cotton-padded jacket / 这被子特别～。This quilt is extremely soft. ❷ gentle; kind; soft:几句～话儿使她心情舒畅多了。These kind words made her feel a lot better.
软技术 ruǎnjìshù soft technology (referring to management, administration, etc.)
软甲龟 ruǎnjiǎguī softshell turtle
软件 ruǎnjiàn ❶〈计算机〉software:～库 software library / ～跟踪方式 software trace mode / ～模型化 software modularity / ～包 software package ❷〈比喻〉quality of personnel, management and services, etc.:这个旅馆的硬件不错,但～跟不上。The hotel is well equipped, but its services are not so good.
软件工程 ruǎnjiàn gōngchéng software engineering
软金属 ruǎnjīnshǔ soft metal
软禁 ruǎnjìn put under house arrest or house confinement:政变领导人据说被～。The coup leaders are said to have been put under house arrest.
软景 ruǎnjǐng 〈戏剧〉backdrop; backcloth
软镜片 ruǎnjìngpiàn soft lens; contact lens
软拷贝 ruǎnkǎobèi 〈电子〉soft copy
软靠 ruǎnkào 〈戏曲〉light-weight armour worn by ancient army commanders
软科学 ruǎnkēxué soft science
软款 ruǎnkuǎn soft; gentle; mild:～的叮咛 gentle advice / 她腰肢不像先前那般～了。Her waist is not so supple as before.
软肋 ruǎnlèi soft rib
软连接 ruǎnliánjiē 〈机械〉flexible joint
软溜溜 ruǎnliūliū ❶ soft; gentle:他肩上挑的担子～地闪动着。The carrying pole on his shoulder swayed gently. ❷ soft and weak; feeble:浑身～地一点劲儿也没有 feel weak all over
软麻工艺 ruǎnmá gōngyì 〈纺织〉❶ bruising (of linen) ❷ batching (of gunny)

软媚 ruǎnmèi gentle and soft; pleasant and likable
软锰矿 ruǎnměngkuàng 〈矿业〉pyrolusite
软绵绵 ruǎnmiānmiān ❶ soft:～的绸料 soft silk (fabric) / 我不喜欢～的音乐。I don't particularly like sentimental music. ❷ weak:卧床几天,我只感到～的,浑身酸痛。Having been confined to bed for a few days, I feel rather weak and ache all over.
软磨 ruǎnmó use soft tactics:经不住他～硬泡,老王终于答应了他的要求。Unable to resist his alternate use of soft and tough tactics, Lao Wang eventually gave in to his demands.
软木 ruǎnmù ❶ *also* "栓皮" shuānpí cork:～塞 cork (as a stopper) ❷ softwood
软木画 ruǎnmùhuà 〈工美〉cork carving; cork picture
软泥 ruǎnní 〈地质〉ooze
软盘 ruǎnpán (short for 软磁盘) diskette; floppy disk (FD)
软片 ruǎnpiàn (a roll of) film
软气 ruǎnqì 〈方言〉❶ weak; mild; soft:你是硬骨头出了名,怎么说出这种～话? How come that you, a well-known hard nosed fellow, made such a wishy-washy statement? ❷ petty annoyances:即使冲撞了她,我也不受这口～! I would not submit to these petty annoyances even if I offended her.
软弱 ruǎnruò weak; feeble; flabby:四肢～无力 be weak in one's limbs / 意志～ be weak-willed / 他性格～,遇事往往犹豫不决。He is weak in character and often wavers where he has to make a decision.
软弱可欺 ruǎnruò-kěqī be weak and easily bullied:不要把我们的克制当做～。Don't take our restraint for weakness.
软弱无能 ruǎnruò-wúnéng weak and incompetent; namby-pamby:我们家怎么出了这么个～的东西! How come we have such a gutless good-for-nothing in our family!
软设备 ruǎnshèbèi *see* "软件"
软食 ruǎnshí soft diet; soft food; pap:老人应当多进一点～。Old people should have more of soft food.
软式飞艇 ruǎnshì fēitǐng blimp; non-rigid airship
软式墙网球 ruǎnshìqiáng wǎngqiú squash rackets; squash
软水 ruǎnshuǐ soft water
软酥酥 ruǎnsūsū limp; weak:这老人两条腿～的,走路要靠拐杖。The old man had to walk with a cane as his legs were limp and unsteady.
软塌塌 ruǎntātā ❶ weak; limp; feeble:她～地说:"我错了。""I am wrong," she said weakly. / 他觉得浑身～的打不起精神。He felt weak all over and could not summon up an ounce of energy. / 八月的太阳把什么都晒得～的,连蝈蝈的叫声也不那么清脆了。Everything languished under the scorching August sun, and even the chirping of the long-horned grasshoppers did not sound so clear and crisp. ❷ unhurried and phlegmatic:他总是～、慢悠悠地不火不急。He is always slow and phlegmatic and has little go in him. / 这个人～的没有刚性。He is a sort of milksop and has no grit in his character. *or* He is a weakling with no will-power.
软瘫 ruǎntān be weak and limp; collapse:他浑身～,像醉了似的。He felt weak and limp all over as if (he were) intoxicated. / 不幸的消息传来后,她就～在地上。She fell inert on the ground on hearing the sad news. / 由于心脏病突发,他的腿脚立刻～下来。Owing to a heart attack, his legs suddenly went limp.
软糖 ruǎntáng jelly drops; soft sweets or candy
软梯 ruǎntī rope ladder
软体动物 ruǎntǐ dòngwù mollusk; mollusc:～学 malacology
软铁 ruǎntiě 〈冶金〉soft iron
软通货 ruǎntōnghuò *also* "软币" soft currency
软土 ruǎntǔ mollisoil
软卧 ruǎnwò 〈交通〉soft berth on a sleeper; soft sleeper:～车厢 soft sleeper carriage / 乘～ travel on a soft sleeper
软武器 ruǎnwǔqì 〈军事〉soft weapon; electronic jamming device; jammer
软席 ruǎnxí 〈交通〉soft or cushioned berth; soft or cushioned seat:～车厢 soft-berth (*or* -seat) carriage
软席卧铺 ruǎnxí wòpù soft-berth carriage; sleeping car with soft berths
软线 ruǎnxiàn 〈电工〉flexible cord
软性 ruǎnxìng softness; pliability; flexibility
软性电影 ruǎnxìng diànyǐng "soft" film
软性读物 ruǎnxìng dúwù light reading
软性推销 ruǎnxìng tuīxiāo soft sell

软性隐形眼镜 ruǎnxìng yǐnxíng yǎnjìng soft (contact) lens
软性印刷电路 ruǎnxìng yìnshuā diànlù 〈电子〉flexible printer circuit
软洋洋 ruǎnyāngyāng 〈方言〉weak; feeble; limp: 他的两只脚～的好像踏在棉花上一样。He feels weak and limp in both legs as if he were stepping on cotton.
软饮料 ruǎnyǐnliào soft drinks
软硬不吃 ruǎn-yìng bùchī yield to neither persuasion nor coercion; be immune to both soft and hard tactics
软硬兼施 ruǎn-yìng jiānshī employ both soft and hard tactics; use a combination of the carrot and the stick: ～，逼得他只好就范。He was forced to surrender by means of cajolery and coercion.
软语 ruǎnyǔ soft words: 温情～ tender and soft words / 吴侬～ pleasantly soft Suzhou dialect; dialects of southern Jiangsu or northern Zhejiang
软玉 ruǎnyù 〈矿业〉nephrite
软玉温香 ruǎnyù-wēnxiāng *also* "软香温玉" soft jade and warm fragrance — feminine charm
软枣 ruǎnzǎo black date
软炸 ruǎnzhá soft-fry: ～虾仁儿 soft-fried shelled shrimp / ～里脊 soft-fried tenderloin
软脂 ruǎnzhī 〈化工〉palmitin
软脂酸 ruǎnzhīsuān 〈化工〉palmitic acid; palmic acid
软指标 ruǎnzhǐbiāo soft target
软着陆 ruǎnzhuólù soft landing: ～装置 soft-lander / 中国成功地实现了经济～。China succeeded in orchestrating a "soft landing" in her economy.
软组织 ruǎnzǔzhī 〈生理〉soft tissue (such as muscles, ligaments, etc.)

ruí

蕤 ruí *see* "葳蕤" wēiruí

ruǐ

蕊(蘂、橤) ruǐ stamen; pistil: 雄～ stamen / 雌～ pistil
橤(繠、蘂) ruǐ 〈书面〉hang low; droop
桵 ruǐ a kind of plant mentioned in ancient books

ruì

锐 ruì ❶ sharp; keen; pungent; acute: 尖～的批评 sharp criticism / 敏～ insightful / 剑锋甚～。The sword has a very keen edge. ❷ vim; vigour; fighting spirit: 养精蓄～，以待来敌 conserve energy and build up strength in anticipation of an enemy invasion ❸ rapid; sharp; drastic: ～增 sharp increase / 久闻其人之名，～欲见之。Because of his reputation, I have long cherished the wish to pay him a visit.
锐不可当 ruìbùkědāng be irresistible: 其锋～ with overwhelming force / 我军～，无坚不摧。Our army is an irresistible force and carries everything before it.
锐度 ruìdù acutance (a measure of the sharpness of the edges of an image)
锐减 ruìjiǎn cut or drop sharply; reduce drastically: 产量～。The output dropped sharply. / 出口～。Exports plummeted.
锐角 ruìjiǎo 〈数学〉acute angle; arris: ～三角形 acute triangle
锐利 ruìlì ❶ (of a knife, dagger, etc.) sharp: ～钢刀 sharp knife; keen-edged sword / ～的爪牙 sharp teeth and claws ❷ (of eyes, remarks, pen, etc.) incisive; keen: ～的观察 keen observation / 我感受到了他论点的～锋芒。I keenly felt the force of his argument.
锐敏 ruìmǐn sensitive; keen: 眼光～ keen eyesight / 听觉～ have a sharp ear / ～的洞察力 penetrating insight / ～地感觉出对方的态度有变 keenly sense the change in the attitude of the other party
锐气 ruìqì dash; drive; push: 他有一股咄咄逼人的～。He has a sort of drive which is peculiarly aggressive. / 不能挫伤群众的～。We shouldn't do anything to lower public morale (*or* dampen people's enthusiasm).
锐器 ruìqì sharp instrument or tool
锐眼 ruìyǎn sharp eyes; 〈比喻〉keen eye: ～识英雄 have a keen eye for discovering able people
锐意 ruìyì strong determination: ～改革 be determined to carry out a reform

瑞 ruì ❶ auspicious; lucky: 祥～之年 auspicious year ❷ (Ruì) a surname
瑞典 Ruìdiǎn Sweden: ～人 Swede; the Swedish / ～语 Swedish (language)
瑞金 Ruìjīn Ruijin, town in Jiangxi Province and capital of the central revolutionary base area in the 1930's
瑞利 Ruìlì Rayleigh (English physicist and mathmatician, born John William Strutt, 1842-1919): ～定律 Rayleigh's law / ～数 Rayleigh number / ～天平 Rayleigh balance
瑞脑 ruìnǎo *also* "冰片" bīngpiàn; "龙脑" lóngnǎo; "莰醇" cǎnchún 〈化学〉borneol; Borneo camphor
瑞气 ruìqì good omen; happy lot; auspicious atmosphere: 霞光～ golden rays and auspicious atmosphere
瑞签 ruìqiān slip of red paper with propitious words (to be put up on the Spring Festival): 新春贴～。We put up slips of red paper with propitious words during the Spring Festival.
瑞士 Ruìshì Switzerland: ～人 Swiss / ～表 Swiss watch
瑞士航空公司 Ruìshì Hángkōng Gōngsī Swissair
瑞士联合银行 Ruìshì Liánhé Yínháng Union Bank of Switzerland, one of the major commercial banks of Switzerland
瑞士银行公司 Ruìshì Yínháng Gōngsī Swiss Bank Corporation, one of the major commercial banks of Switzerland
瑞香 ruìxiāng 〈植物〉winter daphne (*Daphne odora*)
瑞雪 ruìxuě timely snow; auspicious snow; snow: 华北大部地区普降～。There was an extensive fall of snow over most of North China. / 这场～对小麦返青十分有利。This timely snow will be good for the winter wheat to turn green.
瑞雪兆丰年 ruìxuě zhào fēngnián auspicious snow foretells a bumper harvest; snow is the harbinger of an abundant year
瑞芝 ruìzhī glossy ganoderma (*Ganoderma lucidum*) (considered an auspicious omen by the ancients)

睿(叡) ruì 〈书面〉be farsighted
睿哲 ruìzhé 〈书面〉wise and farsighted
睿智 ruìzhì wise and farsighted: ～的眼光 farsighted view / 聪明～，人所不及。No ordinary people can compare with him in intelligence and insight.

汭 ruì 〈书面〉❶ river bend ❷ place where two rivers converge
芮 Ruì a surname
枘 ruì 〈书面〉tenon: 方～圆凿 make a mortise with a round chisel — a square peg in a round hole; incompatible; out of tune; out of one's element
枘凿 ruìzáo *also* "凿枘"〈书面〉❶ mortise and tenon — compatible ❷ (short for 方枘圆凿) at odds
蚋(蜹) ruì buffalo gnat; blackfly

rún

瞤 rún 〈书面〉❶ (of eyelids) twitch: 不知为什么他眼皮有点～。I don't know why his eyelids are twitching. ❷ (of muscles) twitch: 肌肉～酸 pain in the muscle

rùn

闰 rùn 〈天文〉intercalary
闰年 rùnnián leap year; intercalary year

闰日 rùnrì leap day; intercalary day
闰月 rùnyuè leap month; intercalary month

润 rùn ❶ smooth and glossy; moist; sleek: 湿～ moist /嗓音圆～ sweet mellow voice /墨色很～ dark full-bodied ink /珠圆玉～ round as a pearl and sleek as jade — (of singing) sweet and mellow; (of writing) smooth and graceful /雨水丰而草木～。Adequate rainfall is the prerequisite of lush vegetation. ❷ moisten; lubricate: ～嗓子 moisten one's throat /细雨～物。Fine rain moistens everything. ❸ embellish; beautify; touch up: *see* "～色"; "～饰" ❹ profit; remuneration: 利～ profit /每月除工资外，他还可弄些外～。In addition to the monthly pay, he earns extra money on the side. /有人以重～向他索画，他拒绝了。Some people would pay handsomely for his painting, but he turned down their offers.

润笔 rùnbǐ ❶ (of a writing brush) dip in ink ❷ remuneration for a writer, painter or calligraphic artist: ～颇丰。The remuneration offered (for a piece of painting or calligraphy) is pretty handsome.
润肠 rùncháng 〈中医〉 lubricate the intestines — ease constipation
润肺 rùnfèi 〈中医〉 moisten the lungs — facilitate expectoration
润肤剂 rùnfūjì emollient
润肤露 rùnfūlù skin lotion; skin moisturizer
润格 rùngé *also* "润例" 〈旧语〉 scale of fees charged by painters and calligraphers
润滑 rùnhuá lubricate: ～系统 lubricating system /飞溅～法 splash lubrication
润滑剂 rùnhuájì lubricant
润滑油 rùnhuáyóu lubricating or lubrication oil
润滑脂 rùnhuázhī lubricating grease
润例 rùnlì *see* "润格"
润色 rùnsè polish up; touch up: 请把这篇文章～一下。Please have this article touched up. /文章写好后要小心着意～一番。Go over the essay carefully when it is finished. /文章付印前，他作了最后的～。He put the final touches to his essay before he sent it to the press.
润湿 rùnshī ❶ moist; damp; wet: ～的泥土 moist soil ❷ moisten; dampen; wet: 露水～了他的衣服。His clothes were wet with dew.
润饰 rùnshì polish; touch up: 他能拔笔立就，不加～。He could readily finish a piece of writing without changing a word. /书桌～一新。The desk was newly polished and had a beautiful sheen.
润养 rùnyǎng 〈书面〉 nourish; nurture: ～万物 nourish all things on earth
润燥 rùnzào 〈中医〉 moisten the respiratory tract, skin, etc.
润泽 rùnzé ❶ moist; shiny: 雨过天晴，草坪显得青翠～。After the rain, the lawn looked fresh and green under the sun. /天刚黎明，花园里的草木格外～。At dawn, the trees and grass in the garden were dewy and particularly lush. ❷ moisten; lubricate: 细雨～着林间小径。The path in the wood became moist in the fine drizzle.
润资 rùnzī *see* "润笔❷"

ruó

挼 ruó 〈书面〉 finger; knead
see also ruá

挼搓 ruócuo knead; finger; rub: 你这样会把花～坏的。You'll make the flowers wilt if you keep fingering them. /这种料子经不住～。This material won't stand much rubbing.

ruò

爇(焫) ruò 〈书面〉 light (up); burn: ～烛 light a candle

若[1] ruò like; seem; as if: 坚～磐石 firm as rock; rock firm /旁～无人 act as if there was nobody around; have no regard for others; be self-assured; be supercilious /欣喜～狂 be as happy as a lark; go into raptures /～有所思 look as if deep in thought /大智～愚。A person of great wisdom appears slow-witted.

若[2] ruò if: 你～离开，请电话告我。If you leave here, please let me know by telephone. *or* Call me before you leave. /～尽力为之，必当成功。Try your utmost, and you will surely succeed.

若[3] ruò 〈书面〉 you: ～辈 you people
see also rě

若虫 ruòchóng 〈动物〉 nymph
若非 ruòfēi if not; were it not for; but for: ～你的帮助，我是无法完成任务的。I could not have accomplished the task but for your help. /～你提醒，我很可能把它忘了。If you had not reminded me, I might have forgotten about it.
若夫 ruòfū 〈书面〉〈助词〉 (used at the beginning of a sentence to mark a start or to show a contrast) with regard to; as for: 待文王而后兴者，凡民也。～豪杰之士，虽无文王犹兴。Mediocrities were those who rose only after King Wen attained power. As for real talents, they came to the fore even without King Wen.
若干 ruògān ❶ some; certain: 北方～地区遭受干旱。Certain areas in the north are suffering from drought. /我记得～年前他讲过这话。I remember he made such comments years ago. ❷ how many; how much: 存款尚余～? How much of our savings is left?
若果 ruòguǒ if; in case: ～大家都动脑筋的话，一定可以想出好办法。If we pool our ideas (*or* If everybody uses his brains), we can find a way out.
若何 ruòhé what; how: 结果～，不得而知。We are not sure what the outcome will be. *or* The result is yet unknown. /你意～? What do you think?
若即若离 ruòjí-ruòlí be neither close nor distant; keep sb. at arm's length: 他们俩的关系总是～的。Their relationship is always neither warm nor cold. /我不知道他为什么总跟我～的。I don't know why he's always been trying to keep me at arm's length.
若明若暗 ruòmíng-ruò'àn have an indistinct picture of; have a hazy notion about; (of an attitude) be non-committal: 局势至今还是～。The situation still remains murky.
若其 ruòqí 〈书面〉 if; in case
若是 ruòshì if: 他～不赞成，只能撤回动议。If he doesn't agree, I will have to withdraw my motion. /我～你，就接受这个邀请。If I were you, I would accept the offer.
若无其事 ruòwúqíshì as if nothing had happened; calmly; casually: 自己把事情搞糟了，还装出～的样子。He had made a mess of the job, yet he looked as if nothing had happened. /他谈到那次车祸，挺～的。He talked about the car accident with unconcern (*or* indifference). /她捅了娄子，还装作～。Although she had caused all the trouble, she tried to brazen it out.
若要人不知，除非己莫为 ruò yào rén bù zhī, chúfēi jǐ mò wéi if you don't want people to know sth., don't do it; the only way to prevent other people from knowing sth. is to refrain from doing it; murder will out
若隐若现 ruòyǐn-ruòxiàn partly hidden and partly visible; discernible at one moment and gone the next: 远望白云缭绕，峰峦～。Viewed from a distance, the peaks are faintly discernible behind the misty clouds. /晨雾中一只小船在天际～。A small boat loomed faintly on the foggy horizon.
若有所失 ruòyǒusuǒshī feel as if sth. were missing — be distracted; be listless: 他看来～，好像预感到要发生什么事似的。He looked distracted as if having a premonition that something was going to happen.
若有所思 ruòyǒusuǒsī look as if deep in thought; look pensive; be lost in thought: 她坐在窗边，～。I found her sitting by the window, absorbed in thought.

箬(篛) ruò ❶〈植物〉 indocalamus ❷ indocalamus leaf

箬笠 ruòlì broad-brimmed hat made of bamboo splints and leaves; bamboo hat
箬帽 ruòmào broad-brimmed bamboo hat: 一个～蓑衣的渔民在细雨中垂钓。A fisherman in a bamboo hat and palmleaf raincoat is angling in the drizzle.
箬竹 ruòzhú 〈植物〉 indocalamus

偌 ruò (often used in the early vernacular) such; so: 哪里来的～多银子? How is it that there is so much silver (*or* so much money)?

偌大 ruòdà (often used in the early vernacular) of such a big size; so big: ～一个国家 such a large country /～的年纪 so old; so advanced in age (*or* years)

弱 ruò ❶ weak; frail; delicate：他自幼体～。He has been in delicate health since childhood. /我们认为国不分大小强～，应该一律平等。In our opinion, countries, big or small, strong or weak, should all be equal. ❷ young; little：～孙 little grandson /要照顾老～病残。We must take good care of the old, the young, the sick and the handicapped. ❸ inferior; not as good as：他的手艺可不比别人～。He is inferior to nobody in craftsmanship. /你的办事才能略～于他。Your practical ability is not as good as his. ❹〈书面〉die：他的好友又～一个。Another of his good friends has died. ❺ (coming after a number with a fraction) a little less than：八分之一～ a little less than one eighth

弱不禁风 ruòbùjīnfēng too weak to stand a gust of wind; extremely delicate; fragile; frail：这个女孩真是～。This girl is an extremely delicate creature. *or* This girl has a fragile constitution. /她体虚力乏，～。She was so frail that a gust of wind might blow her away, so to speak.

弱不胜衣 ruòbùshèngyī too frail to bear the weight of one's clothes：她病好后～。She is so fragile after her illness that she looks as if she could not carry the weight of her dress.

弱磁场 ruòcíchǎng low-intensity magnetic field

弱点 ruòdiǎn weak point; weakness; failing：临场紧张是他致命的～。His fatal weakness is his inability to overcome nervous tension at the examinations.

弱电 ruòdiàn 〈电工〉weak current; light current：～电缆 weak-current cable /～工程 light-current engineering

弱干扰 ruògānrǎo 〈无线电〉weak jamming

弱冠 ruòguàn initial period of manhood around 20 years old (In ancient times when a man reached 20, he had to perform a ceremony celebrating his manhood by wearing a hat. Later this term was loosely applied to a young man around 20.)：年逋～ just around 20 years old

弱碱 ruòjiǎn 〈化学〉weak base

弱脉 ruòmài 〈中医〉weak pulse

弱拍 ruòpāi 〈音乐〉weak beat; unaccented beat

弱肉强食 ruòròu-qiángshí law of the jungle：～的社会 society characterized by the prevalence of the law of the jungle /那是一个～的黑暗时代。It was a dark period in which the weak were the prey of the strong.

弱视 ruòshì 〈医学〉amblyopia; weak sight：～镜 amblyscope

弱手 ruòshǒu incompetent person

弱酸 ruòsuān 〈化学〉weak acid

弱息 ruòxī 〈书面〉〈谦词〉my child

弱项 ruòxiàng weak event; weak area

弱小 ruòxiǎo small and weak：～的国家 small and weak countries /大国可以任意欺凌～民族的日子已一去不复返了。Gone are the days when big powers could ride roughshod over small and weak nations.

弱信号 ruòxìnhào 〈无线电〉weak signal

弱音器 ruòyīnqì 〈乐器〉mute; sordine

弱智 ruòzhì weak-minded; mentally deficient; retarded：～儿童 (mentally) retarded children

弱智教育 ruòzhì jiàoyù education for the mentally retarded

弱智者 ruòzhìzhě retardate; retardee

箬 ruò 〈古语〉〈植物〉young rush (*Typha japonica*)

S

sā

挲(抄) sā see "摩挲" māsa
see also shā; suō

撒 sā ❶ cast; loosen; let go; let out: ～网 cast one's net /～传单 hand out leaflets /～开缰绳 loosen (or let go) one's rein /我的老板对我很放手,我在他手下可以～开干。My boss allows a lot of freedom, I can make full use of it to get things done. ❷〈贬义〉throw off all restraint; let oneself go; run wild: 他又在家里～酒疯了。He was drunk and disorderly again at home.
see also sǎ

撒巴掌 sā bāzhang 〈方言〉let go; let go one's hold: 不能～不管 can't wash one's hands of the business

撒村 sācūn 〈方言〉use coarse language: ～骂人 shout abuse; swear (at sb.)

撒旦 Sādàn 〈宗教〉Satan; the Devil

撒刁 sādiāo use cunning and shameless tricks; play tricks: 惯于～ often resort to cunning tricks

撒对儿 sāduìr 〈方言〉(often used in the early vernacular) challenge one's opponent by striking a pose

撒疯 sāfēng also "撒风" ❶ act in a silly, joking or drunken manner; run wild: 你撒什么疯呀? Why on earth are you acting like a wilful child? ❷ vent one's spite: 不管你受别人多少气,不该拿我～。Whatever wrong you have suffered, you should not vent your anger (or take it out) on me.

撒哈拉沙漠 Sāhālā Shāmò Sahara Desert, world's largest desert in North Africa

撒豪 sāháo 〈方言〉commit all kinds of despotic outrages: ～称霸 ride roughshod over

撒欢儿 sāhuānr 〈方言〉gambol; frisk; frolic: 这条小狗一看见主人就～。The little dog would frisk (or gambol) at the sight of its master. /孩子们还在院子里～。Some children are still frolicking in the yard. /一群狗撒着欢儿乱跳,莫明其妙地汪汪乱叫。A pack of dogs ran about barking, yapping, and jumping with glee.

撒谎 sāhuǎng 〈口语〉tell a lie; lie: 他惯于～ 。He is always telling lies. or He's given to lying.

撒娇 sājiāo behave like a spoiled child; play the pampered child: 专会使性～ be liable to fits of temper and play the spoiled child /她在奶奶面前一个劲儿～。She acted like a pampered child in the presence of her grandmother.

撒娇撒痴 sājiāo-sāchī pout and flounce: 她不肯走,～,最后还是他屈服。She refused to leave, pouting and flouncing until he had to give in.

撒脚 sājiǎo start (running); take to one's heels

撒酒疯 sā jiǔfēng be roaring drunk; be drunk and act foolishly; be drunk and disorderly: 他端起杯子就～。He will get a bit merry as soon as his lips touch wine.

撒科打诨 sākē-dǎhùn also "插科打诨" chākē-dǎhùn make gags

撒诳 sākuáng lie; tell a lie: 不许撒一个字的诳! Don't you dare tell a lie.

撒拉族 Sālāzú Salar nationality, living in Qinghai and Gansu provinces

撒赖 sālài kick up a row; make a scene; act wildly: ～不认账 shamelessly disavow all responsibility for his actions

撒尿 sāniào 〈口语〉piss; pee; pass water; urinate

撒泼 sāpō make a scene and refuse to be reconciled: 他～打滚地哭闹起来。He made a terrible scene, rolling in the dust, screaming and crying.

撒气 sāqì ❶ (of a ball, tyre, etc.) leak; go soft; get flat; deflate: 轮胎～了。The tyre is deflated. or It is a flat tyre. /车胎又在～。The tyre is leaking again. ❷ vent one's anger or temper: 他在家里拿老婆孩子～。At home he vented his anger on his wife and children. /他觉得到底不好拿朋友～。He found it unwise after all to take it out on his friends.

撒切尔 Sāqiè'ěr Margaret Hilda Thatcher (1925-), first woman prime minister of the United Kingdom from 1979 to 1990

撒扇 sāshàn 〈书面〉folding fan

撒手 sāshǒu let go one's hold; let go of sth.: 你～吧,我搬得了。Let it go, I can manage. /这件事你不能～不管。You should not shy away from the matter like that.

撒手归西 sāshǒu-guīxī go west; go to heaven; kick the bucket; go the way of all flesh

撒手锏 sāshǒujiǎn sudden thrust with the mace to subdue the enemy; 〈比喻〉trump card: 不知他下一步会使出什么～来。No one knows what cards he has up his sleeve.

撒手人世 sāshǒu-rénshì depart this life; pass away

撒腿 sātuǐ take to one's heels; scamper off: ～往家里跑 make straight for home /那匹受惊的马～狂奔起来。The spooked horse started prancing and capering.

撒网 sāwǎng ❶ spread a net; cast a net: ～捕鱼 net fish /我们的部队刚一撒开网,敌人就进了包围圈。Our troops had no sooner laid out a net than the enemy blundered into the encirclement. ❷〈旧语〉give a party on the occasion of a wedding, funeral, birthday, etc., in the hope of collecting presents

撒窝 sāwō open the coop to let out the rooster or hen

撒丫子 sā yāzi also "撒鸭子"〈方言〉take to one's heels; (with a touch of humour) show a clean pair of heels: 你们来到之前,他早就～了。He had made off long before you arrived.

撒野 sāyě act rowdily; behave rudely: 几个小青年在广场上～乱嚷嚷。There are several teenagers scampering and yelling like mad on the square. /你再～,我们就不客气了。Behave yourself or we will get tough with you.

撒呓挣 sā yìzheng 〈口语〉❶ talk in one's sleep: 这孩子白天玩疯了,夜里又咬牙又～。The child frolicked during the day and ground his teeth and raved in his sleep at night. ❷ crazy talk or behaviour: 你是不是～啦,黑灯瞎火的做哪门子饭呀? You must be crazy cooking in complete darkness.

仨 sā 〈口语〉three: ～人 three people /咱们哥儿～ we three pals

sǎ

洒(灑) sǎ ❶ sprinkle; spray: ～香水 spray perfume /往花盆上～点水 sprinkle some water on the potted plant ❷ spill; shed: ～泪而别 part in tears /阳光～遍大地。The land is bathed in sunshine. ❸ (Sǎ) a surname

洒狗血 sǎ gǒuxiě 〈戏曲〉(of actors or actresses) show off one's acrobatic and other skills that have nothing to do with the story or plot of a play

洒家 sǎjiā (used by men in the early vernacular) I; me; myself

洒泪 sǎlèi shed tears: ～告别 part in tears; take a tearful leave /他

~挥毫,写就了这首悲壮的诗。Eyes brimming with tears, he wielded the writing brush and wrote this stirring poem.

洒利　sǎli　〈方言〉free and dexterous

洒落　sǎluò　❶ scatter; strew; trickle down: 花瓣~在地上。The fallen petals are scattered all over the ground. *or* The ground is strewn with petals. /线断了,珠子~在地上。The string snapped and the pearls all fell on the floor. ❷ *see* "洒脱"

洒然　sǎrán　〈书面〉❶ astonished; alarmed ❷ carefree: ~自笑 genial smile

洒洒　sǎsǎ　(of writing) prolific: 洋洋~ prolific; voluminous /这篇文章~万言。The writing runs to an impressive length of ten thousand words.

洒扫　sǎsǎo　sprinkle water (to lay the dust) and sweep the dirt floor; sweep: ~庭除 sweep the courtyard

洒水车　sǎshuǐchē　watering car; sprinkler; spraying car (for cleaning roadways)

洒脱　sǎtuo　free and easy; uninhibited; unrestrained; unaffected: 举止~ have a free and easy manner; look bright and breezy /胸中~ be uninhibited /~的画风 natural and easy style of painting /他的字雄浑~。His style of calligraphy is vigorous and uninhibited. /我觉得他很~。I found his manner very open and free.

洒鞋　sǎxié　❶ slippers ❷ special kind of workmen's cloth shoes with leather toecap and counter or leatherseamed top

靸

sǎ　〈方言〉wear cloth shoes with the backs turned in; shuffle about with the counters of one's shoes trodden down; slipon slippers

靸鞋　sǎxié　❶ slippers ❷ a kind of cloth shoes

撒

sǎ　❶ scatter; sprinkle; spread; broadcast: ~种 sow seeds /~一层糖 spread a layer of sugar ❷ spill; drop: 豆~了一地。The beans are scattered all over the ground. ❸ (Sǎ) a surname

see also sā

撒播　sǎbō　broadcast sowing

撒播机　sǎbōjī　〈农业〉broadcast seeder; broadcaster; planter; grain drill

撒肥机　sǎféijī　〈农业〉fertilizer spreader; manure distributor

撒粉　sǎfěn　〈农业〉dusting

撒粉器　sǎfěnqì　duster

撒镘　sǎmàn　*also* "撒漫"〈旧语〉❶ generous; liberal ❷ (often used in the early vernacular) spend freely; squander

撒眸　sǎmou　〈方言〉look around: 一个老汉站在道旁四下里~着,好像在等人。By the side of the road stood an old man looking all around as if waiting for somebody.

撒散　sǎsan　❶ distribute; spread; give out: ~传单 give out pamphlets ❷ consume; expend: 这件事还得~点钱才能了结。There will also be various expenses to be paid before this matter can be finally settled.

撒施　sǎshī　〈农业〉spread fertilizer over the fields; broadcast (fertilizer)

撒岩粉机　sǎyánfěnjī　〈矿业〉rock duster; rock dust distributor

撒帐　sǎzhàng　〈旧语〉(of women) spread coins, nuts and fruits after the wedding ceremonies were over and the bride and groom seated on the bed

sà

飒

sà　❶ sough; rustle: 寒风~起。The bitter wind was soughing. ❷ wither; wilt: 庭树日衰~。The trees in the yard are withering.

飒然　sàrán　〈书面〉soughing: 风~而起。The wind rose sighing.

飒飒　sàsà　sough; rustle: 风~,木萧萧。The wind was rustling in the trees. /房上雨声~。The rain was pattering against the roof. /在秋风~的傍晚,他独自漫步。He took a leisurely stroll alone in the windy autumn evening.

飒爽　sàshuǎng　〈书面〉of martial bearing; valiant: ~英姿五尺枪。How bright and brave they look, shouldering five-foot rifles.

萨(薩)

Sà　a surname

萨尔瓦多　Sà'ěrwǎduō　El Salvador: ~人 Salvadoran

萨哈林岛　Sàhālíndǎo　*also* "库页岛" Kùyèdǎo　Sakhalin Island, an island in the Sea of Okhotsk, separated by the Tatar Strait from the coast of Russia

萨迦寺　Sàjiāsì　Sagya monastery (in Tibet)

萨克管　sàkèguǎn　〈乐器〉saxophone

萨克号　sàkèhào　〈乐器〉saxhorn

萨拉热窝　Sàlārèwō　Sarajevo, capital of Bosnia-Herzegovena

萨满教　sàmǎnjiào　shamanism: ~巫医 shaman

萨摩亚　Sàmóyà　Samoa: ~人 Samoan /~语 Samoan (language)

萨那　Sànà　Sana'a, capital of Yemen

萨其马　sàqímǎ　a kind of candied fritter

卅

sà　thirty: 五~运动 May 30th Movement (1925)

挲(挱)

sà　〈书面〉attack from the side; make a flank thrust

see also shā

脎

sà　〈化学〉osazone

sāi

塞

sāi　❶ stop; fill in; squeeze in; stuff up: 他把零散的衣物~进箱子里。He packed his clothes and odds and ends into the trunk. /手提包~得满满的。The bag is bulging with things. ❷ stopper: 暖瓶~ thermos-bottle stopper

see also sài; sè

塞包袱　sāi bāofu　〈方言〉bribe; offer a bribe

塞车　sāichē　traffic jam: 这条马路早晚高峰时间~厉害。There is a terrible jam in rush hours along this road.

塞尺　sāichǐ　*also* "厚薄规" hòubóguī　feeler (gauge)

塞规　sāiguī　〈机械〉plug gauge

塞焊　sāihàn　〈冶金〉plug welding

塞环　sāihuán　ring of plug

塞套　sāitào　plug sleeve

塞条　sāitiáo　〈医学〉tent

塞牙　sāiyá　(of food) get stuck between the teeth

塞子　sāizi　stopper; cork; plug; spigot: 软木~ cork

噻

sāi

噻草隆　sāicǎolóng　〈化学〉benzthiazuron; gatinon

噻吩　sāifēn　〈化学〉thiophene

噻唑　sāizuò　〈化学〉thiazole

思

sāi　*see* "于思" yúsāi

see also sī

揌(擡)

sāi　*see* "塞❶" sāi

腮(顋)

sāi　cheek

腮巴　sāibā　*also* "腮巴子"〈方言〉cheek

腮帮子　sāibāngzi　〈口语〉cheek

腮红　sāihóng　rouge; blush

腮颊　sāijiá　cheek

腮托　sāituō　〈乐器〉chin rest (of a violin or viola)

腮腺　sāixiàn　*also* "耳下腺" ěrxiàxiàn　〈生理〉parotid gland: ~切除术〈医学〉parotidectomy

腮腺炎　sāixiànyán　〈医学〉parotitis: 流行性~ epidemic parotitis; mumps /~疫苗 mumps vaccine

腮腺炎性睾丸炎　sāixiànyánxìng gāowányán　〈医学〉mumps orchitis; orchitis parotidea

腮腺硬癌　sāixiàn yìng'ái　parotidoscirrhus

鳃

sāi　gill; branchia

鳃瓣　sāibàn　gill; lamella

鳃盖　sāigài　gill cover

sài

塞

sài　stronghold of strategic importance: 边~ frontier

fortress /守边备～ perform garrison duties on the frontier; guard a frontier fortress; defend the frontier
see also sāi; sè
塞北 Sàiběi *see*"塞外"
塞尔维亚 Sài'ěrwéiyà Serbia:～人 Serb /～克罗地亚语 Serbo-Croatian (language)
塞拉利昂 Sàilālì'áng Sierra Leone:～人 Sierra Leonian
塞纳河 Sàinàhé Seine, a river in northern France from Burgundy to the English Channel
塞内加尔 Sàinèijiā'ěr Senegal:～人 Senegalese /～河 the Senegal
塞浦路斯 Sàipǔlùsī Cyprus:～人 Cypriot
塞舌尔 Sàishé'ěr Seychelles:～人 Seychellois
塞外 Sàiwài beyond the Great Wall:～风光 scenery north of the Great Wall /～江南 lush southern scenery found beyond the Great Wall
塞翁失马,安知非福 sàiwēng shī mǎ, ān zhī fēi fú when the old man on the frontier lost his mare, who could have guessed it was a blessing in disguise — misfortune may be an actual blessing

赛[1] sài ❶ match; game; tournament; competition:篮球～ basketball match (game) /田径～ track and field events /安慰～ consolation event /四分之一决～ quarter-finals /半决～ semi-finals /决～ finals /表演～ exhibition match /对抗～ duel meet /复～ intermediary heat /锦标～ championship contest /乒乓锦标～ ping-pong championships /联～ league /淘汰～ elimination /团体～ team competition /选拔～ tryouts /循环～ round match /小组循环～ group round robin /邀请～ invitation tournament; invitational tournament /预～ preliminary trials /元老～ veterans' event ❷ compete:两个班决定要～一～。The two classes decided to have a competition. /我们要～水平,～风格。We should give full display of our skills and sportsmanship. ❸ be comparable to; surpass:他虽已渐入中年,可是精力～过许多年轻人。He is middle-aged, and yet he compares favourably with young men in vigour and energy.

赛[2] sài 〈迷信〉old practice of offering a sacrifice to gods; worshiping gods:祭～ offer sacrifices to gods
赛贝尔萃取器 Sàibèi'ěr cuìqǔqì 〈化工〉Scheibel extractor; Scheibel column
赛场 sàichǎng site of contest; competition arena; ring; court; rink; ground:～秩序 order at the competition /整个～沸腾了。The whole arena is seething with excitement. /几个排坛老将在～表现不凡。These veteran volleyball players did a superb job in the match.
赛车 sàichē 〈体育〉❶ cycle racing; motorcycle race; automobile race ❷ race car; racing bicycle
赛程 sàichéng 〈体育〉❶ (of racing in competitions) distance:这次自由泳～是二百米。The distance for free style is 200 metres. /获得决赛资格的二十七羽信鸽将从济南市放飞,～空距约五百公里。The 27 racing pigeons entering the finals will be set free in Jinan to cover an approximate straight distance of 500 kilometres. ❷ agenda for competitions:校运会～已经排定。The agenda of the school's sports meet has been worked out. /奥运会～过半,我国获金牌数暂居第四。The Olympic games halfway through, China ranks temporarily fourth in the gold medals.
赛次 sàicì (of sports) heat:男子一千米争先赛已经进行了三个～。Three heats have been held in the men's 1,000m scratch race.
赛会 sàihuì religious procession, usu. with idols, stilts, floats, etc.
赛加羚羊 sàijiā língyáng 〈动物〉saiga (*Saiga tatarica*)
赛力散 sàilìsǎn 〈农业〉phenylmercuric acetate (PMA)
赛璐玢 sàilùfēn cellophane
赛璐纶 sàilùlún cellulon
赛璐珞 sàilùluò celluloid
赛纶 sàilún 〈化工〉saran
赛马 sàimǎ horse racing:德比～日 (UK) Derby Day
赛马总会 sàimǎ zǒnghuì jockey club
赛跑 sàipǎo race:长距离～ long-distance race /一百米～ 100-metre dash /越野～ cross-country race /环城～ round-the-city race
赛区 sàiqū (of sports and other competitions) venue:西部～ (US) west conference (NBA) /北京～ Beijing venue /这次足球邀请赛共有三个～。The football invitational tournament is to be held in 3 venues.
赛社 sàishè 〈旧语〉village festival offering thanks to the gods, esp. after harvest
赛事 sàishì sports competition; match; game:～繁忙 heavily scheduled for competitions /国内外～ tournaments (*or* matches) both at home and abroad; national and international competitions /第一天～中最富有戏剧性的是两位种子选手的一场比赛。The most dramatic game played on the first day of the competition was that between two seeded players.
赛艇 sàitǐng 〈体育〉❶ rowing; yachting ❷ racing boat; shell:单人～ single /单人双桨～ scull /双人双桨～ pair-oared shell /四人双桨～ quadruple scull shell
赛愿 sàiyuàn 〈旧语〉give offerings of thanks for a wish granted
赛珍珠 Sàizhēnzhū Pearl Buck (1892-1973), American Nobel-Prize-winning novelist known for her stories about Chinese life

sān

三 sān ❶ three:～天内写了～篇文章 write three articles in as many days ❷ more than two; several; many; numerous:再～ over and over again; repeatedly /几次～番 time and again; again and again
三八妇女节 Sān-Bā Fùnǚjié International Working Women's Day (March 8)
三八红旗手 sān-bā hóngqíshǒu woman pace-setter
三八式步枪 sānbāshì bùqiāng *also*"三八大盖"38-model rifle (standard Japanese weapon of infantry, used before and during World War II)
三八式干部 sānbāshì gànbù veteran who joined the revolution in 1938; thirty-eighter
三八线 sānbāxiàn 38th parallel (38° north latitude on the Korean Peninsula, the military demarcation line between north and south Korea)
三百六十行 sānbǎi liùshí háng all trades and professions; all walks of life:～,行行出状元。Every profession has its top (*or* number one) expert.
三拜九叩 sānbài-jiǔkòu threefold genuflection with the forehead touching the ground nine times
三般两样 sānbān-liǎngyàng treat people differently; favour some but not others
三班六房 sānbān-liùfáng (in the Ming and Qing dynasties) all the staff of the county magistrate's office
三班制 sānbānzhì three-shift working system:我们是～工作。We work in three shifts.
三板 sānbǎn *also*"舢板"shānbǎn sampan
三胞胎 sānbāotāi triplets
三宝 sānbǎo ❶ three valuable things; three treasures ❷〈佛教〉Triratna — the triad of the Buddha, the dharma and the sanyha
三保太监下西洋 Sānbǎo Tàijiàn Xià Xīyáng *also*"郑和下西洋" Zhèng Hé Xià Xīyáng Expeditions to the Western Ocean (1405-1437), altogether 7 voyages led by eunuch and admiral Zheng He (郑和) on the order of the Ming emperor with a fleet of over 60 ships and some 27,000 naval officers, sailors, officials, businessmen, etc., which reached as far as the east coast of Africa
三北 Sānběi *see*"三北地区"
三北地区 Sānběi dìqū three northern areas, referring to China's northeast, central north and northwest
三倍体 sānbèitǐ 〈生物〉triploid
三边形 sānbiānxíng *see*"三角形"
三边主义 sānbiānzhǔyì trilateralism (referring esp. to the idea of strengthening the relations and cooperation between North America, Western Europe, and Japan)
三不 sānbù policy of "three nos": ❶ (as a policy to encourage free exchange and airing of views) don't pick on others for their faults, don't slap political labels on people, and don't use a big stick (不揪辫子,不扣帽子,不打棍子) ❷ no contact, no talks, no compromise (不接触,不谈判,不妥协) policy of KMT authorities in Taiwan towards the Chinese government before the 1980's ❸ not support Taiwan independence, "two Chinas" or "one China, one Taiwan", nor support Taiwan's participation in international organizations of sovereign states (不支持台湾独立,不支持"两个中国"或"一中一台",不支持台湾加入由主权国家组成的国际组织)

三不管 sānbùguǎn come under no one's jurisdiction; be nobody's business:这一带荒无人烟,位跨两省,历来~。This stretch of uninhabited land joining the two provinces has long been under the jurisdiction of neither.

三不知 sānbùzhī know nothing about the beginning, middle and end of a thing — know nothing at all:一问~ unable to give any answer to the question

三不主义 sānbùzhǔyì *see* "三不❶❷"

三部曲 sānbùqǔ trilogy

三彩 sāncǎi three-colour glazed pottery (esp. of the Tang Dynasty):一只唐~骆驼 a tri-colour pottery camel of the Tang Dynasty

三槽出钢 sāncáo chūgāng 〈冶金〉 three-trough steel tapping technique

三叉戟 sānchājǐ three-pronged spear; trident:~飞机 Trident/~导弹核潜艇〈军事〉Trident nuclear missile submarine

三叉神经 sānchā shénjīng 〈生理〉trigeminal nerve:~痛〈医学〉Fothergill's disease; trigeminal neuralgia; trifacial neuralgia; tic douloureux

三岔路口 sānchà lùkǒu *also* "三岔口" fork in the road; junction of roads

三长两短 sāncháng-liǎngduǎn something untoward; unexpected misfortune or calamity; mishap:您家老人若有个~,我们可担待不起。We could not afford to bear the responsibility should anything unexpected happen to your aged parents.

三朝元老 sāncháo yuánlǎo veteran minister serving under three emperors in succession; official who stays in power under different regimes or administrations

三重 sānchóng triple; threefold:以科学家、教育家和慈善家的~身分 in the triple role of a scientist, educator and philanthropist

三重唱 sānchóngchàng 〈音乐〉(vocal) trio

三重奏 sānchóngzòu 〈音乐〉(instrumental) trio

三春 sānchūn 〈书面〉three months of the spring season

三春柳 sānchūnliǔ *Tamarix chinesis*

三次方程 sāncì fāngchéng 〈数学〉cubic equation

三从四德 sāncóng-sìdé women's three obediences (to father before marriage, to husband after marriage and to son after the death of husband) and four virtues (morality, proper speech, modest manner and diligent work) — spiritual fetters imposed on women in feudal society

三醋酯纤维 sāncùzhǐ xiānwéi 〈纺织〉triacetate

三寸不烂之舌 sāncùn bù làn zhī shé glib tongue; silver tongue; eloquence:他凭着~说服了大家。With his glib tongue he succeeded in persuading others to come around.

三寸金莲 sāncùn jīnlián 〈旧语〉three-*cun* lily feet (referring to women's bound feet)

三大差别 sān dà chābié three major distinctions (that exist between town and country, between industry and agriculture and between manual and mental labour):逐步消灭~ gradually eliminate the distinctions between town and country, industry and agriculture, and manual and mental labour

三大殿 Sāndàdiàn Three Great Halls in the Imperial Palace (the Hall of Supreme Harmony 太和殿, the Hall of Middle Harmony 中和殿 and the Hall of Protecting Harmony 保和殿)

三大法宝 sān dà fǎbǎo three magic weapons (of the Chinese Communist Party for defeating the enemy in the new-democratic revolution), namely, the united front, armed struggle and Party building

三大改造 sān dà gǎizào socialist transformation of agriculture, handicraft industry and capitalist industries (1956)

三大革命运动 sān dà gémìng yùndòng three great revolutionary movements (of class struggle, the struggle for production and scientific experiment)

三大纪律,八项注意 sān dà jìlǜ, bā xiàng zhùyì Three Main Rules of Discipline and Eight Points for Attention of the Chinese People's Liberation Army (The Three Main Rules of Discipline are:1. Obey orders in all your actions; 2. Don't take a single needle or piece of thread from the masses; 3. Turn in everything captured. The Eight Points for Attention are:1. Speak politely; 2. Pay fairly for what you buy; 3. Return everything you borrow; 4. Pay for everything you damage; 5. Don't hit or swear at people; 6. Don't damage crops; 7. Don't take liberties with women; 8. Don't ill-treat captives.)

三大民主 sān dà mínzhǔ democracy in the three main fields (i.e., political, economic and military democracy practised at the company level in the People's Liberation Army)

三大政策 sān dà zhèngcè three cardinal policies of allying with Soviet Russia and with the Chinese Communist Party and supporting the workers and peasants, formulated by Dr. Sun Yat-sen in 1923 as a supplement to his Three People's Principles (三民主义)

三大作风 sān dà zuòfēng three important styles of work of the Party (integrating theory with practice, forging close links with the masses and practising self-criticism)

三代 sāndài ❶ (Sāndài) three earliest dynasties, namely Xia (夏, 21st-16th centuries BC), Shang (商, 16th-11th centuries BC) and Zhou (周, 11th century-256 BC) ❷ three generations (grandfather, father and son):~同堂 three generations living under the same roof

三等兵 sānděngbīng (US Army) private E-1; (US Navy) seaman recruit E-1; (US Air Force) airman third class

三等秘书 sānděng mìshū 〈外交〉third secretary

三点会 Sāndiǎnhuì *see* "三合会"

三点式 sāndiǎnshì bikini (bathing suit)

三碘化物 sāndiǎnhuàwù 〈化学〉triiodide

三叠纪 Sāndiéjì 〈地质〉Triassic Period

三叠系 Sāndiéxì Triassic System

三定 sāndìng three fixed quotas (for production, purchase and marketing of grain)

三冬 sāndōng ❶ winter; the third month of winter (i.e. the twelfth month of the lunar year):正当~,天寒地冻。It was in the depths of winter; the weather was bitter cold and the land was frozen hard. ❷〈书面〉three winters; three years

三度存储器 sāndù cúnchǔqì 〈自控〉three-dimensional memory

三度空间 sāndù kōngjiān 〈哲学〉three dimensional space

三段论法 sānduànlùnfǎ 〈逻辑〉syllogism

三对六面 sānduì-liùmiàn presence of the two interested parties and a third party as the witness

三法 sānfǎ 〈中医〉three therapeutic methods of traditional Chinese medicine (diaphoresis, emetic measures, and purgation and diuresis)

三番五次 sānfān-wǔcì *also* "三番两次" again and again; time and again; repeatedly

三藩之乱 Sānfān Zhī Luàn Rebellion of the Three Vassal Princes, 1673-1681, in the early Qing Dynasty, the three being Wu Sangui (吴三桂) in Yunnan, Shang Kexi (尚可喜) in Guangdong, and Geng Jimao (耿继茂) in Fujian who had all been Ming generals

三反 Sānfǎn *see* "三反运动"

三反运动 Sānfǎn Yùndòng Three Anits, the movement against the three evils (corruption, waste, and bureaucratism within the Party, government, army and mass organizations, 1951-1954)

三方 sānfāng tripartite:~协商 tripartite consultation (*or* discussions)

三废 sānfèi three wastes (waste gas, water and industrial residue):回收~ recycling of the three wastes

三分 sānfēn ❶ 30% — somewhat:让他~ make some concession to him; let him have his way/这小姑娘倒有~机灵。This little girl is quite smart. ❷ divided into three parts; split into three

三分话 sānfēnhuà few words:她只说了~。She scarcely said enough. *or* She didn't say clearly what she really thought. /逢人只说~,未可全抛一片心。〈俗语〉Be reserved in speech, and don't wear your heart on your sleeve.

三分球 sānfēnqiú 〈体育〉(of basketball) three pointer; trey

三分区 sānfēnqū 〈体育〉(of basketball) three point range

三分像人,七分像鬼 sānfēn xiàng rén, qīfēn xiàng guǐ look like three parts a human and seven parts a ghost; look more like a ghost than a human (being)

三坟五典 sānfén-wǔdiǎn most ancient Chinese books or records (prior to 8th century BC)

三伏 sānfú ❶ three ten-day periods of the hot season:~天 dog days ❷ last of the three periods of the hot season

三氟化钚 sānfúhuàbù 〈化学〉PuF_3(plutonium trifluoride)

三复 sānfù 〈书面〉over and over again; repeatedly:~斯言。Think over (*or* Ponder on) my advice.

三副 sānfù 〈航海〉third mate; third officer

三纲五常 sāngāng-wǔcháng three cardinal guides (ruler guides

S

subject, father guides son, and husband guides wife) and five constant virtues (benevolence, righteousness, propriety, wisdom and fidelity) in feudal ethical code

三高农业 sāngāo nóngyè high-yield, high-quality and high-efficiency agriculture

三个臭皮匠,合成一个诸葛亮 sān ge chòupíjiang, héchéng yīge Zhūgě Liàng three cobblers with their wits combined equal Zhuge Liang the master-mind — collective wisdom often proves superior; two heads are better than one:"~"— 这是我们做任何工作都需要强调的。It is necessary to stress collective wisdom in any undertaking.

三个世界 sānge shìjiè three worlds (the first world, the second world and the third world):~的理论 theory of the three worlds

三更半夜 sāngēng-bànyè *also* "半夜三更" in the depths of night

三宫六院 sāngōng-liùyuàn three palaces and six chambers — the imperial harem

三姑六婆 sāngū-liùpó three kinds of middle-aged women, i.e., nuns, women Taoists and women fortune-tellers, and six kinds of elderly women, i.e. women traffickers in human beings, matchmakers, witches, procuresses, women quacks and midwives — women who have no honest occupation and create trouble

三顾茅庐 sāngù-máolú make three personal calls at the thatched cottage (referring to Liu Bei's 刘备 three calls at Zhuge Liang's 诸葛亮 cottage to solicit his help) — repeated and sincere invitations

三光 sānguāng 〈书面〉three luminaries — the sun, the moon and the stars

三光政策 sānguāng zhèngcè policy of "burn all, kill all, loot all" adopted by the Japanese invaders in China (1937-1945)

三辊式开坯机 sāngǔnshì kāipījī three-high bloomer; three-high cogging mill

三辊式轧机 sāngǔnshì zhájī 〈冶金〉three-high mill; three-high rolling mill

三国 Sānguó Three Kingdoms (220-280), namely, Wei (魏, 220-265), Shu Han (蜀汉, 221-263) and Wu (吴, 222-280)

S

三国演义 Sānguó Yǎnyì *The Romance of the Three Kingdoms* by Luo Guanzhong (罗贯中) of the early Ming Dynasty

三国志 Sānguózhì *History of the Three Kingdoms* by Chen Shou (陈寿) of the Western Jin Dynasty

三好 sānhǎo three goods — an honorific title given to students who are good in study, work and physical training:~学生 three-good student

三合板 sānhébǎn three-ply board; plywood

三合房 sānhéfáng *also* "三合院儿" courtyard with houses on three sides

三合会 Sānhéhuì *also* "三点会" Triad, a secret society against the Manchu government operating in the Qing Dynasty

三合土 sānhétǔ 〈建筑〉mixture of lime, sand and clay with water; lime-sand-clay mixture

三合星 sānhéxīng 〈天文〉triple star

三合一 sānhéyī three-in-one

三合银行 Sānhé Yínháng Sanwa Bank Ltd., a major Japanese commercial bank established in 1933

三核苷酸 sānhégānsuān 〈生化〉trinucleotide

三花脸 sānhuāliǎn 〈戏曲〉clown (in Chinese opera)

三化螟 sānhuàmíng 〈农业〉yellow rice borer

三皇五帝 Sānhuáng-Wǔdì Three sage "kings" and five virtuous "emperors" — legendary rulers of antiquity (three sage "kings": Fuxi 伏羲, Suiren 燧人 and Shennong 神农 or Tianhuang 天皇, Dihuang 地皇 and Renhuang 人皇; five virtuous "emperors": Huangdi 黄帝, Zhuanxu 颛顼, Di Ku 帝喾, Tang Yao 唐尧 and Yu Shun 虞舜)

三魂七魄 sānhún-qīpò 〈宗教〉three finer spirits and seven baser instincts that motivate the human body; soul:吓得他~飞天外。He was scared out of his wits.

三级风 sānjífēng 〈气象〉force 3 wind; gentle breeze

三极电子管 sānjí diànzǐguǎn radiotron

三极管 sānjíguǎn 〈无线电〉triode:充气~ gas-filled triode /晶体~ transistor

三极管气体激光器 sānjíguǎn qìtǐ jīguāngqì triode laser

三级火箭 sānjí huǒjiàn three-stage rocket

三级跳远 sānjí tiàoyuǎn 〈体育〉hop, step and jump; triple jump

三级医疗保健网 sānjí yīliáo bǎojiànwǎng three-tiered medical care network

三季稻 sānjìdào triple cropping of rice:这里气候潮湿温暖,宜种~。The climate here is humid and warm and good for triple cropping of rice.

三家村 sānjiācūn ❶ small remote hamlet ❷ (of the mind, one's interests, etc.) provincial; parochial:~学究 village pedant; pedantic scholar /这些话,纯属~语,不足为凭。These remarks which sound purely parochial should not be taken as evidence.

三价 sānjià 〈化学〉trivalence; tribasic:~酸 triatomic acid; tribasic acid /~元素 triad

三驾马车 sānjià-mǎchē ❶ three-horse carriage ❷ troika; triumvirate

三尖瓣 sānjiānbàn 〈生理〉tricuspid valve:~狭窄 tricuspid stenosis

三缄其口 sānjiān-qíkǒu with a closely guarded tongue; with sealed lips; overcautious in speech

三键 sānjiàn 〈化学〉triple bond

三讲 sānjiǎng "three emphases", i. e. emphasis on theoretical study, political awareness and moral rectitude (a measure for Party building):~教育 education on the "three emphases"

三焦 sānjiāo 〈中医〉three visceral cavities housing the internal organs; part of the human body from the tongue to the belly; triple burner:~辨证 analysing and differentiating diseases according to the pathological changes in the three visceral cavities

三角 sānjiǎo ❶ triangle:糖~ steamed triangular bun with sugar filling ❷〈数学〉trigonometry

三角板 sānjiǎobǎn *also* "三角尺" set square

三角测量 sānjiǎo cèliáng triangulation; trigonometrical survey:~标记 triangulation mask /~员 triangulator

三角锉 sānjiǎocuò angle file; triangular file

三角带 sānjiǎodài V-belt; vee belt

三角帆 sānjiǎofān 〈航海〉lateen sail

三角方程 sānjiǎo fāngchéng trigonometric equation

三角鲂 sānjiǎofáng 〈动物〉triangular bream

三角枫 sānjiǎofēng 〈植物〉trident maple (*Acer buergerianum*)

三角港 sānjiǎogǎng estuary; firth

三角刮刀 sānjiǎo guādāo three-cornered scraper; triangular scraper

三角关系 sānjiǎo guānxi triangular relationship

三角函数 sānjiǎo hánshù trigonometric function

三角肌 sānjiǎojī 〈生理〉deltoid (muscle)

三角巾 sānjiǎojīn sling

三角裤 sānjiǎokù panties; briefs

三角恋爱 sānjiǎo liàn'ài love triangle

三角贸易 sānjiǎo màoyì triangular trade

三角帽 sānjiǎomào 〈航空〉delta wing

三角皮带 sānjiǎo pídài belt; cone belt; triangle belt; V-belt

三角藻 sānjiǎopiáo 〈植物〉*Azolla imbricata*

三角旗 sānjiǎoqí pennant; pennon

三角区 sānjiǎoqū 〈生理〉trigone:颈动脉~ carotid trigone /膀胱~ trigone of bladder; vesical trigone

三角铁 sānjiǎotiě ❶〈音乐〉triangle ❷ angle iron; L-iron

三角湾 sānjiǎowān estuary

三角形 sānjiǎoxíng *also* "三边形"〈数学〉triangle:不等边~ scalene triangle /等边~ equilateral triangle /等腰~ isosceles triangle /直角~ right-angled triangle

三角学 sānjiǎoxué 〈数学〉trigonometry

三角翼 sānjiǎoyì 〈航空〉delta wing

三角债 sānjiǎozhài inter-corporate triangular debt; debt chain:清理~ break up the "debt chain"

三角洲 sānjiǎozhōu delta:长江~ Yangtze River Delta

三脚架 sānjiǎojià tripod; tripod mounting; trivet; A-frame

三脚架式钻岩机 sānjiǎojiàshì zuānyánjī 〈机械〉tri-point rock drill

三脚猫 sānjiǎomāo something that is a mere appearance — a person with only a superficial knowledge of the trades

三脚起重机 sānjiǎo qǐzhòngjī 〈机械〉tripod derrick

三教九流 sānjiào-jiǔliú *also* "九流三教" ❶ three religions (Confucianism, Taoism and Buddhism) and nine schools of thought (the Confucians, the Taoists, the *Yin-Yang*, the Legalists, the Logicians, the Mohists, the Political Strategists, the Eclectics and the Agriculturists) ❷ various religious sects and schools of thought ❸ people in various trades; people of all sorts or descriptions:老沈是~

都懂的人。Lao Shen here is well acquainted with every sort of trade.
三街六巷 sānjiē-liùxiàng every street and lane; all over the city: 这件事轰动了～。This has caused a sensation throughout the city. *or* This has become the talk of the town.
三节 sānjié three festivals, a cover term for the Dragon Boat Festival, the Mid-Autumn Festival and the Spring Festival
三节棍 sānjiégùn 〈体育〉cudgel of three linked sections; three-section cudgel
三结合 sānjiéhé three-in-one combination: ～设计小组 three-in-one designing group (consisting of workers, technicians and cadres)/老、中、青～的领导班子 leading group composed of the old, the middle-aged and the young
三九 sānjiǔ *also* "三九天" bitter cold: ～天气 bitterly cold weather /～严寒 inclement winter weather
三九天 sānjiǔtiān third nine-day period after the winter solstice — the depth of winter
三句半 sānjùbàn three-and-a-half-sentence ballad
三句话不离本行 sān jù huà bù lí běnháng be always talking shop: 你们商人～,开口闭口都是生意。You merchants talk shop all the time. *or* Your topic never goes beyond business.
三军 sānjūn ❶ three armed services ❷ army
三 K 党 Sānkèidǎng Ku Klux Klan, a secret US society of white people who try to keep the black population from attaining equality and use terrorism and murder as means to that end
三老 sānlǎo ❶〈旧语〉county official in charge of education ❷〈书面〉octogenarians
三老四严 sānlǎo-sìyán three honests and four stricts (be honest in thought, word and deed and set strict standards for work, organization, attitude and observance of discipline)
三棱 sānléng 〈中药〉*Sparganium stoloniferum*
三棱尺 sānléngchǐ three-square rule; triangular scale
三棱镜 sānléngjìng 〈物理〉(triangular) prism
三连冠 sānliánguàn three successive championships: 这个球队实现了"～"的夙愿。The team realized their long-cherished wish by winning three championships in succession.
三连音符 sānlián yīnfú 〈音乐〉triplet
三联单 sānliándān triplicate form
三联炼钢法 sānlián liàngāngfǎ 〈冶金〉triplex process; triplexing
三联疫苗 sānlián yìmiáo 〈医学〉triple vaccine
三联症 sānliánzhèng triad; trilogy
三磷酸腺甙 sānlínsuān xiàndài adenosine triphosphate (ATP)
三菱电机公司 Sānlíng Diànjī Gōngsī (Japan) Mitsubishi Electric Corporation
三菱银行 Sānlíng Yínháng (Japan) Mitsubishi Bank Ltd.
三菱重工业公司 Sānlíng Zhònggōngyè Gōngsī (Japan) Mistubishi Heavy Industries Ltd.
三令五申 sānlìng-wǔshēn repeated injunctions; repeated orders and instructions: 虽然～,有些人仍不遵守交通规则。Despite repeated injunctions, some people fail to observe traffic regulations.
三硫化物 sānliúhuàwù 〈化学〉trisulfide
三六九等 sān-liù-jiǔděng ❶ of all grades and ranks: 把工作分成～是错误的。It is wrong to regard different kinds of work as indicative of rank or grade. ❷ cold-shoulder sb.: 我退休下来还没几天,这些人就这么～的了。It is not long since I retired, but these people have started cold-shouldering me.
三氯杀螨砜 sānlǜ shāmǎnfēng 〈农业〉tetradiphon; tedion
三乱 sānluàn indiscriminate fines, charges and levies
三轮车 sānlúnchē *also* "三轮儿" tricycle; pedicab: ～夫 pedicabman
三轮摩托车 sānlún mótuōchē motor tricycle; scooter car; motorcycle with side car; three-wheel scooter (cabin); three-wheeler
三轮汽车 sānlún qìchē three-wheeler automobile; three-wheel car
三轮儿 sānlúnr tricycle; pedicab: 蹬～ pedal a pedicab
三麦 sānmài wheat, barley and highland barley
三媒六证 sānméi-liùzhèng 〈旧语〉several match-makers acting as witnesses to an arranged marriage
三昧 sānmèi ❶〈佛教〉samadhi, a Hindu or Buddhist form of two-stage contemplation ❷ secret; trick; knack: 得其～ master the secrets of an art /未解书法～ not grasp the essence of calligraphy
三门干部 sānmén gànbù cadres who began to work in the government straight after graduating from school and have no experience at the grass roots
三门四户 sānmén-sìhù all the doors in a house
三门峡水利枢纽工程 Sānménxiá Shuǐlì Shūniǔ Gōngchéng Sanmenxia Key Water Control Project
三面红旗 sānmiàn hóngqí Three Red Banners (the General Line for Socialist Construction, the Great Leap Forward and the People's Communes, formulated in 1958)
三秒区 sānmiǎoqū 〈体育〉(of basketball) 3-second area or zone; foul lane
三秒违例 sānmiǎo wéilì (of basketball) 3-second-rule violation
三民主义 sānmínzhǔyì the Three People's Principles (Nationalism, Democracy and the People's Livelihood) put forward by Dr. Sun Yat-sen
三明治 sānmíngzhì sandwich
三木武夫 Sānmùwǔfū Miki Takeo (1907-1988), Japanese Prime Minister (1974-1976)
三拇指 sānmuzhǐ 〈方言〉middle finger
三年五载 sānnián-wǔzǎi from three to five years — in a couple of years
三朋四友 sānpéng-sìyǒu many friends
三七 sānqī 〈中药〉pseudo-ginseng (*Panax pseudo-ginseng* var. *noto-ginseng*)
三七开 sān-qīkāi ❶ 30:70 ratio: 这次的奖金,你我～吧。Let's split up the bonus on a thirty to seventy ratio. ❷ seventy-thirty evaluation; evaluation in which the merits outweigh the defects by 7 to 3; 70 per cent achievements and 30 per cent mistakes: 对老李要～。Lao Li should be given a 70-30 evaluation.
三亲六故 sānqīn-liùgù *also* "三亲四友" all the kinsmen and friends
三亲六眷 sānqīn-liùjuàn all the kinsmen
三青子 sānqīngzi 〈方言〉❶ rude and unreasonable; be impervious to reason: 咱们好好说话,谁也别犯～。Let's be reasonable and talk things over sensibly. ❷ rude and unreasonable person: 他是个～,别理他。You'd better leave him alone; he listens to nobody.
三秋 sānqiū ❶〈农业〉three autumn activities (harvesting, ploughing and sowing): 现在正是～大忙季节。Now is the busy period of autumn farming. ❷〈书面〉three autumn months; ninth month in the lunar calendar ❸〈书面〉three years: 一日不见,如隔～。One day away seems as long as three years.
三权分立 sānquán fēnlì separation of powers (i. e. the legislative, executive and judicial powers)
三绕组发电机 sānràozǔ fādiànjī 〈电工〉three-coil dynamo; three-coil generator
三人成虎 sānrén-chénghǔ if three people in the city all say there is a tiger around, you are inclined to believe that it is so; a lie, if repeated often enough, will be accepted as truth
三人行,必有我师 sān rén xíng, bì yǒu wǒ shī if there are three men walking together, one of them is bound to be good enough to be my teacher — everyone around me could teach me something
三人知,天下晓 sān rén zhī, tiānxià xiǎo when something is known to three people, it is public knowledge; when three know it, all know it
三日疟 sānrìnüè 〈医学〉quartan ague or fever; quartan
三三两两 sānsān-liǎngliǎng in twos and threes; by twos and threes; in small groups: 人们～,在园中漫步。People are strolling in the park in twos and threes.
三三五五 sānsān-wǔwǔ in threes and fours
三色版 sānsèbǎn 〈印刷〉three-colour halftone; three-colour block: ～印刷 three-colour printing; trichromatic printing
三色堇 sānsèjǐn 〈植物〉pansy
三色照相机 sānsè zhàoxiàngjī tricolour camera
三生 sānshēng 〈宗教〉three incarnations (past, present and future)
三生石 sānshēngshí 〈迷信〉symbol of predestined relationship (of a person's existence)
三生有幸 sānshēng-yǒuxìng 〈套语〉consider oneself most fortunate (to make sb.'s acquaintance, etc.): 久仰先生清誉,今能一见,～。I have long heard of your reputation, and I consider it a great honour to (be able to) meet you today.
三牲 sānshēng three sacrifices (pig, sheep and ox)
三十二分音符 sānshí'èrfēn yīnfú 〈音乐〉demisemiquaver; thirty-second note

S

三十二开 sānshí'èrkāi thirty-twomo; 32mo
三十六计,走为上计 sānshíliù jì, zǒu wéi shàngjì of all the stratagems, the best is to quit; of all the alternatives, running away is the best
三十年河东,三十年河西 sānshí nián hé dōng, sānshí nián hé xī life full of ups and downs; vicissitudes of life; chequered career
三熟制 sānshúzhì 〈农业〉triple cropping (system)
三刷发电机 sānshuā fādiànjī 〈电工〉three-brush generator
三水铝矿 sānshuǐ lǚkuàng gibbsite
三思 sānsī think carefully; ponder over:事关重大,请你~。As this is a matter of great importance, you had better ponder over it carefully.
三思而行 sānsī'érxíng *also* "三思而后行" think twice; look before you leap; second thoughts are best:对重大事情要~。One must think twice before making an important decision.
…三…四 …sān…sì ❶ *indicating disorder*:说话颠三倒四 be incoherent in speech; speak disconnectedly /几个不三不四的人 some nondescript individuals; some people of dubious character /丢三落四 always be forgetting things; be forgetful ❷ *indicating repetition*:推三阻四 decline with all sorts of excuses /说三道四 make irresponsible remarks /挑三拣四 pick and choose; be picky (*or* choosy)
三潭印月 Sāntán Yìnyuè Three Pools Mirroring the Moon, a scenic site in Hangzhou
三糖 sāntáng 〈生化〉trisaccharide:~酶 trisaccharidase
三体船 sāntǐchuán trimaran
三天打鱼,两天晒网 sān tiān dǎ yú, liǎng tiān shài wǎng go fishing for three days and then dry the nets for two — work off and on:学习外语,贵在坚持,~是学不好的。Perseverance is essential in learning a foreign language; it won't do to work by fits and starts.
三天两头 sāntiān-liǎngtóu 〈口语〉from time to time; almost every day:他~地跟我纠缠,真烦人。I am fed up with him; he annoys me almost every day.
三通 sāntōng ❶〈机械〉tee; tee joint ❷ three-way multiple plug; three-way connecting block ❸ three direct links (in mail, transport and trade) across the Taiwan Strait ❹ (Sān Tōng) formerly referring to the three classical works on ancient Chinese institutions, namely *Tongdian* (通典), *Tongzhi* (通志), and *Wenxian Tongkao* (文献通考)
三通阀 sāntōngfá 〈机械〉triple valve
三通管 sāntōngguǎn three-way pipe
三同 sāntóng three togethers (eating, living and labouring together with the peasants or masses)
三头对案 sāntóu-duì'àn two parties (i. e., the plaintiff and the defendant) and the witness confronting each other in court:咱们可以~,把事情真相弄清楚。Let the three of us put all the cards on the table to thrash out the problem.
三头肌 sāntóujī triceps
三头六臂 sāntóu-liùbì (with) three heads and six arms; three-headed monster with six arms — superhuman power; superman:他再有能耐,时间这么短也是办不了的,难道他有~不成? Capable as he is, he won't be able to accomplish it in such a short time unless he has got (*or* he is endowed with) superhuman abilities.
三头政治 sāntóu zhèngzhì triumvirate
三推六问 sāntuī-liùwèn 〈旧语〉repeated interrogations
三瓦两舍 sānwǎ-liǎngshè (in the Song and Yuan dynasties) brothels and various other public places of entertainment
三围 sānwéi chest, waist and seat measurements
三维空间 sānwéi kōngjiān *also* "三度空间" three-dimensional space
三位一体 sānwèi-yītǐ ❶〈宗教〉Trinity ❷ trinity; organic whole of three; three in one
三…五… sān…wǔ… ❶ many times:三番五次 again and again; time and again ❷ not very large in quantity, number, etc.:三朝五日 in a couple of days; in a few days /三年五载 in a few years
三五成群 sānwǔ-chéngqún in threes and fours; in knots:孩子们~地玩游戏。The children are playing games in threes and fours. /人们~地站着聊天。People are standing in knots chatting.
三峡工程 Sānxiá Gōngchéng Three Gorges Dam Project
三下五除二 sān xià wǔ chú èr neat and quick:这件事若在他手里,~,一下子就会办完。If the matter were in his hands, he would finish it in a jiffy.
三夏 sānxià 〈农业〉❶ three farm activities in summer (planting, harvesting and field management) ❷ three summer months
三鲜 sānxiān three delicacies — delicious ingredients of meat dishes or fillings such as sea cucumber, squid, shrimp and chicken:~汤 three delicacies soup /~水饺 boiled three delicacies dumplings /炒~ three delicacies saute /烩~ braised three delicacies
三弦 sānxián 〈乐器〉*sanxian*, a three-stringed plucked instrument
三线 sānxiàn ❶ third line area; strategic area (regarded in the early 60s as the mainland's rear) ❷ retirement; semi-retirement:许多老干部已退居二线、~。Many veteran cadres have resigned their posts to take up advisory work or retire. ❸〈电工〉three-wire:~变流机 three-wire rotary converter /~发电机 three-wire generator /~制 three-wire system
三项全能运动 sānxiàng quánnéng yùndòng 〈体育〉triathlon
三相 sānxiàng 〈电工〉three-phase:~变压器 three-phase transformer /~电动机 three-phase motor /~发电机 three-phase generator /~电缆 three-phase cable /~制 three-phase system
三硝基甲苯 sānxiāojījiǎběn 〈化学〉trinitrotoluene (TNT)
三心二意 sānxīn-èryì waver and hesitate; be of two minds; be half-hearted; shilly-shally:对于经商,他弟弟决心已定,但他仍~。His brother has decided to go into business but he is of two minds about it. /对会计工作,他是~,不想久干。He is half-hearted about his work as an accountant and does not want to stay long in his job. /~,迟疑不决,必误大事。Indecisiveness and hesitation are bound to bungle one's business. /他办事从来不~。He never dilly-dallies in handling matters.
三芯 sānxìn 〈电工〉three core:~导线 three-core conductor /~电缆 three-core cable; triplex cable /~同轴电缆 triple concentric cable
三星 sānxīng ❶〈天文〉Orion's belt, three bright stars in a short line across the middle of constellation Orion ❷ gods of happiness, wealth and longevity in Chinese folklore
三星电子集团 Sānxīng Diànzǐ Jítuán (ROK) Samsung Group
三性 sānxìng *also* "三自性";"三相"〈佛教〉*trilaksana*
三学 sānxué 〈佛教〉*trisiksa*, referring to the taboos, meditation and wisdom of a Buddhist — the gist of Buddhism
三言二拍 Sānyán-Èrpāi three collections of short stories edited by Feng Menglong (冯梦龙), namely, *Stories to Enlighten the World* (喻世明言), *Stories to Warn the World* (警世通言) and *Stories to Awaken the World* (醒世恒言), and two volumes of *Amazing Stories* (拍案惊奇) edited by Ling Mengchu (凌蒙初), both being authors of the Ming Dynasty
三言两语 sānyán-liǎngyǔ in a few words; in a word or two; casually:他~就能把问题的要点揭示出来。He can highlight the gist of the problem in a few words. /事情很复杂,非~所能说清。The matter is too complicated to be explained in a word or two.
三阳开泰 sānyáng-kāitài *also* "三阳交泰"〈旧语〉(used on New Year's Eve to wish a good year to come) with three *yang* (i.e. the coming of the spring) begins prosperity — the New year ushers in good fortune
三洋电气公司 Sānyáng Diànqì Gōngsī (Japan) Sanyo Electric Co. Ltd.
三氧化二砷 sānyǎnghuà'èrshēn 〈化学〉arsenic trioxide
三氧化物 sānyǎnghuàwù 〈化学〉trioxide
三叶虫 sānyèchóng 〈生物〉trilobite
三一律 sānyīlǜ 〈戏剧〉three unities (i.e. unity of action, unity of time and unity of place)
三一三十一 sān yī sānshíyī share equally among three persons:所付的费用大家~分摊。The expenses are to be shared equally among us.
三用接收机 sānyòng jiēshōujī 〈无线电〉three-way radio
三元 sānyuán ❶ 15th day of the first, seventh and tenth lunar months called respectively *Shangyuan* (上元), *Zhongyuan* (中元) and *Xiayuan* (下元) ❷〈旧语〉lunar New Year's Day ❸ (under the imperial examination system) the one who comes out first successively in the examinations at the provincial capital, the national capital and the palace, winning the titles of *Jieyuan* (解元), *Huiyuan* (会元) and *Zhuangyuan* (状元):连中~ come first in the imperial examinations at all the three levels
三元里抗英斗争 Sānyuánlǐ Kàng-Yīng Dòuzhēng rise of the people of Sanyuanli Village in Guangdong against British aggressors in May 1841 during the Opium War
三源杂交 sānyuán zájiāo 〈农业〉three-way cross

三月 sānyuè ❶ March ❷ third month of the lunar year; third moon
三月街 sānyuèjiē annual fair of the Bai nationality (白族) held at the foot of Diancang Mountain to the west of the city of Dali (大理) in Yunnan Province, which lasts from the 15th to the 20th of the third month by the lunar calendar; other activities besides the exchange of goods including horse-racing, archery contests, and performances of music and dance
三灾八难 sānzāi-bānàn numerous adversities and calamities:人生在世，免不了～。No one is entirely free from misfortune (*or* mishap) in his life.
三藏 Sānzàng 〈佛教〉Tripitaka, the three collections of books making up the Buddhist canon of scriptures
三战两胜制 sānzhàn-liǎngshèngzhì 〈体育〉best of three games
三朝 sānzhāo ❶ third day after matrimony when a bride goes to visit her parents ❷ third day after a child's birth
三朝五日 sānzhāo-wǔrì several days:这个故事～也说不完。It will take more than a few days to tell the story from beginning to end.
三支两军 sānzhī-liǎngjūn three supports and two military actions (support to industry, support to agriculture and support to the broad masses of the Left; exercie military control of certain units or departments and give military training to the students, etc. — tasks given to the PLA during the Cultural Revolution)
三只手 sānzhīshǒu 〈方言〉pickpocket:他遇上了～。His pocket was picked.
三趾鹑 sānzhǐchún 〈动物〉button quail
三趾马 sānzhǐmǎ *Hipparion*, ancient mammal, smaller in size than the modern horse, with three-toed front and hind hoofs
三爪卡盘 sānzhuǎ qiǎpán 〈机械〉scroll chuck
三资企业 sānzī qǐyè three kinds of foreign-invested enterprises or ventures: Sino-foreign joint ventures, cooperative businesses and exclusively foreign-owned enterprises in China
三字经 Sānzìjīng Three-Character Textbook for Beginners or Primer said to be compiled by Wang Yinglin (王应麟) of the Southern Song Dynasty
三自爱国运动 Sānzì Àiguó Yùndòng 〈基督教〉Three-Self Patriotic Movement (i.e. for Self-administration 自治, Self-support 自养, and Self-propagation of the Gospel 自传):中国基督教～委员会 Three-Self Patriotic Movement Committee of the Protestant Churches of China
三自一包 sānzì-yībāo three freedoms and one contract (free markets, private plots, and self-responsibility for gains and losses, and household contract)
三足鼎立 sānzú-dǐnglì stand on three legs like a tripod — tripartite confrontation; tirangular balance of power
三足畸胎 sānzú jītāi 〈医学〉tripus
三座大山 sānzuò dàshān three big mountains (i.e. imperialism, feudalism and bureaucrat-capitalism, which weighed like mountains on the backs of the Chinese people before 1949)

弎 sān see "三" sān

叁 sān (used for the numeral 三 on cheques, etc., to avoid mistakes or alterations) three

毵(毿) sān

毵毵 sānsān 〈书面〉(of hair and twigs, etc.) long and thin:江岸绿柳～。The river is flanked with green hanging willows.

sǎn

糁(糝) sǎn 〈方言〉grains of cooked rice

see also shēn

散 sǎn ❶ come loose; break up; fall apart; not hold together:书箱～了。The bookcase came loose. /～包了。The parcel got torn. /自行车～架了。The bike fell apart. /队伍走～了。The ranks broke up. /这孩子太～，不好好做作业。The child is too lax with his studies and doesn't do his homework regularly. ❷ loose; scattered: ～页 loose pages /一盘～沙 dish of loose sand — in a state of disunity /零～的东西 loose particles; odds and ends /住得～ live far apart ❸ medicine in powder form; medicinal powder:健胃～ digestive powder /中药有汤、～、丸等不同剂型。Traditional Chinese medicine may be in liquid, powder or pill form.

see also sàn

散板 sǎnbǎn ❶ 〈方言〉collapse; fall to pieces ❷ type of music in Beijing opera characterized by less rigid rhythms, i.e. *erhuang sanban*, *xipi sanban*
散兵 sǎnbīng 〈军事〉skirmisher
散兵壕 sǎnbīngháo fire trench
散兵坑 sǎnbīngkēng foxhole; pit
散兵线 sǎnbīngxiàn skirmish line
散兵游勇 sǎnbīng-yóuyǒng stragglers and disbanded soldiers
散诞 sǎndàn ❶ *also* "散淡"〈旧语〉relax; free and unfettered:到园子里～～。Go and relax in the garden. ❷ 〈书面〉be wild in speech and behaviour
散飞子弹 sǎnfēi zǐdàn 〈军事〉wild shot; stray bullet
散匪 sǎnfěi dispersed bandits; straggling bandits:逃进山林的～全部被消灭。All the straggling bandits who had escaped to the mountains were wiped out.
散工 sǎngōng ❶ odd jobs; part-time jobs ❷ part-timer; casual labourer; seasonal labourer

see also sàngōng

散光 sǎnguāng astigmatism:～眼镜 astigmatic glasses
散光计 sǎnguāngjì astigmometer; astigmatometer
散光远视 sǎnguāng yuǎnshì hypermetropic astigmatism
散逛 sǎnguang 〈方言〉saunter; stroll:待在家里闷得慌，出来～～。Feeling terribly bored at home, I've come out for a stroll.
散话 sǎnhuà (often used in the early vernacular) digression; idle talk
散货 sǎnhuò bulk cargo
散货船 sǎnhuòchuán bulk freighter
散记 sǎnjì random notes; sidelights:《旅美～》*Random Notes from North America*
散剂 sǎnjì 〈中药〉powder; pulvis
散架 sǎnjià ❶ collapse; fall to pieces:这张桌子～了。The desk has collapsed. /她浑身酸疼，骨头像散了架似的。Aching all over, she felt as if all her limbs were out of joint. ❷ dissolve; disband; collapse:这个小组要不是你们几个撑着，早就～了。This group would have broken up long ago had it not been for your support.
散件 sǎnjiàn part; piece; component:进口～ imported parts
散劲 sǎnjìn 〈方言〉relax one's efforts; slacken (off):咱们要和他们挑战，谁也不能～。As we are going to challenge them to a competition, none of us should relax our efforts.
散居 sǎnjū live scattered:～户口 residence cards for the individual households /这个民族～于世界各地。People of this nationality live scattered around the world.
散乱 sǎnluàn scattered and disorderly; in a jumble; disorganized:～的头发 dishevelled hair /桌子上～地放着各种文具、书籍。Stationery and books were in a jumble on the desk.
散漫 sǎnmàn ❶ undisciplined; happy-go-lucky:他是个～惯了的人。He is habitually happy-go-lucky. /这个班的学生很～，需要整顿一下。The class is undisciplined; this will have to be properly straightened out. ❷ unorganized; loose; scattered:这文章写得～芜杂。The essay is poorly organized and full of irrelevancies.
散曲 sǎnqǔ type of opera popular in the Yuan, Ming and Qing dynasties with tonal patterns modelled on tunes drawn from folk music
散射 sǎnshè 〈物理〉scattering:～波 scattered wave /～层 scattering layer /～光 scattered light /～粒子 scattering particles /～线 scattered rays /～计 scatterometer /～通讯 scatter communication
散手 sǎnshǒu free-style grappling or fistfight
散碎 sǎnsuì bits and pieces; scrappy:～的银子 bits and pieces of silver /这篇文章的后半部分写得比较～。The second half of this article is rather disjointed.
散套 sǎntào sequence of *sanqu* songs within a particular musical mode
散体 sǎntǐ simple, direct prose style free from parallelism
散文 sǎnwén ❶ prose ❷ literary writings excluding poems, songs, plays and novels
散文诗 sǎnwénshī prose poem
散养 sǎnyǎng (of poultry and livestock) outdoor rearing;

grazing：现代化养鸡场不同于～。A modern mechanized chicken farm is different from outdoor rearing.

散职 sǎnzhí featherbedding or sinecure post; sinecure

散装 sǎnzhuāng in bulk：～白酒 spirits in bulk /～饼干 loose cookies /～货物 bulk cargo; bulk freight /我要买～的糖果，不买整盒的。I want to buy sweets loose, not in a box.

散座 sǎnzuò 〈旧语〉❶ orchestra seats in theatre as distinguished from box seats ❷〈旧语〉non-regular rickshaw customers ❸ seats for individual customers in restaurants

馓 sǎn

馓子 sǎnzi 〈方言〉〈食品〉fried dough twist

伞(傘、❶繖) sǎn

❶ umbrella：雨～ umbrella /旱～ parasol /阳～ parasol; sunshade /打～ hold an umbrella; put the umbrella up /核保护～ nuclear umbrella ❷ sth. shaped like an umbrella：灯～ lamp shade /降落～ parachute /跳～ parachute; bail out ❸ (Sǎn) a surname

伞包 sǎnbāo 〈军事〉pack

伞兵 sǎnbīng parachute troops; parachuter; paratrooper

伞兵部队 sǎnbīng bùduì parachute troops; paratroops

伞兵服 sǎnbīngfú parasuit

伞齿轮 sǎnchǐlún 〈机械〉bevel gear; bevel pinion

伞伐 sǎnfá 〈林业〉shelterwood cutting

伞伐法 sǎnfáfǎ 〈林业〉shelterwood method

伞房花序 sǎnfáng huāxù 〈植物〉corymb

伞骨 sǎngǔ rib

伞降 sǎnjiàng parachute：完成新兵～训练任务 complete a training programme in parachuting for the new recruits /空降兵安全地～到预定地点。The airborne troops were safely parachuted to the designated spot.

伞菌 sǎnjùn 〈植物〉agaric

伞投 sǎntóu drop by parachute; parachute：～炸弹 parachute bomb; parabomb /～杀伤炸弹 parachute fragmentation (bomb) /～照明弹 parachute flare

伞形花序 sǎnxíng huāxù 〈植物〉umbel

伞形科 sǎnxíngkē 〈植物〉carrot family

伞形目 sǎnxíngmù 〈植物〉umbellales

伞形天线 sǎnxíng tiānxiàn 〈无线电〉disc antenna; umbrella antenna

伞衣 sǎnyī 〈军事〉canopy

伞子 sǎnzi 〈方言〉umbrella

sàn

散 sàn

❶ become separate; break up; disperse：我们的诗社～了。Our poetry club has broken up. /天开云～。The sky has cleared up and the clouds have dispersed. /会开到深夜才～。The meeting lasted until midnight. ❷ distribute; scatter; disseminate; give out：把材料～发给听众 distribute the handouts to the audience /天女～花 goddess scattering flowers /从花园里～出一股芬芳的香味。A fragrant smell comes drifting from the garden. ❸ dispel; drive away; let out：一醉～千愁 have a drink to drown one's sorrow /请开窗～～烟。Please open the windows to let the smoke out. /机器待～热冷却后再用。Do not restart the machine till it cools down. /我们到外面走走～～心。Let's go out for a walk just to relieve the boredom of the day. ❹〈方言〉fire; sack; lay off：旧社会资本家随便～工人。In the old society, capitalists laid off workers at will.

see also sǎn

散播 sànbō ❶〈农业〉broadcast; broadcast sowing：～机 broadcast seeder; broadcast sower ❷ disseminate; spread：～怀疑的种子 sow the seeds of suspicion /～谣言 rumour-mongering; spreading rumours /～小道消息 disseminate grapevine information

散布 sànbù spread; disseminate; scatter; diffuse：牛羊～在山坡上吃草。The cattle and sheep are scattered on the mountain slope grazing. /不要～流言蜚语。Don't spread slanderous rumours. /这种错误的观点，大家不要再～了。We should refrain from disseminating these erroneous views.

散步 sànbù take a walk; go for a stroll：早晨她喜欢散散步，做做操。She has the habit of going for a walk and doing exercises in the morning.

散场 sànchǎng (of a theatre, cinema, etc.) empty after the show：电影～了，观众不断涌出。The audience streamed out after the film was over.

散发 sànfā send forth; diffuse; emit; distribute; issue; give out：～传单 distribute leaflets /田野～着泥土润湿的香气。The field is sending forth a fragrant odour of moist earth. /地窖里～着霉烂的气味。There is a musty smell coming from the cellar.

散放 sànfàng send out; send forth; emit：山间野花～着浓郁的香味。The wild flowers at the hillside sent forth a rich perfume (*or* fragrance).

散工 sàngōng knock off; stop work for the day：今天提前～。Today we shall knock off earlier than usual. /河边小路上走过来一群～回村的人。Along the road by the riverside came a group of people just off work and heading for home.

see also sǎngōng

散寒 sànhán 〈中医〉take the chill out of the bone

散会 sànhuì (of a meeting) be over; break up：十点钟才～。The meeting lasted till 10 o'clock. /现在～。The meeting is over. /他宣布～。He declared the meeting adjourned.

散伙 sànhuǒ ❶ (of a group or organization) dissolve; disband：那个业余剧团最近由于经费不足～了。That amateur troupe dissolved recently because of inadequate funding. ❷ (of lovers, husband and wife, partners, etc.) break up; part company：读书社因意见不合而～。The reading club broke up due to differences of opinion.

散结 sànjié 〈中医〉dissipate pent-up feelings or alleviate depression

散开 sànkāi disperse：～队形 dispersed formation /羊群～了。The flock of sheep dispersed.

散课 sànkè 〈方言〉finish class; dismiss the class

散落 sànluò ❶ fall apart; fall down; fall scattered; disperse：风起处树叶纷纷～。The leaves fell in profusion as the wind rose. /花瓣～了一地。The ground is covered with fallen petals. ❷ be scattered：一座座农舍～在田野里。Cottages straggled across the countryside. ❸ not heard of after being scattered：多年战乱，他的家人～异乡。His family was torn asunder by years of war.

散闷 sànmèn drive away one's cares; relieve one's boredom：你应该到各处走动走动，散散闷。I advise you to go visiting some places to refresh yourself.

散热 sànrè dissipate heat：～剂 cooling agent /海水比陆地～慢。Heat dissipates at a lower speed at sea than on land.

散热管 sànrèguǎn ❶ cooling tube ❷ radiating pipe

散热片 sànrèpiàn ❶ cooling fin ❷ radiating fin; radiating rib

散热器 sànrèqì radiator; cooler：～护罩 radiator guard /管式～ tubular radiator

散失 sànshī ❶ scatter and disappear; vanish; be lost; be missing：在那些动荡的年月中，许多珍贵的善本图书～了。Many valuable (*or* rare) books were lost in those turbulent years. /她～多年的儿子终于找到了。Her son who has been missing for years is found at last. ❷ (of moisture, etc.) vaporize; dissipate：夏季，地里的水分很容易～。In summer, the moisture in the fields vaporizes easily.

散水 sànshuǐ 〈建筑〉apron

散摊子 sàn tānzi *also* "散摊儿"〈口语〉break up; dissolve：他们合伙经营的铺子不久就～了。The store which they ran in partnership soon closed down.

散瞳剂 sàntóngjì mydriatic

散亡 sànwáng scatter and disappear; be lost：原稿多已～。Most of the original manuscripts have disappeared.

散席 sànxí (of a dinner party or banquet) end; come to a close; be over

散戏 sànxì (of a theatre, etc.) empty after the show

散心 sànxīn keep from worrying; relieve one's boredom：到公园去散散心 take a walk in the park to relieve one's boredom (*or* ennui)

散学 sànxué 〈方言〉school is over：～回家 go home after school

散佚 sànyì *also* "散轶"；"散逸" get scattered and lost; be missing：著述～殆尽。Practically all his works were lost.

散逸 sànyì ❶〈书面〉be carefree and live in seclusion ❷ disperse; spread：气体向外～。Gas is leaking out. ❸ be missing; get scattered and lost：古籍～。Those ancient works were lost. ❹〈物理〉dissipation：热～ heat dissipation

散溢 sànyì spill; overflow; exude：田野上～着秋熟作物的芳香。The fields exuded the sweet scent of the autumn crops.

散置 sànzhì scatter:案头～着几本画册。A few picture albums lay scattered on the desk.

sāng

丧(喪、丧) sāng funeral; mourning:治～ make funeral arrangements /吊～ pay a condolence call /国～日 national mourning day
see also sàng

丧棒 sāngbàng 〈旧语〉stick held for support by the son of the deceased in a funeral procession

丧服 sāngfú mourning apparel:妇女～ weeds

丧家 sāngjiā family of the deceased; family making funeral arrangements

丧假 sāngjià bereavement leave; compassionate leave

丧礼 sānglǐ obsequies; funeral

丧乱 sāngluàn 〈书面〉disturbance and bloodshed; disaster; calamity

丧门神 sāngménshén *also* "丧门星" god of death — bringer of misfortune:他的脸拉得长长的，像个～。He pulled a long face, like that of the god-of-death.

丧门星 sāngménxīng anyone (esp. a woman) who brings bad luck to someone:婆婆拍打着炕沿骂我是～，克死了他的儿子。Pounding at the edge of the brick bed my mother-in-law called me a jinx, accusing me of having brought death to her son.

丧事 sāngshì funeral affairs; funeral arrangements:节约办～ avoid going to a lot of expense in conducting a funeral

丧帖子 sāngtiězi obituary notice sent by the family of the deceased to relatives and friends

丧仪 sāngyí funeral and burial ceremonies; obsequies

丧葬 sāngzàng burial; funeral:～费 funeral expenses

丧钟 sāngzhōng funeral bell; death knell; knell:教堂响起了～。The knell sounded at the church. /为谁敲～? For whom did the funeral bell toll? /辛亥革命敲响了中国封建皇朝的～。The Revolution of 1911 sounded the death knell of China's feudal monarchy.

丧主 sāngzhǔ person presiding at a funeral ceremony; person in overall charge of the funeral of the deceased; eldest son during a parent's funeral or eldest grandson in absence of eldest son

桑 sāng ❶ white mulberry; mulberry ❷ (Sāng) a surname

桑巴 sāngbā (transliteration) samba (a Brazilian dance of African origin):跳～舞 dance the samba

桑白皮 sāngbáipí 〈中药〉root bark of white mulberry

桑梆 sāngbang 〈方言〉❶ *see* "丧梆" sàngbang ❷ pull a long face:看他那～相儿，也许有不顺心的事。He is pulling a long face. Perhaps there is something on his mind.

桑蚕 sāngcán silkworm

桑弘羊 Sāng Hóngyáng Sang Hongyang (formerly translated as Sang Hung-yang, 152-c.80 BC), politician of the Western Han Dynasty

桑给巴尔 Sāngjǐbā'ěr Zanzibar, capital and port city of Zanzibar Island

桑给巴尔岛 Sāngjǐbā'ěrdǎo Zanzibar Island, an island off the coast of East Africa and part of Tanzania

桑寄生 sāngjìshēng 〈中药〉parasitic loranthus (*Loranthus parasiticus*)

桑间濮上 Sāngjiān-Púshàng Sangjian on the Pu River or Sangjian-on-Pu in the ancient State of Wei — place of illicit love-affairs; lovers' rendezvous

桑那浴 sāngnàyù *also* "桑拿浴" (transliteration) sauna bath; sauna:洗～ take a sauna (bath)

桑农 sāngnóng farmers making a living by planting mulberry trees; mulberry planter

桑皮纸 sāngpízhǐ mulberry (bark) paper

桑螵蛸 sāngpiāoxiāo *also* "螵蛸"〈中医〉dried egg capsule of a mantis

桑葚儿 sāngrènr 〈口语〉mulberry (the fruit)

桑葚 sāngshèn mulberry (the fruit)

桑树 sāngshù white mulberry; mulberry

桑塔纳 Sāngtǎnà Santana, a German car model now made under licence in Shanghai

桑象虫 sāngxiàngchóng mulberry weevil or beetle

桑耶寺 Sāngyēsì Samye Monastery (in Tibet)

桑叶 sāngyè mulberry leaf

桑榆 sāngyú 〈书面〉❶ place where the sun sets — west; evening:失之东隅，收之～ lose in the east and gain in the west; lose on the swings and gain on the roundabouts ❷〈比喻〉waning day; old age; closing years of one's life:～晚景 in the evening of one's life /乐～晚景 enjoy the sunset of one's life

桑榆暮景 sāngyú-mùjǐng sunset glow on mulberry tops — the evening of one's life

桑园 sāngyuán mulberry field

桑梓 sāngzǐ 〈书面〉one's native place:造福～ bring benefit to one's native place (*or* home town)

sǎng

磉 sǎng base of a pillar; pedestal

颡 sǎng 〈书面〉forehead

搡 sǎng 〈方言〉push roughly; shove:推推～～ push and shove /～了他一把 give him a shove /有人把他～了个跟头。Somebody gave him a push, and he fell to the ground.

嗓 sǎng ❶ throat; larynx ❷ voice:哑～儿 hoarse voice

嗓门儿 sǎngménr voice:提高～ lift up one's voice /～小 have a weak voice /扯起～喊 shout at the top of one's voice /她的～又尖又细，我真受不了。I can't stand her shrill voice (*or* her shrieking). /越说～越大，渐渐地就嚷起来了。He raised his voice as he spoke and finally he began to shout.

嗓音 sǎngyīn voice:好～ good voice /～圆润 mellow voice /悦耳的～ sweet (*or* pleasant) voice

嗓音识别 sǎngyīn shíbié voice identification

嗓子 sǎngzi ❶ throat; larynx:清清～ clear one's throat ❷ voice:放开～唱 sing lustily /喉咙疼痛，～沙哑 have a sore throat and a hoarse voice

嗓子眼儿 sǎngziyǎnr throat

sàng

丧(喪、丧) sàng lose:灰心～气 be utterly disheartened
see also sāng

丧梆 sàngbang 〈方言〉❶ *also* "桑梆" sāngbang (of personality, language, etc.) immoderate; ungracious; gruff ❷ offend or hurt (sb.):别拿气话～人。Don't hurt people with offensive (*or* unkind) words.

丧胆 sàngdǎn be terror-stricken; be terrified:闻风～ become terror-stricken (*or* panic-stricken, *or* terrified) at the news /亡魂～ be scared out of one's wits

丧德 sàngdé mean; wicked; morally degenerate:～败俗 corrupt morals /干这种损人利己的事，实在有点～。It's wicked of him to benefit himself at the expense of others.

丧魂落魄 sànghún-luòpò be driven to distraction; be overwhelmed by dread:瞧他那～的样子! Look, how distracted he is! *or* What a distracted look he has! /遭此巨变，怎叫他不～。Afflicted by such a big misfortune, he was shaken to the marrow.

丧家之犬 sàngjiāzhīquǎn *also* "丧家之狗" stray cur:惶惶如～ as forlorn as a lost pup; as scared as a stray cur

丧尽天良 sàngjìn-tiānliáng have no conscience at all; conscienceless:他们是一群滥杀无辜、～的禽兽。They were a horde of heartless beasts who wantonly killed innocent people. /他居然能干出这种～的事来，真是令人发指。Everybody bristled with anger at the ruthlessness of his atrocity.

丧命 sàngmìng lose one's life; meet one's death; get killed:～沙场 be killed on the battlefield (*or* in action) /有一百多人在这次空难中～。Over a hundred people lost their lives in the air crash. /在那次大地震中，他险些～。He had a narrow escape in the disastrous earthquake.

丧偶 sàng'ǒu 〈书面〉 be bereaved of one's spouse, esp. one's wife：中年～是痛苦的事。It is painful to lose one's spouse in middle age.
丧气 sàngqì feel disheartened or depressed; lose heart：灰心～ be utterly disheartened /垂头～ be crestfallen /～话 demoralizing remarks; gloomy talk
丧气 sàngqi 〈口语〉 be ill-starred; be out of luck; have bad luck：今天真～，刚出门就让自行车撞了。What bad luck! I was knocked down by a racing bike just as I stepped into the street.
丧权辱国 sàngquán-rǔguó surrender a country's sovereign rights under humiliating terms; be humiliating; be degrading：～的城下之盟 humiliating treaty concluded under coercion
丧生 sàngshēng meet one's death; get killed; die
丧失 sàngshī lose; forsake; forfeit：～信心 lose heart /～勇气 become discouraged /～理智 take leave of one's senses /～立场 depart from the correct stand /～警惕 be off one's guard; lose one's vigilance /～工作能力 forfeit one's ability to work /～原则 forsake one's principles /～时机 miss the opportunity
丧亡 sàngwáng be killed; be subjugated：吸取这个小国～的教训 draw a lesson from the subjugation of the small nation
丧心病狂 sàngxīn-bìngkuáng frenzied; unscrupulous; perverse：敌人～地杀害了许多善良百姓。The enemy slaughtered a great many innocent people in cold blood.
丧志 sàngzhì demoralized; dispirited; dejected：玩物～ demoralize oneself by indulging in material comforts; pursue a hobby to the point of sapping one's will to make progress

sāo

臊 sāo smell of urine or of a fox; foul smell; stench：这被单有股～味。The sheet smells of urine.
see also sào
臊气 sāoqì foul smell; stink; stench：一身～ have foul smell all over; one's whole body stinks
see also sàoqì

搔 sāo scratch：～头皮 scratch one's head
搔首 sāoshǒu *see* "搔头❶"
搔首踟蹰 sāoshǒu-chíchú scratch one's head in hesitation; be perplexed
搔首弄姿 sāoshǒu-nòngzī *also* "搔头弄姿"（of a woman）pat her own hair in a coquettish manner; be coquettish：你没瞧见她在台上那～的样子？真叫人恶心！Didn't you see her posturing and preening herself on the stage? It's disgusting!
搔头 sāotóu ❶ scratch one's head：～摸腮 scratch one's head and stroke one's cheeks in hesitation; hesitate /这事让人～。This matter is most perplexing. /这案件头绪纷纭，很是～。This case is complicated and baffling. ❷〈旧语〉 hairpin; hair clasp：玉～ jade hair clasp
搔着痒处 sāozhe-yǎngchù scratch where it itches; hit the nail on the head; be just to the point：他的话正好搔着我的痒处。His words struck me as right on the mark.

骚[1] sāo disturb; disrupt; upset：～乱 unrest; riot

骚[2] sāo ❶ (short for《离～》) *Li Sao*, a poem by poet and statesman Qu Yuan (屈原) in the 4th century BC ❷〈书面〉 literary writings

骚[3] sāo ❶ coquettish; obscene：～货 bitch ❷〈方言〉(of certain domestic animals) male：～马 male horse; stallion ❸ *see* "臊" sāo
骚动 sāodòng disturbance; upheaval; turmoil; tumult：引起～ cause (*or* stir up) a disturbance /会场里～起来。The audience was in a tumult. /天下～。The whole country was in a turmoil.
骚话 sāohuà obscene language; obscenities
骚货 sāohuò 〈粗话〉 woman of loose morals; tart; lascivious woman; sexpot
骚客 sāokè 〈书面〉 poet：文人～ man of letters
骚乱 sāoluàn disturbance; turmoil; riot：一阵～的叫喊声 blast of riotous outcries /这几天来，这里～不已。There have been continuous disturbances here in the past few days.
骚闹 sāonào commotion; disturbance：街上一片～。There was a big commotion in the street. /楼上传来～声。A clamour of voices came from upstairs.
骚然 sāorán 〈书面〉 disturbed; tumultuous; turbulent：四海～。The whole country (*or* world) is in turmoil.
骚扰 sāorǎo harass; pester; molest：～社会秩序 upset (*or* disrupt) public order /敌机常来～。The enemy planes often came to harass us. /真不好意思去～他。I hate to go (*or* having to go) and bother him.
骚人 sāorén 〈书面〉 poet：迁客～ demoted officials as well as poets
骚人墨客 sāorén-mòkè literary men; men of letters; literati
骚赛管 sāosàiguǎn 〈医学〉 Southey's tube
骚体 sāotǐ *Sao* style — poetry in the style of *Li Sao*

缫(繅) sāo reel silk from cocoons; reel
缫丝 sāosī silk reeling; reeling; filature：～工厂 reeling mill /～工人 reeler
缫丝机 sāosījī reeling machine; filature

sǎo

嫂 sǎo ❶ elder brother's wife; sister-in-law：兄～ sister-in-law ❷ (form of address for a married woman about one's own age) sister：大～ elder sister; madam
嫂夫人 sǎofūrén (respectful form of address for a familiar friend's wife) your wife; sister：老兄虽然答应了，不知～会不会有意见？Though you have kindly consented, will your wife object?
嫂嫂 sǎosao 〈方言〉 elder brother's wife; sister-in-law
嫂子 sǎozi 〈口语〉 elder brother's wife; sister-in-law

艘 sǎo *see* "莪艘" màosǎo

扫(掃) sǎo ❶ sweep; clear away：～灰尘 clean the dust from; dust /～院子 sweep the courtyard /地～干净了。The floor is swept clean. ❷ wipe out; eliminate; get rid of：一～而光 make a clean sweep of /秋风～落叶 autumn wind sweeping away the fallen (*or* dead) leaves ❸ move along quickly; sweep：他眼睛四下～了一圈。His eyes swept around the place. /她偷偷地～了他一眼。She stole a glance at him. ❹ all put together
see also sào
扫边 sǎobiān minor role in Chinese opera
扫除 sǎochú ❶ clean; clean up：大～ general cleaning; spring cleaning /春节前夕，要进行一次大～。We'll have to clean the rooms thoroughly on the eve of the Spring Festival. ❷ clear away; eliminate; wipe out：～障碍 get rid of the obstacles /～隔阂 clear up misunderstanding /～怀疑 remove doubts (*or* misgivings) /～迷信 eliminate superstition /～害人虫 sweep away pests /～愚昧和贫困 stamp out ignorance and poverty
扫除机 sǎochújī 〈环保〉 sweeper
扫搭 sǎoda 〈方言〉 look at; sweep one's eyes over：他眼睛紧～着我。He looked at me closely.
扫荡 sǎodàng ❶ mop up：～残匪 mop up the remnants of bandits /～与反～的斗争 struggle between mopping-up and anti-mopping-up operations ❷ wipe out; clear up; eliminate：～歪风邪气 combat evil trends and unhealthy practices
扫地 sǎodì ❶ sweep the floor：～恐伤蝼蚁命，爱惜飞蛾纱罩灯。Spare the ants when sweeping the floor, Cover the lamps to save the moth. ❷ (of honour, credibility, etc.) be dragged in the dust; be utterly discredited：名誉～ fall into utter disrepute /威信～ lose all prestige /斯文～ bring disgrace to the intellectuals; damage the reputation of the intellectuals
扫地出门 sǎodì-chūmén be deprived of one's belongings and evicted or driven out; be swept out like rubbish
扫地以尽 sǎodìyǐjìn be swept clean — be completely discredited
扫毒 sǎodú anti-drug campaign
扫房 sǎofáng general house-cleaning; spring cleaning
扫坟 sǎofén sweep a grave — pay respects at sb.'s tomb
扫黄 sǎohuáng anti-pornography campaign
扫祭 sǎojì clean and offer sacrifices at a tomb

扫雷 sǎoléi 〈军事〉 mine sweeping or clearance
扫雷舰 sǎoléijiàn *also* "扫雷艇" minesweeper
扫雷器 sǎoléiqì mine-sweeping apparatus; minesweeper
扫脸 sǎoliǎn lose face; be disgraced:如果他参加比赛，第一个回合就给刷下去了，那岂非～? Wouldn't it be a disgrace if he participated in the contest and then was eliminated in the first round!
扫路机 sǎolùjī *also* "扫路车" 〈环保〉 road sweeper; sweeping machine
扫盲 sǎománg eliminate or wipe out illiteracy:开展～运动 launch a campaign to eliminate illiteracy (*or* an anti-illiteracy campaign)
扫眉 sǎoméi 〈书面〉 paint the eyebrow
扫眉才子 sǎoméi cáizǐ woman poet or scholar
扫描 sǎomiáo ❶〈电子〉 scanning:行～ line scanning /飞点～ flying-spot scanning /锥形～ conical scanning ❷ cast a quick glance; sweep
扫描成像系统 sǎomiáo chéngxiàng xìtǒng scanning imaging system
扫描电子显微镜 sǎomiáo diànzǐ xiǎnwēijìng 〈电子〉 scanning electron microscope
扫描辐射计 sǎomiáo fúshèjì scanning radiometer:多频道微波～ scanning multifrequency microwave radiometer
扫描跟踪 sǎomiáo gēnzōng track-while-scan
扫描激光器 sǎomiáo jīguāngqì scanned-laser
扫描器 sǎomiáoqì scanner
扫描微波分光计 sǎomiáo wēibō fēnguāngjì scanning microwave spectrometer
扫描遥测广度计 sǎomiáo yáocè guǎngdùjì scanning telephotometer
扫描影像 sǎomiáo yǐngxiàng scannogram
扫描造影术 sǎomiáo zàoyǐngshù scanography
扫描周期 sǎomiáo zhōuqī scanning cycle or period
扫灭 sǎomiè exterminate; wipe out:～蝗虫 exterminate locusts /一个月来，～敌军三千余人。More than 3,000 enemy troops have been wiped out in the past month.
扫墓 sǎomù sweep a grave — pay respects at sb.'s tomb (nowadays also referring to the commemorative activities taking place before the tombs of revolutionary martyrs)
扫平 sǎopíng put down; crack down; crush; suppress:～内乱 suppress a revolt
扫气 sǎoqì 〈机械〉 scavenge:～泵 scavenging pump
扫清 sǎoqīng sweep clean:～道路 sweep the road clean — pave the way (for); clear away obstacles (in the way of) /～官气 get rid of bureaucratic airs
扫射 sǎoshè ❶ strafe:敌机向人群～。The enemy aircraft are strafing the crowd. ❷ scan; sweep:他威严的眼光在屋子里～。His stern eyes scanned the room. /探照灯在夜空～。The spotlights swept the dark sky.
扫视 sǎoshì take a sweeping glance:～人群 take a sweeping glance at the crowd of people
扫数 sǎoshù all; whole amount:～还清。The debt was paid in full. /～入库。The whole amount went into the government's coffers.
扫榻 sǎotà 〈书面〉 clean the bed:～以待 tidy up the guest room in anticipation of a visitor
扫堂腿 sǎotángtuǐ *also* "扫腿" way to topple an opponent by a vigorous sweeping movement of the leg
扫听 sǎoting 〈方言〉 find out; inquire; find out in a roundabout way:派出探子去～ send a scout on a reconnaissance mission
扫尾 sǎowěi bring to an end; wind up; round off:～工程 final phase of a project /由我～。I'll duly wind up the work.
扫兴 sǎoxìng dampen one's spirits; spoil sb.'s happiness; feel disappointed:真～! How disappointing! /这种话只能使我们～。These remarks only served to dampen our enthusiasm.
扫雪机 sǎoxuějī *also* "扫雪车" snow sweeper; snowplough; snowplow

sào

梢

sào ❶ conical shape ❷ *also* "锥度" zhuīdù coning; taper
see also shāo

臊

sào shy; bashful; diffident:～得脸红 blush to the ears; blush scarlet /一点儿也不害～ have no sense of shame; not at all shy
see also sāo
臊脸 sàoliǎn 〈方言〉 lose face; be put to shame:你这分明是臊我的脸。You are obviously trying to make a fool of me.
臊气 sàoqì 〈方言〉 have bad luck; be unlucky:真～! How unfortunate!
see also sāoqì
臊子 sàozi 〈方言〉 minced or diced meat (usu. as dressing):羊肉～面 noodles with minced mutton

埽

sào ❶ cylindrical bundle formed by tying up tree twigs, sorghum stalks and stone for use to protect the dykes on the banks of the Yellow River from being washed by flood ❷ water conservancy structure made of many cylindrical bundles

扫(掃)

sào
see also sǎo
扫把 sàobǎ 〈方言〉 *see* "扫帚"
扫帚 sàozhou broom (usu. made of bamboo)
扫帚菜 sàozhoucài 〈植物〉 summer cypress
扫帚高粱 sàozhou gāoliang broomcorn (*Panicum miliaceum*)
扫帚眉 sàozhouméi long and bushy eyebrows:两道～ pair of bushy eyebrows
扫帚星 sàozhouxīng ❶〈天文〉 comet ❷〈贬义〉 woman who brings bad luck; jinx

瘙

sào scabies
瘙痒 sàoyǎng ❶ scabies:后背～。The scabies on the back itch. ❷〈医学〉 pruritus:老年～ senile pruritus

sè

涩(澀、澁)

sè ❶ puckery; astringent:味～苦 taste bitter and puckery /这些又红又亮的柿子不～口。These bright, red persimmons leave no pucker in the mouth. ❷ rough; unsmooth; hard-going:滞～ not move easily /这桌面太粗～。The table's surface is a bit too rough. ❸ (of writing) not smooth; obscure; difficult to read or understand:文句生～，难以卒读。I find the essay heavy going; it is so full of obscurities.
涩剌剌 sèlālā *also* "涩拉拉" very puckery:他眼睛～的，看不了几行字，直打瞌睡。With his eyes screwed up, he dozed off after reading only a few lines.
涩脉 sèmài 〈中医〉 weak, uneven pulse
涩滞 sèzhì not smooth; rough going; not flowing easily:声音～ raucous and halting voice /他文笔～。His writing is not smooth and difficult to read.

塞

sè
see also sāi; sài
塞擦音 sècāyīn 〈语言〉 affricate
塞音 sèyīn 〈语言〉 plosive; stop
塞责 sèzé not do one's job properly:他工作马马虎虎，敷衍～而已。He is sloppy in his work, doing things perfunctorily at best.

瑟

sè 〈乐器〉 *se*, a sixteen-string or twenty-five-string plucked instrument like the zither
瑟瑟 sèsè ❶〈象声〉 (of the wind) rustle:秋风～。The autumn wind is rustling. ❷ shake; tremble:～发抖 be shaking (*or* trembling) all over
瑟缩 sèsuō curl up with cold; cower:全身～ tremble all over with cold /她面色苍白，～在墙角里。She looked pale, cowering in a corner.

啬(嗇)

sè miserly; stingy; mean; close-fisted
啬刻 sèke 〈方言〉 miserly; mean:～鬼 miser; niggard; skinflint

濇(澀)

sè 〈书面〉 *see* "涩" sè

S

穑(穡) sè see“稼穑”jiàsè

色 sè ❶ colour:调～ mix colours /白～ white /原～ primary colour /一辆红～轿车 a red car /不易褪～ colourfast /房间漆成绿～。The room is painted green. /天水一～。The sky and the horizon merged. ❷ look; appearance; countenance; expression:面有喜～ beam with joy /面有难～ show reluctance /她气得脸～都变白了。She turned pale with anger. /泰山崩于前而～不变。Even though Mount Tai collapses before me, I will not bat an eyelid. ❸ kind; sort; description:各～各样的工具 all kinds of tools /各～人等 people of all description (or stripes) ❹ view; scene; scenery:湖光山～ beautiful view of the lake and hills /江～迷茫。The river is covered with mist. ❺ (of precious metals, goods, etc.) quality:这金子成～足。The gold ingot is of pure quality. ❻ woman's beautiful looks:颇有几分姿～ rather pretty /～艺双绝 unrivalled (or peerless) in physical charm and skill /～不迷人人自迷。Good looks do not bewitch one; one bewitches oneself. ❼ erotism:好～之徒 erotic /沉湎酒～ be indulged in drinking and sex

see also shǎi

色标 sèbiāo colour code

色彩 sècǎi ❶ colour; hue; tint; shade:～鲜艳 in bright gay colours; gaudy /～柔和 (in) mellow colours /～缤纷 colourful; riot of colour /增添～ add colour (or lustre) to ❷ emotion; flavour:地方～ local colour /文学～ literary flavour /具有不同政治～的人们 people of various political hues; people from a wide spectrum of political opinions /这个故事带有神秘～。The story has an air of mystery about it.

色彩疗法 sècǎi liáofǎ colour therapy

色层分析 sècéng fēnxī *also*“色谱分析”〈物理〉chromatographic analysis

色层分析法 sècéng fēnxīfǎ chromatography

色层谱 sècéngpǔ 〈物理〉chromatogram

色差 sèchā ❶〈物理〉chromatism ❷〈纺织〉off colour; off shade

色带 sèdài ribbon

色丹岛 Sèdāndǎo Shikotan, one of four islands north of Japan and under Russian jurisdiction but claimed by Japan

色胆 sèdǎn boldness in erotic adventure:～包天 unscrupulous in seeking carnal pleasure; with unbridled lust

色蛋白 sèdànbái 〈生化〉chromoprotein

色道 sèdào 〈方言〉colour:水怎么变成了这～? How come the water has become this colour?

色淀 sèdiàn 〈纺织〉(colour) lake:绯红～ crimson lake /～染料 lake colours /～颜料 mordant pigment

色调 sèdiào tone; hue:冷～ cold tones /～明朗 bright hues /柔和～ subdued hues /这部小说带有浓重的感伤～。The novel is rather sentimental in tone. /这首抒情诗～暗淡。This lyric gives expression to a gloomy sentiment.

色度 sèdù ❶〈物理〉chrominance; chromaticity:～镜 chromoscope /～术 colorimetry ❷ shade of colour:测定肤色～ determine the shade of sb.'s skin

色度计 sèdùjì 〈物理〉colorimeter:光电～ photoelectric colorimeter

色光 sèguāng coloured light:日光通过三棱镜,可见七种～。A prism breaks up white light into seven different colours.

色鬼 sèguǐ 〈贬义〉sex maniac; satyr; lecher; lascivious person:老～ dirty old man; old lecher

色基 sèjī 〈化学〉colour base

色觉 sèjué 〈生理〉colour sense; chromatic vision:～检查 chromatoptometry /～异常 chromatopseudopsis

色觉计 sèjuéjì chromatoptometer; chromatometer

色觉检查表 sèjué jiǎnchábiǎo colour test cards

色拉 sèlā *also*“沙拉”shālā (transliteration) salad:水果～ fruit salad

色拉寺 Sèlāsì Sera Monastery (in Lhasa, Tibet)

色狼 sèláng lecher; wolf; sex maniac

色厉内荏 sèlì-nèirěn fierce of mien but faint of heart; ferocious in appearance but weak within:此人～,不足惧也。The man is an ass in a lion's skin, and we have nothing to fear from him.

色盲 sèmáng 〈医学〉achromatopsia; colour blindness; colour blind

色盲表 sèmángbiǎo colour test cards

色迷迷 sèmīmī look erotic; have lust in the eyes:他～地看着她。He looked at her, his eyes becoming hazy with lust.

色迷 sèmí one who falls for every woman; womanizer; sensualist; a Don Juan

色目人 Sèmùrén (used by the rulers of the Yuan Dynasty to refer to) tribes residing in the western region of China

色品 sèpǐn 〈物理〉chroma; chromaticity

色谱 sèpǔ 〈物理〉chromatogram

色谱法 sèpǔfǎ chromatography

色谱分析 sèpǔ fēnxī chromatographic analysis

色谱仪 sèpǔyí chromatograph

色情 sèqíng pornographic; sex:～电影 pornographic film; porn movie /～文学 erotica; pornography /～作品 pornography; pornographic materials /这部小说～成分太多。There is too much sex in this novel.

色情狂 sèqíngkuáng 〈医学〉erotomania

色球 sèqiú see“色球层”

色球层 sèqiúcéng 〈天文〉chromosphere

色弱 sèruò 〈医学〉tritanomalous vision; colour weakness; chromatelopsia:～患者 tritanope

色散 sèsàn 〈物理〉chromatic dispersion

色色 sèsè all kinds:冬衣～俱全。All kinds of winter wear are available.

色视症 sèshìzhèng 〈医学〉chromatopsia

色授魂与 sèshòu-húnyǔ communion of feelings between man and woman; mutual affection or attachment

色衰爱弛 sèshuāi-àichí passion cools as beauty fades:以色事人者,色衰而爱弛。A woman who finds favour with a man with her good looks will lose it when ageing.

色素 sèsù 〈生物〉pigment:～过多 hyperchromatism /～缺乏 achromasia

色素斑 sèsùbān pigmented spot

色素沉着 sèsù chénzhuó 〈医学〉chromatosis; pigmentation

色素细胞 sèsù xìbāo chromatophore

色素细胞癌 sèsù xìbāo'ái chromoma

色素细胞瘤 sèsù xìbāoliú chromatophoroma

色素性视网膜炎 sèsùxìng shìwǎngmóyán 〈医学〉retinitis

色素痣 sèsùzhì mole

色温 sèwēn colour temperature

色相 sèxiàng ❶ colour phase ❷〈佛教〉outward appearance of things ❸ feminine charm; woman's sexual appeal:以～事人 (of a woman) sell oneself

色艺 sèyì (of women entertainers) charm and skill:～俱佳 outstanding in both charm and skill

色釉 sèyòu coloured glaze

色欲 sèyù sexual desire; sexual passion; lust

色泽 sèzé colour and lustre:～鲜亮 bright and lustrous /这墙壁的～过于暗淡。The colour of the wall is too low.

色织厂 sèzhīchǎng 〈纺织〉yarn-dyed fabric mill

色纸 sèzhǐ coloured paper

色质镜 sèzhìjìng 〈物理〉chromascope

色痣 sèzhì 〈医学〉mole

铯 sè 〈化学〉cesium (Cs):～光灯 cesium vapour lamp/～原子钟 cesium-beam atomic clock (or oscillator) /～源装置 cesium unit

铯原子钟 sèyuánzǐzhōng *also*“铯钟”caesium or cesium clock

sēn

森 sēn ❶ trees growing thickly ❷〈书面〉in profusion ❸ dark; gloomy:阴～可怕 gloomy and horrendous

森冷 sēnlěng dark and cold:～的目光 dark and chilly eyes (or gazes) / 这个地下室～瘆人。We couldn't help shuddering in the dark, cold cellar.

森立 sēnlì stand closely together or in a row:雪峰～。Snow-capped peaks rise closely together.

森列 sēnliè displayed or stacked closely:星辰～ stars in close array

森林 sēnlín forest:～调查 forest survey /～火灾 forest fire /～资源 forest reserves /保护～ forest protection /～抚育 tending of woods; forest care /原始～ primeval forest /茂密的～ thick (or virgin) for-

S

est /～保护区 forestry reserve /～保护队 forest rangers
森林法 sēnlínfǎ forest law
森林覆被率 sēnlín fùbèilǜ percentage of forest cover; forest acreage
森林古猿 sēnlín gǔyuán dryopithecine
森林学 sēnlínxué forestry
森罗殿 sēnluódiàn *also* "阎罗殿" yánluódiàn 〈宗教〉 Palace of the King of Hell or Hades
森罗万象 sēnluó-wànxiàng multifarious; all-inclusive; all-emhracing
森然 sēnrán ❶ (of a wood) dense; close; thick: 成片的高楼～而立。Tall buildings rise like giant trees in a forest. ❷ awesome; awe-inspiring: ～可怖 awesome and terrifying /一块大礁石～屹立在江面上。There is a big terrifying reef standing above the surface of the river.
森森 sēnsēn ❶ dense; thick; heavy; luxuriant: 树影～ darkish shadows of the trees ❷ gloomy; gruesome; ghastly: 阴～的古庙 ghastly-looking ancient temple
森王蛇 sēnwángshé *also* "靛青蛇" diànqīngshé indigo snake (*Drymarchon corais*)
森严 sēnyán solemn; (of guard) strict: 警戒～ heavily guarded; under close guard /等级～ rigid hierarchy /门禁～。The gate is closely guarded. /法度～。The laws are strictly enforced. /两岸高山，～壁立。There are mountains on either side of the river with forbidding cliffs soaring into the air.
森严壁垒 sēnyán-bìlěi *also* "壁垒森严" strongly fortified; strictly defined line of demarcation between two schools of thought or two rival factions: 早已～，更加众志成城。Already our defence is iron-clad, Now our wills unite like a fortress.
森郁 sēnyù thickly overgrown: 林木～ thickly overgrown with trees and bushes

sēng

髻 sēng *see* "鬅髻" péngsēng

僧 sēng Buddhist monk; monk: ～人 monk /高～ eminent monk /落发为～ shave one's head and become a monk; be tonsured as a Buddhist monk
僧道 sēng-dào Buddhists and Taoists; Buddhist monks and Taoist priests
僧多粥少 sēngduō-zhōushǎo *also* "粥少僧多" many monks and little gruel — not enough to go round; inadequate
僧侣 sēnglǚ monks and priests; clergy
僧侣政治 sēnglǚ zhèngzhì theocracy
僧侣主义 sēnglǚzhǔyì fideism
僧尼 sēng-ní Buddhist monks and nuns
僧伽罗 Sēngqiéluó ❶ *also* "僧伽罗人" Sinhalese or Singhalese, majority ethnic group in Sri Lanka ❷ *also* "僧伽罗语" Sinhalese (language); Singhalese; Sinhala ❸ *also* "狮子国" Shīziguó Sinhalam, ancient name for Sri Lanka
僧人 sēngrén Buddhist monk
僧俗 sēng-sú monks and laymen; clerical and secular people
僧徒 sēngtú Buddhist monks
僧衣 sēngyī *kasaya*, outer vestment of a Buddhist monk
僧院 sēngyuàn Buddhist temple; Buddhist monastery
僧众 sēngzhòng Buddhist monks

shā

沙[1] shā ❶ sand: 黄～ yellow sand /流～ quick sand /细～ fine sand /灰～ dust /泥～ silt /飞～走石 sand blowing about and stones hurtling through the air; sandstorm ❷ granulated; powdered: 豆～ bean paste ❸ (Shā) a surname

沙[2] shā (of voice) hoarse; husky: ～音 husky voice /嗓子发～ have a hoarse voice

沙[3] shā tsar: ～皇 tsar; czar
see also shà
沙癌 shā'ái 〈医学〉 psammocarcinoma
沙坝 shābà sandbank; sandbar
沙包 shābāo ❶ sand dune or mound ❷ sandbag
沙暴 shābào sandstorm
沙蚕 shācán sandworm; clam worm; rag worm; mussel worm
沙场 shāchǎng battlefield; battleground: 驰骋～ ride on the battle-field; fight battles at the front /久经～ battle hardened /～老将 sea-soned warrior; veteran /效命～ fight bravely on the battlefield
沙尘 shāchén dust: ～飞扬。A cloud of dust filled the air. /桌椅上布满了厚厚的～。The desks and chairs are covered with a thick layer of dust.
沙虫 shāchóng *also* "星虫" xīngchóng sipunculid worm
沙船 shāchuán large flat-bottomed junk
沙袋 shādài sandbag
沙袋鼠 shādàishǔ wallaby
沙铫子 shādiàozi *also* "沙铫儿" earthern pot
沙丁鱼 shādīngyú sardine
沙俄 Shā-É tsarist or czarist Russia
沙发 shāfā sofa; settee: 单人～ upholstered armchair; sofa /三人～ three-seater settee /两用～ sofa bed /～套 slipcover
沙发床 shāfāchuáng sofa bed; studio couch
沙发椅 shāfāyǐ couch
沙蜂 shāfēng sand wasp
沙肝儿 shāgānr 〈方言〉 spleen of ox, sheep or pig when used as food
沙岗 shāgǎng sand hill; sand bank
沙锅 shāguō earthenware pot; casserole: ～什锦 assorted delica-cies en casserole
沙锅浅儿 shāguōqiǎnr *see* "沙浅儿"
沙果 shāguǒ 〈植物〉 Chinese pear-leaved crabapple
沙海 shāhǎi expanses of desert: 红柳在～里茁壮成长。Red willows thrive in the vast desert.
沙害 shāhài disastrous sandstorms: 治理～ combat and control dis-astrous sandstorms
沙狐 shāhú corsac (fox)
沙化 shāhuà desertification; desert encroachment
沙画 shāhuà *also* "干画" gānhuà sand painting
沙獾 shāhuān sand badger
沙荒 shāhuāng sandy wasteland; sandy waste: 治理～ control the sandy wasteland /北部地区～愈来愈严重。The sandy waste in the north is expanding unchecked.
沙皇 shāhuáng tsar; czar
沙鸡 shājī sandgrouse: 毛腿～ pintail sandgrouse
沙棘 shājí sea buckthorn; sallow thorn
沙迦 Shājiā Sharjiah, the third largest of the member states of the United Arab Emirates
沙浆 shājiāng *also* "砂浆" shājiāng mortar
沙金 shājīn grains of gold mixed in sand; alluvial gold; placer gold
沙坑 shākēng 〈体育〉 jumping pit; sand pit
沙拉 shālā *also* "色拉" sèlā salad
沙梨 shālí 〈植物〉 sand pear
沙里淘金 shālǐ-táojīn obtain grains of gold by washing and siev-ing them from sand — the result obtained is not worth the effort; extract the essence from an abundance of material
沙砾 shālì grit
沙疗 shāliáo sand bath treatment
沙柳 shāliǔ *Salix mongolica*
沙龙 shālóng salon: 社交～ social salon /英语～ English salon /文艺～ artists' salon
沙漏 shālòu sandglass; hourglass: ～计时 use a sand filter for marking the hours
沙罗周期 shāluó zhōuqī 〈天文〉 saros
沙茅草 shāmáocǎo sand reed; beach grass; marram grass
沙门 shāmén 〈佛教〉 *sramana*; Buddhist monk
沙门氏菌 shāménshìjūn salmonella
沙弥 shāmí 〈佛教〉 *sramanera*; Buddhist novice
沙漠 shāmò desert: 塔克拉玛干～ Taklamakan Desert /～带 desert belt /～植被 desert vegetation /～风暴行动 Operation Desert Storm
沙漠化 shāmòhuà desertification
沙漠学 shāmòxué eremology

S

沙漠之舟 shāmò zhī zhōu ship of the desert — the camel
沙鸥 shā'ōu 〈动物〉 sandpiper; shorebirds, any of aquatic birds living by sandy beaches
沙盘 shāpán 〈军事〉 ❶ sand table: ～作业 sand table exercise ❷ plate containing a thin layer of sand, used to practise writing
沙佩维尔事件 Shāpèiwéi'ěr Shìjiàn Sharpeville incident (an incident on 21 March 1960 when security forces fired on a crowd demonstrating against apartheid laws in Sharpeville, a South African Black township)
沙碛 shāqì 〈书面〉 desert
沙浅儿 shāqiǎnr *also* "沙锅浅儿" shallow earthen pot
沙丘 shāqiū (sand) dune: 流动～ shifting dunes
沙瓤 shāráng mushy watermelon pulp
沙壤土 shārǎngtǔ *also* "砂壤土" shārǎngtǔ sandy loam
沙沙 shāshā 〈象声〉 rustle: 风吹过树林，发出～的响声。The wind rustled in the trees. /队伍走在雪地上，～作响。The soldiers mushed along through the snow.
沙山 shāshān sand mountain
沙参 shāshēn 〈中药〉 root of straight ladybell (*Adenophora stricta*)
沙石 shāshí *also* "砂石" shāshí gravel; sandstone
沙鼠 shāshǔ gerbil; sand rat
沙汰 shātài 〈书面〉 eliminate through selection or competition: ～冗员 cut back redundant personnel
沙滩 shātān sandy beach; sand beach; sands: 在～上玩耍 play on the sands
沙滩排球 shātān páiqiú 〈体育〉 beach volleyball
沙滩轻便汽车 shātān qīngbiàn qìchē dune buggy
沙滩椅 shātānyǐ beach chair
沙特阿拉伯 Shātè Ālābó Saudi Arabia: ～人 Saudi Arabian
沙田 shātián sandy lands
沙土 shātǔ sandy soil
沙土植物 shātǔ zhíwù silicicole
沙坨 shātuó *also* "沙坨子" sand hill; sand dune
沙文主义 shāwénzhǔyì chauvinism: 大国～ big-power chauvinism
沙蟹 shāxiè 〈方言〉 ❶ playing cards ❷ play poker
沙噀 shāxùn *also* "刺参" cìshēn a kind of sea cucumber
沙哑 shāyǎ hoarse; husky; raucous: ～的笑声 raucous laugh /感冒后嗓音还有点～ still a bit husky after a recent cold /她把嗓子都喊～了。She shouted herself hoarse.
沙眼 shāyǎn trachoma
沙样瘤 shāyàngliú 〈医学〉 psammoma
沙鱼 shāyú ❶ sandfish ❷ shark
沙浴 shāyù ❶ (of cocks, hens or turkeys) have a cleaning in sand ❷ sand bath
沙浴疗法 shāyù liáofǎ 〈医学〉 psammotherapy
沙灾 shāzāi sandstorm disaster
沙枣 shāzǎo 〈植物〉 narrow-leaved oleaster (*Elaeagnus angustifolia*)
沙蚤 shāzǎo 〈动物〉 sand hopper; sand flea
沙障 shāzhàng sand-break such as made up of weeds, pebbles, bushes, underbrush, etc.
沙螽 shāzhōng Jerusalem cricket; sand cricket
沙洲 shāzhōu shoal; sandbar; sandbank
沙蠋 shāzhú 〈动物〉 lugworm
沙柱 shāzhù dust devil; sand column
沙锥 shāzhuī 〈动物〉 snipe
沙子 shāzi ❶ sand; grit: 米里～多。There is plenty of grit in the rice. /我眼里进～了。I've got a piece of grit in my eye. ❷ small grains; pellets: 铁～ iron pellets; shot
沙钻鱼 shāzuànyú *also* "鱚" xǐ sand borer
沙嘴 shāzuǐ 〈地质〉 sandspit

痧

shā 〈中医〉 cholera, sunstroke and such acute diseases: 拔～ cupping
痧子 shāzi 〈方言〉 measles: 出～ have the measles

裟

shā *see* "袈裟" jiāshā

莎

shā *mostly used in names of places and people*: ～车 Shache (name of a county in Xinjiang)
see also suō
莎鸡 shājī *also* "纺织娘" fǎngzhīniáng long-horned grasshopper; katydid
莎丽 shālì *also* "沙丽" shālì (transliteration) sari; saree
莎笼 shālóng *also* "纱笼" shālóng (transliteration) sarong, Malay and Javanese garment worn by both sexes tucked round the waist or under the armpits
莎士比亚 Shāshìbǐyà William Shakespeare (1564-1616), English dramatist

挲(抄)

shā *see* "挓挲" zhāsha
see also sā; suō

鲨

shā shark
鲨鱼 shāyú *also* "沙鱼" shāyú shark

砂

shā sand; grit
砂泵 shābèng sand pump
砂布 shābù emery cloth; abrasive cloth; sandcloth: 刚玉～ corundum cloth
砂带磨光机 shādài móguāngjī 〈机械〉 belt sander
砂地植被 shādì zhíbèi sand vegetation
砂浆 shājiāng *also* "沙浆" shājiāng; "灰浆" huījiāng 〈建筑〉 mortar: 石灰～ lime mortar /水泥～ cement mortar /～挂面 mortar top
砂礓 shājiāng 〈地质〉 gravel; conglomerate
砂晶 shājīng sand crystal
砂矿 shākuàng placer deposit; placer: 开采～ placer mining; alluvial mining; placering /～工作面 gravel face /～运输 alluvial transport
砂砾 shālì gravel; grit
砂轮 shālún 〈机械〉 emery wheel; grinding wheel; abrasive wheel
砂轮机 shālúnjī grinder
砂囊 shānáng 〈动物〉 gizzard (of a bird)
砂黏土 shāniántǔ sandy clay
砂皮 shāpí 〈纺织〉 emery cloth
砂壤土 shārǎngtǔ *also* "沙瀼土" shārǎngtǔ sandy loam
砂仁 shārén 〈中药〉 fructus amomis
砂糖 shātáng granulated sugar
砂田 shātián sandy land
砂土 shātǔ sandy soil; sand: ～地基 sand foundation
砂箱 shāxiāng 〈冶金〉 sandbox; moulding box
砂心 shāxīn 〈冶金〉 sand core
砂型 shāxíng 〈冶金〉 sand mould
砂型铸造 shāxíng zhùzào sand casting; sand-shell-moulding
砂岩 shāyán sandstone; malmstone
砂眼 shāyǎn 〈冶金〉 sand hole; blowhole; slag pin hole
砂样 shāyàng 〈石油〉 drilling(s); mud cutting(s)
砂纸 shāzhǐ abrasive paper; sand paper: 玻璃～ glass paper /金刚～ emery paper /～打磨 sand papering
砂质岩 shāzhìyán 〈地质〉 arenaceous rock

纱

shā ❶ yarn: 粗支～ low count yarn /细支～ fine count yarn /中支～ medium count yarn /棉～ cotton yarn /经～ warp; twist yarn /纬～ weft; filling yarn /纺～ spinning /浣～ wash cotton ❷ sheer: 尼龙～ nylon sheer ❸ curtain-like products: 钢丝～ wire gauze /塑料～ plastic gauze ❹ textile or fabric products: 泡泡～ seersucker /麦斯林～ sheer muslin
纱包电缆 shābāo diànlǎn 〈电工〉 cotton-covered cable
纱包线 shābāoxiàn cotton-covered wire
纱布 shābù gauze: ～绷带 gauze bandage
纱厂 shāchǎng cotton mill
纱橱 shāchú screen cupboard
纱窗 shāchuāng window screen; screen
纱灯 shādēng gauze lantern
纱锭 shādìng *also* "纺锭" fǎngdìng; "锭子" dìngzi 〈纺织〉 spindle
纱架 shājià 〈纺织〉 creel
纱巾 shājīn gauze kerchief; transparent scarf
纱笼 shālóng *also* "莎笼" shālóng sarong
纱罗 shāluó 〈纺织〉 gauze
纱帽 shāmào *also* "乌纱帽" wūshāmào ❶ gauze hat (worn by an official in feudal society) ❷ 〈比喻〉 public office: 把～丢了 be re-

lieved from office

纱染 shārǎn 〈纺织〉 yarn-dyed

纱线 shāxiàn yarn: ~支数 count of yarn / ~均匀度 yarn evenness / ~上光机 thread polishing machine

纱罩 shāzhào ❶ gauze or screen covering (for food) ❷ mantle (of a gas lamp)

杀(殺) shā

❶ kill; slay; slaughter: 枪~ shoot dead / 他~ homicide / 自~ suicide / 屠~ slaughter / 暗~ assassinate / 误~ manslaughter / 谋~ murder ❷ fight; battle; struggle with; go into battle: 厮~ fight fiercely (often at close quarters) / ~得难解难分 be locked in fierce fighting / ~出重围 fight one's way out of a heavy encirclement / 我们俩~两盘 let's have one or two games of chess ❸ weaken; lessen; reduce; abate: ~暑气 reduce summer heat / 拿人~气 vent one's anger on sb. / ~~他的威风 deflate (*or* blunt) his arrogance / ~歪风邪气 combat evil social trends / 火势稍~。The fire has abated. ❹ end; wind up: ~笔 stop writing ❺ in the extreme; intensely: 气~人了。It drives me mad. / 吓~我了。I was scared to death. / 这真是笑~人也。This would make you laugh yourself silly. ❻ 〈方言〉 smart: 伤口~得慌，我没法睡。The cut hurts so much that I can hardly go to sleep. / 烟把我的眼睛~得难受，看不清楚了。My eyes were smarting from the smoke so that I couldn't see properly.

杀材 shācái *also* "杀才" 〈方言〉〈粗话〉 person deserving death; wretch

杀草强 shācǎoqiáng amitrole

杀场 shāchǎng 〈旧语〉 execution ground

杀虫剂 shāchóngjì *also* "杀虫药" insecticide; pesticide

杀敌致果 shādí-zhìguǒ serve with distinction in war; distinguish oneself in battle

杀伐 shāfá ❶ kill; slaughter; massacre: 互相~ mutual slaughter ❷ fighting; war: ~之声 war cry; battle cry ❸ punish; fix: 他乱扣帽子，打棍子，大行~之能事。He stopped at nothing to fix labels on people and come down on them with a big stick. ❹ boldness; daring and resolution: 他是个有~决断的人。He is a man of bold resolve. / 要不是他有~有决断，这事还不知道怎么收场呢。Had it not been for his daring and resolution, nobody could tell how this matter would have ended.

杀风景 shā fēngjǐng *also* "煞风景" shā fēngjǐng spoil the fun or show: 大家在海滩上正玩得起劲儿，不料下起雨来，真~! It was really disappointing that it suddenly began to rain while we were enjoying ourselves on the beach.

杀害 shāhài murder; kill: ~无辜 kill innocent people / 惨遭~ be murdered in cold blood

杀回马枪 shā huímǎqiāng make a backward thrust at the enemy while pretending to retreat; wheel around and hit back: 趁敌人不备，杀一个回马枪 give the pursuing enemy a Parthian shot / 他很怕同伙~。He was very much afraid of his partners turning against him.

杀蛔虫剂 shāhuíchóngjì ascaricide

杀机 shājī intent to kill: 心藏~ harbour murderous intentions / 他眼里透出~。There was a murderous glint in his eyes.

杀鸡取卵 shājī-qǔluǎn kill the hen to get the eggs; kill the goose that lays golden eggs: 胡乱开采，无异于~。Indiscriminate mining is no different from killing the goose that lays golden eggs.

杀鸡吓猴 shājī-xiàhóu *also* "杀鸡给猴看" kill the chicken to frighten the monkey — punish someone to warn others: 他这样做，有他~之意。What he did was merely making an example of somebody to warn others.

杀鸡焉用牛刀 shā jī yān yòng niúdāo you don't use a butcher's knife or cleaver to kill a chicken: ~，这等小事何须您亲自出马。There is no need to break a butterfly on the wheel (*or* swat a fly with a sledge hammer). You don't have to attend to such minor matters yourself.

杀价 shājià force down the price

杀戒 shājiè Buddhist prohibition against taking life: 大开~ kill by great numbers; massacre; butcher / 出家人不开~。Buddhist monks will not kill. *or* Buddhist monks will refrain from taking life.

杀菌 shājūn kill or destroy bacteria

杀菌剂 shājūnjì germicide; batericide

杀戮 shālù massacre; butcher: 岛上的土人成批被~。The aborigines on the island were slaughtered in large numbers.

杀卵剂 shāluǎnjì ovicide

杀掠 shālüè slaughter and plunder: 当时军阀混战，任意~。In those days the warlords fought among themselves and massacred and plundered the people at will.

杀螨剂 shāmǎnjì acaricide; miticide

杀坯 shāpī 〈方言〉〈粗话〉 person deserving death; wretch

杀气 shāqì ❶ murderous look: 一脸~ with a murderous expression on one's face / 这屋子里充满了~。This is a murderous-looking room. ❷ vent one's ill feeling: 你爱怎么着我不管，别拿我~。What you do is your business. Only don't take it out on me.

杀气腾腾 shāqì-téngténg bellicose; sabre-rattling; murderous: ~的演说 bellicose speech

杀青 shāqīng ❶ 〈旧语〉 heat bamboo strips to prepare them for writing ❷ finalize one's writing, etc.: 他的自传，~甫就。He has just finished his autobiography. / 这部电视剧下月即关机~。The shooting of the whole TV series will be completed next month. ❸ (of green tea) baking process

杀人 shārén homicide; murder: ~偿命 pay with one's life for a murder; a life for a life / ~灭口 kill an eyewitness / ~灭迹 obliterate traces of murder / ~如麻 kill people like flies; commit innumerable murders

杀人不见血 shārén bù jiàn xiě kill a person without spilling a drop of blood; harm a person by underhand means: 他为人阴险歹毒，惯用~的伎俩。He is sinister and vicious, often resorting to subtle but cruel means to achieve his goal.

杀人不眨眼 shārén bù zhǎyǎn kill a person without batting an eyelid; commit murder without blinking an eye: ~的刽子手 ruthless butcher

杀人犯 shārénfàn murderer; manslayer; homicide

杀人放火 shārén-fànghuǒ commit murder and arson: 一伙~无恶不作的匪徒 gang of bandits who commit murder, arson and every crime imaginable

杀人狂 shārénkuáng homicidal maniac

杀人如麻 shārén-rúmá cut men down as one cuts hemp stalks; kill people like flies: 土匪所到之处，~。The bandits committed innumerable murders wherever they appeared.

杀人越货 shārén-yuèhuò murder a person and seize his goods: 他们~，丧尽天良。They kill and loot; they have no conscience at all.

杀伤 shāshāng kill and wound; inflict casualties on: 敌军大部被~后仓皇败退。The enemy retreated in disorder suffering heavy casualties.

杀伤弹 shāshāngdàn 〈军事〉 fragmentation bomb; anti-personnel shell

杀伤力 shāshānglì power of destruction: 这种武器有很强的~。This is a weapon of mass destruction.

杀伤手榴弹 shāshāng shǒuliúdàn 〈军事〉 fragmentation grenade

杀伤卫星 shāshāng wèixīng killer satellite

杀伤武器 shāshāng wǔqì 〈军事〉 anti-personnel weapon

杀伤细胞 shāshāng xìbāo killer cell

杀伤炸弹 shāshāng zhàdàn 〈军事〉 fragmentation bomb; anti-personnel bomb

杀身 shāshēn be killed; lose one's life

杀身成仁 shāshēn-chéngrén sacrifice one's life for the sake of virtue; die for a good cause: 大丈夫当临难不苟，~。A real man will not flinch from death in upholding his lofty ideal.

杀身之祸 shāshēnzhīhuò disaster that costs a person his life: 招来~ court one's own destruction

杀生 shāshēng 〈宗教〉 killing of living things: 佛门戒~。Buddhism preaches that no living things are to be killed.

杀手 shāshǒu ❶ assassin; murderer; killer: 职业~ professional killer ❷ 〈体育〉 steely fingered player; contestant with an iron grip

杀手锏 shāshǒujiǎn *also* "撒手锏" sāshǒujiǎn sudden thrust of the mace — one's trump or master card

杀鼠剂 shāshǔjì rat poison; raticide; rodenticide

杀头 shātóu behead; decapitate; mete out capital punishment

杀威棒 shāwēibàng 〈旧语〉 flogging administered to a culprit with the intention of crushing his spirit upon his first appearance before the magistrate: 打~ flog a culprit severely for the purpose of cowing him; take someone down a peg or two

杀一儆百 shāyī-jǐngbǎi *also* "杀一警百" execute one as a warning to a hundred; punish one as an example to others

杀婴 shāyīng 〈法律〉 infanticide

挲(挱) shā

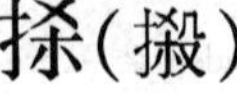

〈书面〉 mix; mingle; blend

S

see also sà

刹 shā put on the brakes; brake; stop:我把车猛地一～。I braked hard. *or* I applied the brakes suddenly. /～住歪风邪气 check an unhealthy tendency
see also chà

刹把 shābǎ handbrake:赶车人一甩缰绳，双手用劲将～往身侧一拉，来了个紧急刹车。With a crack of his whip, the driver pulled the handbrake with all his force so as to bring the cart to an abrupt halt.

刹把 shābà 〈机械〉brake crank

刹车 shāchē *also* "煞车" shāchē ❶ put on the brakes; step on the brake:紧急～ emergency brake /车开到山脚下才～。The driver did not put on the brakes until the car had reached the foot of the mountain. ❷ stop a machine by cutting off the power; turn off a machine:到下班时间了，～吧! It is time to knock off; let's stop the machine! ❸ brake:这辆车的～不灵了。The brakes (of the car) don't work properly. ❹〈比喻〉stop doing sth. instantly:未经批准的项目，已上马的，必须立刻～。All those projects started without prior approval by the leadership must stop at once.

铩(鎩) shā ❶ a kind of spear used in ancient times ❷〈书面〉wreck; destroy; injure; maim

铩羽 shāyǔ with clipped wings:～而归 return with one's wings clipped; come back crestfallen

杉 shā 〈植物〉China fir
see also shān

杉篙 shāgāo 〈建筑〉fir pole

杉木 shāmù China fir

煞 shā ❶ stop; halt; check; brake:收～ stop short /你戏演到这里可以～住了。You'd better stop acting now. ❷ tighten:他弯下腰把鞋带～紧。He bent to tighten the shoestrings. ❸ *see* "杀❸❺" shā
see also shà

煞笔 shābǐ ❶ stop writing (an article, letter, etc.):就此～。I must stop here (*or* now). /还不能～。I can't very well end here. ❷ concluding sentences:文章的～很有力。The concluding remarks of the article are forceful.

煞车 shāchē ❶ *see* "刹车" shāchē ❷ tighten up a load (on a vehicle); lash down

煞风景 shā fēngjǐng *see* "杀风景" shā fēngjǐng

煞气 shāqì *see* "杀气" shāqì
see also shàqì

煞绳 shāshéng rope used to fasten goods on a cart or truck

煞台 shātái 〈方言〉end of performance, show, etc.

煞尾 shāwěi ❶ bring to an end; finish off; round off; complete:我们正做些～工作。We are winding up the work. ❷ last of a sequence of songs in traditional northern drama during the Yuan Dynasty ❸ final stage; end; ending:文章还缺个～。We have yet to add a closing paragraph to this article.

煞性子 shā xìngzi vent anger on an innocent party:你心里烦闷，也别拿我～。Don't vent your spleen (*or* take it out) on me just because you are in a bad mood.

煞账 shāzhàng close accounts

shá

啥 shá 〈方言〉what:有～说～ say what one has to say; speak one's mind /你是～地方人? Where are you from? /你姓～? What's your surname? /这里～也买不着。There is nothing to buy here. /这个电影没～意思。This movie is not very interesting. /要～没～。Practically nothing is available.

啥味呢 sháwèiní cheviot (a kind of sheep, or cloth made from its wool)

啥子 sházi 〈方言〉what:这是～? What is this?

shǎ

傻(儍) shǎ ❶ dull; stupid; muddleheaded:装～ pretend ignorance; act dumb /她真是个～丫头。She is a silly girl indeed. /他有时可能干出～事来的。He is capable of occasional stupidities. ❷ think or act mechanically; be bigoted:他就知道～干。He works hard, and that is all he is good at. ❸ dumbfounded; stunned:吓～了 be frightened out of one's wits; be scared stiff /～了眼儿了 be utterly at a loss /他～站在一边。He stood by, stupified.

傻蛋 shǎdàn 〈粗话〉fool; blockhead; simpleton

傻瓜 shǎguā 〈粗话〉fool; blockhead; simpleton; idiot:你这个～，你讲的是什么? You idiot, what are you talking about?

傻瓜相机 shǎguā xiàngjī foolproof camera; fully automatic camera point-and-shoot (camera)

傻呵呵 shǎhēhē naive; unsophisticated:孩子听故事听得入了神，～瞪大了两只眼睛。The child listened to the story spell-bound, with eager, wide-open eyes. /别看他～的，心里可有数了。He may look like a naive, simple creature, but deep down he always knows what's what.

傻乎乎 shǎhūhū innocent; naive:小孩子抿了抿嘴唇，～地笑了。The child smiled naively with closed lips.

傻话 shǎhuà silly talk; nonsense:你尽说～话。You are talking rubbish.

傻劲儿 shǎjìnr ❶ stupid air or manner:瞧他那～! Look, what a fool he is! ❷ sheer animal strength:光靠～蛮干是不行的，得找窍门。Sheer animal strength won't do. You've got to use your brain.

傻老 shǎlǎo *also* "傻佬"〈方言〉〈讽刺〉simple-minded and slow-witted man

傻老爷们儿 shǎlǎoyéménr 〈戏谑〉simple-minded man; rustic fellow; rube

傻乐 shǎlè 〈方言〉giggle; laugh like an idiot:她躲在一边儿～个没个完。She hid herself in a corner giggling hysterically.

傻里呱唧 shǎliguājī *also* "傻里吧唧" foolish; stupid; dumb:她分明在挖苦他，可他还～，一点不知道。She is obviously mocking him, but he was so dumb that he didn't get it.

傻脸 shǎliǎn ❶〈方言〉be dumbfounded; be stunned:吓傻了脸。He was stunned with fear (*or* scared stiff). ❷ lose face; be disgraced:事情没办成，他觉得怪～的。He felt ashamed of himself for having failed in the attempt.

傻冒儿 shǎmàor 〈方言〉❶ unsophisticated; naive:你出去见见世面，就不会再～了。Go out and see the world, and you will become wiser. ❷ fool; blockhead; simpleton:这个人真是～，上了当还不知道。What a fool he was! He didn't even know that he had played into their hands.

傻气 shǎqì simple; simple-minded; naive:他很老实，带点～。He is very honest and sincere, though he looks a little bit naive.

傻头傻脑 shǎtóu-shǎnǎo look clumsy and stupid:你整天～的，什么事也不操心。You fooled around all day without bothering about anything.

傻笑 shǎxiào laugh like an idiot; giggle; smirk:～小子 silly kid /这孩子也不叫人，光知道～。The child does not know how to greet people, but keeps giggling.

傻眼 shǎyǎn be flabbergasted; be dumbfounded; be stunned:听说考试不及格，他～了。He was dumbfounded when he heard that he had failed (in) the examination. /一拿出逮捕证，他就～了。He was stunned as soon as the arrest warrant was produced. /这下他可～了。He got a real nasty shock this time.

傻样 shǎyàng foolish expression or appearance; silly look:瞧她那～，还想学芭蕾舞! She is so dumb-looking. How can she learn ballet?

傻子 shǎzi fool; nitwit; dunce; simpleton:这孩子一生下来就是个～。The child was born an idiot.

shà

霎 shà very short time; moment; instant:一～ in a split second

霎霎 shàshà 〈象声〉〈书面〉sound of wind and rain:狂风骤起，林木～。Suddenly there arose a gust of strong wind which sent the woods rustling. /林中雨声～。The rain came rustling through the woods.

霎时 shàshí *see* "霎时间"

霎时间 shàshíjiān *also* "霎时" in an instant; in a flash; in a split second; in a jiffy:～雷声大作。A thunderstorm began to rage instantly. /只听一声巨响，～烟尘滚滚，直冲上空。Following a loud re-

port, columns of smoke and dust rose into the sky in a split second.
霎眼 shàyǎn wink; twinkle; very short time:～又是冬天了。In the twinkling of an eye it is winter again.

唼 shà (of water birds, fish, etc.) eat noisily; gnaw; suck: 她把面包渣投进水里,聆听着鱼儿～食的声音。She threw pieces of bread in the water and enjoyed the sound of fish sucking the food.
唼血 shàxuè *see* "歃血" shàxuè
唼喋 shàzhá 〈书面〉sound made by fish, waterfowl, etc., when eating in a group

厦(廈) shà ❶ tall building; mansion:广～ huge mansion /高楼大～ highrise buildings ❷〈方言〉back veranda; porch:前廊后～ front and rear verandas
see also xià

嗄 shà 〈书面〉(of voice) hoarse:她终日号而不～。She yelled endlessly but never got hoarse.
see also á

沙 shà 〈方言〉sift; sieve:把米里的沙子～一～。Sieve out pieces of grit from the rice.
see also shā

歃 shà 〈书面〉suck
歃血 shàxuè *also* "唼血" shàxuè smear the blood of a sacrifice on the mouth (an ancient form of swearing an oath):～为盟 swear loyalty by smearing blood on the mouth; smear the mouth with blood and swear eternal fidelity

啑 shà ❶ *see* "唼" shà ❷ *see* "歃" shà
see also dié

煞[1] shà evil spirit; devil; goblin:凶神恶～ devils; fiends

煞[2] shà very:此事～费踌躇。We made the decision after much deliberation. *or* It took us long to make the decision.
see also shā
煞白 shàbái deathly pale; colourless; ashen; pallid:吓得脸色～ look ghastly pale with fright
煞费苦心 shàfèi-kǔxīn rack one's brains; take great pains; make a painstaking effort:对艺术展览的安排,他们～。They took great pains with the planning of the art exhibition. /为筹办老人大学,他是～。He stinted no effort in setting up a senior citizens' university. /他们～地研究对策。They had to rack their brains to work out counter-measures. /他～地打算把他们拉在一起,但毫无结果。He strained every nerve to bring them together, but to no avail.
煞后 shàhòu 〈口语〉hang back; lag behind:请您～一点儿,让车过去。Please step back a little and make way for the car. /班长带了头,咱们也不能～。Since our team leader has taken the lead, we must not lag behind.
煞气 shàqì ❶ leak:车带～了 have a flat tyre ❷ ferocious mien:一脸～ look ferocious ❸ evil spirit:当时居然有人相信这间屋子有～。Some people even believed then that the house was haunted.
see also shāqì
煞神 shàshén malicious deity or malignant spirit who wreaks havoc
煞有介事 shàyǒujièshì *also* "像煞有介事" xiàng shà yǒu jiè shì swaggering; pretentious:他～地讲了起来。He started to harangue with a show of gravity and dignity.

shāi

酾(釃) shāi *see* "酾[1]" shī

筛[1]**(篩)** shāi ❶ sieve; sifter; screen; riddle:细～ fine sieve /粗～ coarse sieve /滤～ filter sieve /面粉～ flour sifter /煤～ screen; riddle /粮食要过一下～。The grain needs sifting with a sieve. ❷ sieve; sift; screen; riddle:～米 sift rice /～石灰 screen lime /把糠～净 sift away the chaff /～土 riddle earth ❸ eliminate through selection:报考电影学院的人初试就被～下一多半。More than half of the candidates for the film institute were eliminated through the first round of test.

筛[2]**(篩)** shāi ❶ warm a pot of rice wine over a slow fire or in hot water:把酒～一～再喝。Warm the wine before drinking. ❷ pour (wine):她一边说,一边～酒。She poured the wine while talking.

筛[3]**(篩)** shāi 〈方言〉strike (a gong):打鼓～锣 beat drums and strike gongs
筛板 shāibǎn 〈化学〉sieve plate; sieve tray
筛布 shāibù bolting cloth
筛法 shāifǎ 〈数学〉sieve method
筛分 shāifēn screening; sifting; sieving
筛分机 shāifēnjī screening machine
筛粉机 shāifěnjī bolting machine
筛骨 shāigǔ 〈生理〉ethmoidal
筛管 shāiguǎn 〈植物〉sieve tube
筛号 shāihào screen size; screen mesh; mesh number
筛绢 shāijuàn woven fabric of silk, synthetic fibre or metal wire fitted at the bottom of a sieve
筛糠 shāikāng 〈口语〉〈比喻〉shiver; quiver; shudder:吓得～ tremble with fear; shake in one's shoes /浑身颤抖如～ shiver all over
筛析 shāixī sieve analysis; sieving analysis; size analysis
筛洗 shāixǐ screening and washing; shake-out and cleaning; sizing and cleaning
筛屑 shāixiè screen-throughs
筛选 shāixuǎn ❶ screen; sift:～种子 sift seeds /要经过严格～ must go through strict screening /精心～矿石 carefully screen out the ore ❷ selection through competition and elimination at various levels:经过多年的杂交试验,～出瘦肉率高、肥育性能好、经济效益大的瘦肉型猪。After many years of hybridization experiments, we have produced a new breed of pigs which can provide more lean meat, grow faster and bring better economic returns.
筛子 shāizi sieve; sifter; screen:粗眼～ riddle; screen

shǎi

色 shǎi 〈口语〉colour:本～ natural colour /退～ fade /套～〈印刷〉chromatography; colour process /不变～儿 not change colour; colour fast
see also sè
色酒 shǎijiǔ 〈方言〉wine, champagne, etc.:～有舒筋活络的功效。Wine helps to stimulate blood circulation and relax the muscles and joints.
色子 shǎizi *also* "骰子" tóuzi dice:掷～ throw (*or* cast) dice

shài

晒(曬) shài ❶ (of the sun) shine upon:日～雨淋 be weather beaten /太阳～得人直冒汗。We were sweating all over in the scorching sun. ❷ dry in the sun; sun; bask:～太阳 bask in the sunshine; sun oneself /～麦子 dry wheat in the sun /～衣服 air clothes; hang out the washing to dry in the sun /脸给～黑了。The face is tanned. ❸〈方言〉ignore; give the cold shoulder to
晒斑 shàibān 〈医学〉sunburn
晒版 shàibǎn 〈印刷〉plate burning; printing down
晒场 shàichǎng drying yard; sunning ground
晒簟 shàidiàn *also* "晒垫" bamboo mat for drying grains or other farm produce
晒垡 shàifá 〈农业〉sun the earth which has been ploughed up to improve the soil; sun the upturned soil
晒暖儿 shàinuǎnr 〈方言〉bask in the sunshine
晒坪 shàipíng 〈方言〉sunning ground
晒台 shàitái flat roof (for drying clothes, etc.); terrace; balcony
晒田 shàitián *also* "烤田" kǎotián drain and sun paddy fields to

S

strengthen the growth of paddy roots
晒图 shàitú make a blueprint; blueprint
晒图员 shàitúyuán blueprinter
晒图纸 shàitúzhǐ blueprint paper
晒烟 shàiyān sun-cured tobacco
晒盐 shàiyán make salt by evaporating brine in the sun
晒种 shàizhǒng sun seeds to stimulate budding before sowing

shān

羴 shān *also* "膻" shān smell of mutton

膻(羶) shān smell of mutton: 腥～ smell of fish or mutton; fishy / 小土屋里有股～气。The little dirt hut has a strong smell.

扇(❶❷搧) shān ❶ fan: ～炉子 fan a stove / 天太热，她不停地～扇子。It was so hot that she kept fanning herself. / ～～风，凉快多了。The fan has colded me down. ❷ hit with hands; box: 她～了他一耳光。She gave him a box on the ears. *or* She slapped him on the face. ❸ *see* "煽❷" shān
see also shàn
扇动 shāndòng ❶ fan; flap: ～翅膀 flap the wings ❷ *see* "煽动" shāndòng
扇风点火 shānfēng-diǎnhuǒ *see* "煽风点火" shānfēng-diǎnhuǒ
扇风耳 shānfēng'ěr *also* "招风耳" zhāofēng'ěr protruding ears
扇风机 shānfēngjī ventilating fan
扇忽 shānhu *also* "扇乎"〈方言〉❶ flap: 他戴着一顶破皮帽，帽扇没结带，走起路来直～。He had on a worn-out fur cap with loose earflaps that fluttered as he walked. ❷ incite; agitate

S

煽 shān ❶ fan (a fire) ❷ incite; foment; stir up; whip up: 事情是他们～起来的。It was they who instigated the disturbance.
煽动 shāndòng instigate; incite; foment; whip up: ～别人闹事 stir up unrest / ～叛乱 incite a rebellion / ～工潮 whip up a workers strike / 这番话很有～性。These remarks are really inflammatory.
煽风点火 shānfēng-diǎnhuǒ fan the flames — incite people; stir up or instigate trouble: 到处～ whip up a hostile sentiment (*or* a feeling of discontent) among people everywhere / 乘机～ seize the opportunity to stir up trouble / 躲在角落里～ instigate antagonism (*or* rebellion) behind the scenes
煽惑 shānhuò inflame; incite; agitate: ～人心的演说 demagogic speech / 他总～我去做投机生意。He always tries to talk me into speculating. / 我禁不住他的～，做了这件违心的事。At his instigation I did this, quite against my conscience.
煽阴风，点鬼火 shān yīnfēng, diǎn guǐhuǒ fan up evil winds and flames; incite people to violence or rebellion; foment trouble
煽诱 shānyòu incite; agitate

痁 shān 〈古语〉malaria

苫 shān straw mat: 草～子 straw mat
see also shàn

潸(潸) shān 〈书面〉in tears; tearfully
潸然 shānrán 〈书面〉shed tears: 不禁～泪下 cannot refrain from tears
潸潸 shānshān 〈书面〉full of tears; tearful: 泪～ tears streaming down one's cheeks

山 shān ❶ hill; mountain: 高～ high mountain / 登～ climb (*or* scale) a mountain / 登～运动 mountaineering / ～陡。The mountain is steep. ❷ anything resembling a mountain: 冰～ iceberg ❸ bushes in which silkworms spin cocoons: 蚕上～了。The silkworms have gone into the bushes to spin their cocoons. ❹ gable: 房～ side wall of a house ❺ (Shān) a surname
山坳 shān'ào col: 群山环抱的～ col surrounded by mountains
山霸 shānbà 〈旧语〉local tyrant or despot who owned hills and woods and oppressed the local inhabitants
山包 shānbāo 〈方言〉hillock
山背 shānbèi 〈气象〉yamase
山本五十六 Shānběnwǔshíliù Yamamoto Isoroku (1884-1943), Japanese admiral who masterminded the surprise attack on Pearl Harbour on 7 Dec. 1941
山崩 shānbēng landslide; landslip
山崩地裂 shānbēng-dìliè *also* "山崩地坼" mountains collapse and earth cracks — cataclysm; deafening noise
山不转水转 shān bù zhuàn shuǐ zhuàn *also* "山不转路转" if the mountain doesn't move the water does — some change is bound to happen: ～，你我后会有期。Things will change, and we will see each other again one day.
山苍子 shāncāngzǐ 〈中药〉fruit of a cubeb litsea tree (*Litsea cubeba*)
山茶 shānchá 〈植物〉camellia
山茶花 shāncháhuā camellia
山产 shānchǎn wild animals and plants of economic value found in mountains (which provide people with fruits, medicinal herbs, furs, etc.)
山长水远 shāncháng-shuǐyuǎn *also* "山长水阔" far away and difficult of access
山场 shānchǎng 〈方言〉farmland in the mountains: 种～ till land in the mountains
山城 shānchéng town nestling among the mountains; mountain city: 素有～之称的重庆，现在已是交通方便，四通八达的城市了。Mountain-girt Chongqing is now easily accessible thanks to improved transport.
山冲 shānchōng 〈方言〉level land in mountainous regions
山重水复 shānchóng-shuǐfù range upon range of mountains and meandering streams — separated by innumerable barriers: ～疑无路，柳暗花明又一村。The hills and streams have no end, there seem to be no road beyond; But dim with willows, bright with flowers, another village appears — just as the weary traveller despairs of finding a road, a village appears and the shade of willows and riotous flowers beckon; one has a sudden glimpse of hope in the midst of bewilderment
山川 shānchuān mountain and rivers — land; landscape: ～秀丽 beautiful landscape
山鹑 shānchún partridge
山慈姑 shāncígu 〈植物〉edible tulip
山丛 shāncóng mountain chain: 荒僻的～ remote mountains
山村 shāncūn mountain village: 偏僻的～ out-of-the-way mountain village
山丹 shāndān 〈植物〉morningstar lily (*Lilium concolor*)
山道年 shāndàonián 〈药学〉santonin
山地 shāndì ❶ mountainous region; hilly area; hilly country: ～战 mountain warfare ❷ fields on a hill
山地车 shāndìchē mountain bike
山地水文学 shāndì shuǐwénxué orohydrography
山顶 shāndǐng summit or top of a mountain; mountaintop: ～终年积雪。The mountain is snow-capped all the year round.
山顶洞人 Shāndǐngdòngrén 〈考古〉Upper Cave Man, a type of primitive man who lived in the late Old Stone Age or Paleolithic Period about 18 thousand years ago and whose fossil remains were discovered in 1933 at Zhoukoudian (周口店) near Beijing
山东 Shāndōng Shandong (Province)
山东半岛 Shāndōng Bàndǎo Shandong Peninsula
山东梆子 Shāndōng bāngzi Shandong clapper opera, popular in most of Shandong and part of Henan
see also "梆子腔" bāngziqiāng
山东大鼓 Shāndōng dàgǔ *also* "梨花大鼓" líhuā dàgǔ local style of story-telling in Shandong (Province) accompanied by a sort of semi-circular cymbals
山东快书 Shāndōng kuàishū Shandong clapper ballad, popular in Shandong and in north and northeast China
山洞 shāndòng cave; cavern
山豆根 shāndòugēn 〈植物〉subprostrate sophora (*Sophora subprostrata*)
山风 shānfēng ❶ mountain breeze ❷ 〈气象〉wind blown from mountain tops to the bottoms of valleys at night
山峰 shānfēng mountain peak: 险峻的～ precipitous (*or* perilous, *or* craggy) peak / ～耸立。The mountain soars into the sky.
山腹 shānfù half way up a mountain

山旮旯儿 shāngālár *also* "山旮旯子"〈方言〉 out-of-the-way place in the mountains; faraway mountainous area: 这种草药生长在～。This medicinal herb grows in remote mountain areas.
山冈 shāngāng low hill; hillock
山岗子 shāngǎngzi hillock; mound
山高皇帝远 shān gāo huángdì yuǎn *also* "天高皇帝远" remote areas where law and decrees are not strictly enforced
山高水长 shāngāo-shuǐcháng the mountain is high and the river long — far-reaching influence of a noble character, or depth of sb.'s kindness or friendship
山高水低 shāngāo-shuǐdī unexpected misfortune
山高水远 shāngāo-shuǐyuǎn ❶ long way off; far away; distant ❷〈比喻〉unexpected mishap, esp. death: 老人家万一有个～，你们可怎么办啊? What would you do if any mishap should happen to the old man?
山歌 shāngē folk song (sung in the fields or mountains)
山根 shāngēn 〈口语〉foot of a mountain: 到～儿找点水喝 go down the hill and get some water to drink
山梗菜硷 shāngěngcàijiǎn 〈药学〉lobeline: ～中毒 lobelism
山沟 shāngōu ❶ gully; ravine ❷ (mountain) valley ❸ remote mountainous area: 那些年，他一直在～工作。In those years, he was working in the mountainous area.
山狗 shāngǒu 〈动物〉culpeo
山谷 shāngǔ mountain valley
山官 shānguān 〈旧语〉hereditary chieftain administering one or more villages in areas inhabited by the Jingpo or Chingpo (景颇) nationality
山光水色 shānguāng-shuǐsè attractive landscape; beautiful scenery
山国 shānguó ❶ mountainous country: 那是旅游事业很发达的～。That is a mountainous country known for its thriving tourist industry. ❷ mountainous area: 那里群峦起伏，是本省待开发的～。This province has yet to develop the area where a chain of mountain ranges rise and fall in the distance.
山海经 Shānhǎijīng *Book of Mountains and Seas*, a work of folk geography in ancient China (of which fourteen articles are attributed to the Warring States Period, and four to the early Han Dynasty)
山河 shānhé mountains and rivers — the land of a country: 锦绣～ land of enchanting charm and beauty; beautiful land / 祖国～美。Our motherland boasts beautiful mountains and rivers. / 时移世易，～依旧。The land remains as before despite the vicissitudes of life.
山河狸 shānhélí sewellel; mountain beaver (*Aplodontia rufa*)
山和尚 shānhéshang 〈动物〉hoopoe; hoopoo (*Upupa epops*)
山核桃 shānhétao 〈植物〉❶ hickory ❷ hickory nut
山壑 shānhè ❶ valley ❷ gully
山洪 shānhóng mountain torrents: 汹涌的～咆哮而下。Turbulent torrents roared down the mountain.
山户 shānhù person or household living in the mountains
山荒 shānhuāng wasteland in the mountains (as a result of indiscriminate felling of trees)
山回路转 shānhuí-lùzhuǎn winding path along mountain ridges
山火 shānhuǒ fire in the mountains; mountain fire: 严防～是林业工作的头等任务。The prevention of fire in the mountains is a top priority for our work in forestry.
山货 shānhuò ❶ mountain products (such as haws, chestnuts, walnuts, etc.): 这个山乡的集市上到处都是～。Mountain products are everywhere to be found at the country fair. ❷ household utensils made of wood, rattan, bamboo, clay, etc.
山货店 shānhuòdiàn general store
山鸡 shānjī 〈方言〉pheasant
山鸡椒 shānjījiāo 〈植物〉cubeb litsea tree (*Litsea cubeba*)
山积 shānjī 〈书面〉pile mountain high: 货物～。Goods piled up.
山积波委 shānjī-bōwěi affairs piling up like mountains
山脊 shānjǐ mountain ridge
山家 shānjiā household living in the mountains; mountain inhabitants: 他一身～装束。He is dressed like a mountain inhabitant.
山涧 shānjiàn mountain stream
山椒鸟 shānjiāoniǎo minivet
山脚 shānjiǎo foot of a hill or mountain: ～处搭了几个帐篷。A few tents are pitched at the foot of the mountain.
山轿 shānjiào 〈旧语〉sedan (chair)
山结 shānjié area where several mountain ranges converge
山金 shānjīn *also* "脉金" màijīn vein gold: ～矿床 vein gold deposit
山景 shānjǐng mountain view; mountain scene: 看～ admire the mountain scene
山径 shānjìng mountain path: ～曲折。The mountain path twists and turns (*or* zigzags).
山居 shānjū 〈旧语〉live in a mountain hermitage; live in seclusion; lead the life of a hermit or recluse
山口 shānkǒu mountain pass; pass: 这～是通往邻国的咽喉要道。This is the strategic mountain path to a neighbouring country.
山岚 shānlán 〈书面〉mist or haze in the mountains: ～瘴气 mountain haze and miasma / 远处的～时隐时现，飘忽不定。The mist floating about the distant mountains now appears in full view, now disappears altogether.
山狸 shānlí 〈动物〉beaver; mountain beaver (*Aplodontia rufa*)
山梨 shānlí 〈植物〉sorb
山梨糖 shānlítáng 〈生化〉sorbose; sorbin
山理学 shānlǐxué orology
山里红 shānlihóng 〈植物〉large-fruited Chinese hawthorn (*Crataegus pinnatifida* var. *major*)
山梁 shānliáng ridge (of a mountain or hill)
山林 shānlín wooded hills; mountain forest: 我们天一亮就进入～地区。We entered the wooded and hilly lands (*or* regions) when dawn was breaking.
山陵 shānlíng ❶〈书面〉mountain ❷〈旧语〉royal mausoleum; imperial tomb
山岭 shānlǐng mountain ridge or chain
山垄 shānlòng 〈方言〉small patches of level land amid stony hills
山路 shānlù mountain path: ～崎岖。The mountain path is rugged.
山麓 shānlù foot of a mountain: ～冲积平原 alluvial plain at the foot of a mountain range; bajada / ～丘陵 foothill / ～有一片苍翠的松林。There is a green pine grove at the foot of the mountain.
山峦 shānluán mountain chain: 光秃秃的～ barren hills / ～起伏。There is an undulating chain of mountains. / 苍翠的～在云海中忽隐忽现。The emerald mountain is vaguely visible in a sea of clouds.
山萝卜 shānluóbo scabious; scabiosa
山脉 shānmài mountain range; mountain chain: ～纵横 criss-crossed by mountains
山猫 shānmāo leopard cat
山毛榉 shānmáojǔ *also* "水青冈" shuǐqīnggāng 〈植物〉beech
山门 shānmén ❶ gate of a monastery ❷ Buddhism
山盟海誓 shānméng-hǎishì swear eternal love; swear an oath of enduring fidelity: ～，白首不渝。They have sworn eternal love. / 这个人早把他们的～抛到脑后了。He has long forgotten their solemn pledge of mutual fidelity.
山民 shānmín mountain inhabitants; hill folk
山明水秀 shānmíng-shuǐxiù *also* "山清水秀" bright mountains and limpid waters; green hills and clear waters; beautiful scenery: ～的江南 picturesque scenery south of the Yangtze / 这是个～的游览胜地。This is an attractive scenic spot.
山鸣谷应 shānmíng-gǔyìng (of people) find each other very congenial; hit it off
山姆大叔 Shānmǔ Dàshū Uncle Sam — popular name for the United States of America or its government
山奈 shānnài *also* "山萘"〈化学〉cyanide
山南海北 shānnán-hǎiběi ❶ remote places; remote corners of the earth: ～，到处流浪。He has been wandering far and wide. / 无论～，我都要跟你走。No matter where, I'll follow you closely. *or* I'll follow you to the far corners of the earth. ❷ chat aimlessly: ～地神聊 chat about everything under the sun; shoot the breeze (*or* bull)
山南塞北 shānnán-sàiběi north and south over hills and plains: 从此以后，我走遍～，那双袜子，整整穿了三年。After that, trudging north and south over hills and plains, I wore that pair of socks for three whole years.
山炮 shānpào mountain gun; mountain artillery
山棚 shānpéng 〈方言〉❶ mat shed where bundles of straw are placed for silkworms to spin cocoons ❷〈旧语〉decorated archway; make-shift stage for performances
山坪 shānpíng level ground in mountainous regions
山坡 shānpō hillside; mountain slope

S

山气 shānqì mountain mist
山墙 shānqiáng 〈建筑〉gable
山清水秀 shānqīng-shuǐxiù *see*"山明水秀"
山箐 shānqìng 〈方言〉wooded valley
山穷水尽 shānqióng-shuǐjìn where the mountains and the rivers end — be at the end of one's rope or resources; be in predicament: 我现在已经到了~的地步。I am at the end of my tether now.
山丘 shānqiū ❶ hillock: ~起伏。Hillocks rise and fall. ❷〈书面〉tomb; grave
山区 shānqū mountainous area
山泉 shānquán mountain spring: ~丁东 bubbling springs /永不干涸的~ mountain spring which never runs dry; ever-flowing spring
山雀 shānquè tit
山人 shānrén 〈旧语〉❶ hermit or recluse (in feudal China, men of letters and officials sometimes referred to themselves as "*shanren*") ❷ person who makes a living as fortune-teller, diviner, etc.
山上有山 shānshàng-yǒushān ❶ away from home ❷ (often used to refer to) husband
山水 shānshuǐ ❶ water from a mountain: 用~灌溉田地 irrigate the fields with the water from the mountain ❷ mountains and waters; scenery with hills and streams: 两省~相连。The two provinces are linked by common mountains and rivers. /桂林~甲天下。The scenery of Guilin is second to none on earth. ❸〈美术〉traditional Chinese painting of mountains and waters; landscape
山水画 shānshuǐhuà landscape painting; landscape: 这位画家擅长~。This artist is expert in landscape painting.
山水记 shānshuǐjì landscape essay
山塘 shāntáng mountain pond or pool; tarn
山桃 shāntáo mountain peach
山田 shāntián hillside plot
山桐子 shāntóngzǐ 〈植物〉idesia
山头 shāntóu ❶ top of a mountain; hilltop ❷ mountain stronghold; faction: 拉~ form a faction
山头主义 shāntóuzhǔyì mountain stronghold mentality; factionalism; sectarianism
山洼 shānwā depression in the mountains; mountain valley
山外有山 shānwài-yǒushān there's a mountain beyond the mountain — there's always somebody or something better; one should always be modest
山窝 shānwō out-of-the-way mountain area; remote mountain area
山坞 shānwù col or nook in the hills
山西 Shānxī Shanxi (Province)
山西梆子 Shānxī bāngzi Shanxi clapper opera, a local opera popular in Shanxi Province
山系 shānxì 〈地质〉mountain system
山峡 shānxiá gorge; canyon; ravine
山险 shānxiǎn narrow mountain pass; defile: 扼守~ hold a narrow mountain pass
山乡 shānxiāng mountain area: ~人家 inhabitants in a mountainous area /~僻壤 remote mountainous area
山响 shānxiǎng very noisy; deafening; thunderous: 桌子拍得~ pound the desk angrily /拍得门~ knock on the door thunderously
山向 shānxiàng 〈旧语〉direction which a grave faces
山魈 shānxiāo ❶〈动物〉mandrill ❷ legendary one-legged mountain spirit
山鸦 shānyā chough
山崖 shānyá cliff; crag
山羊 shānyáng ❶ goat ❷ *also*"跳跃器" tiàoyuèqì 〈体育〉buck
山羊胡子 shānyáng húzi man's small pointed beard; goatee
山羊绒 shānyángróng cashmere
山阳 shānyáng southern or sunny side of a mountain; adret
山杨 shānyáng 〈植物〉mountain poplar (*Populus davidina*)
山腰 shānyāo *also*"半山腰" bànshānyāo halfway up the mountain
山肴野蔌 shānyáo-yěsù 〈书面〉game and edible wild herbs; local dishes
山摇地动 shānyáo-dìdòng *also*"地动山摇" hills topple and the earth quakes — come with great force and momentum: 喊杀声~。The cry of charge shook the mountains. /大官出行，~。When a big official travels, it is a loud scene.
山药 shānyao ❶〈植物〉Chinese yam ❷〈方言〉potato
山药蛋 shānyaodàn 〈方言〉potato
山野 shānyě ❶ mountains and plains ❷ countryside: ~村夫 country bumpkin; rustic
山阴 shānyīn northern or shady side of a mountain
山阴道上 shānyīn dàoshàng beautiful scenic spots south of the lower reaches of the Yangtze River
山雨欲来风满楼 shānyǔ yù lái fēng mǎn lóu a strong wind blowing in the tower heralds an impending storm in the mountains; a rising wind forebodes a coming storm: 眼前，那里是一种~的形势。At present everything there indicates that a political storm is imminent.
山芋 shānyù 〈方言〉sweet potato
山鹬 shānyù 〈动物〉woodcock
山岳 shānyuè lofty mountains: 云贵一带，~相连。Yunnan and Guizhou provinces are connected by big mountains.
山岳冰川 shānyuè bīngchuān mountain glacier
山晕 shānyùn reaction to high altitudes
山查 shānzhā *see*"山楂"
山楂 shānzhā *also*"山查"〈植物〉❶ (Chinese) hawthorn ❷ haw
山楂糕 shānzhāgāo *also*"山查糕" haw jelly
山楂酱 shānzhājiàng haw jam
山寨 shānzhài fortified mountain village; mountain fortress; mountain fastness
山珍海味 shānzhēn-hǎiwèi *also*"山珍海错" mountain delicacies and seafood delights; delicacies of every kind
山志学 shānzhìxué orography
山中无老虎,猴子称大王 shānzhōng wú lǎohǔ, hóuzi chēng dàwáng the monkey rules the mountain when there is no tiger; in the kingdom of the blind, the one-eyed man rules
山中宰相 shānzhōng zǎixiàng virtuous and talented people who lived in seclusion and refused official posts but who gave counsel when asked by the imperial court
山茱萸 shānzhūyú 〈中药〉fruit of medicinal cornel (*Cornus officinalis*)
山庄 shānzhuāng ❶ mountain village ❷ mountain villa
山子 shānzi 〈方言〉*also*"山子石儿" rockery
山陬海澨 shānzōu-hǎishì 〈书面〉foot of a mountain and side of a sea — remote place
山嘴 shānzuǐ 〈地质〉spur
山鳟 shānzūn cutthroat trout (*Salmo clarki*)

舢 shān sampan

舢板 shānbǎn sampan
舢舨 shānbǎn *see*"舢板"

埏 shān 〈书面〉mix water with clay

芟 shān ❶ mow (grass) ❷ weed out; get rid of; eliminate

芟除 shānchú ❶ mow; weed out; cut down: ~杂草 cutting weeds; weeding ❷ delete; strike out: ~冗词赘句 delete redundant words and sentences; eliminate redundancies
芟秋 shānqiū *also*"删秋" shānqiū weed an autumn field for better crops
芟夷 shānyí *also*"芟荑"〈书面〉❶ uproot wild grass; weed ❷ eliminate (certain forces)
芟荑 shānyí *see*"芟夷"

衫 shān unlined upper garment: 衬~ shirt /衣~ clothes /棉毛~ cotton (*or* interlock) jersey /罩~ overall; dustcoat /恤~ T-shirt /海魂~ jumper /衣~褴褛 be in rags

衫子 shānzi 〈方言〉unlined upper garment

杉 shān 〈植物〉China fir

see also shā

钐 shān 〈化学〉samarium (Sm)

see also shàn

钐中毒 shānzhòngdú samarium poisoning

珊(珊) shān

珊瑚 shānhú coral: ~盆景 coral potted landscape

珊瑚菜 shānhúcài *Glehnia littoralis*
珊瑚虫 shānhúchóng coral polyp; coral worm
珊瑚岛 shānhúdǎo coral island
珊瑚海 Shānhúhǎi Coral Sea, a part of the Pacific lying between Australia, New Guinea and Vanuatu
珊瑚礁 shānhújiāo coral reef
珊瑚树 shānhúshù *Viburnum odoratissimum*
珊瑚在网 shānhú-zàiwǎng coral in the net — talented people are recruited

栅(柵) shān
see also zhà
栅格 shāngé 〈物理〉grid; lattice; cell:～结构 lattice structure /～反应堆 lattice reactor
栅极 shānjí 〈电工〉grid:抑制～ suppressor grid /～电路 grid circuit /～辉光放电管 grid-glow tube
栅控管 shānkòngguǎn 〈电子〉grid control tube
栅漏 shānlòu 〈电子〉grid leak:～检波器 grid-leak detector
栅条管 shāntiáoguǎn 〈电子〉grid tube

跚 shān *see*"蹒跚" pánshān

删(刪) shān delete; strike out; leave out:把这几个字～掉。Leave out those few words. /这一段可以～去。This paragraph can be crossed out. /这篇文章要大～大改。This essay will have to be radically revised.
删除 shānchú delete; remove; cut out; cross out:这本书的后两章已被～。The last two chapters of the book have been cut out.
删除文件 shānchú wénjiàn 〈信息〉delete file; kill file
删定 shāndìng revise and finalize (a manuscript, clause, article, etc.)
删繁就简 shānfán-jiùjiǎn simplify by weeding out superfluities:初稿写成之后,他又～,修改再三,方才定稿。He simplified and revised the first draft again and again before it was finalized.
删改 shāngǎi prune away; revise:略微～ touch up /大加～ make numerous (*or* radical) changes /几经～ revise several times /在～上下功夫 take pains to polish an essay /经过～后文意更显豁。After revision, the theme of the essay stands out more conspicuously.
删减 shānjiǎn abridge or condense an article
删节 shānjié abridge; abbreviate:发表时作了某些～ be slightly condensed before publication /由原本～而来 abridged from the original
删节本 shānjiéběn abridged edition; abbreviated version
删节号 shānjiéhào ellipsis; suspension points; ellipsis dots (……) (...)
删略 shānlüè delete; omit; leave out:前三段似可～为一段。It is advisable to combine the first three paragraphs into one after some deletion. /文稿篇幅过长,须～割爱。The article is a little lengthy and we will have to cut it short, though not without some regret.
删秋 shānqiū *also*"芟秋" shānqiū weed an autumn field for better crops
删润 shānrùn revise and polish a manuscript
删汰 shāntài eliminate; delete; strike off:文章过长,宜略加～。The essay is too long, it needs some trimming.
删削 shānxuē remove; strike out; cut out:必须将一切旁枝末节～以尽。Insignificant details or ideas that tend to branch out must be removed. /编辑不可以胡乱～。Editors must not cut out more from the manuscripts than is absolutely necessary.

姗(姍) shān
姗姗 shānshān slowly; leisurely:～而来 walk towards one in a leisurely fashion
姗姗来迟 shānshān-láichí be slow in coming; arrive late:你为何～? Why are you so late? /今年春天～。This year's spring has arrived late.

shǎn

闪 shǎn ❶ move quickly to one side; dodge:请大家～开,让他们过去。Will you please make way for them. /人群中～开了一条路。The crowd moved swiftly to either side, forming a lane. ❷ twist:路很滑,他身子一～,跌倒了。He tripped and fell, for the road was slippery. ❸ sprain:～了手腕 sprain one's wrist ❹ lightning:我看到夜空正在打～。I saw flashes of lightning in the night sky. ❺ flash:黑暗里～出一个人来。Someone darted out of the darkness. /一个念头～过我的脑子。Suddenly an idea flashed across my mind. ❻ sparkle; shine:空中星光一～一～的。The stars are twinkling in the sky. /你瞧,有什么东西在～。Look, something is sparkling. /有人在门外～起手电。Somebody was using a torchlight outside. ❼〈方言〉leave behind:夜行军时,大家一起走,不要把谁～下。Let's keep close on the night march so nobody will be left behind. ❽ (Shǎn) a surname
闪避 shǎnbì duck; dodge; sidestep:看见一辆轿车疾驰而来,他连忙～。He dodged to one side when he saw a car speeding in his direction.
闪长岩 shǎnchángyán diorite
闪挫 shǎncuò 〈中医〉sudden strain or contusion of a muscle; wrenching and contusion; sprain:～腰痛 wrenched lumbus pain
闪错 shǎncuò mishap and mistake; error; mistake
闪道 shǎndào dodge and get out of the way; make way for:赶快～! Hurry and get out of the way. /闪开道让车过去。Please make way for the car.
闪点 shǎndiǎn 〈化学〉flash point
闪电 shǎndiàn lightning:一道～划破长空。A flash of lightning shot across the sky. /他～般地冲入火中,把孩子救了出来。In a flash, he dashed into the blaze and rescued the child.
闪电战 shǎndiànzhàn lightning warfare; blitzkrieg; blitz
闪动 shǎndòng (of light or objects) move fast; shine off and on; scintillate; flash:烛光～。The candle lights were flashing. /远处有个人影在～。There was the shadow of a man moving back and forth in the distance.
闪躲 shǎnduǒ avoid; dodge; evade:一时～不开,被他撞了一下。I was too slow to dodge and he literally bumped into me. /他有意～我的目光。He deliberately avoided my gaze.
闪光 shǎnguāng ❶ glisten; glitter:萤火虫在草丛中闪着光。Fireflies glowed among the grasses. ❷ flash of light:远处闪着光,也许前头就是村落。Lights are flashing in the distance; maybe, there is a village ahead. /～后接着就是雷声。There was a flash of light followed by a loud crash of thunder.
闪光灯 shǎnguāngdēng ❶〈摄影〉flash (light) (of a camera) ❷ main component of a beacon light (with electric, gas or gasoline light as its source)
闪光对头焊 shǎnguāng duìtóuhàn flash-butt welding
闪光同步 shǎnguāng tóngbù 〈摄影〉flash synchronization; synchronous flash
闪弧 shǎnhú 〈电学〉flashing
闪忽 shǎnhu *also*"忽闪" flash; gleam; glitter
闪击 shǎnjī surprise attack:对敌～ spring a surprise attack on the enemy
闪击战 shǎnjīzhàn *see*"闪电战"
闪开 shǎnkāi get out of the way; step aside quickly; dodge:人们纷纷向两旁～。Many people quickly stepped aside. /房门只～一条缝。The door was only opened a chink.
闪亮 shǎnliàng ❶ glisten; glitter:～的泪珠 glistening tears /这件服装上的小缀片到了台上就会～。These little spangles on the costume will sparkle on the stage. ❷〈方言〉dawn; daybreak:我来到县城时,天才～。It was barely dawn when I arrived at the county seat.
闪露 shǎnlù flash:脸上～出焦虑的神色。Anxiety flashed across his face.
闪络 shǎnluò 〈电工〉flashover; arc-over:～电压 flashover voltage /～试验 flashover test; sparkover test
闪米特人 Shǎnmǐtèrén *also*"闪族" Semites, any of the peoples said to be descended from Shem, son of Noah, including esp. the Jews, Arabs, Assyrians and Phoenicians; Semitic people
闪面 shǎnmiàn 〈方言〉❶ meet; see:两人闪了面,谁也不搭理谁。They cut each other dead when they meet. ❷ show up; appear:近来他在交际场合很少～。He has seldom appeared on social occasions recently.
闪念 shǎnniàn sudden idea flashing across one's mind; flash of inspiration:只是一～,没有深思。It was merely a sudden flash of inspiration; I didn't give the matter serious thought.
闪燃点 shǎnrándiǎn 〈物理〉flash point
闪让 shǎnràng step aside; make way for:给汽车～道路 step aside to let the car pass

S

闪闪 shǎnshǎn sparkle; twinkle; glisten; glitter:此人双目～有凶光。There's a cruel glitter in his eyes. /她双目～有泪痕。Her eyes glistened with tears. /夜空中电光～。Flashes of lightning darted across the night sky.

闪射 shǎnshè blaze; glisten; sparkle:他两眼～着愤怒的光芒。His eyes are ablaze with fury.

闪身 shǎnshēn dodge; step sideways: ～进门 step sideways through the door /他～躲开迎面飞来的石子。He dodged nimbly to evade a flying stone. *or* He dodged a flying stone.

闪失 shǎnshī mishap; accident:这次执行任务,决不能有～。Make sure that the mission is carried out without a hitch.

闪石 shǎnshí 〈矿业〉amphibole

闪烁 shǎnshuò ❶ twinkle; glitter; glimmer; glisten:星光～。The stars twinkled. /灯光～。The lights glimmered. /他额头上～着汗珠。His brow glistened with sweat. ❷ evasive; vague; equivocal; noncommittal:对那件事,他总是闪闪烁烁,不肯说清楚。He is evasive and equivocal on that matter. ❸〈物理〉blinking

闪烁计数器 shǎnshuò jìshùqì scintillation counter; scintillation detector; scintillometer

闪烁其词 shǎnshuò-qící dodge about; evade issues; speak hesitatingly; hedge:他～,令人难以捉摸。He hemmed and hawed, and no one knew what he was driving at.

闪烁扫描 shǎnshuò sǎomiáo scintiscan

闪烁照相图 shǎnshuò zhàoxiàngtú scintiphotogram

闪现 shǎnxiàn flash; appear in a flash; come into view:心中～出希望之光。A ray of hope flashed across his mind.

闪锌矿 shǎnxīnkuàng 〈矿业〉zinc blende; sphalerite

闪眼 shǎnyǎn 〈方言〉❶ dazzling:灯光照得有点～。The lights are a bit dazzling. ❷ holes in ice (on rivers, lakes, etc.):小心冰上的～。Watch out for holes in the ice.

闪耀 shǎnyào glitter; flash; shine; radiate:晴空万里,阳光～。The sun is shining brightly in the clear boundless sky. /她的眼里～着兴奋的光芒。Her eyes flashed with excitement.

闪熠 shǎnyì 〈书面〉glitter; shine; flash; radiate:灯火～。The lights glittered.

闪音 shǎnyīn 〈语言〉flap

闪映 shǎnyìng flash before one:碧波～。The rippling waves sparkled. /雷电忽明忽暗,～着岗哨的身影。The silhouette of the sentry flickered in the flashes of lightning.

闪语族 Shǎnyǔzú Semitic languages group (including Arabic, Hebrew, Aramaic, Amharic, etc.)

闪蒸 shǎnzhēng 〈化工〉flashing; flash vaporization:～分离 flash separation /～釜 flashing kettle; flashing vessel /～室 flash chamber; flash trap; flash vessel

闪蒸塔 shǎnzhēngtǎ flash tower

闪灼 shǎnzhuó shine; glitter; flicker:烛光～。The candlelight flickered. /他那双眼睛～着充满信心和勇敢的光芒。His eyes shone with confidence and courage.

掺(摻) shǎn 〈书面〉hold; grasp:～手 shake hands

see also càn; chān

睒(睒) shǎn blink; wink:飞机一～眼就不见了。The plane vanished in the twinkling of an eye. /一～眼的功夫,他就溜得没影儿了。He slipped out and disappeared in no time.

陕(陝) Shǎn (short for 陕西) Shaanxi Province

陕西 Shǎnxī Shaanxi (Province)

陕西梆子 Shǎnxī bāngzi *also* "秦腔" qínqiāng Shaanxi clapper opera, a local opera popular in Shaanxi Province

shàn

擅 shàn ❶ do sth. without the approval or prior knowledge of one's superior; act on one's own authority:～作主张 act without authorization ❷ be good at; be versed in; be expert in:不～辞令 not have the gift of gab; not be good at speech /～画人物 be expert in painting portraits /不～应酬 not good at socializing; not mix well with people

擅便 shànbiàn 〈书面〉act presumptuously:未敢～,呈请定夺。As I do not wish to presume, I present this matter to you for final decision.

擅长 shàncháng be good at; be expert in; be (well) versed in; be skilled in:他～篆刻。He is skilled in seal cutting. /编藤器是他的～。He is good at weaving rattan utensils. /他有许多～。He is a man of many parts. *or* He is versatile.

擅场 shànchǎng 〈书面〉surpass all others in skill:他以超群的演奏技艺独得～。He surpassed all other contestants with his superb performance.

擅断 shànduàn arbitrary; dictatorial:～孤行 act arbitrarily

擅离职守 shànlí-zhíshǒu be absent from one's post without leave; leave one's post without permission

擅利 shànlì 〈商业〉enjoy monopoly

擅美 shànměi 〈书面〉claim all credit for oneself; get all the credit:～当时 get all the credit of one's time

擅名 shànmíng be well-known; be famous:～一时 enjoy a widespread reputation at the time

擅权 shànquán monopolize power; hold absolute power; assume dictatorial power; usurp power

擅自 shànzì act without authorization:～行动 act presumptuously /～涨价和变相涨价 raise prices without authorization and sometimes in a disguised way /他未经集体讨论～改变了行动方案。He changed the plan of action without collective deliberation.

擅作威福 shànzuò-wēifú (of an official) punish or reward at one's pleasure

嬗 shàn 〈书面〉❶ change; alternation; evolution:汉语古今代～,有很大变化。The Chinese language has gone through great changes from the classical to the modern form. ❷ *also* "禅" shàn abdicate the throne in favour of another person

嬗变 shànbiàn ❶〈书面〉change; evolution:这个展览会显示了中国服装的～。The exhibition is a display of the changes of the Chinese costume. /他认真研究中国古典诗歌之～。He made a serious study of the evolution of classical Chinese poetry. ❷〈物理〉transmutation:自然～ natural transmutation /感应～ induced transmutation

嬗替 shàntì 〈书面〉change and be replaced; evolve:自然科学就是在生产实践和科学实验的基础上,通过各种新旧理论的不断～,而向前发展的。It is on the basis of production and scientific experiments and through the constant evolution of theories with the new replacing the old that natural sciences develop and move forward.

善 shàn ❶ good:～恶分明 distinguish good from evil /改恶从～ give up evil and return to good; mend one's ways /心地～良 kind-hearted /慈眉～目 have a benevolent look /心怀不～ ill-intentioned /与人为～ be sincere and warmhearted towards others /勿以～小而不为,勿以恶小而为之。Do not fail to do a good deed because it is small; do not do a bad deed because it is small. ❷ benevolent act; good deed:行～ do good deeds /劝～规过 advise people to do good and refrain from evil ❸ satisfactory; good:～策 wise move; best policy /尽～尽美 perfect ❹ friendly; kind:相～ be friendly with each other ❺ familiar:面～ look familiar ❻ make a success of; do well:改～ improve /独～其身 give sole attention to improvement of one's own moral character ❼ be good at; be expert in:能言～辩 be able to speak and argue effectively; be eloquent /能歌～舞 good at singing and dancing /～用兵 be versed in the art of war /博学～文 be full of learning and able to write well ❽ properly:～视之 treat sb. with courtesy /～自为谋 consider the matter carefully before making up one's mind /要～自保重 hope that he will take good care of himself ❾ be apt or liable to:多愁～感 be sentimental and susceptible ❿ (Shàn) a surname

善罢甘休 shànbà-gānxiū (often used in the negative) let the matter rest; let it go at that:她哪里肯～。How could she take it lying down? *or* Surely, she won't let the matter go at that.

善报 shànbào reward the good; receive good reward:善人将得～。A good man will be rewarded.

善辈 shànbèi 〈书面〉good people; nice people

善本 shànběn (usu. of a handwritten or block-printed ancient book) reliable text; good edition:～书 rare book (of a good edition)

善变 shànbiàn be apt to change; be fickle:此人多疑～。He is a suspicious and unpredictable character.

善才 shàncái name for famous *pipa* players (in the Tang Dynasty)

善处 shànchǔ 〈书面〉 deal properly with:盼～此事 It is hoped that the matter will be handled with caution.
善待 shàndài treat sb. nicely:～来使 well treat the envoy
善刀而藏 shàndāo'ércáng wipe a sword clean and store it — know where or when to stop
善感 shàngǎn oversensitive; sentimental:多愁～ sentimental
善棍 shàngùn 〈旧语〉 charity racketeer
善果 shànguǒ reward of good deeds; good results:行善事,结～。Reap good results by doing good deeds.
善后 shànhòu properly handle the remaining problems (of an accident, war etc.):做好～工作 properly handle problems that are likely to arise in the aftermath /～事宜由我们负责。We'll take care of the remaining problems.
善静 shànjìng 〈方言〉 (of temperament, attitude, language, etc.) gentle and kind; sincere and honest
善举 shànjǔ 〈书面〉 charitable act:共襄～ make a concerted effort to ensure the success of a charitable activity
善类 shànlèi 〈书面〉 (often used in the negative) good and honest people:此人并非～。The man is not the honest sort.
善良 shànliáng good and honest, kind-hearted; kind:本性～ good and kind by nature /～的心愿 good intentions; best of intentions /她对人一向～。She is always kind to everyone.
善邻 shànlín 〈书面〉 have friendly relations with one's neighbours or neighbouring countries; be a good neighbour
善门 shànmén 〈旧语〉 philanthropic people
善男信女 shànnán-xìnnǚ 〈佛教〉 religious believers; devout men and women:～们不远千里来朝香。Devout believers made light of a thousand-*li* pilgrimage.
善人 shànrén charitable person; philanthropist:～自有天佑。Providence helps good people. /～好欺,善马好骑。Honest people are easy to take advantage of, and good horses are easy to ride.
善善恶恶 shànshàn-wù'è love the good and shun the evil; be clear about what to love and what to hate
善始善终 shànshǐ-shànzhōng begin well and end well; stick it out; see sth. through:希望各位都能～。It is our hope that everybody will stick to the very last now that you have started. /这项工作又难又单调,好些人都不能～。As this kind of task is very difficult and dull, few people can see it through.
善士 shànshì ❶ benevolent person; good man ❷ 〈宗教〉 one who is converted to Buddhism but remains a layman
善事 shànshì good deeds; charitable work
善书 shànshū ❶ rare book; rare edition ❷ book which admonishes people to do good deeds
善堂 shàntáng 〈旧语〉 charity institution which takes in orphans, provides relief to the poor, etc.
善忘 shànwàng forgetful; prone to forget; having a short or bad memory
善为说辞 shànwéishuōcí put in a good word for sb.; intercede for sb.:你见了他,好歹替我～。When you see him, could you put in a good word for me, please?
善心 shànxīn mercy; kindness:我不相信他有一天会发～。I don't think he will one day become kind-hearted.
善行 shànxíng good conduct; kind deed
善意 shànyì good will; good intentions; bona fides:怀有～ with goodwill; out of goodwill /～的忠告 well-meaning advice /答谢他人的～ express appreciation for their kind intentions
善有善报,恶有恶报 shàn yǒu shànbào, è yǒu èbào good will be rewarded with good, and evil with evil; every good or bad deed has its just reward:～;不是不报,时候不到。Good and evil will always be rewarded; it is only a question of time.
善于 shànyú be good at; be versed in; be adept at:～团结群众 know how to rally the broad masses of the people /～交际 be skilful at socializing (*or* striking up acquaintances) /～辞令 have a ready tongue
善与人交 shànyǔrénjiāo be good at making acquaintances or friends
善战 shànzhàn fight like a seasoned soldier; be skilful in battle:这些部队都是英勇～的。These troops are all brave and seasoned warriors.
善终 shànzhōng ❶ die a natural death; die in one's bed; die of old age:此人作恶多端,难得～。This man is steeped in iniquity and will not die in bed. ❷ end well; see sth. through:此事已近尾声,务望～。The matter is drawing to a close. It is our sincere hope that you will manage to see it through.
善自为谋 shànzìwéimóu know how to plan for oneself:情势多变,望君～。The situation is unpredictable. I hope you will take good care of yourself.

墡 shàn white clay

蟮 shàn *see* "曲蟮" qūshan

膳(饍) shàn meals; board:早～ breakfast /午～ lunch /用～ eat one's meals
膳费 shànfèi board expenses
膳食 shànshí meals; food:流质～ liquid diet /半流质～ semiliquid diet /～结构 diet structure
膳宿 shànsù board and lodging:～自理 make one's own board and lodging arrangements; pay for one's own board and lodging

鳝(鱓) shàn eel; finless eel
鳝鱼 shànyú eel; rice paddy eel

缮 shàn ❶ repair; fix; mend:修～ repair /修～内部,暂停开放。Closed under repair. ❷ copy; write out:议定书用汉英两种文字各～一份。The protocol is written in two texts, Chinese and English.
缮发 shànfā copy and dispatch:文件须立刻～。The document is to be copied and dispatched instantly.
缮校 shànjiào copy and check against authoritative text
缮写 shànxiě write out; copy:～清楚 make a clean copy

单(單) Shàn a surname
see also chán; dān

禅(禪) shàn abdicate (from) the throne in favour of another person:受～ accept the abdicated throne
see also chán
禅让 shànràng abdicate the throne in favour of another person
禅位 shànwèi abdicate the throne

墠(壇) shàn 〈旧语〉 level ground as a site for holding rituals

掸(撣) Shàn ❶ reference in Chinese annals to the Dai nationality ❷ one of the Burmese nationalities, most of whom live in the state of Shan
see also dǎn

掞 shàn 〈书面〉 extended; lavish:～张 exaggerate; boast /～丽 ostentatious and flowery (diction)

扇 shàn ❶ fan:折～ folding fan /蒲～ cattail leaf fan; fan /电～ electric fan; ventilator /吊～ pendant fan /宫～ mandarin fan /绢～ silk fan /葵～ palm fan /檀香～ sandalwood fan /羽～ feather fan /通风～ draft fan /团～ round fan (without folds) /落地摇头～ electric vacillating fan with adjustable stand /台～ table fan ❷ leaf:门～ door leaf /隔～ partition ❸ 〈量词〉 *used of windows, doors, etc.*: 一～窗户 a window
see also shān
扇贝 shànbèi *also* "海扇" hǎishàn 〈动物〉 scallop; fan shell:～养殖 scallop culture
扇车 shànchē *also* "风车" fēngchē winnowing machine; winnower
扇骨 shàngǔ *also* "扇骨子" ribs or mount of a fan
扇画 shànhuà fan painting
扇面儿 shànmiànr covering of a fan
扇形 shànxíng ❶ fan-shaped:～窗子 fan-shaped window /～构造 fan structure /他把牌在手上展成～。He fanned out the cards in his hands. ❷ 〈数学〉 sector:园之～ sector of a circle /～扫描 sector scanning
扇形齿轮 shànxíng chǐlún 〈机械〉 sector gear
扇形风 shànxíngfēng 〈气象〉 sector wind

扇形航空发动机 shànxíng hángkōng fādòngjī 〈航空〉fan-type airplane engine
扇叶 shànyè 〈动物〉flabellum
扇坠 shànzhuì pendant attached to a fan
扇子 shànzi fan

骟

shàn castrate; geld; spay: ～马 castrating (*or* gelding) a stud; gelded horse

苫

shàn cover with a straw mat, tarpaulin, etc.: 拿席子把货物～上 cover the cargo with a straw mat
see also shān
苫背 shànbèi (of building) cover straw or mats with plaster to form the base of a roof
苫布 shànbù tarpaulin
苫席 shànxí straw or reed mat

汕

Shàn (short for 汕头) Shantou, Guangdong Province
汕头 Shàntóu Shantou (formerly translated as Swatow), a major port city of Guangdong Province

疝

shàn hernia
疝带 shàndài 〈医学〉truss
疝气 shànqì 〈医学〉hernia: 腹股沟～ inguinal hernia / 脐～ unbilical hernia

讪

shàn ❶ mock; scorn; ridicule: ～笑 ridicule; deride ❷ embarrassed; discomfited; awkward; shamefaced: 脸上发～ look embarrassed
讪谤 shànbàng 〈书面〉malign; slander; vilify; calumniate
讪不搭的 shànbudāde *also* "讪搭搭的" ill at ease; embarrassed; ashamed: 他被我抢白了几句，～笑了笑。At my satirical remarks, he smiled shamefacedly.
讪脸 shànliǎn 〈方言〉(of children) grin roguishly; behave impudently: 不准和爷爷～。Don't play the rogue before grandpa.
讪骂 shànmà rail; hurl abuses: 大声～ rail
讪讪 shànshàn embarrassed; ill at ease; ashamed: 他觉得没趣，只好～地走开了。Feeling snubbed, he left in embarrassment. / 她～地红了脸。She flushed with shame (*or* embarrassment).
讪笑 shànxiào ridicule; scoff; mock; deride: 被人～ be mocked by others / 此言一出，～随之。These words immediately triggered mockery.

赸

shàn 〈书面〉hide oneself; go away; vanish

钐（鐥、釤）

shàn 〈方言〉cut with a sickle: ～草 cut grass with a sickle
see also shān
钐镰 shànlián *also* "钐刀" scythe

赡

shàn ❶ support; keep; provide for: ～家养口 support a family / 收～孤寡 provide for orphaned children and widowed people ❷〈书面〉adequate; sufficient; abundant: 气力不～ lack strength / 典～ copiously quote authoritative works (*or* the classics)
赡养 shànyǎng support; maintain; provide for: ～亲属 support one's family members
赡养费 shànyǎngfèi alimony; support payments

shāng

商[1]

shāng ❶ talk over; discuss; consult: 面～ discuss with sb. in person; consult personally / 洽～ take counsel together / 三方会～ hold a tripartite talk over sth. / ～后再定 make a decision after consultation ❷ trade; commerce; transaction; business: 通～ trade (with) / 经～ be in business / 招～ invite investment ❸ merchant; businessman; salesman; dealer: 小～ pedlar / 客～ travelling trader / 零售～ retailer / 批发～ wholesaler / 外～ foreign businessman / 奸～ profiteer / 坐～ tradesman (as opposite to itinerant merchant); shopkeeper ❹〈数学〉quotient

商[2]

shāng ❶〈音乐〉note of the ancient Chinese five-tone scale, correspond to 2 in numbered musical notation ❷ Heart Constellation of the 28 constellations in ancient astronomy

商[3]

Shāng ❶ Shang Dynasty (c. 17th-11th centuries BC) ❷ a surname
商办 shāngbàn 〈旧语〉privately owned: ～工业 privately-owned industrial enterprises
商标 shāngbiāo trademark: ～图案 trademark design / 假冒～ fake trademarks / 盗用～ usurp a trademark / ～名称 brand name / ～所有权 trademark ownership / ～注册人 trademark registrant / ～专用权 exclusive right to trademark / 这种商品既无～又无生产厂家，一定是伪劣品。These must be shoddy goods as they have no trademark or manufacturer's name on them.
商标法 shāngbiāofǎ trademark law
商标权 shāngbiāoquán trademark ownership; trademark right
商标注册 shāngbiāo zhùcè trademark registration
商埠 shāngbù 〈旧语〉commercial or trading port
商场 shāngchǎng ❶ market; bazaar; mall: 新建的～ newly built market / 规模很大的～ large bazaar / 这是个专营小百货的～。This is a store that sells mainly small articles of everyday use. ❷ large department store ❸ market in a general sense, meaning commercial or business circles, whether of a particular line or more broadly speaking: 经过几年的奋斗，他在～站住了脚。After several years of hard work, he has gained a solid foothold in business. / ～有如战场。The business world is just like a battlefield.
商筹 shāngchóu discuss; consult: ～对策 discuss a countermeasure (*or* countermove)
商船 shāngchuán merchant ship; merchantman: ～船长 master mariner / ～航线 shipping route
商船队 shāngchuánduì mercantile marine; merchant fleet
商店 shāngdiàn shop; store: 百货～ department store / 儿童用品～ children's goods store / 日夜～ day-and-night store / ～橱窗 shopwindow / ～营业时间 shop hours / 开～ run a shop / 国有～ state-owned store / ～的货源充足。The store is well stocked. / ～的信誉最重要。The reputation of a shop is of primary importance.
商调 shāngdiào transfer sb. to another work post through discussion of the two parties concerned; discuss with another unit for the transfer of one of its men
商调函 shāngdiàohán letter requesting transfer of personnel
商定 shāngdìng decide through consultation; arrive at an agreement; agree: 编委会～下一期稿件。The editorial board decided on the articles to be published in the coming issue. / 拆迁的方案已经～。The plan for pulling down the old houses and evacuating the residents has been drawn up through consultation. / 两国首脑会晤日期已经～。The date for the meeting of the heads of the two states has been agreed on.
商队 shāngduì company of travelling merchants; trade caravan: 这支～对活跃城乡贸易起了很好的作用。The trade cavavan played a positive role in invigorating trade between town and country.
商兑 shāngduì 〈书面〉discussion; consultation
商法 shāngfǎ 〈法律〉commercial law; mercantile law
商贩 shāngfàn small retailer; pedlar: 个体～ self-employed vendor / 不法～ law-breaking pedlar
商港 shānggǎng commercial port
商工部 Shānggōngbù (ROK) Ministry of Trade and Industry
商贾 shānggǔ 〈书面〉merchants; businessmen: ～云集。Merchants came in large numbers.
商行 shāngháng trading company; commercial firm
商号 shānghào shop; firm; store; business establishment
商号注册法 shānghào zhùcèfǎ registration of business names act
商户 shānghù *also* "商家" businessman
商会 shānghuì chamber of commerce: ～会长 chairman of the chamber of commerce / ～董事 director of the chamber of commerce
商计 shāngjì discussion; consultation; consideration: 此事尚需～。The matter calls for further consideration.
商检 shāngjiǎn (short for 商品检验) commodity inspection: ～局 commodity inspection bureau / ～部门 commodity inspection departments / ～工作 commodity inspection (work) / ～人员 commodity inspector

商界 shāngjiè business world; commercial circles:他在~交了许多朋友。He made many friends in the world of business. /他与~关系密切。He has close connections (*or* links) with business circles.
商籁体 shānglàitǐ sonnet
商量 shāngliang consult; discuss; exchange views; talk over:~对策 discuss countermeasures /他是以~的口气跟我谈的。He was soliciting my advice when he brought up the matter. /~的结果还没有告诉他们。They have not been informed of the result of the discussion. /有事要同群众~。Consult the masses when something comes up. /这事我们要~一下。We have to talk the matter over.
商路 shānglù trade route:古代,甘肃、新疆有通向西亚的~。In ancient times, there were trade routes in Gansu and Xinjiang leading to western Asia.
商旅 shānglǚ tradesman and traveller:过往~ tradesmen and travellers passing through the place
商民 shāngmín businessmen or trades people (as a class)
商贸 shāngmào business and trade:~企业 business and trading firm
商棚 shāngpéng stall (for selling goods)
商品 shāngpǐn commodity; goods; merchandise:~丰富 great variety of goods; abundant supply of commodities /~交换 exchange of commodities /~制度 commodity system /对路~ marketable commodities /冷背~ unsalable goods /内销~ commodities for home consumption /~价格 commodity price /~库存 commodity stocks; inventory /~列名 commodity entry /~目录 descriptive catalogue /~输出 export of commodities
商品拜物教 shāngpǐn bàiwùjiào commodity fetishism
商品本位 shāngpǐn běnwèi commodity standard
商品贷款 shāngpǐn dàikuǎn commodity credit; commodity loan
商品房 shāngpǐnfáng commercial housing
商品肥料 shāngpǐn féiliào commodity fertilizer
商品化 shāngpǐnhuà commercialization:住房~ commercialize housing
商品货币 shāngpǐn huòbì commodity money
商品检验 shāngpǐn jiǎnyàn commodity inspection
商品检验局 shāngpǐn jiǎnyànjú commodity inspection and testing bureau
商品交易 shāngpǐn jiāoyì commodity transaction
商品交易会 shāngpǐn jiāoyìhuì trade fair; commodities fair
商品交易所 shāngpǐn jiāoyìsuǒ commodity exchange
商品结构 shāngpǐn jiégòu commodity mix; commodity composition
商品经济 shāngpǐn jīngjì commodity economy
商品粮 shāngpǐnliáng commodity grain:~基地 commodity grain base
商品流通 shāngpǐn liútōng circulation of commodities; commodity circulation
商品率 shāngpǐnlǜ commodity rate
商品美元 shāngpǐn měiyuán commodity dollar
商品期权 shāngpǐn qīquán commodity option
商品生产 shāngpǐn shēngchǎn commodity production:~基地 base for the production of commodities
商品市场 shāngpǐn shìchǎng commodity market
商品税 shāngpǐnshuì commodity tax
商品销售市场 shāngpǐn xiāoshòu shìchǎng outlet for goods; market
商品学 shāngpǐnxué merchandising
商品展销会 shāngpǐn zhǎnxiāohuì commodity fair
商品住宅 shāngpǐn zhùzhái commercial residential buildings
商品装潢 shāngpǐn zhuānghuáng commodity decoration; wrapping of goods
商旗 shāngqí merchant flag
商洽 shāngqià take up (a matter) with sb.; discuss:他已来函~。He has brought up the matter in his letter. /产品规格可另行~。The specifications of the products can be discussed separately.
商情 shāngqíng market conditions:~通报 circular on the market conditions
商情晴雨表 shāngqíng qíngyǔbiǎo business barometer
商情研究 shāngqíng yánjiū market research; MR
商情预测 shāngqíng yùcè business forecasting
商榷 shāngquè discuss; consider; deliberate:我想就市场经济问题与同行~。I'd like to discuss with my colleagues the question of market economy. /这个观点值得~。This viewpoint is open to question.
商人 shāngrén businessman; merchant; tradesman; trader
商厦 shāngshà business plaza; commericial building
商事 shāngshì commercial affairs; business matter:~法庭 commercial court /~纠纷 commercial dispute /~诉讼 commercial action /~行为 commercial act /~仲裁 commercial arbitration
商数 shāngshù 〈数学〉quotient
商税 shāngshuì *also* "商业税" business tax
商肆 shāngsì 〈书面〉shop; store
商摊 shāngtān stall
商谈 shāngtán exchange views; talk about; confer; negotiate:~国事 talk about state affairs /这件事如何办,还需多方~。It requires further consultation among all of us on how to handle the problem. /~的气氛非常融洽。The atmosphere of the discussion is very friendly.
商讨 shāngtǎo discuss; consult; deliberate:我们就技术协作问题进行了卓有成效的~。We held fruitful consultations on technical cooperation. /会议还~了两国的经济合作问题。Discussed also at the meeting was the possible economic cooperation between the two countries.
商亭 shāngtíng stall; stand; booth; kiosk:小吃~ snack booth /新建的~ newly-built stalls
商务 shāngwù commercial matters; business affairs:洽谈~ negotiate business affairs /~活动 commercial affairs (*or* activities) /~仲裁 commercial arbitration /~责任 commercial liability
商务参赞 shāngwù cānzàn commercial counsellor
商务处 shāngwùchù commercial counsellor's office
商务代表 shāngwù dàibiǎo commercial or trade representative
商务代表处 shāngwù dàibiǎochù trade representative's office
商务秘书 shāngwù mìshū commercial secretary
商务印书馆 Shāngwù Yìnshūguǎn The Commercial Press (established in 1897)
商务专员 shāngwù zhuānyuán commercial attaché
商学士 shāngxuéshì bachelor of commerce; bachelor of business
商学院 shāngxuéyuàn commercial college; business school
商鞅 Shāng Yāng *also* "商君";"公孙鞅" Gōngsūn Yāng Shang Yang (c.390-338 BC), statesman of the Warring States Period
商鞅变法 Shāng Yāng Biànfǎ political reforms introduced by Shang Yang around 356 BC in the State of Qin to abolish the nine-square system (井田制) and make land private, abolish hereditary privileges of the nobility and encourage farming and fighting for the country, set up a unitary administrative system down to household registration at the grass roots, and unify weights and measures, thus laying the foundations for the State of Qin to become strong and eventually unify China for the first time in history (221 BC)
商鞅量 shāngyāngliàng Shang Yang measure, a standard measure made of bronze introduced by Shang Yang in the State of Qin
商业 shāngyè commerce; trade; business:~部门 commercial department; business sector /~惯例 business practice /~机构 business organization /发展~ expand trade /~不景气 business recession (*or* slump) /合作~ cooperative business /~风险 commercial risks /~汇票 commercial draft /~禁运 commercial embargo /~事务 business affair /~信用 commercial reputation /~注册 commercial registration
商业部 shāngyèbù ministry of commerce; (US) Department of Commerce:~长 minister of commerce; (US) Secretary of Commerce
商业道德 shāngyè dàodé business ethics
商业法 shāngyèfǎ commercial law; business law
商业交易法 shāngyè jiāoyìfǎ law of commercial or business transaction
商业界 shāngyèjiè business circles
商业经济 shāngyè jīngjì business economy
商业经济学 shāngyè jīngjìxué economics of commerce; business economics
商业票据 shāngyè piàojù commercial bill; trade bill; business papers
商业区 shāngyèqū business quarter; commercial district
商业网 shāngyèwǎng commercial network
商业网点 shāngyè wǎngdiǎn network of trading establishments; commercial network
商业危机 shāngyè wēijī commercial crisis

商业卫星 shāngyè wèixīng *also* "商用卫星" commercial satellite
商业信贷 shāngyè xìndài commercial credit
商业信用证 shāngyè xìnyòngzhèng commercial letter of credit
商业银行 shāngyè yínháng commercial bank: ~指数 commercial bank index
商业用语 shāngyè yòngyǔ business terms
商业中心 shāngyè zhōngxīn commercial centre; business centre; shopping centre
商业周期 shāngyè zhōuqī business cycle
商业资本 shāngyè zīběn *also* "商人资本" commercial capital; merchant capital
商议 shāngyì consult; confer; discuss: ~交通安全措施 discuss measures ensuring traffic safety /~会议的准备事宜 confer on arrangements of the meeting /需要双方共同~ require the joint consultation of both sides /他调动的事还得~。His transfer to another job has yet to be discussed. /回去~~。We'll talk the matter over again when we are back.
商誉 shāngyù goodwill; business reputation
商约 shāngyuē commercial treaty
商栈 shāngzhàn inn; caravansary
商战 shāngzhàn ❶ *also* "商业战争" wars fought one after another by Portugal, Spain, England and France between the 15th and 18th centuries to seize colonies and markets in order to win supremacy militarily and in trade ❷ trade war; 〈比喻〉 business competition
商酌 shāngzhuó discuss carefully; consider; deliberate: 这件事是他们三位跟我一起~的。The matter has been carefully discussed by the three of them and me. /讲课的事希望他先跟我~一下。I expect him to have a preliminary discussion with me about his teaching programme.

熵

shāng 〈物理〉 entropy; thermal charge: ~产生 entropy production

墒(䬠)

shāng 〈农业〉 moisture in the soil suitable for the germination of seeds and their growth: 保~ preserve soil moisture for crop growth /抢~ seize the first opportunity to sow while there is still sufficient soil moisture
墒情 shāngqíng soil moisture content: ~好 adequate moisture in the soil for the growth of crops
墒土 shāngtǔ newly ploughed moist soil: 保住~, 按时播种。We must preserve the moist soil and get the sowing done in time.

伤(傷)

shāng ❶ wound; injury: 内~ internal injury; trauma /外~ injury; wound /暗~ invisible (*or* internal) injury /工~ injury suffered on the job; industrial injury /刀~ knife wound /轻~ slight injury /烫~ scald /重~ serious injury /致命~ mortal (*or* fatal) wound /冻~ frostbite /枪~ bullet wound /刺~ stab wound /治~ treat a wound /养~ heal one's wounds /救死扶~ heal the wounded and rescue the dying /死~多人 suffer heavy casualties ❷ injure; wound; hurt: ~身体 impair health /摔了一下, ~了腿 fall down and hurt one's leg /房子倒塌~了人。When the house collapsed, some people were injured. /这就~人感情了。This is hurting people's feelings (*or* wounding people's pride). /谷贱~农。Cheap grain affects farmers. ❸ sad; distressed: 忧~ sad; sorrowful /悲~ sad; heavyhearted ❹ surfeit; overeat: 鸡肉吃~了 sick from eating too much chicken meat ❺ be harmful to; impair: 这无~大体。This is not a matter of high principle. /这真是有~风化。This is indeed an offence against common decency. /这样做无~你学者的威望。To do so would not affect your reputation as a scholar.
伤疤 shāngbā ❶ scar: 他身上有好几处~。His body bears a few scars. /好了~忘了疼。No sooner had the scar tissues formed over the wound than he forgot all about the suffering. ❷ past mistake or humiliation: 不要揭他人~。Don't rake up all that muck about his past.
伤悲 shāngbēi *also* "悲伤" sad; depressed; sorrowful: 少壮不努力, 老大徒~。If you don't exert yourself when young, you'll regret in vain when old.
伤兵 shāngbīng wounded soldier
伤病 shāng-bìng injury and sickness: 本队有几名运动员有~。A couple of players on our team are injured or sick.
伤病员 shāng-bìngyuán sick and wounded soldiers; noneffectives
伤财 shāngcái lose money; waste money: 劳民~ waste money and manpower; exhaust the people and drain the treasury
伤残 shāngcán ❶ (of finished products) damaged; defective: 商品如有~, 保证退换。Replacement is guaranteed if the goods are defective. ❷ handicap; physical disability: ~儿童 handicapped child /他是在一次战役中~的。He got wounded in action and became disabled. ❸ injure; kill: ~人命 kill someone in cold blood
伤残人 shāngcánrén the handicapped; the crippled; the disabled: 国际~奥运会 International Olympic Games for the Handicapped
伤春 shāngchūn grieve over the passing of spring; feel sad in spring: ~的情绪 feeling of sadness evoked by what one sees in spring
伤悼 shāngdào grieve over; mourn for: ~某人的早逝 mourn (*or* grieve) for sb.'s premature death
伤风 shāngfēng catch cold; get or have a cold
伤风败俗 shāngfēng-bàisú violate common decency; corrupt public morals; cause the decay of moral standards: 我没有料到他会做出~的事情来。I never imagined that he would fly in the face of common decency. *or* Never did I imagine that he was capable of such base conduct. /此类事~, 为人所不齿! These things which run counter to human decency are held in utter contempt.
伤俘 shāngfú soldiers wounded and captured in battle; wounded prisoners of war: 对~要进行治疗。Wounded POWs should be given proper medical treatment.
伤感 shānggǎn sick at heart; sentimental; mawkish: 缠绵~ be sorrowful and sentimental /他因儿子早逝而~不已。He kept grieving over his son's premature death. /这不禁使我~万分, 愁肠百结。This gave me feelings of heartbreaking melancholy and anxiety.
伤害 shānghài injure; wound; harm; hurt: ~身体 be harmful to health /~眼睛 hurt one's eyes /~感情 wound one's feelings; offend one's sensibilities /~积极性 dampen one's enthusiasm /人身~ injury /~保险 injury insurance /~中国人民的感情 lacerate the national feeling of the Chinese people; wound the national pride (*or* dignity) of the Chinese people
伤寒 shānghán ❶ 〈医学〉 typhoid fever; typhoid: ~杆菌 typhoid bacillus ❷ 〈中医〉 diseases caused by harmful cold factors; cold damage; febrile diseases
伤寒杂病论 Shānghán Zábìnglùn *Febrile and Other Diseases*, a medical work written by Zhang Zhongjing (张仲景) in the early third century
伤号 shānghào wounded soldier
伤耗 shānghao damage: 蔬菜运输中~太大。Vegetables suffer a good deal of damage in transit.
伤痕 shānghén scar; bruise; gash: 他身上~累累。There are cuts and bruises all over his body. /在人们心中留下一道道深深的~。It leaves deep scars on the public mind. /心灵上的~难以平复。A person's trauma is difficult to heal.
伤痕文学 shānghén wénxué trauma literature
伤怀 shānghuái 〈书面〉 sad; distressed; grieved; sorrowful; broken-hearted
伤筋动骨 shāngjīn-dònggǔ be injured in the sinews or bones; sustain bone injuries; have a fracture: ~一百天。It usually requires about 100 days to recover from bone injuries. /只蹭破了皮, 没有~。It is only a scratch; there is no fracture. /作些人事调整是必要的, 但不能~。It is necessary to make certain personnel changes, but we can't afford to have a fundamental shake-up.
伤酒 shāngjiǔ get sick from too much drink: 他烂醉如泥, 三天~吃不下饭。He got so dead drunk that for the following three days he was too sick to eat.
伤科 shāngkē 〈中医〉 (department of) traumatology
伤口 shāngkǒu wound; cut; gash: 深长的~ gash /脸上的~ cut on the face /包扎~ bind up (*or* suture) a wound /缝合~ sew up (*or* dress) a wound /给~消毒 sterilize a wound /洗~ bathe a wound /~化脓了。The wound is festering. /~发炎。The wound became inflamed. /~愈合了。The wound healed.
伤力 shānglì be injured by excessively heavy physical labour: 他当长工时~落下了个病根儿。He has an old complaint left by excessively heavy work when he was a farmhand.
伤面子 shāng miànzi hurt one's feelings or sensibilities: 办事应当讲原则, 不能怕~。We must adhere to principles in our work and not be afraid to offend people.
伤脑筋 shāng nǎojīn knotty; thorny; troublesome; vexing: 如何又

省钱又把事情办好，还真～。How to do it well as well as economically is indeed a hard nut to crack. /改变她的错误观点还得伤一番脑筋。We must rack our brains to try and persuade her to give up erroneous views. /这孩子的学习是一件～的事。The kid's schooling is a big headache.

伤气 shāngqì ❶〈书面〉feel frustrated; be upset ❷〈中医〉undermine one's constitution; sap one's vitality: 贪杯～。Excessive drinking undermines one's constitution.

伤情 shāngqíng ❶ condition of a wound or injury: ～好转。His injury is getting better. /医生反复察看他的～。The doctor checked on his wound again and again. ❷ sentimental: 抚今追昔，不胜～。Reflecting on the past and present, he was overcome with nostalgia.

伤热 shāngrè (of fruit, vegetables, etc.) no longer fresh; damaged: 这批～的苹果应立即处理。These damaged apples should be disposed of immediately.

伤人 shāngrén ❶ injure sb. ❷ impair one's health ❸ hurt sb.'s feelings; cause sb. distress: 恶语～。Bad language is highly offensive.

伤神 shāngshén ❶ overtax one's nerves; cause great mental strain: 为生计～ strain every nerve trying to make living for oneself (*or* to make ends meet) /过度思虑～。Overtaxing one's brains is harmful to one's nervous system. ❷ sad; distressed: 他因孤独而～。Lonely and friendless, he felt sad. /不值得为无谓的流言而～。You don't have to feel upset about the gossip.

伤生 shāngshēng harmful to life

伤食 shāngshí 〈中医〉dyspepsia caused by excessive eating or improper diet; get sick from overeating: 这孩子～了。The child is suffering from indigestion.

伤势 shāngshì condition of an injury or wound: 经过治疗，～已经减轻。After the treatment, his wound became less serious.

伤逝 shāngshì grieve over the deceased; mourn sb.'s death

伤水 shāngshuǐ get sick from drinking too much water

伤损 shāngsǔn hurt; damage: ～感情 hurt feelings /～树木 damage trees

伤天害理 shāngtiān-hàilǐ in defiance of heaven and human reason; outrageous: ～的勾当 inhuman act; act of gross injustice

伤痛 shāngtòng ❶ grieved; sad; broken-hearted: 懊恼～的面容 look annoyed and sad /她～地哭起来。Broken-hearted, she burst into tears. ❷ ache; be painful: 他忍着浑身的～坐起来。He sat up despite the fact that he was aching all over.

伤亡 shāngwáng injuries and deaths; casualties: 减少～ reduce casualties

伤亡报告 shāngwáng bàogào 〈军事〉report of losses; casualty report

伤心 shāngxīn sad; grieved; sorrowful; broken-hearted: 满腹～事 be eaten up with grief /你要让妈～吗? Do you want to break your mother's heart? /不要～。Don't take it so much to heart. /男儿有泪不轻弹，只因未到～处。A man does not shed tears unless he is really broken-hearted.

伤心惨目 shāngxīn-cǎnmù too ghastly to look at; appalling; horrible: 那情景令人～。It was dreadful to be present on the scene.

伤心事 shāngxīnshì painful memory; agonizing affair; heart-breaking event

伤员 shāngyuán wounded soldier; wounded personnel; the wounded: 抢救～ give emergency (*or* first-aid) treatment to the wounded; rescue the wounded /慰问～ comfort wounded soldiers

汤(湯) shāng

see also tāng

汤汤 shāngshāng 〈书面〉torrentially: 河水～。The river is in full spate.

殇(殤) shāng 〈书面〉die young: 夭～ premature death

觞(觴) shāng 〈考古〉goblet; wine cup; drinking vessel

觞咏 shāngyǒng 〈书面〉compose or chant poems while drinking: 这里曾是文人墨客留连～的地方。This was where men of letters once gathered to compose poems while drinking.

shǎng

赏[1] shǎng

❶ grant or bestow a reward; award: ～了几个小钱 give sb. a few coins as a reward /犒～三军 give an award to the army ❷ reward; bounty; award: 领～ receive an award /悬～缉拿 offer a bounty for the capture of a criminal /论功行～ grant awards to people for their distinguished services (*or* meritorious deeds) /他得了重～。He was given a handsome reward. ❸ (Shǎng) a surname

赏[2] shǎng

❶ admire; enjoy; appreciate: ～月 admire the bright full moon; enjoy the wonderful view of the full moon /～花 feast one's eyes on garden flowers /雅俗共～ appeal to sophisticated and vulgar tastes alike; suit both refined and popular tastes; cater to both highbrow and lowbrow tastes ❷ appreciate; admire: 称～ praise; admire

赏赐 shǎngcì ❶ grant or bestow a reward; award (a prize, title, etc.): ～无度 grant awards indiscriminatingly /老夫人～给她几件首饰。The old lady bestowed a few pieces of jewellery on her. ❷ reward; award: 水、空气和土地是大自然给人类的～。The water, the air and the earth are the bounties of nature for mankind.

赏罚 shǎng-fá rewards and punishments: ～不明 be indiscriminating in one's rewards and punishments

赏罚分明 shǎng-fá fēnmíng be fair and strict in meting out rewards and punishments

赏罚严明 shǎng-fá yánmíng *see* "赏罚分明"

赏封 shǎngfēng 〈旧语〉gift money wrapped up in a piece of red paper

赏格 shǎnggé 〈旧语〉valued price of a reward

赏光 shǎngguāng 〈套语〉accept an invitation: 敬请～。We request the pleasure of your company. *or* We sincerely hope you will honour us with your gracious presence.

赏号 shǎnghào 〈方言〉〈旧语〉individual gift or money

赏鉴 shǎngjiàn appreciate (a work of art): ～书画 appreciate painting and calligraphy /～家 connoisseur

赏金 shǎngjīn money reward; pecuniary reward: 丰厚的～ handsome reward /领取～ collect a reward; claim a reward

赏赉 shǎnglài 〈书面〉bestow or grant a reward

赏览 shǎnglǎn 〈方言〉enjoy; admire (scenery): 他站在临海的一块礁石上任情～。He stood on a rock overlooking the sea, admiring the beauty of the vast stretch of water.

赏脸 shǎngliǎn 〈套语〉grant or do one the honour: 呈献鲜果一篮，务请～。Would you please do me the honour of accepting this basket of fresh fruits?

赏钱 shǎngqian money reward; pecuniary reward; tip: 领～ get money as a reward

赏识 shǎngshí recognize the worth of; praise; appreciate: 备受某人～ be in sb.'s good graces /领导～他办事的效率。The leadership appreciated his efficiency in handling things. /论文受到专家～。The paper (*or* dissertation) was spoken highly of (*or* highly praised) by the experts.

赏收 shǎngshōu 〈套语〉please accept (my gift, etc.)

赏玩 shǎngwán admire the beauty of sth.; be fond of; delight in; enjoy: ～古董 be fond of antiques and curios /～湖对岸夜景 enjoy the night scene across the lake

赏析 shǎngxī make appreciative comments (on literary works, etc.): 唐诗～ appreciative comments on Tang poetry /这是一篇关于李白诗歌～的文章。This is an article that makes an appreciative analysis of Li Bai's poems.

赏心乐事 shǎngxīn-lèshì pleasant and enjoyable experience; happy events

赏心悦目 shǎngxīn-yuèmù pleasing to both the eye and the mind; be a feast for the eye: 春景清新可爱，真是～。The spring scenery, which is fresh and lovely, is a perfect delight to the eye. /踏雪寻梅，可谓～的乐事。To trudge through the snow in search of plum blossoms is really an enjoyable experience.

赏雪 shǎngxuě enjoy a beautiful snow scene

赏月 shǎngyuè enjoy a bright full moon

赏阅 shǎngyuè read for enjoyment, pleasure, or appreciation: 本报将刊出五篇得奖的短篇小说，供读者～。This newspaper will publish the five prize-winning short stories for the benefit of our readers.

S

上 shǎng *see* “上²⑭” shàng
see also shàng

上声 shǎngshēng 〈语言〉*see* “上声” shàngshēng

垧 shǎng land measure equal to fifteen *mu* in most parts of northeast China and three or five *mu* in northwest China

晌 shǎng ❶ part of the day：前半～儿 morning／后半～儿 afternoon／半～，他才憋出个“行”字。It took him a long, long while to mutter the word “OK”. ❷〈方言〉noon：*see* “～觉”

晌饭 shǎngfàn 〈方言〉❶ midday meal; lunch：中午十二时食堂开～。Lunch begins at 12 at the mess. ❷ extra meal in the morning or afternoon during the busy farming season：～送到地头。The extra meal is taken to the fields where the farmers work.

晌觉 shǎngjiào 〈方言〉afternoon nap; siesta：我们夏天有睡～的习惯。We have the habit of taking an afternoon nap in summer.

晌午 shǎngwu 〈口语〉midday; noon：～停工 knock off at midday

shàng

尚¹ shàng ❶ esteem; value; treasure; set great store by：高～ lofty／崇～ uphold; champion; advocate／礼～往来。Courtesy is to be reciprocated. ❷ prevailing custom, habits, etc.：习～ prevailing custom／时～ vogue of the day; fashion ❸（Shàng）a surname

尚² shàng 〈书面〉〈副词〉❶ still; yet：年纪～小 still young／一息～存 as long as one lives; until one breathes one's last／成绩～好。The score is all right.／提出这个问题为时～早。It is too early yet to raise the question.／规章制度～须进一步健全。The rules and regulations will have to be further strengthened.／此项工作～未完成。The task remains to be accomplished（*or* is yet to be done）. ❷ even：老师～不能解释，何必苛求于学生！Even the teacher fails to explain this, why drive students so hard!

尚方宝剑 shàngfāng bǎojiàn imperial sword as a symbol of supreme authority
see also “上方宝剑” shàngfāng bǎojiàn

尚且 shàngqiě 〈连词〉even：这本书我～能看懂，你当然更不成问题。If I can manage to read the book, you will have no difficulty reading it at all.／这种现象科学家～无法解释，我怎么知道呢？Even the scientists cannot account for this, how can you expect me to know about it?

尚书 shàngshū ❶（Shàngshū）*also* “书经” Shūjīng；“书” *Collection of Ancient Texts*, whose compilation is generally attributed to confucius ❷〈历史〉official title in ancient China, corresponding to cabinet minister in the Ming and Qing dynasties：兵部～ minister of the Ministry of War

尚武 shàngwǔ set great store by martial qualities; emphasize military affairs

尚武精神 shàngwǔ jīngshén martial spirit：这个舞蹈表现了一种～。This dance is a striking demonstration of the martial spirit.

尚飨 shàngxiǎng *also* “尚享”〈旧语〉(used at the end of an elegiac address) I beg you to partake of the sacrifice offered

绱（鞝） shàng stitch the sole to the upper：这双鞋还没～完。This pair of shoes are not yet soled.

绱鞋 shàngxié *also* “上鞋” shàngxié sole a shoe

上¹ shàng ❶ upper; up; upward：～嘴唇 upper lip／～半截 upper half／书架的最～一层 uppermost shelf of the bookcase／向～拉 pull upward／从～往下看 overlook／中～水平 above the average; upper middle level／～不～，下不下 be stranded halfway; be in awkward position／～有老，下有小 have both parents and young children to support and take care of ❷ higher; superior; better：至高无～ supreme; paramount／报～级批准 report to a higher level for approval／～情下达 relay information from an upper to a lower level／犯～ offend one's superior／比～不足，比下有余 can pass muster／后来居～。The latecomers surpass the old-timers. ❸ first (part); preceding; previous：～卷 first volume; volume one／～次 last time／～半年 first half of a year／～周末 previous weekend ❹〈旧语〉emperor：～谕 imperial decree ❺ upward：利率～调。The interest rate was readjusted upward.／河水～涨。The river is rising.

上² shàng ❶ go up; mount; board; get on：～山 go up a hill; go uphill／～树 climb up a tree／～车 get on a bus／～船 go aboard a ship; go on board; go on shore; land／～飞机 board a plane; go on board a plane／～台阶 ascend the steps／逆流而～ go upstream; go against the current／能～能下 be ready and able to take a lower as well as a higher post ❷ go to; leave for：～街 go downtown／～剧院 go to the theatre／～东北 leave for the northeast／难得～一次饭馆 rarely eat in a restaurant; seldom eat out ❸ submit; send in; present：～书 submit a letter ❹ forge ahead; press on：迎困难而～ meet difficulties head-on／一拥而～ surge ahead／别害羞，～啊！Come on! Don't be shy. ❺ enter the court：这场球你们五个先～。The five of you will play the first game.／这一幕他先～，我后上。He gets on the stage before me in this scene. ❻ lay on the table：～饭 serve a meal／～菜 serve the dishes ❼ fill; add; supply：～货 replenish the stock of goods／～肥 spread manure; apply fertilizer／～油 refuel／新书～架 put new books on the racks ❽ fix sth. on sth. else：～纱窗 install a screened window／～领子 fix a collar to a garment／给犯人～手铐 have the prisoner handcuffed／门必须～锁。The door must be locked. ❾ apply; paint; put on：～药膏 apply ointment／～漆 paint（sth.）／给机器～油 oil（*or* grease, *or* lubricate）a machine／～光 glaze; polish／颜色～得不匀。The colour is not evenly applied. ❿ be put on record; be carried (in a publication); be published：你的文章已～了学报。Your article has been carried in the school journal.／他的英雄事迹已经～了电影。His heroic deeds have been made the story of a film.／他～了光荣榜。His name is on the honour roll. ⓫ wind; tighten：～表 wind a watch／～螺丝 tighten a screw ⓬ begin work or study at a fixed time：十点～语文课。We have Chinese at 10.／我这星期～夜班。I'm on night shift this week. ⓭ up to; as many as：～千人 no fewer than a thousand people／不～两年，这个村子的农民就富裕起来了。The farmers in the village became moderately well-off within two years.／我～岁数了，记性不好。I'm getting on in years and my memory is failing me. ⓮（*also* shǎng）〈语言〉fall-rising tone, one of the four tones in classical Chinese and the third tone in modern standard Chinese pronunciation

上³ shàng 〈音乐〉note of the scale in *gongchepu*（工尺谱），corresponding to 1 in numbered musical notation
see also “工尺” gōngchě

上 shang ❶ *used after a verb indicating an upward movement*：爬～山顶 reach the summit（*or* the peak of the mountain）／血压升～去了。The blood pressure went up.／预算报～去了。The budget has been submitted to the higher-ups. ❷ *used after a verb indicating that an aim has been achieved*：当～了演员 become an actor（*or* actress）／住～了新房 move into a new apartment／考～了大学 be admitted to a college／点～火 light a fire／加～调料 add some seasoning／安～电话 have a telephone installed／宇航员飞～了太空。The astronauts are flying into space. ❸ *used after a verb indicating the beginning and continuation of an action*：踏～祖国的土地 set foot on the soil of one's motherland／看完电影，大家就议论～了。After the film, we started talking about what we thought of it.／他迷～了电视剧。He is absolutely addicted to TV plays.／我爱～了一位姑娘。I've fallen in love with a girl. ❹ *used after a verb indicating the amount or extent reached or to be reached*：花～一两天时间把这本书看完 spend a day or two finishing the book／每天早晨跑～几公里 run several kilometres every morning／咱俩来下～几盘。Let's have a few games of chess.

上 shang ❶ *used after a noun indicating the surface of an object*：脸～ on the face／身～满是泥 be covered with mud all over one's body／手头～比较紧 be hard up; be short of money／面子～过不去 be embarrassing ❷ *used after a noun indicating the scope of sth.*：会～ at the meeting／书～ in the book／报纸～ in the press／世～ in the world; on earth ❸ *used after a noun, indicating an aspect of sth.*：组织～ organizationally／事实～ as a matter of fact; in reality; actually／实质～ in essence／口头～ in words; verbally; orally／数量～ in quantity／技术～ technologically／首先要从思想～战胜困

难。First all, one must be mentally prepared to surmount the difficulty. *or* Overcome the difficulty first in your mind. /在年龄～他不占优势。He doesn't have the advantage in age.
see also shǎng

上岸费 shàng'ànfèi landing charges

上岸证 shàng'ànzhèng landing permit

上班 shàngbān go to work; be on duty: 每周上五天班 work five days a week /上白班 be on day shift /下午两点～。Work starts at two in the afternoon. /他有好几天没～了。He has been absent from work for many days.

上班族 shàngbānzú office workers

上板儿 shàngbǎnr 〈方言〉(of stores, shops, etc.) put up the shutters — stop doing business

上半场 shàngbànchǎng first half (of a game, etc.): ～54 比 48。The score was 54 to 48 at half time (*or* in the first half).

上半晌 shàngbànshǎng forenoon; morning: 今天～我去医院看病。I am going to the hospital this morning.

上半身 shàngbànshēn upper part of the body; above the waist: ～像 bust

上半时 shàngbànshí *see* "上半场"

上半天 shàngbàntiān before midday; morning

上半夜 shàngbànyè before midnight

上绑 shàngbǎng tie the arms of sb.

上报 shàngbào ❶ appear in the newspapers: 解放军战士舍身救人的事儿～了。The story about the PLA soldier rescuing the child at the risk of his own life is carried in the newspapers. /这事儿一～影响可就大了。This case will have a great impact in society if it is given wide publicity in the press. ❷ report to a higher body; report to the higher-ups: 年终决算已经～。The annual accounts have been reported to the leadership. /有情况及时～。Report immediately if any problem crops up.

上辈 shàngbèi ❶ ancestors; forebears: 听说你家～在明代中过状元。I hear that one of your ancestors came out first in the highest imperial examination in the Ming Dynasty. ❷ elder generation of one's family; one's elders: 家里～都没念过书。None of the elder generation in my family ever had any formal schooling.

上辈子 shàngbèizi ❶ ancestors; forefathers: 我家～在清初由湖南迁到江西。My ancestors moved from Hunan to Jiangxi in the early Qing Dynasty. ❷〈迷信〉previous life: ～积德，下辈子享福。If one does good deeds, one will enjoy happiness in the afterlife (*or* in the next life).

上臂 shàngbì upper arm

上边 shàngbian *see* "上面"

上膘 shàngbiāo (of animals) become fat; fatten: 精心饲养，牲畜就容易～。Farm animals will easily get fattened up if you feed them properly.

上表 shàngbiǎo submit a memorial to the throne

上宾 shàngbīn guest of honour; honoured guest: 视如～ regard sb. as a distinguished guest /待为～ treat sb. as a VIP

上不着天，下不着地 shàng bù zháo tiān, xià bù zháo dì touch neither the sky nor the earth — suspended in midair; stranded halfway

上菜 shàngcài serve food on table; serve the dishes: 咱们已经上了几道菜了？How many courses have been served already?

上苍 shàngcāng Heaven; God: 祷告～ say prayers to God /这是～的赐予。This is a blessing.

上操 shàngcāo go out to drill; be drilling; do exercises

上策 shàngcè best policy; best way out; best thing to do: 就这么呆下去不是～。It would not be the best policy to stay out.

上层 shàngcéng upper strata; higher levels: ～领导 higher leadership /～决策机构 higher decision-making body /～人士 upper circles /决策在～。Decision rests with the higher level.

上层建筑 shàngcéng jiànzhù superstructure: ～领域 realm of the superstructure

上层路线 shàngcéng lùxiàn upper-level line: 走～ get things done through the influence of one's higher connections

上层社会 shàngcéng shèhuì upper strata of society; upper social strata; upper-class society

上谄下骄 shàngchǎn-xiàjiāo *also* "上谄下渎" toady to one's superiors and look down upon those below; flatter those in high position and disdain those of lower ranks

上场 shàngchǎng ❶〈体育〉enter the court or field; participate in the contest: 双方主力运动员都已～。Top players of both teams have entered the court. ❷〈戏剧〉appear on the stage; enter: 他在第四幕才～。He doesn't appear on stage until act four.

上场门 shàngchǎngmén entrance (of a stage)

上朝 shàngcháo ❶ (of courtiers) go to court ❷ (of a sovereign) hold court

上乘 shàngchéng ❶〈宗教〉Mahayana; Great Vehicle ❷ (of literary and artistic works) be of superior quality; be of a high order: 山水画中的～ landscape painting of the highest order /～工作 piece of work of high quality; outstanding work /有～的表演 have turned in a superb performance; have performed superbly

上床 shàngchuáng go to bed; get into bed

上簇 shàngcù (of a silkworm) move up the straw bundle (for cocoon making)

上蹿下跳 shàngcuān-xiàtiào ❶ (of animals) run and jump all over the place: 小松鼠～，寻找食物。The squirrels ran around looking for food. ❷〈比喻〉〈贬义〉run around on sinister errands: 一有机会，他就～，煽风点火。Whenever there is a chance, he would run around stirring up trouble.

上达 shàngdá reach the higher authorities: 使下情～ inform the higher-ups of the situation at lower levels /群情不能～。The public feeling is not properly communicated to the leadership.

上代 shàngdài previous generation; former generations

上党梆子 Shàngdǎng bāngzi one of the local operas in Shanxi Province, popular in its southeastern region

上当 shàngdàng be taken in; be deceived; be cheated; be duped: 我～了，买了个冒牌货。I was fooled when I bought this fake. /年轻人在这方面容易～。Young people are liable to be duped in such matters. /我们不上那个当。We won't walk into that trap.

上灯 shàngdēng light a lamp; turn on the light: ～时分 lighting-up time

上等 shàngděng first class; first rate; superior; top-notch: ～茶叶 high-quality tea /～皮革 quality (*or* superior) leather /～人才 people of top-notch quality

上等兵 shàngděngbīng (Chinese army) private, first class; (Chinese air force) airman, first class; (Chinese navy) seaman, first class; (US army) private, first class; (US & UK marine corps; UK army) lance corporal; (US air force) airman, first class; (UK air force) senior aircraftman; (US navy) seaman; (UK navy) leading seaman

上低音号 shàngdīyīnhào 〈音乐〉baritone

上帝 Shàngdì ❶ Lord on High that governs everything (in ancient Chinese thought) ❷ God

上第 shàngdì 〈书面〉first-class; first-rate; top-notch; superior: 考试列～ be among the best of the successful candidates

上吊 shàngdiào hang oneself

上调 shàngdiào ❶ be transferred to a higher post: 他已经从车间～到厂部了。He has been transferred from a shop to the factory headquarters. ❷ (of funds or material) be transferred to higher authorities for re-allocation
see also shàngtiáo

上冻 shàngdòng freeze: 地已经～了。The ground is frozen. /赶在～以前完工。We have got to finish the work before a freeze sets in.

上都 Shàngdū Shangdu, summer capital of the Yuan Dynasty in today's Inner Mongolia Autonomous Region

上颚 shàng'è ❶ mandible ❷ maxilla (of a mammal); upper jaw

上发条 shàng fātiáo wind (a watch, toy, etc.)

上方宝剑 shàngfāng bǎojiàn *also* "尚方宝剑" shàngfāng bǎojiàn imperial sword (a symbol of supreme authority, investing the bearer with discretionary powers): 可不能拿着～搞独断专行。Never act arbitrarily when you are invested with great powers.

上房 shàngfáng ❶ main rooms (usu. facing south within a courtyard) ❷ wife (as distinguished from concubine in former times)

上访 shàngfǎng seek an audience with the higher authorities to appeal for intervention: 多次来京～ visit Beijing many times to appeal to the leadership for intervention

上坟 shàngfén visit a grave (to honour the memory of the dead)

上粪 shàngfèn apply manure to fields; manure the fields: 多～，多打粮。The more manure we apply, the better the crop.

上风 shàngfēng ❶ windward: 我们站在～头。We stood on the windward side. ❷ advantage; (have) the edge over; superior position; upper hand: 比赛开始时，我队占～。Our team got the upper

hand at the beginning of the game.

上峰 shàngfēng 〈旧语〉superiors; higher-ups: 接到~指示 receive instructions from one's superior

上浮 shàngfú ❶ (of price, wages, etc.) increase: 价格~。The price has gone up. /银行利率~。There has been an increase of the interest rate at the bank. ❷ (of a submarine) come up; surface

上甘岭 Shànggānlǐng Sanggamyong Ridge (in Democratic People's Republic of Korea): ~战役 Battle of Sanggamyong (1952)

上赶着 shànggǎnzhe 〈方言〉cotton up to or fawn on; go out of the way to please: 你干吗老是~跟他亲近呢? Why do you keep cottoning up to him and want to become related to him?

上纲 shànggāng magnify a minor fault as if it were a matter of major principle: ~上线 magnify a person's flaws or mistakes with the intention of fixing a political label on him /是什么就是什么, 别随便~。Take it as it is; don't magnify the error. /这件事上不了纲。This is not a matter of principle.

上岗 shànggǎng ❶ go to duty posts; take up a job: ~职工 staff actually working at their posts / 负责人~抽查。The person in charge went to the various duty posts for a spot check. /只有认真执行售货员守则和服务标准的营业员才能入柜~。Only those who are ready to earnestly observe the rules and the standards of their service can take up jobs behind the counter. ❷〈方言〉seat of honour: 他把老大爷让在~, 两个兄弟陪在下面。He helped the old man to the seat of honour with the two brothers seated on the side.

上高儿 shànggāor go to a high ground: 他一~就头晕。The moment he climbs to a high spot, he gets dizzy.

上告 shànggào ❶ complain or make a complaint to higher authorities; appeal to a higher court: 向纪委~ appeal to the disciplinary committee /越级~ bypass the immediate leadership to appeal (*or* complain) directly to higher levels ❷ report to a higher body: 此事应立即~部长。This matter must be reported to the minister immediately.

上工 shànggōng ❶ go to work: 工人们早八点~。The workers go to work at eight every morning. ❷ start work (on the first day of one's employment): 新雇的保姆明天~。The new nurse starts work tomorrow.

上贡 shànggòng *see* "上供"

上供 shànggòng *also* "上贡" ❶ lay offerings on the altar: 给祖先~ offer up a sacrifice to one's ancestors ❷ grease or oil sb.'s palm (with sth.): 不给他们上点供, 恐怕办不成事。I'm afraid we won't be able to get things done without greasing their palms.

上钩 shànggōu swallow the bait; be enticed; get hooked: 被坏人引诱~ rise to the bait of wicked people; fall into the trap laid by wicked people; be led astray by bad elements /姜太公钓鱼, 愿者~。As is the case of Jiang Ziya fishing in the water, the willing alone swallow the bait.

上古 shànggǔ ancient times; antiquity; remote past

上古史 shànggǔshǐ ancient history

上官 shàngguān ❶ officials at a higher-level department; higher-ups; one's superiors ❷ (Shàngguān) a surname

上馆子 shàng guǎnzi eat in a restaurant; eat out: 轻易不~ rarely eat out

上光 shàngguāng ❶〈纺织〉lustring ❷〈摄影〉ferrotyping ❸ glazing; polishing

上光版 shàngguāngbǎn 〈摄影〉ferrotype plate; ferrotype tin

上光机 shàngguāngjī glazing machine; glazer

上光蜡 shàngguānglà wax polish

上轨道 shàng guǐdào ❶ get on the right track; proceed smoothly: 实验室里的工作已逐步~。The laboratory has gradually got on the right track. /生产还没有完全~。Production is not in full swing yet. ❷〈航天〉be launched into orbit

上国 shàngguó ❶ term used by the states of Wu, Chu, etc., to refer to the dukedoms and principalities of the Central Plains in the Spring and Autumn Period ❷ respectful term used by dependencies to refer to the metropolis ❸〈书面〉capital city of a country

上海 Shànghǎi Shanghai, China's largest city

上海公报 Shànghǎi Gōngbào (short for 中美上海公报) *Sino-US Joint Communiqué* or *Shanghai Communiqué* (concluded in Shanghai on 28 Feb. 1972)

上好 shànghǎo first-class; best-quality; top; tip-top; top-notch: ~的茶叶 best-quality tea /~的棉花 top-notch cotton /~绸缎 superior silks and satins

上颌 shànghé *also* "上颚"〈生理〉upper jaw; maxilla

上呼吸道 shànghūxīdào 〈生理〉upper respiratory tract

上呼吸道感染 shànghūxīdào gǎnrǎn infection of the upper respiratory tract

上户 shànghù 〈旧语〉rich families

上回 shànghuí last time

上火 shànghuǒ ❶〈中医〉suffer from excessive internal heat (with such symptoms as constipation, conjunctivitis, and inflammation of the nasal and oral cavities): 他嘴里起泡, ~了。He has cold sores on his lips because of excessive internal heat. ❷〈方言〉flare up; be upset: 孩子没礼貌, 真让人~。I'm really annoyed with the child for lack of good manners. /不着慌, 也不~。There is no need to be alarmed or get into a temper.

上货 shànghuò ❶ replenish supplies for sale ❷ display goods on shelves: 营业员正忙着~。The shop assistants are busy putting goods on the shelves.

上级 shàngjí high level; high authorities: ~组织 organization at the higher level /~领导 leadership at a higher level /~法院 court above; higher court; superior court /~指示 instruction (*or* order) from above (*or* the higher authorities) /讨好~ curry favour with one's superior /今后她就是你的~。She will be your boss from today.

上计 shàngjì best plan; best way out; best thing to do: 三十六计, 走为~。Of all the stratagems, the best is to run away.

上佳 shàngjiā of superior quality; very good; excellent

上家 shàngjiā person who precedes one in play; (in playing cards) person on one's right; (in mah-jong) person on one's left: 昨天玩扑克, 我是他的~。I was sitting on his right when we were playing cards yesterday.

上尖儿 shàngjiānr 〈口语〉heap up: 到处粮食堆得都~了。The grain was heaped up all around.

上睑 shàngjiǎn 〈生理〉upper eyelid; palpebrae

上江 Shàngjiāng ❶ upper reaches of the Yangtze River ❷ Anhui Province (with Jiangsu as Xiajiang) in the Ming and Qing dynasties

上浆 shàngjiāng 〈纺织〉sizing: 棉布~ starching

上将 shàngjiàng (Chinese army & air force) general; (Chinese navy) admiral; (US & UK armies and marine corps, US air force) general; (US & UK navies) admiral; (UK air force) air chief marshal: 一级~ (Chinese army and air force) general, first class; (Chinese navy) admiral, first class

上交 shàngjiāo turn over to the higher authorities; hand in: 这封批评信应该立即~。This letter of complaint should be communicated to the higher-ups without delay. /矛盾不应~。We should not pass on contradictions (*or* difficulties) to the higher authorities.

上胶 shàngjiāo (in papermaking) sizing

上胶机 shàngjiāojī (in papermaking) gluing machine

上焦 shàngjiāo 〈中医〉part of the body cavity above the diaphragm housing such circulatory, digestive and respiratory organs as the heart, lungs and gullet; upper burner

上缴 shàngjiǎo turn over (revenues, etc.) to the higher authorities: 战利品应全部~。Spoils of war should be handed in with no exception.

上缴利润 shàngjiǎo lìrùn ❶ turn over part of the profits to the higher authorities ❷ that part of the profits turned over to the state

上街 shàngjiē ❶ go shopping; go downtown: 忙得连~的时间都没有 too busy to go shopping ❷ take to the street: ~游行 demonstrate in the streets

上届 shàngjiè previous term; last: ~政协 last committee of the People's Political Consultative Conference /~冠军 defending champion

上界 shàngjiè heaven of heavens; heavenly abode

上紧 shàngjǐn 〈方言〉be quick; without delay: 麦子都熟了, 得~割啦。The wheat is ripe, and we should get it in without delay.

上进 shàngjìn go forward; make progress: 不求~ have no desire to make progress (*or* for improvement)

上进心 shàngjìnxīn desire for improvement: ~不强 no urge to move up; lacking in drive /力求~ strive to excel

上劲 shàngjìn energetically; vigorously; with great gusto: 他学习可~儿啦。He is simply absorbed in his studies. /她越干越~儿。She takes an increasing interest in her work. /他念李白的诗越来越~。He read Li Bai's poems with growing enthusiasm.

上九流 shàngjiǔliú 〈旧语〉people in various respectable trades and with high social status, such as officials, doctors, monks, etc.

上捐 shàngjuān pay tax
上客 shàngkè distinguished guest; guest of honour
上课 shàngkè attend class; go to class; conduct a class; give a lesson or lecture:正在~ lesson in progress /本学期九月一日开始~。School starts on September 1st this term. /那儿正在上大课。There is a lecture going on there. /这两个学生今天没来~。The two students are absent today.
上空 shàngkōng in the sky; high above;overhead:一群信鸽从我们村庄~飞过。A flock of homing pigeons flew over our village. /矿区~烟尘弥漫。A pall of smoke and dust hung over the mining area.
上口 shàngkǒu ❶ be able to read aloud fluently:孩子们才三五岁,读古诗已能琅琅~了。It's amazing that these three-to-five-year old kids can recite the classic poems so fluently. ❷ be easy to read; read smoothly:这篇故事很~。The story makes very smooth reading.
上口字 shàngkǒuzì words in Beijing opera pronounced in the traditional manner
上跨交叉 shàngkuà jiāochā 〈交通〉flyover; overpass
上款 shàngkuǎn name of the recipient (as inscribed on a painting or a calligraphic scroll presented as a gift)
上蜡 shànglà waxing:~机 wax-coating machine; waxing machine
上来 shànglái ❶ at the beginning:~请先讲事情的经过。Please tell us how it all happened first / 他一~就先提要求。He made a request the moment he opened his mouth. ❷〈书面〉to sum up; to put it in a nutshell
上来 shànglai come up:他在楼下看书,一直没有~。He didn't come up because he was busy reading downstairs. /月亮~了。The moon is rising. /锅里的气~了。The pot begins to steam.
上来 shanglai ❶ *used after a verb, indicating a movement either upward or from afar*:从井里爬~一个人。A man climbed up from the well. /他再也追不~了。He will never catch up. /火由地下室着~,越烧越大。The fire started from the basement and soon got out of control. /河里的水漫~了。The river is overflowing. /大家围~问这问那。The crowd gathered around asking all sorts of questions. ❷ *used after a verb, indicating success*:那首诗他念了两遍就背~了。He had read the poem through only twice and then he could recite it. /他们提的问题,我都答~了。I managed to give a correct answer to each of their questions. /究竟为什么,我也说不~。I don't know why! /这种花你叫得上名字来吗? Do you happen to know the name of the flower? ❸〈方言〉*used after an adjective indicating an increase in degree*:天气凉~了。It is getting cold. /天色黑~了。Dusk is gathering.
上联 shànglián first line of a couplet:我说~,你对下联。I'll do the first line of the couplet and you come up with the second. /这幅对子~和下联对得很工整。The two lines of the couplet are perfectly antithetical.
上脸 shàngliǎn ❶ flush from drinking:他一喝酒就~。Whenever he takes a sip of wine, he flushes immediately. ❷ get impudent when complimented:这孩子不懂事,夸他两句他就~。The kid is rather thoughtless; a little praise goes to his head.
上梁 shàngliáng ❶ lay a beam:房子~ have the upper beam laid ❷ (of a building) upper beam
上梁不正下梁歪 shàngliáng bù zhèng xiàliáng wāi If the upper beam is not straight, the lower ones will go aslant; when those above behave unworthily, those below will follow suit; the poison seeps downwards from top:~,中梁不正塌下来。If the upper beam is not straight, the lower ones will go slant and, with a further bent middle beam, the whole edifice will collapse.
上列 shàngliè above-listed; above:~各点要牢记。Keep in mind the above-listed points. /~同学请举手。Will the aforementioned students please raise their hands?
上流 shàngliú ❶ upper reaches (of a river):珠江~ upper reaches of the Zhujiang River ❷ belonging to the upper circles; upper-class; high-society:~阶层 upper (social) strata /~人物 people from high society
上流社会 shàngliú shèhuì polite society; high society; upper classes
上漏下湿 shànglòu-xiàshī dilapidated condition (of a house)
上路 shànglù ❶ begin a journey; start out:他们清早吃了点儿东西就~了。They started off early in the morning after a light breakfast. ❷ on the right track:她工作还没有~。She hasn't got the knack of her job yet.
上马 shàngmǎ ❶ mount a horse ❷ start (a project, etc.):工程定于七月~。The project is due to start in July. /后来这项工程没~。The project was halted later.
上马子 shàngmǎzi *also* "褡裢" dālian〈方言〉❶ long rectangular bag carried across the shoulder ❷ wrestler's jacket
上门 shàngmén ❶ pay a visit; visit; call; drop in:~服务 provide service at one's home; provide home service /送货~ deliver goods to the doorstep /他的夫人如此傲慢,他怎能指望有人~呢? How can he expect anybody to drop in when his wife is so arrogant? ❷ shut the door; bolt the door; lock up for the night ❸ shut up business:杂货店~了。The grocery is closed. ❹ live with one's bride's family after marriage:给闺女找个~的 look for a son-in-law who is willing to marry into the bride's family
上门买卖 shàngmén mǎimai clinch a deal easily; be an easy job
上门女婿 shàngmén nǚxu son-in-law living with the bride's family; living-in son-in-law
上面 shàngmian ❶ upper; above; over; on:木箱下面放被子,~放衣服。The upper part of the wooden case is for clothes, and stored below are quilts. /书架~摆了几件工艺品。There are a few handicraft pieces on the bookshelves. /河~有一座吊桥。A suspension bridge soars across the river. ❷ above-mentioned; above; preceding; foregoing:~一段 preceding paragraph /~提到过 as mentioned above /~几位的表演都非常出色。The performances several of you have just given were superb indeed. ❸ surface of an object:大门~贴着一副对联。A pair of couplets are pasted on the wall. /衣服~沾满了泥。The clothes are stained with mud. *or* The clothes are covered with mud stains. ❹ aspect; respect:在原则问题~大家意见完全一致。We all see eye to eye on issues of principle. /他在国际法~下了很深的功夫。He has done thorough studies in international law. ❺ higher level; higher authorities; higher-ups:~要求我们按期完成任务。The higher authorities demanded that we finish the work in time. /~派他来检查工作。He is sent from above to inspect our work. ❻ elder generation of one's family; one's elders
上命 shàngmìng order or instruction of one's superior:~难违。It is hard to disobey the orders of one's superior.
上年 shàngnián last year; previous year:~收成不如今年好。Last year's harvest was not as good as this year's.
上年纪 shàng niánji be getting on in age:他一~,腿脚就不大灵便了。Advancing in age, he can no longer walk briskly. *or* As he is getting on in years, he has difficulty moving about.
上盘 shàngpán 〈矿业〉hanging wall
上皮 shàngpí 〈生理〉epithelium:~增殖〈医学〉epitheliosis
上皮癌 shàngpí'ái 〈医学〉epithelioma
上皮管型 shàngpí guǎnxíng 〈医学〉epithelial casts
上皮瘤 shàngpíliú 〈医学〉epithelioma:钙化~ benign calcifying epithelioma; calcified epithelioma /毛发~ multiple benign cystic epithelioma /腺性~ glandular epithelioma
上皮炎 shàngpíyán 〈医学〉epithelitis
上皮组织 shàngpí zǔzhī 〈生理〉epithelial tissue
上品 shàngpǐn highest quality; top grade:~名瓷 top-grade porcelain /浙江出产名茶,其中以龙井为~。Zhejiang Province is noted for producing famous brand teas, of which *longjing* is the best.
上坡路 shàngpōlù ❶ uphill road; upward slope:走~ walk uphill /骑车走~真费劲。It really takes a lot of effort to ride a bike up a slope. ❷〈比喻〉upward movement;steady progress; growth:生产走~。Production is on the increase. /他学习上一直走~。He has been making steady progress in his studies.
上铺 shàngpù upper berth
上漆 shàngqī lacquering
上气不接下气 shàngqì bù jiē xiàqì gasp or pant for breath; be short of breath; be out of breath:跑得~ be out of breath from running /~地说 speak incoherently
上腔静脉 shàngqiāng jìngmài 〈生理〉precava; superior vena cava
上情 shàngqíng state of affairs and views of people at higher levels:~及时下达。The views of the higher-ups were transmitted to the lower levels in time.
上穷碧落下黄泉 shàng qióng bìluò xià huángquán search high and low:~,两处茫茫都不见 search high and low, but can never find (sb. or sth.)
上去 shàngqu ❶ go up:顺着山路~ go up along the mountain path /这台子太高,上不去。The platform is too high to ascend. /大家

～跟他握手。Everybody came up to shake hands with him. /你上哪儿去? Where are you going? ❷ move from a lower level to a higher level:这些意见上得去吗? Will these complaints be eventually transmitted to the higher authorities? /工作上不去,我也很着急。I am too worried that our work doesn't move forward. /他年龄大了,上不去了。He is getting old and will not get further promotion.

上去 shangqu ❶ *used after a verb, indicating upward movement*:顺着山坡爬～ climb up along the slope of the hill /一纵身跳～ jump up ❷ *used after a verb, indicating outward or forward direction*:向终点线冲～ dash to the goal /大家连忙向他迎～。Everybody hurried forward to meet him. ❸ *used after a verb, indicating a rise in level*:你们的意见已反映～了。Your views have been forwarded to the higher authorities. /把外贸搞～。We must increase (*or* expand) our foreign trade. ❹ *used after a verb, indicating addition or adhesion*:把所有的力量都使～ exert oneself to the utmost /桌子新刷～一层漆。The table was newly painted.

上圈套 shàng quāntào fall into a trap:上了人家的圈套 fall into sb.'s snare /你不能上他的圈套。You must not play into his hands.

上染率 shàngrǎnlǜ 〈纺织〉 dye-uptake

上人 shàngrén 〈旧语〉 deferential reference to monks

上人 shàngren 〈方言〉 reference to one's parents or grand-parents

上人儿 shàngrénr 〈方言〉 receive patrons:这个店的餐位一天也没上几个人儿。Only a handful of patrons come to the restaurant every day.

上任 shàngrèn ❶ assume an official post; take office:走马～ assume office /新厂长～了。The new director of the factory has taken office. /新官～三把火。A new official applies strict measures. *or* A new broom sweeps clean. ❷ predecessor:～厂长退休了。The former director has retired.

上色 shàngsè best-quality; top-notch:～绿茶 choice green tea

上色 shàngshǎi paint; colour:这些泥人还没～呢。The clay figurines have not been painted yet.

上山 shàngshān ❶ climb mountains; go to mountainous areas:～砍柴 go up the mountain to cut firewood ❷〈方言〉〈婉词〉die and be buried; pass away ❸〈方言〉(of silkworms) go up bundles of straw (to spin cocoons):再过一两天,蚕就要～了。In a day or two, the silkworms will move up the straw bundles.

上山下乡 shàngshān-xiàxiāng (of educated urban youth) go and work in the countryside or mountain areas:文革中,知识青年～,吃了好几年的苦才回城市。During the Cultural Revolution educated young people who went to live and work in the countryside had to endure hardship for several years before they could return to the city.

上赏 shàngshǎng top reward

上上 shàngshàng ❶ very best:～策 best policy /菊花中的～品 chrysanthemums of the topmost grade ❷ before last:～月 month before last

上上下下 shàngshàng-xiàxià high and low; everyone:所里～都知道这件事了。The story has spread through the whole institute. /听到这个消息,家里～都很高兴。All members of the family, old and young, are pleased at the news.

上梢 shàngshāo starting point; initial stage:有～无下梢 have a beginning but no end; start sth. but not finish it

上哨 shàngshào go to the post and stand sentry

上身 shàngshēn ❶ start wearing:这套西服刚～。I'm wearing this suit for the first time. ❷ upper part of the body; above the waist:光着～ stripped to the waist; topless /他～穿着圆领衫。He wore a T-shirt on top. ❸ upper outer garment; blouse; jacket:他穿着白～,黑裤子。He wears a white jacket and black trousers. /她这～太长,得改一改。Her blouse is a bit loose and should be altered to fit her.

上升 shàngshēng ❶ rise; go up; ascend:水位正在～。The water level is going up. /炊烟徐徐～。Wisps of kitchen smoke are curling upwards. /我们乘电梯迅速～到电视塔顶。We took the lift and reached the top of the TV tower in no time. /出生率～。The birth rate is on the rise. ❷ (of grade, degree and amount) go up; increase:气温～。The temperature is going up. /生产大幅度地～。Production is increasing by a large margin. /该国目前处于经济～期。This country is now in a period of economic growth. /这个理论乃是实践经验的～。The theory is a summation of practical experience.

上升角 shàngshēngjiǎo 〈航空〉 angle of climb; angle of ascent

上升气流 shàngshēng qìliú up current; ascending air

上升失速 shàngshēng shīsù advance stall

上升转弯 shàngshēng zhuǎnwān 〈航空〉 pull-up turn

上声 shǎngshēng *also* shǎngshēng ❶ rising tone, the second tone in classical Chinese pronunciation ❷ falling-rising tone, the third tone in modern standard Chinese pronunciation
see also "四声" sìshēng

上士 shàngshì (Chinese army) sergeant, first class; (Chinese air force) technical sergeant; (Chinese navy) petty officer, first class; (US army) sergeant first class; (UK army) staff sergeant; (US navy) petty officer first class; (UK navy) chief petty officer; (US air force) technical sergeant; (UK air force) flight sergeant; (US marine corps) technical sergeant or staff sergeant; (UK marine corps) colour sergeant

上市 shàngshì ❶ go or appear on the market:新蒜快要～了。Fresh garlic will soon be available on the market. /凉席还没～呢。Summer sleeping mats have not yet appeared on the market. /这些西瓜刚～。These watermelons have just come in. ❷ go shopping:～买菜去 go to the food market ❸〈金融〉list; go public:在香港～ be listed in Hong Kong

上市公司 shàngshì gōngsī listed companies

上市股票 shàngshì gǔpiào listed stock or shares

上市规则 shàngshì guīzé listing rules

上世 shàngshì ❶〈书面〉earliest historical periods ❷ last generation:～人 people of the last generation

上视图 shàngshìtú 〈机械〉 top view

上手 shàngshǒu ❶ *also* "上首" left-hand seat; seat of honour:您请坐～。Please take the seat on my left. ❷ *see* "上家" ❸〈方言〉get to work:这事我一个人干就行了,你们就不用～了。I can manage it alone (*or* myself); you don't have to join in. ❹ get started:比赛一～就很激烈。The game was tough-going from the very beginning.

上首 shàngshǒu 〈佛教〉 person among the audience who takes the seat at the head when Buddha preaches — seat of honour

上寿 shàngshòu ❶〈旧语〉highest grade of longevity (90, 100, or 120 years) ❷ drink a toast to longevity:奉觞～ raise the glass and drink a toast to the longevity of sb.

上书 shàngshū ❶〈旧语〉(of an old-style private tutor giving new lessons to his pupils) start teaching:请先生明天～。We would like to ask the master to start teaching tomorrow. ❷ submit a written statement to a higher authority:向市长～ submit a written request to the mayor

上疏 shàngshū submit a memorial to the emperor

上述 shàngshù preceding; mentioned above; above-mentioned:～各条,请切实执行。You are requested to carry out to the letter the regulations mentioned above. /～原则已为国际社会广泛接受。The above-mentioned principles have already been generally accepted by the international community.

上闩 shàngshuān bolt the door:门没有～。The door is not bolted.

上水 shàngshuǐ ❶ feed water to a steam engine, etc.:火车在该站～。Water will be fed to the train at this station. *or* The train will take on water at the station. ❷ upper reaches (of a river):这条江的～流急。The river is turbulent in its upper reaches. ❸ sail upstream:～船 upriver boat /～难行。It is difficult to navigate upstream.

上水 shàngshui 〈方言〉 heart, liver and lungs of an animal, used as food

上水道 shàngshuǐdào water-supply line

上税 shàngshuì pay taxes:刚买的汽车得去～。Tax will have to be paid on a new car.

上驷 shàngsì 〈书面〉 finest horse; thoroughbred horse

上司 shàngsi chief; superior; boss:顶头～ one's immediate chief /看～的眼色行事 take cues from one's boss /在～面前毕恭毕敬 be all attention and deference before one's superior

上诉 shàngsù 〈法律〉 appeal (to a higher court):提出～ lodge (*or* make) an appeal /驳回～ reject (*or* turn down, *or* overrule) an appeal /～程序 procedure for appeal /～理由 reason of appeal /～文件 instrument of appeal /～委员会 board of review

上诉法院 shàngsù fǎyuàn court of appeal; appellate court

上诉庭按察司 Shàngsùtíng Ànchásī (HK) Justice of Appeal (before July 1997)

上诉权 shàngsùquán right of appeal

上诉人 shàngsùrén appellant; petitioner

上诉状 shàngsùzhuàng petition for appeal

上溯 shàngsù ❶ sail or navigate upstream:从九江乘船～武汉 sail upstream from Jiujiang to Wuhan ❷ trace back to; date back to;

date from:这座教堂的历史可～到15世纪中叶。The church dates back to the mid-15th century.

上算 shàngsuàn profitable; economical; worthwhile:买旧车比买新车～。It is more economical to buy a used car than a new one. /这样做挺～。It pays to act the way you did.

上岁数 shàng suìshu 〈口语〉aged; getting on in years

上锁 shàngsuǒ lock:大门已经上了锁,只好从旁门进了。The gate being locked, you can enter only by the side door.

上台 shàngtái ❶ ascend the platform; appear on the stage:～即兴表演 give an impromptu performance on the stage /～讲话 mount the platform to address an audience; go on to the stage to make a speech ❷〈贬义〉assume power; hold sway:～执政 assume office /重新～ resume office; stage a comeback /～不久就下台了 resign shortly after assuming office

上台阶 shàng táijiē make a new round of progress; push sth. to the next plateau:本省的经济工作又上了一个台阶。There has been noticeable progress in the economic work of the province. /让我们的教学水平上一个新台阶。Let's raise the level of our teaching to a new high.

上堂 shàngtáng ❶ go to court; present at the court:～受审 go to the court and stand trial; be on trial ❷〈方言〉(of a teacher) give a lesson or lecture

上膛 shàngtáng ❶〈军事〉load a gun:子弹～。The gun is loaded. ❷〈生理〉palate

上套 shàngtào ❶ harness (draught animals); hitch up an animal to a cart ❷ fall into a trap; be caught in a snare:坏人一勾引,他就上了套儿了。Seduced by bad elements, he fell into the trap.

上腾 shàngténg (of air, gas, etc.) rise:热气～。Steam spouted.

上体 shàngtǐ 〈书面〉upper part of the body:裸露着～ bare or naked to the waist; topless

上天 shàngtiān ❶ go up in the sky; fly skywards:又一颗人造卫星～了。Another man-made satellite was launched. ❷〈婉词〉go to heaven; pass away:老人家昨日～了。The old man (*or* woman) passed away yesterday. ❸ Heaven; Providence; God

上天无路,入地无门 shàngtiān wú lù, rù dì wú mén there is neither road to heaven nor door into the earth — no way of escape; in deep water; cornered

上调 shàngtiáo (of prices) be adjusted upwards; raise:食糖价格～了。The price of sugar has been raised.

see also shàngdiào

上头 shàngtóu 〈旧语〉(of a girl on her wedding day) start wearing her hair in a bun (instead of a plait)

上头 shàngtou ❶ above:从～往下看 look down from above /电视机～布满灰尘。The TV set is covered with dust. ❷ higher authorities:～不批准。The higher authorities did not approve of it. /～变一变,下边乱一片。When people at the top chop and change, there is the devil to pay down here.

上头上脸 shàngtóu-shàngliǎn throw all restraint to the winds:这人你对他和气,他可就～,不知高低了。He is the type that would not know where he stands if you are kind and polite to him.

上吐下泻 shàngtù-xiàxiè throw up on top and purge down below; vomit and have loose bowels

上位 shàngwèi ❶ (usu. of officials) high position; high rank ❷ seat of honour

上味 shàngwèi delicacies; very delicious food

上尉 shàngwèi (Chinese army & air force) captain; (Chinese navy) lieutenant; (US & UK armies, US & UK marine corps, US air force) captain; (US & UK navies) lieutenant; (UK air force) flight lieutenant

上文 shàngwén foregoing paragraphs; preceding paragraphs:见～ see above; see supra /～已有交代。This has been explained in the preceding paragraph(s).

上沃尔特 Shàng-Wò'ěrtè Upper Volta

上屋 shàngwū 〈方言〉main room (usu. facing south) within a courtyard

上无片瓦,下无立锥之地 shàng wú piàn wǎ, xià wú lì zhuī zhī dì *also* "上无片瓦,下无插针之地" have neither a tile over one's head nor a speck of land to stick an awl into — be stony broke

上午 shàngwǔ forenoon; morning

上西天 shàng xītiān 〈宗教〉go to *Sukhavati* or Western Paradise — die; pass away

上下 shàngxià ❶ high and low; old and young:举国～ whole nation /～不通气 lack proper channels of communication between the higher and lower levels /机关里～都很忙。All people in the unit, from the leadership to the staff, are very busy. ❷ from top to bottom; up and down:我～打量着这位客人。I looked the guest up and down. /他浑身～都淋湿了。He was wet through. /新楼～共二十层。The new building is twenty-storeyed. ❸ relative superiority or strength:～难分 hard to tell who is better /不相～ equally matched; about the same ❹ (used after a numerical-classifier compound to designate a rough number) about; nearly; or so; or thereabouts:五十岁～ about fifty years old /这袋粮食有一百斤～。This bag of grain is approximately a hundred kilograms. ❺ go up and down:楼内没有电梯,～很不方便。The building has no lift and it is inconvenient having to climb up and down. /警察仔细观察～车的乘客。Police watched the passengers get on and off the bus.

上下其手 shàngxiàqíshǒu act in an underhand way; resort to deception

上下水 shàng-xiàshuǐ water supply line and sewer:新楼的～还没完工。Work on the water supply line and sewer in the new building has not been completed yet.

上下推委 shàngxià-tuīwěi buck-passing either up or down:哪一级的问题由哪一级解决,不能～。Problems should be solved at whatever level is appropriate without buck-passing either up or down.

上下文 shàng-xiàwén context:脱离～来摘引他的话是很不公正的。It is unfair to quote his remarks out of context.

上下一心 shàngxià-yīxīn the leadership and the rank and file, or the government and the people, are of one mind

上弦 shàngxián ❶〈天文〉first quarter (of the moon) ❷ wind up a clock, toy, etc.

上弦月 shàngxiányuè moon at the first quarter

上限 shàngxiàn upper limit; ceiling:合资企业中,外资～为49%。The upper limit for foreign investment in a joint venture is 49%. *or* Foreign investment in a joint venture cannot exceed 49%.

上线 shàngxiàn raise to the higher plane of struggle over the political line:不要动不动就给人家上纲～,乱扣帽子。Don't criticize people by exaggerating their mistakes at every turn and slap political labels on them right and left.

上宪 shàngxiàn 〈书面〉one's superior; senior officer or official

上香 shàngxiāng burn incense and offer sacrifices (to gods or ancestors); burn joss sticks

上相 shàngxiàng come out well in a photograph; look attractive in photographs; be photogenic:这位姑娘挺～的。The girl is photogenic.

上校 shàngxiào (Chinese army & air force) colonel; (Chinese navy) captain; (US & UK armies and marine corps, US air force) colonel; (US & UK navies) captain; (UK air force) group captain

上鞋 shàngxié *also* "绱鞋" shàngxié sole a shoe; stitch the sole to the upper

上心 shàngxīn 〈方言〉bear or keep in mind; be in earnest; be careful:他只要～,就一定能办到。He can surely do the job only if he is careful enough. /对群众的事要多上点心。We should always keep public interest in mind.

上新世 Shàngxīnshì 〈地质〉Pliocene Epoch

上刑 shàngxíng ❶ torture sb. to extract a confession ❷〈书面〉stiff or severe punishment

上行 shàngxíng ❶〈铁路〉going towards the capital; up; upgoing:～列车 upgoing train; up train ❷ upriver; upstream:～船 upriver boat ❸ official documents submitted to higher authorities:～文 documents to be submitted to the upper levels

上行下效 shàngxíng-xiàxiào the (usu. bad) example set by a person in a leading position will be followed by his subordinates; if a leader sets a bad example, his subordinates will follow suit:～,当头儿的老违反规章制度,事情哪能办好呢? How can things improve when leaders start violating the rules and regulations with their subordinates following suit?

上行线路 shàngxíng xiànlù 〈通信〉uplink

上旋 shàngxuán 〈体育〉top spin:发～球 serve a top-spin ball

上选 shàngxuǎn first-class; first-rate; top-grade; superior:这几件工艺品在展览会上可列为～。These few pieces of handicraft can be rated as top-grade at the exhibition.

上学 shàngxué ❶ go to school; attend school; be at school:收拾好书包,该～去了。Put your things in the satchel. It is time you went to school. /明天放假,不～。Tomorrow is a holiday and there will be

S

no school. ❷ begin school:现在小孩儿～的年龄提前了。Children begin school at an earlier age nowadays.
上旬 shàngxún first ten-day period of a month
上压力 shàngyālì 〈物理〉upward pressure
上眼 shàngyǎn 〈方言〉watch attentively:这是他的拿手节目,同志们～哪! This number is a trick he is especially good at. So watch attentively, comrades!
上眼药 shàng yǎnyào 〈口语〉say bad words about sb.; speak ill of sb.:她小姑子没少给她在婆婆面前～。Her sister-in-law made quite a few malicious remarks about her in front of her mother-in-law.
上演 shàngyǎn put on the stage; stage; perform:不日将～《天下第一楼》。They will put on *Top Restaurant* one of these days. /这出戏正在排练,还没～。The play is not on yet. It is being rehearsed. /剧场正～什么戏? What's on at the theatre?
上演税 shàngyǎnshuì royalty paid by performers to the playwright usually at a set percentage of the box receipts
上扬 shàngyáng go up; increase:纽约股价～,美元汇价下滑。The stock price in New York has gone up and the exchange rate of US dollars has dropped.
上野动物园 Shàngyě Dòngwùyuán Ueno Zoological Garden, the oldest zoo in Japan established in 1882
上夜 shàngyè 〈旧语〉be on night duty:今天该我～。It is my turn to be on night duty today.
上谒 shàngyè 〈书面〉call on (sb. holding high office or an elder)
上衣 shàngyī upper outer garment; jacket
上议院 shàngyìyuàn upper house; (UK) House of Lords
上瘾 shàngyǐn be addicted (to sth.); get into the habit (of doing sth.); be crazy about sth.; get hooked on sth.:吸毒～ be addicted to drugs /他玩电子游戏机～了。He was obsessed with TV games. /这种药吃多了会～。This medicine is habit-forming. /抽烟上了瘾就不好戒了。It is very difficult to give up smoking once the habit is contracted.
上映 shàngyìng show (a film); screen:这部片子多次～,久演不衰。This film has been shown many times and is still very popular.
上游 shàngyóu ❶ upper reaches (of a river):青海地处长江～。Qinghai Province is located in the upper reaches of the Yangtze River. ❷ what is ahead of others; advanced position:力争～ aim high; strive for the best /～无止境。One can always aim higher and still higher. ❸ (of oil industry, etc.) upstream:在天然气～工业上大量投资 make big upstream investments in gas
上游勘探 shàngyóu kāntàn 〈石油〉upstream exploration
上有天堂,下有苏杭 shàng yǒu tiāntáng, xià yǒu Sū-Háng just as there is paradise in heaven, there are Suzhou and Hangzhou on earth
上有政策,下有对策 shàng yǒu zhèngcè, xià yǒu duìcè the higher authorities have policies and the localities have their countermeasures — practice of some local authorities to neutralize the effect of government policies; attempt of those below to get around the policies of their superiors
上釉 shàngyòu 〈化工〉enameling
上谕 shàngyù also "圣谕" shèngyù imperial edict
上元节 Shàngyuánjié Lantern Festival which falls on the 15th day of the first lunar month:～是中国民间的一个重要节日。The Lantern Festival is one of the important festivals among Chinese.
上源 shàngyuán (of rivers) place close to the source or origin:永定河的～有桑干河和洋河两大支流。Near the origin of the Yongding River there are two main tributaries, the Sanggan and the Yanghe rivers.
上院 shàngyuàn upper house; (India) Rajya Sabha
上载 shàngzǎi 〈信息〉upload
上灶 shàngzào cook; do the cooking
上涨 shàngzhǎng rise; go up:洪水正在～。The flood is rising. /牛奶价格～。The price of milk has gone up.
上账 shàngzhàng make an entry in an account book:刚收到的款子已经～了。We have entered in the account the sum of money just received.
上照 shàngzhào 〈方言〉see "上相"
上阵 shàngzhèn go into battle; pitch into the work; play in a game:今晚球赛,咱们一齐～。We are all going to play in tonight's match.
上肢 shàngzhī upper limbs:～麻木无力 feel numb and weak in one's upper limbs
上中农 shàngzhōngnóng also "富裕中农" fùyù zhōngnóng upper-middle peasant
上冢 shàngzhǒng 〈书面〉visit a grave to honour the memory of the deceased
上装 shàngzhuāng ❶ make up (for a theatrical performance):他正在后台～呢。He is making up backstage. ❷ 〈方言〉upper outer garment; jacket:～很合身。The jacket fits you perfectly.
上奏 shàngzòu (of ministers) make an oral presentation to the emperor; present a memorial to the emperor
上座 shàngzuò seat of honour:～留给奶奶。Please reserve the seat of honour for grandma.
上座率 shàngzuòlǜ box-office rate:这部电影～很高。This movie is a box-office success.
上座儿 shàngzuòr (of a cinema, theatre, restaurant, etc.) presence of customers:戏园子里～已到八成。Eighty per cent of the seats of the theatre have been booked.

shang

裳 shang see "衣裳" yīshang
see also cháng

shāo

烧(燒) shāo ❶ set fire to; burn:壁炉～木柴 burn logs in the fireplace /～毁 burn down; destroy /放火～房子 set the house on fire /炭～尽了。The charcoal has been burnt up. ❷ cook; bake; heat:～开水 boil water /～瓷器 bake (*or* fire) porcelain /～暖气 have central heating /炕～热了。The *kang* is heated. ❸ (of culinary art or cooking) stew after frying; fry after stewing:～海参 stewed sea cucumber /～大虾 stewed prawns /红～鲤鱼 carp stewed in brown source ❹ roast; braise:～鸡 roast chicken /～鹅 braised goose /叉～肉 grilled pork ❺ run a fever; have a temperature:～了两天两夜 run a high fever for two days ❻ fever:赶紧给他退～ hurry to bring his temperature down to normal ❼ damage or hurt (due to excessive use of fertilizer, drugs, etc.):肥料太多了～了根了。The roots have been damaged by excessive application of manure. ❽ one's head turned by newly acquired riches:有两个钱就～得不知怎么好了。He is forgetting himself with a fat purse.
烧斑 shāobān burned spot
烧包 shāobāo 〈方言〉get a swollen head because of one's wealth or power; be drunk with success:才当了个小组长,看把你～的! You are only a group leader, and you've gotten too big for your britches.
烧爆 shāobào 〈冶金〉decrepitation
烧杯 shāobēi 〈化学〉beaker (used in a pharmaceutical or chemistry laboratory)
烧饼 shāobing sesame seed cake
烧刀子 shāodāozi also "烧刀" 〈方言〉white spirit (usu. distilled from sorghum or maize)
烧饭 shāofàn 〈方言〉cook rice; do the cooking; prepare a meal
烧高香 shāo gāoxiāng burn joss sticks in worship before the figure or image of Buddha or a god — be blessed or granted a favour; be thankful:你只要不来添麻烦,我就～了,哪里还敢指望你帮忙。I thank God you're not bothering me any more. I certainly don't expect you to help me, far from it! *or* How dare I expect you to lend me a hand?
烧锅 shāoguō glazed steel cooking utensil
烧锅 shāoguo ❶ vat for making liquor ❷ liquor distillery
烧化 shāohuà ❶ cremate ❷ burn (paper, etc. as an offering to the dead)
烧画 shāohuà poker-picture
烧荒 shāohuāng reclaim wasteland by burning wild grass and bushes
烧毁 shāohuǐ burn up; burn down; burn through:手稿已在那次火灾中～。The manuscripts were all destroyed in that fire. /这座楼房被侵略军～了。The building was burned down by invaders.
烧火 shāohuǒ make a fire; build a fire; tend the kitchen fire:～做饭 light a fire to cook rice (*or* dishes)
烧鸡 shāojī roast or baked chicken

烧碱 shāojiǎn 〈化学〉caustic soda
烧结 shāojié sintering; agglomeration; agglutination
烧结玻璃 shāojié bōli sintered glass
烧结厂 shāojiéchǎng sintering plant
烧结法 shāojiéfǎ sintering process
烧结剂 shāojiéjì agglutinant
烧结坩埚 shāojié gānguō sintered crucible
烧结温度 shāojié wēndù sintering temperature
烧结物 shāojiéwù sinter
烧结箱 shāojiéxiāng sinter box
烧酒 shāojiǔ spirit usu. distilled from sorghum or maize:好厉害的～! What a strong spirit or liquor!
烧烤 shāokǎo barbecue:～架 barbecue grill (*or* rack); barbecue / 该国的～很有名。The barbecue of that country is quite famous.
烧垦 shāokěn slash-and-burn cultivation
烧腊 shāolà 〈方言〉pot-stewed fowl, meat, etc. served cold to go with wine
烧蓝 shāolán 〈工美〉enameling; blueing
烧料 shāoliào imitation frosted glass (used to make utensils and handicrafts)
烧麦 shāomai *see* "烧卖"
烧卖 shāomai *also* "烧麦" steamed dumpling with the dough frilled at the top
烧毛 shāomáo 〈纺织〉singeing:煤气～ gas singeing /～工艺 singeing /～机 singeing frame; gassing frame
烧瓶 shāopíng flask (used in a pharmaceutical or chemistry laboratory)
烧伤 shāoshāng 〈医学〉burn:严重～ severe burns /二度～ second-degree burns /他被大火～了。He suffered burns in the fire.
烧蚀锥 shāoshízhuī 〈航天〉ablating cone
烧香 shāoxiāng ❶ burn joss sticks (before an idol):～拜佛 burn incense and pray to Buddha /～许愿 burn incense and make a vow to Buddha ❷ grease sb.'s palm; bribe:办什么事都不～不行。Nothing gets done unless a palm is greased.
烧心 shāoxīn ❶〈医学〉upset stomach; have heartburn:白薯吃多了～。Excessive consumption of sweet potatoes will cause a stomach upset. ❷〈方言〉(of cabbages) turn yellow at the heart:烧了心的大白菜没法吃。The cabbages which turn yellow at the heart are not fit to eat.
烧心壶 shāoxīnhú 〈方言〉tea-urn; samovar; tea-kettle
烧夷弹 shāoyídàn incendiary bomb
烧针 shāozhēn acupuncturel treatment where needles are burnt red at the tip before swift insertion and withdrawal from the skin
烧纸 shāozhǐ 〈迷信〉❶ burn paper money as an offering to the dead ❷ paper money burned for the dead
烧灼 shāozhuó burn; scorch; singe:他们的话像一团火,～着他的心。Their scathing remarks touched him to the quick.
烧灼术 shāozhuóshù 〈医学〉cauterization

鞘

shāo whiplash:鞭～ whiplash
see also qiào

梢

shāo tip; thin end of a twig, etc.:树～ top of a tree /眉～ tip of the brow
see also sào
梢公 shāogōng *see* "艄公" shāogōng
梢林 shāolín 〈方言〉bush; shrub
梢马 shāomǎ *also* "梢子马" draught horse
梢门 shāomen 〈方言〉gate (usu. with gateway) that can let through an animal-drawn vehicle or cart
梢条 shāotiáo branch; twig
梢头 shāotóu ❶ tip of a branch:月上柳～。The moon has risen above the willow trees. /鸟儿在桃树～歌唱。The birds are singing on the twigs of the peach tree. ❷〈林业〉top log
梢尾 shāowěi end:九月～ end of September
梢子 shāozi ❶ tip or end of a branch or anything of similar shape:鞭～ tip of a whip /荆～ tip of a bramble stem ❷〈方言〉main threads (of a complicated affair):摸不着～ be at a loss what to make of the tangle ❸〈方言〉side; flank:偏～ flank ❹〈方言〉boatman
梢子棍 shāozigùn a kind of weapon (a long stick with a short one attached to it by an iron chain); tagged stick
梢子马 shāozimǎ *see* "梢马"

捎

shāo take sth. to or for sb.; bring sth. to sb.:～包东西 take a parcel to sb. /～个好儿 give (*or* pass) one's regards to sb. /给他～个信。Take a message for him.
see also shào
捎搭 shāoda 〈方言〉incidentally; in passing; conveniently:这事我～着就给你办了。I can get it done for you quite conveniently.
捎带 shāodài incidentally; in passing:她不仅为他照管小孩,还～着帮他整理房间。She not only looks after his child but helps him tidy up his room. /这点事儿～着就干完了。This tiny bit of work will be done in a jiffy. /～说一句,戏票已买到了。By the way (*or* Incidentally), I've got a ticket for the play.
捎带脚儿 shāodàijiǎor 〈方言〉without extra trouble; in passing:你要的东西我～就买来了。By the way, I've got you what you want.
捎话 shāohuà take a message to sb.; have a message conveyed to sb.:老师捎了个话,叫他立即到学校去一趟。Here's a message for him — the teacher asks him to come to the school this minute. *or* The teacher sent word that he should come to the school right away.
捎脚 shāojiǎo pick up passengers or goods on the way:请你捎个脚吧。Please give me a lift.
捎手 shāoshǒu 〈方言〉conveniently; in passing:你到了车间,能～把这封信交给主任吗? Could I trouble you to give this letter to the director when you go to the workshop?

蛸

shāo *see* "蟏蛸" xiāoshāo
see also xiāo

筲

shāo pail made of bamboo strips or wood; bucket
筲箕 shāojī basin-like bamboo kitchen utensil (for washing rice)

稍

shāo 〈副词〉a little; a shade; a trifle; slightly:～大一点 a little bigger /～快一点 a bit faster /～好一点 a shade better /～加润色 touch up /～事休息 take a breather /～等一下 wait a minute /～一迟疑,就会丢失机会。Opportunity will slip through your fingers at the slightest hesitation.
see also shào
稍稍 shāoshāo 〈副词〉a little; a bit; slightly:经过一番争夺,他才～占了上风。After an intense competition, he began to gain an edge on his opponent. /把房间～整理一下。Let's straighten up the room a bit.
稍胜一筹 shāoshèng-yīchóu *also* "略胜一筹" lüèshèng-yīchóu a notch or cut above; slightly better:他的英语口语比我～。His spoken English is just a notch better than mine.
稍逊一筹 shāoxùn-yīchóu *also* "略逊一筹" lüèxùn-yīchóu slightly inferior to:她的工作能力比他～。She is somewhat behind him in capability.
稍微 shāowēi 〈副词〉a little; somewhat; a trifle; slightly:～有点粗 somewhat crude /～有点紧张 get a bit nervous or edgy /～休息休息 take a short rest /～想一想就明白了 become clear about sth. when one has given it some thought /～有点眉目。Things are beginning to take shape.
稍为 shāowéi *see* "稍微"
稍许 shāoxǔ 〈副词〉a little; slightly:痛～好了一点 feel a little better
稍纵即逝 shāozòng-jíshì it's gone when the grip is slightly relaxed — transient; fleeting:事机万变,～。The situation is fast changing. If you don't seize the opportunity when it comes, it will be gone (*or* lost) for good.

艄

shāo ❶ stern ❷ rudder; helm:掌～ be at the helm; in control
艄公 shāogōng *also* "梢公" shāogōng ❶ helmsman ❷ boatman

sháo

勺(❶杓)

sháo ❶ spoon; scoop; ladle:漏～ strainer; colander /铁～ iron spoon /不锈钢～ stainless spoon /马～ ladle /炒～ round-bottomed frying pan ❷ *shao*, an old unit of capacity (＝1 centilitre)

S

勺叨 sháodao *also* "勺刀"; "韶刀" sháodao 〈方言〉 chatter; be garrulous: 他喝了两口酒,就～上来了。After a sip or two of the wine, he started to chatter. /他怎么这么勺勺叨叨的讨人嫌。What a nuisance he is, babbling on and on for nothing.

勺口儿 sháokour taste of dishes prepared by a cook; cooking skill of a cook: 您尝尝这位大师傅的～怎么样。Please try some of the dishes prepared by the chef. *or* Let's see what the chef's dishes taste like.

勺鹬 sháoyù 〈动物〉 curlew

勺状软骨 sháozhuàng ruǎngǔ 〈生理〉 cartilage spatulata

勺子 sháozi ladle; scoop

芍 sháo

芍药 sháoyao 〈植物〉 Chinese herbaceous peony

韶 sháo

〈书面〉 beautiful; splendid; magnificent: ～丽 beautiful

韶刀 sháodao *see* "勺叨" sháodao

韶光 sháoguāng 〈书面〉 ❶ beautiful springtime: ～易逝 time passes ❷ 〈比喻〉 glorious youth

韶华 sháohuá 〈书面〉 springtime: ～虚度 idle away one's youth /～不再。Time and tide wait for no man.

韶景 sháojǐng beautiful springtime

韶山 Sháoshān Shaoshan Village (Mao Zedong's birthplace), in Xiangtan County of Hunan Province

韶秀 sháoxiù 〈书面〉 delicate and pretty: 一位～的女郎 graceful girl of delicate features

苕 sháo

〈方言〉 sweet potato: 红～ sweet potato

see also tiáo

shǎo

S

少 shǎo

❶ few; little; scanty; meagre: 人手～ short of hands; short-handed /机会～ have few opportunities /资金～ have little funds /困难不～ have plenty of difficulties /出席人数太～ poor attendance /凶多吉～ bode ill rather than good /～出差错 make less mistakes /～说空话 make no empty promise /你吃那么～,怎么回事? You're only pecking at your food, what's wrong? ❷ be short of; lack; not enough: 缺～钢材 lack steel /～找钱 short change /～个好领导 need a competent leader ❸ lose; be missing: 屋子里～了几把椅子。Some chairs are missing from the room. ❹ owe: ～他的钱都还清了。I've repaid all the money I owed him. ❺ a little while; a minute: 请～候。Wait a moment, please. ❻ stop; cut out: ～废话! Stop talking rubbish! *or* None of your nonsense! /～管闲事。Mind your own business. /～惹事。Don't get into trouble.

see also shào

少安毋躁 shǎo'ān-wúzào don't get impatient; be calm and wait a while: 事情即将有分晓,请君～。Patience is a great virtue. We'll know the outcome soon. *or* The result will come out soon. Will you please wait a little while?

少不得 shǎobudé cannot do without; cannot dispense with; be indispensable: 办这种事～你。We can't do without you in such matters. *or* Your service is indispensable for running the show. /逢年过节,～有些应酬。It is natural that we have social functions to attend on festival days.

少不了 shǎobuliǎo ❶ cannot do without; be bound to; be unavoidable: 以后～还会麻烦你。We may have to trouble you again. ❷ plenty of: 工作开始的时候,困难～。When the work gets started, there will be quite a lot of difficulties.

少待 shǎodài just a moment; wait a minute

少得了 shǎodeliǎo (used in a rhetorical question) can do without; can dispense with: 搞公关～他吗? He is an indispensable person for public relations, isn't he?

少而精 shǎo'érjīng smaller in quantity but better in quality; fewer but better: ～的讲话 concise speech /内容要～。Make it terse and succinct.

少会 shǎohuì 〈套语〉 it's a rare pleasure to see you: 张先生,我们～,您是什么时候到此地的? It's a rare pleasure to meet you, Mr. Zhang. When did you arrive?

少见 shǎojiàn ❶ 〈套语〉 it's a rare pleasure to meet you: ～了,您近来好吗? It's a rare pleasure to see you. How have you been lately? ❷ seldom seen; rare: 这种情景一般很～。Generally speaking, this is quite an unusual case. /他近来很～。He has made himself scarce of late.

少见多怪 shǎojiàn-duōguài to a man who has seen little of the world, everything is remarkable; scanty experience gives rise to many surprises: ～的乡巴佬 ignorant country bumpkin who is easily nonplussed /也许是我～。Perhaps I have seen too little of the world and am unduly curious. /这种做法在这里很平常,用不着～。There is nothing to be surprised at as it's a common practice here.

少间 shǎojiàn 〈书面〉 ❶ in a short time; in a little while; soon: ～便知。We'll (*or* You'll) know in a moment. ❷ (of illness) a little better; somewhat lighter: 病～ the patient is a little better; condition is improving

少刻 shǎokè after a short time; moment later: 客人～就到。The guests will arrive soon.

少劳少得 shǎoláo-shǎodé less pay for less work

少礼 shǎolǐ 〈套语〉 ❶ dispense with formalities: 不必客气,你我～为好。Don't stand on ceremony. ❷ offend; be rude: 对不起,～了。I'm sorry. I have been too rude.

少量 shǎoliàng small amount; little bit; a little; a few: ～的时间 a little time

少慢差费 shǎo-màn-chà-fèi fewer, slower, poorer and less economical: 这种方法～,得不偿失。Being an inefficient and expensive method, it will make us lose more than we gain.

少尿症 shǎoniàozhèng 〈医学〉 oliguria

少陪 shǎopéi 〈套语〉 I must be leaving: 我还有点事,～了。I still have an appointment, I'm afraid I must be going now (*or* I wish to be excused).

少顷 shǎoqǐng 〈书面〉 after a short while; soon; presently: 乌云密布,～风雨大作。Dark clouds blotted out the sky, and presently a fierce rainstorm raged.

少少儿的 shǎoshǎorde just a little; tiny bit; wee bit: 他就希望付出的代价～,而得到的好处却多多的。He hopes to gain as much as possible at the least cost.

少生优生 shǎoshēng-yōushēng (of family planning) have fewer but healthier babies

少时 shǎoshí after a little while; a moment later; presently: ～雨过天晴。After a little while, the rain stopped and the sun broke through.

少数 shǎoshù small number; not many; few; minority: 捣乱的～人 handful of troublemakers /～弃权。A few abstained. /他们是～。They are in the minority. *or* They are a minority. /～服从多数。The minority should be subordinate to the majority.

少数党 shǎoshùdǎng minority party

少数股权 shǎoshù gǔquán minority interest

少数民族 shǎoshù mínzú minority nationality; national minority; ethnic minority: ～地区 areas inhabited by ethnic minorities; minority nationality regions; ethnic minority area; ethnic area /～的风俗习惯 customs and habits of ethnic groups /～的语言 languages of national minorities

少头 shǎotou 〈旧语〉 (of bargaining in trade) possible cut in the price: 这件大衣有什么～没有? Can you cut down the price for this overcoat?

少许 shǎoxǔ 〈书面〉 a little; some; modicum: 菜里放～味精。Season the dish with a little gourmet powder. /把利润分给他～。Give him a small share of the profit.

少言寡语 shǎoyán-guǎyǔ keep to oneself; be reticent; never open one's mouth: 他总是～,闷闷不乐。He always kept to himself and was despondent.

少有 shǎoyǒu rare; exceptional; seldom: 世界～ rare in the world

少云 shǎoyún 〈气象〉 partly cloudy

shào

捎 shào

(of draught animals) draw back a step or two; shy

see also shāo

捎马子 shàomǎzi 〈方言〉 saddlebag

捎色 shàoshǎi (of colour) fade

哨[1] shào

❶ reconnaissance; patrol ❷ sentry post; post: 岗～

sentry post /查～ check on sentry post /放～ be on sentry duty; stand guard; stand sentry ❸〈量词〉contingent; column:一～人马 a contingent of troops

哨[2] shào ❶ (of birds) warble; chirp:鸟在树林里～。Birds are chirping in the woods. ❷〈方言〉idle talk:神聊海～ shoot the bull (*or* breeze) ❸ whistle:口～ whistle

哨棒 shàobàng 〈旧语〉cudgel (carried on the person for self-defence)

哨兵 shàobīng sentry; guard

哨笛 shàodí flageolet

哨岗 shàogǎng sentry post; post

哨马 shàomǎ scout

哨棚 shàopéng *also* "哨棚子" shed serving as a sentry post:当年用石头垒的～还保留得很完整。The stone sentry shed built in those years remains intact.

哨卡 shàoqiǎ check post

哨所 shàosuǒ sentry post; post:前沿～ forward post; outpost /沿途设有五个～。There are five sentry posts along the way.

哨探 shàotàn 〈旧语〉❶ intelligence gathering ❷ scouts

哨位 shàowèi sentry post; post

哨子 shàozi whistle

睄 shào 〈方言〉cast a glance:她～了他一下。She threw a glance at him.

稍 shào

see also shāo

稍息 shàoxī 〈军事〉stand at ease:～! At ease!

潲[1] shào ❶ (of rain) slant in:南～ slant south /西边～雨。The rain is driving in from the west. /快关窗,别让雨～进来。Shut the window, or the rain will slant in. ❷〈方言〉sprinkle; spray:熨衣服前先～点儿水。Please sprinkle some water on the clothes before you iron them.

潲[2] shào 〈方言〉hogwash; swill; slops:猪～ hogwash; swill

潲水 shàoshuǐ 〈方言〉swill; slops; hogwash

潲桶 shàotǒng 〈方言〉bucket for hogwash

少 shào ❶ young; youthful:男女老～ men and women, old and young /老～爷们儿 father and son /年～妇人 young lady /青春年～ (in) the prime of life /老来～ be old but feel young ❷ son of a wealthy family; young master:恶～ young ruffian /阔～ profligate son of the rich /遗～ young man with the mentality of an old fogy; young diehard ❸ (Shào) a surname

see also shǎo

少艾 shào'ài 〈书面〉❶young and beautiful ❷ young and beautiful girl; young beauty

少白头 shàobáitóu ❶ be prematurely grey ❷ young person with greying hair

少不更事 shàobùgēngshì *also* "少不经事" young and inexperienced; green:你真是～,这种人岂能相信! What a greenie you are to have believed such a person! /你毕竟～,这件事处理得不妥当。It was all because of your inexperience that you did not handle the matter properly.

少东家 shàodōngjia 〈旧语〉son of the master or owner; young master

少儿 shào'ér (short for 少年儿童) children:～读物 children's books

少妇 shàofù young married woman

少腹 shàofù 〈中医〉underbelly; lower abdomen

少管 shàoguǎn (short for 少年犯管教) ❶ education of juvenile offenders in reform schools:被送去劳教、～的人近来都有较好的表现。Those offenders and juvenile delinquents sent to institutions for reform and re-education through labour or for correction have acquitted themselves quite well recently. ❷ administer correction and re-education of juvenile offenders

少管所 shàoguǎnsuǒ reformatory for juvenile delinquents

少将 shàojiàng (Chinese army & air force) major general; (Chinese navy) rear admiral; (US & UK armies and marine corps, US air force) major general; (US & UK navies) rear admiral; (UK air force) air vice marshal

少君 shàojūn 〈旧语〉〈敬词〉your son

少林拳 shàolínquán Shaolin boxing, a school of Chinese boxing originated in Shaolin Monastery

少林寺 Shàolínsì Shaolin Monastery, in Songshan (嵩山) of Henan Province

少奶奶 shàonǎinai 〈旧语〉❶ young mistress of the house ❷ your daughter-in-law

少男 shàonán young unmarried man; young boy

少年 shàonián ❶ early youth (from ten to sixteen):他～时代一心想当电影导演。It was his boyhood ambition to become a film director. ❷ boy or girl of that age; juvenile; teenager:～运动员 juvenile players /～业余体校 children's sparetime sports school ❸〈书面〉young man; lad:翩翩～ dashing young man /莫等闲,白了～头,空悲切。Don't lament in vain over the lost chances, when the youthful head turns grey. /他～得志,目中无人。He thought too much of his early success and was getting too big for his boots.

少年班 shàoniánbān class for exceptionally bright minors in a college or university

少年读物 shàonián dúwù juvenile reader

少年犯 shàoniánfàn juvenile delinquent:～教养院 borstal

少年犯罪 shàonián fànzuì juvenile delinquency

少年法庭 shàonián fǎtíng 〈法律〉children's court; juvenile court

少年宫 shàoniángōng children's palace

少年管教所 shàonián guǎnjiàosuǒ reform school; reformatory

少年黑素瘤 shàonián hēisùliú 〈医学〉juvenile melanoma

少年老成 shàonián-lǎochéng ❶ old head on young shoulders:此人年纪虽轻,倒是～。Young as he is, he is fairly mature. ❷ listless young person

少年先锋队 Shàonián Xiānfēngduì Young Pioneers

少年之家 shàonián zhī jiā children's centre; children's club

少女 shàonǚ young girl:～们的共同爱好 shared hobbies of young girls

少尉 shàowèi (Chinese army & air force) second lieutenant; (Chinese navy) ensign; (US & UK armies, US & UK marine corps, US air force) second lieutenant; (US navy) ensign; (UK navy) acting sublieutenant; (UK air force) pilot officer

少先队 shàoxiānduì (short for 少年先锋队) Young Pioneers

少先队员 shàoxiān duìyuán Young Pioneer

少相 shàoxiang look younger than one's age; have a youthful appearance:您长得真～,哪像五十的人呀。You look far younger than a man of fifty.

少小 shàoxiǎo when young:～离家 leave home young

少校 shàoxiào (Chinese army & air force) major; (Chinese navy) lieutenant commander; (US & UK armies and marine corps, US air force) major; (US & UK navies) lieutenant commander; (UK air force) squadron leader

少兴 shàoxing 〈方言〉(of appearance, looks) young

少爷 shàoye 〈旧语〉❶ young master (of the house); young son; 活像个～ very much like a spoiled young man ❷〈敬语〉your son

少爷脾气 shàoye píqi behaviour of a pampered boy:你少跟我发～! Stop behaving like a spoilt young master to me!

少长 shào-zhǎng the youthful and the elderly:～皆宜 fit for the young and the old

少壮 shàozhuàng young and vigorous

少壮不努力,老大徒伤悲 shàozhuàng bù nǔlì, lǎodà tú shāngbēi if one does not work hard when young, it will be useless for him to regret when old; an idle youth, a needy age

少壮派 shàozhuàngpài younger faction or group (in political party or other organizations); powerful rising stars; the up-and-coming; Young Turks

召 Shào a surname

see also zhào

邵 shào *see* "劭❷" shào

邵 Shào a surname

劭 shào 〈书面〉❶ encourage; admonish; exhort:～农 en-

S

courage farming ❷ noble; admirable:年高德～ of venerable age and eminent virtue; venerable

绍[1] shào carry on; keep on; continue:～复大业 inherit and carry on the great cause

绍[2] Shào Shaoxing in Zhejiang Province

绍介 shàojiè introduce:请为～ please introduce me to sb.

绍剧 shàojù Shaoxing opera, a local opera popular in Shaoxing, Zhejiang province

绍兴酒 shàoxīngjiǔ *also*"绍酒" Shaoxing rice wine

shē

樣 shē 〈方言〉mango

樣仔 shēzǐ 〈方言〉mango

奢 shē ❶ luxurious; extravagant; profligate:穷～极欲 (indulge in) luxury and extravagance /骄～淫逸 luxury-loving, loose-living and idle; wallowing in luxury and pleasure; extravagant and dissipated ❷ excessive; inordinate; undue; *see*"～求"

奢侈 shēchǐ luxurious; lavish; wasteful:追求～ seek after an extravagant style of life /反对～ oppose extravagance /～习惯 lavish habits /婚礼极其～。The wedding was extravagant and wasteful.

奢侈品 shēchǐpǐn luxury goods; luxury items; luxuries

奢侈品税 shēchǐpǐnshuì luxury tax

奢华 shēhuá prodigal; luxurious; sumptuous; extravagant:～的生活 extravagant life /建造～宅邸 build a luxurious residence /～的服饰 sumptuous dress and personal adornment

奢丽 shēlì luxurious and resplendent

奢靡 shēmí extravagant; lavish; wasteful:～腐化 be extravagant and corrupted

奢盼 shēpàn extravagant hopes; wild wishes

奢念 shēniàn excessive expectations:心存～ harbour unrealistic expectations

奢求 shēqiú excessive or unreasonable demands

奢望 shēwàng extravagant hopes; wild expectation:抱着～ cherish extravagant hopes /放弃～ give up wishful thinking /对物质的～ hanker after material comforts /对名利的～ inordinate desire for personal fame and gain /这是不可能实现的～而已。This is nothing but an unrealizable wild wish.

奢想 shēxiǎng wild wishes; extravagant hopes; wishful thinking:不存～ cherish no illusion about

奢遮 shēzhē (often used in the early vernacular) outstanding; remarkable; excellent

畲 Shē *see*"畲" Shē

畲 Shē see"畲族"

畲族 Shēzú She nationality, distributed over Fujian, Zhejiang, Jiangxi and Guangdong provinces

畲 shē 〈书面〉〈农业〉burn the grass in the field to fertilize the soil; slash and burn

see also yú

赊 shē buy or sell on credit:～酒 drink on credit

赊购 shēgòu buy on credit:～化肥 buy fertilizers on credit

赊欠 shēqiàn buy or sell on credit; give or get credit:靠～度日 live on credit

赊销 shēxiāo sell on credit:本店～了一大批家电。We sold a large number of electrical appliances on credit.

赊账 shēzhàng ❶ buy or sell on credit; give or get credit:现金交易,概不～。Cash only and no credit. *or* Cash and carry. ❷ outstanding bills or accounts:他有一千美元～。There was an outstanding account of $1,000 against him.

猞 shē

猞猁 shēlì 〈动物〉lynx

shé

蛇(虵) shé snake; serpent:毒～ poisonous snake /蝰～ adder /(青)草～ grass snake /金环～ ring snake /水～ water snake /眼镜～ cobra /蟒～ boa; python /响尾～ rattlesnake /打～ kill a snake /捕～ catch a snake /玩～ charm a snake

see also yí

蛇虫 shéchóng snakeworm

蛇床 shéchuáng 〈植物〉*Cnidium monnieri*

蛇床子 shéchuángzǐ 〈中医〉fruit of *Cnidium monnieri*

蛇胆 shédǎn gallbladder of a snake; snake bile

蛇豆 shédòu *see*"蛇瓜"

蛇毒 shédú 〈医学〉snake venom; venin:～疗法 venomization

蛇根草 shégēncǎo *also*"萝芙木" luófúmù devilpepper

蛇瓜 shéguā *also*"蛇豆" ❶ snake gourd (*Trichosanthes anguina*) ❷ fruit of *Trichosanthes anguina*

蛇管 shéguǎn 〈机械〉hosepipe; coiler

蛇管换热器 shéguǎn huànrèqì hose heat exchanger

蛇管加热器 shéguǎn jiārèqì heating coil

蛇管冷凝器 shéguǎn lěngníngqì coil condenser

蛇颈龟 shéjǐngguī snake-necked turtle

蛇恐怖症 shékǒngbùzhèng 〈心理〉ophidophobia

蛇口蜂针 shékǒu-fēngzhēn snake bite and bee sting — venomous; vicious; malicious

蛇郎中 shélángzhōng 〈方言〉〈中医〉specialist in healing snake bites

蛇麻 shémá *also*"啤酒花" píjiǔhuā 〈植物〉hops

蛇鳗 shémán snake eel

蛇莓 shéméi 〈植物〉Indian strawberry (*Duchesnea indica*); mock-strawberry; snake berry

蛇皮 shépí snakeskin

蛇皮管 shépíguǎn 〈电工〉flexible metal conduit

蛇皮癣 shépíxuǎn 〈医学〉pityriasis

蛇旗 shéqí draco

蛇丘 shéqiū 〈地质〉esker; winding glacial ridge

蛇曲 shéqū 〈地理〉meander

蛇拳 shéquán snake boxing, style of Chinese boxing (with movements like a snake's)

蛇鹈 shétí snakebird; darter

蛇头 shétóu ❶ snake head ❷ ringleader of organized illegal immigration

蛇蜕 shétuì 〈中医〉snake slough; exuviation

蛇纹石 shéwénshí 〈矿物〉serpentine

蛇无头不行 shé wú tóu bù xíng a snake cannot crawl without a head — a group cannot act without a leader:～,抓了他们的首领,就不怕他们了。As a snake can not crawl without its head, there is no need to be afraid of them when their ringleader is locked behind bars.

蛇蜥 shéxī *also*"脆蛇" cuìshé *Ophisaurus gracilis*

蛇蝎 shéxiē snakes and scorpions — heinous people; vipers

蛇蝎心肠 shéxiē-xīncháng venomous as snakes and scorpions:这人～,竟然毒死了亲生子。This man was so fiendish that he even murdered his own son with poison.

蛇行 shéxíng ❶ move in a twisting way on the ground; snake ❷ meander; wind:小溪～,绕林而过。The brook meandered around the woods.

蛇形 shéxíng snakelike; S-shaped

蛇影杯弓 shéyǐng-bēigōng *also*"杯弓蛇影" mistake the reflection of a bow in the cup for a snake — extremely nervous or suspicious

蛇足 shézú foot added to a snake by a fatuous artist — a superfluity:这个结尾,完全是～。The ending is really superfluous.

阇 shé

see also dū

阇梨 shélí monk; senior monk

折 shé ❶ break; split; snap:胳膊摔～了 have one's arm broken /椅子腿～了。The chair leg broke. /树枝突然～断了。The tree branch suddenly snapped. ❷ suffer losses; lose money in business:

不～不赚 break even ❸ (Shé) a surname
see also zhē; zhé
折本 shéběn lose money in business dealings: 他做生意折了本。He suffered losses in business operations.
折秤 shéchèng loss or damage in the course of reweighing the goods
折耗 shéhào damage (to goods during transit, storage, etc.); loss: 可以避免的～ avoidable damage / 过多的～ excessive loss
折钱 shéqián 〈方言〉 lose money

舌

shé ❶ lingua; tongue: 小～ uvula / ～尖口快 sharp-tongued / 长～妇 loquacious woman / 学～ imitate mechanically / 鼓～ engage in loose talk (to stir up trouble) / 嚼～ gossip; chatter ❷ sth. shaped like a tongue: 火～ tongues of flame / 帽～ peak of a cap ❸ clapper
舌癌 shé'ái tongue cancer
舌敝唇焦 shébì-chúnjiāo talk till one's tongue and lips are parched; talk oneself hoarse in pleading, expostulating, etc.: 说得～也无济于事。No matter how hard he pleaded, they just refused to listen.
舌底澜翻 shédǐ-lánfān surging waves under the tongue — gift of the gab; glib tongue; eloquence
舌根 shégēn root of the tongue
舌根音 shégēnyīn *also* "舌面后音" 〈语言〉 velar, such as g, k, h in standard Chinese pronunciation
舌耕 shégēng 〈书面〉 plough with the tongue — teach to make a living
舌尖 shéjiān tip of the tongue
舌尖后音 shéjiānhòuyīn 〈语言〉 blade-palatal, such as zh, ch, sh, r
舌尖前音 shéjiānqiányīn 〈语言〉 dental, such as z, c, s
舌尖音 shéjiānyīn 〈语言〉 apical, such as z, c, s, d, t, n, l, zh, ch, sh, r
舌尖中音 shéjiānzhōngyīn 〈语言〉 blade-alveolar, such as d, t, n, l
舌剑唇枪 shéjiàn-chúnqiāng *also* "唇枪舌剑" battle of words
舌面后音 shémiànhòuyīn 〈语言〉 *see* "舌根音"
舌面前音 shémiànqiányīn 〈语言〉 dorsal, such as j, q, x
舌切除术 shéqiēchúshù 〈医学〉 glossectomy
舌切开术 shéqiēkāishù 〈医学〉 glossotomy
舌人 shérén 〈旧语〉 officials acting as interpreters
舌伤 shéshāng hurt by public opinion: 刀伤好治，～难医。It is easy to heal physical wounds but hard to get over the pain caused by verbal insults.
舌鳎 shétǎ 〈动物〉 tonguefish; tongue sole
舌苔 shétāi 〈中医〉 tongue coating; tongue fur: ～厚 furred tongue / 你的～太厚。There is a thick coating on your tongue.
舌痛 shétòng glossaldynia; glossalgia
舌头 shétou ❶ tongue: 大～ thick-tongued; lisper / 长～ gossiper / 烂～ festered tongue — loquacious person / 嚼～ wag one's tongue; chatter; gossip / 咬～ lisp ❷ enemy soldier captured for the purpose of extracting information from him
舌下神经 shéxià shénjīng lingual nerve; hypoglossal nerve
舌下腺 shéxiàxiàn 〈生理〉 sublingual gland
舌咽神经 shéyān shénjīng glossopharyngeal nerve
舌炎 shéyán 〈医学〉 glossitis
舌蝇 shéyíng *also* "萃萃蝇" cuìcuìyíng tsetse fly
舌战 shézhàn engage in a battle of words; have a verbal battle with; argue heatedly: ～群儒 fight a battle of words with scholar advisers / 展开～ engage in a verbal battle / 会谈中，双方进行了一场激烈的～。During the talks the two sides crossed verbal swords.
舌状花 shézhuànghuā 〈植物〉 lingulate flower
舌子 shézi 〈方言〉 tongue

佘

Shé a surname

shě

舍（捨）

shě ❶ give up; discard; abandon: 难～难分 hard to part with each other / ～此别无他法。There is no other way out. / 四～五入 rounding (off); to the nearest whole number ❷ give alms; dispense charity: ～药 dispense medicine
see also shè
舍本逐末 shěběn-zhúmò attend to trifles to the neglect of essentials: ～，贤哲所非。A sagacious person never seeks after trifles to the neglect of essentials.
舍不得 shěbude be loath to part with or give up; grudge: ～花钱 be loath to spend one's money / 他那么小就离开家，妈妈有点～。He was so young that his mother was reluctant to let him leave home. / 相处久了，～离开。Long-time friends hate to part. / 别～你那点时间啦! Don't be so grudging of that bit of time of yours!
舍不得孩子套不住狼 shěbude háizi tàobuzhù láng one cannot hope to entrap a wolf without risking the life of one's own child — if one wishes to succeed, one has to take great risks
舍得 shěde be ready to part with or give up; not grudge: ～下功夫 not begrudge time spent on sth.; be ready to make efforts / ～吃穿 not grudge (*or* hate) spending money on food and clothes
舍得一身剐，敢把皇帝拉下马 shěde yīshēn guǎ, gǎn bǎ huángdì lāxia mǎ he who fears not being cut to pieces dares to unhorse the emperor
舍己从人 shějǐ-cóngrén give up one's own views and follow those of others'; sacrifice one's own interests to do what others wish
舍己救人 shějǐ-jiùrén save sb. else' life at the risk of one's own: 他做过好几件～的事。He has rescued people several times despite the danger to his own life.
舍己为公 shějǐ-wèigōng sacrifice one's own interests for the sake of the public: 学习他～的精神。Learn from his spirit of self-sacrifice for public good.
舍己为人 shějǐ-wèirén place the interests of others before one's own; be altruistic: 他一向大公无私，～。He is selfless and often sacrifices his own interests for the sake of others.
舍近求远 shějìn-qiúyuǎn *also* "舍近图远" seek far and wide for what lies close at hand: 附近就有一家不错的电器维修店，你们何必～。There is a quite good electrical appliances repair shop nearby. Why do you take the trouble of going all the way to a distant one?
舍车保帅 shějū-bǎoshuài (in chess) give up a rook to save the king — sacrifice minor interests to major ones
舍脸 shěliǎn (be compelled to) cast aside considerations of face: ～求情 (have to) ask for a favour (*or* beg for mercy) unabashedly / 出于无奈，她只好舍着脸向人借贷。She had no choice but to stoop to beg for loans.
舍命 shěmìng risk one's life; be ready to sacrifice oneself: ～相救 come to sb.'s rescue at the risk of one's own life
舍命不舍财 shěmìng bù shěcái would rather part with one's life than one's money: ～的土老财 country miser who treasures his property more than his life
舍命陪君子 shěmìng péi jūnzǐ 〈戏谑〉 keep sb. company at all costs: 我决定～，同你去一趟。I've decided to go there with you and stick it out even at the cost of my life.
舍弃 shěqì give up; forgo; abandon: ～生命 lay down one's life / ～财产 give up one's property / ～幸福 forgo one's happiness / ～职位 relinquish one's post / 甘愿～ abandon of one's own accord; willingly abandon
舍入 shěrù 〈数学〉 rounding off: ～常数 round-off constant / ～误差 rounding error; round-off error / ～指令 round-off order / ～字符 separating character
舍身 shěshēn lay down one's life; sacrifice oneself: ～救国 lay down one's life for (the cause of) national salvation / ～图报 sacrifice oneself to reciprocate sb.'s favour (*or* kindness)
舍生取义 shěshēng-qǔyì sacrifice one's life for a just cause: 君子～，小人则舍生为利。A gentleman dies for a just cause while a mean person risks his life for profit.
舍死忘生 shěsǐ-wàngshēng *also* "舍生忘死" risk one's life: ～，赤心报国 dedicate oneself (*or* give one's all) to the cause of one's country / ～，与坏人斗争。He fought scoundrels in utter disregard of his own safety.
舍我其谁 shěwǒqíshéi if I can't do it, who can: 能担此重任者，～? Who else but me can face up to this heavy responsibility?

shè

涉

shè ❶ wade; ford: 跋山～水 scale mountains and ford

streams; travel across mountains and rivers /～水而过 wade across the water ❷ go through; undergo; experience: ～险 go through perils /～世不深 have scanty experience of life; have seen little of the world ❸ involve; implicate: 干～ interfere in; intervene in /交～ negotiate; make representations /牵～ involve; drag in

涉笔 shèbǐ write with a brush or pen

涉笔成趣 shèbǐ-chéngqù produce an interesting piece of work the moment one sets one's brush to paper; write or paint freely and well

涉渡 shèdù wade across a river; ford a stream

涉及 shèjí involve; relate to; deal with; touch upon: ～三项内容 consist of three items /～思想观念等更广泛的领域 deal with other broad fields like ideology /并不～是非 have nothing to do with right and wrong /不免～时政 would naturally touch upon current policies /～到许多单位 involve many units and institutions /～到他 have something to do with him /～的学科 related subject (*or* discipline) /～的人 those concerned; interested parties /此案～了几个大人物。Several big shots are implicated in the case. /～其他问题。It is related to other issues.

涉览 shèlǎn read casually; browse; skim

涉历 shèlì 〈书面〉 ❶ live through; go through; experience personally: ～三载 what one has gone through in the past three years ❷ do desultory reading; read cursorily: ～经史 read classics and history extensively

涉猎 shèliè do desultory reading; read at random: 广泛～ read extensively /这些史书，我只是～，并未精读。I only made a cursory study of these history books and didn't go deeply into them.

涉禽 shèqín 〈动物〉 wading bird; wader

涉世 shèshì have experience of life; get along in the world; make one's way in the world: ～未深 inexperienced in affairs of the world /青年人～浅，经验不足。Young people are not familiar with the ways of the world.

涉讼 shèsòng be entangled in a lawsuit: ～人 person involved in a lawsuit

涉外 shèwài foreign-related: ～事务 matters relating to foreign nationals, firms, etc. /～部门 foreign-related authorities or department /～经济诉讼 litigation involving foreign businesses

涉外婚姻 shèwài hūnyīn marriage between Chinese and foreigners

涉嫌 shèxián be suspected of being involved or implicated; be a suspect: ～受贿 be suspected of taking bribes

涉险 shèxiǎn ❶ be engaged in an adventure ❷ adventure

涉想 shèxiǎng 〈书面〉 imagine; fancy; indulge in fanciful thinking

涉足 shèzú 〈书面〉 set foot in; enter: ～社会 set foot in society /～仕途 embark on an official career; enter politics

社

shè ❶ organization; agency; society: 报～ newspaper office /新闻通讯～ news agency /杂志～ magazine office /出版～ publishing house /合作～ cooperative; co-op /人民公～ people's commune /结～ form an association (*or* society) ❷ some service units: 旅～ hotel /旅行～ travel service /广告～ advertising agency /茶～ teahouse /总～ head office /分～ branch office ❸ god of the land; sacrifices to him or altars for such sacrifices: 秋～ autumn sacrifice

社办企业 shèbàn qǐyè commune-run enterprise

社队 shèduì people's commune and production brigade, existing in rural areas before China's reform and opening-up

社会 shèhuì ❶ society: 人类～ human society /原始～ primitive society /奴隶～ slave society /封建～ feudal society /资本主义～ capitalist society /文明～ civilized society /黑暗的～ dark society /先进的～ advanced society /稳定的～ stable society /动荡的～ turbulent society /～财富 social wealth /～地位 social status /～福利事业 social (*or* public) welfare services /～环境 social environment /～基础 social basis /～实践 social practice /～制度 social system /～人士 public figures /改造～ change (*or* transform) a society /脱离～ be divorced from society /～不公 social injustice /～不平等 social inequality /～秩序 public order /～公德 social morals /～道德风尚 social moral atmosphere /～阶级 social class /～结构 social structure /～群体 social groups /～舆论 public opinion /～效益 social benefits /～震动 social repercussion ❷ community: ～贤达 community leader

社会办学 shèhuì bànxué all sectors of society giving support to school education

社会保险 shèhuì bǎoxiǎn social insurance

社会保障制度 shèhuì bǎozhàng zhìdù social security system

社会必要劳动 shèhuì bìyào láodòng socially necessary labour

社会存在 shèhuì cúnzài social being: 人的～决定人的社会意识。Man's social being decides his social consciousness.

社会达尔文主义 shèhuì Dá'ěrwénzhǔyì social Darwinism

社会党 shèhuìdǎng socialist party

社会党国际 Shèhuìdǎng Guójì Socialist International, set up in 1951 with headquarters in London

社会调查 shèhuì diàochá social investigation; social survey: 搞～ conduct a social survey /进行～ carry out a social investigation /～的对象 object (*or* subject) of a social survey /～的成果 findings of a social survey

社会发展史 shèhuì fāzhǎnshǐ history of development of society; history of social development

社会分工 shèhuì fēngōng social division of labour; division of labour in society

社会风气 shèhuì fēngqì mood of society; social morals

社会工资 shèhuì gōngzī social wage

社会工作 shèhuì gōngzuò work done for the benefit of the communities in addition to one's regular job; community work: 他担任了许多～。He does a number of community service jobs.

社会公德 shèhuì gōngdé social ethics

社会关系 shèhuì guānxi ❶ one's relatives or relations; one's social connections: ～太复杂 with complicated social relations (*or* connections) /～单纯 with simple social relationships /～牵连太多 too many social connections ❷ human relations in society; social relations

社会化 shèhuìhuà socialization

社会活动 shèhuì huódòng community activities; public activities

社会集团购买力 shèhuì jítuán gòumǎilì institutional purchasing power

社会集资 shèhuì jízī fund raising from various sectors of society

社会教育 shèhuì jiàoyù social education

社会经济制度 shèhuì jīngjì zhìdù socio-economic system

社会科学 shèhuì kēxué social sciences

社会民主党 shèhuì mínzhǔdǎng social democratic party

社会民主主义 shèhuì mínzhǔzhǔyì social democracy

社会名流 shèhuì míngliú noted public figure; eminent person; celebrity: 我们这里很有几位～。There are quite a few luminaries among us (here).

社会青年 shèhuì qīngnián young unemployed: 安置～ make job arrangements for the unemployed youths /～的问题 problems related to the young unemployed /有些～自学成才了。Some unemployed young people have become useful persons by studying on their own.

社会人 shèhuìrén 〈哲学〉 *homo sociologicus*

社会人类学 shèhuì rénlèixué social anthropology

社会沙文主义 shèhuì shāwénzhǔyì social chauvinism

社会生态学 shèhuì shēngtàixué socioecology

社会实践 shèhuì shíjiàn social practice

社会危机 shèhuì wēijī social crisis

社会协商对话制度 shèhuì xiéshāng duìhuà zhìdù system of consultation and dialogue (between groups of people with diverse social interests)

社会心理学 shèhuì xīnlǐxué social psychology

社会形态 shèhuì xíngtài social formation

社会学 shèhuìxué sociology: ～著作 works on sociology /家庭～ sociology of family /比较～ comparative sociology /政治～ political sociology

社会学家 shèhuìxuéjiā sociologist

社会意识 shèhuì yìshi social awareness

社会营销 shèhuì yíngxiāo social marketing

社会语言学 shèhuì yǔyánxué sociolinguistics

社会治安 shèhuì zhì'ān public order: ～条例 regulations on maintenance of public order /～的综合治理 improvement of public order through comprehensive measures

社会制度 shèhuì zhìdù social system

社会主义 shèhuìzhǔyì socialism: ～现代化 socialist modernization /～初级阶段 primary (*or* initial) stage of socialism

社会主义道路 shèhuìzhǔyì dàolù socialist road: 走～ follow or take the socialist road

社会主义法制 shèhuìzhǔyì fǎzhì socialist legal system; socialist legality

社会主义改造 shèhuìzhǔyì gǎizào socialist transformation: 进行～

carry out socialist transformation
社会主义革命 shèhuìzhǔyì gémìng socialist revolution:投入～ be active in socialist revolution
社会主义公有制 shèhuìzhǔyì gōngyǒuzhì socialist public ownership
社会主义集体所有制 shèhuìzhǔyì jítǐ suǒyǒuzhì socialist collective ownership
社会主义建设 shèhuìzhǔyì jiànshè socialist construction:～的规模 scale of socialist construction /～的成就 accomplishments of socialist construction
社会主义建设总路线 shèhuìzhǔyì jiànshè zǒnglùxiàn general line for socialist construction (formulated in 1958), namely, go all out, aim high, and achieve greater, faster, better and more economic results in building socialism:制定～ formulate the general line for socialist construction
社会主义教育运动 Shèhuìzhǔyì Jiàoyù Yùndòng Socialist Education Movement (a nationwide movement to clean things up in the fields of politics, economy, organization and ideology, 1963-1966)
社会主义经济 shèhuìzhǔyì jīngjì socialist economy
社会主义精神文明 shèhuìzhǔyì jīngshén wénmíng socialist culture and ideology; socialist spiritual civilization
社会主义觉悟 shèhuìzhǔyì juéwù socialist consciousness:提高～ heighten one's socialist consciousness (*or* awareness)
社会主义劳动竞赛 shèhuìzhǔyì láodòng jìngsài socialist labour emulation:开展～ launch socialist labour emulation /参加～ participate in socialist labour emulation
社会主义市场经济 shèhuìzhǔyì shìchǎng jīngjì socialist market economy
社会主义所有制 shèhuìzhǔyì suǒyǒuzhì socialist ownership
社会主义物质文明 shèhuìzhǔyì wùzhì wénmíng socialist material civilization
社会主义现代化建设 shèhuìzhǔyì xiàndàihuà jiànshè socialist modernization drive; socialist modernization
社会主义制度 shèhuìzhǔyì zhìdù socialist system:坚持～ adhere to the socialist system
社会总产值 shèhuì zǒngchǎnzhí aggregate social product
社火 shèhuǒ village festive activities, such as dragon lantern dance, lion dance, etc.
社稷 shèjì god of the land and the god of grain — state; country:～神 god of the land and grain /～坛 altar to the god of the land and grain /江山～ state power
社稷之臣 shèjìzhīchén pillar of the state
社交 shèjiāo social life; social contact:擅长～ good mixer /～聚会 social gathering /～活动 social activities
社教 shèjiào (short for 社会主义教育运动) socialist education movement
社科院 Shèkēyuàn (short for 社会科学院) Academy of Social Sciences
社论 shèlùn editorial; leading article; leader:发表～ carry an editorial /撰写～ write a leading article /～阐述了有关政策的精神。The editorial explained the essence of relevant policies.
社评 shèpíng editorial:一篇重要的～ an editorial of great importance
社区 shèqū community:～发展 community development /～研究 community studies /～中心 community centre /旧金山华人～ Chinese-American community in San Francisco
社区康复站 shèqū kāngfùzhàn community rehabilitation centre
社鼠城狐 shèshǔ-chénghú *also* "城狐社鼠" fox in a city wall and rat in a village temple — evildoers with strong backing or influential connections
社团 shètuán mass organization; body of persons:组织～ form a mass organization /文艺性的～ mass organization of art and literature / ～投资者 institutional investor
社团主义 shètuánzhǔyì corporatism
社戏 shèxì 〈旧语〉village theatricals (given on religious occasions):演～ stage village performances during a religious festival
社学 shèxué village school in the Ming and Qing dynasties
社员 shèyuán ❶ commune member:公社～ commune member /～大会 general meeting of commune members ❷ member of a society, club, organization, etc.
社长 shèzhǎng chairman of the board

设 shè ❶ set up; form; establish:～卡 set up a checkpoint /天造地～ work of nature /学院下～六个系。The college has six departments. /汽车给老弱病残～了专座。Special seats are set aside in the bus for the old, sick and handicapped. /系里～了几门新课。The department offered several new courses. /分理处～在北京。The branch office is in Beijing. ❷ work out; design:～计陷害 plot a frame-up; frame a case against sb. ❸ given; supposing:假～ suppose; assume ❹〈书面〉if; in case:～如 if /～有福,当共享。If fortune comes our way, we should share it among us.
设备 shèbèi equipment; installation; facilities; appliances:～精良 well-equipped /机器～ machines and other equipment /厂房～ workshop installations /电教～ audio-visual facilities (for education) /交通运输～ facilities for transport and communication /家用～ household appliances /～更新 updating (of) equipment /～性能 equipment characteristics /～管理 equipment management /原有的～ original equipment /新增的～ additional equipment /～的经费来源 source of funds for equipment
设辞 shècí 〈书面〉excuse; pretext; alibi:他昨日所言,全系～。What he said yesterday was nothing but excuses.
设法 shèfǎ think of a way; try; endeavour:～解决 try to solve /～克服 manage to overcome /正在～ be trying to find out a way /尽量～ do one's best to find a solution /想方～ do everything possible; try every means
设防 shèfáng set up defences; defend with a garrison; fortify:步步～ set up defences at every step /处处～ heavily fortified /～地带 fortified zone /不～城市 unfortified city; open city /以重兵～ heavily garrisoned
设伏 shèfú 〈书面〉lay ambush:～以断敌后路 lay ambush to cut off the enemy's route of retreat
设岗 shègǎng set up sentry posts:街上都临时设了岗,断绝交通。Provisional sentries were posted in the streets and traffic was cut off.
设或 shèhuò 〈书面〉if; in case:～准备不及,会议可改期举行。The meeting can be put off if time is too short for preparations.
设计 shèjì design; devise; plan:～新方案 design a new scheme /～版面 lay out a printed page /～舞蹈动作 design dance movements; choreograph /～服装 design a dress (*or* costume) /精心～ design with great care /重新～ redesign /初步～ draft out a design /根据要求～ design in line with requirements /按照古代建筑的式样～ design modelled on an ancient building /～图纸 design drawing /建筑～ architectural design /舞台～ stage design /～合理 rational design /～得适用大方。The design is practical and natural.
设计洪水 shèjì hóngshuǐ 〈水利〉design flood
设计能力 shèjì nénglì designed capacity
设计人员 shèjì rényuán designer
设计师 shèjìshī ❶ designer:服装～ costume designer; dress designer ❷ architect
设计图 shèjìtú design drawing
设计院 shèjìyuàn designing institute
设局 shèjú set up a trap:～诓骗 lay a plan for swindle
设立 shèlì establish; form; set up:～优秀创作奖 establish an award for works of excellence /～助学金 set up a grant-in-aid
设若 shèruò 〈书面〉supposing; provided:～疏忽大意,便会造成严重后果。If careless, we will suffer grave consequences.
设色 shèsè fill in colours on a sketch; lay paint on canvas; colour:俗艳～ painted in loud colours
设身处地 shèshēn-chǔdì put oneself in sb.'s place; put oneself in another person's shoes; be considerate:他能够将心比心,～地为人家着想。He is very considerate, and can put himself in others' shoes. /～,我认为你还是离开这儿为好。If I were you, I would stay away.
设施 shèshī installation; facilities:市政～ municipal installations /教育～ educational facilities /军事～ military installations /交通～ transport facilities /服务～ service facilities /利用～ utilize facilities /安装～ install facilities
设使 shèshǐ if; supposing that; in case
设想 shèxiǎng ❶ imagine; assume; anticipate:～一种情况 assume a situation /～一套方案 work out a plan /不堪～ too horrifying to contemplate /从最坏的方面～ prepare for the worst /离奇的～ fantastic assumption; fantasy /纯属～ figment of imagination /初步～ tentative plan ❷ have consideration for:为老人～ have consideration for the old /多为青少年～ give more thought to the needs of the

younger generation

设宴 shèyàn give a banquet; provide with a feast; fete:～款待 give a banquet in honour of sb. /～欢迎 give a welcome banquet /～饯行 give a farewell banquet /～洗尘 give a dinner for sb. on his return (from a journey)

设营 shèyíng 〈军事〉quartering; encampment

设营地 shèyíngdì campsite

设营队 shèyíngduì quartering party

设置 shèzhì ❶ set up; put up: ～代销点 set up commission shops /～骗局 lay a trap /～选修课 offer elective or optional courses (in a college or school) /专门～ special establishment ❷ install; fix: ～通风设备 install ventilation facilities /给我～种种障碍 put various obstacles in my way

设座 shèzuò select a venue for a banquet: 明日～前门饭店,宴请外国友人。A banquet will be given at the Qianman Hotel tomorrow in honour of our foreign friends.

赦

shè remit (a punishment); pardon; absolve: 十恶不～ guilty of unpardonable evil; unpardonably wicked /特～ special pardon /大～ general pardon; amnesty /大～国际 Amnesty International

赦令 shèlìng decree for pardon; order of amnesty: 颁发～ issue a decree for pardon

赦免 shèmiǎn remit (a punishment); pardon; absolve: ～某人的罪行 pardon sb. his crime /获得～ be pardoned /实行～ carry out a remission of punishment /～权 power of absolution

赦书 shèshū *see* "赦令"

赦宥 shèyòu 〈书面〉pardon: 揭发同伙,以求～ inform on one's accomplices in order to win pardon

赦罪 shèzuì absolve from guilt; pardon

慑(慴、懾)

shè 〈书面〉fear; dread; coerce: 威～ terrorize with military force; deter /核威～ nuclear deterrence /～于父亲的威严,他不敢反对。Intimidated by the stern dignity of his father, he dared not raise any objection.

慑服 shèfú ❶ submit because of fear; succumb: ～于大自然的威力 submit to the power of nature /他那出奇的冷静～了她。She succumbed to his extraordinary calm. ❷ cow sb. into submission; be awed

摄[1](攝)

shè ❶ take in; absorb; assimilate ❷ take a photo; photo; shoot: 在颐和园拍～外景 location shooting at the Summer Palace /这几张照片～于北京。These photographs were taken in Beijing.

摄[2](攝)

shè 〈书面〉conserve (one's health); keep fit: 善自珍～ take good care of oneself; coddle oneself

摄[3](攝)

shè act for: *see* "～政"

摄动 shèdòng 〈天文〉perturbation

摄理 shèlǐ hold a position in an acting capacity: ～朝政 handle state affairs in an acting capacity

摄谱仪 shèpǔyí 〈物理〉spectrograph

摄取 shèqǔ ❶ absorb; assimilate: ～养分 absorb nourishment /～食物 take in food /～精华 assimilate the essential ❷ take a photo; photo; shoot: ～几个场景 take some photos of the scene /到外景地去～镜头 go for shots in the open

摄生 shèshēng 〈书面〉conserve one's health; keep fit: 善～者 one who knows how to conserve his health /～之道 road to longevity

摄食 shèshí (of animals) feed: ～习性 feeding habit

摄氏度 shèshìdù Celsius; centigrade: 32～ 32°C

摄氏温标 Shèshì wēnbiāo Celsius or centigrade temperature scale

摄氏温度 Shèshì wēndù *see* "摄氏度"

摄氏温度计 Shèshì wēndùjì centigrade thermometer; Celsius thermometer

摄卫 shèwèi 〈书面〉art of conserving life energy or health

摄位 shèwèi act as regent; act for a legitimate ruler

摄像 shèxiàng shoot pictures; make a video recording

摄像管 shèxiàngguǎn camera tube; television camera tube

摄像机 shèxiàngjī video camera: 电视～ television camera

摄像机取景器 shèxiàngjī qǔjǐngqì view finder

摄行 shèxíng 〈书面〉act in some capacity: 部长职务暂时由副部长～。The deputy minister acts provisionally in the minister's capacity.

摄养 shèyǎng art of conserving one's health or keeping fit; hygiene

摄影 shèyǐng ❶ take a photo: ～留念 take a photo as a souvenir; have a souvenir photo taken /特技～ trick photography ❷ shoot a film; film: 内景～ interior shooting /外景～ exterior shooting /全景～ panoramic shooting

摄影比赛 shèyǐng bǐsài photographic competition

摄影测量 shèyǐng cèliáng photographic surveying

摄影地质学 shèyǐng dìzhìxué 〈地质〉photogeology

摄影机 shèyǐngjī camera: 电影～ cinecamera; movie camera; cinematograph /立体～ stereoscopic camera

摄影记者 shèyǐng jìzhě press photographer; cameraman

摄影迷 shèyǐngmí shutterbug

摄影棚 shèyǐngpéng film studio

摄影闪光弹 shèyǐng shǎnguāngdàn 〈军事〉photoflash bomb

摄影师 shèyǐngshī photographer; cameraman

摄影室 shèyǐngshì photographic studio

摄影术 shèyǐngshù photography

摄影展览 shèyǐng zhǎnlǎn photographic exhibition; photo show; picture show

摄影侦察 shèyǐng zhēnchá photographic reconnaissance: ～卫星 photoreconnaissance satellite

摄政 shèzhèng act as regent: 由亲王～ have the prince act as regent

摄政王 shèzhèngwáng prince regent

摄制 shèzhì 〈影视〉produce

摄制组 shèzhìzǔ production unit: ～十分庞大 very large production unit /～分工明确。The production unit has a clear-cut division of responsibility.

摄篆 shèzhuàn 〈旧语〉act as deputy (from 篆 style of Chinese calligraphy used on officials' seals)

厍

shè ❶ 〈方言〉(often used in place names) village ❷ (Shè) a surname

拾

shè 〈书面〉ascend in light steps

see also shí

拾级 shèjí 〈书面〉ascend or walk up, or go up a flight of steps

舍[1]

shè ❶ house: 宿～ dormitory /校～ school buildings ❷ hut: 寒～ my humble house ❸ shed: 牛～ cowshed /猪～ pigsty; pigpen ❹ 〈谦词〉my: ～妹 my younger sister ❺ (Shè) a surname

舍[2]

shè ancient unit of distance equal to 30 *li*: 退避三～ retreat ninety *li* — give way to avoid conflict; keep a good distance from sb.

see also shě

舍间 shèjiān *also* "舍下"〈谦词〉my humble abode; my house: ～离此不远。My humble abode is not far from here. /请到～一叙。I shall be pleased to invite you to my house.

舍监 shèjiān 〈旧语〉proctor of school dormitory; house matron in school; dormitory superintendent

舍利 shèlì *also* "舍利子"〈宗教〉*sarira*, remains from cremation of Buddha's or a saintly monk's body, often in the shape of beads, regarded as most treasured Buddhist relics: 琉璃瓶中藏有十颗～。Ten *sarira* were enshrined in the glazed bottle.

舍利塔 shèlìtǎ stupa; pagoda for Buddhist relics; Buddhist shrine

舍亲 shèqīn 〈谦词〉my relative

舍饲 shèsì raise or rear in pens or folds: 他们引进了一批良种羊,改传统的放牧为采叶～。They bought a fine breed of sheep and, instead of grazing them in the traditional way, raised them in a fold with leaves.

舍下 shèxià *also* "舍间"〈谦词〉my humble abode; my house: ～简陋,请勿见笑。I hope you do not take it as impoliteness to invite you to my humble house. /欢迎光临～。Welcome to my house.

舍营 shèyíng 〈军事〉billeting

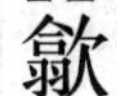

shè

see also xī
歙砚 shèyàn inkslabs produced in Shexian (歙县), Anhui Province from stones quarried in Wuyuan (婺源), Jiangxi Province

射 shè ❶ shoot; fire; eject:～靶 shoot at the target /～出一发炮弹 fire a shell /慢～ slow fire /速～ rapid fire /扫～ strafe /能骑善～ expert at horseback riding and arrow shooting; be a good horseman as well as a crack shot; have high equestrian skills and good marksmanship /弹～器 ejector /弹～椅 ejector seat /别～! Don't shoot! /～人先～马,擒贼先擒王。When shooting a man first shoot his horse; when catching robbers first catch the leader. ❷ discharge in a jet:喷～ spout; spurt; jet /注～ inject /～他一身水 shoot water all over him /～出一股油 spout a stream of oil /～到地上了 spurt to the ground ❸ emit (light, heat, etc.):反～ reflect /辐～ radiate /光芒四～ radiate brilliant light /月光从树梢的空隙里～到地面上。The moon peered through the trees and shed its light on the ground. /从门缝里～进来一道阳光。A beam of sunshine shot into the room through the door which was left ajar. ❹ allude to sth. or sb.; insinuate; intimate:影～ insinuate
射锕 shè'ā 〈化学〉radioactinium (RdAc)
射程 shèchéng range (of fire):有效～ effective range /导弹～ missile fire range /进入大炮～之内 come within range of the guns
射弹 shèdàn projectile
射电谱 shèdiànpǔ radio spectrum
射电天文学 shèdiàn tiānwénxué radio astronomy
射电望远镜 shèdiàn wàngyuǎnjìng radio telescope
射电星 shèdiànxīng radio star
射电源 shèdiànyuán 〈天文〉radio source
射干 shègān 〈植物〉blackberry lily
射击 shèjī ❶ open fire; fire; shoot:～敌人 shoot at the enemy /向手无寸铁的老百姓～ fire a gun at unarmed civilians /开始～ open fire /停止～ stop shooting /～目标 shooting target ❷〈体育〉shooting:苦练～ train hard in shooting /～冠军 shooting champion /飞碟～ claypigeon shooting /多向飞碟～ trapshooting /双向飞碟～ skeet shooting /～技术 marksmanship
射击场 shèjīchǎng shooting range
射击地境 shèjī dìjìng sector of fire
射击孔 shèjīkǒng embrasure; gunport
射箭 shèjiàn ❶ shoot an arrow ❷〈体育〉archery:～场 archery range /～手 archer; bowman /～靶子 rover
射角 shèjiǎo angle of fire; elevation
射界 shèjiè area or field of fire; firing area
射精 shèjīng 〈生理〉ejaculation
射精管 shèjīngguǎn ejaculatory duct
射孔 shèkǒng 〈石油〉perforation
射口 shèkǒu embrasure
射猎 shèliè hunt with bow and arrow; hunt with firearms:酷爱～ ardently love hunting /～能手 good hunter
射流 shèliú 〈物理〉efflux
射流技术 shèliú jìshù fluidics
射流喷口 shèliú pēnkǒu efflux nozzle
射门 shèmén 〈体育〉shoot (at the goal):一次～ a shot /连续～ successive shots /机智地～ shoot resourcefully /～好手 good shooter /擅长～ be good at scoring goals /跳起～ jump shot /反弹～ bounce shot /鱼跃～ dive shot /转身～ pivot shot; turn-around shot
射门手 shèménshǒu goal getter
射频 shèpín radio frequency
射频发电机 shèpín fādiànjī 〈电工〉radio frequency alternator
射频放大器 shèpín fàngdàqì radio frequency amplifier
射铅 shèqiān 〈化学〉radiolead
射手 shèshǒu ❶ shooter; marksman:机枪～ machine gunner /优秀～ excellent marksman; crack shot; sharpshooter /训练～ train shooters ❷〈体育〉goal getter
射束 shèshù 〈电子〉beam:～管 beam tube
射水鱼 shèshuǐyú archer fish
射速 shèsù firing rate
射线 shèxiàn 〈物理〉ray:α～ alpha ray /β～ beta ray /γ～ gamma ray /X～ X-ray /阴极～ cathode ray
射线病 shèxiànbìng radiation sickness
射线疗法 shèxiàn liáofǎ radiotherapy
射线皮炎 shèxiàn píyán 〈医学〉actinodermatitis
射线伤害 shèxiàn shānghài 〈医学〉radiohazard
射线照相 shèxiàn zhàoxiàng 〈物理〉radiograph:～术 radiography
射向 shèxiàng direction of shooting:～准确 shoot straight
射影 shèyǐng projection:～几何 projective geometry
射铀 shèyóu 〈化学〉radio-uranium

麝 shè ❶ musk deer (*Moschus moschiferus*) ❷ musk
麝馥兰香 shèfù lánxiāng breath of musk and the scent of orchids
麝龟 shèguī musk turtle
麝鹿 shèlù musk deer (*Moschus moschiferus*)
麝牛 shèniú musk ox (*Ovibus moschatus*)
麝鼠 shèshǔ muskrat (*Desmana moschata*)
麝香 shèxiāng musk:～草 thyme /～酮 musk ketone
麝香兰 shèxiānglán 〈植物〉grape-hyacinth
麝鼹 shèyǎn 〈动物〉desman
麝雉 shèzhì hoatzin (*Opisthocomus hoazin*)

shéi

谁 shéi *also* shuí ❶ who:今天下午～作报告? Who is the speaker this afternoon? /他们在等～? Who are they waiting for? /这是～的书? Whose book is it? /有～愿意跟我们一起去? Would anyone like to go with us? ❷ (used in a rhetorical question) nobody; no one:难道～都不知道? Is it possible that nobody knows anything about it? /她真对～都讨厌吗? Is it true that she likes no one? /～不说俺家乡好? Who wouldn't speak highly of my hometown? ❸ (used in a supposition or conjecture) somebody; someone:如果有～出来管管,这该有多好! It would be much better if someone came forward to take up the matter! /不知是～把桌上的书拿走了。Someone must have taken the book away from the desk. /～知盘中餐,粒粒皆辛苦。Each grain of rice we ever ate, Cost someone else a drop of sweat. ❹ anyone; anybody; everyone; everybody: (a) *used before* 都 *or* 也:这东西我们～也不愿买。None of us would buy it. /～来都欢迎。Whoever comes will be welcome. (b) *used to denote both the subject and the object*:我们～也不欠～。Neither of us owes anything to the other. *or* We have broken even. /他们俩～也不服～。Neither of them thinks better of the other. (c) *used to refer to the same person*:～笑到最后,～笑得最好。He who laughs last laughs best. /～合适,～就干。Whoever fits the job may take it. *or* Whoever is suited to the job may do it.
谁边 shéibiān where; what place:秦皇岛外打鱼船,一片汪洋都不见,知向～? No fishing boats off Qinhuangdao Are seen on the boundless ocean. Where are they gone?
谁个 shéigè 〈方言〉which person; who:～不说北京好! Who wouldn't speak well of Beijing?
谁何 shéihé 〈书面〉❶ who; what person; any person:不知其～ do not know who he is ❷ question; interrogate:陈利兵而～。Armed with sharp weapons, the soldier questioned every passer-by.
谁们 shéimen 〈方言〉who; what persons:～来了? Who are here? /你那屋里是～? Who are there in your room?
谁人 shéirén who; what person:这是～造的谣? Who started this rumour? /～不知,他是植棉的能手。Everyone knows he is a good hand at planting cotton. /～不知,哪个不晓? It is known to all.
谁谁 shéishéi *used to refer to people whose names need not be mentioned*:乡亲们传着～立了大功,～当了英雄。News about who had rendered meritorious service and who had won the title of "hero" was passing around the village.

shēn

莘 shēn ❶ *see* "莘莘" ❷ (Shēn) a surname
莘莘 shēnshēn 〈书面〉great many; numerous; multitudinous:来自全国各地的～学子,在这所著名的学府里深造。Large numbers of students from different parts of the country pursue advanced studies at this famous university.

深 shēn ❶ going far downward or going well inward from an outer surface; deep:根～叶茂的大树 deep-rooted tree covered with thick foliage /湖很～。The lake is very deep. /他的话太感动人了,使我～铭五内。His words touched me to the depths of my heart. ❷ depth:水～齐胸 breast-deep water /河有多～? What is the depth

S

of the river? ❸ hard to comprehend; difficult:这份地理试题对学生太～了。The geography paper is too difficult (*or* stiff) for the students. /文章揭示的哲理颇～。The truth as expounded in the essay is rather abstruse. ❹ in-depth; incisive; penetrating:艺术家们的表演给我的印象很～。I was deeply impressed by the performance of the artists. /这场大辩论对学术界的影响很～。This great debate had a profound impact on academic circles (*or* in academia). /作者对当前形势作了～刻的分析。The author makes an in-depth (*or* penetrating) analysis of the current situation. /他们对这件事作了～入的调查。They made a thoroughgoing investigation into the matter. ❺ close; intimate:两人是～交。The two are on intimate terms. /他们的交情～得很。They are as thick as thieves. /他同许多作家建立了很～的关系。He has forged a close relationship with many writers. ❻ dark; rich:他穿一套～蓝色的衣服。He is wearing a dark-blue suit. /照片背景颜色太～了些。The background of the photo is a bit dark. ❼ late:～秋下午的阳光显得特别可爱。The afternoon sun in late autumn appears particularly lovely. /夜已～了,四周万籁俱寂。It was in the dead of night, and all nature was quiet and still. ❽ very; keenly; fully:～有同感 share a similar feeling /～得人心 be very popular /我们当时～知世界局势孕育着严重的危机。We were then fully (*or* keenly) aware that the world situation was pregnant with grave crises. /我们～信这种措施定能奏效。We firmly believe that this measure is bound to succeed. /他们～恐自己无法渡过这个难关。They were very much afraid that they might not be able to tide over this difficulty. /他～受群众爱戴。He enjoys the deep love and respect of the public. /我们对灾区人民～表同情。We had profound sympathy for the people of the disaster areas.

深奥 shēn'ào deep; abstruse; unfathomable; recondite:～的原理 abstruse principle /学问～ profound scholarship /他的哲学包括一系列～的观念。His philosophy consists in a series of recondite ideas.

深闭固拒 shēnbì-gùjù shut tight and firmly turn down — reject new things or ideas:～而不肯改悔 reject other people's criticisms and refuse to mend one's ways

S

深播 shēnbō 〈农业〉deep seeding

深不可测 shēnbùkěcè unfathomable; of immeasurable depth or profundity; extremely abstruse:此潭～。The pool is fathomless. /这位大师的国学造诣～。He is a master of profound attainments in Chinese classics and culture.

深藏若虚 shēncáng-ruòxū be exceedingly modest about one's ability or learning:他是个有识之士,～,不露锋芒。He is a man of insight, never seeking to show off his ability. /他虽是个大儒,但～。He was a great scholar, but he was extremely modest and unassuming.

深层 shēncéng ❶ depth:对问题的分析渐入～。The analysis gradually reached the essence of the issue. ❷ deep-going; thorough:～矛盾 deeper (*or* deep-seated) contradictions /分析～原因 make an in-depth analysis of the causes

深层带 shēncéngdài 〈地理〉bathypelagic zone

深长 shēncháng profound:这首诗简朴无华,却是意味～。This poem, though simple and unadorned, has profound implications.

深彻 shēnchè deep and penetrating; profound and thorough:他对美学有较～的研究。He has a thorough and profound knowledge of aesthetics.

深沉 shēnchén ❶ dark; deep:她对他爱得那么～。She loves him so deeply. /夜～。Night deepens. /我们对主人都怀有～的情谊。We all cherished deep feelings for the host. ❷ (of sound or voice) deep; heavy; dull:大提琴～的音调给这支曲子增添了严肃的色彩。The deep notes of the cello gave a solemn touch to the music. /远处传来～的闷雷声。The heavy dull sound of muffled thunder was heard from afar. ❸ concealing one's own feelings; reserved:他只是～地一笑,没有回答我的问题。He didn't answer my question, but only gave a meaningful smile.

深成岩 shēnchéngyán 〈地质〉plutonic rock; plutonite

深成油 shēnchéngyóu 〈石油〉deep oil

深仇大恨 shēnchóu-dàhèn bitter and deep-seated hatred; profound enmity:两家的～是由于争夺一块土地造成的。The bitter feud between the two families arose from their rival claims to a piece of land. /双方因互相鄙视,结下了～。Mutual contempt breeds bitter hatred.

深处 shēnchù depths; recesses; inmost part:密林～有一所寺庙。There is a temple in the depths of the wood. /他在内心～对她有些怨恨。He bears a grudge against her in the innermost recesses of his heart. /我从思想～厌恶他。In my heart of hearts, I do not like him.

深春 shēnchūn late spring

深到 shēndào get to the essence of sth.; be thorough:他对于哲学有～的研究。He is a thorough scholar of philosophy.

深冬 shēndōng severe winter

深度 shēndù ❶ degree of depth; depth:推算～ calculate the depth /探测油层的～ take the soundings of an oil reservoir /矿井的～不够。The mine is not deep enough. ❷ (of work, understanding, etc.) degree of getting to the essence of things; profundity; depth:理解的～ depth of understanding /这篇文章有～。This is a penetrating article. /这篇文章～不够。This essay lacks depth. ❸ degree of development towards a higher stage or level, etc.; depth; profundity (of learning, etc.):向～和广度发展 develop in depth and in width ❹ extremely; deeply; greatly:～近视 extremely myopic (*or* near-sighted)

深度计 shēndùjì depth gauge

深孚众望 shēnfú-zhòngwàng enjoy high prestige among the people; have popular support

深根固柢 shēngēn-gùdǐ *also*"深根固蒂" take deep roots; make sth. firmly rooted and unshakable

深更半夜 shēngēng-bànyè in the depth or dead of night; far into the night:他每天都工作到～。He worked far into the night every day. *or* He always worked till the small hours.

深耕 shēngēng deep culture; deep ploughing; deep tillage:～犁 deep plough; deep-tillage plough

深耕细作 shēngēng-xìzuò deep ploughing and intense cultivation:机械耕作开始以前,我们大力宣传～。We strove to popularize deep ploughing and intense cultivation before mechanized farming was introduced.

深沟高垒 shēngōu-gāolěi deep trenches and high ramparts:～,坚守城池 defend the city behind deep trenches and high ramparts /～,高挂免战牌。Entrenched behind a strong defence, they refused to give or accept battle.

深谷 shēngǔ deep and secluded valley

深固 shēngù deep and solid; profound and firm:他们实现四个现代化的信念更加～。They are even more firmly resolved to work for the success of the four modernizations.

深广 shēnguǎng deep and extensive:影响～ have a profound and far-reaching impact /他们见识～。They have a wide range of experience.

深闺 shēnguī 〈旧语〉women's quarters (in a large household or palace); boudoir:她独处～。She lives in the seclusion of her boudoir.

深海 shēnhǎi deep sea:～探测 deep-sea exploration /～考察 deep-sea observation

深海采矿 shēnhǎi cǎikuàng deep-sea mining

深海测量 shēnhǎi cèliáng bathymetry

深海带 shēnhǎidài abyssal zone

深海平原 shēnhǎi píngyuán abyssal plain

深海潜水器 shēnhǎi qiánshuǐqì bathyscaphe

深海潜水艇 shēnhǎi qiánshuǐtǐng 〈军事〉bathyscaphe; deep submersible vehicle

深海潜望镜 shēnhǎi qiánwàngjìng bathyscope

深海丘陵 shēnhǎi qiūlíng abyssal hill

深海区 shēnhǎiqū abyssal region

深海探测仪 shēnhǎi tàncèyí bathometre; bathymetre

深海遥控潜艇 shēnhǎi yáokòng qiántǐng deep unmanned submersibles (DUMS)

深海研究器 shēnhǎi yánjiūqì deep research vehicle

深海用球形潜水器 shēnhǎiyòng qiúxíng qiánshuǐqì benthoscope; bathysphere

深海鱼 shēnhǎiyú deep-sea fish

深海钻探 shēnhǎi zuāntàn deep-sea drilling (DSD)

深海资源 shēnhǎi zīyuán deep-sea resources

深海作业船 shēnhǎi zuòyèchuán deep-ocean work boat (DOWB)

深壑 shēnhè deep gully or pit

深厚 shēnhòu ❶ deep; profound:两国有着～的传统友谊。A profound traditional friendship exists between the two countries. /他对这里的一草一木都有～的感情。He loves this place dearly, cherishing every single tree and blade of grass here. ❷ solid; thick; deep-seated:他们的群众基础～。They have a solid foundation among the masses. /地上铺着一层～的雪。There is a thick layer of snow on the ground. /他冰雕的功夫～。He is very skilled in (*or* at) ice carving.

or His workmanship in ice-carving is excellent.

深呼吸 shēnhūxī deep breathing：作～ breathe deeply／～有益健康。Deep breathing benefits human health.

深化 shēnhuà go deeper；deepen：认识～ deepening of the process of cognition (or cognitive process)／～体制改革 further the structural reform／大国间矛盾～，会导致严重的后果。Intensification of contradictions among world powers will lead to serious consequences.

深晦 shēnhuì deep and obscure；hard to understand：哲理～。It's an abstruse philosophy.

深加工 shēnjiāgōng intensive processing；downstream processing：～产品 high value added products；downstream products

深涧 shēnjiàn deep gully：高山～ high mountains and deep gullies (or ravines)

深交 shēnjiāo intimate friendship；close friends：两人无甚～。The two friends are not very close.／这个人可以～。He is a friend worthy of trust.／他的熟人不多，～的尤其少。He had few acquaintances and even fewer good friends.

深井 shēnjǐng deep well：～泵 deep well pump

深究 shēnjiū go or probe into (a matter) seriously；get to the bottom of (a matter)；thoroughly investigate：事关重大，必须～。As the matter is of great importance, we have to go into it seriously.／此事不必～。We need not pursue the matter any further.／我未能及时～此事。I have not been able to get to the bottom of the matter in good time.

深居简出 shēnjū-jiǎnchū live in the seclusion of one's own home；live a secluded life；live in isolation from the outside world：他一向～，不大与别人交往。He has all along shut himself up in his own home and has hardly had any social contacts. or He has made himself scarce by cutting himself off from all outside contacts.

深刻 shēnkè ❶ deep；incisive；in-depth：～的评论 incisive comments／这件事有它～的社会根源。This incident has its deep social roots.／他对顺利执行这个政策的因素作了～的分析。He made an in-depth analysis of the factors affecting the implementation of the policy.／这对我们来说是～的教训。This is a profound lesson for us all. ❷ greatly；deeply：我～体会到改革也是一种革命。I fully realize that the present reform is essentially a kind of revolution.／他对自己的失职作了～的检查。He made a sharp self-criticism (or He criticized himself severely) for his dereliction of duty.

深空 shēnkōng 〈物理〉deep space

深空跟踪网 shēnkōng gēnzōngwǎng deep space network (network of ground stations for telemetry, tracking and command for lunar and planetary missions)

深空空间 shēnkōng kōngjiān hyperspace；deep space

深孔内圆磨床 shēnkǒng nèiyuán móchuáng 〈机械〉deep hole grinder

深孔钻床 shēnkǒng zuànchuáng 〈机械〉deep hole drilling machine

深拉 shēnlā 〈机械〉deep drawing：～钢 deep drawing steel

深冷 shēnlěng deep cooling：～设备 deep freezing unit

深冷泵 shēnlěngbèng 〈机械〉cryopump

深冷电缆 shēnlěng diànlǎn 〈电工〉cryogenic cable

深冷温度计 shēnlěng wēndùjì frigorimeter

深秘 shēnmì deep and concealed；profound and abstruse：用思～ abstrusely conceived

深妙 shēnmiào profound；subtle；abstruse and uncanny：义理～ profound argumentation (or reasoning)

深明大义 shēnmíng-dàyì be clear as to principles；know clearly what is right and proper

深谋远虑 shēnmóu-yuǎnlǜ think deeply and plan carefully；be thoughtful and farsighted：～、稳当可靠的战略方针 farsighted and reliable strategy／他总是～，从不草率从事。He always thought things over many times and never acted rashly.／此人一向以～著称。The man is well known for his foresight and circumspection.

深潜船 shēnqiánchuán deep-diving vessel；deep-diving submersible

深潜潜望镜 shēnqián qiánwàngjìng deep submergence periscope

深潜球 shēnqiánqiú bathysphere

深浅 shēnqiǎn ❶ depth：我们还得探明河水的～。We'll have to find out about the depth of the river. ❷ shade (of colour)；hue：这两块布的颜色～稍有不同。The colours of the two pieces of cotton print are of different shades. ❸ proper limits；sense being correct in one's social behaviour；propriety：他这个人说话不知～。He often speaks thoughtlessly and without a sense of propriety.

深切 shēnqiè ❶ profound；cordial；deep：我们向你表示～的谢意。We wish to extend to you our profound thanks.／我们～地怀念周总理。We dearly cherish the memory of late Premier Zhou Enlai. ❷ penetrating and realistic；thorough；deep：对当前的困难，我是有～的感受的。I'm deeply aware of the present difficulties.

深情 shēnqíng profound feeling；deep affection：他～地说到一个人事业的成败是与国家命运息息相关的。He said with deep emotion (or feeling) that the success or failure of a person's career is tied up with (or hinges on) the fate of his country.

深情厚谊 shēnqíng-hòuyì profound friendship：乡亲们的～我们将永远不忘。We will never forget the profound sentiments of friendship that the local people have shown for us.

深秋 shēnqiū late autumn

深入 shēnrù ❶ go deep into；probe into；penetrate into：～实际 be in close contact with social realities／～基层 go deep down to the grass-roots levels／～群众 maintain close ties with the masses／～角色 live the role one is playing／敌人不知道我们正设法诱其～。The enemy didn't realize that we were trying to lure them in deep. ❷ thorough；intensive：～调查 make a thorough investigation／我们应该～思考这个问题，以便找到解决的方法。We should mull over the problem in order to find a solution.／必须在人民群众中～宣传晚婚晚育。It is necessary to carry on intensive publicity on late marriage and late childbirth among the population.

深入浅出 shēnrù-qiǎnchū explain profound or complex ideas in plain terms：这篇文章～，又生动又好懂。This article is full of meat, yet it is graphically written and easy to understand. or This essay explains profound problems in a simple, vivid style.

深入人心 shēnrù-rénxīn strike (or take) root in the hearts of the people；find its way deep into the hearts of the people：这一政策已～。The policy has won popular support.

深山 shēnshān remote mountains：这里是～老林，人迹罕至。These are untraversed mountains and virgin forests.／他们决心剿灭一股盘踞在～的土匪。They were determined to wipe out the gang of bandits entrenched deep in the mountains.

深山穷谷 shēnshān-qiónggǔ remote mountainous areas without human habitation

深水 shēnshuǐ deep water

深水操作人员 shēnshuǐ cāozuò rényuán aquanaut；oceanaut

深水港 shēnshuǐgǎng deepwater port

深水码头 shēnshuǐ mǎtou deepwater wharf

深水炸弹 shēnshuǐ zhàdàn depth charge；depth bomb

深思 shēnsī think deeply about；be deep in thought；ponder on：陷入～ be lost in thought；be deep in meditation／我认为这是值得～的事情。I think this gives plenty of food for thought. or This, I think, provides us with much food for thought.／刚刚发生的情况引起我们～。What has just happened sets us thinking.

深思熟虑 shēnsī-shúlǜ careful consideration；mature deliberation：～的计划 well-thought-out plan／领导经过～之后作出决定。The leaders made the decision after repeated deliberations.

深邃 shēnsuì ❶ going far down from the top or far in from the outside；deep：～的海洋 deep sea；fathomless ocean／～的院子 spacious courtyard ❷ profound；abstruse：这是一部寓意～的小说。This is a novel with a profound message.／这部书包含常人不易理解的～哲理。This book contains abstruse philosophical ideas difficult for the layman to understand.／他们是一些见地～的人。They are people of great insight.

深谈 shēntán have an in-depth conversation；have a deep or penetrating discussion；go deeply into sth.：我们见过面，但没有～。We have met but have not had any serious talk.／这个问题还须大家～一次。We need to have another in-depth discussion on this question.

深通 shēntōng be versed in；understand thoroughly；be an authority or expert on：～诗律 be well versed in poetics

深透 shēntòu deep and thorough；profound：理解～ thoroughly understand／作者在论文中，～地解释了这种现象的社会根源。In the treatise, the author expounds the social roots of the phenomenon with insight.

深望 shēnwàng sincerely hope；devoutly desire；earnestly wish：～阁下注意此事。It is my sincere hope that Your Excellency will pay proper attention to the matter.

深微 shēnwēi close and fine；precise：～玄妙 abstruse／～的哲理 esoteric philosophy

深为 shēnwéi very；greatly；deeply；highly：～不满 be very much

displeased /～庆幸 be greatly rejoiced

深味 shēnwèi ❶ know or realize, or feel deeply:～其言。I feel deeply about what he has expressed in words. ❷ meaningful; significant:这句话别有～。This remark has deep significance.

深文周纳 shēnwén-zhōunà (of feudal officials, judges, etc.) apply the law with the utmost severity to have sb. pronounced guilty; convict sb. by deliberately stretching the law:众所周知,那是个～的判决。This was a case of frame-up, as is well known to all.

深恶痛绝 shēnwù-tòngjué cherish intense hatred for; abhor; detest:他对社会上的丑恶现象～。He hates bitterly the evil practices in society. *or* He hates the evil trends like poison. /他们对这个团伙的罪恶早已～。They have long felt revulsion for the crimes of this gang.

深悉 shēnxī realize fully; be fully aware; know thoroughly:～其中奥妙 know full well what is behind it

深宵 shēnxiāo deep night; late at night; in the small or wee hours of the morning

深心 shēnxīn deep in one's heart; in one's heart of hearts; of one's innermost feelings:发自～的喜悦 heartfelt joy /从这个作品中我们可以看出作者的～。This work reveals the inner world of the writer.

深信 shēnxìn believe strongly; be (deeply) convinced; have deep faith in:～不疑 believe without a shadow of doubt

深省 shēnxǐng *also*“深醒” come to fully realize:这件事不是发人～的吗? Is this not something quite thought-provoking?

深醒 shēnxǐng *see*“深省”

深夜 shēnyè late at night; at midnight; in the small hours of the morning:尽管身体不好,他还是经常工作到～。Despite poor health, he often worked deep into the night. /您～来访,有何见教? Is there something you want to see me about, coming as you are at this late hour of the night?

深意 shēnyì profound meaning; deep implications:领会了这篇文章的～ grasp the deep meaning of the essay /这几行诗似有～。It seems that these few lines have profound implications.

深忧 shēnyōu deep worries

深幽 shēnyōu deep and quiet; deep and secluded:～的山谷 deep and secluded valley

深渊 shēnyuān deep pool; bottomless pit; abyss:如临～ feel like standing on the edge of a bottomless pit — act with extreme caution /他们陷入了苦难的～。They were plunged into the abyss of suffering (*or* misery). /他们觉得自己堕入失望的～,不能自拔。They felt they had fallen into the chasm of despair and could hardly extricate themselves from it.

深源地震 shēnyuán dìzhèn bathyseism

深远 shēnyuǎn profound; far-reaching:搞好这项工作,具有～的历史意义。The success of this work will have profound historic significance. /这个事件将在全世界范围内产生～的影响。This incident is bound to have far-reaching repercussions all over the world.

深造 shēnzào take an advanced course of study; pursue advanced studies:到国外～ go abroad for advanced study /目前农村大部分师资需要～。The majority of teachers in rural areas need further training.

深宅大院 shēnzhái-dàyuàn mansion with many rooms and spacious courtyards:旧日北京城内达官贵人的～不计其数。In the old days, there used to be a great many big mansions occupied by high officials in Beijing.

深湛 shēnzhàn profound and thorough; superb; consummate:～的技巧 superb skill /技艺～ exquisite workmanship /我们钦佩表演艺术家们的～功夫。We admire the consummate skill of the performing artists. /这是一部～的经济学著作。This book on economics is of sound scholarship.

深挚 shēnzhì profound and sincere:～的情谊 profound feeling of friendship /我相信他们之间的感情是～的。I believe that the feelings they cherish for each other are sincere and earnest.

深重 shēnzhòng very grave; extremely serious; critical:罪恶～ be guilty of heinous crimes (*or* all kinds of evils)/灾难～的人民起来反抗殖民统治。The long-suffering people rose in revolt against colonial rule.

燊

shēn 〈书面〉 flaming ablaze; flourishing

莘

shēn

莘莘 shēnshēn 〈书面〉 lush and luxuriant; flourishing:～林木 lush vegetation

娠

shēn 〈书面〉 pregnancy:妊～ pregnancy

申[1]

shēn state; expound; explain:～述自己的立场 explain one's stand (*or* position) /重～自己的观点 reiterate one's views

申[2]

shēn ninth of the twelve Earthly Branches

see also“干支” gānzhī

申[3]

Shēn ❶ another name for Shanghai ❷ a surname

申办 shēnbàn apply for the right to handle sth.; bid:～下届全国运动会 bid for the next national games /～公证 apply for notarization

申报 shēnbào ❶ report to higher authorities:向上级～ submit a report in writing to one's superior /向有关部门～ report to the departments (*or* authorities) concerned /～财产数目 submit a report on the amount of one's property /～户口 apply for residence registration ❷ declare sth. (to the customs):你有～的东西吗? Have you anything to declare? ❸ (Shēnbào) *Shen Bao* (formerly translated as *Shen Pao*), a Shanghai newspaper started in 1872 which ceased circulation in May 1949

申辩 shēnbiàn defend or try to justify oneself; argue or plead one's case:反复～ argue one's case over and over again /一再～ expostulate time and again /被告有～的权利。The accused has the right to defend himself. /被告声称无罪,但他的～是站不住脚的。The defendant pleaded "not guilty", but his argument was not tenable. /我想替他～几句。I would like to say a few words in his defence.

申斥 shēnchì rebuke; reprimand; reprove:服务员因对客人的态度不好,受到旅馆经理的～。The attendants were rebuked by the hotel manager for their unfriendly service to customers. /主任～他的助手未能克尽职责。The director reprimanded his assistant for failing to carry out his duties properly. /父亲～他出言无礼。Father took him to task for his flippant remarks. /母亲因为我逃学把我～了一顿。Mother gave me a dressing down for playing truant.

申饬 shēnchì ❶ *also*“申敕”〈书面〉 warn; admonish; exhort:～前方部队坚守阵地,慎重行事 sternly warn the troops at the front to stick to their positions and act with extreme caution ❷ *see*“申斥”

申理 shēnlǐ 〈书面〉 redress wrong; exonerate; rehabilitate

申领 shēnlǐng obtain by applying for; apply for:～签证 apply for a visa

申令 shēnlìng give orders; order; command:～全国作好一切必要准备,迎击来犯之敌 issue orders to the whole country to make all necessary preparations to fight the invaders

申明 shēnmíng make public; declare; state; avow:～自己的观点 state one's views /～自己的意图 make public one's intentions /～自己的态度 make clear one's attitude /他们公开～自己是支持叛乱分子的。They openly avowed that they were behind the rebels.

申请 shēnqǐng apply for:～加入俱乐部 apply for membership in a club /～离职 ask leave to resign /～执照 apply for a licence /～奖学金 apply for a scholarship /～入(出)境签证 apply for an entry (exit) visa /递交～书 submit an application

申请表 shēnqǐngbiǎo application form

申请国 shēnqǐngguó applicant country

申请人 shēnqǐngrén applicant

申请书 shēnqǐngshū (written) application; petition

申曲 shēnqǔ *also*“沪剧” hùjù Shanghai opera

申申 shēnshēn 〈书面〉❶ relaxed ❷ repeatedly; again and again:～而詈 curse repeatedly

申时 shēnshí period of the day from 3 p.m. to 5 p.m.

申述 shēnshù explain in detail; expound; state:～自己的意见 expound one's views /～反对这个建议的理由 set out reasons for rejecting the proposal /～事情发生的经过 explain in detail exactly what has happened /对自己的主张作详细的～ give a full exposition of one's position

申说 shēnshuō state (reasons); explain:向组长～我昨天缺勤的原因。I explained to the group leader why I was absent yesterday.

申诉 shēnsù ❶ appeal for justice or complain about an injustice to higher authorities or authorities concerned:我认为对我的处理不当,已向上级提出～。I believe the disciplinary measure against me was wrong, so I have appealed to the higher authorities. ❷〈法律〉 pre-

sent one's case in a law court; appeal: ～权 right of appeal / 向上级法院提出～，要求重新审理 appeal to the higher law court for retrial / 法院驳回了他的～。The law court rejected his appeal.

申讨 shēntǎo openly condemn; censure; denounce: ～侵略者的罪行 publicly condemn the criminal acts of the aggressors / 劫机是最严重的犯罪行为，理应加以～。Hijacking ought to be denounced as a most grave crime.

申屠 Shēntú a surname

申谢 shēnxiè acknowledge one's debt of gratitude; express one's appreciation; extend one's thanks: 登门～ pay sb. a visit to extend one's thanks personally / 多承照拂，特此～。I wish to express my gratitude to you for the kindnesses you have showered on me.

申雪 shēnxuě *also* "伸雪" shēnxuě ❶ appeal for vindication ❷ vindicate; redress an injustice; right a wrong: 经过仔细调查，他的冤案终于得到～。He was finally vindicated after a thorough investigation into the case. / 冤屈终会～的。An injustice will eventually be redressed.

申言 shēnyán voice; declare

申冤 shēnyuān ❶ *also* "伸冤" shēnyuān redress an injustice; right a wrong: 他已经～，可以扬眉吐气了。Since the wrong done to him has been righted, he may hold his head high. ❷ appeal for redressing a wrong: 他向领导～。He appealed to the leadership for the injustice to be remedied. / 他决心为小李～。He was determined to right the wrong done to Xiao Li.

申状 shēnzhuàng 〈书面〉 communication or report to one's superior; petition

申奏 shēnzòu present a memorial or report to the throne

珅

shēn 〈书面〉 a kind of jade

砷

shēn 〈化学〉 arsenic (As)

砷化物 shēnhuàwù arsenide

砷黄铁矿 shēnhuángtiěkuàng *also* "毒砂" dúshā arsenopyrite (FeAsS)

砷酸 shēnsuān arsenic acid

砷酸铅 shēnsuānqiān lead arsenate

砷中毒 shēnzhòngdú 〈生理〉 arsenic poisoning

呻

shēn 〈书面〉 chant; recite

呻吟 shēnyín groan; moan; whine: 无病～ moan and groan without being ill; whine without cause; adopt a sentimental pose (in writing) / 病人在床上～。The patient is groaning in bed.

伸

shēn put out; stretch; extend: ～着脖子 crane one's neck / ～舌头 put out one's tongue / ～～腿 stretch one's legs / ～出脚来绊了他一跤 stick out a foot and trip him over / ～出援助之手 extend a helping hand / 林阴大道～向远方。The boulevard extends far into the distance.

伸畅 shēnchàng (spend money) liberally: 也许他花钱太～了。Perhaps he is too liberal with money.

伸大拇哥 shēn dàmugē *also* "伸大拇指头" raise a thumb in admiration: 你为大家伙儿出力，大家伙儿谁不～。We all admire you for what you have done for our benefit.

伸肌 shēnjī 〈生理〉 extensor muscles

伸懒腰 shēn lǎnyāo stretch one's limbs: 他伸伸懒腰，从坐位上站起来就走了。He stretched, got up from his seat and walked out.

伸眉 shēnméi raise eyebrows with pleasure or satisfaction: ～扬气 be in high spirits; feel proud and elated

伸欠 shēnqiàn stretch and yawn

伸手 shēnshǒu ❶ hold out one's hand; 〈比喻〉 stretch out one's hand (as a sign of begging for sth.): 老张～拦住了他。Lao Zhang put out his hand to stop him. / 这个人很不像样，居然向上级～要名誉地位。He is not a decent chap; he has even the cheek to ask for promotion. ❷ meddle: 这是别人的事，我们不能～。This is none of our business. We are not supposed to meddle in it. / 霸权主义者的手伸得太长了。The hegemonists have overextended themselves.

伸手不见五指 shēnshǒu bùjiàn wǔzhǐ so dark that you can't see your own hand in front of you; completely without light: 那是个～的黑夜。It was a pitch-dark night.

伸缩 shēnsuō ❶ lengthen and shorten; stretch out and draw back: 这件东西跟橡皮筋一样可以～。Like rubber bands, these are elastic, too. / 文章尚未定稿，可以有所～。The article is not finalized yet. It may be either lengthened or shortened. ❷ flexibility; modification; latitude: 在原则问题上我们没有～的余地。We are allowed no latitude on the question of principle.

伸缩缝 shēnsuōfèng 〈建筑〉 expansion joint

伸缩三角架 shēnsuō sānjiǎojià extension tripod

伸头 shēntóu crane one's neck; poke one's head; 〈比喻〉 come forward and take action; 〈比喻〉 (of someone who has been suppressed) hold up one's head: 遇事谁也不想～，真没办法。It's simply hopeless, for nobody is willing to come forward when action is needed.

伸头探脑 shēntóu-tànnǎo stretch one's head to peek at; crane's one's neck in an effort to find out: 孩子们都～看热闹。The children craned their necks to watch the fun outside.

伸腿 shēntuǐ ❶ interfere in; step in (to gain an advantage): 他也要往那里头～。He also wanted to step in for personal gain. ❷ 〈口语〉 kick the bucket; turn up one's toes; go west

伸雪 shēnxuě *see* "申雪" shēnxuě

伸延 shēnyán extend; stretch; elongate

伸腰 shēnyāo straighten one's back; hold one's body erect: 时代变了，我们应该伸起腰来。Times have changed and we should straighten our backs and feel proud!

伸冤 shēnyuān *see* "申冤 ❶" shēnyuān

伸展 shēnzhǎn extend; reach; stretch: 修建中的铁路路基一天天向远方～。With each passing day the roadbed of the railway under construction stretched farther and farther into the distance.

伸张 shēnzhāng uphold; promote; stand up for: 必须～国法，打击一切贪污腐化现象。It is essential to enforce the law of the state to combat all forms of corruption and degeneration.

伸张正义 shēnzhāng zhèngyì uphold justice: 打击邪恶，～ combat evil and champion justice

绅

shēn ❶ 〈旧语〉 sash; girdle (as worn by scholars and officials in feudal China) ❷ gentry: 乡～ country gentleman; squire / 开明士～ enlightened gentry / 土豪劣～ local tyrants and evil gentry

绅衿 shēnjīn *also* "绅襟" 〈旧语〉 local gentry; retired officials living in the country

绅粮 shēnliáng 〈方言〉 relatively big landlords

绅耆 shēnqí 〈旧语〉 local gentry and elders

绅商 shēnshāng 〈旧语〉 gentry and business people

绅士 shēnshì gentleman; gentry

绅士协定 shēnshì xiédìng *also* "君子协定" jūnzǐ xiédìng gentleman's agreement

屾

shēn 〈书面〉 two mountains standing side by side

甡

shēn

甡甡 shēnshēn 〈书面〉 great many; large numbers of: 瞻彼中林，～其鹿。Lo and behold, there is many a deer in the dense wood.

诜

shēn

诜诜 shēnshēn 〈书面〉 great many; large numbers of

侁

shēn

侁侁 shēnshēn 〈书面〉 multitude of; numerous

駪

shēn

駪駪 shēnshēn 〈书面〉 great many; numerous: ～征夫。Numerous are the warriors going on the expedition.

身

shēn ❶ body: ～患重病 be seriously ill / 全～疼痛 ache all over / 站起～来 rise; stand up / 翻了一个～ turn over ❷ life: 护～符 protective talisman / 舍～救人 give one's life to rescue others / 杀～成仁 sacrifice one's life to uphold virtue; die a martyr ❸ oneself; personally: 以～作则 set a good example with one's own conduct; be exemplary / 设～处地 put oneself in sb. else's position; be considerate / 置～事外 stay aloof from; be indifferent to / 洁～自好 keep away from immorality; preserve one's purity / 你～为国家干部，应严格要求自己才对。As a government functionary you ought to be strict with yourself. ❹ one's moral character and accomplishment: 修～养性 cultivate one's mind and moral character / 修～法行 elevate one's

S

mind and conduct /立~处世之道 proper way to conduct oneself in society ❺ frame of a structure; body:车~ body of a car /河~ riverbed /机~ fuselage /桥~ upper part of a bridge, including the roadway and the girder truss ❻〈量词〉(of clothes) suit:一~西装 a Western-style suit /这里热,一天要换两~衣服。One has to change twice a day; it is so hot here. ❼ one's lifetime; all one's life:终~ lifelong; all one's life /~后 after one's death

身败名裂 shēnbài-mínglìè bring disgrace and ruin upon oneself; fall into utter disrepute; be thoroughly discredited:落得~ wind up in disgrace and ruin; end up losing all one's standing and reputation /~的可耻下场 come to an ignominious end

身板 shēnbǎn 〈方言〉body; constitution:~儿硬朗 be hale and hearty /老头子的~儿挺结实。The old man is of powerful build.

身边 shēnbiān ❶ at or by one's side; around:他的~围了一群人。A crowd of people gathered around him. /她对~的情况一无所知。She is completely in the dark about what's going on near her. ❷ (have sth.) on one; (take or carry) with one:我很喜欢这件皮大衣,可惜~带钱不多。I really liked the fur coat. It's a pity that I didn't have enough money on me. /他不应该~带着机密文件去娱乐园。He should not have carried confidential documents with him when he went to the amusement park.

身不由己 shēnbùyóujǐ involuntarily; in spite of oneself; not of one's own accord:他喝醉了,~倒在地下。He was drunk and fell on the floor in spite of himself. /你现在是~,只能听他的。You have to listen to him whether you like it or not.

身材 shēncái stature; figure; build:~修长 have a tall and slender figure /~苗条 slender (*or* slim) /中等~ of medium stature /~显得匀称 look well-proportioned /~壮实 of sturdy build

身长 shēncháng ❶ height (of a person) ❷ length (of a garment from shoulder to hemline)

身段 shēnduàn ❶ (woman's) figure:~窈窕 gentle and graceful ❷ (dancer's) posture:练习~ practise posture /花旦的~ posture of an actress of the coquettish type (in Beijing opera)

S

身法 shēnfǎ (of martial arts) techniques or art of manoeuvring the body in self-defence

身分 shēnfen *see* "身份"

身份 shēnfen *also* "身分" ❶ status; capacity; identity:合法~ lawful (*or* legitimate) capacity /暴露~ reveal one's identity /隐瞒~ conceal one's identity /查明~ establish one's identity /证明~ confirm one's identity /以代理人的~发言 speak in the capacity of an agent /进行与外交官~不符的活动 carry on activities incompatible with the status of a diplomat ❷ dignity:你不觉得这样做有失~? Don't you realize that such conduct is beneath your dignity? /你不要忘记了自己的~。You have to uphold your dignity. *or* You have your own dignity to think about. ❸〈方言〉quality (of an article, etc.):这件上衣的~不坏。This jacket is of good quality.

身份证 shēnfenzhèng *also* "身分证" identity or identification card; ID (card)

身高 shēngāo height (of a person):标准的~ of standard height /他~一米八五。He is 185 centimetres tall (*or* in height).

身个儿 shēngèr 〈口语〉stature; figure (esp. height):中等~ of medium height /小小的~ short and slight of stature

身故 shēngù die:因车祸~ die of a car accident /不幸~ pass away unfortunately /父母早已~。My parents died many years ago. *or* My parents have long been dead.

身后 shēnhòu after one's death:~萧条 without money or progeny after one's death /垂名于~ be long remembered by posterity

身怀六甲 shēnhuái-liùjiǎ be pregnant; be with child; be in the family way

身家 shēnjiā ❶ oneself and one's family:~性命 one's own life and the fate of the whole family ❷〈旧语〉class status of one's family; family origin:~清白 come of a good family

身价 shēnjià ❶〈旧语〉selling price of a person 以两百元的~卖给人家 be sold for 200 *yuan* /他的~竟然只值五斗米。Just think that he was only worth 5 *dou* of grain. ❷ social status:抬高~ boost one's own prestige

身价百倍 shēnjià-bǎibèi ❶〈比喻〉have a meteoric rise in social status; receive a tremendous boost in one's position or prestige:一登龙门,~ immediate rise in one's social status (*or* literary fame) with the patronage of the powerful ❷ (in a general sense) (of prices) rise sharply; skyrocket

身架 shēnjià *also* "身架子"〈口语〉human body; stature:这人四十出头,粗壮~,黑红脸膛儿。A man in his early forties, he is of strong build and dark complexion.

身教 shēnjiào teach others by one's own example:言传~ teach by personal example and verbal instruction /老师的~很重要。It is crucial that the teacher should set an example to his pupils.

身教胜于言教 shēnjiào shèngyú yánjiào example is more powerful than precept

身经百战 shēnjīngbǎizhàn have fought a hundred battles; be battle-hardened:他戎马一生,~。Having served in the army all his life, he was a seasoned fighter.

身历 shēnlì go through the experience personally:你如果不是~其境,就不能理解当时情况的艰苦。You could not appreciate the hardship of the situation unless you were actually on the scene.

身历声 shēnlìshēng 〈方言〉*also* "立体声" lìtǐshēng stereophony; stereo

身量 shēnliang 〈口语〉height (of a person); stature:大~ be very tall /小伙子~长得好。The young man is of a strong build.

身临其境 shēnlínqíjìng be present on the scene:《北洋水师》是一部描写中日甲午战争的影片,情节极其生动,使你有~之感。"The Northern Fleet", a film which describes the Sino-Japanese sea battle in 1894, is so graphically realistic that you feel as if you were present on the scene.

身强力壮 shēnqiáng-lìzhuàng (of a person) strong; tough; sturdy; hefty:~的年轻人 strong young man /~的搬运工 robust (*or* hefty) porter /他虽不算年轻,但~,很能干活。Though no longer young, he is still sturdy and good at physical labour.

身躯 shēnqū body; stature:~苗条 be slimly built /~矮小 short in build; of short stature

身热 shēnrè 〈中医〉symptom of feeling feverish all over the body

身上 shēnshang ❶ on one's body:~穿一件连衣裙 wear a woman's dress /我~不舒服。I feel a bit out of sorts. /他~有许多优点。He has many strong points. /我把希望寄托在你们~。My hopes are placed on you. ❷ (have sth.) on one; (carry sth.) with one:我~带了很多钱。I have a lot of money on me. /我~没有带纸笔。I have not got paper and pen with me.

身世 shēnshì one's (often unfortunate) lot; life experience:~悲惨 have led a miserable life

身手 shēnshǒu skill; talent; ability:~不凡 person of uncommon talent /小试~ have a preliminary show of one's skill / 他们现在可以大显~了。Now they can fully display their ability.

身首异处 shēn-shǒu yìchù be decapitated:阿Q竟不明不白地~了。Ah Q was beheaded, not knowing why.

身受 shēnshòu experience personally:~压迫 suffer oppression personally /虽~各种磨难,仍很乐观 remain cheerful after all that one has gone (*or* been) through

身态 shēntài carriage; bearing; demeanour

身体 shēntǐ ❶ body:在平衡木上保持~平衡 keep one's balance on the (balance) beam ❷ constitution; health:~结实 have a tough constitution /~健康 enjoy good health /~瘦弱 thin and weak; bag of bones /~是事业成功的本钱。Good health is essential for the success of a career.

身体力行 shēntǐ-lìxíng earnestly practise what one advocates or preaches:作为领导,凡事都应该~,起表率作用。As a leading cadre, one should work hard and set an example in whatever one does.

身体素质 shēntǐ sùzhì physique; physical constitution

身体钟 shēntǐzhōng body clock (as against biological clock)

身条儿 shēntiáor 〈口语〉stature; height; figure:瘦瘦的~ have a slim stature (or figure) /~匀称 of proportional build; of fine physical proportions

身外之物 shēnwàizhīwù external things; worldly possessions; matters of little consequence:钱财是~。Money and property are mere worldly possessions.

身无长物 shēnwúchángwù have nothing but the necessities of life:他一辈子~。All his life he had few belongings.

身先士卒 shēnxiānshìzú (of a general) lead one's men in charge; (of a leader) be at the forefront of struggle:作战时他总是~,故能所向披靡。He was always at the head of his men in battle, and so his army was invincible.

身心 shēnxīn body and mind:~愉快 enjoy a good health and sound mind

身心二元论 shēnxīn èryuánlùn 〈哲学〉mind-body dualism

身心交瘁 shēnxīn-jiāocuì be worn out both physically and men-

tally

身形 shēnxíng figure; body:健美的～ have a strong and graceful figure

身腰 shēnyāo waist:他挺直了～。He straightened up.

身影 shēnyǐng person's silhouette; form; shape; figure:修长的～ tall and slim /模糊的～ shadowy silhouette /瞧见了他的～ have caught a glimpse of him /他向我走来,他的～越来越清晰了。As he walked towards me, his figure became clearer and clearer.

身孕 shēnyùn pregnancy:她还是第一次有～。This is her first pregnancy. /她怀有～。She is expecting (*or* in the family way).

身在曹营心在汉 shēn zài Cáoyíng xīn zài Hàn live in the Cao camp but with one's heart in the Han camp; though one is physically here, one's mind is elsewhere; be half-hearted

身在福中不知福 shēn zài fú zhōng bù zhī fú people brought up in the midst of happiness often fail to appreciate what happiness really means; you don't know when you are happy:现在有些年轻人总是对什么都不满意,真是～啊! There are some young people nowadays who are always complaining without sensing the happiness they actually enjoy.

身正不怕影儿斜 shēn zhèng bùpà yǐngr xié stand straight and never mind if the shadow inclines — a clear conscience laughs at false accusations

身肢 shēnzhī trunk and limbs; body

身重 shēnzhòng 〈中医〉symptom of having difficulty in moving one's arms and legs

身姿 shēnzī bearing; carriage; demeanour:矫健的～ vigorous carriage

身子 shēnzi 〈口语〉❶ body; physique:我转过～朝外走。I turned round and walked out. /他长期劳累,损坏了～。Years of onerous toil have enfeebled his physique. *or* A laborious life has sapped his strength. ❷ pregnancy:你是个有了～的人,不能过度劳累。You mustn't overwork yourself, now that you are pregnant.

身子骨儿 shēnzigǔr 〈方言〉one's health; physique:您老人家～挺硬朗。You are hale and hearty.

参[1](參、葠、蓡) shēn

general term for ginseng and *dangshen* (*Codonopsis pilosula*), but often referring to ginseng

参[2](參) shēn

one of the twenty-eight constellations

see also cān; cēn

参商 shēnshāng 〈书面〉❶ separation of family members or friends who are not able to meet (*shen* and *shang*, two of the twenty-eight constellations, do not appear in the sky at the same time):我们天各一方,有如～。Living far apart we seldom meet. ❷ do not get along; be on bad terms:兄弟～。The brothers do not get along.

糁(糝、粈) shēn

ground cereal:玉米～儿 ground maize

see also sǎn

鲹(鰺) shēn

scad

shén

神 shén

❶ god; divine being; deity; divinity:有～论 theism /无～论 atheism /多～论 polytheism /瘟～ god of plague /财～ god of wealth /拜～ worship god ❷ man with magic power; supernatural person:料事如～ predict like a prophet; foretell with miraculous accuracy /～鬼莫测 be unpredictable ❸ supernatural; magical; amazing:～效 magical (*or* miraculous) effect /出～入化 reach the acme of perfection; be superb /用兵如～ direct military operations with superior skill /这件事太～了! This really sounds incredible. ❹ spirit; mind; energy:凝～细听 listen with rapt attention /走～ be absent-minded; be preoccupied /安～ calm (*or* soothe) the nerves /提～ refresh oneself /心～不定 have no peace of mind; feel restless /聚精会～ concentrate one's attention, thoughts, etc. (on) /闭目养～ sit in repose with one's eyes closed /～昏意乱 look distracted and confused /费～代问一下。May I trouble you to make inquiries for me? ❺ expression; appearance; look:眼～儿 expression in the eyes /瞧他那精气～儿。Look at his sharp eyes. ❻〈方言〉smart; clever; incredible:这孩子真～! What a clever boy! ❼ (Shén) a surname

神奥 shén'ào mysterious; profound and subtle:这种尖端科学并不～。There's nothing mysterious about these most advanced branches of science.

神不守舍 shénbùshǒushè the soul has departed from its abode; look as if one's mind were unhinged:这一连串的问题把他搞得昏昏沉沉的,简直到了～的程度。The long series of questions dazed him, so much so that he almost went out of his mind.

神不知,鬼不觉 shén bù zhī, guǐ bù jué unknown to god or ghost — (do sth.) without anyone knowing it; in complete secrecy:她想起那天晚上,～地,他突然在她背后出现。She recalled that evening when he had sprung up behind her as if from nowhere.

神采 shéncǎi expression; look:～焕发 beam with health /黑黑的眼睛,洋溢着欣喜的～ dark eyes brimming with joyous expression /焕发出了青春的～ glow with the vigour of youth /她抬起她那没有～的眼睛来。She raised her expressionless eyes.

神采飞扬 shéncǎi-fēiyáng be in fine or good fettle:他满面红光,～,正在侃侃而谈。He spoke with fervour and assurance, looking in ruddy health and fine fettle.

神采弈弈 shéncǎi-yìyì brim with energy and vitality

神差鬼使 shénchāi-guǐshǐ *also* "鬼使神差";"神使鬼差" unexpected happenings; curious coincidence

神扯 shénchě chitchat:他们边走边～着。They chatted aimlessly as they walked along.

神驰 shénchí one's thoughts fly to; range in fancy:～故国 nostalgic thoughts about the ancient kingdom /心往～ be carried away (*or* charmed) by

神出鬼没 shénchū-guǐmò move about like supernatural beings; come and go like a shadow; appear and disappear mysteriously:他大无畏的精神,～的智谋,使敌伪汉奸终日惶恐不安。His dauntless courage and miraculous resourcefulness constantly struck terror into the enemy puppets and traitors.

神创论 shénchuànglùn 〈宗教〉creationism:～者 creationist

神道 shéndào ❶ superstitious belief in ghosts and gods, fortune and misfortune ❷ (sacred) way or path leading to a grave; tomb passage:十三陵～ sacred way leading to the Ming Tombs ❸ *see* "神❶" ❹ (Shéndào) Shinto, native religion of Japan

神道 shéndao 〈方言〉❶ full of spirit:这孩子真～。What a spirited boy! ❷ unexpected; strange:他今天说话神神道道的。He sounds a bit strange today.

神道碑 shéndàobēi stone tablet in front of the tomb passage recording the deeds of the deceased; inscription on such a stone tablet

神道设教 shéndào-shèjiào 〈古语〉(of a monarch, etc.) teach and rule (the people) by imitating the way of deities

神风突击队 Shénfēng Tūjīduì "divine wind corps"; kamikaze corps (Japanese suicide bombers in World War II)

神甫 shénfu *also* "神父";"司铎" sīduó (Roman Catholic or Anglican) father; priest

神工鬼斧 shéngōng-guǐfǔ *also* "鬼斧神工" superlative craftsmanship

神怪 shénguài gods and spirits:～小说 fiction about gods and spirits / ～故事 teratology

神汉 shénhàn sorcerer

神乎其神 shénhūqíshén causing wonder; wonderful; miraculous:吹得～ laud sth. (*or* sb.) to the skies /说得～ paint a fantastic picture of sth.

神乎 shénhu miraculous; fantastic; magical; bizarre:他觉得只有说得～,才能惹人注意。He believed that he could only draw attention by making the story as bizarre as possible.

神户 Shénhù Kobe, seaport for Osaka (大阪) on Honshu Island, Japan

神化 shénhuà deification

神话 shénhuà ❶ mythology:希腊～ Greek mythology ❷ myth; fairy tale:揭穿他们不可战胜的～。Explode the myth of their invincibility. /这听起来像～。This sounds like a fairy tale.

神会 shénhuì comprehend; admire without prior acquaintance:眼前如梦如幻的景象,我只在古典诗词里～过。This is a dream-like scene that I have never come across except in classic poems.

S

神魂 shénhún state of mind; mind:～不安 get the jitters; be upset
神魂不定 shénhún-bùdìng be distraught; be deeply troubled:他前两天就～,似乎有发生某种不祥的预感。He's been deeply perturbed for the last few days as if he had a premonition of evil.
神魂颠倒 shénhún-diāndǎo be infatuated; be in a confused state of mind:我绝没有想到他会为这样一个卖弄风骚的女人而～。I never thought he would lose his head over such a flirtatious woman (*or* such a coquette).
神机妙算 shénjī-miàosuàn wonderful foresight (in military operations, etc.); superb stratagem:谁都佩服诸葛亮的～。Everyone admires Zhuge Liang for his superb stratagems.
神交 shénjiāo ❶ friends with mutual understanding and trust ❷ friendship grown out of mutual admiration without prior acquaintance:～已久 have long cherished admiration for each other without having met
神京 shénjīng 〈旧语〉national capital
神经 shénjīng nerve:～紧张 be on edge; be edgy /～松弛 be relaxed /脑(感觉、听觉、交感)～ cranial (sensory, auditory, sympathetic) nerve /他～有点不正常。He's not all there.
神经病 shénjīngbìng ❶ neuropathy ❷ mental disorder; neurosis:他有点～。He is a bit of a neurotic.
神经错乱 shénjīng cuòluàn mental disorder; be mentally deranged
神经毒气 shénjīng dúqì nerve gas
神经毒素 shénjīng dúsù neurotoxin
神经仿生学 shénjīng fǎngshēngxué 〈生物〉neurobionics
神经放射学 shénjīng fàngshèxué 〈医学〉neuroradiology
神经干 shénjīnggàn 〈生理〉nerve cord
神经工程学 shénjīng gōngchéngxué 〈生物〉neuro-engineering
神经官能症 shénjīng guānnéngzhèng neurosis
神经过敏 shénjīng guòmǐn ❶ neuroticism ❷ neurotic; oversensitive; hypersensitive:跟她说话要小心点,她有点～。Be careful when you speak to her. She is oversensitive.
神经化学 shénjīng huàxué neurochemistry
神经间质炎 shénjīng jiānzhìyán mesoneuritis
神经节 shénjīngjié ganglion
神经解剖学 shénjīng jiěpōuxué neuroanatomy
神经科学 shénjīng kēxué 〈医学〉neurosciences
神经控制论 shénjīng kòngzhìlùn 〈生物〉neurocybernetics
神经末梢 shénjīng mòshāo nerve ending
神经内分泌学 shénjīng nèifēnmìxué 〈医学〉neuroendocrinology
神经生理学 shénjīng shēnglǐxué 〈生理〉neurophysiology
神经衰弱 shénjīng shuāiruò neurasthenia:～的症状 symptoms of nervous breakdown
神经索 shénjīngsuǒ 〈生理〉nerve cord
神经痛 shénjīngtòng neuralgia
神经外科 shénjīng wàikē neurosurgery
神经网络 shénjīng wǎngluò 〈生理〉neural net
神经兮兮 shénjīng-xīxī 〈方言〉nervy; neurotic:这女子有点儿～。She's not quite right in the head. /她还在～地自以为是大明星。She has a bee in her bonnet and believes herself to be a great star.
神经系统 shénjīng xìtǒng nervous system
神经细胞 shénjīng xìbāo nerve cell
神经纤维 shénjīng xiānwéi nerve fibre
神经性皮炎 shénjīngxìng píyán neurodermatitis
神经学 shénjīngxué neurology
神经炎 shénjīngyán neuritis
神经语言学 shénjīng yǔyánxué neurolinguistics
神经原 shénjīngyuán neuron
神经战 shénjīngzhàn war of nerves
神经质 shénjīngzhì nervousness:她是～的人。She is the nervous type.
神经中枢 shénjīng zhōngshū nerve centre
神经阻滞麻醉 shénjīng zǔzhì mázuì 〈医学〉nerve block anesthesia
神龛 shénkān shrine for idols or ancestral tablets
神来之笔 shénláizhībǐ stroke of genius; inspired writing
神力 shénlì superhuman strength; extraordinary prowess:～过人 matchless strength (*or* prowess)
神聊 shénliáo engage in chitchat:他俩天南海北地～起来。The two of them started shooting the breeze.
神灵 shénlíng gods; deities; divinities:～保佑。God bless you.
神领 shénlǐng tacit understanding
神秘 shénmì mysterious; mystical; secretive:表情～ mysterious expression /～的宇宙 unfathomable universe /～的武器 magical weapon /～的微笑 enigmatic smile /这些事对我们并不～。These things are no mystery to us. /他故意把事情搞得很～。He is deliberately trying to mystify people.
神秘化 shénmìhuà mystify; make mystery of
神秘莫测 shénmì-mòcè unpredictable; unfathomable; inscrutable
神秘主义 shénmìzhǔyì mysticism
神妙 shénmiào wonderful; superb; marvellous; ingenious:～的笔力 ingenious brushwork /～的技巧 marvellous skill /～之笔 stroke of genius /～的演奏 superb performance
神灭论 Shénmièlùn *Shen Mie Lun* or *On the Extinction of Spirit* by Fan Zhen (范缜), philosopher of the Southern Dynasties
神明 shénmíng ❶ gods; deities; divinities:奉若～ hold sth. as sacrosanct; make a fetish of sth.; put sb. on a pedestal /祈求～庇护 invoke god's protection; ask a blessing ❷ mental state; spirit:～不衰 remain full of spirit
神农 Shénnóng *also* "神农氏" legendary ruler in ancient China supposed to have introduced agriculture and herbal medicine, also called Yandi or Red Emperor (炎帝)
神农本草经 Shénnóng Běncǎojīng *also* "神农本草" *Shen Nong's Materia Medica* compiled by people of the Qin and Han dynasties in the name of Shen Nong
神农架 Shénnóngjià Shennongjia, a county in Hubei Province, established in 1970:～自然保护区 Shennongjia Nature Reserve
神女 shénnǚ ❶ goddess:～下凡 goddess come to earth /～应无恙,当惊世界殊。The mountain goddess if she is still there Will marvel at a world so changed. ❷〈旧语〉prostitute:～生涯 life of a prostitute; living on immoral earnings
神牌 shénpái spirit tablet; tablet used as the symbol of a deity
神炮手 shénpàoshǒu crack gunner
神品 shénpǐn superb work (of art or literature); masterpiece:人物画中之～ masterpiece of figure painting
神婆 shénpó sorceress; enchantress; witch
神奇 shénqí magical; mystical; wonderful; miraculous:功效～ miraculous (*or* magical) effect /～的人物 legendary figure /～的魅力 magical charm /～的构思 wonderful conception /人物都被渲染上一层～的色彩。The characters are imbued with a sense of mystery and wonder.
神祇 shénqí 〈书面〉gods; deities; divinities
神器 shénqì 〈书面〉❶ imperial throne; political power ❷ magical objects
神气 shénqì ❶ expression; look; air; manner:说话的～ the way one speaks /显出轻蔑的～ assume an air of contempt /露出冷淡的～ display an indifferent expression /一脸不高兴的～ unhappy look written all over the face /老妈妈看见儿子快乐的～,破涕为笑了。Grannie smiled away her tears when she saw the joyous expression on her son's face. ❷ spirited; impressive; vigorous:少先队员们真～! The pioneers look very impressive indeed! /这些年轻人一个个都很～! Every one of these young people appears in high spirits. /越看越～。The more you look at it the more striking it becomes. ❸ putting on airs; cocky; arrogant; overweening:你～什么! What makes you think you're so terrific? /他一度很～,但近来似乎有点泄气了。He was once very cocky, but seems to have been a bit deflated lately. /瞧她那～劲儿。Look, she is as proud as a peacock.
神气活现 shénqì-huóxiàn very cocky; self-important; high and mighty:看他那个～的样子,我就受不了。I can't stand the way he gives himself such grand airs.
神气十足 shénqì-shízú putting on grand airs; very arrogant:他当了县长秘书,显得～。Now that he is secretary to the county magistrate, he looks as proud as punch.
神枪手 shénqiāngshǒu crack shot; dead shot; expert marksman; sharpshooter:不愧是个～ be worthy of the name of expert marksman /名符其实的～ marksman worthy of the name /难得的～ rare sharpshooter
神情 shénqíng air; expression; look:～十分悠闲 assume a carefree air /～大变 suddenly change countenance /～狼狈 look extremely embarrassed /焦急的～ worried expression /～冷漠 look apathetic /他脸上露出绝望的～。His face showed signs of despair.
神曲 shénqū 〈中药〉medicated leaven
神曲 Shénqǔ *Divine Comedy*, by Italian poet Dante Alighieri (1265-1321)

神权 shénquán ❶ religious authority; theocracy:至高无上的～ absolute power of theocracy ❷ divine right:所谓"君王～"就是极端的君主专制的借口。The so-called "divine right of kings" was nothing but a pretext for absolute autocracy.

神人 shénrén ❶ men who attain the Tao (enlightenment and immortality) according to Taoism; immortals:峨嵋山是传说中～居住的地方。Legend has it that Mount E'mei was inhabited by immortals. ❷ person of dignified bearings

神容 shénróng 〈方言〉look; facial features:这一惊吓,他的～大不同平时了。The panic changed his complexion completely.

神色 shénsè expression; countenance; look:～不定 look perturbed /得意的～ complacent look /～仓皇 be panic-stricken /～不变 remain composed /露出羞愧的～ be shamefaced /鄙夷的～ disdainful expression /马上又换了一副关切的～ immediately assume an air of concern

神色自若 shénsè-zìruò be calm and collected; keep one's wits about one; show composure and presence of mind:任凭敌人发疯似地狂叫,他～,旁若无人。He remained unruffled despite the enemies yelling at him like mad.

神伤 shénshāng 〈书面〉dejected; dispirited; listless:黯然～ feel depressed; feel dejected

神社 shénshè ❶ shrine; altar ❷ Shinto shrine; *Jinjia*

神神道道 shénshen-dāodāo *also* "神神叨叨" abnormal in words and deeds; strange in behaviour:这人总是那么～。He is always nervy and nutty.

神圣 shénshèng sacred; holy; consecrated:～的使命 sacred mission /～的自豪感 solemn sense of pride /我国领土～不可侵犯。Our territory is sacred and inviolable.

神圣罗马帝国 Shénshèng Luómǎ Dìguó 〈历史〉Holy Roman Empire (962-1806)

神圣同盟 Shénshèng Tóngméng 〈历史〉Holy Alliance (1815-1830)

神使鬼差 shénshǐ-guǐchāi *see* "神差鬼使"

神思 shénsī state of mind; mental state:～不宁 be upset /～紊乱 be confused

神思恍惚 shénsī-huǎnghū in a trance; beside oneself; distracted:～,心不由主 lose one's presence of mind and be utterly confused

神似 shénsì be alike in spirit or essence:这篇译文不仅形似而且～。The translation agrees with the original both in letter and in spirit. /这幅画像栩栩如生,十分～。The portrait is most vivid and truly lifelike.

神速 shénsù marvellously swift; with lightning speed:～的变化 rapid changes /收效～ yield amazingly quick results /进展～ make speedy progress

神算 shénsuàn ❶ accurate prediction ❷ marvellous stratagem

神髓 shénsuǐ 〈书面〉essence; quintessence; cream:学习先进经验,只得皮毛而失～,就收不到实效。No practical results will be achieved if in studying advanced experience one learns only what is superficial but misses the essence.

神态 shéntài expression; countenance; manner; bearing:～悠闲 look carefree and relaxed /～安详 appear calm and composed /～和蔼可亲 have a genial expression on one's face /～庄肃 have a solemn mien /她的～里,似乎有一种说不出的魅力。There seemed to be an inexpressible charm in her manner.

神通 shéntōng magic powers; immense capabilities:大显～ display one's prowess; give full play to one's ability /干这一行,他可很有些～。He knows all the tricks in this line.

神通广大 shéntōng-guǎngdà be infinitely resourceful:说到探听小道消息,在我们当中数他～。He is a past master at getting information through the grapevine.

神童 shéntóng child prodigy

神往 shénwǎng be carried away; be rapt; be fascinated:令人～的景色 enchanting scenery /草原无边无际,静寂无声,令人～。We were fascinated by the silent boundless expanse of the grassland.

神威 shénwēi martial prowess; invincible strength:巨大的～ towering might /无比的～ invincible might; unrivalled prowess /部队的～令敌人闻风丧胆。The martial prowess of the army struck terror into the hearts of the enemy.

神位 shénwèi spirit tablet; memorial tablet; tablet:设立～ set up a memorial tablet

神巫 shénwū wizard; sorcerer; soothsayer

神武 shénwǔ 〈书面〉wise and mighty; divine and powerful (used mostly to praise emperors, monarchs, generals and prime ministers)

神武门 Shénwǔmén Gate of Divine Prowess of the Palace Museum, Beijing

神武天皇 Shénwǔ Tiānhuáng Jimmu Tenno, the legendary first emperor of Japan (660 BC)

神物 shénwù 〈书面〉❶ wonder; miracle; prodigy; phenomenon:看作～ regard sth. as a wonder ❷ supernatural being; divine being; deity:当作～来供奉 enshrine and worship as a deity

神悟 shénwù 〈书面〉❶ quick to comprehend; intuitive ❷ divine revelation

神仙 shénxian ❶ supernatural being; celestial being; immortal; fairy ❷ person who has the power of clairvoyance:未卜先知的活～ living clairvoyant (who has the power of seeing and understanding future events) ❸ person not encumbered with worldly cares:他过着～一样的生活。He leads a life of blissful happiness, free from care and worry.

神仙葫芦 shénxian húlu 〈机械〉chain block

神仙会 shénxianhuì meeting of immortals — meeting at which the participants express their views freely in an unconstrained atmosphere

神仙美眷 shénxian-měijuàn happily married couple

神仙鱼 shénxianyú angelfish

神像 shénxiàng picture, image, or statue of god or Buddha:大殿里有几百尊～。There are several hundred statues of Buddha in the hall.

神效 shénxiào stunning effect; amazing effectiveness:这种药治胃病具有～。This kind of medicine is extremely efficacious for gastric disease.

神学 shénxué 〈宗教〉theology

神学博士 shénxué bóshì Doctor of Divinity (D.D.)

神学院 shénxuéyuàn theological seminary; school of divinity

神学自由主义 shénxué zìyóuzhǔyì theological liberalism

神医 shényī miracle-working doctor:扁鹊是我国古代的～。Bian Que was a legendary doctor in ancient China who could work miracles.

神异 shényì ❶ gods and spirits:传说此山多～。Legend has it that there were many gods and spirits in this mountain. ❷ magical; supernatural; mystical; miraculous:该书构思～。There seems to be a touch of magic in the conception of the book.

神鹰 shényīng 〈动物〉condor (*Vultur gryphus*)

神勇 shényǒng (of) superhuman bravery

神游 shényóu 〈书面〉feel as if one had personally visited the place; take an imaginary trip to a place:～于太空 as if travelling in outer space /朦胧中,他似乎飞上了仙岛,在那里尽情地～了一番。While half asleep, he seemed to have landed in a fairyland and to be enjoying it to his heart's content.

神佑女王 Shényòu Nǚwáng *God Save the Queen*, the British national anthem

神宇 shényǔ 〈书面〉(a person's) temperament and appearance:两人～迥异。The two people are poles apart in both temperament and appearance.

神韵 shényùn romantic charm (in art and literature):自然的～ natural charm /迷人的～ enchanting grace /独特的～ unique charm /他的许多诗歌颇有～。There is a tinge of romantic charm in many of his poems.

神职人员 shénzhí rényuán clergy

神志 shénzhì consciousness; awareness; senses; mind:～清醒 be in one's right mind; be perfectly sober /～不清 be unconscious /～昏迷 be in a state of delirium; go into a coma /～恍惚 be in a trance /恢复～ regain consciousness; be back to normal; come to

神智 shénzhì mind; intellect; wisdom

神州 Shénzhōu Sacred Land; China:赤县～ China

神主 shénzhǔ 〈旧语〉long and narrow tablet made of wood with the name of the deceased on it, used for enshrinement and worship

神姿 shénzī 〈书面〉expression; graceful bearing

什(甚) shén

see also shí

什么 shénme ❶ *used in the interrogative* (a) *by itself to ask questions*:你～意思? What do you mean? /那是～? What is that? (b) *before a noun to ask who or what*:他是～人? Who is he? /～事儿?

What's the matter? /～书? What book? /他～时候来? When will he come? ❷ *used to refer to anything indefinite*:你想买点～? Would you like to buy anything? /好像发生了～事。It seems that something has happened. ❸ *used to refer to things in general* (a) *before* 也 *or* 都 *to indicate that there is no exception within the limits mentioned*:她～都不说。She refuses to say anything. /这儿他～都喜欢。He likes everything here. /～颜色都行。Any colour will do. (b) *two* 什么 *used one after another to indicate that the first one determines the second*:他演～像～。He acts well in whatever role he plays. /有～就说～。Feel free to say what's on your mind. /学～就干～。Take on what job you are trained for. ❹ *used to express surprise or discontent*:～! 她又请假了? What! She has again asked for leave? /～! 她已经六十岁了,一点也不像。Really? She is sixty already. She doesn't look her age at all. ❺ *used to express censure*:你嚷～? Why all this shouting? /客气～? Don't stand on ceremony! /你说的是～话,一点道理都不讲。What are you talking about? You are most unreasonable. /装～糊涂? Stop playing the fool. ❻ *used to express disagreement with what has been said*:他～谦虚,他只不过虚伪而已。Is he modest? No, he's simply hypocritical. /还散～步呀,你看看都几点了? Take a stroll! Don't you think it's too late for that? ❼ *used before a string of coordinate phrases to indicate an incomplete list*:～弹琴呀,绘画呀,跳舞呀,他全都会。He can play the piano, draw, dance, and what not. /～洗衣呀,做饭呀,收拾屋子呀,她都干得很好。She does a good job of everything: washing clothes, preparing meals and tidying up rooms.

什么的 shénmede and so on; and what not:他不喜欢打球、游泳～,就爱下棋。He doesn't like playing basketball, swimming, or that sort of sport, but loves playing chess. /菜摊上摆满了西红柿、青椒、茄子～。The vegetable stalls are full of tomatoes, green peppers, eggplant, and what not.

shěn

S

沈[1](瀋) Shěn (short for 沈阳) Shenyang

沈[2](瀋) shěn 〈书面〉juice:墨～未干。The ink is still wet.

沈[3] Shěn a surname

沈括 Shěn Kuò Shen Kuo (1031-1095), statesman and scientist of the Northern Song Dynasty

沈铨 Shěn Quán Shen Quan (formerly translated as Shen Ch'uan, 1682-c.1760), traditional brush painter of the Qing Dynasty

沈阳 Shěnyáng Shenyang, the capital city of Liaoning Province

沈腰潘鬓 shěnyāo-pānbìn emaciated and ageing

沈约 Shěn Yuē Shen Yue (formerly translated as Shen Yueh, 441-513), scholar of the Southern Dynasties

沈周 Shěn Zhōu Shen Zhou (formerly translated as Shen Chou, 1427-1509), poet and painter of the Ming Dynasty

审[1](審) shěn ❶ careful; circumspect:～思明辨 discriminate with wisdom /～慎 circumspect ❷ examine; check up; go over:～稿 go over a manuscript (draft) /～批 examine and approve /编～ read and edit ❸ interrogate; try:公～ put sb. on a public trial; stand public trial /～罪犯 interrogate a criminal /候～ wait for trial

审[2](審、讅) shěn 〈书面〉know; be familiar; be aware:～悉 know /未～其详 not be acquainted with the details

审[3](審) shěn 〈书面〉indeed; really:～如是。It's really so.

审办 shěnbàn investigate and handle:此案由地方法院受理～。This case will be submitted to the local court for investigation and trial.

审查 shěnchá examine; check; investigate:～名单 check up on the name list /～计划 examine a plan /～剧本 go over a script /报上级～ submit to higher authorities for further examination

审察 shěnchá ❶ careful observation; watch:他对这些昆虫的生活习性作过认真的～。He has made careful observation of the insects' habits. ❷ examine; investigate; scrutinize:对这事件应该严密地进行～。A careful investigation into the incident should be conducted.

审处 shěnchǔ ❶ try:移交法院～ hand over to the court for trial ❷ examine and decide:此事有关部门正在～。The matter is still under examination and will be subsequently dealt with by the department (*or* authorities) concerned.

审订 shěndìng examine and revise:负责～ be in charge of the revision

审定 shěndìng examine and approve:～经费预算 examine and approve the budget for expenditure /等待上级～ pending examination and approval by higher authorities

审读 shěndú *also* "审阅" check and approve:材料已交主管部门～。The material has been submitted to the department (*or* authorities) in charge for check and approval.

审度 shěnduó study and weigh; deliberate; consider the pros and cons:～时势 size up the current situation; weigh the circumstances

审改 shěngǎi examine and revise; edit:～文稿 revise a manuscript (*or* draft)

审改本 shěngǎiběn draft for examination and revision (before it is sent to the printers)

审干 shěngàn (short for 审查干部) examine cadres' personal histories including family background, work experience and social connections

审核 shěnhé examine and verify:～统计数字 check statistics /～产量 verify output /～账目 audit accounts /负责～ be in charge of examination and verification

审计 shěnjì audit:～人员 auditing personnel /～部门 auditing department /～范围 scope of auditing /～监督 audit supervision /～权限 competence of auditor

审计报告 shěnjì bàogào audit report:有保留意见的～ qualified audit report

审计处 shěnjìchù auditing division or department

审计机构 shěnjì jīgòu auditing body

审计署 shěnjìshǔ auditing administration:中华人民共和国～ Auditing Administration of the People's Republic of China

审计委员会 shěnjì wěiyuánhuì audit committee

审计员 shěnjìyuán auditor

审计长 shěnjìzhǎng auditor general; chief auditor

审计制 shěnjìzhì audit system

审计准则 shěnjì zhǔnzé auditing standards

审校 shěnjiào ❶ examine and revise:～清样 examine and revise the final proof ❷ reviser

审结 shěnjié conclude an investigation:～刑事案件 conclude the investigation of a criminal case

审究 shěnjiū 〈书面〉investigate and handle:此案有关方面正在～。The case is being handled by the department concerned.

审看 shěnkàn examine carefully; look closely into

审理 shěnlǐ 〈法律〉try; hear:～民事纠纷 adjudicate civil disputes /～行政案件 handle administrative cases; conduct administrative proceedings /已交由法院～ have been handed over to court for trial /公开～ public trial

审量 shěnliàng study and assess

审美 shěnměi appreciation of beauty:～标准 aesthetic standards /～观 aesthetic perspective; aesthetic conception (*or* taste)

审判 shěnpàn bring to trial; put on trial; try:进行～ conduct a trial /开始～ commence (*or* open) a trial /～工作 administration of justice /～的过程 trial process /～刑事犯 try a criminal suspect /由军事法庭～ be court-martialled; go on trial before a military tribunal

审判程序 shěnpàn chéngxù judicial procedure

审判机关 shěnpàn jīguān judicial organ

审判权 shěnpànquán judicial authority; jurisdiction

审判员 shěnpànyuán judicial officer; judge

审判长 shěnpànzhǎng presiding judge

审批 shěnpī examine and approve:报请上级主管部门～ submit to the competent authorities at a higher level for examination and approval

审评 shěnpíng examine and evaluate; review and appraise:舆论界对～结果反应强烈。The media reacted strongly to the results of the evaluation.

审慎 shěnshèn cautious; careful; prudent; circumspect:～从事 be prudent in dealing with matters /～地处理问题 handle problems with great caution

审时度势 shěnshí-duóshì judge the hour and size up the situation; take stock of the situation:善于～ be good at reading the signs of the times; be able to make a correct assessment of the situation

审实 shěnshí establish the truth of a matter after investigation:此事一经～,应立即作出处理。Once the matter is confirmed, it should be dealt with promptly.

审视 shěnshì look at sth. or sb. attentively; observe carefully:～片刻 look around carefully for a while /～着周围的人群 watch the crowd milling around

审题 shěntí examine or consider carefully (before writing an article or answering a question):认真～ deliberate (on) the questions

审问 shěnwèn interrogate; question:～嫌疑犯 interrogate some suspects /进行～ conduct interrogation /变相的～ interrogation in disguise

审讯 shěnxùn 〈法律〉❶ interrogate; try:～流氓团伙 interrogate a criminal gang /受到～ be subjected to interrogation ❷ hearing:未经～即定罪 condemn sb. without a hearing

审议 shěnyì consideration; deliberation; discussion:请代表们～ submit sth. to the deputies for examination and approval /～的提案 motion put forward for discussion /正在～中 be under consideration

审议官 shěnyìguān (Japan) deputy vice-minister:外务省～ Deputy Vice-Minister of the Ministry of Foreign Affairs

审议机构 shěnyì jīgòu deliberative body

审阅 shěnyuè check and approve:轮流～ check and approve in turn /～稿件 go over a manuscript /未经本人～不得复印。Not to be printed without being checked by the author.

婶(嬸) shěn

❶ wife of father's younger brother; aunt:三～ third aunt ❷ form of address for a woman about one's mother's age; aunt; auntie:李二～ Second Auntie Li

婶母 shěnmǔ wife of father's younger brother; aunt

婶娘 shěnniáng 〈方言〉wife of father's younger brother; aunt

婶婆 shěnpó husband's aunt

婶婶 shěnshen 〈方言〉wife of father's younger brother; aunt

婶子 shěnzi 〈口语〉wife of father's younger brother; aunt

哂 shěn

〈书面〉smile:不值识者一～ not worth a smile of the discerning /聊博一～ just for your entertainment

哂纳 shěnnà also "哂收"〈套语〉kindly accept (this small gift):送上条幅一帧,望～。I am sending you a scroll which I hope you will kindly accept.

哂笑 shěnxiào 〈书面〉sneer at; ridicule; deride:为行家所～。It incurred the ridicule of the experts.

瞫 shěn

〈书面〉look deep into

谂 shěn

〈书面〉❶ know; be acquainted with:～知 know; be aware of ❷ advise; urge; exhort

谂熟 shěnshú know well; be familiar with

谂悉 shěnxī know; be aware of

矧 shěn

〈书面〉moreover; besides; in addition

shèn

慎 shèn

❶ careful; cautious; prudent:小心谨～ cautious; prudent /谨小～微 overcautious /谨言～行 be discreet in word and action; be prudent with what one says and does /不～ not careful; inadvertent /～之又～ exercise maximum caution ❷ (Shèn) a surname

慎独 shèndú (of self-cultivation in ancient China) guard against all temptations when alone:君子～。A gentleman should behave with caution in solitary circumstances.

慎密 shènmì careful and cautious:经过～研究后作出决定。The decision was made after careful study.

慎终如始 shènzhōng-rúshǐ act prudently from beginning to end

慎重 shènzhòng cautious; careful; scrupulous; discreet:说话～ speak with caution /～行事 act with discretion /问题很微妙,应当～处理。This is a delicate problem which should be handled with care.

甚[1] shèn

❶ very; most; extremely:过～其词 overstate; exaggerate /～冷 extremely cold /～为关切 be most concerned /～为悲痛 be excessively grieved /～为不安 feel very upset /欺人太～ bully others too much; it's going too far ❷ more than:他关心别人～于关心自己。He cares more for others than for himself. /情况恶化,日～一日。The situation was getting worse with each passing day.

甚[2] shèn

〈方言〉what:要它作～? What's the use of it? /姓～名谁? Who is it? /有～说～。Just say what's on your mind. /那有～要紧? What's there to be worried about?

甚低频 shèndīpín 〈通信〉very low frequency (VLF):～电波传播 propagation of very low frequency radio waves

甚短波 shènduǎnbō very short wave

甚而 shèn'ér 〈连词〉even; (go) so far as to:事隔多年,我～连他的名字都记不清了。After a lapse of so many years, I cannot even remember his name.

甚而至于 shèn'érzhìyú see "甚至"

甚高频 shèngāopín 〈通信〉very high frequency (VHF):～电波传播 propagation of very high frequency radio waves

甚或 shènhuò 〈书面〉〈连词〉even; (go) so far as to; so much so that:这个问题,好多人不完全理解,～完全不理解。Few people have a thorough grasp of the question or even a basic understanding of it.

甚近红外区 shènjìn hóngwàiqū very near infrared region

甚且 shènqiě even; (go) so far as to; so much so that:这班人目无所见,耳无所闻,～心无所思。These people see nothing, hear nothing, and even think of nothing.

甚为 shènwéi 〈副词〉very; highly; extremely:～得意 be very much pleased with oneself; feel very satisfied with oneself /这种例子～少见。These instances are very rare indeed.

甚嚣尘上 shènxiāo-chénshàng raise a riotous clamour:读书无用论一时～。The claim that learning is of no use was once rife and rampant. /近来妥协空气又～。Of late, the dust and din of compromise again filled the air.

甚至 shènzhì also "甚至于";"甚而至于"〈连词〉even; (go) so far as to; so much so that:她不仅穿着打扮变了,～连举止言行也和以前判若两人。She's a completely different person, not only in her style of dress but also in her manner and the way she talks and acts.

葚 shèn

see "桑葚" sāngshèn

see also rèn

椹 shèn

see "葚" shèn

see also zhēn

脤 shèn

raw meat offered for sacrifice in ancient times

蜃 shèn

〈动物〉big clam; clam

蜃景 shènjǐng mirage

肾(腎) shèn

❶ also "肾脏";"腰子" yāozi 〈生理〉kidney:～功能 nephritic function ❷〈中医〉testis; testicle

肾癌 shèn'ái renal carcinoma

肾病 shènbìng 〈医学〉nephrosis; nephropathy; nephrodystrophy:～性水肿 nephrotic edema /～综合征 nephrotic syndrome

肾单位 shèndānwèi nephron

肾功能试验 shèngōngnéng shìyàn kidney function test

肾功能衰竭 shèngōngnéng shuāijié kidney failure; renal failure

肾管 shènguǎn nephridium

肾积水 shènjīshuǐ 〈医学〉hydronephrosis

肾绞痛 shènjiǎotòng nephralgia

肾结核 shènjiéhé 〈医学〉nephritic tuberculosis

肾结石 shènjiéshí 〈医学〉kidney stone; renal calculus:～切除术 nephrolithotomy

肾亏 shènkuī 〈中医〉general weakness of the kidney (with symptoms such as fatigue, dizziness and a general weakness of the male sexual prowess); renal weakness

肾瘤 shènliú 〈医学〉nephroma; nephroncus

肾囊 shènnáng 〈中医〉scrotum

肾囊肿 shènnángzhǒng renal cyst

肾气 shènqì 〈中医〉kidney *qi*:～不固 unconsolidation of the

S

kidney-*qi* /～虚 kidney-*qi* deficiency
肾切除术 shènqiēchúshù 〈医学〉nephrectomy
肾上腺 shènshàngxiàn 〈生理〉adrenal gland; adrenal
肾上腺瘤 shènshàngxiànliú suprarenoma
肾上腺素 shènshàngxiànsù adrenaline; suprarene
肾上腺炎 shènshàngxiànyán 〈医学〉hypernephritis; paranephritis
肾衰竭 shènshuāijié 〈医学〉kidney failure; renal failure
肾细胞癌 shènxìbāo'ái 〈医学〉renal-cell carcinoma; clear-cell carcinoma; Grawitz's tumour
肾下垂 shènxiàchuí 〈医学〉nephroptosis
肾性血尿 shènxìng xuèniào 〈医学〉renal hematuria
肾炎 shènyán nephritis
肾移植 shènyízhí kidney transplantation
肾硬化 shènyìnghuà 〈医学〉nephrosclerosis
肾盂 shènyú 〈生理〉renal pelvis
肾盂肾炎 shènyú shènyán pyelonephritis
肾盂炎 shènyúyán pyelitis
肾脏 shènzàng kidney:～有病 have kidney disease /切除有病的～ excise the diseased part of the kidney /换一个～ change a kidney
肾周炎 shènzhōuyán 〈医学〉paranephritis

胂

shèn 〈化学〉arsine
胂酸 shènsuān 〈化学〉arsonic acid

渗(滲)

shèn ooze; seep; leak:～干了 have seeped dry /屋里～进了水。Water has seeped into the room. /血往外～。Blood was oozing from the wound. /污水朝里～。The foul water is leaking in.
渗出液 shènchūyè 〈医学〉exudate
渗氮 shèndàn 〈冶金〉nitride:～钢 nitrided steel /～炉 nitriding furnace
渗铬 shèngè 〈冶金〉chromize:～钢 chromized steel
渗沟 shèngōu sewer
渗井 shènjǐng *see* "渗坑"
渗坑 shènkēng seepage pit
渗凉 shènliáng chill:他刚一进冷库就觉得浑身～～的。The moment he stepped into the cold storage, he was chilled all over.
渗流 shènliú ooze; seep
渗漏 shènlòu seepage; leakage
渗漏损失 shènlòu sǔnshī 〈水利〉seepage loss
渗铝 shènlǚ 〈冶金〉aliting; aluminizing; alumetizing:～处理 calorizing /～钢 alumetized steel; aluminized steel
渗滤 shènlǜ 〈化学〉percolation; filtration
渗滤白土 shènlǜ báitǔ 〈石油〉percolation clay
渗滤器 shènlǜqì percolator
渗硼 shènpéng 〈冶金〉boriding
渗入 shènrù ❶ permeate; seep into:山顶的泉水～洞里,洞里满是泥浆。The spring water from the mountaintop seeped into the cave which was full of slurry. ❷〈贬义〉penetrate; infiltrate; invade:警惕这些坏思想的～ be on guard against infiltration of these pernicious ideas
渗色 shènsè 〈纺织〉bleeding
渗水试验 shènshuǐ shìyàn infiltration test
渗碳 shèntàn 〈冶金〉carburization; cementation:表面～ superficial cementation; surface cementation /固体～ pack carburizing /气体～ gas carburization; cementation by gases /～烧结 carbusintering
渗碳钢 shèntàngāng 〈冶金〉carburized steel; cementated steel
渗碳剂 shèntànjì 〈冶金〉carburizer; carburization material
渗碳炉 shèntànlú cementation furnace
渗碳体 shèntàntǐ 〈冶金〉cementite
渗透 shèntòu ❶ osmosis ❷ permeate; seep; soak:～了雨水 be soaked in rain /～了衣服 clothes soaked through /～的原因 reason for the seepage /～的状况 conditions of the seepage /森林里～着湿润泥土和野花的气息。The forest was filled with the tang of wet earth and wild flowers. ❸ (mostly used in connection with abstract things) infiltrate:经济～ economic infiltration /文化～ cultural infiltration /思想～ ideological infiltration /政治～ political infiltration
渗透法 shèntòufǎ osmose process
渗透剂 shèntòujì penetrant; penetrating agent
渗透率 shèntòulǜ penetration coefficient
渗透平衡 shèntòu pínghéng osmotic equillibrium
渗透速度 shèntòu sùdù seepage speed or velocity
渗透性 shèntòuxìng permeability
渗透压 shèntòuyā 〈物理〉osmotic pressure
渗透战术 shèntòu zhànshù infiltration tactics
渗析 shènxī *also* "透析" tòuxī 〈化学〉dialysis:～器 dialyzer
渗血 shènxuè 〈医学〉hemorrhage; staxis

瘆(瘮)

shèn terrify; horrify:～人 make one sick with revulsion; be nauseating /使人发～ make one's hair stand on end /感到很～ feel appalled

shēng

声(聲)

shēng ❶ sound; voice; noise:风～ sound of wind /吵闹～ loud noise; uproar; hubbub; din /人～ voice /犬吠～ bark /大～叫卖 loudly hawk one's wares /高～歌唱 sing lustily /寂然无～ silent; silent and still /别出～。Keep quiet. /言为心～。Words are the voice of the mind. /我得大～喊大家才能听得见。I had to shout to be heard. ❷〈量词〉*used for sounds*:听见了几～鸡叫 hear a cock crow several times ❸ make a sound; state:不～不响 keep quiet; remain silent (*or* speechless) ❹ fame; reputation:～施千里 (enjoy) a widespread reputation /～震寰宇 become known far and wide; gain resounding fame ❺ initial consonant (of a Chinese syllable):双～ alliteration ❻ tone:平～ level tone /仄～ oblique tone /四～ four tones in classical and modern Chinese
声辩 shēngbiàn argue; justify; explain away:极力～ do one's utmost to justify oneself /在那种情况下,他不得不为自己～。Under those circumstances he had to say something to defend himself.
声波 shēngbō 〈物理〉sound wave; acoustic wave:～的频率 frequency of sound waves
声波记录仪 shēngbō jìlùyí voice printer
声波照相法 shēngbō zhàoxiàngfǎ 〈物理〉phonophotography
声部 shēngbù 〈音乐〉part (in concerted music):～的配合必须协调。There must be perfect harmony among the different parts of the music.
声叉 shēngchā tuning fork
声场 shēngchǎng sound field; acoustic field
声称 shēngchēng profess; claim; state; assert:他竟敢公然～自己是学术权威。He has the impertinence to claim that he was an academic authority. /他～对这笔肮脏交易毫无所知。He professed to know nothing about the dirty deal. /他们～实际上已掌握了这种技术。They asserted that they had practically mastered the technique.
声传输 shēngchuánshū 〈物理〉transmission of sound; sound transmission:～线 acoustic line
声创伤 shēngchuāngshāng acoustic trauma
声存储器 shēngcúnchǔqì 〈电子〉acoustic memory or storage
声达 shēngdá 〈通信〉sound-radar
声带 shēngdài ❶ vocal chords ❷ (of a film) sound track
声导 shēngdǎo 〈物理〉acoustical conduction:～率 acoustic conductivity /～纳 acoustic admittance
声道 shēngdào sound track:单～ single sound track /双～ double sound track /混～ mixed (sound) track(s)
声调 shēngdiào ❶ tone; voice note:～高昂 in an impassioned tone /～激越 in a clear and sonorous voice /提高～ raise one's voice /改变～ change one's tone ❷〈语言〉tone of a Chinese character:掌握普通话的～ grasp the tones of *putonghua* (*or* standard Chinese pronunciation) /这两个中文词的拼音相同,但～不同。The two Chinese words have the same phonetic transcriptions but different tones. *see also* "四声" sìshēng
声东击西 shēngdōng-jīxī make a feint to the east and attack in the west; take sb. unawares:他惯于～,转移别人的视线。He would feint and pretend to move in one direction while going in another so as to divert people's attention.
声发射 shēngfāshè 〈物理〉acoustic emission
声符 shēngfú 〈语言〉phonetic element of a Chinese pictophonetic character (e.g. 青 in 菁 and 同 in 铜)
声辐射计 shēngfúshèjì 〈物理〉acoustic radiator
声共振 shēnggòngzhèn 〈物理〉acoustic resonance:～器 acoustic resonator
声光 shēngguāng fame; prestige; repute
声光表演 shēngguāng biǎoyǎn *son et lumière*
声光滤波器 shēngguāng lǜbōqì acousto-optic filter

声光摄影术 shēngguāng shèyǐngshù sonophotography
声光学 shēngguāngxué 〈物理〉acoustooptics
声华 shēnghuá 〈书面〉fame; popularity
声迹 shēngjì sound track
声价 shēngjià fame; reputation:抬高~ raise sb's reputation; enhance the fame of sb. or sth./他是戏剧界里~迅速上升的一颗明星。He is a rapidly rising star in the theatrical firmament.
声价十倍 shēngjià-shíbèi *also* "声价百倍" meteoric rise in fame or position
声接收机 shēngjiēshōujī 〈电子〉acoustic receiver
声抗 shēngkàng 〈物理〉acoustic reactance
声控 shēngkòng audio-controlled; sound-activated:这里的部分喷泉为~,可以随着音频率的变化喷出不同形状的水花。Some of the fountains here are controlled by acoustics and their sprays vary with the changing frequencies of music.
声口 shēngkǒu 〈方言〉❶ accent:听他的~,不是北方人。Judging from his accent, he is not from the north. ❷ tone; note:他话中一副含冤叫屈的~。There was a note of complaint in what he said.
声浪 shēnglàng ❶〈物理〉sound wave; acoustic wave ❷ voice; din; clamour:喝彩的~ wave of applause /人群中掀起一股巨大的~。A tremendous clamour burst out from the crowd.
声泪俱下 shēnglèi-jùxià speaking while tears are streaming down; in a tearful voice:他~地叙述他遭受的苦难。In a tearful voice, he described the misery he had endured./她同我谈到她童年的不幸经历时,不禁~。She could not refrain from tears when she spoke to me about the unhappy experience of her childhood. /他激动得~。He was so moved that tears gushed out as he talked.
声门 shēngmén 〈生理〉glottis
声名 shēngmíng fame; reputation:~鹊起 rapid rise in fame /~显赫 of great renown
声名狼藉 shēngmíng-lángjí have a bad name; fall into disrepute; be totally discredited:~的贪官污吏 notorious corrupt official
声明 shēngmíng ❶ state; declare:严正~ solemnly declare /正式~ officially state /公开~ publicly announce /~作废 declare sth. invalid (*or* null and void) ❷ statement; declaration:外交部的~ statement by the Ministry of Foreign Affairs /联合~ joint statement /中英关于香港问题的联合~ Sino-British Joint Declaration on the Question of Hong Kong (1984) /发表~ issue (*or* make) a statement
声母 shēngmǔ 〈语言〉initial consonant (of a Chinese syllable):汉语拼音共有二十一个~。There are altogether 21 consonants in the Chinese phonetic alphabet. /汉语拼音时~在前,韵母在后。In Chinese phonetic transcriptions, consonants come before simple or compound vowels.
声呐 shēngnà sonar (sound navigation and ranging):~传输 sonar transmission /~发射器 sonar projector /~接收机 sonar receiver /~设备 sonar set
声呐浮标 shēngnà fúbiāo 〈军事〉sonobuoy
声纳 shēngnà 〈物理〉acoustic susceptance
声囊 shēngnáng 〈动物〉vocal sac
声能 shēngnéng 〈物理〉acoustic energy; sound-energy
声能电话机 shēngnéng diànhuàjī 〈通信〉sound-powered telephone
声能学 shēngnéngxué 〈物理〉sonics
声旁 shēngpáng 〈语言〉*see* "声符"
声频 shēngpín 〈物理〉acoustic frequency
声频电报 shēngpín diànbào 〈通信〉acoustic telegraphy
声谱 shēngpǔ 〈物理〉sound spectrum
声谱仪 shēngpǔyí sound spectrograph
声气 shēngqì ❶ information; message:互通~ exchange information; keep in touch with each other ❷〈方言〉voice; tone:他的~有点嘶哑。He is a bit hoarse. /她用细细的~跟我们说话。She spoke to us in a soft voice.
声腔 shēngqiāng tune
声强 shēngqiáng 〈物理〉sound intensity
声强计 shēngqiángjì phonometer
声桥 shēngqiáo 〈物理〉sound bridge
声情 shēngqíng voice and emotional appeal:~激越 loud and strong voice
声情并茂 shēngqíng-bìngmào sing in a good voice and with much expression:她的演唱~,扣人心弦。Her beautiful voice coupled with its strong emotional appeal makes her singing deeply fascinating.
声请 shēngqǐng *also* "申请" shēnqǐng make an application; apply
声全息 shēngquánxī 〈物理〉acoustic holography
声嚷 shēngrǎng shout loudly:他吓得连~几句都不敢。He was too frightened even to make a noise.
声喏 shēngrě say "Yes, sir"
声色 shēngsè ❶ voice and countenance:不动~ maintain one's composure; stay calm and collected ❷ (of art performance, etc.) style; colour:这出戏他演得别具~。He performed the opera with a distinctive style of his own. ❸ vigour; energy; spirit:他的演唱为晚会增添了~。His songs added spirit to the evening party. ❹〈书面〉women and unhealthy music:沉溺于~ wallow in sensual pleasures /迷恋~ be fond of woman and song
声色俱厉 shēngsè-jùlì look stern and sound severe; be stern in voice and countenance:~地提出质问 question sternly
声色犬马 shēngsè-quǎnmǎ *also* "声色狗马" (of life style) sensual pleasures:不为~所迷惑 remain impervious to sensual enticements
声势 shēngshì power; influence; impetus; momentum:虚张~ make a show of strength; bluff and bluster /大造~ build up great momentum /普法宣传的~逐渐形成。The campaign to spread knowledge about law is gaining impetus. /一霎时,他感到自己仿佛又回到了家族~赫赫的时代。He felt as if transported back to the heyday of his family.
声势浩大 shēngshì-hàodà great in strength and momentum; gigantic in scale:~的示威 massive (*or* gigantic) demonstration /声势日渐浩大 gain momentum every day
声输出 shēngshūchū sound output
声说 shēngshuō tell; state or present (reasons); explain:他明知吃了亏也无法~。Though he knew perfectly well that he had been put at a disadvantage, he had no way to tell about it.
声嘶力竭 shēngsī-lìjié shout oneself hoarse; shout oneself blue in the face; be exhausted from shouting:哭得~ cry oneself hoarse; one's voice gets husky as a result of crying /他已经~,再也讲不下去了。Exhausted from shouting, he could no longer speak.
声诉 shēngsù appeal; tell; recount; relate:~思乡之情 tell about one's homesickness
声速 shēngsù *also* "音速" yīnsù 〈物理〉velocity or speed of sound:这种新型战斗机的巡航速度为~的二倍。The cruising speed of this new-type fighter is Mach two.
声损失 shēngsǔnshī acoustic loss
声态 shēngtài voice and sentiment:凡有所叙述,皆能在纸上见其~。A writer is bound to reveal his own sentiments in what he puts to paper.
声讨 shēngtǎo denounce; condemn; decry:~流氓杀人犯的罪行 condemn the crimes of hooligans and murderers /愤怒~ indignantly denounce /公开~ publicly decry /义正词严地~ denounce with the force of justice
声讨会 shēngtǎohuì denunciation meeting
声望 shēngwàng popularity; prestige; repute:享有很高的国际~ enjoy high international prestige /~日隆 have a rising reputation /他~很高,而且名实相符。He is in high repute, and very deservedly so.
声威 shēngwēi ❶ fame; renown; prestige:震慑于他的~ be awe-stricken by his fame and influence ❷ power; strength; momentum:畏惧其~ cower before his domineering power
声威大震 shēngwēi-dàzhèn gain great fame and high prestige; gain resounding fame:战胜世界冠军队后,我队~。Our team won high renown after beating the world champion.
声纹 shēngwén sound track
声闻九皋 shēngwén-jiǔgāo enjoy great prestige; be held in high esteem
声问 shēngwèn 〈书面〉❶ news; tidings ❷ fame; reputation
声吸收 shēngxīshōu sound absorption
声息 shēngxī ❶ (often used in the negative) sound; noise:什么~也没有。All was quiet and still. ❷ information; message:我们应互通~。We should keep each other informed of what is going on. /上下级要经常互通~。The higher and lower levels should be in frequent contact with each other.
声响 shēngxiǎng sound; noise:机器发出很大的~。The machine makes a tremendous noise. /楼梯上传来脚步的~。There came the sound of footsteps on the stairs. /那天夜里,我们听见炮弹爆炸的~。We heard loud reports of gun shells that night.
声像 shēngxiàng 〈物理〉sound image

S

声像错位 shēngxiàng cuòwèi slippage of sound to picture; sound and picture out of sync

声学 shēngxué acoustics: 超~ ultrasonics / 几何~ ray acoustics; geometrical acoustics / 建筑~ architectural acoustics

声学工程 shēngxué gōngchéng acoustical engineering

声压 shēngyā 〈物理〉acoustic radiation pressure; acoustomotive pressure

声言 shēngyán assert; claim; state; declare: 他~自己正直无私。He claimed that he was upright and selfless.

声扬 shēngyáng make public; disclose; publicize: 此事不可~。Hush it up.

声音 shēngyīn sound; voice: 这位歌唱家~洪亮。The singer has a deep, sonorous voice. / 我们能清楚地听见大厅里谈笑的~。We could hear distinctly the sound of laughing and talking in the hall.

声域 shēngyù vocal range; voice register

声誉 shēngyù reputation; fame; honour; prestige: 享有很高的~ enjoy great prestige / 为祖国赢得了~ win credit for the country / 维护国家的~ defend the honour of the country / 这样做他就玷污了自己的~。By so doing he has tarnished his own reputation.

声誉鹊起 shēngyù quèqǐ quickly become known: 五十出头时他~。In his early fifties, he gained a fast-growing reputation.

声誉卓著 shēngyù zhuózhù be famous; be widely known; enjoy an excellent reputation: 他是一位大儒,晚年~。He was a great scholar who attained a high repute late in life.

声冤 shēngyuān voice grievances; ask for the righting of wrongs

声援 shēngyuán show support for; support: 呼吁~ appeal for support / 各方纷纷~。Support came from all quarters.

声源 shēngyuán 〈物理〉sound event

声乐 shēngyuè 〈音乐〉vocal music: ~家 singer; vocalist / 她~的造诣很深。She is an accomplished vocalist.

声韵 shēngyùn ❶ rhyme and tone of words; voice; sound: ~铿锵 sound sonorous and powerful ❷ (of Chinese) consonants and vowels

S

声韵学 shēngyùnxué *also* "音韵学" yīnyùnxué 〈语言〉phonology: ~家 phonologist

声张 shēngzhāng (often used in the negative) make public; reveal; disclose: 你最好不要把这件事~出去。You had better keep your mouth shut about the matter. / 他们想尽一切办法不把这个秘密~出去。They tried their best to avoid disclosure of the secret.

声障 shēngzhàng 〈物理〉sound or sonic barrier

声振动 shēngzhèndòng 〈物理〉acoustic vibration

声震 shēngzhèn acoustic shock

声震区 shēngzhènqū bang-zone

声子 shēngzǐ 〈物理〉phonon: ~带 phonon band / ~发射 phonon emission

声阻 shēngzǔ 〈物理〉acoustic resistance

声阻抗 shēngzǔkàng acoustic impedance

声罪致讨 shēngzuì-zhìtǎo denounce or condemn the crimes of one's opponent or enemy

生[1]

shēng ❶ give birth to; bear; deliver: 平安地~了一个女孩 be safely delivered of a baby girl / ~了第二胎 give birth to a second child / ~得很顺利 have an easy delivery / ~儿育女 give birth to and rear children ❷ be born: ~于天津 be born in Tianjin / ~来就有的权利 birthright ❸ grow: 自~自灭 emerge of itself and perish of itself; run one's course / 杂草丛~ be overgrown with weeds ❹ existence; life: 起死回~ bring (sb.) back to life; perform a miraculous cure / ~的伟大,死的光荣 live a great life and die a glorious death / ~得光明,死得磊落 live honourably and die honourably / 人~在世应有所作为。One should accomplish something worthy in one's life. / ~当为人杰,死亦为鬼雄。One should live a hero's life and die a martyr's death. ❺ living; livelihood: 营~ make a living / 国计民~ national economy and people's livelihood ❻ life: 杀~ take animal life / 舍~取义 lay down one's life for a just cause / 虎口余~ have a narrow escape / 了此残~ terminate one's remaining years; end one's wretched life; commit suicide ❼ life span; life time; (throughout) one's life: 一~一世 all one's life; life time / 前半~ first half of one's life / 素昧平~ have never met before ❽ living; alive: 栩栩如~ life-like; to the life ❾ cause; engender; give rise to: ~疮 get (*or* develop) sores / 从没~过冻疮 have never had chilblains / ~出好多是非 cause a lot of troubles / 她又~出什么花样来? What new tricks has she been up to? ❿ light (a fire): ~炉子 light a stove / 这火得~到三月份。We have to keep the stove burning till March. / 火~得旺。The fire is burning brightly. ⓫ (Shēng) a surname

生[2]

shēng ❶ unripe; immature; green: ~瓜 unripe melon / ~柿子 green persimmon; unripe persimmon / 不太~。It's almost ripe. ❷ raw; uncooked: ~鱼 raw fish / 半~不熟 half cooked / 黄瓜~吃最香。Cucumbers are best eaten raw. ❸ crude; raw; unprocessed: *see* "~丝"; "~石灰" ❹ unfamiliar; new; strange: 面~ look unfamiliar / 欺~ bully or cheat outsiders / 我头一次到这里,很~。I am new here. ❺ stiff; unnatural: ~造词语 forging new words and expressions; unnatural coinages / ~拼硬凑 jumble together (disconnected words and phrases); dish up (unrelated facts) ❻ (used before certain words expressing emotions and feelings) very: ~怕同行批评 be very afraid of criticism from one's colleagues

生[3]

shēng ❶ pupil; student: 师~员工 teachers, students and administrative staff / 师~比例 teacher-student ratio / 毕业~ graduates / 门~ pupil; disciple / 考~ candidate for an entrance examination; examinee / 招~ recruit (*or* enrol) new students ❷ 〈旧语〉learned man; scholar; intellectual: 书~ scholar; intellectual / 儒~ Confucian scholar; learned man ❸ male role in traditional opera: 老~ *laosheng*, the role of older men (usu. scholars or officials) / 小~ *xiaosheng*, the role of young men (usu. scholars) / 武~ *wusheng*, the role of warriors ❹ *suffix of certain nouns referring to people*: 先~ Mr.; sir; gentleman; teacher / 晚~ I (used when speaking to an elder or a senior) / 后~ young man; lad

生[4]

shēng *suffix of certain adverbs*: 好~为难 be in an extremely embarrassing or difficult situation / 偏~这样 as luck would have it / 怎~是好? What's to be done?

生搬硬套 shēngbān-yìngtào copy mechanically or follow blindly in disregard of specific conditions; apply mechanically: 反对任何~的作法 oppose any mechanical copying / 习惯于~ be in the habit of parroting others

生编 shēngbiān fabricate; cook up: 这些情节是~的。It's a cock-and-bull story.

生变 shēngbiàn bring trouble or misfortune in the wake: 事不宜迟,迟则~。There should be no delay in handling the matter, or it might give rise to unforeseen trouble.

生病 shēngbìng fall ill; be taken ill: 经常~ often fall ill / 又~了 be taken ill again / 假装~ pretend to be ill; sham (*or* feign) illness; malinger

生不逢时 shēngbùféngshí *also* "生不逢辰" born under an unlucky star; born at the wrong time: 有~之叹 pity oneself for being born in the wrong age

生财 shēngcái ❶ amass wealth; make money: ~有方 have the knack of making money / ~之道 way of making money; way of accumulating wealth / 和气~。Good manners bring riches. ❷ 〈方言〉furniture and miscellaneous articles used in shops

生财有道 shēngcái-yǒudào 〈贬义〉be good at making money; have a or the knack of making money: 他做生意门路多,迅速致富,可谓~。Good at wheeling-and-dealing as a businessman, he soon got rich. He was really expert at making money.

生菜 shēngcài ❶ 〈植物〉romaine; romaine lettuce; cos lettuce: ~往往生吃。Romaine is usually eaten raw. ❷ raw vegetables: 厨房里,~熟菜要分开放。Raw vegetables and cooked dishes should be kept separate in the kitchen.

生产 shēngchǎn ❶ 〈经济〉produce; make; manufacture: 工业~ industrial production / 农业~ agricultural production / 提高~ increase production / 从事~ be engaged in production / ~粮食 produce grain / ~机器 manufacture machines / ~设备 production equipment (*or* facilities) / ~潜力 productive potentialities; latent productive capacity / 大规模地~ produce on a large scale / 成批~ serial production; mass production / ~恢复正常。Production is back to normal. / ~不合标准。Production is not up to standard. / 过去某些工厂不顾市场需要大量~质量低劣的产品。In the past, some factories churned out shoddy products regardless of market demand. ❷ give birth to a child: 听说她最近~了。I hear she has just had a baby.

生产成本 shēngchǎn chéngběn cost of production

生产大队 shēngchǎn dàduì (under a people's commune) production brigade

生产单位 shēngchǎn dānwèi production unit
生产定额 shēngchǎn dìng'é production quota
生产队 shēngchǎnduì (under a production brigade) production team
生产方式 shēngchǎn fāngshì mode of production: 先进的～ advanced mode of production /采取集体的～ adopt a collective mode of production
生产工具 shēngchǎn gōngjù 〈经济〉tool of production: 被淘汰的～ obsolete production tools
生产关系 shēngchǎn guānxì 〈经济〉relations of production: 先进的～与落后的生产力的矛盾 contradictions between the advanced relations of production and the backward productive forces
生产过剩 shēngchǎn guòshèng overproduction: 造成～ cause overproduction
生产合作社 shēngchǎn hézuòshè producers' cooperative: 蔬菜～ vegetable producers' cooperative
生产基金 shēngchǎn jījīn fund for production; production fund: ～不得挪用。Production funds are not to be appropriated for other purposes.
生产建设兵团 shēngchǎn jiànshè bīngtuán production and construction corps
生产劳动 shēngchǎn láodòng productive labour
生产力 shēngchǎnlì 〈经济〉productive forces
生产率 shēngchǎnlǜ productivity: 提高～ raise productivity /劳动～ labour productivity
生产能力 shēngchǎn nénglì production capacity: 充分发挥现有设备的～ tap fully the production capacity of the existing equipment; tap the existing equipment to its maximum capacity
生产手段 shēngchǎn shǒuduàn means of production
生产线 shēngchǎnxiàn production line: 这种专用设备～是我国自行设计、制造的。This production line for specialized equipment is designed and produced in China.
生产销售一体化 shēngchǎn xiāoshòu yītǐhuà vertical integration; integration of production and marketing
生产要素 shēngchǎn yàosù essential factors of production (e.g. skilled workers, equipment, funds, technologies, resources, etc.)
生产责任制 shēngchǎn zérènzhì production responsibility system
生产指标 shēngchǎn zhǐbiāo production target
生产资本 shēngchǎn zīběn productive capital; production capital
生产资料 shēngchǎn zīliào 〈经济〉means of production: 必需的～ necessary means of production /个人的～ private means of production /～的所有权 ownership of the means of production
生产自救 shēngchǎn zìjiù support oneself through work relief (usu. after a natural disaster); make a living with one's own hands: 组织灾民～ help people in a stricken area to restore production and make a living with their own hands
生产总值 shēngchǎn zǒngzhí total output value
生辰 shēngchén birthday
生辰八字 shēngchén-bāzì 〈旧语〉Eight-Characters used in fortune telling, etc.
see also "八字" bāzì
生成 shēngchéng ❶ produce; form: 台风的～ shaping (*or* development) of typhoon ❷ inborn; by nature: 他～的一张巧嘴。He was born with a glib tongue. ❸〈书面〉raise; rear: 报～之德 repay sb. for bringing one up
生成程序 shēngchéng chéngxù generator; generating routine
生成物 shēngchéngwù 〈化学〉product; resultant
生成语法 shēngchéng yǔfǎ 〈语言〉generative grammar
生齿 shēngchǐ 〈书面〉number of people (as in the family, etc.): ～日繁 have a growing family; have an expanding population
生词 shēngcí new word: ～表 word list; vocabulary list
生祠 shēngcí 〈旧语〉memorial hall or temple set up for a living official
生凑 shēngcòu manage to gather or bring together; round up: 他～了几个朋友去庆贺他上司的生日。He rounded up some friends to celebrate his superior's birthday.
生存 shēngcún subsist; survive; live: ～的权利 right to live /～的意志 will to live; resolve to live /民族的～ national survival /适者～ survival of the fittest /人类离开空气便不能～。Man cannot subsist without air.
生存斗争 shēngcún dòuzhēng struggle for survival
生存环境 shēngcún huánjìng living environment
生存竞争 shēngcún jìngzhēng *see* "生存斗争"
生存空间 shēngcún kōngjiān (as in Nazi theory) lebensraum (living space)
生存能力 shēngcún nénglì viability
生存农业 shēngcún nóngyè subsistence farming
生存权 shēngcúnquán right of existence; right to life; right to subsistence
生存资料 shēngcún zīliào means of subsistence
生旦净丑 shēng-dàn-jìng-chǒu male role, female role, painted-face role and comic role (the four main roles in traditional Chinese opera)
生地 shēngdì ❶ strange land; alien land ❷〈农业〉virgin soil; uncultivated land: 开垦～ reclaim virgin land /那儿有不少～。There is a lot of uncultivated land there. ❸〈中药〉*also* "生地黄" dried rhizome of rehmannia (*Rehmannia glutinosa*)
生地黄 shēngdìhuáng *see* "生地❸"
生动 shēngdòng graphic; vivid; life-like; lively: 情节～。The plot is gripping. /这部小说是以人物描写～出名的。The novel is well known for its vivid characterization. /故事文笔～。The story is written in a lively style. /人物塑造得十分～。The characters are graphically portrayed.
生动活泼 shēngdòng-huópo vivid and vigorous; vivacious: ～的样子 vivacious look /～的政治局面 lively and dynamic political situation
生端 shēngduān 〈书面〉provoke incidents: 滋事～ create disturbances and provoke incidents /不得借故～。It is forbidden to stir up trouble under any pretext.
生而知之 shēng'érzhīzhī be born wise; have inborn knowledge: ～者,天下少见。Few men are born wise.
生发 shēngfā multiply; breed; develop: 一切皆由此～而来。All has grown out of this.
生法 shēngfǎ 〈方言〉think of a way (to do sth.): 你生个法儿搞点吃的来。Do what you can to get us something to eat.
生发灵 shēngfàlíng hair tonic; hair regrowth liniment
生发油 shēngfàyóu hair oil; hair tonic: 从不使用～ never use hair tonics /这个厂生产多种～。This factory produces many kinds of hair oil.
生番 shēngfān 〈贬义〉savage; barbarian: 吃人～ cannibal
生防 shēngfáng (short for 生物防治) biological control
生分 shēngfen estranged; separated: 两人的感情明显地～了。They are clearly estranged from each other.
生风 shēngfēng ❶〈书面〉(of wind) rise; blow ❷ create disturbances: 借故～ create disturbances under some pretext /遇事～ cause trouble whenever there is a chance
生俘 shēngfú capture (alive); take prisoner
生父 shēngfù one's own father (as distinct from adoptive or foster father); biological father
生父母 shēngfùmǔ biological parents; bio-parents
生根 shēnggēn take or strike root; put down roots: 他的主张已在群众心中～。His ideas have taken root in the minds of the people.
生光 shēngguāng 〈天文〉third contact (of a solar or lunar eclipse)
生果 shēngguǒ 〈方言〉fruit
生花之笔 shēnghuāzhībǐ *also* "生花妙笔" gifted pen; brilliant style of writing
生化 shēnghuà (short for 生物化学) biochemistry: ～燃料电池 biochemical fuel cell /～制品 biochemical product
生化净化 shēnghuà jìnghuà 〈生化〉biochemical purification
生化形态学 shēnghuà xíngtàixué biochemorphology
生化学 shēnghuàxué biochemistry; biochemics
生化氧化 shēnghuà yǎnghuà 〈生化〉biochemical oxidation
生还 shēnghuán return alive; survive: 他们冲进火海,无一～。They rushed into a sea of flames and none of them returned alive.
生荒地 shēnghuāngdì *also* "生地"; "生荒"〈农业〉virgin soil; uncultivated land
生活 shēnghuó ❶ life: 经济～ economic life /城市～ city life; urban life /农村～ village life; rural life /～的哲理 philosophy of life ❷ live: 他们二十年来一直～在一起。They have lived together for the last twenty years. ❸ survive; exist; subsist: 他在高山缺氧的条件下坚强地～着。He subsisted tenaciously under oxygen-deficient high-altitude conditions. ❹ livelihood; living: ～优裕 be well off; live in easy circumstances /改善～ improve livelihood /～幸福 live in blissful happiness; live a happy life; live happily ❺〈方言〉work (used mainly to refer to industrial, agricultural and handicraft work): 做～ do manu-

S

al labour; work
生活必需品 shēnghuó bìxūpǐn daily necessities; necessaries of life
生活补助 shēnghuó bǔzhù allowance or subsidy for living expenses
生活待遇 shēnghuó dàiyù *also* "物质待遇" wùzhìdàiyù material benefits
生活方式 shēnghuó fāngshì way of life; life style: ~不变。The life-style will remain unchanged.
生活费 shēnghuófèi living expenses; allowance: 申请~ apply for an allowance for living expenses /~指数 cost of living index /我们的~足够了。We have enough to cover living expenses.
生活费用 shēnghuó fèiyòng cost of living: ~调整 cost-of-living-adjustment (COLA)
生活福利 shēnghuó fúlì welfare; welfare benefits
生活关 shēnghuóguān ❶ test of austere living conditions: 过好~ stand the test of a rigorous life ❷ temptations of evil in easy circumstances: 把牢~ resist the temptations of evil when living in easy circumstances
生活环 shēnghuóhuán life cycle
生活环境 shēnghuó huánjìng surroundings; environment
生活经验 shēnghuó jīngyàn experience of life; life experience: ~丰富 know much of the world
生活垃圾 shēnghuó lājī 〈环保〉consumer waste
生活来源 shēnghuó láiyuán source of income
生活能力 shēnghuó nénglì 〈生物〉viability
生活史 shēnghuóshǐ 〈生物〉life history
生活水平 shēnghuó shuǐpíng standard of living; living standard
生活条件 shēnghuó tiáojiàn living conditions
生活习惯 shēnghuó xíguàn habits and customs
生活细节 shēnghuó xìjié trifling matters of everyday life; domestic trivia
生活周期 shēnghuó zhōuqī 〈生物〉life cycle
生活资料 shēnghuó zīliào means of subsistence; means of livelihood; consumer goods: ~的来源 source of means of subsistence /必要的~ necessary means of subsistence /丰富充足的~ abundance of consumer goods
生活作风 shēnghuó zuòfēng conduct; behaviour: ~有问题 lead a dissipated life
生火 shēnghuǒ ❶ make or light a fire: ~做饭 light a fire to prepare a meal /火车~待发。The fire (for the steam engine) has been lit and the train is ready to start. ❷ stoker
生货 shēnghuò unprocessed local products
生机 shēngjī ❶ hope of life, success, etc.: 一线~ off chance of survival /只要有一线~,你都应该奋斗下去。You should struggle on as long as there is still a gleam of hope. ❷ life; vigour; vitality: 恢复~ regain vigour /一片~ a scene of vitality /春天的大草原充满了~。The vast grasslands are full of life in the spring.
生机盎然 shēngjī-àngrán vibrant with life; overflowing with vigour: 冬去春来,大地~。With the advent of spring the land is vibrant with life.
生计 shēngjì (means of) livelihood; living: 维持~ eke out a living; make (both) ends meet /~无着 have no means of livelihood /我离开故乡时,家里一切~全断。By the time I left my hometown, the family was at the end of its rope.
生忌 shēngjì birthday of a deceased person
生姜 shēngjiāng 〈口语〉ginger
生胶 shēngjiāo raw rubber; caoutchouc
生津 shēngjīn 〈中医〉promote the secretion of saliva or body fluid: 这药可以~止渴。The medicine promotes the secretion of saliva and quenches thirst.
生境 shēngjìng 〈生物〉habitat; biotope
生就 shēngjiù be born with; be gifted or endowed with: ~一副倔脾气 be born stubborn /~一张利嘴 have the gift of a sharp tongue
生聚 shēngjù 〈书面〉(of a nation) grow in population and wealth
生聚教训 shēngjù-jiàoxùn the people and army work with one heart to wipe out national humiliation and defeat the enemy by building up their strength
生角 shēngjué male role (as of a scholar or official) in traditional Chinese opera: 他是京剧里演~的。He plays a male role in Beijing opera.
生客 shēngkè stranger: 别麻烦,我又不是~。Don't bother. I am no stranger here.
生恐 shēngkǒng fear; be afraid; lest: ~得罪人。I am afraid people might take offence. /~大家不赞成这主意。I fear that people will not approve of the idea. /他~自己在这桩丑闻中受到牵累。He dreaded that he might get involved in the scandal.
生圹 shēngkuàng tomb built before one's death
生拉硬拽 shēnglā-yìngzhuài ❶ drag sb. along kicking and screaming: 妹妹终于~地把姑妈请了来。My sister managed to get auntie here literally by dragging her along. ❷ *also* "生拉硬扯" draw a forced analogy; make a farfetched comparison; stretch the meaning: 不能把两个毫不相干的问题~地搅在一起。We should not mix two totally irrelevant issues and give a strained interpretation.
生来 shēnglái (of people) ever since one's birth; from childhood: 姑娘~就淘气。The girl has been naughty since her babyhood.
生老病死 shēng-lǎo-bìng-sǐ birth, age, illness and death — all the problems of one's life; lot common to all people
生冷 shēnglěng uncooked, cold food: 忌食~。Avoid eating anything raw or cold.
生离死别 shēnglí-sǐbié part never to meet again; part for ever: 那真是~的情景。It was really a scene of final separation.
生理 shēnglǐ physiology: ~缺陷 physiological defect or deficiency /~现象 physiological phenomenon /~特点 special physiological qualities; physiological characteristics /植物~ plant physiology
生理节律 shēnglǐ jiélǜ circadian rhythm
生理器官 shēnglǐ qìguān 〈生理〉bio-organ
生理心理学 shēnglǐ xīnlǐxué physiological psychology
生理学 shēnglǐxué physiology
生理盐水 shēnglǐ yánshuǐ 〈药学〉physiological saline; normal saline
生力军 shēnglìjūn ❶ fresh troops; fresh reinforcements: 调来一支~ have a new batch of troops move in ❷ new force; new blood: 需要~ need some new blood /成为~ constitute a new force /中青年科技人员是国防攻坚的~。Young and middle-aged scientists constitute a vital contingent in our major efforts to strengthen national defence.
生利 shēnglì ❶ yield profit; make profit ❷ accrue interest; bear interest
生粮 shēngliáng uncooked food grains (usually those carried by soldiers on march)
生料 shēngliào raw material: 储备大批~ store up large quantities of raw materials
生灵 shēnglíng ❶ 〈书面〉common people: 拯救~于水火 rescue the people from the depths of misery /残害~ trample the people underfoot ❷ life; living thing: 大森林里有许多可爱的小~。There are lots of lovely little creatures in the forests.
生灵涂炭 shēnglíng-tútàn the common people are plunged into the abyss of untold suffering: 化干戈为玉帛,以免~ bury the hatchet and restore peace so as to avoid the destruction of people's lives and property
生龙活虎 shēnglóng-huóhǔ full of animal spirits; full of vim and vigour; bursting with energy: ~似的青年人 young people brimming with energy /他工作起来~,总是抢挑重担。He was dynamic and vigorous, and would always take on the heaviest load of work.
生路 shēnglù ❶ means of livelihood: 另谋~ seek some other means of livelihood; look for another job ❷ way out (of a desperate situation): 杀出一条~ fight one's way out (as of an encirclement) /给他一条~ leave sb. a way out
生煤 shēngméi unburnt coal
生闷气 shēng mènqì sulk; be pettish: 我只好一个人~。I could only nurse my anger by myself.
生猛 shēngměng 〈方言〉(of fish, etc.) live; alive; full of life: ~海鲜 shellfish fresh from the sea; fresh seafood
生米煮成熟饭 shēngmǐ zhǔchéng shúfàn the rice is cooked — what is done cannot be undone; it can't be helped: 如今,~,后悔已无济于事了。What's done can't be undone, and there's no use crying over spilt milk. /这事必须马上决定,等到~,就来不及了。We have to make a prompt decision, otherwise it will be too late when the rice is already cooked. /反正~,大家都已经认可了。Anyway it was already a *fait accompli*, accepted by everybody.
生面 shēngmiàn ❶ new situation, pattern or form: 别开~ start sth. new (*or* original); break a new path; break fresh ground; blaze a trail ❷ 〈方言〉unfamiliar face: 听众里有不少是~的青年学生。There are quite a lot of unfamiliar students among the audience. ❸

dough:她跟妈妈要了块～,自己擀饼。She got some dough from her mother and started making cakes by herself.
生民 shēngmín 〈书面〉the people; the populace
生命 shēngmìng life:新的～ new life; new lease on life /政治～ political career/保护人民的～、财产安全 safeguard or protect the people's lives and property /火星上至今还没有发现～。No life has been found on Mars so far. /病人的～岌岌可危。The patient is critically ill. /我把这件事看做～攸关的问题。I regarded this as a matter of life and death.
生命保险 shēngmìng bǎoxiǎn life insurance
生命保障系统 shēngmìng bǎozhàng xìtǒng life-support system
生命科学 shēngmìng kēxué life science
生命力 shēngmìnglì vitality; life-force: 充满～ be full of vital power /无限的～ boundless vitality
生命率 shēngmìnglǜ vital rates
生命权 shēngmìngquán right to life
生命线 shēngmìngxiàn lifeline; lifeblood:这项政策极其重要,实际上是一切工作的～。This policy is of vital importance; it is in fact the lifeblood of all our work. /保证这条工作的～畅通无阻。We must make sure that this lifeline of our work is unimpeded.
生命现象 shēngmìng xiànxiàng biological phenomenon
生命学 shēngmìngxué 〈生物〉biotics
生母 shēngmǔ one's own mother (as distinct from an adoptive or foster mother)
生怕 shēngpà for fear that; so as not to; lest: ～打扰别人 so as not to disturb others /我们～他改变了主意。We fear that he may change his mind.
生皮 shēngpí rawhide; untanned hide
生僻 shēngpì uncommon; rare; obscure: ～字 rare word /～的术语 rarely used term
生平 shēngpíng ❶ all one's life:老人的～不详。Little is known about the old man's life. /他～为人正直耿介。He was upright and straightforward all his life. ❷ ever since one's birth:这种事是他～最不愿做的。This is the last thing he would ever like to do.
生漆 shēngqī raw lacquer
生气 shēngqì ❶ get angry; be furious:懒得～ not bother to be angry /瞎～ be in a blind rage /有点～ be a little put out /～的原因 cause of one's rage /～的样子 look piqued (*or* offended) /现在不必～。There is no need to get carried away now. /一提起他的名字就叫人～。The very mention of his name makes my blood boil. /我一想到这件事,心里就～。It makes me see red just thinking of it. ❷ life; vitality: ～蓬勃 full of vigour (*or* vitality); dynamic /他没有～。He is quite dead. /一篇文章,若无描写,则干瘪枯燥,毫无～可言。If an article contains no description, it is dry as dust with no vitality to speak of.
生气勃勃 shēngqì-bóbó dynamic; vigorous; full of vim and vigour: 一群～的青年男女 a group of energetic young people
生前 shēngqián during one's lifetime: 完成死者～未竟的事业 accomplish what the deceased had not been able to do during his lifetime /～的理想 unfulfilled ideal (of sb. who is dead)
生擒 shēngqín capture (alive); take prisoner: ～匪首 capture the bandit chieftain alive
生擒活捉 shēngqín-huózhuō capture alive; arrest:持枪的杀人嫌疑犯被～。The gunman was apprehended as a suspect.
生趣 shēngqù joy of life:小家伙给全家增添了不少～。The child has added a lot of joy to the life of the whole family. /这些花朵给荒凉的山谷平添了几分～。These flowers lend some joy of life to the desolate valley.
生全 shēngquán save life; keep alive
生人 shēngrén ❶ be born:他是 1966 年～。He was born in 1966. ❷ stranger:小姑娘怕见～。The little girl is shy of strangers.
生日 shēngrì birthday:过～ keep (*or* observe) a birthday /庆祝(纪念)某人的～ celebrate (*or* commemorate) sb.'s birthday /～快乐! Happy birthday!
生荣死哀 shēngróng-sǐ'āi be honoured while living and mourned when dead (usually in praise of a respected deceased person)
生桑之梦 shēngsāngzhīmèng be near the end of one's life; one's days are numbered
生色 shēngsè add colour to; give lustre to:这位著名歌星的演唱,为我们的晚会～不少。The performance of the famous singer lent much lustre to our (evening) party (*or* soirée).
生涩 shēngsè (of language) difficult and lacking in fluency; jerky; crude: 语言～,极不自然。The language is difficult and affected. /句子显得～难懂。The sentences are jerky and difficult to understand.
生杀予夺 shēngshā-yǔduó possess the power of life and death over:当时,军阀们掌握着～的大权。At that time the warlords held the absolute power to punish and execute innocent people at will.
生晒参 shēngshàishēn sun-dried ginseng
生身 shēngshēn give birth to:～娘 one's own mother
生身父母 shēngshēn fùmǔ one's own parents; one's biological parents:视为～ regard (*or* look upon) them as one's own parents
生生 shēngshēng ❶ multiply or breed unceasingly:保护生物,使之～不息。We must protect living beings so that they will multiply endlessly. ❷ generation after generation: ～因果〈宗教〉preordained fate from generation to generation ❸ compel; be compelled to; under compulsion:生活的重担～地压在他的肩上。He was weighed down with the need to earn a living. ❹ *used after nouns and adjectives as a suffix*:虎气～ full of vigour /好～ well and healthy /活～地被打死 literally beaten to death
生生世世 shēngshēng-shìshì generation after generation; for ever and ever:～永不忘 will live forever in the memory of the people
生生性性 shēngshēng-xìngxìng 〈方言〉be sensible; be intelligent: 你要教他～,用心读书。Teach him to be a good boy at school.
生石膏 shēngshígāo *also* "石膏" plaster stone
生石灰 shēngshíhuī *also* "煅石灰" duànshíhuī quick lime
生势 shēngshì (of plants) growth; the way a plant is growing
生事 shēngshì create trouble; foment disturbance:专门造谣～ be always spreading rumours and making troubles /他们偏偏找定了我们家来～。They have to pick on our family to kick up a row.
生手 shēngshǒu sb. new to a job; green hand:我是个～,请多指教。I'm new to the job. I hope you'll advise me whenever you can. /我们在工作中要照顾～。We have got to take care of new employees in our work.
生受 shēngshòu ❶ (mostly used in the early vernacular) embarrass; put to trouble: ～你。Thanks for the trouble you've taken for me. ❷ (mostly used in the early vernacular) go through hardships; take great pains:今后休辞～。Make nothing of hardships from now on. ❸ accept; take:他不好意思～人家这样的厚礼。He was embarrassed to take such generous gifts.
生疏 shēngshū ❶ unfamiliar:人地～ be unfamiliar with the place and have very few friends there /业务～ be lacking in professional knowledge or training; not know the ropes ❷ out of practice; rusty:我的法语有点～了。My French is a bit rusty. /我的驾车技术～了。I'm a bit out of practice behind the steering wheel. ❸ not as close as before; getting more distant:他们的关系～了。Their relations are not as good as they should be. /她怎么显得这样～? How could she be so distant?
生水 shēngshuǐ unboiled water
生丝 shēngsī raw silk; silk: ～的加工 processing of raw silk
生死 shēngsǐ ❶ life and death: ～未卜 be poised between life and death ❷ share weal and woe: ～兄弟 sworn friend
生死存亡 shēngsǐ-cúnwáng life or death; survival or destruction; (matter of) vital importance: ～的斗争 life-and-death struggle; desperate struggle /～的关头 critical juncture
生死关头 shēng-sǐ guāntóu moment when one's life or fate hangs in the balance
生死攸关 shēngsǐ-yōuguān be of life and death: ～的大事 matter of life and death
生死与共 shēngsǐ-yǔgòng go through thick and thin together: ～的战友 comrades-in-arms going through thick and thin; battle companions sharing a common fate
生死之交 shēngsǐzhījiāo persons who swear eternal friendship; fast friends; sworn friends:他们结为～。They became bosom friends until death.
生态 shēngtài organism's biological and life habits; modes of organic life and their relation to the environment; ecology: ～因素 ecological factor /～破坏 ecological damage /～管理 eco-management
生态变异 shēngtài biànyì ecocline
生态工程 shēngtài gōngchéng ecoengineering
生态环境 shēngtài huánjìng ecological environment: ～保护 protection of ecological environment
生态监测 shēngtài jiāncè ecological monitoring
生态旅游 shēngtài lǚyóu ecotourism

生态灭绝 shēngtài mièjué ecocide
生态难民 shēngtài nànmín ecological refugees
生态农业 shēngtài nóngyè ecoagriculture
生态平衡 shēngtài pínghéng ecological balance; balance of nature
生态气候 shēngtài qìhòu ecoclimate: ～学 ecological climatology
生态汽车 shēngtài qìchē eco-car
生态圈 shēngtàiquān ecosphere
生态系统 shēngtài xìtǒng ecosystem
生态型 shēngtàixíng ecotype
生态学 shēngtàixué ecology: ～家 ecologist
生态政策 shēngtài zhèngcè ecopolicy
生铁 shēngtiě pig iron
生铜 shēngtóng 〈冶金〉pig copper
生徒 shēngtú pupil; disciple; follower
生土 shēngtǔ 〈农业〉immature soil
生吞活剥 shēngtūn-huóbō swallow sth. raw and whole; copy mechanically; accept sth. uncritically: 学习理论, 决不能～, 死背条文。In the study of a theory, one should never swallow it raw and whole or learn its dogmas by rote.
生外 shēngwài 〈方言〉not close enough; not familiar with: 你只是少来两回, 怎么倒～起来了。There is no reason why you should feel less at home here just because you have made fewer visits than before.
生物 shēngwù living thing; organism: 各种各样的～ all kinds of living things / 超显微镜～ ultramicroscopic organism / 浮游～ plankton / 微～ micro-organism; microbe / 海洋～ marine organism
生物材料 shēngwù cáiliào biomaterial
生物舱 shēngwùcāng 〈航天〉biopak
生物测定系统 shēngwù cèdìng xìtǒng biometric system: 眼睛虹膜扫描是所有～最可靠的一种。Iris scans are the most secure of all biometric systems.
生物测定学 shēngwù cèdìngxué biometrics
生物层 shēngwùcéng biostrome
生物带 shēngwùdài biozone
生物地层学 shēngwù dìcéngxué biostratigraphy
生物地理学 shēngwù dìlǐxué biogeography
生物地球化学 shēngwù dìqiú huàxué biogeochemistry
生物电化学 shēngwù diànhuàxué bioelectrochemistry
生物电流 shēngwù diànliú 〈生理〉bioelectric current
生物电子学 shēngwù diànzǐxué bioelectronics
生物多元化 shēngwù duōyuánhuà biodiversity
生物发生律 shēngwù fāshēnglǜ biogenetic law; recapitulation theory
生物反馈 shēngwù fǎnkuì biofeedback
生物防治 shēngwù fángzhì 〈农业〉biological control
生物辐射伤害调查 shēngwù fúshè shānghài diàochá 〈航天〉biological investigation of radiation damage
生物感测器 shēngwù gǎncèqì biosensor
生物工程 shēngwù gōngchéng *also* "生物工艺学" biotechnology
生物工程学 shēngwù gōngchéngxué biological engineering; bioengineering
生物固氮 shēngwù gùdàn biological nitrogen fixation
生物光 shēngwùguāng bioluminescence
生物航天学 shēngwù hángtiānxué bioastronautics
生物合成 shēngwù héchéng biosynthesis
生物化学 shēngwù huàxué biochemistry
生物环 shēngwùhuán biocycle
生物环境 shēngwù huánjìng biological environment
生物计算机 shēngwù jìsuànjī biocomputer
生物技术 shēngwù jìshù biotechnology
生物架 shēngwùjià 〈航天〉biorack
生物碱 shēngwùjiǎn 〈化学〉alkaloid
生物礁 shēngwùjiāo bioherm
生物节律 shēngwù jiélǜ biological rhythm
生物科学 shēngwù kēxué biological sciences
生物恐怖主义 shēngwù kǒngbùzhǔyì bioterrorism
生物控制论 shēngwù kòngzhìlùn biocybernetics
生物力学 shēngwù lìxué biomechanics
生物量 shēngwùliàng biomass
生物疗法 shēngwù liáofǎ biotherapy
生物膜 shēngwùmó biomembrane
生物能 shēngwùnéng 〈物理〉bioenergy
生物能量学 shēngwù néngliàngxué bioenergetics
生物气候学 shēngwù qìhòuxué bioclimatology
生物气体 shēngwù qìtǐ *also* "沼气" zhǎoqì biogas
生物气象学 shēngwù qìxiàngxué biometeorology
生物区 shēngwùqū biotic division
生物圈 shēngwùquān biosphere
生物群落 shēngwù qúnluò biocommunity
生物群系 shēngwù qúnxì biome
生物燃料 shēngwù ránliào biofuel: ～电池 biofuel cell
生物色素 shēngwù sèsù biochrome
生物生产力 shēngwù shēngchǎnlì biological productivity
生物生态学 shēngwù shēngtàixué bioecology
生物素 shēngwùsù biotin
生物体 shēngwùtǐ organism; bion
生物卫星 shēngwù wèixīng biosatellite
生物武器 shēngwù wǔqì 〈军事〉biological weapons
生物物理学 shēngwù wùlǐxué biophysics
生物学 shēngwùxué biology: 主修～ major in biology / ～家 biologist / 古～ palaeontology / ～平衡 biological balance
生物岩 shēngwùyán biogenic rock; biolith
生物遥测器 shēngwù yáocèqì biotelemeter
生物药剂学 shēngwù yàojìxué biomedicine
生物语言学 shēngwù yǔyánxué biolinguistics
生物战 shēngwùzhàn 〈军事〉biological warfare
生物政治 shēngwù zhèngzhì biopolitics
生物制品 shēngwù zhìpǐn 〈医学〉biological product: 广泛利用～ make extensive use of biological products
生物钟 shēngwùzhōng biological clock; biochronometer; living clock: 调节～ regulate the biological clock / ～紊乱。The biological clock is in disorder.
生物种群 shēngwù zhǒngqún biological population
生物周期 shēngwù zhōuqī biological periodicity
生息 shēngxī ❶ bear interest: 把钱存在银行～ deposit money in a bank to earn interest / ～资本 interest-bearing capital ❷ 〈书面〉live; exist: 自古以来, 我们的祖先就劳动、～、繁殖在这块土地上。From ancient times our forefathers laboured, lived and multiplied on this land. ❸ 〈书面〉grow; propagate; procreate: 休养～ recuperate and multiply ❹ 〈书面〉cause to grow: ～力量 build up one's strength
生隙 shēngxì 〈书面〉provoke incidents; create disturbances; cause friction between (people): 借故～ create disturbances under a pretext
生相 shēngxiàng ❶ look; appearance; expression: 她～好, 又活泼。She is pretty and sprightly. ❷ *see* "生肖"
生橡胶 shēngxiàngjiāo *also* "生胶" raw rubber; caoutchouc
生消 shēngxiāo (of natural phenomena) appear and disappear: 寒潮的～过程 formation and disappearance of a cold wave
生肖 shēngxiào *also* "属相" shǔxiang any of the twelve animals (rat, ox, tiger, rabbit, dragon, snake, horse, sheep, monkey, rooster, dog and pig), representing the twelve Earthly Branches, used to symbolize the year in which a person is born
生效 shēngxiào come or go into force; take effect; become effective: 自批准之日起～ go into effect from the date of ratification / 此命令立即～。The order takes immediate effect. / 法律昨天开始～。The law came into force yesterday. / 条约签字后立即～。The treaty will become effective immediately upon signature.
生心 shēngxīn be oversensitive; be suspicious: 他让我不要跟你说这件事, 怕你～。He asked me not to mention this to you lest you should have some misgivings.
生性 shēngxìng one's nature; one's natural disposition: ～刚直 be upright and outspoken by nature / ～难改。It is difficult to change one's nature.
生锈 shēngxiù get rusty; rust: 防止～ prevent rust / 这把刀容易～。The knife rusts (*or* gets rusty) easily.
生涯 shēngyá career; life: 教书～ teaching career / 卖文～ live by one's pen; earn a living by writing; take to writing as a profession / 戎马～ one's career as a soldier; military career / 坎坷的～ life full of frustrations / 艰难的～ difficult life
生衍 shēngyǎn 〈书面〉multiply; breed; produce
生养 shēngyǎng 〈口语〉give birth to; bear: 奶奶～了哥儿仨, 我爹是老二。Grandmother gave birth to three sons, and father was the middle one.
生药 shēngyào dried medicinal herbs: 收集～ collect dried medici-

nal herbs
生药学 shēngyàoxué pharmacognosy
生业 shēngyè occupation; livelihood:不事～ have no job; be jobless; be idle
生疑 shēngyí be suspicious:容易使人～ easily arouse distrust /避免别人～ avoid suspicion /不由得不～ cannot help being suspicious
生意 shēngyì flourishing growth; life and vitality:洋溢着一片～ brimming with life and vigour /大自然的无限～ boundless vitality of nature
生意 shēngyi ❶ business; trade; deal:同几乎所有国家和地区做～ do business with nearly all countries and regions /做成一笔～ make a deal; strike a bargain /做珠宝～ deal in jewellery; have a jewellery business /～兴隆。Trade is brisk. *or* Business is flourishing. /～萧条。Business is bad (*or* slack). /那是一桩赔本～。It is a losing business. ❷〈方言〉occupation; job; work:停～ dismiss; sack
生意经 shēngyijīng knack of doing business; business expertise:懂～ have a knack of doing business; have a shrewd business sense
生意人 shēngyirén businessman
生硬 shēngyìng ❶ unnatural; not smooth; not polished; crude:用字～ unnatural (in) wording /文章写得有点～。The writing needs to be polished. /这个典故用得太～。This is not an apt allusion. ❷ blunt; rigid; crude; stiff:作风～ inflexible in one's style /说话～ speak harshly (*or* bluntly) /态度～ take a rigid attitude /～做作 rigid and affected /～牵强 stringent and farfetched /动作～。The action is stiff.
生油 shēngyóu ❶ unboiled oil ❷〈方言〉peanut oil
生油层 shēngyóucéng 〈石油〉source bed
生鱼片 shēngyúpiàn sashimi (sliced raw fish eaten as delicacy in Japanese cuisine)
生育 shēngyù give birth to; bear; beget:实行计划～ practise family planning /节制～ practise (*or* exercise) birth control /～年龄 child-bearing age /不能～ be unable to have children; be sterile
生育低谷 shēngyù dīgǔ baby bust: ～出生者 baby busters; Generation X
生育酚 shēngyùfēn vitamin E
生育高峰 shēngyù gāofēng baby boom; the bulge:～出生者 baby boomer
生育力 shēngyùlì fecundity; fertility:～差异 differential fertility
生育率 shēngyùlǜ fertility rate
生员 shēngyuán *also*“秀才”xiùcai people who passed the imperial examination at the county level in the Ming and Qing dynasties
生源 shēngyuán source of students; source of school enrolment:～枯竭。The source of students has exhausted. /～不足。There aren't enough applicants.
生源说 shēngyuánshuō 〈生物〉biogenesis
生造 shēngzào coin (words and expressions):他并不想～简化字，只是他不会写罢了。He did not intend to coin simplified Chinese characters; it was just that he could not write properly. /他的作品里常有～的词语。Poor coinages are often found in his writing.
生造词 shēngzàocí coinage
生长 shēngzhǎng ❶ grow:小麦的～期 growth (*or* growing) period of wheat /这种树在山区～良好。This species of trees grows well in mountainous areas. ❷ grow up; be bred up:他出生在上海，～在四川。He was born in Shanghai but grew up in Sichuan.
生长点 shēngzhǎngdiǎn 〈植物〉growing point
生长硅膜晶体管 shēngzhǎng guīmó jīngtǐguǎn 〈电子〉grown-film silicon transistor
生长激素 shēngzhǎng jīsù 〈生理〉somatotropin; growth hormone
生长率 shēngzhǎnglǜ growth rate
生长轮 shēngzhǎnglún growth ring
生长期 shēngzhǎngqī growth or growing period
生长素 shēngzhǎngsù 〈农业〉auxin
生长型晶体管 shēngzhǎngxíng jīngtǐguǎn 〈电子〉grown transistor
生殖 shēngzhí reproduce:分裂～ reproduction by division /有性～ sexual reproduction /无性～ asexual reproduction
生殖洄游 shēngzhí huíyóu 〈动物〉breeding migration
生殖孔 shēngzhíkǒng gonopore
生殖率 shēngzhílǜ reproduction rate
生殖泌尿系统 shēngzhí mìniào xìtǒng 〈生理〉genitourinary system; urogenital system
生殖器 shēngzhíqì *also*“性器官”xìngqìguān 〈生理〉reproductive organs; genitals:～崇拜 phallicism
生殖系统 shēngzhí xìtǒng reproductive system
生殖细胞 shēngzhí xìbāo germ cell
生殖腺 shēngzhíxiàn gonad; genital gland:～导管 gonaduct /～发育不全 hypogenitalism
生猪 shēngzhū pig; hog:繁殖～ breed pigs /饲养～ raise pigs
生字 shēngzì new words:预习～ preview new words /记住～ commit new words to memory /～表 list of new words

甥 shēng sister's son; nephew

甥女 shēngnǚ sister's daughter; niece

笙 shēng 〈乐器〉*sheng*, a reed pipe wind instrument:善于吹～ be good at playing the *sheng* /鼓瑟吹～ play both the *se* (an ancient Chinese plucked instrument) and the *sheng*

笙歌 shēnggē 〈书面〉playing instruments and singing songs:～达旦 with music and singing all through the night
笙管乐 shēngguǎnyuè music made with traditional Chinese wind instruments, such as the *bili* (觱篥) or the flute, to the accompaniment of the drum, the cymbals, the Chinese violin, the gong, etc.
笙磬同音 shēngqìng-tóngyīn work together in perfect harmony; be on intimate terms
笙珊瑚 shēngshānhú organ-pipe coral (*Tubipora*)

牲 shēng ❶ domestic animal ❷ offering of an ox, sheep, pig, etc. as a sacrifice; animal sacrifice:三～ three sacrificial animals /献～ offer animal sacrifice

牲畜 shēngchù livestock; domestic animal:繁殖～ breed livestock /饲养～ raise livestock
牲畜车 shēngchùchē 〈铁路〉livestock wagon; stock wagon or car
牲粉 shēngfěn 〈化学〉animal starch; glycogen
牲口 shēngkou draught animal; beast of burden:贩卖～ deal in draught animals
牲口贩子 shēngkou fànzi cattle dealer
牲口棚 shēngkoupéng stock barn; livestock shed
牲灵 shēnglíng 〈方言〉draught animals; beasts of burden

胜 shēng *also*“肽”tài peptide

see also shèng

狌 shēng 〈书面〉*see*“鼪”shēng

see also xīng

鼪 shēng 〈书面〉yellow weasel

升[1](昇、❷陞) shēng ❶ rise; hoist; go up; climb:太阳从东方～起。The sun rises in the east. /旗子～上去了。The flag has been hoisted. /气温～高了。The temperature has gone up. /价格～得真快。Prices have been soaring. ❷ promote; elevate:～为局长 be promoted (to be) director /连～三级 be promoted to a position three levels higher /老～不上去 always fail to ascend the official ladder /这孩子今年又～不了级。This year the child again failed to go up to the next grade. /～了半天他才是个科长。For all the fuss about promotion, he became only a section chief.

升[2] shēng ❶ litre (l.):一～汽油 a litre of petrol (*or* gas) /一下子就喝了两～啤酒 drink two litres of beer in one breath ❷ *sheng*, a unit of dry measure for grain (=1 litre):三～小麦 three *sheng* of wheat /十～为一斗。Ten *sheng* equals one *dou* (a unit of dry measure for grain=1 decalitre) ❸ *sheng* measure:用～量比用秤称方便。It's easier to weigh grain with a *sheng* than with a balance.

升班 shēngbān go up to the next grade (in school)
升沉 shēng-chén ups and downs; rise and fall:宦海～ rise and fall of an official; ups and downs of a political career; chequered official career
升船机 shēngchuánjī ship lift
升调 shēngdiào 〈语言〉rising tune or tone
升斗小民 shēngdǒu-xiǎomín poor people; peck-and-hamper people

S

升发 shēngfā get rich and win promotion

升幅 shēngfú extent of increase; rise:粮价～不大。There is a moderate rise in the price of grain. /今年空调器产量～较大。The production of air-conditioners rose by a big margin this year.

升高 shēnggāo go up; ascend; rise:千千万万人从电视上看火箭迅速～。Millions of TV viewers watched the rocket soar higher and higher. /最近几天气温～了不少。In the past few days the temperature has gone up sharply.

升格 shēnggé promote; upgrade:由县市～为省辖市 be upgraded from a county town to a city directly under the provincial government /两国外交关系～为大使级 upgrade the diplomatic relations between the two countries to ambassadorial level /这个机构已由司级～为部级。The status of this unit has been raised from a department to a ministry.

升汞 shēnggǒng 〈化学〉mercuric chloride

升官 shēngguān be promoted; move up (the official ladder)

升官发财 shēngguān-fācái win promotion and get rich; rise in position and fortune:贪图～ hanker after power and money /追求～ jockey for power and wealth

升轨 shēngguǐ rail lift

升号 shēnghào 〈音乐〉sharp (♯)

升华 shēnghuá ❶ sublimate:容易～ get sublimated easily /～为水蒸汽 be sublimated to steam ❷ raising of things to a higher level; distillation; sublimation:生活的艺术～ artistic distillation of life

升华干燥 shēnghuá gānzào lyophilization

升华热 shēnghuárè heat of sublimation; latent heat of sublimation

升级 shēngjí ❶ go up (one grade, etc.); promote:同意她～ approve her promotion ❷ (of war, etc.) escalate:世界各国人民对这一地区战争的～深为关切。People the world over are gravely concerned about the escalation of war in this region.

升级换代 shēngjí-huàndài (of manufactured goods) updating and upgrading:在市场竞争中，轻工业产品的～加快。The upgrading and updating of light industrial products accelerate in the face of market competition.

S

升降 shēng-jiàng rise and fall; go up and down

升降舵 shēngjiàngduò 〈航空〉elevator

升降机 shēngjiàngjī elevator; lift

升降奖惩 shēng-jiàng-jiǎng-chéng promotion and demotion, reward and punishment

升结肠 shēngjiécháng 〈生理〉colon ascendens

升空 shēngkōng (of astronautics, rocketry, etc.) go up into the sky; lift-off

升力 shēnglì ❶ lift ❷〈航空〉elevating force; lift:～面 lifting surface

升幂 shēngmì 〈数学〉ascending power; increasing power:～级数 ascending power series

升平 shēngpíng peace:～气象 peaceful atmosphere

升旗 shēngqí hoist or raise a flag:～时间 time of flag-raising

升迁 shēngqiān be transferred to a higher position in a new department:得到～ get promoted to a new unit /屡次～ be repeatedly transferred to higher positions in new departments /他十年没有～。He remained where he was for ten years.

升任 shēngrèn be promoted to the post of:他～连长了。He was promoted to (the post of) company commander.

升势 shēngshì 〈金融〉upward trend; revaluation:美元～回落。The rising dollar began to drop.

升水 shēngshuǐ 〈经济〉premium

升水率 shēngshuǐlǜ premium rate

升堂入室 shēngtáng-rùshì *also* "登堂入室" dēngtáng-rùshì pass through the hall into the inner chamber — reach the level of high scholarly attainments:做学问不长期下苦功夫，怎能～? How can one hope to acquire high proficiency in his special field of study without working hard and long?

升腾 shēngténg leap or creep up; rise:热气～的咖啡 steaming hot coffee /江面上～起一层白蒙蒙的浓雾。A thick white fog crept up from the river.

升天 shēngtiān ❶ ascend heaven; die ❷ go up into the sky; lift-off:卫星～。The satellite was sent up (to space).

升温 shēngwēn rise in temperature;〈比喻〉become warm:两国关系开始～。The bilateral relations began to warm up. /目下计算机需求～。There's a rising demand for computers. *or* The computer market is booming.

升限 shēngxiàn 〈航空〉ceiling:～高度 ceiling height

升学 shēngxué go to a school of a higher grade:～人数 number of students going to higher schools

升学率 shēngxuélǜ proportion of students entering schools of a higher grade

升压 shēngyā 〈电学〉step up; boost

升压变压器 shēngyā biànyāqì step-up transformer

升压器 shēngyāqì booster

升涨 shēngzhǎng rise; grow; run high:群众对体育运动的热情一直在～。The public enthusiasm for sports has been on the rise.

升帐 shēngzhàng 〈书面〉(mostly used in the early vernacular, now used figuratively) (of a marshal or commander-in-chief) call a meeting of generals in his command tent to discuss military matters or issue military orders; take command:钢铁～。(a slogan used in 1958) Let iron and steel take command in the national economy.

升值 shēngzhí 〈经济〉(upward) revalue; appreciate:日元～ appreciation of Japanese yen /英镑现在～。The pound sterling is being revalued.

升擢 shēngzhuó promote:～高任 be promoted; be appointed to a higher post /他已～为少将。He has been promoted to the rank of major general.

shéng

绳(繩) shéng ❶ rope; cord; string:麻～ hemp rope /草～ straw rope /线～ cotton rope /钢～ steel cable /用～儿绑上 bind sth. with a rope /牵一根～儿 pull a rope ❷〈书面〉restrict; restrain; punish: *see* "～之以法" ❸〈书面〉continue; carry on: *see* "～其祖武" ❹ (Shéng) a surname

绳鞭技 shéngbiānjì 〈杂技〉(do) tricks with a whip; (perform) feats with a whip

绳操 shéngcāo cord dance (as a kind of artistic gymnastics)

绳伎 shéngjì ❶ *also* "绳技"〈杂技〉rope-walking; rope-dancing ❷〈旧语〉female tightrope walker:江湖卖艺的～ itinerant female tightrope walker

绳锯木断 shéngjù-mùduàn saw with a rope and fell a tree — little strokes fell great oaks:一日一钱，千日千钱，～，水滴石穿。Enough feathers can sink a boat, and many a little makes a mickle.

绳捆索绑 shéngkǔn-suǒbǎng tie or truss sb. up (mostly criminals) with a rope

绳缆 shénglǎn mooring rope; hawser; cable

绳墨 shéngmò ❶ carpenter's line marker ❷〈书面〉rules; rules and regulations:不守～ not be bound by rules and regulations

绳其祖武 shéngqízǔwǔ carry on the cause of one's forefathers

绳愆纠谬 shéngqiān-jiūmiù expose and rectify errors

绳趋尺步 shéngqū-chǐbù 〈书面〉behave according to decorum; be decorous; be on one's best behaviour

绳绳 shéngshéng 〈书面〉❶ continuous; unending:众力～可劈山。Even a mountain can be split into two if everybody keeps up the effort. ❷ cautious; prudent

绳枢瓮牖 shéngshū-wèngyǒu wretched living conditions; impoverished family

绳索 shéngsuǒ rope; cord:挣脱捆住手脚的～ break loose from the ropes binding one's hands and feet

绳套 shéngtào ❶ cord loop; cord noose:绞架上的～ cord loop on the gallows; hangman's noose ❷ leather cord or hemp rope used for tying draught animals

绳梯 shéngtī rope ladder:利用～攀登 use a rope ladder to climb up

绳戏 shéngxì 〈旧语〉〈杂技〉tightrope or wirerope walking:～表演者 tightrope walker; tightrope dancer; ropewalker

绳藓 shéngxiǎn cord moss

绳正 shéngzhèng 〈书面〉correct sb.'s mistakes:多有～ make lots of corrections

绳之以法 shéngzhīyǐfǎ punish sb. in accordance with the law; prosecute and punish according to law:对贪污受贿的官员要～。Corrupt officials must be brought to justice.

绳子 shéngzi cord; rope; string

shěng

省[1] shěng ❶ economize; save; be frugal:能～则～ economize wherever possible /～出五元钱 have saved five *yuan* /～些力气 conserve one's strength /我们得～着点用。We have to be more economical. ❷ omit; delete; leave out: ～这两个字 leave out these two words /～掉不少麻烦 save a lot of trouble /～一道手续 omit one procedure /这句话不能～。This sentence cannot be dispensed with. /这道工序可以～。This step can be eliminated from the process. ❸ shortened form (of words and expressions):"联合王国"是"大不列颠及北爱尔兰联合王国"之～。"United Kingdom" is short for "the United Kingdom of Great Britain and Northern Ireland".

省[2] shěng ❶ province:河南～ Henan Province /～长 governor of a province /～政协 provincial people's political consultative conference /～妇联 provincial women's federation /～级机关 Party and government organizations at the provincial level /河北～电视台 Hebei provincial TV station ❷ capital of a province:进～ go to the capital of a province ❸ (of Japan) ministry:大藏～ Ministry of Finance /厚生～ Ministry of Health and Welfare /通产～ Ministry of International Trade and Industry /文部～ Ministry of Education
see also xǐng

省便 shěngbiàn convenient and trouble-saving:贪图～ hanker after convenience and simplicity /～的作法 convenient way of doing things /这样做较为～。Done this way it is quite simple.

省城 shěngchéng provincial capital

省吃俭用 shěngchī-jiǎnyòng save money on food and expenses; live frugally; be thrifty:养成～的习惯 cultivate a habit of living frugally /提倡～的作风 advocate the practice of thrift in everyday life /这些钱是他们～积蓄起来的。They saved all this money by economizing on daily expenses. /他想,～几年,必能有个住的地方。He thought that by skimping and saving for a few years he would have a roof over his head.

省得 shěngde so as to avoid:明天你们去长城时多穿点衣服,～冷。Put on more clothes when you visit the Great Wall tomorrow so you won't be cold.

省督 Shěngdū (Canada) Lieutenant Governor

省份 shěngfèn province:许多～连年丰收。There have been bumper harvests for years on end in many provinces.

省港大罢工 Shěng-Gǎng Dàbàgōng Strike of the Workers of Guangzhou and Hong Kong in 1925 in support of the May 30th Movement against imperialism

省会 shěnghuì *also* "省城" provincial capital

省俭 shěngjiǎn 〈方言〉 thrifty; frugal:她过日子很～。She lives frugally.

省界 shěngjiè provincial boundaries

省劲 shěngjìn save effort; save labour:你如果通过这条渠道办事,就会～儿得多。It would save a good deal of effort if you are to handle the matter through this channel. /用棍子撬比手搬～儿多了。A crowbar would make the work much easier than your hands.

省力 shěnglì save effort; save labour: ～的办法 labour-saving method

省略 shěnglüè leave out; delete; omit:此段标志着故事的转折,绝对不可～。The episode that marks a turning point in the story should by no means be omitted. /这个句子的主语可以～,因为上下文很清楚。The subject of the sentence can be left out as it is clearly understood in the context.

省略符号 shěnglüè fúhào ellipsis

省略规则 shěnglüè guīzé default rule

省略号 shěnglüèhào ellipsis; suspension points; ellipsis dots (…… or ...)

省略句 shěnglüèjù elliptical sentence

省略值 shěnglüèzhí omitted value; default value

省免 shěngmiǎn avoid; dispense with:这套繁缛的旧礼节都～了。These outmoded overelaborate formalities were all dispensed with.

省钱 shěngqián save money:这样办既省力又～。This saves effort as well as money.

省却 shěngquè ❶ save; economize:这样做,可以～不少时间。Much time can be saved this way. ❷ remove; avert; rid sb. of:～许多不必要的烦恼 rid people of many unnecessary worries

省事 shěngshì ❶ save trouble; make things easy; simplify matters:力求省点事 do everything possible to make things simpler /怎么办～就怎么办。Do it in the simplest way possible. ❷ more convenient; handy:搬家托给搬家公司较为～。A more convenient way of house moving is to hire the service of a moving company.

省属 shěngshǔ directly under the jurisdiction of a provincial government:～单位 units directly under the provincial government

省委 shěngwěi provincial Party committee:～书记 secretary of a provincial Party committee /～常委 member of a provincial Party standing committee

省心 shěngxīn save worry or anxiety:孩子有老人照顾,我～多了。With the child taken care of by its grandparents, I have a load taken off my mind.

省优 shěngyōu (of manufactured goods) superior quality by standards of a province; superior quality product of a province:获得国优、部优、～称号的名牌产品 famous brand products awarded the title of national, ministerial or provincial superior goods

省油灯 shěngyóudēng 〈方言〉 oil-saving lamp — person who causes the least trouble:这姑娘心眼儿多,可不是个～。The girl is shrewd and is obviously not easy to handle.

省垣 shěngyuán 〈书面〉 provincial capital

省治 shěngzhì 〈旧语〉 provincial capital

眚 shěng 〈书面〉 ❶ eye ailment or disease; film; cataract ❷ adversity; calamity; disaster ❸ fault; mistake:不以一～掩大德。Do not obliterate a person's great virtue on account of a single fault.

瘖 shěng 〈方言〉 thin; emaciated

shèng

晟 shèng 〈书面〉 ❶ bright; light:旭日大～。The morning sun is very bright. ❷ vigorous; prosperous; flourishing

盛 shèng ❶ flourishing; thriving; prosperous:全～时期 time of great power and influence; flourishing period; heyday /牡丹花～开。The peonies are blooming. ❷ vigorous; energetic; aggressive:气焰极～ very aggressive /火势很～。The fire is blazing. ❸ magnificent; grand; solemn: *see* "～举" ❹ rich, sumptuous:丰～的早餐 heavy breakfast ❺ profuse; profound: *see* "～意" ❻ popular; prevalent; extensive:此风很～。This trend is quite conspicuous. ❼ greatly; deeply:～夸 praise lavishly; laud to the skies ❽ (Shèng) a surname
see also chéng

盛产 shèngchǎn rich in; teem with:～水果 abound with fruits /这个地区～石油。This region is rich in oil. /洞庭湖～鱼虾。Lake Dongting teems with fish and shrimp.

盛称 shèngchēng highly praise; speak highly of:游客～太湖的风光。The visitors were full of praise for the wonderful views on Taihu Lake.

盛传 shèngchuán be on everyone's lips; spread far and wide; be circulated extensively; be widely known:这个地区～着他的英雄事迹。His heroic deeds are on everyone's lips in this region. /～他将担任学院院长。The rumour is widely circulated that he will be appointed president of the institute.

盛大 shèngdà grand; majestic; magnificent: ～节日 grand festival /～典礼 stately ceremony /～晚宴 magnificent feast /～的欢迎 rousing welcome

盛德 shèngdé high moral character: ～若虚 a man of illustrious morals is always modest; a man of virtue is always unassuming

盛典 shèngdiǎn grand ceremony; great occasion:举行～ hold a grand ceremony /躬逢～ be present in person on the grand occasion

盛纺 shèngfǎng soft plain-weave silk fabric produced at the township of Shengze (盛泽), Wujiang County(吴江县), Jiangsu Province

盛服 shèngfú 〈书面〉 splendid attire; festive or formal dress; (in) full dress

盛会 shènghuì distinguished gathering; grand assembly:主持这个～ preside over this distinguished gathering /妇女的～ grand assem-

S

bly by women /直播~的实况。The grand gathering will be televised live.

盛极必衰 shèngjí-bìshuāi everything starts to decline after it has reached zenith

盛极而衰 shèngjí'érshuāi fall from the pinnacle of one's power:这次叛乱使这个王朝~。The rebellion caused the monarchy to fall from the peak of its power.

盛极一时 shèngjí-yīshí be in fashion or be the craze for a time; be all the rage at the moment:赌博之风在农村~。For a time gambling was rampant in the countryside. /摇滚乐在青年中曾~。Rock music used to be a fad among young people. /这些倾向~。These trends were once prevalent.

盛季 shèngjì busy season; peak period:旅游~ busy season for tourism; tourist season

盛景 shèngjǐng grand occasion; spectacular scene

盛举 shèngjǔ great undertaking or enterprise; worthy undertaking:共襄~ let all people join in this great undertaking; lend common support to this magnificent event

盛开 shèngkāi be in full bloom:到处是~的鲜花。Flowers are blooming everywhere.

盛况 shèngkuàng grand occasion; spectacular affair:庙会的~ spectacular event of a temple fair

盛况空前 shèngkuàng kōngqián exceptionally or unusually grand occasion:奥运会的开幕式~。The opening ceremony of the Olympic Games was an exceptionally grand occasion.

盛名 shèngmíng high fame or reputation:久负~ have long enjoyed a great reputation

盛名之下,其实难副 shèngmíng zhī xià, qí shí nán fù a high reputation is hard to live up to; one's ability often falls short of one's reputation:~,我并没有人们说的那么大的本领。As one often falls short of one's reputed ability, I am really not as capable as people say.

盛年 shèngnián robust years of a person's life (between thirty and fifty); prime of life; prime:~难再。Youth comes but once in a lifetime. *or* The prime of life will never return. *or* One cannot stay in the prime of his life for ever. /~不重来,一日难再晨。A man cannot always be at the prime of his life; a day is past before morning comes again.

盛怒 shèngnù rage; fury:~之下拂袖而去 go off in a huff

盛期 shèngqī peak period; high season:这个地区的棉花已进入开花结铃的~。In this area it is already the high season for cotton to bloom and have bolls.

盛气凌人 shèngqì-língrén with overweening airs; domineering; arrogant:~地训斥别人 dress sb. down imperiously /他骄傲自满,~。He is arrogant, conceited and domineering.

盛情 shèngqíng great kindness; kind hospitality; boundless generosity:~厚谊 great hospitality and deep friendship /受到~款待,至深感荷。I am very grateful for the generous hospitality accorded me.

盛情难却 shèngqíng-nánquè would be ungracious not to accept a kind offer:这次研讨会~,我不能不参加。It would be ungracious of me not to accept the kind invitation to the symposium.

盛秋 shèngqiū eighth month by the lunar calendar; height of autumn; mid-autumn

盛世 shèngshì time of prosperity; flourishing age; heyday:恭逢~ come upon a flourishing age /生于~ be born into the halcyon days /太平~ times of peace and prosperity; times of peace

盛事 shèngshì grand occasion; great event:不朽之~ great, immortal event /体坛~ grand occasion in sports

盛暑 shèngshǔ sweltering summer heat; very hot weather; dog days; height of summer:~严冬 in sultry summer and freezing winter /~难耐。It's hard to endure the intensive heat. /~时节。It is the peak of summer.

盛衰 shèng-shuāi prosperity and decline; wax and wane; rise and fall; ups and downs:关心民族的~ be concerned with the prosperity of a nation /~兴废 vicissitudes; ups and downs; rise and fall /关系到国家的~。It's a matter of prosperity or decline for the country. /现在这条路线是否真正得以贯彻,将关系这个时期文学的~。Whether the present line is really implemented determines the wax and wane of literature in this era.

盛衰荣辱 shèngshuāi-róngrǔ prosperity and decline, glory and humiliation; rise and fall; ups and downs; vicissitudes of life:国家的~与每个人的命运息息相关。The fate of the individual hinges on the prosperity or otherwise of the state.

盛夏 shèngxià peak of summer; midsummer:~将至。The peak of summer is drawing near. /~已过。Midsummer is past.

盛行 shèngxíng be very popular; be current or rife; be in vogue:日益~ become increasingly popular /今年又一次~超短裙。Miniskirts are once again in vogue this year. /通俗音乐~。Pop music is all the rage now.

盛行风 shèngxíngfēng 〈气象〉prevailing wind

盛行一时 shèngxíng-yīshí in vogue for a time; prevalent for a time

盛筵 shèngyán grand banquet; sumptuous or lavish dinner:~易散。Like a grand banquet, good times do not last long.

盛筵难再 shèngyán-nánzài a sumptuous dinner seldom repeats itself; grand gatherings do not take place every day; a happy get-together is hard to come by

盛颜 shèngyán 〈书面〉appearance of a person in the prime of life

盛宴 shèngyàn *also* "盛筵" grand banquet; sumptuous dinner; magnificent spread:~招待 hold a grand banquet in honour of sb.

盛业 shèngyè great cause; grand undertaking

盛意 shèngyì great kindness; generosity; magnanimity:有负~ fail to live up to sb.'s high expectations; be unworthy of sb.'s generosity /~难却。It's hard to decline a kind invitation (*or* offer).

盛誉 shèngyù great renown; high reputation:享有~ enjoy a high reputation; be of great renown

盛赞 shèngzàn speak of sb. or sth. in glowing terms; highly praise; extol:~两国人民的友谊 extol the friendship between the two peoples /~工艺品的精巧样式 be full of praise for the delicate styles of the handicraft articles

盛馔 shèngzhuàn feast; sumptuous meal

盛装 shèngzhuāng splendid attire; rich dress; Sunday or holiday best:穿着~ be dressed in splendid attire /舞会~ gorgeous attire for a ball /全城披上节日的~。The whole city is splendidly decorated for the festive occasion.

盛壮 shèngzhuàng strong; sturdy; robust:正当~之年 in the prime of life

棄 shèng *see* "乘" shèng

see also chéng

乘[1] shèng historical records of the State of Jin (晋) during the Spring and Autumn Period; historical records in general:史~ annals of history; historical records /野~ unofficial history

乘[2] shèng war chariot drawn by four horses in ancient times:千~之国 state with a thousand chariots /元戎十~。The chief general had ten chariots.

see also chéng

乘舆 shèngyú 〈书面〉❶ carriage and utensils used by the emperor or king — emperor or king ❷ (used in a general sense) horse-drawn carriage or cart

剩(賸) shèng surplus; leftover; remnant:~菜 leftover dishes /~货 surplus wares /资料~了好几本。Quite a few copies of the reference material have been left over. /一点儿不~。Not a bit remained. /机关人员过~。The unit is overstaffed.

剩磁 shèngcí 〈物理〉residual magnetism; remanence; remanent magnetism:~测定 residual magnetism measurement /~法 residual method /~感应 remanence

剩水残山 shèngshuǐ-cánshān *also* "残山剩水" reduced territories of a nation after invasion by a foreign power:南宋小朝廷在~间寻欢作乐。The wretched royal court of the Southern Song Dynasty indulged in sensual pleasures in its reduced territories.

剩下 shèngxia be left (over); remain; stay:~的人 remaining people /还~什么? What is left? /~的东西都收拾好了。All the rest has been put in order. /~的人没有几个了。Only a handful of people stayed behind. /~的票都给人了。All the spare tickets have been given away.

剩余 shèngyú surplus; remainder:~用品 surplus articles /~的粮食 surplus grain /~的人员 remaining personnel /略有~。There is a small surplus.

剩余产品 shèngyú chǎnpǐn surplus products：分配～ allot surplus products /处理～ dispose of surplus products
剩余磁场 shèngyú cíchǎng remanent field
剩余电离 shèngyú diànlí residual ionization
剩余电路 shèngyú diànlù residual circuit
剩余价值 shèngyú jiàzhí 〈经济〉surplus value：创造～ produce surplus value /剥削～ exploit surplus value /占有～ possess surplus value
剩余劳动 shèngyú láodòng 〈经济〉surplus labour
剩余设备能力 shèngyú shèbèi nénglì excess capacity
剩余物资 shèngyú wùzī surplus materials

胜[1]（勝） shèng ❶ victory；success：战～ win (a battle)；triumph /得～ win a victory；be victorious /以巧取～ win by ingenuity /乘～前进 advance on the crest of a victory；push on in the flush of victory /得～回朝 returning to the capital to report on one's victory；triumphal return /我队以全～的成绩荣获冠军。Our team won the championship by winning every match in the tournament. ❷ win victory over (sb. or sth.)；defeat：以少～多 defeat sb. who is superior in number /人定～天 man can conquer nature；man will triumph over nature /屡战屡～ have fought many battles and won every one of them；score one victory after another /无往不～ be ever-victorious；be invincible /甲队～乙队。Team A beat team B. ❸ surpass；be superior to；be better than；get the better of：略～一筹 slightly better or superior /事实～于雄辩。Facts speak louder than words. /实际行动～过空洞的言词。Practical action is better than empty talk. ❹ superb；wonderful；beautiful：引人入～ be fascinating；be enchanting

胜[2]（勝） shèng be equal or up to；can bear：不～其烦 be pestered beyond endurance /防不～防 be difficult or impossible to prevent (*or* ward off) /美不～收 so many beautiful things that one simply can't take them all in /数不～数 be too numerous to count；countless /不～枚举 too numerous to mention individually (*or* one by one)

胜[3]（勝） shèng 〈古语〉woman's hair ornament：方～ slanting hair decoration
see also shēng

胜败 shèng-bài victory or defeat；success or failure：不计～ not fuss over victory or defeat /～未卜。It is uncertain whether we will succeed or not.
胜败乃兵家常事 shèng-bài nǎi bīngjiā chángshì for a military commander, winning or losing a battle is a common occurrence；a military commander would not fuss over a battle won or lost：～，何须为一战失利而烦恼。Victories and defeats are nothing out of the ordinary to a soldier；one shouldn't feel frustrated by just one loss.
胜不骄，败不馁 shèng bù jiāo, bài bù něi neither be dizzy with success nor lose heart because of failure
胜朝 shèngcháo preceeding dynasty (conquered and destroyed)：～遗老 die-hards of the defunct dynasty
胜地 shèngdì famous scenic spot：旅游～ scenic spot for tourists /避暑～ summer resort /开辟新的观光～ open up new tourist spots
胜负 shèng-fù victory or defeat；success or failure；outcome (of a war, etc.)：决一～ fight to see who is the stronger；fight it out /～未决。It is uncertain who will emerge the victor and who the loser. /～尚难预料。It's difficult to predict who will be the winner.
胜概 shènggài 〈书面〉beautiful scenery；most enjoyable or pleasant view
胜过 shèngguo excel；surpass；be better than：莫道昆明池水浅，观鱼～富春江。Do not say the waters of Kunming Lake are too shallow, For watching fish they are better than Fuchun River.
胜会 shènghuì 〈书面〉❶ distinguished gathering；grand meeting；great festive occasion：此等～难得一见。Such a grand gathering is very rare. ❷ lofty enthusiasm；exquisite zest；ennobling interest
胜迹 shèngjì renowned historical site：我国有数不尽的名山～。There are numerous famous mountains and historical sites in our country.
胜景 shèngjǐng beautiful scenery or landscape
胜境 shèngjìng ❶ place commanding a glorious view：名山～ well-known mountains and scenic spots ❷ (of a literary or artistic work) excellent mood；beautiful mood
胜局 shèngjú victory；success：～已定。The battle is as good as won. *or* The match is in the bag. *or* Victory is a foregone conclusion.
胜利 shènglì ❶ victory；triumph；success：取得～ win a victory /～在望。Victory (*or* success) is in sight. ❷ (of a task, etc.) attain the goal as planned：谈判～结束。The negotiation ended in success. /我们～地完成任务。We have accomplished our task.
胜利果实 shènglì guǒshí fruits of victory：篡夺～ appropriate the fruits of victory /摘取～ pluck the fruits of victory
胜利者 shènglìzhě winner；victor；champion
胜券 shèngquàn confidence in victory：～在握 success is within one's grasp /稳操～ be certain of victory
胜任 shèngrèn competent；equal to：力能～ be equal to the task /力不～ be incompetent for (the job)
胜任愉快 shèngrèn-yúkuài be fully competent；be well qualified：对于此事可以～者，竟无一人。There isn't even a single person who can fill the post with credit.
胜如 shèngrú surpass；be better than：他热情接待我们，～亲兄弟。He received us with a warmth surpassing that between blood brothers.
胜似 shèngsì superior to；surpass：～亲人 be dearer than one's own family members /不是春光，～春光。Unlike spring's splendour, Yet surpassing spring's splendour.
胜诉 shèngsù win a lawsuit or court case：～的一方 prevailing party /～人 winner of a lawsuit /他的案子终于～。He has gained (*or* won) his case at last.
胜算 shèngsuàn 〈书面〉stratagem which ensures success；tactic that enables one to prevail over one's opponent：操～ be sure to win
胜游 shèngyóu pleasant trip；enjoyable visit
胜友 shèngyǒu good friends；bosom friends：～如云 good friends hailed together as thick as clouds
胜仗 shèngzhàng victorious battle；triumph：打了一次大～ win a big battle；score a great victory
胜状 shèngzhuàng 〈书面〉beautiful scenery or landscape

圣（聖） shèng ❶ holy；sacred：我国领土神～不可侵犯。Our territory is sacred and inviolable. ❷ sage；master：诗～ poet among poets；poet of genius /书～ calligrapher of the first magnitude /棋～ master chess player ❸ sage；saint；*see* "～贤" ❹ emperor：～驾 his (*or* her) majesty /～恩 his (*or* her) majesty's kindness /面～ face his (*or* her) majesty ❺〈宗教〉holy：朝～ pilgrimage；hadj /麦加朝～ pilgrimage to Mecca /～父、～子、～灵 Father, Son and Holy Spirit (*or* Ghost)

圣保罗 Shèngbǎoluó Sao Paulo, the largest city in Brazil
圣彼得大教堂 Shèngbǐdé Dàjiàotáng Saint Peter's Basilica, Roman Catholic basilica in the Vatican City
圣饼盒 shèngbǐnghé 〈宗教〉pyx；pix (vessel in which the consecrated bread of the Eucharist is kept)
圣布赖德杯 Shèngbùlàidébēi 〈体育〉St. Bride Vase (top award for men's singles of the World Table Tennis Championships)
圣餐 shèngcān 〈宗教〉Holy Communion；Communion：领受～ take (*or* receive) Holy Communion
圣但尼 Shèngdànní Saint-Denis, capital of the island of Réunion in the Indian Ocean
圣诞 shèngdàn ❶〈旧语〉birthday of Confucius ❷ Christmas, the birthday of Jesus Christ：～礼物 Christmas gifts
圣诞节 Shèngdànjié Christmas；Christmas Day：欢度～ celebrate Christmas Day with jubilation /～前夜 Christmas Eve
圣诞卡 shèngdànkǎ Christmas card
圣诞老人 Shèngdàn Lǎorén Santa Claus；Father Christmas
圣诞树 shèngdànshù Christmas tree
圣地 shèngdì ❶〈宗教〉Holy Land；Holy City ❷ sacred place；shrine：革命～ sacred place of the revolution
圣地亚哥 Shèngdìyàgē Santiago, capital of Chile
圣多美 Shèngduōměi Sao Tome, capital of Sao Tome and Principe
圣多美和普林西比 Shèngduōměi Hé Pǔlínxībǐ Sao Tome and Principe, an African island state
圣多明各 Shèngduōmínggè Santo Domingo, capital and chief port of the Dominican Republic
圣父 Shèngfù ❶〈基督教〉God the Father ❷ Holy Father (the

S

Pope) ❸〈旧语〉term of respect for the emperor's father (who has abdicated in his favour)

圣公会 Shènggōnghuì 〈基督教〉Anglican Church; Church of England; Episcopal Church

圣公宗 Shènggōngzōng 〈基督教〉Anglicanism; Anglican Church

圣躬 shènggōng 〈旧语〉emperor's health: ～违和。His majesty was unwell.

圣何塞 Shènghésài San Jose, capital and chief port of Costa Rica

圣赫勒拿岛 Shènghèlènádǎo Saint Helena Island

圣胡安 Shènghú'ān San Juan, capital and chief port of Puerto Rico

圣火 shènghuǒ holy fire: 点燃奥运会～ light the holy fire for the Olympic Games

圣基茨和尼维斯联邦 Shèngjīcí Hé Níwéisī Liánbāng the Federation of St. Kitts and Nevis, a Latin-American island state

圣济总录 Shèngjì Zǒnglù *A General Compendium on Medicine*, compiled between 1111 and 1117 during the Song Dynasty

圣洁 shèngjié holy and pure: ～的心灵 pure heart

圣经 Shèngjīng Holy Bible; the Bible; Holy Writ; (Holy) Scriptures

圣经会 Shèngjīnghuì 〈基督教〉Bible Society

圣经贤传 shèngjīng-xiánzhuàn 〈旧语〉Confucian classics: 熟读～ be very familiar with the Confucian classics

圣灵 shènglíng 〈宗教〉Holy Ghost; Holy Spirit

圣灵节 Shènglíngjié Whitsunday; Pentecost

圣卢西亚 Shènglúxīyà Saint Lucia

圣马力诺 Shèngmǎlìnuò San Marino: ～人 San Marinese

圣庙 shèngmiào shrine for Confucius; temple; shrine: 朝～ go on a pilgrimage to the shrine of Confucius /瞻仰～ pay homage at the temple of Confucius

圣明 shèngmíng of great insight and wisdom (flattering epithet for the emperor): ～天子 wise emperor

S

圣母 shèngmǔ ❶ female deity; goddess ❷ (Blessed) Virgin Mary; Madonna: 信仰～ believe in the Virgin Mary /祈求～ pray to the Virgin Mary /《～颂》*Ave Maria*

圣母军 Shèngmǔjūn 〈宗教〉Legion of Mary (founded on 7 Sept. 1921 in Dublin)

圣母升天节 Shèngmǔ Shēngtiānjié 〈宗教〉assumption of Mary

圣母圣心会 Shèngmǔ Shèngxīnhuì 〈宗教〉Congregation of Immaculate Heart of Mary

圣母堂 Shèngmǔtáng Lady chapel

圣母像 Shèngmǔxiàng Madonna

圣牌 shèngpái metal medals with pictures of Jesus, Mary, angels or saints on them (worn by Catholics)

圣皮埃尔和密克隆群岛 Shèngpí'āi'ěr Hé Mìkèlóng Qúndǎo (French) St. Pierre and Miquelon Islands, south of Newfoundland in North America

圣品 shèngpǐn excellent works; best writings

圣乔治 Shèngqiáozhì St. George's, capital of Grenada in the West Indies

圣人 shèngrén 〈旧语〉❶ sage (such as Confucius); wise man: ～门前卖字 show off one's petty cleverness before a wise man; display one's smattering of knowledge before a sage /没有天生的～。No one was born wise. ❷ Your Majesty (the way to address a monarch by his officials in feudal China)

圣人无常师 shèngrén wú chángshī sages have no constant tutors; a sage has more than one teacher

圣萨尔瓦多 Shèngsà'ěrwǎduō San Salvador, capital of El Salvador

圣上 shèngshàng His or Her Majesty

圣诗班 shèngshībān choir: ～指挥 choirmaster

圣事论 shèngshìlùn 〈宗教〉doctrine of sacrament

圣手 shèngshǒu great master: 堪称棋坛～ can rightly be called a master chess player /草书～ one who writes a beautiful cursive hand

圣水 shèngshuǐ holy water

圣所 shèngsuǒ holy place

圣坛 shèngtán chancel

圣体 shèngtǐ ❶〈旧语〉body of the emperor ❷〈宗教〉Holy Communion; Eucharist

圣徒 shèngtú 〈宗教〉saint

圣文森特和格林纳丁斯 Shèngwénsēntè Hé Gélínnàdīngsī St. Vincent and the Grenadines, an island state in Latin America

圣贤 shèngxián sages and men of virtue: 人非～，孰能无过? Men are not all saints, so how can they be free from error?

圣训 shèngxùn ❶〈旧语〉imperial decree; admonitions of a sage ❷〈宗教〉(in the terminology of Chinese Muslims) recorded words and deeds of Mohammed (c. 570-632), founder of Islam

圣药 shèngyào efficacious medicine: 灵丹～ miraculous cure; panacea

圣约翰 Shèngyuēhàn St. John's, capital of Antigua and Barbuda

圣谕 shèngyù imperial decree

圣战 shèngzhàn holy war; jihad; crusade: ～者 crusaders; holy warrior

圣旨 shèngzhǐ imperial edict: 这是老板的"～"，我们不敢违反。This is the "edict" of the boss which we dare not go against.

圣子 shèngzǐ ❶〈基督教〉Son of God; Jesus Christ ❷ saintly son; son who is an emperor

shī

湿(濕、溼) shī wet; moist; damp; humid: 空气～ moist air /用～布擦窗子 wipe the windows with a damp cloth /空气增～器 air humidifier/地上很～，昨夜一定下雨了。It must have been raining last night, for the ground is very wet. /屋里潮～。It is damp in the room. /我全身～透了。I got drenched to the skin.

湿痹 shībì 〈中医〉arthritis with fixed pain caused by dampness

湿病 shībìng 〈中医〉dampness-induced diseases

湿答答 shīdādā dripping wet; drenched

湿地 shīdì wetland

湿毒 shīdú 〈中医〉noxious dampness: ～疮 eczema of shank

湿度 shīdù ❶ humidity: 绝对～ absolute humidity /相对～ relative humidity /～高 high humidity /～低 low humidity /空气～ air humidity /空气太干燥，我们得设法增加～。The air is too dry, and we must try to increase humidity by some means. ❷ moisture: 土壤的～ soil moisture

湿度比 shīdùbǐ psychrometric ratio

湿度表 shīdùbiǎo hygrometer; hygrograph; moisture meter

湿度测量术 shīdù cèliángshù hygrometry

湿度调节器 shīdù tiáojiéqì humidistat

湿度图 shīdùtú hygrogram

湿度指数 shīdù zhǐshù humidity index

湿法冶金 shīfǎ yějīn hydrometallurgy

湿纺 shīfǎng 〈纺织〉wet spinning

湿腐 shīfǔ wet rot

湿乎乎 shīhūhū *also* "湿呼呼" moist; damp; wet: 雨后场院上～的。The threshing ground was swampy after the rain. /他额头上有汗，～的。His forehead was wet with sweat. /这双袜子～的。This pair of socks is damp. *or* These socks are damp.

湿季 shījì damp season; wet season

湿津津 shījīnjīn wet or damp with sweat; sweaty: 她走了七八里山路，浑身有点～的。After walking seven or eight *li* in the mountain she felt damp all over.

湿冷 shīlěng damp and chilly; dank; clammy: ～的地下室 cold and damp cellar /我不习惯南方冬天的～气候。I can't stand the clammy winter in the south.

湿淋淋 shīlínlín dripping wet; soaking wet; drenched: 全身～的 be drenched through /刚捞上来的水草，～的。The water plants just dredged up from the river are dripping wet.

湿漉漉 shīlùlù *also* "湿渌渌" wet; damp: ～的台阶 wet steps /墙壁摸上去～的。The walls feel damp.

湿蒙蒙 shīmēngmēng moist; damp; humid: ～的田野 damp fields /清凉的夜空，渗着～的水气。The night sky was clear and cool, and the air moist with vapour.

湿婆 Shīpó (of Hinduism) Siva: ～派 Sivaism

湿气 shīqì ❶ moisture; dampness: 这里～太重。It is too damp here. ❷〈中医〉eczema; fungus infection of hand or foot

湿热 shīrè ❶ damp and hot; muggy: ～的天气 muggy weather ❷〈中医〉damp heat: ～腹痛 abdominal pain due to damp heat /～内蕴 retention of damp heat in the interior

湿润 shīrùn moist; damp: ～的泥土 damp soil /～的天气 humid weather /～的海风 moist breeze from the sea /他眼眶～了。His eyes moistened. /他用舌头～了一下嘴唇。He moistened his lips with his tongue.

湿水货 shīshuǐhuò water-damaged goods
湿透 shītòu be wet through; soaked; be drenched: 全身～ wet from top to toe; soaked to the skin/眼泪～了她的手巾。Her handkerchief was wet through with tears. /他的上衣被汗水～。His jacket is drenched with sweat.
湿泻 shīxiè *also* "洞泄" dòngxiè; "濡泻" rúxiè〈中医〉damp diarrhoea
湿选 shīxuǎn 〈矿业〉wet separation
湿癣 shīxuǎn exudative dermatitis
湿郁 shīyù 〈中医〉retention of dampness in the interior
湿疹 shīzhěn 〈医学〉eczema

诗

shī poetry; verse: 写～ write (*or* compose) poetry /吟～ recite poetry /抒情～ lyric poetry; lyrics /叙事～ narrative poetry /史～ epic /散文～ poem in prose /田园～ pastoral poetry; idyll /十四行～ sonnet /情～ love (*or* amorous) poem /古体～ classical poetry /自由～ free verse /赞美～ hymn /打油～ doggerel /无韵～ blank verse /有韵～ rhymed verse /～的用语 poetic diction /～穷而后工 an impoverished poet tends to attain skill; adversity makes for (poetic) excellence /～中有画，画中有～。There is painting in poetry just as there is poetry in painting .
诗碑 shībēi stele inscribed with poems
诗才 shīcái gift as a poet; talent for poetry
诗风 shīfēng style of poem: 他的～淡雅清新。His poetic style is fresh and quietly elegant.
诗歌 shīgē poems and songs; poetry: ～欣赏 appreciation of poems; poetry appreciation /古典～ classical poetry
诗格 shīgé ❶〈书面〉rules of prosody ❷ style of poetry: ～不高 (a poem written in) rather vulgar style
诗豪 shīháo great poet; great master in poetry
诗话 shīhuà ❶ notes and comments on poets and poetry; notes on classical Chinese poetry: 作为研究中国文学的学者，他很喜欢读～。As a student of Chinese literature, he was very fond of reading comments on classical poetry. ❷ vernacular stories interspersed with poems, which can be used as materials for ballad singing
诗集 shījí collection or anthology of poems: 现代英语～ modern English verse /杜甫～ collection of Du Fu's poems; collected poems of Du Fu; authology of Du Fu's poems
诗节 shījié stanza
诗经 Shījīng *The Book of Songs*, or *Classic of Poetry*, China's first ancient poem collection
see also "五经" Wǔjīng
诗境 shījìng artistic conception of a poem; poetic atmosphere or setting
诗句 shījù verse; line: 清新的～ fresh verse /这些都是经常为人引用的～。These lines are often quoted. *or* These are oft-quoted lines.
诗剧 shījù drama in verse; poetic drama
诗礼 shīlǐ *The Book of Songs* (诗经) and *The Rites* (礼经) (i. e. *The Ritual of Zhou*《周礼》, *The Book of Etiquette*《仪礼》), classics an old-time scholar must read: ～之家 highly cultured family
诗礼传家 shīlǐ-chuánjiā old family of literary scholars
诗律 shīlǜ rules of prosody; rules of verse form
诗谜 shīmí riddle in verse form
诗篇 shīpiān ❶ poem: 这是影响深远的～。This is a poem with farreaching influence. ❷ inspiring story: 这一场群众斗争谱写了一部悲壮的～。This mass struggle was in itself a solemn and stirring epic.
诗品 Shīpǐn ❶ *Grades of Poetry*, critigue of poetry written by Zhong Rong (钟嵘) of the Southern Dynasties ❷ work of the same name written by Sikong Tu (司空图) of the Tang Dynasty
诗情 shīqíng poetic charm
诗情画意 shīqíng-huàyì poetic beauty: 富有～的景色 idyllic scene; picturesque scenery
诗趣 shīqù appeal of a poem: 富于～ full of poetic appeal
诗人 shīrén poet: 浪漫主义～ romantic poet /桂冠～ poet laureate /女～ woman poet /～的气质 makings (*or* temperament) of a poet
诗社 shīshè poetry club or society
诗圣 shīshèng (title given to a great poet such as Du Fu of the Tang Dynasty) sage poet; poet among poets
诗史 shīshǐ ❶ history of poetry: 中国～ history of Chinese poetry ❷ poems reflecting the times and thus having historical significance: 杜甫的许多诗歌被称为"～"。Many of Du Fu's poems have been called "history through poetry".
诗书 shīshū ❶ *The Book of Songs* (诗经) and *Collection of Ancient Texts* (尚书) ❷ classics in general
诗书门第 shīshū-méndì scholarly family
诗思 shīsī poetic inspiration; poetic thoughts: 门外的喧嚷打断了我的～。My thoughts in composing the poem were interrupted by the noises outside.
诗薮 Shīsǒu *Collection of Poems*, a work of critical analysis of poems and poets by Hu Yinglin (胡应麟) of the Ming Dynasty
诗坛 shītán circle of poets: ～新星 new star in poetic circles
诗仙 shīxiān (title given to a poet of exceptional talent and natural grace such as Li Bai of the Tang Dynasty) fairy poet; poetic genius; poet immortal
诗兴 shīxìng poetic inspiration; poetic mood: ～全无 not be in a poetic mood /～迸发 feel greatly inspired to write poetry
诗选 shīxuǎn selected poems
诗学 shīxué poetics
诗意 shīyì poetic quality; poetic sentiment: ～盎然 brimming with poetic sentiment /这给这次演出增添了～。This would give poetic lustre to the theatrical performance.
诗余 shīyú another name for *ci* (词) — Chinese poetic genre (with varied tonal patterns and sentence lengths)
诗韵 shīyùn ❶ rhyme (in poetry) ❷ rhyming dictionary
诗章 shīzhāng poem
诗钟 shīzhōng 〈旧语〉game in composing verses with given words before a coin hanging by a piece of string from an inch of burning incense drops onto a bronze tray below and rings the end of the allowed time
诗宗 shīzōng poet of poets; great master in poetry: 一代～ great poet held in high esteem by the poets of the time
诗作 shīzuò poems; verses

酾[1] (釃)

shī *also* shāi ❶〈书面〉purify by a filter: ～酒 purify wine by a filter ❷〈方言〉pour (wine or tea)

酾[2] (釃)

shī 〈书面〉dredge (rivers and canals): ～二渠，以引其河 dredge two canals to channel water from the river

蓍

shī 〈植物〉alpine yarrow (*Achillea alpina*)

师[1] (師)

shī ❶ teacher; master: 教～ teacher; schoolmaster (schoolmistress) /～徒 master and apprentice (*or* disciple) /尊～爱生 respect teachers and cherish students /良～益友 good teacher and helpful friend/困难是严～。Difficulty is a severe teacher. /严～出高徒 An outstanding student comes from a strict teacher. ❷ model; example; guide: 前事不忘，后事之～。Lessons learned from the past (*or* Past lessons, if not forgotten,) can guide one in the future. ❸ person skilled in a certain profession or trade: 画～ painter; artist /农艺～ agronomist /会计～ accountant /工程～ engineer /技～ technician /律～ lawyer /厨～ cook; chef /医～ doctor /理发～ barber; hairdresser ❹ courtesy title for a Buddhist monk or Taoist priest: 法～ Master (a title of respect for a Buddhist or Taoist priest) /禅～ Zen master /大～ Grand Master (title for a Buddhist monk *or* Taoist priest, as well as for a certain class of chess player) ❺ of one's master or teacher: *see* "～母" ❻〈书面〉learn; follow: ～古 take the ancients as one's model /～其所长 learn from sb. 's strong points /各～其师，转相教海。We may study under different masters, but then we can always exchange experience with each other. ❼ (Shī) a surname

师[2] (師)

shī ❶ division (of an army): 装甲～ armoured division /骑兵～ cavalry division /步兵～ infantry division /坦克～ tank division ❷ troops; army: 雄～ mighty army /班～回朝 troops return from the front after a victory; recall one's troops from the front /出～不利 lose the first battle (*or* game); be unsuccessful in one's first attempt
师表 shībiǎo 〈书面〉paragon of virtue and learning: 堪称～ may be called a model of virtue and learning for others /万世～ teacher of all ages (traditional title for Confucius)
师部 shībù 〈军事〉division headquarters
师承 shīchéng ❶ the way in which a disciple receives training in

a specific school: ~梅派 be trained in the Mei Lanfang School (in Beijing opera) ❷ pass on from master to disciple: 学有~ learn from one's own master/这些艺术家虽各有~，但也广泛学习别家长处。Though these artists received their training under different masters, they have learned extensively from other schools.

师出无名 shīchū-wúmíng dispatch troops without a just cause; do something without proper reason: ~，非惟不胜，乃自危之道也。Fighting for an unjust cause would bring nothing but destruction upon oneself.

师道尊严 shīdào-zūnyán dignity or honour of the teaching profession

师德 shīdé teacher's professional ethics: ~规范 code of teacher's professional ethics /对新教师进行~教育 initiate the new teachers in the professional ethics of their work

师弟 shīdì ❶ male junior fellow apprentice or pupil ❷ son of one's master (younger than oneself) ❸ father's apprentice or pupil (younger than oneself) ❹ teacher and pupil

师法 shīfǎ 〈书面〉❶ model oneself after (a great master); take as a model; imitate: ~古人 imitate the ancients /~前辈 follow the example of the older generation ❷ knowledge or skill passed down from master to disciple: 不失~ not forget the skill taught by one's master

师范 shīfàn ❶ teacher-training school; normal school: ~学院 teachers college; normal college ❷〈书面〉model: 为世~ be a model for the people

师范教育 shīfàn jiàoyù teacher-education; teacher-training

师范学校 shīfàn xuéxiào normal school; teacher-training school

师父 shīfu ❶ *see* "师傅" ❷ polite form of address to a Buddhist monk or nun or a Taoist priest or nun

师傅 shīfu ❶ master who gives instruction in any trade, business or art: 尊敬~ respect the master /这位艺术家自愿作她的~。The artist was willing to be her teacher. ❷ polite title for one with accomplished skill usu. in a trade or handicraft: 木匠~ carpenter /理发~ barber /老~ old master workman

师傅领进门，修行在个人 shīfu lǐngjìn mén, xiūxíng zài gèrén *also* "师父领进门，修行在个人" while a master initiates one in a trade, the perfection of one's skill depends on oneself; a master teaches the trade, but apprentice's skill is self-made

师公 shīgōng ❶ master of one's master ❷ wizard; sorcerer

师姑 shīgū Buddhist nun

师姐 shījiě ❶ female senior fellow apprentice or pupil ❷ daughter of one's master or teacher older than oneself ❸ father's female apprentice or pupil older than oneself

师老兵疲 shīlǎo-bīngpí troops fighting for a long time are lacking in combat effectiveness: 连年征战，~。Years of war exhausted the soldiers.

师妹 shīmèi ❶ female junior fellow apprentice or pupil ❷ daughter of one's master or teacher younger than oneself ❸ father's female apprentice or pupil younger than oneself

师门 shīmén ❶ residence of one's master or teacher: 半年不入~ not call on the master at home for six months ❷〈旧语〉form of address to the examiner official used by successful candidates in the highest imperial examination ❸ teacher or his guidance in general: 同出~ under the guidance of the same teacher /数年来学业荒疏，有负于~的期许。In the past few years I have neglected my studies, thus failing to live up to my teacher's expectations.

师母 shīmǔ wife of one's teacher or master

师娘 shīniáng 〈口语〉wife of one's teacher or master

师婆 shīpó *also* "师婆子" sorceress; witch

师生 shī-shēng teacher and student: ~关系 teacher-student relationship /~员工 teachers, students, administrative personnel and workers

师事 shīshì 〈书面〉acknowledge as one's teacher or master: 他多年来~这位教授。He has been studying under the professor for years.

师徒 shītú ❶ master and apprentice; teacher and student: ~关系 master-apprentice (*or* teacher-student) relationship /~合同 indentures ❷〈书面〉soldier

师团 shītuán 〈军事〉division

师心自用 shīxīn-zìyòng *also* "师心自是" be opinionated; be obstinate; be conceited: 学者大病，在于~。The major failing of a scholar is conceit.

师兄 shīxiōng ❶ male senior fellow apprentice or pupil ❷ son of one's master older than oneself ❸ father's male apprentice older than oneself

师兄弟 shīxiōngdì ❶ fellow apprentices ❷ male apprentices of the same master

师训 shīxùn instructions of a teacher

师训班 shīxùnbān (short for 师资训练班) teacher training class or course

师爷 shīye (popular term for 幕友) private assistant attending to legal, fiscal or secretarial duties in a *yamen*; private adviser (for a ranking official): 钱粮~ private assistant attending to economic and financial affairs /刑名~ private adviser on legal matters

师友 shī-yǒu teachers and friends

师长 shīzhǎng ❶〈敬词〉teachers: 不负~们的谆谆教诲 not be unworthy of the earnest instruction by one's teachers ❷〈军事〉division commander

师直为壮 shīzhí-wéizhuàng an army fighting for a just cause has high morale; an army is strong when fighting for a just cause

师专 shīzhuān teachers training school; normal school

师资 shīzī (used collectively) teaching staff; faculty; teachers: ~缺乏 be short of teachers /我们需要干练的行政人员，但更缺乏高水平的~。we need good administrators, but we need qualified teachers even more.

鲕(鰤) shī 〈动物〉amberjack; yellowtail

鲕鲈 shīlú 〈动物〉pikeperch; sauger

狮(獅) shī lion (*Panthera leo*): 母~ lioness /睡~ sleeping lion

狮虎 shīhǔ liger

狮毛猴 shīmáohóu *also* "狨猴" rónghóu; "绢猴" juānhóu 〈动物〉lion marmoset; lion monkey

狮身人面像 shīshēn-rénmiànxiàng sphinx

狮头鹅 shītóu'é lion-head goose, a native species of Guangdong Province that is large and stocky, and the male bird has black sarcomas on its face

狮子 shīzi lion

狮子鼻 shīzibí pug nose

狮子搏兔 shīzi-bótù (like) a lion pouncing on a hare — go all out even when fighting a weaker enemy or tackling a minor problem; not take anything lightly

狮子大开口 shīzi dà kāikǒu ❶ make an excessive demand; demand an exorbitant price: 你真是~，一斤西红柿别人卖一元，你竟敢要五元。You're demanding a sky-high price indeed. The market price for tomatoes is one *yuan* a *jin*, and you ask for five *yuan*. ❷ talk big; brag

狮子狗 shīzigǒu pug-dog

狮子头 shīzitóu large meatball (usu. fried in deep oil before being braised with vegetables): 红烧~ large meatballs braised in soy sauce

狮子舞 shīziwǔ lion dance: 表演~ perform or present a lion dance

狮子鱼 shīziyú snailfish; sea snail

狮子座 Shīzizuò *also* "狮子星座"〈天文〉Leo

鸸 shī 〈动物〉nuthatch

嘘 shī 〈叹词〉*used to stop sb. from doing sth. or to drive sb. or sth. away*: ~，别有响声! Sh (*or* Hush)! Be quiet!
see also xū

失 shī ❶ suffer loss of; lose: 不计个人得~ in disregard of personal gains or losses /顾此~彼 attend to one thing and lose sight of another; have too many things to attend to at the same time /证件挂~ report the loss of one's identity papers ❷ lose hold of; let slip; miss: 坐~良机 miss (*or* lose) a good opportunity /行为~检 be indiscreet in one's behaviour /万无一~ one hundred percent secure; foolproof /马~前蹄。The horse lost its footing. ❸ get lost: 迷~方向 lose one's bearings /~群的羔羊 lamb that has wandered away from the flock ❹ fail to achieve one's end: 大~所望 be greatly disappointed ❺ deviate from the normal: 有~常态 be somewhat abnormal /大惊~色 turn pale from fear /有~身份 be incompatible with one's status ❻ break (a promise); go back on (one's word): 有~信誉 damage one's reputation ❼ mishap; defect; error: *see* "~政"; "~辞"

失败 shībài ❶ be defeated; lose (a war, game, etc):～者 loser / 遭到惨重～ meet one's Waterloo; suffer a crushing defeat /招致～ bring defeat upon oneself; invite defeat /彻底～ come a cropper /正视～ face up to one's defeat /不甘心～ not resign (*or* reconcile) oneself to one's defeat /不为～所吓倒 be undaunted by failure or defeat /我队在这场网球赛中～了。Our team lost the tennis game. ❷ fail:注定要～ be doomed to failure /他的婚姻～了。His marriage was a failure. /计划～了。The plan was a washout. *or* The plan came unstuck.

失败情绪 shībài qíngxù defeatist sentiments

失败是成功之母 shībài shì chénggōng zhī mǔ failure is the mother of success

失败主义 shībàizhǔyì defeatism:～者 defeatist

失策 shīcè ❶ miscalculate; be unwise; be ill-advised:你借债结婚是～的。It was unwise of you to get into debt for the wedding. ❷ wrong tactics; miscalculation:严重的～遭致灾难性的后果。The grave miscalculation brought about disastrous consequences. /工作上的～,给这项工程造成了巨大的浪费。A wrong decision regarding the project caused tremendous waste.

失察 shīchá neglect one's supervisory duties; commit an oversight:一时～ momentary negligence /必须追究领导者～的责任。It is necessary to look into the matter of neglect of duty on the part of those in charge.

失常 shīcháng not normal; abnormal; odd:态度～ behave strangely; not be one's usual self /精神～ mentally deranged; not in one's right mind /操作～ operate (*or* run) abnormally /比赛中发挥～ be out of form in the competition /你的神经有点～。Your nerves are a little upset.

失晨之鸡 shīchénzhījī cock that fails to crow — accidental error; occasional neglect of duty

失宠 shīchǒng lose favour; be in disfavour; be disgraced:这位大臣～后,被放逐到远方。The minister was exiled to a remote place when he fell into disgrace.

失出 shīchū 〈书面〉 err in imposing unduly light penalty; fail to give any penalty at all

失传 shīchuán no longer existing; not extant:久经战乱,有些古书早已～。Some ancient books have been lost through the successive turmoils of war and disorder. /那是一种～的民间艺术。It was a lost folk art. /古时有些医道已经～了。Some ancient arts of healing have not been handed down from past generations.

失辞 shīcí 〈书面〉 use wrong or discourteous words; make improper utterances; be indiscreet

失次 shīcì not in proper order; incoherent

失聪 shīcōng become deaf:右耳～ deaf in the right ear

失措 shīcuò lose one's presence of mind; be at a loss as to what to do:茫然～ be at a total loss /仓皇～ be disconcerted; lose one's head /惊慌～ be frightened out of one's senses; be panic-stricken

失错 shīcuò make a mistake from oversight:有经验的导演也有～的时候。Even an experienced film director may sometimes err from oversight.

失单 shīdān list of lost articles; slip showing items of lost property

失当 shīdàng improper; inappropriate; indiscreet:言语～ speak indiscreetly /问题在于安排～。The problem lies in inappropriate arrangement. /我们在这件事情上用人～。We have not chosen the right person to handle this matter.

失盗 shīdào *also* "失窃" be burgled or burglarized; have sth. stolen; suffer loss by theft:邻居家～了。The house of one of our neighbours was burgled (*or* burglarized).

失道寡助 shīdào-guǎzhù an unjust cause finds scant support; he who is unjust enjoys little support

失德 shīdé 〈书面〉 fault; offence; sin

失地 shīdì ❶ lose territory:屡战屡败,连连～。The country suffered repeated defeats in the war and lost much of its land to the enemy. ❷ lost territory:收复～,保卫祖国 recover lost territory and defend the homeland /我们支持该国人民收复～的斗争。We support the people of that country in their struggle to regain their lost territories.

失掉 shīdiào ❶ lose:～联络 lose contact; be out of touch /～勇气 lose heart /～理智 be out of one's mind; lose one's mind /～知觉 become unconscious; lose consciousness; fall into a coma ❷ miss; let slip:～时机 let slip an opportunity /他们～了一个宝贵的机会。They squandered a valuable opportunity.

失而复得 shī'érfùdé regain what is lost:手表～。The watch was lost and found again.

失分 shīfēn lose points (in a game):甲队连连～。Team A lost points in quick succession.

失风 shīfēng have an accident; meet with a mishap; go wrong:他让那一回的～吓破了胆,现在什么事都不想干。Scared out of his wits by that accident, he shies away from doing anything now. /想不到他这次又失了风。Unexpectedly, things went wrong for him again this time.

失格 shīgé ❶ exceeding what is proper; inappropriate; not befitting one's position or not suited to the occasion:～的话 inappropriate remarks ❷ lose face:他这次可大大～了。This time he brought deep disgrace on himself.

失和 shīhé fail to get along well; become estranged:婆媳～。The old lady and her daughter-in-law are not on the best of terms. /夫妻～。The man and his wife fell out with each other. /这两个朋友已经多年～了。The two friends have been estranged from each other for years. /两国关系～。Relations between the two countries have become strained.

失衡 shīhéng lose balance:产销～ imbalance between production and marketing /心理～ mental disequilibrium

失怙 shīhù 〈书面〉 lose one's father when young; be orphaned

失欢 shīhuān fall into disfavour; be out of favour

失慌 shīhuāng 〈方言〉 flurried; flustered; confused:她听见隔壁墙倒屋塌的声音,失失慌慌就往门外跑。Hearing the noise of collapsing walls next door, she rushed out of the door in a fluster.

失悔 shīhuǐ regret; repent:毫不～ have no regrets; remain unrepentant /由于措施不当,功败垂成,甚为～。I very much regret the inappropriate measures which caused defeat on the verge of success.

失婚 shīhūn 〈方言〉 have lost one's spouse:～的妇人 widow

失魂 shīhún lose one's wits; become muddled or muddle-headed:自见了那个女人之后,他就好像失了魂。He has been obsessed with that woman since he saw her.

失魂落魄 shīhún-luòpò be panic-stricken; be scared out of one's wits; be terrified within an inch of one's life:他～地坐在书桌旁边。He sat at his desk, looking distraught. /她～地呆望着这一切。She gaped distractedly at all this. /他们把她吓得～。They terrified her within an inch of her life.

失火 shīhuǒ catch fire; be on fire:调查～的原因 investigate the cause of the fire

失机 shījī (used usu. in sports) loss of opportunity:他们几个长传处理不当,以致～。They did not handle the long passes properly and lost many scoring opportunities. /前锋配合不密切,导致～。Lack of cooperation between the forwards caused the loss of successive opportunities for scoring.

失计 shījì *see* "失策"

失记 shījì 〈书面〉 lose the memory of; forget:年远～ have lost the memory of sth. with the passage of time

失检 shījiǎn commit an indiscretion; be careless in one's personal conduct:行为～ indiscreet in behaviour; indiscreet/出言～ make indiscreet remarks

失脚 shījiǎo lose one's footing; lose one's balance; slip:～摔倒 trip and fall over /他爬山时～跌倒,受了重伤。He lost his footing while climbing up a mountain and fell down seriously injured.

失教 shījiào overlook education (of one's children); give inadequate parental guidance

失节 shījié ❶ lose one's integrity; be disloyal; turncoat:宁可杀头,亦不～投降。Better be killed than lose one's integrity by surrendering to the enemy. ❷〈旧语〉(of a woman) lose one's chastity

失禁 shījìn 〈医学〉 incontinence:大小便～ incontinence of faeces and urine; double incontinence

失惊 shījīng be startled; be astonished; be taken aback; be shocked:有人从背后打他一下,他～地回头去看。Startled by the slap on his back, he turned and looked back.

失惊打怪 shījīng-dǎguài *also* "失惊打张" be surprised or alarmed at a trivial matter; make a fuss:就为打碎一只碗,也值得这样～! Why make such a fuss merely over a broken bowl!

失敬 shījìng 〈套语〉 show inadequacy; be sorry:没有去机场迎接您,实在～。I am awfully sorry for not having met you at the airport. /没有一下子认出你来,～了。Forgive me for failing to recognize you at once.

S

失据 shījù lose base of support: 进退～ be in a dilemma / 神魂～ in a state of utter stupefaction

失控 shīkòng out of control; runaway: 通货膨胀～ runaway inflation / 防止局势～ prevent the situation from getting out of hand / 别把车开得太快，当心～。You're driving much too fast; the car might career out of control. / 老人手足～，从梯子上摔了下来。The old man lost his balance and fell from the ladder.

失口 shīkǒu slip of the tongue: 不慎～ make a slip of the tongue / 谨防～泄密 guard against leaking secrets inadvertently

失礼 shīlǐ ❶ breach of etiquette; impoliteness; discourtesy: 行为～ act against social etiquette; commit a faux pas / 讲话～ speak impolitely / 这是他的严重～。This is a serious breach of etiquette on his part. / 他这样做是非常～的。It was most impolite of him to do so. / 她觉得这样做有些～。She thought this somewhat uncivil. ❷〈套语〉 excuse me for any impropriety, lack of manners, etc. on my part: ～之处，务请原谅。I ask you to forgive me if you found me lacking in proper etiquette. / 恐怕我们对您太～了。I'm afraid we have to ask your forgiveness.

失利 shīlì suffer a setback; be defeated: 谈判～ suffer a setback in negotiation / 初战～ lose the first battle (*or* game) / 敌人几次～后匆忙退却。The enemy beat a hasty retreat after several reverses.

失恋 shīliàn be disappointed in love; be jilted: 经历～的痛苦 suffer from a disappointment in love

失灵 shīlíng not work (properly); be out of order; be ineffective: 发动机～了。The motor is out of order. / 机器运转～。The machine is not working properly. / 奖金发得太滥就～了。Bonuses will not be effective if they are paid indiscriminately.

失路 shīlù ❶ lose one's way; go astray ❷〈书面〉〈比喻〉 not be successful in one's career; not have one's ambition fulfilled; be thwarted in one's ambition

失露 shīlù 〈方言〉 let out; betray; reveal: ～机密 reveal secrets

失律 shīlǜ 〈书面〉 ❶ (of troops) breach of discipline during a march ❷ suffer a defeat (in war); lose (a battle or war): 数战皆～。They lost several battles.

失伦 shīlún illogical in sequence; incoherent: 言语～ speak incoherently

失落 shīluò lose: ～身份证 lose one's identity card / ～的一代 lost generation

失落感 shīluògǎn sense of loss; feeling of being left out; feeling of being abandoned and alone: 退休之初，他一度产生过～。Upon retirement, he felt, for a while, being left out.

失迷 shīmí lose one's bearings; get lost: 半道～方向 get lost on the way

失密 shīmì give away official secrets as a result of carelessness; leak out confidential information: 部分～ partial leakage (of sth.) / 严重～事件 serious (*or* grave) leak / 谨防～ guard against leakage of state secrets

失眠 shīmián (suffer from) insomnia; sleeplessness: 长期～ chronic insomnia / 患～症 have (*or* suffer from) insomnia / ～症患者 insomniac / 老人彻夜～。The old man lay awake (*or* did not get a wink) all night. / 那时我老是～。I was plagued by insomnia in those days.

失明 shīmíng lose one's sight; be unable to see; go blind: 双目～ go blind in both eyes / 右眼～ lose the sight of one's right eye; be blind in the right eye

失能性毒剂 shīnéngxìng dújì 〈军事〉 incapacitating agent

失黏 shīnián make a mistake in tones in a poem or rhythmical prose

失陪 shīpéi 〈套语〉 take leave ahead of others: 我有个约会，得先走一步，～了。Excuse me, but I must be leaving now. I have an appointment with somebody.

失窃 shīqiè *also* "失盗" be burglarized; have things stolen; suffer loss by theft: 近来这个地区连续发生了几起～案。There have been several burglaries in the neighbourhood recently. / 珠宝的～引起很大震动。The theft of the jewels caused much consternation.

失去 shīqù lose; forfeit: ～自制力 lose one's self-control / ～耐心 get impatient / ～机会 miss an opportunity / 他担心局面～控制。He is worried that the situation is getting out of hand. / 他鲁莽从事，从而～了我们对他的信任。By acting rashly, he has forfeited our confidence. / 合同已～时效。The contract is no longer effective. / 他～一切希望。He was bereft of all hope.

失却 shīquè 〈书面〉 lose; miss; let slip: ～了它存在的意义 lose its *raison d'être*

失群 shīqún (of man or animal) leave the collective or group: 迷途～ lose one's way and leave one's group / ～的孤雁 solitary wild goose that has left (*or* strayed from) the flock

失容 shīróng 〈书面〉 ❶ neglect one's looks due to illness or fatigue: 憔悴～ wan and sallow without make-up ❷ turn pale; lose colour: 矍然～ turn pale in astonishment

失入 shīrù 〈书面〉 impose undeserved penalty or improperly heavy penalty

失润 shīrùn ❶ not mellow and full; husky: 嗓音有些～。Her voice sounded not quite mellow and full. ❷ not smooth; rough; coarse: 皮肤～ roughened skin

失散 shīsàn be scattered: 他终于见到了～多年的弟弟。At last he saw his brother with whom he had lost touch for years. / 一家人在战乱中～。The family were scattered in the confusion of war.

失色 shīsè ❶ lose colour; be discoloured: 一张年久～的办公桌 old desk that has lost its original colour ❷ lose countenance; turn pale: 惊愕～ turn pale (*or* white) with consternation / 一言而使四座～。The remark shocked all the people present.

失闪 shīshan mishap; accident: 你要是有个～，我们怎么办? What if anything should happen to you?

失墒 shīshāng (of soil) lose moisture; lack moisture: 冬春无雪无雨，土地～严重。It has not rained or snowed from winter to spring, leaving the soil seriously insufficient in moisture content.

失少 shīshǎo lacking; missing; deficient: 这一段删掉后，不仅不会～什么，反而能收到更好的艺术效果。With this paragraph deleted, nothing will be lost while the artistic effect will be heightened.

失身 shīshēn (of a woman) lose one's virginity; lose one's chastity

失神 shīshén ❶ negligent; inattentive; absent-minded: 稍一～就会出差错。Even a moment's inattentiveness would cause errors. *or* If you get absent-minded for a moment, you are liable to commit errors. ❷ out of sorts; in low spirits; dejected: 他看来有点～，是不是出了什么事? He looks a bit out of sorts; what is wrong with him?

失慎 shīshèn ❶ not prudent; careless: 言语～ make indiscreet remarks ❷〈书面〉 cause a fire through carelessness: 王家～，使街坊们蒙受相当大损失。The fire which broke out in the Wangs' home caused considerable damage to the neighbourhood.

失声 shīshēng ❶ cry out involuntarily: 她吓了一跳，不觉～地叫了起来。Startled, she cried out involuntarily. ❷ lose one's voice: 悲从中来，痛哭～ feel sadness welling up and cry oneself hoarse

失失慌慌 shīshī-huānghuāng 〈方言〉 flurried; flustered; in a hurry: 他为着赶火车，～吃了半碗饭就走了。In his haste to catch the train he left after taking only half a bowl of rice.

失时 shīshí miss the season; let slip or let go the opportunity: 收割～ miss the harvest season / 医治～ belated treatment to an illness

失实 shīshí be without foundation; inaccurate; untrue: 显系传闻～。Evidently the rumour has no foundation in fact. / 报道～。The report was a gross misrepresentation of the truth.

失势 shīshì lose power and influence; be out of power: 突然～ suddenly fall into disgrace / 他不无伤感地意识到他自己已经～了。He sadly came to realize that his power had waned.

失事 shīshì (have an) accident: 火车～ train accident / 轮船～ shipwreck / 那次飞机～中，有一百多旅客和十二名机组人员丧生。The plane crash took a toll of over 100 passengers and twelve crew members.

失恃 shīshì 〈书面〉 lose one's mother in childhood

失收 shīshōu ❶ crop failure: 今年此地小麦～。The year's wheat crop in this area has failed. ❷ (of writings) what should be included is left out: 这位作家的全集中有好几篇散文～。Quite a few pieces of prose are not included in the collected works of the writer.

失手 shīshǒu ❶ accidentally drop; make a slip of the hand: ～杀人 killing sb. unintentionally; manslaughter/ 他一～把玻璃盘打碎了。He accidentally lost hold of the glass plate and broke it. / 在击剑比赛中，他不慎～刺伤对手。In the fencing match, he stabbed and injured his opponent by mistake. ❷ (unexpected) loss or defeat: 赛场～ lose the game unexpectedly / 这次围棋赛中，一名老将～于新手。A master of *Weiqi* was defeated by an upcoming star in the game.

失守 shīshǒu fall; be taken: 阵地～。The position was lost to the enemy. / 要塞～。The fortress fell into enemy hands. / 这座城市的～是战争的转折点。The fall of the city was a turning point in the war.

失水 shīshuǐ ❶ out of water: 神龙～。〈比喻〉 The emperor lost his power. ❷ lack of water; deprivation or loss of body fluid; dehydra-

S

tion:病人因严重～，进入休克状态。The patient has lapsed into coma owing to a serious loss of body fluid.
失溲 shīsōu 〈中医〉incontinence of urine
失速 shīsù 〈航空〉stall:～滑翔 stalled glide /～颤振 stall flutter/飞机突然～。The plane suddenly stalled.
失算 shīsuàn miscalculate; misjudge; misread:他一向精明，这次却～了。Clever as he had always been, he misread the situation this time. /这一步～了。That was a miscalculated move. /一着～，顿使全盘处于劣势。The moment he made the wrong move, he found himself at a disadvantage in the chess game.
失所 shīsuǒ displaced; homeless:流离～ be uprooted and homeless; wander about homeless
失态 shītài forget oneself; not be one's usual self; be ill-mannered in one's behaviour:举止～ deviate from one's normal behaviour; behave oddly /我昨晚酒后～，请各位见谅。Please excuse me for behaving foolishly under the influence of alcohol last night.
失体 shītǐ ❶ improper manners; breach of etiquette ❷ substandard; deformed:草书～，难以辨认。Written in a deformed cursive hand, the note is hardly legible.
失调 shītiáo ❶ imbalance:购销～ imbalance between purchases and sales /营养比例～ unbalanced nutrition /近来雨水～ abnormal rainfall /人口增长与经济增长比例～。The population growth is out of proportion to the economic growth. ❷ lack of proper care and rest:病后～ lack of proper care and rest after an illness ❸〈无线电〉maladjustment:频率～ maladjustment of frequency
失拖 shītuō 〈方言〉be disappointed in love
失望 shīwàng lose hope; lose confidence; despair; be discouraged or disappointed:强烈的～情绪 intense disappointment /结果令人～。The result was very disappointing (*or* discouraging). /老人对儿子彻底～了。The old man has lost all hopes in his son. /诗人在～之余隐退乡间了。In despair the poet retired to the country and led the life of a recluse. /他对自己的前途从来没有悲观～过。He was never pessimistic (*or* despondent) about his future.
失物 shīwù lost article; lost property:寻找～ look for lost articles /归还～ return lost property to its owner /～招领 advertise for the owner of a lost article; articles found, please contact; found (used as the title of notice)
失物招领处 shīwù zhāolǐngchù lost property office; lost-and-found (office)
失误 shīwù fault; muff; faulty move; mistake:传球～ faulty pass /接球～ muff a ball; miss a ball /发球～ serving fault /计算～ error in calculation /外交～ diplomatic faux pas /开局就出现了～。It was a faulty gambit.
失陷 shīxiàn (of cities, territory, etc.) fall; fall into enemy hands; be lost to the enemy:重镇～ fall of an important city
失效 shīxiào ❶ lose efficacy; cease to be effective:过期～ cease to be effective after the specified date /药品保管不善容易～。Medicines are apt to lose efficacy if not carefully kept. ❷ (of a treaty, agreement, etc.) be no longer in force; be invalidated:自动～ automatically cease to be in force /～支票 invalid cheque /～提单 stale bill of lading /～日期 date of expiry; expiration date /宣布合同～ declare the contract null and void /这张证明业已～。This certificate is invalid.
失笑 shīxiào laugh in spite of oneself; cannot help laughing; cannot refrain from laughing:不禁哑然～ can hardly suppress a smile; cannot help smiling
失谐 shīxié 〈无线电〉detuning; mismatching:～天线 dumb aerial
失信 shīxìn break one's promise; go back on one's word; lose credibility:决不～ never go back on one's word /～于人 break faith with others /我决不～。I'm a man of my word.
失信于民 shīxìnyúmín (of a government) lose the confidence of the people; lose credibility with the public:凡是答应的事都要办到，不可～。The government should keep its promise and must not lose credibility with the people.
失修 shīxiū be in bad repair; fall into disrepair; become neglected:老屋年久～。The old house has fallen into disrepair over the years. *or* The house is poorly maintained.
失学 shīxué cannot afford to go to school; be obliged to discontinue one's studies:不少青少年～。Many teenagers are unable to attend school. /她十岁就～了。She had to drop out of school at the age of ten.
失血 shīxuè loss of blood; hemorrhage:被害者因～过多而死亡。The victim died as a result of excessive loss of blood.
失言 shīyán *also* "失口" make an indiscreet remark:无意中～ let drop an inappropriate remark unintentionally /他后悔自己～。He regretted having said something he shouldn't have said.
失业 shīyè lose one's job; be out of work; be made redundant:～津贴(救济金) unemployment benefit /～救济基金 relief fund for the unemployed /长期～ chronic unemployment /季节性～ seasonal unemployment
失业保险 shīyè bǎoxiǎn employment insurance
失业率 shīyèlǜ rate of unemployment
失业者 shīyèzhě unemployed people; the jobless
失仪 shīyí commit a breach of etiquette:我怕喝醉了在人家面前～。I don't want to get drunk and commit a breach of etiquette before so many people. /她提醒我在外宾面前不要～。She told me not to forget myself before the foreign guests.
失宜 shīyí 〈书面〉inappropriate; improper:措辞～ inappropriate wording; unhappy choice of words /此事处置～，可能产生严重后果。The mishandling of the matter could have serious consequences.
失意 shīyì be frustrated; be disappointed:政治上～ be frustrated in politics; suffer setbacks in one's political career /情场～ be disappointed in love
失音 shīyīn 〈医学〉loss of all but whispered voice; aphonia
失迎 shīyíng 〈套语〉fail to meet a guest personally:原来是你，～了。So it's you. Excuse me for not greeting you at the gate.
失语 shīyǔ ❶〈书面〉indiscreet remark:酒后～ make indiscreet remarks under the influence of the alcohol ❷ difficulty in speech; inability to speak:病后～ be unable to speak clearly and coherently after a major illness
失语症 shīyǔzhèng 〈医学〉loss of ability to use or comprehend words; aphasia
失约 shīyuē fail to keep an appointment:因故～ fail to keep one's appointment for some reason /第一次见面，千万不能～。You must not break the appointment since this is your first meeting with him.
失责 shīzé fail to do one's duty:事情办得不如意，是我～。The matter has not been well handled. It is all my fault.
失张失志 shīzhāng-shīzhì *also* "失张失智" lose one's head; be frightened:她这般前言不搭后语，～，内中必有缘故。She is talking incoherently and acting oddly. There must be something wrong with her.
失着 shīzhāo unwise move; wrong move:这盘棋我很有几个～。I made quite a few faulty moves in the chess game. /他在这件事中屡次～。He made a series of unwise moves in this matter.
失真 shīzhēn ❶ (of voice, images, etc.) lack fidelity or exactitude; not be true to the original:情节～。The story is lacking in verisimilitude. ❷ *also* "畸变" jībiàn 〈无线电〉distortion:频率～ frequency distortion /声频信号谐波～ audio-frequency harmonic distortion /图像～ image fault /～度 distortion factor
失政 shīzhèng 〈书面〉misgovernment
失之东隅，收之桑榆 shī zhī dōngyú, shōu zhī sāngyú what is lost in the morning is made up in the evening; what you lose on the swings you gain on the roundabouts; it's all swings and roundabouts
失之毫厘，谬以千里 shī zhī háolí, miù yǐ qiānlǐ an error the breadth of a single hair can lead you a thousand *li* astray — a small discrepancy leads to a great error
失之交臂 shīzhī-jiāobì *also* "交臂失之" miss by a split second:我与他那天都在火车站，却没有见面，真是～。Though we were both at the railway station that day, we just missed each other. /他怎能让这样的好机会～呢? How could he let such a good opportunity slip through his fingers?
失职 shīzhí negligence of one's duty; dereliction of duty:严重～ gross negligence of duty /由于值班人员的～，盗贼才得以进入银行。The thieves succeeded in entering the bank because those on duty had neglected their duties.
失重 shīzhòng 〈物理〉weightlessness; zero gravity; weight loss:～状态 state of weightlessness /在～条件下 when there is zero gravity
失重错视 shīzhòng cuòshì agravic illusion
失重疗法 shīzhòng liáofǎ zero-gravity therapy
失主 shīzhǔ owner of lost property:找不到车子的～。The owner of the stolen car is nowhere to be found.

失坠 shīzhuì lose:这使他树起久已～的自信。This has restored his long-lost self-confidence.

失踪 shīzōng be missing; disappear:突然～ suddenly disappear / 战争～人员 personnel missing in action (MIA) /他的神秘～在京城引起震动。His mysterious disappearance caused a stir in the capital. / 海轮失事,旅客五十多人死亡,十多人～。More than 50 passengers died and a dozen or more passengers were missing in the shipwreck.

失足 shīzú ❶ lose one's footing; miss one's step; slip:他在冰上～滑倒了。He slipped on the ice and fell over. /小孩～从桥上落入水中。The child lost his footing and fell from the bridge into the water. / 老人～从楼梯上摔了下来。The old man missed his step and fell down the stairs. ❷ (often of a moral nature) take a wrong step in life; commit a serious error in life; go astray:～的姑娘 fallen girl /一～成千古恨。One false step brings eternal remorse.

失足青年 shīzú qīngnián young offender of the law; juvenile delinquent:挽救～ reform juvenile delinquents

施

shī ❶ execute; carry out; put into practice:无计可～ have no strong card to play; be at the end of one's resources /发号～令 issue orders /软硬兼～ use both soft and hard tactics ❷ exert; exercise; impose:～加巨大压力 exert tremendous pressure /～暴力 use violence /～暴政 practise tyranny ❸ bestow; grant; hand out; give:布～ alms giving /～不望报 bestow favours without expecting anything in return ❹ use; apply:～农家肥 spread farmyard manure /略～脂粉 apply a little rouge and powder (to one's face) ❺ (Shī) a surname

施暴 shībào ❶ use violence:歹徒在光天化日下向一小贩～。The thug violently attacked a pedlar in broad daylight. ❷ rape:此人企图向一女青年～。The man attempted to rape a young girl.

施恩 shī'ēn *also* "施惠" grant favours (to others); bestow favours on; be kind:～图报非君子。It is ungentlemanly to bestow favours on others in the hope of getting something in return.

施法 shīfǎ ❶〈书面〉enforce laws and decrees ❷ (of Taoist priests, wizards, sorcerers, etc.) perform magic arts

施放 shīfàng let off; discharge; fire:～烟火 put on a display of fireworks; let off fireworks /大量～催泪弹 fire a large number of tear-gas shells /～毒气 discharge poisonous gas /～烟幕〈比喻〉throw up a smokescreen

施肥 shīféi spread manure; apply fertilizer:给麦苗～ apply fertilizer to wheat seedlings /合理～ rational application of fertilizers; rational fertilization

施工 shīgōng construction:～单位 unit in charge of construction / ～人员 builders; construction workers /～工地 construction site /～蓝图 blueprints for the construction /～方案 working plan /～进度 progress of construction /～程序 order of construction /～重地,闲人免进。Construction Site. No Admittance Except On Business. /前面道路～,车辆绕行。Detour. Road Under Repair Ahead. /楼房正在～。The building is under construction. /水库尚未～。Construction has not yet started on the reservoir.

施工缝 shīgōngfèng 〈建筑〉construction joint

施工图 shīgōngtú working drawing

施加 shījiā exert; inflict:～政治压力 exert political pressure on sb.; bring political pressure to bear on sb. /～影响 exercise one's influence on sb. /～刑罚 inflict punishment; mete out punishment

施教 shījiào teach; educate; guide; instruct:严格～ give rigorous instruction /现场～ on-the-spot guidance (*or* instruction)

施救 shījiù rescue:紧急～ administer emergency first aid /不及～ too late for any rescue measures

施控系统 shīkòng xìtǒng controlling system

施乐公司 Shīlè Gōngsī (US) Xerox Corporation

施礼 shīlǐ bow; salute

施力点 shīlìdiǎn 〈物理〉point of application

施耐庵 Shī Nài'ān Shi Nai'an, novelist of the late Yuan and early Ming dynasties and author of *Heroes of the Marshes* (水浒传)

施舍 shīshě give or dole out alms; give in charity:～物 dole; handout /～粮食 give food in charity /乐意～ be glad to give alms / 靠～度日 live on charity (*or* handouts) /乞求～ beg (for) alms /拒绝接受～ refuse alms (*or* charity) /～先及亲友。Charity begins at home. /每天～三次,为饥饿的失业者供应食物。Food was provided for hungry unemployed people three times a day.

施设 shīshè 〈书面〉decorate; arrange

施施 shīshī 〈书面〉❶ leisurely; slowly:～而行 walk at a slow pace ❷ complacently; proudly:他～然走进来,显出很自得的样子。He walked in with an air of complacency, looking very much pleased with himself.

施事 shīshì 〈语言〉doer of the action in a sentence; agent

施特劳斯 Shītèláosī Johann Strauss the younger (1825-1899), Austrian composer known as "the waltz king"

施威 shīwēi exhibit one's power; throw one's weight about:他官不大,可最爱向黎民百姓～。Petty official as he was, he just loved to lord it over the common people.

施为 shīwéi ❶〈书面〉what one does; action; behaviour; conduct:不得妄有所～。It is forbidden to act arbitrarily. ❷ put to use; give play to

施洗 shīxǐ administer baptism; baptize:给新入教者～ baptize new believers (*or* converts)

施刑 shīxíng ❶ mete out punishment; carry out a sentence ❷ apply torture:旧时县官审问犯人,往往首先～。In feudal days, magistrates often began hearing a case by applying torture to the defendant.

施行 shīxíng ❶ put in force; carry out; execute; implement:～考勤办法 implement a set of rules for checking work attendance /～细则 rules for implementation /本规定自公布之日起～。These regulations will come into force upon promulgation. /所有命令都立即～了。All orders were immediately executed. ❷ perform; effect; administer:顺利地～手术 perform a surgical operation successfully /～输液 administer infusion (to a patient) /～人工降雨 induce artificial rainfall /～飞机播种 sow seeds by plane

施药 shīyào dispense free medicine to the poor

施医 shīyī provide free medical service for the poor; treat poor patients free of charge

施用 shīyòng use; apply:～化妆品 use (*or* apply) cosmetics /～国产材料 use Chinese-manufactured (*or* home-made) materials /～范围有限 be of limited application /～有机肥料是改良土壤的基本方法之一。Application of organic fertilizer is one of the basic methods for the improvement of soil.

施与 shīyǔ grant; bestow:～小恩小惠 bestow petty favours; dole out sops

施斋 shīzhāi give food to monks or nuns; give food to a monastery

施展 shīzhǎn put to good use; give full play to; display:～雄才 give full play to one's talent /～抱负 strive to realize one's ambition /～谋略 bring into full play one's tactics and resourcefulness / ～离间伎俩 resort to the tactics of sowing discord to effect disintegration

施诊 shīzhěn *also* "施医" give free medical treatment (to the poor)

施赈 shīzhèn give relief (as in a famine); give alms:向灾区～ give relief to victims in disaster areas

施政 shīzhèng governing; governance:～方针 policies (*or* principles) for running an institution or government; administrative policies /～纲领 programme for governance; administrative programme

施粥 shīzhōu give free porridge to the poor

施主 shīzhǔ ❶ (monks' or priests' form of address for) those who give money or food to the monastery or Taoist temple; patron; benefactor:慷慨的～ munificent benefactor /无名的～ anonymous benefactor ❷〈物理〉donor:～性杂质〈电子〉donor

施助 shīzhù aid financially; subsidize:此事全赖亲友～。This has been made possible thanks to financial assistance from our friends and relatives.

绝

shī 〈书面〉a kind of rather coarse silk fabric

尸(❶屍)

shī ❶ corpse; dead body; carcass:死～ dead body; corpse /干～ mummified corpse /验～ postmortem; autopsy / 借～还魂 (of a dead person's soul) find reincarnation in another's corpse; (of sth. evil) revive in a new guise /行～走肉 living corpse / 政治僵～ political mummy ❷〈古语〉person who sat behind the altar, acting as the deceased during the performance of the sacrificial rites

尸斑 shībān 〈医学〉ecchymosis in lower parts of corpse

尸变 shībiàn *also* "诈尸" zhàshī 〈迷信〉mysterious rising of a corpse

尸袋 shīdài body bag

尸骨 shīgǔ ❶ skeleton; bones of the dead: ～无存。No bones of the dead are left. ❷ remains; dead body: ～未寒 (while) sb.'s remains are scarcely cold yet
尸骸 shīhái skeleton
尸横遍野 shīhéngbiànyě field littered with corpses: 一场恶战之后, ～。When the battle was over, the field was strewn with dead bodies.
尸检 shījiǎn autopsy
尸谏 shījiàn admonish one's emperor (lord or master) at the cost of one's own life; remonstrate with the emperor by sending a memorial and committing suicide
尸解 shījiě (of a Taoist immortal) separate from bodily remains and become a spirit
尸居余气 shījū-yúqì be sinking fast; be a living corpse; be lifeless and good-for-nothing: 这个人～, 形神已离。This person is a mere living corpse.
尸蜡 shīlà well-preserved corpse
尸亲 shīqīn family and relatives of the deceased in a murder case
尸身 shīshēn corpse; dead body: 检验～ postmortem examination; necropsy
尸首 shīshou dead body; corpse
尸体 shītǐ corpse; dead body; cadaver; carcass: 保存～ preserve a corpse / 捐献～ donate one's remains / 辨认～ identify a corpse / ～鉴定 identification of the dead body
尸体检验 shītǐ jiǎnyàn necropsy; autopsy
尸体解剖 shītǐ jiěpōu autopsy; postmortem examination; dissection of a cadaver
尸体内部检查 shītǐ nèibù jiǎnchá internal postmortem examination
尸体剖检 shītǐ pōujiǎn ptomatopsia; ptomatopsy
尸位 shīwèi 〈书面〉occupy a position without doing any work: ～误国 do a disservice to one's country if one doesn't do any real work while holding a post
尸位素餐 shīwèi-sùcān hold on to one's post while doing nothing; hold down a job without doing a stroke of work: 有人～, 不以为耻。There are people who are not ashamed of themselves when they practically do nothing in their posts.
尸注 shīzhù 〈中医〉consumption; tuberculosis

鸤 shī

鸤鸠 shījiū (in ancient Chinese writing) cuckoo

虱(蝨) shī louse: 体～ body louse / 毛～ crab louse

虱病 shībìng infestation with lice; pediculosis; phthiriasis
虱多不痒, 债多不愁 shī duō bù yǎng, zhài duō bù chóu when one is covered with lice, one doesn't itch; when one is up to one's ears in debt, one stops worrying
虱蝇 shīyíng louse fly
虱子 shīzi louse: 头上长～ have lice in one's hair / 许多难民身上长满～。Many of the refugees had on clothes infested with lice.

鲺 shī 〈动物〉carp louse; fish louse

shí

实(實) shí ❶ solid; full: 这是个～心球。It's a solid ball. / 冰冻～了。The ice is frozen solid. / 把窟窿用土填～了。Fill up the hole with earth. ❷ real; true; actual; sincere: 虚～ false and true — the actual situation (usu. as of the opposing side) / 货真价～ genuine goods at a fair price / 真心～意 truly and wholeheartedly; sincerely / 据～交待 tell (us) the truth / 眼见为～。Seeing is believing. ❸ reality; actuality; fact: 名副其～ live up to the name; be worthy of the name; in name and in fact / 有名无～ in name but not in fact / 言过其～ exaggerate; overstate ❹ fruit; seed: 春华秋～ blossom in spring and bear fruit in autumn; be beautiful in appearance and virtuous in substance / 其～可食。Its fruit is edible.

实报实销 shíbào-shíxiāo be reimbursed for what one actually spends; be reimbursed for one's expenses: 掌握～的原则 go by the principle of reimbursing all actual expenses involved / 一切费用可以～。All the expenses incurred can be refunded.
实逼处此 shíbī-chǔcǐ be forced by the circumstances to do what one does; have no option under the circumstances: 他们仇恨你们, 亦～, 是你们实行高压政策的结果。Because of your high-handed policy, they have no choice but to hate you.
实变函数 shíbiàn hánshù function of real variable; real variable function
实才 shícái *also* "实材"〈书面〉❶ real ability ❷ person of real ability
实测 shícè survey or inspection with instruments
实诚 shícheng 〈口语〉honest; frank: ～话 truth / 这个人～, 答应了的事不会做不到的。He is an honest man and will be as good as his word.
实处 shíchù where it really matters: 把措施落到～ put the measure into practice; carry the measure through
实词 shící 〈语言〉notional word
实打实 shídǎshí hundred percent true; genuine: ～地说吧 tell us nothing but the truth / ～的硬功夫 genuine hard-won skill
实弹 shídàn 〈军事〉❶ (of rifles, guns, etc.) loaded: 荷枪～ carry a loaded rifle ❷ live shell; live ammunition: ～射击 ball firing; combat firing; firing practice; range practice / ～演习 practice with live ammunition / ～战斗演习 combat practice
实地 shídì ❶ on-the-spot; field: ～调查 carry out on-the-spot investigations / 深入～了解情况 go deep down and learn on the spot how things are / ～勘测 on-the-spot or field survey / ～训练 field training / ～演习 field exercise ❷ steadfast; practical and steady: ～去做 do sth. in a practical manner / 要提倡脚踏～的作风。It is necessary to encourage the down-to-earth work style.
实繁有徒 shífányǒutú 〈贬义〉men like this abound; there are plenty of people like this or him: 目前, 靠不正当手段致富者～。Currently there are plenty of people getting rich by illegitimate means.
实感 shígǎn genuine feelings; real sentiments: 真情～ true feelings
实干 shígàn do solid work: 提倡～精神 promote the spirit of doing solid work / ～、苦干加巧干 work energetically, perseveringly and ingeniously
实干家 shígànjiā man of action
实根 shígēn 〈植物〉real root
实话 shíhuà truth: 听～ hear the truth; want the truth / 供出～ confess the truth / 说～, 他确实不如以往结实了。Truth to tell, he is no longer as strong as before.
实话实说 shíhuà-shíshuō speak the plain truth; call a spade a spade: ～, 这件事与他们无关。To be perfectly frank, they have nothing to do with the matter.
实惠 shíhuì ❶ real benefit; material gain: 捞取～ get real benefit / 让农民从改革中得到～ let the peasants really benefit from the reform / 讲究～ think in terms of material gain; be practical-minded ❷ substantial; solid; practical: 经济～ inexpensive and practical; economical and serviceable / 经济～的家具 utility furniture / 这家小餐厅比许多大饭店要～得多。The food is much cheaper and more substantial in this small restaurant than in many big ones.
实火 shíhuǒ 〈中医〉symptoms of fever such as high temperature, thirstiness, constipation, etc.
实祸 shíhuò real disaster or misfortune: 此事无实惠而有～。This will bring no substantial benefit but only real disaster.
实际 shíjì ❶ reality; actual practice: 接触～ be in touch with reality / 脱离～ lose contact (*or* be out of touch) with reality; be divorced from reality / 符合～ correspond to (*or* accord with) reality / 从～出发 proceed from actual conditions; be realistic / 理论和～相结合 unity of theory and practice / ～上 as a matter of fact; in fact; in reality; actually / 理论联系～ integrate theory with practice ❷ real; true; actual; concrete: ～文化水平 real (*or* actual) level of education / ～办法 concrete measures; practical means / ～生活 real life; everyday life / ～增长 growth in real terms / ～成本 actual cost; real cost / ～需求 effective demand / ～敌对行为 active hostilities / ～现金支出 out-of-pocket expenses ❸ practical; realistic: ～应用 practical application / 不切～的空洞言词 empty talk / 计划订得不～。The plan is not realistic. / 讲话讲得很～。What he said was quite practical.
实际工资 shíjì gōngzī 〈经济〉real wages
实际汇价 shíjì huìjià 〈经济〉effective rate (of exchange)
实际控制线 shíjì kòngzhìxiàn 〈军事〉line of actual control: 两国将以现在的～为基础开始边界谈判。The two countries will open negotiations on the boundary question on the basis of the current line of actual control.

实际年利率 shíjì niánlìlǜ 〈金融〉annualised percentage rate
实际伤害 shíjì shānghài 〈法律〉real injury
实寄封 shíjìfēng envelope of a posted letter (in philately)
实绩 shíjì deeds; real achievements; concrete results: 做出～ show tangible results / 根据每人的工作～予以奖励 reward each person according to the actual work he (*or* she) has done / 这本选集是他近年来创作上的～。This collection testifies to his latest achievements in writing.
实价 shíjià actual price; net price: 明码～，童叟无欺。(as in a shop advertisement) We sell at marked net prices and are equally honest with all customers, including the aged and children.
实践 shíjiàn ❶ put into practice; carry out; implement: 他决心把这个方案付诸～。He was determined to put the plan into practice. / 他没有资金来～自己的计划。He has no funds to carry out his project. ❷ practice: ～是检验真理的唯一标准。Practice is the sole criterion for testing truth.
实践出真知 shíjiàn chū zhēnzhī genuine knowledge comes from practice; practice gives birth to true knowledge
实践论 Shíjiànlùn *On Practice*, philosophical thesis written by Mao Zedong in 1937
实践性 shíjiànxìng practicality; practicalness
实景 shíjǐng realistic view (as distinguished from "setting")
实据 shíjù substantial evidence; actual proof: 真凭～ ironclad evidence / 提供～ produce factual proof / 我们并无～可以证明他是有罪的。We have no substantial evidence to prove that he is guilty.
实况 shíkuàng what is actually happening: 大会～ actual proceedings of the rally / 这次选举的～报道 live coverage of the election
实况录音 shíkuàng lùyīn live recording; on-the-spot recording
实况转播 shíkuàng zhuǎnbō live broadcast; live transmission; live telecast; field pick-up
实牢 shílao 〈方言〉honest; dependable: 他这个人挺～，就是太死板。He is honest, only a bit rigid in his ideas.
实力 shílì strength; power: 增强经济～ build up economic strength / 消耗敌人的～ wear down the enemy's effective strength / 军事～ military power (*or* strength) / 国防～ national defence capabilities
实力地位 shílì dìwèi position of strength
实力政策 shílì zhèngcè policy of strength
实利 shílì actual benefit: ～主义 utilitarianism
实例 shílì concrete example; example: 举出～ cite a living (*or* concrete) example / 这样的～不胜枚举。Innumerable examples of this kind might be adduced. *or* Examples like this are too many to enumerate.
实录 shílù ❶〈书面〉factual record; faithful record: 这本日记是他晚年生活的～。This diary is a faithful record of the last years of his life. ❷ annals that record the big events in the reign of an emperor; personal record of the deeds of one's ancestors ❸ record the facts or what has actually happened
实录电影 shílù diànyǐng *cinéma vérité*
实落 shíluo 〈方言〉❶ honest: 他有点执拗，对人心地可～。Though a little obstinate, he is honest and true to people. ❷ (of state of mind) at peace; free from anxiety: 听他这样一说，我心里才感到～。After hearing his remarks, I felt relieved. ❸ precise; exact: 你究竟哪天动身，请告诉我个～的日子。Let me know exactly the day of your departure (*or* on which day you are leaving). ❹ firm; solid: 这把椅子做得可真～。This chair is of a very strong make.
实脉 shímài 〈中医〉forceful pulse
实名制 shímíngzhì real name system for personal bank account
实模铸造法 shímú zhùzàofǎ 〈冶金〉cavityless casting
实情 shíqíng actual state of affairs; real situation; truth: 我们必须掌握这里的～。We must keep ourselves informed of what is going on here. / 必须了解～才能作出决定。We have to find out the true state of affairs before we can make any decision.
实情实理 shíqíng-shílǐ true state of affairs; truth: 我说的都是～，决不骗你。To be honest with you, I've told nothing but the truth.
实权 shíquán real power: 掌握～的人 person who wields real power; man with the clout / 赋予某人～ invest real power in sb.; invest sb. with real power
实缺 shíquē 〈旧语〉official position with clearly defined duties; vacancy; opening
实生 shíshēng (of nursery stock, etc.) raised directly from planted seeds
实生苗 shíshēngmiáo 〈农业〉seedling
实施 shíshī put into effect; implement; enforce: ～婚姻法 implement the Marriage Law / ～合同 carry out a contract / ～他的政治主张 put his political ideas into practice / 派工作组到各地检查政策的～情况 send working groups to various places to check up on the implementation of a policy / 严格～学校的规章制度 strictly enforce the rules and regulations of the school / 负责计划的～ be responsible for the execution of a plan / 这项法律将于明年1月1日起～。This law will go into effect on January 1 next year.
实时 shíshí real time: ～数据处理 real time data processing
实实 shíshí really; in fact; indeed: 我～不知此事，所以才问你。I am asking you because I really don't know anything about it.
实事 shíshì ❶ actual thing; fact: 此剧取材于京城～。This play was based on what really happened in the capital. ❷ deeds; solid work; practical work: 做～ do solid (*or* practical) work / 为大众办十件～ try to accomplish ten specific projects for the welfare of the public / 他是一个干～的人。He is a man of action. *or* He is a man who likes to get down to brass tacks. / 少讲空话，多办～。Less empty talk, more practical deeds.
实事求是 shíshì-qiúshì seek truth from facts; be realistic and truthful: ～的态度 practical and realistic approach (*or* attitude) / ～地制定计划 draw up a realistic plan / 我们无论做何种工作，都应该～。Whatever we do, we must base ourselves on facts. / 我是～派。I'm a realist, or as we put it, I seek truth from facts.
实收款项 shíshōu kuǎnxiàng proceeds of sale
实数 shíshù ❶〈数学〉real number ❷ actual amount or number: ～是多少? What is the actual figure?
实说 shíshuō tell the truth; speak frankly; talk straight: 实话～ tell the truth; talk straight; be quite blunt / 他到底出了什么事，请你～。Please tell us straight out what happened to him.
实体 shítǐ ❶〈哲学〉substance: ～性 substantiality / ～形式 substantial form / ～主义 substantialism ❷〈法律〉entity: 独立的政治～ independent political entity / 经济～ economic entity
实体法 shítǐfǎ 〈法律〉substantive law
实物 shíwù ❶ material object; real object: 用～进行教学 make use of samples to carry out classroom instruction / 收集～标本 collect specimens; collect samples / ～教学 object lesson ❷ in kind: ～赔偿 reparation in kind / ～证据 tangible evidence / 用～进行交换 exchange by barter / 提供～援助 provide aid in kind ❸〈物理〉matter
实物地租 shíwù dìzū 〈经济〉rent in kind
实物工资 shíwù gōngzī wages in kind
实物幻灯机 shíwù huàndēngjī epidiascope
实物奖 shíwùjiǎng bonus or reward in kind
实物交易 shíwù jiāoyì barter; barter trade; trade in kind: 两国边境居民经常进行～。The inhabitants on both sides of the border often barter with each other.
实物税 shíwùshuì tax in kind
实习 shíxí practice; fieldwork; field trip: 毕业～ graduation field work / 教学～ teaching practice
实习工厂 shíxí gōngchǎng factory for training purposes
实习护士 shíxí hùshi nurse being trained and still on probation; probationer
实习记者 shíxí jìzhě student journalist
实习技术员 shíxí jìshùyuán technician on probation
实习教师 shíxí jiàoshī student teacher; trainee teacher
实习领事 shíxí lǐngshì student consul
实习期 shíxíqī period of probation; internship
实习生 shíxíshēng trainee; interne
实习医生 shíxí yīshēng interne
实现 shíxiàn realize; achieve; bring about: ～计划 fulfil a plan / ～远景规划 carry out a long-term programme / 努力～四化 strive for the realization (*or* success) of the four modernizations / ～优质高产 attain the goal of top quality and high output (in production) / ～安定团结 bring about (*or* achieve) stability and unity / ～统一祖国的大业 accomplish the task of unifying the country / 我的愿望～了。My wish came true. / 他的希望从未～。His hopes never materialized.
实像 shíxiàng 〈物理〉real image
实效 shíxiào actual effect; substantial benefit: 讲求～ stress actual results / 确有～ be really effective / 给国民经济的发展带来～ bring substantial benefits to the development of the national economy / 决议的～部分 operative part of a resolution / 工作要注重～。Actual effects should be sought in one's work. / 这些办法没有取得～。These

measures produced no practical results.

实心 shíxīn ❶ sincere; earnest: ~话 sincere words; words from the bottom of one's heart ❷ solid: ~地板 solid floor /~汤圆 dumplings made of glutinous rice flour without any filling inside /这种铁球是~的。These iron balls are solid.

实心球 shíxīnqiú *also* "药球" yàoqiú 〈体育〉 medicine ball

实心实意 shíxīn-shíyì honest and sincere; true and earnest: ~为群众办事 serve the masses wholeheartedly

实心眼儿 shíxīnyǎnr ❶ honest; conscientious ❷ honest person

实行 shíxíng put into practice; carry out; practise; implement: ~计划生育 practise family planning /~停火 implement a cease-fire /~必要的监督 exercise necessary supervision /~科学管理 carry out scientific management /~共产党领导的多党合作和政治协商制度 institute the system of multi-party cooperation and political consultation under the leadership of the Communist Party/新税法已经~。The new tax regulations have come into effect. /这里~五天工作制。A five-day working week has been introduced here. /计划能不能~还是个问题。Whether the plan can be put through or not is still a question.

实性人 shíxìngrén honest person

实学 shíxué real learning; sound scholarship: 真才~ real ability and learning

实言 shíyán truth: ~相告 tell the truth; speak frankly; to be honest

实验 shíyàn experiment; test: 科学~ scientific experiment (*or* experimentation) /做~ make a test; conduct an experiment /通过~证明理论的正确性 prove by experiment the correctness of the theory /用动物做~ experiment on animals /~报告 laboratory report /~数据 experimental data

实验动物 shíyàn dòngwù animal used as a subject for experiment, such as a guinea pig

实验式 shíyànshì *also* "最简式" zuìjiǎnshì chemical equation

实验室 shíyànshì laboratory

实验心理学 shíyàn xīnlǐxué experimental psychology

实验学校 shíyàn xuéxiào experimental school

实验员 shíyànyuán laboratory technician

实验战略导弹 shíyàn zhànlüè dǎodàn experimental strategic missile (ESM)

实业 shíyè industry and commerce; business; enterprise: 振兴~ promote industry and commerce /~救国 save the nation through industrial development

实业家 shíyèjiā industrialist; big businessman

实业界 shíyèjiè industrial and commercial circles; business community

实益 shíyì real benefit

实意 shíyì sincere; heartfelt: 真心~ genuinely and sincerely; wholeheartedly

实蝇 shíyíng fruit fly

实用 shíyòng ❶ practical use or application: 有些学问不能要求~。Certain branches of learning are not expected to be of immediate practical use. ❷ practical; pragmatic; applied; functional: ~工艺美术 applied industrial arts /~建筑 functional architecture

实用美术 shíyòng měishù applied fine arts

实用文 shíyòngwén 〈旧语〉 practical writing (e.g. official documents, notices, etc.)

实用主义 shíyòngzhǔyì ❶〈哲学〉 pragmatism: ~者 pragmatist /~法学 pragmatic jurisprudence /~政策 pragmatic policy ❷ expediency: 我们不搞~。Our policy is not based on expediency. *or* We do not act by expediency.

实在 shízài ❶ true; honest; practical: 这人很~。He is honest and down-to-earth. /这个想法很~。The idea is practical. /内容~。The content is substantial. ❷ really; in all conscience: 我~不了解他。I really don't know anything about him. /我~敬佩他的能力。I have in all conscience the greatest esteem for his ability. /那家伙~讨厌。That fellow is a perfect nuisance. /那~太好了! That's just wonderful! *or* It's simply terrific! /他说话~太啰嗦。He is far too long-winded. ❸ in fact; in reality: 他表面上同意,心里~并不同意。He pretended to agree, but really he didn't. ❹〈哲学〉 reality: 主观~ subjective reality /客观~ objective reality

实在 shízai 〈方言〉 (of work) done in real earnest; well done: 小伙子干活儿~。The young man is a careful (*or* good) worker. /他的工作总是做得很~。His work is always well done.

实在法 shízàifǎ 〈法律〉 positive law (in contrast with 自然法 natural law)

实在论 shízàilùn 〈哲学〉 realism

实则 shízé in actual fact; in reality: 他说起来头头是道,~什么也不会做。He talks as if he knew everything, but when it comes to actual practice he is an ignoramus.

实战 shízhàn actual combat or fighting: 用~的标准衡量 be measured by the criteria of actual combat /二次大战中他当了三年兵,却从未参加过~。Though he was a soldier for three years in World War II, he never saw action.

实战演习 shízhàn yǎnxí combat exercise with live ammunition

实着 shízhao 〈口语〉 steady; sound; peaceful; dependable: 孩子睡~了。The child is sound asleep. /这个年轻人总是不~。This young man is not reliable.

实证 shízhèng actual or concrete evidence: 出示~ produce concrete evidence

实证主义 shízhèngzhǔyì 〈哲学〉 positivism: ~者 positivist

实症 shízhèng *also* "实证" 〈中医〉 excess syndrome — a case of an otherwise physically strong patient running a high fever or suffering from such disorders as stasis of blood, constipation, etc.

实职 shízhí position with actual duties or work

实至名归 shízhì-míngguī the name follows the reality — fame is a reflection of real achievements

实质 shízhì substance; essence; gist: ~性问题 matters of substance /~证据 material (*or* substantive) evidence /问题的~ crux (*or* heart) of the matter; essence of the question /文件的精神~ gist of the document /他的讲话没有~性内容。His speech has no substance. /双方会谈有了~性进展。Substantive progress has been achieved in the talks between the two sides.

实字 shízì 〈语言〉 notional word

实足 shízú full; exact; solid: ~工资 full wages /~年龄 exact age /~走了十公里 walk a full ten kilometres /到会的~五十人。There were no fewer than fifty people at the meeting. /他~讲了三小时。He talked for a good three hours.

识(識) shí

❶ know: 大字不~一个 unable to read a single character; absolutely illiterate /素不相~ have never met; not be acquainted with each other ❷ knowledge; learning: 常~ general (*or* elementary) knowledge; common sense /博~ learned; erudite /远见卓~ foresight and sagacity /见多~广 experienced and knowledgeable /有~之士 person with breadth of vision; person of insight; knowledgeable person /~穷天下 (possess) infinite wisdom and intelligence /~事明理 show good sense

see also zhì

识拔 shíbá recognize the ability of and promote (a person): 他以工作优异为领导所~。He was promoted because the leaders recognized his merit.

识辨 shíbiàn identify; recognize; discern: ~风向 determine the direction of the wind; see which way the wind blows /提高~能力 improve the power of discernment

识别 shíbié distinguish; discern; identify: ~真伪 distinguish between truth and falsehood; tell the false from the genuine /~人才 spot a man of talent /善于~人 know how to judge people /~笔迹 identify sb.'s handwriting /指纹~ fingerprint identification /~各种杂草 differentiate varieties of weeds /~伪学者 see through pseudo-scholars /图像~ pattern recognition

识别标记 shíbié biāojì identification mark(ing)

识别力 shíbiélì discernment

识才 shícái know real talents; value men with outstanding abilities: ~善教 spot talents and know how to bring out the best in them

识大体,顾大局 shí dàtǐ, gù dàjú have the fundamental principles and overall situation in mind

识度 shídù 〈书面〉 with insight and magnanimity; knowledgeable and broad-minded: 博学有~ learned man of insight and magnanimity

识货 shíhuò be able to tell good from bad; know what's what; be knowledgeable: ~的买主 buyer (*or* customer) who knows what is what; knowledgeable customer /不怕不~,就怕货比货。Don't fear it won't be appreciated if it stands well up to comparison. *or* Don't worry about the lack of appreciation for your goods; comparison with other goods will bring out their worth.

识家 shíjiā knowledgeable customer: 今天画展来的可都是~。Those

S

you see at today's painting exhibition are all specialists.

识见 shíjiàn 〈书面〉knowledge and experience:此人颇有~。He is a man of great insight.

识荆 shíjīng 〈书面〉〈敬词〉have the honour of making your acquaintance; be flattered to get acquainted with you:素不~。I have never had the pleasure of meeting you before. /今日~,三生有幸。I feel very much honoured to get acquainted with you today.

识力 shílì power of discernment; power of discrimination

识量 shíliàng 〈书面〉knowledge and tolerance; insight and magnanimity:~狭小 narrow-minded

识虑 shílǜ knowledge and consideration; insight and understanding:~过人 excel in knowledge and understanding

识面 shímiàn 〈书面〉meet; see

识破 shípò see sb. as he or she really is; see through; penetrate: ~阴谋 see through a conspiracy /~某人的伪装 penetrate sb.'s disguise /~两面派 see a double-dealer in his true colours

识趣 shíqù behave or respond sensibly in a delicate situation; be judicious:不~ be tactless /她~地走开了。She had the good sense to walk away. /我以前还夸他~呢。I used to give him credit for being sensible.

识时务者为俊杰 shí shíwù zhě wéi jùnjié a person is wise who understands the signs of the times; those who bow to objective necessity are wise people

识途老马 shítú-lǎomǎ old horse that knows the way — man of experience; wise old bird; old hand:你还得我这样的~来点拨。You need a wise old bird like me to show you the ropes.

识文断字 shíwén-duànzì be able to read and write; be literate:自幼~ have learned to read and write since childhood /这青年~,工作定能胜任。The young man is educated and will certainly be competent for the job.

识闲 shíxián (often used in the negative) idle; not occupied; not busy:他起早贪黑地工作,一年四季不~。All the year round he keeps himself busy from morning till night.

识相 shíxiàng 〈方言〉showing good sense; be sensible; be tactful: 奉劝你还是~点,不要再纠缠了。You'd better be more sensible and quit. /他倒是~,一句话都不说。He had enough sense to keep his mouth shut. /好一个不~的家伙! What a tactless fellow!

识羞 shíxiū (often used in the negative) feel ashamed; have a sense of shame:这样不~的人少见。Seldom do we see such a shameless person. /她一点也不~。She is not in the least ashamed of herself.

识阈效应 shíyù xiàoyìng 〈商业〉threshold effect

识者 shízhě 〈书面〉the knowledgeable; those in the know; experts:文中不当之处,有待~教正。The author humbly welcomes comments by the knowledgeable on what needs improvement in this article.

识字 shízì learn to read; become literate:读书~ read and write

识字班 shízìbān literacy class

识字课本 shízì kèběn reading primer; elementary reader

十 shí ❶ ten:~本书 ten books /~年 ten years; decade /~周年 tenth anniversary; ten whole years /产品数量比七年前增加~倍。Production increased ten-fold in seven years. /可能性只有~分之一。The chances may well be one in ten. /~个人~样性。There are as many personalities as the number of people. ❷ topmost; highest:~足 100 per cent; complete

十八般武艺 shíbā bān wǔyì skill in wielding the 18 kinds of weapons (in the traditional Chinese armoury) — skill in various fields of work:~,样样精通 be skilful in the use of each and every one of the 18 weapons; be an all-rounder; be versatile

十八层地狱 shíbā céng dìyù bottom or depths of hell:被打入~ be cast into utter darkness and misery

十八开金 shíbā kāijīn 18-carat gold

十八罗汉 shíbā luóhàn 〈佛教〉eighteen arhats:~的塑像栩栩如生。The statues of the eighteen arhats are as vivid as life.

十边地 shíbiāndì small plots of land by the sides of houses, roads, etc.:充分利用~ make full use of small plots of land around houses and by the sides of roads and ponds

十病九痛 shíbìng-jiǔtòng weak and ailing

十不闲儿 shíbùxiánr *also*"什不闲儿" shíbùxiánr a kind of ballad singing, accompanied by gong, drum, etc.

十步芳草 shíbù-fāngcǎo *also*"十步之内,必有芳草" you can always find fragrant grass within a distance of ten steps — talent can be found everywhere

十成九稳 shíchéng-jiǔwěn *also*"十拿九稳" ninety per cent sure; practically certain:他认为办成这件事~。He was quite certain that he could get the job done.

十大功劳 shídàgōngláo 〈中药〉Chinese mahonia (*Mahonia fortunei*)

十滴水 shídīshuǐ 〈药学〉"10 drops", a popular liquid medicine for summer ailments, esp. sun-stroke, with each dose generally consisting of ten drops

十冬腊月 shídōng-làyuè tenth, eleventh, and twelfth months of the lunar year — the coldest months of the year:这个老农民终年劳累,~也不得休息。The old farmer toiled all the year round, not even taking a day off in winter.

十恶不赦 shí'è-bùshè be too wicked to be pardoned; guilty of unpardonable evil; guilty beyond forgiveness:~的罪犯 unpardonable criminal /~的坏蛋 totally depraved scoundrel /~的罪行 outrageous atrocities; heinous crimes

十二分 shí'èrfēn exceedingly; extremely:~地高兴 be overwhelmed with joy /我~地感谢你。I owe my deepest gratitude to you. /我对这个安排感到~的满意。I am really very much satisfied with the present arrangement.

十二红 shí'èrhóng 〈动物〉Japanese waxwing

十二黄 shí'èrhuáng 〈动物〉waxwing

十二级风 shí'èrjífēng 〈气象〉force 12 wind; hurricane

十二进制 shí'èrjìnzhì duodecimal notation

十二开 shí'èrkāi 〈印刷〉duodecimo; 12mo (twelvemo)

十二码球 shí'èrmǎqiú *also*"点球" diǎnqiú penalty kick

十二门徒 shí'èr méntú 〈宗教〉twelve apostles (of Jesus Christ)

十二平均率 shí'èr píngjūnlǜ 〈乐器〉twelve-tone equal temperament

十二生肖 shí'èr shēngxiào *also*"十二属相" twelve symbolic animals representing the Earthly Branches, namely, the rat, ox, tiger, rabbit, dragon, snake, horse, sheep, monkey, rooster, dog and pig

see also"生肖" shēngxiào

十二月 shí'èryuè ❶ December:~党人 Decembrist (of 19th century Russia) ❷ twelfth month of the lunar year; twelfth moon

十二指肠 shí'èrzhǐcháng 〈生理〉duodenum

十二指肠癌 shí'èrzhǐcháng'ái cancer of the duodenum

十二指肠溃疡 shí'èrzhǐcháng kuìyáng duodenal ulcer

十二指肠切除 shí'èrzhǐcháng qiēchú duodenectomy

十二指肠炎 shí'èrzhǐchángyán duodenitis

十番锣鼓 shífān luógǔ *see*"十番乐"

十番乐 shífānyuè *also*"十番" folk music played by a band with ten different musical instruments

十方 shífāng 〈佛教〉ten directions — east, west, south, north, southeast, northeast, southwest, northwest, above and below

十分 shífēn 〈副词〉fully; very; most; extremely:~兴奋 very excited (*or* agitated) /~悲痛 deeply grieved /~关心 be extremely concerned /~无知 be utterly ignorant /~正常 absolutely normal / ~重视 attach great importance; pay close attention / ~珍贵 be most valuable; cherish dearly /~感谢 thank sb. from the bottom of one's heart /~仇视 intensely hate /会见在~友好的气氛中进行。The meeting proceeded in a most friendly atmosphere.

十分话 shífēnhuà what one really thinks or feels; sincere words: 早先他有什么话都愿说给我听,近来他对我也不说~。He used to tell me everything on his mind, but lately he hasn't taken me into his confidence.

十风五雨 shífēng-wǔyǔ *also*"五风十雨" frequent timely rains — favourable weather; good weather for the crops:今年是~,年景不会错。As the weather is so favourable, there will be a good harvest this year.

十个指头有长短 shíge zhǐtou yǒu chángduǎn the fingers are different in length — you can't expect people to be all the same

十行俱下 shíháng-jùxià read ten lines at a glance — read very fast

十级风 shíjífēng 〈气象〉force 10 wind; whole gale

十佳 shíjiā ten best:这是一部 1992 年的~电影。This was one of the ten best films of 1992.

十戒 shíjiè 〈佛教〉Ten Prohibitions

十诫 shíjiè 〈宗教〉Ten Commandments; Decalogue

十锦 shíjǐn *also* "什锦" shíjǐn assorted; mixed
十进币制 shíjìn bìzhì decimal currency; decimal coinage
十进对数 shíjìn duìshù 〈数学〉decimal logarithm
十进数 shíjìnshù decimal number; decimal numeration
十进制 shíjìnzhì 〈数学〉decimal system; decimal scale: ~记数法 decimal notation /~运算 decimal arithmetic /~分类法 decimal classification /~补码 ten's complement /~反码 nine's complement
十里洋场 shílǐ-yángchǎng 〈旧语〉foreign concession or settlement in Shanghai; general reference to Shanghai
十六分音符 shíliùfēn yīnfú 〈音乐〉semiquaver; sixteenth note
十六进数 shíliùjìnshù sexadecimal number; sexadecimal numeration
十六进制 shíliùjìnzhì sexadecimal system; sexadecimal scale
十六开 shíliùkāi 〈印刷〉sixteenmo; sextodecimo; 16mo: 把纸裁成~ cut paper into sixteenmo
十六烷 shíliùwán 〈化学〉cetane
十魔九难 shímó-jiǔnàn continued tribulations or sufferings; hardship upon hardship
十目所视,十手所指 shí mù suǒ shì, shí shǒu suǒ zhǐ many accusing fingers and angry eyes — one cannot do anything wrong without being exposed: ~, 他觉得心中不安稳。With many eyes watching and many fingers pointing, he felt ill at ease (*or* on tenterhooks) all the time.
十拿九稳 shíná-jiǔwěn *also* "十拿九准" 90 per cent sure; practically certain; as good as settled: 他得冠军是~的。He is almost certain to win the championship. /她考入大学~。She has a ten-to-one chance of passing the national college entrance examinations. /他们觉得他当选议员是~的。They felt that his election to the Congress was almost in the bag.
十年动乱 shínián dòngluàn decade of turmoil; ten turbulent or chaotic years (a reference to the Cultural Revolution of 1966-1976)
十年寒窗 shínián-hánchuāng *also* "十年窗下" (of a scholar's life in imperial China) ten years' study at a cold window — a student's long years of hard work; prolonged perseverance in one's studies in spite of hardships: 古人有"~无人问, 一举成名天下知"的说法。It was said in former times that an unknown scholar working hard at his studies for ten long years would become a celebrity the moment he passed the imperial examination.
十年九不遇 shí nián jiǔ bù yù not once in ten years; once in a blue moon; very rare: ~的旱灾 exceptionally serious drought /这么热的夏天, 真是~。Such a hot summer is quite unprecedented. *or* Hot summers like the one we're having are rare indeed.
十年内战 shínián nèizhàn Ten-Year Civil War (Second Revolutionary Civil War, 1927-1937)
十年树木,百年树人 shí nián shù mù, bǎi nián shù rén 〈谚语〉it takes ten years to grow trees, but a hundred to cultivate people: ~, 我们不能丝毫忽视教育。As it takes a long time to bring up people of talent, we cannot afford to neglect education in the least.
十全 shíquán perfect: 普天下找不出~的事。There is nothing perfect in the world.
十全十美 shíquán-shíměi be perfect (in every way); be the acme of perfection; be the paragon of excellence: 世上没有~的人。Nobody is perfect.
十三点 shísāndiǎn 〈方言〉❶ foolish; nutty: 这个人有点~。The guy is a little weird. ❷ dunce; nitwit: 他女儿是个~, 你别理会她。His daughter is a little under normal. Don't take her seriously.
十三经 Shísānjīng Thirteen Classics of Confucianism, namely *The Book of Changes* (易经), *Collection of Ancient Texts* (书经), *The Book of Songs* (诗经), *The Ritual of Zhou* (周礼), *The Book of Etiquette* (仪礼), *The Book of Rites* (礼记), *Zuo Zhuan* (左传), *The Gongyang Commentary* (公羊传), *The Guliang Commentary* (穀梁传), *The Analects* (论语), *The Book of Filial Piety* (孝经), *Er Ya* (尔雅) and *The Book of Mencius* (孟子)
十三陵 Shísānlíng Ming Tombs (tombs of 13 Ming emperors built outside Beijing from the 15th to 17th centuries)
十三辙 shísānzhé 〈语言〉thirteen major rhyming categories of words for certain local operas and folk singing performances
十室九空 shíshì-jiǔkōng nine houses out of ten are deserted — a scene of desolation (as after a plague or war): 经过这次战乱, 那个繁华的城市已经~。After the war, the once prosperous city was almost deserted.
十死一生 shísǐ-yīshēng in a very critical or precarious situation
十四行诗 shísìhángshī sonnet
十万八千里 shíwàn bāqiān lǐ one hundred and eight thousand *li* — an extremely long distance: 相差~ be poles apart /就学问而论, 我比他差了~。In terms of knowledge (*or* scholarship), I am miles behind him. /孩子的世界与成人世界的差别不啻~。The child's world is vastly different from that of the adult.
十万火急 shíwàn-huǒjí posthaste; most urgent (capitalized when used as a mark on dispatches): ~的情况 extra-urgent matter /~的军情 military information of utmost urgency /他~地前去营救他们。He went posthaste to their rescue.
十五个吊桶打水,七上八下 shíwǔ ge diàotǒng dǎ shuǐ, qī shàng bā xià have one's heart clanging like fifteen buckets in a single well, seven going up and eight down — have one's heart pounding with uncertainty, fear or turmoil: 他的心总是像~, 静不下来。His mind was in a turmoil and he couldn't calm down.
十项全能运动 shíxiàng quánnéng yùndòng 〈体育〉decathlon: ~员 decathlete /现代~包括 100 米跑、跳远、铅球、跳高、400 米跑、110 米跨栏、铁饼、撑竿跳、标枪和 1500 米跑等项目。The modern decathlon consists of the 100-metre dash, broad jump, shot-put, high jump, 400-metre run, 110-metre hurdles, discus-throw, pole-vault, javelin-throw and 1,500-metre run.
十羊九牧 shíyáng-jiǔmù nine shepherds tending ten sheep — too many government officials; too many chiefs and not enough Indians; bloated bureaucracy: ~, 其令难行; 一国三公, 何所适从? With too many officials on top, no order could be effectively carried out, and who should we follow if three princes were reigning in the state?
十一 Shí-Yī October 1, National Day of the People's Republic of China
十一级风 shíyījífēng 〈气象〉force 11 wind; storm
十一月 shíyīyuè ❶ November ❷ eleventh month of the lunar year; eleventh moon
十月 shíyuè ❶ October ❷ tenth month of the lunar year; tenth moon
十月革命 Shíyuè Gémìng October Revolution (occurring in Russia on 25 October 1917, according to the Russian calendar, but 7 November 1917, by the Gregorian calendar)
十之八九 shí zhī bājiǔ *also* "十有八九" in nine cases out of ten; very likely: ~要下雨。It's going to rain. /~他今天不会来了。Most likely he won't come today. /这个谣言~是她传出来的。In all likelihood, she is the person to have started the rumour.
十指连心 shízhǐ-liánxīn the fingers are linked to the heart — what happens to children is of special concern to parents: ~话不假, 儿行千里母担忧。As it is sure that all the fingers are linked to the heart, the mother is worried about her son when he is thousands of *li* away from home.
十姊妹 shízǐmèi 〈植物〉multiflora rose (*Rosa multiflora*)
十字镐 shízìgǎo pick; pickaxe; mattock
十字花科 shízìhuākē 〈植物〉mustard family; Cruciferae
十字架 shízìjià cross; crucifix
十字接头 shízì jiētóu cruciform joint; X-conn (X-connection); X-joint
十字街头 shízì-jiētóu crisscross streets; busy streets: 徘徊在~ hesitate at the crossroads /离开象牙之塔, 走向~ leave the ivory tower for the mundane world
十字军 Shízìjūn ❶ Crusades, military expeditions by the European Christian countries to recover the Holy Land from the Muslims in the Middle Ages: ~骑士 knights of the Crusades /~东征 eastern expeditions of the Crusades ❷ crusading army; crusades: ~战士 crusader
十字路口 shízì lùkǒu crossroads: 来到~ come to a crossroads /~的红绿灯 traffic lights at an intersection /处于人生的~ be at the crossroads of one's life
十字轴 shízìzhóu cross axle
十足 shízú ❶ hundred percent; pure; out-and-out; sheer: ~赤金 pure gold; 24-karat gold /~的书呆子 hundred per cent bookworm (*or* pedant) /~的骗局 out-and-out fraud /~的讨厌鬼 downright nuisance /~的官僚主义 bureaucracy pure and simple /~的强盗逻辑 sheer gangster logic /~的伪君子 utter hypocrite /~的笨蛋 unmitigated fool (*or* idiot) /~的市侩作风 consummate philistinism ❷ full: 神气~ put on grand airs; be on one's high horse /派头~ put on quite a show /威风~ have an imperious bearing /傲气~ be puffed

S

up with haughty airs /官气～ assume bureaucratic airs /具有～的理由 have ample reason; be well founded /这～地证明他们是一伙胆小鬼。It fully proves that they are just a pack of cowards.

十足类 shízúlèi 〈动物〉 decapods (*Decapoda*)

什 shí ❶〈书面〉ten:～百 tenfold or hundredfold /～九 nine tenths ❷ assorted; varied; sundry:家～ home utensils and furniture ❸〈旧语〉(of books) sections or chapters; ten poems or ten pieces of writing forming one volume:篇～ poems ❹〈旧语〉file of ten soldiers; squad

see also shén

什不闲儿 shíbùxiánr *also* "十不闲儿" shíbùxiánr *shibuxianr*, folk art form with singing to the accompaniment of musical instruments such as gongs, drums and cymbals

什件儿 shíjiànr ❶ duck or chicken giblets:烩～ braised giblets ❷〈方言〉metal accessories fixed on trunks, carriages, swords, etc.:黄铜～ brass accessories

什锦 shíjǐn assorted; mixed:～糖 assorted candy /素～ assorted vegetarian's delights /～拼盘 mixed cold dish /～果酱 mixed fruit jam

什锦锉 shíjǐncuò set of various types of files or rasps

什器 shíqì household utensils

什物 shíwù articles for everyday use; odds and ends; sundries:处理无用的～ dispose of the junk

什袭 shíxí 〈书面〉carefully pack and preserve:～而藏 carefully stored away

什叶派 Shíyèpài 〈宗教〉Shiite sect (of Islam)

什一税 shíyīshuì tithe

石 shí ❶ stone; rock; pebble:碎～ crushed stone (*or* rock); macadam /吸铁～ loadstone /滑～ talcum; talc /花岗～ granite /浮～ pumice /电～ calcium carbide /矸～ waste (stone) /化～ fossil /鹅卵～ pebble /矿～ ore /火～ flint/采～场 stone quarry /～墙 stone wall /～堤 stone embankment (*or* dyke) ❷ stone inscription:金～ inscriptions on ancient bronzes and stone tablets /～经 inscriptions of classics or scriptures on stone /勒～ inscribe on a stone tablet ❸ stone needle used in ancient times to cure diseases:药～ medicines and stone needles (for acupuncture) ❹ (Shí) a surname

see also dàn

石斑鱼 shíbānyú grouper

石板 shíbǎn ❶ slabstone; flagstone; flag:～路 flagging; flagstones /～桥 flagstone bridge /铺～ pave with flagstone /～蓝 slate blue /～瓦 roofing slate ❷ (for writing) slate:用～练字 practise writing on a slate

石版 shíbǎn 〈印刷〉stone plate:～印刷 lithographic printing

石版画 shíbǎnhuà lithograph

石碑 shíbēi stone tablet; stele:在墓前竖块～ erect a stone tablet before a grave

石笔 shíbǐ slate pencil

石壁 shíbì rock cliff:～上面刻着各种栩栩如生的佛像。The cliff side was carved with various kinds of life-like Buddhist figures. /更立西江～,截断巫山云雨,高峡出平湖。Wall of stone will stand upstream to the west, To hold back Wushan's clouds and rain Till a smooth lake rises in the narrow gorges.

石鳖 shíbiē 〈动物〉chiton

石菖蒲 shíchāngpú 〈植物〉grass-leaved sweetflag (*Acorus gramineus*)

石沉大海 shíchéndàhǎi (disappear) like a stone dropped into the sea:他这一走,如～,音讯全无。Like a stone dropped into the sea, he simply disappeared without a trace. *or* There has been no news whatever about him since he left.

石莼 shíchún 〈植物〉sea lettuce (*Ulva lactuca*)

石达开 Shí Dákāi Shi Dakai (formerly translated as Shih Ta-K'ai, 1831-1863), one of the leaders of the Taiping Heavenly Kingdom

石担 shídàn 〈体育〉barbell with stone weights

石刁柏 shídiāobǎi 〈植物〉asparagus (*Asparagus officinalis*)

石貂 shídiāo 〈动物〉stone marten (*Martes foina*)

石雕 shídiāo stone carving; stone sculpture:擅长～ be skilled in stone carving (*or* sculpture) /～像 stone statue

石碓 shíduì treadle-operated tilt hammer for hulling rice

石墩 shídūn carved block of stone used as a stool

石蛾 shí'é caddisfly

石耳 shí'ěr rock tripe (*Umbilicaria*)

石方 shífāng cubic metre of stonework:土～ earth and stone work /一万～ ten thousand cubic metres of stonework

石坊 shífāng stone memorial archway or gateway

石舫 shífǎng stone or marble boat (in gardens)

石膏 shígāo gypsum; plaster stone:生～ gypsum plaster stone /熟～ plaster; plaster of Paris /他右腿上了～。His right leg was in a plaster cast.

石膏绷带 shígāo bēngdài plaster bandage

石膏床 shígāochuáng plaster bed

石膏粉 shígāofěn gesso

石膏灰胶纸夹板 shígāohuījiāozhǐ jiābǎn 〈建筑〉sheetrock

石膏夹板 shígāo jiābǎn plaster splint

石膏浆 shígāojiāng gypsum plaster

石膏像 shígāoxiàng plaster statue; plaster figure

石工 shígōng ❶ masonry ❷ *also* "石匠" stonemason; mason

石拱桥 shígǒngqiáo stone arch bridge

石鼓文 shígǔwén 〈考古〉inscriptions on drum-shaped stone blocks believed to have been made during the Warring States Period

石棺 shíguān sarcophagus

石磙 shígǔn *also* "碌碡" liùzhou stone roller

石海 shíhǎi 〈地质〉felsenmeer

石河 shíhé 〈地质〉rock stream

石斛 shíhú 〈中医〉noble dendrobium (*Dendrobium nobile*), the stem of which is used as medicine

石花菜 shíhuācài agar-agar, a kind of seaweed; agar (*Gelidium cartilagineum*)

石花胶 shíhuājiāo *also* "琼脂" qióngzhī;"洋粉" yángfěn agar-agar, a kind of jelly or powder extracted from the seaweed

石化 shíhuà 〈地质〉petrify; lithify:～林 Petrified Forest (in eastern Arizona, USA)

石化作用 shíhuà zuòyòng petrifaction

石灰 shíhuī lime:生～ calcium lime; caustic (*or* quick) lime /熟～ white (*or* slaked, *or* drowned) lime /～熔烧 lime-roasting

石灰华 shíhuīhuá *also* "钙华" gàihuá 〈地质〉travertine; tufa

石灰浆 shíhuījiāng lime white

石灰砂浆 shíhuī shājiāng lime mortar

石灰石 shíhuīshí lime-rock; limestone

石灰水 shíhuīshuǐ limewater

石灰水泥 shíhuī shuǐní 〈建筑〉grappler cement:～砂浆 lime-and-cement mortar

石灰岩 shíhuīyán limestone

石灰窑 shíhuīyáo lime-burning kiln; lime-kiln

石灰质 shíhuīzhì 〈地质〉calcareous; calcarious:～土 calcareous soil

石灰质砂岩 shíhuīzhì shāyán calcareous sandstone

石火 shíhuǒ flash of flint sparks — the shortness or brevity of life

石鸡 shíjī 〈动物〉chukar

石级 shíjí stone stairs or steps

石家庄 Shíjiāzhuāng Shijiazhuang, the capital of Hebei Province

石见穿 shíjiànchuān *also* "石打穿";"紫参" zǐshēn *Salvia chinensis*

石匠 shíjiang stonemason; mason

石蜐 shíjié *also* "龟足" guīzú *Pollicipes mitella*, a kind of marine crustacean

石芥花 shíjièhuā toothwort

石经 shíjīng ❶ Confucian classics engraved on stone tablets (usually by orders of emperors) ❷ Buddhist sutras engraved on stone tablets

石决明 shíjuémíng 〈中药〉abalone shell used as medicine

石坎 shíkǎn ❶ regulating dam built of stone ❷ steps cut into a rocky mountain; stone-hewn steps

石刻 shíkè carved stone; stone-engraving; stone inscription:～文字 inscriptions on carved stone /山崖上发现了古代～。Ancient inscriptions were discovered on a cliff.

石窟 shíkū rock cave; grotto:～寺 cave temple /龙门～ Longmen Grottoes (at Luoyang, Henan Province) /云冈～ Yungang Grottoes (at Datong, Shanxi Province)

石窟画 shíkūhuà cave painting

石块 shíkuài (piece of) stone:～切割机 stone-cutter /用～垒墙 build a wall with stones /示威者向警察扔～。The demonstrators threw rocks at the police.

石砬子 shílázi *also* "石头砬子"〈方言〉projecting rock; crag; boulder
石蜡 shílà paraffin wax:～试验 paraffin test /用～封果酱罐子 seal jars of jam with paraffin wax
石蜡烃 shílàtīng alkane paraffin hydrocarbon
石蜡油 shílàyóu paraffin oil
石雷 shíléi stone-shelled mine (used by people in revolutionary base areas during the War Against Japanese Aggression, 1937-1945)
石砾 shílì gravel; shingle
石栗 shílì 〈植物〉candlenut:～树 candlenut tree
石料 shíliào (as raw material) stone; rock:～堆 rockpile /人造～ imitation stone or rock (used as building material)
石林 Shílín Stone Forest, in Lunan County (路南县) of Yunnan Province
石流 shíliú 〈地质〉rock stream; rock glacier
石硫合剂 shíliú héjì 〈农业〉lime sulfur:～是一种有效的杀虫剂。Lime sulfur is an effective insecticide.
石硫磺 shíliúhuáng *also* "硫磺" liúhuáng 〈中医〉sulphur
石榴 shíliu 〈植物〉pomegranate (*Punica granatum*):～花开红艳艳。When pomegranates blossom, they are a blaze of brilliant red.
石榴红 shíliuhóng garnet (colour); garnet-red
石榴裙 shíliuqún garnet-red skirt (usu. used to refer to a woman's charms):拜倒在她的～下 prostrate oneself before a woman's garnet-red skirt — be captivated by her beauty
石榴石 shíliushí 〈矿业〉garnet:～砂纸 garnet paper
石榴属 shíliushǔ 〈植物〉*Punica*
石龙芮 shílóngruì *Ranunculus sceleratus*
石龙子 shílóngzǐ 〈动物〉skink (any of the family of lizards):～科 *Scincidae* /～属 *Eumeces*
石绿 shílǜ green pigment made from malachite; mineral green
石煤 shíméi bone coal
石棉 shímián asbestos:～制品 asbestos product /～手套 asbestos gloves
石棉癌 shímián'ái 〈医学〉asbestos cancer
石棉板 shímiánbǎn 〈建筑〉asbestos board
石棉布 shímiánbù asbestos cloth
石棉衬里 shímián chènlǐ 〈机械〉asbestos lining
石棉肺 shímiánfèi 〈医学〉asbestosis
石棉瓦 shímiánwǎ (short for 石棉水泥瓦)〈建筑〉fibrotile; asbestos shingle; asbestos tile
石末沉着病 shímò chénzhuóbìng *also* "硅肺" guīfèi silicosis
石漠 shímò rock desert; stony desert
石墨 shímò graphite:涂～ cover with graphite; graphitize
石墨电极 shímò diànjí graphite electrode
石墨坩埚 shímò gānguō black-lead crucible
石墨减速剂 shímò jiǎnsùjì 〈核物理〉graphite moderator
石墨慢化反应堆 shímò mànhuà fǎnyìngduī 〈核物理〉graphite moderated reactor
石墨气冷反应堆 shímò qìlěng fǎnyìngduī 〈核物理〉gas-graphite reactor
石墨润滑剂 shímò rùnhuájì graphite lubricant
石墨纤维 shímò xiānwéi graphite fibre
石墨铀堆 shímòyóuduī 〈核物理〉graphite-uranium pile
石墨炸弹 shímò zhàdàn 〈军事〉graphite bomb
石磨 shímò millstone
石楠 shínán 〈植物〉Chinese photinia (*Photinia serrulata*)
石脑油 shínǎoyóu naphtha
石女 shínǚ woman with a hypoplastic vagina
石破天惊 shípò-tiānjīng rock-shattering and heaven-shaking — (of music, writing, etc.) remarkably original and forceful; staggering:这位教授在学术研究中每多～之语，皆能发人神智。In his academic research, the professor has made many original and penetrating remarks which were quite thought-provoking.
石栖动物 shíqī dòngwù 〈动物〉petrocoles
石器 shíqì stone implement; stone artifact; stone vessel:古墓中发现有各种～。Various kinds of stone artifacts were discovered in the ancient tomb.
石器时代 shíqì shídài 〈考古〉Stone Age:旧～ Paleolithic (*or* Old Stone) Age; Paleolithic Period /新～ Neolithic (*or* New Stone) Age; Neolithic Period /中～ Mesolithic Age; Mesolithic Period /～之后是青铜时代。The Stone Age was followed by the Bronze Age.
石桥湛山 Shíqiáozhànshān Ishibashi Tanzan (1884-1973), Japanese Prime Minister (1956-1957)
石青 shíqīng azurite (a blue pigment made of azure stone for use in traditional Chinese painting)
石蕊 shíruǐ ❶〈植物〉reindeer lichen; reindeer moss ❷〈化学〉litmus:～蓝 litmus blue /～试验 litmus test
石蕊试纸 shíruǐ shìzhǐ litmus paper
石山羊 shíshānyáng mountain goat; rocky mountain goat; *Oreamnos americanus*
石生植物 shíshēng zhíwù chomophyte
石首鱼 shíshǒuyú 〈动物〉croaker; surf fish:～科 *Sciaenidae* /～属 *Sciaena* /黄鱼是我国沿海常见的一种～。The yellow croaker is a common surf fish found in China's coastal seas.
石松 shísōng 〈植物〉club moss; lycopod; *Lycopodium clavatum*:～粉 lycopodium powder
石松鼠 shísōngshǔ 〈动物〉rock squirrel (*Sciurotamias davidianus*)
石蒜 shísuàn 〈植物〉short-tube lycoris (*Lycoris radiata*), whose stem and roots are used as medicine:红白两色的～花 red and white flowers of short-tube lycoris
石髓 shísuǐ stalactite
石笋 shísǔn 〈地质〉stalagmite:岩洞中～林立。There is a forest of stalagmites in the cave.
石锁 shísuǒ 〈体育〉stone dumbbell in the form of an old-fashioned padlock
石胎 shítāi 〈医学〉lithopedion
石炭 shítàn 〈旧语〉coal
石炭纪 Shítànjì 〈地质〉Carboniferous Period
石炭酸 shítànsuān 〈化学〉carbolic acid; phenol
石炭系 Shítànxì 〈地质〉the Carboniferous:～的煤层 Carboniferous coal beds; Carboniferous seams of coal
石涛 Shí Tāo *also* "原济" Yuánjì Shi Tao (formerly translated as Shih T'ao, 1642-1707), a Buddhist monk and painter of early Qing Dynasty
石头 shítou stone; rock:～房子 stone house /～墙 stone wall /采～ quarry stones /凿～ cut stone /搬起～砸自己的脚 lift a rock only to drop it on one's own toes /心里好像一块～落了地 feel as though a load has been taken off one's mind; feel greatly relieved
石头掌 shítouzhǎng 〈植物〉living-rock cactus
石头子儿 shítouzǐr 〈口语〉small stone; cobble; pebble:我的鞋里有几粒～。Some pieces of grit have got into my shoes. /～那么点小事，不值得挂心。It isn't worth your while to worry about such a trifling matter.
石硪 shíwò flat stone rammer with ropes attached at the sides
石蟹 shíxiè fossil crab (as an ingredient in traditional Chinese medicine)
石盐 shíyán rock salt; halite
石燕 shíyàn 〈考古〉*Spirifer*
石羊 shíyáng *also* "岩羊" yányáng 〈动物〉bharal; blue sheep
石印 shíyìn lithographic printing; lithography:～印刷品 lithograph; lithoprint
石印机 shíyìnjī lithographic press
石印石 shíyìnshí lithographic stone
石印术 shíyìnshù lithography
石印油画 shíyìn yóuhuà oleograph
石印照相制版 shíyìn zhàoxiàng zhìbǎn lithophotogravure
石印纸 shíyìnzhǐ lithographic paper
石英 shíyīng quartz:乳～ milk quartz /紫～ violet quartz /～坩埚 silica crucible
石英玻璃 shíyīng bōli quartz glass
石英电子表 shíyīng diànzǐbiǎo *also* "石英表" quartz watch
石英电子钟 shíyīng diànzǐzhōng *also* "石英钟" quartz clock
石英晶体 shíyīng jīngtǐ quartz crystal
石英卤钨灯 shíyīng lǔwūdēng 〈摄影〉quartz tungsten halogen light
石英砂 shíyīngshā quartz sand; arenaceous quartz
石英谐振器 shíyīng xiézhènqì quartz resonator
石英岩 shíyīngyán 〈地质〉quartzite
石英质砂岩 shíyīngzhì shāyán quartzose sandstone
石蝇 shíyíng stonefly
石油 shíyóu petroleum; oil:沥青基～ asphalt-based petroleum /石蜡基～ paraffin-based petroleum /开采～ tap (*or* produce) oil /发现～ strike oil /～储藏量 oil reserve; oil deposit /海上～ offshore oil

石油柏油 shíyóu bǎiyóu 〈建筑〉petroleum tar
石油地质学 shíyóu dìzhìxué petroleum geology
石油工程 shíyóu gōngchéng petroleum engineering
石油工业 shíyóu gōngyè oil industry; petroleum industry
石油管路 shíyóu guǎnlù *also* "石油管道" petroleum pipeline
石油化工厂 shíyóu huàgōngchǎng petrochemical works
石油化学 shíyóu huàxué petrochemistry: ~产品 petrochemical products; petroleum chemicals /~工业 petrochemical industry
石油勘探 shíyóu kāntàn petroleum prospecting
石油蜡 shíyóulà petroleum wax
石油沥青 shíyóu lìqīng petroleum pitch
石油美元 shíyóu měiyuán petro-dollar
石油醚 shíyóumí petroleum ether
石油气 shíyóuqì petroleum gas: 液化~ liquefied petroleum gas (LPG)
石油输出国组织 Shíyóu Shūchūguó Zǔzhī *also* "欧佩克" Ōupèikè Organization of Petroleum Exporting Countries (OPEC): ~部长级会议 OPEC ministerial meeting
石油运移 shíyóu yùnyí oil migration
石油钻井 shíyóu zuànjǐng oil drilling well
石油钻台 shíyóu zuàntái derrick floor
石鱼 shíyú stonefish (*Synaceja verrucosa*)
石陨石 shíyǔnshí meteoric stone; stony meteorite
石陨星 shíyǔnxīng 〈天文〉aerolith
石凿 shízáo bolster; inch-tool
石指甲 shízhǐjia *also* "垂盆草" chuípéncǎo stringy stonecrop (*Sedum sarmentosum*)
石钟 shízhōng stone chimes
石钟乳 shízhōngrǔ *also* "钟乳石" stalactite: 岩洞顶上挂着形同冰凌的~。Stalactites, shaped like icicles, were hanging from the roof of the cave.
石竹 shízhú 〈植物〉China pink (*Dianthus chinensis*): ~科 caryophyllaceae /~木 pinkwood /~色 dianthus /香~ *also* "康乃馨" carnation /~红 carnation red
石柱 shízhù ❶〈地质〉stone pillar or column, formed when a stalactite joins a stalagmite in a cave ❷ stela
石子 shízǐ cobblestone; cobble; pebble: ~路 cobblestone street; cobbled road /愿作一粒铺路的~ be willing to serve the public like a paving cobblestone — be willing to work for a cause in an obscure and unselfish manner
石梓 shízǐ 〈植物〉gumhar (*Gmelina arborea*)
石作 shízuō 〈旧语〉stonemason's workshop
石作 shízuò masonry

炻 shí

炻器 shíqì ceramic product with qualities between porcelain and pottery; stoneware

鼫 shí 〈古语〉flying squirrel

湜 shí 〈书面〉(of water) limpid; clear

寔 shí 〈书面〉❶ place; lay: ~于平地 place sth. on the level ground ❷ real; true: 这些都是眼前~事。These were events which occurred right before our very eyes. ❸ this

时(時) shí

❶ time; times; days: 古~ in ancient times /旧~ in old times /唐~ during the Tang Dynasty /在校~ when at school /儿~ in one's childhood /那~ at that time; in those days /生逢其~ be born at the right time /盛极一~ be in vogue (for a time); be all the rage /此一~, 彼一~ what is right for one time may be wrong for another; times are different /何~返校? When do you return to school? ❷ fixed time: 按~上班 go to work on time /赴约从不准~ be never punctual for appointments /定~就寝 go to bed at a fixed hour ❸ season: 四~ four seasons /~货 goods of the season /应~水果 fruit in season ❹ current; present: ~下 at present; currently ❺ fashion: 入~ in vogue ❻ one of the 12 periods into which the day was divided in ancient times: 子~ 11 p.m. - 1 a.m. /丑~ 1-3 a.m. /寅~ 3-5 a.m. /卯~ 5-7 a.m. /辰~ 7-9 a.m. /巳~ 9-11 a.m. /午~ 11 a.m.-1 p.m. /未~ 1-3 p.m. /申~ 3-5 p.m. /酉~ 5-7 p.m. /戌~ 7-9 p.m. /亥~ 9-11 p.m. ❼ hour: 报~ (of clock) strike the hour; (of people) tell or announce the hour /从上午十~到下午三~半 from 10 a.m. to 3:30 p.m. ❽ opportune moment; opportunity; chance: 失~ lose the opportunity; miss the chance /千载一~ chance of a lifetime; chance in a million ❾ occasionally; now and then; from time to time: 不~之需 things which may be needed from time to time /学而~习之 learn sth. and review it every now and then ❿ (used in pairs) now... now...; sometimes... sometimes...: ~断~续 on and off /~快~慢 sometimes fast, sometimes slow /~起~伏 rise and fall at different times; have frequent ups and downs /~喜~忧 one's moods alternate between happiness and gloom ⓫〈语言〉tense: 现在~ present tense /完成~ perfect tense ⓬ (Shí) a surname

时报广场 Shíbào Guǎngchǎng Times Square, New York
时辈 shíbèi 〈书面〉well-known personages; figures of the time; contemporaries
时弊 shíbì social evils of the day: 抨击~ lash out at the social evils /他的批评切中~。His criticism of present-day evils hits home.
时变 shíbiàn ❶ changing situation; domestic or international developments: 通达~ keep abreast of the latest developments ❷ change of seasons
时病 shíbìng ❶ ills of the times; current evils: 针砭~ criticize the ills of the times ❷ seasonal ailment
时不可失 shíbùkěshī must not let slip an opportunity: ~, 机不再来。Opportunity knocks only once. *or* Opportunity does not wait.
时不时 shíbùshí 〈方言〉from time to time; every now and then: 我们~地碰碰头。We meet once in a while. /我~去看场电影。I go to the cinema from time to time. /他~去探望老母亲。He visits his elderly mother every now and then.
时不我待 shíbùwǒdài time and tide wait for no man: 任务紧迫, ~。As the task is urgent, we can't afford to wait.
时不我与 shíbùwǒyǔ *also* "岁不我与" suìbùwǒyǔ time has run out; we have missed a golden opportunity, and we can only chew the bitter cud of regret
时不宜迟 shíbùyíchí there is no time to lose: 抢救大熊猫, ~。There is no time to be lost in rescuing the giant panda.
时不再来 shíbùzàilái once lost the opportune moment will not come again
时不常儿 shíbuchángr 〈方言〉often; from time to time: 他~来串门聊天儿。From time to time he would drop in for a chat.
时差 shíchā ❶〈天文〉equation of time ❷ time difference; jet lag: 适应~ get accustomed to the time difference /受~的影响 be affected by jet lag /你~倒过来了吗? Have you got over your jet lag? /两国间的~为七小时。The time difference between the two countries is seven hours.
时差反应 shíchā fǎnyìng jet lag; jet fatigue
时常 shícháng often; frequently; again and again: 我~来打扰你, 很不好意思。I am very sorry to have troubled you so often. /你~来帮助我, 我很感激。I am very obliged to you for the kind help you have accorded me from time to time.
时辰 shíchen ❶ one of the 12 two-hour periods into which the day was traditionally divided, each being given the name of one of the 12 Earthly Branches: 约莫有两个~ for about 4 hours ❷ time; right time: ~不到。It is not yet time. /~不早了。It is getting late.
时代 shídài ❶ age; era; epoch: 青铜~ Bronze Age /三国~ period of the Three Kingdoms /维多利亚~ Victorian Age /动荡的~ turbulent times /~精神 spirit of the times; zeitgeist /一项划~的发现 epoch-making discovery /~潮流 trend of the times; tendency of the day /开辟人类历史的新~ usher in a new era (*or* epoch) in human history /跟上~ keep abreast of the times /~不同, 风气不同。Other times, other manners. ❷ period in one's life; years: 青年~ youth /少年~ adolescence; boyhood /儿童~ childhood /少女~ girlhood /大学~ college years /一生中的黄金~ golden times in one's life /艰难的~ hard times
时代周刊 Shídài Zhōukān *Time*, a news weekly published in the United States since 1923
时点 shídiǎn point of time; exact time up to a certain point
时调 shídiào popular folk tunes or ditties (some of which have developed into folk singing with orchestral accompaniment): 江苏~ Jiangsu tunes
时段 shíduàn period of time: 秋季是该市旅游的黄金~。Autumn is the city's best tourist season.
时而 shí'ér ❶ from time to time: 远处~传来歌声。Sounds of

singing could be heard from afar every now and then. ❷(used in pairs) now... now...; sometimes... sometimes...:初秋时节,～热,～冷,气候变化无常。The weather is fickle in early autumn — one moment it's quite warm, the next it becomes chilly.

时分多址 shífēn duōzhǐ 〈信息〉time division multiple access (TDMA)

时分 shífèn time:午夜～ at midnight /黎明～ at dawn; at daybreak /掌灯～ at dusk; at twilight /三更～ at the third watch; in the dead of the night

时乖运蹇 shíguāi-yùnjiǎn *also* "时乖命蹇" down on one's luck; have the hand of fate against one; be born under an unlucky star:他～,只得以年老多病为理由,提出辞职。He had a run of bad luck and had to resign on the grounds of age and failing health.

时光 shíguāng ❶ time:消磨～ while away one's time /～还早。It's still early. ❷ period:他是抗日战争～入党的。He joined the Party during the Anti-Japanese War. ❸times; years:度过一段极为快乐的～ have a jolly good time / 过去的美好～ good old days /最辉煌的～ finest hour

时过境迁 shíguò-jìngqiān circumstances change with the passage of time; times have passed, and circumstances have altered:～,这部书现在已经无人过问了。With the passage of time the book finds very few readers now. /虽然已经～,但我仍清楚地记着那美好的岁月。I still recall vividly those wonderful days although a good deal of change has taken place since then.

时号 shíhào time signal

时好 shíhào fashion; craze; fad

时候 shíhou ❶ (the duration of) time:收割的～ harvest time /他去了多少～? How long has he been away? /他的好～已经过去了。His halcyon days are over. ❷ (a point in) time; moment:就在这～ just at this moment /他来的正是～。He came in the nick of time. /是～了,该走了。It is time we left.

时会 shíhuì special circumstances at the time:迫于～ as a result of the prevailing circumstances

时或 shíhuò from time to time; every now and then:他在院子里来回走着,～抬起头来望着星空。While pacing back and forth in the courtyard, he looked up at the starry sky from time to time.

时机 shíjī opportunity; opportune moment:错过～ miss a chance /珍惜～ treasure the opportunity /选择～ choose the right time or moment /～一到 when the time comes; at the opportune moment /在适当的～说适当的话 say the right thing at the right time /这一步,～选择得好! That was a well-timed move. /掌握～很重要。Timing is important.

时计 shíjì 〈天文〉chronometer; time-piece

时际 shíjì time; period; occasion:朋友们通常在节日的～聚在一起。Friends usually get together on festive occasions.

时季 shíjì season:割早稻的～ season for harvesting early rice

时价 shíjià current price:季节不同,蔬菜的～也不一样。The prices of vegetables vary from season to season.

时间 shíjiān ❶ (the concept of) time:～观念 sense of time /～与空间 time and space /这一设计经受了～的考验。This design has stood the test of time. ❷ (the duration of) time:办公～ office hours /业余～ spare time /夏令～ summer time /缩短所需的～ cut down the time required /获得喘息的～ gain breathing space /要多少～? How long will it take? /～剩下不多了。There isn't much time. ❸ (a point in) time:北京～15 点 15:00 Beijing time /出发～ departure time /～已到。Time is up.

时间表 shíjiānbiǎo timetable; schedule

时间词 shíjiāncí 〈语言〉temporal words:时间连接词 temporal conjunction

时间效率 shíjiān xiàolǜ time efficiency

时间性 shíjiānxìng timeliness:这种文章～强,要赶快刊出。Topical articles have to be published in time. /这件工作没有什么～,可以慢慢去做。You may take your time, for there is no deadline for this job.

时间知觉 shíjiān zhījué 〈心理〉time perception

时艰 shíjiān 〈书面〉difficult times; hard times; national crisis:共济～ work together to tide over current difficulties

时角 shíjiǎo 〈天文〉hour angle

时节 shíjié ❶ season:秋收～ autumn harvest season /春播～ spring-sowing season /清明～ around the Qing Ming festival /仲夏～ during mid-summer /金秋～ golden autumn season /三十一年还旧国,落花～读华章。Back in the old capital after thirty-one years, At the season of falling flowers I read your polished lines. ❷ time:岁月不居,～如流。Seasons succeed each other and time flies.

时局 shíjú current political situation:扭转～ reverse the course of events; bring about a change in the current situation /～动荡不安。The situation was volatile. /～孕育着危机。The situation was pregnant with danger.

时刻 shíkè ❶ hour; moment; occasion:关键～ critical moment /在这个庄严的～ on this solemn occasion; at this solemn hour /一生中最幸福的～ happiest moment of one's life /在重大的历史～ at an important historical juncture ❷ constantly; always; at all times:～保持清醒的头脑 always keep a cool head /时时刻刻关心群众利益 constantly keep the people's interest at heart /～不忘自己是人民的勤务员。Never forget for a single moment that you are a servant of the people.

时刻表 shíkèbiǎo timetable; schedule:作息～ daily schedule /火车～ railway timetable; train schedule /夏令～ summer timetable (*or* schedule)

时空 shíkōng time and space:～关系 relation between time and space

时款 shíkuǎn fashion:～的衣着 fashionable dress; modish clothes

时来运转 shílái-yùnzhuǎn fortune is smiling at sb.; time has moved in one's favour:他终于～,由职员提升为经理。The wheel of fortune had turned in his favour; he was promoted from a clerk to a manager.

时令 shílìng season:正当～ be in season /不合～ be out of season /～的变化 change of the seasons /～已交初冬。It is already early winter.

时令 shíling 〈方言〉*see* "时令病"

时令病 shílìngbìng seasonal disease

时令不正 shílìng-bùzhèng abnormal or unseasonable weather:目下～,三伏天这么凉。The weather is a bit abnormal. It's much too chilly for mid-summer.

时令河 shílìnghé seasonal river

时流 shíliú 〈书面〉contemporaries; scholars of the times

时论 shílùn public opinion of the time

时髦 shímáo fashionable; stylish; latest:衣着～ be fashionably dressed /赶～ keep up with the fashion; follow the fashion /～的话题 topic of the day /短裙不再～。Short skirts are no longer in vogue. /眼下穿长筒靴极为～。High boots are all the rage right now.

时派 shípai ❶ fashion; prevailing custom or practice ❷ fashionable; stylish; in vogue

时评 shípíng commentaries on current events:写一篇国际～ write a commentary on the current international situation

时期 shíqī period; stage:新的历史～ new historical stage /过渡～ transitional period /殖民统治～ during the colonial rule /和平～ peacetime /战争～ wartime /鼎盛～ zenith of prosperity; height of power

时气 shíqi 〈方言〉❶ momentary luck:他真有～。He is really lucky. ❷ epidemic due to abnormal change of weather

时穷节乃见 shí qióng jié nǎi xiàn integrity stands out in times of adversity; adversity brings out the best in man

时区 shíqū time zone:北京处在东八～。Beijing is located in the eighth time zone east of Greenwich.

时圈 shíquān hour circle

时人 shírén ❶ people of our time; contemporaries:～有诗为证。We can quote poems by our contemporaries as evidence. ❷〈旧语〉people most active for the period

时日 shírì ❶ time; date:他离家颇有～了。He has been away from home for quite some time. /假以～,此项措施定可见效。Given time, this measure will prove effective. ❷ relatively long period of time:尚需～ require more time

时尚 shíshàng fashion; vogue; fad:开创新～ set new fashions (*or* fads) /穿着合乎～ dress in fashion /穿西装成了一种～。Western-style clothes are in vogue.

时时 shíshí often; constantly; again and again:～记起 often recall or call to mind /～告诫自己 constantly caution oneself against /～处处以身作则 set an example for others in all matters; practise what one preaches on all occasions

时世 shíshì ❶ times; era; epoch:艰难～ hard (*or* difficult) times ❷ present-day society:不识～ have little understanding of the contemporary society

时式 shíshì (of clothes, etc.) up-to-date style; latest fashion:～装潢 modish decoration /～服装 garments of the latest fashion

S

时事 shíshì current affairs; current events:请人作～报告 ask sb. to give a talk on current events /讨论国际～ discuss current international affairs /～手册 handbook on current affairs

时事通讯社 Shíshì Tōngxùnshè (Japan) Jiji News Agency

时势 shíshì current situation; prevailing circumstances; trend of the times:不明～ do not see the current situation clearly; be blind to the trend of the times; be not clear about the way things are going /合乎～潮流 keep up with the trend of the times /顺应～ move with the times

时势造英雄 shíshì zào yīngxióng the times produce their heroes; the hero is a product of his time:是英雄造时势,还是～? Is it the hero who makes the times, or do the times make the hero?

时俗 shísú prevalent custom of the time:～崇尚节俭。Thrift was the prevailing virtue of the day.

时速 shísù speed per hour; hourly speed:正常～ normal speed /最高～ maximum speed per hour /～限制 speed limit /保持55英里的～ keep to a speed of 55 miles per hour /客轮以平均25海里的～行驶。The passenger ship sails at an average speed of 25 nautical miles an hour.

时态 shítài 〈语言〉tense:～的呼应 sequence of tenses

时文 shíwén ❶ literary essays required at imperial examinations (particularity in reference to the eight-part essay, a literary composition prescribed for the imperial civil service examinations) ❷ popular literary style:这两年小品文成了～。The familiar essay has been all the vogue in recent years.

时务 shíwù prevalent circumstances; trend of the times:不识～ show no understanding of the times; do not know what's best for one /识～者为俊杰。Whosoever understands the times is a great man. *or* A wise man submits to circumstances.

时下 shíxià currently; at present; right now:～纯棉织物旺销。Pure cotton fabrics sell well at present.

时鲜 shíxiān (of vegetables, fruits, etc.) in season:～果蔬 fruits and vegetables just in season

时贤 shíxián 〈书面〉wise men of virtue and reputation of the time; eminent persons; public figures

时限 shíxiàn time limit; deadline:确定最后～ set final deadline /工程必须在～内完成。The project must be completed within the time limit.

时宪书 shíxiànshū 〈旧语〉almanac

时效 shíxiào ❶ effectiveness for a given period of time:标明药品的～ medicines marked with expiry dates ❷〈法律〉prescription; limitation:～中断 interruption of prescription /依据～取得财产 acquire property by prescription /诉讼～ limitation of actions ❸〈冶金〉ageing:～化 ageing

时效处理 shíxiào chǔlǐ ageing

时效法 shíxiàofǎ 〈法律〉statute of limitations

时效硬化 shíxiào yìnghuà 〈冶金〉age-hardening

时新 shíxīn stylish; fashionable; trendy:～服装 trendy clothes /～的式样 modern (*or* up-to-date) style /展销会上的女式服装都是～款式。Women's garments at the trade fair were quite stylish.

时兴 shíxīng fashionable; popular; voguish:现在桥牌很～。Bridge is now very popular. /你那种思想已经不～了。That concept of yours is out of date. /那时正～长裙子。Long skirts were then all the vogue.

时行 shíxíng see "时兴"

时序 shíxù course of the seasons; seasons; times:～推移,秋去冬来。With the change of seasons, autumn is gone and winter has now set in.

时序分析 shíxù fēnxī 〈商业〉time-series analysis

时序计算机 shíxù jìsuànjī time sequential computer

时彦 shíyàn 〈书面〉persons of ability and integrity; well-known public figures

时谚 shíyàn popular sayings of the time; prevailing mottos or proverbs

时样 shíyàng latest fashion:女式服装～变换频繁。Fashions in women's dress are constantly changing.

时宜 shíyí what suits the occasion:不合～ be not appropriate to the occasion; be out of keeping with the times; be inappropriate /切合～ be compatible with the times; be appropriate

时移势迁 shíyí-shìqiān with the passage of time, the entire situation has changed; times have changed, so have the circumstances:～,旧办法不灵了。Things are quite different now, and the old method won't work any more.

时移俗易 shíyí-súyì customs vary with the times

时议 shíyì 〈书面〉critical views of contemporary thinkers

时疫 shíyì epidemic

时雨 shíyǔ timely rain

时域 shíyù time domain

时誉 shíyù current reputation

时运 shíyùn luck; fortune:走～ have good luck

时运不济 shíyùn-bùjì have bad luck:～,命途多舛 be out of luck and ill-fated

时运亨通 shíyùn-hēngtōng have all the luck:他～,诸事顺遂。He has the best of luck, and everything goes well with him.

时针 shízhēn ❶ hands of a clock or watch ❷ hour hand:～指向八点整。The hour hand pointed exactly to eight. /把～往前(后)拨一小时。Set the clock or watch forward (backward) by an hour.

时政 shízhèng 〈旧语〉current political situation; current political affairs:陈述～利弊 present one's views on politics and government

时值 shízhí ❶〈乐器〉duration; time value ❷ current price or value

时钟 shízhōng clock:～刚敲过十二下。The clock has just struck twelve.

时装 shízhuāng ❶ fashionable dress; latest fashions:冬季～ winter fashions /～款式 fashion style /～杂志 fashion magazine ❷ modern clothing (in contrast to ancient costumes):有些人总不爱看～京剧。Some people do not like to see Beijing operas with players in modern costume.

时装表演 shízhuāng biǎoyǎn fashion show:～队 modelling team

时装模特儿 shízhuāng mótèr fashion model; mannequin

时装商店 shízhuāng shāngdiàn fashion house

时装设计师 shízhuāng shèjìshī fashion designer

时装展览 shízhuāng zhǎnlǎn fashion exhibition

埘(塒) shí 〈书面〉chicken roost built into a wall

莳(蒔) shí

see also shì

莳萝 shíluó dill (*Anethum graveolens*):～子油 dill seed oil

鲥(鰣) shí

鲥鱼 shíyú hilsa herring; reeves shad

拾[1] shí

❶ pick up (from the ground); gather; collect:～起手绢 pick up the handkerchief /～到钱包一个 find a purse left by sb. somewhere /～麦穗 glean stray ears of wheat /～柴禾 gather crop stalks (as fuel) /俯～即是 be extremely common; can be found everywhere ❷ put in order; clean:把苹果～进筐里 put the apples into a basket /把桌子～干净。Clean the table.

拾[2] shí

ten (used for the numeral 十 to avoid mistakes or alterations)

see also shè

拾波线圈 shíbō xiànquān 〈物理〉pick-up loop

拾掇 shíduo ❶ tidy up; clean up; put in order:饭后～餐具 tidy up after dinner /～房间 tidy (up) a room /～院子 clean up a courtyard /请把文件～一下。Please put the papers in order. /屋子里～得整整齐齐的。The room was kept clean and tidy. ❷ repair; mend; fix:～收音机 fix a radio /～钟表 repair watches and clocks ❸ settle with; take to task; punish:我非～～他不可。I must teach him a lesson.

拾荒 shíhuāng collect firewood and scraps:～度日 eke out one's livelihood by collecting scraps

拾芥 shíjiè 〈书面〉as if picking up a blade of grass from the ground; as easy as pie:视夺冠如～ regard the championship as an easy trophy for one

拾金不昧 shíjīn-bùmèi not pocket the money one picks up; return money found:学校表扬一批～的小学生。The school authorities have commended a number of pupils who returned the money they found.

拾零 shílíng news in brief; snippets of news; highlights:奥运会～ highlights of the Olympic Games

拾取 shíqǔ pick up; gather; collect:～花瓣 pick up petals /在沙滩上～贝壳 collect shells on a beach

拾趣 shíqù collect bits and pieces of sth. interesting (usu. used as titles):《熊猫~》*Panda Delights*
拾人涕唾 shírénțituò *also*"拾人唾余" repeat what others have said or written; parrot others' views; plagiarize:此书论从史出,非~者。Based on historical facts, the book is quite solid and original in its ideas.
拾人牙慧 shírényáhuì pick up remarks from others and pass them off as one's own:切忌~ never pick up sb.'s remarks and pass them off as samples of one's own wit or wisdom /此乃平庸之作,~而已。The work is rather mediocre and is a mere rehash of stale ideas.
拾物 shíwù lost articles found by other people
拾物招领处 shíwù zhāolǐngchù lost and found (office); lost property office
拾遗 shíyí ❶ appropriate lost property; pocket lost articles:道不~,夜不闭户(as evidence of good public order and high moral standards in society) articles left by the wayside are never appropriated and doors need not be bolted at night ❷ make good or make up for omissions
拾遗补阙 shíyí-bǔquē make good omissions and shortcomings
拾音 shíyīn pickup:~头 pickup head /~极限 pickup limit /~插头 phono plug /~插座 phono jack
拾音器 shíyīnqì 〈电学〉sound pickup; pickup; adapter:立体声~ stereo pickup /~放大器 pickup amplifier

食(❼蚀) shí ❶ eat:多~蔬菜,少~肥肉 eat more greens and less fat /~多倒胃口 overeating kills one's appetite /不~人间烟火 not eat human food; be other-worldly /不劳动者不得~。He who does not work, neither shall he eat. ❷ have one's meal:废寝忘~(be so absorbed as to) forget food and sleep ❸ live on:~天子俸禄 live on salaries granted by the emperor /自~其力 live by one's own labour (*or* by the sweat of one's brow) ❹ food; meal:主~ staple food /副~ non-staple food /面~ food made of wheat flour /素~ vegetarian food /肉~ meat /熟~ cooked food /零~ between-meal nibbles; snacks ❺ feed:鸡~儿 chicken feed ❻ edible:~油 edible oil; cooking oil ❼ eclipse:日~ solar eclipse /月~ lunar eclipse /全~ total eclipse /环~ annular eclipse /偏~ partial eclipse
see also sì
食变星 shíbiànxīng 〈天文〉eclipsing variable
食补 shíbǔ eat nutritious food:药补不如~。Taking food as tonic is better than taking tonic medicine.
食不甘味 shíbùgānwèi *also*"食不知味" eat without relish; have no appetite for food:寝不安席,~ sleep fitfully and eat without appetite
食不果腹 shíbùguǒfù have not enough to eat; be ill-fed:那时候穷人过着衣不遮体、~的生活。In those days, the poor had rags on their backs and little in their bellies.
食不下咽 shíbùxiàyàn unable to eat or swallow (food) — be heavy-hearted
食不厌精,脍不厌细 shí bù yàn jīng, kuài bù yàn xì very exacting about one's food (originally, the expression means just the opposite — eating rice not necessarily of the best quality nor meat finely minced)
食草动物 shícǎo dòngwù herbivorous animal; herbivore:牛羊同属~。Both cattle and sheep are herbivores.
食虫动物 shíchóng dòngwù insectivorous animal; insectivore:许多鸟类属~。Many birds are insectivores.
食虫虻 shíchóngméng robber fly
食虫目 shíchóngmù insectivora
食虫植物 shíchóng zhíwù insectivorous plant; carnivorous plant
食道 shídào *also*"食管"〈生理〉esophagus; gullet
食而不化 shí'érbùhuà eat without digesting — read without comprehension:学习理论知识,要避免~。In learning theoretical knowledge, one should avoid swallowing it without understanding.
食饵 shí'ěr bait (for fish)
食分 shífēn 〈天文〉magnitude of eclipse; degree of obscuration
食粪动物 shífèn dòngwù coprophagous animal:最名副其实的~要数屎壳郎虫了。The dung beetle is the most truly coprophagous animal.
食粪鱼 shífènyú scat
食俸 shífèng *also*"食禄"〈旧语〉salary:~一千石 with the salary of one thousand *piculs* of grain
食腐动物 shífǔ dòngwù saprophagous or saprozoic animal; scavenger
食古不化 shígǔ-bùhuà swallow ancient learning without digesting it; follow the ancients blindly:他的迂腐是由于~。His pedantry results from his uncritical acceptance of ancient learning.
食管 shíguǎn *also*"食道"〈生理〉esophagus; gullet:一根鱼骨卡在她的~里。A fishbone lodged in her gullet.
食管癌 shíguǎn'ái 〈医学〉cancer of the esophagus
食管痉挛 shíguǎn jìngluán esophagismus
食管镜 shíguǎnjìng esophagoscope:~检查 esophagoscopy
食管扩张 shíguǎn kuòzhāng 〈医学〉esophagectasia
食管旁囊肿 shíguǎnpáng nángzhǒng 〈医学〉paraesophageal cyst
食管切除术 shíguǎn qiēchúshù 〈医学〉esophagectomy
食管胃吻合术 shíguǎn wèi wěnhéshù 〈医学〉esophagogastrostomy
食管炎 shíguǎnyán 〈医学〉esophagitis
食管赘瘤 shíguǎn zhuìliú 〈医学〉esophageal neoplasm
食猴雕 shíhóudiāo 〈动物〉monkey-eating eagle
食火鸡 shíhuǒjī 〈动物〉cassowary
食积 shíjī 〈中医〉dyspepsia; indigestion
食既 shíjì 〈天文〉second contact of an eclipse
食尽鸟投林 shí jìn niǎo tóu lín when food is gone, birds return to the woods:好一似~,落了片白茫茫大地真干净! When the food is gone the birds return to the woods; all that's left is emptiness and a great void.
食径 shíjìng 〈天文〉eclipse path
食具 shíjù tableware; dinner service:一套~ dinner-set; set of tableware
食客 shíkè ❶ person sponging on an aristocrat; hanger-on (of an aristocrat):养了大批~ keep large numbers of hangers-on ❷ patrons or customers of a restaurant
食口 shíkǒu (of a family) number of people to provide for:家中~众多 have a large family to feed (*or* support)
食粮 shíliáng food grain; food:保证~的供应 ensure supplies of food grains /精神~ nourishment for the mind /煤是工业的~。Coal is the lifeblood of industry.
食量 shíliàng capacity for eating; appetite:~大 be a big (*or* heavy) eater /~惊人 have an enormous appetite /~小 be a light (*or* small) eater; have a small appetite
食疗 shíliáo dietotherapy; food therapy:对病人采用~ treat patients with dietotherapy
食料 shíliào foodstuff
食糜 shímí 〈生理〉chyme
食品 shípǐn foodstuff; food; provisions:罐头~ tinned (*or* canned) food /方便~ convenience food /家常~ homely food /速冻~ fast-frozen food /天然~ natural food /保健~ health food /营养~ nutritious food /代用~ substitute food /~杂货店 grocery /~加工 food processing /~保藏 food preservation /~储藏 food storage /~工艺 food technology
食品工业 shípǐn gōngyè food industry
食品规则 shípǐn guīzé *Codex Alimentarius* (the code of laws governing food standards, food hygiene, additives, etc.)
食品化学 shípǐn huàxué food chemistry
食品结构 shípǐn jiégòu composition of diet
食品添加剂 shípǐn tiānjiājì food additive
食品微生物学 shípǐn wēishēngwùxué food microbiology
食谱 shípǔ ❶ recipe; cookbook:家常~ everyday recipe /中国~ Chinese cookery book /按照~烹饪 follow a recipe ❷ menu:拟定~ plan (*or* draw up) a menu /一周的~ menu of the week /病号~ menu for invalids
食前方丈 shíqián-fāngzhàng have food spread out one hundred square feet in front — live in luxury; be in clover
食亲财黑 shíqīn-cáihēi 〈方言〉greedy and selfish; avaricious:千万别跟这种~的人交朋友。Take care not to befriend such a rapacious person.
食顷 shíqǐng 〈书面〉duration of a meal
食人俗 shírénsú cannibalism
食肉动物 shíròu dòngwù carnivorous animal; carnivore:狗、猫、狮子、老虎等均属于~。Dogs, cats, lions, tigers, and the like are carnivorous.
食肉目 shíròumù 〈动物〉carnivora
食肉寝皮 shíròu-qǐnpí want to eat sb.'s flesh and sleep on his hide — hate sb. so much as to want to tear him limb from limb:她痛恨这

恶棍，恨不得～。Her hatred for the villain was such that she wished she could hack him to pieces.

食肉植物 shíròu zhíwù carnivorous or insectivorous plant; insectivore

食少事烦 shíshǎo-shìfán eat little and overwork — won't live very long

食甚 shíshèn 〈天文〉 middle or maximum phase of an eclipse

食尸动物 shíshī dòngwù necrophage

食双星 shíshuāngxīng 〈天文〉 eclipsing binary

食宿 shí-sù board and lodging：安排～ make arrangements for board and lodging／提供～ provide lodging with meals／～自理 make one's own arrangements for room and board／～方便 have easy access to board and lodging; provide a convenient board and lodging service

食堂 shítáng mess hall; canteen：军官～ officers' mess／学生～ canteen for students／自助～ cafeteria／去～吃饭 go to the dining hall

食糖 shítáng sugar

食蚊鱼 shíwényú mosquito fish; gambusia

食物 shíwù food; victuals：高蛋白～ high-protein food／清淡的～ light food／营养丰富的～ nourishing (*or* nutritious) food／易变质的～ perishable food／猎取～ hunt for food／～循环 food cycle

食物变态反应 shíwù biàntài fǎnyìng food allergy

食物金字塔 shíwù jīnzìtǎ food pyramid

食物链 shíwùliàn *also* "营养链" yíngyǎngliàn food chain; food cycle

食物摄入 shíwù shèrù 〈动物〉 food intake：每日～量 daily food intake

食物污染 shíwù wūrǎn food pollution

食物中毒 shíwù zhòngdú 〈医学〉 food poisoning

食相 shíxiàng 〈天文〉 phase of an eclipse

食性 shíxìng ❶〈动物〉 feeding habits or patterns：动物种类不同，它们的～也各不相同。Feeding habits vary from animal to animal. ❷ one's preference for food：他一家三口，～各不相同。The three members of the family each have a different taste for food.

食血动物 shíxuè dòngwù sanguivorous animal; haematophagous animal

食言 shíyán break one's promise：决不～ never go back on one's promise; be as good as one's word

食言而肥 shíyán'érféi break one's promise out of selfish considerations; break faith with sb.：他是个有名的～者，如何能信任他呢？How can we trust him? He is notorious for breaking his promises whenever it suits him.

食盐 shíyán table salt; salt

食洋不化 shíyáng-bùhuà mechanically copy anything foreign

食蚁兽 shíyǐshòu anteater：～没有牙齿，它们用细长的舌头舔食蚂蚁。Anteaters have no teeth but use their threadlike tongues to lick ants.

食蚁针鼹 shíyǐ zhēnyǎn (ant-eating) echidna

食邑 shíyì *also* "食土"〈历史〉 fief town

食用 shíyòng ❶ eat; consume：面包已不新鲜，不宜～。The bread is not fresh enough for human consumption.／这种食物不易消化，老年人不便～。This stuff is difficult to digest and not fit for old people. ❷ edible：～植物 edible plant; food plant／～蜗牛 edible snail／～鱼 food fish

食用碱 shíyòngjiǎn baking soda

食用菌 shíyòngjùn edible fungus

食用色素 shíyòng sèsù food colouring

食油 shíyóu edible oil; cooking oil

食玉炊桂 shíyù-chuīguì food as costly as jade and firewood as precious as cassia — extremely high cost of living

食郁 shíyù 〈中医〉 indigestion; dyspepsia

食欲 shíyù appetite：～旺盛 have a good appetite／促进～ sharpen (*or* whet) (one's) appetite／～不振 have a poor appetite; have a jaded appetite

食欲障碍 shíyù zhàng'ài 〈医学〉 dysorexia; appetite disorder

食之无味，弃之可惜 shí zhī wúwèi, qì zhī kěxī the food is not palatable enough, but one would hesitate to throw it away

食指 shízhǐ ❶ index finger; forefinger ❷〈书面〉 number of people in a family：～浩繁 have many mouths to feed／～众多 have a big family to support

食治 shízhì 〈中医〉 food therapy; diet therapy

食茱萸 shízhūyú 〈植物〉 ailanthus prickly ash (*Zanthoxylum ailanthoides*)

蚀 shí ❶ lose; erode; corrode：～光了本钱 lose all one's capital (in business)／久经风雨侵～ long eroded by wind and rain／铁易锈～。Iron corrodes easily.／酸会腐～金属。Acid eats into (*or* erodes) metal. ❷ eclipse

蚀本 shíběn lose one's capital; lose money in business：～出售 sell at a loss／～生意 business running at a loss; losing proposition; unprofitable deal／他不善经营，几次～。As he has no business sense, he has lost money in several deals.／你去经商，准定蚀光老本。It would be throwing away your capital if you were to go into business.

蚀变 shíbiàn alteration

蚀财 shícái lose property

蚀耗 shíhào lose; wear out：～了老本 lose one's capital

蚀刻 shíkè etching：铜版～ etching on copper sheet／～艺术 art of etching／～机 etching machine／～剂 etcher; etchant／～印刷 etch printing／～版 etching plate／～针 etching needle／～电路 etched circuit／～试验 etching test

蚀损 shísǔn lose; depreciate：上次出门做生意，他又～了不少钱。He lost quite a lot of money again on his last business trip.

shǐ

豕 shǐ 〈书面〉 pig; hog; swine

豕突狼奔 shǐtū-lángbēn *also* "狼奔豕突" rush like a boar and run like a wolf; run about like wild beasts; rampage in total disorder

史 shǐ ❶ history：古代～ ancient history／中世纪～ medieval history／近代～ modern history／现代～ contemporary history／编年～ chronicles; annals／断代～ dynastic history／通～ general history／简明～ concise (*or* brief) history／野～ unofficial records of history／秘～ secret history／思想～ history of ideas; intellectual history／家～ family history／有～以来 since the beginning of recorded history／名垂青～ be crowned with eternal glory in history; go down in history ❷〈古语〉 official in charge of historical records; official：太～ chief imperial historian／御～ imperial censor／女～ woman official ❸ (Shǐ) a surname

史不绝书 shǐbùjuéshū history abounds with such instances：统治集团内部父子兄弟相残的事～。History is full of patricide and fratricide among the ruling clique (*or* the royal family).

史部 shǐbù history as the second of the four divisions of ancient Chinese library collection

see also "四部" sìbù

史册 shǐcè historical records; annals; history：载入民族解放斗争的～ go down (*or* be recorded) in the annals of national liberation struggles／韦布作为第一个游过英吉利海峡的人而名垂～。Webb made history as the first man to swim across the English Channel.

史抄 shǐchāo extracts from history：唐代～ extracts from the history of the Tang Dynasty

史迪威 Shǐdíwēi Joseph Warren Stilwell (1883-1946), US general who served in China during World War II

史官 shǐguān official historian; historiographer

史馆 shǐguǎn office of the historiographer in ancient China

史话 shǐhuà historical account; historical narrative (usu. used as titles of books)：《辞书～》 *A Narrative History of Dictionaries*

史籍 shǐjí historical records; history：通晓～ be well-versed in historical records／整理～ edit historical records

史记 Shǐjì *Shi Ji* or *Historical Records*, by Sima Qian (司马迁, c.145 or c.135 -? BC) of the Western Han Dynasty

史迹 shǐjì historical site; historical relics：早期文明的～ relics of an early civilization／～的保护 preservation of historical sites

史剧 shǐjù historical drama or play

史可法 Shǐ Kěfǎ Shi Kefa (1601-1645), patriotic general of the Ming Dynasty, who died after Yangzhou(扬州) was captured by the Manchus

史料 shǐliào historical materials; historical data：收集～ gather historical data and materials／关于太平天国运动的丰富～ abundant historical materials on the Taiping Revolution

史略 shǐlüè outline of history; historical synopsis：《中国小说～》 *A Brief History of Chinese Fiction*

史论 shǐlùn essays on history; historical essay

史沫特莱 Shǐmòtèlái Agnes Smedley (1890-1950), US journalist and writer who wrote books about China's revolution, including *The Great Road* (a biography of Marshal Zhu De)

史评 shǐpíng historical criticism:撰写~ write historical criticism / 《六国论》是一篇著名的~。*On Six States* is a celebrated piece of historical criticism.

史前 shǐqián prehistoric:珍贵的~文物 precious relics of prehistoric times /~动物 prehistoric animal

史前考古学 shǐqián kǎogǔxué prehistoric archaeology

史前历史学 shǐqián lìshǐxué protohistory

史前人 shǐqiánrén prehistoric man

史前学 shǐqiánxué prehistory

史乘 shǐshèng 〈书面〉historical works; history

史诗 shǐshī epic; event resembling the epic in grandeur and scope:民族~ national epic /《伊利亚特》是一部惊天动地的英雄~。*Iliad* is a heroic epic of earth-shaking significance.

史识 shǐshí historian's knowledge and insight

史实 shǐshí historical fact:丰富的~ wealth of historical facts

史事 shǐshì what happened in history; historical events; history

史书 shǐshū historical records; history:编纂~ compile a history / 参考~ consult historical records

史坛 shǐtán historical circles; community of historians

史通 Shǐtōng *Comments on Works of History*, written by Liu Zhiji (刘知几) of the Tang Dynasty

史无前例 shǐwúqiánlì without precedent in history; unprecedented; unparalleled:~的盛况 spectacle without precedent in history; spectacle of unprecedented grandeur /其规模之大,是~的。It was unparalleled in scale.

史学 shǐxué science of history; historiography:~著作 historiographic works /~研究 study of historiography /~家 historian; historiographer

史帙 shǐzhì history; historical records

使[1] shǐ ❶ send; have (sb. do sth.):~某人去执行任务 send sb. on a mission /~人去请医生 send for a doctor ❷ use; employ; exert; apply:劲往一处~ direct all efforts towards one goal /~出一切办法 employ all available means /~完一卷胶卷 use up a whole roll of film /~高压锅做饭 cook rice in a pressure pot /~绝招 play one's best (*or* trump) card /能~一下你的自行车吗? May I use your bike? ❸ make; cause; help; enable:~工程蒙受巨大损失 cause enormous losses to the project /~他改变主意 make him change his mind /~合同作废 invalidate the contract /采取措施~企业恢复活力 take measures to enable the enterprise to recover its vitality (*or* to rejuvenate the enterprise) /这场雨~空气变得新鲜。The rain cleaned up the air. ❹ 〈书面〉if; supposing:纵~ even if; even though

使[2] shǐ envoy; emissary; messenger:特~ special envoy /公~ minister /大~ ambassador /信~ courier; messenger /出~国外 be accredited to a foreign country; be sent abroad as an envoy /遣~媾和 send an emissary to negotiate peace

使绊儿 shǐbànr *also* "使绊子" ❶ (of Chinese wrestling) trip the opponent with a leg trick ❷ injure others by devious (often covert) means; try to trip sb. up; put a spoke in sb.'s wheel:嘴上说话比蜜甜,暗中~算计人 talk with honey on one's lips while scheming against others in secret /他对新计划不满意,尽在暗中~。He was dissatisfied with the new plan and secretly did everything he could to obstruct it.

使不得 shǐbude ❶ cannot be used; be useless:情况变了,老办法~了。Since circumstances have changed, the old approach no longer works. ❷ be undesirable or impermissable; must not be done:你重感冒刚好,加班可~。You've just recovered from a bad cold; it won't do to work overtime.

使不惯 shǐbuguàn unfamiliar with; unaccustomed to:这种香皂我~。The toilet soap doesn't agree with me.

使不了 shǐbuliǎo ❶ more than one needs:这么多的碗我家~。My family doesn't need that many bowls. ❷ cannot use:计算机我~了。I don't know how to use the computer.

使臣 shǐchén envoy; diplomatic envoy; representative of a country sent abroad

使出 shǐchū use; exert; expend:~全力 exert oneself to the utmost /~最后的招数 play one's last card /~惯用的伎俩 be up to the same old trick

使出浑身解数 shǐchū húnshēn xièshù 〈俗语〉use all one's skill; do all one can:这盘棋,我~也还是战不过他。I couldn't beat him in the chess game despite my best effort.

使得 shǐde ❶ can be used; will work:虽然把儿断了,但茶壶仍~。Although the handle is broken, the teapot is still serviceable. /这台录音机~使不得? Does the tape-recorder work all right? ❷ will do; be feasible:这样做才~。This is the way to do it. /这个办法如何~? I don't think this method is feasible (*or* practicable). ❸ make; cause; bring about:~大家了解事实真相 make the facts (*or* truth) known to everyone /责任制的实施~生产有了很大的提高。The implementation of the responsibility system brought about a great increase in production. /是什么~他改变主意的? What made him change his mind? /他的一席话~我深受感动。I was deeply moved by his words.

使馆 shǐguǎn diplomatic mission; embassy:大~ embassy /公~ legation /各国驻京~ diplomatic missions in Beijing /~外交人员 diplomatic staff of a mission /~馆长 head of a mission /~馆舍 premises of a mission; chancellery

使坏 shǐhuài be up to mischief; play a dirty trick; create trouble:你又在使什么坏? What mischief are you up to again? /有人在我们背后~。Someone is making trouble for us behind our backs. /我不是存心给他~。I didn't mean to create difficulties for him.

使坏水儿 shǐ huàishuǐr supply evil ideas; make mischievous suggestions:他明装老实,暗地~。Putting on the appearance of a simple-minded man, he is hatching sinister plots secretly.

使唤 shǐhuan ❶ order about or around:一辈子听他妻子~ be at his wife's beck and call all his life /他把助手们~来~去,那架势真叫人看不入眼。The way he orders his assistants around has caused many eyebrows to be raised. ❷ use; manage; handle:~起来很容易 be easy to use (*or* handle) /这匹马不听生人~。This horse won't obey a stranger.

使唤丫头 shǐhuan yātou maidservant; maid

使假 shǐjiǎ use things of inferior quality to pass off as good ones; practise fraudulence

使节 shǐjié diplomatic envoy; envoy:各国驻华~ diplomatic envoys (accredited) to China /友好~ goodwill envoy; envoy of friendship / 文化~ cultural envoy /~旅行 diplomatic tour

使劲 shǐjìn exert oneself; make efforts:一齐~ exert strength in unison; work in concert /尽量~ exert all one's strength; do one's utmost /~跑 run as fast as one can /~哭 cry one's eyes out /~摇头 shake one's head vigorously /他使出吃奶的劲也搬不动这箱子。He strained every muscle to move the box, but in vain.

使君子 shǐjūnzǐ 〈中药〉fruit of Rangoon creeper (*Quisqualis indica*)

使力 shǐlì exert one's utmost; do sth. with might and main:~敲打 knock with all one's strength

使领馆 shǐ-lǐngguǎn diplomatic and consular missions; embassies and consulates:我驻美~ Chinese diplomatic and consular missions in the United States

使令 shǐlìng 〈书面〉❶ order about ❷ person to be ordered about; servant

使妈 shǐmā 〈方言〉maidservant; female attendant; maid

使命 shǐmìng mission:秘密~ secret mission /特殊~ special mission /肩负外交~前往伦敦 go to London on a diplomatic mission /完成历史~ accomplish a (*or* one's) historic mission

使女 shǐnǚ maidservant; housemaid; maid:作~ work as a maid

使气 shǐqì be swayed by personal feelings; lose one's temper:任性~ headstrong and easily swayed by personal feelings

使钱 shǐqián spend money:他~很大方。He is liberal with money. / 她再困难也不使别人的钱。However hard up she is, she would not use what is not her own money.

使然 shǐrán make it so; it's because:这家工厂效益不高,主要是体制~。The low efficiency of the factory is due to its structural defects. /这孩子之所以四体不勤,实为父母娇惯~。It's really the parents' pampering that has produced such a lazy child.

使生效 shǐ shēngxiào 〈法律〉bring into force; give effect to; validate

使失效 shǐ shīxiào 〈法律〉vitiate; invalidate; nullify

使徒 shǐtú 〈宗教〉apostle:~法规 apostolic canons /~宪典 apostolic constitutions

S

使徒公教会 Shǐtú Gōngjiàohuì 〈宗教〉Catholic Apostolic Church

使团 shǐtuán diplomatic mission; diplomatic corps: 参加～活动 attend functions of the diplomatic missions /～长 dean (*or* doyen) of the diplomatic corps

使性 shǐxìng *also* "使性子" 〈口语〉throw a tantrum; fly off the handle: 小时候,她特别爱～。She often threw a tantrum when she was a child. /有话慢慢说,何必～? Speak calmly if you have anything to say; why fly off the handle? /好啦,好啦,别～了。Come, come, don't be cross any more.

使眼色 shǐ yǎnsè wink: 我一个劲儿向你～,你没觉察到。I kept winking at you, but you did not notice it.

使羊将狼 shǐyángjiànglláng make a sheep lead a pack of wolves — doomed to failure; courting disaster

使役 shǐyì work (an animal): ～耕畜要得当。Draught animals must be used properly.

使用 shǐyòng make use of; use; resort to; employ: ～一切现有材料 employ all available materials /～计策 resort to stratagem /学会～微机 learn to use a personal computer /合理～人才 make rational use of talented people /他在工作中～了统计方法。He applied statistical methods in his work. /新装配线已投入～。The new assembly line has already gone into operation.

使用额 shǐyòng'é expenditures; disbursements

使用国 shǐyòngguó user state

使用价值 shǐyòng jiàzhí 〈经济〉use value: 具有很高的～ have high use value; be of great use

使用率 shǐyònglǜ rate of utilization

使用面积 shǐyòng miànjī 〈建筑〉usable floor area

使用权 shǐyòngquán 〈法律〉right of use; right to use sth.

使用寿命 shǐyòng shòumìng service life (of a machine, etc.)

使用说明书 shǐyòng shuōmíngshū operation instructions; user's manual

使用资本 shǐyòng zīběn capital employed

使者 shǐzhě emissary; envoy; messenger: 和平～ emissary of peace /友好～ goodwill messenger (*or* envoy)

S

驶

shǐ ❶ (as of a vehicle) go or pass quickly; speed: 顺风疾～ speed before the wind /飞～而去 speed by; fly past ❷ sail; drive; ride: ～出河湾 sail out of the estuary /沿公路行～ drive along a highway /谨慎驾～! Drive with caution! /机车～进车站。The locomotive pulled into the station. /公共汽车因机器故障停～。The bus is suspended for engine trouble.

驶离 shǐlí 〈航海〉layoff

矢[1]

shǐ arrow: 流～ stray arrow

矢[2]

shǐ take an oath; vow; swear: ～忠 vow one's allegiance /～死不二 pledge unswerving allegiance (*or* faith) unto death

矢[3]

shǐ excrement; faeces

矢不虚发 shǐbùxūfā *also* "矢无虚发" without a single arrow missing the target; with every arrow hitting the target

矢车菊 shǐchējú 〈植物〉cornflower (*Centaurea cyanus*)

矢口 shǐkǒu state emphatically; insist

矢口抵赖 shǐkǒu-dǐlài categorically deny (one's guilt or mistake): 在人证物证面前,他依然～。Despite all the witnesses and evidence, he refused categorically to admit his guilt.

矢口否认 shǐkǒu-fǒurèn flatly disavow: ～事先知道这个计划 categorically deny prior knowledge of the plan

矢量 shǐliàng *also* "向量" xiàngliàng 〈数学〉〈物理〉vector: ～比 vector ratio /～场 vector field /～功率 vector power /～空间 vector space /～图 vector diagram; vectogram /～分析 vector analysis /～尖头 terminus /风～ wind vector /切变～ shear vector

矢石 shǐshí (used as weapons in ancient battles) arrows and stones: 亲冒～ brave the arrows and stones in battle /～如雨。The arrows and stones came down like a shower.

矢志 shǐzhì pledge oneself; swear; vow: ～不屈 swear not to yield /～为国捐躯 pledge oneself to die for the country

矢志不移 shǐzhì-bùyí *also* "矢志不渝" vow to adhere unswervingly to one's chosen course; pledge steadfast devotion to a cause: 革命信念～ remain staunchly loyal to one's revolutionary faith

矢忠 shǐzhōng 〈书面〉swear to be loyal to: ～祖国 pledge loyalty to one's motherland

屎

shǐ ❶ excrement; faeces; dung; stool: 鸡～ chicken droppings /马～ horse dung /拉～ empty the bowels; shit /验～ stool examination /～尿 stool and urine ❷ secretion (of the eye, ear, etc.): 耳～ earwax /眼～ eye discharge; gum in the eyes

屎壳郎 shǐkelàng 〈方言〉dung beetle

屎坑 shǐkēng country-style public toilet; dung pit

屎粒化石 shǐlì huàshí 〈地质〉faecal pellets

屎盆子 shǐpénzi 〈方言〉〈比喻〉bad reputation; evil doing: 自己做的丢人事,哪能把～往别人头上扣! How can you shift on to another's shoulders the blame for your own disgrace!

屎棋 shǐqí *also* "臭棋" chòuqí 〈讽刺〉(of chess) rotten move

始

shǐ ❶ begin; commence; start: 周而复～ go round and begin again; go round and round; move in cycles /全～全终 stick to sth. to the very end; finish what has been started /自～至终 from beginning to end; from start to finish /～料不及 come as a surprise; be unexpected ❷ 〈书面〉only then; not...until: 展览至晚十时～毕。The exhibition was not closed until 10 p.m. /领带熨烫之后,～能恢复原状。Only after ironing can the tie be restored to its original shape.

始爆器 shǐbàoqì primer

始创 shǐchuàng originate; initiate; pioneer: 乒乓球运动～于十九世纪末。Table tennis as a sport was initiated towards the end of the 19th century.

始而 shǐ'ér 〈副词〉first; at first (usu. followed by 继而, 终于, etc.): ～惊愕,继而欢喜 first surprised, then pleased

始发站 shǐfāzhàn starting station; terminal: 这趟列车的～ starting station of the train /15 路公共汽车的～ terminal of Bus No.15

始沸点 shǐfèidiǎn bubble point

始基 shǐjī foundation; beginning: 他这篇短篇小说,奠定了创作事业的～。This short story laid the foundation of his career in creative writing.

始料 shǐliào original expectations: 工作进行的顺利为～所不及。The smooth progress in this work is something unexpected. *or* The work progressed more smoothly than expected.

始料所及 shǐliào-suǒjí as has been expected: 这些情况多为～。These developments are well within our expectations.

始乱终弃 shǐluàn-zhōngqì desert a girl after seducing her

始末 shǐ-mò start to finish; beginning and end; whole story: 事情的～ whole story from beginning to end /事故的～ ins and outs of an accident /我已经弄清楚了这一事件的～。I've found out what the affair was all about.

始新世 Shǐxīnshì 〈地质〉Eocene Epoch

始业 shǐyè beginning of a school year: ～式 inaugural ceremony for a new school year

始终 shǐzhōng from beginning to end; from start to finish; throughout: 我～反对这种做法。I'm against this practice from beginning to end. /物价～保持稳定。Prices remained stable throughout. /他一生～保持谦虚谨慎的作风。He remained modest and prudent all his life. /我～认为我们会成功的。I knew all along that we were going to make it.

始终不懈 shǐzhōng-bùxiè unremitting; indefatigable; tireless: ～地做好本职工作 make unremitting efforts to do one's work well /～地保持警惕 maintain unflagging vigilance; be always on one's guard (*or* alert)

始终不渝 shǐzhōng-bùyú unswerving; steadfast; constant: ～地坚持和平共处五项原则 adhere unswervingly to the five principles of peaceful co-existence /他对祖国对人民忠心耿耿,～。He remained loyal to his country and people to the end of his life.

始终如一 shǐzhōng-rúyī constant; unchanging; consistent: 他是中国人民～的朋友。He has been a consistent friend to the Chinese people. /她～地致力于科学研究。She devoted herself unremittingly to science. /多年来他朴实的文风～。He has adhered to a plain style of writing all these years.

始祖 shǐzǔ ❶ first ancestor; earliest ancestor: 人类的～ first ancestor of mankind ❷ originator or founder (of a school of thought, etc.): 屈原是"楚辞"的～。Qu Yuan is the father of Chu poetry. ❸ primitive animals

始祖马 shǐzǔmǎ eohippus; dawn horse (*Hyracotherium eohippus*)

始祖鸟 shǐzǔniǎo archaeopteryx

始作俑者 shǐzuòyǒngzhě creator of a bad precedent:～,其无后乎? Those who invented wooden or earthen figurines to be buried with the dead would have no male offspring — those who start a bad practice are guilty of a most heinous crime.

shì

室 shì ❶ room:教～ classroom /大教～ lecture hall /寝～ bedroom /浴～ bathroom; shower room /阅览～ reading room /会客～ reception room /起居～ sitting room ❷ administrative subdivision (of an agency, organization, institution, corporation, etc.); office: 办公～ office; administrative office; staff office /科～ sections and offices; basic-level administrative units /收发～ mailroom /医务～ clinic /教研～ teaching and research office (*or* department) /实验～ laboratory /电教～ audio-visual teaching laboratory (*or* office) /财务～ finance office (*or* section, *or* department) /编辑～ editorial office (*or* department) ❸ shop (in a hotel, department store, etc.): 美容～ beauty shop (*or* parlour, *or* salon) ❹ wife:妻～ wife /继～ second wife (after the first one dies) ❺ family:皇～ royal family ❻ cavity:脑～ ventricles of the brain ❼ one of the twenty-eight constellations

室间隔缺损 shìjiàngé quēsǔn 〈医学〉ventricular septal defect

室内 shìnèi indoor; interior:～运动 indoor sport /～网球场 indoor tennis court /～照明 interior illumination /～装潢 interior decoration /～健身脚踏车 exercycle

室内乐 shìnèiyuè 〈音乐〉chamber music

室内乐队 shìnèi yuèduì chamber orchestra

室内植物 shìnèi zhíwù house plant

室女 shìnǚ 〈旧语〉maiden; virgin

室女座 Shìnǚzuò 〈天文〉Virgo (one of the 12 zodiacal constellations)

室外 shìwài outdoor; outside:～活动 outdoor activities /～天线 outside aerial (*or* antenna)

市 shì ❶ market:菜～ food market /早～ morning market /集～ fair /黑～ black market /上～ be on the market; be in season ❷ buying and selling; business transaction:开～ (of a shop) reopen after a cessation of business; first transaction of a day's business /罢～ shopkeepers' strike /互～ trade with each other ❸ city; municipality:上海～ city of Shanghai; Shanghai municipality /都～ metropolis; big city /城～ city; town /～中心 city centre; downtown area /～政府 municipal government ❹ administrative units (i.e. ordinary cities as well as cities directly under the jurisdiction of the State Council) ❺ pertaining to the Chinese system of weights and measures: *see* "～里";"～寸"

市布 shìbù unbleached plain cotton cloth

市曹 shìcáo 〈书面〉❶ market place; downtown area ❷ officials in charge of shops and stores ❸ public square (where punishment of criminals was carried out in ancient times):斩于～ was beheaded in the public square

市廛 shìchán 〈书面〉stores in a market or street; bazaar

市场 shìchǎng marketplace; market; bazaar:买方～ buyer's market /卖方～ seller's market /劳务～ service market /黄金～ gold market /股票～ stock market /外汇～ foreign exchange market; international exchange market /现货～ spot market /期货～ futures market /房地产～ real estate market /超级～ supermarket /大型超级～ hypermarket /自由～ free market /农贸～ free market selling farm produce /整顿～ rectify (*or* straighten up) the market (including penalizing illegal business dealings) /扩大～ expand (*or* broaden, *or* extend) the market /控制～ control (*or* command) the market /操纵～ rig the market /垄断～ corner (*or* forestall) the market /搞活～ activate (*or* enliven, *or* invigorate) the market /～不景气 slump; recession /～供应紧张 strained market supply /～秩序 market order /～概况 market profile /～波动 market fluctuation /～繁荣。The market is flourishing. /～活跃。Business is brisk.

市场份额 shìchǎng fèn'é market share

市场管理 shìchǎng guǎnlǐ market management

市场供应 shìchǎng gōngyìng market supplies

市场行情 shìchǎng hángqíng market quotation

市场机制 shìchǎng jīzhì market mechanism

市场价格 shìchǎng jiàgé market price

市场进入障碍 shìchǎng jìnrù zhàng'ài barrier to entry

市场经济 shìchǎng jīngjì market-oriented economy; market economy

市场社会主义 shìchǎng shèhuìzhǔyì *also* "自由社会主义" zìyóu shèhuìzhǔyì market socialism

市场体系 shìchǎng tǐxì network of markets

市场调节 shìchǎng tiáojié regulation by market forces

市场细分 shìchǎng xìfēn 〈商业〉market segmentation; differentiated marketing

市场信息 shìchǎng xìnxī market information

市场需求 shìchǎng xūqiú market demand

市场预测 shìchǎng yùcè market forecasting

市场准入 shìchǎng zhǔnrù market access

市秤 shìchèng Chinese scale of weights

市尺 shìchǐ *chi*, a unit of length ($=\frac{1}{3}$ metre)

市寸 shìcùn *cun*, a unit of length, equal to 0.1 *chi* (市尺) or to 3.333 centimetres, or 1.312 inches

市撮 shìcuō *cuo*, a traditional unit of capacity, equal to 0.001 *sheng* (市升), or to 1 mililitre or 0.002 pint

市石 shìdàn *dan*, a unit of dry measure of grain (=1 hectolitre)

市担 shìdàn *dan*, a unit of weight (=50 kilograms)

市电 shìdiàn electricity produced mainly for lighting in city residential areas:～电源 municipal power supply

市斗 shìdǒu *dou*, a unit of dry measure for grain (=1 decalitre)

市恩 shì'ēn ingratiate oneself with; curry favour with

市房 shìfáng 〈方言〉house facing the street which can be converted into a shop

市分 shìfēn ❶ *fen*, a unit of length ($=\frac{1}{300}$ metre) ❷ *fen*, a unit of weight ($=\frac{1}{2,000}$ kilogram) ❸ *fen*, a unit of area (=0.0066 hectare)

市府 shìfǔ (short for 市政府) municipal government

市合 shìgě *ge*, a unit of dry measure for grain ($=\frac{1}{10}$ litre)

市棍 shìgùn rascals; scoundrels; riffraffs of a city or market place

市毫 shìháo ❶ *hao*, a unit of length ($=\frac{1}{30,000}$ metre) ❷ *hao*, a unit of weight ($=\frac{1}{200,000}$ kilogram)

市虎 shìhǔ 〈比喻〉rumours and slanders:遂怀～之疑 suspicion aroused by repeated rumours and slanders

市花 shìhuā flower of a city; city flower

市徽 shìhuī emblem of a city; city emblem

市惠 shìhuì 〈书面〉dispense favours in order to win popularity

市集 shìjí ❶ fair ❷ small town

市价 shìjià market price:～平稳。Market prices remain stable. /～暴涨。Market prices skyrocketed (*or* shot up). /～暴跌。Market prices plummeted. /～回升。Market prices are picking up (*or* rising again).

市郊 shìjiāo suburb; outskirts:住在～ live in a suburban district /近年来许多人都搬住～。In recent years many people have moved into the suburbs.

市街 shìjiē downtown streets

市斤 shìjīn *jin*, a unit of weight ($=\frac{1}{2}$ kilogram)

市井 shìjǐng 〈书面〉marketplace; town

市井无赖 shìjǐng wúlài street rough or thug

市井小人 shìjǐng xiǎorén philistine; vulgar villain

市井之徒 shìjǐngzhītú philistine; vulgar bumpkin

市侩 shìkuài vulgar and detestable person; philistine:一帮～ gang of philistines

市厘 shìlí ❶ *li*, a unit of length ($=\frac{1}{3,000}$ metre) ❷ *li*, a unit of weight ($=\frac{1}{20,000}$ kilogram)

市里 shìlǐ *li*, a unit of length (=0.5 kilometre)

市立 shìlì municipal:～学校 municipal school

市两 shìliǎng *liang*, a unit of weight ($=\frac{1}{20}$ kilogram)

市面 shìmiàn ❶ market:～上店铺林立,好不红火。Shops and stalls lined up in the market, a sign of brisk business. /他们都是～上的人,懂得什么叫商业信用。They are all business people, they know what business credibility means. ❷ market conditions; business situation:～繁荣。Business is flourishing. *or* The market is brisk. /～萧条。Business is slack. *or* The market is dull.

市民 shìmín urban residents, townspeople

市民文学 shìmín wénxué literature for burghers (in late medieval times); low-brow literature; plebeian literature

市亩 shìmǔ *mu*, a unit of area (=0.066 hectare)

市内电话 shìnèi diànhuà local telephone service; local (phone)

S

call

市钱 shìqián *qian*, a unit of weight (= $\frac{1}{200}$ kilogram)

市情 shìqíng ❶ general conditions of a city ❷ market conditions

市顷 shìqǐng *qing*, a unit of area (= 6.667 hectares)

市区 shìqū city proper; downtown area:～街道纵横。Streets criss-cross the city proper. /～至少有两个大型购物中心。There are at least two large shopping centres in the downtown area.

市区重建 shìqū chóngjiàn urban renewal

市日 shìrì (of townships) day of fair; fair day

市容 shìróng appearance of a city:参观～ visit places of interest in the city; go sightseeing in the city; have a look around the city /影响～ have an adverse effect on the general appearance of the city /北京的～更美了。As a metropolitan city, Beijing is becoming even more beautiful.

市勺 shìsháo *shao*, a unit of dry measure for grain, equal to 0.01 *sheng*

市升 shìshēng *sheng*, primary unit of dry measure for grain (= 1 litre)

市声 shìshēng street noise:恬静的乡村没有那种扰人的～。There is no annoying street noise (*or* din) in this quiet village.

市树 shìshù tree of a city; city tree

市丝 shìsī ❶ *si*, a unit of length (= $\frac{1}{300,000}$ metre) ❷ *si*, a unit of weight (= $\frac{1}{2,000,000}$ kilogram)

市肆 shìsì 〈书面〉shop; store

市委 shìwěi municipal Party committee:～机关 municipal Party organizations (*or* agencies) /～书记 secretary of the municipal Party committee

市引 shìyǐn *yin*, a unit of length (= 33.3333 metres)

市盈率 shìyínglǜ 〈金融〉price/earning ratio; P/E ratio

市用制 shìyòngzhì *see* "市制"

市长 shìzhǎng mayor

市丈 shìzhàng *zhang*, a unit of length (= 3.3333 metres)

市招 shìzhāo shop sign; signboard

市镇 shìzhèn towns; small towns

市政 shìzhèng municipal administration:～当局 municipal authorities /～建设 municipal construction; urban construction / ～债券 municipal bond (in the USA)

市政工程 shìzhèng gōngchéng municipal works; municipal engineering (project)

市制 shìzhì *also* "市用制" Chinese system of weights and measures

柿(梯) shì persimmon

柿饼 shìbǐng dried persimmon

柿蒂 shìdì 〈中药〉calyx and receptacle of a persimmon

柿漆 shìqī persimmon paint

柿霜 shìshuāng 〈中药〉powder on the surface of a dried persimmon

柿子 shìzi ❶ persimmon tree ❷ persimmon (fruit):这些～软而不涩。These are soft persimmons that leave no pucker in the mouth.

柿子椒 shìzijiāo sweet bellpepper

铈 shì 〈化学〉cerium (Ce)

谥(謚) shì ❶ title given to an emperor, noble, minister, etc. after his death for his achievements:～号 posthumous title /汉武帝～"武"。Emperor Wu of the Han Dynasty was given the posthumous title of "Wu" (mighty). ❷ call; name:～之为激进主义 call it radicalism

视(眡、眎) shì ❶ look; view:熟～无睹 pay no attention to a familiar sight; turn a blind eye to; ignore /怒～ glare at; glower at /正～ face squarely; look squarely at ❷ regard; look upon; treat:蔑～ despise; scorn; show contempt for /鄙～ disdain; despise; hold in contempt /重～ attach importance to; pay attention to; lay stress on /敌～ be hostile to /～为例外 make an exception of ❸ inspect; examine; watch:监～ keep sb. under surveillance /巡～ go on an inspection tour

视财如命 shìcái-rúmìng worship money as if it were one's life:他是个～的吝啬鬼。He is a miser who looks upon wealth as his life.

视差 shìchā 〈物理〉❶ visual error ❷ parallax:～角 angle of parallax

视察 shìchá ❶ inspect:～工作 inspect sb.'s work / ～基层 inspect the grass-roots units (*or* units at the grass-roots level) ❷ examine; look carefully at:～地形 examine (*or* survey) the terrain /～灾情 tour (*or* investigate) the afflicted areas; make an investigation of the damages caused by the disaster

视察团 shìchátuán inspection team; inspectorate

视察员 shìcháyuán inspector

视场 shìchǎng field of vision; (in optics) range of response

视唱 shìchàng sightsinging

视唱练耳 shìchàng liàn'ěr solfeggio

视程 shìchéng 〈气象〉visual range

视窗操作系统 shìchuāng cāozuò xìtǒng 〈信息〉Windows

视窗 98 shìchuāng Jiǔbā Windows 98, a computer software by Microsoft

视地平 shìdìpíng 〈天文〉apparent horizon

视而不见 shì'érbùjiàn look but see not; turn a blind eye to:要尊重事实,不能～。One should respect the facts, not shut one's eyes to them. /～,听而不闻 look but see not, listen but hear not — turn a blind eye or deaf ear to sth.

视轨道 shìguǐdào 〈天文〉apparent orbit

视角 shìjiǎo ❶ visual angle; angle of view ❷ angle from which one looks at a problem; approach; perspective:以一种新的～来观察这个问题 look at the matter from a new angle /作者善于从多种～反映客观世界。The writer is good at reflecting the objective world from different perspectives.

视界 shìjiè field of vision; visual field

视景 shìjǐng vista:飞机降落时,机场的～不断变换。The vista keeps changing before the eyes of the pilot while the plane is landing.

视距 shìjù apparent distance; stadia:～达一千米以上 apparent distance of over 1,000 metres /～不良 poor visibility /～一般 average visibility

视觉 shìjué 〈生理〉sense of sight; visual sense; vision:～敏锐 have an acute sense of sight; have a keen eyesight /～器官 visual organ /～缺陷 defects of vision

视觉感受器 shìjué gǎnshòuqì visual sensor

视觉污染 shìjué wūrǎn visual pollution

视觉误差 shìjué wùchā collimation error

视觉象 shìjuéxiàng 〈心理〉visual image

视觉印象 shìjué yìnxiàng 〈心理〉eye or visual impressions

视觉暂留 shìjué zànliú persistence of vision

视觉障碍 shìjué zhàng'ài trouble in one's eyesight; dysopia; dysopsia

视力 shìlì power of vision; eyesight:～好 have good eyesight /～差 have poor (*or* bad) eyesight /保护～ protect one's eyesight /丧失～ lose one's eyesight /老人～快不行了。The old man's eyesight is failing. /他的～提高了些。His eyesight has improved a little.

视力表 shìlìbiǎo visual chart

视力测验 shìlì cèyàn eyesight test

视力敏度 shìlì mǐndù 〈医学〉visual acuity

视亮度 shìliàngdù 〈天文〉apparent luminance; apparent brightness

视面 shìmiàn 〈天文〉visual magnitude

视频 shìpín 〈物理〉video frequency:～鉴别 video discrimination /～时差 video time-base /～增益 video gain

视频随机存取存储器 shìpín suíjī cúnqǔ cúnchǔqì 〈电子〉video ram (VRAM)

视如敝屣 shìrú-bìxǐ regard as a pair of worn-out shoes; cast aside as worthless; regard as of no importance:这些资料十分可贵,不应～,一焚了之。These data are too important to be regarded as worthless and be committed to the fire.

视如草芥 shìrú-cǎojiè *also* "视如土芥" regard as not worth a straw; look upon as dirt; consider sth. worthless

视如粪土 shìrú-fèntǔ look upon as filth and dirt; have the greatest contempt for:视功名如粪土 regard fame and power as beneath one's contempt

视如己出 shìrú-jǐchū regard sb. as one's own child; treat sb. as if he were one's own:把前妻之子～ regard her stepson as her own

视如寇仇 shìrú-kòuchóu regard or look upon sb. as one's enemy:视直言极谏者如寇仇 regard an out-spoken counsellor as a mortal foe

视若无睹 shìruòwúdǔ take no notice of what one sees; shut one's eyes to; be oblivious to; disregard:决不能对社会上的不良倾向～。We

should never turn a blind eye to the unhealthy tendencies in society.

视弱 shìruò have congenital weak eyesight

视色素 shìsèsù 〈生理〉visual pigment

视神经 shìshénjīng 〈生理〉optic nerve

视神经萎缩 shìshénjīng wěisuō optic atrophy

视神经炎 shìshénjīngyán optic neuritis

视事 shìshì 〈书面〉(of officials) attend to business after assuming office; assume office:就职～ take office and begin to attend to one's duties /因病不能～ unable to assume the duties of office because of illness

视死如归 shìsǐrúguī look upon death without flinching; meet one's death like a hero; face death unflinchingly:～的大无畏精神 indomitable death-defying spirit /三军之士～。Men of the three armed services were ready to lay down their lives for the cause.

视听 shì-tīng what one sees and hears; personal observation; mental horizons; public opinion:混淆～ throw dust in people's eyes; confuse the public; mislead the people /以正～ clarify matters to the public; ensure a correct understanding of the matter /组织赴经济特区参观,以广～ organize visits to the special economic zones in order to broaden people's horizons

视听电话 shì-tīng diànhuà video telephone; videophone

视听教材 shì-tīng jiàocái audio-visual materials; audio-visuals

视听教具 shì-tīng jiàojù audio-visual aids

视听教学 shì-tīng jiàoxué audio-visual instruction

视听中心 shì-tīng zhōngxīn audio-visual centre

视同等闲 shìtóng-děngxián regard or treat lightly; regard as unimportant; belittle:工人们把当头烈日和四五级的风沙～。The workers made light of working under the scorching sun or in the teeth of a force 4 or 5 sandstorm.

视同儿戏 shìtóng-érxì treat (a serious matter) as an issue of little importance; take (something serious) lightly; trifle with:这是关系到我们民族利益的大事,千万别～。This is a matter of vital interest to our nation and must on no account be taken lightly.

视同路人 shìtóng-lùrén *also* "视同陌路" regard as a stranger:他把过去的许多亲密朋友～。He treated many of his former close friends as mere strangers.

视图 shìtú 〈机械〉view:～数据 viewdata /前～ front view /侧～ side view /上～ top view

视网膜 shìwǎngmó 〈生理〉retina

视网膜镜 shìwǎngmójìng retinoscope

视网膜脱落 shìwǎngmó tuōluò 〈医学〉detached retina; retinal detachment

视网膜炎 shìwǎngmóyán retinitis

视为 shìwéi regard as:～知己 regard sb. as a bosom friend

视为具文 shìwéi-jùwén regard sth. as a mere scrap of paper

视为畏途 shìwéi-wèitú regard it as a dangerous road to take — be afraid to do sth.; be afraid to press forward in the face of difficulties:在经商成为热门的时候,他却～。When everybody was scrambling to go into business, he regarded it as a dangerous path to take.

视线 shìxiàn ❶ line of vision; line of sight (in surveying):扰乱～ interfere with sb.'s view /挡住～ obstruct the view ❷ attention:他这样做不过是为了转移人们的～。He did this simply to divert people's attention to something else.

视星等 shìxīngděng 〈天文〉apparent magnitude

视学 shìxué 〈旧语〉educational inspector

视野 shìyě field of vision:～开阔 have a wide (*or* broad) vision /～狭窄 have a narrow (*or* tunnel) vision /开拓～ broaden (*or* enlarge) one's horizons

视译 shìyì sight translation or interpretation

视阈 shìyù ❶〈生理〉visual threshold ❷ *also* "视域" vision:这次出国开阔了我的～。This trip abroad has opened up new vistas for me.

视在功率 shìzài gōnglǜ 〈物理〉apparent output

视紫质 shìzǐzhì *also* "视网膜紫质" shìwǎngmó zǐzhì 〈生理〉visual purple; rhodopsin

式

shì ❶ type; style; fashion:发～ hair style; hairdo /中～ Chinese style /西～ Western style /新～ new type; new style /老～ old-fashioned; outdated /手提～打字机 portable typewriter ❷ pattern; form; model:法～ pattern; model /版～ type ❸ ceremony; celebration; ritual:开幕～ opening ceremony /闭幕～ closing ceremony /阅兵～ military review; military parade ❹ formula:方程～ equation /分子～ molecular formula ❺〈语言〉mood; mode:命令～ imperative mood /条件～ conditional mood

式量 shìliàng 〈化学〉(chemical) formula weight

式微 shìwēi 〈书面〉decline in power or wealth:家道～ the family fortunes declined; the family has gone down in the world /国运～ the country was on the decline

式样 shìyàng style; design; type; model:～齐全 in all styles; of various designs (*or* descriptions); whole (*or* satisfactory) variety of /～美观大方 elegant and in good taste; graceful-looking /新颖的～ novel style /奇怪的～ strange (*or* odd) style /古老～的家具 imitation antique furniture /新潮～的服装 garments of the latest fashion; trendy dress /最新～的小汽车 car of the latest model /不同～的皮鞋 leather shoes of different designs

式子 shìzi ❶ posture:他练太极拳,很讲究～。He is very particular about his posture when doing *taiji* boxing. ❷ formula:先列出～再计算。Write down the formula before you start to calculate.

试

shì ❶ try; attempt; test:～新车 test drive a new car /～穿新衣 try on a new dress /一～身手 try one's hand /初～锋芒 show one's ability or display one's talent for the first time /～～这方法行不行 try and see if the method works /我叫你～～我的厉害! I'll give you a taste of my prowess. *or* I'll teach you a lesson! ❷ examination; test:笔～ written examination /口～ oral examination; viva voce; viva /初～ preliminary examination /复～ final examination

试巴 shìba 〈口语〉try; test:骑车并不难,上来～～。It is not at all difficult to ride a bicycle. Come and have a try.

试办 shìbàn run an enterprise, etc. on a trial basis; run a pilot scheme:～工厂 run a pilot plant

试笔 shìbǐ try one's hand at writing, painting or calligraphy:～之作 one's virgin piece of writing or painting

试表 shìbiǎo 〈口语〉take sb.'s temperature; measure the temperature or heat of one's body

试播 shìbō trial broadcast; trial telecast

试场 shìchǎng examination hall or room

试车 shìchē trial run; test run

试点 shìdiǎn ❶ conduct an experiment at selected points; launch a pilot project:这种方法～之后再推广也不迟。You may as well do a pilot survey before you try to popularize the method. ❷ place where an experiment is made; experimental unit:～班 experimental class /实行学分制,你校是～。The credit system will be tried out in your school.

试电笔 shìdiànbǐ *also* "电笔"〈电工〉test pencil; screw driver with voltage tester

试飞 shìfēi ❶ test flight; trial flight:～驾驶员 test pilot /进行～ carry out a trial flight /～结果表明飞机性能良好。The test flight showed that the performance of the plane was very good. ❷ preflight; exploratory flight

试工 shìgōng (of a workman or servant) on probation:～期六个月 be on six-month probation

试管 shìguǎn 〈化学〉test tube:～架 test-tube stand (*or* rack, *or* support)

试管实验 shìguǎn shíyàn test-tube experiment

试管婴儿 shìguǎn yīng'ér test-tube baby

试航 shìháng ❶ trial trip; trial voyage or flight; shakedown cruise or flight ❷ shake down (a ship or an airplane)

试剂 shìjì *also* "试药"〈化学〉reagent

试金法 shìjīnfǎ assaying

试金石 shìjīnshí touchstone; lydian stone:逆境是友谊的～。Adversity is the touchstone of friendship.

试镜头 shì jìngtóu screen test

试卷 shìjuàn examination paper; test paper:出地理～ set a geography paper /批改～ go over the examination papers; mark the examination papers

试看 shìkàn ❶ try sth. and see how it works:这台彩电,商店让我先～一个月。The shop-owners gave me a month to try out the TV set before I paid for it. ❷ just see:～谁能战胜这个强队? Let's wait and see who will beat this strong team? /军民团结如一人,～天下谁能敌? If the army and the people are united as one, who in the world can match them?

试射 shìshè 〈军事〉fire for adjustment; trial fire

试生产 shìshēngchǎn trial production

试手 shìshǒu ❶ (of a workman or servant) on probation ❷ have a try; give it a try
试探 shìtàn probe; explore; find out: ～水的深浅 fathom the depth of the water /～虚实 try to find out the strength (of an opponent, etc.)
试探 shìtan sound out; feel out: 进行～ put out feelers; try to find out /～对方的态度 sound out the other side
试探气球 shìtàn qìqiú trial balloon
试探性 shìtànxìng trial; exploratory; probing: ～提问 probing question /～谈判 exploratory talks
试题 shìtí examination questions; test questions: 出～ set examination questions /物理～特难。The physics paper was extremely tough.
试跳 shìtiào 〈体育〉 trial jump; trial dive
试帖 shìtiě ❶ test in classics in the civil service examination in the Tang Dynasty ❷ *also* "试帖诗" composition of poetry in the civil service examination of ancient China
试图 shìtú attempt; strive; try: 敌人～抵抗, 但为时已晚。The enemy attempted to put up a resistance but it was too late.
试问 shìwèn we should like to ask; it may well be asked: ～你有什么资格干涉别人的事? May we ask what right you have to interfere in other people's business?
试想 shìxiǎng (used in a rhetorical question to imply mild reproach) just think; just imagine: ～一下, 这事的结果会多么严重! Just think of the serious consequences it may bring. *or* Just imagine how serious the consequences might be. /～, 群众对这样的处理会有何种想法。Just imagine what the public will think of the settlement of the case. /～, 他对此事能一无所知吗? Fancy him not knowing anything about it!
试销 shìxiāo placing goods on trial sale; trial marketing; trial sale: ～商品 commodities for trial marketing (*or* on trial sale) /～专柜 trial sale counter
试行 shìxíng try out: ～六小时工作制 try out a six-hour day (*or* workday) /责任制的～时间 time set for the implementation of the system of job responsibility on a trial basis /这个规定已由厂务会议通过～。At the board meeting of the factory the rule was approved for trial implementation.
试选样品 shìxuǎn yàngpǐn 〈机械〉 pilot model
试演 shìyǎn trial performance (of plays, operas, etc.): 今天～新排的话剧。There will be a trial performance of the new stage play today.
试验 shìyàn ❶ experiment; trial; test: 科学～ scientific experiment /药物～ pharmaceutical test /部分禁止核～ partial nuclear test ban /～汽车性能 test the car's performance /～新方法 try out a new method ❷ 〈旧语〉 examination
试验场 shìyànchǎng proving ground; testing ground
试验农场 shìyàn nóngchǎng experimental farm; pilot farm
试验田 shìyàntián ❶ experimental plot; experimental field: 棉花～ experimental cotton plot ❷ 〈比喻〉 experimental unit; experiment
试验性工厂 shìyànxìng gōngchǎng pilot plant
试样 shìyàng ❶ try on (clothes, shoes, etc.) ❷ test (sample)
试药 shìyào *also* "试剂" 〈化学〉 reagent
试营销 shìyíngxiāo test marketing
试映 shìyìng 〈影视〉 preview: ～新片《红楼梦》 give a preview of the new film *A Dream of Red Mansions*
试用 shìyòng try out; on probation: ～期 probationary period /～人员 person on probation; probationer /产品还属于～性质。The products are still on trial. /经理雇用了一个秘书, ～两个月。The manager has hired a secretary who will be on probation for two months.
试用本 shìyòngběn trial edition (put out to solicit comments)
试用品 shìyòngpǐn trial products
试院 shìyuàn 〈旧语〉 imperial examination hall
试运转 shìyùnzhuǎn 〈机械〉 test run; trial run; running-in
试纸 shìzhǐ 〈化学〉 test paper: 姜黄～ turmeric test paper /石蕊～ litmus test paper /万用～ universal test paper
试制 shìzhì trial-produce; trial-manufacture: ～新产品 trial-manufacture new products /～小组 trial-production group /～工作 development work /这种新型录音机～成功了。The new tape recorder's trial production was successful.
试种 shìzhòng plant experimentally: ～经济作物 grow cash crops on a trial basis

栻 shì instrument for divination in ancient China

拭 shì wipe away; wipe; remove: 拂～ wipe off; whisk /擦～ clean /～泪 wipe (away) one's tears
拭除 shìchú remove; wipe out; dust off: 用毛刷轻轻～附在上面的灰尘 gently remove the surface dust with a brush
拭目以待 shìmùyǐdài wait and see; look forward to (the fulfilment of one's wish): 他们能否实现诺言, 我们将～。We shall wait and see if they will keep their promise.

轼 shì 〈书面〉 wooden handrail in the front of an ancient carriage

弑 shì 〈书面〉 murder (one's sovereign or parent): ～君 murder one's sovereign; commit regicide

奭 shì ❶ 〈书面〉 grand; magnificent ❷ (Shì) a surname

示 shì show; produce; notify; instruct: 出～身份证 produce one's identity card /告～ notice /显～ show; demonstrate; manifest /暗～ drop a hint /明～ state explicitly /指～ instruct; indicate /请～ ask for instructions /承～二诗, 均已拜读。I have carefully read the two poems you showed me.
示波管 shìbōguǎn 〈电学〉 oscilloscope tube
示波器 shìbōqì 〈电学〉 oscillograph; oscilloscope
示恩 shì'ēn *also* "示惠" show favour to sb.: 他这个人很敏感, 你千万不要有任何～的表示。You should by all means avoid letting him know you are showing him favour, as he is very sensitive.
示范 shìfàn set an example; demonstrate; show: 作～ give a demonstration; demonstrate /～动作 demonstration /～操纵机器 show how to operate the machine /～教学 teach sth. by demonstration /起～作用 play an exemplary role
示复 shìfù 〈书面〉 give instructions in reply; await a reply: 兹事体大, 亟盼～。Instructions are urgently awaited, as this is a matter of great importance.
示功器 shìgōngqì 〈机械〉 indicator
示功图 shìgōngtú 〈机械〉 indicator card; indicator diagram
示寂 shìjì 〈宗教〉 (of monks) die; expire; pass away
示警 shìjǐng alert to danger; give a warning; warn: 鸣枪～ fire a warning shot; give a warning by firing a shot /拉铃或亮红灯～ give an alarm by ringing a bell or by flashing a red light
示例 shìlì give typical examples; give instances; give a demonstration
示人 shìrén show sth. to others; let others have a look at sth.; make known: 他珍藏的古董从不轻易～。His collection of antiques has never been shown to others easily.
示弱 shìruò show signs of weakness; take sth. lying down: 不甘～ refuse to yield; unwilling to be outdone /决不～ will never give in
示威 shìwēi ❶ demonstrate; hold a demonstration: 学生～ student demonstration /自发性～ spontaneous demonstration /和平～ peaceful demonstration /～群众 demonstrators /为声援罢工工人而～ hold (*or* stage) a demonstration in support of the workers on strike ❷ put on a show of force; display one's prowess: 陈兵边境向邻国～ mass troops along the borders to flex one's muscles to the neighbouring countries
示威游行 shìwēi yóuxíng demonstration; parade; march
示温涂料 shìwēn túliào thermopaint
示意 shìyì signal; hint; motion; gesture: 用手势～ speak by gesture; give a hint with a gesture /以目～ wink at sb.; tip sb. the wink /警察～他站住。The policeman motioned him (*or* gestured to him) to stop. /首长～他进来。The senior official motioned him in.
示意图 shìyìtú ❶ sketch map: 机器安装～ illustrated instructions for installing the machine /市政工程～ sketch map of the municipal works /城市交通～ city transport map ❷ 〈机械〉 schematic diagram or drawing: 发动机～ diagram of the engine
示振仪 shìzhènyí vibroscope
示众 shìzhòng publicly expose; punish before the public: 游街～ parade sb. through the streets (as a punishment)
示踪测定 shìzōng cèdìng tracer determination
示踪物 shìzōngwù 〈物理〉 tracer

示踪元素 shìzōng yuánsù 〈物理〉tracer element
示踪原子 shìzōng yuánzǐ labelled atom; tagged atom; tracer

士 shì ❶〈古语〉bachelor ❷ social stratum between senior officials (大夫) and the common people (庶民) in ancient China ❸ scholar; intelligentsia: ～农工商 scholars, farmers, artisans and merchants ❹ soldier; armyman; serviceman: 战～ soldier /将～ officers and men ❺ noncommissioned officer: 上～ (UK) staff sergeant; (US) sergeant first class /中～ sergeant /下～ corporal ❻ person trained in a specified field: 助产～ midwife /护～ nurse /医～ doctor /谋～ adviser /斗牛～ bullfighter ❼ (praiseworthy) person: 烈～ martyr /勇～ brave fighter; warrior /骑～ knight /志～ person of high ideals and integrity /义～ high-minded or chivalrous man; person dedicated to a righteous cause /绅～ gentleman /壮～ hero; warrior ❽ bodyguard, one of the pieces in Chinese chess ❾ (Shì) a surname

士别三日，刮目相看 shì bié sān rì, guā mù xiāng kàn scholar who has been away for three days must be looked at with new eyes; scholar should be judged in a new light when he reappears after an absence

士兵 shìbīng rank-and-file soldier; rank and file; private

士大夫 shìdàfū scholar-officials; literati (in feudal China)

士可杀而不可辱 shì kě shā ér bùkě rǔ a scholar may be killed but not be insulted; a scholar prefers death to humiliation

士林 shìlín 〈书面〉intelligentsia; academic world: 交游～ make friends with scholars

士流 shìliú 〈书面〉men of letters; scholars in general

士敏土 shìmǐntǔ cement

士女 shìnǚ ❶ young men and women: ～如云。Men and women gathered in crowds. ❷ *see* "仕女❷" shìnǚ

士气 shìqì morale; spirit: 激励～ boost (*or* heighten) the morale /保持旺盛的～ keep one's pecker up /影响～ affect the morale /瓦解～ demoralize /～高昂。The morale is high. /～低落。The spirits sag. *or* The morale is sinking low.

士人 shìrén 〈旧语〉scholar

士绅 shìshēn gentry: 开明～ enlightened gentry

士师记 Shìshījì *The Book of Judges*, the seventh book of *The Old Testament*

士为知己者死 shì wèi zhījǐzhě sǐ *also* "士死知己" a true knight dies for his friend: ～，女为悦己者容。A gentleman will die for one who appreciates his worth; a woman will beautify herself for one who dotes on her.

士子 shìzǐ scholars; students

士卒 shìzú soldiers; privates: 身先～ (of an officer) fight at the head of his men; lead the charge

士族 shìzú influential and privileged family of scholar-officials (which came into existence during the Eastern Han, Wei, Jin, and Northern and Southern dynasties)

仕 shì ❶ hold an official post; be an official: ～家子弟 sons (*or* children) of officials /学而优则～。A good scholar will make an official (a Confucian doctrine). ❷ bodyguard, one of the pieces in Chinese chess

仕宦 shìhuàn be an official: ～之家 official's family

仕进 shìjìn 〈书面〉work one's way up by embarking on an official career: 在封建时代，许多知识分子只求～。In feudal times many intellectuals sought to improve their social status by entering into officialdom.

仕路 shìlù *see* "仕途"

仕女 shìnǚ ❶ maid in an imperial palace; maid of honour ❷ *also* "士女" shìnǚ 〈美术〉painting or portraying beautiful women — a genre in traditional Chinese painting: 善绘古装～ be good at painting beauties in ancient costumes

仕途 shìtú 〈书面〉official career: 走～捷径 take a short cut to officialdom /～沉浮 ups and downs of an official career

恃 shì ❶ rely on; count on; depend on: 有～无恐 be unscrupulous because one has powerful backing; feel secure in the knowledge that one has something to fall back upon ❷〈书面〉mother: 失～ have lost one's mother

恃才傲物 shìcái-àowù think too highly of oneself and be arrogant; be conceited and overweening: ～，落拓不羁 be overweening, unconventional and uninhibited /有些年轻人，认为自己有才华，常～。Some young people who consider themselves talented often get conceited and contemptuous of others.

恃德者昌，恃力者亡 shìdézhě chāng, shìlìzhě wáng those who rely on virtue will thrive, while those who rely on force will perish

恃强凌弱 shìqiáng-língruò use one's strength to bully the weak; play the bully: 有的国家在国际事务中常常～。In international affairs, there are countries that often play the bully.

恃势凌人 shìshì-língrén use one's power to bully others; be domineering

侍 shì wait upon; attend on; serve: ～茶～水 serve tea and drink

侍从 shìcóng attendants; retinue

侍从副官 shìcóng fùguān aide-de-camp (ADC); aide: 身后跟着许多～ be followed by many ADCs

侍儿 shì'ér 〈书面〉maid; maidservant

侍奉 shìfèng wait upon; attend upon; serve: ～箕帚 perform the duties of a wife /他～这个孤寡老人就像～父母一样。He looks after the old childless widow as if she were his own mother.

侍候 shìhòu wait upon; take care of; look after; attend: ～伤病员 attend the sick and wounded /～老人 look after one's aged parents or grandparents /～得周到 take good care of /难～ be hard to please

侍郎 shìláng vice-president of one of the Six Boards (六部) in the Ming and Qing dynasties

侍立 shìlì stand in attendance; stand by respectfully: ～一旁 stand at sb.'s side in attendance

侍弄 shìnòng ❶ attend (crops, livestock, poultry, etc.): ～庄稼 attend one's crops /～两头大母猪 take care of two fat sows ❷ repair; fix: ～电视机 fix a TV set

侍女 shìnǚ maidservant; maid

侍卫 shìwèi ❶ bodyguard ❷ imperial bodyguard

侍养 shìyǎng support and wait upon (one's parents, elders, etc.)

侍役 shìyì servant

侍应生 shìyìngshēng 〈旧语〉young odd-job man working in a bank, etc.

侍者 shìzhě attendant; servant; waiter: 餐厅～ waiter /旅馆～ bellboy

螫 shì 〈书面〉sting

螫针 shìzhēn sting (of a bee or other insects)

世(卋) shì ❶ lifetime; life: 一生一～ lifetime; all one's life /生生～～永不忘 will be remembered by posterity (*or* from generation to generation) ❷ generation: 他的第九～孙 ninth in descent from him; his descendant in the ninth generation /四～同堂 four generations under one roof ❸ from generation to generation: ～交 long-standing friendship between two families ❹ form of address among people who maintain good family relations: ～伯 older friend of one's father /～叔 younger friend of one's father /～弟 son of father's friend, younger than oneself ❺ age; era; time: 今～ at the present time; nowadays /近～ modern times /盛～ age of prosperity; heyday /乱～ troubled times; turbulent years ❻ world; society: 盖～无双 unparalleled (*or* unrivalled) in the world; peerless; second to none /公诸于～ make sth. public; make sth. known to the world /～有伯乐，然后有千里马。A talented man will remain obscure unless somebody appreciates his talent and is in a position to help him. ❼〈地质〉epoch: 古新～ Palaeocene Epoch ❽ (Shì) a surname

世弊 shìbì maladies of the present-day world

世变 shìbiàn changes in the world; vicissitudes: 饱经～ having experienced the vicissitudes of life

世仇 shìchóu ❶ family feud; vendetta: 两家结下了～。The two families have been feuding with each other for generations. /～难解。A family feud is difficult to resolve (*or* settle). ❷ sworn enemy (in a family feud)

世传 shìchuán be handed down from generation to generation; be known for generations: ～秘方 secret recipe handed down through generations

世次 shìcì (of people or family members) order of seniority

S

世代 shìdài ❶ long period of time; many, many years: 这些故事不知流传了多少~。These stories have been in circulation for God knows how many years. ❷ generation after generation; for generations: ~书香 (from) a long line of scholars / 他家在此定居已有好些~了。His family has lived here for generations.

世代交替 shìdài jiāotì 〈生物〉 alternation of generations

世代相传 shìdài-xiāngchuán pass on from generation to generation: 这个故事在当地~。The story has been passed on from generation to generation in the locality.

世道 shìdào manners and morals of the time; ways of the world: ~变了。Things are not what they were. / ~真的变了。You don't know what the world is coming to.

世道人心 shìdào-rénxīn social morality and popular feelings: 这些腐朽思想贻害~。These decadent ideas are bad for social morals.

世风 shìfēng 〈书面〉 public morals and mores; morals of the world: ~日下。The moral degeneration of the world is going from bad to worse. *or* Public morals are deteriorating day by day.

世故 shìgù ways of the world: 饱经~的人 man well versed in the ways of the world; experienced person / 不懂人情~ inexperienced in life

世故 shìgu worldly-wise; shrewd; crafty: 老头儿很~。The old chap is quite a smooth (*or* slippery) character. / 他年纪虽不大, 但处世却~得很。Though young, he knows how to get along in this world.

世纪 shìjì century: 公元前5~ 5th century BC / 18~后期 late 18th century / 19~中叶 mid-19th century / 19~80年代 the 1880's / 进入21~ enter the 21st century / 20~即将结束。The 20th century is drawing to an end.

世纪末 shìjìmò end of the century; *fin de siècle*

世家 shìjiā ❶ noble family; old and well-known family: ~子弟 children of influential families / 他出身于名门~。He comes of an eminent family. ❷ hereditary house of a noble (in the *Historical Records*): 《楚~》 *The Hereditary Houses of the State of Chu* ❸ family in which a special skill has been handed down from generation to generation: 梨园~ family of Beijing opera singers; Beijing opera family

S

世间 shìjiān world; society: ~万事万物都在不断变化。All things in the world are changing.

世交 shìjiāo ❶ long-standing friendship between two families: 他们两家是多年的~。The two families have had good traditional relations for many years. *or* There is a long-standing friendship between the two families. ❷ old family friends: 黄先生与我是~。Mr. Huang and I are old family friends.

世界 shìjiè ❶ world: 创造新~ create a new world / 认识~ know (*or* understand) the world / 改造~ change the world / ~之大, 无奇不有。It takes all sorts to make a world. ❷ 〈宗教〉 universe: 大千~ boundless universe ❸ all over the world: 放眼~ have the whole world in view / 轰动~ cause a sensation throughout the world; shake the world (*or* earth) / ~风云变幻 world situation is fast changing (*or* volatile) / 主宰~ dominate the world ❹ existing conditions of society: 难道他们还不知道~已经变了, 他们再也不能横行霸道了? Don't they realize that the times have changed and that they can no longer ride roughshod over others with impunity? ❺ scope; realm: 现实~ real world; world as it is; world as you find it / 客观~ objective world / 男人的~ men's world / 精神~ mental world / 内心~ inner world / 童话~ fairyland

世界版权公约 Shìjiè Bǎnquán Gōngyuē Universal Copyright Convention (1952)

世界报 Shìjièbào *Le Monde*, a French daily first published in 1944 in Paris

世界博览会 Shìjiè Bólǎnhuì World's Fair; World Fair

世界大战 shìjiè dàzhàn world war: 第一次~ First World War (1914-1918); World War I / 第二次~ Second World War (1939-1945); World War II

世界观 shìjièguān world outlook

世界冠军 shìjiè guànjūn world champion

世界纪录 shìjiè jìlù world record

世界贸易 shìjiè màoyì world commerce or trade

世界名著 shìjiè míngzhù world classics

世界末日 shìjiè mòrì end of the world; doomsday; judgement day

世界气象组织 Shìjiè Qìxiàng Zǔzhī World Meteorological Organization (WMO)

世界人权宣言 Shìjiè Rénquán Xuānyán Universal Declaration of Human Rights (1948)

世界时 shìjièshí 〈天文〉 universal time

世界市场 shìjiè shìchǎng world market: 打入~ get into (*or* enter) the world market / 在~上竞争 compete in the world market

世界水平 shìjiè shuǐpíng world standard or level

世界卫生组织 Shìjiè Wèishēng Zǔzhī World Health Organization (WHO)

世界舞台 shìjiè wǔtái world arena

世界银行 Shìjiè Yínháng World Bank

世界舆论 shìjiè yúlùn world opinion

世界语 Shìjièyǔ Esperanto

世界知识产权组织 Shìjiè Zhīshi Chǎnquán Zǔzhī World Intellectual Property Organization (WIPO)

世界主义 shìjièzhǔyì cosmopolitanism

世局 shìjú international situation: ~如此, 实在令人担忧。As it is, the world situation is really a cause for anxiety.

世路 shìlù vicissitudes of life; life's journey: ~风波 vicissitudes of life

世论 shìlùn current criticism; prevailing public opinion

世面 shìmiàn various aspects of society; world; life: 经风雨, 见~ face the world and brave the storm / 没见过~ have not seen much of the world; be inexperienced

世亲 shìqīn kinsfolk for generations

世情 shìqíng ways of the world: 不懂~ ignorant of the ways of the world; inexperienced in life / ~冷暖 fickleness of the world (*or* of human relationships) / ~如纸。Human relationships are but paper-thin (*or* wafer-thin).

世人 shìrén people at large; common people: ~的看法 common views / ~的眼光 in the eyes of the common people; by common standard / 遭到~的唾骂 be spurned by the people

世上 shìshàng in the world; on earth: 长江后浪推前浪, ~新人胜旧人。As in the Yangtze River the waves behind drive on those ahead, so each new generation excels the last one.

世上无难事 shìshàng wú nánshì there is nothing difficult under the sun: ~, 只怕有心人。Nothing in the world is difficult for one who sets his mind on it. *or* Perseverance is the road to success. / ~, 只要肯登攀。Nothing is hard in this world If you dare to scale the heights.

世事 shìshì affairs of the world: 不谙~ be ignorant of worldly affairs / ~艰难。Human life is full of twist and turns. / ~繁杂。Worldly matters are many and complex. / ~洞明皆学问, 人情练达即文章。A grasp of mundane affairs is genuine knowledge; understanding of worldly wisdom is true learning.

世说新语 Shìshuō Xīnyǔ *New Collection of Anecdotes of Famous Personages* written by Liu Yiqing (刘义庆) of the Southern Dynasties

世俗 shìsú ❶ customs and traditions; social conventions; vulgar or commonplace thing: ~之见。These are the views of the philistines. ❷ secular; worldly

世态 shìtài ways of the world: ~人情 ways of the world

世态炎凉 shìtài-yánliáng people are warm or cold, depending on whether one is successful or not — the snobbish ways of the world: 饱受~之苦 experience much fickleness of human relationships

世途 shìtú life's journey: ~坎坷 life's journey full of frustrations; life of hardships

世外 shìwài away from this world; out of this world; away from this mortal life

世外桃源 shìwài-táoyuán Land of Peach Blossoms — an imaginary ideal world; beautiful retreat; haven of peace and happiness; Shangri-La: 他对喧嚣的人世感到厌倦, 渴望寻个~的去处。He is tired of the hustle and bustle of the world and longs for a haven of peace.

世务 shìwù affairs of the world; current affairs; trends of the world: 不达~ ignorant of the trends of the world; inexperienced in society

世袭 shìxí hereditary: ~爵位 hereditary title of nobility / ~领地 fief patrimony / ~制度 hereditary system

世系 shìxì pedigree; genealogy; lineage

世相 shìxiàng ways of the world

世兄 shìxiōng son of father's friend, older than oneself

世医 shìyī doctor of traditional Chinese medicine with generations' experience of medical practice

世议 shìyì 〈书面〉public opinion
世谊 shìyì friendship spanning two or more generations
世运 shìyùn course of events; rise and fall of nations
世子 shìzǐ eldest son of the emperor by his empress; crown prince; eldest son of a feudal prince by his princess
世族 shìzú (in feudal China) influential family of generations' standing; family of traditional importance

贳 shì 〈书面〉❶ hire; rent; let ❷ buy or sell on credit; give or get credit: ～酒 buy wine on credit ❸ deal with leniently; remit (a punishment); pardon: 对犯法者不稍～ show no mercy to offenders (*or* lawbreakers)
贳器店 shìqìdiàn 〈方言〉shop with utensils for hire

嗜 shì have a liking for; take to; be addicted to: ～酒成性 be addicted to alcohol /～书成癖 be fond of reading to a fault
嗜好 shìhào hobby; addiction; habit: 有打麻将的～ be very fond of playing mah-jong /～烟酒 be addicted to smoking and drinking /不良～ harmful habit /读小报成了他的新～。Reading tabloids has become his new hobby.
嗜痂之癖 shìjiāzhīpǐ eccentric taste: 此人有～，专爱看那些最下流低级的黄色小说。This fellow has a depraved taste for the most vulgar porn stories.
嗜酒狂 shìjiǔkuáng alcoholic
嗜眠 shìmián somnolence
嗜杀成性 shìshā-chéngxìng bloodthirsty; sanguinary; trigger-happy: 审判那些～的法西斯强盗 put those bloodthirsty fascist bandits on trial
嗜血 shìxuè bloodthirsty; bloodsucking: ～成性 be bloodthirsty; kill without batting an eyelid
嗜血菌 shìxuèjūn haemophilus
嗜欲 shìyù desire for the satisfaction of the senses (of sight, hearing, smell, taste, etc.); lust: 节制～ curb one's desire for the pleasure of the senses; abstain from sensual pleasures /满足～ gratify sensual desires

莳(蒔) shì ❶〈方言〉transplant: ～秧 transplant rice shoots ❷〈书面〉plant; cultivate: ～花 raise flowers
see also shí

事 shì ❶ matter; affair; thing; business: 家～ family affairs /国～ affairs of state /私～ private business /公～ public business /无关紧要的～ matter of no consequence /把坏～变成好～ turn a bad thing into a good one /就～论～ deal with sth. on its merits /～有凑巧 as luck would have it /～有蹊跷 sense something fishy; smell a rat /～关人命。A man's life is involved. /～属两难。It is difficult either way. *or* We are caught in a dilemma. /遇～要冷静。Stay cool if any problem crops up. /这是怎么回～儿? What is all this about? /这不碍～儿。It doesn't matter. /～无不可对人言。There is nothing we should hold back from others. /～到如今，恐怕也只有听天由命了。Things have come to such a pass that I am afraid we'll have to resign ourselves to fate. ❷ trouble; difficulty; accident: 肇～ have an accident /闹～ make trouble; cause trouble /胆小怕～ timid and overcautious /造谣生～ create trouble by spreading rumours /多～之秋 troubled times /平安无～。All is well. /别怕，没什么了不起的～。Don't be afraid, there is nothing serious. ❸ job; task; work: 谋～ look for a job; seek employment ❹ responsibility; involvement: 你别急，这里没有你儿子的～儿。Don't worry. Your son is not involved in the trouble. ❺〈书面〉attend upon; wait upon; serve: ～母至孝 wait upon one's mother with great filial piety; be a filial son /仰～俯畜 support one's parents and wife and bring up one's children; support the whole family ❻ go in for; be engaged in: 从～文学创作 go in for literary writing /不～正业 lead an idle life /终日无所～事 loaf about all day ❼〈方言〉way; means; measure: 老等着也不是～儿，得想法儿找到他。It won't do to keep waiting here, we have to think of a way to get hold of him.
事半功倍 shìbàn-gōngbèi half the work with twice the result: 力求收到～的效果 strive to achieve twice the result for half the effort /此事由他经手，必能收～之效。Since the matter is in his hands, he will certainly achieve more with less effort.
事倍功半 shìbèi-gōngbàn twice the work with half the result: 这样做岂不是～吗? Isn't this to get half the result with twice the effort? /因粗心大意造成～。Owing to carelessness we only achieved half the result for double effort.
事必躬亲 shìbìgōngqīn see or attend to everything oneself; give personal attention to everything, big or small: 他处处带头，～。He takes the lead in all matters and attends to everything. /你作为一个领导，无须～。As a leader, you don't have to take care of every single thing personally.
事变 shìbiàn ❶ incident: 西安～ Xi'an Incident (of 1936) /七七～ July 7 Incident of 1937 (*or* Marco Polo Bridge Incident of 1937) ❷ emergency; eventuality; exigency: 万一发生～ in case of emergency /应付突然～的能力 ability to cope with all eventualities (*or* contingencies) ❸ course of events; events: 我们必须了解～的内部联系。We must look into the inner connections of events in all their changing aspects.
事不关己，高高挂起 shì bù guān jǐ, gāogāo guàqǐ let things drift or go hang if they do not affect one personally; stand or remain aloof from things of no immediate concern to oneself
事不过三 shìbùguòsān not tolerate anything undesirable that has happened more than three times: ～，我不能再原谅他了。I can no longer forgive him for he has let me down repeatedly.
事不宜迟 shìbùyíchí lose no time in doing sth.; attend to the matter immediately; the matter brooks no delay: ～，必须迅作决定。Procrastination is the thief of time and we must decide at once. /～，迟则生变。It must be done without delay, or something untoward might happen. *or* There is not a moment to lose, for delay may bring unwelcome change.
事出有因 shìchū-yǒuyīn it is by no means accidental; no smoke without fire: ～，查无实据。There must be something behind it, but investigation revealed no evidence (*or* but no evidence has been found after investigation). *or* Investigation was justified but revealed no evidence against anybody.
事到临头 shìdàolíntóu when things reach a climax; when the situation becomes critical: ～，他不知所措。When things come to a head, he is at a loss what to do.
事典 shìdiǎn ❶〈书面〉encyclopedia (of precedents, events, institutions and laws) ❷ reference book (on special subjects)
事端 shìduān disturbance; trouble; incident; undesirable event: 发生这起～的原因还在调查之中。The causes of the incident were being looked into.
事功 shìgōng 〈书面〉success or achievement in work: 急于～ be anxious for success in one's work; be overanxious to achieve instant results
事故 shìgù accident; mishap: 造成～ bring about (*or* cause) an accident /防止～ avert (*or* prevent) accidents /减少～ reduce the accidents /工伤～ industrial accident /交通～ traffic accident /责任～ accident due to negligence /医疗～ faulty medical or surgical treatment; surgical accident /意外～ unforeseen accident /～频率 accident frequency /～责任者 person responsible for the accident; culprit /～损失赔偿 accident compensation /～报告书 accident report
事故由子 shìgù-yóuzi 〈方言〉❶ disturbance; incident: 他净惹～。He is always creating disturbances (*or* causing troubles). ❷ *also* "事故由儿" pretext; excuse: 他怕惹麻烦，借个～溜走了。Afraid to get into trouble, he made off under some pretext.
事过境迁 shìguò-jìngqiān events have passed and the situation has changed; things change with the passage of time: 过去的那些恩怨早已～，你又何必提它。The old scores have already become things of the past; there is no need for you to bring them up again.
事后 shìhòu after the event; afterwards: ～才通知当事人 notify the person concerned only after the event; not inform the person concerned until after the event /～补救 take remedial measures afterwards /～看来 with hindsight /～总结教训 find out what lessons can be drawn from the incident
事后诸葛亮 shìhòu Zhūgě Liàng wise after the event; belated wisdom; I-told-you-so attitude: 别当～。Don't vaunt your after-the-fact wisdom. *or* Don't be a Monday morning quarterback. /的确，事情的发展证明他太傻了，但是当～还不容易! Of course as things turned out he had been a fool, but anyone could be wise after the event.
事机 shìjī ❶ secret; confidential matter: ～不密，消息很快传出去了。The secret was not well kept, and it was not long before it was leaked out. ❷ opportunity; opportune moment: 不失～ seize the opportunity /口陈～ tell sb. the time for an action

事迹 shìjì deed; merit; achievement:生平~ one's life story /英雄~ heroic exploits /介绍他的模范~ give an account of his exemplary deeds

事假 shìjià leave of absence (to attend to private business):请半天~ ask for half-day leave of absence /批准~ grant sb. leave of absence

事件 shìjiàn incident; particular event:历史~ historical event /政治~ political event /流血~ bloody (*or* sanguinary) incident; bloodshed /中毒~ case of poisoning /爆炸~ explosion /偶然~ accident /发生了不幸~。An untoward incident occurred.

事理 shìlǐ reason; sense; logic:不合~ unreasonable; insensible /晓以~ bring sb. to his senses through reasoning

事例 shìlì case; example; instance:具体~ specific case /生动的~ telling (*or* graphic) example /举出一个恰当的~ cite a case in point

事略 shìlüè biographical sketch; biographical note:生平~ brief biographical account

事前 shìqián before the event; in advance; beforehand:~通知 notify in advance; give prior (*or* advance) notice /~请示 ask for instructions beforehand /~准备好 be prepared in time /~谁也不知道。No one knew anything about it before the event.

事情 shìqing ❶ affair; matter; question; business:内部的~ internal affairs /亟待解决的~ questions that require immediate settlement /骗人的~ fraud or hoax /~的真相 truth of the matter; truth; facts of the case /~的内幕 inside story; what goes on behind the scenes /~的始末 whole story /~不简单。This is not as simple as it seems to be. ❷ accident:不能马虎,出了~就麻烦了。Try to be very careful, or you'll get into trouble if anything untoward should happen. ❸ work; occupation:在公司里找了一个~ get a job in the company

事权 shìquán power; authority

事实 shìshí fact:铁的~ hard (indisputable) facts /既成~ fait accompli; accomplished fact /无视~真相 shut one's eyes to facts; refuse to see the truth /夸大~ overstate the case; exaggerate /歪曲~ distort (*or* pervert) facts /摆~,讲道理 state the facts and reasons; present the facts and reason things out /~果真如此吗? Is this really the case? /传闻与~不符。The rumour going around does not tally with reality.

事实上 shìshíshang in fact; really; as a matter of fact:~的承认 *de facto* recognition /~的控制 actual control /你说的情况~不存在。What you said does not really exist.

事实胜于雄辩 shìshí shèngyú xióngbiàn facts speak louder than words; a single fact is worth a shipload of arguments; reality is stronger than rhetoric

事事 shìshì ❶ everything:~如意。Everything came off satisfactorily. *or* Everything goes well. /~都要小心。You have got to be careful in anything you do. ❷〈书面〉be engaged in; be occupied with:无所~ loafing about; doing nothing

事势 shìshì trends; situation; state of affairs:他看到~不好,便想抽身走掉。Seeing that things were taking an unfavourable turn (*or* going against him), he tried to make himself scarce. /真没想到~竟然弄到如此地步。Who would have expected such a turn in the situation!

事素 shìsù 〈哲学〉event

事态 shìtài state of affairs; developments; situation:~有所缓和。Things have somewhat smoothed down (*or* eased). /他们企图扩大~。They attempted to aggravate the situation. /我们密切注意~的发展。We are closely following (*or* watching) the development of events. /~如何发展,很难预料。It's hard to anticipate how things will work out.

事体 shìtǐ 〈方言〉❶ affair; thing; matter:明白~ have good sense; be sensible; know what's what ❷ accident; mishap:车间里出了~。There was an accident in the workshop. ❸ work; occupation:托人找个~做 ask sb. to find one a job

事头 shìtóu 〈方言〉❶ boss ❷ work:我这儿没~了,你先回去吧。You may go now. There is nothing more to do.

事头婆 shìtóupó 〈方言〉boss' wife

事务 shìwù ❶ work; affair; routine:行政~ administrative work; administration /私人~ private affairs /日常~ daily routine /~繁忙 be tied up with work; be snowed under with work /主持日常~ be in charge of everyday routine ❷ general affairs:~科 general affairs section

事务次官 shìwù cìguān (Japan) permanent vice-minister:外务省~ Permanent Vice-Minister of the Ministry of Foreign Affairs

事务所 shìwùsuǒ office:建筑师~ architect's office

事务员 shìwùyuán office clerk

事务主义 shìwùzhǔyì routinism:~者 person bogged down in the quagmire of trivial routine matters

事物 shìwù thing; object; reality:客观~ objective reality /新~ new things /~的发展规律 law of the development of things /任何~都是可以认识的。Nothing is beyond cognition. /~都是一分为二的。Everything divides into two. *or* Everything has its positive and negative sides.

事先 shìxiān in advance; prior to; beforehand:~联系 get in touch in advance /~防范 take precautions /~警告 forewarn /没有上级的~同意,任何人都无权做出这个决定。Nobody has the right to make such a decision without the prior consent of the higher-ups.

事项 shìxiàng item; point; matter:注意~ items for attention /有关~ relevant issues /补充~ additional points /安全~ safety matters /保密~ security regulations

事象 shìxiàng images; how things look:作品所描写的~,生动逼真。The book presents a vivid and life-like image of everything it depicts.

事业 shìyè ❶ cause; task; undertaking; career:革命~ revolutionary cause /建设~ task of construction /科学文化~ scientific and cultural undertakings /交通运输~ public transport /旅游~ tourist trade; tourist industry; tourism /献身于~ dedicate oneself to a cause /断送了一生的~ ruin (*or* blast) one's life career /搞~的人 career-minded person; career man or woman ❷ institution:福利~ welfare services /公用~ public utilities

事业单位 shìyè dānwèi public institution; institution

事业费 shìyèfèi operating expenses

事业心 shìyèxīn dedication or devotion to one's work:~不强 lack responsibility or devotion (to one's work) /他有很强的~。He is a highly dedicated (*or* motivated) person.

事宜 shìyí (usu. used in official documents, laws and decrees, etc.) matters concerned; relevant matters:讨论教改~ discuss matters concerning educational reform /商量住宿~ discuss the problem of accommodation

事由 shìyóu ❶ origin of an incident; specifics of a matter:问清~ gain a clear idea of the whole story; know the whys and wherefores of the matter /交代~ specify the particulars of a matter ❷ (used in official documents) main content; gist ❸ excuse; pretext:找个~离开会场 find an excuse to leave the meeting ❹〈方言〉job; employment:找~ look for a job

事与愿违 shìyǔyuànwéi things run counter to one's wishes:由于措施不当,结果~。As they failed to take proper measures, things did not turn out the way they wished (*or* things went contrary to their wishes).

事在人为 shìzàirénwéi all success hinges on human effort; human effort is the decisive factor:~,只要你努力,就有成功的希望。It all depends on your effort. If you try hard enough, there is hope of success.

事主 shìzhǔ ❶ victim of a crime:~向派出所报了案。The injured party reported the case to the police station. ❷〈旧语〉family holding wedding or funeral ceremonies

事状 shìzhuàng what has taken place; events; happening:诸书大多偏重~,少所铺叙。Most books stress what actually took place with little elaboration.

誓

誓 shì ❶ take an oath; swear; vow; pledge:海~山盟 lovers' vow to be true to each other forever /~同生死 swear to share weal and woe with somebody ❷ solemn promise; oath; vow:宣~ take an oath; swear; make a vow; make a pledge:信~旦旦 make a solemn vow; pledge in all sincerity

誓不罢休 shìbùbàxiū vow not to stop; swear not to rest:此仇不报,~。We'll never give up until we have avenged the wrong.

誓不两立 shìbùliǎnglì swear not to exist together with sb. under the same heaven; be implacably hostile; be irreconcilable:~的两大派 two utterly antagonistic factions

誓词 shìcí oath; vow; pledge

誓师 shìshī ❶ rally to pledge resolution before going to war:~北伐 (of the Northern Expeditionary Army) pledge resolution before starting (*or* launching) the Northern Expedition ❷ take a solemn pledge at a mass rally:~大会 meeting to pledge mass effort for the

accomplishment of an important task

誓死 shìsǐ pledge one's life; vow to die (for a cause):～捍卫祖国的边疆 pledge to fight to the death in defending the frontiers of one's country /～不屈 would rather die than surrender; be unbending

誓死不二 shìsǐ-bù'èr pledge to remain true to death:他对自己献身的事业,有～的决心。He is resolved to dedicate himself to the cause all through his life.

誓言 shìyán oath; pledge:立下～ swear an oath /决不违背～ will never go back on one's pledge

誓愿 shìyuàn vow; pledge:许下从头再来的～ make a pledge to start all over again

誓约 shìyuē vow; oath; solemn promise:信守～ keep one's pledge; keep a vow; be faithful to one's vow

逝

shì ❶ pass:韶光易～。Time flies. ❷ die; pass away:母早～。His mother died early.

逝世 shìshì pass away; die; become dead:～的噩耗 sad (*or* grievous) news of sb.'s death /溘然～ pass away suddenly /～二十周年纪念日 20th anniversary of sb.'s death /他不幸三年前因病～。To our great sorrow, he died of illness three years ago.

逝者如斯 shìzhě-rúsī time passes like the flow of water:子在川上曰:"～夫! 不舍昼夜。"It was by a stream that the Master said, "Thus do things flow away, day and night!"

势(勢)

shì ❶ power; force; strength; influence:得～ be in power; get the upper hand /失～ lose power and influence /人多～众 dominate by sheer force of number; many hands provide great strength /仗～凌人 bully people on the strength of one's high position or powerful connections; take advantage of one's power or connections with influential people to bully others /趋炎附～ play up (*or* cater) to those in power; curry favour with the powerful; be obsequious ❷ momentum:来～甚猛 come with tremendous force /乘着商业繁荣的～头 on the momentum of a business boom /以泰山压顶之～ bear down on sb. with the weight of Mount Tai; overwhelm sb. ❸ outward appearance of a natural object or phenomenon:地～平坦 level terrain /山～险峻。The mountain is high and precipitous. /火～得到了控制。The fire has been brought under control. ❹ situation; state of affairs; circumstances; tendency:趁～ take advantage of a favourable situation /采取守～ be on the defensive; assume the defensive /发起攻～ launch an offensive /大～所趋 trend of the times; general trend /～在必然 inevitably; as a matter of course /趋～明显 marked (*or* pronounced) tendency /局～变化难以预料。It is difficult to predict how the situation will develop. *or* The future course of events is hard to predict. /大～已去。The game is as good as lost. ❺ sign; gesture:作手～ make a sign with the hand; gesture /装腔作～ put on airs and graces ❻ male genitals:去～ castration

势必 shìbì certainly will; be certain to:你这样做～脱离群众。What you are doing is sure to alienate you from the public.

势不得已 shìbùdéyǐ be forced by circumstances; can't help doing

势不可当 shìbùkědāng irresistible; overwhelming:～地冲向敌阵 make a forceful (*or* an overpowering) charge on the enemy /历史潮流～。The historical trend is irresistible. /～的泥石流卷走了桥墩。The rapid mud-rock flow swept away the pier.

势不两立 shìbùliǎnglì mutually exclusive; diametrically opposite; irreconcilable:两大派～。The two factions are irreconcilable. /科学与迷信是～的。Science is diametrically opposed to superstition.

势成骑虎 shìchéngqíhǔ in the position of one riding a tiger — unable to get down but dangerous to go on; circumstances make it difficult for one to back down; be caught between the devil and the deep blue sea

势单力薄 shìdān-lìbó small in number and meagre in strength; not enough manpower and resources:～,难有作为 not have enough strength and resources to accomplish anything

势家 shìjiā 〈旧语〉influential family

势均力敌 shìjūn-lìdí be evenly matched in strength:一场～的篮球赛 close basketball match /这是一场～的较量。This is a close contest (*or* an evenly-matched trial of strength).

势力 shìli force; power; influence:进步～ progressive forces /邪恶～ demonic influences; evil forces /习惯～ force of habit /削弱反对派的～ weaken (*or* reduce) the power of the opposition; lessen (*or* impair) the influence of the opposition /他有不可小视的～。He is a force to be reckoned with.

势力范围 shìli fànwéi sphere of influence:视这一地区为其～ regard this part of the world as its sphere of influence

势利 shìli snobbish:～透顶 too much of a snob; extremely snobbish

势利眼 shìliyǎn ❶ snobbish attitude; snobbishness; snobbery:这种～的人不可交。One shouldn't make friends with such a snobbish person. ❷ snob:远近闻名的～ notorious snob

势能 shìnéng *also* "位能" wèinéng 〈物理〉potential energy

势派 shìpai 〈方言〉❶ ostentation and extravagance:瞧人家那～多大! Look! What airs they give themselves! ❷ situation; circumstances:要看事情发展的～。It all depends on how things develop.

势穷力竭 shìqióng-lìjié in dire straits with one's strength exhausted

势如破竹 shìrúpòzhú be like splitting bamboo; carry all before one:部队长驱直入,～。The army drove straight in, carrying all before them.

势所必然 shìsuǒbìrán as a matter of course; certainly:深化改革,～。Deepening reforms is an inevitable trend.

势态 shìtài position; situation:善观～ know which way the wind blows /处于有利的～ be in an advantageous position

势头 shìtou impetus; momentum; situation; tendency:雨的～更大了。It is raining with a vengeance. /风的～有所减弱。The wind has subsided (*or* abated). /必须扼制这股不健康的～。It is necessary to check the unhealthy tendency. /工业生产出现增长的～。Industrial production shows signs of an upturn (*or* is picking up). /他发现～不对。He found the odds were against him. *or* He sensed that he was at a disadvantage.

势位 shìwèi power and position; position and influence:～显赫 very powerful and influential

势焰 shìyàn power and arrogance:～嚣张 be puffed up with pride; be swollen with arrogance /～熏天 overbearing arrogance

势要 shìyào 〈书面〉those in power; the influential and the mighty:～之家 influential family

势在必行 shìzàibìxíng be imperative (under the circumstances); become unavoidable:改革开放,～。It is imperative to carry out reforms and open to the outside world. /教学改革,～。Educational reforms must be carried out without delay.

势子 shìzi 〈方言〉gesture; posture; stance:他站起来做出要走的～。He stood up and made as if he was leaving.

势族 shìzú influential and powerful clan

是[1]

shì ❶ correct; right; true:大～大非 major matters of right and wrong /今～昨非 (realize that) one was wrong before but right now /实事求～ seek truth from facts /自以为～ consider oneself always in the right; be self-opinionated /一无～处 have no merit whatsoever to speak of /这就是你的不～了。That's your fault. ❷ 〈书面〉justify; uphold; praise:各～其是 each tries to justify what he considers correct /口～心非 say one thing and mean another ❸ yes; right:～,我一定去。Yes, I'll go there. /这是你要的那本书吗? 正～。Is this the book you want? That's right. ❹ (Shì) a surname

是[2]

shì 〈书面〉this; that:由～可知 thus it follows (that...); this shows /～岁华北大旱。Northern China suffered a serious drought that year. /～时风雨大作。Just then a strong wind rose and the rain began pouring down.

是[3]

shì ❶ *used as "verb to be" in emphatic form when the predicative is a noun*:巴金～《家》的作者。Ba Jin is the author of *Family*. /鲁迅～周树人的笔名。Lu Xun is a pseudonym (*or* penname) of Zhou Shuren. /他最佩服的就～你。Of all the people, you are the one he admires most. ❷ *used with* 的 *to indicate classification*:这套家具～新买的。The set of furniture was bought (*or* acquired) recently. /这台机器～从国外进口的。The machine was imported from abroad. /他～来找你的。He is here to see you. ❸ *used to indicate the state or condition of the subject*:北半球～冬天,南半球～夏天。While it is winter in the northern hemisphere, it is summer in the southern hemisphere. /他～一片诚心。He is completely sincere (*or* all sincerity). ❹ *used to indicate existence*:满身～汗 sweat all over /满脸～泪 one's cheeks were bathed in tears; tears streamed

S

down one's cheeks /学校左边～邮局，前边～马路，后边～一条小河。There is a post office to the left of the school, a road in front of it, and a small river behind it. *or* To the left of the school is a post office, in front of it a road, and behind it a small river. ❺ *used in between two identical nouns or verbs in two or more similar patterns to indicate distinction*：他～他，我～我，我们谁也管不着谁。We have our own wills, he and I, neither is the other's master. /昨天～昨天，今天～今天，情况是在不断地变化。Events are moving very fast; what was true yesterday may not be so today. /这个人言行不一，说～说，做～做。This man's deeds do not match his words; he never practises what he preaches. ❻ *used to indicate concession*：书～好书，可惜贵了点儿。It's true that this is a good book, but it's a bit too expensive. /这房子老～老，但离商店近，采购方便。Indeed, the house is old, but as it is close to the stores, it is convenient for shopping. ❼ *used at the beginning of a sentence for the sake of emphasis*：～谁教你这样做的？Who taught you this? *or* Who told you to do this? /～这位解放军战士救了你。It was this PLA man who saved you (*or* your life). ❽ *used before a noun to indicate each and everyone of the kind*：～人都会犯错误。Every man is liable to error. *or* No one is free from error. /～孩子他都喜爱。He loves all children. /～亲三分向。Blood is thicker than water. ❾ *used before a noun to indicate fitness or suitability*：屋里的家具都放得不～地方。The furniture in the room is put exactly where it should not be. /你来的正～时候。You've come just in the nick of time. *or* You can't have come at a better time. /她穿这条裙子很～样。The dress looks very becoming on her. ❿ *used in an alternative and negative question*：你～看电视还～听音乐？Would you like to watch TV or listen to music? /你～病了不～？You are ill, aren't you? /他不～出国了吗？Hasn't he gone abroad? ⓫ *pronounced emphatically to indicate certainty*：她爸爸～不同意她和小刘来往。Her father disapproves of her having anything to do with Xiao Liu. /这件事他～不知道。He certainly doesn't know this. /她～很努力的。She does work hard.

S

是的 shìde ❶ yes; right; just so; that's it ❷ as; like

是凡 shìfán every; any; all：～他的事，我一概不过问。I never bother myself about any of his business.

是非 shìfēi ❶ right and wrong; truth and falsehood：～不明 unable to tell right from wrong; have no sense of right and wrong /判断～ decide (*or* judge) what is right and what is wrong /～界限 dividing line between right and wrong /颠倒～ *also* "混淆～" confuse truth and falsehood; confound right with wrong; turn things upside down ❷ quarrel; dispute; trouble：搬弄～ tell tales; sow discord /挑拨～ foment discord; stir up trouble /～之人 controversial person /卷进了～的旋涡 get oneself entangled in a dispute

是非曲直 shìfēi-qūzhí rights and wrongs; truth and falsehood; merits and demerits：不分～ fail to distinguish between right and wrong; confuse truth and falsehood /评论～ comment on the rights and wrongs of a case /根据～断案 decide the case on its merits /～，一目了然。It is clear at a glance who's right and who's wrong.

是非窝 shìfēiwō *see* "是非之地"

是非之地 shìfēizhīdì place where one is apt to get into trouble; trouble-spot：～，不可久留。One should not hang on (*or* tarry) in a place where one can easily get into a fix.

是非自有公论 shìfēi zìyǒu gōnglùn the public will judge the rights and wrongs of the case; public opinion is the best judge of who is right and who is wrong：事实俱在，我相信～。As all the facts are available, I believe public opinion will be the best judge.

是否 shìfǒu whether or not; whether; if：他～同意，我还不清楚。I am not yet clear whether he agrees or not. /这个方案～可行，还得大家讨论才能决定。Whether the plan is feasible will have to be decided through discussion.

是个儿 shìgèr 〈口语〉match; equal：跟他掰腕子，你～吗？Are you his match in hand wrestling? /和他下象棋，我敢说你不～。I bet you are no match for him in Chinese chess.

是古非今 shìgǔ-fēijīn praise the past to condemn the present; extol the ancient and disparage the modern

是可忍，孰不可忍 shì kě rěn, shú bùkě rěn if this can be tolerated, what else cannot：他们如此欺负弱小国家，～！They have so brazenly bullied weak and small nations. If this can be put up with, then what else cannot!

是味儿 shìwèir 〈口语〉❶ have the right flavour; suit one's taste：这四川凉面做得可真～。The Sichuan cold noodles are really very delicious. ❷ feel better; feel more comfortable：得知他病危的消息，我心里真不～。I was very distressed to hear that he was critically ill. /这场足球赛看得很～。It was really a treat to watch that football match.

是样儿 shìyàngr 〈口语〉stylish：她做的衣服都挺～。The dresses she has made are all quite stylish (*or* trendy).

是正 shìzhèng 〈书面〉check and correct; put right; rectify：～文字 check and correct the scripts

释[1]（釋）

shì ❶ explain; expound; elucidate：注～ annotation; explanatory notes ❷ clear up; dispel; remove：前嫌冰～。All previous ill will has melted into thin air. /心中疑云顿～。The misgivings clouding one's mind were instantly dispelled. ❸ let go; be relieved of：如～重负 as if relieved of a heavy load; feel a sense of relief ❹ release; set free; put down：保～出狱 be released on bail; be bailed out /假～ be released on parole

释[2]（釋）

Shì (short for 释迦牟尼) Sakyamuni; Buddhism：～门 Buddhism

释典 shìdiǎn 〈佛教〉Buddhist Scripture

释读 shìdú 〈书面〉conduct research on and explain the texts of ancient writing

释放 shìfàng ❶ release; acquit; set free：刑满～ be released upon completion of a sentence /提前～ be released before one's sentence expires (*or* before the end of the official period of imprisonment) /～裁定书 rulings of acquittal /～出狱令 order of release /～证书 release certificate ❷ 〈物理〉release：～原子能 release atomic energy

释怀 shìhuái (usu. used in the negative) (of sentiments such as love, hatred, sorrow, happiness, etc.) disappear; vanish：当年离别的情景使我久久不能～。Memories of our parting (many) years ago remain long and fresh in my mind.

释迦牟尼 Shìjiāmóuní Sakyamuni (565-486 BC), founder of Buddhism

释教 Shìjiào Buddhism

释卷 shìjuàn put down a book：手不～ always have a book in one's hand; be engrossed in one's studies; be a diligent reader /书中情节曲折离奇，令人不能～。The book is so involved and fascinating that one finds it hard to put it down.

释老 Shì-Lǎo Buddhism and Taoism

释然 shìrán 〈书面〉no longer be worried; feel relieved; feel at ease：心中顿觉～ feel relieved immediately

释手 shìshǒu relax the hold; let go：爱不～ have a great liking for sth. and find it hard to part with it; be too fond of sth. to let go of it; fondle admiringly /不忍～ can hardly bear to put (sth.) down

释俗 shìsú explain in simple language：新名词要～。A new expression must be explained in simple terms.

释文 shìwén ❶ (usu. used in titles of books) explanation：《楚辞～》*Explanation of Poetry of Chu* ❷ transcribe the text of ancient writing

释疑 shìyí dispel doubts; explain difficult points：跟他谈谈，好让他～ talk with him so as to clear up his doubts /老师的责任之一是～。One of the teacher's duties is to explain difficult points to the students.

释义 shìyì explain the meaning (of a word, etc.)：给古文～ explicate classical Chinese writing

释藏 Shìzàng *also* "三藏" Sānzàng Tripitaka

释战草 shìzhàncǎo loosestrife

释重 shìzhòng be relieved of a heavy burden

释子 shìzǐ 〈书面〉monks; Buddhist followers

筮

shì 〈古语〉practise divination with alpine yarrow

澨

shì 〈书面〉water margin

噬

shì bite：吞～ swallow up /反～ make a false counter charge; hurl back an accusation

噬菌体 shìjūntǐ 〈生物〉bacteriophage; phage

噬脐莫及 shìqí-mòjí it's impossible to bite one's own navel — it's impossible or too late to save the situation; repentance is too late：事在预防，待羽翼成后，便～。It is important to take preventive measures; once an evil force is allowed to come into its own, it'll be too late to repent. /今不为曲突徙薪之计，后必有～之忧。Failure to take

precautions today will surely lead to irrevocable disaster (*or* irreparable loss) tomorrow.

噬人鲨 shìrénshā white shark (*Carcharodon carcharias*)

噬食 shìshí swallow; devour

噬细胞 shìxìbāo phagocyte

适[1](適) shì ❶ fit; suitable; appropriate; proper: ~于孕妇服用的药品 medicine fit for pregnant women /~于孩子观看的电视剧 TV plays suitable for children ❷ right; opportune: 正要找他,在路上~与他碰上了。I was looking for him when I ran into him on the way. /~逢元旦。It happened to be New Year's Day. ❸ comfortable; well; at ease: 身体略感不~ feel a bit under the weather (*or* slightly indisposed) /舒~的环境 comfortable environment

适[2](適) shì ❶ go; follow; move towards: 无所~从 be at a loss what to do; be at a loss whom to turn to /~他处 go to his place ❷〈书面〉(of a woman) get married; marry: 其女~张家。His daughter married Zhang's son.

适才 shìcái just now: ~还听他说到你。I heard him talking about you only a moment ago.

适当 shìdàng suitable; proper; appropriate; right: ~的场合 appropriate occasion /~的方式 proper way /~的人选 suitable candidate; suitable choice for (a position); right person (for a job) /繁简~ neither too simple nor too elaborate; just right /~的批评 reasonable (*or* well-founded) criticisms /~处罚 punishment commensurate with the offence /~的权限 due authority /~的休息 adequate rest /~的活动 moderate exercise /~的限制 necessary restriction /这个时候找他是不~的。It was not an opportune time to see him now.

适得其反 shìdé-qífǎn turn out to be just the opposite of what one wished; run counter to one's desire; be just the opposite: 这努力大抵是徒劳的,而且还~。This is a futile attempt; what's more, it is counterproductive. /拔苗助长,~。Trying to help the shoots grow by pulling them upward is only to kill them. /体育锻炼有助于身体健康,但运动量过大则~。Physical exercise helps one keep fit, but too much of it will produce the opposite effect.

适度 shìdù appropriate; proper; to a moderate degree: ~的营养 proper nutrition /~的睡眠 right amount of sleep /体育活动对一般人来说以~为好。For most people, it's better to do a moderate amount of physical exercise.

适逢其会 shìféng-qíhuì happen to be present on the occasion; turn up at the opportune moment: 我是来巧了,~,才看了这场演出。I came at the right time to watch the performance.

适航性 shìhángxìng (of an aircraft) airworthiness; (of a ship) seaworthiness

适合 shìhé suit; fit; befit: ~国情 be suited to the conditions of the country /~周围的环境 fit in with the surroundings /~各人的口味 suit everyone's taste; be to everybody's liking /~个人需要 suit (*or* serve) individual needs /不~这种场合的言论 remarks not befitting the occasion /你认为他~做新闻工作吗? Do you think he is cut out (*or* fit) for journalistic work? /这东西太贵,不~工薪阶层的购买力。The thing is too expensive for the salaried class.

适婚 shìhūn suitable age for marriage; (legally) marriageable age: ~青年 youth of marriageable age

适间 shìjiān just now; just a moment ago: 想起~发生的事情,他好久不能平静。Recalling what had just happened, he couldn't calm down for quite some time.

适可而止 shìkě'érzhǐ refrain from going too far; know when and where to stop; must not exceed proper limits: 凡事都应~,不能太过了。One should keep from going too far in whatever one does. *or* One should not overdo it.

适口 shìkǒu agreeable to the taste; pleasant to taste; palatable: 饭菜~。The food is palatable.

适来 shìlái 〈书面〉just now; a moment ago: ~何人在此喧哗? Who made such a big noise here just now?

适量 shìliàng just the right amount: 小学生作业应当~。Primary school pupils should be assigned only a reasonable amount of homework. *or* The homework assigned to primary school pupils should be kept within reasonable limits. /用药必须~。Medicine must be taken in moderate doses.

适龄 shìlíng of the right age: ~儿童都上学了。Children of school age all go to school now. /村里~青年大都参军了。Most young people of military age in the village have joined the army.

适路 shìlù meet the need: 大学里开设~对口的新专业。In the universities and colleges new disciplines geared to practical needs have been introduced.

适巧 shìqiǎo by chance; by coincidence: 我刚要去找他,~他回来了。He came back just when I was about to go and look for him.

适切 shìqiè suitable; fitting; appropriate; proper: 这个比喻用在这里非常~。This metaphor fits in very well here.

适人 shìrén 〈书面〉(of women) marry; get married

适如 shìrú just as; just like: 事情~他所说的那样。Things turned out just as he had predicted.

适时 shìshí in good time; timely; seasonable: ~春耕 begin spring ploughing in good time /~的忠告 piece of seasonable advice /~劝告他注意身体 give him timely advice that he should keep close watch on his health

适体 shìtǐ fit: 这套西服穿起来很~。This suit fits very well.

适销 shìxiāo have a ready market: ~对路 (of commodities) salable; fit for sale /~商品 commodities that sell well in the market; salable goods /这个厂积极抓~对路的产品,经营效益不断提高。The factory has paid special attention to the production of goods that have a ready market, and there has been a steady increase in its profit.

适宜 shìyí suitable; proper; fit; appropriate: 气候~ genial climate /条件~ suitable conditions /剪裁~ (of a garment) well-cut out; well-tailored /穿戴~ be properly dressed; be in proper attire /~技术 appropriate technology /~的环境 favourable environment /这种补品~于老年人服用。This kind of tonic is good for elderly people. /他~当教师。He has the makings of a teacher. /她不~学外语。She has no aptitude for foreign languages.

适意 shìyì agreeable; pleasant; enjoyable; comfortable: 大热天洗个冷水澡,~极了。I feel very refreshed after a cold bath in such hot weather.

适应 shìyìng suit; adapt; fit: ~工作的需要 meet the requirements of one's work /~当地生活习惯 adapt (oneself) to the local way of life /~形势的需要 cater to the needs of the circumstances /到新地方总有个~过程。It takes one some time to adjust to a new place. /他的~能力很强。He is very adaptable. *or* He can adapt to any situation easily. /各项工作都应~经济改革的需要。All work should be geared to the needs of economic reform. /上层建筑要与经济基础相~。The superstructure should correspond with the economic base.

适应性 shìyìngxìng 〈生物〉adaptability

适应症 shìyìngzhèng 〈医学〉indication

适用 shìyòng suit; be applicable: ~范围 scope (*or* sphere) of application /马克思主义的基本原理是普遍~的。The fundamental tenets of Marxism are universally applicable. /安全驾驶的各项规定对司机都~。The rules of safe driving apply to all motorists. /我们必须制定一些~于沿海地区不同情况的政策。We must work out some policies suited to the different conditions in coastal areas.

适用性 shìyòngxìng applicability

适者生存 shìzhě shēngcún 〈生物〉survival of the fittest

适值 shìzhí 〈书面〉just when: ~期终考试 just when I was having the term-end examinations /重返故乡,~中秋佳节。It was on the Moon Festival that I returned to my home town.

适中 shìzhōng ❶ proper; appropriate; moderate: 长短~ of moderate length /高矮~ of middle (*or* average) height /试题难度~。The test paper was of average difficulty. ❷ (of place) well situated: 地点~ be well (*or* conveniently) situated; be in a fine location

似 shì
see also sì

似的 shìde 〈助词〉*used after a noun, a pronoun, or a verb to indicate similarity*: 像血~那么红 as red as blood /他好像顿时年轻了~。He looks as if he had suddenly become young again. /她高兴得什么~。She looks immensely happy.

氏 shì ❶ family name; surname: 王~兄弟 Wang brothers ❷ née: 李张~ Mrs. Li, née Zhang ❸ *used after famous persons such as scientists, inventors, etc.*: 华~表 Fahrenheit thermometer /李~定理 Li Siguang's theorem ❹〈书面〉one's kinsfolk: 舅~ (maternal) uncle
see also zhī

S

氏族 shìzú clan:～公社 clan commune /～社会 clan society /～制度 clan system /～贵族 gentile noble

舐

shì 〈书面〉lick:老牛～犊 a cow licks her calf

舐犊情深 shìdú-qíngshēn deep affection towards one's children; parental love

舐痔 shìzhì 〈书面〉lick piles (of VIPs) — be obsequious; show sycophancy; lick someone's boots:～吮痈 suck the piles and ulcers of another person — play the bootlicker

饰

shì ❶ adorn; dress up; polish; hide:粉～ gloss over; whitewash /文～ cover up (one's mistakes) /文章还需修～一下。The essay needs polishing. /他竭力掩～自己的真实意图。He tried very hard to conceal his true intentions. ❷ decoration; ornaments:首～ women's personal ornaments; jewelry /服～ clothes and ornaments /头～ adornments for one's hair; ornaments for the head; headdress /窗～ window decorations ❸ play the role or act the part of a dramatic character:她在《红楼梦》里～林黛玉。She plays the role of Lin Daiyu in *A Dream of Red Mansions*.

饰菜 shìcài garnish

饰词 shìcí excuse; pretext

饰品 shìpǐn head ornaments; jewels:黄金～ gold ornaments

饰物 shìwù ❶ ornaments; jewelry:佩戴着珍贵的～ wear precious jewelry /她头上缀满了亮晶晶的～。She is wearing a lot of sparkling hair adornments. *or* She is crowned with glittering hair ornaments. ❷ ornaments; decorations:墙上挂着一些雅致的～。Some elegant decorations are hung on the wall.

饰演 shìyǎn act; play the part of:他在京剧《武松打虎》中～武松。He acted (the part of) the hero Wu Song in the Beijing opera *Wu Song Kills the Tiger*.

S

shi

殖

shi *see* "骨殖" gǔshi

see also zhí

匙

shi *see* "钥匙" yàoshi

see also chí

shōu

收(収)

shōu ❶ bring in; gather together; put in proper place:～网 draw (*or* haul) in the net /～帆 take in sail /～起桌上的纸笔 gather together paper and pencils on the desk /把晾干的衣服～进来 bring in dried washing /～票 collect tickets /～了不少有用的成语 contain quite a lot of useful idioms /～好工具 stow the tools away /把桌上的盘子～走 clear away the dishes from the table ❷ recover; retrieve:～回 recover; take back /把矿山、油田～归国有 nationalize mines and oilfields ❸ collect (revenues); charge (fees):～会费 collect membership dues /～房租 collect rent /～管理费 charge a service fee /分文不～ without charging a single cent; free of charge /税～ tax revenues ❹ reap; harvest:～庄稼 harvest (*or* gather in) crops /提前～玉米 reap the maize (*or* corn) ahead of schedule /抢～ rush in the harvest /秋粮丰～ good autumn harvest /歉～ crop failure; poor harvest ❺ receive; accept:～到许多生日礼物 receive many birthday presents /请～下这个小礼品作个纪念。Please accept this little gift as a souvenir. /王师傅～他当了徒弟。Master Worker Wang accepted him as his apprentice. /该大学今年～一百五十名研究生。The university will enrol 150 graduate students this year. ❻ restrain; control:～泪 restrain one's tears; stop crying or weeping /～不住了 get out of control /一发而不可～。Once it gets started, there is no way of holding it back. /过完春节,我可得～～心、好好念点书了。After the Spring Festival I'll have to keep a grip on myself and get down to my studies. ❼ arrest; take into custody; put in jail or prison:～拿 put under arrest; arrest /～进教养院 put in a correctional institution /～入监狱 put in jail (*or* prison) ❽ end; stop:去晚了,早市已经～了。When we got there, the morning market had already closed. /今天出工早,现在就～了吧。As we started work fairly early this morning, we may as well call it a day now.

收报 shōubào receive a telegram:～员 telegrapher

收报机 shōubàojī (telegraphic or radiotelegraphic) receiver

收编 shōubiān incorporate into one's own forces:～地方部队 incorporate local armed forces (into the national armed forces, etc.)

收兵 shōubīng ❶ withdraw troops; call off a battle:鸣金～ beat the gongs to recall the troops /不获全胜,决不～。We will not withdraw our forces till complete victory. ❷〈比喻〉wind up; bring to an end:不达目的,誓不～。We shall not stop trying till our goal is attained.

收藏 shōucáng collect; store up:～文物 collect cultural relics /～军火 store up munitions /请把这份文件～好。Please put this document in the filing cabinet for safekeeping.

收藏家 shōucángjiā collector (of books, antiques, curios, etc.)

收操 shōucāo 〈军事〉bring drill to an end; end drilling

收操号 shōucāohào bugle call to dismiss; recall

收场 shōuchǎng ❶ wind up; end; stop:草草～ wind sth. up hastily or perfunctorily /这事如何～? How should we end it all? *or* How is this going to end? /你的表演早该～了。It's high time you put an end to (*or* stopped) these antics of yours. ❷ ending; conclusion:出乎意料的～ unexpected denouement /不会有好～ will come to no good end

收车 shōuchē drive or pull back carts or trucks when the transport job is done:下班时间到了,该～了。It's time to knock off and drive the truck back.

收成 shōucheng harvest; crop:～很好 good harvest; bumper harvest /苹果～不好 have a poor crop of apples /鱼虾～不坏 have a good catch of fish and shrimps /今年玉米～要创新记录。This year's maize crop will set a new record.

收存 shōucún receive and keep; keep:老王出差了,我替他～这封信吧。You can leave the letter with me as Lao Wang is away on a business trip.

收到 shōudào receive; get; achieve:～一张汇单 receive a money order /～回信 get a reply /～预期的效果 achieve the desired (*or* hoped-for) results

收发 shōufā ❶ receive and dispatch:～文件 receive and dispatch documents ❷ dispatcher (of documents or mail)

收发报 shōufābào receive and transmit telegrams

收发报机 shōufābàojī transmitter-receiver; transceiver

收发室 shōufāshì office for incoming and outgoing mail; mail office

收方 shōufāng debit side; debit

收房 shōufáng 〈旧语〉take a maidservant as one's concubine

收放 shōufàng receive and keep; keep:所有文件都～在档案柜里。All documents are kept in the filing cabinet.

收费 shōufèi collect fees; charge:他管～。He is in charge of collecting fees. /游艇出租,每小时～五元。The rowboats are for hire at 5 *yuan* per hour. /这个我们不～。We don't charge anything for that. *or* This is free of charge.

收费厕所 shōufèi cèsuǒ pay toilet

收费电话 shōufèi diànhuà pay phone

收费电视 shōufèi diànshì subscription television; pay TV

收费高速公路 shōufèi gāosù gōnglù toll expressway

收风 shōufēng time for prisoners to return to their cells after being let out for fresh air

收伏 shōufú *see* "收服"

收服 shōufú *also* "收伏" subdue and bring under control; win over:这个部落被～后,宣告臣服皇帝。The subdued tribe proclaimed allegiance to the emperor.

收抚 shōufǔ ❶ take in and console:～难民 house (*or* take in) refugees ❷ take in and raise; have sb. in one's care:～孤儿 adopt an orphan /～被遗弃的女婴 foster (*or* be foster-parent to) a deserted baby girl

收复 shōufù recover; regain; recapture:～失地 recover lost territory /～阵地 recapture a position

收港 shōugǎng return to port:现在还有渔船没有～,我不能离开岗位。I can't leave my post when there are still a number of fishing boats not yet back in port.

收割 shōugē reap; harvest; gather:～水稻 reap in (*or* gather, *or* harvest) paddy /～一百亩玉米要多少时间? How long does it take to reap 100 *mu* of maize?

收割机 shōugējī harvester; reaper:联合～ combine harvester /玉米～ maize harvester

收工 shōugōng stop work (for the day); knock off: 按时～ stop work on time /我们下午五点～。We shall knock off at five in the afternoon.
收购 shōugòu buy; purchase; procure: ～旧家具 buy used furniture /～额 value of purchase /～价格 purchasing (*or* procurement) price /以合理价格～棉花 purchase (*or* buy) cotton at a fair price
收购站 shōugòuzhàn purchasing station or centre
收骨 shōugǔ bury the dead
收管 shōuguǎn collect and preserve; safekeep: ～文物 collect and preserve cultural relics
收归 shōuguī restore (title to sth., etc.); regain; recover: 土地～国有。Land was nationalized.
收后付款 shōuhòu fùkuǎn payable on receipt
收回 shōuhuí ❶ regain; recover; recall: ～主权 regain sovereignty (over...) /～港口 recover (*or* regain) a port /～贷款 recall (*or* retrieve) a loan /～投资 recoup one's investment (*or* capital outlay) /～财产 evict (sb.) and recover (property) ❷ withdraw; rescind: ～所说的话 take back one's statement /他后来～了对她的指控。He withdrew the charges he had made against her.
收回成命 shōuhuí chéngmìng rescind or countermand an order; revoke a command
收活 shōuhuó ❶ (of repair shops, processing departments, etc.) take orders from customers: 这家服装加工厂近来～不多。This garment factory has received very few orders recently. ❷〈方言〉stop work for the day; knock off: 今天早点～。Let's knock off early today.
收货凭单 shōuhuò píngdān consignment sheet
收货人 shōuhuòrén consignee: ～地址 consignee's address
收获 shōuhuò ❶ gather (a crop); reap; harvest: 春天播种,秋天～ sow in the spring and reap in the autumn /～的季节到了。The harvest season has come. /南方的水稻一年可以～三次。In the south there can be 3 crops of rice a year. ❷ gains; rewards; results: 一次很有～的夏令营活动 very rewarding camping activity /不下功夫,焉有～。No pain, no gain. /我跑了两趟,毫无～。I made two fruitless trips. /我们搜索了一整天,但毫无～。We searched all day in vain.
收获量 shōuhuòliàng harvest yield; yield
收集 shōují bring together; collect; gather: ～古玩字画 collect antiques, calligraphy works and paintings /～情报 gather information; collect intelligence /这位经济学教授正忙着为他的下一部著作～数据。The economics professor is busy accumulating data for his next book.
收集系统 shōují xìtǒng〈石油〉gathering system
收监 shōujiān put behind bars; imprison: ～候审 take into custody to await trial
收检 shōujiǎn check and put in order: 秘书把寄来的文件一一～。The secretary checked and arranged all the incoming papers.
收件人 shōujiànrén addressee; consignee
收缴 shōujiǎo ❶ take over; confiscate; capture: ～敌人的武器 capture the enemy's arms /他的非法收入已被全部～。All his illegal gains were confiscated. ❷ levy; collect: ～私藏的枪支弹药 collect illegally-held guns and ammunition /～税款 levy taxes
收紧 shōujǐn tighten up: ～包围圈 tighten up the encirclement
收进 shōujìn incorporate; include: 这个新词没有～词典里。This new word is not incorporated in the dictionary.
收据 shōujù receipt: 领货～ receipt for freight /装货～ shipping receipt
收据簿 shōujùbù receipt book
收看 shōukàn watch (TV): ～"新闻联播"节目 watch the National TV Network Newscast /请继续～。Please stay tuned. *or* Please stay with us.
收看率 shōukànlǜ audience ratings: 高～ high audience ratings /电视～下降 drop in television viewing /全国～晚间增加百分之一,白天下降了百分之三。There was a one percent rise nationwide in evening viewing and a three percent decline in daytime viewing.
收口 shōukǒu ❶ (as in knitting) binding off: 毛衣的袖子差几针就～了。The cuff of the woollen sweater will be bound off with a few more stitches. /编筐的功夫在～。The craftsmanship (*or* skill) of basket-weaving lies in the casting off. ❷ (of a wound) close up; heal: 刀伤～儿了。The cut has healed.
收款机 shōukuǎnjī cash register
收款人 shōukuǎnrén payee
收扩两用机 shōu-kuò liǎngyòngjī receiver-amplifier
收揽 shōulǎn ❶ win over (through bribery or demagoguery): ～民心 buy popular support ❷〈书面〉bring under control: 难以～ hard to control /为特权者所～ be under the thumb of the privileged
收礼 shōulǐ accept a present or gift: 概不～。No gifts accepted.
收理 shōulǐ put in order: ～农具 put the farm tools in order
收镰 shōulián end the harvest season; finish the harvest (of): 今年的早稻～早。The reaping of rice ended earlier this year than last.
收敛 shōuliǎn ❶ weaken; diminish; disappear: 夕阳已经～了它的余晖。The radiance of the setting sun has diminished. /她脸上不耐烦的表情顿时～了。Her impatient look suddenly disappeared. ❷ show restraint: 她本来讲话都是那么没大没小的,现在已有所～。She used to be frivolous, but now she has learnt to bridle her tongue. ❸〈医学〉shrink (body tissues); check (flow of blood or other secretions); stanch ❹〈数学〉convergence: ～算法 convergence algorithm /～条件 condition of convergence /～半径 convergence radius /～级数 convergent series
收敛药 shōuliǎnyào *also* "收敛剂" astringent
收殓 shōuliàn lay a body in a coffin; prepare a corpse for burial; bury: 当年祖父去世后,多亏乡亲们～了他。When grandpa died, it was his fellow villagers who buried him.
收留 shōuliú undertake the care of; take in: 那孤儿被一对老夫妻～了。An old couple offered to take care of the orphan. /他们已无力再～更多难民了。They can no longer afford to take in more refugees.
收拢 shōulǒng ❶ draw in; gather together: 把晾在场上的麦子～起来 gather together the wheat being sunned on the threshing ground /弹簧拉过了头,就再也不能～了。A spring will lose its elasticity once it is overstretched. ❷ win over (with money or other favours): ～人心 court popularity; win people over by dispensing favours
收录 shōulù ❶ employ; recruit; enlist: ～旧部 reemploy one's former subordinates /被工厂～为会计 be recruited as an accountant in the factory ❷ collect (in an anthology, etc.); include: 这本选集～了他的主要作品。All his major works are included in the anthology. ❸ receive and record: ～电台的晚间新闻 record the evening news broadcast
收录两用机 shōu-lù liǎngyòngjī *also* "收录机"〈无线电〉radio cassette tape recorder; radio-recorder: 双卡～ double-cassette radio-recorder
收罗 shōuluó collect; recruit: ～材料 collect materials (esp. research and information materials) /～人才 scout for competent personnel
收买 shōumǎi ❶ purchase; buy: ～股票 buy stocks ❷ bribe; buy over; buy off; buy up: ～政府官员 bribe government officials /为了个人目的而～一些人 buy over some people for one's own purposes
收买人心 shōumǎi-rénxīn buy popular support; court popularity: 不要用小恩小惠的手段～。Don't try to win people's support by bestowing small favours.
收没 shōumò confiscate: 财产～归官。His property was confiscated by the government.
收纳 shōunà take in; accept: 如数～ accept (a sum of money, etc.) as indicated /他前去投奔舅父,谁知舅父不肯～他。He sought shelter with his uncle who, to everybody's surprise, refused to take him in.
收盘 shōupán〈经济〉(as of an exchange) closing quotation: ～出价 closing bid /～价 closing price; closing quotation /昨天～时,美元汇率开始反弹。There was a rebound in the closing rate of the US dollar yesterday.
收篷 shōupéng〈方言〉shorten sail; haul in sail; finish; conclude: 趁势～ make a timely withdrawal
收票员 shōupiàoyuán ticket collector
收起 shōuqǐ ❶ pack up; pick up: 他～书包回家去。Picking up his satchel, he started for home. ❷ give up; cut out; stop: 除非他们～那套骗人花招,不然我们就要毫不客气地予以揭露。Unless they give up their chicanery, we shall expose them without mercy. /～你的那一套谬论吧。Cut out your nonsense. /～你的如意算盘吧! No more of your smug calculations!
收讫 shōuqì (as on a bill of lading, an invoice, etc.) paid (in full); received (in full): ～章 receipt stamp /在账单上注明～ receipt a bill /费用～。Expenses paid.
收清 shōuqīng receive in full: ～旧债 receive payment for all old debts; collect all old debts /货款～。Payment (for a supply of goods) received in full.

收秋 shōuqiū autumn harvest：农民们忙着～。The farmers are busy with their autumn harvest.
收取 shōuqǔ get payment：～附加费 impose a surcharge
收容 shōuróng take in and provide for：～难民 accept refugees; feed and house refugees
收容所 shōuróngsuǒ collecting post (for stray soldiers, etc.); house for refugees; refugee camp
收入 shōurù ❶ take in; include; incorporate：将文件～档案 file a document; place a document on file /词典修订版～了许多新词语。Many new expressions are incorporated in the revised edition of the dictionary. /把散乱的书籍～书柜。Put the scattered books in the bookcase. ❷ income; revenue; earnings; proceeds：个人～ personal income /现金～ cash income /国家～ state revenue /外汇～ earnings in foreign exchange /毛～ gross income; gross earnings /净～ net income; net earnings /捐税～ tax proceeds /～和支出 revenue and expenditure; receipts and expenditure /～过分悬殊 excessive income disparity
收入不均 shōurù bùjūn income inequality
收入分配 shōurù fēnpèi income distribution：～结构 pattern of income distribution
收入税 shōurùshuì income tax; receipt tax
收入效应 shōurù xiàoyìng income effect; revenue effect
收涩 shōusè 〈中医〉 astringent or styptic treatment (for spontaneous sweating, seminal emission, chronic diarrhoea, anal prolapse, uterine bleeding, etc.)
收煞 shōushā *also* "收杀" stop; end：刮了一夜的大风，直到天明方才～。The wind raged all night and didn't subside until daybreak.
收梢 shōushāo 〈方言〉 wind up; stop; end up：事情闹得收不了梢。Things got out of control, and now there is no way to stop them.
收摄 shōushè restrain oneself：他～了心神，不再胡思乱想。He put a tighter rein on his thoughts and refrained from going off into wild flights of fancy.
收审 shōushěn detain for interrogation：依法～ detain sb. for interrogation according to law /他无理殴打保安人员，已被～。He has been detained for hitting the public security man without provocation.
收生 shōushēng midwifery
收生婆 shōushēngpó midwife
收尸 shōushī bury the dead
收湿性 shōushīxìng 〈化学〉 hygroscopicity
收市 shōushì (of a market) close：这家农贸市场每天什么时候～？When does this agricultural produce market close every day?
收市行情 shōushì hángqíng closing quotations
收视 shōushì viewing：～效果 viewing effect
收视率 shōushìlǜ rating (of a TV programme)
see also "收看率"
收拾 shōushi ❶ put in order; tidy up; clear away; get ready：把书架上的书～一下 put the books on the shelves in order /～房间 tidy up a room /～桌子 clear up a table /～床铺 make the bed /～残部，东山再起 collect the remnant troops and stage a comeback /不可～ unmanageable; out of hand /～行装 pack one's luggage; pack up one's things (for travel) /她在～明天野餐用的东西。She's getting things ready for tomorrow's picnic. /这一堆脏东西我来～。I'll clean up the mess. ❷ repair; mend; fix：～拉锁 repair a zipper /～皮包 mend a leather briefcase (*or* handbag) ❸ settle with; punish：～这个坏蛋 settle with the scoundrel /一定要好好～～这帮流氓。We will teach these hooligans a good lesson. ❹ eliminate; get rid of：这楼里的老鼠全叫我们～了。We've killed all the rats in this building.
收拾残局 shōushi-cánjú pick up the pieces：这里的残局怕不大好收拾。It might not be easy to clear up the mess here.
收受 shōushòu receive; accept：他从不～病人的任何礼物。He won't accept any gifts from his patients.
收受人 shōushòurén recipient
收束 shōushù ❶ collect; restrain：～心思 collect one's thoughts; restrain one's wandering mind ❷ bring to an end; wind up：我想他正在～他的讲话呢。I think he is winding up his speech. ❸ pack (for a journey)：～行李 pack(up) one's luggage
收缩 shōusuō ❶ contract; shrink; reduce：这东西晒干了会～。It contracts as it becomes dry. /毛料用热水洗会～。Woollen cloth shrinks in hot water. ❷ draw back; tighten up：～开支 cut spending /敌人将主力～到几个中心城市里。The enemy withdrew their main forces into a few key cities. /全身肌肉一下子～起来。All his muscles were tightened up immediately. ❸ 〈生理〉 systole：心脏的～与舒张 systole and diastole (of the heart)
收缩比 shōusuōbǐ contraction ratio
收缩量 shōusuōliàng shrinkage
收缩率 shōusuōlǜ shrinkage
收缩期 shōusuōqī 〈生理〉 (of the heart) systole (as against diastole)：～杂音 systolic murmur
收缩系数 shōusuō xìshù coefficient of contraction
收缩压 shōusuōyā 〈生理〉 systolic pressure
收摊儿 shōutānr pack up the stall for the day; wind up a day's business or the work on hand：天色渐晚，小贩们纷纷～了。It was getting late, and the vendors began packing up their stalls one after another. /这次普查工作可以～了。Now we can wind up the work on the survey.
收条 shōutiáo receipt：打个～ make (*or* write) out a receipt
收听 shōutīng listen (in)：～天气预报 listen in to a weather forecast /～实况广播 listen to a live broadcast /你的收音机能～福州台吗？Can you get Radio Fuzhou on your radio set? /请继续～。Please stay tuned.
收托 shōutuō admit (babies or children) to nursery or childcare centre：这个托儿所共～五十个幼儿。This childcare centre has admitted a total of 50 preschool children.
收尾 shōuwěi ❶ final phase (of a project, etc.)：完成工程的～工作 bring to an end the final phase of a project; wind up a project ❷ concluding paragraph (of an article, etc.); ending：可以看出，故事的～有些草率。The ending of the story shows signs of hasty work.
收文 shōuwén incoming dispatches or correspondence：登记～时间 register the time of arrival of incoming dispatches
收文簿 shōuwénbù register or log of incoming dispatches
收系 shōuxì 〈书面〉 arrest; take into custody; imprison：～囹圄 be thrown into prison; be put behind prison bars
收夏 shōuxià reap summer harvest; harvest summer crops
收降 shōuxiáng receive or accept surrender：前次战役里～了敌军三万人。Thirty thousand enemy troops surrendered in the last battle.
收效 shōuxiào yield or produce an effect：～明显 produce (*or* bring) notable results; be quite effective /～甚微 produce very little effect; be quite ineffectual /投资少，～快 small investments with quick returns
收歇 shōuxiē ❶ stop; subside; abate：夜已深，市区喧闹声渐渐～了。It was midnight, and the hustle and bustle of the downtown area had gradually abated. ❷ 〈方言〉 stop operation; close down：由于市场萧条，国外不少工厂～了。Because of a slumping market many factories abroad have closed down.
收心 shōuxīn ❶ get into the frame of mind for work or study：马上就要开学，你也该收收心了。The new term is about to begin. It's time you settled down and got ready for serious study. ❷ have a change of heart; convert to a different view：～向善 repent and turn over a new leaf
收信人 shōuxìnrén recipient (of a letter); addressee
收押 shōuyā take into custody; detain：～嫌疑犯 take a suspect into custody; detain a suspect
收养 shōuyǎng take in and bring up; take into one's family; adopt：～遗孤 adopt sb.'s orphan /～关系 adoptive relationship
收养法 shōuyǎngfǎ law of adoption
收养继承人 shōuyǎng jìchéngrén 〈法律〉 heir by adoption
收养人 shōuyǎngrén adopter
收益 shōuyì income; profit; proceeds; returns：获得巨大～ reap huge profits /～递减 diminishing returns /～账户 income account /～债券 income bond /这次演出的全部～ entire earnings (*or* proceeds) of the performance
收益率 shōuyìlǜ rate of return; earning rate; yield rate
收音 shōuyīn ❶ (of an auditorium, etc.) have good or bad acoustics：音乐厅的～效果极佳。The acoustics of the concert hall are excellent. *or* The concert hall has excellent acoustics. ❷ (of radio) reception：天气坏时～效果不佳。Reception is poor in bad weather.
收音电唱两用机 shōuyīn diànchàng liǎngyòngjī radiogramophone
收音机 shōuyīnjī radio (set); wireless (set)：便携式～ portable radio /落地式～ console radio /～手表 radio watch
收载 shōuzǎi include and record：书中～了许多民间验方。A great number of proved recipes circulated among the people are recorded in the book.
收摘 shōuzhāi harvest; pick：～草莓 pick strawberries

收账 shōuzhàng ❶ enter into accounts; charge to accounts ❷ collect payments of bills

收针 shōuzhēn (in knitting) decrease; cast off the stitches: 袖子够长了，该～了。It's time to cast off the stitches; the sleeve is long enough.

收支 shōu-zhī revenue and expenditure; income and expenses: ～平衡 balance of revenue and expenditure / ～不平衡 payments imbalance; payments disequilibrium / ～账目 income and expenditure accounts; balance sheet / 使～相抵 make both ends meet; break even

收支包干 shōu-zhī bāogān (of an enterprise) be responsible for one's own revenue and expenditure; be responsible for balancing one's budget

收支差额 shōu-zhī chā'é 〈经济〉 balance of payment

收支逆差 shōu-zhī nìchā unfavourable balance of payments; balance of payments deficit

收执 shōuzhí ❶ (of a certificate, etc.) be issued for safekeeping: 交给当事人～ be given to the party concerned for safekeeping ❷ receipt (issued by a government agency)

收治 shōuzhì ❶ (of hospitals) admit for treatment: 这个医院增加床位，～病人。The hospital has increased its beds to admit more patients for treatment. ❷〈书面〉 arrest and punish

shóu

熟 shóu 〈口语〉 *see* "熟" shú
see also shú

shǒu

守 shǒu ❶ guard; defend; garrison: ～边疆 guard the frontier / 失～ (of a city, etc.) be occupied by the enemy; fall / ～大门 keep the gate / 据～阵地 hold a position / 驻～海岛 stationed on an island ❷ keep watch; watch over; look after: 他在山头连续～了两天。He kept watch at the hilltop for two days running. / 母亲整夜～着生病的孩子。The mother watched over the sick child all night. ❸ observe; abide by; adhere: 严～纪律 observe discipline strictly / 恪～条约 abide by a treaty scrupulously / ～规矩 play by the rules; behave oneself properly / ～本分 act according to one's status; know one's place / 不要～着老一套不放。It won't do to always stick to the old ways. ❹ by the side of; next to; near: ～着山的地方可多种果树。Plant more fruit trees where there are hills. / 她～着婶子过一辈子。She stayed with her aunt all her life.

守备 shǒubèi garrison; defence: 我们必须加强首都的～。We must strengthen the defence of the capital.

守备部队 shǒubèi bùduì garrison force; garrison

守兵 shǒubīng garrison force; garrison troops

守财奴 shǒucáinú miser; tightwad; skinflint

守场员 shǒuchǎngyuán 〈体育〉 fielder

守车 shǒuchē 〈铁路〉 guard's van; caboose: ～车长 van guard

守成 shǒuchéng 〈书面〉 maintain the achievements of one's forefathers or predecessors; carry on an undertaking started by one's predecessors: 创业难，～亦不易。While it is difficult to blaze a new path, it is by no means easy to keep it open. / 他足以～，但难以创业。He is good enough to carry on what has been started, but not good at pioneering work.

守敌 shǒudí enemy defending or garrisoning a place

守法 shǒufǎ obey or observe the law; be law-abiding: 遵纪～ observe discipline and abide by the law / 奉公～是每个人的义务。Everyone is duty-bound to obey the law.

守法户 shǒufǎhù law-abiding firm

守分 shǒufèn behave properly and correctly; be content with one's lot in life

守服 shǒufú observe mourning for one's parent

守宫 shǒugōng (old name for 壁虎) gecko; house lizard

守寡 shǒuguǎ remain a widow; live in widowhood: 她～一辈子，好不容易把儿子拉扯大。Being a widow most of her adult life, she had tremendous difficulty bringing her son up.

守恒 shǒuhéng 〈物理〉 conservation: ～性质 conservative property / ～方程 conservation equation

守恒定律 shǒuhéng dìnglǜ 〈物理〉 conservation law: 能量～ law of conservation of energy

守候 shǒuhòu ❶ wait for; await; expect: ～着选举的结果 wait for the results of the election ❷ watch over; look after: 日夜～着患病的婆母 watch day and night over her sick mother-in-law

守护 shǒuhù guard; protect; defend: ～着祖国的海疆 guard the territorial waters of the homeland / ～天使 guardian angel

守护神 shǒuhùshén ❶〈宗教〉 patron saint; guardian angel; tutelary spirit ❷〈信息〉 daemen; demon

守活寡 shǒu huóguǎ *also* (in certain areas) "守生寡" married woman living by herself away from her husband for a long time; grass widow: 丈夫在外国学习，她在家～。Her husband was studying abroad while she lived as a grass widow at home.

守家 shǒujiā ❶ mind the house; look after the house ❷ guard family property

守将 shǒujiàng commanding general or officer in charge of the defence of a city or strategic spot

守节 shǒujié 〈旧语〉 ❶ preserve chastity or not remarry (after the death of her betrothed or husband): 在封建社会里，～被认为是妇女的一种美德。In feudal society, it was considered a virtue not to remarry after one's husband's death. ❷ (of a subject, etc.) remain loyal (to former emperor or dynasty); preserve one's integrity

守经达权 shǒujīng-dáquán be flexible while adhering to principles

守旧 shǒujiù ❶ stick to old ways; be a stickler for old practices; be conservative: 衣着～的人 conservative dresser / 老年人容易～。Old people tend to stick to old ways. ❷〈戏曲〉 backcloth; backdrop

守旧派 shǒujiùpài old-liner; stickler for old ways; stick-in-the-mud; old fogey

守军 shǒujūn defending troops; defenders: 城里的～ defending troops in town

守空房 shǒu kōngfáng (of a married woman) stay home alone

守口如瓶 shǒukǒu-rúpíng keep one's mouth shut; have one's lips sealed; be tight-mouthed: 他对此事～。He remained tight-lipped about it. / 在敌人面前，他～。He said nothing when he was interrogated by the enemy.

守垒员 shǒulěiyuán 〈体育〉 baseman

守擂 shǒulèi (as of martial contests) (be ready to) take on a challenger and maintain one's dominance: ～成功 beat the challenger and keep the championship

守灵 shǒulíng stand guard at the bier; keep vigil beside the coffin: 轮流在灵堂～ take turns in keeping vigil in the mourning hall

守门 shǒumén ❶ stand guard at the door or gate: ～人 doorkeeper; concierge ❷〈体育〉 keep goal

守门员 shǒuményuán goalkeeper

守谱 shǒupǔ 〈方言〉 behave properly and correctly; know one's place; be content with one's lot in life: 这个姑娘挺～，像个过日子的人。This girl keeps her place and seems to be the type that knows how to manage household affairs.

守钱虏 shǒuqiánlǔ miser

守丧 shǒusāng keep vigil or observe mourning (for the deceased): 为父亲～ observe mourning for one's deceased father

守哨 shǒushào sentry; guard

守身 shǒushēn keep one's integrity intact

守身如玉 shǒushēn-rúyù keep one's reputation as spotless as jade; maintain one's integrity like a piece of flawless jade

守时 shǒushí be punctual

守视 shǒushì guard; watch over

守势 shǒushì defensive: 处于～ be on the defensive / 采取～ assume the defensive; stand on the defensive / 变～为攻势 move from the defensive to the offensive

守岁 shǒusuì stay up all night on New Year's Eve: 除夕，全家欢聚一起～。The family had a happy reunion on New Year's Eve and stayed up to see the Old Year out and the New Year in.

守土 shǒutǔ 〈书面〉 defend one's territory: ～有责 be duty-bound to defend the territory of one's country / 将士们冒死～。The soldiers defended our land at the risk of their lives.

守望 shǒuwàng keep watch: 收获时节到了，人们搭起小棚子，在瓜田里～。When the harvest season approached, people would put up makeshift sheds and keep watch over the melon patches.

守望台 shǒuwàngtái watchtower

守望相助 shǒuwàng-xiāngzhù (formerly of neighbouring villages) keep watch and help defend each other: 两村人和睦相处，～。People in the two neighbouring villages lived in harmony and pledged to

S

render each other help and protection.

守卫 shǒuwèi keep safe; guard; defend:～边疆 defend (*or* guard) national borders /部队严密地～着总统府。The troops guarded the presidential palace closely.

守孝 shǒuxiào observe mourning for one's deceased parent:在封建时代,父母死了,儿子要～三年。In feudal times, the son was required to observe mourning for three years when a parent died.

守信 shǒuxìn keep or be true to one's word; be trustworthy:办事～ be reliable (*or* dependable) in one's work

守业 shǒuyè *see* "守成"

守夜 shǒuyè *also* "守更" keep watch or vigil at night:那时,盗匪横行,村里人组织起来,轮流～。As bandits and thieves ran rampant, the villagers organized themselves and took turns in keeping watch at night.

守御 shǒuyù defend; guard:～有方 put up an effective defence

守约 shǒuyuē ❶ keep a promise; stick by contract; honour a pledge ❷ keep an appointment

守则 shǒuzé rules; regulations:学生～ rules and regulations for students /工作～ work regulations

守贞 shǒuzhēn keep one's chastity

守正不阿 shǒuzhèng-bù'ē *also* "守正不挠" uphold justice or stick to fairness despite pressure; be unbending in upholding justice:为人～ upright person

守职 shǒuzhí be duty-conscious; stick to one's duty:～尽责 be committed to one's duties

守制 shǒuzhì mourning system (practised in feudal China), according to which one was to stay at home (and stayed away from office if one was an official) for 27 months without receiving guests after one's parent's death

守株待兔 shǒuzhū-dàitù stand by a tree stump waiting for a hare to dash itself against it — wait for a windfall; trust foolishly to chance and luck:成功靠自己去努力争取,决不可～,寄希望于偶然机遇。We should strive for success and must not wait for it to happen to us, pinning our hopes on chance and luck.

S

首[1] shǒu ❶ head:回～ look back; look round; turn round /昂～ hold one's head high /搔～ scratch one's head /翘～〈书面〉raise one's head and look /枭～〈书面〉cut off a person's head; behead /皓～〈书面〉hoary head ❷ first; foremost; supreme:荣登榜～ come out first in the list of successful candidates /成绩为全班之～ be a top student in the class; rank first in the class; be at the head of the class ❸ head; boss; leader; chief:以…为～ headed by sb.; with sb. as the leader /国家元～ head of state /匪～ bandit chieftain; rebel leader /罪魁祸～ arch-criminal; chief culprit; ring leader ❹ first of all; first (to do sth.); *see* "～倡";"～义" ❺ bring charges against sb.:自～ (of a criminal) surrender oneself; give oneself up /出～ inform against sb. /～告 start court action by lodging a complaint ❻ (Shǒu) a surname

首[2] shǒu 〈量词〉*used for poems and songs*:三～民歌 three folk songs /《唐诗三百～》*300 Tang Poems*

首倡 shǒuchàng initiate; begin; start:～和平共处五项原则 initiate the Five Principles of Peaceful Coexistence

首车 shǒuchē first bus or train:15 路公共汽车～是几点? What time is the first No. 15 bus?

首创 shǒuchuàng initiate; originate; invent; pioneer:～一种新学说 initiate a new doctrine or theory /～一种新印刷机 originate a new printing-machine /缺乏～进取精神 lack initiative (*or* the creative spirit) and enterprise /据说指南针为黄帝所～。Legend has it that the Yellow Emperor invented the compass.

首次 shǒucì for the first time; first:～航行 first (*or* maiden) voyage /～上演某部话剧 first performance; (of a play) première /1969 年人类～登上月球。Man landed on the moon for the first time in 1969.

首当其冲 shǒudāng-qíchōng be the first to suffer the impact (of a disaster, etc.); bear the brunt:山洪下来,这个村子总是～。The village is always the first to be affected whenever mountain torrents occur. /出了岔子挨批评时,他总是～。When anything goes wrong, he always bears the brunt of criticism.

首都 shǒudū capital (of a country)

首都体育馆 Shǒudū Tǐyùguǎn Capital Gymnasium (in Beijing)

首恶 shǒu'è arch-criminal; principal or prime culprit:严惩～分子 punish the principal culprits severely /～必办,胁从不问,立功受奖。The chief criminals shall be punished without fail, those who are accomplices under duress shall go unpunished, and those who perform deeds of merit shall be rewarded.

首发式 shǒufāshì ceremony celebrating the first publication of a book; inaugural ceremony for launching a publication

首犯 shǒufàn arch-criminal; chief criminal; principal culprit

首府 shǒufǔ ❶〈旧语〉prefecture where the provincial capital is located ❷ capital city of a province, a prefecture or an equivalent administrative division ❸ capital of a dependency or colony

首富 shǒufù richest family or person of a place:他家是本镇的～。His family is the wealthiest in this town.

首钢 Shǒugāng (short for 首都钢铁公司) Capital Iron and Steel Works (in Beijing)

首告 shǒugào report an offence; inform against

首功 shǒugōng first-class merit:破获此案,他立了～。He won a first-class merit citation for cracking the case.

首航 shǒuháng maiden or first flight; maiden or first voyage:1992 年,中国国际航空公司班机～万象。Air China made its maiden flight to Vientiane in 1992.

首航式 shǒuhángshì inaugural flight ceremony

首户 shǒuhù wealthiest family in the locality

首级 shǒují chopped-off head ("首" means "head" in classical Chinese, and "级" means "grade". According to the law of the Qin Dynasty, a soldier was to be promoted according to the number of the enemy's heads he had chopped off in battle, each head being counted as a grade.)

首季 shǒujì first quarter of a year:这个煤矿提前完成了国家～产煤计划。This coal mine has fulfilled state production quota for the first quarter ahead of schedule.

首届 shǒujiè first session; first:本市～运动会 first sports meet of this city /该校～毕业生 first graduates of the school

首肯 shǒukěn nod approval or assent; approve; consent:得到领导的～ obtain the approval of the leaders

首揆 shǒukuí 〈书面〉prime minister; premier

首领 shǒulǐng ❶〈书面〉head and neck:保全～ keep alive ❷ chieftain; leader:他是起义军的～。He was the leader of the insurrectionary army.

首难 shǒunàn 〈书面〉be the first to rise in revolt or launch an attack

首脑 shǒunǎo head; leader:政府～ head of government /～机关 leading body /～会议 meeting (*or* conference) of heads of state or government; summit meeting (*or* conference); summit /～人物 leading figure (*or* personage)

首七 shǒuqī 〈旧语〉seventh day after a person's death

首屈一指 shǒuqū-yīzhǐ come first on the list; come out first; rank first:他的技术在全厂是～的。His skill is second to none in the plant.

首任 shǒurèn first to be appointed to an office:美国～驻华大使 first US ambassador accredited to China /中华人民共和国～驻联合国代表 first permanent representative of the People's Republic of China to the United Nations

首日封 shǒurìfēng first-day cover (a special envelope with new commemorative stamps and postmark affixed on the first day of their issue):～图案为总工会成立大会会场。The picture on the first-day cover is that of the meeting hall where the Federation of Trade Unions was founded.

首善之区 shǒushànzhīqū 〈书面〉best of all places — national capital

首事 shǒushì 〈书面〉❶ matter of cardinal or prime importance; priority matter ❷ be first to rise in revolt or launch an attack ❸ first person to rise in revolt or launch an attack

首饰 shǒushi jewellery:她佩带着钻石耳环、珍珠项链等各种贵重～。She wore a pair of diamond earrings, a pearl necklace and various other expensive pieces of jewellery.

首饰店 shǒushidiàn jeweller's shop; jewellery store

首饰盒 shǒushihé jewellery case or box

首鼠两端 shǒushǔ-liǎngduān be in two minds; hesitate; shilly-shally:此人办事,常～,犹豫不决。He is indecisive, being always in two minds about what to do. /在是与非之间,岂容～! There is no room for shilly-shallying in matters of right and wrong.

首途 shǒutú 〈书面〉begin a journey; set out on a journey:翌日～

set out on a journey the next day /代表团～来华。The delegation has left for China.

首陀罗 Shǒutuóluó Sudra; Shudra (Hindu worker caste)

首尾 shǒu-wěi ❶ head and tail; first and last; beginning and end:～相连 with head and tail linked together; continuous without interruption; in an unbroken line /敌军中伏,～不能相顾。The enemy force having been ambushed, its vanguard was cut off from its rear. ❷ from beginning to end; from start to finish:这次旅行,～一共一个多月。The trip lasted over a month from beginning to end. /这样大的工程～只用了大半年的时间。It took only a little more than six months to complete such a big project.

首位 shǒuwèi first place; first priority:放在～ put in the first place; place before everything else; give first priority to /居全国～ be number one (*or* first) in the country

首乌 shǒuwū 〈中药〉 *also* "何首乌" héshǒuwū tuber of multiflower knotweed (*Polygonum multiflorum*)

首乌藤 shǒuwūténg 〈中药〉 vine of multiflower knotweed

首席 shǒuxí ❶ seat of honour:请在～入坐。Please be seated at the head of the table. *or* Please take the seat of honour. ❷ chief:～法官 chief judge; chief justice /～检察官 chief inspector; chief procurator /～监事 chief supervisor /～秘书 principal secretary /～仲裁员 chief arbitrator /～小提琴 first violin; first fiddle

首席按察司 shǒuxí ànchásī (HK) chief justice (before 1 July 1997)

首席财务官 shǒuxí cáiwùguān chief financial officer (CFO)

首席馆员 shǒuxí guǎnyuán No. 2 in a diplomatic mission; senior member of the diplomatic staff next to the head of a mission

首席信息官 shǒuxí xìnxīguān chief information officer (CIO)

首席营运官 shǒuxí yíngyùnguān chief operating officer (COO)

首席知识官 shǒuxí zhīshíguān chief knowledge officer (CKO)

首席执行官 shǒuxí zhíxíngguān chief executive officer (CEO)

首先 shǒuxiān ❶ first:～发言 be the first to take the floor; be the first to speak; speak first ❷ in the first place; first of all; first:～,让我代表全厂工人向你们表示热烈欢迎。Let me, first of all, extend to you a warm welcome on behalf of all the workers of the factory. /～,你是否有权这样做? Do you have the right to do so in the first place?

首相 shǒuxiàng prime minister; premier

首选 shǒuxuǎn first chosen; first elected:～演员 first chosen actor /球队的～队员 first on the select players list /当教师是我的～职业。Teaching is my first preference as a profession.

首演 shǒuyǎn première (of a play, dance, etc.):该团即将在人民剧场～这出新编历史剧。The troupe is ready for the forthcoming première of this new historical play at the People's Theatre.

首要 shǒuyào ❶ of the first importance; primary; first:～条件 primary condition /～原因〈法律〉first cause /～战犯 arch-criminal; chief war criminal ❷ leader; chief:政府～ government leaders /商界～ leading businessmen /今天这个会可以说是～云集。Today's meeting is a galaxy of leading figures.

首要分子 shǒuyàofènzǐ major culprit; ringleader

首夜权 shǒuyèquán *also* "初夜权" chūyèquán droit de seigneur (the right of a lord to sleep with a vassal's bride on her wedding night)

首义 shǒuyì 〈书面〉 be the first to rise in revolt:辛亥～ take the lead in launching the Revolution of 1911

首映 shǒuyìng first show or première (of a film)

首映式 shǒuyìngshì ceremony for the first show (of a film); première:影片《红楼梦》的～在首都影剧院举行。The première of the film *A Dream of Red Mansions* was held in the Capital Cinema.

首战 shǒuzhàn first battle or game:～告捷 win the first battle or game /～失利 lose the first battle or game /～打成平局。The first game ended in a draw.

首长 shǒuzhǎng senior officer or official; leading cadre:各部～ heads of the ministries (*or* departments under the Party's Central Committee) /师～ commanders of a division

首长级 shǒuzhǎngjí (HK) directorate grade:～官员 directorate rank officer

首长席 shǒuzhǎngxí VIP seats or box

首座 shǒuzuò ❶ *also* "首坐" seat of honour (at a banquet) ❷ senior monk in a Buddhist sanctuary

艄

shǒu stem; (of a ship) bows

艄楼 shǒulóu forecastle

艄柱 shǒuzhù stempost:～锚 stem anchor

手

shǒu ❶ hand:握～ shake hands /挥～ wave one's hand; wave /～巧 deft (*or* skilful) with one's hands /双～叉腰 with arms akimbo /赤～空拳 with bare hands; bare-handed; unarmed ❷ hold in one's hand; possess:人～一册。Everyone has a copy. /这种说明书可以人～一份。There is a copy of the manual (available) for everyone. ❸ handy; easy to carry:～折 notebook recording deliveries, orders, payments, etc. ❹ personally; in person:～植 plant personally /～订 personally edit ❺ ability; stratagem:大显身～ give full play to one's abilities /心狠～辣 wicked and merciless ❻ 〈量词〉 *of skill or proficiency*:学一～真功夫 learn some genuine skill /写一～好字 write a beautiful hand ❼ expert of some occupation or job:舵～ helmsman; steersman /鼓～ drummer /水～ seaman; sailor /猎～ hunter /射～ shooter; marksman; archer /竖琴～ harpist; harper /神炮～ crack gunner /歌～ singer /多面～ versatile person; all-rounder /巧～ dab hand /能～ skilled (*or* good) hand; crackerjack /红旗～ "red-banner" pace-setter /棋逢对～ meet one's match in chess or other contests /扒～ pickpocket

手巴掌 shǒubāzhang ❶ palm ❷ 〈方言〉 glove:他拿走了几副～儿。He took a few pairs of gloves with him.

手把手 shǒubǎshǒu instruct or pass on knowledge and skills, etc. in person:我是他～教出来的。He taught me personally.

手版 shǒubǎn *also* "手板" ❶ tablet held with both hands (by emperor and ministers) at court ❷ visiting card

手板 shǒubǎn ❶ 〈方言〉 palm:～上放着一枚硬币 hold a coin in one's palm ❷ *see* "手版"

手板儿 shǒubǎnr bamboo or birch, formerly used for punishing school-pupils; ferule:他是个顽皮孩子,上学时常常因淘气吃～。As he was a naughty boy, he was often beaten with a birch for his antics at school.

手膀 shǒubǎng *also* "手膀子" 〈方言〉 arm

手刨 shǒubào hand plane

手背 shǒubèi back of a hand

手本 shǒuběn ❶ (used in the Ming and Qing dynasties) visiting card; name card ❷ *see* "手册"

手笔 shǒubǐ ❶ sb.'s writing, calligraphy or painting; hand:书名题签是茅盾的～。The title of the book is in Mao Dun's handwriting. /这篇杂文似乎出自大家～。This essay seems to have come from the hand of a great master. ❷ literary or artistic skill:不愧大家～ be worthy of a great master ❸ style (in doing sth. or spending money):他～阔。He is very liberal with money. *or* He is fond of doing things in grand style.

手臂 shǒubì ❶ arm:～上挎着个篮子 carry (*or* have) a basket on one's arm /～上中了枪 be shot in the arm /马蜂蜇了～ be stung on the arm by a wasp /～伸得太长 stretch one's arm too far; overstep one's authority or proper domain ❷ 〈比喻〉 aide; assistant:他是部长的得力～。He is the minister's right-hand man.

手边 shǒubiān on hand; at hand:我～儿现款不多了。I don't have much cash on hand. /你要的那张画,不在～,等以后给你。The picture you want is not at hand, and I'll give it to you later. /我～儿没有零钱。I've no change on me.

手表 shǒubiǎo wrist watch:～指针 watch hand /～机心 movement of a watch; watch movement

手柄 shǒubǐng 〈机械〉 hand lever; hand shank:活动～ flexible (*or* free) handle

手脖子 shǒubózi 〈方言〉 wrist

手不释卷 shǒubùshìjuàn never seen without a book in one's hand; be an avid reader:她勤奋好学,经常～。She's so studious that she is rarely seen without a book in her hand.

手不稳 shǒubùwěn 〈方言〉 have an itchy finger — have an itch to steal small things:听说这人～。They say the man is light-fingered.

手簿 shǒubù handbook; manual:测量～ handbook on surveying

手彩 shǒucǎi 〈口语〉 (of gambling or jugglery) skill in sleight of hand; skill in cunning moves:耍～儿 play tricks

手册 shǒucè ❶ handbook; manual:教师～ teacher's handbook (*or* manual) /速记～ shorthand manual /旅游～ tourist guide /《英语语法～》 *A Handbook of English Grammar* ❷ record book; workbook:工作～ workbook /劳动～ worker's book

手长 shǒucháng seize every opportunity to grab money or power; have a finger in every pie; be grasping

S

手抄 shǒuchāo copy by hand：～默诵 copy by hand and read silently — study diligently／恭楷～一部 make a carefully handwritten copy

手抄本 shǒuchāoběn handwritten copy：这部小说的～曾在民间长期流传。Handwritten copies of the novel circulated among the people for a long time.

手车 shǒuchē *also*"手推车" handcart；pushcart；dolly

手持 shǒuchí hand；in hand：～送话器 hand microphone／～兵器 hand weapon；shoulder weapon

手持式焊工面罩 shǒuchíshì hàngōng miànzhào handshield；handscreen

手钏 shǒuchuàn 〈方言〉bracelet

手创 shǒuchuàng personally establish

手锤 shǒuchuí （usu. small-sized）hammer

手戳 shǒuchuō 〈口语〉private seal；signet：请在收条上盖上～。Please apply your private seal to the receipt. *or* Please put your personal seal on the receipt.

手刺 shǒucì 〈旧语〉（as a practice of officialdom）visiting card written by the caller himself

手锉 shǒucuò 〈机械〉hand file or rasp

手搭凉棚 shǒudā-liángpéng *also*"手打遮阳" shade the eye from the sun by lifting a hand and holding it horizontally against the forehead：他站在路口，～向前张望。Standing at the crossing, he was looking around with a lifted hand shading his eyes.

手大 shǒudà be liberal with money

手到病除 shǒudào-bìngchú cure a patient by a touch of the hand （said in praise of a doctor or a trouble-shooter）

手到擒来 shǒudào-qínlái *also*"手到擒拿" stretch out your hands and it is within your grasp；be a breeze or walkover：要收拾他们几个坏蛋还不是～？Nothing would be easier than to settle with these few scoundrels.／一个星期内完成这样简单工作真是～。It would be a snap to get such simple work done in a week.

手倒立 shǒudàolì 〈体育〉handstand：做～ stand on one's hands；do a handstand／单～ stand on one hand

手底下 shǒudǐxia *see*"手下"

手颠 shǒudiān hand tremor

手电筒 shǒudiàntǒng *also*"手电" electric torch；flashlight；torch light

手订 shǒudìng personally lay down：～条例 regulations laid down by sb. personally

手定 shǒudìng personally draft or work out（plans, procedures, documents, etc.）

手动 shǒudòng 〈机械〉hand；hand-operated：～冲压机 hand-punch／～焊接机 hand-held welder／～起重机 hand-screw；hand-jack

手动装置 shǒudòng zhuāngzhì 〈机械〉hand-gear

手短 shǒuduǎn be unable to handle matters impartially after accepting people's gifts or bribes：拿了人家的～，吃了人家的嘴软。A person who accepts gifts or an invitation to dinner is not likely to act impartially.

手段 shǒuduàn ❶ means；measure；method；way：法律～ legal means／通讯～ means of communication／解决问题的～ ways of solving problems／使用行政～ take administrative measures／采取合法的斗争～ adopt legal forms of struggle／通过艺术～ through artistic medium／作为最后的～ as the（*or* a）last resort／不择～ by fair means or foul；by hook or by crook；unscrupulously／使用强制～ use coercive method；resort to coercion ❷ trick；wiles；artifice：耍～ play tricks／采取欺骗～ by deceit／拙劣～ clumsy trick／善于用～ good at using artifice ❸ skill；ability：～高强 highly skilled／他在推销产品方面很有～。He knows the ropes in sales promotion.

手法 shǒufǎ ❶ skill；technique：国画的白描～ line drawing technique of Chinese painting／夸张～ hyperbole／倒叙～ flashback／艺术表现～ means of artistic expression／写作～ writing method／独具匠心的导演～ ingeneous directing technique ❷ trick；gimmick；artifice：欺骗～ deceptive tactics／卑劣的～ dirty trick；despicable gimmick／宣传～ propaganda ploy（*or* gimmick）／惯用的～ customary（*or* habitual）practice；same old trick

手风 shǒufēng 〈方言〉luck at gambling as in playing cards：～不顺 be out of luck（in playing mah-jong or cards）

手风琴 shǒufēngqín accordion：六角～ concertina

手扶拖拉机 shǒufú tuōlājī walking tractor

手斧 shǒufǔ hand-axe；hand-adze；adze

手感 shǒugǎn 〈纺织〉feel；handle：～好 have a nice feel；feel nice／～柔软 have a soft handle（*or* feel）／有些化纤织物的～不比天然材料差。The feel of some synthetic fabrics compares favourably with that of natural materials.

手高手低 shǒugāo-shǒudī allowing for slight differences（when dividing things by hand）：这筐苹果匀成十堆，～的，大致差不多就行了。Divide this basket of apples into ten portions；as long as they are about equal, it'll be all right.

手稿 shǒugǎo original or holograph manuscript：最近又发现两篇老舍的～。Two more original Lao She manuscripts have been found lately.

手工 shǒugōng ❶ handwork：上～课 have a lesson in handwork／收～费 collect payment for（a piece of）handwork done ❷ by hand；manual：～劳动 manual（*or* hand）labour／～操作 operated（*or* done）by hand；of manual operation／～排版 hand-set／～水饺 handmade *jiaozi*（dumplings with meat and vegetable stuffing）❸〈口语〉charge for（a piece of）handwork done：料子不一样，做衣服的～也不同。The charge for tailoring varies with the material.

手工工具 shǒugōng gōngjù hand tool

手工提花织机 shǒugōng tíhuā zhījī draw loom

手工业 shǒugōngyè handicraft industry；handicraft：～生产 handicraft production／～作坊 handicraft workshop／～者 handicraftsman

手工业生产合作社 shǒugōngyè shēngchǎn hézuòshè handicraft producers' cooperative

手工艺 shǒugōngyì handicraft art or skill；handicraft

手工艺工人 shǒugōngyì gōngrén craftsman；artisan

手工艺品 shǒugōngyìpǐn articles of handicraft art；handicrafts：精美的～ exquisite handicraft work；piece of fine handicraft workmanship

手鼓 shǒugǔ 〈乐器〉hand drum；tabor

手函 shǒuhán letter written in longhand；personal letter

手翰 shǒuhàn 〈书面〉handwritten letter

手黑 shǒuhēi 〈方言〉be unscrupulous；resort to wicked tricks：心狠～ be cruel and vicious；be merciless and wicked

手滑 shǒuhuá 〈书面〉act rashly or wilfully

手机 shǒujī 〈通信〉mobile phone；cellular phone

手疾眼快 shǒují-yǎnkuài *also*"眼疾手快" quick of eye and deft of hand；sharp-sighted and neat-handed：那警察～，当场就把小偷抓住了。The policeman was so agile and swift that he arrested the pickpocket red-handed.

手记 shǒujì ❶ take notes personally：我～了他的讲话。I put down all he said myself. ❷ minutes made by one personally：我聆听过他的教诲，并留下了这份～。I once attended his lectures and made these notes myself.

手技 shǒujì ❶ handicraft；manual skill ❷（of acrobatics）sleight of hand；jugglery

手迹 shǒujì original calligraphic work or painting：这是鲁迅先生的～。This is an original calligraphic work by Lu Xun.

手简 shǒujiǎn 〈书面〉handwritten personal letter or note

手脚 shǒujiǎo ❶ movement of limbs；motion：～利落 dexterous；nimble；agile／～勤快 quick and industrious／毛手毛脚 careless（in handling things）；inattentive and clumsy／大手大脚 extravagant；wasteful／他年纪大了，～也慢了。He is getting on in years and moves slowly. ❷〈方言〉trick：暗中弄～ play dirty tricks on the sly／这件事有人做了～。Someone must have juggled things on this matter.

手脚干净 shǒujiǎo-gānjìng honest in money matters：手脚不干净 be sticky-fingered；be questionable in money matters；seek minor illicit gains／找个～的人做司库 find an honest person to serve as treasurer

手紧 shǒujǐn ❶ close or tight with money；tightfisted；stingy：她一向～得很。She is always closefisted. ❷ *also*"手头儿紧" short of money：我近日～。I am broke（*or* hard up）lately.

手劲儿 shǒujìnr （muscular）strength of the hand；grip：他的～真大。He has a very powerful grip.

手巾 shǒujin ❶ towel：热～ hot towel ❷〈方言〉handkerchief：绣花～ embroidered handkerchief

手巾架 shǒujinjià towel rack

手锯 shǒujù handsaw

手卷 shǒujuàn 〈美术〉hand scroll

手绢 shǒujuàn handkerchief

手铐 shǒukào handcuffs：戴～ wear handcuffs／给…戴上～ put

handcuffs on sb.; handcuff sb.
手控 shǒukòng manual control
手快 shǒukuài deft of hand:她～,干活灵巧。She has nimble hands and works real fast.
手拉葫芦 shǒulā húlu 〈机械〉chain block
手拉手 shǒulāshǒu hand in hand:两个小姑娘～地走进屋来。Hand in hand, the two girls came into the room.
手拉锁 shǒulāsuǒ drawback lock
手辣 shǒulà be vicious or unscrupulous:心狠～ be merciless and vicious
手雷 shǒuléi 〈军事〉antitank grenade
手力千斤顶 shǒulì qiānjīndǐng 〈机械〉hand jack
手零脚碎 shǒulíng-jiǎosuì ❶ light-fingered; thievish ❷ be active and busy; bustle about (all day long)
手令 shǒulìng order or instruction in one's own handwriting
手榴弹 shǒuliúdàn hand grenade; grenade:催泪～ teargas grenade /铝热剂～ thermite grenade /燃烧～ incendiary grenade /杀伤～ fragmentation grenade /～投掷场 grenade (practice) range /～防护圈 grenade net
手笼 shǒulóng muff
手炉 shǒulú handwarmer
手轮 shǒulún 〈机械〉handwheel
手锣 shǒuluó *also* "小锣" xiǎoluó small gong
手慢 shǒumàn slow-moving; slow in action:这个人～,老赶不上趟儿。This fellow is so slow that he is always behind schedule in whatever he does.
手忙脚乱 shǒumáng-jiǎoluàn be thrown into confusion; be in a frantic rush; be in a great bustle:你办事这么～,准会出错的。You are liable to make mistakes if you go about your business in such a flurry. /一个独生子就搞得全家～。This only child kept the whole family running round in circles.
手铆 shǒumǎo 〈机械〉hand-riveting /～机 hand-riveting machine
手闷子 shǒumènzi 〈方言〉(leather or cotton-padded) handwarmers or gloves
手面 shǒumiàn how one spends money (liberal or stingy):～较紧 rather tightfisted (*or* stingy) /他一向～阔绰。He has always been liberal with money.
手民 shǒumín 〈书面〉typesetter
手民之误 shǒumín zhī wù typographical error; misprint
手模 shǒumó fingerprint
手磨机 shǒumòjī 〈矿业〉hand-mill
手拿把掐 shǒuná-bǎqiā *also* "手拿把攥" certain of success; in the bag:他们小组人多,技术又好,完成这项任务～。With so many people and such superior skills, this group can fulfil the task without fail.
手黏 shǒunián sticky fingers — have kleptomanic tendency
手帕 shǒupà handkerchief; hankie:～舞 handkerchief dance
手捧子 shǒupěngzi 〈方言〉handcuffs
手胼足胝 shǒupián-zúzhī 〈书面〉callouses have formed on one's hands and feet — result of hard manual labour:他们的先人～,使这片荒地成为良田。Their ancestors reclaimed the wasteland and toiled strenuously to convert it into fertile fields.
手蹼 shǒupǔ webbed gloves
手旗 shǒuqí handflag; semaphore flag
手气 shǒuqì luck at gambling, etc.:她今天～好。Luck is with her today. /我的～背透了。I'm just down on my luck.
手钳 shǒuqián hand vice; (pair of) pliers
手枪 shǒuqiāng pistol:标准～ standard pistol /气～ air pistol /自动～ automatic pistol /左轮～ revolver /自选～〈体育〉free pistol
手枪慢加速比赛 shǒuqiāng mànjiāsù bǐsài 〈体育〉centre-fire pistol
手枪射程 shǒuqiāng shèchéng pistol shot
手枪射击场 shǒuqiāng shèjīchǎng pistol range; pistol course
手枪速射 shǒuqiāng sùshè 〈体育〉rapid-fire pistol
手枪套 shǒuqiāngtào holster
手巧 shǒuqiǎo handy with needlework; deft; dexterous:心灵～ clever and deft
手勤 shǒuqín diligent (with one's hands); hardworking:她～脚快,整天都不闲着。She is so hardworking that she bustles about all day long without a break.
手轻 shǒuqīng handle gently; not use too much force:花瓶易碎,～一点。Handle the fragile vase with care.
手球 shǒuqiú ❶ handball:～场 handball field /～运动员 handball player ❷ handball (a foul in sports):～在足球赛中是技术犯规。Handball is a technical foul in football matches.
手刃 shǒurèn stab to death; kill with a knife:～仇敌 kill an enemy by one's own hand
手软 shǒuruǎn be soft-hearted; lack firmness:心慈～ be soft-hearted and irresolute /一定要彻底揭露两面派,我们决不能～。Double-dealers should be thoroughly exposed, and we must on no account show them any mercy.
手刹车 shǒushāchē hand brake
手生 shǒushēng lacking in practice and skill; out of practice:我过去钢琴弹得还可以,现在～了。I used to play the piano fairly well, but I'm out of practice now.
手势 shǒushì gesture; sign; signal:打～ make a gesture; gesticulate; sign /聋哑人用～进行交谈。Deaf-mutes converse by signs. /他作～让大家安静。He signed (*or* gestured) to them to be quiet. /乐队指挥作～请全体队员起立。The conductor signalled the orchestra to rise.
手势信号 shǒushì xìnhào arm-and-hand signal
手势语 shǒushìyǔ sign language
手书 shǒushū ❶ write in one's own hand:他欣然命笔,～唐诗一首相赠。He gladly set pen to paper and inscribed a Tang poem for me. ❷ personal letter:拜读～ have the pleasure of reading sb.'s letter
手术 shǒushù surgical operation:妇科～ gynecological operation /腹腔～ abdominal operation /动～ perform an operation; (of a patient) undergo (*or* have) an operation /～成功。The operation is successful.
手术刀 shǒushùdāo scalpel
手术刀包 shǒushùdāobāo surgical kit
手术麻醉师 shǒushù mázuìshī anaesthetist for an operation
手术室 shǒushùshì operating room; operating theatre
手术台 shǒushùtái operating table
手术死亡率 shǒushù sǐwánglǜ operative mortality rate
手松 shǒusōng (concerning money etc.) freehanded; liberal:他花钱一向～。He has always been openhanded.
手谈 shǒután 〈书面〉play *weiqi*:我每夜与他～。I played *weiqi* with him every evening.
手套 shǒutào gloves; mittens:毛线～ woollen gloves /棉～ cotton-padded gloves /毛里～ fur-lined gloves /无指～ mittens /拳击～ boxing gloves; mitts /棒球～ baseball gloves; mitts
手提 shǒutí ❶ carry with one's hand:肩挑～ carry things on one's shoulders or with one's hands /他～两件行李。He carried two pieces of luggage in his hands. ❷ portable:～兵器 hand weapons; hand arms /～打字机 portable typewriter /～式机枪 sub-machine gun; tommy-gun /～行李 hand luggage; hand baggage
手提包 shǒutíbāo handbag; bag
手提步话机 shǒutí bùhuàjī walkie-talkie; handie-talkie
手提电话 shǒutí diànhuà *also* "移动电话" yídòng diànhuà; "大哥大" dàgēdà cellular phone; mobile phone
手提摄像机 shǒutí shèxiàngjī walkie-lookie
手提箱 shǒutíxiāng suitcase
手条子 shǒutiáozi 〈方言〉tricks; artifice:别看他一副善良的样子,为了达到自己的目的,他可以使出毒辣的～。His kindly countenance is deceptive. He could resort to ruthless means to achieve his goal.
手帖 shǒutiě handwritten note
手头 shǒutóu ❶ on hand; at hand:～的事不少 have a lot of work on hand; have one's hands full /参加研讨会时,～可以带一些资料。When you attend the seminar, it might be a good idea to take some reference materials with you. /时间到了,快放下～的工作去开会吧。It's time to wind up your work and go to the meeting. ❷ one's present financial situation:～宽裕 be in easy circumstances; be quite well off; have plenty of money to spend /～拮据 be in straitened circumstances; be hard up; be hard pressed for money ❸ writing or other abilities:～快 be quick in writing; be a fast pen /～麻利 neat and able
手头字 shǒutóuzì 〈旧语〉simplified Chinese character
手推播种机 shǒutuī bōzhǒngjī 〈农业〉hand seeder unit
手推车 shǒutuīchē *also* "手车" handcart; wheelbarrow
手推磨 shǒutuīmò quern
手推婴儿车 shǒutuī yīng'érchē pushchair; light baby carriage; bassinet or basket crib on wheels; stroller
手袜 shǒuwà 〈方言〉gloves
手腕 shǒuwàn ❶ wrist ❷ artifice; finesse; stratagem:耍～ play

tricks; resort to stratagems; use an artifice /政治～ political stratagem (*or* artifice) /外交～ diplomatic finesse; diplomatic skill /卑鄙的～ contemptible ploy (*or* trick) /欺骗～ deceit; double-crossing /他比一般贪官更贪婪,更有～。He is greedier and more deceitful than the average corrupt official.

手腕子 shǒuwànzi wrist

手纹 shǒuwén lines of the palm

手无寸铁 shǒuwúcùntiě without any weapon in one's hand; barehanded; unarmed:向～的群众施暴 use force against unarmed masses

手无缚鸡之力 shǒu wú fù jī zhī lì not strong enough even to truss up a chicken; physically very weak; feeble:那老头～,竟然抓住了那四个窃贼! Imagine a frail old man actually captured those four burglars!

手舞足蹈 shǒuwǔ-zúdǎo dance for joy:他饮了几杯酒,不禁～起来。He drank several cups of wine and could not help jumping for joy.

手下 shǒuxià ❶ under the leadership or direction of:他～有不少能人。He has many able people working under him. /强将～无弱兵。There are no weak troops under an able general. ❷ at hand:书不在～,以后我拿给你看。I haven't got the book at hand; I'll show it to you later. ❸ one's financial condition:～不宽裕 be short of money; be in straitened circumstances ❹ at the hands of sb.:～照顾着点儿 not hit or attack as hard as one could; pull one's punches /～毫不留情 show no mercy; give no quarter

手下败将 shǒuxià-bàijiàng opponent one has beaten; one's vanquished foe; one's defeated adversary:下棋他是我的～。I often beat him on the chessboard.

手下留情 shǒuxià-liúqíng show or have mercy; be lenient:对这个坏蛋～就是对好人的残忍。Mercy towards (*or* To have mercy on) a thug like him means cruelty towards honest citizens. /他还年轻,我们对他多少有点～。We made an allowance for his young age.

手下人 shǒuxiarén 〈旧语〉❶ subordinates ❷ servants

手相 shǒuxiàng lines of the palm by which palmists tell one's fortune:看～ read the palm /看～者 palmist

手相术 shǒuxiàngshù palmistry; chiromancy

手携手 shǒuxiéshǒu hand in hand:心连心,～ heart to heart, hand in hand

手写 shǒuxiě write personally; take notes personally:口问～ ask questions and write down the replies personally

手写识别 shǒuxiě shíbié handwriting recognition

手写体 shǒuxiětǐ handwritten form; script

手心 shǒuxīn ❶ (centre of one's) palm:急得他～都出汗了。He was so worried that even his palms became sweaty. /～手背都是肉。(often used to show that there is no discrimination against one child in favour of another) Palm or back of the hand, it's all one's flesh and blood. ❷ range of one's control:谁也逃不出他的～儿。Nobody can get out of his control.

手续 shǒuxù procedure; formalities:入会～ admission procedure /入学～ registration procedure /～齐全 (with) all formalities gone through /～未完 the formalities have not been completed /～繁琐 overelaborate procedures; over-complex procedures /简化～ simplify procedures

手续费 shǒuxùfèi service charge; commission

手癣 shǒuxuǎn 〈医学〉tinea manus; fungal infection of the hand

手眼 shǒuyǎn trick; artifice

手眼通天 shǒuyǎn-tōngtiān be a past master at playing tricks:这人～,跟部长也能说上话。He is full of wiles and even has access to the minister.

手痒 shǒuyǎng have an itch to do sth.:看见别人放鞭炮,他就～。He was itching to have a go himself when he saw others setting off firecrackers.

手摇 shǒuyáo operated by hand; motivated by hand

手摇泵 shǒuyáobèng hand pump

手摇发电机 shǒuyáo fādiànjī hand generator

手摇风琴 shǒuyáo fēngqín barrel organ

手摇计算机 shǒuyáo jìsuànjī 〈计算机〉hand calculator

手摇离心机 shǒuyáo líxīnjī 〈机械〉hand centrifuge

手摇铃 shǒuyáolíng handbell

手摇破碎机 shǒuyáo pòsuìjī 〈机械〉hand-crusher

手摇起重机 shǒuyáo qǐzhòngjī 〈机械〉hand travelling crane

手摇曲柄机 shǒuyáo qūbǐngjī 〈机械〉brace and bit; brace

手摇跳汰机 shǒuyáo tiàotàijī 〈矿业〉hand jig

手摇钻 shǒuyáozuàn 〈机械〉hand drill; wimble

手艺 shǒuyì craftsmanship; workmanship; skill:～高超 superb workmanship /～粗糙 crude craftsmanship /学门～ learn a trade /没想到这位名教授做菜的～还真不错呢! I never imagined that the famous professor was also a good cook.

手艺人 shǒuyìrén craftsman

手淫 shǒuyín masturbation; self-abuse

手印 shǒuyìn ❶ impression of the hand; hand-print:作案现场留下了几个明显的～。A few impressions of the hand were visible at the scene of the crime. ❷ thumbprint; fingerprint:按～ put one's thumbprint (to a document, etc.) /验证～ verify a fingerprint

手语 shǒuyǔ sign language; dactylology

手谕 shǒuyù handwritten directive (as from one's superior or elder):下达～ issue (*or* deliver) a hand-written directive to lower levels

手泽 shǒuzé 〈书面〉handwriting or articles left by one's forefathers

手札 shǒuzhá 〈书面〉personal letter in longhand

手闸 shǒuzhá hand brake

手章 shǒuzhāng private seal; signet

手掌 shǒuzhǎng palm:～印 palm print

手掌心 shǒuzhǎngxīn ❶ centre of the palm ❷ control:你怎么做也跳不出我的～。However you try, you'll still be under my thumb.

手杖 shǒuzhàng walking stick; stick; cane

手诏 shǒuzhào imperial edict in the emperor's own handwriting

手折 shǒuzhé 〈旧语〉❶ memo presented to one's superior ❷ account book (of a merchant) in accordion form

手植 shǒuzhí plant (a tree, etc.) personally:这棵树是贵国总理来访时～的。This tree was personally planted by the premier of your country on his visit here.

手纸 shǒuzhǐ toilet paper; tissue

手指 shǒuzhǐ finger:～尖 fingertip /～麻木 numbness of fingers

手指甲 shǒuzhǐjia fingernail

手指头 shǒuzhǐtou 〈口语〉finger

手指头肚儿 shǒuzhǐtoudùr finger cushion

手指字母 shǒuzhǐ zìmǔ dactylology; manual alphabet

手治疗法 shǒuzhìliáofǎ 〈医学〉chiropractic

手重 shǒuzhòng use too much force; heavy-handed:护士打针时～了些,孩子疼得哭了。The nurse jabbed the needle a little too hard when she gave the injection, and the child cried from pain.

手肘 shǒuzhǒu ❶〈方言〉elbow ❷〈旧语〉manacles

手镯 shǒuzhuó bracelet:一对玛瑙～ pair of agate bracelets

手足 shǒuzú ❶ hand and foot; limbs:～抽搐〈医学〉tetany /～徐动症〈医学〉athetosis ❷ brothers:～之情 brotherly (*or* fraternal) affection; fraternity /情同～ close like brothers; feeling as if sb. was one's own brother /他二人俨然同胞～。The two of them are as close as blood-brothers.

手足无措 shǒuzú-wúcuò at a loss (as to what to do); in helpless confusion:吓得～ be helpless with fear /弟子二人不敢近身,面面相觑,～。His two disciples dared not take another step closer. They looked at each other in consternation.

手钻 shǒuzuàn hand drill

手作 shǒuzuò handicrafts; various handicraft trades

shòu

狩

shòu 〈书面〉hunting (esp. in winter)

狩猎 shòuliè hunting; venery:～季节 hunting season /～队 professional hunting team /～袋 game bag /～衫 hunting shirt

兽(獸)

shòu ❶ beast; brute; animal:野～ wild animal (*or* beast) /猛～ beast of prey /禽～ birds and beasts; 〈比喻〉beasts /～聚鸟散 (as of a loosely assembled group) scramble and scatter like beasts and birds ❷ beastly; bestial:衣冠禽～ beast in human shape (*or* clothing)

兽环 shòuhuán door-knocker (on doors of old mansions) shaped like the head of a beast with a ring in its mouth

兽类 shòulèi (when contrasted with birds, etc.) beasts; (when contrasted with humans) animals

兽力车 shòulìchē animal-drawn cart

兽王 shòuwáng king of beasts — lion

兽行 shòuxíng ❶ brutal act; brutality; bestial behaviour:谴责敌人

的～ denounce the savagery of the enemy /对俘虏滥施～ subject captives to wanton brutality ❷ act of lust
兽性 shòuxìng brutish nature; beast in a man: ～不改 one's brutish nature remains unchanged /～发作 (when) the beast in one gets the upper hand
兽药 shòuyào veterinary medicine; medicine for animals
兽医 shòuyī veterinary surgeon; veterinarian; vet
兽医学 shòuyīxué veterinary medicine; veterinary science
兽医院 shòuyīyuàn veterinary hospital
兽医站 shòuyīzhàn veterinary station
兽疫 shòuyì animal disease or epidemic; epizooty
兽疫学 shòuyìxué epizootiology
兽欲 shòuyù animal desire; bestial lust: 发泄～ let off one's bestial lust

寿(壽、夀) shòu ❶ long life; longevity: 人～年丰 people live long and harvests are good; have a long life and a good year /福～双全 enjoy both fortune and longevity ❷ life; age: 高～ long life; longevity; your venerable age /长～ long life; longevity /短～ short life /～同彭祖 be as old as Methuselah ❸ birthday: 做～ (usu. of middle-aged or elderly people) celebrate a birthday; hold a birthday party /祝～ congratulate sb. on his or her birthday; toast sb.'s long life (at his/her birthday celebrations) /拜～ offer birthday felicitations (*or* congratulations) ❹〈书面〉congratulate sb. on his or her birthday: 以酒为～ drink to sb.'s longevity ❺〈婉词〉(sth. prepared before one's death) for burial: ～板 coffin boards ❻ (Shòu) a surname
寿斑 shòubān liver-coloured spot on the face or other parts of the skin (as a result of ageing); senile speckle or plaque
寿比南山,福如东海 shòu bǐ nánshān, fú rú dōnghǎi (complimentary or congratulatory expression for elderly people) may you live to be as old as Zhongnan Mountain and may your happiness be as deep as the Eastern Sea
寿材 shòucái coffin (usu. prepared before one's death)
寿辰 shòuchén birthday (of a middle-aged or elderly person): 昨天是祖父九十～。Yesterday was grandpa's ninetieth birthday.
寿诞 shòudàn *see* "寿辰"
寿光鸡 shòuguāngjī Shouguang chicken — variety of chicken known for its meat and eggs, first bred in Shouguang County, Shandong Province
寿酒 shòujiǔ birthday wine; wine drunk at a birthday party: 吃杯～ drink a toast at a birthday party; attend a birthday feast
寿考 shòukǎo 〈书面〉long life; longevity: 富贵～ wealth, high rank and longevity
寿礼 shòulǐ birthday present
寿联 shòulián congratulatory couplets presented to a person on his or her birthday; longevity couplets
寿面 shòumiàn noodles eaten to symbolize longevity on one's birthday; birthday or longevity noodles
寿命 shòumìng life-span; life; lifetime: 平均～ average life-span; life expectancy /延长～ prolong sb.'s life /～不长 have a short life; die young /机器～ service life of a machine /电视机～ lifetime of a television set /粒子～ particle lifetime /～试验 length-of-life test
寿木 shòumù *see* "寿材"
寿器 shòuqì coffin prepared before one's death; coffin
寿山石 shòushānshí agalmatolite; pagodite; figure stone
寿数 shòushu 〈迷信〉one's destined lifespan
寿司 shòusī sushi, a Japanese dish of rolls of cold rice flavoured and garnished
寿算 shòusuàn 〈书面〉destined lifespan of a person
寿堂 shòutáng ❶〈书面〉hall where the coffin is placed before being sent to a cemetery; hall where sacrifices are offered to the deceased ❷〈书面〉graveyard built before one's death ❸ hall where well-wishers come to offer congratulations to a person on his or her birthday
寿桃 shòutáo ❶ birthday peach (offered as a birthday present or eaten at birthday celebrations) ❷ (peach-shaped) birthday cake
寿头 shòutóu 〈方言〉clumsy and stupid fellow; sucker; blockhead
寿险 shòuxiǎn life insurance
寿限 shòuxiàn life expectancy: 随着生活条件的改善,人类的～还要延长。With increasingly better living conditions, man's life expectancy will extend still further.
寿星 shòuxing ❶ god of longevity ❷ elderly or sometimes middle-aged person whose birthday is being celebrated
寿穴 shòuxué tomb or graveyard (prepared for one who is still alive): 那皇帝三十多岁就开始营造～。The emperor started to have his tomb built when he was in his thirties.
寿筵 shòuyán birthday party; birthday feast
寿衣 shòuyī graveclothes; cerements; shroud
寿藏 shòuzàng 〈书面〉graveyard built during a person's lifetime
寿幛 shòuzhàng sheets of silk presented to a person on his or her birthday
寿终 shòuzhōng die of old age: 其人年过八旬,以～。He died at the ripe old age of eighty-plus.
寿终正寝 shòuzhōng-zhèngqǐn die of old age; die a natural death: 老人安详地～。The old man died peacefully. /那杂志出到第三期便～了。The magazine stopped after the publication of its third issue.

受 shòu ❶ receive; accept: ～鼓舞 be inspired; be encouraged /接～训练 undergo training /病人～到最好的照顾。The patient received the best of care. ❷ suffer; sustain; be subjected to: ～伤害 sustain an injury /～委屈 suffer a wrong or an injustice; be wronged /～歧视 be subjected to discrimination; be discriminated against /～训斥 get a dressing down /～责骂 get a scolding; be scolded /～重伤 be seriously wounded /由于军事失利,指挥员～到各方严厉的批评。The commander came under serious criticism from all quarters for military setbacks. ❸ stand; endure; bear; tolerate: 真够～的。This is really hard to put up with. *or* This is a bitter pill to swallow. /在外面多跑跑也是好的,比在家里～闲气好多了。Running around outside is much better than sitting at home being sniped at. ❹〈方言〉pleasant; agreeable: ～吃 pleasant to the taste; tasty
受病 shòubìng catch or contract a disease; become sick; fall ill: 喝生水会～的。You may fall ill by drinking unboiled water.
受不了 shòubuliǎo cannot stand or bear: 疼得～ can't stand the pain /这点苦他也～。Even this little hardship was too much for him.
受不起 shòubuqǐ dare not accept; not deserve; cannot endure: 你怎么这点儿委屈也～? Why can't you put up with such a slight inconvenience? /你的礼我可～。I don't deserve your gift.
受潮 shòucháo get moist; become damp: 连日阴雨,东西容易～。As it's raining for days on end, things easily become damp. /切勿～! Keep from moisture!
受宠 shòuchǒng receive a favour; be indebted to sb. for a favour
受宠若惊 shòuchǒng-ruòjīng receive a favour with joy and surprise; be overwhelmed by an unexpected favour; feel extremely flattered: 他被邀请主持一次重要的学术会议,真觉得～。He felt immensely flattered when he was asked to chair an important academic conference.
受挫 shòucuò be foiled or defeated; suffer a setback: 多次～而不气馁 not lose heart despite repeated setbacks /敌人的图谋～。The enemy was foiled in his attempt.
受得了 shòudeliǎo can stand or bear: 你怎么～她那份尖刻? How can you tolerate that biting sarcasm of hers?
受敌 shòudí be under enemy attack: 四面～ come under enemy attack on all sides /腹背～ be attacked front and rear
受罚 shòufá be punished; be fined: 违章～ be fined for violating the regulations
受粉 shòufěn 〈植物〉be pollinated: 许多花都通过蜜蜂～。Many flowers are pollinated by bees.
受雇人 shòugùrén employee
受过 shòuguò bear the blame (due to sb. else): 他这是代我～。He took the blame for the mistake I made.
受害 shòuhài fall victim; be affected; be afflicted: ～不浅 suffer a great deal; be seriously affected /～的一方 aggrieved party; injured party /这次风灾严重,～的人数近五千。The cyclone disaster was very serious and the number of victims came close to 5,000.
受害行为学 shòuhài xíngwéixué victimology
受害者 shòuhàizhě sufferer; victim: 无辜～ innocent victim
受寒 shòuhán be chilled; catch a chill: 腿～了。He caught a chill in the leg. *or* His legs were chilled.
受旱 shòuhàn suffer from drought; be drought-stricken: 天久不雨,庄稼普遍～。The crops suffered extensively from the long dry spell.
受话器 shòuhuàqì (telephone) receiver
受欢迎的人 shòuhuānyíngde rén 〈外交〉*persona grata*: 不～ *per-*

S

sona non grata

受贿 shòuhuì take or accept bribes: ～行为 act of accepting bribes /行贿～ offer and take bribes /贪污～ corruption and bribery /那个警察经查清未～。The policeman was cleared of bribery.

受惠 shòuhuì receive benefits; benefit by

受惠国 shòuhuìguó 〈外交〉beneficiary country; beneficiary

受货人 shòuhuòrén consignee; vendee

受祸 shòuhuò be hit by disaster; suffer damage

受激发射 shòujī fāshè 〈物理〉stimulates emission

受激态 shòujītài 〈物理〉excited state

受夹板气 shòu jiābǎnqì be blamed by both parties; come under criticism by both sides: 你们两个都不肯让步，我在中间～。Neither of you is ready for a compromise, with me caught in between.

受奖 shòujiǎng receive rewards; be rewarded: 他曾多次立功～。He has been repeatedly rewarded for the meritorious deeds he performed.

受教 shòujiào be taught; receive instruction or guidance; have the benefit of sb.'s advice

受戒 shòujiè 〈佛教〉be initiated into monkhood or nunhood: 落发～ have one's head shaved (*or* tonsured) and become a monk or nun

受惊 shòujīng frightened; scared; startled: 对不起，让你～了。I'm sorry to have startled you. /马～了，发疯似的奔跑。The horse was frightened and galloped like mad.

受精 shòujīng be fertilized; be inseminated: 体内(外)～ internal (external) fertilization /异体～ cross-fertilization /自体～ self-fertilization

受精卵 shòujīngluǎn fertilized egg; zygote: ～移植 zygote transplant

受精素 shòujīngsù fertilizin

受窘 shòujiǒng be embarrassed; be caught in an awkward situation: 他当场～，不知怎么说才好。He felt embarrassed on the spot and was at a loss what to say.

受看 shòukàn ❶ good to look at; nice-looking: 这块花布～。This cotton print is really pretty. ❷ feel proud or honoured: 孩子不争气，大人脸上也不大～。Parents feel small when their children misbehave.

受苦 shòukǔ suffer; have a tough time: ～多年 have a tough time over the years /他受不了这份苦。He cannot endure such hardships.

受苦受难 shòukǔ-shòunàn lead a life of hardships and sufferings

受款人 shòukuǎnrén payee; beneficiary

受亏 shòukuī 〈方言〉lose; suffer loss

受累 shòulěi be implicated or incriminated (on account of sb. else): 无辜～ be incriminated or implicated without cause /不忍别人～ can't bear to implicate others on one's account

受累 shòulèi be put to much trouble; cause inconvenience to: 这么远来看我，让您～了。Thank you for taking the trouble to come such a long way to see me.

受冷 shòulěng catch cold

受礼 shòulǐ receive a gift; get a present

受理 shòulǐ ❶ accept and handle: ～托运业务 handle consignments of goods ❷ 〈法律〉accept and hear (a case): ～案件 accept and hear a case; take up a case /～控诉 accept a complaint /～诉状 accept a petition /市中级法院决定不～此案。The municipal intermediate court decided to throw the case out.

受凉 shòuliáng catch cold

受领 shòulǐng accept; receive; take: ～任务 accept a task (*or* an assignment) /你们的心意我～了，东西可不能收下。I appreciate your kind regard, but I can't accept your gift.

受命 shòumìng receive instructions or an assignment: ～办理此事 receive instructions to handle the matter /～于危难之际 receive the assignment in times of dire peril

受难 shòunàn suffer calamities or disasters; undergo great sufferings; be in distress: 受苦～的人们 people in a difficult and miserable plight; wretched of the earth /地震～者 victims of an earthquake /劳苦大众～的时代已经过去了! Gone are the days when the toiling masses lived in misery and distress.

受难曲 Shòunànqǔ the Passion (a musical setting of the sufferings of Christ from the Last Supper to his death on the cross)

受盘 shòupán *also* "接盘" jiēpán (of industrialists and merchants) buy up a business (including all its assets such as buildings, machines, equipment, stocks, etc.)

受骗 shòupiàn be deceived; be cheated; be taken in: 这是假货，我们～了! This is a fake. We've been taken in! /他上当～，加入了一个走私集团。He was deceived into joining a gang of smugglers.

受票人 shòupiàorén drawee

受聘 shòupìn ❶ 〈旧语〉(the bride's family) accept betrothal gifts (from the bridegroom's family) ❷ accept invitation to take a job: 他～当了排球教练。He accepted the job of a volleyball coach.

受气 shòuqì be bullied; be made to suffer: 他受不了老板的气，决定辞职。He could no longer stand the way he was treated by his boss and decided to quit.

受气包 shòuqìbāo person anyone can vent his spite upon; one who always takes the rap; whipping boy: 他成了他老婆的～。He serves as the whipping boy for his wife.

受穷 shòuqióng suffer from poverty; be poverty-stricken: 他祖父一辈子～。His grandfather lived in poverty all his life.

受屈 shòuqū be wronged; suffer an injustice

受权 shòuquán be authorized; be empowered: ～处理某事 be empowered to handle sth. /～发表声明 be authorized to issue a statement

受让人 shòuràngrén 〈法律〉assignee

受热 shòurè ❶ be exposed to heat; be heated: ～器 thermoreceptor; heat receiver /这种药不能～或受潮。Keep this medicine from heat and damp. ❷ be affected by the heat; have heatstroke or sunstroke

受辱 shòurǔ be insulted; be mortified; suffer humiliation: 宁死不～ would rather die than suffer humiliation

受禅 shòushàn ascend the throne abdicated by the emperor

受伤 shòushāng be injured; be wounded: 他背部～。His back was injured. *or* He was wounded in the back. /她腰部受重伤。She sustained a severe injury in the waist.

受赏 shòushǎng receive an award; be rewarded: 立功～ be rewarded for meritorious deeds /岂敢无功～! How can I accept a reward when I have not done anything worthwhile! *or* I'm afraid I don't deserve the reward.

受审 shòushěn be tried; stand trial; be on trial: 出庭～ be tried at a court; stand trial at a court /他因杀人而～。He was tried for homicide.

受使 shòushǐ be good to use; be handy; work well: 这支新钢笔挺～的。This new fountain pen writes very well.

受事 shòushì 〈语言〉object of the action in a sentence

受暑 shòushǔ suffer from heatstroke or sunstroke

受胎 shòutāi *also* "受孕" become pregnant; be impregnated; gestate; conceive

受胎率 shòutāilǜ pregnancy rate; fertility rate; 〈畜牧〉conception rate

受听 shòutīng good to hear; pleasant to the ear; sound nice (sweet, etc.): 这曲子～。This is a beautiful melody. /你说这话我还～。The way you put it sounds right to me.

受托 shòutuō be commissioned; be charged; be entrusted (with a task): ～给图书馆买书 be commissioned to buy books for the library; be asked to buy books for the library /～照看他的孩子 be entrusted with the care of sb.'s children /受人之托，忠人之事 try one's best to do what one is entrusted to do

受托国 shòutuōguó 〈外交〉mandatory country

受托人 shòutuōrén 〈法律〉trustee; fiduciary

受洗 shòuxǐ 〈宗教〉receive baptism; be baptized: ～仪式 baptism /孩子已～，取名玛丽。The child was baptized Mary. /他～为天主教徒。He was baptized a Catholic.

受降 shòuxiáng accept a surrender: 部队开进城市～。The army marched into the city to accept the surrender of the enemy.

受刑 shòuxíng be put to torture; be tortured: ～不过，屈打成招。He confessed to false charges under torture.

受学 shòuxué be taught by a teacher; study under the guidance of a teacher

受血者 shòuxuèzhě receptor; donee; recipient

受训 shòuxùn receive or undergo training; be trained: 正在～的新兵 recruits that are receiving training

受押人 shòuyārén 〈法律〉pledgee; mortgagee

受业 shòuyè 〈书面〉❶ learn from a teacher: ～弟子 sb.'s student or disciple /我～于这位画家多年。I studied under the painter for quite a few years. ❷ 〈谦词〉your pupil

受遗赠人 shòuyízèngrén 〈法律〉devisee; legatee

S

受益 shòuyì benefit from; profit by:这本书使我～非浅。I benefited a great deal from the book. *or* The book benefited me greatly. /你的忠告使我～良多。I have profited much by your advice. /水库的～地区很大。A vast area is serviced by the reservoir.
受益人 shòuyìrén 〈法律〉beneficiary
受益税 shòuyìshuì benefit tax
受益信托 shòuyì xìntuō benefit trust
受用 shòuyòng enjoy; benefit from; profit by:我们且～这里的荷香月色好了。Now we can enjoy the beauty of lotuses and moonlight here.
受用 shòuyong (often used in the negative) feel comfortable; gratifying:你这些事办得叫人不～。The way you did it made me sick.
受用不尽 shòuyòng-bùjìn profit by sth. all one's life:这些书使我～。I shall benefit from these books for the rest of my life.
受援 shòuyuán receive aid:～项目 aid project
受援国 shòuyuánguó 〈外交〉recipient country
受阅 shòuyuè (of troops, etc.) be reviewed
受孕 shòuyùn become pregnant; gestate; conceive
受灾 shòuzāi be hit by a natural calamity; be disaster-stricken:～群众 people afflicted by a natural calamity (*or* disaster) /～地区 disaster area; stricken (*or* afflicted) area / 这次冰雹使大片庄稼～。Large tracts of standing crops were damaged by the hailstones.
受赠人 shòuzèngrén donee
受之无愧 shòuzhī-wúkuì deserve sth.; be worthy of sth.; accept with a good conscience:劳动模范的称号,他～。He deserves the title of "model worker".
受之有愧 shòuzhī-yǒukuì not deserve sth.; be unworthy of sth.:却之不恭,～。To decline would be disrespectful, but to accept is embarrassing.
受知 shòuzhī 〈书面〉be recognized (for one's talent, etc.); win recognition; be appreciated
受制 shòuzhì ❶ be controlled; be under control:～于人 be under sb.'s control or command ❷ suffer hardships; endure rough conditions:我～受够了! I have had enough of it!
受主 shòuzhǔ 〈电子〉acceptor:～密度 acceptor density /～级 acceptor level /～杂质 acceptor impurity /～原子 acceptor atom
受阻 shòuzǔ be hindered or blocked; meet with obstruction:计划～ plan be blocked /施工～ construction be halted (*or* obstructed) /因交通～,不能按时到达。Owing to the traffic jam, we couldn't arrive on time.
受罪 shòuzuì suffer hardships; endure rough conditions; have a hard time:坏人当道,好人～。When evil people are in power, good people suffer.

授 shòu ❶ award; present; vest; confer:～以博士学位 confer a doctoral degree /～以勋章 present a decoration /～以某人权力 vest sb. with power (*or* authority) /～以骑士爵位 confer a knighthood (upon sb.); knight sb. /～以劳动模范称号 award sb. the title of "model worker"; the title of "model worker" is conferred upon sb. ❷ teach; instruct; tell:口～ pass on (skill, etc.) orally; dictate (a letter, etc.) /函～ teach by correspondence /面～机宜 personally instruct sb. on the line of action to pursue; give confidential briefing /～以秘诀 give sb. a secret formula or recipe
授粉 shòufěn 〈植物〉pollinate; pollenize:人工～ artificial pollination /～媒介 pollinator; pollenizer /绝大多数植物靠昆虫或风～。Most plants are pollinated with the help of insects or wind.
授计 shòujì confide a stratagem to sb.; tell sb. a scheme:暗地～与人 secretly tell sb. a plan of action
授奖 shòujiǎng award or confer a prize:授予头奖 award sb. the first prize /由首长～ prize to be presented by the leadership /邀请名人～ invite celebrities to award (*or* hand out) prizes
授精 shòujīng insemination:人工～ artificial insemination
授课 shòukè give lessons; give lectures:他在夜大～。He teaches at the night college.
授命 shòumìng ❶〈书面〉give or lay down one's life; sacrifice oneself:临危～ lay down one's life in time of danger /～疆场 die on the battlefield; die in action ❷ give orders; authorize:～组阁 authorize sb. to organize the cabinet
授权 shòuquán empower; authorize; delegate power to:～外交部发表声明 authorize the foreign ministry to make a statement /～秘书长进行斡旋 empower the secretary-general to mediate /～行为 act of authorization /～范围 scope of authority /经～的官员 authorized officer
授权立法 shòuquán lìfǎ delegated legislation
授权书 shòuquánshū letter of authorization; letter of attorney; power of attorney
授权制度 shòuquán zhìdù 〈法律〉empowerment
授人以柄 shòurényǐbǐng give sb. a handle (against oneself):言多必失,～。If you talk too much, you tend to make errors and give people a handle against yourself.
授时 shòushí ❶〈天文〉time service ❷〈旧语〉issue the official calendar
授时信号 shòushí xìnhào time signal
授室 shòushì 〈书面〉take a bride; take a wife
授首 shòushǒu 〈书面〉(of a traitor or robber) be beheaded:法场～ be beheaded on the execution ground /敌酋～。The enemy chieftain was killed in action.
授受 shòu-shòu give and receive; offer and accept:私相～ give and accept in private; illegally pass things between individuals /男女～不亲〈旧语〉(according to Confucian rules of etiquette) man and woman should not touch each other when giving and receiving something
授衔 shòuxián confer a title or rank (on sb.)
授勋 shòuxūn confer or award an order, a decoration or a medal
授业 shòuyè 〈书面〉teach; tutor
授艺 shòuyì teach sb. a skill
授意 shòuyì incite or inspire (sb. to do sth.); suggest an idea (to sb.):某人～写的文章 article inspired by sb. /这些都是谁～的? Who's behind all this? /一定有人～他干这些蠢事。He must have been put up to doing such stupid things.
授予 shòuyǔ confer; award:～学位 confer a degree (upon sb.) /～奖状 award sb. a certificate of merit /～人 grantor /～物 grant

绶 shòu coloured silk ribbon (usu. attached to an official seal or a medal):印～〈旧语〉seal with its silk ribbon /解～而去 return the official seal (i.e. resign) and leave
绶草 shòucǎo ladies' tresses (*Spiranthes lancea*)
绶带 shòudài coloured silk ribbon (attached to an official seal or a medal); cordon (worn as a sash of honour or an ornament):这位老将军戴了许多～。The old general wore many ribbons on his chest.
绶带鸟 shòudàiniǎo paradise flycatcher

瘦 shòu ❶ thin; slim; emaciated:清～ thin; lean /干～ skinny; bony /面黄肌～ sallow and emaciated /骨～如柴 be a bag of bones /～猴似的 thin and shrivelled; skinny /～得皮包骨 be all skin and bones /千金难买老来～。To remain slim at old age is more than money can buy. ❷ lean:～肉 lean meat /～肉率 cutability /挑肥拣～〈贬义〉pick the fat or choose the lean — choose whatever is to one's advantage; be choosy ❸ fitting too closely; tight:我穿这条裤子裤腿嫌～,能不能放出点来? This pair of trousers is somewhat tight for me at the legs. Can you have them let out? ❹ not fertile; poor; barren:～田 poor soil; infertile land
瘦巴 shòuba *also* "瘦巴巴" thin; emaciated; skinny; lean:～脸 thin face
瘦瘪 shòubiě thin and sunken:～的嘴 thin and depressed lips
瘦长 shòucháng tall and thin; lanky:～的裤腿儿 long slim trouser legs /～的身材 tall, slender figure /他是个～个儿。He's a lanky fellow.
瘦高挑儿 shòugāotiǎor 〈方言〉tall and slender figure; tall, slender person
瘦骨嶙峋 shòugǔ-línxún be thin and bony; be a bag of bones:他望着她～的背影,无限同情地沉思起来。As he beheld her wasted figure, he was lost in thought and full of sympathy.
瘦刮刮 shòuguāguā *also* "瘦括括" very skinny; emaciated
瘦果 shòuguǒ 〈植物〉achene
瘦活儿 shòuhuór 〈方言〉energy-consuming, badly paid job
瘦瘠 shòují ❶ thin and weak:～的身体 be thin and weak ❷ (of land, soil, etc.) poor; barren:把～的荒山改造成富饶的果木园 turn barren hills into rich orchards
瘦金体 shòujīntǐ style of Chinese calligraphy originated by Emperor Huizong (Zhao Ji) of the Song Dynasty, featuring thin and sturdy strokes
瘦精精 shòujīngjīng *also* "瘦筋筋" very thin; emaciated
瘦劲 shòujìng (of Chinese calligraphy) thin but sturdy (strokes):

S

书法～. style of calligraphy which features thin but vigorous strokes
瘦溜 shòuliu 〈方言〉slim; slender; thin: 他身材～，动作灵活。He is of slender build and very agile.
瘦煤 shòuméi lean coal; meagre coal
瘦俏 shòuqiào (of figure) slender and pretty
瘦缺 shòuquē poorly paid job; unprofitable post
瘦弱 shòuruò thin and weak; frail: ～的老人 frail old man
瘦损 shòusǔn lose weight; become thin or emaciated: 由于疾病的折磨，他一天天～起来。He grew thinner than ever as a result of his illness.
瘦西湖 Shòuxīhú Slender West Lake (in Yangzhou 扬州 of Jiangsu Province)
瘦小 shòuxiǎo thin and small: 身材～ of a slight build /～的妇人 woman of small stature
瘦型体质 shòuxíng tǐzhì of the thin type; ectomorph
瘦削 shòuxuē very thin; emaciated; gaunt: ～的面孔 gaunt (*or* haggard) face /双肩～ lean shoulders
瘦硬 shòuyìng slender and yet tough: 书贵～。In Chinese calligraphy, thin but powerful strokes are valued the most. /亭子角上～的松枝直指天空。The fine and strong twigs of the old pine tree round the corner of the pavilion point upwards to the sky.
瘦子 shòuzi lean or thin person

售

shòu ❶ be on sale; sell: 出～ sell; put on sale; offer for sale /零～ sell by retail; retail /抛～ dump (large stocks of merchandise in the market) /寄～ consign for sale; put up for sale in a secondhand shop /代～ be commissioned to sell sth. /转～ sell what one has bought /四处兜～ go around peddling (*or* hawking) sth. ❷ 〈书面〉carry out (intrigues, tricks, etc.): 以～其奸 carry out one's evil design /其计不～ one's plan falls through
售后服务 shòuhòu fúwù service after sale; after-sale service; aftersales; customer service: 改善和加强～ improve and strengthen after-sale service
售后回租 shòuhòu huízū 〈商业〉sale-and-leaseback
售货 shòuhuò sell or vend goods: ～车 sales wagon /～报价 selling offer; offer /～确认书 sale confirmation
售货机 shòuhuòjī vending machine
售货员 shòuhuòyuán shop assistant; salesclerk; salesman: 女～ saleswoman; salesgirl; shopgirl
售价 shòujià selling price: ～太高。The price is too high. /实际～低于账面价值。The actual selling price is below book value.
售卖 shòumài sell: ～食品杂货 sell groceries /沿街～ peddle or hawk along the streets
售票处 shòupiàochù ticket office; booking office (at a railway station); box office (at a theatre, etc.)
售票口 shòupiàokǒu ticket window; wicket (of a ticket office)
售票员 shòupiàoyuán ticket seller; (of a bus) conductor or conductress; (of a railway station or airport) booking-office clerk; (of a theatre) box-office clerk

shū

梳

shū ❶ comb: 木～ wooden comb /电热～ electric heat comb /细齿～ fine-tooth comb ❷ comb one's hair, etc.: 你的头发要好好～一～。Your hair needs a good comb.
梳篦 shūbì thick and fine-tooth comb
梳辫子 shū biànzi ❶ plait or braid one's hair; wear plaits; put one's hair into plaits or braids: 那小姑娘梳两条辫子。The little girl wears her hair in two plaits. ❷ 〈比喻〉sort sth. out: 把问题梳梳辫子。Sort out the problems.
梳骨螺 shūgǔluó Venus comb
梳理 shūlǐ ❶ 〈纺织〉carding ❷ comb: ～头发 comb one's hair /给猫～毛结 combed out the knots in the cat's fur /把思路～清楚 organize one's ideas
梳拢 shūlǒng ❶ comb (hair, etc.): ～蓬乱的头发 comb one's tousled hair ❷ 〈旧语〉(of prostitutes) receive a patron for the first time
梳拢婆 shūlǒngpó matchmaker; go-between
梳掠 shūlüè comb (beard, hair, etc.)
梳麻机 shūmájī carding machine (for hemp, flax, etc.); dresser
梳麻器 shūmáqì 〈农业〉hemp comb
梳毛 shūmáo carding
梳毛机 shūmáojī wool card
梳棉 shūmián 〈纺织〉carding: ～间 carding room
梳棉机 shūmiánjī 〈纺织〉carding machine (for cotton, kapok, etc.)
梳头 shūtóu comb one's hair: ～洗脸 comb one's hair and wash one's face
梳洗 shūxǐ wash and dress: ～后穿上礼服 put on a dinner jacket after washing and dressing oneself /～得漂漂亮亮 be clean, tidy and smart as a new pin
梳洗用具 shūxǐ yòngjù toilet articles
梳妆 shūzhuāng dress and make up
梳妆打扮 shūzhuāng-dǎban make oneself up; be dressed up; dress smartly
梳妆台 shūzhuāngtái dressing table
梳子 shūzi comb

疏[1]（疎）

shū ❶ dredge (a river, etc.): 禹～九河。Yu (reputed founder of the Xia Dynasty) dredged nine rivers (in order to prevent floods). ❷ thin; loose; sparse; scattered: ～发 thin hair /苗～ sparse seedlings /～网 loose net /～雨 scattered showers /稀～的村落 thinly scattered (*or* isolated) villages /～柳寒烟 some sparse willow trees and a frosty sky ❸ (of family or social relations) distant: 亲～有别 treat differently those who are close to oneself and those who are not ❹ not familiar with: 业务荒～ become rusty in one's professional skills /人地生～ be unfamiliar with the place and the people; be a stranger in the land ❺ negligent; careless: 粗～ careless; inattentive ❻ scanty; inadequate; meagre: 才～学浅 have little talent and less learning /志大才～ have lofty aspirations but inadequate talent ❼ thin out; disperse; scatter: *see* "～财仗义" ❽ (Shū) a surname

疏[2]

shū ❶ memorial to the emperor: 上～ present a memorial to the emperor /奏～ memorial to the throne ❷ detailed annotation: 注～ notes and commentaries
疏不间亲 shūbùjiànqīn outsiders cannot succeed in driving a wedge between insiders; blood is thicker than water: 俗话说～，你我终是外人，最好别管他的家事。As the saying goes, "Blood is thicker than water", we are after all outsiders and should not get involved in his family affairs.
疏财仗义 shūcái-zhàngyì *also* "仗义疏财" be generous in giving aid to poor people
疏淡 shūdàn ❶ thin and light; simple and elegant: 白云～ thin, white clouds /梅花～多姿。The plum blossoms are quietly elegant. ❷ distant and faint; become estranged and indifferent: 由于志趣不同，他们的感情有些～了。They have become estranged due to different aspirations and interests.
疏宕 shūdàng 〈书面〉untrammelled; unconventional; carefree: ～不拘 free and easy
疏导 shūdǎo ❶ dredge: ～运河 dredge a canal ❷ direct; regulate: ～交通 direct the flow of traffic
疏放 shūfàng 〈书面〉❶ unbridled; self-indulgent: 他为人～。He always lets his passion carry him away. ❷ (of writing) not constrained by conventional style, form, etc.: 文笔～ write in an unconventional style
疏港 shūgǎng regulate the flow of ships and cargoes in a port
疏隔 shūgé become estranged: 由于长期不在一起生活，他们的感情有些～了。As a result of long separation, they have become estranged.
疏果 shūguǒ 〈农业〉fruit thinning
疏忽 shūhu carelessness; neglect; negligence; oversight: 他们将这次车祸归咎于司机的～。They imputed the accident to the driver's carelessness. /一个小小的～酿成这场灾难。A slight neglect led to the tragedy. /错误是～造成的。The mistake was the result of an oversight. /领导～了这个问题。The leadership has overlooked this problem.
疏花 shūhuā 〈农业〉flower thinning
疏剪 shūjiǎn prune (bushes, etc.); prune away (branches, etc.)
疏解 shūjiě ❶ mediate: 老师从中～，他俩才消除了误会。It was the teacher's mediation that helped remove the misunderstanding between them. ❷ make sth. less difficult (bitter, etc.); ease up; mitigate: 扩大运输能力，～客流 expand the existing carrying capacity

in order to cut down the number of stranded passengers
疏浚 shūjùn dredge: ～航道 dredge the waterways /～泵 dredge pump
疏开 shūkāi 〈军事〉 extend; disperse; deploy: ～操练 extended order drill /～地域 dispersed area /～队形 dispersed formation; extended order; open order (*or* formation); route formation /～机场 dispersed airfield /～距离 extended distance /～配置 disposition in open order; dispersed deployment /～突击 attack in open order /～阵地 dispersal site /～纵队 open column
疏狂 shūkuáng 〈书面〉 uninhibited; untrammelled; unconventional
疏旷 shūkuàng open; spacious: ～的野景 open country scene
疏阔 shūkuò 〈书面〉 ❶ careless; not well conceived: 天下初定,制度～。Order had just been achieved in the country, and there were many loopholes in rules and regulations. ❷ drift apart; become estranged: 交往～ be estranged from each other ❸ unrealistic; impractical: ～之论 pedantic views; pedantry /思虑～ unrealistic thinking ❹ long separation: 兄弟～。Brothers have parted for a long time.
疏懒 shūlǎn careless and lazy; indolent; lackadaisical: 他生性～。He was born careless and lazy.
疏朗 shūlǎng ❶ thin and clear: 须眉～ thin beard and eyebrows /夜空中闪烁着疏疏朗朗的几点星光。A few stars glistened in the night sky. ❷ sanguine; cheerful: 胸怀渐渐～了。Little by little he became happier.
疏冷 shūlěng ❶ 〈书面〉 sparse and desolate: 古槐～。A few ancient Chinese scholartrees stood far and between. ❷ estranged; not close: 随着时间的推移,他们的感情越发～了。They became further alienated as time went by.
疏理 shūlǐ put to order; disentangle (a confused situation): ～商品的流通渠道 unclog and readjust channels for commodities
疏漏 shūlòu careless omission; slip; oversight; negligence: 防止～ guard against careless omissions; avoid slips /校对中有不少～。There are quite a few oversights in the proofreading.
疏略 shūlüè 〈书面〉 ❶ carelessness; oversight: 他工作多有～。There are quite a few careless errors in his work. ❷ sketchy; inadequate: 会议的记录过于～。The minutes of the meeting are too sketchy (*or* leave out too many important details).
疏落 shūluò thinly distributed; sparse; scattered: ～的晨星 scattered morning stars /山上的树长得疏疏落落的。The trees on the hill were sparse. /山脚下疏疏落落有几座房子。At the foot of the mountain there were a few houses here and there.
疏慢 shūmàn 〈书面〉 neglect; treat coldly; cold-shoulder
疏密 shūmì density; spacing: ～相间 of alternate density /～有致 be well spaced
疏苗 shūmiáo thin out seedlings (young shoots, etc.)
疏排 shūpái 〈印刷〉 white-out
疏浅 shūqiǎn ❶ crude and shallow: 才学～ 〈谦词〉 of limited scholarship ❷ not be close; drift apart: 关系～ not close to each other
疏散 shūsàn ❶ sparse; scattered; dispersed: ～的渔村 scattered fishing villages ❷ evacuate; vacate; disperse: ～人口 evacuate residents /～队伍 disperse the troops /～机场 dispersed airfield /～区 evacuated area
疏神 shūshén one's mind is wandering; be absent-minded; be careless: 携带这样贵重东西,千万不能～。You can never be too careful when you bring such valuables with you.
疏失 shūshī careless mistake; thoughtless error; remissness: 这是我的～。It is my fault. /我们要防止工作中的遗漏～。We must guard against careless mistakes in work.
疏松 shūsōng ❶ loose; puffy: ～的蛋糕 puffy cake /土质～ porous soil /骨质～ osteoporosis; rarefaction of bone ❷ loosen: ～土壤 loosen the soil
疏松结缔组织 shūsōng jiédì zǔzhī 〈生理〉 loose connective tissue
疏通 shūtōng ❶ dredge; remove obstacles from: ～沟渠 dredge the ditches /～管道 remove obstacles from the pipe ❷ mediate between two parties; remove misunderstanding: ～关系 mediate between two parties /～感情 remove misunderstanding
疏脱 shūtuō ❶ 〈书面〉 careless ❷ 〈旧语〉 (prisoner's) escape caused by the warder's dereliction of duty
疏挖 shūwā dredge: ～运河 dredge a canal
疏稀 shūxī few and scattered; few; thin; sparse
疏懈 shūxiè negligent; neglectful; lazy: 他对待工作严肃认真,从不～。He is a very conscientious worker who never neglects his duties.
疏于 shūyú be neglectful about; neglect to do sth.; fail to do sth. out of negligence: ～防守 fail to strengthen defence; be neglectful about defence /～职守 negligent of one's duties /～管教 lax in discipline (*or* guidance) /～研究 neglect one's research
疏虞 shūyú 〈书面〉 carelessness; oversight: 倘有～,干系不小。An oversight may lead to serious consequences.
疏远 shūyuǎn alienate; drift apart; become estranged: 互相～ be estranged from each other /他的愚蠢行为使朋友们与之～。His foolish behaviour alienated his friends. /她和丈夫逐渐～,最后终于分居了。She and her husband gradually drifted apart until they separated.
疏运 shūyùn direct and expedite transport: 搞好港口物资～。Expedite the transport of materials in the port.
疏质骨 shūzhìgǔ 〈生理〉 cancellous bone

蔬 shū vegetables: 菜～ vegetables /布衣～食 coarse clothes and simple fare
蔬菜 shūcài vegetables; greens; greenstuff: ～栽培 vegetable growing; vegetable farming /～作物 vegetable crop /～轮作 vegetable crop rotation /～园艺 vegetable gardening /～农场 (US) truck farm
蔬菜学 shūcàixué olericulture
蔬果 shūguǒ vegetables and fruits

枢(樞) shū ❶ hinge; pivot: 支～ pivot /流水不腐,户～不蠹。Running water is never stale and a door-hinge is never worm-eaten. ❷ hub; centre of activity or importance: 神经中～ nerve centre /兰州是西北～要之地。Lanzhou is the most important city of northwest China.
枢杆 shūgǎn hinged arm
枢机 shūjī ❶ 〈旧语〉 key position or institution: 处～之要 hold a key post in the government /国家～ key state institution (*or* agency) ❷ 〈书面〉 key to the problem; crux or heart of the matter: 耳目乃心之～。Ears and eyes are the pivot of the mind.
枢机主教 shūjī zhǔjiào cardinal
枢接 shūjiē pin joint
枢密大臣 shūmì dàchén (UK) member of the privy council; privy councillor
枢密院 Shūmìyuàn ❶ 〈历史〉 Supreme Military Council (907-1368) ❷ (UK) Privy Council
枢纽 shūniǔ pivot; hub; axis; key: 交通～ hub of communications /水利～工程 key water control (*or* conservancy) project /抓住工作的～ grasp the key link in work /控制战略～ get hold of the strategic point (*or* place)
枢纽断层 shūniǔ duàncéng 〈地质〉 hinge fault
枢要 shūyào 〈书面〉〈旧语〉 central administrative department: 任典～ be in charge of the central administrative department
枢轴 shūzhóu pivot; gudgeon; king journal; weigh bar shaft: 垂直～ pintle
枢椎 shūzhuī 〈生理〉 axis: 骨骼的～是脊骨。The axis of the skeleton is the spinal column.

叔 shū ❶ father's younger brother; uncle: 三～ Uncle No. 3; father's second younger brother /堂～ father's younger male cousin (bearing the same surname) /表～ father's younger male cousin (bearing a different surname) ❷ form of address for a man about one's father's age; uncle: 王大～ Uncle Wang ❸ husband's younger brother: 小～子 husband's younger brother /～嫂二人一块去。She and her younger brother-in-law went there together. ❹ third son in the family: 伯仲～季 first, second, third and fourth sons in the family
叔胺 shū'àn 〈化学〉 tertiary amine
叔伯 shūbai relationship between cousins of the same grandfather or great-grandfather: ～姐妹 first or second female cousins on the paternal side; cousins
叔父 shūfù father's younger brother; uncle
叔公 shūgōng ❶ (paternal) uncle of one's husband ❷ 〈方言〉 (paternal) grandfather's younger brother; great uncle
叔母 shūmǔ wife of father's younger brother; aunt
叔婆 shūpó ❶ aunt of one's husband ❷ 〈方言〉 *see* "叔祖母"
叔叔 shūshu ❶ 〈口语〉 father's younger brother; uncle ❷ uncle (a

child's form of address for any young man one generation his or her senior)：解放军～ uncle PLA
叔岳 shūyuè uncle of one's wife
叔子 shūzi husband's younger brother; brother-in-law
叔祖 shūzǔ (paternal) grandfather's younger brother; great uncle
叔祖母 shūzǔmǔ wife of (paternal) grandfather's younger brother; great aunt

淑 shū 〈书面〉kind and gentle; fair; graceful; pretty：贤～ (of a woman) virtuous
淑德 shūdé female virtue
淑静 shūjìng (of women) quiet and gentle
淑均 shūjūn kind and fair：性行～ have a kind and fair disposition
淑美 shūměi (of a woman) refined and beautiful
淑女 shūnǚ 〈书面〉fair maiden; virtuous woman; noble lady：窈窕～ pretty woman
淑质 shūzhì virtue; moral excellence

菽(尗) shū beans：麦～不辨 can't tell wheat from beans — ignorant of common things
菽麻 shūmá sunn; sunn hemp; Indian hemp (*Crotalaria juncea*)
菽水承欢 shūshuǐ-chénghuān be a dutiful son to one's parents even in poverty — poor but filial
菽粟 shūsù (general term for) grain：布帛～ cloth and grain

摅(攄) shū 〈书面〉❶ express; give expression to：各～己意。Each freely expresses his or her own views. ❷ prance; bounce

殊 shū ❶ different; divergent：悬～ differ widely; be poles apart / 二人秉性各～。The two have entirely different dispositions. ❷ outstanding; special; unusual：获此～荣 win (*or* receive) exceptional honour ❸〈书面〉very much; exceedingly; really：文笔～佳 write extremely well; be an outstanding writer / 体魄～健 be in excellent health / ～感悲痛 feel deeply grieved ❹〈书面〉break off; cut off
殊不知 shūbùzhī ❶ who knows that... (contrary to what others say)：人们都说这趟火车历来准时，～今天就误点了。They say this train is very punctual, but it is behind schedule today. ❷ little imagine; hardly expect (contrary to what one oneself has thought)：原以为会受到热情接待，～竟吃了闭门羹。I thought I would receive a warm welcome; I never dreamt that I would be denied entrance.
殊方 shūfāng 〈书面〉❶ with different purposes and interests; going in different directions：好恶～ tastes differ; have different likes and dislikes ❷ strange lands; distant places：～异物 strange lands and exotic things
殊功 shūgōng outstanding exploits; remarkable achievement：立～ render meritorious service
殊绩 shūjì distinguished service; outstanding merit：以～而被提拔 be promoted because of one's outstanding performance
殊绝 shūjué rare; very special; outstanding; remarkable：风韵～ exceptional charm / ～的功勋 illustrious exploit; extraordinary achievement
殊荣 shūróng special honour; unusual honour
殊深轸念 shūshēn-zhěnniàn express deep concern; be very solicitous about
殊死 shūsǐ ❶ desperate; life-and-death：～抵抗 put up a desperate resistance / ～战斗 fight a last-ditch battle; fight to the bitter end ❷〈古语〉penalty of decapitation
殊途同归 shūtú-tóngguī reach the same goal by different routes; all roads lead to Rome：两个人的做法虽然不同，但～，结果还是一样的。The two have different approaches to the problem, but as all roads lead to Rome, the result will be the same.
殊效 shūxiào special effect：此药治关节炎有～。This medicine is specially effective for arthritis.
殊勋 shūxūn 〈书面〉outstanding merit; eminent service：屡建～ render distinguished services time and again
殊异 shūyì ❶ different; distinct：由于掌握材料的不同，研究方法的～，这两位学者得出的结论不一样。Different data and approaches led the two scholars to different conclusions. ❷ special; extraordinary：～的事迹 extraordinary achievement; distinguished service
殊遇 shūyù special treatment; great kindness：不忘～之恩 never forget the special favour you have bestowed on me
殊致 shūzhì 〈书面〉❶ differ; be different：褒贬～ get a mixed reception; receive both praise and censure ❷ spectacular view; wonderful scenery
殊姿 shūzī 〈书面〉❶ exceedingly graceful manner; unusual charm ❷ distinctive bearing

姝 shū 〈书面〉❶ pretty; beautiful：姿颜～丽 good-looking; beautiful / 静女其～。The girl is very attractive. ❷ beauty：绝代之～ peerless beauty

输[1] shū ❶ transport; transmit; convey：这些棉花将～往国外。The cotton will be transported abroad. / 这个电网把电～到这个地区的各个城市。This network carries electric power to all the cities in the region. ❷〈书面〉make a gift of; contribute money; donate：捐～ contribute; donate / ～财助战 donate money for the war effort

输[2] shū lose; be beaten; suffer defeat：认～ admit defeat; throw in the towel / 决不服～ refuse to admit defeat; not be reconciled to defeat / ～得精光 lose all money (*or* every cent) at gambling / 我们～给了客队。We were beaten by the visiting team.
输布 shūbù 〈中医〉circulation and distribution of vital energy, blood, body fluids, etc. in the human body
输诚 shūchéng 〈书面〉❶ express one's sincerity：～结交 make friends in all sincerity ❷ surrender; capitulate
输出 shūchū ❶ send out：血液从心脏～，经血管分布到全身组织。Blood flows out of the heart and is carried to different organs of the body through blood vessels. ❷ export：向日本～原料 export raw materials to Japan / 劳务～ export of labour (*or* services) / ～品 export / ～口岸 loading port / ～限额 export quota / ～管制 export control ❸ give off; emit; (of electricity) output：～能量 emit energy / ～信号 sent out signals / ～电流 output current / ～电路 output circuit / ～电压 output voltage / ～电阻 output resistance
输出端数 shūchū duānshù fan-out
输出端子 shūchū duānzǐ 〈电子〉output terminal
输出港 shūchūgǎng port of export; outport
输出功率 shūchū gōnglǜ output power
输出开关 shūchū kāiguān out switch
输出数据 shūchū shùjù data-out
输出许可证 shūchū xǔkězhèng export licence or permit
输电 shūdiàn transmit electricity：～系统 transmission system / 线路修复，开始向山区～。The circuit has been repaired and begun to transmit electricity to the mountain area.
输电量 shūdiànliàng transmission capacity
输电塔 shūdiàntǎ 〈电工〉power transmission tower
输电网 shūdiànwǎng *also* "电网" power transmission network; grid system
输电线路 shūdiàn xiànlù transmission line
输家 shūjia loser in a game or gamble
输将 shūjiāng 〈书面〉contribute money; donate：慷慨～ make liberal (*or* generous) contributions
输精管 shūjīngguǎn 〈生理〉spermatic duct; deferent duct; *vas deferens*; *ductus deferens*
输精管结扎术 shūjīngguǎn jiézāshù vasoligation
输精管精囊炎 shūjīngguǎn jīngnángyán vasovesiculitis
输精管切除术 shūjīngguǎn qiēchúshù deferentectomy; vasectomy
输精管炎 shūjīngguǎnyán deferentitis; spermatitis
输捐 shūjuān pay; contribute：～军饷 contribute to the pay and provisions for soldiers
输理 shūlǐ right is not on one's side：你们在这个关键问题上～了。You are in the wrong on this key issue.
输卵管 shūluǎnguǎn 〈生理〉oviduct; Fallopian tube; *salpinx uterina*
输卵管积水 shūluǎnguǎn jīshuǐ hydrosalpinx
输卵管结扎术 shūluǎnguǎn jiézāshù tubal ligation
输卵管绝育 shūluǎnguǎn juéyù 〈医学〉tubal sterilization
输卵管卵巢切除术 shūluǎnguǎn luǎncháo qiēchúshù salpingo-oophorectomy
输卵管切除术 shūluǎnguǎn qiēchúshù deferentectomy; vasectomy

输卵管妊娠 shūluǎnguǎn rènshēn salpingocyesis; tubal gestation; tubal pregnancy
输卵管系膜 shūluǎnguǎn xìmó mesosalpinx
输卵管炎 shūluǎnguǎnyán salpingitis
输煤管 shūméiguǎn coal chute
输纳 shūnà 〈书面〉pay money or goods to the authorities: ~钱粮 pay money or submit grains as taxes to the authorities
输尿管 shūniàoguǎn 〈生理〉ureter
输尿管囊肿 shūniàoguǎn nángzhǒng ureterocele
输尿管石病 shūniàoguǎnshíbìng ureterolithiasis
输尿管石切除术 shūniàoguǎnshí qiēchúshù ureterolithotomy
输尿管狭窄 shūniàoguǎn xiázhǎi ureterostenosis
输尿管炎 shūniàoguǎnyán ureteritis
输钱 shūqián lose money at gambling
输入 shūrù ❶ bring in: 把河水~蓄水池 channel water from the river into the reservoir ❷ import; introduce: ~机床 import machine tools / ~额 amount of imports / ~限额 import quota; import control / ~登记证明书 registration certificate of import / 从国外~了许多先进技术。Many sophisticated technologies have been introduced from abroad. ❸ 〈电学〉〈计算机〉input: 把数据~电脑 input the data / ~程序 input routine; loading routine / ~子程序 input (*or* loading) subroutine / ~文件 input file / ~字段 input field / ~字块 input block / ~电路 input circuit / ~电压 input voltage / ~电阻 input resistance
输入端数 shūrù duānshù fan-in
输入端子 shūrù duānzǐ input terminal
输入港 shūrùgǎng port of import; port of entry
输入功率 shūrù gōnglǜ input power
输入输出 shūrù shūchū import/outport; I/O: ~分析 I/O analysis
输入数据 shūrù shùjù data-in
输入许可证 shūrù xǔkězhèng import licence
输沙率 shūshālǜ 〈水利〉silt discharge
输水道 shūshuǐdào aqueduct
输送 shūsòng carry; transport; send; convey: 往农村~货物 send (*or* transport) goods to the rural area / 给边疆地区~了大批技术人员 provide the border areas with large numbers of technical personnel / ~新鲜血液 infuse new blood
输送泵 shūsòngbèng transfer pump
输送带 shūsòngdài conveyer belt: ~系统 belt system
输送机 shūsòngjī conveyer
输血 shūxuè ❶ 〈医学〉blood transfusion: 已给病人~。The patient has been given a blood transfusion. / 她自愿为伤员~。She offered to give her blood to help the wounded soldier. ❷ give aid and support; shore up; give sb. a shot in the arm: 对贫困地区, 只~是远远不够的, 更重要的是帮助他们造血。For the poor areas, mere aid is far from enough. What is more important is to help people there find ways to aid themselves.
输血操作者 shūxuè cāozuòzhě transfusionist
输血者 shūxuèzhě blood doner
输氧 shūyǎng 〈医学〉oxygen therapy: 病人需要立即~。The patient needs oxygen therapy immediately.
输液 shūyè 〈医学〉infusion
输赢 shūyíng ❶ gain or loss; defeat or victory (in a game, etc.): 这两个球队憋足了劲要较量一番, 非见个~不可。Bursting with energy, each of the two teams is determined to fight it out and outplay the other. ❷ (of gambling) gains and losses: 这伙赌徒, 一夜就有十几万元的~。These gamblers gain or lose money in (*or* on) the order of over one hundred thousand *yuan* a night.
输油泵 shūyóubèng fuel delivery pump
输油管 shūyóuguǎn petroleum pipeline; oil line
输油软管 shūyóu ruǎnguǎn oil hose
输纸辊 shūzhǐgǔn 〈印刷〉feed rollers
输嘴 shūzuǐ admit mistake or defeat in argument: 你不~, 我就叫你下不了台。Admit defeat, or else I will put you on the spot.

毹

shū *see* "氍毹" qúshū

倏(倐)

shū 〈书面〉swiftly: ~已三月。Three months have passed without my knowing it. *or* How time flies! Three months have elapsed!
倏地 shūdì swiftly; suddenly: ~不见。It disappeared suddenly.
倏尔 shū'ěr 〈书面〉swiftly; suddenly; in the twinkling of an eye: ~雨雪纷纷。All of a sudden rain, mixed with snow, came down.
倏忽 shūhū swiftly; abruptly; unexpectedly: 海上天气, ~万变。Weather at sea changes in the twinkling of an eye.
倏然 shūrán 〈书面〉❶ abruptly; all of a sudden: ~一阵暴雨。Suddenly it poured. ❷ swift; quick: 一道流星, ~而逝。In a twinkling, the meteor was lost from sight.

儵

shū *see* "倏" shū

殳

shū ❶ ancient weapon made of bamboo ❷ (Shū) a surname

抒

shū ❶ give voice to; express; convey: 直~胸臆 frankly express one's feelings / 以~其愤 voice one's anger / 畅~己见 air one's views freely ❷ relieve; alleviate
抒发 shūfā express; voice; convey: ~义愤 give voice to one's indignation / 这首诗~了诗人的爱国热忱。The poem expresses the ardent patriotism of the poet. / 这支歌~了全国人民的壮志豪情。This song conveys the aspiration and determination of the whole nation.
抒怀 shūhuái express one's feelings: 凭栏~ lean against a railing and unbosom oneself to nature / 春日~ express one's sentiments on a spring day
抒情 shūqíng express or convey one's emotion: ~歌曲 lyric song / 借景~ convey one's emotion by describing the scenery
抒情散文 shūqíng sǎnwén lyric prose
抒情诗 shūqíngshī lyric poetry; lyrics
抒写 shūxiě describe; express: ~怀念故国的情思 describe the longings for his native land / ~郁积在内心的悲愤 give vent to his pent-up grief and indignation

舒

shū ❶ stretch; relax; unfold; free from (oppressed feeling, etc.): ~腰伸臂 lean back and stretch one's arms / 心境宽~ entirely free from worry; carefree / ~了一口气 heave a sigh of relief ❷ 〈书面〉easy; leisurely: ~步 walk unhurriedly ❸ (Shū) a surname
舒伯特 Shūbótè Franz Schubert (1797-1828), Austrian composer
舒畅 shūchàng entirely free from worry; relaxed; happy: 心情~ feel happy; have ease of mind
舒迟 shūchí slow and leisurely
舒服 shūfu ❶ comfortable; pleasant: 舒舒服服地过日子 lead a comfortable life; live in ease and comfort / 我坐在这儿挺~。I'm quite comfortable sitting here. ❷ be well: 他今天不大~。He is out of sorts today. / 你哪儿不~? What's wrong with you?
舒缓 shūhuǎn ❶ slow; leisurely: 动作~ slow in motion / 节拍~的歌声 singing in slow tempo ❷ relaxed: 语调~ in a mild tone / 他的心情好像~了一些。He seemed to be in a more relaxed mood. ❸ (of slopes) flattish; gentle: 他从~的斜坡上慢慢走了下来。He walked slowly down the gentle slope.
舒筋活络 shūjīn-huóluò 〈中医〉stimulate the circulation of the blood and cause the muscles and joints to relax
舒筋活血 shūjīn-huóxuè 〈中医〉soothe the sinew and quicken the blood; relax the muscles and stimulate the blood circulation
舒卷 shūjuǎn 〈书面〉roll back and forth: ~自如 roll back and forth freely / 青烟~。The blue smoke is curling up.
舒快 shūkuài happy; free from worry: 精神~ feel happy and at ease / 在温泉洗完澡, 觉得浑身~。A bath in the hot spring made him feel totally refreshed.
舒曼 Shūmàn Robert Alexander Schumann (1810-1856), German composer
舒眉展眼 shūméi-zhǎnyǎn unknit the brows and stretch the eyes — be cheerful; feel very happy; show pleasure: 这个小姑娘~的, 真叫人喜欢。The little girl has such a beaming face that everyone likes her.
舒齐 shūqí 〈方言〉all ready; all in order: 种子已经准备~, 明天可以播种了。With the seeds all ready, sowing can start tomorrow. / 房子虽然不宽绰, 可是拾掇得舒舒齐齐的。The house, though not very big, is kept in good order.
舒气 shūqì ❶ get a breathing space; have a respite; take a breather: 他喝下两口水, 才慢慢舒过气来。After taking a sip or two of water, he slowly recovered. ❷ relax; relax one's efforts: 险情排除, 大家才算舒了口气。They did not relax their efforts until the dangerous situation was brought under control. ❸ vent one's spleen; work off one's anger: 你只知道发牢骚~, 一点儿也不考虑后果。All you care

S

to do is to grumble and let off steam regardless of the consequences.

舒散 shūsàn ❶ limber (oneself) up; relax one's muscles:坐久了要起来～～。Take a stroll after sitting up for so long. ❷ shake off one's weariness and tedium:心里闷得慌,到外面～一下。I feel so depressed and would like to relax a bit outdoors.

舒声 shūshēng 〈语言〉(of classical Chinese) level tone, falling-rising tone and falling tone

舒适 shūshì easy; comfortable; cosy; snug:～的环境 easy circumstances /生活～ live a comfortable life; lead a life of ease and comfort /房子里又暖和又～。The room was warm and cosy. /大家～地坐在壁炉前。We all sat snug in front of the fireplace.

舒适带 shūshìdài comfort zone; comfort standard temperature (approximately 20°-24°C)

舒爽 shūshuǎng comfortable and refreshed:听了这些话,他感到心头～了不少。Hearing those remarks, he felt much better.

舒松 shūsōng comfortable and relaxed:今日休会,我才～一点。I'm able to ease up a bit today as the meeting is adjourned. /在疗养院里,他感到～。He was feeling relaxed in the sanatorium. /他在林间散步,看上去非常～。He was strolling in the woods, looking very easygoing and comfortable.

舒泰 shūtài comfortable; at ease; carefree:他休息了一会儿,觉得心头还是不～。He rested a while but still felt unwell. /他觉得没有什么问题了,舒舒泰泰地在一把椅子上坐下。Seeing that everything was taken care of, he sat down comfortably.

舒坦 shūtan comfortable; carefree:心里很～ feel at ease /浑身不～ feel very uncomfortable

舒帖 shūtiē comfortable; at ease:浑身～ (feel) relaxed all over

舒头探脑 shūtóu-tànnǎo pop one's head in and look about (usu. sneakily)

舒心 shūxīn 〈方言〉happy; contented:父母都很～。My parents are well pleased and happy. /他们笑得多么～。They are having a hearty laugh. /退休工人过着～的日子。The retired workers are living a happy and contented life.

舒徐 shūxú leisurely; slow:小溪的水～地流淌。The little brook flows slowly.

舒意 shūyì 〈方言〉feel happy; be pleased:他们俩是自由恋爱结的婚,没有一点不～的地方。They fell in love and got happily married of their own free will with absolutely nothing to hamper their happiness.

舒展 shūzhǎn ❶ unfold; smooth out:一夜之间,花苞就～开来。The bud broke into bloom overnight. /他眉头～了,脸上的皱纹也～了。He unknitted his eyebrows and the wrinkles on his face also smoothed out. ❷ limber up; stretch:～一下筋骨 stretch one's limbs ❸ comfortable; at ease:～畅快 have ease of mind

舒张 shūzhāng 〈生理〉diastole

舒张期杂音 shūzhāngqī záyīn 〈医学〉diastolic murmur

舒张压 shūzhāngyā 〈医学〉diastolic pressure

纾

shū 〈书面〉❶ relieve; alleviate; free from:毁家～难 give all one has to help the state meet the crisis /～人之忧 relieve sb. from anxiety ❷ procrastinate; delay:～死 slow death ❸ well-to-do; comfortably off:由于国家大力扶持,农家得以小～。Thanks to assistance from the state, the farmers are now a little better off.

书(書)

shū ❶ write; record:振笔直～ take up the pen and write quickly /大～特～ record in letters of gold; record boldly /罄竹难～ (of crimes, etc.) too numerous to record ❷ style of calligraphy; script:楷～ regular script /草～ characters executed swiftly and with strokes flowing together; cursive hand /隶～ official script, an ancient style of calligraphy current in the Han Dynasty, simplified from *xiaozhuan* (小篆) /行～ running hand /篆～ seal character (a style of Chinese calligraphy often used on seals) /法～ model calligraphy; 〈敬词〉your (esteemed) calligraphy ❸ book:一套丛～ a series of books; collection /古～ ancient books /经～ Confucian classics /线装～ thread-bound (Chinese) book /小人儿～ picture-story book /工具～ reference book /教科～ textbook /兵～ book on the art of war /类～ reference books with material taken from various sources and arranged according to subjects /禁～ banned book /读～破万卷,下笔如有神。Read ten thousand books and you write like magic. /～山有路勤为径。Diligence is the only way to acquire learning. *or* There is no royal road to learning. ❹ letter; epistle:家～ letter to or from home /情～ love letter /休～ formerly a letter by husband divorcing his wife /血～ letter written in one's own blood (expressing one's last wish, hatred, determination, etc.) ❺ official paper; document:递交国～ present one's letter of credence (*or* credentials) /申请～ (written) application /批准～ instrument of ratification /证明～ certificate; testimonial /协定～ protocol /起诉～ indictment; bill of complaint /委托～ trust-deed /白皮～ white paper; white book

书案 shū'àn 〈书面〉writing desk

书办 shūbàn 〈旧语〉clerk in government office

书包 shūbāo satchel; schoolbag

书包带 shūbāodài book strap (of school children)

书报 shūbào books and newspapers

书背 shūbèi back of a book; spine

书本 shūběn book:～知识 book learning (*or* knowledge)

书不尽言 shūbùjìnyán (used at the end of a personal letter) I still have a lot more to say:～,言不尽意。I have to leave off now, though I still have a lot more to say.

书册 shūcè book:考生不得夹带～入考场。Examinees are not allowed to bring books into the examination room.

书茶馆儿 shūcháguǎnr 〈旧语〉teahouse with professional storytelling

书场 shūchǎng public gathering place where professional entertainers perform storytelling, cross talk, etc.

书呈 shūchéng 〈旧语〉letter written to one's superior

书痴 shūchī *see* "书呆子"

书橱 shūchú bookcase

书春 shūchūn write Spring Festival or lunar New Year couplets

书呆子 shūdāizi pedant; bookworm:一副～气 look like a bookworm; be bookish /读死书会变成～。Studying mechanically will turn you into a pedant.

书丹 shūdān write (with red ink) for stone inscription:～于碑 carve an inscription on a tablet

书单 shūdān book list:老师给我们开了个～。The teacher has prepared a book list for us.

书挡 shūdǎng bookend

书到用时方恨少 shū dào yòng shí fāng hèn shǎo it is when you are applying what you have learned from books that you wish you had read more:～,事非经过不知难。You regret your deficiency in learning only when it comes to applying what you have learned; you realize the difficulties of a task only when you try to get it done.

书店 shūdiàn bookshop; bookstore; bookseller's:旧～ second-hand bookshop

书牍 shūdú 〈书面〉letter

书蠹 shūdù ❶ bookworm ❷ 〈比喻〉pedant; bookworm

书段 shūduàn (of professional storytelling) episode

书法 shūfǎ penmanship; calligraphy:～练习 drills to improve one's handwriting /～展览 calligraphy exhibition /～比赛 calligraphy contest

书法家 shūfǎjiā calligrapher

书坊 shūfāng 〈旧语〉place serving as both a printing house and a bookshop

书房 shūfáng study

书扉 shūfēi (of books) title page

书肺 shūfèi book lung (of certain insects)

书稿 shūgǎo (of writings) script

书槅子 shūgézi *also* "书格子" bookshelf

书贾 shūgǔ 〈旧语〉book dealer; bookseller

书鼓 shūgǔ small drum used to accompany versified storytelling

书馆 shūguǎn ❶ 〈旧语〉private school set up at home ❷ 〈旧语〉bookshop ❸ 〈方言〉teahouse with professional storytelling

书柜 shūguì book cabinet; bookcase

书函 shūhán ❶ 〈旧语〉sack for letters ❷ letter:～敬悉。Your letter is received (*or* has come to hand).

书翰 shūhàn 〈书面〉❶ Chinese calligraphy:工～ excel in Chinese calligraphy ❷ letter (of correspondence); letter writing

书号 shūhào book number:国际标准～ ISBN (International Standard Book Number)

书后 shūhòu postscript

书画 shūhuà painting and calligraphy:擅长～ good at painting and calligraphy

书会 shūhuì ❶ (in the Yuan and Ming dynasties) guild of authors of traditional Chinese operas, versified stories, etc. ❷ calligraphers' gathering; calligraphy promotion gathering:去年在北京举行～，中日两国书法家欢聚一堂，当众挥毫。At the meeting to promote calligraphy held in Beijing last year, Chinese and Japanese calligraphers gathered together and wielded their writing brushes in demonstrations on the spot.

书籍 shūjí books; works; literature:收藏～ collect books /科技～ books on science and technology /军事～ military literature /文学～ literary works

书脊 shūjǐ *also*"书背" spine (of a book)

书记 shūji ❶ secretary:党委～ secretary of the Party committee /团委～ secretary of the (Communist Youth) League committee /总～ general secretary ❷ clerk;〈法律〉recorder:～员〈法律〉clerk (of a court)

书记处 shūjichù secretariat

书家 shūjiā calligrapher; calligraphist

书架 shūjià bookshelf; bookrack

书柬 shūjiǎn *see*"书简"

书简 shūjiǎn *also*"书柬" letters; correspondence

书经 Shūjīng *also*"书";"尚书" Shàngshū *Collection of Ancient Texts*

see also"五经" Wǔjīng

书局 shūjú publishing house; press; bookshop; bookstore:线装～ bookshop selling thread-bound (Chinese) books

书卷 shūjuàn book (from its ancient form of a scroll)

书卷气 shūjuànqì (of an intellectual) air of cultivated refinement; cultured; polished:他言谈话语间带有几分～。He talked in a somewhat scholarly manner.

书刊 shūkān books and periodicals:～登记 books registration /～登记证 certification; books registration /～审查(制度) censorship of books (system)

书靠 shūkào bookend

书壳 shūké cardboard slipcase

书口 shūkǒu fore edge

书库 shūkù stack room; stacks

书立 shūlì bookend

书吏 shūlì〈旧语〉government clerk

书林 shūlín〈书面〉forest of books — treasury of books

书录 shūlù index containing such data as the editions, illustrations, commentaries and sources of a certain book or certain publications

书簏 shūlù ❶ bamboo bookcase ❷〈书面〉person who reads a lot but fails to put his knowledge to good use; pedant

书帽 shūmào (of professional storytelling) opening remarks before the programmed episode begins

书眉 shūméi top of a page; top margin:在～上写了不少批语 write many comments on the top margin

书迷 shūmí ❶ bookworm; book fiend ❷ professional storytelling fan

书面 shūmiàn written; in written form; in writing:～鉴定 written evaluation; written appraisal /～判决 written judgment /～凭据 written confirmation /～证据 documentary evidence; evidence in writing; literal proof /～裁定 written verdict /总理在机场发表了～讲话。The Prime Minister issued a written statement at the airport.

书面合同 shūmiàn hétong contract in writing; written contract

书面语 shūmiànyǔ written language; literary language

书名 shūmíng title of a book; title

书名号 shūmínghào punctuation marks used in Chinese to enclose the title of a book or an article (《 》); double angle brackets

书名页 shūmíngyè title page

书目 shūmù ❶ booklist; title catalogue:参考～ list of reference books; bibliography ❷ (of folk art forms) various kinds of popular entertainment

书脑 shūnǎo book back; spine of the binding

书皮 shūpí book cover; jacket; dust cover; cover:塑料～ plastic cover /～设计 design of book cover

书皮纸 shūpízhǐ paper for covering books

书评 shūpíng book review:撰写～ write a book review

书启 shūqǐ〈书面〉letter of correspondence

书契 shūqì〈书面〉characters; script

书签 shūqiān ❶ title label pasted on the cover of a Chinese-style thread-bound book ❷ bookmark; bookmarker

书商 shūshāng bookseller

书社 shūshè ❶〈旧语〉bookclub of men of letters ❷ publishing house:齐鲁～ Qilu Publishing House

书生 shūshēng intellectual; scholar:白面～ pale intellectual /文弱～ frail scholar

书生气 shūshēngqì bookishness:他～十足，完全脱离实际。Bookish and naive in the extreme, he is completely divorced from reality.

书生之见 shūshēngzhījiàn pedantic view:你这是～，纸上谈兵。Your approach is completely pedantic and unrealistic.

书市 shūshì book market:社科～将于月底举行。There will be a book fair at the end of the month, selling books on social sciences.

书手 shūshǒu〈旧语〉copyist; scribe; amanuensis

书塾 shūshú old-style private school

书肆 shūsì〈书面〉bookshop

书摊 shūtān bookstall; bookstand:摆～ set up a bookstall /逛～ go to a bookstand

书坛 shūtán ❶ calligraphers' circles ❷ professional storytellers' circles

书套 shūtào slipcase

书体 shūtǐ style of calligraphy

书亭 shūtíng book-kiosk; bookstall

书童 shūtóng boy servant of a scholar; page boy

书屋 shūwū ❶〈旧语〉study ❷ bookstore (also used in names of bookshops)

书物 shūwù books and other things concerned with books

书香 shūxiāng family having a noted scholar or scholars in earlier generations:世代～ be a scholar-gentry family for generations

书香门第 shūxiāng-méndì family having a noted scholar or scholars in the previous generations; scholar-gentry family:出身于～ come from a family of scholars

书写 shūxiě write:～对联 write couplets /～规则 rules for writing /～错误〈法律〉clerical error

书写纸 shūxiězhǐ writing paper

书心 shūxīn (of a page in a book or magazine) type area

书信 shūxìn letter; correspondence; written message:～格式 form of a letter /互通～ keep up a correspondence

书信电 shūxìndiàn letter cable

书信体 shūxìntǐ epistolary style:采用～ adopt the epistolary style /～小说 epistolary novel

书信炸弹 shūxìn zhàdàn letter bomb

书页 shūyè page

书衣 shūyī〈书面〉book jacket

书淫 shūyín〈书面〉book fiend; book lover

书影 shūyǐng printed matter that indicates the type form or partial content of books and periodicals

书寓 shūyù〈方言〉〈旧语〉euphemism for a high-class brothel

书院 shūyuàn〈旧语〉academy of classical learning

书札 shūzhá〈书面〉letters; correspondence:爱情～ love letters /烈士～ letters by martyrs

书斋 shūzhāi study

书展 shūzhǎn book fair:这次～展出了图书近一万种。Approximately 10,000 titles were on display at the book exhibition. /我们出版社参加了在上海举行的国际～。Our publishing house participated in the international book fair held in Shanghai.

书证 shūzhèng ❶ (of writings and notes) written examples of the origin, meaning and usage of a word or phrase ❷〈法律〉written evidence such as letters, pamphlets, contracts, books of account, etc., including material evidence in general

书帙 shūzhì〈书面〉book jacket

书中自有黄金屋，书中自有颜如玉 shūzhōng zìyǒu huángjīnwū, shūzhōng zìyǒu yánrúyù〈旧语〉golden houses and beautiful wives can be found through study

书桌 shūzhuō writing desk; desk

书子 shūzi〈方言〉letter of correspondence

shú

孰 shú〈书面〉❶ who:人非圣贤，～能无过? No one is a saint, so who can be entirely free from error? /～能当之? Who is capable of such a job? *or* Who can face up to the task? ❷ which; who:～是

～非 which is right and which is wrong /～得～失 who wins and who loses ❸ what:是可忍,～不可忍? If this can be tolerated, what cannot?

熟 shú ❶ ripe:催～ accelerate the ripening (of fruit) /早～西瓜 early-ripe watermelon /瓜～蒂落。When a melon is ripe it falls off its stem — things will be easily settled when conditions are ripe. ❷ cooked; done:～肉 cooked meat /烂～ thoroughly cooked; know sth. thoroughly /半生不～ half-cooked /生米煮成了～饭。The rice is done — fait accompli. ❸ processed; wrought: *see* "～铁" ❹ frequently seen or heard; well-known; familiar:听起来耳～ sound familiar /耳～能详 what's frequently heard can be repeated in detail; often heard and well remembered /我们俩很～。We know each other quite well. ❺ skilled; experienced; versed in:技术纯～ highly skilled /驾轻就～ drive a light carriage on a familiar road — be able to handle a job with ease because one has had previous experience ❻ deeply; profoundly:深思～虑 ponder deeply (over sth.); give careful consideration (to sth.) /孩子睡得很～。The child is fast (*or* sound) asleep.

see also shóu

熟谙 shú'ān 〈书面〉be familiar with; be well versed in:～时事 be well acquainted with current events /对他家情况～ be quite familiar with his family situation

熟菜 shúcài cooked food; prepared food

熟道 shúdào familiar route

熟地 shúdì ❶ cultivated land:把生荒变成～。Turn virgin soil into cultivated land. ❷ *also* "熟地黄"〈中药〉prepared rhizome of rehmannia (*Rehmannia glutinosa*)

熟读 shúdú read carefully over and over again:～唐诗三百首,不会吟诗也会吟。After learning three hundred Tang poems, one can try one's hand at poetry, even if one is not a poet.

熟惯 shúguàn be skilful at; have the knack of; be practised in:她～了这个活计。She has become skilful at the job.

熟化 shúhuà ❶〈农业〉cultivating:～地 cultivated land ❷ ripening ❸ ageing:糖浆～ ageing of syrup

熟荒 shúhuāng *also* "熟荒地"〈农业〉land under cultivation in the past; once cultivated land; abandoned cultivated land

熟货 shúhuò 〈商业〉local manufactures; finished native products

熟记 shújì learn by rote; commit to memory; memorize:要～所有公式。Memorize all the formulas.

熟见 shújiàn often seen:人所～,不足为奇。It is a common occurrence, and there is nothing peculiar about it.

熟客 shúkè frequent visitor:他是这里的～,不必太客气。There is no need to stand on ceremony. He is a frequent visitor here.

熟练 shúliàn skilled; expert; practised; proficient:动作～ skilful in action /～的打字员 proficient typist /业务～ well versed in one's professional work; be in practice /他是个沉稳～的司机。He is a steady and skilled driver. /她使用计算机非常～。She is thoroughly practised in computer skills.

熟练工 shúliàngōng journeyman; skilled worker

熟练劳动 shúliàn láodòng skilled labour

熟料 shúliào ❶〈冶金〉grog; chamotte ❷〈建筑〉clinker

熟路 shúlù familiar route; beaten track:走～ take a familiar route /轻车～ (drive in) a light carriage on a familiar road — (do) sth. one knows well and can manage with ease /我们沿一条～穿过森林。We followed a well-beaten path through the forest.

熟虑 shúlǜ consider carefully:深思～ careful consideration; much deliberation

熟门熟路 shúmén-shúlù familiar road and familiar door — things that one is well acquainted with:他对这里～的。He knows his way around here.

熟眠 shúmián 〈书面〉sleep soundly; be fast asleep; fall into a deep slumber

熟能生巧 shúnéngshēngqiǎo skill comes from practice; practice makes perfect; the more you practise, the more you improve

熟年 shúnián year of good harvests; good year; bumper year

熟皮 shúpí processed hides; tanned hides; leather

熟漆 shúqī lacquer

熟人 shúrén acquaintance; friend:他全国各地都有～。He has acquaintances in all parts of the country.

熟稔 shúrěn 〈书面〉very familiar with; on intimate terms with

熟石膏 shúshígāo plaster of Paris

熟石灰 shúshíhuī slaked lime

熟食 shúshí cooked food; prepared food

熟视无睹 shúshì-wúdǔ pay no heed to; turn a blind eye to; ignore:对这些歪风邪气可不能～。We must not shut our eyes to those unhealthy trends and evil practices. /他对手下追求享受的倾向～。He dismissed the tendency among his subordinates to pursue sensual pleasures as a matter of no consequence.

熟识 shúshi be well acquainted with; be conversant with:～的朋友 close friend /不甚～此地的风俗习惯 not familiar with the customs here /他～水性。He is an expert swimmer.

熟手 shúshǒu practised hand; old hand:干这工作,他是～。He is an old hand at the job.

熟睡 shúshuì sleep soundly; be fast or sound asleep

熟丝 shúsī 〈纺织〉boiled-off silk

熟思 shúsī give serious thought to; ponder deeply; mull over; consider carefully:此事非同小可,当～之。This is no small matter, and I'll give serious thought to it.

熟烫 shútang 〈口语〉(of fruits, melons) damaged; spoiled:这些苹果都折腾得～了。These apples are all spoiled in the process of handling.

熟铁 shútiě wrought iron

熟铜 shútóng wrought copper

熟土 shútǔ 〈农业〉mellow soil

熟悉 shúxī know sth. or sb. well; be well acquainted with:～情况 know the ropes /～某一问题 know a subject inside out /～地形 be well acquainted with the terrain /～多种语言 have several languages at one's fingertips

熟习 shúxí be skilful at; be familiar with; be practised in:～欧洲的历史 have an intimate knowledge of European history /～计算机技术 be well versed in computer technology /～企业管理 be practised in business management

熟橡胶 shúxiàngjiāo vulcanized rubber

熟语 shúyǔ 〈语言〉idiom; idiomatic expression

熟知 shúzhī know very well; know intimately:～此中奥妙 know very well what's behind sth. /～底细 know the inside story; know the ins and outs of sth.

熟字 shúzì words already learned; familiar words

塾 shú 〈旧语〉private or family school:私～ old-style private school /村～〈旧语〉village school /家～〈旧语〉family school

塾师 shúshī tutor of a private or family school

赎(贖) shú ❶ redeem; ransom:到当铺～首饰 redeem the jewellery from a pawnshop; take the jewellery out of pawn /～回被绑架的人 ransom a kidnapped person ❷ atone for (a crime):～罪 atone for one's crime /此人罪不可～。He is beyond redemption.

赎当 shúdàng redeem a pawned article

赎价 shújià ransom price for a hostage; ransom

赎金 shújīn ransom money; ransom:绑架他人索取～ hold a person to (*or* for) ransom

赎买 shúmǎi redeem; buy back; buy out

赎买政策 shúmǎi zhèngcè policy of redemption; buying out policy

赎身 shúshēn (of slaves, girls, prostitutes, etc.) redeem or ransom oneself; buy back one's freedom

赎刑 shúxíng 〈法律〉buy freedom from punishment by law in ancient China

赎罪 shúzuì atone for one's crime:将功～ perform meritorious services to atone for one's crime

赎罪券 shúzuìquàn indulgence (a formal practice of the medieval Roman Catholic Church)

赎罪日 Shúzuìrì 〈宗教〉Yom Kippur; Day of Atonement

赎罪书 shúzuìshū penitential book

秫 shú *kaoliang*; (Chinese) sorghum

秫秸 shújiē *also* "秫稻" *kaoliang* stalk

秫米 shúmǐ husked sorghum

秫秫 shúshú 〈方言〉*kaoliang*; (Chinese) sorghum

shǔ

数(數) shǔ ❶ count:～钱 count money /屈指可～ can

be counted on one's fingers — very few /让我们把选票~一~。Let's count the votes. ❷ be particularly conspicuous by comparison:全班成绩~他最好。He is considered the best in the class. /姐妹中最漂亮的要~大姐了。The eldest one is the prettiest of the sisters. ❸ enumerate; list:悉~〈书面〉enumerate in full detail /~其罪 list the crimes sb. has committed

see also shù; shuò

数白论黄 shǔbái-lùnhuáng count white (i.e. silver) and yellow (i.e. gold) — fuss about money

数不胜数 shǔbùshèngshǔ too many to be counted; countless; innumerable:这位老工人为群众做的好事~。The old worker did numerous good deeds for others.

数不过来 shǔbuguòlái too many to be counted; countless:过往车辆多得~。There is incessant traffic in the street.

数不清 shǔbuqīng too numerous to count; incalculable:草原上~的牛羊。There are numberless cattle and sheep on the prairie.

数不上 shǔbushàng *see*"数不着"

数不着 shǔbuzháo not count as outstanding, important, etc.:论技术,在组里可~我。I cannot compare with others of the team in skill.

数叨 shǔdao 〈方言〉*see*"数落"

数得上 shǔdeshàng *see*"数得着"

数得着 shǔdezháo *also*"数得上" be counted among the best:他是我们村里~的热心肠。He is among the most warm-hearted people of our village.

数点 shǔdiǎn count by pointing at (things):小弟弟坐在我身边,~着天上的星星。Little brother sat beside me, counting the stars in the sky.

数典忘祖 shǔdiǎn-wàngzǔ be well acquainted with the historical facts of other countries but not one's own; disown one's forefathers; forget one's ancestral origin:这些先生们满嘴高论,可惜多是~。Those gentlemen hold forth about the history of other nations, but much to our regret, they are entirely ignorant of their own. /搞建筑的人不能~。Architects mustn't forget the traditions of their own country.

数冬瓜道茄子 shǔ dōngguā dào qiézi *see*"数葫芦道茄子"

数伏 shǔfú start of hot summer days or dog days; beginning of the three hottest ten-day periods of the year

数黑论黄 shǔhēi-lùnhuáng *also*"数黄论黑";"论黄数黑" irresponsible talk; gossip

数葫芦道茄子 shǔ húlu dào qiézi chatter; twaddle:他~地说个没完。He rattled on endlessly.

数九 shǔjiǔ nine periods (of nine days each) following the winter solstice:~严冬 coldest days of the year /~天是滑冰的好季节。The cold days after the Winter Solstice are the best time for skating.

数九寒天 shǔjiǔ-hántiān days after the Winter Solstice — coldest days of the year

数来宝 shǔláibǎo 〈戏曲〉rhythmic storytelling to the accompaniment of clapper

数落 shǔluo 〈口语〉❶ scold sb. by enumerating his wrongdoings; reproach; reprove:事情没做好,父亲直~我。Father gave me a good dressing down for failing to make a good job of it. ❷ cite one example after another; list; enumerate:一件一件地~开了 start enumerating the items

数米而炊 shǔmǐ'érchuī count the grains of rice before cooking it — do useless trifles; be contemptibly parsimonious; be hard up:我如今穷得~。I'm penniless now. /他是个~的吝啬鬼。He is extremely tight-fisted.

数念 shǔniàn enumerate one by one; read sentence by sentence:车间主任~了一遍得奖者的名字。The director of the workshop enumerated all the names of those to be awarded. /这首歌谣,到如今这位老人还常向晚辈们~着呢。Even today the old man often recites this ballad to the youngsters sentence by sentence.

数贫嘴 shǔ pínzuǐ be garrulous:听这个~的,不知又要编派哪一个呢! What a glib tongue! God knows who he is going to gibe at next!

数数儿 shǔshùr count; reckon:这孩子很小就会~。The child knew how to count when he was very small.

数说 shǔshuō ❶ enumerate; list:~自己的难处 list all the difficulties one is up against ❷ rebuke; reproach:~手下人的鲁莽 rebuke one's subordinates for their rudeness

数算 shǔsuàn calculate; figure; check the number or amount:蒸了一锅馒头,他~着,来干活的一个人合仨。He made a number of steamed buns, and figured each worker would get three.

数往知来 shǔwǎng-zhīlái one can predict the future when one knows the past

数一数二 shǔyī-shǔ'èr be among the very best; be one of the best:这所大学是全国~的高等学府。This university ranks as one of the most prestigious institutions of higher learning in the country.

暑

shǔ summer heat; hot weather:盛~ height of the summer; sweltering summer days /酷~ intense heat of the summer /中~ get sunstroke; get heatstroke; suffer heat exhaustion /防~ heatstroke prevention /到海边避~ be away for the summer holidays at seaside /寒来~往 as the seasons change; as time passes

暑假 shǔjià summer vacation; summer holidays:我们每年七月放~。Our summer vacation starts in July every year.

暑期 shǔqī summer vacation; summer:~学校 summer school /~夏令营 summer camp /你~有何安排? What's your plan for the summer vacation?

暑气 shǔqì summer heat; heat:~逼人。The summer heat is oppressive.

暑热 shǔrè hot summer weather; swelter of the summer days

暑天 shǔtiān hottest days of the year; dog days

暑瘟 shǔwēn 〈中医〉febrile diseases in summer, including encephalitis B, dysentery, malignant malaria, etc.

署[1]

shǔ ❶ government office; office:官~ government office /海关总~ customs head office; customs bureau; (China) General Administration of Customs /专员公~ prefectural commissioner's office ❷ make arrangements for; arrange; prepare:部~下届会议 make arrangements for the next conference ❸ stand proxy for; act as deputy:由办公厅主任~副部长事。The director of the general office will act as the deputy of the vice-minister during the latter's absence.

署[2]

shǔ affix one's name to; sign:签~条约 sign a treaty /~上自己的名字 sign; sign one's name

署理 shǔlǐ handle by proxy; act as deputy:~日常部务 handle day-to-day affairs of the ministry during the minister's absence

署名 shǔmíng affix one's name to; put one's signature to; sign:~人 the undersigned /这封信没有~。The letter is unsigned.

署名文章 shǔmíng wénzhāng signed article:报上对这件事发表了~。The newspaper carried a signed article concerning the matter.

署长 shǔzhǎng head of an administrative bureau

薯(藷)

shǔ potato; yam:白~ sweet potato /红~ sweet potato /马铃~ potato /木~ cassava /豆~ yam bean

薯莨 shǔliáng *also*"茨莨" cíliáng 〈植物〉dye yam (*Dioscorea cirrhosa*)

薯莨绸 shǔliángchóu 〈纺织〉gambiered Guangdong gauze

薯芋类作物 shǔyùlèi zuòwù tuber crops

薯蓣 shǔyù *also*"山药" shānyao 〈植物〉yam (*Dioscorea batatas*)

曙

shǔ 〈书面〉break of day; daybreak; dawn:天将~。It's almost dawn. *or* The day is dawning.

曙光 shǔguāng first light of morning; daylight:和平的~ dawn of peace /天边露出一线~。The first sign of daylight appears on the horizon. /黑暗即将过去,~就在前头。Dark night will soon disappear and dawn is right ahead.

曙色 shǔsè light of early dawn:~浸染了山峰。The mountain peak is washed by the light of early dawn.

蜀

Shǔ ❶ name of a state in the Zhou Dynasty, located in the Chengdu area of Sichuan ❷ (short for 蜀汉) Shu Han ❸ another name for Sichuan Province

蜀道难 shǔdàonán the roads in Sichuan are hilly and rugged:蜀道之难,难于上青天。It is as difficult to negotiate the narrow paths of Sichuan as it is to climb up to heaven.

蜀汉 Shǔ Hàn Kingdom of Shu Han (221-263), one of the Three Kingdoms

蜀锦 shǔjǐn Sichuan brocade

蜀葵 shǔkuí 〈植物〉hollyhock (*Althaea rosea*)

蜀犬吠日 shǔquǎn-fèirì Sichuan dogs bark at the sun (because it's a rare sight in that misty region) — ignorant people are easily surprised
蜀黍 shǔshǔ *kaoliang*; sorghum
蜀绣 shǔxiù Sichuan embroidery:～与湘绣、苏绣齐名。Sichuan embroidery equals Hunan and Suzhou embroideries in beauty and splendour. *or* Sichuan embroidery is as famous as Hunan and Suzhou embroideries.
蜀中无大将,廖化作先锋 Shǔzhōng wú dàjiàng, Liào Huà zuò xiānfēng in the land of the blind, the one-eyed man is king

黍 shǔ *see* "黍子"
黍子 shǔzi broomcorn millet (*Panicum miliaceum*)

鼠 shǔ mouse; rat:老～ rat; mouse /家～ rat /胆小如～ as timid as a mouse; chicken-hearted
鼠辈 shǔbèi mean creatures; rascals; scoundrels:无知～! Ignorant mean creatures!
鼠标 shǔbiāo 〈计算机〉 mouse
鼠疮 shǔchuāng 〈中医〉 scrofula
鼠窜 shǔcuàn scamper off like a rat; scurry away:抱头～ cover the head and scurry off like a frightened rat /狼狈～ flee in panic like a rat
鼠窜狼奔 shǔcuàn-lángbēn *also* "狼奔鼠窜" run hither and thither like rats and wolves
鼠袋鼠 shǔdàishǔ rat kangaroo
鼠胆 shǔdǎn chicken-hearted; lily-livered; cowardly
鼠肚鸡肠 shǔdù-jīcháng *also* "小肚鸡肠" xiǎodù-jīcháng narrow-minded; mean; petty
鼠海豚 shǔhǎitún porpoise
鼠害 shǔhài damage caused by rats
鼠耗 shǔhào loss (of grains, etc.) caused by rats
鼠夹 shǔjiā mousetrap
鼠立死 shǔlìsǐ 〈药学〉 crimidine
鼠笼 shǔlóng 〈电工〉 squirrel-cage
鼠笼式电动机 shǔlóngshì diàndòngjī squirrel-cage motor
鼠目寸光 shǔmù-cùnguāng a mouse can see only an inch; see only what is under one's nose; lack foresight:～的势利小人 short-sighted snobbish scoundrel
鼠鸟 shǔniǎo coly; mousebird
鼠窃 shǔqiè petty theft
鼠窃狗偷 shǔqiè-gǒutōu *also* "鼠窃狗盗" filch like rats and snatch like dogs — play petty tricks on the sly; commit petty theft
鼠曲草 shǔqūcǎo *also* "清明菜" qīngmíngcài 〈植物〉 affine cudweed (*Gnaphalium affine*)
鼠鲨 shǔshā ratfish
鼠伤寒 shǔshānghán mouse typhus
鼠蛇 shǔshé rat snake
鼠兔 shǔtù pika; mouse-hare; whistling hare; piping hare
鼠尾巴草 shǔwěibacǎo mousetail
鼠尾草 shǔwěicǎo sage (*Salvia officinalis*)
鼠尾蝠 shǔwěifú mouse-tailed bat
鼠蹊 shǔxī 〈生理〉 groin
鼠咬热 shǔyǎorè 〈医学〉 rat-bite fever
鼠疫 shǔyì *also* "黑死病" hēisǐbìng plague:淋巴腺～ bubonic plague /～,又名黑死病,曾在中古欧洲流行过。The plague, also known as the Black Death, once raged in medieval Europe.
鼠子 shǔzi 〈方言〉 mouse; rat

癙 shǔ 〈书面〉 fall ill from worry and distress:～忧 illness caused by anxiety

属(屬) shǔ ❶ category:金～ metal /非金～ nonmetal ❷〈生物〉 genus:猫～ *Felis* /亚～ subgenus ❸ come within one's jurisdiction:部～ troops under one's command; subor-dinates /附～单位 unit (*or* organization) affiliated or attached to another; subsidiary unit /中央直～机关 departments directly under the Party Central Committee /这个县～河北省。This county is now within the jurisdiction of Hebei Province. ❹ belong to; be part of:这幅画～我。This painting belongs to me. *or* I own this painting. /老虎～猫科。A tiger is a member of the cat family. /他～"鹰"派。He is a "hawk". ❺ family members; dependants:家～ family members; (family) dependants /眷～ family dependants; man and wife /直系亲～ direct dependants /军～ soldier's dependants; armyman's family /烈～ members of a revolutionary martyr's family ❻ be:情况～实 prove to be true /实～非法 be definitely unlawful /纯～虚构 sheer fabrication; out-and-out fabrication ❼ be born in the year of (one of the 12 animals):姐姐～马,妹妹～羊。The elder sister was born in the Year of the Horse, and the younger sister in the Year of the Sheep.
see also zhǔ
属地 shǔdì possession; dependency; colony:这些岛屿一度曾是美国～。These islands were once a colony of the United States.
属国 shǔguó vassal state; dependent state
属吏 shǔlì 〈旧语〉 secretaries and assistants to an official; subordinates
属僚 shǔliáo subordinates
属土 shǔtǔ dependent territory:英国～公民 British Dependent Territories Citizens (BDTCs)
属下 shǔxià subordinates
属相 shǔxiang *also* "生肖" shēngxiào 〈口语〉 any of the 12 symbolic animals used to denote the year of one's birth
see also "十二生肖" shí'èr shēngxiào
属性 shǔxìng attribute; property:运动是物质的～。Motion is an attribute of matter.
属于 shǔyú belong to; be part of:这座山～张村。This hill belongs to Zhang Village. /功劳～大家。The credit should go to all of us. /民主～上层建筑。Democracy is part of the superstructure. /这些是～政府职责范围的事。These responsibilities rest with the government. /生命～人只有一次。A man has but one life. /最后胜利一定～我们。We are confident final victory will be ours.
属员 shǔyuán subordinates of a superior official; officials under a superior authority

shù

澍 shù 〈书面〉 timely rain:天云晦合,须臾～雨。A timely rain fell at dusk.

树(樹) shù ❶ tree:果～ fruit tree /槐～ Chinese scholartree /柳～ willow /圣诞～ Christmas tree /摇钱～ legendary tree that sheds coins when shaken;〈比喻〉 ready source of money /植～ plant trees /植～节 Arbor Day ❷ plant; cultivate:～之以桑 plant mulberries in the fields /十年～木,百年～人。It takes ten years to grow trees, but a hundred years to cultivate people. ❸ hold up; set up; establish:～典型 hold sb. up as model /～榜样 set an example /有所建～ score achievements /独～一帜 fly one's own colours — create a school of one's own ❹ (Shù) a surname
树碑立传 shùbēi-lìzhuàn 〈贬义〉 glorify sb. by erecting a monument to him and writing his biography — build up sb.'s prestige by an overdose of praise:为人歌功颂德,～ sing sb.'s praises and try to build up his public image
树杈 shùchà *also* "树杈子" crotch (of a tree)
树串儿 shùchuànr 〈方言〉〈动物〉 willow warbler
树丛 shùcóng grove; thicket; shrubbery
树大根深 shùdà-gēnshēn a big tree has deep roots — influential and firmly entrenched
树大阴宽 shùdà-yīnkuān the bigger the tree, the bigger its shade — a powerful man can easily offer protection to his followers
树大招风 shùdà-zhāofēng 〈俗语〉 a tall tree catches the wind — a person of great reputation often comes under attack:～,名大招忌。Detraction pursues the great.
树袋熊 shùdàixióng *also* "考拉" kǎolā 〈动物〉 koala
树倒猢狲散 shù dǎo húsūn sàn when the tree falls the monkeys scatter — when an influential person falls from power, his hangerson disperse; a sinking ship is deserted by rats:他失势后,～,所有朋友都离他而去。When he fell into disgrace, all his acquaintances deserted him.
树敌 shùdí make enemies; arouse hostility; antagonize:到处～ make enemies everywhere /不可～过多。One mustn't antagonize too many people (*or* create too many enemies).
树蔸 shùdōu 〈方言〉 root of a tree; tree stump
树墩 shùdūn *also* "树墩子" tree stump; stump

树蜂 shùfēng 〈动物〉wood wasp

树干 shùgàn tree trunk; trunk

树高千丈,叶落归根 shù gāo qiānzhàng, yè luò guī gēn a tree may grow ten thousand feet high, but its leaves fall back to the roots — a person residing away from home eventually returns to his native soil; one who lives long in an alien land wished to return and be buried in one's home town

树疙瘩 shùgēda 〈方言〉tree stump or root (after the trunk is cut off)

树挂 shùguà 〈气象〉(soft) rime; hoarfrost; icicles (from tree branches)

树冠 shùguān crown (of a tree):~覆盖 crown cover /~平均直径 crown mean diameter /~疏伐 crown thinning /~修剪 pollarding

树海 shùhǎi sea of trees — big forest

树行子 shùhàngzi rows of trees; tree plantation

树胶 shùjiāo gum (of a tree)

树胶肿 shùjiāozhǒng 〈医学〉gumma

树节 shùjié *also* "树疤" burl; branch knot

树棵子 shùkēzi 〈方言〉grove; thicket

树懒 shùlǎn 〈动物〉sloth

树篱 shùlí quickset-hedge; brush hurdle

树立 shùlì set up; build up; establish:~全局观念 adopt an overall point of view /~新的道德标准 set new moral standards /~信心 establish confidence /~威信 be built up; build up a good reputation / ~远大的理想 set up a lofty ideal

树凉儿 shùliángr *also* "树阴凉儿" cool shade of a tree (in summer):在~里歇一会儿。Let's take a rest in the shade of the tree.

树林 shùlín *also* "树林子" woods; grove

树龄 shùlíng age of tree; tree age

树码 shùmǎ *also* "树码子" 〈方言〉twigs used for grafting

树莓 shùméi *Rubus* spp. (its edible varieties being *R. idaeus*, *R. occidentalis* and *R. Palmatus*)

树棉 shùmián *also* "印度棉" yìndùmián tree cotton (*Gossypium arboreum*)

树苗 shùmiáo sapling

树杪 shùmiǎo 〈书面〉tip of a tree; treetop

树木 shùmù trees:~密度 density of trees /~生长 arboreal growth /~园 arboretum

树木年代学 shùmù niándàixué dendrochronology (study of the annual rings of trees, used esp. to date past events)

树木学 shùmùxué dendrology

树木栽培 shùmù zāipéi arboriculture

树木整形术 shùmù zhěngxíngshù topiary

树木志 shùmùzhì silva

树皮 shùpí bark

树皮布 shùpíbù bark cloth

树皮画 shùpíhuà 〈美术〉bark picture

树鼩 shùqú 〈动物〉tree shrew

树人 shùrén 〈书面〉nurture or bring up men of ability; educate the young:教育是为了~。The purpose of education is to cultivate the young.

树梢 shùshāo tip of a tree; treetop

树蛇 shùshé tree snake

树身 shùshēn tree trunk

树势 shùshì shape of a tree:老树经过修剪可以恢复~,促其多萌芽,多分枝。Pruning keeps an old tree in shape and promotes budding and branching.

树熟儿 shùshóur 〈方言〉ripe fruit on a tree

树薯 shùshǔ *also* "木薯" mùshǔ cassava

树趟子 shùtàngzi *also* "树行子" rows of trees

树蛙 shùwā 〈动物〉tree frog

树蜥 shùxī *Calotes versicolor*, a kind of tree-climbing lizard

树藓 shùxiǎn tree moss

树熊猴 shùxiónghóu potto; bush bear; tree bear

树丫 shùyā *also* "树桠" branch; crotch (of a tree)

树鸭 shùyā whistling duck; tree duck

树叶 shùyè tree leaves

树液 shùyè sap:~循环 circulation of sap

树艺 shùyì aboriculture

树阴 shùyīn shade (of a tree)

树阴凉儿 shùyīnliángr *see* "树凉儿"

树欲静而风不止 shù yù jìng ér fēng bù zhǐ the tree craves calm, but the wind will not subside — all things take their own course independent of people's will; things will not occur as one wishes

树栽子 shùzāizi sapling

树葬 shùzàng burial on a tree (custom of some minority nationalities)

树枝 shùzhī branch; twig

树脂 shùzhī resin:醇酸~ alkyd resin /环氧~ epoxy resin /合成~ synthetic resin /离子交换~ ion exchange resin /中性~ resinene

树脂化石 shùzhī huàshí fossil resin

树脂胶合板 shùzhī jiāohébǎn compo board; resin bonded plywood

树脂漆 shùzhīqī lacquer-type organic coating

树脂酸 shùzhīsuān resinic acid

树脂整理 shùzhī zhěnglǐ 〈纺织〉resin finishing

树种 shùzhǒng ❶ varieties of trees:阔叶~ broadleaf tree /针叶~ conifer ❷ seeds of trees

树桩 shùzhuāng ❶ *also* "树桩子" stump of a tree ❷ dwarf tree (as used in potted landscape)

树籽 shùzǐ seeds of trees

竖[1](竪、豎)

shù ❶ vertical; straight up; upright; perpendicular:~柱 upright post /字~着写 write vertically downward from the top /横七~八 in disorder ❷ set upright; put up; erect; stand:~旗杆 erect a flagstaff /把竹竿~起来 get the bamboo pole to stand up ❸ vertical stroke (in Chinese characters):你写的这个字缺一~。One vertical stroke is missing from the character you've written.

竖[2](竪、豎)

shù 〈书面〉young servant:童~ boy servant /内~ palace eunuch

竖臣 shùchén small palace attendant

竖笛 shùdí 〈乐器〉recorder

竖宦 shùhuàn eunuch

竖脊肌 shùjǐjī erector spinae

竖井 shùjǐng 〈矿业〉(vertical) shaft:~矿 shaft mine

竖立 shùlì erect; raise; stand:~一座纪念碑 erect a monument /宝塔~在山顶。The pagoda stands on the top of the hill.

竖起 shùqǐ hold up; erect; stand up:~广告牌 erect a billboard /~大拇指 holding up one's thumb in approval; thumbs up /~衣领 turn up the collar /~风帆 hoist the sails /~耳朵听 prick up one's ears / ~脊梁 brace up /吓得毛发都~来了 one's hair stands on end with fear

竖琴 shùqín 〈乐器〉harp:~手 harper; harpist

竖蜻蜓 shù qīngtíng 〈方言〉handstand

竖式钢琴 shùshì gāngqín upright piano

竖子 shùzǐ 〈书面〉❶ boy; lad ❷〈贬义〉mean fellow; fellow; bloke:~不足与谋。That fellow is not worthy to be taken into our confidence.

裋

shù

裋褐 shùhè 〈书面〉coarse cloth clothes

潄

shù gargle; rinse:洗~ wash one's face and rinse one's mouth

潄口 shùkǒu rinse the mouth; gargle:饭后~ rinse your mouth after meals

潄口杯 shùkǒubēi glass or mug for mouth-rinsing or teeth-cleaning; tooth glass

潄口剂 shùkǒujì gargle

庶[1]

shù ❶ multitudinous; myriad:富~ rich and populous /~物 every kind of creature; all things of the universe /~类 various kind of animals; various things of life /~多 very much ❷〈书面〉common people; the populace:众~ the populace

庶[2]

shù 〈旧语〉of or by the concubine (as distinguished from the wife): *see* "~子"

庶[3]

shù 〈书面〉so that; so as to; in order to:~保… in order to ensure... /~不致误 so as to keep away from mistakes /~不至于

S

谬辖 with a view to avoiding confusion
庶出 shùchū (as distinguished from 嫡出) be born of a concubine
庶乎 shùhū 〈书面〉it is hoped; hopefully:～无过。Hopefully it may be free of error.
庶几 shùjī *also* "庶几乎";"庶乎"〈书面〉〈连词〉so that; so as to:～可免于难 so as to avert disaster
庶民 shùmín 〈书面〉common people; man in the street:王子犯法,与～同罪。All men are equal in the eyes of the law, not excepting royal princes.
庶母 shùmǔ concubine of one's father
庶人 shùrén 〈书面〉common people; commoners:夺去爵位,废为～。He was deprived of his title of nobility and reduced to a commoner.
庶室 shùshì concubine
庶务 shùwù 〈旧语〉❶ general affairs; business matters:管理机关～ in charge of the general affairs of the organization /～科 business section or division ❷ person in charge of business matters
庶政 shùzhèng (various) affairs of the government
庶子 shùzǐ (as distinguished from 嫡子) son of a concubine
庶族 shùzú (in feudal society) clan of commoners

数(數) shù

❶ number; figure:次～ number of times/人～ number of people /两位～ double digit number /～以万计 number in the tens of thousands /如～归还 return sth. in full /心中有～ know what's what ❷〈数学〉number:偶～ even number /奇～ odd number /未知～ unknown number /常～ constant /有理～ rational number /无理～ irrational number /～域 number field /～系 number system ❸〈语言〉number:单～ singular number / 复～ plural number ❹ fate; destiny:天～ predestination /气～已尽。One's days are numbered. /在～难逃。There's no escape from one's fate. *or* What is destined cannot be avoided. ❺ several; a few:～种版本 several editions /～年之后 a few years later ❻ *used before certain numerals or quantifiers to indicate an approximate number*:千～斤大米 around a thousand *jin* of rice
see also shǔ; shuò

数表 shùbiǎo mathematical table
数词 shùcí 〈语言〉numeral:序～ ordinal number /基～ cardinal number
数额 shù'é number; amount:～不大 small number; not many /限制～ limit the amount
数据 shùjù data:基础～ basic data /计算～ calculation data /预算～ budget data /原始～ raw data /科学～ scientific data
数据保护 shùjù bǎohù 〈信息〉data protection
数据操作语言 shùjù cāozuò yǔyán data manipulation language
数据处理 shùjù chǔlǐ data processing
数据存储系统 shùjù cúnchǔ xìtǒng data-storage system
数据存取 shùjù cúnqǔ data access:～方式 data access method
数据代码 shùjù dàimǎ data code
数据档案 shùjù dàng'àn data file
数据电话 shùjù diànhuà data phone
数据读出器 shùjù dúchūqì data reader
数据分析 shùjù fēnxī data analysis
数据管理系统 shùjù guǎnlǐ xìtǒng data management system
数据计算机 shùjù jìsuànjī data computer
数据记录 shùjù jìlù data logging
数据检查 shùjù jiǎnchá data check
数据库 shùjùkù database; data bank:～管理系统 database management system (DBMS)
数据输入 shùjù shūrù data entry; data input
数据通信系统 shùjù tōngxìn xìtǒng data communication system (DCS):～-1800 DCS-1800
数据纸 shùjùzhǐ data sheet
数据终端 shùjù zhōngduān data terminal
数控 shùkòng 〈自控〉numerical control (NC); digital control:总体～ total numerical control /～设备 numerical control equipment /～程序设备 NC programming device /～磁带 NC tape
数理化 shù-lǐ-huà (short for 数学,物理,化学) mathematics, physics and chemistry:学好～,走遍天下都不怕。〈俗语〉If you learn your math, physics and chemistry well, you've no fear about finding a job anywhere.
数理经济学 shùlǐ jīngjìxué mathematical economics
数理理论 shùlǐ lǐlùn mathematical theory
数理逻辑 shùlǐ luójí *also* "符号逻辑" fúhào luójí mathematical logic
数理统计学 shùlǐ tǒngjìxué mathematical statistics
数理物理学 shùlǐ wùlǐxué mathematical physics
数理语言学 shùlǐ yǔyánxué mathematical linguistics
数理哲学 shùlǐ zhéxué mathematical philosophy
数理主义 shùlǐzhǔyì mathematicism
数量 shùliàng quantity; amount; volume:分配～ quantity allotted / 消耗～ quantity consumed /～贸易配额 quantitative trade quota /～贸易限额 quantitative trade restriction /～成本 volume cost /～指标 quantitative index
数量词 shùliàngcí 〈语言〉numeral-classifier compound (as 一次,两个,三本)
数量分布 shùliàng fēnbù quantitative distribution
数量化理论 shùliànghuà lǐlùn quantitative theory
数量级 shùliàngjí order of magnitude
数量经济学 shùliàng jīngjìxué quantitative economics
数量控制 shùliàng kòngzhì quantity control
数列 shùliè 〈数学〉ordered series of numbers
数论 shùlùn 〈数学〉number theory
数码 shùmǎ ❶ numeral:阿拉伯～ Arabic numerals /罗马～ Roman numerals ❷ numerical code; number; amount:这次进货的～比以前大得多。We have stocked more in our shop this time than before.
数码照相机 shùmǎ zhàoxiàngjī digital camera
数目 shùmù sum; number; amount:请给我一个准确的～。Please give me the exact number. /这是一个不小的～。That's an enormous sum.
数目字 shùmùzì *see* "数字"
数位 shùwèi 〈数学〉digit:～移误 slide error
数系 shùxì 〈数学〉number system
数学 shùxué mathematics:～归纳法 mathematical induction /～近似 mathematical approach /～投影 mathematical projection /～规划 mathematical programming /～模拟 mathematical simulation /～模型 mathematical model /纯～ pure mathematics /应用～ applied mathematics /模糊～ fuzzy mathematics /～家 mathematician
数学哲学 shùxué zhéxué philosophy of mathematics
数值 shùzhí 〈数学〉numerical value:～演算 arithmetic operation /～法分析 numerical method analysis /～积分 numerical integration /～级数 numerical series /～解 numerical solution /～微分 numerical differentiation /～文字 numerical literal
数值天气预报 shùzhí tiānqì yùbào numerical weather forecast
数制 shùzhì number representation system; methods of computation on various numerical bases, such as binary system (base 2) or decimal system (base 10)
数轴 shùzhóu 〈数学〉number axis
数珠 shùzhū 〈佛教〉beads
数字 shùzì *also* "数目字" ❶ numeral; figure; digit:阿拉伯～ Arabic numerals /汉字～ Chinese numerical character ❷ numerical symbol ❸ quantity; amount; figure:这是个天文～。This is an astronomical figure.
数字编码 shùzì biānmǎ digital coding; numeric coding
数字地球 shùzì dìqiú 〈信息〉Digital Earth, a multi-resolution, three-dimensional representation of the Earth accessible through a computer and a special headset:～的具体应用 applications of Digital Earth / 为建设～项目数据库作出贡献 make one's contribution towards building databases for the Digital Earth project
数字电视 shùzì diànshì digital TV
数字分频器 shùzì fēnpínqì digital frequency divider
数字分析器 shùzì fēnxīqì digital analyzer
数字蜂窝 shùzì fēngwō digital cellular
数字高级移动电话系统 shùzì gāojí yídòng diànhuà xìtǒng 〈通信〉D-AMPS (digital advanced mobile phone system)
数字化 shùzìhuà digitization:～装置 digitizer /～自动驾驶仪 digital autopilot
数字辉光管 shùzì huīguāngguǎn 〈电子〉digitron
数字计算机 shùzì jìsuànjī digital computer
数字控制 shùzì kòngzhì digital or numerical control
数字控制系统 shùzì kòngzhì xìtǒng digital control system
数字录音 shùzì lùyīn digital sound recording
数字通讯 shùzì tōngxùn digital communication
数字显示 shùzì xiǎnshì digital display or presentation:～电子手表 digital display electronic watch

数罪并罚 shùzuì bìngfá 〈法律〉concurrent punishment for several crimes; cumulative punishment

数罪并合 shùzuì bìnghé 〈法律〉joinder of offences; merger of offences

术(術) shù ❶ art; skill; craft; technique:美～ fine arts /巫～ witchcraft; sorcery /骑～ horsemanship; equestrian skill /擅长拳～ be good at Chinese boxing /医～高明 excellent medical skill /不学无～ have neither learning nor skill /魔～ magic; conjuring ❷ method; tactics; trick:心～ calculation; scheming /战～(military) tactics /权～ political chicanery /骗～ deceitful trick; ruse /智～ trickery; stratagem
see also zhú

术科 shùkē subject or course in military training or physical training

术士 shùshì ❶ Confucian scholar ❷ *also* "方士" fāngshì necromancer; alchemist

术业 shùyè 〈书面〉academic skills; one's studies

术语 shùyǔ technical terms; terminology:政治～ political terms /语言学～ linguistic terminology /统一英语语法～ standardize the terminology of English grammar

述 shù state; relate; narrate; recount:阐～ expound; explain /～人之言 relate other's words; tell what someone else has said /讲～事情的经过 give an account of what happened /陈～意见 state one's views /申～自己的看法 explain in detail one's own ideas /叙～平生之经历 recount one's personal history or deeds /上～各项 above-mentioned items

述而不作 shù'érbùzuò retell or expound the works of one's predecessors without contributing new ideas:～,信而好古 only repeat what has been said by one's predecessors and prefer to believe in things ancient

述怀 shùhuái pour out one's feelings; unburden one's heart:七十～ personal reflections at the age of seventy

述评 shùpíng review; commentary:时事～ critical review of current affairs /经济～ economic review /本报记者～ commentary by our correspondent

述说 shùshuō state; recount; relate; narrate:～事情的经过 give an account of the event; recount the incident /～他的委屈 pour out his grievances

述职 shùzhí report on one's work; report:大使回国～。The ambassador has returned for consultations.

钵 shù 〈书面〉long needle

束 shù ❶ bind; tie; bundle up:开车要～好安全带 wear seat belt when driving ❷ 〈量词〉bundle; bunch; sheaf:一～红玫瑰 a bouquet of red roses /一～文稿 a sheaf of manuscripts /一～草 a bundle of straw /一～青丝 a tuft of black hair ❸ beam:光～ beam /电子～ electron beam ❹ control; contain; restrain:无拘无～ uninhibited /～身自爱 treasure one's own good name and act within the bounds of propriety ❺ (Shù) a surname

束发 shùfà tie up one's hair;〈旧语〉ceremony of capping a boy at the age of fifteen

束缚 shùfù tie; bind up; fetter; shackle:～了生产力的发展 impede (*or* hinder) the development of productive force /受封建制度的～ be fettered by the feudal system /打破旧框框的～ smash the shackles of old convention

束射管 shùshèguǎn 〈电子〉beam tube

束身 shùshēn ❶ self-control; restraint:～自修 self-cultivation ❷ bind oneself:～投案 give oneself up to the police

束身藏拙 shùshēn-cángzhuō hide one's inadequacy by keeping quiet

束手 shùshǒu have one's hands tied; be at one's wits' end; be helpless:群医～。No doctor could offer any advice.

束手待毙 shùshǒu-dàibì sit idly by waiting for destruction; resign oneself to death:与其～,不如决一死战。We would rather put up a last-ditch fight than resign ourselves to fate.

束手就擒 shùshǒu-jiùqín allow oneself to be caught without putting up a fight; be unable either to escape or to resist

束手束脚 shùshǒu-shùjiǎo timid and hesitant; over-cautious:你这般～,怎能有所作为? What could you accomplish if you always try to play safe (*or* if you're afraid of taking the smallest risks)?

束手无策 shùshǒu-wúcè feel simply helpless; be at a loss what to do; be paralyzed:足智多谋的他,一时竟也～了。He used to be very resourceful, but now he finds himself at the end of his tether.

束狭 shùxiá (of waterways) narrow:河谷～,仅十米左右。The valley is narrow, only ten metres or so in width.

束脩 shùxiū 〈旧语〉private tutor's remuneration or emolument

束胸 shùxiōng woman's old-fashioned girdle for flattening the breasts

束腰 shùyāo ❶ girdle the waist ❷ girdle

束之高阁 shùzhīgāogé lay aside on a high shelf; shelve; pigeonhole:这个重要建议,可惜被他们～了。It's a shame that they put aside such an important proposal.

束装 shùzhuāng 〈书面〉pack up:～就道 pack and set out on a journey

戍 shù defend; garrison:卫～ garrison

戍边 shùbiān garrison the frontiers:～部队 garrison at the frontier

戍鼓 shùgǔ garrison drum

戍楼 shùlóu watchtower

戍守 shùshǒu garrison; guard

戍役 shùyì 〈旧语〉military service at border regions (often as a way of exile)

戍卒 shùzú 〈旧语〉frontier guard

墅 shù villa:别～ villa

腧(俞) shù

腧穴 shùxué acupuncture point; acupoint

恕 shù ❶ forbearance (as advocated by Confucius); consideration for others:忠～之道 doctrine of loyalty and consideration for others; forgiveness /～道 principle of reciprocity; do unto others as you wish others to do unto you ❷ forgive; pardon; excuse; allow for:宽～ forgive /饶～ forgive; pardon ❸ 〈套语〉excuse me; beg your pardon:～我无知 please forgive my ignorance /～草。(used at the end of a handwritten letter) Forgive my scrawl. /～我直言,那是胡说八道。Excuse me for being blunt, but that is simply nonsense.

恕不奉陪 shùbùfèngpéi excuse me for not keeping you company

恕难从命 shùnáncóngmìng forgive me for not complying with your wishes

恕宥 shùyòu 〈书面〉forgive; pardon:量情～ grant pardon according to actual circumstances

恕罪 shùzuì pardon an offence; forgive a sin:招待不周,万望～。Forgive us for not having provided a better service.

shuā

刷[1] shuā ❶ brush:牙～ toothbrush /发～ hairbrush /鞋～ shoe brush /板～ scrub brush /鬃～ bristle brush /油漆～ paintbrush ❷ brush; scrub; clean; daub:～鞋 brush (*or* clean) shoes /～墙 whitewash (*or* clean) a wall /～油漆 varnish (sth.); paint (sth.) /～布告 paste up a notice (*or* post) /～白 wash until sth. is white; whitewash /冲～ scour; wash out /粉～ whitewash ❸ 〈比喻〉expel; discharge; eliminate (through selection or competition):他经常破坏劳动纪律,让厂里给～了。He was expelled from the factory for repeated breaches of work discipline. /他在比赛的第一轮就给～下来了。He was eliminated in the first round of the competition.

刷[2](唰) shuā 〈象声〉swish; rustle:树叶被风吹得～～地响。The leaves rustled in the wind. /地里一片寂静,只听见镰刀～～地割麦声。Silence reigned in the field, except for the swishing of sickles among the wheat.
see also shuà

刷拉 shuālā 〈象声〉rustle; swish:～一声,一只小鸟从树上飞走了。Swish, a bird flew off the tree.

刷洗 shuāxǐ scrub; scour; clean:～墙壁 scrub the walls /～地板上的油渍 scour the grease off the floor /～洗涤槽 clean a sink

刷新 shuāxīn renovate; refurbish:～门面 repaint the front (of a

S

shop, etc.); give (the shop, etc.) a face-lift /～世界记录 break a world record

刷牙子 shuāyázi 〈方言〉toothbrush

刷印 shuāyìn print:木版～线装古书 block-printed and thread-bound ancient Chinese books

刷子 shuāzi brush; scrub:头发～ hairbrush /衣服～ clothes brush

shuǎ

耍 shuǎ ❶〈方言〉play:这可不是～的! This is no joke! *or* It's no joking matter! /有功夫到我家来～。Come and visit me when you're free. ❷ play or juggle with; manipulate:～枪 playing with a spear; spearplay /～狗熊 perform tricks with a bear; put on a bear show /～狮子 perform lion dance ❸ give play to; behave (in an unsavoury manner):～鬼把戏 play a dirty trick; be up to mischief /～阴谋 hatch a conspiracy; brew a plot; conspire /～两面派 resort to double-dealing tactics; be Janus-faced /～派头 make a show of importance; put on airs ❹ play with:～女人 play with the affections of a woman; womanize /我让他给～了。I was fooled by him. ❺ (Shuǎ) a surname

耍把戏 shuǎ bǎxì ❶ perform jugglery, magic, or similar show:～的 juggler; variety actor /他只好靠～混日子。He had to make a living as a juggler. ❷ play tricks:别跟我～了。None of your little tricks, please. /到底你在耍什么把戏呀? What gimmick are you up to?

耍把 shuǎba 〈方言〉wield; brandish; flourish:这孩子成天拿着枝木枪～。The kid is wielding a wooden gun (*or* spear) all day long.

耍笔杆 shuǎ bǐgǎn 〈贬义〉wield a facile pen; be skilled in literary tricks:他这个人就会～儿,别的什么也不行。He is no good at anything but churning out literary trash.

耍叉 shuǎchā *also*"耍锤"〈方言〉create trouble for sb.:你今儿个跟我～,我可饶不了你。I won't let you off easily for causing me so much trouble.

耍刺儿 shuǎcìr 〈方言〉find fault with; deliberately make things difficult for; nitpick:这个人老实,从来不会～。He is honest and straightforward and never try to make things difficult for others.

耍单儿 shuǎdānr 〈方言〉wear thin clothes in cold weather:别净～,留神冻着。Put on warmer clothes or you'll catch cold before you know it.

耍逗 shuǎdòu play with; tease; tantalize:他高兴了就哼几句山西梆子,或者～～孩子。When he was in high spirits, he would sing an aria or two from a Shanxi local opera or play with the children.

耍骨头 shuǎ gǔtou 〈方言〉❶ crack jokes:人家说正经事呢,你别在这儿～。None of your foolishness, please; we're talking business here. ❷ deliberately make trouble; be mischievous:你再敢到这里～,可是找不自在。If you dare try to be funny here, you are only doing yourself a mischief.

耍鬼 shuǎguǐ 〈方言〉play tricks; do mischief:捣乱～ play tricks and cause trouble

耍孩儿 shuǎhái'er *also*"嗨嗨调" hāihāidiào;"咳咳腔" hāihāiqiāng local opera popular in northern Shanxi Province and in Inner Mongolia

耍横 shuǎhèng 〈方言〉rude and unreasonable; arbitrary; peremptory:你受了批评没地方撒气,到我面前～来啦! You think you can take it out on me because you got a dressing-down and have nowhere to vent your spleen?

耍猴儿 shuǎhóur ❶ put on a monkey show ❷〈比喻〉make fun of; play tricks on; tease; kid:别以为我拿你～,我说的可都是实话。Don't think that I'm kidding you. I'm telling you nothing but the truth.

耍花枪 shuǎ huāqiāng play tricks; be up to tricks; play games (with sb.)

耍花腔 shuǎ huāqiāng use honeyed words; sweet-talk:你别在这儿跟我～。Don't you try to sweet-talk me.

耍花样 shuǎ huāyàng play tricks

耍花招 shuǎ huāzhāo ❶ display showy movements in *wushu* (武术); show off one's cleverness or skill ❷ play tricks; resort to deception:他这人老～,不可轻信。Don't trust him; he's always up to one trick or another.

耍滑 shuǎhuá *also*"耍滑头" try to shirk work or responsibility; dodge:这些人是～的老手。They are past masters in passing the buck.

耍奸 shuǎjiān *see*"耍滑"

耍赖 shuǎlài *also*"耍赖皮";"耍无赖" act in a brazen manner (trying to break a promise, dodge a responsibility, etc.):欠债要还,～是不行的。A debt must be paid, and there is no way to disown it.

耍流氓 shuǎ liúmáng bully, harass or insult people by shameless, indecent and base means; take liberties with women:他居然大吵大闹,耍起流氓来。He went so far as to make a terrible scene and acted exactly like a scoundrel.

耍蛮 shuǎmán 〈方言〉be fierce and arrogant; be rude and unreasonable

耍闹 shuǎnào romp; skylark; have horseplay:孩子们在院子里嘻嘻哈哈地～着。The children were having fun in the courtyard, laughing and joking merrily.

耍弄 shuǎnòng ❶ play tricks:～花招 be up to tricks ❷ make a fool of; make fun of; pull sb.'s leg:你是不是在～我? Are you trying to make a fool of me? *or* Are you pulling my leg?

耍排场 shuǎ páichang show off one's wealth; be given to ostentation and extravagance

耍盘子 shuǎ pánzi 〈杂技〉plate-spinning; disc-spinning

耍脾气 shuǎ píqi get into a huff; be in a fit of the sulks; be in a touchy mood:你怎么老～? Why are you always so touchy? /不要耍小姐脾气。Don't behave like a spoilt princess. /有话好好讲,耍什么脾气? Reason things out if you think you are right. You don't have to fly off the handle like this!

耍飘儿 shuǎpiāor 〈方言〉play the coquette; flirt

耍贫嘴 shuǎ pínzuǐ 〈方言〉shoot off one's mouth; be loquacious; be garrulous:去,去! 少～! Away with you and shut up! /这出相声怎么跟～的似的? This is more of a loquacious play than a comic dialogue!

耍泼 shuǎpō 〈方言〉make a terrible scene without provocation:～放刁 ready to kick up a row and behave like a scoundrel

耍钱 shuǎqián 〈方言〉gamble

耍俏 shuǎqiào play the coquette; flirt

耍趣 shuǎqù make fun of sb.; hold sb. up to ridicule:我说过～人的话吗? Did I ever poke fun at anyone?

耍人 shuǎrén make fun of others; play tricks on other people

耍舌头 shuǎ shétou 〈方言〉show off one's eloquence; talk glibly:世事变了,凭～吃不开啦。The world has changed, and nowadays nobody can get along by mere rhetoric.

耍手段 shuǎ shǒuduàn *also*"耍手腕" resort to tricks; use artifices:此人不光明正大,喜欢～。He is not open and aboveboard; he is given to chicanery. /你要耍什么手段我还不知道? You think I don't know what tricks you have up your sleeves?

耍手艺 shuǎ shǒuyì make a living by some skill; be a craftsman:～的 craftsman /解放前,他耍了二十多年手艺。He made a living by his craft for over twenty years before liberation.

耍死狗 shuǎ sǐgǒu 〈方言〉act shamelessly:在确凿的证据面前,他仍然～,不肯认罪。He shamelessly but stubbornly refused to admit his guilt, even when evidence had been produced against him.

耍态度 shuǎ tàidu fly into a temper; get into a huff:有话好好说,不能～。Say what you have got to say, but don't get excited.

耍坛子 shuǎ tánzi 〈杂技〉juggle with jars:下面一个节目是～。Then next show is a jar balancing act.

耍玩 shuǎwán ❶ play; enjoy oneself; have fun:小孩掏出那个小铁匣子～了一阵子。The boy took out the small iron box and played with it awhile. ❷ make fun of; play tricks on; tease:这一番话可把他～得哭笑不得。He was so embarrassed by the bantering remarks that he didn't know whether to cry or laugh.

耍威风 shuǎ wēifēng vaunt one's authority or power; flaunt one's seniority or superiority:什么人这样～呀? Who's putting on such a big show of authority?

耍无赖 shuǎ wúlài *also*"耍赖" act shamelessly; behave capriciously and unreasonably:喝完酒没钱付账,他开始～。Having no money to pay for the drinks he has had, he began to kick up a row.

耍戏 shuǎxi 〈方言〉play tricks on; make fun of:不要～人! Don't play tricks on me!

耍线儿 shuǎxiànr (of puppet show) pull the strings

耍笑 shuǎxiào ❶ laugh and joke; have fun:他们～得真开心。They laughed and joked and had a lot of fun. *or* They had a lot fun, laughing and joking. ❷ make fun of; pull sb.'s legs:那个调皮学生故意～老师,把他的眼镜儿藏起来。That naughty pupil played a prank on

his teacher by hiding his glasses.

耍心眼儿 shuǎ xīnyǎnr make use of one's petty cleverness to gain profit:她这个人太会～。She is a very calculating person. /这事你老老实实办好,别跟我～。Do it conscientiously. Don't you try to be smart with me.

耍熊 shuǎxióng 〈方言〉act shamelessly; behave brazenly:你少和我～。Don't you try to brazen it out before me. /他一上路就耍起熊来,说什么也不走了。No sooner had we started on our journey than he became obstinate, refusing to move an inch.

耍子 shuǎzi 〈方言〉have fun; have a good time

耍嘴皮子 shuǎ zuǐpízi ❶ talk glibly or slickly; show off one's eloquence:这个人就会～。He is a slick talker all right. /他喜欢～。He likes to show off his eloquence. ❷ engage in empty talk; pay lip service:不用你～,有本事你就试试。None of your lip service. Show your talent by getting down to work.

shuà

刷 shuà 〈方言〉select; pick; pick and choose:咱们打这堆梨里～出去几个大的给奶奶。Let us pick a few large pears from this batch for Grandma.

see also shuā

刷白 shuàbái 〈方言〉white; ashen; pale:吓得脸色～ turn (*or* be) pale with fear /月亮把大地照得～。The earth was flooded with the silvery light of the moon.

刷利 shuàli 〈方言〉agile; nimble:小伙子三下两下爬到树上,动作～得像猴子一样。With a few quick moves, the young boy climbed up the tree like a monkey.

刷亮 shuàliàng 〈方言〉very bright:灯光～。The lights were dazzling.

刷溜 shuàliu 〈方言〉agile; quick

shuāi

衰 shuāi decline:年老体～ aged and frail /未老先～ be prematurely aged /家道日～。The family is declining. /风势渐～。The wind has gradually abated.

see also cuī

衰败 shuāibài decline; wane; fall into disrepair:国势～。The influence of the nation was waning. /战后该国呈现一片～的景象。After the war, the country was in a state of decay.

衰惫 shuāibèi 〈书面〉weak and tired; feeble and weary:身体～不堪 extremely weak and tired; overcome with fatigue; exhausted

衰敝 shuāibì decline; decay:国力～ decline of national strength /生产～ production has fallen off /体力～ one's strength has been sapped

衰变 shuāibiàn 〈物理〉decay; disintegrate:粒子的～ decay (*or* disintegration) of particles /～模式 decay mode /～链 decay chain /～率 rate of decay /～常数 decay constant

衰病 shuāibìng weak and ailing:～残年 in one's ailing old age; aging and ailing

衰残 shuāicán ❶ decline and degenerate:～的菊花 withered chrysanthemums ❷ old and disabled; aging and handicapped

衰草 shuāicǎo wilted grass:～败叶 wilted grass and withered leaves

衰耗 shuāihào drain; decline; attenuate; deteriorate:他气力～殆尽。His strength is draining away.

衰减 shuāijiǎn ❶ weaken; worsen; diminish:精力～ be debilitated /体力日渐～ get weaker physically ❷〈物理〉attenuate; decay; degenerate:～器 attenuator /～失真 attenuation distortion /～因数 attenuation factor /～均衡器 attenuation equalizer /～律 decay law /～时间 decay time

衰竭 shuāijié 〈医学〉exhaustion; prostration:全身～ general prostration /呼吸～ prostration of breathing /心力～ heart failure

衰老 shuāilǎo old and feeble; aged; decrepit:近年来他～得多了。He has aged a lot in recent years.

衰陵 shuāilíng 〈书面〉decline; degenerate; go downhill:国势～。The nation was on the decline.

衰落 shuāiluò decline; deteriorate; go downhill:经济～ decline of the economy /家境～ reduced family circumstances /封建制度日渐～。The feudal system was on the wane (*or* decline).

衰落产业 shuāiluò chǎnyè declining industry

衰迈 shuāimài old and weak; senile:年已～ be aging and ailing

衰疲 shuāipí weak and weary; enervated:精力～ be enervated /～的神情 look frail and weary

衰弱 shuāiruò ❶ weak; frail; feeble:久病之后身体～ emaciated after a long illness /神经～ neurasthenia ❷ flag; decline in vigour:在我军反击下,敌军攻势已经～。Under our counterattack, the enemy offensive is petering out.

衰飒 shuāisà 〈书面〉❶ decline; be on the wane:庭树日益～。Trees are turning gaunt in the courtyard. ❷ dejected; depressed; frustrated:颓唐～ become frustrated and despondent

衰世 shuāishì age of decline or decadence

衰瘦 shuāishòu weak and thin:身体～ be all skin and bones

衰损 shuāisǔn (of health) be enervated

衰替 shuāitì 〈书面〉decline; wane:王朝日益～乃必然之势。The decline of the dynasty was inevitable.

衰颓 shuāituí weak and dejected; degenerate:精神～ be dejected (*or* dispirited)

衰退 shuāituì decline; fail; physically deteriorate:视力～ deteriorating eyesight /体力～ decline in physical strength /记忆力～ failing memory /意志～ one's will is waning /经济～ economic recession (*or* decline)

衰亡 shuāiwáng decline and fall; wither away; become extinct:第三帝国的～ decline and fall of the Third Reich /濒于～的绝境 verge on extinction

衰微 shuāiwēi 〈书面〉decline; wane:民族～ decline of a nation

衰萎 shuāiwěi wilt; wither:被霜打过的野草渐渐～下来。Nipped by the frost, the weeds gradually wilted.

衰歇 shuāixiē 〈书面〉decline and come to an end

衰谢 shuāixiè (of flowers, plants, hair, beard, etc.) past bloom; thinning out:百花～。All the flowers are withered. /他已鬓发～。His hair has thinned.

衰朽 shuāixiǔ 〈书面〉feeble and decaying; decrepit:～的封建王朝 decaying feudal dynasty /～残年 be feeble from age and illness; reach a decrepit old age

衰颜 shuāiyán age-worn face; withered face

摔(❶蹿) shuāi ❶ fall or tumble (after losing one's balance):老人一个趔趄,～了个跟头。The old man staggered and fell headlong. /她从楼梯上～下来了。She tumbled down the stairs. ❷ hurtle down; plunge; crash:姑娘脚下一滑,～到了井里。The girl slipped and fell hurtling down the well. /突然风筝一个倒栽葱从空中～下来。The kite took a sudden downward plunge from the sky. /飞机冒着黑烟～下来了。The plane crashed in a trail of black smoke. ❸ (cause to) fall and break:我不小心把玻璃杯～破了。I accidentally dropped a glass and broke it. /暖瓶～了个粉碎。The thermos (flask) tumbled and was smashed to pieces. /她一发脾气就～东西。She breaks things when she gets into a fit. ❹ throw; hurl; fling:把对手～倒在地 throw (*or* fling) one's opponent to the ground /孩子把书包往桌上一～。The boy threw (*or* flung) his school bag on the table. /他把门一～,走了。He slammed the door and left. /他还给我～电话呢! He simply hung up on me! ❺ beat; knock:把炊帚上的水～一～。Beat the water off the pot-scouring brush.

摔打 shuāida ❶ strike; beat; knock:他进去前～了一下他衣服上的灰尘。He beat the dust off his coat before he entered. /把鞋子上的泥～～。Knock the dirt off your shoes. ❷ temper oneself by roughing it:从困难环境中～出来 temper oneself in difficult circumstances

摔跟头 shuāi gēntou ❶ trip and fall; go head over heels; tumble:当心,别～! Watch your step and don't trip up. /路很滑,他摔了好几个跟头。The road was slippery, and he tumbled several times. ❷ come a cropper; make a blunder:谦虚谨慎,工作中就可以少～。Modesty and prudence help one avoid blunders in one's work.

摔跤 shuāijiāo ❶ tumble; slip and fall:那孩子跑着跑着绊了一下,摔了一跤。The child tripped and fell as he ran. ❷ come a cropper; fall into an error:不听别人劝,这次他摔了跤。Ignoring his friends' advice, he made a blunder. ❸〈体育〉wrestling:～运动 wrestling /～运动员 wrestler

摔耙子 shuāi pázi throw up one's job; wash one's hands of sth.:意见归意见,你可不能～。You may have different opinions, but you shouldn't throw up your job because of it.

S

shuǎi

甩 shuǎi ❶ swing; sway; wave: ～胳膊 swing one's arms / 鞭子～得响。The whip cracked. /演员的水袖～得真漂亮。The actress (in classical Chinese opera) waves her long sleeves in a most graceful manner. /她傲慢地把辫子一～,愤愤地冲出房间。With a proud wave of her pigtail, she stormed out of the room. ❷ throw; fling; hurl: ～手榴弹 throw (*or* fling) hand grenades /她把书包～给他。She flung the satchel to him. ❸ throw off; leave behind: 把钉梢的人～掉 throw off a pursuer (*or* tail) /我们等他一下吧,别把他一个人～在后面。Let's wait awhile for him so as not to leave him too far behind. /他把女朋友～了。He gave his girl friend the brush-off. *or* He jilted his girl friend.

甩包袱 shuǎi bāofu cast off burden; get a load off one's back: 国有企业要甩掉那些社会包袱,才能轻装前进。State-owned enterprises must be relieved of the many social burdens before they can take off again.

甩车 shuǎichē 〈铁路〉 uncouple (a railway coach or coaches from the locomotive)

甩搭 shuǎida *also* "甩打" swing; throw; toss; fling: 他把胳膊一～,头也不回就走了。With a swing of the arm, he left without looking back.

甩发 shuǎifà (of Chinese opera) long, hanging wig worn by actors who swing such hair to show anxiety

甩干 shuǎigān spin-dry; tumble-dry

甩开膀子 shuǎikāi bǎngzi do all one can; go all out; go full steam ahead: ～大干 go full steam ahead with one's work /～抓生产 go all out to boost production

甩脸子 shuǎi liǎnzi 〈方言〉 pull a long face; be in a fit of the sulks: 你不高兴,也不用跟我～。You may be in a foul mood, but you don't have to sulk in front of me.

S

甩卖 shuǎimài sell at a reduced price; have a markdown sale; dump: 清仓大～ clearance sale; rummage sale /不惜血本大～ dump goods at a loss

甩腔 shuǎiqiāng speak with a drawl

甩手 shuǎishǒu ❶ swing one's arms: 她甩着手走了过来。She came up swinging her arms. ❷ throw up (one's job, etc.); wash one's hands (of sth.): 他一概不管,～走了。He washed his hands of it all and left.

甩手操 shuǎishǒucāo arm swinging exercise

甩手掌柜 shuǎishǒu zhǎngguì 〈口语〉 "hands-off" boss — boss who merely gives general instructions but keeps his hands off any practical work; "do-nothing" guy — one who merely watches or talks but does nothing useful (as in a team or a household)

甩湾 shuǎiwān 〈方言〉 (of rivers, roads, etc.) curve; bend; turn: 这条河从西南流向东北,在村外形成一个大～。This river flows from southwest to northeast, forming a big bend outside the village.

甩闲话 shuǎi xiánhuà *also* "甩闲腔" deliberately make complaints which are meant for the ear of sb.

甩线 shuǎixiàn string attached to a fishing rod; fishing line; fishline

甩袖子 shuǎi xiùzi swing one's sleeves — wash one's hands of (work, matter, etc.): 他～不干了。He has washed his hands of the business.

甩站 shuǎizhàn (of a public bus) fail to pull up at a stop; miss a stop

甩子 shuǎizǐ 〈方言〉 (of fish, insect, etc.) lay eggs

甩子 shuǎizi horsetail whisk

shuài

率[1] shuài ❶ lead; command: ～队入场 lead one's team into the arena (sportsground, auditorium, or similar venue) /～师北上 lead one's troops north /～兵百万 command a million troops ❷ 〈书面〉 follow; comply; conform: ～彼淮浦 follow the Huai River

率[2] shuài ❶ hasty; rash; impetuous: 粗～ rough and careless; ill-conceived /～忽应战 engage the enemy in haste ❷ frank; straightforward; forthright: 真～ sincere and candid /坦～ frank; outspoken ❸ 〈书面〉 in general; generally; usually: ～皆如此。This is generally the case. ❹ handsome; good-looking

see also lǜ

率常 shuàicháng 〈书面〉 generally speaking; on the whole; in the main: ～如此。This is often the case.

率尔 shuài'ěr rashly; hurriedly; hastily: ～成章 composed (*or* written) in haste (often used self-depreciatingly)

率尔操觚 shuài'ěr-cāogū ❶ wield a facile pen ❷ write offhand or carelessly: 其文亦颇有～者。Even he has a few carelessly written articles.

率领 shuàilǐng lead; head; command: ～所部增援守城部队 lead one's troops to reinforce the city garrison /～代表团出访非洲十国 lead (*or* head) a delegation on a tour of ten African countries /由他～的访问团 visiting group headed by him /～雄师百万 command a powerful army of one million

率马以骥 shuàimǎyǐjì lead horses with a fine steed — let able or talented people take the lead

率然 shuàirán casually; hastily: ～回答 answer casually

率兽食人 shuàishòu-shírén ride roughshod over the people; be tyrannical

率土之滨 shuàitǔzhībīn over all this land; territory of a state

率先 shuàixiān take the lead in doing sth.; be the first to do sth.: ～响应 be the first to respond to (a call, etc.)

率性 shuàixìng ❶ simply; just: 因为找不到躲雨的地方,他～就脱掉上衣迎着暴风雨大踏步前进。Finding no shelter, he simply took off his coat and strode ahead in the teeth of the raging storm. ❷ wilful; self-willed; headstrong: 他由于～行事,不知吃了多少苦头。He has suffered God knows how much because of his mullish obstinacy.

率意 shuàiyì 〈书面〉 at will; on the spur of the moment: ～而行 act as one pleases; follow one's bent

率由旧章 shuàiyóujiùzhāng follow precedents; act in conformity with the existing or established rules; follow old ways

率真 shuàizhēn honest and sincere: 待人～ be frank and sincere towards others

率直 shuàizhí frank and straightforward: 心地～ outspoken and straightforward by temperament /～陈词,敬希见谅。Forgive me for making such a blunt statement.

蟀 shuài see "蟋蟀" xīshuài

帅[1](帥) shuài ❶ commander in chief: 元～ marshal; (in ancient times) supreme commander /主～ commander in chief /大元～ generalissimo /最高统～ supreme commander /亲自挂～ take command personally /舍车保～ (in Chinese chess) sacrifice a chariot to save the king; sacrifice a lesser figure to save the ringleader ❷ (Shuài) a surname

帅[2](帥、率) shuài handsome; graceful; smart: 小伙子长得真～。What a handsome young man! /他的字写得很～。He writes a beautiful hand. /你穿这身衣服挺～。You look really smart in this suit. /这几个跟头翻得干净利落,真～! These somersaults were neatly done. They were just terrific!

帅才 shuàicái person of remarkable leadership abilities who can be entrusted with overall command (of an army, enterprise, undertaking, etc.)

帅旗 shuàiqí flag of a commander in chief

帅气 shuàiqi handsome; elegant; graceful: 他这身打扮很～。He is elegantly (*or* smartly) dressed. /他竟然写出这么～的好字! Can you imagine that he should be able to write such a graceful hand?

帅印 shuàiyìn seal of a commander in chief

shuān

闩(櫄) shuān bolt; latch; beam used to bar a door: 门～ door bolt /铁～ iron bolt /从里面把门～好 bolt the door on the inside

栓 shuān ❶ bolt; plug: 消火～ fire hydrant; fire plug ❷ ri-

fle bolt ❸ stopper; cork; anything resembling a cork or stopper
栓剂 shuānjì 〈药学〉suppository
栓皮 shuānpí 〈林业〉cork (outer covering of the cork oak)
栓皮栎 shuānpílì oriental oak (*Quercus variabilis*)
栓皮树 shuānpíshù 〈植物〉cork tree
栓塞 shuānsè 〈医学〉embolism:静脉～ venous embolism /肺～ pulmonary embolism /脑～ cerebral embolism /～形成 embolization
栓子 shuānzǐ 〈医学〉embolus

拴 shuān ❶ tie; bind; fasten:把马～在树上 tie (*or* tether, *or* hitch) a horse to a tree /箱子上～个行李牌 tie a luggage tag to a suitcase /用铁链～住 fasten with an iron chain ❷〈比喻〉be bogged down:今年我被一个科研项目～得死死的。I have been bogged down by a research project this year. /人心用钱是～不住的。Money cannot buy people's affection.
拴绑 shuānbǎng tie up; bind; truss up:把行李～在自行车上 tie up the luggage on the bicycle
拴车 shuānchē 〈方言〉❶ buy carts or (horse-drawn) carriages:秋后,村里一户农民添了一台拖拉机,还拴了两辆大车。After the autumn harvest, one farmer in the village bought a tractor and two carts. ❷〈旧语〉run a shop to rent out rickshaws:～的 be in the rickshaw-renting business
拴持 shuānchi *also* "拴插"〈方言〉bring up; look after (children):你妈从小把你～这么大,很不容易。Your mother had a hard time bringing you up.
拴缚 shuānfù tie up; bundle up:～包裹 tie up the parcel
拴马桩 shuānmǎzhuāng hitching post
拴系点 shuānxìdiǎn tie-down point
拴线 shuānxiàn (of the Dai nationality) bless sb. by tying the person's hands with white threads

shuàn

涮 shuàn ❶ rinse:～手 rinse one's hands /～瓶子 rinse out a bottle /这床单至少～三遍。Give the sheet at least three rinses. ❷ scald (thin slices of meat, etc.) in boiling water; dip-boil:～海鲜 dip-boil sea food ❸〈方言〉trick; fool; deceive:我让他～了。I was tricked by him.
涮锅子 shuànguōzi dip-boil slices of meat and vegetables in a chafing dish
涮羊肉 shuànyángròu instant-boiled mutton; dip-boiled mutton slices

shuāng

霜 shuāng ❶ frost:早～ early frost /晚～ late frost /结了～的窗户 frosted window /昨晚下了～。There was a frost last night. /田野铺满了～。The fields have frosted over. ❷ frostlike powder:糖～ frosting; icing /盐～ salt efflorescence /杏仁～ almond powder ❸ white; silver; hoar:～锋 shining edge of a knife /两鬓飞～ grey (*or* hoary) temples /艰难苦恨繁～鬓。Hardships and sorrows are greying my temples.
霜晨 shuāngchén frosty morning:西风烈,长空雁叫～月。Fierce the west wind, Wild geese cry under the frosty morning moon.
霜点 shuāngdiǎn frost point
霜冻 shuāngdòng frost
霜度 shuāngdù 〈气象〉degrees of frost
霜害 shuānghài frostbite; frost damage:遭受～的农作物 frost-bitten crops
霜花 shuānghuā ❶ frostwork ❷ (soft) rime
霜降 Shuāngjiàng ❶ Frost's Descent, 18th seasonal division point, marking the sun's position at 210° on the ecliptic ❷ day marking such a seasonal division point, usu. falling on the 23rd or 24th of October ❸ period lasting from such a seasonal point till the next one (Beginning of Winter 立冬)
see also "节气" jiéqì; "二十四节气" èrshísì jiéqì
霜霉病 shuāngméibìng 〈农业〉downy mildew
霜期 shuāngqī 〈气象〉frost season
霜天 shuāngtiān frosty sky; frosty weather:万类～竞自由。Under freezing skies a million creatures contend in freedom. /万木～红烂漫。Forests blaze red beneath the frosty sky.
霜条 shuāngtiáo 〈方言〉ice-lolly; popsicle; ice-sucker
霜叶 shuāngyè red leaves; autumn maple leaves:～红于二月花。Autumn maple leaves are even redder than spring flowers.

鹴 shuāng *see* "鹔鹴" sùshuāng

孀 shuāng widow:孤～ widow /遗～ widow /居～多年 live in widowhood for many years
孀妇 shuāngfù 〈书面〉widow:孤苦伶仃的老～ old widow, lonely and helpless
孀居 shuāngjū 〈书面〉be a widow; live in widowhood:年仅三十即～ be widowed at the age of 30

骦 shuāng *see* "骕骦" sùshuāng

鹴 shuāng *see* "鹔鹴" sùshuāng

骦 shuāng *see* "骕骦" sùshuāng

双(雙、隻) shuāng ❶ two; twin; both; dual:～行道 two-way road (*or* street) /举～手赞成 vote aye with both hands — agree completely or support unreservedly /～引擎战斗机 twin-engined fighter plane /～推力发动机 dual-thrust motor /～目失明 blind in both eyes; lose the sight of both eyes /盖世无～ unrivalled; second to none ❷〈量词〉pair:一～手 a pair of hands ❸ even:～号座位 even-numbered seats /书的～(数)页 even pages of a book ❹ double; twofold:～份儿 double portion /～折射 double refraction /～倍 twofold; double ❺ (Shuāng) a surname
双百方针 shuāngbǎi fāngzhēn (short for "百花齐放,百家争鸣"的方针) policy of letting a hundred flowers blossom and a hundred schools of thought contend
双棒儿 shuāngbàngr 〈方言〉twins
双胞胎 shuāngbāotāi twins
双背书 shuāngbèishū 〈金融〉double endorsement
双倍体 shuāngbèitǐ amphiploid
双边 shuāngbiān bilateral:～谈判 bilateral negotiation /～协定 bilateral agreement /～合同 bilateral contract /～交易 bilateral transaction /～进口配额 bilateral import quota
双边贸易 shuāngbiān màoyì bilateral trade; two-way trade:～互惠主义 bilateralism /～及支付协定 bilateral trade and payment agreement /～总量 total volume of bilateral trade
双边主义 shuāngbiānzhǔyì bilateralism
双宾语 shuāngbīnyǔ 〈语言〉double object
双波段 shuāngbōduàn 〈电子〉two-waveband
双层 shuāngcéng double-deck; double-layered:～公共汽车 double-deck bus; double-decker /～立交桥 double-deck fly-over (*or* over-pass) /～床 double-decker /～玻璃窗 double window; double-glazed window /～胶合板 two-ply board /"～"税制 "two-tier" tax system /儿童～床 bunk bed
双翅目 shuāngchìmù diptera:～昆虫 dipter; dipteran /～昆虫学家 dipterist
双重 shuāngchóng double; dual; both; twofold:～标准 double standard /内部和外部的～压力 both internal and external pressure /～性 dual nature; duality /起～作用 serve a dual purpose /受帝国主义和封建主义的～压迫 suffer from the twofold oppression of imperialism and feudalism /～交配 double mate /～曝光 double exposure /～熔点 double melting point /～X射线源 binary X-ray source /～效应 double effect
双重保险 shuāngchóng bǎoxiǎn double insurance
双重承认 shuāngchóng chéngrèn dual recognition
双重代表权 shuāngchóng dàibiǎoquán 〈外交〉dual representation
双重国籍 shuāngchóng guójí dual nationality
双重汇率 shuāngchóng huìlǜ two-tier exchange rate; dual exchange rate
双重间谍 shuāngchóng jiàndié double agent
双重领导 shuāngchóng lǐngdǎo dual leadership
双重人格 shuāngchóng réngé dual personality
双重星系 shuāngchóng xīngxì binary galaxy; double galaxy
双重征税 shuāngchóng zhēngshuì double taxation:避免～协定

agreement to avoid double taxation
双重主权 shuāngchóng zhǔquán dual sovereignty
双唇音 shuāngchúnyīn 〈语言〉bilabial (sound)
双打 shuāngdǎ 〈体育〉doubles:获男子(女子)~冠军 win the men's (women's) doubles / 男女混合~ mixed doubles / ~运动员 doubles player
双滴虫 shuāngdīchóng diplomonad
双端引线 shuāngduān yǐnxiàn 〈电工〉double end
双耳效应 shuāng'ěr xiàoyìng binaural effect
双方 shuāngfāng both sides or parties; two parties or sides:交战~ both belligerents / 劳资~ both labour and capital / 缔约国~ both signatory states; two contracting parties / ~当事人 both litigants; both parties / 照顾~的利益 take into consideration the interest of both parties
双峰驼 shuāngfēngtuó 〈动物〉two-humped camel; Bactrian camel
双幅 shuāngfú double width:这块毛料是单幅还是~的? Is this woolen cloth single or double width?
双缸洗衣机 shuānggāng xǐyījī two-tub washing machine; semi-automatic washing machine
双岗 shuānggǎng sentry post with two guards; double-sentry post
双杠 shuānggàng 〈体育〉parallel bars
双工 shuānggōng 〈通信〉duplex; diplex:~器 duplexer
双宫丝 shuānggōngsī 〈纺织〉doupion (silk); douppioni
双钩 shuānggōu 〈美术〉tracing the contour of the strokes of a character
双挂号 shuāngguàhào registered mail requiring the receiver's receipt
双关 shuāngguān having a double meaning:语意~ speak with a double meaning
双关语 shuāngguānyǔ pun; word play
双管 shuāngguǎn double-barrelled / ~猎枪 double-barrelled shotgun / ~式摄像机 twin-barrel camera / ~立式喷雾器 duplex vertical sprayer / ~直接回水(供暖)系统 two-pipe direct-return system / ~竖笛 double flageolet
双管齐下 shuāngguǎn-qíxià paint with a brush in each hand — work along two lines; do two things simultaneously:厂长一手抓生产,一手抓科研,~。The factory director makes great effort to promote both production and scientific research.
双光眼镜 shuāngguāng yǎnjìng bifocal glasses
双轨 shuāngguǐ double track:~铁路 double-track railway
双轨制 shuāngguǐzhì double-track system (as in education or pricing):价格~ two-tiered price system; double-track price system of official and market prices / ~并轨 replace the dual price system by a single-price system
双号 shuānghào even numbers:报数,~出列! Count off! Even numbers step forward! / ~由此入场 even numbers entrance
双铧犁 shuānghuálí double-shared plough; double furrow plough
双簧 shuānghuáng *also* "双镬"〈戏曲〉two-man comic show in which the front man does the acting while the one hiding behind him does the speaking:演~ *also* "唱~" give a two-man comic show; collaborate closely; work hand in glove (with)
双簧管 shuānghuángguǎn 〈乐器〉oboe
双季稻 shuāngjìdào double cropping of rice; double-harvest rice
双髻鲨 shuāngjìshā 〈动物〉hammerhead (*Sphyrna lewini* or *Sphyrna zygaena*)
双肩挑 shuāngjiāntiāo shoulder or bear responsibility for both teaching or other professional work and administrative work:~干部 teacher (researcher, technician, etc.) and administrator at the same time
双交 shuāngjiāo *also* "双杂交"〈农业〉double cross:~种 double cross hybrid
双镜头反光照相机 shuāngjìngtóu fǎnguāng zhàoxiàngjī 〈摄影〉twin-lens reflex (TLR)
双卡 shuāngkǎ double cassette tape recorder
双款 shuāngkuǎn upper and lower inscriptions (both dedication and signature) for a painting, etc.
双礼 shuānglǐ 〈旧语〉simultaneous bow by bride and groom to elders on wedding day:受~ receive the salutations of the bride and groom
双联体 shuāngliántǐ Siamese twins
双料 shuāngliào of reinforced material; extra quality: ~冠军 champion with two first prizes / ~坏蛋 out-and-out scoundrel / 这个搪瓷盘子是~的。This enamel plate is made of reinforced material.
双陆 shuānglù ancient chess game
双轮 shuānglún ❶〈体育〉double round:~射箭 double round archery ❷ two-wheeled:~推车 two wheeler
双轮双铧犁 shuānglún-shuānghuálí two wheeled double-shared plough
双面 shuāngmiàn two-sided; double-edged; reversible: ~刀片 double-edged razor blade / ~凹 bi-concave / ~凸 bi-convex / ~加热 sandwich heating
双面式上衣 shuāngmiànshì shàngyī reversible coat
双面绣 shuāngmiànxiù double-faced embroidery
双面摇纱机 shuāngmiàn yáoshājī double reeling frame
双面印刷机 shuāngmiàn yìnshuājī perfecting press; perfector
双面织物 shuāngmiàn zhīwù reversible cloth; reversibles
双名法 shuāngmíngfǎ binomial nomenclature
双目望远镜 shuāngmù wàngyuǎnjìng binoculars
双目显微镜 shuāngmù xiǎnwēijìng binocular microscope
双抢 shuāngqiǎng rush-harvesting and rush-sowing:~季节 rush-harvesting and rush-sowing season; time when farmers have to harvest the ripe crop and sow a new crop in a rush
双亲 shuāngqīn both parents:他~健在。Both of his parents are still living and in good health.
双亲家庭 shuāngqīn jiātíng two-parent family or household
双球菌 shuāngqiújūn 〈微生物〉diplococcus
双曲函数 shuāngqū hánshù hyperbolic function
双曲几何 shuāngqū jǐhé hyperbolic geometry
双曲面 shuāngqūmiàn 〈数学〉double curved surface; hyperboloid: ~齿轮 hypoid gear / ~图 hyperbolic chart
双曲线 shuāngqūxiàn 〈数学〉hyperbola:~导航 hyperbolic navigation / ~幅度 hyperbolic amplitude / ~天线 hyperbolic antenna
双全 shuāngquán enjoy a double blessing; possess both of two complementary qualities:父母~ with both parents still living / 儿女~ have a son and a daughter / 福寿~ enjoy happiness as well as longevity / 智勇~ endowed with both wisdom and courage / 文武~ be adept with both the pen and the sword
双人床 shuāngrénchuáng double bed
双人房 shuāngrénfáng double-bedded room; twin-bedded room
双人舞 shuāngrénwǔ dance by two people; duet; pas de deux
双日 shuāngrì even days (of the month)
双身子 shuāngshēnzi 〈口语〉pregnant woman
双生 shuāngshēng twins:~姐妹(兄弟) twin sisters (brothers) / ~孢子 didymospore / ~水母属 Diphyes / (同卵)全等~ identical twins / 非全等~ unidentical twins (*or* fraternal twins)
双声 shuāngshēng 〈语言〉phrase having two or more characters with the same initial consonant (as 公告 gōnggào, 方法 fāngfǎ); alliteration
双声道 shuāngshēngdào dual track; double track:~磁带录音机 double-track tape recorder
双十二事变 Shuāng-Shí'èr Shìbiàn *also* "西安事变" Xī'ān Shìbiàn Xi'an Incident of 12 December 1936
双手 shuāngshǒu both hands:~合十 put both palms together (as a Buddhist greeting) / ~拱让 surrender sth. submissively; hand sth. on a silver platter / ~反绑 tie sb.'s hands behind his back / 藏族姑娘~向贵宾献上哈达。A Tibetan girl presented a *hada* with both hands to the distinguished guest.
双输 shuāngshū lose-lose:形成~局面 result in a lose-lose situation
双数 shuāngshù even number
双双 shuāngshuāng in pairs; both:情侣~ pair of lovers / ~进入大厅 walk into the hall in pairs / 我校男女队~获得冠军。The men's and women's teams of our school both won the championships.
双宿双飞 shuāngsù-shuāngfēi (of lovers) always keep each other's company (like birds flying and nestling together):愿如池中鸳鸯鸟,~过一生。How I wish we could spend all our lives together like the mandarin ducks in the pool!
双糖 shuāngtáng 〈化学〉disaccharide
双体船 shuāngtǐchuán *also* "双体艇" catamaran
双瞳剪水 shuāngtóng-jiǎnshuǐ clear, beautiful eyes of a pretty girl
双筒望远镜 shuāngtǒng wàngyuǎnjìng binoculars; field glasses
双喜 shuāngxǐ double happiness:~临门。Two happy events occur

at the same time. /他去年真是～，结了婚，又取得了博士学位。He had a double cause for rejoicing last year: he was happily married and earned his doctorate.

双下巴 shuāngxiàba double chin: 他胖得都有～了。He's grown so fat that he's got a double chin.

双响 shuāngxiǎng firecracker which explodes twice; double-bang firecracker

双向 shuāngxiàng two-way; bidirectional; bilateral: ～交流 two-way (*or* bilateral exchange) /～电视 two-way television /～波形 bidirectional wave-form /～电路 bilateral circuit /～公差 bilateral tolerance /～晶体管 bidirectional transistor /～天线 bilateral antenna /～线 bidirectional line

双向飞碟射击 shuāngxiàng fēidié shèjī 〈体育〉skeet shooting

双向开关 shuāngxiàng kāiguān two-way switch

双向选择 shuāngxiàng xuǎnzé two-way selection, referring to employer and employee choosing each other in a job market

双薪 shuāngxīn double pay: 发～ issue double pay

双星 shuāngxīng ❶〈天文〉double star; binary star ❷ Cowherd (Altair) and Weaving-Girl (Vega) — two stars representing true eternal love

双姓 shuāngxìng (of Chinese family names) two-character surname

双学位 shuāngxuéwèi double BA degree

双眼井 shuāngyǎnjǐng twin-mouthed well

双眼皮 shuāngyǎnpí double-fold eyelid: 割～ undergo an operation for double-fold eyelids

双氧水 shuāngyǎngshuǐ *also* "过氧化氢溶液" guòyǎnghuàqīng róngyè; "二氧化氢溶液" èryǎnghuàqīng róngyè 〈药学〉hydrogen peroxide solution

双翼机 shuāngyìjī biplane

双音节词 shuāngyīnjiécí 〈语言〉disyllabic word; disyllable

双赢 shuāngyíng win-win: 这是一个～的办法。This is a win-win proposition.

双拥 shuāngyōng (short for 拥军优属、拥政爱民) support the army and give preferential treatment to families of revolutionary armymen and martyrs, and support the government and cherish the people

双鱼座 Shuāngyúzuò 〈天文〉Pisces

双语 shuāngyǔ bilingual: ～教学 bilingual teaching

双语词典 shuāngyǔ cídiǎn bilingual dictionary

双元音 shuāngyuányīn 〈语言〉diphthong

双月刊 shuāngyuèkān bimonthly (publication)

双增双节 shuāngzēng-shuāngjié raise production and revenue, cut waste and expenditure

双职工 shuāngzhígōng man and wife both working; double income couple; working couple: ～家庭 two-earner household; two-income family /"小饭桌"解决了许多～家庭的困难。Setting up a neighbourhood lunch table for children solves a lot of problems for working couples.

双周刊 shuāngzhōukān biweekly; fortnightly

双绉 shuāngzhòu 〈纺织〉crêpe de Chine

双子叶植物 shuāngzǐyè zhíwù 〈生物〉dicotyledon

双子座 Shuāngzǐzuò 〈天文〉Gemini: ～流星群 Geminids /～U 型星 U Geminorum star

双座 shuāngzuò two-seater; double-seater: ～飞机 two-seater aircraft

shuǎng

爽[1] shuǎng ❶ bright; clear; fresh: 神清气～ feel fresh and clear-headed /秋高气～的日子 fine clear autumn day ❷ frank; straightforward; forthright: 生性～直 frank or forthright by nature ❸ feel well: 身体不～ feel unwell; be under the weather /精神为之一～ feel exhilarated /人逢喜事精神～。Morale soars in happy times.

爽[2] shuǎng make a mistake; deviate: 毫厘不～ not deviating the least bit; free from the slightest error /屡试不～ prove effective after repeated trials

爽畅 shuǎngchàng comfortable and happy: 身心～ feel comfortable and happy

爽脆 shuǎngcuì ❶ (of voice) clear and melodious: 她说一口～的上海话。She speaks a clear and melodious Shanghai dialect. ❷ (of character) frank; straightforward; (of action) agile; quick; with alacrity: 哥哥干活那～劲儿谁也比不了。No one can compare with my brother in labour enthusiasm. ❸ (of food) crispy and refreshing: 生拌黄瓜吃起来～。Tossed fresh cucumbers are crispy and nice to eat.

爽当 shuǎngdang 〈口语〉efficient and able; quick and neat: 办事～ be efficient in work

爽的 shuǎngde *also* "爽得"〈方言〉simply; just; may as well: 既是你要去，我～就陪你走一趟。Since you insist on going, I may as well go with you.

爽健 shuǎngjiàn agile and sturdy: 她年纪在五十岁上下，硬朗～，显出一副豁达干练的样子。She is about fifty, full of vim and vigour, a woman who appears both broad-minded and efficient.

爽捷 shuǎngjié deft; dexterous; with alacrity: 举止～ act quickly and straightforwardly /他～地回答了我的问题。He answered my questions readily.

爽垲 shuǎngkǎi 〈书面〉(of topography) open and high

爽口 shuǎngkǒu refreshing: 这凉拌菜吃着挺～。The cold dish is tasty and refreshing.

爽快 shuǎngkuai ❶ refreshed; happy; feel good: 把这话说出来，心里～多了。Having poured out what was on my mind, I felt a good deal better. ❷ frank; straightforward; forthright: 办事～ be forthright in doing sth.; do sth. without fuss /他是个～人。He is a frank and outspoken person. /他～地承认了错误。He readily admitted his mistakes. /我就喜欢她这个～劲儿。I like her for her openness and dynamism.

爽朗 shuǎnglǎng ❶ bright and clear: 金秋季节，天气～。The sky is bright and clear in the golden autumn. /院子里比屋里～得多了。It's much brighter in the courtyard than in the room. ❷ frank and cheerful; hearty: 阵阵～的笑声 peals of hearty laughter /这姑娘很～。The girl is frank and open.

爽利 shuǎnglì quick and efficient; brisk and neat: 动作～ be agile in one's movements /这人干什么都～。He is efficient in whatever he does.

爽亮 shuǎngliàng ❶ clear and loud: 嗓音～ have loud and clear voice ❷ cheerful; sanguine; optimistic: 他心里是～的。He is cheerful and broad-minded.

爽目 shuǎngmù pleasing to the eye; nice-looking: 清晰～ clear and pleasant /浅黄的楼房在蔚蓝天空的衬托下，显得格外～。The light yellow buildings look especially nice against the bright blue sky.

爽气 shuǎngqì ❶〈书面〉fresh air; crisp air: 西山朝来，致有～。The morning air from the Western Hills is fresh and crisp. ❷〈方言〉*see* "爽快"

爽然 shuǎngrán 〈书面〉feel lost; be at a loss

爽然若失 shuǎngrán-ruòshī feel perplexed, not knowing what to do

爽身粉 shuǎngshēnfěn talcum powder

爽声 shuǎngshēng clear and loud voice: 看着孩子的立功喜报，老人家～大笑。Looking at the bulletin announcing his son's meritorious service, the old man laughed heartily.

爽失 shuǎngshī 〈书面〉failure; error; mistake

爽适 shuǎngshì fresh and comfortable; cool and refreshing: ～的凉风 cool refreshing breeze /雨后空气清新，使人感觉～。After the rain the air was clear and refreshing.

爽心 shuǎngxīn pleased; cheerful; gratified

爽心悦目 shuǎngxīn-yuèmù refreshing to the heart and pleasing to the eye; refreshing; pleasing: 园中百花盛开，令人～。The blooming flowers in the garden is a refreshing and heartening sight.

爽信 shuǎngxìn 〈书面〉fail to keep one's promise; fail to honour one's word: 决不～ will never go back on one's word

爽性 shuǎngxìng might just as well: 既已晚了，～不去了。Since it is already late, we might just as well not go. /只剩下一页了，～抄完了再吃饭吧。There is only one page left. I might as well finish copying it before dinner.

爽意 shuǎngyì pleased; satisfied; cheerful: 大家笑得那样～。Everyone laughed heartily.

爽约 shuǎngyuē 〈书面〉fail to keep an engagement; break an appointment: ～于人 fail to keep an appointment with sb.

爽直 shuǎngzhí frank; straightforward; open: 生性～ frank and straightforward by nature /为人～ be open and straightforward

塽 shuǎng 〈书面〉high place that faces the sun

shuí

谁 shuí see "谁" shéi

shuǐ

水 shuǐ ❶ water:淡～ fresh water /海～ sea water /硬～ hard water /软～ soft water /洪～ flood /活～ running water; flowing water /死～ stagnant water /茶～ tea ❷ river:湘～ Xiangshui River ❸ general term for rivers, lakes, seas, etc.; water:青山绿～ green hills and clear water /一衣带～ narrow strip of water /细～长流 a small stream flows far — accomplish something little by little /～上人家 boat dwellers ❹ liquid:药～liquid medicine; medicinal liquid; lotion /香～ perfume /汽～ aerated drinking water; soft drink /柠檬～ lemonade /橘子～ orangeade /胶～ glue /糖～ syrup /泪～ tears; teardrop /脑积～ hydrocephalus ❺ additional cost; extra income:贴～ agio /外～ extra income /油～ extra income and benefits ❻ times of washing:这件衣服才洗过两～就不能穿了! The dress can no longer be worn after it has been washed only twice. ❼ (Shuǐ) a surname

水案 shuǐ'àn (of division of labour among cooks) jobs such as washing vegetables, cutting open and cleaning fish, chicken, etc. (as distinguished from 白案 "cooking that deals with staple food" and 红案 "cooking that deals with meat and vegetable dishes")

水坝 shuǐbà dam:修～ build a dam

水霸 shuǐbà person who extorts money from people by controlling the water source or water conservancy facilities; water despot

S

水柏枝 shuǐbǎizhī 〈植物〉German tamarisk

水半球 shuǐbànqiú 〈地理〉water hemisphere

水保护 shuǐbǎohù 〈环保〉water conservation

水饱儿 shuǐbǎor 〈方言〉feel full after taking food with a lot of liquids in it:他喝了一大碗粥，落了个～。He felt full after taking a large bowl of porridge.

水泵 shuǐbèng water pump:～扬程 pump head

水笔 shuǐbǐ ❶ stiff-haired writing brush ❷ water-colour paintbrush ❸〈方言〉(fountain) pen

水标 shuǐbiāo watermark

水表 shuǐbiǎo water meter:查～ read the water meter /～井 water meter chamber

水鳖 shuǐbiē 〈植物〉frogbit (*Hydrocharis morsus-ranae*)

水鳖子 shuǐbiēzi 〈动物〉apus

水滨 shuǐbīn waterside; water front; shore

水兵 shuǐbīng seaman; sailor; bluejacket:年轻的～ young seamen

水波 shuǐbō wave; ripple:～不兴 without even a ripple /～粼粼 clear ripples

水玻璃 shuǐbōli 〈化工〉water glass; sodium silicate

水簸箕 shuǐbòji ❶ (of water conservancy works) small, dustpan-shaped earth dykes built along a slope ❷〈方言〉footrests for the passenger on a rickshaw or pedicab

水布植物 shuǐbù zhíwù hydrochore

水彩 shuǐcǎi watercolour

水彩画 shuǐcǎihuà 〈美术〉watercolour (painting)

水彩颜料 shuǐcǎi yánliào watercolours

水彩纸 shuǐcǎizhǐ watercolour paper

水仓 shuǐcāng 〈矿业〉sump

水槽 shuǐcáo water channel; trough; water slide:～运输 flume

水草 shuǐcǎo ❶ pasture and water:～丰美 (place) with plenty of water and lush pasture /牧民逐～而居。The herdsmen live where there is water and pasture. *or* The nomads rove about for water and pasture. ❷ waterweeds; water plants:湖里长满～。The lake is full of water plants.

水涔涔 shuǐcéncén ❶ (of eyes) bright and intelligent:小姑娘吃惊地闪着～的大眼睛。The little girl's bright and intelligent eyes shone in surprise. ❷ (of things) soaked:他脱下棉衣，露出～的衬衣。He took off his cotton-padded coat and revealed his soaked shirt.

水层 shuǐcéng water layer:深～ deep water /浅～ shallow water /鲣鱼、鲐鱼等各依季节的不同而生活在不同的～中。Tuna, chub mackerel and other fishes live in different layers of water in different seasons.

水虿 shuǐchài 〈动物〉nymph of the dragonfly, etc.

水产 shuǐchǎn aquatic product:～丰富 be abundant in aquatic products /～资源开发 development of aquatic (*or* fishery) resources

水产品 shuǐchǎnpǐn aquatic product

水产养殖 shuǐchǎn yǎngzhí aquaculture

水产养殖场 shuǐchǎn yǎngzhíchǎng aquafarm

水产业 shuǐchǎnyè aquatic products industry; fishery

水厂 shuǐchǎng waterworks

水车 shuǐchē ❶ waterwheel ❷ old-fashioned water-powered mechanical device ❸ watercart; water wagon ❹〈方言〉fire engine

水车前 shuǐchēqián *also* "龙舌草" lóngshécǎo century plant

水尘 shuǐchén water dust

水丞 shuǐchéng *also* "砚滴" yàndī tiny pot holding water on an ink slab

水成岩 shuǐchéngyán 〈地质〉aqueous rock; hydrogenic rock

水城 shuǐchéng city by or astride a river or by sea

水程 shuǐchéng journey by boat, water, river, etc.; voyage

水池 shuǐchí pond; pool; cistern

水池式反应堆 shuǐchíshì fǎnyìngduī 〈核物理〉aquarium reactor

水池子 shuǐchízi ❶ pond; pool; cistern ❷ sink

水尺 shuǐchǐ 〈水利〉water gauge

水处理 shuǐchǔlǐ 〈化学〉water treatment:～设备 water treatment facilities

水搋子 shuǐchuāizi plunger

水床 shuǐchuáng 〈医学〉hydrostatic bed; water bed

水锤 shuǐchuí water hammer:～泵 hydraulic ram

水蝽 shuǐchūn 〈动物〉water treader

水磁学 shuǐcíxué 〈物理〉hydromagnetism

水次 shuǐcì 〈书面〉waterside:亭临～ the pavillion is located by the river (*or* lake, etc.)

水葱 shuǐcōng *Scirpus tabernaemontani*

水淬 shuǐcuì water quenching or hardening

水淬钢 shuǐcuìgāng water-hardened steel

水淬碎玻璃 shuǐcuì suìbōli quenched cullet

水淬硬化 shuǐcuì yìnghuà 〈冶金〉water-hardening

水袋 shuǐdài water bag

水荡 shuǐdàng ❶ shallow lake ❷ pool; puddle:路上到处都是泛着黄泥浆的～。There are muddy puddles all along the road.

水到渠成 shuǐdào-qúchéng where water flows, a channel is formed — when conditions are ripe, success is assured:此事尚需时间，时间一到，自然～。It is only a matter of time. When the right time arrives, success is sure to come.

水道 shuǐdào ❶ water course:～变迁 shifting of waterways /～测量 hydrographic survey /省内～纵横。The province is crisscrossed with rivers and water courses. ❷ waterway; water route:走～去武汉 go to Wuhan by water ❸〈体育〉lane in a swimming pool:第三～ lane No. 3

水道学 shuǐdàoxué hydrography

水稻 shuǐdào paddy (rice); rice:～秧田 rice seedling bed /我国南方盛产～。Southern China abounds in rice.

水稻插秧机 shuǐdào chāyāngjī rice or paddy transplanter

水稻二化螟 shuǐdào èrhuàmíng 〈动物〉rice-stem borer (*Chilo suppressalis*)

水稻土 shuǐdàotǔ rice or paddy soil

水稻象鼻虫 shuǐdào xiàngbíchóng rice or water weevil

水滴石穿 shuǐdī-shíchuān *also* "滴水穿石" dripping water wears through rock; constant effort brings success; little strokes fell great oaks

水底电缆 shuǐdǐ diànlǎn submarine cable; subaqueous cable

水底生物 shuǐdǐ shēngwù benthon; benthos

水底隧道 shuǐdǐ suìdào underwater tunnel

水地 shuǐdì ❶ *also* "水浇地" irrigated land ❷ paddy field

水电 shuǐdiàn ❶ water and electricity:～供应 water and electricity supply /楼内～设备齐全。The building is well equipped with water and electricity facilities. ❷ hydropower; hydroelectricity:～资源 hydroelectric resources

水电费 shuǐdiànfèi charges for water and electricity

水电站 shuǐdiànzhàn hydroelectric (power) station; hydropower station

水淀 shuǐdiàn shallow lake

水殿 shuǐdiàn ❶ palace or hall overlooking water ❷ emperor's pleasure-boat

水貂 shuǐdiāo 〈动物〉mink:～皮帽 mink fur cap

水斗 shuǐdǒu ❶ *also*"水斗子" wicker or rattan basket used for fetching water ❷ funnel-shaped part at the top of a rain pipe or downspout

水豆腐 shuǐdòufu 〈方言〉very soft beancurd (usually kept in water)

水痘 shuǐdòu 〈医学〉varicella; chicken pox:出～ contract chicken pox

see also"水花❷"

水碓 shuǐduì water-powered trip-hammer (for husking rice)

水盾草 shuǐdùncǎo fanwort; water shield

水遁 shuǐdùn escape by water

水发 shuǐfā (of food) water saturated:～青豆 water-saturated green peas /～玉兰片 slices of water-saturated bamboo shoots

水法 shuǐfǎ water law

水饭 shuǐfàn ❶ porridge made of cooked rice and water or soup:小米绿豆～ porridge of cooked millet with mung beans ❷〈旧语〉porridge; gruel

水飞蓟 shuǐfēijì 〈植物〉milk thistle (*Silybum marianum*)

水肥 shuǐféi manure of fermented night-soil with water added

水肺 shuǐfèi aqualung

水粉 shuǐfěn ❶ a kind of cosmetic ❷〈方言〉soaked noodles made from beans or sweet potatoes

水粉画 shuǐfěnhuà 〈美术〉gouache:擅长～ be good at gouache painting

水分 shuǐfèn ❶ moisture content:～充足 adequate moisture ❷ exaggeration; overstatement:这个话里有～。The remark must be taken with a grain of salt. /他们的统计材料不实,～很大。Their statistics were not reliable, for they were much overblown.

水风琴 shuǐfēngqín hydraulis

水封 shuǐfēng water seal; liquid seal:～储气器 water sealed gas holder

水浮莲 shuǐfúlián 〈植物〉water lettuce; water cabbage

水蝮蛇 shuǐfùshé 〈动物〉water mocassin; cottonmouth (*Agkistrodon piscivorus*)

水疙瘩 shuǐgēda pickled or salted rutabaga

水阁 shuǐgé waterside pavillion

水工 shuǐgōng (short for 水利工程) irrigation works; water conservancy project or works

水工建筑 shuǐgōng jiànzhù hydraulic structure

水工学 shuǐgōngxué hydraulic engineering

水沟 shuǐgōu ditch; drain; gutter:挖～ dig a ditch

水垢 shuǐgòu scale; incrustation:除去暖水瓶里的～ scour out a flask /～净化器 scaler

水鸪鸪 shuǐgūgū 〈口语〉wood-pigeon

水臌 shuǐgǔ 〈中医〉ascites

水关 shuǐguān ❶ drainhole at base of a city wall, etc. ❷ water gate

水管 shuǐguǎn ❶ waterpipe:热～ hot-water pipe /～式锅炉 tubulous boiler; water tube boiler /～堵塞。The waterpipe gets clogged. ❷〈生理〉aqueduct

水龟 shuǐguī terrapin; *Clemmys mutica*

水龟虫 shuǐguīchóng water scavenger beetle

水柜 shuǐguì ❶ water tank:机车～ water tank in the locomotive ❷〈方言〉reservoir; cistern ❸〈旧语〉shop counter

水锅 shuǐguō boiler

水锅炉反应堆 shuǐguōlú fǎnyìngduī 〈核物理〉water-boiler reactor

水国 shuǐguó 〈书面〉area crisscrossed with rivers and dotted by lakes; watery region

水果 shuǐguǒ fruit:～蛋糕 fruit cake /此地盛产～。The place produces plenty of fruits.

水果罐头 shuǐguǒ guàntou tinned or canned fruit

水果鸡尾酒 shuǐguǒ jīwěijiǔ fruit cocktail

水果软糖 shuǐguǒ ruǎntáng fruit jelly

水果糖 shuǐguǒtáng fruit drops

水害 shuǐhài flood; flood disaster

水旱 shuǐ-hàn ❶ flood and drought:旧社会人民遇到～的年头儿四处逃荒。In the old society people had to flee from famine in times of flood and drought. ❷ water and land:～码头 centre for transport by land and by water

水合 shuǐhé *also*"水化"〈化学〉hydration

水合水 shuǐhéshuǐ hydrate water

水合物 shuǐhéwù hydrate

水合运动 shuǐhé yùndòng hydration movement

水鹤 shuǐhè water crane (a railroad device that supplies water for steam locomotives)

水红 shuǐhóng bright pink; cerise:～色的连衣裙 bright pink blouse

水喉 shuǐhóu 〈方言〉(water) tap; faucet

水壶 shuǐhú ❶ kettle ❷ canteen ❸ watering can

水葫芦 shuǐhúlu 〈植物〉water hyacinth

水浒传 Shuǐhǔzhuàn *Heroes of the Marshes* or *Water Margin*, a Chinese novel of the early Ming Dynasty by Shi Nai'an (施耐庵)

水花 shuǐhuā ❶ water spray; foam; froth:汽艇划破平静的湖面,船头闪着一团团晶莹的～。The motorboat sped across the tranquil lake, throwing up glittering foam round its bow. ❷〈方言〉varicella; chicken pox; water pox:出～ have chicken pox

水华 shuǐhuá water bloom; marine bloom

水化 shuǐhuà hydration; aquation

水化酶 shuǐhuàméi hydrase

水化物 shuǐhuàwù 〈化学〉hydrate

水化氧化物 shuǐhuà yǎnghuàwù hydrated oxide

水桦 shuǐhuà river birch; red birch; water birch (*Betula nigra*)

水患 shuǐhuàn flood; inundation:连年～ be flooded for years

水荒 shuǐhuāng shortage of water or water supply

水会 shuǐhuì 〈旧语〉nongovernmental fire-fighting organization; volunteer fire brigade

水火 shuǐhuǒ ❶ fire and water — two things diametrically opposed to each other; mutual contrariety:势如～ mutual antagonism ❷ extreme misery:救民于～之中 save the people from the abyss of misery ❸ (often used in the early vernacular) human excrement

水火不相容 shuǐhuǒ bù xiāng róng be absolutely irreconcilable as fire and water:两种观点～,不可调和。The two views are diametrically opposed to each other and can not be reconciled.

水火地 shuǐhuǒdì disaster-ridden land; land affected by either flood or drought

水火棍 shuǐhuǒgùn 〈旧语〉club used by *yamen* runners (painted red at one end and black at the other)

水火无交 shuǐhuǒ-wújiāo (of an official) honest and incorruptible

see also"水米无交"

水火无情 shuǐhuǒ-wúqíng floods and fires are inexorable

水货 shuǐhuò smuggled goods:由香港转口而来的～ goods smuggled in via Hong Kong

水鸡 shuǐjī ❶ aquatic bird; water bird ❷ frog ❸ *also*"水鸡子"〈方言〉like a drenched chicken; soaked through; drenched and bedraggled:雨不停地下,大家淋得～儿似的。The rain fell without letup and everyone was soaked through and through.

水碱 shuǐjiǎn scale; incrustation; thermonatrite

水浆 shuǐjiāng soup; drinks:病人已经～不进。The patient can no longer take even soup or water.

水饺 shuǐjiǎo boiled dumplings

水脚 shuǐjiǎo 〈方言〉cost of water transport

水窖 shuǐjiào water cellar or pit (usually built in arid areas or places where the water tastes bitter on China's loess plateau)

水解 shuǐjiě 〈化学〉hydrolysis:这东西不能～。These substances cannot resolve in water.

水解产物 shuǐjiě chǎnwù hydrolysate

水解蛋白 shuǐjiě dànbái 〈药学〉protein hydrolysate

水解酶 shuǐjiěméi hydrolase

水解器 shuǐjiěqì hydrolyzer

水解质 shuǐjiězhì hydrolyte

水津津 shuǐjīnjīn damp with perspiration or moisture:他浑身是汗,～的。He was damp all over with sweat.

水经注 Shuǐjīngzhù *Commentary on the Waterways*, a classic work of geography written by Li Daoyuan (郦道元) of the Northern Wei Dynasty (386-534)

水晶 shuǐjīng crystal; rock crystal; quartz:～镜片 crystal lens

水晶包 shuǐjīngbāo steamed dumpling stuffed with lard and sugar

水晶玻璃 shuǐjīng bōli crystal (glass)

水晶灯笼 shuǐjīng dēnglong (of people) very shrewd and discerning

水晶宫 shuǐjīnggōng Crystal Palace (of the Dragon King)
水晶棺 shuǐjīngguān crystal sarcophagus
水晶兰 shuǐjīnglán Indian pipe; pinesap; corpse plant; fitroot; fit plant; *Monotropa uniflora*
水晶体 shuǐjīngtǐ 〈生理〉 crystalline lens
水井 shuǐjǐng water well
水景 shuǐjǐng water scene:这几处喷泉不仅是优美的~，而且还能改变局部地区的小气候。These fountains not only make beautiful water scenery but can also improve the weather in the locality.
水警 shuǐjǐng police in charge of public order on rivers, etc.; water police
水韭 shuǐjiǔ quillwort
水酒 shuǐjiǔ watery wine (said modestly by a host of his own wine):喝一杯~ drink a glass of wine
水军 shuǐjūn 〈旧语〉 waterborne troops
水客 shuǐkè 〈旧语〉 ❶ boatman ❷ merchant who travels to obtain shop supplies and act as messenger for other people
水坑 shuǐkēng puddle; pool; water hole:大雨过后，路上到处是~。The downpour left lots of puddles in the road.
水寇 shuǐkòu robbers and bandits haunting rivers and lakes
水库 shuǐkù reservoir:修~ build a reservoir / ~容量 reservoir capacity / ~养鱼 fish culture in reservoir
水裤 shuǐkù waders
水牢 shuǐláo water dungeon:私设~ set up an illegal water dungeon
水老鸹 shuǐlǎogua *also* "水老鸦" 〈方言〉〈动物〉 cormorant
水涝 shuǐlào waterlogging
水涝地 shuǐlàodì waterlogged land
水雷 shuǐléi 〈军事〉 (submarine) mine:敷设~ submarine mining / ~密布的水域 heavily mined waters / ~区 submarine mine zone / ~舰 mine vessel / ~清扫 mine dragging; mine sweeping
水冷 shuǐlěng water-cooling:~系统 water-cooling system / ~式发动机 water-cooled engine / ~堆 〈核物理〉 water-cooled reactor / ~器 hydrocooler; water chiller
水礼 shuǐlǐ gifts of fruit and sweets
水力 shuǐlì waterpower; hydraulic power:~充填 〈矿业〉 hydraulic mine filling; hydraulic filling / ~冲挖 hydraulic excavation; hydraulic extraction / ~运输 hydrotransport
水力发电 shuǐlì fādiàn hydroelectric generating
水力发电站 shuǐlì fādiànzhàn hydroelectric (power) station; hydropower station
水力发动机 shuǐlì fādòngjī water motor; water engine
水力井下泵 shuǐlì jǐngxiàbèng 〈石油〉 hydraulic bottom-hole pump
水力开采 shuǐlì kāicǎi hydraulicking; hydraulic mining
水力学 shuǐlìxué hydraulics
水力资源 shuǐlì zīyuán hydroelectric resources or potential; waterpower resources
水利 shuǐlì ❶ water conservancy:改进~设施 improve water conservancy facilities ❷ irrigation works; water conservancy project
水利部 shuǐlìbù ministry of water resources
水利工程 shuǐlì gōngchéng irrigation works; water conservancy project or works
水利工程学 shuǐlì gōngchéngxué hydraulic engineering
水利灌溉网 shuǐlì guàngàiwǎng irrigation network
水利化 shuǐlìhuà build irrigation works on a vast scale; bring all farmland under irrigation
水利建设 shuǐlì jiànshè construction or building of water control or conservancy projects
水利枢纽 shuǐlì shūniǔ 〈水利〉 key water control project
水利资源 shuǐlì zīyuán water resources
水帘 shuǐlián screen of water (as in waterfall); cascade:密密的~挡住了人们的视线。A thick screen of water blocks everything out of sight.
水量 shuǐliàng ❶ flow or volume of water:~越多，推动水轮机的力量越大。The bigger the flow and volume of water, the greater the force to propel the water turbine. ❷ 〈方言〉 swimming skill:她~不好。she is a poor swimmer.
水疗 shuǐliáo 〈医学〉 hydrotherapy; hydropathy:~疗养院 hydropathic establishment; hydropathic
水疗法 shuǐliáofǎ hydrotherapy
水淋淋 shuǐlīnlīn dripping with water:他爬上岸来，浑身~的。He climbed ashore dripping with water.
水羚 shuǐlíng waterbuck; kob
水灵 shuǐling 〈方言〉 ❶ (of fruit, greens, etc.) fresh and juicy:这梨~清甜。The pear is juicy and sweet. ❷ (of appearance) bright and beautiful; spirited and pretty:一双眼睛又大又~ a pair of big, bright and beautiful eyes
水流 shuǐliú ❶ rivers; streams; waters:湖南省有湘、资、沅、澧四大~。There are four major rivers in Hunan Province, namely the Xiang, Zi, Yuan and Li. ❷ current; course; flow:~湍急 swift flow; torrent / ~平缓 slow and steady flow / ~量 water flow
水流花谢 shuǐliú-huāxiè water has flown and flowers have withered — deserted scene; irrevocable decline
水流星 shuǐliúxīng 〈杂技〉 spinning bowls of water; water meteors
水榴石 shuǐliúshí hydrogarnet
水溜 shuǐliù 〈建筑〉 eaves gutter
水龙 shuǐlóng ❶ 〈植物〉 *Jussiaea repens* ❷ fire hose; hose
水龙带 shuǐlóngdài hose
水龙骨 shuǐlónggǔ 〈植物〉 wall fern; golden locks
水龙卷 shuǐlóngjuǎn 〈气象〉 waterspout
水龙头 shuǐlóngtóu (water) tap; faucet; spigot; bibcock:开(关)~ turn on (off) the tap / 别让~开着白流。Don't leave the water faucet running.
水漉漉 shuǐlūlū *also* "水渌渌" wet; moist; damp:这孩子像是刚哭过，眼眶里~的。The child must have just wept as his eyes are still wet.
水陆 shuǐ-lù ❶ land and water:~并进 advance by both land and water; combined attack by army and navy ❷ delicacies from land and sea:~俱陈 provide with dainties of every kind
水陆交通线 shuǐ-lù jiāotōngxiàn land and water communication lines
水陆联运 shuǐ-lù liányùn water-land transshipment: ~车 flexivan
水陆联运码头 shuǐ-lù liányùn mǎtou dock for joint land and water transport service
水陆两用 shuǐ-lù liǎngyòng amphibious
水陆两用车 shuǐ-lù liǎngyòngchē amphibian
水陆两用船 shuǐ-lù liǎngyòngchuán alligator
水陆两用飞机 shuǐ-lù liǎngyòng fēijī amphibious aircraft
水陆两用履带装甲车 shuǐ-lù liǎngyòng lǚdài zhuāngjiǎchē 〈军事〉 amtrack
水陆汽车 shuǐ-lù qìchē 〈交通〉 amphibious automobile; amphicar
水陆坦克 shuǐ-lù tǎnkè amphibious tank
水陆运输 shuǐ-lù yùnshū transport by water and land
水鹿 shuǐlù *also* "马鹿" mǎlù; "麖" jīng sambar; *Cervus unicolour*
水路 shuǐlù waterway; water route:由上海到大连走~更方便。It's more convenient to travel from Shanghai to Dalian by water.
水铝矿 shuǐlǚkuàng 〈矿业〉 gibbsite
水绿 shuǐlǜ light green:~色的窗帘 light green curtain
水轮 shuǐlún waterwheel
水轮泵 shuǐlúnbèng (water) turbine pump:~站 (water) turbine-pump station
水轮发电机 shuǐlún fādiànjī water turbogenerator; hydrogenerator
水轮机 shuǐlúnjī hydraulic or water turbine
水落 shuǐluò 〈方言〉 eaves gutter
水落管 shuǐluòguǎn 〈建筑〉 downspout; downpipe; fallpipe; water-spout
水落归槽 shuǐluò-guīcáo the overflowing flood falls back into the river — a weight on one's mind has been removed:他听到这个好消息，心里才~，十分高兴。Hearing the good news, he was relieved of a burden on his mind and felt very happy.
水落石出 shuǐluò-shíchū when the water subsides the rocks emerge — the whole thing is out in the open; the truth is fully revealed:把案子查个~ get to the bottom of the case / 事情没~，决不罢休。We would not rest until the matter has been thoroughly cleared up.
水幔 shuǐmàn screen of water
水蟒 shuǐmǎng anaconda
水煤气 shuǐméiqì 〈化学〉 water gas
水霉 shuǐméi water mold; fish molds

水镁石 shuǐměishí brucite
水门 shuǐmén ❶ water valve ❷〈方言〉sluice gate; watergate
水门事件 Shuǐmén Shìjiàn (US) Watergate Affair (1972)
水门汀 shuǐméntīng 〈方言〉cement
水虻 shuǐméng 〈动物〉soldier fly; stratiomyiid
水锰矿 shuǐměngkuàng manganite
水米无交 shuǐmǐ-wújiāo never take even such simple things as rice and water from others — (of an official) be free from corruption; not associated with each other; having no contacts with each other:我与他～，毫不相干。I have no connection with him whatsoever.
水密 shuǐmì 〈机械〉watertight:～结合 watertight joint /～性 watertightness
水密舱 shuǐmìcāng watertight compartment
水蜜桃 shuǐmìtáo honey peach
水绵 shuǐmián 〈植物〉pond scum; spirogyra
水面 shuǐmiàn ❶ water surface:～跑道 fairway /～供气式潜水装置 hookah-type diving apparatus /～减压 surface decompression /～上漂着无数的落花。On the water floated numerous fallen flowers. ❷ water area; area of waters:我国可以养鱼的～很大。China has vast water areas suitable for fish breeding.
水面侦察雷达 shuǐmiàn zhēnchá léidá 〈军事〉anti-surface-vessel radar
水磨 shuǐmó polish with a waterstone:～砖的地面 floor paved with waterstone-polished tiles
see also shuǐmò
水磨工夫 shuǐmó gōngfu patient and meticulous work; painstaking effort:编纂词典要有～。The compilation of a dictionary requires conscientious work.
水磨石 shuǐmóshí 〈建筑〉terrazzo:～墙 terrazzo wall
水墨画 shuǐmòhuà 〈美术〉ink and wash; wash painting:～山水 mountains and rivers in wash painting /中国～ Chinese ink and wash
水磨 shuǐmò ❶ watermill:一扇大～ a big watermill ❷ grind grain, etc. fine while adding water:～年糕 New Year cake made from finely ground glutinous rice flour
see also shuǐmó
水母 shuǐmǔ 〈动物〉jellyfish; medusa
水木清华 shuǐmù-qīnghuá secluded and beautiful garden with woods, flowers and ponds; quiet and beautiful scenery:这座花园～，入内如置身江南胜地。Once inside the beautiful garden, one feels as if at a scenic spot south of the Yangtze River.
水囊 shuǐnáng water pocket; hyponome
水囊瘤 shuǐnángliú 〈医学〉hygroma
水囊肿 shuǐnángzhǒng 〈医学〉hydrocele
水能 shuǐnéng hydroenergy
水能载舟,亦能覆舟 shuǐ néng zài zhōu, yì néng fù zhōu *also* "载舟覆舟" zàizhōu-fùzhōu while the waters can keep a boat afloat, they can also overturn it — a warning to the ruler to pay attention to popular feelings
水泥 shuǐní cement:高标号～ high-quality cement /加气～ air-entrained cement /矿渣～ blast-furnace cement; blast furnace slag cement /～地 cement floor /～墙 cement wall /～路 concrete road /～库 cement bunker
水泥泵 shuǐníbèng cement pump
水泥标号 shuǐní biāohào cement mark; cement grade; strength of cement
水泥厂 shuǐníchǎng cement plant
水泥船 shuǐníchuán concrete boat; plastered boat; concrete ship
水泥钉 shuǐnídīng steel nails for use on a cement wall; cement nail
水泥喷枪 shuǐní pēnqiāng concrete gun
水泥瓦 shuǐníwǎ cement tile
水泥研磨机 shuǐní yánmójī cement mill
水泥窑 shuǐníyáo cement kiln
水泥砖 shuǐnízhuān cement brick
水碾 shuǐniǎn water-powered roller (for grinding grain)
水鸟 shuǐniǎo aquatic bird; water bird:～飞翔在湖面上。Water birds are flying over the lake.
水牛 shuǐniú (water) buffalo
水牛果 shuǐniúguǒ buffalo berry; rabbit berry (*Shepherdia argentea*)
水牛儿 shuǐniúr 〈方言〉snail
水暖 shuǐnuǎn ❶ device of heating by radiator ❷ general term for tap water and heating facilities:～设备 tap water and heating facilities
水暖工 shuǐnuǎngōng plumber:他在学校当～。He works as a plumber in the school.
水沤 shuǐ'ōu bubbles on surface of water
水排 shuǐpái 〈冶金〉〈古语〉instrument to start bellows with hydropower
水牌 shuǐpái board for erasable account entry in a shop
水泡子 shuǐpàozi 〈方言〉small lake
水疱 shuǐpào blister:手上烫了个～。Several blisters emerged on the hand from scalding. /～化脓了。The blister is festering.
水疱疹 shuǐpàozhěn vesicular exanthema
水培法 shuǐpéifǎ aquaculture; hydroponics
水皮儿 shuǐpír 〈方言〉surface of water:茶叶漂在～上。The tea leaves are floating on the water.
水漂儿 shuǐpiāor ducks and drakes:打～ play ducks and drakes
水漂生物 shuǐpiāo shēngwù pleuston
水瓢 shuǐpiáo (gourd) water ladle:一把木制的～ a wooden water ladle /用葫芦当～ use a bottle gourd as water ladle /把竹筒做成～ make a water ladle from a bamboo tube
水平 shuǐpíng ❶ horizontal; level:～方向 horizontal orientation /～梯田 level terraced field; level terrace /～距离 horizontal distance ❷ standard; level:生活～ standard of living; living standard /文化～ education level; cultural level /业务～ professional standard /提高对环保的认识～ enhance one's awareness of environmental protection /提高管理～ improve one's art of management /～高 high calibre
水平差 shuǐpíngchā 〈地理〉inclination
水平等高线 shuǐpíng děnggāoxiàn 〈地理〉contours of water table
水平飞行 shuǐpíng fēixíng horizontal or level flight
水平沟 shuǐpínggōu horizontal ditch
水平轰炸 shuǐpíng hōngzhà 〈军事〉horizontal or level bombing
水平洄游 shuǐpíng huíyóu horizontal migration
水平角 shuǐpíngjiǎo horizontal angle
水平贸易 shuǐpíng màoyì 〈经济〉horizontal trade
水平面 shuǐpíngmiàn ❶ water level ❷ horizontal plane; level (surface)
水平起飞 shuǐpíng qǐfēi horizontal take-off (HTO)
水平扫描 shuǐpíng sǎomiáo horizontal scanning
水平线 shuǐpíngxiàn horizontal line; level line
水平仪 shuǐpíngyí level; levelling instrument
水苹 shuǐpíng 〈植物〉duckweed
水泼不进,针插不进 shuǐ pō bù jìn, zhēn chā bù jìn watertight and impenetrable:～的独立王国 independent kingdom that seals itself off entirely from the outside — region or department that refuses to obey the central authority
水芪草 shuǐqícǎo water milfoil
水气胸 shuǐqìxiōng hydropneumothorax; pneumohydrothorax
水汽 shuǐqì vapour; steam; moisture
水枪 shuǐqiāng ❶〈矿业〉giant; monitor; nozzle; water pistol ❷ fire-fighting device
水橇 shuǐqiāo *also* "滑水橇" huáshuǐqiāo water ski
水橇运动 shuǐqiāo yùndòng water skiing
水芹 shuǐqín 〈植物〉water parsnip; *Oenanthe javanica*
水禽 shuǐqín 〈动物〉waterfowl; water bird; aquatic bird
水青冈 shuǐqīnggāng *also* "山毛榉" shānmáojǔ 〈植物〉beech (*Fagus longepetiolata*)
水青树 shuǐqīngshù beech
水情 shuǐqíng 〈水利〉regimen:观察～ regimen observation
水球 shuǐqiú 〈体育〉water polo:～比赛 water polo match /打～ play water polo
水曲柳 shuǐqūliǔ 〈植物〉northeast China ash; Manchurian ash
水渠 shuǐqú ditch; canal; water channel:开～ open a ditch /整治～ realignment of a canal
水圈 shuǐquān 〈地理〉hydrosphere
水溶胶 shuǐróngjiāo hydresol
水溶液 shuǐróngyè 〈化学〉aqueous solution
水乳交融 shuǐrǔ-jiāoróng well blended as milk and water — complete compatibility; perfect harmony:彼此～，情投意合。The relationship between them is one of perfect harmony and congeniality. /宾主谈得～。The talk between the host and guest is a meeting

of minds like milk mingling with water.
水软化 shuǐruǎnhuà 〈化工〉water softening
水色 shuǐsè water colour
水杉 shuǐshān 〈植物〉dawn redwood; metasequoia (*Metasequoia glyptostroboides*)
水上芭蕾 shuǐshàng bāléi 〈体育〉figure swimming
水上飞机 shuǐshàng fēijī seaplane; hydroplane
水上飞行 shuǐshàng fēixíng overwater flight
水上滑翔机 shuǐshàng huáxiángjī hydroglider
水上机场 shuǐshàng jīchǎng 〈航空〉seadrome
水上居民 shuǐshàng jūmín boat dwellers
水上旅馆 shuǐshàng lǚguǎn aquatel; floating hotel
水上运动 shuǐshàng yùndòng 〈体育〉aquatic sports; water sports: ～会 aquatic sports meet /开展～ go for aquatic sports
水上侦察机 shuǐshàng zhēnchájī scouting seaplane
水筲 shuǐshāo 〈方言〉(wooden or bamboo) water bucket
水蛇 shuǐshé water snake: ～星座〈天文〉Hydrus
水蛇腰 shuǐshéyāo very slender waist
水深火热 shuǐshēn-huǒrè deep water and scorching fire — abyss of suffering; extreme misery; dire distress: 人民陷于～之中。The people were trapped in an abyss of misery. /内战使全国人民处于～的境地。The civil war has plunged the whole nation into the depths of suffering.
水深计 shuǐshēnjì fathometer
水生动物 shuǐshēng dòngwù aquatic animal
水生根 shuǐshēnggēn water root
水生甲虫 shuǐshēng jiǎchóng water beetle
水生平原 shuǐshēng píngyuán 〈地理〉aquiprata
水生生物 shuǐshēng shēngwù aquatic; aquatic life; hydrobois
水生学 shuǐshēngxué hydrobiology
水生植物 shuǐshēng zhíwù water or aquatic plant; hydrophyte: ～群系 aquatic formation (*or* vegetation)
水声学 shuǐshēngxué 〈物理〉marine acoustics
水声遥测 shuǐshēng yáocè underwater acoustic telemetry
水师 shuǐshī 〈旧语〉navy: 北洋～ Northern Navy /～提督〈旧语〉commander-in-chief of the navy
水虱 shuǐshī 〈动物〉beach louse; bosmina
水蚀 shuǐshí 〈矿业〉aquatic erosion
水势 shuǐshì flow of water; rise and fall of floodwater: ～汹涌 turbulent flow of water /上流～趋缓。The flood on the upper reaches of the river was abating (*or* subsiding).
水手 shuǐshǒu seaman; sailor: 老～ old sailor
水手长 shuǐshǒuzhǎng boatswain
水鼠 shuǐshǔ water rat
水刷石 shuǐshuāshí 〈建筑〉granitic plaster
水松 shuǐsōng 〈植物〉China cypress (*Glyptostrobus pensilis*)
水损 shuǐsǔn damage by water
水塔 shuǐtǎ water tower: 高耸的～ water tower standing tall and erect
水獭 shuǐtǎ 〈动物〉otter
水獭呢 shuǐtǎní 〈纺织〉beaver cloth
水潭 shuǐtán puddle; pool: 深～ deep pool
水塘 shuǐtáng pool; pond: 早已干涸的～ long dried-up pond /荷花盛开的～ pond covered with lotus in full bloom
水体 shuǐtǐ waters; body of water: ～污染 water-body pollution
水天一色 shuǐtiān-yīsè the water and the sky blend into one colour (said of great stretches of water): 那洞庭湖真个波涛万顷，～。The Dongting Lake is a vast expanse of water, which merges with the horizon far beyond.
水田 shuǐtián paddy field: 扩大～面积 enlarge the paddy field
水田耙 shuǐtiánbà paddy field harrow
水田芥 shuǐtiánjiè water cress (*Nasturtium officinale*)
水田犁 shuǐtiánlí paddy field plough
水汀 shuǐtīng 〈方言〉steam; central heating
水听器 shuǐtīngqì hydrophone
水桶 shuǐtǒng pail; bucket: 一担～ two buckets (carried on a shoulder pole)
水头 shuǐtóu ❶〈水利〉head; water head: ～落差 head fall ❷ flood peak; peak of flow: 打了一口～很旺的井。Dig a well with a high peak of flow.
水土 shuǐtǔ ❶ water and soil: 森林能保持～。Forests can preserve water and soil. ❷ natural environment and climate: 一方～养一方人。Man is conditioned by the natural environment he lives in.
水土保持 shuǐtǔ bǎochí 〈农业〉conserve water and top soil: 注意～的工作 lay emphasis on water and soil conservation
水土不服 shuǐtǔ bùfú not accustomed to the environment and climate of a new place; not acclimatized or acclimated: 这病起自～。The ailment stems from lack of acclimatization.
水土流失 shuǐtǔ liúshī soil erosion: 防止～ prevent the soil from eroding away
水团 shuǐtuán water mass
水豚 shuǐtún capybara; water hog (*Hydrochoerus*)
水洼 shuǐwā puddle; charco; water hole
水湾 shuǐwān arm; bay
水汪 shuǐwāng 〈方言〉*also* “水汪子” water pit
水汪汪 shuǐwāngwāng ❶ (of land, field, etc.) covered with water; wet through ❷ (of children's or young women's eyes) clear and intelligent: 一对～的大眼睛 a pair of clear and intelligent eyes
水网 shuǐwǎng network of rivers
水位 shuǐwèi ❶ water level: 高～ high water level /确定～ ascertain the water level /超过警戒～ be over and above the flood-warning level /～线 waterline ❷ water table; groundwater level
水位报警器 shuǐwèi bàojǐngqì 〈水利〉high and low water alarm
水位计 shuǐwèijì fluviograph
水文 shuǐwén hydrology: ～调查 hydrologic survey /～工作者 hydrologist /～设计 hydrologic design /～资料 hydrological data
水文地理学 shuǐwén dìlǐxué hydrography
水文地质学 shuǐwén dìzhìxué hydrogeology; geohydrology
水文队 shuǐwénduì hydrological team
水文年鉴 shuǐwén niánjiàn hydraulic yearbook
水文气象学 shuǐwén qìxiàngxué hydrometeorology
水文图 shuǐwéntú hydrograph; hydrographic chart or map
水文学 shuǐwénxué hydrology; hydrography
水文预报 shuǐwén yùbào hydrologic forecast
水文站 shuǐwénzhàn hydrometric station; hydrologic station
水污染 shuǐwūrǎn water pollution or contamination
水雾 shuǐwù spray
水螅 shuǐxī 〈动物〉hydra
水洗 shuǐxǐ washing; rinsing
水洗布 shuǐxǐbù washed cloth; washed denim: ～牛仔裤 washed jeans
水洗牢度 shuǐxǐ láodù 〈纺织〉wash fastness
水系 shuǐxì river system; hydrographic net: 长江～ Yangtze River system /珠江～ Pearl River system
水下 shuǐxià underwater; undersea: ～作业 underwater operation /～岸坡 offshore slope
水下爆炸 shuǐxià bàozhà underwater explosion
水下弹道学 shuǐxià dàndàoxué 〈军事〉hydroballistics
水下电视 shuǐxià diànshì underwater television
水下对空导弹 shuǐxià duìkōng dǎodàn underwater-to-air missile (UAM)
水下发射 shuǐxià fāshè underwater launching
水下焊接 shuǐxià hànjiē underwater welding
水下视觉 shuǐxià shìjué underwater vision
水下油井 shuǐxià yóujǐng 〈石油〉underwater well
水下远程导弹系统 shuǐxià yuǎnchéng dǎodàn xìtǒng underwater or undersea longrange missile system (ULMS)
水下照明 shuǐxià zhàomíng underwater lighting
水仙 shuǐxiān 〈植物〉narcissus
水险 shuǐxiǎn 〈经济〉marine insurance
水藓 shuǐxiǎn water moss; brook moss; fountain moss
水线 shuǐxiàn waterline: 超越～ surmount the waterline /低于～ below the waterline /高出～ above the waterline
水乡 shuǐxiāng region of rivers and lakes: 富饶美丽的～ beautiful and richly endowed region of rivers and lakes /从小生长在江南～ be brought up in the south of the lower reaches of the Yangtze River
水箱 shuǐxiāng water tank
水蝎 shuǐxiē water scorpion
水泻 shuǐxiè 〈医学〉watery diarrhoea: 他早上忽然～起来。He suddenly had watery diarrhoea in the morning.
水泄不通 shuǐxiè-bùtōng not even a drop of water could trickle through; be very crowded; be packed with people: 把守得～ tightly guarded /广场上挤得～。The square is swarming with people.
水榭 shuǐxiè waterside pavilion: 幽静典雅的～ quiet and elegant

waterside pavilion
水星 Shuǐxīng 〈天文〉Mercury
水性 shuǐxìng ❶ skill in swimming: 精于～ good swimmer; be good at swimming ❷ depth, velocity of flow and other characteristics of a river, lake, etc.: 熟悉嘉陵江的～ be familiar with the characteristics of Jialing River in terms of its depth, currents, etc.
水性涂料 shuǐxìng túliào 〈化工〉 water-based paint; water-thinned paint; water-dilutible paint
水性杨花 shuǐxìng-yánghuā (of women) fickle and lascivious; of easy virtue; of loose morals
水秀 shuǐxiù (of appearance) bright and beautiful; radiant and vivacious: 小姑娘长得十分～。The little girl is pretty and vivacious.
水袖 shuǐxiù long white silk sleeves used in performance of classical Chinese operas and dances: 挥舞～ swing the long white silk sleeves
水锈 shuǐxiù ❶ scale; incrustation: 除去～ remove the scale ❷ water stain (in water vessels)
水选 shuǐxuǎn (of seeds or minerals) dressing by washing
水靴 shuǐxuē wellington (boots); rubber boots: 长筒～ high (leg) rubber boots
水循环 shuǐxúnhuán water circulation; water cycle
水压 shuǐyā hydraudic or water pressure: ～锻造 hydraulic forging /～太低,水上不去。The water is unable to go up because of low hydraulic pressure.
水压机 shuǐyājī hydropress
水压计 shuǐyājì hydraulic gauge
水鸭 shuǐyā teal
水涯 shuǐyá waterside
水烟 shuǐyān shredded tobacco for water pipes: 抽～ smoke a water pipe
水烟袋 shuǐyāndài *also* "水烟筒"; "水烟斗" water pipe
水烟筒 shuǐyāntǒng water pipe; hooka; hookah
水眼 shuǐyǎn ❶ mouth of a spring; spring ❷ 〈医学〉 hydrophthalmos
水杨 shuǐyáng 〈植物〉bigcatkin willow
水杨醇 shuǐyángchún 〈化学〉salicyl alcohol; orthohydroxybenzyl alcohol
水杨柳 shuǐyángliǔ bigcatkin willow
水杨梅 shuǐyángméi avens
水杨酸 shuǐyángsuān 〈化学〉salicylic acid
水杨酸钠 shuǐyángsuānnà sodium salicylate
水杨盐 shuǐyángyán salicylate
水杨中毒 shuǐyáng zhòngdú 〈医学〉salicylism
水样 shuǐyàng water sample
水舀子 shuǐyǎozi ladle; dipper; scoop
水冶 shuǐyě 〈冶金〉hydro-metallurgy
水翼船 shuǐyìchuán hydrofoil craft; hydrofoil; jet foil
水银 shuǐyín 〈化学〉mercury; quicksilver
水银灯 shuǐyíndēng mercury-vapour lamp; mercury-arc lamp; mercury lamp
水银气压表 shuǐyín qìyābiǎo 〈气象〉 mercury or mercurial barometer
水银温度计 shuǐyín wēndùjì 〈气象〉mercury or mercurial thermometer
水银中毒 shuǐyín zhòngdú mercurial poisoning; mercurialism; hydrargyrism
水银柱 shuǐyínzhù mercury column
水印 shuǐyìn ❶〈美术〉watercolour block printing ❷ watermark: ～检验器 watermark detector ❸ water stain ❹〈方言〉〈旧语〉formal seal or stamp of a shop
水莹莹 shuǐyīngyīng *also* "水盈盈" clear and bright; radiant and velvety: 一双～的眼睛 a pair of radiant and velvety eyes
水有源,树有根 shuǐ yǒu yuán, shù yǒu gēn every river has its source and every tree its roots — nothing happens without a cause
水浴 shuǐyù water bath: ～疗法 hydrotherapy
水域 shuǐyù waters; water area; body or mass of water: 内陆～ inland waters /国际～ international body of water; international waters /～辽阔 vast expanse of water
水源 shuǐyuán ❶ source of a river; headwaters; waterhead: 高山冰川是长江、黄河等大河流的～。Glaciers in high mountains are headwaters of such large rivers as the Yangtze and Yellow River. ❷ source of water; water source: 这个大水库是本市的～。The big reservoir is the source of water supply to the city.
水运 shuǐyùn water transport: ～的物资 supplies transported by water /～网 water transport network /～部门 water transport authorities /～费 water transport fees; waterage
水运码头 shuǐyùn mǎtou port handling river or ocean cargo
水运仪象台 shuǐyùn yíxiàngtái water-driven astronomical clock tower, ancient Chinese astronomical instrument made in 1092 in the Northern Song Dynasty
水灾 shuǐzāi flood; inundation: ～的救援工作 flood-relief work /～面积 flood-stricken area /今年有不少地区发生～。Flood has hit quite a few regions this year.
水栽法 shuǐzāifǎ *also* "水栽培"〈农业〉water culture; hydroponics
水葬 shuǐzàng water burial: 按当地风俗进行～ give a water burial according to the local customs
水蚤 shuǐzǎo water flea
水藻 shuǐzǎo algae
水灶 shuǐzào 〈方言〉shop that sells hot and boiled water and tea
水泽 shuǐzé region with many rivers, lakes and swamp areas
水闸 shuǐzhá sluice; watergate: 开启～ lift the sluice /～另门 slacker
水战 shuǐzhàn fighting on the water: 在海面上发生了大规模的～。A large-scale battle took place on the sea.
水涨船高 shuǐzhǎng-chuángāo 〈俗语〉 when the river rises the boat goes up: 钞票发多了, 物价就上涨, ～嘛。Prices rise in proportion to currency in circulation, like boats going up with the level of the water. /随着文艺的普及, 群众的欣赏水平也～。The level of appreciation of the masses keeps improving with the popularization of literary arts.
水针疗法 shuǐzhēn liáofǎ 〈中医〉 acupuncture therapy with medicinal injection
水圳 shuǐzhèn 〈方言〉ditches in the fields
水蒸气 shuǐzhēngqì steam; water vapour
水至清则无鱼 shuǐ zhì qīng zé wú yú when the water is too clear there are no fish — one should not demand absolute purity: ～, 人至察则无徒。When the water is too clear, there are no fish; if a person is too critical, he has no friends.
水质 shuǐzhì water quality: ～优良 water of high quality /～化学 hydrochemistry /～卫生控制 water hygiene control
水质保护 shuǐzhì bǎohù 〈环保〉water quality protection: 采取～的措施 take measures to protect the water quality
水质监测 shuǐzhì jiāncè 〈环保〉water quality surveillance; water quality monitoring: ～船 water quality monitoring ship /～器 water monitor
水质污染 shuǐzhì wūrǎn water pollution or contamination: ～严重 serious water pollution /防止～ prevent the water from being polluted
水蛭 shuǐzhì leech: ～疗法 hirudinization /～吸血法 leeching
水蛭病 shuǐzhìbìng 〈医学〉hirudiniasis
水雉 shuǐzhì jacana; lily-trotter; lotus bird
水中捞月 shuǐzhōng-lāoyuè fish for the moon in the water — cry for the moon; make impractical or vain efforts: 你在这件事上花力气, 等于～。Your efforts on this matter are all in vain, like fishing for the moon in the water.
水中月,镜中花 shuǐ zhōng yuè, jìng zhōng huā *also* "水月镜花" moon in the water, flowers reflected in the mirror — sth. within sight but beyond reach; sth. unattainable; sth. unreal; illusion: 我当年的这些念头都成了～。All the ideas I toyed with then have proved chimerical.
水肿 shuǐzhǒng 〈医学〉oedema; dropsy: 出现～ have dropsy
水珠 shuǐzhū drop of water: 早晨菜叶上都挂着～。In the morning dew drops glisten on the vegetable leaves.
水珠子 shuǐzhūzi 〈口语〉drop of water: 落下几滴～。A few drops of water have fallen down.
水竹 shuǐzhú *also* "烟竹" yānzhú *Phyllostachys congesta*
水注 shuǐzhù tiny pot holding water for ink slab
水柱 shuǐzhù *also* "水柱子" water column; water sprout
水准 shuǐzhǔn ❶ horizontal plane; level (surface): ～测量 levelling ❷ level; standard: 文化～ standard of education; cultural level /生活～高于一般人 living standard that is above average
水准点 shuǐzhǔndiǎn bench mark
水准面 shuǐzhǔnmiàn level surface; level plane
水准器 shuǐzhǔnqì spirit level

S

水准仪 shuǐzhǔnyí surveyor's level; levelling instrument; gradienter
水渍 shuǐzì water stain
水渍险 shuǐzìxiǎn 〈经济〉with particular average (WPA)
水族 shuǐzú ❶ (Shuǐzú) Sui nationality, living mainly in Guizhou Province ❷ aquatic animals
水族馆 shuǐzúguǎn aquarium
水钻 shuǐzuàn diamond

shuì

说 shuì try to persuade or bring round: 游～ go around drumming up support for one's views; peddle an idea; canvass; lobby
see also shuō; yuè

帨 shuì ancient scarf that looks like today's handkerchief

税 shuì ❶ tax; duty; revenue: 营业～ business tax /所得～ income tax /版～ royalty (on books) /通过～ toll; transit fee /关～ customs duty; tariff /进口(出口)～ import (export) duty /累进～ progressive tax (*or* taxation) /印花～ stamp duty (*or* tax) /附加～ surtax; additional tax; supertax /捐～ taxes and levies /工商～ industrial and commercial taxes /人头～ capitation (*or* poll) tax /从价～ *ad valorem* tax /减～ tax abatement; tax mitigation /增值～ value added tax (VAT) /免～ tax exemption /交～ pay taxes /收～ collect taxes /抽～ levy a tax /偷～ evade taxes /漏～ evade payment of a tax; tax evasion /欠～ back taxes; arrears of taxes /退～ tax rebate; tax refund /补～ pay an overdue tax ❷ (Shuì) a surname
税单 shuìdān tax return; tax receipt
税额 shuì'é amount of tax to be paid: ～计算 computation of tax
税法 shuìfǎ tax law
税负 shuìfù tax burden: 减轻～ reduce tax burden
税赋 shuìfù tax liabilities; tax obligation
税关 shuìguān 〈口语〉customs
税基 shuìjī tax base
税金 shuìjīn tax dues
税捐 shuìjuān taxes and levies
税款 shuìkuǎn tax payment; taxation; tax: ～收入 tax revenue /～摊销 amortization of taxes /～调节 tax adjustment /～滞纳罚金 penalty tax /收到～一千元 have collected 1,000 *yuan* in taxes /补纳～一万元 pay an overdue tax of 10,000 *yuan*; pay a tax of 10,000 *yuan* that has been evaded
税利 shuì-lì tax and profit paid by enterprises to competent government authorities
税利分流 shuì-lì fēnliú separation of taxes and profits — a reform measure to enable enterprises to retain profits after paying taxes (instead of handing over all earnings to the state under the planned economy)
税率 shuìlǜ rate of taxation; tax rate; tariff rate: 按规定的～纳税 pay taxes at the regulated tax rate /～为百分之五 5% tax rate /～表 table of tax rates; tax table; tariff schedule
税目 shuìmù tax items; taxable items
税契 shuìqì 〈旧语〉title deed
税卡 shuìqiǎ 〈旧语〉check posts for taxation
税收 shuìshōu tax revenue: 工业的～ industrial tax revenue /～抵免 tax credit /～附加 tax surcharge /～减免 reduction and exemption of taxes /～漏洞 tax loophole /～特惠 tax privilege; tax preference /～支出 tax expenditure
税收政策 shuìshōu zhèngcè tax policy
税务 shuìwù taxation: ～代理人 tax agent /～当局 tax authority /～罚款 tax penalty /～管理 tax administration /～署 (US) Internal Revenue Service
税务庇护 shuìwù bìhù tax shelter
税务稽查员 shuìwù jīcháyuán inspector of taxes
税务局 shuìwùjú tax bureau: 北京～ Beijing Tax Bureau
税务员 shuìwùyuán tax collector; revenue agent: 当～ be a tax collector
税源 shuìyuán source of tax revenue
税印 shuìyìn tax seal
税则 shuìzé tax regulations: ～分类 classification of taxes /～委员会 tariff commission (*or* board)
税制 shuìzhì tax system; taxation: 累进～ progressive taxation /单一～ unitary tax system /复合～ compound tax system /～改革 tax reform /～修改 tax revision
税种 shuìzhǒng categories of taxes; items of taxation

睡 shuì sleep: ～着了 be (*or* fall) asleep /熟～ sleep soundly; sleep like a log /～过了 oversleep /午～ afternoon nap; nap after lunch; siesta /打瞌～ doze off; fall into a doze /鼾～ snore away soundly /早～早起 early to bed, early to rise /他习惯于晚～。He is used to going to bed late at night.
睡菜 shuìcài buckbean
睡袋 shuìdài sleeping bag: 鸭绒～ eiderdown sleeping bag; (duck's) down sleeping bag /躺在～里 lie inside a sleeping bag
睡虎子 shuìhǔzi 〈讽刺〉sleepyhead
睡觉 shuìjiào sleep: 披衣而～ sleep with one's clothes on /老想～ feel sleepy (*or* drowsy) all the time /昨晚没～。I stayed awake all last night.
睡裤 shuìkù sleeping pants; pyjama or pajama trousers
睡懒觉 shuì lǎnjiào get up late; sleep in
睡莲 shuìlián 〈植物〉water lily: 池中盛开着粉色和白色的～。Both pink and white water lilies are in full bloom on the pond.
睡帽 shuìmào nightcap
睡梦 shuìmèng sleep; slumber; dream: 一阵雷声把他从～中惊醒了。He was roused from sleep by a clap of thunder. /～中的情景依然历历在目。Flashes of his dream still leap up vividly in his mind.
睡眠 shuìmián sleep: ～剂 sleeping draught /～时间 sleeping time /～病 sleeping sickness /～过度 hypersomnia /～不足 insufficient sleep
睡眠疗法 shuìmián liáofǎ 〈医学〉physiological sleep therapy: 采用～ use physiological sleep therapy
睡魔 shuìmó 〈比喻〉strong desire to go to sleep; extreme drowsiness: 惊走～ wake up (from sleep) with a start /～袭来。Drowsiness came over me.
睡袍 shuìpáo nightgown
睡铺 shuìpù bed; sleeping berth; sleeper
睡容 shuìróng look sleepy; be sleepy-eyed: 惺忪～ eyes heavy with slumber; sleepy-eyed /半夜里值班人的脸上都现出～来。All those on night duty are sleepy-eyed.
睡鲨 shuìshā sleeper shark; Greenland shark (*Somniosus microcephalus*)
睡鼠 shuìshǔ dormouse; glirid
睡乡 shuìxiāng state of being asleep; dreamland: 很快进入～ be quick in falling asleep
睡相 shuìxiàng posture in sleep
睡鞋 shuìxié 〈旧语〉women's sleeping slippers (usually with soft-soles and red in colour)
睡醒 shuìxǐng wake up: 一觉～已经是早上八点钟了。I didn't wake up until 8 o'clock in the morning.
睡眼 shuìyǎn eyes heavy with slumber; sleepy-eyed
睡眼惺忪 shuìyǎn-xīngsōng sleepy-eyed; eyes heavy with sleep; eyes fogged with sleep: 他衣冠不整，～地走出屋来。Sloppily dressed, he walked out, eyes heavy with sleep.
睡衣 shuìyī night clothes; pyjamas; pajamas: 买了一件～ buy a pair of pyjamas /舒适的～ comfortable night clothes
睡椅 shuìyǐ deck or reclining chair; sling chair: 藤～ rattan deck chair
睡意 shuìyì sleepiness; drowsiness: 毫无～ not sleepy at all /～顿消。The sleepiness disappeared all of a sudden.

shǔn

楯 shǔn 〈书面〉railings; banisters; balustrade
see also dùn

吮 shǔn suck: ～乳 suck milk /吸～ suck; absorb
吮吸 shǔnxī suck: ～手指头 suck fingers /～老百姓的血汗 bleed the ordinary folks white /狮子贪婪地～猎物的血。The lion greedily sucked the blood of its prey.
吮痈舐痔 shǔnyōng-shìzhì suck the ulcers and piles of another

person — play the lickboot; practise sycophancy or servile flattery: 溜须拍马、～的小人 bootlicking sycophant
吮咂 shǔnzā suck:～血液 suck blood

shùn

舜 Shùn *also* "虞舜" Yúshùn Shun, name of a legendary sage monarch in ancient China
舜日尧年 Shùnrì-Yáonián time of peace and prosperity
瞬 shùn wink; twinkling:一～即逝 vanish in a flash /刹那间的沉寂～即被一阵钟声打破。In the twinkling of an eye, the silence was dispelled by the ringing of bells.
瞬变 shùnbiàn 〈无线电〉〈电工〉transient:～电阻 transient resistance /～压力 transient pressure /～反应 transient response /～波 transient wave /～电流 transient current /～特性分析器 transient analyser
瞬间 shùnjiān in the twinkling of an eye:一颗流星～即逝。A meteor disappeared in a flash.
瞬间需氧量 shùnjiān xūyǎngliàng immediate oxygen demand
瞬刻 shùnkè in a twinkling:～万变 undergoing a myriad of changes in the twinkling of an eye; fast-changing /～不停地转动 revolve without a moment's pause
瞬目 shùnmù blink (eyes); wink
瞬时 shùnshí ❶ shortly:～火光冲天。Flames shot skyward in a moment. ❷〈物理〉instant; instantaneous:～电流 instantaneous current
瞬时磁化 shùnshí cíhuà flash magnetization
瞬时电热水器 shùnshí diànrèshuǐqì instantaneous water heater
瞬时速度 shùnshí sùdù instantaneous velocity
瞬时性 shùnshíxìng instantaneity
瞬时值 shùnshízhí instantaneous value
瞬态 shùntài 〈物理〉transient; transient state:～电抗 transient reactance /～失真 transient distortion /～场 transient fields /～故障 transient fault
瞬息 shùnxī twinkling; in a flash:死寂的李宅，～间便恢复了生气。The deathly still Li house came back to life again in a flash.
瞬息万变 shùnxī-wànbiàn undergo a myriad of changes in an instant; change rapidly:山地的气候～。The climate in the mountains is changeable.
瞬载 shùnzài transient load
瞬子 shùnzǐ 〈物理〉instanton
顺 shùn ❶ in the same direction as; along with:～时针方向转动钥匙 turn a key clockwise / 气球～风飘来。The balloon came flying with the wind. /今天风～，船到得早。Sailing with the wind, today's boat arrived earlier than usual. ❷ along:～着马路朝前走 walk along the road /水～沟流。Water runs along the ditch. ❸ arrange; sort out:把头发～一～ smooth the hair /把卡车都～过来 bring the truck alongside ❹ act at one's convenience; take the opportunity:～嘴就说了出来 slip from one's mouth /～致最崇高的敬意。I avail myself of this opportunity to express (*or* renew) to you the assurances of my highest consideration. /～手关灯。Turn off the lights when you go out. ❺ suitable; agreeable:事情进行得不～意。Things did not turn out as he had wished. /文章读起来很～口。The essay reads smoothly. /这衣服看着～眼。The dress looks pleasing. ❻ in good luck; successfully:流年不～ unlucky year /事儿办得挺～。The matter was successfully handled. ❼ in sequence:～序入场 enter the hall one by one /比赛遇雨～延。The match will be postponed accordingly in case of rain. ❽ obey; yield to; submit to:归～ come over and pledge allegiance /孝～ show filial obedience to one's parents; be filial /对她百依百～ be docile and obedient to her; cater to her every wish /你怎么总～着他? How can you always do as he wishes? ❾ (Shùn) a surname
顺坝 shùnbà 〈水利〉longitudinal dike
顺变 shùnbiàn 〈书面〉accept or bow to the change:～节哀 face the untoward happening and restrain one's grief
顺便 shùnbiàn incidentally; in passing:～提醒大家一下 remind you by the way /～说一句 in passing; incidentally /你有空请～来一趟。Please come over at your convenience. *or* Drop in when you are free. /请你进城时～给我买支钢笔。Please buy a pen for me when you go to town if it doesn't give you too much trouble.
顺差 shùnchā favourable balance; surplus:外贸～ favourable balance of trade /国际收支～ favourable balance of payments; balance of payments surplus /变逆差为～ turn deficit to surplus
顺产 shùnchǎn 〈医学〉natural labour
顺畅 shùnchàng smooth; unhindered:水流～ smooth flow of water /念得非常～ read very smoothly /呼吸～ breathe easily /文笔～ facile style
顺磁 shùncí 〈物理〉paramagnetic:～共振 paramagnetic resonance /～体 paramagnet /～性 paramagnetism /～振子 paramagnon
顺次 shùncì in order; in proper sequence; successively:根据报名先后～安排 make arrangements one by one in order of entry /～应诊 see patients one after another /房间～编号。The rooms are serial-numbered.
顺从 shùncóng obey; comply with; yield to:～父母的意思 do as parents wish /～领导的愿望 comply with what the leaders want /～民心 fall in with the popular will /～地点头 nod obediently
顺带 shùndài incidentally; in passing:～捎点东西来。Bring something with you if it doesn't inconvenience you too much.
顺当 shùndang smoothly; harmoniously; without a hitch:事情办得很～。Things went smoothly.
顺导 shùndǎo guide sb. or steer sth. along the right track:他有了转变，就应加以～。We should help him on now that he has taken a turn for the better.
顺道 shùndào ❶ on the way:～拜访一位朋友 visit a friend when one is on his way to see somebody else ❷ direct route
顺丁橡胶 shùndīng xiàngjiāo 〈化工〉butadiene rubber; cis-polybutadiene
顺耳 shùn'ěr pleasing to the ear:爱听～的话 like to listen to what sounds pleasing
顺访 shùnfǎng visit on the way; visit conveniently; stop over:～北京 make a stopover visit to Beijing
顺风 shùnfēng get before the wind; have a favourable wind; have a tail wind:～扯篷 sail with the wind — take advantage of /一路上我骑自行车正好～。I cycled with the wind all the way. /祝你一路～。Have a pleasant journey. *or* Have a good trip. *or* Bon voyage.
顺风吹火 shùnfēng-chuīhuǒ *also* "因风吹火" yīnfēng-chuīhuǒ things done without much effort; work made easy by outside help; taking advantage of favourable conditions:这是～的事，何乐而不为。I was only too glad to do it, for I could take it in my stride.
顺风耳 shùnfēng'ěr ❶ person in traditional Chinese novels who can hear distant voices ❷ someone who is well informed:她可是我们机关里的～。She is a well informed person in our unit. ❸ old-fashioned megaphone or loudhailer
顺风转舵 shùnfēng-zhuǎnduò trim one's sails to the wind; take one's cue from changing conditions:这个人很善于～。The man is good at chopping around with the wind. *or* This one knows which way the wind blows. *or* The man is a weathercock.
顺服 shùnfú obey; submit; yield:她对父母历来～。She is always obedient to her parents.
顺竿儿爬 shùngānrpá chime in with sb. in order to please him; readily fall in with other people's wishes:"～"成了升官的秘诀。Chiming in sycophantly with one's superiors has become the best way to get promotion in officialdom.
顺光 shùnguāng 〈摄影〉frontlighting
顺和 shùnhe (of speech, attitude, etc.) smooth and comforting; affable:语气～ speak in a genial tone
顺脚 shùnjiǎo ❶ conveniently or without extra trouble; on the way:请～捎回来一点青菜。Bring back some fresh vegetables if it's not too much trouble for you. ❷ direct route
顺境 shùnjìng favourable circumstances:中年以后，渐入～。Things began to pick up when he passed middle age.
顺口 shùnkǒu ❶ read smoothly:改过的这段台词比原来～多了。The revised actor's lines read more smoothly than the previous ones. ❷ speak casually; say offhandedly:对这样重要的问题，他竟然不加思索～就答应了。He agreed on such an important matter without a second thought. /他很会说相声，～就能来一段。He is so good at comic-dialogue that he can make impromptu ones. ❸〈方言〉suit one's taste; be palatable:这个菜的味道很顺他的口儿。He likes the taste of the dish.
顺口搭音 shùnkǒu-dāyīn chime in with others; echo what others

say; readily agree：他不晓得说什么好，只好～应酬了几句。Not knowing what to say, he could only echo what others were saying in order to be polite.

顺口溜 shùnkǒuliū doggerel; jingle：他会编～。He can make up doggerel verse.

顺理成章 shùnlǐ-chéngzhāng (of a statement, argument, etc.) logical; coherent; well reasoned：这样做～，不必再考虑了。There's no need for further consideration because it is a matter of course.

顺利 shùnlì smoothly; favourably; successfully：～时要谨慎。In time of success, prudence is required. /谈判一开始就不～。The negotiation hit a snag at the very outset. /我们一行～地抵达西安。Our party arrived at Xi'an without a hitch.

顺溜 shùnliu 〈方言〉❶ in good order; tidy：几句外语说得非常～ speak a foreign language very fluently /头发梳得很～。The hair is neatly combed. /这篇文章写得很～。The essay is well organized. /屋里的东西摆得顺顺溜溜的。Everything in the room is in apple-pie order. ❷ smoothly; without a hitch：小两口生活美满，日子过得很～。The young couple enjoyed a happy life. /这次旅游一路都很～。Everything went smoothly during this tour. ❸ obedient; pliant：姐妹几个中就数她最～。She is the most compliant one among the several sisters.

顺路 shùnlù *also* "顺道儿"；"顺脚" ❶ on the way：你去城里买东西，可以～去看看妈妈。You may drop in at mum's on your way to the town for shopping. ❷ direct route：去百货大楼这么走～。This is the most direct route to the department store.

顺民 shùnmín 〈贬义〉〈旧语〉those who are docile and pledge allegiance to foreign invaders or submit to the authority of new rulers：典型的～ typical yes-man

顺气 shùnqì 〈口语〉(of state of mind, mood, etc.) happy; free from worry; satisfied：他真倒霉，一进城就碰上了一件不～的事。What bad luck he had! The moment he went downtown he came across something unpleasant.

顺情 shùnqíng reasonable; amenable to reason; conform to propriety：～顺理 in comformity with propriety and reason /～说好话 say nice things in accordance with propriety

顺势 shùnshì ❶ take advantage of an opening：他趁着人多，～溜进了剧场。He sneaked into the theatre through the crowd. ❷ conveniently：～买些生活用品 buy some daily necessities at one's convenience

顺势疗法 shùnshì liáofǎ 〈医学〉homoeopathy

顺适 shùnshì ❶ smoothly and satisfactorily：他们～地过着美满的生活。They lived a happy life free of all worries. /事情正如他料想的那么～。Things turned out to be quite satisfactory just as he had expected. ❷ conform to; comply with：他思想保守，不能～时代潮流。Being conservative in his views, he could hardly keep pace with the times.

顺手 shùnshǒu ❶ smoothly; easily; without difficulty：工作进行得很～。The work goes smoothly. /手续办得不够～。There has been some difficulty in going through formalities. ❷ without extra trouble：请～关灯。Please turn off the lights when you go out. /他～从书架上取下一本书递给我。He picked a book from the shelf and gave it to me. ❸ do sth. as a natural sequence; in passing：你擦完桌子，把桌上的文具～也收拾一下吧! After wiping the desk, please put the stationery there in order. ❹ handy; convenient and easy to handle：这网球拍使起来挺～。This tennis racket is very handy.

顺手牵羊 shùnshǒu-qiānyáng lead away a goat in passing — pick up sth. on the sly; walk off with sth.; take sth. by stealth; pilfer：从水果摊上他～地拿起一个苹果吃了起来。He just picked up an apple from the fruit stall and began to eat.

顺受 shùnshòu live with; tolerate; accept sth. as it is; submit to circumstances：逆来～ meekly submit to oppression, maltreatment, etc. /他对于这一切，只是默默在～着。He just put up with all this in silence.

顺水 shùnshuǐ downstream; with the current：～而下 go downstream /顺风～好行船。It's easy to sail with the wind and the stream (*or* to drift with the current).

顺水人情 shùnshuǐ-rénqíng favour done at little or no cost to oneself：做个～，把这些用不着的东西送人吧! As it costs you nothing, do him a favour and give him all these things you have no use for.

顺水推舟 shùnshuǐ-tuīzhōu push the boat along with the current — swim with the tide; go with the flow：这事他既已应允了，我也乐得～。He has already agreed to it, and I'm only too glad to follow suit.

顺遂 shùnsuì go satisfactorily; go smoothly：事事～ everything goes well

顺坦 shùntan 〈方言〉smoothly; successfully; without a hitch：他家的日子过得不～。Life has not always been easy for his family.

顺藤摸瓜 shùnténg-mōguā follow the vine to get the melon — track down sb. or sth. by following clues; hunt for sb. or sth. by following the traces：他们～，破获了一个盗窃团伙。Tracking down the culprit by the clues, they uncovered a ring of thieves.

顺我者昌，逆我者亡 shùnwǒzhě chāng, nìwǒzhě wáng those who submit will prosper; those who resist shall perish (usually said of the arbitrary, brutal rule of a tyrant)

顺铣 shùnxǐ 〈机械〉down milling or cutting; climb milling or cutting

顺心 shùnxīn happy; satisfactory：生活过得挺～ lead (*or* enjoy) a happy life /世上哪有那么多～事? How can everything be to your liking in this mundane world?

顺行 shùnxíng 〈天文〉posigrade (orbital motion in the same direction that the earth is moving from west to east)

顺序 shùnxù ❶ sequence; order：按安排好的～发言 speak in the arranged order /干什么事也得有个先后～。Everything must be done in sequence. ❷ in proper order; in turn; in succession：～上车 get on the bus in proper order /～自我介绍 introduce oneselves in turn

顺序处理 shùnxù chǔlǐ 〈自控〉sequential processing

顺序检索 shùnxù jiǎnsuǒ 〈自控〉sequential search

顺叙 shùnxù (of writing, films, etc.) arranged in chronological order or time sequence

顺驯 shùnxùn tame and docile

顺延 shùnyán postpone accordingly：演出时间因故～一天。The performance is postponed till tomorrow for some reason.

顺眼 shùnyǎn pleasing to the eye; pleasant to look at：这种服装看着挺～。This dress looks pleasing. /这人怪模怪样看着很不～。The odd appearance of the man is an eyesore (*or* is offensive to the eye).

顺意 shùnyì to one's liking; as one wishes; satisfactory：他遇到不～的事就好发火儿。He is apt to fly into a rage when something goes against his wishes.

顺应 shùnyìng follow; comply with; conform to：～时代潮流 conform to the trend of the times; keep up with the march of events /～民心 follow the wishes of the people /～大多数人的要求 comply with the majority will

顺证 shùnzhèng 〈中医〉serious case that improves steadily; favourable pathocondition

顺治 Shùnzhì Shunzhi, title of the reign (1644-1661) of Aisin Gioro Fulin (爱新觉罗·福临), 1st emperor of the Qing Dynasty after reunifying China, called reverently Qing Shizu (清世祖) after death

顺砖 shùnzhuān 〈建筑〉stretcher：～砌合 stretching bond; stretcher bond

顺嘴 shùnzuǐ ❶ read smoothly ❷ say offhandedly

shuō

说 shuō ❶ speak; talk; say：～得多做得少 much talk but little action; a giant in word but a dwarf in deed /你真会～笑话! You're joking! /我不会～日语。I can't speak Japanese. /有什么～什么。Speak out what's in your mind. /你～得有道理。You have a point there. /那未免～得太轻了。That's putting it too mildly. /他能～会道，我～不过他。I am no match for him as he is such a glib talker (*or* has such a clever tongue). /这回我们可～到一块儿了。For once we very well see eye to eye. ❷ give an explanation; explain：请他把道理～清楚。Ask him to state his reasons clearly. /～～你不去的理由。Please explain why you refused to go. /为什么非得这么做不可，得跟大家～一～。You have to tell us why it must be done this way. ❸ theory; views; doctrine：著书立～ write books to expound a theory /自圆其～ justify oneself /不拘泥于成～ break free of conventional wisdom (*or* ready theories) /日心～ heliocentric theory ❹ scold; criticise：他被母亲～了一顿。His mother gave him a good dressing-down (*or* talking-to). /把他～哭了。He was scolded into tears. ❺ act as go-between or matchmaker; introduce：～了个女朋友 be introduced to a girlfriend /她很小就～了婆家。She was engaged when she was a little girl. ❻ hint; indicate; refer to：他的话似乎～的是你。His

remarks seem to target on you. /这部电影的主题是～有志者事竟成。The theme of this film points to the moral that where there is a will, there is the way.
see also shuì; yuè

说白 shuōbái spoken parts in an opera:大段～ long speeches in an opera

说白了 shuōbáile put it bluntly; talk straight

说部 shuōbù 〈旧语〉 novels or books of anecdotes

说不得 shuōbude ❶ too shocking to say; unspeakable; unmentionable:这种话太难听，可～! These words sounded too rude (*or* offensive) and are taboo. ❷ not know how to put it; be scandalous:他的人品坏得～。He is a total scandal. ❸〈方言〉 have nothing to say; have to comply with:她坚持要单独去，我也～。Since she insisted on going alone, I had to agree.

说不定 shuōbudìng perhaps; maybe; possibly:～她早知道这事了。Maybe she was already aware of this. /～他不愿去了。Perhaps he is unwilling to go there.

说不过去 shuōbuguòqù cannot be justified or explained away; be unreasonable:这样好的单位，她还不满意，实在有点～了! She really has no excuse for being unsatisfied with such a good work unit.

说不来 shuōbulái ❶cannot see eye to eye (with sb.); cannot get along (with sb.):他们俩一向～。The two of them are never on good terms with each other. ❷〈方言〉 not know how to say it; be beneath one to say it:这种低三下四的话儿我～。It is beneath me to say such self-debasing things.

说不清 shuōbuqīng cannot explain sth. clearly:秀才碰到兵，有理～。When a scholar meets a soldier, it's no use arguing with the latter. *or* A scholor can't reason with a soldier.

说不上 shuōbushàng ❶ cannot say for sure:他是哪个学校毕业的，我可～。I can't tell for sure which school he graduated from. /这东西～是好是坏。I'm not sure whether it is good or bad. ❷ be not worth mentioning:我跟他认识，可～熟悉。I just have a nodding acquaintance with him.

说不下去 shuōbuxiàqù find it difficult to finish what one wants to say

说不着 shuōbuzháo ❶ not appropriate or necessary to mention:我根本不知道这件事儿，这些话你跟我～。I know nothing whatsoever about this. You are barking up the wrong tree. ❷ (conversation) disagreeable:他两个总闹别扭，～话。The two are always at odds with each other and can never speak without quarrelling.

说曹操曹操就到 shuō Cáo Cāo Cáo Cāo jiù dào mention Cao Cao and there he is — speak of the devil (and he is sure to appear):真是～，大家正在这儿夸你能干，你就来了。Just as the saying goes, talk of an angel and you will hear the fluttering of his wing. As we are praising your capabilities, you come on the scene.

说长道短 shuōcháng-dàoduǎn comment on other people's merits and demerits; gossip:我才不怕别人～呢! I simply don't care about what others say behind my back!

说唱 shuōchàng genre of popular entertainment consisting mainly of talking and singing such as comic dialogue, etc.

说唱文学 shuōchàng wénxué *also* "讲唱文学" jiǎngchàng wénxué literary entertainment in a form of storytelling and ballad singing

说穿 shuōchuān expose; disclose:一语～ lay bare the truth with one penetrating remark; hit the nail on the head /～了他的心事 reveal what's weighing on his mind /～了，你就是想多捞回扣。To put it bluntly, what you want is to get more kickbacks.

说辞 shuōcí alibi; excuse:编～ make up excuses; find a pretext

说大话 shuō dàhuà brag; boast; talk big; blow one's own horn or trumpet:～也不脸红 not feel ashamed when talking big /光～不干实事。All hot air, no real action. *or* All bark and no bite.

说到底 shuōdàodǐ in the last analysis; in reality; at bottom:～还是你自己不行。To be quite frank, you're not good at it.

说到钱，便无缘 shuō dào qián, biàn wúyuán to ask for money is to end friendship:常言说:"～。"一提到借路费，亲友们果然便不答碴儿了。As the saying goes that money may turn friends into foes, his relatives all fell silent the moment he said he wanted to borrow some money to cover his travelling expenses.

说到做到 shuōdào-zuòdào do what one says; match one's deeds to one's words; practise what one preaches; live up to one's word:他历来守信用，～。He is a man of his word.

说道 shuōdào say:妈妈～:"芳芳是妈妈的好孩子。" Mom said, "Fangfang is mama's good child."

说道 shuōdao 〈方言〉 ❶ say:事情已经真相大白，你还有什么可～的? Now that everything is clear, what else do you have to say? ❷ discuss; talk about:这件事你一定得跟领导～～，再作决定。You should discuss this matter with the leaders before making any decision. ❸ reason; cause:他为什么突然改变主意，这里头肯定有～。Why did he change his mind all of a sudden? There must be something behind it.

说…道… shuō… dào… *used before two parallel or similar adjectives or numerals to indicate the quality of various remarks*:说亲道热 make warmhearted remarks /说张道李 gossip about this or that person /说苦道难 pour out one's woes

说得过去 shuōdeguòqù justifiable; passable; about average; so-so:情面上～ be acceptable without wounding people's sensibilities /他的驾驶技术还～。His driving skill is passable.

说得来 shuōdelái ❶ can get along; be friendly with:他跟全班同学都能～。He can get along well with all his classmates. ❷〈方言〉 can speak:上海话我也～。I can also speak Shanghai dialect.

说得着 shuōdezháo ❶ appropriate or necessary to mention:你没有说错，这些话都是～的。You were right; what you said is relevant. ❷ agreeable; congenial:他俩很～。They two hit it off with each other.

说定 shuōdìng decide; settle; agree on:这件事就这样～了。The matter is as good as settled.

说东道西 shuōdōng-dàoxī chatter or rattle away on a variety of topics:两位亲家正在亲热地～。The two mothers-in-law were warmly chattering away about various things.

说短论长 shuōduǎn-lùncháng *see* "说长道短"

说法 shuōfǎ expound Buddhist doctrine:讲经～ expound Buddhist doctrine and scripture

说法 shuōfa ❶ way of saying a thing; wording; formulation:劝你还是变个～。I'd advise you to say it in another way. /这个意思可以有三种～。This idea can find expression in three different ways. ❷ statement; view; argument:我不同意他的～。I don't agree with his statement. /关于地震的成因，现在～不一。There are different theories about the cause of earthquakes. /这种～看起来似乎有理。The argument seems plausible. ❸ solution or settlement (agreeable to both parties of a dispute, etc.); (justifiable) explanation; (equitable) judgment:讨个～ demand an explanation; ask for an equitable judgment /我想请贵商场给个～。I think your department store should come up with a solution. /这事儿总得有个～。After all, you'll have to suggest a settlement of this matter.

说服 shuōfú persuade; convince; bring round; talk sb. over:～群众 convince the masses /要～，不要压服。Resort to persuasion, not coercion. /他终于被我～。At last I brought him round. /事实最有～力。Facts speak louder than words.

说好 shuōhǎo reach an agreement or understanding:两人～一起去游长城。The two of them have arranged to visit the Great Wall together. /这事你放心，我已经跟她～了。You may rest assured on it; I've settled everything with her.

说好说歹 shuōhǎo-shuōdǎi try every way to persuade or convince:任你～，他就是不肯。In spite of all that was said, he was not convinced.

说合 shuōhe ❶ bring two or more parties together; help bring about:～买卖 make a deal ❷ talk over; exchange views; discuss:咱们先得～～。We must put our heads together beforehand. ❸ mediate a settlement; reconcile

说和 shuōhe mediate a settlement; make peace between; compose a quarrel:你去给他们从中～。Go and patch things up between them, will you?

说黑道白 shuōhēi-dàobái make free and frivolous comments or remarks:对这事～者比比皆是。There are plenty of irresponsible and frivolous comments on this matter.

说话 shuōhuà ❶ speak; talk; say:这姑娘太爱～。This girl is too talkative. /我还是不～为妙。I had better keep my mouth shut. /气得她说不出话来。She was too angry to say anything. /～应该算话。One should always keep one's word. /～要兑现。One should put one's money where one's mouth is. ❷ chit-chat; chat; talk:几个朋友难得有机会在一起～。It was rare for these few friends to have time to chat together. ❸ gossip; censure:这样做，你难道不怕别人～? Aren't you afraid what you've done might set people talking? ❹ in a minute; right away:你们别急，饭菜～就得。Don't worry, the meal will be ready in a jiffy. /我～就来。I'm coming. *or* I shan't be a

S

minute. ❺〈方言〉remark; word; talk: 他这句～很合理。He made a reasonable remark. *or* What he said sounded reasonable. ❻ storytelling in the Tang and Song dynasties

说黄道黑 shuōhuáng-dàohēi *also* "论黄数黑" lùnhuáng-shǔhēi criticize; find fault with: 他这人喜欢～，无中生有。He is fond of nitpicking and often makes up stories out of thin air.

说谎 shuōhuǎng tell untruths; lie: 不能～。One shouldn't tell lies. / 这些不实数字表明这个单位在～。These false figures give the lie to the claims of this unit.

说教 shuōjiào ❶〈宗教〉deliver a sermon; preach ❷〈比喻〉preachify; preach: 空洞的～是不解决问题的。Empty preaching doesn't solve any problem at all.

说开 shuōkāi ❶ explain: 你索性把事情的原委跟他～了，免得他猜疑。You might as well tell him the whole story lest he become suspicious. ❷ (of words, phrases, idioms, etc.) become current: 这个词儿已经～了，大家也都懂得了。This term has already become current, and everyone knows what it means.

说客 shuōkè ❶ person good at persuasion: 这个人足智多谋，能说会道，是个好～。This man is a persuasive talker, for he is both resourceful and eloquent. ❷〈贬义〉person often sent to win sb. over or enlist his support through persuasion; lobbyist

说口 shuōkǒu (mostly used in the early vernacular) boast; brag

说口 shuōkou spoken prologue to song-and-dance duet (二人转), ballad singing, etc.

说来 shuōlái come to speak of it: ～大家都是乡里乡亲的，我理应帮忙。Come to speak of it, we should help each other as we are all townspeople.

说来话长 shuōlái-huàcháng it's a long story: 此事～。It takes time to tell the whole story.

说来说去 shuōlái-shuōqù repeat over and over; say again and again: ～一句话，这种事我们不能做。To put it in a nutshell, we simply cannot do anything like this.

说理 shuōlǐ ❶ reason things out; reason; argue: 我说了半天理，他们才同意。It took us quite a long while to talk them into it. ❷ (often used in the negative) listen to reason; be reasonable; be sensible: 你们～不～? Don't you listen to reason?

说漏嘴 shuōlòuzuǐ inadvertently blurting out; slip of the tongue: 一下子～了。It's an unexpected slip of the tongue.

说媒 shuōméi act as a matchmaker: 给他～ to make a match for him / ～的人 matchmaker

说明 shuōmíng ❶ explain; illustrate; show: ～事实真相 explain how things stand; tell the truth / ～原因 give reasons / 用事实～ illustrate with facts / 有件事我必须～清楚。There is one thing I must make absolutely clear. ❷ explanation; directions; caption: 图片的～很扼要。The caption under the picture is very explicit. ❸ prove; show; uphold: 事实～这种观点是错误的。The facts have proved that the opinion is wrong.

说明书 shuōmíngshū booklet of directions; guidebook; (technical) manual; synopsis (of a play or film): 产品～ directions of a product

说明文 shuōmíngwén expository writing; exposition: 学写～ learn to write expositions

说破 shuōpò tell what sth. really is; reveal; disclose: 无意～隐私 inadvertently betray secrets; let the cat out of the bag / 有意～ intentional disclosure

说破嘴 shuōpòzuǐ talk oneself hoarse: 你～他也不会改。He would not mend his ways, even if you talked yourself hoarse.

说千道万 shuōqiān-dàowàn *also* "说一千，道一万" keep repeating one's views: 你～，他也不动心。He remained unmoved even though you had stated your views thousands of times.

说亲 shuōqīn be a matchmaker: 给儿子～ make a match for one's son

说情 shuōqíng plead for mercy for sb.; put in a good word for; intercede for sb.: 求人给女儿～ ask sb. to intercede for one's daughter / 代为～ plead on sb.'s behalf

说三道四 shuōsān-dàosì make irresponsible remarks; gossip: 不怕别人～ not be afraid of other's gossip

说啥 shuōshá whatever one may say: ～老头子也不同意这门亲事。For all our efforts to convince him the old man refused to agree to the proposed marriage.

说舌 shuōshé gossip; tell tales

说时迟，那时快 shuō shí chí, nàshí kuài (in old-style novels) in the twinkling of an eye; before one can say Jack Robinson

说是 shuōshì it is said; they say: 他要请几天假，～家里有急事。He asked for a few days off, saying he had some urgent family matters to attend to. / 电台广播了，～今天下午下雨。According to the weather forecast, it is going to rain this afternoon.

说书 shuōshū storytelling: ～的人 storyteller / 他特别喜欢听～。He likes to listen to storytelling very much.

说死 shuōsǐ fix definitely; make it definite; make sth. dead certain: 咱们～了，下午三点钟在车站会齐。Let's make it definite — we'll meet at the railway station at 3 p.m.

说帖 shuōtiě 〈旧语〉aide-mémoire; talking points

说头儿 shuōtour ❶ something to talk about: 这件事还有个～。There still remains something to be said about it. ❷ excuse; pretext: 他真不虚心，别人指出他的错误他都有～。He is so immodest that he always has an excuse when others point out his mistakes.

说妥 shuōtuǒ come to an agreement; agree: 一切条件都必须事先～。We must come to an agreement on all the terms beforehand.

说文解字 Shuōwén Jiězì *Origin of Chinese Characters*, the earliest Chinese dictionary by Xu Shen (许慎, c.58-c.147) of the Eastern Han Dynasty

说戏 shuōxì explain the plot of a play to the cast or give directions by demonstration acts

说下 shuōxia fix; settle; agree on: 咱们先～，到时候可不能反悔。Let's settle on this now and don't you go back on your word when the time comes.

说闲话 shuō xiánhuà ❶ gossip; complain: 有意见当面提，别在背后～。Air your opinions openly instead of complaining or gossiping at one's back. / 办事要公平，免得别人～。We must be fair in whatever we do so that we'll not give anyone cause for complaint. ❷ talk casually about; prattle; chat: 老人们茶余饭后总爱在一起～。Old people like to chat together at their leisure.

说咸道淡 shuōxián-dàodàn gossip; engage in idle talk

说项 shuōxiàng put in a good word for sb.; intercede for sb.; plead: 他最爱替人～。He is fond of acting as a pleader.

说笑 shuōxiào talking and laughing: 院子里传来了同学们的～声。The students can be heard chatting and laughing in the courtyard. / 大家在一起说说笑笑，高兴极了。All the people are talking animatedly and laughing merrily.

说笑话 shuō xiàohuà ❶ tell a joke or a funny story: 让爷爷给我们说个笑话。Let Grandpa tell us a funny story. ❷ make fun of; tease; kid: 他是在跟你～，你怎么就当真了呢? Why take him seriously? He's only joking.

说一不二 shuōyī-bù'èr mean what one says; stand by one's word; always keep one's promise: 他是个～的人。He is a man of his word.

说着玩儿 shuōzhewánr joking; not serious in what one says: 这可不是～的事。It's no joking matter.

说嘴 shuōzuǐ ❶ talk big; brag; boast: 谁也别～，有本事比比看。Let's not have any boasting. Have a match and see who is the best. ❷〈方言〉argue; wrangle; quarrel: 他有和人～的毛病。One of his shortcomings is that he likes to pick quarrels with people.

shuò

数（數） shuò 〈书面〉often; frequently; repeatedly: 频～ frequently; again and again; repeatedly; often
see also shǔ; shù

数见不鲜 shuòjiàn-bùxiān *also* "屡见不鲜" lǚjiàn-bùxiān what is often seen; common occurrence; nothing new: 这种现象在这里～。This kind of phenomenon is very common here.

数脉 shuòmài 〈中医〉rapid pulse (of more than 90 beats per minute)

朔¹ shuò ❶ new moon ❷ first day of the lunar month

朔² shuò north: 威震～土 win resounding fame in the north; inspire awe in the north / ～风呼啸。The north wind is whistling.

朔方 shuòfāng 〈书面〉north

朔风 shuòfēng 〈书面〉north wind: 凛冽的～ freezing (*or* icy) north wind

朔日 shuòrì first day of the lunar month
朔望 shuòwàng first and fifteenth days of the lunar month; new moon and full moon; syzygy: 潮汐的大小随～而变化。Spring tides come with the new and full moon.
朔望潮 shuòwàngcháo spring tide
朔望月 shuòwàngyuè 〈天文〉lunar month; lunation; synodic month
朔月 shuòyuè new moon

蒴 shuò sesame; capsule: 芝麻～ capsule
蒴果 shuòguǒ 〈植物〉capsule

槊 shuò ancient spear, which has a fairly long pole: 横～赋诗 write poems with spear drawn

搠 shuò 〈旧语〉stab; poke: ～了他一枪 stab him with a spear / 一枪朝他～去 stab at him with a spear

硕 shuò big; large: ～大无比 gigantic / 丰～ plentiful and substantial; rich / 肥～ big and fleshy
硕大 shuòdà huge; enormous: ～的身躯 of huge build
硕大无朋 shuòdà-wúpéng of unparalleled size; colossal; huge: 海上,太阳像一个～的火球,正在向地平线慢慢沉落。Looking like a massive fire ball over the sea, the sun was gradually setting towards the horizon.
硕果 shuòguǒ rich fruits; tremendous achievements: 结～ bear rich fruits / ～压枝 trees overhung with fruits / 科研的～ great scientific achievements
硕果仅存 shuòguǒ-jǐncún rare survival: 这是本城内～的一家大茶馆了。This is the only existing big teahouse in the town.
硕士 shuòshì master: 获得～学位 get a master's degree / ～研究生 postgraduate studying for a master's degree; postgraduate student / 文学～ Master of Arts / 理学～ Master of Science / 工程学～ Master of Engineering
硕学 shuòxué 〈书面〉❶ scholarly; erudite ❷ learned man; scholar
硕学通儒 shuòxué-tōngrú great learned scholar: 这样的～健在的不多了。Very few great men of learning are still alive today.
硕壮 shuòzhuàng big and strong: 身体～ big and strongly built / ～的果实 large and rich fruit

稍 shuò 〈书面〉see "槊" shuò

烁(爍) shuò bright; brilliant; shining: 闪～ twinkle; glimmer: 光～如电 be shining like lightning
烁亮 shuòliàng bright; brilliant; shining: ～的马刀 gleaming sabre
烁烁 shuòshuò shine; glitter; sparkle: 红灯～ glittering red lights / 光焰～ sparkling lights and flames

铄[1](鑠) shuò 〈书面〉❶ melt (metal, etc.): 众口～金 public clamour can confound right and wrong ❷ waste away; weaken

铄[2](鑠) shuò see "烁" shuò
铄石流金 shuòshí-liújīn *also* "流金铄石" (hot enough to) melt stone and metal — intense heat; sweltering

妁 shuò see "媒妁" méishuò

sī

斯 sī ❶〈书面〉this; here: ～时 this time (*or* moment) / 贪婪如～ as greedy as this; this greedy / 以至于～ come to such a pass / 生于～, 长于～ be born and bred here ❷〈书面〉then; thus: 知惧如是, ～不亡矣。Had they been vigilant enough, they would not have been vanquished. ❸ (Sī) a surname
斯大林 Sīdàlín Joseph Vissarionovich Stalin (1879-1953)
斯德哥尔摩 Sīdégē'ěrmó Stockholm, capital of Sweden
斯芬克斯 Sīfēnkèsī Sphinx, a mythological monster with a human head and the body of a lion
斯堪的纳维亚 Sīkāndìnàwéiyà Scandinavia: ～半岛 Scandinavian Peninsula / ～航空公司 Scandinavian Airline System (SAS)
斯拉夫人 Sīlāfūrén Slav
斯拉夫语 Sīlāfūyǔ Slavic (language): ～系 Slavic language family
斯里兰卡 Sīlǐlánkǎ Sri Lanka: ～人 Sri Lankan
斯洛伐克 Sīluòfákè Slovakia: ～共和国 Republic of Slovakia / ～人 Slovak; Slovakian / ～语 Slovak (language) / ～矿山 Slovak ore mountains
斯洛文尼亚 Sīluòwénníyà Slovenia: ～共和国 Republic of Slovenia / ～人 Sloven
斯密 Sīmì Adam Smith (1723-1790), Scottish philosopher and economist
斯内伦远距视力表 Sīnèilún yuǎnjù shìlìbiǎo Snellen's test-chart
斯涅耳定律 Sīniè'ěr dìnglǜ 〈物理〉Snell's law (a law of refraction)
斯诺 Sīnuò Edgar Parks Snow (1905-1972), American journalist who visited Yan'an in 1936 and later wrote *Red Star Over China* and a number of other books on China
斯特拉斯堡 Sītèlāsībǎo Strasbourg, a city in northeast France where sessions of the European Parliament are held
斯特朗 Sītèlǎng Anna Louis Strong (1885-1970), American journalist and writer who interviewed Mao Zedong in 1946 in Yan'an
斯瓦希里语 Sīwǎxīlǐyǔ 〈语言〉Swahili (language)
斯威士兰 Sīwēishìlán Swaziland: ～人 Swazi
斯韦思林杯 Sīwéisīlínbēi 〈体育〉Swaythling Cup (top award for men's team event of World Table Tennis Championships)
斯文 sīwén 〈书面〉❶ learning; culture ❷ learned person; scholar: 有辱～ disgrace to learned persons / 假冒～ pretend to be learned; pretend to be a scholar
斯文 sīwen refined; gentle: 举止～ refined behaviour / 说话～ gentle speech / ～得有点做作 too refined to be natural; genteel / 他这个人斯斯文文的, 哪能干这种粗活? Refined gentleman that he is, how could he do such rough work?
斯文败类 sīwén-bàilèi dregs or scum of the literati
斯文扫地 sīwén-sǎodì learning and refinement are swept into the dust; (one's) scholarly dignity is thoroughly degraded: 博士到小馆子里去涮盘洗碗, 岂不是～? Isn't it disgraceful for Ph. D. s to wash dishes in cheap restaurants?
斯须 sīxū 〈书面〉short time or while; a moment: ～而没 disappear (*or* vanish) in a moment

澌 sī 〈书面〉totally; completely
澌灭 sīmiè 〈书面〉totally disappear; completely vanish

凘 sī 〈书面〉floating ice (as on a river during the spring thaw); ice floe: 流～ drifting ice on a thawing river; ice floe

厮[1](廝) sī (often used in the early vernacular) ❶ male servant: 小～ page boy; page ❷ fellow; guy: 这～ this guy / 那～ that fellow

厮[2](廝) sī each other; together: ～混在一起 fool (*or* hang) around together / ～敬～爱 love and respect each other / 耳鬓～磨 close childhood friendship (between a boy and a girl)
厮搏 sībó come to blows; fight; wrestle: 他俩滚在地上～开了。They rolled on the ground, wrestling with each other.
厮缠 sīchán pester; worry
厮打 sīdǎ come to blows; exchange blows; tussle: 互相～ tussle with each other / 不分青红皂白地～起来 come to blows without asking why (*or* without rhyme or reason)
厮混 sīhùn ❶〈贬义〉live together; mix in company; be together: 他整天和那些不三不四的人～。He hangs around with persons of dubious background all day. ❷ mix: 人的喊声、马的叫声、枪声～在一起了。One could hear all round people shouting, steeds neighing and gunfire resounding.
厮杀 sīshā fight at close quarters; engage in hand-to-hand combat: ～得不可开交 be engaged in fierce hand-to-hand fighting
厮守 sīshǒu keep together; stay with each other; rely on each other: ～一辈子 keep each other's company all one's life; be lifelong companions / 母女俩～在一起过日子。Clinging to each other, mother and daughter lived on their own.

斯熟 sīshú be well acquainted with; know well:他们俩渐渐～了，成了一对好朋友。Gradually they came to know each other well and became good friends.

撕

sī tear; rend; rip:从墙上～下招贴画 tear a poster from the wall /把信封～开 slit the envelope open /～了几封旧信 tear up some old letters /把衣服～开了 rend one's garments /～下布告 rip down a notice /你这块衣料什么时候～的? When did you buy this piece (of cloth)?

撕巴 sība 〈方言〉tear:他把纸～～扔了。He tore up a piece of paper and threw it away.

撕扯 sīchě tear; rip:他一怒之下把来信～成碎片。In his anger he tore the letter to pieces.

撕毁 sīhuǐ tear up; scrap:～过去的情书 tear up old love-letters /～合同 scrap a contract

撕掳 sīlu ❶ break up (a fight):他好不容易才把两个打架的人～开。It was not without difficulty that he separated the pair from fighting each other. ❷ *also* "撕罗" handle or deal with (difficult matter):这几天他只顾～这桩事，顾不及别的闲事了。These past few days he has been busy attending to this business and has had no time for anything else.

撕票 sīpiào (of kidnappers) kill a hostage (as when they fail to get the ransom they ask for)

撕破 sīpò tear; rip:裤子～了。The trousers are torn.

撕破脸 sīpòliǎn quarrel openly:既～了，说话也就不管轻重了。Since the quarrel became open, they no longer cared what they said to each other.

嘶[1]

sī 〈书面〉❶ (of horses) neigh ❷ hoarse:声～力竭 hoarse and exhausted

嘶[2]

sī whistle

嘶喊 sīhǎn shout:连声～ shout repeatedly

嘶叫 sījiào shriek; neigh:她尖声～起来。She screamed. /远处传来战马的～声。From a distance came the neighing of battle steeds.

嘶鸣 sīmíng (of donkey, horse, etc.) neigh; bray:战马～。War horses neigh.

嘶啸 sīxiào scream; whizz; whistle

嘶哑 sīyǎ hoarse:发出一声～而颤抖的哭叫 utter a hoarse, tremulous wail /喊得嗓子都～了 shout oneself hoarse

蛳(螄)

sī *see* "螺蛳" luósi

思

sī ❶ think; consider; ponder:沉～ meditate; be lost in thought; ponder deeply /追～ think back /深～熟虑 give careful consideration to; think over carefully /三～而后行 think thrice before you act; look before you leap ❷ think of; long for; miss:相～ yearning for one's lover; lovesickness /～悠悠，恨悠悠 endless longing and heart sickness ❸ wish; hope; desire:～归 wish to go home; be homesick /穷则～变 poverty gives rise to a desire for change ❹ train of thought:文～敏捷 quick-witted in writing /哀～缕缕 sad memories; grief-stricken reflections ❺ (Sī) a surname

see also sāi

思辨 sībiàn ❶〈哲学〉reasoning ❷ *also* "思辩" think and analyze:他的谈话闪烁着博学和～的光彩。He showed profound learning and brilliant analytical ability in his speech. *or* His conversation is sparkling with wit and erudition.

思辩 sībiàn *see* "思辨❷"

思潮 sīcháo ❶ trend of thought; current of thought:文艺～ literary trend (*or* current) /新～ new trend (*or* current) of thought /极左～泛滥 ultra-leftist currents of thought were rampant ❷ (surging) thoughts:～翻滚 thoughts surging in one's mind

思春 sīchūn (of a young girl) have thoughts of love

思忖 sīcǔn 〈书面〉ponder; consider; mull over:暗自～ ponder to oneself /露出～的表情 show a thoughtful expression

思凡 sīfán (as of deities or fairies in tales or of monks or nuns in real life) long for the secular life:这出戏写的是一个尼姑～的故事。The play is about a nun who longs to lead a secular life.

思古 sīgǔ recall the past; be nostalgic:发～之幽情 have nostalgic musings over the past

思过 sīguò ponder over one's mistakes; feel remorse; repent:闭门～ shut oneself up and ponder over one's mistakes; ponder over one's mistakes in seclusion; meditate on one's own faults behind closed doors

思旧 sījiù think of old friends (times, etc.); remember old friends (times, etc.); be nostalgic:～之情 feeling of nostalgia

思考 sīkǎo think deeply; ponder; consider:～问题 mull over (*or* consider) a problem /具有独立～的能力 be able to think independently /经过认真～的回答 carefully-considered answer

思力 sīlì mental power:～衰退 decline of one's mental power

思恋 sīliàn remember or think of fondly:～故乡 think fondly of one's native place; be homesick

思量 sīliang ❶ consider; turn sth. over in one's mind:仔细～ consider sth. carefully /反复～ turn sth. over in one's mind again and again /～利弊 weigh the advantages and disadvantages ❷〈方言〉think of; long for; miss:断不了对家乡的～ cannot help missing one's home town /大伙儿正～你呢! We were all thinking of you! /不～，自难忘。Though not often thinking of you, naturally I cannot forget.

思路 sīlù train of thought; line of thinking:打断～ interrupt sb.'s train of thought; lose one's thread of thought /顺着这个～想下去 follow this line of thought /符合逻辑的～ logical way of thinking /～开阔 broad vision; broad-mindedness /开拓改革新～ develop new ideas for reform

思虑 sīlǜ consider; reflect on; deliberate:～周到 be thoughtful (*or* considerate); be circumspect /～重重 be lost in contemplation

思摸 sīmo think; ponder; mull over:我～了好久，觉得这事还是非解决不可。I have been turning the matter over in my mind for some time and I am convinced that we have to find a settlement.

思谋 sīmóu think over; consider:～自己的出路 ponder over one's prospects

思慕 sīmù think of with esteem or longing; admire:～他为人正直 admire him for his integrity /引起了人们对童年时代的～ arouse fond reminiscences of their childhood

思念 sīniàn think of; miss:～祖国 think of (*or* miss) one's motherland /～故友 miss one's old friends

思前想后 sīqián-xiǎnghòu think over again and again; mull over; ponder over:他～，难下决心。He gave the matter plenty of thought and still found it hard to make a decision.

思情 sīqíng nostalgia

思如泉涌 sīrúquányǒng *also* "思若泉涌" ideas gushing out like spring water; ideas teeming in one's head

思索 sīsuǒ think deeply; reflect; ponder:～人生 ponder on the meaning of life /苦苦～ think long and hard; do some hard thinking /无暇～ have no time for reflection

思惟 sīwéi *see* "思维"

思维 sīwéi *also* "思惟"❶ thought; thinking:～敏捷 quick-witted /形象～ thinking in (terms of) images /人类的～ human thought /抽象～ abstract thought /逻辑～ logical thinking /锻炼～能力 train one's thinking ability /～的规律 law of thinking /～的方式 mode of thinking /～的过程 thinking process ❷ think; consider; weigh:～得失 consider the gains and losses; weigh the pros and cons

思贤若渴 sīxián-ruòkě (of a ruler) thirst for or yearn for the assistance of talented people; be eager to enlist able people

思乡 sīxiāng think of one's native place longingly; miss one's hometown; be homesick:老人动了～之情。The old man began to miss his hometown. *or* The old man became homesick.

思想 sīxiǎng ❶ thought; thinking; ideology:文艺～ thought on art and literature /毛泽东～ Mao Zedong Thought /悲观～ pessimistic thinking; pessimism /解放～ emancipate (*or* unfetter) one's mind /提高～ have a better understanding of /搞通～ straighten out one's thinking /～顾虑 sth. that is weighing on one's mind; burden on one's mind; misgivings /～革命化 revolutionization of one's ideology /有～准备 be mentally prepared /吸取先进的～ absorb advanced (*or* progressive) ideas ❷ idea:打消了跳槽的～ give up the idea of changing one's job /产生了出国深造的～ form (*or* conceive) an idea of doing further studies abroad /从不掩饰真实的～ never conceal one's true thoughts ❸ think of; consider:这些事很值得～一番。This matter is worth careful consideration. *or* The matter gives much food for thought. /她日夜～着年迈的双亲。She missed her aged parents day and night.

思想包袱 sīxiǎng bāofu sth. weighing on one's mind; mental burden:放下～ get rid of what is weighing on one's mind

思想道德建设 sīxiǎng dàodé jiànshè drive to raise people's ideological and moral standards
思想动向 sīxiǎng dòngxiàng ideological trend
思想斗争 sīxiǎng dòuzhēng ideological struggle; mental struggle or conflict; heart or soul searching
思想方法 sīxiǎng fāngfǎ way of thinking; mode of thinking
思想改造 sīxiǎng gǎizào ideological remoulding
思想疙瘩 sīxiǎng gēda knot in one's mind; hang-up
思想根源 sīxiǎng gēnyuán ideological cause or root
思想工作 sīxiǎng gōngzuò ideological work: 做细致的～ do painstaking ideological work
思想家 sīxiǎngjiā thinker: 孔子是我国古代伟大的～。Confucius was a great thinker of ancient China.
思想检查 sīxiǎng jiǎnchá check on one's thinking; examine one's wrong ideas
思想见面 sīxiǎng jiànmiàn candid exchange of ideas
思想建设 sīxiǎng jiànshè ideological building
思想交锋 sīxiǎng jiāofēng confrontation of ideas
思想教育 sīxiǎng jiàoyù ideological education: 加强～ strengthen ideological education
思想界 sīxiǎngjiè realm of ideology
思想禁区 sīxiǎng jìnqū ideologically forbidden zone
思想境界 sīxiǎng jìngjiè ideological level
思想觉悟 sīxiǎng juéwù political consciousness or awareness
思想库 sīxiǎngkù think tank (a centre or institute for theoretical studies and research in solving problems of society, science and technology)
思想烙印 sīxiǎng làoyìn ideological brand or imprint
思想路线 sīxiǎng lùxiàn ideological line
思想认识 sīxiǎng rènshi ideological understanding: 这是～问题，不是政治立场问题。It is a question of understanding, not one of political position (*or* attitude).
思想水平 sīxiǎng shuǐpíng ideological level
思想体系 sīxiǎng tǐxì ideological system; ideology: 儒家的～ ideological system of the Confucian school / 马克思主义～ Marxist ideology
思想问题 sīxiǎng wèntí problem arising from erroneous thinking; ideological problem: 解决～ untie the knot in one's heart
思想性 sīxiǎngxìng ideological content or level
思想修养 sīxiǎng xiūyǎng ideological cultivation
思想意识 sīxiǎng yìshi ideology
思想政治工作 sīxiǎng zhèngzhì gōngzuò ideological and political work
思想作风 sīxiǎng zuòfēng way of thinking: 端正～、工作作风和生活作风 straighten out the style of one's thinking, work and life
思绪 sīxù ❶ train of thought; line of thinking: ～万千 be lost in a myriad of thoughts / ～如潮 with one's mind surging like a turbulent river; in an agitated mood / 打断～ interrupt one's train of thought / 理清～ sort out one's thoughts ❷ feeling; mood: 厌倦的～ weary feelings / ～不宁 feel anxious (*or* worried)
思议 sīyì comprehend; conceive; imagine: 不可～ inconceivable; unimaginable; incredible / 难于～ difficult to understand; can hardly imagine

楒

sī

楒仔 sīzǐ *also* "淋漓柯" línlíkē 〈植物〉 a kind of evergreen conifer

罳

sī *see* "罘罳" fúsī

锶

sī 〈化学〉 strontium (Sr): ～90 strontium 90 / 氧化～ strontium oxide; strontia

偲

sī
see also cāi

偲偲 sīsī 〈书面〉 learn from each other by exchanging views: 朋友之间切切～ (of friends) compare notes and learn from each other

飔

sī 〈书面〉 cool wind

篤

sī

篤簩竹 sīláozhú a kind of bamboo with thin skin and slender sections, used for making furniture

缌

sī 〈书面〉 fine linen

厶

sī 〈书面〉 *see* "私" sī

私

sī ❶ personal; private: ～函 personal (*or* private) letter / 隐～ private matters; privacy / 公～分明 make a clear distinction between public and private interests ❷ selfish: 自～自利 selfish; self-centred / 大公无～ selfless; unselfish ❸ secret; stealthy; private: 窃窃～语 talk in whisper; whisper ❹ illicit; illegal; unlawful: 走～ smuggle / ～盐 smuggled salt; contraband salt / ～酒 bootleg liquor; moonshine / ～运军火 (engage in) gun-running / ～贩鸦片 opium-trafficking / ～藏武器 unlawful possession of weapons
私帮 sībāng small clique: 搞宗派，立～ form a small clique and engage in factional activities
私奔 sībēn elope: 与情人～ (of a girl) elope with one's lover
私弊 sībì corrupt practice; malpractice: 为官清正，毫无～ be an honest official without a taint of corruption
私藏 sīcáng ❶ private collection; private property: ～巨万 with immense wealth ❷ keep or possess illegally: ～违禁品 possess contraband goods
私产 sīchǎn private property; personal possession: 将非法占有的～归还个人 return illegally-held private property to its owners
私娼 sīchāng unlicensed prostitute: 取缔～ ban prostitutes; prohibit prostitution
私仇 sīchóu personal enmity or grudge: 结下～ incur (sb.'s) personal enmity / 公报～ settle a personal grudge in the name of public interests; retaliate against a personal enemy by abusing public power
私党 sīdǎng (member of) clique or faction privately formed to further selfish interests
私倒 sīdǎo private profiteering
私德 sīdé personal morals; personal integrity: 缺乏～ lack personal morals (*or* integrity) / ～失检 have a poor moral character
私觌 sīdí 〈书面〉 meet in private; make a rendezvous
私邸 sīdǐ *also* "私第" private residence (of a high official): 用公费修建～ build a private residence with public funds
私底下 sīdǐxia in secret; in private: 大家～早就在议论这件事了。People have been talking about this matter among themselves for quite some time.
私第 sīdì private residence
私斗 sīdòu struggle over private ends; engage in personal strife
私法 sīfǎ 〈法律〉 private law; *jus privatum*: 国际～ private international law / ～行为 private law act
私贩 sīfàn illicit sale of commodities in government monopoly; smuggle
私方 sīfāng (of joint state-private enterprise) private ownership (as distinguished from 公方): ～代表 representative of private ownership / ～人员 personnel representing private ownership
私房 sīfáng private housing; private residence: 这是一幢～。This is a privately-owned house.
私房 sīfang ❶ private savings (as distinct from family or public funds): ～钱 private savings of a family member ❷ secret; confidential: 说～话 talk in confidence; exchange confidences; have a tête-à-tête
私访 sīfǎng (as of an official, etc.) visit secretly; inspect in disguise: 微服～ make a secret visit (*or* inspection trip) in disguise; travel incognito / ～受害人家属 visit the family of the victim in secret
私愤 sīfèn personal spite or grudge: 发泄～ vent personal grudges
私股 sīgǔ private share (as in a joint state-private enterprise)
私馆 sīguǎn old-style private school
私孩子 sīháizi 〈口语〉 child born out of wedlock; illegitimate child; bastard
私和 sīhé settle a dispute in private instead of taking it to court; settle out of court: ～人命 compound a case of homicide
私话 sīhuà confidential talk: 咱们说句～，可不许告诉别人。This is just between you and me. Don't tell anybody else.
私会 sīhuì secret meeting of lovers; lovers' rendezvous; tryst
私惠 sīhuì personal benefits

私活 sīhuó moonlighting：拼命干～ be a hard moonlighter

私货 sīhuò smuggled goods; contraband (goods)：买卖～ trade in smuggled goods / 贩运～ traffic in contraband goods

私己 sījǐ ❶〈旧语〉private savings, money or things of a family member ❷ private pocket：旧社会老百姓的捐款往往入了官吏的～。In the old society donations from the people often went into the pockets of officials. ❸ (often used in the early vernacular) in private; secretly

私家 sījiā ❶ private; in private capacity; non-official：～住宅 private residence / ～侦探 private detective ❷ one's own home：在～闲坐 stay at home without a job; stay in without employment

私见 sījiàn ❶ personal prejudice; personal bias：他对我久有～。He has long had personal grudges against me. ❷ personal views：略陈～ briefly express one's personl point of view

私交 sījiāo personal friendship：两人有～。The two of them are personal friends. / 我们在学术观点上虽然常不一致，但～一向不错。Though we often differ in academic views, we have always been on good terms with each other personally.

私窠子 sīkēzi *see* "私窝子"

私立 sīlì privately run; private：～医院 privately-run hospital / ～学校 private school; (UK) public school

私利 sīlì selfish interests; personal gain：图谋～ seek personal gain; pursue one's selfish interests / 贪图～ greedy for personal profit

私了 sīliǎo settle in private; settle out of court; compound：你看，这事是公了还是～? What do you say? Shall we go to court or settle it in private? / 刑事案件不能～。Criminal cases cannot be compounded.

私囊 sīnáng one's own purse：中饱～ fill one's own purse; line one's pockets; feather one's nest

私念 sīniàn selfish motives or ideas：心存～ harbour selfish motives

私情 sīqíng ❶ (as contrasted with public interests, etc.) personal friendship; personal sentiments：不徇～ not swayed (*or* influenced) by personal sentiments / 不顾～ despite personal friendship ❷ illicit or secret love：儿女～ young people's secret love

私曲 sīqū 〈书面〉❶ injustice：性耿介，无～。He was straightforward by nature and always fair and just. ❷ private view; personal wish; personal feeling

私人 sīrén ❶ private：～财产 private property / ～开业 private practice ❷ personal：～关系 personal relations / ～恩怨 personal friendships and enmities; personal gratitudes and resentments ❸ personal friend, relative or protégé：滥用～ fill a post with one's own man; practise nepotism

私人代表 sīrén dàibiǎo personal representative

私人电台 sīrén diàntái private radio station

私人经济 sīrén jīngjì private sector of the economy

私人广告 sīrén guǎnggào personal ad or advertisement

私人劳动 sīrén láodòng 〈经济〉individual labour

私人秘书 sīrén mìshū private secretary

私人企业 sīrén qǐyè private enterprise

私商 sīshāng ❶ private business ❷ businessman; merchant

私设公堂 sīshè gōngtáng set up an illegal court; form a kangaroo court

私生活 sīshēnghuó one's private life：～方面不大检点 inappropriate behaviour in one's private life

私生子 sīshēngzǐ illegitimate child; child born out of wedlock; bastard

私史 sīshǐ 〈旧语〉unofficial history (compiled by private persons)

私事 sīshì private affairs; personal matters：处理～ deal with one's private affairs / 因～请假两天 ask for a 2-day leave to attend to one's personal matters

私淑 sīshū 〈书面〉regard sb. one never studied under as one's teacher

私淑弟子 sīshū dìzǐ self-styled disciple (of a master one never studied under)

私塾 sīshú old-style tutorial school：年少时读过～ attended an old-style tutorial school in one's childhood / ～先生 tutor of an old-style private school

私逃 sītáo escape; abscond：畏罪～ escape (*or* abscond) to avoid punishment

私通 sītōng ❶ have secret ties with; collude secretly with：～土匪 collude secretly with the bandits ❷ illicit intercourse; liaison (between man and woman); adultery：～有夫之妇 have a liaison with a married woman

私图 sītú 〈书面〉personal scheme

私吞 sītūn embezzle; misappropriate：～公款 embezzle public funds

私窝子 sīwōzi *also* "私窠子"〈旧语〉unlicensed or unregistered prostitute

私下 sīxià *also* "私下里" in private; in secret：～决定 make a secret (*or* private) decision / ～进行调解 mediate in private / ～了结 settle out of court

私相授受 sīxiāngshòushòu give and take (bribes, gifts, property, etc.) in private; transfer (funds, property, etc.) in an underhand or illicit manner：断不能以公物～。It is impermissable to give and take public property as gifts in private.

私枭 sīxiāo ❶〈旧语〉salt smuggler ❷ smuggler; drugpusher

私心 sīxīn ❶ heart; innermost being：我～非常高兴，没有虚此一行。I am very happy that the trip was most rewarding. / 他这种公而忘私的精神，使我～非常佩服。I admire him whole-heartedly for his selfless spirit. ❷ selfish motives; selfishness：～太重 be extremely selfish

私心话 sīxīnhuà words spoken in confidence：他们俩悄悄地说了几句～。They privately exchanged a few words in confidence.

私心杂念 sīxīn-zániàn selfish ideas and personal considerations：说穿了，还是他那个～在作怪。To be quite blunt, it's all due to his selfishness.

私信 sīxìn personal correspondence; private letter

私行 sīxíng ❶ (of an official) private trip; trip on personal business ❷ act in secret or privately：～交易 secret deal / ～察访 investigate privately (*or* incognito)

私刑 sīxíng extralegal punishment or torture (as meted out by a kangaroo court)：滥用～ mete out harsh extralegal punishment / ～处死 lynch

私休 sīxiū settle dispute without going through government (as distinguished from 官罢)

私蓄 sīxù private savings：～不少 have a lot of private savings

私学 sīxué privately-run school

私议 sīyì gossip; comment in private：窃窃～ exchange whispered comments

私谊 sīyì personal friendship：～甚厚 have close personal friendship

私益 sīyì personal interest

私营 sīyíng privately operated; privately run; private：～企业 private enterprise / ～商店 private shops

私有 sīyǒu privately owned; private：～房产权 private ownership of a house / 绝不能把公家财产占为～。One should never turn public property into one's private possession.

私有财产 sīyǒu cáichǎn private property

私有观念 sīyǒu guānniàn private ownership mentality

私有化 sīyǒuhuà privatize; denationalize

私有制 sīyǒuzhì private ownership：生产资料～ private ownership of the means of production

私语 sīyǔ ❶ whisper; speak in a low voice：窃窃～ talk in whispers / 夜半无人～时 when all was quiet at midnight, they talked heart to heart ❷ talk in confidence; speak in private：窃听～ eavesdrop on private conversation

私欲 sīyù selfish desire：满足～ satisfy (*or* gratify) one's selfish desires

私怨 sīyuàn personal grudge：了结～ end a personal grudge

私运 sīyùn smuggle：经海关～货物 smuggle goods through the customs

私章 sīzhāng personal seal; signet：加盖～ stamp one's personal seal / 刻～ carve a personal seal (*or* signet)

私衷 sīzhōng 〈书面〉personal feelings：倾吐～ unbosom oneself

私自 sīzì without permission; on the sly：～动用公款 use public funds without permission / ～买卖 buy or sell without authorization

司

sī ❶ take charge of; attend to; operate; manage：各～其职。Each attends to his own work. *or* Every man plays his own part. / 各有所～。Each has his tasks. ❷ department (under a ministry)：外交部新闻～ Information Department of the Ministry of Foreign Affairs / 地质部人事～ Personnel Department of the Ministry of Geology ❸ official in charge of a department; official：税务

~〈旧语〉commissioner of tariffs and taxes /上~ superior (official) /有~ official in charge; official concerned /布政~ (HK before July 1997) Chief Secretary /律政~ (HK before July 1997) Attorney General ❹ (Sī) a surname
司泵员 sībèngyuán pump man; pumper
司晨 sīchén 〈书面〉herald the break of day; be a harbinger of dawn:牝鸡~,惟家之索。A hen that crows at dawn invites disaster. *or* It is the misfortune of a family (*or* a country, etc.) to be ruled by a woman.
司铎 sīduó *also* "神甫" shénfu Catholic father; priest
司舵 sīduò ❶ at the helm ❷ helmsman
司法 sīfǎ administration of justice; judicature:~调查 judicial investigation
司法部 sīfǎbù ministry of justice; department of justice:中华人民共和国~ Ministry of Justice of the People's Republic of China /美国~ US Department of Justice
司法部门 sīfǎ bùmén judicial department; judiciary
司法程序 sīfǎ chéngxù judicial process
司法独立 sīfǎ dúlì judicial independence; independence of judicature
司法否决权 sīfǎ fǒujuéquán judicial veto
司法管辖 sīfǎ guǎnxiá judicial control:~范围 judicial limits
司法机关 sīfǎ jīguān judicial organ
司法鉴定 sīfǎ jiàndìng expert testimony or evidence
司法界 sīfǎjiè judicial circles; judicial world; the bar
司法权 sīfǎquán ❶ judicial powers ❷ jurisdiction
司法人员 sīfǎ rényuán judicial official; law officer
司法院 sīfǎyuàn Judicial *Yuan* (China before 1949):~院长 president of the Judicial *Yuan*
司各特 Sīgètè Sir Walter Scott (1771-1832), Scottish novelist and poet
司号 sīhào ❶ bugle; blow the bugle ❷ bugler; trumpeter
司号员 sīhàoyuán bugler; trumpeter
司阍 sīhūn 〈书面〉concierge; doorkeeper; janitor
司机 sījī driver; chauffeur:公共汽车~ bus driver /出租车~ taxi driver /火车~ engine driver; locomotive engineer /配有(专职)~的小轿车 chauffeured car /~室 (driver's) cab
司空 sīkōng ❶〈历史〉Minister of Public Works ❷ (Sīkōng) a surname
司空见惯 sīkōng-jiànguàn common sight; common occurrence; commonplace:这种款式一年前还算新奇,如今已是~了。A novelty a year ago, this style is now a commonplace.
司寇 sīkòu ❶〈历史〉Minister of Justice:大~ Minister of Justice ❷ (Sīkòu) a surname
司库 sīkù treasurer:当选为基金会的~ be elected treasurer of the foundation
司令 sīlìng commander; commanding officer:海军~ navy commander /兵团~ commander of an army (*or* army corps) /总~ commander-in-chief
司令部 sīlìngbù command; headquarters
司令官 sīlìngguān commander; commanding officer
司令台 sīlìngtái reviewing stand
司令员 sīlìngyuán commander; commanding officer:空军~ air force commander /军区~ commanding officer of a military region
司炉 sīlú stoker; fireman
司马 sīmǎ ❶〈历史〉Minister of Defence; Minister of War:大~ Minister of Defence ❷ (Sīmǎ) a surname
司马光 Sīmǎ Guāng Sima Guang (formerly translated as Ssu-ma Kuang, 1019-1086), statesman and historian of the Northern Song Dynasty
司马迁 Sīmǎ Qiān Sima Qian (formerly translated as Ssu-ma Ch'ien, c.145 *or* c.135-? BC), historian and scholar of the Western Han Dynasty
司马相如 Sīmǎ Xiāngrú Sima Xiangru (formerly translated as Ssu-ma Hsiang-ju, 179-118 BC), *fu* prose writer of the Western Han Dynasty
司马昭之心,路人皆知 Sīmǎ Zhāo zhī xīn, lùrén jiē zhī every man in the street is aware of Sima Zhao's intent — the villain's design is obvious to all
司南 sīnán (in ancient China) southward-pointing instrument — prototype of the compass:~车 southward-pointing cart
司事 sīshì 〈旧语〉person in general charge or in charge of the accounts; clerk performing miscellaneous duties; factotum
司书 sīshū 〈旧语〉official copyist or scribe
司替林 sītìlín 〈化学〉stearic acid
司徒 sītú ❶〈历史〉Minister of Land and People (in charge of registration of cultivated land, settlement and corvée):大~ (in certain dynasties) prime minister ❷ (Sītú) a surname
司徒雷登 Sītúléidēng John Leighton Stuart (1876-1962), American diplomat
司务 sīwù ❶ (in the Ming and Qing dynasties, 1368-1911) official performing miscellaneous duties in *yamen* ❷ workman with special skills:厨~ cook; chef
司务长 sīwùzhǎng company quartermaster:他在部队当~。He serves as a company quartermaster in the army.
司线员 sīxiànyuán 〈体育〉linesman
司药 sīyào pharmacist; druggist; chemist:在药房当~ work as a druggist in a pharmacy
司仪 sīyí master of ceremonies; MC:担任~ serve as MC
司长 sīzhǎng director of a department (in a ministry)
司账 sīzhàng 〈旧语〉treasurer; cashier
司钻 sīzuàn driller:副~ assistant driller

丝(絲) sī ❶ silk:缫~ silk reeling; filature /生~ raw silk /真~ genuine silk /人造~ artificial silk; rayon /绢~ spun silk /桑蚕~ mulberry silk /柞蚕~ fussa(h) silk ❷ anything threadlike:钢~ steel wire /铅~ galvanized wire /钨~ tungsten filament /肉~ shredded meat /烟~ cut tobacco; pipe tobacco ❸ one ten-thousandth of certain units of measure ❹ unit of weight (= 0.0005 grams) ❺ unit of length (= 0.0033 millimetres) ❻ tiny bit; least bit:一~不苟 not be the least bit negligent; be very strict (*or* meticulous) /一~不挂 nude; stark naked /一~亮光 thread of light /露出一~笑容 reveal (*or* betray) a trace of smile /晴空飘着几~白云。Traces of white cloud are floating in the clear sky.
丝氨酸 sī'ānsuān serine
丝包线 sībāoxiàn 〈电学〉silk wire — metal wire insulated with silk
丝虫 sīchóng 〈动物〉filaria
丝虫病 sīchóngbìng filariasis
丝绸 sīchóu silk cloth; silk:~服装 silk clothes; silk /~被面 silk quilt cover /江浙一带盛产~。Silk is produced in large amounts in Jiangsu and Zhejiang provinces.
丝绸之路 sīchóu zhī lù *also* "丝路"〈历史〉Silk Road
丝带 sīdài silk ribbon; silk braid; silk sash:礼品上系着一条漂亮的~。The gift is tied with a pretty silk ribbon.
丝带木 sīdàimù ribbon tree
丝恩发怨 sī'ēn-fàyuàn gratitude for the slighest favour received or hatred for the slightest wrong suffered; hatred
丝杠 sīgàng 〈机械〉guide screw; leading screw
丝杠车床 sīgàng chēchuáng leading screw lathe
丝糕 sīgāo steamed corn cake:蒸~ steam corn cakes /枣泥~ steamed corn cake with jujube-paste
丝瓜 sīguā loofah (*Luffa cylindrica*); towel gourd; sponge gourd; dishcloth gourd:种植~ plant towel gourd /~秧 loofah (*or* towel gourd) sprout /~藤 luffa vine /~叶 luffa leaf /~络 loofah; luffa; vegetable sponge
丝光 sīguāng silky lustre (of mercerized cotton fabrics):~处理 mercerization
丝光机 sīguāngjī mercerizing range; mercerizer
丝光棉 sīguāngmián mercerized cotton
丝光沙线 sīguāng shāxiàn mercerized yarn
丝毫 sīháo (used generally in the negative) slightest amount or degree; least bit; at all:没有~危险 not the slightest risk; not dangerous at all /没有~意义 completely meaningless /~不爽 not err by a hair's breadth; tally in every detail; be perfectly right /林中没有~声音。Not a sound is heard in the forest. /他并没有受到~伤害。He was not a tiny bit hurt.
丝极 sījí 〈电学〉filament
丝兰 sīlán izote; Adam's needle (*Yucca flaccida*)
丝栎 sīlì silk oak; silky oak
丝萝 sīluó (in old-style poetry) bond of matrimony; marriage
丝米 sīmǐ decimillimetre (dmm. = $\frac{1}{10,000}$ metre)
丝绵 sīmián silk floss (usu. used as wadding):~被 silk-floss wadded quilt /~袄 silk-floss wadded (*or* quilted) jacket

丝棉木 sīmiánmù *also* "白杜" báidù *Euonymus bungeana*
丝绒 sīróng velvet; velour：黑～长裙 long black velvet skirt /～窗帘 velvet curtain
丝丝入扣 sīsī-rùkòu (as in weaving) with all threads neatly tied up — (of literary composition or artistic performance) done with flawless skill; done to perfection：歌喉婉转，～。The voice is sweet and the singing perfect.
丝丝拉拉 sīsi-lālā off and on; intermittently; fitfully：小雨～地下个没完。It kept drizzling intermittently. /他～病了有半年多。He has been ill off and on for over six months now.
丝袜 sīwà silk stockings; silk socks
丝网 sīwǎng 〈印刷〉silk screen
丝网印刷 sīwǎng yìnshuā screen printing
丝网印刷机 sīwǎng yìnshuājī screen process press
丝网印刷术 sīwǎng yìnshuāshù silk-screen process
丝微 sīwēi very small; very little; slight; subtle：在～之处可看出他工作是多么细心、认真。One can see how meticulous and conscientious he is, even down to tiny details.
丝弦 sīxián ❶ silk string (for a musical instrument) ❷ local opera popular in the Shijiazhuang (石家庄) region of Hebei Province
丝线 sīxiàn silk thread (for sewing); silk yarn：彩色～ coloured silk thread (*or* yarn) /用～绣花 embroider with silk thread /纺～ spin silk yarn
丝腺 sīxiàn silk gland
丝织品 sīzhīpǐn ❶ silk fabrics ❷ silk knitwear
丝竹 sīzhú ❶ traditional stringed and woodwind instruments：～乐 ensemble of such instruments ❷ music
丝状 sīzhuàng threadlike; filiform; filamentous：～毛 filiform hair /～体 filament /～病毒 filamentous virus
丝锥 sīzhuī *also* "螺丝攻" luósīgōng 〈机械〉screwtap; tap：粗制～ taper tap /中～ second tap /精～ bottoming tap /～扳手 tap wrench /～磨床 tap-grinding machine

咝（噝）

sī 〈象声〉(of shells and bullets) whistle：四周子弹～～飞过，他仍然从容不迫地继续观察敌情。With bullets whistling all around, he remained calm and went on with his observation of the enemy movements.

鸶（鷥）

sī *see* "鹭鸶" lùsī

sǐ

死

sǐ ❶ die; cease to live; be dead：饿～ die of hunger; starve to death /毒～ kill with poison; poison /横～ die a violent death /装～ play possum /假～ pretend to be dead; feign death;〈医学〉suspended animation /送～ court death /安乐～〈医学〉euthanasia /～而有知 if the dead should know /～而无憾 die without regret /～而不僵 dead but not yet showing signs of rigor mortis; retaining remnants of former influence, power or wealth /～无牵挂 die content; rest content in one's grave /～不足惜 death is not too high a price (for sth.); (sb.) deserves death /半～不活 half dead, half alive; dead-alive /视～如归 accept death with perfect equanimity; face death with a smile /宁～不屈 prefer death to humiliation /人皆有～。Death comes to all men. /人～万债休。〈俗语〉Death pays all debts. *or* Death squares all accounts. /～了张屠夫，不吃浑毛猪。Even if Butcher Zhang dies, we won't have to eat the hog with its hair. *or* No man is indispensable. /～到临头。One's last hour has come. *or* Death is at hand. ❷ to the death：拼命～战 fight to the death /～守阵地 defend a position to the death; hold a position at all costs /敢～队 dare-to-die squad (of soldiers) ❸ determinedly; adamantly; unyieldingly：～不改悔 die impenitent; be absolutely unrepentant (*or* incorrigible) /～不讲理 stubbornly refuse to listen to reason; be impervious (*or* dead) to reason /～不回头 wilfully refuse to mend one's ways; remain absolutely unrepentant /～不要脸 be dead to all sense of shame; be utterly shameless; have no sense of shame ❹ very; extremely：忙～了 be extremely busy; be as busy as a bee /气～了 be very angry; be enraged /恨～了 hate like poison /咸～了 terribly salty /饿得要～ as hungry as a wolf; famished /穷得要～ extremely poor; as poor as a church mouse /渴得要～ be parched with thirst; be dying for a drink /～要面子 be extremely anxious to keep up appearances /～要面子活受罪 suffer excruciatingly from trying hard to save face /他怎么把这事忘得～～的呢？How could he clean forget this? *or* How could he forget all about it? ❺ implacable; deadly; irreconcilable：～冤家 irreconcilable foe; sworn enemy ❻ fixed; rigid; stereotyped; inflexible：～工资 fixed salary (*or* wages) /～规矩 hard and fast rule /～教条 lifeless dogma /～脑筋 one-track mind /把窗钉～ nail a window fast /～啃书本 try to memorize what one reads without thinking /统得过多过～ rigid and excessive control /期限现在不讲～。No deadline is set for the time being. *or* We won't set a rigid time-limit now. ❼ impassable; closed：把门堵～ seal (*or* stop) a door /把这条水沟拦～ dam up a ditch /这是一条～巷。This is a blind alley.

死巴巴 sǐbābā fixed; unmoving; fastened：她眼睛～地盯着他。She stared at him fixedly.
死巴 sǐba 〈口语〉rigid; inflexible：这个人太～。He is far too rigid.
死板 sǐbǎn rigid; stiff; unpliant; inflexible：表情～ rigid (*or* stiff) expression /语言～ stiff language /人很～ inflexible person /办事～ not know how to be adaptable in one's work
死别 sǐbié be parted by death; part forever：生离～ part never to meet again
死不瞑目 sǐbùmíngmù would not close one's eyes when one dies; would not rest easy in one's grave; die with regret or grievance：不达目的，～。I won't rest in my grave if I can't achieve my goal.
死产 sǐchǎn 〈医学〉stillbirth
死沉 sǐchén ❶ very heavy：这箱书～～的。This box of books is awfully heavy. ❷ very quiet; silent：战地一片～的气氛。Silence reigned over the battlefield.
死沉沉 sǐchénchén ❶ very heavy：～的枕木 very heavy sleeper ❷ still as death; very quiet：～的荒原上不见人的踪影。Not a single soul could be seen in the silent wilderness. ❸ (of looks) sombre; glum：他脸色～的，一句话也不说。He looked glum and would not even say a word.
死党 sǐdǎng sworn supporter; diehard follower：结成一伙～ form a ring of sworn followers
死当 sǐdàng 〈旧语〉invalid overdue pawn ticket
死得其所 sǐdéqísuǒ die a worthy death：人生有死，～，夫复何恨。Death befalls all men. I will have no regret if I die for a worthy cause.
死等 sǐděng wait without end; wait indefinitely
死敌 sǐdí deadly or mortal enemy; sworn enemy; implacable foe：把他视为～ regard him as one's sworn enemy
死地 sǐdì fatal position; deathtrap：必欲置之～而后快 (hate sb. so much that one) cannot be happy with anything less than sb.'s death /置之～而后生 confront sb. with the danger of death so that he will fight to survive
死点 sǐdiǎn 〈机械〉dead centre;〈电学〉dead spot;〈生物〉dead point：～发火 dead centre ignition
死读书 sǐdúshū study mechanically; read without thinking; be a bookworm：～的学习方法决不可取。A mechanical way of learning is undesirable.
死对头 sǐduìtou sworn enemy; deadly foe：没想到这一对～又见面了。As luck would have it, the two irreconcilable opponents found themselves confronting each other again.
死而后已 sǐ'érhòuyǐ until one's death; to the end of one's days：鞠躬尽瘁，～ work with selfless devotion until one's heart ceases to beat
死而无怨 sǐ'érwúyuàn die without regret or remorse：为人民而死，～。If I am to die for the people, I'll do so without regret.
死工夫 sǐgōngfu great exertion; sheer hard work：下～ work really hard
死谷 Sǐgǔ Death Valley, a deep arid desert basin in southeast California
死光 sǐguāng ❶ death ray：～武器 death-ray weapon ❷ all dead：敌人都～了。All the enemy soldiers were dead.
死鬼 sǐguǐ ❶ (used to curse a person or as a term of endearment) devil：你这～，藏到什么地方去了？You devil! Where have you been hiding all this time? ❷ dead person
死海 Sǐhǎi Dead Sea, a bitter salt lake in the Jordan Valley on the Jordan-Palestine border：～古卷 Dead Sea Scrolls (discovered from 1947 onward)
死耗 sǐhào news of a person's death

死胡同 sǐhútòng blind alley; impasse; dead end:我找不到创作上的出路,正在~里打转转。I am at a dead end in my writing and cannot find a way out.
死话 sǐhuà remark made with a note of finality
死缓 sǐhuǎn (short for 死刑缓期执行)〈法律〉death sentence with a two-year reprieve; stay of execution:他被判~。He was sentenced to death with a two-year reprieve.
死灰 sǐhuī dying embers; cold ashes:心如~ (of persons) be in total despair
死灰复燃 sǐhuī-fùrán dying embers flaring up again;〈贬义〉resurgence or revival of sth. that has been regarded as dead or dying:封建迷信活动在这一地区竟又~了。Superstitious and feudal activities have again surfaced in this area.
死魂灵 Sǐhúnlíng *Dead Souls*, a masterpiece by Nikolai Gogol, Russian writer, in 1842
死活 sǐhuó ❶ life or death; lot; fate:他们只管赚钱,一点也不顾别人的~。Bent upon profit, they don't care a damn about others. ❷〈口语〉anyway, simply:他~不同意。He simply wouldn't agree. 明天我~不去见那个人。I refuse to see that man tomorrow, come what may.
死火山 sǐhuǒshān extinct or dead volcano
死记 sǐjì memorize mechanically; memorize by rote; learn by heart
死记硬背 sǐjì-yìngbèi learn by rote; memorize mechanically:只知~是学不好外语的。One cannot master a foreign language by rote memory alone. /~不是学习的好方法。Memorizing without understanding is not a good way of learning.
死忌 sǐjì anniversary of a person's death
死寂 sǐjì〈书面〉deathly stillness or silence:枪声过后,山谷一片~。After the gunshots died away, a deathly stillness filled the valley. /夜深人静,一片~。Night was deep and a deathlike silence reigned.
死角 sǐjiǎo ❶〈军事〉dead angle; blind angle; dead space ❷ spot or corner as yet unaffected by a movement, current of thought, prevailing custom, etc.; backwater:室内卫生的~ dirty corner in an otherwise clean room
死校 sǐjiào proof reading based on the original script only
死节 sǐjié〈书面〉die a martyr's death; die for honour; (of widow) die for loyalty to her deceased husband
死结 sǐjié fast knot:打个~ tie a fast knot /这问题成了他心上的一个~,很难一下子解开。This has formed a fast knot on his mind and is hard to untie in a short time.
死劲儿 sǐjìnr (with) all one's strength or might; (with) might and main:他~跑,终于得了冠军。Running for all his worth, he came first in the race. /同学们用~拉,终于把船拉回了岸边。Using all their strength the students at last dragged the boat back to the bank.
死晶体 sǐjīngtǐ dead crystal
死静 sǐjìng deathly still:院里漆黑~,没有一点儿声响。It was pitch dark and deathly still in the courtyard. You could have heard a pin drop. /大街小巷~~的,不见一个人影。The streets and lanes were dead still and completely deserted.
死局 sǐjú (of chess) lost game
死扣儿 sǐkòur fast knot
死库容 sǐkùróng dead storage (of a reservoir)
死拉活拽 sǐlā-huózhuài drag by force:他~,硬把我拽进屋里了。He dragged me into the room against my will.
死牢 sǐláo death row; death house; death cell
死劳动 sǐláodòng materialized labour
死老虎 sǐlǎohǔ〈贬义〉slain tiger — person no longer in power and rather helpless
死里逃生 sǐlǐ-táoshēng escape by the skin of one's teeth; have a narrow escape; be a close shave; be out of the jaws of death:他~,从敌占区来到这里。He had a narrow escape from the enemy-occupied area.
死理 sǐlǐ rigid and inflexible rules; dogma:认~ stick to rigid and inflexible rules /他老是咬住他的~不放。He always clings to his lifeless dogmas.
死力 sǐlì (with) all one's strength; (with) might and main:拼~ strain every effort; exert one's utmost /~拦住惊马 stop a runaway horse with all one's strength /~反抗 resist with might and main; fight back tooth and nail
死路 sǐlù blind alley; dead end; road to ruin or destruction:若不回头,~一条。If you don't mend your ways, you are sure to meet your doom.
死马当作活马医 sǐmǎ dàngzuò huómǎ yī doctor a dead horse as if it were still alive — not give up for lost; make a last attempt to save a hopeless situation:事已至此,只有~了! Since things have come to such a sorry pass, all we can do is to redeem the situation as best we can.
死面 sǐmiàn unleavened dough:~饼 flat cake made of unleavened dough
死灭 sǐmiè die (out); become extinct
死命 sǐmìng ❶ doom; death:制敌于~ deal the enemy a deathblow; send the enemy to his doom ❷ desperately; recklessly:~呼救 shout desperately for help /~逃跑 run as fast as one's legs can carry one; run for one's dear life
死模活样 sǐmú-huóyàng half dead, half alive; listless
死难 sǐnàn die in an accident, etc.:~烈士 martyr /这次飞机失事中的~人员 those who were killed in the air-crash
死脑筋 sǐnǎojīn ❶ inflexible view; old-fashioned ideas ❷ old fogey; one-track mind:你真是个典型的~,办事一点也不知变通。You must have a typical one-track mind as you are so inflexible in whatever you do.
死皮赖脸 sǐpí-làiliǎn thick-skinned; utterly shameless; brazen-faced:这人真讨厌,总是~地缠着别人。The man is quite a nuisance; he keeps pestering others shamelessly.
死期 sǐqī time of death; day of doom:~将近。Death is imminent.
死棋 sǐqí dead piece or fatal move in a game of chess; hopeless case:下了一步~ make a stupid move /走活了一盘~ save a hopeless situation
死气沉沉 sǐqì-chénchén lifeless; spiritless; listless; stagnant:打破~的局面 change radically a lifeless state of affairs /这个年轻人~的,没有一点朝气。This young man looked so spiritless and devoid of vigour. /改革给~的企业带来了生机。Reforms brought life to the stagnant enterprise.
死气白赖 sǐqìbáilài *also* "死乞白赖"〈方言〉pestering; importunate:~地跟别人要钱 pester sb. for money /~地向她讨好 toady to her shamelessly
死契 sǐqì irrevocable title deed or contract
死钱 sǐqián ❶ money that does not make profit or yield interest ❷ regular income of fixed amount
死囚 sǐqiú condemned prisoner; convict sentenced to death and awaiting execution:~牢房 condemned cell; death cell; death row /~看守人 deathwatch
死球 sǐqiú〈体育〉(of baseball, rugby, etc) dead ball; (of ice hockey, etc.) icing:~区 (of billiards) anchor space /~线 (of rugby) dead-ball line
死去活来 sǐqù-huólái half dead, half alive; more dead than alive:哭得~ sob one's heart out; cry one's eyes out /他被折磨得~。He was tortured within an inch of his life.
死人 sǐrén ❶ dead body; corpse:~崇拜 necrolatry /活~ walking corpse /枪战后,街上遍地都是~。The street was strewn with dead bodies after the shootout. ❷〈戏谑〉devil; lazy-bones:快起来干活,你这个~! Get up and start work, you lazybones!
死伤 sǐshāng the dead and the wounded; casualties:~惨重 heavy casualties; heavy toll of lives
死神 sǐshén god in charge of deaths — death:经过抢救,终于把病人从~的手里夺回来。The emergency treatment saved the patient from the jaws of death.
死生有命,富贵在天 sǐ-shēng yǒu mìng, fùguì zài tiān as life and death are a matter of destiny, so wealth and honour are the will of heaven; as life and death are preordained by fate, so wealth and rank are decreed by heaven
死尸 sǐshī corpse; dead body:火化~ cremate a dead body
死士 sǐshì〈书面〉dare-to-die soldier
死事 sǐshì〈书面〉die for the affairs of the state
死守 sǐshǒu ❶defend to the death; put up a last-ditch resistance:~制高点 defend the height (*or* commanding elevation) to the death ❷ obstinately cling to; stick fast to:~封建礼教 (obstinately) cling to feudal etiquette and ethics
死水 sǐshuǐ stagnant water; standing water:一潭~ a pool of stagnant (*or* standing) water; stagnant and lifeless condition /心如~ with one's mind as settled as standing water; in utter despair /~微澜。Stagnant water hardly ripples.
死说活说 sǐshuō-huóshuō try to persuade by all means; impor-

S

tune incessantly：我～也没说动他的心。However hard I tried, I failed to persuade him.

死胎 sǐtāi 〈医学〉stillborn foetus; stillbirth：生下一个～ have a stillbirth /～不下 retention of a dead foetus

死土 sǐtǔ 〈农业〉dead soil

死亡 sǐwáng death; doom; extinction：～事故 fatal accident /正在一步步走向～ head step by step for doom (*or* extinction) /～原因不明。The cause of the death is unknown.

死亡抚恤金 sǐwáng fǔxùjīn death benefits

死亡鉴定 sǐwáng jiàndìng verification of death

死亡率 sǐwánglǜ death rate; mortality：婴儿～ infant mortality rate/医疗条件的改善使～大大降低。Improved medical service has brought about a drastic drop in mortality.

死亡人名册 sǐwángrén míngcè death roll

死亡统计 sǐwáng tǒngjì necrology

死亡线 sǐwángxiàn verge of death：在～上挣扎 struggle for existence on the verge of death; struggle for survival

死亡学 sǐwángxué thanatology

死亡证 sǐwángzhèng death certificate

死无对证 sǐwúduìzhèng the dead cannot bear witness; dead men tell no tales：这事～，看来要成悬案了。Since the dead cannot bear witness, the case may have to be suspended.

死无葬身之地 sǐ wú zàngshēn zhī dì die without a burial place — die without a decent burial; come to a bad end：弄得～ die in disgrace

死相 sǐxiang disgusting expression, speech and deportment, make-up, etc. (sometimes a teasing remark in disgust by a girl or wife to a man)：一脸～ be expressionless

死心 sǐxīn abandon the idea altogether; cherish no more illusions：姑娘仍然不～。The girl simply wouldn't give up the idea. /这回，他可死了心了。After this, he cherished no more illusions.

死心塌地 sǐxīn-tādì totally; completely; with all one's heart：～的反动分子 die-hard (*or* out-and-out) reactionary /～地为侵略者卖命 be dead set (*or* hell-bent) on serving the aggressors /尽管他有不少缺点，她还是～地爱他。Despite his faults, she loved him with all her heart.

S

死心眼儿 sǐxīnyǎnr ❶ stubborn; mullish：真是一个～的孩子! What a stubborn child! ❷ person with a one-track mind：她从小就是个～。She has been pigheaded ever since she was a little girl.

死信 sǐxìn ❶ news of sb.'s death; obituary：惊悉某人的～ be shocked to learn about the death of someone ❷ dead letter：她把两百多封～都设法投递出去了。She managed to resurrect over two hundred dead letters.

死刑 sǐxíng 〈法律〉capital punishment; death penalty; death sentence：判处～ sentence sb. to death /执行～ execute a death sentence /～缓刑 death sentence with a reprieve

死刑犯 sǐxíngfàn 〈法律〉condemned criminal or prisoner; prisoner under death sentence; death-row prisoner

死性 sǐxing inflexible; obstinate：你干吗那么～，非走这步棋? Why are you so obdurately bent on taking this move?

死讯 sǐxùn news of sb.'s death; obituary notice

死因 sǐyīn cause of death：～证明书 certificate of the cause of death /～调查 coroner's inquest; death inquiry

死因裁判官 sǐyīn cáipànguān (HK) coroner

死因研究庭 Sǐyīn Yánjiūtíng (HK) Coroner's Court

死硬 sǐyìng stiff and inflexible; intransigent; diehard：态度～ intransigent attitude

死硬派 sǐyìngpài *also* "死硬分子" diehard

死友 sǐyǒu 〈书面〉friends sworn to the death

死有应得 sǐyǒuyīngdé deserve to be condemned to death; deserve death

死有余辜 sǐyǒuyúgū even death would not be sufficient punishment; the crime calls for more than death：罪行累累，～。The man has committed countless crimes, and even death is too good for him.

死于非命 sǐyú-fēimìng die an unnatural or a violent death：没想到他竟然因车祸而～。We were shocked to learn of his violent death in a car accident.

死凿儿 sǐzáor 〈方言〉❶ headstrong; obstinate; inflexible：你别犯～，什么事都要看宽一点儿。Don't you get so mulish again. You mustn't take everything so seriously. ❷ stubborn character; mule：他是一个～，怎么劝他也不听。He is too stubborn to listen to advice.

死战 sǐzhàn ❶ life-and-death battle：决一～ wage a life-and-death struggle ❷ fight to the death：只有～才有脱险的可能。Only by fighting to the death will it be possible to escape danger.

死仗 sǐzhàng tough battle; formidable task

死账 sǐzhàng dead loan; dead account

死者 sǐzhě the dead; the deceased; the departed：～姓名 name of the dead (*or* deceased)

死症 sǐzhèng disease beyond cure; incurable malady; fatal disease

死罪 sǐzuì ❶ capital offence or crime：赦免他的～ absolve sb. from capital punishment /～可免，活罪难逃。Your capital offence may be pardoned, but some physical punishment is due. ❷〈套语〉please pardon me：手下人失察，造成这场误会，～，～。This misunderstanding was caused by my men who neglected their duties. Please do pardon me for that.

sì

禩 sì *also* "祀" sì offer sacrifices to the gods or one's ancestors

肆[1] sì wantonly; wilfully; unbridledly：放～ throw restraint to the winds; be unbridled (*or* unscrupulous) /大～挥霍 wantonly squander; spend (money) like water /大～泛滥 run rampant /大～宣扬 sing loudly the praises of; trumpet with great vigour /～口谩骂 swear like a trooper; use profane language freely

肆[2] sì four (used for the numeral 四 on cheques, etc. to avoid mistakes or alterations)

肆[3] sì 〈书面〉shop：茶楼酒～ teahouses and wineshops /市～ shop; store

肆口 sìkǒu talk without restraint (in scolding, abusing, etc.)：～诋毁 abuse outrageously without restraint /～讥讽 ridicule at will /～大骂 let loose a torrent of abuse; shout abuse

肆力 sìlì 〈书面〉do all one can; exert one's utmost：～农事 apply oneself to farming

肆虐 sìnüè indulge in wanton destruction; wreak havoc; persecute：蚊虫～。Mosquitoes and insects ran rampant. /春夏之间更是风沙～的季节。Wind and dust do their worst in late spring and early summer.

肆扰 sìrǎo wantonly harass; wilfully disturb：～四邻 wantonly harass one's neighbourhood

肆无忌惮 sìwújìdàn reckless and unbridled; unscrupulous：～地攻击 mount a brazen attack /～地违法乱纪 violate law and discipline wantonly

肆行 sìxíng wanton; unbridled：～劫掠 indulge in wanton plunder /～无忌 act in a reckless, unbridled manner

肆意 sìyì brazenly; recklessly; wilfully：～污蔑 slander recklessly /～嘲弄 ridicule unscrupulously /～歪曲事实真相 wilfully distort the truth /～破坏他国领土完整 wantonly encroach upon the territorial integrity of another country

肆应 sìyìng 〈书面〉able to get on well with people：善于～ be good at socializing; be a good mixer /～之才 ability to get along well with other people /周旋～ mix with (people); move in (society, circles, etc.); socialize

寺 sì ❶〈历史〉central government organ; ministry：大理～ Imperial Court of Justice (in charge of reviewing cases and sentences, sometimes divided into 左～ and 右～ "Left Court and Right Court") /大理～卿 Chief Justice of the Imperial Court /太常～ Ministry of Ceremonies and Worship ❷ temple; mosque; monastery：佛～ Buddhist temple /摩尼～ Manichean temple /清真～ *also* "礼拜～" mosque /喇嘛～ lamasery /大昭～ Jokhang Monastery /扎什伦布～ Tashi Lhunpo Monastery /甘丹～ Gahdan (*or* Gyadan) Monastery /哲蚌～ Drepung Monastery/～产 property (*or* real estate) owned by a monastery or temple or mosque /～舍 temple (mosque, etc.) premises

寺观 sìguàn Buddhist and Taoist temples; temples in general

寺庙 sìmiào temple; altar for gods or well-known historical figures

寺人 sìrén 〈旧语〉palace attendant; eunuch
寺院 sìyuàn temple; monastery; cloister
寺主 sìzhǔ abbot

四[1] sì ❶ four: 二加二等于～ Two plus two equals four. ❷ (Sì) a surname

四[2] sì 〈音乐〉note of the scale in *gongchepu* (工尺谱), corresponding to 6 in numbered musical notation

四…八… sì…bā… *used before two similar words to indicate all sides or directions*: 四乡八镇 all towns and villages / 四停八当 be very well-disposed; have everything ready / 四维八德 four principles and eight virtues — moral foundations of a society
四胞胎 sìbāotāi quadruplets
四倍体 sìbèitǐ 〈生物〉tetraploid
四边 sìbiān (on) four sides: ～都被矮墙围着 surrounded by short walls on all sides / ～围着不少人 with many people around
四边形 sìbiānxíng tetragon; quadrangle; quadrilateral: 画一个～ draw a quadrilateral / 平行～〈数学〉parallelogram
四不拗六 sìbù'àoliù the few is no match for the many
四不像 sìbùxiàng ❶〈动物〉(Pere) David's deer (*Elaphurus davidianus*); *milu* (麋鹿) ❷ nondescript; neither fish, flesh, nor fowl: 他说话既不是普通话, 也不是四川话, 简直是～。He spoke a nondescript dialect, neither standard Chinese nor Sichuan dialect.
四部 sìbù standard library classification into four categories in ancient China: 经 Confucian classics, 史 history, including geography, 子 philosophy (other than Confucian) and the arts and sciences, and 集 collected literary works (by subject or author); later also called 四库 (a reference to the four vaults where the classics, history, philosophy and collected works are kept respectively)
四称 sìchèn (of articles, objects, etc.) properly arranged and placed or laid out; (of appearance, body figure, etc.) well-proportioned; well-balanced: 房间里家具虽然简单, 但安排得很～。The furniture, though simple, was properly placed and arranged. / 她的身段长得挺～。She is of proportional build. *or* She has a shapely figure.
四冲程 sìchōngchéng four-cycle; four-stroke: ～发动机 four-stroke engine; Otto engine
四重唱 sìchóngchàng 〈音乐〉(vocal) quartet: 女声～ female quartet / 表演～ sing a quartet
四重奏 sìchóngzòu 〈音乐〉(instrumental) quartet: 弦乐～ string quartet / 演出～ play a quartet
四出 sìchū go all around: ～活动 move about in all directions / 游击队经常在夜间～打击敌人。The guerrillas often moved here and there at night, dealing blows at the enemy.
四处 sìchù all around; far and near; everywhere: ～打听 make inquiries everywhere / ～蔓延 run wild in all directions / ～游说 go around to "sell an idea"; go about drumming up support; barnstorm / ～奔波 go hither and thither / ～寻找 search high and low; look into every nook and cranny
四川 Sìchuān Sichuan (Province)
四川盆地 Sìchuān Péndì Sichuan Basin
四川清音 Sìchuān qīngyīn Sichuan ballad singing
四磁头录像机 sìcítóu lùxiàngjī quadruplex videotape recorder
四次方程 sìcì fāngchéng quartic equation
四大 sìdà ❶ (short for 大鸣, 大放, 大辩论, 大字报) speak whatever one likes, air views without limit, hold mass debates and write big-character posters; speak out, air views and hold debates in a big way and write big-character posters ❷〈佛教〉four elements of earth, water, fire and air
四大发明 sì dà fāmíng ancient China's four great inventions, namely, the compass, gunpowder, paper-making and printing
四大皆空 sìdà-jiēkōng 〈佛教〉everything in this world is void; all is vanity
四大金刚 Sì Dà Jīngāng (popular term for 四大天王) Four Heavenly Guardians at the entrance to a Buddhist temple
四大名旦 sì dà míngdàn four great *dan* actors in Beijing opera (i.e. Mei Lanfang 梅兰芳, Cheng Yanqiu 程砚秋, Xun Huisheng 荀慧生 and Shang Xiaoyun 尚小云)
四大天王 Sì Dà Tiānwáng Four *Devarajas* whose statues are often placed at the entrance of a Buddhist temple as guardians
四等分 sìděngfēn quartering
四谛 sìdì 〈佛教〉Four Noble Truths (suffering 苦, the cause of suffering 集, the extinction of suffering 灭 and the way leading to the extinction of suffering 道)
四点分析 sìdiǎn fēnxī 〈经济〉swot analysis(strength, weakness, opportunity and threat)
四叠体 sìdiétǐ 〈生理〉corpora quadrigemina
四方 sìfāng ❶ four directions (north, south, east and west); all sides; all quarters: 奔走～ run hither and thither / ～分散 disperse in all directions / ～游客 tourists from everywhere / ～响应。Response came from every quarter. ❷ square or cubic: 长着一张～脸 with a square face / 四四方方的金属匣子 square metal box / ～晶系 tetragonal system
四方步 sìfāngbù solemn and measured stride: 他迈着不紧不慢的～走进大厅。He walked into the hall with a leisurely and measured stride.
四方联 sìfānglián block of four stamps still attached
四分五裂 sìfēn-wǔliè fall apart; be rent asunder; disintegrate: ～的局面 situation of disunity (*or* disintegration) / 执政党内部已经～。The ruling party has disintegrated from within. *or* The ruling party has split up.
四分音符 sìfēn yīnfú 〈音乐〉crotchet; quarter note
四分之一决赛 sìfēnzhīyī juésài 〈体育〉quarter-finals
四伏 sìfú lurk everywhere: 危机～ danger lurks on every side
四个现代化 sìgè xiàndàihuà Four Modernizations (i.e. of industry, agriculture, national defence, and science and technology)
四顾 sìgù look around: 茫然～ look around, feeling at a loss / ～无人。Nobody is seen around.
四轨 sìguǐ 〈无线电〉four-track; four channel: ～录音放音 quadraphony; quadraphonics
四国 Sìguó Shikoku, smallest of the four main islands of Japan
四海 sìhǎi four seas — whole country; whole world: ～飘零 drift (*or* wander) from one place to another; lead a wandering life / 放之～而皆准 be universally applicable (*or* true) / ～一家 the whole country (*or* nation) is one family / ～同悲 the whole nation is grief-stricken / ～鼎沸 the whole country (*or* world) is in a tumult / ～承平 there is peace and stability throughout the country / 我们来自五湖～。We hail from all corners of the country.
四海升平 sìhǎi-shēngpíng peace in the country or world: ～, 国泰民安。The country is prosperous and the people live in peace.
四海为家 sìhǎi-wéijiā ❶ all corners of the earth belong to the emperor; achieve perfect unity within the empire; make the country a big family ❷ make one's home wherever one is; lead a wandering life
四海之内皆兄弟 sìhǎi zhī nèi jiē xiōngdì all men are brothers within the Four Seas
四害 sìhài four pests (rats, bedbugs, flies and mosquitoes): 除～ wipe out the four pests
四合 sìhé closed in on all sides; close in all around: 暮色～。Dusk is closing in (all around).
四合房 sìhéfáng *see* "四合院"
四合院 sìhéyuàn traditional, residential compound with houses around a courtyard; courtyard house; quadrangle: 北京的～别具一格。The quadrangles in Beijing have a distinctive style of its own.
四呼 sìhū 〈语言〉(of traditional Chinese rhyming) four categories of rhyming vowels, i.e. 齐齿呼 syllables with i as the final or its beginning, such as 坚 jiān; 合口呼 syllables with u as the final or its beginning, such as 关 guān; 撮口呼 syllables with ü as the final or its beginning, such as 捐 juān; and 开口呼 syllables not with i, u or ü as the final or its beginning, such as 肝 gān
四胡 sìhú traditional Chinese four-stringed fiddle
四化 sìhuà (short for 四个现代化) Four Modernizations (of agriculture, industry, national defence, and science and technology): 实现～的宏伟目标 realize the grand goal of the four modernizations / ～建设 modernization drive
四环素 sìhuánsù 〈药学〉tetracycline: ～药片 tetracycline tablets / ～软膏 tetracycline ointment
四级风 sìjífēng 〈气象〉force 4 wind; moderate breeze: 今天刮～。There's a moderate breeze today.
四级管 sìjíguǎn 〈无线电〉tetrode
四季 sìjì four seasons: ～不凋 bloom throughout the year / ～如春 like spring all the year round / 景色～宜人。The view is delightful in all seasons. / 这是棵～常青树。This tree remains green throughout

S

the year. *or* This tree is an evergreen.
四季豆 sìjìdòu kidney bean
四季海棠 sìjì hǎitáng 〈植物〉Chinese flowering crabapple
四季花 sìjìhuā representative flowers of the four seasons: peony (spring), lotus (summer), chrysanthemum (autumn) and plum (winter)
四季节 Sìjìjié 〈宗教〉Ember Days (four periods of three days each, set apart for fasting and prayer by the Roman Catholic, Anglican and other churches, being the Wednesday, Friday and Saturday following the first Sunday in Lent, Whitsunday, September 14 and December 13)
四季青 sìjìqīng 〈中药〉Chinese holly leaf
四郊 sìjiāo suburbs; outskirts
四郊多垒 sìjiāo-duōlěi there are many camps round the city — enemy forces closing in on all sides; critical situaiton:如今～,正是男儿效命之时。The enemy forces are closing in on all sides. It is the time for men to render their service to the country.
四脚八叉 sìjiǎo-bāchà *also*"四仰八叉"〈口语〉(sleep) on one's back with arms and legs stretched out; (lie) sprawling:孩子～地躺在炕上,睡得正香呢。Lying with his arms and legs stretched out comfortably, the child was sound asleep.
四脚朝天 sìjiǎo-cháotiān fall backwards with one's hands and legs in the air:摔了个～ fall flat on one's back /忙得～ be run (*or* rushed) off one's feet (in one's work)
四脚蛇 sìjiǎoshé 〈口语〉lizard
四近 sìjìn all around; close by:～都是山。There are mountains all around.
四旧 sìjiù "four olds" (old ideas, old culture, old customs and old habits, all of which came under attack during the Cultural Revolution):破～ do away with the "four olds"
四开 sìkāi 〈印刷〉quarto
四开本 sìkāiběn quarto
四库 sìkù *see*"四部"
四库全书 Sìkù Quánshū Complete Library in the Four Branches of Literature, compiled in 1772-1782 at the order of Emperor Qianlong (乾隆)
四类分子 sìlèifènzǐ ❶ four categories of politically undesirable people (landlords, rich peasants, counterrevolutionaries and bad elements) ❷ person belonging to one of the above catagories
四联单 sìliándān quadruplicate form
四邻 sìlín one's close neighbours:搅得～不安 create quite a disturbance in the neighbourhood /与～和睦相处 be on good terms with one's neighbours; enjoy good-neighbourly relations
四邻八舍 sìlín-bāshè all the neighbours; whole neighbourhood:～都来帮他的忙。All the neighbours came to his help.
四六风 sìliùfēng 〈医学〉umbilical tetanus of newborn babies
四六体 sìliùtǐ 〈文学〉euphuistic style of parallel constructions, known for pairs of sentences of four and six characters
四六文 sìliùwén a kind of rhythmical prose with parallel constructions consisting of pairs of sentences of four and six characters
四轮驱动 sìlún qūdòng four-wheel drive:～汽车 four-wheel drive car
四面 sìmiàn (on) four sides; (on) all sides:～环山 be surrounded by hills /～埋伏 lie in ambush on all sides
四面八方 sìmiàn-bāfāng all directions; all quarters; all around; everywhere:奔向祖国的～ go to all parts of the country /从～汇集到北京 come to Beijing from all corners of the country
四面出击 sìmiàn-chūjī hit out in all directions; attack on all sides simultaneously
四面楚歌 sìmiàn-chǔgē be exposed to attack on all sides; be utterly isolated:他已陷入了～的困境。He has been hopelessly isolated.
四面受敌 sìmiàn-shòudí be completely encircled by the enemy; be exposed to enemy attacks on all sides
四面体 sìmiàntǐ tetrahedron; tetrahedroid
四拇指 sìmuzhǐ 〈方言〉third finger; ring finger
四旁 sìpáng ❶ back and front, left and right; in the neighbourhood:～无人。Nobody is around. ❷ "four sides" (i.e. house side, village side, roadside and waterside):～绿化 green the "four sides" (as part of an afforestation campaign)
四平八稳 sìpíng-bāwěn methodical and well-balanced; stable and dependable; overcautious and lacking in initiative:他办事一向～,极少出错。He is always stable and dependable, and rarely makes a mistake. /他的讲话～,毫无新意。His speech was overcautious and devoid of any original ideas.
四鳍旗鱼 sìqí qíyú *also*"枪鱼" qiāngyú spearfish
四起 sìqǐ rise from all directions:喊声～。Cries rose from all directions. /谣言～。Rumours came thick and fast. *or* There was rumour everywhere.
四清运动 Sìqīng Yùndòng *also*"社会主义教育运动" Shèhuìzhǔyì Jiàoyù Yùndòng "four clean-ups" movement (a movement to purify politics, economy, organization and ideology, 1963-1966)
四人帮 Sìrénbāng "Gang of Four": Jiang Qing (江青), Zhang Chunqiao (张春桥), Wang Hongwen (王洪文) and Yao Wenyuan (姚文元) — ringleaders of the ultra-leftists in the Cultural Revolution (1966-1976)
四人皮艇 sìrén pítǐng 〈体育〉kayak four
四散 sìsàn scatter or disperse in all directions:～奔逃 flee in all directions
四舍五入 sìshě-wǔrù 〈数学〉rounding (off); to the nearest whole number:～法 rounding-off method
四声 sìshēng 〈语言〉❶ four tones of classical Chinese pronunciation (i.e. 平声, 上声, 去声, and 入声) ❷ four tones of modern standard Chinese pronunciation (i.e. 阴平"-", 阳平"ˊ", 上声"ˇ", and 去声"ˋ") ❸ tone
四声道 sìshēngdào 〈无线电〉four-track; four-channel:～立体声 quadraphony; quadraphonics; quadruple stereophone /～录音 four-track recording /～立体声收音机 stereo four-channel receiver
四时 sìshí four seasons:～鲜果 fresh fruit of the season; fresh fruit in season
四时八节 sìshí-bājié four seasons (spring, summer, autumn and winter) and eight solar terms (the Beginning of Spring, the Beginning of Summer, the Beginning of Autumn, the Beginning of Winter, the Vernal Equinox, the Autumnal Equinox, the Summer Solstice and the Winter Solstice)
四书 Sìshū Four Books (i.e. the four major Confucian classics: *The Great Learning*《大学》, *The Doctrine of the Mean*《中庸》, *The Analects of Confucius*《论语》and *Mencius*《孟子》):熟读～五经 be well versed in the Four Books and Five Classics
四体 sìtǐ ❶〈书面〉four limbs; arms and legs ❷ *see*"四体书"
四体不勤,五谷不分 sìtǐ bù qín, wǔgǔ bù fēn 〈贬义〉can neither use one's four limbs nor tell the five grains apart; can neither do physical work nor distinguish rice from wheat:～的书呆子 bookworm who is divorced from productive labour
四体书 sìtǐshū four major styles of Chinese calligraphy (i.e. 正 the regular script, 草 the cursive script, 隶 the official script and 篆 the seal character)
四通八达 sìtōng-bādá extend in all directions; be accessible from all directions:这是个～的商埠。It is a commercial port accessible from all directions. *or* This is a trading port with links to all parts of the country.
四通阀 sìtōngfá four-way valve
四头肌 sìtóujī 〈医学〉quadriceps
四外 sìwài all around (esp. in an open place); in all directions:～空无一人。There was not a soul all around. /～一片黄澄澄的麦子。Expanses of golden wheat extended in all directions.
四望 sìwàng look around:放眼～ look around /～无人。Nobody is seen around.
四围 sìwéi all round:房子～都是竹子。All round the house are bamboo groves.
四维 sìwéi ❶ the four basic virtues (of Confucian ethics:礼 propriety, 义 justice, 廉 integrity and 耻 honour) ❷〈书面〉southeast, northeast, southwest and northwest ❸〈中医〉four limbs; arms and legs ❹ four dimensions:～时空 four-dimensional space-time /～宇宙 four-dimensional universe /～几何学 four-dimensional geometry
四维空间 sìwéi kōngjiān 〈物理〉four dimensional space; fourth dimension
四下里 sìxiàli *also*"四下" all around:～一片漆黑。It was pitch-dark everywhere. /～一看全是些不认识的人。Looking around, he saw strangers only. /～都找遍了,也没个人影。We searched high and low, and not a soul was to be seen.
四仙桌 sìxiānzhuō old-fashioned square table for four (with one person at each side)
四乡 sìxiāng country surrounding a town or city:街上挤满了进城购物的～农民。The streets were crowded with farmers who came in

from the neighbouring country for shopping.
四项基本原则 sìxiàng jīběn yuánzé Four Cardinal Principles (i.e. adherence to the socialist road, the people's democratic dictatorship, the leadership of the Communist Party, and Marxism-Leninism and Mao Zedong Thought)
四象 sìxiàng groups of constellations in ancient China, each consisting of seven, showing directions: the *Canglong* or Dragon(苍龙) in the east, the *Baihu* or White Tiger(白虎) in the west, the *Zhuque* or Vermillion Bird (朱雀) in the south and the *Xuanwu* or Black Warrior (玄武) in the north
四言诗 sìyánshī classical poetry with four characters to a line, popular before the Han Dynasty
四仰八叉 sìyǎng-bāchà *see* "四脚八叉"
四野 sìyě vast expanses of open country: ~渺无人迹。There was not a trace of man on the vast expanses of open country.
四有 sìyǒu cherish lofty ideals, foster moral integrity, have a good education and observe discipline: ~新人 new generation of people with lofty ideals, moral integrity, good education and a strong sense of discipline
四月 sìyuè ❶ April ❷ fourth month of the lunar year; fourth moon
四则 sìzé 〈数学〉four fundamental operations of arithmetic (i.e. addition, subtraction, multiplication and division): ~运算 arithmetic calculation / ~题 arithmetic problem
四战之地 sìzhànzhīdì *also* "四战之国" place exposed to attack on all sides
四诊 sìzhěn 〈中医〉four methods of diagnosis (i.e. 望 observation of the patient's complexion, expression, movements, tongue, etc., 闻 auscultation and olfaction, 问 interrogation and 切 pulse feeling and palpation)
四肢 sìzhī four limbs; arms and legs: ~健全 be sound in body; be physically sound / ~麻痹 quadriplegia; tetraplegia
四至 sìzhì four boundaries of a piece of land or a construction site
四致 sìzhi 〈方言〉appropriate; fitting; proper: 砌上围墙，栽上花草，小院就更~了。This would be a proper garden when flowers are planted and an enclosure built round.
四周 sìzhōu all around: 出了地铁车站，她看见~都是高楼大厦。Emerging from the subway station, she saw high-rise buildings all around.
四周围 sìzhōuwéi 〈口语〉all around; on all sides
四足动物 sìzú dòngwù quadruped; tetrapod
四座 sìzuò all the people present: ~哗然。The audience burst into an uproar.

泗[1]

sì 〈书面〉nasal mucus; snivel: 涕~横流 tears and snivel streaming all over

泗[2]

Sì Sishui River
泗州戏 sìzhōuxì *also* "拉魂腔" lāhúnqiāng Sizhou opera (a local opera popular in the Huai River area and named after its place of origin Sizhou or present-day Sixian, Anhui Province)

驷

sì 〈书面〉❶ team of four horses ❷ horse
驷不及舌 sìbùjíshé even a team of four horses cannot overtake and recover what is said
驷马 sìmǎ 〈书面〉team of four horses: 一言既出，~难追。Even four horses cannot take back what one has said — what has been said cannot be unsaid. *or* A word spoken is past recalling.
驷马高车 sìmǎ-gāochē carriage drawn by four horses — powerful and influential people

兕

sì 〈书面〉female rhinoceros

食

sì 〈书面〉bring food to; feed
see also shí

饲

sì *see* "饲" sì

耜

sì 〈古语〉❶ spade-shaped farm tool ❷ ploughshare-shaped instrument

佀

sì ❶ *see* "似" sì ❷ (Sì) a surname

似

sì ❶ similar; like; approximate: 近~ be approximate; be similar / 酷~ exactly like; as like as two peas / 貌~ look alike in appearance / 如狼~虎 as ferocious as wolves and tigers / 归心~箭 anxious to return home as soon as possible; eager to dart homeward / ~胶如漆 like glue and lacquer — deep love / 我们双方在这些问题上的观点是一致或相~的。Our two sides hold identical or similar views on these questions. ❷ look; seem; appear: ~属可行 seem feasible ❸ indicating superiority: 一天好~一天 get better day by day / 不是春光，胜~春光。It is more beautiful than the spring scene though spring is not at hand.
see also shì
似曾相识 sìcéngxiāngshí seem to be familiar: 她在人群中看见了一位~的年轻人。She spotted a young man in the crowd whom she thought she had met before.
似…非… sì…fēi… *used before the same word to indicate both similarity and dissimilarity*: 似亲非亲 have some kind of kinship / 似雾非雾 something that looks like fog / 似梦非梦 something like a dream; dreamy / 似醉非醉 be in a half-drunken state
似乎 sìhū it seems that; as if; seemingly: 天~要下雨了。It looks as if it's going to rain. *or* It looks like rain. / 他~有一肚子的苦恼。He seems to be very vexed.
似箭离弦 sìjiànlíxián run away or fly like an arrow: 那车~地在高速公路飞驰。The car was speeding along the highway.
似梦初醒 sìmèngchūxǐng as though waking out of a dream: 等到真相大白，她才~，知道自己上了当。Only after the truth came out did she see the light and knew that she had been fooled.
似是而非 sìshì'érfēi apparently true but actually false; specious: ~的推理 specious reasoning; sophistry / 这个说法有点~。This is plausible argument.
似水年华 sìshuǐniánhuá *also* "似水流年" time passes as swiftly as flowing water; youth will not endure

姒

sì 〈古语〉❶ elder sister ❷ 〈古语〉wife of husband's elder brother ❸ (Sì) a surname

涘

sì 〈书面〉water front; water margin

俟(竢)

sì 〈书面〉wait: ~机出击 wait for the right moment to attack / 一~修改完毕，即可交稿。We will send the manuscript to the publisher as soon as we finish revising it.
see also qí
俟河之清 sìhézhīqīng wait for the Yellow River to run clear — hardly possible: ~，人寿几何? One cannot live long enough to see the Yellow River flow clear.

嗣

sì ❶ succeed, inherit: ~君 succeed to the throne ❷ heir; inheritor; descendant: 继~ adopting sb. as one's son; heir; inheritor / 绝~ without male offspring (*or* heir) / 子~ son; male offspring / 后~ descendant; offspring
嗣后 sìhòu 〈书面〉hereafter; subsequently; afterwards; later on
嗣位 sìwèi succeed to the throne

觇

sì 〈书面〉peep at; spy on

笥

sì 〈书面〉square bamboo-plaited basket or suitcase

伺

sì keep watch; await; observe: 窥~ be on watch for; watch and wait (for a chance to act)
see also cì
伺察 sìchá spy on; reconnoitre; trace secretly: ~动静 trace movements secretly; spy out the land
伺服 sìfú 〈电学〉servo: ~传动 servo-drive / ~电动机 servo-motor; actuating motor / ~放大器 servo-amplifier / ~泵 servo-pump / ~阀 servo-valve / ~控制机构 servo-control mechanism
伺机 sìjī watch for one's chance: ~而动 wait for the opportune moment to act / ~报复 find some way to take revenge (on)
伺隙 sìxì wait for an opening; watch for one's chance: ~进攻 wait for an opportunity to attack / ~乘虚 wait for the opportune

moment and take advantage of an opening

饲 sì ❶ raise; breed; rear ❷ forage; feed：打草储～ cut grass as fodder
饲槽 sìcáo bunk; manger; feeding trough
饲草 sìcǎo forage grass
饲料 sìliào forage; fodder; feed：猪～ pig feed
饲料粉碎机 sìliào fěnsuìjī feed or fodder grinder
饲料加工厂 sìliào jiāgōngchǎng feed-processing plant
饲料作物 sìliào zuòwù forage or feed crop
饲喂 sìwèi raise or rear (animals)
饲养 sìyǎng raise, rear：～家禽 raise (*or* rear) poultry /～牲口 raise livestock
饲养场 sìyǎngchǎng feed lot; dry lot; farm
饲养动物 sìyǎng dòngwù animals that are raised by man (such as ox, horse, mule, donkey, pig, honey bee, etc.) or are used for experiment (frog, guinea pig, etc.) or have commercial values (weasel, fox, etc.)
饲养业 sìyǎngyè livestock or poultry farming
饲养员 sìyǎngyuán stockman; poultry raiser; animal keeper (in a zoo)
饲育 sìyù feed; raise

巳(巳) sì sixth of the twelve Earthly Branches
巳时 sìshí period of the day from 9 a.m. to 11 a.m.

祀 sì 〈书面〉 offer sacrifices to gods or ancestors：奉～ offer sacrifices to gods or ancestors /～祖 offer sacrifices to the spirits of one's ancestors /～孔 hold a memorial ceremony for Confuscius

sōng

S

松[1] sōng ❶ pine：马尾～ masson pine /苍～ green pines /白皮～ lacebark pine /赤～ Japanese red pine /白果～ ginkgo pine /罗汉～ yew podocarpus /红～ Korean pine /水～ Chinese cypress; *Glyptostrobus pensilis* /落叶～ larch /油～ Chinese pine /～柏常青 remain evergreen as the pine and cypress; the pine and cypress stay evergreen /～鹤延年 live as long as the pine and crane ❷ (Sōng) a surname

松[2]**(鬆)** sōng ❶ not firm; loose; slack：螺丝钉～了。The screw has come loose. /把绳子放～点儿。Slack the rope. *or* Give the rope more play. ❷ loosen; relax; relieve; slacken：～～皮带 loosen the belt a little bit /～了一口气 heave a sigh of relief /不能～劲儿 shouldn't relax effort ❸ not hard up; well off：现在他手头～多了。He is much better off now. ❹ light and flaky; fluffy; soft：蓬～ puffy; fluffy /沙土～～的 soft sand /这木头质地太～。The wood is too soft. /酥饼～脆。The cake is light and crisp. ❺ untie：～扣儿 unbutton /快～手 let go ❻ dried meat floss, dried minced meat：鱼～ dried fish floss
松巴 sōngbā sompa, square-headed Tibetan shoes
松绑 sōngbǎng ❶ untie a person ❷ free a person or an organization from unnecessary restrictions：给企业～ free enterprises from unwarranted control; delegate greater powers to enterprises
松冰 sōngbīng rubber ice：～团 lolly ice
松冰山 sōngbīngshān sugar berg
松饼 sōngbǐng muffin
松弛 sōngchí ❶ limp; flabby; loose; slack：脸上肌肉～ flaccid facial muscles /他心神一阵～，竟然沉沉地睡着了。He relaxed into a sound sleep. /绷带～地吊着。The bandage is hanging loosely. ❷ lax, not strict：纪律～ be lax in discipline
松弛素 sōngchísù relaxin
松脆饼 sōngcuìbǐng shortbread; shortcake
松丹宁酸 sōngdānníngsuān pinitannic acid; *pinus tannic*
松貂 sōngdiāo pine marten
松动 sōngdòng ❶ become less crowded：密集的人群突然开始～了。The packed crowd suddenly began to fall away. ❷ not hard up：这几天他手头不很～。He has been a bit hard up these days. ❸ become loose：门牙～。The front teeth have come loose. ❹become flexible：立场～ softening in one's stance /双方的口气都在～。Both sides have become a bit more flexible. /两国关系有所～。There is a thaw in the relations between the two countries. *or* Relations between the two countries have eased a bit (*or* become less strained).
松度 sōngdù looseness
松泛 sōngfan comfortable; relaxed：睡了一觉，他觉得～多了。After a good sleep, he felt much relaxed.
松果体 sōngguǒtǐ 〈生理〉 pineal body; pineal gland; *epiphysis cerebri*：～瘤 pinealoma
松果腺 sōngguǒxiàn *see* "松果体"
松果眼 sōngguǒyǎn 〈生理〉 pineal eye
松虎 sōnghǔ 〈方言〉 pine moth
松花 sōnghuā *also* "皮蛋" pídàn; "变蛋" biàndàn preserved egg：～蛋 preserved egg
松花江 Sōnghuājiāng Songhua or Sungari River in northeast China：我的家在～上。I live by the Songhua River.
松缓 sōnghuǎn relax; calm down：紧张的空气顿时～下来。The tension eased instantly.
松鸡 sōngjī capercaillie; grouse
松焦油 sōngjiāoyóu 〈化工〉 pine tar
松节油 sōngjiéyóu 〈化工〉 turpentine (oil); gum turpentine; spirits of turpentine; gum spirits; turps
松节油中毒 sōngjiéyóu zhòngdú terebinthinism
松紧 sōngjǐn degree of tightness
松紧带 sōngjǐndài elastic cord; elastic：买一米～儿 buy one metre of elastic cord
松劲 sōngjìn relax one's efforts; loosen up; slacken (off)：千万不能～。Never relax efforts. /考试后学生们往往会产生～情绪。Students tend to slacken off after the exam.
松口 sōngkǒu ❶ relax one's bite and release what is held; let go the bite：再不～我的手指头就要被你咬断了。You are going to bite my finger off if you don't stop it. ❷ be less intransigent; moderate; relent：我相信他会～让你去的。I believe he will relent and let you go. /他宁死也不～。Even death won't make him open his mouth.
松快 sōngkuai ❶ at ease; relieved：心情～ have ease of mind; feel happy /这会儿觉得～多了。I feel much better now. /任务完成后，她感到一阵～。She felt much relieved after the job was done. ❷ less crowded：屋里家具不多，住着还算～。The room can be considered spacious, as there isn't much furniture in it. ❸ feel relaxed; relax：工作到此为止，让大家～～吧。Let's call it a day and relax a bit.
松萝 sōngluó beard lichen; beard moss; *Usnea barbata*
松毛虫 sōngmáochóng pine caterpillar：～蛾 pine moth
松明 sōngmíng pine torches
松明木 sōngmíngmù torchwood
松气 sōngqì relax one's efforts; slacken：我们的事业正处在关键时刻，千万不能～。We must not relax our efforts when the future of our cause hangs in the balance.
松墙 sōngqiáng *also* "松墙子" fence of Chinese juniper, cypress, etc.
松球 sōngqiú 〈植物〉 pinecone
松雀 sōngquè *also* "蜡嘴雀" làzuǐquè; "锡嘴雀" xīzuǐquè pine grosbeak
松仁 sōngrén pinecone kernel; pine nut kernel
松茸 sōngróng *see* "松蕈"
松软 sōngruǎn ❶ soft; spongy; loose：～的土地 spongy soil ❷ feeble; weak：他病了，感到浑身～。He is ill and feels weak.
松散 sōngsǎn ❶ loose; not firm or compact：～的土质 porous soil /一头～的披肩发 fell of hair hanging loose to one's shoulders /文章的结构～。The article is loosely organized. /几棵小树～地分布在画面上。A few small trees are drawn here and there on the canvas. ❷ inattentive; wandering：学生上课时为什么显得～？How come the students cannot concentrate in class?
松散 sōngsan relax; ease up：饭后散散步会使身子～些。A stroll after meals helps one relax physically.
松手 sōngshǒu loosen one's grip; hold less tight; let go：千万不能～，否则会掉下来的。Don't loosen your grip, otherwise you will fall down.
松鼠 sōngshǔ squirrel：树上有一只可爱的小～。There's a lovely little squirrel on the tree.
松鼠猴 sōngshǔhóu squirrel monkey
松树 sōngshù pine tree; pine：～的精神 spirit of fortitude as symbolized by the pine tree
松爽 sōngshuǎng refreshed; comfortable：他吃了药，身上才觉得～

了一点。He felt somewhat refreshed only after he had taken the medicine.

松松垮垮 sōngsong-kuǎkuǎ ❶ (of structure) not solid or compact：一张～的桌子 a rickety table ❷ lax and undisciplined; slack and perfunctory：训练时～，比赛时一定吃败仗。Lax in training, the team is certain to come to grief in the tournament.

松塔 sōngtǎ ❶〈方言〉pinecone ❷〈中药〉cone of lacebark pine

松涛 sōngtāo soughing of the wind in the pines

松土 sōngtǔ 〈农业〉break up and loosen the soil; scarify the soil：～犁 pulverator plough

松土机 sōngtǔjī loosener; scarifier

松下电气工业公司 Sōngxià Diànqì Gōngyè Gōngsī (Japan) Matsushita Electric Industrial Co., Ltd.

松闲 sōngxián idle; unoccupied; not busy：秋收一完，农活就～点了。As soon as autumn harvesting is finished, there will be less farm work.

松香 sōngxiāng rosin; colophony

松香精 sōngxiāngjīng rosin spirit

松香清漆 sōngxiāng qīngqī rosin vanish

松香酸 sōngxiāngsuān abietic acid

松香油 sōngxiāngyóu retinol; rosin oil

松懈 sōngxiè ❶ slacken; slack：工作～ laxity in one's work /～的情绪 slack mood /学习刻苦，从不～ never slack off in one's studies ❷ undisciplined; weak-willed：斗志～ lack the will to fight /戒备～ lax security ❸ cool and indifferent; uncoordinated：团结涣散，关系～。They are disunited and stand aloof from one another.

松心 sōngxīn relaxed; carefree：家务有儿媳妇操持，婆婆就～了。With the daughter-in-law attending to household chores, the mother-in-law felt relaxed.

松蕈 sōngxùn pine mushroom：拾～ pick up pine mushrooms

松鸦 sōngyā jay

松烟 sōngyān pine soot (best for making Chinese ink)

松烟墨 sōngyānmò Chinese ink made from pine soot; pine-soot ink

松油 sōngyóu pine oil

松赞干布 Sōngzàngānbù Songtsam Gambo (c. 617-650), King of the Tubo Kingdom (吐蕃王朝) in Lhasa in the 7th century, who first introduced Buddhism and Tang culture in Tibet

松针 sōngzhēn pine needle：～油 pine needle oil

松脂 sōngzhī rosin; pine gum：～制品 naval stores

松子 sōngzǐ ❶ pine nut：采摘～ pluck pine nuts ❷〈方言〉pine nut kernels：～糖 candies with pine nut kernels

松嘴 sōngzuǐ 〈口语〉*see*"松口"

淞 Sōng Songjiang River (also known as Wusongjiang River), a tributary of the Yangtze River：～沪抗战 Anti-Japanese War of 1932 in Shanghai

凇 sōng *see*"雾凇" wùsōng

菘 sōng 〈古语〉Chinese cabbage

菘菜 sōngcài 〈方言〉Chinese cabbage

菘蓝 sōnglán woad; *Isatis tinctoria* var. *indigotica* (its root "板蓝根" bǎnlángēn is a medicinal herb; its leaf "大青叶" dàqīngyè is a medicinal herb and dye)

忪 sōng *see*"惺忪" xīngsōng
see also zhōng

嵩（崧） sōng 〈书面〉❶ high mountain ❷ (of mountains) high, lofty

嵩山 Sōngshān Mount Song or Songshan Mountain (in Henan Province) — the Central Sacred Mountain (中岳)

sóng

㞞（㞞） sóng ❶ seminal fluid; semen ❷ (of persons) weak and incompetent; good-for-nothing：这人真～。He is a namby-pamby.

㞞包 sóngbāo good-for-nothing：我就不信你这么～！I don't believe you are such a nitwit!

sǒng

竦 sǒng ❶〈书面〉respectful; deferential：～然起敬 hold somebody in high esteem ❷ fear, dread：战～而却 be frightened and retreat from battle ❸ *see*"耸" sǒng

悚 sǒng 〈书面〉fear, dread

悚惧 sǒngjù fear; dread; be terrified; feel frightened

悚然 sǒngrán terror-stricken; terrified; horrified：毛骨～ with one's hair standing on end /～而立 stand up terrified

扨（搜） sǒng ❶〈书面〉stand upright, stand firm：～身直立 stand erect ❷〈方言〉push：～来～去 push around

怂（慫） sǒng 〈书面〉frightened：～兢 alarmed; scared; panic-stricken

怂恿 sǒngyǒng instigate; incite; foment; egg on：～学生闹事 instigate a student riot

耸（聳） sǒng ❶ towering; high; lofty：高～入云 tower into the clouds; tower to the skies /高～的纪念碑 towering monument /双颧高～ with high cheek bones ❷ alarm; attract (attention)：～耳倾听 prick up one's ears

耸拔 sǒngbá shoot high up; rise straight up：群峰～ peaks soar skyward

耸动 sǒngdòng ❶ shrug (one's shoulders)：她～着肩膀哭泣不止。She sobbed away, her shoulders shaking. ❷ create a sensation：～视听 intend to cause a sensation

耸壑昂霄 sǒnghè-ángxiāo remarkable talent; the best and the brightest

耸肩 sǒngjiān shrug one's shoulders

耸立 sǒnglì tower aloft; rise high：高楼～ high-rise buildings /宝塔～在西山之巅。A pagoda towers aloft on top of the Western Hill.

耸人听闻 sǒngréntīngwén deliberately try to create a sensation：～的新闻 sensational news /～的言论 alarmist talk

耸入云霄 sǒngrù-yúnxiāo tower to the skies：～的雪山 soaring snow mountains

耸身 sǒngshēn jump; leap：～跳过水洼 leap a puddle

耸听 sǒngtīng blow things up so as to create a sensation：危言～ startling statement creates a sensation; say frightening things just to cause alarm

耸峙 sǒngzhì tower aloft; stand erect：峭壁～。The cliffs stand towering to the skies.

sòng

宋[1] Sòng ❶ name of a kingdom in the Zhou Dynasty, covering the area of today's Shangqiu (商丘) of Henan Province ❷ Song Dynasty (420-479), one of the Southern Dynasties, founded by Liu-yu (刘裕) ❸ Song Dynasty (960-1279), founded by Zhao Kuangyin (赵匡胤) ❹ a surname

宋[2] sòng *also*"味" sòng sone, a unit of subjective loudness

宋词 sòngcí *ci* poetry of the Song Dynasty

宋干节 Sònggānjié Sonkran Festival; Water-Sprinkling Festival in Thailand, Laos, etc.

宋江起义 Sòng Jiāng Qǐyì Song Jiang Rebellion, an uprising led by Song Jiang in 1110 in today's Shandong and Hebei provinces, upon which is based the novel *Heroes of the Marshes* (水浒传)

宋锦 sòngjǐn imitation Song brocade

宋庆龄 Sòng Qìnglíng Mme Soong Ching Ling (1893-1981), Honorary President of the People's Republic of China

宋体字 sòngtǐzì Song typeface, a standard typeface first used in the Ming Dynasty but popularly attributed to the Song Dynasty：他会写～。He can write Song typeface.

宋应星 Sòng Yìngxīng Song Yingxing (1587-c.1661), scientist of

the Ming Dynasty and author of *Exploitation of the Works of Nature*（天工开物）
宋玉 Sòng Yù Song Yu, poet of the State of Chu in the Warring States Period

咪 sòng 〈旧语〉 *see* "宋²" sòng

讼 sòng ❶ bring a case to court：听～ try a case / 诉～ lawsuit; litigation / 胜～ win a lawsuit (*or* court case) ❷ debate; dispute; argue：聚～纷纭 arguing back and forth without coming to an agreement; disparity of views without any consensus
讼案 sòng'àn case in court：了结～ close a case in court
讼词 sòngcí lawsuit; legal case：包揽～ monopolize legal practice; engage in legal pettifoggery
讼棍 sònggùn legal pettifogger; shyster
讼师 sòngshī 〈旧语〉 legal counsel
讼事 sòngshì lawsuit; litigation

颂 sòng ❶ praise; extol; acclaim; laud：称～ praise; eulogize / 歌～ sing the praises of ❷ express good wishes (usu. in letters)：敬～夏安。Wish you a pleasant summer. ❸ one of the three sections in *The Book of Songs*（诗经）consisting of sacrificial songs ❹ ode; paean; panegyric; eulogy：《橘～》*Ode to the Tangerine*
颂词 sòngcí ❶ complimentary address or message; eulogy ❷ 〈外交〉 speech delivered by an ambassador on presentation of his credentials
颂歌 sònggē song; ode; paean：友谊的～ ode to friendship / 唱～ sing the praises of
颂古非今 sònggǔ-fēijīn eulogize the past at the expense of the present; extol the past and condemn the present
颂美 sòngměi praise; eulogize; laud：～祖国的大好山河 eulogize (*or* glorify) the beautiful mountains and rivers of the motherland
颂扬 sòngyáng eulogize; laud; extol：～祖国 extol one's motherland
颂谀 sòngyú praise profusely; toady to; fawn upon：满口～ full of flattery
颂赞 sòngzàn extol; laud; eulogize：～人民英雄 laud people's heroes
颂祝 sòngzhù express good wishes

送 sòng ❶ send; deliver; carry：播～ broadcast; transmit / 抄～ make a copy for / 递～ send; deliver / 分～ distribute / ～文件 dispatch a document / 信～错了。The letter was sent to a wrong place (*or* person). ❷ give as a present; offer; give：奉～ offer as a gift / 赍～ 〈书面〉 send sb. sth. as a present / 赠～ give as a present; present as a gift / 转～ make a present of what one has been given ❸ see sb. off or out; go along with; accompany：护～ escort; convoy / 欢～ see off; send off / 解～ send under guard / 目～ watch sb. go / 扭～ seize sb. and hand him over to the police / 遣～ repatriate; send back / 押～ send under escort; escort / ～朋友 see one's friends off / ～妻子上班 accompany one's wife to her office or workplace / ～她一段路 walk with her part of the way / 把孩子～进幼儿园 take a child to kindergarten / ～客出门 see a guest to the door; walk a guest to the gate / ～回家去 see sb. home / 用车接～ ride sb.
送报员 sòngbàoyuán messenger
送别 sòngbié see sb. off
送殡 sòngbìn take part in a funeral procession; attend a funeral
送风机 sòngfēngjī 〈机械〉 forced draught blower; blower
送话器 sònghuàqì 〈电学〉 microphone
送还 sònghuán give back; send back; return：把失物～原主 return the lost article to its owner
送货 sònghuò deliver goods：～上门 deliver goods to the doorstep of a customer; provide home delivery service / ～回单 delivery receipt / ～人 delivery man / ～清单 consignment invoice / ～簿 delivery book
送交 sòngjiāo dispatch; deliver; hand over：～书信 deliver letters / 把小偷～派出所 hand the thief over to the police station
送旧迎新 sòngjiù-yíngxīn see off the old and welcome the new; ring out the old year and ring in the new
送君千里，终须一别 sòng jūn qiānlǐ, zhōng xū yī bié 〈俗语〉 even though you may escort your friend a thousand *li*, yet you must part in the end：～，诸位就此留步吧。Please don't bother to come any further. However far you accompany me, we have to say goodbye to each other in the end.
送客 sòngkè see a visitor out：～出门 see a guest to the door / ～到码头 see a guest off at the wharf
送款员 sòngkuǎnyuán cashboy
送礼 sònglǐ give presents; send gifts：请客～ give dinners and send gifts (in order to curry favour or to get things done)
送殓 sòngliàn accompany the bereaved family in seeing the deceased encoffined
送命 sòngmìng lose one's life; get killed; die：我险些在那场车祸中送了命。I had a narrow escape in that car accident.
送气 sòngqì 〈语言〉 aspirated
送气音 sòngqìyīn aspirated sound; aspirate
送亲 sòngqīn escort the bride by her family to the bridegroom's home or the wedding party
送情 sòngqíng ❶ convey one's affection：眉目～ cast amorous glances ❷ 〈方言〉 give sb. a present：逢年过节总得给亲友家送点情。I find it necessary to present gifts to my friends and relatives on New Year's Day and other festive occasions.
送人情 sòng rénqíng ❶ deliberately do sb. a good turn to curry his favour：用公款～ curry favour with others by spending public money ❷ 〈方言〉 give gifts
送三 sòngsān *also* "接三" jiēsān 〈迷信〉 holding of Buddhist or Taoist rites on the third day after the death of the deceased in order to absolve the latter of sins and send him or her to heaven
送丧 sòngsāng attend a funeral; take part in a funeral procession：不少人给逝者～。Many people attended the funeral of the deceased.
送上门 sòngshàngmén deliver sth. to the doorsteps：哪有那么多～的好事! How can there be so many windfalls?
送上西天 sòngshàng-xītiān 〈口语〉 send somebody to heaven or to his death：把进犯的敌人～。Wipe out the invading enemies.
送审 sòngshěn submit (report, article, etc.) to one's superior or the competent departments for examination and approval or for examination and revision：～稿 draft submitted for examination and approval
送死 sòngsǐ 〈口语〉 court death：我们不能白白去～。We must not die in vain.
送往迎来 sòngwǎng-yínglái see off those who depart and welcome those who arrive; speed the parting guests and welcome the new arrivals; engage in the work of reception：这些～的事占了他不少时间。It took him a lot of time to do reception work.
送瘟神 sòng wēnshén send away the god of plague — get rid of sb. or sth. unwanted or unpleasant：举杯～。Raise our glasses to bid farewell to the god of plague.
送信儿 sòngxìnr 〈口语〉 convey a message; send word; go and tell：她有急事不能马上回家，劳你给她家里送个信儿。Would you go and tell her family that she is unable to return home right now for some urgent business?
送行 sòngxíng ❶ see sb. off; bid sb. farewell; wish sb. bon voyage：上车站为弟弟～ see one's younger brother off at the station ❷ give a send-off party：特意举行宴会给她～ give a send-off banquet in her honour / ～仪式 sending-off ceremony
送葬 sòngzàng join a funeral procession
送灶 sòngzào 〈旧语〉 ceremony of sending off (on the 23th of the 12th lunar month) the kitchen god on his annual trip to heaven with foods, drinks, etc. offered as sacrifices
送站 sòngzhàn see sb. off at the (railway) station：姐姐远行，爸爸去～。My elder sister is going on a long journey. Father has gone to the railway station to see her off.
送终 sòngzhōng look after a dying parent or other senior member of one's family; arrange for the burial of a deceased parent or elder relative：养老～ provide for and attend upon the old

诵 sòng ❶ read aloud; declaim; chant：朗～ read aloud with expression; recite / 吟～ chant; recite ❷ recite：背～ recite; repeat from memory / 过目成～ be able to recite sth. after reading it over once; have a photographic (*or* very retentive) memory ❸ state; relate; narrate：传～ be on everybody's lips; be widely read / 群臣～功，请刻于石。All the ministers extolled the emperor's feats and requested that they be carved in stone.

诵读 sòngdú read aloud; chant: ～经文 read aloud the scripture
诵习 sòngxí 〈书面〉study: ～经典 study the classics

sōu

溲 sōu 〈书面〉urinate: 一日数十～ urinate dozens of times a day
溲疏 sōushū 〈植物〉*Deutzia scabra*
溲血 sōuxiě 〈中医〉haematuria

廋 sōu 〈书面〉hide; conceal; remain under cover; stay hidden: 人焉～哉? Where can the man hide himself?
廋辞 sōucí *also* "廋词"〈书面〉evasive words; phrase with hidden meaning; riddle; puzzle
廋语 sōuyǔ 〈书面〉riddle; puzzle; enigma: 善说～ be good at asking riddles

搜(❶**蒐**) sōu ❶ look for; collect; gather: 锐意穷～ be determined to collect sth. ❷ search: ～于国中 search all over the country
搜捕 sōubǔ search and arrest: ～逃犯 track down an escaped convict
搜查 sōuchá search; ransack; rummage; scout for: ～毒品 search for drugs /～房间 ransack the room /在屋内～赃物 rummage the house for stolen goods (*or* spoils, *or* loot)
搜查证 sōucházhèng search warrant
搜肠刮肚 sōucháng-guādù think very hard; cudgel one's brains: 他～地想办法, 却怎么也想不出好点子来。He racked his brains for a solution but failed to come up with any good idea.
搜刮 sōuguā forcibly seize; extort; expropriate; fleece: ～钱财 extort money and valuables /～民脂民膏 rob the people of their wealth; fleece the people
搜集 sōují collect; gather; solicit: ～邮票 collecting stamps; philately /～资料 gather data /～意见 solicit opinions from
搜检 sōujiǎn search (for illegal goods)
搜剿 sōujiǎo search for and wipe out: ～残敌 search for and exterminate remnant enemy troops
搜缴 sōujiǎo search and confiscate: ～私藏的枪支弹药 search and seize illegally possessed firearms and ammunition
搜劫 sōujié search and loot; ransack: 匪帮到处～粮食。The bandit gang searched for and grabbed away food grain wherever they went. *or* The bandits ransacked every house for grain.
搜括 sōukuò *see* "搜刮"
搜罗 sōuluó collect; gather; recruit: ～人才 recruit qualified or competent personnel; scout for talent /～材料 collect materials
搜拿 sōuná hunt and arrest: ～嫌疑犯 track down and arrest suspects
搜求 sōuqiú seek; hunt: ～信息 seek information
搜山 sōushān comb the mountains
搜身 sōushēn search by passing the hands over the body; search the person; make a body search; frisk: ～检查 subject a person to search
搜索 sōusuǒ search; comb; hunt for; scout around: ～残敌 comb for remnants of the enemy forces /在头脑中～准确的字眼 search one's mind for the right word /在丛林中～ search in the jungle /～救援 reconnoitre and rescue
搜索飞行 sōusuǒ fēixíng scouting flight
搜索机 sōusuǒjī search aircraft
搜索枯肠 sōusuǒ-kūcháng cudgel or rack one's brains (for fresh ideas or felicitous expressions): 我～也没想出一个好句子来。After beating my brains out, I still can't think of a good sentence.
搜索天线 sōusuǒ tiānxiàn search antenna
搜索引擎 sōusuǒ yǐnqíng 〈信息〉search engine
搜讨 sōutǎo 〈书面〉explore; seek: 广为～ seek far and wide /～遗闻 search for anecdotes from the past
搜寻 sōuxún search for; hunt; seek: 留心地～ make a careful search /两人四下～。The two men searched for it everywhere.
搜腰包 sōu yāobāo search sb.'s pockets; search sb. for money and valuables: 武装匪徒到处～。The armed robbers searched everybody they met for money and valuables.

嗖 sōu *also* "飕" sōu 〈象声〉whiz: 子弹～～地飞过头顶。The bullets whizzed over his head.

螋 sōu *see* "蠼螋" qúsōu

锼 sōu 〈方言〉engrave; carve (on wood): 家具上的花纹是～出来的。The patterns on the furniture are engraved.
锼弓子 sōugōngzi 〈方言〉fretsaw; scroll saw

艘 sōu 〈量词〉*of ships*: 五～货轮 five freighters (*or* cargo ships, *or* cargo vessels)
艘次 sōucì 〈量词〉vessel-time

飕[1] sōu 〈方言〉(of wind) make sth. dry or cool: 梨让风～干巴了。The pears dried up in the wind. /冷风直～脖子。Cold wind was blowing into the neck.

飕[2] sōu *see* "嗖" sōu
飕飗 sōuliú 〈书面〉sound of wind

馊 sōu sour; spoiled: 菜～了。The dish has spoiled. *or* The dish smells a bit off. /这主意多～! What a lousy idea! /这办法～透了! A nasty way of doing things, isn't it?
馊点子 sōudiǎnzi *see* "馊主意"
馊主意 sōuzhǔyi rotten idea; lousy idea

蒐 sōu 〈书面〉❶ hunt; hold spring or autumn hunt ❷ review troops ❸ seek; search for; collect

sǒu

嗾 sǒu ❶ sounds made to incite a dog ❷ 〈书面〉incite (a dog) by making such sounds: ～犬伤人 set a dog on sb. ❸ instigate; abet
嗾使 sǒushǐ incite; instigate; abet: ～人群纵火行凶 incite a mob to arson and violence /受别人～ act on sb.'s instigation /揭露幕后～者 expose the person behind the scenes; unmask the hidden instigator

薮(**藪**) sǒu 〈书面〉❶ lake overgrown with grass ❷ gathering place (of fish, beasts, etc.); den; haunt: 罪恶的渊～ breeding ground of crime; sink (*or* den) of iniquity
薮泽 sǒuzé 〈书面〉marsh; swamp: 山林～ mountain forests and overgrown marshes

擞(**擻**) sǒu *see* "抖擞" dǒusǒu
see also sòu

叟(**叜**) sǒu old man: 童～无欺 not cheating even children and old people; absolutely honest or fair /老～ old man /智～ wise old man

瞍 sǒu 〈书面〉❶ pupilless and blind ❷ blind person

sòu

嗽 sòu cough: 干～ dry cough

擞(**擻**) sòu 〈方言〉poke the fire (to make the ashes fall through the grating); rake: 把炉子～一～ poke (*or* rake) the fire
see also sǒu

sū

窣 sū *see* "窸窣" xīsū

苏[1](**蘇**) sū perilla: 紫～ purple perilla (*Perilla frutes-

cens var. crispa) /白～ common perilla

苏²(蘇) sū threads hanging down:流～ tassel

苏³(蘇、甦) sū revive; come to; become conscious:万物在春天里复～。Spring brings life back to everything.

苏⁴(蘇) Sū ❶(short for 苏州) Suzhou:～州评弹 storytelling and ballad-singing in Suzhou dialect /上有天堂,下有～杭。Suzhou and Hangzhou are like paradise on earth. ❷(short for 江苏) Jiangsu Province:～北 northern Jiangsu (i. e. part of Jiangsu north of the Yangtze River) ❸ a surname

苏⁵(囌) sū *see* "噜苏" lūsu

苏⁶(蘇) sū ❶ soviet ❷(Sū)(short for 苏联) Soviet Union or USSR (1922-1991):中～关系 Sino-Soviet relations /～欧地区 Soviet Union and Eastern Europe

苏⁷(蘇) sū *sou*, the smallest denomination of former French money

苏爱人 Sū'àirén Scotch-Irish

苏氨酸 sū'ānsuān threonine

苏白 sūbái ❶ Suzhou dialect:她会说一口地道的～。She speaks pure Suzhou dialect. ❷ lines in Kunqu or Beijing opera that are spoken in Suzhou dialect

苏必利尔湖 Sūbìlì'ěrhú Lake Superior, one of the five Great Lakes of North America and the largest freshwater lake in the world

苏菜 sūcài southern Jiangsu (Province) cuisine

苏长岩 sūchángyán 〈地质〉 norite

苏打 sūdá *also* "纯碱" chúnjiǎn soda:小～ sodium bicarbonate /～饼干 soda biscuit; soda cracker /～汽水 soda water; soda pop /～面包 soda bread

苏打石 sūdáshí nahcolite

苏丹 sūdān ❶ sultan ❷(Sūdān) the Sudan:～共和国 Republic of the Sudan /～人 Sudanese /～语 Sudanic

苏堤 Sūdī Su Causeway, named after Su Dongpo (苏东坡) in Hangzhou

苏俄 Sū-É ❶ Soviet Russia — Russia after the October Revolution of 1917 ❷(short for 俄罗斯苏维埃联邦社会主义共和国) Russian Soviet Federated Socialist Republic

苏菲教 Sūfēijiào Sufism:～派穆斯林 Sufi

苏格拉底 Sūgélādǐ Socrates (469-399 BC), Greek philosopher:～的问答法 Socratic method

苏格兰 Sūgélán Scotland:～人 Scot; Scotsman; the Scottish /～㹴 Scottish terrier /～威士忌酒 Scotch whiskey /～帽 Glengarry /～场 Scotland Yard, headquarters of the London Police

苏合香 sūhéxiāng 〈中药〉 storax (*Liquidambar orientalis*):～醇 styracitol /～英 styracin

苏黄米蔡 Sū-Huáng-Mǐ-Cài Su Shi (苏轼), Huang Tingjian (黄庭坚), Mi Fu (米芾) and Cai Xiang (蔡襄), four noted calligraphers of the Song Dynasty

苏活 sūhuó bring or come back to life; revive; resuscitate

苏剧 sūjù one of the local operas in Jiangsu Province

苏黎世 Sūlíshì Zurich, the largest city in Switzerland:～湖 Lake Zurich

苏里南 Sūlǐnán Surinam:～人 Surinamese

苏联 Sūlián Soviet Union — the Union of Soviet Socialist Republics (1922-1991):～人 Soviet citizen; Soviet /～的解体 disintegration of the Soviet Union

苏门答腊 Sūméndálà Sumatra, second largest island of Indonesia:～人 Sumatran

苏门羚 sūménlíng 〈动物〉 serow

苏木 sūmù *also* "苏方" sappan wood; haematoxylon (*Caesalpinia Sappan*):～精 *also* "～素" haematoxylin

苏气 sūqi 〈方言〉 good-looking and natural; debonair; chic:他穿得尽管讲究,可并不～。Though well-dressed, he does not look debonair. /在县城里她是一个顶～出色的人。In the county town she is a most pretty and outstanding girl.

苏秦 Sū Qín Su Qin (? -284 BC), politician and strategist of the Warring States Period, who sought to unite all the other warring states against the State of Qin (秦) and was chosen leader of the alliance, which later was wrecked by the stratagems of Qin as well as the selfish intrigues among the other states

苏区 Sūqū Soviet Area (established in China during the Second Revolutionary Civil War, 1927-1937)

苏生 sūshēng come to oneself; resuscitate; revive:春回大地,万木～。Now that spring is here, a myriad trees and flowers have come back to life.

苏轼 Sū Shì Su Shi (formerly translated as Su Shih, 1037-1101), alias Su Dongpo (苏东坡), writer and calligrapher of the Song Dynasty

苏颂 Sū Sòng Su Song (1020-1101), astronomer and pharmacologist of the Song Dynasty

苏铁 sūtiě *also* "铁树" tiěshù 〈植物〉 sago palm; cycas (*Cycas revoluta*):～时代 age of cycads /～蕨 cycad fern /～素 cycasin

苏瓦 Sūwǎ Suva, capital of Fiji

苏维埃 sūwéi'āi soviet; soviet government or regime:中央～ Central Soviet Government /～政权 Soviet political power /最高～ (as of the USSR) Supreme Soviet

苏武 Sū Wǔ Su Wu(139-60 BC), sent on a mission to Xiongnu (匈奴) and detained in today's Lake Baikal region for nineteen years without submission, known since as a symbol of national integrity

苏息 sūxī 〈书面〉 ❶ come back to life; revive ❷ rest; recuperate

苏醒 sūxǐng revive; come to; regain consciousness:手术后病人～了。The patient came to after the operation. /春天大地～了。The earth revived in spring.

苏绣 sūxiù Suzhou embroidery:～艺术享誉中外。Suzhou embroidery is world-famous.

苏伊士运河 Sūyīshì Yùnhé Suez Canal (built in 1859-1869 in Egypt)

苏州码子 Sūzhōu mǎzi *also* "草码" cǎomǎ Suzhou numerals, formerly used in business, such as 〡, 〢, 〣, 〤, 〥, 〦, 〧, 〨, 〩, 十

苏子 sūzǐ perilla-seed

酥 sū ❶〈古语〉 butter (made from cow's or mare's milk):以～点画 paint a picture with butter ❷ crisp; fluffy:～皮点心 crisp-skinned pastry /～糖 crunchy candy /香～鸭 savoury, crisp duck /龙虾～ lobster-shaped candy ❸ shortbread; shortcake:芝麻～ sesame shortbread /桃～ walnut kernel shortbread /牛角～ horn-shaped shortcake /蛋奶～ soufflé /乳～ junket ❹ limp; weak; frail; soft:全身发～ feel weak all over

酥脆 sūcuì crisp:这种饼干很～。This biscuit is crisp and crunchy.

酥麻 sūmá limp and numb:两手～ one's hands feel weak and numb

酥软 sūruǎn limp; weak; soft:四肢～ feel weak in the limbs

酥松 sūsōng (of soil, etc.) loose; porous:～的石灰层 layer of porous limestone

酥胸 sūxiōng soft and fair-skinned breasts (of a woman)

酥油 sūyóu butter

酥油茶 sūyóuchá buttered tea

酥油花 sūyóuhuā (Tibetan artifact) coloured butter figurines, trees and flowers, birds and animals, etc.

稣 sū revive; come to

sú

俗 sú ❶ custom; practice; convention:习～ custom; convention /陋～ unsavoury or undesirable practice or custom /民～ folk custom; folkway /民～学 folklore /移风易～ change prevailing customs and habits; bring about a change in morals and mores /入乡随～。When in Rome, do as the Romans do. ❷ popular; common; ordinary:通～ popular (language, style, etc.) /雅～共赏 (of a work of art or literature) appeal to both the more and the less cultured; suit both refined and popular tastes ❸ vulgar; boorish:脱～ free from vulgarity; not bound by conventions /粗～ vulgar; coarse; crude /庸～ vulgar; philistine ❹ secular; lay:僧～ monks and lay-

men; clergy and laity /还～〈佛教〉resume secular life
俗不可耐 súbùkěnài unbearably vulgar; hopelessly boorish:～的广告画 poster of low taste
俗称 súchēng ❶ be generally called or termed:马铃薯～土豆儿。Potato is commonly known as "土豆儿" in Chinese. ❷ popular name
俗词语 súcíyǔ 〈语言〉vulgarism
俗话 súhuà popular saying; common saying; proverb:～说,欲速则不达。As the saying goes, "more haste, less speed." /这句～尽人皆知。This adage is known to all.
俗家 sújiā ❶ (used in the case of a Buddhist or Taoist monk) original family:这位法师～姓王。The Buddhist Master's original family name is Wang. ❷ laymen; secular:～打扮 in secular dress
俗讲 sújiǎng (in the Tang Dynasty) preach Buddhist sutras with storytelling
俗例 súlì common practices; customary rules
俗名 súmíng ❶ popular name; local name ❷ original name of a person before he or she becomes a Buddhist or Taoist monk or nun
俗气 súqi inelegant:显得～ look vulgar /这件衣服样式太～。The dress is in rather poor taste.
俗曲 súqǔ *also* "俚曲" lǐqǔ 〈旧语〉folk songs
俗人 súrén ❶ layman (as distinguished from a clergyman) ❷ vulgarian; philistine
俗尚 súshàng prevailing custom or fashion:服饰随～而易。Dress and personal adornment change with the fashions.
俗套 sútào ❶ conventional etiquette:废除～ do away with conventional etiquette (*or* formalities) ❷ convention; stereotype:不落～ conform to no conventional pattern; depart from the beaten track
俗体字 sútǐzì nonstandard popular form (of a Chinese character)
俗文学 súwénxué ancient Chinese popular literature (such as ballads, songs, storytelling, and the local operas since the Song and Yuan dynasties)
俗务 súwù chores; routines; everyday matters:屏弃～ dispense with the routines
俗物 súwù unrefined person or thing; vulgarian; philistine
俗语 súyǔ *also* "俗话" popular saying; folk adage:言简意赅的～ compendious popular saying /广泛流传的～ widely known folk adage
俗乐 súyuè 〈旧语〉popular music
俗子 súzǐ *also* "俗人" man in the street:凡夫～ ordinary people; the common run of people
俗字 súzì *see* "俗体字"

sù

宿[1] sù ❶ put up for the night; stay overnight:夜～于农家 put up for the night at a farmhouse /住～ stay; get accommodation /借～ ask for a night's lodging; stay overnight at sb. else's place /露～ sleep in the open; bivouac /归～ home to return to; end-result /留～ put up a guest for the night; have sb. stay the night /食～ food and lodging ❷ (Sù) a surname

宿[2] sù 〈书面〉❶long-standing: *see* "～志","～诺" ❷ old; veteran:耆～ venerated elder (of a community)
see also xiǔ; xiù
宿弊 sùbì long-standing malpractice or evil; age-old malady:～一清。The age-old malady was done away for good. /～难除。It is difficult to get rid of long-standing malpractices.
宿逋 sùbū 〈书面〉long-standing debt:～未偿。The long-standing debt has yet to be paid.
宿草 sùcǎo 〈书面〉grass grown over the year(s) (mostly that on graves), a term usually used in mourning a deceased friend
宿娼 sùchāng go whoring; visit prostitutes
宿仇 sùchóu feud; old grievance:不忘～ hard to forget an old grievance
宿处 sùchù quarters; lodging
宿敌 sùdí *also* "夙敌" sùdí old enemy
宿分 sùfèn (of superstition) destiny; lot; fate
宿根 sùgēn 〈植物〉biennial or perennial root:～植物 perennial plant
宿憾 sùhàn *also* "宿恨" old grudge; old grievance; deep-rooted rancour
宿疾 sùjí long-standing disease; old trouble:～未愈 not recover from a prolonged illness /～难医。It is difficult to cure a chronic disease.
宿见 sùjiàn long-held opinion; established views
宿将 sùjiàng veteran general:久经沙场的～ battle-tested veteran general
宿酒 sùjiǔ intoxication lasting overnight; hangover:～未醒 not yet sober from the effects of last night's drinking
宿命论 sùmìnglùn 〈哲学〉fatalism:～者 fatalist
宿诺 sùnuò *also* "夙诺" sùnuò long-given promise
宿儒 sùrú learned old scholar
宿舍 sùshè living quarters; dormitory; hostel:家属～ living quarters for staff with families /单身～ living quarters for unmarried staff /集体～ dormitory /学生～ students' hostel
宿世 sùshì 〈佛教〉previous life; last incarnation
宿头 sùtóu place to stop over for the night; inn:错过了～ have missed the chance to find lodging /再不快走,就赶不上～了。We won't be able to find a place to stop over for the night if we don't hurry.
宿土 sùtǔ earth on the root of a plant (when it is transplanted):带有～的花草易活。A plant is easier to survive when it is transplanted with some earth on its root.
宿昔 sùxī 〈书面〉❶ all along; habitually in the past:～之友 long-time friend ❷ short time:～而死 short lived
宿夜 sùyè stop over for the night:在野地搭帐篷～。They put up tents and spent the night in the wilderness.
宿营 sùyíng (of troops) take up quarters; pitch a tent;camp:到野外～ go camping; bivouac /～地 camp site
宿缘 sùyuán 〈佛教〉causation or inheritance from previous existence; predestined relationship:前世～ cause going back to previous incarnation
宿怨 sùyuàn *also* "夙怨" sùyuàn old grudge; old score:多年的～ long-standing grudge /积下～ incur lasting hatred /了结～ settle an old score
宿愿 sùyuàn *also* "夙愿" sùyuàn long-cherished wish:实现到国外深造的～ realize one's long-cherished wish of pursuing further studies abroad
宿债 sùzhài old debt; unrepaid debt:偿还～ pay an old debt
宿志 sùzhì 〈书面〉long-cherished aspirations
宿主 sùzhǔ 〈生物〉host:中间～ intermediate host /终～ final host /～地层 host formation /～颗粒 host grain
宿醉 sùzuì intoxication lasting overnight; hangover:～头仍重 still feel dizzy from the hangover

蹜 sù
蹜蹜 sùsù 〈书面〉walk briskly:～而前 walk on briskly

缩 sù
see also suō
缩砂密 sùshāmì 〈植物〉*Amomum xanthioides*

溯(泝、遡) sù ❶ go up (a stream, etc.):～流而上 go up a river or stream; go upstream ❷ trace back; recall; recollect:上～ trace back to /追～往事 recall past events /～及既往原则〈法律〉principle of retroactivity /追～效力〈法律〉retroactive effect
溯源 sùyuán trace to the source:追本～ track down the origin; trace to the source; get to the root of the problem

愬 sù 〈书面〉*see* "诉" sù

塑 sù ❶ model; sculpture; mould:彩～ colour modelling; painted sculpture /泥～ clay sculpture /雕～ carve and mould; sculpture /面～ dough modelling ❷ plastic:涂～壁纸 plastic wallpaper
塑封 sùfēng plastic-coated:～文件夹 plastic-coated documents folder
塑化剂 sùhuàjì plasticizer
塑建 sùjiàn sculpture and put up:～烈士铜像 mould a bronze statue of the martyr
塑胶 sùjiāo synthetic resin; plastic cement
塑炼 sùliàn plasticate

S

塑炼机 sùliànjī plasticator
塑料 sùliào plastic:～桌布 plastic tablecloth /通用～ general-purpose plastics /工程～ engineering plastics /氟～ fluoroplastics /泡沫～ foam (*or* foamed) plastics /硬～ rigid plastics /软～ mild (*or* soft) plastics
塑料薄膜 sùliào bómó plastic film; plastic sheeting
塑料袋 sùliàodài plastic bag
塑料胶布带 sùliào jiāobùdài plastic adhesive tape
塑料热合机 sùliào rèhéjī plastic welder
塑料上镀 sùliào shàngdù plastic plating
塑料添加剂 sùliào tiānjiājì plastic additive
塑料贴面 sùliào tiēmiàn plastic-face overlays
塑料贴面板 sùliào tiēmiànbǎn plastic veneer
塑料印版 sùliào yìnbǎn 〈印刷〉plastic (printing) plate
塑料雨衣 sùliào yǔyī plastic raincoat
塑料炸弹 sùliào zhàdàn plastic bomb
塑料制品 sùliào zhìpǐn plastic product; plastic ware; plastics
塑像 sùxiàng statue:英雄的～ statue of a hero /石膏～ plaster statue; plaster figure /半身～ bust
塑性 sùxìng 〈物理〉plasticity:～变形 plastic deformation /～黏土 plastic clay
塑性分析 sùxìng fēnxī plastic analysis
塑性化 sùxìnghuà plastification
塑性金属陶瓷复合材料 sùxìng jīnshǔ táocí fùhé cáiliào plasticmetal-ceramic composite
塑性炸药 sùxìng zhàyào plastic explosive; high-explosive plastics
塑性指数 sùxìng zhǐshù plasticity index
塑造 sùzào ❶ model; mould:～头像 mould (*or* model) a head ❷ portray; create:～生动鲜明的形象 create vivid and clear-cut images /～人物的灵魂 portray a character's soul

谡

sù 〈书面〉rise; stand up
谡谡 sùsù tall and straight:～长松 tall, straight pines

诉

sù ❶ tell; narrate; relate:告～ tell; inform /陈～ state; narrate ❷ complain; speak out what is on one's mind:倾～ pour out (one's feelings, troubles, etc.); unburden oneself of /～委屈 air (*or* vent) one's grievances /～衷情 unbosom oneself; pour out one's heart; reveal one's innermost feelings ❸ accuse; sue:控～ accuse; denounce /上～ appeal (to a higher court) /起～ bring a suit (*or* action) (against sb.); sue; prosecute /公～ public prosecution /胜～ win a lawsuit (*or* court case) /～诸法律 go to law; have recourse to law; start (*or* take) (legal) proceedings /～诸武力 resort to force; appeal to arms /"杰克逊～魏德"案 "Jackson v. Wade"
诉辩 sùbiàn 〈法律〉pleading
诉告 sùgào complain (of hardships); air grievances; lodge complaint against
诉苦 sùkǔ vent one's grievances; pour out one's woes:向父母～ pour out one's grievances to one's parents /～会 meeting for pouring out grievances (against injustices, etc.)
诉权 sùquán right to bring a suit or lodge an administrative complaint against sb.
诉述 sùshù tell; relate; recount:～经历 recount the experience
诉说 sùshuō give an account of; tell; recount:～身世 tell one's life story /～内心的苦恼 recount one's worries; tell one's troubles /～事情的经过 give an account of how sth. happened
诉讼 sùsòng 〈法律〉lawsuit; litigation; accusation:对他提出～ bring a lawsuit against him /撤销～ withdraw an accusation; drop a lawsuit /提出版权～ take (*or* start) copyright proceedings /民事～ civil lawsuit /刑事～ criminal lawsuit /～费 court costs; expense of a lawsuit
诉讼程序 sùsòng chéngxù judicial proceedings; litigation procedure
诉讼代理人 sùsòng dàilǐrén agent *ad litem*; legal representative; process attorney
诉讼当事人 sùsòng dāngshìrén litigant
诉讼法 sùsòngfǎ procedural law
诉讼豁免 sùsòng huòmiǎn immunity from suit
诉讼权利 sùsòng quánlì procedural rights
诉讼时效 sùsòng shíxiào limitation of action; prescription of action
诉讼条例 sùsòng tiáolì rules of procedure
诉因 sùyīn 〈法律〉cause of lawsuit; cause of action
诉冤 sùyuān vent one's wrong; air or pour out one's grievances
诉愿 sùyuàn lodge an administrative complaint
诉状 sùzhuàng 〈法律〉plaint; indictment; petition:递交～ file (*or* submit) a plaint /代写～ write out a plaint (for sb.)

素

sù ❶ white:～衣～服 white clothing (as a sign of mourning) ❷ plain; simple; quiet:衣着朴～ plainly dressed /～妆淡描 simple make-up ❸ (as opposed to meats) vegetables, fruits, etc.:吃～ *also* "茹～" be a vegetarian; be on a vegetarian diet /两荤一～ two meat dishes and one vegetable dish /～面 noodles with vegetable trimmings /～香肠 prosage ❹ native: *see* "～质" ❺ basic element:色～ pigment /因～ factor; element /元～ element /维生～ vitamin /要～ essential factor; key element ❻ habitually; of long standing:～望 (one's) usual (*or* customary) reputation /安之若～ bear (*or* regard) with equanimity
素白 sùbái plain and white
素不相识 sùbùxiāngshí do not know at all; have never met:他二人～。The two are complete strangers. /飞机把我带到了这～的他乡。The plane has brought me to this alien land.
素材 sùcái source material (of art and literature); material:收集创作～ gather material for one's creative work
素菜 sùcài vegetable dish:～馆 vegetarian restaurant
素餐 sùcān ❶ vegetarian meal:富有特色的～ distinctive vegetarian meal ❷ be a vegetarian:老人常年～。The old man is a total vegetarian. ❸〈书面〉get one's pay without doing any work:尸位～ hold a job without doing a stroke of work
素常 sùcháng as a rule; usually; ordinarily:他～不爱运动。As a rule he is not keen on sports. /～他都要工作到深夜。Usually he would work far into the night.
素车白马 sùchē-báimǎ plain carriage and white horse (formerly used in a funeral procession or on a similar occasion); funeral; burial
素淡 sùdàn quiet (colour):衣着～ dress in quiet colours
素封 sùfēng 〈书面〉rich without ranks:～之家 wealthy family without ranks
素服 sùfú white clothing (usually as a sign of mourning)
素裹 sùguǒ 〈书面〉dressed in white:红装～ clad in white and adorned in red
素混凝土 sùhùnníngtǔ plain concrete
素交 sùjiāo friendship of long standing; old friend
素洁 sùjié plain and white:池中的白莲花是那么的～，雅致。The white lotus flowers in the pond look very clean and elegant.
素净 sùjing plain and neat; quiet (colour):～的灰衬衫 plain grey shirt /花色～的裙子 skirt in quiet colours
素酒 sùjiǔ ❶ wine served at a vegetarian feast ❷〈方言〉vegetarian feast
素来 sùlái always; regularly:他～讲信用。He always keeps his word.
素绫 sùlíng thin silk of plain colours ordinarily used for mourning; white silk sometimes used for painting
素昧平生 sùmèi-píngshēng have never met before:我和您～，您是怎么知道我的姓名的? I have never had the honour of making your acquaintance. How do you get to know my name?
素面 sùmiàn ❶ vegetarian noodles; plain noodles ❷ in one's natural state or features; without adornment or disguise:～朝天 (as of a woman) present oneself to the emperor without make up; face the public without adornment or disguise; present oneself as one really is
素描 sùmiáo ❶〈美术〉sketch:～写生 sketch from nature (*or* life) /～簿 sketchblock; sketchpad; sketchbook ❷ literary sketch:采用～的手法勾画人物 sketch out the characters (of a novel, etc.)
素坯 sùpī fired unglazed pottery; biscuit
素朴 sùpǔ ❶ simple and unadorned:一张～生动的脸 a simple yet lively face ❷ rudimentary; undeveloped (esp. philosophical ideas):～的观念 rudimentary concept /～唯物主义 naive materialism
素日 sùrì generally; ordinarily; usually:妈妈～难得进城。Mother seldom goes to town. /他～不爱说话。He is a man of few words.
素什锦 sùshíjǐn assorted vegetables dish
素食 sùshí ❶ vegetarian diet:老年人宜～。A vegetarian diet agrees with elderly people. ❷ take vegetarian food:～者 vegetarian /～主义 vegetarianism

素手 sùshǒu ❶ soft, fair-skinned hands ❷ empty-handed
素数 sùshù 〈数学〉prime number:～对 prime pair /～分布律 law of distribution of primes
素昔 sùxī usually; ordinarily; so far:我们～没有往来。We had no contacts in the past.
素习 sùxí ❶ usual habit ❷ usually know well or be skilful at
素席 sùxí vegetarian feast:今天的宴会有两桌～。There are two vegetarians' tables at today's feast.
素心 sùxīn ❶ one's true mind or intention; cherished ambition or wish:与～相违 against one's cherished wish ❷ simple and honest:～人 simple and honest person
素馨 sùxīn 〈植物〉jasmine:～油 jasmine oil /～木 jasminewood
素性 sùxìng one's nature; one's disposition or temperament:～端方,言行不苟。He is by nature upright and discreet in speech and conduct.
素雅 sùyǎ simple but elegant; quiet but tasteful:衣着～大方 dressed in a simple but elegant style
素养 sùyǎng level of (artistic, educational, etc.) attainment; qualities:文学～ literary attainments /音乐～ musical accomplishments /国民～ qualities of the citizenry /他在数学上很有～。He is well versed in mathematics.
素因子 sùyīnzǐ 〈数学〉prime factor; prime divisor
素油 sùyóu vegetable oil
素友 sùyǒu true and honest friend
素愿 sùyuàn cherished ambition or wish:～得偿 have achieved (*or* realized) one's long cherished ambition
素月 sùyuè brilliant moon
素志 sùzhì 〈书面〉long cherished ambition or aspiration:～不改 always cherish lofty aspirations
素质 sùzhì ❶ quality:运动员的心理～ psychological quality of an athlete /孩子的先天～ inherent qualities of a child /全面提高企业的～ comprehensive improvement of the performance of enterprises /科学文化～ cultural and scientific levels /思想道德～ ideological and ethical standards ❷ 〈医学〉diathesis
素质教育 sùzhì jiàoyù (as distinguished from 应试教育) quality-oriented education; education aimed at all-round development (of students)
素珠 sùzhū 〈方言〉〈佛教〉beads
素装 sùzhuāng white garments; simple and elegant dress:一身～ dressed in white; be in simple but elegant dress
素子 sùzi ❶ wine vessel ❷ *see* "嗉子❶"

愫 sù 〈书面〉true feeling; sincerity:情～ sincere feelings; true sentiments

嗉(膆) sù crop (of a bird)
嗉子 sùzi ❶ *also* "嗉囊";"素子" sùzi crop (of a bird) ❷ 〈方言〉wine flask made of tin or porcelain

速[1] sù ❶ fast; rapid; swift; quick:～胜 quick victory; immediate success /兵贵神～ speed is the soul of war /母病,～归。(telegraph) Mother ill, return at once. ❷ speed; velocity; tempo:风～ wind speed; wind velocity /光～ velocity of light /音～ velocity of sound /加～进行 step up; accelerate /减～ slow down; decelerate /超～ exceeding the speed limit; speeding /初～ initial velocity /全～ full speed /失～〈航空〉stall

速[2] sù 〈书面〉invite:不～之客 uninvited guest; gate-crasher
速成 sùchéng achieve by quick methods; speed up:～教学法 speeded-up teaching method /～识字法 quick method of achieving literacy /工农～中学 shorter-term secondary school for workers and farmers /世界上有些事情是不可能～的。Certain things just cannot be achieved by quick methods.
速成班 sùchéngbān accelerated course; crash course
速冻 sùdòng quick-freeze:～食品 quick-frozen food
速度 sùdù ❶〈物理〉velocity:初～ initial velocity /匀～ uniform velocity /逃逸～ *also* "第二宇宙～"〈航天〉escape velocity /轨道～ orbital velocity /巡航～ cruising speed /加～ acceleration ❷〈音乐〉tempo ❸ speed; rate; pace; tempo:国民经济增长～ rate of growth of the national economy /科学发展的～惊人。Science developed by leaps and bounds.
速度比 sùdùbǐ velocity ratio
速度不足 sùdù bùzú underspeed
速度场 sùdùchǎng velocity field
速度滑冰 sùdù huábīng *also* "速滑"〈体育〉speed skating
速度计 sùdùjì velocimeter; speed indicator; speedometer
速度向量 sùdù xiàngliàng velocity vector
速记 sùjì *also* "速记法" shorthand; stenography; speedwriting
速记打字机 sùjì dǎzìjī stenograph
速记员 sùjìyuán stenographer
速决 sùjué quick decision
速决战 sùjuézhàn war or battle of quick decision
速可眠 sùkěmián 〈药学〉seconal; secobarbital sodium
速率 sùlǜ speed; rate:冷却～ rate of cooling /感光～ exposure speed /打印～ line feed (speed) /～计 ratemeter /～陀螺 rate gyroscope
速尿剂 sùniàojì 〈药学〉furosemide
速溶 sùróng quick to dissolve; instant:～茶 instant tea /～咖啡 instant coffee
速射 sùshè 〈军事〉rapid fire:～武器 rapid-fire weapon
速射炮 sùshèpào quick-firing gun; quick-firer
速生丰产林 sùshēng fēngchǎnlín fast-growing, high-yield timber forest
速食米 sùshímǐ instant rice
速食面 sùshímiàn instant noodles
速算 sùsuàn short-cut counting; rapid calculation
速逃星 sùtáoxīng 〈天文〉runaway star
速调管 sùtiáoguǎn 〈无线电〉klystron:～放大器 klystron amplifier
速效 sùxiào quick acting:～伤风胶囊 quick-cold-relieving capsule /～药 medicine that produces quick results; quick-acting medicine /～洗涤剂 quick-acting detergent
速效肥料 sùxiào féiliào 〈农业〉quick-acting fertilizer
速写 sùxiě ❶ rough, quickly made drawing; sketch:画～ draw sketches /一张人像～ sketch of a portrait ❷ written sketch:新闻人物～ sketch of a news figure
速战速决 sùzhàn-sùjué battle of quick decision:一场～的战斗 fight a battle of quick decision /他二人从恋爱到结婚不足一个月,真算得上～。From the time they fell in love to the time they got married, it is only a matter of a few weeks. It's real fast work!

觫 sù *see* "觳觫" húsù

馃 sù 〈书面〉food in a tripod, an ancient cooking vessel

蔌 sù 〈书面〉vegetable:山肴野～ mountain food and wild vegetables; game and edible herbs (as food)

嗀 sù *see* "麗嗀" lùsù

簌 sù
簌簌 sùsù ❶〈象声〉rustle:风中竹声～。Bamboo leaves were rustling in the wind. ❷ (tears) streaming down:她的眼泪～地流个不停。Her tears kept streaming down. ❸ shiver:他全身～地抖。He was shivering all over.

粟 sù ❶ millet ❷ (Sù) a surname
粟米 sùmǐ 〈方言〉maize; corn
粟疹 sùzhěn 〈生理〉miliaria
粟子 sùzi 〈方言〉millet

傈 sù *see* "傈僳族" Lìsùzú

夙 sù 〈书面〉❶ early in the morning:～夜 morning and night; day and night ❷ long-standing; of yore; old: *see* "～怨"
夙仇 sùchóu ❶ enemy of long standing; old enemy ❷ long-running enmity:～未报 old scores yet to be settled
夙敌 sùdí *also* "宿敌" sùdí old foe or adversary
夙诺 sùnuò *also* "宿诺" sùnuò long-given promise
夙日 sùrì usually; ordinarily; at ordinary times:～过从甚密。Ordinarily they keep close touch with each other.
夙世 sùshì 〈佛教〉previous existence:～因缘 causation (*or* inheritance) from previous existence; predestined relationship /～冤家

S

enemies of a previous existence
夙嫌 sùxián long-standing enmity; old grudge: 捐弃～ let bygones be bygones
夙兴夜寐 sùxīng-yèmèi rise early and retire late — be hard at work day and night; be very industrious
夙夜 sùyè morning and night; all the time: 他～期望着做一名医生。Day and night he dreamed of becoming a doctor.
夙夜匪懈 sùyè-fěixiè work diligently day and night: 他立志读书，～。He studies hard, engrossed in books day and night.
夙因 sùyīn 〈迷信〉 predestined relationship
夙怨 sùyuàn *also* "宿怨" sùyuàn old grudge; old score: 了却～ settle an old score
夙愿 sùyuàn *also* "宿愿" sùyuàn long-cherished wish: ～得偿 realize one's long-cherished wish

肃(肅) sù

❶ respect; esteem: ～～ respectfully / 待长者不～ not show enough respect for the elderly ❷ solemn; sombre: 严～ solemn; serious; grave ❸ eliminate; eradicate: ～贪 root out corruption
肃反 sùfǎn (short for 肃清反革命) elimination of counterrevolutionaries: ～运动 movement for the elimination of counterrevolutionaries; movement to crack down on counterrevolutionaries
肃静 sùjìng solemn silence: ～地站立 stand in solemn silence / 请～! Keep quiet, please!
肃立 sùlì stand respectfully; rise as a mark of respect: ～致敬 stand in salute / 全体～，默哀三分钟。All rose to observe three minutes' silence.
肃穆 sùmù ❶ solemn and quiet; grave: ～的陵园 solemn cemetery (*or* mausoleum) ❷ respectful and genial: 神情庄重～ look respectful and congenial
肃清 sùqīng eliminate; clean up; root out: ～封建思想 eradicate feudal ideas and concepts / ～贪官污吏 get rid of (*or* eliminate) corrupt officials / ～残匪 mop up remnant bandits / ～敌人的据点 clean up (*or* capture) enemy strongholds
肃然 sùrán respectful: ～生畏 be struck with awe; stand in awe of
肃然起敬 sùrán-qǐjìng be held in profound respect: 他的高风亮节令人～。He is held in high esteem for his noble character and sterling integrity.
肃杀 sùshā 〈书面〉 cold and lifeless: 秋气～ cold and lifeless atmosphere of late autumn

鹔(鷫) sù

鹔鹴 sùshuāng *also* "鹔鹩" water bird mentioned in ancient books
鹔鹩 sùshuāng *see* "鹔鹴"

骕(驌) sù

骕骦 sùshuāng *also* "骕骥" fine horse mentioned in ancient books
骕骥 sùshuāng *see* "骕骦"

suān

酸[1] suān

❶ 〈化学〉 acid: 抗坏血～ ascorbic acid; vitamin C / 柠檬～ citric acid / 醋～ acetic acid / 盐～ hydrochloric acid / 硫～ sulphuric acid / 硝～ nitric acid / ～化作用 acidization ❷ sour; vinegary; tart: ～杏儿 sour apricot / 胃～过多 acid indigestion; acidity / 卖酒不说酒～。A wine seller never complains that his wine is sour. *or* One is prone to blow one's own trumpet. ❸ sick at heart; feel sad; grieved: 感到心～ feel sad / 辛～的一生 miserable life; bitter experience of one's life ❹ of impoverished pedantic scholars in the old days: 寒～的样子 miserable and shabby / 一副穷～相 look every inch an impoverished pedant

酸[2](痠) suān

prickling sensation; ache: 腰～背疼 have a backache; have a pain in the back / 手脚发～ feel painful in the limbs / 手写～了。My hand aches from writing.
酸败 suānbài (of fat, meat, fish, etc.) turned sour; rancid
酸鼻 suānbí have an irritated sensation in the nose; feel like crying; be grieved: 令人～ make one want to cry out of pity
酸不唧 suānbujī ❶ taste just a little bit sour: 这果子～儿的，好吃。This fruit has a nice tart taste. ❷ exhausted; fatigued: 浑身～的 feel weary all over
酸不拉唧 suānbulājī *also* "酸拉吧唧" disgustingly sour: 这种杏儿～的，不好吃。This kind of apricot is too sour to the taste.
酸不溜丢 suānbuliūdiū 〈方言〉 be of a sour taste; (of persons) sour; cynical: ～的味道 tart flavour / ～的样子 look disappointed and bitter / 这菜～的，真难吃。The dish tastes too sour for human consumption. / 这人真讨厌，～的! That chap is cynical and gets on your nerves.
酸菜 suāncài pickled vegetables; sauerkraut; pickles: 腌～ make pickled vegetables / 爱吃～ like to eat pickles / ～汤 Chinese sauerkraut soup
酸槽 suāncáo acid tank
酸潮 suāncháo 〈生理〉 acid tide
酸尘 suānchén acid dust
酸橙 suānchéng lime (*Citrus aurantifolia*)
酸处理 suānchǔlǐ 〈石油〉 acid treatment; acidation
酸楚 suānchǔ grieved; painful; distressed: 心中感到～ feel grieved / ～的心情 painful feeling / ～的样子 look distressed
酸脆 suāncuì 〈冶金〉 acid brittleness
酸度 suāndù 〈化学〉 acidity
酸腐 suānfǔ ❶ (of odour) sour and rotten: 食品已～变质。The foods have gone bad and become smelly. ❷ pedantic: 这人过于～。The man is dull and dogmatic.
酸腐病 suānfǔbìng sour rot
酸腐蚀 suānfǔshí acid corrosion
酸酐 suāngān 〈化学〉 acid anhydride
酸根 suāngēn 〈化学〉 acid radical
酸哽 suāngěng feel sad and choke with sobs: ～难言 choking with sobs and too grieved to speak
酸化 suānhuà acidify; acidulate
酸化剂 suānhuàjì 〈化学〉 acidifier; acidulant
酸化器 suānhuàqì 〈化学〉 acidifier
酸基 suānjī 〈化学〉 acyloxy; acidic group
酸碱催化 suānjiǎn cuīhuà 〈化学〉 acid-base catalysis
酸碱滴定法 suānjiǎn dīdìngfǎ 〈化学〉 acid-base titration
酸碱度 suānjiǎndù pH value
酸碱工业 suānjiǎn gōngyè acid-base industry: 大力发展～ energetically develop the acid-base industry
酸碱中和 suānjiǎn zhōnghé acid-base neutralization
酸解 suānjiě 〈化学〉 acidolysis
酸苦 suānkǔ grieved; bitter; miserable: ～的心情 feel grief-stricken / 历尽～ have experienced untold bitter sufferings / 提起旧社会的遭遇，老大娘心头一阵～。As she recounted her sufferings in the old society, the old woman felt a gnawing pain in her heart.
酸困 suānkùn (of the body) aching and exhausted: 浑身～ dog-tired and aching all over
酸辣酱 suānlàjiàng chutney, an Indian condiment made of fruits or vegetables, vinegar, spices, sugar, etc.
酸辣汤 suānlàtāng vinegar-pepper soup; hot and sour soup: 本店的～远近驰名。The vinegar-pepper soup served in this restaurant is known far and wide. / 泰国的～颇具特色。The Thai hot and sour soup has a distinctive flavour.
酸懒 suānlǎn 〈方言〉 (of body) aching and tired: 只觉全身～ be aching all over and overcome with fatigue / 四肢～ feel sore in all limbs
酸溜溜 suānliūliū ❶ sour taste or smell: 一股～的气味 sour smell / 这话梅～的，很好吃。The preserved plum, pleasantly sour, tastes good. ❷ aching: 我累极了，周身～的难受。I am tired to death and aching all over. ❸ feeling sadly envious: 看见他俩亲密的样子，心里总有点～的感觉。I could not refrain from feeling sadly envious when I found them so chummy with each other. ❹ pedantic: 这位先生满嘴之乎者也，～的。That man talked like a pedant, his speech full of archaisms.
酸麻 suānmá ache and feel numb from overexertion: 走了一天山路，腿都～了。As he had walked all day in the mountains, his legs ached and felt numb.
酸马奶 suānmǎnǎi koumiss: 请喝一杯～。Have a cup of koumiss, please.
酸梅 suānméi smoked plum; dark plum
酸梅汤 suānméitāng sweet-sour plum juice
酸尿 suānniào 〈医学〉 aciduria
酸凝树脂 suānníng shùzhī 〈化学〉 acid-cured resin

酸牛奶 suānniúnǎi yoghurt; sour milk:～不仅富于营养，还有助于消化。Sour milk is not only nutritious, but helps digestion as well.
酸曲 suānqǔ 〈方言〉 love song
酸溶液 suānróngyè acid solution
酸软 suānruǎn aching and limp:周身～无力 aching and sluggish all over / 四肢～没劲儿 feel listless
酸涩 suānsè ❶ sour and puckery:这柿子太～了。The persimmons are sour and puckery. ❷ feel sore in the eyes (owing to eyestrain):眼睛～。My eyes are sore.
酸式盐 suānshìyán 〈化学〉 acid salt
酸疼 suānténg *see* "酸痛"
酸甜苦辣 suān-tián-kǔ-là sour, sweet, bitter, hot — joys and sorrows of life, esp. sorrows; vicissitudes of life:他这一辈子，什么～没尝过! In his life he has experienced all kinds of sweet and bitter feelings (*or* ups and downs).
酸甜儿 suāntiánr sour-sweet
酸痛 suāntòng ache:关节～ have pain in the joints / 手腕～。The wrist aches. / 跑得腿肚子～。My legs are sore from walking.
酸头儿 suāntóur 〈口语〉 tart:这种苹果略带～。This kind of apple has a slightly tart flavour.
酸味 suānwèi tart flavour:这饭已有～，不能吃了。The cooked rice has turned sour (*or* gone bad) and is not fit to be eaten.
酸文假醋 suānwén-jiǎcù feigned elegance; affected manners:大凡一个人，总别～的才好。It is advisable not to affect a man of elegance and learning.
酸污染 suānwūrǎn 〈环保〉 acid pollution
酸雾 suānwù acid mist
酸洗 suānxǐ 〈冶金〉 pickling; acid pickling
酸洗试验 suānxǐ shìyàn acid washing test
酸洗液 suānxǐyè pickle; pickle liquor; acid wash
酸心 suānxīn ❶ sick at heart; grieved; distressed:这出戏看了叫人～。This play makes people feel very sad. ❷ sour the stomach; suffer from heartburn:白薯吃多了～。Eating too many sweet potatoes sours the stomach.
酸辛 suānxīn sad; grieved:～地哭泣 cry bitterly / ～的生活 sad and miserable life / 有谁能知道她的～? Who knows how much she has gone through?
酸性 suānxìng acidity; acidness:〈化学〉～染料 acid dyes / ～物质 acidoid / ～油 acid-stage oil / 〈冶金〉～钢 acid steel; Bessemer steel / ～炼钢法 acid process
酸性反应 suānxìng fǎnyìng acid reaction
酸性试验 suānxìng shìyàn acid test
酸性岩 suānxìngyán acidic rock
酸性转炉 suānxìng zhuànlú acid converter; Bessemer converter:～炼钢法 acid converter process
酸血症 suānxuèzhèng 〈医学〉 acidaemia
酸雨 suānyǔ acid rain; acid precipitation
酸枣 suānzǎo *also* "棘" jí wild jujube:～汁 wild jujube juice / ～树 wild jujube tree / ～林 wild jujube grove
酸渣 suānzhā 〈化工〉 acid-sludge
酸沼 suānzhǎo bog
酸值 suānzhí 〈化学〉 acid value; acid number
酸酯 suānzhǐ 〈化学〉 acid ester
酸中毒 suānzhòngdú 〈医学〉 acidosis

狻 suān

狻猊 suānní legendary fierce animal

suàn

蒜 suàn

also "大蒜" dàsuàn ❶ garlic:大～ garlic / 一辫～ a braid of garlic / 一挂～ a string of garlic / 一头～ a head of garlic / ～味肠 garlic sausage / 青～ young garlic stalk and leaves / 糖～ garlic in syrup ❷ bulb of this plant
蒜瓣儿 suànbànr garlic clove:他一次吃了三个～。He ate three garlic cloves at a time.
蒜毫 suànháo *see* "蒜薹"
蒜黄 suànhuáng blanched garlic leaves:肉丝炒～ shredded pork stir-fried with blanched garlic leaves
蒜苗 suànmiáo garlic pedicel or shoot:肉片炒～ meat slices stir-fried with garlic shoot / 这～又鲜嫩又便宜。The garlic pedicels are both fresh and tender, and cheap, too.
蒜泥 suànní mashed garlic:把蒜瓣捣成～。Mash the garlic. / 凉拌茄子应加点～。Cooled steamed eggplant should go with mashed garlic.
蒜素 suànsù 〈化学〉 allicin
蒜薹 suàntái pedicel or shoot of garlic (edible when it is tender):这～真嫩。The garlic pedicel is very tender.
蒜头 suàntóu head or bulb of garlic:这个～真大! What a big head of garlic!

筭 suàn

〈书面〉 *see* "算" suàn

算(祘) suàn

❶ calculate; estimate; reckon:笔～ written calculation; do a sum in writing / 珠～ arithmetic by abacus / 概～ rough estimate / 心～ mental arithmetic; do sums in one's head / 口～ oral calculation; chant out the result while doing the sum in one's head / 反复～ check the calculation over and over again / 从头～ calculate (*or* count) from the very beginning / 认真～ make a serious reckoning / ～一下住宿费 make up the accommodation bill / ～伙食费 tot up the cost of board / ～～这一周共用了多少钱 check how much was spent this week / ～清了 one's bill is paid / ～得快 calculate fast; do the calculation fast / ～错了 make a wrong calculation ❷ count; include; figure in:一起～进去 count everything up / 你们去北戴河，可得把我也～上。Count me in when you go to Beidaihe. / 把他～进去，一共有五人。There are 5 people, including him. / ～上星期天，也只剩三天了。There are only three days left even if Sunday is included. ❸ plan; figure; calculate:暗自盘～ calculate in one's mind; figure sth. to oneself / 暗～ plot against / 又失～了 misjudge (*or* miscalculate) again / 打～去北京 plan to go to Beijing ❹ think; suppose; reckon:～起来，他今天该到家了。I suppose he'll arrive home today. / 我～准了，她今天一定会来。I am sure that she will come today. / 从表现看，我～她这次准能考上。Judging from her performance, I think she will be successful in the examination. ❺ regard as; consider; count as; take for:他～我们这里的专家。He is to be counted (*or* regarded) as one of our experts here. / 他处处照顾大家，～是我们的老大哥了。Taking care of all of us, he is just as good as our elder brother. / 今天不～太热。I don't think it is too hot today. / 孩子们是闹着玩儿，不～打架。The children are just playing for fun; they are not fighting. / 碰上这个不讲理的人，～我倒霉! It's really bad luck to have met such an unreasonable chap. / 今天这顿饭～我请客。This meal is on me. ❻ count; carry weight; be effective:说话～话 make good one's promises; mean what one says; be as good as one's word / 他说话从来不～数儿。He never keeps his promise. / 在我们家，只有妈妈说了～。In the whole family Mum's words alone count. *or* Mum wears the trousers in our house. ❼ (followed by 了) come, come; let it be:～了，～了，不理他就是了。Come, come, just leave him alone. / 他不愿意就～了，何必再求他。We might as well do without him if he is reluctant. There's no need to bother him again. ❽ due to; on account of; in the end; finally:这一次～他运气好，没被人抓着。It was due to his good luck that he was not caught red-handed. / 矛盾～解决了。The problem was solved after all.
算草 suàncǎo rough formula in doing mathematical calculations:先列出～儿 list rough calculation formula first
算尺 suànchǐ slide rule
算得 suàndé consider; regard as; count as:～是一员干将 can be regarded as a go-getter
算法 suànfǎ 〈数学〉 algorithm; way of calculation:有多种～ have many ways of calculation / 简便的～ simple calculation; simple and convenient algorithm
算卦 suànguà practise divination
算计 suànji ❶ calculate; reckon; figure:～总人数 work out the total number of people / ～需要的劳动力 figure out the labour force needed / 你好好～一下，这个月剩下的钱够不够花消? Check carefully to see if enough money is left this month. ❷ think; consider; plan:他正～着利用暑假回老家一次。He is thinking of making a trip to his hometown during the summer vacation. / 他在～兼职的事。He is contemplating moonlighting. / 究竟该选谁，他要好好地～一下。He will carefully think it over as to exactly whom he should vote for. ❸ expect; figure; estimate:我～着孩子这两天该来信了。I expect to hear from my son one of these days. / 你～一下领导对这件事会怎么处理? Can you figure out how the leadership is going to handle the

matter? ❹ plot; scheme; intrigue：他心眼儿真坏，老是～别人。He is so evil-minded that he is always plotting against others.

算计儿 suànjìr 〈方言〉plan; design：过日子要有个～。Planning is important for managing a household.

算经十书 Suànjīng Shíshū *Ten Mathematical Manuals*, ten important mathematical works in ancient China

算旧账 suàn jiùzhàng *also* "算老账" settle an old account or score：我不想跟他～。I'm not intending to make him pay an old debt. /新账旧账一起算！All scores, old and new, shall be paid (*or* cleared) off.

算命 suànmìng fortune-telling：他很喜欢给别人～。He is fond of telling fortunes for others.

算命先生 suànmìng xiānsheng fortune-teller：我们不是～，不知道将来会怎样。We are no clairvoyants; we don't know what will happen in the future.

算盘 suànpan ❶ abacus：学习打～ learn to use an abacus ❷ scheme; design：个人的小～ selfish designs (*or* calculation) /如意～ wishful thinking; smug calculations /他对这件事满口应承，是有他自己的～的。He readily gave his consent to the matter out of ulterior motives.

算盘子儿 suànpanzǐr oblate beads of an abacus

算式 suànshì equation：先列出～ write out the equation first /～的顺序排列 sequence of an equation

算是 suànshì presumably; at last：她想进重点大学的愿望今年～可以实现了。At last, her wish to go to a key university will come true this year. /不管怎样，你也～一个长辈，怎能这样对待他？In any case, you're presumably of the elder generation. How could you treat him that way (*or* like that)?

算术 suànshù arithmetic：学～ learn arithmetic /做～ do sums /教～ teach arithmetic /～题 arithmetic problem; sum

算术级数 suànshù jíshù 〈数学〉arithmetic progression

算术平均值 suànshù píngjūnzhí 〈数学〉arithmetic average or mean

算术运算 suànshù yùnsuàn arithmetic operation

算术中项 suànshù zhōngxiàng arithmetic mean

算数 suànshù ❶ count; hold; stand; carry weight：中国人说话是～的。We Chinese people mean what we say. /例外的情况不～。Exceptions do not count. /如今有了新制度，旧制度不～了。Now that we have new regulations, old ones no longer hold (*or* stand). ❷ until：学会了才～。You must keep on learning until you master it.

算题 suàntí mathematical exercises; computational problems

算无遗策 suànwúyícè plan very carefully with every conceivable possibility taken into account：他的安排～，众人口服心服。His meticulous arrangements have won him general acclaim.

算学 suànxué ❶ mathematics ❷ arithmetic

算账 suànzhàng ❶ do or work out accounts; balance the books; make out bills：一笔一笔地～ settle accounts one by one /他～又快又准，谁都比不上他。As far as doing accounts is concerned, nobody can match him in speed and accuracy. ❷ square accounts with; settle scores with; get even with：你别得意得太早，咱们改日再～！Don't laugh too soon. I'll get even with you some other time! /我以后再跟你～！I'll make you pay for this! /总有跟他们～的一天！The day will come when we will settle accounts with them!

算子 suànzǐ 〈数学〉operator：微分～ differential operator /～代数 operator algebra /～方程 operator equation

算总账 suàn zǒngzhàng square the whole accounts with sb.：～的一天 day of reckoning /目前只能隐忍，等日后再跟那家伙～。We have to put up with it for now, but we will square the whole accounts with that villain later (*or* we will make that villain pay for it later).

suī

荽

suī *see* "芫荽" yánsui

眭

suī ❶〈书面〉gaze thoughtfully at：～然而视 gaze intently at ❷ (Suī) a surname

睢

suī ❶ *see* "恣睢" zìsuī ❷ (Suī) a surname

虽(雖)

suī 〈书面〉❶ though; although：房间～不大，但收拾得干净整齐。Though small, the room is clean and tidy. /人～小，志气却很大。He is very ambitious despite his youth. /为了工作，～累也心甘。I am most willing to work hard to get the job done. ❷ even if; even though：为民造福，～苦犹荣。To work for the well-being of the people is a matter of great honour, even though one has to go through a lot of hardships.

虽然 suīrán though; although：我～喜欢古诗，但不会做诗。Though I like classical poetry, I can't write poems. /这孩子～小，但却很懂事。Young as he is, the child is very sensible. /这事影响太大，～事情本身并不严重。The matter is not serious by itself, but it has great repercussions. /～不少人都劝过她，但她还是不同意跟他和解。She still refuses to make it up with him despite exhortations from many people.

虽说 suīshuō 〈口语〉though; although：～他英语不怎么好，但也还能叫人听懂。Though he does not speak English well, he still can make himself understood. /你～是开玩笑，但也讲得太过分了。This is going too far even though you're joking.

虽死犹生 suīsǐ-yóushēng still live in the hearts of the people though dead：烈士们～。The martyrs will always live in our memory (*or* hearts).

虽则 suīzé though; although：～题目并不难，但数量太多，两小时做不完。The examination paper is not very stiff, but the questions are too many to be finished in two hours.

尿

suī urine：尿了一泡～ make water; urinate

see also niào

尿泡 suīpao *see* "尿脬"

尿脬 suīpao *also* "尿泡"〈方言〉bladder

suí

遂

suí *see* "半身不遂" bànshēn-bùsuí

see also suì

隋

Suí ❶ Sui Dynasty (581-618) ❷ a surname

随(隨)

suí ❶ follow：紧～ follow closely /～父母旅游 travel with one's parents /尾～ tail behind; tag along after; follow at sb.'s heels; shadow /快～我来。Follow me quick. *or* Come along with me quick. /你～我去吧！Come with me! /～着时代的改变，人们的观念也有了改变。People's ideas change with the change of the times. ❷ comply with; adapt to; go along with：～风而舞 dance in the wind /吃什么都成，我～你。I'll take whatever you like (to eat). ❸ let (sb. do as he likes); do at one's convenience; act at one's discretion：～你怎么说，我都不会改变自己的主意。No matter what you say, I won't change my mind. /这几本书～他挑。He is free to choose from among these books. /参加不参加，～你决定好了。It's up to you whether you take part in it or not. ❹ along with (some other action)：他～口喊出了她的名字。He blurted out her name without thinking. ❺〈方言〉look like; be similar; resemble：这女孩子的眼睛～她爸爸。The girl takes after her father: she has the same eyes. ❻ (Suí) a surname

随笔 suíbǐ ❶ informal essay; familiar essay; sketches：我很爱读郁达夫写的～。I like informal essays by Yu Dafu very much. ❷ jottings; short notes：记～ jot down notes

随便 suíbiàn ❶ at one's convenience; at one's discretion; at one's pleasure：客随主便。A guest should suit the convenience of the host. /随你的便。Suit yourself. *or* Do as you please. ❷ as much or as little as one wishes; free; informal：～座谈一下 have a free talk (*or* an informal talk) /～唱 sing whatever you like /～吃 please help yourself /～谈谈看法 make some random remarks /这些材料，你们可以～看，～抄。You are free to read or copy these materials. /有问题能～提问吗？Are we free to ask any questions? ❸ at will; at random; without consideration or care; casually：～中止合同 break the contract at will /工作随随便便 be slipshod in one's work /大家可以～些，别太拘束。Make yourselves at home. /写文章应对读者负责，不能随随便便。The author should take his writing seriously as he is ultimately responsible to his readers (*or* as he must hold himself responsible to his readers). ❹ any; anyhow; no matter (what, when, how, etc.)：只要穿着大方，～哪种颜色都行。Any colour will do so long as the dress looks in good taste. /他爱京剧，～哪种唱法他都

喜欢。He likes Beijing opera, no matter what style of singing it may be.

随波逐流 suíbō-zhúliú drift with the tide or current:凡事都必须有主见，不能～。One should have ideas of one's own, and not follow others blindly. /喜欢～的人往往容易犯错误。Those who like to swim (*or* float) with the stream are apt to make mistakes.

随常 suícháng usual; ordinary; common:她带了两件～的衣服作为替换。She took with her two dresses for everyday wear for change.

随处 suíchù in all places; everywhere; anywhere:果皮不能～乱扔。Peel should not be littered around. /这种电池～可买到。This kind of battery is available everywhere.

随从 suícóng ❶ accompany or follow (one's superior); go along with:～大军渡江南下 go south across the Yangtze River with the army /～代表团团长出访莫斯科 accompany the leader of the delegation to Moscow ❷ retinue; suite; entourage:带着一大帮～ accompanied by a large entourage

随大溜 suí dàliù *also* "随大流" drift with the stream; follow the herd:他办事向来是～。He always does as others do./看来这事只能～了。It seems that we have to conform to the majority will on this issue.

随带 suídài ❶ going along with; together with:信封内～照片两张。Two photos are enclosed in the envelope. /出售家电应～说明书。Electric home appliances should be sold together with the operation manual. ❷ have sth. taken along with one; take along:每位旅客可以～行李二十公斤。Each passenger is allowed to take along 20 kilos of luggage with him.

随地 suídì all over the places; everywhere; anywhere:禁止～吐痰! No spitting! /垃圾不能～乱扔。Don't litter. /果皮、纸屑几乎～都是。Peel and waste paper are littered almost everywhere.

随动件 suídòngjiàn 〈机械〉 follower

随方就圆 suífāng-jiùyuán go with the trend; be pliant

随访 suífǎng ❶ accompany (one's superior) on a visit:～记者 accompanying reporter /外交部长出访，～的有部长夫人及外交部官员。Accompanying the Foreign Minister on the visit are his wife and some officials from the Foreign Ministry. ❷ follow-up visit by a doctor to his patients after treatment:王大夫坚持～观察，积累了大量材料。Dr. Wang used to visit his patients after treatment and accumulated a lot of data.

随份子 suí fènzi ❶ contribute one's share as part of a group gift ❷ *also* "出份子" chū fènzi bring money with oneself to a wedding party, funeral, etc.

随风倒 suífēngdǎo bend with the wind — be easily swayed (by whichever side that has more power or influence); be a weathercock:墙头草，～。Grass on the top of the wall bends with the wind. /不要～。Don't be swayed easily.

随风转舵 suífēng-zhuǎnduò trim one's sails; take one's cue from changing conditions
see also "顺风转舵" shùnfēng-zhuǎnduò

随感 suígǎn random thoughts:《～录》*Random Thoughts*

随行就市 suíháng-jiùshì fix prices according to market changes:小贩出售蔬菜，可以～，按质论价。Vendors may sell their vegetables at varying prices based on different qualities and market conditions. /粮油议购价格可参考集市价格，本着～，略低于集市价格的原则确定。The negotiated purchasing prices of cereals and oil may fluctuate with reference to the market prices but should be a bit lower than the latter.

随和 suíhe amiable; obliging; easygoing:性情～ be amiable (*or* genial) /待人～ be obliging to people /老师傅的样子挺～。The veteran worker looks kindly.

随后 suíhòu soon after:你刚出去，电话～就来了。The telephone call came soon after (*or* the moment) you left. /大家先喝茶，饭菜～就得。Have some tea first. The meal will be ready in a minute.

随机 suíjī ❶ 〈统计〉 random ❷ 〈数学〉 stochastic

随机变数 suíjī biànshù 〈统计〉 random variable

随机抽样 suíjī chōuyàng random sampling; stochastic sampling

随机存取存储器 suíjī cúnqǔ cúnchǔqì 〈计算机〉 random access memory (RAM)

随机过程 suíjī guòchéng random process; stochastic process

随机应变 suíjī-yìngbiàn act according to circumstances; be resourceful:幸亏他能～，否则事情就要闹大了。But for his resourcefulness, the whole thing might have gone out of control. /总之要～，要机警，要沉着。Just do what seems best. Keep your wits about you, and keep cool.

随即 suíjí immediately; presently; right away:听到报警，民警～登车奔赴出事地点。On hearing the alarm, the police immediately got into their vehicles and hurried to the scene of the accident. /汽笛一响，轮船～起航。The ship set sail right after the steam whistle was sounded.

随记 suíjì random notes:《采访～》*Random Notes of an Interview*

随驾 suíjià follow the emperor's carriage; be in the emperor's entourage:～出征 go on an expedition with the emperor

随军 suíjūn follow the army (in its movements)

随军记者 suíjūn jìzhě war correspondent

随军家属 suíjūn jiāshǔ families of officers accompanying the army; camp family

随口 suíkǒu speak thoughtlessly; blurt out; shoot off one's mouth:～之言 words that escape one's lips; offhand remarks /这几个相声演员真行，～就来一段儿。These cross talkers are really terrific; they are able to perform a comic dialogue impromptu. /他办事一贯认真，从不～许诺别人。He takes everything seriously and never makes promises lightly.

随群 suíqún do as others do:他这个人有点怪，当然也不～。He is a bit eccentric and of course not gregarious. /你怎么事事不～? Why are you always so withdrawn?

随群逐队 suíqún-zhúduì follow the herd; lack in originality

随人俯仰 suírén-fǔyǎng be at sb.'s beck and call; do sb.'s bidding; follow sb. servilely

随身 suíshēn (carry) on one's person; (take) with one; personally:出差时，各种证件都应～带着。One should personally carry all the credentials on one's business trips. /行李可托运，这包书可要～带着。The luggage can be checked, but you should take this bag of books with you. /我～没带多少钱。I haven't got much money on me.

随身听 suíshēntīng walkman

随身行李 suíshēn xíngli personal luggage

随声附和 suíshēng-fùhè echo what others say; chime in with others' opinion:我最讨厌那些不加思索而～的人。I hate those who chime in with others thoughtlessly. /由于多人～，他的意见在会上占了上风。As the majority had no particular opinion of its own, his views prevailed at the meeting.

随时 suíshí ❶ at any time; at all times; whenever:欢迎你～来玩儿。You are welcome to come (*or* drop in) at any time. /只要你愿意，我～都可奉陪。Call me any time you want; I am always ready. /碰到麻烦可～来找我。Come to me whenever you are in trouble. /～准备歼灭入侵之敌 be ready at all times to wipe out any invaders ❷ whenever necessary; whenever possible; as the occasion demands:～调整工作进度 adjust the progress of the work as the occasion demands /～改正缺点 rectify shortcomings as soon as they occur /战士们准备～出击。The soldiers are ready to launch an attack whenever necessary.

随时随地 suíshí-suídì at any time and in any place; at all times and in all places:～与指挥部联系 keep in contact with the headquarters at all times and places

随侍 suíshì 〈书面〉 ❶ be in the attendance of an elder ❷ attendant

随手 suíshǒu conveniently; immediately; without extra trouble:～拈来 pick up at random /～扔进抽屉 toss sth. casually into the drawer /～打开电视机 turn on the TV right away /～把门关上。Shut the door behind you.

随顺 suíshùn obey; comply with; yield to; be obedient to:姑娘对妈妈一向～。The daughter is always docile and obedient to her mother.

随俗 suísú comply with convention; do as everybody else does:入乡～。When in Rome, do as the Romans do.

随…随… suí…suí… *used before two verbs or two verbial phrases to indicate that one action is immediately followed by the other*:随叫随到 be available at any time; be on call at any hour /随到随走 come and go all the time /随看随画 keep on drawing while observing /随印随发 hand out sth. as it is printed /随到随修，立等可取。Repairs are being done while you wait.

随同 suítóng accompany; go with; be accompanying:～总理出国访问 accompany the premier on a visit abroad; visit other countries as members of the premier's entourage /～好友一起旅游 go on a tour with one's good friends

随喜 suíxǐ ❶ 〈佛教〉 be willing to give donations ❷ indicate one's

S

willingness to join others in the fun, etc.：～拍手喝彩 clap and cheer with others /～，～！也算我一份。Count me in when you send the gifts. ❸〈旧语〉visit temples

随乡入乡 suíxiāng-rùxiāng *also*"入乡随乡" when in Rome do as the Romans do：常言说："～。"现在到了你们这儿，我就听你的。As the saying goes, when in Rome do as the Romans do. Now that I am here, I am at your disposal.

随想曲 suíxiǎngqǔ 〈音乐〉caprice; capriccio

随心 suíxīn ❶ follow one's inclinations; have one's own way：作息～ have one's own way of arranging work and rest /她在图书馆～阅读各种书籍。She browsed among (*or* through) the books in the library. ❷ find sth. satisfactory; be pleased or satisfied with：干这工作～。I am pleased with the job I am doing. /这件衣服挺～的。This dress is very much to my liking.

随心所欲 suíxīnsuǒyù follow one's inclinations; have one's own way; do whatever one likes：你年纪不小了，哪能还像过去那样～，想干什么就干什么呢？You're no longer a child. How can you still do whatever you like as you used to? /工作上的事情不能～，要掌握原则。Nobody can do his work entirely in the way his interest guides him. In fact, he should have certain principles to go by.

随行 suíxíng ❶ accompany sb. on a trip：这次省长下乡巡视，只有一名秘书～。This time the provincial governer only took his secretary with him on his inspection tour of the rural areas. ❷ entourage; suite; party：代表团团长及其～一共五人 the head of the delegation and his party, five people all told

随行人员 suíxíng rényuán entourage; retinue; party：总理的～ premier's entourage /总统及其～ president and his party

随宜 suíyí as one pleases or chooses; comply with propriety：拙作请您～改正。Please correct my writing as you see fit.

随意 suíyì freely; at will; as one pleases：～地说 speak freely /～地看他一眼 cast a casual look at him /～吵闹 quarrel without any reason /～捏造谎言 wantonly make up stories; spin yarns freely /～侮辱别人 let loose a stream of abuse against people /～走动 walk around at will

随意肌 suíyìjī 〈生理〉voluntary muscle

随意任情 suíyì-rènqíng do as one's interest leads one; be free and unrestrained

随语生解 suíyǔ-shēngjiě explain a difficult idea in context

随遇而安 suíyù'ér'ān feel at home wherever one is; take the world as one finds it; be able to adapt oneself to different circumstances：到边疆旅游，只要能找到住处，大家也就～，不计较什么条件了。During a sightseeing trip to the frontier, we would feel satisfied if we could find accomodation and nobody would complain of the conditions. /他那个人～，不图名，不贪利。Ready to take the world as it is, he cares neither for fame nor for gain (*or* he is indifferent to either fame or gain).

随遇平衡 suíyù pínghéng 〈物理〉indifferent equilibrium

随员 suíyuán ❶ staff members of a delegation; suite; retinue; entourage ❷ attaché：～领事 attaché consul

随葬 suízàng be buried with the dead

随葬物 suízàngwù *also*"随葬品" funerary objects; burial articles：古墓中发现不少～。A lot of funerary objects have been found in the ancient tombs.

随着 suízhe along with; following：～时代的发展 with the development of times /～改革、开放政策的实施，我国人民的生活水平迅速提高。Following the implementation of China's reform and open policy, the living standards of the Chinese people have improved rapidly. /～经济发展，环境和生态保护的问题将更加突出。Alongside economic advances, the problem of environment and ecological protection will become more conspicuous than ever.

随珠弹雀 suízhū-tánquè kill a bird with a precious pearl — gain a trifle at great cost; the loss outweighs the gain

绥

suí 〈书面〉❶ peaceful ❷ bring peace to; pacify

绥靖 suíjìng pacify; appease：～四方 bring peace and order to the country

绥靖政策 suíjìng zhèngcè 〈贬义〉appeasement policy

绥靖主义 suíjìngzhǔyì 〈贬义〉doctrine of appeasement

suǐ

髓

suǐ ❶ *also*"骨髓" gǔsuǐ marrow：红骨～ red marrow ❷ something like marrow：脑～ brains /脊～ spinal marrow (*or* cord) /齿～ dental pulp ❸〈植物〉pith

髓瘤 suǐliú 〈医学〉myeloma

髓腔 suǐqiāng 〈生理〉pulp cavity; medullary cavity

髓细胞 suǐxìbāo 〈医学〉myelocyte

髓细胞生成 suǐxìbāo shēngchéng myelopoiesis

髓细胞增多症 suǐxìbāo zēngduōzhèng medullosis

髓组织 suǐzǔzhī myeloid tissue

suì

谇

suì 〈书面〉❶ scold; berate：逐而～之 chase sb. away with curse /催赋者打门而～。The tax-collector knocked the door open and scolded the house-owner for tax evasion. ❷ counsel a soverign against a royal decision

碎

suì ❶ broken pieces：粉～ shatter to smithereens /破～ break sth. into pieces; crush /打～ smash to pieces ❷ break：粉身～骨 have one's body smashed to pieces — die the most cruel death /～了一个碗 break a bowl /～成灰 grind into ash /窗户玻璃～了。The glass of the window is broken. /猿声～客心。The cry of the apes broke my heart. ❸ broken; fragmentary; scattered：～布片 oddments of cloth /～纸屑 scraps of paper /～金屑玉 bits of gold and powder of jade — fragmentary pieces of excellent literature /～土块 broken clod /琐～ trifling; trivial /零～ odds and ends ❹ garrulous; gabby; talkative：闲言～语 gossip /这人嘴太～。He is a regular chatterbox.

碎布 suìbù cloth waste; macerated fabric; rag

碎步儿 suìbùr quick short steps：踏着～ walk with quick short steps

碎催 suìcuī 〈方言〉errand-boy

碎花 suìhuā fine and dense flower pattern：～布 cotton print in a fine and dense flower pattern

碎裂 suìliè break to pieces; crackle：酒瓶～。The wine bottle cracked.

碎米蕨 suìmǐjué lip fern

碎尸 suìshī ❶ dismember a body ❷ dismembered body：～奇案 mysterious case of a dismembered body

碎尸万段 suìshī-wànduàn cut up sb.'s body into ten thousand pieces：把他～也不解我心头之恨。Even tearing him to shreds wouldn't be enough to vent my hatred.

碎石 suìshí 〈建筑〉crushed stone; broken stones

碎石混凝土 suìshí hùnníngtǔ 〈建筑〉crushed stone concrete

碎石机 suìshíjī stone crusher

碎石路 suìshílù macadam road; broken stone road

碎石器 suìshíqì 〈医学〉lithotrite

碎石术 suìshíshù 〈医学〉lithotrity

碎屑岩 suìxièyán clastic rock

碎音 suìyīn 〈音乐〉acciaccatura

碎纸机 suìzhǐjī shredder

碎嘴子 suìzuǐzi 〈方言〉❶ chatter; jabber; prate：他又犯～了。He jabbered away again. ❷ garrulous person; chatterbox

睟

suì 〈书面〉❶ smooth：～面 smooth cheeks ❷ (of colour) pure

遂[1]

suì ❶ gratify; satisfy; fulfil：顺～ go well; go smoothly ❷ succeed：劫机未～ abortive hijack /不～ fail to materialize /政变未～。The *coup d'état* aborted.

遂[2]

suì 〈书面〉then; thereupon; hence：劳动后出了一身汗，头痛～止。I had a good sweat after doing some physical labour, and my headache disappeared.

see also suí

遂心 suìxīn after one's own heart; to one's liking; satisfied：诸事～ be satisfied with everything; find everything satisfactory /～所欲 do as one likes

遂意 suìyì to one's liking; as one wishes：你要买的都给你买来了，这回可遂了你的意了吧？You must be fully satisfied that you've got everything you want to buy.

遂愿 suìyuàn have one's wish fulfilled; achieve what one wishes: 我们总不可能事事都～。We can hardly expect to fulfil all our wishes.

邃 suì 〈书面〉❶ (of time or space) remote; distant: 深～ deep; remote / 幽～ deep and quiet ❷ profound; deep: 精～于学 profound learning

邃密 suìmì ❶ deep: 屋宇～。The houses extend far inwards. ❷ profound; recondite: ～的理论 abstruse theory

燧 suì ❶ flint ❷ 〈古语〉 beacon fire

燧发机 suìfājī flintlock

燧木取火 suìmù-qǔhuǒ get fire from wood by friction

燧人氏 Suìrénshì legendary figure in ancient China supposed to have discovered fire

燧石 suìshí flint: ～玻璃 flint glass

穟 suì 〈书面〉 *see* "穗" suì

隧 suì 〈书面〉 tunnel

隧道 suìdào tunnel: 打通～ open up a tunnel / 开凿～ dig a tunnel / 秦岭～ Qinling Tunnel / 海底～ seabed tunnel

隧道管 suìdàoguǎn 〈电子〉 tunneltron

隧道式退火炉 suìdàoshì tuìhuǒlú 〈冶金〉 tunnel furnace

隧道效应 suìdào xiàoyìng 〈电子〉 tunnel effect

隧洞 suìdòng *see* "隧道"

岁(歲、嵗、歳) suì ❶ year: 今～ this year / 来～ next year / 去～ last year / 年年～～花相似，～～年年人不同。While flowers remain the same year after year, people keep changing all the time. ❷ 〈量词〉 year (of age): 周～ one full year of life / 这孩子五～了。The child is aged five. / 那匹马是三～口。The horse is three years old. ❸ age: 虚～ nominal age / 足～ real age (in contrast to nominal age) / ～老根弥壮，阳骄叶更阴。The roots become much firmer when the tree grows old, The leaves seem more shady under the blazing sun. ❹ 〈书面〉 time: ～不我与。Time and tide wait for no man. ❺ 〈书面〉 year's harvest: 歉～ lean year / 丰～ year of bumper harvest; good (*or* bumper) year

岁差 suìchā 〈天文〉 preccession of the equinoxes

岁出 suìchū state expenditure in a fiscal year (as opposed to "岁入" suìrù)

岁初 suìchū beginning of the year

岁除 suìchú 〈书面〉 last day of the year; New Year's Eve: 白发催年老，青阳逼～。White hairs remind one of one's advancing age, And the spring sun is chasing the old year out.

岁寒三友 suìhán-sānyǒu three friends in winter — the pine, the bamboo and the plum (which do not wither in winter)

岁寒松柏 suìhán-sōngbǎi only when winter comes do people realize that the pine and cedar are evergreen — adversity reveals man's virtue

岁口 suìkǒu age of draught animals: 四～的驴 four-year old donkey / 这匹马～老些。This horse is a bit too old.

岁阑 suìlán 〈书面〉 end of the year

岁杪 suìmiǎo 〈书面〉 end of the year: ～无事。Nothing happened towards the end of the year.

岁暮 suìmù 〈书面〉❶ the year is drawing to an end: ～日短。The days grow shorter at the close of the year. ❷ ageing; advanced in years: ～之人 old man

岁入 suìrù state revenue in a fiscal year (as opposed to 岁出)

岁时 suìshí four seasons; seasons

岁收 suìshōu state revenue in a fiscal year

岁首 suìshǒu 〈书面〉 beginning of the year

岁首节 Suìshǒujié 〈宗教〉 Rosh Hashanah, important holiday of Judaism celebrated at the beginning of the Jewish New Year

岁数 suìshu 〈口语〉 age; year: 父亲是上了～的人了。Father is getting on in years. / 他今年多大～了? How old is he now?

岁星 Suìxīng ancient name for the planet Jupiter

岁修 suìxiū annual repairs

岁序 suìxù 〈书面〉 sequence of the change of years: ～更新 change of years

岁月 suìyuè years: 在漫长的～中 during the long years; over the years / 艰苦的～ hard times / 难忘的～ unforgettable years; memorable time / 动乱的～ years of chaos; time of turmoil; time of storm and stress / 十年的～ ten years; whole decade / ～易逝。How time flies. / ～无情。Time is inexorable. / ～流逝，不可复追。Time past cannot be recalled. *or* Lost time is never found again.

岁朝 suìzhāo 〈书面〉 first day of the first lunar month

穗[1](❷繐) suì ❶ ear of grain; spike: 抽～ heading; earing / 秀～儿 put forth flowers or ears / 谷～ ear of cereal / 麦～ ear of wheat / 稻～ ear of rice ❷ tassel; fringe: 绒～ nap fringe / 丝～ silk tassel / 宫灯上的彩～ colourful fringes on palace lanterns

穗[2] Suì ❶ another name for Guangzhou: 明日抵～ to arrive in Guangzhou tomorrow ❷ a surname

穗花牡荆 suìhuā mǔjīng 〈植物〉 chaste tree (*Agnus castus*); monk's pepper tree; wild lavender (*Vitex agnuscastus*)

穗花油 suìhuāyóu spike oil

穗烂 suìlàn ear rot

穗选 suìxuǎn 〈农业〉 ear selection

穗轴 suìzhóu spike-stalk

穗状花序 suìzhuàng huāxù 〈植物〉 spike

穗子 suìzi ❶ ear of grain: 高粱～ ear of sorghum ❷ tassel; fringe: 彩灯下坠着红～。The bottom of the coloured lantern is fringed with red tassels.

祟 suì ❶ 〈迷信〉 evil spirit; ghost ❷ act like an evil spirit; haunt; plague: 鬼鬼～～ sneaking; furtive; stealthy / 作～ exercise an evil influence on

sūn

飧(飱) sūn 〈书面〉 supper; dinner: 饔～不继 have no other meals after breakfast; be poverty-stricken

孙(孫) sūn ❶ grandson: 祖～三代 three generations / ～儿 grandchild ❷ generations below that of the grandchild: 曾～ great-grandson / 玄～ great-great-grandson / 重～女 great-granddaughter / 孔子的二十世～ 20th generation of Confucius ❸ relative belonging to grandchild's generation: 外～ daughter's son; grandson / 侄～ brother's grandson; grandnephew; greatnephew ❹ second growth of plants: 稻～ new rice shoots grown from the old stalk / ～竹 new shoots of bamboo from the old stump ❺ (Sūn) a surname

孙膑 Sūn Bìn Sun Bin, descendant of Sun Wu, military strategist of the Warring States Period and author of *Sun Bin on the Art of War* (孙膑兵法)

孙女 sūnnǚ granddaughter: 老人只有一个亲～。The old man has only one granddaughter of his own.

孙女婿 sūnnǚxu granddaughter's husband; grandson-in-law

孙权 Sūn Quán *also* "孙仲谋"; "吴大帝" Wú Dàdì Sun Quan (182-252), founder of the Kingdom of Wu during the Three Kingdoms Period

孙思邈 Sūn Sīmiǎo Sun Simiao (581-682), medical scientist of the Tang Dynasty

孙武 Sūn Wǔ Sun Wu, great military strategist of the late Spring and Autumn Period, called Sun-tzu (孙子) in respect, author of *Master Sun's Art of War*

孙悟空 Sūn Wùkōng protean Monkey King in the novel *Pilgrimage to the West*: ～跳不出如来佛的手心 like the Monkey King who cannot jump out of Buddha's palm — be unable to extricate oneself from sb.'s control

孙媳妇 sūnxífu grandson's wife; granddaughter-in-law

孙中山 Sūn Zhōngshān Sun Yat-sen (1866-1925), leader of China's modern democratic revolution

孙子 Sūnzǐ Sun-tzu or Master Sun, venerable title for Sun Wu (孙武)

孙子兵法 Sūnzǐ Bīngfǎ *Sun-tzu's Art of War* or *Master Sun's Art of War*, China's ancient classic on military strategy

孙子 sūnzi grandson

荪(蓀) sūn aromatic plant referred to in ancient Chinese books

S

狲(猻) sūn see "猢狲" húsūn

sǔn

损 sǔn ❶ decrease; diminish; lose: 磨～ wear and tear /耗～ consume; deplete /亏～ loss; deficit /～有余而补不足 cut the unnecessary surplus to make up for the deficiency ❷ harm; injure: 有～于党的利益 be detrimental to the Party's interests /以～人开始, 以害己告终 begin with injuring others and end up ruining oneself /满招～。Pride goes before a fall. ❸ damage: 一张破～不堪的桌子 a badly damaged desk ❹〈方言〉sarcastic; biting; caustic; cutting: see "～人" ❺〈方言〉mean; shabby; vicious: 这个方法可够～的! This is a dirty trick. /这人办事真～! He is mean in doing business.

损兵折将 sǔnbīng-zhéjiàng have one's generals and soldiers either killed or wounded; sustain heavy losses

损德 sǔndé cause damage to one's virtue; do wrong

损公肥私 sǔngōng-féisī also "损公肥己"; "损公利己" line one's pocket at the expense of the public; feather one's nest at public expense

损害 sǔnhài harm; impair; damage; injure: ～身体 impair one's health /～视力 bad for one's eyes /～人民的利益 infringe upon (*or* be detrimental to) the interests of the people /～党的形象 harm the Party's image /～名誉 ruin one's reputation; blacken one's name /～威信 damage one's prestige /～庄稼 be harmful to crops /～信用 discredit /～保险 insurance of damage /～赔偿 compensation for damages; damages

损耗 sǔnhào ❶ loss; wear and tear; consumption: 能源的～增加。The loss of and drain on energy have increased. ❷〈商业〉wastage; spoilage; shrinkage: 注意物资的～ pay attention to the wastage of materials /防止搬运的～ prevent transport damages /～的程度 extent of damage

S

损耗费 sǔnhàofèi cost of wear and tear

损耗率 sǔnhàolǜ 〈商业〉proportion of goods damaged

损坏 sǔnhuài damage; break: ～机器 damage machines /故意～路标 destroy road marks deliberately /轻微地～ slight damage /修复～的汽车 fix a damaged car

损毁 sǔnhuǐ damage; destroy: ～树木近万株。About ten thousand trees were destroyed.

损人 sǔnrén ❶〈方言〉deride; ridicule; hurt sb. with mean words: 你有意见直说, 干吗～? State your views outright. Why so sarcastic? /他动不动就～, 也经常被别人损。He loves to make caustic remarks, and others pay him in his own coin. ❷ cause material damage to others

损人利己 sǔnrén-lìjǐ harm others to enrich oneself; profit at the expenses of others: 应该公而忘私, 不能～。Be selfless instead of benefiting oneself at others' expense. /人们都讨厌那些～的人。We all dislike selfish people.

损伤 sǔnshāng ❶ harm; damage; hurt; injure: 肌肉～了 pull one's muscle /脑子～了 injure one's brain /自尊心被～了 hurt one's self-esteem (*or* self-respect) /～筋骨 be injured in the sinews or bones; have a fracture /～了群众的积极性 dampen the enthusiasm of the masses /这次事故使他的身体大受～。This incident seriously harmed his health. ❷ loss: 主力～殆尽。The main force has suffered grievous losses. /兵力～严重。The military forces were seriously depleted.

损失 sǔnshī lose: ～飞机两架 lose two planes /～了威信 blow to one's prestige /～的物资和人力 lost materials and human resources /～额 amount of loss /～率 loss rate /造成～ cause losses /遭受～ incur losses /弥补～ make up for the losses /赔偿～ compensate the losses /无法挽回的～ irrecoverable losses

损益 sǔnyì ❶ increase and decrease: 严格按药方配药, 不可随意～。Strictly follow the prescription in making up a medicine, and do not add or subtract. ❷ profit and loss; gains and losses: ～分配 division (*or* distribution) of profit and loss /～持平 the profit keeps in balance with the loss; break even /～相抵。The gains offset the losses.

损益比 sǔnyìbǐ profit and loss ratio

损益表 sǔnyìbiǎo profit and loss account

损益计算书 sǔnyì jìsuànshū statement of profit and loss; operating statement

笋(筍) sǔn bamboo shoot: 竹～ shoots of *mao* bamboo /嫩～ tender bamboo shoots /春～ bamboo shoots in spring /冬～ winter bamboo shoots /石～ stalagmite /芦～ asparagus /～炒虾仁 fried shelled shrimps with bamboo shoots /乡办企业如雨后春～般蓬勃发展起来。Township enterprises have sprung up like mushrooms.

笋鞭 sǔnbiān subterranean stem of bamboo

笋干 sǔngān dried bamboo shoots: 腌制了不少～ salt a lot of bamboo shoots /晒～ dry bamboo shoots

笋瓜 sǔnguā 〈植物〉winter squash; *Cucurbita mazima*

笋鸡 sǔnjī young chicken; broiler; spring chicken: 辣子炒～ young chicken sautéed with hot pepper /炸～ fried spring chicken

笋尖 sǔnjiān tender tips of bamboo shoots: 鲜嫩可口的～。The tender tips of bamboo shoots are fresh and delicious.

笋席 sǔnxí mat made of bamboo strips

笋子 sǔnzi ❶〈方言〉bamboo shoot ❷ also "榫子" sǔnzi tenon

簨 sǔn frame for suspending chime stones and drums in ancient China

隼 sǔn also "鹘" hú 〈动物〉falcon: ～形目 falconiformes

榫 sǔn tenon

榫接 sǔnjiē joggle joint; joggle

榫舌 sǔnshé joint tongue; feather piece; key protrusion

榫头 sǔntou tenon

榫眼 sǔnyǎn mortise

榫凿 sǔnzáo socket chisel; mortise chisel

榫子 sǔnzi tenon

sùn

潠 sùn 〈书面〉gush; spout; spurt

suō

莎 suō

see also shā

莎草 suōcǎo 〈植物〉nutgrass flatsedge (*Cyperus rotundus*)

桫 suō

桫椤 suōluó 〈植物〉spinulose tree fern (*Cyathea spinulosa*)

挲(抄) suō see "摩挲" mósuō

see also sā; shā

娑 suō

娑罗树 suōluóshù 〈植物〉sal tree (*Shorea robusta*); sala

娑罗双树 suōluó shuāngshù twin sal trees (Legend has it that Sakyamuni attained nirvana in between the twin sal trees.)

缩 suō ❶ become smaller; contract; shrink: ～了两寸 have shrunk two inches /这种衣服～长短, 不～肥瘦。This kind of clothes shrinks in length, not in width. /金属遇冷即～。Metal contracts as it gets cool. ❷ draw back; withdraw: 龟～ shrink back like a turtle drawing in its head and legs /～成一团 huddle oneself up /老鼠～进洞子里。The rat shrank back into the hole. ❸ withdraw; fall back; retreat: 畏～ flinch; recoil in fear /紧～ reduce; tighten; retrench /紧～政策 policy of retrenchment /～到后边儿 shrink to the back /遇到困难他从不往后～。He never retreats before difficulties.

see also sù

缩编 suōbiān ❶ (of troops or institutions) reduce the size of the staff: ～机构 trim organizations /部队～ cut back military forces /我们机关的～工作已经完成。Our institution has already been streamlined. ❷ cut down the number of pages; reduce the length (of a piece of writing): 这个电视剧已由原来的十集～为六集。The TV drama has been shortened from 10 to 6 parts.

缩脖子 suō bózi pull in one's neck; shrink back; flinch from (difficulty, etc.): 碰上困难, 咱可不能～。We must not flinch from difficulty.

缩尺 suōchǐ reduced scale; scale

缩尺模型 suōchǐ móxíng scale model

缩尺图 suōchǐtú scale drawing

缩短 suōduǎn shorten; reduce; curtail; cut down: ～工期 shorten the time limit for a project /～时间 cut down the time /～日程 cut one's schedule /～差距 reduce the differences; narrow the gap /～假期 curtail one's holidays /～一半 cut sth. down by half

缩短战线 suōduǎn zhànxiàn shorten the battle line; narrow the scope of activity: 缩短基本建设战线 curtail (*or* slash) capital construction

缩放仪 suōfàngyí pantograph

缩合 suōhé 〈化学〉condensation

缩合反应 suōhé fǎnyìng condensation reaction

缩合剂 suōhéjì condensing agent

缩合物 suōhéwù condensation compound

缩减 suōjiǎn reduce; economize; cut: ～经费 reduce (*or* cut) funds /～开支 cut back on spending /～职工人数 retrench the staff /大胆～ bold cut /～进口 curtail import /～会议 have fewer meetings

缩聚 suōjù 〈化学〉condensation polymerization

缩聚物 suōjùwù condensation polymer

缩裂 suōliè shrinkage crack

缩手 suōshǒu ❶ draw back one's hand ❷ shrink (from doing sth.); stop: 工作刚铺开，哪能一下子就～? How can we back down (*or* backpedal) as the work has just started? /必需立即～。We must stop doing this immediately.

缩手缩脚 suōshǒu-suōjiǎo ❶ shrink with cold: 冻得他们一个个都～的。All of them shrank with cold. ❷ be overcautious; timid: 干工作就应该大刀阔斧，不能～。One should be bold and resolute, and not overly cautious, in work.

缩水 suōshuǐ *also* "抽水" chōushuǐ (of cloth through wetting) shrink: 这布不～。This kind of cloth doesn't shrink in the wash.

缩水甘油 suōshuǐ gānyóu glycide; epihydrin alcohol

缩水率 suōshuǐlǜ shrinkage

缩头虫 suōtóuchóng 〈动物〉bamboo worm

缩头缩脑 suōtóu-suōnǎo ❶ recoil; shrink; flinch: 为什么他在人多的场合里总是～的? Why does he become so withdrawn when there are a lot of people around? ❷ be timid or fainthearted; shrink from responsibility: 他太胆小，干什么事都是优柔寡断，～的。Being such a timid person, he is always indecisive and shies away from responsibility.

缩微 suōwēi microform

缩微技术 suōwēi jìshù micrography; micrographics

缩微胶卷 suōwēi jiāojuǎn microfilm

缩微胶片 suōwēi jiāopiàn microcopy; microfiche

缩微照片 suōwēi zhàopiàn microfilm; microphotograph

缩小 suōxiǎo reduce; lessen; diminish; shrink: ～面积 reduce size /～包围圈 tighten up the ring of encirclement /～差距 narrow the gap /～率 minification /～像 reduced image

缩写 suōxiě ❶ abbreviation: 采用～的办法 abbreviate ❷ abridge (literary works, esp. novels)

缩写本 suōxiěběn abridged edition or version: 我读过《简爱》的～。I've read the abridged edition (*or* version) of *Jane Eyre*.

缩写签字 suōxiě qiānzì initials

缩衣节食 suōyī-jiéshí *also* "节衣缩食" economize on food and clothing; lead a frugal life

缩印 suōyìn reprint books in a reduced format: 请把这张招贴画～一下。Please reprint this poster in a reduced format.

缩印机 suōyìnjī reduction printer

缩影 suōyǐng epitome; miniature: 一幅～ miniature /这是历史的～。This is the epitome of history.

缩语 suōyǔ abbreviation; abbeviated expression

缩语字典 suōyǔ zìdiǎn abbreviations dictionary

蓑(簑) suō

蓑草 suōcǎo 〈方言〉〈植物〉Chinese alpine rush (*Eulaliopsis binata*)

蓑笠 suōlì large straw or palm-bark rain hat: 孤舟～翁，独钓寒江雪。In a lonely boat, on the freezing waters, an old man wearing a large straw hat is fishing in the snow alone.

蓑衣 suōyī straw or palm-bark rain cape: 披～ put on a straw rain cape /编织～ knit straw rain capes /他抄起一件～就冲进大雨中去了。Picking up a straw rain cape, he rushed out into the heavy rain.

嗍 suō

suck: ～手指头 suck fingers /～奶头 suck the nipples

嗦 suō

❶ *see* "哆嗦" duōsuo ❷ *see* "啰嗦" luōsuo

羧 suō

〈化学〉carboxyl

羧基 suōjī 〈化学〉carboxyl; carboxyl group: ～反应 carboxyl reaction /～酶 carboxylase /～肽酶 carboxypeptidase

羧酸 suōsuān 〈化学〉carboxylic acid: ～皂 carboxylic soap /～酯 carboxylic eater

梭 suō

shuttle: 金～银～ gold and silver shuttles /木～ wooden shuttles /无～织机 shuttleless loom /穿～往来 shuttle back and forth; shuttle visit /穿～外交 shuttle diplomacy /穿～轰炸 shuttle bombing /光阴荏苒，日月如～。Time flies like an arrow.

梭镖 suōbiāo spear: 玩～ play with a spear /投掷～ throw a spear /～队 spear corps

梭罗 Suōluó Henry David Thoreau (1817-1862), American writer

梭罗河 Suōluóhé Solo River (in Indonesia)

梭梭 suōsuō 〈植物〉sacsaoul (*Holoxylon ammodendron*)

梭心 suōxīn cop latch

梭心夹子 suōxīn jiāzi bobbin hook

梭形细胞 suōxíng xìbāo spindle cell

梭巡 suōxún 〈书面〉move around to watch and guard; patrol: 沿马路～ patrol along the street /有人在立交桥上～。Somebody is patrolling on the flyover.

梭鱼 suōyú (redeye) mullet

梭状芽孢杆菌 suōzhuàng yábāo gǎnjūn *also* "梭菌" clostridium: ～感染 clostridial infection

梭子 suōzi ❶〈纺织〉shuttle: 织布～ weaving shuttles ❷ cartridge clip: 把～装满子弹 load the cartridge clip with bullets /安上～ fix the cartridge clip ❸〈量词〉(of ammunition) clip: 一～子弹 a whole clip of ammunition /给他一～ fire a whole clip at him

梭子蟹 suōzixiè *also* "蝤蛑" yóumóu swimming crab

梭子鱼 suōziyú *also* "魣" yú barracuda; pike

唆 suō

instigate; abet; incite: 教～ instigate; stir up /调～ incite /教～犯 abettor

唆弄 suōnong incite; instigate; sow discord: ～是非 foment discord

唆使 suōshǐ instigate; foment; abet: ～学生罢课 incite students to boycott the class /～党徒捣乱 instigate henchmen to make trouble /～小贩抬价 abet pedlars in raising prices /受到坏人的～ at the instigation of evil persons /暗中～ covert instigation

睃 suō

look askance at; cast a sidelong glance at: 偷偷地～了他一眼 steal a glance at him

suǒ

索[1] suǒ

❶ large rope or chain: 钢～ steel chain /麻～ hempen rope /缆～ thick rope; cable /船～ ship's rigging /绞～ (the hangman's) noose /绳捆～绑 tie up (with ropes and chains) /铁～桥 chain bridge ❷ (Suǒ) a surname

索[2] suǒ

❶ search, look for: 搜～ search for; hunt for; scout around /摸～ grope for; feel about /按图～骥 look for a steed with the aid of its picture — try to locate sth. by following up a clue ❷ demand; ask: 勒～ extort; blackmail /～价 ask a price; charge /～债 demand debt payment /～债人 claimant

索[3] suǒ

〈书面〉❶ solitary; all by oneself: 离群～居 live in solitude ❷ dull; insipid: *see* "～寞"

索偿 suǒcháng claim reimbursement; demand compensation: ～银行 reimbursement bank

索道 suǒdào cableway; ropeway: 高架～ telpher /有～供游人上下山。Tourists may go up and down the mountain by the cableway.

索尔兹伯里 Suǒ'ěrzībólǐ Salisbury, former name of Harare, capital of Zimbabwe

索非亚 Suǒfēiyà Sofia, capital of Bulgaria
索贿 suǒhuì extort bribes:向卖方~ extort bribes from the seller /~受贿 solicit or accept bribes
索价 suǒjià ask a price; charge:~过高 ask too high a price
索结 suǒjié Blackwall hitch
索解 suǒjiě search for an explanation (of words, phrases, etc.) or a solution (of a problem, etc.):~人生的意义 explore the purpose (*or* meaning) of life /他这一番话实在叫人难以~。His remarks defy any explanation (*or* are beyond me).
索居 suǒjū live alone (like a hermit):~独处 live all alone by oneself; live in seclusion
索具 suǒjù rigging
索礼 suǒlǐ extort a "gift" (in return for a favour)
索伦石 suǒlúnshí 〈矿业〉suolunite
索马里 Suǒmǎlǐ Somalia:~人 Somali /~语 Somali (language)
索密痛 suǒmìtòng 〈药学〉somedon
索寞 suǒmò *also* "索莫";"索漠"〈书面〉❶ depressed; dejected; downhearted:神情~ look depressed; be crestfallen ❷ lonely; desolate; bleak and chilly:山上杂草丛生, 异常~。Overgrown with weeds, the hill looks extremely desolate.
索尼公司 Suǒní Gōngsī (Japan) Sony Corporation
索赔 suǒpéi claim damages; claim indemnity:~委员会 claims board /~人 claimer; claimant /~一千元 claim for one thousand *yuan* /拒绝~ reject the claim
索桥 suǒqiáo cable bridge; chain bridge
索求 suǒqiú demand; claim; seek:~过多 ask for too much
索取 suǒqǔ ask for; demand; exact:~报酬 ask for remuneration /~欠款 demand the payment of a debt /~赔款 extort an indemnity /向大自然~财富 wrest wealth from nature
索然 suǒrán depressed; in low spirits; insipid:兴趣~ uninterested; low-spirited
索然寡味 suǒrán-guǎwèi flat and insipid; dull and dry:这篇文章被他们删改得~了。The article reads flat after their revision.
索索 suǒsuǒ ❶〈象声〉rustle; whispering sound:她走路时绸裙~作响。Her silk skirt rustled as she walked. /雨~地下着。It was drizzling softly. ❷ shiver; tremble:他吓得脸色苍白, ~发抖。He was so frightened that he looked pale and was shivering all over. /他累得~地摇晃着, 说什么也爬不上这座山。He was so tired that his steps began to falter, and he could not for the life of him climb to the top of the hill.
索韦托惨案 Suǒwéituō Cǎn'àn Soweto Massacre (16 June 1976 in South Africa)
索性 suǒxìng may (might) as well:既然大家都不走, ~一起干完再休息。Since nobody will leave, we might as well finish the work before having a rest. /人太少没意思, 这次活动~取消算了。It's rather disappointing that so few people are coming, so we'd better cancel the gathering.
索要 suǒyào demand; ask for; extort:~财物 extort money and things
索引 suǒyǐn *also* "引得" yǐndé index:地名~ gazetteer /目录~ catalogue index /作者~ author index /汉语拼音音节~ index of Pinyin syllable /笔画~ index of strokes of Chinese characters /熟悉这些书名~ be familiar with the title index
索隐 suǒyǐn search for hidden meanings; expose, unearth or expound something concealed, hidden or obscure:探赜~ delve into the abtruse; unravel mysteries /~行怪 look for the abstruse and behave eccentrically
索诈 suǒzhà extort; blackmail; racketeer:肆意~ wantonly blackmail
索子 suǒzi 〈方言〉rope; chain:套上一根粗~ tied with a large rope /地上放着一条麻~。A hempen rope was lying on the ground.

琐

suǒ ❶ trivial; insignificant; petty:繁~ loaded down with trivial details /烦~哲学 scholasticism ❷ lowly; humble:猥~ (of behaviour) vulgar; boorish; (of appearance) wretched; miserable
琐事 suǒshì trifles; trivial matters; trivialities:家务~ household chores /谈些日常~ talk trivialities
琐碎 suǒsuì petty; trifling; trivial:~事务 trifling matter; petty affairs /材料太~。The materials are too fragmentary. /尽忙于这些~事儿, 没时间学习。Busy with odd jobs, I have no time to study.
琐琐树 suǒsuǒshù 〈植物〉saxaul (*Haloxylon ammodendron*)
琐尾流离 suǒwěi-liúlí (of one's situation) change from favourable to unfavourable
琐闻 suǒwén bits of news; scraps of information:社会~ scraps of social news
琐细 suǒxì trifling; trivial:无论多么~的事儿, 她都是一丝不苟地认真对待。She is always very conscientious in what she does, however trivial it may be.
琐屑 suǒxiè 〈书面〉trifling; trivial:他认为秘书的工作太~。He thinks that the work of a secretary is too trivial.
琐杂 suǒzá trifling; trivial:~事 trifles

唢

suǒ
唢呐 suǒnà *suona* horn, a woodwind instrument:吹~ play the *suona* horn /~表演艺术家 *suona* horn player

锁

suǒ ❶ lock:铁~ iron lock /自动~ automatic lock /弹簧~ spring lock /保险~ safe lock /门~ door lock /暗~ built-in lock /挂~ padlock /拉~儿 zip fastener; zipper /一把钥匙开一把~ one key to one lock /上了~ locked ❷ lock (up):~自行车 lock the bicycle /他把孩子~在家里了。He locked the child up at home. /他双眉紧~, 满面愁容。With knitted brows, he looks terribly sad. ❸ sth. which resembles a lock:石~〈体育〉stone dumbbell in the form of an old-fashioned padlock ❹ chains:枷~ yoke; chains; shackles; fetters ❺ lockstitch:~扣眼儿 do a lockstitch on a buttonhole /~花边 lockstitch a lace /拿丝线~ lockstitch with silk thread /~得密 dense lockstitch
锁匙 suǒchí 〈方言〉key
锁定 suǒdìng 〈电子〉locking:~开头 locking switch
锁肛 suǒgāng 〈生理〉aproctia
锁骨 suǒgǔ 〈生理〉clavicle; collarbone:~中线 midclavicular line
锁国 suǒguó close the country to the outside world:实行~政策 pursue a closed-door policy /闭关~ close the country to international intercourse
锁合 suǒhé closure; closing component
锁簧 suǒhuáng 〈机械〉locking spring
锁匠 suǒjiang locksmith
锁紧 suǒjǐn 〈机械〉locking:自~ self-locking /~垫圈 lock washer
锁具 suǒjù lockset
锁链 suǒliàn *also* "锁链子" ❶ chain ❷ shackles; fetters; yoke:戴上~ be tied in chains /砸碎~ smash the shackles /解开束缚思想的~ get rid of the trammels that fetter one's mind /砸烂封建礼教的~ shatter the yoke of the feudal ethical code
锁眼 suǒyǎn lock hole
锁阳 suǒyáng 〈中药〉Chinese cynomorium (*Cynomorium songaricum*)
锁钥 suǒyuè ❶ key:搞好双方关系的~ key to improving the relationship between the two sides ❷ strategic gateway:北门~ strategic gateway on the northern border

所(听)

suǒ ❶ place:住~ dwelling place; one's residence; one's domicile /安身之~ place to settle down /各得其~ each in his proper place; each has a role to play /流离失~ wander about homeless ❷ place of garrison during the Ming Dynasty (now used only in place names, e.g. 后~ Housuo in Shanxi Province) ❸ *used as a name of an institution or other organization*:研究~ research institute /派出~ local police station; police post; police substation /招待~ guest house; hostel /律师事务~ law office /诊疗~ clinic ❹〈量词〉*of house, school, buildings, etc.*:一~楼房 a building /两~民宅 two civilian houses /这~幼儿园 this kindergarten ❺〈助词〉(a) *used together with* 为 *or* 被, *to indicate passive construction*:为人~不齿 be held in contempt /为好奇心~驱使 be driven by one's curiosity /被他的谎言~欺骗 be taken in by his lies (b) *used before a verb followed by a noun which is the receiver of the action*:我~敬佩的老师 the teacher I admire /大家~谈的看法 the views expressed by various people /他~采取的行动 the actions he has taken (c) *used in the* "是…的" *sentence structure for emphasis*:她是广大青年~喜爱的歌星。She is a singer loved by many young people. /世界杯足球赛的决赛情况是全世界的球迷~最关心的。The final match of the World Cup is what all the football fans in the world care about most. (d)〈书面〉*used before a verb to form a compound object*:闻~未闻 unheard-of /大失~望 to one's great disappointment /众~周知 known

to all /～答非～问 irrelevant answer /各有～长，各有～短 each has its strong points and weak ones (e) *used after* 有 *or* 无 *to form* "有所…" (meaning to some extent) *or* "无所…" (meaning all-inclusive) *structure*：有～发明 have some inventions to one's credit /有～增长 have increased somewhat /无～用心 not give serious thought to anything; remain idle /无～不知 omniscient ❻ (Suǒ) a surname

所部 suǒbù troops under one's command：率～投诚 surrender with one's troops

所长 suǒcháng what one excels in; one's strong point：唱歌是她的～。Singing is her forte.
see also suǒzhǎng

所得 suǒdé income; earnings; gains：劳动～ earnings through labour /在这场较量中，该国～不多，所失甚大。That country gained little but lost a great deal in that contest.

所得税 suǒdéshuì income tax：交纳～ pay income tax /收取～ collect income tax /～法 income tax law /～申报表 income tax return /～抵免 income tax credit /～税率 income tax rate

所费不赀 suǒfèi-bùzī incur a good deal of expense：此项工程历时十余年，～。That project lasted over ten years at great cost.

所见所闻 suǒjiàn-suǒwén what one sees and hears：我刚到农村时，～无不觉得新鲜。Everything I saw and heard was fresh to me when I first went to the countryside.

所罗门群岛 Suǒluómén Qúndǎo Solomon Islands, a country consisting of a group of islands in the South Pacific

所属 suǒshǔ ❶ what is subordinate to one or comes under one's command：外交部～单位 departments and other offices under the Ministry of Foreign Affairs /海军～舰队 fleets under the naval command ❷ what one belongs to or is affiliated with：向～派出所报案 report the crime to the local police station

所谓 suǒwèi ❶ what is called：～分析，就是分析事物的内在矛盾。Analysis means to analyse the inherent contradictions of things. /～"阳春白雪"，就是指那些高深的、不够通俗的文学艺术。By highbrow art and literature we mean literary works that are too profound and far above the head of the ordinary reader. ❷ so-called (implying disagreement or disapproval)：如果过分强调个人的～"兴趣"，那就不合适了。It won't be proper to overemphasize the so-called personal interests. /难道这就是～的"革新"? Is this the so-called innovation?

所向披靡 suǒxiàng-pīmǐ (of troops) carry all before one; be irresistible：这支部队奋勇杀敌，～。The soldiers fought courageously and swept away all obstacles.

所向无敌 suǒxiàng-wúdí all-conquering like a (hot) knife through butter; invincible

所向无前 suǒxiàng-wúqián carry all before one; break all enemy resistance：这是一队骁勇善战、～的骑兵。This group of cavalrymen are valiant and invincible in battle.

所以 suǒyǐ ❶ (conjunction used to indicate cause and effect) so; therefore; the reason why; because (a) *used in the latter half of a sentence to indicate effect*：临行匆忙，～来不及向你辞行了。I left in a hurry, so I didn't come to say goodbye to you. /一连几天下雨，～最近气候比较凉爽。As it has rained continuously for several days, the weather is fairly cool recently. (b) *used between the subject and the predicate in the first half of a sentence to stress the subject matter that needs to be explained with the explanation given in the latter half of the sentence*：这个电视剧之～受欢迎，是因为它内容生动，富有教育意义。The reason why this TV drama is so popular is that it is vivid and thought-provoking (*or* educational). /我们～赞成这个提案，是因为它反映了人民的共同愿望。We support the proposal because it reflects the common wishes of the people. (c) *the cause is stated in the first half of sentence, followed by* "是…所以…的原因（缘故）" *in the second half of the sentence*：土壤含有水分和养料，这就是作物～能够生长的原因。There are water and nutrition in the soil; that's why crops can take root. (d) 〈口语〉 *used separately to indicate cause or reason*：～呀！要不然我怎么会同意选他呢? Well, that's just the point, otherwise I wouldn't have elected him. ❷ *used in set phrases as an object*：忘乎～ forget oneself /不知～ not know what is the matter (*or* what to do)

所以然 suǒyǐrán the whys and wherefores：知其然而不知其～ know the how but not the why; know what is done but not why it is done /看不出这里面的～。I don't see the whys and wherefores of the matter. /他说了半天，也没有说出个～来。He talked a lot but you are none the wiser.

所有 suǒyǒu ❶ own; belong to：公司的一切财产都归集体～。All the property of the company is owned by the collective. /土地属国家～。All land belongs to the state. ❷ possessions：倾其～ give everything in one's possession; give one's all ❸ all：～的问题都解决了。All the problems have been solved. /他把～的稿费都捐给了儿童福利事业会。He donated all the payment he received for his book to the welfare project for children.

所有格 suǒyǒugé 〈语言〉 possessive case

所有权 suǒyǒuquán 〈法律〉 proprietary rights; ownership; title：～归个人 ownership being vested in individuals; private ownership /～属国家 the proprietary rights belong to the state /集体的～ collective ownership /房屋的～ ownership of a house /～说明书 certificate of title /～的丧失 loss of ownership /～的转让 transfer of ownership /～与经营权分离 separate ownership from management (authority)

所有人 suǒyǒurén owner

所有制 suǒyǒuzhì system of ownership; ownership：全民～ ownership by the whole people /生产资料～的变革 reform of the system of ownership of the means of production /～结构 pattern (*or* structure) of ownership

所在 suǒzài ❶ place; site; location：古迹众多的～ place of many historical relics /一个较偏僻的～ an out-of-the-way place ❷ where; 原因～ the reason why; exact cause /这是他的聪明～。This is where his intelligence works. /这是人民的力量～。This is where the strength of the people lies.

所在地 suǒzàidì location; seat; site：～法 *lex situs*

所在多有 suǒzài duōyǒu there is plenty of such things; can be found everywhere：此类弊病，～。One finds this kind of malpractice everywhere.

所长 suǒzhǎng head of an institute, office, etc.
see also suǒcháng

所致 suǒzhì be caused by; be the result of：他的病是劳累过度～。His illness was due to overexertion.

所作所为 suǒzuò-suǒwéi what one has done; one's behaviour; one's conduct：我的～经得起大家的检查。What I have done can bear close scrutiny. /他的～很不像个学者。His behaviour does not befit his position as a scholar.

璅 suǒ 〈书面〉 *see* "琐" suǒ

鏁 suǒ 〈书面〉 *see* "锁" suǒ

T

tā

他 tā ❶ *referring to the third person singular, now usu. male*:～是我同班同学的父亲。He is the father of my classmate. /我已经很久没有见到～了。I haven't seen him for a long time. /一个人要是不懂得学习别人的长处,～就将一事无成。Whoever fails to learn from others' strong points will accomplish nothing. /这里的每个人都有～自己的特长。Everyone here has their own special skill. ❷ *used between a verb and a numeral as a form word*: 咬～一口 have a bite / 唱～几句京剧 sing a few lines of Beijing opera / 买～几公斤尝尝。Buy several kilos and have a taste. /好好揍～几下。Give it a good thrashing. ❸ other; another; some other: 此病别无～法可治。There's no other cure for this disease. /此人已～调。The person has been transferred to another unit. /毫无～求。There is no other demand at all.

他动 tādòng propelled by an external force

他动词 tādòngcí *also* "及物动词" jíwù dòngcí 〈语言〉transitive verb

他动轴 tādòngzhóu driven shaft

他方 tāfāng elsewhere; another place: ～求食 seek a living elsewhere /远走～ leave for a faraway place /久在～,度日如年。A long stay in an alien country makes days wear on like years.

他故 tāgù another cause:必有～ must have another cause /若有～,一定明言相告。If there were other reasons, I would certainly let you know.

他加禄语 Tājiālùyǔ Tagalog (language of the Philippines)

他冷式电机 tālěngshì diànjī separately-cooled motor

他励 tālì 〈电工〉separate excitation: ～电动机 separately excited motor /～发电机 separately excited generator

他妈的 tāmāde 〈粗话〉damn it; hell; shit; fuck:去～! To hell with it! /你～想干什么? What the hell are you up to? /～,又晚了。Shit, we're late again.

他们 tāmen *referring to the third person plural, usu. of male or indefinite gender*:～家 their family /～单位 their unit /～祖孙俩相依为命。The grandfather and the grandson depended on each other for survival. /～湖南人喜欢吃辣的。People from Hunan Province like hot dishes (*or* food). /系主任～在开会。The dean and others are at a meeting.

他年 tānián ❶ another year; in the future:救命之恩,～定当报答。In the future, I would certainly requite your kindness of saving my life. ❷〈书面〉past:忆～之事 recall the past

他人 tārén another person; other people; others:非法闯入～住宅 break into other people's houses illegally /～暗中相助 secret help from others /事必躬亲,不假手～ see (*or* attend) to everything oneself without seeking others' help /这是我们两人之间的事,～最好不要干涉。This is something that concerns us two only. Nobody should try to interfere.

他日 tārì 〈书面〉❶ some other time or day; some day; later on:以备～之用 set aside for future use /希望我们～能够再度相逢。I hope we shall meet again some day. ❷ some time in the past; ever before:其得意非～可比。He is more complacent than ever before.

他杀 tāshā 〈法律〉homicide:从种种迹象看,像是自杀,但不排除～的可能性。By all appearances this was a suicide, but the possibility of a homicide should not be ruled out.

他山攻错 tāshān-gōngcuò *also* "他山之石,可以攻玉" there are other hills whose stones may serve to polish the jade; advice from or example by others may help one overcome one's shortcomings:看来我们必须～,引进别人的经验。It seems we must learn from others' experiences for our own benefit.

他伤 tāshāng injuries inflicted by other people:死者身上的伤痕显然是～所致。The wounds on the body were obviously caused by assaults.

他谁 tāshéi 〈书面〉who; whom:心中凄苦告～? To whom could I pour out my misery? /万千隐情告～? Who could possibly share my myriads of secrets?

他生 tāshēng next life: 只好～报答大恩 have to requite sb.'s kindness in the next life

他乡 tāxiāng place far away from home; alien land: ～遇故知 run into an old friend in a distant land /久在异国～ live long in an alien land /～虽好,不是久留之地。A foreign land, however fine, is not an ideal place for permanent stay.

他志 tāzhì 〈书面〉ulterior motives; different plan:素有～ long cherish other plans; long have ulterior motives /岂有～? How could I have disloyal ideas?

她 tā 〈代词〉❶ *referring to the third person singular of female gender*:～丈夫 her husband /～获得了女子单打冠军。She won the women's singles championship. ❷〈比喻〉*used to refer to sth. one esteems or treasures, e.g. one's motherland, national flag, hometown, etc.*

她们 tāmen 〈代词〉*referring to the third person plural of female gender*:～是中国女性中的佼佼者。They are outstanding among the Chinese women.

它(牠) tā *referring to the third person singular and nonhuman*:她拾起地上的报纸,把～放回桌上。She picked up the newspaper from the ground and put it back on the table. /这条牛请你把～拉走。Please lead away this ox.

它们 tāmen *referring to the third person plural and nonhuman*:保护野生动物,做～的朋友。Protect wildlife and be their friends.

铊 tā 〈化学〉thallium (Tl)

铊化物 tāhuàwù 〈化学〉thallide

铊氧硫晶体管 tāyǎngliú jīngtǐguǎn 〈电子〉thallofide cell

铊中毒 tāzhòngdú 〈医学〉thallotoxicosis

溻 tā 〈方言〉(of clothes, etc.) become soaked with sweat; (of sweat) soak (clothes):梦中醒来,汗水～湿了床单。He awoke from the dream to find the bed sheet soaked with sweat. /烈日下行走,背心都～了。Walking in the scorching sun, he felt that his vest was drenched in sweat.

遢 tā *see* "邋遢" lāta

褟[1] tā 〈方言〉hem or sew (lace or tassel):～花边的床罩 lace-hemmed bedspread /～边的桌布 laced tablecloth /裙子的下摆～了花边。The lower hem of the skirt is laced.

褟[2] tā *also* "汗褟儿" hàntār singlet

塌 tā ❶ collapse; crumble; fall down:老屋年久失修,院墙都～了。The old building was long out of repair. Even the courtyard

wall had collapsed./房子旧得都快～了。The house was so dilapidated that it was on the verge of crumbling down. ❷ sink; subside; droop:看看病中的妻子两颊一天天～下去,他的心如刀割。It stabbed him to the heart to see the cheeks of his sick wife sink day by day. ❸ ease; calm down; settle down:这两天心～不下来,思绪很乱。My mind has been in a turmoil these days, and I could not set it at ease. /～下心来,认真把作业做完。Get down to finishing your homework in earnest.

塌鼻子 tābízi snub nose; flat nose:～小孩 snub-nosed child

塌车 tāchē *also* "榻车" tàchē 〈方言〉large handcart

塌翅 tāchì dejected like a bird drooping its wings; crestfallen:垂头～的没精气神儿 be crestfallen and dispirited /仕途～ feel dejected in one's official career

塌方 tāfāng *also* "坍方" tānfāng cave in; collapse; landslide:入夜以后,洪水陡涨,大坝出现～。The flood rose suddenly after night fell, and a section of the dam collapsed./前方有一段公路因暴雨～了。There was a landslide in the highway ahead because of the rainstorm.

塌架 tājià ❶ (of a house) collapse; crumble; cave in:后花园的凉亭～了。The gazebo in the back garden collapsed. /这栋房子年久失修,快～了。The house has been neglected for years and is fast falling to pieces. ❷〈比喻〉collapse; fall from power:警察局长因参与贩毒而～。The police superintendent lost his post because of his involvement in drug-trafficking.

塌棵菜 tākēcài *also* "太古菜" tàigǔcài broadleafed mustard

塌落 tāluò fall down; collapse:暴雨中,天花板突然～。All of a sudden, the ceiling gave in during the rainstorm.

塌实 tāshi *also* "踏实" tāshi ❶ steady and sure; steadfast; stable:学习认真、～ be conscientious and persevering in one's study; be a conscientious student /这样～、肯干的人不多见。Such steady and hard-working people are rare. ❷ free from anxiety; at peace:这几件事干完了,我心里才觉得～。Having finished the work, I had my mind set at rest. /他昨天夜里睡不～。He did not sleep well last night.

塌塌米 tātāmǐ tatami, Japanese mattress placed on the floor

塌台 tātái collapse; fall from power:～人物 downfallen figure; the down-and-out /～将军 deposed general /他因丑闻而～,并受到选民的谴责。He fell from power after the scandal and was condemned by voters.

塌陷 tāxiàn subside; sink; cave in:脸色苍白,两颊～ with pale complexion and sunken cheeks /路基～。The roadbed sank. /地壳～。The earth's crust has subsided.

塌心 tāxīn 〈方言〉settle down; calm down:这孩子干什么都塌不下心来。The child can't set his mind to anything. /他心里有事,干活也不～。With something on his mind, he can't concentrate on his work.

塌秧 tāyāng 〈方言〉❶ (of grass, vegetables, etc.) droop:入春以来,老天没下过一点雨,园子里的菜都～了。There has not been a single drop of rain since spring, and vegetables in the garden have all drooped. ❷ dejected; crestfallen:小伙子这几天～啦! The young guy has become listless these days.

塌中 tāzhōng 〈戏曲〉(of opera singer) voice breaks down during middle age

缗

tā 〈书面〉tie; bind:以索～之 tie sth. with a rope

嚃

tā 〈书面〉drink

趿

tā *see* "趿拉"

趿拉 tāla wear shoes with the backs turned in; shuffle about with the backs of one's shoes trodden down; wear shoes as slippers:整天～着一双破鞋 shuffle about all day in a pair of worn-out shoes /鞋都～坏了 tread one's shoes to pieces /他～着鞋就出去了。He went out with the backs of his shoes turned in.

趿拉板儿 tālabǎnr 〈方言〉*also* "呱哒板儿" guādabǎnr wooden slippers; clogs

趿拉儿 tālar 〈方言〉slippers:皮～ leather slippers /草～ straw slippers

踏

tā

see also tà

踏实 tāshi *see* "塌实" tāshi

tǎ

涾

tǎ (old name for 焦油)〈化学〉tar

塔(墖)

tǎ ❶〈佛教〉Buddhist pagoda; pagoda:佛～ Buddhist pagoda /舍利～ stupa; pagoda for Buddhist relics; Buddhist shrine ❷ tower:铁～ iron tower /水～ water tower /灯～ lighthouse; beacon /金字～ pyramid /纪念～ monument /炮～ gun turret /钻～ boring tower; derrick /合成～ synthetic tower /提纯～ purifying column (*or* tower) /蒸馏～ distillation column (*or* tower) ❸ (Tǎ) a surname

塔车 tǎchē 〈电工〉tower wagon

塔吊 tǎdiào tower crane

塔夫绸 tǎfūchóu 〈纺织〉taffeta

塔灰 tǎhuī 〈方言〉cobwebs and dirt under a ceiling:天花板上的～落了下来。The dirt on the ceiling is falling off.

塔吉克斯坦 Tǎjíkèsītǎn Tadzhikistan:～人 Tajik

塔吉克族 Tǎjíkèzú Tajik nationality, living in the Xinjiang Uygur Autonomous Region

塔克拉玛干沙漠 Tǎkèlāmǎgān Shāmò Taklamakan Desert, China's largest desert in Xinjiang

塔里木河 Tǎlǐmùhé Tarim River, China's longest inland river in Xinjiang

塔里木盆地 Tǎlǐmù Péndì Tarim Basin, China's largest inland basin in Xinjiang

塔林 tǎlín ❶ pagoda forest, tombs of Buddhist monks near a temple ❷ (Tǎlín) Tallinn, capital of Estonia

塔楼 tǎlóu ❶ tower building ❷ turret

塔轮 tǎlún 〈机械〉cone pulley; stepped pulley

塔桥 tǎqiáo tower bridge

塔什干 Tǎshígān Tashkent, capital of Uzbekistan

塔式 tǎshì tower-type:～打浆机 tower beater /～干燥机 tower drier /～锅炉 updraft boiler /～建筑 tower building /～净化器 tower purifier /～浓缩器 tower concentrator /～起重机 tower crane (*or* hoist) /～酸洗机 tower pickle /～炉〈冶金〉tower furnace

塔斯社 Tǎsīshè TASS, official news agency of the former Soviet Union, merged with the Russian Telegraphic Information Agency in 1992 and renamed Itar-Tass (俄通－塔斯社, or 俄塔社)

塔塔尔族 Tǎtǎ'ěrzú Tatar nationality, living in Xinjiang

塔台 tǎtái 〈航空〉control tower

塔钟 tǎzhōng tower clock

獭

tǎ 〈动物〉otter:水～ (common) otter /海～ sea otter /旱～ marmot /～皮大衣 otter fur overcoat

獭褐 tǎhè 〈书面〉otter-skin overcoat

獭冠 tǎguān 〈书面〉otter-skin hat

獭祭 tǎjì 〈书面〉writer's parade of allusions in literary composition (as an otter spreads fish about):为文多～,不足为法。An empty parade of allusions is no example to follow in writing.

鳎

tǎ 〈动物〉*also* "鳎目鱼" sole

tà

沓(澾)

tà 〈书面〉slippery:路陡苔～。The path is steep and the mosses are slippery.

闼(闥)

tà 〈书面〉door; small door; wicket gate:禁～ palace gate /排～直入 push the door open and stride in (without knocking)

挞(撻)

tà 〈书面〉flog; whip:鞭～ flog; lash /～罚 punishment by whipping

挞伐 tàfá 〈书面〉send armed forces to suppress; send a punitive expedition against:大张～ launch attacks by sending huge armed forces; attack on a large scale

佻(僋) tà see "佻佻" tiāotà

拓(搨) tà make rubbings from (inscriptions, pictures, etc. on stone tablets or bronze vessels):老教授把断碑上的文字小心地～了下来。The old professor carefully made rubbings from the inscription on the broken stone tablet.
see also tuò

拓本 tàběn book of rubbings:这是本很珍贵的金石～。This is a valuable album of the rubbings of ancient bronze and stone carvings.

拓片 tàpiàn rubbing (from a stone tablet or bronze vessel):金石～ rubbings of ancient bronze and stone carvings / 泰山石刻～ rubbings of stone carvings on Mount Tai

拓印 tàyìn 〈印刷〉rubbing

嗒 tà
see also dā

嗒然 tàrán 〈书面〉disheartened; dejected; despondent; depressed:～若失 deeply despondent

嗒丧 tàsàng dejected; dispirited; depressed:老人～着脸走了。The old man went away with a gloomy face.

阘 tà
see also dá

阘懦 tànuò 〈书面〉lowly and spineless

阘茸 tàróng 〈书面〉❶ mean; worthless; contemptible ❷ mean and contemptible person

榻 tà long, narrow and low bed; couch:病～ sick bed / 藤～ rattan (*or* cane) couch / 同～而卧 sleep in the same bed; share a bed / 贵宾下～之处,离海边不远。The hotel where the distinguished guests stay is not far from the beach.

榻车 tàchē see "塌车" tāchē

榻榻米 tàtàmǐ see "塌塌米" tātāmǐ

蹋 tà ❶ tread; stamp:其舞～地为节。The dance requires you to stamp your feet to beat time. ❷ 〈书面〉kick:～鞠 kick the ball

艡(艌) tà 〈书面〉big ship

逻 tà see "杂逻" zátà

沓 tà 〈书面〉crowded; repeated:重～ repeated / 纷至～来 come thick and fast; keep pouring in / 他这个人办起事来有些拖～。He is dilatory in doing things.
see also dá

沓潮 tàcháo tidal water:～如山而来。The tide is coming like a mountain.

沓乱 tàluàn numerous and disorderly; cluttered:～的树影 disorderly tree shadows

沓沓 tàtà confusing; hurried:车骑～ fast-moving traffic

沓杂 tàzá *also* "杂沓" numerous and disorderly:文字～。The writing is redundant and poorly organized.

沓至 tàzhì come in a continuous stream; come thick and fast; keep pouring in:宾客～。Guests come in a continuous stream.

踏 tà ❶ step on; tread; stamp:～出几行脚印 leave several footprints by treading / ～上通往故乡的路 set foot on the way to one's hometown / 脚～实地 be earnest and down-to-earth / ～上新的工作岗位 take up a new post / 请勿践～绿地。Keep off the lawn. *or* No stamping on the lawn. ❷ go to the spot (to make an investigation or survey): see "～勘";"～看"
see also tā

踏板 tàbǎn ❶ footboard; step (usu. on a car, train, etc.) ❷ footstool (usu. placed beside a bed) ❸ springboard (usu. for long-jump) ❹ treadle; footrest:缝纫机～ treadle of a sewing machine ❺ 〈音乐〉pedal (of a piano, etc.):强音～ damper (*or* loud) pedal / 弱音～ soft pedal

踏步 tàbù ❶ mark time:～走 marking time / ～不前 remain where one is ❷ 〈方言〉flight of steps

踏查 tàchá make an on-the-spot survey:～路线 make an on-site survey of a route

踏春 tàchūn go sightseeing in spring:到郊外去～ go for an outing in spring

踏凳 tàdèng *also* "踏脚凳"〈方言〉footstool (usu. placed beside a bed)

踏访 tàfǎng see "踏看"

踏歌 tàgē beat time to a song with feet; song accompanied by dancing

踏勘 tàkān ❶ make an on-the-spot survey (of a railway line, construction site, etc.):～油田 make an on-the-spot survey of an oil field ❷ make a personal investigation on the scene:～现场 make a personal investigation on the spot / 逐一～ make field investigations one by one

踏看 tàkàn go to the spot to make an investigation; make an on-site survey:～地形 go to the spot to make a survey of the terrain / 总工程师亲临工地～。The chief engineer went to the construction site himself to make a survey.

踏破铁鞋 tàpò-tiěxié wear out a pair of iron shoes — travel far and wide in search of sth.:～无觅处,得来全不费功夫。You can wear out iron shoes in fruitless search, whereas you may hit on what you need without even looking for it. *or* Find by sheer luck what one has searched for far and wide.

踏青 tàqīng go for a walk in the country in spring (when the grass has just turned green):在山间随处可见～的人群在野餐。Crowds taking an outing in the country in spring were seen picnicking here and there on the hillside.

踏踏 tàtà 〈象声〉clatter of a horse's hoofs; clip-clop:马蹄～,车声隆隆 clip-clop of horse hoofs and rumble of carts

踏雪 tàxuě walk in the snow:～寻梅 look for plum blossoms while walking in the snow — try to find inspiration for writing

踏月 tàyuè walk in moonlight:～归来 return in the moonlight

踏足 tàzú set foot:～社会 set foot in society

tāi

苔 tāi see "舌苔" shétāi
see also tái

胎[1] tāi ❶ foetus; embryo:胚～ embryo / 死～ stillborn baby / 怀～ become (*or* be) pregnant / 双胞～ twins / 堕～ have an (induced) abortion / 投～ be reincarnated in a new body / 祸～ root of the trouble; cause of the disaster ❷ birth; farrow:生过两～ have given birth to two babies / 一～下了十二、三只小猪 deliver about a dozen piglets at a litter (*or* at one farrow) / 头～生了个姑娘。The first baby was a girl. / 这是第三～了。This is the third birth. ❸ padding; stuffing; wadding:棉花～ cotton padding of a quilt / 鸭绒～的冬装 winter dress stuffed with down / 腈纶～的被子 quilt padded with acrylic ❹ roughcast (in the making of china, cloisonné, etc.):铜～ bronze roughcast / 泥～儿菩萨 Bodhisattva of clay roughcast

胎[2] tāi tyre:车～ tyre / 内～ inner tube (of a tyre) / 外～ cover (of a tyre); tyre / 给轮～充气 inflate the tyres

胎动 tāidòng quickening; movement of the foetus

胎动不安 tāidòng bù'ān 〈中医〉movement of the foetus causing pain in the lower abdomen as a sign of approaching miscarriage

胎毒 tāidú 〈中医〉skin infections of a newborn infant such as boils, blisters, eczema, etc. considered to be caused by febrile toxin inherited from the mother

胎儿 tāi'ér foetus; embryo:～石化〈医学〉calcified foetus / ～窒息 foetal asphyxia

胎儿学 tāi'érxué 〈医学〉fetology

胎发 tāifà foetal hair; lanugo

胎记 tāijì birthmark

胎教 tāijiào prenatal conditioning of the foetus (as by music, etc.)

胎具 tāijù *also* "胎模" ❶ model ❷ matrix

胎块 tāikuài 〈生理〉mole

胎里富 tāilǐfù one who is born rich; person born with a silver spoon in his mouth
胎里坏 tāilǐhuài one who is born bad; innate bad guy
胎里素 tāilǐsù born vegetarian
胎毛 tāimáo foetal hair; lanugo
胎膜 tāimó 〈生理〉foetal membrane:～早破 premature rupture of foetal membrane
胎盘 tāipán 〈生理〉placenta:～早期剥离 abruptio placentae /～滞留 retention of placenta /～溶素〈生化〉placentolysin /前置～ placenta praevia /粘连～ adherent placenta
胎盘结构 tāipán jiégòu placentation
胎盘瘤 tāipánliú placentoma
胎盘炎 tāipányán placentitis
胎气 tāiqi 〈中医〉❶ nausea, vomiting and oedema of legs during pregnancy ❷ nourishing ether for the foetus:动了～ disturb the foetus
胎球蛋白 tāiqiúdànbái 〈生化〉fetuin
胎生 tāishēng 〈动物〉viviparity:鲸鱼是一种～哺乳动物。The whale is a kind of viviparous mammal.
胎生动物 tāishēng dòngwù viviparous animal; vivipara
胎位 tāiwèi 〈医学〉position of a foetus; presentation:～正常 normal presentation /～不正性难产 malpresentation /～倒转术 version
胎样心音 tāiyàng xīnyīn 〈医学〉embryocardia
胎衣 tāiyī (human) afterbirth
胎痣 tāizhì 〈生理〉birthmark
胎座 tāizuò 〈植物〉placenta

tái

臺 tái ❶ see "台¹" tái ❷ (Tái) a surname

薹¹ tái 〈植物〉a kind of sedge

薹² tái bolt of garlic, rape, etc.:蒜～ garlic bolt /韭～ bolt of (Chinese) chives

儓 tái 〈旧语〉runner in a government office

台¹(臺、❻檯、枱) tái ❶ tower:塔～ control tower /炮～ fort; battery /瞭望～ watch tower; lookout ❷ platform; stage; terrace:站～ platform /月～ railway platform /亭～楼阁 pavilions /戏～ stage /舞～ stage; arena /看～ bleachers; stand /擂～ ring (for martial contest); arena /观礼～ reviewing stand; visitors' stand /主席～ rostrum; platform /登～表演 take the stage and perform /下～ exit (from the stage); fall from power ❸ stand; support:镜～ dressing table /灯～ lampstand /烛～ candlestick ❹ anything shaped like a platform, stage or terrace:井～ well platform/印～ ink pad; stamp pad /砚～ inkstone; inkslab /窗～ windowsill/阳～ balcony /柜～ counter; bar ❺〈量词〉(a) *used of a stage performance or properties on a stage*:一～音乐舞蹈节目 a musical and dance performance /一～布景 a setting (b) *used of a mechanical device or a machine*:一～电扇 an electric fan /一～收录机 a tape-recorder /两～刨床 two planers ❻ table; desk:写字～ (writing) desk /工作～ (work) bench /梳妆～ dressing table /乒乓球～ ping-pong table ❼ station; service:广播电～ broadcasting station /电视～ television broadcasting station /长途电话～ trunk call service; long distance (phone) service; toll board

台² tái 〈敬词〉you; your:兄～ you /～教 your advice /～驾 your presence /谨遵～命 obey your instructions

台³ Tái ❶ (short for 台湾) Taiwan: *see* "～办"; "～胞" ❷ a surname

台⁴(颱) tái *see* "台风"

台班 táibān amount of work done by a truck or a machine in a working day:一辆卡车一个～要付三百元租金。One has to pay 300 *yuan* as rent for a truck doing a full day's work.
台办 Táibàn (short for 国务院台湾事务办公室) Taiwan Affairs Office of the State Council
台胞 Táibāo compatriots of or from Taiwan:海外～ Taiwan compatriots abroad /近年来,许多～来大陆寻根。In recent years, many compatriots from Taiwan come to the mainland to seek their roots.
台刨 táibào 〈机械〉bench plane
台北 Táiběi Taibei or Taipei, capital of Taiwan Province
台本 táiběn playscript with stage directions; stage playscript:～初稿 draft playscript with stage directions /修改～ revise a stage playscript /导演～ director's playscript
台笔 táibǐ pen with a support placed on a table
台币 táibì Taiwan dollar:新～ New Taiwan dollar (NT dollar)
台标 táibiāo TV station logo
台布 táibù tablecloth
台步 táibù 〈戏曲〉gait of an actor or actress on the stage:走～ move in the stylized gait on the stage /～是戏曲演员的基本功。Gait is the basic skill of a Chinese opera actor (*or* actress).
台秤 táichèng ❶ *also* "磅秤" bàngchèng platform scale; platform balance ❷ *also* "案秤" ànchèng counter scale
台词 táicí actor's lines:背～ recite one's lines /对～ practise lines on each other /提～ prompt actor's lines
台单 táidān 〈方言〉tablecloth
台灯 táidēng desk lamp; table lamp; reading lamp
台地 táidì 〈地质〉platform; tableland; mesa
台独 Táidú "Taiwan independence":近年来,台湾某些政治势力的"～"言论十分嚣张。In recent years, some political forces in Taiwan have been rampant in advocating "Taiwan independence".
台度 táidù 〈旧语〉dado
台端 táiduān 〈敬词〉(used chiefly in correspondence) you; your esteemed self:谨聘～为本社顾问。We respectfully invite you to be consultant to this Society.
台风 táifēng 〈气象〉typhoon:强～ violent typhoon /～动向 typhoon movement /～警戒线 typhoon detective line /～路径 typhoon track
台风儿 táifēngr stage manners:这位老艺术家为青年演员树立了好～。The old performer has set good stage manners for young actors and actresses.
台风眼 táifēngyǎn typhoon eye
台甫 táifǔ 〈敬词〉your personal name:敢问尊姓～? May I know your name?
台辅 táifǔ 〈书面〉prime minister's post in feudal China:久居～ have long held the prime minister's office
台虎钳 táihǔqián 〈机械〉bench vice
台基 táijī base of a structure above ground
台驾 táijià 〈敬词〉you; your esteemed self:我在寒舍恭候～。I'll respectfully waiting for you at home.
台鉴 táijiàn 〈套语〉(used right after the salutation on an old-fashioned letter) please read my letter:王明先生～ Attention of Mr. Wang Ming
台铰 táijiǎo 〈机械〉table-hinges
台阶 táijiē ❶ flight of steps; steps leading up to a house, etc.:每几年上一个新～ scale a new height (*or* make a marked advance) every few years /从山脚到寺庙,共有三百六十级～。There are altogether 360 steps leading from the foot of the mountain to the temple. ❷ chance to extricate oneself from a predicament:我们给他留个～,让他自己下吧。Let's give him a chance to back down. /自己找个～儿下吧。Find an out for yourself. ❸〈矿业〉〈地质〉〈机械〉bench:～爆破 bench blasting /～熔岩 bench lava (*or* magma) /～齿轮 stepped gear wheel
台锯 táijù 〈机械〉bench saw
台览 táilǎn *see* "台鉴"
台历 táilì desk calendar
台联 Táilián (short for 台湾同胞联谊会) All-China Federation of Taiwan Compatriots
台盟 Táiméng (short for 台湾民主自治同盟) Taiwan Democratic Self-Government League
台面 táimiàn ❶〈方言〉aboveboard; on the table:你的话能拿到～上说吗? Can you make public what you've told me just now? ❷〈方言〉all the money on a gambling table:～大 high-stakes gamble ❸〈电子〉mesa:～型晶体管 mesa transistor
台命 táimìng 〈敬词〉your instruction; your order:谨遵～。I shall respectfully follow your instructions.
台盘 táipán 〈方言〉❶ dishes served at a banquet ❷ social engage-

ment
台钳 táiqián 〈机械〉bench clamp
台球 táiqiú ❶ billiards ❷ billiard ball ❸〈方言〉table tennis; ping-pong
台扇 táishàn 〈电工〉desk fan
台商 táishāng Taiwan business people
台上 táishang holding an official position; in power
台式焊机 táishì hànjī 〈机械〉bench welding machine
台式计算机 táishì jìsuànjī desk computer or calculator; desk-top computer or calculator; desk calculating machine
台属 Táishǔ family members of Taiwan compatriots:在京的～代表,应邀出席了晚会。Representatives of family members of our Taiwan compatriots attended the evening party in Beijing on invitation.
台毯 táitǎn table rug
台田 táitián 〈农业〉raised fields; platform fields
台湾 Táiwān Taiwan (Province of China):～同胞 Taiwan compatriots
台湾海峡 Táiwān Hǎixiá Taiwan Strait
台下 táixià out of (political) power; out of office:这两个党,一个在台上,一个在～。One of these two parties is in power (*or* government), and the other in opposition.
台榭 táixiè pavilion on a terrace:公园中心湖的北岸建了许多楼阁～。To the north of the lake in the centre of the park were built many pavilions and kiosks.
台钟 táizhōng 〈方言〉desk clock
台柱 táizhù *also*“台柱子” leading light; pillar; cornerstone; mainstay:他是我们剧团的～。He is the pillar of our troupe. /研究所里的几个～全让人用高薪挖走了。The institute has lost several of its best research fellows by the outside offer of higher pay. *or* Several of the best research fellows of the institute have been enticed away by the offer of better remuneration.
台资 táizī investment from Taiwan; Taiwan capital:～企业 Taiwan-invested enterprise
台子 táizi ❶ ping-pong or billiards table ❷〈方言〉table; desk:我如今是成人了,可以上～陪客人吃饭了。I am a grown-up now, and can keep the guests company at dinner table. ❸ platform; stage:戏～ stage /窗～ windowsill
台钻 táizuàn 〈机械〉bench drill

炱

tái soot:煤～ coal soot /烟～ soot /松～ pine soot

苔

tái 〈植物〉liverwort; moss; lichen
see also tāi
苔藓 táixiǎn *Hepaticae* and *Musci*; moss; lichen; liverwort:～丛生 overgrown with moss
苔藓虫 táixiǎnchóng bryozoan; polyzoan; ectoproct
苔藓植物 táixiǎn zhíwù bryophyte
苔癣 táixuǎn 〈医学〉lichen:扁平～ lichen planus /毛发～ lichen pilaris /荨麻疹性～ lichen urticatus /～样硬化 lichenification
苔原 táiyuán 〈地理〉tundra

抬(擡)

tái ❶ lift; raise:把椅子～起来 lift (up) the chair /～高物价 jack up (*or* raise) prices /～头挺胸 raise one's head and throw out one's chest; chin up and chest out /他～手就打人。He raised his hand to hit others without the least provocation. /你叫她,她连眼皮也不～。She did not even lift her eyes when you called her. ❷ (of two or more persons) carry; move:～伤员 carry the wounded /这张床两人都～不动。Even two people are not able to move the bed. /桌子太沉,请帮我～一下。The table is very heavy. Please help me with it. ❸ argue for the sake of arguing:只要一商量事情,他俩就～起来没完。Whenever they discuss something, they argue for hours on end. ❹〈量词〉*used of what is carried by two persons*:一～担架 one stretcher /三～嫁妆 three trunkfuls of dowry
抬爱 tái'ài favour and take good care of:多蒙～,不胜感谢。Many thanks for your favour and kindness.
抬秤 táichèng giant steelyard worked by three persons, with two lifting the steelyard on a shoulder pole and the third adjusting the weight
抬杠 táigàng ❶ argue for the sake of arguing; quarrel; bicker:他存心和我～。He was trying to pick a quarrel with me. /兄弟之间～拌嘴是常有的事。Arguing and bickering are quite common between brothers. ❷〈旧语〉carry a coffin on stout poles
抬高 táigāo promote; raise; heighten:～身份 enhance one's status /打击别人,～自己 build up oneself by belittling others
抬阁 táigé a kind of folk amusement with a couple of little boys sitting or standing on a wooden framework (carried by others) playing their parts in opera stories
抬盒 táihé 〈旧语〉large gift container (carried by two persons)
抬价 táijià jack or force up prices; hike up prices:随意～,坑害顾客 hike prices at the expense of customers /时近年节,小商小贩乘机～。As the New Year holidays are drawing near, peddlers are taking the occasion to jack up prices.
抬肩 táijian *also*“抬裉” half the circumference of the sleeve where it joins the shoulder
抬轿子 tái jiàozi ❶ carry a sedan chair ❷ lick sb.'s boots; flatter; fawn on:上面喜欢听颂歌,下面就有人～。When higher-ups like to be flattered, there will be sycophants below.
抬举 táijǔ lift:冷空气把暖空气～起来。Hot air is lifted by cold air.
抬举 táiju praise or promote to show favour; favour:不识～ not know how to appreciate favours /承蒙～,不胜感激。I am very grateful for your generosity. /我是大家～上去的。I was promoted on the strength of your generous recommendation.
抬裉 táikèn 〈方言〉*see*“抬肩”
抬筐 táikuāng large basket for earth or manure (to be carried by two persons)
抬升 táishēng (of terrain or air current) rise:青藏高原在持续～。The Qinghai-Tibet Plateau has been rising all the time. /气流受山脉阻拦被迫～。The air current rises due to mountain obstruction.
抬手 táishǒu ❶ raise one's hand ❷ be magnanimous; be generous; not be too hard on sb.:都是我的不是,还请您高抬贵手。It's all my fault. Please forgive me for my oversight.
抬头 táitóu ❶ raise one's head:他脸红得抬不起头来。He was blushing so much that he found it hard to raise his head. ❷ gain ground; rise; look up:今生今世休想～。Don't imagine that you can rise again in this life. /奖罚分明,正气才能～。Healthy trends can prevail (*or* gain ground) only when we are strict with rewards and penalties. /我们不能让封建迷信思想重又～。We must prevent feudalistic superstitious belief from rearing its ugly head again. ❸〈旧语〉begin a new line as a mark of respect, when mentioning the addressee in official correspondence, etc. ❹ (on receipts, bills, etc.) name of the buyer, payer or receiver, or space for filling in such a name:收据～写什么? What name shall I put down on the bill as the payer?
抬头不见低头见 táitóu bùjiàn dītóu jiàn be bound to see much of each other; frequently see each other:乡里乡亲的,～,别把关系弄僵了。As fellow villagers who see each other every day, don't let our relationship turn sour. /都是熟人,～的,何必发这么大火! There is no need for you to flare up like this as we are all quite familiar with each other.
抬头纹 táitóuwén wrinkles on one's forehead

跆

tái
跆藉 táijí *also*“跆籍”〈书面〉❶ stamp; step:兵相～。The soldiers stepped on each other in a stampede. ❷ offend; affront:～贵势 offend the high and mighty
跆拳道 táiquándào 〈体育〉tae kwon do — Korean boxing (which allows use of legs and feet, as well as arms and hands)

鲐

tái 〈动物〉chub mackerel

邰

Tái a surname

骀

tái 〈书面〉inferior horse; broken-down nag:驽～ inferior horse; mediocre person
see also dài

tǎi

呔(奤、嗿)

tǎi 〈方言〉speak with an accent differ-

ent from the local one
see also dāi

tài

泰 tài ❶ safe; secure; peaceful:身体康~ in good health /否极~来。Out of the depth of misfortune comes bliss. ❷ extreme; most:~古 remote antiquity ❸〈书面〉excessive; too much:俭财用,禁侈~。Be thrifty. Don't be extravagant. ❹(Tài) a surname

泰斗 tàidǒu (short for 泰山北斗) Mount Tai and the Big Dipper (respectful epithet for a person of distinction); leading scholar of the time:画坛~ leading painter /刘老是海内闻名的医学~。Mr. Liu is an outstanding doctor in medical circles throughout the country.

泰阿倒持 Tài'ē-dàochí *see* "太阿倒持" tài'ē-dàochí

泰戈尔 Tàigē'ěr Rabindranath Tagore (1861-1941), Indian poet, writer and artist, winner of Nobel Prize for literature (1913)

泰国 Tàiguó Thailand:~人 Thailander; Thai

泰和 tàihé 〈书面〉peaceful and harmonious:天下~ peace and harmony throughout the country

泰姬陵 Tàijīlíng Taj Mahal, mausoleum of white marble at Agra, India, built in 1632-1648 by the fifth emperor of the Mogul dynasty for his wife Arjumand Banu, known as Mumtaz Mahal ("ornament of the palace")

泰勒 Tàilè ❶ Brook Taylor (1685-1731), English mathematician:~定理 Taylor's theorem ❷ Frederick Winslow Taylor (1856-1915), American industrial engineer, pioneer of "time and motion" study ❸ Zachary Taylor (1784-1850), 12th President of the United States (1849-1850) ❹ John Tyler (1790-1862), 10th President of the United States (1841-1845)

泰勒级数 Tàilè jíshù 〈数学〉Taylor series

泰勒拉丝法 Tàilè lāsīfǎ 〈冶金〉Taylor process; Taylor method

泰米尔人 Tàimǐ'ěrrén Tamil, people inhabiting southern India and northern Sri Lanka

泰然 tàirán calm; composed; self-possessed:处世~ conduct oneself calmly in worldly affairs /神情~ with composure; at ease /他坐在那里~地喝茶谈笑。He sat there calmly chatting over tea.

泰然处之 tàirán-chǔzhī *also* "处之泰然" take calmly; bear with equanimity:情况再复杂,他也能~。No matter how complicated the situation is, he remains cool and collected. /遇事不惊,~,这是他性格的一大特点。He is characteristically composed and unruffled whatever happens.

泰然自若 tàirán-zìruò behave with perfect composure; be self-composed:面对眼前一大堆的困难,他竟~,应付自如。Who would have expected that he could handle the situation with perfect ease in the face of such difficulties? /他临危不惧,显出一副~的神气。He betrayed no fear in times of danger, putting on an air of perfect composure.

泰山 tàishān ❶(Tàishān) Mount Tai; Taishan Mountain (a symbol of great weight or import):有眼不识~ have eyes but fail to see Taishan Mountain; entertain an angel unawares /重如~,轻如鸿毛 be as weighty as Mount Tai or as light as a feather ❷ father-in-law

泰山北斗 Tàishān-Běidǒu *see* "泰斗"

泰山鸿毛 Tàishān-hóngmáo Mount Tai and a feather:死有~之异。Deaths are as different as the disparity between Mount Tai and a feather.

泰山压顶 Tàishān-yādǐng bear down with the weight of Mount Tai:以~之势击敌于措手不及 make a surprise attack on the enemy with the force of an avalanche /他是~不弯腰的硬汉子,硬压是压不住他的。He is a dauntless unyielding man and won't give in to any kind of pressure.

泰山压卵 Tàishān-yāluǎn like Mount Tai crushing an egg — with absolute superiority:我军长驱直入,如~,敌人毫无抵抗能力。Our army drove straight in with overwhelming force and met with little enemy resistance.

泰水 tàishuǐ mother-in-law

泰晤士报 Tàiwùshìbào *The Times*, British newspaper since 1785

泰晤士河 Tàiwùshìhé Thames, river of southern England flowing through London

泰西 Tàixī the West; the Occident:~各国 Western countries; European countries

泰语 Tàiyǔ Thai (language)

太 tài ❶ highest; greatest; remotest: *see* "~空";"~学" ❷ extreme; most: *see* "~古" ❸ most senior; great:~夫人〈敬词〉mother of another person ❹ (a) over; too; excessively:这个~大了,我不要。This is too big for me. /她~相信自己了。She is over-confident of herself. /这孩子~娇气。The child is pampered. (b) extremely; terribly; very:他这话~有意思了。His remarks are extremely interesting. /大熊猫~可爱了。The panda is very lovely indeed. /这出戏~激动人心了。The play is most exciting. /你来得~好了。You have come at a perfect time. (c) (used in the negative) very; quite; too:不~热情 not too enthusiastic; lukewarm /不~令人满意 not very satisfactory /这件事办得不~好。This matter wasn't handled very well. /你这样做不~合适吧? Don't you think what you did was not quite proper? ❺ (Tài) a surname

太白星 Tàibáixīng *also* "金星" Jīnxīng 〈天文〉Venus; Vesper

太半 tàibàn 〈书面〉greater half:敌军死伤~。The better part of the enemy have either been killed or wounded.

太仓一粟 tàicāng-yīsù grain of millet in the barn; drop in the ocean; drop in the bucket:地球在宇宙中不过是~。The earth is but a drop in the bucket in the universe. /这点钱对他来说不过是~。This much money is just peanuts to him.

太阿 Tài'ē name of a famous sharp sword; power:~在握 hold the sword in one's hand—wield state power

太阿倒持 Tài'ē-dàochí *also* "倒持太阿";"泰阿倒持" Tài'ē-dàochí hold the sword by the tip — surrender one's power to another at one's own peril:历史上大权旁落、~的事例屡见不鲜。There are plenty of cases in history of surrendering one's power to another at one's own peril.

太妃 tàifēi imperial concubine of the deceased emperor

太妃糖 tàifēitáng taffy; toffee

太公 tàigōng 〈方言〉great-grandfather

太公钓鱼,愿者上钩 Tàigōng diàoyú, yuànzhě shànggōu *also* "姜太公钓鱼,愿者上钩" (invite one to) walk into a trap with one's eyes wide open, like the fish rising to Jiang Taigong's hookless and baitless line; offer or accept sth. as a calculated risk; do sth. of one's own free will:这是~。又没人请你,是你自己找上门来,你能怪谁? Who can you blame for it since you asked for trouble yourself, like the fish rising to Jiang Taigong's hookless and baitless line?

太古 tàigǔ remote antiquity:~久远之事 something in the remote past (*or* antiquity)

太古菜 tàigǔcài 〈方言〉*also* "塌棵菜" tākēcài broadleafed mustard

太古代 Tàigǔdài 〈地质〉Archean or Archaeozoic Era

太古界 Tàigǔjiè 〈地质〉Archean Group or Erathem

太和 tàihé universal peace and harmony

太和殿 Tàihédiàn Hall of Supreme Harmony, in the Palace Museum of Beijing

太后 tàihòu mother of an emperor; empress dowager; queen mother

太湖 Tàihú Taihu lake, freshwater lake of over 2,000 square kilometres, lying across Jiangsu and Zhejiang provinces

太湖石 tàihúshí Taihu Stone (a kind of porous stone from Taihu Lake famous for use in rockeries)

太皇太后 tàihuángtàihòu grandmother of the emperor

太极 tàijí quintessence of the universe; Supreme Ultimate; the Absolute

太极拳 tàijíquán *taijiquan* or t'ai chi ch'uan, a kind of traditional Chinese shadow boxing:打~ do *taijiquan*

太极图 tàijítú diagram of cosmological scheme; *Taiji* symbol, consisting of a circle with S-shaped dividing line between white or light, or *yang* and black or dark, or *yin* halves

太监 tàijiàn (court) eunuch

太空 tàikōng firmament; outer space:~探险 venture into space /~奥秘 space mystery /~垃圾 space junk (*or* trash) /~车 space vehicle /~实验室 (US) Skylab (manned space station launched on 19 May 1973) /~环境模拟实验室 space environment simulation laboratory

太空病 tàikōngbìng space sickness

太空人 tàikōngrén ❶ spaceman ❷〈戏谑〉Hong Kong businessman shuttling between Hong Kong and a foreign land where his wife and family reside

太空梭 tàikōngsuō space shuttle

太空探测器 tàikōng tàncèqì 〈航天〉deep-space probe
太空衣 tàikōngyī *also* "太空服" spacesuit
太空站 tàikōngzhàn space station
太罗斯卫星 Tàiluósī wèixīng 〈航天〉Tiros satellite (television infrared observation satellite)
太庙 tàimiào Imperial Ancestral Temple, to the east of Tian An Men of Beijing, now housing the Working People's Cultural Palace
太平 tàipíng peace and tranquillity:天下~ universal peace and tranquillity /~世界 peaceful world /时局不~。The situation is far from tranquil. /不把这些恶势力除掉,这一方人就休想~! There can be no peace for the people here without eradicating these evil forces.
太平车 tàipíngchē 〈方言〉heavy cart with four wheels
太平斧 tàipíngfǔ hydrant hatchet
太平鼓 tàipínggǔ ❶ drum with iron rings attached to its handle ❷ folk dance by women dancing and beating drums at the same time
太平花 tàipínghuā 〈植物〉Beijing mockorange (*Philadelphus pekinensis*)
太平间 tàipíngjiān mortuary; morgue
太平龙头 tàipíng lóngtóu fire hydrant; fire plug
太平门 tàipíngmén emergency exit
太平鸟 tàipíngniǎo 〈动物〉waxwing
太平绅士 tàipíng shēnshì (HK) Justice of the Peace
太平圣惠方 Tàipíng Shènghuìfāng *Classified Compendium of Prescriptions*, medical collection compiled by Wang Huaiyin (王怀隐) and others of the Northern Song Dynasty in 992
太平盛世 tàipíng-shèngshì times of peace and prosperity:我辈生在~,又当有为之年,岂能无所作为? How can people of our generation who were born in times of peace and prosperity and are in the prime of life attempt nothing and accomplish nothing?
太平水缸 tàipíng shuǐgāng vat filled with water for use in case of fire
太平梯 tàipíngtī fire escape
太平天国 Tàipíng Tiānguó Taiping Heavenly Kingdom (1851-1864), established by Hong Xiuquan (洪秀全) and his followers:~革命 Taiping Revolution (1851-1864, largest of peasant uprisings in Chinese history)
太平无事 tàipíng-wúshì all is well; everything is all right:现今的世界,并非~。Today's world is not all that peaceful.
太平洋 Tàipíngyáng Pacific (Ocean)
太平御览 Tàipíng Yùlǎn *Taiping Imperial Encyclopedia*, completed in 983 on the authorization of Emperor Taizong (太宗) of the Northern Song Dynasty
太婆 tàipó 〈方言〉great-grandmother
太上皇 tàishànghuáng ❶ "super-emperor", a title assumed by an emperor who abdicated in favour of his son ❷ super-sovereign; overlord; backstage ruler:外国顾问成了这个国家的~。The foreign advisers became overlords of the country.
太上老君 Tàishàng Lǎojūn respectful form of address for Laozi or Lao-tzu by Taoists
太甚 tàishèn go too far:逼人~ be overly aggressive /牢骚~ have too many complaints /欺人~。That's going too far.
太师椅 tàishīyǐ old-fashioned wooden armchair
太史公 Tàishǐgōng respectful name for Sima Qian or his father Sima Zhao, well-known Chinese historians, also used by Sima Qian to refer to himself when giving comments in *Historical Records* (史记)
太守 tàishǒu 〈旧语〉chief of a prefecture; prefect
太岁 tàisuì ❶ (Tàisuì) ancient name for the planet Jupiter ❷ (Tàisuì) legendary God living underground ❸ local tyrant or bully:县城里有名的~ notorious despot in the county town
太岁头上动土 tàisuì tóushang dòng tǔ break ground where *Taisui* (an earthly god) presides — provoke sb. far superior in power or strength:你想找死,竟敢在~! You dare to defy me? Are you asking for trouble?
太太 tàitai ❶〈旧语〉wife of an imperial official ❷〈旧语〉respectful title for the mistress of the house ❸ Mrs.; madame:住在隔壁的张~ Mrs. Zhang nextdoor ❹ (used with my, your, his, etc.) wife; Mrs.:我~跟李~中学时是同学。My wife and Mrs. Li were classmates in middle school. ❺〈方言〉great-grandparent
太瓦 tàiwǎ 〈电工〉TW; terawatt (equal to 10^{12}W)
太翁 tàiwēng ❶ great-grandfather ❷ grandfather
太息 tàixī 〈书面〉heave a deep sigh:抚卷~ heave a deep sigh while reading /掩涕~ hide one's tears and heave a heavy sigh
太虚 tàixū 〈书面〉❶ great void:~幻境 great void; dreamland (*or* fairyland) ❷ heaven; universe
太学 tàixué 〈旧语〉Imperial College:许多朝代都在京城设立~。The Imperial College was established in the capital in many a dynasty.
太阳 tàiyáng ❶ sun:~偏西。The sun slanted to the west. /~从西边出来。Pigs might fly. ❷ sunlight; sunshine; sun:几个老汉靠墙坐着晒~。Some old men are sitting against the wall basking in the sun. /这块地背~,不长庄稼。This piece of land is always in the shade, therefore no crop will grow on it. ❸ temples (of head)
太阳常数 tàiyáng chángshù solar constant
太阳大气 tàiyáng dàqì solar atmosphere
太阳灯 tàiyángdēng 〈医学〉sunlamp; sunlight lamp
太阳地儿 tàiyángdìr 〈方言〉place where there is sunshine; sunny spot:房前~ sunny spot in front of the house /大晌午站在~里,也不嫌热? Don't you feel hot standing under the scorching sun at noon?
太阳电池 tàiyáng diànchí solar cell
太阳帆 tàiyángfān 〈航天〉solar sail
太阳风 tàiyángfēng solar wind
太阳辐射 tàiyáng fúshè solar radiation
太阳光激励激光器 tàiyángguāng jīlì jīguāngqì 〈物理〉sun-pumped laser; solar-excited laser
太阳光谱 tàiyáng guāngpǔ 〈物理〉solar spectrum
太阳黑子 tàiyáng hēizǐ 〈天文〉*also* "日斑" rìbān; "黑子" sunspot
太阳活动 tàiyáng huódòng solar activity
太阳活动周 tàiyáng huódòngzhōu solar cycle
太阳镜 tàiyángjìng sunglasses
太阳历 tàiyánglì solar calendar
太阳炉 tàiyánglú solar furnace
太阳帽 tàiyángmào sun-helmet; topi
太阳目视镜 tàiyáng mùshìjìng 〈天文〉helioscope
太阳能 tàiyángnéng solar energy:~发电 solar electric power generation /~电话 solar telephone /~发动机 solar engine /~加热器 solar (radiation) collector /~蒸发器 solar still /~转换器 solar converter
太阳年 tàiyángnián solar year
太阳鸟 tàiyángniǎo sunbird
太阳日 tàiyángrì solar day
太阳时 tàiyángshí solar time
太阳室 tàiyángshì solar house
太阳探测器 tàiyáng tàncèqì solar probe
太阳同步轨道 tàiyáng tóngbù guǐdào 〈航天〉sun-synchronous orbit
太阳窝 tàiyángwō 〈方言〉temples (of head)
太阳系 tàiyángxì solar system
太阳穴 tàiyángxué temples (of head):这孩子好认,左边~上有颗痣。The child can easily be identified. There is a mole on his left temple.
太阳耀斑 tàiyáng yàobān solar flare
太阳鱼 tàiyángyú 〈动物〉sunfish
太阳月 tàiyángyuè solar month
太阳灶 tàiyángzào solar energy stove; solar cooker
太爷 tàiyé ❶ (paternal) grandfather:你家老~在家吗? Is your grandpa at home? ❷〈方言〉(paternal) great-grandfather
太医 tàiyī ❶ imperial physician ❷〈方言〉doctor
太医署 tàiyīshǔ 〈旧语〉imperial academy of medical science
太阴 tàiyīn ❶〈方言〉moon ❷〈天文〉lunar:~周 lunar cycle
太阴历 tàiyīnlì lunar calendar
太阴年 tàiyīnnián lunar year
太阴月 tàiyīnyuè lunar month; lunation
太原 Tàiyuán Taiyuan, capital of Shanxi Province
太子 tàizǐ crown prince
太子港 Tàizǐgǎng Port-au-Prince, capital of Haiti
太子参 tàizǐshēn 〈中药〉radix pseudostellariae

汰

tài discard; eliminate:裁~冗员 lay off surplus personnel (*or* staff); streamline; make redundant /优胜劣~ survival of the fittest
汰遣 tàiqiǎn 〈书面〉eliminate and repatriate; make redundant and send home:~返乡 discharge and send sb. home /~归田 be sent home to till the land

态(態) tài ❶ form; state; condition; appearance:形～ shape; morphology /状～ state; situation /神～ expression; manner; bearing; mien /体～ posture; carriage /时～ tense /动～ trends; developments; dynamic state /固～ solid state /液～ liquid state /气～ gaseous state /病～ morbid state /丑～ buffoonery /故～复萌 slip back into one's old ways; revert to type /事～的发展出乎人们的意料。The course of events was quite unexpected. ❷〈语言〉voice:主动语～ active voice /被动语～ passive voice

态度 tàidu ❶ how one conducts oneself; manner; bearing:～大方 be natural and poised /～诚恳 be sincere /～傲慢 be arrogant; put on airs /发～ fly into a rage /耍～ lose one's temper; get into a huff ❷ how one views (sth. or sb.) and acts (on it or him); attitude; approach:学习～ attitude towards study /工作～扎实 have a down-to-earth approach towards one's work /～鲜明 clear-cut stand /在事实面前,他的～有很大转变。He changed his attitude considerably in the face of facts. /请在这个问题上表明你们的～。Please make clear your position on this matter. /我们要以公平的～处理这件事情。We must be fair in handling the matter.

态势 tàishì posture; state; condition; situation:战略～ strategic situation (*or* posture) /经济～ economic condition /分析敌方的～ analyze the military posture of the enemy /我军摆开全线进攻的～。Our army was poised for an all-out attack.

酞 tài 〈化学〉phthalein

酞氨苄青霉素 tài'ānbiàn qīngméisù 〈药学〉talampicillin

酞酐 tàigān 〈化学〉phthalic anhydride; acid phthalic anhydride

酞化青 tàihuàqīng 〈化工〉phthalocyanine

酞酸 tàisuān 〈化学〉phthalic acid:～盐 phthalate /～酯 phthalate ester

钛 tài 〈化学〉titanium (Ti)

钛白 tàibái *also* "钛白粉"〈化学〉titanium white; titanium dioxide

钛钢 tàigāng 〈冶金〉titanium steel

钛酸 tàisuān 〈化学〉titanic acid; titanic hydroxide:～盐 titanate /～钡 barium titanate

钛碳铁 tàitàntiě 〈冶金〉ferrocarbon titanium

钛铁 tàitiě 〈冶金〉ferrotitanium

钛铁矿 tàitiěkuàng ilmenite; titanic iron ore

钛质电容器 tàizhì diànróngqì 〈电工〉titanium condenser

肽 tài 〈化学〉peptide

肽酶 tàiméi 〈生化〉peptase; peptidase

tān

坍(坤) tān collapse; fall; crumble; cave in:房～了。The house collapsed. /院墙～了。The courtyard wall fell down. /洪水一冲,靠近河边的房子全～了。The house along the river bank crumbled down with the coming of the floodwater.

坍方 tānfāng cave in; collapse; landslip

坍架 tānjià collapse; crumble down

坍圮 tānpǐ 〈书面〉collapse; fall down; crumble down:亭阁～,花木凋零,后院已是面目全非了。The pavilions had collapsed, and the flowers and trees were either withered or fallen. The backyard looked almost beyond recognition.

坍缩 tānsuō (of a heavenly body) collapse

坍缩星 tānsuōxīng *also* "黑洞" hēidòng collapsar; black hole

坍塌 tāntā cave in; fall down; collapse:堤岸～。The embankment collapsed. /断墙～。The broken wall fell down. /窑顶～。The kiln top caved in. /麦垛～。The stock of wheat crumpled.

坍台 tāntái 〈方言〉❶ (of enterprises, etc.) collapse; fail; fold:苦心经营了一辈子的企业,想不到还是～了。To my sorrow the enterprise collapsed after a lifetime of painstaking efforts I put in. /这次试验决不能～。The forthcoming test must not be allowed to fail. ❷ lose face; bring humiliation upon oneself; fall into disgrace:当众～,这是他最不能忍受的了。Losing face in public, this is the last thing he can put up with. /几十年头一回～,他感到无地自容。He felt too ashamed to show himself after being disgraced for the first time in his life.

坍陷 tānxiàn subside; sink; cave in:地层～。The stratum has sunk. /暴雨过后,路面有好多处～。After the rainstorm, the road surface caved in at several places.

啴(嘽) tān

see also chǎn

啴啴 tāntān 〈书面〉(of draught animals) pant

贪 tān ❶ corrupt; venal:性～ be avaricious /倡廉肃～ promote honest and clean government and eliminate corruption /～货弃命 lose one's life through avarice ❷ have an insatiable desire for; be greedy:～吃～喝 be greedy (*or* gluttonous) for food and drink /～睡 be an insatiable sleeper /起早～黑 work hard from dawn to dusk ❸ covet; seek; hanker after:～小便宜 covet small gains; be keen on getting things on the cheap /～名图利 pine after fame and money

贪杯 tānbēi be too fond of drinking (liquor):～误事 bungle one's mission by excessive drinking /他一向～,见酒不要命。He is too fond of drinks and can even give up life for wine.

贪鄙 tānbǐ 〈书面〉impudently greedy; avaricious and despicable:如此～小人! Such a vile and covetous character!

贪财 tāncái money-mad; money-grubbing:～好色之徒 person lusting for money and women

贪残 tāncán greedy and cruel:～成性 greedy and cruel by nature

贪馋 tānchán ❶ greedy; gluttonous:她从小～,爱吃个零食什么的。She has been fond of eating from childhood, always nibbling between meals. ❷ insatiable; avid:他～地读着一本著名的小说。He read a famous novel avidly.

贪大求全 tāndà-qiúquán go in for grandiose projects; go after the grandiose:办企业不能～,否则就会造成人力物力的浪费。One shouldn't go after the grandiose in running an enterprise, for that would mean waste of human and material resources.

贪得无厌 tāndé-wúyàn inordinately greedy; insatiably avaricious:我一会儿请你写,一会儿又请你画,所求甚多,竟是～了。I have asked you for your calligraphy, then your painting. Perhaps I am asking too much of your generosity.

贪黩 tāndú 〈书面〉corruption; graft:地方官个个～,老百姓苦不堪言。The local officials were all corrupt and took graft, so the people were in deep water.

贪多嚼不烂 tānduō jiáo bù làn 〈俗语〉bite off more than one can chew:书不可不读,但也不能像你这样～。Reading is imperative, but it shouldn't be overdone, or you'll bite off more than you can chew.

贪多务得 tānduō-wùdé seek and acquire knowledge in a wide field of subjects:他这种孜孜以求,～的精神很受导师的赞赏。His assiduity in study and insatiable thirst for knowledge have won high praise from his tutor.

贪官 tānguān corrupt official:～污吏 corrupt officials; venal officials /在旧社会～多如牛毛。In the old society there were no end of corrupt officials.

贪狠 tānhěn greedy and ruthless:～的野心家 greedy and ruthless careerist

贪贿 tānhuì be corrupt and take bribes:他在任职期间,～共达数十万元之多。During his term in office, he took bribes worth hundreds of thousands of *yuan*.

贪贿无艺 tānhuì-wúyì be insatiable for bribes

贪婪 tānlán ❶ avaricious; greedy; rapacious:～的吸血鬼 greedy blood-sucker /～地为自己谋取私利 rapaciously seek self-interest ❷ insatiable; greedy; avid:～地闻着花香 smell a flower greedily /～地吸着新鲜空气 take a deep breath of fresh air /他捧着那本书,～地看了又看。He held the book in his hands reading avidly.

贪恋 tānliàn be reluctant to part with; hate to leave; cling to:～舒适的生活 be loathe to give up ease and comfort /～小家庭 cling to one's own family /～功名利禄 be greedy for honour, fame, money and rank /他～这园中的奇花异草,久久不愿离去。He lingered in the garden for a long time, gazing rapturously at exotic flowers and rare herbs.

贪墨 tānmò 〈书面〉corrupt:～败度 take bribes and bend the law /～成风。Corruption has run wild.

贪青 tānqīng (of crops) remain green (when it is time to turn yellow and grow ripe)

贪求 tānqiú covet; hanker after:～无度 be covetous beyond bounds /～富贵 hanker after wealth and position

贪权 tānquán power-mad; greedy for power:～窃柄 be greedy for and usurp power /随着地位的变化,他的～之心也越发膨胀了。With

T

changes in his position, his lust for power has become inflated more than ever.

贪色 tānsè be crazy about women; womanize; indulge in sex

贪生 tānshēng 〈贬义〉 prefer life to honour; stay alive at all costs

贪生怕死 tānshēng-pàsǐ cravenly cling to life instead of braving death; crave for nothing but saving one's hide; be mortally afraid of death: ~,临阵脱逃 sneak away at a critical juncture to save one's own skin / 原来你是个~之徒。What a dastardly coward you are!

贪天之功 tāntiānzhīgōng lay claim to what others have achieved; arrogate to oneself the merits of others; claim credit for what one has done nothing to deserve: ~,据为己有 arrogate to oneself what others have achieved

贪图 tāntú seek; hanker after; be greedy for; covet: ~安逸 seek ease and comfort / ~享乐 hanker after pleasure / 我~凉快,不料竟着凉感冒了。I enjoyed the cool too long and caught a cold.

贪玩 tānwán be crazy about play; be excessively fond of play: 这孩子~,学习成绩不好。The child cares for nothing but play and gets poor marks in school.

贪污 tānwū corruption; graft; embezzlement: ~腐败 corruption and degeneration / ~公款 embezzlement of public funds / ~盗窃 engage in graft and theft; embezzle and steal (state property) / ~犯 grafter; embezzler / ~分子 person guilty of corruption; grafter; embezzler

贪污腐化 tānwū-fǔhuà corrupt and degenerate

贪污受贿 tānwū-shòuhuì embezzlement and bribe-taking; corruption

贪小失大 tānxiǎo-shīdà covet a little and lose a lot; seek small gains but incur big losses; be penny-wise and pound-foolish: ~,后悔莫及。It is too late to repent big losses which resulted from coveting small gains.

贪心 tānxīn ❶ greed; avarice; rapacity: ~太大 unlimited avarice / 无法满足的~ insatiable greed ❷ greedy; avaricious; insatiable; voracious: 他变得越来越~了。He has become increasingly voracious.

贪欲 tānyù covetous desire; avarice; greed: 为了迎合他的~,一份份重礼送到他的家中。In order to cater to his avarice, expensive gifts were sent to his home one after another.

贪赃 tānzāng take bribes; practise graft: ~受贿 practise graft and take bribes / ~舞弊 engage in graft and fraudulent practices / ~徇私 practise graft and favouritism

T

贪赃枉法 tānzāng-wǎngfǎ take bribes and bend the law; pervert justice for bribes: 此人~,声名狼藉。The man became notorious for his perversion of justice after taking bribes. / 恶吏~,滥杀无辜。Evil officials took bribes, bent the law and indiscriminately killed the innocent.

贪占 tānzhàn embezzle: ~公家财产 embezzle public property / ~教育经费 embezzle education funds

贪嘴 tānzuǐ greedy (for food); gluttonous: ~的毛病 bad habit of being too greedy for food

猹

tān a kind of legendary animal

怹

tān 〈方言〉 *courtesy form of* 他: "老爷子好啊?" "~还挺硬朗。" "How is your father?" "He is still going strong."

滩(灘)

tān ❶ beach; sands: 海~ seabeach; beach / 盐~ salina; saltmarsh / 沙~ sand bank; sands / 河~地 floodland (along a river); floodplain ❷ shoal: 险~ dangerous shoals / 暗~ hidden shoal / 急流湍~ shoals and rapids

滩地 tāndì beachland; floodland; floodplain

滩簧 tānhuáng a form of storytelling in rhymes (performed at teahouses, partly sung, partly acted, popular in southern Jiangsu and northern Zhejiang provinces)

滩头 tāntóu sand bank; sandy beach: ~阵地 beach position

滩头堡 tāntóubǎo 〈军事〉 beachhead

滩涂 tāntú low beach

滩羊 tānyáng a kind of sheep famous for its pelt, bred in Ningxia

瘫(癱)

tān paralysis: 偏~ hemiplegia / 瘋~ paralysis / 吓~了 faint with fear; paralysed with fright

瘫巴 tānba 〈方言〉 paralysed: 他给吓~了。He was paralysed by fear. / 那台机床被捅~啦。The machine tool broke down as a result of careless operation.

瘫倒 tāndǎo fall down as if paralysed: ~在床 bedridden with paralysis / 他摔~在地。He fell, paralysed, to the ground.

瘫痪 tānhuàn ❶ *also* "风瘫" fēngtān paralysis; palsy: ~在床 be confined to bed because of paralysis / 四肢~ quadriplegia; four-limb paralysis; totally paralysed / 他下身~已有两年了。He has been paralysed from the waist down for two years. ❷ be paralysed; break down; be at a standstill: 在台风袭击下,那里的交通运输全部陷于~。When the typhoon struck, transport there was at a total standstill. / 领导班子~。The leadership does not function any more. / 大罢工导致该国整个社会生活的~。The general strike in that country led to the total breakdown of social life.

瘫软 tānruǎn (of arms, legs, etc.) weak and limp: ~无力 weak and limp / 双腿~ feel weak at the knees / 他双眼紧闭,~在沙发上。With closed eyes, he lay in the sofa feeling extremely weak.

瘫子 tānzi person suffering from paralysis; paralytic

瘫坐 tānzuò sit as if paralysed: ~一旁 sit on the side as if paralysed

摊(攤)

tān ❶ spread out; unfold: 桌子上~着好几本书。Quite a few books were spread out on the desk. / 希望你们把问题都~到桌面上来。I hope you will put all the problems on the table. ❷ vendor's stand; booth; stall: 菜~儿 vegetable stand; vegetable stall / 书~儿 bookstand / 旧货~ secondhand goods stall / 练~儿 manage a booth; be a street vendor / 摆地~儿 be a street vendor / 收~儿 shut up shop; wind up the day's business ❸ 〈量词〉 *used of sth., usu. pasty or liquid, that is spread out*: 一~泥 a mud puddle / 一~积水 a pool of water / 一~工作 a whole lot of work ❹ fry batter in a thin layer: ~鸡蛋 make an omelet / 他在集市上~鸡蛋煎饼。He makes egg pancakes at the market. ❺ take a share in; share: 这笔钱~到每个人头上不过二、三元。If the sum is shared by everyone, it amounts to only two to three *yuan* each. / ~钱买礼物。Each contributes some money for gifts. / 把任务分~到小组。Assign the tasks to different groups. ❻ (usu. of sth. unpleasant) befall; happen to: 倒霉的事全叫我~着了。Bad luck always befalls me. / 他好像~上什么不愉快的事了! It seems something unpleasant has happened to him.

摊场 tāncháng spread harvest grain on a threshing ground; ted grain

摊车 tānchē pedlar's stand and cart: 取缔无照~ ban unlicensed pedlar's stands and carts

摊档 tāndàng 〈方言〉 stall; stand; vendor's stand

摊点 tāndiǎn stand; booth: 夜市~ night market booth / 这个农贸市场共有四百多个~。The farm-produce market boasts a total of more than 400 vending stands.

摊贩 tānfàn street pedlar; street vendor: 无照~ unlicensed street pedlar / 路边有几个~在张罗生意。Some street vendors are soliciting customers on the roadside.

摊还 tānhuán 〈金融〉 amortization: ~期 amortization period

摊牌 tānpái ❶ lay one's cards on the table ❷ 〈比喻〉 show one's hand; have a showdown: 不到紧要时刻不~ refrain from showing one's hand till the crucial moment / 到了该向他们~的时候了。It's time to have a showdown with them.

摊派 tānpài apportion (expenses, work, etc.); portion or share out: ~任务 apportion tasks / ~捐款 portion out donations / 合理~ rational allotment / 禁止向农民乱~钱和粮。It is prohibited to arbitrarily collect money and food grain from farmers.

摊棚 tānpéng canopy for a vendor's stand or stall; booth

摊晒机 tānshàijī 〈农业〉 tedder

摊商 tānshāng vendor; pedlar: 零售百货的~ general retail vendor / 对摊点和~要加强管理 tighten control over pedlars and their stalls

摊市 tānshì stall quarters; open-air market: 早晚~ morning and evening mart

摊手 tānshǒu loosen one's grip; let go: 他一~,水桶就掉到井里去了。He loosened his grip and the bucket fell into the well. / 抓紧了,你别~! Hold tightly and don't let go!

摊售 tānshòu sell at a vendor's stand: ~廉价商品 sell cheap goods in a booth / 摆在路边~ peddle goods at the roadside / 办理~营业执照 go through the formalities for obtaining a vendor's licence

摊头 tāntóu 〈方言〉 booth; stall; vendor's stand

摊位 tānwèi vendor's stand; booth; stall: 增加售货~,方便群众生活 set up more selling stands to suit people's convenience / 本镇共有~、摊点二百多个。There are over 200 vendors' stands and booths

throughout the town.

摊销 tānxiāo 〈经济〉 amortization

摊子 tānzi ❶ vendor's stand; booth; stall: 旧货～ junk vendor's stand / 杂货～ grocery stall / 摆～ sell goods at a stand ❷ the way sth. is set out; structure of an institution; set-up: 别把～铺得太大了。Don't do things on too large a scale. / 谁也收拾不了这个烂～。No one is able to clear up this mess.

tán

檀 tán ❶ *also* "青檀" qīngtán 〈植物〉 wingceltis (*Pteroceltis tatarinowii*) ❷ (Tán) a surname

檀板 tánbǎn hardwood clappers

檀香 tánxiāng 〈植物〉 white sandalwood; sandalwood: ～木 sandalwood / ～扇 sandalwood fan / ～油 sandalwood oil / ～皂 sandal soap

檀香山 Tánxiāngshān Honolulu, capital of Hawaii, US

檀口 tánkǒu (of women) light red lips: ～低吟 hum showing light red lips / ～一笑 move the light red lips to give a winsome smile

檀郎 tánláng handsome man

檀越 tányuè (used by a Buddhist monk or nun to address a lay donor or, by extension, any lay person) benefactor; alms giver

弹（彈） tán ❶ catapult; spring; bounce: 反～球 rebounded ball / 石子从墙上反～到他脑门上。The stone bounced off the wall and hit his head. ❷ fluff; tease: ～丝棉 fluff (*or* tease) silk floss / ～被套 fluff cotton wadding ❸ flick; flip: 把袖子上的灰尘～掉 flick the dust off one's sleeve / ～玻璃球 flip glass beads; play marbles ❹ play (a stringed musical instrument); pluck: ～吉他 play the guitar / ～三弦 pluck the *sanxian* / 对牛～琴 play the lute to a cow — talk over sb.'s head; cast pearls before swine / 老调重～ strike up a hackneyed tune; harp on the same old tune ❺ elastic; resilient; springy: *see* "～簧" ❻ assail or attack (with words); lash out at: 讥～ lash out at

see also dàn

弹拨 tánbō play; pluck: 她从墙上取下琵琶，坐在床上轻轻地～着。She took the *pipa* from the wall, sat on the bed and began to pluck it gently.

弹拨乐器 tánbō yuèqì plucked (stringed) instrument

弹唱 tánchàng plucking and singing: ～小曲 sing a ballad while playing a stringed instrument

弹词 táncí 〈戏曲〉 storytelling (in Suzhou dialect) to the accompaniment of stringed instruments

弹榧子 tán fěizi snap one's fingers: 轻轻弹了一个榧子 snap one's fingers lightly / ～，吹口哨，剧场里乱成一团。There was great confusion in the theatre with people snapping their fingers and whistling.

弹冠相庆 tánguān-xiāngqìng congratulate each other and dust off their old official's hats (in anticipation of fat jobs upon hearing of a mutual friend's appointment to a high post); congratulate each other on the prospect of getting good appointments: 新总统上台，竞选班底的人～。The new president was sworn in, while his campaigning staff congratulated each other on their success.

弹劾 tánhé ❶ (in a monarchy) supervisory official's report on the crimes of officials; censure ❷ impeach (a public official): ～总统 impeach the President

弹花 tánhuā flick the cotton with a bow and make it fluffy; fluff the cotton: ～行业 cotton-fluffing trade

弹花机 tánhuājī cotton fluffer

弹簧 tánhuáng *also* "绷簧" bēnghuáng spring: 回动～ return spring / 保险～ relief spring / 圈式～ coil spring / ～闩 spring bolt / ～掣子 spring catch

弹簧秤 tánhuángchèng spring balance

弹簧床 tánhuángchuáng spring bed

弹簧钢 tánhuánggāng spring steel

弹簧绞链 tánhuáng jiǎoliàn spring hinge

弹簧减震器 tánhuáng jiǎnzhènqì spring buffer; spring bumper

弹簧门 tánhuángmén swing door

弹簧圈 tánhuángquān spring coil; coil spring

弹簧锁 tánhuángsuǒ spring lock

弹铗 tánjiá flick the handle of a sword; 〈比喻〉 turn (to sb.) for help; seek help

弹纠 tánjiū 〈书面〉 impeach; censure: ～奸佞 impeach wicked and sycophantic officials

弹空说嘴 tánkōng-shuōzuǐ brag out of the void; brag out of thin air: ～不算数。Bragging does not count. / ～，有谁相信? Who believes such hot air?

弹泪 tánlèi shed tears: ～向人述冤情 pour out one's grievances with tears streaming down the cheeks

弹力 tánlì elastic force; elasticity; resilience; spring: ～极限 maximum elasticity; elastic limit / ～大，拉力强 great elastic and pulling force

弹力计 tánlìjì elastometer

弹力尼龙 tánlì nílóng stretch nylon

弹力纱 tánlìshā stretch yarn

弹力袜 tánlìwà stretch socks

弹黏度 tánniándù 〈物理〉 elasticoviscosity

弹球 tánqiú (play) marbles

弹球机 tánqiújī pinball machine

弹球戏 tánqiúxì pinball

弹射 tánshè ❶ launch (as with a catapult); catapult; shoot off; eject ❷ 〈书面〉 pick faults and criticize; censure: ～时弊 criticize the present social evils and malpractices

弹射器 tánshèqì catapult ejector

弹射坐椅 tánshè zuòyǐ ejection or ejector seat

弹射座舱 tánshè zuòcāng ejection capsule

弹塑性 tánsùxìng 〈物理〉 elastoplasticity: ～材料 elastic-plastic material

弹跳 tántiào spring; bounce; jump up: ～力 jumping capacity

弹跳板 tántiàobǎn springboard

弹涂鱼 tántúyú 〈动物〉 mudskipper

弹性 tánxìng ❶ elasticity; resilience; spring; elastic strength: 这个弹簧失去～了。The spring has lost its elasticity. ❷ 〈比喻〉 elastic; resilient; flexible: 他这个指示～太大，不好掌握。This instruction of his is too flexible to be handled well.

弹性波 tánxìngbō elastic wave

弹性极限 tánxìng jíxiàn elastic limit

弹性计 tánxìngjì elastometer

弹性抗 tánxìngkàng 〈物理〉 elastic reactance

弹性模量 tánxìng móliàng modulus of elasticity: ～比 modular ratio / ～试验 elasticity modulus test

弹性上班时间 tánxìng shàngbān shíjiān flexible hours of work; flexitime

弹性生产 tánxìng shēngchǎn flexible manufacturing

弹性塑料 tánxìng sùliào resilient plastic

弹性体 tánxìngtǐ elastomer

弹性外交 tánxìng wàijiāo flexible or elastic diplomacy

弹压 tányā suppress; put down; quell: ～学生运动 suppress a student movement / ～群众示威 quell a mass demonstration / ～造反的农民 subdue rebellious farmers / 出动警察进行～ send police for suppression

弹指 tánzhǐ (as quick as a) snap of the fingers: ～光阴 quick passage of time; twinkling of an eye

弹指之间 tánzhǐzhījiān in a flash; in the twinkling of an eye; in an instant: ～三十年过去了。Thirty years passed in a flash.

弹奏 tánzòu ❶ play (a stringed musical instrument); pluck: ～琵琶 pluck the *pipa* / ～乐曲 play music / ～钢琴 play the piano ❷ 〈书面〉 impeach an official before the emperor

痰 tán phlegm; sputum: 咳～ cough out phlegm; expectorate / 吐～ spit

痰喘 tánchuǎn 〈中医〉 phlegmatic asthma: ～多日 have asthma for days due to excessive phlegm / 夜里～不宁 suffer from chronic phlegmatic asthma at night

痰厥 tánjué 〈中医〉 coma due to blocking of the respiratory system

痰迷心窍 tánmíxīnqiào blinded judgment: 你一定是～啦! 找他做什么? You must be blind in your judgment. Why are you looking for him?

痰气 tánqì 〈方言〉 ❶ mental disorder ❷ apoplexy

痰桶 tántǒng spittoon (usu. in the shape of a bucket)

痰盂 tányú spittoon; cuspidor

痰郁 tányù 〈中医〉 phlegm stasis in the body

谈 tán ❶ talk; speak; chat; discuss: ～家常 talk about everyday (*or* commonplace) matters; engage in small talk; chit-chat /

T

高~阔论 talk volubly or bombastically; engage in highfalutin talk / 洽~ hold talks; negotiate / ~~心里的想法 speak one's mind / 此公颇为健~。This man is a good talker. / 请大家~一~投资的问题。Please let us discuss the investment problem. ❷ what is said or talked about; tale; story: 海外奇~ traveller's tale; fantastic tale; tall story / 老生常~ commonplace; platitude / 传为笑~ become a standing joke ❸ (Tán) a surname

谈柄 tánbǐng ❶ laughing stock; object of ridicule: 传为~ be a standing joke / 被人当作~ become an object of ridicule ❷ 〈旧语〉 horsetail whisk (one holds while talking)

谈不到 tánbudào *also* "谈不上" nothing like; out of the question: 我刚入门, 还~深入了解。I have just learned the rudiments, and have nothing like in-depth knowledge. / 我们彼此相交日浅, 还~有什么交情。We have just gotten to know each other, and there is no long-standing friendship to speak of.

谈不来 tánbulái not get along well; not hit it off: 两人一向~。The two have never got on together.

谈到 tándào speak of; talk about; refer to; mention: 一~故乡, 我就想起儿时的情景。The mere mention of my hometown reminds me of my childhood. / 我们上次~的问题很多。We talked about many issues last time.

谈得到 tándedào *also* "谈得上" take into consideration; consider: 找到了工作才~安家。I won't be able to consider setting up house until I've found a job. / 有了稳定的政治局面, 才~发展。Development is out of the question without political stability.

谈得来 tándelái get along well; hit it off: 在这个问题上我们有共同语言, 很~。We have common language on that question and get along well with each other.

谈锋 tánfēng gusto or enthusiasm (with which one talks); volubility; eloquence: ~甚健 talk with much gusto; be a good talker; have the gift of the gab / ~不减当年 no less eloquent than before / ~犀利 incisive in conversation

谈何容易 tánhéróngyì easier said than done; no easy job; by no means easy: 一月内办成此事, ~! It's no easy job to get this done in one month!

谈虎色变 tánhǔ-sèbiàn turn pale at the mention of a tiger; get jittery at the mere mention of something terrifying

谈话 tánhuà ❶ conversation; talk; chat: 小声~ talk in a low voice / 一边~, 一边喝茶 chat over tea / 注意~的方式方法 pay attention to the way you talk to others / 很有兴趣地听两个孩子的~ listen with great interest to the conversation between two children ❷ statement: 在机场发表书面~ make a written statement at the airport

谈唠 tánlào 〈方言〉 chat; chitchat: 两人一见面就~起来。The two started chatting as soon as they met.

谈论 tánlùn discuss; talk about: ~他人隐私 talk about other people's private life; tell tales of other's secrets / ~天下大事 discuss world affairs (*or* events)

谈判 tánpàn negotiations; talks: 举行~ hold talks; conduct negotiations / 停战~ truce talks / 边界~ border negotiations / ~破裂 breakdown of the talks / 第二轮~ second round of talks / ~桌 conference table / ~双方 both sides in the talks / ~地点和~时间 negotiation venue and timetable / 两国政府今年的贸易~进展顺利。The trade talks between the two governments proceeded smoothly this year.

谈判心理 tánpàn xīnlǐ psychology of negotiation

谈判语言 tánpàn yǔyán negotiating language

谈情说爱 tánqíng-shuō'ài courting

谈说 tánshuō discuss; talk about: ~旧事 talk about things of the past

谈天 tántiān chat; make conversation: 饭后~ chat after a meal / 在一起~ get together for a chat

谈天说地 tántiān-shuōdì talk of everything under the sun; chat randomly; ramble about sth.; talk discursively: 人们聚在一起, ~, 好不开心。People gathered together and chatted with great gusto.

谈吐 tántǔ style of conversation: ~不俗 have an elegant style of conversation / 衣着~ way of dress and conversation / ~不雅 vulgar style of conversation / ~粗俗 coarse talk

谈闲天 tán xiántiān chat; make conversation: 老人感到寂寞时, 便到邻居家里~。The old man often goes to the neighbour's for a chat when he feels lonely.

谈笑 tánxiào talk and laugh: 他们~了一阵, 便走了。They chatted and laughed for a while and then left.

谈笑风生 tánxiào-fēngshēng talk cheerfully and humorously: ~, 旁若无人 talk merrily as if there were no one else present / 这位外长在接见外宾时, 总是那样从容大方, ~。When receiving foreign guests, the Foreign Minister is always poised and elegant, and talks with wit and humour.

谈笑自若 tánxiào-zìruò *also* "谈笑自如" continue one's gay chatter with great composure; go on talking and laughing as if nothing had happened: 临危不乱, ~ remain calm in the face of danger and go on talking as cheerfully as ever / ~, 气度不凡 go on talking and laughing with graceful (*or* elegant) bearing

谈心 tánxīn have a heart-to-heart talk: 彼此~ have heart-to-heart talks with each other / 交心~ open one's heart to another / 促膝~ sit side by side and talk intimately; have a hearty talk

谈兴 tánxìng mood to talk; talking mood: ~正浓 be rapturously engaged in conversation; talk with great zest

谈叙 tánxù chat; chitchat; talk together: 兄弟~别情。The brothers talked about what had happened to each other after they parted. / 咱俩多年不见了, 这回得好好~~。Since we haven't met each other for years, let's have a good chat.

谈玄 tánxuán ❶ talk about the "Profound Theory" of Laozi and Zhuangzi (in the period of Wei, Jin and the Southern dynasties) ❷ metaphysics; philosophy: ~之风 tendency of talking in the abstract / 文人墨客好~。Men of letters often indulge in abstract talk. / 少~, 多务实。Less theorizing and more practical work.

谈言微中 tányán-wēizhòng speak tactfully but to the point; make one's point implicitly: 老刘的玩笑话~, 点到了他的要害。Jokingly and tactfully Old Liu made his point, touching him on the raw.

谈助 tánzhù 〈书面〉 topic of conversation: 录此逸闻, 聊作~。I've put this anecdote on record just as a topic of conversation. / 所言多为不经之谈, 姑作~而已! What was said is mostly hearsay and serves only as a topic of idle talk!

谈资 tánzī matter for gossip; subject of a conversation: 茶余饭后的~ subject of chatting at one's leisure

锬

tán 〈书面〉 lance; spear

倓

tán 〈书面〉 calm; tranquil

坛[1](壇)

tán ❶ altar; platform: 天~ Temple of Heaven (in Beijing) / 月~ Altar to the Moon (in Beijing) / 点将~ altar used to call the muster roll of officers and assign them tasks / 登~拜将 get on to the altar and hold the ceremony of appointing a general ❷ raised plot of land for planting flowers, etc.; terrace: 花~ (raised) flower bed ❸ organization set up by a secret society to worship gods in a rally ❹ (sports or literary) circles; world: 影~ movie world; film circles / 诗~ poetry circles / 体~ sports world / 球~ ball-playing world; ball-playing circles; ball-players / 乒~ table tennis circles / 棋~ chess circles

坛[2](墰、罈、壜、罎)

tán ❶ earthen jar; jug: 酒~ wine jug ❷ 〈量词〉: 一~酒 a jug of wine / 两~醋 two jars of vinegar

坛坛罐罐 tántán-guànguàn pots and pans; household goods; personal possessions: 杂货架子上摆满了~。The grocery shelves are stacked with pots and pans. / 近几年他的生活有很大改善, 家里的~也逐渐多起来了。There has been great improvement in his life in recent years and he has acquired more and more household goods now.

坛子 tánzi earthen jar: 泡菜~ earthen jar for pickling vegetables

昙(曇)

tán covered with clouds; cloudy: 彩~ colourful clouds

昙花 tánhuā 〈植物〉 broad-leaved epiphyllum (*Epiphyllum oxypetalum*)

昙花一现 tánhuā-yīxiàn flower briefly as the broad-leaved epiphyllum; last only briefly; be a flash in the pan: 在历史上~ last briefly in history / 此人不过是当今文坛上~的人物。The person was only a transient figure in the contemporary literary scene.

醰

tán 〈方言〉 (usu. used in place names) pool; pond

覃 tán ❶〈书面〉deep:～思 deep in thought ❷ (Tán) a surname
see also Qín

潭 tán ❶ deep pool; pond:一～死水 pond of stagnant water/一泓清～ pond of limpid water/龙～虎穴 dragon's pool and tiger's den — danger spot ❷〈方言〉pit; depression:泥～ mire; morass; quagmire/水～ puddle; pool

潭第 tándì 〈书面〉〈敬词〉your residence

潭府 tánfǔ 〈书面〉❶ abyss ❷〈敬词〉your residence

燂 tán 〈方言〉heat over fire

谭 tán ❶ *see*"谈" tán ❷ (Tán) a surname

谭嗣同 Tán Sìtóng Tan Sitong (1865-1898), reformist thinker and one of the leaders of the Reform Movement of 1898, who gave his life for his cause

醰 tán 〈书面〉(of wine) rich; mellow

澹 tán
see also dàn

澹台 Tántái a surname

tǎn

菼 tǎn *also*"荻" dí 〈书面〉〈植物〉*Miscanthus sacchariflorus*, a kind of reed

毯 tǎn blanket; rug; carpet:毛～ woolen blanket/地～ rug; carpet/壁～ tapestry/线～ cotton (*or* thread) blanket/满铺的地～ wall-to-wall carpet

毯子 tǎnzi blanket

忐 tǎn

忐忑 tǎntè perturbed; mentally disturbed:心情～ feel disturbed/他脸上露出～的样子。The expression on his face betrayed his fidgets (*or* perturbation).

忐忑不安 tǎntè-bù'ān uneasy; fidgety; mentally upset:行情变化使这位经理～。The manager felt apprehensive about the price fluctuations on the market.

袒 tǎn ❶ leave (the upper part of the body) uncovered; be stripped to the waist; have one's shirt unbuttoned:～腹 leave one's belly uncovered ❷ be biased towards; shield; shelter:左～ take sides with; be partial to/裁判员明显地偏～对方。The referee was obviously biased in favour of the other side.

袒护 tǎnhù be partial to; protect; shield:无原则地～ be partial to sb. at the expense of principle/你这样～他,实际上是害了他。You are in fact doing him harm by shielding him.

袒露 tǎnlù uncover; reveal; expose:～后背 expose one's back/～上身 be stripped to the waist/～心声 reveal one's inner thoughts

袒胸露背 tǎnxiōng-lùbèi (of a woman) expose one's neck and shoulders; be décolleté:我这么大年岁,穿～的连衣裙合适吗? I don't think it's proper for me, at my age, to wear that décolleté dress.

坦 tǎn ❶ level; even; smooth:平～ (of land, etc.) level; smooth ❷ open; frank; candid: *see*"～率" ❸ calm; collected; composed:舒～ comfortable; at ease

坦白 tǎnbái ❶ honest; frank; candid:襟怀～ honest and aboveboard/为人～,心地无私 be candid and unselfish/我～地告诉你 to be frank with you/我从他那里得到的是～诚挚的答复。I got a straightforward and sincere reply from him. ❷ confess; make a confession; own up:彻底～ make a clean breast of (one's wrongdoings)/～从宽,抗拒从严 be lenient to those who confess their crimes and severe to those who do not/他～了自己的贪污事实。He owned up to the embezzlement.

坦步 tǎnbù walk at a leisurely pace:林中～ walk at a leisurely pace in the woods/～当车 walk over leisurely instead of riding in a carriage; walk rather than ride

坦诚 tǎnchéng frank and honest; sincere and candid:～相见 be straightforward and honest towards each other; bare one's heart (*or* soul) to sb./～的话语 frank, sincere remarks

坦荡 tǎndàng ❶ (of a road, etc.) broad and level:～的大道 level highway/辽阔、～的草原 vast and open grassland/～肃穆的广场 open and majestic square ❷ magnanimous; big-hearted:胸怀～ big-hearted; magnanimous/～高洁的心灵 generous and noble mind/君子坦荡荡。A man of a noble character is always magnanimous.

坦腹东床 tǎnfù-dōngchuáng (become) a son-in-law

坦噶尼喀 Tǎngáníkā Tanganyika, continental part of Tanzania

坦噶尼喀湖 Tǎngáníkāhú Lake Tanganyika, world's longest freshwater lake, in East Africa

坦怀 tǎnhuái honest; candid:～待人 be honest with others/～之言 sincere words

坦缓 tǎnhuǎn even; gradual; level:～的山坡 gradual mountain slope/一片布满荆棘的、～的开阔地 flat ground full of brambles

坦克 tǎnkè (transliteration) tank:反～自行火炮 tank destroyer/防～障碍物 tank barrier (*or* obstacle)/小～ tankette/高射～ anti-aircraft tank/空降～ airborne tank/重型～ heavy tank/～乘员 tank crew/～手 tankman; tanker

坦克兵 tǎnkèbīng *also*"装甲兵" zhuāngjiǎbīng tank or panzer forces; tankman

坦平 tǎnpíng level; flat; even:地面～ level ground

坦然 tǎnrán calm; composed; unperturbed; having no misgivings:～答对 reply calmly and confidently/他显得那样～、从容。He looked composed and unhurried.

坦然自若 tǎnrán-zìruò calm and confident; completely self-assured:任凭那女人暴跳如雷,他始终～,从容对待。Though the woman stamped with fury, he was perfectly composed and handled the situation calmly and confidently.

坦桑尼亚 Tǎnsāngníyà Tanzania:～人 Tanzanian

坦实 tǎnshí frank and honest; candid and sincere:他的回答很～。He gave a candid reply.

坦率 tǎnshuài candid; frank; straightforward:～直言 speak without reservation; state outright/双方在友好而又～的气氛中会谈。The two sides held talks in a cordial and frank atmosphere./他的谦虚和～给我留下了深刻的印象。His modesty and candour left a deep impression on me.

坦爽 tǎnshuǎng outspoken; forthright; frank; candid:我感激他的～。I am grateful for his straightforwardness.

坦坦 tǎntǎn broad and even:大道～ broad and level avenue/～荒原 broad expanse of wildness

坦途 tǎntú level road; highway:视若～ regard as an easy path; consider (sth.) plain sailing/人生没有～。No one's life is without twists and turns.

坦言 tǎnyán say or speak candidly:～优劣 say candidly which is better; point our merits and faults frankly

坦赞铁路 Tǎn-Zàn Tiělù Tanzam Railway (Tanzania-Zambia Railway, 1860.5 kilometres long), largest Chinese aid project in Africa, completed 1970-1976

坦直 tǎnzhí ❶ level and straight:～的柏油马路 smooth and straight asphalt road ❷ frank; forthright; outspoken:他为人热情～。He is warmhearted and outspoken.

坦挚 tǎnzhì candid and sincere; frank and open:他对我的批评十分～。He was quite candid and sincere in criticizing me.

钽 tǎn 〈化学〉tantalum (Ta)

钽电容器 tǎndiànróngqì 〈电工〉tantalum capacitor

钽膜微型电路 tǎnmó wēixíng diànlù 〈电子〉tantalum-film microcircuit

钽丝灯 tǎnsīdēng 〈电工〉tantalum lamp

钽酸盐 tǎnsuānyán 〈化学〉tantalate

钽铁矿 tǎntiěkuàng 〈矿业〉tantalite

tàn

探 tàn ❶ try to find out; explore; sound; prospect:试～ sound out; put out a feeler/～消息 try to find out information/勘～ exploration; prospecting/钻～ (exploration) drilling ❷ scout;

T

agent; spy; detective: 密～ secret agent; spy /坐～ enemy agent planted within one's own ranks; stoolpigeon ❸ visit; call on: *see* "～亲"; "～丧" ❹ stretch forward; crane: ～头张望 crane one's neck and look around /他从窗外～进头来。He popped his head in at the window. ❺〈方言〉concern oneself with; take an interest in: ～闲事 meddle in other people's business

探案 tàn'àn investigate a case: ～小说 detective story

探宝 tànbǎo look for treasure; prospect for mineral deposits: 深山～ prospect for mineral deposits in remote mountains

探本穷源 tànběn-qióngyuán *also* "探本溯源" trace to the source; get to the root of the matter: 他决心对这个问题作～的研究。He made up his mind to get to the root of the matter.

探测 tàncè survey; sound; probe: ～星空奥秘 probe into the mysteries of the space /～对方用意 sound the other party out /经过～,摸清了这个湖的深度。They found out the depth of the lake after surveying it.

探测器 tàncèqì sounder; probe; detector: 电离层～ ionospheric sounder /空间～ space probe /月球～ lunar probe; lunar survey probe /激光～ laser detector /宇宙尘～ cosmic-dust detector /电子～ electronic detector /故障～ fault detector

探查 tànchá reconnoitre; scout: ～敌情 gather intelligence about the enemy

探察 tànchá reconnoitre; scout: ～地形 make a reconnaissance of the terrain

探访 tànfǎng ❶ seek by inquiry or search; search: ～新闻 seek news stories /～珍禽异兽 search for rare birds and animals ❷ call on; visit: ～亲友 pay a visit to one's relatives and friends /～病友 visit a wardmate /我们来这里旅行,目的是～古迹。The purpose of our travel here is to seek out historic sites.

探风 tànfēng inquire about sb. or sth.; fish for information: 我们已经派出几个人到各地～。We have sent out several persons to various places to gather information.

探戈 tàngē (transliteration) tango: ～舞曲 tango music; tango tune

探海锚 tànhǎimáo admiralty creeper

探海球 tànhǎiqiú bathysphere

探海艇 tànhǎitǐng bathyscaphe

探花 tànhuā number three successful candidate in the national civil examinations in imperial China

T

探家 tànjiā go home to visit one's family: 去年冬天,他探过一次家。Last winter, he returned on home leave. /在～的日子里,他参观了附近的一些工厂。He visited a number of nearby factories during his temporary stay at home on leave.

探监 tànjiān visit a prisoner

探井 tànjǐng ❶〈矿业〉prospect or test pit; exploring or exploratory shaft ❷〈石油〉test well; exploratory well: 野猫～ wildcat rig

探究 tànjiū make a thorough inquiry; probe deeply into: ～成因 make a thorough inquiry into the contributing factors /～事故发生的原因 look into the causes of an accident /～事物的内部联系 find out the internal relations of things

探勘 tànkān *also* "勘探" exploration; prospecting

探看 tànkàn ❶ pay a visit; visit; call on: 去医院～病人 visit a patient in the hospital ❷ watch; look carefully at; observe: 四处～了一下,没发现什么 peer in all directions without finding anything unusual

探空 tànkōng 〈气象〉sounding; air sounding: 无线电～ radio sounding /～气球 sounding balloon /～火箭 atmospheric rocket probe; altitude probe; sounding rocket; rocket sounder

探空仪 tànkōngyí 〈气象〉sonde: 臭氧～ ozone sonde /雷达～radar sonde

探口气 tàn kǒuqi *also* "探口风" try to ascertain or find out sb.'s opinions or feelings; sound sb. out: 想方设法～ try to find out what a person thinks (*or* feels) by every possible means /想～,反而被别人摸了底 try to sound sb. out only to be felt out instead

探矿 tànkuàng go prospecting (for mineral deposits); prospect: ～局 prospecting bureau /～大队 prospecting team /为～踏遍山山水水 traverse the length and breadth of the land to prospect for ore

探雷 tànléi detect or locate a mine

探雷器 tànléiqì mine detector

探骊得珠 tànlí-dézhū writing which keeps to the point: 在这十几篇文章中,惟有这一篇称得上～。Among a dozen articles this is the only one that is to the point.

探路 tànlù find out the way to a place: 你先去探探路,我们随后就来。You go first to find out the way and we will follow later.

探马 tànmǎ (often used in the early vernacular) scout cavalryman

探秘 tànmì probe the secrets; explore the mysteries: 海底～ probe the secrets of the seabed /宇宙～ explore the mysteries of the universe

探明 tànmíng ❶ find out: ～敌人的动向 find out the enemy's movements /这条路我已～,大家都随我来。I have made a reconnaissance of this road, please everybody follow me. ❷ ascertain; verify: 我们用了一年的时间,～了油田的面积和储量。We spent a year's time ascertaining the area and deposit of the oilfield. /这种矿的分布情况,尚未彻底～。The distribution of the mine has not yet been fully verified.

探摸 tànmō fumble; grope; grope for: 把手伸到口袋中～ put one's hand into the pocket to grope for sth. /～了半天,什么也没有找到 fumble for a long time without finding anything

探囊取物 tànnáng-qǔwù like taking sth. out of one's pocket; as easy as winking; like duck soup: 他办这件事如～,你无需多虑。He will handle the matter as easily as falling off a log. There is no need to worry.

探亲 tànqīn go home to visit one's family; go to visit one's relatives: 报销～路费 reimburse travelling expenses on home leave /他已十年未回老家～了。It is ten years since he last went back to his hometown to visit his relatives.

探亲假 tànqīnjià family leave; home leave

探求 tànqiú seek; pursue; search: 努力～ strive to seek /～不懈 search unremittingly /他努力～真理的精神使他在同事中赢得了很高声誉。His pursuit for truth has won him great respect among his colleagues.

探区 tànqū prospecting area

探丧 tànsāng 〈方言〉visit the bereaved to offer one's condolences; pay a condolence call

探伤 tànshāng 〈冶金〉detection of defects; flaw detection; crack detection: 无损～ non-destructive testing

探伤法 tànshāngfǎ 〈冶金〉defectoscopy

探伤仪 tànshāngyí 〈冶金〉flaw detector; detectoscope

探身 tànshēn lean forward; bend over: ～向门里望了一下 lean forward to have a look at what is inside the door

探胜 tànshèng make a tour of the scenic spots: 西山～ make a tour of the Western Hills

探视 tànshì ❶ visit: ～病人 visit a patient /～时间 visiting hours (in a hospital) /遵守～的有关规定 observe the relevant regulations concerning visiting patients ❷ look; peer: 向窗外～ look out of the window

探试 tànshì *also* "试探" probe; sound out

探索 tànsuǒ explore; probe; seek: ～人生道路 explore the path one should follow in life /～战争的原因 probe the causes of war /～真理 seek truth /刻苦～ pursue assiduously /终生～,死而不悔 devote one's whole life to the exploration of sth. without remorse /人类总是在～中前进的。The human race always advances by trial and error.

探讨 tàntǎo investigate; examine; inquire; probe: 这个问题正在～中,目前还不能下结论。The problem is being looked into, therefore no conclusion can be drawn at this time. /最近许多经济学家都在对经济体制改革作进一步的～。Recently many economists are further examining the question of economic structural reform.

探条 tàntiáo iron probing rod

探听 tàntīng try to find out; inquire about; sound out: ～消息 inquire about sb. or sth.; fish for information /～对方对新建议的看法 sound out the views of the other party on the new proposals /～小道消息 nose about for grapevine news /已有好几个人来～新所长任命的消息。Several people have made inquiries about the appointment of a new director of the institute.

探头 tàntóu ❶ pop one's head in; crane one's neck: 他从窗口～看了一下,不见屋里有人。He popped his head into the window and saw no one in the room. /太阳从云里探出头来。The sun emerged from behind the clouds. ❷〈物理〉probe: 感应式～ inductive probe /静电～ electrostatic probe /球形～ spherical probe

探头探脑 tàntóu-tànnǎo pop one's head in and look about; pry about furtively: 要进来就进来,不要在外面～。Come in if you like, don't just pop your head in and look about. /黄昏时分,我看见一个外

地模样的人在胡同里～。At dusk, I saw a person who didn't look like a local resident prying furtively in the alley.

探望 tànwàng ❶ look; glance:四处～ look all around /不时～几眼 shoot a glance every now and then /他向门外～,看看她来了没有。He looked out of the door to see if she had come. ❷ visit:～老同学 visit one's old schoolmate /～师长 pay a visit to one's teachers /办完公事后,我准备顺便回家～父母。After finishing my business, I would like to go to my hometown to see my parents on my way back.

探纬针 tànwěizhēn 〈纺织〉feeler

探问 tànwèn ❶ make (cautious) inquiries about; question tentatively; ask:～有关情况 make inquiries about relevant information /她用～的眼光看着我。She looked at me inquiringly. ❷ visit; inquire after:～老前辈 visit one's seniors /此次路过武汉,没有登门～他,只通了个电话。Passing through Wuhan this time, I only made a phone call instead of paying him a visit.

探析 tànxī inquire into and analyze:《疑难病症～》*Inquiry into and Analysis of Difficult and Complicated Diseases*

探悉 tànxī ascertain; discover; learn; find out:这些背景情况,他们大约已经～。Perhaps they have already obtained the background information they need.

探险 tànxiǎn explore; make explorations; venture into the unknown:南极～ antarctic exploration /～生活 exploration career /～笔记 exploration notes

探险队 tànxiǎnduì exploring party; expedition

探险家 tànxiǎnjiā explorer:那个大沙漠使～望而生畏。The great desert struck awe into the explorers.

探向器 tànxiàngqì direction finder

探信 tànxìn 〈口语〉ask about sb.; inquire about sb.:他走后十几天无消息,我只好打长途～。I had to inquire about him by making a trunk (*or* long distance) call when he was not heard from for more than ten days after his departure.

探寻 tànxún seek; search after; search for; look for:～真理 seek truth /～地下矿藏 prospect for underground mineral resources /那架直升飞机在低空盘旋,～降落地点。The helicopter was circling at a low altitude, searching for a place to land.

探询 tànxún *see*"探问"

探幽 tànyōu 〈书面〉❶ probe into profound truth:～析微 inquire into the abstrusities or esoterica ❷ search for beautiful scenery:～揽胜 visit places of scenic beauty

探鱼仪 tànyúyí fish detector; fish-finder

探源 tànyuán trace to its source; get at the root of the matter:寻本～ get to the bottom of sth. /探水要～ find water by tracing to its source

探赜索隐 tànzé-suǒyǐn probe into profound truth; unravel mysteries:～,期在必得 be determined to find out the abstruse truth /～,成果甚丰 make a fruitful inquiry into a profound mystery

探照灯 tànzhàodēng searchlight:～的光焰 radiance of a searchlight

探针 tànzhēn probing pin; probe:离子～ ion probe /～测量 probe measurement /高压～〈电工〉high-voltage probe

探针式高温计 tànzhēnshì gāowēnjì probe-type pyrometer

探知 tànzhī get to know sth. after inquiry:我终于从他口中～了一些重要消息。Finally I got some important information after sounding him out.

探子 tànzi ❶ scout:派出～四处刺探情报 send scouts everywhere to collect intelligence (*or* spy out the land) ❷ thin tube used to extract samples of food grains, etc.

叹(嘆、歎)

tàn ❶ sigh:悲～ sigh mournfully; lament /长吁短～ moan and groan ❷ recite (poetry) with a cadence; chant:咏～ intone; chant; sing ❸ exclaim in admiration; acclaim; praise:赞～不已 be full of praise; sigh continuously in admiration /～为天下之奇观 admire and praise sth. as a wonderful sight on earth

叹词 tàncí 〈语言〉interjection; exclamation

叹服 tànfú admire sincerely; gasp in admiration:令人～ compel (*or* command) admiration /这部作品高超的艺术手法令行家～。The experts all gasped in admiration for the artistic excellence of the work.

叹观止矣 tànguānzhǐyǐ *see*"叹为观止"

叹号 tànhào exclamation mark (!)

叹绝 tànjué admire as superb or unique:其唱腔之美让人～。Her beautiful singing is simply matchless.

叹气 tànqì sigh; heave a sigh:叹了一口气 heave a sigh /有些人在困难面前只会唉声～。Some people do nothing but sigh in despair before difficulties.

叹赏 tànshǎng admire; praise; express admiration for:～不止 admire without end /～不绝 keep on praising /人们啧啧～这茶的清香。People were profuse in their praise of the tea for its fragrance.

叹惋 tànwǎn 〈书面〉heave a pitiful sigh; sigh sorrowfully:～再三 sigh again and again

叹为观止 tànwéi-guānzhǐ *also*"叹观止矣" hail or acclaim as the acme of perfection:这样精彩的表演,令人～。The wonderful performance was hailed as the acme of perfection. *or* What could outshine such wonderful performance?

叹息 tànxī 〈书面〉heave a sigh; sigh:扼腕～ clench one's own wrist and sigh /不知为什么,她近来老是愁眉苦脸地～。I wonder why she has been grieving all the time with knitted brows. /她为失去一次进修的机会而～。She regretted the loss of an opportunity to further her studies.

叹惜 tànxī sigh with regret; find (sth.) a pity:功亏一篑,令人～。Regrettably, it falls short of success for lack of a final effort.

叹羡 tànxiàn 〈书面〉gasp in admiration; highly praise:万分～ gasp in indescribable admiration /他在学业上的成就,令他的朋友们～。His friends all greatly admired his achievements in study.

炭(炭)

tàn ❶ charcoal; carbon:木～ charcoal /～厂 charcoal works; charcoal mill /泥～ peat ❷ charcoal-like thing ❸ 〈方言〉coal:挖～ dig coal

炭笔 tànbǐ charcoal pencil; crayon

炭肺 tànfèi 〈医学〉anthracosis

炭黑 tànhēi 〈化工〉black; carbon black

炭黑涂料 tànhēi túliào 〈化工〉charcoal blacking

炭化 tànhuà carbonize;〈冶金〉charring:～层 charring layer

炭画 tànhuà 〈美术〉charcoal drawing:～铅笔 carbon pencil

炭火 tànhuǒ charcoal fire

炭墼 tànjī (usu. cylindrical) charcoal briquette

炭精 tànjīng ❶ charcoal product ❷ artificial charcoal and graphite

炭精棒 tànjīngbàng carbon rod; carbon

炭精灯 tànjīngdēng arc lamp; arc light

炭疽 tànjū 〈农业〉anthrax:～病 anthracnose /棉～病 anthracnose of cotton

炭坑 tànkēng 〈方言〉coal pit; charcoal kiln

炭粒传声器 tànlì chuánshēngqì 〈通信〉carbon microphone

炭篓子 tànlǒuzi ❶ charcoal basket ❷ 〈方言〉flattery:只要给他戴上～,他就高兴得不知东南西北了。He is easily befuddled by flattery.

炭面子 tànmiànzi coal dust; soot

炭盆 tànpén charcoal brazier

炭窑 tànyáo charcoal kiln

碳

tàn 〈化学〉carbon (C)

碳棒 tànbàng 〈电工〉carbon rod; crayon

碳氮共渗 tàn-dàn gòngshèn 〈冶金〉carbonitriding; gas cyaniding; nicarbing

碳氮化物 tàndànhuàwù carbonitride

碳电池 tàndiànchí 〈化工〉carbon cell

碳电极 tàndiànjí 〈电工〉carbon resistor rod

碳定年法 tàndìngniánfǎ *see*"碳14断代法"

碳酐 tàngān 〈化学〉carbonic anhydride

碳钢 tàngāng 〈冶金〉carbon steel:低～ low carbon steel /高～ high carbon steel

碳膏 tàngāo 〈电工〉carbon paste

碳黑 tànhēi 〈化学〉carbon black

碳弧 tànhú 〈电工〉carbon arc:～焊 carbon arc welding /～切割 carbon cutting

碳化 tànhuà 〈冶金〉carburize; carbonize:～作用 carbonization

碳化钙 tànhuàgài calcium carbide

碳化硅 tànhuàguī carborundum; silicon carbide

碳化氢 tànhuàqīng carburetted hydrogen

碳化物 tànhuàwù carbide; carbonide; carburet:～刀具 carbide cutter /～金属陶瓷 carbide cermet

碳精 tànjīng 〈电工〉carbon:～避雷器 carbon protector; carbon arrester

碳精棒 tànjīngbàng carbon stick or rod

碳精电极 tànjīng diànjí carbon electrode; baked carbon
碳链聚合物 tànliàn jùhéwù 〈化学〉carbon chain polymer
碳霉素 tànméisù 〈生化〉carbomycin
碳片 tànpiàn carbon plate: ～避雷器 carbon-plate lightning arrester
碳氢化合物 tànqīng huàhéwù 〈化学〉hydrocarbon
碳14断代法 tàn-shísì duàndàifǎ C14 dating; carbon-14 dating; carbon-dating
碳刷 tànshuā 〈电学〉carbon brush
碳水化合物 tànshuǐ huàhéwù 〈化学〉carbohydrate
碳丝 tànsī 〈电学〉carbon filament
碳丝灯 tànsīdēng carbon lamp
碳素钢 tànsùgāng 〈化学〉carbon steel
碳素工具钢 tànsù gōngjùgāng 〈冶金〉carbon tool steel; ordinary tool steel
碳酸 tànsuān 〈化学〉carbonic acid: ～同化作用 carbonic acid assimilation
碳酸钙 tànsuāngài calcium carbonate
碳酸钠 tànsuānnà sodium carbonate; soda
碳酸气 tànsuānqì carbon dioxide; chokedamp
碳酸氢氨 tànsuānqīng'ān 〈化学〉ammonium hydrogen carbonate
碳酸氢钠 tànsuānqīngnà 〈化学〉sodium bicarbonate; baking soda
碳酸氢盐 tànsuānqīngyán 〈化学〉bicarbonate
碳酸盐 tànsuānyán 〈化学〉carbonate
碳酰基 tànxiānjī *also*"羰" tāng 〈化学〉carbonyl (group)

tāng

汤(湯) tāng ❶ hot water; boiling water: 温～ hot water /盆～ bathtub cubicle /赴～蹈火 go through fire and water /扬～止沸 try to stop water from boiling by scooping it up and pouring it back — an ineffectual remedy ❷ (now used usu. in place names) hot spring: 小～山 Little Hot Spring Hill ❸ water in which sth. has been boiled: 饺子～ dumpling water /米～ rice soup /姜～ ginger tea ❹ soup; broth: 鸡～ chicken soup /肉～ broth /鸡蛋～ egg soup /豆腐～ soybean soup ❺ liquid preparation of medical herbs; decoction: 柴胡～ decoction of Chinese thorowax root (with other ingredients) ❻ (Tāng) *also*"成汤" Chéngtāng Tang, founder of the Shang Dynasty ❼ (Tāng) a surname
see also shāng
汤包 tāngbāo steamed dumplings filled with minced meat and gravy
汤饼 tāngbǐng noodle soup: ～之喜 celebration of a child's birth by eating noodle soup
汤饼会 tāngbǐnghuì *also*"汤饼筵";"汤饼宴"〈旧语〉noodle-soup feast — celebration on the third day of a baby's birth with noodles in soup as a token for a long life
汤菜 tāngcài *also*"抱子甘蓝" bàozǐ gānlán Brussels sprouts
汤池 tāngchí ❶ *also*"金城汤池" jīnchéng-tāngchí impregnable fortress ❷ hot-water bathing pool
汤匙 tāngchí tablespoon; soup-spoon
汤罐 tāngguàn water pitcher on the kitchen range
汤锅 tāngguō ❶ butcher's cauldron in a slaughterhouse ❷ slaughterhouse
汤壶 tānghú *also*"汤婆子" metal or earthen hot-water bottle
汤火 tānghuǒ 〈书面〉hot water and flames; chaos caused by war: ～之灾 disaster due to war; scourge of war /不避～ make light of chaos caused by war
汤镬 tānghuò cauldron for boiling a man alive in ancient times: 不避～ not shrink (*or* flinch) from a boiling cauldron; defy death
汤剂 tāngjì 〈中医〉decoction (of herbal medicine); herb soup; medicinal broth
汤加 Tāngjiā Tonga: ～人 Tongan
汤料 tāngliào soup stock
汤面 tāngmiàn noodles in soup
汤沐 tāngmù 〈书面〉have or take a bath; bathe; immerse
汤婆子 tāngpózi 〈方言〉*see*"汤壶"
汤泉 tāngquán 〈古语〉hot spring
汤儿事 tāngrshì 〈方言〉❶ be perfunctory; go through the motions; muddle through: 要干就来真格的,不能～。If you want to do something, pitch in. You mustn't just go through the motions. ❷ unpractical trifles; trifling talk: 他净说些～,没什么要紧的。He always talks about trifles, nothing serious.
汤色 tāngsè colour or tone of the tea (water) (for testing the quality of tea leaves): ～明亮 bright and clear colour of the tea
汤勺 tāngsháo soup ladle
汤水 tāngshuǐ ❶ water in which sth. has been boiled ❷ 〈方言〉boiling water; hot water
汤头 tāngtóu 〈中医〉prescription for a medical decoction: ～歌诀 medical recipes in jingles; prescription in rhyme
汤团 tāngtuán 〈方言〉stuffed dumplings made of glutinous rice flour served in soup
汤碗 tāngwǎn soup bowl
汤药 tāngyào 〈中医〉decoction of medicinal ingredients
汤圆 tāngyuán (usu. stuffed) dumplings made of glutinous rice flour served in soup: 豆沙～ dumplings with sweet bean meal filling

铴(鐋) tāng
铴锣 tāngluó small brass gong

耥 tāng weed and loosen the soil (in a paddy field)
耥耙 tāngbà 〈农业〉paddy-field harrow
耥稻 tāngdào weed and loosen the soil with a harrow in a paddy field

趟 tāng *see*"蹚" tāng
see also tàng

嘡 tāng 〈象声〉loud ringing sound (of gongs, shots, etc.): 锣鼓～～不断。The sound of gongs kept ringing.
嘡啷 tānglāng 〈象声〉loud ringing sound; clang: ～一声,他的脸盆摔在地上了。His washbasin fell onto the ground with a loud clang.

蹚[1](蹅) tāng wade; ford: 他～着水出去了。He waded his way out. /满街上都是水,我的两只鞋都～湿了。The street was covered with water and my shoes were all wet through.

蹚[2](蹅) tāng 〈农业〉turn the soil and dig up weeds (with a hoe, etc.)
蹚道 tāngdào *also*"蹚路"〈方言〉explore the way; spy out the land: 由他先去～。He will go and find out about things first.
蹚浑水 tāng húnshuǐ 〈方言〉follow others' bad example; get involved (in sth. undesirable): 你千万不要毁自己,跟着别人～。Don't ruin yourself by following evil ways. /我可不蹚这趟浑水。I won't get involved in all this trouble.

镗 tāng *see*"嘡" tāng
see also táng

羰 tāng *also*"碳酰基" tànxiānjī 〈化学〉carbonyl (group)
羰基 tāngjī 〈化学〉carbonyl (group): ～键 carbonyl bond (*or* link)
羰酸 tāngsuān 〈化学〉carboxylic acid

táng

唐[1] táng ❶ exaggerative; bombastic; boastful: ～大无验 sheer bragging; braggadocio ❷ in vain; for nothing; to no avail: 功不～捐。The effort will not be in vain.

唐[2] Táng ❶ legendary dynasty established by Yao (尧) ❷ Tang Dynasty (618-907): ～律 laws of the Tang Dynasty /～代诗人李白 poet Li Bai of the Tang Dynasty ❸ Later Tang (923-936) ❹ a surname
唐餐 tángcān Chinese meal; Chinese food or cooking
唐菖蒲 tángchāngpú *also*"剑兰" jiànlán 〈植物〉gladiolus (*Gladiolus gandavensis*)
唐棣 tángdì *also*"棠棣" tángdì 〈书面〉a kind of white poplar
唐古拉山 Tánggǔlāshān Danggula Mountains, in the Tibet Autonomous Region

唐花 tánghuā *also* "堂花" tánghuā hothouse flower
唐人 tángrén people in the Tang Dynasty; Chinese people: ～遗风 customs handed down from the Tang Dynasty
唐人街 tángrénjiē Chinatown
唐三彩 tángsāncǎi 〈考古〉 tricoloured glazed pottery of the Tang Dynasty; Tang tricolour
唐诗三百首 Tángshī Sānbǎishǒu *Three Hundred Poems of the Tang Dynasty*, compiled by Sun Zhu (孙洙, 1711-1778) of the Qing Dynasty
唐宋八大家 Táng-Sòng bādàjiā eight prose masters of the Tang and Song dynasties (namely, Han Yu 韩愈, Liu Zongyuan 柳宗元, Ouyang Xiu 欧阳修, Su Xun 苏洵, Su Shi 苏轼, Su Zhe 苏辙, Zeng Gong 曾巩 and Wang Anshi 王安石)
唐宋传奇集 Táng-Sòng Chuánqíjí *Short Stories of the Tang and Song Dynasties*, compiled by Lu Xun (鲁迅)
唐突 tángtū *also* "搪突" tángtū 〈书面〉 ❶ brusque; rude; abrupt: 行事～ blunt in behaviour /～而入 break in abruptly ❷ slight; tamper with; treat irreverently: ～古人 slight the ancients /～名家手笔 take liberties with a famous person's handwriting
唐寅 Táng Yín *also* "唐伯虎" Táng Bóhǔ Tang Yin (1470-1523), painter of the Ming Dynasty
唐装 tángzhuāng Chinese costume

溏 táng half congealed; viscous

溏便 tángbiàn 〈中医〉 semiliquid or unformed stool
溏心 tángxīn (of eggs) with a soft yolk: ～儿松花 preserved egg with a jelly-like yolk /我就不爱吃～儿鸡蛋。I just don't like soft-boiled eggs.

糖 (❶醣) táng ❶ a kind of organic compound: 果～ fructose /葡萄～ glucose /乳～ milk sugar /单～ monose; monosaccharide /双～ disaccharide /多～ polysaccharide ❷ sugar: 白～ sugar /红～ brown sugar /冰～ crystal sugar; rock candy /方～ cube sugar; lump sugar /砂～ granulated sugar /麦芽～ malt sugar; maltose ❸ sweets; candy: 水果～ fruit drops /奶油夹心～ sweets with cream centre /软～ jelly drops

糖包 tángbāo steamed bun stuffed with sugar
糖厂 tángchǎng sugar refinery
糖醋 tángcù sugar and vinegar; sweet and sour: ～排骨 sweet and sour spareribs /～鱼 fish in sweet and sour sauce
糖代谢 tángdàixiè 〈生理〉 glycometabolism
糖甙 tángdài *also* "糖苷" 〈化学〉 glucoside
糖弹 tángdàn (short for 糖衣炮弹) 〈比喻〉 sugar-coated bullet
糖蛋白 tángdànbái 〈生化〉 glucoprotein: ～酶 glucoproteinase
糖坊 tángfáng sugar workshop
糖房 tángfáng *also* "糖寮"; "榨寮" zhàliáo sugar workshop
糖分解 tángfēnjiě 〈生理〉 glycolysis
糖苷 tánggān 〈生化〉 glycoside: ～酶 glycosidase
糖膏 tánggāo massecuite; fillmass
糖瓜 tángguā melon-shaped maltose
糖果 tángguǒ sweets; candy; sweetmeats: ～店 sweet shop; candy store; confectionery
糖葫芦 tánghúlu sugar-coated haws on a stick
糖化 tánghuà 〈化学〉 saccharification: ～饲料 saccharified pig feed; fermented feed
糖姜 tángjiāng sugared ginger
糖浆 tángjiāng ❶ medicinal syrup: 咳嗽～ cough syrup ❷ syrup
糖精 tángjīng saccharin; gluside
糖类 tánglèi 〈化学〉 carbohydrate
糖量计 tángliángjì 〈化学〉 saccharometer; saccharimeter
糖寮 tángliáo 〈方言〉 *see* "糖房"
糖料作物 tángliào zuòwù 〈农业〉 sugar crop
糖萝卜 tángluóbo ❶〈口语〉 beet ❷〈方言〉 preserved carrot
糖酶 tángméi 〈生化〉 carbohydrase
糖蜜 tángmì molasses
糖尿病 tángniàobìng diabetes: ～患者 diabetic
糖槭 tángqì 〈植物〉 sugar maple (*Acer Saccharum*)
糖人 tángrén sugar doll; sugar figure
糖三角 tángsānjiǎo triangular steamed bun stuffed with sugar
糖色 tángshǎi melted brown sugar: 上～ cook meat, etc. with melted brown sugar (to make it dark brown)
糖食 tángshí sweetmeats
糖霜 tángshuāng ❶ layer of white sugar (on some food); icing; frosting ❷〈方言〉 white sugar
糖水 tángshuǐ syrup: ～菠萝 pineapples in syrup
糖酸 tángsuān 〈生化〉 glucic acid
糖蒜 tángsuàn garlic in syrup; sweetened garlic
糖稀 tángxī thin malt sugar
糖血症 tángxuèzhèng 〈医学〉 glycohemia
糖衣 tángyī sugar-coating: 小儿服用的药片多有～。Pills meant for children are mostly sugar-coated.
糖衣炮弹 tángyī pàodàn 〈比喻〉 sugar-coated bullet: 提防各种各样的～的侵袭。One should guard against assaults by sugar-coated bullets of various kinds.
糖饴 tángyí maltose; malt sugar
糖原 tángyuán 〈生化〉 glycogen: ～酶 glycogenase /～病〈医学〉 glycogenosis
糖脂 tángzhī glycolipid
糖纸 tángzhǐ printed wrapping paper for sweets; candy wraps

瑭 táng 〈书面〉 a kind of jade

塘 táng ❶ dyke; embankment: 河～ river embankment /海～ seawall ❷ pool; pond: 荷～ lotus pond /池～ pond; pool /苇～ reed pond ❸ hot-water bathing pool: 洗澡～ bathhouse; public baths ❹〈方言〉 stove chamber: 火～ stove-chamber of blazing coal

塘报 tángbào 〈历史〉 ❶ urgent military information ❷ court bulletin in the Qin Dynasty
塘肥 tángféi pond sludge used as manure
塘鳢 tánglǐ 〈动物〉 sleeper
塘泥 tángní pond sludge; pond silt
塘虱 tángshī *also* "胡子鲇" húzinián a kind of catfish
塘堰 tángyàn *also* "塘坝" small reservoir (in a hilly area)

赯 táng red complexion: 紫～脸 dark red cheeks

搪[1] táng ❶ ward off; fend off; keep out: ～寒 keep out the cold /～饥 allay one's hunger /设一道篱障给地里的菜～～风 built up a fence for vegetables in the fields to ward off the wind ❷ evade; shirk; do perfunctorily: ～事 do something perfunctorily /～账 put off a creditor

搪[2] táng spread (clay, paint, etc.) over; daub: ～炉子 line a stove with clay

搪[3] táng *also* "镗" táng boring

搪瓷 tángcí enamel: ～碗 enamel bowl /～器皿 enamelware
搪瓷钢板 tángcí gāngbǎn 〈建筑〉 enamelled pressed steel
搪缸机 tánggāngjī 〈机械〉 cylinder borer; cylinder boring machine
搪磨 tángmó 〈机械〉 honed finishing: ～机 honer /～头 hone
搪塞 tángsè stall off; do perfunctorily: 他想用几句官腔来～我。He tried to stall me with official jargon. /她纠缠不休, 我只好找话～。She pestered me endlessly, and I had to stall her off with a few vague remarks.
搪突 tángtū *see* "唐突" tángtū

螗 táng 〈古语〉 a kind of cicada

饄 táng *see* "糖" táng

堂 táng ❶ main room of a house: *see* "～屋" ❷ hall or room for a specific purpose: 音乐～ concert hall /佛～ family hall for worshipping Buddha /灵～ mourning hall /礼拜～ church /礼～ auditorium ❸〈旧语〉 court of law; principal hall in a *yamen*: 大～之上 in the court /升～ (of a magistrate, etc.) hold court; bring the accused to the court and begin the trial ❹ *used in a hall's name*: 积善～ Benevolence Hall ❺ *used in a shop's name*: 同仁～ Tongren Medicine Shop ❻ *used to indicate relationship between cousins, etc. with the same paternal grandfather or great-grandfather*: ～侄子 nephews on the paternal side; nephews /～兄妹 cousins on the paternal side; cousins ❼〈量词〉 (a) *for sets of furniture*: 一～西式家具 a set of western-styled furniture (b) *for classes in school*: 两～

课 two periods (of class) /一～数学课 a math class (c)〈旧语〉*for appearances in court*：过了两～ appear twice in court (to be tried); have been through two sessions (of a trial) (d) *for mural paintings, stage scenes, etc.*：两～内景 two indoor scenes /一～壁画 a fresco

堂奥 táng'ào 〈书面〉❶innermost recess of a house ❷ interior of a country：～之内 in the interior of a country ❸ depth of thought or knowledge; profundities; 未登～ not acquire profound knowledge / 师从名家而登～ be a student of a famous scholar and become well versed in a branch of knowledge

堂而皇之 táng'érhuángzhī ❶ open; overt; public; making no secret of sth.：他是凭着一张伪造的出入证～进来的。He swaggered in with a forged pass. ❷ in a grand style or way：讲出一套～的理论来 come out with an impressive theory

堂房 tángfáng relationship between cousins, etc. with the same paternal grandfather or great-grandfather

堂鼓 tánggǔ 〈戏曲〉a kind of drum

堂倌 tángguān *also* "堂官"〈旧语〉waiter; boy

堂号 tánghào 〈旧语〉name of a hall or of a household：三槐堂是他家的～。Three Pagoda Tree Hall is the name of his house.

堂花 tánghuā *also* "唐花" tánghuā hothouse flower

堂皇 tánghuáng ❶ grand; stately; magnificent：富丽～ magnificent palace hall ❷ highfalutin; high-sounding：～的理由 high-sounding pretext /把自己的要求掩饰得很～ gloss over one's selfish demands with highflown rhetoric

堂会 tánghuì 〈旧语〉performance by hired actors and actresses at a home gathering for celebration：唱～(of professional actors or actresses) sing at a private home celebration

堂客 tángke ❶ lady guest：此系家宴，单请～。It is a family dinner and only lady guests are invited. ❷〈方言〉woman ❸〈方言〉wife：送～回娘家 escort the wife back to her parents' home /小伙子娶了个漂亮的～。The young man married a beautiful girl.

堂上 tángshàng ❶ parents：～健在。My parents are still living and in good health. ❷〈旧语〉*used by one who is being tried to refer to magistrates or judges* ❸〈旧语〉courtroom; courthouse

堂堂 tángtáng ❶ dignified; impressive：相貌～ dignified looks ❷ having noble aspirations and boldness of vision：～中华儿女 Chinese men and women with high aspirations and bold vision /～男子汉 man worthy of the name; real man; he-man ❸ imposing; awe-inspiring; formidable：～军威 formidable prestige of an army; awe-inspiring demonstration of military strength

堂堂正正 tángtáng-zhèngzhèng ❶ open and aboveboard：为人～ upright person /我的话～，不怕人听。My remarks are open and aboveboard, so I don't care who may be listening. ❷ impressive or dignified in personal appearance：～，举止不俗 be impressive-looking and good-mannered

堂屋 tángwū ❶ central room of the main wing (of a one-storey Chinese traditional courtyard house consisting of several wings) ❷ main wing of a courtyard house

堂戏 tángxì ❶ performance at a home gathering for celebration ❷ one of the Hubei operas

堂子 tángzi ❶ site for the imperial family of the Qing Dynasty to worship God ❷〈方言〉〈旧语〉euphemistic term for brothel

棠 táng ❶〈植物〉birchleaf pear (*Pyrus betulaefolia*) ❷ (Táng) a surname

棠棣 tángdì ❶ Chinese bush cherry ❷ *also* "唐棣" tángdì a kind of white poplar ❸ *also* "常棣" chángdì 〈书面〉〈比喻〉brother

棠梨 tánglí *also* "杜梨" dùlí 〈植物〉birchleaf pear (*Pyrus betulaefolia*)

樘 táng ❶ door or window frame：门～ door frame /窗～ window frame ❷〈量词〉*used of doors or windows with their frames*：一～玻璃门 a pair of glass doors /两～双扇窗 two pairs of double-leaf windows

螳 táng mantis

螳臂当车 tángbì-dāngchē *also* "螳臂挡车" mantis trying to stop a chariot — overrate oneself and try to hold back an overwhelmingly superior force：～，自不量力 acting just like a mantis trying to stop a chariot, not taking a proper measure of oneself

螳螂 tángláng *also* "刀螂" dāolang 〈动物〉mantis

螳螂捕蝉，黄雀在后 tángláng bǔ chán, huángquè zài hòu 〈俗语〉the mantis stalks the cicada, unaware of the oriole behind — covet gains ahead without being aware of danger behind

镗 táng *also* "搪" táng 〈机械〉boring

see also tāng

镗床 tángchuáng 〈机械〉boring machine; boring lathe; borer：坐标～ jig boring machine

镗刀 tángdāo 〈机械〉boring cutter; boring tool

镗孔 tángkǒng 〈机械〉bore hole; boring

膛 táng ❶ thorax; chest：开～ cut open its chest ❷ enclosed space inside sth.; chamber：枪～ bore (of a gun) /灶～ chamber of a cooking stove /前～枪 muzzle-loader

膛式炉 tángshìlú 〈冶金〉hearth furnace

膛线 tángxiàn *also* "来复线" láifùxiàn 〈军事〉rifling

膛音 tángyīn big chest voice：他说起话来，～很大，语调铿锵有力。He speaks sonorously in a big chest voice.

膛子 tángzi 〈方言〉stove chamber

饧（餳） táng 〈书面〉*see* "糖" táng

see also xíng

tǎng

淌 tǎng drip; trickle; shed：脸上汗珠直往下～。Sweat was dripping from his face. /嘴里～着血。Blood trickled down from the mouth. /水龙头坏了，～得满屋是水。The tap broke, so water ran all over the house. /小河～水。The river is brimming over. /溪水日夜流～。The brook is flowing day and night.

惝 tǎng *also* chǎng

惝恍 tǎnghuǎng *also* chǎnghuǎng ❶ disappointed; unhappy ❷ blurry-eyed; unclear

倘（儻） tǎng if; supposing; in case：～有难处，请及时相告。If you have any difficulty, please don't hesitate to let me know.

see also cháng

倘或 tǎnghuò if; in case; supposing：他～有个三长两短，我可担待不起。If anything untoward should happen to him, I won't be able to shoulder the responsibility.

倘来之物 tǎngláizhīwù unexpected or undeserved gain; windfall：～不可求。One should not seek any undeserved gain.

倘然 tǎngrán *see* "倘若"

倘若 tǎngruò if; supposing; in case：～有误，请予指正。Please point out any possible mistakes so that they can be corrected. /～客人不来怎么办？What shall we do if the guests fail to turn up?

倘使 tǎngshǐ if; supposing; in case：～你这次不去，以后恐怕就没有机会了。I am afraid there won't be another chance if you don't go this time.

躺 tǎng lie; recline; rest：一根扁担横～在地上。A carrying pole lies across on the ground. /他靠着墙根，斜～在地上。He reclined on the ground against the corner of the wall. /父亲在医院里整整～了三个月。Father was confined to the hospital for three whole months.

躺倒 tǎngdǎo lie down：他感到头晕，不由自主地～在地上。He felt dizzy and couldn't help falling onto the ground.

躺倒不干 tǎngdǎo-bùgàn stay in bed and refuse to do anything more — refuse to shoulder responsibilities any longer

躺柜 tǎngguì long low box with a lid on top; chest

躺尸 tǎngshī 〈粗话〉lie stiff in bed, like a corpse：成天～，真是个懒骨头。You lie stiff in bed just like a corpse all day. What a lazybones!

躺椅 tǎngyǐ deck chair; sling chair

镋（钂） tǎng ancient military weapon with a long handle, resembling a fork

傥(儻) tǎng ❶ *see* "倘" tǎng ❷ *see* "倜傥" tìtǎng

傥荡 tǎngdàng 〈书面〉dissolute; dissipated; unconventional:～不拘 unconventional and unrestrained; untrammelled

帑 tǎng 〈书面〉funds in the state treasury:公～ public funds / 国～ state treasury funds

帑藏 tǎngzàng 〈书面〉state treasury

tàng

烫(燙) tàng ❶ scald; burn:他的脚被开水～伤了。His foot was scalded by boiling water. /他嘴上～了个泡。His mouth got a blister through being scalded (*or* burnt). ❷ iron; heat up in hot water; warm:～衣服 iron (*or* press) clothes /请把黄酒～一～。Please heat the rice-wine. /他每晚睡前都～～脚。He bathed his feet in hot water every day before going to bed. ❸ very hot; scalding; steaming hot:这杯茶真～! The tea is boiling hot! /水太～,过会儿再喝。The water is steaming hot. You'd better drink it later. ❹ perm; have one's hair permed:她的头发～得很漂亮。She had a darling perm.

烫发 tàngfà give or have a permanent wave; perm

烫花 tànghuā *also* "烙花" làohuā 〈工美〉branded flowers

烫金 tàngjīn 〈印刷〉gilding; bronzing:布面～ cloth gilt /～封面 gilt cover /～套色 gilding colour process

烫金机 tàngjīnjī 〈印刷〉gilding press; bronzing machine

烫蜡 tànglà polish with melted wax; wax (a floor, etc.):～地板 waxed floor /～打光 waxing and polishing

烫面 tàngmiàn dough made with boiling water:～饺 dumplings made of dough prepared with boiling water

烫伤 tàngshāng scald:～舌头 scald one's tongue

烫手 tàngshǒu thorny; troublesome; knotty:他感到这个问题有些～。He felt that this was a sticky business.

烫头 tàngtóu give or have a permanent wave; perm

烫印机 tàngyìnjī 〈印刷〉thermoprinting machine

趟 tàng ❶〈量词〉*used of a trip, etc., or a vehicle that makes a trip*:他打算到西安去一～。He plans to make a trip to Xi'an. /昨晚上我找了你三～。Yesterday evening I went three times to look for you. /今日还有一～从上海来的车。There is another train from Shanghai. ❷ (marching) ranks:差一点儿跟不上～ almost lag behind ❸〈方言〉〈量词〉*used of sth. that stands or is arranged in a row*:两～桌子 two rows of tables /一～栏杆 a railing /几～大字 several rows of big characters
see also tāng

趟马 tàngmǎ 〈戏曲〉series of stylized movements imitating the riding of a horse in Beijing opera

tāo

涛(濤) tāo great waves; billows:江～滚滚 rolling waves of the river /波～汹涌 surging waves /林～ soughing of the wind through a forest

掏(搯) tāo ❶ take out; draw out; pull out; fish out:从口袋里～出钥匙 take keys out of one's pocket /～鸟窝 take young birds (*or* eggs) out of a nest; go bird's-nesting /～耳朵 pick one's ears /～兜的小偷 pickpocket; pilferer /他的钱包儿被～了。His wallet was stolen. /这场戏是他～的钱。He treated us to the theatre. ❷ dig (a hole, etc.); hollow out; scoop out:在山坡上～一个洞 make a hole in the slope /～防空洞 dig air-raid shelter

掏槽 tāocáo 〈矿业〉cutting

掏底 tāodǐ try to find out the bottom line; sound sb. out:他想方设法掏我的底。He tried every means to find out my real intentions.

掏坏 tāohuài 〈方言〉be up to mischief; play a dirty trick:不和他～ not do the dirty on him /对于张大哥,只准帮忙,不准掏一点坏。You are only allowed to help Brother Zhang and not to play tricks on him.

掏灰 tāohuī 〈方言〉dig coal:～的小工 unskilled coal-digger /他是～工人。He is a coal miner.

掏窟窿 tāo kūlong 〈方言〉run or get into debt:月头乱花钱,月底～ spend money like water at the beginning of each month and run into debt at the end /他折腾了半天,还得～。He got into debt despite his great effort to make ends meet.

掏摸 tāomō ❶ draw out; pull out; take out:从炕洞里～出一根火筷子 fish out a poker from the flue of the *kang* ❷ steal:夜间出来～东西 come out to steal during the night

掏心 tāoxīn confide one's secrets (to another); open one's heart (to sb.):说句～的话,你真不该那样对他。To be quite frank, you should not have treated him like that.

掏腰包 tāo yāobāo ❶ pay out of one's own pocket; foot a bill:～请客 invite guests to dinner out of one's own pocket /这顿饭我～。This meal is on me. ❷ pick sb.'s pocket:当场抓住一个～的。A pickpocket was caught red-handed. /真倒霉,碰上了～的。What bad luck! My pocket was picked.

滔 tāo inundate; flood:白浪～天 whitecaps running high

滔滔 tāotāo ❶ torrential; surging:～巨浪 torrential huge waves /～洪水 surging flood ❷ keeping up a constant flow of words:此人～善辩。The guy can talk on and on in a flow of eloquence.

滔滔不绝 tāotāo-bùjué words tumble out in a flood; pour out words in a steady flow:他～,有声有色地讲述自己的经历。He talked on and on graphically describing his own experience.

滔天 tāotiān ❶ (of billows, etc.) dash to the skies:～巨浪 huge waves running high /小船被～大浪冲走了。The small boat was washed away by surging waves. ❷ heinous; monstrous:～之罪 monstrous crime /此人罪恶～,民愤极大。The person has committed towering crimes and earned the bitter hatred of the people.

滔天大罪 tāotiān-dàzuì heinous crime; monstrous crime; towering crime

韬(韜、弢) tāo 〈书面〉❶ sheath; bow case ❷ hide; conceal:～迹 lie low; hide one's light ❸ art of war:六～ six strategies

韬笔 tāobǐ 〈书面〉stop writing:钳口～ hold one's tongue and write nothing /独步文坛,群才～ be so outstanding in literary circles that other men of letters bemoan their inadequacy in writing

韬光养晦 tāoguāng-yǎnghuì hide one's capacities and bide one's time:～,静而待变 hide one's capacities and await a favourable turn of events (*or* bide one's time)

韬晦 tāohuì 〈书面〉conceal one's true features or intentions; lie low:～之计 ruse of concealing one's true features /～于乱世 lie low in turbulent times

韬略 tāolüè military strategy:～过人 excel in military strategy /颇有～的军事家 good military strategist

韬声匿迹 tāoshēng-nìjì hide one's light and live in seclusion:～于乱世 hide one's light and live in retreat in turbulent times /～,以求自安 seek ease of mind by hiding one's light and leading a secluded life

绦(縧、絛、縚) tāo silk ribbon; silk braid

绦虫 tāochóng 〈动物〉taenia; tapeworm:～类 cestode /杀～药 taeniacide

绦虫病 tāochóngbìng 〈医学〉taeniasis; cestodiasis; tapeworm disease:牛肉～ taenia saginata /猪肉～ taenia solium

绦子 tāozi silk ribbon; silk braid

饕 tāo 〈书面〉greedy; gluttonous:老～ glutton; gourmand

饕戾 tāolì 〈书面〉greedily fierce and perverse:为人～ be greedily fierce and perverse

饕餮 tāotiè ❶ *taotie*, a mythical ferocious animal ❷ ferocious and cruel person:～之人 fierce and gluttonous person /～贪昧 fierce and greedy ❸ voracious eater; glutton; gourmand

饕餮纹 tāotièwén 〈考古〉*taotie* design

叨 tāo be favoured with; get the benefit of; receive:谬～重任。I have been entrusted with the heavy responsibility.
see also dāo; dáo

叨光 tāoguāng 〈套语〉much obliged to you:又来府上～,多有打扰。I'm much obliged to you for letting me come and inconvenience you

again. /客居期间,时来～,特表感谢。I am much obliged to you for your kindness to receive my frequent calls during my stay here.

叨教 tāojiào 〈套语〉many thanks for your advice:～多日,受惠不浅。Thank you very much. I have benefited a great deal from you during my stay here.

叨陪 tāopéi 〈套语〉accompany; keep sb. company:～末座 feel flattered to keep you company

叨窃 tāoqiè 〈书面〉〈谦词〉be incompetent for a post:～重任 be entrusted with an important task beyond one's ability /～非据 incompetently hold a post

叨扰 tāorǎo 〈套语〉thank you for your hospitality:多有～,不胜感激。Thank you very much for your hospitality. /承蒙接待,又要～数日了。I am very grateful to you for your kind reception. I am afraid I have to bother you again for a few days.

叨沓 tāotà 〈书面〉be greedy and lax (in government, etc.):～获罪 be punished for avaricе and dereliction of duty

叨越 tāoyuè 〈书面〉improperly take sth. as one's own:妄求～covet improperly /～无厌 inordinate desire for sth.

táo

梼(檮) táo

梼昧 táomèi 〈书面〉〈谦词〉ignorant; benighted:自惭～ think oneself ignorant (*or* benighted)

梼杌 táowù legendary fierce beast with a man's face, tiger's paws and boar's tusks, which never runs away from fighting; fierce, vicious person

洮 Táo Taohe River in Gansu Province

洮汰 táotài cleanse; wash away

洮砚 táoyàn precious inkstone (made of stones from the Taohe River)

逃(迯) táo ❶ run away; escape; flee; take to one's heels:溃～ escape in disorder; flee helter-skelter /临阵脱～ run away on the eve of a battle /动物园里～出去一只猴子。A monkey escaped from the zoo. ❷ evade; dodge; shirk; escape:难～法网 be unable to escape from the punishment of law /那个走私者没有～过海关的检查。The smuggler could not evade the customs inspection.

逃奔 táobèn run away (to another place); flee:～他乡 run away to an alien land /一路～ flee all the way /败军连夜向南～。The defeated army scurried south the very night.

逃避 táobì escape; evade; shun; shirk:～责任 shirk responsibility /～现实是懦弱的表现。To shun reality is a sign of cowardice. /他想～,可是追捕的人已经卡住他的去路。He wanted to escape but the pursuers had blocked his way out.

逃兵 táobīng ❶ army deserter; deserter:抓～ catch army deserters ❷ sb. who flinches from difficulty:在工作中不能当～。One should not shrink from difficulty in one's work. /困难再大我们也决不当～。We should not flinch no matter how great the difficulty is.

逃窜 táocuàn run away in panic; flee in disorder:狼狈～ flee helter-skelter /四处～ scurry in all directions

逃遁 táodùn flee; escape; run away:～远方 escape to a distant place /双方在城里交火,老百姓纷纷向四面八方～。The belligerent sides exchanged fire in the city, causing the people to flee in all directions.

逃反 táofǎn flee turmoil or scourge of war:因～而流落在外 wander destitute far from home to avoid the scourge of war

逃犯 táofàn escaped criminal or convict:捕获～ catch escaped criminals /通缉～ order the arrest of a criminal at large

逃荒 táohuāng flee from famine; get away from a famine-stricken area:～要饭 flee from famine and go begging

逃汇 táohuì evade foreign exchange control; keep foreign exchange illegally

逃婚 táohūn run away from an arranged marriage:～在外 flee home to avoid an undesirable marriage

逃课 táokè play truant; cut class:分析学生～的原因 analyze why the students do not attend classes

逃命 táomìng run or flee for one's life:在～时,他把随身衣物都丢光了。While fleeing for his life, he lost all his personal belongings.

逃难 táonàn flee from a calamity; be a refugee:南京沦陷前,这一家～出来,到贵阳已经精疲力竭了。The family fled from Nanjing before it fell into the hands of the Japanese aggressors, and were completely worn out when they arrived at Guiyang.

逃匿 táonì escape and hide; go into hiding:武警在山区搜剿～的土匪。The armed police were tracking down the hidden bandits in this hilly region.

逃跑 táopǎo run away; flee; take flight; take to one's heels:临阵～ desert on the eve of a battle; sneak away at a critical juncture /这个小长工是忍无可忍才～出来的。The young farm labourer ran away when he found life there almost unbearable.

逃跑主义 táopǎozhǔyì flightism (advocacy, practice or habit of running away from the battlefield or from difficulties)

逃票 táopiào not buy a ticket when riding in a bus or travelling by train, boat, etc.; get a free-ride

逃散 táosàn become separated in flight:寻找～的弟妹 look for one's brother and sister separated in flight

逃生 táoshēng flee or run for one's life; escape with one's life:死里～ barely escape with one's life; have a narrow escape; have a close shave (*or* call) /虎口～ have a hair's breath escape; escape by the skin of one's teeth

逃世 táoshì live the life of a recluse; retire from the world

逃税 táoshuì evade or dodge a tax:～漏税 tax evasion

逃死 táosǐ flee a fatal disaster; flee for life

逃脱 táotuō ❶ succeed in escaping; make good one's escape; get clear of:半路～ make one's escape on the way /侥幸从虎口～ have a narrow escape by sheer luck ❷ shake off; free oneself from; cast off:～罪责 shake off one's responsibility for an offence /～不了法律的惩罚 cannot possibly elude the punishment of law

逃亡 táowáng become a fugitive; flee from home; go into exile:抗战期间,他一家～到了南洋。During the Anti-Japanese War, his family fled to southeast Asia.

逃席 táoxí quit or duck out of a banquet unnoticed (for fear of getting drunk); take French leave:～而归 return before the banquet is over /～而去 take French leave in the middle of a banquet

逃学 táoxué play truant; cut class:无故～ play truant for no reason /他是个调皮的爱～的小学生。He is a naughty truant pupil.

逃逸 táoyì 〈书面〉escape; flee; abscond:对这伙凶残的罪犯,务必一网打尽,不使一人～。These ruthless criminals must be rounded up at one fell swoop without letting a single one escape.

逃逸速度 táoyì sùdù 〈航天〉escape velocity

逃债 táozhài evade debts; dodge a creditor

逃之夭夭 táozhīyāoyāo decamp; slip away; take to one's heels; show a clean pair of heels:深夜,他们两人～,不知去向。They slipped away in the dead of night and were heard of no more.

逃走 táozǒu run away; flee; escape; take to one's heels:～了事 wind up by running away /这家公司的一个会计卷巨款～了。An accountant of this company absconded with an enormous sum.

逃罪 táozuì escape from the law:无所～ can hardly escape from the punishment of the law

鼗(鞉、鞀) táo 〈书面〉drum-shaped rattle; rattle drum

桃 táo ❶ peach:投～报李 give a plum in return for a peach — return gift for gift ❷ peach-shaped thing:棉～ cotton boll ❸ walnut:～酥 walnut shortbread

桃符 táofú ❶ peachwood charms against evil (hung on the gate on the lunar New Year's Eve in former times) ❷ Spring Festival couplets

桃脯 táofǔ preserved peach

桃红 táohóng pink:～衬衫 pink blouse

桃红柳绿 táohóng-liǔlǜ pink peaches and green willows — beautiful spring scenery of green trees and colourful flowers:～,春色宜人 attractive spring colours

桃花 táohuā peach blossom

桃花粉 táohuāfěn rouge

桃花米 táohuāmǐ inferior rice

桃花扇 Táohuāshàn *Peach Blossom Fan*, a play written by Kong Shangren (孔尚任,1648-1718) of the Qing Dynasty

桃花心木 táohuāxīnmù mahogany

桃花雪 táohuāxuě snow when the peaches blossom; spring snow

桃花汛 táohuāxùn *also*"桃汛";"春汛" chūnxùn spring flood

桃花鱼 táohuāyú minnow
桃花源 Táohuāyuán *also*“桃源” Arcadia; Shangri-la; haven of peace and simple living
桃花运 táohuāyùn ❶ (used of men) luck in love; romance:眼下他走了～,几个姑娘都爱上了他。He is being lucky in love at the moment as several girls have taken a fancy to him. ❷ luck (in general):短篇小说交了～。Short stories are all the rage now.
桃胶 táojiāo peach gum
桃李 táolǐ peaches and plums; one's pupils or disciples:～盈门 one's house is crowded with pupils — have numerous pupils (*or* disciples)
桃李不言,下自成蹊 táolǐ bù yán, xià zì chéng xī the peach and the plum do not speak, yet a path is worn beneath them — a man of true worth attracts admiration:王先生忠厚少言,但～,其道德、学问名垂一时,为世人所景仰。Mr. Wang is a man of honesty and few words, yet he has won the admiration of all and sundry for his integrity and erudition.
桃李满天下 táolǐ mǎn tiānxià have pupils everywhere:这个四十年前的青年人,如今已是满头银丝,～。A young man forty years ago, he is now hoary-headed with pupils in all parts of the country.
桃仁 táorén ❶〈中药〉peach kernel ❷ walnut meat; shelled walnut
桃腮杏眼 táosāi-xìngyǎn peach-like cheeks and almond-shaped eyes — beauty of a woman
桃色 táosè ❶ peach colour ❷ *pertaining to an illicit affair*:～新闻 newspaper reports of illicit love stories /～事件 romance incident; affair /～纠纷 romance dispute
桃树 táoshù peach (tree)
桃汛 táoxùn *see*“桃花汛”
桃子 táozi peach

咷

táo scream; yell:号～ cry bitter tears; cry loud with abandon

桃

táo

桃黍 táoshǔ 〈方言〉Chinese sorghum

匋

táo *see*“陶”táo

淘[1](❷掏)

táo ❶ wash in a pan or basket:沙里～金 pan out gold; panning ❷〈方言〉seek or buy sth. in a second-hand shop or a flea market:～旧书 buy used books ❸ clean out; dredge:～粪池 remove night soil from a manure pit /把缸里的脏东西～出来 dredge the dirt from the vat

淘[2]

táo ❶ tax (a person's energy):～费精力 tax one's energy ❷〈方言〉naughty; mischievous:这孩子～得要命。The child is extremely mischievous.
淘河 táohé *also*“鹈鹕”tíhú;“塘鹅”táng'é〈动物〉pelican
淘换 táohuan look for; try to get:这件皮大衣是我好不容易～来的。I acquired this fur coat after much effort. /你从哪～来这些希罕物件? Where did you lay hands on these rarities?
淘金 táojīn 〈矿业〉wash (for gold):～热 gold rush
淘矿机 táokuàngjī 〈矿业〉vanner; vanning machine
淘箩 táoluó basket for washing rice in
淘米 táomǐ wash rice in a pan or basket
淘气 táoqì ❶ naughty; mischievous:～鬼 mischievous imp; regular little mischief /～包 mischievous imp (*or* elf) /～的孩子 naughty child ❷〈方言〉lose one's temper (over a trifle):不值得为这件小事～。It is not worth getting angry at such a trivial matter. /何必～自寻烦恼? Why should you fret over trifles?
淘神 táoshén 〈口语〉trying; bothersome:这件事太让人～了。The matter is extremely bothersome. /天天有这些～的事儿。No day is free from such nuisances.
淘汰 táotài eliminate through selection or competition:他们在前几轮比赛中～过一些强队。They eliminated some strong teams in the first few rounds. /当年的许多文章让时间给～了。Many essays of those days have become out of date with the passage of time.
淘汰赛 táotàisài elimination series; elimination match
淘析 táoxī *also*“淘洗”〈矿业〉elutriation:～器 elutriator
淘选 táoxuǎn 〈矿业〉panning; elutriation;〈化学〉levigation:～铲 van

萄

táo grapes:～酒 grape wine /～糖 grape sugar

酶

táo *see*“酕酶”máotáo

啕

táo cry loudly; wail:嚎～大哭 wail loudly; cry one's eyes out

陶[1]

táo ❶ pottery; earthenware:彩～ coloured (*or* painted) pottery /黑～ black pottery ❷ make pottery ❸ cultivate; mould; nurture; educate:熏～ exert a gradual uplifting influence on; nurture ❹ (Táo) a surname

陶[2]

táo contented; happy:以浊酒自～ be content with bad liquor /～情适性 please oneself and be happy
陶车 táochē moulding device in the process of making chinaware
陶瓷 táocí pottery and porcelain; ceramics:～工 potter /～业 ceramics; ceramic industry /～器皿 porcelain ware
陶瓷片 táocípiàn 〈考古〉potsherd
陶瓷学 táocíxué ceramics
陶管 táoguǎn 〈建筑〉earthenware pipe
陶弘景 Táo Hóngjǐng Tao Hongjing (456-536), Taoist thinker and medical scientist of the Southern Dynasties
陶匠 táojiàng potter
陶钧 táojūn 〈书面〉❶ potter's wheel ❷ mould character as a potter moulds clay:～之力 efforts to cultivate people's mind /师承多年,一任～ have been sb.'s pupil for years and follow his every instruction
陶粒 táolì 〈建筑〉ceramsite:～混凝土 ceramsite concrete
陶轮 táolún potter's wheel
陶坯 táopī greenware
陶器 táoqì pottery; earthenware
陶犬瓦鸡 táoquǎn-wǎjī valueless object; rubbish; trash:～,何惜之有? Why do you feel pity for such trash? /～,何用之有? What's the use of this rubbish?
陶然 táorán happy and carefree:～自乐 be happy and content with one's lot /～亭 Pavilion of Happiness and Ease (in Beijing)
陶式反坦克导弹 táoshì fǎntǎnkè dǎodàn 〈军事〉TOW (tube-launched optically-tracked wire-guided anti-tank missile)
陶塑 táosù pottery figure; pottery statue
陶陶 táotáo happy; drunk:山水之乐,其乐～ extremely delighted at the beauty of mountains and rivers
陶土 táotǔ 〈矿业〉potter's clay; pottery clay; kaolin
陶文 táowén 〈考古〉inscription on pottery
陶冶 táoyě ❶ make pottery and smelt metal ❷ exert a favourable influence (on a person's character, etc.); mould:～情操 refine a person's sentiment /感谢恩师多年～之功 be grateful to one's teacher for his benign influence over the years
陶俑 táoyǒng pottery figurine; terracotta figurine
陶渊明 Táo Yuānmíng Tao Yuanming (c. 376-427), poet of the Eastern Jin Dynasty
陶铸 táozhù 〈书面〉❶ (of potters and blacksmiths) mould and form (utensils) ❷educate and train (talents):～贤才 train talented persons /～后学 educate young people
陶醉 táozuì be intoxicated (with success, etc.); revel in:～在湖光山色之中 be intoxicated with the landscape of lakes and mountains /～在春光美景之中 revel in the beauty of spring

绹

táo ❶〈书面〉rope ❷〈方言〉bind with rope

tǎo

讨

tǎo ❶ send armed forces to suppress; send a punitive expedition; fight:南征北～ fight north and south /征～ go on a punitive expedition /举兵～逆 send an armed force against the traitors ❷ denounce; decry; condemn:声～ denounce ❸ demand; ask for; beg for:～房租 demand the payment of rent ❹ marry (a woman):～老婆 take a wife; get married ❺ incur; court; invite:自～没趣儿 court a rebuff for oneself ❻ discuss; discourse; study:研～

T

deliberate; study and discuss /探～ inquire into; probe into; approach (a subject)

讨保 tǎobǎo look for bail; get bail:～出狱 be out on bail

讨吃 tǎochī beg for food; be a beggar

讨底 tǎodǐ sound sb. out; find out the bottom line; find out sb.'s true intentions:你到城里跟他讨个底。You'd better go to the town and sound him out.

讨伐 tǎofá send armed forces to suppress; send a punitive expedition against:～叛逆 send armed forces to put down a rebellion /亲自～ personally command troops on a punitive expedition

讨饭 tǎofàn beg for food; be a beggar:四处～ go begging from place to place /背井离乡,～为生 leave one's native place and live by begging

讨好 tǎohǎo ❶ try to please; ingratiate oneself with; fawn on; curry favour with:～上司 try to please one's superior; curry favour with one's boss /～巴结人 fawn on others /～卖乖 show off one's cleverness and ingratiate oneself ❷ (often used in the negative) be rewarded with a fruitful result; have one's labour rewarded:吃力不～的事 thankless, laborious job /反正怎么做也讨不了他的好。Whatever you do would find no favour in his eyes.

讨还 tǎohuán demand the return of sth.; get sth. back:～欠债 get one's debt repaid

讨还血债 tǎohuán-xuèzhài make sb. pay a blood debt

讨价 tǎojià ask or demand a price:漫天～ ask (*or* demand) an exorbitant price /～太高 ask too high a price

讨价还价 tǎojià-huánjià bargain; haggle:在集市上买东西,就是要～。You have to bargain at a bazaar. /经过激烈的～,双方终于达成妥协。Both sides finally came to a compromise after heated bargaining. /对分配给她的工作任务,她从来不～。She never haggles over the work assigned to her.

讨贱 tǎojiàn 〈方言〉not appreciate a favour and ask for trouble

讨教 tǎojiào ask for advice; consult:向专家～ turn to an expert for advice

讨究 tǎojiū further observe and study; investigate:工作中还有许多值得～的问题。There are still many problems in our work that require further study. *or* There is still much room for improvement in our work.

讨口 tǎokǒu 〈方言〉go begging; be a beggar

讨脸 tǎoliǎn ingratiate oneself with; fawn on; toady to; curry favour with

讨论 tǎolùn discuss; talk over:～问题 discuss an issue /～要点 key points for discussion /～得很激烈 have a heated discussion /现在我们可以结束～了。We can now bring the discussion to a close.

讨论会 tǎolùnhuì discussion; symposium:学术～ academic discussion; scientific conference; symposium /最近学校要召开本学期的科学～。The school is going to hold this semester's academic symposium.

讨米 tǎomǐ 〈方言〉beg for food; be a beggar:穷得沿街～ be destitute and have to beg from door to door

讨便宜 tǎo piányi seek undue advantage; try to gain on the cheap; look for a bargain:想方设法～ try every possible means to gain sth. at the expense of others /人家也不是傻瓜,你休想去～。Nobody is a fool. Don't try to seek undue advantages.

讨平 tǎopíng send armed forces to suppress:～叛乱 send armed forces to quell (*or* quash) a rebellion /～叛匪 send armed forces to suppress the rebels

讨乞 tǎoqǐ beg alms; beg:流落异乡,～多年 wander destitute far from home and beg for years

讨气 tǎoqì get angry; court or look for trouble:讨了一肚子气 get extremely angry

讨巧 tǎoqiǎo act artfully to get what one wants; get the best for oneself at the least expense; achieve success by a short cut; choose the easy way out:练基本功必须扎扎实实,不可～。You must work solidly at basic exercises. There's no short cut. /哪有那么多～的事儿? Where can you find so much luck?

讨俏 tǎoqiào give a sense of wit:她的表演幽默、轻松,善于～。Her performance is humorous, lively, and often leaves the audience with a sense of wit.

讨亲 tǎoqīn 〈方言〉take a wife; get married:～的人马吹吹打打进了村口。The people accompanying the bridegroom have entered the village piping and drumming.

讨情 tǎoqíng 〈方言〉plead or intercede for sb.; beg for a favour or for pardon:上门～ come to plead for sb. (*or* oneself) /代人～ intercede for sb.; beg (for mercy) on sb.'s behalf

讨饶 tǎoráo beg for mercy; ask for forgiveness:一再～ ask again and again for forgiveness /这个孩子从不认输,也从不向人～。The child never admits defeat, nor does he beg for mercy.

讨扰 tǎorǎo 〈套语〉thank you very much for your hospitality:多有～,感激不尽。I can never thank you enough for your hospitality.

讨人嫌 tǎorénxián *see* "讨嫌"

讨生活 tǎo shēnghuó make a living; muddle along; drift along:在码头～,混口饭吃 eke out a living working at the wharf /这年头～不易。It's not easy to make a living nowadays.

讨嫌 tǎoxián *also* "讨人嫌" be a nuisance; be disagreeable or annoying:你少干这种～的事情。Stop being such a nuisance. /那孩子好搞恶作剧,真～。The child is always up to some mischief. What a bother!

讨厌 tǎoyàn ❶ disagreeable; disgusting; repugnant:他说话啰里啰嗦的,真～! He is far too long-winded. It's very annoying! ❷ hard to handle; difficult; troublesome; nasty:处理车祸是一件～的差事。Handling car accidents is a nasty job. /这项工程很～,进展太不顺利了。The project is rather troublesome and makes little headway. ❸ dislike; loathe; be disgusted with:我十分～他那种虚假的作风。I simply detest his pretentious manner. /他～春天的风沙。He hates the windy and dusty weather in spring.

讨袁运动 Tǎo Yuán Yùndòng *also* "护国运动" Hùguó Yùndòng expedition against warlord Yuan Shikai (1915-1916, after the latter declared himself emperor)

讨债 tǎozhài demand payment of a debt; ask for payment of debt

讨债鬼 tǎozhàiguǐ ❶ child who dies young ❷ person who squanders the money of his family; prodigal; spendthrift

讨账 tǎozhàng ❶ ask for payment of debt ❷ 〈方言〉claim payment due (for some purchase or service)

韬 tǎo

韬黍 tǎoshǔ 〈方言〉Chinese sorghum

tào

套 tào

❶ sheath; case; cover; slipcover:书～ slipcover for a book /剑～ sword's sheath /手～ glove /外～ overcoat ❷ cover with; slip over or on; encase in:～上一件蓝上衣 slip on a blue coat /给计算机～上罩子 put a cover over the computer ❸ that which covers (garments, shoes, etc.): *see* "～袖"; "～鞋" ❹ overlap; interlock; interlink:工序一环～一环 be closely linked in the working procedure ❺ (usu. used in place names) bend of a river; curve in a mountain range:河～ Great Bend of the Yellow River ❻ 〈方言〉cotton padding or wadding; batting:被～ cotton padding of a quilt; quilt padding /棉花～ cotton wadding /丝绵～ silk wadding ❼ 〈方言〉put cotton, silk wadding, etc. into bedclothes and sew up ❽ traces; harness:牲口～ harness for a draught animal /大车～ cart harness ❾ harness (an animal); hitch up (an animal to a cart):让我来～这匹马。Let me harness (*or* hitch up) this horse. ❿ illegally purchase (state-controlled commodities): *see* "～汇" ⓫ knot; loop; noose:活～儿 slip knot; running knot /双～结 double knot /用绳子做个～儿 make a loop with string ⓬ model on or after; copy; imitate:～着人家的调子写 model after another's tune in writing /这些办法不能在我们这里硬～。These measures cannot be copied (*or* applied) here mechanically. ⓭ convention; formula; stereotype:虚～ mere formalities /俗～ conventionalities; stereotype /老一～管理办法 old formula of management; conventional management ⓮ coax a secret out of sb.; pump sb. about sth.; sound out:她把小李的秘密～出来了。She has pumped the secret out of Xiao Li. /你是想～我的话。You are trying to trick me into telling you the secret. ⓯ try to win (sb.'s friendship); draw over to one's side:这个采购员正在想方设法与工厂～关系。The purchasing agent is trying his best to get in well with the factory. ⓰ set; suit; suite:成～设备 complete set of equipment; complete plant ⓱ 〈量词〉*used of series or sets of things*:一～餐具 a dinner set /一～两居室的住房 a two-room flat /新出版的一～儿童读物 a set of newly published children's books /他买了一～家具。He bought a suite of furniture. ⓲ use the tap or screw die to cut a thread

套版 tàobǎn 〈印刷〉❶ register ❷ process plate; colour plate

套包 tàobāo *also*"套包子" collar for a horse
套裁 tàocái cut (usu. two or more dresses) out of a piece of cloth in a way to make optimum use of the material
套菜 tàocài semi-finished dish:出售～ sell semi-finished dishes /～专柜 counter for semi-finished dishes
套餐 tàocān table d'hôte; set meal:吃～ eat table d'hôte
套层蒸馏器 tàocéng zhēngliúqì 〈化工〉 jacketed still
套车 tàochē harness an animal to a cart:车把式套好了车。The cart-driver harnessed the animal to the cart. /明天大伙儿～上路。Tomorrow we'll get ready with our carts and start off.
套垫 tàodiàn upholstery
套阀 tàofá 〈机械〉 sleeving valve
套房 tàofáng ❶ small room opening off another; inner room ❷ suite; apartment; flat:高级旅馆～ stately hotel suite /总统～ presidential suite
套服 tàofú *also*"套装" suit (in which the jacket and trousers — or skirt — are of the same colour, cloth, weave, etc.): 西装～ western-style suit /毛料～ suit of woollen cloth
套耕 tàogēng make deep furrows in the soil with two ploughs, one following the other
套购 tàogòu fraudulently purchase (state-controlled commodities); illegally buy up:～外汇 illegally purchase foreign exchange
套管 tàoguǎn jacket tube; casing pipe; sleeve; bush:绝缘～ insulating bush /～接头 sleeve tube connector; sleeve joint /～天线 sleeve antenna /～式电容器 bushing type condenser /～测井 casing log /～程序 casing programme /～头储罐 casinghead tank
套红 tàohóng (of newspaper) print part of a page with red ink, such as masthead or title:报头～ newspaper masthead printed in red
套话 tàohuà ❶ polite, conventional verbal exchanges; conventionalities ❷ empty talk; empty formula:大会发言要开门见山,把～、空话去掉。At any meeting, one should come straight to the point, getting rid of all empty formulae and verbiage.
套环 tàohuán 〈机械〉 lantern ring
套换 tàohuàn get sth. illegally: ～外汇 get foreign currency through illegal channels
套汇 tàohuì ❶ illegal procurement of foreign exchange: ～汇率 cross rate of exchange ❷ engage in arbitrage (of foreign exchange); arbitrage: ～商 arbitrageur /～账户 arbitrage account
套枷 tàojiā ox yoke
套间 tàojiān ❶ apartment; flat ❷ room opening off another; inner room
套交情 tào jiāoqing try to be in good with:一见面,先～ try to establish friendship from the start
套近乎 tào jìnhu *also*"拉近乎" lā jìnhu try to form ties with; cotton up to:咱们公事公办,～也没用! Business is business. It's no use trying to cotton up to me!
套裤 tàokù trouser legs worn over one's trousers; leggings
套犁 tàolí *see*"套耕"
套礼 tàolǐ ❶ conventional courtesies ❷ 〈旧语〉 set of gifts presented at social gatherings: 备好～ get ready the set of gifts for guests
套利 tàolì 〈金融〉 arbitrage:股票～ arbitrage of stocks
套利基金 tàolì jījīn *also*"对冲基金" duìchōng jījīn 〈金融〉 hedge fund
套耧 tàolóu till between rows for close planting
套路 tàolù established series of movement in martial arts or *wushu*
套马 tàomǎ ❶ harness a horse to a cart ❷ lasso a horse
套马杆 tàomǎgān *also*"套马杆子" lasso pole
套曲 tàoqǔ 〈音乐〉 divertimento: ～形式 cyclical (*or* cycle) form
套取 tàoqǔ obtain through illegal transactions:法律禁止所有～外汇的活动。All foreign currency transactions through illegal channels are banned by law.
套裙 tàoqún suit of clothes for women (including a skirt); woman's suit
套色 tàosè 〈印刷〉 chromatography; colour process
套色版 tàosèbǎn process plate; colourplate
套色木刻 tàosè mùkè coloured woodcut
套衫 tàoshān *also*"套头衫" pullover:男～ man's pullover /羊毛～ woollen sweater
套绳 tàoshéng ❶ harness ❷ lasso; noose
套数 tàoshù ❶ cycle of songs in traditional opera ❷ series of skills and tricks as in *wushu* ❸ conventional remark; stereotyped statement; conventionality
套索 tàosuǒ lasso; noose
套套 tàotao 〈方言〉 method; approach:老～ same old stuff; hackneyed stuff /年年有新～。There are new approaches each year.
套筒 tàotǒng ❶ a kind of old-fashioned rifle ❷ 〈机械〉 bush; sleeve; muff; thimble; jacket:汽缸～ cylinder sleeve; cylinder bush; cylinder jacket /～扳手 box spanner (*or* wrench); socket wrench; sleeve-pipe wrench /～活塞泵 sleeve pump /～联轴节 muff coupling; sleeve coupling
套头基金 tàotóu jījīn *see*"套利基金"
套头交易 tàotóu jiāoyì 〈金融〉 hedging
套问 tàowèn find out by asking seemingly casual questions; tactfully sound sb. out:经不住对方几句～,他就讲了实话。A few seemingly casual questions drew the truth out of him. /他想方设法地～,也没问出个所以然来。Despite all his tactful inquiry he didn't succeed in finding out the truth.
套鞋 tàoxié overshoes; rubbers; galoshes
套袖 tàoxiù oversleeve
套印 tàoyìn 〈印刷〉 chromatography:彩色～ process printing /～本 chromatograph edition
套用 tàoyòng apply mechanically; use indiscriminately; copy:别人再成功的经验,也不可机械地～。One must not apply others' experience mechanically, however useful it may be elsewhere.
套语 tàoyǔ ❶ polite formula: 见面寒暄,说了半天～ exchange words of greeting and polite expressions for quite some time ❷ conventional remark; platitude
套种 tàozhòng *also*"套作"〈农业〉 interplanting:间作～ intercropping and interplanting
套轴 tàozhóu 〈机械〉 sleeve spindle
套装 tàozhuāng *also* "套服" suit; clothes: 西服～ western-style suit
套子 tàozi ❶ sheath; case; sleeve; cover:沙发～ sofa cover /电视机～ TV set cover /靠垫～ cushion case ❷ 〈方言〉 cotton padding or wadding; batting:丝绵～ silk padding /棉花～ cotton padding ❸ conventional or stereotyped remark:俗～ conventional pattern; convention /老～ same old stuff; same old story ❹ snare; trap:他设下～等着你去钻。He has laid a trap for you to walk into.
套作 tàozuò 〈农业〉 interplanting

tè

忑 tè *see*"忐忑" tǎntè

特[1] tè ❶ special; unusual; exceptional; extraordinary:能力～强 of outstanding ability /这本书～贵。The book is unusually expensive. ❷ for a special purpose; specially:我～来车站接你。I have come to the station specially to meet you. ❸ secret agent; spy:敌～ enemy agent

特[2] tè 〈书面〉 but; only:此～匹夫之勇耳。This is mere foolhardiness.

特[3] tè (short for 特斯拉) 〈物理〉 tesla, unit of magnetic flux density

特别 tèbié ❶ special; uncommon; distinctive; peculiar: ～的关系 special relationship /～的设计 original design / ～的味道 peculiar flavour /这件衣服的式样很～。The cut of this dress is rather distinctive. ❷unusually; uncommonly; extraordinarily: 数量～小 of an unusually small amount /他说笑话的本领～大。He is extraordinarily good at cracking jokes. /屋子收拾得～干净。The house looks spotlessly clean after tidying up. ❸ going out of one's way to (do sth.); especially: 经理～邀请他参加会议。The manager specially asked him to take part in the meeting. ❹ especially; particularly; in particular:他喜欢郊游,～是骑车郊游。He likes outings to the suburbs, especially by bicycle.
特别法 tèbiéfǎ 〈法律〉 special law; *jus speciale*
特别会议 tèbié huìyì special meeting; special session
特别监护病房 tèbié jiānhù bìngfáng intensive care unit (ICU)
特别快车 tèbié kuàichē express train; special express; express

T

特别联大 tèbié Liándà special session of the UN General Assembly
特别提款权 tèbié tíkuǎnquán special drawing right (SDR)
特别条款 tèbié tiáokuǎn special clause
特别行政区 tèbié xíngzhèngqū special administrative region (SAR)：香港～ Hong Kong Special Administrative Region (HKSAR)
特别许可证 tèbié xǔkězhèng special licence
特产 tèchǎn special local product; speciality：南方～ specialities (*or* special local products) of the south /土～ special local product /杭州～龙井茶驰名中外。Dragon Well Tea, a special product of Hangzhou, is well known all over the world.
特长 tècháng what one is skilled in; strong point; forte; speciality：到了那里你可以充分发挥你的～了。You can give full play to your special skill after going there. /这个人有缺点，但也有～。The person has his strong points though he also has shortcomings. /这个学生在书法方面有～。The student is particularly good at calligraphy.
特出 tèchū outstanding; prominent; remarkable; extraordinary：～的贡献 outstanding contributions /他在数学研究上取得了～的成绩。He has extraordinary achievements to his credit in mathematical research.
特此 tècǐ 〈套语〉*used in official correspondence or documents*：～函告。You are hereby informed by letter. /你的申请业已批准，～奉告。It is hereby notified that your application has been approved.
特大 tèdà especially or exceptionally big; extra large (XL)：～新闻 particularly big news /他穿～号皮鞋。He wears extra large size shoes. /今年本省发生了百年未见的～水灾。This year, the province witnessed the worst flood ever in a hundred years.
特等 tèděng special grade or class; top grade; ace：～奖 special award /～战斗英雄 special class combat hero /～舱 stateroom; de luxe cabin /～射手 crack shot; expert marksman
特地 tèdì for a special purpose; specially：～写信问候 write specially to send regards /～前来看望 come specifically to visit /为了解决这个问题，他们～开会研究。They are holding a meeting for the express purpose of solving this problem.
特点 tèdiǎn characteristic; distinguishing or unique feature; peculiarity; trait：精神病人的心理～ psychological characteristics of a mental patient /抓住事物的～ grasp the distinctive features of a thing /这座大厦具有我国的民族风格和～。The tower building is well-known for its Chinese style and unique construction.
特定 tèdìng ❶ specially designated or appointed：～的任务 specially designated task ❷ specific; specified; given：这是在～的历史条件下制定的政策。This was the policy formulated under given historical conditions. /作者给人物描绘了一个～的生活环境。The author provided a specified environment for the character.
特氟隆 tèfúlóng 〈化工〉(transliteration) teflon
特高频 tègāopín 〈电子〉extremely high frequency
特高强度钢 tègāoqiángdùgāng 〈冶金〉extra-high tensile steel：～丝 extra-high strength wire
特高压 tègāoyā 〈电工〉extra-high tension (EHT); extra-high voltage (EHV)
特工 tègōng secret service：～人员 special agent; secret service personnel; spy /～组织 secret service; spy organization
特供 tègōng special supply
特古西加尔巴 Tègǔxījiā'ěrbā Tegucigalpa, capital of Honduras
特护 tèhù ❶ special nursing：～病房 special-nursing ward /～病人 specially cared patient /～处理 special-nursing treatment ❷ special nurse
特化 tèhuà 〈生物〉specialization
特惠 tèhuì 〈商业〉special preference; indulgence：～贸易 preferential trade /～税率 concessionary rate of tax
特惠待遇 tèhuì dàiyù special treatment; preferential treatment
特惠关税 tèhuì guānshuì preferential tariff
特惠制 tèhuìzhì 〈商业〉preferential system：普遍～ universal preferential system
特混舰队 tèhùn jiànduì (naval) task force
特级 tèjí special grade or class; superfine：～啤酒 superfine beer /～厨师 special-grade chef; chef of a special classification
特急 tèjí extra urgent：～电报 extra-urgent telegram; flash message /～件 extra-urgent papers (*or* documents)
特辑 tèjí ❶ special number or issue of a periodical：小说～ special issue of novels /报告文学～ special number of reportage ❷ special collection：外国电影故事～ special collection of foreign film stories
特技 tèjì ❶ stunt; trick：～跳伞 trick parachuting /飞车～ stunt cycling /～表演 stunt (performance) ❷〈影视〉special effects：～镜头 trick shot /～摄影 trick photography
特技飞行 tèjì fēixíng stunt flying; aerobatics
特技演员 tèjì yǎnyuán stunt man; stunt woman
特价 tèjià special offer; bargain price; sale：～供应 supply at a lower price than usual /～批发 wholesale at a bargain price /～商品 cheap goods /～商品部 bargain counter
特警 tèjǐng special police; special policeman
特刊 tèkān (of a journal, brochure, promotional magazine, etc.) special issue or number; special：国际博览会～ special number of the international fair /新年～ New Year special issue
特快 tèkuài ❶ express：～邮件 express mail /～业务 express (*or* urgent) business ❷ (short for 特别快车) special express; express train：5 次～列车 express No.5
特快专递 tèkuài zhuāndì express mail service (EMS)
特困户 tèkùnhù destitute household
特拉维夫 Tèlāwéifū Tel Aviv, or Tel Aviv-Jaffa, chief city and seaport of Israel on the Mediterranean coast
特立独行 tèlì-dúxíng independently minded; not drift with the tide; not follow the general trend：～的伟大诗人 great poet with an independent mind /在那样的压力下，他能～，令人钦佩。He is very much admired for his courage to stand firm and not to bend to such great pressure.
特立尼达和多巴哥 Tèlìnídá Hé Duōbāgē Trinidad and Tobago, country in the West Indies
特例 tèlì special case：罕见的～ rare, special case /有史以来无此～。This is unprecedented in history. /星期日不放假，对于学校这是～。No holiday on Sunday; this is something special for a school.
特洛伊 Tèluòyī Troy：～战争 Trojan war /～木马 Trojan horse
特命全权大使 tèmìng quánquán dàshǐ ambassador extraordinary and plenipotentiary
特命全权公使 tèmìng quánquán gōngshǐ envoy extraordinary and minister plenipotentiary
特派 tèpài specially appointed：～记者 special correspondent; accredited journalist /～张同志前来办理此案。I am sending specially Comrade Zhang to handle this case.
特派员 tèpàiyuán commissioner：～公署 commissioner's office /外交部驻港～ commissioner of the Foreign Ministry in Hong Kong
特批 tèpī with special approval or authorization
特遣部队 tèqiǎn bùduì task force
特区 tèqū special zone：经济～ special economic zone
特屈儿 tèqū'ér 〈化学〉(transliteration) tetryl
特权 tèquán privilege; prerogative; perquisite：～地位 privileged position (*or* status) /外交～ diplomatic privileges /他的～思想很严重。He has a very serious "special privilege" mentality.
特任 tèrèn ❶ appoint by presidential order ❷〈旧语〉first rank in the four-echelon officialdom of China before 1949
特软钢 tèruǎngāng 〈冶金〉extra soft steel
特色 tèsè characteristic; distinctive feature or quality：法国～的面包 bread with distinctive French flavour; French bread /建设有中国～的社会主义 build socialism with Chinese characteristics /这台歌舞极富东方～。These songs and dances were exceptionally rich in oriental flavour.
特设 tèshè ad hoc：～委员会 ad hoc committee /～机构 ad hoc organ
特赦 tèshè special pardon; special amnesty：宣布～ announce a special amnesty /～罪犯 grant a special pardon to criminals
特赦令 tèshèlìng decree or writ of special pardon or amnesty
特赦权 tèshèquán 〈法律〉prerogative of mercy
特使 tèshǐ special envoy：外交～ diplomatic envoy /联合国～ UN emissary
特首 tèshǒu Chief Executive (of Hong Kong or Macao Special Administrative Region)
特殊 tèshū special; particular; uncommon; exceptional：～条件 specific condition /～材料 particular material /这种现象很～。This phenomenon is rather unusual (*or* exceptional). /这个女人打扮得很～。The woman dressed up in a peculiar way.
特殊钢 tèshūgāng 〈冶金〉special steel
特殊化 tèshūhuà become privileged：杜绝～的现象 put an end to the practice of personal privileges /有权的人容易搞～。People in

power are apt to become privileged.
特殊教育 tèshū jiàoyù special education for the handicapped
特殊性 tèshūxìng particularity; peculiarity; speciality; specific characteristic:分配工作时要考虑到妇女的～。We must take into consideration the particular needs of women while assigning them jobs.
特斯拉 tèsīlā 〈物理〉tesla (unit for measurement of the intensity of magnetic induction)
特体 tètǐ (of human build or figure) uncommonly large or fat:～服装 clothes of uncommon size
特为 tèwèi for a special purpose; specially; going out of one's way to (do sth.):我今天～起个早给你送行。I got up early this morning specially to see you off.
特务 tèwù special task or duties:～连 special task company
特务 tèwu special or secret agent; spy:～活动 espionage /～机关 secret service; espionage agency /派遣～ send spies
特效 tèxiào specially good effect; special efficacy:～药 specific drug; specific; effective cure /～配方 effective prescription /对各类肠道疾病具有～。The medicine has specially good effect on various intestinal diseases.
特写 tèxiě ❶ feature article or story; feature:人物～ feature article on a person /～专辑 special collection of feature stories /新闻～ news features ❷〈影视〉close-up:～镜头 close-up (shot) /面部～ face close-up
特型演员 tèxíng yǎnyuán typecast actor
特性 tèxìng specific property or characteristic:～鲜明 striking characteristics /具有明显的～ with distinctive features /勤劳勇敢是我们这个民族的～。Bravery and industriousness are the specific properties of our nation.
特许 tèxǔ special permission:～证书 special permit; letters patent /进口这批机械,得到了有关方面的～。The import of these machines was specially licensed by the appropriate authorities.
特许公司 tèxǔ gōngsī chartered company
特许经营商店 tèxǔ jīngyíng shāngdiàn franchise store
特许权 tèxǔquán 〈法律〉chartered right; franchise:购买经营快餐的～ buy a fast-food franchise
特压 tèyā 〈化工〉extreme pressure:～添加剂 extreme pressure additive
特邀 tèyāo specially invite:～演员 specially invited actor (*or* actress); guest actor (*or* actress)
特异 tèyì ❶ exceptionally good; excellent; superfine:以～成绩升入大学 enter university with an excellent performance (*or* extraordinary record) /功效～ excellent efficacy ❷ peculiar; distinctive:～的格调 distinctive style
特异反应性 tèyì fǎnyìngxìng 〈医学〉idiosyncrasy; atopy:～皮炎 atopic dermatitis
特异功能 tèyì gōngnéng extra-sensory perception (ESP)
特异质 tèyìzhì *also* "特异反应";"特异素"〈医学〉idiosyncrasy
特意 tèyì for a special purpose; specially:～问好 send special regards /～来帮忙 come specially to help /～制造麻烦 deliberately make trouble
特有 tèyǒu peculiar; characteristic:本地～的风俗 customs peculiar to this locality /他表现出了青年人～的朝气。He displayed the characteristic vigour of youth.
特约 tèyuē engage by special arrangement:～记者 special correspondent /～维修店 special repair shop /～演员 guest actor (*or* actress) /～评论员 special commentator /～他参加讨论会 specially invite him to take part in the symposium
特征 tèzhēng characteristic; feature; trait:地理～ geographical features /时代～ characteristics of the times /这种文化表现出我们民族的～。The culture is an expression (*or* manifestation) of our national traits.
特指 tèzhǐ refer in particular to:我的发言并不是～某人某事,而是指一种普遍的现象。My speech is not directed at any particular person or incident, but at a widespread phenomenon.
特制 tèzhì specially made:～产品 special product /～商品 specially-produced goods
特质 tèzhì (of people) special quality:在他身上仍保留着某些农民的淳朴的～。We can see in him some of the simplicity and honesty characteristic of the farmers.
特种 tèzhǒng special type; particular kind:～部队 special armed units
特种兵 tèzhǒngbīng special troops
特种出版物 tèzhǒng chūbǎnwù SP (special publications)
特种工艺 tèzhǒng gōngyì special arts and crafts; special handicraft products
特种合金钢 tèzhǒng héjīngāng 〈冶金〉special alloy steel
特种邮票 tèzhǒng yóupiào special stamp
特装本 tèzhuāngběn 〈印刷〉edition binding; publisher's binding

忒 tè 〈书面〉error; mistake:差～ error
see also tēi; tuī

铽 tè 〈化学〉terbium (Tb)

蟘(螣) tè 〈古语〉small insect destroying rice seedlings or young sprouts

慝 tè 〈书面〉evil; wickedness; viciousness

te

脦 te *also* de *see* "肋脦" lēde *also* lēte

tēi

忒 tēi
see also tè; tuī
忒儿 tēir 〈方言〉〈象声〉flap (as of wings of a bird):鸽子～一声飞了。With a flap of its wings the dove flew off.

tēng

熥 tēng heat up by steaming or baking:～馒头 heat steamed bread /把昨天剩下的饺子～一～。Heat up the dumplings left over from yesterday.

鼟 tēng 〈象声〉*used to describe the sound of a drumbeat*:把鼓擂得～～响 thump the drum

téng

誊(謄) téng transcribe; copy out:你这篇作文的字迹太潦草,请～写后交上去。Your handwriting in the composition is almost illegible. Make a clean copy and hand it in.
誊录 ténglù transcribe; copy out:～稿件 transcribe a manuscript /照原样～ make a clean copy of the draft
誊清 téngqīng make a fair copy of:～稿 clean copy /把底稿～ make a fair copy of the draft
誊写 téngxiě transcribe; copy out:～来稿 copy out a contribution (received by an editor) /～课堂笔记 copy out one's notes
誊写版 téngxiěbǎn 〈印刷〉stencil
誊写钢版 téngxiě gāngbǎn steel plate for cutting stencils
誊写蜡纸 téngxiě làzhǐ stencil paper
誊写油墨 téngxiě yóumò stencil ink
誊印社 téngyìnshè mimeograph service
誊正 téngzhèng make a fair copy of:他取出用红稿纸～的文稿。He took out the manuscript, a fair copy made on the red ruled paper.

螣 téng
螣蛇 téngshé 〈古语〉legendary snake that can fly

鰧 téng 〈动物〉stargazer

滕 Téng ❶ name of a state during the Zhou Dynasty, in what is now Tengzhou (滕州) in Shandong Province ❷ a surname

藤(籐) téng ❶ vine:瓜～ melon vine /顺～摸瓜 follow the vine to get the melon — track sth. (*or* sb.) down by following

T

clues ❷ cane; rattan: ～箱 cane suitcase; rattan trunk /～篮 rattan basket

藤本植物 téngběn zhíwù 〈植物〉 liana; liane; vine

藤编 téngbiān ❶ use rattan or cane to make suitcases, trunks, chairs, etc. ❷ rattan basketwork; rattan work

藤编织品 téngbiānzhīpǐn rattan basketwork

藤壶 ténghú 〈动物〉 barnacle

藤黄 ténghuáng 〈植物〉 ❶ garcinia ❷ gamboge ❸gamboge yellow

藤黄胶 ténghuángjiāo 〈化工〉 gamboge; gum cambogia

藤萝 téngluó 〈植物〉 Chinese wistaria (*Wisteria sinensis*)

藤牌 téngpái cane or rattan shield; shield: ～兵 soldier holding a rattan shield

藤球 téngqiú 〈体育〉 Sepak Takraw (Thai rattan ball game)

藤圈操 téngquāncāo hoop gymnastics

藤条 téngtiáo rattan

藤蔓 téngwàn vine: 葡萄～ grapevines

藤子 téngzi 〈口语〉 ❶ vine ❷ cane; rattan

滕

téng 〈书面〉 ❶ seal off; restrain ❷ rope

腾

téng ❶ gallop; jump; bound; prance: 浪花涌～ waves surging turbulently /万马奔～ ten thousand horses galloping ahead; all going full steam ahead /万众欢～。Millions of people rejoice. ❷ rise; ascend; soar: 浓烟升～ billows of thick smoke rising ❸ make room; clear out; release; vacate: ～出这间房子放东西 vacate the room for storage /～出一个人来专门干这件事 release one person to do this job full time /这件事等～出手来再干。We'll see to the matter when we are not occupied. ❹ *used after a verb denoting repeated action*: 倒～ do sth. over and over again /扑～ (of the heart) throb /闹～ clamorous; noisy /这些想法一直在脑子里翻～。These ideas have been tossing about in my mind. ❺ (Téng) a surname

腾达 téngdá 〈书面〉 ❶ move upward; rise; ascend: 烈焰～ fierce fire flaring up ❷ (of career) soar aloft: 飞黄～ make rapid advances in one's career; have a meteoric rise

腾飞 téngfēi ❶ fly about; soar: 石壁上的雕龙～起舞,十分生动。The dragon on the stone wall was so vividly carved that it seemed to be flying about. ❷ rapid development; take-off: 经济～ rapid economic development; take-off /这一代将是～的一代。This generation will witness a leap forward.

腾沸 téngfèi seethe with excitement; boil over: 热血～ one's blood boils

腾格里沙漠 Ténggélǐ Shāmò Tengger Desert, in north China

腾贵 téngguì (of prices) shoot up; soar; skyrocket: 物价～。The prices shoot up.

腾欢 ténghuān be joyous; roar with joy: 万众～。Millions of people roared with joy.

腾蛟起凤 téngjiāo-qǐfèng of rich and varied talent: ～,文才盖世 of unparalleled and richly endowed talent

腾空 téngkōng soar; shoot up; rise high into the air; rise to the sky: 机场上,一架架战鹰～而起。One fighter after another soared into the sky at the airport.

腾落指数 téngluò zhǐshù 〈金融〉 advance/decline ratio

腾挪 téngnuó ❶ transfer (funds etc.) to other use; divert: 这项农业贷款,不得～。The loan earmarked for agriculture mustn't be misappropriated. ❷ move sth. to make room: 把这些大木箱～开才能摆床。We should move away these big wooden boxes to make room for the bed.

腾迁 téngqiān vacate and move elsewhere: ～户 households to vacate /～的住户得到妥善安排。Households who had vacated their original houses were properly attended to.

腾闪 téngshǎn dodge; evade: ～不及 be too late to dodge

腾腾 téngténg steaming; seething: 热气～的馒头 steamed bread just out of a steamer tray /山顶上雾气～。The mountain top is hazy with mist. /敌军杀气～直奔市郊而来。The enemy troops advanced towards the city suburbs with blood in their eyes.

腾退 téngtuì vacate (a room or house) and return it to the owner: ～被挤占的住房 vacate squatted housing and return it to the owner

腾骧 téngxiāng 〈书面〉 gallop; prance: 万马～ ten thousand horses galloping ahead; going full steam ahead

腾笑 téngxiào arouse laughter; invite ridicule: ～国际 be laughed at around the world; become an international joke

腾涌 téngyǒng rapid flow; rushing current: 洪水～。The flood rushed ahead.

腾踊 téngyǒng ❶ jump; leap; bound ❷ (of prices) go up; soar; skyrocket

腾跃 téngyuè ❶ jump; leap; bound: ～奔驰 leap forward speedily ❷ 〈书面〉 (of prices) go up; soar; skyrocket: 谷价～。The grain prices shot up.

腾越 téngyuè jump over: 大河～千山万壑,向东奔去。The big river flows eastward, cutting through and surmounting thousands of mountains and crags.

腾云驾雾 téngyún-jiàwù ❶ mount the clouds and ride the mist — speed across the sky; levitate: ～的神仙 celestial beings speeding across the sky ❷ feel giddy or dizzy: 坐在飞驰的车内,有～的感觉 feel giddy in the speeding car /不要被好听的话捧得～,忘乎所以。Don't be carried away when you hear a few words of praise. /他听数学报告感觉如～一般。He felt totally at sea when he attended a maths lecture.

疼

téng ❶ ache; pain; hurt; be sore: 头～脑热 headache and fever /肚子～ stomachache /腰酸腿～ have a sore back and aching legs; be aching all over /我的牙真～。My tooth is really hurting. ❷ love dearly; adore; be fond of; dote on: 招人～的孩子 lovable (*or* lovely) child; endearing child /她最～小儿子。She dotes on her youngest son.

疼爱 téng'ài be very fond of; love dearly: ～子女 be very fond of one's children /～丈夫 love one's husband dearly /过分～ dote on

疼怜 ténglián be very fond of; love dearly: ～孩子 love the child dearly

疼痛 téngtòng pain; ache; hurt: 伤口发炎,十分～。The wound is hurting a lot because it has become inflamed. /越来越～。It's becoming more and more painful. /我的左手掌火辣辣地～。My left palm hurts extremely.

疼惜 téngxī love dearly and take pity on: 她母亲去世后,父亲对她格外～。The father has loved her all the more dearly since her mother's death.

tī

梯

tī ❶ ladder; steps; stairs: 楼～ staircase /软～ rope ladder /自动扶～ escalator ❷ equipment which functions as a ladder or stairs: 电～ lift; elevator ❸ anything shaped like a staircase; terraced: *see* "～田"

梯次队形 tīcì duìxíng 〈军事〉 echelon formation

梯度 tīdù ❶ slope; gradient ❷ 〈物理〉 gradient; change of temperature, atmospheric pressure, density, speed, etc. in a certain time unit or within a certain distance

梯度风 tīdùfēng gradient wind

梯队 tīduì ❶ 〈军事〉 echelon formation; echelon: 命令第二～投入战斗 order the second echelon to throw itself into the battle ❷ echelon or line of successor: 培养干部队伍的第三～ build up the third echelon of cadres /女排第二～ second echelon (*or* line) formation of the women's volleyball team

梯恩梯 tī'ēntī 〈化学〉 trinitrotoluene (TNT): ～当量 〈军事〉 TNT equivalent

梯河 tīhé river with dams built on it

梯级 tījí ❶ stair; step ❷ terraced water conservancy project or works

梯己 tīji *also* "体己" tīji ❶ private savings: 她手头好像还有点～。She seemed to have some private savings on hand. ❷ intimate; confidential: ～话 words said in confidence /老太太很想身边有个～人。The old lady wishes to have a confidante at her side.

梯媒 tīméi introducer; sponsor: 以推荐信为～ use a letter of recommendation as the introducer

梯牧草 tīmùcǎo 〈植物〉 timothy (*Phleum pratense*)

梯气 tīqi *see* "梯己"

梯山航海 tīshān-hánghǎi scaling mountains and crossing seas — take long, arduous voyages: ～,历尽艰险 take long, arduous voyages and go through all kinds of hardships and dangers /～,不远万里而来 make a long, arduous journey to visit (sb.)

梯田 tītián 〈农业〉 terraced fields; terrace

梯形 tīxíng 〈数学〉 (US) trapezoid; (UK) trapezium

梯形翼 tīxíngyì trapezoidal wing; tapered airfoil

梯子 tīzi stepladder; ladder

锑 tī 〈化学〉antimony; stibium (Sb)

锑合金 tīhéjīn 〈冶金〉antimony alloy

锑化物 tīhuàwù 〈化学〉antimonide; stibide; stibnide

锑铅合金 tīqiān héjīn 〈冶金〉antimony or antimonial lead

锑酸 tīsuān 〈化学〉antimonic acid: ～盐 antimonate; stibate; stibnate

锑铜矿 tītóngkuàng 〈矿业〉horsfordite

锑中毒 tīzhòngdú 〈医学〉stibialism; antimony poisoning

擿 tī 〈书面〉expose; unmask; bring to light; lay open: 发奸～伏 expose crafty and evil practices

see also zhì

剔 tī ❶ clean with a pointed instrument; pick (meat from bones): 把肉～得干干净净 pick the bones clean ❷ pick (as from a crack or fissure): ～牙缝儿 pick one's teeth / ～指甲 pick one's fingernails ❸ pick out and reject; get rid of: 挑～ nit-pick; be hypercritical; be fastidious / 把坏鸡蛋～出来 pick out the bad eggs ❹ rising stroke (in Chinese characters)

剔除 tīchú reject; delete; remove; get rid of: ～错字病句 get rid of misprints and ungrammatical sentences / ～那些与主题无关的情节。Delete those plots which have nothing to do with the theme.

剔灯 tīdēng pick the wick: ～送水,夜半伴读 carry tea to sb. and pick the wick in the lamp while accompanying him reading at midnight

剔红 tīhóng *also* "雕红漆" diāohóngqī carved lacquerware

剔透 tītòu bright and limpid; transparent: 晶莹～ be sparklingly bright; crystal clear / 玲珑～ exquisitely carved; beautifully wrought

剔庄货 tīzhuānghuò goods sold at reduced prices; shop-soiled or sub-standard goods

踢 tī kick; play (football): ～毽子 kick the shuttlecock (as a game) / 拳打脚～ cuff and kick / 他自小爱～足球。He loved to play football since childhood. / 我～后卫。I play fullback. / 他把老母亲～出了家门。He drove his old mother out of his house.

踢跶 tīdā 〈象声〉rattle: 他在地板上～～地踱起步来。He stepped, tap-tap, to and fro on the floor.

踢跶 tīda ❶ kick at random; wear carelessly: 布鞋已经～出好几个窟窿。The cloth shoes were worn out with holes. ❷ squander: 不把这个家～穷你不甘心呀! You won't feel satisfied unless you've squandered the family fortune!

踢蹬 tīdeng ❶ kick at random: 这女孩比男孩还爱动,一天到晚老～。The girl never keeps her legs still and is even more restless than a boy. ❷ throw one's money about; spend freely; squander: 他不几年就把祖上的产业～光了。He squandered his forbears' property in just a few years' time. ❸ handle; conduct; deal with; dispose of: 好不容易才把这些鸡毛蒜皮的事～完了。It taxed my patience to get these trivial matters settled.

踢肩 tījiān one after another; in succession; running: ～生了两个女儿 give birth to two daughters in close succession / 喜讯～而至。Happy tidings keep pouring in. / 客人～而来。Guests arrived one after another.

踢脚板 tījiǎobǎn *also* "踢脚线"〈建筑〉skirting board; skirtboard

踢脚绊手 tījiǎo-bànshǒu dodder along; stagger along: 一路上～的 dodder along all the way / ～的狼狈相 stagger along and cut a sorry figure of oneself

踢皮球 tī píqiú ❶ kick a ball; play children's football ❷ kick sth. back and forth like a ball; pass the buck: 事情已上报了半年,上级单位互相～,至今未见回音。The matter was submitted to the higher authorities half a year ago; however, there has been no reply yet because they have been passing the buck to each other.

踢踏 tītà 〈象声〉footfall; footsteps: 午睡时他被一阵～～的声音惊醒了。He suddenly woke up from his nap at the footsteps.

踢踏 tīta ❶ wear: 敌人扛起枪,～着大马靴走了。The enemy soldier put his rifle on the shoulder, and pounded off in large riding boots. ❷ squander (property): 把一份家当～个精光。The family fortune was dissipated with nothing left.

踢踏舞 tītàwǔ step dance; tap dance

踢腾 tīteng *see* "踢蹬"

踢天弄井 tītiān-nòngjǐng be naughty or mischievous up to the hilt: 一天到晚～,惹是生非 be mischievous to the hilt and stir up trouble all day / 这孩子～,什么嘎事都干。The little imp stops at nothing to do mischief.

体(體) tī

see also tǐ

体己 tīji *see* "梯己" tīji

鷉 tī *see* "鸊鷉" pìtī

tí

啼(嗁) tí ❶ cry; weep aloud: 哀～ cry with despair / ～天哭地 wail with great sorrow ❷ crow; caw: 鸡～ cocks crow / 鸟～ birds sing / 猿～ apes jabber

啼号 tíháo cry; weep aloud; wail; howl

啼饥号寒 tíjī-háohán cry from hunger and cold; wail in hunger and cold: 子女缠膝,～。The children were wailing in hunger and cold before their parents.

啼叫 tíjiào ❶ (of birds and beasts) sing or howl: 树枝上的乌鸦不住地～。The crows squawked incessantly in the twigs. ❷〈方言〉cry; wail

啼哭 tíkū cry; wail: 孩子在妈妈怀里～。The baby cried in his mother's lap.

啼鸣 tímíng (of birds) tweet; warble: 雄鸡在～。The cock is crowing.

啼泣 tíqì cry; wail; weep: 雨下个不停,好像在为死难的战友～。It rained incessantly as if weeping for the martyrs.

啼笑皆非 tíxiào-jiēfēi not know whether to laugh or cry; find sth. both laughable and irritating: 他的玩笑开得过分了,弄得我～。His joke was overdone, making me ill at ease.

蹄(蹏) tí hoof: 马～ horse's hoofs / 猪～ pig's trotters / 马不停～ without any rest

蹄筋 tíjīn tendons of beef, mutton or pork: 炖～ stewed tendons

蹄髈 típǎng 〈方言〉uppermost part of a leg of pork

蹄铁 títiě 〈冶金〉horseshoe: ～钢 horseshoe bar

蹄形磁铁 tíxíng cítiě 〈电学〉horseshoe magnet

蹄子 tízi ❶〈口语〉hoof ❷〈方言〉leg of pork ❸〈旧语〉〈粗话〉(used of a woman) bitch: 你这个小～。You little bitch.

鹈 tí

鹈鹕 tíhú *also* "淘河" táohé; "塘鹅" táng'é 〈动物〉pelican

绨 tí a kind of thick silk

see also tì

荑 tí 〈书面〉❶ (of grass) sprouts ❷ tare

see also yí

醍 tí

醍醐 tíhú 〈古语〉finest cream; 〈佛教〉supreme truth: 如饮～ as if drinking the finest cream

醍醐灌顶 tíhú-guàndǐng be filled with wisdom; be enlightened; suddenly feel refreshed: 他的一席话如同～,使我明白了其中的道理。What he said enlightened me on the truth of the matter.

题 tí ❶ topic; subject; title; problem: 小标～ subtitle / 习～ exercise / 议～ subject under discussion; items on the agenda / 问～ question; problem; issue / 离～万里 stray far away from the subject; be wide of the mark / 还有三道～没做 have three more problems to do; have three problems left ❷ write; inscribe: ～照 sign one's photo (*or* picture) ❸ (Tí) a surname

题跋 tíbá ❶ preface and postscript ❷ short comments, annotations, etc. on a scroll (of painting or calligraphy)

题本 tíběn a kind of memorial to the ruler in the Ming and Qing dynasties

题壁 tíbì ❶ write a line or a poem on the wall ❷ characters or

poems written on the wall:洞里有历代文人墨客的～。Literati through the ages left their calligraphy or poems on the cave walls.

题材 tícái subject matter; topic; theme:农村～ theme on the rural scene /～新颖 original in the choice of subject (*or* theme) /这位作家的作品～广泛。The author writes about a wide range of subjects. *or* The works of the author cover a wide range of subjects.

题词 tící ❶ write words of encouragement, appreciation or commemoration:～记游 write a few words to remember the trip ❷ inscription; dedication:展厅正中墙上悬挂着国家领导人的～。On the centre-wall of the exhibition hall hung the inscriptions by state leaders. ❸ foreword:这部书的～文字不长,却是一篇绝妙的文章。The foreword of the book, short as it may be, is an excellent essay.

题额 tí'é write an inscription on a horizontal board:横匾由名家～。The horizontal board bears an inscription written by a celebrity.

题花 tíhuā title design

题记 tíjì ❶ preface ❷ short remarks at the beginning of an article; summary; abstract

题解 tíjiě ❶ explanatory note on the title or background of a book:这个古文选本的每篇文章都有～。There are explanatory notes on the title of each article in this selection (*or* anthology) of classical Chinese prose. ❷ key to exercises or problems:《高中物理～》*Key to Physics Exercises for Senior Secondary School*

题库 tíkù examination question bank

题款 tíkuǎn name of author, writer, painter or recipient inscribed on a painting or a piece of calligraphy presented as a gift

题名 tímíng ❶ inscribe one's name; autograph:在本人著作上～ autograph one's own work /～留念 give one's autograph as a memento ❷ name of a title:这本书的～为《平凡者之歌》。The title of this book is *Song of the Common Man*. *or* The book is entitled *Song of the Common Man*.

题目 tímù ❶ title; name; subject; topic:小说的～ title of the novel /讲演的～ subject of the speech /专辑的～ title of the special number ❷ exercise problem; examination question:考试时看清～要求 read carefully the instructions of exam questions during the examination /注意～内容和要求 pay attention to the contents and requirements of the exercise problems

题签 tíqiān ❶ write the title of a book on a label to be stuck on the cover ❷ label with the title of a book on it

题外话 tíwàihuà digression; what is mentioned in passing:这都是～了。I have sidetracked (*or* digressed). *or* I have mentioned this in passing.

题写 tíxiě write; inscribe:～书名 inscribe (*or* write) the title of the book

题旨 tízhǐ ❶ meaning or theme embodied in the title (of an article) ❷ meaning of the theme of literary and artistic works:～深远 have a profound artistic meaning

题字 tízì ❶ write; inscribe:挥笔～ wield the brush to write sth. /请来宾～ ask the guests to write in the visitors' book ❷ inscription:扉页上有作者的亲笔～。The title page of the book is autographed by the author.

提 tí ❶ carry (in hand with arm hanging down):肩挑手～ carry (things) on the shoulder and in the hand /手～行李 hand-luggage /左手～着公文包,右手～着衣箱 carry a briefcase in the left hand and a suitcase in the right ❷ move upward; lift; raise; promote:一只手～起来 lift with one hand /～为船长 promote to the rank of captain /从河里～水 draw water from a river /将问题～到原则高度来分析 analyse a problem from the high plane of principle /该把这件事～到议事日程上来了。It's time (that) this matter was put on the agenda. ❸ move to an earlier date or time; move up (a date); advance:选举日期已～到十一月初。The date of the election has been moved up to early November. ❹ offer for consideration; put forward; raise:～倡议 put forward a proposal /～条件 make (*or* raise) a condition; put forward a condition /～问题 ask (*or* raise) a question /～几点看法 make a few comments /～意见 make comments and suggestions; make criticisms (*or* complaints) ❺ draw; take out; withdraw; extract:从银行里～一万元 withdraw 10,000 *yuan* from the bank ❻ bring or take out from prison under escort; summon:～犯人 take out a convict from prison (under escort) ❼ speak about; bring up; mention; refer to:重～往事 bring up an old score; recall a past event /他～到了应该注意的事项。He mentioned the items that need attention. ❽ dipper; ladle:油～ oil-dipper /酒～ wine-dipper ❾ *also* "挑" tiǎo rising stroke (in Chinese characters) ❿ (Tí) a surname

see also dī

提案 tí'àn motion; proposal; draft resolution:讨论中的～ motion under discussion (*or* debate) /建设性的～ constructive proposal /一零一号～ (as in the UN) draft resolution 101 /关于安置难民的～ draft resolution on the resettlement of refugees /～国 sponsor country (of a resolution); sponsor /共同～国 co-sponsor /～审查委员会 motions examination committee

提拔 tíba promote; raise:由办事员～为经理 promote sb. from a staffer to a manager /破格～ break a rule to promote sb.; promote sb. as an exceptional case /他最近已被～担任团长。He has recently been raised to the rank of a regimental commander.

提包 tíbāo handbag; shopping bag; bag; valise

提笔 tíbǐ take up one's pen; start writing; begin to put down in black and white

提拨 tíbo 〈方言〉 remind; warn; call attention to:这件事多亏你及时～。I can't thank you enough for reminding me of this in time. /一经～,大家也就清楚了。A word of warning made us see things clearly.

提倡 tíchàng advocate; promote; champion; encourage:～节俭 advocate frugality /～国货 promote home (*or* domestic) products /～教育事业 champion the cause of education /～敬老爱幼 foster respect for the aged and love for the young /～晚婚晚育,优生优育 encourage late marriage, late birth, prenatal and post-natal care /这种减少能源消耗的新方法特别值得～。This new method of economizing energy deserves special encouragement (*or* promotion).

提成 tíchéng deduct or take a percentage (from a sum of money, etc.); take a cut:按合同～ deduct a percentage of money according to a contract /～数额 amount (to be) deducted

提出 tíchū put forward; raise; propose; set forth:～异议 make an objection; take exception /～程序问题 raise a point of order /～新方案 propose (*or* set forth) a new plan /～决议草案 put forward (*or* table) a draft resolution /～一种新的理论 advance a new theory /～解决办法 come up with (*or* propose) a solution /～问题 ask a question /～忠告 offer a piece of advice /～严重警告 give (*or* serve) a serious warning /～强烈抗议 lodge a strong protest (with sb.) /～更高标准 set higher standards /～辞职 send in (*or* tender) one's resignation /～入会申请 hand in (*or* submit) an application for membership /希望你们对自己～更严格的要求。I hope you'll set stricter demands on yourselves. /新的历史时期对我们～了新的挑战。The new historical period poses new challenges to us.

提纯 tíchún purify; refine:～复壮〈农业〉 purify and rejuvenate /～器 purifier /酒精～ alcohol purification /～金属 refine a metal

提词 tící 〈戏剧〉 prompt:幕后～ prompt behind the scenes /～人 prompter

提单 tídān *also* "提货单" bill of lading (B/L):直达～ direct bill of lading /联运～ through bill of lading /～正本 original bill of lading /～副本 duplicate bill of lading

提灯 tídēng hand lantern; lantern:～游行 lantern procession

提调 tídiào ❶ direct; dispatch; control:现场～ direct (*or* control) on the spot /在工地专管～ work exclusively as dispatcher on the work site ❷ dispatcher; controller:～员 dispatcher /总～ chief dispatcher

提兜 tídōu 〈口语〉 handbag; shopping bag; valise:绣花～ embroidered handbag

提督 tídū ❶ 〈旧语〉 military commander (usu. in a province or region):水师～ naval commander ❷ 〈书面〉 supervise:～学政 supervise education and examinations

提法 tífǎ the way sth. is put; formulation; manner of presentation; wording:这个～值得商榷。This formulation is open to question. /这不仅是～问题,也是实质问题。It's not just a matter of wording; it is also a matter of substance. /文中～多有不妥。The article contains quite a few inappropriate remarks.

提干 tígàn ❶ promote (a worker) to the status of an official:他不久前～,当了科长。He was promoted (from a worker) to be a section head not long ago. ❷ promote (to a higher position):突击～的做法是十分有害的。It is a very harmful practice to promote officials in a rush.

提纲 tígāng outline:汇报～ outline for a report /讨论～ outline for discussion

提纲挈领 tígāng-qièlǐng grasp a net by the headrope or a coat by

the collar — concentrate on the main points; bring out the essentials; give the gist:他对问题的阐述可谓～，简明扼要。He brought out the essentials of the problem in succinct language. /这篇发言虽长，但～，眉目清楚。This speech, though a bit long, did focus on the main points and was well organized.

提高 tígāo raise; lift; boost; improve:～嗓门 lift one's voice /～价格 raise (*or* mark up) prices /～经济效益 improve economic performance; increase economic efficiency /～劳动者素质 better the quality of the work force /～投资效益 improve investment returns /～业务水平 raise the professional (*or* technical) level; increase professional (*or* technical) competence /～觉悟 heighten one's political awareness /～士气 boost one's morale /～警惕 enhance (*or* heighten) one's vigilance /～认识 deepen one's understanding /～勇气 pluck up one's courage /～收入 augment one's income /人民的生活水平有了大幅度的～。The living standards of the people have improved (*or* risen) by a big margin. /我国的国际声望不断～。Our country's prestige in the world has grown steadily.

提供 tígōng provide; supply; furnish; offer:～食宿 provide room and board (*or* board and lodging) /～优质服务 offer quality service /为当地工业～廉价劳动力 supply cheap labour for local industries; supply the local industries with cheap labour /～确凿证据 furnish conclusive evidence /～无私援助 give (*or* provide) disinterested aid (*or* assistance) /～思考材料 provide food for thought /～解开这个奥妙的线索 afford a clue to the mystery /～资金 fund; finance /～方便 facilitate; make things easy

提灌 tíguàn pump (water) for irrigation:～设备 pumping equipment

提行 tíháng 〈印刷〉begin a new line:～另起 begin a new line; start another line /～符号 sign on a new line

提盒 tíhé tiered lunchbox with a handle and two or more (usu. round) compartments one on top of the other; tiered box (for carrying pastry, etc.)

提花 tíhuā 〈纺织〉jacquard weave:～织机 jacquard loom /～枕巾 jacquard pillow cover /～被面 jacquard quilt cover /～线毯 jacquard cotton blanket

提婚 tíhūn *see* "提亲"

提货 tíhuò pick up goods; take delivery of goods:～通知 cargo delivery notice /～报关代理人 delivery and customs agent /～担保书 letter of guarantee for production of bill of lading /到码头～ pick up goods at the wharf /请于本周内来机场～。Please come and take delivery of the goods at the airport within this week.

提货单 tíhuòdān *see* "提单"

提肌 tíjī 〈生理〉levator (muscles)

提及 tíjí mention; refer to:我不记得曾经～此事。I don't remember ever mentioning this.

提级 tíjí promote (sb. to a higher rank or level):～不提薪 be promoted to a higher rank without any raise in salary (*or* any pay raise)

提价 tíjià increase or raise prices; mark up prices:适当～ raise prices by an appropriate margin /～商品 goods sold at raised prices /～过高 excessive price increase (*or* hike) /禁止私自～。No unauthorized price hike is allowed.

提交 tíjiāo submit; refer:～该机构解决 refer (sth.) to that institution for solution /～仲裁 submit (sth.) for arbitration /～表决 put (sth.) to the vote /报告已～上级机关审批。The report has been submitted to the higher authorities (*or* the higher body) for examination and approval. /本条约应～全国人民代表大会予以批准。The present treaty is subject to ratification by the National People's Congress (*or* shall be submitted to the NPC for ratification).

提款 tíkuǎn draw or withdraw money (from a bank):～单 withdrawal ticket /～通知 advice of drawing /按时～ draw money regularly

提拉 tílā 〈体育〉lift:～球 lifting the ball

提篮 tílán hand basket

提炼 tíliàn extract and purify; abstract; refine:～过程 refining process /～原油 refine crude oil /从石英中～金子 extract gold from quartz /～率 rate of extraction /创作即是作家对生活素材～加工和艺术再创造的过程。The process of creative writing means that the writer has to refine and recreate in artistic form the source materials he has gathered from life.

提梁 tíliáng handle (of a basket, pot, etc.); straps (of a handbag, etc.); loop handle

提梁卣 tíliángyǒu 〈考古〉ewer with a loop handle

提留 tíliú deduct a part from the whole (for oneself); retain a portion (of sth.):企业可以～一定比例的利润作为公积金。The enterprise may deduct and keep a certain proportion of the profit as public accumulation fund.

提名 tímíng nominate:组织～ be nominated by an organization /群众～ be nominated by the rank and file /～人 nominator /被～人 nominee /～委员会 nomination committee /赢得～ win a nomination /～某人为理事会理事 nominate sb. for the board /被一致～为董事长 be unanimously nominated as chairman of the board

提名奖 tímíngjiǎng nomination:奥斯卡～ nomination for an Oscar

提念 tíniàn 〈方言〉mention; speak of:这位就是我常～的李医生。This is the Dr. Li I've often spoken of.

提起 tíqǐ ❶ mention; speak of; bring up:自你走后，我们大家经常～你。We have often spoken of you since you left. /别再～这事了。Don't bring this up again. ❷ raise; arouse; boost; brace up:～精神，迎接挑战。Brace yourself up for the challenge. ❸ put forward; initiate; institute:～诉讼 bring (*or* institute) a suit; institute legal proceedings /～公诉 initiate a public prosecution

提前 tíqián do (sth) in advance or ahead of time; move or shift to an earlier date; move up (a date); advance:～完成任务 accomplish a task ahead of time /把文件～送去 send (*or* deliver) the documents in advance (*or* beforehand) /～释放犯人 release a convict before his (*or* her) sentence expires /～召开会议 convene (*or* hold) a meeting before the due time /会期如果～，请尽早通知我们。Please let us know as early as possible if the date for the meeting is moved up. /预计汛期将～到来。The flood season is forecast to begin earlier this year.

提前偿付 tíqián chángfù prepayment

提前量 tíqiánliàng 〈军事〉lead

提挈 tíqiè 〈书面〉❶ lead; take with one; marshal:～妻儿 take one's wife and children with one /～全军 marshal all one's army (*or* forces) ❷ guide and support; give guidance and assistance to:～后辈 give guidance and help to younger people /～下级 recommend one's subordinates for higher positions

提亲 tíqīn *also* "提亲事" make a proposal of marriage on behalf of a young man's, or sometimes a girl's, family:托人～ ask a third party to make a proposal of marriage on one's behalf /媒人～ propose marriage through a matchmaker

提琴 tíqín any instrument of the violin family; fiddle:小～ violin /中～ viola /大～ violoncello; cello /低音～ double bass; contrabass /～手 fiddler; violinist

提请 tíqǐng ask for; submit to; refer to:～仲裁 submit sth. to arbitration; institute arbitration proceedings /～董事会审批 submit (a proposal, etc.) to the board of directors for deliberation and approval /～撤消案件 make a motion for dismissal /组织委员会～全体代表注意会议日程。The organizational committee called the attention of all the delegates to the timetable of the conference.

提取 tíqǔ ❶ draw; withdraw; pick up; collect:～行李 pick up (*or* collect) one's luggage /～存款 draw money from a bank; withdraw a bank deposit /～货物 pick up goods; take delivery of goods ❷ extract; abstract; recover:从矿石中～金属 extract metals from ores /从谷物中～酒精 distil alcohol from grain

提取器 tíqǔqì extractor

提取塔 tíqǔtǎ extraction column

提任 tírèn promote (to a certain post):～为市教育局长 be promoted to director of the municipal bureau of education

提神 tíshén invigorate; refresh; give a lift:～健脑 refresh oneself and invigorate the function of the brain /～补气 lift one's spirits and build up one's vital energy /他很想抽支烟提提神。He wanted very much to have a smoke and give himself a lift. / 浓咖啡有～作用。Strong coffee is invigorating (*or* stimulating).

提审 tíshěn ❶ bring (a suspect, etc.) before the court; bring to trial; fetch or bring in for interrogation:～被告 fetch the defendant (*or* accused) for interrogation /～罪犯 bring a criminal before the court /当堂～ interrogate at court ❷ review (a case tried by a lower court, etc.):～前案 review a past case /～悬案 review an outstanding law case /越级～ bypass the immediate higher court to review a case

提升 tíshēng ❶ promote:～两级 raise (*or* promote) by two grades /～有功人员 promote those who have rendered meritorious service ❷ hoist; elevate:～设备 hoist; elevator /～设施 elevating fa-

T

cilities
提升平车 tíshēng píngchē 〈矿业〉dukey
提示 tíshì point out; prompt: ～要点 point out the main points; brief sb. on the key points /阅读～ reading guide /老师让一个学生回答问题时，其他人不得给他～。When one student is called upon to answer the teacher's questions, the others must not prompt him.
提手 tíshǒu handle (of a basket, bag, etc.)
提说 tíshuō 〈方言〉mention; speak of
提头儿 títóur be the first to speak of sth; start the ball rolling; break the ice: 有人一～，大家就你一言我一语地议论开了。Once the ice was broken, everybody started talking about the matter.
提味 tíwèi make (food, dish, etc.) palatable or appetizing (by adding condiments); season: 撒点胡椒粉提提味儿。Add some pepper to make it more appetizing.
提问 tíwèn ask or put a question; quiz: 课堂～ put questions to students in class /～方式 way to ask a question /拒不回答记者们的～ refuse to answer the reporters' questions
提线木偶 tíxiàn mù'ǒu marionette
提箱 tíxiāng *also*"手提箱" shǒutíxiāng suitcase
提携 tíxié ❶ lead (a child, etc.) by the hand; guide and support: ～晚辈 guide and help one's juniors /～年轻人 give advice and assistance to young people ❷ 〈书面〉join hands; cooperate: 互相～ work together; help each other (in getting promotions)
提心 tíxīn worry; be concerned: 她最～这件事。This is what troubles her most. /家里孩子有人照看，你不必～。You don't have to worry about your child; there's someone to look after her at home.
提心吊胆 tíxīn-diàodǎn *also*"悬心吊胆" xuánxīn-diàodǎn have one's heart in one's mouth; be on tenterhooks; be in constant fear: 一路上～ have the jitters all the way /～，寝食不安 have one's heart in one's mouth and be worried waking or sleeping /他～，一夜未眠。He was on tenterhooks and lay awake the whole night.
提醒 tíxǐng remind; alert; warn; call attention: ～大家注意环境卫生 call (everybody's) attention to environmental sanitation /～过路行人走地下人行通道 remind the passers-by to take the underground walkway (*or* underpass)/交通警察～司机不要超过时速限制。The traffic police warned drivers not to exceed the speed limit.
提选 tíxuǎn select; pick; choose: ～方案 selection scheme /～程序 selection procedure /～优良品种 select fine varieties
提讯 tíxùn bring (a prisoner, etc.) before the court; bring to trial; fetch for interrogation: ～多次 fetch and interrogate (a detainee) repeatedly /～要犯 bring an important criminal to trial
提要 tíyào ❶ sum up the main points; wrap up; synopsize: 全篇～如下。The main points are summed up as follows. ❷ précis; summary; abstract; synopsis: 全文～ abstract of an article /全书～ synopsis (*or* capsule summary) of a book
提要钩玄 tíyào-gōuxuán grasp the essentials; extract the essence
提掖 tíyè 〈书面〉promote; guide and support: ～后进 guide and help one's juniors (*or* subordinates); promote juniors
提议 tíyì ❶ propose; suggest; move: 我现在～为我们双方的合作与友谊干杯。I now propose a toast to cooperation and friendship between our two sides. /她～将决议草案付诸表决。She moved that the draft resolution be put to vote. /与会者一致～成立一个特别委员会。The participants were unanimous in proposing the setting up of a special committee. ❷ proposal; motion: 该～在大会获得多数通过。The proposal was adopted at the conference by a majority. /根据主席的～，会议休会。The meeting adjourned on the motion of the chairman.
提早 tízǎo shift to an earlier time; be earlier than planned or expected; do (sth.) in advance or ahead of time: 冬天～降临了。Winter is upon us earlier than usual. /已经宣布这次访问将～结束。It has been announced that this visit will end earlier than planned. /如果会议不开，请你～通知大家。Please let everybody know in advance if the meeting is cancelled.
提制 tízhì obtain through refining; refine; distil; extract: 玫瑰油由玫瑰花瓣～而得。Rose oil is extracted from rose-petals.
提子 tízi 〈方言〉dipper; ladle

鹈 tí

鹈鴂 tíjué 〈古语〉cuckoo

鳀(鮷) tí 〈动物〉anchovy

猑 tí *see*"灵猑" língtí

騠 tí *see*"駃騠" juétí

缇 tí 〈书面〉(of colour) orange

tǐ

体(體、躰) tǐ

❶ body; part of the body; limb: 人～ human body /肢～ limb /遗～ remains /五～投地 be on all fours; prostrate oneself before sb. (in admiration) /～弱多病 weak and ill; valetudinarian ❷ substance; state of a substance: 固～ solid /液～ liquid /气～ gas /集～ collective /个～ individual /本～ noumenon; thing-in-itself /天～ celestial body ❸ style; form: 字～ form of a written (*or* printed) character; style of calligraphy /草～ characters executed swiftly and with strokes flowing together; cursive hand /文～ type of writing; literary form; style /旧～诗 old-style poem; classical poetry /应用文～ practical writing ❹ personally do or experience sth.; put oneself in another's position: 身～力行 earnestly practise what one preaches ❺ system; regime: 政～ system of government /国～ state system ❻ 〈语言〉aspect (of a verb): 进行～ progressive aspect /完成～ perfect aspect
see also tī
体壁 tǐbì 〈动物〉body wall: 胚～ somatopleure
体表 tǐbiǎo ❶ body surface: ～面积 body surface area /～寄生虫 epizoon ❷ body thermometer
体裁 tǐcái type or form of literature; genre: 文学～ literary form; genre
体操 tǐcāo gymnastics: 器械～ gymnastics on (*or* with) apparatus /艺术～ artistic gymnastics /徒手～ freestanding exercise /自由～ floor (*or* free) exercise /健美～ callisthenics /～运动员 gymnast /～健将 master of gymnastics
体操表演 tǐcāo biǎoyǎn gymnastic exhibition or display
体操服 tǐcāofú gym outfit; gym suit
体操器械 tǐcāo qìxiè gymnastic apparatus
体察 tǐchá experience and observe; be understanding and sympathetic: ～下情 know what is going on at the lower levels /～百姓疾苦 be aware of the hardships of the common people /深入～情况 be ready to look into matters with an open mind; not be prejudiced in sizing up situations
体尝 tǐcháng have personal experience of; experience: 他终于～到了生活的艰辛。He finally experienced the hardships of life.
体词 tǐcí 〈语言〉(in Chinese grammar) general term for nouns, pronouns, numerals and classifiers
体大思精 tǐdà-sījīng (as of a book) extensive in scope and penetrating in thought; broad in conception and meticulous in execution: 这部中国小说史，～，征引宏富。Extensive in scope and meticulous in execution, this history of Chinese fiction provides a wealth of source materials.
体电阻 tǐdiànzǔ 〈电子〉bulk resistor
体锻标准 tǐduàn biāozhǔn (short for 国家体育锻炼标准) National Standards for Physical Training
体罚 tǐfá corporal or physical punishment: ～学生 punish students physically /严禁～。Corporal punishment is strictly prohibited.
体法 tǐfǎ (of poems, paintings, etc.) mode; style; rules and patterns: ～师承名家高手。The style was modelled after a great master's. /～自有神韵。The style stands out with its unique charm.
体范 tǐfàn (of literary works) form; style; model; pattern: ～合时 be appropriate (in style) to the occasion /拘泥～，墨守成规 adhere to form and conventions punctiliously
体改 tǐgǎi (short for 体制改革) structural reform; institutional reform; restructuring
体改委 tǐgǎiwěi (short for 体制改革委员会) commission for structural reform
体格 tǐgé ❶ physique; build; constitution: ～健壮 of strong physique (*or* constitution); of strong (*or* powerful) build ❷ bodily form; build; figure: ～匀称 of proportional build /从类人猿进化到人，～发生了明显的变化。Man underwent marked changes in bodily form as he evolved from the anthropoid ape.

体格检查 tǐgé jiǎnchá health check-up; physical examination: 定期～ regular health check-up (*or* physical examination)

体会 tǐhuì know or learn from experience; realize: 个人～ personal experience (*or* understanding) /两者的差别,只能在工作实践中去慢慢～。Gradually you'll see the difference between the two through your work. /你最近到开发区访问有什么～? What have you learned from your recent tour of the development zone?

体积 tǐjī volume; bulk; size: ～大 bulky; large in size /水箱的～ volume of the water tank /～密度 volume density /～黏度 bulk viscosity /这种计算机～不大,便于携带。Computers of this kind are small and handy.

体积吨 tǐjīdūn 〈交通〉 measurement ton or tonnage

体积膨胀 tǐjī péngzhàng 〈物理〉 volume expansion

体架 tǐjià 〈方言〉 build; figure: ～魁梧 of powerful build; powerfully built; heavyset

体检 tǐjiǎn (short for 体格检查) physical examination; health check-up: 全面～ general (*or* overall) physical examination /每年例行～ annual physical check-up

体节 tǐjié 〈动物〉 body segment

体镜 tǐjìng 〈医学〉 somascope

体力 tǐlì physical or bodily strength; physical power: ～过人 possess unusual physical power /～充沛 be full of (physical) strength /～测试 test of physical strength /耗费～和心血 be a drain on one's strength and energy

体力劳动 tǐlì láodòng physical or manual labour: ～者 physical worker; manual labourer /～与脑力劳动 physical and mental labour /从事～ do physical labour

体例 tǐlì stylistic rules and layout; style: 印刷～ style sheet; style book /～说明 note to the style /～要求 style requirement /统一～ unify the style of the writing

体量 tǐliàng size (of building); scale: 整个建筑虽然～不大, 却别有风格。Though not large in scale, the building boasts a style of its own.

体谅 tǐliang show understanding and sympathy; make allowances: ～对方的难处 allow for the difficulties of the other party /相互～ show understanding and sympathy for each other /～人 make allowances for others; be understanding

体貌 tǐmào figure and (facial) features: ～俊秀 have a handsome figure and face /～相似 resemble each other in carriage and looks

体面 tǐmian ❶ dignity; prestige; face: 有失～ be a loss of face; be beneath one's dignity; lose one's dignity /保全对方的～ save the face of the other side /有碍～ be detrimental to one's dignity; impair one's dignity; be embarrassing ❷ honourable; creditable; respectable: 不～的行为 disgraceful (*or* disreputable) conduct; indecency /～的职业和家庭 decent job and respectable family /～的和平 peace with honour ❸ good-looking; smart: 长得～、大方 have good looks and ease of manner /他穿上这套西服显得真～。He looks smart in this suit.

体脑倒挂 tǐ-nǎo dàoguà manual labour is paid more than mental labour — irrational structure of distribution

体能 tǐnéng physical strength (as displayed in sports); stamina: ～测试 test of physical strength

体念 tǐniàn give sympathetic consideration; be understanding: ～对方的为难之处 give sympathetic consideration to the other side's difficulty; be understanding of their difficulty /～他人的疾苦 be concerned about the sufferings of others

体膨胀 tǐpéngzhàng 〈物理〉 volume expansion: ～系数 coefficient of volume expansion

体魄 tǐpò physique; physical health: ～强健 be physically strong; have a tough constitution /锻炼～ build up one's physique; go in for physical training /健康的～ healthy body

体气 tǐqì ❶〈方言〉 moral character; nature: ～和脾气都好 have a high moral character as well as a gentle temperament ❷〈方言〉 physical health; physique: ～虚弱 be in frail health ❸〈书面〉 moral tone (of writing, etc.): ～高雅 have a refined moral tone; be refined and noble in taste

体腔 tǐqiāng 〈生理〉 body cavity; coelom: ～动物 coelomate /～管 coelomoduct /～口 coelomostome /～液 coelomic fluid /～镜 celioscope; coelioscope /～镜检查 celioscopy /～内移植 intra-coelomic graft

体热 tǐrè body heat

体虱 tǐshī 〈动物〉 body louse

体式 tǐshì ❶ form of characters: 手写～ cursive hand; handwritten form /印刷～ printed form; print hand ❷〈书面〉 form of literary work; genre; style: ～划一 uniform in style (*or* form) /～的变化 variations in form (*or* genre) /文章～不同。The articles differ in style.

体势 tǐshì form; pattern: 草书打破了方块字的～。The cursive hand breaks the traditional form of Chinese characters.

体视 tǐshì 〈物理〉 stereo: ～摄影机 stereo camera /～显微镜 stereomicroscope /～望远镜 stereotelescope; telestereoscope /～镜 stereoscope /～光学 stereoptics /～半径 radius of stereoscopic vision; stereoscopic radius

体态 tǐtài posture; carriage; bearing: ～柔美 supple and elegant carriage /～轻盈 lithe and graceful bearing /～健美 vigorous and handsome carriage

体坛 tǐtán sports circles; sports world: ～纵横 across the sports world /～新秀 new sports star /～逸事 anecdotes concerning sports circles /～盛事 grand event in the sports world; grand sports meet

体贴 tǐtiē show consideration; give every care; be considerate: ～而又温柔 considerate and gentle

体贴入微 tǐtiē-rùwēi look after with great care; be extremely considerate or thoughtful: 她视病人如同自己的亲人, 对他们～。She regards her patients as her own flesh and blood and looks after them with meticulous care (*or* cares for them with great solicitude).

体统 tǐtǒng decorum; propriety; decency: 不成～ most improper; downright outrageous /有失～ be against decorum (*or* decency); be disgraceful /成何～! What impropriety! *or* How disgraceful!

体外式起搏器 tǐwàishì qǐbóqì 〈医学〉 external pacemaker

体外受精 tǐwài shòujīng 〈生理〉 external fertilization; *in vitro* fertilization

体外循环 tǐwài xúnhuán 〈生理〉 extracorporeal circulation: ～心脏手术 open-heart surgery

体委 tǐwěi (short for 体育运动委员会) commission for physical culture and sports; sports commission

体位 tǐwèi 〈医学〉 posture; position: ～整合 postural integration /～引流法 postural drainage /～低血压 postural hypotension

体味 tǐwèi savour; chew; appreciate: ～他的话的含义 savour the implication of his remarks; chew his words /～到其中甘辛 appreciate the difficulty and pleasure of sth. /～到人情冷暖 learn the ways of the world; realize the inconstancy of human relationships

体温 tǐwēn (body) temperature: ～曲线 temperature curve /～过高 hyperthermia /～过低 hypothermia /量～ take one's temperature

体温计 tǐwēnjì (clinical) thermometer

体无完肤 tǐwúwánfū ❶ have cuts and bruises all over the body; be a mass of bruises: 伤痕累累, ～ be a mass of bruises and wounds /被打得～ be covered with cuts and bruises ❷ be thoroughly revised; be scathingly refuted: 他的论点被驳得～。His argument was scathingly refuted. /文章被改得面目全非, ～。The article was revised beyond recognition.

体惜 tǐxī understand and sympathize; care: ～民间疾苦 be sympathetically concerned about the hardships of the people /～死难遗属 sympathize with the bereaved /～民心、民力 understand the people's sentiments and cherish their resources

体系 tǐxì system; setup: 思想～ ideological system /商业～ business setup (*or* network) /防御～ defence structure /等级～ hierarchy /自成～ build up (*or* develop) one's own system; constitute a system in oneself

体系建筑 tǐxì jiànzhù 〈建筑〉 system building; industrialized building

体细胞 tǐxìbāo 〈生物〉 soma; somatic cell; somatoplasm; body cell: ～染色体 somatochrome; somatic chromosome /～重组 somatic recombination /～分离 somatic segregation /～突变 somatic mutation

体现 tǐxiàn embody; manifest; reflect; give expression to: 具体的～ concrete embodiment (*or* manifestation) /～全貌 reflect the complete (*or* overall) picture /～新工艺的优越性 give expression to (*or* manifest) the superiority of the new technology /这是他对工作高度负责的～。This shows his high sense of responsibility towards his work.

体相 tǐxiàng physiognomy

体校 tǐxiào (short for 体育学校) sports school; gymnastic school: 少年～ sports school for children

体刑 tǐxíng corporal or physical punishment: 废除～ abolish (*or*

prohibit) corporal punishment

体形 tǐxíng physical shape; bodily form; somatotype: ～怪异 grotesque in shape /～优美 of graceful figure /～难看 of repulsive form; unshapely

体型 tǐxíng type of build or figure: ～不同 different types of figure /～匀称 be of proportional build; have a well-rounded figure /～相似 of similar build /～躺椅 contour couch

体性 tǐxìng character; temperament; nature: 想要跟他共处，首先要懂得他的～。It is essential for one to know his temperament if one wants to get along with him.

体恤 tǐxù understand and sympathize; concern oneself; show solicitude: ～百姓 show solicitude for the common people; concern oneself with the welfare of the common people /～下情 be understanding of the situation of one's inferiors; understand how things are at the grass roots

体恤衫 tǐxùshān (transliteration) T-shirt

体癣 tǐxuǎn 〈医学〉 ringworm of the body; tinea corporis

体循环 tǐxúnhuán 〈生理〉 systematic circulation; greater circulation

体验 tǐyàn learn through personal experience; learn through practice; experience: 亲身～ personal experience; first-hand experience /～生活 observe and learn from real life /这种感情我还没有～过。I have never experienced such feelings.

体液 tǐyè body fluid; humour: ～病理学 humoral pathology /～免疫性 humoral immunity /水样～ aqueous humour /玻璃状～ vitreous humour

体育 tǐyù ❶ physical culture; physical training; physical education: ～课 physical education (PE) /～教研室 PE teaching and research section /～教材 PE teaching material /～锻炼标准 standards for physical training /～工作者 physical educator; PE worker ❷ sports: ～科学 sports science /～卫生 sports hygiene /～医学 sports medicine /～爱好者 sports enthusiast; sports fan /～十佳 top ten sports stars; ten best sportsmen and sportswomen /～用品 sports goods /军事～ military sports

体育场 tǐyùchǎng stadium; sportsground

体育道德 tǐyù dàodé sportsmanship

体育馆 tǐyùguǎn gymnasium; gym

体育疗法 tǐyù liáofǎ physical exercise therapy

体育用品 tǐyù yòngpǐn sports goods; sports requisites

体育运动 tǐyù yùndòng sports; physical culture: 群众性～ mass sports activities /参与性～ participatory sports /观赏性～ spectator sports /～荣誉奖章 Medal of Honour for Sports /～委员会 commission for physical culture and sports

体院 tǐyuàn (short for 体育学院) sports institute or college

体胀系数 tǐzhàng xìshù coefficient of volume expansion or dilatation

see also "膨胀系数" péngzhàng xìshù

体针 tǐzhēn 〈中医〉 body acupuncture

体征 tǐzhēng pathological (bodily) sign

体制 tǐzhì ❶ system (of organization); set-up; regime: 国家～ state system /外汇管理～ foreign exchange regime /领导～ leadership set-up /～结构 institutional structure /～不健全 imperfect system of organization; faulty institutions ❷ 〈书面〉 (of literary works) form; pattern; genre: 突破传统的诗词～，发展新诗格律 break through the traditional poetic patterns and develop rules and forms of a modern prosody

体制改革 tǐzhì gǎigé structural reform; institutional reform; restructuring: 经济～ reform of the economic structure; restructuring of the economy; economic restructuring /教育～ structural reform of education

体制改革委员会 tǐzhì gǎigé wěiyuánhuì commission for structural reform

体质 tǐzhì physique; constitution: ～下降 declining physique /增强～ improve (*or* build up) one's physique /～因人而异。Constitution varies from one person to another.

体质人类学 tǐzhì rénlèixué physical anthropology

体重 tǐzhòng (body) weight: ～不足 underweight /～过重 overweight /～增加 put on weight; gain weight /～减轻 lose weight /过去他～有 150 公斤上下。He used to weigh around 150 kilograms.

tì

涕

tì ❶ tear: 破～为笑 smile through one's tears /相对垂～ face each other, weeping /痛哭流～ weep bitterly; cry one's heart out ❷ mucus of the nose; snivel

涕泪 tìlèi ❶ tears: ～纵横 with tears streaming down one's face ❷ tears and snivel: ～俱下 shed tears and snivel; have tears and mucus flowing down together

涕零 tìlíng shed tears; weep: 感激～ shed tears of gratitude; be moved to tears of gratitude /～如雨 with tears streaming down like rain

涕泣 tìqì 〈书面〉 weep: 相对～ weep face to face /～不语 weep in silence /～沾襟 weep till the front of one's jacket is wet with tears; shed endless bitter tears

涕泗 tìsì 〈书面〉 tears and snivel: ～横流 with tears and snivel flowing down one's face

涕泗交流 tìsì-jiāoliú *also* "涕泗交下"; "涕泗交颐" tears and snivel streaming down at the same time: 老人～地向我们讲述她儿子惨死的情况。Tears streamed down the old lady's cheeks when she was telling us the story of her son's tragic death.

涕泗滂沱 tìsì-pāngtuó *see* "涕泗交流"

悌

tì 〈书面〉 love and respect for one's elder brother: 孝～ filial piety and fraternal love

剃

tì shave: ～胡子 have a shave; shave oneself /～发修行 have one's head shaved and become a monk (*or* nun)

剃齿 tìchǐ 〈机械〉 gear shaving: ～机 gear-shaving machine

剃刀 tìdāo razor

剃刀鲸 tìdāojīng blue whale

剃度 tìdù 〈佛教〉 tonsure: ～出家 be tonsured /～为尼 take the tonsure and become a nun

剃光头 tì guāngtóu ❶ have one's head shaved: 夏天～凉快。It makes one cool to have one's head shaved in summer. ❷ (as in an examination or contest) lay an egg; fail miserably: 这场球他们输得真惨: 〇比五，给剃了个大光头。The game was a catastrophe: they laid an egg by losing zero to five.

剃头 tìtóu ❶ have one's head shaved: ～刀 shaver /电动～刀 electrical shaver ❷ have one's hair cut; have a haircut: ～师傅 barber

剃须刀 tìxūdāo razor

剃须膏 tìxūgāo shaving cream

剃枝虫 tìzhīchóng 〈动物〉 armyworm

绨

tì a kind of blended silk or rayon and cotton fabric: 线～ rayon and cotton fabric

see also tí

替[1]

tì ❶ take the place of; replace; substitute for: 他下月就要离开，得找个人～他。He is leaving next month. We must find someone to replace him (*or* take his place). /你身体不舒服，我～你去吧! Let me go in your place since you're not feeling well. ❷ for; on behalf of: ～人受罪 suffer for sb. else /～人送礼 present a gift on sb.'s behalf /～父报仇 avenge one's father /先～别人着想 think about the interests of others first /～你担心 feel worried for your sake

替[2]

tì 〈书面〉 decline; fall: 历代兴～ rise and fall of dynasties /百年兴～ vicissitudes of a century

替班 tìbān work in place of sb.: 找人～ find a replacement (*or* substitute) /～的工人 replacement worker /有人病了时，主任往往亲自～。The director often worked as a replacement when anyone was ill.

替补 tìbǔ substitute for; replace: ～队员 substitute (player); alternate; understudy /～疗法 replacement therapy /请某人～他 ask sb. work as a substitute (*or* replacement) for him

替代 tìdài substitute (for); replace; supersede: 进口～ import substitution /～进口产品 import substitute /～疗法 substitution therapy /～能源 alternate energy /不可～ irreplaceable /用塑料～木料 replace wood by plastics; substitute plastics for wood /任何人都～不了他的历史作用。No one could have replaced him in the role he played in history.

替工 tìgōng ❶ work as a (temporary) substitute: 安排人～ find sb. as a temporary substitute /本月～三次 work as a temporary substitute three times this month /～记录 replacement record ❷ temporary substitute (worker): 按有关规定给～报酬 pay the substitutes

according to the relevant regulations
替古人担忧 tì gǔrén dānyōu worry about the ancients (e.g. while reading history); concern oneself with the fate of the ancients; waste one's energy by worrying needlessly
替换 tìhuan replace; substitute for; take the place of:轮流～ do sth. in turn; take turns (in doing sth.); relieve each other by turns / 让10号～2号 substitute No. 10 for No. 2 /已经决定由他～王师傅当班长。It has been decided that he will replace Wang as team leader. / 必须立即派人～那些超时工作的拖拉机手。We must immediately send people to relieve those tractor drivers who have been working overtime. /他随身只带了一套～的衣服。He brought with him only one change of clothes.
替换材料 tìhuan cáiliào alternate material
替角儿 tìjuér understudy
替身 tìshēn ❶ substitute; replacement; stand-in:当～ serve as a replacement ❷ scapegoat; fall guy:代人受罚的～ fall guy; whipping boy/他一有错就想找～。He always tries to find a scapegoat whenever he makes a mistake.
替身演员 tìshēn yǎnyuán stunt man or woman; stand-in
替手 tìshǒu ❶ work in sb.'s place; substitute; replace:女儿大了,家务上可以给母亲替替手了。Now that her daughter has grown up, she can do some of the housework in her place. ❷ substitute; replacement:你先干收发,等一有了～就给你安排别的工作。Please work as receptionist for the time being. We'll assign you another job, as soon as a replacement is available.
替死鬼 tìsǐguǐ 〈口语〉scapegoat; fall guy:没想到我倒成了他的～。I had never thought that I would become his scapegoat.
替天行道 tìtiān-xíngdào (usu. used as a slogan for rebelling against a dynasty) carry out the Way of Heaven; enforce justice on behalf of Heaven; act as agent for Heaven
替续器 tìxùqì *also* "继电器" jìdiànqì relay
替罪羊 tìzuìyáng *also* "替罪羔羊" scapegoat; whipping boy:错误政策的～ scapegoat who takes the blame for a wrong policy

趯
tì 〈书面〉jump; leap

薙
tì 〈书面〉❶ remove weeds; weed ❷ shave

惕
tì cautious; watchful:警～ be vigilant; be on alert
惕厉 tìlì *also* "惕励" watchful; alert; on guard:日夜～ be on the alert day and night
惕惕 tìtì 〈书面〉afraid; fearful:心怀～ feel misgivings; be fearful at heart
惕息 tìxī dare not breathe — be scared to death:～从命 obey fearfully

裼
tì 〈书面〉baby clothes
see also xī

殢
tì 〈书面〉❶ be held up ❷ be perplexed and pestered

逖(逷)
tì 〈书面〉far away; distant

嚏
tì 〈书面〉sneeze
嚏喷 tìpen sneeze

俶
tì
see also chù
俶傥 tìtǎng *see* "倜傥" tìtǎng

倜
tì
倜然 tìrán 〈书面〉❶ uncommon; out-of-the-ordinary; outstanding:～举荐 specially recommend; recommend highly ❷ aloof; detached; distant; indifferent:～而去 leave in an unconcerned manner
倜傥 tìtǎng *also* "俶傥" tìtǎng 〈书面〉free and easy of manner; unconventional:～不群 unconventional and aloof /风流～ unrestrained and overflowing with talent; unconventional and romantic

屉(屜)
tì ❶ food steamer with several trays; steamer tray:～帽 lid (*or* cover) of a steamer /一～包子 a trayful of steamed stuffed buns ❷ *see* "屉儿" ❸ 〈方言〉drawer:五～柜 chest of drawers
屉儿 tìr removable seat (of a chair) or top (of a bedstead), usu. made of woven rattan, steel wires, coir ropes, etc.
屉子 tìzi ❶ (one of) a set of removable trays (in furniture or a utensil) ❷ *see* "屉儿" ❸ 〈方言〉drawer

tiān

天
tiān ❶ sky; heaven:蓝～ blue sky /九重～ Ninth Heaven; highest of heavens /满～星斗 star-studded sky ❷ overhead: *see* "～窗"; "～桥" ❸ day:～～ every day /昨～ yesterday /大白～ in broad daylight /七～七夜 seven days and nights ❹ period of time in a day; time of day:正午～ high noon /～刚黑。It's just turned dark. /～还早,喝杯茶再走。It's early yet. Have a cup of tea before you go. ❺ season:冬～ winter /梅雨～ rainy season (usu. in April and May in the middle and lower reaches of the Yangtze River) /三九～ coldest days of winter (third nine-day period after the Winter Solstice) ❻ weather:下雪～ snowy weather /晴～ sunny day; fine day /阴～ overcast sky; cloudy day ❼ inborn; innate; inherent; natural:先～ congenital; a priori; innate ❽ nature:战～斗地 combat nature /人定胜～。Man will conquer nature. ❾ Heaven; God:～哪! Good Heavens! *or* Mercy on us! /谢～谢地! Thank Heaven! /上～保佑。May God be with me. *or* God help me. /～亡我也! It's God's will that I shall fail (*or* perish). /老～可怜可怜吧! Heaven pity us! ❿ celestial abode of gods; heaven; paradise:归～ go to heaven; die
天安门 Tiān'ānmén Tian An Men (the Gate of Heavenly Peace of the Imperial Palace of Beijing)
天安门广场 Tiān'ānmén Guǎngchǎng Tian'anmen Square (in central Beijing)
天半 tiānbàn in mid air; in the air:风烟滚滚来～。Smoke billowed with the wind in mid air.
天宝 Tiānbǎo Tianbao, second reign title (742-756) of Li Longji (李隆基,685-762), 6th emperor of the Tang Dynasty, called reverently Tang Xuanzong (唐玄宗) after death:～十年 in the tenth year of Tianbao (751 AD)
天崩地裂 tiānbēng-dìliè *also* "天崩地坼" the skies fall and the earth cracks:地震时,～,房倒屋塌。The quake sent the houses tumbling down with such deafening sounds, as if the skies were falling and the earth cracking. /～的社会大变革,彻底改变了神州大地。Earth-shaking social transformation thoroughly changed the outlook of China.
天边 tiānbiān ❶ ends of the earth; remotest places:家乡远在～,何时能归? When shall I be back home, my far, far away old home? ❷ horizon:～一抹朝霞。A streak of rosy dawn was breaking over the horizon.
天兵 tiānbīng ❶ troops from heaven:～天将 soldiers and generals from heaven ❷ 〈比喻〉invincible army:号称"～" claim to be "an invincible army" /～怒气冲霄汉。The wrath of the Heaven's armies soars to the clouds. ❸ 〈旧语〉imperial army; government troops
天禀 tiānbǐng 〈书面〉natural gift; natural endowments; talent:～过人 be endowed with outstanding talents /～聪颖 bright and talented
天波 tiānbō *also* "空间波" kōngjiānbō sky wave; spatial wave; space wave:～传播 sky wave propagation; sky wave transmission /～干扰 sky wave trouble /～效应 sky wave effect /～高频雷达 sky wave HF radar
天不变,道亦不变 tiān bùbiàn, dào yì bùbiàn Heaven changeth not; likewise, the Way changeth not
天不负人 tiānbùfùrén Heaven never fails the faithful; Heaven always rewards the faithful; all is for the best
天不假年 tiānbùjiǎnián *also* "天不假人" god does not give one a long enough life (to accomplish one's mission or task); one's life is unfortunately cut short (before one accomplishes one's mission or task); unfortunately good people do not always live long:可惜～,一位科学奇才在他崭露头角时便与世长辞了! Unfortunately those whom the gods love die young, and we have lost a rare scientist when he has just begun to show his remarkable talent.
天不绝人 tiānbùjuérén *also* "天无绝人之路" Heaven would not drive a man to the wall; Heaven would not fail a man (when he is

T

in desperate straits)

天不怕,地不怕 tiān bù pà, dì bù pà fear neither Heaven nor Earth; fear nothing at all; be dauntless:他是一条~的硬汉子。He is a tough guy who fears nothing and no one.

天不作美 tiānbùzuòměi *also* "天公不作美" Heaven is not cooperative; the weather is not helpful (to one's plans); the weather lets us down:~,连日大风使我的长城之游不能不作罢。The weather was bad, and the continuous windstorm spoiled my plan to visit the Great Wall.

天才 tiāncái ❶ genius; talent; gift:艺术~ artistic genius; gift for art / ~儿童 gifted child; child prodigy / ~的构思和创作 ingenious plotting and creation / 这人自幼便有绘画~。He had an aptitude for drawing as a boy. ❷ man of genius; genius:画坛~ master in painting / 足球~ football genius / 被人誉为神奇的"~" be reputed as a "prodigy"

天才教育 tiāncái jiàoyù genius education

天才论 tiāncáilùn theory of innate genius

天蚕 tiāncán 〈动物〉giant silkworm; wild silkworm:~蛾 giant silkworm moth

天差地远 tiānchā-dìyuǎn *also* "天悬地隔"〈比喻〉vastly different; worlds or poles apart; far off the beam:~,无可比拟。The two are poles apart and cannot be mentioned in the same breath. / ~,不可企及。It is far off the beam and unattainable.

天产 tiānchǎn natural or native product:~富饶 abound in natural products

天长地久 tiāncháng-dìjiǔ enduring as heaven and earth; everlasting and unchanging:友谊~ everlasting friendship; eternal friendship / 两地相思,~。Time and distance did not dull the everlasting yearning between the two lovers.

天长日久 tiāncháng-rìjiǔ after a long, long time; as the years go by:他们在这个热带国家定居下来,~,逐渐习惯了当地的生活。After they settled down in the tropical country, it took them a long time to get used to the life there.

天朝 tiāncháo ❶ (formerly of the dominant Chinese dynasty) Celestial Empire; Heavenly Kingdom; Heavenly Court:"~心理" Heavenly Kingdom complex ❷ (title used by the Taipings, 1853-1864) Kingdom of Heavenly Peace; Heavenly Kingdom

天朝田亩制度 Tiāncháo Tiánmǔ Zhìdù System of Land Ownership of the Heavenly Kingdom, a programmatic document promulgated in 1853 which was to abolish feudal land ownership under the Taiping regime but was not put into practice

T

天车 tiānchē *also* "行车" hángchē 〈机械〉overhead travelling crane; shop traveller:~滑道 crane runway

天成 tiānchéng (as if) produced by heaven; springing from nature; natural:~佳偶 perfect match (*or* marriage) made by Heaven / 音韵~ natural and perfect metre / 文章本~,妙手偶得之。All excellent writings come spontaneously as if from heaven; even good writers hit upon them but once in a while.

天秤座 Tiānchèngzuò 〈天文〉Libra; the Balance

天池 tiānchí ❶〈古语〉sea ❷〈天文〉name of a star ❸ Heavenly Pond, name of any of the lakes on top of Tianshan (天山) in Xinjiang, Baitou Mountain (白头山) in Jilin, or Guancen Mountain (管涔山) in Shanxi

天愁地惨 tiānchóu-dìcǎn miserable situation; melancholy atmosphere

天窗 tiānchuāng ❶〈建筑〉skylight:打开~说亮话 frankly speaking; let's not mince matters; let's call a spade a spade / 太阳透过~照进屋里。The sun is peeping in through the skylight. ❷〈旧语〉blank (left in a newspaper to show sth. has been suppressed by censorship):开~ leave a blank (in a newspaper)

天赐 tiāncì sent by heaven or God:~之物 godsend / ~甘霖 heaven-sent rain; auspicious rain / ~良缘 heaven-ordained marriage; match arranged by God / 有机会出国进修,对于这位自学成才的工程师可谓~良机。The opportunity to study abroad was a godsend to the self-taught engineer.

天从人愿 tiāncóngrényuàn heaven granting man's wish; by the grace of God; God willing:~,事事如意。By the grace of God, everything turned out as one wished. / 倘若~,明年此时这项任务就可大功告成了。God willing, the task would have been accomplished with every success by this time next year.

天打雷轰 tiāndǎ-léihōng *also* "天打雷劈";"天打五雷轰" (usu. used in swearing) be stricken by thunder; be punished by God:我若对你有二心,~! Strike me dead if I'm found unfaithful to you!

天大 tiāndà as big as the heavens; extremely big:~的事 extremely important (*or* serious) matter / ~的好事 wonderful luck; unqualified blessing / 你就是有~的本事,恐怕也施展不开。However capable you are, you probably can do nothing in the circumstances.

天道 tiāndào ❶〈哲学〉(in ancient Chinese philosophical terminology) Way of Heaven — either referring to objective laws governing nature and its development or regarded as manifestations of God's will:上逆~,下违人常 run counter to the ways of both Heaven and man — be grossly unjust; be outrageous ❷〈方言〉weather:山里的~,说变就变。The weather in these mountainous areas is extremely changeable. / 看~,说不定会下雨。It looks like rain.

天道好还 tiāndào-hǎohuán The Way of Heaven goes in a circle; Heaven is bound to come around and punish evildoers

天敌 tiāndí 〈生物〉natural enemy

天底 tiāndǐ 〈天文〉nadir

天底下 tiāndǐxia 〈口语〉under heaven; under the sun; in the world; on earth:~什么新鲜事都有。There is no lack of strange things in this world. / ~哪有这么不讲理的人! There can be no one more impervious to reason! *or* What an unreasonable man!

天地 tiāndì ❶ heaven and earth; world; universe:~万物 all creatures in the universe; everything in the world / 狂风暴雨,~混沌一片。All was thrown into murky chaos as the storm raged. ❷ field of activity; sphere; world:儿童~ children's world / 军事~ (a TV programme) military world / 开辟科技兴农的新~ open up a new sphere (*or* vista) by developing agriculture through science and technology / 人人都有自己生活的~。Everyone lives in his own circle. ❸〈方言〉wretched situation; plight:没想到竟落到这般~! Never thought things could have come to such a (sorry) pass!

天地不容 tiāndì-bùróng *also* "天地难容" cannot be tolerated by heaven or earth; cannot escape the punishment of heaven and earth; Heaven forbid

天地会 Tiāndìhuì Heaven and Earth Society (a secret popular group organized in the early Qing Dynasty for overthrowing the Manchus and restoring the Ming Dynasty, later renamed the Three-In-One or Triad Society to carry on anti-Qing activities in collaboration with the Taipings)

天地良心 tiāndì-liángxīn *also* "天理良心" in my soul of souls; in all honest truth; in all fairness:我的所作所为对得起~。I have a clear conscience in whatever I do. / ~! 这可不是我的本意。Honestly, this is not what I meant.

天地头 tiāndìtóu 〈印刷〉top and bottom margins of a page; upper and lower margins of a page:留出~来 leave enough margin both at the top and bottom / 在~处写批注 write annotations and commentaries in the top and bottom margins; put (*or* write) down marginalia

天帝 tiāndì God of Heaven (supreme god in Chinese legend)

天电 tiāndiàn 〈电学〉atmospherics; spherics; static:~干扰 static disturbances; statics / ~观测 spherics observation

天顶 tiāndǐng ❶ sky:飞机在~上盘旋。A plane was hovering above. ❷〈天文〉zenith:~角 zenith angle / ~等距投影〈地理〉zenithal equidistant projection

天鹅 tiān'é *also* "鹄" hú swan; *Cygnus*:小~ cygnet / ~羽绒 swansdown / ~舞 swan dance /《天鹅湖》*Swan Lake* / ~之歌 swan song

天鹅绒 tiān'éróng velvet

天鹅座 Tiān'ézuò 〈天文〉Cygnus; Northern Cross

天蛾 tiān'é 〈动物〉sphingid; hawkmoth; sphinx

天恩 tiān'ēn 〈旧语〉emperor's benevolence or kindness; imperial bestowal:~浩荡。The kindness of the emperor is boundless. / ~殊绝。The imperial bestowal is out of the ordinary.

天翻地覆 tiānfān-dìfù *also* "地覆天翻" heaven and earth turning upside down; earth-shaking:~的事件 earth-shaking event / 打它个~ fight one's way in and turn everything upside down; smash up everything / 闹个~ make an awful disturbance; raise hell / 日行月移,~。Tremendous changes took place as time went by.

天方 Tiānfāng 〈旧语〉Arab countries in the Middle East; Arabia

天方教 Tiānfāngjiào 〈旧语〉Islam

天方夜谭 Tiānfāng-yètán ❶ (Tiānfāng Yètán) *Arabian Nights Entertainments* or *The Thousand and One Nights*, a series of anonymous stories in Arabic, now known all over the world ❷ cock-and-bull story; most fantastic tale:我不相信会有这件事,这是~! I don't believe it. It is simply incredible.

天分 tiānfèn natural gift; special endowments; talent: ～甚高 uncommonly gifted (*or* talented) /很有～ be endowed with unusual talents; be unusually talented

天府之国 tiānfǔzhīguó (usu. used in referrence to Sichuan Province) land of abundance; land of plenty

天赋 tiānfù ❶ endowed by nature; inherent; innate: ～才智 innate ability and wisdom /～神力 extraordinary strength endowed by nature ❷ natural gift; talent; endowments: ～过人 be uncommonly (*or* remarkably) talented /成功不能光靠～。Success does not depend on talent alone.

天赋人权 tiānfù rénquán natural right; inalienable right: ～论 the theory (*or* concept) of the inalienable rights of man

天干 tiāngān *also* "十干" shígān ten Heavenly Stems, used as serial numbers and also in combination with the twelve Earthly Branches to designate years, months, days and hours

天罡 Tiāngāng *also* "天罡星" (in ancient Chinese astronomy) Big Dipper; Plough

天高地厚 tiāngāo-dìhòu ❶ (of kindness and love) profound; deep: ～的恩情 profound kindness ❷ (usu. used after 不知) how high the sky and how deep the earth; immensity of the universe; complexity of things: 不知～ not understand the complexity of things; think too much of oneself; have an exaggerated opinion of one's own abilities

天高皇帝远 tiān gāo huángdì yuǎn 〈俗语〉 the sky is high and the emperor far away; law and government are far from here; when the cat's away, the mice will play: 咱这里是个～, 谁也管不着的地方。This is a place beyond the reach (*or* power) of law and government.

天高气爽 tiāngāo-qìshuǎng the sky is high and the air fresh; it's a fine breezy day with clear skies

天戈 tiāngē ❶ 〈书面〉 imperial troops: ～所指, 莫不归顺。Where the invincible imperial troops marched, all rebel forces surrendered and pledged allegiance. ❷ (Tiāngē) *also* "玄戈" Xuángē 〈天文〉 one of the stars of the Herdsman

天鸽座 Tiāngēzuò 〈天文〉 Columba

天各一方 tiāngèyīfāng (of a family or friends) be far apart: 你我此别, ～, 不知相会又在何日! We shall part and live in different corners of the world, not knowing when to meet again!

天工 tiāngōng *also* "天功" work of Heaven; performance of the Creator; work of nature: 巧夺～ (of superb workmanship) surpass nature's creations

天工开物 Tiāngōng Kāiwù *Tian Gong Kai Wu* or *Exploitation of the Works of Nature*, a work of science and technology of the Ming Dynasty

天公 tiāngōng ruler of heaven; God; weather: ～善体人意。The weather seemed to know our wishes. /我劝～重抖擞, 不拘一格降人材。O Heaven! Bestir yourself, I beseech you, And send down men of all the talents.

天公不作美 tiāngōng bù zuòměi *see* "天不作美"

天公地道 tiāngōng-dìdào absolutely fair; exactly as it should be: 事情办得～, 人人都满意。The matter was handled fairly and reasonably to the satisfaction of all.

天宫 tiāngōng heavenly palace: 孙悟空大闹～ the Monkey King wreaking havoc in the Heavenly Palace (an episode from *Pilgrimage to the West*)

天沟 tiāngōu 〈建筑〉 channel or trough along or under the lower edge of a roof to carry off rain water; gutter

天狗 tiāngǒu ❶ (in legends) beast like a racoon dog ❷ dog-shaped star

天狗螺 tiāngǒuluó 〈动物〉 a kind of mollusc

天光 tiānguāng ❶ daylight; time of the day: ～刚露出鱼肚白。It is just turning light. *or* Day is only just breaking. /鸡叫头遍, ～还早呢。The cock is crowing for the first time. It's early yet. ❷ sunlight; sunbeam; sunshine: ～普照大地。The sun illuminates every corner of the land. /明湖映～。The limpid lake water reflected the myriad of colours in the sky. ❸ 〈方言〉 morning

天癸 tiānguǐ 〈中医〉 menstruation: ～至 beginning of menstrual function /～竭 menopause

天国 tiānguó ❶ kingdom of Heaven: 地上～ kingdom of Heaven on earth /灵魂升入～ one's soul goes to the kingdom of Heaven ❷ utopia; paradise: 人间～ paradise on earth

天寒地冻 tiānhán-dìdòng so cold that the ground is fozen; freezing: ～的天气 icy weather

天汉 Tiānhàn 〈书面〉 Milky Way

天河 Tiānhé (general term for 银河) Milky Way; Galaxy

天河石 tiānhéshí amazon stone; amazonite

天黑 tiānhēi ❶ dusk; evening: ～前他就到家了。He got home before dark (*or* evening). ❷ dark; dim: ～看不清楚。It was too dark to see clearly.

天候 tiānhòu weather: 全～公路 all-weather road /全～战机 all-weather fighter /全～飞行 all-weather flight

天花 tiānhuā ❶ *also* "痘" dòu; "痘疮" dòuchuāng 〈医学〉 smallpox: ～病毒 pox virus /～疫苗 smallpox vaccine; anti-smallpox vaccine; glycerinated vaccine virus ❷ stamen of maize

天花板 tiānhuābǎn ceiling

天花粉 tiānhuāfěn 〈中药〉 root of Chinese trichosanthes (*Trichosanthes Kirilowii*)

天花乱坠 tiānhuā-luànzhuì (according to a Chinese legend, Heaven was once so deeply touched by the preaching of Monk Yunguang 云光法师 during the reign of Emperor Wu of the Liang Dynasty, that it rained flowers) give an extravagantly colourful description: 说得～ give an exaggerated account of sth.; shoot one's mouth off

天荒地老 tiānhuāng-dìlǎo *also* "地老天荒" until heaven and earth get old; for a long, long time: ～, 石碑上的字迹已难辨识了。After such a long period of time, the inscription on the stone tablet was hardly recognizable.

天皇 tiānhuáng ❶ Son of Heaven; emperor ❷ emperor of Japan; mikado; tenno: 明仁～ Akihito Tenno; Emperor Akihito /～制度 Tennoism

天回日转 tiānhuí-rìzhuǎn passage of time: ～, 其谢如矢。Time passes as swiftly as a flying arrow.

天昏地暗 tiānhūn-dì'àn *also* "天昏地黑" ❶murky sky over a dark earth; dark all round: 狂风夹着暴雨, 一时～。It turned dark all round for a moment, as a fierce wind swept by accompanied by a torrential rain. ❷ chaos and darkness: 奸臣当道, ～, 民不聊生。With treacherous courtiers in power, the country was plunged into a state of chaos and darkness, and the people were deprived of their means of livelihood. ❸ awfully; terribly; violently; like hell: 哭得个～ wail like hell

天火 tiānhuǒ 〈口语〉 fire started by lightning or other natural cause

天机 tiānjī ❶ God's design; secret of providence: ～难测 unpredictable secret of providence ❷ nature's mystery; important secret: 一语道破了～ lay bare the truth with one penetrating remark

天机不可泄露 tiānjī bùkě xièlòu 〈俗语〉 one must not reveal the design of God; one must not give away a heavenly secret: ～, 到时你便自知。No design of God should be divulged prematurely, and you will know in time.

天鸡 tiānjī (legendary) heavenly cock whose crow arouses the crowing of all cocks on earth

天极 tiānjí ❶ 〈天文〉 celestial pole: ～仪 polar telescope ❷ 〈书面〉 horizon: 黄沙滚滚来～。Clouds of dust rolled over from beyond the horizon.

天疾 tiānjí congenital defect or disease

天际 tiānjì 〈书面〉 horizon: 莽莽原野一直伸向～。The vast wilderness stretched as far as the horizon. /～星光闪烁。The stars were twinkling over the horizon.

天假良缘 tiānjiǎliángyuán heaven-sent opportunity; chance of a lifetime

天骄 tiānjiāo proud or favorite son of Heaven — a reference to the chief of Xiongnu (a minority nationality) in the Han Dynasty, later used in reference to rulers of certain northern minority nationalities: 一代～成吉思汗 Genghis Khan, proud son of Heaven for his time

天角 tiānjiǎo ❶ forehead: ～隆起 have a protruding forehead ❷ corner of the sky: ～一星 solitary star hanging in a corner of the sky /～风云乍起。All of a sudden a storm broke out on the far horizon.

天芥菜 tiānjiècài garden heliotrope: ～属 heliotrope /～精 heliotropin

天津 Tiānjīn Tianjin (formerly translated as Tientsin), major city in North China and one of the four municipalities directly under the State Council

天津条约 Tiānjīn Tiáoyuē Treaties of Tianjin or Tientsin, unequal treaties signed between the Qing Government and the imperialist

T

powers of Tsarist Russia, the United States, Great Britain and France respectively during the Second Opium War (1856-1860)

天经地义 tiānjīng-dìyì principle of heaven and earth; unalterable truth: 种瓜得瓜, 种豆得豆, 这是~的事情。As one sows, so shall one reap — this is an unalterable truth. /按照中国伦理观念, 子女赡养父母是~的道理。According to Chinese ethics, it is only right and proper for adult children to provide for their parents.

天井 tiānjǐng ❶ courtyard (enclosed by housing or walls); patio ❷ uncovered skylight in a traditional house: ~沟 ditch under uncovered skylight ❸ 〈矿业〉 raise: 通风~ air raise

天可汗 Tiānkèhán Heavenly Emperor — title of Tang Taizong (唐太宗, or Li Shimin 李世民, 599-649, second emperor of the Tang Dynasty) used by monarchs of northwestern ethnic minorities

天空 tiānkōng sky; heavens: 蔚蓝的~ blue sky; azure sky /布满乌云的~ overcast sky /~景色 skyscape /~滤光片〈摄影〉 sky filter /~实验室 skylab; space laboratory /~海阔 as boundless as the sea and the sky; of infinite capacity; with a magnanimous mind

天葵 tiānkuí 〈植物〉 *Semiaquilegia adoxoides*

天籁 tiānlài 〈书面〉 sounds of nature: 此时明月当空, ~俱寂。A bright moon was above and tranquillity reigned.

天籁自鸣 tiānlài-zìmíng ❶ sound of nature (such as wind, water, birds, etc.) ❷ chant or sing to oneself

天蓝 tiānlán sky blue; azure: ~色 sky blue; cerulean /~石 lazulite; blue spar

天狼星 Tiānlángxīng 〈天文〉 Sirius: ~光谱 Sirian spectrum

天朗气清 tiānlǎng-qìqīng clear sky and fresh air

天老儿 tiānlǎor albino

天老爷 tiānlǎoye *also* "老天爷" Heavens; God

天理 tiānlǐ ❶ heavenly principles — ethics as propounded by the Song Confucianists: 灭人欲, 存~ eradicate human desires and maintain the heavenly principles (ethical slogan of the Song Confucianists) ❷ (plain) justice: 有违~ this is incompatible with justice; justice would not tolerate this /上合~, 下顺人情 conform to both heavenly principles and human ethics

天理教 Tiānlǐjiào *also* "八卦教" Bāguàjiào Society of Heavenly Principles, a branch of the White Lotus Society (白莲教), which came into existence after the parent society's armed uprising in the mid-18th century failed and which later launched anti-Manchu uprisings in Beijing and Henan

T

天理难容 tiānlǐ-nánróng justice would not tolerate this; heaven forbid: 赚这种昧心钱, ~! It goes against justice to make that dishonest money!

天理昭彰 tiānlǐ-zhāozhāng Heaven's laws are manifest in themselves; justice will overtake all crimes: 这个恶贼也有今天, 真是~! As Heaven will eventually settle all accounts, that bastard has at last got what he deserves!

天良 tiānliáng conscience: 丧尽~ conscienceless; heartless: ~发现 be stung by conscience; one's better nature asserts itself /~未泯 retain a shred of conscience; be not totally lost to conscience

天亮 tiānliàng daybreak; dawn: ~时出发 start off at daybreak (*or* dawn)

天料木 tiānliàomù 〈植物〉 *Homalium cochinchinensis*

天灵盖 tiānlínggài top of skull; crown (of the head)

天龙座 Tiānlóngzuò 〈天文〉 Draco; Dragon

天炉座 Tiānlúzuò 〈天文〉 Fornax

天伦 tiānlún 〈书面〉 natural bonds and ethical relationships between members of a family: 父子~ natural bonds and ethical relationship between father and son; love between father and son

天伦之乐 tiānlúnzhīlè family love and happiness; (esp.) happiness of a family living together: 一家人共享~。The family were happy together.

天罗地网 tiānluó-dìwǎng nets above and snares below; tight encirclement; inescapable net (of law, etc.): 难逃~ difficult (*or* impossible) to break through the tight encirclement /武警在逃犯隐藏处布下了~。A dragnet was spread by the armed police around the escaped convict's hiding place.

天麻 tiānmá 〈中药〉 tuber of elevated gastrodis (*Gastrodia elata*)

天马行空 tiānmǎ-xíngkōng like a heavenly steed soaring across the skies; vigorous and unconstrained in style: ~, 笔意纵横 write in a free and powerful style /~, 独往独来 be a loner like a heavenly steed soaring across the skies in solitude

天门 tiānmén ❶ 〈旧语〉 gate to the Heavenly Palace ❷ gate to an imperial or royal palace ❸ centre of forehead ❹ (in Taoist terminology) heart; mind

天门冬 tiānméndōng *also* "天冬草" 〈植物〉 lucid asparagus (*Asparagus cochinchinensis*): ~酰胺〈生化〉 asparagine /~氨酸〈生化〉 aspartic acid /~氨酸酶〈生化〉 aspartase

天名精 tiānmíngjīng 〈植物〉 *Carpesium abrotanoides*

天明 tiānmíng daybreak; dawn: ~鸡啼。The cock crows at dawn.

天命 tiānmìng God's will; mandate of heaven; destiny; fate: ~无常。The mandate of heaven is inconstant. /宿命论者认为~不可违。Fatalists hold that man cannot challenge fate.

天幕 tiānmù ❶ canopy of the heavens; sky: 乌云布满了~。Black clouds blotted out the sky. *or* The sky was overcast. /~之下是一片大草原。Under the canopy of the sky lies a vast stretch of grassland. ❷ backdrop (of a stage): ~上呈现出百花吐艳、百鸟争鸣的春天景象。The backdrop presented a spring scene with flowers blooming in a riot of colours and birds singing cheerfully. /两束灯光射向~。Two beams of light shot forth towards the backcloth (*or* backdrop).

天南地北 tiānnán-dìběi *also* "天南海北" ❶ far apart; poles apart: ~, 两地相思。Living far apart, the couple yearned for each other endlessly. ❷ from different places or areas; from all over: 观光的游客来自~。The tourists came from different parts of the country and the world. ❸ about a wide range of things; rambling: ~地闲谈 chat about everything under the sun

天南星 tiānnánxīng 〈植物〉 jack-in-the-pulpit (*Arisaema consanguineum*)

天年 tiānnián ❶ natural span of life; one's allotted span; one's natural life: 安享~ spend one's last years in peace /得尽~ die a natural death; live one's full span ❷ 〈方言〉 year's harvest: 今年~不好。Crops were bad this year. ❸ 〈方言〉 times; days; years: 兵荒马乱的~, 家家都不好过。Life was difficult for everyone in those years of war.

天牛 tiānniú 〈动物〉 longicorn; long-horned beetle

天怒人怨 tiānnù-rényuàn wrath of God and resentment of man; widespread indignation and discontent: ~, 民心丧尽。The regime lost all popular support and faced widespread indignation and discontent.

天女散花 tiānnǚ-sànhuā goddess strewing flowers down from heaven: 雪花飘飞, 似~。The snowflakes were dancing about as if a goddess were strewing flowers over the earth.

天疱疮 tiānpàochuāng 〈医学〉 pemphigus

天棚 tiānpéng ❶ 〈建筑〉 ceiling: ~灯 ceiling lamp ❷ *also* "凉棚" liángpéng awning or canopy, usu. made of reed matting and bamboo poles

天平 tiānpíng balance; scales: 分析~〈化学〉 analytical balance

天平动 tiānpíngdòng 〈天文〉 libration: ~轨道 libration orbit /~点 libration point /月球的~ libration of the moon

天启 Tiānqǐ Tianqi, title of the reign (1621-1627) of Zhu Youjiao (朱由校), 16th emperor of the Ming Dynasty, called reverently Ming Xizong (明熹宗) after death

天气 tiānqì ❶ weather: 这里的~变化无常。The weather here is changeable. /~转暖。It's getting warm. /只要~好, 明天我们就按计划破土动工。Weather permitting, we shall break ground tomorrow as scheduled. ❷ 〈方言〉 (point of) time: ~不早了, 到此为止吧。It's getting late and let's call it a day.

天气图 tiānqìtú weather map; synoptic chart

天气形势预报 tiānqì xíngshì yùbào weather prognostics

天气学 tiānqìxué synoptic meteorology

天气预报 tiānqì yùbào weather forecast: ~员 weatherman; weathergirl; weathercaster

天堑 tiānqiàn river or channel hard to cross; natural moat; chasm: ~难通。The natural barrier permits no easy passage. /一桥飞架南北, ~变通途。A bridge will fly to span the north and the south, Turning a deep chasm into a thoroughfare.

天桥 tiānqiáo ❶ platform bridge; overpass; overhead walkway; overhead crosswalk: 过街~ pedestrians' overpass (across a street) ❷ 〈体育〉 bridge

天琴座 Tiānqínzuò 〈天文〉 Lyra

天青 tiānqīng reddish black

天青石 tiānqīngshí celestine; celestite

天穹 tiānqióng vault of heaven; firmament: ~如盖。The firmament looks like a canopy. /~之下, 原野苍苍。Under the vault of

heaven lies a vast expanse of open country.

天球 tiānqiú 〈天文〉celestial sphere:～地平圈 celestial horizon

天球赤道 tiānqiú chìdào celestial equator

天球仪 tiānqiúyí celestial globe

天球子午圈 tiānqiú zǐwǔquān celestial meridian

天球坐标 tiānqiú zuòbiāo celestial coordinates

天区 tiānqū 〈天文〉area of the celestial sphere

天趣 tiānqù natural appeal or charm; (usu. of literary writing or work of art) appeal:～盎然 appealing; full of charm /曲尽～之妙。The tune is most appealing. *or* It is a most charming tune.

天阙 tiānquè ❶ (legendary) celestial palace ❷ imperial palace; royal or imperial court; imperial capital

天然 tiānrán natural:～冰 natural ice /～珍珠 natural pearl /～色 natural tint (*or* colour) /～露头〈地质〉natural outcrop /～盟友 natural ally /～有机化合物 natural organic compound /～屏障 natural barrier; natural cover for defence /～牧地 natural pasture /～淘汰 natural selection /～伪装 natural camouflage; natural mask

天然磁铁 tiānrán cítiě natural magnet

天然堤 tiānrándī natural levee

天然港 tiānrángǎng natural harbour

天然更新 tiānrán gēngxīn 〈林业〉natural regeneration; self-restoration

天然碱 tiānránjiǎn trona

天然免疫 tiānrán miǎnyì *also* "自然免疫" zìrán miǎnyì congenital immunity; native immunity

天然牧地 tiānrán mùdì natural pasture

天然气 tiānránqì natural gas:干～ dry gas; poor gas /湿～ wet gas; rich gas /～井 gas well; gasser /～田 gas field /～净化 natural gas purification /～提纯 natural gas refining /液化～ liquefied natural gas

天然气回注 tiānránqì huízhù 〈石油〉gas injection

天然丝 tiānránsī natural silk

天然汽油 tiānrán qìyóu 〈石油〉natural gasoline:～工厂 natural-gasoline plant /～回收厂 cycle plant

天然橡胶 tiānrán xiàngjiāo natural rubber

天然铀 tiānrányóu native or natural uranium:～反应堆 natural uranium reactor

天壤 tiānrǎng 〈书面〉❶ heaven and earth:～间烟雨朦朦,混沌一片。Heaven and earth seem blended together in the misty rain. *or* It looks hazy all around in the misty rain. ❷ high heaven and deep sea; poles apart:兄弟俩的境遇,有若～。His lot was utterly different from that of his brother.

天壤之别 tiānrǎngzhībié *also* "天渊之别";"天壤之隔" as far apart as heaven and earth; worlds or poles apart; world of difference:这五星级宾馆的设施与小客栈相比,自有～。There's of course a world of difference between this five-star hotel and an unknown small inn in terms of amenities.

天人 tiānrén ❶〈书面〉heaven and man; way of heaven and way of man:～合一 theory that man is an integral part of nature; harmony of man with nature /～相应 correspondence between man and heaven; communication (*or* interaction) between man and nature ❷ "heavenly person" — genius or beauty

天人之际 tiānrénzhījì relationship between heaven and man (fundamental thesis in classical Chinese philosophy); relationship between natural phenomena and human affairs

天日 tiānrì sky and sun; light:重见～ once more see the light of day; be freed (*or* delivered) from oppression (*or* persecution) /难见～ can hardly see the light of day again; can hardly regain freedom (*or* see the injustice redressed)

天色 tiānsè colour of the sky; time of the day (as shown by the colour of the sky); weather:～微明。The sky is faintly light with the dawn. /～还早,你再睡一会儿。It's early yet. You can sleep a little longer. /看～要起风了。It seems the wind is rising.

天上 tiānshàng sky; heavens:月亮高挂～。The moon hung high in the sky. /～有雨地下湿。〈俗语〉The ground is wet when it rains. *or* There is no smoke without fire.

天上人间 tiānshàng-rénjiān heaven and earth; in heaven and in the world; world of difference:流水落花春去也,～! Flowing water, fallen blossoms — spring has gone away now, As far as heaven from the land of man.

天神 tiānshén god; deity:～之怒 wrath of gods /～降临。Some celestial spirits have descended from heaven.

天生 tiānshēng born; inborn; inherent; innate:～的本领 inborn (*or* innate) capabilities /～的艺术家 born artist /～尤物 born siren; sex kitten /～的不爱说话 be quiet by nature /她～双目失明。She was born stone-blind. /～我才必有用。There must be a use for my talent since it is Heaven that has endowed me with it.

天生桥 tiānshēngqiáo *also* "自然桥" zìránqiáo 〈地理〉natural bridge

天师 Tiānshī "Heavenly Master" — title used by Taoists for Zhang Ling (alias Zhang Daoling 张道陵) in the Eastern Han Dynasty, founder of the *Wudoumi* (five *dou* of rice) sect of Taoism, as well as his heirs; grand master of the Taoists

天时 tiānshí ❶ season; climate:种庄稼要看～。Farming should be done in season. ❷ timeliness; opportunity:～、地利、人和 good timing, geographical convenience and harmonious human relations; opportune time, advantageous terrain and popular support; favourable climatic, geographical and human conditions /～不如地利,地利不如人和。Opportunity is important, even more so is geographical convenience, but most important of all is popular support. ❸ weather:～不顺,久旱无雨。The weather has been abnormal as there has been long-drawn-out drought. ❹ time:～尚早。It's still early.

天使 tiānshǐ ❶〈宗教〉angel ❷ envoy sent by the emperor; imperial envoy

天授 tiānshòu divine; natural:～皇权 divine imperial power /～神威 natural martial prowess

天书 tiānshū ❶〈迷信〉book or epistle from heaven or a heavenly immortal ❷ abstruse or illegible writing:他的字跟～一样难认。His writing is as illegible as hieroglyphics. /谁也读不懂这篇～似的文章。Nobody can understand this article, which reads like double Dutch. ❸〈旧语〉imperial edict

天数 tiānshù 〈迷信〉predestination; fate; predestined disaster or tragedy:～难逃。Nobody can escape his fate. /此乃～,无可如何。This is a predestined disaster and nothing can be done about it.

天顺 Tiānshùn Tianshun, title of the reign (1457-1464) of Zhu Qizhen (朱祁镇), 8th emperor of the Ming Dynasty, called reverently Ming Yingzong (明英宗) after death

天塌地陷 tiāntā-dìxiàn ❶ heaven falls and earth crumbles; both heaven and earth collapse:这次地震发生时犹如～,一下子就毁了整个城市。When the earthquake occurred, it was as if both heaven and earth collapsed, and the entire city was demolished in an instant. ❷ extremely serious; terribly grave:～的事,他也要等到明天再说。However grave the matter was, he would put it off until the next day.

天台 tiāntái ❶ (Tiántái) name of a mountain in Zhejiang Province ❷ *also* "天中" (Taoist terminology) nose

天台乌药 Tiāntái wūyào *also* "乌药" root of three-nerved spice bush (*Lindera strychnifolia*)

天坛 Tiāntán Temple of Heaven (in Beijing)

天坛座 Tiāntánzuò 〈天文〉Ara

天堂 tiāntáng ❶ heaven:灵魂升入～ one's soul ascends to heaven — die /～的召唤 call from heaven ❷ paradise; ideal life:人间～ paradise on earth /如进～ as if in heaven ❸〈方言〉top of forehead

天梯 tiāntī tall ladder; scaling-ladder

天体 tiāntǐ celestial body; star:～摄影望远镜 astrograph /～测量 astrometry /～测量仪 astrometer

天体导航 tiāntǐ dǎoháng celestial navigation

天体地质学 tiāntǐ dìzhìxué astrogeology

天体光谱学 tiāntǐ guāngpǔxué astronomical spectroscopy; astrospectroscopy

天体力学 tiāntǐ lìxué celestial mechanics

天体生物学 tiāntǐ shēngwùxué astrobiology

天体物理学 tiāntǐ wùlǐxué astrophysics

天体演变学 tiāntǐ yǎnbiànxué *also* "天体起源学"〈天文〉cosmogony

天体照相仪 tiāntǐ zhàoxiàngyí astrograph

天天 tiāntiān every day; daily; day in, day out:～读 practice of setting aside a certain amount of time every day to study Mao Zedong's works during the Cultural Revolution /好好学习,～向上。Study well and make progress every day.

天条 tiāntiáo ❶〈迷信〉laws of heaven:因触犯～而被贬落人间的仙女 fairy maiden banished to the earth because of violation of the laws of heaven ❷ Heavenly Commandments (set by the Taipings, 1851-1864)

T

天庭 tiāntíng ❶ middle of the forehead: ～开阔 broad forehead / ～饱满 full forehead ❷ (used in fairy tales and myths) abode of deities; heavenly court ❸ imperial or royal abode; imperial or royal residence

天头 tiāntóu top or upper margin of a page: ～甚宽 broad margin at the top of a page / ～留有批注 with annotations and commentaries written in the top margin of a page

天外 tiānwài ❶ beyond the horizon; beyond the earth; in the outer space; extraterrestrial: ～来客 visitor from outer space; ET / ～文明 extraterrestrial civilization ❷ highest and farthest place; sky of the skies: 魂飞～ one's soul flitting away to nowhere; be scared to death ❸ totally unexpected: 事出～。This has fallen out of the blue. *or* It is totally unexpected.

天外有天 tiānwài-yǒutiān there is always another heaven beyond this one — there is no limit to the universe; however strong, or clever, or learned you are, there is always someone stronger, or cleverer, or more learned; nothing is final: ～, 人上有人。As the sky is the limit to knowledge, so there is always someone more learned.

天王 tiānwáng ❶ Son of Heaven — emperor: ～老子〈口语〉emperor ❷ Celestial Emperor —title of Hong Xiuquan (洪秀全), leader of the Kingdom of Heavenly Peace (1851-1864) ❸ (in mythology) god; deity: 托塔李～ Taoist Deity Li who held a pagoda on his palm

天王星 Tiānwángxīng 〈天文〉Uranus

天网恢恢 tiānwǎng-huīhuī the net of Heaven has large meshes: ～, 疏而不漏。The net of Heaven has large meshes, but it lets nothing through. *or* God's mill grinds slow but sure. *or* Justice has a long arm.

天威 tiānwēi 〈书面〉❶ power of heaven; power of the emperor ❷ magical power; divine prowess

天文 tiānwén astronomy: ～观测 astronomical observation / ～大地测量 astronomical geodesy / ～地震学 astronomical seismology / ～常数 astronomical constant / ～测时 astronomical time determination

天文表 tiānwénbiǎo pocket chronometer; box chronometer; marine chronometer

天文单位 tiānwén dānwèi 〈天文〉astronomical unit (149,567,892 km)

天文导航 tiānwén dǎoháng celestial navigation

天文地质学 tiānwén dìzhìxué astrogeology

天文馆 tiānwénguǎn planetarium

天文光度学 tiānwén guāngdùxué astronomical photometry

天文年历 tiānwén niánlì astronomical yearbook; astronomical almanac

天文气象学 tiānwén qìxiàngxué astrometeorology

天文时 tiānwénshí astronomical time

天文数字 tiānwén shùzì astronomical figure; enormous figure

天文台 tiānwéntái (astronomical) observatory

天文望远镜 tiānwén wàngyuǎnjìng astronomical telescope

天文卫星 tiānwén wèixīng astronomical satellite

天文学 tiānwénxué astronomy: 航海～ nautical astronomy / 恒星～ stellar astronomy / 空间～ space astronomy / 球面～ spherical astronomy / 射电～ radio astronomy / ～家 astronomer

天文仪 tiānwényí astroscope

天文照相术 tiānwén zhàoxiàngshù astrophotography

天文制导 tiānwén zhìdǎo celestial guidance

天文钟 tiānwénzhōng astronomical clock; chronometer

天无二日 tiānwú'èrrì there is but one sun in the sky — there cannot be two kings in a country or two bosses in an office, etc.: ～, 人无二主。As there is but one sun in the sky, so there can be only one unrivalled ruler in one country.

天无绝人之路 tiān wú jué rén zhī lù Heaven never drives a man to the wall; Heaven will always leave a door open; every cloud has a silver lining: ～, 只要我们有信心, 总有办法闯过这道难关。God does not shut all doors; so long as we have confidence, we can surely find a way out of these difficulties.

天物 tiānwù produce of nature; natural resources: 暴殄～ squander the produce of nature; waste natural resources mindlessly

天下 tiānxià ❶ land under heaven; world; country: ～为家 make one's home everywhere; take the whole country as one's abode / ～汹汹 chaos under heaven; general disorder / ～闻名 known throughout the country (*or* world); world-famous; of national renown / ～大事 world affairs; major events in the country / ～奇闻 most fantastic tale; most absurd thing on earth; unheard-of absurdity / ～事总难十全十美。Nothing can ever be perfect in this world. / 有理走遍～。Nothing can be more convincing than reason. ❷ rule; domination; state power: 打～ conquer the country; seize state power / 人民的～ government (*or* rule) by the people; country where the people are their own masters

天下本无事, 庸人自扰之 tiānxià běn wú shì, yōngrén zì rǎo zhī though peace reigns over the land, stupid people create trouble for themselves; stupid people always make much ado about nothing; all is well with the world, only the ignorant will fuss over nothing

天下大乱 tiānxià-dàluàn great disorder under heaven; big upheaval throughout the country or world: ～, 军阀争雄。The whole country was thrown into disorder, with the warlords fighting for hegemony.

天下大势 tiānxià-dàshì historical trend: 话说～, 分久必合, 合久必分。〈旧语〉(formerly used by storyteller in beginning an account of historical incidents) Speaking of the general trend of things under heaven, there is bound to be unification after prolonged division, and division after prolonged unificaiton.

天下大治 tiānxià-dàzhì great order across the land

天下第一 tiānxià-dìyī first under heaven; peerless; unequalled; second to none: 其草书可称当今～。He is the best calligrapher of cursive script in China today.

天下奇闻 tiānxià-qíwén most fantastic tale; unheard-of absurdity

天下太平 tiānxià-tàipíng peace reigns throughout the world or country; the world or country is at peace: ～, 人民安乐。The country was at peace, and the people lived in happy contentment. / 我只求～, 大家相安无事。All I want is just peace and harmony for everybody.

天下为公 tiānxià-wéigōng (originally derived from legendary utopia where the aging monarch relinquished power in favour of sb. better qualified rather than his own son) the world or country for all; the whole world or country as one community

天下文章一大抄 tiānxià wénzhāng yī dà chāo all writings in the world are copyings

天下乌鸦一般黑 tiānxià wūyā yībān hēi all crows are black—evil people are the same all over the world; in every country dogs bite

天下无不散之筵席 tiānxià wú bù sàn zhī yánxí all feasts must break up at last; all good things must come to an end: ～, 我们又何必为暂别而伤心? As no nice things last forever, why should we feel sad about a temporary separation?

天下无敌 tiānxià-wúdí invincible; ever-victorious; all-conquering: 剑术～ of matchless swordsmanship

天下无难事, 只怕有心人 tiānxià wú nánshì, zhǐpà yǒuxīnrén nothing in the world is difficult for one who sets his heart on it; where there is a will, there is a way; it is dogged that does it: "～", 只要我们努力去做, 就一定能办成。"Where there is a will, there is a way". We can accomplish any task so long as we exert ourselves.

天下无双 tiānxià-wúshuāng unparalleled in the world; peerless; unique: 秦家有女, 姿容～。The Qins have a daughter, who is beautiful beyond compare.

天下兴亡, 匹夫有责 tiānxià xīngwáng, pǐfū yǒu zé every man has a duty towards his country; everyone is responsible for the fate of his country

天下一家 tiānxià-yījiā all under heaven are of one family; all men are brothers

天仙 tiānxiān goddess; fairy maiden; beauty: ～下凡 goddess (*or* fairy maiden) who has descended to the world / 貌如～ as beautiful as a goddess (*or* fairy maiden)

天仙子 tiānxiānzǐ 〈中药〉henbane seed (*Hyoscyamus niger*)

天险 tiānxiǎn natural barrier or obstacle: 扼守～ hold (*or* guard) a strategic natural barrier / 飞越～ fly over a natural barrier; cross a natural barrier with lightning speed

天线 tiānxiàn antenna; aerial: 定向～ beam (*or* directional) antenna / 拉杆～ *also* "套筒式～" telescopic antenna / 室外～ outside antenna / 鞭状～ whip antenna / ～波束 *also* "～射束" antenna beam / ～插口 *also* "～插座" socket (*or* jack) for antenna / ～座 antenna pedestal; antenna mount / ～磁心 antenna core / ～接头 antenna terminal / ～导线 antenna conductor / ～接线 antenna connection / ～电路 antenna circuit; radiating circuit / ～反射器 antenna reflector / ～稳定系统 antenna stabilization system / ～定向控制 antenna orientation control / ～有效长度 effective antenna length / ～噪声 antenna

T

noise

天线阵 tiānxiànzhèn antenna array

天香国色 tiānxiāng-guósè *also* "国色天香" heavenly fragrance and national beauty — originally in reference to the peony, later often to beautiful women; peerless beauty：这女子虽非～，倒也袅袅婷婷。Although not extraordinarily beautiful, the girl is slim and graceful.

天象 tiānxiàng ❶ astronomical phenomena; celestial phenomena：夜观～ observe astronomical phenomena at night ❷ changes of wind and cloud：根据～预测天气变化 forecast the weather according to changes of wind and cloud

天象仪 tiānxiàngyí planetarium

天晓得 tiānxiǎode 〈方言〉God or Heaven knows; nobody can tell：～他什么时候来。Nobody knows when he will show up. /～什么时候会下雨。God knows when it will rain. /～他为什么要来。Why is he here? Beats me.

天蝎座 Tiānxiēzuò 〈天文〉Scorpio; Scorpius

天心 tiānxīn ❶ meridian position in the sky; zenith：太阳升到了～。The sun has risen to its zenith. *or* The sun has reached the meridian. ❷ mind of Heaven; God's will：上合～，下合民意 accord with both God's will and the desire of the people ❸〈旧语〉desire or wish of the emperor：～难测。The mind of the emperor is unfathomable. ❹ *also* "摆轴" bǎizhóu axle of balance wheel (in a watch or clock)

天行赤目 tiānxíng chìmù 〈中医〉red and swollen eyes; conjunctivitis

天性 tiānxìng natural instinct; nature：父子～ natural bonds between father and son /～宽厚 be generous and tolerant by nature

天幸 tiānxìng providential luck; narrow escape; close shave：他大难不死，实乃～。It was really providential luck for him to survive the catastrophe. /那场大火烧毁了整个商店，～他还有些积蓄存在别处。The entire shop burnt down in the fire. Fortunately, he had stowed away some savings elsewhere.

天旋地转 tiānxuán-dìzhuǎn ❶ heaven and earth turn round — earthshaking changes occur：形势变化之大，有如～。Tremendous changes have taken place as if both heaven and earth had been transformed. ❷ (feel as if) the sky and earth were spinning round; be very dizzy：他只觉得～，两脚不稳。He felt as if the sky and earth were spinning round, and could hardly walk steadily. ❸ kick up a fierce row：他俩吵了个～。They had a hell of a row.

天悬地隔 tiānxuán-dìgé *see* "天差地远"

天涯 tiānyá end of the world; remotest place on earth：远在～，近在咫尺 seemingly at the end of the earth but actually close at hand /～相逢 meet by chance at a place far from home /流落～ wander destitute far from home /～咫尺。It is but a small world.

天涯比邻 tiānyá-bǐlín *also* "天涯若比邻" (of friends) though living in different corners of the world, yet close (at heart) like nextdoor neighbours; be close to each other though physically far apart：海内存知己，天涯若比邻。A bosom friend afar brings a distant land near.

天涯海角 tiānyá-hǎijiǎo *also* "天涯地角" end of the earth; remotest corners of the earth：～，人各一方 (of family members, friends or lovers) live far apart from each other /～难找寻。It is nowhere to be found, not even in the remotest corners of the earth. /此次分别，又是～。When we part this time, we will once again be living far away from each other.

天阉 tiānyān (of man) natural impotency; naturally impotent person

天要下雨，娘要嫁人 tiān yào xiàyǔ, niáng yào jiàrén 〈俗语〉if it threatens to rain and your mother wishes to remarry — so be it; there's no use worrying about an inevitable occurrence：～，任它去吧！Since it is certain to happen, we may just as well let it go at that.

天爷 tiānyé Heaven; God

天衣无缝 tiānyī-wúfèng seamless heavenly robe — (usu. of literary work, etc.) perfect; flawless：落笔缜密，～。His writing was meticulous and flawless.

天意 tiānyì 〈迷信〉will of Heaven; God's will：～莫测。The will of Heaven is unpredictable (*or* unfathomable). /～不可违。God's will is inviolable. /你认为万事自有～，我坚信人定胜天。You think everything is determined by Heaven, but I firmly believe man can conquer nature.

天鹰座 Tiānyīngzuò 〈天文〉Aquila

天有不测风云 tiān yǒu bùcè fēngyún a sudden storm may arise at any moment; the weather is unpredictable; something unexpected may happen any time：～，人有旦夕祸福〈谚语〉in nature there are unexpected storms and in life unpredictable vicissitudes; man's fortune is as unpredictable as the weather; the unexpected always happens in life as well as in nature

天宇 tiānyǔ ❶ sky; heaven：歌声响彻～。The singing rang through the skies. /大雾弥漫～。The sky was clouded by a dense fog. ❷〈书面〉world; country：平定～，统一四海 seize state power and reunify the country /～安定，人民和乐。The country enjoys stability and the people live in peace and harmony.

天渊 tiānyuān 〈书面〉like high heaven and deep sea; poles apart：相去有如～ as wide asunder as the poles

天渊之别 tiānyuānzhībié *see* "天壤之别"

天缘 tiānyuán heavenly opportunity; happy coincidence; predestined marriage or firendship：～巧合 happy coincidence

天运 tiānyùn 〈书面〉❶ mandate of heaven; God's will; destiny; fate ❷ movement of celestial bodies

天灾 tiānzāi natural disaster or calamity：连年～ successive years of natural disaster /～过后 in the wake of a natural calamity

天灾人祸 tiānzāi-rénhuò natural calamities and man-made misfortunes; natural and man-made disasters：～纷至沓来。Natural and man-made disasters came in quick succession.

天葬 tiānzàng celestial burial (by which bodies are cut up and fed to birds of prey)

天造地设 tiānzào-dìshè created by nature; heavenly; ideal：～的一对 ideal couple /～的度假胜地 heavenly holiday resort

天真 tiānzhēn ❶ innocent; simple and unaffected; artless：～活泼 innocent and lively /～可爱 simple and lovely /～无邪 innocent and pure /～少女 ingénue ❷ naive; childish：～的想法 naive idea /他待人处世太～了。He was too simple-minded in dealing with people.

天真烂漫 tiānzhēn-lànmàn innocent and artless：多么～的小姑娘！What an innocent girl!

天之骄子 tiānzhījiāozǐ God's favoured son; unusually lucky person：如今有些大学生自诩为～。Some college students today consider themselves the elite.

天知道 tiānzhīdao Heaven knows; God knows; nobody knows：～那是怎么回事。God knows what it's all about.

天知地知，你知我知 tiānzhī-dìzhī, nǐzhī-wǒzhī 〈俗语〉between you and me and the gatepost; nobody knows besides you and me：此事只有～，不得外传。This is strictly between you and me, no one else should know about it.

天职 tiānzhí bounden duty; mission：神圣的～ sacred duty (*or* mission) /应尽的～ what one is duty bound to fulfil; bounden duty

天轴 tiānzhóu ❶〈机械〉line shaft ❷〈天文〉celestial axis

天诛地灭 tiānzhū-dìmiè be destroyed by heaven and earth; stand condemned by God; may Heaven strike one dead：人神共怒，～ stand condemned by God and man /～，情理难容。God forbid such gross injustice. /我若违背誓言，～！Heaven strike me dead, if I betray my pledge!

天竹 tiānzhú *also* "南天竹" nántiānzhú 〈植物〉nandina

天竺 Tiānzhú 〈旧语〉India：～僧人 Indian monk

天竺鲷 tiānzhúdiāo 〈动物〉cardinal fish

天竺葵 tiānzhúkuí 〈植物〉pelargonium (*Pelargonium hortorum*)

天竺鼠 tiānzhúshǔ 〈动物〉guinea pig; cavy

天主 Tiānzhǔ (of Catholicism) God; Jehovah

天主教 Tiānzhǔjiào Catholicism：罗马～会 Roman Catholic Church /～徒 Catholic /～堂 Catholic church; Catholic chapel

天主堂 tiānzhǔtáng Catholic church or chapel

天助 tiānzhù God's help; divine blessing; unexpected luck：～与人助 blessing from Heaven and help from man /～我也。It is a blessing from Heaven. *or* It is pure luck. /自助者～。God helps those who help themselves.

天姿 tiānzī ❶ natural appearance or look：奇花异卉，各呈～。All the wonderful and rare flowers presented their various natural beauty. ❷〈书面〉natural gift; natural endowments

天姿国色 tiānzī-guósè exceptional beauty; extraordinarily beautiful woman

天资 tiānzī natural gift; natural endowments; talent：过人～ extraordinary natural endowments; unusual talent /～聪慧 bright and talented

T

天子 tiānzǐ Son of Heaven — the emperor
天子门生 tiānzǐ ménshēng 〈旧语〉one who won the first place in the palace examination personally given by the Emperor under the imperial examination system
天字第一号 tiānzì dì-yī hào number one in the world; A-1; par excellence:～的大傻瓜 greatest fool on earth /～的新闻人物 most sensational figure in the news
天纵 tiānzòng 〈书面〉Heaven-bestowed; gifted (usu. used in compliments paid to an emperor):此～之英作也! This is a gifted piece of writing!
天纵之才 tiānzòngzhīcái outstanding talent
天足 tiānzú 〈旧语〉(of women) unbound, natural feet
天尊 tiānzūn 〈佛教〉honorific title of Buddha;〈道教〉deity; divinity:原始～〈道教〉Original Divinity
天作孽,犹可违;自作孽,不可活 tiān zuònìè, yóu kě wéi; zì zuònìè, bùkě huó 〈谚语〉if disasters come from nature, something can be done to counter them; but if they are of one's own making, one is done for
天作之合 tiānzuòzhīhé heaven-made match; predestined marriage:你们是～的一对良缘。Yours is a happy marriage predestined by God.

添

tiān ❶ add; get or give more; increase:～柴 add firewood (to the fire); put in more firewood /～饭 get more rice (to eat); serve more rice /～衣服 put on (*or* buy) more clothes /～了白发 grow greyer /～了三台电脑 acquire three (more) computers /～双筷子 lay another pair of chopsticks (for an unexpected guest) /～一道菜 order another course (of food at a meal) /新～的服务项目 newly-introduced item of service /锦上～花 make what is good still better /上了年岁的人容易～病。Old people contract illness easily. ❷〈方言〉have (a baby):老两口新～了个孙子。The old couple had a grandson recently.
添办 tiānbàn add to one's possessions; get more; acquire:～家具 get more furniture; acquire new furniture
添补 tiānbu replenish; supplement; get more:～冬衣 replenish one's winter clothes; buy new winter clothes /～些文具 get a fresh supply of stationery; get more stationery /～两台自动售货机 buy (*or* acquire) two more slot machines
添彩 tiāncǎi add honour or glory to; do credit to:增色～ make more attractive (*or* glamorous) /为祖国～ bring honour to one's motherland /为母校～ be a credit to one's Alma Mater
添仓 tiāncāng *see*"填仓"tiáncāng
添丁 tiāndīng 〈旧语〉have a baby (esp. a boy) born into the family:～之喜 happy occasion of having a baby boy born into the family / 恭喜～添财。〈套语〉Best wishes for having more sons (born into the family) and acquiring a greater fortune.
添堵 tiāndǔ 〈方言〉increase sb.'s vexations; be upsetting; be a bother:你这不是给我～吗? Aren't you complicating matters for me?
添坟 tiānfén add earth to the grave of the deceased on Pure Brightness Day (清明节, usu. falling in early April) to show one's respect and concern
添福添寿 tiānfú-tiānshòu increase one's happiness and longevity; be more blessed and live longer:祝您～,多子多孙!〈套语〉Wish you greater happiness and longevity, with an ever multiplying family!
添加 tiānjiā add; increase:故事框架已有了,只要～细节。Now that we've got the plot, all we need is to add the details. /工作忙,需要～人手。We need more hands to do the work.
添加法 tiānjiāfǎ additive process
添加剂 tiānjiājì 〈化学〉additive:有些食物～会导致癌症。Some food additives may cause cancer.
添乱 tiānluàn 〈口语〉increase the confusion or chaos; add to the trouble:说是帮忙,其实尽给我们～了。He said he was helping us; actually, he gave us more trouble.
添设 tiānshè instal or set up more; increase:～商业网点 set up more shops and sales outlets /～安全设备 instal additional safety equipment
添手垫脚 tiānshǒu-diànjiǎo lend a hand to; offer help to:必须找几个～的朋友。It's necessary to get a few friends to help.
添盆 tiānpén 〈旧语〉(of well-wishers) throw coins of luck into the bathtub at the ceremony of bathing the newborn baby on the third day after its birth
添箱 tiānxiāng 〈旧语〉❶ (as of relatives and friends of the bride) add to the dowry; give wedding presents or money to the bride:吉期将近,来～的亲友络绎不绝。Relatives and friends called one after another to present wedding gifts to the bride as the wedding day drew close. ❷ wedding presents given to the bride:这两对樟木箱是舅舅送的～。The two pairs of camphorwood trunks were wedding presents from the bride's uncle.
添油加醋 tiānyóu-jiācù *see*"添枝加叶"
添枝加叶 tiānzhī-jiāyè *also*"添油加醋";"添油加酱" garble a story by adding trimmings to it (to inflame the audience); embellish or embroider a story:她把路上听来的话,又～地说了一遍。She repeated and embroidered what she had heard on the way.
添置 tiānzhì add to one's possessions; acquire; buy:～结婚用品 get things needed for wedding /近几年来这个村不少人家都～了高档家用电器。In recent years many families in the village have bought high-grade household electrical appliances.
添砖加瓦 tiānzhuān-jiāwǎ do what little one can; do one's bit:为家乡的发展～ do what little one can for the development of one's home town

黇

tiān
黇鹿 tiānlù 〈动物〉fallow deer

tián

甜

tián ❶ sweet; honeyed:～羹 sweet custard /～而不腻 sweet but not cloying; agreeably sweet /～妹子 sweet girl; charming girl /话说得真～! What sweet words! ❷ (of sleep) sound:～～地睡一觉 have a refreshing sleep; sleep soundly
甜不唧 tiánbujī slightly sweet; sweetish:这里的泉水～儿的挺好喝。The spring water here tastes nice and sweet.
甜不梭 tiánbusuō 〈方言〉unpleasantly sweet:这蛋糕～的,我不爱吃。I don't like the sweet taste of the cake.
甜菜 tiáncài *also*"糖萝卜"tángluóbo;"菾菜"tiáncài ❶ beet; sugar beet:～花叶病 beet mosaic ❷ beetroot:～糖 beet sugar /～丝 beet cossette /～渣 beet pulp
甜菜苷 tiáncàigān 〈生化〉betanin
甜橙 tiánchéng Chinese orange; sweet orange (*Citrus sinensis*)
甜点 tiándiǎn sweet pastry; dessert:～厨师 chef specializing in making sweet pastry; sweet pastry cook /今天的～是什么? What's today's dessert?
甜度 tiándù sweetness:～不够 not sweet enough
甜柑 tiángān *also*"甜橙" sweet orange
甜杆儿 tiángǎnr sweet tender stalk of maize, broomcorn millet, etc.
甜甘 tiángan (of one's words, etc.) gentle and pleasant; sweet:她的小嘴儿真～。She has a honeyed tongue.
甜高粱 tiángāoliang sorgo; sorgho
甜瓜 tiánguā muskmelon
甜活儿 tiánhuór easy and well-paid job; cushy job
甜和 tiánhuo 〈方言〉gratify; please; satisfy:别净拿好话～人,我还得看你的行动啊。Don't try to sweet-talk me; I'll see what you do.
甜椒 tiánjiāo 〈植物〉sweet pepper; pimiento (*Capsicum annuum*)
甜津津 tiánjīnjīn pleasantly sweet:～的味道 pleasantly sweet flavour /～的大蜜桃 luscious honey peaches
甜酒酿 tiánjiǔniàng sweet fermented glutinous rice *see also*"醪糟"láozāo
甜菊 tiánjú *also*"甜叶菊" *Stevia rebaudiana*:～甙 Stevia glucoside /～糖 Stevia sugar
甜露酒 tiánlùjiǔ liqueur
甜美 tiánměi ❶ sweet; luscious:这橙子多汁而～。These oranges are juicy and sweet. ❷ pleasant; refreshing:～的爱情 tender love / 睡的很～ have a sound sleep /打了个～的盹儿 have a refreshing nap; have one's beauty sleep
甜蜜蜜 tiánmīmī ❶ sweet:糖水～的。The sugar water tastes sweet. ❷ happy; pleasant:日子过得～的 lead a happy life
甜蜜 tiánmì sweet; happy:～的生活 happy life /～的微笑 sweet smile /沉浸在～的爱情之中 head over heels in love
甜面酱 tiánmiànjiàng *also*"甜酱" sweet sauce made of fermented flour
甜腻腻 tiánnīnī sweet and cloying; overly sweet:～的蛋糕 overly

sweet cake /～的笑容 saccharine smile; suave smile
甜品 tiánpǐn sweetmeats: 制作～ process sweetmeats /～专柜 sweetmeats counter
甜软 tiánruǎn (of voice) sweet and soft
甜润 tiánrùn sweet and mellow; sweet and pleasant: ～的唱腔 (in Chinese opera) sweet and mellow tune; sweet and pleasant singing /清凉～的空气 cool, refreshing air
甜食 tiánshí sweet food; sweetmeats: 爱吃～ have a sweet tooth / 小～ sweet snacks /饭后～ dessert
甜适 tiánshì comfortable; cosy: 过着～的生活 live in ease and comfort
甜爽 tiánshuǎng sweet and refreshing: 味道～ sweet and tasty
甜水 tiánshuǐ ❶ fresh water; sweet water: ～井 fresh (*or* sweet) water well ❷ happiness and comfort: 生活在～里 live a happy and comfortable life
甜睡 tiánshuì sleep soundly; be fast asleep
甜丝丝 tiánsīsī ❶ pleasantly sweet: ～的苹果 sweet apple /这米酒～的。This rice wine tastes sweet. ❷ *also* "甜滋滋" pleased; gratified; happy: 母亲心里～的。Mother felt pleased.
甜酸苦辣 tián-suān-kǔ-là *also* "酸甜苦辣" sweet, sour, bitter and hot — all kinds of flavours; all the sweets and bitters of life; entire spectrum of life experiences: 尝遍了人生的～ taste all the sweets and bitters of life; go through the whole range of life's vicissitudes
甜酸儿 tiánsuānr tartly sweet: ～的橘子 tartly sweet tangerine
甜头 tiántou ❶sweetish taste; pleasant flavour: 吃起来有点～ taste somewhat sweet ❷ (as an inducement) benefit; sop: 尝到了～ draw benefit from sth.; appreciate the good of sth. /给他点儿～。Let him take a cut of the benefit. *or* Throw him a few sops.
甜味 tiánwèi sweet taste: 这种药略带～。This medicine tastes somewhat sweet (*or* has a sweetish taste).
甜香 tiánxiāng ❶ fragrant and sweet: 味道儿～ taste delicious ❷ sound: 睡得～ have a sound sleep; sleep like a baby
甜馨 tiánxīn sweet and fragrant: ～的梦 sweet dream
甜芽菜 tiányácài sweet vernal grass; vernal grass
甜言蜜语 tiányán-mìyǔ ❶ sweet words and honeyed phrases; sweet talk: 满口～ spout sweet words; wag a honeyed tongue /我可不信他的～。I won't be taken in by his fine words. ❷ sweet-talk; wheedle: 别～的了，还是拿出点实际行动吧。Don't try to sweet-talk us; do something practical! /他为人耿直，不会～。Honest and upright, he is not good at sweet talk.
甜叶菊 tiányèjú *see* "甜菊"
甜玉米 tiányùmǐ sweet corn
甜滋滋 tiánzīzī ❶ pleasantly sweet ❷ pleased; gratified; happy
甜嘴蜜舌 tiánzuǐ-mìshé mouth fine words; be honey-mouthed: 想要什么快说吧，不用和我～的了！Whatever you want, out with it. No need to wag your honeyed tongue at me!

阗

tián 〈书面〉be filled with; be full of: 喧～ noisy and crowded /宾客～门。The house is filled with guests.
阗咽 tiányè 〈书面〉gather noisily

填

tián ❶ fill; stuff; stop up: ～土 fill in earth /用羽毛～靠垫 stuff a cushion with feathers /～饱肚子 fill the belly; be adequately fed /～海造田 fill in the sea to reclaim land; reclaim land from the sea /义愤～膺 be filled with righteous indignation ❷ replenish; supplement; complement: 这个空缺由他补～。He is to fill the position (*or* vacancy). ❸ write; fill in; fill out: ～表 fill in (*or* fill out) a form /～调查表 fill out a questionnaire /数字～错了。Wrong figure was filled in.
填报 tiánbào fill in a form and submit it to the leadership or higher authorities: ～财政情况 submit a financial report /～每学年教学工作量 make an annual report of one's actual teaching load
填补 tiánbǔ fill (a vacancy, gap, etc.): ～空额 fill a vacancy /～政治真空 fill a political vacuum /～空白 fill in a gap /～亏空 make up a deficit
填仓 tiáncāng *also* "添仓" tiāncāng 〈旧语〉put grain into one's bin as a sign of good luck (on the 25th day of the first lunar month): ～节 Grain-bin-filling Festival (25th day of the first lunar month)
填充 tiánchōng ❶ fill up; stuff: ～作用 filling effect /～物 infilling; filler; packing material ❷ fill in the blanks (as in a test paper): ～测试 cloze test /这回考卷有几道冠词～题。The test paper had a few problems on filling in blanks with articles.
填充塔 tiánchōngtǎ 〈石油〉packed column or tower
填词 tiáncí compose a poem to a given tune of *ci* (词); write words to a given melody: 善于～ good at writing *ci* poetry
填堵 tiándǔ fill up; stop up: ～河堤决口 fill up a breach in the river dyke /用一种新型材料～高炉裂缝 stop up cracks in the blast furnace with a new material
填发 tiánfā fill in (a certificate, etc.) and distribute: ～新生录取通知书 fill in letters of admission the names of newly recruited students /～身份证 fill out and issue ID cards
填方 tiánfāng 〈建筑〉fill: ～断面 fill section
填房 tiánfáng (of a woman) marry a widower
填房 tiánfang woman who marries a widower: 给人做～ become the wife of a man after his previous wife's death; marry a widower
填空 tiánkòng ❶ fill a vacant position; fill a vacancy: ～补缺 fill vacancies and supply deficiencies ❷ *see* "填充❷"
填窟窿 tián kūlong 〈口语〉make up a deficit; supply a shortage: 他一年拼命挣钱～，还是欠了一屁股债。Although he worked desperately throughout the year to make up the deficits, he found himself sunken in debt at year's end.
填料 tiánliào packing; stuffing; padding; filling: ～函 gland box; stuffing box /～金属 filler metal /～橡胶 loaded rubber /塑料～ plastic packing (*or* filling)
填密 tiánmì 〈机械〉packing; densification: 液压～ hydraulic packing /～函 packing box; caulk /～片 sheet packing; caulking piece; packing piece
填平 tiánpíng fill and level up: 把沟～ fill up a ditch /～补齐 fill up gaps
填塞 tiánsè fill up; stop up: ～洞隙 fill up holes and cracks /～心灵上的空虚 fill a spiritual vacuum
填石 tiánshí rockfill: ～坝〈建筑〉rockfill dam
填书 tiánshū *also* "填篆" style of calligraphy usually used for engraving seals
填闲作物 tiánxián zuòwù 〈农业〉catch crop
填写 tiánxiě fill in; write: ～会客登记簿 fill in the visitor's register / 请在这里～你的身分证号码。Please write your ID (*or* identification) number here.
填鸭 tiányā ❶ force-feed a duck; cram ❷ force-fed duck
填鸭式教学法 tiányāshì jiàoxuéfǎ cramming or force-feeding method of teaching
填字游戏 tiánzì yóuxì crossword puzzle

恬

tián 〈书面〉❶ quiet; tranquil; peaceful; calm: ～和 quiet and gentle ❷ not care at all; be indifferent; remain unperturbed: ～不为意 remain unruffled (*or* unperturbed); be indifferent (*or* nonchalant); could not care less
恬不为怪 tiánbùwéiguài (with regard to unhealthy tendency or abnormality) be not surprised at all; not wonder in the least; be not disturbed or shocked
恬不知耻 tiánbùzhīchǐ be lost to all sense of shame; have no sense of shame; be shameless: ～的家伙 shameless person
恬淡 tiándàn ❶ indifferent to fame or gain: ～一生 remain indifferent to fame and gain all one's life; seek neither fame nor wealth all one's life /～寡欲 be contented and quiet with few worldly desires; be contented and indifferent to worldly gain ❷ quiet; tranquil; serene: ～的生活 quiet life /～的环境 tranquil surroundings
恬静 tiánjìng quiet; serene; peaceful; tranquil: 性格～ have a quiet disposition; be quiet and withdrawn by nature /～舒适的环境 peaceful and pleasant environment
恬美 tiánměi serene and beautiful; quiet and charming: 她的心境像春天一样～。Her mood was serene and beautiful like the spring. *or* She was in a quiet and charming mood like the spring.
恬谧 tiánmì 〈书面〉quiet; tranquil; serene; peaceful: ～的夜晚 serene (*or* tranquil) night
恬然 tiánrán 〈书面〉unperturbed; calm; collected; nonchalant: ～处之 remain unruffled /～自若 be calm and collected; be unperturbed and nonchalant
恬适 tiánshì 〈书面〉quiet and comfortable: ～幽雅的套间 quiet, comfortable and tastefully decorated apartment (*or* suite)

湉

tián
湉湉 tiántián 〈书面〉(of a river) calm; quiet; sluggish: 河水～。

T

The river flowed quietly.

菾 tián

菾菜 tiáncài *also* "甜菜" tiáncài beet; beetroot

田[1] tián ❶ (cultivated) land; farmland; cropland; field: 水～ irrigated land /稻～ paddy field; paddy /耕～ plough a field /解甲归～ be demobilized (and go back to farm) ❷ field (of ores, etc.): 煤～ coal field /油～ oil field /天然气～ gas field ❸ (Tián) a surname

田[2] tián 〈书面〉 *also* "畋" tián go hunting

田岸 tián'àn 〈方言〉 low bank of earth between fields; ridge

田鳖 tiánbiē 〈动物〉 giant water bug; fish killer

田产 tiánchǎn land property

田塍 tiánchéng 〈方言〉 low bank of earth between fields; ridge: ～小路 narrow ridge pathway /～交错。Ridges crisscross in the fields.

田畴 tiánchóu 〈书面〉 farmland; cultivated land; fields: ～一望无际 boundless stretch of farmland

田唇 tiánchún 〈方言〉 ridge between fields

田地 tiándì ❶ field; farmland; cropland: 在～里劳作 toil in the fields /多少年来，农民离不开～。For ages, farmers could never be separated from farmland. ❷ wretched situation; pass; plight: 他怎么会弄到这步～? How come he got into such a sorry plight? /事情简直到了不可收拾的～! The matter is just getting out of control! /她还不至于无耻到这般～! I don't think she is that shameless!

田畈 tiánfàn 〈方言〉 farmland; land

田凫 tiánfú 〈动物〉 lapwing

田父 tiánfǔ 〈书面〉 aged peasant or farmer

田赋 tiánfù 〈旧语〉 land tax: 征收～ collect land tax /交～，服劳役 pay land tax and do corvée labour

田埂 tiángěng low bank of earth between fields; ridge: 修～ build (*or* repair) ridges in the fields

田鸡 tiánjī 〈动物〉 ❶ sora; sora rail ❷ (common name for 青蛙) frog

田基 tiánjī 〈方言〉 low bank of earth between fields; ridge: 筑～ build low banks of earth between fields /～路 field-ridge pathway

田家 tiánjiā farmer's family; farmhouse: ～子 farm boy; farmer's son; country boy /～生活 life on the farm (*or* in the countryside); country life; rural life

田间 tiánjiān field; farm: ～劳动 field labour; farm work /～小道 path in the fields

田间持水量 tiánjiān chíshuǐliàng 〈农业〉 field (moisture) capacity

田间管理 tiánjiān guǎnlǐ field management: 加强～ do a better job of field management

田菁 tiánjīng 〈植物〉 sesbania

田径 tiánjìng 〈体育〉 track and field: ～选手 track-and-field competitor

田径队 tiánjìngduì track and field team

田径全能运动 tiánjìng quánnéng yùndòng all-round athletics

田径赛 tiánjìngsài track and field meet

田径项目 tiánjìng xiàngmù track and field event

田径运动 tiánjìng yùndòng track and field sports; athletics

田坎 tiánkǎn low bank of earth between fields; ridge

田客 tiánkè 〈旧语〉 tenant farmer

田猎 tiánliè 〈书面〉 hunting: ～于野 go hunting in open country

田鹨 tiánliù 〈动物〉 paddy-field pipit

田垄 tiánlǒng ❶ low bank of earth between fields; ridge ❷ raised land for cultivation in wet fields; ridge

田螺 tiánluó 〈动物〉 river snail

田陌 tiánmò path between fields: ～上有成排的杨树。There are rows of poplar trees on the paths between the fields.

田亩 tiánmǔ land; fields: ～荒芜。The land lay waste. /～干裂。The fields were dry and cracked.

田纳西 Tiánnàxī Tennessee, state in central southeastern United States

田七 tiánqī 〈中药〉 pseudo-ginseng (*Panax pseudo-ginseng* var. *notoginseng*)

田契 tiánqì title deed for land

田缺 tiánquē 〈方言〉 opening in a field for irrigation: 开～ dig an opening for watering a field

田赛 tiánsài 〈体育〉 field event: 每人最多可以报名参加两项～、三项径赛项目。Every competitor at most can enter for two field events and three track events.

田舍 tiánshè 〈书面〉 ❶ land and houses ❷ farmhouse ❸ farmer's household

田舍郎 tiánshèláng 〈书面〉 young farmer; farm boy

田舍翁 tiánshèwēng 〈书面〉 old farmer: 做一名～，这是他的平生之愿。His lifelong wish is to be a farmer.

田鼠 tiánshǔ field mouse; vole: 普通～ field vole /～杆菌 vole bacillus

田田 tiántián 〈书面〉 (of lotus leaves floating on water) graceful: 莲叶何～。How graceful the floating lotus leaves are!

田头 tiántóu ❶ edge of field: 坐在～地边 sit by the fields ❷ 〈方言〉 field: 男女老少奋战在～。Men and women, old and young, were working hard in the fields.

田野 tiányě field; open country: 烟雨茫茫的～ vast fields (*or* expanse of farmland) shrouded in rain and mist /～似锦。The land is as beautiful as a tapestry.

田野工作 tiányě gōngzuò (in scientific research, etc.) field work

田园 tiányuán fields and gardens; countryside: ～秀丽 beautiful countryside /～生活 idyllic life; pastoral life /～风光 rural scenery /～荒芜 lands lie waste /绿色的～ green fields /～之乐 idyllic happiness

田园诗 tiányuánshī idyll; pastoral poetry: ～诗人 pastoral poet /优美的～ beautiful idyll

田月桑时 tiányuè-sāngshí time for fieldwork; busy farming season: ～未得闲 have no leisure in the busy farming season

田中角荣 Tiánzhōngjiǎoróng Kakuei Tanaka (1918-1993), Japanese Prime Minister in 1972-1974

田中奏折 Tiánzhōng Zòuzhé Tanaka Memorial to the Throne (presented by then prime minister Giichi Tanaka on 25, July 1927, laying the blueprint for later Japanese aggression against China and East Asia by occupying China's Manchuria and Inner Mongolia as the first step)

田主 tiánzhǔ 〈旧语〉 owner of land property; landowner

田庄 tiánzhuāng ❶ country estate ❷ 〈方言〉 peasant household; countryside: ～人家 peasant family

田字草 tiánzìcǎo 〈植物〉 clover fern

田租 tiánzū farm rent

钿 tián 〈方言〉 ❶ coin: 铜～ copper coin; money; fund ❷ money: 几～? How much is it? ❸ sum of money: 本～ capital
see also diàn

畋 tián 〈书面〉 go hunting

佃 tián 〈书面〉 ❶ till; cultivate: 亦～亦渔 engage in both farming and fishing ❷ *also* "畋" tián go hunting
see also diàn

佃作 tiánzuò tillage; cultivation; farming: ～之时 time for cultivation; farming season

tiǎn

忝 tiǎn 〈书面〉〈谦词〉 be unworthy of the honour; have the honour (though not worthy of it): ～列门墙 have the honour to be a student of sb.'s (*or* yours) /才疏学浅，～官日久。I have the honour, though I'm lacking both in talent and learning, to have held an official position for a long time.

舔 tiǎn lick; lap: 把盘子～干净 lick a plate clean /～光碟子里的牛奶 (of a dog, etc.) lap up the milk in a saucer /猫～爪子。The cat licked her paws.

舔屁股 tiǎn pìgu 〈粗话〉 lick sb.'s ass — lick sb.'s boot; fawn servilely: 他自以为财大气粗，我才不去给他～呢! He may brag about his wealth but I, for one, won't lick his boot!

𫗭 tiǎn 〈书面〉 lure; bait; seduce: 以利～之 entice with benefits; lure with promise of gain

淟 tiǎn 〈书面〉 filthy; dirty

洟汩 tiǎngǔ 〈书面〉buried and lost：～于乱世 buried and lost in turbulent times

洟浊 tiǎnzhuó 〈书面〉turbid; foul; filthy：风俗～ have corrupt customs

惧 tiǎn 〈书面〉be ashamed

惧墨 tiǎnmò 〈书面〉shamefaced and tongue-tied：～而谢 blush for shame and apologize

腆 tiǎn ❶ rich; sumptuous; plentiful：不～之国 needy country / 不～之田 barren land ❷〈方言〉protrude; stick or thrust out：～着肚子 bulge one's belly / ～着胸脯 stick out one's chest

靦 tiǎn ❶〈书面〉ashamed ❷ brazen：～着脸 brazen it out

靦颜 tiǎnyán 〈书面〉❶ shamefaced; ashamed ❷ brazen; shameless：～惜命 save one's life at the cost of one's honour; barter honour for life

覥 tiǎn 〈书面〉❶ facial; faced ❷ shamefaced; ashamed
see also miǎn

殄 tiǎn extirpate; exterminate：暴～天物 waste nature's produce (such as grain) mindlessly; squander natural resources / 武～暴逆 get rid of the tyrant by force

殄灭 tiǎnmiè 〈书面〉wipe out; eliminate：～匪徒 wipe out the bandits

tiàn

掭 tiàn ❶ dip (the brush) in ink and shape (it) properly against the inkstone：饱～浓墨 (brush) dipped with thick ink ❷〈方言〉poke：～灯心 clip the wick (of an oil lamp)

tiāo

祧 tiāo 〈书面〉❶ keep up one's ancestral shrine; be heir to：兼～ be heir to both one's father and one's uncle ❷ move (forefathers' memorial tablets) into the ancestral shrine：不～之祖 ancestor who does not deserve a place in the ancestral shrine

挑[1] tiāo ❶ choose; select; pick：从这些衬衣中～两件 choose two from these shirts / ～一张最好的画 select (*or* pick) the best picture / 任～任选。Take your choice. / 把发霉的花生～出来。Pick out the rotten peanuts. ❷ find (fault); pick (holes); be fastidious：～错 find fault; pick holes / 爱～毛病 be fault-finding (*or* nit-picking)

挑[2] tiāo ❶ carry on the shoulder with a pole; shoulder：～一担水 carry two buckets of water on the shoulder pole / ～重担 shoulder a heavy load; assume heavy responsibilities ❷ carrying pole with its load; load carried on a shoulder pole：挑～儿 shoulder a carrying pole with its loads / 杂货～儿 two baskets of sundry goods carried on a shoulder pole ❸〈量词〉*used of loads carried on the shoulder pole*：一～子新鲜蔬菜 two baskets of fresh vegetables carried on a shoulder pole
see also tiǎo

挑饬 tiāochi 〈方言〉nit-pick; be captious

挑刺儿 tiāocìr 〈方言〉find fault; nit-pick; be captious：爱～的人 captious (*or* nit-picking) person / 你不要老是成心～。Don't always find fault with people.

挑担 tiāodàn ❶ carrying pole with its baskets or loads ❷ carry loads on a pole：～上街卖菜 carry loads of vegetables on a pole and peddle them in the streets

挑肥拣瘦 tiāoféi-jiǎnshòu pick the fat or choose the lean — choose whichever is to one's personal advantage; be choosy：～，招人讨厌 be invidiously choosy / 做工作总有困难，哪能～？There're bound to be difficulties in one's work. How can one pick and choose all the time? *or* There're always hard nuts in your work. You've got to take the rough with the smooth.

挑夫 tiāofū 〈旧语〉porter

挑拣 tiāojiǎn pick; pick and choose：～杂物 pick over odds and ends / 她买东西总爱挑挑拣拣的。She is fastidious about her shopping.

挑脚 tiāojiǎo carry luggage or goods for a fee; work as a porter：～的 porter / 在车站～为生 make a living working as a railway porter

挑礼 tiāolǐ be particular or fussy about etiquette; reproach sb. for a faux pas：不去拜年，她会～的。You must not forget to make a New Year call on her, for she is fussy about etiquette.

挑毛剔刺 tiāomáo-tīcì nit-pick; be captious：她这个人呀，你就是白送她东西，她也要～。She is so nit-picking that she would look a gift horse in the mouth if you gave her one.

挑三拣四 tiāosān-jiǎnsì pick and choose; be choosy：都是上等货色，不用～的。These are all quality goods. There is no need to pick and choose.

挑食 tiāoshí *also* "挑嘴" have a partiality for certain kinds of food; be particular about what one eats：他不～，有什么就吃什么。He is not choosy about food and eats whatever is available.

挑剔 tiāoti nit-pick; be captious; be fastidious：过分～ be extremely fastidious; be captious to the hilt / 无可～ beyond criticism; faultless

挑选 tiāoxuǎn choose; select; opt for; pick out：～合适人选 select suitable candidates / 从这些书中～ choose among these books / 每种尺寸都有许多型号可供～。There is a wide choice of patterns for each size. *or* Each size has a great variety of patterns for you to choose from.

挑眼 tiāoyǎn 〈方言〉find fault; be fastidious (usu. about formalities, etc.)：举行婚礼该做的咱们都要做到，不能让女方亲属～。We must do whatever is required for the wedding, and give the bride's family no cause for complaint.

挑字眼儿 tiāo zìyǎnr find fault with the wording; be fastidious about choice of words：有些老师爱～。Some teachers are overly particular about choice of words.

挑子 tiāozi carrying pole with its load; load carried on a shoulder pole

挑嘴 tiāozuǐ *see* "挑食"

佻 tiāo frivolous; flippant; giddy

佻薄 tiāobó 〈书面〉frivolous; flippant; giddy：为人～ be frivolous (*or* flippant) / ～浪子 philanderer

佻巧 tiāoqiǎo 〈书面〉❶ frivolous and cunning; unreliable：～小人 unreliable frivolous person ❷ (of diction) full of fine words and frivolous expressions; flowery and flippant：文词～ flippant, flowery language

佻㒓 tiāotà 〈书面〉frivolous; loose; flippant

tiáo

条(條) tiáo ❶ twig：枝～ branches and twigs / 柳～ willow twig; wicker / 荆～ twig of the chaste tree ❷ long narrow piece; strip; slip：纸～ strip of paper / 病假～ sick-leave slip / 便～ brief informal note / 面～ noodles ❸ long and slender in pattern or shape; stripe; streak：花～布 stripe cloth ❹ item; article：律～ articles of a regulation ❺ order：井井有～ in perfect order; well-organized; shipshape ❻〈量词〉(a) *used with sth. narrow or thin and long*：一～毒蛇 a poisonous serpent / 四～腿 four legs / 两～鱼 two fish (b) *used with bar-shaped objects*：一～肥皂 a bar of soap / 一～香烟 a carton of cigarettes (c) *used with itemized or abstract nouns*：一～新闻 a piece (*or* an item) of news / 几～建议 several proposals (*or* suggestions) / 一～心 be of one mind (d) *used with towels, quilts, clothes, etc.*：一～毛巾 a towel / 一～床单 a sheet / 一～裤衩 a pair of undershorts

条案 tiáo'àn *also* "条几" long narrow table

条播 tiáobō 〈农业〉drilling：～沟 drill furrow / ～行距 drill spacing / ～栽培 drill culture / ～法 drilling method

条播机 tiáobōjī 〈农业〉seed drill; drill

条播开沟犁 tiáobō kāigōulí 〈农业〉drill furrow opener

条材 tiáocái 〈冶金〉bar stock：～轧机 bar mill

条畅 tiáochàng 〈书面〉(of writings) smooth and well organized; fluent and well-knit：文笔～ of fluent and coherent writing

条陈 tiáochén ❶ present item by item; state or expound point by point：～如下 state point by point as follows ❷〈旧语〉written proposal to one's superior; official report or memorandum：上一～ sub-

T

mit a report to one's superiors /撰拟～ draft a memorandum

条凳 tiáodèng bench

条分缕析 tiáofēn-lǚxī analyse point by point; make a careful and detailed analysis:～，言之成理 make a careful and detailed analysis in a rational and convincing way

条幅 tiáofú vertically-hung scroll; scroll:草书～ scroll of cursive-hand calligraphy /展开～ unroll a scroll /卷起～ roll up a scroll

条钢 tiáogāng 〈冶金〉bar iron; bar steel; merchant steel:商品～ merchant bar iron; merchant steel /～轧机 merchant mill

条格平布 tiáogé píngbù 〈纺织〉gingham

条贯 tiáoguàn 〈书面〉proper arrangement; systematic presentation; orderliness:～分明 clear and systematic

条规 tiáoguī (itemized) rules and regulations

条痕 tiáohén 〈矿业〉streak; roping; snailing

条几 tiáojī long narrow table

条件 tiáojiàn ❶ condition; term; factor; circumstance:不利的～ unfavourable factor /主客观～ subjective factors and objective circumstances; subjective and objective conditions /生活～ living conditions /贸易～ terms of trade /为国家独立准备～ prepare the ground for national independence /那些行星不具备生命存在的～。Conditions are not fit for life on those planets. ❷ requirement; prerequisite; qualification:先决～ prerequisite; precondition /入学～ entrance (*or* enrolment) requirement /军人的基本～ basic requirements (*or* qualifications) of a soldier /不附带任何～ with no strings attached /在对等～下 on condition of reciprocity; on a reciprocal basis /具备从事这项工作的所有～ be fully qualified for the job /他同意做这项工作，～是我们不得干预。His agreement to do the work is conditional upon our commitment not to interfere. ❸ situation; state; condition:他身体～很好。He is in excellent condition physically. *or* He's in the pink of health. /这家工厂～好:工人素质不错，设备也比较先进。This factory is in a favourable situation with its well-qualified work force and relatively up-to-date equipment.

条件变量 tiáojiàn biànliàng conditional variable

条件刺激 tiáojiàn cìjī 〈生理〉conditioned stimulus

条件从句 tiáojiàn cóngjù 〈语言〉conditional clause

条件反射 tiáojiàn fǎnshè 〈生理〉conditioned reflex

条件概率 tiáojiàn gàilǜ conditional probability:～分布 conditional probability distribution /～密度 conditional probability density

T

条件句 tiáojiànjù 〈语言〉conditional sentence

条件期望 tiáojiàn qīwàng 〈数学〉conditional expectation:～值 conditional expectation

条块 tiáokuài vertical and horizontal lines of leadership, management, control, or coordination; functional departments of a higher or central government and of local governments:～管理体制 system of management through both vertical lines of leadership (from central ministries to their corresponding departments at lower levels) and through horizontal lines of leadership (from local, i.e. provincial, prefectural, county governments to said departments); system of management through both vertical functional lines and horizontal administrative lines; management both by central ministries and by local governments

条块分割 tiáokuài fēngē create barriers between central ministries and local governments; sever links between various departments and regions:～的流通体制 system of distribution with unrelated jurisdictions of central ministries and local governments

条块结合 tiáokuài jiéhé integration of leadership by central ministry with leadership by local government; integration of departments and regions at various levels:～，块块为主 combine central and local leadership, with emphasis on the latter /～，条条为主 combine central and local leadership with central ministries playing the main role

条款 tiáokuǎn clause; article; provision:最惠国～ most-favoured-nation clause /仲裁～ clause of arbitration /保留～ clause reséré /法律～ legal provision

条理 tiáolǐ proper arrangement; systematic presentation; orderliness; method:～化 methodization /～不清 badly organized; unmethodical; disorderly /有～的人 methodical person /～井然的讲话 well-organized presentation /他干什么事都很有～。He is a man with an orderly mind.

条例 tiáolì regulations; rules; ordinances:保密～ security regulations /工会～ rules and regulations of labour unions /奖惩～ rules for rewards and penalities /交通管理～ traffic ordinance /试行～ tentative regulations; experimental regulations

条令 tiáolìng 〈军事〉regulations:内务～ routine service regulations /战斗～ combat regulations /纪律～ disciplinary regulations

条码 tiáomǎ *also* "条形码" bar code:～化 adoption of bar codes; popularization of bar codes

条目 tiáomù ❶ clauses and subclauses (in a formal document):分列～ list in clauses and subclauses ❷ entry (in a dictionary):～过于繁琐 have over-elaborate entries

条绒 tiáoróng *also* "灯心绒" dēngxīnróng corduroy

条施 tiáoshī 〈农业〉apply (fertilizer, etc.) along furrows

条石 tiáoshí rectangular stone slab

条鳎 tiáotǎ 〈动物〉striped sole

条田 tiáotián strip-shaped fields

条条 tiáotiao ❶ rules and regulations; conventions:在奖罚方面要订一些～。Rules and regulations should be formulated for rewards and punishment. ❷ vertical lines of leadership or organization from higher to lower levels:要处理好～和块块的关系 properly handle the relations between various levels of government as well as between different regions and departments

条条框框 tiáotiao-kuàngkuang 〈贬义〉rules and regulations; conventions and restrictions; various taboos:打破～的束缚 break down the trammels of outmoded conventions /～太多，办事效率低。Too many taboos and restrictions result in inefficiency.

条文 tiáowén article; clause:～范例 standard clause /～规定 stipulations /详细～ detailed articles

条纹 tiáowén stripe; streak:～衬衫 streaky shirt; striped shirt

条纹布 tiáowénbù striped cloth; stripe

条形 tiáoxíng *also* "线形" xiànxíng linear:～保险丝 band fuse /～导线 strip conductor

条形码 tiáoxíngmǎ *also* "条码" bar code:～标志 bar code label /～读出器 bar code reader /印～的商品 bar-coded commodity

条锈病 tiáoxiùbìng 〈农业〉stripe rust; yellow rust

条约 tiáoyuē treaty; pact; covenant:军事～ military pact /经贸～ trade treaty /友好合作～ treaty of friendship and cooperation /不平等～ unequal treaty /双边～ bilateral treaty /多边～ multilateral pact /和平～ peace treaty /停战～ armistice treaty /～义务 treaty obligation /～保障 treaty protection /签署～ sign a treaty /批准～ ratify a treaty

条约法 tiáoyuēfǎ law of treaties; law derived from treaty obligations

条子 tiáozi ❶ strip:布～ strip of cloth /纸～ narrow strip of paper; slip of paper ❷ brief informal note:给讲演人递～ pass a note to the speaker /各级领导都不得私自批～、讲人情。Leaders at all levels are forbidden to send in notes or speak on anybody's behalf without official approval. ❸〈方言〉gold bar

鲦(鰷、鯈) tiáo

鲦鱼 tiáoyú *also* "鳘鲦" cāntiáo *Hemiculter leucisculus*

调[1] tiáo

❶ suit well; fit in perfectly; be harmonious or propitious:风～雨顺 good weather for the crops; propitious weather /起居失～ ailment caused by an irregular life-style ❷ mix; regulate; adjust:～颜色 mix colours /～酒 mix a drink /～电视天线 adjust a TV antenna /～高价格 adjust a price upwards /把钢琴～一～ tune the piano ❸ mediate; reconcile; arbitrate:劝～ persuade and mediate; reconcile through mediation

调[2] tiáo

❶ tease; provoke; dally: *see* "～笑"; "～戏" ❷ abet; instigate; incite; *see* "～唆"

see also diào

调拨 tiáobō sow dissension; provoke; alienate:～两国之间的关系 drive a wedge between the two countries

see also diàobō

调处 tiáochǔ mediate; arbitrate:～武装冲突 mediate in hostilities /～双方的纠纷 arbitrate between the two sides in their dispute

调词架讼 tiáocí-jiàsòng abet sb. in filing a suit:～，从中取利 profit from inciting legal proceedings

调达 tiáodá adjust; regulate; smooth:～气血 regulate the flow of vital energy and blood

调挡 tiáodǎng 〈机械〉gear shift

调幅 tiáofú 〈无线电〉amplitude modulation (AM):～编码 ampli-

tude-modulation coding /～波 amplitude-modulated wave; AM wave /～干扰 AM jamming /～检波器 amplitude-modulation detector /～度 factor of amplitude-modulation; modulation factor; modulation

调羹 tiáogēng spoon

调光器 tiáoguāngqì light modulator

调和 tiáohé ❶ be or put in harmonious proportion; regulate; blend; mix:～肝脾〈中医〉harmonize the liver and spleen; regulate the functions of the liver and spleen /色彩～ harmonious (*or* well-matched) colours /雨水～ well-distributed rainfall /地毯和壁纸配得很～。The carpet blends in well (*or* goes well) with the wallpaper. ❷ mediate; reconcile:从中～ mediate; act as a mediator /～各种利害冲突 reconcile various conflicting interests ❸ compromise; make concessions:～行为 conciliatory behaviour; appeasement /原则问题不可能～。No concession is possible in matters of principle. /没有～的余地。There is no room for compromise. ❹〈数学〉harmonic:～比 harmonic ratio /～方程 harmonic equation; Laplace equation /～分割 harmonic division; harmonic section /～函数 harmonic function /～级数 harmonic progression; harmonic series /～平均数 harmonic mean

调和漆 tiáohéqī mixed paint:磁性～ mixed varnish paint /油性～ mixed oleopaint

调护 tiáohù convalescent care; care of a patient during convalescence; nursing:住院～ be hospitalized for special care /～病人恢复健康 nurse a patient back to health

调级 tiáojí promote (sb.) to a higher wage scale; raise sb.'s salary or wage

调剂 tiáojì ❶ make up or fill a prescription ❷ adjust; regulate:～商品供应 regulate the supply of commodities /～余缺 adjust surpluses and deficiencies; regulate supply and demand /～生活 enliven (*or* enrich) one's life

调价 tiáojià readjust prices; (often) raise prices:各种粮食从明日起～。The prices of all food grains will be raised as of tomorrow.

调减 tiáojiǎn adjust and reduce:～投资项目 curtail investment projects

调浆 tiáojiāng 〈纺织〉size mixing:～设备 size mixing equipment /～机 paste mixer

调焦 tiáojiāo 〈摄影〉focusing:～镜头 focusing lens

调教 tiáojiào ❶ teach; train; discipline:～学前儿童 teach preschool children /～顽皮的孩子 discipline mischievous children ❷ tame; break in; domesticate:～劣马 tame a vicious horse /～牲口 break in draught animals

调节 tiáojié regulate; adjust; control:～体温 adjust (*or* regulate) body temperature /～货币流通 regulate money supply /～电容 control capacitance /～电压 regulating resistance /这张课桌可根据学生的身高加以～。This desk is adjustable to the height of the schoolchild.

调节器 tiáojiéqì regulator; adjuster; controller

调节税 tiáojiéshuì regulatory tax

调解 tiáojiě mediate; arbitrate; make peace:～劳资纠纷 mediate in a labour dispute /～合同纠纷 arbitrate a quarrel over a contract /～分歧 iron out differences /通过～解决冲突 resolve a conflict through mediation /～人 mediator; peacemaker

调经 tiáojīng 〈中医〉regulate menstrual function; regulate menstruation

调侃 tiáokǎn ridicule; scoff; mock; banter:～他人 hold others up to ridicule; scoff at (*or* mock) others /善于～ be good at banter

调控 tiáokòng regulate and control:～设备 controlling apparatus /～手段 controlling mechanism /宏观～ macro-control

调理 tiáoli ❶ nurse (a patient, etc.):～病人 nurse the sick /细心～ nurse with meticulous care ❷ take care of; look after:精心～伙食 take great care of one's diet; painstakingly prepare the food ❸ teach; train; break in; discipline:～警犬 train police dogs ❹〈方言〉make fun of; play tricks on; fool; tease:～老实人 tease (*or* fool) an honest guy ❺〈生物〉opsonize:～素 opsonin /～指数 opsonic index /～作用 opsonic action; opsonization

调料 tiáoliào condiment; seasoning; flavouring:～瓶 cruet; castor /～瓶架 cruet-stand; castor

调弄 tiáonòng ❶ make fun of; play tricks on; tease; dally:～良家妇女 take liberties (*or* dally) with a respectable woman /～乡下人 play tricks on country folks ❷ fix; adjust:喜欢～钟表 fond of tinkering at clocks and watches /～了半天，也没把机器修好 fail to repair a machine despite much work on it ❸ instigate; stir up:～家人不和 sow discord among family members /～两人吵架 stir up a quarrel between the two of them

调配 tiáopèi mix; blend:～颜料 mix paints (*or* dyes) /～几服草药 prepare a few doses of herbal medicine
see also diàopèi

调皮 tiáopí ❶ naughty; mischievous:你这个小～! You little mischief! /四、五岁正是～的年龄。Children at four or five are extemely naughty. /告诉孩子别～。Tell the boy to behave himself. ❷ unruly; recalcitrant:～的小马驹 skittish pony /此人一贯～，不好好干工作。He has always been recalcitrant and never done a stroke of honest work. ❸ tricky; smart-alecky:做学问必须老老实实，来不得半点～。Scholarship requires honest work and admits of no smart-aleckism.

调皮捣蛋 tiáopí-dǎodàn mischievous; troublesome; recalcitrant:几个～的球迷在制造事端。Some recalcitrant football fans are making trouble.

调频 tiáopín 〈电学〉❶ adjust frequency (of a receiver) or output (of a generator) ❷ frequency modulation (FM):～广播波段 frequency-modulation band /～雷达 frequency-modulated radar /～收音机 FM receiver /～电台 FM radio station /～立体声 FM stereo

调情 tiáoqíng flirt; dally:～作乐 take pleasure in flirtation; amuse oneself by flirting

调人 tiáorén mediator; peacemaker:请～评理 turn to a mediator for arbitration

调三窝四 tiáosān-wōsì *also* "调三斡四" sow discord; stir up disputes; make mischief:～，搬弄是非 tell tales and stir up trouble

调色板 tiáosèbǎn palette

调色刀 tiáosèdāo palette knife

调色碟 tiáosèdié colour-mixing tray or dish

调色 tiáoshǎi 〈美术〉toning; colour-mixing:～剂 toner

调栅 tiáoshān tuned grid

调摄 tiáoshè 〈书面〉take good care of oneself (after an illness); recuperate one's health by resting and taking nourishing food; be nursed back to health

调试 tiáoshì ❶ preliminary or shakedown test; trial run:新机器装好后要进行～。The new machine must go through trial runs after installation. ❷〈计算机〉debugging:～程序 debugging program

调速发电机 tiáosù fādiànjī 〈电工〉velodyne

调速器 tiáosùqì 〈机械〉governor; speed controller:～联动装置 governor linkage

调唆 tiáosuo incite; abet; instigate:～青少年犯罪 abet teenagers in crime /～两家不和 drive a wedge between the two families; set the two families against each other /～是非 stir up trouble; sow discord

调停 tiáotíng ❶ mediate; intervene; act as an intermediary:从中～ mediate (*or* offer one's good offices) between two parties /～争端 mediate (*or* intervene in) a dispute ❷ (often used in the early vernacular) take care; look after; arrange

调位 tiáowèi 〈机械〉positioning

调味 tiáowèi flavour; dress; season:在汤里加点胡椒～ flavour the soup with pepper

调味番茄酱 tiáowèi fānqiéjiàng ketchup

调味品 tiáowèipǐn condiment; flavouring; seasoning

调味瓶 tiáowèipíng castor; cruet

调温 tiáowēn thermoregulation

调温箱 tiáowēnxiāng controlled temperature cabinet; thermoregulator

调戏 tiáoxì take liberties with (a woman); dally; assail (a woman) with obscenities:～妇女 take liberties with a woman

调弦 tiáoxián tune (up) a stringed instrument

调相 tiáoxiàng phase adjustment;〈电学〉phase modulation (PM):～常数 phase modulation constant; PM constant /～机 phase modifier; phase converter

调笑 tiáoxiào make fun of; poke fun at; tease:尽情～ make fun to one's heart's content /相互～ poke fun at each other; make fun of each other

调协 tiáoxié coordinate; harmonious; concerted:正副科长的工作不～。The section chief and his deputy do not cooperate well in work.

调谐 tiáoxié ❶ harmonious:上下～ harmonious relations (*or* harmony) between the leader and the led ❷ tune; resonate; syntonize:～旋钮 tuning knob /～范围 tuning range /～电路 tuned circuit /～滤波仪 tuned filter

调蓄 tiáoxù store (water in a reservoir or lake) and regulate (the volume of flow in the lower reaches):新修的水库可以～一亿立方的水。The new reservoir can store 100 million cubic metres of water.
调谑 tiáoxuè make fun of; poke fun at; tease:严肃场合不可肆意～。It is bad form to banter on serious occasions.
调训 tiáoxùn tame; break in:一批军马正在～。A number of horses are being broken in for combat use.
see also diàoxùn
调压 tiáoyā adjust pressure;〈电学〉regulate voltage:～变压器 regulating transformer /～阀 pressure regulating valve /～式振荡器 voltage-tuning oscillator
调压器 tiáoyāqì 〈电工〉〈机械〉pressure regulator; voltage regulator
调养 tiáoyǎng take good care of (sb. or oneself after an illness); build up one's health or convalesce by rest and by taking nourishing food; nurse back to health:静心～ recuperate by resting and nourishment /病虽然已经好了，但病人身体仍然虚弱，需要好好～才是。It is essential to nurse the patient back to health as he is still weak and frail after the illness.
调音 tiáoyīn 〈音乐〉tuning:演出前为钢琴～ tune the piano before a performance
调音台 tiáoyīntái 〈电子〉sound console
调匀 tiáoyún mix or blend evenly:饮食～ regular diet /雨水～ well-distributed rainfall /涂料已经～。The paint is well blended.
调帧器 tiáozhēnqì 〈电子〉framer
调整 tiáozhěng adjust; readjust; regulate; revise:～工资 readjust wages (usu. upwards); raise wages /～汇率 readjust exchange rates /～人力 redistribute (*or* realign) manpower /～供求关系 regulate supply and demand /～计划 revise a plan /～生产方向 re-orient production /～产品结构 readjust the product mix /～作息时间 make changes in the work schedule /～政府结构 restructure government institutions /～、巩固、充实、提高 readjustment, consolidation, filling out and raising standards
调整杆 tiáozhěnggǎn 〈机械〉adjusting rod
调整器 tiáozhěngqì 〈机械〉adjuster:自动松紧～ automatic slack adjuster
调脂弄粉 tiáozhī-nòngfěn apply rouge and powder; dress and make up:她一天到晚只知道～。She was obsessed with her own make-up and dress all day long.
调治 tiáozhì recuperate under medical treatment:安心～ quietly recuperate under medical treatment
调制 tiáozhì ❶ mix; concoct:～饲料 mix fodder ❷〈电子〉modulation:～器 modulator /脉冲～ pulse modulation /音频～ audio modulation /振幅～ amplitude modulation /～电平 modulation level /～间隙 modulation gap ❸ blend and make; make by mixing:～药丸 blend and make medicinal pills /～鸡尾酒 prepare a cocktail
调制解调器 tiáozhì jiětiáoqì 〈信息〉modulator-demodulator (MODEM)
调资 tiáozī adjustment of wages (usu. upwards):给职工评级～ grade the staff and raise their wages accordingly
调嘴学舌 tiáozuǐ-xuéshé *also*"调嘴弄舌" gossip; tell tales:不要背地里～。Don't gossip behind people's backs. *or* Don't backbite.

蜩 tiáo
〈古语〉cicada
蜩螗 tiáotáng 〈书面〉noisy; disorderly; in confusion:国事～ there is turmoil throughout the country; the country is in a state of chaos

迢 tiáo
迢迢 tiáotiáo far away; remote:千里～来到北京 come to Beijing from a thousand *li* away (*or* from afar)
迢遥 tiáoyáo 〈书面〉far away; remote:旅途～ long journey
迢远 tiáoyuǎn far away; remote:路途艰难而～。The road is arduous and long.

髫 tiáo
〈书面〉child's hanging hair:垂～之年 childhood /垂～小儿 little child with hanging hair
髫龄 tiáolíng 〈书面〉childhood
髫年 tiáonián 〈书面〉childhood

苕 tiáo
〈植物〉Chinese trumpet creeper
see also sháo
苕子 tiáozi 〈植物〉a kind of rush plant, whose stem can be used for broomstick

龆 tiáo
〈书面〉shed the milk teeth
龆龀 tiáochèn 〈书面〉❶ child ❷ childhood
龆年 tiáonián early childhood (about seven or eight)

岧(岹) tiáo
岧岧 tiáotiáo 〈书面〉high; lofty
岧峣 tiáoyáo 〈书面〉(of a mountain) high; lofty

笤 tiáo
笤帚 tiáozhou whisk broom

tiǎo

窕 tiǎo
see"窈窕"yǎotiǎo

挑 tiǎo
❶ pick, push or hold up with a pole or stick; raise:从水里把帽子～起来 pick up a hat from the water with a pole /～着灯笼 hold a lantern on a stick /酒店门口的竹竿上高～着一面酒幌子。A streamer was flying at the top of a bamboo pole outside the wineshop. ❷ poke; prick:～火 poke a fire /～灯心 trim the lampwick /～刺 pick out a splinter (as from one's finger) /问题～开了。The problem is now out in the open. ❸ (in embroidery) cross-stitch:～针 cross-stitching ❹ stir up; instigate; foment:～得兄弟不和 sow discord between the brothers; set the brothers against each other /小两口吵架全是他～的。The young couple fell out at his instigation. ❺ rising stroke (one of the basic strokes of Chinese characters)
see also tiāo
挑棒游戏 tiǎobàng yóuxì jackstraws
挑拨 tiǎobō instigate; incite; stir up trouble; sow or foment discord:～是非 stir up trouble by spreading lies; foment discord /～同事不和 sow dissension among colleagues
挑拨离间 tiǎobō-líjiàn sow dissension; stir up trouble; incite or play off one against the other; drive a wedge (between):～，破坏民族团结 undermine national unity by fomenting discord /～的小人 vicious backbiter
挑大梁 tiǎo dàliáng ❶ (of an actor or actress) play the leading role ❷ shoulder a major responsibility; play a key role; be a mainstay:中青年教员～。The younger and middle-aged teachers are the mainstay now.
挑灯 tiǎodēng ❶ pick the lampwick:～夜读 pick the lampwick and read late into the night; read by lamplight during the night ❷ hang a lamp high; raise a lantern or torch:～夜战 fight by torchlight; work late into the night
挑动 tiǎodòng ❶arouse; foment; provoke:～好奇心 arouse one's curiosity /～是非 stir up trouble; foment a dispute ❷ instigate; incite; abet:～两国之间的武装冲突 instigate armed conflicts between the two countries /～一部分人斗另一部分人 incite people to struggle against each other; set one group of people against another
挑逗 tiǎodòu provoke; tease; tantalize; dally:～寻衅 pick a quarrel /～妇女 dally with a woman; take liberties with a woman /孩子喜欢～动物。Children like to tease animals. /他正在生气，别～他! Don't provoke him; he's already in a huff.
挑费 tiǎofei 〈口语〉daily expenses; household expenditure:两口之家～轻。It is not expensive to keep a family of two.
挑花 tiǎohuā cross-stitch work
挑祸 tiǎohuo 〈口语〉make trouble; foment discord:有人背后～。Someone is stirring up trouble behind our backs.
挑明 tiǎomíng bring into the open; lay open; lay bare:～他们之间的关系 lay bare their relationship /这事她迟早要知道，现在索性～算了。She will get to know this sooner or later; why don't we tell her right now?
挑弄 tiǎonòng ❶ stir up; provoke:～是非 stir up ill will (between two parties); foment discord ❷ make fun of; play tricks on; tease
挑起 tiǎoqǐ provoke; incite; instigate:～争端 provoke a dispute /～他们对外国人的敌意 arouse their hostility towards aliens

挑三窝四 tiǎosān-wōsì *also*"调三窝四" tiáosān-wōsì sow discord; tell tales; foment dissension:这两个人打起来，就因为他在中间～。The two came to blows all because of his incitement.
挑事 tiǎoshì 〈口语〉stir up trouble; sow discord:～包 trouble-maker
挑唆 tiǎosuo incite; abet; foment; instigate:～人们闹事 incite (*or* instigate) people to riot; incite (*or* foment) a riot /暗中～ stir up trouble behind the scenes
挑头 tiǎotóu be the first; take the lead; take the initiative:他～儿向领导提意见。He was the first to voice complaints against the leadership. /不管谁～，我们都会跟着干。Whoever takes the lead, we will follow.
挑衅 tiǎoxìn provoke:～者 provocateur /武装～ armed provocations /～行为 provocative act /他的讲话无疑是在～。His speech was undoubtedly a provocation.
挑战 tiǎozhàn ❶ throw down the gauntlet; challenge to battle:接受～ take up the gauntlet; accept a challenge /向对手发出～ issue a challenge to one's adversary (*or* rival) ❷ challenge to a contest:富有～性的任务 challenging assignment /规定～条件 set terms for a challenge /机遇与～并存 there exist both opportunities and challenges
挑战书 tiǎozhànshū letter of challenge; challenge
挑战者号 Tiǎozhànzhěhào (US) Challenger (space shuttle)
挑治疗法 tiǎozhì liáofǎ 〈中医〉prick or pick therapy
挑痔疗法 tiǎozhì liáofǎ 〈中医〉hemorrhoid pricking (therapy)
挑嘴 tiǎozuǐ tell tales; gossip

朓 tiǎo 〈旧语〉appearance of the moon in the west at the end of a lunar month

斢 tiǎo 〈方言〉exchange; swap; change
斢换 tiǎohuàn 〈方言〉exchange; swap; change:～谷种 swap seeds

tiào

眺 tiào look into the distance from a high place:登高远～ ascend a height to enjoy a distant view
眺台 tiàotái gazebo
眺望 tiàowàng look into the distance from a high place:站在山顶～大海 overlook the sea from the top of a mountain

跳 tiào ❶ jump; leap; bounce; spring:～过小溪 jump (over) a stream /高兴得直～ jump for (*or* with) joy /他猛地～了起来。He sprang to his feet. /纵身～过墙头 clear the wall in one jump /上窜下～ go up and down to make contacts; run around on sinister errands /皮球～得很高。The rubber ball bounced high. /小女孩连蹦带～地走了。The little girl bounced away. /他在这个关键问题上～了出来，破坏我们的计划。He came out into the open on this key issue to disrupt our plans. ❷ move up and down; beat; pulsate:他的脉搏～得很快。His pulse was beating rapidly. /她害怕得心口直～。Her heart was throbbing with fear. /左眼～财，右眼～祸。〈迷信〉When one's left eyelid twitches, it means good fortune; when one's right eyelid twitches, it forebodes misfortune. ❸ skip (over); make omissions:～两行往下读 skip (*or* jump) two lines and read on / ～针 (in knitting) drop stitches /隔三～两地把书读了一遍 skim through a book
跳班 tiàobān (of a pupil) skip a grade
跳板 tiàobǎn ❶ gangplank; gangway:乘客经过～，陆续下船。The passengers filed down the gangplank while disembarking. ❷ springboard; diving board:三米～ three-metre springboard ❸ (traditional game for ethnic Korean girls) "seesaw jumping", with one girl jumping up and down on her end of the seesaw to bounce up the girl standing on the other end, who will then take her turn to jump and bounce up the former
跳板跳水 tiàobǎn tiàoshuǐ springboard diving
跳布扎 tiào bùzhá *also*"跳神";"打鬼" dǎguǐ (as of Tibetan lamas) dance to drive out demons on religious festivals
跳槽 tiàocáo ❶ (of stable-kept livestock) go to another trough for fodder ❷ abandon one job for another; job-hop:～经商 drop one's occupation to go in for business /他一心想～，找个更好的工作。He likes to job-hop and is intent on hunting for better employment.
跳场 tiàochǎng dancing carnival — popular festival of the Miao nationality, usu. held in the first month of the lunar year, with men and women playing reedpipes and dancing around flowered poles
跳虫 tiàochóng 〈动物〉springtail; snowflea
跳跶 tiàoda ❶ beat; pulsate; hop:心～个不停。The heart keeps throbbing. /麻雀在场院上～觅食。Sparrows hopped about on the threshing ground looking for food. ❷ be on the hop; bustle about:召开运动会的事儿全仗他一个人～。He bustled about preparing for the sportsmeet single-handed. /一家人的生活就靠他一个人～。The whole family depended upon him as the only breadwinner.
跳弹 tiàodàn 〈军事〉ricochet:～轰炸 ricochet bombing; skip bombing /～射击 ricochet fire
跳荡 tiàodàng move up and down; beat; pulsate; swing:快乐的心随着歌声～。Merry hearts were beating to the accompaniment of the singing. /她～着两根小辫子跑来跑去。She ran about with her pigtails swaying back and forth.
跳动 tiàodòng move up and down; beat; pulsate:心脏停止～。One's heart ceases to pulsate. /眼皮不断～。One's eyelids keep twitching.
跳端公 tiào duāngōng 〈方言〉sorcerer's dance in a trance
跳房子 tiào fángzi *also*"跳间" hopscotch, a children's game
跳发球 tiàofāqiú 〈体育〉jump-serving
跳高 tiàogāo 〈体育〉high jump:撑杆～ pole vault; pole jump /俯卧式～ straddle jump; straddle /背越式～ backstyle; Fosbury flop /滚式～ Western layout /剪式～ Eastern layout /～架 jumping standard /～运动员 high jumper
跳行 tiàoháng ❶ skip a line (in reading or transcribing):抄写时小心不要～。Be careful not to skip a line in copying. /读～了 miss a line in reading ❷ start a new line in writing:～顶格书写。Start a new line and leave no space at the beginning. ❸ change to a new occupation:～做小买卖 quit one's job and start a small business
跳级 tiàojí *also*"跳班" (of pupils) skip a grade:学习成绩卓异者允许～。Students with outstanding academic achievements are permitted to skip a grade.
跳加官 tiào jiāguān 〈旧语〉〈戏曲〉side-show that opens a performance, or is inserted into a performance upon the arrival of dignitaries, performed by an actor wearing a mask and a red robe and holding a sign invoking blessings for the audience
跳间 tiàojiān hopscotch
跳脚 tiàojiǎo stamp one's foot:急得～ stamp with impatience /事情得慢慢办，你再～也没用。You've got to take your time; there's no use stamping your foot.
跳脚舞 tiàojiǎowǔ *also*"打跳" dǎtiào;"对脚舞" duìjiǎowǔ stamping dance — folk dance of the Yi nationality featuring various footsteps
跳进黄河洗不清 tiàojìn Huánghé xǐbuqīng even if one jumped into the Yellow River, one could not wash oneself clean — there's nothing one can do to clear one's name; find it impossible to clear oneself:这件事我有口难辩，跳进黄河也洗不清。I can't possibly clear myself, for I'm unable to offer an explanation of how it all happened.
跳井 tiàojǐng jump into the well to commit suicide:～投河 commit suicide by throwing oneself into a well or river
跳栏 tiàolán 〈体育〉hurdle race; the hurdles:～运动员 hurdler
跳雷 tiàoléi 〈军事〉bounding mine
跳梁 tiàoliáng *also*"跳踉" jump up and down; perform antics; be rampant:～乡里 lord it over one's townsmen
跳梁小丑 tiàoliáng-xiǎochǒu buffoon who performs antics; contemptible scoundrel
跳踉 tiàoliáng *see*"跳梁"
跳楼 tiàolóu jump from a building to commit suicide:～价 distress price /这次股票暴跌，不知有多少人要～! I wonder how many people are going to commit suicide during the present stock market crash!
跳楼货 tiàolóuhuò 〈口语〉distress merchandise
跳马 tiàomǎ 〈体育〉❶ vaulting horse ❷ horse-vaulting
跳猫子 tiàomāozi 〈方言〉rabbit; hare
跳蝻 tiàonǎn 〈动物〉nymph of a locust
跳皮筋儿 tiào píjīnr *also*"跳猴皮筋"(a children's game) skipping and dancing over a chain of rubber bands; rubber-band skipping
跳频 tiàopín 〈电子〉frequency hopping

跳棋 tiàoqí Chinese chequers; Chinese draughts; halma
跳球 tiàoqiú 〈体育〉jump ball
跳伞 tiàosǎn parachute; bail out: ～门 bailout door /～运动员 parachutist; parachuter /～是我最喜欢的运动。Parachute-jumping is my favourite sport.
跳伞区 tiàosǎnqū parachute drop area
跳伞塔 tiàosǎntǎ parachute tower
跳神 tiàoshén ❶ sorcerer's dance in a trance ❷ *see* "跳布扎"
跳绳 tiàoshéng rope skipping: 几个小姑娘在操场上～。A few little girls were skipping ropes on the playground.
跳虱 tiàoshī 〈方言〉flea
跳鼠 tiàoshǔ 〈动物〉jerboa
跳水 tiàoshuǐ ❶〈体育〉dive: ～运动 fancy diving; diving /～运动员 diver /～表演 diving exhibition /花式～ fancy diving /高难度～ variety diving /直体～ straight header /屈体～ pike dive; jackknife /转体～ twist dive /向前～ front dive /向后～ back dive; reverse dive /臂立～ handstand dive ❷〈方言〉throw oneself into water to commit suicide
跳水池 tiàoshuǐchí diving pool
跳台 tiàotái diving tower; diving platform: 十米～ ten-metre diving platform /～滑雪 sky jumping
跳台跳水 tiàotái tiàoshuǐ platform diving; high diving
跳汰 tiàotài 〈矿业〉jigging: ～洗选机 jig washer /～选矿法 jigging /～选煤 coal jigging
跳腾 tiàoteng ❶ jump; hop; beat ❷ be on the hop; bustle about: 看他那身力气，多能～！He is bursting with energy and is on the hop all the time.
跳舞 tiàowǔ ❶ dance: 我们在节日期间～唱歌。We dance and sing songs on festivals. ❷ go to the ball: 女士们都穿晚礼服去～。The ladies were all dressed in long gowns for the ball.
跳舞厅 tiàowǔtīng dancing hall
跳箱 tiàoxiāng 〈体育〉❶ box horse; vaulting box ❷ jump over the box horse
跳鞋 tiàoxié (spiked) jumping shoes
跳远 tiàoyuǎn 〈体育〉long jump; broad jump: 三级～ hop, step (*or* skip) and jump
跳月 tiàoyuè moon dance — festive singing and dancing in the moonlight performed by young people of the Miao or Yi nationalities
跳跃 tiàoyuè jump; leap; bound: ～前进 leap forward /～运动 jumping exercise /～现象 jump phenomenon /～进化〈生物〉saltatory evolution
跳跃病 tiàoyuèbìng ❶〈医学〉jumping disease ❷〈兽医〉louping ill
跳跃器 tiàoyuèqì *also* "山羊" shānyáng 〈体育〉buck
跳跃着陆 tiàoyuè zhuólù 〈军事〉rebound landing
跳蚤 tiàozao *also* "蛇蚤" gèzao; "跳虱" flea
跳蚤市场 tiàozao shìchǎng flea market
跳闸 tiàozhá 〈电工〉trip; tripping: 过载～ overload trip; circuit breaker /电压过高～ overvoltage trip /自动～ automatic tripping
跳闸开关 tiàozhá kāiguān 〈电工〉trip switch
跳闸装置 tiàozhá zhuāngzhì tripgear
跳字 tiàozì 〈印刷〉rising type; rising space

粜（糶） tiào sell (grain): ～米 sell rice

tiē

怗 tiē 〈书面〉suppress; put down

帖¹ tiē ❶ submissive; pliant; obedient: 服服～～ docile and obedient /俯首～耳 be all obedience; be servile ❷ proper; steady; secure: 办事妥～ do things properly; handle matters well

帖² Tiē a surname

see also tiě; tiè
帖服 tiēfú 〈书面〉docile and obedient; submissive
帖帖 tiētiē 〈书面〉quiet; serene: ～而坐 sit quietly /天下～无事。All is quiet in the country.

萜 tiē 〈化学〉terpene

贴¹ tiē ❶ paste; stick; glue; attach: 剪～ clip and paste /～宣传画 paste up a poster /～邮票 stick on a stamp /在身分证上～照片 stick one's photo on one's ID card /把这几张报纸～在一起 glue the newspapers together /～布告 put up a bulletin (*or* notice) / 在行李上～标签 label one's luggage ❷ cling to; keep close to; press or nestle closely to: 湿衬衫～在背上 wet shirt clinging to one's back /～着妈妈睡 nestle closely to one's mother in one's sleep /～墙放把椅子 place a chair against the wall /～着耳朵小声说 murmur in sb.'s ear / 两个工厂～得很近。The two factories lie close to each other. ❸ subsidize; help (out) financially: 上大学时，父母每月～他五十块钱。When he was at college, his parents gave him fifty *yuan* every month to help him out. /这个项目需要不少资金，他的积蓄全～进去还不够。The project required a large investment; not even all his savings would be enough. ❹ subsidy; allowance; grant: 粮～ food allowance /车～ traffic allowance ❺〈量词〉*used of medicated plaster*: 一～膏药 a piece of medicated plaster

贴² tiē *see* "帖¹" tiē

贴边 tiēbiān ❶ be connected with; be relevant to; be involved in: 说话不～ make irrelevant remarks; be off (*or* beside) the point / 我跟这件事儿不～。I am not involved in this. *or* I have nothing to do with this. ❷ hem; border (of a garment): 有～的窗帘 hemmed curtain /衬衣短了点儿，加个～。The blouse is a little short and needs an extra hem.
贴标签 tiē biāoqiān 〈比喻〉(of comments or criticisms) slap on a label without making a concrete analysis; label
贴标签机 tiēbiāoqiānjī 〈机械〉labeller; labelling machine
贴饼子 tiēbǐngzi corn or millet cake baked on a pan
贴补 tiēbu ❶ subsidize; help (out) financially: ～家用 help out with the daily expenses (of one's family); help pay the family expenses /每月～父母一百元 give 100 *yuan* each month to one's parents as subsidy ❷ eke out by drawing on one's savings: 靠存款～生活 make ends meet by drawing on one's savings
贴旦 tiēdàn 〈戏曲〉secondary female character
贴兜 tiēdōu *also* "明兜" míngdōu patch pocket
贴合 tiēhé link closely; integrate: 夜来了，平原上的天和地完全～在一起。Night fell on the plain, and the horizon became indiscernible. / 做计划要～具体情况。Plans must be made to suit the specific conditions.
贴花 tiēhuā 〈纺织〉appliqué
贴画 tiēhuà ❶ New Year picture; poster ❷ picture on a match box
贴换 tiēhuan trade in: ～一台缝纫机要多少钱? How much do I have to pay if I trade in my old sewing-machine for a new one?
贴黄 tiēhuáng 〈旧语〉stick a piece of yellow paper on the imperial edict for any changes made in it; write further comments on yellow paper stuck onto a petition or memorandum to the emperor
贴己 tiējǐ ❶ intimate; close: ～的人 close friend; confidant(e) /～话 intimate words; confidences /她对张大娘表现出十分～的样子。She seemed as if she were very close to Aunt Zhang. ❷〈方言〉private savings: ～钱 private savings of a family member; pin money /她把～首饰卖了，贴补家用。She sold her jewelry to help out with the family expenses.
贴金 tiējīn ❶ gild: 给佛像～ cover the statue of Buddha with gold foil ❷ touch up; prettify: 往自己脸上～ put feathers in one's own cap; blow one's own trumpet
贴金漆 tiējīnqī gold size
贴近 tiējìn ❶ press close to; nestle up against: ～耳边低语 whisper in sb.'s ear /把折叠椅～墙根码好。Stack up the folding chairs against the wall. /文学家要～生活，写出广大读者喜闻乐见的作品。Writers should get close to life and create works that are well received by vast numbers of readers. ❷ intimate; close: ～的人 sb. close to one; trusted follower; confidant(e)
贴脸 tiēliǎn wooden strip or board used to seal up the space between a window-frame and a wall
贴邻 tiēlín next-door neighbour; close neighbour
贴面 tiēmiàn face; facing: 大理石～的圆柱 marble-faced column /柚木～的家具 teak-faced furniture /～胶合板 faced plywood /～砖 face

brick; face tile /～塑料 formica /～材料 facing
贴面舞 tiēmiànwǔ cheek-to-cheek dancing: 跳～ dance cheek to cheek
贴面砖 tiēmiànzhuān 〈建筑〉 furring brick
贴谱 tiēpǔ apt; appropriate; to the point: 分析～ sound analysis / 这些话不～。These remarks are off the mark.
贴切 tiēqiè (of words) apt; fitting; suitable; appropriate; proper: ～的表达方法 apt (*or* appropriate) expression /十分～的词 le mot juste /他写文章总是反复琢磨，力求每个词都用得～。He writes with great deliberation as he tries his best to use every word in its proper place.
贴晌 tiēshǎng 〈方言〉 near noon: 天已～。It is almost noon.
贴身 tiēshēn ❶ next to the skin: ～内衣 underwear; underclothes / ～穿了件布褂 wear a cotton shirt next to the skin /把钱放在～的衣兜里 put money in the pocket of one's underclothes ❷ fit nicely; be a good fit: 他裁的衣服穿着～。The clothes he cut out fit well. ❸ personal: ～丫环 personal maid /～保镖 personal bodyguard
贴实 tiēshi ❶ solid; sound; down-to-earth: 干活很～ work in a down-to-earth manner; work conscientiously /这孩子从小就看着很～。I found the boy (*or* The boy seemed to be) very conscientious even as a child. ❷ free from anxiety; at peace; at ease: 这消息弄得他心里不～。The news unsettled him. ❸ 〈方言〉 close; intimate: 他跟队长很～。He is on intimate terms with the team-leader. *or* He's a pal of the team-leader. ❹ 〈方言〉 sturdy; robust: 他显得身子骨很～。He looked strong and sturdy.
贴水 tiēshuǐ 〈金融〉 ❶ pay an agio ❷ agio; currency exchange; premium: ～率 agio
贴题 tiētí relevant; pertinent; to the point: 不～的话不说 make no irrelevant remarks /简洁、～ brief but to the point /文章写得很～。The article is very pertinent.
贴体 tiētǐ 〈方言〉 fit: 这身制服很～。The uniform fits nicely.
贴息 tiēxī 〈金融〉 ❶ pay a discount when cashing a promissory note ❷ discount for cashing a promissory note; discount (as on a promissory note)
贴现 tiēxiàn 〈金融〉 discount (as on a promissory note): 期票～ discount on a promissory note; time discount /～掮客 discount broker /～利息 discount interest /～窗口 discount window
贴现率 tiēxiànlǜ discount rate
贴现市场 tiēxiàn shìchǎng discount market
贴现银行 tiēxiàn yínháng discount bank
贴心 tiēxīn intimate; close: ～话 words spoken in confidence; confidences /～人 intimate (*or* bosom) friend; trusted companion; confidant(e) /他虽贵为天子，却没有一个～的人。Emperor though he was, he had not a single person he could confide in.

tiě

帖 tiě ❶ invitation: 下～ send an invitation /请～ invitation / 谢～ card of thanks; thank-you note ❷ 〈旧语〉 card on which are written the hour, date, month and year of one's birth (traditionally used for betrothal, etc.); age card: 庚～ age card /换～定亲 (of a couple) become engaged by exchanging their age cards /换～弟兄 sworn brothers (who exchanged age cards) ❸ note; card: 字～儿 brief note ❹ 〈方言〉 〈量词〉 *used of Chinese herbal medicine*: 几～草药 a few doses (*or* draughts) of herbal medicine
see also tiē; tiè
帖木儿 Tiěmù'ér Timur or Tamerlane (1336-1405), Mongol conqueror
帖子 tiězi ❶ invitation ❷ age card ❸ note; card: 名～ visiting card

铁(鐵、銕) tiě ❶ iron; ferrum (Fe): ～锅 iron wok / 钢～ iron and steel /镔～ wrought iron /生～ pig iron; cast iron /磁～ magnet /马口～ tinplate /马蹄～ horseshoe /打～ forge iron; work as a blacksmith /炼～ iron-smelting /斩钉截～ resolute and decisive / 点～成金 touch iron and turn it into gold; turn sth. crude into sth. of great value ❷ arms; weapon: 手无寸～ completely unarmed; bare-handed ❸ hard or strong as iron: ～打的汉子也吃不消。It is too much even for an iron man. ❹ violent; harsh; cruel: ～血政策 blood-and-iron policy /～的统治 iron-handed rule; tyranny ❺ ironclad; indisputable; unalterable: ～的事实 hard fact; ironclad evidence /～的纪律 iron discipline ❻ serious; solemn: ～着脸 look stern ❼ (Tiě) a surname
铁案如山 tiě'àn-rúshān case borne out by ironclad evidence; ironclad case: 证据确凿，～ ironclad case supported by conclusive evidence
铁板 tiěbǎn iron plate; sheet iron
铁板钉钉 tiěbǎn-dìngdīng be very sure; be absolutely certain: 这次足球比赛，我认为甲队获胜是～了。I think team A is sure to win the football match. /事实俱在，～，不容抵赖。The evidence is conclusive and brooks no denial.
铁板一块 tiěbǎn-yīkuài monolithic bloc: 这个同盟绝不是～。This alliance is by no means a monolithic bloc.
铁板租 tiěbǎnzū 〈旧语〉 fixed land rent regardless of natural disasters
铁笔 tiěbǐ ❶ cutting tool used in carving seals, etc. ❷ stylus for cutting stencils; stencil pen
铁箅子 tiěbìzi ❶ grate (as of a stove) ❷ gridiron; grill
铁壁铜墙 tiěbì-tóngqiáng *also* "铜墙铁壁" wall of iron and bronze — bastion of iron; impregnable fortress
铁饼 tiěbǐng 〈体育〉 ❶ discus throw ❷ discus
铁驳 tiěbó iron barge
铁蚕豆 tiěcándòu roasted broad bean
铁杵磨成针 tiěchǔ móchéng zhēn an iron pestle can be ground down to a needle; perseverance will prevail; little strokes fell great oaks: 只要功夫深，～。So long as one works hard enough at it, even an iron pestle can be ground down to a needle. *or* Persistent effort leads to success.
铁窗 tiěchuāng ❶ window with iron grating ❷ prison bars; prison: ～生活 life behind bars; prison life
铁窗风味 tiěchuāng-fēngwèi prison life; life behind bars: 尝到了～ come to know the taste of prison life
铁磁 tiěcí 〈物理〉 ferromagnetic: ～半导体 ferromagnetic semicouductor /～探伤器 ferromagnetic crack detector /～示波器 ferrograph /～探测器 ferroprobe /～体 ferromagnet
铁磁共振 tiěcí gòngzhèn 〈物理〉 ferromagnetic resonance
铁磁性 tiěcíxìng ferromagnetism
铁搭 tiědā *also* "铁锴" 〈方言〉 rake with three to six teeth
铁锴 tiědā *see* "铁搭"
铁打 tiědǎ ironclad; solid; sturdy: ～的江山 unshakable state power /他有一副～的身体。He is as strong as a horse.
铁丹 tiědān *also* "红土子" hóngtǔzi a kind of dark red or light red pigment
铁蛋白 tiědànbái 〈生化〉 ferritin
铁刀木 tiědāomù 〈植物〉 *Cassia siamea*
铁道 tiědào railway; railroad: 高架～ aerial railway; elevated railroad /地下～ underground (railway); tube; subway
铁道兵 tiědàobīng 〈军事〉 railway engineering corps
铁道部 tiědàobù ministry of railways
铁道炮兵 tiědào pàobīng railway artillery
铁电 tiědiàn 〈物理〉 ferroelectric: ～材料 ferroelectric material /～晶体 ferroelectric crystal /～效应 ferroelectric effect
铁电陶瓷 tiědiàn táocí 〈电工〉 ferroelectric ceramics
铁电现象 tiědiàn xiànxiàng 〈物理〉 ferroelectricity
铁定 tiědìng ironclad; fixed; indisputable; unalterable: ～的局面 unalterable situation /事情已经～，没有争论余地。The matter has been decided finally and allows of no dispute.
铁矾土 tiěfántǔ 〈矿业〉 bauxite
铁饭碗 tiěfànwǎn iron rice bowl; secure job: 打破～ break the iron rice bowl; abolish the system of lifetime employment /端着～ have a lifelong job
铁杆 tiěgǎn ❶ reliable; loyal: ～卫士 loyal guards ❷ stubborn; inveterate; dyed-in-the-wool: ～保皇派 dyed-in-the-wool royalist /～汉奸 out-and-out traitor ❸ of guaranteed high yield; sure-fire: ～庄稼 guaranteed high-yielding crop /～收入 guaranteed income
铁哥们儿 tiěgēmenr 〈口语〉 sworn or close friend; faithful pal; crony
铁工 tiěgōng ❶ ironwork ❷ ironworker; blacksmith
铁工资 tiěgōngzī fixed salary
铁公鸡 tiěgōngjī iron cock; stingy person; miser: 那老头儿是个一毛不拔的～。That old man is such a miser that no one could get a penny from him.
铁箍 tiěgū iron hoop

T

铁骨铮铮 tiěgǔ-zhēngzhēng staunch and unyielding; with iron determination: 他是一个~的汉子，在困难面前从来不低头。He is a man of true calibre and never bows to difficulties.
铁钴合金 tiěgǔ héjīn 〈冶金〉 ferrocobalt
铁拐李 Tiěguǎi Lǐ Li with the Iron Crutch, one of the legendary eight immortals who cross the sea to the fairy island
铁观音 tiěguānyīn Tieguanyin, a variety of oolong (乌龙) tea
铁管 tiěguǎn iron pipe; iron tube
铁轨 tiěguǐ rail: 路基已经修好，就等着铺~了。With the roadbed built, all that is left is the laying of rails (*or* tracks).
铁柜 tiěguì iron or steel chest; strongbox; safe
铁海棠 tiěhǎitáng 〈植物〉 crown of thorns; Christ-thorn (*Euphorbia splendens*)
铁汉 tiěhàn *also* "铁汉子" man of iron; man of iron will; person of strong determination: 好一条刚强的~! What a man of strong will!
铁合金 tiěhéjīn 〈冶金〉 ferroalloy; iron alloy
铁黑 tiěhēi ❶〈化工〉 iron oxide black ❷ iron-black
铁红 tiěhóng iron oxide red
铁花 tiěhuā 〈工美〉 ornamental work of iron; iron openwork
铁画 tiěhuà 〈工美〉 iron picture
铁画银钩 tiěhuà-yíngōu (of calligraphy) vigorous and powerful
铁环 tiěhuán iron hoop: 滚~ trundle a hoop; play with (*or* roll) a hoop
铁黄 tiěhuáng iron oxide yellow
铁灰 tiěhuī dark grey
铁活 tiěhuó ironwork: 加工~ process ironwork / 干~ make iron articles; work as an ironsmith
铁基合金 tiějī héjīn 〈冶金〉 iron-base alloy
铁蒺藜 tiějíli 〈军事〉 caltrop
铁甲 tiějiǎ ❶ mail; armour: ~战袍 coat of mail / ~骑兵 armoured cavalry / 身披~ wear armour; be clad in armour ❷〈军事〉 armour for vessels, vehicles, etc.
铁甲车 tiějiǎchē armoured car; armoured vehicle
铁甲虫 tiějiǎchóng 〈动物〉 army weevil (*Hispa armigera*)
铁甲舰 tiějiǎjiàn ironclad warship; ironclad
铁将军 tiějiāngjūn 〈戏谑〉 door lock: 我昨天到你家，不料~把门。I called at your house yesterday, only to find the door locked fast.
铁匠 tiějiang blacksmith; ironsmith
铁匠铺 tiějiangpù smithy; blacksmith's shop
铁脚板 tiějiǎobǎn iron soles; toughened feet: 南征北战，练就了他一双~。Frequent marching toughened his feet.
铁紧 tiějǐn very tight or close: 门关得~ shut the door tight / 事情瞒得~ keep a matter very close (*or* in complete secrecy)
铁军 tiějūn iron army; invincible army
铁铠 tiěkǎi mail; armour
铁矿 tiěkuàng ❶ iron ore: ~砂 iron ore ❷ iron mine: 富~ high-grade iron mine
铁矿石 tiěkuàngshí iron ore
铁兰 tiělán 〈植物〉 Spanish moss; black moss; long moss; vegetable horsehair (*Tillandsia usneoides*)
铁力木 tiělìmù 〈植物〉 ferreous mesua (*Mesua ferrea*)
铁链 tiěliàn iron chain; shackles
铁流 tiěliú ❶ flowing molten iron: 灼热的~从炉门奔泻而下。Rolling molten iron poured down from the furnace opening. ❷ strong army; invincible force: ~转战千里，所向无敌。The great army marched from one place to another, carrying everything before it.
铁路 tiělù railway; railroad: ~标志 railway sign / ~部门 railway department / ~运输 railway (*or* rail) transport; railway transportation; shipping by rail / ~货物周转量 goods moved by rail; volume of railway freight / ~旅客周转量 volume of railway passenger transport / ~通车里程 railway traffic mileage / ~营业里程 mileage of railway lines in service / 国际~联运 international railway through transport / 宽轨~ broad-gauge railway / 窄轨~ narrow-gauge railway / 高架~ aerial railway; elevated railroad / 市郊~ suburban railway / 洲际~ transcontinental railway / 电气化~ electric railway / 铺~复线 double-track a railway
铁路岔线 tiělù chàxiàn railway siding
铁路道口 tiělù dàokǒu railway crossing
铁路干线 tiělù gànxiàn trunk railway
铁路公路两用桥 tiělù-gōnglù liǎngyòngqiáo (railway and highway) combined or dual-use bridge
铁路路基 tiělù lùjī railway bed
铁路网 tiělùwǎng railway network
铁路线 tiělùxiàn railway line
铁路油槽车 tiělù yóucáochē rail tank car; rail tanker
铁马 tiěmǎ ❶ armoured horses; cavalry: 金戈~ shining spears and armoured horses — symbol of war in ancient times ❷ tinkling pieces of metal hanging from the eaves of pagodas, temples, etc.
铁门 tiěmén ❶ iron gate ❷ grille
铁闷子 tiěmènzi *also* "铁闷子车" boxcar
铁面无私 tiěmiàn-wúsī impartial and incorruptible; just and stern: ~的法官 impartial and incorruptible justice
铁木真 Tiěmùzhēn Timujin (1167-1227), Mongol conqueror, proclaimed Genghis Khan or Jenghiz Khan (成吉思汗) in 1206
铁幕 tiěmù "Iron Curtain", a term used by the West after World War II to refer to the barrier to the passage of persons and information between the former Soviet Union (together with its East European allies) and the West
铁娘子 tiěniángzi iron lady
铁鸟 tiěniǎo airplane; aeroplane
铁牛 tiěniú iron ox; tractor
铁皮 tiěpí iron sheet: 洋~ tinplate / 白~ galvanized iron (sheet) / 黑~ black sheet (iron) / ~箱子 iron-plated case (*or* box)
铁骑 tiěqí 〈书面〉 cavalry: 三千~ three thousand cavalrymen
铁器 tiěqì ironware: ~加工 ironware processing
铁器时代 tiěqì shídài Iron Age
铁锹 tiěqiāo spade; shovel
铁青 tiěqīng ashen; livid; ghastly pale: 脸色~ turn deadly pale; turn livid
铁拳 tiěquán iron fist; mailed fist; powerful attack: 握紧~ clench one's powerful fist / 来犯之敌被我边防部队的~击得溃不成军。Our frontier troops dealt the invaders a smashing blow.
铁券 tiěquàn inscribed metal pledge of the emperor conferring special privileges on a deserving minister or prince
铁人 tiěrén iron man; person of exceptional physical and moral strength
铁纱 tiěshā wire gauze; wire cloth: ~罩 iron gauze cover; wire gauze guard
铁砂 tiěshā ❶〈矿业〉 iron sand ❷ shot (in a shotgun cartridge); pellets
铁杉 tiěshān 〈植物〉 Chinese hemlock (*Tsuga chinensis*)
铁石心肠 tiěshí-xīncháng be iron-hearted; have a heart of stone; be hard-hearted: 在这种人间悲剧面前，~也要落泪。Seeing such a tragedy, even a hard-hearted man could not hold back his tears.
铁树 tiěshù (common name for 苏铁) 〈植物〉 sago cycas (*Cycas revoluta*)
铁树开花 tiěshù-kāihuā iron tree in blossom; something seldom seen or hardly possible: 他的癌症治好了，这真是~。It was virtually a miracle that his cancer was cured.
铁水 tiěshuǐ molten iron; liquid iron: ~包 foundry ladle / ~穿漏 molten iron breakout
铁丝 tiěsī iron wire: ~筐 iron wire basket
铁丝网 tiěsīwǎng ❶ wire netting; wire meshes ❷ wire entanglement: 有刺~ barbed wire entanglement
铁素体 tiěsùtǐ 〈冶金〉 ferrite: ~不锈钢 ferritic stainless steel; stainless iron / ~化 ferritization / ~可锻铸铁 ferritic malleable / ~铸铁 ferrite cast iron
铁酸盐 tiěsuānyán 〈化学〉 ferrite
铁算盘 tiěsuànpan iron abacus — meticulous calculation; competent accountant; shrewd person: 他是远近闻名的~。His astuteness in business is widely known in this area.
铁索 tiěsuǒ cable; iron chain: ~吊车 cable car
铁索桥 tiěsuǒqiáo chain bridge
铁塔 tiětǎ ❶ iron pagoda; iron tower: 埃菲尔~ Eiffel Tower ❷〈电学〉 pylon; transmission tower
铁塔广播天线 tiětǎ guǎngbō tiānxiàn 〈无线电〉 broadcast-tower antenna
铁塔天线 tiětǎ tiānxiàn 〈无线电〉 pylon antenna; mast antenna
铁碳合金 tiětàn héjīn 〈冶金〉 iron-carbon alloy
铁蹄 tiětí iron heel — rule by force; tyrannical rule: ~下的歌女 girl singer under the iron heel / 在征服者的~下挣扎 struggle under the despotic rule of the conquerors
铁铜合金 tiětóng héjīn 〈冶金〉 iron-copper

铁桶 tiětǒng metal pail or bucket; metal drum: ～江山 solid state power / 包围得～似的 be tightly encircled
铁托 Tiětuō Josip Bozr Tito (1892-1980), Yugoslav statesman: ～分子 Titoist (Tito's follower)
铁腕 tiěwàn iron hand: ～人物 iron-handed person; strong man / ～统治 rule by an iron hand; high-handed rule
铁锨 tiěxiān shovel; spade
铁苋菜 tiěxiàncài 〈植物〉 *Acalypha australis*
铁线订书机 tiěxiàn dìngshūjī wire stitcher; wire stitching machine
铁线蕨 tiěxiànjué *also* "铁线草" 〈植物〉 venushair; maidenhair; venus'-hair fern (*Adiantum capillus-veneris*)
铁线莲 tiěxiànlián 〈植物〉 clematis (*Clematis florida*)
铁屑 tiěxiè iron filings; iron chippings and shavings
铁心 tiěxīn ❶ steel one's heart; make up one's mind irrevocably; be unshakable in one's determination: 姑娘～要嫁他。The girl has made up her mind to marry him. / 我是铁了心，不完成学业不回去。I'm adamant in my determination not to return until I complete my education. ❷ 〈电学〉 (iron) core: ～线圈 ironcore coil; ironcore choke; magnet coil / ～变量器 ironcore transformer; core transformer; core-type transformer
铁锈 tiěxiù iron rust
铁血 tiěxuè be iron-willed and ready to sacrifice oneself: ～男儿 strong-willed and valiant man
铁血宰相 Tiěxuè Zǎixiàng Iron Chancellor (nickname for Otto Von Bismarck, 1815-1895, chancellor of Germany 1871-1890)
铁盐 tiěyán molysite
铁砚 tiěyàn iron inkslab: 磨穿～ wear through the iron inkslab; study assiduously
铁氧体 tiěyǎngtǐ ferrite: ～开关 ferrite switch / ～波导 ferrite waveguide / ～磁棒天线 ferrite-rod antenna / ～磁体 ferrimagnet / ～磁头 ferrite head / ～磁心 ferrite core; ferramic core
铁衣 tiěyī coat of (iron) mail
铁陨石 tiěyǔnshí iron meteorite
铁则 tiězé ironclad rule; cast-iron rule
铁砧 tiězhēn anvil
铁铮铮 tiězhēngzhēng firm as iron; staunch: ～的汉子 man of iron will; man of true calibre / ～的誓言 solemn pledge; inviolate oath
铁证 tiězhèng ironclad proof; irrefutable evidence: 这是无法否认的～。The evidence is irrefutable.
铁证如山 tiězhèng-rúshān irrefutable, conclusive proof; ironclad evidence: ～，无可抵赖 undeniable ironclad evidence
铁中铮铮 tiězhōng-zhēngzhēng 〈比喻〉 finest among metals; most distinguished among people; person of true calibre; organization of unusual quality

tiè

餮 tiè 〈书面〉 greedy for food; gluttonous: 饕～ mythical ferocious gluttonous beast; voracious eater; greedy person

帖 tiè book containing models of handwriting or painting for learners to copy: 字～ book of models of calligraphy; calligraphy models / 临～ copy a model of calligraphy / 画～ book of model paintings (*or* drawings); painting models / 碑～ book of rubbings (from stone inscriptions)
see also tiē; tiě

tīng

汀 tīng 〈书面〉 low, level land along a river; spit of land: 沙～ sandbar; sand shoal
汀线 tīngxiàn line track (of a seashore)
汀洲 tīngzhōu sand shoal

厅(廳、庁) tīng ❶ hall: 宴会～ banquet hall / 会议～ conference hall / 音乐～ concert hall / 舞～ dance hall; ballroom / 餐～ dining hall; restaurant / 休息～ lounge; foyer / 客～ drawing room; living room; parlour ❷ office: 国务院办公～ General Office of the State Council ❸ department under the provincial government: 财政～ department of finance / 水利～ water conservancy department / 民政～ civil affairs department / ～长 head of a department (under a provincial government)
厅房 tīngfáng 〈方言〉 hall; parlour
厅事 tīngshì hall (usu. of an official building or institution)
厅堂 tīngtáng hall; chamber
厅子 tīngzi 〈方言〉 drawing room; parlour

听[1](聽、聴) tīng ❶ listen; hear: ～音乐 listen to music / 偏～偏信 listen to only one side; be partial / ～不清 be hard of hearing / 在分机上～电话 listen in on the extension / 收～北京广播电台 tune in to Radio Beijing / 偷～别人的私房话 eavesdrop on a private conversation / 幻～ acousma; acouasm / 这句话～起来有道理。This remark sounds reasonable. / 废话太多，实在～不下去。I can hardly put up with all this rubbish (*or* verbiage). / 对不起，我没～清。Pardon, I didn't catch your words. *or* Sorry, I didn't quite get it. ❷ heed; obey: 谁也不～ obey (*or* heed) no one / 言～计从 always follow sb.'s advice; do whatever sb. says / 不～劝告 turn a deaf ear to advice / 一切行动～指挥 act on every order; follow every order ❸ 〈书面〉 administer; manage: 兼～万事 take care of many things simultaneously

听[2](聽、聴) tīng let be; allow: 此事～你处理。I'll leave the matter to you. / 悉～尊便。Do whatever you like. *or* As you please.

听[3](聽、聴) tīng 〈方言〉 tin; can: 三～咖啡 three tins of coffee
听壁脚 tīng bìjiǎo *also* "听壁角" 〈方言〉 eavesdrop
听便 tīngbiàn as one pleases; please yourself: 存取～。Feel free to make or draw a deposit (at this bank).
听蹭儿 tīngcèngr 〈方言〉 attend an opera without pay; gatecrash (a theatre, etc.)
听差 tīngchāi 〈旧语〉 manservant; footman; office boy
听窗 tīngchuāng *also* "听房" (as a folk custom) eavesdrop outside the bridal chamber
听从 tīngcóng obey; heed; follow; comply with: ～教诲 heed sb.'s admonition (*or* instruction) / ～指挥 obey orders / ～劝告 follow sb.'s advice / ～祖国的召唤 respond to (*or* answer) the call of the motherland
听道 tīngdào 〈生理〉 auditory canal
听断 tīngduàn 〈书面〉 try a case; hear a case: 善于～ be good at trying cases; be a wise judge
听而不闻 tīng'érbùwén listen but hear not; hear but pay no attention; turn a deaf ear to: 对群众的疾苦～，视而不见 remain indifferent to the people's problems / 他沉入遐想，对眼前的喧闹～。Lost in reverie, he was oblivious of the hubbub around him.
听房 tīngfáng *see* "听窗"
听风是雨 tīngfēng-shìyǔ *also* "听见风就是雨" no sooner has one heard the wind than one believes it is raining; speak or act merely upon hearsay; be oversensitive; be credulous
听骨 tīnggǔ 〈生理〉 ear bones
听喝 tīnghē 〈口语〉 at sb.'s disposal; at sb.'s service; at sb.'s beck and call: 我们是～的，别的事一概不问。We follow orders and ask no question. / 你说怎么干就怎么干，全听你的喝。We're at your disposal; whatever you say goes.
听候 tīnghòu wait for (a decision, settlement, etc.); be pending: ～指示 wait for instructions / ～调遣 be ready to do sb.'s bidding / 将犯人还押，～最后判决。The suspect is to be remanded pending the final sentence (*or* remanded to custody pending final sentencing).
听话 tīnghuà heed what an elder or superior says; be obedient: ～的孩子 well-behaved (*or* obedient) child / 不要哭了，～! Stop crying and be a good boy!
听话儿 tīnghuàr wait for a reply: 领导正在考虑你的申请，过几天你再～。The leaders are considering your application and will let you know their decision in a few days.
听话听音儿 tīnghuà-tīngyīnr 〈口语〉 listen for the tone, not just the words; listen for the meaning behind what sb. says; grasp what is actually meant; understand the implication of sb.'s remarks: 俗话说"～"，他的意思你还不明白? As the saying goes, the tone is more

T

meaningful than the words. Don't you understand what he is implying?

听会 tīnghuì attend or go to a meeting as a visitor：今天来～的人很多。There was a good turnout at today's meeting.

听见 tīngjian hear：～有人读书 hear sb. reading out loud／耳语的声音小得几乎听不见 whisper in a scarcely audible voice

听讲 tīngjiǎng ❶ listen to a talk；attend a lecture：专心～ listen to a lecture attentively／慕名来～的很多。Many came out of admiration for the famous speaker. ❷〈方言〉be told；hear of：这事儿你是眼见还是～？Did you see it or only hear of it？

听觉 tīngjué 〈生理〉sense of hearing；audition：～不灵 hard of hearing；poor hearing／～灵敏（have）sharp hearing／～受损 one's hearing is impaired／～越来越差 one's hearing gets worse／～造成的幻象 auditory hallucination

听课 tīngkè ❶（as of a student）attend a lecture or class ❷（as of another teacher）visit or sit in on a class

听力 tīnglì ❶ hearing：恢复～ regain one's hearing／丧失～ lose one's hearing ❷ aural or listening comprehension（in language acquisition）：～测验 listening comprehension test／英语～课 English listening comprehension class

听命 tīngmìng ❶ submit to the will of Heaven；resign oneself to one's fate；trust to luck；let things run their own course：对此我无能为力，只好～了。I can do nothing about it and have to resign myself to fate. ❷ take orders（from）；be at sb.'s command：～于人 follow sb.'s orders；be at sb.'s command／俯首～ be at sb.'s beck and call／甘心～ resign oneself to taking orders

听凭 tīngpíng allow；let（sb. do as he pleases）：～命运的摆布 bow to fate；be at the mercy of fate／去与不去，～你自己作主。It's all up to you whether to go or not.／一切～他处理。Everything has been left to his discretion.

听其言观其行 tīng qí yán guān qí xíng listen to what a person says and watch what he does；judge people by their deeds，not just by their words：要～，然后再下结论。We should base our judgment not only on what sb. says，but also on what he does.

听其自然 tīngqízìrán let things take their own course；let matters slide：什么事情都～，还要你这个经理做什么？What's the point of having you as the manager if you merely let everything take its own course？

T

听起来 tīngqilai sound；ring：这样安排～还算合理。The arrangement sounds quite reasonable.／他的话～有假。His words rang false.

听墙根 tīng qiánggēn eavesdrop

听取 tīngqǔ listen to：～工作报告 listen to a work report／校方将～教授们对新教学大纲的意见。The university leadership will solicit the professors' comments on the new teaching programme.

听任 tīngrèn 〈书面〉allow；let（sb. do as he pleases）：～自流 let things drift（*or* slide）／～调遣 be at sb.'s command／～宰割 place oneself at sb.'s mercy／～命运摆布 resign oneself to one's fate／你不能～他自行其是。You mustn't allow him to do whatever he wants.

听上 tīngshang 〈方言〉believe：千万别～了他的话。Never believe what he says.

听神经 tīngshénjīng 〈生理〉auditory or acoustic nerve

听审 tīngshěn ❶（of the accused）wait for a trial：在押～ be in custody waiting for the trial ❷（of the public）attend a trial as a visitor：法院开庭那天，～的格外多。The day the trial was conducted，there was an unusually big audience at the court.

听声 tīngshēng 〈方言〉eavesdrop

听事 tīngshì 〈书面〉❶（of a monarch or regent）hold court；administer affairs of state：五日一～ hold court every five days／升堂～（of a magistrate in ancient times）hold court to conduct a trial ❷ *also* "厅事" tīngshì hall

听书 tīngshū listen to a（professional）storyteller；go to a storytelling session：咱们不看戏，到茶馆里～吧。Let's go and listen to storytelling in a teahouse instead of attending the opera.

听顺 tīngshùn 〈方言〉heed；comply with：～他的话 follow his advice；comply with what he says

听说 tīngshuō ❶ be told；hear of：我～他挺能干。I hear that he is an able man.／这件事我是第一次～。This is the first time that I have heard of it.／他出国的消息只是～而已。It is mere hearsay that he has gone abroad. ❷〈方言〉be obedient：不～不听劝的人 stubborn person who won't listen to anybody

听说法 tīngshuōfǎ 〈语言〉aural-oral method；aural-lingual method

听讼 tīngsòng 〈书面〉hold a trial；hear or try a case：～折狱，可无审邪？How could one be anything but prudent in hearing and deciding a case？

听随 tīngsuí obey；allow：～尊便。Do as you please.

听天由命 tīngtiān-yóumìng submit to the will of Heaven；resign oneself to one's fate；trust to luck：事情到了这一步，只好～。Now that things have come to such a pass，we can do nothing but trust to luck.

听筒 tīngtǒng ❶（telephone）receiver ❷〈电学〉headphone；earphone ❸〈医学〉stethoscope

听头儿 tīngtour worth listening to：这地方戏没～。This local opera is boring.

听闻 tīngwén 〈书面〉hearing；what one hears：耸人～ deliberately exaggerated so as to create a sensation；sensational／骇人～ appalling；shocking／以广～ broaden the range of what one hears；enrich one's knowledge／追录沿途～ write down the stories one heard on one's trip

听戏 tīngxì go to a traditional opera

听写 tīngxiě dictation：～练习 dictation exercise／～能力 ability at taking dictation／教师给全班学生～。The teacher gave dictation to the class.

听信 tīngxìn ❶ wait for information：一有情况我就会告诉你，你在家～儿吧。If anything crops up，I'll let you know. Please stay at home and wait. ❷ believe what one hears：～谎言 believe a lie／～一面之词 trust one-sided stories

听阈 tīngyù 〈物理〉threshold of audibility；threshold of hearing；auditory threshold

听诊 tīngzhěn 〈医学〉auscultation：～把脉 feel sb.'s pulse and auscultate

听诊器 tīngzhěnqì stethoscope

听证 tīngzhèng hear（the evidence of litigants）

听证会 tīngzhènghuì hearing：委员会将在一些大城市举行一系列～。The committee（*or* commission）will hold a series of hearings in some major cities.

听政 tīngzhèng （of a monarch or regent）hold court；administer affairs of state：垂帘～（formerly of a woman regent）hold court from behind a screen；administer state affairs in the name of a child emperor；hold power behind the scenes

听之任之 tīngzhī-rènzhī let sth.（undesirable，evil，etc.）go unchecked；take a laissez-faire attitude；let matters drift：此种不良现象，岂能～？How can we let such bad practices go unchecked？*or* How can one shut one's eyes to such unhealthy tendencies？

听众 tīngzhòng audience；listeners：吸引大批～ attract a large audience／～来信 letters from the audience；listeners' letters

听装 tīngzhuāng tinned；canned：～饼干 canned biscuits（*or* crackers）

听子 tīngzi 〈方言〉tin；can：香烟～ cigarette tin／咖啡～ coffee can

鞓 tīng 〈书面〉leather belt or sash

桯 tīng ❶ shaft of an awl ❷ small bedside table used in ancient China

桯子 tīngzi ❶ shaft of an awl ❷ floral axis of a vegetable

烃（烴） tīng 〈化学〉hydrocarbon：长链～ long chain hydrocarbon／开链～ open chain hydrocarbon／闭链～ closed chain hydrocarbon／芳～ aromatic hydrocarbon／～转化 hydrocarbon conversion／～聚合油 hydrocarbon polymer oil／～类树脂 hydrocarbon resin

烃黑 tīnghēi 〈化工〉hydrocarbon black

烃基 tīngjī 〈化学〉hydrocarbon radical：～醇 hydrocarbon alcohol

烃气 tīngqì 〈化学〉hydrocarbon gas

烃类转化炉 tīnglèi zhuǎnhuàlú 〈化工〉hydrocarbon performer furnace

tíng

亭[1] tíng ❶ pavilion；kiosk：湖心～ pavilion in the middle of a lake；mid-lake pavilion ❷ stall；stand；booth；kiosk：书～ bookstall／报～ newsstand／电话～ telephone booth／邮～ postal kiosk／岗～ sentry box；police box

亭[2] tíng 〈书面〉well-proportioned; well-balanced
亭戍 tíngshù sentry post; frontier station
亭亭 tíngtíng 〈书面〉❶ tall and erect; upright:新荷数株～立于水面之上。Out of the water stood a few lotus blooms, fresh and graceful. ❷ *also* "婷婷" tíngtíng gracefully slim; gracefully erect
亭亭如盖 tíngtíng-rúgài (of a tree) standing tall with a canopy of leaves:路旁树木～,好像在向行人挥手致意。Tall trees on the roadside spread their drooping canopies as if greeting the passers-by.
亭亭玉立 tíngtíng-yùlì (of a girl or tree) be slim and graceful; stand gracefully tall and erect
亭午 tíngwǔ 〈书面〉midday; noon:～时分 noontime
亭匀 tíngyún *also* "停匀" tíngyún 〈书面〉well-balanced; well-proportioned
亭子 tíngzi (usu. without walls) pavilion; kiosk; gazebo
亭子间 tíngzijiān 〈方言〉small poorly-lit back room between two flights of stairs; cubby; cubbyhole

渟 tíng 〈书面〉(of water) stagnate

葶 tíng
葶苈 tínglì 〈植物〉*Roripa montana*

停[1] tíng ❶ stop; cease; halt; pause:汽车突然～了下来。The car came to a sudden halt. /风止雨～。The wind died and the rain ceased. ❷ stop over; stay:我在北京只能～两天。I can stop only for two days at Beijing. /你可以中途～三次。You can make three stopovers on the way. ❸ (of cars) be parked; (of ships) lie at anchor:禁止～车。No parking. /港口～了不少轮船。Quite a few steamboats were anchored in the harbour. ❹ ready; settled: *see* "～妥"

停[2] tíng part (of a total); portion:三～人马损了一～。One third of the troops were lost.
停摆 tíngbǎi (of a pendulum) come to a standstill; stop:咱们不能让日常工作～。We mustn't let routine work come to a standstill.
停办 tíngbàn stop working; cease operation; close down:这所业余学校现已～。The spare-time school has closed down. /逾期～。Nothing overdue will be processed.
停闭 tíngbì close down; shut down; go out of business:商店因资金短缺而暂时～。The shop was temporarily shut down for lack of funds.
停表 tíngbiǎo *also* "马表" mǎbiǎo stopwatch
停泊 tíngbó anchor; berth:～港 port of call /军舰在近海处～。The warship is anchored (*or* lying at anchor) offshore. /这个港口可以～十多艘轮船。The harbour can berth over a dozen vessels. /你们的集装箱船～在一号码头。Your container ship is berthed at wharf (*or* pier) No. 1.
停泊处 tíngbóchù berth; dock; anchorage; roadstead
停泊费 tíngbófèi anchorage dues
停泊权 tíngbóquán right of anchorage
停产 tíngchǎn stop production:～转产 stop production or change the line of production /～待料 stop production to wait for raw materials /～整顿 stop production to strengthen discipline; stop production to improve working conditions
停车 tíngchē ❶ stop; pull up:每站～十分钟。There is a ten-minute stop at every station. ❷ park:～处 parking lot /～收费计 parking meter ❸ (of a machine) stall; stop working:～维修 stop a machine for maintenance /今天下午车间～检修。The workshop stops production this afternoon for an overhaul.
停车场 tíngchēchǎng car park; parking lot; parking area
停当 tíngdang ready; settled:收拾～ put everything in order; finish packing /商量～ finish consultations; talk sth. over fully /大家准备～,只待出发。We are all ready to go.
停电 tíngdiàn power cut; power failure; blackout:全市～ blackout of the whole city /又～了,快发动备用发电机。There's another power cut. Start the reserve generator immediately!
停顿 tíngdùn ❶ stop; halt; pause; be at a standstill:陷入～状态 be at a standstill; come to a standstill /工作～不前。The work stagnated. /谈判～了下来。The negotiations have been suspended. ❷ pause (in speaking):他～了一下,又继续讲下去。He paused and went on speaking. *or* He hesitated before going on with his talk.
停放 tíngfàng park; place:广场上～着好几百辆自行车。Hundreds of bicycles were parked on the square. /烈士的遗体～在大厅中央,周围摆满了鲜花。Amidst fresh flowers, the hero's remains were placed at the centre of the hall.
停飞 tíngfēi grounding of aircraft:全部军用飞机一律～。All military aircraft were grounded without exception.
停风 tíngfēng 〈冶金〉blowing out
停工 tínggōng stop work; shut down:～待料 stop work for lack of materials /这次事故使车间～三天。The accident caused the workshop to suspend production for three days.
停航 tíngháng suspend air or shipping service:班机因机械故障～。The flight was cancelled due to mechanical trouble. /风浪太大,渡轮均已～。The waves were so high that all the ferries suspended their shipping service.
停火 tínghuǒ ceasefire:～谈判 negotiations for a ceasefire /～线 ceasefire line /达成～协议 reach an armistice agreement
停机 tíngjī ❶ (of a film, TV play, etc.) finish shooting ❷ (of an airplane) park ❸〈计算机〉halt; stop calculation:～指令 halt instruction; stop instruction /～问题 halting problem
停机坪 tíngjīpíng aircraft parking area; parking apron; tarmac
停建 tíngjiàn suspend construction:～项目 suspended project
停经片 tíngjīngpiàn 〈纺织〉dropper
停刊 tíngkān (of a newspaper, magazine, etc.) stop publication; close; cease:～整顿 suspend publication for a shake-up /本刊从下期起～。This magazine will cease with the next issue.
停靠 tíngkào (of a train) stop; (of a ship) berth:列车～在二号站台。The train stopped at platform No. 2. /江边有个～小船的码头。There was a berth by the river for small vessels.
停靠港 tíngkàogǎng port of call
停课 tíngkè suspend classes; stop classes:～考试 stop regular classes to have examinations /因暴风雪学校～一天。The school was closed for a day because of the snowstorm.
停灵 tínglíng keep a coffin (in a temporary shelter) before burial
停留 tíngliú ❶ stay for a time; stop; lay over; remain:在小城～一夜 stay (*or* stop) overnight in a small town ❷ remain; continue; proceed (as before):不能～在目前的水平上 cannot remain at the present level /研究工作尚～在试验阶段。The research is still proceeding on an experimental (*or* trial) basis. /请勿在此～。Please keep moving.
停留时间 tíngliú shíjiān 〈环保〉retention period
停妻再娶 tíngqī-zàiqǔ 〈旧语〉divorce one's wife and remarry
停球 tíngqiú 〈体育〉stop the ball:跑动中～ stop the ball on the run
停赛 tíngsài ❶ (of a match or sports meet) stop; halt:因雨暂时～ (of a match) stop temporarily because of the rain ❷ be temporarily disqualified from contests:～两年 be disqualified from contests for two years
停尸间 tíngshījiān *also* "停尸室" morgue; mortuary
停食 tíngshí 〈中医〉gastric disorder; indigestion
停手 tíngshǒu stop (doing sth.); cease:忙得一会儿也不能～ have one's hands full
停水 tíngshuǐ cut off the water supply; cut off the water:今天全天～。There will be no water supply for the whole day. /这半年～的现象少见了。Water cut-offs have been rare in the past six months.
停妥 tíngtuǒ be all set; be well arranged; be in order:收拾～后,他即赶赴车站。After he had put everything in order, he hurried off to the station. /事情联系～后,我会及时通知你。As soon as the matter is all set (*or* properly arranged), I'll let you know.
停息 tíngxī stop; cease:大风～了。The high wind died down.
停闲 tíngxián (often used in the negative) stop; let-up; free time:几天没有～ do not take a rest for several days; there is no let-up for days
停歇 tíngxiē ❶ stop doing business; close down:这家商场～了两周,最近又开业了。The shopping mall reopened recently after a two-week closedown. ❷ stop; cease; halt:毫不～地工作 work non-stop /从早到晚全无～。There is no letup from morning till night. ❸ stop for a rest; rest:他们晌午在小树林里～。They rested in a grove during the lunch break. /鸟儿～在树上。Birds perched in the tree.
停辛伫苦 tíngxīn-zhùkǔ through all kinds of hardships and difficulties
停薪留职 tíngxīn-liúzhí retain one's position with one's salary suspended; obtain an indefinite leave of absence from one's work unit
停学 tíngxué ❶ stop going to school; drop out of school:因病～

T

drop out of school on account of illness ❷ suspend (sb.) from school：他因醉酒闹事而被～。He was suspended from school for getting drunk and rioting.

停业 tíngyè ❶ temporarily stop doing business; close temporarily：年终盘点，～一天。Close for the day for clearing inventories at year-end. ❷ wind up a business; go out of business; close down：～甩卖 closing sale /因经营不善而～ close down due to mismanagement

停匀 tíngyún *also* "亭匀" tíngyún 〈书面〉 well-proportioned; well-balanced：体态～ have a well-proportioned figure; have a shapely (*or* fine) figure /字体疏密～ well-proportioned characters

停云落月 tíngyún-luòyuè 〈比喻〉 think of absent friends or relatives; miss one's friends or relatives afar：老来常有～之思。One tends to miss old friends and acquaintances when one gets old.

停战 tíngzhàn armistice; truce; ceasefire; cessation of hostilities：～谈判 armistice talks (*or* negotiations) /～协定 armistice; truce agreement /下达～命令 issue a ceasefire order

停诊 tíngzhěn (of doctors) stop examining patients; (of a hospital, etc.) close：医院门诊部春节～一天。The out-patient department closes for one day on the Spring Festival.

停职 tíngzhí suspend sb. from his duties：～检查 be temporarily relieved of one's post and asked to make a self-criticism /～停薪 suspend sb. from his post and stop his pay

停止 tíngzhǐ stop; cease; end; halt：～使用 stop using /～操作 stop operation /～进攻 call a halt to an attack /～一切挑衅活动 cease all the provocations /～供应 cut off (*or* suspend) the supply /～谈判 discontinue the negotiations /～一切论战 end all polemics

停滞 tíngzhì stagnate; be at a standstill; bog down：扭转生产～的局面 reverse the stagnation of production /思想～ be close-minded; be rigid in one's thinking /经济～。The economy is stagnant (*or* at a standstill).

停滞不前 tíngzhì-bùqián stagnate; be at a standstill：工作～。There is no progress in the work. *or* Work has stagnated.

停滞膨胀 tíngzhì péngzhàng (shortened as 滞胀) 〈经济〉 stagflation

停潴 tíngzhū (of water) be held up; be blocked

婷 tíng

婷婷 tíngtíng *also* "亭亭" tíngtíng 〈书面〉 gracefully erect; gracefully slim：～而立 (of a woman) stand slim and graceful

廷 tíng court of a monarch; seat of a monarchical government：宫～ palace; royal (*or* imperial) court; court /朝～ royal (*or* imperial) court; royal (*or* imperial) government /明～ the Ming court; the Ming government /内～ imperial household (*or* residence) /教～ the Vatican; the Holy See /～魁〈旧语〉number one successful candidate in the highest civil examinations held in the imperial palace

廷布 Tíngbù Thimphu, capital of Bhutan

廷试 tíngshì highest imperial examination presided over by the emperor (held in the imperial palace)

廷杖 tíngzhàng (punishment in ancient China) flogging of an official at the imperial court

庭 tíng ❶ hall：大～广众 (before) a big crowd; (on) a public occasion ❷ front courtyard; front yard：前～后院 front courtyard and back garden /门～若市 courtyard as crowded as a marketplace; much visited house (*or* place) ❸ law court：开～ open a court session; call the court to order /出～ appear in court /民～ civil court /～外和解 settle out of court

庭除 tíngchú courtyard：洒扫～ clean (*or* sweep) the courtyard

庭审 tíngshěn try; interrogate：～笔录 minutes of a court trial /～日 court day

庭训 tíngxùn 〈书面〉 parental instruction

庭园 tíngyuán flower garden (attached to a house); grounds

庭院 tíngyuàn courtyard：～森森 heavily-wooded courtyard

庭院经济 tíngyuàn jīngjì courtyard economy

庭院树 tíngyuànshù courtyard tree

庭长 tíngzhǎng president of a law court or tribunal; presiding judge

霆 tíng thunderbolt：雷～ thunderclap; thunderbolt; thunder-like rage

莛 tíng stem of a herb, etc.：麦～儿 stalks of wheat

蜓 tíng *see* "蜻蜓" qīngtíng

tǐng

町 tǐng 〈书面〉 ❶ raised path as border between farm fields ❷ farmland; field ❸ Japanese measure of length (= 119 yards)

町町 tǐngtǐng 〈书面〉 even; level; smooth：其地～。The land was level.

珽 tǐng 〈书面〉 jade tablet held in two hands by an official when received in audience by the emperor

梃 tǐng ❶ 〈书面〉 stick; club ❷ frame：门～ door frame /窗～ window frame ❸ 〈方言〉 pedicel; flower stalk

see also tìng

梃子 tǐngzi frame (of a door or window)

颋 tǐng 〈书面〉 upright; straight

挺[1] tǐng ❶ hard and straight; erect; stiff：笔～的军服 well-pressed army uniform /直～～地站着 stand still and stiff; stand erect ❷straighten up (physically); stick out; protrude：～起胸膛来。Throw out your chest! *or* Square your shoulders. /他胖得肚子都～出来了。He is so stout that his belly bulges out. ❸ endure; bear; hold out; stick out：他累得有点～不住了。He was so tired that he could not hold out any more. /你有病别硬～着。Don't brave it out when you are ill. /这场病他怕是～不过去了。It seems he will not survive his illness. ❹ outstanding; striking; prominent：好一个英～的小伙子！What a handsome young man! ❺ very; rather; quite：～和气的老人 kind old man /谈得～痛快 have a delightful talk

挺[2] tǐng 〈量词〉 *used of machine guns*：一～机枪 a machine gun

挺拔 tǐngbá ❶ tall and straight; towering：公路两旁一排杨树，～苍翠。On either side of the road stand a row of poplar trees, tall, straight and verdant. ❷ steady and forceful; powerful：笔力～ steady, forceful strokes (in handwriting or drawing) /身体～有力 of strong, stalwart build

挺杆 tǐnggǎn 〈机械〉 tappet：阀门～ valve tappet /～扳手 tappet wrench /～间隙 tappet clearance

挺括 tǐngguɑ 〈方言〉 (of cloth, paper, etc.) stiff and smooth; (of clothes) well-pressed; trim

挺进 tǐngjìn (of troops) boldly drive on; thrust into; press ahead; push forward：～大别山 press onward to the Dabie Mountains

挺劲 tǐngjìng tall, straight and forceful：～的古松 towering, old pines

挺举 tǐngjǔ 〈体育〉 clean and jerk

挺俊 tǐngjùn tall and graceful; of a tall and graceful figure

挺立 tǐnglì stand upright; stand erect：昂首～ stand erect with one's chin up /青松迎风～。The pine trees stood upright against the wind.

挺身 tǐngshēn straighten one's back; stand up (instead of cowering)：～反抗 rise in resistance; bravely resist; stand up to (an enemy, etc.) /～迎接艰难困苦 brave difficulties and hardships

挺身而出 tǐngshēn'érchū step forward bravely; rise courageously; come out boldly：那时候，曾经有多少仁人志士～，奋起救国。At that time, many patriots rose bravely in defence of the nation.

挺尸 tǐngshī 〈粗话〉 lie stiff and sleep like a dead body：他在屋里～，外面的事什么也没听见。He was sleeping like a corpse in the room and didn't hear anything outside.

挺实 tǐngshi strong; sturdy; solid; tough：～的腰膀 of a sturdy build

挺脱 tǐngtuō 〈方言〉 ❶ vigorous; strong; forceful：文字～ vigorous language /这匹马真～！What a spirited horse! ❷ stiff and smooth; neat and firm：他穿这身衣服很是～大方。He looks smart in this well-

pressed suit.

挺胸凸肚 tǐngxiōng-tūdù ❶ throw out one's chest and belly; be full of vigour; be spirited ❷ throw one's weight about; be arrogant or self-satisfied

挺秀 tǐngxiù towering; tall and graceful; elegant:字体～ write an elegant hand

挺直 tǐngzhí stick out; hold erect; straighten up: ～腰板儿 straighten up; square one's shoulders /脖子伸得～ hold one's neck straight; hold one's head high

挺撞 tǐngzhuàng 〈方言〉contradict (one's elder or superior); talk back

铤

tǐng 〈书面〉(walk or run) quickly

see also dìng

铤而走险 tǐng'érzǒuxiǎn risk danger in desperation; make a reckless move:发财的欲望使得他～。Hunger for wealth led him to make a reckless move. *or* Greed made him desperate.

侹

tǐng 〈书面〉level and straight

艇

tǐng ❶ (light) boat; skiff:汽～ steamboat /游～ yacht; pleasure boat ❷ (light) naval vessel:潜水～ submarine /炮～ gunboat /登陆～ landing craft

艇子 tǐngzi 〈方言〉light boat; skiff

脡

tǐng 〈书面〉❶ long, narrow strip of dried meat ❷ straight

tìng

梃

tìng ❶ poke (an iron rod between the leg skin and the flesh of a slaughtered pig before blowing air into the space between the flesh and skin so as to separate them and pump up the skin for cleansing):～猪 poke an iron rod under the leg skin of a slaughtered pig ❷ iron rod or bar used for the above purpose

see also tǐng

tōng

恫(痌)

tōng 〈书面〉disease; sickness; pain

see also dòng

恫瘝在抱 tōngguān-zàibào be concerned with the hardships of the people; have the sufferings of the people at heart:～的好官 good official who cares about hardships of the people

通

tōng ❶ open; through:公路现在～了。The highway is now open. /隧道打～了。The tunnel has been driven through. /我给他打电话,但是打不～。I tried to call him but couldn't get through. /此路不～。〈交通〉Dead end. *or* No thoroughfare. /他想～了。He has come round to the idea. *or* Now he's got it. /这行得～吗? Will this work? ❷ open up or clear out by poking; poke: ～烟囱 sweep a chimney /～炉子 poke the fire (in a stove) /～下水道 clear out a sewer ❸ lead to; head for; go to:四～八达 extend in all directions; be linked by rail and road to various parts of the country /直～车 through train /这条高速公路直～天津。This expressway leads (*or* goes) straight to Tianjin. /条条大路～罗马。〈谚语〉All roads lead to Rome. ❹ connect; link; communicate: ～着的屋子 connecting rooms; rooms that open into each other /暗～款曲 communicate in secret; send secret messages; keep up secret contacts /沟～情况 keep (each other) informed /互～有无 each supplies what the other needs; supply each other's needs /买～中间人 bribe (*or* buy off) the middleman ❺ notify; inform; tell: 互～消息 keep each other informed /事先～个气儿 brief (*or* notify) sb. in advance /～名报姓 introduce oneself /～个电话 give sb. a ring; give sb. a call; call (*or* phone) sb. up ❻ know; understand; comprehend:精～业务 know one's work inside out /～英、法语 have a good command of English and French /博古～今 conversant with things past and present; erudite and informed /无师自～ self-taught /不～情理 impervious to reason; unreasonable ❼ authority; expert; past master:美国～ expert on the United States /中国～ old China hand; Sinologue /万事～ know-all; versatile person ❽ logical; coherent; correct:文字不～ ungrammatical and incoherent writing ❾ general; ordinary; common:普普～～ common; commonplace; routine ❿ all; entire; whole:～夕不寐 lie awake all night (*or* the whole night) /～算起来费用约为200美元。The cost totals around 200 dollars. ⓫〈书面〉〈量词〉*used of documents, letters, telegrams, etc.*:一～文书 a document; an official dispatch /一～电报 a telegram /手书两～ two letters hand-written by sb. ⓬ (Tōng) a surname

see also tòng

通报 tōngbào ❶ (usu. of higher authorities) cite or announce in a dispatch or circular; circulate a notice or dispatch: ～表扬 cite (sb.) for commendation in an official dispatch; circulate a notice of commendation /～如下 announce the following in an official dispatch; circulate a notice as follows /在有关范围内～ circulate a dispatch (*or* notice) among those concerned ❷ circular; dispatch; notice:发～ circulate a notice /关于商品价格的～ circular on commodity prices ❸ (usu. used in academia) bulletin; journal:《化学～》*Chemical Journal* /《医学～》*Medical Journal* ❹ make known; report; inform:这个新情况要立刻向有关单位～。The new development must be reported immediately to the institutions concerned. ❺ introduce (oneself); give (one's name): ～姓名 give one's name; introduce oneself / ～宾客 (of usher, etc.) announce the names and titles of guests

通便 tōngbiàn catharsis; purgation; easing of constipation; purging of the bowels

通便剂 tōngbiànjì 〈医学〉laxative; cathartic

通禀 tōngbǐng report to one's superior or master:烦请～。May I trouble you to report to your master?

通病 tōngbìng common failing or defect; prevalent problem:官僚机构的～ failings common to all bureaucracies /旧机制的～ common defect of the old mechanism

通才 tōngcái all-round or versatile person; universal genius; generalist:～教育 liberal education; general education /难得的～ rare all-rounder

通草 tōngcǎo 〈中药〉stem pith of the rice-paper plant (*Tetrapanax papyriferus*)

通常 tōngcháng general; common; usual; normal:～的做法 usual (*or* common) practice /这是一种～的情况。This is quite a normal case. /我～晚饭后散步。I usually take a walk after supper. /这种机会～是很难有的。This is a rare opportunity.

通畅 tōngchàng ❶ unobstructed; free; clear:呼吸～ easy breathing /干渠～。The main canal is clear. /水流～。The water flows smoothly (*or* freely). ❷ easy and smooth; fluent:文笔～ smooth (*or* fluent) writing

通车 tōngchē ❶ (of a railway or highway) be open to traffic; be commissioned:～典礼 open-to-traffic ceremony /这条高速公路两年之内～。The expressway will be open to traffic within two years. ❷ have (vehicle) traffic; have transport service:因天气缘故本线不～。Service on this route is temporarily suspended due to the bad weather. /清除泥石流后即可～。Traffic will be restored as soon as the mud slide is cleared away.

通彻 tōngchè thoroughly understand; be well versed in:～经义 have a thorough understanding of the Confucian classics /～人情世故 be well versed in the ways of the world; be worldly-wise; be sophisticated

通称 tōngchēng ❶ be generally called; be generally known as:乌贼～墨斗鱼。Cuttlefish is generally known as inkfish. ❷ non-technical term or reference; general term; popular name:水银是汞的～。Quicksilver is the non-technical term (*or* popular name) for mercury.

通诚 tōngchéng confess (before god, Buddha, etc.):～祷告 confess and pray

通达 tōngdá be understanding; be sensible: ～事理 reasonable; sensible /～之士 person of good sense

通道 tōngdào ❶ thoroughfare; passageway; road:运输～ transport thoroughfare /盘山～ winding mountain road ❷〈自控〉channel:～程序 channel program /～传输能力 *also* "～容量" channel capacity /～脉冲 channel pulse /～干扰 interference between channels /～共用性 channel affinity /～命令 channel command /～同步器 channel synchronizer

通敌 tōngdí collude or collaborate with the enemy; work for the

T

enemy (in secret); have illicit relations with the enemy:有~嫌疑 be suspected of being a collaborationist (*or* collaborator)

通典 Tōngdiǎn *Cyclopaedia of Institutions*, a multi-volumed reference book on ancient Chinese political, social and cultural institutions up to the mid-8th century, compiled by Du You (杜佑) of the Tang Dynasty

通电 tōngdiàn ❶ set up an electric circuit; electrify; energize:这条线路不~。This electric line is cut off. /这个偏远的山村最近~了。Electricity reached the outlying mountain village recently. ❷ send a circular telegram; publish an open telegram:~起义 send a circular telegram to announce an uprising /~全国 publish an open telegram to the nation ❸ circular or open telegram:发出~ issue an open telegram; send a circular telegram /大会~ circular telegram of the congress

通牒 tōngdié diplomatic note:最后~ ultimatum

通都大邑 tōngdū-dàyì big city; metropolis

通读 tōngdú ❶ read over or through; read from cover to cover:~全文 read the text through ❷ understand (what one reads); comprehend:~诸子百家 be well versed in the works of various schools of thought and their exponents

通断开关 tōng-duàn kāiguān 〈电工〉 on-off or on-and-off switch

通房 tōngfáng ❶〈书面〉 connecting rooms ❷〈旧语〉 maidservant serving also as a concubine; maid-concubine

通匪 tōngfěi collude with bandits; work for bandits (in secret); have illicit relations with bandits

通分 tōngfēn 〈数学〉 reduction of fractions to a common denominator

通风 tōngfēng ❶ ventilate:~设备 ventilation equipment (*or* installation) /~系统 ventilation (*or* ventilating) system /~除尘 remove dust through ventilation /改善车间的~条件 improve the ventilation of a workshop /冬天室内要注意~。Rooms must be well ventilated in winter. ❷ divulge information; tip off:事先肯定有人给他通了风。Someone must have tipped him off beforehand. ❸ be well ventilated:屋子~,空气新鲜。The room is well ventilated with fresh air. /炉子~不良。The furnace does not draw well.

通风报信 tōngfēng-bàoxìn divulge or furnish secret information; tip off:防止有人给嫌疑人~。Guard against anybody tipping off the suspect.

通风管道 tōngfēng guǎndào ventilating or ventilation duct; air-duct

通风机 tōngfēngjī ventilation machine; ventilator; fanner

通风井 tōngfēngjǐng ventilation shaft; air shaft; air-well

通风口 tōngfēngkǒu vent; air vent

通告 tōnggào ❶ give public notice; announce (in a circular, etc.):~周知 make a public announcement /~有关人士 give notice to people concerned /谨~如下 it is hereby announced as follows ❷ public notice or announcement; circular:发出~ give public notice /张贴~ put up a notice

通功易事 tōnggōng-yìshì share out the work and cooperate with one another; make a division of labour:~,以羡补不足 share out the work and cooperate in order to make up for each's shortcomings with the other's merits

通共 tōnggòng in all; altogether; all told:~才来了三个人。All told, only three people turned up. /全镇~只有两家小酒馆。There are only two small pubs in the whole town.

通古斯 Tōnggǔsī Tungus; Tunguz:~人 Tungus /~语 Tungus /~语族 Tungusic language family

通关 tōngguān ❶ finger-guessing game — a drinking game at feasts ❷〈旧语〉 official document issued to various localities ❸ go through the Customs; be cleared by the Customs:这批货物尚未~。These goods have not been cleared by the Customs yet.

通关节 tōng guānjié circumvent (laws, rules, regulations, etc.) by bribery:这人靠~做了几笔大生意。This fellow struck a few lucrative business deals by buying off the authorities concerned.

通观 tōngguān take a comprehensive view:~全书 take the book as a whole /~全局 take stock of the overall situation /~上述所列事实 make a general assessment of the facts listed above; put all the above listed facts together

通国 tōngguó throughout the country; nationwide; countrywide:~上下 entire nation (from top leaders to the man in the street) /~一致 whole nation united as one

通过 tōngguò ❶ pass (through); cross; traverse:~人行桥 cross the foot bridge /~边境 cross the border /~华北平原 traverse the North China Plain /队伍~主席台。The procession passed by the rostrum. /一股暖流~我的全身。A warm current ran through me. /一慢二看三~。(watchword for drivers) Slow down and look round before you go ahead. ❷ adopt; pass; carry:~决议 pass a resolution /~提案 adopt a motion /以全票~ be carried unanimously /没有~论文答辩 fail in the oral defence of one's dissertation; flunk one's oral defence ❸ by means of; by way of; by; through:~合法手段 by legal means /~外交途径 through diplomatic channels /~译员进行交谈 talk to each other through an interpreter /~座谈征求意见 hold group discussions to solicit opinions /~谈判解决争端 settle a dispute by negotiations ❹ ask the consent or approval of:~上级 seek the approval of one's superior /~群众讨论作出的决定 decision made after consulting people at the grass roots

通航 tōngháng be open to navigation or air traffic:首次~ be open to air traffic (*or* navigation) for the first time; make a maiden voyage (*or* flight) /直接~ direct air service (*or* link); direct shipping service /~水域 navigable waters /~河道 navigable channel; navigable riverway

通好 tōnghǎo 〈书面〉(of nations) have friendly relations:两国世代~。The two countries had friendly relations for generations.

通红 tōnghóng *also* tònghóng very red; red through and through:~的太阳 glowing sun /他气得满脸~。He turned crimson with rage. /晚霞把天空映得~。The sky was aglow in the evening sunlight.

通话 tōnghuà ❶ communicate by telephone:为了交换信息,他俩每天都~一次。The two of them make a daily call to exchange information. ❷ converse; communicate:彼此方音太重,难以~。Due to their heavy dialects, they could hardly communicate with each other. /我们都不懂对方的母语,只好借助英语~。Neither of us understood the mother tongue of the other, so we conversed in English.

通话计时器 tōnghuà jìshíqì peg count meter

通婚 tōnghūn be or become related by marriage; intermarry:两姓世代~。The (extended) families had intermarried for generations.

通货 tōnghuò 〈经济〉 currency; current money:硬~ hard currency /自由~ convertible currency /~回笼 withdrawal (*or* recall) of currency /~贬值 depreciation of currency /~升值 appreciation of currency /~自由兑换 currency convertibility

通货紧缩 tōnghuò jǐnsuō deflation (of currency):~政策 deflational policy; tight money policy

通货膨胀 tōnghuò péngzhàng inflation (of currency):恶性~ galloping (*or* runaway) inflation /控制~ control inflation /~率 rate of inflation /~压力 inflation pressure /~政策 inflationary policy; loose money policy /通货再膨胀 reflation

通缉 tōngjī order the arrest (of a criminal at large); list as wanted:~逃犯 issue the order to arrest a criminal at large /~令 order for arrest (of a runaway criminal) /~名单 wanted list /~布告 wanted poster

通家 tōngjiā 〈书面〉❶ families of intimate friendship:~之谊 intimate familial friendship ❷ expert; virtuoso:他经过刻苦自学成了古代史~。Through painstaking studies, he has become an expert in ancient history.

通家之好 tōngjiāzhīhǎo 〈书面〉 intimate relationship between two families (as though they were one family)

通假 tōngjiǎ (of Chinese characters) interchangeable with other characters and representative of homophones:~字 character used for an interchangeable one or to represent a homophone /同音~ character used to represent a homophone /我国古书中~现象很多。Use of homophones of interchangeable characters was common in ancient Chinese writings.

通奸 tōngjiān commit adultery; fornicate; have illicit sexual intercourse:~者 adulterer; adulteress; fornicator /~行为 adultery

通间 tōngjiān connecting rooms:东厢房共有三间,两个~,一个单间。There are three rooms in the east wing, two connecting and one separate.

通鉴 Tōngjiàn (short for 资治通鉴) *Historical Events Retold as a Mirror for Government*, first chronological general history of China (from 403 BC to 959 AD), written by Sima Guang (司马光, 1019-1086)

通解 tōngjiě ❶〈书面〉 thoroughly understand; be well versed in:~经义 be well versed in Confucian classics ❷〈数学〉 general solution

通今博古 tōngjīn-bógǔ *also* "博古通今" conversant with things past and present; erudite and informed: 她是个～的才女。She is a woman scholar conversant with ancient and modern learning.

通经 tōngjīng ❶ be well versed in Confucian classics: 博学～之士 erudite scholar well versed in Confucian classics ❷〈中医〉stimulate or restore menstrual flow (by emmenagogues or acupuncture): 活血～ invigorate circulation of blood and stimulate menstrual flow /～理气 stimulate menstrual flow and regulate the flow of vital energy by removing obstructions

通款 tōngkuǎn make peace: 两国～ make peace between the two countries /～修好 make peace and foster cordial relations

通栏 tōnglán that which goes across the whole breadth or length of a newspaper, magazine or book: ～标题 banner headline; banner; streamer

通览 tōnglǎn read through; take an overall view; look at as a whole: ～全书 read through the book; take the book as a whole /～上下五千年 look back on the past five thousand years as a whole

通礼 tōnglǐ commonly accepted etiquette or ritual

通力 tōnglì make a concerted effort; pitch in for sth. together: ～解决 work together to solve a problem

通力合作 tōnglì-hézuò make a concerted effort; fully cooperate; give full cooperation (in doing sth.): 此事他一定会与你～的。He will certainly do everything possible to cooperate with you on this matter.

通例 tōnglì ❶ general rule; usual practice: 节假日不办公,是各机关的～。As a rule, government offices close on public holidays. /有函必复是公文往来的～。Official letters usually require reciprocity. ❷〈书面〉general law or principle

通连 tōnglián be connected; lead to: 与卧室～的小客厅 small drawing room off the bedroom /～花园的小径 path leading to the garden

通联 tōnglián (short for 通讯联络) communications and liaison: 搞好～工作,保证信息畅通 do a good job of communications and liaison to ensure the smooth passage of information

通亮 tōngliàng well-illuminated; brightly lit: 探照灯照得～的广场 square illuminated by searchlight /灯笼把庭院照得～。The courtyard was brightly lit by lanterns.

通量 tōngliàng 〈物理〉flux: 磁～ magnetic flux /～畸变 flux distortion /～折射 flux reflections /～变化周期 flux period

通令 tōnglìng issue a circular order; issue a general order: ～全国 issue a circular order to the whole nation /～嘉奖 issue an order (*or* citation) of commendation /执行国务院的～ carry out the circular order issued by the State Council

通路 tōnglù ❶ thoroughfare; passageway; route: 横贯草原的～ route through the grassland /这是连接两个城镇的唯一～。This is the only passageway between the two towns. ❷ channel; passage; path: ～衰减〈通信〉path attenuation /～失真系数 channel distortion coefficient /经脉,中医指人体内气血运行的～。In traditional Chinese medicine the term *jingmai* refers to the passages through which vital energy circulates in the human body.

通路子 tōng lùzi get things done by using one's influence: 找个～的人 try to get help from sb. who has the right connections

通论 tōnglùn ❶ well-rounded argument; convincing idea or thesis: 此乃人生真谛之～。This argument reveals the true meaning of life. ❷ general survey: 《现代中国文学～》*Survey of Modern Chinese Literature* /《史学～》*An Introduction to History*

通脉 tōngmài 〈中医〉❶ promote blood circulation by invigorating vital energy ❷ promote lactation

通名 tōngmíng ❶ (often used in traditional opera or fiction) announce one's name: 来将～! (formula used to address each other before unknown generals fight each other) Announce who you are, enemy general! ❷ general term; popular name

通明 tōngmíng well-illuminated; brightly lit: 广场灯火～。The square was ablaze with lights.

通谋 tōngmóu conspire together; scheme with each other: ～投敌 conspire (together or with each other) to defect to the enemy side

通年 tōngnián throughout the year; all the year round: ～辛劳 toil throughout the year /～卧病在床 be confined to bed all the year round

通盘 tōngpán overall; all-round; comprehensive: ～考虑 take the overall situation into account; consider from every possible angle /～筹划 work out a comprehensive plan

通票 tōngpiào through ticket

通铺 tōngpù wide bed (often *kang* in north China) for several people: 小旅店的单间都住满了,我们三个人只好睡～。Since there were no single rooms available in the inn, we three had to share a wide bed with others.

通起 tōngqǐ 〈方言〉in all; altogether; all told: ～只有三挂大车。There were only three carts altogether.

通气 tōngqì ❶ aerate; ventilate: ～性差 poorly ventilated (*or* aerated) ❷ be in touch or communication with each other; keep each other informed: 互不～ be out of touch (*or* communication) with each other; exchange no information /互相～,紧密配合 keep each other informed and cooperate closely /这件事他没跟我～,我一无所知。I'm completely in the dark about this as he told me nothing about it.

通气孔 tōngqìkǒng air vent; vent

通窍 tōngqiào understand things; be sensible or reasonable: 一点就～ understand at the slightest intimation; readily take the hint /说了半天也不～ fail to understand sth. despite repeated explanations

通勤 tōngqín regular transport service (for staff); shuttle or commuter service (for staff): ～船 commuter ship for staff /～票 commuter's ticket /跑～ (of train, etc.) be in regular commuter service for staff; commute from and to work

通勤车 tōngqínchē commuter train (for staff)

通情 tōngqíng ❶ understanding; reasonable; sensible: 妈妈是～的,只要你把事情讲清,她就会原谅你。Mother is reasonable and will forgive you when you explain it clearly. ❷ understand the affection and love between the sexes: 尚未～ not yet understand love and affection between men and women; be innocent about love

通情达理 tōngqíng-dálǐ showing good sense; sensible; reasonable: ～之人 man of sense; reasonable man /～地商量解决办法 find a sensible solution to the problem /～,善解人意 be sensible and considerate (*or* understanding)

通衢 tōngqú thoroughfare; highway: ～大道 thoroughfare; highway

通权达变 tōngquán-dábiàn be flexible and untrammelled by conventions; adapt oneself to circumstances; act as the occasion requires: 在～上,谁也比不上他。There is no match for him in adapting to circumstances. *or* His ready adaptability to circumstances is unmatched.

通人 tōngrén 〈书面〉person of wide experience and sound scholarship; learned and flexible person; rounded scholar; Renaissance man: ～达才 versatile scholar of great erudition and understanding

通融 tōngrong ❶ stretch rules or get around regulations to accommodate sb.; make an exception in sb.'s favour: 这是原则问题,我们无法～。This is a matter of principle on which we can make no exception. /罚款的事,向队长认个错,或许可以～。Go to the team-leader and admit your mistake; maybe he will stretch the rules over the fine. ❷ accommodate sb. with a short-term loan: 您能不能～五百块钱? Could you lend me five hundred *yuan* as a favour?

通儒 tōngrú 〈旧语〉profound Confucian scholar; erudite person on the classics

通商 tōngshāng (of nations) have trade relations: ～条约 trade treaty; treaty of commerce /～口岸 trading port; open port; 〈旧语〉treaty port (under unequal treaties during late Qing Dynasty) /五口～ open five ports to trade with foreign powers

通商产业省 Tōngshāng Chǎnyèshěng (Japan) Ministry of International Trade and Industry (MITI)

通身 tōngshēn whole body; all over: ～上下 all over the body /～是伤 be covered with wounds

通史 tōngshǐ comprehensive history; general history: 中国～ general history of China

通市 tōngshì 〈旧语〉(of nations) have trade relations; be open to foreign trade: 边境～ open the border for trade /边民～已久。Border people of the two countries have carried on trade with each other for a long time.

通式 tōngshì 〈化学〉general formula

通事 tōngshì 〈旧语〉translator; interpreter

通书 tōngshū ❶ almanac ❷〈旧语〉notice from the bridegroom's family to the bride's about the date of wedding

通顺 tōngshùn clear and coherent; smooth: 语言～ coherent language /这段话欠～。This paragraph does not read quite smoothly.

通司 tōngsī 〈方言〉❶ translator; interpreter ❷ guide

通俗 tōngsú popular; common; easy; simple: ～文学 popular liter-

T

ature /～文化 popular culture /～小报 tabloid /～上口 easy to read (*or* sing) /～易懂 easy to understand; easily understood /文字～ simple in language /～地说明了环境保护的重要性 explain the importance of environmental protection in simple terms

通俗读物 tōngsú dúwù books for general readership; popular literature

通俗歌曲 tōngsú gēqǔ popular songs; pop songs

通俗歌星 tōngsú gēxīng pop star

通俗化 tōngsúhuà popularize

通泰 tōngtài *also* "通太" ❶〈方言〉clear; lucid ❷ comfortable and refreshed:一身～ feel comfortable and refreshed

通体 tōngtǐ ❶ entire; whole:～透明的宝石 completely transparent gem ❷ all over the body:～湿透 be wet through and through

通天 tōngtiān ❶ exceedingly high or great:罪恶～ towering crime /你有～之能也解决不了这个问题。You would not be able to solve the problem even if you had superhuman skills. ❷ have direct access to the highest authorities:～人物 person with direct access to the highest authorities

通条 tōngtiao ❶ poker (for a stove) ❷ cleaning rod (for a gun)

通通 tōngtōng *also* "通统" all; entirely; wholly; completely:～售出 all (*or* completely) sold out /财物～丢失 lose all one's belongings /～带回家里 bring the whole lot home; bring them all home /院子内外～收拾干净了。The courtyard has been tidied up both within and without. /他立下遗嘱,把财产～给了他的女儿。He made his will to leave everything to his daughter.

通同 tōngtóng collude; gang up:～一气 act in collusion with each other; work hand in glove; be in league /～舞弊 act fraudulently in collusion with sb.; gang up to cheat

通统 tōngtǒng *see* "通通"

通透 tōngtòu penetrating; thorough:道理讲得～。The reason was clearly explained. *or* The argument was explained thoroughly.

通途 tōngtú〈书面〉thoroughfare; major road; main street:变天堑为～ turn a natural barrier into a thoroughfare

通侻 tōngtuō *see* "通脱"

通脱 tōngtuō *also* "通侻"〈书面〉flexible and unconventional; not punctilious:～豪爽 unconventional and straightforward /～不羁 flexible and unrestrained /～之才 man of unconventional talent

通脱木 tōngtuōmù〈植物〉rice-paper plant (*Tetrapanax papyriferus*)

通问 tōngwèn〈书面〉communicate by letter; correspond (with each other):书信～ communicate by letter /久未～ have not corresponded with each other for quite some time

通显 tōngxiǎn〈书面〉hold high positions; be illustrious and influential:七世～ have held high positions for seven generations

通项 tōngxiàng〈数学〉general term

通宵 tōngxiāo all night; whole night; throughout the night:～失眠 suffer from insomnia all night; spend a sleepless night /～服务 offer all-night service; be open the whole night /玩个～ make a night of it (playing cards, etc.) /赶稿子熬了个～ stay up the whole night writing an article

通宵达旦 tōngxiāo-dádàn all night long; throughout the night:～地工作 work all night long (*or* throughout the night)

通晓 tōngxiǎo thoroughly understand; be well versed in; be proficient in:～音律 be proficient in musicology /～世故 know the ways of the world; be worldly-wise /～三国文字 have a good command of three languages /～大义 understand the higher principles of justice; know right from wrong

通心粉 tōngxīnfěn macaroni

通信 tōngxìn ❶ communicate by letter; correspond:～录 address book /两人～多年。They have kept up correspondence for years. ❷ telecommunications:数字～ digital communication /～工程 communication engineering; communication project

通信保密 tōngxìn bǎomì〈军事〉communication or traffic security

通信兵 tōngxìnbīng〈军事〉signal corps or unit; signalman

通信部队 tōngxìn bùduì signal unit

通信处 tōngxìnchù mailing address

通信鸽 tōngxìngē homing pigeon; carrier pigeon

通信连 tōngxìnlián signal company

通信联络 tōngxìn liánluò〈军事〉signal communication; communications and liaison

通信犬 tōngxìnquǎn messenger dog

通信枢纽 tōngxìn shūniǔ signal or communication centre

通信卫星 tōngxìn wèixīng communication satellite; radio relay satellite; radio satellite:～公司 (US) COMSAT (Communication Satellite Corporation) /通信技术卫星 CTS; communications technology satellite

通信员 tōngxìnyuán messenger; orderly

通信中继线 tōngxìn zhōngjìxiàn communication relay station

通行 tōngxíng ❶ pass through; go through:无害～〈法律〉innocuous passage /自由～ pass freely; have free passage /前方施工,停止～。Road works ahead. Closed to traffic. /巷子太窄,卡车不～。The lane is too narrow for trucks. /此巷(或此路)不～。No thoroughfare. *or* Dead end. ❷ current; common; general:～的办法 current practice; general (*or* common) practice /全国～教材 nationally used textbooks /全省～的规定 regulation applicable throughout the province

通行费 tōngxíngfèi toll

通行能力 tōngxíng nénglì traffic capacity

通行权 tōngxíngquán right of way:无害～ right of innocuous passage

通行税 tōngxíngshuì transit duty; toll

通行无阻 tōngxíng wúzǔ open and unobstructed; open to traffic; accessible to public:这条公路经过抢修,现已～。After rush repairs the road is now reopened to traffic. /也不知道有什么神通,他干什么事情都能～。He succeeded in everything he did, as if by some magic power.

通行证 tōngxíngzhèng pass; permit; safe-conduct; laissez-passer:军事～ military pass /边境～ border pass /临时～ provisional pass (*or* permit) /特别～ special pass (*or* permit)

通性 tōngxìng general character; generality:高级动物的～ characteristic common to all higher animals

通宿 tōngxiǔ all night; whole night; throughout the night:聊了一个～ chat all night; spend the whole night chatting /～值班 be on duty the whole night

通学生 tōngxuéshēng〈旧语〉day student; nonresident student

通讯 tōngxùn ❶ communication:～理论 communication theory /～设备 communication apparatus (*or* equipment) /～码 communication code /～线路 communication line /无线电～ radio (*or* wireless) communication /微波～ microwave communication /红外线～ infrared ray communication /激光～ laser communication /地外信息～ communication with extraterrestrial intelligence ❷ correspondence; reportage; news report or dispatch:农村～ dispatch from rural areas /人物～ feature article about outstanding figures /旅游～ tourism report /新华社海外～ Xinhua overseas correspondence /很有魅力的～ absorbing piece of reportage

通讯录 tōngxùnlù address book

通讯赛 tōngxùnsài〈体育〉correspondence match

通讯社 tōngxùnshè news agency; news or press service:新华～ Xinhua News Agency

通讯网 tōngxùnwǎng communication network:建立～ establish (*or* set up) a communication network

通讯员 tōngxùnyuán reporter; (press) correspondent:特约～ special reporter /业余～ amateur correspondent; sparetime reporter /战地～ war correspondent

通夜 tōngyè all night; whole night; throughout the night:办公室灯光～未灭。The light in the office was on throughout the night.

通译 tōngyì〈旧语〉❶ translate; interpret ❷ translator; interpreter

通用 tōngyòng ❶ in common use; common; current; general:～软件 common software /～程序 general program; generalized program /～机械 general machinery; general machine /～机床 universal machine tool /～指令〈计算机〉universal command /～机器人 all-purpose robot; universal robot /～资产负债表 all-purpose balance sheet /～分类账 regular ledger /全国～教材 national textbook ❷ interchangeable:这两个字可以～。These two words are interchangeable.

通用电气公司 Tōngyòng Diànqì Gōngsī (US) General Electric Company (GE)

通用化 tōngyònghuà universalization; standardization

通用货币 tōngyòng huòbì current money

通用机械厂 tōngyòng jīxièchǎng general or universal machine works

通用件 tōngyòngjiàn universal part; standardized part

通用汽车公司 Tōngyòng Qìchē Gōngsī (US) General Motors Corporation (GM)

T

通用移动电信业务 tōngyòng yídòng diànxìn yèwù universal mobile telecoms service (UMTS)
通用语言 tōngyòng yǔyán language in common use; commonly used language; common language; lingua franca: 通用商业程式语言 common business-oriented language (COBOL) /在这个部族杂居的非洲国家,法语是他们的～。French is the common language (*or* lingua franca) of this African country inhabited by numerous tribes.
通用月票 tōngyòng yuèpiào monthly ticket for all urban and suburban lines
通邮 tōngyóu accessible by postal communication: 两岸间直接～ direct postal service between the two sides of the Taiwan Strait /这个山村到 1980 年才～。The mountain hamlet was not accessible by postal communication until 1980.
通则 tōngzé general rule: 民法～ general rules of civil law
通知 tōngzhī ❶ notify; inform; advise: ～有关各方 inform all the parties concerned /除非另行～ unless otherwise advised /～他们赶快派车。Tell them to send a car at once. ❷ notice; circular; message: 书面～ written message (*or* notice) /发～ send out (*or* dispatch) a notice /我接到了开会的～。I have received notice of the meeting.
通知存款 tōngzhī cúnkuǎn 〈金融〉 deposit at call; deposit at notice
通知贷款 tōngzhī dàikuǎn 〈金融〉 call loan: ～利率 call rate
通知书 tōngzhīshū ❶ notice: 终止条约～ notice of termination of a treaty; notice of denunciation ❷〈商业〉 letter of advice; advice note
通直 tōngzhí straight: 树干～。The tree trunk is straight.
通志 Tōngzhì *General History*, from legendary times to the Sui Dynasty, best known for its 20 chapters on institutions, compiled by Zheng Qiao (郑樵, 1103-1162), a historian of the Southern Song Dynasty

嗵

tōng 〈象声〉 thump; thud: ～～的脚步声 thudding footfalls; heavy footsteps /他的心～～直跳。His heart was thumping.

tóng

童 (❸僮)

tóng ❶ child: 孩～ child /神～ child prodigy /牧～ cowherd; shepherd boy /报～ newspaper boy /学～ schoolboy /～言无忌 children say what they think (without fear); children and fools speak the truth; take no offence at a child's babble ❷ virgin: ～身 (usu. of a man) virgin /～男子 virgin man ❸〈旧语〉 page-boy: 书～儿 boy servant waiting on a scholar (*or* serving in the study) /家～ page-boy ❹ bare; bald; barren: ～枯 dried up and barren; bleak and desolate ❺ (Tóng) a surname
童騃 tóng'ái 〈书面〉 young and naive
童便 tóngbiàn 〈中药〉 urine of boys under twelve
童工 tónggōng child labourer; child labour: 非法雇用～ illegally hire child labour
童话 tónghuà children's story; nursery story; fairy tales: ～故事 fairy tale /～世界 world in children's stories; wonderland
童婚 tónghūn child marriage
童伶 tónglíng 〈戏曲〉 child actor or actress
童蒙 tóngméng 〈书面〉 childish ignorance: ～时代 innocent childhood /～识字课本 primer for children; reader for children
童男 tóngnán ❶ virgin boy ❷ under-age boy
童年 tóngnián childhood: 天真的～时代 innocent childhood /～的伙伴 friend from childhood; childhood playmate /～生活 life as a child; childhood life
童牛角马 tóngniú-jiǎomǎ hornless oxen and horned horses; fictious things; groundless hearsay: 你说的全是～之事。What you've said is just a cock-and-bull story.
童女 tóngnǚ ❶ virgin girl ❷ under-age girl
童仆 tóngpú 〈书面〉 houseboy and manservant; servants: ～成群 with numerous servants
童趣 tóngqù child's interest; childish delight; innocent playfulness (as of a child): 饶有～ full of childish playfulness; interesting in a childish way
童山 tóngshān bare hills: ～秃岭 bare hills and mountains
童山濯濯 tóngshān-zhuózhuó bare and barren hills; hills denuded of vegetation
童参 tóngshēn 〈中药〉 radix pseudostellaria
童生 tóngshēng 〈旧语〉 (in the Ming and Qing dynasties) scholar who has not yet passed the examination at the county level; candidate for primary civil examination: 白发～ grey-haired untitled scholar
童声 tóngshēng child's voice: ～合唱 children's chorus /说话～气的 speak in a child's (*or* childlike) voice
童叟无欺 tóngsǒu-wúqī cheat neither the old nor the young; be honest with all customers: 货真价实,～ guarantee quality goods and reasonable prices for all customers
童心 tóngxīn heart like a child's; childlike innocence; childlike delight or playfulness: ～未泯 retain a childlike heart; retain traces of childlike innocence (*or* playfulness)
童星 tóngxīng child star
童颜 tóngyán (of old men) rosy complexion like a child's: 老人虽年过八旬,不改～。Though in his eighties, the old man still has a ruddy complexion.
童颜鹤发 tóngyán-hèfà *also* "鹤发童颜" have grey hair but a ruddy complexion; look youthful in old age
童养媳 tóngyǎngxí girl brought up in the family of her future husband; child daughter-in-law; child bride
童谣 tóngyáo children's folk rhyme or song; nursery rhyme
童音 tóngyīn child's voice
童贞 tóngzhēn (esp. of a woman) virginity; chastity
童真 tóngzhēn childlike naivety; innocence
童稚 tóngzhì ❶ child: 笑得像～一样 laugh like a child; laugh in a childlike manner ❷ naivety; innocence: 我们怎样抚慰孩子～天真的心呢? How can we soothe these innocent children?
童装 tóngzhuāng children's garment
童子 tóngzǐ boy; lad
童子鸡 tóngzǐjī 〈方言〉 young chicken; broiler; cockerel
童子军 tóngzǐjūn boy scout: 女～ girl guide; girl scout
童子痨 tóngzǐláo 〈中医〉 children's tuberculosis

潼

tóng
潼关 Tóngguān Tongguan, county in Shaanxi Province and a strategic pass on the Yellow River

橦

tóng 〈古语〉 silk cotton tree; kapok tree

曈

tóng
曈昽 tónglóng 〈书面〉 light at daybreak
曈曈 tóngtóng 〈书面〉 ❶ brilliance of the rising sun: 初日～ bright rising sun ❷ (of eyes) glisten; glimmer; flash: 双目～ flashing eyes

瞳

tóng pupil (of the eye)
瞳孔 tóngkǒng 〈生理〉 pupil: ～放大 have one's pupils dilated; mydriasis /～扩大剂 mydriatics /～缩小 myosis /～收缩剂 myotics /～麻痹 pupilatonia; pupilloplegia /～间距离 interocular distance /～括约肌 sphincter pupillae
瞳人 tóngrén *also* "瞳仁" pupil (of the eye): 蓝灰色的～ greyish-blue pupils /一双～,明如秋水。Her limpid eyes are as clear as autumn waters.
瞳子 tóngzǐ pupil (of the eye)

朣

tóng
朣朦 tóngméng 〈书面〉 dim; poorly illuminated

同

tóng ❶ same; identical; alike; similar: 相～ same; identical /异～ similarities and differences /等～ equate; put on the same par /混～ confuse; mix up /大～小异 alike except for minor differences; very much the same /性格不～ of different dispositions /车～轨,书～文。Wheels for all carriages are of the same gauge and the same characters are used in all writings. ❷ be the same as; be similar to; be alike: ～上所言 as mentioned above /视～路人 regard as a total stranger /不～凡响 extraordinary; out of the common run ❸ share; do together; have in common: 一～前往 go (*or* set out) together /陪～ accompany /～进退 (of colleagues taking the same stand over an issue) advance or withdraw together; stay on or quit together ❹〈介词〉 with: ～父母在一起 with one's parents /～有关各方会谈 talk with all parties concerned /～自然灾害作斗争 fight against natural disasters /理论～实践相结合 combine theory and practice /～专家商量 consult the experts ❺〈介词〉 as...as; like; as: 她长得～母亲一样漂亮。She is as pretty as her mother. /今天的工作～

T

往常一样。Today's work is the same as before. ❻〈方言〉〈介词〉for:这张照片她一直~你保存着。She's kept the photo for you all this time. /我~你出这口气。Let me avenge your wrongs. ❼〈连词〉and; as well as:张先生~丁小姐都是上海人。Both Mr. Zhang and Miss Ding are from Shanghai. ❽ (Tóng) a surname

同案 tóng'àn ❶〈旧语〉(in the Ming and Qing dynasties) *xiucai* scholars who passed the county imperial examination in the same year ❷ be involved in the same law case:~的还有一个本地人。A native of this city is also involved in the case.

同案犯 tóng'ànfàn suspect or criminal involved in the same criminal case; companion in crime; accomplice

同班 tóngbān ❶ in or of the same class:中学时,他们同校不~。They studied at the same secondary school but were not in the same class. ❷ classmate:我俩大学是~。We two were classmates at college.

同伴 tóngbàn companion:~关系 companionship /童年时代的~ childhood companion; childhood playmate /志趣相投的~ congenial companion /书籍是他朝夕相处的~。Books keep him company day and night.

同胞 tóngbāo ❶ born of the same parents:一母~ born of the same mother /~兄妹 full brothers and sisters /~手足 born of the same parents ❷ fellow countryman; compatriot:海外~ overseas compatriots /台湾~ compatriots in Taiwan

同辈 tóngbèi of the same generation; peer:~群体 peer group /~中最为杰出 most outstanding in one's generation; stand head and shoulders above one's peers

同病 tóngbìng suffer from the same illness; experience the same hardships:~异治〈中医〉treat the same disease in different ways

同病相怜 tóngbìng-xiānglián those who have the same illness sympathize with each other; fellow sufferers commiserate with each other; be in the same boat:他俩遭遇同样坎坷,难免~。As fellow sufferers, the two of them sympathized with (*or* felt for) each other.

同步 tóngbù ❶〈物理〉synchronism:载波~ carrier synchronization /~操作 synchronous operation (*or* working) /~传动,~传播 synchronous transmission ❷ coordinate in time or progress; synchronize; keep simultaneous:~建设 synchronized construction /画面与声音不~。The image does not synchronize with the sound. /实现产值和利润的~增长 bring about simultaneous increases in output value and profits

同步电动机 tóngbù diàndòngjī synchronous motor

同步放映机 tóngbù fàngyìngjī synchronized film projector

同步光纤网 tóngbù guāngxiānwǎng 〈通信〉synchronous optical network (SONET)

同步轨道 tóngbù guǐdào geostationary orbit:地球~ earth-synchronous orbit; geostationary orbit /~卫星 geostationary equatorial orbit (GEO)

同步回旋加速器 tóngbù huíxuán jiāsùqì 〈物理〉synchrocyclotron

同步加速器 tóngbù jiāsùqì 〈物理〉synchrotron

同步卫星 tóngbù wèixīng *also* "地球同步卫星" dìqiú tóngbù wèixīng synchronous satellite; geostationary satellite:地球同步通讯卫星 geostationary telecommunications satellite

同侪 tóngchái 〈书面〉of the same generation; peer

同仇敌忾 tóngchóu-díkài share a bitter hatred of the enemy; be filled with a common hatred (for the enemy):万众一心,~ be all of one mind and filled with a common hatred for the enemy /全国人民~,共御外侮。Sharing a bitter hatred of the aggressors, the whole nation rose in united resistance.

同窗 tóngchuāng ❶ study in the same school or class:~之谊 friendship between fellow students /~好友 intimate classmate /~十年,情同手足 study in the same class for ten years like brothers ❷ schoolmate; classmate:~相聚 alumni gathering; class reunion

同床共枕 tóngchuáng-gòngzhěn share the same bed (and the same pillow); be bedfellows or sex partners:十年~的恩爱夫妻 couple who have been happily married for a decade

同床异梦 tóngchuáng-yìmèng same bed, different dreams — be strange bedfellows; be thrown together with each having a different purpose; hide different purposes behind the semblance of accord:他们~,各怀鬼胎。They were strange bedfellows, each harbouring his own sinister design.

同党 tóngdǎng ❶ belong to the same party or organization:他是不是和你~? Does he belong to your party? ❷ member of the same party or organization; confederate; accomplice:他的三个~ three members of his gang; his three accomplices

同道 tóngdào ❶ person of the same belief or conviction; people with the same ideal:我们是事业上的~。We work for the same cause. ❷ person of the same trade or occupation:他常与~切磋技艺。He often consults with other people in the trade to improve his skill. ❸ take the same route; travel together:两人~赴美。The two of them went to the United States together.

同等 tóngděng of the same class, rank, or status; on an equal basis or footing:~就业机会 equal employment opportunity /~地位 equal in status; on an equal footing /~效力 equally effective; equally valid; equally authentic /~学历 equivalent education /合同对签字各方具有~约束力。The contract is equally binding on all signatories.

同等学力 tóngděng xuélì have the same educational level (as regular graduate or student of certain academic qualifications):取得大学本科~ attain the same educational level as a regular college graduate

同调 tóngdiào person of the same taste; person holding the same view or ideal:引为~ regard (sb.) as sharing one's taste, opinion, or ideal

同恶相济 tóng'è-xiāngjì evildoers collude with each other; the wicked help the wicked:这伙人~,狼狈为奸。They ganged up in evil-doings, abetting and helping each other.

同犯 tóngfàn partner in a crime; confederate; accomplice

同房 tóngfáng ❶ share a room; be roommates:~住宿的几个年轻人 youngsters who share the same room ❷〈婉词〉(of husband and wife) sleep together; have sexual intercourse:久未~ (of a couple) have not had sex for quite some time ❸ of the same branch of an extended family:~兄弟 brothers of the same family branch

同分异构 tóngfēn-yìgòu 〈化学〉isomerization:~体 isomer; isomeride /~酶 isomerase /~现象 isomerism

同父异母 tóngfù-yìmǔ born of the same father but a different mother:~兄弟 half-brother /她们姐妹俩~。The two sisters were born of the same father but different mothers.

同甘共苦 tónggān-gòngkǔ share weal and woe; share comforts and hardships; go through thick and thin together:一对~的老夫妻 old couple who have been through thick and thin together /干部必须与群众~。Cadres must share the comforts and hardships of the masses.

同甘苦,共患难 tóng gānkǔ, gòng huànnàn go through thick and thin together; share weal and woe; share comforts and hardships:~的战友 comrades-in-arms sharing weal and woe; fellow fighters through thick and thin together

同感 tónggǎn same feeling or impression;〈心理〉consensus:颇有~ feel very much the same /~反应 consensual reaction

同根 tónggēn of the same root; born of the same parents:~词〈语言〉word of the same root; conjugate /异姓~ full brothers with different surnames; sworn brothers of different surnames /本是~生,相煎何太急? We sprang from the selfsame root; Why should you kill me with anger hot?

同庚 tónggēng of the same age:~好友 bosom friends of the same age

同工同酬 tónggōng-tóngchóu equal pay for equal work:男女应该~。Men and women ought to enjoy equal pay for equal work.

同工异曲 tónggōng-yìqǔ *also* "异曲同工" sing different tunes but with equal skill — take different approaches but achieve equally good results

同功酶 tónggōngméi *also* "同工酶"〈生化〉isoenzyme

同构 tónggòu 〈数学〉isomorphism:~群 isomorphic groups

同归殊途 tóngguī-shūtú *also* "殊途同归" reach the same goal by different routes; all roads lead to Rome

同归于尽 tóngguīyújìn perish together; end in common ruin:与敌人~ die together with the enemy /他死了,一切计划,一切希望,也~。He died, all his plans and expectations gone with him.

同行 tóngháng ❶ be of the same trade or occupation:原来你我~。So you and I are of the same trade. ❷ person of the same trade or occupation:~嫉妒 professional jealousy /~是冤家。People of the same occupation are enemies.

see also tóngxíng

同好 tónghào person of the same taste or inclination:将作品公诸~ show one's works to friends who share the same interest

同呼吸,共命运 tóng hūxī, gòng mìngyùn share a common lot:与人民群众~ identify oneself with the masses of the people

同化 tónghuà assimilate:民族~ national assimilation /~现象 as-

similatory phenomenon /邻近～〈语言〉proximate assimilation /～组织 assimilating tissue /～效应 assimilation effect /～率 assimilability

同化政策 tónghuà zhèngcè policy of national assimilation

同化作用 tónghuà zuòyòng 〈生物〉assimilation

同伙 tónghuǒ ❶ work in partnership; collude (in doing evil): ～打劫 loot in collusion; work together in a robbery ❷ partner; confederate; fellow gangster: 这个坏蛋手下有几个～。The rascal has several followers.

同极 tóngjí homopolar: ～磁铁 homopolar magnet /～发电机 homopolar generator

同居 tóngjū ❶ live together: 他曾跟儿子～过,两年后搬了出来。He lived with his son but moved out two years later. ❷ cohabit: 两人～五个月后分手了。The two of them parted after five months' cohabitation. /她刚认识这个人才两个星期就跟他～了,不是太草率了吗? Wasn't it rash of her to move in with a man she had known only two weeks?

同科 tóngkē 〈旧语〉candidates who passed the imperial civil examination at the same time

同空间 tóngkōngjiān isospace

同乐 tónglè share joy; fraternize: ～晚会 (as organized by people of different positions or occupations) evening party; get-together /军民～。The army fraternized with the people. *or* The soldiers and civilians had a happy get-together.

同类 tónglèi ❶ of the same kind; similar: ～事物 similar matters; things of a (*or* same) kind /～意识 consciousness of kind /把这些书分一下,～的放在一起。Sort out the books and group them by category. ❷ people or things of the same category: ～交配 homogamy /～相食 cannibalism /～相求。Like attracts like. /～不相残。Dog does not eat dog.

同类色 tónglèisè similar colours

同类项 tónglèixiàng 〈数学〉like terms; similar terms

同里 tónglǐ 〈书面〉person from the same village, town or province; fellow villager, townsman or provincial

同量素 tóngliàngsù *also* "同量异位数";"同量异序数" isobar: ～原子 isobaric atom

同僚 tóngliáo 〈旧语〉colleague; fellow official: 这位是我的～。This is my colleague.

同龄 tónglíng in the same age group; of the same age; contemporary: 他是我的～人。He is my contemporary. /我和新中国～。I was born in the year when the People's Republic of China was founded.

同流合污 tóngliú-héwū go along with evil trend; wallow in the mire with sb.; associate with a vile person: ～,越陷越深 wallow in the mire with evil elements and sink deeper and deeper /他一辈子从来没有与那些败类～。He never associated with such scum in his life.

同路 tónglù go or travel the same way: ～回家 go the same way (as sb.) to get home /～远行 go with sb. on a long journey

同路人 tónglùrén fellow traveller: 他曾是革命的～。He was once a fellow traveller in the revolution.

同伦 tónglún 〈数学〉homotopy

同门 tóngmén 〈旧语〉❶ learn from the same teacher or master: ～受业 be taught by the same teacher ❷ classmate: 那位教授是我父亲的～。That professor used to be my father's classmate.

同盟 tóngméng ❶ allied; joint ❷ alliance; league: 军事～ military alliance /民主～ (one of the parties allied with the Chinese Communist Party) Democratic League /几个国家结成松散的～。A few countries formed (*or* entered into) a loose alliance. /他们订下了攻守～。They made a pact to shield each other. *or* They pledged not to betray each other.

同盟罢工 tóngméng bàgōng joint strike

同盟国 tóngméngguó ❶ ally; allied nations ❷ (in World War I) the Central Powers ❸ (in World War II) the Allies

同盟会 Tóngménghuì (short for 中国革命同盟会) *Tongmenghui* — Chinese Revolutionary League (established by Dr. Sun Yat-sen in 1905)

同盟军 tóngméngjūn allied forces; allies

同盟条约 tóngméng tiáoyuē treaty or pact of alliance

同名 tóngmíng of the same name or title: ～同姓 namesake /根据～小说改编 be adapted from a novel of the same title

同谋 tóngmóu ❶ conspire (with sb.); scheme or plot together: 这起抢劫事件是窃贼和佣人～干的。The thieves conspired with the servant in the robbery. ❷ confederate; accomplice: 他是这起刑事案件的主要～。He was the ringleader in the criminal case.

同谋犯 tóngmóufàn co-conspirator; accessary; accomplice

同母异父 tóngmǔ-yìfù born of the same mother but a different father: ～姐妹 half-sister

同年 tóngnián ❶ same year: 他们～毕业。They graduated in the same year. /铁路大桥～十月竣工。The construction of the railway bridge was completed in October of the same year. ❷ 〈方言〉of the same age: 两家的孩子正好～。The children of the two families happened to be of the same age. ❸ 〈旧语〉candidates who passed the imperial examination in the same year

同袍 tóngpáo ❶ 〈旧语〉fellow soldier in the same army; comrade-in-arms ❷ 〈书面〉bosom friend

同期 tóngqī ❶ corresponding period: 产量超过去年～水平。The output surpassed that of the corresponding period of the last year. ❷ same year or class (in school, etc.): ～毕业生 graduates of the same class /他们同校～。They entered the same school in the same year. ❸ synchronism: ～性 synchronism /～录音〈影视〉synchronization /～管理 synchronized management /～复孕〈生理〉superfecundation

同衾共枕 tóngqīn-gòngzhěn share the same quilt and pillow; sleep together; have sexual intercourse

同情 tóngqíng sympathize with; show sympathy for: ～者 sympathizer /～落泪 shed tears of compassion /～穷人 show sympathy for the poor /博得他人的～ win other's sympathy /对他的处境,我深表～。I deeply sympathize with him in his plight.

同情罢工 tóngqíng bàgōng sympathetic or sympathy strike

同情心 tóngqíngxīn sympathy; compassion; fellow feeling

同人 tóngrén *also* "同仁" colleague: 当年,常有二三～到他家聚会。At that time, a couple of his colleagues would often come to his house for a party.

同仁 tóngrén *see* "同人"

同日而语 tóngrì'éryǔ (usu. used in the negative) mention in the same breath; put on the same par: 两者不可～。The two cannot be mentioned in the same breath. *or* They are not on the same level.

同上 tóngshàng (often used in filling out a form) ditto; *idem*: ～第101页。*Idem*, p.101. *or* Ditto, p.101. /通讯地址～。The address is the same as the above. *or* (when filling in a form) Address: ditto.

同生死,共患难 tóng shēngsǐ, gòng huànnàn go through fire and water together: ～的一对恩爱夫妇 loving couple who share difficulties and hardships

同声 tóngshēng ❶ speak at the same time; speak simultaneously ❷ with the same voice; in unison: ～歌颂 sing the praises (of sb.) in unison; praise with the same voice /～一哭 (as over the death of a hero or tragedy of a virtuous character) shed tears of grief together; be moved to tears of compassion simultaneously

同声传译 tóngshēng chuányì simultaneous interpretation: 八种语言的～设备 facilities for simultaneous interpretation in eight languages

同声相应,同气相求 tóng shēng xiāng yìng, tóng qì xiāng qiú people of the same inclination or taste tend to group themselves together; like attracts like

同时 tóngshí ❶ at the same time; concurrently; meanwhile; in the meantime: ～并举 develop simultaneously; undertake at the same time /～输入、输出 simultaneous input and output /与此～,还提出了改善劳动条件的建议。In the meantime, suggestions were made to improve the working conditions. ❷ moreover; besides; in addition; furthermore: 任务重要,～也很艰巨。The task is arduous as well as important. /我们肯定了他的成绩,～又指出了一些不足之处。While acknowledging his achievements, we pointed out his deficiencies.

同事 tóngshì ❶ work in the same place; work together: 我们同过事。We once worked together. ❷ colleague; fellow worker: 找～帮忙 turn to one's colleagues for help

同室操戈 tóngshì-cāogē family members drawing swords on each other — internal or fratricidal strife; internecine feud: ～,易招外患。Internal strife tends to invite foreign invasion.

同素异形 tóngsù-yìxíng allotropism; allotropy: ～体 allotropic substance; allotrope /～变化 allotropic change

同岁 tóngsuì ❶ of the same age: 咱俩～。You and I are of the same age. ❷ 〈旧语〉successful candidates in the same imperial examination

同榻 tóngtà sleep in the same bed; share a bed: 老友重逢,～长谈。United after a long separation, the two old friends shared a bed

chatting far into the night.
同位 tóngwèi 〈语言〉apposition：～名词 appositive noun
同位角 tóngwèijiǎo 〈数学〉corresponding angle
同位数 tóngwèishù 〈数学〉isotopic mumber
同位素 tóngwèisù 〈化学〉isotope：放射性～ radioisotope /～分离 isotope separation /～扫描器 radioisotope scanner /～探伤仪 isoscope /～污染 isotope contamination /～治疗 isotope therapy /～内照射治疗 internal isotope therapy /～地质年龄测定 isotopic (geological) age determination /～生产堆 isotope production reactor /～化学 isotope chemistry
同位素量 tóngwèisùliàng isotopic mass
同位素学 tóngwèisùxué isotopy
同位通信卫星 tóngwèi tōngxìn wèixīng geosynchronous communication satellite
同位语 tóngwèiyǔ 〈语言〉appositive：～从句 appositive clause
同位元素 tóngwèi yuánsù isotopic element
同温层 tóngwēncéng *also* "平流层" píngliúcéng 〈气象〉stratosphere：～电视 stratovision /～加油机〈航空〉stratotanker
同屋 tóngwū share a room; be a roommate：上大学时，他跟我～。I was his roommate at college.
同喜 tóngxǐ 〈套语〉thank you for your congratulations
同系 tóngxì 〈化学〉homology：～对 homologous pair
同系聚合物 tóngxì jùhéwù polymer homologue
同系物 tóngxìwù homologue
同乡 tóngxiāng person from the same village, town or province; fellow villager, townsman or provincial：听口音，你和熊先生是～吧？By your accent, you must be from the same town as Mr. Xiong.
同乡会 tóngxiānghuì association of fellow provincials or townsmen
同相 tóngxiàng 〈物理〉homophase; inphase：～电流 inphase current /～信号 inphase signal
同心 tóngxīn ❶ with one heart; of like mind and spirit：～结 true "lovers' knot" (tied together by lovers) /～锁 "lovers' lock" (locked on to sth. to show the bond of love of a couple) /二人～，其利断金。When united, two people can be a formidable force. *or* Unity is strong enough to cut metals. ❷ concentric; homocentric：～断层〈地质〉concentric faults /～阀 concentric valve /～食〈天文〉concentric eclipse /～透镜 concentric lens /～线圈 concentrically wound coil /～环形山构造〈天文〉concentric ring structure /～式汽化器 concentrically built carburetter
同心度 tóngxīndù 〈机械〉concentricity
同心戮力 tóngxīn-lùlì *also* "同心协力" unite in a concerted effort; make a concerted effort：～，共赴国难 be united in a concerted effort to counter the national calamity /全国上下，～。The whole nation is united in the common cause.
同心同德 tóngxīn-tóngdé be of one heart and one mind; be dedicated heart and soul to the same cause：～的战友 dedicated comrades-in-arms /全国人民～为实现四个现代化而奋斗。United as one, the people of the whole country are striving for the success of the modernization drive.
同心协力 tóngxīn-xiélì *also* "同心合力" work in full cooperation and with unity of purpose; work together with one heart; make concerted efforts：我们必须～迎战强敌。We must make concerted efforts to fight against the formidable enemy.
同心圆 tóngxīnyuán 〈数学〉concentric circles
同行 tóngxíng travel together：～的伙伴 travel companion; fellow traveller /有三名记者与省长～。Three reporters accompanied the provincial governor on the trip.
see also tóngháng
同型 tóngxíng 〈生物〉homomorphous：～分裂 homotypic division /～抗原 isotypes /～染色体 homomorphic chromosome /～生殖 homogenesis /～性瘤〈医学〉homologous tumor
同性 tóngxìng ❶ of the same sex：～子女 children of the same sex ❷ of the same nature or character; like：～电 like electricity /～极 like pole /异性相吸，～相斥。Two unlike electric charges attract each other, while two like ones repel each other.
同性恋 tóngxìngliàn *also* "同性恋爱" homosexuality：～者 homosexual /女～者 lesbian /男～者 gay /～运动 (in Western countries) gay movement
同姓 tóngxìng of the same surname：这个村里的人大多～。Most of the villagers have the same surname.
同学 tóngxué ❶ be in the same school：他们～三年。They studied in the same school for three years. ❷ fellow student; schoolmate：同班～ classmate /新～ new schoolmate; freshman (*or* freshwoman) /老～ former schoolmate (*or* classmate) /他是我的大学～。He used to be my schoolmate at college. ❸ form of address used in speaking to a student：请问这位～，到学生宿舍怎么走？Excuse me, could you tell me where the student dormitory is?
同学录 tóngxuélù schoolmates' address book
同砚 tóngyàn 〈旧语〉schoolmate; classmate
同样 tóngyàng same; equal; alike; similar：～高明 equally wise (*or* clever) /～尺寸的衬衣 shirts of the same size /～形状的建筑 buildings alike in shape /我们的看法是～的。We share the same views. /赞成的意见要听，～，反对的意见也要听。We must listen to dissenting views as well as those in our favour. /理工科的学生～需要学一点文史知识。Science students also need learn something about literature and history (*or* humanities).
同业 tóngyè ❶ same trade or business：～价 trader's price /～交易 trader's transaction /～折扣 trader's discount /～共济。People of a trade help one another. ❷ person of the same trade or business：诸位～！Fellow businessmen!
同业工会 tóngyè gōnghuì trade council; trade association; guild
同一 tóngyī ❶ same; identical：～命运 same fate /～观点 identical view ❷ identity; unity
同一律 tóngyīlǜ 〈逻辑〉law of identity
同一性 tóngyīxìng 〈哲学〉identity
同义 tóngyì 〈语言〉synonymy：～性 synonymy /～复合词 synonym-compound
同义词 tóngyìcí synonym
同意 tóngyì agree; concur; consent; approve：～书 letter of consent /～任命〈外交〉agrément /表示～ express one's agreement /一致～ agree unanimously; achieve (*or* reach) unanimity (on sth.) /一致～的文本 agreed text /我们～他的意见。We agreed with him (*or* to his opinion). /双方～这项裁决。The two sides concurred on the ruling. /经理～了他们的要求。The manager consented to their request. /代表们最后还是～了这项建议。The delegates adopted the proposal at last. /经过领导～后，上月开始生产。With the approval of the leadership production started last month.
同音词 tóngyīncí 〈语言〉homophone; homonym
同寅 tóngyín ❶〈旧语〉fellow official; colleague in office ❷〈方言〉of the same age：～兄弟 brothers of the same age (referring to one's bosom friends)
同余 tóngyú 〈数学〉congruence：～数 congruent numbers
同源 tóngyuán homology; isogeny：～蛋白质 homologous protein /～移植 homologous graft /～发生 isogenesis; homogeny /～器官 homologous organ /～染色体 homologous chromosome /～火山 homologous volcano /～嫁接 isogenetic graft /～疗法原则〈心理〉isopathic principle /～岩 congenetic rock /～词 cognate words /～多倍体 autopolyploid
同志 tóngzhì ❶ comrade：～关系 comradeship /革命尚未成功，～仍须努力。The revolution is yet to be accomplished and our comrades must continue to work hard. ❷ form of address on Chinese mainland：互称～ call each other comrade /～，请问几点钟了？Comrade, what time is it please?
同治 Tóngzhì Tongzhi, title of the reign (1862-1874) of Aisin Gioro Zaichun (爱新觉罗·载淳, 1856-1874), 8th emperor of the Qing Dynasty with his mother the Empress Dowager Cixi (慈禧) actually in control, called reverently Qing Muzong (清穆宗) posthumously
同治中兴 Tóngzhì Zhōngxīng Tongzhi Restoration, a period when the peasant uprisings (such as the Taiping Revolution) were suppressed, the Self-Strengthening Movement was launched by influential officials among the Qing ruling circles, and relative stability ensued for the dynasty
同种 tóngzhǒng of the same race：同文～ be of the same race and use the same script (*or* written language)
同舟共济 tóngzhōu-gòngjì cross a river in the same boat — pull together in times of trouble; people in the same boat should help each other：～，以渡时艰 pull together in times of trouble to tide over the difficult period /在当前情况下，你我除了～，别无出路。Under the circumstances, we have no option but to continue our efforts and help each other out.
同轴 tóngzhóu coaxial：～圈 coaxial circles /～线 coaxial line /～波导 coaxial waveguide /～传输 coaxial transmission /～电路 coaxial circuit /～共振器 coaxial resonator /～扬声器 coaxial speaker

同轴电缆 tóngzhóu diànlǎn coaxial cable
同宗 tóngzōng of the same clan or lineage; having common ancestry:～兄弟 cousins of the same clan /同姓不一定～。Those who have the same surname do not necessarily belong to the same clan.
同宗配合 tóngzōng pèihé 〈植物〉homothallism
同族 tóngzú ❶ of the same clan; having common ancestry:～人 fellow clansman ❷ of the same race
同族元素 tóngzú yuánsù 〈化学〉homotope

茼 tóng

茼蒿 tónghāo 〈植物〉crowndaisy (*Chrysanthemum coronarium*)

桐 tóng 〈植物〉❶ paulownia ❷ tung tree ❸ phoenix tree

桐酸 tóngsuān 〈化学〉eleostearic acid
桐油 tóngyóu tung oil
桐油树 tóngyóushù (popular term for 油桐) tung tree
桐子 tóngzǐ seed of the tung tree

酮 tóng 〈化学〉ketone:～胺 ketoamine /～醇 keto-alcohol; acyloin /～酸 ketonic acid

酮醇酶 tóngchúnméi 〈生化〉ketolase
酮尿 tóngniào 〈医学〉ketonuria
酮醛 tóngquán 〈化学〉keto-aldehyde
酮酸 tóngsuān 〈化学〉keto acid; ketonic acid:～裂解酶〈生化〉ketoacid-lyase /～中毒〈医学〉ketoacidosis
酮糖 tóngtáng 〈生化〉ketose:～尿 ketosuria
酮体 tóngtǐ 〈生化〉ketone body; acetone body

峒 tóng *see* "崆峒" Kōngtóng
see also dòng

铜 tóng copper (Cu):紫～ red copper /黄～ brass /青～ bronze /白～ copper-nickel alloy /自然～ native copper /硫酸～ cupric sulphate /～锭 copper ingot /～号 brass trumpet /～溶金属 copper-soluble metal

铜氨 tóng'ān *also* "铜铵" cuprammonium
铜氨人造丝 tóng'ān rénzàosī cuprammonium rayon; copper rayon
铜氨纤维素 tóng'ān xiānwéisù cuprammonium cellulose
铜氨液 tóng'ānyè cuprammonium solution
铜板 tóngbǎn ❶〈方言〉copper coin; copper:从口袋里抓出一把～来 produce a handful of copper coins from the pocket ❷ copper clappers (a kind of percussion instrument)
铜版 tóngbǎn 〈印刷〉copperplate
铜版画 tóngbǎnhuà 〈美术〉copperplate etching or engraving; copperplate
铜版印刷 tóngbǎn yìnshuā copperplate printing
铜版印刷机 tóngbǎn yìnshuājī copperplate press; etching press
铜版纸 tóngbǎnzhǐ art printing paper
铜币 tóngbì copper coin
铜钹 tóngbó *also* "铜拔" brass cymbals
铜锤 tóngchuí 〈戏曲〉"bronze-hammer" — painted-face, male character specializing in singing
铜电缆 tóngdiànlǎn 〈电工〉copper cable
铜钢 tónggāng 〈冶金〉copper steel
铜鼓 tónggǔ bronze drum
铜管乐 tóngguǎnyuè music by brasswind instrument
铜管乐队 tóngguǎn yuèduì brass band
铜管乐器 tóngguǎn yuèqì brasswind instrument; brasswind
铜硅合金 tóngguī héjīn 〈冶金〉cuprosilicon
铜焊 tónghàn copper brazing:～缝 brazed seam /～料 brazing solder /～条 copper-welding rod
铜合金 tónghéjīn 〈冶金〉copper alloy
铜壶滴漏 tónghú dīlòu (a kind of ancient Chinese water clock) copper clepsydra
铜活 tónghuó ❶ brass or copper fittings, accessories, etc.:修理～ repair copper fittings ❷ work in copper; coppersmithing:他干得一手好～。He is an excellent coppersmith.
铜匠 tóngjiang coppersmith
铜筋铁骨 tóngjīn-tiěgǔ with brass muscles and iron bones — having a body of iron; tough and strong:～,浑身是劲 having an iron body bursting with energy
铜镜 tóngjìng bronze mirror
铜扣子 tóngkòuzi brass button
铜矿 tóngkuàng ❶ copper ore:～石 copper ore ❷ copper mine
铜蓝 tónglán 〈矿业〉covellite; indigo copper
铜绿 tónglǜ 〈化学〉verdigris
铜锰合金 tóngměng héjīn 〈冶金〉cupromanganese
铜模 tóngmú *also* "字模" zìmú 〈印刷〉matrix; (copper) mould
铜模雕刻机 tóngmú diāokèjī matrix-cutting machine
铜镍合金 tóngniè héjīn 〈冶金〉cupronickel
铜牌 tóngpái 〈体育〉bronze medal:～得主 bronze medal winner; bronze medalist
铜器 tóngqì bronze; brass; copper ware
铜器时代 tóngqì shídài 〈考古〉Bronze Age
铜钱 tóngqián copper cash; copper coin
铜墙铁壁 tóngqiáng-tiěbì *also* "铁壁铜墙" bastion of iron; impregnable fortress; tower of strength:我军阵地有如～,敌人是攻不破的。Our troops' position is impregnable to enemy assault.
铜丝 tóngsī 〈冶金〉copper wire
铜钿 tóngtián 〈方言〉copper cash; money
铜头蛇 tóngtóushé *also* "铜头蝮蛇"〈动物〉copperhead
铜头铁额 tóngtóu-tiě'é bronze head and iron forehead — brave and intrepid; doughty; valiant
铜驼荆棘 tóngtuó-jīngjí bronze camel amid brambles — desolute scene under foreign rule
铜像 tóngxiàng bronze statue
铜臭 tóngxiù stink of money:满身～ stinking with money; filthy rich /沾上了～ be possessed by the desire for wealth
铜锈 tóngxiù *see* "铜绿"
铜元 tóngyuán *see* "铜圆"
铜圆 tóngyuán *also* "铜元" copper coin; copper
铜章墨绶 tóngzhāng-mòshòu 〈旧语〉bronze seal with a black silk ribbon attached to it — (position of) county magistrate
铜子儿 tóngzǐr 〈口语〉copper coin; copper

侗 tóng 〈书面〉childish; ignorant
see also Dòng

仝 tóng ❶ *see* "同" tóng ❷ (Tóng) a surname

砼 tóng concrete

佟 Tóng a surname

彤 tóng ❶〈书面〉red:红～～ bright red /～弓 red-painted bow ❷ (Tóng) a surname

彤闱 tóngwéi imperial palace
彤云 tóngyún 〈书面〉❶ red clouds:太阳刚刚落山,峰顶上还留着一抹～。The sun has just set, with a patch of red cloud lingering over the mountain-top. ❷ dark clouds (before a snow):严冬天气,～密布。The winter sky was darkly clouded.

tǒng

统[1] tǒng ❶ continuum or order of interrelated things; system; genealogy:系～ system; scheme /血～ blood relationship; genealogy /传～ tradition; heritage /正～ orthodoxy; legitimism /法～ legally constituted authority ❷ all; entirely; together:～归一人掌握 all under the control of one person; entirely at the disposal of one person /～算起来,有十个人要走。Altogether, ten people are leaving. ❸ lead; command; control:～兵打仗 lead soldiers into battle /～雄师百万 command a mighty army of a million men /～得过死 exercise rigid and excessive control ❹〈地质〉series:更新～ Pleistocene series

统[2] tǒng tube-shaped part of an article of clothing, etc.:皮～子 fur lining for a coat /长～靴 high boots

统舱 tǒngcāng (passenger accommodation on board a ship) steerage:～客票 steerage ticket /～旅客 steerage passenger /坐～ go (*or* travel) steerage
统称 tǒngchēng ❶ be called by a joint name; be grouped together

under a generic or common name：小号、圆号、长号等～为铜管乐器。Trumpets, French horns and trombones are often referred to as brasswind instruments. ❷ general designation or term：粮食是小麦、玉米等农作物的～。Grain is a general term for wheat, corn and other cereal crops.

统筹 tǒngchóu make overall plans; plan as a whole; coordinate in an overall manner：～全局 take the whole situation into account and plan accordingly /～规划 overall planning /～安排 comprehensive arrangement /～医疗 subsidized medical care under a coordinated plan; cooperative medical care /全书由他～，大家分头撰写。He will be in overall charge of the book and assign each of us a part of it to write.

统筹兼顾 tǒngchóu-jiāngù unified planning with due consideration for all concerned; making overall plans by taking all factors into consideration; overall planning and all-round consideration：项目涉及各方面的利益，需要～。Since various interests are involved in the project, overall plans must be made for it with due consideration for all concerned.

统带 tǒngdài ❶ command; lead：～重兵 command massive forces ❷ regimental commander (in the Qing Dynasty)

统共 tǒnggòng altogether; in all：这个处～只有十几个人。There are altogether a dozen people in this division.

统购统销 tǒnggòu tǒngxiāo *also*"统购包销" state monopoly for purchase and marketing (of grain, cotton, etc.); unified purchase and sale by the state

统管 tǒngguǎn unified management; centralized control：大学的行政和教学业务工作由校长～。The president has overall control over the administration and teaching at the university.

统货 tǒnghuò 〈商业〉gradeless and uniformly-priced commodities

统计 tǒngjì ❶ statistics：官方～ official statistics /人口～ census; vital statistics /综合国力～ statistics on overall national strength /据部分～ according to some statistics /～资料 statistical data /～抽样 statistical sampling /～方法 statistical method /～权重 statistical weight /～精度 statistical accuracy ❷ add up; count：～与会人数 count up the number of people present at the meeting /～选票 count the votes

统计地图 tǒngjì dìtú statistical map

统计概率 tǒngjì gàilǜ statistical probability

统计力学 tǒngjì lìxué statistical mechanics

统计数字 tǒngjì shùzì statistical figures; statistics

统计图表 tǒngjì túbiǎo statistical graph, chart, or table

统计推断 tǒngjì tuīduàn 〈数学〉statistical inference

统计物理学 tǒngjì wùlǐxué statistical physics

统计学 tǒngjìxué statistics：～家 statistician

统计员 tǒngjìyuán statistician

统建 tǒngjiàn build or construct in a systematic way; build or construct under overall planning：～工程 construction project under overall planning /集资～住宅区 raise funds to build residential quarters in a systematic way

统考 tǒngkǎo (short for 统一考试) uniform or unified examination：全国～ nationwide unified examinations /语文～ unified examination in Chinese

统括 tǒngkuò sum up; conclude：～全文大意 sum up or give the main ideas of the text

统揽 tǒnglǎn be in overall charge; exercise overall management; handle in an all-round manner：～施工任务 be in overall charge of the construction project /～全校总务 manage all the general services in the school

统领 tǒnglǐng ❶ command; lead：～各路人马 command a joint force ❷ commander; leader：大～ commander-in-chief

统配 tǒngpèi unified distribution (by the state)：～物资 materials earmarked for unified distribution by the state /～包销 state monopoly of distribution and marketing /～煤矿 coal mine whose output is under unified distribution by the state; coal mine under central planning

统铺 tǒngpù *also*"通铺" tōngpù wide bed for a number of people (as in barracks, hostels, etc.)

统摄 tǒngshè 〈书面〉have under one's command; control; govern; direct：～三军 command the armed forces /～全局 control the overall situation

统收统支 tǒngshōu tǒngzhī unified (state) control over income and expenditure; centralized control over earnings and spendings; unified collection of revenue (from state-owned enterprises) and coverage of (their) expenditure

统属 tǒngshǔ subordination：～关系 relations of subordination /不相～ not subordinate to one another

统帅 tǒngshuài ❶ commander-in-chief; commander：三军～ commander of the armed forces (*or* armed services) /最高～ supreme commander ❷ *see*"统率"

统帅部 tǒngshuàibù supreme command：～后备部队 general reserves

统率 tǒngshuài *also*"统帅" command; lead：～所部增援友军 lead one's troops to aid friendly forces /不久，将军就要～部队出征了。The general will soon lead his army into battle.

统通 tǒngtōng all; entirely; completely

统统 tǒngtǒng all; completely; entirely：除了值班人员，其余的人～下班了。Everybody has knocked off except the person on duty. /屋里屋外我～打扫了。I have given the house a through cleanup.

统系 tǒngxì system; scheme

统辖 tǒngxiá have under one's jurisdiction; exercise control over：该市～五个区十三个县。The municipality has five districts and thirteen counties under its jurisdiction. /这个部～的部门实在不少。The ministry has got quite a few departments under it.

统销 tǒngxiāo unified marketing

统一 tǒngyī unify; unite; integrate：～全国 unify the country /～行动 seek unity of action; coordinate actions; act in unison /～认识 reach common understanding; reach consensus /～步调 take concerted action /～口径 work out (*or* prepare) a unified (*or* uniform) statement (on a question or problem) /对立的～ unity of opposites /内容和形式的～ unity of content and form /理论与实践的～ integration of theory with practice /规定不～ lack of coherence in regulation; incoherent (*or* contradictory) regulations /～调配 unified (*or* centralized) allocation /～的意见 unanimity (*or* consensus) of opinion /～的多民族国家 unitary multinational state /～基金 (UK) consolidated fund /～命令语言 uniform command language /～输入处理 integrated data processing (IDP) /～发票 uniform invoice /～书号 standard book number

统一管理 tǒngyī guǎnlǐ uniform management

统一经营 tǒngyī jīngyíng unified or centralized management

统一商法法典 Tǒngyī Shāngfǎ Fǎdiǎn (US) Uniform Commercial Code

统一税 tǒngyīshuì flat tax; consolidated tax

统一体 tǒngyītǐ 〈哲学〉entity; unity

统一性 tǒngyīxìng 〈哲学〉unity

统一战线 tǒngyī zhànxiàn united front：结成最广泛的爱国～ form the broadest patriotic united front

统御 tǒngyù *also*"统驭"〈书面〉control; master

统战 tǒngzhàn (short for 统一战线) united front：～部 United Front Work Department /～政策 united front policy /～策略 united front tactics /～人士 personage included in the united front /进行～ try to win (sb.) over to one's united front; apply united front tactics (to sb.)

统治 tǒngzhì ❶ rule; control：高压～ high-handed rule /极权～ totalitarian rule (*or* control) /殖民～ colonial rule /～者 ruler ❷ dominate：旧中国，小农经济占～地位。In old China small-scale peasant economy farming dominated the national economy. /严寒～北国大地。Bitterly cold weather prevails all across north China.

统治董事 tǒngzhì dǒngshì governing director

统治阶级 tǒngzhìjiējí ruling class

统制 tǒngzhì control：经济～ economic control /外汇～ foreign exchange control /～经济 command economy /～货币市场 exercise control over the money market /～主义 dirigisme

筒（筩） tǒng

❶ section of thick bamboo：竹～ thick bamboo tube ❷ thick tube-shaped object：枪～ barrel of a gun /电～ (electric) torch; flashlight /话～ microphone; telephone transmitter; megaphone /气～ inflator; bicycle pump /笔～ brush pot /邮～ pillar-box; mailbox ❸ tube-shaped part of clothing or accessories：袜～儿 leg of a stocking /袖～儿 sleeve /长～靴 long (*or* high) boots

筒管 tǒngguǎn *also*"线轴" xiànzhóu 〈纺织〉bobbin：～丝 bobbin filament

筒裤 tǒngkù straight-legged trousers

筒裙 tǒngqún straight skirt

筒式干燥器 tǒngshì gānzàoqì 〈机械〉drum dryer; cylinder dry-

T

ing machine

筒瓦 tǒngwǎ arched tile; semicircular tile

筒形锅炉 tǒngxíng guōlú barrel boiler

筒状花 tǒngzhuànghuā *also* "管状花" guǎnzhuànghuā 〈植物〉tubular flower

筒子 tǒngzi tube or tube-shaped object：靴～ leg of a boot

筒子楼 tǒngzilóu storeyed building with a long corridor through the middle of each floor lined by dormitories on either side and without private kitchens or lavatories

桶

tǒng tub; pail; bucket; keg; barrel：水～ water pail / 塑料～ plastic bucket / 汽油～ petrol drum / 火药～ powder keg / 饭～ rice bucket; 〈比喻〉fat-head / 七～原油大约相当于一公吨。Seven barrels of crude are more or less equivalent to one metric ton.

桶匠 tǒngjiang cooper

捅(通)

tǒng ❶ poke; stab：～炉子 poke the fire (in a stove) / 把铁丝从门缝里～过去 poke the wire through the door crack / 他背上被人～了一刀。He was stabbed in the back. ❷ touch; nudge; push (with one's hand or elbow)：用胳膊肘～人 give sb. a nudge / 我悄悄地～了他一下。I nudged him on the quiet. / ～～他，别叫他睡着了。Give him a push or he will fall asleep. ❸ disclose; leak; give away; let out：他把内情～出去了。He disclosed (*or* leaked) the inside story. / 只要把秘密向外一～，就够他受的。He will get into real trouble if the secret is out.

捅咕 tǒnggu 〈口语〉❶ touch：电这玩艺儿，不懂可别瞎～。You'd better keep yourself away from electricity if you know nothing about it. / 你没事儿～那东西干什么？What are you tampering with that for? ❷ stir up; instigate; egg on：～别人 egg on others (in sth. undesirable) / 他就爱到处～个事儿。He likes to stir up trouble everywhere.

捅娄子 tǒng lóuzi *also* "捅漏子" 〈口语〉make a mess of sth.; make a blunder; get into trouble：不小心捅了娄子 make a careless blunder / 你又要给我～？You are getting me into trouble again, aren't you?

捅马蜂窝 tǒng mǎfēngwō stir up a hornet's nest; bring a hornet's nest about one's ears：谁让你招他，这不是～吗？You chose to provoke him. Weren't you stirring up a hornet's nest?

tòng

恸(慟)

tòng 〈书面〉❶ deep sorrow; grief; agony：悲～ grieved; sorrowful ❷ cry out loud; wail：～哭 wail; cry one's heart out / 不禁大～ cannot but wail loudly

同

tòng *see* "胡同" hútòng

see also tóng

衕

tòng *see* "衚衕" hútòng

痛

tòng ❶ ache; pain：牙～ (have a) toothache / 胃～ (have a) stomach-ache / 肚子～ (have a) bellyache; tummyache / ～得打滚 writhe with pain / 全身酸～ be sore all over / ～不可支 unbearably painful / 我的脚很～。My foot hurts badly. ❷ sadness; grief; sorrow：哀～ grief; sorrow / 悲～欲绝 be stricken with infinite sorrow; grieve deeply ❸ extremely; deeply; thoroughly; bitterly：～加斥责 denounce sharply; reproach deeply; haul over the coals

痛痹 tòngbì 〈中医〉arthritis

see also "寒痹" hánbì

痛不欲生 tòngbùyùshēng grieve to the extent of wishing to die; be overwhelmed with sorrow：他暮年丧爱子，～。He almost went mad with grief when he lost his darling son in his declining years.

痛陈 tòngchén make a strong statement; state in energetic terms：～民间疾苦 voice the hardships of the people with profound feelings

痛斥 tòngchì make a stinging attack; scathingly denounce：～卖国贼 denounce a traitor scathingly / ～谬论 thoroughly refute a fallacy

痛楚 tòngchǔ pain; anguish; distress; suffering：～难言 anguish too great for words (*or* too embarrassing to mention) / 倾诉内心的～ pour out one's innermost sufferings

痛处 tòngchù sore spot; tender spot：触及～ touch sb.'s sore spot; touch sb. on the raw / 被人击中～ be stung to the quick

痛打 tòngdǎ beat mercilessly or soundly：～一顿 give sb. a good (*or* sound) beating; tan sb.'s hide / ～落水狗 beat the cur mercilessly even when he's fallen into the water; be relentless with evil people even if they are down

痛悼 tòngdào mourn deeply; grieve over：～死难烈士 mourn deeply over the martyrs

痛定思痛 tòngdìng-sītòng recall a painful experience (as a reminder or warning); draw a lesson from a bitter experience; bring home a painful lesson：～，痛何如哉! Nothing could possibly exceed my anguish when I recall the painful experience!

痛愤 tòngfèn hate bitterly; intensely detest：切齿～ gnash one's teeth in hatred

痛风 tòngfēng 〈医学〉gout：～性关节炎 gouty arthritis / ～石 〈医学〉tophus; chalkstone

痛改前非 tònggǎi-qiánfēi earnestly repent and reform oneself; sincerely mend one's way; thoroughly rectify one's errors; make a clean break with one's (past) misdeeds：～，重新做人 sincerely mend one's ways and begin one's life anew (*or* turn over a new leaf)

痛感 tònggǎn ❶ keenly feel; be keenly aware (of sth.)：～经验不足 keenly feel one's lack of experience / 工作中的诸多失误，使他～不安。He was grievously upset by the errors in his work. ❷ sense of pain：失去～ lose the sense of pain / 这里有无～？Do you feel pain here? *or* Does it hurt here?

痛恨 tònghèn hate bitterly; utterly loathe：～不已 harbour endless hatred / ～在心 nurse a bitter hatred at heart / 万般～ detest in every possible way / 对腐败现象十分～ feel a deep (*or* abiding) hatred for corruption

痛悔 tònghuǐ regret deeply; bemoan; rue：～平生 regret the way one has spent one's life; rue one's wasted life / ～前非 deeply regret one's past errors; repent bitterly of one's past misdeeds / 他对自己的过失深感～。He felt extremely guilty (*or* was filled with remorse) for his mistake.

痛击 tòngjī strike relentless blows at; deal a heavy or hard blow to：迎头～ deal head-on blows; strike at sb. head-on / ～侵略者 strike a telling blow at the aggressors / 连连～对手 shower crushing blows on one's rival

痛歼 tòngjiān wipe out; destroy; annihilate：～入侵之敌 annihilate the invaders

痛经 tòngjīng 〈医学〉dysmenorrhoea

痛疚 tòngjiù be stung by remorse or compunction; have a guilty conscience：为犯错误而感到～ be stung by remorse (*or* compunction) about making a mistake / 内心～不安 have a guilty (*or* troubled) conscience

痛觉 tòngjué 〈生理〉sense of pain：～迟钝 〈医学〉hypalgesia; hypalgia / ～过敏 〈医学〉hyperalgia / ～计 algometer / 背部有～ feel a pain in the back / 割伤的地方，用手一按，就有明显的～。A mere touch on the cut feels extremely painful (*or* causes great pain). / 伤口仍有～。The wound still hurts.

痛哭 tòngkū cry or weep bitterly; wail：放声～ cry loudly and bitterly; wail in grief / 听到这不幸的消息，人人失声～。Everybody burst out crying upon hearing the sad news.

痛哭流涕 tòngkū-liútì weep or shed bitter tears; cry one's heart out：他～地检讨自己的罪过。He cried his heart out when he came clean about his crimes.

痛苦 tòngkǔ pain; agony; distress; suffering：万分～ be very distressing; suffer infinite agony / 这一段～的经历，他永生难忘。He will never forget the painful experience for the rest of his life.

痛快 tòngkuai ❶ happy; delighted; joyful; gratified：～一时 indulge in momentary pleasure (*or* gratification) / 看着心里～ delighted at the sight of sth. / 全家团聚，她倍感～。She was overjoyed at the happy reunion of the family. / 他这话叫人听了不～。What he said annoyed people. ❷ to one's heart's content; to one's great satisfaction：吃个～ eat to one's heart's content; eat one's fill / 痛痛快快地睡个觉 have a refreshing sleep ❸ frank and direct; forthright; straightforward：说话～ speak with complete frankness; not mince one's words / 众人之中，数他最～。He is the most frank and direct of all the people around. / 他这个人性子～。He is a straightforward man.

痛快淋漓 tòngkuai-línlí unrestrained and forceful; vigorous：骂得～ give a good dressing-down / 他提起笔来，～地写了一大篇。He took up his pen and wrote a whole essay at a stretch (*or* at one go).

T

痛骂 tòngmà scold severely; curse roundly; tell off scathingly; give a good scolding:遭人～ be given a good telling-off; be told off scathingly
痛切 tòngqiè with great agony; most sorrowfully; keenly:～地认识到自己的错误 realize one's mistake with great agony /～感到自己的不足 feel one's deficiency keenly /他诚恳检讨,言辞～。He made sincere and remorseful self-criticisms.
痛诉 tòngsù speak with grief; painfully pour out:～他的不白之冤 speak painfully of his unrighted wrong
痛恶 tòngwù bitterly detest; dislike intensely; abhor; loathe:令人～ be abhorrent /官场腐败深为人民所～。Official corruption is bitterly detested by the people.
痛惜 tòngxī deeply regret; feel remorse for; deplore:深为～ deeply deplore /～之情 great regret /眼看着庄稼枯死,谁能不～呢? It is heart-rending to watch helplessly the dying crops.
痛心 tòngxīn pained; distressed; saddened; grieved:深感～ be deeply grieved; feel deep regret /事情糟到这种地步,令人～。It is distressing to see that things have come to such a sorry pass.
痛心疾首 tòngxīn-jíshǒu with bitter hatred; with great resentment:这种奢靡之风,令人～。People bitterly resented the widespread debauchery and extravagance.
痛心入骨 tòngxīn-rùgǔ intensely painful; extremely sad:抨击时弊,～ make scathing attacks on existing social ills /我每与友人谈及此事,莫不～。Everybody feels immensely pained whenever I talk about it with my friends.
痛痒 tòngyǎng ❶ sufferings; hardships; difficulties:关心百姓的～ be concerned with the hardships of the common people ❷ importance; consequence:无关～ of no consequence; of little account /不关～的小事情,何必去计较呢? Why bother yourself with such inconsequential trifles?
痛痒相关 tòngyǎng-xiāngguān be closely connected; share a common lot:这事跟他～,他怎能不着急? How could he feel easy when the matter is of great concern to him?
痛饮 tòngyǐn drink one's fill; drink to one's heart's content:为胜利～ drink to victory; toast victory
痛阈 tòngyù 〈医学〉threshold of pain
痛责 tòngzé scold harshly; denounce scathingly:他办事不力,遭到～。He was severely reprimanded for his failure to deal with the matter properly.

T

通 tòng 〈量词〉*referring to action*:发了一～议论 make a torrent of comments /大吵大闹一～ make quite a big scene /胡吹一～ shoot off one's mouth /臭骂一～ haul sb. over the coals /打了儿子一～ give his son a good beating
see also tōng
通红 tònghóng *see* "通红" tōnghóng

tōu

偷(❺媮) tōu ❶ steal; pilfer; pinch; filch:～几块面包 pilfer a few pieces of bread /她的自行车让人～走了。Her bicycle was stolen. ❷ thief; pilferer; burglar:小～ thief; pickpocket /惯～ hardened thief ❸ stealthily; secretly; on the sly; surreptitiously: *see* "～看";"～跑";"～猎" ❹ take (time) off; find (time):～点功夫学外语 find time to learn a foreign language /忙里～闲 snatch a little leisure from a busy life ❺ seek temporary ease; muddle along: *see* "～安";"～生"
偷安 tōu'ān seek temporary ease:苟且～ seek only temporary ease and comfort /～于一时 enjoy ease for the time being; muddle along for a while
偷薄 tōubó frivolous; flirtatious; unkind:其人～好辩。He is a frivolous glib talker.
偷馋抹嘴 tōuchán-mǒzuǐ take food on the sly:改不了～的坏毛病 cannot give up the bad habit of petty pilfering
偷盗 tōudào steal; pilfer; filch:～公共财物 steal public property /～犯 thief; pilferer
偷渡 tōudù stealthily cross (a blockaded river, etc.):～国境 steal across a national border; cross the border illegally; steal out of (*or* into) a country /～入境 steal into a country; enter a country illegally (*or* steathily)
偷惰 tōuduò 〈书面〉perfunctory and lazy:～成性 be hopelessly lazy
偷儿 tōu'ér 〈方言〉petty thief; pilferer; pickpocket
偷工减料 tōugōng-jiǎnliào do shoddy work and use inferior material; scamp work and stint material; jerry-build:这家公司～,损害顾客利益。This company damaged its customer's interests with shoddy products.
偷寒送暖 tōuhán-sòngnuǎn curry favour (with ladies) on the sly; do everything to please one's mistress; act as a secret go-between (for illicit affairs)
偷汉子 tōu hànzi *also* "偷汉" (of a married woman) carry on a clandestine love affair with a man; have a secret lover; commit adultery
偷合苟容 tōuhé-gǒuróng *also* "偷合取容" pander to others in order to shelter oneself:～之事,吾不为也。It's not my way to toady to other people for survival.
偷换 tōuhuàn supersede surreptitiously; substitute stealthily; replace secretly:～概念 substitute a concept stealthily; tamper with (*or* distort) a concept
偷活 tōuhuó drag out an ignoble existence; live a meaningless life
偷鸡不成蚀把米 tōu jī bùchéng shí bǎ mǐ 〈俗语〉try to steal a chicken only to end up losing the rice; go for wool and come back shorn
偷鸡摸狗 tōujī-mōgǒu ❶ steal; pinch; pilfer:那几年穷,免不了干些～的事。Want occasionally drove him into petty theft in those years. ❷ (of a man) have illicit love affairs with women:从年轻时起,他就有拈花惹草、～的毛病。He has been prone to philandering since his youth.
偷奸取巧 tōujiān-qǔqiǎo resort to chicanery or opportunism to serve oneself:他这个人专会～,干事全凭一张嘴。A man of slick tongue, he always resorted to chicanery for personal gain.
偷看 tōukàn look secretly; peep; peek:从门孔里～ peek through the keyhole /～新娘子 peep at the bride
偷空 tōukòng take time off (from work to do sth. else); snatch a moment:～回家看看 snatch a moment to return home for a short visit /～打个盹 snatch a doze
偷懒 tōulǎn loaf on the job; be lazy:这孩子学习总～。The boy is always lazy in his studies.
偷老婆 tōu lǎopo (of a man) steal someone's wife — commit adultery
偷垒 tōulěi 〈体育〉steal a base; steal
偷梁换柱 tōuliáng-huànzhù steal beams and pillars and replace them with rotten timber — commit a fraud; substitute sth. (usu. inferior) for sth. else:他们采取～的手段,拿别厂的产品冒充本厂的参评。They cheated by passing other factories' products off as their own for quality appraisal.
偷猎 tōuliè poach:～者 poacher /～自然保护区里的鹿 poach deer on a nature reserve
偷漏 tōulòu evade (taxes):～税款 evade taxes /查禁～ ban (*or* prohibit) tax evasion
偷摸 tōumō steal; pinch; pilfer:他这个人～成性。Stealing has become his second nature.
偷跑 tōupǎo 〈体育〉jump the gun; run away stealthily; sneak
偷期 tōuqī 〈书面〉(of lovers) make a secret rendezvous; arrange a secret meeting or tryst
偷巧 tōuqiǎo skimp by avoiding what is difficult and time-consuming; resort to trickery to serve oneself:做～的事儿 gain by duplicity; play tricks to further one's interests
偷窃 tōuqiè steal; pilfer:～罪 crime of theft; larceny /因～坐牢 be imprisoned for stealing (*or* larceny)
偷情 tōuqíng carry on a clandestine love affair:男女～ (of a man and woman) have a secret love affair
偷秋 tōuqiū steal a ripening autumn harvest crop
偷人 tōurén carry on a clandestine love affair:～养汉 (of a woman) have an affair; commit adultery
偷生 tōushēng drag out an ignoble existence:～于乱世 lead a meaningless life in the turbulent world /忍辱～ live in humiliation
偷手 tōushǒu hold back a trick or two (in showing one's abilities)
偷税 tōushuì evade taxes:～漏税 tax evasions /～罚款 impose a forfeit (*or* fine) on tax evaders /采取造假账的手段～ evade taxes by way of false accounts
偷天换日 tōutiān-huànrì steal the sky and change the sun — commit a gigantic fraud:～,欺骗世人 mislead the public by sheer

chicanery
偷听 tōutīng listen in stealthily; eavesdrop:～父母谈话 eavesdrop on one's parents' conversation
偷偷 tōutōu stealthily; secretly; covertly; surreptitiously:～溜出宿舍 sneak out of one's dormitory /～儿看了一眼那张照片 steal a look at the picture
偷偷摸摸 tōutōu-mōmō furtively; secretly; surreptitiously; covertly:～干坏事 be engaged in covert evildoing /这又不是什么见不得人的事,何必～? It's quite open and aboveboard. Why all this secrecy?
偷袭 tōuxí sneak attack; sneak raid; surprise attack:～成功 bring off a sneak raid /～敌营 launch a surprise attack on an enemy camp
偷暇 tōuxiá *see* "偷闲❶"
偷闲 tōuxián ❶ snatch a moment of leisure; take time off; find time:忙里～ snatch a little leisure from a busy life /～出游 allow oneself a bit of time for a sightseeing tour ❷〈方言〉loaf on the job; be idle:一天到晚就会～,不干正事 idle around all day long and never do a stroke of honest work
偷香窃玉 tōuxiāng-qièyù *also* "窃玉偷香" (of a man) have illicit sexual relations; fool around with women; philander
偷眼 tōuyǎn steal a glance; take a furtive glance:～看人 steal a look at sb.
偷营 tōuyíng make a surprise attack on an enemy camp; raid an enemy camp:～劫寨 attack an enemy camp by surprise
偷越 tōuyuè stealthily cross; slip through:～国境 illegally cross a national border
偷嘴 tōuzuǐ take food on the sly

tóu

头(頭)¹ tóu ❶ head:从～到脚 from head to foot; from tip to toe; from top to bottom ❷ hair; hair style:洗～ wash one's hair; have a shampoo /剃～ have a haircut /染～ dye one's hair /推个平～ have a crewcut ❸ top; tip; end:山～ top of a hill; hilltop /笔～ tip of a pen; pen point /桥～ either end of a bridge /两～尖尖 with sharp points at both ends /村西～ west end of a village /坟～ grave mound ❹ beginning; end:开个好～ make a good beginning /万事起～难。Beginning is always difficult. /事情说了个～,没说尾。The story has no ending. /到～来她仍是孤身一人。She was left alone in the end. ❺ remnant; leftover; end:布～儿 leftover of a bolt of cloth; odd bits of cloth /粉笔～儿 chalk stub (*or* stump) /烟～儿 cigarette end (*or* butt, *or* stub) ❻ chief; head; boss:车间的～儿 head of a workshop /工～ foreman /他是我们的～儿。He is our boss. ❼ side; aspect:两～讨好 try to please both sides /一心挂两～ have divided loyalties /驼子跌跟头,两～不落实〈俗语〉like a hunchback falling down with neither the head nor the feet touching the ground — fall between two stools /他俩是对～。They are enemies. ❽ number one; first:～回 for the first time ❾ leading: *see* "～羊"; "～马" ❿ (used before a numeral or a classifier) first:～趟车 first train /～两周 first two weeks /鸡叫～遍 when the cock first crows; at the first crow of a cock ⓫〈方言〉(used before 年 or 天) previous; last: *see* "～天"; "～年" ⓬ right before; prior to:～五点起床 get up before five o'clock ⓭ (used between two numerals) about; around:十～八块钱 about eight or ten *yuan* ⓮〈量词〉(a) *used with domestic animals*:十～牛 ten heads of cattle /两～驴 two donkeys (b) *used with garlic*:两～蒜 two bulbs of garlic

头(頭)² tou ❶ *noun suffix* (a) *used with a noun*:骨～ bone /石～ stone /苗～ symptom of a trend; suggestion of a new development (b) *used with a verb*:想～ sth. worth thinking about; idea /接～儿 contact (c) *used with an adjective*:准～儿 accuracy /苦～儿 foretaste of bitterness; hardship ❷ *suffix of a noun of locality*:前～ front /后～ behind; rear; back /里～ inside /外～ outside
头版 tóubǎn front page (of a newspaper):～头条 headline news on the front page; banner (headline) /～责任编辑 editor responsible for the front page
头半天 tóubàntiān morning; forenoon:～抓紧干 work hard in the morning
头孢氨苄 tóubāo'ānbiàn *also* "苯甘孢霉素" běngānbāoméisù〈药学〉cefalexin; cephalexin
头孢菌素 tóubāojūnsù〈药学〉cephalosporin
头孢霉素 tóubāoméisù *also* "先锋霉素" xiānfēngméisù〈药学〉cephalothin:～II cephaloridine
头边 tóubian〈方言〉in front; ahead:咱们～是谁呀? Who's ahead of us?
头彩 tóucǎi first prize in a lottery:得了个～ win first prize in a lottery
头筹 tóuchóu first; championship:拔取～ come out first; win the championship
头寸 tóucùn〈商业〉❶ cash; liquidity:～缺 run short of cash ❷ money market; money supply:～紧。Money is tight. *or* Money is in short supply.
头大 tóudà〈方言〉with dilated head; having a headache; troubled:一动笔写文章,他就～了。Writing always gives him a bad headache.
头道 tóudao〈方言〉cause; reason:猜来猜去,总猜不出个～来 fail to figure it out despite much guesswork
头灯 tóudēng〈矿业〉head lamp
头等 tóuděng first-class; first-rate:～奖 first prize /坐～舱 travel first-class /～品 first-rate (*or* top quality) goods /～重要任务 task of prime importance; major task /～人才 first-rate personnel; best qualified person; most talented person /这家饭店是～的。This is a five-star hotel.
头等大事 tóuděng dàshì matter of prime importance; major event:眼下县里的～是抓好春耕生产。The most important task of the county government at the moment is to do a good job in the spring sowing.
头顶 tóudǐng top or crown of the head
头发 tóufa hair (on the human head):有些白～ have some grey hairs /～夹子 hairpin; hairclip; bassette /～定型喷剂 hairspray /～护养专家 hairologist
头发菜 tóufacài *also* "发菜" hair weeds; black moss
头房 tóufáng main room of a hotel:上好的～ best rooms of a hotel /留下三间～,给远道来的客人。Please keep (*or* reserve) three main rooms for the guests coming from afar.
头风 tóufēng〈中医〉headache; migraine
头缝儿 tóufèngr parting (of combed hair):偏～ side parting /中～ centre parting /不分～ without parting /他的～在右边。His hair parted on the right.
头伏 tóufú *also* "初伏" chūfú ❶ first *fu*, the first of the three ten-day periods of the hot season ❷ first day of the first *fu*
头盖 tóugài ❶ skull; cranium ❷ red head scarf or gauze worn by the bride at her wedding
头盖骨 tóugàigǔ〈生理〉cranium; skull
头高头低 tóugāo-tóudī〈口语〉approximate measure on the scale; slight difference:～的,不用计较。There is no need to be exact to an ounce.
头功 tóugōng ❶ first contribution; first meritorious performance:抢～ vie to be the first to perform meritorious service ❷ first-class merit:立了～ win a first-class merit citation
头骨 tóugǔ skull; cranium
头号 tóuhào ❶ number one; size one:～铅字 size one type /～新闻 headline news /～儿笨蛋 greatest fool; unmitigated idiot ❷ first-rate; top quality:～面粉 top-grade flour
头花 tóuhuā〈工美〉headdress flower
头昏 tóuhūn dizzy; giddy:感到～ feel one's head swimming
头昏脑胀 tóuhūn-nǎozhàng feel dizzy or giddy:工作忙得他～。He is reeling from overwork.
头昏眼花 tóuhūn-yǎnhuā with one's head swimming and one's eyes blurred; dizzy:太阳晒得我～。I felt dizzy in the blazing sun.
头髻 tóujì hair bun or coil
头家 tóujiā ❶ host of a gambling party who takes a percentage or cut of the winnings ❷ banker in a gambling party ❸ (in mah-jong, card, dice or games, etc.) player whose turn comes just before:他是我的～。He is before me. ❹〈方言〉shopkeeper; proprietor; boss
头奖 tóujiǎng first prize (in a contest; etc.):在演讲比赛中得～ win the first prize in a speech contest
头角 tóujiǎo talent or brilliance (of a young person):崭露～ make a brilliant show of one's talent
头角峥嵘 tóujiǎo-zhēngróng (of a youth) brilliant; outstanding:此子～,前途无量。This is a very promising young man with a bright future.
头巾 tóujīn ❶ head-covering (for men in ancient clothes) ❷

T

scarf; kerchief: 包～ turban

头巾气 tóujīnqì pedantry: 他这个人～太重。He is hopelessly pedantic.

头颈 tóujǐng 〈方言〉 neck

头壳 tóuké *also* "头脑壳"〈方言〉 head; head capsule

头口 tóukǒu 〈方言〉 draught animal; beast of burden: 养了些～ keep (*or* raise) some cattle

头会箕敛 tóukuài-jīliǎn heavy taxation: ～, 民不堪命。People can hardly make both ends meet under the heavy burden of taxation.

头盔 tóukuī (steel) helmet

头佬 tóulǎo 〈方言〉 foreman; overseer

头里 tóuli ❶ in front; ahead: 处处走在～ take the lead in everything / 他在～走, 大家在后面紧紧跟着。He walked ahead and all the others followed closely behind. ❷ in advance; beforehand: 我先把话说在～。Let me make this clear in advance. / 这些事我～都交代过。I told you all this beforehand. ❸ 〈方言〉 ago; before; formerly; previously: 十年～到处都唱这个歌。The song was very popular ten years ago.

头脸 tóuliǎn ❶ head and face: ～好几天没有梳洗了 have not combed one's hair and washed one's face for quite a few days ❷ face; features; appearance: 好半天我才看清他的～。It took me quite some time to recognize him. ❸ dignity; face: 他是地方上有～的人。He is a local big shot.

头领 tóulǐng leader; chief; commander: 义军～ commander of the righteous army

头颅 tóulú head: 抛～, 洒热血 sacrifice oneself (for a just cause)

头鲈鱼 tóulúyú silver-spotted grunt

头路 tóulù ❶ first-class; top quality; top-notch; tip-top: 上好的～货 best-quality goods ❷ 〈方言〉 parting hair ❸ 〈方言〉 clue; main threads: 理不出～来 be unable to get things straight / 乱七八糟的, 没个～。It's a complete mess (*or* a mare's nest) with no thread to follow. ❹ 〈方言〉 job; way or connections (for getting sth. done): 找～ job hunt; hunting for a job / 他干此事有～。He knows how to get this done.

头马 tóumǎ lead horse

头门 tóumén exterior gate; outer gate

头面人物 tóumiàn rénwù prominent figure; magnate; bigwig; big shot: 这几年他成了～。He has become a VIP in recent years.

头面 tóumian 〈旧语〉 woman's head ornament or headgear: 一副～ a set of headgear

头名 tóumíng first place; the best (in a profession): ～状元 number one successful scholar (in the palace civil service examination) / 这次马拉松赛他跑了个～。He came in first in the marathon race.

头明 tóumíng 〈方言〉 just before daybreak or dawn: ～咱们就动身上路。We are to set out before daybreak.

头目 tóumù 〈贬义〉 head of a gang; ringleader; chieftain: 大～ ringleader / 小～ sub-group leader in a gang / 总～ No. 1 chieftain

头目人 tóumùrén 〈方言〉 leader: 他是村里的～儿。He is the village head.

头难 tóunán 〈方言〉 difficult beginning: 凡事～, 做起来就好了。The first step is always difficult, and it becomes easier once you get started.

头脑 tóunǎo ❶ brains; mind: ～清楚 have a clear mind; be clear-headed / 有～ have plenty of brains; be resourceful / ～发热 be over-optimistic; cherish impractical grandiose ideas / ～冷静 have a cool head / 有商业～的人 commercially minded people; people who have a head for business; people with a business sense / 四肢发达, ～简单 sturdily built, but simple-minded / 被胜利冲昏～ get carried away by success; be swell-headed with success ❷ main thread; clue: 丈二金刚, 摸不着～ cannot make head or tail of sth.; be quite puzzled; be in the dark ❸ 〈口语〉 chief; chieftain; leader; head: ～人物 top leader

头年 tóunián ❶ first year: 三年的工程看～。The first year is of crucial importance for a three-year project. ❷ last year; previous year; year before: 那是你～答应过的事。That's what you promised last year.

头牛 tóuniú lead cattle

头帕 tóupà 〈方言〉 scarf; kerchief

头牌 tóupái 〈旧语〉〈戏曲〉 plate or board on which the leading actor's or actress's name is written: 挂～ be the leading actor or actress on the plate / ～花旦 leading actress (in Beijing opera)

头皮 tóupí ❶ scalp: ～针 scalp acupuncture / 硬着～走上讲台 screw up one's courage and walk onto the platform / 硬着～顶住 grim and bear it ❷ *also* "头皮屑" dandruff; scurf: ～多 plenty of dandruff / 去～ cure (sb.'s) dandruff

头破血流 tóupò-xuèliú (be hit until) one's head is covered with bumps and bruises — be badly battered; be (beaten) black and blue; 〈比喻〉 be thoroughly beaten: 在铁的事实面前碰得～ butt one's head against a wall of ironclad facts

头七 tóuqī first seven days after sb.'s death

头前 tóuqián ❶ in front; at the head; ahead: 他在～引路。He is leading the way ahead. / 楼房～新栽了两排小杨树。Two rows of young poplar trees were recently planted in front of the building. ❷ in the past; previously: ～这个地方还是很荒凉的。It was quite desolate here in the past.

头钱 tóuqián commission taken from the winnings of a gambling party

头秋 tóuqiū right before the autumn harvest: ～得把场院整理好了。The threshing ground must be cleaned (*or* straightened) up before the autumn harvest.

头球 tóuqiú header: ～破门 head the ball into the goal

头人 tóurén tribal chief; headman

头纱 tóushā gauze headscarf

头晌 tóushǎng 〈方言〉 before noon; in the morning

头上安头 tóushàng-āntóu meaningless repetition; redundancy: 形容词用得太多, ～, 何不去掉。It is needless repetition to use too many adjectives, and we may just as well leave them out.

头上长疮, 脚底流脓 tóushàng zhǎng chuāng, jiǎodǐ liú nóng 〈俗语〉 with boils on the head and feet running with pus — rotten through and through: 他可是个～的流氓。He is an out-and-out rascal.

头生 tóushēng ❶ first birth: 她是～, 不免有些紧张。It was her first delivery and she could not but feel a bit nervous. ❷ firstborn: ～丫头 firstborn daughter / ～子 firstborn son ❸ firstborn child; first child: 他是妈妈的～。He is his mother's firstborn.

头绳 tóushéng ❶ string for binding a plait or bun: 红～ red hair string / 扎～ tie one's hair with a piece of string ❷ 〈方言〉 knitting wool

头虱 tóushī head louse

头式 tóushì hair style; hairdo

头饰 tóushì ornament for the head; headdress; headgear

头势 tóushi 〈方言〉 momentum; tendency; look of things

头水 tóushuǐ ❶ top-quality: ～货 top-notch goods ❷ (of articles and utensils) first use ❸ (of clothes) first washing: 这件毛衣刚洗了～就短了好多。The sweater shrank a lot after the first washing. ❹ first irrigation: 地已浇过～。The fields have been irrigated once.

头胎 tóutāi firstborn

头套 tóutào actor's headgear; wig: 戴～ wear a wig

头疼 tóuténg (have a) headache: 感到～ have a headache / 这件事真让人～。It is a big headache.

头疼脑热 tóuténg-nǎorè headache and slight fever; slight illness: ～, 浑身无力 feel ill and weak / ～不算病。It's just a slight indisposition.

头天 tóutiān ❶ day before; yesterday: ～的事我直到早上才想起来。Not until the morning did I remember the incident that happened the day before. ❷ first day: 新学徒～上工。It's the first day of work for the new apprentice.

头挑 tóutiāo choicest: 这些瓜果都是～。These are the choicest fruits.

头条新闻 tóutiáo xīnwén front-page headline; top story of the newspaper: 这件事成了报纸上的～。The story made front-page headline in the press.

头童齿豁 tóutóng-chǐhuō hairless and toothless; senile; decrepit: ～, 老之将至。With hair gone and teeth falling out I am aging rapidly.

头痛 tóutòng (have a) headache: 感冒～ have a cold and headache / 让人～的事情 knotty (*or* thorny) problem / 通货膨胀是件令政府非常～的事。Inflation was a big headache of the government.

头痛医头, 脚痛医脚 tóutòng yī tóu, jiǎotòng yī jiǎo treat the head when the head aches, treat the foot when the foot hurts — treat the symptoms but not the disease; scratch the surface without getting to the root of things; apply or prescribe mere palliatives: 出了事故得抓根儿, 不能～。One should get to the root of an accident once it occurs instead of taking stopgap measures only.

头头是道 tóutóu-shìdào clear and logical; closely reasoned and well argued:讲得～ argue convincingly /说起来～,做起来满不是那么一回事 coherent and cogent in speech but quite different in action
头头儿 tóutour 〈口语〉boss; head; chief:新来的～ new boss
头陀 tóutuó mendicant Buddhist monk
头晚 tóuwǎn last night; previous night:～的会开到后半夜。The meeting last night went on till the small hours.
头尾 tóuwěi ❶ head and tail:～相连。The head and the tail are connected. ❷ beginning and end:会议～他都参加了。He sat through the meeting. ❸ main threads; clue:问不出个～ fail to get a relevant answer /等他的事有个～再说 wait until he gets things into shape
头午 tóuwǔ 〈方言〉near noon
头先 tóuxiān 〈方言〉❶ before; in the past; in the beginning:你～不是这样说的。You didn't say so at first. ❷ in the front; ahead:～领路 lead the way ❸ just now:他～还在,不会走远。He was around a moment ago and can't be far away.
头衔 tóuxián title:光荣的～ glorious title /世界冠军的～ world championship; title of world champion
头像 tóuxiàng head portrait or sculpture:青铜～ head sculpture in bronze /封面上印着诗人的～。There is a head portrait of the poet on the front cover.
头屑 tóuxiè dandruff; scurf:去～香波 shampoo that will cure dandruff; shampoo for scurf
头囟儿 tóuxìnr 〈方言〉fontanel
头行人 tóuxíngrén 〈方言〉leader; bell-wether
头胸部 tóuxiōngbù 〈动物〉cephalothorax
头须 tóuxū hair and beard:～渐白。His hair and beard are turning grey.
头绪 tóuxù main threads (of sth. complicated); clue:毫无～ have no clues to follow; be in a complete mess /案子有了～。We are beginning to get somewhere in the case. /事情复杂,一时尚找不出～。The matter is too complicated to straighten out right now. /办工厂的计划有些～了。The plan to set up a factory is beginning to take shape.
头癣 tóuxuǎn 〈医学〉favus of the scalp
头雁 tóuyàn lead wild goose
头羊 tóuyáng bell-wether; lead sheep or goat
头由 tóuyóu pretext:找些～儿跟人搭话 try to find some excuse to start a conversation with sb.
头油 tóuyóu hair oil; pomade
头晕 tóuyūn dizzy; giddy; fainting
头针疗法 tóuzhēn liáofǎ 〈中医〉head-acupuncture therapy
头重脚轻 tóuzhòng-jiǎoqīng with one's head growing heavy and one's feet growing light; top-heavy; dizzy:～的官僚机构 top-heavy bureaucracy /他感冒刚好,有些～的。He has just recovered from a cold and still feels heavy-headed.
头状花序 tóuzhuàng huāxù 〈植物〉capitulum; head
头子 tóuzi chieftain; chief; boss:土匪～ bandit chief /流氓～ gangleader
头足动物 tóuzú dòngwù cephalopod

投

tóu ❶ throw; toss; fling; hurl:～球 throw a ball ❷ put in; drop:把烟头～进烟灰缸 drop a cigarette stub into the ash tray ❸ throw oneself into (a river, well, ect. to commit suicide): *see* "～河"; "～井" ❹ project; cast; fling:月光从窗外～进来。The moon shone through the windows. /灯光将女孩身影～在墙上,显得很大。The light projected the girl's enlarged shadow on the wall. /她向他～去绝望的目光。She cast a look of despair at him. ❺ send; dispatch; deliver:把稿件～给当地的一份报纸 send contributions to a local newspaper ❻ go to; enter; join:弃暗～明 forsake darkness for light ❼ fit in with; agree with; be congenial to:情～意合 find each other congenial; fall in love with each other /气味相～ share each other's likes (*or* tastes) ❽ approaching; before: *see* "～明"; "～暮"
投案 tóu'àn give oneself up or surrender oneself to the police:～自首 surrender oneself to the police and confess one's crime
投保 tóubǎo buy insurance; insure:人寿～ buy life insurance /财产～ have one's property insured /货物安全～ insure one's goods against risks /～单 insurance policy /向当地一家保险公司～ be insured with a local insurance company
投保方 tóubǎofāng insured party; (insurance) policy holder
投奔 tóubèn go to (a friend or a place) for shelter:～亲友 go to one's relatives and friends for help /无处～ have nowhere to turn to
投笔从戎 tóubǐ-cóngróng throw aside the writing brush and join the army; renounce the pen for the sword; give up academic pursuits for a military career:～,报效祖国 cast aside the pen and take up the sword in defence of one's motherland
投畀豺虎 tóubì-cháihǔ throw (an evildoer) among beasts of prey — feel strong indignation (against):～,方解心头之恨。Only by throwing the evildoer among wolves and tigers can we appease our rankling hatred.
投币式公用电话 tóubìshì gōngyòng diànhuà coin-operated phone; pay phone; prepay-set; coin box telephone:～机 coin box; coin box set /～亭 coin-box pay station
投鞭断流 tóubiān-duànliú if the cavalrymen threw their whips into the river, it would be enough to stem the current — have a large and powerful army
投标 tóubiāo submit a tender; enter a bid:～建坝 bid for the construction of the dam /公开～ public tender; open tender /～人 bidder; tenderer /～书 tender; bid
投镖 tóubiāo ❶ dart; dart throwing ❷ throw a dart
投产 tóuchǎn go into operation; put into production; commission:大规模～ go into large-scale (*or* mass) production /核电厂即将～。The nuclear power plant will soon go into operation. *or* It will soon be commissioned.
投诚 tóuchéng (of enemy troops, rebels, bandits, etc.) surrender; cross over:向我方～ come over to our side /主动～ surrender of one's own accord
投弹 tóudàn ❶ drop a bomb; bomb; bombard:向军事目标～ drop bombs on military targets /敌机向平民区～。The enemy planes bombarded the civilian residential quarters. ❷ throw a hand grenade:～训练 training in grenade-throwing
投弹高度 tóudàn gāodù 〈军事〉release altitude
投弹角 tóudànjiǎo 〈军事〉dropping angle
投弹器 tóudànqì 〈军事〉bomb rack control; bomb release mechanism
投弹手 tóudànshǒu bombardier; grenadier
投敌 tóudí go over to the enemy; defect to the enemy:变节～ commit betrayal and defect to the enemy
投递 tóudì deliver:～邮件 deliver mail /无法～的信 dead letter /无法～,寄回原处。Undeliverable, returned to the sender.
投递员 tóudìyuán *also* "邮递员" yóudìyuán postman; letter or mail carrier; mailman
投店 tóudiàn put up at an inn; stay the night at an inn
投放 tóufàng ❶ throw in; put in:向池里～鱼苗 put fry into the pond ❷ put (money) into circulation; invest:通货～ money supply /在纺织业～大量资金 invest heavily in the textile industry ❸ put goods on the market:把多种商品～市场 supply the market with a variety of goods
投分 tóufèn 〈书面〉be alike in temperament; be congenial with each other
投稿 tóugǎo submit a piece of writing for publication; contribute (to a newspaper or magazine):向学术杂志～ send a contribution to an academic journal /本次征文,欢迎各界人士积极～。All are welcome to contribute to the coming special issue.
投稿人 tóugǎorén contributor
投戈 tóugē 〈书面〉lay down arms:解甲～ take off one's armour and lay down one's arms; be demobilized
投工 tóugōng put in labour:动员农民增加向农田水利事业投资～。The farmers are encouraged to increase their capital and labour input in agricultural water conservancy projects.
投函 tóuhán write a letter (to a newspaper, etc.):向报界～ send letters to the press
投合 tóuhé ❶ agree; get along:这两个人很～。The two of them are hitting it off. ❷ cater to:～大众口味 cater to the public taste
投河 tóuhé throw oneself into the river; drown oneself in the river
投壶 tóuhú throw arrows into a vase (an ancient game played at a banquet, in which the loser must drink as a penalty)
投缳 tóuhuán 〈书面〉put one's neck into a noose; hang oneself
投簧 tóuhuáng ❶ (of a key) fit (a lock):新配的钥匙～,很好用。The newly-made key fits the lock perfectly. ❷ be practical; work well:这一招包管～。This trick is sure to work.
投机 tóujī ❶ congenial; agreeable:彼此一向～ have long found each other congenial /话不～半句多。Even one word is too much

when the conversation gets disagreeable. ❷ speculate; profiteer; seek private gain by hook or by crook: ～行为 speculations / 做股票～生意 speculate in stocks / ～钻营 seek personal gain by opportunism and trickery

投机倒把 tóujī-dǎobǎ engage in speculation and profiteering: ～, 牟取暴利 seek huge profits by speculation / ～的不法分子 lawbreaking speculators (*or* profiteers)

投机分子 tóujīfènzǐ opportunist; careerist

投机取巧 tóujī-qǔqiǎo seize every chance to gain advantage by trickery; be opportunistic: 在政治上～ indulge in political thievery

投机商 tóujīshāng speculator; profiteer

投寄 tóujì send by mail; mail; post: ～信件 send a letter; mail a letter / ～包裹 send a parcel by mail

投井 tóujǐng throw oneself into a well; commit suicide by jumping into a well

投井下石 tóujǐng-xiàshí *also* "落井下石" luòjǐng-xiàshí drop stones on someone who has fallen into a well; hit a person when he's down

投军 tóujūn join the army; enlist: 有志于～ make up one's mind to join the army

投考 tóukǎo sign up for an examination: ～大学 sign up for a college entrance examination / ～不中 fail (*or* flunk) an entrance examination

投靠 tóukào go and seek sb.'s patronage: 卖身～ barter away one's honour for sb.'s patronage / ～敌人 throw in one's lot with the enemy; sell out to the enemy; turn renegade / 无亲友可～ have no one to turn to / 他先后～过许多人。He sold himself to quite a few people.

投篮 tóulán 〈体育〉 shoot (a basket): 近距离～ close-in shoot / 远距离～ long shot / 跳起～ jump up and shoot / ～不准 inaccurate shooting / ～命中 shoot and score a hit / 单手～ one-hand shot / 勾手～ hook shot / 反手～ reverse lay-in (*or* lay-up) / 急停～ stop shot / ～命中率 shooting average

投料 tóuliào feeding: ～器 feeding apparatus

投袂而起 tóumèi'érqǐ rise with a flick of one's sleeve — show one's indignation; go into action: 国难当头, 万众～。The people rose in action in the face of the national crisis.

投明 tóumíng before dawn: ～起身 rise before dawn

投暮 tóumù towards dusk: ～归家 return home at dusk

投票 tóupiào vote; cast a vote: ～赞成 vote for; vote in favour of / ～反对 vote against / ～表决 take a vote; decide by ballot / 无记名～ secret ballot / ～否决 vote down / ～通过 vote through / 人们成群结队前往～。People are going to the polls in great numbers.

投票权 tóupiàoquán suffrage vote; right to vote

投票日 tóupiàorì polling day; voting day; election day

投票箱 tóupiàoxiāng ballot box

投票站 tóupiàozhàn polling booth or station; the polls

投其所好 tóuqísuǒhào cater to sb.'s likes or tastes: ～, 引诱上钩 lure sb. by playing up to him

投契 tóuqì 〈书面〉 see eye to eye; get along well; be congenial: 言谈甚为～ have an agreeable conversation

投洽 tóuqià agree; be compatible; hit it off: ～的朋友 congenial friends

投枪 tóuqiāng javelin; (throwing) spear

投亲 tóuqīn go and live with relatives; seek refuge with relatives: ～靠友 seek shelter with relatives and friends

投入 tóurù ❶ throw into; put into: ～生产 put into production; go into operation / 全身心地～工作 devote oneself heart and soul to one's work; bury oneself in one's work / ～使用 put to use; commission / ～训练 throw (oneself) into training / 在这项工程上～大量资金 invest heavily in this project ❷ do sth. with concentration; be engrossed (in sth.): 他工作不甚～。He doesn't quite concentrate on his work. *or* He isn't quite engrossed in his work. ❸ input; investment: 农业～ agricultural input / 教育～ input into education / ～产出关系 input-output relationship

投射 tóushè ❶ throw; cast; fling: 举起标枪, 奋力～ raise one's javelin and throw it vigorously ❷ project (a ray of light, etc.); cast: 月光～到一望无际的草地上。The moon cast its rays over the vast grassland (*or* prairie). / 观众对他～出愤怒的目光。The audience looked at him with anger.

投身 tóushēn throw oneself; plunge: ～于争取民族独立的斗争 plunge into the struggle for national independence / ～教育事业 dedicate oneself to educational work

投生 tóushēng ❶ 〈迷信〉 be reincarnated in a new body; be reborn: ～富贵人家 be reborn in a wealthy and influential family ❷ seek a livelihood away from one's home: 异国～ make a living in an alien land

投师 tóushī seek instruction from a master; become the disciple of a master: ～学艺 learn skill (*or* a trade) from a master / ～于名艺术家门下 become the student of a well-known artist

投石问路 tóushí-wènlù cast a stone to find out whether one should proceed; send out a trial balloon; sound out: 他提出的这几个问题显然是～。He raised these questions obviously as a trial balloon.

投手 tóushǒu 〈体育〉 pitcher: ～犯规 balk

投售 tóushòu sell on the market: ～新棉 sell new cotton on the market

投书 tóushū deliver or send a letter; write to (a newspaper, etc.)

投鼠忌器 tóushǔ-jìqì hesitate to pelt a rat for fear of smashing the dishes (beside it) — refrain from taking action against an evildoer for fear of harming good people: 对这个人要依法定罪, 不可因有损其父而～。This man must be punished by law, even though his father might be affected in the process.

投顺 tóushùn surrender and pledge allegiance

投诉 tóusù complain: ～法院 appeal to a court / 处理顾客～ handle customer complaints

投宿 tóusù seek temporary lodging; put up for the night: 去旅店～一晚 put up at an inn for one (*or* the) night

投胎 tóutāi 〈迷信〉 be reincarnated

投桃报李 tóutáo-bàolǐ give a plum in return for a peach — return present for present; exchange favours; repay a favour: ～, 外交常礼。Reciprocity is part of diplomatic protocol.

投纬 tóuwěi 〈纺织〉 picking: 每分钟～数 picks per minute

投闲置散 tóuxián-zhìsǎn leave unused; let (sb. or sth.) stay idle; be given an official post without real power: 这几年～, 他在单位很不得意。He has been unhappy these years in an official post of no consequence.

投降 tóuxiáng surrender; capitulate: 缴械～ lay down one's arms and surrender; give oneself up to sb. / 无条件～ unconditional surrender

投降派 tóuxiángpài capitulator; capitulationist

投降书 tóuxiángshū instrument of surrender or capitulation

投降主义 tóuxiángzhǔyì capitulationism

投向 tóuxiàng direction; orientation: 购买力的新～ new orientation of purchasing power on the market

投效 tóuxiào 〈书面〉 offer one's services: ～祖国 serve one's motherland / ～无门 have no chance to render one's service

投药 tóuyào ❶ medicate; prescribe: ～量 dosage ❷ apply poison: ～灭鼠 poison rats

投医 tóuyī seek medical advice; go to a doctor: ～求药 seek medical treatment

投影 tóuyǐng ❶ projection: 极～ polar projection / 墨卡托地图～ Mercator (map) projection ❷ shadow: 灯光将花瓶的～打在窗户上。The light cast the shadow of the vase on the window.

投影电视 tóuyǐng diànshì projection television

投影机 tóuyǐngjī overhead projector

投影几何学 tóuyǐng jǐhéxué 〈数学〉 projective geometry

投影图 tóuyǐngtú 〈机械〉 projection drawing

投映 tóuyìng reflect; mirror: 晚霞～在平静的湖面上。The evening glow is mirrored in the calm lake.

投邮 tóuyóu send by mail; post

投缘 tóuyuán congenial; agreeable: 两人十分～。The two of them hit it off well.

投掷 tóuzhì throw; fling; hurl: ～标枪 throw a javelin / ～项目 throw event / ～硬币 toss a coin / ～炸弹 throw a bomb; drop a bomb

投置 tóuzhì throw into; put into: ～于火热的斗争中 throw oneself into a fiery struggle

投注 tóuzhù throw (energy, etc.) into: 把全副精力～到工作里 devote oneself to one's work

投资 tóuzī ❶ invest; put in (money, etc.): ～百万元 invest one million *yuan* / ～建厂 invest to build a factory; invest in a factory / ～办学 make an investment in education ❷ money or fund invested; investment; input: 国家～ state investment / 需要一笔～ need a capital investment / ～效益 returns on an investment / 收回～ recoup

capital outlay (*or* input) /智力～ intellectual investment; investment in education
投资场所 tóuzī chǎngsuǒ investment outlet; field or venue for investment
投资法 tóuzīfǎ investment law
投资公司 tóuzī gōngsī investment company
投资环境 tóuzī huánjìng investment environment; investment climate
投资基金 tóuzī jījīn investment fund
投资人 tóuzīrén investor
投资市场 tóuzī shìchǎng investment market
投资信托公司 tóuzī xìntuō gōngsī investment trust
投资银行 tóuzī yínháng investment bank
投资政策 tóuzī zhèngcè investment policy
投资组合 tóuzī zǔhé 〈金融〉investment portfolio:～分析 portfolio analysis
投足 tóuzú 〈书面〉how one lifts one's foot; gait:他一举手,一～,都展现出非凡的气度。Every gesture he makes shows his dignified bearing.

骰

tóu dice
骰骨 tóugǔ 〈生理〉cuboid
骰子 tóuzi 〈方言〉dice:掷～ throw the dice /骨质的～ bone dice

tǒu

敨

tǒu 〈方言〉❶ spread out; unfold; open up:～开铺盖卷 unfold the bedding roll ❷ shake off:～一～衣服上的土 shake the dust off the clothes

钭

Tǒu a surname

tòu

透

tòu ❶ penetrate; pass through; seep or leak through:～水 leaky /不～水 waterproof /门缝里～出一线光。Light came in through the crack in the door. /阳光～过树叶照在地上。Sunlight shone through tree leaves and fell upon the ground. /这件事要～过表面看实质。We must see through the appearance to get at the essence of the matter. ❷ tell secretly; leak:～信息 tip sb. off /把底～给他 give him the bottom line /～出一点风声 drop a hint or two /秘密～出去了。The secret leaked out. ❸ thoroughly; in a penetrating way; clearly:一点就～ realize at the slightest hint /把事情说～了 give a thorough explanation of sth. /摸～了某人的脾气 get to know sb. through and through /了解～了 know (sb. or sth.) inside out ❹ to saturation; to the extreme; fully; completely:糟～了 extremely bad /火～了 very angry /恨～了 hate sb.'s guts /麻烦～了 too much trouble; big headache /湿～了 wet through; soaked to the skin /荒唐～了 absolutely ridiculous; absurd to the extreme /这场雨总算下～了。We got a real good soaker this time, thank God. ❺ appear; look; show:他脸上～出惊异的神情。He appeared quite amazed. /这话软里～硬。There is toughness in this seemingly soft remark. /小伙子～着机灵。The boy has a smart look.
透彻 tòuchè penetrating; thoroughgoing; thorough:～的分析 penetrating analysis /对事情了解得很～ understand sth. thoroughly; have sth. at one's fingertips /把自己的观点讲得很～ express oneself very well; drive home one's point
透翅蛾 tòuchì'é 〈动物〉clearwing (moth)
透底 tòudǐ reveal the bottom line; tell the inside story:不小心透了底 unwittingly give away the secret; let the cat out of the bag /向报界～ release inside information to the press
透雕 tòudiāo 〈工美〉fretwork
透顶 tòudǐng 〈贬义〉thoroughly; absolutely; downright; extremely:荒唐～ absolutely ridiculous; absurd in the extreme /腐败～ extremely corrupt; rotten to the core /糊涂～ downright wooly-minded
透风 tòufēng ❶ let in air; aerate; ventilate:打开门窗～。Open the doors and windows to let in fresh air. /这房子夏天～。The house is well ventilated in summer. /房门裂了条缝,有点～。There was a crack in the door and the wind blew through. ❷ air (sth.):把衣服挂起来透透风 hang up the clothes to air ❸ divulge a secret; leak:他事先没有向我～。He did not leak anything to me beforehand. *or* He didn't tell me anything in advance. /这事早透了风。This has long become an open secret.
透骨 tòugǔ ❶ piercing to the bones; biting:冷得～ piercing cold /北风吹来～寒。The north wind chills one to the bone. ❷ penetrating; deep:看得～ see through
透汗 tòuhàn profuse sweat; copious perspiration:出了一身～ be sweated all over; have a good sweat; be dripping with sweat
透河井 tòuhéjǐng well that is connected to a river
透话 tòuhuà hint; tip off; drop or give a hint:他～要买这所房子。He hinted that he was going to buy the house.
透镜 tòujìng 〈物理〉lens:凹～ concave lens /凸～ convex lens /分光～ beam-splitting lens /复合～ compound lens
透光 tòuguāng 〈物理〉transparent:～度 transparence (*or* transparency)
透亮儿 tòuliàngr allow light to pass through:玻璃窗～。Light gets in through the window panes.
透亮 tòuliang ❶ bright; transparent:又宽敞又～的房间 spacious and bright room ❷ clear; obvious:经他一指点,我～多了。Thanks to his explanation, it's much clearer to me now.
透漏 tòulòu divulge; let out; leak; reveal:～机密 let out (*or* betray) a secret /消息～后,报界一片哗然。The leak touched off an uproar in the press. /内部情况不许～。Inside information should be kept secret.
透露 tòulù divulge; leak; disclose; reveal:～风声 leak (*or* disclose) information /～真相 reveal the truth /～计划 divulge the plan /我对他们～过这个计划。I told them something about this plan.
透明 tòumíng transparent:～液体 transparent liquid /半～ translucent /不～ opaque /～丝巾 diaphanous silk scarf /～衣服 see-through dress /～电话机 see-through telephone
透明度 tòumíngdù transparency; diaphaneity:增加～ increase transparency in work
透明计 tòumíngjì diaphanometer
透明接口 tòumíng jiēkǒu transparent interface
透明漆 tòumíngqī celluloid paint; clear lacquer
透明塑料 tòumíng sùliào transparent plastic
透明体 tòumíngtǐ 〈物理〉transparent body
透明纸 tòumíngzhǐ cellophane paper; cellophane
透辟 tòupì penetrating; sharp; incisive; thorough:～的话语 incisive remarks /讲解～ explain penetratingly
透平机 tòupíngjī *also* "涡轮机" wōlúnjī turbine
透气 tòuqì ❶ let air in or through; aerate; ventilate:不～的房间 stuffy room /把被子拿出去透透气 give the bedding an airing /开门～。Open the door and let in some fresh air. ❷ breathe freely:憋得透不过气来 feel suffocated /到室外透透气 take air in the open; go outdoors and breathe in fresh air ❸ tell; inform; tip off:这件事我们要给他透点气儿。We should let him know of the matter.
透气薄膜 tòuqì bómó breathable film
透气性 tòuqìxìng 〈纺织〉(air) permeability
透热疗法 tòurè liáofǎ diathermy
透热性 tòurèxìng 〈物理〉diathermancy; diathermaneity
透闪石 tòushǎnshí 〈地质〉tremolite
透墒 tòushāng (of soil) have sufficient moisture
透射 tòushè ❶ penetrate; pass through:阳光从窗口～进来。Sunlight came in through the window. ❷〈物理〉transmission:定向～ regular transmission
透视 tòushì ❶ perspective:三点～ three-point perspective ❷〈医学〉fluoroscopy; roentgenoscopy; X-ray examination:肺部～ have one's chest X-rayed / ～结果 X-ray result ❸ see clearly:～西方民主的实质 see through the essence (*or* nature) of Western democracy
透视比 tòushìbǐ 〈物理〉transmittance
透视率 tòushìlǜ 〈物理〉transmissivity
透视缩短 tòushì suōduǎn foreshortening
透视图 tòushìtú picture or drawing in perspective; perspective drawing
透熟 tòushú know well; be familiar:这一条水路我～。I'm very familiar with this water route. /他的脾性我摸得～。I know him inside out.
透水层 tòushuǐcéng 〈地质〉pervious bed; permeable stratum
透脱 tòutuō 〈方言〉clever; sharp; bright; intelligent:这个人～,办

T

事也挺利落。This man is very smart and gets things done quite neatly.
透析 tòuxī *also*“渗析”shènxī 〈医学〉dialysis：～疗法 dialysis therapy
透析器 tòuxīqì 〈医学〉dialyser
透析蒸馏 tòuxī zhēngliú 〈化工〉perdistillation
透心儿凉 tòuxīnrliáng ❶ chill through; chill to the marrow：一场秋雨，把我浇了个～。The autumn rain chilled me to the bone. ❷〈比喻〉bitterly disappointed; thoroughly disillusioned：你早晚得～。You'll be totally disillusioned sooner or later.
透信 tòuxìn leak out news; tip off：如果有什么变化，你最好给我透个信儿。You'd better let me know if there is any change.
透穴 tòuxué 〈中医〉penetration puncture
透雨 tòuyǔ saturating or soaking rain; soaker：庄稼需要一场～。The crops need a soaking rain.
透支 tòuzhī ❶ overdraw; make an overdraft：～账户 overdrawn account / 请求银行～ ask the bank to allow an overdraft / 同意～ authorize overdrafts / ～利息 overdraft interest ❷ overspend; have a deficit ❸ draw one's salary in advance：～薪金 anticipate one's pay
透支制 tòuzhīzhì overdraft system

tū

突 tū ❶ dash forward; charge; sprint：狼奔豕～ run like wolves and rush like boars — run about like beasts ❷ all of a sudden; abruptly; unexpected：他的名声～降。His popularity plummeted. ❸ projecting; protruding; sticking out：高高地～起 tower high ❹〈书面〉chimney：灶～ chimney / 曲～徙薪 bend the chimney and remove the firewood (to prevent a possible fire); take precautions against any possible danger
突变 tūbiàn ❶ sudden change：事态～ abrupt change in the situation / 风云～，军阀重开战。Sudden veer of wind and rain, The warlords are clashing anew. ❷〈哲学〉leap：在认识上从渐变到～ from a gradual change to a leap in the process of cognition ❸〈生物〉mutation：隐性～ recessive mutation / 自发～ spontaneous mutation / ～体 mutant / ～子 muton
突出 tūchū ❶ charge out of; break through：～包围圈 break through an encirclement ❷ protruding; projecting; prominent：颧骨～ prominent cheekbones / 悬崖～ projecting cliffs / 下巴～ pointed chin ❸ outstanding; salient; conspicuous：矛盾～ sharp contradiction / 成绩～ outstanding achievements; conspicuous success / ～的特点 salient feature / 表现～ be an outstanding example ❹ give prominence to; stress; emphasize：～难点 stress the difficult points / ～个人 push oneself forward; place oneself in the spotlight / ～主题 bring the main theme into bold relief
突出部 tūchūbù 〈军事〉salient
突发 tūfā erupt; burst out; break out：～事件 unexpected incident / 枪声～。There was a sudden burst of gunfire.
突飞猛进 tūfēi-měngjìn advance by leaps and bounds; forge ahead rapidly; advance with seven-league strides; make giant strides：经济发展～ forge ahead in economic development / 学业～ make remarkable progress in one's studies
突击 tūjī ❶ make a sudden and violent attack; assault：～敌阵 make a sudden and violent attack on the enemy positions ❷ make a concentrated effort to finish a job quickly; make a rush; do a crash job：～完成任务 make a rush on the task / ～修路 do a crash job of constructing a road / ～任务 rush job; shock work / 考试前～复习英语 bone up on English before the examination
突击点 tūjīdiǎn 〈军事〉point of assault
突击队 tūjīduì shock brigade; shock team; ad hoc team formed for performing an urgent task
突击手 tūjīshǒu shock worker
突击战术 tūjī zhànshù shock tactics
突骑 tūqí dashing cavalry：铁甲～ armoured cavalrymen
突进 tūjìn charge; press onward：向敌军左翼～ charge at the enemy's left wing
突厥 Tūjué Tujue or Turk, ethnic nationality in ancient north China：～人 Turk; Turki / ～语 Turki
突尼斯 Tūnísī ❶ Tunisia：～人 Tunisian ❷ Tunis, capital of Tunisia
突破 tūpò ❶ break through; make or effect a breakthrough：～封锁线 break through a blockade ❷ surmount; break; top：～难关 overcome a difficulty; break the back of a tough job / 生物学上的重大～ major breakthrough in biology ❸〈体育〉score a goal after breaking through the opponent's defence
突破地区 tūpò dìqū 〈军事〉area of penetration or breakthrough
突破点 tūpòdiǎn 〈军事〉breakthrough point; point of penetration
突破口 tūpòkǒu 〈军事〉breach; gap
突破上篮 tūpò shànglán 〈体育〉break：快捷～ fast break
突起 tūqǐ ❶ break out; suddenly appear：狂风～。A strong wind sprang up. / 异军～。A new force has suddenly come to the fore. ❷ rise high; tower：峰峦～，巍巍耸立。Ridges and peaks tower into the sky. ❸ protuberance; swelling
突然 tūrán suddenly; abruptly; unexpectedly：～事变 eventuality; contingency / ～转身 turn about abruptly / ～停止 stop (*or* pull up) short / ～痛哭起来 burst into tears / 消息来得～。The news came unexpectedly. / 政策～变了。The policy changed all of a sudden. / 这事对我来说有些～。This is all too sudden for me. / 他～大笑。He broke out laughing.
突然袭击 tūrán-xíjī surprise attack：向敌军发起～ launch a surprise attack on enemy troops
突如其来 tūrúqílái arise suddenly; come all of a sudden：～的事态变化，使大家感到震惊。The sudden change in the situation shocked everybody.
突突 tūtū 〈象声〉：我吓得心～地跳。My heart went pit-a-pat out of fear. / 拖拉机～地驶过。The tractor chugged along.
突围 tūwéi break through an encirclement：组织第二次～ make a second attempt to break through an encirclement / ～脱险 break through a ring of encirclement to safety
突兀 tūwù ❶ lofty; towering：山石～。Rocky peaks thrust themselves towards the sky. ❷ sudden; abrupt; unexpected：事情来得～，令人措手不及。The unexpected event caught everybody unawares.
突袭 tūxí surprise attack：～敌营 launch a surprise attack on an enemy camp
突现 tūxiàn appear suddenly; emerge unexpectedly：美丽的景色～在眼前。A beautiful landscape suddenly came into view.

葖 tū *see*“蓇葖”gūtū

凸 tū protruding; bulging; raised; convex：～花面料 dress material with a raised floral design / 挺胸～肚 throw out one's chest and bulge one's belly / 凹～不平 rough and uneven
凸岸 tū'àn 〈地质〉convex bank
凸版 tūbǎn 〈印刷〉relief printing plate：～胶印机 letterset printing machine / ～轮转机 rotary letterpress machine / ～平台印刷机 cylinder flat bed machine / ～印刷 letterpress; relief (*or* typographic) printing
凸版纸 tūbǎnzhǐ relief printing paper
凸窗 tūchuāng bay window
凸度 tūdù 〈物理〉camber; protuberance
凸极发电机 tūjí fādiànjī salient pole generator
凸轮 tūlún 〈机械〉cam：推动～ actuating cam / 急升～ quick lift cam / ～轴 cam shaft / ～发动机 cam engine
凸面镜 tūmiànjìng 〈物理〉convex mirror
凸透镜 tūtòujìng 〈物理〉convex lens
凸缘 tūyuán 〈机械〉flange：环状～ collar flange / 接头～ joint flange / ～管 flanged tube (*or* pipe) / ～机 flange (*or* flanger) / ～型电动机 flange motor / ～型钢 flanged section

秃 tū ❶ bald; bare：头顶～了 get bald / ～尾巴鸡 bare-tailed chicken / 这人头全～了。The man is as bald as a coot. ❷ barren; bare：荒山～岭 barren hills / ～树 bare trees; defoliated trees ❸ blunt; unpointed：钢笔尖～了。The pen is blunt. *or* The tip of the pen is worn out. ❹ incomplete; deficient; unsatisfactory：这小说煞尾太～。The novel seems a bit lame at the end.
秃笔 tūbǐ bald writing brush; poor writing ability; low skill at composition：用～写不好字。A worn-out pen does not write well. / ～难以胜任。A poor writer (like me) can hardly do the job.
秃疮 tūchuāng 〈方言〉favus of the scalp; tinea favosa
秃顶 tūdǐng ❶ get bald; bald：四十多岁开始～了 start to bald at forty ❷ bald head：～上只有几根头发 a few hairs on the bald head
秃发病 tūfàbìng 〈医学〉alopecia

秃鹫 tūjiù *also*“坐山雕”zuòshāndiāo (cinereous) vulture

秃噜 tūlu 〈方言〉❶ get loose; come undone:你的鞋带～了。Your shoelace is loose. ❷ drop; fall off or away; come off:这张老羊皮的毛儿都～了。The old sheepskin has worn off. ❸ droop; drag; hang down:裙子～地了。The skirt is dragging on the ground. ❹ make an indiscreet remark; make a slip of the tongue:我们要留神，别把话说～了。We should take care not to shoot our mouths off. *or* We must beware of slips of the tongue. ❺ use up; exhaust:把钱花～了 overspend one's money /饭吃～了。The meal is all eaten up.

秃瓢 tūpiáo bald head:他剃了个～儿。He has a shaven head.

秃山 tūshān barren or bare mountain

秃头 tūtóu ❶ bareheaded:他秃着个头出去了。He went outside bareheaded. ❷ baldhead ❸ baldheaded man; baldy

秃子 tūzi ❶ baldhead; baldy ❷〈方言〉favus of the scalp

秃子当和尚——将就材料 tūzi dāng héshang — jiāngjiu cáiliào let a baldhead serve as a monk—use as a make-do:他们让我做这件事，真是“～”。I am not the right person for the job. They have chosen me as a mere fill-in.

秃子头上的虱子——明摆着 tūzi tóushàngde shīzi — míngbǎizhe like a flea on a baldhead — perfectly clear:这中间的原由是～。The reason can't be clearer.

tú

徒[1] tú ❶ on foot: *see*“～步”;“～涉”❷ bare; empty: *see*“～手”❸ merely; just only: ～有其名 in name only /家～四壁 have nothing but the bare walls in one's house; be utterly destitute ❹ in vain; to no avail; futile: ～费精力 waste one's energy; make futile efforts /～自惊扰 frighten oneself without reason; become needlessly alarmed /～劳无益 work in vain ❺ (Tú) a surname

徒[2] tú ❶ apprentice; pupil; disciple:门～ pupil; disciple /学～ apprentice /尊师爱～ respect the teacher and cherish the student ❷ (of a religion) believer; follower:信～ believer; devotee /佛教～ Buddhist /基督教～ Christian ❸〈贬义〉clique member:纳粹党～ member of the Nazi Party ❹〈贬义〉person; fellow:赌～ gambler /歹～ rascal; evildoer; bandit /匪～ bandit /叛～ renegade /囚～ prisoner /亡命～ desperado /好事之～ troublemaker /不法之～ lawbreaker ❺〈书面〉(prison) sentence; imprisonment

徒步 túbù on foot:～而去 go away on foot /～旅行 travel on foot; hike /～行军 (of troops) march

徒弟 túdi apprentice; disciple; pupil

徒费唇舌 túfèi-chúnshé waste one's breath

徒歌 túgē 〈书面〉sing without musical accompaniment

徒工 túgōng apprentice

徒唤奈何 túhuàn-nàihé utter helpless cries; cry to no avail

徒劳 túláo useless or futile effort; fruitless labour:～之举 futile effort /～此行 fruitless journey

徒劳往返 túláo-wǎngfǎn hurry back and forth for nothing; make a trip in vain:几次～，毫无收获。It was a fruitless trip with no gain at all.

徒劳无功 túláo-wúgōng *also*“徒劳无益”make a futile effort; work to no avail:联系了几次，都是～，白费力气。The attempted contacts all ended in failure. What a waste of energy!

徒乱人意 túluàn-rényì can only bring confusion and worry to people

徒然 túrán ❶ futile; in vain; for nothing; to no avail:～耗费时间 waste one's time /～表白了半天，她一句也听不进去。All the explanations fell on deaf ears, and she simply wouldn't listen. ❷ only; merely; simply:如果这样做，～有利于敌方。Such a move can only help the enemy.

徒涉 túshè 〈书面〉wade through; ford:～江河 wade through rivers

徒手 túshǒu bare-handed; unarmed:～搏斗 fight bare-handed (*or* with bare hands)

徒手操 túshǒucāo free-standing exercises

徒属 túshǔ followers; adherents:招集～ call one's adherents together

徒孙 túsūn disciple's disciple; pupil's pupil

徒托空言 tútuō-kōngyán make empty promises; pay lip service:但愿你不是～，应付我们。Hopefully you are not making empty promises to fool us.

徒跣 túxiǎn 〈书面〉walk barefoot:免冠～ remove one's hat and shoes

徒刑 túxíng 〈法律〉imprisonment; (prison) sentence:有期～ specified (prison) sentence /无期～ life imprisonment (*or* sentence) /判处五年～，缓期两年执行 give a five years prison sentence suspended for two years

徒有虚名 túyǒu-xūmíng *also*“徒有其名”have an undeserved reputation:说是合资企业，其实～。The enterprise is a joint-venture only in name. /他这人～，并无实学。He is not much of a scholar and simply has an unearned reputation.

徒长 túzhǎng 〈农业〉excessive growth (of branches and leaves); spindling

徒子徒孙 túzǐ-túsūn 〈贬义〉disciples, adherents and followers; hangers-on and their spawn:他手下有一帮～听命于他。He has a gang of followers at his beck and call.

瘏 tú 〈书面〉illness; disease

屠 tú ❶ slaughter (animals for food):～牛宰羊 butcher cows and sheep ❷ massacre; butcher: *see*“～城”;“～戮”❸ (Tú) a surname

屠伯 túbó butcher; ruthless ruler

屠场 túchǎng slaughterhouse

屠城 túchéng massacre the inhabitants of a captured city

屠刀 túdāo butcher's knife:放下～，立地成佛 lay down the cleaver and become a Buddha; attain salvation as soon as one stops doing evil

屠夫 túfū butcher; ruthless despot or ruler:他为人凶残，被人称作“～”。He is nicknamed “butcher” for his ruthless cruelty.

屠格涅夫 Túgénièfū Ivan Sergievich Turgenev (1818-1883), Russian writer

屠户 túhù butcher

屠龙 túlóng skill of killing the dragon — impractical skill:～之技 superb, but impractical skill

屠戮 túlù 〈书面〉slaughter; massacre; kill indiscriminately:～无辜 massacre the innocent

屠门大嚼 túmén-dàjué *also*“过屠门而大嚼”guò túmén ér dàjué start munching when passing the butcher's — feed on illusions

屠杀 túshā massacre; butcher; slaughter; kill indiscriminately:敌兵～了所有的俘虏。The enemy soldiers massacred all the prisoners of war.

屠苏 túsū ❶ a kind of plant ❷ a kind of wine formerly drunk on Chinese New Year's Day ❸ house; thatched cottage

屠宰 túzǎi butcher; slaughter:～牲畜 slaughter animals; butcher fat stock

屠宰场 túzǎichǎng slaughterhouse; butchery; abattoir

屠宰率 túzǎilǜ dressing percentage

屠宰税 túzǎishuì tax on slaughtering animals

菟 tú *see*“於菟”wūtú

see also tù

图(圖) tú ❶ picture; drawing; diagram; chart:绘～ draw a picture /地～ map /挂～ hanging chart /看～识字 learn to read through pictures /制～ make a drawing (*or* chart) /描～ trace designs /构～ composition of a picture /地形～ topographic map /天气～ weather map; synoptic chart /示意～ sketch-map /草～ (rough) sketch; draft /蓝～ blueprint /插～ illustration; plate ❷ scheme; plan; seek; pursue:弃旧～新 discard the old and strive for the new ❸ covet; desire; be after:只～一时痛快 be after momentary satisfaction (*or* gratification) / 唯利是～ be intent on nothing but profit; make profit above all else /只～苟安，不求进取 be content with momentary comfort without any thought of further progress ❹ intention; intent:良～ good intention /宏～大略 great plan and broad strategy /另有他～ have different plans ❺〈书面〉draw; paint:绘影～形 draw sb.'s picture

图案 tú'àn pattern; design:几何～ geometrical pattern /～设计 pattern design /花卉～ floral designs /～玻璃 figured plate (*or* sheet) glass /装饰～ decorative pattern; ornamental design

图案操 tú'àncāo 〈体育〉callisthenic performance forming patterns

T

图板 túbǎn drawing board
图版 túbǎn 〈印刷〉plate (for printing photos, maps, illustrations, etc.)
图版纸 túbǎnzhǐ enamelled paper
图报 túbào try to repay sb.'s kindness; try to requite sb. for his kindness: 感恩～ be grateful for sb.'s kindness and try to repay it
图表 túbiǎo chart; diagram; graph: 统计～ statistical chart (*or* table) / 示意～ illustrative chart / 绘制～ draw a chart / 附有～说明 with illustrative diagrams
图波列夫 Túbōlièfū Andrey Nikolayevich Tupolev (1888-1972), father of Russian aviation: 图 24 飞机 Tu-24 plane
图财害命 túcái-hàimìng *also* "谋财害命" móucái-hàimìng murder for money
图谶 túchèn book of prophecy or omen: ～之说, 不足为信。Books of prophecy are not worth believing.
图存 túcún seek one's survival: 救亡～ save the nation from subjugation and ensure its survival; national salvation
图钉 túdīng drawing pin; thumbtack
图画 túhuà drawing; picture; painting: 画～ draw a picture
图画文字 túhuà wénzì 〈语言〉picture writing; pictographic script
图画纸 túhuàzhǐ drawing paper
图籍 tújí 〈书面〉map of territory and register of population
图记 tújì ❶ seal; stamp: 古画上印有收藏者的～。The old painting bears the seal of its collector. ❷ mark; sign; symbol
图件 tújiàn general name for maps, atlas, blueprints, design drawings, etc.
图鉴 tújiàn illustrated or pictorial handbook: 《哺乳动物～》*Pictorial Handbook of Mammals*
图解 tújiě ❶ diagram; graph; figure: 彩色～ coloured diagrams / 附有～ with illustrations ❷ 〈数学〉graphic solution: ～法 graphic method
图景 tújǐng ❶ scene in a picture or painting: 画中的～似曾相识。The scene in the painting looks familiar. ❷ view; prospect: 田园生活的～ idyllic (*or* pastoral) scenery
图卷 tújuàn picture scroll: 历史～panorama of history / 为歌颂红军的伟大历史功绩, 画家集体创作了长征～。The painters jointly created the Long March scroll in praise of the Red Army's historic achievements.
图赖 túlài ❶ try to repudiate (debts) ❷ blackmail; falsely incriminate: ～好人 incriminate innocent people
图利 túlì seek personal gains; try to make a profit; profiteer
图例 túlì legend (of a map, etc.); key
图录 túlù ❶ album that contains pictures of antiques ❷ *also* "图箓" 〈书面〉book of prophecy
图论 túlùn 〈数学〉graph theory
图谋 túmóu ❶ plot; scheme; conspire: ～反叛 conspire to rebel ❷ stratagem; trap: 另有～ have other plans / 中了他的～ fall into his trap
图谋不轨 túmóu-bùguǐ hatch a sinister plot; engage in underhand activities
图囊 túnáng chart sack; bag for atlas: 军用～ military bag
图片 túpiàn picture; photograph: ～说明 caption / ～展览 photo (*or* picture) exhibition / ～社 picture service
图谱 túpǔ collection of illustrative plates; atlas: 动物～ faunal atlas / 植物～ floral atlas / 历史～ historical atlas
图穷匕首见 tú qióng bǐshǒu xiàn *also* "图穷匕见" when the map is unrolled, the dagger is revealed — the real intention is revealed in the end
图示 túshì graph; graphic expression; graphics; graphic representation: ～比例尺 graphic scale / ～符号 graphic character; graphical symbol / ～器 graphic instrument / ～终端〈计算机〉graphic terminal
图书 túshū books: 中文～ books in Chinese / 外文～ foreign language books / 社科～ books on social sciences / 科技～ science books / ～资料 books and reference materials / ～目录 catalogue of books; library catalogue / ～管理员 librarian / ～阅览室 reading room
图书 túshu seal; stamp
图书馆 túshūguǎn library: 国家～ national library / 公共～ public library / 专业～ special library / 学校～ school library / ～网 library network / ～书目数据库 library database
图书馆学 túshūguǎnxué library science
图书学 túshūxué bibliology
图说 túshuō illustrated manual; pictorial handbook: 《天体～》*Illustrated Handbook of Celestial Bodies*
图腾 túténg totem
图腾崇拜 túténg chóngbài totem worship; totemism
图腾柱 túténgzhù totem pole
图瓦卢 Túwǎlú Tuvalu, island state in the southwest Pacific
图文并茂 túwén-bìngmào (of publications) excellent in both pictures and language
图文传真 túwén chuánzhēn fax; facsimile transmission
图希 túxī 〈方言〉seek; want; try; attempt: ～得到好处 seek personal gains / 赶脚的～个脚钱。What the cart-driver wants is a service fee.
图像 túxiàng picture; image: ～清 clear image / 立体～〈电子〉stereopicture / ～识别 pattern recognition / ～分类 image classification / ～注记 image annotation / ～压缩 image compression / ～增强 image enhancement / ～处理 image processing / ～修复 image restoration / ～分段 image segmentation / ～改造 image transformation
图像传输 túxiàng chuánshū image transmission
图形 túxíng ❶ graph; figure: 绘制～ draw a graph / 显示～ display a figure ❷ (short for 几何图形) geometric figure
图形识别 túxíng shíbié 〈自控〉pattern recognition
图形用户界面 túxíng yònghù jièmiàn 〈信息〉graphical user interface (GUI)
图样 túyàng pattern; design; draft; drawing: 机器～ draft for a machine / 加工～ processing draft / 建筑～ architectural blueprint
图章 túzhāng seal; stamp: 刻制～ engrave a seal / 盖上～ affix one's seal (to sth.); seal; stamp / 塑料～ plastic stamp / 玉石～ jade seal
图纸 túzhǐ blueprint; drawing: 施工～ working drawing / 工程～ blueprint for a project
图志 túzhì illustrated records, annals or gazeteers: 《郡县～》*Illustrated Annals of the Prefectures and Counties*

涂[1](塗)

tú ❶ spread; apply; smear: ～漆 apply a coat of paint; paint / ～色 apply (*or* spread) colour / 在面包上～果酱 spread some jam on the bread ❷ scribble; daub; scrawl: 在墙上乱～乱画 scribble (*or* scrawl) on the wall; deface the wall with graffiti ❸ blot out; cross out; erase: ～掉错字 cross out wrong words / ～去一行 delete a line

涂[2](塗)

tú ❶ 〈书面〉mud; slush: *see* "～炭" ❷ sea shoal; shallows: 围～造田 reclaim land from the sea ❸ way; road; route: 道听～说 hearsay; rumour; gossip

涂[3](涂)

Tú a surname

涂层 túcéng coat; coating: 减磨～ friction coat / 反雷达～ antiradar coating / ～材料 coating; enamel / ～磁带 coated magnetic tape
涂改 túgǎi alter; modify; change: ～原文 tamper with the original text / 随意～ change at random / ～液 correction fluid
涂画 túhuà smear over; daub; paint in a slipshod manner: 我当年～的几张花卉他至今还保留着。He still keeps the pictures of flowers I daubed years ago.
涂绘 túhuì ❶ paint: 油纸伞上～着色彩鲜艳的图案。Colourful patterns are painted on the oilpaper umbrella. ❷ smear over; daub; paint in a slipshod manner
涂料 túliào coating; paint: 防腐～ anticorrosive paint / 耐火～ refractory coating / 透气～ paint that can breathe
涂抹 túmǒ ❶ daub; smear; paint: ～油漆 daub paint / 栅栏～了绿漆。The fence is painted green. ❷ scribble; scrawl: 信手～ doodle / 胡乱～ scribble aimlessly
涂片 túpiàn 〈医学〉smear: 血～ blood smear
涂漆 túqī paint coating; painting
涂饰 túshì ❶ cover with paint, lacquer, colour wash, etc.: ～七彩之色 cover with seven colours ❷ daub (plaster, etc.) on a wall; whitewash: ～墙壁 whitewash a wall
涂刷 túshuā daub with a brush; brush: 给家具～清漆 varnish the furniture
涂说 túshuō *also* "道听途说" dàotīng-túshuō hearsay; gossip
涂炭 tútàn 〈书面〉❶ mud and ashes — utter misery; severe suffering: 生灵～。The people are plunged into misery and suffering. ❷ make (people) suffer: ～百姓 wreak havoc among the people
涂写 túxiě scribble; scrawl: ～污染 graffiti pollution / 不要在墙上

～标语。Don't scribble slogans on the wall.
涂鸦 túyā 〈谦词〉poor handwriting; scrawl; graffiti; chicken tracks:～之作 my poor handwriting
涂乙 túyǐ 〈书面〉prune (an essay, etc.); delete and alter:多有～,敬请斧正。I have made quite a few revisions in the article, and hope to receive your generous correction.
涂泽 túzé 〈书面〉gloss over; cover up; whitewash; embellish (oneself); apply cosmetics
涂脂抹粉 túzhī-mǒfěn apply powder and paint; prettify; whitewash; embellish

途 tú way; road; route; path:旅～ journey /长～ long distance /沿～ along the way (*or* road) /～中 on the way; en route /中～而废 give up halfway /路～遥远 long way to go /长～跋涉 long trek
途程 túchéng road; way; course:人生的～ course of life /人类进化的～ evolution of mankind
途次 túcì 〈书面〉stopover; traveller's lodging:～不胜寂寞 feel terribly lonely while staying in a tavern
途经 tújīng by way of; via:～北京去东北 go to the Northeast by way of Beijing /去山村的路上～一条大河。There is a big river on the way to the mountain village.
途径 tújìng way; path; channel; avenue: 外交～ diplomatic channels /通过私人～ through personal connections /寻找解决问题的～ seek a solution to the problem /探索一条新～ explore a new path (*or* avenue) /通过各种～开展文化交流 carry out cultural exchanges by various means
途路 túlù 〈书面〉road; path; way; journey
途人 túrén 〈书面〉passer-by; stranger

荼 tú 〈古语〉❶ bitter edible plant ❷ white flower of reeds, etc.:如火如～ like a raging fire
荼毒 túdú 〈书面〉afflict with great suffering; torment:～百姓 plunge the people into the abyss of misery; wreak great havoc among the people
荼毒生灵 túdú-shēnglíng plunge the people into the depth of suffering
荼蘼 túmí *also* "酴醾" túmí 〈植物〉roseleaf raspberry (*Rubus rosaefolius* var. *Coronarius*)
荼毗 túpí 〈佛教〉cremation of a deceased monk

酴 tú 〈书面〉yeast (for making wine)
酴醾 túmí ❶ double-fermented wine ❷ *see* "荼蘼" túmí

腯 tú 〈书面〉fat
腯肥 túféi pig offered at sacrificial rites

圕 túshūguǎn library (written as a single character, but pronounced as three syllables, used only in writing or signboards)

tǔ

土 tǔ ❶ soil; earth; dust:表～ topsoil /黑～ black soil; black earth /红～ red soil /沃～ fertile (*or* rich) soil /瘠～ lean (*or* poor) soil /黄～ loess /黏～ clay /壤～ loam /碱性～ alkaline soil /冲积～ alluvial land /盐渍～ saline soil /中性～ neutral soil /腐殖～ humus /他的大衣上满是～。His overcoat is covered with dust. ❷ land; ground; territory:国～ country's territory;land /领～ territory; domain /疆～ territory ❸ local; native; indigenous: *see* "～产";"～人";"～著" ❹ home-made; local; indigenous:～办法 indigenous methods /～设备 crude, home-made equipment /～方子 handed-down recipe; home remedy ❺ unrefined; unenlightened; crude; rustic:衣服样子～ rustic dress /他长得真～。He looks like a country bumpkin. /她说话太～。She speaks in crude language. ❻ (raw) opium:烟～ opium ❼(Tǔ) a surname
土坝 tǔbà 〈水利〉earth-filled dam; earth dam
土白 tǔbái 〈方言〉local, colloquial expression; local dialect
土邦 tǔbāng native state:在英国统治下的印度曾有过五百六十二个半独立的～。There were 562 semi-independent states in India under British rule.
土包 tǔbāo ❶ mound; hillock ❷〈方言〉*see* "土包子"
土包子 tǔbāozi 〈贬义〉clodhopper; (country) bumpkin; coarse person; crude guy
土豹 tǔbào *also* "鵟" kuáng 〈动物〉buzzard
土崩瓦解 tǔbēng-wǎjiě disintegrate; crumble; fall to pieces; collapse like a house of cards:顷刻之间～ collapse instantly /内讧导致这个联盟的～。Internal strife led to the disintegration of the alliance.
土鳖 tǔbiē 〈动物〉ground beetle
土拨鼠 tǔbōshǔ 〈动物〉marmot
土布 tǔbù handwoven or handloomed cloth; homespun cloth
土蚕 tǔcán 〈方言〉❶ larva of a noctuid ❷ grub
土产 tǔchǎn ❶ be produced locally:本地～的西瓜不怎么甜。Watermelons produced in the locality are not very sweet. ❷ local or native product:各地的～ local products of various areas /～门市部 local produce store / 经销～distribute local products /蜡染布是云南的～。Wax-printed cloth is a special product of Yunnan Province.
土场 tǔchǎng 〈方言〉dirt ground (in front of a farmer's house)
土地 tǔdì ❶ land; soil:～贫瘠 poor land /肥沃的～ fertile land; good soil /～使用权 land-use right /～资源 land resources /～租赁 land leasing /～集中 concentration of landholding /耕耘～ till the land /市政建设征用～ expropriate land for municipal works ❷ territory; area:～辽阔 vast territory
土地 tǔdi *also* "土地爷";"土地老" local god of the land; village god:一方～一方神。Every place has its own god.
土地报酬递减率 tǔdì bàochou dìjiǎnlǜ law of diminishing returns on land
土地法 tǔdìfǎ land law; agrarian law
土地分红 tǔdì fēnhóng dividend on land shares
土地改革 tǔdì gǎigé land reform; agrarian reform
土地革命战争 Tǔdì Gémìng Zhànzhēng Agrarian Revolutionary War (1927-1937)
see also "第二次国内革命战争" Dì-èr Cì Guónèi Gémìng Zhànzhēng
土地管理署 Tǔdì Guǎnlǐshǔ (HK) Land Authority
土地税 tǔdìshuì land tax
土地证 tǔdìzhèng land certificate; land deed
土地制度 tǔdì zhìdù land system
土地庙 tǔdimiào tiny temple housing the village god
土电影 tǔdiànyǐng 〈方言〉slide show
土豆 tǔdòu potato:炸～片 crisps;(US) chips /炸～条 chips;(US) French fries
土遁 tǔdùn (of certain spirits in myths) disappear into the earth; run away and become invisible
土耳其 Tǔ'ěrqí Turkey:～人 Turk / ～语 Turkish (language)
土耳其浴 tǔ'ěrqíyù Turkish bath
土垡 tǔfá 〈方言〉soil block; clod
土法 tǔfǎ indigenous method; local method; traditional method:～加工 process with indigenous methods /～治病 treat an illness with a folk recipe /～上马 get on the job with local methods
土方 tǔfāng ❶ cubic metre of earth ❷ earthwork:～工程 earthwork ❸〈中医〉folk recipe; home remedy:收集～儿 collect (*or* seek) folk prescriptions / ～儿能治大病。Folk recipes may work wonders for some serious illnesses.
土房 tǔfáng *also* "土房子" adobe house
土肥 tǔféi farmyard manure
土匪 tǔfěi bandit; brigand
土粉子 tǔfěnzi 〈方言〉chalk
土粪 tǔfèn muck; dung; compost
土风 tǔfēng ❶ local ballad ❷ local custom
土风舞 tǔfēngwǔ (old name for 民间舞) folk dance
土蜂 tǔfēng 〈动物〉scoliid (*Scoliidae*)
土改 tǔgǎi (short for 土地改革) land reform; agrarian reform
土岗 tǔgǎng *also* "土岗子" hillock; mound
土疙瘩 tǔgēda *also* "土圪垯"〈方言〉lump of earth; clod
土埂 tǔgěng *also* "土埂子" low bank of earth between fields; earth ridge
土工建筑物 tǔgōng jiànzhùwù 〈建筑〉earth structure
土工学 tǔgōngxué 〈建筑〉geotechnics
土狗子 tǔgǒuzi 〈方言〉mole cricket
土圭 tǔguī ancient Chinese sundial for telling solar terms
土棍 tǔgùn village bully; ruffian; scoundrel:流氓～ hooligan; gangster
土豪 tǔháo local tyrant or despot:打～,分田地 fight the local

T

despots and redistribute the land
土豪劣绅 tǔháo-lièshēn local tyrants and evil gentry; despotic landlords
土猴 tǔhóu 〈方言〉a kind of insect injurious to peanuts
土话 tǔhuà also "土语" local dialect
土皇帝 tǔhuángdì local despot; local tyrant:横行乡里的～ local tyrant who rides roughshod over people of the locality
土黄 tǔhuáng colour of loess; yellowish brown; sallow:～色的墙壁 yellowish brown walls /她脸色～,身体瘦弱。She looks sallow and thin.
土蝗 tǔhuáng a kind of locust
土混混 tǔhùnhun 〈方言〉local bully; ruffian; scoundrel:～出身 begin life as a local bully
土货 tǔhuò local product; native produce:从乡下带回来几样～ bring from the country a few local products
土箕 tǔjī dustpan
土墼 tǔjī 〈方言〉sun-dried mud brick; adobe
土籍 tǔjí place where a family has lived for generations:居民～ residents whose families have lived in the same area for generations
土家语 Tǔjiāyǔ Tujia language
土家族 Tǔjiāzú Tujia or Tuchia nationality (distributed over Hunan and Hubei provinces)
土建 tǔjiàn civil engineering:～工程 civil engineering project
土阶茅屋 tǔjiē-máowū earth steps and thatched cottage; simple and crude house:昔日～,今日高堂大厦。Where there used to be thatched cottages, high-rise buildings now stand.
土芥 tǔjiè 〈书面〉dirt and grass; trifle:视如～ regard as mere dirt
土坎 tǔkǎn also "土坎子" earth bank or ridge:在～上挖一个洞 dig a hole in the earth ridge
土炕 tǔkàng heatable adobe sleeping platform; adobe *kang*:躺在～上暖暖和和的 feel quite warm lying on the adobe *kang*
土库曼斯坦 Tǔkùmànsītǎn Turkmenistan:～人 Turkman
土狼 tǔláng aardwolf (*Proleles dristatus*)
土牢 tǔláo dungeon:囚身于～之中 be held in a dungeon /打入～ be thrown into a dungeon
土老财 tǔlǎocái country moneybags
土老儿 tǔlǎor 〈旧语〉country bumpkin; rustic
土老冒儿 tǔlǎomàor 〈贬义〉see "土包子"
土垒 tǔlěi earth rampart
土礼 tǔlǐ gift of native products
土沥青 tǔlìqīng natural asphalt; natural bitumen
土粒 tǔlì 〈农业〉soil grain; soil particle
土里土气 tǔlitǔqì rustic; uncouth; coarse; cloddish:他嫌我浑身～。He cold-shouldered me, because I appeared cloddish to him.
土鲮鱼 tǔlíngyú also "鲮" líng dace
土龙 tǔlóng 〈方言〉earthworm
土路 tǔlù dirt road
土埋半截 tǔmái-bànjié have one foot in the grave: ～的年龄 very old
土馒头 tǔmántou grave; tomb
土霉素 tǔméisù 〈药学〉terramycin; oxytetracycline
土名 tǔmíng popular name; local name
土模 tǔmú clay mould
土木 tǔmù building; construction:大兴～ go in for large-scale building (*or* construction)
土木工程 tǔmù gōngchéng civil engineering:他在大学是学～的。He majored in civil engineering in the university.
土木形骸 tǔmù-xínghái natural appearance:～,天资自然 be in an unadorned natural state
土牛 tǔniú mound; pile of earth (on a dyke, prepared against possible breaches)
土牛木马 tǔniú-mùmǎ earthen ox and wooden horse—shape without soul; useless person or thing
土偶 tǔ'ǒu clay idol
土坯 tǔpī sun-dried mud brick; adobe
土平 tǔpíng 〈方言〉level; destroy:敌人把村子打了个～。The enemies razed the village to the ground.
土坪 tǔpíng 〈方言〉level ground; flat ground
土坡 tǔpō slope
土气 tǔqi ❶ rustic style; uncouth bearing; cloddish manner:他可没一点农村孩子的～。He has none of the uncouthness of a country boy. ❷ rustic; uncouth; countrified:穿着～ be dressed like a bumpkin /家具式样～,质地却很好。The furniture looks rustic in design but has excellent quality.
土墙 tǔqiáng earthen wall; cob wall
土丘 tǔqiū hillock; mound
土壤 tǔrǎng soil:耕作～ cultivated soil /原始～ initial soil /肥沃的～ fertile soil /～改良 soil improvement; soil amelioration /～湿度 soil moisture /～通气性 soil aeration /～污染 soil pollution /～质地 soil texture /～渗透性 soil permeability /～肥力 soil fertility /孕育战争的罪恶～ vile soil for (*or* hotbed of) wars
土壤保持 tǔrǎng bǎochí soil conservation
土壤化学 tǔrǎng huàxué soil chemistry
土壤力学 tǔrǎng lìxué 〈建筑〉soil mechanics
土壤生态学 tǔrǎng shēngtàixué edaphology
土壤学 tǔrǎngxué soil science; pedology
土人 tǔrén native; aborigine
土色 tǔsè ashen; pale:面如～ turn deadly pale
土生土长 tǔshēng-tǔzhǎng locally born and bred; born and brought up on one's native soil:～的作家 native writer
土石方 tǔshífāng cubic metre of earth and stone:～量 earth and stone work
土司 tǔsī ❶ system of appointing national minority hereditary headmen in the Yuan, Ming and Qing dynasties ❷ such a headman; chieftain
土丝 tǔsī raw silk reeled with local methods; home-reeled silk
土俗 tǔsú ❶ local custom:按当地的～安葬 bury sb. according to the local custom ❷ vulgar; coarse:～的语言 vulgar language /～不堪 coarse and unrefined
土特产 tǔtèchǎn local speciality; local specialty
土头土脑 tǔtóu-tǔnǎo cloddish; unsophisticated:真是个～的人! What a hillbilly!
土头 tǔtou 〈方言〉soil quality:～薄 poor (*or* sterile) soil /～壮 rich (*or* productive) soil
土豚 tǔtún 〈动物〉aardvark; African ant bear (*Orycteropus afer*)
土围子 tǔwéizi fortified village
土卫 Tǔwèi 〈天文〉satellite of Saturn; Saturnian satellite:(all the following are in order of closeness to Saturn except for Janus, which is the closest but was discovered last) ～一 Mimas /～二 Enceladus /～三 Tethys /～四 Dione /～五 Rhea /～六 Titan /～七 Hyperion /～八 Iapetus /～九 Phoebe /～十 Janus
土温 tǔwēn 〈农业〉soil temperature
土物 tǔwù local or native product:收购～ purchase local products
土戏 tǔxì ❶ traditional opera of the Tujia nationality ❷ a kind of opera of the Zhuang nationality
土星 Tǔxīng also "镇星" Zhènxīng 〈天文〉Saturn:～光环 Saturn's rings /～工作舱 Saturn workshop
土腥气 tǔxīngqì also "土腥味儿" smell of the earth:菠菜没洗干净,尝起来有一股～。The spinach was not washed clean, leaving an earthern taste in the mouth.
土性 tǔxìng soil's property (of providing plants with nutrients and moisture)
土燕 tǔyàn also "燕鸻" yànhéng swallow plover; pratincole
土洋并举 tǔ-yáng bìngjǔ use both indigenous and foreign methods; use both traditional and modern methods
土洋结合 tǔ-yáng jiéhé combine indigenous and foreign methods; combine traditional and modern methods
土仪 tǔyí 〈书面〉gift of native product:～微薄,不成敬意。Please accept the meagre gifts of our native produce.
土宜 tǔyí 〈书面〉❶ suitability of soil (to various crops, etc.) ❷ local or native product
土音 tǔyīn local accent:一口～ speak with a strong local accent /～难改 hard to change one's accent
土语 tǔyǔ local or colloquial expression; local dialect:满口～ speak in one's dialect
土元 tǔyuán 〈方言〉〈中医〉ground beetle (*Eupolyphage sinensis*)
土葬 tǔzàng burial (of the dead) in the ground; burial
土造 tǔzào produce or make with indigenous methods:～手榴弹 home-made grenade
土政策 tǔzhèngcè local policies (often opposed to those laid down by the central authorities)
土纸 tǔzhǐ hand-made paper
土质 tǔzhì soil texture; soil property:～肥沃 fertile soil
土冢 tǔzhǒng grave mound:～之上杂草丛生。The grave mound is

overgrown with weeds.
土著 tǔzhù original inhabitant; aboriginal; aborigine:印地安人是美洲的～。The "Indians" were the original inhabitants of the American continents.
土专家 tǔzhuānjiā self-taught expert; local expert
土族 Tǔzú Tu nationality (living mainly in Qinghai Province)

吐 tǔ ❶ spit:～鱼刺 spit out a fishbone /狗嘴里～不出象牙。A dog's mouth emits no ivory. *or* A filthy mouth can't utter decent language. ❷ emit; send out; put forth:春蚕～丝。Spring silkworms spin silk. /机枪～着火舌。The machine gun was spitting fire. /这口气不～不快。I must find a way to vent my anger on this matter. *or* I will not bottle this up. ❸ say; tell; pour out:～字清楚 enunciate clearly /谈～ style of conversation /～真情 unbosom oneself; tell the truth
see also tù
吐哺 tǔbǔ stop in the middle of eating — be eager to welcome a guest:～握发 stop in the middle of eating or washing one's hair — be eager to meet and recruit talented people
吐翠 tǔcuì 〈书面〉look fresh and green:杨柳～。The willow trees are all in green.
吐胆倾心 tǔdǎn-qīngxīn speak one's mind; open one's heart; pour out one's true feelings:～之言 words from the bottom of one's heart /面对知己,怎能不～? How can I withhold anything from my bosom friend?
吐蕃 Tǔfān Tibetan regime in ancient China
吐凤 tǔfèng *also* "吞凤" tūnfèng be good at writing:～之才 gifted writer
吐刚茹柔 tǔgāng-rúróu dread the strong and bully the weak
吐根 tǔgēn 〈植物〉ipecac (*Cephaelis Ipecacuanha*):～碱〈药学〉emetine /～酸〈药学〉ipecacuanhic acid
吐根素 tǔgēnsù 〈药学〉emetine
吐故纳新 tǔgù-nàxīn get rid of the stale and take in the fresh; exhale the old and inhale the new:人的思想要不断～。One should always discard outmoded views and embrace new ideas. /我们的组织要～。We should absorb new blood into our organization while retiring old members.
吐话 tǔhuà utter words — permit:头头儿～了,让我们去办这件事。The boss has given us the green light to do the work.
吐决 tǔjué 〈书面〉make policy or a strategic decision:临危～ make a strategic decision in time of danger
吐口 tǔkǒu ❶ tell; reveal:死活不～ doggedly refuse to tell the truth ❷ say in approval
吐苦水 tǔ kǔshuǐ pour out one's bitterness:向知心朋友～ pour out grievances to one's close friend /他有一肚子苦水没处吐。He is full of complaints but has nowhere to turn to.
吐鲁番盆地 Tǔlǔfān Péndì Turpan Depression (in the Xinjiang Uygur Autonomous Region)
吐露 tǔlù reveal; tell:～心扉 unbosom oneself; pour out one's heart
吐露真情 tǔlù-zhēnqíng unbosom oneself; tell the truth
吐气 tǔqì ❶ feel elated after unburdening oneself of resentment; feel elated and exultant:终会有～伸冤的一天。The day will surely come when the injustice is redressed. ❷〈语言〉aspirated:～音 aspirated sound
吐气扬眉 tǔqì-yángméi *also* "扬眉吐气" feel elated and exultant; be proud and happy
吐弃 tǔqì spurn; discard; cast aside; reject:万人～ spurned by the people
吐绶鸡 tǔshòujī *also* "火鸡" huǒjī turkey
吐属 tǔshǔ 〈书面〉style and manner of conversation:～脱俗 refined manner of conversation
吐丝草 tǔsīcǎo *Lygodium japonicum*
吐诉 tǔsù tell; pour out one's heart, etc.:～苦衷 pour out one's troubles /我向他～了学医的决心。I told him my determination to study medicine.
吐穗 tǔsuì 〈农业〉earing (up); heading (of cereal plants)
吐痰 tǔtán spit; expectorate:请勿随地～。No spitting.
吐絮 tǔxù 〈农业〉opening of bolls; boll opening:棉花～ cotton plants opening bolls /杨柳～。The willow trees are developing catkins.
吐艳 tǔyàn 〈书面〉take on brilliant colours; be riotous with colour:寒梅～。The winter plum trees are in full blossom. /朝阳～。The morning sun shines in a riot of colour.
吐谷浑 Tǔyùhún national minority in ancient China, living in present Gansu and Qinghai provinces
吐字 tǔzì pronounce; articulate:～清楚 clear articulation

钍 tǔ thorium (Th)
钍石 tǔshí thorite

tù

吐 tù ❶ vomit; retch; throw up:呕～ vomit; throw up /又～又泻 vomit and have loose bowels /恶心想～ feel sick; retch; feel like vomiting (*or* throwing up) ❷ give up unwillingly; disgorge:～退赃款 return stolen money
see also tǔ
吐法 tùfǎ 〈中医〉emetic measures — inducing vomit
吐酒石 tùjiǔshí 〈药学〉tartar emetic
吐沫 tùmo saliva; spittle; spit:～乱飞 emit saliva in all directions /满口～ foaming with saliva
吐血 tùxiě spitting blood; haematemesis
吐泻 tù-xiè vomiting and diarrhoea
吐赃 tùzāng disgorge ill-gotten gain

兔（兎） tù hare; rabbit:家～ rabbit /野～ hare /小白～ bunny /玉～ Jade Hare — moon
兔唇 tùchún 〈医学〉harelip; cleft lip:这孩子长了～。The child is harelipped.
兔毫 tùháo writing brush made of rabbit's hair
兔灰 tùhuī 〈方言〉colour of grey rabbit; pale grey:～色的毛衣 sweater of pale grey
兔起鹘落 tùqǐ-húluò the moment a hare is flushed out, the falcon swoops down — be agile; have a ready pen
兔儿爷 tùryé ❶ clay toy rabbit for the Mid-Autumn Festival ❷ pederast
兔死狗烹 tùsǐ-gǒupēng the hounds are killed for food once all the hares are bagged — trusted aides are eliminated when they have outlived their usefulness
兔死狐悲 tùsǐ-húbēi the fox mourns the death of the hare — like grieves for like:～,物伤其类。Just as the fox saddens at the death of the hare, one feels for one's own kind.
兔狲 tùsūn 〈动物〉steppe cat (*Felis manul*)
兔脱 tùtuō 〈书面〉run away like a hare; escape by a fluke; flee:敌人侥幸～。The enemy made a narrow escape.
兔眼 tùyǎn 〈医学〉lagophthalmus; lagophthalmos; hare-eyed
兔崽子 tùzǎizi 〈粗话〉brat; bastard
兔子 tùzi hare; rabbit
兔子不吃窝边草 tùzi bù chī wōbiān cǎo a rabbit doesn't eat the grass near its own hole (for its own protection) — even a villain doesn't harm his nextdoor neighbours
兔子尾巴长不了 tùzi wěiba chángbuliǎo 〈贬义〉the tail of a rabbit can't be long — sth. won't last long; sb.'s days are numbered:这个独裁者的统治是～。The dictator's days are numbered.

堍 tù ramp of a bridge:两头桥～ both ends of a bridge

菟 tù
see also tú
菟丝子 tùsīzǐ *also* "菟丝" 〈中药〉seed of Chinese dodder (*Cuscuta chinensis*)

tuān

湍 tuān 〈书面〉❶ (of a current) rapid; torrential: *see* "～流"❷ rapids; rushing waters:急～ rushing current /飞～ swift waters; cliffside waters
湍急 tuānjí (of a current) rapid; torrential:江水～ turbulent river /～的河水 swift flow of the river
湍流 tuānliú ❶〈书面〉swift current; rushing waters; torrent;

T

rapids：～奔泻。The swift current is rushing forward. ❷〈物理〉turbulent flow；turbulence：～强度 turbulence intensity

湍流层 tuānliúcéng 〈气象〉turbosphere

tuán

抟(漙) tuán dewy：朝露～～。The morning dew is heavy.

抟(摶) tuán ❶〈书面〉hover；circle；spiral：鹏鸟～扶摇而上。The roc is spiralling upwards. ❷ roll sth. into a ball；roll：～泥为人 (of legendary goddess) roll mud into men；make men out of earth

抟弄 tuánnong see "团弄" tuánnong

团(團、❷糰) tuán ❶ round；circular：～城 round city /～～坐下 sit down in a circle ❷ dumpling：汤～ boiled rice dumplings ❸ roll into a ball；roll：～煤球 roll briquets /～纸团儿 roll paper into a ball /～泥球儿玩 have fun rolling mud balls ❹ sth. shaped like a ball or a circle；roundish mass：纸～儿 paper crumpled up into a ball /棉花～儿 cotton ball /抱成～儿 hang together；stick together /围成～儿 form a mass round；cluster round /缩成～儿 curl up into a ball /一～糟 complete mass ❺ unite；assemble；conglomerate：see "～结"；"～聚" ❻ group；circle；organization：参观～ visiting group /旅游～ tourist group /剧～ drama troupe /乐～ orchestra；band /马戏～ circus /代表～ delegation；mission；deputation ❼〈军事〉regiment：～参谋长 regimental chief of staff ❽ political organization for teenagers；(short for 中国共产主义青年团) the Communist Youth League of China；the League：入～ join the League；be admitted to the League /退～ withdraw from the League；give up league membership /～籍 League membership /～旗 flag of the Communist Youth League；League flag /～徽 emblem of the Communist Youth League；League emblem /～委 committee of the Communist Youth League (at a college, etc.)；League committee /儿童～ Children's Corps ❾〈旧语〉village-level government ❿〈量词〉：一～毛线 a ball of knitting wool /一～面 a lump of dough /一～废纸 a ball of waste paper /一～乱麻 a mass of intangled flax yarn；a mess

团拜 tuánbài (during a festival) mutual greetings or congratulations in a group：春节～ gather together to exchange greetings during the Spring Festival /参加～ participate in mutual greetings in a group

团匾 tuánbiǎn 〈方言〉big round shallow basket for raising silkworms

团丁 tuándīng 〈旧语〉member of a local militia group；local militiaman

团队 tuánduì group；corps；team：旅游～ tourist group /体育～ sports team

团队精神 tuánduì jīngshén *esprit de corps*；team spirit

团队协作 tuánduì xiézuò teamwork

团防 tuánfáng 〈旧语〉local militia controlled by landlords or merchants

团粉 tuánfěn cooking starch

团凤 tuánfèng round phoenix design or pattern：绣着～的披风 cloak embroidered in round phoenix patterns /七彩～的图案 multi-coloured phoenix design

团花 tuánhuā (painted or embroidered) round flower pattern：～缎子马褂儿 satin mandarin jacket with embroidered round flower patterns

团伙 tuánhuǒ gang；ring：打击流氓～ crack down on criminal gangs

团箕 tuánjī round flat wicker or bamboo vessel for holding grains

团结 tuánjié unite；rally：～广大群众 unite the broad masses of the people /～各界人士 unite people from all circles (*or* walks of life) /～一致 unite as one /搞好～ achieve (*or* strengthen) unity /～友好的气氛 atmosphere of solidarity and friendship /～的大会 meeting of unity /安定～的政治局面 political unity and stability /～、紧张、严肃、活泼 united, alert, earnest and lively /～就是力量。Unity is strength.

团聚 tuánjù ❶ reunite：合家～ family reunion /今日分手后，何日再～？When shall we be reunited after today's separation? ❷ gather；assemble：组织和～千千万万群众 organize and assemble thousands upon thousands of people /一伙人～在街头。A band of people gathered on the street. /几位老人～而坐。Some old people sat together.

团课 tuánkè (Communist Youth) League class；League lecture

团矿 tuánkuàng 〈冶金〉nodulizing；briquetting

团粒 tuánlì 〈农业〉granule：～结构 granular structure / 呈～状的土壤 granular soil

团练 tuánliàn 〈旧语〉local militia controlled by landlords or merchants：地主～武装 local landlord militias /办～ set up (*or* organize) a local militia

团练使 tuánliànshǐ 〈历史〉military commander of a district or prefecture in the Tang and Song dynasties

团龙 tuánlóng round dragon design or pattern：雕刻～的玉器 jade-ware carved in round dragon designs (*or* patterns)

团拢 tuánlong 〈方言〉❶ hold or gather together；rally：我总算把他～住了。I finally managed to hold him. /他要把这个家～住，不让它四分五裂。He wanted to hold the family together and avoid a split-up. ❷ huddle up；curl up：他～在炕上呼呼地睡着了。He curled up on the *kang* and started snoring immediately.

团圞 tuánluán also "团栾"〈书面〉❶ (of the moon) round：一轮～的明月 bright round moon ❷ reunite；hold or gather together；be together：合家～ reunion of the whole family /～到老 live together into old age

团年 tuánnián (of a family) reunite or gather together for the Spring Festival：～饭 family reunion dinner /～酒 family reunion wine /吃顿～的饺子 have dumplings to celebrate the family reunion

团弄 tuánnong also "抟弄" tuánnong 〈方言〉❶ roll into a ball；roll：～泥巴 roll mud (*or* clay) ❷ manipulate；hoodwink；deceive：～老实人 manipulate an honest man /～公众 deceive the general public

团瓢 tuánpiáo 〈方言〉round thatched hut

团脐 tuánqí ❶ abdomen of a female crab：几只～的大肥蟹 several large crabs with round abdomens ❷ female crab：～比尖脐肥。Female crabs have got more flesh than male ones.

团契 tuánqì 〈基督教〉fellowship；communion

团日 tuánrì day on which Communist Youth League organizations hold activities；League day：～活动 League day activities

团扇 tuánshàn moon-shaped fan；round fan：绢丝～ round spunsilk fan /纤巧精致的～ delicate moon-shaped fan

团体 tuántǐ organization；group；society；team：群众～ mass organization /学术～ academic society /～入口 group entrance /～保险 group insurance /～精神 *esprit de corps*

团体操 tuántǐcāo group callisthenics

团体冠军 tuántǐ guànjūn team title

团体票 tuántǐpiào group ticket

团体赛 tuántǐsài team competition

团体项目 tuántǐ xiàngmù team event

团头 tuántóu 〈旧语〉leader of a group of coroners, coffin-carriers or beggars

团头鲂 tuántóufáng also "武昌鱼" wǔchāngyú；"团头鳊" blunt-snout bream (*Megalobrama amblycephala*)

团头团脑 tuántóu-tuánnǎo round fleshy head；corpulent build：长得～的 of corpulent build

团团 tuántuán ❶ round：～的小脸 little round face ❷ round and round；all round：～围住 surround completely；encircle；cluster round /围着火炉～坐好 sit in a circle around the stove

团团簇簇 tuántuán-cùcù in a cluster or swarm：同学们～地跑向操场，观看篮球赛。Students swarmed to the sports ground to watch the basketball game. /花渐渐开得～的了。By and by, flowers were blooming in clusters.

团团转 tuántuánzhuàn go round and round；move in a circle：急得～ pace about in an agitated state of mind；be on tenterhooks with anxiety /忙得～ be up to one's ears in work

团鱼 tuányú also "鳖" biē soft-shelled turtle

团员 tuányuán ❶ member of a group or delegation：访问团～ member of a visiting group /文工团～ member of an art troupe ❷ member of the Communist Youth League of China；League member：共青～ Communist Youth League member /～证 League membership card /全体～大会 general meeting of League members

团圆 tuányuán ❶ reunion：夫妻～ reunion of husband and wife /～饭 family reunion dinner /一家人团团圆圆，红红火火地过日子 have the

whole family living together in prosperity and harmony ❷ round; circular:～脸、大眼睛的胖孩子 chubby child with a round face and big eyes
团圆节　Tuányuánjié　Mid-Autumn or Moon Festival (15th day of the 8th lunar month, when a family is supposed to gather together and eat moon-cakes in celebration)
团圆媳妇　tuányuán xífu　〈方言〉〈旧语〉daughter-in-law raised in the family as a child; child daughter-in-law; child bride
团藻　tuánzǎo　〈植物〉volvox
团长　tuánzhǎng　❶〈军事〉regimental commander ❷ head or leader of a delegation, troupe, etc.
团支部　tuánzhībù　Communist Youth League branch
团子　tuánzi　dumpling:糯米～ dumpling made of glutinous rice /菜～ cornmeal dumpling with vegetable stuffing /饭～ rice ball /玉米面～ corn bread
团总支　tuánzǒngzhī　general branch of the Communist Youth League
团组织　tuánzǔzhī　organization of the Communist Youth League
团坐　tuánzuò　sit in a circle:促膝～ sit side by side in a circle /围炉～ sit around the stove in a circle

tuǎn

疃（畽） tuǎn　(usu. used in place names) village:柳～ Liu Village /王～ Wang Village

tuàn

彖 tuàn　〈书面〉judge; assert
彖辞　tuàncí　*also*"卦辞" guàcí　commentary on the meaning of different combinations of the trigrams (as in *The Book of Changes*)

tuī

忒 tuī　*also* tēi　〈方言〉too; awfully:街上人～多。The street is just too crowded. /天气～热。It's awfully hot.
see also tè

推 tuī　❶ push; shove; thrust:～门而入 push the door open and enter /～一把 give a push /～铅球 put the shot /把堆在大门口的垃圾～走 remove the rubbish heap at the gate /他把我～开。He shoved me aside. ❷ turn a mill or grindstone; grind:～点儿玉米面 grind some cornmeal ❸ cut; pare; plane; mow:～草机 mowing machine; mower /用推土机～土 use a bulldozer to move earth; bulldoze ❹ push forward; promote; advance; apply:～向高潮 push to a climax ❺ infer; deduce:类～ reason by analogy; analogize /以一～十 deduce ten from one /～情度理 consider the circumstances and infer the reasons ❻ decline; yield; give:～梨让枣 decline the pears and jujubes (in favour of one's brothers, etc.) /解衣～食 yield (*or* give) one's own food and clothing (to the needy); share all one has (with friends, etc.) ❼ push away; shift; shirk:～来～去 each pushes sth. away to the other; give the runaround /～开责任 shake off (*or* shirk) one's responsibility; pass the buck /～个一干二净 shift all blame onto others /～病不去 beg off on the pretext of illness /～作不知 pretend not to know ❽ put off; delay; postpone:总是今天～明天 always put off till tomorrow /往后～几天 postpone for a few days ❾ hold in esteem; praise highly: *see* "～重"; "～崇" ❿ elect; choose; recommend:～贤让能 recommend the worthy and make way for the talented /～他为代表 choose him to be their representative /被～为研究室主任 be elected head of the research group
推扳　tuībān　*also*"推班"〈方言〉no good; bad; poor:我的耳朵～,请大点儿声说。My ears are not good. Please speak louder. /这把椅子的质量真～。The chair is of very bad quality.
推板　tuībǎn　farm tool with a long handle fixed with a rectangular board at one end (for spreading out or gathering together grain on the threshing ground)
推刨　tuībào　〈方言〉plane
推本溯源　tuīběn-sùyuán　*also*"推本穷源" trace the origin; ascertain the cause; get to the bottom:～,不难得出正确的结论。One can draw the right conclusion by tracing the origin of the matter.
推波助澜　tuībō-zhùlán　make a stormy sea stormier; add fuel to the fire; pour oil on the flames:～,惟恐天下不乱 stir up trouble by adding fuel to the fire /事情已经够乱的了,你就别再～了。Things are bad enough as they are. Don't make them even worse.
推测　tuīcè　infer; conjecture; guess:据有关情况～ infer according to relevant information /这仅是我的～。This is only my guess (*or* conjecture).
推阐　tuīchǎn　examine and explain
推陈出新　tuīchén-chūxīn　evolve or bring forth the new from the old; weed through the old to bring forth the new:百花齐放,～。Let a hundred flowers blossom, and bring forth the new by weeding through the old.
推诚相见　tuīchéng-xiāngjiàn　open one's heart (to sb.); treat with sincerity; deal with in good faith:彼此～ treat each other with sincerity / 朋友之间应～,无话不谈。Friends should open their hearts to each other and talk without reserve.
推迟　tuīchí　put off; postpone; defer:一再～ put off again and again /～几周再作决定 defer the decision for several weeks /庆典～数日。The celebration will be postponed for a few days.
推斥　tuīchì　〈物理〉repulsion:～力 repulsion; repulsive force
推崇　tuīchóng　hold in esteem; praise highly; extol:～备至 full of praise (for sb.) /人们对他所做的研究工作十分～。People hold him in high esteem for his research.
推出　tuīchū　introduce; promote; initiate; come out with:～改革方案 introduce a reform programme /～最新产品 promote latest products /隆重～ initiate in a grand way /～新排剧目 stage a new play (*or* opera) /这家商场最近又～促销的新招。This shop has recently employed a new gimmick for sales promotion.
推辞　tuīcí　decline; refuse; turn down:一再～ decline repeatedly / 婉言～ decline graciously; turn down politely
推戴　tuīdài　〈书面〉support (sb. in assuming leadership, etc.):竭诚～ wholeheartedly support sb. (in assuming leadership) /受众人～ enjoy popular support (for assuming office or leadership)
推挡　tuīdǎng　〈体育〉half volley with push:正手～ forehand half volley with push /下旋～ backspin half volley with push
推宕　tuīdàng　procrastinate; shelve; lay aside:不容～ allow of no procrastination
推导　tuīdǎo　deduce:从错误的前提～出错误的结论 deduce the wrong conclusion from the wrong premise
推倒　tuīdǎo　❶ push over; overturn; topple:把桌子～了 overturn a table /把他～了 push him over; shove him to the ground ❷ repudiate; overthrow; cancel; reverse:～旧政权 overthrow an old regime /～不切实际的计划 repudiate (*or* cancel) an impractical plan /～重来 replace with sth. new; start all over again /～陈说 repudiate an old theory /～一切不实之词 reject all falsehoods
推定　tuīdìng　❶ elect; choose:大家～他当下一次的大会主席。He was chosen by general consensus to preside over the next meeting. ❷ conclude by conjecture; infer:踏勘现场后,他～这是谋杀而非自杀。He concluded after investigating the scene that it was murder, not suicide. ❸〈法律〉constructive:～欺诈〈法律〉constructive fraud /～藐视法庭行为〈法律〉constructive contempt (of court) /～全损〈商业〉constructive total loss
推动　tuīdòng　push forward; promote; encourage; give impetus to:～力 motive (*or* driving) force /～生产力的发展 promote the development of productive forces /～彼此的交往 encourage mutual exchanges /～文体活动的进一步开展 further develop recreational and sports activities
推断　tuīduàn　infer; deduce:根据有关事实～ draw inferences based on relevant facts /令人信服的科学～ convincing scientific deduction
推度　tuīduó　infer; conjecture; guess:私下～ conjecture in private / 妄加～ make improper inferences
推恩　tuī'ēn　〈书面〉extend benevolence or kindness; extend favours:～及弟子 extend favours to the children and junior relatives (of one's supporters) /～及禽兽 extend one's benevolence (*or* kindness) to birds and beasts
推而广之　tuī'érguǎngzhī　by logical extension; in the same way; by the same token; likewise:这个道理～,可以运用到为人处世。This principle is also applicable to one's behaviour in society.
推翻　tuīfān　❶ overthrow; overturn; topple; undo:～殖民统治 overthrow the rule of colonialism /～旧政府 bring down (*or* topple) an old government ❷ repudiate; cancel; reverse:～错误的结论 re-

T

verse a wrong conclusion /～旧学说 repudiate an old theory /～协议 repudiate (*or* cancel) an agreement /～原方案 abolish the original plan

推服 tuīfú admire; consider as better than oneself:诚心～ admire in all sincerity /众所～ be held in esteem by all

推杆 tuīgǎn 〈机械〉push rod; pusher; pusher bar; pushover:～式送料 pusher feed /～输送机 pushbar conveyor /～提升机 pushbar booster

推毂 tuīgǔ 〈书面〉help to achieve; recommend for a post

推故 tuīgù give a reason or pretext:他～不来了。He begged off by giving a pretext.

推广 tuīguǎng popularize; spread; extend:～普通话 popularize *putonghua* (the common spoken Chinese) /～先进经验 spread (*or* popularize) advanced experience /迅速～和应用新的工艺 rapidly extend and apply new technologies

推及 tuījí extend by analogy; extend; analogize:～其余 extend to the rest; generalize /～有关方面 extend to the parties concerned (*or* to the relevant questions)

推己及人 tuījǐ-jírén put oneself in the place of another; do onto others as you would be done by; be considerate:将心比心,～ feel for others and be considerate

推挤 tuījǐ ❶ push; shove:人群～得你喊我叫。People thronged together, pushing and yelling. ❷〈书面〉push aside; squeeze out:受到～ be elbowed out

推见 tuījiàn imagine; guess; reckon:不难～ not hard to imagine /由此小事,可以～其为人坦诚。One can conclude from such trifles that he is an honest and aboveboard person.

推荐 tuījiàn recommend:～作品 recommend literary works /极力～ endorse strongly

推奖 tuījiǎng commend; praise:他的著作颇受同行～。His work was highly spoken of by his colleagues.

推襟送抱 tuījīn-sòngbào open one's heart; lay one's heart bare; treat with sincerity:～,诚以待人 lay one's heart bare and treat people with sincerity

推进 tuījìn ❶ push or carry forward; promote; give impetus to:～到新的高度 push to a new high /有力地～了两国贸易往来 give great impetus to the trade exchanges between the two countries /～科技成果的应用 promote the application of achievements in scientific research ❷〈军事〉move forward; push; drive:前锋部队迅速～。The vanguard troops pushed forward rapidly. /战线已～到长江一线。The battlefront moved forward to the Yangtze River. ❸〈物理〉propel; thrust:～功率 thrust power /～喷管 propelling nozzle /～系数 propulsive coefficient

推进舱 tuījìncāng 〈航天〉propulsion module (part of a space vehicle containing fuel tanks, rocket engine and related equipment)

推进剂 tuījìnjì propellant; propulsor

推进力 tuījìnlì propulsive force; driving power; thrust

推进器 tuījìnqì propeller

推究 tuījiū examine; study:～成因 examine the contributing factors /其中的道理值得～。It is worth going into the causes of the matter.

推举 tuījǔ ❶ choose; recommend; elect:～贤才 recommend virtuous and talented people /受到众人的～ be chosen by all /～为代表 choose (*or* elect) sb. one's representative /大家～他去有关部门交涉。They chose him to negotiate with the departments concerned. ❷〈体育〉clean and press; press:～一百四十六公斤 press 146 kilograms /～项目已从举重运动中取消。The press has been cancelled as a weightlifting event.

推拒 tuījù refuse; decline; turn down:她说这话并没有～的意思。She did not mean to refuse by these words.

推勘 tuīkān study and collate:～文义 study and collate a text /经他一番～,才知道这是一篇伪托的作品。After carefully collating the work, he found it to be a forgery.

推口 tuīkǒu 〈方言〉offer or give as an excuse (for not doing sth.); plead:她～有事不去。She gave the excuse of another appointment for not going. /你可以～说不知道。You may plead ignorance of this matter.

推理 tuīlǐ 〈逻辑〉inference; reasoning; ratiocination:间接～ indirect reasoning /演绎～ deduction /～能力 power of reasoning; reason /～小说 ratiocinative novel /写议论文离不开～。Reasoning is an essential element of argumentation.

推力 tuīlì ❶ motive or driving force; incentive ❷ propulsion; thrust:螺旋桨～ propeller thrust /喷气发动机～ jet thrust /～室 thrust chamber /～载荷 thrust load /～系数 thrust coefficient

推聋装哑 tuīlóng-zhuāngyǎ *also* "推聋做哑" pretend to be deaf and dumb; pretend to be ignorant; feign ignorance

推论 tuīlùn inference; deduction; corollary:有力的～ forceful inference /令人叹服的～ deduction which compels admiration

推磨 tuīmò turn a millstone

推拿 tuīná 〈中医〉massage; manipulation:～疗法 naprapathy; massage /～师 massager

see also "按摩" ànmó

推盘 tuīpán 〈方言〉offer (house, shop, etc.) for sale

推迁 tuīqiān 〈书面〉❶ (of time) elapse; pass:日月～ with the lapse (*or* passage) of time; as time goes by ❷ find an excuse to put off; stall:～不已 keep postponing

推敲 tuīqiāo weigh (one's words); deliberate:～再三 weigh one's words repeatedly /经得起～ can stand close scrutiny /这篇文章的结构还得好好～一下。We should give more thought to the organization of this article.

推切式牛头刨 tuīqiēshì niútóubào 〈机械〉push-cut shaper

推求 tuīqiú find out (from what is known); inquire; study:潜心～ inquire into sth. with great concentration /他力图～对方此举的动机。He tried hard to find out what was behind the opponent's decision to make such a move.

推却 tuīquè refuse; decline; turn down:借故～ decline with an excuse; beg off /执意～邀请 firmly refuse (*or* decline) an invitation

推让 tuīràng decline (a position, favour, etc.) out of modesty; yield; submit:互相～ submit (*or* yield) to one another /有意～ deliberately decline (a favour, etc.)

推人犯规 tuīrén fànguī 〈体育〉pushing:因～受黄牌警告 receive a yellow card for pushing

推三宕四 tuīsān-dàngsì delay again and again; procrastinate time and again

推三阻四 tuīsān-zǔsì *also* "推三推四" make excuses and create obstacles; make all sorts of excuses; give the runaround:～,执意不肯 firmly decline with all sorts of excuses /～,一点儿也不爽快 be always ready with excuses and never come to the point in a straightforward manner /别跟我～的,我不吃这一套! Don't you give me the runaround. I won't stand for it.

推搡 tuīsǎng push and shove:他被～着,来到这间屋子里。He was pushed into this room. /走到门口,姑娘们互相～着,谁也不肯先进去。Approaching the door, the girls pushed and shoved and no one wanted to enter first.

推事 tuīshì 〈旧语〉judge (at a court of law)

推说 tuīshuō ❶〈方言〉offer as an excuse (for not doing sth.); plead:他～有病,没有参加今天的会。He pleaded illness for not coming to today's meeting. ❷ infer; deduce:～其意 infer its meaning

推算 tuīsuàn calculate; estimate; reckon:根据有关数据～ calculate on the basis of relevant figures /～结果 result of calculation /据我～,她这时应该到家了。I reckon she should be home by now.

推索 tuīsuǒ *see* "推求"

推搪 tuītáng 〈方言〉offer as an excuse (for not doing sth.); plead; procrastinate:他一再～,拒不搬迁。He offered every possible excuse and would not move out of the place.

推涛作浪 tuītāo-zuòlàng make a stormy sea stormier; stir up trouble; fan the flames of disorder:～,混水摸鱼 create disturbances and fish in troubled waters /～,扩大事态 stir up trouble and aggravate the situation

推头 tuītóu 〈口语〉❶ have a haircut:推平头 have a crew cut /推光头 have one's head shaved ❷ cut sb.'s hair (with clippers)

推土机 tuītǔjī bulldozer

推托 tuītuō offer as an excuse (for not doing sth.); plead:借故～ find an excuse to decline /有意～ try to get out of sth. by offering excuses /她既有～之意,我看就算了。Since she's bent on declining it, we'd best not press her.

推脱 tuītuō evade; dodge; shirk:～责任 evade (*or* shirk) responsibility; shift blame onto others

推挽 tuīwǎn ❶〈书面〉recommend; introduce:感谢先生～玉成。I am most grateful for your recommendation and help, sir. ❷〈电学〉push-pull:～电路 push-pull circuit /～变压器 push-pull transformer /～晶体管 push-pull transistor

推委 tuīwěi *also* "推诿" shift (blame, responsibility, etc.); pass the buck:～于人 shift responsibility onto others; pass the buck to

T

sb. else /～罪责 shirk responsibility (for an accident, killing, etc.)

推问 tuīwèn question; interrogate; examine minutely:在严词～之下,他不得不认罪。Under close interrogation, he had to plead guilty.

推详 tuīxiáng examine; study:～起来,他的话很有道理。If you think it over, what he said is quite reasonable.

推想 tuīxiǎng imagine; deduce; reckon:合情合理的～ reasonable deduction /不难～。It's not hard to imagine.

推销 tuīxiāo promote sales; market; sell; peddle:～商品 promote the sale of goods /广为～ market widely /廉价～ reduce the price to promote sales; sell at a low price /～员 salesman

推销术 tuīxiāoshù 〈商业〉salesmanship; selling techniques

推卸 tuīxiè shirk; evade; shift off:负有不可～的责任 have an unshirkable (*or* unavoidable) responsibility

推谢 tuīxiè decline with an excuse:假意～ decline insincerely /何必如此～? Why turn it down like this?

推心置腹 tuīxīn-zhìfù open one's heart (to sb.); place full confidence (in sb.); confide (in sb.):～,促膝而谈 confide in sb. and have a heart-to-heart talk /很久没有听到这种～的话了。We have long missed such heartfelt remarks.

推行 tuīxíng carry out; pursue; introduce:～新方法 introduce a new method /～新措施 carry out new measures /在国际关系中～强权政治 pursue a policy of power politics in international relations

推许 tuīxǔ have a high regard for; hold in esteem:交口～ unanimously have a high regard (for sb.)

推选 tuīxuǎn elect; choose:～代表 choose representatives /～他为秘书长 elect him secretary-general

推寻 tuīxún examine; study; scrutinize:细细地～他说这话的意思 reflect closely on his remarks

推延 tuīyán put off; postpone:无故～ put off for no reason at all /会议往后～三天。The meeting will be postponed for three days.

推演 tuīyǎn infer; deduce:正确的前提～出正确的结论。Correct conclusions can only be deduced from true premises.

推移 tuīyí (of time) elapse; pass; (of a situation, etc.) develop; evolve:随着时间的～ with the lapse (*or* passage) of time; as time goes by /日月～ as time passes /时局的～ developments in current affairs

推移质 tuīyízhì 〈水利〉bed load

推展 tuīzhǎn push forward; advance:～太空计划 advance a space programme /沉积的泥沙填满了海湾,促使海岸向前～。The bay was silted up with deposits, pushing the coastline forward.

推知 tuīzhī infer; deduce; reckon:知道了气压的分布可以～风的分布。The distribution of wind can be inferred from the distribution of atmospheric pressure.

推重 tuīzhòng think highly of; hold in esteem:为人～ be held in high esteem

推子 tuīzi hair-clippers; clippers

推尊 tuīzūn hold in esteem; praise highly

蓷 tuī 〈古语〉〈植物〉motherwort (*Leonurus heterophyllus*)

tuí

僓(僓) tuí *see*“虺僓”huītuí

穨 tuí 〈书面〉*see*“颓”tuí

隤 tuí 〈书面〉*see*“颓”tuí

颓 tuí ❶ collapse; crumble; become dilapidated or ruined:～井残垣 ruined wells and crumbling walls ❷ declining; decadent; decayed:衰～ weak and declining /白发～颜 grey hair and aged complexion ❸ dejected; dispirited: *see*“～唐”;“～丧”

颓败 tuíbài decline; decay; become corrupt:～的景象 scene of decline and decay /政风日渐～。Politics is becoming increasingly corrupt. /故园～不堪,全非昨日景象。Hopelessly dilapidated, the old garden is not what it used to be.

颓放 tuífàng 〈书面〉dissolute; degenerate; abandoned:为人～,不拘礼法 dissolute and heedless of etiquette and morality /从那以后他便日渐～,再也振作不起来。From then on, he became more and more abandoned, unable to brace himself up again.

颓废 tuífèi decadent; dissipated; degenerate:～的生活 dissipated life /～派 decadent school; decadents

颓风 tuífēng degenerate manners; decadent customs:～日甚。Decadent customs are becoming increasingly widespread. /～不可长。Degenerate manners must not be allowed to go unchecked.

颓坏 tuíhuài collapse; be ruined:房屋～。The house fell into ruins.

颓景 tuíjǐng scene of decline and decay:故园一派～。The old residence is a scene of dilapidation.

颓老 tuílǎo old and feeble; decrepit

颓龄 tuílíng *also*“颓年”declining years:～自哀 grieve over one's declining years /～自娱 amuse oneself in old age /～易丧 may die at any moment in old age

颓靡 tuímǐ downcast; dejected; decadent:～放纵的生活 downcast, dissolute life /～之音 decadent music

颓圮 tuípǐ 〈书面〉collapse; topple down; fall into decay:古刹～。The old temple has fallen into decay.

颓然 tuírán 〈书面〉dejected; disappointed:～不振 become dejected and listless /看到这种情景,大家都不禁游兴～。Everybody was disappointed to see this and lost interest in the tour.

颓丧 tuísàng dejected; dispirited; listless:士气～ be demoralized /近来他～得很。He has been dispirited lately.

颓势 tuíshì declining tendency; decline:力挽～ do one's utmost to turn the tide in one's favour

颓塌 tuítā collapse; crumble; topple down:～的房屋 collapsed house /那道土墙,因年久失修,一段一段地～了。The earthen wall had been in disrepair for years and crumbled part by part.

颓唐 tuítáng ❶ dejected; dispirited; disconsolate:暮色沉沉,～沮丧 feel lethargic and disconsolate in the deepening dusk /少年～ be dispirited despite one's youth ❷〈书面〉decline; decay:家境～ decline of one's family fortune; family decline

颓萎 tuíwěi listless; dispirited; dejected:精神～ dispirited and inert

颓朽 tuíxiǔ decayed; rotten:古墓中的棺椁已全部～。The coffins in the ancient tomb were all rotten.

颓阳 tuíyáng 〈书面〉setting sun

颓垣断壁 tuíyuán-duànbì crumbling walls and ruined houses — a scene of decay or devastation; debris:战后到处是～。After the war there were ruins everywhere.

颓运 tuíyùn 〈书面〉declining luck; decline

tuǐ

腿 tuǐ ❶ leg:前～ foreleg /后～ hind leg /大～ thigh /小～ shank; calf /玉～ (of women) beautiful legs /罗圈～ bowlegs; bandy legs /铁～ legs that never tire — good walker (*or* runner) /～酸 have stiff legs /迈不开～ too weak (*or* tired) to walk;〈比喻〉be bound hand and foot /～勤手快 deft of hand and tireless in running around ❷ leglike support; leg:床～ legs of a bed /三条～的凳子 three-legged stool ❸ ham:云～ Yunnan ham

腿绑 tuǐbǎng 〈方言〉puttee:把～裹紧 tighten the puttees

腿带 tuǐdài leg wrappings

腿肚子 tuǐdùzi calf (of the leg):～抽筋 get a cramp in the calf

腿花 tuǐhuā clubbing of one's legs as punishment in ancient China:当堂打了一百～ be clubbed on the legs a hundred times at court

腿脚 tuǐjiǎo legs and feet; ability to walk:～有病 have ailing legs and feet /～不便 have difficulty walking /老人～倒还利落。The old man still moves briskly.

腿快 tuǐkuài quick-footed; swift-footed

腿懒 tuǐlǎn reluctant to move around; lazy about paying visits

腿勤 tuǐqín on one's toes all the time; tireless in running round:他这个人～,常到同事家串门。He is tireless in running round and often calls on his colleagues.

腿弯子 tuǐwānzi 〈方言〉hollow of the knee; back of the knee

腿腕子 tuǐwànzi ankle

腿子 tuǐzi ❶〈方言〉leg:～粗 brawny legs ❷ hired thug; lackey; henchman

tuì

蜕 tuì ❶ slough off; exuviate; *see*“～化”❷ exuviae;

slough:蛇～snake slough /蝉～ cicada exuviae ❸ (of birds) moult ❹ 〈道教〉 shed one's body; pass away

蜕变 tuìbiàn ❶ change qualitatively; transform; transmute; degenerate:～成不法分子 degenerate into a lawless person /形势～,不可收拾。The worsening situation is getting out of control. ❷ 〈物理〉 decay:感生～ induced decay /自发～ spontaneous decay

蜕化 tuìhuà ❶ slough off; exuviate:蚕不食不动,看样子快要～了。The silkworms seem to be sloughing off as they don't eat and move. ❷ degenerate

蜕化变质 tuìhuà-biànzhì degenerate:～分子 degenerate /此人追求享乐,终于～为贪污分子。This man craved sensual pleasure and became a grafter in the end.

蜕膜 tuìmó 〈生理〉 decidua:～瘤 deciduoma /～炎 deciduitis

蜕皮 tuìpí 〈动物〉 slough; exuviate; ecdysis:～素 ecdysone

侻

tuì 〈书面〉 handsome; beautiful; agreeable; suitable

see also tuō

退

tuì ❶ move backwards; back up; retreat:进一步,～两步 one step forward, two steps backwards /进～两难 difficult to advance or retreat; in a dilemma /倒～几步 step back a few paces; back up a few steps /～无可～ be left with no room for retreat; there is no place to retreat to /～而求其次 have to take the second best; settle for one's second choice ❷ cause to move back; withdraw; remove:～敌 get the enemy to retreat (*or* withdraw); repulse the enemy /～保 withdraw one's guaranty; cease to act as guarantor /把磁带～出来 remove the tape from the cassette ❸ retire from; quit; adjourn:～归林下 retire from public life /～思补过 quit one's position in order to repair the wrong one has done; retire to amend one's error /～而让贤 withdraw in favour of more competent people ❹ decline; recede; decrease: ～汗 arrest perspiration; stop sweating /水～了。The water has receded. *or* The flood is over. ❺ return; give back; refund:把这份礼～了。Return this gift. ❻ cancel; retract; break off:～掉合同 cancel a contract

退保值 tuìbǎozhí surrender value

退避 tuìbì withdraw and keep off; keep out of the way; yield:～再三 yield (to sb.) time and again /～不及 have no time to get out of the way

退避三舍 tuìbì-sānshè retreat ninety *li* — give way to sb. to avoid a conflict; keep a good distance (from sb.); avoid like a plague:～,不与争锋 retreat and avoid a conflict /碰见这样不讲理的人,我们只好～了。With such an unreasonable person, we have to keep out of his way.

退兵 tuìbīng ❶ retreat; withdraw troops:火速～ retreat posthaste ❷ force the enemy to retreat; repulse:～之计 plan for repulsing the enemy

退步 tuìbù ❶ lag or fall behind; retrogress:学习～ lag behind in one's studies /他的工作显然～了。Clearly, he is not doing so well in his work as he used to. ❷ make a concession; give in; give way:双方都～,就不至于冲突起来。If both sides had made some concessions, there would have been no conflict. ❸ room for manoeuvre; leeway:留个～ leave some room for manoeuvre; leave some leeway /不留～ leave no other option; burn one's boats

退仓 tuìcāng return a leased warehouse to its owner

退场 tuìchǎng leave (an arena, sportsground, theatre, etc.); exit:运动员～。The athletes march out. /今晚的演出到此结束,请观众～。The performance is over. Goodnight, everybody.

退朝 tuìcháo adjourn an imperial court session; declare such a session over

退潮 tuìcháo ebb tide; ebb:～时分 ebb time /涨潮～ rising tide and ebb tide; ebb and flow

退出 tuìchū withdraw from; secede; leave; quit:～比赛 withdraw from a competition; scratch /～工会 withdraw from the trade union /～联邦 secede from the union /～一个学术团体 leave an academic society /～会场 walk out of a meeting /～历史舞台 step down from the stage of history

退磁 tuìcí *also* "去磁" qùcí 〈物理〉 demagnetize

退党 tuìdǎng withdraw from or quit a political party

退佃 tuìdiàn (of a landlord) cancel a tenancy; evict a tenant:～之风 prevailing practice of cancelling tenancies /赶下种的时候强迫～,咱们还有什么活路? How could we make a living when we're evicted during the sowing season?

退耕 tuìgēng let cultivated land revert to its natural state; stop cultivating (land); let lie fallow:因地制宜,～还林 reforest some of the cultivated land in line with the local conditions

退股 tuìgǔ withdraw shares (from a joint-stock company)

退关 tuìguān (of an exporter, etc.) cancel a declaration (of goods already cleared by customs)

退化 tuìhuà ❶ degenerate; retrograde; retrogress:机能～ functional retrogradation /智力～ intellectual retrogression /品种的～与复壮 degeneration and rejuvenation of strains /～突变 retrogressive mutation /随着外界条件的变化而～ degenerate with the change of the environment ❷ worsen; become worse:干部素质～ worsening quality of cadres /学习成绩～ backslide in one's studies

退还 tuìhuán return:～原主 return sth. to its owner /原物无损～ return sth. intact /～抗议照会 reject a protest note

退换 tuìhuàn exchange or replace a purchase; refund or exchange:照章～ replace a purchase in accordance with the regulations /要求～ seek a replacement /如属质量问题,保证～。Replacement is guaranteed for any faulty product. /货物售出,概不～。All sales are final. No refunds or exchanges.

退回 tuìhuí ❶ return; send back:～余款 return the balance /用毕请立即～。Send it back after use, please. /无法投递,～原处。Undeliverable, returned to sender. ❷ go or turn back:～原地待命 go back to where one was for further orders /原路～ go (*or* turn) back along the route one took /大雪封山,一行人只好～。As all the mountain roads were blocked by snow, they had to turn back.

退婚 tuìhūn break off an engagement:女方～。The girl's family (*or* the girl) broke off the engagement.

退火 tuìhuǒ 〈冶金〉 annealing:～钢 annealed steel /～炉 annealer; annealing oven; annealing furnace /～铸件 annealed casting

退伙 tuìhuǒ ❶ 〈旧语〉 withdraw from an underworld gang ❷ cancel an arrangement to eat at a mess; withdraw from a mess:办理～手续 go through the procedure for cancelling an arrangement to eat at a mess; handle such cancellations /下月～ withdraw from the mess as from next month

退货 tuìhuò return merchandise or goods:产品质量差,买主纷纷～。Many goods were returned for their poor quality.

退浆 tuìjiāng 〈纺织〉 desize:～工艺 desizing

退居 tuìjū ❶ retreat; withdraw:～二线 give up an active (*or* responsible) post but remain at work as adviser, etc.; retreat to the second line of work /～幕后 retire backstage; withdraw behind the scene ❷ go down (in rank, quality, etc.); decline:该厂产品质量已～二等。The products of the factory have declined to second-rate in quality.

退壳 tuìké 〈军事〉 ejection:～器 extractor; ejector

退路 tuìlù ❶ route or line of retreat:沿着～设下标记 make signs along the route of retreat /我们的～被敌军切断了。Our retreat was cut off by enemy troops. ❷ room for manoeuvre; leeway:留个～ leave some leeway; keep another option open; not burn one's boats /改革方案业已出台,我们没有～,只有努力把工作做好。With the reform programme initiated, we have no alternative but to carry it out to the best of our ability.

退落 tuìluò ❶ recede; ebb:潮水～。The tide receded (*or* ebbed). ❷ decline:他的作品反映了当时社会的～。His works give expression to the decline of society at the time.

退赔 tuìpéi return what one has unlawfully taken or pay compensation for it:责令～ order sb. to return (*or* pay for) what he has unlawfully taken /彻底～ do a thorough job of making compensations; compensate for everything one has unlawfully taken

退票 tuìpiào return a ticket; get a refund for a ticket; cancel a reservation:～手续 procedures for getting a refund for a ticket /～处 ticket-refund window (*or* office) /按原价～ get a full refund for a ticket

退坡 tuìpō fall off; backslide; retrograde:～思想 falling off of revolutionary will (*or* zeal); ideological backsliding /在困难和挫折面前,有些人～了。Some people shrink back before difficulties and setbacks.

退钱 tuìqián refund; reimburse:这份报纸停刊了,应立即向订户～。The newspaper has stopped publication, and the subscribers should be refunded (*or* reimbursed) at once.

退亲 tuìqīn *see* "退婚"

退青 tuìqīng (of rice seedlings) turn from dark to light green

退却 tuìquè ❶ 〈军事〉 retreat; withdraw:暂时的～ temporary re-

T

treat /全军～ general retreat (of an army) /全线～ retreat all along the line ❷ hang back; shrink back; flinch: ～不前 flinch and not press forward /看见这么多陌生的面孔,他想～,于是放慢了脚步。Seeing so many strange faces, he wanted to hang back and so slowed his steps.

退让 tuìràng ❶ step back; step aside; make way: ～贤路〈书面〉yield one's position (*or* office) to more talented people; resign in favour of abler people /骑车人～不及,被汽车撞倒。The cyclist was run down before he had a chance to get out of the way. ❷ make a concession; yield; give in: 稍作～ yield a little /在这个问题上,我们决不能～。We can make no concessions on this matter.

退热 tuìrè *see* "退烧"

退色 tuìshǎi fade: 越洗越～ fade with each washing /塑料制品久晒会～。Plastics' colours fade if long exposed to the sun.

退烧 tuìshāo *also* "退热" bring down or allay a fever; (of a person's temperature) come down: 打针～ have (*or* give) an injection to bring down the fever; give (*or* have) an antipyretic injection / ～后,他感到舒服了。He felt much better when the fever was gone.

退烧药 tuìshāoyào antipyretic

退守 tuìshǒu retreat and make a defence: ～新的阵地 retreat and defend a new position /～待援 retreat and wait for reinforcements

退税 tuìshuì 〈经济〉drawback; tax rebate; tax refund; tax reimbursement: 进口原料加工后再出口时可以～。A drawback can be made (on custom duties) on imported materials when they are re-exported later as processed products. /有不少项目到年终都可以～。There are quite a few items for which tax rebates can be obtained at the end of the year.

退缩 tuìsuō shrink back; flinch; cower: ～不前 flinch; shrink back /在这种关键时刻决不能畏惧～。One must never flinch from difficulty at a critical juncture like this.

退堂 tuìtáng 〈旧语〉(of a magistrate) adjourn a court session: ～! Court adjourned! /～鼓 (beating of) drum announcing adjournment of court; retreat /打～鼓 beat a retreat

退庭 tuìtíng adjourn the court: 法官宣布～。The judge declared the adjournment of the court (*or* declared the court adjourned).

退团 tuìtuán withdraw from a youth league (esp. the Communist Youth League); give up League membership: 超龄～ withdraw from a youth league as one is overage /勒令～ order sb. to give up membership in a youth league (as a milder punishment than expulsion)

退位 tuìwèi give up the throne; abdicate: ～让贤 give up the throne in favour of a better qualified person /～诏书 imperial abdication edict /通过政变,迫使总统～ unseat the president through a *coup d'état*

退伍 tuìwǔ retire or be discharged from active military service; be demobilized; leave the army: 光荣～ leave the army with honour; receive an honourable discharge /～返乡 leave the army and return to one's native village /～军人 demobilized soldier; ex-serviceman; veteran /～证书 demobilization certificate

退席 tuìxí leave a banquet or a meeting; walk out: 中途～ leave a meeting before it is over; walk out /醉而～ get drunk and leave a banquet /一一～ file out of a meeting (*or* banquet) /借故～ find some excuse and leave (a meeting, etc.) /有事提前～ quit half way for some urgent business /气愤地～ walk out angrily

退闲 tuìxián 〈书面〉retire and live an idle life

退行 tuìxíng ❶ retrogress; degenerate: 老年性机体功能～ senile functional retrogradation of the body ❷ (of celestial bodies) back away (from earth)

退省 tuìxǐng 〈书面〉self-examination; self-questioning

退休 tuìxiū retire: ～职工 retired workers and staff /因病～ retire due to illness /提前～ retire before the retirement age /～反聘 recruit sb. in retirement; hire a retired person /～顶替 replace one's parent on his (*or* her) retirement

退休金 tuìxiūjīn retirement pay; pension

退休年龄 tuìxiū niánlíng retirement age

退休人员 tuìxiū rényuán retiree; retired personnel; the retired

退学 tuìxué leave school; drop out; discontinue one's schooling: 因病～ drop out of school due to poor health /勒令～ order sb. to leave school (as a milder punishment than expulsion)

退押 tuìyā (esp. of a landlord during the land reform) return (tenant's) deposit

退养 tuìyǎng (of workers and staff of a collective enterprise) retire

退役 tuìyì ❶ retire from active military service; be released on completing the term of reserve: ～军官 retired officer /～军人 ex-serviceman /这位上校已～。The colonel has retired. ❷ (of outdated weapons) be taken out of service; be withdrawn from inventory; decommission: ～航母 decommissioned aircraft carrier /这种型号的战斗机已～了。This type of fighter planes are no longer in service. ❸ (esp. of athletes) retire: ～后,他开始当教练。He became a coach after retirement as an athlete.

退隐 tuìyǐn 〈旧语〉(of an official) retire from public life; go into retirement: ～山林 retire from public life and live in seclusion among the hills /～生活 retired and secluded life

退有后言 tuìyǒuhòuyán overtly agree but covertly oppose; comply in public but oppose in private; speak ill of sb. behind his back: 当面谀顺,～ flatter sb. to his face but speak ill of him behind his back

退约 tuìyuē withdraw from a treaty; denounce a convention

退赃 tuìzāng give up or disgorge ill-gotten gain: 责其～ enjoin sb. to disgorge ill-gotten gain /清赃～ assess sb.'s graft (*or* booty) and order him to surrender it /～之后,他才有了如释重负的感觉。He felt relieved of a heavy load after surrendering the ill-gotten goods.

退职 tuìzhí resign or be discharged from one's (usu. permanent) work; quit working: ～人员 people who have resigned from their permanent work /主动～ resign of one's own accord /～报告 application for resignation

退职金 tuìzhíjīn severance pay; dismissal pay; retirement pay; retirement benefit

退走 tuìzǒu retreat; withdraw: 迅速～ withdraw speedily /主动～ retreat of one's own accord; take the initiative to retreat

煺(燵、㨃) tuì scald (a pig, chicken, etc.) in order to remove hairs or feathers: ～毛 remove the hairs or feathers (of a pig, chicken, etc.) /～猪 remove the hairs of a pig

褪 tuì ❶ take off (clothes); shed (feathers): ～去冬装 take off winter clothes /小鸡～了黄毛。The chicks have shed their yellow down. ❷ (of colour) fade

see also tùn

褪色 tuìshǎi fade

tūn

吞 tūn ❶ swallow; devour; gulp down: 狼～虎咽 gobble up; wolf down; devour ravenously /囫囵～枣 swallow dates whole; read without understanding /～刀吐火 (in magic) swallow knives and spit fire /～敌之势 so overwhelming as to make the enemy cower / 气可～牛 of great mettle; full of daring /人心不足蛇～象 be as greedy as a snake trying to swallow an elephant ❷ seize; take (illegal) possession of; annex: 独～ take exclusive possession of /侵～ embezzle; misappropriate; swallow up; annex

吞并 tūnbìng annex; seize; take over: ～别国领土 seize another country's territory /～弱小国家 annex (*or* gobble up) a small and weak country /～了十几家公司 annex (*or* take over) a dozen companies /无耻～ impudent annexation

吞剥 tūnbō swallow up and exploit: ～弱国 annex and exploit a weak country /～民财 grab the property of the people; embezzle public property

吞吃 tūnchī ❶ swallow up; gulp down: 大口～ wolf down ❷ embezzle; misappropriate: ～公款 misappropriate public money

吞恨 tūnhèn suffer a wrong silently; nurse a grievance in private: ～多年 nurse a grievance for years /终生～ suffer a wrong which is never redressed for the rest of one's life

吞金 tūnjīn swallow gold (to commit suicide): ～自杀 commit suicide by swallowing gold

吞灭 tūnmiè conquer and annex; gobble up: ～邻国 conquer and annex a neighbouring country /一口～ gobble up at one go

吞没 tūnmò ❶ embezzle; misappropriate: ～公款 misappropriate (*or* embezzle) public money /变相～ misappropriate in a disguised manner ❷ (of floods, etc.) swallow up; submerge; engulf: 被无边的夜色所～ enveloped (*or* submerged) in complete darkness /小小的筏子顷刻之间便被巨浪～了。In a flash, the tiny raft was engulfed in the

T

waves. /狂暴的山洪～了一切。The raging mountain torrents swallowed up everything in their path.

吞舌 tūnshé bite one's tongue; hold one's tongue; be tongue-tied: 钳口～ hold one's tongue; keep one's mouth shut

吞声 tūnshēng 〈书面〉gulp down or suppress one's sobs; choke down one's tears; dare not cry out: 忍气～ swallow insults and humiliations silently; eat humble pie /～饮泣 choke down one's tears; sob bitterly and silently /惟有～而已 cannot but gulp down one's sobs /相对～ sob silently face to face

吞食 tūnshí swallow; devour; gulp down: ～一尽 gobble up /一口～ swallow up at one go /蟒蛇正在～小兔。A python is devouring a rabbit.

吞蚀 tūnshí embezzle; swallow up: 远山逐渐被黑夜～。Slowly the remote mountain peaks were wrapped in the darkness of the night.

吞噬 tūnshì devour; gobble up; engulf: 大火～了整座庙宇。The fire engulfed the entire temple. /黑暗～了大地。The land is shrouded in darkness. /他巧妙地～了属于弟妹们的财产。He slyly appropriated the wealth that belonged to his brothers and sisters.

吞噬细胞 tūnshì xìbāo 〈生理〉phagocyte

吞噬作用 tūnshì zuòyòng 〈生理〉phagocytosis

吞酸 tūnsuān 〈中医〉sudden rise (to the pharynx) and swallowing of gastric acid; reflux of gastric acid

吞吐 tūntǔ ❶ take in and send out in large quantities; (of a port, etc.) handle: ～货物 handle cargoes /车站日夜～着来往旅客和货物。There are comings and goings of passengers and cargoes 24 hours a day at the railway station. ❷ hesitate in speech; hum and ha: ～其词 hesitate in speech; hum and ha /其言～含混。He spoke hesitantly.

吞吐港 tūntǔgǎng port; harbour: 横滨是东京的～。Yokohama is the port of Tokyo.

吞吐量 tūntǔliàng handling capacity (of a harbour); volume of freight handled

吞吞吐吐 tūntūn-tǔtǔ speak hesitantly or falteringly; hum and ha; mutter and mumble: ～，不知所云 mutter and mumble without making anything clear; speak hesitantly and unintelligibly /～的样子让人看了着急 hum and ha in such a way as to make listeners thoroughly nervous

吞咽 tūnyàn swallow: ～食物 swallow food /～困难 have difficulty swallowing; 〈医学〉dysphagia /话到嘴边又～下去了。He hesitated when about to speak up.

吞咽功能 tūnyàn gōngnéng 〈生理〉deglutition

吞云吐雾 tūnyún-tǔwù blow a cloud; smoke opium or tobacco: 有几个人在办公室里～。Some people are smoking in the office.

吞占 tūnzhàn invade and occupy; take illegal possession of; seize: ～别国领土 invade and occupy the territory of another country /～别人的房屋 seize (*or* usurp) sb. else's house

暾 tūn 〈书面〉newly-risen sun: 朝～ early morning sun

tún

屯 tún ❶ gather; collect; store up: 聚草～粮 collect grain and fodder (for an army); store up army provisions ❷ station (troops); quarter (troops): 驻～ be stationed; be quartered ❸ (often used in place names) village: 小～ Xiaotun Village (in Henan Province)

see also zhūn

屯兵 túnbīng station troops; quarter troops: ～边城 quarter troops in a frontier town /～戍边 station troops to guard the frontier

屯积 túnjī hoard (for speculation); corner (the market)

屯集 túnjí assemble; gather; collect: ～粮草 collect grain and fodder (for an army)

屯聚 túnjù assemble (troops); gather together: ～兵马 assemble military forces /～三千人马 gather together three thousand troops

屯垦 túnkěn station troops to open up wasteland: ～戍边 station troops to guard the frontier and cultivate the frontier areas /～之策 policy of stationing troops to guard the frontier as well as open up the frontier areas

屯绿 túnlǜ Tunxi green — quality green tea grown in Tunxi (屯溪) region of Anhui Province

屯落 túnluò 〈方言〉village

屯守 túnshǒu garrison; defend: ～边疆 garrison the frontier

屯戍 túnshù garrison; defend

屯田 túntián have garrison troops or newly settled peasants open up wasteland for cultivation of food grains — a policy introduced in the Han Dynasty during the first and second centuries BC

屯卫 túnwèi station troops to defend: ～京师 garrison the capital /～要地 quarter troops to defend strategic points

屯扎 túnzhā station (troops); quarter (troops): ～于此 be stationed here /重兵～ be heavily guarded

屯驻 túnzhù *also* "驻屯" station; quarter; garrison: ～大军 quarter a strong army

屯子 túnzi 〈方言〉village

忳 tún

忳忳 túntún 〈书面〉distressed; weighed down with sorrow or worry

囤 tún store up; hoard: ～货 store goods /～粮 hoard grain

see also dùn

囤积 túnjī hoard (for speculation); corner (the market): ～粮食 hoard grain; corner the grain market

囤积居奇 túnjī-jūqí hoarding and cornering; hoarding and speculation: ～，操纵市场 engage in hoarding and cornering the market /奸商～，大发国难财。Unscrupulous merchants made fat profits hoarding and speculating during the national crisis.

囤集 túnjí store; store up: 窑洞里～着满满的粮食。The cave is filled with grain.

囤聚 túnjù gather and store; store up: ～干鲜海味 store up both dry and fresh sea food

鲀 tún *also* "河豚" hétún globefish; balloonfish; puffer

饨 tún *see* "馄饨" húntun

豚(豘) tún suckling pig; pig: 家养鸡～ raise chickens and pigs at home

豚草 túncǎo ragweed: ～属 ambrosia

豚儿 tún'ér *also* "豚子"; "豚犬" 〈谦词〉my worthless son or child

豚肩 túnjiān pig's thigh or rump: 后～ pig's butt

豚鹿 túnlù 〈动物〉hog deer (*Axis porcinus*)

豚鼠 túnshǔ guinea pig; cavy: ～属 Cavia /～麻痹症 guinea-pig paralysis

豚蹄禳田 túntí-rángtián pray for a bumper harvest with pig's feet as sacrificial offerings — offer a little but seek a lot: ～之举 act which offers a little but expects to gain a lot /～，所望甚多 be bent on gaining much at a little expense

豚尾猴 túnwěihóu 〈动物〉pig-tailed macaque (*Macaca nemestrina*)

臀 tún buttock; rump

臀部 túnbù buttock: ～受伤 wounded in the buttocks /～肥大 fat buttocks; fat bottom

臀肌 túnjī gluteus muscles

臀尖 túnjiān (pig's) rump: 前～ front rump /后～ back (*or* hind) rump; butt

臀鳍 túnqí 〈动物〉anal fin

臀围 túnwéi hipline

臀疣 túnyóu 〈动物〉monkey's ischial callosities; monkey's seat pads

tǔn

氽 tǔn 〈方言〉❶ float; drift: 木板～在水上。Planks are drifting on the water. /人～水上。People are floating on the river. ❷ deep-fry: 油～馒头片 fried slices of steamed bread

tùn

褪 tùn ❶ (as of one's limbs) slip out of sth.: ～下手镯子 slip

off a bracelet ❷〈方言〉keep or hide in the sleeve:～着手 keep one's hands in the sleeves / 袖子里～着一封信 hide a letter in one's sleeve
see also tuì

褪去 tùnqù take off:～冬装 take off one's winter clothes

褪套儿 tùntàor ❶ break loose (of a leash, etc.); free oneself; get oneself free:狗～跑了。The dog broke loose and ran away. ❷ shake off responsibility:这事大家都有责任,谁也甭想～。Everybody is involved in this case and no one can shake off responsibility.

tuō

捝 tuō 〈书面〉❶ free or extricate oneself; release ❷ omit; err

侻 tuō 〈书面〉❶ simple:其行～而顺情。His behaviour is simple and natural. ❷ suitable; proper; appropriate ❸ *see* "通侻" tōngtuō
see also tuì

脱 tuō ❶ shed (hair, skin, etc.); lose; come off:头发几乎～光 lose most of one's hair; become almost bald /～骨烧鸡 roast chicken whose bones have become separate from the meat ❷ take off; cast off:～帽 take off one's hat /～衣就寝 undress for bed ❸ escape from; extricate oneself from; get out of:摆～ break away from; free (*or* extricate) oneself from /逃～ make good one's escape /～出樊笼 get out of the cage; shake off the yoke /～弓之箭 arrow shot from a bow ❹ miss out (words); omit; elide:～扣落襻 miss this and that; deal with sth. in a careless way /这里～了一行。One line is missing here. ❺〈书面〉neglect; slight:轻～ flippant /无礼则～。Lack of courtesy amounts to a slight. ❻〈书面〉supposing; in case:～有遗漏 in case there are omissions ❼ (Tuō) a surname

脱靶 tuōbǎ miss the target (in shooting practice):多次～ repeatedly miss the target /打了十发,有五发～ shoot ten bullets, of which five missed the target

脱班 tuōbān be late for work; (of a bus, train, etc.) be behind schedule:统计～人数 count the number of people who are late for work /火车～了。The train is behind schedule.

脱膊 tuōbó barebacked; stripped to the waist:～上阵 go into battle stripped to the waist

脱产 tuōchǎn be released from production or one's regular work to take on other duties:～干部 cadre not engaged in production /半～ be released from production for half the time /～学习 be released from work for study

脱出 tuōchū get out of; free or extricate oneself from; veer (from an orbit, etc.):～常规 veer from the normal course /～困难局面 extricate oneself from a difficult situation

脱除 tuōchú get rid of; extricate oneself from:～危险 extricate oneself from danger

脱垂 tuōchuí 〈医学〉prolapse:脐带～ prolapse of the cord /子宫～ prolapse of uterus (*prolapsus uteri*)

脱党 tuōdǎng disconnect oneself from a political party (esp. the Communist Party of China); quit or leave a political party; forfeit party membership:自动～ disconnect oneself from a party (i. e. the CPC) of one's own accord /长期～ forfeit one's party membership through long-standing disconnection from a party

脱档 tuōdàng out of sale; sold out; not in supply:长期～ sold out for a long time /暂时～ out of stock for the time being /紧俏商品常常～。Goods in great demand are often out of sale.

脱发 tuōfà loss of hair;〈医学〉trichomadesis:～症 trichomadesis /年老～ senile trichomadesis /因病～ lose hair owing to illness

脱肛 tuōgāng 〈医学〉prolapse of anus:腹泻～ diarrhoea leading to prolapse of anus /～痔 hemorrhoid complicated by prolapse of anus

脱稿 tuōgǎo (of a manuscript) be completed:～付梓 (of a manuscript) be completed and sent to the press /～日期 date for completing a manuscript

脱钩 tuōgōu be separated or disconnected from; cut one's ties with; delink:人权与贸易～ delinkage (*or* uncoupling) of human rights from trade /经营性企业必须与党政机关～。All profit-making enterprises must cut their ties with government or Party organizations.

脱谷 tuōgǔ thresh; hull; shell:不久可能有雨,这些稻子要抓紧～。Have this paddy threshed as soon as possible, for the rains may be coming.

脱谷机 tuōgǔjī 〈农业〉threshing machine; huller; sheller

脱冠 tuōguān *also* "挂冠" guàguān remove one's official hat; resign one's office:～而去 give up one's official position and leave /～归隐 resign one's office to live a secluded life

脱硅 tuōguī 〈冶金〉desiliconization

脱轨 tuōguǐ derail:～事故 derailment /地铁三节车厢～。Three subway cars derailed.

脱滑 tuōhuá shirk responsibility or work; act in a slick way:～偷懒 shirk responsibility and loaf on the job /临阵～ desert on the eve of a battle; sneak away at a critical juncture

脱货 tuōhuò out of stock; sold out:这种药暂时～,四五天后才能运到。This medicine is temporarily out of stock; it will arrive in four or five days.

脱机 tuōjī 〈计算机〉off-line:～存储器 off-line storage (*or* memory) /～计算机 off-line computer /～输入装置 off-line input device

脱籍 tuōjí 〈旧语〉(of women sold or sentenced to become singsong girls or prostitutes) be officially released from the profession:～从良 quit the profession as a singsong girl (*or* prostitute) and be accepted into a good family

脱痂 tuōjiā 〈医学〉decrustation

脱浆 tuōjiāng 〈纺织〉desize:～工艺 desizing /～轧布机 desizing mangle

脱缰之马 tuōjiāngzhīmǎ like a runaway horse; uncontrollable; running wild:思绪如～ let one's thoughts (*or* imagination) run wild /通胀失控,势如～ uncontrollable runaway inflation /山洪突来,有如～。The mountain torrent burst forth like a runaway horse.

脱胶 tuōjiāo ❶ (of parts joined with gum or glue) come unglued; come unstuck; come apart:桌面～了。The table surface has come unstuck. /地板革～。The synthetic flooring has come unglued. /皮鞋～了。The upper and sole came apart. ❷〈化工〉degum:生丝～ degumming of raw silk

脱节 tuōjié come apart; be split; be disjointed; be out of line:因焊接不牢而～ come apart due to faulty welding /言论与实际行动～。Theory is divorced from practice.

脱静电作用 tuōjìngdiàn zuòyòng destaticization

脱臼 tuōjiù 〈医学〉dislocation

脱壳机 tuōkéjī huller; sheller

脱空 tuōkōng ❶ come to naught; abort; fail; fall through:希望～ one's hope comes to nothing ❷〈方言〉lie; resort to deception:～汉 liar

脱口 tuōkǒu say sth. unguardedly; blurt out:～骂人 blurt out abuses /她～说了这么一句。She said these words without thinking.

脱口成章 tuōkǒu-chéngzhāng *also* "出口成章" chūkǒu-chéngzhāng words flow from one's mouth as from the pen of a master; speak beautifully:这个人果然是～,文不加点。The man is a master conversationalist and his words can be written down as an essay without the slightest alteration.

脱口而出 tuōkǒu'érchū say unwittingly; blurt out; let slip:不假思索,～ blurt out without thinking /～,话多有失。If one says much without thinking, one is likely to make many slips of the tongue.

脱蜡 tuōlà 〈石油〉dewaxing

脱懒 tuōlǎn loaf on the job; be lazy:他素来勤快,从不～。He is always diligent and never loafs on the job.

脱离 tuōlí cut oneself from; break away from; be divorced from:～群众 cut oneself off from the masses; be divorced from the masses /～实际 lose contact with reality; be divorced from reality /～包围圈 break away from the encirclement /～父子关系 break off relation (*or* cut ties) as father and son /～革命 drop out of (*or* quit) the revolutionary ranks /～苦海 be rid of this troublesome life; escape from the human world of woes /～危险 be out of danger /～困境 extricate oneself from a dilemma /～接触 disengage /～虎口 escape from peril /他的计划～实际,根本行不通。His plan is impractical and won't work at all.

脱离速度 tuōlí sùdù *also* "宇宙速度" yǔzhòu sùdù second cosmic velocity

脱粒 tuōlì 〈农业〉threshing; shelling

脱粒机 tuōlìjī thresher; sheller

脱沥青 tuōlìqīng 〈石油〉deasphalting

脱磷 tuōlín 〈化学〉dephosphorization:～石油 dephosphorized oil

T

脱硫 tuōliú desulphurize; sweeten
脱漏 tuōlòu be left out; be dropped; be omitted; be missing:文字～ missing words /无一字～ without a single word left out /前胸～三针。Three stitches were dropped on the chest (in knitting). /此文～甚多。There are many omissions in this article.
脱落 tuōluò ❶ drop; fall off or away; come off:成片毛发～ one's hair falls off in patches /墙纸～了。The wall paper peeled off. /他的牙齿已全部～。All his teeth have come out. /上衣有两个扣子～了。The jacket has lost two buttons. ❷ (of writings) omit:字句～ omissions of words and sentences (in an article)
脱略 tuōlüè 〈书面〉❶ unrestrained; slighting; carefree:～细行 not bother about small matters; not be punctilious ❷ (of writings) omission; ellipsis
脱盲 tuōmáng eliminate illiteracy; wipe out illiteracy; become literate; learn to read and write:～率 rate of those who have learnt to read and write among the illiterate /她三年前才～,如今已能写小说了。Though she learnt to read and write only three years ago, she can write stories now.
脱毛 tuōmáo ❶ lose hair or feathers; moult; shed:骆驼～了。The camels have shed. /这只公鸡～脱得很厉害。This cock is moulting badly. ❷ depilate:～剂 depilatory /～作用 depilation
脱卯 tuōmǎo ❶ miss roll call ❷ out of mortise; disjointed:～之处 flaw; fault /老大的～,怎么你也看不出来? How could you fail to see such obvious flaws?
脱帽 tuōmào take off or raise one's hat (in respect):～致敬 salute sb. by taking off one's hat /～默哀 bare one's head and mourn in silence
脱敏 tuōmǐn 〈医学〉desensitize; hyposensitize:～剂 desensitizer /～药 desensitizer /～牙膏 desensitizing tooth-paste
脱模 tuōmú 〈冶金〉drawing of patterns; demoulding:～油 mould oil /～板 stripper plate
脱泡 tuōpào 〈纺织〉deaeration:～桶 deaerator
脱坯 tuōpī mould adobe blocks:和泥～ prepare some clay to mould adobe blocks /～三千 mould three thousand adobe blocks
脱皮 tuōpí slough off or shed skin; exuviate:晒得～ (skin) peels off due to sunburn /～掉肉地干活 work so hard as to neglect one's own health; work like mad
脱贫 tuōpín cross the threshold from poverty; get rid of poverty; become prosperous:～致富 shake off poverty and attain prosperity; get rid of poverty and become rich /～规划 plans to eliminate poverty
脱坡 tuōpō (of a dike or dam) have its banks collapsed or washed away (by floodwater):大坝～了。The dam collapsed. /堤岸两处～。Two sections of the dike were washed away.
脱期 tuōqī (esp. of a periodical) fail to come out on time; miss the deadline:因故～ fail to come out on time for some reason /一再～ miss the deadline again and again /～告示 notice on delayed publication /～交货 delay delivery
脱浅 tuōqiǎn (of ships) get out of a stranded position; be no longer stranded
脱氢 tuōqīng 〈化学〉dehydrogenation:～醋酸 dehydroacetic acid /～醋酸钠 sodium dehydroacetate /～酶 dehydrogenase; dehydrase
脱洒 tuōsǎ 〈书面〉free and easy; unrestrained:～不俗 free and easy; unconventional
脱色 tuōsè ❶ decolour; decolourize:～剂 decolourant; decolourizer /～工艺 decolourizing technology ❷ fade:永不～ colour-fast /衣服～了。The colour of the clothes faded.
脱涩 tuōsè remove astringent taste (of persimmons):柿子～之后才甜软。Persimmons become sweet and soft after their astringent taste is removed.
脱身 tuōshēn get away; get free; extricate oneself:一时脱不了身 can't get away for the time being /～之计 plan that helps one to extricate oneself /～而走 give sb. the slip; escape secretly
脱手 tuōshǒu ❶ slip out of the hand; let go; let slip:不小心～了 slip from one's hand while one is inattentive /箱子～砸了脚。The handle slipped from his grip and the trunk dropped on his foot. ❷ get off one's hands; dispose of; get rid of; sell:稿子你是什么时候～的? When did you get the manuscripts off your hands? *or* When did you finish the manuscripts? /货色不佳,不好～。These goods are difficult to dispose of because of their poor quality. /这批童装全部～了。That batch of children's clothes have all been sold.
脱水 tuōshuǐ ❶ 〈医学〉loss of body fluids; dehydration:～症状 symptoms of dehydration /病人～。The patient suffered a loss of body fluids. ❷ 〈化学〉dehydration; dewatering:～后储藏 store sth. after dehydration ❸ 〈方言〉(of paddy fields) be depleted of water; suffer a drought:大田～。The fields have dried up.
脱水机 tuōshuǐjī hydroextractor; whizzer
脱水冷冻 tuōshuǐ lěngdòng dehydrofreezing
脱水蔬菜 tuōshuǐ shūcài dehydrated vegetable
脱俗 tuōsú free from vulgarity; refined:一生～,处世清高 free from vulgarity and above worldly considerations throughout one's life
脱粟 tuōsù 〈书面〉brown rice; unpolished rice:～之饭 cooked brown rice
脱酸 tuōsuān 〈化工〉deacidify
脱榫 tuōsǔn (of furniture) have a loose joint:～了。The mortising has come loose.
脱胎 tuōtāi ❶ 〈工美〉process of making bodiless lacquerware:～漆器 bodiless lacquerware ❷ emerge from the womb of; be born out of; be derived from:这首歌～于陕北信天游。The song is derived from *xintianyou*, a folk song of northern Shaanxi. /这支交响乐～于一首二胡独奏曲。The symphony evolved out of an *erhu* solo.
脱胎瓷 tuōtāicí bodiless chinaware
脱胎换骨 tuōtāi-huàngǔ cast off one's old self; be reborn; thoroughly remould oneself; undergo a radical transformation:～,重新做人 thoroughly remould oneself and turn over a new leaf /～,面目一新 be thoroughly transformed and take on an entirely new look
脱碳 tuōtàn 〈冶金〉decarburize:～剂 decarburizer
脱逃 tuōtáo run away; break free; escape; flee:临阵～ flee from battle /途中历尽艰辛,他才侥幸得以～。Going through all kinds of hardships and dangers, he finally made a narrow escape.
脱体 tuōtǐ 〈方言〉(of an illness) be cured; be over:他的病快要～了。He has almost recovered from his illness.
脱兔 tuōtù (fast as) a fleeing hare:动如～ move fast as a fleeing hare /～之势 with the momentum of a fleeing hare — sharp and swift
脱位 tuōwèi *also* "脱臼"〈医学〉dislocation:关节～ joint dislocation /摔伤～ fall and suffer a dislocation
脱误 tuōwù omissions and errors:刊正～之处 publish corrigenda for omissions and errors
脱屣 tuōxǐ 〈书面〉cast-off slippers; sth. of no consequence:视如～ regard as worn-out shoes; cast aside as worthless
脱险 tuōxiǎn escape or be out of danger:虎口～ escape mortal danger; survive a disaster /侥幸～ have a narrow escape /病人正在抢救,尚未～。The patient is being given emergency treatment, but is not yet out of danger.
脱销 tuōxiāo out of stock; sold out:市场～ not available on the market /一时～ temporarily out of stock /商品～了。The goods are sold out.
脱孝 tuōxiào be out of the period of mourning
脱卸 tuōxiè shake off; shirk:～罪责 shirk responsibility for an offence (*or* crime) /百般～ try in every possible way to shake off (one's responsibility, etc.)
脱盐 tuōyán 〈化工〉desalt; desalinize
脱氧 tuōyǎng 〈化学〉deoxidate; deoxidize:～剂 deoxidizer; deoxidant
脱氧核糖 tuōyǎng hétáng 〈生化〉deoxyribose
脱氧核糖核酸 tuōyǎng hétáng hésuān deoxyribonucleic acid (DNA):～聚合酶 DNA polymerase /～酶 deoxyribonuclease; DNase
脱衣舞 tuōyīwǔ striptease:～女 stripteaser /～夜总会 striptease nightclub
脱易 tuōyì rash; impetuous; indiscreet:为人～ rash by nature; indiscreet in character
脱颖而出 tuōyǐng'érchū talent will reveal itself in a prominent way (like the point of an awl sticking out through a bag); (of talented person) rise from obscurity; become prominent:各种人才～。Various kinds of talented people have come into prominence. /这次比赛中,有许多年轻选手～。A host of young players came to the fore in the competition.
脱羽 tuōyǔ (of birds) moult:百鸟～ birds of various kinds have moulted /～季节 moulting season
脱证 tuōzhèng 〈中医〉exhaustion of vital energies at the critical stage of an illness; exhaustion syndrome
脱脂 tuōzhī defat; degrease:～牛奶 skim milk; nonfat milk
脱脂剂 tuōzhījì 〈皮革〉degreasing agent

脱脂棉 tuōzhīmián absorbent cotton
脱脂奶粉 tuōzhī nǎifěn skim milk powder; nonfat dried milk
脱脂乳 tuōzhīrǔ skim milk; nonfat milk
脱脂纱布 tuōzhī shābù absorbent gauze

拕 tuō 〈书面〉 *see* "拖" tuō

拖 tuō ❶ pull; tug; drag; haul: ~来~去 drag about; pull and haul / ~舟下水 pull (*or* drag, *or* haul) a boat into the water / ~人入股 drag sb. in as a shareholder; get sb. to invest / ~地板 mop the floor / 长裙~在地上 long skirt trailing on the ground / 汽船~着五条驳船。The steamer was towing five barges. / 这工作把人都~垮了。This job will simply wear me down! ❷ drag behind one: ~着个尾巴 trail a tail behind one / ~着根辫子 wear a pigtail down one's back / ~了一屁股债 be weighed down with debts; be deep in debt ❸ drag on; delay; postpone; procrastinate: 这件事还得~两个月才能办。The matter will drag for another two months. / 再~天就黑了。It will get dark if there's further delay. / 你真能~时间。You really know how to dillydally!

拖把 tuōbǎ *also* "拖布"; "墩布" dūnbù mop; swab: ~头 mop head
拖驳 tuōbó barge; lighter: 几只~上装满了粮食。A few barges were loaded to the brim with grain.
拖布 tuōbù *see* "拖把"
拖步 tuōbù 〈套语〉 trouble; bother: 多有~, 感谢不尽。How can I thank you enough for the trouble you've taken on my behalf?
拖铲 tuōchǎn 〈建筑〉 dragscraper: ~挖土机 dragshovel
拖车 tuōchē trailer
拖船 tuōchuán ❶ tugboat; (steam) tug; towboat: ~员工 tugman ❷ barge; lighter
拖床 tuōchuáng sledge (over ice and snow)
拖床 tuōchuang sledge for carrying farm tools in the fields
拖带 tuōdài ❶ pull; tow; haul: 一次~四节车辆 pull four carriages at one go / 新型车辆~灵活, 平稳安全。This new type of vehicle is manoeuvrable in traction, and stable and safe. ❷ 〈方言〉 be burdened by or with: 受老婆孩子的~ be burdened with one's family
拖宕 tuōdàng 〈书面〉 delay; procrastinate: ~不付 keep delaying the payment / ~时日 delay indefinitely
拖斗 tuōdǒu trailer
拖儿带女 tuō'ér-dàinǚ have one's children with one; have family burden: 她一个人~, 起五更, 熬半夜, 真不容易。She has to rise before dawn and stay up late in order to bring up the children herself. It is no easy thing to do!
拖粪 tuōfèn 〈方言〉 mop
拖杆起重机 tuōgǎn qǐzhòngjī 〈机械〉 gib crane; jib crane
拖挂 tuōguà pull; tow; haul: 拖拉机可以~犁、耙等农具。A tractor can haul a plough, a rake, or some such farm tool.
拖挂车 tuōguàchē 〈交通〉 towed vehicle; trailer
拖后腿 tuō hòutuǐ hinder or impede sb.; hold sb. back; be a drag on sb.: 不要~。Don't try to hold others back! / 这个问题不解决, 势必拖我们计划的后腿。If not properly solved, this will surely hinder our plans. / 全厂有几个落后班组, 工作一贯~。There are a few backward groups which have long been a drag on the whole factory.
拖家带口 tuōjiā-dàikǒu *also* "拖家带眷" have a family to take care of; have family burden: 他~的, 日子过得不易。Life is not easy for him as he has a family to provide for.
拖拉 tuōlā dilatory; slow; sluggish: 办事从不拖拖拉拉 never be dilatory in doing things; never drag one's heels in one's work / ~成性 sluggish by habit / ~成风 tendency to be dilatory
拖拉机 tuōlājī tractor: 手扶~ walking tractor / 轮带式~ wheeled tractor / 履带式~ tracked tractor; caterpillar tractor / ~厂 tractor plant / ~手 tractor driver / ~站 tractor station
拖累 tuōlěi encumber; burden; implicate: 家务~ burdened with household chores / 受孩子~ be tied down by children / 这件事~了你, 真对不起。I'm extremely sorry that you're implicated in this.
拖轮 tuōlún tugboat; tug; towboat
拖磨 tuōmó 〈方言〉 delay; drag on; procrastinate: 他没钱还账, 只好~着。Having no money to repay the debt, he had to resort to procrastination.
拖泥带水 tuōní-dàishuǐ messy; untidy; sloppy; slovenly: 办事~ slovenly in handling matters / ~的文章 sloppy writing / 说话干脆, 从不~ come straight to the point and never beat about the bush
拖欠 tuōqiàn fail to pay; be behind in payment; be in arrears; default: ~房租 be in arrears with rent / ~公款 hold public funds back (usu. for private use) / ~日久 be a long time behind in payment / 有意~不还 deliberately default on payment
拖腔 tuōqiāng 〈戏曲〉 drag out a word in singing
拖人下水 tuōrén-xiàshuǐ drag sb. into the water (i. e. trouble, crime, degradation, etc.) with one; get sb. into trouble; make an accomplice of sb.; corrupt sb.: 设圈套~ lay a trap to implicate sb. in an evil venture / 难道只许你~, 不许我救人上岸? How can you expect to drag people down into the mud wilfully while I'm not allowed to help them out of it?
拖三拉四 tuōsān-lāsì *also* "拖三阻四" procrastinate by one pretext or another; give the run-around: 有些人对群众求上门的事, 常常~。Some officials would procrastinate by one pretext or another even when people pay personal visits to seek help.
拖神 tuōshén 〈方言〉 rogue; hoodlum; hooligan
拖沓 tuōtà dilatory; sluggish: 工作作风~ dilatory style of work / 文字~冗长 dilatory and long-winded writing / 毫不~ free from sluggishness
拖堂 tuōtáng (of a teacher) not dismiss the class on time; drag on the class: 下课铃响了, 他还在滔滔不绝地~。Although the bell had gone, he still kept talking volubly and wouldn't dismiss the class.
拖腿 tuōtuǐ hinder; impede; hold back; be a drag: 你干你的, 我决不~。Go ahead with your work; I would not hold you back. / 快给我们原料, 否则就拖住我们的腿了。Supply us with the raw materials as soon as possible, or you'll be impeding our work.
拖网 tuōwǎng trawlnet; trawl; dragnet: ~鱼船 trawler
拖尾巴 tuō wěiba ❶ hinder; impede; hold back; be a drag: 他们不敢回来, 怕家里人~。They dared not return for fear that their families would hold them back. ❷ leave sth. undone; leave loose ends: 这工程还拖了个尾巴。There still remain some loose ends in the project.
拖鞋 tuōxié slippers
拖延 tuōyán delay; postpone; put off; procrastinate: 一味~ put off again and again / ~时日 play for time; stall (for time) / 不得~交货。No delay in delivery is permitted.
拖延策略 tuōyán cèlüè delaying ploy (in negotiation)
拖延战术 tuōyán zhànshù delaying or stalling tactics
拖曳 tuōyè drag; pull; tow: ~一门重炮 drag a heavy gun / ~一辆大车 tow a large cart
拖引船 tuōyǐnchuán towing vessel
拖油瓶 tuōyóupíng 〈贬义〉 ❶ (of a woman) remarry and bring a child of a previous marriage ❷ child of a previous marriage living with the family of one's second husband
拖债 tuōzhài be behind in debt repayment; be in arrears with debt repayment; default on debt: 不~ not to default on debts / 他拖的债还没有还清。He has not cleared off his outstanding debts.

乇 tuō (now written as 托) torr (measurement of pressure)

托[1] tuō ❶ hold up; hold in the palm; support with the hand or palm: 单手~起 hold up with one hand / 用力~着 support with all one's strength / 一只手~着下巴 cup one's chin in one's hand / 和盘~出 reveal (*or* tell) everything; hold nothing back; make a clean breast ❷ sth. serving as a support: 枪~ stock (*or* butt) of a rifle / 茶~儿 saucer / 木头~儿 wooden support / 日历~儿 calendar-book stand ❸ serve as a foil; set off: 烘云~月 paint clouds to set off the moon / 衬~ make sth. stand out by contrast; set off / 烘~ (in painting) add shading around an object to make it stand out; set off

托[2] **(託)** tuō ❶ ask; beg; entrust: ~人关照 ask sb. for a favour / 我只好央~他去为我说情。I'll have to beg him to put in a word for me. / 此人可~大事。This is someone you may entrust important business with. ❷ give as a pretext; plead: *see* "~病"; "~故" ❸ count upon; rely on; owe to: ~古改制 carry out reforms in the name of ancient precedents; quote classical principles to institute a reform

托[3] tuō (formerly written as 乇) torr (measurement of pressure)

托板 tuōbǎn 〈建筑〉 fascia

T

托庇 tuōbì rely upon sb. (usu. one's elder or an influential person) for protection:～于人 rely upon sb. for protection; be under sb.'s protection /幸有长辈～,我这才找到一份工作。Thanks to my elders, I was able to find a job.

托病 tuōbìng pleading illness; on pretext of illness:～不出 shut oneself up on pretext of illness /～不见 plead illness as an excuse for not meeting sb. /～不去 beg off on account of illness

托钵 tuōbō (as of mendicant monks) beg for alms:云游四方,～而行 roam about begging for alms /久病无依,～四邻 go begging of one's neighbours due to one's prolonged illness and lack of a livelihood

托钵僧 tuōbōsēng 〈基督教〉(mendicant) friar;〈伊斯兰〉calender

托词 tuōcí *also* "托辞" ❶ find a pretext; use a subterfuge; make an excuse:～不予办理 decline to handle sth. on some pretext /～婉拒 graciously decline with an excuse ❷ pretext; excuse; subterfuge:寻找～ look for an excuse (*or* pretext) /外交上常以有病为～。A common subterfuge in diplomacy is illness.

托辞 tuōcí *see* "托词"

托大 tuōdà ❶ put on airs; be presumptuous:他待人谦恭,从不～。He is always modest and never puts on airs. ❷ (often used in the early vernacular) careless; negligent

托底 tuōdǐ 〈方言〉❶ reassured; confident:见他回来,我的心～了。I was relieved to see him back. /群众听了这句话,都托了底,敢说话了。Hearing these words, the people felt reassured and dared to speak out. ❷ tell the truth; give the bottomline:谈到婚事,她只好向妈妈～了。Speaking of her marriage, she had to tell her mother the truth.

托地 tuōdì suddenly; abruptly; unexpectedly:他～跳过来,一把抓住我的衣领。He suddenly jumped over and seized me by the collar.

托儿所 tuō'érsuǒ nursery; kindergarten; childcare centre; crèche

托尔斯泰 Tuō'ěrsītài Lev Nikolayevich Tolstoy (1828-1910), Russian writer known for *War and Peace* and other masterpieces

托福 tuōfú ❶〈套语〉thanks to you:托您老的福,我们一家都平安。Thank you for your concern. My family and I are all safe and sound. /临走,他一再说"～"。As he was to leave, he said "thanks" again and again. ❷ (transliteration) TOEFL (Test of English as a Foreign Language)

托福考试 tuōfú kǎoshì TOEFL test

托付 tuōfù entrust; commit to sb.'s care:她把孩子～给邻居。She entrusted her child to the care of her neighbour. /这是老人临终时的～。That was the old man's request right before his death.

托孤 tuōgū (as of a dying monarch to a minister, etc.) entrust one's orphan to sb.'s care

托故 tuōgù give a pretext; make an excuse:～退席 leave a banquet (*or* meeting) on a pretext /～不来 give an excuse for not coming; beg off with a pretext

托管 tuōguǎn trusteeship:由英国～ under British trusteeship

托管地 tuōguǎndì trust territory; mandated territory

托管国 tuōguǎnguó trustee

托管理事会 tuōguǎn lǐshìhuì trusteeship council

托管领土 tuōguǎn lǐngtǔ trust territory

托管区 tuōguǎnqū mandated area; trust territory

托管制度 tuōguǎn zhìdù trusteeship

托灰板 tuōhuībǎn 〈建筑〉hawk

托疾 tuōjí 〈书面〉plead illness; on a pretext of illness:～推辞 refuse on an excuse of illness

托架 tuōjià 〈机械〉bracket:气泵～ air-pump bracket /夹紧～ clamp bracket /角形～ angle bracket

托靠 tuōkào 〈方言〉entrust; commit to sb.'s care

托克劳群岛 Tuōkèláo Qúndǎo Tokelau Islands, a group of islands between Kiribati and Western Samoa in the western Pacific Ocean

托拉斯 tuōlāsī 〈经济〉trust

托赖 tuōlài (often used in the early vernacular) rely upon sb. (usu. one's elder or an influential person) for protection

托里拆利真空 Tuōlǐchāilì zhēnkōng 〈物理〉Torricellian vacuum

托洛茨基 Tuōluòcíjī Leon Trotsky (1879-1940), an early leading member of the Bolshevik party, expelled by Stalin in 1927 and exiled in 1929:～分子 Trotskyite

托洛茨基主义 Tuōluòcíjīzhǔyì Trotskyism (mainly his theories of world revolution and permanent revolution)

托门子 tuō ménzi try to find channels through which to wangle a favour; look for ways to enlist an influential person's help:～,拉关系 try to enlist help wherever possible and cozy up to influential people

托梦 tuōmèng 〈迷信〉(as of the ghost of one's kith and kin) appear in one's dream and make a request or a revelation:～于人 appear in sb.'s dream and make a request (*or* revelation)

托名 tuōmíng use sb. else's name for one's own purpose; do sth. in sb. else's name:～行骗 practise fraud in sb. else's name /～之作 work written under sb. else's name; fake

托墨 tuōmò (of writing paper) hold the ink so that it does not run

托派 Tuōpài ❶ Trotskyite; Trotskyist:～分子 Trotskyite; Trotskyist ❷〈戏谑〉TOEFL buff

托盘 tuōpán (serving) tray

托腔 tuōqiāng (of musical accompaniment in a Chinese opera) set off or provide suitable accompaniment for the singing of an actor or actress:他拉胡琴没有花招,～托得很严。Never trying to show off in playing the *huqin*, he does his best to set off the singing of the actor (*or* actress).

托儿 tuōr 〈方言〉lure in a swindle; decoy; come-on:这个店雇～坑蒙顾客。The store hired a come-on to cheat customers.

托人情 tuō rénqíng *also* "托情" ask an influential person to help arrange sth.; gain one's end through pull; seek the good offices of sb.:～办私事 ask an influential person to arrange a private matter for one /这件事托了人情,才办妥了。We got it done only after obtaining the help of an influential person.

托身 tuōshēn ❶ find accommodation or a place to live in:暂且在此～。I might just as well find shelter here. /半生无有～之处。I wandered from place to place for half my life. ❷ seek a living:～无术 be unable to make a living

托生 tuōshēng 〈迷信〉be reincarnated (in a new body); be reborn:希望来世～一个好去处 hope to be reborn in a better place in the next life /～为富家子 be reincarnated as a child of a wealthy family

托收 tuōshōu 〈商业〉collection:～票据 bill for collection /～承付 (as of an entrusted bank) collection and payment

托熟 tuōshú not stand on ceremony due to familiarity; feel familiar enough not to bother about etiquette:彼此一见面,他便有些～。At their first meeting, he felt so close to him as not to bother about etiquette. /因为～,两人见面便没有讲俗礼。As they felt familiar with each other, they dispensed with conventional etiquette when they met.

托叶 tuōyè 〈植物〉stipule

托幼 tuōyòu nursery and kindergarten:～教育 preschool education /从事～事业 work in nurseries and kindergartens

托运 tuōyùn consign for shipment; check:～行李 check one's baggage /～物 consignment /慢件～ (consign) by ordinary delivery /快件～ (consign) by express delivery /把行李直接～到纽约 check one's baggage through to New York

托运人 tuōyùnrén consignor

托嘱 tuōzhǔ ask; beg; entrust:信中一再～ ask (*or* request) repeatedly in the letter /～之言 request; entreaty

托子 tuōzi base; stand; support:枪～ rifle butt (*or* stock) /花瓶～ vase support (*or* holder) /雕花木～ carved wooden base

托足 tuōzú 〈书面〉gain a foothold; find shelter

托座 tuōzuò 〈建筑〉bracket

侂(侘、任) tuō 〈书面〉entrust to the care or safekeeping (of sb.)

tuó

沱 tuó ❶〈方言〉(often used in place names) small bay in a river:朱家～ Zhu Family Bay ❷ (of tears) stream down like rain:出涕～若 let loose a flood of tears

沱茶 tuóchá bowl-shaped compressed mass of tea leaves produced in Sichuan or Yunnan

坨 tuó ❶ (of food made of flour) stick together:面条～了。The noodles have stuck together. ❷ lump; heap:肉～儿 lump of meat

坨子 tuózi lump; heap:盐～ lump of salt /泥～ lump of mud; clod /礁石～ reef crag

柁 tuó 〈建筑〉girder

酡 tuó 〈书面〉(of one's face) be flushed with drink:～然 be flushed with drink

酡颜 tuóyán 〈书面〉complexion flushed with drink

砣(❶铊) tuó ❶ movable or sliding weight of a balance or steelyard ❷ stone rooler ❸ cut or polish jade with an emery wheel:～了一个玉杯 polish jade into a cup

砣子 tuózi emery wheel for cutting or polishing jade

跎 tuó *see* "蹉跎" cuōtuó

佗 tuó 〈书面〉carry or bear on the back:以马～食 carry grain on horseback

鮀 tuó

鮀鼥 tuóbá 〈古语〉marmot

鸵 tuó ostrich (*Struhio camelus*)

鸵鸟 tuóniǎo ostrich

鸵鸟政策 tuóniǎo zhèngcè ostrich policy; ostrichism:他们实行～,对这个长期存在的事实装做看不见。Resorting to ostrichism, they just turned a blind eye to this long-standing problem.

陀 tuó 〈书面〉hill; hillock

陀螺 tuóluó spinning top:抽～ whip a top

陀螺动力学 tuóluó dònglìxué gyrodynamics

陀螺罗盘 tuóluó luópán gyrocompass

陀螺仪 tuóluóyí 〈航空〉gyroscope; gyro; gyroscopic drift

驼 tuó ❶ camel:～毛 camel's hair / 单峰～ dromedary; Arabian camel / 双峰～ Bactrian camel ❷ hunchbacked; humpbacked:老年背～ be hunchbacked from old age

驼背 tuóbèi ❶ hunchbacked; humpbacked:～老人 hunchbacked old man ❷〈方言〉hunchback; humpback:张～ Hunchback Zhang

驼峰 tuófēng ❶ hump (of a camel) ❷〈交通〉hump:～调车场 hump yard / ～调车法 hump switching

驼工 tuógōng person who works a camel; camel driver

驼铃 tuólíng camel bell

驼鹿 tuólù *also* "堪达罕" kāndáhǎn; "犴" hān 〈动物〉elk; moose

驼绒 tuóróng ❶ camel's hair:～大氅 overcoat made of camel's hair / ～毛线 camel wool ❷ *also* "骆驼绒" luòtuoróng camel hair cloth

驼色 tuósè colour of camel's hair; light tan

驼羊 tuóyáng 〈动物〉llama

驼子 tuózi 〈口语〉hunchback; humpback

堶 tuó 〈书面〉brick

橐[1](槖) tuó 〈书面〉a kind of bag

橐[2](槖) tuó 〈象声〉:～～的皮靴声 thudding of leather boots

橐驼 tuótuó 〈书面〉camel

鼍(鼉) tuó *also* "鼍龙"; "扬子鳄" yángzǐ'è 〈动物〉(popularly known as 猪婆龙) Chinese alligator

陁 tuó 〈书面〉*see* "盘陁" pántuó

驰 tuó 〈书面〉*see* "驼" tuó

驮 tuó carry or bear on the back:～了一口袋面 carry a sack of flour on one's back / 肩扛背～ carry on one's back or shoulder

see also duò

驮鞍 tuó'ān pack saddle

驮畜 tuóchù *also* "驮兽" pack animal

驮轿 tuójiào sedan-chair carried on an animal's back:坐在～上上山 go uphill in a sedan-chair carried on a pack animal's back

驮筐 tuókuāng pannier:装了一～水果 fill a pannier with fruit / ～装满了。The panniers are full to the brim.

驮篓 tuólǒu pannier

驮马 tuómǎ pack horse

tuǒ

庹 tuǒ ❶〈量词〉arm spread — about 5.5 feet or 1.7 metres ❷ (Tuǒ) a surname

鬌 tuǒ *see* "鬈鬌" wǒtuǒ

椭(橢) tuǒ ellipse

椭率 tuǒlǜ 〈数学〉ellipticity

椭面 tuǒmiàn 〈数学〉ellipsoid

椭球 tuǒqiú ellipsoid:～坐标 ellipsoidal coordinates / ～投影 elliptical projection

椭球函数 tuǒqiú hánshù ellipsoidal harmonics

椭球体 tuǒqiútǐ spheroid; ellipsoid:～泛光灯 ellipsoidal floodlight / ～聚光灯 ellipsoidal spotlight

椭圆 tuǒyuán 〈数学〉❶ ellipse; oval:～齿轮 elliptical gear / ～轨道 elliptical orbit / ～形办公室 Oval Office (of the US President) ❷ ellipsoid

椭圆截面 tuǒyuán jiémiàn oval cross section

椭圆体 tuǒyuántǐ ellipsoid

椭圆星云 tuǒyuán xīngyún elliptical nebula

椭圆柱面 tuǒyuánzhùmiàn elliptic cylinder

椭圆椎面 tuǒyuánzhuīmiàn elliptic cone

妥 tuǒ ❶ appropriate; suitable; sound; proper:稳～ safe; reliable / 欠～ not proper; not quite satisfactory / ～为处理 deal with sth. properly / 意见～否 whether an idea is sound or not ❷ (often used after a verb) ready; settled; resolved; finished:车已雇～。The taxi is ready. / 住房已租～。A deposit has been paid for the room. / 货已购～。The goods have been purchased.

妥便 tuǒbiàn suitable and convenient:这个解决办法很～。This is an appropriate and convenient solution.

妥布霉素 tuǒbùméisù 〈药学〉tobramycin

妥当 tuǒdang appropriate; proper; suitable:～的方法 proper method / 又～又安全 both appropriate and safe / 一切均安排～。Everything has been well arranged (*or* prepared).

妥靠 tuǒkào reliable; dependable; trustworthy:～的人选 trustworthy (*or* reliable) candidate / 是否～,还望斟酌。Please consider again whether it is reliable.

妥善 tuǒshàn appropriate; proper; well arranged:下岗职工已得到～安排。Appropriate arrangements have been made for those who are laid off. / 要～地处理同对方的关系问题。We should properly handle our relationship with the other side.

妥实 tuǒshí solid and proper; practical and reliable:提出～可行的意见 make proper and practical suggestions

妥适 tuǒshì appropriate; fitting; proper:这种贵重的物品须保藏在～的地方。Such valuables should be kept in a proper place.

妥帖 tuǒtiē fit and proper; appropriate; fitting:文字～ proper wording; happy choice of words / ～的译文 apt translation / 这些事他都办～了。He has made all necessary arrangements. / 请勿担心,我自有～安排。Don't worry. I know how to get things fixed.

妥协 tuǒxié come to terms; compromise:双方～的结果 outcome of mutual concessions / ～性 tendency towards compromise (*or* accommodation) / 看来两国未能就这些问题达成～。It seems that no compromise has been reached between the two countries.

tuò

拓 tuò ❶ open up; develop; reclaim:开～一条新马路 construct a new street ❷ (Tuò) a surname

see also tà

拓跋宏 Tuòbá Hóng Tuoba Hong (467-499), emperor of the

T

Northern Wei Dynasty, called reverently Wei Xiaowendi (魏孝文帝) after death
拓地 tuòdì 〈书面〉expand one's territory: ～千里 expand the territory far and wide by thousands of *li*
拓荒 tuòhuāng open up virgin soil; reclaim wasteland: 高原～ reclaim wasteland on a plateau /～边境 open up virgin soil in a border area /～者 pioneer; pathbreaker; trailblazer
拓宽 tuòkuān broaden; extend: ～研究的范围 broaden (*or* extend) the scope of one's research /～思路 expand one's ideas; broaden one's horizon /～人行道 broaden a pavement
拓落 tuòluò 〈书面〉❶ be frustrated; be disappointed: 为官～ be frustrated in one's official career ❷ broad; vast: ～大度 broad-minded
拓扑学 tuòpūxué 〈数学〉topology
拓展 tuòzhǎn expand; extend; develop: ～视野 extend one's field of vision; extend one's horizon /～市场 expand one's market
拓殖 tuòzhí occupy and colonize

柝(欜) tuò 〈书面〉watchman's clapper or knocker: 击～ strike a clapper

跅 tuò

跅弛 tuòchí 〈书面〉dissolute; dissipated: ～之士 dissipated person; person who leads a life of debauchery

萚(蘀) tuò 〈书面〉fallen bark or leaves

箨(籜) tuò 〈书面〉sheaths of bamboo shoots

唾 tuò ❶ saliva; spittle: ～沫 saliva; spittle ❷ spit; expectorate: 力～数尺之远 spit a distance of several *chi* /～了一口唾沫 give a spitting ❸ show one's contempt (by spitting): *see* "～骂"; "～弃"

唾壶 tuòhú spittoon
唾骂 tuòmà spit on and curse; spurn: 万人～ be spat on and cursed by the common people /为世人所～ be spurned by the general public
唾面自干 tuòmiàn-zìgān be spat on the face and let the spittle dry without wiping — sign of extreme obsequiousness or composure; swallow an insult in meek submission; be composed even when people make one angry: ～, 世人不忍 be spat on the face and let the spittle dry — sth. most people can't tolerate /～, 无济于事。It's no use turning the other cheek.
唾沫 tuòmo saliva; spittle: 吐了一口～ spit /直咽～ keep swallowing saliva
唾沫星子 tuòmoxīngzi spray of saliva: 说到得意处, 嘴里直喷～。He got so excited that he sprayed saliva while speaking.
唾弃 tuòqì contemn; spurn; treat with contempt: 为世人所～ be contemned by the people
唾手可得 tuòshǒu-kědé get or win with hands down; be extremely easy to obtain: ～之物 something extremely easy to get /胜利～。The victory can easily be won. /敌人阵地～。We would seize the enemy position without much effort.
唾涎 tuòxián saliva
唾液 tuòyè saliva: 分泌～ secrete saliva /满口～ (with one's mouth) full of saliva
唾液腺 tuòyèxiàn *also* "唾腺" salivary gland
唾余 tuòyú sb. else's insignificant phrases or opinion: 拾人～ pick up phrases from sb. and pass them off as one's own
唾掌 tuòzhǎng spit in one's palm — extremely easy: ～之劳 sth. as easy as spitting in one's palm; easy job; duck soup /天下～可定。It's as easy as pie to stabilize the country.

魄 tuò variant for pò as in "落魄" luòpò

see also bó; pò

T

wā

洼(窪) wā ❶ low-lying; hollow; depressed: 低～地 low-lying land /坑坑～～ full of potholes ❷ depression; low-lying area: 水～儿 water-logged depression /山～ depression in a mountain ridge; col

洼地 wādì depression; low-lying area: 填平～ fill up a depression /～排水不良。Low-lying land does not drain well.

洼下 wāxià near to the ground; low-lying: 地势～ low-lying land (*or* terrain)

洼陷 wāxiàn depressed; sunken: 路面～ sunken surface of a road /眼眶～ sunken orbit

洼子 wāzi depression; hollow: 水～ water-logged depression

哇 wā ❶〈象声〉*used to indicate sound of crying, etc.*: ～地哭出声来 cry out loud; burst out crying /～地吐了一地 vomit all over the ground ❷〈书面〉decadent: 淫～之音 sexy music

see also wa

哇啦 wālā *also*"哇喇"〈象声〉din; uproar: ～～地乱叫 raise a hullabaloo /他一进门就～～地抱怨起来。Hardly had he entered the room when he started complaining loudly.

哇喇 wālā *see*"哇啦"

哇哇 wāwā 〈象声〉cry; caw: 小孩～地哭了起来。The little child sent forth a cry. /一开门就听见老鸦在树上～叫。We heard the crows cawing noisily in the trees when we opened the door.

蛙(鼃) wā frog: 青～ frog /牛～ bullfrog /～科动物 ranid /井底之～ frog in a well — person with a very parochial outlook (*or* a very narrow vision)

蛙人 wārén frogman

蛙式打夯机 wāshì dǎhāngjī frog rammer

蛙泳 wāyǒng 〈体育〉breaststroke; frog style or stroke: ～蹬腿 frog (*or* breaststroke) kick; whip kick /反～ breaststroke on the back /高航式～ "high sail" breaststroke /～运动员 breaststroker

挖 wā ❶ dig; excavate; scoop: ～战壕 dig a trench (*or* an entrenchment) /～洞 dig (*or* excavate) a hole /～耳朵 pick one's ears /在花园里～出一箱古钱币 unearth a box of ancient coins in the garden /～出潜藏的奸细 ferret (*or* winkle) out hidden spies /～思想根源 analyse the ideological root /～塘泥 scoop up sludge from a pond /～人才 lure talents (to one's institution from another) /恐怖分子～掉了人质的眼睛。The terrorists gouged out the eyes of the hostage. ❷〈方言〉scratch; claw: 他脸被人～破了。His face was scratched (by someone).

挖补 wābǔ mend by covering a damaged place; patch: 爸爸的这件旧皮袄需要～一下。Father's worn-out fur jacket needs mending.

挖槽机 wācáojī 〈机械〉groover

挖兜 wādōu inset pocket

挖耳 wā'ěr 〈方言〉earpick

挖方 wāfāng 〈建筑〉earthwork and stonework dug; cubage of excavation

挖根 wāgēn dig up by the roots; pull up by the roots; root out; uproot

挖沟机 wāgōujī ditcher; trench digger

挖角儿 wājuér 〈口语〉lure away a star performer (from a rival company or troupe)

挖掘 wājué excavate; unearth; tap: ～古墓 excavate ancient tombs /～出一批珍贵文物 unearth a large number of precious historical relics /～科研的潜力 tap potentials for scientific research /要注意～这些诗词的意境。Try to bring out the subtle meaning and nuances of these poems.

挖掘机 wājuéjī excavator; navvy; steam shovel: 斗式～ bucket excavator /履带式～ caterpillar (*or* tracked) excavator /步行式～ walking excavator /拉索式～ dragline excavator /液压～ hydraulic excavator

挖空心思 wākōng-xīnsī 〈贬义〉rack or cudgel one's brains: ～为自己的错误行径辩护 cudgel one's brains trying to justify one's wrong behaviour

挖苦 wāku speak sarcastically or ironically; taunt: 他拿这事可把我～了一顿。He made sarcastic remarks about me on that account. /她～他出了洋相。She taunted him for having cut such a sorry figure. /你没听出来那是～你的? Don't you realize that it was a dig at you?

挖苦话 wākuhuà sarcastic remark; ironic thrust

挖泥船 wāníchuán dredger; dredge

挖潜 wāqián exploit latent potentialities; tap potentials: 想方设法～ try every means to bring all potentialities into full play

挖墙脚 wā qiángjiǎo 〈口语〉undermine the foundation (of sth.); cut the ground from under sb.'s feet: 这个集体很团结，谁也无法挖他们的墙脚。This is a closely united team that nobody could do anything to undermine its solidarity. /我们决不干那种～的缺德事。We will never stoop so low as to cut the ground from under someone's feet.

挖肉补疮 wāròu-bǔchuāng *also*"剜肉医疮" wānròu-yīchuāng cut out a piece of flesh to treat a boil — a cure worse than the ailment

挖土机 wātǔjī *see*"挖掘机"

凹 wā *also*"洼" wā (used in place names) concave; hollow: 核桃～ Hetaowa (Walnut Hollow — a place in Shanxi Province)

see also āo

窊 wā *also*"洼" wā (used in place names) concave; hollow: 南～子 Nanwazi (South Hollow — a place in Shanxi Province)

娲(媧) wā *see*"女娲" Nǚwā

啘[1] wā 〈方言〉〈助词〉*used for affirmation or emphasis*

啘[2] wā 〈中医〉retch

wá

娃 wá ❶ baby; child: 女～儿 baby girl ❷〈方言〉newborn animal: 狗～ puppy /猪～ piglet; pigling

娃娃 wáwa baby; child: 胖～ chubby (*or* plump) child /泥～ clay doll /小～ baby /～脸 baby face

娃娃床 wáwachuáng bed for a young child; crib; cot

娃娃亲 wáwaqīn child betrothal (arranged by the children's parents): 有些农村还流行～，给双方带来许多麻烦。Child betrothals, still common in some villages, often land both parties in trouble.

W

娃娃生 wáwashēng 〈戏曲〉baby *sheng* — child actor who performs the role of a teenager in traditional Chinese opera
娃娃鱼 wáwayú giant salamander
娃崽 wázǎi 〈方言〉baby; child; kid
娃子 wázi ❶〈方言〉baby; child：这个～真淘气。The child is very naughty. ❷〈方言〉newborn animal：猪～ piglet; pigling ❸〈旧语〉slave (esp. among the minority nationalities in the Liangshan Mountains in the past)

wǎ

瓦[1] wǎ ❶ tile：砖～ bricks and tiles / 脊～ ridge tile / 石～ tilestone / ～碴儿 broken tiles / 红墙绿～ ochre walls and green tiles / 片～无存 not a single tile remains; be razed to the ground ❷ made of baked clay; earthen：～盆 earthen basin
瓦[2] wǎ (short for 瓦特)〈电学〉watt
see also wà
瓦当 wǎdāng 〈考古〉eaves tile
瓦房 wǎfáng tile-roofed house
瓦釜雷鸣 wǎfǔ-léimíng earthen pot making a lot of noise (instead of copper bells) — man without virtue or talent usurping a high position and lording it over others; worthless politicians are in power while good men are out
瓦岗军 Wǎgāngjūn Wagang Army, peasant army of Henan that rose against the Sui Dynasty and played a vital role in its overthrow
瓦工 wǎgōng ❶ bricklaying, tiling or plastering：新房子的～已经完成。The bricklaying, tiling and plastering for the new house have been completed. ❷ bricklayer; tiler; plasterer
瓦棺 wǎguān earthen coffin in ancient times
瓦罐 wǎguàn earthen jar
瓦灰 wǎhuī dark gray：穿一身～色衣裤 in a suit of dark gray clothes
瓦匠 wǎjiang bricklayer; tiler; plasterer
瓦解 wǎjiě fall apart; collapse; crumble; disintegrate：～敌军 cause the enemy forces to fall apart / 反动政权已经全部～。The reactionary regime has totally collapsed.
瓦解冰消 wǎjiě-bīngxiāo *also* "冰消瓦解" melt like ice and break like tiles; disintegrate; dissolve
瓦块 wǎkuài fragments of tiles; broken tiles
瓦剌 Wǎlà name used for western Mongolian tribes during the Ming Dynasty
瓦蓝 wǎlán azure; bright blue; sky-blue：～的天空，没有一丝云彩。The sky is blue and clear without a cloud.
W
瓦楞 wǎléng ❶ *see* "瓦垄" ❷ corrugated：～帽 (formerly worn by common people) hat with a depression along the middle
瓦楞铁皮 wǎléng tiěpí corrugated (sheet) iron
瓦楞纸 wǎléngzhǐ corrugated paper
瓦楞子 wǎléngzi *see* "瓦垄子"
瓦砾 wǎlì rubble; debris：这座建筑物被烧得只剩下一片～。The building was reduced to debris by the fire.
瓦亮 wǎliàng polished; shiny：～的晴天 bright sunny day / 擦得油光～的自行车 well-polished bike
瓦垄 wǎlǒng *also* "瓦楞"〈建筑〉corrugated ridges of tiles on a roof
瓦垄子 wǎlǒngzi *also* "瓦楞子" popular term for blood clam, ark shell, etc. whose shell is used as traditional medicine
瓦努阿图 Wǎnǔ'ātú Vanuatu, country consisting of a group of islands in the southwest Pacific
瓦圈 wǎquān rim (as of a bicycle or cart wheel)
瓦全 wǎquán live in dishonour; drag out an ignoble existence：宁为玉碎，不为～ would rather die in honour than live in shame
瓦舍 wǎshè ❶ tile-roofed house ❷ *also* "瓦子" (in the Song and Yuan dynasties) entertainment district
瓦时 wǎshí 〈电学〉watt-hour
瓦斯 wǎsī gas：毒～ poisonous gas / ～爆炸 gas explosion / ～筒 gas cylinder / ～监控系统 methane monitoring system / ～警报系统 gas alarm / ～油〈化工〉gas oil
瓦斯炉 wǎsīlú gas stove
瓦松 wǎsōng 〈植物〉*Orostachys fimbriatus*
瓦特 wǎtè 〈电学〉watt
瓦特计 wǎtèjì wattmeter
瓦特小时 wǎtè xiǎoshí 〈电学〉watt-hour：～计 watt-hour meter
瓦头 wǎtóu outward edge of an eaves-tile
瓦砚 wǎyàn tile-inkstone (made from palace tile)
瓦窑 wǎyáo tile kiln

佤 Wǎ *see* "佤族"
佤族 Wǎzú Va nationality, living in Yunnan Province

wà

袜(襪、韤) wà socks; stockings; hose：一双短～ a pair of socks / 尼龙～ nylon socks / 毛～ woollen socks / 连裤～ panty hose; tights / ～底子 (usu. with hand-stitched patches) reinforced soles of socks
袜厂 wàchǎng hosiery
袜船 wàchuán 〈方言〉cloth slippers (worn inside shoes)
袜带 wàdài suspenders; garters
袜底儿 wàdǐr sole of a sock
袜套 wàtào socks; ankle socks
袜筒 wàtǒng leg of a stocking
袜子 wàzi socks; stockings; hose
瓦 wà cover (a roof) with tiles; tile：房子就等～瓦了。The house is ready for the tiling of the roof.
see also wǎ
瓦刀 wàdāo bricklayer's cleaver
嗢 wà 〈书面〉❶ swallow：～咽 swallow ❷ laugh
嗢噱 wàjué 〈书面〉laugh loudly; guffaw
膃 wà
膃肭 wànà 〈书面〉obese; corpulent
膃肭脐 wànàqí 〈中药〉penis and testes of the ursine seal used as medicine
膃肭兽 wànàshòu *also* "海狗" hǎigǒu 〈动物〉fur seal; ursine seal

wa

哇 wa 〈助词〉*variant of* 啊 *when preceded by words ending phonetically in* u *or* ao：你别哭～。Couldn't you stop crying, eh? / 多好～！Wonderful!
see also wā

wāi

歪 wāi ❶ askew; tilted; inclined; slanting：镜子挂～了。The mirror is hung askew. / 柱子～了。The column is not erect. / 他～着头仔细瞧这幅画。He scrutinized the picture with his head tilted to one side. ❷ lie on one's side to rest：他忙了一夜，才～下，你们就来了。He was busy working the whole night and had just lain down to rest when you came. ❸ improper; unethical; evil：说得轻点，这也是个～主意。The idea is unethical, to say the least. ❹〈方言〉domineering; despotic：这家伙在乡下可～得很呢。The fellow is a genuine local despot in the village.
歪才 wāicái perverted genius or talent
歪缠 wāichán bother persistently; pester; plague：别跟我～，我不会答应你的。Stop pestering me! I won't agree.
歪词儿 wāicír unreasonable talk; false reasoning：他这个人正事不干，～倒挺多。Although he never does a stroke of decent work, he is always ready with lame and self-righteous excuses.
歪打正着 wāidǎ-zhèngzháo hit the mark by a fluke; win success by mere chance; have a stroke of serendipitous luck：他这次获奖不过是～。He won the award by a fluke. / 他有点福气，往往能～。He is a lucky guy who often gets what he wants, though not quite deservedly.
歪道 wāidào ❶ evil ways; depraved way of life：年纪轻轻的，可要

注意不走～。As you are young, you must particularly guard against temptations to evil. ❷ *also* "歪道道儿" evil or wicked idea; dirty trick:这家伙脑袋里装的尽是～。The guy is full of dirty tricks.

歪风 wāifēng evil wind; unhealthy trend or practice:狠刹～ put an end to unhealthy practices resolutely

歪风邪气 wāifēng-xiéqì evil winds and noxious influences; harmful trends and sinister practices:抵制～ oppose (*or* boycott) harmful trends and sinister practices

歪号 wāihào 〈方言〉nickname

歪话 wāihuà lie; untruth:明明没那宗事,要叫我说～,我不干。That is not true, and I won't be made to lie about it!

歪楞 wāileng 〈方言〉tilt:他～着脑袋争辩。He was arguing with his head tilted to one side.

歪理 wāilǐ lame argument; false reasoning; sophistry:～邪说 sophistries and heresies /这个家伙又精又滑,善讲～。Cunning as a fox, the fellow is adroit at sophistry.

歪路 wāilù crooked path or course; dishonest practices or means:发家致富走正路还是走～,这是一个严肃的问题。It is a matter of grave consequence whether we follow the right course or resort to crooked means in order to get rich.

歪门邪道 wāimén-xiédào crooked ways or means; dishonest practices:这个人尽搞～。The chap is for ever getting involved in shady deals.

歪扭 wāiniǔ twisted; crooked; askew:他的嘴有些～。His mouth was slightly twisted.

歪派 wāipai 〈方言〉blame wrongly; shift blame on; do wrong to:自己弄糟的事,别～别人。Don't try to shift the blame on to others for the mess you've made yourself. *or* Don't try to blame others for what you did.

歪七扭八 wāiqī-niǔbā *also* "歪七竖八";"歪七斜八" twisted out of shape; crooked; askew:字写得～ write a poor hand; scrawl /喝了酒,走路～ stagger along after drinking /他没做过～的见不得人的事。He has never done anything that he is ashamed of.

歪曲 wāiqū ❶ distort; misrepresent; twist:～某人的话 twist what sb. says /不容许任意地～事实。Deliberate distortions of facts are not allowed. *or* We won't allow the facts to be deliberately distorted. /这篇文章～了原作的主旨。This article misrepresents the theme of the original work. /改动几处数据就可能～整个调查的结果。A few altered figures would skew the result of the survey. ❷ crooked; askew; aslant:面部～ distorted face

歪诗 wāishī inelegant verse; doggerel:我那几首～不值一提。Those doggerels of mine are not worth mentioning. /他能写几句～。He can write verses of a sort.

歪歪倒倒 wāiwai-dǎodǎo ❶ unsteady:他一声不响,～地上了床。Quietly he staggered into bed. ❷ crooked; aslant; twisted:字写得～的 write a poor hand; scrawl

歪歪扭扭 wāiwāi-niǔniǔ crooked; askew; twisted:～的两排牙齿 two rows of uneven teeth /～的字体 sprawling handwriting

歪斜 wāixié crooked; askew; aslant:～不平的石板路 crooked uneven flagstone road /风把树吹得～了。The tree bent (*or* leant) in the wind. /房子～得厉害。The house leant conspicuously to one side. /书摆得歪歪斜斜的。The books were stacked in a haphazard way. /他歪歪斜斜地向前挪了几步。He staggered a few steps forward.

歪嘴和尚 wāizuǐ héshang monk with a wry mouth — person who deliberately distorts things (e.g. policies and decrees of the country or instructions of the higher authorities)

喎

wāi 〈叹词〉hey; well:～,你住在哪儿? Well, where do you live?

喎(喎)

wāi (of the mouth) awry

喎僻不遂 wāipì-bùsuí 〈中医〉facial paralysis and hemiplegia resulting from apoplexy

喎斜 wāixié (of the mouth and the eyes) awry:口眼～ with both the mouth and the eyes awry

wǎi

搲

wǎi scoop up; ladle out:从水桶里～水 ladle out water from a bucket

崴(❸踒)

wǎi ❶ rugged (mountain) path ❷ (used in place names) bend (in a river or mountain range) ❸ sprain; twist:～了脚 sprain one's ankle

see also wēi

崴泥 wǎiní be bogged down in mire; land in trouble:事情拖下去要～。Further delay will cause trouble. /这下子他可崴了泥了。Now he is in deep water.

崴子 wǎizi 〈方言〉(usually used in place names) bend (in a river or mountain range):三道～ *Sandao Waizi* (Third Bend — a place in Jilin Province)

wài

外[1]

wài ❶ outer; outside:～城 outer city /～壕 outer trench /～膜 outer membrane /城～ outside the city /大门～ outside the gate /～脆里嫩 crisp on the outside but tender within /从～向里推 shove in /围得里三层,～三层 (of a crowd) surround sth. ring upon ring /女主内,男主～。〈旧语〉The woman takes charge inside the home, while the man handles everything outside. ❷ other (than one's own):～村 other villages /～校学生 students from other schools /出门在～ be away from home /～出谋生 leave home to seek a living ❸ foreign; external; alien:～轮 foreign steamer; foreign ship (*or* vessel) /涉～事务 foreign-related matters (*or* affairs) /古今中～ ancient and modern, Chinese and foreign; at all times and in all countries /中～合资 joint venture /对～开放 open to the outside world /～为中用 make foreign things serve China /中～关系 relations between China and foreign countries; China's relations with foreign countries /对～贸易 foreign trade; external trade /改善～商投资环境 improve the environment for overseas investments in China ❹ (relatives) of one's mother, sisters or daughters:～亲 wife's or mother's relatives; relatives on mother's or wife's side /～姑〈方言〉wife's mother; mother-in-law ❺ not of the same family, class, organization, etc.; not closely related:～客 visitor who is not a relative or friend; guest /见～ regard as an outsider /电话不～借。This telephone is not for public use. ❻ besides; moreover; in addition; beyond:百里之～ beyond a hundred *li*; over one hundred *li* away /预算～开支 extra-budgetary expenditure /中国除汉族～,还有五十多个兄弟民族。There are over fifty nationalities besides the Hans in China. /主客之～,另有七位陪客。Apart from the guest of honour, there were seven other guests at the dinner. /饭菜～加酒水共七十五元。The dinner came to 75 *yuan* including the beverages. ❼ unofficial: *see* "～号";"～传"

外[2]

wài 〈戏曲〉role of an elderly man

外摆线 wàibǎixiàn 〈数学〉epicycloid:～轮〈机械〉epicycloid wheel

外办 wàibàn (short for 外事办公室) foreign affairs office; foreign relations office; (at a school) international programme

外邦 wàibāng 〈书面〉foreign country

外币 wàibì (short for 外国货币) foreign currency:～账户 foreign currency account /～兑换处 foreign currency exchange section (*or* counter) /～申报表 currency declaration /不准倒卖～。Trading in foreign currencies without a permit is forbidden.

外边 wàibian ❶ outside; out:～正在下雨。It is raining outside. /房子～有个花园。There is a garden in front of the house. /～有人敲门。Someone is knocking at the door. ❷ away from where one lives or works:他在～住了好多年。He has lived away from home for many years. /我儿子在～上大学。My son is away at college. ❸ exterior; outer; outside:水管～涂了一层银粉。The water pipe is coated with a layer of silver paint. /箱子～捆了一道绳子。The trunk is tied up with a rope.

外表 wàibiǎo (outward) appearance; exterior; surface; veneer:从～上看 judging by appearances /～粗糙 have a rough surface; look coarse /～老实,骨子奸诈 appear honest but be inwardly full of cunning and deceit /～上道貌岸然,一肚子男盗女娼 pose always as a gentleman of high morals but actually have no shame or scruples /他虽很自负,～上却显得彬彬有礼。He is a conceited man with a veneer of good manners.

外宾 wàibīn foreign guest or visitor:接待～ receive foreign

W

guests /～接待室 reception room for foreign guests
外部 wàibù ❶ outside; external; extraneous:～条件 external conditions /～联系 external relations /～世界 outside (*or* external) world /～敌人 enemies from without ❷ exterior; outer; surface:～装修 exterior decoration; outside finish /～形状 exterior shape /～标记 external label
外部程序式计算机 wàibù chéngxùshì jìsuànjī externally programmed computer
外部存储 wàibù cúnchǔ external (memory) storage
外部电源 wàibù diànyuán external power source
外部董事 wàibù dǒngshì outside director
外部辐射 wàibù fúshè external radiation
外部裂化 wàibù lièhuà 〈化工〉extraneous cracking
外部注气 wàibù zhùqì 〈石油〉external gas injection; crestal injection; gas-cap injection
外埠 wàibù town or city other than where one is:～邮件 out-of-town mail /本市生产的啤酒在～也很畅销。Beer made here sells well in other cities too.
外财 wàicái special earnings; extra income:人无～不富。〈俗语〉You have to have extra earnings to get rich. /他这几年颇发了点～。In the past few years, he has made quite a pile in his spare time.
外层 wàicéng outer; outer-field:～旋转发电机 outer-field generator
外层空间 wàicéng kōngjiān extra-atmospheric space; outer space:～导弹 outer-space missile /～法 law of outer space /～生命 exolife
外层空间生物学 wàicéng kōngjiān shēngwùxué *also* "宇宙生物学" yǔzhòu shēngwùxué; "外空生物学" exobiology:～家 exobiologist
外层焰 wàicéngyàn 〈化学〉outer flame
外差 wàichā 〈电学〉heterodyne:～检波器 heterodyne detector /～频率 heterodyne frequency /～式分析仪 heterodyne analyser /超～superheterodyne
外差因素 wàichā yīnsù externality
外场 wàicháng used to socializing and grandeur:他是个～人,人头儿挺广。He is a socialite with a wide circle of acquaintances. /她～了一辈子,如何能安于孤独? She was used to socializing and the grand style all her life. How could she content herself with a life of solitude?
外场 wàichǎng ❶〈体育〉outfield:～手 outfielder ❷ (in drama or opera) front-stage:～椅 front-stage chair ❸ field round the runway of an airfield
外钞 wàichāo foreign money or banknote; foreign currency
外臣 wàichén 〈旧语〉❶ term used to refer to oneself by an official of a feudal state before the king of another ❷ vassal ❸ local government offical
外齿轮 wàichǐlún external gear
外出 wàichū ❶ be not in; be not at home ❷ go out (esp. to another city or town) on business
外出血 wàichūxuè 〈医学〉external haemorrhage
外传 wàichuán ❶ spread; leak:这件事不要～。Don't let it out. ❷ it is said; they say:～他要当科长。It is said that he is going to be the section chief.
see also wàizhuàn
外串 wàichuàn be a guest performer
外存储器 wàicúnchǔqì 〈计算机〉external storage; file (storage):～信息处理机 file processor
外错角 wàicuòjiǎo alternate exterior angle
外大气层 wàidàqìcéng exoatmosphere
外大气层杀伤飞行器 wàidàqìcéng shāshāng fēixíngqì 〈军事〉(US) Extra-atmospheric Kill Vehicle, a 140-centimeter-long, 54 kilogram device carried on a booster rocket designed to destroy a launched missile
外代数 wàidàishù 〈数学〉exterior algebra
外带 wàidài ❶ tyre:前轮的～破了。There was a puncture in the tyre of the front wheel. ❷ in addition; as well; besides:这个小店出售日用品,～传呼电话。The small shop sells daily necessities and handles messages for the public phone as well. /这个人长得其貌不扬,还～有点口吃。The man is plain; in addition, he speaks with a slight stutter.
外待 wàidài treat as an outsider:你在我们这儿干,不会有人～你的。While you are working here, none of us will treat you as an outsider.
外道 wàidào 〈佛教〉unorthodox sect; heterodoxy:邪魔～ evil and unorthodox ways
外道儿 wàidàor indecent behaviour; affair:搞邪魔～ do sth. indecent or illegal; resort to indecent or illegal devices (*or* means) /他有了～了。He is having an affair with someone.
外道 wàidao stand on ceremony; treat (sb.) very ceremoniously as if to keep sb. at arm's length:您这么客气就显得～了。Please don't stand on ceremony, or else you'll be keeping us at a distance. /家常便饭,没特别为您准备,千万别～。It is just pot-luck, nothing special. Do help yourself.
外倒转术 wàidàozhuǎnshù 〈医学〉external version (in childbirth)
外敌 wàidí foreign enemy:～入侵 foreign aggression (*or* invasion)
外地 wàidì part of the country other than where one is; other places:去～视察 make an inspection tour of other parts of the country /他家住在～。His family live in another city.
外典 wàidiǎn 〈宗教〉non-Buddhist classics and scriptures
外电 wàidiàn dispatch or report from a foreign news agency:此事～已有报道。This has been reported by foreign news agencies.
外电路 wàidiànlù 〈电学〉external circuit
外调 wàidiào ❶ transfer (materials or personnel) to other localities or institutions:晋煤～ transport coal from Shanxi (to other provinces) /我们单位的技术骨干已～了不少。Many of our key technical staff have been transferred to other institutions. ❷ investigate an internal case through outside channels:内查～ make investigations both within and without a unit
外毒素 wàidúsù 〈医学〉exotoxin
外耳 wài'ěr 〈生理〉external ear; outer ear
外耳成形术 wài'ěr chéngxíngshù otoplasty
外耳道 wài'ěrdào external auditory meatus
外耳门 wài'ěrmén porus austicus externus
外耳炎 wài'ěryán otitis externa
外翻足 wàifānzú 〈医学〉talipes valgus
外藩 wàifān 〈旧语〉❶ prince with fief in border province ❷ vassal
外放 wàifàng (of officials in ancient China) post or be posted in a province
外分泌 wàifēnmì 〈生理〉exocrine; eccrine; external secretion:～腺 exocrine gland; eccrine gland /～学〈医学〉exocrinology; eccrinology
外稃 wàifū 〈植物〉lemma
外敷 wàifū apply externally (ointment, etc.):～药 medicine for external application /～内服 for external application or to be taken orally
外感 wàigǎn 〈中医〉disease caused by external factors such as cold, heat, dampness, draught, etc.; exopathic affection:～腰痛 exopathic lumbago /～内滞 external irritation and internal congestion
外港 wàigǎng outport:神户是大阪的～。Kobe is the outport of Osaka.
外高加索 Wàigāojiāsuǒ Transcaucasia, a region to the south of the Caucasus Mountains:～人 Transcaucasian
外稿 wàigǎo contribution from outside an institution; paid paper work from outside one's institution
外割函数 wàigē hánshù 〈数学〉exsecant
外公 wàigōng 〈方言〉maternal grandfather
外公切线 wàigōngqiēxiàn exterior common tangent
外功 wàigōng *Wushu* exercises to strengthen the muscles and bones
外骨骼 wàigǔgé exoskeleton
外观 wàiguān outward appearance; exterior:这些手表～不错,但不知是否走得准。These watches are all splendid in appearance, but we don't know whether they keep good time.
外观图 wàiguāntú outside drawing; outside view
外官 wàiguān 〈旧语〉government official posted in a place other than the capital; official in the provinces
外国 wàiguó foreign country:～朋友 foreign friend /～报界 foreign press /～干涉 foreign intervention (*or* interference) /从～回来 return from a foreign country; return from abroad /具有～风味 exotic
外国法 wàiguófǎ foreign law
外国公债 wàiguó gōngzhài foreign bond

外国管辖权 wàiguó guǎnxiáquán foreign jurisdiction
外国货 wàiguóhuò foreign commodity or goods
外国居民 wàiguó jūmín foreign or alien resident
外国军事基地 wàiguó jūnshì jīdì foreign military base
外国留学生 wàiguó liúxuéshēng foreign student
外国侨民 wàiguó qiáomín foreign national
外国人 wàiguórén foreigner; alien: ～居留证 residence permit for foreigners
外国文学 wàiguó wénxué foreign literature
外国语 wàiguóyǔ foreign language: ～学院 foreign languages institute /～学生 foreign language major (*or* student)
外国驻华机构 wàiguó zhù Huá jīgòu foreign institutions in China
外国驻华使领馆 wàiguó zhù Huá shǐ-lǐngguǎn foreign diplomatic and consular missions in China
外国租界 wàiguó zūjiè foreign settlement or concession
外果皮 wàiguǒpí 〈植物〉exocarp
外海 wàihǎi pelagic sea (between the ocean and the coastal waters): 开发～渔场 develop pelagic fishery
外行 wàiháng ❶ lay; uninitiated; nonprofessional: ～话 lay language /内战内行,外战外～ in one's element when fighting internal war, out of one's element when it comes to fighting external war; good at fighting one's own countrymen but poor at fighting foreigners /这纯系～话。This is purely nonprofessional advice. ❷ layman; novice; nonprofessional: 变～为内行 turn a layman into an expert /他对服务行业却是个十足的～。He was a complete novice in the service trade. /办教育,我可是个～。I am rather ignorant about education. /～看热闹,内行看门道。While laymen are keen to watch the excitement, the initiated appraise and admire the skill.
外号 wàihào nickname: 给人乱取～ give nicknames to others irresponsibly /此人～智多星。He is nicknamed "wizard".
外话 wàihuà 〈方言〉utterances made as if by a stranger: 咱们自己人没～。As friends, we should not speak like strangers.
外踝 wàihuái 〈生理〉external malleolus
外患 wàihuàn foreign aggression: ～不断 continuous foreign aggression /内忧引来～。Internal disturbances led to foreign invasion.
外汇 wàihuì foreign exchange; foreign currency: ～收入 foreign exchange earnings (*or* revenue) /～交易 foreign exchange transactions /～经纪人 exchange broker /～管理法令 exchange control regulations /～管理机构 exchange control authorities /～限额 exchange quota /～转移证 exchange surrender certificate /～留成 percentage of foreign exchange earnings to be kept by the company or factory (apart from what is handed over to the state); foreign exchange retention
外汇储备 wàihuì chǔbèi foreign exchange reserve
外汇行情 wàihuì hángqíng exchange quotations
外汇率 wàihuìlǜ exchange rate
外汇平准基金 wàihuì píngzhǔn jījīn exchange stabilization fund
外汇评价 wàihuì píngjià par of exchange; exchange parity
外汇券 wàihuìquàn (short for 外汇兑换券) foreign exchange certificate (FEC)
外汇市场 wàihuì shìchǎng foreign exchange market: 外汇调剂市场 foreign exchange swap market
外婚制 wàihūnzhì exogamy, the custom of marrying only outside one's own tribe or clan
外活 wàihuó ❶ processing job (form outside); external order: 接～ accept processing jobs or orders (apart from one's regular production schedule) ❷ extra work with pay; moonlighting: 他常常干～。He often moonlights.
外货 wàihuò foreign goods; imported goods
外祸 wàihuò foreign aggression: ～频仍。Foreign aggression was frequent.
外激素 wàijīsù 〈生化〉ecto-hormone
外籍 wàijí ❶ having one's permanent residence registered somewhere else; not being a local: ～人 person from another city or province ❷ foreign nationality: ～教师 foreign teacher /～劳工 foreign labour /～华人 foreign national of Chinese origin (*or* descent, *or* extraction) /～军团 foreign legion /～船 vessel of foreign registry
外寄生物 wàijìshēngwù ectoparasite
外加 wàijiā additional; extra; plus: 邮购图书须～书价5%的邮费。Books by mail order require an additional five per cent for postage.
外加电压 wàijiā diànyā applied voltage
外家 wàijiā ❶ home or family of one's maternal grandparents ❷ 〈方言〉family or home of a married woman's parents ❸〈书面〉wife's parents' home ❹ house of a concubine who lives apart from the legal wife ❺〈旧语〉such a concubine or kept woman
外间 wàijiān ❶ outer room: ～是客厅。The outer room serves as a parlour. ❷ external world (as opposed to one's family, unit, etc.); outside circles: 关于此事,～颇有传闻。There have been all sorts of rumours abroad about this. /～传闻,不可尽信。One must not give full credence to rumours.
外江 wàijiāng 〈方言〉other parts of the country: ～佬 nonlocal guy
外交 wàijiāo diplomacy; foreign affairs: ～部 Ministry of Foreign Affairs; Foreign Ministry /～部长 Minister of (*or* for) Foreign Affairs; Foreign Minister /～学院 Foreign Affairs College /～官 diplomat /～人员 diplomatic personnel /～信袋 diplomatic pouch; diplomatic bag /～信使 diplomatic courier /～人员服务局 diplomatic personnel service bureau /穿梭～ shuttle diplomacy /度假～ vacation diplomacy /过境～ transit diplomacy/金钱～ money diplomacy /金元～ dollar diplomacy /乒乓～ ping-pong diplomacy /炮舰～ gunboat diplomacy /实用～ pragmatic diplomacy /实质～ substantial diplomacy
外交庇护 wàijiāo bìhù diplomatic asylum
外交病 wàijiāobìng diplomatic illness or sickness
外交承认 wàijiāo chéngrèn diplomatic recognition
外交程序 wàijiāo chéngxù diplomatic procedure
外交辞令 wàijiāo cílìng diplomatic language or parlance
外交大臣 Wàijiāo Dàchén (UK) Foreign Secretary; Secretary of State for Foreign and Commonwealth Affairs
外交代表 wàijiāo dàibiǎo diplomatic representative
外交地位 wàijiāo dìwèi diplomatic status
外交法 wàijiāofǎ diplomatic law
外交关系 wàijiāo guānxi diplomatic relations: 建立大使级～ establish diplomatic relations at ambassadorial level /～升格 upgrade diplomatic relations /断绝～ severance of diplomatic relations; diplomatic rupture /恢复～ resumption of diplomatic relations /中止～ suspension of diplomatic relations
外交官名册 wàijiāoguān míngcè diplomatic list
外交官衔 wàijiāo guānxián diplomatic rank
外交惯例 wàijiāo guànlì diplomatic practice
外交国务大臣 Wàijiāo Guówù Dàchén (UK) Minister of State for Foreign and Commonwealth Affairs
外交护照 wàijiāo hùzhào diplomatic passport
外交豁免权 wàijiāo huòmiǎnquán diplomatic immunities
外交季刊 Wàijiāo Jìkān *Foreign Affairs*, a US political quarterly published since 1922
外交家 wàijiāojiā diplomat; diplomatist
外交交涉 wàijiāo jiāoshè diplomatic representations
外交界 wàijiāojiè diplomatic circle
外交礼节 wàijiāo lǐjié diplomatic protocol
外交签证 wàijiāo qiānzhèng diplomatic visa
外交使节 wàijiāo shǐjié diplomatic envoy
外交特权 wàijiāo tèquán diplomatic prerogative; diplomatic privilege
外交途径 wàijiāo tújìng diplomatic channels: 通过～解决争端 settle an issue through diplomatic channels
外交团 wàijiāotuán diplomatic corps: ～团长 dean (*or* doyen) of the diplomatic corps
外交文件 wàijiāo wénjiàn diplomatic document
外交文书 wàijiāo wénshū diplomatic correspondence; diplomatic documentation
外国斡旋 wàijiāo wòxuán diplomatic good offices
外交政策 wàijiāo zhèngcè foreign policy: 独立自主的和平～ independent foreign policy of peace
外交制裁 wàijiāo zhìcái diplomatic sanction
外交姿态 wàijiāo zītài diplomatic gesture or overture
外角 wàijiǎo 〈数学〉exterior angle
外教 wàijiào (short for 外籍教师) foreign teacher
外接圆 wàijiēyuán 〈数学〉circumscribed circle; circumcircle
外界 wàijiè of the external or outside world; outside: ～舆论 public opinion /～人士 the public /～影响 outside influence /向～征求意见 solicit comments and suggestions from the public /断绝了与～的联系 be cut off from the external world /他对～的情况一点也不了解。He is totally ignorant of what is happening in the outside world. /飞机的机身必须承受～的空气压力。The fuselage of an airplane must

W

be able to withstand outside air pressure.
外景 wàijǐng outdoor scene; scene shot on location; exterior: ~镜头 exterior shot / 拍~ film the exterior; shoot a scene on location / 到黄山选~ go to Huangshan Mountain for outdoor scenes
外径 wàijìng 〈机械〉external diameter; outside or outer diameter: 齿轮~ outside diameter of gear / ~尺寸 outside dimension / ~规 outside calipers / ~千分尺 outside micrometer
外舅 wàijiù 〈书面〉father-in-law
外卡 wàikǎ 〈体育〉wild card: 他是这场锦票赛惟一持~参赛的运动员。He is the only wild-card player competing in the championships.
外卡钳 wàikǎqián 〈机械〉outside callipers
外科 wàikē 〈医学〉surgical department: ~医生 surgeon / ~手术 surgical operation / ~病房 surgical ward / ~结 surgeon's knot / 临床~ clinical surgery / 矫形~ orthopaedic surgery; plastic surgery
外科学 wàikēxué surgery
外科正宗 Wàikē Zhèngzōng *Orthodox Treatise on Surgery*, written in 4 volumes in 1617 by Chen Shigong (陈实功) of the Ming Dynasty
外壳 wàiké outer covering; case; shell; husk: 电视机~ case of a TV set / 手表的~ case of a wrist watch / 热水瓶~ outer casing of a thermos flask / 种子的~ husk of a seed / 蜗牛的~ shell of a snail
外客 wàikè visitor or guest who is an outsider
外空 wàikōng (short for 外层空间) outer space: ~武器 weapon deployed in outer space
外空法 wàikōngfǎ law of the outer space
外寇 wàikòu invading enemy; invader: 团结一致, 共御~ unite to resist foreign invaders
外快 wàikuài *also* "外水" extra profit; extra earnings: 捞~ wangle extra income; make an extra penny / 他每月挣不少~。He has quite a lot of extra earnings every month.
外来 wàilái outside; foreign; extraneous: ~人 person from another place; non-native / ~影响 foreign (*or* outside) influence / ~干涉 foreign interference (*or* intervention) / ~侵略者 foreign aggressor
外来户 wàiláihù household from another place; non-native
外来继承人 wàilái jìchéngrén 〈法律〉extraneous heir
外来语 wàiláiyǔ word borrowed from a foreign language; word of foreign origin; foreign word; loanword
外力 wàilì ❶ outside force or power; outside or external influence: 借~以自重 strengthen one's position with the help of outside force ❷ 〈物理〉external force: ~功 external work
外联网 wàiliánwǎng 〈信息〉extranet
外流 wàiliú outflow; drain: 资源~ resource outflow / 黄金~ gold bullion outflow / 科技人员~ outflow of scientific and technical personnel / 人才~ brain drain
外流河 wàiliúhé river that flows (directly or indirectly) into the sea
外路 wàilù from other places; non-local: ~人 person from another place; non-local person / ~客商 merchants from other cities; non-native businessman
外露 wàilù ❶ show; display; demonstrate: 凶相~ look most ferocious; display all one's ferocity / 他性格内向, 从不~。He is an introvert and is never demonstrative. / 高手的绝技决不轻易~。An expert rarely reveals his unique skills. ❷ 〈地质〉outcropping: ~层 outlier
外轮 wàilún foreign ship
外螺纹 wàiluówén 〈机械〉external screw thread; external thread: ~磨床 external thread grinder
外卖 wàimài take-out: ~店 take-out restaurant / 兼营~ have a subsidiary take-out service
外贸 wàimào (short for 对外贸易) foreign trade; external trade: ~部 Ministry of Foreign Trade / ~部门 foreign trade department or establishment / ~经营权 power (*or* authorization) to engage in foreign trade / ~专业公司 specialized foreign-trade corporation / ~仲裁 foreign trade arbitration
外貌 wàimào appearance; looks: ~纤弱 look slim and delicate / ~像羊, 内心是狼 wolf in sheep's clothing / 从~看, 他可能是个老工人。Judging by his appearance, he may be a veteran worker.
外面 wàimiàn exterior; surface; outward appearance: 这座楼看~很坚固。The building looks quite solid.
外面 wàimian outside; out: 到~去散步 go out for a walk / ~有人等你。Someone is waiting for you outside. / 他家通常每周要在~吃几次饭。His family usually eat (*or* dine) out several times a week.
外面儿光 wàimiànrguāng deceptively smooth appearance; outward show; veener: 这个人做事只求~。Whatever he does, he is only interested in slick appearances.
外酶 wàiméi 〈生化〉exoenzyme
外膜 wàimó 〈生理〉adventitia; tunica adventitia; extima
外…内… wài… nèi… outwardly... but inwardly...: 外方内圆 be outwardly stern but inwardly kind / 外刚内柔 a rough (*or* stern) appearance hides a gentle heart / 外松内紧 relaxed in appearance but alert in reality / 外善内奸 fair without but false within; friendly behaviour hiding evil intentions
外内项比 wài-nèixiàngbǐ 〈数学〉extreme and mean ratio
外胚层 wàipēicéng 〈生物〉ectoderm: ~体型 ectomorph
外胚乳 wàipēirǔ 〈生物〉perisperm
外胚叶 wàipēiyè 〈生物〉epiblast; ectoblast
外皮层 wàipícéng 〈植物〉exodermis
外婆 wàipó 〈方言〉maternal grandmother
外戚 wàiqī relative of a king or emperor on his mother's or wife's side; king's or emperor's in-law: ~擅权 abuse of power by relatives of the king's (*or* emperor's) mother or wife
外企 wàiqǐ (short for 外资企业) foreign enterprise; enterprise with external funding
外气 wàiqi 〈方言〉as polite as a stranger: 老朋友可不兴~。Let's not stand on ceremony since we're old friends.
外欠 wàiqiàn ❶ external debt: 已无~ owe no more debts ❷ remaining debt: 两相抵消后, ~二十元。After offsetting the two items (*or* On balance), there is 20 *yuan* on the debit side.
外强中干 wàiqiáng-zhōnggān outwardly strong but inwardly brittle; strong in appearance but weak in reality; fierce of mien but faint of heart: 别看他长得胖, 其实~, 浑身是病。Despite his stout build, he is actually quite weak and suffers from all sorts of diseases. / 那家大公司表面很红火, 但亏空不少, 不免有点~了。Prosperous as the big company appears, it is heavily in debt and may well be described as "outwardly strong, inwardly weak".
外侨 wàiqiáo foreign national or resident; alien: 该国~人口众多。The country has a large alien population. / ~必须遵守居住国的法律。Foreign residents must abide by the laws of their host country.
外切 wàiqiē 〈数学〉externally tangent: ~形 circumscribed figure / ~多边形 circumscribed polygon
外勤 wàiqín ❶ work done in the field (as distinct from work in the office or at the headquarters): 跑~ do fieldwork / ~记者 field reporter / ~人员 field staff / ~补贴 fieldwork allowance ❷ field personnel; fieldworker
外倾 wàiqīng *also* "外向"〈心理〉extroversion
外圈 wàiquān 〈体育〉outer lane; outside lane
外燃机 wàiránjī 〈机械〉external-combustion engine
外人 wàirén ❶ person not a member of one's group, etc.; outsider; stranger: 你们家的事儿, 我这个~不好多插嘴。As an outsider, it would be improper for me to comment on your family matters. / 此事总要办得严密, 免得~说长道短。The matter must be handled with all circumspection lest people gossip about it. / 他不是~, 对他不必保密。He is one of us, and there is no need to keep anything from him. ❷ foreigner; alien
外任 wàirèn 〈口语〉hold a position in the provinces: 放个~ be appointed to a post in the provinces
外柔内刚 wài'róu-nèigāng soft outside but hard inside — outwardly gentle but inwardly tough; iron fist in a velvet glove
外伤 wàishāng injury; wound; trauma: 腿受~ be wounded in the leg / ~病 traumatism / ~性休克 traumatic shock
外伤性肺病 wàishāngxìng fèibìng 〈医学〉traumatic pneumonosis
外伤学 wàishāngxué traumatology
外商 wàishāng foreign merchant or businessman: ~投资企业 enterprises with overseas investment
外设 wàishè 〈信息〉peripheral
外伸 wàishēn 〈机械〉overhang: ~臂 overhanging arm
外肾 wàishèn 〈中医〉testicles; scrotum: ~肿硬 indurated swelling of scrotum
外生殖器 wàishēngzhíqì 〈生理〉external reproductive organs; external genitals
外省 wàishěng other province than one's own: ~人 person from another province; non-local
外甥 wàisheng ❶ sister's son; nephew ❷ 〈方言〉daughter's son; grandson

外甥打灯笼 wàisheng dǎ dēnglong nephew carrying a lantern to give light to his uncle — same as before (a pun on 照舅 and 照旧, which are homophones in Chinese):他的老毛病改了几天,过后还是～—照舅(旧)。He gave up his bad habits for a while, only to relapse into his old self soon afterwards.
外甥女 wàishengnǚ ❶ sister's daughter; niece ❷〈方言〉daughter's daughter; granddaughter
外史 wàishǐ unofficial history; anecdotal account:《儒林～》*The Scholars* (novel written by Wu Jingzi 吴敬梓 of the Qing Dynasty)
外事 wàishì ❶ foreign affairs; external affairs:～部门 foreign affairs department ❷ outside affairs:他～从不对家人提及。He never discusses outside affairs with his family.
外事办公室 wàishì bàngōngshì *also* "外办" foreign affairs office
外事工作 wàishì gōngzuò foreign service
外事活动 wàishì huódòng public functions concerning foreigners
外事局 wàishìjú bureau of foreign affairs
外事口 wàishìkǒu all units dealing with foreign affairs considered as a sector (of government functions):分管～ be responsible for all foreign affairs (in the government)
外事小组 wàishì xiǎozǔ leading group in charge of foreign affairs
外饰 wàishì exterior decoration:该楼～颜色黄绿相间,色调柔和。Decorated in alternating yellows and greens, the building displays charming exterior.
外室 wàishì 〈旧语〉kept woman or mistress (living apart from legal wife)
外手 wàishǒu (when driving a vehicle or operating a machine) right-hand side
外首 wàishǒu 〈方言〉outside; out
see also "外头"
外水 wàishuǐ extra income or earnings
外孙 wàisūn daughter's son; grandson
外孙女 wàisūnnǚ daughter's daughter; granddaughter
外孙子 wàisūnzi 〈口语〉daughter's son; grandson
外胎 wàitāi tyre (of a wheel)
外台秘要 Wàitái Mìyào *Essentials of Medical Theories and Prescriptions*, compiled in 752 by Wang Tao (王焘) of the Tang Dynasty
外逃 wàitáo flee to some other place; flee the country:～分子 deserter; fugitive /战端一起,居民纷纷～。Residents fled pell-mell as soon as hostilities broke out.
外套 wàitào ❶ overcoat ❷ coat; outer garment
外听道 wàitīngdào *also* "外耳道"〈生理〉external auditory meatus
外头 wàitou 〈口语〉outside; outdoors; out:咱们到～去溜达溜达。Let's go out for a stroll. /～很黑。It's pitch-dark outside. /围墙～就是大街。The street is just beyond the wall.
外推 wàituī 〈数学〉extrapolation
外围 wàiwéi periphery:～视野 peripheral field /扫清～ wipe out peripheral obstacles or fortifications (as before attacking the main target); pave the way (for undertaking the main task) /皇城～是道护城河。The imperial city is surrounded by a moat.
外围防线 wàiwéi fángxiàn outside defence line; outer defence line
外围工事 wàiwéi gōngshì 〈军事〉outwork
外围设备 wàiwéi shèbèi peripheral equipment:～接口 peripheral component interface (PCI)
外围组织 wàiwéi zǔzhī peripheral organization
外文 wàiwén foreign language:～书报 foreign language books and newspapers; foreign language publications /这部著作已有多种～译本。The work has been translated into several foreign languages.
外文出版社 Wàiwén Chūbǎnshè Foreign Languages Press
外文干部 wàiwén gànbù official engaged in foreign language work; one who uses foreign languages in one's work
外屋 wàiwū outer room:沙发放在～。The sofa is in the outer room.
外侮 wàiwǔ foreign aggression; external aggression:～内患 foreign invasion and domestic turbulence
外务 wàiwù ❶ matters not within the scope of one's job:屏绝～ exclude or put aside all extraneous matters (to concentrate on sth.) ❷ external affairs; foreign affairs:～繁忙 be busily engaged in foreign affairs
外务大臣 wàiwù dàchén minister of foreign affairs
外务省 Wàiwùshěng (Japan) Ministry of Foreign Affairs
外务相 Wàiwùxiàng (Japan) Minister of Foreign Affairs
外骛 wàiwù 〈书面〉be distracted by what is irrelevant to one's work or business:驰心～ be absorbed in irrelevant things (to the neglect of one's duty or work)
外弦 wàixián 〈乐器〉outside string (of a fiddle)
外县 wàixiàn county other than one's own
外线 wàixiàn ❶〈军事〉exterior lines:～作战 fighting on exterior lines; exterior-line operation ❷ outside (telephone) connections:拨～ dial an outside number /～不通 cannot make outside connections; cannot get through to an outside number /～占线。The outside line is busy. ❸〈旧语〉person making outside contacts for a secret organization; contact
外乡 wàixiāng another part of the country; some other place (than one's own):飘泊～ drift about in a strange place; wander from place to place /这里住着几个～人。Some people from other places live here.
外向 wàixiàng ❶〈心理〉extroversion:性格～的人 extrovert ❷ export-oriented
外向型经济 wàixiàngxíng jīngjì export-oriented economy
外相 Wàixiàng (short for 外务相) Foreign Minister
外项 wàixiàng 〈数学〉extreme term; extreme
外销 wàixiāo for sale abroad or in other parts of the country:～产品 product for export; product for sale in other parts of the country /这个厂生产的电机大部分～。Most of the electric motors produced in this factory are for export.
外心 wàixīn ❶ unfaithful or disloyal intentions (usu. of husband and wife or sovereign and subject):他感觉到妻子有了～。He has a vague feeling that his wife is no longer the devoted wife she was. ❷〈数学〉circumcentre
外星人 wàixīngrén extraterrestrial being (ET)
外星系 wàixīngxì external galaxy
外行星 wàixíngxīng 〈天文〉outer planet; superior planet
外形 wàixíng external form; contour; appearance:～奇特 present a bizarre exterior; look bizarre
外姓 wàixìng (people) of a different surname:他在张庄是～。He is not of the same surname as most of the people in Zhang village.
外延 wàiyán 〈逻辑〉denotation; extension:～意义 denotating meaning
外延型晶体管 wàiyánxíng jīngtǐguǎn epitaxial transistor
外焰 wàiyàn *also* "外层焰"〈化学〉outer flame
外秧 wàiyāng 〈方言〉person not of one's group, clan or locality
外扬 wàiyáng spread; publicise:家丑不可～ keep quiet family scandals; not air dirty linen in public /不可～的家丑 skeleton in the cupboard
外洋 wàiyáng ❶〈旧语〉foreign country:他早年就到～去了。He went abroad in the early years of his life. ❷〈旧语〉foreign currency ❸ blue water; outer ocean
外爷 wàiyé 〈方言〉maternal grandfather
外衣 wàiyī ❶ coat; jacket; outer clothing; outer garment:～的样式 style of outer garments /你把这件～穿上,免得着凉。Please put on this jacket so as not to catch cold. ❷ outward show; semblance; appearance; facade:在合法～的掩盖下搞违法勾当 carry out unlawful activities behind a facade of legitimacy
外逸层 wàiyìcéng 〈气象〉exosphere
外溢 wàiyì ❶ (of money, wealth, etc.) outflow; drain:金钱～ outflow of money ❷ (of liquid) overflow; spill:污水～ overflow of waste water /杯里的啤酒～。The beer in the glass spilt over.
外因 wàiyīn ❶〈哲学〉external cause or factor:内因为第一位,～为第二位。The internal cause is primary while the external cause is secondary. ❷〈中医〉exopathic factor (such as draught, cold, heat, dampness, etc.)
外阴 wàiyīn 〈生理〉vulva:～炎 vulvitis /～搔痒 pruritus vulvae
外引内联 wàiyǐn-nèilián absorb investment from abroad and establish cooperative relations at home
外用 wàiyòng 〈药学〉external use or application:～药 external medicine /～药水 lotion /只能～,不得内服 for external use only
外语 wàiyǔ foreign language:～教学 foreign language teaching /～学习班 foreign language class or course /～系 department of foreign languages /主攻～ major in a foreign language /用～讲课 conduct a class in a foreign language; lecture in a foreign tongue
外域 wàiyù 〈书面〉foreign lands:～习俗 foreign (*or* exotic) custom

外遇 wàiyù extra-marital affair:她怀疑丈夫有～。She suspects that her husband is carrying on with another woman. *or* She suspects her husband of having an affair with another woman.
外圆 wàiyuán excircle:～车削 external cutting /～珩磨机 external honing machine
外圆磨床 wàiyuán móchuáng cylindrical grinder; external grinding machine; plain grinder:普通～ plain external grinding machine
外圆内方 wàiyuán-nèifāng round outside but square inside — outwardly gentle but inwardly stern; easy going in manners but strict on matters of principle
外援 wàiyuán ❶ foreign aid; outside help; external assistance:不依靠～ not rely on external (*or* international) assistance ❷〈体育〉foreign player:该队有两名得力～。The team has two skilful foreign players.
外源河 wàiyuánhé 〈地理〉exotic stream
外在 wàizài external; outside; extrinsic:～力量 external force /～原因 external cause
外在论 wàizàilùn 〈哲学〉externalism
外在性 wàizàixìng externalism; externality
外债 wàizhài external debt; foreign debt:无力偿还～ be unable to repay (*or* have to default on) external debts /这个国家的～高达千亿美元。The country has run into a foreign debt of 100 billion US dollars.
外展肌 wàizhǎnjī 〈生理〉abductor
外展神经 wàizhǎn shénjīng 〈生理〉abducens nerve
外长 wàizhǎng (short for 外交部长) foreign minister:副～ vice foreign minister /～助理 assistant foreign minister /～即将出访中东。The foreign minister will soon visit (*or* be on a visit to) the Middle East.
外找儿 wàizhǎor 〈旧语〉extra income
外罩 wàizhào ❶ outer garment; overall; mantle; robe ❷ dust-coat; cover:玻璃～ glass cover
外痔 wàizhì external piles or haemorrhoids
外周神经系统 wàizhōu shénjīng xìtǒng 〈生理〉peripheral nervous system
外专局 Wàizhuānjú (short for 外国专家局) Bureau of Foreign Experts Affairs
外传 wàizhuàn ❶〈旧语〉commentaries on the Confucian classics ❷ unofficial biography or history
see also wàichuán
外资 wàizī foreign capital or fund; foreign investment:引进～ absorb foreign capital; lure foreign investment
外资企业 wàizī qǐyè foreign enterprise; foreign-funded enterprise
外子 wàizǐ 〈书面〉my husband
外族 wàizú ❶ not of the same clan:～人 person from another clan ❷ foreigner; alien:沦为～的殖民地 be reduced to the status of a foreign colony ❸ of a nationality (other than one's own):～的习俗 customs and habits of other nationalities
外祖父 wàizǔfù maternal grandfather; grandpa
外祖母 wàizǔmǔ maternal grandmother; grandma

wān

豌 wān

豌豆 wāndòu pea:～粉 peameal /～汤 pea soup /～属 *Pisum*
豌豆黄 wāndòuhuáng pea flour cake
豌豆象 wāndòuxiàng 〈动物〉pea weevil

剜 wān

cut out; gouge out; scoop out:凶残的奴隶主～掉了奴隶的双眼。The brutal master had the slave's eyes gouged out.
剜肉医疮 wānròu-yīchuāng *also* "剜肉补疮";"挖肉补疮" wāròu-bǔchuāng cut out good flesh to patch up an ulcer — resort to a remedy worse than the ailment; adopt a stopgap measure at the expense of long-term interests:这是一种～的办法，令人痛心。This is a deplorable case of robbing Peter to pay Paul.

蜿 wān

蜿蜒 wānyán ❶ (of snakes, etc.) wriggle; twist:那蛇奔草丛～而去。The snake wriggled its way towards the thick growth of grass. ❷ wind; spiral; zigzag; meander:～的山路 winding mountain path /～流淌的小河 meandering stream /河渠依着山势曲折～。The irrigation canal zigzags along the mountain.

帵 wān

帵子 wānzi 〈方言〉leftover of the cloth after a garment is cut out

弯(彎) wān

❶ curved; roundabout; tortuous; crooked:苹果压～了枝条。The branches were so laden with apples that they were weighed down. /月儿～～照九洲。The earth is bathed in the silvery rays of the crescent moon. ❷ make crooked or curved; bend; flex:～腰拾起东西 bend over to pick up sth. (from the ground) /～铁丝 bend a piece of wire /伸伸腿，～～腰 stretch one's legs and bend one's waist ❸ turn; curve:拐～儿 round a bend; turn a corner /转～抹角 beat about the bush /这根竹竿有个～儿。The bamboo pole is curved. ❹〈书面〉bend; draw:盘马～弓 ride round and round bending one's bow; assume an impressive posture but take no action
弯板机 wānbǎnjī 〈冶金〉plate bender; press brake; bending rolls
弯刀 wāndāo tulwar
弯度 wāndù bend; camber; curvature
弯钢机 wāngāngjī 〈冶金〉〈建筑〉steel-bender
弯弓 wāngōng draw a bow; bend a bow:～射雕 draw a bow to shoot at a vulture
弯拱 wāngǒng 〈建筑〉camber arch
弯管 wānguǎn bent tube:～锅炉 bent tube boiler /～接头 corner joint; union elbow
弯管器 wānguǎnqì hickey
弯轨机 wānguǐjī jim crow; rail bender
弯路 wānlù ❶ winding road; tortuous path:前面有段～。There are a lot of twists and turns in the road ahead. ❷ detour; roundabout course:这几年，我们走了不少～。In the past few years, we made quite a few detours in our work.
弯扭 wānniǔ winding; zigzag; crooked:狭窄～的小街 crooked street /字写得弯弯扭扭，真难看。The characters are shapeless, twisted and unsightly.
弯曲 wānqū ❶ winding; meandering; zigzag; crooked:～的羊肠小道 winding path /这块木板已～变形。The board is warped. ❷〈机械〉bend; curve; flexure:～半径 bend radius /～机 bending machine /～理论 flexure theory /～强度 flexural strength /～试验 bending test /～应力 bending stress /～时空 curved space-time
弯蜷 wānquán bend and twist:那个杂技演员能够十分灵巧地把身体～起来。The acrobat could bend and twist his body with great agility.
弯条机 wāntiáojī 〈冶金〉bar bender
弯头 wāntóu 〈机械〉bend; elbow (pipe or joint); bight:回转～ return bend /接合～ joint elbow /～螺丝刀 offset screwdriver
弯月形透镜 wānyuèxíng tòujìng 〈物理〉meniscus lens
弯折机 wānzhéjī 〈机械〉bar folder
弯子 wānzi ❶ *also* "弯儿" bend; turn; curve:转～ round a bend; undergo a change of heart (*or* mind) ❷〈方言〉spiked or pointed pole with a hook

湾(灣) wān

❶ bend in a stream:天下黄河几十几道～? How many bends are there in the Yellow River? ❷ gulf; bay; estuary:港～ estuary /孟加拉～ Bay of Bengal /海～ (Persian) Gulf ❸ cast anchor; anchor; moor:把船～在背风处。Moor the boat to leeward.
湾泊 wānbó moor; berth:岸边～着两艘大船。Two large vessels are lying at anchor along the bank.
湾鳄 wān'è 〈动物〉estuarine crocodile (*Crocodilus porosus*)

塆(壪) wān

(usu. used in names of villages) level plot in a mountain gully; glen:张家～ Zhangs' Glen
塆坳 wān'ào 〈方言〉level plot in the mountains; glen:～里有座农家小院。A farmer's house lies in the glen.

wán

完 wán

❶ intact; entire; whole:体无～肤 have cuts and

bruises all over the body; be a mass of bruises; 〈比喻〉be torn to pieces /覆巢之下自无～卵。When a bird's nest is overturned, no egg can remain intact. ❷ exhaust; finish; use up:油箱的汽油快～了。The gas in the tank is almost exhausted (*or* finished). /米吃～了。We have run out of rice. ❸ end; finish; be over; be through:文章写～后至少要看两遍。After you have finished writing your essay, you should read it over at least twice. /这件事还没有～呢，你不能走。The thing is not over yet; you must not leave. /他的发言马上就～了。He will soon be through with his speech. *or* He is coming to an end (in his speech). /摔下去命就～了。You will kill youself if you fall down. ❹ pay:税款早已～清。The tax has been paid long since. ❺ (Wán) a surname

完备 wánbèi all; complete; perfect:资料～ have complete data /设施～ have all necessary facilities /手续～ have completed all the formalities /条件尚不～。The conditions are not yet ripe.

完毕 wánbì finish; complete; end; be over:诸事～。Everything is ready. /仪式～。The ceremony is over. /工作尚未～。The work still remains unfinished.

完璧归赵 wánbì-guīzhào return the jade intact to the State of Zhao (from which it was brought); return sth. to its owner in perfect condition:你放心，你那两件东西不日就可～。You can rest assured that those two articles will be returned to you in perfect condition shortly.

完成 wánchéng accomplish; complete; finish; fulfil:～使命 complete one's mission /～工作 finish the work /～计划 fulfil a plan /按期～任务 carry out (*or* perform) a task on schedule /提前～ complete ahead of schedule /未～的杰作 unfinished masterpiece

完蛋 wándàn be done for; be ruined; be finished:这家公司快要～了。The company was on the verge of collapse. *or* It was on its last legs. /你这么下去会～的。You are doomed if you go on behaving like this.

完稿 wángǎo finish a piece of writing; have the draft ready:大作何时～? When will you be through with your writing? *or* When will the draft be ready?

完工 wángōng complete a project; finish doing sth.:工程按期～。The project was completed on schedule. /隧道～以后就开始铺轨。After the tunnel work is finished, we will start laying the track.

完好 wánhǎo intact; unimpaired; whole; in good condition:物归原主，～无损 return sth. intact to its rightful owner /机器使用五年，仍基本～。After five years in operation the machine was still in fairly good shape.

完婚 wánhūn *also* "完姻"〈书面〉consummate a marriage; get married:业已～ already married /择吉日为儿子～ choose an auspicious day for the son's wedding

完结 wánjié end; conclude; be over; finish:生命总是要～的。Life's journey ends sooner or later. /你要有思想准备，事情决不会这样简单就～。You have to be mentally prepared, for the matter cannot be disposed of so easily.

完井 wánjǐng 〈石油〉well completion

完具 wánjù 〈书面〉complete; perfect:首尾～ complete from beginning to end

完聚 wánjù 〈书面〉gather together; be reunited:长期离散的一家人，最后得以～。The family were finally reunited after a long separation.

完竣 wánjùn (of a project, etc.) finish; complete:扩建工程～。The extension project has been completed. /军队整编～。The troops have been reorganized.

完粮 wánliáng 〈旧语〉pay a grain tax:～纳税 (formerly of a peasant) pay taxes both in kind and in money

完了 wánliǎo bring or come to an end; realize:～一桩心愿 realize a cherished wish

完满 wánmǎn successful; perfect:世间的事物，多不如人们所设想的那么～。Nothing in this world is as perfect as people expect. /大会～结束。The conference came to a successful close.

完美 wánměi perfect; consummate; superb:她的杂技表演，在技巧上达到惊人的～程度。She displayed an amazingly superb skill in her acrobatic performance.

完美无缺 wánměi-wúquē *also* "完美无疵" perfect; impeccable; flawless:获奖的小说不都是～的。All prize winning novels are not flawless.

完密 wánmì well-organized:这篇文稿写得不够～，还要修改。The draft article is not well-organized (*or* lacks coherence), it needs touching up.

完全 wánquán complete; entire; whole; full:～四边形〈数学〉complete quadrilateral /～数〈数学〉perfect number /～真菌〈植物〉perfect fungus /～错误 entirely wrong /～正确 absolutely correct; perfectly right /～不同 totally dissimilar; have nothing in common /～相反 exact opposite; just the opposite; diametrically opposed /～无效 null and void /～相同 identical /不～统计 incomplete statistics /你～误解了我们的意思。You completely misunderstood our intention. /那～是另外一回事。That is quite a different story (*or* a different kettle of fish).

完全变态 wánquán biàntài 〈生物〉complete metamorphosis

完全燃烧 wánquán ránshāo complete combustion

完全停机 wánquán tíngjī 〈计算机〉dead halt

完全小学 wánquán xiǎoxué *also* "完小" six-grade primary school

完全叶 wánquányè complete leaf

完人 wánrén perfect man:金无足赤，人无～。As no gold is 100 percent pure; so no man is perfect and flawless. /只有伟人、巨人，没有～、圣人。There exist in the world great men and giants, but no perfect men or saints.

完善 wánshàn ❶ perfect; ideal; consummate:日趋～ be perfected (*or* improved) day by day /装备～的工厂 well-equipped factory /还有许多不～的地方需要改进。There is still much room for improvement. ❷ make perfect; perfect; improve:～管理制度 perfect the management /不断地～自己 continual self-improvement

完胜 wánshèng 〈体育〉win a perfect or complete victory (over sb.); thoroughly defeat:以三比零～对手 defeat the rival team 3 to 0

完事 wánshì finish; be done; get through; come to an end:忙到半夜才～ not finish (*or* not be done) until midnight /你去向她道个歉，不就～了吗? Why don't you go and apologize to her to get it over and done with?

完熟 wánshú (of cereal crops) final ripening stage

完税 wánshuì pay tax:～货价 price after tax /～凭证 tax payment receipt

完小 wánxiǎo *see* "完全小学"

完整 wánzhěng complete; entire; integral; intact:一套～的仪器 a complete set of instruments /领土～ territorial integrity /主权～ full sovereignty /只有这部书～地保存下来了。This is the only book preserved intact. /文章层次清楚，结构～。The article is coherent and well organized. /对全书先要有个～的印象。You must have an overall idea of the book in the first place.

完足 wánzú comprehensive; complete:措辞适当，语意～ appropriately-worded and well-expressed

烷

wán alkane:甲～ methane /乙～ ethane /丙～propane /丁～ butane /～酸 alkanoic acid

烷醇 wánchún 〈化学〉alkanol:～胺 alkanolamine

烷化 wánhuà *also* "烷基化"〈化工〉alkylation:～汽油 gasoline alkylate

烷基 wánjī 〈化工〉alkyl:～胺 alkylamine /～醇 alkylol /～锌 zinc alkyl /～金属 metal alkyl /～纤维素 alkylcellulose

烷烃 wántīng *also* "石蜡烃" shílàtīng alkane:～醛 alkanal

烷氧基 wányǎngjī 〈化学〉alkoxy; alkoxyl:～化作用 alkoxylation /～锆 zirconium alkoxide /～有机硅烷 alkoxyorganosilane

玩[1]

wán ❶ play; have fun; joke; amuse or enjoy oneself:逗孩子～儿 play with a child /～得很开心 have a very good time /闹着～儿 do sth. for fun; be joking /这可不是闹着～儿的。This is no joking matter. /没事请来～儿。Please drop in whenever you are free. ❷ play (a game or instrument):～儿足球 play football /～儿纸牌 play cards /～儿吉他 play the guitar ❸ use; employ; resort to (improper means, tricks, etc.):甭～这套把戏。Stop playing such tricks. /敌人又在～花招儿。The enemy is resorting to crafty manoeuvres again.

玩[2]（翫）

wán ❶ trifle with; toy with; treat lightly:～人丧德 denigrate one's virtues by playing tricks on others /寇不可～ never drop (*or* lower) one's guard against the enemy's plot ❷ enjoy; appreciate; find pleasure in:游～ go sight-seeing /凭栏～月 lean against the balustrades admiring the moon ❸ object for appreciation; curio:古～ curio; antique /珍～ rare curio

玩法 wánfǎ trifle with law

W

玩忽 wánhū neglect; ignore; trifle with:～职守 dereliction of duty

玩话 wánhuà words said in jest; joke:你以为我说的是～，不，这是事实。Do you think I was joking? No, I was telling the truth.

玩火 wánhuǒ play with fire:教育孩子们不要～ teach children not to play with fire

玩火自焚 wánhuǒ-zìfén who plays with fire shall perish by it; who sows the wind shall reap the whirlwind

玩具 wánjù toy; plaything:～手枪 toy pistol /电动～ power-driven (*or* electric) toy /～商店 toyshop

玩具熊 wánjùxióng teddy bear

玩乐 wánlè make merry; have fun; amuse oneself:终日～ make merry all day

玩弄 wánnòng ❶ play with; juggle with; show off:她低着头，～手上的手帕。She bent her head and fiddled with the handkerchief she was holding. /这是肺腑之言，决不是～词句。These words are from the bottom of my heart. Believe me, I was not going in for rhetoric. ❷ play fast and loose with; dally with; trifle with:～感情 play fast and loose with another's feelings (*or* affections) /～女性 womanize ❸ resort to; engage in; employ (tricks, etc.):～各种手段 resort to every artifice /～两面手法 engage in double-dealing tactics; be a double-dealer /～政治手腕 employ political stratagems /～权术 play politics

玩偶 wán'ǒu doll; toy figurine

玩器 wánqì curio:古董～ antique curio

玩儿不转 wánrbuzhuàn 〈口语〉 cannot manage; find sth. too much for one:这个人真没用，这么点小事都～。The chap is thoroughly worthless; he can't even get such trivial things done properly. /你不是说这事特别容易吗？怎么样，～了吧？Didn't you say it was as easy as pie? Well, finding it a little too much now, aren't you?

玩儿得转 wánrdezhuàn can manage; be able to handle:这几项工作他～。He is able to get these jobs done.

玩儿坏 wánrhuài 〈方言〉 be up to mischief; play a dirty trick; stab sb. from behind:这人爱～，得防着点儿。We have to be on our guard against him; he is always up to some trick or other.

玩儿命 wán'rmìng gamble or play with one's life; do things recklessly:这小子打起架来真～。When the boy fights, he is reckless of the consequences. /别这么～，还有的是时间嘛。Don't carry on like mad. There's plenty of time yet.

玩儿票 wánrpiào perform (Chinese opera) as an amateur:他玩儿了好几年票才下海。He performed as an amateur for quite a few years before he finally became a professional singer (*or* actor).

玩儿去 wánrqù get lost; clear off; away with sb.:你想在我跟前摆谱，～！Trying to be bossy over me? Forget it.

玩儿完 wánrwán 〈口语〉 the jig is up:这只小狗～了。The jig is up for the puppy. /不听我的话，你迟早要～！If you don't listen to me, you will be finished for good sooner or later!

玩儿真的 wánrzhēnde 〈口语〉(do sth.) for real:要么不干，要干就～。Do it for real or forget it.

玩赏 wánshǎng enjoy; admire; take pleasure or delight in:～山景 enjoy (*or* admire) the mountain scenery /无心～ be in no mood to enjoy sth. /反复～一件古玩 take delight in examining an antique repeatedly /园中有许多可供～的花木。The garden boasts many flowers and trees which are a delight to visitors.

玩世不恭 wánshì-bùgōng defy all ethical values; disdain worldly affairs; be cynical:他似乎用～的态度对待生活。He seems to be taking a cynical attitude towards life.

玩耍 wánshuǎ play; frolic; have fun; amuse oneself:小时候我们在一起～。We used to play together in our childhood. *or* We were childhood playmates.

玩索 wánsuǒ ponder; mull; ruminate:～词句的义蕴 ponder over the implications of the words and phrases

玩味 wánwèi ponder; chew the cud; ruminate:这首诗颇耐～。This poem is well worth pondering.

玩物 wánwù plaything; toy

玩物丧志 wánwù-sàngzhì sensuous pleasures sap lofty aspirations; sensuous luxury blunts the edge of determination; if you indulge in pleasures, you'll forget your high aims in life

玩狎 wánxiá 〈书面〉 dally with; play with

玩笑 wánxiào joke; jest:开某人的～ play a (practical) joke on sb.; make fun of sb. /这两个小孩常在一起～。The two children are playmates, often joking with each other. /这是个善意的～。That was a well-intentioned jest. /开～要适可而止。You shouldn't carry a joke too far.

玩兴 wánxìng mood for a good time:他们～正浓，天却下起雨来了。They were thoroughly enjoying themselves when it began to rain.

玩意儿 wányìr *also* "玩艺儿"〈口语〉❶ toy; plaything:她的书桌上总摆着几件小～。There are always a few toys on her desk. ❷ (of *quyi*, acrobatics, etc.) (item of) performance:这是多年不见的～，值得一看。Such a performance has not been seen for years. It is well worth watching. ❸ thing; creature:那是什么～？从没见过。What's that newfangled gadget? Never saw one before. /他可真不是个～。He is an utter scoundrel.

抏 wán 〈书面〉 frustrate; consume; exhaust

顽[1] wán ❶ stupid; foolish; dense; insensate:冥～ thickheaded; stupid /～石 hard rock; insensate stone ❷ stubborn; persistent:愚～ ignorant and stubborn /刁～ sly and perverse ❸ naughty; mischievous

顽[2] wán *see* "玩[1]" wán

顽磁 wáncí 〈物理〉 remanence:～性 magnetic retentivity

顽敌 wándí stubborn enemy; inveterate foe

顽钝 wándùn 〈书面〉❶ dull and obtuse; thickheaded:质性～ dull and obtuse by nature ❷ lacking in integrity; unprincipled:～无耻的嗜利者 shameless, unprincipled profit-seeker ❸ not sharp; blunt:良医之门多疾人，砥砺之旁多～。As a good doctor draws a crowd of patients to his door, so there is always a pile of blunt knives beside the whetstone waiting to be sharpened.

顽梗 wángěng pigheaded; perverse:～不化 incorrigibly stubborn; diehard

顽固 wángù ❶ obstinate; stubborn; self-willed; headstrong:～态度 stubborn attitude /老～ mulish old man (*or* woman); muleheaded old fogey /这个人思想～，不容易说服。The man is opinionated and not susceptible to persuasion. ❷ bitterly opposed to change or progress; bigoted; diehard:～的右翼分子 hardline rightist ❸ (of disease) chronic and stubborn:这病～得很，不易根治。This is a stubborn disease hard to eradicate.

顽固不化 wángù-bùhuà incorrigibly obstinate; dyed in the wool:～的反动派 dyed-in-the-wool reactionaries /～的犯罪分子 hardened criminal /在这件事情上，老头儿很固执，简直有点～了。The old man is inflexible on this matter, and incorrigibly so.

顽固分子 wángùfènzǐ diehard; diehard element

顽固派 wángùpài diehard; dyed-in-the-wool conservative

顽疾 wánjí stubborn, chronic disease; persistent ailment

顽健 wánjiàn 〈书面〉〈谦词〉 well:我向来多病，自离退以来，稍觉～。I used to be something of an invalid but have been stronger since my retirement.

顽抗 wánkàng put up a stubborn resistence:负隅～ fight stubbornly with one's back to the wall; put up a desperate struggle /残敌还在～。Remnants of the routed enemy are resisting desperately.

顽廉懦立 wánlián-nuòlì turn the dishonest into honest people and fill the drifters with ambition

顽劣 wánliè stubborn and wicked; naughty and unruly:秉性～ stubborn and wicked by nature /～异常 unusually naughty and unruly

顽民 wánmín (derogatory term formerly used by rulers for disobedient subjects who clung to the overthrown dynasty or for people who did not bow to their government) inveterate trash

顽皮 wánpí naughty; mischievous:很～的男孩 very naughty boy /那孩子～地向我做起鬼脸来。The boy made faces at me mischievously.

顽强 wánqiáng indomitable; staunch; steadfast; tenacious:～的毅力 indomitable will; great willpower /与病魔～地搏斗 carry on a tenacious struggle against illness /沙漠是人类最～的自然敌人之一。The desert is one of mankind's most inexorable enemies in nature.

顽躯 wánqū 〈书面〉〈谦词〉 my health:～粗健。I am in fairly good health.

顽石点头 wánshí-diǎntóu (be so persuasive as to make) the insensate stones nod in agreement:他的言词恳切，真可使～。His advice was so sincere and earnest that it could even make the stones, as it were, nod in agreement. /你这样苦口婆心，顽石也会点头。Your earnest and well-intentioned words would even melt a heart of

stone.
顽童 wántóng naughty child; urchin
顽癣 wánxuǎn 〈中医〉stubborn dermatitis (e.g. neurodermatitis)
顽症 wánzhèng stubborn, chronic disease; persistent ailment: ～下霸药，乱世用重典。As a persistent disease requires a strong remedy, so do turbulent times call for draconian legislation.

刓 wán ❶〈书面〉cut (edges and angles); round off: ～方为圆 cut a square into a round; turn a man of strong character into a slick worldly-wise person ❷ carve or cut (as with a knife)

丸 wán ❶ ball; pellet: 弹～ pellet; shot; bullet /泥～ mud ball ❷ pill; bolus: 蜜～ bolus made of powdered Chinese medicine and honey /每天服两次，每次服一～。Take one pill each time, twice a day.
丸剂 wánjì pill
丸药 wányào pill or bolus of Chinese medicine
丸子 wánzi ❶ round mass of food; ball: 肉～ meatball /鱼～ fishball ❷ pill or bolus of Chinese medicine

汍 wán
汍澜 wánlán 〈书面〉shed tears: 泪雨～ all tears; in tears

纨 wán 〈书面〉fine silk fabrics
纨绔 wánkù *see* "纨袴"
纨袴 wánkù *also* "纨绔"〈书面〉profligate son of the rich; fop; dandy: ～子弟 beau; coxcomb; playboy
纨扇 wánshàn round silk fan
纨素 wánsù 〈书面〉white, fine ganze

wǎn

莞 wǎn
see also guān; guǎn
莞尔 wǎn'ěr 〈书面〉smile: ～一笑 give a winsome smile

皖 Wǎn another name for Anhui Province: ～北 northern Anhui
皖南事变 Wǎnnán Shìbiàn South Anhui Incident — large-scale anti-Communist incident in 1941, in which the Communist-led New Fourth Army was perfidiously ambushed by the Kuomintang army in southern Anhui when the two sides were allies fighting Japanese aggression

脘 wǎn *also* "胃脘" wèiwǎn gastral cavity

绾 wǎn coil up: 头上～个发髻 coil up (*or* tie up) one's hair /把米口袋～起来，扛在肩上 tie a knot at the top of the rice bag and put it on the shoulder
绾毂 wǎngǔ 〈书面〉hub of communications: ～要道 important communication hub (*or* centre) /此地～数省，自古为军事重镇。As a hub of communications linking several provinces, the area has been a strategic point since ancient times.

宛[1] wǎn ❶ winding; circuitous; tortuous ❷ (Wǎn) a surname

宛[2] wǎn 〈书面〉as if: ～在水中 as if in the middle of a river /音容～在 as if the person were still alive
宛妙 wǎnmiào ❶ (of scenery) winding and graceful: 园中亭台花竹，布置～。The pavilions, terraces, flowers and bamboos are beautifully laid out along winding paths in the garden. ❷ *also* "婉妙" wǎnmiào (of voice) sweet
宛然 wǎnrán as if; as though: ～在目 as if before one's very eyes /群山笼罩着一层薄雾，～一幅秀丽的水墨画。Shrouded in thin mist, the mountain range looks as if it were a Chinese painting.
宛如 wǎnrú just like; as if: 江水迂回曲折，～一条碧绿的玉带。The river meanders like a green jade belt. /当时情景～昨日。I remember the occasion as if it were yesterday.
宛若 wǎnruò just like; as if: ～天仙 as beautiful as a fairy maiden /那棵榕树枝叶繁茂，～巨大的绿伞。The luxuriant banyan looks like a huge green umbrella.
宛似 wǎnsì just like; as if: 灯光在黑夜中闪烁着绚烂的色彩，～百花园中的艳丽花朵。Lights flashed colourfully in the darkness of night just like so many beautiful flowers in a garden.
宛延 wǎnyán winding; zigzag; meandering: ～起伏的山峦 winding and undulating hills
宛转 wǎnzhuǎn ❶ *also* "辗转" zhǎnzhuǎn toss about; pass through (many places) ❷ *also* "婉转" wǎnzhuǎn tactful; sweet; agreeable

惋 wǎn 〈书面〉heave a sigh; sigh: 叹～ sigh with regret; sigh sympathetically
惋伤 wǎnshāng sigh with sorrow; lament
惋叹 wǎntàn sigh mournfully or regretfully: ～的音调 sigh in a mournful tone
惋惜 wǎnxī feel sorry; sympathize: 他在商业中失去许多机会，我深感～。I sympathize with him for his lost opportunities in business. /那个运动员最后没有冲刺上去而痛失冠军，大家深为～。We all felt sorry for the athlete who failed to win the championship (*or* come in first) for lack of one final effort. /古瓶碎了，她十分～。She grieved over the broken old vase.

琬 wǎn 〈书面〉fine jade

菀 wǎn *see* "紫菀" zǐwǎn
see also yù

碗(椀、盌) wǎn ❶ bowl: 汤～ soup bowl /一～饭 a bowl (*or* bowlful) of rice /茶～ tea cup /铁饭～ iron rice-bowl; secure job /～橱 cupboard /洗～机 dishwasher ❷ bowl-like vessel or object: 轴～儿 axle-bowl
碗柜 wǎnguì cupboard
碗式磨粉机 wǎnshì mòfěnjī 〈机械〉bowl-mill pulverizer
碗碗腔 wǎnwǎnqiāng local opera in Shaanxi Province
碗盏 wǎnzhǎn bowls and dishes; crockery

畹 wǎn 〈古语〉land measure, equivalent to 30 *mu* or 2 hectares (about 6 acres)

婉 wǎn ❶ mild; restrained; tactful: ～劝 plead (with sb.) tactfully ❷〈书面〉gentle; meek: 和～ gentle; kind ❸〈书面〉graceful; elegant: ～容 lovely features; graceful manners
婉辞 wǎncí ❶ *also* "婉词" gentle or courteous words; euphemisms: ～推却 decline courteously /"坦率的讨论"在外交上往往是"分歧"或"争执"的～。"Candid discussion" in diplomatic language is often a euphemism for "disagreement" or "dispute". ❷ graciously decline; politely refuse: ～高薪聘请 decline an offer of a high salary
婉和 wǎnhé tactful and mild; gentle: 语气～ in a tactful and mild tone
婉丽 wǎnlì 〈书面〉❶ beautiful; attractive; lovely: 姿容～ good-looking; lovely; beautiful ❷ (of poems) graceful: 词句清新～。The lines are fresh and graceful.
婉娈 wǎnluán 〈书面〉(of manners, etc.) graceful: ～的舞姿 graceful dancing
婉曼 wǎnmàn 〈书面〉gentle and graceful: ～的话语 gentle words
婉媚 wǎnmèi 〈书面〉tender and charming: 容貌～ charming features
婉妙 wǎnmiào *also* "宛妙" wǎnmiào (of one's voice) sweet and beautiful: ～的歌声 sweet song
婉曲 wǎnqū ❶ indirect; roundabout: 我～地请求他帮我一次忙。I hinted to him that I needed his help. *or* I asked him in a roundabout way if he could help me out for once. ❷〈书面〉subtle sentiments; innermost feelings: 倾诉～ reveal one's innermost feelings
婉商 wǎnshāng consult in a tactful or polite manner: 这件事不可逼他太紧，要同他～。You shouldn't press him too hard in this matter; it is essential to consult with him tactfully.
婉顺 wǎnshùn (of women) gentle and agreeable; meek: 性情～ have a mild disposition
婉娩 wǎnwǎn 〈书面〉meek; docile: ～听从 obey meekly

W

婉谢 wǎnxiè courteously decline; politely refuse: 我～了他们的邀请。I politely declined their invitation.
婉言 wǎnyán gentle remarks; tactful expressions: ～谢绝 decline gently /～劝阻 try to dissuade tactfully
婉约 wǎnyuē 〈书面〉 subtle and restrained: ～其辞 use restrained language; speak with restraint
婉转 wǎnzhuǎn *also* "宛转" wǎnzhuǎn ❶ mild and indirect; tactful; gentle: 他对我的责备很～。He reproached me mildly. /你说话～一点不行吗? Couldn't you be a little more tactful with your remarks? /请把事情～地告诉他们。Would you mind breaking the news to them gently? ❷ sweet and agreeable: 林中有黄鹂～啼鸣。Orioles are singing sweetly in the woods.

挽[1] (❹❺輓)

wǎn ❶ draw; hold; pull: ～弓 draw a bow /她紧紧地～着他的胳膊。She held his arm tightly in hers. ❷ reverse; retrieve: 力～狂澜 make vigorous efforts to turn the tide ❸ roll up: ～着裤腿 with one's trouser legs rolled up ❹ tow; draw: ～车 tow a vehicle; pull a cart (*or* carriage) ❺ lament or elegise (the deceased): 哀～ lament (over sb.'s death) /敬～ (formula on wreaths, etc.) with deep condolences (from sb.)

挽[2]

wǎn *see* "绾" wǎn
挽畜 wǎnchù draught animal; draft horse
挽词 wǎncí *also* "挽辞" elegiac words; elegy
挽额 wǎn'é elegiac tablet or board
挽歌 wǎngē dirge; elegy: ～低唱 sing a dirge in a low voice
挽回 wǎnhuí ❶ retrieve; recover; redeem; recoup: ～错误 redeem an error /～名誉 redeem (*or* recover) one's reputation (*or* honour) /～面子 save face /造成不可～的损失 cause irretrievable losses /局势已无可～。The situation is beyond (*or* past) retrieval. ❷ take back; recover (economic rights and interests): 话已说出, 无法～。You cannot take back what you have said.
挽救 wǎnjiù save; deliver; rescue: ～一名溺水男子 rescue a man from drowning /为～民族危亡而献身 sacrifice one's life for the salvation of one's nation
挽具 wǎnjù harness (for a draught animal)
挽力 wǎnlì (of a draught animal) pulling force: 改良马种, 提高～和速度 improve the breeds of horses for greater pulling force and speed
挽联 wǎnlián elegiac couplet
挽留 wǎnliú urge sb. to stay: 真心～ sincerely urge (*or* press) sb. to stay on /他要走了, 我们实在～不住。He is leaving, as we have not been able to persuade him to stay.
挽马 wǎnmǎ draught horse; harness horse
挽诗 wǎnshī elegiac poem
挽幛 wǎnzhàng large, oblong sheet of silk or cloth bearing an elegy

W

晚

wǎn ❶ evening; night; night time: 明～ tomorrow evening; tomorrow night /傍～ dusk /从早到～ from morning till night /～十点 ten in the evening; 10 p.m. /下～儿〈口语〉towards evening; at dusk; at nightfall ❷ far on in time; late: ～明 late Ming (Dynasty) /睡得～ stay up late; go to bed late /起得～ get up late; sleep late /大器～成 great minds mature late ❸〈地质〉upper; neo-: ～奥陶世 Upper Ordovician (about 440 million years ago) /～侏罗世 Upper Jurassic (about 155 million years ago) /～白垩世 Upper Cretaceous (about 90 million years ago) /～古生代 Neopaleozoic ❹ behind time; late (for sth.): 公共汽车～了半小时。The bus was half an hour late. /现在去是不是～了? Is it too late to start off now? ❺ succeeding; junior: *see* "～娘"; "～辈" ❻ (used in correspondence to refer to oneself as a self-depreciatory term) your humbly: ～弟 your humble younger brother; I or me ❼〈书面〉latter; latter life: 岁～ latter life; evening of one's life ❽ (Wǎn) a surname
晚安 wǎn'ān 〈套语〉(usu. used in translations from western works) good night
晚班 wǎnbān night shift: 上～ be on night shift /下～ be off night shift
晚半天儿 wǎnbàntiānr 〈方言〉 *also* "晚半晌儿" towards dusk: ～才回家 arrive home towards dusk
晚报 wǎnbào evening paper
晚辈 wǎnbèi younger generation; (sb.'s) junior: 您先请, 我是～。After you. I'm your junior. /我们这些～应该继承他的事业。We of the younger generation should carry on his unfinished work.
晚边 wǎnbiān 〈方言〉towards evening; at dusk; at nightfall
晚餐 wǎncān supper; dinner: 用～ have dinner (*or* supper) /吃～的时候 at supper time; over dinner (*or* supper)
晚场 wǎnchǎng *also* "夜场" yèchǎng evening show; evening performance: 人们喜欢看～。Generally, people prefer evening shows (to matinées).
晚车 wǎnchē night train: 坐～去天津 take a night train to Tianjin; get to Tianjin by night train
晚炊 wǎnchuī make a fire and cook supper: ～时刻 time to prepare supper
晚春 wǎnchūn late spring: ～作物 late spring crop
晚祷 wǎndǎo 〈宗教〉 evensong; vespers; compline: ～曲 vesper music
晚稻 wǎndào late rice
晚点 wǎndiǎn (of train, ship, plane, etc.) late; behind schedule: ～运行 run (*or* travel) behind schedule /～十五分钟 be fifteen minutes late (*or* behind schedule) /这趟车发车～半小时。The train was delayed for departure by half an hour. /从上海来的班机～了。The flight from Shanghai is delayed (*or* late).
晚点名 wǎndiǎnmíng 〈军事〉evening roll call
晚饭 wǎnfàn supper; dinner: 吃～ have supper (*or* dinner)
晚会 wǎnhuì evening entertainment; soirée; social evening; evening party: 联欢～ (get-together) evening party /营火～ campfire party /春节～ Spring Festival party
晚婚 wǎnhūn marrying at a mature age; late marriage: ～率 rate of late marriages
晚间 wǎnjiān (in the) evening; (at) night: ～新闻 evening (TV) news /各电视台的～节目很丰富。TV stations provide a great variety of programmes in the evening.
晚节 wǎnjié ❶ integrity or honour in one's later years: 保持～ maintain one's integrity (*or* honour) till the end of one's life /～不终 ruin one's integrity (*or* honour) in one's later years ❷〈书面〉one's remaining years; sunset of life
晚近 wǎnjìn in recent years; over the last few years: 计算机较普遍的使用, 在我国是～的事了。It is only in recent years that computers came into wide use in our country.
晚景 wǎnjǐng ❶ evening scene: 海边的～叫人流连忘返。The evening scene at the seaside is beautiful enough to make people linger. ❷ life or circumstances in old age: 这位老人～凄凉。The old man led a miserable and dreary life in old age.
晚境 wǎnjìng one's circumstances in old age
晚课 wǎnkè (of monks, etc.) evening chanting of scripture
晚礼服 wǎnlǐfú black tie; full evening dress
晚恋 wǎnliàn love at a mature age
晚年 wǎnnián old age; one's later or remaining years: 幸福的～ happy old age /凄苦地度过～ spend one's remaining years in hardship and misery /他只希望～生活安定。All he longs for is a peaceful life in his old age. /他的演技～达到了炉火纯青的地步。He attained perfection in the performing arts late in life.
晚娘 wǎnniáng 〈方言〉stepmother: ～待她很好。Her stepmother treats her kindly.
晚期 wǎnqī later period; (of diseases, etc.) terminal stage: 20世纪～ in the late 20th century; towards the end of the 20th century /～拉丁语 late Latin /癌症～ terminal stage of cancer; terminal cancer /这是他～的作品。This is one of his later works.
晚秋 wǎnqiū ❶ late autumn; late in the autumn: 时近～ approaching late autumn /～萧瑟, 草木凋零。Trees and grasses are withered in bleak late autumn. ❷ late-autumn crop: 收～ get in the late-autumn crops
晚秋作物 wǎnqiū zuòwù late-autumn crop
晚晌 wǎnshǎng 〈方言〉evening: ～饭 supper; dinner
晚上 wǎnshang (in the) evening; (at) night: ～有演出。There is a performance this evening. /～再谈吧。Let's talk it over tonight.
晚生 wǎnshēng 〈书面〉(used by a younger man to refer to himself while addressing a senior person) your humble pupil; junior: ～后辈 younger generation; junior
晚世 wǎnshì 〈书面〉modern times; latter days: 到了～, 这类事情颇为多见。Things of this kind have become common occurrences in modern times.
晚熟 wǎnshú 〈农业〉late-maturing: ～性 late maturity /～品种

late-maturing variety /～作物 late-maturing crop
晚霜 wǎnshuāng late frost
晚岁 wǎnsuì 〈书面〉old age; one's later or remaining years
晚田 wǎntián 〈方言〉late-autumn crop
晚霞 wǎnxiá sunset glow; sunset clouds:～逝去,夜幕降临。Dusk prevailed over the receding sunset glow. /西天浮着玫瑰色的～。Rosy sunset clouds are floating in the western sky.
晚香玉 wǎnxiāngyù 〈植物〉tuberose (*Polianthes tuberosa*)
晚学 wǎnxué ❶〈书面〉(used by a younger man to refer to himself while addressing a senior person) your humble pupil; junior ❷ attend school at old age ❸〈方言〉afternoon classes:放～ finish afternoon classes /上～ go to (*or* attend) afternoon classes
晚宴 wǎnyàn evening feast; dinner
晚疫病 wǎnyìbìng late blight
晚育 wǎnyù late childbirth
晚造 wǎnzào late crop:～玉米 late maize (*or* corn) /～大丰收 bumper harvest of late crops
晚照 wǎnzhào sunset glow; evening glow

娩

wǎn *see* "婉娩" wǎnwǎn
see also miǎn

wàn

忨

wàn 〈书面〉have an insatiable desire for; be greedy; covet

蔓

wàn tendrilled vine:瓜～儿 melon vine /扁豆～儿 hyacinth bean vines /顺～摸瓜 follow the vine to get the melon — track down sb. or sth. by following clues
see also mán; màn

万(萬)

wàn ❶ ten thousand:十～ hundred thousand /百～ million /～～ hundred million /十～～ thousand million; billion /～把人 some ten thousand people /～里挑一 one in ten thousand /～分之一 one ten-thousandth /～倍 ten thousand times; ten thousand-fold ❷ very great number; multitude; myriad:～邦 all countries; all nations /～里长空 boundless sky /～木争荣 all trees and shrubs vie in splendour /家财巨～ be worth millions; be very wealthy /十～火急 posthaste; Most Urgent (as a mark on dispatches) /一本～利 bring (*or* make) a ten-thousand-fold profit; make a big profit with a small capital ❸ absolutely; under all circumstances:～不能 absolutely cannot; can by no means; must not on any account /～无此理 cannot be true under any circumstances ❹ (Wàn) a surname
see also mò

万安 wàn'ān ❶〈书面〉perfectly sound; surefire:～之计 completely safe plan; surefire plan ❷ (often used in the early vernacular) rest assured; feel relieved:您老只管～。Please rest easy, venerable senior.
万般 wànbān ❶ all kinds:虽遇～阻力,仍坚持进行 forge ahead despite all kinds of obstacles /～皆下品,惟有读书高。〈旧语〉To be a scholar is to be at the top of society while all other careers are inferior. *or* Scholars are superior to all other walks of life. ❷ exceedingly; extremely:～惆怅 extremely melancholy; disconsolate /～困苦 in extreme hardship; in dire straits
万般无奈 wànbān-wúnài have no alternative whatsoever; have no choice but:我这样做也是出于～。I did it because I had no other choice (*or* no option).
万变不离其宗 wàn biàn bù lí qí zōng cling to one's original purpose or position despite a myriad changes; the method may vary but the principle remains the same; use ten thousand guises to serve a single purpose:这号人的表现形形色色,但～,目的都是不劳而获。Although people of this type may vary one from another in appearance, there is one thing about them which essentially remains the same, namely, they all want to profit by other people's toil.
万不得已 wànbùdéyǐ only when it is absolutely necessary; as a last resort:～的办法 last-ditch plan; last resort /这些贵重物品,非～他不肯轻易变卖。He won't sell these valuables except out of absolute necessity. /不到～,头儿不会亲自出马。The boss won't take up the matter himself unless he absolutely has no choice.
万次闪光灯 wàncì shǎnguāngdēng 〈摄影〉multitime flash lamp
万代 wàndài throughout the ages:千秋～ throughout the ages; eternally
万端 wànduān multifarious; innumerable:变化～ multifarious (*or* kaleidoscopic) changes /思绪～ be swamped by a myriad of thoughts /感慨～ a multitude of feelings rush to one's mind; be overwhelmed with a myriad of feelings
万恶 wàn'è ❶ absolutely vicious; iniquitous; nefarious:～不赦 vicious beyond redemption; iniquitous /～的侵略战争 vicious war of aggression /～的种族隔离制度 iniquitous (*or* nefarious) system of racial segregation (*or* apartheid) ❷ all evil; myriad wrongdoings:～之源 source of all evil; root of all evil /～淫为首。〈旧语〉Of all vices, lewdness is the worst.
万方 wànfāng ❶ all parts (of the country or world):～多难 troubles occur all over the land (*or* world) /～同庆 (occasion or festival) be celebrated everywhere ❷ (as of one's bearing, etc.) of varied splendour; of myriad graces:仪态～ (be) graceful in all aspects
万分 wànfēn very much; exceedingly; extremely:～激动 be very excited /～焦急 be much worried; feel extremely anxious /～热情 be exceedingly enthusiastic; be full of enthusiasm /～欣喜 be wild with joy; go into raptures /～悲痛 be overwhelmed by grief; be greatly grieved
万夫不当 wànfū-bùdāng *also* "万夫莫当" even 10,000 men are not one's match; be unmatched (in valour, etc.):～之勇 be peerless in valour; be a man of unsurpassed courage
万福 wànfú 〈旧语〉curtsy
万感 wàngǎn all sorts of feelings; mixed feelings:～交集 all sorts of feelings converge in one's heart
万古 wàngǔ throughout the ages; for ever and ever; eternally:斯人斯事,～不灭。He and his deeds will be remembered throughout the ages.
万古长存 wàngǔ-chángcún last forever; go on forever; be everlasting
万古长青 wàngǔ-chángqīng remain fresh forever; be everlasting; be eternal
万古流芳 wàngǔ-liúfāng leave a good name in history; be remembered throughout the ages
万古霉素 wàngǔméisù 〈药学〉Vancomycin
万古千秋 wàngǔ-qiānqiū throughout the ages; eternally
万贯 wànguàn ten million cash; large fortune:～家财 be worth millions /腰缠～ be a millionaire; have pots of money
万国 wànguó all nations; all countries
万国博览会 wànguó bólǎnhuì international exhibition; world exposition
万国邮政联盟 Wànguó Yóuzhèng Liánméng Universal Postal Union (UPU)
万户侯 wànhùhóu marquis with a fief of ten thousand households; high-ranking official or noble
万花筒 wànhuātǒng kaleidoscope
万汇 wànhuì 〈书面〉all things on earth
万机 wànjī myriad or numerous affairs of state:日理～ attend to numerous affairs of state every day; be occupied with a myriad of state affairs /～待理 a myriad of state affairs call for attention
万家灯火 wànjiā-dēnghuǒ lamps and candles of a myriad households; myriad twinkling lights (as of a city):展现在眼前的是～的夜景。Before our eyes emerged a night scene of a myriad twinkling lights. /船靠岸时已是～了。When the ship docked, night had fallen with lights twinkling in a myriad households.
万家生佛 wànjiā-shēngfó 〈旧语〉(used in praise of an official) living Buddha to ten thousand households — a benefactor to all
万箭攒心 wànjiàn-cuánxīn *also* "万箭穿心" grief-stricken as if ten thousand arrows had pierced one's heart:她听到儿子死去的消息,犹如～。She was so overwhelmed by her son's death that she felt as if ten thousand arrows had pierced her heart.
万劫不复 wànjié-bùfù beyond redemption; doomed forever:倘使连这一点反抗精神都没有,岂不就成～的奴才了! Without this bit of rebellious spirit, one would be an abject flunkey forever.
万金油 wànjīnyóu ❶ *Tiger Balm*, a balm for treating headaches, scalds and other minor ailments ❷ Jack of all trades (and master of none):～干部 Jack-of-all-trades cadre (*or* official)
万钧 wànjūn ten-thousand *jun* or three hundred thousand *jin* —

W

very heavy; very powerful:雷霆～ as powerful as a thunderbolt

万籁 wànlài all kinds of sound

万籁俱寂 wànlài-jùjì all (of nature's) sounds are hushed; all is quiet; silence reigns everywhere:夜里～,只听到滴答的钟声。It was night and silence reigned supreme. All one could hear was the ticking of the clock.

万类 wànlèi all things or creatures on earth:洪钧陶～。All living creatures are nurtured by Nature.

万里长城 Wànlǐ Chángchéng Great Wall (built on and off from 3rd century BC to 16th century AD, and over 13,400 *li* or 6,700 kilometres in its total length)

万里长征 wànlǐ chángzhēng ❶ ten-thousand-*li* journey; very long journey:过去的工作只不过像～走完了第一步。What has been done is only the first step in a ten-thousand-*li* march. ❷ Long March (referring to the 25,000 *li* or 12,500 kilometre march made by the Chinese Worker-and-Peasant Red Armies from Jiangxi and other southern provinces to northern Shaanxi in 1934-1935)

万历 Wànlì Wanli, title of the reign (1573-1620) of Zhu Yijun (朱翊钧,1563-1620), 14th emperor of the Ming Dynasty, called reverently Ming Shenzong (明神宗) after death

万灵节 Wànlíngjié (in Catholicism) All Soul's Day, usu. on 2 November

万流景仰 wànliú-jǐngyǎng be admired by all; command universal respect

万隆 Wànlóng Bandung, city in western Java, Indonesia:～精神 spirit of the Bandung Conference; Bandung spirit (of peaceful co existence)

万隆会议 Wànlóng Huìyì Bandung Conference, held in Bandung of Indonesia in 1955 and attended by delegates from 29 countries of Asia and Africa

万马奔腾 wànmǎ-bēnténg like ten thousand horses galloping ahead; going full steam ahead:风卷着雪花,～似的,从山顶上呼啸而来。The howling wind and snowstorm swept down from the top of the mountain, with the momentum of ten thousand stampeding horses. /工农业生产出现了～的新局面。There emerged a new situation in which industrial and agricultural production went full steam ahead.

万马齐喑 wànmǎ-qíyīn ten thousand horses stand mute — lack of vitality; apathy:～的时代已经过去了。Gone for ever is the era when "ten thousand horses were all muted".

万米 wànmǐ ten thousand metres; myriametre:～波〈电子〉myriametric wave /～赛跑 ten-thousand-metre race

万民 wànmín all the people; common people:消息传来,～欢腾。All the people rejoiced at the news. /四野萧条,～涂炭。The common people were plunged into an abyss of misery while the fields were laid to waste.

W

万民伞 wànmínsǎn 〈旧语〉(presented as souvenir to a departing magistrate or governor to express gratitude and appreciation) silk parasol hung with strips signed by great numbers of people

万目睽睽 wànmù-kuíkuí *also* "众目睽睽" zhòngmù-kuíkuí with all eyes staring; with everybody watching:～之下 in the public eye; with all eyes watching /～,难以逃脱 be unable to escape with everybody watching

万难 wànnán ❶ hardly possible; very difficult:～从命 impossible to do as requested; unable to comply with your request /～挽回 irreversible; irretrievable; beyond redemption /～更改 leave no room for modifications; admit of no alteration whatever /～幸免 cannot survive (*or* escape) by any chance ❷ all difficulties:排除～ surmount all difficulties /纵有～,也要完成任务。We will accomplish the task no matter what difficulties there may be.

万能 wànnéng ❶ omnipotent; all powerful:"金钱～。"Money will do anything. *or* Money makes the mare (to) go. ❷ universal; all-purpose; versatile:～分度头 universal dividing head /～工具机 all-purpose machine /～拖拉机 multipurpose tractor; versatile tractor /～机械手 general-purpose manipulator

万能刨 wànnéngbào universal plane

万能刨床 wànnéng bàochuáng universal planer

万能表 wànnéngbiǎo *see* "万用表"

万能胶 wànnéngjiāo all-purpose adhesive

万能磨床 wànnéng móchuáng universal grinder

万能润滑脂 wànnéng rùnhuázhī all-purpose grease

万能铣床 wànnéng xǐchuáng universal milling machine

万能钥匙 wànnéng yàoshi master-key; passkey

万能轧机 wànnéng zhájī universal mill

万年 wànnián ten thousand years; throughout the ages; eternity:遗臭～ leave a bad name for all eternity

万年历 wànniánlì perpetual calendar

万年青 wànniánqīng 〈植物〉❶ evergreen ❷ Japanese rohdea (*Rohdea japonica*)

万念俱灰 wànniàn-jùhuī *also* "万念俱焚" with all hopes dashed to pieces; totally disillusioned with life; tired of earthly life:想到这里,她不禁～。At the thought of this, she was totally disillusioned with life. /他把～的老王说动了心。He stirred up the enthusiasm of Lao Wang, who had resigned all hope.

万千 wànqiān myriad; numerous; multifarious:造就～的科学人材 train myriads of scientists /感慨～ be overcome with a multitude of feelings /变化～ undergoing multifarious changs; changing all the time /气象～ scene of kaleidoscopic splendour

万顷 wànqǐng (of area) immerse stretch; vast expanse:碧波～ vast expanse of water /～良田 immense stretch of fertile land

万全 wànquán completely safe; surefire:计出～ work out a foolproof (*or* surefire) scheme

万全之策 wànquánzhīcè *also* "万全之计" completely safe plan; surefire plan:这件事难有～。There is no absolutely foolproof plan for the matter.

万儿八千 wànr-bāqiān about ten thousand:这两年你攒了个～的吧? You have saved about ten thousand *yuan* in the past two years, haven't you?

万人 wànrén ten thousand people; numerous people; all and sundry:～唾骂 be despised and cursed by all and sundry /～景仰 be universally admired and revered /～莫敌 outmatch ten thousand warriors; have no match in valour

万人坑 wànrénkēng large pit used for burial of numerous corpses; mass grave

万人空巷 wànrén-kōngxiàng the whole town turns out (to welcome sb. or celebrate some event):城里～,争看火炬接力队伍从大街跑过。The whole town turned out to watch the torch-relay pass through the main street.

万牲园 Wànshēngyuán Garden of Ten Thousand Animals, former name of the Beijing Zoo

万圣节 Wànshèngjié *also* "诸圣节" Zhūshèngjié 〈基督教〉All Saints Day (1 Nov.)

万世 wànshì thousands of generations; all ages:～不灭 last for ten thousand generations; last forever /～不易 remain immutable for all eternity; be everlasting /～留芳 leave a good name in history; be held in high esteem throughout the ages /此～一时也,机不可失。This is a once-in-a-lifetime chance; we mustn't miss it.

万世师表 wànshì-shībiǎo model (teacher) for all ages:孔子历来被称作"～"。Confucius has always been esteemed as the model teacher for all ages.

万事 wànshì all things; everything:～如意 realize all one's wishes; have good luck in everything; "May all go well with you!" /～不求人 never turn to anybody for help; be totally self-reliant /～均妥。Everything is in place (*or* in order). /～不由人。Nothing ever turns out as one wills.

万事大吉 wànshì-dàjí everything is just fine; all's well and propitious:祝您～! May all go well with you! /如果以为一生都会～,你就大错特错了。You are sadly mistaken if you think everything in your life will ever go off without a hitch.

万事亨通 wànshì-hēngtōng everything goes well:时来运转,～。Time moves in my favour, and luck is always on my side. /不敢说～,只不过有些事办起来比你顺畅点。I cannot say that everything goes well with me, but I do manage some matters more smoothly than you.

万事俱备,只欠东风 wànshì jù bèi, zhǐ qiàn dōngfēng everything else is ready, all that is needed is fair wind; all is on hand except what is crucial:有不少事～,到头来还是办不成。Many things are aborted for lack of what is crucial, although everything else is in place.

万事起头难 wànshì qǐtóu nán *also* "万事开头难" getting things started is always difficult; everything is difficult at the start

万事通 wànshìtōng *also* "百事通" bǎishìtōng know-it-all; know-all:你找他也许能行,这个人是个～。Maybe you can turn to him for help; he is Mr. Know-It-All.

万寿山 Wànshòushān Longevity Hill (in the Summer Palace of

Beijing)

万寿无疆 wànshòu-wújiāng (formula for wishing sb. longevity) infinitely long life:祝～ wish sb. a long, long life

万水千山 wànshuǐ-qiānshān myriad rivers and thousand mountains — diverse and difficult terrain of a vast area or distance; ten thousand crags and torrents; trials of a long journey:～,路途遥远 journey over a very long distance /他走遍了祖国的～。He travelled all over the country. *or* He traversed the length and breadth of the land.

万死 wànsǐ die ten thousand deaths:罪该～ deserve to die ten thousand deaths /～犹轻 ten thousand deaths cannot atone for the crime /～一生 one-in-ten-thousand chance for survival; almost no chance to survive

万死不辞 wànsǐ-bùcí willing to risk a thousand deaths (for a noble cause):国家有用我之处,我当～。I'm willing to risk any danger if my country needs me.

万岁 wànsuì ❶ long live:世界和平～! Long live world peace! ❷ (term of deference for the emperor) His majesty; Your majesty:～爷〈口语〉His majesty; Your majesty

万万 wànwàn ❶ hundred million:千千～ milions upon millions /我国农民超过八～。The rural population in our country exceeds eight hundred million. ❷ (used in the negative) absolutely; on no account:～不可失信 absolutely must not break one's promise /～骄傲不得 must not get conceited on any account /～没有这个道理。This is absolutely unjustifiable. /他～没有想到自己会落到这个田地。Never did he imagine that he would come to this.

万维网 wànwéiwǎng World Wide Web (WWW); Web

万位 wànwèi 〈数学〉myriabit:～存储器〈计算机〉myriabit memory

万无一失 wànwúyīshī have every chance of success; not the least danger of anything going wrong; run no risk at all; be perfectly safe:这样安排,～。Things are so arranged as to rule out the slightest danger of anything going wrong. *or* This is a surefire plan. /他们的安全～。Their security is guaranteed without the least risk. *or* They are perfectly safe.

万物 wànwù all things on earth; all creatures:人为～之灵。Man is the wisest of all creatures on earth.

万向 wànxiàng 〈机械〉universal:～阀 universal valve /～接头 universal coupling; universal joint; cardan joint /～钳 universal vise /～轴 cardan shaft /～架 gimbal

万象 wànxiàng ❶ every phenomenon on earth; all manifestations of nature:包罗～ all-embracing; all-inclusive /～回春 nature revives with the return of spring; all life revives in spring ❷ (Wànxiàng) Vientiane, capital of Laos

万象更新 wànxiàng-gēngxīn everything looks fresh and gay; everything takes on a new look:初春时节,～。It's early spring, a fresh start for all living things.

万幸 wànxìng very lucky or fortunate; in good luck; by sheer luck:东西虽受了点损失,但未伤人,总算～。Fortunately we had no casualties despite some loss of property.

万姓 wànxìng ten thousand names — common people; the masses

万言书 wànyánshū ten-thousand-word memorial; long memorial:上～ submit a long memorial (to the emperor, etc.)

万一 wànyī ❶ one ten-thousandth; very small portion:我那首诗未能表达这种心情于～。My poem is but a most inadequate reflection of such sentiments. ❷ contingency; emergency; eventuality:以防～ be ready for all eventualities; be prepared for the worst /不怕一万,就怕～。〈俗语〉One should always prepare for the worst even if it is unlikely to happen. ❸〈连词〉(just) in case; if by any chance:～下雨,还去不去? In case it rains, will you go? /～出点差错,我们也有应急的办法。We have got contingency plans if anything should go wrong by any chance. ❹ what if:～他不来呢? What if he doesn't come?

万应锭 wànyìngdìng 〈中药〉Universal Tablet — patent medicine for common ailments such as indigestion, heat-strokes and sores

万应灵丹 wànyìng-língdān elixir for all ills; panacea:世上哪有什么～。There can be no such thing as an elixir for all ills.

万用 wànyòng versatile; universal:～控制器 universal controller /～自动测试设备〈电子〉versatile automatic test equipment

万用表 wànyòngbiǎo *also* "万能表"〈电工〉avometer; multimeter; universal meter

万有引力 wànyǒu yǐnlì 〈物理〉universal gravitation:～定律 law of universal gravitation

万元户 wànyuánhù household or person with an annual income of ten thousand *yuan*; (often used in the 1980's to mean) well-off person or family

万丈 wànzhàng lofty; bottomless; infinite:～光芒 shine with boundless radiance; shine in all one's splendour /气焰～ overweening arrogance /高楼～平地起。〈谚语〉A tall building has to rise from the ground. *or* Great oaks from little acorns grow.

万丈深渊 wànzhàng-shēnyuān bottomless pit; vast chasm; abyss

万众 wànzhòng millions of people; the masses:～景仰 be esteemed by millions of people; command universal veneration; be held in high esteem by the public /～欢腾 all people dance for joy; there is nationwide jubilation

万众一心 wànzhòng-yīxīn millions of people united as one; all of one heart and one mind:举国上下,～。The entire nation is united as one.

万状 wànzhuàng in all manifestations; in every way; in the extreme:惊恐～ be extremely frightened; be scared out of one's wits /危险～ be in great danger; be hanging by a thread

万紫千红 wànzǐ-qiānhóng riot or blaze of colour:节日的公园,花团锦簇,～。During holidays the park is a blaze of colour with all its flowers and festoons.

腕 wàn wrist:～关节 wrist joint

腕骨 wàngǔ carpus; carpale; carpal bone:～骨折 fracture of carpal bone

腕力 wànlì ❶ wrist strength or power:～击球 (in golf) wrist shot ❷ ability (to get things done); finesse:胆识～ vision and ability; courage and finesse

腕儿 wànr *also* "大腕儿" dàwànr 〈口语〉star (usu. referring to actors, singers, etc.); mainstay (in a theatrical troupe, etc.)

腕下垂 wànxiàchuí 〈医学〉wristdrop

腕子 wànzi wrist:手～ wrist /腿～ ankle /扳～ wrist-wrestling (*or* arm wrestling)

腕足 wànzú peduncle; tentacle:～纲 *Brachiopoda*

腕足动物 wànzú dòngwù brachiopod

wāng

汪[1] wāng ❶〈书面〉(of water) deep and wide: *see* "～洋" ❷ (of liquids) collect; gather; accumulate:眼里～着泪水 eyes brimming with tears /路上～了些水。Puddles of water gathered on the road. ❸〈方言〉puddle:泥水～ muddy puddle ❹〈量词〉*used for liquid*:一～清水 a puddle of clear water ❺ (Wāng) a surname

汪[2] wāng 〈象声〉bark; yap; bow-wow

汪汪 wāngwāng ❶ tears welling up; brimming with tears; tearful:两眼泪～ (with) tearful eyes ❷〈书面〉(as of water) vast; immense:～湖面 vast expanse of a lake /气度～ have a magnanimous bearing ❸〈象声〉bark; yap; bow-wow:狗～叫。A dog is barking.

汪克尔发动机 Wāngkè'ěr fādòngjī Wankel engine

汪洋 wāngyáng ❶ (of water) vast; immense; boundless:～大海 boundless ocean /～一片 a vast expanse of water ❷〈书面〉(of sb.'s mind) broad; magnanimous:～大度 with immense generosity /～浩博 (of sb.'s learning or mind) vast as the boundless sea

汪子 wāngzi 〈口语〉stretch or puddle (of water):一～水 a puddle of water /水～ puddle or pool

尪(尩) wāng 〈书面〉❶ bent calves, back or chest ❷ thin and weak; frail

尪羸 wāngléi 〈书面〉thin and weak; frail; feeble

尪怯 wāngqiè 〈书面〉timid; cowardly:性～ cowardly by nature

wáng

亡(亾) wáng ❶ flee; escape; run away:流～ flee; be in exile ❷ lose; be lost:消～ wither away; die out /～戟得矛 lose a halberd and get a spear — the gains offset the losses /名存实～ cease to exist except in name; exist in name only /唇～齿寒 if the lips are gone, the teeth will feel cold ❸ die; pass away; perish:夭～

W

die young /家破人～ with one's family broken up, some gone away, some dead ❹ deceased; dead:～友 deceased friend /～者 the deceased /悼～ mourn for the dead ❺ fall; subjugate:衰～ decline and fall /兴～ rise and fall (of a country) /～无日矣!〈书面〉It will not be long before the nation is subjugated. *or* The country is doomed.

亡故 wánggù die; perish; pass away:怀念～的亲人 one's thoughts go to those family members who have passed away /他于上月不幸～。To our sorrow, he died last month.

亡国 wángguó ❶ subjugate a nation; cause a state to perish ❷ subjugated country; conquered nation:～之民 people of a subjugated country or a conquered nation /～之君 monarch who caused or witnessed the fall of his dynasty; overthrown monarch

亡国灭种 wángguó-mièzhǒng conquer the country and destroy its people; suffer national subjugation and genocide

亡国奴 wángguónú slave of a foreign conqueror; person without a country; vanquished people

亡国之音 wángguózhīyīn music or tune presaging the fall of a state; decadent music or tune

亡魂 wánghún soul of a deceased person; ghost:超度～ expiate the sins of the dead; deliver souls from the purgatory

亡魂丧胆 wánghún-sàngdǎn be frightened out of one's wits; be terrified; be terror-stricken:吓得～ be frightened (*or* scared) out of one's wits

亡魂失魄 wánghún-shīpò be panic-stricken; be at a loss; be stupefied:他～地坐着,有如一块木头。He sat stupefied as if turned into a wooden figure.

亡灵 wánglíng soul of a deceased person; ghost; spectre

亡命 wángmìng ❶ flee; escape; seek refuge; go into exile:～他乡 flee one's hometown /～国外 seek refuge abroad; live in exile ❷ desperate; reckless:～歹徒 desperate thug

亡命之徒 wángmìngzhītú desperate scoundrel; desperado:对这种～决不能宽饶。We must not be softhearted to such desperate scoundrels.

亡失 wángshī lost; missing:前代名画,多已～。Most of the valuable ancient paintings have been lost.

亡血 wángxuè 〈中医〉massive or frequent haemorrhage

亡羊补牢 wángyáng-bǔláo mend the fold after a sheep is lost:～,犹未为晚。It is not too late to mend the fold even after some sheep have been lost. *or* Better late than never.

亡阳 wángyáng 〈中医〉loss or depletion of *Yang* — prostration caused by runaway perspiration or vomiting and diarrhoea

亡佚 wángyì 〈书面〉lost; missing:这几本书久已～。These books have long been lost.

亡阴 wángyīn 〈中医〉loss or depletion of *Yin* — coma and convulsion caused by high fever and excessive perspiration, massive haemorrhage, or excessive vomiting and diarrhoea

W

王 wáng ❶ king; monarch; sovereign:帝～ king; emperor /女～ queen ❷ duke; prince:亲～ prince /～妃 princess; consort of a prince ❸ head; chief:占山为～ occupy a hill to act as a lord /霸～ overlord /魔～ tyrant; despot; Prince of the Devils ❹ first or largest of its kind:蜂～ queen bee /猴～ monkey king /蚁～ queen ant ❺〈书面〉senior; grand:～父 grandfather /～母 grandmother ❻ best; strongest:～牌 trump card ❼ (Wáng) a surname

see also wàng

王安石 Wáng Ānshí Wang Anshi (formerly translated as Wang Anshih, 1021-1086), writer, philosopher and statesman of the Northern Song Dynasty

王安石变法 Wáng Ānshí Biànfǎ reform instituted by Wang Anshi as prime minister, 1070-1076, to resolve social conflicts and financial crisis

王八 wángba ❶ (popular term for 乌龟 or 鳖) turtle; tortoise ❷〈粗话〉cuckold ❸〈旧语〉pimp; pander

王八蛋 wángbadàn 〈粗话〉bastard; son of a bitch:这些～跑到家里等着跟我要账。These bloody bastards I owed money to crowded round the door waiting for me.

王不留行 wángbùliúxíng 〈中医〉seed of cowherb (*Vaccaria segetalis*)

王朝 wángcháo dynasty; royal or imperial court:封建～ feudal dynasty /清～ Qing Dynasty /法鲁克～ (Egypt) Farouk Monarchy (1936-1952) /汉诺威～ (Britain) House of Hanover (1714-1901)

王充 Wáng Chōng Wang Chong (formerly translated as Wang Chung, 27-c.97), philosopher of the Eastern Han Dynasty

王重阳 Wáng Chóngyáng Wang Chongyang (1113-1170), founder of the Quanzhen Sect of Taoism (全真道)

王储 wángchǔ crown prince

王船山 Wáng Chuánshān *see* "王夫之"

王岱舆 Wáng Dàiyú Wang Daiyu (c. 1570-1660), Islamic scholar of the Ming and Qing dynasties

王道 wángdào kingly way; benevolent government:儒家主张～,反对霸道。The Confucian school is in favour of kingly way as opposed to the way of might.

王道 wángdao 〈方言〉❶ fierce; intense; strong:这药～,可别多吃。This is strong medicine. Take it in moderate doses. ❷ perverse to reason; unreasonable; high-handed:这人真～,张口就骂人。What a rude fellow! He'd call names as soon as he speaks.

王法 wángfǎ ❶〈旧语〉state law ❷ law of the land; law:目无～ lawless; law-defiant; defying the law /～无情。The law knows no mercy.

王夫之 Wáng Fūzhī Wang Fuzhi (formerly translated as Wang Fu-chih, 1619-1692), also named "王船山", philosopher of the late Ming and early Qing dynasties

王府 wángfǔ residence of a prince:恭亲王～ Residence of Prince Gong /北京还有几处清代～。There are still a few residences of Qing princes in Beijing.

王公 wánggōng princes and dukes; nobility:～大臣 princes, dukes and ministers /～贵族 nobility; aristocracy /～贵戚 princes and princesses of the royal family

王宫 wánggōng (imperial) palace

王顾左右而言他 wáng gù zuǒ-yòu ér yán tā the king looked right and left, and spoke of sth. else — be evasive; dodge the issue:一接触到正题,他就～。He became evasive each time I tried to bring up the matter.

王官 wángguān court official

王冠 wángguān (imperial or royal) crown

王国 wángguó ❶ kingdom:比利时～ Kingdom of Belgium /约旦哈希姆～ Hashemite Kingdom of Jordan ❷ realm; domain; sphere:数学的～ domain of mathematics /从必然～到自由～ from the realm of necessity to the realm of freedom /独立～ personal fiefdom; private preserve /这里仍然是自行车的～。This remains a world of bicycles.

王侯 wánghóu princes and marquises; nobility; aristocracy

王后 wánghòu queen; queen consort

王蔧 wánghuì 〈古语〉〈植物〉summer cypress (*Kochia scoparia*)

王浆 wángjiāng royal jelly

王莲 wánglián Amazon royal water lily (*Victoria regia*)

王莽改制 Wáng Mǎng Gǎizhì Institutional reform introduced to relieve social unrest by Wang Mang (45 BC-23 AD), who eventually set up a short-lived Xin Dynasty (新朝,8-23 AD)

王冕 Wáng Miǎn Wang Mian (formerly translated as Wang Mien, 1287-1359), painter of the Yuan Dynasty

王母娘娘 Wángmǔ Niángniang (popular term for 西王母) Queen Mother of the Western Heavens, a legendary figure of the Taoist mythology

王牌 wángpái trump card; ace:～军 elite troops; ace fighting units; crack units /～飞行员 ace pilot /这是他手中的一张～。It is his trump card.

王婆卖瓜,自卖自夸 Wángpó mài guā, zì mài zì kuā 〈俗语〉ring one's own bell; blow one's own trumpet

王清任 Wáng Qīngrèn Wang Qingren (1768-1831), medical scientist of the Qing Dynasty

王权 wángquán right of the crown; royal right

王实甫 Wáng Shífǔ Wang Shifu (formerly translated as Wang Shihfu, c.1250-1337?), dramatist of the Yuan Dynasty and author of *The West Chamber* (西厢记)

王室 wángshì ❶ royal family:～宗亲 relative of a royal family ❷ royal court; imperial court:～法律顾问 (UK) Queen's Counsel (QC) /～训令 (UK) Royal Instructions

王守仁 Wáng Shǒurén Wang Shouren (formerly translated as Wang Shou-jen, 1472-1528), also named "王阳明", philosopher of the Ming Dynasty

王叔和 Wáng Shūhé Wang Shuhe, medical scientist of the Wei Kingdom and the Western Jin Dynasty

王水 wángshuǐ 〈化学〉aqua regia

王孙 wángsūn prince's descendants; offspring of the nobility:～

公子 descendent of a noble family
王太后 wángtàihòu queen mother
王维 Wáng Wéi Wang Wei (701-761), poet and painter of the Tang Dynasty
王唯一 Wáng Wéiyī Wang Weiyi, acupuncturist and court physician of the Northern Song Dynasty
王位 wángwèi throne:继承～ succeed to the throne (*or* crown) / 登上～ ascend the throne / 篡夺～ usurp the throne / ～继承人 successor to the throne
王羲之 Wáng Xīzhī Wang Xizhi (formerly translated as Wang Hsi-chih, 303-361), calligrapher of the Eastern Jin Dynasty
王仙芝起义 Wáng Xiānzhī Qǐyì Peasant uprising led by Wang Xianzhi towards the end of the Tang Dynasty
王献之 Wáng Xiànzhī Wang Xianzhi (formerly translated as Wang Hsien-chih, 344-386), calligrapher of the Eastern Jin Dynasty
王小二过年,一年不如一年 Wáng Xiǎo'èr guònián, yī nián bùrú yī nián 〈俗语〉 go from bad to worse every year; be on the decline:他家的境况真是～。His family fortunes are on the decline from year to year.
王阳明 Wáng Yángmíng *see* "王守仁"
王爷 wángye His or Your Highness:谢～恩典。Thank Your Highness for the favour.
王昭君 Wáng Zhāojūn Wang Zhaojun, or Wang Qiang (王嫱), lady-in-waiting at the Western Han court who volunteered to marry the chief of Xiongnu (匈奴) in 33 BC and helped to strengthen the Han Dynasty's friendly ties with countries of the Western Regions (西域)
王子 wángzǐ prince; king's or emperor's son:～犯法,与庶民同罪。If a prince violates the law, he must be punished like an ordinary person. *or* All offenders are punishable by law, be they princes or commoners.
王族 wángzú persons of royal lineage; imperial kinsmen
王佐之才 wángzuǒzhīcái talent to assist a monarch in governing the state:此公非寻常之辈,有～。This man is out of the common; he has the ability to serve as counsellor to the top leadership.

wǎng

往 wǎng ❶ go:寒来暑～ as summer goes and winter comes; as time passes / 来～频繁 frequent contacts ❷ in the direction of; towards:～下扔 throw down / ～外走 go out / ～下说 go on talking / ～后靠 lean back / ～西不远就到了。Go westwards and you'll be there in a short while. / 公路通～山里。The road leads up into the mountain. / 汽车从车站直接开～机场。The bus goes directly from the station to the airport. ❸ former; past; previous:以～ before; formerly; in the past / 一如既～ as always; as before; as in the past; as has always been
往常 wǎngcháng as before; as one used to do in the past:今天的会同～有点不同。Today's meeting was a bit different from the previous ones. / 老人～早上要散一回儿步。The old man used to take a walk early in the morning. / 她像～一样,进门先换鞋。As usual, she changed her shoes before she entered.
往初 wǎngchū 〈书面〉 in ancient times; in remote antiquity
往返 wǎngfǎn travel to and fro; hurry back and forth:徒劳～ make a fruitless trip; hurry back and forth for nothing / ～要半天时间。It'll take half a day to get there and back. / 为这件事,他～奔走了半年。He was rushed off his feet for half a year on that account. / 我每天乘车～于住处与办公室之间。I commute between home and office every day.
往返票 wǎngfǎnpiào return ticket; round-trip ticket:从北京到天津,单程票八元,～十五元。The price is 8 *yuan* single from Beijing to Tianjing and 15 *yuan* return.
往复 wǎngfù ❶ move back and forth; repeat oneself; 〈机械〉 reciprocate:循环～ repeat itself in cycles / 四时～ the four seasons repeat themselves in cycles / ～泵 reciprocating pump / ～运动 reciprocating movement; alternating motion; advance and return movement / ～式发动机 reciprocating engine; reciprocal motor / ～输送机 reciprocating conveyor / ～转子发动机 reciprocating rotary piston engine / ～磨床 reciprocating grinder / ～式轧机 〈冶金〉 reciprocating rolling mill ❷ contact; intercourse; exchange (of visits):书信～ exchange of correspondence; written communications; communicating by writing (*or* letter)
往古 wǎnggǔ 〈书面〉 in ancient times; in remote antiquity:～来今 since ancient times / ～的史迹 site or relics of remote antiquity
往后 wǎnghòu from now on; henceforth; later on; in the future:～的天气就会越来越冷了。It will be colder and colder from now on. / ～我们还计划买辆汽车呢。We plan to buy a car in the future.
往还 wǎnghuán contact; dealings; exchange; intercourse:偶有诗画～ keep in touch by occasionally sending each other poems and paintings / 两校人员经常～。The staff of the two schools have frequent contacts.
往迹 wǎngjì the past; past event; thing of the past:一切都成了～。All these have become things of the past.
往来 wǎnglái ❶ come and go:我们看到许多青年～于旅馆门口。We saw many young people coming and going at the gate of the hotel. ❷ contact; exchange; dealings; intercourse:有贸易～ have trade contacts / 加强同别国的友好～ strengthen friendly exchanges with other countries / 我虽然同他们有～,但关系不算密切。Though I have dealings with them, we are not on intimate terms.
往来账 wǎngláizhàng *also* "往来账户" current account; open or running account
往年 wǎngnián in former years; previously:和～不同 different from previous years / 今年收成比～好。We have had better harvests this year than before.
往前 wǎngqián ❶ in the past; past:～的事不要再提了。Let's forget about the past. *or* Let bygones be bygones. ❷ ahead; forward:～走 go forward / 只有～看,才能增强信心。Only by looking forward (*or* ahead) can we strengthen our confidence.
往日 wǎngrì in former days; in the past:～无仇,今日无冤。We had no enmity against each other before, nor have we today. / 这个湖泊～的自然之美已完全消失了。The natural beauty which characterized the lake is gone forever.
往时 wǎngshí before; in the past; in former times:他还像～一样健谈。He is as good a talker as he used to be.
往事 wǎngshì past events:～如烟。The past has vanished (from memory) like smoke. *or* What in past, is past. / ～历历在目。The past is still fresh in one's memory. / 这些～我已经记不大起来了。I can hardly recollect these past events. / ～不堪回首。I can't bear to look back. / 我们可以在一起谈谈同学时代的～。We have many reminiscences of our college days to talk over together.
往天 wǎngtiān 〈方言〉 formerly; in the past:～这时他早回来了。Normally he would have long been back by now.
往往 wǎngwǎng often; frequently; usually:她～为了点小事生气。She often gets angry over trivial matters. / 他～工作到深夜。He usually works late into the night.
往昔 wǎngxī in former times; in those days:一如～ as in the past / 追忆～,形迹相亲,情同手足。I recall that in those days we were attached to each other like brothers.

枉 wǎng ❶ crooked; warped:矫～过正 straighten the crooked to excess; exceed the proper limits in righting a wrong; overdo sth. in righting a wrong ❷ twist; bend; pervert:*see* "～法" ❸ treat unjustly or badly; wrong:诬～ lay a false charge against sb. / 你太冤～他了。You are doing him a gross injustice. ❹ in vain; to no avail; uselessly; vainly:～活了一辈子 live one's life in vain; waste one's whole life / 不～此行。This trip was not made in vain. *or* It is well worth the trip.
枉尺直寻 wǎngchǐ-zhíxún do sth. a little out of the straight in order to accomplish a greater good; make a minor concession for a major gain
枉道 wǎngdào ❶ take a roundabout course or route; go roundabout:他去车站时～看望了一个朋友。He made a detour to see a friend on his way to the railway station. ❷ 〈书面〉 please sb. by crooked means; curry favour with sb. in a devious way
枉道事人 wǎngdào-shìrén bend the law for sb.'s benefit; fawn on sb. unscrupulously
枉断 wǎngduàn pervert the law in settling a lawsuit
枉法 wǎngfǎ pervert the law:贪赃～ take bribes and bend the law / 大干～之事 wantonly pervert the course of justice
枉费 wǎngfèi waste; try in vain; be futile; be of no avail:～工夫 waste one's time / ～钱财 throw away good money for nothing / 他的一切心血都～了。All his efforts were wasted (*or* of no avail, *or* to

W

no purpose).

枉费唇舌 wǎngfèi-chúnshé waste one's breath:你不必～,再去求他了。You needn't waste your breath pleading with him.

枉费心机 wǎngfèi-xīnjī rack one's brains in vain; scheme to no avail; try in vain:他的挑拨只不过是～罢了。His scheme to sow discord will be of no avail. /事实证明,你们是～。Facts prove that you are only making futile efforts (*or* have been baying at the moon).

枉顾 wǎnggù 〈书面〉〈敬词〉your visit or company:承蒙～,不胜荣幸。It is a great pleasure to have you with us. *or* Your company is our great pleasure and honour.

枉己正人 wǎngjǐ-zhèngrén be crooked oneself yet try to set others straight; lecture others while setting a bad example oneself:～,这怎么可能呢? If he is crooked himself, how can he possibly set others straight? *or* If he is not honest and upright, how can he correct others?

枉驾 wǎngjià 〈书面〉〈敬词〉❶ pleasure of sb.'s company; honour of sb.'s presence; honour to invite:兹定于三月七日上午九时至十一时举行国际问题研讨会,敬请～光临。The pleasure of your company is hereby requested at a seminar on international affairs on March 7 from 9:00 to 11:00 a.m. ❷ (used to urge the party addressed) pay a special visit to:如能～前往,他将十分感激。He will be very grateful if you can pay a special call on him.

枉口拔舌 wǎngkǒu-báshé (often used in the early vernacular) talk nonsense; wag one's tongue too freely

枉临 wǎnglín *see*"枉顾"

枉然 wǎngrán futile; useless; to no purpose:政策再好,落实不了也～。Any policy, however wise, will come to nothing if not implemented.

枉杀无辜 wǎngshā-wúgū kill an innocent person wantonly

枉死 wǎngsǐ die uncleared of a false charge:～鬼 victim of a frame-up

枉自 wǎngzì in vain; for nothing:～费了半天劲,什么也没办成。I have been working hard at it the whole morning for nothing. /绿水青山～多,华佗无奈小虫何! So many green streams and blue hills, but to what avail? This tiny creature left even Hua Tuo powerless!

罔[1]

wǎng 〈书面〉deceive:～上 deceive the monarch

罔[2]

wǎng 〈书面〉no; not:置若～闻 take no heed of; turn a deaf ear to /药石～效 beyond medical cure

罔替 wǎngtì 〈书面〉not to change; not to be replaced:世袭～ to be inherited without any change; be hereditary

惘

wǎng feel frustrated; be in a trance:怅～ distracted; listless; melancholy

惘然 wǎngrán frustrated; lost; disappointed:～而返 return disappointed

惘然若失 wǎngrán-ruòshī feel lost; be listless:他精神恍惚,～。He was assailed by a disconcerting sense of loss. /这不幸的消息使他～,什么也干不下去。The bad news left him listless and unable to do anything.

辋

wǎng wheel rim (of a cart)

蝄

wǎng

蝄蜽 wǎngliǎng *see*"魍魉"wǎngliǎng

魍

wǎng

魍魉 wǎngliǎng *also*"蝄蜽"wǎngliǎng demons and monsters

网(網)

wǎng ❶ net (for fishing or catching birds):拖～ trawl net; trawl; dragnet /兜～ bag net; stake net /撒～ cast a net (into the water) /结～ mesh a net /起～ haul a net /在河上张～捕鱼 net a river for fish ❷ net-like object:发～ hairnet /蜘蛛～ cobweb /排球～ volleyball net /情～ meshes of love ❸ network:交通～ network of transport /灌溉～ network of irrigation /通讯～ communication network /商业～ business network ❹〈信息〉network; web; (esp.) Internet:计算机联～ networking of computers /上～ access the Internet; be on line / ～吧 Internet café; cyberbar /因特～ Internet /万维～ WWW (World Wide Web) /～上采购 shopping on Internet; web (*or* Internet) shopping /～上营销 web (*or* Internet) marketing ❺ catch with a net; net:～住一条鱼,一只鳖 net a fish and a turtle /～鸟儿 net birds ❻ cover or enclose as with a net; enmesh:田野～着一层白雾。The fields are shrouded in a thin mist.

网斑病 wǎngbānbìng 〈植物〉net blotch:大麦～ net blotch of barley (*Helminthosporium teres*)

网玻璃 wǎngbōli reticulated glass

网虫 wǎngchóng 〈信息〉Internet buff; web enthusiast; Internet geek

网点 wǎngdiǎn network:商业～ commercial network; network of trading establishments /服务～ network of service centres

网兜 wǎngdōu string bag

网纲 wǎnggāng warp; head rope (of a fishing net)

网格 wǎnggé 〈建筑〉lattice; lattice work; latticing

网关 wǎngguān 〈信息〉gateway

网获量 wǎnghuòliàng haul; catch

网际协议 wǎngjì xiéyì Internet protocol (IP)

网巾 wǎngjīn mesh hair kerchief; hairnet

网景 Wǎngjǐng Netscape (US company)

网具 wǎngjù fishing gear or tackle

网开三面 wǎngkāisānmiàn *also*"网开一面" leave three sides of the net open — give sb. a way out; be lenient or merciful:对愿改悔者都要～。We should give a way out to (*or* be leinent to) those who repent.

网扣 wǎngkòu needle lace:沙发～ needle lace cover for a sofa

网篮 wǎnglán basket with netting on top; net-topped basket

网漏吞舟 wǎnglòu-tūnzhōu 〈比喻〉the meshes of the law are so large that giant fish could slip through — criminals escape from the net of justice if the law is too lax

网路 wǎnglù 〈电工〉network:四端～ four-terminal (*or* four-pole) network /～继电器 network relay /～控制盘 network control-board

网罗 wǎngluó ❶ fishing net; bird trap ❷ enlist the services of; recruit:～人才 enlist talented people; scout for talent /～亲信 recruit trusted followers /～死党 scrape together one's sworn followers

网络 wǎngluò ❶ net-like object ❷ system; network:邮政～ postal network /这个城市已经形成合理的经济～。This city has established a rational economic network. ❸ network; web; cyber-:有源～ active network /无源～ passive network /计算机～ computer network (*or* web) /金融～ financial web /～布置图 network plan /～系统 network system

网络冲浪 wǎngluò chōnglàng surfing the net; net surfing

网络分析计算机 wǎngluò fēnxī jìsuànjī network analyzer

网络服务器 wǎngluò fúwùqì network server

网络管理 wǎngluò guǎnlǐ network management (NM):～员 web master

网络化 wǎngluòhuà networking

网络计算 wǎngluò jìsuàn network computing:～时代 network computing age

网络计算机 wǎngluò jìsuànjī network computer

网络技术 wǎngluò jìshù network technology

网络经济 wǎngluò jīngjì *also*"电子经济" diànzǐ jīngjì cyber-economy

网络空间 wǎngluò kōngjiān *also*"电子空间" diànzǐ kōngjiān cyberspace

网络扩展 wǎngluò kuòzhǎn roll-out

网络浏览器 wǎngluò liúlǎnqì web browser

网络世界 wǎngluò shìjiè cyberworld

网络文化 wǎngluò wénhuà cyberculture

网络新闻传输协议 wǎngluò xīnwén chuánshū xiéyì net news transfer protocol (NNTP)

网络闲聊 wǎngluò xiánliáo chat:～室 chat room (a system for chatting on the Internet) /～组 chat group /～电话服务 chatline

网络信息中心 wǎngluò xìnxī zhōngxīn network information centre (NIC)

网络运行中心 wǎngluò yùnxíng zhōngxīn network operation centre (NOC)

网霉素 wǎngméisù 〈生化〉reticulin

网民 wǎngmín one who access the Internet; net citizen; netizen; cyber citizen

网膜 wǎngmó ❶〈生理〉omentum:～切除术 omentectomy /～固定术 omentopexy /大～ epiploon /大～缝定术 epiplopexy /大～炎 epiploitis ❷ (short for 视网膜) retina

网屏 wǎngpíng *also* "网版"〈摄影〉mesh screen
网球 wǎngqiú tennis: 草地～ lawn tennis /硬地～ hard court tennis /打～play tennis /～明星 tennis star /～拍 tennis racket /～场 tennis court /一打～ a dozen tennis balls
网上交易 wǎngshàng jiāoyì online transaction
网坛 wǎngtán tennis circles
网细胞 wǎngxìbāo 〈生理〉reticular cell
网箱养鱼 wǎngxiāng yǎngyú net-pen fish culture
网眼 wǎngyǎn *also* "网目" mesh
网址 wǎngzhǐ Internet address; website
网状脉 wǎngzhuàngmài 〈植物〉netted veins; reticulated veins: ～叶 net-veined leaf; reticulate leaf
网状内皮瘤 wǎngzhuàng nèipíliú 〈医学〉reticuloendothelioma
网状纤维 wǎngzhuàng xiānwéi 〈生理〉reticular fibre
网状组织 wǎngzhuàng zǔzhī ❶〈生理〉reticulum; reticular tissue ❷〈冶金〉net structure; network structure
网坠 wǎngzhuì bottom weight
网子 wǎngzi ❶ net: 渔～ fishnet /蜘蛛～ spider web; cobweb ❷ net-like object: 头发～ hairnet

wàng

忘 wàng forget; escape one's memory; neglect: 贵人多～事 a man of importance has a short memory; the higher the post, the worse the memory /～了给他打电话。I forgot to ring him up. /别～了在困难中帮助过你的人。Remember those who have helped you in difficult times. /客人把钱包～在旅馆里了。The guest left his purse in the hotel.
忘本 wàngběn forget one's class origin; forget one's past suffering: 生活富裕了不能～。One should not forget one's past sufferings when one becomes well off.
忘掉 wàngdiào forget; fail to remember or recall; let slip from one's mind: 面向未来，但不要～过去。Look forward to the future, but don't forget the past. /～过去那些不愉快的回忆吧。Let those unhappy memories stop haunting you.
忘恩负义 wàng'ēn-fùyì have no feeling of gratitude; be ungrateful; bite the hand that feeds one: 这简直是～! This is pure ingratitude! /他不是那种～的人! He never forgets a favour. *or* He is not the ungrateful sort!
忘乎所以 wànghū-suǒyǐ *also* "忘其所以" forget oneself; have one's head in the clouds; get swollen-headed: 兴之所至，～ be carried away by one's impulse; let one's jest get the better of oneself /此人骄横到了～的程度。He is so arrogant that he has forgotten what he is.
忘怀 wànghuái forget; no longer worry about; dismiss from one's mind: 童年是我一生中最难～的岁月。The childhood years were the most unforgettable of my life. /那句刺耳的话语使他数月不能～。These words so jarred on his nerves that, for several months, he could not dismiss them from his mind.
忘机 wàngjī 〈书面〉not be given to calculation or trickery — stand aloof from worldly success
忘记 wàngjì ❶ forget; cannot recall: 这些事儿，难道你都～了? Have you clean forgotten all this? /我～这句话是谁说的了。I cannot remember who said these words. ❷ overlook; neglect: 不要～你作为工会会员的责任。Don't neglect your duties as a member of the trade union.
忘旧 wàngjiù forget old friends (after making new ones)
忘年交 wàngniánjiāo *also* "忘年之交"; "忘年之好" friendship between generations; good friends despite great disparity in age: 结为～ become good friends despite the difference in age
忘情 wàngqíng ❶ be unruffled by emotion; be detached; be indifferent: 难以～ remain sentimentally attached ❷ let oneself go; enjoy with abandon: 他～地引吭高歌。He sang lustily to his heart's content. *or* He let himself go, singing lustily.
忘却 wàngquè forget: 他连做人的尊严都～了。He went so far as to forget his dignity as a man.
忘我 wàngwǒ be selfless: ～地劳动 toil selflessly; work untiringly /迷人的音乐，把人们引进了一个～的境界。The audience listened spellbound to the enchanting music.
忘形 wàngxíng be beside oneself (with glee, etc.); have one's head turned; be puffed up: 他得意～，成了众矢之的。He was so smug and self-satisfied that he became the target of public ridicule.
忘性 wàngxing forgetfulness: 我的～大。I am very forgetful. *or* I have a poor memory. /瞧你这～儿! What a (poor) memory (you've got)!

妄 wàng ❶ absurd; ridiculous; preposterous: 虚～ unfounded; fabricated /愚～ ignorant but self-important; stupid but conceited /狂～ wildly arrogant ❷ presumptuously; excessively; rashly: 作为一个局外人，我想最好不要～加评论。As an outsider, I think I had better refrain from any indiscreet (*or* rash) comments. /结局如何，殊难逆料，谁也不愿～加揣测。The outcome is hard to predict, and nobody would wish to hazard a guess. /在这种情况下，你不要～作主张。Under such circumstances, you should not risk offering any advice.
妄称 wàngchēng make a presumptuous claim: 发表了两首小诗，就～自己是诗人。With only two short poems to his credit, he claimed to be a poet.
妄动 wàngdòng rash action; reckless action; ill-considered move: 做事切不可～。One mustn't be rash in action. /值此多事之秋，我们不宜轻举～。In such troubled times, we should think twice before we move.
妄断 wàngduàn rush into a conclusion; jump to a conclusion
妄口巴舌 wàngkǒu-bāshé (often used in the early vernacular) talk nonsense; wag one's tongue too freely
妄念 wàngniàn wild fancy; fanciful or absurd idea: 他对那位时装模特儿动了～。He takes a wild fancy to that fashion model. /消除～，脚踏实地，方能成功。To succeed, one must give up all fanciful notions and be down-to-earth.
妄求 wàngqiú make an inappropriate request; make an unwarranted demand: 对于物质享受，要视客观条件而定，不可～。One should not ask for material comforts regardless of the objective conditions.
妄取 wàngqǔ get wrongfully; take without permission: 我们是人民的勤务员，从不向人民～一针一线。As servants of the people, we will never take anything from the people wrongfully, not even a needle or a piece of thread.
妄人 wàngrén 〈书面〉ignorant and impudent person: 这是～的信口开河。This is an irresponsible remark of an impudent, ignorant person.
妄说 wàngshuō nonsense; absurd remark: 无知～，不足为信。This is the remark of an ignoramus, not to be taken seriously.
妄图 wàngtú try in vain; make a futile attempt: ～篡夺最高领导权 try in vain to usurp the supreme power /～行凶 attempt to commit murder or physical assault
妄为 wàngwéi take reckless action (in defiance of the law or public opinion); commit all kinds of outrages: 胆大～ be reckless and act wildly /恣意～ behave unscrupulously; act recklessly
妄下雌黄 wàngxià-cíhuáng make unwarranted changes in others' writing; make irresponsible remarks or comments: 书未读通，岂可～? How could you make such irresponsible comments (about others' writings) when you don't half understand them?
妄想 wàngxiǎng vain hope; futile attempt; wishful thinking: ～统治世界 vainly hope to dominate the whole world /以为天上会掉下馅饼来，这是痴心～。It is wishful thinking that apple pies will fall from the sky. /你一点希望也没有! 不要～! You haven't got a ghost of a chance! Don't fool yourself with fantasies!
妄想狂 wàngxiǎngkuáng 〈医学〉paranoia: ～患者 paranoid
妄想型精神分裂症 wàngxiǎngxíng jīngshén fēnlièzhèng 〈医学〉paranoid schizophrenia
妄言 wàngyán *see* "妄语"
妄言妄听 wàngyán-wàngtīng speak offhandedly and listen casually; neither the speaker nor the hearer is in earnest
妄语 wàngyǔ ❶ tell lies; talk nonsense: ～诓人 cheat by lying /出家人不打～。Buddhist monks are not supposed to tell lies. ❷ rave and rant: 痴言～ ranting rigmarole /他一生无～。He never made any improper remarks throughout his life.
妄自菲薄 wàngzì-fěibó belittle oneself; unduly humble oneself; have a sense of inferiority: 一味～，就会丧失志气。If a person always humbles himself unduly, he will become a man without any serious purpose in life.
妄自尊大 wàngzì-zūndà be overweening or overbearing; be self-important or arrogant; have too high an opinion of oneself: 他稍一出名，便～。He got swollen-headed with slight fame. /一个人固然不可以～，但也不可妄自菲薄。One should not overrate oneself, nor should

W

one belittle oneself.

望[1] wàng ❶ look or gaze into the distance; look far ahead: ～着对岸 look at the other bank; look across the river /登高～远 ascend high and look far ahead /一～无际 stretch as fas as the eye can see ❷ call on; pay a visit; visit: 看～ call on sb. /拜～ call to pay one's respects /探～病人 visit a patient (in hospital) ❸ hope; expect; look forward to: 渴～ thirst for; long for; yearn for /～回信 look forward to a reply /～早日归来 expect sb. to be back soon /大失所～ be greatly disappointed; to one's great disappointment /胜利在～。Final victory is in sight. ❹ reputation; fame; prestige: 声～ fame /威～ prestige /德高～重 be of noble character and high prestige ❺ hatred; hate: 怨～ bear (*or* have) a grudge (against sb.) ❻ sign flag: *see* "～子" ❼ 〈介词〉 to; towards: ～东走 go eastwards /他～我们点头微笑。He smiled and nodded to us. ❽ 〈书面〉 (of age) approaching; near; almost: 我已是～五十的人了。I'm approaching fifty. ❾ (Wàng) a surname

望[2] wàng ❶ full moon ❷ 15th (occasionally 16th or 17th) day of the lunar month: 朔～ first and fifteenth day of the lunar month; syzygy

望板 wàngbǎn 〈建筑〉 roof boarding

望尘莫及 wàngchén-mòjí be so far behind that one can only see the dust raised by the rider ahead — fall way behind; be far too inferior: 他的文史知识之丰富，是一般同学～的。His knowledge of literature and history is far better than that of his fellow students.

望穿秋水 wàngchuān-qiūshuǐ gaze with eager expectation; look forward with impatient expectancy: ～，不见夫君还家，潸潸泪似麻。Gazing eagerly at the horizon, she caught no sight of her husband returning, and tears began to stream down her cheeks.

望断 wàngduàn 〈书面〉 look as far as the eye can see: 天高云淡，～南飞雁。The sky is high, the clouds are pale, We watch the wild geese flying south till they vanish.

望而却步 wàng'érquèbù shrink back at the sight (of sth. dangerous or difficult); recoil; flinch: 这项任务很艰苦，它已经使许多人～。The task is so hard that many have flinched.

望而生畏 wàng'érshēngwèi be terrified or awed by the sight (of sb. or sth.); panic at the sight; look with fear; stand in awe: 老头子那严峻的面容，使人～。People were awed by the old man's stern look.

望风 wàngfēng be on the lookout (for a group of people carrying on secret activities); keep watch; stay watching: 他在盗窃团伙里充当～的角色。He served as a lookout for the gang of thieves.

望风捕影 wàngfēng-bǔyǐng *also* "望风扑影"; "捕风捉影" bǔfēng-zhuōyǐng speak or act on hearsay evidence; go on a wild goose chase

望风而逃 wàngfēng'értáo flee at the mere sight of sb.: 我军声势浩大，敌人～。We were so powerful that enemy troops fled at the mere rumour of our approach.

望风披靡 wàngfēng-pīmǐ flee pell-mell or helter-skelter at the mere sight of sb.; flee at sight: 我军挥戈南指，敌军～。Our troops switched southward and the enemy fled helter-skelter before us.

望果节 Wàngguǒjié *also* "旺果节" Wàngguǒjié Ongkor Festival or Good Harvest Festival, traditional Tibetan festival falling in late July or early August

望衡对宇 wànghéng-duìyǔ 〈书面〉 live very close to each other: 两家～，经常来往。As close neighbours, the two families visited each other frequently.

望加锡海峡 Wàngjiāxī Hǎixiá Makassar Strait, stretch of water separating Borneo and Sulawesi and linking the Sulawesi Sea and the Java Sea

望江南 wàngjiāngnán 〈植物〉 coffee senna (*Cassia occidentalis*)

望楼 wànglóu watchtower; lookout tower

望梅止渴 wàngméi-zhǐkě look at plums to quench thirst — console oneself with false hopes; feed on fancies: 把摆脱经济困难的希望寄托于别国的施舍上，那无异于～。It is sheer fantasy to pin hopes on foreign aid for getting out of economic difficulties.

望门 wàngmén old and well-known family; distinguished or prominent family: 出身～ come from a prominent family

望门寡 wàngménguǎ 〈旧语〉 betrothed woman who remains unmarried after her fiance dies: 这可怜的老妇人守了一辈子～。The poor old woman remained unmarried all her life after her fiance died.

望门投止 wàngmén-tóuzhǐ stop over wherever there is a house; be desperate for accommodation

望其项背 wàngqíxiàngbèi (often used in the negative) can see sb.'s neck and back; be equal to sb.; be a match for sb.: 我等难以～。It is difficult for us to rival with him.

望日 wàngrì 15th (sometimes 16th or 17th) day of a lunar month, when there is a full moon

望天树 wàngtiānshù 〈植物〉 *Parashorea cathayensis*

望天田 wàngtiāntián fields which are at Heaven's mercy — fields that depend on rainfall for watering

望头 wàngtou 〈方言〉 good prospects; good hope: 今年庄稼长势好，丰收有～了。The crops are growing well and the prospects for a bumper harvest are good.

望望然 wàngwàngrán 〈书面〉 ❶ be reluctant to leave or part ❷ look disappointed or ashamed: ～而去 go away looking disappointed; depart with a look of disappointment (*or* embarrassment)

望文生义 wàngwén-shēngyì take the words at their face value; interpret without real understanding: 你的解释违背本意，有～之嫌。Your interpretation departs from the original meaning; you seem to have taken it too literally.

望闻问切 wàng-wén-wèn-qiè 〈中医〉 four methods of diagnosis in traditional Chinese medicine — observation (of the patient's complexion, expression, movements, tongue, etc.), auscultation and olfaction, interrogation, and pulse feeling and palpation

望厦条约 Wàngxià Tiáoyuē Wangxia Treaty (1844), first unequal treaty imposed upon the Qing government by the US

望乡台 wàngxiāngtái ❶ 〈旧语〉 terrace, natural or man-made, where one tries to see one's home in the distance ❷ 〈迷信〉 terrace in hell where the deceased could see their homes in the distance

望眼欲穿 wàngyǎn-yùchuān wear out one's eyes looking for sb.'s return; gaze anxiously till one's eyes are overstrained; look forward earnestly: 读着妻子的来信，我仿佛看到了她那依门而待，～的样子。While reading the letter from my wife, I seemed to see her gazing anxiously into the distance expecting me at the door any minute.

望洋兴叹 wàngyáng-xīngtàn lament one's smallness before the vast ocean — bemoan one's inadequacy in the face of a great task; feel powerless and frustrated: 面对世界科技迅速发展的形势，我们不可～，而应奋力追赶。Faced with the rapid development of science and technology in the world, we should not feel frustrated, but should instead strive to catch up.

望远镜 wàngyuǎnjìng telescope: 反射～ reflecting telescope; reflector /射电～ radio telescope /双筒～ binoculars; field glasses /天文～ astronomical telescope /(剧场用)小～ opera glasses /折射～ refracting telescope; refractor /～瞄准器 telescopic sight / ～镜头 telephoto lense

望远镜学 wàngyuǎnjìngxué telescopy

望远显微镜 wàngyuǎn xiǎnwēijìng telemicroscope

望月 wàngyuè *also* "满月" mǎnyuè full moon

望诊 wàngzhěn 〈中医〉 observation (of the patient's complexion, expression, movements, tongue, etc.) as one of the four diagnostic methods in traditional Chinese medicine

望砖 wàngzhuān roofing brick

望子成龙 wàngzǐ-chénglóng long to see one's son become a dragon — hope one's children will have a bright future; long to see one's children succeed in life

望子 wàngzi sign flag: 酒～ wine-shop sign flag

望族 wàngzú distinguished family; prominent family

王 wàng 〈书面〉 (of a monarch) reign over (a kingdom): ～天下 reign over the country
see also wáng

旺 wàng ❶ prosperous; thriving; flourishing; vigorous: 炉火正～ roaring fire (in a stove or furnace); raging flames /草原上人畜两～。Both men and livestock on the prairie are thriving. /庄稼长势很～。The crops are flourishing. ❷ 〈方言〉 plenty; abundant

旺炽 wàngchì (of fire) blazing: ～的火焰 blazing fire /希望之火似乎又～了。The fire of hope seems to be burning brightly once again.

旺发 wàngfā (of fish) multiply rapidly; grow vigorously; prosper: 渔汛～ schools of fish multiplying rapidly /现在正是绿肥作物的～期。This is the prime growing season for green manure crops.

旺果节 Wàngguǒjié *see*“望果节” Wàngguǒjié

旺季 wàngjì peak period; busy season：营业～ peak period of a business /水果～ fruit season /旅游～ busy tourist season

旺健 wàngjiàn strong and healthy; vigorous：精力～ be full of vim and vigour

旺年 wàngnián 〈方言〉(of fruit trees) good year; bumper year; on-year

旺盛 wàngshèng exuberant; vibrant; vigorous：精力～的年轻人 vigorous young man /～的工作热情 great enthusiasm for work /士气～ high morale /求知欲～ thirst for knowledge /我的游兴益发～起来。My interest in travel was further aroused.

旺实 wàngshi 〈方言〉vigorous; dynamic; exuberant：大家的干劲更～了。We all worked even more vigorously.

旺相 wàngxiàng 〈方言〉prosperous; vigorous：火势～。The fire was burning vigorously. /这里的红花草长得特别～。The lucerne here is extremely lush.

旺销 wàngxiāo sell well：～商品 goods that have a ready market; salable commodities /家用电器出现～势头。Home appliances were in great demand.

旺月 wàngyuè busy season：眼下正是销售～。It is brisk marketing season.

wēi

威 wēi ❶ impressive strength; mighty force; prowess：军～ military prowess; might of an army /声～ renown; prestige /示～ show off one's strength; hold a demonstration /扬我国～ demonstrate our national might (*or* strength) /耀武扬～ make a show of one's strength; swagger around /～震群雄 domineer over other gallant men with power and prestige ❷ by force or by sheer strength：*see*“～胁”；“～慑”

威逼 wēibī compel or threaten by force; coerce：～恫吓 coerce and intimidate /以死相～ threaten with death

威逼利诱 wēibī-lìyòu *also*“威迫利诱” alternate coercion with cajolery; combine threats with inducements; use both the carrot and the stick：～不能动摇他的决心。No coercion or cajolery can shake his will (*or* determination).

威德 wēidé 〈书面〉power and benevolence; punishment and reward：～并用 resort to both force and beneficence

威尔刚 wēi'ěrgāng *also*“伟哥” wěigē Viagra, US brand name of medicine for sexual impotence or erectile dysfunction

威尔士 Wēi'ěrshì Wales, southwestern part of the United Kingdom

威风 wēifēng ❶ power and prestige; awe-inspiring bearing or manners：耍～ throw one's weight about; be overbearing /我队昨天在比赛场上大显～。Our team demonstrated overwhelming power and skill in yesterday's match. /怎么灭自己志气，长他人～? Why deflate our own morale and boost others' arrogance? ❷ imposing; impressive; awe-inspiring; majestic-looking：小伙子们穿上军装真～。How impressive those young men are in army uniform!

威风凛凛 wēifēng-lǐnlǐn have an awe-inspiring bearing; have a commanding presence; be majestic-looking：这队人马全身披挂，～，杀气腾腾。The troops were all in full armour, looking most imposing and menacing. /他～，确有一副军人气概。He is majestic-looking and has a military bearing about him.

威风扫地 wēifēng-sǎodì with every shred of one's prestige swept away — thoroughly dishonoured; with one's dignity in the dust：这支球队连连败北，～。This team has been beaten repeatedly and lost all prestige.

威骇 wēihài intimidate; deter：靠言语是～不住那些亡命徒的。Words are no deterrent to those desperadoes.

威吓 wēihè intimidate; threaten; browbeat; bully：我们死都不怕，难道还怕～吗? Since we do not fear death, how can we fear intimidation?

威赫 wēihè power and prestige：～一时的权臣 once powerful and influential courtier

威克岛 Wēikèdǎo Wake Island, an atoll in the north central Pacific and a US military and commercial base

威棱 wēiléng 〈书面〉prestige; influence：～远震四方 have high prestige and widespread influence

威力 wēilì (formidable) power; force; might：～无比 have matchless power /显示舆论的～ demonstrate the might of public opinion

威厉 wēilì 〈书面〉stern and authoritative：他双目炯炯，～逼人。He has bright piercing eyes and is rather awe-inspiring.

威烈 wēiliè ❶ fierce; violent：～的北风 fierce north wind ❷〈书面〉great power; power and authority

威灵 wēilíng 〈书面〉❶ fame and prestige; power and authority ❷ gods; deities; divinities

威灵仙 wēilíngxiān 〈中药〉root of Chinese clematis (*Clematis Chinensis*)

威猛 wēiměng powerful and valiant：这些部族人体格高大，粗壮～。The tribesmen are of high stature, sturdy and intrepid.

威名 wēimíng prestige or fame (based upon one's martial renown or military exploits)：～扬天下 one's fame spreads far and wide

威尼斯 Wēinísī Venice or Venezia, city of northeast Italy built on numerous islands linked by canals and bridges：～人 Venetian /《～商人》*The Merchant of Venice*, play by Shakespeare (1596)

威迫 wēipò *see*“威逼”

威权 wēiquán authority; power：炫耀～ flaunt one's authority or power

威容 wēiróng solemn looks; stately or majestic countenance

威慑 wēishè deter：～力量 deterrent force; deterrent /～政策 policy of deterrence /核～ nuclear deterrence /起～作用 produce a deterrent effect

威士忌 wēishìjì whisky; whiskey：苏格兰～ Scotch whisky

威势 wēishì power and influence：树立个人～ foster one's personal authority and influence /酷暑的～有增无减。The intense heat of high summer has been steadily on the increase.

威斯汀豪斯电器公司 Wēisītīngháosī Diànqì Gōngsī *also*“西屋公司” Xīwū Gōngsī Westinghouse Electrical Corporation, US manufacturer of electrical equipment

威妥玛-翟理斯拼音法 Wēituǒmǎ-Zháilǐsī pīnyīnfǎ Wade-Giles Romanization, phonetic spelling system of Chinese characters created by Westerners after 1859

威望 wēiwàng prestige：中国的国际～不断提高。China's international prestige is growing steadily.

威武 wēiwǔ ❶ might; force; power：～不能屈，富贵不能淫 be neither intimidated by force nor seduced by wealth or rank ❷ powerful; mighty; impressive：～雄壮 full of power and grandeur; mighty and splendid /仪表～ impressive bearing

威武不屈 wēiwǔ-bùqū unyielding in the face of brutal force; not submit to force：他视死如归，～。He looked death calmly (*or* squarely) in the face and refused to be subdued by force.

威胁 wēixié threaten; menace; intimidate; imperil：～利诱 intimidation and bribery; coercion and bribery; carrot and stick /～到本地区的安全 threaten the security of this region /面临死亡的～ faced with the menace of death /她既不为利诱，也不惧～。She had neither risen to the bait nor knuckled under to threats.

威信 wēixìn prestige; popularity; public trust：领导者的～ prestige of leaders /～很高 be highly prestigious /群众～很低 be rather unpopular /他在群众中的～几乎赶上了老王。His standing with the public was almost on a par with Lao Wang.

威信扫地 wēixìn-sǎodì have one's prestige swept into the dust; lose popular trust; be completely discredited：封建政府腐败无能，～。The feudal government was corrupt and incompetent and lost all popular trust. /他已经～了。His dignity and prestige have been swept into the dust. *or* He has been thoroughly discredited.

威压 wēiyā coerce; oppress; treat high-handedly：～良民 ride roughshod over honest, law-abiding citizens

威严 wēiyán ❶ dignified; imposing; august; awe-inspiring：～的目光 awe-inspiring eyes /他看起来很～。He looks very dignified. ❷ awe; prestige; dignity：保持尊长的～ keep up an elder's prestige /检阅场面的～盛大，给了我很深的印象。The august and grand occasion of military inspection made a deep impression on me.

威仪 wēiyí impressive and dignified manner：～凛然 awe-inspiring dignified bearing

威重 wēizhòng 〈书面〉dignified; stately; majestic; awe-inspiring

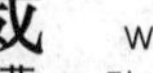 wēi

葳蕤 wēiruí 〈书面〉(of plants) luxuriant; lush：一片～的柚林 luxuriant shaddock orchard /合欢树～盛开。Silk trees are in lush blossom.

揻 wēi 〈方言〉bend:～钩儿 make a hook

崴 wēi
see also wǎi

崴嵬 wēiwéi 〈书面〉(of mountains) lofty and towering

煨 wēi ❶ cook over a slow fire; stew; simmer:～鸡 stewed chicken /罐～牛肉 beef stewed in casserole ❷ roast in fresh cinders:～白薯 roast sweet potatoes in fresh cinders

椳 wēi 〈书面〉door socket

偎 wēi snuggle up to; nestle in; lean close to:依～在一起 snuggle together /婴儿～在母亲的怀里。The baby nestled in the mother's arms.

偎傍 wēibàng snuggle up to; lean close to:孩子～在母亲身旁。The child snuggled up to the mother.

偎抱 wēibào hold in one's arms; embrace; hug; cuddle:老大娘笑眯眯地～着小孙女。The old woman cuddled her granddaughter with a broad smile on her face. /映山红正在盛开,像一片片彩霞把巉岩峭壁轻轻～着。The azalea was in full blossom as if softly embracing the precipice like rosy clouds.

偎红倚翠 wēihóng-yǐcuì visit prostitutes; go whoring

偎贴 wēitiē (of one's body) lean close to:女儿～在母亲身边。The daughter leaned close to her mother.

偎窝子 wēi wōzi 〈方言〉habitually rise late; sleep late:星期天早上她总是～。She usually sleeps late on Sunday mornings.

偎依 wēiyī snuggle up to; cuddle up to; lean close to:偎偎依依 hold each other closely swaying to and fro /他们在寒风中紧紧地～着。They hugged each other in the cold wind.

偎倚 wēiyǐ curl up to; lean close to; snuggle up to:三个孩子～着在说悄悄话儿。The three children snuggled up together, talking in whispers.

鳂 wēi 〈动物〉holocentrid, a kind of tropical sea fish

隈 wēi 〈书面〉(of a hill, river, etc.) bend:山～ mountain recess /城～ city corner

溦 wēi 〈书面〉drizzle

微 wēi ❶ minute; tiny:～差 tiny difference /细～ minute; tiny /低～ lowly; humble /稍～ a little; a bit /轻～ slight; light /些～ slightly; a trifle /～感不适 feel a bit out of sorts /人～言轻。The words of the lowly carry little weight. ❷ one millionth part; micro-: see "～安"; "～米" ❸ decline; weaken:式～ on the decline ❹ profound; abstruse; esoteric: see "～妙"

微安 wēi'ān 〈电学〉microampere:～计 microammeter

微巴 wēibā 〈物理〉microbar

微波 wēibō microwave:～管 microwave tube /～区 microwave region /～集成电路 microwave integrated circuit /～雷达 microwave radar /～通信 microwave communication /～通信网 microwave network /～预警雷达 microwave early warning radar /～干扰测量法 microwave interferomery /～边缘探测法 microwave limb sounding /～断面测量 microwave profiling

微波测高器 wēibō cègāoqì microwave height finder

微波测距仪 wēibō cèjùyí tellurometre

微波激射器 wēibō jīshèqì MASER (microwave amplification by stimulated emission of radiation)

微波接收机 wēibō jiēshōujī microwave receiver

微波理疗机 wēibō lǐliáojī microwave therapeutic apparatus

微波炉 wēibōlú microwave oven

微波散射计 wēibō sǎnshèjì microwave scatterometer

微波扫描辐射计 wēibō sǎomiáo fúshèjì microwave scanning radiometer

微波锁定 wēibō suǒdìng 〈电子〉microlock

微波遥感器 wēibō yáogǎnqì microwave remote sensor

微薄 wēibó little; meagre; scanty:～的收入 meagre income (*or* earnings) /竭尽自己～的力量 exert what little strength one has; do what little one can; do one's bit

微不足道 wēibùzúdào not worth mentioning; insignificant; negligible:～的成绩 negligible achievement /～的小纪念品 small present as a memento; little souvenir /～的小人物 insignificant man; person of no consequence; nonentity; nobody /我的作用是～的。My contribution is not worth mentioning. /这点钱～。That's just chicken feed. *or* This is peanuts.

微尘学 wēichénxué koniology; coniology

微程序 wēichéngxù 〈计算机〉microprogram:～设计 microprogramming /～设计语言 microprogramming language /～控制计算机 microprogrammable computer; microprogrammed computer

微处理机 wēichǔlǐjī microprocessor; microprocessing unit:～中央处理部件 microprocessor central processing unit /～的编译程序语言 microprocessor compiler language

微穿孔 wēichuānkǒng 〈机械〉micropunch

微词 wēicí *also* "微辞"〈书面〉complaint; covert criticism:人们对他颇有～。People complained about him a lot in private. /字里行间略有～。There is a bit of veiled criticism between the lines. *or* You'll discover a kind of implied criticism if you read between the lines.

微代码 wēidàimǎ 〈计算机〉microcode:～指令系统 microcode instruction set

微地貌 wēidìmào micro-topography; configuration of an area

微地形学 wēidìxíngxué 〈地理〉micro-geomorphology

微电机 wēidiànjī 〈电工〉micromotor; micro-machine:～控制台 micromotor control

微电脑 wēidiànnǎo micro-computer; personal computer (PC)

微电子 wēidiànzǐ microelectronic:～集成电路 microelectronic integrated circuit

微电子技术 wēidiànzǐ jìshù microelectronic technique

微电子学 wēidiànzǐxué microtronics; microelectronics

微雕 wēidiāo *also* "微刻" microsculpture; microcarving:～艺术 art of microcarving

微动物 wēidòngwù 〈动物〉animalcule

微法拉 wēifǎlā 〈电学〉microfarad

微分 wēifēn 〈数学〉differential:完全～ complete differential /中间～ intermediate differential /三角～ trigonometric differential /～分析 differential analysis /～法 differentiation

微分几何 wēifēn jǐhé differential geometry

微分器 wēifēnqì differentiator

微分学 wēifēnxué 〈数学〉differential calculus

微风 wēifēng ❶ breeze:～细雨 gentle breeze and fine rain /～拂面。A light breeze was stroking my face. ❷〈气象〉gentle breeze

微蜂窝 wēifēngwō 〈通信〉microcellular:微～ picocellular

微伏 wēifú microvolt:～表 microvolter; microvoltmeter

微服 wēifú 〈书面〉in plain clothes; incognito:～私访 (of officials) travel incognito on a fact-finding mission

微观 wēiguān microcosmic; microscopic:～组织〈冶金〉microscopic structure; microstructure

微观经济 wēiguān jīngjì microeconomy

微观经济学 wēiguān jīngjìxué microeconomics

微观粒子 wēiguān lìzǐ microparticle

微观世界 wēiguān shìjiè microcosmos; microcosm

微观物理学 wēiguān wùlǐxué 〈物理〉microphysics

微观现象 wēiguān xiànxiàng 〈物理〉microphenomenon

微观语言学 wēiguān yǔyánxué microlinguistics

微管 wēiguǎn 〈生物〉microtubule

微光电视 wēiguāng diànshì 〈电子〉LLLTV (low light level television)

微光束 wēiguāngshù 〈物理〉microbeam

微焊 wēihàn 〈电子〉microwelding

微合金 wēihéjīn microalloy:～型晶体管 microalloy-type transistor

微亨利 wēihēnglì 〈电学〉microhenry; one millionth of a henry

微乎其微 wēihūqíwēi very little; insignificant; next to nothing; negligible:两者差别～。There is very little difference between the two. /成功的机会～。The chances for success are very slim indeed. /王室的权力是～。The power of the royal house was practically nil.

微火 wēihuǒ gentle heat; slow fire

微机 wēijī 〈计算机〉microcomputer:～操作 microcomputer operation /～处理 microcomputer processing

微积分 wēijīfēn 〈数学〉infinitesimal calculus; calculus:～学 infinitesimal calculus; calculus

微寄生物 wēijìshēngwù 〈微生物〉microparasite

微件焊接 wēijiàn hànjiē 〈电子〉microwelding
微贱 wēijiàn humble; lowly; obscure:出身～ be of humble origin
微晶 wēijīng 〈物理〉microcrystal; microlite:～结构 microcrystalline structure
微刻 wēikè *see* "微雕"
微孔 wēikǒng micropore:～塑料薄膜 microporous plastic sheet
微利 wēilì small profit; low profit:～行业 low-profit profession (*or* industry)
微粒 wēilì 〈物理〉particle; corpuscle:～说 theory of particles; corpuscular theory /核～回降〈物理〉nuclear fallout
微量 wēiliàng microscale; trace:～测定 microdetermination; microestimation /～分析 microchemical-analysis; microanalysis
微量化学 wēiliàng huàxué microchemistry
微量天平 wēiliàng tiānpíng microbalance
微量元素 wēiliàng yuánsù trace element; microelement
微脉 wēimài 〈中医〉weak pulse
微茫 wēimáng 〈书面〉indistinct; faint; dull; dim:～的星光 faint starlight /月色～ dim moonlight /海洋～的景色 hazy view of the sea /眼神～ blurred eyesight
微米 wēimǐ micron
微妙 wēimiào delicate; sensitive; subtle:处境～ be in a delicate situation /感情上的～变化 subtle emotional change /用词上的～差别 nuances of wording /问题相当～。It's a rather sensitive issue.
微明 wēimíng dim or faint light:在～的晨曦中,他们沿河边漫步。In the first faint rays of the morning sun, they were strolling along the river.
微模 wēimó 〈电子〉micromodule:～程序 micromodular program / ～电子学 micromodule electronics
微末 wēimò trifling; immaterial; insignificant:～的作用 insignificant role /～的成功 success of little consequence /～之事,不值挂齿。Such trifling matters are not worth mentioning.
微漠 wēimò indifferent; apathetic; nonchalant:～的悲哀 faint grief
微气候 wēiqìhòu local climate
微气象计 wēiqìxiàngjì micrometeorograph
微切削加工 wēiqiēxiāo jiāgōng 〈电子〉micromachining
微驱动 wēiqūdòng 〈计算机〉microdrive
微热 wēirè 〈医学〉low fever:他有～。He has a slight fever.
微软公司 Wēiruǎn Gōngsī (US) Microsoft Corporation
微软件 wēiruǎnjiàn 〈计算机〉microsoftware
微弱 wēiruò faint; feeble; thin; weak:～的灯光 faint (*or* dim) lamplight /～的脉息 feeble pulse /～低沉的声音 low and weak (*or* thin) voice /瘦小～的身躯 weak and emaciated body /昏迷不醒,气息～ be in a coma, breathing faintly /以～的多数当选 be elected by a slender (*or* narrow) majority /甲队对乙队的优势是极其～的。Team A has a very tenuous advantage over Team B.
微生态学 wēishēngtàixué microecology
微生物 wēishēngwù microorganism; microbe:～农药 microbial pesticide
微生物学 wēishēngwùxué microbiology
微缩 wēisuō microform:～风景区 micro-scenic spot
微调 wēitiáo ❶〈电子〉fine-tuning; vernier tuning:～发动机〈航天〉vernier engine /～火箭发动机 vernier rocket /～电容器〈电工〉trimmer capacitor; trimmer condenser; vernier condenser ❷ adjust slightly; fine-tune:工资～ slight raise of salary /与该国关系进行～ fine-tune relations with that country
微微 wēiwēi ❶ slight; faint:～一笑 give a faint smile /她的双手～颤抖。Her two hands trembled slightly. ❷ tiny; very small:春风～地拂在她的脸上。A spring breeze stroked her face softly. ❸ micromicro-; pico-:〈电学〉～法拉 micromicrofarad; picofarad /～秒 picosecond
微微了了 wēiwēi-liǎoliǎo 〈方言〉very little:只剩下～几个钱了。There are only a few pence left.
微熹 wēixī 〈书面〉(of light) faint:～的曙光 faint rays of the morning sun
微细 wēixì very small; fine; minute:～的神经和血管 very small nerves and blood vessels /～的区别 fine distinction /他对这些～的地方也很认真。He is meticulous even about such minute details.
微纤维 wēixiānwéi 〈生物〉microfibril
微小 wēixiǎo small; little; fine; tiny:～的进步 slight progress /影响极其～ of little influence /～的沙粒 fine sands /～的损失 minor loss /哪怕是一点～的错误也不放过。He will not overlook even the smallest mistake.
微小系统 wēixiǎo xìtǒng 〈物理〉microsystem
微笑 wēixiào smile:会心地～ smile understandingly /报以～ respond with a smile /她眼睛里露着～。There was a smile in her eyes. /老师赞许地～了。The teacher smiled approval. /她脸上漾起一丝～。Her face brightened into a smile.
微笑服务 wēixiào fúwù serve with smiles:提倡～ promote smile-service
微笑外交 wēixiào wàijiāo smile diplomacy
微行 wēixíng (of an emperor or a high official) go on a (fact-finding) tour in plain clothes; travel incognito
微型 wēixíng miniature; mini-:～雕刻 microsculpture /～电视 microtelevision /～管〈电子〉microminiature tube; microtube /～组件〈电子〉micromodule; chip
微型出租车 wēixíng chūzūchē minicab
微型处理机 wēixíng chǔlǐjī 〈计算机〉microprocessor
微型电路 wēixíng diànlù microcircuit:微型印刷电路 microprinted circuit
微型电子计算机 wēixíng diànzǐ jìsuànjī microcomputer
微型飞机 wēixíng fēijī diminutive plane
微型公共汽车 wēixíng gōnggòng qìchē minibus
微型化 wēixínghuà microminiaturization; miniaturization
微型集成电话设备 wēixíng jíchéng diànhuà shèbèi 〈通信〉MITE (miniaturized integrated equipment)
微型计算机 wēixíng jìsuànjī personal computer; microcomputer
微型技术 wēixíng jìshù microtechnology
微型汽车 wēixíng qìchē minicar; mini; subcompact:～运动 karting
微型小说 wēixíng xiǎoshuō mininovel; one-page novel
微型照相机 wēixíng zhàoxiàngjī microcamera; minicam
微血管 wēixuèguǎn (blood) capillary
微循环 wēixúnhuán 〈生理〉microcirculation:～系统 microcirculatory system
微言 wēiyán 〈书面〉❶ subtle words or remarks ❷ words with concealed or hidden meaning
微言大义 wēiyán-dàyì subtle words with a profound message; deep meaning in pithy remarks
微恙 wēiyàng slight illness; ailment; indisposition:偶染～ happen to be indisposed (*or* under the weather)
微音器 wēiyīnqì *also* "传声器" chuánshēngqì; "话筒" huàtǒng; "麦克风" màikèfēng microphone; mike; mic
微震 wēizhèn ❶ slight shock ❷〈地质〉〈物理〉microseism:～学 microseismology
微阻计 wēizǔjì ducter

薇

wēi 〈古语〉common vetch

委

wēi

see also wěi

委蛇 wēiyí ❶ *see* "逶迤" wēiyí ❷ comply with; yield to:虚与～ pretend politeness and compliance

逶

wēi

逶迤 wēiyí *also* "委蛇" wēiyí 〈书面〉winding; curving; meandering:群山～ meandering mountain range /溪水欢快地向山下～流去。The stream meanders merrily downhill. /人们沿着崎岖的山路～而行。People walked up the hill along the rugged winding path.

巍

wēi towering; soaring; lofty:崔～ towering; lofty

巍峨 wēi'é towering; lofty; majestic:～的山岭 lofty mountains / ～的天安门城楼 majestic Tian An Men /珠穆朗玛峰高踞于～的群峰之上。Mount Qomolangma stands towering over all the lofty peaks.
巍然 wēirán towering; grand; majestic:庙外,两株苍松～而立。Standing majestic outside the temple were two dark-green pine trees. /一栋五十层大厦～耸立在河边。A fifty-storeyed mansion tower aloft at the riverside.
巍然屹立 wēirán-yìlì stand lofty and firm; tower majestically:庐山～在长江之滨。Lushan Mountain (*or* Mount Lu) stands loftily by the Yangtze River. /社会主义中国～在世界东方。Socialist China

stands rock-firm in the east of the world.

巍巍 wēiwēi towering; lofty: ～昆仑 towering Kunlun Mountains /～的高楼大厦连成一片。High-rise buildings stand side by side.

危 wēi ❶ danger; hazard; peril: 转～为安 turn peril into safety /乘人之～ take advantage of sb.'s predicament ❷ endanger; jeopardize; imperil: ～及生命的疾病 disease that may endanger one's life /～及治安的行动 acts that jeopardize public security /一场大火,～及四邻。A big fire broke out that brought damage to the entire neighbourhood. ❸ dying: 垂～ be critically ill; be dying ❹〈书面〉high; precipitous; sheer: ～峰 precipitous peak ❺〈书面〉proper; erect; upright: *see* "～坐" ❻ twelfth of the twenty-eight constellations in ancient astronomy ❼ (Wēi) a surname

危城 wēichéng ❶〈书面〉city with very high walls ❷ besieged city (soon to fall into enemy hands)

危辞耸听 wēicí-sǒngtīng *see* "危言耸听"

危殆 wēidài 〈书面〉in great peril; in jeopardy; in a critical state: 情况～ in a precarious situation /生命～之时 when one's life is in danger (*or* at stake); when one's life hangs by a thread /其统治地位日渐～。His rule was increasingly in peril.

危地马拉 Wēidìmǎlā Guatemala: ～人 Guatemalan /～城 Guatemala City (the capital)

危笃 wēidǔ 〈书面〉be critically ill: 病势～ be critically ill /伤员生命～。The wounded soldier's life was in danger.

危房 wēifáng house or building in dangerous state; crumbling house; ramshackle building: 拆除～ demolish a ramshackle house

危害 wēihài harm; imperil; endanger; jeopardize: ～公众 harm the public /～大局 jeopardize the overall situation /～人民生命财产 imperil the people's lives and property /～公共卫生 impair public sanitation /～社会秩序 disrupt public order /～国家安全 be detrimental to (*or* threaten) national security /～人民利益 damage the interests of the people

危害性 wēihàixìng harm; perniciousness: ～极大 tremendously harmful or dangerous / 贩卖毒品对社会的～极大。Drug trafficking does great harm to society.

危机 wēijī time of great difficulty or danger; crisis: 信用～ credibility crisis /能源～ energy crisis /周期性经济～ recurrent economic crisis /处于～之中 in the grip of crisis /转嫁～ shift the consequences of a crisis onto others

危机感 wēijīgǎn crisis awareness; sense of crisis

危机四伏 wēijī-sìfú beset with crises; with danger lurking in every direction: 该国～,政权面临崩溃。The country was crisis-ridden and its government on the verge of collapse.

危及 wēijí harm; endanger; jeopardize; imperil: ～生命 endanger sb.'s life /～国家安全 jeopardize national security

危急 wēijí critical; precarious; in imminent danger; in a desperate situation: 病势～ be gravely (*or* dangerously) ill /～存亡之秋 at a most critical moment or time (in a nation's history) /情况～ faced (*or* confronted) with imminent danger /到了～关头,你得挺身而出。When the chips are down, you'll have to step forward.

危境 wēijìng dangerous situation or state: 身处～ be confronted with a dangerous situation; be in danger

危局 wēijú dangerous or precarious state; hazardous or desperate situation: 挽救～ save a dangerous situation /独撑～ be left alone to cope with a precarious situation

危惧 wēijù worry and fear; be anxious and afraid: 无丝毫～之意 show no sign of worry or fear

危楼 wēilóu 〈书面〉highrise building: 百尺～ building of over hundreds of feet high

危难 wēinàn danger and disaster; peril and calamity: 他受命于～之际。His appointment came at a time of danger and adversity. *or* He was asked to take charge when danger was imminent. /～之中见真情。A friend in need is a friend indeed. *or* A friend is best found in adversity.

危迫 wēipò critical; desperate: 情况～。The situation is touch-and-go.

危浅 wēiqiǎn 〈书面〉dying; critically ill; at one's last gasp: 人命～,朝不保夕。She is in her last hours and may not live to the end of the day.

危如累卵 wēirúlěiluǎn as hazardous as a pile of eggs; in an extremely precarious situation: 国势岌岌,～。The situation of the nation is as precarious as a pile of eggs. *or* The country is in an extremely critical situation.

危若朝露 wēiruòzhāolù precarious as the morning dew (which will soon evaporate at sunrise) — fast approaching one's doom; dying

危途 wēitú dangerous road or path: 他身入～而犹未察觉。He is pursuing a dangerous course without being aware of it.

危亡 wēiwáng in peril; in hazard; at stake: 民族～的关键时刻 at a critical moment when the nation's very existence is at stake (*or* when the nation's fate hangs in the balance)

危险 wēixiǎn dangerous; perilous; risky: ～的境地 perilous situation /冒着生命～救火 fight a fire at the risk of one's life /～区 danger zone /～标志 danger sign /有电,～! Danger! Electricity! /欧洲经济萧条的～日益加剧。The danger of an economic recession was on the increase in Europe.

危险品 wēixiǎnpǐn dangerous goods or articles; dangerous materials

危险信号 wēixiǎn xìnhào danger signal

危险性 wēixiǎnxìng danger; dangerous nature

危象 wēixiàng alarming symptoms (of a disease): 高血压～ dangerous symptoms of high blood pressure /病情恶化,～环生。The patient was getting worse with all kinds of dangers appearing.

危言 wēiyán ❶〈书面〉blunt words: ～危行 speak bluntly and act honestly ❷ say frightening things; exaggerate things: ～惑众 exaggerate in order to confuse (*or* mislead) the public; confuse (*or* mislead) the people by demagogy

危言耸听 wēiyán-sǒngtīng say frightening things to produce a great sensation; exaggerate things just to scare people; make a sensational statement; make an alarmist speech: 言过其实,有～之嫌。It is an overstatement aimed probably at producing a sensational effect. /这不过是～而已,不足为虑。This is nothing but alarmist talk, not to be taken seriously.

危在旦夕 wēizàidànxī hang by a thread; be in imminent danger; be on the verge of death or destruction: 战争一触即发,形势～。The situation was hanging by a thread, for war might break out any moment.

危症 wēizhèng dangerous symptom or case

危重 wēizhòng seriously or dangerously ill: ～病人 serious or dangerous case

危坐 wēizuò 〈书面〉sit bolt upright: 围炉～ sit up around a fire /正襟～ straighten one's dress and sit bolt up right

wéi

为¹(為、爲) wéi ❶ do; act; perform: 尽力而～ do one's best; do everything one can /偶一～之 do sth. occasionally (*or* once in a while, *or* by chance) /奋发有～ diligent and full of promise ❷ take as; serve as; act as; work as: 以法律～准绳。Take law as the yardstick. /以此～证。This will serve as a proof. /他被选～市长。He was elected mayor. /民以食～天。The first and foremost need of the people is food. ❸ become; turn: 化险～夷 turn danger into safety /化整～零 break up the whole into parts /转忧～喜。Worry turns into pleasure. ❹ be; mean; make: 学习期限～一年。The total length of schooling is one year. /三人～一组。Three makes a group. /一年～三百六十五天。One year consists of 365 days.

为²(為、爲) wéi 〈介词〉*often used together with* 所: ～风雪所阻 be held up by a snowstorm; be snowed up /～人所称道 be praised by others

为³(為、爲) wéi 〈书面〉〈助词〉(often used with 何) why, what for: 何后期～? Why come after the scheduled time? /何以伐～? What need have you to attack it?

为⁴(為、爲) wéi ❶ *used after certain single-character adjectives to form adverbs to indicate "extent", "scope", etc.*: 广～流传 spread far and wide /大～增加 increase greatly /深～感动 be deeply moved ❷ *used after certain single-character adverbs to strengthen the tone*: 极～幸福 extremely happy /更～重要 even more important /甚～特殊 very extraordinary indeed

see also wèi

为非作歹 wéifēi-zuòdǎi do evil; commit misdeeds and crimes; perpetrate outrages: ~的家伙 evildoer / 他们所反对的只是那帮假借上帝名义来~的人。They merely opposed those who used the name of God to cover up their own evildoing and crimes.

为富不仁 wéifù-bùrén rich and cruel; wealthy and heartless: ~, 为仁不富。The rich are not benevolent, the benevolent are not rich.

为害 wéihài harm; hurt: 这种害虫对农作物~最大。This kind of pest does the greatest harm to crops.

为患 wéihuàn bring disaster; be a curse or scourge: 洪水~ be scourged by floods / 人满~ be burdened with over-population; be over-populated; be overcrowded

为力 wéilì make an effort: 易于~ be easy to do / 这件事他是无能~的。He is in no position to do anything about it.

为难 wéinán ❶ be embarrassed; feel awkward or uneasy: 左右~ feel ill at ease one way or the other / 这是使人感到~的事。This is something embarrassing. / 她真的很~。She is really in a dilemma. ❷ make things difficult for: 不要再~他了。Don't make things difficult for him any more.

为期 wéiqī within or for a certain period of time; by a certain date: 以三月~ not to exceed three months / 这次运动会~一周。The sports meet is scheduled to last one week. / 工程全部完工~尚远。The day is still far off when the project will be completed. *or* There is still a long way to go before the project is completed.

为期不远 wéiqī-bùyuǎn not in the distant future; not far off (in time): 五十周年校庆~了。The fiftieth anniversary of the school is drawing near.

为人 wéirén be; behave; conduct: ~和善 be kind and gentle; be genial / ~正派 be a decent man / ~不做亏心事, 半夜不怕鬼敲门。〈俗语〉He who has done nothing with a bad conscience will not panic when there is a knock at the door at midnight. *or* No troubled conscience, no fear.

为人处世 wéirén-chǔshì way one conducts oneself in society: 他的~是无可指摘的。His conduct is impeccable.

为人师表 wéirén-shībiǎo be an examplary teacher; be worthy of the name of teacher; be a paragon of virtue and learning

为善最乐 wéishàn-zuìlè it is a great pleasure to do good: ~, 读书便佳。Philanthropic acts are a great pleasure and reading an enjoyment.

为生 wéishēng earn one's living: 以卖画~ make a living by selling (one's own) paintings / 行医~ earn a living as a medical practitioner

为时 wéishí in terms of time: 再从头干起, ~太晚。It is too late to start afresh.

为时过早 wéishí-guòzǎo premature; too early; too soon; far ahead of time: 现在开始~。It is too early to begin now. / 说这种话尚~。It is still premature to pass such judgement.

为首 wéishǒu headed by; led by; with sb. as the leader: 以一位副总理~的越南政府代表团昨日抵达北京。A Vietnamese government delegation headed by a deputy premier arrived in Beijing yesterday. / 这个施工队以他~。The construction team is led by him.

为数 wéishù add up to; amount to; number: ~可观 considerable in number or quantity / ~不少 quite a few; numerous / ~甚微 amount to very little

为所欲为 wéisuǒyùwéi do as one pleases; do whatever one likes; have one's own way; follow one's bent: 当年, 慈禧太后一个人大权独揽, ~。In those days, the Empress Dowager Cixi arrogated all authority to herself and had her own way in everything.

为伍 wéiwǔ associate with; mix with: 与一些不三不四的人~ hang around with some dubious characters / 羞与~ think it beneath one to associate with sb.

为限 wéixiàn be within the limit of; not exceed; be no more than: 以二十人~ no more than twenty persons / 三天~ within three days / 有效期以三个月~ good for three months only / 一次取款额以五百元~。Each time one can draw up to 500 *yuan*.

为止 wéizhǐ till; up to: 迄今~ to this day; so far; up to now / 到上月底~ up to the end of last month / 这件事就到此~。Let the matter rest. / 今天到此~。Let's call it a day.

为重 wéizhòng attach great importance to; treasure; stress: 以国家利益~ put the national interest first / 以团结~ value solidarity above everything else / 以大局~ set store by the overall interests

为主 wéizhǔ give first place to; give priority to: 以自力更生~ rely mainly on oneself; give priority to self-reliance / 大家一起干, 但以你~。Let's do the job together, with you playing the major role.

韦(韋)

wéi ❶〈书面〉leather; hide ❷ (Wéi) a surname

韦编三绝 wéibiān-sānjué 〈比喻〉study diligently; be an avid reader (Confucius studied *The Book of Changes* over and over again, so that the leather thongs binding the bamboo slips on which the book was inscribed were broken three times)

韦伯 wéibó ❶〈物理〉weber ❷ (Wéibó) Max Weber (1864-1920), German sociologist whose best work is *Protestant Ethic and the Spirit of Capitalism* (1904-1905)

韦地亚钻头 Wéidìyà zuàntóu 〈矿业〉Widia bit

韦尼克脑病 Wéiníkè nǎobìng 〈医学〉Wernicke's encephalopathy

韦太姆手术 Wéitàimǔ shǒushù 〈医学〉Wertheim's operation

闱(闈)

wéi ❶ palace's side gate: 宫~ living quarters of a palace ❷ hall of the imperial (civil service) examination: 春~ spring examination / 秋~ autumn examination / 入~ enter the imperial examination hall

闱墨 wéimò (in the Qing Dynasty) successful papers printed as models for candidates for the imperial examinations to learn from

违(違)

wéi ❶ oppose; disobey; violate: 阳奉阴~ overtly agree but covertly oppose; comply in public but oppose in private; feign compliance / ~令者军法从事。He who disobeys orders shall be courtmartialled. ❷ part with; leave: 久~ not have seen sb. for a long time

违碍 wéi'ài taboo; ban; prohibition: ~字句 taboo words and expressions

违拗 wéi'ào not comply with; disobey; defy: 不可~ not to be defied (*or* disobeyed) / ~旨意 disobey an imperial order / ~父命 act against one's father's wishes

违背 wéibèi violate; contravene; go against; run counter to: ~良心 go against one's conscience / ~协议 violate an agreement / ~法律 contravene the law; be illegal; commit an offence / ~道德标准 run counter to the norms of morality / ~诺言 go back on one's word; break a promise / ~事实 be contrary to (*or* fly in the face of) the facts

违别 wéibié part; leave; bid farewell

违法 wéifǎ break or violate the law; be illegal: ~行为 illegal activity; unlawful practice / ~分子 law-breaker / ~搜查 illegal search; search without a warrant / 知法~ violate the law knowingly / 这样做是~的。This is against the law. / 有法必依, ~必究。Laws must be obeyed and offenders prosecuted.

违法乱纪 wéifǎ-luànjì commit malfeasance; violate the law and discipline: ~行为 acting against the law and discipline; unlawful act / 严防国家工作人员~ be strictly on guard against violations of the law and discipline by public functionaries

违反 wéifǎn violate; contravene; go against; run counter to: ~操作规程 act contrary to the rules of operation / ~协议 violate an agreement / ~人民利益 infringe upon the interests of the people / ~劳动纪律 disregard (*or* failure to observe) labour discipline / ~实事求是的原则 be not in conformity with the principle of seeking truth from facts / ~信托义务 commit a breach of trust / ~合同 breach of contract / ~诺言 break a promise / ~常识 go against common sense / ~常态 be contrary to common practice; abnormal / ~中国的国情 depart from the realities in China

违犯 wéifàn violate; infringe; contravene; act contrary to: ~校规 violate the school regulations / ~国法 break the law of the state / ~纪律 breach the discipline

违和 wéihé 〈婉词〉(in reference to the person addressed) have a minor ailment; be indisposed: 贵体~, 这次就不打扰了。As you are not feeling well, I shall come next time.

违纪 wéijì violate the discipline: ~行为 act of breach of discipline

违教 wéijiào 〈书面〉〈谦词〉not have the benefit of sb.'s instructions: ~已久。I have long been denied the benefit of your instructions.

违禁 wéijìn violate a ban: 有意~ deliberately violate a ban / ~品 contraband (goods)

违抗 wéikàng disobey; defy: ~领导 defy the higher-ups (*or* the leadership, *or* one's superiors); be insubordinate / 他的指示谁也不敢~。Nobody dares to challenge his instructions.

W

违例 wéilì ❶ contrary to or different from the usual practice:不该～另搞一套 should not act in contradiction to the established regulations; should not deviate from the usual practice ❷〈体育〉breach of rules:发球～ breach the service rules

违令 wéilìng disobey orders; act in defiance of orders:～者一律开除! Those who disobey orders shall be dismissed without exception.

违逆 wéinì violate; breach:～军令 go against military orders

违忤 wéiwǔ 〈书面〉violate; defy; disobey

违误 wéiwù (used in officialese) disobey orders and cause delay:令到之日即办,不可～。The order must be acted upon the day it is received; no deviation or delay will be permitted.

违宪 wéixiàn against the constitution; unconstitutional:宣布～ declare sth. unconstitutional

违心 wéixīn against one's conscience; contrary to one's convictions:说了些～的话 uttered a few words against one's conscience; make some insincere remarks /我觉得说这样的话太～了。It goes against the grain for me to make such remarks.

违心之论 wéixīnzhīlùn words uttered against one's conscience; insincere talk; untruthful statement:我不能敷衍迎合,作～。I won't just try to please them and say things against my better judgement.

违言 wéiyán 〈书面〉❶ grudge; complaint ❷ improper words; unreasonable remarks

违约 wéiyuē ❶ break a contract; violate a treaty or accord, agreement, deed, charter, etc.:～霸占 seize (*or* occupy) in violation of an agreement (*or* treaty) /～者受罚。The party who does not honour the agreement is subject to a fine. ❷ go back on one's words; break off an engagement

违章 wéizhāng break rules and regulations:～操作 operate a machine contrary to the instructions /～建筑 building put up in defiance of rules and regulations; unauthorized construction

围(圍) wéi

❶ enclose; surround; besiege:～而歼之 besiege and annihilate /人～得水泄不通 be tightly packed /把围巾～得严严实实的 wear the scarf tightly round the neck /包～ surround; encircle; besiege; close in on /突～ break through an encirclement ❷ all round; around:房子周～植了树。Trees were planted around the house. /四～都是鲜花。There are flowers all around. ❸ measurement of certain parts of body:腰～ waistline /胸～ chest measurement /三～ (of women) measurements ❹〈量词〉(a) hand span:腰大十～ waist of ten hand spans (b) arm span:千年古树,粗可十～。A thousand year ancient tree can grow as thick as ten arm spans.

围抱 wéibào surround:纪念碑耸立在松柏～之中。The monument stood erect among the pine and cypress trees.

围脖儿 wéibór 〈方言〉scarf; muffler:如今年轻人又兴围～了。Scarfs have again become popular among young people today.

W

围捕 wéibǔ surround and catch; round up:～逃犯 hunt down an escapee /～鱼群 round up a shoal of fish

围场 wéichǎng royal hunting ground

围城 wéichéng ❶ encircle a city; besiege a city:～战 battle of besiegement ❷ besieged city:被困～ trapped in a besieged city

围簇 wéicù surround tightly or closely; gather round:看着～在身边的孩子们,他高兴得笑出声来。Looking at the children closely round him, he laughed happily.

围点打援 wéidiǎn-dǎyuán *also*"围城打援" beseige an enemy stronghold in order to strike at enemy reinforcements

围堵 wéidǔ close in and intercept:四面～ close in on all sides /～政策 policy of containment

围攻 wéigōng ❶ besiege and attack; lay siege to:～城堡 lay siege to a castle /围而不攻 surround without attacking ❷ jointly speak or write against; launch convergent attacks on:屡遭～ come under incessant attacks from all sides /轮番～ subject sb. to repeated converging attacks

围观 wéiguān surround and watch:～的群众 (crowd of) onlookers /～陌生人很不礼貌。It isn't good manners to crowd round and stare at a stranger.

围裹 wéiguǒ wrap up; wrap in:老师脱下大衣,把刚从水中救起的小孩～起来。The teacher took off his overcoat and wrapped up the child that had just been rescued from drowning.

围湖造田 wéihú zàotián (build dikes to) reclaim land from lakes; reclaim lake bottomland for planting crops

围护 wéihù surround to protect:几名保镖～着部长挤出人群。Several bodyguards escorting the minister pushed their way out of the crowd.

围击 wéijī surround and attack; lay siege to

围歼 wéijiān surround and annihilate:～残敌 surround and wipe out the remnant enemy troops

围剿 wéijiǎo encircle and suppress:粉碎敌人的～ smash the enemy's encirclement /调动大军进行～ dispatch large numbers of troops to carry out suppression /反～ the struggle (*or* operations) against an encirclement campaign; anti-encirclement struggle

围巾 wéijīn scarf; muffler:围好～ put a scarf round the neck

围聚 wéijù gather from all around:店门前～了不少看热闹的人。A large crowd of onlookers gathered in front of the shop.

围垦 wéikěn enclose tideland for cultivation; (build dikes to) reclaim land from marshes

围困 wéikùn lay siege to; besiege; hem in; pin down:长期～的战术 tactic of staging a prolonged siege /被～的县城 county town under siege /五万军民被大水～。Fifty thousand civilians and servicemen were surrounded by the flood water.

围栏 wéilán fence:无～草场 fenceless pasture

围猎 wéiliè close in and hunt

围领 wéilǐng 〈方言〉muffler; scarf:围上～ put on a muffler

围拢 wéilǒng crowd around; close in:大家～来看这几幅画。They all crowded round to look at the paintings. /这帮歹徒发现警察向他们～,拔腿就跑。The gang of thugs took to their heels when they saw police closing in on them.

围炉 wéilú sit around a fire:～小酌 sit around a fire drinking

围埝 wéiniàn earth dike (to prevent flooding)

围屏 wéipíng multi-leaf screen; folding screen

围棋 wéiqí *weiqi*, or encirclement chess, a game of chess played with black and white pieces on a board of 361 crosses; go:下一盘～ play a game of go /他是一位九段的～大师。He is a level 9 *weiqi* master. *or* He is a ninth-dan go-master.

围枪 wéiqiāng 〈方言〉shot-gun; hunting gun or rifle; fowling piece

围墙 wéiqiáng enclosure; enclosing wall

围裙 wéiqún apron

围绕 wéirào ❶ round; around:直升机～着山头盘旋。The helicopter was hovering round (*or* circling over) the hilltop. /地球～太阳运转。The earth revolves round the sun. ❷ centre on; revolve round:会议～着战争与和平的问题进行讨论。The discussion at the meeting revolved round (*or* centred on) the question of war and peace.

围网 wéiwǎng purse seine (a large net that encloses a school of fish and is then closed at the bottom); purse net:～渔船 purse seiner; purse boat

围魏救赵 wéiwèi-jiùzhào besiege the State of Wei to rescue the State of Zhao — relieve the besieged by besieging the base of the besiegers

围岩 wéiyán 〈矿业〉country rock; surrounding rock

围堰 wéiyàn cofferdam; coffer

围腰 wéiyāo ❶ *also*"围腰子" waist protector; waistpad ❷〈方言〉apron

围寨 wéizhài *also*"围砦" stockaded or walled-up village

围桌 wéizhuō (formerly used in a wedding, funeral or sacrificial ceremony) table curtain

围子 wéizi ❶ defensive wall; stockade surrounding a village:土～ fortified village /墙～ village stockade ❷ dike against flooding ❸ curtain:床～ bed curtain /桌～ table curtain

围嘴儿 wéizuǐr bib

围坐 wéizuò sit round sb. or sth.; sit in a circle:孩子们～在老爷爷身边,听他讲故事。The children sat round the grandpa listening to his story.

帏(幃) wéi

❶ *also*"帷" wéi curtain ❷〈古语〉perfume bag

圩 wéi

dike; embankment:筑～ build a dike /～埂 earth dike

see also xū

圩岸 wéi'àn dike; dyke

圩堤 wéidī dike or dyke against flooding in lowlands

圩田 wéitián diked low-lying paddy fields; polder

圩垸 wéiyuàn protective embankment in lakeside areas

圩子 wéizi ❶ protective embankment(s) surrounding low-lying fields ❷ village defensive wall; stockade surrounding a village

硙(磑) wéi

硙硙 wéiwéi 〈书面〉 high; towering

嵬 wéi

〈书面〉 tower aloft; rise up: ～然 towering; loftily

嵬嵬 wéiwéi 〈书面〉 lofty; towering: 群峰～ towering peaks

惟[1] wéi

❶ only; solely; alone: ～一无二 only one /～真理是从 follow truth alone ❷ but; only that: 他品学兼优, ～身体稍差。He excels both in character and scholarship, only that he is weak physically.

惟[2] wéi

〈书面〉〈助词〉 *used before year, month and day*: ～公元一千九百五十年 in the year of 1950

惟[3] wéi

thinking; thought; idea: 思～ (now usu. written as 思维) thinking

惟独 wéidú *also* "唯独" wéidú only; alone: 大家都按时到校, ～他一人迟到。Everybody else arrived at school in time; he was the only one that turned up late. /他几乎没有什么爱好, ～对钓鱼兴趣很大。He has almost no other hobbies than fishing.

惟恐 wéikǒng *also* "唯恐" wéikǒng for fear that; lest: ～落后于别人 lest one should lag behind others /～对客人照顾不周 be afraid that the guest is not well attended to /～天下不乱 desire to see the world plunged into turmoil; be always ready to stir up trouble

惟利是图 wéilì-shìtú *also* "唯利是图" wéilì-shìtú seek nothing but profit; work exclusively for profit; be bent solely on profit; put profit before everything else; be interested only in material gains: ～的奸商 profiteer bent solely on profit

惟妙惟肖 wéimiào-wéixiào *see* "维妙维肖" wéimiào-wéixiào

惟命是从 wéimìng-shìcóng *also* "唯命是听" wéimìng-shìtīng always do as one is told; be always ready to take orders (as from one's superior): 对领导～ be absolutely obedient to one's superior /他表面上～, 心里却不以为然。He is obedient outwardly, but he has reservations. /他对她凡事都只有～而已。He can only answer "yes" to everything she says.

惟其 wéiqí 〈书面〉〈连词〉 because; as; since: 冬天日短, ～短, 就更要抓紧时间学习。Winter days are short; that is why we should try all the more to make good use of the time to study.

惟我独尊 wéiwǒ-dúzūn *also* "唯我独尊" wéiwǒ-dúzūn overweening; extremely conceited; lording it over all others: 当领导的不能～, 容不得不同意见。Leaders should not be overbearing and intolerant of dissenting views.

惟一 wéiyī *also* "唯一" wéiyī only; sole; unique: ～人选 only candidate /～选择 no other alternative; only choice /～理由 sole reason /实践是检验真理的～标准。Practice is the sole (*or* the one and only) criterion of truth.

惟有 wéiyǒu only; alone: ～团结奋斗, 方能渡过难关。Only through united efforts can we tide over our present difficulties. /～斗争, 才能胜利。Struggle, and struggle alone, can ensure victory. /～他感到不满意。Everyone was satisfied except him.

唯 wéi

only; solely; alone: ～实 base oneself only on reality; proceed from objective realities /～书 rely solely on books and documents /～条件论 view that everything depends entirely on conditions /～此为大。This alone is the most important.

see also wěi

唯成分论 wéichéngfènlùn theory of the unique importance of class origin; theory that nothing counts but one's class background

唯恐 wéikǒng *see* "惟恐" wéikǒng

唯理论 wéilǐlùn 〈哲学〉 rationalism

唯利是图 wéilì-shìtú *see* "惟利是图" wéilì-shìtú

唯灵论 wéilínglùn 〈哲学〉 spiritualism

唯美主义 wéiměizhǔyì aestheticism

唯名论 wéimínglùn 〈哲学〉 nominalism

唯命是听 wéimìng-shìtīng *see* "惟命是从" wéimìng-shìcóng

唯能说 wéinéngshuō 〈物理〉 energetics

唯生产力论 wéishēngchǎnlìlùn doctrine of the unique importance of productive forces (used in the Cultural Revolution to denounce any effort to give priority to the national economy)

唯我独尊 wéiwǒ-dúzūn *see* "惟我独尊" wéiwǒ-dúzūn

唯我主义 wéiwǒzhǔyì 〈哲学〉 solipsism

唯武器论 wéiwǔqìlùn theory that weapons alone decide the outcome of war

唯物辩证法 wéiwù biànzhèngfǎ 〈哲学〉 materialist dialectics

唯物论 wéiwùlùn 〈哲学〉 materialism: ～的反映论 materialist theory of reflection

唯物史观 wéiwù shǐguān 〈哲学〉 materialist conception of history; historical materialism

唯物主义 wéiwùzhǔyì 〈哲学〉 materialism: 辩证～ dialectical materialism /机械～ mechanical materialism /历史～ historical materialism /庸俗～ vulgar materialism /～者 materialist

唯心论 wéixīnlùn 〈哲学〉 idealism

唯心史观 wéixīn shǐguān 〈哲学〉 idealist conception of history; historical idealism

唯心主义 wéixīnzhǔyì 〈哲学〉 idealism: ～先验论 idealist apriorism

唯信仰论 wéixìnyǎnglùn 〈宗教〉 solifidianism: ～者 solifidian

唯一性 wéiyīxìng uniqueness: ～定理〈数学〉 uniqueness theorem

唯意志论 wéiyìzhìlùn view that will decides everything; 〈哲学〉 voluntarism

帷 wéi

curtain

帷薄不修 wéibó-bùxiū 〈书面〉〈婉词〉 (of an official's family) promiscuity; promiscuousness; incest

帷幔 wéimàn *see* "帷幕"

帷幕 wéimù *also* "帷幔" heavy curtain: ～徐徐拉开, 戏开始了。As the curtain slowly rises, the opera begins. /拉开了新时代的～。The curtain rises on a new era.

帷幄 wéiwò 〈书面〉 army tent: 运筹于～之中, 决胜于千里之外。Strategies devised in the command tent will ensure victory in the far-away battlefield.

帷帐 wéizhàng bed curtain; mosquito net

帷子 wéizi curtain: 床～ bed curtain /车～ cart curtain /窗～ window curtain

维[1] wéi

❶ bind; tie up; hold together ❷ keep; maintain; safeguard; uphold ❸ (Wéi) a surname

维[2] wéi

thought; thinking

维[3] wéi

dimension: 三～空间 three-dimensional space /直线是一～的, 平面是二～的。A line has one dimension and a plane two dimensions.

维持 wéichí ❶ keep; uphold; maintain; preserve: ～生命 keep alive; preserve life /～现状 maintain the status quo; let things go on as usual /～原判 affirm the original judgement; uphold the original verdict (*or* sentence) /～治安 keep the peace; maintain public order; maintain law and order /～生产 continue production /～生活 support oneself or one's family; make a living; make both ends meet ❷ protect; safeguard; support: 亏他暗中～, 我们才得安全抵达。We arrived safe and sound thanks to his secret support.

维持和平部队 wéichí hépíng bùduì peace-keeping force

维持会 wéichíhuì order-maintenance committee; caretaker committee; "peace preservation association" (local quisling organization during the War of Resistance Against Japanese Aggression, 1937-1945)

维多利亚湖 Wéiduōlìyàhú Lake Victoria, largest lake in Africa

维多利亚瀑布 Wéiduōlìyà Pùbù Victoria Falls, spectacular cataract on the River Zambezi in southern Africa

维尔京群岛 Wéi'ěrjīng Qúndǎo Virgin Islands (in the Caribbean Sea): 美属～ American Virgin Islands /英属～ British Virgin Islands

维管束 wéiguǎnshù 〈植物〉 vascular bundle

维护 wéihù safeguard; preserve; defend; uphold: ～社会公德 uphold civic virtues /～公共利益 safeguard public interests /～国家的主权和独立 defend national sovereignty and independence /～民族尊严 vindicate national honour; defend national dignity /～法律的严肃性 stand up for the dignity of the law /～交通安全 ensure traffic safety /～安定团结 maintain unity and stability

维纶 wéilún *also* "维尼纶"; "维尼龙" 〈纺织〉 polyvinyl alcohol fibre

维棉布 wéimiánbù 〈纺织〉 vinylon and cotton blend

维妙维肖 wéimiào-wéixiào *also*“惟妙惟肖”wéimiào-wéixiào remarkably true to life; absolutely lifelike; vivid; graphic:把人物的神采刻画得～ vividly portray the looks and spirit of the characters / 这个细节写得～。The details are graphically portrayed.
维尼纶 wéinílún vinylon
维生 wéishēng make a living:他以卖水果～。He made a living by selling fruit.
维生素 wéishēngsù vitamin:～A vitamin A / 复合～B vitamin B complex
维生素过多症 wéishēngsù guòduōzhèng hypervitaminosis
维生素缺乏症 wéishēngsù quēfázhèng 〈医学〉 vitamin-deficiency; avitaminosis
维氏硬度 Wéishì yìngdù 〈冶金〉 Vickers-hardness:～试验 Vickers hardness test / ～数 Vickers hardness number
维数 wéishù 〈数学〉 dimension; dimensionality:～论 dimension theory
维他命 wéitāmìng (old transliteration for) vitamin
维提岛 Wéitídǎo Viti Levu, largest island of Fiji
维吾尔语 Wéiwú'ěryǔ Uygur language
维吾尔族 Wéiwú'ěrzú Uygur, nationality living in the Xinjiang Uygur Autonomous Region:他们是～。They are Uygurs.
维系 wéixì hold together; keep up; maintain:～人心 keep up popular morale / 一根无形而坚强的纽带把他们～在一起。An invisible but strong tie links them together.
维新 wéixīn reform; modernization:～派 reformist; reformer / ～势力 reformist elements (*or* forces) / ～运动 reform movement / 戊戌～ Constitutional Reform and Modernization of 1898 / 日本明治～ Meiji Reform of Japan (1868)
维修 wéixiū keep in (good) repair; service; maintain:～队 service team; maintenance group / ～费 maintenance cost (*or* fee, *or* charge); upkeep; service charge / ～工 maintenance worker / ～住房 maintain a house / ～设备 maintenance equipment / ～手册 servicing manual / 设备～得很好。The equipment is in good repair. / 机器～得很差。The machines are out of repair.
维修工艺学 wéixiū gōngyìxué terotechnology
维也纳 Wéiyěnà Vienna, capital of Austria:～人 Viennese
维族 Wéizú (short for 维吾尔族) Uygur

桅 wéi mast:船～ mast
桅灯 wéidēng ❶〈航海〉 masthead light; range light ❷ barn lantern
桅顶 wéidǐng masthead
桅杆 wéigān ❶ mast:～起重机 mast crane / ～式天线 mast antenna ❷ tall mast for installing signal, antenna, etc.
桅樯 wéiqiáng mast

W

wěi

亹 wěi
亹亹 wěiwěi 〈书面〉❶ diligent; industrious ❷ move forward

芳(蔿、蔿) Wěi a surname

伪(僞、僞) wěi ❶ false; counterfeit; fake; bogus:虚～ hypocritical / 作～ fake; forge / 真～难辩。It is difficult to tell what is false from what is true. ❷ puppet; collaborationist; quisling:～政权 puppet regime / ～政府 illegitimate government
伪币 wěibì ❶ counterfeit money; counterfeit banknote; forged banknote; spurious coin ❷ money issued by a puppet or quisling government
伪钞 wěichāo counterfeit banknote
伪顶 wěidǐng 〈矿业〉 fake roof
伪经 wěijīng forged classic; fake scripture
伪军 wěijūn ❶ puppet or quisling army; puppet troops:他参加过～。He once joined a puppet army. ❷ puppet or quisling soldier:杀伤～五百余人 kill or wound over 500 quisling troops
伪君子 wěijūnzǐ hypocrite:欺世盗名的～ hypocrite that angles for fame
伪科学 wěikēxué pseudo-science
伪劣 wěiliè counterfeit and inferior:～商品 counterfeit and shoddy merchandise; fake and shoddy goods; inferior-quality products
伪善 wěishàn pretending to be virtuous; hypocritical:～者 hypocrite / ～行为 hypocritical conduct; hypocrisy / 事实揭露了他那～的嘴脸。Facts have revealed his true features as a hypocrite.
伪饰 wěishì false embellishment; pretence; affectation:～之辞 pretentious remark
伪书 wěishū ancient book of dubious or questionable authenticity; ancient book found to have been forged, incorrectly dated, or attributed to a wrong author
伪托 wěituō forge ancient art or literary works; palm modern works off as ancient ones:先秦的某些著作是后人～编写的。Some of the pre-Qin works were forgeries by people of later times.
伪学 wěixué false learning; heterodoxy
伪造 wěizào fake; forge; falsify; fabricate; counterfeit:～火车票 forge a train ticket / ～账目 doctor (*or* falsify) accounts / ～身分证 fabricate (*or* falsify) an ID card / ～公章 falsify a public seal / ～的文件 spurious (*or* fake, *or* forged) document; pseudograph / ～现场 simulate a scene
伪造品 wěizàopǐn fake; forgery; counterfeit
伪造罪 wěizàozuì forgery
伪证 wěizhèng 〈法律〉 false witness, testimony or evidence; perjury:犯有～罪 be guilty of perjury; give false testimony / 作～ bear false witness; give fake testimony
伪指令 wěizhǐlìng 〈计算机〉 pseudo-order; pseudo-instruction; quasi-instruction
伪撰 wěizhuàn forge ancient art or literary works; forge writings by other people:这是～之作。This is a forged work.
伪装 wěizhuāng ❶ pretend; feign; disguise:～成一名黑社会人物 disguise oneself as someone from the underworld / ～革命,混进党内 pretend to be revolutionary and sneak into the Party / 他～中立,欺骗了不少人。His feigned neutrality deceived quite a few people. ❷ disguise; guise; mask:一旦剥去～,他只不过是个卑鄙无耻的小人。Once his mask is stripped off, he is nothing but a mean and despicable rascal. ❸ camouflage:～工事 camouflaged works / 天然～ natural camouflage / 人工～ artificial camouflage / 迷彩～ colour camouflage / 前面的山脚下是加了～的炮兵阵地。At the foot of the hill was the artillery position under camouflage. / 卡车已用竹枝～起来。The truck was camouflaged with bamboo.
伪足 wěizú 〈动物〉 pseudopodium
伪作 wěizuò ❶ art or literary work done by usurping sb. else's name (esp. that of a well-known artist or writer of the past) ❷ art or literary work published in one's own name but actually done by sb. else

炜(煒) wěi 〈书面〉 bright

玮(瑋) wěi 〈书面〉❶ a kind of jade ❷ rare; valuable; precious:明珠～宝 bright pearls and valuable jewels

苇(葦) wěi reed:芦～ reed
苇箔 wěibó reed matting
苇丛 wěicóng reed grove; cluster of reeds:小船隐蔽在～里。The small boat hid in the (thicket of) reeds.
苇荡 wěidàng *also*“芦荡”lúdàng reed marsh:～是游击队出没的好地方。The reed marsh was an ideal place for guerrilla operations.
苇塘 wěitáng reed pond
苇席 wěixí reed mat
苇子 wěizi reed

暐(暐) wěi 〈书面〉 (of light) very bright; brilliant

韪(韙) wěi *see*“不韪”bùwěi

伟(偉) wěi ❶ great:雄～ magnificent / 宏～ grand; lofty ❷〈书面〉 strong and handsome:魁～ tall and broad-shouldered; gigantic in stature; stalwart / 身～ (man of) prowess / ～男 big muscular man
伟岸 wěi'àn 〈书面〉 big and tall:身材～ be tall and strong / 村头长着两棵挺拔～的松树。Standing straight in front of the village were two towering big pine trees.

伟大 wěidà great; lofty; mighty: ～的功绩 outstanding achievement /～的事业 noble cause (*or* undertaking) /～的国家, ～的人民 great country, great people
伟哥 wěigē *also* "威尔刚" wěi'ěrgāng Viagra, US brand name of medicine for sexual impotence or erectile dysfunction
伟观 wěiguān magnificent view; majestic scene; spectacular sight: 钱塘江潮是我国自然～之一。The Qiantang River tide is one of the magnificent sights in China.
伟绩 wěijì great feat; outstanding exploit; brilliant achievement: 他们的丰功～永垂青史。Their great achievements will go down in the annals of history.
伟晶岩 wěijīngyán 〈地质〉 pegmatite
伟举 wěijǔ great act or undertaking: 空前的～ unprecedented act of great significance
伟力 wěilì great force; tremendous strength: 科技的～还没有充分发挥出来。The great force of science and technology has yet to be brought into full play.
伟丽 wěilì ❶ grand; sublime; magnificent: ～的宫殿 majestic palace /～的云海 magnificent sea of clouds /～的山景 grand view of the mountains /～的前程 splendid future ❷ beautiful; handsome: 仪容～ beautiful appearance and graceful bearing
伟论 wěilùn informed opinion; enlightened or intelligent view
伟人 wěirén great man: 革命～ great revolutionary /一代～ great man of the generation
伟业 wěiyè great cause; noble undertaking: 建一代之～ undertake the great cause of the time /～丰功 heroic exploits and great achievements

韡(韡)

wěi 〈书面〉 bright; rich and beautiful

纬(緯)

wěi ❶ 〈纺织〉 weft; woof: 经～ warp and weft ❷ 〈地理〉 latitude: 南～25° 25 degrees south latitude /北～54° 54 degrees north latitude ❸ (short for 纬书) augury (book): 谶～ divination and augury
纬编 wěibiān 〈纺织〉 weft knitting: ～针织物 weft-knit fabric
纬度 wěidù 〈地理〉 latitude: 低～ (at) low latitudes /高～ (at) high latitudes / ～线 latitude line; parallel
纬密 wěimì weft density
纬纱 wěishā 〈纺织〉 woof; pick; filling
纬书 wěishū augury book (of the Han Dynasty)
纬线 wěixiàn ❶ 〈纺织〉 weft ❷ 〈地理〉 parallel *see also* "纬度"

痏

wěi 〈书面〉 sore; wound

鲔

wěi ❶ yaito tuna ❷ 〈古语〉 sturgeon

蒍

wěi ❶ Chinese slender-leaved polygala ❷ (Wěi) a surname

唯

wěi 〈书面〉 yea
see also wéi
唯唯喏喏 wěiwěi-nuònuò be a yesman; be servile: 在领导面前～ be a yesman before one's superiors; never say no to one's bosses

委[1]

wěi ❶ entrust; delegate; appoint: ～以要职 appoint sb. to an important post ❷ throw away; discard; cast aside: 将信～地而去 cast the letter on the ground and leave ❸ shift; shirk; transfer: *see* "～过"; "～罪" ❹ (short for 委员会 or 委员) committee; committee member: 县～ county Party committee /政～ political commissar /编～ editorial board; member of the board /常～ standing committee; member of a standing committee

委[2]

wěi indirect; circuitous; roundabout: ～婉其辞 speak in a mild and roundabout way; be tactful in wording

委[3]

wěi 〈书面〉 ❶ accumulate; gather: *see* "～积" ❷ end; lower reaches: 原～ beginning and end (of sth.) /穷源竟～ trace sth. to its source; get to the bottom of sth.

委[4]

wěi listless; depressed; dejected: *see* "～顿"; "～靡"

委[5]

wěi 〈书面〉 actually; definitely; certainly: ～实不错。It is really not bad.
see also wēi
委顿 wěidùn tired; exhausted; weary; fatigued: 彻夜未眠, 颇觉～。As I did not sleep a wink last night, I feel rather tired.
委过 wěiguò *also* "诿过" wěiguò shift blame on to sb.: 这是你的责任, 可不能～于他。This is your fault and you shouldn't blame it on him.
委积 wěijī 〈书面〉 accumulate; amass; heap or pile up; keep in reserve: 问题～如山, 一时难以理出头绪来。Problems have accumulated like a mountain and it is impossible to sort them out presently.
委决不下 wěijué-bùxià be hesitant and unable to reach a decision: 他一时～, 跑来找我出主意。Unable to make a decision himself, he came to ask me for advice.
委令 wěilìng 〈旧语〉 order of appointment
委靡 wěimǐ *also* "萎靡" wěimǐ listless; lethargic; dispirited; dejected: 神志～ dispirited; dejected; in low spirits /你要去掉那种消极的思想和～的情绪。You should overcome your own inertia and apathetic mood. /我们没有理由这样～。There is no reason why we should wallow in misery.
委靡不振 wěimǐ-bùzhèn dispirited; lethargic; in low spirits; dejected and apathetic: 人们不应因困难和挫折而～。One should not be daunted by difficulties or setbacks.
委内瑞拉 Wěinèiruìlā Venezuela: ～人 Venezuelan
委派 wěipài appoint; delegate; dispatch; send: ～他向基层单位征求意见。He was sent to solicit opinions from the grassroots units.
委弃 wěiqì cast aside; discard; get rid of as useless; give up: ～不顾 cast aside as useless; give up /～恶习 get rid of one's bad habits
委曲 wěiqū ❶ (of roads, rivers, etc.) winding; meandering; tortuous: ～婉转的小溪沿山而下。The stream wound its way downhill. ❷ 〈书面〉 whole story; ins and outs: 告知～ tell sb. what has happened
委曲求全 wěiqū-qiúquán stoop to compromise; compromise for the general interests: 在原则问题上, 他一向据理力争, 决不～。On questions of principle, he would argue strongly on just grounds and never stoop to compromise. /忍辱负重, ～, 这不是每个人都能做到的。Not everybody can endure humiliation and make compromises for the general good.
委屈 wěiqu ❶ feel wronged or aggrieved; nurse a grievance: 倾吐心中的～ pour out one's grievances /她觉得很～, 禁不住哭了。She felt wronged and cried in spite of herself. ❷ put to great inconvenience; do (sb.) wrong: 这件事可真～你了。I'm afraid this has put you to great inconvenience. *or* I'm sorry you have had to go through all this. /对不起, 只好～你再跑一趟了。I am sorry. You'll have to take the trouble of going there again.
委任 wěirèn ❶ appoint: ～某人担任某职 appoint sb. to an office / ～代理 agency by mandate /～行为 act of commission ❷ 〈旧语〉 fourth rank in the four-echelon officialdom of China before 1949
委任书 wěirènshū certificate of appointment or deputation
委任统治 wěirèn tǒngzhì mandate: ～地 mandated territory /～国 mandatory power
委任状 wěirènzhuàng certificate of appointment
委身 wěishēn 〈书面〉 stoop; force oneself to: ～事人 stoop to serve sb.
委实 wěishí actually; really; indeed: ～如此。That's what it is. / ～难办 it's indeed a hard nut to crack /～记不起了。I really don't remember.
委琐 wěisuǒ ❶ trifling; trivial; petty: 不为～之事而烦心 not to be worried about trivial matters ❷ wretched; miserable
委托 wěituō entrust; trust; commission: ～保险 trust insurance / ～代理 agency by agreement /我们完全可以～他来办这件事。We may well entrust him with the work. /他把房子～给朋友看管。He entrusted his house to the care of a friend. / 这事就～你办了。I leave the matter to you.
委托人 wěituōrén trustor
委托商店 wěituō shāngdiàn commission shop; commission house
委托书 wěituōshū trust deed; certificate of entrustment; power of attorney
委托责任 wěituō zérèn fiduciary duty
委婉 wěiwǎn *also* "委宛" mild and roundabout; tactful: 态度诚恳, 语气～ earnest in attitude and moderate in tone /～动听 mild and

W

pleasant /他语言～,批评严厉。His harsh criticism was couched in polite terms.

委婉语 wěiwǎnyǔ 〈修辞〉euphemism

委员 wěiyuán ❶ member of a committee; committee member:中央委员会～ member of the Central Committee /支部委员会～ member of a branch committee ❷〈旧语〉person entrusted with specific tasks; commissar

委员会 wěiyuánhuì committee; commission; council:国家发展计划～ State Development Planning Commission /中国共产党中央～ Central Committee of the Chinese Communist Party /常务～ standing committee /筹备～ preparatory committee /调查～ committee of enquiry /市政～ city council

委员长 wěiyuánzhǎng chairman (of a committee); president:人大常委会～ chairman of the Standing Committee of the NPC

委罪 wěizuì *also* "诿罪" wěizuì shift the blame; put the blame on sb. else

痿

wěi 〈中医〉paralysis:下～ paralysed in one's leg(s) /阳～ (sexually) impotent

痿症 wěizhèng 〈中医〉flaccid paralysis; motor impairment as shown by weakness and numbness of the limbs, etc.

诿

wěi shift (the responsibility or blame) to sb. else; shirk:推～ shift responsibility onto others; pass the buck /执事不～上。One should not shirk one's responsibility and blame one's boss.

诿过 wěiguò shift blame (onto others):出了问题,绝不可～于人。One should never shift the blame onto others if something goes wrong.

诿卸 wěixiè 〈书面〉shirk; dodge:～责任 shirk responsibility /任务再重也不可～。However arduous the task may be, we should not fight shy of it.

诿罪 wěizuì *see* "委罪" wěizuì

萎

wěi ❶ wither; wilt; fade:枯～ wither ❷ decline:气～ deflated; flat (tyre) /买卖～了。Business is slack. /价钱～下来了。Prices have dropped.

萎顿 wěidùn *also* "委顿" wěidùn tired; exhausted; fatigued

萎黄 wěihuáng ❶ withered and yellow:～的树叶 withered and yellow leave(s) ❷ haggard and pallid; haggard and sallow:面色～ haggard and pallid face

萎黄病 wěihuángbìng 〈植物〉chlorosis

萎落 wěiluò ❶ wither and fall:草木～。The grass withered and leaves fell from trees. ❷ on the wane; on the decline:国力～。The national power declined. /久病～。His strength was on the wane after a lingering disease.

萎靡 wěimǐ *also* "委靡" wěimǐ dejected; in low spirits

萎蔫 wěiniān wilting:花儿一天不浇水就～了。If not watered just for one day the flower will wilt.

萎弱 wěiruò weak; faint; feeble:性格～ weak in character /～的声音 (in) a faint voice /爷爷体力日渐～。Grandpa got feebler with each passing day.

萎缩 wěisuō ❶ wither; shrivel; shrink:昨天才开花,不料今天就～了。It began to flower yesterday and has now withered, quite unexpectedly. ❷ dejected; listless:神情～ in low spirits; dispirited ❸〈经济〉shrink; sag; contract:经济已出现～的趋势。Signs of economic decline have appeared. /生产～,民生凋敝。Production sagged and life was hard. /商品市场交易～。Trade fell off in the commercial markets. ❹〈医学〉atrophy:肝～ hepatatrophy; atrophy of liver /视神经～ optic atrophy /肌肉～ amyotrophy; muscular atrophy /婴儿～症 atrepsy; athrepsia (*or* athrepsy)

萎缩性鼻炎 wěisuōxìng bíyán atrophic rhinitis

萎缩性胃炎 wěisuōxìng wèiyán gastratropia; atrophic gastritis

萎陷 wěixiàn 〈医学〉collapse:肺～ collapse of the lung /～疗法 collapse therapy

萎谢 wěixiè wither; wilt; fade:秋风萧瑟,草木～。The autumn wind is soughing and the plants have all withered. /花朵因缺水而～。The flowers are wilting from lack of water.

隗

Wěi a surname

see also Kuí

颀

wěi 〈书面〉(usu. used in personal names) quietness

猥

wěi ❶ numerous; multifarious; miscellaneous:～滥 excessively numerous /～杂 miscellaneous ❷ base; lewd; lascivious; salacious:贪～ greedy and base

猥鄙 wěibǐ 〈书面〉base and mean; despicable:～小人 mean and despicable person

猥辞 wěicí *also* "猥词" obscene language; salacious words

猥獕 wěicuī (often used in the early vernacular) ugly looking; hideous; vulgar and ungainly:他身材矮小,长相～。He is short, and looks ugly and vulgar.

猥贱 wěijiàn base and humble; lowly

猥劣 wěiliè 〈书面〉base; mean; despicable:～手段 mean trick /～行径 base conduct

猥陋 wěilòu 〈书面〉*see* "猥鄙"

猥琐 wěisuǒ *also* "委琐" wěisuǒ (of appearance, manners, etc.) wretched; dreadful:此人衣着考究而相貌～。This person is elegantly dressed but of wretched appearance.

猥屑 wěixiè 〈书面〉base; mean; abject; contemptible:～的勾当 dirty deal or action /行为～ sordid conduct; base action /其人～。He is a mean person.

猥亵 wěixiè ❶ lewd; obscene; salacious:言行～ obscene in words and conduct /～的言语 salacious words ❷ act indecently towards a female; take liberties with; harass:～妇女行为 sexual harassment

尾

wěi ❶ tail; rear:鱼～ fishtail /牛～ oxtail /马～ ponytail /(汽车)～箱 rear trunk; car trunk; boot; luggage boot /船～ stern ❷ sixth of the 28 constellations into which the celestial sphere was divided in ancient Chinese astronomy ❸ end:从头至～ from beginning to end; from start to finish /首～相连 (join) end to end /排～的是小王。The one at the end of the queue (*or* line) is Xiao Wang. /故事收～部分需要改动。The ending of the story needs some alterations. ❹ remaining part; remainder; remnant:扫～工程 final phase of a project /收～工作由我做。I'll wind up the work. ❺〈量词〉*used of fish*:有鱼数百～。There are hundreds of fish.

see also yǐ

尾巴 wěiba ❶ tail:猪～ pigtail /狐狸～ foxtail /狗摇～ dog wagging its tail /夹着～做人 pull one's horn in; tuck one's tail between one's legs /～翘上了天 be very cocky; be overweening /老板们～翘得老高,毫无妥协之意。Their tails up, the bosses were in no mood for compromise. ❷ tail-like part:彗星～ tail of a comet /队伍长得～都拐过弯去了。The tail of the queue extended round the corner. ❸ remaining part of sth.:这件事你要干得干净利落,不要留～。You should do the job properly, leaving no loose ends for others to tidy up. *or* You should get it done properly so as not to leave behind a mess to be cleaned up later. ❹ person that shadows sb.; person that tags along; tail:要设法甩掉～。You should try to throw off (*or* get rid of) your tail. ❺ person who follows sb. servilely or is sb.'s appendage:你怎么老当别人的～? Why do you always follow others servilely?

尾巴主义 wěibazhǔyì tailism

尾大不掉 wěidà-bùdiào the tail wagging the dog; (of an organization) too cumbersome to be effective:这个国家地方势力超过中央,委实是～。The local authorities of that country have exceeded the central government in power; this is really a case of the tail wagging the dog.

尾灯 wěidēng tail or rear light (of a car, bus, plane, etc.); stern light (of a ship)

尾动脉 wěidòngmài caudal artery

尾工 wěigōng final phase of a project; tail end of a project

尾骨 wěigǔ 〈生理〉coccyx, tailbone

尾骨肌 wěigǔjī coccygeus muscle

尾管 wěiguǎn 〈机械〉tailpiece; tailpipe

尾后 wěihòu 〈方言〉at the end (of sth.); in the end:大家听到～,都忍不住笑起来。We couldn't help laughing towards the end of the story. /～还有许多事情要做。Much remains to be done after that.

尾花 wěihuā fill-in drawings at the end of a chapter in a book where there is blank space

尾击 wěijī attack (an enemy) from behind; raid the (enemy) rear:～来犯之敌,拖住敌人,掩护主力部队安全转移。Attack the back part of the invading enemy to tie them down so that our main force can shift in safety.

尾迹 wěijì jet trace

尾矿 wěikuàng 〈矿业〉tailings; refuse ore
尾流 wěiliú 〈物理〉wake flow:～理论 wake stream theory
尾闾 wěilǘ ❶〈书面〉mouth of a river; lower reaches ❷〈中医〉sacrum; coccyx; end of coccyx
尾轮 wěilún tail-wheel (of an airplane)
尾门式播种机 wěiménshì bōzhǒngjī 〈农业〉endgate seeder
尾牌 wěipái rear number plate; rear licence plate
尾期 wěiqī final phase; last or final stage:雨季已近～,旱季即将开始。The rainy season is drawing to its end and the dry season will soon set in.
尾鳍 wěiqí tail fin; caudal fin
尾气 wěiqì tail exhaust
尾欠 wěiqiàn ❶ owe a small balance:现付三千,～二百。With the payment of 3,000, there is a small balance of 200. ❷ balance due; remainder of a debt or levy:～下月还清。The balance due will be cleared next month.
尾梢 wěishāo end; tail end:冬季的～ end of winter /这根竹子的～相当粗。This bamboo's tapering end is rather thick.
尾参 wěishēn *also*"玉竹" yùzhú 〈植物〉*Polygonatum odoratum*
尾声 wěishēng ❶〈戏曲〉coda, last tune of a play or set of tunes ❷〈音乐〉epilogue:快板乐章的～ epilogue of allegro ❸ ending of a literary work:这部小说的～写得很动人。The ending of the novel is very touching. ❹ end; close:大战～ towards the end of the war /会议已近～。The meeting is drawing to a close.
尾数 wěishù ❶ number after the decimal point ❷ odd amount in addition to the round number of a credit balance or of settled accounts:外面的欠款只有一点～未收回。Only an odd amount of the arrears has not been collected. ❸ last number of a multidigital figure
尾水 wěishuǐ tailwater:～渠(as of a hydropower station) tailrace; tailwater channel /～池 tailpond; tail bay
尾随 wěisuí tail behind; tail; tag along after; follow at sb.'s heels:他～那个女人进了商店。He followed the woman into the shop.
尾卸 wěixiè end-dumping:～式车身 end (*or* rear) dump body /～式自动倾卸车 end tipper
尾须 wěixū 〈动物〉cercus
尾翼 wěiyì 〈航空〉tail unit; tailplane; empennage
尾音 wěiyīn last syllabic sound of a word or sentence
尾蚴 wěiyòu 〈动物〉cercaria:～性皮炎 cercarial dermatitis
尾脂腺 wěizhīxiàn uropygial gland
尾轴 wěizhóu 〈机械〉trailing axle; tail shaft
尾追 wěizhuī in hot pursuit; hot on the trail:～不舍 in hot pursuit of sb.; hot on the trail of sb. /部队接受了～歼敌的任务。The army unit was ordered to pursue and annihilate the enemy.
尾椎骨 wěizhuīgǔ 〈生理〉caudal vertebra
尾子 wěizi 〈方言〉❶ final phase or end (of sth.) ❷ odd amount in addition to the round number (usu. of a credit balance or settled accounts)
尾座 wěizuò 〈机械〉tailstock

艉
wěi stern

娓
wěi

娓娓 wěiwěi (talk) tirelessly; (speak) interestingly:～而谈 talk in an informal and friendly fashion /这普通的道理,由他～谈来,竟把我吸引住了。It was only plain truth, but he talked about it so vividly that I just got carried away.
娓娓动听 wěiwěi-dòngtīng speak most interestingly; sound pleasing and attractive; be very pleasant to the ear:他谈得～,引人入胜。He spoke with absorbing interest and the audience listened spellbound.

骫
wěi 〈书面〉bend; crook; pervert:～曲 stoop to compromise /～法 pervert the law
骫骳 wěibèi 〈书面〉bent; tortuous

wèi

为(為、爲)
wèi ❶〈书面〉be on the side of; help; support:他虽年少,但勇于～人。Young as he is, he is always ready to help others. ❷ on behalf of; for the benefit of; in the interest of:～祖国做出新的贡献 make new contributions to the motherland /请～我向主人表示谢意。Please convey my appreciation to the host. /谢谢你～我操这么多心。Thank you for all the trouble you have taken on my behalf. ❸ for (the purpose or sake of):～保卫世界和平而斗争 strive to safeguard world peace /我这样做,不～名利～尽责。I am doing this not for fame or gain but for doing my duty. /～慎重起见,再让技术员来检查一下。To be on the safe side, ask the technician to check again. ❹ to:此事请勿～外人道。Please say nothing of this (*or* Don't breathe a word about it) to other people. ❺ because; for; on account of:～什么如此激动? Why get so worked up?
see also wéi
为此 wèicǐ to this end; for this reason; for this purpose; in this connection:～而奋斗不止 strive persistently to this end /～,我们付出了极大的代价。For this, we have paid a high price.
为国捐躯 wèiguó-juānqū give up or sacrifice one's life for one's country; die for one's country:数百名将士～。Several hundred officers and men laid down their lives for the country. /烈士为国慷慨捐躯。The martyr died a glorious death for his country.
为何 wèihé why; for what reason:～不早说? Why didn't you say it sooner?
为虎傅翼 wèihǔ-fùyì *also*"为虎添翼" give wings to a tiger — lend assistance or support to an evildoer; add to the influence of a villain:如果让敌人从我们这里窃走尖端军事技术,那无异～。It is lending support to the enemy if we let them steal our sophisticated military technology.
为虎作伥 wèihǔ-zuòchāng play the jackal to the tiger; help a villain in evildoing:～的刀笔吏 hack writer in the service of a tyrant /此人一贯～,人人切齿。As the man is always acting as a cat's paw, he has earned himself the intense hatred of the public.
为了 wèile for; for the sake of; with a view to; in order to:～方便读者,阅览室星期天也开放。For readers' convenience, the reading-room is open on Sundays as well. /～便于理解,我先举几个例子。To make it easier to understand, I'll give you a few examples first. /～祖国美好的明天,让我们加倍努力吧。Let's redouble our efforts for the bright future of our motherland.
为民除害 wèimín-chúhài rid the people of an evil; remove a scourge for the people:我们一定要抓获这伙惯盗,～。We must capture these hardened thieves so as to rid the people of a scourge.
为民请命 wèimín-qǐngmìng plead in the name of the people; pose as a spokesman of the people:装着～的样子 strike an attitude of pleading for the people
为人作嫁 wèirén-zuòjià sew sb. else's trousseau — make bridal clothes for others to wear; toil for others without reaping any reward in return:你这样辛辛苦苦,全是～! You are just slaving for others!
为什么 wèishénme why; why is it that; how come:～一定要写这么长呢? why did you have to write so long? /你～这么晚才来? How is it that you came so late? /这件事你至今不明确表态,到底～? You have so far not made your position clear on this matter. What for?
为我之物 wèiwǒzhīwù 〈哲学〉thing-for-us
为渊驱鱼,为丛驱雀 wèi yuān qū yú, wèi cóng qū què drive the fish into deep waters and the sparrows into the thickets — force one's friends into the enemy's camp:我们决不能干～的蠢事。We must not do such stupid things as to drive our friends to the enemy's side.
为着 wèizhe for; for the sake of:他这样做完全是～你好。It is entirely for your good that he has done it.

未[1]
wèi 〈副词〉❶ not yet:什么时候动身,尚～最后确定。The date of departure has not been finally decided yet. /我生在内地,～见过大海。As I was born and brought up in the interior, I have never seen the sea. ❷ not; no:前途～可限量 have boundless prospects /～置可否 neither "yes" nor "no"; non-committal

未[2]
wèi eighth of the twelve Earthly Branches
see also"干支" gānzhī
未爆弹 wèibàodàn 〈军事〉dud
未必 wèibì may not; by no means; not necessarily:这样做～好。It may not be advisable to do it the way you want to. /他的意见～正确。His opinion is not necessarily correct.

未便 wèibiàn not be in a position to; find it hard or inconvenient to: ～多说 not advisable to say more /～声张 find it inappropriate to make sth. public /他有些为难,我也～勉强。He showed some reluctance and I could hardly press him to act against his own wish. /这是老李负责的,我～决定。I am not in the position to decide as this is in Lao Li's charge.

未卜 wèibǔ unpredictable; unforeseen: 前途～ have an unpredictable future; face an uncertain prospect

未卜先知 wèibǔ-xiānzhī know without consulting the oracle — have foresight; foresee; need no crystal ball to see: 我虽不能～,但也能料定你此行必无结果。Though I am no prophet, I predict that your trip will be fruitless.

未曾 wèicéng not; never: ～听说过的事 something unheard of /此点我～想到。I had never thought of this before. /～开言泪先流。Tears rolled down one's cheeks before one could speak a word.

未尝 wèicháng ❶ not; never: 这种艰苦的生活,我们这些人都～经历过。None of us has ever experienced such hardships. ❷ *used before a negative to denote a mild affirmative*: 这样解释也～不可。Such an interpretation is by no means impossible. /这番话～没有道理。These words are not without reason. /我看他这样做～不是好心。I think he may be well-intentioned in doing this.

未成年 wèichéngnián not come of age yet; be under age: ～人 minor

未达一间 wèidá-yījiàn almost; nearly: 他与那位世界冠军相比,不过～罢了。Compared with the world champion, he is almost on a par with him.

未定 wèidìng uncertain; not definite; undecided; undefined: 主意～ not yet decided what to do /大局～。The situation is still uncertain.

未定稿 wèidìnggǎo draft

未定界 wèidìngjiè undefined boundary; undelineated boundary

未定之天 wèidìngzhītiān remain undecided: 此事成败尚在～。It is hard to tell whether the matter will end in success or failure. *or* The future of this matter still hangs in the balance.

未敢苟同 wèigǎn-gǒutóng beg to differ; disagree: 你提出的这个方案,我～。I'm sorry, but I can't agree with the proposal you put forward. /他的做法我～。I could hardly agree with the way he did it.

未婚 wèihūn unmarried; single: ～青年 unmarried young people /～子女 unmarried sons and daughters /～母亲 single mother

未婚夫 wèihūnfū fiancé

未婚妻 wèihūnqī fiancée

未及 wèijí ❶ too late (to do sth.); not enough time (to do sth.): 他～说完,孩子已经跑开了。The child had run away before he finished his words. ❷ have not reached or touched: 你所说的只是事情的表面,而～于实质。What you've said touches only the surface of things, not their essence.

未几 wèijǐ ❶ not long afterwards; soon after: ～他便一命呜呼。He died soon after. ❷ not many; not much; just a little; just a few: 所剩～。There isn't much left.

未竟 wèijìng unfinished; unaccomplished: 完成先辈～之业 fulfil the unfinished tasks of the older generation; carry forward the unfinished work of one's predecessors

未竟之志 wèijìngzhīzhì ideal or ambition not yet realized: 完成这部著作,乃先父的～。It is my late father's unrealized aspiration to finish this book. /深望后辈完成我～。I ardently hope that my children and my children's children will carry on my unfinished tasks.

未决 wèijué unsettled; pending; outstanding: 议而～ be still under discussion (*or* consideration); reach no conclusion after deliberation /这件事一直悬而～。The matter remains unsettled. *or* The issue is still pending.

未决犯 wèijuéfàn prisoner awaiting trial; culprit; unconvicted prisoner

未可 wèikě should in no case; must not: ～小视 should in no case underestimate /～冒然行事 must not act rashly /～乐观 give no cause for optimism; there's hardly anything to be optimistic about

未可厚非 wèikě-hòufēi give no cause for much criticism; be not altogether inexcusable: 他这样做也是迫不得已,～。What he did was by no means inexcusable since he had no alternative. /我想请大家对我们的计划提点意见,这想法大概～吧? I think it is by no means out of order to ask people to favour us with their comments on our plan.

未来 wèilái ❶ coming; approaching: 在～的几小时内还会有较强的余震。There will be pretty strong tremors within the next few hours. /胜负就在～的两三天内见分晓。The outcome will be made known in a couple of days, be it success or failure. ❷ future; tomorrow: ～的世界 world of tomorrow /光明的～ bright future

未来学 wèiláixué futuristics; futurology

未来主义 wèiláizhǔyì futurism: ～者 futurist

未老先衰 wèilǎo-xiānshuāi prematurely senile; old before one's time: 生活的折磨,使她～。Suffering from a hard life, she looks older than her age. /他是壮年而无壮年的神采,～。Although he is in the prime of life, he lacks energy and vigour and is prematurely aged.

未了 wèiliǎo unfinished; outstanding: ～工作 unfinished work /～的手续 uncompleted formalities /一桩～的心事 sth. still weighing on one's mind /还有一些杂务～。There're still some trivial matters to attend to.

未了公案 wèiliǎo-gōng'àn unsettled matter; outstanding issue: 他们之间尚有一段～。There is still some outstanding issue between them.

未免 wèimiǎn ❶ rather; a bit too; a little: 这房间～小了一点。This room is a bit too small. /这事你～欠考虑。Perhaps you didn't give sufficient thought to the matter. /你的顾虑也～多了些。You are perhaps a little overcautious. ❷ would naturally; unavoidably: 这件事这样简单处理,群众～会有意见。People would of course complain if the case should be settled so summarily. /当众训斥,～使他难堪。He would be very much embarrassed if he were to be scolded in public.

未能 wèinéng fail to; have not been able to: ～挽回败局 unable to retrieve a defeat

未能免俗 wèinéng-miǎnsú be unable to rise above the conventions or customs; cannot but conform to conventionality: 许多场合下,我们都～。On many occasions, we cannot but bow to conventional practice.

未然 wèirán not yet materialize: ～之事 sth. not yet accomplished /与其补救于已然,不如防范于～。Prevention is better than cure.

未时 wèishí period of the day from 1 p.m. to 3 p.m.

未始 wèishǐ *see* "未尝❷"

未遂 wèisuì not accomplished; unfulfilled; abortive: 行刺～ attempted assassination /政变～ abortive coup d'état /心愿～ one's wish remains unfulfilled

未遂犯 wèisuìfàn one who attempts to commit a crime

未遂罪 wèisuìzuì 〈法律〉attempted crime; attempt

未完 wèiwán unfinished; uncompleted: ～待续 to be continued /疗程～,不能出院。You cannot leave the hospital halfway through the course of treatment.

未亡人 wèiwángrén 〈旧语〉(used by a widow) I; me

未详 wèixiáng unknown: 作者生平～。The life of the author is unknown. /死因～。The cause of the death is not clear.

未央 wèiyāng 〈书面〉not ended: 夜～。The night is not yet over.

未雨绸缪 wèiyǔ-chóumóu repair the house before it rains; save for a rainy day; take preventive measures: 沿江一带须～,事先做好防汛的一切准备。Every precaution must be taken against a possible flood in areas along the river.

未知量 wèizhīliàng 〈数学〉unknown quantity

未知数 wèizhīshù ❶〈数学〉unknown number ❷ unknown; not sure; uncertain: 这次报考,我能否录取,还是个很大的～。It is quite uncertain whether I can pass the entrance examination and get enrolled.

味

wèi ❶ taste; flavour: 风～儿 local (*or* special) flavour (of food, etc.) /苦～儿 bitter taste /膻～儿 smell of mutton /走～儿 lose flavour /口～ taste ❷ smell; scent; odour: 香～儿 sweet smell; fragrance; aroma /异～儿 peculiar odour ❸ interest; relish: 人情～ human interest; human touch /韵～ lingering charm; lasting appeal /说得津津有～ talk with great relish ❹ dishes; food: 腊～ cured meat, fish, etc. /山珍海～ delicacies from land and sea ❺ distinguish the flavour of; reflect on: 玩～ ponder; ruminate /耐人寻～ afford food for thought ❻〈量词〉ingredient (of a Chinese medicine prescription): 这个方子里共有八～药。This prescription specifies eight medical herbs.

味道 wèidao ❶ taste; flavour: 这菜咸淡适宜,～鲜美。This dish is nice and tastes delicious. /这菜有一股苦涩的～。This vegetable has a bitter taste. /他的话里含着讽刺的～。There was a touch of sarcasm in his remark. /她心里有股辛酸的～。She had a feeling of bitterness. ❷ interest: 日子越过越有～。We feel an ever greater sense of joy in our life as time goes by. ❸〈方言〉odour; smell

味精 wèijīng *also* "味素" monosodium glutamate (MSG); gourmet powder
味觉 wèijué sense of taste
味蕾 wèilěi 〈生理〉 taste bud
味美思 wèiměisī Vermouth, a kind of wine
味气 wèiqi 〈方言〉 smell; odour:~难闻 smell foul (*or* bad); have a bad smell (*or* odour)
味素 wèisù *see* "味精"
味同嚼蜡 wèitóngjiáolà like chewing tallow or wax; as dry as dust:读这种诗~。Reading such poems is like chewing tallow. /听他的报告~。His report is as dull as ditchwater.

辖 wèi 〈古语〉 copper cylinder for capping end of the axle of a cart

畏 wèi ❶ fear; dread:大无~的精神 fearless (*or* dauntless) spirit /望而生~ awe-inspiring; forbidding /~之如虎 fear sth. (*or* sb). as if it were a tiger ❷ admire:敬~ respect /后生可~! What an admirable young man!
畏避 wèibì avoid out of fear; recoil from; shrink from; flinch from:子侄们见了他无不~。His sons and nephews would all flinch at his sight.
畏怖 wèibù 〈书面〉 fear; dread:心怀~ be in fear
畏服 wèifú obey in fear:其威严令人~。People were overawed by his dignified bearing.
畏光 wèiguāng 〈医学〉 photophobia
畏忌 wèijì fear and distrust; apprehensions; misgivings:他对你早就存有~之心。He has long had misgivings about you.
畏惧 wèijù fear; dread; be afraid:无所~ be fearless /在困难面前~退缩 flinch in the face of difficulties /怀疑和焦虑最后变成~。Doubt and anxiety changed into dread.
畏难 wèinán be scared of difficulty:他正视困难而不~。He faces difficulties squarely without fear.
畏怯 wèiqiè timid; timorous; cowardly:在他面前,姑娘有些~。The girl was a bit timid with him. /他~地后退了两步。He stepped back in cowardly fear.
畏首畏尾 wèishǒu-wèiwěi be afraid of things ahead as well as behind; be full of misgivings:像你这样~,哪里有一点年轻人的朝气! You are so overcautious that you seem to have lost the dashing spirit of youth!
畏缩 wèisuō recoil; cringe; shrink; flinch:孩子~在母亲身后,不敢上前。The child, hidden behind his mother, was afraid to step forward.
畏缩不前 wèisuō-bùqián recoil in fear; cower; hang back:~,坐失消灭敌人的时机。They hesitated to move and lost the opportunity to wipe out the enemy.
畏途 wèitú 〈书面〉 dangerous road; perilous undertaking:视为~ regard as a dangerous road to take; be afraid to undertake
畏葸 wèixǐ 〈书面〉 timid; frightened; afraid:~退缩 recoil in fear /~不前 be afraid to advance
畏友 wèiyǒu friend who inspires both awe and respect; revered friend:这本书是我的严师~。For me, this book is a strict teacher and a revered friend. /听听~的意见,往往可以使自己头脑清醒。Advice from an esteemed friend often has a sobering effect.
畏罪 wèizuì dread punishment for one's crime:~自杀 commit suicide for fear of punishment /~携款潜逃 abscond with the money to avoid punishment

碨(硙) wèi 〈方言〉 millstone

喂[1] wèi 〈叹词〉 (of greeting) hello; hey:~,你有什么事吗? Hello, what can I do for you? /~,小方,什么时候了,还不出发? Hey, Xiao Fang, isn't it high time we started off?

喂[2]**(餵、餧)** wèi ❶ give food to; feed:~牲口 feed draught animals ❷ spoonfeed:~孩子 feed a child /给病人~药 spoonfeed medicine to a patient
喂料 wèiliào feed (cattle, etc.):嘿,老头子,早该给牛~啦! Hey, old man, you should have fed the cattle long ago.
喂奶 wèinǎi ❶ give or feed milk ❷ breastfeed; suckle; nurse
喂青 wèiqīng feed green fodder (to cattle, etc.)
喂食 wèishí give food to people or animals:定时~ feed at fixed time
喂养 wèiyǎng feed; breed; raise; keep:她用自己的奶水~这个孤儿。She breastfed the orphan herself. /小林精心~着几只鸽子。Xiao Lin kept some pigeons with great care. /这水兵是海洋~大的。The sailor was raised on the sea.

胃 wèi ❶ stomach ❷ seventeenth of the 28 constellations in ancient Chinese astronomy *see also* "二十八宿" èrshíbāxiù
胃癌 wèi'ái cancer of the stomach; stomach cancer; gastric carcinoma
胃病 wèibìng stomach trouble; gastric disease; gastropathy
胃肠炎 wèichángyán gastroenteritis
胃出血 wèichūxuè gastric haemorrhage; gastrorrhagia
胃穿孔 wèichuānkǒng gastric or stomach perforation
胃呆 wèidāi indigestion
胃蛋白酶 wèidànbáiméi 〈生理〉 pepsin:~原 pepsinogen
胃电图 wèidiàntú 〈医学〉 electrogastrogram:~描记器 electrogastrograph
胃毒剂 wèidújì 〈农业〉 stomach poison
胃结肠炎 wèijiéchángyán 〈医学〉 gastrocolitis
胃痉挛 wèijìngluán 〈医学〉 gastrospasm
胃镜 wèijìng gastroscope:~检查 gastrocopy
胃口 wèikǒu ❶ appetite:~一向好 always have a good appetite /近来~欠佳 have had a poor appetite recently ❷ liking; fancy:旅游活动适合我的~。Travelling is to my liking. ❸ 〈比喻〉 ambition; appetite:他的~很大。He has a wild ambition.
胃溃疡 wèikuìyáng gastric ulcer; ulcer in the stomach
胃扩张 wèikuòzhāng dilatation of the stomach; gastrectasis
胃酶 wèiméi 〈生化〉 gastric enzyme
胃气胀 wèiqìzhàng 〈医学〉 hoven; bloat
胃切除术 wèiqiēchúshù gastrectomy
胃石 wèishí 〈医学〉 gastrolith:~病 gastrolithiasis
胃酸 wèisuān hydrochloric acid in gastric juice:~过多 hyperchlorhydria; hyperacidity /~过少 hypochlorhydria; hypoacidity
胃痛 wèitòng stomach-ache; gastralgia
胃脘 wèiwǎn 〈中医〉 gastral cavity:~痛 stomach-ache
胃萎缩 wèiwěisuō 〈医学〉 gastratrophia
胃下垂 wèixiàchuí ptosis of the stomach; gastroptosis
胃腺 wèixiàn 〈生理〉 gastric gland:~炎〈医学〉 gastradenitis
胃炎 wèiyán gastritis
胃液 wèiyè 〈生理〉 gastric juice:~腺 peptic glands
胃灼热 wèizhuórè *also* "烧心" shāoxīn 〈医学〉 heartburn

渭 Wèi Weihe River, a tributary of the Yellow River:~河流域 Weihe River valley (in Shaanxi)

谓 wèi ❶ say:勿~言之不预也。Don't say I have not warned you in time. ❷ call; name; mean:称~ appellation; title /何~人造卫星? What is meant by man-made satellite?
谓词 wèicí ❶ 〈逻辑〉 predicate ❷ predicate
谓语 wèiyǔ 〈语言〉 predicate:复合~ compound predicate

猬(蝟) wèi 〈动物〉 hedgehog
猬集 wèijí 〈书面〉 (of matters) as numerous as the spines of a hedgehog:百感~。All sorts of feelings welled up in one's mind.

遗 wèi 〈书面〉 offer as a gift; make a present of:~之以书 make a present of books
see also yí

魏 Wèi ❶ State of Wei (403-225 BC), one of the Warring States, covering today's northern Henan, eastern Shaanxi, southwestern Shanxi and southern Hebei ❷ one of the Three Kingdoms (220-265 AD), covering today's provinces in the Yellow River valley and Hubei, Anhui, northern Jiangsu and central Liaoning ❸ Northern Wei Dynasty (386-534 AD) ❹ a surname
魏碑 wèibēi ❶ tablet inscriptions of the Northern Dynasties (386-581 AD) ❷ calligraphy represented by aforesaid inscriptions, regarded as a model by later calligraphers
魏玛共和国 Wèimǎ Gònghéguó Weimar Republic, German re-

W

public in 1919-1933 (named after the Consititution drawn up at Weimar in 1919)

魏阙 wèiquè 〈比喻〉royal or imperial court: 身在江海,心驰~ very much concerned with state affairs though an ordinary citizen

魏源 Wèi Yuán Wei Yuan (1794-1857), thinker, historian and man of letters of the Qing Dynasty

魏征 Wèi Zhēng Wei Zheng (580-643), statesman of the early Tang Dynasty

位 wèi ❶ place; location; seat: 方~ location /床~ bed (in hospital, hostel, etc.) /岗~ (one's) post /各就各~。On your marks! ❷ position; rank; status: 爵~ rank of nobility; title of nobility /名~ fame and position /学~ degree /~极人臣 get (*or* rise) to the highest official position ❸ throne: 即~ come to the throne; be enthroned /在~ be on the throne; reign /退~ give up the throne; abdicate ❹〈数学〉place; figure; digit: 个~ unit's place /十~ ten's place /百~ hundred's place /算到小数点后三~ calculate to three decimal places ❺〈信息〉bit ❻〈量词〉*used in deferential reference to people*: 诸~先生 Gentlemen /各~女士 Ladies /列~代表 Delegates /还有三~没到。There are three more yet to come. ❼ (Wèi) a surname

位次 wèicì ❶〈旧语〉status; position ❷ order of seats; seating arrangement: ~卡 place card

位错 wèicuò 〈物理〉dislocation

位分 wèifen social status; hierarchical position: 此人在学术界~极高。He ranks very high in the academic circles.

位觉 wèijué sense of balance

位能 wèinéng 〈物理〉potential energy

位矢 wèishǐ 〈物理〉position vector

位势米 wèishìmǐ 〈气象〉geopotential metre

位望 wèiwàng 〈书面〉position and prestige; status and fame: 在社会上颇有~ enjoy a high prestige in society

位相 wèixiàng *also* "相位"〈物理〉phase: ~角 phase angle

位移 wèiyí 〈物理〉displacement

位于 wèiyú be located; be situated; lie: 泰国~东南亚中南半岛中部。Thailand is situated at the centre of the Indo-Chinese peninsula of southeast Asia.

位置 wèizhi ❶ seat; place; location: 请按指定的~入席。Will everybody please take his (*or* her) designated seat at the table. /他把书放回原来的~上。He put back the book where he took it. /找到了地下水的~。The underground fountain has been located. ❷ position; place: 占有重要~ hold an important position (*or* place) /他站在领导~上,说话不能不慎重。As a leader he has to speak cautiously. ❸ post; position; job: 谋到处长的~ get a post (*or* job) as division chief /她希望能够找到一个小学教员的~。She hopes to find a job as a primary school teacher.

位子 wèizi seat; place; position: 留个~ reserve a seat /占个~ keep a seat /他很看重科长的~。He attaches great importance to the position of a section chief.

䜅(讆、𧬘) wèi 〈书面〉unfounded; fabricated: ~言 unfounded remarks

卫¹(衛、衞) wèi ❶ defend; guard; protect: 防~ defend /守~ guard /护~ protect ❷ place for stationing troops in the Ming Dynasty

卫²(衛、衞) Wèi ❶ name of a dukedom in the Zhou Dynasty ❷ a surname

卫报 Wèibào *The Guardian*, British daily newspaper published since 1821

卫兵 wèibīng guard; bodyguard

卫道 wèidào defend traditional morality: ~者 moral defender /~士 apologist

卫队 wèiduì bodyguards; armed escort: 皇室~ royal bodyguards /总统~ armed escort for the president; presidential guards /~长 captain of the guards

卫顾 wèigù escort and attend to; act as bodyguard in attendance: 他一路小心~着老将军。All the way he carefully escorted and attended to the old general.

卫护 wèihù defend; protect; guard: ~着祖国的海疆 guard the coastal areas and territorial seas of the motherland

卫矛 wèimáo 〈植物〉winged euonymus (*Euonymus alatus*)

卫冕 wèimiǎn 〈体育〉maintain one's coronet; keep the championship in one's hand: 男子队能否~,就看这场比赛了。The success or failure of the men's team to defend its championship hinges on this match.

卫气营血辨证 wèiqì yíngxuè biànzhèng 〈中医〉analysing, differentiating and judging the development of a (usually febrile) disease by studying the four conditions of the human body: superficial resistance, nutrition, vital function and blood; defence, *qi*, construction, and blood pattern identification; four-aspect pattern identification

卫青 Wèi Qīng Wei Qing (? -106 BC), renowned general of the Western Han Dynasty

卫生 wèishēng ❶ good for one's health; hygienic; sanitary: ~人员 health worker /~知识 hygienic knowledge /既适用又~ both convenient and hygienic /饭馆搞得很~。The restaurant is of high hygienic standards. /这种吃法不~。This eating habit is bad for the health. ❷ hygiene; sanitation: 讲~ pay attention to hygiene /环境~ environmental sanitation /个人~ personal hygiene

卫生部 wèishēngbù Ministry of Public Health

卫生带 wèishēngdài sanitary towel; sanitary napkin

卫生队 wèishēngduì medical unit; medical team

卫生防疫站 wèishēng fángyìzhàn sanitation and antiepidemic station

卫生工程学 wèishēng gōngchéngxué health or sanitary engineering

卫生间 wèishēngjiān toilet; WC; rest room

卫生巾 wèishēngjīn feminine napkin

卫生局 wèishēngjú public health bureau

卫生科 wèishēngkē health section

卫生裤 wèishēngkù 〈方言〉sweat pants

卫生棉 wèishēngmián cotton wool

卫生棉球 wèishēng miánqiú Q-tip

卫生球 wèishēngqiú camphor ball; moth ball

卫生设备 wèishēng shèbèi sanitary facilities or equipment

卫生室 wèishēngshì clinic

卫生田 wèishēngtián 〈讽刺〉unmanured farmland or field

卫生学 wèishēngxué hygiene; hygienics

卫生衣 wèishēngyī 〈方言〉sweat shirt

卫生油 wèishēngyóu 〈方言〉cotton-seed oil

卫生员 wèishēngyuán medical orderly; paramedic

卫生院 wèishēngyuàn township or county hospital; hospital

卫生纸 wèishēngzhǐ toilet paper

卫士 wèishì guard; bodyguard; escort: 铁道~ railroad policeman

卫戍 wèishù garrison: ~部队 garrison force /~司令部 garrison headquarters /~区 garrison command /这个部队担任~首都的任务。The army unit is charged with the task of garrisoning the capital.

卫校 wèixiào medical school

卫星 wèixīng ❶〈天文〉satellite; moon: 土星有十颗~。Saturn has ten moons. ❷ sth. that has the function of a satellite: ~城市 satellite town ❸ artificial satellite; man-made satellite: 发射~ launch a satellite /~侦察 reconnoitre by satellite /气象~ weather satellite; meteorological satellite /通讯~ communications satellite /人造地球~ man-made earth satellite /大气~ aeronomy satellite (AEROS) /航空~ aeronautical satellite (AEROSAT) /技术应用~ applications technology satellite /天体观测~ celestial observation satellite /直接广播~ direct broadcasting satellite /预警~ early-warning satellite /地球观察~ earth observation satellite /地球资源~ earth resources satellite /环境监测~ environmental monitoring satellite /绕地轨道测地~ geodetic earth orbiting satellite /同步~ geostationary satellite /红外天文~ infrared astronomical satellite /截击~ interceptor satellite /多任务~ multi-mission satellite /导航~ navigation satellite /无源~ passive satellite /有源~ active satellite /"立体"~ Stereosat (satellite for high resolution, stereoscopic remote sensing data) /同步通讯~ synchronous communications satellite /宇宙辐射~ cosmic radiation satellite /反射~ reflecting satellite /~跟踪和数据收集网 satellite tracking and data acquisition network

卫星测位中心 wèixīng cèwèi zhōngxīn satellite situation centre

卫星城 wèixīngchéng satellite town

卫星地球站 wèixīng dìqiúzhàn earthstation

卫星电话 wèixīng diànhuà satphone

卫星电视 wèixīng diànshì television (programmes) (transmitted) by satellite; satellite TV:～教育 education by way of satellite television; educational satellite TV programmes
卫星国 wèixīngguó satellite state; satellite country
卫星天线 wèixīng tiānxiàn satellite antenna
卫星田 wèixīngtián 〈比喻〉(used during the 1958 Great Leap Forward Movement) satellite fields — agricultural fields with record-breaking (usu. false) yields
卫星通信 wèixīng tōngxìn satellite communication; satcom
卫星微波辐射计 wèixīng wēibō fúshèjì satellite microwave radiometer

尉 wèi ❶ ancient official title:太～ imperial minister in charge of military affairs ❷ (military rank) junior officer:少～ second lieutenant /中～ lieutenant /上～ captain ❸ (Wèi) a surname
see also yù
尉官 wèiguān junior military officer

慰 wèi ❶ console; soothe; comfort:安～ console and comfort /劝～ soothe /聊以自～ take as a consolation; find consolation (in sth.) ❷ feel relieved:快～ be pleased /顷悉康复,至感欣～。I am relieved to learn of your recovery.
慰安 wèi'ān solace; comfort:从中得到些许～ take (*or* seek) some comfort (in sth.) /自我～ solace oneself (with sth.)
慰安妇 wèi'ānfù comfort woman (in World War II, the Japanese government ran frontline brothels, pressganging women from Korea, China, the Philippines and Indonesia to serve as "comfort women")
慰抚 wèifǔ *also* "抚慰" console; soothe
慰藉 wèijiè 〈书面〉consolation; comfort:使大娘感到～的是儿子终于考上了大学。It came as a big comfort to the old woman that her son was finally admitted to the university.
慰劳 wèiláo bring gifts in recognition of service rendered:～品 gifts /～筑路民工 bring gifts to the road construction workers
慰留 wèiliú (try to) persuade sb. to stay:再三～ repeatedly try to persuade sb. to stay; repeatedly ask sb. to stay
慰勉 wèimiǎn comfort and encourage:好言～ give well-intentioned consolation and encouragement /这位老人常来～我,劝我不要着急。This old man often came to comfort me, telling me not to worry.
慰问 wèiwèn express sympathy and solicitude; show gratitude and appreciation; extend regards or greetings; salute:～信 letter of sympathy; sympathy note /～团 group sent to convey regards and appreciation /～灾区人民 express sympathy and solicitude for the people of disaster-stricken areas /～军烈属 convey greetings to the families of soldiers and martyrs /写信～ write a letter expressing one's appreciation and sympathy /我们代表全市人民来～你们。We have come to extend our gratitude and appreciation to you on behalf of all the people of the city.
慰唁 wèiyàn express condolences:葬礼中,亲朋们纷纷前来向她表示～。Her relatives and friends came one after another to condole with her at the funeral.
慰悦 wèiyuè feel relieved:病人情况好转,甚感～。The patient's recovery filled me with relief.

蔚 wèi 〈书面〉❶ luxuriant; grand; magnificent:～为大国 great country in all its magnificence ❷ colourful:云蒸霞～ rise of colourful clouds
蔚蓝 wèilán azure; sky blue:～天幕 blue canopy of the sky /～的天空 azure sky
蔚起 wèiqǐ 〈书面〉flourishing; mushrooming:乡镇工业～。Township industries are flourishing.
蔚然 wèirán exuberant; flourishing:几年前栽的树苗,现已～成林。The saplings planted a few years ago have grown into an exuberant wood.
蔚然成风 wèirán-chéngfēng *also* "蔚成风气" become common practice; be the prevailing trend; become the order of the day:广大职工的业余学习已～。It has become a common practice (*or* phenomenon) for staff and workers to take up sparetime study.
蔚为大观 wèiwéi-dàguān present a splendid sight; offer a spectacular view:展出的千盆兰花～。The hundreds of potted orchids presented a splendid sight.

罻 wèi 〈书面〉net for catching birds

鳚 wèi 〈动物〉blenny

wēn

温 wēn ❶ warm; lukewarm; tepid:～水 lukewarm water; warm water ❷ temperature:气～ atmospheric temperature /体～ temperature (of the body) /高～ high temperature /常～ conventional temperature ❸ warm up; heat up (to a moderate degree):～酒 warm up the wine /把中药～一～再喝 warm up the medicinal brew before you drink it ❹ gentle; meek; tender: *see* "～顺"; "～情" ❺ review; revise:～书 review one's lessons /重～旧梦 revive an old dream; relive past happiness ❻ *see* "瘟" wēn ❼ (Wēn) a surname
温饱 wēnbǎo have enough to eat and wear:不得～ not have enough food and clothing /仅足～ just enough to keep body and soul together /～问题 problem of (adequate) food and clothing /～型 just having (*or* providing) enough to eat and wear
温标 wēnbiāo 〈物理〉thermometric scale:华氏～ Fahrenheit's thermometric scale /摄氏～ Celsius' thermometric scale /开氏～ Kelvin's thermometric scale
温差 wēnchā difference in temperature; range of temperature:昼夜～ difference in temperature between day and night /这里四季～不大。The temperature here does not vary much throughout the year.
温差电 wēnchādiàn 〈物理〉thermoelectricity:～堆 thermopile /～检波器 thermodetector
温差电池 wēnchā diànchí thermoelectric cell; thermoelectric generator
温床 wēnchuáng ❶〈农业〉hotbed:～播种 frame seeding /～栽培 frame culture; hotbed culture ❷〈比喻〉hotbed; breeding ground:奢侈常是腐化堕落的～。Luxury is often the breeding ground for corruption and degeneration.
温存 wēncún ❶ be attentive; give tender attention (mostly to a person of the opposite sex):他时时送她鲜花,～备至。He would give her flowers every now and then, and shower attentions on her. ❷ affectionate; kind; gentle; tender:性格～ temperamentally gentle and considerate
温带 wēndài temperate zone:～气候 temperate climate /～雨林 temperate rainforest
温度 wēndù temperature:绝对～ absolute temperature /室内～ indoor temperature /室外～ outdoor temperature /～变化 temperature variation /～记录法 thermography
温度计 wēndùjì *also* "温度表"〈气象〉thermograph; thermometer:光学～ optical thermograph /电阻～ resistance thermograph /摄氏～ centigrade (*or* Celsius) thermometer /华氏～ Fahrenheit thermometer /寒暑～ weather thermometer /体温～ clinical thermometer /～多少度? What does the thermometer read?
温法 wēnfǎ 〈中医〉(making the patient's internal organs active by) warming and stimulation
温服 wēnfú 〈中药〉(of medical decoction) to be taken lukewarm
温哥华 Wēngēhuá Vancouver, city and seaport of British Columbia, on the west coast of Canada
温故知新 wēngù-zhīxīn learn the new while re-studying the old; gain new insights through reviewing old material; recalling the past helps one understand the present:这本书我反复阅读,往往能收到～的效果。I always gained new insights every time I re-read the book. /不忘记过去的教训,才能～。We do not forget the past lessons so that we may be better able to understand the present.
温和 wēnhé ❶ (of weather) temperate; mild; moderate:～的阳光 warm sunshine /昆明气候～,四季如春。Kunming has a pleasant climate with moderate temperature all the year round. ❷ (of temperament, attitude or language) gentle; mild; complaisant:性情～ genial disposition /语气～ mild tone /她态度～,容易接近。She is gentle in manner and easy of approach.
see also wēnhuo
温和派 wēnhépài moderates
温厚 wēnhòu gentle and kind; sincere and considerate; good-natured:为人～ be kind and sincere

温乎乎 wēnhūhū neither cold nor hot; fairly warm：这茶～的正好喝。The tea is lukewarm and nice to drink.
温乎 wēnhu slightly warm：米饭还有点～。The rice is still somewhat warm.
温和 wēnhuo lukewarm; warm：饭还～呢，快吃吧。The food is still warm, please help yourself. /他怕是刚起床，被窝里还有点～。He may have just got up as his bed is still warm.
see also wēnhé
温静 wēnjìng gentle and quiet：～的姑娘 girl of gentle and quiet disposition
温居 wēnjū housewarming：～宴 housewarming party
温觉 wēnjué 〈生理〉sense of heat
温良 wēnliáng gentle and kind：她举止娴雅，性情～。She has a graceful manner and a gentle disposition.
温良恭俭让 wēn-liáng-gōng-jiǎn-ràng temperate, kind, courteous, restrained and magnanimous; kind and gentle in disposition and refined in manners
温暖 wēnnuǎn mild; warm：室内～如春。It is mild as spring indoors. /同志们的关怀～了我的心。The concern of my comrades warmed my heart.
温疟 wēnnüè 〈中医〉ague; malaria
温谱图 wēnpǔtú *also* "温度记录"〈物理〉thermogram
温情 wēnqíng tender affection：～的目光 tender glance /她～地目送我走出家门。She followed me with tender eyes as I walked out of home.
温情脉脉 wēnqíng-mòmò full of tender feeling：她～地看了小伙子一眼。She cast an amorous glance at the young man.
温情主义 wēnqíngzhǔyì 〈贬义〉undue leniency or soft-heartedness; sentimentalism：小资产阶级～ petty-bourgeois sentimentalism
温泉 wēnquán hot spring：～泥 fango
温热 wēnrè warm; hot
温柔 wēnróu gentle and soft; sweet：～的少女 gentle young girl /～地一笑 give a sweet smile /声音～而甜润 soft and sweet voice /海水抚摩着细软的沙滩，发出～的刷刷声。The sea water stroked the fine sandy beach, producing a soft murmuring sound. /在明净的月光下，洞庭湖显得特别～、平静。The Dong Ting Lake looked unusually peaceful and calm under the bright moonlight.
温柔敦厚 wēnróu-dūnhòu gentle and kindly：根据中国传统，诗的灵魂是～，怨而不怒。According to Chinese tradition, the essence of poetry is gentleness and kindliness, an expression of emotion with restraint.
温柔乡 wēnróuxiāng land of tenderness — place where a man can find solace in feminine charms; euphemism for a harem or brothel
温软 wēnruǎn ❶ soft; gentle; mild：～的语调 soft voice; mild tone ❷ warm and soft：～的被子 warm and soft quilt
温润 wēnrùn ❶ (of disposition, attitude and lauguage) gentle; soft; cordial：性情～ of a gentle disposition /～的面容 kindly complexion ❷ warm and moist：气象～ humid and warm climate /～的海风习习吹来。The wind from the sea came warm and moist. ❸ fine and smooth：玉质～ fine and smooth jade
温湿 wēnshī (of climate) mild and moist; temperate
温湿计 wēnshījì 〈气象〉hygrothermograph
温湿指数 wēnshī zhǐshù temperature-humidity index (THI)
温室 wēnshì hothouse; greenhouse; glasshouse; conservatory：～育苗 nurse seedlings in hothouses
温室气体 wēnshì qìtǐ greenhouse gas：控制～的排放 control greenhouse gas emissions /主要的～有二氧化碳、甲烷、氮氧化物等。Carbon dioxide, methane and nitrous oxide are among the major greenhouse gases.
温室效应 wēnshì xiàoyìng greenhouse effect; gradual warming of earth's atmosphere said to be caused by increased carbon dioxide in the air
温淑 wēnshū 〈书面〉(of a woman) tender and kind
温顺 wēnshùn submissive; docile; meek; tame：她～地低下头去。She lowered her head meekly. /那马又～又平稳。That horse is both obedient and steady. /那条大河爱变脸，一时～，一时狂暴。The river is very changeable, sometimes tame, sometimes wild.
温汤 wēntāng ❶ lukewarm water ❷〈书面〉hot spring
温汤浸种 wēntāng jìnzhǒng 〈农业〉hot water treatment of seeds
温吞 wēntun *see* "温暾"
温暾 wēntun *also* "温吞"〈方言〉❶ (of liquid) lukewarm; tepid：～水 lukewarm water ❷ (of speech, diction, etc.) not neat; not to the point：～之谈 irrelevant talk
温婉 wēnwǎn ❶ (of voice or tone) soft and mild：她说话亲切～。She speaks softly and earnestly. *or* She is soft-spoken and has a cordial tone. ❷ (mostly applicable to women) amiable and mild; meek and gentle：～可亲 amiable and affable
温文 wēnwén (of temper, manner, speech, etc.) mild; gentle：～有礼 mild and courteous /～儒雅 gentle and refined; urbane and graceful
温文尔雅 wēnwén-ěryǎ gentle and cultivated; cultured; refined：～的学者 refined scholar /言谈举止～ gentle and refined both in speech and deportment
温习 wēnxí review; revise：学过的知识要常～。You ought to frequently review what you have learnt.
温馨 wēnxīn mild fragrance; warmth：～的气息 mildly fragrant smell /～的情谊 warm friendship
温煦 wēnxù ❶ warm; mild：阳光明媚，天气～清新。The sun is bright, and the air is warm and refreshing. /时已深秋，昆明仍～如春。It is late autumn, but Kunming is still as mild as spring. ❷ warm and cordial：～的目光 with a kind and cordial eye
温血动物 wēnxuè dòngwù warm-blooded animal
温驯 wēnxùn (of animals) docile; meek; tame：一群～的小羊 a flock of tame sheep
温雅 wēnyǎ gentle and graceful; urbane and refined：态度～ graceful manners
温针 wēnzhēn 〈中医〉warm-needle acupuncture therapy
温中 wēnzhōng 〈中医〉warming the stomach and biles (by using mild medicine)：～补虚 warm the stomach and biles, and supply deficiencies

薀 wēn

薀草 wēncǎo 〈方言〉water weeds

瘟 wēn

❶〈中医〉acute communicable disease：春～ spring epidemic /鸡～ chicken pest /猪～ swine fever; hog cholera ❷ (of traditional operas) dull; insipid; vapid：这出戏太～。This play is simply vapid. /情节松，人物也～。The plot is loose and characters dull.
瘟病 wēnbìng 〈中医〉seasonal epidemic
瘟神 wēnshén god of plague：送～ bid farewell to the god of plague /街坊四邻像碰到～一样躲避这两个浑小子。Everybody in the neighbourhood shunned the two rascals as they would the god of plague.
瘟生 wēnshēng 〈方言〉weakling; good-for-nothing：你这个～，一见生人就结巴。You good-for-nothing, why do you always stammer before strangers.
瘟头瘟脑 wēntóu-wēnnǎo muddle-headed; confused：他这个人～的，别把事情办糟了。He is muddle-headed and I hope he will not spoil the show.
瘟疫 wēnyì pestilence; plague
瘟疹 wēnzhěn infectious diseases such as scarlet fever, typhus, etc. with rashes on the skin

榅 wēn

榅桲 wēnpo 〈植物〉quince (*Cydonia oblonga*)

辒 wēn

辒辌 wēnliáng 〈古语〉sleeping carriage, also used as a hearse

鳁 wēn

鳁鲸 wēnjīng 〈动物〉sea whale; rorqual

wén

文 wén

❶ character; writing; inscription; script：阴～ characters cut in intaglio /甲骨～ "oracle bone" inscriptions (of the Shang Dynasty); inscriptions on bones or tortoise shells /钟鼎～ inscriptions on ancient bronze objects ❷ language：外～ foreign languages /法～ French /语～ Chinese ❸ literary composition; article; writing：作～ composition /征～ solicit articles (*or* essays) /公～ official document /祭～ funeral oration; elegiac address /一纸空～ mere scrap of paper /以～会友 cultivate friends (*or* friendships) through

writing ❹ literary or classical language: 半～半白 half literary and half vernacular / 这句话太～。This sentence is too bookish. ❺ culture; civilization: *see* "～化"; "～明" ❻ liberal arts; humanities: 我是学～的。I am a student of liberal arts. ❼〈旧语〉etiquette; formal ritual: 繁～缛节 overelaborate formalities; red tape / 虚～ mere formality ❽ civilian; civil: *see* "～职"; "～官"; "～修武备" ❾ soft; mild; refined: *see* "～静"; "～火" ❿ *used to refer to certain natural phenomena*: 天～ astronomy / 水～ hydrology ⓫ tattoo: ～了双颊 have one's cheeks tatooed (as a sign of punishment in ancient China) ⓬ cover up; paint over; explain away: ～过 gloss over one's fault ⓭〈量词〉unit of ancient coins: 一～钱 a cent / 一～不名 penniless ⓮ (Wén) a surname

文案 wén'àn ❶〈旧语〉official documents, letters, etc.; files; archives: 未处理的～堆积如山。There were piles upon piles of unprocessed files. ❷ archivist

文本 wénběn text; version: 这个文件有中、日两种～。This document has both Chinese and Japanese versions. / 两种～具有同等效力。Both texts are equally valid (*or* authentic).

文笔 wénbǐ style of writing: ～优美 write beautifully / ～犀利 wield a trenchant pen

文不对题 wénbùduìtí irrelevant to the subject; beside the point; not pertinent; wide of the mark: 你的回答～。Your answer is not to the point. / 他大发宏论，其实全然～。He held forth at great length, but was wide of the mark.

文不加点 wénbùjiādiǎn never blot a line in writing; need no revision; have a facile pen: 写文章，～的情况不多见。It is rare that one can write copiously without changing a word.

文部省 Wénbùshěng (Japan) Ministry of Education

文才 wéncái literary talent; aptitude for writing: 这个人品德好，～也好。He is a man of both moral integrity and literary talent.

文采 wéncǎi ❶ rich and bright colours: ～斑斓的贝壳 multicoloured sea shells ❷ literary grace; literary gift: 此人颇有～，又多情善感。He is a man of literary taste and sentimental reflection.

文昌鱼 wénchāngyú〈动物〉lancelet

文场 wénchǎng ❶ strings and winds in a traditional opera band ❷ a kind of folk art with several persons singing to the accompaniment of the dulcimer, popular in parts of Guangxi. ❸ place where the literati gather ❹ hall for imperial examinations

文抄公 wénchāogōng〈戏谑〉plagiarist

文成公主 Wénchéng Gōngzhǔ Princess Wencheng (? -680) of the Tang Dynasty, who in 641 married Songtsam Gambo (松赞干布, 617? -650), king of Tubo (吐蕃, ancient name for Tibet), and introduced Tang culture into Tibet

文丑 wénchǒu〈戏曲〉clown or buffoon specialized in comic dialogue and acting (as distinguished from acrobatics)

文辞 wéncí *also* "文词" ❶ diction; language: ～华丽 flowery language; ornate diction ❷ articles and essays: 他以工于～而闻名。He is well known for his prose.

文从字顺 wéncóng-zìshùn readable and fluent; coherent and smooth: 写文章先求～。Readability and fluency are the first requirements in writing.

文代会 wéndàihuì (short for 文学艺术工作者代表大会) congress of writers and artists

文旦 wéndàn〈方言〉pomelo (fruit)

文档 wéndàng archives

文典 wéndiǎn〈书面〉❶ model in diction: 言成～。One's words became a classic in diction. ❷ ancient books and records; classics: 博览～ be well versed in the classics

文电 wéndiàn telegram; telegraphic text

文斗 wéndòu (used in the Cultural Revolution) verbal struggle; arguing without coming to blows

文牍 wéndú ❶ official documents and correspondence: ～冗繁 lengthy and copious official documents; too much red tape ❷〈旧语〉scribe; copyist: 这位老先生在旧法院里当过～。The old gentleman used to work in the court as a scribe before liberation.

文牍主义 wéndúzhǔyì red tape: 要消灭～，还得进行大量工作。Much work remains to be done to do away with red tape.

文法 wénfǎ ❶ grammar: ～不通 grammatically incorrect; wrong in grammar ❷〈旧词〉written laws and decrees

文法学校 wénfǎ xuéxiào〈历史〉grammar school, a kind of selective state secondary school in Britain with a mainly academic curriculum

文贩 wénfàn〈贬义〉person hawking articles and other writings (usually of the cheap kind) for a profit

文房 wénfáng ❶〈书面〉study: ～清玩 elegant and refined antiques, ornaments, etc. in the study ❷〈旧语〉secretarial section of a government office

文房四宝 wénfáng sìbǎo four treasures of the study — writing brush, ink stick, ink slab and paper

文风 wénfēng style of writing: 整顿～ rectify the style of writing

文风不动 wénfēng-bùdòng *also* "纹风不动" wénfēng-bùdòng not give way at all; be absolutely still: 一锤砸下去，那冻土竟～。The frozen earth did not give way at all under the hammer strike. / 树梢～，天闷得叫人喘不过气来。It was a stifling day; there was not a breath of wind and even the treetops did not wave.

文稿 wéngǎo manuscript; draft: 草拟～ draft a document / 修改～ revise a draft (*or* manuscript) / 这些～很珍贵，应妥为保存。These manuscripts are very valuable and should be kept with great care.

文告 wéngào proclamation; declaration; bulletin; statement: 发布～ issue a proclamation

文革 Wéngé (short for 文化大革命) Cultural Revolution: ～小组 leading group for the Cultural Revolution

文蛤 wéngé〈动物〉clam

文工团 wéngōngtuán song and dance ensemble; art troupe; cultural troupe

文攻武卫 wéngōng-wǔwèi (used in the Cultural Revolution) attack with the pen and defend with the sword

文官 wénguān civil official; civil servant: ～考试 examination for the civil service / ～制度 civil service (system) / ～政府 civil government

文冠果 wénguānguǒ〈植物〉shiny-leaved yellowhorn (*Xanthoceras sorbifolia*)

文过饰非 wénguò-shìfēi conceal mistakes and gloss over wrongs; cover up one's errors; explain away and whitewash mistakes: 他也有缺点错误，但从不～。He has shortcomings and mistakes too, but he never tries to cover them up.

文翰 wénhàn〈书面〉❶ article; essay; writing ❷ official documents and correspondence: 专掌～ in charge of official documents

文豪 wénháo literary giant; great writer; eminent author: 一代～ great writer of his (*or* her) time

文虎 wénhǔ literary riddle

文化 wénhuà ❶ civilization; culture: 新～ new culture / 大众～ popular culture / 亚～ subculture / 外来～ foreign culture / 传统～ traditional culture / ～领域 domain of culture / ～生活 cultural life / ～交流 cultural exchanges / ～浸透 cultural infiltration / ～事业 cultural undertakings / ～工作者 cultural worker ❷〈考古〉ancient culture or civilization: 仰韶～ Yangshao Culture / 龙山～ Longshan Culture ❸ education; schooling; literacy: 学习～ acquire an elementary education; acquire literacy; learn to read and write / ～课 literacy class / ～教养 education and upbringing / 有～ literate

文化部 wénhuàbù Ministry of Culture

文化参赞 wénhuà cānzàn cultural counsellor; cultural attaché

文化层 wénhuàcéng〈考古〉cultural stratum

文化程度 wénhuà chéngdù *also* "文化水平" educational level: 下一代农村人口的～要比现在高。The next generation of the rural population will be better educated.

文化大革命 Wénhuà Dàgémìng (short for 无产阶级文化大革命) Great Cultural Revolution (1966-1976)

文化地理学 wénhuà dìlǐxué cultural geography

文化宫 wénhuàgōng palace of culture; cultural palace: 劳动人民～ Labouring People's Palace of Culture

文化馆 wénhuàguǎn cultural centre

文化界 wénhuàjiè cultural circles

文化经济学 wénhuà jīngjìxué cultural economics

文化景观 wénhuà jǐngguān cultural landscape; cultural panorama: ～使文化艺术与自然景观融为一体。This cultural panorama is an excellent interweaving of art and culture with natural landscape.

文化买办 wénhuà mǎibàn person selling foreign culture in the service of colonialism; cultural comprador

文化人 wénhuàrén ❶ (used mainly during and after the War of Resistance Against Japanese Aggression) person engaged in cultural work ❷ intellectual; man of letters; literati

文化人类学 wénhuà rénlèixué cultural anthropology

文化沙漠 wénhuà shāmò cultural desert

W

文化社会学 wénhuà shèhuìxué cultural sociology
文化生态学 wénhuà shēngtàixué cultural ecology
文化史 wénhuàshǐ cultural history
文化市场 wénhuà shìchǎng cultural products market
文化水儿 wénhuàshuǐr 〈口语〉education; schooling; literacy:我～低,工作中经常碰到困难。As I have had little formal schooling, I often come across difficulties in work.
文化下乡 wénhuà xiàxiāng (of urban people and institutions) disseminate culture and knowledge in the countryside; popularize education and hygiene in the rural areas:组织科普书籍巡回书市是～的一种好形式。A good method to disseminate culture and knowledge in the countryside is to organize roving stores of books on popular science.
文化遗产 wénhuà yíchǎn cultural heritage; cultural legacy:世界～cultural heritage of the world
文化遗址 wénhuà yízhǐ site of ancient cultural relics; remains of an ancient culture:红山～ site of Hongshan Culture
文化用品 wénhuà yòngpǐn stationery
文化站 wénhuàzhàn cultural centre
文化专员 wénhuà zhuānyuán 〈外交〉cultural attaché
文化专制主义 wénhuà zhuānzhìzhǔyì cultural autocracy or tyranny
文话 wénhuà polished or cultured remarks
文汇报 Wénhuìbào *Wen Hui Bao*, Chinese daily newspaper first published in 1938 in Shanghai; (HK) *Wen Wai Po*
文火 wénhuǒ slow fire; gentle heat:红烧猪肉要用～。Use a slow fire to braise pork in soy sauce.
文集 wénjí collected works:《郁达夫～》*Collected Works of Yu Dafu*
文籍 wénjí writings; publications; books:有关这段历史的～多已散失。Most of the books concerned with this period of history are lost.
文件 wénjiàn ❶ official documents and correspondence; papers; file:中共中央～ document of the CCP Central Committee /机密～ classified document /～夹 file (folder)/～袋 documents pouch; dispatch case /～柜 filing cabinet /～编号 reference (*or* serial) number of a document /把去年的～清理归档。Sort out last year's papers and have them properly filed. ❷ article or work concerning political studies, academic research and current affairs; document:理论学习～ articles for theoretical study /纲领性～ programmatic document /这是指导当前工作的重要～。It is an important document guiding the current work. ❸〈信息〉file:～服务器 file server
文件传送协议 wénjiàn chuánsòng xiéyì 〈信息〉FTP (file transfer protocol)
文教 wénjiào (short for 文化教育) culture and education:～部门 cultural and educational institutions /发展～事业 develop culture and education; promote the cause of culture and education
文教界 wénjiàojiè cultural and educational circles
文景之治 Wén-Jǐng Zhī Zhì peace and prosperity during the reign of Emperors Wen and Jing (179 BC-140 BC) of the Western Han Dynasty
文静 wénjìng gentle and quiet:她的一举一动,都显得那么～。She is so gentle and quiet in her demeanour. *or* She has such a gentle demeanour.
文句 wénjù sentences of an article or essay; diction; language:～流畅。The language is fluent. /～不通。The sentences are ungrammatical.
文具 wénjù stationery:～店 stationer's; stationery shop
文据 wénjù written pledge (including receipt, IOU, contract, etc.)
文康广播科 Wénkāng Guǎngbōkē (HK) Recreation and Culture Branch
文科 wénkē liberal arts:～教材 teaching materials for liberal arts /报考～ take the entrance examination for liberal arts colleges
文库 wénkù series of books issued in a single format by a publisher; library:《少年～》*Children's Library*
文侩 wénkuài phrase-monger
文莱 Wénlái Brunei:～苏丹国 Sultanate of Brunei
文理 wénlǐ unity and coherence in writing:～通顺 be logical and coherent; make smooth reading /～不通 be illogical and ungrammatical
文联 wénlián literary federation:中国～ China Federation of Literary and Art Circles
文林 wénlín 〈书面〉galaxy of literary talent; literati
文律 wénlǜ ❶ temperament or rules of essays ❷〈书面〉law
文脉 wénmài (of an essay) organization:此文～不清。This article is poorly organized.
文盲 wénmáng illiterate person; illiterate:半～ semi-illiterate /扫除～ wipe out illiteracy
文面 wénmiàn 〈书面〉tattoo one's face; have a tattoo on one's face
文庙 wénmiào Confucian temple
文名 wénmíng literary fame:苏氏兄弟都有～。The Su brothers were all renowned for their literary achievements.
文明 wénmíng ❶ civilization; culture:古代～ ancient civilization /现代～ modern civilization /精神～ spiritual civilization; ethical and ideological progress /物质～ material civilization ❷ civilized; civil:～国家 civilized country (*or* nation) /～社会 civilized society /～古国 country with an ancient civilization /～居住小区 model residential subarea /～礼貌月 civic virtues month /～公约 agreement (*or* regulations) on civic virtues / 威武～之师 mighty and well-disciplined army /讲话这么粗鲁是不～的行为。It is bad manners talking so rudely. /讲话要放～些。Keep a civil tongue in your head. /有必要强调～礼貌。It is necessary to stress good manners and good behaviour. ❸ modern and western:～结婚 modern-style marriage
文明棍 wénmínggùn (walking) stick
文明经商 wénmíng jīngshāng be courteous and honest in business dealings
文明戏 wénmíngxì early modern drama (prevalent in Shanghai and contiguous areas in the early years of the 20th century)
文墨 wénmò ❶ writing; literacy:粗通～ barely know the rudiments of writing ❷ of mental labour:～事儿 mental work
文墨人 wénmòrén intellectual:他是个～,不会干粗活。He is an intellectual incapable of heavy physical labour.
文痞 wénpǐ hack scoundrel who deliberately tries to confuse right and wrong by phrase-mongering:～小丑 literary buffoon
文凭 wénpíng diploma:混～ muddle along to get a diploma; wangle a diploma
文气 wénqì force or cohesion of writing:～贯通 cohesive writing
文气 wénqi 〈方言〉gentle and reserved:这小伙子～得很。The young man has very gentle and smooth manners.
文契 wénqì contract for real estate transactions; title-deed; lease
文情 wénqíng literary grace and emotional appeal; content and language:～并茂 beautiful in both sentiment and expression; excellent in both content and language
文丘里管 wénqiūlǐguǎn *also* "文氏管"〈物理〉venturi (tube)
文曲星 wénqǔxīng legendary god in charge of imperial examinations and literary affairs;〈比喻〉renowned man of letters
文人 wénrén man of letters; scholar:～学者 literary scholars; men of letters /无聊～ boring scribbler /帮闲～ literary hack /～墨客 literati
文人画 wénrénhuà (used in Chinese art history) paintings by scholars and officials
文人无行 wénrén-wúxíng men of letters are lacking in moral character; the literati are a bunch of debauched people
文人相轻 wénrén-xiāngqīng scholars tend to look down upon each other; writers often disparage one another:～,自古而然。Scholars have scorned each other since time immemorial. /他们俩的笔墨官司,正应了一句古话:～。The polemic between the two has confirmed an old saying:writers tend to think poorly of one another.
文如其人 wénrúqírén the writing mirrors the writer; the style is the man; like (the) author, like (the) book
文弱 wénruò gentle and frail:～的白面书生 frail-looking, pale-faced intellectual
文山会海 wénshān-huìhǎi mountains of documents and seas of meetings; endless documents and innumerable meetings:讲实效,不搞～。Emphasize practical results and do away with endless documents and meetings.
文身 wénshēn tattoo
文史 wénshǐ literature and history:～知识 knowledge about literature and history /～资料 historical accounts of past events
文史馆 wénshǐguǎn Research Institute of Culture and History
文史通义 Wénshǐ Tōngyì *General Interpretation of Historiography*, setting forth principles and criteria for writing history, by

Zhang Xuecheng (章学诚, 1738-1801), historian and thinker of the Qing Dynasty

文士 wénshì man of letters; scholar

文氏管 wénshìguǎn 〈物理〉 venturi (tube)

文饰 wénshì ❶ polish; refine: 语言还粗糙些, 需加～。The language is still a little crude and needs some touching up. ❷ conceal; cover up; gloss over: 错误就是错误, 无须～。Mistakes are mistakes, and there is no need to cover them up.

文书 wénshū ❶ documents; official dispatches ❷ scribe; copyist; secretary: 我在这个团当过二年～。I served as secretary in this regiment for two years.

文殊 Wénshū *also* "文殊师利" 〈佛教〉 Manjusri, a Bodhisattva of Mahayana Buddhism: ～菩萨 Bodhisattva Manjusri

文思 wénsī thread of ideas in writing; train of thought in writing: ～敏捷 have a ready pen; wield a facile pen / ～枯竭 one's creative flow dries up; run out of ideas to write about; be literarily sterile

文坛 wéntán literary world; literary arena; literary circles; world of letters: ～新人 new figure in the literary world / ～盛会 grand occasion for literary circles; gathering of celebrated literary figures

文韬武略 wéntāo-wǔlüè military expertise; military strategy

文体 wéntǐ ❶ type of writing; literary form; genre: ～学 stylistics / 记叙～ narration / 议论～ argumentation / 实用～ practical writing ❷ (short for 文娱体育) recreation and sports: 开展～活动 promote recreational and sports activities

文天祥 Wén Tiānxiáng Wen Tianxiang (1236-1283), patriot and writer of the Southern Song Dynasty

文恬武嬉 wéntián-wǔxī the civil officials are indolent and the military officers frivolous; the entire officialdom, both civil and military, wallows in luxury and dissipation: 承平日久, 朝中大臣, ～。Peace had prevailed so long that the entire officialdom, both civil and military, were dissipated and corrupt.

文玩 wénwán ornamental object

文网 wénwǎng ❶ 〈书面〉 net of justice; arm of the law ❷ 〈旧语〉 ban on the free expression of thought

文武 wén-wǔ ❶ civil accomplishments and military prowess: ～兼备 be well versed in both polite letters and martial arts ❷ 〈书面〉 cultural and military achievements; peaceful and coercive means: ～并用 use both persuasion and coercion ❸ 〈书面〉 ministers and generals: 满朝～ all the ministers and generals of the imperial court / ～官员 civil officials and officers of the armed services

文武双全 wén-wǔ shuāngquán be well versed both in civil and military affairs; be fit for both physical exertion and intellectual pursuit; be adept with both pen and sword

文物 wénwù cultural relic; historical relic: 出土～ unearthed cultural relics / 国家～局 State Bureau for the Preservation of Cultural and Historical Relics

文物保护 wénwù bǎohù preservation of cultural relics; protection of historical relics

文戏 wénxì Chinese opera focusing on singing and acting as distinguished from that with acrobatic fighting as its main feature; gentle show: ～、武戏一齐上 give performance both of singing and of acrobatic fighting; use both persuasion and coercion

文献 wénxiàn document; literature: 历史～ historical documents / 科技～ literature of science and technology / 革命～ revolutionary literature / 医学～ medical literature / ～时滞 literature time lag / ～老化 documental ageing / ～数据库 document data bank

文献记录片 wénxiàn jìlùpiàn documentary (film)

文献通考 Wénxiàn Tōngkǎo *A Critical History of Institutions*, a study of the evolution of Chinese institutions up to the end of the 12th century, esp. those of the Song Dynasty, written by historian Ma Duanlin (马端临, c. 1254-1323)

文协 wénxié (short for 文学艺术工作者协会) association of literary and art circles

文心雕龙 Wénxīn Diāolóng *The Literary Mind and the Carving of the Dragon*, classic work of literary criticism by Liu Xie (刘勰, c. 465-c. 532) of the Liang Dynasty, one of the Southern Dynasties

文胸 wénxiōng 〈方言〉 brassiere; bra

文秀 wénxiù gentle and charming; delicate: ～的面孔 delicate features

文选 wénxuǎn selected works; literary selections: 活页～ loose-leaf literary selections / 《邓小平～》 *Selected Works of Deng Xiaoping*

文学 wénxué literature: 英国～史 history of English literature / ～艺术 art and literature / ～家 writer; man of letters / ～作品 literary works / ～遗产 literary heritage / ～流派 schools of literature / ～传统 literary tradition / ～批评 literary criticism / 古典～ classical literature / 当代～ contemporary literature / 纯～ belles-lettres

文学革命 wénxué gémìng literary revolution

文学士 wénxuéshì bachelor of arts (BA)

文学语言 wénxué yǔyán ❶ standard speech or language ❷ literary language

文雅 wényǎ elegant; graceful; cultured; polished: 谈吐～ talk in refined taste / 这件素净的衣服穿在她身上, 更显出她的～了。She looks even more elegant and graceful in this quiet-coloured dress.

文言 wényán classical Chinese

文言文 wényánwén writings in classical Chinese; classical style of writing: 他读～没有困难。He has no difficulty reading classical Chinese.

文以载道 wényǐzàidào (traditional criterion for literary criticism) literature is a vehicle of the Way or Confucian ideas; writings are meant to convey truth; men write to expound truth

文艺 wényì art and literature: ～工作 work in the artistic and literary fields / ～工作者 art and literary workers; artists and writers / ～思潮 trend of thought in art and literature / ～观点 views on art and literature / ～政策 policy on art and literature / ～团体 art and literature organization; theatre troupe / ～座谈会 forum (*or* symposium) on art and literature / ～队伍 ranks (*or* contingent) of artists and writers / ～战线 on the art and literary front

文艺复兴 Wényì Fùxīng Renaissance (in 14th-17th centuries in Western Europe)

文艺黑线 wényì hēixiàn (used in the Cultural Revolution) sinister or revisionist line in art and literature

文艺会演 wényì huìyǎn *also* "文艺汇演" theatrical festival; joint performance

文艺节目 wényì jiémù programme of entertainment; theatrical items; theatrical performance

文艺界 wényìjiè art and literary circles; world of art and literature

文艺批评 wényì pīpíng art and literary criticism: ～家 art (*or* literary) critic

文艺社会学 wényì shèhuìxué sociology of art and literature

文艺思想 wényì sīxiǎng thought on art and literature

文艺心理学 wényì xīnlǐxué art and literary psychology

文艺学 wényìxué study of art and literature

文艺语言 wényì yǔyán language of art and literature; literary language

文友 wényǒu literary friend or associate: 他和几个～计划搞个刊物。He and several literary associates of his are planning to publish a journal.

文娱 wényú cultural recreation; entertainment: ～活动 recreational activities / ～设施 entertainment facilities

文苑 wényuàn literary circles; world of literature

文苑英华 Wényuàn Yīnghuá *Choice Blossoms from the Garden of Literature*, an encyclopedic collection of one thousand volumes compiled by Li Fang (李昉, 925-996) and others of the Northern Song Dynasty

文约 wényuē contract; deed; charter: 订有～。A contract has been signed.

文责 wénzé author's responsibility for his own writings: ～自负。The author takes sole responsibility for his own views.

文摘 wénzhāi ❶ extracts from articles or books ❷ abstract; digest: 《新华～》 *Xing Hua Abstracts* / 《～报》 *Press Résumé* / 《读者～》 *Reader's Digest* / 《～周刊》 *Weekly Digest*

文战 wénzhàn ❶ 〈旧语〉 imperial examination ❷ battle of words; written controversy or polemic: 一场～打了三年。The written polemic lasted three years.

文章 wénzhāng ❶ essay; article: 这个集子共有十二篇～。There are twelve essays in this collection. / 这是一篇与众不同很有特色的～。This is a unique article. ❷ literary works or compositions; writings: ～乃不朽之盛事。Literature is a great undertaking that has the stamp of immortality. ❸ hidden meaning; implied meaning; implication: 我知道这里有～。I know there is an insinuation here. / 猜不透这番话里的～。I can't make out what's behind all this talk. / 其中大有～。There is much more to it than meets the eye. ❹ way

W

(of doing sth.); room (for doing sth.); elbow room:关于改进服务,还大有~可做。There is much room for improvement in our service.

文证 wénzhèng written evidence; evidence on paper

文职 wénzhí civilian post:担任~ hold a civilian post; be in the civil service /~官员 civil officials; civilian staff

文治 wénzhì 〈书面〉statesmanship; statecraft; achievements in running public affairs:以~兴邦 develop the country through improved civil administration

文治武功 wénzhì-wǔgōng (outstanding) statecraft and (brilliant) military exploits:~缺一不可。Cultural and military achievements are both indispensable.

文质彬彬 wénzhì-bīnbīn suave; urbane; quiet and scholarly:~的书生 quiet scholarly young man; young man of the quiet scholarly type /~,然后君子。One can only be a true gentleman when one has both polish and substance.

文绉绉 wénzhōuzhōu genteel; bookish:你说话总是那么~的! You are always talking like a book.

文竹 wénzhú 〈植物〉asparagus fern (*Asparagus plumosus*)

文字 wénzì ❶ characters; script; writing:表形~ pictography; pictogram; hieroglyph /表意~ ideography; ideogram /表音~ alphabetic writing /楔形~ cuneiform characters ❷ written language:~宣传 written propaganda /学好祖国的语言~。Learn to speak and write one's native language well. /他精通几种~。He has a good command of several languages. ❸ writing (mostly referring to form and style):~简练 written in a concise style

文字处理机 wénzì chǔlǐjī *also* "文字处理器" word processor

文字方程 wénzì fāngchéng 〈数学〉literal equation

文字改革 wénzì gǎigé reform of a writing system

文字交 wénzìjiāo pen friends; literary friends or associates

文字学 wénzìxué philology

文字游戏 wénzì yóuxì play on words; juggle with terms:玩弄~ play on words; pun

文字狱 wénzìyù 〈历史〉imprisonment or execution of an author for writing sth. (often taken out of context) considered offensive by the imperial court; literary inquisition:大兴~ go in for literary inquisitions in a big way

文宗 wénzōng 〈书面〉writer whose works are accepted as paragons; master writer:百代~ long established master writer

炆

wén 〈方言〉cook food on a slow fire

雯

wén 〈书面〉patterned clouds

蚊

wén mosquito:黑斑~ yellow-fever mosquito /疟~ malarial mosquito / 摇~ midge; chironomid

蚊虫 wénchóng mosquito

蚊母树 wénmǔshù 〈植物〉*Distylium racemosum*, evergreen tree indigenous in China

蚊蚋 wénruì mosquito

蚊香 wénxiāng mosquito-repellent incense; mosquito coil incense:电~ electric mosquito repellent

蚊帐 wénzhàng mosquito net:~纱 mosquito netting

蚊子 wénzi mosquito

纹

wén ❶ pattern:花~ patterns ❷ line; vein; grain:波~ ripple /指~ loops and whorls on a finger; finger print /裂~ crack /鱼尾~ crow's-feet /额~ lines on one's forehead /皱~ lines (on one's face); wrinkles; furrows /细~木 fine-grained wood

纹板 wénbǎn 〈纺织〉card; pattern card; figure sheet:~冲孔机 card puncher; card nipper /~架 cradle /~链 pattern chain

纹波电压 wénbō diànyā 〈电工〉ripple voltage

纹瓷 wéncí crackleware

纹理 wénlǐ veins; grain:这些叶子有清晰的淡红色的~。These leaves have clear, reddish veins./这块大理石的~很美。The marble has a very beautiful grain.

纹路 wénlu lines; grain:这里的山岩有一条条平行排列的~。The mountain rocks here have parallel lines on them.

纹缕 wénlǚ veins; grain:条形~ striped veins

纹饰 wénshì patterns engraved or painted on wares; engraved or painted patterns:殷周青铜器~展 exhibition of Yin and Zhou patterned bronzes

纹丝 wénsī (usu. used in the negative) least or slightest (amount or degree); tiny bit:未受~影响 not affected at all

纹丝不动 wénsī-bùdòng absolutely still or motionless:他笔挺地坐着,~。He sat bolt upright without moving a muscle.

纹样 wényàng decorative patterns (on wares)

纹银 wényín 〈旧语〉fine silver; sterling silver:十足~ pure silver /~百两 hundred taels of sterling silver

纹章学 wénzhāngxué heraldry

闻

wén ❶ hear:早有耳~ have long heard of; have long got wind of /~一可以知二 hear the beginning and know the end /百~不如一见 seeing for oneself is a hundred times better than hearing from others; seeing is believing ❷ news; story; anecdote:传~ rumour; hearsay /新~ news /奇~ fantastic story /趣~ anecdote ❸ 〈书面〉well-known; renowned; famous: *see* "~人" ❹ repute; reputation:令~ good repute /秽~ ill repute /默默无~ be unknown to the public; be forgotten; sink into oblivion ❺ smell:看起来、~起来、吃起来都不错。It looks fine, smells good and tastes nice. ❻ (Wén) a surname

闻达 wéndá 〈书面〉fame and publicity:不求~ seek no fame

闻风而动 wénfēng'érdòng act without delay on hearing the news; take action as soon as one hears about the matter; answer a call with immediate action:这次搞卫生,各单位都能~。Every unit responded enthusiastically to the call for improved public hygiene.

闻风而逃 wénfēng'értáo run away or take to one's heels on getting wind of sth:清兵只要望见太平军的影子,就~。The Qing troops fled pell-mell before actually catching sight of the Taipings.

闻风丧胆 wénfēng-sàngdǎn become terror-stricken or panic-stricken at the news:我军向前挺进,敌人~。The enemy were scared to death on hearing the news of our advance.

闻过则喜 wénguò-zéxǐ feel happy when one learns of one's errors; be glad to have one's errors pointed out:他常常以~来自勉。He often reminds himself that one should feel thankful for any unfavourable criticism.

闻鸡起舞 wénjī-qǐwǔ 〈比喻〉rise at cockcrow and practise martial arts — exert oneself to the utmost for a worthy cause

闻见 wénjiàn knowledge; information; experience; what one sees and hears:~甚浅 ill-informed; inexperienced /我生长在穷村僻壤,~有限。My experience is limited as I was born and brought up in a remote country town.

闻见 wénjian ❶ smell:她~一股烧焦的味道。She smelled something burning. ❷ hear:~风就要防备雨。You'd better be prepared for the rain when you hear the wind blowing.

闻名 wénmíng ❶ be familiar with sb.'s name; know sb. by repute:久闻大名,如雷贯耳。Your name has long resounded in my ears. ❷ well-known; celebrated; famous; renowned:举世~的大作家 great writer enjoying an international reputation /遐迩~的医生 doctor well-known far and near /中国菜~于世界。Chinese cuisine is world-famous.

闻名不如见面 wénmíng bùrú jiànmiàn knowing a person by repute is not as good as seeing him in the flesh:~,见面胜似闻名。〈套语〉Knowing a person by repute is certainly inadequate. Now that I have met you, I know you more than deserve your reputation.

闻人 wénrén ❶ well-known figure; eminent person; luminary; celebrity:他是本地的~。He is one of the celebrities in this locality. ❷ (Wénrén) a surname

闻所未闻 wénsuǒwèiwén unheard of:~的故事 unheard-of story /这些新鲜事我~。These are things I have never heard of before.

闻听 wéntīng 〈方言〉hear:他~客人到了楼下,便急忙出来迎接。As soon as he heard the guests arrive downstairs, he hurried to meet them.

闻悉 wénxī 〈书面〉hear; learn; be informed; come to one's knowledge:~火箭升空,兴奋之至。On hearing about the successful launching of the rocket, we got very excited.

闻讯 wénxùn hear the news:~赶来 rush over after hearing the news

闻一知十 wényī-zhīshí learn one thing and understand ten things — good at drawing analogies; be very bright

闻诊 wénzhěn 〈中医〉auscultation and smelling, one of the four methods of diagnosis

see also "四诊" sìzhěn

wěn

抆 wěn 〈书面〉wipe:～泪 wipe tears from one's eyes

紊 wěn dishevelled; disorderly; confused:有条不～ in an orderly way; in apple-pie order; methodically; systematically

紊动 wěndòng 〈物理〉turbulent fluctuation; turbulent motion

紊流 wěnliú 〈物理〉turbulence; turbulent flow:～热交换 turbulent heat transfer

紊流煤粉燃烧器 wěnliú méifěn ránshāoqì turbulent burner

紊乱 wěnluàn disorder; chaos; turmoil; confusion:思想～ confused thoughts /秩序～ in a state of turmoil /局势～ chaotic situation /肠功能～ functional disorder of the intestines /心律～ arrhythmia /工作一片～。The work was in complete disarray. /许多书在桌子上～地堆着。The books are piled haphazardly on the desk.

稳(穩) wěn ❶ steady; firm; steadfast:站～ stand firm /坐～ sit tight /把舵掌～ take the helm steadily /这椅子放不～。This chair is unsteady. /她立场～,从不随风倒。She is steadfast in her stand (*or* position) and never bends with the wind. ❷ calm; staid; sedate:这个人很～。He is very calm and self-possessed. ❸ sure; certain:十拿九～ quite sure; practically certain; in the bag /他～拿冠军。He is certain to win the championship. ❹ stabilize; calm; put at ease:～住局势 stabilize the situation /你想法儿把他～住,不要让他跑了。Try your best to steady him down and prevent him from slipping away.

稳便 wěnbiàn ❶ fitting and proper:这些事一刀切,恐怕不够～。It is not proper to handle all matters in rigid conformity with rules, I'm afraid. ❷ (often used in the early vernacular) as you please; as you like

稳步 wěnbù with steady steps; steadily:～发展 develop steadily /我们怀着极大信心～进入 21 世纪。We'll stride into the 21st century with great confidence.

稳操胜券 wěncāo-shèngquàn *also*"稳操左券";"稳操胜算" be sure to win; be certain of victory; have full assurance of success:这次足球赛北京队可以～。The Beijing Team is sure to win in the football match.

稳产 wěnchǎn stable yield:这是～高产田。This is a field with a stable and high yield. /促进农作物～高产。Promote high and stable yields of crops.

稳当 wěndang ❶ reliable; dependable; secure; safe:办事～ be reliable in doing things ❷ steady; sure; stable:孩子走得很～。The child walks quite steadily. /他的双杠,动作无可挑剔,落地也稳稳当当。He was perfect on the parallel bars and his dismount was steady.

稳定 wěndìng ❶ firmly established; stable; steady:生活～ stable life /社会～ social stability /产量～增长 steady growth in output /经济～而健康地发展。The economy is developing steadily and healthily. /人心～。The popular feeling remains unruffled. ❷ stabilize; calm; steady:～物价 stabilize prices /～血压 stabilize one's blood pressure /首先要～她的情绪。We must try to calm her down first. ❸ stability:化学性能～ stability of chemical property /钠的性能极不～。Sodium has a very unstable property.

稳定度 wěndìngdù 〈物理〉stability

稳定剂 wěndìngjì 〈化学〉stabilizer

稳定流 wěndìngliú 〈物理〉*also*"定常流" dìngchángliú stable current

稳定平衡 wěndìng pínghéng 〈物理〉stable equilibrium

稳定装置 wěndìng zhuāngzhì 〈化学〉stabilization plant

稳固 wěngù ❶ firm; solid; stable:～的基础 solid foundation /～的政权 stable government /～的职业 stable (*or* secure) job ❷ stabilize; consolidate:～统治地位 stabilize one's rule (*or* position) /～经济基础 consolidate the economic foundation

稳厚 wěnhòu honest and down-to-earth:他为人朴实～。He is honest, sincere and down-to-earth.

稳弧装置 wěnhú zhuāngzhì 〈电工〉arc stabilizer

稳获 wěnhuò sure or certain to get; have full assurance of:我队三战皆捷,～冠军。We've won all the three matches and the Cup is a sure thing. *or* We've got three wins and the championship is in the bag.

稳健 wěnjiàn ❶ firm; stable; steady:老人的步子仍然很～。The old man is still walking with steady steps. ❷ steady; sure; reliable:他办事一向～。He is level-headed and steady in whatever he does. /随着年龄的增长,他变得～多了。He became more experienced and more sure of himself as he grew older.

稳健派 wěnjiànpài moderates

稳静 wěnjìng quiet and unhurried:她态度总是那么～。She is always clam and unhurried in manner.

稳练 wěnliàn steady and skilful:操作～ operate with a steady and skilful hand

稳流 wěnliú 〈物理〉steady flow

稳拿 wěnná be certain of success:这事交给他办～。The matter will be in safe hands if you entrust it to him. /他～金牌。He is a sure-fire gold medalist.

稳拿把攥 wěnná-bǎzuàn 〈方言〉sure; certain:他长跑得第一是～的事。It is certain that he will be the champion in the long-distance race.

稳婆 wěnpó 〈旧语〉midwife

稳如泰山 wěnrú-Tàishān as stable as Mount Tai; rock-firm:洪水冲来,大坝屹立不动,～。Though battered by the floodwater, the dam remained rock-firm.

稳实 wěnshi steady and sure; free from anxiety; at ease:士兵们迈着～的步伐前进。The soldiers marched forward with steady steps. /听到这个消息我心里怎么也～不下来。I could hardly set my mind at ease after hearing the news.

稳态 wěntài 〈物理〉steady state; stable state:～电流 steady-state current /～反应堆 〈核物理〉steady-state reactor

稳帖 wěntiē proper; correct:一切都办得很～。All is done properly.

稳妥 wěntuǒ safe; reliable; trustworthy:商量一个～的解决办法 work out a sound method to solve the problem /要交给一个～的人去办。This must be left to a trustworthy person. /这样处理比较～可靠。It is safer and more reliable to act the way it is suggested.

稳压 wěnyā 〈电工〉stabilized voltage; voltage regulation:～电源 stabilized voltage (*or* power) supply /～管 stabilivolt

稳压器 wěnyāqì 〈物理〉manostat;〈电工〉voltage regulator; voltage stabilizer

稳扎稳打 wěnzhā-wěndǎ ❶ make steady progress and strike sure blows:我们的方针是～,不求速效。Our policy is to go ahead steadily and strike sure blows, not to seek quick results. /～,沉着应战。Move ahead steadily and meet the challenge calmly. ❷ go about things steadily and surely:整顿工作一直在～地进行。The consolidation work has been going on quite steadily. /他做事～,不慌不忙。He handles his work (*or* goes about his business) in an unhurried, matter-of-fact fashion.

稳扎扎 wěnzhāzhā steady; measured:他不慌不忙,～地直往前方走去。He walked unhurriedly but steadily ahead into the distance.

稳重 wěnzhòng steady; discreet; prudent:态度～大方 have a steady and easy manner /他做事十分～。He acts with utmost discretion.

稳住阵脚 wěnzhù zhènjiǎo hold one's position; secure a foothold:在强手面前,广东队决定先～,然后相机反攻。Faced with a strong opponent, the Guangdong team decided to hold its position first and counter-attack when opportunities arose.

稳庄 wěnzhuang 〈口语〉staid and serious; steady and reliable:毛头小伙子,办事不太～。He is young and green, not quite steady and reliable in getting anything done.

稳准狠 wěn-zhǔn-hěn sure, accurate and relentless:～地打击一小撮犯罪分子。Deal sure, accurate and relentless blows at the handful of criminal elements.

稳坐钓鱼船 wěn zuò diàoyúchuán sit tight in the fishing boat — remain calm and hold one's ground:任凭风浪起,～ sit tight in the fishing boat despite the rising wind and waves; face danger with calm and confidence; hold one's ground despite pressure and opposition

刎 wěn cut one's throat:自～ cut one's own throat; commit suicide

刎颈交 wěnjǐngjiāo *also*"刎颈之交" friends who are ready to die for each other; tested friends; bosom friends:结为～ become devoted friends

吻(脗) wěn ❶ lips：接～ kiss ❷ touch by the lips；kiss：～了一下小宝宝 kiss the baby／～别 kiss sb. goodbye ❸〈动物〉muzzle；snout

吻合 wěnhé ❶ be identical；fit perfectly；coincide；tally：看法～ have identical views／上下～。The upper part fits in perfectly with the lower part.／现金与账目相～。The cash tallies with the account. ❷〈医学〉anastomose：～术〈医学〉anastomosis

吻兽 wěnshòu （decorative）animal sculptures（on roof ridges）

wèn

问 wèn ❶ seek information from；ask；inquire：询～ inquire／～电话号码 ask for a telephone number／明知故～ ask a question when one already has the answer／所答非所～ give an irrelevant answer to a question ❷ ask after；inquire after：代我向他致～。Please ask after him for me. *or* Please give him my best regards.／探～病人 inquire after a patient ❸ interrogate；question；examine：～口供 interrogate someone／～成死罪 sentence sb. to death after interrogation／胁从不～。The accomplice under duress shall not be punished. ❹ hold responsible；intervene：不闻不～ be indifferent to sth.／唯你是～。I'll hold you responsible for it.／这件事你去过～一下。Will you see to（*or* take care of）the matter? ❺ from：我想～你借本书。I'd like to borrow a book from you.／你没～他借过钱? Didn't you borrow money from him?／你～我要，我～谁要去? You ask me for it but then whom am I to ask? ❻（Wèn）a surname

问安 wèn'ān （usu. to elders）pay one's respects；visit sb. as a token of respect；wish sb. good health：他常到伯父家去～。He often goes to his uncle's to pay his respects.／我向老奶奶～。I wish Granny good health.

问案 wèn'àn try a case；hear a case；try a criminal

问卜 wènbǔ 〈迷信〉seek answers from divination：求神～ turn to a deity for help and seek answers from divination

问长问短 wèncháng-wènduǎn ask about this and that；make solicitous inquiries：母亲一直坐在儿子身边，～。All the time the mother sat beside her son asking all kinds of solicitous questions about him.

问答 wèndá questions and answers：演讲后安排了～。The speech will be followed by a question and answer session.

问道于盲 wèndàoyúmáng ask the way from a blind person — seek advice from one who can offer none：你向他诗歌的问题，这实在是～。When you asked him about poetry，it was seeking enlightenment from an ignoramus.

问鼎 wèndǐng ❶ intend to seize power：有～之心 have the ambition to seize state power ❷ try to win a championship：他在决赛中负于对手，痛失～的机会。He was defeated in the final，regrettably losing the championship.

问官 wènguan 〈旧语〉interrogator；inquisitor

问寒问暖 wènhán-wènnuǎn inquire with concern about sb.'s well-being；make solicitous inquiries about sb.'s health：别后他常来信～。After parting he often wrote to ask how I was getting on.

问好 wènhǎo send one's regards；say hello；extend greetings：向你父母～。Please say hello to your parents.／代我向大家～。Please extend my greetings to everybody.／老同学们要我向你～。The old classmates asked me to send you their regards.

问号 wènhào ❶ question mark；interrogation mark（?）❷ unknown factor；unsettled problem：他能不能解决这个问题，我脑子里打～。Whether he can solve the problem remains a question in my mind.／他这病好不好得了，还是个～。Whether he can recover from his present illness is still unknown.

问候 wènhòu send one's respects or regards；extend greetings；send best wishes：写信去～ write a letter of greetings／～军烈属 convey greetings to the families of armymen and martyrs／请代为～。Please send my best regards（*or* best wishes）to him. *or* Please remember me to him.

问话 wènhuà ask；inquire；question：处长找你～，你怎么不赶快去? Why don't you go immediately to see the division chief，who wants to ask you about something?

问津 wènjīn 〈书面〉（used mostly in the negative）make inquiries（as about the situation or the price of sth.）：这么贵的东西，我不敢～。I don't even dare to ask about the price of such expensive stuff.／～者不多。Few people make inquires about it.／这个店的服务态度不好，很少有人～。The reason the shop has attracted few customers is its poor service record.

问荆 wènjīng 〈植物〉meadow pine（*Equisetum arvense*）

问卷 wènjuàn questionnaire：～调查 investigation by questionnaire

问柳寻花 wènliǔ-xúnhuā *also* "寻花问柳" visit prostitutes；go whoring

问名 wènmíng 〈旧语〉written inquiry（sent by the groom's family to the bride's for her name，birthdate，etc.）

问难 wènnàn repeated question and debate（in academic studies）：质疑～ raise doubts and difficult questions for discussion；raise queries

问世 wènshì ❶ be published；come out：他的新著将于明年～。His new work will be published next year.／一套大型历史丛书即将～。A comprehensive history series will soon come out. ❷ be available in the market；be marketed：一种新型轿车～。A new type of sedan is now available in the market.

问事 wènshì ❶ inquire：向服务台的小姐～ inquire of the receptionist（about sth.）❷ attend to business；concern oneself with sth.；bother oneself about sth.：他年老多病，已不再～。He is ageing and ailing，and no longer concerns himself with the work.

问事处 wènshìchù information desk；inquiry office

问俗问禁 wènsú-wènjìn inquire about the customs and taboos of a land

问题 wèntí ❶ question：～单 questionnaire／他善于思考，也善于提出～。He is a thoughtful person and good at asking the right questions. ❷ problem；issue；matter：思想～ ideological problem／住房～ housing problem／共同关心的～ issue of common concern（*or* interest）／节电～ matters concerning economization on electricity／争吵解决不了任何～。Disputes will get you nowhere.／这个办法很解决～。This method worked very well. ❸ crucial point；key：计划已经定好了，～是怎样落实。The plan has been worked out，but the thing is how to carry it out.／生活中可写的东西是很多的，～在善于发掘和提炼。There are many things in life that one can write about，but the point is how to explore and select them. ❹ trouble；mishap；something wrong：好久没有听到他的消息了，一定发生了什么～。Something must have gone wrong. We haven't heard from him for so long.／昨天游泳，差点出了～。We nearly ran into trouble yesterday while swimming.

问心 wènxīn examine one's conscience；introspect：何以～? How can you face your own conscience?

问心无愧 wènxīn-wúkuì have a clear conscience；not have a guilty conscience：我自觉没有做错事，～。I have done nothing wrong，nothing to be ashamed of.／她觉得～。She felt she harboured no feelings of guilt. *or* She felt she had a clear conscience.

问心有愧 wènxīn-yǒukuì feel a twinge of conscience；suffer a qualm of conscience；have a guilty conscience：你这样做，不觉得～吗? Don't you feel ashamed of yourself acting the way you did?

问询 wènxún inquire；ask：车祸发生后，亲朋同事纷纷打电话～。After the traffic accident，many relatives，friends and colleagues telephoned to make inquiries.

问讯 wènxùn ❶ inquire；ask：她投过来～的眼光。She shot an inquiring look at me.／～吴刚何所有，吴刚捧出桂花酒。Wu Kang，asked what he can give，Serves them a laurel brew.／情况到底如何，无从～。There is no way of finding out how things stand. ❷ send one's respects；extend greetings：互致～ exchange greetings／他向老者很客气地～。He greeted the old man politely. ❸（of Buddhist monks and nuns）greet by putting one's palms together in front of oneself：那僧人向他打个～。The monk greeted him with his palms put together.

问讯处 wènxùnchù information office；inquiry desk

问斩 wènzhǎn 〈旧语〉behead；decapitate

问诊 wènzhěn 〈中医〉interrogation or inquiry，one of the four methods of diagnosis
see also "四诊" sìzhěn

问罪 wènzuì denounce；condemn：大兴～之师 denounce sb. publicly for his crimes（*or* serious errors）

揾 wèn 〈书面〉❶ press with fingers ❷ wipe：～泪 wipe one's tears；wipe one's tears away

璺 wèn crack（on glassware or earthenware）：玻璃瓶裂了一道～。The glass bottle has a crack.／打破沙锅～到底。When the earth-

en pot breaks, it cracks all the way to the bottom — keep asking questions until one gets to the bottom of the matter.

wēng

翁 wēng ❶ old man：富～ rich old man; wealthy old man /渔～ old fisherman /白发谁家～媪？Who can they be, that elderly couple with whitening hair? ❷ father：乃～ your father /尊～ your father ❸ husband's father; (woman's) father-in-law: *see* "～姑" ❹ wife's father: *see* "～婿" ❺ (Wēng) a surname

翁姑 wēng-gū 〈书面〉husband's parents; woman's parents-in-law

翁茸 wēngróng 〈书面〉(of plants) luxuriant; exuberant; flourishing

翁婿 wēng-xù father-in-law and son-in-law：～相处融洽。He and his son-in-law got on very well.

翁仲 wēngzhòng carved stone or bronze figure; engraved stone figure (usu. in front of a tomb)

鞥 wēng 〈方言〉boot leg

鞥靴 wēngxuē cotton padded high boots

嗡 wēng 〈象声〉buzz; hum; drone：蚊子老是在耳边～叫。Mosquitoes were buzzing around my ears. /他说话～～的，听众都快睡着了。He droned on, almost putting the audience to sleep. /我走进大厅时，就听见人们～～的交谈声。When I walked into the hall, I found a crowd buzzing with conversation.

嗡子 wēngzi *also* "京二胡" jīng'èrhú Beijing opera fiddle whose timber ranges between those of *jinghu* and *erhu*

鹟 wēng 〈动物〉flycatcher

鳉 wēng 〈动物〉a kind of sea fish (*Cirrhitus pinnulatus*)

wěng

滃 wěng 〈书面〉❶ (of water or spring) gush：清泉～然涌出。The clear spring gushed. ❷ (of clouds) rise：黑云～起。Dark clouds emerged.

塕 wěng 〈方言〉❶ with dust blown about; dusty ❷ dust

蓊 wěng 〈书面〉(of vegetation) lush; luxuriant

蓊勃 wěngbó 〈书面〉vigorous; exuberant：香气～ full of fragrance; exuberating rich perfume

蓊郁 wěngyù 〈书面〉lush and green; luxuriant：～苍翠的竹林 lush and green bamboo grove /松柏～于山峰。Pines and cypresses grew luxuriantly on the mountain-top. /荷塘四周，长着许多树，蓊蓊郁郁的。The lotus pond is surrounded by lush green trees.

wèng

蕹 wèng

蕹菜 wèngcài *also* "空心菜" kōngxīncài water spinach

瓮(甕、❶罋) wèng ❶ earthen jar：酒～ wine jar /泡菜～ jar for pickling vegetables; pickle jar ❷ (Wèng) a surname

瓮城 wèngchéng small town or citadel outside a city gate, reinforcing the defence of the city; enceinte of a city gate

瓮棺 wèngguān funeral urn

瓮声瓮气 wèngshēng-wèngqì in a low muffled voice：这汉子说话～的。The chap speaks in a low, muffled voice.

瓮中之鳖 wèngzhōngzhībiē turtle in a jar — caught in a trap; bottled up：猎人们逐渐缩小包围圈，恶狼成了～。The hunters slowly tightened the ring of encirclement and the ferocious wolf was like a rat in a trap (*or* a turtle in a jug).

瓮中捉鳖 wèngzhōng-zhuōbiē catch a turtle in a jar — go after an easy prey; be sure of success; be a walkover：敌人与主力的联系被切断，我军～之势已成。As the enemy have been cut off from the main part of their army, we will have them netted in no time.

齆 wèng

齆鼻儿 wèngbír ❶ speak with a twang due to a stuffy nose ❷ person who speaks with a twang

wō

挝(撾) wō *see* "老挝" Lǎowō

see also zhuā

涡(渦) wō whirlpool; maelstrom; eddy：旋～ eddies of water; vortex

涡场 wōchǎng 〈物理〉vortex field; vorticity field

涡虫 wōchóng 〈动物〉turbellarian worm; turbellarian

涡电流 wōdiànliú *see* "涡流❸"

涡动 wōdòng 〈气象〉eddy turbulence; vortex or whirling motion：～速度 eddy velocity

涡核 wōhé 〈物理〉vortex core

涡流 wōliú ❶ *also* "旋流" xuánliú circular movement of a fluid; whirling of a fluid; eddy ❷ whirlpool; vortex; eddy ❸ *also* "涡电流" 〈物理〉eddy current; vortex flow

涡轮 wōlún turbine

涡轮泵 wōlúnbèng turbopump

涡轮发电机 wōlún fādiànjī turbogenerator

涡轮机 wōlúnjī *also* "透平机" tòupíngjī turbine：航空～ aviation turbine

涡轮螺旋浆发动机 wōlún luóxuánjiǎng fādòngjī turboprop

涡轮喷气发动机 wōlún pēnqì fādòngjī turbojet

涡轮叶片 wōlún yèpiàn turbine blade

涡轮增压器 wōlún zēngyāqì 〈机械〉turbocharger; turbosupercharger

涡轮轴 wōlúnzhóu turboshaft

涡轮钻 wōlúnzuàn 〈石油〉turbodrill

涡扇发动机 wōshàn fādòngjī 〈航空〉fanjet; turbofan

涡旋 wōxuán whirlpool; vortex; eddy：河流拐弯的地方有～，小心别被卷进去。The river has whirlpools at the bend; take care not to be drawn into them.

窝(窩) wō ❶ nest：鸟～ bird's nest /蚂蚁～ ant's nest /蜜蜂～ honeycomb /马蜂～ hornet's nest /狗～ kennel / 鸡～ hencoop; roost ❷ lair; den; haunt：匪～ bandits' lair /贼～ thieves' den ❸ 〈方言〉place or space occupied：他站在那儿半天不动～儿。He stood there for a long time without budging. /这自行车挡道儿，给它挪挪～儿。This bicycle is in the way; let's move it away. ❹ hollow part of the human body or a place; pit：心～儿 pit of the stomach /山～儿 mountain hollow /眼～儿 eye socket /酒～儿 dimple ❺ harbour; shelter; shield: *see* "～藏" ❻ huddle up; curl up; stay still：把头～在衣领里 bury one's head in the collar /～在屋里生闷气 be in the sulks behind closed doors ❼ hold in; check：心里有火，可不能总～着。One must not bottle up one's anger for too long. ❽ bend：用铁丝～个衣架。Bend the wire into a coat hanger. /别把照片～了。Don't bend (*or* crease) the photo. ❾ 〈量词〉litter; brood：一～下了四只猫 bear four kittens at a litter /一～小鸭 a brood of ducklings

窝瘪 wōbiě sunken; hollow：～的两腮 hollow cheeks /脸上窝窝瘪瘪 shrivelled (*or* wizened) face

窝憋 wōbie 〈方言〉❶ unhappy; worried：事情好久未能处理，心里老觉得～得慌。I cannot help feeling exasperated, as the matter has remained unsettled for so long. ❷ be cooped up：整个冬天我都～在小屋里。I was cooped up in my tiny room all winter. /她一天到晚不得不～在家，无聊透了。She was bored stiff having to stay at home all day long. ❸ lacking in space; cramped：这间屋子太～。This room is too cramped.

窝脖儿 wōbór 〈方言〉❶ 〈旧语〉porter; carrier：本行是～ be a porter by occupation ❷ *also* "窝脖子" rebuff; snub：他会上吃了个～。He was rebuffed at the meeting.

窝藏 wōcáng conceal; harbour; shelter：～逃犯 shelter escaped convicts /～赃物 harbour stolen goods /～枪支 conceal firearms

窝巢 wōcháo ❶ nest; lair; den：捣毁鸟的～跟射杀鸟类同样犯法。Destroying birds' nests, like shooting the birds, is against the law.

W

❷ (as of bandits) lair; den; haunt:攻占敌人～ storm and capture the enemy's lair

窝点 wōdiǎn lair; den; hideout:贩毒～ hideout of drug-traffickers

窝匪 wōfěi give shelter to a bandit:有人告他～。He was charged with giving shelter to bandits.

窝风 wōfēng lacking fresh air; stuffy:这个院子四周都是高层建筑,很～。Surrounded by tall buildings, the courtyard is all blocked up and stuffy.

窝工 wōgōng enforced idleness (due to poor organization of work); hold-up in the work:～时间 downtime /窝了半天工。Work was held up for half a day as a result of poor organization.

窝弓 wōgōng trap crossbow (for shooting big game)

窝火 wōhuǒ simmering with rage; forced to bottle up one's anger:你说～不～? Isn't this vexing? *or* Isn't it upsetting?

窝集 wōjí 〈方言〉 woody marshland

窝家 wōjiā *also* "窝主" person who harbours criminals, loot or contraband goods; fence

窝眍眼 wōkōuyǎn 〈方言〉 sunken eyes

窝里斗 wōlidòu *also* "窝儿里斗"〈口语〉 internecine strife; infighting:两位厂长就热中于～。The two directors of the plant are keen on nothing but infighting.

窝里反 wōlifǎn *also* "窝儿里反"〈口语〉 (as within a clan or clique) internal strife; domestic conflict; infighting:战斗还没打响,敌人先～了。The enemy started fighting among themselves before we launched the attack.

窝里横 wōlihèng *also* "窝儿里横"〈方言〉 rude and arbitrary at home only:这小子是个～,一出去就成熊包。The man is a lord at home but a chicken outside.

窝囊 wōnang ❶ helpless vexation or annoyance:心里实在～ feel helplessly vexed (*or* exasperated) /何必在这儿受这份～气! I (*or* You) don't have to stay here just to be annoyed. /这事让人～! What a botched job! ❷ weak and cowardly; good-for-nothing; hopelessly stupid:怎么就不敢说呢,你可真～! Why were you afraid to say so? What a weakling you are!

窝囊废 wōnangfèi 〈方言〉 good-for-nothing; worthless wretch; cowardly weakling:他是一棍子打不出屁来的～! He is an out and out good-for-nothing!

窝盘 wōpán (often used in the early vernacular) win sb. over by fair means or foul:你想想吧,要是天长日久,叫他把你～住了,什么底儿不掏给他? Just think it over. If he gets hold of you with the passage of time, he'll twist you round his little finger.

窝棚 wōpeng shack; shed; shanty:临时搭起的～ makeshift sheds

窝铺 wōpù shed for sleeping

窝气 wōqì simmering rage; pent-up anger:他窝着一肚子气。He was simmering with rage. /又冷又饿,一进家门就挨老婆一顿臭骂,心中更加～。Cold and hungry, he came back home, only to get a dressing-down from his wife, which aggravated his pent-up rage.

窝缩 wōsuō crouch; huddle up; curl up:她在冰冷黑暗的墙角里～着,混身发抖。She crouched in an icy dark corner, trembling all over.

窝头 wōtóu *also* "窝窝头" steamed bread of coarse grain; corn bun

窝窝 wōwo 〈方言〉 ❶ steamed bread of coarse grain; corn bun:艾～ steamed sticky rice bun with sweet filling ❷ small and shallow pit; hollow:泥～ small mud puddle

窝心 wōxīn 〈方言〉 depressed; dejected; feeling low after being wronged or offended:喝了两杯～酒 gulp down two cups of wine in a very bad mood /那件事想起来就～。I have a gnawing pain whenever I think of the incident.

窝心气 wōxīnqì bottled-up anger; pent-up rage:我受不了这个～。I cannot get over this bottled-up rage. *or* My pent-up rage threatens to explode.

窝赃 wōzāng harbour or transfer loot or contraband goods:她犯了～罪。She committed the offence of harbouring loot.

窝种 wōzhǒng 〈方言〉 artificial incubation (of silkworm eggs):村民们开始～了。The villagers began the silkworm incubation.

窝主 wōzhǔ *see* "窝家"

窝子 wōzi ❶〈方言〉 place; space:老在一个地方坐～,真没意思! It's rather depressing having to stay put in the same old place! ❷ dibbling hole; hole for dibbling:点播的～要事先挖好。Holes should be prepared in advance for dibbling. ❸〈方言〉 hut; shanty:土坯～ adobe hut

莴(萵) wō

莴苣 wōjù lettuce

莴笋 wōsǔn asparagus lettuce

蜗(蝸) wō snail

蜗杆 wōgǎn 〈机械〉 worm:双头～ double-thread worm /分度～ indexing worm /～轴 worm shaft /～传动 worm drive

蜗居 wōjū 〈书面〉 ❶ humble abode:他就栖身在这几平方米的～里。He lives in this humble abode of just a few square metres. ❷ live in a small place:～斗室 confine oneself to a small room /那时我们全家～在一间小小的阁楼里。My whole family then had to live in a small attic.

蜗轮 wōlún 〈机械〉 worm gear; worm wheel; snail wheel

蜗牛 wōniú snail

蜗行牛步 wōxíng-niúbù 〈比喻〉 move like a snail or an ox — at a snail's pace; snail-paced:这样～,何年才能搞完! If we continue to work at such a snail's pace, when shall we finish it!

蜗旋 wōxuán wind; spiral:塔内壁有石阶,～而上。There is a staircase winding up the pagoda inside.

倭 Wō 〈旧语〉 Japan

倭瓜 wōguā 〈方言〉 pumpkin; cushaw

倭寇 Wōkòu 〈历史〉 Japanese pirates (operating in Chinese coastal waters from the 14th century to the 16th century)

踒 wō sprain; strain:～了脚脖子 sprain one's ankle /钢笔尖～了。The nib of the pen is bent.

喔 wō 〈象声〉 cock's crow:雄鸡～～叫。The cock is crowing. Cock-a-doodle-doo!

wǒ

髮 wǒ

髮髯 wǒtuǒ 〈书面〉 (of a woman's hair-coil) pretty

我 wǒ 〈代词〉 ❶ I; me; my:～有～的爱好。I have my own interest. /～见犹怜。(said of a beautiful woman by another woman) Even I cannot help loving her upon seeing her. ❷ we; us; our:～校 our school /敌～矛盾 contradiction between ourselves and the enemy /亡～之心 design (*or* intention) to subjugate our country ❸ (used with 你) one; people:大家你一言～一语地说开了。With everyone joining in, people started talking among themselves. /这几个人你让～,～让你,让个没完。These people each kept declining and offering it to the other. /这样你来～往互相报复,疙瘩越结越大。Hatred deepens as they keep returning revenge for revenge. ❹ self:忘～劳动 work selflessly /依然故～ be one's old self; remain unchanged

我辈 wǒbèi we; us:～青年当奋发有为。We young people should work hard and aim high.

我见 wǒjiàn my view or opinion; my personal view:计划经济之～ my views on the centrally-planned economy

我们 wǒmen ❶ we; us; our:～两国人民 people of our two countries; our two peoples /～俩都去了。We both went. /让～干吧。Let us get down to work. ❷〈口语〉 I; me; my:～那口子 my wife (*or* husband) /你这么不讲道理,让～怎么办? What can I possibly do about it since you are so unreasonable? ❸ *used to mean those addressed*:老师对学生说:"你要记住,～是学生,～的主要任务是学习。" The teacher told her students: "You must remember that you are students, and your principal task is study."

我行我素 wǒxíng-wǒsù do whatever one pleases; go one's own way no matter what others may say:任凭我怎么劝说,她半句也听不进,始终～。No matter how I tried to bring her around, she just wouldn't listen but did whatever she pleased.

我字当头 wǒzì-dāngtóu me-first mentality

wò

涴 wò 〈方言〉 stain; make dirty

沃 wò ❶ irrigate; pour (water):如汤～雪 like melting snow with hot water — easy task ❷ (of soil) fertile; rich:肥田～地 fertile land; rich land ❸ (Wò) a surname
沃尔沃汽车公司 Wò'ěrwò Qìchē Gōngsī *Volvo Aktiebolaget*, Swedish car manufacturer
沃壤 wòrǎng rich soil
沃饶 wòráo rich and abundant:～的土地 rich and fertile land
沃土 wòtǔ fertile land
沃衍 wòyǎn 〈书面〉(of land) level and fertile
沃野 wòyě rich fields:～千里 vast (*or* unbounded) rich fields; vast expanse of fertile land

斡 wò 〈书面〉revolve; gyrate; rotate
斡旋 wòxuán mediate; use one's good offices:～争端 mediate a dispute /居中～ mediate between the two sides (*or* parties) /由于他的～,我们在这个问题上达成了协议。With his good offices (*or* Thanks to his mediation), we reached agreement on this matter.

卧(臥) wò ❶ lie:仰～ lie on one's back /～不安席 have no peace of mind; be distracted ❷〈方言〉get babies to lie down:把小孩儿～在炕上 let the baby lie on the *kang* ❸ (of animals or birds) crouch; sit:鸡～在窝里。The chickens were in the coop. /猫～在炉子旁边。The cat was sitting beside the stove. ❹ for sleeping in: *see* "～房"; "～铺" ❺ sleeping berth:硬～ hard berth; hard sleeper /软～ soft berth; soft sleeper ❻〈方言〉poach (eggs):～两个鸡子儿 poach two eggs
卧病 wòbìng be confined to bed; be bedridden:～在床 be ill in bed; be laid up in bed; be bedridden
卧舱 wòcāng sleeping cabin
卧车 wòchē ❶ sleeping car; sleeping carriage; sleeper ❷ automobile; auto; car; sedan
卧床 wòchuáng ❶〈方言〉bed ❷ lie in bed:～不起 be very ill; be critically ill /～休息 bed rest /医生嘱咐每天饭后至少～半个小时。The doctor asked him to lie in bed for half an hour at least after each meal.
卧倒 wòdǎo drop to the ground; take a prone position:～! (word of command) Lie down! *or* Hit the ground!
卧底 wòdǐ 〈方言〉serve as a planted agent:先派两个人去～。Have two agents planted there first.
卧冬 wòdōng ❶ (of a boat, ship, etc.) anchor for winter:～期长达六个月。The ships' winter anchoring is as long as six months. ❷〈方言〉〈旧语〉(of a peasant) do odd jobs in town during slack winter season
卧房 wòfáng *see* "卧室"
卧佛 wòfó reclining Buddha:～寺 Temple of Reclining Buddha (in Beijing)
卧轨 wòguǐ lie on the rails (to stop the train or commit suicide):～自杀 commit suicide by lying on the rails /～抗议 (of demonstrators) lie on the rails in protest
卧柜 wòguì 〈方言〉horizontal cabinet or chest; lowboy.
卧果儿 wòguǒr 〈方言〉❶ poach an egg ❷ poached egg:吃俩～ have two poached eggs
卧具 wòjù bedding
卧龙 wòlóng reclining dragon — person of unusual talent living in seclusion
卧龙自然保护区 Wòlóng Zìrán Bǎohùqū Wolong Reservation, about 200,000 square kilometres in Sichuan Province for protecting pandas and other rare species
卧铺 wòpù sleeping berth; sleeper:坐～ travel on a sleeper; take a sleeper
卧射 wòshè 〈军事〉prone fire
卧式 wòshì 〈机械〉horizontal:～发动机 horizontal engine /～镗床 horizontal boring machine /～锅炉 horizontal boiler /～吹炉〈冶金〉barrel converter
卧室 wòshì *also* "卧房" bedroom:里间是～。The inside one is the bedroom.
卧榻 wòtà 〈书面〉bed:～之侧,岂容他人鼾睡。How can one put up with people snoring at one's bedside? — No one would tolerate others encroaching on one's own preserve.
卧薪尝胆 wòxīn-chángdǎn sleep on firewood and taste gall — endure self-imposed hardships (to strengthen one's resolve to achieve some ambition or to avenge a national humiliation):～,奋发图强 be resolved to undergo all possible hardships in an effort to make one's country strong /他给我讲了～的故事。He told me the story of the defeated Prince of Yue (越) who slept on firewood and frequently tasted gall to remind himself of his humiliation and steel his determination to avenge it.
卧椅 wòyǐ 〈方言〉deck chair; sling chair
卧游 wòyóu 〈书面〉read interesting and graphic travels; look at such pictures (*or* documentaries)
卧甑 wòzèng 〈冶金〉horizontal retort:～式炼锌法 horizontal retort process
卧姿 wòzī 〈体育〉prone position

硪 wò flat stone or iron rammer with ropes attached at the sides:打～ tamp (*or* pound) with such a rammer

肟 wò 〈化学〉oxime

渥 wò 〈书面〉❶ wet; moisten ❷ deep; profound:～恩 great kindness
渥太华 Wòtàihuá Ottawa, capital of Canada

握 wò ❶ take in one's hand; hold; grasp:～紧拳头 clench one's fist /～着方向盘 hold the steering wheel; sit behind the steering wheel ❷ have; possess:手～大权 wield great power
握把 wòbà 〈方言〉handle
握别 wòbié part with a handshake:他们在入口处～。They parted with a handshake at the check-point.
握管 wòguǎn 〈书面〉set pen to paper; write:～疾书 take up one's pen (*or* writing brush) and write vigorously
握力 wòlì gripping power; grip
握力器 wòlìqì 〈体育〉spring-grip dumb-bell
握拳 wòquán make a fist; clench one's fist:～透爪 clench one's fist with fury
握蛇骑虎 wòshé-qíhǔ hold a snake and ride a tiger — be in a very precarious situation
握手 wòshǒu shake hands; clasp hands:与贵宾～ shake hands with the guest of honour /他俩默默地～告别了。The two of them held each other by the hand and then parted in silence.
握手言欢 wòshǒu-yánhuān have a congenial handshake; chat cheerfully after making up a quarrel; patch up a quarrel and be friends again; bury the hatchet

龌 wò
龌龊 wòchuò ❶ unclean; dirty; filthy:～的水池 dirty pond /满口～话 full of dirty language; foul-mouthed ❷ base; sordid:卑鄙～ mean and sordid /他这种～的行为受到公众普遍谴责。He was universally denounced for his base, shameful behaviour. ❸ narrow-minded; petty

幄 wò 〈书面〉tent:帷～ army tent

wū

於 wū 〈书面〉〈叹词〉sigh
see also Yū
於乎 wūhū *also* "呜呼" wūhū alas
於戏 wūhū *also* "呜呼" wūhū alas
於菟 wūtú 〈古语〉tiger

污(汙、汚) wū ❶ dirt; muck; filth:粪～ dung /去～粉 cleanser /藏垢纳～〈比喻〉shelter evil people and evil deeds ❷ dirty; filthy; foul:～水 dirty water /～名 bad name ❸ corrupt; dishonest:贪～ corruption; graft ❹ defile; vilify; smear:玷～ stain; sully; tarnish /奸～ rape; violate
污点 wūdiǎn ❶ stain; spot:他西服上沾了～。He got stains on his suit. /镜子上有～。There are spots on the mirror. ❷ blemish; defect; smirch:历史～ blemish in one's record
污毒 wūdú dirty and injurious to health; noxious; rotten:这些是要

W

倾倒的～食物。This rotten food is to be thrown away.
污垢 wūgòu dirt; filth:洗去～ wash off the filth /这个锅底有一层～。The bottom of the pot is covered with a layer of dirt.
污痕 wūhén stain; smear; smudge: ～累累 have countless smudges; have a long bad record
污秽 wūhuì 〈书面〉❶ dirty; filthy; foul: ～的现象 unhealthy phenomenon /环境～。The surroundings are filthy. /语言～,不堪入耳。The language was dirty and coarse and unbearably offensive to the ear. ❷ dirt; filth:洗刷掉旧时留下的～ wash away the filth left over from old times
污迹 wūjì stain; smear; smudge:去掉衣服上的～ get the stain off one's clothes /他以为一生清白,没有～。He thinks he is a man of impeccable (*or* spotless) character.
污吏 wūlì corrupt official; dishonest official
污蔑 wūmiè ❶ vilify; smear; slander:竭尽～之能事 stop at nothing in spreading lies and slanders ❷ stain; sully; tarnish:他并非坏人,可是别人却百般～他。He is not a bad sort, but people are deliberately trying to sling mud at him (*or* tarnish his name) in every way.
污泥 wūní mud; mire; sludge:荷花出于～而不染。Though rooted in mire, the lotus emerges unstained from the filth.
污泥浊水 wūní-zhuóshuǐ mud and sludge; filth and mire:滚滚洪流,洗刷乾坤,涤荡着～。The torrential waters surged forward washing away the sludge and filth off the earth.
污七八糟 wūqībāzāo *see* "乌七八糟" wūqībāzāo
污染 wūrǎn pollute; contaminate: 环境～ environmental pollution /空气～ air pollution /水～ water contamination /大气层～ atmospheric pollution /放射性～ radioactive contamination /飘尘～ floating dust pollution; airborne dust pollution /噪音～ noise pollution /工业粉尘～ industrial dust pollution /精神～ spiritual pollution; idealogical contamination /～社会风气 debase social morals /～地带 contaminated zone /防治～ prevention of pollution /水源已被放射性物质～。The water has been contaminated by radioactive material. /有毒的工业废料已经把这条河～了。The river has been defiled by toxic industrial waste.
污染报警系统 wūrǎn bàojǐng xìtǒng pollution warning system
污染计数计 wūrǎn jìshùjì contamination counter
污染气象学 wūrǎn qìxiàngxué (air) pollution meteorology
污染生物学 wūrǎn shēngwùxué pollution biology
污染物 wūrǎnwù pollutant; contaminant
污染源 wūrǎnyuán source of pollution
污染指示生物 wūrǎn zhǐshì shēngwù pollution indicating organism
污辱 wūrǔ ❶ humiliate; affront; insult:这句话是对知识分子的～。This remark is an insult to the intellectuals. ❷ sully; tarnish: ～他的名声 sully sb. reputation (*or* good name)
污水 wūshuǐ foul or polluted water; waste water; sewage; slops: ～坑 puddle of foul water /生活～ domestic sewage /工业～ industrial sewage /～管道 sewage conduit; sewer line
污水车 wūshuǐchē cesspit emptier; cesspool emptier tank; cesspoolage truck
污水处理 wūshuǐ chǔlǐ sewage disposal; sewage treatment: ～厂 sewage treatment plant
污水灌溉 wūshuǐ guàngài sewage irrigation
污水净化 wūshuǐ jìnghuà sewage purification
污损 wūsǔn smear and damage; vandalize: ～名胜古迹是犯罪行为。Vandalism at scenic spots and historical sites is a criminal act.
污浊 wūzhuó ❶ (of air, water, etc.) dirty; muddy; filthy:空气～ foul air /一潭～不堪的死水 puddle of filthy stagnant water ❷ dirt; filth:把地上的这些～扫除掉。Sweep away all this filth off the floor.
污渍 wūzì stain; smear

洿

wū 〈书面〉❶ low-lying land: ～池 low-lying pond ❷ dig a pond or a pool

圬(杇)

wū 〈书面〉❶ trowel used by a bricklayer ❷ plaster a wall:粪土之墙,不可～也。A dirt wall cannot be whitewashed.
圬工 wūgōng 〈旧语〉bricklaying; plastering; tiling

恶(惡)

wū 〈书面〉❶ *see* "乌²" wū ❷ 〈叹词〉*used to indicate surprise*: ～,是何言也! Oh! What a remark is this?
see also ě; è; wù

巫

wū ❶ shaman; witch; wizard:女～ witch /在阴谋策划方面,他与哥哥比真是小～见大～。In scheming behind the scenes, he is a dwarf compared with his elder brother who is a real giant. ❷ (Wū) a surname
巫婆 wūpó witch; sorceress
巫神 wūshén wizard; sorcerer
巫师 wūshī *also* "巫士" wizard; sorcerer
巫术 wūshù witchcraft; sorcery:伏都～ voodooism
巫统 Wūtǒng UMNO (short for United Malays National Organization, ruling party of Malaysia)
巫医 wūyī witch doctor

诬

wū accuse falsely; slander: ～良为盗 accuse innocent people of stealing; falsely charge people with robbery /辩～ defend sb. (*or* oneself) against a false charge /反～ make a false countercharge; accuse falsely (instead of admitting one's error)
诬谤 wūbàng slander; vilify; smear
诬告 wūgào falsely accuse; bring a false charge against; trump up a charge against: ～案件 trumped-up case; frame-up /～无辜是犯罪行为。It is a criminal act to bring a false charge against innocent people.
诬告罪 wūgàozuì 〈法律〉crime of false charge
诬害 wūhài injure by spreading false reports about; calumniate; frame: ～好人 calumniate good people; bring false charges against innocent people
诬控 wūkòng falsely charge; lodge a false accusation against; trump up a charge against
诬赖 wūlài falsely incriminate or accuse:你别～人! Don't you incriminate me!
诬蔑 wūmiè slander; defame; malign; smear:造谣～ spread rumours in order to vilify; spread calumny and slanders /事实揭穿了他们的～。Facts have given the lie to their rumour mongering.
诬枉 wūwǎng slander and do wrong to:这是对无辜者的～。This is slandering the innocent and treating them most unjustly.
诬陷 wūxiàn produce false evidence against; frame a case against; frame (up):受到莫须有的～和迫害 be framed and persecuted /推倒一切～不实之词 repudiate all the slander and libel that have been heaped on sb.
诬栽 wūzāi incriminate sb. with false evidence:把自己的罪行都～到别人身上 shift one's crime onto others; bring charges against sb. when one is guilty oneself
诬指 wūzhǐ trump up a charge against; invent or make up a story against

兀

wū
see also wù
兀秃 wūtu *see* "乌涂" wūtu

乌¹(烏)

wū ❶ crow: 月落～啼。The crows cawed when the moon went down. /爱屋及～ love of a house extends to love of the crows on its roof — when you love a person you love everything about him; love me, love my dog ❷ black; dark: ～发 glossy black hair ❸ (Wū) a surname

乌²(烏)

wū 〈书面〉(often used in a rhetorical question) what; how: ～能苟活? How can I live on in degradation?
see also wù
乌暗 wū'àn dark:天空布满～的浓云。The sky was full of dark clouds. *or* The sky was overcast.
乌鲳 wūchāng 〈动物〉black pomfret
乌沉沉 wūchénchén dark; black: ～的烟雾 black smog
乌灯黑火 wūdēng-hēihuǒ dark; unlit:村子里～,四周静悄悄的。Not a house was lit in the village; it was silent and still all around.
乌洞洞 wūdòngdōng pitch-dark:山野里～的,什么也看不见。One could see nothing in the pitch-dark hills.
乌尔都语 Wū'ěrdūyǔ Urdu
乌饭树 wūfànshù oriental blueberry (*Vaccinium bracteatum*)
乌飞兔走 wūfēi-tùzǒu rotation of the sun and the moon — swift

W

passage of time:天上~，人间古往今来。While the sun and the moon shuttle across the sky, time goes by eternally on earth.
乌干达 Wūgāndá Uganda:~人 Ugandan
乌骨鸡 wūgǔjī black-boned chicken
乌龟 wūguī ❶ tortoise:~壳 tortoise shell ❷ cuckold
乌龟壳 wūguīké 〈比喻〉〈贬义〉❶ pill-box (of the enemy):敌人缩进了~。The enemy withdrew into their pill-boxes. ❷ (enemy) tank:敌人坐着~，不断向我方开炮。The enemy tanks kept firing at our positions.
乌合之众 wūhézhīzhòng sheep without a shepherd — disorderly or motley crowd; rabble; mob:他们是一群~，不堪一击。Sheep without a shepherd, they can hardly withstand a single assault.
乌黑 wūhēi pitch-black; jet-black:~的辫子 jet-black braids /眼前一片~。It was pitch-dark all around. /脸晒得~。His face was very much tanned.
乌红 wūhóng dark red
乌呼 wūhū *also* "呜呼" wūhū alas
乌金 wūjīn ❶ coal ❷〈中药〉(Chinese) ink
乌金釉 wūjīnyòu *wujin* glaze; black bronze glaze
乌桕 wūjiù 〈植物〉Chinese tallow tree
乌克兰 Wūkèlán Ukraine:~人 Ukrainian /~语 Ukrainian (language)
乌拉 wūlā *also* "乌喇" ❶ corvée labour formerly imposed on serfs in Tibet ❷ *wula* labourer
see also wùla
乌拉尔 Wūlā'ěr Ural:~山脉 Ural Mountains; the Urals
乌拉圭 Wūlāguī Uruguay:~人 Uruguayan
乌拉圭回合 Wūlāguī Huíhé Uruguay Round (eighth and longest round of talks on the General Agreement on Tariffs and Trade, or GATT, lasting on and off from Sept. 1986 to Oct. 1994 with the first session held in Uruguay and finally leading to the establishment of WTO on 1 Jan. 1995 to replace GATT)
乌兰巴托 Wūlánbātuō Ulan Bator, capital of Mongolia
乌兰浩特 Wūlánhàotè Ulan Hot, city in Inner Mongolia
乌兰牧骑 wūlánmùqí mobile Inner Mongolian performing troupe (moving around on horseback)
乌蓝 wūlán dark blue:~的天空，闪着几颗星星。There are a few stars twinkling in the dark blue sky.
乌榄 wūlǎn 〈植物〉Chinese black olive (*Canarium pimela*)
乌鳢 wūlǐ *also* "乌鱼"; "黑鱼" hēiyú 〈动物〉snakehead; snakeheaded fish
乌亮 wūliàng glossy black; jet-black:把皮鞋擦得~ polish the black leather shoes till they shine /油井喷出~的石油。Glossy darkish petroleum gushed out of the oil well.
乌溜溜 wūliūliū (of eyes) dark and liquid:~的一双大眼睛 sparkling, big black eyes
乌龙茶 wūlóngchá oolong tea:听装~在日本很时髦。Tinned oolong tea is very popular in Japan.
乌鲁木齐 Wūlǔmùqí Ürümqi, capital of the Xinjiang Uygur Autonomous Region
乌梅 wūméi *also* "酸梅" suānméi smoked plum; dark plum:~丸〈中药〉dark plum pill
乌霉 wūmei *also* "乌米"〈方言〉〈农业〉smutted crop (sorghum, maize, wheat, etc.)
乌木 wūmù 〈植物〉❶ ebony ❷ dark heavy wood
乌娘 wūniáng 〈方言〉newly hatched silkworms
乌鸟私情 wūniǎo-sīqíng *also* "乌鸟反哺" legend has it that a young crow feeds the old — filial piety:~，愿乞终养。I beg your Majesty to allow me to retire and take care of my grandmother for the remainder of her life.
乌篷船 wūpéngchuán dark-awninged boat
乌七八糟 wūqībāzāo *also* "污七八糟" wūqībāzāo ❶ in a horrible mess; in great disorder; all in a jumble:满屋子都是~的东西。The room is in a terrible clutter. ❷ obscene; dirty; salacious:这本书的内容~。The book is atrociously obscene in content.
乌漆墨黑 wūqī-mòhēi pitch-dark; pitch-black:洞里~，伸手不见五指。It was pitch-dark in the cave and you couldn't see your own hand before you.
乌青 wūqīng dark blue:她嘴唇冻得~。Her lips were blue with cold.
乌纱帽 wūshāmào ❶ black gauze hat (worn by an imperial official to indicate his position) ❷〈比喻〉official post:眼看着保不住自己的~了 be on the verge of losing one's official post
乌苏里江 Wūsūlǐjiāng Wusuli River (major tributary of Heilongjiang River)
乌头 wūtóu 〈中药〉rhizome of Chinese monkshood (*Aconitum carmichaeli*)
乌涂 wūtu *also* "兀秃" wūtu ❶ (of drinking water) warm; lukewarm:~水不好喝。Lukewarm drinking water is unpalatable. ❷ sluggish; hesitant; indecisive:他办事太~。He is always tardy in getting anything done.
乌托邦 wūtuōbāng Utopia:~的理想 Utopian ideal (*or* dream) /这个计划是个~，根本实现不了。The plan is based on a utopian fancy, which is hardly realizable.
乌压压 wūyāyā dense or dark mass:朝前方看去，只见~一片人头攒动。In the distance was a dark mass of human sea.
乌鸦 wūyā crow:天下~一般黑。Crows are black the world over. *or* In every country dogs bite. *or* Evil people are equally bad everywhere in the world
乌烟瘴气 wūyān-zhàngqì foul atmosphere; pestilential atmosphere:这帮人又喝酒，又猜拳，闹得满屋子~。Drinking and finger-guessing, these people turned the room into a living hell.
乌药 wūyào 〈中药〉root of three-nerved spicebush (*Lindera strychnifolia*)
乌油油 wūyōuyōu shining black:~的辫子 shining black ponytail /泥土~的，十分肥沃。Shiny and black, the soil is very fertile.
乌有 wūyǒu 〈书面〉nothing; naught; fiction:化为~ come to nothing (*or* naught) /子虚~ made-up story; story made out of thin air /~先生 fictitious gentleman
乌鱼 wūyú *also* "乌鳢" snakehead; snakeheaded fish
乌鱼蛋 wūyúdàn egg gland of the cuttlefish, used as food:~汤 soup with cuttlefish egg glands
乌云 wūyún ❶ black cloud; dark cloud:满天~。The sky is covered with dark clouds. /~密布。Black clouds blotted out the sky. /他脸上好像忽然蒙上了一层~。His face suddenly clouded over. ❷〈比喻〉sinister situation:战争的~ dark clouds of war ❸〈比喻〉women's black hair
乌糟糟 wūzāozāo 〈方言〉❶ foul; filthy:~的天气 foul weather /~的马路 filthy road ❷ unpalatable:饭菜做得~的。The food is badly cooked. ❸ disorderly; messy:会开得~的，吵吵嚷嚷，乱成一团。The meeting was a mess; it was all noise but no order.
乌枣 wūzǎo smoked jujube; black jujube
乌贼 wūzéi *also* "乌鲗"; "墨鱼" mòyú; "墨斗鱼" mòdǒuyú 〈动物〉cuttlefish; inkfish
乌鲗 wūzéi *see* "乌贼"
乌珠 wūzhū 〈方言〉black pupil (of the eye)
乌孜别克斯坦 Wūzībiékèsītǎn Uzbekistan
乌孜别克族 Wūzībiékèzú Uzbek nationality, living in the Xinjiang Uygur Autonomous Region
乌紫 wūzǐ dark purple:~的桑葚 dark purple mulberry fruit /脸冻得~ one's face blue from cold

呜(嗚)

呜(嗚) wū 〈象声〉hoot; toot:雾中汽笛在~~叫。A horn hooted in the fog. /司机们等急了，把喇叭按得~~响。The drivers tooted their horns to show their impatience at the delay. /汽车~的一声疾驶过去了。The car sped past with a zoom.
呜呼 wūhū *also* "乌呼" wūhū ❶〈书面〉〈叹词〉alas; alack:~！此人之心何其毒也！Alas! What a venomous person he is! ❷ die:一命~ give up the ghost; kick the bucket
呜呼哀哉 wūhū-āizāi ❶〈旧语〉(used in an elegy) alas:~，伏维尚飨。(formula to end an elegy) Such being my sorrow, do rest in peace. ❷ be dead and gone; die:仔细一看，那人早已~了。On a closer look, I found the man stone dead. /老头得了癌症，隔不好久，就~，一命归阴了。The old man got cancer and not long afterwards, alas, he passed away.
呜噜 wūlū 〈象声〉utter indistinctly; mumble:~~地大哭起来 slobber indistinctly /谁也听不清他在~些什么。Nobody could make out what he was mumbling.
呜囔 wūnang speak indistinctly through a stuffy nose; mumble:他说话~得厉害。He was mumbling abominably.
呜咽 wūyè 〈书面〉❶ sob; whimper:她在悲伤地~。She was whimpering with grief. /他说不下去了，呜呜咽咽地哭了起来。He broke down and started sobbing. ❷ (of wind, stream, stringed instrument, etc.) mourn; wail; weep:风声~凄厉。The wind was

wailing.

钨(鎢) wū tungsten; wolfram (W):～合金 tungsten alloy /～锰矿 huebnerite

钨钒钢 wūfángāng Vasco steel

钨钢 wūgāng tungsten steel; wolfram steel

钨铬钢 wūgègāng tungstenchrome steel

钨极惰性气体保护焊 wūjí duòxìng qìtǐ bǎohùhàn (tungsten-inert-gas arc welding TIG)

钨砂 wūshā tungsten ore

钨丝 wūsī tungsten filament:～灯 tungsten lamp

钨酸 wūsuān tungstic acid:～盐 tungstate /～钙 calcium tungstate /～镁 magnesium tungstate /～钠 sodium tungstate; sodium wolframate

钨铁 wūtiě ferrotungsten:～矿 ferberite

钨氩管 wūyàguǎn tungar:～充电器 tungar charger

邬(鄔) Wū a surname

屋 wū ❶ house:房～ house; building; housing /草～ thatched house (*or* hut) ❷ room:堂～ central room (of a traditional Chinese house); middle room /里～ inner room /外～ outer room

屋场 wūchǎng 〈方言〉hamlet; village (usually with the inhabitants bearing one or a few surnames)

屋顶 wūdǐng roof; housetop:～毡 roofing felt /～板 roofing slate /大～ overhanging roof /曲线～ curved roof /扇形～ arched roof /四坡～ hipped (*or* hip) roof /人字～ gabled roof /平～ flat roof /螺旋式小园～ spiral cupola

屋顶花园 wūdǐng huāyuán roof garden

屋脊 wūjǐ ridge of a roof; roof:人称帕米尔高原为世界～。The Pamir Plateau is called the roof of the world.

屋架 wūjià roof truss

屋里人 wūlirén *also* "屋里的"〈方言〉wife; (the, his, your, etc.) missus:我屋里的不在家。The missus is not in. /他那个～可是个传话筒子。That good wife of his is a real gossip.

屋漏更遭连夜雨 wū lòu gèng zāo liányèyǔ 〈俗语〉like a leaky house exposed to a night-long pouring rain — misfortune never comes singly

屋面 wūmiàn 〈建筑〉roofing:瓦～ tile roofing /～板 roof boarding /钢筋混凝土～ reinforced concrete roofing

屋上架屋 wūshàng-jiàwū 〈比喻〉house over another house — redundant or overlapping organizations; unnecessary duplication

屋舍 wūshè house; building; cottage

屋头 wūtou 〈方言〉❶ house; building:昨天晚上他还到我～来过。He came to my house yesterday evening. ❷ room:请～坐。Come on in, please.

屋檐 wūyán eaves:～天线 eaves aerial

屋宇 wūyǔ 〈书面〉house; building:鼓乐齐鸣，声震～。Loud music and drumbeats reverberated throughout the house. /古寺傍山，～重重。An ancient temple stood at the foot of the mountain with houses clustered all around.

屋子 wūzi room:两间～ two rooms

wú

无(無) wú ❶ not have; be without; have nothing or nil:虚～ nihility; nothingness /从～到有 grow out of nothing; start from scratch /一～所有 have nothing at all; be penniless /～病而死 die without illness /有名～实 in name but not in reality; titular; nominal /家～隔宿之粮 live from hand to mouth /学～止境。There is no limit to learning. /全境陷入了～秩序的状态。Disorder reigned everywhere. /童叟～欺。Deal honestly with every customer, be he a child or an oldster. ❷ not; un-; a-; in-:～须重申 not necessary to reiterate /～足轻重 insignificant; of little consequence; negligible ❸ regardless of; irrespective of; no matter whether, what, etc.:国～大小，一律平等。All nations, big or small, are equal. ❹ do not; must not
see also mó

无碍 wú'ài not harm; not affect:～健康 do no harm to health; not be detrimental to health /～大局 not affect the situation as a whole /试试也～。There's no harm trying.

无伴奏 wúbànzòu without (instrumental) accompaniment; unaccompanied:～歌曲 unaccompanied song /～合唱 a cappella

无被花 wúbèihuā 〈植物〉flower without calyx; naked flower

无被选举权 wúbèixuǎnjǔquán *also* "无被选举资格"〈法律〉ineligibility (for election):不少国家有35岁以下公民～的法律规定。It is stipulated by law in quite a few countries that citizens under 35 are ineligible for election.

无比 wúbǐ incomparable; unparalleled; matchless; exceeding:威力～ unmatched in power; tremendously powerful /～幸福 height of happiness /～激动 extreme excitement /～优越 unparalleled (*or* incomparable) superiority

无边 wúbiān boundless; limitless; vast:～的荒野 boundless wilderness /宽大～ over-lenient /～落木萧萧下。Ceaselessly, rustling leaves are falling.

无边无际 wúbiān-wújì boundless; limitless; immense; vast:～的草原 boundless (*or* vast) expanse of grassland /白浪滔滔，～。Surging billows stretch as far as the eye can see. /闪电消失，一切又被～的黑暗吞没了。As soon as the flash of lightning vanished, the universe was lost once again in the limitless darkness.

无柄叶 wúbǐngyè 〈植物〉sessile leaf

无病呻吟 wúbìng-shēnyín moan and groan without being ill; pine and whine without cause:作者的感情真挚，决非装腔作势的～。It's a revelation of the author's true feelings and by no means an affected pose.

无补 wúbǔ *also* "无裨" of no help; of no avail:空言～。Empty talk is of no avail. /这个想法脱离实际，于事～。The idea is unpractical and will not help matters.

无补于事 wúbǔyúshì of no avail; to no (useful) purpose:不但～，反而会把事情搞糟。It won't do any good; on the contrary, it will make things even worse.

无不 wúbù without exception; invariably; all:～拍手称快。All without exception were overjoyed. /～为之惋惜。Everybody was sorry for him. /～表示愤慨。People were invariably indignant.

无猜 wúcāi innocent; unsuspecting:两小～ two innocent childhood playmates

无差别曲线 wúchābié qūxiàn 〈经济〉indifference curve

无差异市场 wúchāyì shìchǎng 〈商业〉undifferentiated marketing

无产阶级 wúchǎnjiējí proletariat:～国际主义 proletarian internationalism /流氓～ lumpen proletariat

无产阶级文化大革命 Wúchǎnjiējí Wénhuà Dàgémìng (shortened as 文化大革命 or 文革) Great Proletarian Cultural Revolution (1966-1976)

无产阶级专政 wúchǎnjiējí zhuānzhèng dictatorship of the proletariat; proletarian dictatorship

无产者 wúchǎnzhě proletarian:全世界～，联合起来! Workers of the world, unite!

无肠公子 wúcháng gōngzǐ 〈书面〉(nickname for 螃蟹) crab

无常 wúcháng ❶ variable; changeable; fickle:喜怒～ capricious; volatile /天气变化～。The weather is changeable (*or* unpredictable). ❷〈宗教〉impermanence:人生～ impermanence of life ❸〈迷信〉ghost supposed to come and take away a person's soul upon death:白～ White *Wuchang* /黑～ Black *Wuchang* ❹〈婉词〉pass away; die:一旦～ once one passes away

无偿 wúcháng free; gratis; gratuitous:提供～经济援助 render economic assistance gratis; give free economic aid /～调用 commandeer /～让与 voluntary conveyance /～劳动 work without remuneration; unpaid labour

无偿付能力 wú chángfù nénglì 〈经济〉insolvent:～的工厂 insolvent factory

无成 wúchéng unaccomplished; unfulfilled:一事～ nothing is accomplished /毕生～ achieve nothing all one's life; be a complete failure

无耻 wúchǐ shameless; brazen; brash; impudent:卑鄙～ base and shameless /～行径 impudent act /～吹捧 brazenly lavish praise on sb.

无耻之徒 wúchǐzhītú shameless person; person with no sense of shame

无耻之尤 wúchǐzhīyóu brazen in the extreme

无酬劳动 wúchóu láodòng 〈经济〉unpaid labour

无出其右 wúchūqíyòu be surpassed by no one; be second to none:文学巨匠，～ be a peerless literary master

无触点 wúchùdiǎn 〈机械〉contactless:～传感器 contactless pick-up /～控制龙门刨床 contactless controlled double housing planer

无从 wúcóng have no way (of doing sth.); be unable (to do sth.):～知晓 in no position to find out; impossible to know /～谈起 not know where to start /这句话的出处已～查考。There is no way of discovering the source of (*or* the chapter and verse for) this remark.

无大无小 wúdà-wúxiǎo ❶ *also* "无小无大" old and young:这项补助,～,人人有份。Everyone will get the subsidy, old and young. ❷ (of young people) fail to show proper respect for elders:这孩子在长辈面前～。The child didn't know how to behave properly towards elder people.

无担保债券 wúdānbǎo zhàiquàn 〈金融〉debenture (bond)

无党派人士 wúdǎngpài rénshì person without party affiliation; nonparty personage; Independent

无道 wúdào unprincipled; without morals:国君～,天下大乱。When a monach was a man without morals, the country would be in chaos.

无敌 wúdí unmatched; invincible; invulnerable; unconquerable:所向～ carry all before one in every battle; be always invincible /英勇～ valiant and ever-victorious /～于天下 unmatched anywhere in the world

无底洞 wúdǐdòng (often used as a metaphor) bottomless pit:填不满贪官的～。Corrupt officials' greed is like a bottomless pit that can never be filled up.

无地自容 wúdì-zìróng can find no place to hide oneself (for shame); wish that one could sink through the ground (for shame); look for a hole to crawl into; feel utterly ashamed:羞愧得～ feel too ashamed to show one's face /在这些大学者面前,他真感到～。He felt small in the company of such learned scholars.

无的放矢 wúdì-fàngshǐ shoot an arrow without a target; shoot at random; be totally irrelevant:～的空谈 irrelevant, idle talk /写文章不可～。When writing, one must have a clear purpose in mind. /有些同志却在搞"～",乱放一通,这样的人就容易把事情弄坏。Some comrades, however, are "shooting without a target", shooting at random, and such people are liable to harm our cause.

无调性 wúdiàoxìng 〈音乐〉atonality

无定形 wúdìngxíng shapeless; amorphous:～硫 amorphous sulphur /～泥炭 amorphous peat /～植物 amorphophyte /～碳 a-graphitic carbon

无定形体 wúdìngxíngtǐ 〈物理〉amorphous solid

无冬无夏 wúdōng-wúxià *also* "无冬历夏" be it winter or summer — all (the) year round; during the whole year; throughout the year:他有眼病,～总是戴着墨镜。He has eye trouble and wears dark glasses all the year round. /他们～地苦干了三年。They worked at it for three whole years without a break.

无动于衷 wúdòngyúzhōng unmoved; detached; indifferent; impassive:她对他的关怀～。She was quite unmoved by his solicitude. /看着自己人身受毒刑,你能～? How can you remain indifferent at the sight of your comrades being tortured? /什么话我都得听,什么脸色我都得看,我能做到～。I've got used to all kinds of remarks and facial expressions. I take nothing to heart.

无独有偶 wúdú-yǒu'ǒu 〈贬义〉it is not unique but has its counterpart; there is another to match it (in stupidity, cruelty, etc.); (strange as it may seem,) things never come singly but in pairs:真是～,世界上竟然还存在一个跟他一样心狠手黑的人,而且还是个女人。Strange enough, there exists in this human world another who is as wicked and ruthless as he is and who is, moreover, a member of the fair sex.

无毒不丈夫 wúdú bù zhàngfū 〈旧语〉ruthlessness is the mark of a truly great man

无毒蛇 wúdúshé nonpoisonous snake

无度 wúdù immoderate; inordinate; excessive:挥霍～ squander wantonly; be excessively extravagant /荒淫～ excessive debauchery

无端 wúduān without rhyme or reason:～生事 deliberately make trouble (*or* kick up a row) /～受罚 be punished (*or* fined) for no fault of one's own /～生气 flare up without provocation

无恶不作 wú'è-bùzuò stop at no evil; commit all manner of crimes:横行霸道,～ ride roughshod over the people and stop at no evil /当年,这一带有一个鱼肉乡民、～的土豪。There was then a local tyrant who cruelly oppressed the villagers and committed all sorts of crimes.

无法 wúfǎ unable; incapable; powerless:～履行 unable to fulfil (*or* perform) /～分析 defy analysis /～形容 beyond description; indescribable /～辨认 irrecognizable; undecipherable /～逃避的责任 inescapable (*or* unshirkable) responsibility /～解决的难题 insoluble problem /～投递,退回原处。Undeliverable, return to sender. /她陷入了～抑制的痛苦之中。She was plunged into a state of uncontrollable grief.

无法无天 wúfǎ-wútiān be absolutely lawless; defy laws human or divine; run wild; be outrageous:他在县城做出许多～的事情来。He committed numerous lawless acts in the county town. /要拿点厉害的出来对付这群～的东西。We've got to get tough with those bums; they are simply violating all laws, human and divine.

无方 wúfāng not in the proper way; incompetent; not knowing how:领导～ incompetent leadership /经营～ mismanage /教子～ not able to educate one's children properly

无妨 wúfáng there is no harm; have no reason not to; may or might as well:交涉的情况～跟大家吹吹风。You may as well give them a briefing on the negotiations. /病已好多了,下床走动走动也～。You are much better now, and there's no harm in getting up and moving about a bit. /有意见～直说。Feel free to speak out if you have anything on your mind.

无纺织布 wúfǎngzhībù 〈纺织〉non-woven fabric; adhesive-bonded fabric

无非 wúfēi nothing but; no more than; merely; only:她们谈的～是家常话。They talked about nothing but the trivialities of everyday life. /送你这本书,～要你培养对英语的兴趣。I give you this book in the hope of helping you cultivate an interest in English.

无风 wúfēng windless; calm:赤道～带 the doldrums /～三尺浪。There are big, lumpy waves even on calm days.

无风不起浪 wúfēng bù qǐ làng there are no waves without wind; where there's smoke, there's fire; there is no smoke without fire:他静下心来,仔细一想,又觉得～,不由得担心起来。On reflection, he realized that there must be some reason for these rumours, and he became worried.

无风带 wúfēngdài calm belt; calm zone

无峰骆驼 wúfēng luòtuo llama

无缝钢管 wúfèng gāngguǎn seamless steel tube or pipe:～厂 seamless steel tubing mill

无氟冰箱 wúfú bīngxiāng freon-free refrigerator

无干 wúgān have nothing to do with; be of no concern to:这事与他～,全是我的责任。I am to blame; it has nothing to do with him. /与他～的事他从不过问。He never bothers about anything that does not concern him. /不必多问,与你～! Shut up! It's none of your business.

无告 wúgào ❶ helpless; having no one to turn to for help or redress:穷苦～的老人 poor helpless old man ❷ 〈书面〉helpless person:哀怜～ pity the helpless

无工不富 wúgōng-bùfù there is no prosperity (in the countryside) without development of rural industry

无公害 wúgōnghài 〈环保〉pollution free; nuisance free:～蔬菜 pollution-free vegetable /～工艺 nuisanceless technology

无功 wúgōng 〈电工〉reactive:～电流 reactive current /～电压 reactive voltage /～力率 reactive power /～元件 reactive element

无功受禄 wúgōng-shòulù get a reward that one does not earn or deserve:～,寝食不安。Undeserved (*or* Unmerited) rewards make one feel uneasy day and night. /无功不受禄。One must accept no reward which one does not deserve.

无辜 wúgū ❶ innocent; guiltless:～百姓 innocent people /～的一方〈法律〉innocent party /～受害 be injured (*or* harmed) without giving provocation /事实证明她是～的。Facts proved her innocent. ❷ innocent (person):迫害～ persecute innocent people /株连～ implicate the innocent (in a criminal case)

无故 wúgù without cause or reason:～缺席 be absent without reason /～骂人 swear at people without provocation

无怪 wúguài *also* "无怪乎" small wonder; not to be wondered at:他去外地了,～老见不着他。He's been out of town; no wonder I haven't seen him around for so long.

无关 wúguān have nothing to do (with sb. or sth.); be irrelevant:这与你～。It has nothing to do with you. *or* It's none of your business. /他尽看些与自己业务～的书。He is always reading books unrelated to the subject he majors in.

无关大局 wúguān-dàjú not affecting the overall situation; of little

W

consequence; insignificant:～的决定 decision of no consequence /～的措施 measure that will have little bearing on the overall situation

无关宏旨 wúguān-hóngzhǐ not of cardinal principle; of no great importance:～的问题 issue of no cardinal principle; side-issue /～的区区小事 trivial matter

无关紧要 wúguān-jǐnyào of no importance; inessential; immaterial:说些～的话 make some inconsequential remarks / ～的事物 irrelevance /把文章～的段落删去 delete non-essential paragraphs from an article

无关痛痒 wúguān-tòngyǎng unimportant; irrelevant; pointless:～的批评 superficial (*or* irrelevant) criticism /结尾的改动决不是～的枝节问题。The alteration of the ending is by no means an insignificant side-issue.

无官一身轻 wú guān yīshēn qīng out of office, out of cares; feel carefree without official duties:～,退休后多年的失眠症竟自消失了。Now that he had retired, his long-time insomnia was gone.

无光漆 wúguāngqī 〈化工〉lustreless paint; flat paint; flat varnish

无规 wúguī 〈物理〉random;〈化学〉atactic:～介质 random media /～共聚物 random copolymer /～取向 random orientation /～聚合物 atactic polymer

无轨 wúguǐ ❶ trackless:～矿井 trackless mine ❷〈口语〉(short for 无轨电车) trolleybus:三路～ Trolleybus No.3

无轨电车 wúguǐ diànchē trackless trolley; trolleybus

无国籍 wúguójí stateless:～人 stateless person; stateless alien /减少～状态公约 Convention on the Reduction of Statelessness (30 Aug. 1961)

无害 wúhài harmless; innocuous; without evil intentions:～误差 harmless error /于人～ harmless to people /用意～ mean no harm / ～昆虫 innocuous insect /～转让 innocuous conveyance /～气体〈环保〉innocuous gas

无害通过 wúhài tōngguò 〈法律〉innocent passage

无何 wúhé 〈书面〉❶ soon afterwards; before long:居～,则致资累巨万。He amassed a huge fortune not long after taking up residence there. ❷ nothing much; nothing else:自度～。He reckoned that there was not much to worry about.

无何有之乡 wúhéyǒu zhī xiāng (imaginary) nowhere; dreamland

无核 wúhé ❶ non-nuclear; nuclear-free:～国家 *also* "无核武器国家" non-nuclear country; non-nuclear-weapon state ❷ seedless; stoneless:～葡萄干 seedless raisins

无核化 wúhéhuà denuclearize; make nuclear-free

无核区 wúhéqū *also* "无核武器区" nuclear(-weapon)-free zone

无恒 wúhéng lacking in perseverance; inconstant; inconsistent:学忌～。Lack of perseverance is to be guarded against in learning. /～则大事难成。Great accomplishments are hardly possible without tenacity. /政策～则失民心。Inconsistent policies alienate the people.

无后 wúhòu without male offspring; having no son to carry on the family line:不孝有三,～为大。〈旧语〉Of the three kinds of unfilial acts in the world, the greatest is not to have a son to carry on the family line.

无后坐力炮 wúhòuzuòlìpào 〈军事〉recoilless gun

无花果 wúhuāguǒ 〈植物〉fig

无华 wúhuá unadorned; unornamented:质朴～ simple and unadorned

无话不谈 wúhuà-bùtán take each other into their confidence; keep no secrets from each other; be in each other's confidence:他俩是～的知交。They are very close friends who hide nothing from each other. /他对我～。He shares confidences with me about everything.

无机 wújī 〈化学〉inorganic; mineral:～黏结剂 inorganic binder; mineral binder bond

无机肥料 wújī féiliào inorganic fertilizer; mineral fertilizer

无机化合物 wújī huàhéwù inorganic compound; mineral compound

无机化学 wújī huàxué inorganic chemistry

无机界 wújījiè inorganic world

无机染料 wújī rǎnliào inorganic dye

无机树脂 wújī shùzhī inorganic resin

无机酸 wújīsuān inorganic acid

无机物 wújīwù inorganic matter; inorganic substance; mineral

无机盐 wújīyán inorganic salt

无机液体激光器 wújī yètǐ jīguāngqì inorganic liquid laser; neodymium liquid laser

无稽 wújī unfounded; fantastic; preposterous; absurd:荒诞～ absurd; incredible /～之尤 absolutely absurd; height of absurdity

无稽之谈 wújīzhītán unfounded rumour, pure and simple; sheer nonsense:这种～不值一驳。Such nonsense is not worth rebutting.

无及 wújí too late; belated:悔之～ too late to repent

无级 wújí 〈机械〉stepless:～调速 stepless speed regulation /～变速 infinitely variable speed

无几 wújǐ ❶ very few; very little; not much; hardly any:两者相差～。The difference between the two is negligible. *or* There is not much difference between them. /他们已经喝了很多,瓶里所剩～了。They had consumed a good deal, and there was little left in the bottle. /快半夜了,街上行人寥寥～。It was nearly midnight, and there were few pedestrians in the street. ❷〈书面〉not long afterwards; soon after:～,其人已渺。The man disappeared soon after. *or* It was not long before the man vanished without a trace.

无脊椎动物 wújǐzhuī dòngwù invertebrate; invertebrata

无计可施 wújì-kěshī at one's wit's end; at the end of one's tether:左思右想,～。We cudgeled our brains trying to find a way out, but to no avail.

无计名投票 wújìmíng tóupiào secret ballot:通过～选举产生 elect by secret ballot

无记名债券 wújìmíng zhàiquàn 〈金融〉bearer bond

无际 wújì boundless; infinite:一望～ stretch as far as the eye can see; stretch to the horizon /蓝天之下,大海～。The sea merged into the azure sky on the horizon.

无济于事 wújìyúshì of no avail; to no effect:这晚他睡不着了,吃三片安眠药也～。He could not fall asleep even after taking three sleeping tablets. /事到如今,骂娘也～。It is useless shouting curses at this late hour.

无家可归 wújiā-kěguī homeless; displaced:～的难民 homeless refugee; displaced person /流落他乡,～ wander from place to place homeless

无价之宝 wújiàzhībǎo *also* "无价宝" priceless treasure; invaluable asset:这些陈列的艺术品都是～。The works of art on display are all priceless treasures. /这些儿童读物是我女儿的～。These children's books are my daughter's invaluable assets.

无坚不摧 wújiān-bùcuī carry all before one; be ever-victorious; be all-conquering:～的队伍 invincible army

无间 wújiàn 〈书面〉❶ not hiding anything from each other; very close to each other:他俩亲密～。The two are bosom friends. ❷ without interruption or interval; continuously:勤学苦练,寒暑～。Study diligently and practise hard all the year round. ❸ not distinguish; make no difference:～是非 not distinguish between right and wrong

无疆 wújiāng limitless; infinite; boundless; endless:万寿～ longevity; long life

无阶级社会 wújiējí shèhuì classless society

无尽 wújìn endless; infinite; limitless:无穷～的智慧 inexhaustible wisdom /无穷～的草原 infinite stretch of grassland

无尽无休 wújìn-wúxiū ceaseless; infinite:～的烦恼 endless worries

无精打采 wújīng-dǎcǎi listless; lackadaisical; downcast; in low spirits:～地回到家中 come back home in low spirits /那老太太叹一口气,～地继续缝补她的衣服。The old woman sighed while she was lazily mending her clothes. /她忽然注意到女儿垂着头～地立在窗前。She suddenly found her daughter standing by the window looking listless and tired.

无咎无誉 wújiù-wúyù deserving neither censure nor praise; middling; commonplace

无拘无束 wújū-wúshù unconstrained; unrestrained:～、自由自在的田园生活 free and unrestrained idyllic life /～地各抒己见 express one's views freely /会谈的气氛是～的。The discussion was conducted in an unconstrained atmosphere.

无菌 wújūn 〈生物〉germ-free; aseptic:～装罐 aseptic canning

无菌操作法 wújūn cāozuòfǎ aseptic operation

无菌隔离室 wújūn gélíshì germ-free isolation unit

无菌牛奶 wújūn niúnǎi germ-free milk

无菌培养基 wújūn péiyǎngjī axenic culture medium

无可比拟 wúkě-bǐnǐ incomparable; unparalleled; unrivalled; unmatched:～的优越条件 incomparable advantages /有史以来～的大变化 changes unparalleled in history

无可不可 wúkě-bùkě ❶ be good at whatever one lays one's hand to; the sky is the limit:家务事、地里活,她样样都行,真称得上～了。Household chores or field work, she is good at every job

imaginable. As one might say, the sky is the limit. ❷ not know what to do (due to excitement, joy, etc.):老人家搬进新房子，喜欢得～。Having moved into their new house, the old couple were too overjoyed to know what to do.

无可非议 wúkě-fēiyì beyond reproach; above criticism; blameless; unimpeachable:其动机是～的。His motives are beyond reproach.

无可奉告 wúkě-fènggào no comment

无可厚非 wúkě-hòufēi *also* "未可厚非" wèikě-hòufēi give no cause for much criticism (though not without faults or shortcomings):作者的动机～，但客观效果却与其初衷不符。The author's motives gave little cause for criticism, but the effect did not turn out as he had expected.

无可讳言 wúkě-huìyán there is no denying the fact that...:～，他应该对这次失误负责。Undeniably, he should be held responsible for the mistake.

无可救药 wúkě-jiùyào incurable; incorrigible; irremediable:～的病 incurable disease /此人已堕落到～的程度。The man has degenerated beyond cure. *or* He is beyond redemption.

无可奈何 wúkě-nàihé have no alternative; be helpless; have no choice; have no way out:～的苦笑 sad, helpless smile /我们～，只得应允。We had no alternative but to agree. /他又恨又怕，但又～。Angry and fearful as he was, there was nothing he could do about it. /她看见他微微地摇头，脸上现出一种～的表情。She saw him shake his head slightly with an expression of helplessness on his face.

无可奈何花落去 wúkě nàihé huā luòqù flowers fall off, do what one may — be in irreversible decline or hopeless predicament

无可挽回 wúkě-wǎnhuí irretrievable; irredeemable; irrevocable:声誉已～。The reputation is past redemption. /局面已～了。It is impossible to retrieve the situation.

无可无不可 wúkě-wúbùkě make no difference; not care one way or another:这件事对我来说～。It makes no difference to me. *or* Either yes or no, it doesn't matter really.

无可争辩 wúkě-zhēngbiàn indisputable; unquestionable; irrefutable:～的当代最伟大的音乐家 irrefutably the greatest musician of our time /～的道理 incontrovertible argument

无可置疑 wúkě-zhìyí beyond doubt or question; indubitable; unquestionable:～的真理 indubitable truth /这个消息千真万确，～。The information is accurate and beyond doubt.

无孔不入 wúkǒng-bùrù 〈贬义〉never missing any opportunity; all-pervasive:～的思想渗透 all-pervasive ideological infiltration /他们对第三世界国家的掠夺是～的。They never miss an opportunity to plunder third-world countries.

无愧 wúkuì have a clear conscience; feel no qualms; be worthy of (sth.):当之～ be worthy of sth. /问心～ feel no qualms upon self-examination /"鸿儒"称号，他当之～。He fully deserves the title of "venerable scholar". *or* He is worthy of the name of "venerable scholar".

无赖 wúlài ❶ shameless; brazen:耍～ act shamelessly; brazen it out /～行为 shameless (*or* despicable) behaviour ❷ *also* "无赖汉"; "无赖子" hooligan; scoundrel:他常跟一些流氓～混在一起。He often hangs around with some hooligans.

无俚 wúlǐ 〈书面〉bored:闲坐～ sit idle and bored

无理 wúlǐ ❶ unreasonable; unwarranted; unjustifiable:～挑衅 unjustifiable provocation /～干涉 unwarranted interference /～要求 unreasonable demand /～谴责 groundless censure /有理走遍天下，～寸步难行。With justice on your side, you can go anywhere unhindered; without it, you can't move a single step. ❷〈数学〉irrational

无理方程 wúlǐ fāngchéng irrational equation

无理根 wúlǐgēn irrational root

无理函数 wúlǐ hánshù irrational function

无理取闹 wúlǐ-qǔnào wilfully make trouble; be deliberately provocative; kick up a row for no reason at all:他们是在～。They are being deliberately provocative.

无理式 wúlǐshì irrational expression

无理数 wúlǐshù irrational number

无力 wúlì ❶ beyond one's power; powerless; unable; incapable:～应付这个局面 powerless to cope with the situation /这个问题我～解决。It is not in my power to work out a solution to the problem. ❷ lack strength; feel weak; be debilitated:四肢～ feel weak in one's limbs /病后软弱～ be frail after an illness /说话有气～ speak wearily; speak in a faint voice

无力偿付 wúlì chángfù insolvency

无梁殿 wúliángdiàn beamless hall

无两 wúliǎng matchless; peerless; unmatched:这个人跑百米的速度，目前天下～。This man is matchless in the 100-metre dash at the moment.

无量 wúliàng measureless; immeasurable; limitless; boundless:前途～ have boundless prospects /功德～ render a great service to mankind /～纲数〈数学〉dimensionless number

无量寿佛 Wúliàngshòufó *also* "阿弥陀佛" Ēmítuófó 〈佛教〉*Amitabha*; *Amitayus*

无聊 wúliáo ❶ bored; dull:他觉得生活很～。He feels his life is as dull as ditchwater. /休假的时间一长，反而觉得～。One becomes bored when a vacation lasts too long. ❷ senseless; silly; vulgar:说了许多～的话 talk a lot of nonsense /这事真～。This is absolutely senseless. /一天到晚尽谈吃穿，太～了。It is silly talking about food and clothing all the time.

无聊赖 wúliáolài 〈书面〉infinitely bored; frustrated:她～地翻着一本画册。She leafed through a pictorial, looking bored. /她～地在那里坐了一会儿。She sat there for a while numb with ennui.

无虑 wúlǜ ❶〈书面〉about; roughly:参加此次讨论会的～百十人。As many as a hundred people or so participated in the seminar. ❷ have nothing to worry about:无忧～ free from care; carefree

无论 wúlùn whatever; however; whenever; regardless of:～何时何地 whenever and wherever /～怎样忙 no matter how busy; however busy /～多大年岁 regardless of age /～是男是女 regardless of sex /～天晴下雨 rain or shine /～成与不成，后天一定告诉你。Whatever the outcome, I'll let you know the day after tomorrow.

无论如何 wúlùnrúhé in any case; at any rate; whatever happens; under any circumstances:～都要保持冷静。Keep calm whatever happens. /～这个问题要马上考虑。At any rate, the problem calls for immediate attention. /～你明天不能走。You must not leave tomorrow in any case.

无脉 wúmài 〈医学〉asphygmia

无米之炊 wúmǐzhīchuī cook a meal without rice; make bricks without straw:巧妇难为～。Even the cleverest housewife can't cook a meal without rice.

无冕之王 wúmiǎnzhīwáng king without a crown — man without a title but very influential (often used to refer to a reporter)

无面见江东父老 wú miàn jiàn Jiāngdōng fùlǎo one feels ashamed to go back and see people of one's hometown again (because one has failed to get anywhere)

无名 wúmíng ❶ nameless:～小溪 nameless stream ❷ unknown to the world:～作家 unknown (*or* obscure) writer ❸ indefinable; inexpressible; indescribable:产生一种～的紧张空气 indefinable air of tension

无名高地 wúmíng gāodì unnamed hill

无名氏 wúmíngshì anonymous person or writer

无名帖 wúmíngtiě 〈书面〉anonymous letter

无名小卒 wúmíng xiǎozú nobody; small potato:文学界的～ obscure figure in the literary circles

无名英雄 wúmíng yīngxióng unsung hero:～纪念碑 monument to unsung heroes; monument to the unknown warriors (*or* soldiers)

无名指 wúmíngzhǐ ring finger; third finger

无名肿毒 wúmíng zhǒngdú 〈中医〉nameless sore or boil

无明火 wúmínghuǒ *also* "无名火" inexplicable anger:～起。An inexplicable anger flares up (in sb.). /提起这件事他就～冒三丈。He always flies into a rage at the mere mention of the incident.

无模铸造 wúmó zhùzào 〈冶金〉containerless casting

无乃 wúnǎi 〈书面〉〈副词〉*used in a rhetorical question to indicate gentle disapproval or disagreement*:～不可乎? That won't do, will it? /～后乎? Is that not too late?

无奈 wúnài ❶ cannot but; have no alternative or choice but:我出于～才作了妥协。I had no option but to compromise. /这也是～的事。That could not be helped. ❷ unfortunately; but:～他不听我的劝告。Unfortunately he refused to take my advice. /本想今天去郊游，～天不作美，只好改期。We planned to go on an excursion today, but as the weather is not cooperative, we have to postpone it.

无奈何 wúnàihé ❶ cannot do anything about:这件事已经决定，我也～。As a decision has been made about the matter, I can't do anything about it. ❷ be in a helpless situation; have no alternative:～只得再去一趟。I was compelled to make another trip to the place.

无脑畸胎 wúnǎo jītāi 〈医学〉anencephalia

无能 wúnéng incompetent; inept; incapable: 软弱～ weak and inept / 缺乏决断是～的表现。Indecisiveness is a sign of incompetence.

无能为力 wúnéngwéilì not be in one's power to help; incapable of doing anything to help; powerless: 解决这样复杂的问题，我实在～。I am really in no position (*or* It's beyond my power) to solve this complicated problem.

无宁 wúnìng rather than
see also "毋宁" wúnìng

无农不稳 wúnóng-bùwěn there is no stability without agricultural development

无匹 wúpǐ 〈书面〉❶ have no spouse; have no companion; be unmarried ❷ matchless; unparalleled; peerless: 举世～ peerless in the world / ～的威力 matchless power

无偏无党 wúpiān-wúdǎng impartial; fair: 赏罚～。Justice is done in both rewards and punishments.

无期徒刑 wúqī túxíng life imprisonment: 被判处～ be sentenced to life imprisonment; be given a life sentence

无其数 wúqíshù 〈口语〉countless; innumerable: 他家珠宝就存了～。His family was in possession of innumerable pieces of jewellery.

无奇不有 wúqí-bùyǒu there is no lack of strange things; extraordinary things abound (in this world): 世界之大，～。Nothing is too strange in this wide world.

无千无万 wúqiān-wúwàn 〈方言〉thousands: ～的彩色气球飞向天空。Thousands of coloured balloons flew up to the sky.

无牵无挂 wúqiān-wúguà free from worldly cares; carefree

无铅 wúqiān leadless; unleaded; lead-free: ～玻璃 LFG (lead-free glass) / ～汽油 unleaded gasoline

无前 wúqián ❶ invincible; unconquerable: 所向～ carry all before one; be invincible / 一往～ press forward with indomitable courage ❷ unprecedented: 成绩～ unprecedented achievement / 诗人兴会更～。And the poet is inspired as never before.

无巧不成书 wú qiǎo bù chéng shū it is coincidence that makes a story; what a coincidence; as luck would have it: 真是～。说曹操，曹操就到。What a coincidence! Talk of the devil, and here he is now (*or* and the devil is sure to appear).

无巧不巧 wúqiǎo-bùqiǎo luckily; fortunately; by sheer luck: 我到车站送人，真是～，一位二十年未见的老朋友也在送客。What a coincidence that while I saw someone off at the railway station, an old friend of mine I had not seen for twenty years was also seeing people off there!

无情 wúqíng ❶ unfeeling; heartless; merciless: 冷酷～ cruel and unfeeling; cold and heartless / ～无义 heartless and faithless ❷ merciless; ruthless: ～的嘲讽 bitter satire / ～揭露 mercilessly expose / 水火～。Floods and fires have no mercy for anybody. / 他这个人翻脸～。He is the sort of person who could turn against a friend as if he were an utter stranger. / 法律是～的。Law is inexorable.

无穷 wúqióng infinite; limitless; boundless: ～的潜力 inexhaustible potential / 此事如不妥善处理则后患～。The matter, if not handled properly, will give rise to endless trouble in the future.

无穷大 wúqióngdà 〈数学〉infinitely great; infinity

无穷级数 wúqióng jíshù 〈数学〉infinite series

无穷无尽 wúqióng-wújìn infinite; boundless; endless; limitless: 知识的海洋是～的。The sea of knowledge is boundless. / 宇宙是～的，它的运动也是～的。The universe is infinite; so is its movement.

无穷小 wúqióngxiǎo 〈数学〉infinitely small; infinitesimal

无趣 wúqù feel snubbed: 自讨～ ask for a snub

无权 wúquán have no right or authority; be powerless: ～过问 have no authority to intervene / 有职～ hold a title but no real power / 涉外事务，～处理 have no right to handle foreign-related matters

无权追索 wúquán zhuīsuǒ 〈法律〉without recourse

无拳无勇 wúquán-wúyǒng have neither physical strength nor courage: 一个～的小人物 weak and cowardly small fry

无缺 wúquē complete; intact; flawless; perfect: 保存完整～ be kept intact / 完美～ perfect; flawless / 金瓯～〈比喻〉territorial integrity

无人 wúrén ❶ unmanned: ～宇宙飞船 unmanned spaceship / ～驾驶潜水装置 robot submarine ❷ without population; not populated: ～区 no man's land; depopulated zone ❸ self-service: ～售书处 self-service book stall / ～售票公共电汽车 bus without a conductor

无人采煤工作面 wúrén cǎiméi gōngzuòmiàn 〈矿业〉manless coalface

无人地带 wúrén dìdài 〈军事〉no man's land

无人驾驶 wúrén jiàshǐ pilotless: ～飞机 pilotless aircraft; unmanned plane / ～高空侦察机 pilotless high-altitude reconnaissance plane

无人问津 wúrén-wènjīn have no bidders; no one takes any interest in it: 这项研究是冷门，几乎～。This research project receives little attention, and no one seems to have taken any interest in it.

无人值班变电所 wúrén zhíbān biàndiànsuǒ 〈电工〉unattended substation

无任 wúrèn 〈书面〉extremely; exceedingly; immensely: ～欢迎 be extremely welcome / ～感荷 be very much obliged

无任所大使 wúrènsuǒ dàshǐ ambassador-at-large; roving ambassador: 文化事务～ (US) Ambassador-at-Large for Cultural Affairs

无日 wúrì ❶ (when followed by 不) every day; continuously: ～不在念中 have always been in one's thoughts ❷〈书面〉before long; soon: 祸至～。It will not be long before disaster strikes.

无日无夜 wúrì-wúyè day and night; continuously: ～地工作 work round the clock

无如 wúrú *see* "无奈❷"

无砂铸造 wúshā zhùzào 〈冶金〉sandless casting

无伤大雅 wúshāng-dàyǎ involving no major principle; not affecting the main aspect; immaterial: 布景设计虽有缺点，但～。The design of the setting is not free from flaws, but that does not matter much.

无上 wúshàng supreme; uppermost; paramount; highest: ～光荣 highest honour / 至高～ supreme; paramount / 其中自有～的乐趣。One would find infinite joy in it.

无神论 wúshénlùn atheism: ～者 atheist

无生代 Wúshēngdài 〈地质〉Azoic Era

无生物 wúshēngwù inanimate object; non-living matter

无生殖力 wúshēngzhílì agenesis; agenesia; infertility

无声 wúshēng noiseless; still; silent: 悄然～ noiseless; silent / ～打字机 noiseless typewriter / 此时～胜有声。Silence here speaks more eloquently than words.

无声片儿 wúshēngpiānr 〈口语〉silent film

无声片 wúshēngpiàn *also* "默片" mòpiàn silent film

无声手枪 wúshēng shǒuqiāng pistol with a silencer

无声无臭 wúshēng-wúxiù unknown; little known; obscure: 不甘心～地过一辈子 not be resigned to living in obscurity all one's life; not want to remain obscure in life / 他虽然～地度过一生，但他并无遗憾。Although he has remained little known all his life, he doesn't seem to regret it.

无绳电话 wúshéng diànhuà cordless (phone)

无失真 wúshīzhēn 〈通信〉distortionless; undistorted: ～传输 undistorted transmission / ～输出 undistorted output

无师自通 wúshī-zìtōng self-taught: 有些技艺不可能～。Certain skills cannot be learnt without a master. / 他勤奋好学，～，懂得了两门外语。He is very diligent and has taught himself two foreign languages.

无时无刻 wúshí-wúkè all the time; at every moment; always: 宇宙万物～不在发展变化。Everything in the universe is changing unceasingly.

无事不登三宝殿 wú shì bù dēng sānbǎodiàn never go to the temple for nothing; call on sb. only on business or only when one needs his help: 他是个"～"的人。He is the sort of person who "only goes to the temple when he is in trouble." / 我是～。I wouldn't come to you if I hadn't something to ask of you.

无事忙 wúshìmáng fuss about things which are not properly one's own duties; make much ado about nothing: 他这个人就是～，整天瞎跑。He was rushed off his feet, busy about things outside his own province all day long.

无事生非 wúshì-shēngfēi create trouble out of nothing; stir up unnecessary trouble; create difficulty where none exists: 我最讨厌～。What I hate most is making trouble out of nothing. / 这个人就爱～。This man is apt to be deliberately provocative.

无视 wúshì shut one's eyes to; ignore; disregard; defy: ～人民疾苦 shut one's eyes to the sufferings of the people / ～别国主权 disregard the sovereignty of other countries / ～法纪 defy law and discipline / ～人民意志 fly in the face of the will of the people

无殊 wúshū 〈书面〉no different (from...); just the same: 就人性而言，今古～。As far as human nature is concerned, there is no difference between past and present.

W

无熟料水泥 wúshúliào shuǐní 〈建筑〉clinker-free cement

无数 wúshù ❶ innumerable; untold; countless:～的财宝 innumerable treasures /死伤～ (suffer) countless casualties ❷ not know for certain; not be sure; be uncertain:心中～ not know for certain; not sure /他是怎样的人, 你有数～啊? Have you any idea what sort of person he is?

无双 wúshuāng unparalleled; unrivalled; unmatched; matchless:盖世～ absolutely unrivalled /英勇～ have no match in valour (*or* strength); be unmatched in valour (*or* strength)

无霜 wúshuāng 〈气象〉frostless:～带 frostless zone; green belt; verdant zone

无霜期 wúshuāngqī frost-free period; frostless season

无水 wúshuǐ 〈化学〉anhydrous:～酒精 absolute alcohol; anhydrous alcohol /～剂 anhydrous solvent /～酸 anhydrous acid

无丝分裂 wúsī fēnliè *also*"直接分裂" zhíjiē fēnliè 〈生物〉amitosis

无私 wúsī selfless; unselfish; disinterested:大公～ selfless and impartial /～援助 (give) disinterested assistance /铁面～的法官 incorruptible, unbiased judge

无私有弊 wúsī-yǒubì be under suspicion though one is innocent

无私有意 wúsī-yǒuyì *see*"无私有弊"

无似 wúsì 〈书面〉❶ extremely:振奋～ greatly encouraged /钦佩～ deeply admire ❷〈谦词〉incapable; unworthy:小可～, 难当此殊荣。I am unworthy of the special honour you bestow on me.

无算 wúsuàn 〈书面〉countless; infinite; innumerable:死伤～ countless casualties

无损 wúsǔn ❶ do no harm:争论～于友谊。Argument is not detrimental to friendship. ❷ not damaged; intact:完好～ remain intact

无损检验 wúsǔn jiǎnyàn 〈机械〉NDT (non-destructive testing)

无梭织机 wúsuō zhījī 〈纺织〉shuttleless loom

无所不包 wúsuǒbùbāo all-embracing; all-inclusive:他的哲学是～的。His philosophy is all-embracing.

无所不及 wúsuǒbùjí be in no way inferior to:比起老张来, 他～。He is in no way inferior to Lao Zhang.

无所不可 wúsuǒbùkě anything will do; it will be all right, one way or the other:你要这么办, 我也～。If you insist, I'll not object in any way.

无所不能 wúsuǒbùnéng omnipotent; very capable:他从小聪明伶俐, ～。Bright and clever as a boy, he proved capable in everything he undertook.

无所不谈 wúsuǒbùtán (as among good friends) nothing is kept secret:他俩私交甚厚, 平日～。The two of them were on the best of terms and shared their private views about anything under the sun. *or* As great friends, they shared each other's confidences.

无所不通 wúsuǒbùtōng know all:十八般武艺, ～ be skilful in using each and every one of the 18 (traditional) weapons; be versatile /琴、棋、书、画～ be good at musical instruments, chess, calligraphy and painting

无所不为 wúsuǒbùwéi stop at nothing; commit all kinds of evils:敌军杀人放火, ～。Killing and burning, the enemy troops stopped at nothing. /这个人有权时～, 失势时奴性十足。He is the sort of official who will stop at nothing to benefit himself when in power and act slavishly when in disgrace.

无所不用其极 wú suǒ bù yòng qí jí go to any length; resort to every conceivable means; stop at nothing:为夺帝位, 弑父杀兄, ～。To usurp the throne, he committed every conceivable crime, including murdering his father and brother. /某些报纸对他的讽刺嘲骂, ～。Some newspapers did their utmost (*or* spared no efforts) to hold him up to ridicule and mockery.

无所不有 wúsuǒbùyǒu have everything:社会上千奇百怪, ～。There are all sorts of strange things in this world. /植物园内, 千树万木, 奇花异草, ～。In the botanical garden there is a great variety of trees, flowers, herbs and what not.

无所不在 wúsuǒbùzài universal; ubiquitous; omnipresent:矛盾～。Contradictions are universal.

无所不知 wúsuǒbùzhī know everything; be omniscient:在信教的人们看来, 神是～的。To religious people God is omniscient. /国内外大事, 他～。He is knowledgeable about very major event that is happening at home or abroad.

无所不至 wúsuǒbùzhì ❶ penetrate everywhere; pervade:在他们的生活里, 宗教影响～。Religious influence penetrates every nook and cranny of their lives. ❷ spare no pains (to do evil); be capable of anything; stop at nothing:吃喝嫖赌, ～ go dining, wining, whoring, gambling, and what not

无所措手足 wú suǒ cuò shǒu zú not know where to put one's hands or feet — be at a loss (as to) what to do:他当时完全没有料到会受批评, 弄得～。He was criticized when he least expected it, and he was at a loss what to do.

无所事事 wúsuǒshìshì be occupied with nothing; fool around; idle away one's time:游手好闲, 终日～ fool around all day without doing a stroke of decent work /你是不是要我呆在这儿, 终日～? You want me to stay here twiddling my thumbs, don't you?

无所适从 wúsuǒshìcóng not know which way to turn; be at a loss what to do:领导意见不一, 下面～。As the leaders were divided, the rank and file did not know whom to turn to. /他一会儿这么说, 一会儿那么说, 搞得大家～。He spoke differently on different occasions so that everybody got confused, not knowing what to do.

无所畏惧 wúsuǒwèijù fearless; intrepid; dauntless; undaunted:～的坚强斗士 undaunted tough fighter

无所谓 wúsuǒwèi ❶ cannot be designated as; not deserve the name of; not make much of:有些事是～对错的。Some things cannot be designated as right or wrong. /只是一些粗浅的体会, ～经验。These are just my impressions, nothing much to draw upon. /野外实习还得照常进行, ～晴天不晴天。Rain or shine, the field practice will have to go on as usual. ❷ care nothing; not take seriously; be indifferent:一副～的样子 look blasé (*or* indifferent) / 去不去, 我～。I don't really care whether we go or not. /她参加就行, 是否真有兴趣就～了。It mattered little if she was really interested, as long as she participated in it. /对这件事, 不要采取～的态度。You shouldn't take the "devil-may-care" sort of attitude towards this problem.

无所用心 wúsuǒyòngxīn not give serious thought to anything; remain idle:饱食终日, ～ be sated with food and remain idle all day

无所作为 wúsuǒzuòwéi attempt nothing and accomplish nothing; be in a state of apathy:克服～的思想 put an end to lethargy; get rid of ideas of helplessness /安于现状者是～的。Those who are satisfied with things as they are will accomplish nothing.

无炭钢 wútàngāng carbon-free steel

无题 wútí no title:～诗 poem without a title

无条件 wútiáojiàn unconditional; without conditions; with no strings attached:～投降 unconditional surrender /～撤军 unconditional troop withdrawal /～承兑 absolute acceptance /～担保 absolute guaranty /～转让 absolute conveyance; absolute assignment

无条件报价 wútiáojiàn bàojià unconditional offer (in negotiation)

无条件反射 wútiáojiàn fǎnshè 〈生理〉unconditioned reflex

无痛分娩 wútòng fēnmiǎn 〈医学〉painless childbirth; painless labour

无头案 wútóu'àn *also*"无头公案" case without clues; unsolved mystery:这种～, 谁都不愿意管。Nobody would like to put himself in charge of a case without clues. /这是历史上的一件无头公案。That is an unsolved mystery in history.

无头苍蝇 wútóu cāngying 〈比喻〉(scurrying aimlessly) like a headless fly:瞧这家伙到处乱钻, 成了～。Look! That guy scurries here and there — all to no purpose.

无头告示 wútóu gàoshi ambiguous official notice; writing that does not have a clear idea or purpose

无投票股权 wútóupiào gǔquán non-voting share

无土农业 wútǔ nóngyè soil-less agriculture

无土栽培 wútǔ zāipéi 〈农业〉soil-less cultivation:作物的～ soil-less cultivation of plants

无往不利 wúwǎng-bùlì be ever-successful:具备了这些条件, 工作起来就能～。With these qualifications, one will be successful in whatever one does.

无往不胜 wúwǎng-bùshèng ever-victorious; always triumphant; invincible:充分发动群众, 依靠群众, 我们就会无往而不胜。By fully relying on and mobilizing the masses, we shall be invincible.

无往不在 wúwǎng-bùzài present everywhere; omnipresent:迷信的说法是, 人死后魂灵犹存, 而且～。Superstition has it that when people die, their souls remain and are present everywhere.

无妄之灾 wúwàngzhīzāi uncalled-for calamity:他遭了一场～, 散步时被一颗流弹击中。An unexpected misfortune fell upon him; he was hit by a stray bullet while taking a stroll.

无望 wúwàng hopeless; impossible:成功～ no chance of success /治愈～ beyond cure /事情已经～。The matter is hopeless.

无微不至 wúwēi-bùzhì meticulously; with great care; in every

W

possible way: ~的照料 meticulous care / 他关心人真是~。He was the sort who would take pains over the smallest details in his concern for others.

无为 wúwéi (as a Taoist concept of life) do nothing; let things take their own course: 清静~ living in seclusion and doing nothing; quietude and inaction

无为而治 wúwéi'érzhì govern by doing nothing that is against nature; govern by non-interference

无味 wúwèi ❶ unpleasant to taste; tasteless; unpalatable: 这菜做得淡而~。This dish is vapid and unpalatable. / 食之~, 弃之可惜。It is unappetizing and yet one would hesitate to throw it away. ❷ dry; dull; insipid; uninteresting: 枯燥~ dry as dust; insipid / 索然~ uninspiring / 平淡~ flat and uninteresting

无畏 wúwèi fearless; courageous; dauntless: 大~的革命精神 dauntless revolutionary spirit / 无私~的战士 selfless, intrepid fighters

无谓 wúwèi meaningless; worthless; pointless; senseless: ~的冒险举动 meaningless (*or* senseless) risks / 避免作~的争论 avoid senseless polemics

无文字社会 wúwénzì shèhuì nonliterate society

无污染 wúwūrǎn 〈环境〉 pollution-free: ~能源 pollution-free energy

无污染工艺 wúwūrǎn gōngyì pollution-free technology

无…无… wú… wú… ❶ *used before two parallel characters, similar or identical in meaning, to achieve emphasis*: 无休无止 boundless; limitless / 无亲无故 without relatives or friends / 无根无据 groundless / 无声无息 silent; still; quiet / 无了无休 endless; on and on / 无情无绪 in low spirits; gloomy / 无缘无故 without rhyme or reason; for no reason at all ❷ *used before two parallel characters, contrasting in meaning, to show the range of effect*: 无大无小 whether big or small; equally / 无冬无夏 be it winter or summer; all the year round / 无日无夜 day and night; round the clock

无物 wúwù without content; empty: 言之~ empty talk / 眼空~ consider everyone and everything beneath one's notice; be supercilious / 空洞~ devoid of content; without substance

无误 wúwù free from error; all correct: 准确~ accurate and correct / 查核~ verify that all is in order; be verified / 捐款已全部上交~。All donations have been duly turned over to the higher authorities.

无息贷款 wúxī dàikuǎn interest-free loan

无息票债券 wúxīpiào zhàiquàn 〈金融〉 zero-coupon bond

无隙可乘 wúxì-kěchéng *also* "无懈可乘"; "无机可乘" no crack to drive a wedge in; no chink in one's armour; no loophole or opening to exploit; no vulnerability or weakness to take advantage of: 我们要加强防范, 使他们~。We must be on the alert, so that they could find nothing to take advantage of.

W

无瑕 wúxiá flawless; without blemish: 完美~ perfect; flawless / 白璧~ flawless white jade; impeccable integrity (*or* reputation)

无暇 wúxiá have no time; be fully occupied or engaged: ~过问 have no time to attend to it / ~前往 too busy to go

无限 wúxiàn infinite; limitless; boundless; unlimited: ~热诚 boundless enthusiasm / ~忠诚 absolute loyalty / ~光明 infinitely (*or* incomparably) bright / ~愤慨 unbridled indignation / ~的创造力 inexhaustible creative power / 他短暂的生命, 放出了~光辉。Short as his life was, it was one of everlasting splendour. / 字里行间流露出~深情。The words and phrases were full of deep feelings.

无限大 wúxiàndà *see* "无穷大"

无限公司 wúxiàn gōngsī *also* "无限责任公司" unlimited company

无限花序 wúxiàn huāxù indefinite inflorescence

无限期 wúxiànqī indefinite duration: ~罢工 strike of indefinite duration / 动议~搁置 shelve a motion *sine die* / 访问~推迟 postpone a visit indefinitely

无限上纲 wúxiàn shànggāng (of criticism) exaggerate: 动不动就给人家~ criticize people in most exaggerated terms at the slightest opportunity

无限小 wúxiànxiǎo *see* "无穷小"

无限制 wúxiànzhì unrestricted; unbridled; limitless; unlimited: ~扩大编制 enlarge (*or* expand) the staff without restriction

无线电 wúxiàndiàn ❶ radio: ~交换台 radio exchange / ~技师 radioman / ~噪声 *also* "射频噪声" radio noise / ~播音室 radio studio / ~测距 radio rangefinding / ~定位 radiolocation; radiofix / ~控制 wireless control; radio control / ~指令 radio command / 用~联系 communicate by radio ❷ radio set: 修理~ repair a radio set / 听~ listen to the radio / 从~上听到 hear on the radio

无线电报 wúxiàn diànbào wireless telegram; radio-telegram: 发~ send (*or* transmit) a radio-telegram

无线电波 wúxiàn diànbō radio wave

无线电测向器 wúxiàndiàn cèxiàngqì radio direction finder; radio goniometer

无线电传真 wúxiàndiàn chuánzhēn radiophotography; radiofacsimile: ~机 fax (machine)

无线电导航 wúxiàndiàn dǎoháng radio navigation: ~台 radio navigation station / ~系统 radio navigation system / ~信标 radio range beacon

无线电电子学 wúxiàndiàn diànzǐxué radio-electronics

无线电发射机 wúxiàndiàn fāshèjī radio transmitter; transmitter

无线电干扰 wúxiàndiàn gānrǎo radio jamming

无线电跟踪 wúxiàndiàn gēnzōng radio tracking

无线电工程 wúxiàndiàn gōngchéng radio engineering: ~师 radio engineer

无线电话 wúxiàn diànhuà radiotelephone: 便携式~ (popularly known as 大哥大) cellular phone; mobile phone

无线电频谱 wúxiàndiàn pínpǔ *also* "无线频谱" radio spectrum: ~分配 radio spectrum allocation

无线电视 wúxiàn diànshì radiotelevision

无线电收发两用机 wúxiàndiàn shōufā liǎngyòngjī radio transmitter-receiver; transceiver

无线电收音机 wúxiàndiàn shōuyīnjī radio receiver; radio set

无线电台 wúxiàn diàntái radio station

无线电探空仪 wúxiàndiàn tànkōngyí radiosonde

无线电天文学 wúxiàndiàn tiānwénxué radio astronomy

无线电通信 wúxiàndiàn tōngxìn radio communication; wireless communication

无线电信标 wúxiàndiàn xìnbiāo radio-beacon; radiophare: ~监视站 radio-beacon monitor station

无线电遥测 wúxiàndiàn yáocè radio telemetry

无线电遥控 wúxiàndiàn yáokòng radio-telecontrol: ~反潜艇攻击机 DASH (drone anti-submarine helicopter)

无线电业余爱好者 wúxiàndiàn yèyú àihàozhě amateur radio operator; ham

无线电运动 wúxiàndiàn yùndòng 〈体育〉 radio transmission and reception (as a sport)

无线电侦察 wúxiàndiàn zhēnchá radio reconnaissance; reconnaissance by radio

无线电侦听 wúxiàndiàn zhēntīng radio intercept

无线话筒 wúxiàn huàtǒng wireless microphone

无效 wúxiào of or to no avail; ineffective; invalid; null and void: 过期~ invalid upon expiration / 宣布~ declare invalid (*or* null and void); invalidate; nullify / 医治~ fail to respond to medical treatment; medical treatment proves to be ineffective / 该决议对我方~。The resolution is invalid for our side.

无效分蘖 wúxiào fēnniè 〈农业〉 ineffective tillering

无效劳动 wúxiào láodòng ineffectual work; fruitless or useless labour

无邪 wúxié without evil intentions; innocent: 天真~ innocent

无屑加工 wúxiè jiāgōng 〈机械〉 non-chip finish; chipless machining

无懈可击 wúxiè-kějī leaving no room for criticism; with no chink in one's armour; unassailable; impregnable: 叙述得头头是道, ~。The story was well told, leaving no room for criticism. / 事情办得细密周到, ~。The thing was done with meticulous care, leaving no loopholes whatsoever.

无心 wúxīn ❶ not in the mood for; not inclined to: ~恋战 have no desire to continue fighting / ~开玩笑 be in no joking mood / 他忙得连他最喜欢的电影也~去看。He was so busy that he was not in the mood even for his favourite movies. ❷ not intentionally; not on purpose; unwittingly; inadvertently: 他~伤害了你的感情。He did not mean to hurt your feelings. / 言者~, 听者有意。Although the remark is inadvertent, it is taken seriously. *or* A casual remark sounds deliberate to a suspicious listener. *or* A careless word may provide important information to an attentive listener. ❸ 〈机械〉 centreless; coreless: ~磨床 centreless grinder / ~珩床 centreless honing machine / ~感应电炉 coreless induction furnace

无行 wúxíng 〈书面〉 lacking in virtues; immoral in conduct: 有才~

have ability but not moral integrity

无行为能力 wú xíngwéi nénglì 〈法律〉incompetence:~者 incompetent

无形 wúxíng ❶ invisible; intangible; incorporeal:~罗网 invisible net /~进(出)口 invisible import (export) /~贸易 invisible trade /~财产 incorporeal (*or* intangible) property /~价值 intangible value /~权利 intangible right /~损失 non-physical (*or* invisible) loss /~资本 incorporeal capital ❷ *see* "无形中"

无形教会 wúxíng jiàohuì 〈宗教〉invisible church

无形损耗 wúxíng sǔnhào invisible or intangible depreciation

无形物 wúxíngwù intangibles

无形中 wúxíngzhōng imperceptibly; unnoticeably; virtually:我们~成了竞争对手。Imperceptibly, we became rivals. /这些做法~成了惯例。These procedures have virtually become conventional practice.

无形资产 wúxíng zīchǎn intangible assets

无性 wúxìng 〈生物〉without sex or sex organs; asexual

无性繁殖 wúxìng fánzhí asexual or vegetative propagation; cloning

无性分离 wúxìng fēnlí asexual split

无性更新 wúxìng gēngxīn asexual regeneration

无性生殖 wúxìng shēngzhí asexual reproduction

无性世代 wúxìng shìdài asexual generation

无性杂交 wúxìng zájiāo asexual hybridization

无休止 wúxiūzhǐ ceaseless; endless; perpetual:~的争论 unending argument /~的烦恼 endless vexation

无须 wúxū *also* "无需";"无须乎" need not; be not necessary; not have to:~细说。There is no need to go into details. /~再讨论了。No further discussion is called for. /~再抄一遍。You don't have to make a clean copy. /~你多嘴。Keep your mouth shut.

无血手术 wúxuè shǒushù 〈医学〉bloodless operation

无涯 wúyá boundless; endless; infinite:~的草原 endless (*or* vast) grassland /~的幻想 boundless imagination; infinite fantasy

无烟工业 wúyān gōngyè smokeless industry (referring to tourism, etc.)

无烟火药 wúyān huǒyào smokeless powder; ballistite

无烟煤 wúyānméi anthracite:~粉 anthracite duff /~化 anthracitization

无言以对 wúyányǐduì *also* "无言可对" not know what to say in reply:他问得我~。He bombarded me with questions, to which I could hardly find any reply.

无颜见江东父老 wú yán jiàn Jiāngdōng fùlǎo *see* "无面见江东父老"

无焰燃烧 wúyàn ránshāo covered or shielded fire

无氧酸 wúyǎngsuān *also* "氢酸" qīngsuān hydric acid

无恙 wúyàng 〈书面〉in good health; well; secure; safe:安然~ safe and sound /别来~? I trust everything has been getting on well with you since we last met.

无业 wúyè ❶ jobless; unemployed ❷ propertyless:全然~ not have a stick of property

无业游民 wúyè yóumín jobless riffraff; vagrant

无依无靠 wúyī-wúkào have no one to turn to (in difficult times); be helpless:这孩子父母双亡,~。The child has lost both parents and has no one to depend on. /小树~,在狂风中摇曳着。The unsupported sapling swung to and fro in the fierce wind.

无遗 wúyí leaving out nothing; completely; thoroughly:暴露~ be thoroughly exposed /破坏~ be completely wrecked; be reduced to total debris /一览~ take in (*or* cover) everything at a glance; command an entire view (of...) /囊括~ sweep up everything; be all inclusive

无遗嘱法 wúyízhǔfǎ 〈法律〉law of intestacy

无疑 wúyí beyond doubt; certainly; undoubtedly:确定~ ascertain (*or* confirm) beyond any shadow of doubt /深信~ be certain; firmly believe /这~是一种巧合。This is undoubtedly a coincidence.

无已 wúyǐ 〈书面〉❶ no end of; endless; ceaseless:诛求~ ceaseless extortion ❷ have no choice but; cannot but:时有恶霸地痞相扰,~,老丈遂携女移居他处。Having often been harrassed by local despots and thugs, the old man had no alternative but to move elsewhere with his daughter.

无以复加 wúyǐfùjiā could not be more...; be in the extreme:荒唐到了~的地步 absurd in the extreme; height of absurdity /其手段之残忍,~。The means adopted couldn't be more cruel.

无以为生 wúyǐwéishēng have nothing to live on; have no means of supporting oneself:他失业在家,~。He lost his job and had nothing to live on.

无艺 wúyì 〈书面〉❶ without criteria or norms:用人~ have no criteria for official appointments ❷ without limit; immoderate; excessive:贪欲~ excessive greed

无异 wúyì no different from; same as:这种行为与狂人~。Such behaviour is no different from that of a maniac. /对自己的同志采取过"左"政策,~于将他们推向敌人一边。To adopt an ultra-left attitude towards our own comrades is tantamount to pushing them over to the enemy side.

无异议 wúyìyì without demur

无益 wúyì unprofitable; futile; useless; no good:徒劳~ all in vain; all to no avail /说也~ words are useless /于事~ not help matters

无意 wúyì ❶ not intend (to do sth.); have no intention (to do sth.); not be inclined:~干涉 have no intention to intervene /~卷入这场派性斗争 not mean to get involved in this factional strife ❷ not deliberately; inadvertently; unwittingly; accidentally:~中发现了一个秘密 discover a secret by accident /~遗漏 innocent omission /她打破花瓶是~的。She broke the vase inadvertently.

无意识 wúyìshí unconscious:~地望了她一眼 glance at her unconsciously /想不到我一句~的话,竟伤害了她的感情。I didn't realize that I had unknowingly hurt her feelings by an inadvertent remark.

无翼鸟 wúyìniǎo *also* "几维鸟" jīwéiniǎo;"鹬鸵" yùtuó kiwi

无垠 wúyín boundless; limitless; vast:浩渺~的宇宙 boundless universe /漠漠~的原野 vast open country

无影灯 wúyǐngdēng 〈医学〉shadowless lamp

无影无踪 wúyǐng-wúzōng disappear without a trace; melt into thin air:那件事我已忘得~了。I have clean forgotten about it. /野外没有半个人影儿,连山禽走兽都~了。The terrain was desolate, without a trace of either man or beast in the wilderness. /匪徒登上山头时,小分队已~了。When the bandits reached the top of the mountain, not a shadow of the detachment could be found.

无庸 wúyōng *also* "毋庸" wúyōng no need to

无用 wúyòng useless; of no avail; no good:~之辈 good-for-nothing

无用功 wúyònggōng 〈物理〉useless work

无用能 wúyòngnéng 〈机械〉unavailable energy

无忧无虑 wúyōu-wúlǜ free from care; free from anxieties:~的年轻人 care-free youngster /那时,生活虽然清贫,倒也~。Poor as we were then, we had few worries.

无由 wúyóu 〈书面〉not be in a position (to do sth.); have no way (of doing sth.):他们的意见分歧~解决。There is no way of resolving their differences. /这个问题不解决,生产便~增长。Production can in no way grow before the problem is solved.

无油断路器 wúyóu duànlùqì 〈电工〉oil-less circuit-breaker

无油螺杆式压缩机 wúyóu luógǎnshì yāsuōjī 〈机械〉oil-free rotary screw compressor

无余 wúyú have nothing left:揭露~ thoroughly expose /一览~ take in everything at one glance

无与伦比 wúyǔlúnbǐ unique; incomparable; without parallel; unparalleled:~的成就 unique achievement /~的贡献 unparalleled contribution /此物工艺精美,~。It is exquisitely made and incomparably beautiful.

无原则 wúyuánzé involving no principle; trivial:~纠纷 dispute that has nothing to do with principles; dispute over trivial matters; petty squabble

无援 wúyuán without aid or support; supportless:孤立~ be isolated and cut off from support (*or* reinforcements)

无缘 wúyuán ❶ be destined not to; have no chance to; not have the good fortune (of doing sth.):~相识 be destined (*or* fated) not to make sb.'s acquaintance; not have had the pleasure of making sb.'s acquaintance /他与艺术~。He is not destined for the arts. *or* He is not interested in the arts. /解放前穷人的孩子与学校是~的。Children from poor families had little chance to go to school before liberation. ❷ have no way of doing (sth.):此事我虽愿帮忙,但一时~插手。I am ready to help but have no way of doing so at the moment.

无缘无故 wúyuán-wúgù without rhyme or reason; for no reason at all:~地发脾气 get into a temper for no reason at all /你为何~骂

人？How could you call people names without any provocation?
无源 wúyuán 〈无线电〉passive：～天线 passive antenna /～雷达 passive radar /～反射器 passive reflector /～系统 passive system /～元件 passive element
无源之水，无本之木 wú yuán zhī shuǐ, wú běn zhī mù water without a source, tree without roots; things without solid foundation：脱离生活，文艺创作就将是～。Divorced from life, literary creation is like water without a source, or a tree without roots.
无韵诗 wúyùnshī blank verse
无章可循 wúzhāng-kěxún have no rules and regulations to go by：这类问题～，很难处理。It is hard to tackle issues of this kind, as there are no rules (*or* regulations) for them.
无照营业 wúzhào yíngyè 〈商业〉trade without a licence; interlope：～者 interloper
无政府主义 wúzhèngfǔzhǔyì ❶ anarchism：～者 anarchist /～状态 anarchy; chaos /～思潮 anarchist ideas; anarchism ❷ undisciplined behaviour or idea：这简直是～。This is sheer defiance of discipline.
无知 wúzhī ignorant：愚昧～ ignorant and stupid; benighted /～而又狂妄 shallow but arrogant /～之辈 ignoramus /这种态度说明对现代企业如何运转全然～。This attitude is based on total ignorance of how modern enterprises work.
无止境 wúzhǐjìng endless; limitless; boundless：学～。There's no end to learning.
无中生有 wúzhōng-shēngyǒu create out of nothing; fabricate out of thin air; be fictitious：～的海外奇谈 cock-and-bull story /这完全是～。This is sheer fabrication (*or* imagination). *or* This is purely fictitious. /他们可会制造舆论了 — 不一定完全～，却把一分事实夸大成十分。They know how to shape public opinion — not necessarily by total fabrications, but highly exaggerated accounts.
无重力 wúzhònglì 〈宇航〉agravic; weightless：～状态 null-gravity state; weightlessness
无着 wúzhuó have no assured source：衣食～ have no means of livelihood; be unable to make one's own living
无籽 wúzǐ seedless：～果 seedless fruit
无足轻重 wúzúqīngzhòng of little importance or consequence; trivial; insignificant：～的事情 matter of little consequence /～的问题 trivial question /～的损失 insignificant (*or* minor) loss
无阻 wúzǔ unblocked; unobstructed：畅通～ be open and unobstructed; pass unimpeded /风雨～ regardless of the weather; rain or shine
无罪 wúzuì innocent; not guilty：宣判～ acquit sb. of a crime /～释放 set free with a verdict of "not guilty"; release upon acquittal /任何人在未被宣告为犯罪以前应被推定为～。One should be presumed innocent before one is proved guilty.
无罪推定原则 wúzuì tuīdìng yuánzé 〈法律〉principle of presumption of innocence
无坐力炮 wúzuòlìpào *also* "无后坐力炮" recoilless gun

芜(蕪) wú 〈书面〉❶ overgrown with weeds：田园将～。The fields will lie waste. ❷ land overgrown with weeds：平～ open country overgrown with weeds ❸ 〈比喻〉mixed and disorderly; superfluous; useless：举要删～ keep the essential and cut out the superfluous /去～存菁 eliminate the dross and retain the essence; discard the useless and absorb the significent
芜鄙 wúbǐ (of writings) disorganized and vulgar：辞义～ poor in organization and vulgar in diction
芜词 wúcí superfluous word; redundant wording
芜秽 wúhuì overgrown with weeds; gone to seed：荒凉～ desolate and overgrown with weeds
芜菁 wújīng *also* "蔓菁" mánjing 〈植物〉turnip
芜劣 wúliè 〈书面〉(of writings) poorly organized and bad in style：此稿～，难以卒读。Poor in organization and overall qualities, the manuscript is hardly readable.
芜杂 wúzá (usu. of writings) mixed and disorderly; confused：内容尚可，惟词句颇多～处。It can pass muster in terms of content, but it is rather wordy.

鹀 wú 〈动物〉bunting

吾 wú ❶〈书面〉I; we：～友 my friend /～日三省～身。I examine myself three times a day. ❷ (Wú) a surname
吾辈 wúbèi 〈书面〉we; us
吾侪 wúchái 〈书面〉we; us
吾人 wúrén 〈书面〉we; us

梧 wú 〈植物〉Chinese parasol
梧桐 wútóng Chinese parasol (tree)

唔 wú *see* "咿唔" yīwú

铻 wú *see* "锟铻" Kūnwú

鼯 wú
鼯鼠 wúshǔ 〈动物〉flying squirrel

吴(吳) Wú ❶ name of a kingdom in the Zhou Dynasty, with its territory covering present southern Jiangsu and northern Zhejiang ❷ name of one of the Three Kingdoms, embracing middle and lower reaches of the Yangtze ❸ region covering southern Jiangsu and northern Zhejiang ❹ a surname
吴承恩 Wú Chéng'ēn Wu Cheng'en (1504?-1582), writer of the Ming Dynasty and author of *Pilgrimage to the West* (西游记)
吴丹 Wúdān U Thant (1909-1974), Burmese diplomat, UN Secretary-General from 1961 to 1971
吴道子 Wú Dàozǐ Wu Daozi, painter of the Tang Dynasty
吴哥窟 Wúgēkū Angkor Wat (ruins of the greatest temple of the Khmers)
吴哥艺术 Wúgē yìshù Angkor art, including Angkor town and Angkor Wat, built round the 11th century, representing the height of ancient Khmer culture
吴广 Wú Guǎng Wu Guang (? -208 BC), one of the leaders of a peasant uprising towards the end of the Qin Dynasty
see also "陈胜吴广起义" Chén Shèng-Wú Guǎng Qǐyì
吴敬梓 Wú Jìngzǐ Wu Jingzi (formerly translated as Wu Ching-tzu) (1701-1754), writer of the Qing Dynasty and author of *The Scholars* (儒林外史)
吴牛喘月 wúniú-chuǎnyuè Wu buffalo would pant at the sight of the moon — have excessive fear due to suspicion
吴起 Wú Qǐ Wu Qi (? -381 BC), military strategist, reformer, and prime minister of the State of Chu during the Period of the Warring States
吴下阿蒙 Wúxià-Āméng one who has only superficial knowledge; person of little learning
吴语 Wúyǔ Wu dialect, varieties of which are spoken in Shanghai, southeastern Jiangsu and most of Zhejiang
吴茱萸 wúzhūyú 〈植物〉*Evodia rutaecarpa*, whose unripe seeds are used in Chinese medicine

蜈 wú centipede
蜈蚣 wúgong 〈动物〉centipede (*Lithobius centipeda*)
蜈蚣草 wúgongcǎo 〈植物〉ciliate desert-grass (*Eremochloa ciliaris*)

毋 wú ❶〈书面〉no; not：～妄言。Do not lie. /临财～苟得。Do not forget honour and integrity at the sight of gain. /～因小失大。Do not try to save a little at the expense of a lot. ❷ (Wú) a surname
毋宁 wúnìng *also* "无宁" wúnìng 〈副词〉rather... than...：说他的成功是由于天才，～说是由于勤奋。His success was due not so much to his talent as to his diligence. /与其坐而论道，～起而行动。Let's act instead of talking idly about principle.
毋庸 wúyōng *also* "无庸" wúyōng need not; be unnecessary：～置疑 beyond all doubt; doubtless; undoubtedly /～置辩。There is no need to explain (*or* argue).
毋庸讳言 wúyōng huìyán to be frank; (there is) no need for reticence：～，我们的工作确实存在不少问题。There is no denying (the fact) that we have quite a few problems in our work.
毋庸赘述 wúyōng zhuìshù need not elaborate：这件事大家都清楚，～。As it's clear to everybody, there is no need to go into details.

wǔ

武[1] wǔ ❶ military; of military strength:～力 military strength; force /尚～ promote military affairs; attach importance to military strength /动～ resort to force; come to blows /偃～修文 desist from military affairs and promote culture and education ❷ (of) martial arts; *wushu*:比～ compete in *wushu* (*or* the martial arts) ❸ bold and powerful; valiant; fierce:威～ valiant and majestic /勇～ brave and powerful ❹ (Wǔ) a surname

武[2] wǔ 〈书面〉(half a) footstep:踵～ follow in the footsteps (of sb.); follow on the heels (of sb.); follow suit

武把子 wǔbǎzi 〈方言〉〈戏曲〉❶ actor or actress playing a martial role ❷ weapons used in such performances ❸ acrobatic fighting

武备 wǔbèi 〈书面〉 military preparedness; military strength; (state of) national defence:加强～ strengthen national defence /～不修。National defence has been neglected.

武昌起义 Wǔchāng Qǐyì Wuchang Uprising (10 Oct. 1911) *see also* "辛亥革命" Xīnhài Gémìng

武昌鱼 wǔchāngyú blunt-snout bream (*Megalobrama amblycephala*)

武场 wǔchǎng 〈戏曲〉percussion instrument accompaniment

武丑 wǔchǒu *also* "开口跳" kāikǒutiào 〈戏曲〉acrobatic clown

武打 wǔdǎ 〈戏曲〉acrobatic fighting; kung fu fighting

武打片 wǔdǎpiàn martial arts movie; kung fu movie

武旦 wǔdàn 〈戏曲〉actress playing a martial role

武斗 wǔdòu resort to fist-fighting or (armed) violence:挑动～ incite a violent conflict

武断 wǔduàn ❶ make an arbitrary decision or assertion:事情是不是这样,我不敢～。I can't say for sure that this is true. ❷ arbitrary:～的结论 arbitrary conclusion ❸〈书面〉settle a dispute arbitrarily by one's power or authority:～乡曲 settle local disputes arbitrarily

武夫 wǔfū ❶ man of valour:赳赳～ valiant and stalwart man ❷ warrior; military man:一介～ mere soldier

武工 wǔgōng *also* "武功" acrobatic skill:这位演员的～底子深厚。This actor is well versed in acrobatic skills.

武工队 wǔgōngduì (short for 武装工作队) armed working team (operating in enemy-occupied areas during the War of Resistance Against Japanese Aggression, 1937-1945)

武功 wǔgōng ❶〈书面〉military feats or exploits:文治～ achievements in government and military affairs /～显赫 outstanding military exploits ❷ martial arts; *wushu*; kung fu:他练过～。He has learned martial arts. ❸ *see* "武工"

武官 wǔguān ❶ military officer:文官不要钱,～不怕死。(traditional criterion of good government) Civilian officials seek no personal gains while military officers are not afraid of death. ❷ military attaché:陆军～ military attaché /海军～ naval attaché /空军～ air attaché

武官处 wǔguānchù military attaché's office

武汉 Wǔhàn Wuhan (triple city consisting of Wuchang, Hankou and Hanyang in Hubei Province):～长江大桥 Wuhan Yangtze River Bridge

武行 wǔháng 〈戏曲〉acrobatic actor playing a supporting role

武花脸 wǔhuāliǎn 〈戏曲〉actor with a "painted face", playing a martial role

武火 wǔhuǒ intense or high heat in cooking, etc.:炒菜要用～,炖东西却是要用文火的。Intense heat is necessary for stir-frying, while slow fire is good for simmering.

武将 wǔjiàng military officer; general

武警 wǔjǐng (short for 武装警察) armed police:～部队 (contingent of the) armed police

武净 wǔjìng *see* "武花脸"

武举 wǔjǔ ❶ imperial examinations specializing in military knowledge and skill ❷ one who passed the provincial imperial examinations in military knowledge and skill:～出身 start as a successful candidate in the provincial military examinations

武剧 wǔjù *see* "武戏"

武科 wǔkē imperial examinations specializing in military knowledge and skill

武库 wǔkù armoury; arsenal:核～ nuclear arsenal

武力 wǔlì ❶ (brute) force:～镇压 suppress (*or* put down) by force ❷ armed force; military strength:诉诸～ resort (*or* appeal) to force /使用～或以～相威胁 use or threat of force /炫耀～ show of force /～行为 act of force /我们不赞成使用～解决争端。We are not in favour of using force as a means to settle disputes.

武林 wǔlín martial arts circles:～新秀 promising young person in martial arts /～高手 master of martial arts

武庙 wǔmiào temple of martial valour (devoted to Guan Yu 关羽 or Guan Yu and Yue Fei 岳飞 jointly)

武器 wǔqì ❶ weapon; arms:常规～ conventional weapon /非常规～ non-conventional weapon /轻～ small arms; light weapon /重～ big arms; heavy weapon /核～ nuclear weapon /大规模毁灭性～ weapon of mass destruction /激光～ laser weapon /化学～ chemical weapon /生物～ biological weapon /缴获了大批～ capture a lot of arms /～交易 *also* "军火贸易" arms deal; arms trade ❷ sth. used as a weapon:石油～ oil weapon /思想～ ideological weapon /学会使用批评和自我批评这一～ learn to use criticism and self-criticism as a weapon

武器禁运 wǔqì jìnyùn arms embargo

武器库 wǔqìkù arsenal; armoury

武器制导及跟踪设备 wǔqì zhìdǎo jí gēnzōng shèbèi WGT (weapon guidance and tracker)

武器装备 wǔqì zhuāngbèi weaponry: 最新式～ state-of-art weaponry

武人 wǔrén soldier

武生 wǔshēng 〈戏曲〉actor playing a martial role

武师 wǔshī 〈旧语〉teacher or master of martial arts; kung fu master

武士 wǔshì ❶〈古语〉palace guard ❷ man of prowess; warrior; knight:～俑 burial figure in the shape of a warrior; warrior figure ❸ (in ancient and medieval Japan) samurai

武士道 wǔshìdào (in ancient and medieval Japan) bushido

武士债券 wǔshì zhàiquàn 〈金融〉samurai bond

武术 wǔshù *wushu*; martial arts; kung fu: ～大师 *wushu* master; master of martial arts /～队 *wushu* team; martial arts team /～表演 *wushu* performance; martial arts show /练～ learn (*or* practise) martial arts

武松 Wǔ Sōng Wu Song, character in the classical novel *Heroes of the Marshes* (《水浒》), otherwise translated as *Water Margin* or *All Men Are Brothers*), known for his prowess and traditionally regarded as a typical hero of great valour

武坛 wǔtán *wushu* circles; realm of martial arts:中国～ Chinese *wushu* circles /～新星 new star in martial arts

武戏 wǔxì 〈戏曲〉military piece; piece full of acrobatic fighting

武侠 wǔxiá chivalrous swordsman

武侠小说 wǔxiá xiǎoshuō tales of roving knights; martial arts novel; kung fu novel

武艺 wǔyì *wushu* skill; martial arts skill; kung fu skill:～高强 adept in *wushu* (*or* kung fu) skills /有一身好～ good at martial arts (*or* kung fu) skills

武则天 Wǔ Zétiān Empress Wu Zetian (formerly translated as Wu Tse-tien, c. 624-705), only empress in Chinese history who ruled China from 690 to 705 under the dynastic title of Zhou (周), which reverted to Tang upon her abdication

武职 wǔzhí position of a military officer:担任～ serve as an army officer; serve in the armed forces /～人员 military staff (*or* officer)

武装 wǔzhuāng ❶ arms; military equipment; battle outfit or gear:全副～ (in) full battle gear /～人员 armed personnel /～对峙 armed confrontation /～护卫 armed escort /～挑衅 armed provocation /～泅渡 swim across (a river, etc.) in battle gear /解除～ disarm ❷ arm; equip:用现代化装备～部队 arm the troops with modern weaponry ❸ armed forces:地主～ armed forces of the landed class /人民～ the people's armed forces

武装部队 wǔzhuāng bùduì armed forces

武装冲突 wǔzhuāng chōngtū armed conflict or clash

武装带 wǔzhuāngdài Sam Browne (belt)

武装斗争 wǔzhuāng dòuzhēng armed struggle

武装干涉 wǔzhuāng gānshè armed intervention

武装警察 wǔzhuāng jǐngchá armed police

武装力量 wǔzhuāng lìliàng armed forces; military power

武装起义 wǔzhuāng qǐyì armed uprising

武装侵略 wǔzhuāng qīnlüè armed aggression

武装中立 wǔzhuāng zhōnglì armed neutrality

珷 wǔ

珷玞 wǔfū *also* "碔砆" wǔfū 〈书面〉 jade-like stone

碔 wǔ

碔砆 wǔfū *see* "珷玞" wǔfū

鹉 wǔ *see* "鹦鹉" yīngwǔ

庑(廡) wǔ 〈书面〉 side room or building in a traditional compound house; wing: 东～ east wing /居～下，为人赁舂。The hired hand lived in a small side room husking rice.

庑殿 wǔdiàn side building (on either side of the main hall); wings

怃(憮) wǔ 〈书面〉 ❶ tender affection ❷ frustration; disappointment

怃然 wǔrán 〈书面〉 disappointed; melancholy: ～不乐 feel depressed /～长叹 sigh mournfully

妩(嫵、娬) wǔ

妩媚 wǔmèi (of a flower, woman, etc.) lovely; attractive; charming: ～一笑 with a winsome smile /柳树婀娜多姿，～极了。The willows swaying gracefully in the breeze are a most lovely sight.

舞 wǔ ❶ dance: 歌～ song and dance /集体～ group dance /独～ solo dance /双人～ pas de deux /红绸～ red silk dance /秧歌～ *yangko* dance /腰鼓～ drum dance /芭蕾～ ballet /交际～ ballroom dancing; social dancing /狐步～ fox trot /华尔兹～ waltz /探戈～ tango /霹雳～ break dance /脱衣～ strip tease /恰恰～ cha-cha /桑巴～ samba /伦巴～ rumba /土风～ folk dance /草裙～ hula-hula ❷ move about as if in a dance; dance: 载歌载～ singing and dancing /轻歌曼～ singing merrily and dancing gracefully; soft music and graceful dancing /眉飞色～ (with) dancing eyes and radiant face; enraptured; exultant /手～足蹈 dance for joy /群魔乱～ demons and monsters dancing like mad; evil spirits of all kinds dancing in riotous revelry ❸ dance with sth. in one's hands: ～剑 (perform) swordplay /～龙灯 (perform) the dragon lantern dance /～狮子 (perform) the lion dance ❹ flourish; wave; brandish; wield: 手～双刀 brandish (*or* sway) two swords /张牙～爪 bare fangs and show paws — make threatening gestures ❺ play with: ～文弄墨 show off one's literary skill; juggle with words ❻ 〈方言〉 get: 先～点饭吃了再干。Let's get sth. to eat before we continue.

舞伴 wǔbàn dancing partner (usu. for ballroom dancing); partner

舞弊 wǔbì embezzlement; malpractice; fraudulent practice: 徇私～ fraudulence (*or* cheating) for selfish purposes /考试～被抓住 be caught cheating in an examination

舞步 wǔbù dancing step: ～轻盈 graceful dancing steps

舞场 wǔchǎng commercial dance hall: ～活跃人物 ballroom (*or* dancing) buff

舞池 wǔchí dance floor

舞蹈 wǔdǎo dance: 表演～ perform a dance /古典～ classical dance /～动作 dance movement /～设计 choreography /～编导者 choreographer /～音乐 dance music /今晚节目以～为主。Tonight's programme consists mainly of dances. /孩子们在快活地～。The children are dancing merrily.

舞蹈病 wǔdǎobìng 〈医学〉 chorea

舞蹈家 wǔdǎojiā dancer: 芭蕾舞～ ballet dancer /民间舞～ folk dancer

舞动 wǔdòng wave; shake; brandish: ～手中的红旗 wave the red flag in one's hand

舞会 wǔhuì dance; ball: 周末～ weekend dance /化装～ fancy dress ball /举行～ hold (*or* give) a dance (*or* ball)

舞技 wǔjì dance skill: ～娴熟 consummate skill in dancing

舞剧 wǔjù dance drama; ballet: 民族～ folk dance drama /芭蕾～ ballet

舞客 wǔkè guest or customer at a commercial dance hall

舞美 wǔměi (short for 舞蹈美术) stage art; stagecraft: ～设计 stage art design /～专家 stage artist

舞迷 wǔmí dance fan or fiend

舞弄 wǔnòng ❶ flourish; brandish; wield: ～大刀 brandish (*or* flourish) a long-handled sword ❷ 〈方言〉 do; make: 他想做个鸟笼子，可是自己不会～。He wanted to make a bird cage, but didn't know how.

舞女 wǔnǚ dancing-girl; dance-hostess; taxi dancer

舞谱 wǔpǔ dance notation

舞曲 wǔqǔ dance music; dance

舞台 wǔtái stage; arena: ～生涯 stage career /～照明 stage illumination; lighting /～布景 (stage) scenery; décor /～指示 stage directions /～设计 stage design /～效果 stage effect /～工作人员 stage hand /～监督 stage manager (*or* director); stage /搬上～ present on the stage; stage /旋转～ revolving stage /政治～ political arena (*or* scene, *or* stage) /国际～ international arena /历史～ stage of history; historical stage

舞台记录片 wǔtái jìlùpiàn stage documentary

舞台美术 wǔtái měishù stage art; stagecraft

舞台音乐 wǔtái yīnyuè theatrical music

舞厅 wǔtīng ❶ ballroom; dance hall ❷ *see* "舞场"

舞坛 wǔtán dance circles: ～新人崭露头角。Young and promising dancers are making their début.

舞文弄墨 wǔwén-nòngmò ❶ *also* "舞文弄法" pervert the law by playing with legal phraseology: ～的讼棍 legal trickster adept at perverting the law ❷ engage in phrase-mongering: 这是一篇没有真情实感的～之作。This is merely a phrase-mongering sort of work, devoid of true emotion. /此事照直写来就清楚，～反而不美。Better write this in a simple and straightforward language. Too much embellishment would only spoil it.

舞榭歌台 wǔxiè-gētái *also* "歌台舞榭" music and dance halls

舞星 wǔxīng ace dancer

舞俑 wǔyǒng burial figure in the shape of a dancer; dancing figurine

舞踊 wǔyǒng *see* "舞蹈"

舞艺 wǔyì dance skills: 其～冠绝一时。She was unparalleled in the art of dancing in her time.

舞姿 wǔzī manner or carriage in dancing: ～翩翩 dance lightly and gracefully

五[1] wǔ five: ～岁 five years old /～路无轨(电车) No.5 trolleybus /～口之家 family of five /～集电视连续剧 five-part TV serial

五[2] wǔ 〈音乐〉 musical notation on the traditional Chinese musical scale, equivalent to the numbered musical notation "6"

五爱 wǔ'ài "Five Loves", referring to love for the motherland, the people, physical labour, science, and public property

五霸 Wǔbà *also* "五伯" five hegemons of the Spring and Autumn Period, generally referring to Huangong of Qi (齐桓公), Wengong of Jin (晋文公), Zhuangwang of Chu (楚庄王), Helü of Wu (吴王阖闾), and Goujian of Yue (越王勾践)

五百年前是一家 wǔbǎi nián qián shì yījiā (we) belonged to the same family or clan 500 years ago; share the same surname (and so may be descendants of the same ancestors): 你姓牛，我也姓牛，你我～。Since your name is also Niu, we must have descended from the same family five hundred years ago.

五保 wǔbǎo five guarantees in Chinese rural areas, namely, food, clothing, medical care, housing and burial expenses: ～户 household (of infirm and childless old people) enjoying the five guarantees

五倍子 wǔbèizǐ 〈中药〉 Chinese gall; gallnut

五倍子虫 wǔbèizǐchóng 〈中药〉 gall maker

五倍子酸 wǔbèizǐsuān gallic acid

五棓子 wǔbèizǐ *see* "五倍子"

五边形 wǔbiānxíng pentagon

五步蛇 wǔbùshé 〈动物〉 long-noded pit viper

五彩 wǔcǎi ❶ five colours — blue, yellow, red, white and black ❷ multicoloured: ～旗帜 multicoloured flags and pennants

五彩缤纷 wǔcǎi-bīnfēn blazing with colour; having all the colours of the rainbow; colourful: 公园里繁花似锦，～。The blooming flowers in the park are a riot of colour.

五常 wǔcháng ❶ five cardinal virtues in traditional Chinese ethics: *ren* (仁, benevolence), *yi* (义, justice), *li* (礼, propriety), *zhi* (智, wisdom) and *xin* (信, honour) ❷ *see* "五伦" ❸ *see* "五行"

五重唱 wǔchóngchàng 〈音乐〉 vocal quintet

五重奏 wǔchóngzòu 〈音乐〉 instrumental quintet

W

五次方程 wǔcì fāngchéng 〈数学〉quintic equation
五大湖 Wǔdàhú Great Lakes, five large interconnected lakes (Superior, Michigan, Huron, Erie, and Ontario) in North America
五大三粗 wǔdà-sāncū tall and brawny: ～的汉子 tall and brawny fellow
五代 Wǔdài Five Dynasties, which ruled the Yellow River Basin and neighbouring regions 907-960 (Later Liang, 907-923; Later Tang, 923-936; Later Jin, 936-946; Later Han, 947-950; and Later Zhou, 951-960)
五帝 Wǔdì five virtuous "emperors" — legendary rulers in prehistoric China: Huangdi (黄帝), Zhuanxu (颛顼), Di Ku (帝喾), Tang Yao (唐尧) and Yu Shun (虞舜)
五冬六夏 wǔdōng-liùxià in summer and winter alike; despite heat and cold; all the year round: ～, 他整日赶着羊群去放牧。In summer and winter alike, he was out all day grazing his flock of sheep.
五斗橱 wǔdǒuchú *also* "五屉柜" chest of drawers
五斗米 wǔdǒumǐ five decalitres of rice — petty salary or paltry sum of money: 不为～折腰 refuse to hold a petty office for a paltry salary; would rather starve than bow low for a paltry sum of money
五斗米道 Wǔdǒumǐdào *Wudoumi* sect of Taoism, established by Zhang Daoling (张道陵) towards the end of the Eastern Han Dynasty
五毒 wǔdú ❶ five poisonous creatures (sometimes used in traditional Chinese medicine): scorpion, viper, centipede, house lizard and toad ❷ "five evils", first used in the Five Antis Movement (五反运动) to refer to bribery, tax evasion, theft of state property, cheating on government contracts, and stealing of state economic secrets: ～俱全 guilty of all "five evils"; engaged in all kinds of unlawful acts; steeped in all iniquities
五短三粗 wǔduǎn-sāncū short and sturdy: 他生得～, 浓眉大眼。He was short and sturdy, with thick eyebrows and big eyes.
五短身材 wǔduǎn shēncái short in body and limbs: 此人～, 面色黝黑。He is short and dark of complexion.
五反运动 Wǔfǎn Yùndòng Five Antis Movement (political movement launched in 1952 to combat the "five evils")
五方 wǔfāng east, west, north, south and centre — everywhere: ～之民, 言语不通, 嗜好不一。People from different places have difficulty communicating with each other, and they have their own likes and dislikes.
五方杂处 wǔfāng-záchǔ inhabited by people of all sorts: 省会之地, ～。The provincial capital is inhabited by people of every description.
五分制 wǔfēnzhì five-grade marking system, using 5, 4, 3, 2 and 1 to represent respectively "excellent", "good", "fair", "poor" (*or* "fail") and "very poor"
五分钟热度 wǔfēnzhōng rèdù *also* "三分钟热度" sānfēnzhōng rèdù short-lived enthusiasm; flash in the pan: 他什么事都干不长, 只有～。He can hardly stay long in any job; his enthusiasm lasts only five minutes (*or* is like a flash in the pan).
五风十雨 wǔfēng-shíyǔ *also* "十雨五风" good weather (for the crops); favourable weather
五服 wǔfú ❶ 〈旧语〉five styles of mourning apparel indicating different relationships between the wearer and the deceased ❷ kinship (that can still be traced to a common ancestor): 没出～ (one's) kith and kin / 出了～的远房亲戚 very distant cousin; second cousin thrice removed
五更 wǔgēng ❶ five watches of the night (from dusk to dawn) ❷ fifth watch of the night; just before dawn: ～侵早起, 更有早行人。There are always people who get up earlier than you, though you rise at dawn — there is no cause for complacency, for you might be excelled by other people at any time.
五供 wǔgòng utensils (usu. five pieces) for holding sacrificial offerings; five oblation utensils
五古 wǔgǔ ancient poem with five characters to each line
五谷 wǔgǔ five cereals — rice, two kinds of millet, wheat and beans; food crops in general: ～杂粮 all kinds of food grains
五谷不分 wǔgǔ-bùfēn cannot tell one cereal from another: 四体不勤, ～ can neither toil with one's four limbs nor tell the five cereals apart
五谷丰登 wǔgǔ-fēngdēng abundant harvest of all food crops
五官 wǔguān ❶ five sense organs — ears, eyes, mouth, nose and body ❷ facial features: ～不正 have irregular features
五官端正 wǔguān-duānzhèng have regular features
五光十色 wǔguāng-shísè of all hues and colours; of all kinds; multifarious: 溪水清澈, 游鱼和水底～的小石头都看得清清楚楚。In the limpid stream, the fish swimming below and pebbles of all shapes and colours at the bottom are clearly discernible.
五行八作 wǔháng-bāzuō all trades and businesses: 上个世纪, 这一带商业发达, 会聚着～的人们。It was a flourishing commercial area in the last century, where people of all trades and professions congregated. / 这个人～全能来两下子。This guy is a veritable jack of all trades.
五好家庭 wǔhǎo jiātíng "five-good" family, an honorary title awarded to model families in the movement to strengthen socialist ethics in the 1980's (A "five-good" family should do well in the following five areas: 1) abiding by the law; 2) conscientious study and participation in public activities; 3) family planning and education of the children; 4) domestic harmony and good relationship with neighbours; and 5) security, sanitation and frugality in household management.)
五合板 wǔhébǎn five-layer plywood
五湖四海 wǔhú-sìhǎi five lakes and four seas — all corners of the land: 来自～的宾客 guests from all over the country / 要搞"～", 不搞山头主义。We must draw talents from every part of the country and discard "mountain-stronghold mentality" (*or* narrow-minded sectarianism).
五花八门 wǔhuā-bāmén multifarious; kaleidoscopic; of all sorts: 书摊上摆放的杂志～。There are all sorts of magazines at the bookstall. / 这个人的鬼点子～, 使人莫测高深。He had so many tricks up his sleeve that no one knew exactly what he was up to.
五花大绑 wǔhuā dàbǎng have one's hands and arms tied behind one's back (by the same rope that is looped around one's neck)
五花马 wǔhuāmǎ multicoloured horse
五花肉 wǔhuāròu streaky pork
五花羊 wǔhuāyáng multicoloured goat
五黄六月 wǔhuáng-liùyuè fifth and sixth lunar months, the hottest time of the year: ～不做工, 十冬腊月喝西风。If one doesn't work in summer, one will be hard up in winter.
五荤 wǔhūn five strongly flavoured vegetables, such as garlic, leek, scallion, shallot, etc.: 不食～ eat no strongly-flavoured vegetables
五级风 wǔjífēng *also* "清劲风" qīngjìngfēng force 5 wind; fresh breeze
五极管 wǔjíguǎn 〈电子〉pentode: 五极晶体管 pentode transistor
五脊六兽 wǔjǐ-liùshòu 〈方言〉*also* "五积六受" be ill at ease; be on tenterhooks: 老太太气得～, 上气不接下气。The old lady was so agitated by anger that she was gasping for breath. / 他长期病休, 闲得～的。He has been on sick leave for so long that he is fed up with lying idle all day.
五加 wǔjiā 〈植物〉slender acanthopanax (*Acanthopanax gracilistylus*)
五加皮 wǔjiāpí ❶ bark of slender acanthopanax, used as Chinese medicine ❷ *Wujiapi*, medicinal liquor made from the bark of slender acanthopanax steeped in liquor
五价 wǔjià 〈化学〉pentavalent; quinquevalent
五讲四美三热爱 wǔjiǎng sìměi sānrè'ài "five emphases, four beauties and three loves" — norms advocated in the movement to build socialist ethics in the 1980's (The "five emphases" refer to emphasis on civility, courtesy, sanitation, orderliness, and morality. The "four beauties" refer to beauty of soul, speech, behaviour, and environment. The "three loves" refer to love of the homeland, socialism and the Communist Party.)
五角大楼 Wǔjiǎo Dàlóu Pentagon (headquarters of the US Department of Defence)
五角星 wǔjiǎoxīng five-pointed star
五金 wǔjīn ❶ five metals — gold, silver, copper, iron and tin ❷ metals; hardware: 小～ metal fitting (such as nails, botts, etc.) / ～店 hardware store / ～商 dealer in hardware; hardware dealer; ironmonger / ～公司 hardware company
五经 Wǔjīng Five (Confucian) Classics — *The Book of Changes* (易), *Collection of Ancient Texts* (书), *The Book of Songs* (诗), *The Rites* (礼), and *The Spring and Autumn Annals* (春秋)
五绝 wǔjué classical poem with four five-character lines, following a strict tonal pattern and rhyme scheme

see also "绝句" juéjù

五口通商 Wǔkǒu Tōngshāng five commercial ports of Guangzhou (广州), Fuzhou (福州), Xiamen (厦门), Ningbo (宁波) and Shanghai (上海) opened by the Qing Government to the foreign powers under compulsion after the Opium War (1840-1842)

五劳七伤 wǔláo-qīshāng *also* "五痨七伤"〈中医〉"five lesions" (of the heart, liver, spleen, lungs and kidneys) and "seven injuries" (as caused to the spleen by overeating, to the liver by rage, to the kidneys by lifting heavy weights and sitting long on wet ground, to the lungs by wearing too little and taking cold food and drinks, to the heart by sorrow and anxiety, to the body by abrupt weather changes, and to the consciousness by immoderate fear); poor health and ailments in general

五雷轰顶 wǔléi-hōngdǐng be thunderstruck: 这消息犹如～, 把他惊傻了。Like a bolt from the blue, the news stuck him dumb.

五类分子 wǔlèifènzǐ five categories of people regarded as "public enemies" before the late 1970's, namely, landlords, rich peasants, counter-revolutionaries, bad elements (morally degenerate people) and "Rightists" (those condemned for "opposing socialism" in 1957-1958)

五里雾 wǔlǐwù 〈比喻〉thick fog; total mystery: 他的话弄得我不知所措, 如堕～中。What he said was beyond me; I was completely mystified.

五敛子 wǔliǎnzǐ 〈中药〉fruit of carambola (*Auerrhoa carambola*)

五粮液 wǔliángyè Five-Grain Liquor, famous brand of liquor made from five kinds of grain (produced at Yibin 宜宾, Sichuan Province)

五灵脂 wǔlíngzhī 〈中医〉dried dung of *Trogopterus xanthipes* used as medicine

五零四散 wǔlíng-sìsàn scatter or disperse in all directions: 枪声一响, 吓得人们～, 拼命奔逃。The crowd stampeded at the report of a gun, running for dear life.

五岭 Wǔlǐng Five Ridges (of Yuecheng, Dupang, Mengzhu, Qitian and Dayu) lying across the borders between Hunan and Jiangxi on the one hand, and Guangxi and Guangdong on the other: ～逶迤腾细浪。The Five Ridges wind like gentle ripples.

五律 wǔlǜ classical poem with eight five-character lines, following a strict tonal pattern and rhyme scheme

see also "律诗" lǜshī

五氯硝基苯 wǔlǜ xiāojīběn 〈农业〉pentachloronitrobenzene (PCNB)

五伦 wǔlún five cardinal relationships in traditional ethics — those between monarch and subject, father and son, husband and wife, among brothers and among friends

五马分尸 wǔmǎ-fēnshī *also* "五牛分尸" (ancient torture and capital punishment by tying the victim's head and each of his limbs to a horse and driving the five horses in different directions to tear him to pieces; 〈比喻〉tear or break sth. to pieces; divide up

五内 wǔnèi 〈书面〉viscera: ～俱裂 feel as if one's bowels had been cut through; feel intense pain or anger

五内如焚 wǔnèi-rúfén *also* "五内俱焚" feel as if one's viscera were on fire; be rent with grief; be torn by deep anxiety: 愁得～ be rent with anxiety

五年计划 wǔnián jìhuà five-year plan: 第一个～期间 during the First Five-Year Plan period (1952-1957)

五七干校 Wǔ-Qī gànxiào May Seventh Cadre School, farm-school for government officials, teaching staff and students of colleges and universities, etc. to temper themselves through labour in accordance with Mao Zedong's "May 7 directive" issued during the Cultural Revolution

五禽戏 wǔqínxì Five-Animal Exercise (patterned upon the movements of the tiger, deer, bear, ape and bird, first created by Hua Tuo 华佗, a famous Chinese physician of the Eastern Han Dynasty)

五权宪法 wǔquán xiànfǎ constitution providing for a five-branch government (i. e. the legislative, executive, judicial, supervisory and civil examination branches — the idea was first introduced in 1906 and later elaborated in 1924 by Dr. Sun Yat-sen)

五日京兆 wǔrì-jīngzhào be in office for a short time only; be a lame-duck outgoing office holder: 对这件事, 我这个～已经无能为力了。As I'll soon leave office, I'm really unable to do anything about it.

五卅运动 Wǔ-Sà Yùndòng May 30th Movement, revolutionary movement protesting against imperialist slaughter of Chinese demonstrators in foreign concessions of Shanghai on 30 May 1925

五色 wǔsè five colours — blue, yellow, red, white and black: ～无主 one's face turns now crimson, now pale — be flustered / ～痢〈中医〉dysentry with multicoloured stool / ～主病〈中医〉diagnostic significance of the five colours (as shown in the patient's complexion, etc.) / ～旗 five-coloured flag (national flag of the Republic of China from 1911 to 1927)

五色斑斓 wǔsè-bānlán riot of colour; all the colours of the rainbow

五声音阶 wǔshēng yīnjiē 〈音乐〉five-tone musical scale; pentatonic scale

五十步笑百步 wǔshí bù xiào bǎi bù one who retreats fifty paces laughs at one who retreats a hundred; the pot calls the kettle black: 你干得也不怎么样, 何必～。Stop criticizing others, for you are behaving no better than the pot calling the kettle black.

五世其昌 wǔshì-qíchāng 〈旧语〉(often used to congratulate a newly-wed couple) may the family multiply and prosper for generations to come

五四青年节 Wǔ-Sì Qīngniánjié Youth Day (May 4th), in commemoration of the May 4th Movement of 1919

五四运动 Wǔ-Sì Yùndòng May 4th Movement (1919), political and cultural movement against imperialism and feudalism

五体投地 wǔtǐ-tóudì prostrate oneself on the ground (in admiration); be knocked out with admiration: 佩服得～ admire sb. from the bottom of one's heart / 你今天的手段, 连魔鬼也会～。Even Satan would be knocked out with admiration for the tricks you played today.

五维空间 wǔwéi kōngjiān five-dimensional space; quintuple space

五味 wǔwèi five flavours — sweet, sour, bitter, pungent and salty; all sorts of flavours: ～偏嗜 addiction to one of the five flavours

五味子 wǔwèizǐ 〈中药〉fruit of Chinese magnoliavine (*Schisandra*): 北～ *Schisandra chinensis* / 华中～ *Schisandra sphenanthera*

五线谱 wǔxiànpǔ 〈音乐〉staff; stave

五香 wǔxiāng five spices — prickly ash, star aniseed, cinnamon, clove and fennel; spices: ～豆 spiced beans / ～鱼 spiced fish / ～豆腐干 spicy bean cheese / ～牛肉干 dried spicy beef

五项运动 wǔxiàng yùndòng *also* "五项全能"〈体育〉pentathlon

五小工业 wǔxiǎo gōngyè five small industries — small-scale factories or mines that produce iron and steel, coal, machinery, chemical fertilizers, and cement by using local resources

五星红旗 Wǔxīng Hóngqí Five-Star Red Flag, national flag of the People's Republic of China

五星级 wǔxīngjí five-star: ～豪华宾馆 five-star luxury hotel

五星上将 wǔxīng shàngjiàng five-star general: 空军～ (US) general of the air force

五刑 wǔxíng (in ancient China) five cardinal forms of punishment — tattooing the face (墨), cutting off the nose (劓), cutting off the feet (剕), castration (宫), and decapitation (大辟)

五行 wǔxíng five elements (metal 金, wood 木, water 水, fire 火 and earth 土) — a theory used by ancient Chinese philosophers to explain the origin of the world, by physicians of traditional Chinese medicine to make pathological diagnoses, and by superstitious people in fortune-telling: ～相生。The five elements produce (*or* promote) one another (in the order of wood, fire, earth, metal, water, and wood again). / ～相克。The five elements subdue (*or* repel) one another (in the order of water, fire, metal, wood, earth and water again).

五行学说 wǔxíng xuéshuō 〈中医〉theory of the five elements

五旬节 Wǔxúnjié *also* "圣临节" Shènglínjié Pentecost

五言诗 wǔyánshī poem with five characters to a line

五颜六色 wǔyán-liùsè of various colours; multicoloured; colourful: ～的气球 balloons of various colours / ～的服装 colourful costumes

五羊城 Wǔyángchéng City of Five Rams — nickname for Guangzhou (广州)

五一 Wǔ-Yī (short for 五一国际劳动节) May Day

五一国际劳动节 Wǔ-Yī Guójì Láodòngjié International Labour Day (May 1); May Day

五音 wǔyīn ❶〈音乐〉five notes of the ancient pentatonic scale: ～

不全 have a poor ear and voice; be a poor singer ❷〈语言〉five points of consonant articulation
五元合金 wǔyuán héjīn 〈冶金〉quinary alloy
五月 wǔyuè ❶ May ❷ fifth month (of the lunar year); fifth moon
五月花 wǔyuèhuā mayflower:～号 the Mayflower ship carrying the Pilgrim fathers to North America in 1620
五月节 Wǔyuèjié *also* "端午节" Duānwǔjié Dragon Boat Festival (fifth day of the fifth month of the lunar year)
五岳 Wǔyuè Five Sacred Mountains (for worship in traditional Chinese culture): Taishan Mountain or Mount Tai (泰山), the Eastern Sacred Mountain in Shandong; Hengshan Mountain or Mount Heng (衡山), the Southern Sacred Mountain in Hunan; Huashan Mountain or Mount Hua (华山), the Western Sacred Mountain in Shaanxi; Hengshan Mountain or Mount Heng (恒山), the Northern Sacred Mountain in Shanxi; Songshan Mountain or Mount Song (嵩山), the Central Sacred Mountain in Henan
五脏 wǔzàng five internal organs — heart, liver, spleen, lungs and kidneys
五脏六腑 wǔzàng-liùfǔ all the internal organs of the human body; vital organs:她感到～像让什么扯着似地阵阵发痛。She felt stabbing pains going through her vital organs. /他可把你的～摸透了。He understands you through and through. *or* He knows you inside out.
五指 wǔzhǐ five fingers — thumb, index finger, middle finger, third or ring finger and little finger:伸手不见～ so dark that you can't see your own fingers; pitch dark
五中 wǔzhōng 〈书面〉internal organs of the human body; innermost being:～无主 indecisive; totally at a loss /铭感～ deeply grateful; thank sb. from the bottom of one's heart
五洲 wǔzhōu whole world; everywhere in the world; the world over:来自～四海的国际友人 foreign friends who come from various parts of the world
五子棋 wǔzǐqí gobang:下盘～ play a game of gobang
五族 wǔzú five (major) ethnic groups; five nationalities (Hans, Manchus, Mongolians, Huis and Tibetans):～共和 republic based upon the five (major) nationalities (ethnic principle introduced by Dr. Sun Yat-sen for the Republic of China born in 1912)

伍

wǔ ❶ basic five-man unit of the army in ancient China; army:队～ troops; ranks /行～ army; rank and file /入～ join the army; enlist /退～ retire from active military service; be demobbed /退～军人 demobilized soldier; ex-serviceman; veteran ❷ company:相与为～ keep company with sb. /乐与为～ glad to keep sb. company; happy to be with sb. /落～ fall behind (the others or the times) ❸ five (used for the numeral 五 to avoid mistakes or alterations) ❹ (Wǔ) a surname
伍的 wǔde 〈方言〉and what not; and so on:什么椅子、凳子～都搬走了。The chairs, stools, and what not have all been taken away. /要是扭着、碰着～可不好。It would be bad to get strained, or bruised, or whatever.

捂(摀)

wǔ cover; seal; hide; muffle:用手～住鼻子 cover one's nose with one's hand /～汗 be heavily dressed (*or* covered in bed) in order to sweat (out a cold, etc.) /她用厚毛巾～着电话,免得惊醒了孩子。She muffled the telephone with a thick towel lest the child be awakened. /想～住人家的嘴是办不到的。It's impossible to seal other people's lips.
捂盖子 wǔ gàizi keep the lid on; cover up the truth; conceal:采取～的办法不解决问题。It won't help to cover up the truth. /他们越是～,我们就越是要揭盖子。The more they try to keep the lid on, the more we would have the truth revealed.
捂捂盖盖 wǔwǔ-gàigài 〈方言〉hide; conceal; keep from being known or seen:男子汉在妻子面前～的就不对了。It is wrong for a man to conceal what he does and feels from his wife. /做人要诚实,有错不能～的。One should be honest and never try to cover up one's mistakes.
捂眼 wǔyan 〈方言〉blinkers (for draught animals)
捂扎 wǔzha 〈方言〉fiddle with

牾

wǔ 〈书面〉contradict; go against; run counter to:抵～ contradict /～意 go against sb.'s wish

午

wǔ ❶ seventh of the twelve Earthly Branches *see also* "干支" gānzhī ❷ noon; midday:中～ noon /上～ morning /下～ afternoon /正～ (at) high noon /你们～间休息吗? Do you have a lunch break? *or* Do you take a nap at noon?
午餐 wǔcān lunch; noon meal; midday meal
午餐肉 wǔcānròu luncheon meat:火腿～ ham luncheon meat
午错 wǔcuò (often used in the early vernacular) just after noon time; a little past noon
午饭 wǔfàn lunch; noon meal; midday meal:早饭吃饱,～吃好,晚饭吃少。Breakfast should be substantial, lunch nutritious and supper light.
午后 wǔhòu afternoon:天气预报,～有雷雨。According to the weather forecast, there will be a thunderstorm this afternoon.
午间 wǔjiān noon; midday:～新闻 midday news (*or* broadcast)
午觉 wǔjiào afternoon nap; noontime snooze; siesta:许多人有睡～的习惯。Many people are in the habit of taking an afternoon nap. /他来时,我～睡醒了。I was through napping when he came.
午刻 wǔkè *see* "午时"
午前 wǔqián forenoon; before noon; morning:我们必须于二十日～到达。We must arrive on the morning of the 20th.
午时 wǔshí 7th period in the ancient 12-period time keeping schedule — from 11:00 a.m. to 1:00 p.m.
午睡 wǔshuì ❶ *also* "午觉" afternoon nap; noontime snooze; siesta:～时间,请勿打扰。Nap time. Do not disturb. /～打个盹也能使人整个下午都有精神。Even a catnap after lunch keeps one energetic the whole afternoon. ❷ take or have a nap after lunch:我要～了。I'm going to take a nap (*or* have a short siesta).
午休 wǔxiū noon break; midday rest; lunch hour:～时间,不得喧哗。Keep quiet during the noon break. /每天有一小时～时间。There is an hour's lunch break every day.
午宴 wǔyàn feast at noon; luncheon:设～招待 give a luncheon in sb.'s honour
午夜 wǔyè midnight:战斗于～打响。The battle broke out at midnight.

忤(啎)

wǔ ❶ disobedient; unfilial ❷ on bad terms; uncongenial:与人无～ bear no ill will against anybody; get along well with everybody
忤逆 wǔnì unfilial; disobedient (to one's parents):～不孝 filial impiety /～之子 disobedient (*or* unfilial) son /～长辈 be defiant to one's seniors

迕

wǔ 〈书面〉❶ encounter:与友人相～ encounter one's friend(s) ❷ disobedient; defiant:违～ be defiant

仵

wǔ ❶〈旧语〉*yamen* employee whose duty was to find out the cause of a person's death at a trial; coroner ❷ (Wǔ) a surname
仵工 wǔgōng 〈方言〉one who carries or buries the deceased; funeral helper
仵作 wǔzuò 〈旧语〉coroner

侮

wǔ insult; humiliate; bully:外～ foreign aggression /欺～ bully; insult /不可～ not to be bullied; not to be insulted
侮骂 wǔmà abuse; swear (at sb.); call names
侮慢 wǔmàn slight; treat disrespectfully; humiliate:恣意～ deliberately slight
侮蔑 wǔmiè be scornful; show disdain; treat with contempt:他的话并无丝毫～之意。There was no suggestion of contempt in his remark.
侮弄 wǔnòng bully and tease:受人～ be bullied and made a fool of
侮辱 wǔrǔ insult; humiliate; affront; subject to indignities:～人格 affront to sb.'s dignity /～名誉 insult to sb.'s reputation /觉得受了～ feel insulted (*or* humiliated)

wù

鋈

wù 〈书面〉❶ copper-nickel alloy; white copper ❷ plating; gilding:～器 gilded ware; gold-plated utensil

W

误(悞)

wù ❶ mistake; error: 严重舛～ blunder /错～ mistake; error /勘～表 errata; corrigenda /笔～ slip of the pen /口～ slip of the tongue /～传 false information /耽搁总比失～要好。Delay is preferable to error. ❷ miss; delay: ～了末班车 miss the last bus /～了两小时 be delayed for 2 hours /磨刀不～砍柴工。Deliberating is not delaying. ❸ harm; damage: ～人不浅 do no little harm to other people /聪明反被聪明～。Clever people may fall victim to their own cleverness. ❹ by mistake; accidentally: ～触忌讳 break a taboo by mistake

误班 wùbān be late for work; miss work: 我上周生病，误了三天班。I was ill and absent from work for three days last week.

误餐 wùcān miss a meal: ～补贴 compensation for missing a meal; subsidy for eating out (while on business)

误差 wùchā error; tolerance: ～范围 range of error /平均～ mean error; average error /方位～ error in bearing /瞄准～ error of sighting /绝对～ absolute error /累积～ accumulated (*or* aggregate) error /容许～ tolerated error /～极小的精密仪器 precision instrument with a very close tolerance /～不超过千分之零点五 with a tolerance of less than half a thousandth /这种表年～不到一秒。The yearly error of the watch is within one second.

误差函数 wùchā hánshù error function

误差率 wùchālǜ rate of error

误场 wùchǎng (of an actor, etc.) miss a performance

误车 wùchē ❶ (of vehicles or drivers) run into a traffic jam; be delayed: 由于交通拥挤，这条路上有时会～两个小时。Owing to heavy traffic, you could sometimes be delayed for 2 hours driving on this road. ❷ miss a bus or train: 因为临时有急事，他那天～了。He missed the train that day because of some last-minute business he had to attend to.

误打误撞 wùdǎ-wùzhuàng 〈口语〉 by accident; as luck would have it: ～，他竟然跑了个第一。As luck would have it, he won first place in the race. /我们～，竟然在大街上相遇了。We ran into each other in the street.

误导 wùdǎo mislead; lead astray: 某些新闻媒体～了舆论。Public opinion was led astray by some mass media.

误点 wùdiǎn late; overdue; behind time; behind schedule: 这趟火车经常～。This train is often behind schedule. /由于遇上洪水，17 次直快～12 小时。Through Train No. 17 was 12 hours late due to the flood.

误工 wùgōng ❶ cause delay in work: 施工现场狭小，常常～。As the construction site is too small, work is often delayed. ❷ be late for, or absent from work: 他今年一天也没有～。He has never been absent from work this year.

W

误国 wùguó damage national interests; harm the country: 奸臣～ treacherous officials harm the country /误党～ damage the interests of the Party and the state

误会 wùhuì misunderstand; misinterpret; mistake; misconstrue: 引起～ cause (*or* lead to) misunderstanding /消除～ remove (*or* dispel) misunderstanding /你～我了。You misunderstood me. /这可是个老大的～! What gross misconception!

误解 wùjiě misread; misunderstand; miscomprehend: 你～了我的用心。You misread my intentions. /你的话，他～了。He misunderstood what you said. /这纯属～。This is sheer misunderstanding.

误卯 wùmǎo late for roll-call; late: 他从来没请过假误过卯。He never asked for leave or was late for work.

误谬 wùmiù error; mistake; falsehood: ～百出。There are countless errors.

误期 wùqī miss the deadline; exceed the time limit: 由于工程～，我们公司被罚款。Our company is fined for missing the deadline for the project.

误区 wùqū "area of error" — long-standing mistaken idea or concept: 引导人们走出～ help people get rid of the long-standing mistaken ideas

误人子弟 wùrénzǐdì lead young people astray; mislead the younger generation

误入歧途 wùrù-qítú go astray; be misled: 他受人愚弄，～。He was deceived and led astray.

误杀 wùshā 〈法律〉 manslaughter: 这是故杀而非～。This is premeditated murder, not manslaughter.

误伤 wùshāng accidentally injure: ～好人 harm (*or* injure) an innocent person by accident (*or* mistake) /他在一次军事演习中被流弹～，不治而亡。He was hit by a stray bullet in a military exercise and died consequently.

误事 wùshì bungle or spoil matters (as through delay, oversight, etc.): 他常因酗酒而～。He often bungles matters through drunkenness. /请放心，误不了你的事。You may rest assured that there won't be any delay in the matter.

误听 wùtīng wrongly believe what one hears: ～谗言 be misled by lies

误信 wùxìn wrongly believe; be misled: 不能～那套谬论。One should not be taken in by those fallacies.

误诊 wùzhěn ❶ make or give a wrong diagnosis: 把肺炎～为感冒 diagnose pneumonia as a common cold ❷ miss the chance for timely diagnosis and treatment: 因离医院太远而～。No timely treatment was possible as the hospital was too far away.

恶(惡)

wù ❶ dislike; loathe; detest; hate: 憎～ hate /厌～ detest; abhor; be disgusted with /可～ disgusting; loathsome; distasteful /个人好～ one's personal likes and dislikes ❷ 〈中医〉 aversion: ～风 aversion to wind / ～食 aversion to food

see also ě; è; wū

恶寒 wùhán 〈中医〉 aversion to cold

恶热 wùrè 〈中医〉 aversion to heat

恶湿居下 wùshī-jūxià dislike dampness but make one's abode in low-lying land — one's action at variance with one's wish

寤

wù 〈书面〉 ❶ wake up ❷ *see* "悟" wù

寤寐 wùmèi awake or asleep: ～以求 crave day and night

痦(疬)

wù

痦子 wùzi naevus; mole: 她脸上有颗～。There is a mole on her face.

悟

wù realize; become aware; awaken: 领～ comprehend; grasp /执迷不～ obstinately stick to a wrong course; refuse to listen to reason /若有所～ seem to realize; seem enlightened

悟彻 wùchè thoroughly understand or realize: ～佛理 thoroughly grasp Buddhism /他在晚年～了这一终身大错，隐退田园。He woke up to this error of his lifetime in old age and retired to the countryside.

悟道 wùdào comprehend the way of truth; realize the truth of a doctrine or religion

悟会 wùhuì understand; realize; comprehend: 对其原理渐有～ come to understand the fundamental tenets gradually

悟解 wùjiě understand; comprehend: 他这句话我很久才～过来。It took me quite some time to realize what he meant.

悟性 wùxìng power of understanding; comprehension: ～差 poor comprehension; slow wit /惊人的～ amazingly good understanding (*or* comprehension)

焐

wù warm up: 用开水把黄酒～热了再喝。Warm up the rice wine in hot water before you drink it. /天太冷，写字前先用热水袋～～手。It's so cold. Warm your hands with a hot-water bottle before you start to write.

晤

wù meet; encounter; interview; see: 会～外宾 meet (*or* see) a foreign guest /有暇请来一～。Come and see me when you are free.

晤对 wùduì 〈书面〉 meet; see: ～片时 meet for a while

晤见 wùjiàn meet; see; interview: 承蒙～，不胜感激。I am most grateful to you for granting me an audience.

晤聚 wùjù meet; get together: 每年～一次 get together once a year

晤面 wùmiàn meet; see: 我们已多年未曾～了。We haven't seen each other for many years now.

晤商 wùshāng meet and discuss: 此事你我日后～。We shall discuss it when we meet later.

晤谈 wùtán meet and talk; have a talk or discussion; interview: ～甚欢 have a cordial talk (*or* discussion) /我们～的机会还很多。We shall have plenty of time to meet and talk with each other.

兀

wù 〈书面〉 ❶ rising to a height; lofty; towering: 巉岩突～ crags rise precipitously ❷ (of a hill) barren; bald

see also wū

兀傲 wù'ào 〈书面〉 overweening; supercilious; arrogant; haughty:性情～ arrogant by nature
兀的 wùdì ❶ (often used in the early vernacular) this; such:觑了他～模样。I found him in such a (wretched, agitated or angry) state. ❷ (often used in the early vernaculer) how; why:这般热天气，～不晒杀人! It's so hot! Why, you could get roasted in the sun! ❸〈方言〉suddenly; abruptly:隔壁的门～砰然一声，走出来一个人。All of a sudden, the door of the next room banged open and somebody came out.
兀鹫 wùjiù 〈动物〉griffon vulture
兀立 wùlì stand errect; tower:一座大山～眼前。A huge mountain towered ahead. /山石～如柱。Rocks stood erect like so many pillars.
兀臬 wùniè *see* "杌陧" wùniè
兀然 wùrán ❶ rise towering; stand steadfast:～端坐 sit erect in one's seat /山峰～耸立。The peaks rise towering (above the plain, etc.). ❷ suddenly; all of a sudden:他～而止，不再往下说了。He stopped talking all of a sudden. ❸ be in a trance; be in a stupor:～而醉 be in a drunken stupor
兀突 wùtū unexpectedly; suddenly:事情来得那么～，使我惶惑不安。It all happened so unexpectedly that I felt most uneasy and perplexed.
兀兀 wùwù ❶ motionless; still:他～地坐着，似乎全神贯注地看书。He sat motionless in his seat, apparently engrossed in reading. ❷〈书面〉untiringly diligent:～以穷年 work hard all the year round ❸〈书面〉be in a trance; be in a stupor:醉～ be in a drunken stupor
兀自 wùzì 〈方言〉still:～不动 remain motionless /～坐在那里。He sat there quiet and still.
兀坐 wùzuò sit up straight:～不语 sit bolt straight without saying a word

靰 wù

靰鞡 wùla *see* "乌拉" wùla

杌 wù (usu. small) stool

杌凳 wùdèng (usu. small) stool
杌陧 wùniè *also* "兀臬" wùniè; "阢陧" wùniè 〈书面〉(of a situation, state of mind, etc.) restless; unstable; uneasy:数日来，我一直～不安。I have been feeling uneasy for several days.
杌子 wùzi (usu. small) stool

扤 wù 〈书面〉shake; convulse

屼 wù 〈书面〉(of a hill etc.) barren; bald

鹜 wù *see* "鹣鹜" nièwù

阢 wù

阢陧 wùniè *see* "杌陧" wùniè

戊 wù fifth of the ten Heavenly Stems
see also "干支" gānzhī
戊胺 wù'àn 〈化学〉amylamine; pentylamine
戊巴比妥 wùbābǐtuǒ 〈药学〉amobarbital:～钠 nembutal; pentobarbital sodium
戊醇 wùchún 〈化学〉pentanol; amyl alcohol
戊酸 wùsuān 〈化学〉pentanoic acid; pentanoate; valeric acid
戊烷 wùwán 〈化学〉pentane:～灯 pentane lamp /～精炼 pentafining /～馏除器 depentainizer /～喹〈药学〉pentaquine
戊烯 wùxī 〈化学〉amylene; pentene
戊戌变法 Wùxū Biànfǎ *also* "戊戌维新" Reform Movement of 1898 (the year of Wuxu in the Chinese chronology), launched by Kang Youwei (康有为) and other reformers under the auspices of Emperor Guangxu (光绪) and suppressed by the Empress Dowager Cixi (慈禧)

务(務) wù ❶ task; affair; business:国～ state affair /公～ official business /任～ task; assignment /总～ general affairs /杂～ odd jobs; miscellaneous affairs /业～ professional work; business ❷ apply oneself to; be engaged in; go in for:～商 go in for commerce; go into business /当～之急 pressing matter of the moment; urgent matter; task of top priority ❸〈旧语〉outpost of a tax office (now used as part of a place name) ❹ must; be sure to:～请准时出席。Be sure to be present on time. /陈言～去。All clichés must be deleted. ❺ (Wù) a surname
务本 wùběn direct one's efforts towards the basic tasks; attend to the fundamentals
务必 wùbì must; be imperative to; be sure to:各项规章制度～严格执行。All rules and regulations must be strictly implemented. /～按期到达。Be sure to arrive in time.
务工 wùgōng ❶ be engaged in industrial or engineering work ❷ in-put:土地好，～不多，收益颇丰。On good land, a moderate in-put will bring considerable return.
务农 wùnóng go in for farming; be a farmer; work in the fields:高中毕业后我打算回家～。I am going to return to the countryside and be a farmer after graduating from secondary school.
务期 wùqī be imperative; be sure to (do sth.):～全歼来犯之敌。Be sure to wipe out all the invading enemy troops.
务求 wùqiú be sure to have sth. done; ensure:此事～按期完成。It is imperative to fulfil the task as scheduled.
务实 wùshí ❶ deal with concrete matters:今天只讨论总的原则，先不～。Today, we shall confine ourselves to general principles only, and not take up any specific matters. ❷ pragmatic:～主义 pragmatism /～主义者 pragmatist /～精神 spirit of realism; pragmatism
务使 wùshǐ see to it that; make sure; ensure:～大家正确认识这点。Make sure that everyone understands this correctly.
务须 wùxū must; be essential to; be sure to:～今天将此信寄出。See to it that this letter gets posted today. /～掌握文件的精神实质。It is essential to grasp the spirit of the document.
务虚 wùxū discuss principles or ideological guidelines (in contrast with concrete matters); discuss matters from a plane of principle:理论～会 meeting to discuss theoretical and cognitive problems /先～，后务实。Discuss principles before concrete matters.
务要 wùyào must; be sure to:～结伴而行。Be sure to travel in a group.
务育 wùyù 〈方言〉cultivate; foster; breed:～庄稼 cultivate crops /～果树 raise fruit trees
务正 wùzhèng (usu. used in the negative) do a proper or honest job; engage in honest business:此人素不～。He's never done an honest job.

雾(霧) wù ❶ fog; mist:烟～ smog /晓～ morning mist /大～ heavy fog /晨有薄～。There was a mist in the morning. /秋～凉风冬～雪。An autumn fog presages a cold wind and a winter fog a snow. ❷ fine spray:喷～器 sprayer
雾霭 wù'ǎi 〈书面〉mist; haze:～茫茫 vast veil of mist /乳白色的～轻笼着大地。A milky-white haze enveloped the land.
雾标 wùbiāo 〈交通〉fog buoy
雾沉沉 wùchénchén covered by mist or fog; fog-bound:山上～的模糊一片。The hill-top was hidden in a mist.
雾滴 wùdī 〈环保〉fog drop; fog drip
雾谷 Wùgǔ Foggy Bottom (nickname for the US Department of State, which is located in a neighbourhood so named)
雾号 wùhào *also* "雾笛"〈交通〉fog signal; fog horn; fog siren
雾虹 wùhóng *also* "白虹" báihóng 〈气象〉fogbow
雾化 wùhuà atomize; aerosolize; nebulize:～粉 atomized powder
雾化器 wùhuàqì atomizer; diffuser
雾里看花 wùlǐ-kànhuā *also* "雾中看花" ❶ (of old people) see or watch flowers through misty eyes ❷ see hazily; have a hazy idea or impression:只是～，凭想当然去处理，没有不失败的。One is bound to fail if one relies on hazy impressions and takes everything for granted.
雾茫茫 wùmāngmāng foggy; misty; hazy:～的山路上什么也看不清。Everything on the mountain path was blurred in the mist.
雾气 wùqì fog; mist; vapour:车间里～太大。There is too much vapour in the workshop.
雾凇 wùsōng *also* "树挂" shùguà 〈气象〉rime
雾腾腾 wùtēngtēng with a rising or surging fog; foggy:湖面上～的。There was a surging fog over the lake.
雾钟 wùzhōng fog bell:雾中停泊的船只鸣响～以示位置。A ship at anchor in a fog indicates its position by ringing its fog bell.

勿 wù (usu. used in imperative sentences) no; not:～妄语。No lying. *or* Do not rant. /切～上当! Beware of swindlers! /请～打

W

扰。Do not disturb. /请～喧哗。Be quiet, please.
勿忘草 wùwàngcǎo *also* "勿忘我草" forget-me-not
勿谓言之不预 wù wèi yán zhī bù yù do not complain that you have not been forewarned; do not forget my warning
勿以恶小而为之,勿以善小而不为 wù yǐ è xiǎo ér wéi zhī, wù yǐ shàn xiǎo ér bù wéi do no evil because it is a small evil; do not leave a good undone because it is a small good

芴

wù 〈化学〉fluorene

物

wù ❶ thing; creature; matter; material: 读～ reading matter /货～ goods; commodity /产～ product; outcome; result /宝～ treasure /动～ animal /宠～ pet /信～ token; keepsake /～各有主。Everything has its rightful owner. ❷ outside world as distinct from oneself; people other than oneself; other people: 超然～外 be above wordly considerations ❸ content; essence; substance: 空洞无～ be without substance; absolutely nothing in terms of content
物产 wùchǎn product; produce: 地域广大, ～丰富 vast in territory and plentiful in products
物腐虫生 wùfǔ-chóngshēng worms infest decayed matters; worms breed in decaying matter — internal weakness invites external aggression: ～, 疑起谗入。As worms breed in rotten matter, calumny finds refuge in a suspicious heart.
物阜民安 wùfù-mín'ān *also* "物阜民康" goods are in plentiful supply and the people are happy; the country has plenty of products and the people live in contentment
物故 wùgù 〈书面〉pass away: 双亲～已久。Both his parents passed away long ago.
物归原主 wùguīyuánzhǔ return sth. to its rightful owner: 这幅名画一度被盗, 现已～。This famous painting, once stolen, has been returned to its original owner.
物耗 wùhào consumption of goods and materials: 降低～ reduce the consumption of materials
物候 wùhòu phenology: ～学 phenology /～学家 phenologist /～研究 phenological study
物华天宝 wùhuá-tiānbǎo good products from the earth are nature's treasures: 这个地区～, 人杰地灵。The area is blessed with a favourable climate, fertile land, rich resources and outstanding talents.
物化 wùhuà 〈书面〉pass away
物化劳动 wùhuà láodòng *also* "死劳动" sǐláodòng 〈经济〉materialized labour
物换星移 wùhuàn-xīngyí *also* "星移物换" things change with the passing of years; the seasons change: 寒来暑往, ～。Things change with the passing of the years, as the seasons follow each other.
物活论 wùhuólùn *also* "万物有生论" wànwù yǒushēnglùn 〈哲学〉hylozoism
物极必反 wùjí-bìfǎn things turn into their opposites when they reach the extreme; things negate themselves when they reach their limits; no extremes will hold long: ～, 压迫愈甚, 反抗愈烈。As things turn into their opposites when they reach the extreme, the worst oppression arouses the fiercest resistance.
物价 wùjià (commodity) price: 调整～ regulate (*or* adjust) prices /提高～ raise prices /稳定～ stabilize prices /哄抬～ jack up prices /～失控 prices get out of control; runaway prices /～冻结 price freeze /严格～纪律 strictly enforce price regulations /～飞涨。Prices skyrocket (*or* soar).
物价补贴 wùjià bǔtiē subsidy to make up for price rises
物价统计 wùjià tǒngjì statistics of prices
物价政策 wùjià zhèngcè pricing policy
物价指数 wùjià zhǐshù price index: 物价总指数 general price index /物价上涨指数 index of price rises
物件 wùjiàn object; thing; article: 储藏室里堆满了零碎～。The store-room is cluttered with odds and ends.
物尽其用 wùjìnqíyòng put things to best use; let all things serve their proper purposes: 人尽其才, ～ tap every person's talents and everything's uses to the maximum; make the best use of every person and thing
物镜 wùjìng 〈物理〉objective lens
物理 wùlǐ ❶ 〈书面〉innate laws of things: 穷究～ thoroughly investigate the innate laws of things /其～鲜为人知。Its actual workings are known to few people. ❷ physics: 理论～ theoretical physics /应用～ applied physics /固体～ solid physics /液体～ liquid physics /～测量 physical measurement /～环境 physical environment /～试验 physical test /～显影 physical development
物理变化 wùlǐ biànhuà physical change
物理常数 wùlǐ chángshù physical constant
物理地质学 wùlǐ dìzhìxué physical geology
物理化学 wùlǐ huàxué physical chemistry
物理量 wùlǐliàng physical quantity
物理疗法 wùlǐ liáofǎ physical therapy; physiotherapy
物理性质 wùlǐ xìngzhì physical property
物理学 wùlǐxué physics: 低温～ low temperature physics /高能～ high energy physics /地球～ geophysics /天体～ astrophysics /原子～ atomic physics /原子核～ nuclear physics /量子～ quantum physics /～家 physicist
物理诊断 wùlǐ zhěnduàn physiodiagnosis
物力 wùlì material resources: 爱惜人力、～。Use manpower and material resources sparingly.
物力维艰 wùlì-wéijiān the production of things is no easy job: 一粥一饭, 当思来之不易; 半丝半缕, 恒念～。One should bear in mind that every meal and every piece of clothing is hard to come by.
物料 wùliào goods and materials: 包装～ packaging materials /防汛抢险～ materials for flood prevention and emergency use
物美价廉 wùměi-jiàlián of excellent quality and reasonable price; cheap and fine
物品 wùpǐn article; goods; product: 日用～ article for everyday use /免税～ duty-free articles (*or* goods) /应上税～ dutiable articles /贵重～ valuables /私人～ personal belongings; personal effects /零星～ sundries; odds and ends /违禁～ contraband
物情 wùqíng the way things are: 世态～ ways of the world
物权 wùquán 〈法律〉real right; right over something: ～行为 juristical act of real right /～诉讼 action *in rem*; action of real right
物色 wùsè look for; recruit; seek; choose: ～经济管理人才 look for (*or* recruit) trained personnel in business management /～人选 seek a proper candidate
物伤其类 wùshāngqílèi all beings grieve for their fellows' misfortunes; like feels for like: 兔死狐悲, ～。As the fox mourns when the hare dies, so all beings grieve for their own kind.
物神 wùshén 〈宗教〉fetish
物事 wùshì ❶ 〈书面〉matter; thing: 作何～? What does it serve as? ❷ 〈方言〉visible thing; object; article: 啥～? What's it?
物是人非 wùshì-rénfēi things remain the same but the people are gone; the scenery remains as before, but human affairs have changed
物态 wùtài 〈物理〉state of matter
物态方程 wùtài fāngchéng equation of state
物探 wùtàn physical exploration
物体 wùtǐ body; substance; object: 发光～ luminous body /绝缘～ insulator /固态～ solid substance
物外 wùwài 〈书面〉above or outside worldly matters: 她生性孤傲, 超然～。Proud and aloof, she transcended worldly considerations.
物望 wùwàng popular trust or confidence: ～所归 enjoy popular trust
物物交换 wù-wù jiāohuàn barter: ～是原始社会的重要交换形式。Barter is the main form of exchange in primitive society.
物象 wùxiàng ❶ change in the behaviour of an animal or the property of an object, reflecting changing circumstances: 我国劳动人民常将～作为预测天气变化的辅助手段。The labouring people of China often use changes in natural phenomena as a supplementary means in weather forecasting. ❷ image: 模写～ copy an image
物像 wùxiàng reflection; image: 烛光通过小孔, 可在墙上映出倒置的～。A candlelight may, through a tiny hole, cast an upside-down reflection on a wall.
物业 wùyè real estate; property: ～管理 property management
物以类聚 wùyǐlèijù like attracts like; birds of a feather flock together: ～, 人以群分 things of a kind come together, people of a mind form a group; birds of a feather flock together
物以稀为贵 wù yǐ xī wéi guì when a thing is rare, it becomes precious; rare things are precious; scarcity enhances value
物议 wùyì criticism from others: 不屑于～ ignore criticism by others /～沸腾 popular criticisms are boiling /小心谨慎, 免遭～。Take care to avoid public censure.
物欲 wùyù desire or yearning for material comfort: 人的～永远无法

满足。Human desire for material comfort is insatiable.

物证 wùzhèng material evidence; *probatio mortua*: ～化验 test of material evidence / 人证、～俱在,罪犯供认不讳。Confronted with witnesses and material evidence, the suspect admitted his crime (*or* pleaded guilty).

物质 wùzhì ❶ matter; substance: 导电～ conductive substance / 矿～ mineral substance / ～第一性,意识第二性。Matter is primary and consciousness is secondary. ❷ material: ～财富 material wealth / ～奖励 material reward / ～利益 material gains / 改进～条件 improve material conditions

物质不灭定律 wùzhì bùmiè dìnglǜ law of the conservation of matter

物质刺激 wùzhì cìjī material incentive

物质鼓励 wùzhì gǔlì material reward; material incentive

物质基础 wùzhì jīchǔ material base

物质生活 wùzhì shēnghuó material life

物质世界 wùzhì shìjiè physical world; material world

物质损耗 wùzhì sǔnhào *also* "有形损耗" yǒuxíng sǔnhào material loss

物质文明 wùzhì wénmíng material civilization

物质性 wùzhìxìng materiality

物质运动 wùzhì yùndòng motion of matter

物种 wùzhǒng 〈生物〉species: ～特征 species characteristic / ～种群 species population

物种起源 Wùzhǒng Qǐyuán *On the Origin of Species by Means of Natural Selection* (usu. called *The Origin of Species*), by Charles Robert Darwin (1809-1882)

物主 wùzhǔ rightful owner (usu. of sth. lost or stolen)

物资 wùzī goods and materials: 战略～ strategic materials / 出口～ goods for export / ～交流 interflow (*or* exchange) of commodities / ～分配 distribution of materials / ～管理 control of goods and materials / ～丰富 rich supply of commodities

乌(烏) wù

see also wū

乌拉 wùla *also* "靰鞡" wūla leather boots lined with dried *wula* sedge, worn in northeast China

see also wūlā

乌拉草 wùlacǎo 〈植物〉*wula* sedge

坞(塢、隖) wù

❶ depressed place; hollow: 山～ valley; col ❷ structure tall on all sides that keep out the wind: 船～ dock / 花～ sunken flower-bed ❸〈书面〉small castle; fort: 村～ village fort

鹜 wù

〈书面〉duck: 趋之若～ go after sth. like a flock of ducks; go after in a swarm; scramble for sth.

婺 Wù

❶ Wujiang River (in Jiangxi Province) ❷〈旧语〉prefecture in Zhejiang Province (now Jinhua Prefecture)

婺剧 wùjù Wu opera (local opera popular in Jinhua Prefecture, Zhejiang Province)

婺绿 wùlǜ superior green tea produced in Jiangxi Province

骛 wù

〈书面〉❶ move about freely and quickly: 趺马驰～ go for a gallop ❷ go after; seek for; pursue: 好高～远 reach for what is beyond one's grasp; aim too high / 驰心旁～ have one's mind wandering elsewhere; be distracted / 外～ not concentrate on one's duty (*or* business); be distracted by sth. irrelevant; be inattentive

W

X

xī

羲 xī a surname

爔 xī 〈书面〉 *see*“曦”xī

曦 xī 〈书面〉 sunlight (usu. in early morning):朱～烁河堤。A red sun is shining over the river bank.

曦光 xīguāng sunlight in early morning:东方天空泛出淡紫色的～。A light violet sunlight peeped through the sky in the east. /天色清明,～在树。The sky was cloudless and the trees were bathed in the faint rays of the morning sun.

熹 xī ❶〈书面〉dawn; daybreak ❷ brightness

熹微 xīwēi 〈书面〉(of morning sunlight) faint; pale; dim:凌晨,窗外透出～晓色。At first dawn, faint rays appeared outside the window. /远处一座高大建筑矗立在～的晨光里。A tall building was seen in the distance towering in the pale light of dawn.

熺 xī *see*“熹”xī

譆 xī 〈书面〉cry of anguish; lament

噫 xī 〈书面〉sigh

嘻 xī ❶〈书面〉〈叹词〉*used to show one's surprise*:～,不意人间有此美景! Oh, What a surprise to find such beautiful scenery on earth! ❷〈象声〉*sound of laughing*:她冲我～～一笑。She giggled at me. /～～,桂珍姐,你在看什么,该不是情书吧? Aha, sister Guizhen, you aren't reading a love letter, are you?

嘻和 xīhe *also*“嬉和”xīhe 〈口语〉amiable expression and pleasant words; sweet-talk:你去递个～儿,事情就好办了。Everything will be alright if only you'll say a few pleasant words. /你低声下气地和管事的人～～,问题就解决了。The problem will be solved if you take a low posture and sweet-talk (*or* butter up) those in charge.

嘻里呼噜 xīlihūlu *also*“稀里呼噜”xīlihūlu 〈象声〉sound of snoring or slurping (as when gulping down porridge)

嘻闹 xīnào *see*“嬉闹”xīnào

嘻皮笑脸 xīpí-xiàoliǎn *also*“嘻皮赖脸” *see*“嬉皮笑脸”xīpí-xiàoliǎn

嘻嘻哈哈 xīxī-hāhā ❶ laughing and joking; laughing merrily; jolly; light-hearted:成天～的 jolly all day long /～,大大咧咧 light-hearted and careless /大家～地闹了一个晚上。They enjoyed themselves the whole night, laughing and joking. ❷ not serious or earnest; happy-go-lucky; careless:对待这样的大事情,～的可不行! It won't do if you treat such important things casually (*or* carelessly).

嘻笑 xīxiào *see*“嬉笑”xīxiào

僖 xī 〈书面〉happy and joyous

嬉 xī 〈书面〉play; have fun:文恬武～。(as of a decadent dynasty) The civil officals are too lazy to work while the military are bent on fun. /业精于勤,荒于～。Learning is perfected through diligence and lapses by neglect.

嬉和 xīhe *see*“嘻和”xīhe

嬉闹 xīnào *also*“嘻闹”xīnào laughing and joking; romp; frolic:一群放了学的小学生,在胡同里追逐着,～着。After school, a group of pupils chased after each other in the lane, laughing and joking. /姑娘们～了一阵,开始安静下来。The girls turned quiet after having a romp.

嬉皮士 xīpíshì hippie; hippy:一副～打扮 dressed like a hippie /六十年代后期是美国～运动的顶峰阶段。The hippie movement in the United States reached its peak in the late 1960's.

嬉皮笑脸 xīpí-xiàoliǎn *also*“嘻皮笑脸”xīpí-xiàoliǎn grin cheekily; smile and grimace; be comically cheerful:他那么大岁数了,还能成天和你们小孩子们～吗? How could a man of his age grin and grimace with children like you all day?

嬉耍 xīshuǎ play; have fun; amuse oneself:孩子们光着脚在河边～。Children were playing bare-footed by the river. /猴子在树枝上蹿跳～。Monkeys were jumping about in the trees, amusing themselves.

嬉戏 xīxì 〈书面〉play; sport; frolic:小鸭在池水中～。Ducklings were playing about in the pond. /课间,孩子们在操场上～。During the break, the children were frolicking on the playground. /国家处在危急关头,可是那群男女还在调情～,醉生梦死。The country is in crisis, but those men and women are leading a decadent life, flirting and playing all the time.

嬉笑 xīxiào laugh and play; laugh and frolic:一路～ laugh and frolic (*or* play) all the way /她心里不乐,看到别人～的样子,越发恼怒起来。Unhappy herself, she became even more angry at seeing others laugh and play.

嬉笑怒骂 xīxiào-nùmà mirth, laughter, anger and curses — various moods of life; earthy depictions of such moods:～皆成文章。Mirth or laughter, bouts of anger or strings of curses — all makes excellent writing (under sb.'s pen). /他的文章～,兼而有之。One finds both merry laughter and angry denunciations in his writings.

嬉怡 xīyí 〈书面〉happy; cheerful; blissful:他跟人谈话时总是带着～的微笑。He always smiles cheerfully when he talks to others.

嬉游 xīyóu play; sport:孩子们在湖边～。Children are playing by the lake.

嬉游曲 xīyóuqǔ 〈音乐〉divertimento

昔 xī past; former:今～ past and present /往～ past; former times; days bygone /～酒 old wine; mellow wine /今非～比。There is no comparing the present with the past. *or* The present is a far cry from the past.

昔年 xīnián 〈书面〉(in) former years; (in) the past:时过境迁,～的这些小事,如今早已忘却。With the passage of time, such trivialities of the past have long escaped my memory.

昔人 xīrén people of the past; past generation; ancient people:～的告诫,我辈不可忘记。We should not forget the admonitions of past generations.

昔日 xīrì past days; former times; bygone days:～之游 past trip /～同窗 former classmate /这个小镇恢复了～的繁华。This small town has regained its former prosperity.

昔时 xīshí former times; past days; days of yore:张先生是我～旧友,请多加关照。As Mr. Zhang is an old friend of mine, please take care of him as much as you can.

昔岁 xīsuì last year; previous year:入春以来,祖母身体竟大不如～。Since the beginning of this spring Grandmother has been much weaker than last year.

昔者 xīzhě 〈书面〉❶ former times; past days ❷ yesterday

惜 xī ❶ value; cherish; appreciate:珍～ treasure; cherish;

value / ～春 cherish one's youth / ～财 be careful with one's money; cherish one's possessions / 惺惺～惺惺。People with like minds appreciate each other. ❷ regret; have pity; feel sorry: 痛～ deeply regret; deplore / 怜～ have pity on; care tenderly for / 深～我的一番苦心,不为你所理解。What a shame you don't appreciate my painstaking efforts. / 这件衣服质量不错,可～样式旧了一点。This dress is of high quality, but the pity is that its style is somewhat out of fashion. ❸ stint; spare; grudge: 不～工本 spare no expense / 不～一切 grudging nothing; at all cost / 偷生～死 cling to life and be scared of death; live dishonestly to save one's skin

惜别 xībié be reluctant to part; hate to see sb. go; find it hard to take leave (of sb): 依依～ hate to part from sb. (*or* each other); find it difficult to tear oneself away from sb. (*or* away from each other) / ～之时 when parting reluctantly (from sb. or each other); when it is time to part / 他向朋友挥手致意,脸上充满了～的表情。As he was waving goodbye to his friends, his expression showed how hard he was finding it to part.

惜寸阴 xī cùnyīn cherish or treasure every minute: 人生宜当～。One must cherish every minute of one's life.

惜福 xīfú cherish one's good fortune; not squander when one has plenty: 有些年轻人只会乱花钱,不知道～。Some young people tend to spend money extravagantly, having no idea that they should not squander when they have plenty.

惜老怜贫 xīlǎo-liánpín *also* "怜贫惜老" care for the aged and sympathize with the poor: ～的传统美德 traditional virtue of caring for the aged and sympathizing with the poor / 我们老太太最是～的,比不得那些狂三诈四的人。The Old Lady is goodness itself to the old and needy. She's not haughty and high-handed like some people.

惜力 xīlì be sparing of one's energy; grudge or spare one's efforts: 干活不～ never spare oneself in work; spare no efforts in one's work / 只要你不～,什么活儿学不会? Nothing will be too difficult for you to learn so long as you don't stint in your efforts.

惜怜 xīlián be tender and considerate; love and care for: 她的遭遇令人～。Her suffering calls for compassion and consideration.

惜吝 xīlìn stint; spare; grudge: 毫不～ without stint; unstintingly; freely

惜墨如金 xīmò-rújīn regard one's ink as if it were gold; be extremely prudent about one's work (such as writing, calligraphy, or painting): 他对自己的作品总是改了又改,删了又删,真可谓～了。He is extremely prudent about his work, revising and condensing it again and again after it is completed.

惜售 xīshòu sell reluctantly; be unwilling or reluctant to sell; refrain from selling: ～待涨 be unwilling to sell in expectation of a price rise / 板栗集市价格持续上升,个体商贩抬价争购,农民益加～。As the price of Chinese chestnuts kept rising in the market and merchants competed with each other by offering higher prices, farmers were all the more reluctant to sell.

惜阴 xīyīn treasure and make full use of every minute; cherish one's time

惜玉怜香 xīyù-liánxiāng be tender to the fair sex (usu. pretty girls): 这莽汉亦有～之情。Though the man is boorish, he is tender to pretty women.

惜指失掌 xīzhǐ-shīzhǎng try to save a finger only to lose the whole hand — try to save a little only to lose a lot

腊

xī 〈书面〉dried meat
see also là

熙

xī 〈书面〉❶ brightness; light ❷ happy and content: ～事 auspicious (*or* happy) event / ～笑 happy and contented smile / 众人～～。Everyone is happy and contented. ❸ amiable; lovely; pleasant: ～春 happy spring; lovely spring ❹ prosperous; flourishing: ～朝 prosperous reign or age; prosperous and peaceful reign

熙和 xīhé ❶〈书面〉peaceful and happy ❷ warm; genial: ～的南风 warm south wind

熙来攘往 xīlái-rǎngwǎng *see* "熙熙攘攘"

熙攘 xīrǎng bustling with activity: ～的人群 bustling crowds / 节日的集市,一派～欢乐的气氛。The festival fair is bathed in a bustling, joyful atmosphere.

熙提 xītí 〈物理〉stilb — unit of brightness equal to one candle per square centimeter of a surface

熙熙攘攘 xīxī-rǎngrǎng bustle about; bustle with activity: ～,摩肩接踵 crowds of people bustling about and jostling against each other; hustle and bustle of large crowds / 他们来到乡政府,只见门前～,好像办喜事,热闹非常。When they reached the townhall, they saw large crowds of people milling around as if a wedding ceremony were going on. / 车站的候车室里,南来北往的旅客～。The waiting room of the train station was packed with swarms of passengers arriving or departing all the while. / 大街上车马如云,行人～。The street was a sea of carriages and pedestrians.

膝

xī knee: 护～ knee pad; kneecap / 盘～ cross one's legs / 屈～ go down on one's knees; genuflect; surrender / 把孩子抱在～上 hold a child in one's lap

膝盖 xīgài knee; kneecap; patella: 塘里的水已没～了。The water in the pond is already knee-deep.

膝盖骨 xīgàigǔ *also* "髌骨" bìngǔ kneecap; kneepan; patella

膝盖损断 xīgài sǔnduàn 〈医学〉patellar fracture

膝关节 xīguānjié knee joint; *articulatio genus*: ～炎 gonitis; gonarthritis

膝腱 xījiàn patellar tendon

膝腱反射 xījiàn fǎnshè 〈医学〉knee jerk; knee reflex; patellar reflex

膝髁 xīkē 〈方言〉kneecap; patella

膝瘤 xīliú 〈医学〉gonatocele; gonyoncus

膝内翻 xīnèifān 〈医学〉gonyectyposis; bow leg; *genu varum*; out knee

膝上计算机 xīshàng jìsuànjī lap-top computer

膝上型文字处理机 xīshàngxíng wénzì chǔlǐjī lap-top word processor; lap-top

膝头 xītou 〈方言〉knee

膝外翻 xīwàifān 〈医学〉gonycrotesis; knock-knee; *genu valgum*; in knee

膝下 xīxià ❶ respectful term of address for one's parents or sometimes grandparents in letter-writing: 父母大人～ my beloved parents ❷ state of having children: ～只有一女 have an only daughter / ～犹虚 be still childless

膝行 xīxíng 〈书面〉move forward on one's knees (showing one's fear or supplication for favour, pardon, help, etc.); grovel: ～而前 move forward on one's knees

膝痒搔背 xīyǎng-sāobèi scratch the back while the knee is itching — miss the point entirely; be irrelevant: 这种～的做法,是解决不了问题的。This method is completely irrelevant and solves no problem.

西

xī ❶ west: 路～ on the western side of the street (*or* road) / 人各东～ be a long way from each other / 住在城～ live west of the city / 声东击～ make a feint to the east and attack in the west / 从这儿往～走三百米就到了。Go west for 300 metres and you'll be there. ❷ (Xī) the Occident; the West: 中～合璧 good combination of Chinese and Western elements / 学贯中～ be versatile both in Chinese and Western learning ❸ (Xī) a surname

西安 Xī'ān Xi'an, capital of Shaanxi Province

西安事变 Xī'ān Shìbiàn *also* "双十二事变" Shuāng Shí'èr Shìbiàn Xi'an Incident (of 12 Dec. 1936, when two Kuomintang generals, Zhang Xueliang 张学良 and Yang Hucheng 杨虎城, detained Chiang Kai-shek in Xi'an, to force him to cease the civil war, unite with the Chinese Communist Party and form a national united front against Japanese aggression)

西班牙 Xībānyá Spain: ～人 Spaniard / ～语 Spanish / ～斗牛 Spanish bullfighting / ～内战 Spanish Civil War (1936-1939)

西半球 xībànqiú Western Hemisphere

西北 xīběi ❶ northwest: ～方向 in the northwest / ～西 west-northwest; northwest by west / 古寺在县城～二十公里。The old temple lies 20 kilometres to the northwest of the town. ❷ (Xīběi) northwest China; the Northwest: ～边疆 northwestern border / ～民歌 folk songs of northwest China

西北风 xīběifēng northwest wind; northwesterly (wind)

西边 xībian west: ～下雨东边晴。It rained in the west but shone in the east. / 风从～刮过来。Winds blow from the west.

西宾 xībīn 〈旧语〉(as a complimentary term of address) staff adviser or family tutor

西伯利亚 Xībólìyà Siberia: ～人 Siberian / ～虎 Siberian tiger / ～冻原 Siberian tundra

西柏林 Xībólín West Berlin, a state of the Federal Republic of Germany forming an enclave within the German Democratic Republic until the unification of Germany in 1990
西捕 xībǔ 〈旧语〉Western police or policeman (in the foreign concessions of old China)
西部片 xībùpiàn Wild West movie; cowboy movie; western
西部作家 Xībù zuòjiā writer of northwest China; writer of the Northwest
西餐 xīcān Western-style food; Western food; European food: 吃～ have Western food / 这家饭店有～部。There is a restaurant providing Western-style food in this hotel.
西餐馆 xīcānguǎn restaurant serving Western food; Western-style restaurant
西厂 Xīchǎng Western Depot, secret service organization of the Ming Dynasty
西点 xīdiǎn ❶ Western-style pastries ❷ (Xīdiǎn) (US) West Point: ～军校 West Point Military Academy
西法 xīfǎ in the Western style; in the Western way: ～洗染 Western-style laundering and dyeing / ～制作 manufacture in the Western way
西番莲 xīfānlián 〈植物〉❶ passion-flower (*Passiflora caerulea*) ❷ dahlia
西方 xīfāng ❶ west: 大门朝着～ with the door (*or* gate) facing the west / 残月挂在～。A waning moon was hovering in the western sky. ❷ (Xīfāng) the West; the Occident: ～国家 Western countries / ～世界 Western world ❸ *also* "西方净土"〈佛教〉happy land in the west; western paradise: ～极乐世界 Western Paradise
西方石油公司 Xīfāng Shíyóu Gōngsī Occidental Petroleum Corporation, US oil and gas producing company
西非 Xī Fēi West Africa
西非国家经济共同体 Xī Fēi Guójiā Jīngjì Gòngtóngtǐ Economic Community of West African States (ECOWAS), established in 1975
西风 xīfēng ❶ west or westerly wind; autumn wind: ～扫落叶 autumn wind sweeping fallen leaves / ～残照 setting sun in the west wind / 正～落叶下长安，飞鸣镝。The west wind scatters leaves over Chang'an, And the arrows are flying, twanging. ❷ Western style; Western practice; Western culture: ～东渐。The Western influence was extending to the East. *or* The Western culture was spreading to the East. ❸ decadent forces; decaying influences: 不是东风压倒～，就是～压倒东风。Either the East wind prevails over the West wind or the West wind prevails over the East wind.
西风带 xīfēngdài 〈地理〉westerlies
西凤酒 xīfèngjiǔ Xifeng liquor — famous brand of liquor produced at Liulin (柳林), Fengxiang (凤翔) County, Shaanxi Province
西弗吉尼亚 Xīfújíníyà West Virginia, an eastern state of the United States
西服 xīfú Western-style clothes; Western suit: ～革履 dressed in a spotless Western suit and leather shoes / ～套装 suit of Western-style clothes / ～上衣 Western-style jacket

西服料 xīfúliào suiting (for Western-style clothes)
西府海棠 xīfǔ hǎitáng 〈植物〉midget crabapple
西宫 xīgōng ❶〈旧语〉western palaces where the emperor's concubines lived: ～娘娘 Lady of the Western Palaces (complimentary term for the emperor's secondary wife) ❷〈旧语〉imperial concubine
西贡 Xīgòng Saigon, former name of Ho Chi Minh City, Viet Nam
西谷椰子 xīgǔ yēzi *also* "米树" mǐshù 〈植物〉sago palm
西瓜 xīguā watermelon: ～田 watermelon field / ～子 watermelon seed
西哈努克 Xīhānǔkè King Norodom Sihanouk (1922-), Head of State of Cambodia
西汉 Xī Hàn Western Han Dynasty (206 BC-24 AD)
西河大鼓 xīhé dàgǔ variety of *dagu* popular in Hebei and Henan provinces
西红柿 xīhóngshì tomato: ～汁 tomato juice / ～酱 ketchup; tomato sauce / 奶油～汤 cream tomato soup / ～炒鸡蛋 stir-fried eggs with tomatoes
西葫芦 xīhúlu 〈植物〉pumpkin; summer squash
西湖 Xīhú West Lake, Hangzhou
西化 xīhuà westernize: "全盘～" "total westernization"; "wholesale westernization"
西画 xīhuà Western painting
西晋 Xī Jìn Western Jin Dynasty (265-316)
西经 xījīng 〈地理〉west longtitude: ～180度 longtitude 180°W
西康 Xīkāng former province covering parts of present Tibet and Sichuan
西口 xīkǒu passes in the western sections of the Great Wall: 走～ Go Beyond the Great Wall (as a refugee) — title for a popular folk song of northwest China
西历 xīlì 〈旧语〉Western calendar; Gregorian calendar
西力生 xīlìshēng 〈农业〉ceresan
西陵 Xīlíng Western Qing Mausoleums in Yixian County (易县) of Hebei
西门 Xīmén a surname
西门子 xīménzǐ 〈电学〉siemens (the SI unit of electrical conductance)
西门子公司 Xīménzǐ Gōngsī Siemens AG, German electrical company
西门子炉 xīménzǐlú 〈冶金〉Siemens furnace
西蒙斯圆锥破碎机 Xīméngsī yuánzhuī pòsuìjī 〈矿业〉Symons cone (disk) crusher
西米 xīmǐ *also* "西谷米" sago: ～粉 sago flour
西面 xīmiàn west: 大会堂在纪念碑～。The Great Hall is to the west of the Monument.
西奈半岛 Xīnài Bàndǎo Sinai Peninsula, mostly desert, at the north end of the Red Sea, now part of Egypt
西南 xīnán ❶ southwest: ～南 south-southwest / ～非 Southwestern Africa / 卢沟桥在北京的～郊。Lugou Bridge (otherwise called Marco Polo Bridge) is situated in the southwestern suburbs of Beijing. ❷ (Xīnán) southwest China; the Southwest: ～边陲 southwestern frontiers
西南非洲 Xīnán Fēizhōu South-West Africa, former name of Namibia: ～人民组织 South-West African People's Organization (SWAPO)
西南风 xīnánfēng southwest wind; southwestly (wind)
西南联合大学 Xīnán Liánhé Dàxué *also* "西南联大" South-West Associated University (formed by combining Peking, Tsinghua and Nankai universities during the War of Resistance Against Japanese Aggression)
西宁 Xīníng Xining, capital of Qinghai Province
西欧 Xī Ōu Western Europe: ～联盟 West European Union / ～共同市场 West European Common Market
西欧司 Xī-Ōusī Department of West European Affairs, Ministry of Foreign Affairs
西皮 xīpí 〈戏曲〉*xipi*, one of the major tunes in such traditional Chinese operas as Beijing opera
西人 xīrén 〈旧语〉Westerner
西撒哈拉 Xīsāhālā Western Sahara, former Spanish colony on the Atlantic coast of Northwest Africa until 1976
西萨摩亚 Xīsàmóyà Western Samoa, island country in the southwest Pacific
西赛罗 Xīsàiluó Marcus Tulius Cicero (106 BC-43 BC), Roman prose-writer and public speaker
西沙尔麻 xīshā'ěrmá *also* "剑麻" jiànmá sisal (*Agave sisalana*)
西沙群岛 Xīshā Qúndǎo Xisha Islands (called Paracel Islands by Westerners)
西晒 xīshài (of a house, room, etc.) facing west and exposed to the afternoon sun: 这房间当～。This room is hot on summer afternoons due to its western exposure.
西施 Xīshī ❶ *also* "西子" name of a famous beauty in the late Spring and Autumn Period ❷ beautiful woman; beauty: 情人眼里出～。Beauty is in the eyes of the beholder.
西式 xīshì Western-style: ～糕点 Western-style pastries / ～家具 Western-style furniture
西天 xītiān 〈宗教〉❶ (ancient Buddhist name for) India ❷ Western Paradise: 上～ go to the Western paradise; go west; die
西王母 Xīwángmǔ (popularly known as 王母娘娘) Xiwangmu — Grand Old Lady of the West, a deity in ancient Chinese myths
西维因 xīwéiyīn 〈农业〉sevin; carbaryl
西魏 Xī Wèi Western Wei Dynasty (535-556), one of the Northern Dynasties

西文 xīwén 〈旧语〉Western language; Western words
西西 xīxī *also* "毫升" háoshēng c.c. (cubic centimetre)
西西里 Xīxīlǐ Sicily, a large triangular island in the Mediterranean Sea separated from mainland Italy by the Strait of Messina
西席 xīxí *also* "西宾" 〈旧语〉❶ family tutor ❷ private staff of an official
西夏 Xī Xià Western Xia Dynasty of the Dangxiang nationality (党项族) reigning over part of northwest China (1038-1227)
西厢记 Xīxiāngjì *The West Chamber*, play written by Wang Shifu (王实甫) of the Yuan Dynasty
西学 xīxué (term used in late Qing for natural and social sciences of Western countries) Western learning: ~东渐 Western learning spreading to the East / 崇尚~ advocate Western learning
西雅图 Xīyǎtú Seattle, Pacific port and industrial city in the State of Washington, US
西亚 Xī Yà West Asia: ~北非司 Department for West-Asian and North-African Affairs, Ministry of Foreign Affairs
西洋 Xīyáng ❶ (term used in late Qing and early Republican days) the West; the Occident; Western world: ~各国 Western countries / ~文学 Western literature / ~文明史 history of Western civilization ❷ (a term used in the Yuan and Ming dynasties) Western Seas, i.e. seas and lands west of the South China Sea (west of longitude 110°E): 郑和七下~ Zheng He's seven voyages to the Western Seas (1406-1433)
西洋画 xīyánghuà Western painting
西洋记 Xīyángjì (short for《三宝太监西洋记通俗演义》) *Adventure to the Western Seas*, novel of the Ming Dynasty
西洋景 xīyángjǐng *also* "西洋镜" ❶ peep show ❷ camouflaged dishonest dealing; hanky-panky; trickery: 拆穿~ expose sb.'s tricks; strip off sb.'s mask
西洋人 xīyángrén Westerner
西洋参 xīyángshēn *also* "花旗参" huāqíshēn 〈中药〉American ginseng (*Panax quinquefolium*)
西洋史 xīyángshǐ history of the West; history of Western countries
西药 xīyào Western medicine
西医 xīyī ❶ Western medicine (as distinguished from traditional Chinese medicine) ❷ doctor of Western medicine
西印度群岛 Xīyìndù Qúndǎo West Indies, group of islands largely in the Caribbean Sea, extending from the coast of Florida in North America to that of Venezuela in South America
西游记 Xīyóujì *Pilgrimage to the West* or *Journey to the West*, fiction about Tang Seng's (唐僧) pilgrimage to the West, written by Wu Cheng'en (吴承恩) of the Ming Dynasty
西语 xīyǔ Western language: ~系 department of Western languages
西域 Xīyù (term used in the Han Dynasty for areas west of Yumenguan, including present Xinjiang and parts of Central Asia) Western Regions: 张骞通~ Zhang Qian's missions to the Western Regions (138-115 BC)
西元 xīyuán (now called 公元) 〈旧语〉Western calendar; Gregorian calendar
西乐 xīyuè Western music
西岳 Xīyuè Western Sacred Mountain (another name for 华山 Mount Hua in Shaanxi Province)
see also "五岳" Wǔyuè
西崽 xīzǎi 〈旧语〉"Western whelp" — derogatory term for waiter or houseboy in the employ of Westerners; boy
西藏 Xīzàng Xizang; Tibet: ~人 Tibetan / ~自治区 Tibet Autonomous Region
西藏学 Xīzàngxué Tibetology
西藏野驴 Xīzàng yělǘ 〈动物〉kiang
西爪哇 Xīzhǎowā Jawa Barat or West Java, Indonesia
西周 Xī Zhōu Western Zhou Dynasty (11th century BC-771 BC)
西装 xīzhuāng Western-style clothes
西子 Xīzǐ *also* "西施" name of an ancient beauty: 欲把西湖比~，淡妆浓抹总相宜。For varied charms the West Lake well may I compare, To Xizi, who, adorned or not, alike was fair.
西子湖 Xīzǐhú *see* "西湖"

恓 xī

恓惶 xīhuáng ❶〈书面〉scared and vexed ❷〈方言〉poor and miserable; impoverished: 日子过得~ lead an impoverished life; live in poverty and misery
恓恓 xīxī 〈书面〉lonesome; lonely: ~终日 be lonesome all day

粞 xī

❶〈书面〉broken rice ❷〈方言〉chaff; husk

茜 xī

(sometimes pronounced qiàn) *used in female names, esp. when transliterating foreign names*
see also qiàn

栖 xī

see also qī
栖栖 xīxī 〈书面〉unsettled; restless

硒 xī

〈化学〉selenium (Se)
硒醇 xīchún 〈化学〉selenol
硒电池 xīdiànchí 〈化学〉selenium cell; selenium photocell; selenium conductive photocell
硒鼓 xīgǔ 〈机械〉selenium-coated drum
硒化物 xīhuàwù 〈化学〉selenide
硒酸 xīsuān 〈化学〉selenic acid / ~钠 sodium selenate / ~盐 selenate
硒整流器 xīzhěngliúqì 〈电子〉seletron
硒中毒 xīzhòngdú 〈医学〉selenosis

牺(犧) xī

〈书面〉beast of pure colour used for sacrifice; sacrifice: ~牛 sacrificial cattle
牺牲 xīshēng ❶〈古语〉beast slaughtered for sacrifice; sacrifice ❷ sacrifice oneself; lay down one's life: 流血~ shed one's blood or lay down one's life / 为有~多壮志，敢教日月换新天。Bitter sacrifice strengthens bold resolve Which dares to make sun and moon shine in new skies. ❸ give up; sacrifice: 自我~的精神 spirit of self-sacrifice; selfless spirit / 你为子女们作了多大的~! What a great sacrifice you have made for your children! / 他~了许多休息时间去指导学棋的少年儿童。He spent a lot of his spare time teaching children to play chess. / 不能为了眼前这点小利而~长远利益。One must not pursue such petty immediate profits at the expense of long-term interests.
牺牲品 xīshēngpǐn victim; prey; sacrifice: 她几度挣扎，还是成了旧势力的~。Though she put up a struggle several times, she eventually fell a victim to the forces of tradition.
牺尊 xīzūn 〈考古〉ancient Chinese wine vessel in the shape of a sacrificial ox; ox-shaped drinking vessel

舾 xī

舾装 xīzhuāng ❶ fittings of a ship ❷ fit up a ship

醯 xī

〈书面〉vinegar

析 xī

❶ divide; separate; resolve: ~产 divide property / ~箸〈书面〉break up the household; split up the family / 分崩离~ fall to pieces; disintegrate / 条分缕~ make a careful and detailed analysis ❷ analyse; dissect: 辨~ differentiate and analyse / 解~几何 analytical geometry / 疑义相与~ analyse a dubious point together ❸ (Xī) a surname
析出 xīchū ❶ analyse; dissect: 认真~的结论 conclusion drawn through earnest analysis / 这样做，后果不难~。It's not difficult to infer the consequences of such a course of action. ❷〈化学〉separate out: ~结晶 separate out crystals
析爨 xīcuàn 〈书面〉set up separate kitchens; (of family members) live separately from each other
析居 xījū live separately: 兄弟~ brothers live separately (instead of living under the same roof as when their parents were alive)
析像管 xīxiàngguǎn 〈电子〉image dissector
析疑 xīyí 〈书面〉resolve a doubt; clear up an uncertainty: 一一~ resolve (*or* clear up) one doubtful point after another / 请专家给学员们~ invite experts to resolve the students' questions
析义 xīyì expound the meaning (of a word)

淅 xī

〈书面〉wash rice: ~米 wash rice
淅沥 xīlì 〈象声〉(as of wind, rain or falling leaves) rustle; patter: 秋雨~ patter of autumn rains / 外面是淅淅沥沥的落叶声。The contin-

uous rustle of falling leaves could be heard outside.

淅飒 xīsà 〈象声〉rustle; crackle:雨点打在树叶上,淅淅飒飒地响。Rain drops kept pattering on the tree leaves.

淅淅 xīxī 〈象声〉(as of wind, rain, snow, etc.) rustle; patter; whistle:雨～地下个不停。It kept drizzling. /雪花打在窗子上～作响。Snowflakes fell rustling against the window panes.

晰(晳) xī clear; distinct; explicit:明～的印象 lucid impression /发音清～ clear pronunciation

皙 xī 〈书面〉light-complexioned; fair-skinned:白～ light-complexioned; pale

菥 xī

菥蓂 xīmì *Thlaspi arvense*, a kind of medicinal herb

蜥 xī lizard:巨～ giant lizard

蜥甲 xījiǎ lizard beetle; langurid beetle

蜥尾草 xīwěicǎo 〈植物〉lizard's tail; water dragon (*Saururus cernuus*)

蜥蜴 xīyì 〈动物〉lizard

巇 xī *see* "险巇" xiǎnxī

裼 xī 〈书面〉strip to the waist:袒～ strip to the waist

see also tì

锡[1] xī ❶ tin; stannum (Sn):～罐 tin can; tin /焊～ soldering tin ❷ (Xī) a surname

锡[2] xī 〈书面〉bestow; grant:～恩 grant a favour /～福 bestow happiness /～命 give an order

锡安山 Xī'ānshān Zion, mount in Jerusalem and site of King David's palace and temple

锡伯族 Xībózú Xibe nationality, living in the Xinjiang Uygur Autonomous Region and Liaoning Province

锡铂钯矿 xībóbǎkuàng 〈矿业〉atokite

锡箔 xībó tinfoil paper (used as offerings to ghosts)

锡焊料 xīhànliào 〈冶金〉tin solder; pewter solder

锡合金 xīhéjīn 〈冶金〉tin alloy

锡化物 xīhuàwù 〈冶金〉stannide

锡婚 xīhūn tin wedding anniversary — 10th wedding anniversary

锡匠 xījiang tinsmith

锡金 Xījīn Sikkim:～人 Sikkimese

锡剧 xījù *also* "常锡文戏" Cháng-Xī wénxì Wuxi opera; local opera popular in southern Jiangsu and Shanghai

锡克教 Xīkèjiào Sikhism, a monotheistic religion based in the Punjab, India:～信徒 Sikh

锡矿 xīkuàng tin ore; tin mine

锡镴 xīla 〈方言〉❶ soldering tin ❷ tin

锡兰 Xīlán Ceylon, former name of Sri Lanka (until 1972)

锡兰肉桂 Xīlán ròuguì *also* "桂皮" guìpí Ceylon cinnamon (*Cinnamomum zeylanicum*)

锡林浩特 Xīlín Hàotè Xilin Hot, city in Inner Mongolia

锡器 xīqì tinware

锡壳试验 xīqiào shìyàn 〈医学〉Schick test (reaction)

锡石 xīshí 〈矿业〉cassiterite; tinstone (SnO_2)

锡酸 xīsuān 〈化学〉stannic acid:～钠 sodium stannate /～盐 stannate

锡烷 xīwán 〈化学〉stannane

锡杖 xīzhàng 〈宗教〉stick headed with a tin ring, used in Buddhist services

锡纸 xīzhǐ tinfoil; silver paper

吸 xī ❶ inhale; breathe in; draw:～风饮露 inhale wind and drink dew — (of Taoist priest, etc.) abstain from food /～入凉气 inhale cold air /～烟斗 draw (*or* drag) at one's pipe; smoke a pipe ❷ absorb; suck up:～音 absorb sound /～血 suck blood /这种纸～墨性能好。This paper absorbs ink well. /拿块海绵把水～干。Get a sponge to soak up the water. ❸ attract; draw to oneself:磁铁上～着几根针。The magnet has attracted several needles.

吸尘器 xīchénqì vacuum cleaner; vacuum

吸虫 xīchóng fluke; trematode

吸虫病 xīchóngbìng 〈医学〉distomiasis; trematodiasis:肠～ intestinal distomiasis /肺～ pulmonary distomiasis /血～ hemic distomiasis; schistosomiasis

吸顶灯 xīdǐngdēng lamp affixed to the ceiling

吸毒 xīdú drug taking; drug addiction:～成瘾 be addicted to drug

吸毒者 xīdúzhě drug addict; narcotic addict

吸风冷却塔 xīfēng lěngquètǎ 〈机械〉induced-draft cooling tower

吸附 xīfù absorb:～作用 adsorption /～化合物 adsorption compound

吸附剂 xīfùjì absorbent

吸附器 xīfùqì absorber

吸附汽油 xīfù qìyóu absorption gasoline

吸附水 xīfùshuǐ absorbed water

吸管 xīguǎn straw (for sipping liquid); suction pipe; sucker or sucking pipe

吸积 xījī 〈天文〉acretion:～理论 acretion theory

吸力 xīlì suction; attraction:磁性～ magnetic attraction /地心～ terrestrial gravity; force of gravity /抽水泵利用～抽水。Pumps work by suction. /月球和太阳对海水的～引起潮汐。The attraction of sea water by the moon and the sun causes tides.

吸力计 xīlìjì suction gauge

吸溜 xīliu 〈方言〉slurp:他端着碗粥使劲～,就像饿了三天一样。He held a bowl of gruel and slurped it greedily, as if he had gone without food for three days. /职业介绍所门口排队的人越来越多,不少人都冻得直～。The line before the employment agency was ever-lengthening, and many people were shivering with cold.

吸滤器 xīlǜqì Nutsch filter; suction strainer

吸墨纸 xīmòzhǐ blotting paper; blotter:用～把墨吸干。Soak up the ink with a blotter.

吸奶器 xīnǎiqì milk-pump; breast pump

吸泥泵 xīníbèng dredge pump

吸盘 xīpán ❶ 〈动物〉sucking disc; sucker ❷ 〈机械〉suction cup

吸气 xīqì 〈机械〉aspiration; air-breathing; inspiration; insprium:～泵 aspirator pump /～计 〈医学〉inspirometer /～式导弹 〈军事〉air-breathing missile

吸取 xīqǔ absorb; inhale; draw; assimilate:～知识 absorb knowledge /～教训 learn one's lesson /～新鲜空气 inhale fresh air /～养料 draw nourishment

吸热 xīrè absorption of heat; endotherm

吸热反应 xīrè fǎnyìng 〈化学〉endothermic reaction

吸热器 xīrèqì thermal absorber; heat absorber

吸入 xīrù suction:～管 suction chute /～汽化器 suction-type carburetor /～式分级机 suction sorter /～式排种器播种机 suction seeder

吸声 xīshēng sound absorption or absorbing:～材料 sound-absorbing material; acoustic absorbent /～建筑 acoustic construction /～器 sound absorber; acoustical damper

吸湿 xīshī moisture-absorbing

吸湿剂 xīshījì hygroscopic agent; moisture absorbent

吸湿性 xīshīxìng hygroscopicity; moisture absorbency

吸食 xīshí suck:用吸管～果汁饮料 suck fruit juice with a straw /～毒品 use (*or* take) drugs

吸收 xīshōu ❶ absorb; assimilate; take in; draw:木炭～气体。Charcoal absorbs gas. /隔音板～声音。Sound-insulating board takes in sound. /弹簧～震动。Springs absorb shock. /他吃得虽多,但～不好。He is not good at assimilating food though he eats a lot. ❷ recruit; receive; enrol; admit:协会～新成员。The association enrols (*or* admits) new members. /歌咏队最近～她入队。She has just been admitted into the chorus.

吸收比 xīshōubǐ absorptance

吸收不良综合征 xīshōu bùliáng zōnghézhēng malabsorption syndrome

吸收光谱 xīshōu guāngpǔ *also* "暗线光谱" ànxiàn guāngpǔ 〈物理〉absorption spectrum:～分析仪 absorption spectrometer

吸收剂 xīshōujì absorbent

吸收率 xīshōulǜ absorptivity

吸收塔 xīshōutǎ 〈化学〉absorption tower

吸收体 xīshōutǐ absorber

吸收障碍 xīshōu zhàng'ài 〈医学〉malabsorption

吸收作用 xīshōu zuòyòng absorption

吸水 xīshuǐ water-absorbing:～泵 suction pump /～管 suction duct (*or* pipe) /～率 water-absorbing capacity; water absorption /～性 water-absorbing capacity (*or* quality); water absorption /～纸 absorbent paper
吸吮 xīshǔn suck; absorb:～手指上的血 suck blood from a finger / 孩子～母亲的奶汁。The baby is sucking the milk of its mother.
吸铁石 xītiěshí loadstone; lodestone; magnet
吸筒 xītǒng suction tube
吸血蝠 xīxuèfú vampire bat
吸血鬼 xīxuèguǐ bloodsucker; vampire
吸压泵 xīyābèng 〈机械〉combined suction and force pump
吸烟 xīyān smoke:禁止～区 no-smoking area /～有害健康。Smoking is harmful to health.
吸烟室 xīyānshì smoking room
吸烟区 xīyānqū smoking area
吸扬式挖泥船 xīyángshì wānǐchuán cutterhead dredger; discharging dredger; pipeline dredger; pump dredger; hydraulic dredge
吸音板 xīyīnbǎn 〈建筑〉acoustic board
吸音绒布 xīyīn róngbù 〈建筑〉hush cloth
吸音贴砖 xīyīn tiēzhuān 〈建筑〉acoustolith tile
吸引 xīyǐn attract; draw; appeal to; fascinate:～力 attraction; fascination /展销会上的工艺品～了许多顾客。The handicraft products at the exposition attracted the attention of many customers. /我们被晚会上精彩的文艺节目～住了。We were fascinated by the excellent performances at the soirée. /这些画把他强烈地～住了。These paintings appealed to him enormously. *or* These paintings held him spellbound. /这里的山水以其巨大的魅力～着海内外无数游客。With their beautiful scenery, the mountains and streams here draw countless tourists from other parts of the country and from foreign lands.
吸引器 xīyǐnqì 〈医学〉suction apparatus; aspirator

蠵 xī

蠵龟 xīguī loggerhead turtle

觿 xī 〈书面〉bodkin made of horn or ivory used in ancient days to undo knots

奚 xī ❶〈书面〉*interrogative word meaning why, how, where, what, etc.*:～取? What (*or* Which) shall we take? /～如? How about it? /水～自至? Where does the water come from? /子～哭之悲也? Why are you crying so bitterly, sir? ❷ (Xī) a surname
奚落 xīluò taunt; ridicule; jeer at; scoff at:受人～ be taunted; be scoffed at /他从这番话里听出有～自己的意思。He sensed in these words an implied jeer at himself. /她受不住这样的～。She couldn't bear such ridicule.
奚幸 xīxìng *see*"傒倖" xīxìng

溪 xī small stream; brook; rivulet:～水潺潺 gurgling stream /清～ clear brook /～谷 small valley /～边照影行,天在清～底。Walking by the stream, fair reflections I see; At the bottom of the clear water lies the sky above me.
溪涧 xījiàn mountain stream; mountain brook:两山之间是一条曲折的～。There was a winding brook between the two mountains.
溪流 xīliú stream; brook; rivulet:欢快的～ lively rivulet /～蜿蜒 the stream winds along /～清澈,游鱼可数。The water in the brook was so limpid that the fish sporting in it could be counted.
溪瓢羹 xīpiáogēng *Cynanchum glaucescens*, a kind of medicinal herb

鸂 xī

鸂鶒 xīchì 〈古语〉water birds resembling the mandarin duck and drake

磎 xī 〈书面〉*see*"溪" xī

蹊 xī 〈书面〉footpath:桃李不言,下自成～。Peaches and plums do not talk, yet the world beats a path to them — a man of true worth attracts admiration without advertising.
see also qī

蹊径 xījìng 〈书面〉path; way; shortcut:独辟～ blaze a new path for oneself; develop a new style (*or* method) of one's own /另辟～ look for another way; seek a different solution or shortcut

谿 xī ❶ *see*"溪" xī ❷ *see*"勃谿" bóxī

谿谷 xīgǔ 〈书面〉mountain valley
谿壑 xīhè 〈书面〉ravine; gully; valley:～之心,贪而无厌 sb.'s greed is like a gully that can never be filled; be insatiably greedy /～之中花树错落。The ravine is dotted with flowers and trees.
谿卡 xīkǎ manor or feudal estate in pre-reform Tibet, usually associated with a lamaist temple or monastery
谿刻 xīkè 〈书面〉caustic; petty:心怀～ petty-minded

徯 xī *see*"勃徯" bóxī

傒 xī

傒倖 xīxìng *also*"奚幸" xīxìng (often used in the early vernacular) vexation; worry

鼷 xī

鼷鼠 xīshǔ mouse

徯 xī 〈书面〉❶ wait:～待 await; expect ❷ *also*"蹊" xī path

希[1] xī hope:尚～笑纳。It is hoped that you will graciously accept it. /敬～指教。Your advice is hereby earnestly solicited.

希[2] xī rare; scarce; uncommon:～客 rare guest

希伯来语 Xībóláiyǔ Hebrew (language)
希贵 xīguì *also*"稀贵" xīguì rare and precious:～植物 rare and valuable plant
希罕 xīhan *also*"稀罕" xīhan ❶ rare; scarce; unusual; uncommon:～的东西 rare object; rare sight; something precious /集邮很有意思,不过能得到一枚有价值的邮票却是～事儿。Although stamp collecting is interesting in itself, you get a valuable stamp only once in a blue moon. ❷ value as a rarity; treasure; cherish:我才不～你的臭钱呢。谁～,你给谁! I couldn't care less about your lousy money. Give it to anyone who does! ❸ rare thing or sight; rarity:他从城里弄回来几条金鱼,准备让孩子们看～儿。He brought back some goldfish from town as a rarity which the children would enjoy watching.
希冀 xījì 〈书面〉yearn for; desire; aspire after:老人多年来～的,就是儿子能成为一名医生。What the old man had yearned for over the years was for his son to become a doctor. /她～能够重新得到从前那样的愉悦。She wished she could regain the happiness she had had before.
希腊 Xīlà Greece:～人 Greek /～语 Greek (language) /～正教会 Greek Orthodox Church
希腊字母 Xīlà zìmǔ Greek alphabet;Greek letter
希奇 xīqí *also*"稀奇" xīqí rare; peculiar; strange; curious:～古怪 curious and bizarre; fantastic /城里出了件～事。A strange thing happened in town.
希企 xīqǐ 〈书面〉yearn for; hope for:～美好的未来 yearn for a bright future
希求 xīqiú ❶ hope to get:～大家的帮助 hope to get help from you all ❷ wish; hope; expectation:他现在除了念书,没有别的～。Now he desires nothing but an opportunity to study.
希少 xīshǎo few; scarce
see also"稀少" xīshǎo
希世 xīshì extremely rare
希世珍宝 xīshì zhēnbǎo rare treasure
希特勒 Xītèlè Adolf Hitler (1889-1945), German dictator and leader of Nazi (National Socialist Party of Germany)
希图 xītú harbour the intention of; try to; attempt to:他们操纵市场,～牟取暴利。They manipulated the market in the hope of getting exorbitant profits. *or* They tried to get exorbitant profits by cornering the market. /我这样做,并不～得到报偿。I did not do this for a reward.
希望 xīwàng ❶ hope; wish; expect:～大家好自为之。It is to be hoped that everyone will do his best. /～你早日恢复健康。I wish you an early recovery. /他～赢得冠军。He wanted to win the championship. /～你常来做客。Please drop in whenever you have time. ❷

hope; expectation:战争使他们的～落空了。War shattered (*or* dashed) their hopes. /～又在他心里燃烧起来了。He is burning with hope again. /有没有～把老人治好? Is there any chance to cure the old man? ❸ person or thing that is likely to bring success:他现在是我们唯一的～了。He is now our only hope.

希望工程 xīwàng gōngchéng Project Hope, a project to enlist popular support to help children of poor families receive schooling

希希罕儿 xīxihǎnr 〈方言〉rare object:大家一看,这可是个～,都在那里纳闷儿。Taking a look, they found it was a rare object they had never seen before and were filled with wonder.

希有 xīyǒu rare; seldom
see also "稀有" xīyǒu

希珍 xīzhēn *also* "稀珍" xīzhēn rare and valuable

悕 xī 〈书面〉grief

烯 xī 〈化工〉alkene:乙～ ethane; olefiant gas

烯丙基 xībǐngjī 〈化学〉allyl group

烯丙树脂 xībǐng shùzhī 〈化学〉allyl resin

烯醇 xīchún 〈化学〉enol:～化 enolization /～酶〈生化〉enolase

烯烃 xītīng 〈化学〉alkene; olefin(e):～共聚物 olefin copolymer /～树脂 olefin resin

豨 xī 〈古语〉swine; hog

豨莶 xīxiān 〈中药〉common St. Paul's wort (*Siegesbeckia orientalis*)

唏 xī ❶〈书面〉sigh ❷〈叹词〉*used to show surprise*:～! 你这出的什么洋相! Hey! What a fool you are making of yourself!

唏里呼噜 xīlihūlū *see* "稀里呼噜" xīlihūlū

唏里哗啦 xīlihuālā *see* "稀里哗啦" xīlihuālā

唏嘘 xīxū 〈书面〉*also* "欷歔" xīxū sob

晞 xī 〈书面〉❶ dry:白露未～ before the morning dew is dry ❷ dawn; first light of day:东方未～ before daybreak

睎 xī 〈书面〉❶ watch from a height or a distance:登西山而～北京城 climb the West Hill and watch Beijing from the top ❷ admire; esteem

稀 xī ❶ rare; scarce; unusual; uncommon:～世之宝 extremely rare treasure /年过古～ over seventy years old; rather old ❷ sparse; thinly scattered:一株叶少枝～的老树 old tree with few leaves and sparse branches /地上～～地长着一些草。The ground is sparsely dotted with grass. /东方欲白,月落星～。Before dawn breaks in the east, the moon sets and the stars diminish. ❸ watery; diluted; thin:～泥 thin mud; slime /～粥 watery porridge; gruel /农药和～了。We've added too much water to the pesticide. /你吃稠的,我喝～的。When you have solid food, give me some gruel to eat. *or* When you make sth. substantial, I'll be contented with what you leave over. ❹ (used to modify certain adjectives) very; extremely: *see* "～烂";"～松" ❺ sth. watery; sth. thin:糖～ syrup; molasses

稀巴烂 xībalàn smashed to pieces; broken to bits:砸它个～ smash it to smithereens

稀播 xībō 〈农业〉thin sowing

稀薄 xībó rare; thin:高原空气～。Air is rare on a high plateau. /月光透过～的雾气照在地上。Moonlight filters on the ground through a thin mist.

稀薄气体 xībó qìtǐ rarefied gas; low density gas:～动力学 rarefied gas dynamics

稀饭 xīfàn (usu. made of rice or millet) gruel; porridge:小豆～ rice porridge with red beans /过去,北京人的早餐多是馒头～就咸菜。People in Beijing used to breakfast on steamed bread, rice gruel and pickles.

稀贵 xīguì *also* "希贵" xīguì rare and valuable

稀罕 xīhan *see* "希罕" xīhan

稀糊烂 xīhulàn ❶ pulpified; reduced to a paste:小豆粥熬得～。The red bean porridge was cooked to a paste. ❷ completely crushed or routed:把敌人打得～ crush (*or* rout) the enemy completely ❸ hard pressed:农活一紧,他爷俩就忙个～。When farm work was pressing, the father and son would be terribly busy.

稀货 xīhuò rare commodity; scarcity; scarce good

稀客 xīkè rare visitor:侯先生,总有三年没来了吧,真是～。What a rare guest, Mr. Hou. It must be three years since you last came.

稀拉 xīla ❶ sparse; few and far between:～的枯草 sparse, dead grass ❷〈方言〉careless; sloppy:作风～ sloppy style of work

稀烂 xīlàn ❶ completely mashed; pulpy:炖得～ stewed to a pulp ❷ *also* "稀巴烂" smashed to pieces; broken to smithereens:鸡蛋掉到地上摔了个～。The egg smashed to pieces when it dropped on the ground.

稀朗 xīlǎng (as of light or stars) scattered but bright:夜半时分,星光～。There were a few scattered bright stars at midnight.

稀里光当 xīliguāngdāng ❶ watery; thin:我只喝了两碗～的大米粥。I only had two bowlfuls of watery rice porridge. ❷ sloppy and careless:他上学时～的,后来当了工人还是松松垮垮的。Happy-go-lucky as a student, he became a careless and sloppy worker later on.

稀里呼噜 xīlihūlū 〈象声〉slurp; snore:他端着碗粥,～地喝起来。He held up a bowl of gruel and slurped it. /他～地睡得很香。He was snoring in a sound sleep. /大家披着雨衣从院子里～地跑出来。With raincoats on, we rushed out of the courtyard noisily.

稀里糊涂 xīlihútú ❶ not knowing what is what; at sea; muddle-headed:这道题他讲了两遍,我还是～。I'm still at sea (*or* befuddled) though he has explained the problem twice. ❷ careless; casual:一天到晚～地混日子 muddle along carelessly day by day /没有在会上认真讨论,就～地通过了这项决议。The resolution was adopted in a most casual manner without any serious deliberation at the meeting.

稀里哗啦 xīlihuālā *also* "稀溜哗啦"〈口语〉❶〈象声〉patter; crash:雨～下了起来。The rain began pouring down. /房子～倒塌。The house collapsed with a crash. ❷ be smashed to pieces; be routed completely:桌子上的菜盘饭碗打了个～。The plates and bowls on the table were smashed to pieces.

稀里马虎 xīlimǎhu careless; thoughtless:念书可不能～的。One must never be careless in one's studies.

稀料 xīliào diluent; thinner

稀溜溜 xīliūliū (of gruel, soup, etc.) thin; watery:一碗～的粥 bowl of thin porridge /～的一锅汤 pot of watery soup

稀落 xīluo scattered; sparse:草坪周围有几棵～的桃树。Scattered around the lawn were a few peach trees. /枪声～了。The shooting was dying down.

稀漆剂 xīqījì 〈化工〉lacquer diluent

稀奇 xīqí *also* "希奇" xīqí rare; peculiar; strange

稀缺 xīquē scarce; lacking; in short supply

稀溶液 xīróngyè 〈化学〉diluted solution

稀散元素 xīsàn yuánsù 〈矿业〉scattered element

稀少 xīshǎo *also* "希少" xīshǎo few; rare; scarce; hardly any:顾客～ have few customers /人烟～ sparsely populated /这种矿物非常～。The mineral is quite rare. /夜深了,街上关门闭户,行人～。It was late at night, with all doors closed and hardly any pedestrians in the streets.

稀湿 xīshī very wet; soaking wet:雨继续在下,他身上淋得～。The rain continued and he was soaked to the skin.

稀世 xīshì *also* "希世" xīshì rare on earth:～之珍 rare treasure

稀释 xīshì dilute; attenuate:～酒精 diluted alcohol

稀释测定 xīshì cèdìng 〈化学〉dilution metering

稀释剂 xīshìjì 〈化学〉diluent; thinner

稀释液 xīshìyè 〈化学〉dilution

稀疏 xīshū few and far between; scattered; thin; sparse:～的雪花 scattered snowflakes /～植被 sparse vegetation; thin vegetation /～的枪声 sporadic firing; scattered shots /他头发逐渐～了。His hair's getting thin on top. *or* He is starting to go bald. /草原～地散布着几座蒙古包。The grassland was dotted with a few yurts.

稀疏霉素 xīshūméisù 〈药学〉sparsomycin

稀松 xīsōng ❶ lax; not strict:作风～ lax style of work ❷ poor; sloppy:这家具活儿做得太～。The quality of this furniture is just too poor. /他们哥儿几个干起活来哪个也不～。None of these brothers is a sloppy worker. ❸ unimportant; trifling; trivial:她就是那么个小心眼儿,好记那些～事儿。She is so petty that she never forgets those trivial matters. ❹ thin; loose:泥土～。The soil is loose and thin. /农活儿～时,村上的人就纷纷进县城找活儿干。When farm work slackened, most of the villagers would go to the county-seat to hunt for temporary jobs.

稀酸 xīsuān 〈化学〉diluted acid;稀硫酸 dilute sulfuric acid

稀碎 xīsuì in pieces; in bits:玻璃杯摔了个～。The glass was bro-

ken to pieces.

稀汤寡水 xītāng-guǎshuǐ (as of gruel, soup, etc.) watery and tasteless:这也叫豆腐脑儿? 全是~的酱油汤! Do you call this jellied bean curd? It's watery soy sauce soup, pure and simple!

稀土 xītǔ rare earth:~矿物 rare-earth mineral /~磁体 rare-earth magnet /我国是~资源最丰富的国家,~储量约占世界已知总储量的百分之八十。China has the richest rare-earth resources in the world, accounting for about 80% of the world's total known deposits.

稀土金属 xītǔ jīnshǔ 〈化学〉rare-earth metal

稀土元素 xītǔ yuánsù 〈化学〉rare-earth element

稀稀拉拉 xīxilālā *also* "稀稀落落" ❶ sparse; scattered:~的观众 sparse audience; scattered crowd /雨~地下了起来。It began raining sporadically. /几年前他的头发就有点~的了。His hair began to thin a few years ago. ❷ sloppy; poorly organized:这支~的队伍怎么打仗? How can such sloppy troops fight? /今天的大会开的~。Today's meeting was quite a flop.

稀血症 xīxuèzhèng hydraemia

稀有 xīyǒu *also* "希有" xīyǒu rare; uncommon:十月天下大雪在这儿并不是~的事。Heavy snowfalls in October are by no means rare here.

稀有金属 xīyǒu jīnshǔ 〈化学〉rare metal

稀有气体 xīyǒu qìtǐ 〈化学〉noble gas; rare gas:~包括氦、氖、氩、氪等。Among rare gases are helium (He), neon (Ne), argon (Ar), krypton (Kr), etc.

稀有元素 xīyǒu yuánsù 〈化学〉rare element

稀糟 xīzāo 〈方言〉rotten; very bad:这种产品的质量~到家了。This product is just rotten.

稀珍 xīzhēn *also* "希珍" xīzhēn rare and valuable

欷 xī

欷歔 xīxū *also* "唏嘘" xīxū 〈书面〉sob:~不止 keep on sobbing /相对~ sob and sigh to each other

郗 Xī

a surname (pronounced Chī as used in ancient books)

兮 xī

〈书面〉〈助词〉:风萧萧~易水寒。The wind soughs and sighs while the water in the Yi River chills. /祸~福所倚,福~祸所伏。Good fortune lieth within bad; bad fortune lurketh within good.

悉[1] xī

all; entirely:事情的发展,未能~如人意。Things didn't turn out entirely as one might have desired. /文中所见错字,~予纠正。Please correct all the misspellings in the article. /一切~听尊便。Do just as you please. *or* Please suit your convenience.

悉[2] xī

know; understand; learn; be informed:获~ have heard; have learnt /欣~ be glad to learn /洞~ know clearly; understand thoroughly /来函收~。Your letter has come to hand.

悉力 xīlì do one's utmost; go all out; spare no effort:~协助 go all out to help; assist with might and main

悉尼 Xīní Sydney, largest city and port of Australia

悉数 xīshǔ enumerate in full; make a complete list:品种繁多,不可~。There are too many varieties to list. /诸如此类的事实难以~。Such facts are too many to enumerate.

悉数 xīshù 〈书面〉all; each and all:~归公 turn in everything to the state /所需之款,已~寄去。We have sent you the full amount of what you required.

悉心 xīxīn devote all one's attention; exercise the greatest care:~照料 look after sb. with the utmost care; take the utmost care of sb. /~钻研技术 devote all one's attention to the study of technology (*or* the perfection of one's skill)

窸 xī

窸窣 xīsū 〈象声〉rustle:她走路时,裙子~作响。Her skirt rustled when she walked.

蟋 xī

蟋蟀 xīshuài *also* "促织" cùzhī; "蛐蛐儿" qūqur 〈动物〉cricket:斗~ cricket fight

蟋蟀草 xīshuàicǎo 〈植物〉yard grass; goose grass

嘻 xī

嘻嗦 xīsuō *see* "窸窣" xīsū

翕 xī

〈书面〉❶ amiable; docile ❷ fold; close; furl

翕动 xīdòng *also* "噏动" xīdòng 〈书面〉(as of lips, etc.) open and close alternately:嘴唇~ one's lips keep moving

翕然 xīrán 〈书面〉❶ (usu. of one's actions and words) conform; accord:~从之 obey willingly ❷ stable; peaceful:境内~ stable domestic situation

翕张 xīzhāng 〈书面〉open and close alternately:双目~ with one's eyes opening and closing alternately

噏 xī

〈书面〉❶ *see* "吸" xī ❷ furl; fold; close

噏动 xīdòng *see* "翕动" xīdòng

歙 xī

〈书面〉breathe; inhale

see also shè

息 xī

❶ breath:喘~ gasp for breath /窒~ suffocate /奄奄一~ at one's last gasp; on one's last legs /瞬~万变 myriad changes occur in the twinkling of an eye ❷ news:互通声~ keep each other informed (*or* posted) ❸ cease; stop; end:自强不~ make unremitting efforts to improve (*or* strengthen) oneself /川流不~ flow in an endless stream /偃旗~鼓 lower the banners and muffle the drums — cease all activities /生命不~,战斗不止 fight as long as one is alive; fight to one's last breath ❹ rest; break:安~ rest; go to rest /小~ have a short rest; take a short break /作~时间 timetable for work and rest ❺ grow; breed; multiply:休养生~ rest and build up strength; recuperate and multiply ❻ interest:月~ monthly interest /股~ dividend /还本付~ repay capital and interest /年~四厘 at an annual interest of four percent ❼〈书面〉one's children:无有子~ have no children; be childless ❽ (Xī) a surname

息兵 xībīng cease fire; stop fighting; end hostilities:两国~。The two countries ceased to fight each other.

息肩 xījiān 〈书面〉❶ put down one's burden; be relieved of responsibilities:我年事已高,该~了。As I am getting on in years, I should be relieved of my responsibilities. ❷ stay; sojourn:坎坷一生,无~之地 have no place to stay after going through a lifetime of frustrations and setbacks

息交绝游 xījiāo-juéyóu break off one's contacts with the world; go into seclusion:~,闭门谢客 go into seclusion and decline to receive visitors

息率 xīlǜ rate of interest

息男 xīnán one's own son

息怒 xīnù cease to be angry; calm one's anger:请君~。Please don't be angry. /过了许久,他才渐渐~。It was a long time before his wrath subsided.

息女 xīnǚ one's own daughter

息票 xīpiào interest coupon

息钱 xīqián 〈方言〉interest

息黥补劓 xīqíng-bǔyì mend one's ways; turn over a new leaf

息肉 xīròu *also* "瘜肉" xīròu 〈医学〉polyp; polypus:鼻~ adenofibroma edematodes /~性鼻炎 polypous gastritis

息事宁人 xīshì-níngrén ❶ patch up a quarrel and reconcile the parties concerned; pour oil on troubled waters:我们不是当事人,只能两边劝说,以求~。As a third party, we can only try to get the two sides to patch up their quarrel and effect a reconciliation. ❷ make concessions to avoid trouble; pacify sb. by meeting him halfway; gloss things over to stay on good terms:他总是抱着~的态度,避免和同事发生争执。He would always try to placate his colleagues and avoid disputes with them.

息讼 xīsòng end a lawsuit

息息相关 xīxī-xiāngguān *also* "息息相通" be closely related; be closely bound up:~,亲如一家 be as closely linked as people from the same family /"大河有水小河满"— 这句话充分说明了个人利益与集体利益~。The saying that "the tributaries never run dry when there is water in the main river" fully indicates the close relationship between one's personal interests and those of one's community. /生命的起源和水~,水是生命的摇篮。The emergence of life goes hand in hand with water; water is the cradle of life.

息心 xīxīn ❶〈方言〉feel relieved; be at ease: 听说孩子的伤势很轻,家里人都～了。All the family were relieved at the news that the boy's injury was slight. ❷〈书面〉dispel distracting thoughts (from one's mind)
息影 xīyǐng 〈书面〉live in retirement; go into seclusion: ～乡间,以娱余生 go into seclusion in the countryside and enjoy one's remaining years happily
息战 xīzhàn stop fighting; end hostilities: 双方有～的愿望。Both sides wished to have a ceasefire.
息止 xīzhǐ cease; end; stop: 无～地劳作 toil (*or* work) ceaselessly

瘜 xī

瘜肉 xīròu *see* "息肉" xīròu

熄 xī

extinguish (a fire); put out (a light): 把灯～了睡觉吧。Put out the light and go to sleep. /炉子～了。The fire in the stove went out.
熄灯 xīdēng turn off or put out the light: ～就寝 put out the light and go to bed /学生宿舍每晚十一时～。Lights in the student dorms are turned off at eleven every evening.
熄灯号 xīdēnghào lights-out; taps
熄风 xīfēng 〈中医〉subdue endogenous wind (i.e. relieve vertigo, tremor, convulsion, epilepsy, etc. by administering traditional medicine)
熄弧 xīhú 〈电工〉arc blowout: ～器 arc-arrester
熄火 xīhuǒ ❶ (of an engine, etc.) stop working; go dead: 引擎～,车停在路上。The engine went dead and the car stopped on the road. /火车就要驶进终点站,司机正在～。As the train was pulling into the station, the driver was cutting the engine. ❷ put out (a fire); extinguish: ～后,砖窑里温度仍然很高。The temperature in the brick-kiln remained high after the fire was put out.
熄灭 xīmiè extinguish; put out; go out: 灯光～了。The lights went out. /他连忙～了烟,站起身来走了。He immediately put out his cigarette, stood up and left. /希望的火花～了。Sparks of hope are extinguished.

螅 xī

also "水螅" shuǐxī hydra

夕 xī

❶ sunset; dusk: 朝不保～ not know at dawn what may happen at dusk — be in a precarious state /朝令～改 issue an order in the morning and rescind it in the evening — make unpredictable changes in policy ❷ evening; night: 危在旦～ be on the verge of death (*or* destruction); hang by a thread /国庆节前～ on the eve of National Day
夕晖 xīhuī sunlight at dusk; rays of the setting sun; brilliance of the sunset: 最后一抹～为炊烟代替,我们在小镇的一处旅社投宿了。When the smoke from cooking fires replaced the last rays of the setting sun, we stopped at an inn in the small town.
夕暮 xīmù dusk; sunset
夕烟 xīyān evening smoke and mist: ～袅袅。Evening smoke and mist curled upward.
夕阳 xīyáng setting sun: ～西下 sun setting in the west /～残照 last rays of the setting sun /～如血。The glow of the setting sun was crimson as blood. /～无限好,只是近黄昏。As the sun sets, unrivalled in its splendour, Pity is that the dusk is fast approaching.
夕阳工业 xīyáng gōngyè sunset industry; fading industry: ～与朝阳工业 fading industries and rising industries
夕阳市场 xīyáng shìchǎng sunset market; declining market
夕照 xīzhào glow of the setting sun; evening glow: 青山～,风景依旧。In the evening glow, the green hills are as beautiful as ever. /～把山冈染上了一层金色。The setting sun painted the hillock a golden hue.

汐 xī

tide during the night; night tide: 潮～ tide

穸 xī

see "窀穸" zhūnxī

矽 xī

(old name for 硅)〈化学〉silicon (Si): ～尘 silicious dust /～化 silicification
矽肺 xīfèi (old name for 硅肺)〈医学〉silicosis; pneumosilicosis: ～结核 silicotubercolosis
矽钢 xīgāng (old name for 硅钢)〈冶金〉silicon steel

犀 xī

rhinoceros
犀角 xījiǎo rhinoceros horn
犀利 xīlì keen; sharp; incisive; trenchant: ～的眼睛 sharp eyes /～的笔触 trenchant pen; incisive style /啊,电! 你这宇宙中最～的剑呀! Ah, lightning! Keenest sword of the universe!
犀鸟 xīniǎo hornbill
犀牛 xīniú rhinoceros

樨 xī

see "木樨" mùxi

娭 xī

〈书面〉*see* "嬉" xī
see also āi

xí

席(❶蓆) xí

❶ mat: 芦～ reed mat /篾～ mat made of (thin) bamboo strips /凉～ mat for summer /枕～ pillow mat /炕～ mat for *kang* (*or* earthen bed) ❷ seat; place; box: 就～ take one's seat; be seated (at a dinner or conference table) /离～ leave the (dinner or conference) table /首～ seat at the head of a table; seat of honour; chief /被告～ defendant's seat; dock /原告～ plaintiff's (*or* prosecutor's) seat /证人～ witness box (*or* stand) /旁听～ visitor's seats; public gallery /记者～ seats for the press /列～ attend as a nonvoting delegate; be present /坐无虚～ all the seats are taken; be packed to capacity /缺～ be absent /退～ leave (a dinner or meeting); walk out ❸ seat in parliament: 执政党在议会中占有二百五十～。The ruling party has 250 seats in the parliament. ❹ feast; banquet; dinner: 筵～ banquet; feast /还～ return dinner /摆了一桌～ give a feast (*or* dinner) /～间祝酒 make a toast during dinner ❺〈量词〉: 一～话 a talk /摆了十几～酒 order more than a dozen tables for the feast (*or* dinner) ❻ (Xí) a surname
席不暇暖 xíbùxiánuǎn not sit long enough to warm the seat; be in a tearing hurry; be as busy as a bee: ～,来去匆匆。He is constantly on the move, coming and going in a tearing hurry. /他整天～,怎能有时间去顾及他的子女的学习呢? As he is busy the whole day, how would he find time to concern himself with the studies of his children?
席草 xícǎo 〈植物〉*Scirpus triangulatus*
席次 xícì order of seats; seating arrangement; one's seat as arranged: 正式宴会前,礼宾官员都要安排～。Protocol officers have to make seating arrangements before an official dinner. /客人依～入坐。The guests took their assigned seats.
席地 xídì on the ground or floor: ～而坐 sit on the ground (*or* floor) /～幕天 take the earth (*or* ground) for a mat and the sky for a tent — take a broad view of the world; be broad-minded
席间 xíjiān at or during a feast: ～宾主频频为两国的友好关系而举杯。During the feast the hosts and guests raised their glasses (*or* proposed toasts) time and again to the friendly relationship between the two countries.
席卷 xíjuǎn roll up like a mat; carry everything with one; sweep across; engulf: ～天下 conquer the whole country in a sweep /～而逃 make a clean sweep and decamp; make off with everything one can lay hands on /改革的浪潮正～全国各地。An upsurge of reform is sweeping across the country. /一场经济衰退～各国。An economic recession engulfed various countries.
席勒 Xílè Friedrich Schiller (1759-1805), German dramatist and poet
席梦思 xímèngsī (transliteration from simmons, a brand name) inner-spring mattress
席面 xímiàn ❶ feast; banquet: ～常开,宾客如云。Banquets are held frequently and crowds of guests entertained. ❷ food presented at dinner: ～精美无加,来客无不赞叹。Guests all gasped at the superb food served at dinner.
席篾 xímiè thin strips of the skin of bamboo, reed or sorghum stalks (used for making mats)
席棚 xípéng mat shed or boarding (put up temporarily)
席位 xíwèi seat (at a conference, in a legislative assembly, etc.): 在议会选举中获得过半数～ win over half of the seats in a parliamen-

tary election
席纹组织 xíwén zǔzhī 〈纺织〉hopsack weave; mat weave
席状矿床 xízhuàng kuàngchuáng 〈地质〉sheet deposit
席子 xízi mat

觋 xí 〈书面〉wizard; sorcerer

檄 xí ❶ (in ancient times) official summons to arms; official proclamation (denouncing a usurper, traitor, etc.): 传～声讨 spread a summons to arms against sb.; publish an official proclamation denouncing sb. / 羽～ (in ancient times) urgent dispatch (with a feather attached to indicate its urgency) calling men to arms ❷〈书面〉announce or denounce in such a call or proclamation: ～讨 issue an official denunciation (against sb.) / ～喻 issue an official announcement (to the local officials and people at large)
檄书 xíshū see "檄文"
檄文 xíwén official call to arms; written summons to arms; official denunciation (against the enemy, etc.): 战斗的～ call to arms / 一篇词锋锐利的讨逆～ trenchant manifesto against the traitors / 讨伐封建专制制度的～ manifesto condemning the feudal authoritarian regime

袭[1] (襲) xí ❶ raid; attack: 空～ air raid / 侵～ invade; attack / 奔～ make a long-range raid / 奇～ make a surprise attack / 寒气～人。The nip in the air chills one to the bone. ❷ (Xí) a surname

袭[2] (襲) xí ❶ follow the pattern of; carry on as before; copy: 沿～ carry on without change / 抄～ plagiarize; copy; borrow indiscriminately / 承～ inherit and carry on / 世～ inherit (from generation to generation) ❷〈书面〉〈量词〉: 一～棉衣 a suit of cotton-padded clothes
袭夺 xíduó ❶ attack and take by surprise (an unprepared city, etc.) ❷〈地质〉(of rivers) capture: ～湾 elbow of capture
袭封 xífēng (in feudal times) inherit a rank or title
袭击 xíjī spring an attack on; attack by surprise; raid: 1941 年 12 月 7 日日本海空军～珍珠港。The Japanese air force and navy made a surprise attack on Pearl Harbor on 7 December 1941. / 南方各省遭到洪水的～。The southern provinces were hit by the floods.
袭爵 xíjué see "袭封"
袭取 xíqǔ ❶ take by surprise: ～敌营 attack and take an enemy camp by surprise ❷ take over (something that has long been popular among the people): 作者～一个广为流传的民间传说,改编成这部电视连续剧。The author took a popular folk tale and turned it into the present TV series.
袭扰 xírǎo make harassing attacks; harass: ～敌人后方 harass the enemy rear / 苦遭蚊虫～ be pestered by mosquitoes / 土匪四处～。The bandits made harassing raids everywhere.
袭用 xíyòng take over (something that has long been used in the past); follow: ～古方,配制丸药 make pills according to an age-old prescription / ～成说 follow an accepted theory or formulation / ～故技 use the old tactics; repeat an old trick
袭占 xízhàn attack and take by surprise: ～敌军前沿阵地 attack and take an enemy forward position by surprise

媳 xí daughter-in-law: 儿～ daughter-in-law / 弟～ younger brother's wife; sister-in-law / 童养～ girl raised in the family of her future husband; child bride / 婆～ mother-in-law and daughter-in-law / 翁～ father-in-law and daughter-in-law
媳妇 xífù ❶ *also* "儿媳妇儿" érxífur daughter-in-law; son's wife: 老太太和～的关系很好,一家人和和睦睦。The old lady gets along well with her daughter-in-law, and the whole family lives in perfect harmony. ❷ wife of a relative of a generation younger than oneself: 侄～ nephew's wife / 孙～ grandson's wife / 兄弟～ wife of one's younger brother; sister-in-law
媳妇儿 xífur 〈方言〉❶ wife: 娶～ (of a man) take a wife; get married / 小伙子有个漂亮的～。The young guy has got a pretty wife. ❷ young married woman: 村里的大姑娘小～们 young women of the village, married and unmarried

习 (習) xí ❶ study; learn; review; practise: ～画 practise painting / 学～ learn / 自～ study by oneself / 实～ practice; fieldwork / 演～ military drill or exercise / 补～ take lessons after school or work / 温～功课 review one's lessons ❷ be accustomed or used to; be inured to; be familiar with: 不～夜战 not inured to night fighting; not good at night fighting ❸ habit; custom; convention; usual practice: 陈规陋～ outmoded conventions and invidious customs / 相沿成～ become a custom through long usage ❹ (Xí) a surname
习兵 xíbīng 〈书面〉❶ train troops ❷ be well versed in the art of war
习非成是 xífēi-chéngshì accept the erroneous as right as one grows accustomed to it: 对错误的东西无动于衷、～,后果不堪设想。To remain indifferent to wrongdoings and accept them as right would lead to disastrous consequences.
习惯 xíguàn ❶ be accustomed to; be used to; be familiar with: ～于戎马生涯 be inured (*or* accustomed) to army life / ～于早睡早起 be in the habit of keeping early hours / 北京这样干冷的天气,许多人不～。Many people just can't get used to Beijing's dry and cold weather. / 在幼儿园里待了几天以后,我的孩子就～了。After a few days, my child felt quite at home in the kindergarten. ❷ habit; custom; convention; usual practice: 生活～ way of life / 民族～ national customs / ～势力 force of habit / ～用语 favourite or habitual wording / ～性流产 habitual abortion / 养成～ form a habit (*or* the habit of doing sth.) / 他染上了酗酒的～。He has become addicted to alcohol. *or* He has become an alcoholic.
习惯成自然 xíguàn chéng zìrán habit makes things natural; habit is second nature; the force of habit is irresistible: 俗话说"～",毛病一旦形成就不好改了。As the proverb goes, "Habit is second nature", a bad habit once formed is difficult to get rid of.
习惯法 xíguànfǎ common law; customary law: ～婚姻 common-law marriage
习惯继承人 xíguàn jìchéngrén heir by custom
习好 xíhào addiction; habit: ～饮酒 be addicted to drinking; take to drinking
习见 xíjiàn (of things) commonly seen: 这种情况已为人们所～。This is no uncommon occurrence.
习气 xíqì bad habit; bad practice: 官僚～ practices of bureaucracy; bureaucratism / 不要沾染酗酒的坏～。Don't fall into the bad habit of excessive drinking.
习染 xírǎn 〈书面〉❶ contract (a bad habit); get into (evil ways): 恶习一经～,难以根除。Once contracted, a bad habit is hard to eradicate (*or* break). ❷ bad habit: 这少年有小偷小摸的～。The boy is in the bad habit of pilfering.
习尚 xíshàng common practice; custom: 受人尊敬的民族一定具有优良的～。A respected nation must have excellent customs.
习俗 xísú custom; practice; convention: 社会～ social convention / 民间～ popular practice; folk tradition / 赛龙舟的～ custom of holding dragon-boat races / ～移人。Customs and habits make people different.
习题 xítí exercise (in school work); sum: ～解答 key to exercises / 做～ do an exercise; do a sum
习习 xíxí (of the wind) blow gently: 清风～。A refreshing breeze was blowing gently. / 湖上微风～,水波不兴。As there was only a gentle breeze, the water in the lake remained unruffled.
习性 xíxìng habits and characteristics; temperament: 生活～ habits and characteristics (as of an animal); way of life / 飞蛾有趋光的～。Moths are in the habit of going after light. *or* Moths characteristically are attracted to light.
习焉不察 xíyān-bùchá too accustomed to sth. to call it into question; failing to see anything wrong in what one is used to: 他指出的这些弊端确实存在,但人们已经～。Such malpractices as he exposed did exist, but people were too used to them to raise any question. / 人们对于常见的事物往往难免～。It is only natural that people usually do not question what they are accustomed to.
习以为常 xíyǐwéicháng be accustomed or used to; be in or get into the habit of: 他对说谎似乎已经～了。He seems to be in the habit of telling lies. / 走这么多路,对老人来说是～的。The old man was accustomed to such long walks. / 这样嘈杂的环境,父亲已经～了。Father was used to such noisy surroundings.
习艺 xíyì learn a skill or craft: 他从小学徒,～多年。He was apprenticed as a child and learned his trade for years.
习用 xíyòng be in the habit of using; habitually use: 习见～,不足为

怪。What is commonly seen is habitually used; there's nothing strange about that. /导演在这部电影中舍弃了许多～手法，艺术上很有新意。Discarding many conventional devices, the director of the film was quite inventive in artistic creation.

习用语 xíyòngyǔ idiom

习与性成 xíyǔxìngchéng habits form one's character; habits become second nature：俗话说："～。"坏毛病往往由坏习惯而来。As the saying goes, "Habits become second nature", and one's vices are often derived from one's bad habits.

习语 xíyǔ *see* "习用语"

习字 xízì practise penmanship or calligraphy

习字帖 xízìtiè copybook; calligraphy model

习作 xízuò exercise in composition, painting, etc.：刻苦～ apply oneself to exercises; work hard to improve (one's writing, painting, etc.) through practice /这些是作者早年的～。These are the author's early exercises. /送上～数篇，盼指正。Here are some of my immature works for your criticism.

霫 xí

霫霫 xíxí 〈书面〉(of rain) drip; patter

隰 xí

❶〈书面〉low, wet land ❷〈书面〉newly cultivated farmland ❸ (Xí) a surname

xǐ

喜 xǐ

❶ happy; delighted; joyful; pleased：欢～ happy; delighted /狂～ wild with joy /大～ very much pleased /幸～ fortunately; luckily /惊～交加 be pleasantly surprised /沾沾自～ feel complacent; be pleased with oneself /～溢眉梢 be radiant with joy; eyes lit up with joy /转悲为～ grief turns into joy /～忧参半 be torn between joy and sorrow; be partly glad and partly worried /～迁新居 happily move into new housing /～结良缘 consummate a marriage happily; tie the nuptial knot ❷ happy event (esp. wedding); auspicious occasion：道～ congratulate (sb. on a happy occasion); offer felicitations /双～临门 be blessed with double happinesses /～上加～ two happy events come one after the other ❸ pregnancy：害～ be pregnant; showing symptoms of pregnancy /恭喜你，你媳妇儿有～啦。Congratulations. Your wife is expecting (*or* in the family way). ❹ be fond of; love; like; have a partiality for：～游泳 like swimming /～人奉承 be fond of flatteries /好大～功 crave greatness and success; have a fondness for the grandiose /猴子性～模仿人的动作。Monkeys have a natural inclination for imitating human beings. ❺ (as of growing environment for some plant or cooking requirements for some food) be prone to; agree with; require：～光 photophilous /～阴 sciophilous; heliophobous /～阳 heliophilous /～氮 nitrophilous /萝卜～荤，最好和肉一块儿炖。As turnips taste better with lard, it is better to stew them with pork.

喜爱 xǐ'ài love; have a liking for; be fond of; be keen on：～体育运动 be keen on sports; be fond of sports /～交际 love company; be sociable /十分～阅读文艺作品 be an avid reader of literary works /各种文摘报刊受到读者的～。Digests of various types are popular with the readers. /这孩子真招人～。What a lovely child!

喜报 xǐbào bulletin of glad tidings; report of good news：立功～ bulletin announcing sb.'s meritorious service; citation /～频传。Reports of good news keep pouring in.

喜报神 xǐbàoshén harbinger of good news：哦！原来你有个～，事情都知道了。So a little bird told you everything.

喜病 xǐbìng pregnancy (with all its "indispositions")：害～ show symptoms of early pregnancy (such as morning sickness)

喜不自胜 xǐbùzìshèng be delighted beyond measure; be transported with joy; be unable to restrain oneself for joy; be overjoyed：他获悉后～，不由得多喝了两杯。He was overjoyed to learn the news and had a drop too much. /宝玉听了，～，走来恭恭敬敬磕了几个头。Baoyu, only too glad to comply, came over and kowtowed respectfully.

喜车 xǐchē car or carriage used to meet the bride at her home and take her to the bridegroom's home for wedding; wedding car or carriage：披红戴绿的～ wedding cars draped in red and green silks

喜冲冲 xǐchōngchōng be radiant with joy; look exhilarated：他～地跑回家去。He rushed back home with happiness written all over his face. /有什么好事，这么～的？What happy occasion makes you so excited?

喜出望外 xǐchūwàngwài be overjoyed (at unexpected good news, etc.); be pleasantly surprised：接到这所著名大学的入学通知书，他不禁～。He was pleasantly surprised to receive a letter of admission to the famous university. /盼望已久的事情突然降临，他难免有些～。He couldn't help being overwhelmed with joy when what he had long hoped for came true all of a sudden.

喜从天降 xǐcóngtiānjiàng unexpected piece of good fortune; godsend; windfall：几十年下落不明的叔叔突然从海外回来了，真是～！What a godsend to see his uncle return from abroad, as nothing had been known of his whereabouts for dozens of years!

喜蛋 xǐdàn red painted egg (presented to friends on birth of baby, etc.)

喜房 xǐfáng 〈方言〉❶ wedding chamber ❷ room (in a residence) temporarily used as a delivery room

喜封 xǐfēng packet of gift money (usu. wrapped in crimson paper) given away to guests, etc. on a happy occasion：打开～一看，大红纸内包着二十元钱。Upon opening the crimson-paper packet, he found twenty *yuan* inside. /主人派人分发～，一人一份。The host had packets of gift money distributed, one for each guest.

喜歌 xǐgē 〈旧语〉song sung on a happy occasion (wedding, etc.)

喜歌剧 xǐgējù comic opera

喜光植物 xǐguāng zhíwù *also* "阳性植物" yángxìng zhíwù photophilous plant; sun plant

喜果 xǐguǒ ❶ "happy nuts" — peanuts, dates, etc. distributed among guests at an engagement or wedding ceremony, or among relatives and friends afterwards ❷〈方言〉red painted egg (presented to friends on birth of baby, wedding, etc.)

喜好 xǐhào like; love; be fond of; be keen on：他对曲艺有特殊的～。He is especially fond of *quyi*. /我姐姐酷爱音乐，却不大～体育。My sister loves music but is not so keen on sports.

喜欢 xǐhuan ❶ like; love; be fond of; be keen on：～看足球赛 like watching football matches /讨某人～ win sb.'s favour; make sb. happy /～训人 love to lecture people; be fond of preaching /最不～扯谎 loathe (*or* detest) lying /他渐渐看出哥哥也～她。Gradually he noticed that his brother had a soft spot for her, too. ❷ happy; delighted; elated; filled with joy：喜喜欢欢过春节 jubilantly celebrate the Spring Festival /听到她病愈的消息，我们好不～。We were elated at the news of her recovery.

喜酒 xǐjiǔ wine drunk at a wedding feast; wedding feast：请人吃～ invite sb. to one's wedding feast /平时我不大喝酒，但今天你这杯～我非喝不可。I don't drink usually, but this glass of wine I must drink to celebrate your wedding.

喜剧 xǐjù comedy：～作家 comedist /情景～ situation comedy /性格～ comedy of character /风俗～ comedy of manners /～演员 comedian /～女演员 comedienne

喜乐 xǐlè happiness; joy; delight：有什么可～的事情，快说出来，让大家高兴高兴。What is the happy news? Out with it and let everybody rejoice.

喜联 xǐlián antithetical couplets (written on scrolls, etc.) hung on walls at a wedding; wedding couplets

喜马拉雅山脉 Xǐmǎlāyǎ Shānmài the Himalayas

喜脉 xǐmài 〈中医〉pulsebeat showing symptoms of pregnancy

喜眉笑眼 xǐméi-xiàoyǎn one's eyes and brows twinkling with delight; all smiles：这几天高兴，她逢人便～的。As she was in a happy mood recently she greeted everyone with a smiling face. /这孩子长得～的。The child has a lovely smiling face.

喜娘 xǐniáng 〈旧语〉woman serving as bride's attendant

喜怒哀乐 xǐ-nù-āi-lè happiness, anger, grief and joy — the whole gamut of sentiments：他的一身，就是大众的一体，～，无不相通。He identified himself with the common people, sharing their joy and anger, their pleasure and sorrow. /此人～不形于色。He never shows his feelings. *or* He is quite an inscrutable person.

喜怒无常 xǐnù-wúcháng subject to changing moods; volatile; capricious：正值更年期，她的脾气更加～。Her temper became even more unpredictable as she was in her climacteric. *or* Being in her climacteric, she was even more capricious than before. /他的那位上司～。That boss of his is a man of moods.

喜期 xǐqī wedding day

喜气 xǐqì cheerful look or expression; joyful atmosphere; festive

mood：满脸～ be radiant with joy; be all smiles

喜气洋洋 xǐqì-yángyáng full of joy; radiant with happiness; jubilant：人人～，欢呼雀跃。Everyone was in high spirits, shouting and jumping for joy. /全国人民～地迎来了新的一年。Filled with jubilation, people throughout the country ushered in the new year. /整个广场歌声嘹亮，～。The whole square was alive with singing and rejoicing.

喜钱 xǐqian money distributed on a happy occasion：分送～ distribute money on a happy occasion

喜庆 xǐqìng ❶ calling for celebration; arousing jubilation：今天是个～的日子，我们要玩个痛快。As this is a day for jubilation, let's enjoy ourselves as much as we can. /大礼堂里一片～气氛。An atmosphere of rejoicing and festivity prevailed in the auditorium. ❷ occasion for celebration; happy event：结婚～ wedding celebration

喜鹊 xǐque *also* "鹊"〈动物〉magpie

喜人 xǐrén gratifying; heartening; satisfactory：～的成果 satisfactory result /～的秋雨 welcome autumn rain /麦苗长势～。The wheat is growing luxuriantly. /这孩子鬼得～。The child is a lovely artful devil.

喜容 xǐróng ❶ happy expression; joyful look：她脸上一点～儿都没有。There is not a trace of a smile on her face. ❷〈旧语〉portrait

喜丧 xǐsāng funeral arrangements of sb. who lived to a very old age

喜色 xǐsè happy expression; joyful look：面带～ wear a happy expression or joyful look /他面有～。He was beaming with joy.

喜沙植物 xǐshā zhíwù psammophilous plant

喜上眉梢 xǐshàng-méishāo beam with delight; be radiant with joy

喜事 xǐshì ❶ happy event; joyous occasion; glad tidings：～临门。A great happiness descended upon the house. /人逢～精神爽。A happy event brings joy to people. *or* A happy occasion raises people's spirits. ❷ wedding：办～ hold a wedding ceremony

喜树 xǐshù *Campotheca acuminaa* (garden plant believed to have cancer-curing properties)

喜堂 xǐtáng hall where a wedding ceremony takes place; wedding hall

喜糖 xǐtáng "happy-sweets" (offered to guests at or after a wedding)

喜帖 xǐtiě *also* "喜帖子"〈旧语〉invitation card for a wedding celebration

喜慰 xǐwèi be gratified; be pleased：母亲听到我获奖的消息，心中十分～。Mother was most gratified to hear that I had won the prize.

喜温植物 xǐwēn zhíwù thermophile; thermophilic or thermophilous plant

喜闻乐见 xǐwén-lèjiàn love to see and hear; love：我们应该提倡人民～的作品。We should promote works that the people love. /这是个青年人～的电视节目。This TV programme is popular among young people.

喜相 xǐxiang〈方言〉amiable expression; pleasant look：这人虽然不怎么好看，可是总那么～。Though he is not good-looking, he has a pleasant look.

喜笑颜开 xǐxiào-yánkāi (as of one's face) light up with happiness or pleasure; be wreathed in smiles; beam with pleasure or joy：孩子们一见到这位喜剧演员就～。Kids would beam at the sight of the comedian. /他看罢来信，不觉～，一天忧愁都化为乌有了。After he finished reading the letter he was all smiles, and the anxiety he had felt all day vanished.

喜新厌旧 xǐxīn-yànjiù *also* "喜新厌故" love the new and loathe the old — be off with the old love and on with the new; be fickle in one's affection：这个女孩子总是～，爱情不专一。The girl kept abandoning the old for the new and could never be constant in love.

喜形于色 xǐxíngyúsè be visibly pleased; be radiant with joy; (as of one's face) light up with pleasure or joy：此人每有惬意之事，便～，手之舞之，足之蹈之。Whenever he was pleased with something, he would be radiant with joy, dancing, leaping and gesticulating. /他～地把刚听到的消息告诉我们。Beaming with pleasure, he told us the news he had just learnt.

喜幸 xǐxìng〈书面〉happy; delighted：～之事 happy occasion or event

喜兴 xǐxing〈方言〉happy; joyful：～事儿 happy event /～劲儿 happy or joyful expression /过个～年 celebrate a joyful New Year /今天他显得格外精神和～。He looks exceptionally happy and spirited today.

喜讯 xǐxùn happy news; good news; glad tidings：～频传 good news keeps pouring in /～传来，欢声雷动。The glad tidings were received with thunderous cheers. /～很快传遍全城。The happy news quickly spread all over the city.

喜盐植物 xǐyán zhíwù halophile; halophilous plant

喜阳植物 xǐyáng zhíwù heliophilous plant; heliophile

喜洋洋 xǐyángyáng beaming with pleasure or joy; radiant：心里～ with joy in one's heart /个个脸带笑，家家～ with smiles on every face and joy in every house

喜阴植物 xǐyīn zhíwù sciophilous or heliophobous plant

喜吟吟 xǐyínyín joyful; pleased：看他那～的样子，定有什么美事。Judging from his pleased look, he must have some happy news for himself.

喜盈盈 xǐyíngyíng happy; pleased：丰衣足食～ happy with plentiful food and clothing /全家团聚～ joyful family reunion

喜雨 xǐyǔ seasonable rain; spell of welcome rain：～连降，丰收在望。Plenty of seasonable rain promises a good harvest.

喜雨植物 xǐyǔ zhíwù ombrophile; ombrophilous plant

喜悦 xǐyuè delightful; happy; joyous：他那～之情，难以言传。His joy (*or* happiness) is beyond words. /他两眼放射出～的光芒。His eyes were radiant with delight.

喜跃 xǐyuè jump for joy

喜幛 xǐzhàng large oblong sheet of red silk with inscriptions of blessing, presented as a wedding gift

喜蛛 xǐzhū a kind of long-bodied and long-legged spider

喜滋滋 xǐzīzī feeling pleased; full of joy：心里～ be filled with joy /听别人的夸奖，他不由得～的。He couldn't help feeling pleased on hearing people's kind words.

喜子 xǐzi *see* "蟢子" xǐzi

禧（釐）

xǐ auspiciousness; happiness; jubilation：恭贺新～。(I wish you a) Happy New Year! /年～ season's greetings; Happy New Year

蟢

xǐ

蟢子 xǐzi *also* "喜子" xǐzi a kind of long-bodied and long-legged spider

鳍

xǐ *also* "沙钻鱼" shāzuànyú〈动物〉sand borer

缅（纚）

xǐ silk hair ribbon

see also lí

葸

xǐ〈书面〉fear; dread; be scared：畏～不前 be too scared to press forward; hang back (*or* recoil) in fear

洗

xǐ ❶ wash; bathe; clean：拆～ wash (padded coat, quilt, etc.) after removing the padding or lining; unpick and wash /干～ dry-clean /盥～ wash one's hands and face /浆～ wash and starch /淋～ drip wash /梳～ wash and dress /～伤口 bathe a wound /～磁头 clean a magnetic head (as of a VCR set) /碧空如～ cloudless blue sky /一贫如～ penniless; in utter destitution ❷〈基督教〉baptize：领～ be baptized; receive baptism ❸ redress; remedy; right：～冤 right a wrong; remedy an injustice ❹ clear away; eliminate：清～ purge; comb out ❺ kill and loot; sack：～城 sack a city and massacre its inhabitants /土匪血～了这个山村。The bandits plunged the mountain village into a bloodbath. *or* The bandits massacred the inhabitants of the mountain village. ❻ develop (a film)：～一卷胶卷 develop a roll of film /～两张相片 have two photos printed ❼ erase (a recording)：他的那段讲话已经～了。That part of his speech has been erased (from the tape). ❽ shuffle (cards, etc.)：～骨牌 shuffle the dominoes /把这副牌好好～～一下。Give the cards a good shuffle. ❾ small vessel or tray for washing (writing) brushes

see also Xiǎn

洗布机 xǐbùjī〈纺织〉cloth washing machine

洗槽 xǐcáo〈化学〉washing tank; washtrough; sink

洗肠 xǐcháng intestinal lavage

洗尘 xǐchén wash away the dust — give a dinner of welcome (to a visitor from afar)：设便宴为某人～ give an informal dinner to welcome sb. (upon his arrival or return)

洗荡 xǐdàng wash clean; wash away: 那年发大水,村子被～一空。That year a flood washed the village clean. *or* Everything in the village was washed away by a flood that year.
洗涤 xǐdí wash; rinse: 在溪水里～衣裳 wash clothes in a stream / 早晨,经过一场大雨～的香山,显出特有的清新明朗。After a heavy rain, the Fragrant Hill appeared especially clean and bright in the morning.
洗涤槽 xǐdícáo washing tank; sink; washtrough
洗涤粉 xǐdífěn washing powder
洗涤剂 xǐdíjì detergent
洗涤碱 xǐdíjiǎn washing soda; sal soda
洗涤器 xǐdíqì washing appliance; washer; scrubber
洗涤塔 xǐdítǎ 〈化学〉 washing tower
洗耳恭听 xǐ'ěr-gōngtīng listen with respectful attention; lend an attentive ear; be all ears: 说吧,我～。Go ahead! I'm all ears. / 我们应该～民众对这件事的感想。We should be attentive (*or* listen) to the sentiments of the man in the street about this matter.
洗发剂 xǐfàjì shampoo
洗剂 xǐjì 〈药学〉 lotion
洗碱 xǐjiǎn *see* "洗盐"
洗脚礼 xǐjiǎolǐ 〈基督教〉 washing of feet; foot-washing
洗劫 xǐjié loot; ransack; sack: 村子被匪徒们～一空。The village was sacked by the bandits.
洗洁净 xǐjiéjìng liquid detergent
洗井 xǐjǐng 〈石油〉 flushing (of a well)
洗矿 xǐkuàng 〈矿业〉 ore wash: ～槽 trough washer; strake / ～机 ore washer / ～水 washwater / ～台 (ore) washing table
洗礼 xǐlǐ ❶ baptism: 给某人施～ administer (*or* give) baptism to sb. ❷ severe test; baptism: 经受炮火的～ receive the baptism of fire; go through the test of battle (*or* war) / 他是一位饱受战争、多次出生入死的老兵。He is an old soldier who has repeatedly braved death and gone through the test of war.
洗礼堂 xǐlǐtáng 〈基督教〉 baptistery
洗脸盆 xǐliǎnpén washbasin; washbowl
洗练 xǐliàn *also* "洗炼" (as of speech, writing, etc.) neat; succinct; terse: 文字～ succinct language / 剧情紧凑～。The plot is well-knit.
洗毛 xǐmáo 〈纺织〉 scouring
洗毛机 xǐmáojī 〈纺织〉 wool-scouring machine; wool-washing machine
洗煤 xǐméi coal washing
洗煤厂 xǐméichǎng coal washery; coal cleaning plant
洗煤机 xǐméijī coal washer
洗面膏 xǐmiàngāo (facial) cleansing cream
洗脑 xǐnǎo brainwashing; indoctrination
洗牌 xǐpái shuffle cards or dominoes
洗片 xǐpiàn develop or process (a film)
洗片机 xǐpiànjī developing machine
洗钱 xǐqián money laundering (i. e. transferring money obtained from crime to a bank or to a legitimate business, etc. so as to disguise its source)
洗染店 xǐrǎndiàn laundering and dyeing shop; cleaners and dyers
洗三 xǐsān traditional custom of bathing a baby on the third day of its birth
洗手 xǐshǒu ❶ (as of a gangster, robber, etc.) stop doing evil and reform oneself: 痛改前非,～不干 thoroughly reform oneself and hang up one's axe ❷ wash one's hands of sth.; give up (a vocation, hobby, etc.): 他在海外从商多年,打算就此～归国。Having engaged in business abroad for years, he thought of retiring and returning to his native land. ❸ go to the lavatory; use the restroom
洗手间 xǐshǒujiān lavatory; toilet; bathroom; restroom
洗漱 xǐshù wash one's face and rinse one's mouth
洗刷 xǐshuā ❶ wash and brush; scrub: ～浴盆 wash and brush a bathtub / ～地板 scrub the floor ❷ wash off; remove; clear oneself of (opprobrium, guilt, etc.): ～自己 vindicate oneself / 她决心用诚实的劳动～自己心灵上的污渍。She made up her mind to wash away the stain on her conscience by honest labour.
洗涮 xǐshuàn wash and rinse: 把蔬菜倒进池子里～干净。Put the vegetables in the basin and give them a thorough rinse.
洗头 xǐtóu wash one's hair; shampoo: 请给我～。I want to have my hair washed. *or* Give me a shampoo.
洗碗碟机 xǐwǎndiéjī dish-washing machine; dishwasher
洗胃 xǐwèi 〈医学〉 gastric lavage
洗心革面 xǐxīn-gémiàn *also* "革面洗心" turn over a new leaf; start one's life afresh; reform oneself thoroughly: ～,重新做人 reform oneself thoroughly and begin one's life anew / ～,迷途知返 realize one's errors and turn over a new leaf
洗选 xǐxuǎn 〈矿业〉 washing: ～法 washing process / ～厂 washery / ～机 washer / ～设备 washing apparatus (*or* appliance)
洗雪 xǐxuě wipe out (a disgrace); redress (a wrong): ～耻辱 wipe out a humiliation / ～沉冤 redress a long-standing wrong; clear sb. of a long-standing false charge
洗盐 xǐyán 〈农业〉 desalinize soil by flooding or leaching
洗眼杯 xǐyǎnbēi eyecup
洗眼剂 xǐyǎnjì collyrium; eyewash
洗衣 xǐyī wash clothes; do one's washing: ～工人 washerwoman; washerman
洗衣板 xǐyībǎn washboard
洗衣店 xǐyīdiàn *also* "洗衣房" washhouse; laundry; dry cleaner
洗衣粉 xǐyīfěn washing powder
洗衣机 xǐyījī washing machine; washer
洗衣刷 xǐyīshuā wash brush
洗印 xǐyìn 〈摄影〉 develop and print; process
洗印机 xǐyìnjī (film) processor
洗浴 xǐyù take a bath: ～室 bathroom / 洗海水浴 go for a bathe in the sea; go bathing in the sea
洗澡 xǐzǎo have or take a bath; bath: 用冷水～ take a cold bath; bath in cold water / 给孩子～ bath the child; give the child a bath
洗澡间 xǐzǎojiān bathhouse; bathroom
洗澡盆 xǐzǎopén bathtub
洗澡塘 xǐzǎotáng bath pool
洗濯 xǐzhuó wash; cleanse: 在溪水中～ wash in a stream / ～污垢 cleanse filth

铣

xǐ 〈机械〉 milling: 端～ face milling / 逆～ conventional milling; up milling / 排～ gang milling / 平～ plain milling / 顺～ down milling; climb milling
see also xiǎn
铣床 xǐchuáng mill; miller; milling machine: 成形～ milling and shaping machine; profile (*or* shaping) machine; profile milling machine; profiler / 专用～ production miller (*or* milling machine)
铣刀 xǐdāo 〈机械〉 mill; milling cutter; milling tool: 成形～ profile milling cutter; profile cutter
铣工 xǐgōng ❶ milling (work): ～车间 milling machine shop; milling shop ❷ miller; miller hand; milling machine operator
铣镗两用机床 xǐ-táng liǎngyòng jīchuáng 〈机械〉 milling and boring machines
铣削 xǐxiāo work (metal, etc.) with milling machine
铣钻两用机床 xǐ-zuàn liǎngyòng jīchuáng 〈机械〉 milling and drilling machines

徙

xǐ ❶ move (from one place to another); migrate: 迁～ move to another place; migrate / 流～ drift about / ～迁之累 fatigue of moving from one place to another ❷ 〈书面〉 be transferred to another official post
徙边 xǐbiān 〈书面〉 banish (prisoners) to a border region: 坐罪～ be exiled to the border areas
徙居 xǐjū move house; change one's residence; migrate: ～内地 move to the hinterland; move up-country / 举家～江西。The whole family moved to Jiangxi.
徙倚 xǐyǐ 〈书面〉 linger in hesitation; wander about irresolutely: ～不忍离去 hesitate to tear oneself away / 回望故里,～良久。He lingered for a good while as he looked back at his hometown.
徙宅忘妻 xǐzhái-wàngqī move one's residence but forget (to take along) one's wife — attend to the superficial and neglect the essentials; be penny-wise but pound-foolish

葸

xǐ 〈书面〉 fivefold increase: 倍～ several times; severalfold

屣

xǐ 〈书面〉 shoes; slippers; sandals: 视如敝～ regard as of no importance or as useless (as worn-out shoes) / 倒～而迎 slip on one's shoes hurriedly to extend one's welcome

玺(璽)

xǐ imperial or royal seal: 符～ emperor's seal / 玉

～ jade seal /国～ seal of the emperor; seal of state; great seal /～书 document with imperial (*or* royal) seal /掌～大臣 minister in charge of imperial seals; (UK) Lord Privy Seal

枲 xǐ male nettle-hemp; hemp

枲麻 xǐmá *also* "花麻" huāmá male nettle-hemp

xì

禊 xì 〈古语〉sacrificial festival held at water's edge in spring and autumn (when participants drink to heaven and chase away evil spirits)

卌 xì forty

赩 xì 〈书面〉red (colour)

睎 xì 〈书面〉(of eyes) roll; rove

隙(隟) xì ❶ crack; rift; chink; crevice: 孔～ small opening; hole /门～ crack in the door /冰川裂～ crevasse /白驹过～ (glimpse of) a white colt flashing past a chink in a wall — evanescent or transient /～大而墙坏。The wall will collapse if the crack in it grows bigger. ❷ gap; interval: 空～ interval; gap /农～ interval between busy seasons in farming ❸ loophole; opening; opportunity: 寻～ look for a loophole (*or* opportunity) /可乘之～ opening to take advantage of ❹ discord; rift; grudge: 嫌～ ill will; grudge /与人有～ have a quarrel with sb.; bear sb. a grudge

隙地 xìdì vacant or unoccupied place; open space: 门前房后的～ open spaces around a house /广场上人山人海, 几无～。The square was swarming with people, with hardly any space.

隙缝 xìfèng chink; crack: 秃鹰穴巢筑在悬崖峭壁的～中。Vultures make their nests in the cracks of precipices.

隙罅 xìxià 〈书面〉crack; crevice

虩 xì

虩虩 xìxì 〈书面〉frightened; scared

舄 xì ❶〈书面〉shoe ❷ see "潟" xì ❸ (Xì) a surname

舄卤 xìlǔ see "潟卤" xìlǔ

潟 xì 〈书面〉saline soil

潟湖 xìhú 〈地理〉lagoon

潟卤 xìlǔ 〈书面〉saline-alkaline land or soil

阋(鬩) xì 〈书面〉quarrel; fight: 兄弟～墙。Brothers fight each other. *or* There is strife at home.

系[1](❹係、❺-❽繫) xì ❶ system; series; line: 水～ river system /根～ root system /山～ mountain chain (*or* system) /银河～ Milky Way; Galaxy /父～ of paternal line; patriarchal /母～ of maternal line; matriarchal /直～亲属 lineal relative /旁～亲属 collateral relative ❷ department; faculty: 中文～ Chinese department /土木工程～ department of civil engineering ❸〈地质〉system: 泥盆～ Devonian system /志留～ Silurian system ❹ relate to; rely on: 观瞻所～ relating to the appearance of a place; having to do with the impressions a place leaves on visitors /成败所～ success or failure hinges on this; stand or fall by this /维～人心 maintain popular support; keep up one's popularity ❺ be concerned; feel solicitous: *see* "～恋"; "～念" ❻ tie up and carry; fasten and pull up; fasten and lower down: 从地窖里把白薯～上来 pull sweet potatoes up from a cellar /从后窗口～了一个皮箱下来。A leather suitcase was let down from the back window. ❼ tie; fasten: ～马 tether a horse /械～ put in fetters /解铃还待～铃人。Let him who tied the bell (on the tiger) take it off. *or* He who caused the problem has to solve it. ❽ take into custody; jail: ～狱 be put in prison /囚～ imprison; incarcerate

系[2](係) xì 〈书面〉be: 确～实情。It is indeed the truth. /纯～无中生有。This is sheer fabrication. /此种花生～山东名产。This kind of peanut is a famous product of Shandong Province.

see also jì

系绊 xìbàn trammels; fetters; yoke: 为琐事～ be tied down with trivialities

系泊锚 xìbómáo 〈船舶〉mooring anchor

系船浮筒 xìchuán fútǒng 〈船舶〉mooring buoy

系词 xìcí ❶〈逻辑〉copula ❷〈语言〉copulative verb; link verb

系风捕影 xìfēng-bǔyǐng *also* "捕风捉影" bǔfēng-zhuōyǐng chase the winds and clutch at shadows — make groundless accusations; speak or act on hearsay

系缚 xìfù 〈书面〉tie; fasten; bind up: 冲破旧观念的～ break the bonds of conventional ideas

系累 xìlěi ❶ burden: 他家劳力强, ～少, 比较富裕。With more able-bodied persons to work and fewer dependents to feed, his family is comparatively well off. ❷ fetters; yoke

系恋 xìliàn be attached to; be reluctant to leave: ～家乡 be reluctant to leave one's hometown

系列 xìliè series; set: 进行一～科学观测 make a series of scientific observations /～产品 set of products /运载～ vehicle series /～电视剧 TV series

系列化 xìlièhuà seriate; serialize

系列片 xìlièpiàn serial: 电视～ TV serial

系留 xìliú 〈船舶〉moor; mooring: ～索 mooring line; hawser /～塔 mooring mast /～柱 mooring post

系留水雷 xìliú shuǐléi 〈军事〉moored mine

系念 xìniàn 〈书面〉be concerned about; feel solicitous or anxious about: ～在心 have (sth. or sb.) on one's mind /小诗反映了母亲对游子的深切～之情。This little poem reflects the deep concern of a mother for her son who is away.

系谱 xìpǔ pedigree; genealogy

系谱树 xìpǔshù genealogical tree; family tree

系谱学 xìpǔxué genealogy

系囚 xìqiú 〈书面〉prisoner; captive

系数 xìshù 〈数学〉coefficient: 摩擦～ coefficient of friction /膨胀～ coefficient of expansion /相关～ coefficient of correlation /光学～ optical coefficient

系统 xìtǒng system; setup: 显示～ display system /通信～ communication system /党、政、军～ Party, government and military setups /灌溉～ irrigation system /密码～ latched system /消化～〈生理〉digestive system; alimentary system /呼吸～〈生理〉respiratory system /心血管～〈生理〉cardiovascular system /进行～的分析 undertake systematic analysis /～地学习无线电基础知识 learn the ABC of radio technology systematically

系统分析 xìtǒng fēnxī systems analysis

系统工程 xìtǒng gōngchéng systems engineering; systematic engineering

系统功能 xìtǒng gōngnéng system capability

系统管理理论 xìtǒng guǎnlǐ lǐlùn theory of system administration

系统化 xìtǒnghuà systematize

系统集成 xìtǒng jíchéng system integration

系统科学 xìtǒng kēxué system science

系统论 xìtǒnglùn systematology; systems theory

系统码 xìtǒngmǎ 〈计算机〉system code

系统设计 xìtǒng shèjì systems design

系统外存储器 xìtǒng wàicúnchǔqì 〈计算机〉system file

系统性 xìtǒngxìng systematic nature; system

系统学 xìtǒngxué systematology; systematics

系维 xìwéi maintain; hold together

系柱 xìzhù 〈船舶〉bitt

系子 xìzi 〈方言〉string or rope attached to a container or weight: 箩筐～ ropes attached to a bamboo basket /秤锤～ string for the sliding weight of a steelyard

饩(餼) xì 〈书面〉❶ grain; fodder; provisions: 献～ contribute (*or* present) provisions /马～ feed for horses ❷ live animal; animal for sacrifice; raw meat: ～羊 sacrificial lamb; lamb for sacrifice ❸ present (food) as a gift: ～粟 present millet

肸 xì 〈书面〉glare at; glower at: 瞋目～之 stare (at sb.) angrily

郤 xì ❶ see "隙" xì ❷ (Xì) a surname

X

绤 xì 〈书面〉coarse linen

戏(戲、戯) xì ❶ play; sport; have fun: 鸳鸯～水 mandarin ducks and drakes playing about in water / 视同儿～ regard as child's play; treat lightly; trifle with ❷ make fun of; joke with: 调～ take liberties with (a woman) / ～用 use humorously ❸ drama; opera; play; show: 京～ Beijing opera / 马～ circus show / 把～ acrobatics; juggling / 傀儡～ puppet show / 唱～ sing in an opera; be an actor or actress / 排～ rehearse a play / 看～ go to the theatre (*or* opera) / 点～ select a piece for performance / 压轴～ last item that serves as the climax of a theatrical programme / 好～连台 stage one good play after another / 拿手好～ best piece; forte; speciality / 逢场作～ play (*or* act) according to the circumstances; join in the fun when the occasion arises / 这场～演得真没劲。It was such a dreadful performance. / 好～还在后头呢。The best part of the show is yet to come.

see also hū

戏班 xìbān *also* "戏班子" old-style theatrical troupe: 进～ join a theatrical troupe (as an apprentice)

戏报子 xìbàozi 〈旧语〉playbill

戏本 xìběn *also* "戏本子" script of a play or opera

戏场 xìchǎng 〈旧语〉theatre; opera house

戏称 xìchēng ❶ call (sb.) jokingly: 人们～这姑娘为"假小子"。People jokingly call her "tomboy". ❷ joking nickname

戏出儿 xìchūr figurine or painting of a character from a play or opera

戏词 xìcí (actor's) lines or part

戏单 xìdān programme of a play or opera

戏德 xìdé actor's ethics: 这位戏曲艺术家很有～。This opera actor is a man of strong professional ethics.

戏法 xìfǎ juggling; sleight of hand; tricks; magic: 变～ juggle; conjure; perform a trick (*or* sleight of hand) / 你别跟我变～了, 你的用意我还不清楚吗? Don't play tricks with me. How could I fail to see what you are up to?

戏份儿 xìfènr 〈旧语〉actor's share of earnings from a performance

戏馆子 xìguǎnzi 〈旧语〉theatre or opera house

戏剧 xìjù ❶ drama; play; theatre: 古典～ classical drama; classical theatre / 现代～ modern drama; modern theatre / ～评论 dramatic criticism ❷ text or script of a play

戏剧家 xìjùjiā playwright; dramatist

戏剧界 xìjùjiè theatrical circles

戏剧文学 xìjù wénxué dramatic literature

戏剧性 xìjùxìng dramatic: 局势发生了～的变化。The situation changed dramatically. / 他们俩的悲欢离合很富有～。The joys and sorrows, partings and reunions of the couple are very dramatic.

戏乐 xìlè make merry; have fun; amuse oneself; play: 尽情～ engage in merry-making as much as one likes; play to one's heart's content / ～笑语 talk and laugh merrily

戏楼 xìlóu 〈旧语〉stage built for shows in an ancestral hall or temple

戏路 xìlù *also* "戏路子" ability to act different types of characters: ～窄 have limited ability to perform different types of characters / 她～宽, 正反两种人物都能扮演。She is a versatile actress, able to play both virtuous and evil characters.

戏码 xìmǎ 〈旧语〉catalogue of theatrical performances

戏迷 xìmí theatre-goer; theatre fan: 这个停演多年的剧目吸引了许多～。As the play had not been performed (*or* staged) for years, it attracted a lot of theatre-goers. 一群～在公园的一角有拉有唱, 自得其乐。A number of theatre fans amused themselves singing and playing theatrical instruments in a corner of the park.

戏目 xìmù *also* "剧目" jùmù item or piece of theatrical performance

戏弄 xìnòng make fun of; play a prank on; tease; kid: 成心～别人 deliberately make fun of others / 我不知道他是在称赞我, 还是～我。I don't know whether he is praising me or just pulling my leg.

戏评 xìpíng dramatic criticism; dramatic review

戏情 xìqíng plot or scenario of a play or opera

戏曲 xìqǔ ❶ traditional opera: 地方～ local opera / 传统～ traditional opera / ～改革 reform of traditional opera / ～作家 writer for traditional opera / ～作品 works in traditional opera / ～演员 traditional opera singer ❷ singing parts in *chuanqi* (传奇) and *zaju* (杂剧)

戏曲片儿 xìqǔpiānr screen adaptation of a traditional or local opera

戏曲片 xìqǔpiàn documentary film or film adaptation of a traditional opera

戏耍 xìshuǎ ❶ play tricks on; make fun of: 他可不是好～的。He is not to be made fun of (*or* trifled with). ❷ play; amuse oneself: 终日～, 不务正业 idle about all day and do no decent work

戏台 xìtái stage: 今晚有剧团来演出, 人们正在打谷场上搭～。As a theatrical troupe is coming to perform tonight, people are putting up a makeshift stage on the threshing ground.

戏谈 xìtán humorous or playful comments

戏文 xìwén ❶ *also* "南戏" nánxì southern drama ❷ *see* "戏词" ❸ traditional opera: 听～ go to the theatre; see an opera

戏侮 xìwǔ insult sb. by making fun of him; insult: 有意～ insult deliberately / 迹近～ be tantamount to an insult

戏匣子 xìxiázi 〈方言〉gramophone; phonograph; radio

戏箱 xìxiāng trunk for costumes and other accessories (for a theatrical performance)

戏笑 xìxiào ❶ laughter; banter: 一阵～ burst of laughter ❷ laugh at; ridicule: 不要～人! Don't laugh at people.

戏谑 xìxuè banter; crack jokes: 善～ good at bantering / 一阵～, 引得大家开怀大笑。The playful conversation made everyone laugh heartily.

戏言 xìyán joke; playful words; humorous remarks: 军中无～。No joke is allowed in the army. / 几句～, 你不必介意。That was only a wisecrack (*or* playful remark). Please don't take it seriously.

戏眼 xìyǎn most interesting scene or part of a play

戏衣 xìyī stage costume

戏园子 xìyuánzi 〈旧语〉playhouse; theatre; opera house

戏院 xìyuàn theatre

戏照 xìzhào photo of a person in stage costume: 报刊杂志上常有这位女演员的～。Photos of this actress in stage costume often appear in newspapers and magazines.

戏装 xìzhuāng theatrical or stage costume

戏子 xìzi 〈旧语〉〈贬义〉player; actor or actress

虩 xì 〈书面〉sad; sorrowful; painful: ～然泪下 cry sadly; shed sad tears

屃(屭) xì *see* "赑屃" bìxì

细 xì ❶ thin; slender; fine: ～毛线 thin knitting wool / ～腰 slender waist / ～～的雨丝 fine light rain / ～如发丝 as thin as a hair ❷ narrow; thin: 小河～得像一根腰带。The brook is so narrow that it looks like a waistband. / 满天的星, 一钩～到几乎看不见的月亮。In the star-studded sky there was a crescent so thin as to be hardly visible. ❸ in small particles; fine: ～沙 fine sand / ～面 fine flour / 磨得很～的咖啡 finely ground coffee / 他额上沁出一层～汗珠。Fine beads of sweat broke out on his forehead. ❹ (of one's voice) thin and soft: ～声 thin voice / 箫声愈颤愈～。The sound of the bamboo flute became softer with each vibration. ❺ fine; superb; exquisite; delicate: ～瓷 fine porcelain / 粗粮～作 make delicacies out of coarse (food) grains / 这衣服的做工很～。This dress is exquisitely done. ❻ careful; prudent; meticulous; detailed: ～察 investigate or examine carefully / 胆大心～ bold but prudent / 粗中有～ usually careless, but quite sharp at times; casual in most matters, but subtle in some / 这件事的具体情况我没有～打听。I didn't make a detailed inquiry into this matter. ❼ minute; tiny; trivial; trifling: 微～ very small; tiny / 琐～ trifling; trivial ❽〈方言〉young; little: ～娃子 little boy / ～妹子 little girl

细胞 xìbāo cell: 癌～ cancer cell / 白～ white blood cell; leucocyte / 红～ red blood cell; erythrocyte / ～融合 cell fusion / ～构造 cell structure / ～呼吸 cellular respiration / ～组织 cellular tissue

细胞壁 xìbāobì cell wall

细胞分裂 xìbāo fēnliè cell division; mitosis

细胞工程 xìbāo gōngchéng cellular engineering

细胞核 xìbāohé nucleus

细胞化学 xìbāo huàxué cytochemistry

细胞膜 xìbāomó cell membrane

细胞器 xìbāoqì organelle

细胞生态学 xìbāo shēngtàixué cytoecology

X

细胞体 xìbāotǐ cell body
细胞学 xìbāoxué cytology
细胞学说 xìbāo xuéshuō cell theory
细胞液 xìbāoyè cell sap
细胞质 xìbāozhì cytoplasm
细胞周期 xìbāo zhōuqī cell cycle
细刨 xìbào 〈机械〉smoothing plane: ~床 smoothing planer; smoothing planing machine
细别 xìbié ❶ minute or fine difference; subtlety; nuance: 区分两个词之间的~ distinguish the nuances between the two words /仔细看,不难看出~。It is not difficult to see the minute differences upon careful examination. ❷ differentiate carefully: 难以~ hard to differentiate to the finest detail
细布 xìbù fine cloth; muslin
细部 xìbù detail (of a drawing): 人物画的~ details of a figure painting
细菜 xìcài vegetable out of season and in short supply
细长 xìcháng long and thin; tall and slim: ~的身材 tall and slender figure /~的柳条 long and thin willow twigs /~的眼睛 long and narrow eyes /村东有条~的小路,直通山口。To the east of the village there is a long and narrow path leading straight to the mountain pass.
细齿 xìchǐ 〈机械〉serration: 内~ internal serration /外~ external serration /~拉刀 serration broach /~螺母 serrated nut
细川护熙 Xìchuānhùxī Morihiro Hosokawa (1938-), Japanese Prime Minister (1993-1994)
细大不捐 xìdà-bùjuān cast away nothing, big or small; leave nothing out: 他办事稳重、谨慎,~,悉记在心。He is prudent and cautious and keeps track of everything, big or small.
细底 xìdǐ ins and outs; exact circumstances: 不知~ not know the exact details
细点 xìdiǎn delicate refreshments; fine pastry
细度 xìdù fineness: ~指数 fineness index (numerical)
细发 xìfa 〈方言〉fine; delicate: 又~又鲜艳的棉布 fine and bright-coloured cotton cloth /这活做得多~。How delicate the work is.
细纺 xìfǎng finespun: ~布 finespun cloth /~车间 fine-spinning shop
细高挑儿 xìgāotiǎor 〈方言〉tall and slender figure or person: 孟康是个~,长脖子小脑袋。Meng Kang is tall and slender, with a long neck and a small head.
细工 xìgōng fine workmanship; delicate work: 骨雕是~活儿。Bone carving requires fine workmanship.
细故 xìgù trivial matter; triviality; trifle: 性情豁达,不同~ have a generous disposition and never bother about trivial matters /不必计较~。Don't mind trifles.
细活 xìhuó job requiring fine workmanship or meticulous care; skilled work; fine and delicate work: 慢工出~儿。Slow work yields fine products. /他粗活~都能干。He is good at all work, skilled or unskilled.
细火 xìhuǒ slow fire; soft fire: 把白薯放在炉灶上用~烤。Put the sweet potatoes around the cooking range and bake them over a slow fire (*or* gentle heat).
细嚼慢咽 xìjiáo-mànyàn chew one's food well before swallowing it; eat one's meal slowly
细节 xìjié details; specifics; particulars: 要从大处着眼,不必纠缠~。Keep your eyes on the overall goals and do not get bogged down in the particulars. /侦探办案时不能忽略任何一个~。Detectives cannot afford to neglect any detail in handling a case.
细究 xìjiū get to the bottom of (a matter); probe into (a matter): ~起来你我都有责任。If we investigate the matter thoroughly, neither of us could shirk responsibilities.
细菌 xìjūn 〈微生物〉bacterium; germ: 抗酸~ acid-fast bacteria /嗜酸~ acidophilic bacteria /需氧~ acrobic bacteria /厌氧~ anaetobic bacteria /产色~ chromagenic bacteria /发光~ photogenetic bacteria /产气~ aerogenic bacteria /~培养 germiculture /~感染 bacterial infection
细菌病 xìjūnbìng 〈医学〉bacteriosis
细菌弹 xìjūndàn 〈军事〉B-bomb; bacteria bomb
细菌肥料 xìjūn féiliào 〈农业〉bacterial fertilizer; bacterial manure
细菌疗法 xìjūn liáofǎ bacteriotherapy
细菌农药 xìjūn nóngyào bacterial pesticide
细菌武器 xìjūn wǔqì bacteriological weapon; germ weapon
细菌性肺炎 xìjūnxìng fèiyán bacterial pneumonia
细菌性痢疾 xìjūnxìng lìji bacillary dysentery
细菌性瘤 xìjūnxìngliú bacteriophytoma
细菌学 xìjūnxué bacteriology: ~家 bacteriologist
细菌战 xìjūnzhàn bacteriological or germ warfare
细粮 xìliáng (as opposed to 粗粮 coarse grains) fine grains — wheat flour and rice, etc.
细溜溜 xìliūliū slender and long; slim and tall: ~的身材 tall and slender figure /~的面条 long thin noodles
细脉 xìmài 〈中医〉thready pulse
细毛 xìmáo fine, soft fur (such as otter or mink)
细毛羊 xìmáoyáng fine-wool sheep
细蒙蒙 xìméngméng *also* "细濛濛" drizzly; misty: ~的春雨 fine spring drizzle
细眯眯 xìmīmī squinting: ~的眼睛 squinting eyes
细密 xìmì ❶ fine and closely woven; close: 这种布比那种布~。This kind of cloth is more closely woven than that one. /这块大理石质地~,花纹美丽。This piece of marble is of close texture and beautiful grain. ❷ with great precision and care; meticulous; detailed: 思维~ think meticulously /观察~ be careful in observation /文章的分析欠~。The article lacks detailed analysis.
细描 xìmiáo (as in literature) minute description
细民 xìmín 〈书面〉common people; people of low status
细磨 xìmó 〈机械〉fine grinding; finish grinding: ~料 finer abrasive /~机 finishing mill
细目 xìmù ❶ detailed catalogue: 商品~ detailed catalogue of commodities ❷ specific item; particular detail: 讨论计划的~ discuss the details of a plan
细木工 xìmùgōng ❶ joinery ❷ joiner; cabinetmaker
细嫩 xìnèn fine; delicate; tender: ~的新梢 tender shoot /这种鱼的肉很~。This fish is quite tender.
细腻 xìnì ❶ fine and smooth; delicate: 瓷纹~ delicate porcelain texture ❷ exquisite; superb; minute: 文笔~ exquisite writing; refined language /~的表演 superb performance /刻画~ depict to a nicety /感情~ of fine sentiments
细皮嫩肉 xìpí-nènròu *also* "细皮白肉" delicate skin and soft flesh — being fragile or delicate: 他长得~的,没干过力气活。He is delicate and has never done a stroke of manual work.
细巧 xìqiǎo exquisite; fine; dainty; delicate: ~的胸针 delicate brooch /~的手工 fine (*or* delicate) craftsmanship /玲珑~的玉雕 exquisitely wrought jade carvings
细切削 xìqiēxiāo fine cut
细情 xìqíng details; particulars: 先告诉你个大概,~等一会儿再说吧。I'll give you a general idea first, and the details can wait.
细人 xìrén 〈书面〉❶ ignorant and mean person ❷ person of low status ❸ waiting maid; concubine
细绒线 xìróngxiàn fingering yarn
细柔 xìróu soft and slender; gentle and soft: ~的声音 soft voice /~的垂柳 slender weeping willow /~光洁的皮革 soft and shining leather
细软 xìruǎn ❶ jewelry, expensive clothing and other valuables: 收拾~,准备出逃 pack up one's valuables to flee ❷ soft and slender: ~的柳条 soft and slender willow branches
细润 xìrùn fine and smooth: 皮肤~ fine, delicate skin
细弱 xìruò thin and delicate; thin and fragile: 声音~ thin and weak sound; feeble voice /~的嫩芽 thin and fragile sprouts /~的呼吸声 feeble breathing
细沙轮 xìshālún 〈机械〉fine wheel
细纱 xìshā 〈纺织〉spun yarn
细纱车间 xìshā chējiān 〈纺织〉spinning workshop
细纱锭 xìshādìng ring spindle
细纱机 xìshājī spinning frame
细声细气 xìshēng-xìqì in a gentle, quiet voice; soft-spoken: 这个小伙子说话~的,像个女孩。This young man speaks in a soft voice like a girl.
细石器 xìshíqì 〈考古〉microlith
细石器文化 xìshíqì wénhuà 〈考古〉microlithic culture
细事 xìshì small matters; trifles; trivialities: 他从不计较~。He never fusses about trifles.
细瘦 xìshòu thin and small: ~的手臂 small and thin arm
细水长流 xìshuǐ-chángliú ❶ plan for the long term to avoid running short: 收入多了也不能挥霍浪费,还是~的好。One shouldn't be

extravagant even if one earns more than before. It's better to economize so as to avoid running short. ❷ go about sth. little by little without let-up; work persistently:学习要～,功夫下多了才会有收获。One should be persistent in one's study. It always takes time and effort to make progress.

细水牛 xìshuǐniú 〈方言〉 cow that drinks water slowly

细说 xìshuō ❶ *also* "细谈" narrate in detail:～分晓 go into details; give a detailed account /此是后话,不必～。These are subsequent happenings and need not be recounted here. ❷ 〈书面〉 gossip; garbled story

细碎 xìsuì small and broken; in fine scraps:～的石子 small, broken stones /～的脚步声 sound of light and hurried footsteps

细琐 xìsuǒ petty; trivial; trifling

细谈 xìtán *also* "细说" talk in detail:咱们坐下～吧。Let's sit down and talk it over in detail.

细条 xìtiao *see* "细挑"

细挑 xìtiao *also* "细条" tall and slim:～个儿 tall and slender figure or person

细微 xìwēi tiny; minute; slight; subtle:～的进步 slight progress /～的差别 subtle distinction; nuance /～之处 niceties; subtleties /作家观察得多么～,多么深入啊! How meticulous and deep-going the author is in his observations! /他的声音很～,似乎连说话的气力也没有了。His voice was so feeble that he seemed too weak to say a word.

细味 xìwèi *also* "细玩" 〈书面〉 think carefully; ponder; ruminate:不暇～ too busy to think it over carefully /～其言 ruminate on sb.'s words

细纹锉刀 xìwén cuòdāo 〈机械〉 fine file; smooth cut

细纹木 xìwénmù fine-grained wood

细细儿 xìxìr ❶ very thin; very fine:把胡萝卜切得～的 cut the carrots into fine shreds ❷ with a lot of care; in great detail:你～地跟我说一说。Tell me the details.

细香葱 xìxiāngcōng 〈植物〉 chive (*Allium schoenoprasum*)

细小 xìxiǎo very small; wee; tiny; trivial:～的枝条 tiny twigs /～的缝隙 small crack /声音～ in a thin voice /～的事情 trivial matters; trifles

细心 xìxīn meticulous; careful; attentive:～倾听 listen attentively /～照顾 care for sb. tenderly /～观察 be very observant /他这个人事事都～。He is careful in everything he does. /～的妻子看出了丈夫情绪异常。The attentive wife saw that her husband was not in his usual mood.

细辛 xìxīn 〈中药〉 root of Chinese wild ginger (*Asarum sieboldii*)

细行 xìxíng 〈书面〉 trivial matters of conduct:不拘～ not care about trivialities; not be prudish

细伢子 xìyázi 〈方言〉 child; kid

细腰 xìyāo (usu. of women) slender waist:楚王好～,宫中多饿死。The King of Chu loved slim women, so many of his royal concubines died of abstinence from food.

细雨 xìyǔ drizzle; fine rain:～蒙蒙 misty drizzle /～纷纷 steady drizzle /～霏霏 light drizzle /斜风～ light breeze and drizzling rain /毛毛～下了一晚上。It drizzled all night.

细语 xìyǔ speak gently or softly; whisper:轻声～ speak gently; speak in a soft, low voice

细乐 xìyuè ❶ traditional Chinese stringed and wind instruments ❷ music produced by such instruments

细匀 xìyún smooth and delicate:肌肤～ have smooth and delicate skin

细则 xìzé detailed rules and regulations; bylaws:工作～ rules and regulations of work /实施～ rules and regulations for implementation

细账 xìzhàng itemized account; detailed account:算～ give sth. careful consideration; weigh the pros and cons carefully

细针密缕 xìzhēn-mìlǚ fine, close stitches — delicate needlework; meticulous work:灯下,母亲～给将要出远门的儿子缝制冬衣。By the lamp, a mother was sewing a winter jacket in fine, close stitches for her son who was leaving for a far-away place. /有关措施安排得～,十分稳妥。Meticulous and reliable measures have been taken.

细支纱 xìzhīshā 〈纺织〉 fine yarn

细枝末节 xìzhī-mòjié petty details; non-essentials:工作要抓住要害,不能只注意～。Instead of paying attention to minor details only, one must grasp the crucial points in one's work.

细致 xìzhì ❶ careful; meticulous; precise; painstaking:～周到的安排 careful and thoughtful arrangements /深入～的工作作风 deep-going and painstaking style of work /认真～地调查研究 earnest and careful investigation and study ❷ fine; exquisite; delicate:花纹～的大理石 delicately veined marble

细琢 xìzhuó fine-pointed dressing; fine-pointed finish

细子龙 xìzǐlóng 〈植物〉 *Amesiodendron chinense*

细作 xìzuò 〈旧语〉 spy; secret agent; agent

xiā

瞎 xiā ❶ blind:～了左眼 blind in the left eye /他的右眼～了。His right eye is blind. ❷ groundlessly; foolishly; to no avail:～讲一气 talk groundlessly; shoot one's mouth off /～猜一通 make wild (*or* random) guesses /来～气 do sth. foolishly /～干 go it blind; fly blind /～操心 worry for nothing ❸ fail to detonate or explode; misfire; go dud:炮炮不～,发发命中。Without a single dud, the shells all hit the target. ❹ 〈方言〉 (as of seeds) fail to sprout or bud:天干地旱,麦子～了。It was so dry that the wheat failed to sprout. ❺ 〈方言〉 waste; spoil; lose:白～了一个名额 waste a candidature /好菜让他给做～了。He spoiled a good dish. ❻ 〈方言〉 (as of thread, etc.) become tangled:瞧,毛线都～了,针哪里去了? Look, the knitting wool is all in a tangle! Where are the knitting needles?

瞎掰 xiābāi 〈方言〉 ❶ work to no purpose; work in vain; waste one's effort:天没黑就点灯,这不是～吗? Isn't it sheer waste to turn on the lights before it's dark? ❷ talk nonsense; talk groundlessly:根本没有这事儿,你别听他～。There is nothing of the kind. Don't listen to his rubbish.

瞎白货 xiābáihuo *also* "瞎白话" 〈俗语〉 speak at random; talk irresponsibly:别以为我在～,这种事我见多了! Don't think I'm making up stories; I've seen enough of things like this.

瞎扯 xiāchě ❶ talk irresponsibly; talk rubbish:抓紧时间干活吧,别～了! Get on with your work and stop talking rubbish! ❷ spin; gossip; waffle:别听他～! Don't listen to his gossip! /老同学凑在一起,～了一夜,兴致可高了。The former classmates were so happy about their reunion that they spun the long yarn the whole night.

瞎吹 xiāchuī brag wildly; boast irresponsibly:亩产一万斤粮食,那是～。It was a wild boast to claim a harvest of 10 thousand *jin* of grain per *mu*. /说了就得办,你可别～! Do as you promise. Don't just brag.

瞎点子 xiādiǎnzi 〈俗语〉 impractical idea; wild notion:有的人专门热衷于出～,干蠢事。Some people are keen on offering impractical ideas and trying out foolish things.

瞎胡勒 xiāhúlēi 〈方言〉 talk groundlessly; talk irresponsibly; talk rubbish:这个人一天到晚～,太不可靠了。This guy is just too unreliable; he talks nothing but rot all the time.

瞎话 xiāhuà untruth; story; lie:睁眼说～ lie blazenly; tell a barefaced lie /说来也怪,有的傻瓜就爱信他的～。Strange enough some suckers swallow his stories readily.

瞎混 xiāhùn muddle along:我这几年一事无成,～呗! I have achieved nothing all these years, just muddling along. /他干脆不上班,专和一伙不三不四的人～。He simply stopped going to work and hung around with a batch of dubious characters.

瞎火 xiāhuǒ fail to detonate or explode; be a dud; misfire:他一扣板机,手枪～了。He pulled the trigger but the pistol misfired. /打了五发炮弹,其中一发是～。One of the five shells that were fired was a dud.

瞎聊 xiāliáo talk at random; engage in chitchat:你别以为我在～,句句都是真话。Don't think I'm telling a tall story. What I said is nothing but the truth. /你们几个还不回家,～什么呢? Why don't you guys go home? What on earth are you gossiping about?

瞎忙 xiāmáng fuss about nothing; be all fuss and feathers:我这个人,一天到晚～。I've been busy from morning till night, but all for nothing.

瞎猫逮住死耗子 xiāmāo dǎizhù sǐhàozi a blind cat stumbled on a dead rat — by sheer luck

瞎蒙 xiāmēng wild guess:你是～上了。You got it by sheer guesswork. *or* You just stumbled on it.

瞎摸合眼 xiāmohéyǎn *also* "瞎摸糊眼" where or when it is too dark to see clearly; not seeing clearly where one is going:～的,掉了根针可怎么找呀? How can you find a needle you dropped, when you can hardly see clearly? /他～地往外跑,差点让门槛儿绊了一跤。He tried to get out, not looking where he was going, tripped over the

threshold and almost fell.

瞎奶 xiānǎi ❶ retracted nipple; unprotrusive nipple; flat nipple ❷ nipple that gives no milk; dry breast

瞎闹 xiānào act senselessly; mess about; fool around: 原来你～了半天，连要求也不问问清楚！So you were messing about all the time without finding out about the requirements! / 不按操作规则加工零件，这不是～吗？Isn't it sheer madness to process parts in disregard of the operating rules? / 几个学生正在～，教室里乱哄哄的。The classroom was in a mess as a few students were playing rough house.

瞎炮 xiāpào *also* "哑炮" yǎpào unexploded dynamite or shell; dud: 清除～ remove unexploded dynamite (*or* duds)

瞎三话四 xiāsān-huàsì 〈方言〉 talk irresponsibly; talk rubbish; says who: 他都二十好几了，还成天～，说话没个准。Though he is going on for thirty now, he is still shooting his mouth off all day long with hardly a grain of truth in what he says.

瞎说 xiāshuō talk irresponsibly; talk rubbish: ～一通 talk all rubbish / 睁眼～ tell a barefaced lie; lie brazenly

瞎说八道 xiāshuōbādào *also* "胡说八道" húshuōbādào talk sheer nonsense; talk rubbish; says who: "那溪里到处是鳟鱼。" "～，我从来没有见过谁在那里捕到鳟鱼。" "That brook is full of trout." "Says who. I never saw anybody catch trout there."

瞎信 xiāxìn *also* "盲信" mángxìn dead letter

瞎眼 xiāyǎn blind: ～老汉 blind old man / 怪我当初瞎了眼，没有看出他是个骗子。It was all my fault; I was so blind that I did not see he was a swindler.

瞎指挥 xiāzhǐhuī give arbitrary and impracticable directions; mess things up by giving wrong orders; command at whim: 领导～，下面怎能不乱套？How can the subordinates help being confused if the higher-ups issue orders at whim?

瞎诌 xiāzhōu 〈方言〉 make up a wild story; spin a yarn; talk irresponsibly: 别～了！Don't pull stories out of thin air! *or* Stop making up wild stories! / 睁着眼睛～，也不怕别人笑话？Why do you tell such barefaced lies? Don't you have any sense of shame?

瞎抓 xiāzhuā do things without a plan; go about sth. in a haphazard manner; grasp anything within reach without knowing what to do with it: ～一气，不得要领 go about sth. in a haphazard manner without knowing how to handle it

瞎字儿不识 xiāzìr bùshí unable to read a single word; completely illiterate: 我～，看不了信。I cannot read the letter as I'm completely illiterate.

瞎子 xiāzi ❶ blind person ❷ 〈方言〉 *also* "瞎籽" blind seed or ear (of corn, etc.)

瞎子点灯白费蜡 xiāzi diǎn dēng báifèi là lighting a candle for a blind man — sheer waste: 你跟他说这些全是～。You're simply wasting your breath by talking to him about the matter.

瞎子摸象 xiāzi-mōxiàng a blind man feels an elephant — be unable to learn the whole picture: 我们大家眼下都是～，等调查清楚了再讨论吧。At present, we are still in the dark. Let's discuss it after further investigation.

瞎子摸鱼 xiāzi-mōyú a bind person gropes for fish — act blindly or heedlessly: 再这样～摸下去，实在太危险了！It would be very dangerous if we continued to act blindly.

虾(蝦) xiā

shrimp: 毛～ shrimp / 对～ prawn / 龙～ lobster / 卤～ salted shrimps / 青～ freshwater shrimp / 油焖大～ braised prawns / 炸～球 fried prawn balls / ～荒蟹乱 panic among shrimps and crabs — omen of war and great disturbance

see also há

虾兵蟹将 xiābīng-xièjiàng shrimp soldiers and crab generals — numerous (but ineffectual) followers or troops: 他们纠合一些～，多次对我边境进行骚扰。Mustering a few ineffectual troops, they harassed our frontier areas time and again.

虾干 xiāgān dried shrimps

虾蛄 xiāgū mantis shrimp; squilla

虾酱 xiājiàng shrimp paste

虾红素 xiāhóngsù 〈生化〉 astacene; astacin

虾米 xiāmi ❶ dried, shelled shrimps ❷ 〈方言〉 small shrimp: ～汤 shrimp soup / 大鱼吃小鱼，小鱼吃～。Big fish eat small fish, while the latter feed upon small shrimps — the competition is to the mighty.

虾皮 xiāpí *also* "虾米皮" dried small shrimps

虾青素 xiāqīngsù 〈生化〉 astaxanthin

虾仁 xiārén shelled fresh shrimps; shrimp meat: 清炒～ sauté shrimp meat / ～吐司 shrimp meat and croutons / 芙蓉～ shrimp meat with eggwhite

虾油 xiāyóu shrimp sauce

虾子 xiāzǐ shrimp roe; shrimp eggs: ～酱油 shrimp-roe soy sauce / ～酱 shrimp roe paste

虾子 xiāzi 〈方言〉 shrimp

鰕 xiā

see "虾" xiā

呷 xiā

〈方言〉 sip; drink: ～了一口酒 take a sip (*or* drink) of wine

see also gā

xiá

峡(峽) xiá

gorge: 山～ gorge / 地～ isthmus / 海～ strait; channel / 长江三～ Three Gorges of the Yangtze; Yangtze Gorges

峡谷 xiágǔ gorge; canyon: 大～ (US) Grand Canyon / ～阶地 canyon bench / ～急流 dalles

峡江 xiájiāng cove

峡口 xiákǒu 〈地理〉 narrows

峡湾 xiáwān 〈地理〉 fiord: ～谷 fiord valley

侠(俠) xiá

❶ person adept in martial arts and given to chivalrous conduct; chivalrous swordsman: 游～ roaming swordsman (given to chivalrous conduct); knight-errant / 剑～ practised swordsman / 武～小说 novel about such swordsmen; kung fu novel ❷ chivalrous: 行～仗义 perform chivalrous actions and uphold justice

侠肝义胆 xiágān-yìdǎn chivalrous and fearless: 此人～，疾恶如仇。A man of chivalry and justice, he hates social evils like poison.

侠骨 xiágǔ 〈书面〉 chivalrous frame of mind

侠客 xiákè person adept in martial arts and given to chivalrous conduct; chivalrous swordsman

侠气 xiáqì lofty sense of honour and courage; heroic spirit: 一身～ brimming with a heroic spirit / 父亲年轻时好结交朋友，颇有几分～。When he was young, father liked to make friends and had rather a lofty sense of honour and courage.

侠士 xiáshì practised swordsman; gallant person

侠义 xiáyì having a strong sense of justice and ready to help the weak; having a lofty sense of honour and gallantry; chivalrous: ～之人 man with a strong sense of justice and ready to help the weak; man of honour and courage / ～心肠 chivalrous temperament: 古称燕赵多～之士。Legend has it that Hebei Province is the home of many outstanding men of honour and gallantry.

狭(狹) xiá

of small width; narrow: ～路曲巷 narrow crooked alleyway / 宽～适度 right breadth; appropriate width / 坡陡路～，行路艰难。The steep slope and narrow path made walking difficult.

狭隘 xiá'ài ❶ narrow: 山势险要，只有一条～的盘山小道可通山顶。The mountain was difficult of access with only a narrow winding path leading to the summit. ❷ narrow and limited; parochial; illiberal: ～经验主义 narrow empiricism / ～民族感情 illiberal nationalist sentiments / ～集团 small exclusive clique / 走出～的圈子 step out of narrow confines / 他心胸～，目光短浅。He is parochial and short-sighted.

狭隘民族主义 xiá'ài mínzúzhǔyì narrow or parochial nationalism

狭长 xiácháng long and narrow: ～地带 long, narrow strip of land

狭路相逢 xiálù-xiāngféng (of adversaries) meet face to face on a narrow path — come into unavoidable confrontation; confront each other face to face: 仇人～，分外眼红。When enemies meet face to face on a narrow path, their eyes blaze with hate. / 刘岱引一队残军，夺路西走，正撞见张飞，～，急难回避。Fleeing with a company of defeated soldiers, Liu Dai got clear of the fight but stumbled right upon Zhang Fei. Escape was impossible.

狭小 xiáxiǎo narrow and small; cramped: 气量～ narrow-minded; intolerant of the views of others / ～的院子 small courtyard / ～的办公室 cramped little office / 老人在～的阁楼上养了一群鸽子。The old man raised a flock of pigeons in the poky attic.

狭邪 xiáxié *also* "狭斜"〈书面〉crooked, narrow alleyways where prostitutes live; red-light district：～中人物 people living in or visiting a red-light district /～小说 novel about brothels and prostitutes
狭心症 xiáxīnzhèng 〈医学〉stenocardia; angina pectoris *see also* "心绞痛" xīnjiǎotòng
狭义 xiáyì narrow sense：从～的角度看 taken (*or* viewed) in a narrow sense
狭义相对论 xiáyì xiāngduìlùn 〈物理〉special theory of relativity; special relativity
狭窄 xiázhǎi ❶ narrow; cramped：一条又肮脏又～的胡同 dirty and narrow alley ❷ narrow and limited：心地～ narrow-minded; insular; parochial /见识～ limited in knowledge and narrow in experience; ill-informed and narrow-minded /生活的天地太～ live within narrow confines ❸〈医学〉stenosis; stricture：尿道～ stricture of urethra
狭窄射线 xiázhǎi shèxiàn 〈物理〉narrow-beam
狭窄性骨盆 xiázhǎixìng gǔpén contracted pelvis

陿(陿)

xiá ❶ *see* "狭" xiá ❷ *see* "峡" xiá

辖(鎋、舝)

xiá ❶ linchpin ❷ have jurisdiction over; be under one's command; administer; govern：管～ have... under one's jurisdiction; administer /直～市 municipality directly under the central government /西线方面军下～两个兵团，拥兵三十万。The Western Front Army has two armies under its command with 300,000 men.
辖区 xiáqū area or district under one's jurisdiction
辖制 xiázhì restrain; check; control：受人～ be under sb.'s command (*or* control) /～太严 exercise too rigid control; exercise too much restraint

黠

xiá 〈书面〉sly; crafty; cunning：狡～ crafty; cunning /鬼～ sly; crafty /桀～ ferocious and crafty /～智 crafty; cunning
黠棍 xiágùn crafty ruffian
黠慧 xiáhuì 〈书面〉intelligent and crafty; smart and cunning：～无比 incomparably shrewd and crafty; extremely sly
黠吏 xiálì villainous and crafty official

柙

xiá cage for wild beasts, formerly also used for felons

匣

xiá small box or case; casket：梳头～儿 dressing case /一～点心 a box of pastry
匣式开关 xiáshì kāiguān 〈电工〉box switch
匣子 xiázi ❶ small box or case; casket ❷〈方言〉Mauser pistol
匣子枪 xiáziqiāng *also* "匣枪"；"匣子"〈方言〉Mauser pistol

狎

xiá be improperly familiar; indulge in flirtations or intimacies：～弄 treat with improper intimacy /～近 take liberties with
狎妓 xiájì visit a brothel; have fun with a prostitute：～出游 go on a trip accompanied by prostitutes
狎客 xiákè customer at brothel; prostitute's client
狎昵 xiánì be improperly familiar：态度～ have an improperly familiar manner /过分～ be too familiar; be improperly intimate
狎亵 xiáxiè be disrespectfully familiar; take liberties with (a woman)：亲昵而不～ affectionate but not disrespectfully familiar

祫

xiá 〈旧语〉(of emperors) perform grand rites in honour of one's ancestors in the Imperial Ancestral Temple

遐

xiá 〈书面〉❶ far; remote; distant：～布 spread far and wide /～眺 look as far as the eye can see ❷ lasting; durable; long：～福 enduring blessing or happiness
遐迩 xiá'ěr 〈书面〉far and near; far and wide：景德镇的瓷器，～皆知。Jingdezhen is widely known for its porcelain.
遐迩闻名 xiá'ěr-wénmíng be known far and near; enjoy great renown：～的哈蜜瓜 famous Hami melons
遐龄 xiálíng advanced age
遐思 xiásī reverie; day-dream：～冥想 reveries and meditations /～悠悠 be far away in one's reveries /沉浸在～之中 lost in thought; deep in one's day-dreams
遐想 xiáxiǎng reverie; day-dream; (wild) fancy：引人～ give play to one's fancy /无边的～ wild, fanciful thoughts

霞

xiá rosy clouds; morning or evening glow：朝～ rosy sunrise; glow of sunrise; sunrise clouds /彩～ rosy (*or* roseate) clouds /烟～ mists and clouds (as at twilight)
霞光 xiáguāng rays of morning or evening sunlight：旭日初升，～万道。The rising sun emits a myriad of rays.
霞帔 xiápèi (in ancient times) embroidered shawl or cape for a woman of noble rank：凤冠～ phoenix-shaped tiara and embroidered cape
霞石 xiáshí 〈矿业〉nepheline

瑕

xiá flaw (in a piece of jade); defect; drawback; shortcoming：白璧微～ tiny flaw in a piece of white jade; flaw in sth. otherwise perfect
瑕不掩瑜 xiábùyǎnyú one flaw cannot obscure the splendour of the jade — small defects cannot obscure virtues; drawbacks do not overshadow achievements：这部小说尽管艺术上有不足之处，但～，在反映现实的深度和广度上有口皆碑。Despite its weaknesses in artistry, the novel's defects cannot obscure its virtues. It is universally praised for its deep-going and extensive depictions of reality.
瑕疵 xiácī flaw; defect; blemish：多有～ have quite a few flaws (*or* defects)
瑕玷 xiádiàn 〈书面〉blemish; stain; taint; defect：～难免，不可苛求。As blemishes and defects are unavoidable, one should not be overcritical.
瑕瑜互见 xiáyú-hùjiàn have defects as well as merits; have both strengths and weaknesses：文章草成，难免～，不尽如意。As the article was written in a hurry, it must have defects as well as merits and leave much to be desired. /她心里清楚，丈夫有毛病，也有优点，～，不能太苛求。She knew in her heart that her husband was a composite of strengths and weaknesses and she shouldn't be nitpicking.

暇

xiá free time; spare moment; leisure：余～ spare time; leisure /自顾不～ be unable even to fend for oneself (much less take care of others); have enough to do looking after oneself; be busy enough with one's own affairs /应接不～ play host to a constant stream of visitors (customers, etc.); be up to one's ears in work; be too busy to make a proper response /无～兼顾家务 be too busy (with work) to attend to household chores
暇日 xiárì day of leisure; free time：晚年无事，～常与诗画为伴。I am quite free in my old age and often spend my leisure writing poetry and painting.
暇逸 xiáyì 〈书面〉be leisurely and carefree：退休之后，生活～ lead a leisurely and carefree life after retirement
暇豫 xiáyù 〈书面〉leisurely and comfortable：晚景～ lead a peaceful and happy life in old age

xià

下[1]

xià ❶ below; under; underneath; down：零～ below zero; sub-zero /一般水平之～ below (the) average /普天之～ all under the sun /水～一百米 one hundred metres under water (*or* beneath the water) /楼～ downstairs /山～ at the foot of the hill /～嘴唇 lower lip /上有父母，～有儿女 with parents above and children below — have to support both one's parents and children ❷ lower; inferior; poor：*see* "～级"；"～策" ❸ next; latter; later：～星期一 next Monday /～半年 latter (*or* second) half of the year ❹ down; downward：沿着山道往～走 walk down a mountain path ❺ *used in collocations indicating circumstances, extent, situation, etc.*：名～ under sb.'s name /属～ (sb.'s) subordinate /在"援助"的幌子～ on the pretext of "aid" /在集中指导～的民主 democracy under centralized guidance /在某人的指导和帮助～ with sb.'s guidance and help /在不利的情况～ under (*or* in) unfavourable circumstances ❻ *used in collocations indicating a particular time or season*：节～ during a holiday (*or* festival) /眼～ at the moment; at present; right now /年～有几个朋友来访。During the lunar New Year festival some friends will call on me. ❼ *used after a numeral to indicate orientation or position*：两～相思 miss each other /四～无人 with nobody around /两～里都愿意 both sides are willing

下[2] xià ❶ go down; descend; alight; get off: ～火车 get off (*or* disembark from) a train /～床 get out of bed /～楼 go (*or* come) downstairs /～河 get down into a river /顺河而～ go down a river; go downstream ❷ (of rain, snow, etc.) fall: ～雪天 snowy day /～大雨。It's raining heavily (*or* hard). /昨天～了一场雹子。There was a hail yesterday. *or* It hailed yesterday. ❸ issue; deliver; send: ～战书 deliver a letter of challenge /～调令 issue an order of transfer /～指示 give an instruction /局里刚～通知,明天开会。The bureau has just given (*or* served) notice that there will be a meeting tomorrow. ❹ go (down) to: 上山～乡 go and work in the countryside or mountainous areas /～连当兵 (of officers) go down to a company and serve in the ranks (to get firsthand experience) /～基层 go to the grass roots /～馆子 go and eat in a restaurant; eat out; dine out /～厨房 go into the kitchen — (help to) cook a dish or meal /干部～车间劳动。Cadres go to workshops to take part in manual labour. ❺ exit; leave: ～火线 leave the front (*or* battlefield) /这场戏完后从右边门儿～。After the scene, exit from the right door. /下半场,教练让六号～,换上了二号。During the second half, the coach replaced No. 6 with No. 2. ❻ put in; cast: ～赌注 lay bets (*or* stakes) /～饺子 put dumplings in (a pot); cook dumplings /舍得～作料 not stint the condiments ❼ play (board) games: 咱俩～两盘。Let's play chess for a while. ❽ take away; take off; unload; dismantle: ～某人的枪 take away sb.'s gun; disarm sb. /把门～下来 take down the door /～螺丝钉 remove the screw ❾ form (an opinion); draw (a conclusion); give (a definition): ～判断 form an opinion; pass a judgement /～保证 make a pledge /～批语 write comments on a document, etc. ❿ apply; use: ～筷子吃饭 use one's chopsticks and start eating ⓫ (of animals) give birth to; lay: ～小猪 give birth to a litter of piglets; be in litter ⓬ capture; seize; take: 连～三城 capture three cities in succession; defeat three adversaries in a row ⓭ give in; yield: 相持不～ neither side would give in (*or* yield) ⓮ finish (work, etc.); leave off: ～早班 come off morning shift /～晚自习的铃声响了。The bell rang for the end of the evening homework session. ⓯ (usu. used in the negative) less than: 不～十次 no less than ten times /死伤不～千人。The casualties numbered a thousand at least.

下[3] xià *also* "下子" ❶ 〈量词〉 *used to indicate repetition of action*: 敲了两～门 give a couple of knocks on the door /擦一～饭桌 mop up the table /打了三～手心 give three strikes on the palm /休息一～ take a rest /想了一～ after thinking it over ❷ 〈方言〉〈量词〉 *used to indicate the volume of a container*: 杯子里装了半～白酒。The glass of liquor was half-full. /这么大的海碗,他竟然吃了三～。With this huge bowl, he ate three bowlfuls. ❸ *used after* 两 *or* 几 *to indicate one's ability or skill*: 他真有两～! He really can show you a thing or two! *or* He is really capable! /就这么几～,你还逞能? You want to show off with such pitiful skill?

下 xia (used after a verb) ❶ *to indicate downward motion*: 坐～ sit down /走～山冈 walk down a hillock /跳～卡车 jump off the truck /我晚上一躺～就做梦。I start dreaming as soon as I lie down every evening. ❷ *to indicate room or space*: 这间教室起码能坐～八十人。This classroom can seat (*or* hold) at least eighty people. /就这么半条炕,哪能睡～一家子人? How can the whole family sleep on only half of the *kang*? ❸ *to indicate completion or consequence of an action*: 脱～皮鞋,换上拖鞋 take off the leather shoes and put on the slippers /准备～各种应变方案 get ready plans for all eventualities /定～锦囊妙计 work out a wise plan (for an emergency, etc.)

下巴 xiàba ❶ lower jaw ❷ chin

下巴颏儿 xiàbakēr 〈口语〉 chin

下摆 xiàbǎi lower hem of a gown, jacket or skirt

下拜 xiàbài kneel down; bend the knee; make obeisance to

下班 xiàbān come or go off work; knock off: 提前～ knock off ahead of time /已经～ be off duty (*or* work) /下夜班 be off night shift /如有急病,～后也可以找这位医生。For emergency cases, the doctor can be reached after hours.

下板儿 xiàbǎnr 〈方言〉 take off door- and window-shutters — open shop: 年关节下生意正好,隔壁杂货铺没～,没准出事了? It's the height of the New Year season, but the grocery nextdoor has not yet opened. Has something gone wrong by any chance? /当学徒也真不易,半夜歇下,天不亮又要～,准备当天的买卖。It was really a hard job to be an apprentice, going to bed at midnight and getting up before daybreak to open the shop and get everything ready for the day's business.

下半辈子 xiàbànbèizi latter half of one's life; rest of one's life; one's remaining years: 他正在想～怎么个活法。He was just thinking about how to spend the latter half of his life.

下半场 xiàbànchǎng second half (of a game): 主力队员～才上场。The top players were not fielded until the second half of the game.

下半旗 xià bànqí *also* "降半旗" jiàng bànqí fly a flag at half-mast: ～志哀 fly a flag at half-mast as a sign of mourning

下半晌 xiàbànshǎng 〈口语〉 afternoon: ～,天下起了大雨。A heavy rain began to fall in the afternoon.

下半身 xiàbànshēn lower part of the body; below the waist

下半时 xiàbànshí second half (of a game): ～客队反攻,进了两个球。In the second half, the guest team launched an offensive and scored two goals.

下半天 xiàbàntiān afternoon

下半夜 xiàbànyè time after midnight; latter half of the night; wee hours: 他有工作到～的习惯。He was in the habit of working until after midnight.

下辈 xiàbèi ❶ future generations; offspring ❷ younger generation of a family: ～尊敬长辈。The younger generation esteems the elder.

下辈子 xiàbèizi next life; next incarnation: ～也不忘您的大恩大德。I won't forget your great kindness even in my next life.

下本儿 xiàběnr *also* "下本钱" invest: 现下父母在教育孩子上大都舍得～。Most parents nowadays invest liberally in their children's education. *or* Most parents nowadays stint nothing in investing in their children's education.

下笔 xiàbǐ put pen to paper; begin to write or paint: 难以～ find it hard to put pen to paper /～立就 write with ease and finish forthwith /～如有神 write with inspiration; write quickly and powerfully; write like an angel

下笔成章 xiàbǐ-chéngzhāng whatever one writes turns into a fine essay; write an essay at one go; write quickly and skilfully: 才思敏捷,～ have a facile imagination and great literary acumen

下笔千言,离题万里 xiàbǐ qiānyán, lítí wànlǐ 〈俗语〉 a thousand words from the pen in a stream, but ten thousand *li* away from the theme — write quickly but stray from the theme; write a lot but miss the point; be verbose and irrelevant: 这种～的文章,实在难以卒读。I find it difficult to read articles that drag on and on without making a point.

下边 xiàbian *see* "下面"

下不为例 xiàbùwéilì not be taken as a precedent; must not happen again: 只此一次,～! Just this once. Don't let it occur again! /这是特殊情况,保证～。This is quite an exceptional case; I won't do it again.

下不来 xiàbulái ❶ refuse to come down: 他一犯病就持续发高烧,总也～。Whenever he falls ill, he will run a high fever and his temperature won't come down for some time. ❷ cannot accomplish or succeed: 你要盘这个店,没有三、四十万元～。You won't be able to buy this shop over for less than 300,000 to 400,000 *yuan*. ❸ feel awkward or embarrassed: 你说话也太厉害了,总让人脸上～。You are so sharp-tongued that people feel embarrassed at your words.

下不来台 xiàbuláitái be unable to back down with grace; be on the spot; be unable to extricate oneself from a predicament: 事情闹到这种地步,两方都觉得～。Since things have come to such a pass, both sides find it hard to back down.

下不去 xiàbuqù 〈方言〉 embarrass; make things difficult for; go against: 别多心,他不会跟你～的。Don't be suspicious. He won't try to embarrass you.

下部 xiàbù ❶ lower part; latter half ❷ lower part of the body; below the waist

下操 xiàcāo ❶ have drills: 这几天,天天头顶着月亮～,一跑就是十几里地。These days we have started drilling in the moonlight, running for more than ten *li* at one go. ❷ finish drilling: 学员们刚～,正在宿舍整理内务。The cadets have just finished drilling and are tidying up their dormitories.

下策 xiàcè bad plan; unwise move; worst option or alternative: 不得已才出此～ have no alternative but to resort to this /实为～。This is really an unwise move. *or* This is really the worst thing to do.

下层 xiàcéng lower levels; lower strata: 深入～ go down to the grass-roots level; go to lower-level units /社会～ lower strata of society /～工作人员 lower-level functionaries

下茶 xiàchá 〈书面〉(as of the boy's family) present a gift of tea (to the girl's family) as token of betrothal; present betrothal gifts: ～定婚 present gifts as a token of the consummation of a betrothal

下场 xiàchǎng ❶〈戏剧〉go off stage; 〈体育〉leave the playing field; exit: 谢完幕就～了 go off the stage after answering the curtain call /在下半时～ leave the playing field in the second half of a match ❷〈旧语〉sit for an official examination: 多次～，屡试不中 take the official examination time and again but fail each time /应试的举子依次～。The examinees filed in for the examination.

下场门 xiàchǎngmén exit (of a stage)

下场头 xiàchǎngtou 〈方言〉end; fate

下场 xiàchang 〈贬义〉end; fate: 不会有好～ come to no good end / 这是他应有的～。This serves him right.

下车伊始 xiàchē-yīshǐ the moment one alights from the official carriage; as soon as one takes up one's official post: ～，他便哇啦哇啦地发号施令。He gave out orders right and left the moment he took office.

下沉 xiàchén sink; go under; subside; submerge: 敌舰在剧烈的爆炸声中慢慢～。The enemy warship sank slowly amidst terrific explosions. /一遇危险，潜水艇即刻～。At the first sign of danger the submarine will submerge. /由于地基～，木塔开始向西北倾斜。As the foundations subsided, the wooden tower began to lean to the northwest.

下乘 xiàchéng ❶ *also* "小乘" xiǎochéng 〈佛教〉Hinayana; Little Vehicle ❷ (as of literary or artistic work) of low order; of poor quality: ～之作 inferior work; work of low (artistic) quality

下程 xiàchéng (often used in the early vernacular) ❶ gift of money to help cover travelling expenses; gift: 走时又送些～与他。Upon departure he was given some money to help cover his travelling expenses. ❷ give a farewell dinner: 预备～酒饭。A farewell dinner was prepared.

下处 xiàchu temporary lodging during a trip: 途经荒野，～难寻。It's difficult to find temporary lodging when travelling through a wilderness.

下穿交叉 xiàchuān jiāochā 〈交通〉underpass; undercrossing

下船 xiàchuán ❶ go ashore; disembark: 乘客一个个～，上岸观光。Passengers disembarked one by one and went sightseeing. ❷〈方言〉get into (a boat); embark; go on board: 大家依次剪票～。All the passengers had their tickets punched and embarked on the ship in proper order.

下垂 xiàchuí ❶ hang down; sag; droop: 双手～ with both hands drooping /肥大的豌豆荚沉甸甸地～着。The large pea pods hung down heavily. ❷〈医学〉prolapse: 子宫～ prolapse of the uterus; metroptosis /胃～ gastroptosis

下存 xiàcún (of a sum) remain after deduction: 贵号昨天提了七千元，～四万三千。As your company drew out seven thousand *yuan* from this account yesterday, there is forty-three thousand left. /这笔款子～数额还有八千元。The balance of this account is 8,000 *yuan*.

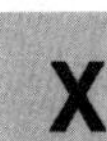

下达 xiàdá transmit or release to lower levels: ～命令 issue an order (*or* command) to lower levels /～任务(或指标) assign a task (*or* quota) /～文件 release a document

下蛋 xiàdàn lay eggs: ～鸡 layer /海龟通常在沙中～。Sea tortoises usually lay eggs in the sand.

下道 xiàdao 〈口语〉off-colour; near or close to the bone: 该死的，说着说着又～了。Damn you. You are being vulgar again in no time!

下得 xiàde *also* "下的" (often used in the early vernacular) be hardhearted enough; bear: 怎～便撇了你远走高飞。How could I bear to leave you behind and flee far away?

下得去 xiàdequ 〈方言〉❶ (usu. used in the negative or interrogative) feel at ease; bear: 扔下老人没人管，你心里～吗? Don't you feel sorry to leave your aged parents behind without anyone to take care of them? *or* Can you bear to desert your aged parents? ❷ tolerable; passable; not too bad: 他的长相还～。He is not really ugly. *or* He is passable as far as looks go.

下等 xiàděng low-grade; poor; inferior: ～客房 cheap room (at an inn, etc.) /～原料 inferior raw material

下等人 xiàděngrén persons of lower social status; lower orders

下地 xiàdì ❶ go to the fields: ～劳动 go to work in the fields ❷ get out of bed; leave a sick bed: 老人一到冬天就犯病，很少～。The old man would fall ill in winter and be confined to bed most of the time. /有小病别老躺着，多～活动活动。When you are slightly indisposed, you'd better get up and move about as much as you can, instead of staying in bed all day long. ❸〈方言〉(of a baby) recently born

下第 xiàdì ❶〈书面〉low-grade; poor; inferior: 置之于～ put in a low grade; regard sth. as inferior ❷ *also* "落第" luòdì 〈旧语〉fail in an official examination: ～而归 return home after failing in the official examination

下店 xiàdiàn put up at an inn: ～投宿 put up at an inn for the night

下调 xiàdiào transfer to a lower-level work unit
see also xiàtiáo

下跌 xiàdiē fall; drop; go down: 河水～ drop of the water level in a river /价格～ prices fall /调高利率以制止英镑～ raise interest rates to halt the pound's slide (*or* decline) /股票价格直线～。Stock prices plummeted.

下定 xiàdìng ❶〈旧语〉(of the boy's family) present gifts (to the girl's family) to finalize the betrothal: 去年～，今年迎娶。With the betrothal entered into last year, the wedding is to be held this year. ❷ advance payment (for a purchase or rent)

下碇 xiàdìng cast anchor; anchor: 船老大把船拐进河湾，靠近岸边～。The boatman sailed his boat into the river bend and anchored near the bank.

下毒 xiàdú put poison into; poison: 这个丧心病狂的家伙，居然往井里～! This villain went so far as to poison the well!

下毒手 xià dúshǒu strike a vicious blow; lay murderous hands: 背后～ stab sb. in the back /自己的亲生儿子，你也下得了毒手? Would you go so far as to lay murderous hands on your own son?

下颚 xià'è lower jaw; mandible; maxilla

下法 xiàfǎ 〈中医〉purgation — making the patient evacuate what is harmful or superfluous

下凡 xiàfán (of gods or immortals) descend to the world: 仙女～ fairy maiden descending to the world; celestial beauty coming down to earth

下饭 xiàfàn ❶ go with rice: 那时日子过得苦，顿顿就着萝卜干～。Life was hard in those days. We had only dried turnips to go with rice from one meal to another. ❷ go well with rice: 这是酒菜儿，不～。This dish goes well with wine, but not with rice. ❸〈方言〉food other than grain, such as vegetables, eggs and meat: 母亲从集市上带回些～来，好准备明天待客。Mother bought some food at the market-place to entertain guests the next day.

下方 xiàfāng ❶ below; underneath: 泉水的～有一块平地。There is some flat ground below the spring. ❷ (in contrast to "heaven") earth: ～各路妖魔 all kinds of demons on earth

下房 xiàfáng servants' room; servants' quarters: 几间～ several rooms for servants

下放 xiàfàng ❶ transfer to a lower level: 把权力～给企业 transfer power to the enterprises /～审批权限 delegate the power of examination and approval to the lower levels ❷ send (cadres, etc.) to work at the grass-roots level or to do manual labour in the countryside or in a factory: 那几年，父亲被～到一个偏远的山村。In those years, my father was sent to a remote mountain village to work.

下放干部 xiàfàng gànbù cadre sent to work at a lower level or to do manual labour in the countryside or in a factory

下风 xiàfēng ❶ leeward; downwind: 站在～处 stand to leeward / 猎人蹑手蹑脚地从～处接近了母鹿。The hunter approached the roe gingerly from downwind. ❷ inferior or disadvantageous position: 甘拜～ candidly admit defeat; throw in the towel /客队首场失利，暂时处于～。Having lost the first game, the visiting team is for the time being at a disadvantageous position.

下浮 xiàfú drop; decrease: 电视机价格全面～。There was an overall drop in the prices of TV sets.

下腹 xiàfù 〈生理〉hypogastrium: ～联胎 hypogastropagus

下腹部 xiàfùbù underbelly; weak or vulnerable part (of a place, plan, etc.)

下疳 xiàgān 〈医学〉chancre: 软～ chancroid

下岗 xiàgǎng ❶ come or go off (sentry) duty: 战士～了。The soldier came off sentry duty. ❷ (as of a technician or worker) be removed from a post; be made redundant; be laid off: ～人员安置工作 outplacement (of laid-off workers or personnel) /干不了的，一律～培训。Those who are incompetent must all be removed from their posts for further training. /安排好～职工的再就业工作。Proper ar-

rangements must be made to re-employ redundant (*or* laid-off) workers.

下岗分流 xiàgǎng fēnliú lay off workers and reposition redundant personnel

下工 xiàgōng ❶ stop work; knock off:～的铃声响了。The bell rang for knocking off. ❷〈旧语〉(of an employee) dismiss; fire; discharge:他因病被厂主～。He was dismissed for illness by the factory owner. ❸〈旧语〉mediocre doctor of medicine; quack doctor

下工夫 xià gōngfu *also* "下功夫" put in time and energy; take pains; exert oneself:我在她身上没少～,谁知她就是不理我。Although I have taken no small pains with her, she just wouldn't pay any attention to me. /只有～,才能提高写作水平。One cannot expect to improve one's writing unless one works hard at it.

下官 xiàguān ❶〈旧语〉(as of an official in depreciating self-reference) I; me:～有失远迎,恕罪,恕罪。Please pardon me for failing to welcome you when you arrived. ❷ subordinate; inferior

下跪 xiàguì kneel down; be on bended knees:～磕头 go down on one's knees and kowtow /～求饶 beg for mercy on one's knees /请将双膝弯曲,呈～的姿势。Please bend your knees and crouch down as if kneeling.

下锅 xiàguō put (rice, vegetables, etc.) into the cooking pan:菜已～。The vegetables are already in the pot. /没米～。There is no rice left to cook. /企业不能光"等米～",还要"找米～"。An enterprise can't simply "wait for rice to come"; it should also "look for rice to cook".

下国 xiàguó ❶〈旧语〉vassal state; small country ❷〈书面〉〈谦词〉my country; this country

下海 xiàhǎi ❶ go to sea; put out to sea:～游泳 go swimming (*or* bathing) in the sea /趁着早潮～ put out to sea on the early morning tide ❷ (of fishermen) go fishing in the sea:头次～,难免晕吐。It is hardly avoidable to feel dizzy and vomit on one's first trip at sea. ❸ (of an amateur) turn career performer:他当了多年票友,常有～之心。Having been an amateur for years, he often thought about becoming a professional actor. ❹〈旧语〉become a prostitute, etc. ❺ (of people from other walks of life) go in for business; become a businessman:他辞职～已有三年了。It is three years since he resigned and became a businessman.

下颌 xiàhé *also* "下颚";"下巴"〈生理〉lower jaw; mandible

下颌骨 xiàhégǔ lower jawbone; mandible

下颌关节 xiàhé guānjié mandibular joint; *articulatio mandibularis*

下黑儿 xiàhēir 〈方言〉dusk; twilight:当天～,他才回到家里。He did not return home that day until dusk.

下户 xiàhù 〈旧语〉poor people; paupers

下怀 xiàhuái one's heart's desire:正中～ be just what one wants; be after one's heart

下回 xiàhuí next chapter; next session; next time:欲知后事如何,且听～分解。If you wish to know what follows, please read the next chapter.

下级 xiàjí lower level; subordinate:～机关 government organization at a lower level /～军官 lower-ranking (*or* junior) officer /～单位 subordinate units /～服从上级。The lower level is subordinate to the higher level. *or* The subordinates should obey their superiors. /我是他多年的～。I have worked under him for years.

下家 xiàjiā ❶ (in mah-jong, card game or drinker's wagers) person next in turn to play:该～出牌了。It's time for the next person to play. ❷〈方言〉〈谦词〉my humble house:～敝陋,不意贵客光临。I didn't expect the presence of such distinguished company at my shabby, humble house.

下家伙 xià jiāhuo 〈口语〉use weapons:两伙人在街上～对打,看样子要拼个你死我活。The two gangs were fighting each other with weapons in the street, and it seemed that they'd fight to the bitter end.

下嫁 xiàjià 〈旧语〉(as of a princess or a girl of noble family) marry a man of lower rank; marry below or beneath oneself:父亲家世代布衣,当年母亲算是～了。As father was born of a commoner family, it could be said that mother married beneath herself.

下贱 xiàjiàn ❶〈旧语〉low; humble:出身～ be of low birth /卑微～的家庭 low, humble family ❷ mean; low-down; obscene:无耻～的东西 shameless, mean bird /～货 lowly person; slut /语言～,长相粗俗 with obscene language and coarse appearance

下江 Xiàjiāng lower reaches of the Yangtze River:～人 native of one of the provinces on the lower reaches of the Yangtze River /～官话 mandarin with a strong accent of one of the provinces on the lower reaches of the Yangtze

下降 xiàjiàng descend; fall; decline; decrease:收入～ falling income /气温～ drop in the temperature /生活水平～ standard of living declines; have a lower standard of living; become worse off /威信～ prestige declining /地下水位～。The underground water table is going down. /进入淡季以来,日营业额平均～10.6%。Since the beginning of the slack season, the volume of daily sales has decreased (*or* dropped) 10.6% on average.

下降风 xiàjiàngfēng katabatic wind; fall wind

下焦 xiàjiāo 〈中医〉that part of the body cavity below the umbilicus housing the bladder, kidneys and bowels; lower burner

下脚 xiàjiǎo ❶ get or gain a foothold; plant one's foot:无处～ be unable to get a foothold; have nowhere to plant one's foot /屋里摆满了家具,连～的地方都没有。The room was so full of furniture that one could hardly step into it. ❷ leftover bits and pieces; leftovers; waste:～棉 cotton waste

下脚货 xiàjiǎohuò leftover goods (usu. of inferior quality); shopworn or shopsoiled goods

下脚料 xiàjiǎoliào leftover bits and pieces (from processed industrial material)

下街 xiàjiē go into the street (to sell goods or be a street-performer):为方便居民,他推着车～售货。He pushed his wheelbarrow from street to street, selling things to the inhabitants at a more convenient distance. /她自小跟着师傅走码头,～卖艺。From childhood onward, she followed her master from port to port, performing in the streets.

下届 xiàjiè next session or term:～政府的首要任务是降低通货膨胀率。The primary task of the next government is to bring down inflation.

下界 xiàjiè ❶ (of gods or immortals) descend to the world:天神～ gods descending to the world ❷ (in contrast with "heaven") world of mortals; world of man:～凡夫俗子 ordinary mortals of the world

下劲 xiàjìn put in time and energy; make an effort; strain oneself:干活舍得～ spare no effort in work /如不是有求于人,他也就不会这样～了。He would not try so hard if he were not asking for a favour.

下井投石 xiàjǐng-tóushí *also* "下井落石" throw stones at one who has fallen in a well; hit a man when he is down:千万不可～。Never hit a man when he is down. /这种～的事也是人干的? How can a man throw stones at one who has fallen in a well?

下九流 xiàjiǔliú 〈旧语〉people from the lower walks of life, such as performers, porters, trumpeters, and others engaged in "lowly" occupations:各路～是这家下等酒馆的常客。This cheap wine shop was frequented by people from the lower walks of life. /公子也不长进,专和～交往,也不怕辱没了祖宗。The young master doesn't seem to have high aspirations either. He is keen on associating with people of low social status, and does not care if he brings disgrace to his ancestors.

下酒 xiàjiǔ ❶ drink wine (with sth.); (of dishes) go with wine:来二两白干,再来一盘牛肉～。Bring me two *liang* of liquor and a dish of beef to go with the drink. ❷ go well with wine:每到周末,母亲都替父亲准备下几样～的好菜。On weekends, mother would prepare for father some dishes that went well with wine.

下酒菜 xiàjiǔcài dish that goes well with wine

下颏儿 xiàkēr 〈方言〉chin

下课 xiàkè dismiss class; finish class:五点的电影,～后再去也不迟。The film will be on at five, so we won't be late if we go there after class. /现在～是不是还早点? Isn't it too early to dismiss the class right now?

下口 xiàkǒu ❶ open one's mouth to eat or bite:把西瓜切开,要不无从～。Have the melon sliced so that we can eat it. ❷ (often used in the early vernacular) dish that goes well with rice and wine:酒家,明日多备些～,我家主人请客。Hi, chef, prepare more dishes tomorrow; my master wants to invite some guests to dinner.

下苦 xiàkǔ 〈方言〉(usu. of manual labour) exert oneself; work hard:～劳动 exert oneself in physical labour; work hard

下筷 xiàkuài apply one's chopsticks to the food — start eating; help oneself:有鱼有肉的,他还嫌没菜～! There is fish and meat on the table, yet he still complains that he does not have nice food to eat!

X

下款 xiàkuǎn name of a donor, painter or author (usu. inscribed in the lower corner of a painting or a calligraphic scroll); signature of a writer at the end of a letter

下来 xiàlai ❶ come down:从山坡上～ come down from a hillock / 部里～了一位司长视察工作。A department director of the ministry has come to inspect the work here. ❷ (of crops, fruits, vegetables, etc.) be ripe enough to harvest:再有半个月白薯就要～了。The sweet potatoes will be harvested in half a month. /玉米一时还下不来。The maize won't be ripe for a while yet.

下来 xialai ❶ *used after a verb to indicate a downward direction or a movement from far to near*:把绳子上晾的衣服都收～。Get in all the clothes on the line. /洪水冲过堤岸流～。The flood water overflowed the embankment. /上级又派～新的任务了。The higher authorities have assigned us new tasks again. ❷ *used after a verb to indicate a continuation from the past to the present or from start to finish*:编者把历代流传～的民歌辑为一集。The editor compiled into a volume folk songs handed down from generation to generation. /本地首届马拉松赛跑,所有参赛的选手,都坚持～了。In the first local marathon race, all the participants persisted to the end. ❸ *used after a verb to indicate the completion or result of an action*:雨看样子一时停不～。It seems that the rain won't stop for a while yet. /留～的就这么几个人,你看着派活吧! These are the only people left. Assign them whatever work you see fit. /把有关情况详细记录～。Make a detailed record of all the relevant circumstances. ❹ *used after an adjective to indicate increasing degree*:病人的脉搏弱了～。The patient's pulse became weaker and weaker. /天色暗了～,林中响起了风声。As it got darker, a rising wind could be heard in the woods.

下礼 xiàlǐ present gifts:临近吉期,～的人络绎不绝。As the wedding day drew near, people came in a continuous stream to present gifts.

下里巴人 xiàlǐ-bārén Song of the Rustic Poor (a folk song of the State of Chu during the period of the Warring States); popular or lowbrow art or literature (in contrast with 阳春白雪):现在是"阳春白雪"和"～"统一的问题,是提高和普及的问题。The question now is how to bring about unity between "The Spring Snow" and the "Song of the Rustic Poor", between higher standards and popularization. /普通老百姓更喜欢～的民歌和地方戏剧。Common people prefer popular folk songs and local operas.

下里 xiàli *used after a numeral to indicate orientation or position*:两～用力一挤 press hard from both sides /演员被热心的观众四～团团围住。The actors and actresses were surrounded by the enthusiastic audience on all sides.

下力 xiàlì exert oneself; make efforts; do all one can:～人 man who exerts himself; toiler /这件事他下了大力。He did all he could on the matter.

下联 xiàlián second line of an antithetic couplet:只见～写道:"恩爱夫妻百年长。" And the second line of the couplet reads:"An affectionate couple enjoys a long life." /我出上联,你对～。I'll offer the first line of a couplet, and you'll match it in the second.

下僚 xiàliáo 〈书面〉 lower-ranking official; subordinate

下列 xiàliè listed or mentioned below; following; ensuing:我想提出～几点。I would like to make the following points. /请～人员准时出席会议。The people listed below are requested to attend the meeting on time.

下劣 xiàliè 〈书面〉 base; mean; despicable:背叛朋友的～行为 despicable act of betraying a friend

下令 xiàlìng give orders; order; instruct:～紧急集合 give orders for an emergency muster /师部～突击营凌晨五时发起攻击。The division headquarters ordered the shock battalion to launch the attack at five a.m.

下流 xiàliú ❶ lower reaches (of a river):黄河～各省 provinces on the lower reaches of the Yellow River ❷ 〈旧语〉 of low or inferior rank:君子恶居～。A gentleman loathes to be of inferior rank. ❸ low; base; obscene; dirty: ～话 salacious remarks; obscene language; obscenities /～无耻 low and shameless /行为～ base act / 少开这样～的玩笑! Don't crack such blue jokes!

下落 xiàluò ❶ whereabouts:逃犯～不明。The whereabouts of the escaped prisoner is unknown. ❷ drop; fall; decline:降落伞在空中缓缓～。The parachute dropped gradually through the air. /股市连连～后又略有回升。The stock market is picking up a bit after a continuous decline.

下马 xiàmǎ ❶ get off a horse; dismount from a horse:～受缚 dismount from the horse and give oneself up to be bound /躬身～ bend at the waist and dismount ❷ discontinue (a project, etc.):～单位 unit that has become defunct, superseded, or redundant /很多基建工程不得不～。Many capital construction projects had to be discontinued (*or* abandoned).

下马看花 xiàmǎ-kànhuā dismount to view the flowers — stay at the grass roots or a given place over a period of time and get a deeper understanding of the situation there:检查工作要～,不能走马观花。When engaged in inspection and checkup, one must dismount to view the flowers instead of giving them a hurried glance on horseback. *or* To do a good job of inspection and checkup, one must carry out thoroughgoing investigation and study, rather than skim over things superficially.

下马威 xiàmǎwēi severity shown by an official on assuming office; show of strength at first contact:打他个～ administer sb. a heavy blow at the very first encounter /上任伊始,他就来了个～。He made a display of his authority the moment he was installed in his job. /不给你个～看看,你不知道我的厉害! If I don't show you my strength right at the beginning, you won't know that I'm not to be trifled with.

下毛毛雨 xià máomaoyǔ ❶ drizzle:天刚黑就下起了毛毛雨。It had scarcely got dark when it began to drizzle. ❷ break (some bad news) little by little; criticize or scold gently:先给他下点毛毛雨,让他有个思想准备。Break this to him little by little so that he can be mentally prepared. /他这个人脸皮厚得很,～对他根本不起作用。He is so thick-skinned that gentle criticism would not produce any effect on him.

下面 xiàmian ❶ below; under; beneath; underneath:图片～有详细的文字说明。There is a detailed caption below the picture. /老人把钱藏在床垫～。The old man hid the money under the mattress. ❷ coming immediately after; next; following:～该谁看病了? Who's the next to see the doctor? /～几个人,你务必把他们请来见我。Please make sure that the following people come to see me. /～请张先生作报告。Now let's invite Mr. Zhang to give his lecture. *or* Now Mr. Zhang. ❸ lower level:～的同志对情况最了解,要认真听取他们的意见。As comrades at the lower levels are most familiar with the real situation, you must take their opinions seriously. /这个报告的精神要及时向～传达。The gist of this report must be conveyed to the rank and file in time.

下奶 xiànǎi stimulate the secretion of milk; promote lactation:产妇吃炖猪蹄能～。Stewed pig's trotters help puerperal (*or* puerperant) women stimulate the secretion of milk.

下女 xiànǚ 〈旧语〉 woman of low social status; maid servant:几个粗使的～吓得胆战心惊。The maids-of-all-work were trembling with fear.

下皮 xiàpí 〈生理〉 hypodermis

下品 xiàpǐn low-grade; inferior:画中～ inferior painting

下聘 xiàpìn present betrothal gifts:周家～,要娶的是张家二小姐。The Zhous are delivering betrothal gifts to the second daughter of the Zhangs.

下坡 xiàpō ❶ 〈方言〉 go to the fields (to do farm work):～锄草 go to the fields to hoe up weeds ❷ go down a slope; go downhill:～容易上坡难。It is easy to go downhill but difficult to go uphill. /学习上稍有放松,成绩就要走～。If you slacken your efforts a bit in your studies, your grades will go down.

下坡路 xiàpōlù ❶ downhill path; downhill journey:一出村口就是一段～。There is a downhill path right outside the village. ❷ decline; deteriorate:那时我们的关系就开始走～了。Our relations in those days were already deteriorating (*or* on the decline).

下铺 xiàpù lower berth or bunk

下棋 xiàqí play chess; have a game of chess:喜欢～ love to play chess; be keen on chess /下象棋 play Chinese chess /下盲棋 play blind /下一盘围棋 have a game of *weiqi* (*or* go)

下气 xiàqì in a calm voice; in a humble voice:低声～ speak in a low, humble voice /我～求他,他还是不答应。Though I begged him stoopingly, he turned me down all the same.

下欠 xiàqiàn ❶ still owing; outstanding:他还款五十元,～五十元。He has paid back 50 *yuan*, with 50 *yuan* still outstanding (*or* owing). /～的八十元,下月还清。Next month I will return the 80 *yuan* I still owe. ❷ sum still owing; outstanding sum:借款业已还清,无有～。The debt has been paid up with nothing outstanding.

下腔静脉 xiàqiāng jìngmài 〈生理〉 inferior vena cava:～综合征〈医

学〉inferior vena cava syndrome; inferior mediastinal syndrome

下情 xiàqíng ❶ conditions at the lower levels; circumstances and sentiments of the common people or one's subordinates: ～上达 make the situation at the lower levels known to the higher authorities; report the circumstances and sentiments of the common people to the higher-ups / 体察～ observe and understand what is going on at the lower levels ❷〈谦词〉my situation; my circumstances; my state of mind: 录此～,请君详察。I've written down my circumstances for your detailed examination.

下丘脑 xiàqiūnǎo 〈生理〉hypothalamus

下去 xiàqu go down; get off; descend: 你腿脚不便,还是我～锁门吧! As you have difficulty walking, let me go downstairs to lock the door. / 月台上没有卖食品的,你不用～了。Since there are no food-pedlers on the platform, there is no need for you to get off. / 领导干部每月要～几天。Leading cadres should go down to the grass roots for a few days each month.

下去 xiaqu ❶ *used after a verb to indicate a descending motion or going away from near to afar*: 把这块大石头推～! Push the big rock down. / 过了两天,山洪才慢慢退了～。It was two days before the flood began to recede little by little. / 一定要把敌人的嚣张气焰压～。We must crush (*or* deflate) the enemy's arrogance. / 把这个闹事的带～! Take this trouble-maker away! ❷ *used after a verb to indicate a continuation*: 说～ go on (speaking) / 这所学校应继续办～。The school must be maintained. / 你再不能这样混～了! You mustn't muddle along like this any more! / 把老一辈开创的事业继续～,这是我国人民的共同愿望。It is the common wish of our people to carry on the cause pioneered by the older generation. ❸ *used after an adjective to indicate an increasing degree*: 都过了八月了,看样子天气还要热～。Though August is over, it seems to be getting still hotter. / 病人的情况一天天坏～。The patient is getting worse and worse.

下人 xiàrén ❶ *also* "底下人" dǐxiarén 〈旧语〉servant: 人面前哪有咱们当～说话的份儿! How can we servants speak before company? ❷〈方言〉children or grandchildren: 我们要给～作表率。We must set a good example for our children.

下三烂 xiàsānlàn *also* "下三滥"; "下三赖"〈方言〉❶ mean; dirty; low: 我哪里就那样～,给这种人去跑腿儿。How could I stoop so low as to run errands for such people? / 他一来就胡说八道,满嘴～。He started talking nonsense the minute he came in, mouthing dirty words all the time. ❷ despicable good-for-nothing or ne'er-do-well: 这几个都是街上面的～,好吃懒做惯了。These are the ne'er-do-wells of the neighbourhood, lazy to the core and greedy. ❸ cheap prostitute: 你满世界打听打听,老娘又不是～! Go and find out for yourself! This lady is no cheap prostitute.

下山 xiàshān ❶ go down a hill: 老人带着孙子,慢慢～去了。The old man walked slowly downhill, taking his grandson with him. / 这些土匪经常～抢劫附近村庄。The bandits often left their mountain hideouts to raid the nearby villages. ❷ (of the sun) set: 太阳已经～了。The sun is set.

下晌 xiàshǎng 〈方言〉afternoon: 我～有空,帮你家浇地吧。I'm free in the afternoon; let me help your family water the fields.

下梢 xiàshāo ❶ end: 木棍的～越来越细。The wooden stick tapers down. ❷ (often used in the early vernacular) ending; outcome: 落了个死无葬身之地的～ end up by dying without a burial place; come to a bad end

下哨 xiàshào be off sentry duty; leave lookout post: 新战士～后,又去帮大娘挑水。Being off sentry duty, the new recruit carried water for the old granny.

下身 xiàshēn ❶ lower part of the body: 这人上身长,～短,体型十分难看。With a long torso and short legs, the man has a grotesque figure. ❷ private parts: 他逛了几年烟花巷,败了家业,连自己的～也烂了。Having frequented brothels for years, he not only squandered his patrimony but actually had his genitals rotted. ❸ trousers: 这套衣服～有些长。The trousers of this suit are a bit long.

下神 xiàshén 〈迷信〉(as of a witch) invoke a spirit or an immortal: ～时,那巫婆浑身乱抖,口里念念有词。While invoking spirits and immortals, the witch would tremble all over and mutter incantations.

下生 xiàshēng be born; come into the world: 婴儿在子夜～。The baby was born at midnight.

下剩 xiàshèng 〈口语〉be left: ～的储备 remainder of the reserves (*or* store) / ～的就是老弱妇孺了。There are only the old and the weak left, as well as women and children.

下湿 xiàshī low-lying and wet: 开沟挖渠,改造～地 transform low-lying, wet land by digging drainage ditches

下士 xiàshì (US & UK army and marine corps, or UK air force) corporal; (UK navy) petty officer second class; (US navy) petty officer third class

下市 xiàshì ❶ off season: 立秋后西瓜～。Water melons go off season when autumn sets in. ❷ close shop: 太阳老高这家铺子就～了。The shop closed for the day well before sunset.

下世 xiàshì ❶ pass away; die: 先父于昨日午时～。My father passed away at noon yesterday. ❷ next life; next incarnation: ～为奴,以报大恩。I'll be your servant in my next life to repay your great kindness. ❸〈方言〉be born; come into the world: 我当兵那会儿,你还没～呢! When I joined the army, you weren't even born.

下手 xiàshǒu ❶ put one's hand to (a job, etc.); start; begin; set about: 无从～ have no idea where to start; not know how to begin ❷ *also* "下首" right-hand (seat): 正房北屋的～是两间下人住的平房。On the right-hand side of the south-facing master room, there are two one-storey house for servants. / 他～坐的是一位中年妇女。Sitting next to him was a middle-aged woman. ❸ *see* "下家" ❹〈口语〉assistant; helper: 给人打～ act as sb.'s assistant (*or* helper); assist sb. / 工地上的人看我个儿小,让我打～。Seeing that I was short, people on the building site made me their helper.

下首 xiàshǒu *also* "下手" right-hand seat

下书 xiàshū 〈书面〉deliver a letter: 派人前来～ send sb. to deliver a letter

下属 xiàshǔ subordinate: 关心他～的生活 be concerned with the everyday needs of those working under him / ～无不钦佩。The subordinates without exception were filled with admiration.

下水 xiàshuǐ ❶ (cause a ship, etc. to) move into the water; be launched: ～典礼 launching ceremony / 下半年将有三艘新船～。Three new ships will be launched in the second half of the year. ❷ (of textiles, fabrics, etc.) be soaked in water: 买来的布料最好先下下水再做衣服。It's better to soak the cotton cloth in water before making the dress. / 这件衬衣～后明显地变小了。The shirt shrank visibly after washing. ❸ engage in evildoing; fall into evil ways: 有十几名公职人员被拖～。More than a dozen civil servants were enticed into evildoings. ❹ downriver; downstream: 路虽远,若是乘～船,有三天也到了。Though it is a long way to go, we can make it in three days if we take a boat down the river.

下水 xiàshui (cooked as food) offal; entrails: 猪～ pig's offal; pig's entrails; tripe and chitterlings

下水道 xiàshuǐdào sewer; drain: ～系统 sewer system; sewerage / ～检查井 sewer man-hole

下死点 xiàsǐdiǎn 〈机械〉bottom dead centre

下死劲 xià sǐjìn with all one's might; with might and main: ～地干活 work with all one's might; exert one's utmost in work / 小姑娘～把我拉住,不让我走。The little girl seized hold of me with all her strength and would not let go.

下宿 xiàsù 〈方言〉put up (for the night); stay; get accommodation: ～处 place where one stays; temporary quarters or lodgings / 山里人家少,天黑了也没找到一个～的地方。As there weren't many households in the mountain village, I failed to find a place to stay though it had already grown dark.

下榻 xiàtà 〈书面〉stay (at a place during a trip); find accommodation: 在国宾馆～ stay at the state guesthouse

下台 xiàtái ❶ step down from the stage or platform: 老先生在女儿的搀扶下下了台。The old gentleman stepped down from the platform leaning on his daughter's arm. / 演员们还未～,观众已经一哄而散了。Hardly had the actors left the stage when the audience dispersed in a hubbub. ❷ hand over power; leave office: 被赶～ be driven out of office; be thrown out / ～后隐居山村 retire to a secluded life in the mountains after leaving office (*or* after falling out of power) ❸ (usu. used in the negative) get out of a sorry plight or an embarrassing situation: 没法～ unable to extricate oneself from an embarrassing situation with good grace / 叫人下不了台 embarrass sb.; put sb. on the spot

下台阶 xià táijiē back down with good grace; extricate oneself (from a predicament): 自己～ have to extricate oneself from a predicament / 给他个～的机会。Give him an opportunity to back out with good grace. *or* He was given a nail to hang his hat on.

下堂 xiàtáng ❶〈方言〉finish class: ～后马上回家 go back home as soon as class is over ❷〈旧语〉(of a woman) be divorced or deserted

(by her husband)

下体 xiàtǐ 〈书面〉❶ lower part of the body ❷ private parts; genitals

下田 xiàtián go to the fields (to work):～插秧 go to transplant rice seedlings in the fields

下调 xiàtiáo reduce; lower:～利率 reduce interest rates /自下月起,家用电器零售价～1%。Beginning next month, retail prices of household electrical appliances will be reduced by one percent.
see also xiàdiào

下帖 xiàtiě send or deliver an invitation card:有人～请老爷赴宴。An invitation card was delivered for the master to attend a banquet.

下同 xiàtóng (often used in notes or brackets) similarly hereinafter; same below:凡用蓝铅笔修改处均删去。～。Leave out what has been revised in blue pencil; the same applies below.

下头 xiàtou *see* "下面 ❶❸"

下晚儿 xiàwǎnr 〈口语〉near dusk; towards evening:～天下起了大雪。It began to snow heavily by dusk.

下网 xiàwǎng 〈信息〉off-line

下痿 xiàwěi 〈中医〉paraplegia

下文 xiàwén ❶ what follows in an article or book; later in an article or book:～将进一步说明。More about this later. /此处姑且存疑,～详述。Let's leave the doubts for the time being, for they are going to be explained in detail in the ensuing chapters (*or* paragraphs). ❷ later development; outcome; result; sequel:事情没这么简单,还有～哩! The matter was not so simple; there was a sequel to it. /我托你的事情多少天了,怎么还没～? It's been days since I asked you for help. How come there's been no result? /报告递上去半年了,一直没有～。The report was submitted six months ago, but so far nothing's been heard of it.

下问 xiàwèn ask someone who is less learned or of lesser status than oneself:不耻～ not feel ashamed to ask and learn from one's subordinates (*or* from those who are less learned than oneself) /屈尊～ stoop to inquire; deign to ask

下午 xiàwǔ afternoon

下细 xiàxì 〈方言〉carefully; attentively:我～一想,还是他说的对。Thinking it over carefully, I realized that he was right.

下下 xiàxià ❶ most inferior; lowest:～策 most undesirable policy or plan /抽了个～签 draw the worst lot ❷ (of time) after the next:～月 month after the next

下弦 xiàxián 〈天文〉last or third quarter (of the moon)

下弦月 xiàxiányuè moon at the last or third quarter

下限 xiàxiàn lower limit; prescribed minimum; floor (level):征文要求以八百字为～,以一千五百字为上限。Solicited articles should be more than 800 characters, but less than 1,500. /书中所辑人物传记以第一次鸦片战争为～。This book collects biographies of historical figures who lived before the first Opium War.

下陷 xiàxiàn sink; subside; cave in:眼眶～ sunken eyes /地基～ subsidence of the foundation (of a building) /在地震中～的矿井很快修复了,并恢复了生产。The mines which caved in during the earthquake were soon restored, and production resumed.

下乡 xiàxiāng go to the countryside (to work or settle):我十五岁～,在兵团呆了十二年。I went to the countryside at the age of 15 and stayed in a production and construction corps (state farm organized along military lines under the leadership of PLA men) for 12 years.

下乡知识青年 xiàxiāng zhīshi qīngnián (often shortened as 下乡知青) educated urban youth who worked and settled in the countryside before the 1980's

下泻 xiàxiè ❶ (of water) flow downward:～不畅 not flow downward freely; not drain well ❷ (of prices, etc.) fall steeply; plummet:当地货币对美元汇价一路～。The local currency has been plummeting against the American dollar. ❸ loose bowels; diarrhoea:上吐～ vomit and have loose bowels

下泄 xiàxiè (of water current) flow or rush downward:洪峰正沿江～。The flood peak (*or* crest) is moving down the river. /冲出峡口,江水～,声势陡长。Once out of the gorge, the river current rushed down with abruptly increasing momentum.

下行 xiàxíng ❶〈铁路〉away from the capital Beijing; down:103次列车是～车,这种季节乘客不会太多。No. 103 is a down train, and won't have a lot of passengers at this time of the year. ❷ downriver; downstream:江轮～至湖口,正是下半夜。It was just after midnight when the ship got to Hukou in its voyage down the river. ❸ (of a document) to be issued to the lower levels:～公文 official document issued to the lower levels

下行线路 xiàxíng xiànlù 〈信息〉downlink

下旋 xiàxuán 〈体育〉underspin; backspin

下学 xiàxué finish classes; finish school:～后做作业 do homework after school /一到～的时候,小院子里顿时热闹起来。As soon as school was over, the small courtyard would be bustling with noise and excitement. /那时我还小,没人照看,天天跟着姐姐上学、～。I was little at the time and had no one to look after me, so I followed elder sister going to school and returning from it every day.

下旬 xiàxún last ten-day period of a month:本月中、～将有寒流出现。There will be cold currents in the second and third ten-day periods of the month.

下压力 xiàyālì 〈物理〉downward pressure

下咽 xiàyàn swallow; gulp down:这碗汤药实在难以～。This bowl of herb decoction is too difficult to get down. /这种粗劣的食物,让人如何～? How can people swallow such coarse food?

下腰 xiàyāo ❶ bend down:她～抱起孩子。She bent down to pick up the child. ❷ (of martial arts) bend backwards as far as possible

下药 xiàyào ❶ prescribe medicine:要不是碰见一个高明的大夫对症～,我这病早给耽误了。I would have missed the best time to cure my illness if I hadn't had a good doctor who prescribed the right remedy. ❷ put in poison:罪犯～时被当场抓获。The criminal was caught red-handed putting in the poison.

下野 xiàyě (as of a ruler or politician) fall from power; retire from the political arena:被迫～ be forced to relinquish power; be forced to step down /～之后出洋考察 go abroad on a study tour after retiring from the political arena /选举后执政党～。The ruling party fell from power after the election.

下夜 xiàyè go on night patrol:打更～ patrol the streets (neighbourhood, etc.) and announce the watches of the night /～看青 go on night patrol and watch over the ripening crop

下议院 xiàyìyuàn *also* "下院" lower house; lower chamber; (UK) House of Commons

下意识 xiàyìshí subconscious:母亲～地紧紧抓住父亲的手,半天没有说一句话。Holding tight father's hands subconsciously, mother was speechless for a long time. /她～地重复了一句。She repeated the sentence without thinking.

下游 xiàyóu ❶ lower reaches (of a river):～十几处码头他都有熟人。He's got acquaintances in the more than a dozen ports on the lower reaches. /顺着河沟,我们徒步向～走去。We walked downstream along the brook. ❷ backward position; lagging behind:甘居～ be resigned to being backward /劳动竞赛进入高潮,二车间暂处～。The labour emulation drive is reaching a climax, with No.2 workshop lagging behind for the time being. ❸〈经济〉downstream

下游产品 xiàyóu chǎnpǐn downstream product

下游产业 xiàyóu chǎnyè downstream industry (e.g. industry of refining, distribution, or marketing of oil and its derived products):投资于～ invest in downstream industries

下游炼油 xiàyóu liànyóu downstream refining

下余 xiàyú remnant; remaining:～的钱 money left over; balance (of an account, etc.) /～的活儿,我们几个全包了! We'll take care of the remainder of the work.

下狱 xiàyù be put behind bars; be thrown into prison; be imprisoned:被捕～ be arrested and put in prison /他出来没几天又～了。He was thrown into prison again only days after he was released.

下载 xiàzǎi 〈信息〉download

下葬 xiàzàng be buried or interred:～之时 day of the burial /先父～之后,母亲又病倒了。Mother fell ill after father was buried.

下账 xiàzhàng enter into the account book:检查组查出了几笔没～的款子。The inspection team discovered several sums of money that hadn't been entered into the account book.

下诏 xiàzhào issue an imperial edict:～退位 issue an imperial edict of abdication

下肢 xiàzhī 〈生理〉lower limbs; legs:～轻瘫 paraparesis

下中农 xiàzhōngnóng lower-middle-peasant:～出身(be) of lower-middle-peasant origin

下种 xiàzhǒng sow (seeds):雨后～ sow seeds after a rain

下注 xiàzhù lay down a stake (in gambling); stake:把手中的钱全下了注 stake all one's money

下箸 xiàzhù start eating with chopsticks:满桌的海味山珍,一时无从～。The dinner table was so full of delicacies from the land and the sea that it was hard to decide where to start eating.

下装 xiàzhuāng remove theatrical makeup and costume：～之后，我们才看清扮演包公的竟是一位女性。We did not realize that it was an actress who played the part of Bao Gong until she removed her makeup and costume.

下坠 xiàzhuì ❶ (of objects) fall; drop ❷〈医学〉straining (at stool); bearing down; tenesmus

下子 xiàzǐ ❶ sow seeds ❷ lay eggs

下子 xiàzi *see* "下[3]"

下钻 xiàzuàn run the drilling tool into a well

下作 xiàzuo ❶ low; mean; indecent; obscene：无耻～的手段 brazen, low-down trick／如此～，世上罕见。Such meanness is rare. ❷〈方言〉greedy; ravenous; gluttonous：没见过吃东西这样～的人。I've never seen such a greedy eater before. ❸〈方言〉assistant; helper：打～ act as assistant or helper

吓(嚇) xià

frighten; terrify; scare; intimidate：～跑 scare (sb.) away／～人一跳 give sb. a start／～得屁滚尿流 frighten the pants off (sb.); be terror-stricken／别～着孩子。Don't frighten the child.／～得发抖 shake (*or* tremble) with fear; shake in one's shoes／～死我了。I had my heart in my mouth. *or* I was scared stiff.／他见这么多人，脸都～白了。He blanched at the sight of such a large crowd.

see also hè

吓唬 xiàhu frighten; scare; bluff：别～我！Don't try to frighten me.／这是～人的。This is merely a bluff. *or* It's just a scarecrow.／别担心，我只不过～～他。Don't worry. I was only putting the wind up him.

吓人 xiàrén terrifying; appalling; frightening：山洞又深又黑，真～。The cave was deep and dark; it was frightening.／他一脸凶相，长得真～！With his ferocious features, he was so terrifying!

夏[1] xià

summer：初～ early summer／立～ beginning of summer (7th seasonal division point)／仲～ midsummer／炎～ hot summer; height of summer／盛～ height of summer; midsummer／苦～ *also* "疰～" loss of appetite and weight and general lassitude in summer／消～ offset the effects of summer; spend the summer at leisure; take a summer holiday／三～ three summer jobs on the farm (planting, harvesting and field management)／～末 end of summer; late summer

夏[2] Xià

❶ Xia Dynasty (c. 21st-c. 16th century BC) ❷ ancient name for China：华～ China ❸ a surname

夏播 xiàbō summer sowing：～时节 summer-sowing season

夏布 xiàbù grass cloth; ramie cloth：老式的～衣服 old-fashioned clothes made from grass cloth

夏锄 xiàchú hoeing fields in summer; summer hoeing

夏宫 xiàgōng summer palace

夏管 xiàguǎn field management in summer; summer field management：做好～工作，力争秋季丰收。Do a good job of field management in summer for a bumper autumn harvest.

夏圭 Xià Guī Xia Gui (formerly translated as Hsia Kui), painter of the Southern Song Dynasty

夏侯 Xiàhóu a surname

夏候鸟 xiàhòuniǎo summer resident or bird

夏季 xiàjì summer：～萎缩病 summer dwarf／～牧场 summer pasture／～休闲 summer fallow／这些羊群～在高原牧场放牧。These flocks of sheep summer on the plateaus.

夏景天 xiàjingtiān 〈方言〉summer：～日头毒，地里的庄稼都晒蔫了。In summer, crops in the fields droop under the blazing sun.

夏枯草 xiàkūcǎo 〈中药〉selfheal; prunella (*Prunella vulgaris*)

夏历 xiàlì traditional Chinese calendar; lunar calendar

夏粮 xiàliáng grain crops harvested in summer：～丰收在望。A good harvest of summer grain crops is expected.

夏令 xiàlìng ❶ sum-mer; summer-time：～食品 food for the summer; summer food／～时装 summer fashions／～香肠 summer sausage／～白宫 Summer White House／时值～，我们几个结伴北上。It was summer-time and some of us travelled together to the north. ❷ summer weather：春行～ summer weather in spring; exceptionally warm days in spring

夏令时 xiàlìngshí summer time (ST); daylight saving time

夏令营 xiàlìngyíng summer camp

夏炉冬扇 xiàlú-dōngshàn stoves in summer and fans in winter — inappropriate measure

夏眠 xiàmián *also* "夏蛰"〈动物〉aestivation

夏普公司 Xiàpǔ Gōngsī (Japan) Sharp Corporation

夏日 xiàrì ❶ summer; summer-time; days of summer ❷〈书面〉sun in summer：～炎炎 scorching summer sun

夏时制 xiàshízhì *also* "夏令时" summer time (ST); daylight saving time：实行～ be on daylight saving time

夏收 xiàshōu ❶ summer harvesting：帮助农民～ help the farmers with the summer harvest／～农忙时节 busy season for summer harvesting; busy harvesting season in summer ❷ summer harvest：～比去年增长一成。The summer harvest this year was 10 percent more than that of last year.

夏熟 xiàshú ripen in summer：～作物 crop that ripens in summer; summer crop

夏天 xiàtiān summer

夏娃 Xiàwá Eve (the first woman, according to the Bible)

夏威夷 Xiàwēiyí Hawaii, a state of the US comprising a chain of islands in the North Pacific：～人 Hawaiian

夏衣 xiàyī summer clothing; summer wear

夏耘 xiàyún 〈书面〉summer hoeing：～人倍忙。People are all the busier with summer hoeing.

夏蛰 xiàzhé aestivation：～动物 aestivator

夏至 Xiàzhì ❶ Summer Solstice, 10th seasonal division point, marking the sun's position at 90° on the ecliptic ❷ day marking such a seasonal division point, usu. falling on the 21st or 22nd of June ❸ period lasting from such a seasonal division point till the next one (Slight Heat 小暑)

see also "节气" jiéqì; "二十四节气" èrshísì jiéqì

夏至草 xiàzhìcǎo 〈植物〉*Lagopsis supina*, a kind of medicinal herb：欧～ horehound

夏至点 xiàzhìdiǎn first point of Cancer; Summer Solstice

夏至线 xiàzhìxiàn *also* "北回归线" běihuíguīxiàn Tropic of Cancer

夏种 xiàzhòng summer sowing：～作物 crop sown in summer／～时节 summer sowing season

夏装 xiàzhuāng *see* "夏衣"

厦(廈) xià

see also shà

厦门 Xiàmén Xiamen or Amoy, Fujian Province

唬 xià *see* "吓" xià

see also hǔ

罅 xià

〈书面〉crack; chink; crevice; rift：石～ crack (*or* crevice) in a rock／窗～ crack in the window

罅封 xiàfēng 〈书面〉chink; crack; crevice：临江巨石，近水颇多～。The big rocks by the river have many crevices facing the water.

罅缝 xiàfèng 〈书面〉crack; chink; rift

罅漏 xiàlòu 〈书面〉crevice; loophole; gap; deficiency：～之处，尚待订补。There are deficiencies and shortcomings to be remedied (in future editions).／此事尚有～，容我三思。Please allow me to ponder on it, for there are still some loopholes.

罅隙 xiàxì 〈书面〉crevice; cleft; fissure; flaw：日光穿过树叶的～照下来。The sun shines through the cracks of the leaves.／石多～，空中多窍。There are many crevices in the rock, which is hollow and full of holes.

xiān

籼(秈) xiān

籼稻 xiāndào long-grained non-glutionous rice; *indica* rice

籼米 xiānmǐ polished long-grained non-glutinous rice

仙(僊) xiān

celestial being; immortal; fairy：天～ celestial being; fairy／狐～ fox-fairy／酒～ great drinker／诗～ immortal poet／修～ (usu. by making and taking elixirs) cultivate oneself to become an immortal／～才 genius; immortal talent／山不在高，有～则名。It matters not whether a mountain is tall or low, its fame

will spread far and wide as long as there is an immortal dwelling on it. *or* Substance far outweighs appearance.
仙丹 xiāndān immortality pill; elixir of life: 炼~ (as of an alchemist or Taoist) make elixir of life
仙方 xiānfāng 〈迷信〉prescription made by an immortal; magical prescription
仙风道骨 xiānfēng-dàogǔ have divine poise and sagelike features; be elegant in an other-worldly way: 此人长得~, 飘逸洒脱。With his elegant poise and sagelike features, the man seemed to be free and easy without a single care in the world.
仙姑 xiāngū ❶ female immortal or celestial being: 何~是传说中的"八仙"之一。Sister He is one of the legendary "Eight Immortals". ❷ *also* "道姑" dàogū sorceress: 村后住着个~, 以装神弄鬼为生。A sorceress lived at the back of the village, who made her living by "invoking" ghosts and spirits.
仙鹤 xiānhè ❶ red-crowned crane; stork: ~挺立在水中 red-crowned crane standing erect in the water ❷ (as in fairy tales) white crane or stork raised by immortals: 那神仙骑着~隐入云端。Riding a white crane, the immortal disappeared into the clouds.
仙鹤草 xiānhècǎo *also* "龙牙草" lóngyácǎo 〈中药〉hairyvein agrimony (*Agrimonia pilosa*)
仙后座 Xiānhòuzuò 〈天文〉Cassiopeia
仙家 xiānjiā ❶ divine abode ❷ immortal; celestial being: 传说蓬莱乃~所住之地。Penglai Island is said to be the abode of immortals.
仙界 xiānjiè abode of immortals; fairyland; paradise
仙境 xiānjìng fairyland; wonderland; paradise: 如入~ as if in a wonderland / 美如~ as beautiful (*or* gorgeous) as fairyland
仙客来 xiānkèlái 〈植物〉cyclamen (*Cyclaminos*)
仙灵脾 xiānlíngpí 〈植物〉longspur epimedium (*Epimedium macranthuns*)
仙茅 xiānmáo 〈中药〉*Curculigo rhizome* (herb whose stem and root are used as medicine)
仙女 xiānnǚ young female immortal; fairy maiden: ~下凡 fairy maiden descending to the world
仙女座 Xiānnǚzuò 〈天文〉Andromeda
仙品 xiānpǐn of outstanding grade or rank; of rare excellence or quality: 画中~ painting of unusual excellence / 茶中~ very best tea
仙人 xiānrén celestial being; immortal: 请~指点迷津 ask an immortal for advice as to how to get out of a dilemma
仙人鞭 xiānrénbiān 〈植物〉snake cactus (*Nyctocereus serpentinus*)
仙人果 xiānrénguǒ 〈植物〉prickly pear
仙人球 xiānrénqiú 〈植物〉globose cactus; bulbous cactus
仙人跳 xiānréntiào 〈旧语〉confidence trick by which a girl (i.e. "fairy") is used as a decoy to cheat a man out of money and jewels
仙人掌 xiānrénzhǎng 〈植物〉cactus (*Opuntia dillenii*): ~科 *Cactaceae* / ~属 *Opuntia*
仙人柱 xiānrénzhù (formerly used by the Oroqen nationality in northeastern China) Oroqen tepee
仙山 xiānshān mountain inhabited by immortals; elfland's hill
仙山琼阁 xiānshān-qiónggé jewelled palace in elfland's hills: 烟霭萦绕的~ fairy mountain draped in mist and haze
仙逝 xiānshì 〈婉词〉pass away: 贾夫人~扬州城。The lady Jia passed away at Yangzhou.
仙桃 xiāntáo peach of immortality in Chinese mythology
仙童 xiāntóng fairy (messenger) boy
仙王座 Xiānwángzuò 〈天文〉Cepheus
仙乡 xiānxiāng 〈敬词〉your hometown: 请问~何处? May I ask where your hometown is? *or* Where are you from, please?
仙游 xiānyóu go to fairyland — pass away; die
仙姿 xiānzī fairy-like appearance or look; ethereal beauty: ~绰约 graceful, fairy-like poise / 如此~, 人间少有。Such ethereal beauty is rare on earth.
仙子 xiānzǐ ❶ female immortal; fairy maiden: 牡丹~ Peony Fairy ❷ immortal; celestial being

氙

xiān 〈化学〉xenox (Xe): 六氟化~ xenox hexafluoride
氙灯 xiāndēng *also* "氙氧灯" xenon lamp

祆

xiān
祆教 Xiānjiào *also* "拜火教" Bàihuǒjiào Zoroastrianism

莶(薟)

xiān *see* "豨莶" xīxiān

暹

xiān
暹粒 Xiānlì Siemreab, major city in northwest Cambodia
暹罗 Xiānluó Siam — former name for Thailand: ~湾 Gulf of Siam / ~猫 Siamese cat / ~孪生子 *also* "联体双胞胎" liántǐ shuāng bāotāi Siamese twins

跹(躚)

xiān *see* "翩跹" piānxiān

铦(銛)

xiān 〈书面〉sharp: ~利 sharp; pointed

先

xiān ❶ early; earlier; before; in advance: ~到灶头~得食 he who arrives early gets served first; the early bird catches the worm / 你乘公共汽车, 我骑自行车, 看谁~到家。Let's see who gets home sooner (*or* earlier, *or* first), you by bus or I by bike. / 他~说不去, 后来改变了主意。He said he wouldn't go at first but changed his mind later. / 你~别急, 我帮你打听打听。Don't start worrying yet, I'll go and inquire for you. / 他每次都抢~发言。He always seizes the first opportunity to speak. / 您~。After you. ❷ older generation; ancestor; forefather: 祖~ ancestors; forefathers ❸ deceased; late: ~母 my late mother / ~总统 late president ❹ earlier on; before: 你~怎么不来找我呀? Why didn't you consult me earlier? / 这里的环境比原~好多了。The environment here is much better than before. ❺ (Xiān) a surname
先辈 xiānbèi ❶ older generation: 这件东西是~一代代传下来的。This heirloom has been handed down in the family from generation to generation. ❷ ancestors; forefathers; forerunners: 踏着~的足迹前进 advance in the footsteps of one's forerunners / 牢记~遗训 bear in mind the teachings of one's ancestors
先妣 xiānbǐ 〈书面〉my late or deceased mother
先鞭 xiānbiān be the first; take the lead; get ahead (of others): 首着~ be the first (to do sth.); take the lead (in sth.); have (*or* get) a head start
先不先 xiānbuxiān 〈方言〉first of all (often used in enumerating one's reasons, etc.): ~就有人极力反对。First of all, there were some people who did their best to oppose this.
先慈 xiāncí 〈书面〉my late or deceased mother
先打击能力 xiāndǎjī nénglì 〈军事〉first-strike capability
先导 xiāndǎo ❶ lead the way; be in the van: 十辆摩托车~, 车队浩浩荡荡地驶过长安街。With ten motorcycles leading the way, the motorcade passed through the Chang'an Avenue in style. ❷ guide; forerunner; predecessor; precursor: 民众的~ guide for the masses / 挫折往往是成功的~。A setback is often the precursor of success.
先帝 xiāndì previous emperor; late emperor: 宣读~遗诏 announce the edict of the late emperor
先睹为快 xiāndǔ-wéikuài consider it a pleasure to be among the first to read or watch: 观众争相购票, 以求~。People scrambled for tickets so as to be among the first to watch the performance.
先端 xiānduān 〈植物〉tip (of a leaf, flower, fruit, etc.)
先发制人 xiānfā-zhìrén gain the initiative by striking first; steal a match on one's rival; forestall the enemy; preempt: ~的战争 pre-emptive war / ~袭击 pre-emptive strike (*or* attack) / 他~, 抢在他的对手之前宣布参加竞选。He stole a march on his rival by announcing his candidacy first.
先锋 xiānfēng pioneer; vanguard; van: 开路~ pathbreaker; pioneer / 起~模范作用 play an exemplary vanguard role / 打~ fight in the van; take the lead; be a trailblazer (*or* pathbreaker)
先锋队 xiānfēngduì vanguard: 少年~ Young Pioneers / 北上抗日~ vanguard column to go north and fight Japanese aggression / 攻打敌人碉堡的~ shock squad to attack an enemy pillbox / 共产党是工人阶级的~。The Communist Party is the vanguard of the working class.
先锋霉素 xiānfēngméisù *also* "头孢菌素" tóubāojūnsù 〈药学〉cephalosporin: ~I 号 *also* "头孢菌素 I 号" cephalothin / ~II 号 *also* "头孢菌素 II 号" cephaloridine
先锋派 xiānfēngpài avant-garde
先夫 xiānfū my late husband: ~未曾留下半点遗产。My late husband left no property for us.
先父 xiānfù my late father
先公后私 xiāngōng-hòusī subordinate one's personal interests to

X

public interests:当干部的,理所当然应~。Government officials must as a matter of course put public interests before their personal interests.

先寒武纪时期 Xiānhánwǔjì shíqī 〈地质〉 Precambrian era

先河 xiānhé source; precedent; forerunner:开现代"新红学"的~ break a path for present-day studies of *A Dream of Red Mansions*

先后 xiānhòu ❶ early or late; from first to last; priority order; priority:爱国不分~。Whether one joins the ranks of patriots early or late, one is equally welcome. /要解决的问题很多,应当排排队,分分~缓急。As there are so many problems to be solved, it is necessary to put them in priority order. ❷ in succession; one after another:我们在农村搞调查研究,~到过三个村。When we were conducting investigations and study in the countryside, we went to three villages successively. /你~三次来函,我们都已收到了。We received your three letters, sent at different times. /他和他的弟弟们~都参军了。He and his brothers joined the army one after another.

先…后… xiān… hòu… first... and then...; at first... but later...;... before...:先付款,后发货 payment must be made before delivery of goods /先国后家 the state comes before the family; put the country before one's family /先难后易 tackle the difficult before the easy; crack the hard nut first /先易后难 tackle the easy before the difficult; begin by attacking the easier problems /先有耕耘后有收获。One must sow before one can reap.

先机 xiānjī opportunity of vital importance to the future:巧夺~ seize a critical opportunity cleverly /~占领高地 capture a commanding height at an opportune moment (*or* before the enemy)

先见之明 xiānjiànzhīmíng ability to anticipate what is coming; prophetic vision; foresight:具有~的政治家 provident statesman /如果没有你的~,我们这回一定要吃亏了。But for your foresight, we would have got the worst of it. /他对大多数事情都有~。He has a long head on most matters.

先进 xiānjìn ❶ advanced:~技术 advanced technology /~事迹 meritorious (*or* exemplary, *or* praiseworthy) deed /管理~ advanced (*or* sophisticated) management ❷ advanced individual or collective:争当~ strive to be an advanced (*or* model) worker; strive to be a pace-setter /后进赶~ those behind trying to catch up with those ahead

先进工作者 xiānjìn gōngzuòzhě advanced or model worker

先进集体 xiānjìn jítǐ pace-setting or advanced units

先决 xiānjué prerequisite:足够的师资力量是办好学校的~条件之一。An adequate teaching staff is one of the prerequisites (*or* preconditions) for the success of a school.

先觉 xiānjué person of foresight; prophet:孙中山先生是中国民主革命的~者。Dr. Sun Yat-sen was a prophet of the Chinese Democratic Revolution.

先君 xiānjūn 〈书面〉 my late father

先考 xiānkǎo 〈书面〉 my deceased or late father

先来后到 xiānlái-hòudào in the order of arrival; first come, first served:凡事要讲个~,等车也得排队。In everything we do there is precedence in order of arrival. If you want to take the bus, you have to queue up. /小馆里只有两口锅,跑山的人很多,得有个~嘛! The inn has only two cauldrons and there are many people travelling in the mountains. It is a case of "first come, first served".

先礼后兵 xiānlǐ-hòubīng a gentleman first and a warrior second; words before blows; using peaceful means before resorting to force:咱们还是~,谈判不成,再发动攻击不迟。Words before blows. There will be plenty of time for us to launch the offensive if the negotiations fail.

先例 xiānlì precedent:遵循~ follow a precedent /尽管无~可援,我们也能打赢这场官司。Though we have no precedents to go by, we are sure to win the case all the same.

先烈 xiānliè martyr:遗承~的事业 carry on the cause left behind by the martyrs /缅怀革命~ cherish the memory of revolutionary martyrs

先令 xiānlìng ❶ (British and other) shilling ❷ (Austrian) schilling:一奥地利~值一百格罗申。One schilling is worth 100 groschen.

先民 xiānmín 〈书面〉❶ ancestors; forefathers; forbears ❷ ancient sages

先母 xiānmǔ my late or deceased mother

先农坛 Xiānnóngtán Altar of the God of Agriculture, Beijing

先期 xiānqī earlier on; in advance:~收缩〈医学〉 premature contraction; extrasystole /~录音〈影视〉 prescoring /名单已~公布。The name list had been published in advance (*or* at an earlier date).

先前 xiānqián in the past; before; previously:他的风湿病比~好多了。His rheumatism is much better than before. /这儿~是一片荒原。Previously, it was a wilderness here.

先遣 xiānqiǎn sent in advance:~队 advance party /~部队已进入阵地。The advance troops are in position.

先秦 Xiān Qín before Qin Dynasty; pre-Qin (usu. the Spring and Autumn Period and the Warring States Period, 770-221 BC):~史 pre-Qin history of China

先驱 xiānqū pioneer; forerunner; trailblazer:~者 pioneer; forerunner; harbinger /~工业 pioneer industry /发展新针疗法的~ pioneer (*or* trailblazer) in the development of the new acupuncture therapy

先人 xiānrén ❶ ancestor; forefather:刘先生的~几代都在镇上做绸缎生意。Mr. Liu's ancestors had been silk drapers in the town for generations. ❷ late father:家父和李府的~有过八拜之交。My father and Mr. Li's late father were sworn brothers.

先人后己 xiānrén-hòujǐ place oneself after others; put other people's interests above one's own:有关个人福利的事,我们要做到~。On matters concerning personal welfare, we must put others before ourselves.

先容 xiānróng 〈书面〉 introduce and praise in advance; put in a good word in advance:为之~ put in a good word for sb. in advance

先入为主 xiānrù-wéizhǔ first impressions are strongest; preconceived ideas keep a strong hold; be prejudiced or preoccupied:既有了~的成见,他就很难听进别人的意见。With preconceived ideas firmly entrenched in his mind, he found it hard to accept other people's advice. /新到一个单位,凡事不可~。As a newcomer, you should be on your guard against any bias.

先入之见 xiānrùzhījiàn preconceived idea or notion; prejudice; preconception:有了~,你就不可能作出正确的判断。It's impossible for you to arrive at sound judgement when you're prejudiced.

先声 xiānshēng precursor; herald; harbinger:1915年的"新文化运动"是五四运动的~。The New Culture Movement of 1915 heralded (*or* was a harbinger of) the May Fourth Movement (of 1919).

先声夺人 xiānshēng-duórén forestall one's opponent by a show of strength; overawe others by displaying one's prowess:比赛开始后不久,甲队~,首先攻入一球。Team A got the jump on their rivals in the first minutes of the game by scoring a goal.

先生 xiānsheng ❶ teacher:同学们喜欢听王~讲唐诗。The students liked to hear Mr. Wang, their teacher, explaining Tang poetry. ❷ mister (Mr.); gentleman; sir:主席~! Mr. chairman! /女士们,~们! Ladies and gentlemen! /对不起,~。I'm sorry, sir. /人家是进过洋学堂的~,见过大世面。He is a gentleman who has been educated in foreign schools and has seen the world. ❸ (used together with personal pronouns) husband:我~在报馆当差。My husband works for a newspaper. /你们家~真是好脾气。Your husband is really good-natured. ❹〈方言〉 doctor:孩子发烧了,快请~看看。The child is running a fever. Please send for the doctor at once. ❺〈旧语〉 bookkeeper; accountant:在商号里当~ work as bookkeeper in a firm ❻〈旧语〉 *used to refer to people engaged in storytelling, fortune-telling, geomancy, etc.*:算命~ fortune-teller /风水~ geomancer

先世 xiānshì forefathers; forebears; ancestors:刘家的~中过举人,方圆数十里,很有名气。One of the forefathers of the Lius had been a successful candidate in the imperial civil examination at the provincial level and a household word for dozens of *li* around.

先室 xiānshì 〈旧语〉 my late wife

先是 xiānshì formerly; originally; at first:两国停火以后,边民~小有贸易来往,数月之后,情况才恢复正常。After hostilities ceased between the two countries, inhabitants of the border areas started trade exchanges in a small way; it was only several months later that everything returned to normal.

先手 xiānshǒu (in chess) have the initiative; be on the offensive:~棋下成了后手棋。One's offensive play was reduced to the defensive.

先天 xiāntiān ❶ congenital; inbred; inborn:~缺损 congenital defect (*or* deficiency) /~性梅毒 congenital syphilis /~性卵巢发育不全 ovarian agenesis /~愚型 mongolism /~的责任感 inbred sense of duty ❷〈哲学〉 *a priori*; innate:人的高尚品德不是~就具备的,而是后天培养教育的结果。Man's noble character is not innate; it is attained through education and nurture.

先天不足 xiāntiān-bùzú be congenitally deficient; suffer from an inherent shortage:这孩子～，后天又失调，体质很差。The boy has a poor constitution, born a weak baby and having been poorly nourished later. /这所研究所筹备之时即～，代表性、权威性都较差。Being poorly founded from its inception, the research institute is not so representative or authoritative.

先天下之忧而忧，后天下之乐而乐 xiān tiānxià zhī yōu ér yōu, hòu tiānxià zhī lè ér lè *also* "先忧后乐" be the first to worry about the affairs of the state and the last to enjoy oneself; be concerned with state affairs before others, but enjoy oneself only after everyone else has done so; be the first to endure hardships and the last to enjoy comforts

先天性白痴 xiāntiānxìng báichī 〈医学〉 congenital idiocy

先天性疾病 xiāntiānxìng jíbìng congenital disorders

先天性免疫 xiāntiānxìng miǎnyì congenital immunity

先天性缺陷 xiāntiānxìng quēxiàn birth defect

先天性心脏病 xiāntiānxìng xīnzàngbìng congenital heart disease

先头 xiāntóu ❶ vanguard; van:～部队 vanguard /～骑兵连 advance cavalry company ❷ before; formerly; previously:我～去找过她，但她不在家。I went to her place before, but she was not in. /他～在上海读书，而后去了新疆。He previously studied in Shanghai; later he went to Xinjiang. /我～没想到他会来。I didn't expect to see him here. ❸ in advance; ahead; in front:把关心孤寡老人放在～ give priority to care for childless aged people

先王 xiānwáng former kings or sovereigns

先下手为强 xiān xiàshǒu wéi qiáng 〈谚语〉 he who strikes first gains the upper hand:～，后下手遭殃。He who strikes first prevails; he who strikes late fails. *or* Hit first and win, strike second and lose. /他们～，占领了港口。They beat their enemy to it by occupying the harbour first.

先贤 xiānxián wise man of the past; sage:～遗训 teachings of past wise men /历代～ wise men of past generations /～祠 temple of sages

先小人后君子 xiān xiǎorén hòu jūnzǐ be a (calculating) villain first and a (magnanimous) gentleman afterwards; specify (the harsh) terms before showing courtesy:咱们～，把租金讲定了再住房，免得日后生麻烦。Let's allow impoliteness to precede courtesy and settle on the rent before moving in so as to avoid future trouble.

先行 xiānxíng ❶ go ahead of the rest; start off before the others; precede:兵马未动，粮草～。Food and fodder should go ahead of troops and horses — preparations should always precede the main part of work. /这次进军，以工兵团～。This expedition will be spearheaded by the engineers corps. ❷ beforehand; earlier; in advance:～准备 make preparations beforehand /我们想～举办培训班。We intend to run training classes in advance. ❸ commander of an advance unit or vanguard:此次东征，他出任～。He is commander of the vanguard force for this eastward campaign.

先行官 xiānxíngguān commander of an advance unit; vanguard:交通运输是国民经济的～。Communications and transport are the vanguard of the national economy.

先行者 xiānxíngzhě pioneer; forerunner:中国民主主义革命的伟大～ great pioneer for China's democratic revolution

先兄 xiānxiōng my deceased elder brother

先严 xiānyán 〈书面〉 my deceased father

先验 xiānyàn 〈哲学〉 a priori; transcendental:～知识 a priori knowledge /社会意识决定于社会存在，而不是主观的，～的。Social consciousness is determined by social being; it is not inherent or a priori.

先验方法 xiānyàn fāngfǎ transcendental method

先验论 xiānyànlùn 〈哲学〉 apriorism

先意承志 xiānyì-chéngzhì do what one's parents, etc., would like one to do before being told so; curry favour by anticipating other's wishes:这孩子从小就懂事，～，很得大人欢心。Sensible and understanding as a child, he was very much in favour with his elders. /此人极善～，迎合人心，上上下下关系都搞得很好。As he is well versed in anticipating other people's wishes and humouring everybody, he is on very good terms with all his superiors and subordinates.

先斩后奏 xiānzhǎn-hòuzòu execute the criminal first and report to the emperor afterwards — act first and report afterwards; do sth. without prior approval from one's superiors:他常常～，一意孤行，大家居然也奈何他不得。He often acted without prior approval or consultation, and would cling obstinately to his own course. However, nobody could do anything about him.

先张 xiānzhāng 〈建筑〉 pretension:～法混凝土 pretensioned concrete /～法预应力混凝土 pretensioning prestressed concrete /～管道 pretensioned pipe

先兆 xiānzhào omen; portent; sign; indication:不祥的～ ill omen /暴风雨的～ indications (*or* signs) of an impending storm /这是战争的～。This portends war.

先兆惊厥 xiānzhào jīngjué 〈医学〉 *see* "先兆子痫"

先兆流产 xiānzhào liúchǎn early signs of miscarriage or abortion; threatened miscarriage or abortion

先兆症状 xiānzhào zhèngzhuàng precursor

先兆子痫 xiānzhào zǐxián 〈医学〉 pre-eclampsia

先哲 xiānzhé great thinker of the past:历代～ sages through the ages /～名言 celebrated dicta (*or* sayings) of great thinkers of the past

先知 xiānzhī ❶ person of foresight:人类的～ those with foresight among the human race ❷ 〈宗教〉 prophet:古希伯来人的～ prophet of the ancient Hebrews

先知先觉 xiānzhī-xiānjué ❶ person of foresight or vision ❷ having foresight:不要以为别人都浑浑噩噩，只有自己～。Don't think you alone possess foresight while everybody else is muddle-headed!

先祖 xiānzǔ 〈书面〉 ❶ ancestor ❷ my deceased grandfather

酰

xiān *also* "酰基" 〈化学〉 acyl

酰胺 xiān'àn 〈化学〉 acylamide; amides:～酶〈生化〉 amidase /～水解酶 amidohydrolase /～植物 amide plant

酰化 xiānhuà 〈化学〉 acylate

酰基 xiānjī 〈化学〉 acyl

鲜

xiān ❶ fresh; new:～牛肉 fresh beef /～啤酒 fresh (*or* new) beer ❷ bright-coloured; bright:这些围巾颜色真～! How bright these scarves are! ❸ delicious; tasty:这鸡汤很～。This chicken broth is delicious. ❹ delicacy:时～ vegetables (fruits, etc.) just in season; delicacies of the season /尝～ have a taste of something (that is a delicacy) ❺ aquatic food:鱼～ fresh fish /本店供应海～。Delicious seafood is served at this restaurant. ❻ (Xiān) a surname

see also xiǎn

鲜卑 Xiānbēi Xianbei or Sienpi, ancient nationality inhabiting areas in present northeast China and Inner Mongolia, establishing the Northern Wei, Northern Qi and Northern Zhou dynasties successively in the 4th-6th centuries

鲜脆 xiāncuì fresh and crisp:～的甜瓜 fresh and crisp muskmelon

鲜果 xiānguǒ fresh fruit

鲜红 xiānhóng bright red; scarlet:～的朝霞 scarlet dawn /～的颜色 bright red /夕阳把满山的枫叶照得～。The setting sun painted the mountain and its maple leaves scarlet.

鲜花 xiānhuā fresh flowers; flowers:～的世界 world of flowers /时值严冬，花房中各色～争奇斗艳。In the greenhouse all kinds of flowers are competing in beauty and colour even in the freezingly cold winter.

鲜货 xiānhuò fresh product (such as fruit, vegetable, aquatic product, or medicinal herb):商店的柜台上摆满了各色～。The counter of the store is lined with all kinds of fresh fruits. /这家水产商店总有～出售。Fresh seafood is always available in the aquatic food store.

鲜活 xiānhuó vivid; lively:～的个性 lively personality (*or* character) /这一切，～地出现在我眼前。All these emerged vividly in my mind's eye.

鲜活 xiānhuo ❶ (fish, flowers, etc.) fresh:～商品 perishable commodities /～的水产品 fresh aquatic products /那花朵含着露水，多～呀。How fresh the flowers look with the dewdrops still on them! ❷ bright-coloured:这块布料的颜色很～。This cloth is bright-coloured.

鲜洁 xiānjié fresh and clean:空气～ fresh air /～的百合花 fresh and clean-looking lily

鲜京企业集团 Xiānjīng Qǐyè Jítuán (ROK) Sunkyong Ltd.

鲜丽 xiānlì bright-coloured and beautiful:衣着～ be beautifully dressed in bright colours /色彩～的壁画 bright-coloured frescos

鲜亮 xiānliang 〈方言〉 ❶ (of colours) bright and shining:天空是一片～的蓝色。The sky is a bright shining blue. /这件毛衣的颜色真～。How bright and beautiful this sweater is! ❷ pretty; beautiful:姑娘这一打扮，就显得更～了。The girl looks prettier when she is dressed up.

鲜灵 xiānling 〈方言〉bright and fresh：浇了水之后，麦苗更～了。After being watered, the wheat sprouts looked all the more fresh. /他买了一条鲜鲜灵灵、活蹦乱跳的大鲤鱼。He bought a fresh-looking, bouncing carp.

鲜绿 xiānlǜ vivid green; bright green：～的秧苗 bright green rice seedlings

鲜美 xiānměi ❶ delicious; tasty：这道菜味道～，远近驰名。This dish is known far and wide for its delicious taste. ❷〈书面〉fresh and beautiful：公园里花草～，群蝶飞舞。Flowers and plants in the park look fresh and beautiful, with numerous butterflies fluttering about them.

鲜明 xiānmíng ❶ (of colour) bright; shiny：色调～ in bright hue /战旗～耀眼。The battle banners were dazzlingly bright. ❷ clear-cut; sharp; distinct：线条～ be in clear-cut contours /观点～ present a clear-cut viewpoint /个性～ have a distinctive personality (*or* character) /爱憎～ be unequivocal about what one loves and what one hates /～的民族风格 distinct national style /～的对比 striking (*or* sharp) contrast

鲜嫩 xiānnèn fresh and tender：～的竹笋 fresh and tender bamboo shoots

鲜浓 xiānnóng bright and rich in colour：猩红毛毯，色泽～。The scarlet woollen blanket is bright and rich in colour.

鲜皮 xiānpí 〈皮革〉fresh hide; greenhide

鲜润 xiānrùn fresh and smooth; fresh and moist：～的红花 fresh and moist red flowers

鲜甜 xiāntián fresh and sweet; sweet and delicious：～的哈蜜瓜 fresh and sweet *hami* melons

鲜血 xiānxuè blood：～淋漓 drenched with blood; dripping with blood /～浇灌的友谊之花 flowers of friendship nourished by blood

鲜妍 xiānyán bright-coloured; bright and beautiful

鲜艳 xiānyàn *also* "鲜妍" bright-coloured; gaily-coloured; bright and beautiful：～的颜色 bright colours /～的彩虹 bright and beautiful rainbow /她打扮得非常～。She is dressed in gay colours. /牡丹花开得格外～。Peonies are blooming in all their splendour.

鲜艳夺目 xiānyàn-duómù dazzlingly beautiful; resplendent; brilliant; radiant：漫山遍野的映山红，～。Resplendent azaleas are flowering all over the hills.

鲜衣怒马 xiānyī-nùmǎ be dressed in fine clothes and ride on well-groomed horses — lead a life of luxury; wallow in luxury

鲜于 Xiānyú a surname

忺

xiān 〈书面〉pleased; gratified; happy

掀

xiān ❶ lift (a cover, lid, etc.); open up; turn over：～门帘 lift a door curtain /～开井盖 take the lid (*or* cover) off the well /～开书的封面 turn over the cover of a book; open a book /马把骑手～了下来。The horse has thrown its rider. ❷ convulse; rock; shake：白浪～天 white waves heaving to the sky; white breakers leaping skywards

掀动 xiāndòng ❶ start; unleash; launch：～战争 start a war ❷ move; set in motion：老人的嘴唇～了几下。The old man's lips moved several times. /这件事在他心中～着激愤波澜。This event stirred up waves of indignation in his mind.

掀风鼓浪 xiānfēng-gǔlàng stir up a turmoil or upheaval; make trouble：有人躲在背后～，惟恐天下不乱。Someone is trying to incite a turmoil behind the scenes, craving nothing short of nationwide chaos. /那些有成见的人，～，挑拨两大民族间的感情。People who are prejudiced are doing all they can to make trouble and stir up ill feeling between the two great nations.

掀起 xiānqǐ ❶ lift; raise：～锅盖 lift the lid off a pot ❷ surge (up); cause to surge：狂风～了惊涛骇浪。The gust caused terrifying waves to surge up. /暴风～漫天黄沙。The storm blew yellow sand all over the sky. ❸ launch; start; set off：～新的热潮 set off a new mass fervour /如何评价这部书，～了一场辩论。A debate has been launched as to how to appraise the book.

掀腾 xiānteng be in a tumult; turn into a tumult; convulse：在暴风雪中，整个牧场～着蒙蒙雪浪。The snowstorm turned the whole pasture into a tumult of misty snow waves.

掀天揭地 xiāntiān-jiēdì stir the heavens and shake the earth — be overwhelming in one's power; be of far-reaching influence：～的人才 man capable of earth-shaking deeds; man of great talents /～的力量 overwhelming force; earth-shaking power

掀涌 xiānyǒng be turbulent; seethe：波浪～ turbulent waves

锨(杴、枚)

xiān shovel; spade：铁～ shovel; spade /木～ wooden winnowing shovel

纤(纖)

xiān fine; tiny; minute：空气中漂浮着～埃。Fine dust is floating in the air.

see also qiàn

纤长 xiāncháng slender and long：～的手指 slender and long fingers

纤尘 xiānchén fine dust：春风拂起～。A breeze of spring wind raised fine dust.

纤尘不染 xiānchén-bùrǎn be not soiled by a particle of dust; be spotlessly clean; maintain one's original integrity or purity：海滨～ immaculate beaches /他在财税部门工作三十年，两袖清风，～。Although he has worked in the financial and taxation departments for over three decades, he remains uncorrupted and spotlessly clean.

纤度 xiāndù 〈纺织〉fibre number; size

纤毫 xiānháo finest hairs; minutest details or particles：没有～的差别 not the least (*or* slightest) difference /～毕见 distinct in the minutest details /～不爽 accurate (*or* correct) down to the smallest (*or* last) detail

纤介 xiānjiè *also* "纤芥"〈书面〉tiny detail; minute particle：无～之失 free from the slightest error or fault

纤毛 xiānmáo 〈生物〉cilium：～运动 ciliary movement

纤毛虫 xiānmáochóng 〈动物〉infusorian

纤美 xiānměi slender and pretty; delicate and beautiful：～的手迹 delicate, beautiful handwriting

纤密 xiānmì fine-woven; meticulous; detailed：～的刺绣 finely embroidered piece; fine embroidery /针脚～ close stitches

纤巧 xiānqiǎo delicate; exquisite：一双～的手 a pair of delicate hands /这件玉器雕镂～。This jadeware is exquisitely carved.

纤柔 xiānróu soft and delicate：～的长发 soft and delicate long hair

纤弱 xiānruò slender and fragile; delicate：～的身影 slim and fragile figure; delicate figure /～之身 delicate health

纤手 xiānshǒu (formerly of a woman) soft delicate hands：她伸出～，折下一枝梅花。Stretching out her soft delicate hand, she picked a branch of plum blossom.

纤瘦 xiānshòu small and thin; slim and fragile; delicate：身体～ be of slim, fragile physique /～的手 small, thin hand; delicate hand

纤微 xiānwēi minute; tiny, infinitesimal：～的过失 tiny mistake

纤维 xiānwéi fibre; staple：天然～ natural fibre /合成～ synthetic fibre /人造～ man-made fibre /光学～存储器 fibre-optic memory /～结构复合材料〈机械〉filamentary structural material /～增强复合材料 fibre reinforced composite /～激光器 fibre laser

纤维癌 xiānwéi'ái 〈医学〉fibrocarcinoma

纤维板 xiānwéibǎn 〈建筑〉fibreboard; fibrous slab

纤维变性 xiānwéi biànxìng fibrosis

纤维玻璃 xiānwéi bōli fibreglass

纤维蛋白 xiānwéi dànbái 〈生化〉fibrin

纤维蛋白原 xiānwéi dànbáiyuán 〈生化〉fibrinogen

纤维隔音板 xiānwéi géyīnbǎn acoustic-celotex (board); acoustic-celotextile

纤维光缆 xiānwéi guānglǎn fibre-optic cable

纤维光学 xiānwéi guāngxué fibre optics

纤维集束 xiānwéi jíshù collection of filaments

纤维镜 xiānwéijìng 〈医学〉fibrescope：结肠～ fibrecolonoscope /胃～ fibregastroscope

纤维瘤 xiānwéiliú 〈医学〉fibroid; fibroma

纤维强化金属 xiānwéi qiánghuà jīnshǔ fibre-strengthening metal

纤维石膏板 xiānwéi shígāobǎn fibrous plaster

纤维束 xiānwéishù fibre bundle; 〈纺织〉tow：光导～ fibre-optic bundle

纤维素 xiānwéisù 〈生化〉cellulose：～酶 cellulase /～酸 cellulosic acid /～甲醚〈化学〉methyl cellulose /～树脂 cellulosic resin

纤维素分解菌 xiānwéisù fēnjiějūn 〈生化〉cellulose-decomposing bacterium; cellvibrio

纤维增强塑料 xiānwéi zēngqiáng sùliào fibre-reinforced plastics

纤维织炎 xiānwéizhīyán 〈医学〉fibrofascitis; fibrositis

纤维脂肪瘤 xiānwéi zhīfángliú 〈医学〉fibrolipoma (FRP)

纤维植物 xiānwéi zhíwù fibre plant

纤悉 xiānxī 〈书面〉detailed; meticulous：途中所记，甚为～。What

was recorded during the trip was very detailed.

纤悉无遗 xiānxī-wúyí *also* "纤悉不遗"; "纤屑无遗" with no detail unnoticed or omitted; down to the minutest detail: 搜刮民财，～ plunder the possessions of the people lock, stock and barrel

纤细 xiānxì slim; slender; fine; tenuous: 笔画～ written (*or* drawn) in a fine hand /～的身材 slim build (*or* figure) /她的手～白嫩。Her white hands are slender and tender.

纤纤 xiānxiān 〈书面〉long and slender; delicate: 十指～ with long, slender fingers

纤小 xiānxiǎo fine; little; delicate: 画面上的小燕，显得～轻盈。The young swallows in the picture appeared delicate and graceful.

纤屑 xiānxiè 〈书面〉details; trivia: 丁宁备至，～无遗 give such thoughtful advice as to leave no detail unmentioned

纤秀 xiānxiù fine and elegant: 写得一笔～的小楷 write a fine elegant hand

纤妍 xiānyán slender and beautiful

纤腰 xiānyāo (a woman's) slender waist

纤指 xiānzhǐ (a woman's) delicate fingers

騫 xiān 〈书面〉(of birds) fly

xián

舷 xián side of a ship or plane; board: 左～ port /右～ starboard /船～ side of a ship (*or* boat) /干～〈船舶〉freeboard /干～甲板 freeboard deck

舷边 xiánbiān 〈船舶〉gunwale

舷窗 xiánchuāng porthole

舷门 xiánmén 〈船舶〉gangway

舷梯 xiántī ❶ (of a ship, etc.) gangway ladder; gangway: 登上～ mount the gangway /放下～ lower the gangway /收起～ raise the gangway ❷ (of a plane) ramp

舷外发动机 xiánwài fādòngjī 〈船舶〉outboard motor; outboard engine

弦(❷絃) xián ❶ bowstring: 弓～ bowstring /箭在～上 the arrow is on the bow — poised to strike; reaching a point of no return like an arrow on the bowstring ❷ string of a musical instrument; chord (sometimes used figuratively to refer to one's wife): 断～ have the string of one's instrument broken — one's wife dies /续～ put a new string on one's instrument — (of a man) remarry; (of a woman) sb.'s second wife /忍泪不能歌，试托哀～语。With tears in my eyes I cannot sing, So I try to let the dolorous lute (string) speak on my behalf. /知音少，～断有谁听? Who would listen to my broken string, Since I have no understanding friend? ❸ spring (of a watch, etc.): 闹钟忘了上～。I forgot to wind up the alarm clock. ❹〈数学〉chord ❺〈数学〉hypotenuse

弦板腔 xiánbǎnqiāng a kind of shadow play popular in parts of Shaanxi and Gansu provinces

X

弦歌 xiángē sing to stringed accompaniment

弦脉 xiánmài 〈中医〉taut pulse

弦诵 xiánsòng 〈书面〉(as in traditional Confucian studies) sing to stringed accompaniment and read aloud: ～不辍 keep on singing and reading aloud; study uninterruptedly

弦索 xiánsuǒ 〈旧语〉stringed instruments

弦外之音 xiánwàizhīyīn overtones; implication; innuendo: 谁都不难听出他这一番话的～。No one failed to get the meaning behind his words. /韩云程懂得许总经理的～: 这事工程师和工务主任也有责任。Han Yuncheng understood what General Manager Xu was implying: the engineer and the works manager were also responsible.

弦线 xiánxiàn string of a musical instrument

弦月 xiányuè crescent; half moon

弦乐队 xiányuèduì 〈音乐〉string orchestra; string band

弦乐器 xiányuèqì 〈音乐〉stringed instrument

弦柱 xiánzhù post or neck to which the strings of a musical instrument are attached

弦子 xiánzi three-stringed plucked instrument

弦子戏 xiánzixì *also* "柳子戏" liǔzixì 〈方言〉variety of Shangdong local opera

闲(閒) xián ❶ not busy; idle; leisurely; unoccupied: 吃～饭 not earn one's keep; be an idler /游手好～ loaf; gad about; live in idleness /退休后，我就清～了。I'll be at leisure after retirement. ❷ not in use; unoccupied; free; lying idle: 这台缝纫机一直～着，你拿去用吧。Take this sewing-machine for your use; it has been lying idle. ❸ spare time; leisure: 农～ slack farming season /余～ spare time; leisure /偷～ snatch a moment of leisure /消～ pass one's leisure /今天我哪得～陪你看电影去。How can I afford time to see a film with you today? ❹ informal; irrelevant; random; idle: 莫管～事! Don't muddle in what is none of your business! *or* Mind your own business!

闲白 xiánbái 〈方言〉idle talk; chat: 扯～ chat; chit-hat

闲笔 xiánbǐ what is irrelevant in writing; digression: 文中几处～均应删去。Cut out all the digressions in the article.

闲步 xiánbù walk leisurely; take a stroll: 沿着海滨～ stroll along the beach

闲不住 xiánbuzhù refuse to be idle; always keep oneself occupied: 这庄稼汉手脚总也～。The farm hand simply cannot stay idle.

闲常 xiáncháng 〈方言〉usually; in general; as a rule: 他～在家里爱养些花草。He usually likes to grow flowers and plants at home.

闲扯 xiánchě chat; chit-chat; twaddle: 别听他～! Don't listen to his twaddle! /她与那陌生人～几句，以免他感到冷落。She made conversation with the stranger so that he would not feel left out.

闲打牙 xiándǎyá 〈方言〉indulge in idle talk; chit-chat; twaddle: 我一天忙到晚，没有工夫跟你～。I am busy from morning till night and have no time to chit-chat with you.

闲荡 xiándàng saunter; stroll; idle; loaf: 整天四处～ saunter about all day

闲房 xiánfáng vacant house or room: 我们家没有～。We have no vacant (*or* unoccupied) rooms in the house. /～出租。Rooms to let.

闲工夫 xiángōngfu spare or free time; leisure: 这两天腾不出～来。I haven't been able to snatch a moment of leisure these days.

闲官 xiánguān one holds an official post with little to do; holder of a sinecure

闲逛 xiánguàng saunter; stroll; loaf; gad about: 这孩子无人管束，任其～。The child was left to gad about at his pleasure.

闲汉 xiánhàn person without legitimate occupation; loafer: 一帮～ bunch of loafers /老爷子专有几个～陪着下棋。The old gentleman had a few hangers-on to play chess with.

闲花野草 xiánhuā-yěcǎo *also* "野草闲花" ❶ weeds and wild flowers: 山坡上长着许多不知名的～。The mountain slope is covered by many nameless weeds and wild flowers. ❷ women of easy virtue; prostitutes: 慎勿沾染～。Be careful not to get involved with loose women.

闲话 xiánhuà ❶ digression; cackle: ～少说! Cut the cackle! *or* Save your breath to cool your porridge. /～少说，言归正传。(often used in traditional storytelling) Enough of this digression, let's return to our story. *or* However, to continue the story. /他讲课时～太多。He digresses too often when he lectures. ❷ complaint; gossip: 说某人的～ gossip about sb. /怎么招来这么多～? Why all this complaint? /不要怕人家说～，咱们要坚持干下去。Don't be afraid of the gossip. Let's stick to our course. ❸〈书面〉engage in idle talk; talk casually; chat: ～家常 chat about daily life; chit-chat

闲寂 xiánjì 〈书面〉deserted and quiet; unoccupied and still: 园中～无人。The garden was totally deserted and quiet.

闲静 xiánjìng leisurely and tranquil; quiet; undisturbed: 旷野～ quiet open country /举止潇洒而～ deport oneself in an unrestrained and leisurely manner

闲居 xiánjū stay at home idle: ～半生，一事无成 stay idle for half a lifetime with nothing accomplished

闲磕牙 xiánkēyá 〈方言〉indulge in idle talk; chatter; chit-chat: 一边晒太阳，一边～ chatter in the sun /他们半夜半夜地～。They would chit-chat late into the night.

闲空 xiánkòng free or spare time; leisure: 不得～ have no spare time /趁他有～你再去找他。Go and call on him when he is free.

闲聊 xiánliáo chat; gossip: ～了一通 have a chat /一些老头儿坐在树阴下边喝茶边～。Some old men were shooting the breeze over their cups of tea under a tree.

闲磨牙 xiánmóyá indulge in idle argument; chit-chat; twaddle: 这会儿我没工夫跟你～。I don't have time to indulge in idle argument with you right now.

闲盘儿 xiánpánr ❶ what is not one's business; trivia:他没工夫管这些～。He had no time for such trivia. ❷ idle chatter; chitchat; gossip:她只要一空就爱扯～。She liked to gossip whenever she had the opportunity. /我不能再听这些～。I can't stand all this idle talk. *or* I've had enough of all this tittle-tattle.

闲篇 xiánpiān 〈方言〉idle talk or chatter; irrelevant talk; gossip:这都是～儿,你别往心里去。This is mere gossip. Don't take it to heart.

闲频 xiánpín 〈电子〉idle(r) frequency

闲气 xiánqì anger about trifles; uncalled-for abuse:你何必跟他生这份～! You don't have to be angry with him over such a trifle! /她就是为这个缘故,受了不少的～。She took a good deal of uncalled-for abuse for that very reason.

闲弃 xiánqì unoccupied; unused:把～的空房辟为阅览室 turn an unoccupied room into a reading room

闲钱 xiánqián 〈口语〉spare money; spare cash:日子好过了,人人兜儿里有几个～。As life is easier now, everybody has some spare cash in his or her pocket.

闲情逸致 xiánqíng-yìzhì *also* "闲情雅趣" cultivated pleasures of a leisurely life; leisurely, carefree mood:别人忙得要死,你还有～听音乐? How can you have the leisure and mood for enjoying music when everybody else is so busy? /这样一来,刚才的～便一扫而空,心情变得沉重起来。This incident immediately swept away my leisurely and carefree mood of a moment before and my heart grew heavy again.

闲人 xiánrén ❶ idle or unoccupied person; idler:大～ one who has absolutely nothing to do; total idler /开工之后,队里就抽不出一个～了。When the project starts, there will be no one to spare on the team. ❷ person not concerned:～免进。No admittance except on business. *or* Off limits to unauthorized personnel. *or* Admittance to staff only.

闲散 xiánsǎn ❶ free and leisurely; at a loose end:他～惯了,一时受不了约束。Being used to a free and easy life, he found it hard, for a while, to submit to restraint and discipline. ❷ scattered and unused; idle:～人员 idle people /～资金 idle capital /充分利用～土地 make full use of scattered plots of unused land

闲时 xiánshí free time; leisure time:他～爱养花。He enjoys raising flowers in his leisure time. /～到我这里来玩儿。Please drop in when you're free.

闲事 xiánshì ❶ matter not of one's concern; other people's business:少管～! None of your business! *or* Mind your own business! /爱管～的人 one who likes to poke one's nose into other people's business; busybody ❷ unimportant matter; trifle:他很忙,不要用这些～去打扰他。He is very busy; don't bother him with such trifles.

闲是闲非 xiánshì-xiánfēi idle talk; chit-chat:别人的那些～我连听都不愿听。I wouldn't like to hear idle gossip about other people.

闲适 xiánshì leisurely and comfortable; easy and carefree:～的心情 leisurely and comfortable mood; feeling of leisure and comfort /生活～ lead an easy and carefree life

闲书 xiánshū light reading:看～ do light reading; read for amusement

闲谈 xiántán chat; chit-chat:终日～,无所事事 chit-chat all day without doing a stitch of work

闲田 xiántián vacant field

闲庭 xiántíng quiet, tranquil courtyard or garden:～信步 stroll in a quiet, tranquil courtyard (*or* garden)

闲玩 xiánwán *also* "闲耍" have fun at one's leisure; amuse oneself in a leisurely manner:他们喜欢在花园里～。They like to amuse themselves in the gardens.

闲文 xiánwén digression; irrelevant writing:这段譬喻切中要害,并非～。This parable is not a digression; it is very much to the point.

闲暇 xiánxiá free time; leisure:了无～ have no spare time at all /趁此～,补读报纸 use leisure time to bring oneself up to date in news

闲闲 xiánxián 〈书面〉❶ self-possessed; unruffled; at ease:十亩之间兮,桑者～兮。Mulberry planters were enjoying some leisure after working on ten *mu* of land. ❷ ample; wide:大知～。Great knowledge is ample.

闲心 xiánxīn leisurely mood:没有～开玩笑 be in no mood for jokes /我要能有这份～,我的身体也就好了。If I were in such a leisurely mood, I would be well again.

闲雅 xiányǎ *also* "娴雅" xiányǎ easy; graceful; elegant

闲言碎语 xiányán-suìyǔ *also* "闲言冷语";"闲言闲语" ❶ unrelated trivia; digressions:～不用讲,表一表好汉武二郎。(in storytelling) Digressions apart, let us move on to our hero Wu Song. ❷ groundless accusations or complaints (usu. behind people's backs); sneering remarks; gossip:背地里散布～ gossip behind sb. back /不要听了几句～就打退堂鼓。Don't beat a retreat just because of some jeering remarks.

闲逸 xiányì 〈书面〉leisurely and carefree:～地踱步 take a leisurely stroll

闲游 xiányóu saunter; stroll; loaf:他们在外～了一小时左右。They strolled around for an hour or so. /他对～渐渐感到厌倦了。He is becoming weary of loafing.

闲员 xiányuán surplus personnel; redundant staff:裁汰～ reduce redundant personnel

闲月 xiányuè slack farming month:冬春～ slack (farming) months in winter and spring /田家少～,五月人倍忙。Farmers have few slack months and are extremely busy in May.

闲云野鹤 xiányún-yěhè floating clouds and wild cranes — persons who live in leisure and ease untrammelled by worldly affairs, often referring to hermits and Taoist priests in the past:退休之后的他如～,无拘无束。After retirement, he leads a leisurely life, free from all worldly cares.

闲杂 xiánzá without fixed duties; irrelevant; redundant:～人员 people without fixed duties; miscellaneous personnel /精简～人员,提高工作效率 cut redundant staff to raise (working) efficiency /～人员不得入内。Off limits to unauthorized personnel.

闲杂儿 xiánzár 〈方言〉❶ irrelevancies; digressions:你们别听～了,还是做作业吧。Don't listen to irrelevancies any more; better do your homework. ❷ unimportant matters; trivialities:一天到晚净是忙～ be busy with trivialities from morning till night

闲在 xiánzai 〈方言〉at leisure; leisurely and carefree:你今天怎么这样～呀? How come you are so leisurely and carefree today? /等～的时候,咱俩再好好叙谈一番。Let's have a good talk when we're free.

闲章 xiánzhāng informal seal (usu. bearing a proverb or quotation one enjoys); seal for one's own amusement

闲职 xiánzhí official post with little to do (thus with little power); sinecure:他只是挂了个～,并不具体管事。His post being just nominal (*or* a sinecure), he is not really in charge of anything.

闲置 xiánzhì leave unused; let sth. lie idle; gather dust:～不用 let sth. lie idle /～设备 standby (*or* idle) equipment /这套进口设备已～了三年,造成了很大的浪费。This set of imported equipment has been left unused for three years, causing great waste.

闲坐 xiánzuò sit back for a chat; sit idly and enjoy one's leisure:在邻居家～了一会儿 sit and chat for a while at the neighbour's

痫(癇)

xián 〈医学〉癫～ epilepsy

痫症 xiánzhèng epilepsy

鹇(鷴)

xián see "白鹇" báixián

娴(嫺)

xián 〈书面〉❶ refined; elegant:幽～ quiet and elegant; poised and quiet ❷ adept; skilled; well-versed:～于交际 be a good mixer; be sociable /不～工笔画 not skilled in traditional fine-brushwork painting

娴静 xiánjìng gentle and quiet:温顺～ meek and gentle /性情～,体态柔弱 with a gentle disposition and a fragile carriage

娴淑 xiánshū refined and kind-hearted:～端庄 refined and dignified in manner

娴熟 xiánshú adept; skilled; well-versed:笔法～ versed in wielding the brush (as in writing or drawing) /棋艺～ adept at chess /他～的演奏博得了热烈的掌声。His skilful performance (of a musical instrument) won warm applause.

娴习 xiánxí familiar; well-versed:～礼仪 be well-versed in etiquette /～英美文学 be well-read in English and American literature

娴雅 xiányǎ *also* "闲雅" xiányǎ (of a woman) refined; graceful; elegant:举止～ refined in manner /～斯文 elegant and gentle

嫌

xián ❶ suspicion:涉～ be under suspicion; be suspected /有贪赃之～ be suspected of corruption ❷ ill will; hard feeling; spite; grudge:消释前～ remove previous ill will (*or* resentment); bury the hatchet ❸ dislike; loathe; complain:讨人～ get oneself dis-

X

liked; be unpopular /大家～价钱太贵，都不愿买。Considering the price too high, no one wanted to buy. /文章写得很好，就是～长了一点。The article is well-written, only it's a bit long.

嫌猜 xiáncāi dislike and suspicion: 消释～ dispel suspicion and dislike

嫌烦 xiánfán not want to take the trouble; regard as too much bother; consider troublesome: 伺候老人她从来没嫌过烦。She never regarded it as a burden to take care of aged people. /你自己做饭，不～吗？Don't you think it's too much trouble to do the cooking yourself?

嫌肥挑瘦 xiánféi-tiāoshòu *also* "挑肥拣瘦" tiāoféi-jiǎnshòu dislike the fat and choose the lean — choose only what is to one's personal advantage; be choosy or fussy: ～，难以满足 choosy and hard to please

嫌乎 xiánhu *also* "嫌唬"〈方言〉dislike; mind; complain: 他苦活脏活啥也不～。He never minds how hard and dirty the work is. /她～丈夫个子太矮。She complains of her husband being too short.

嫌忌 xiánjì 〈书面〉be suspicious and jealous: 有些人总是～比自己能干的人。Some people are always suspicious and jealous of those who are abler than they.

嫌怕 xiánpà 〈方言〉dislike; fear

嫌弃 xiánqì dislike and shun; cold-shoulder: 遭人～ be disliked and avoided; be cold-shouldered /他虽有错，但～他也不对。It is wrong to give him the cold shoulder even though he has made some mistakes.

嫌酸植物 xiánsuān zhíwù oxyphobe

嫌恶 xiánwù abhor; detest; loathe: 令人有～之感 arouse one's loathing

嫌隙 xiánxì ill feeling; animosity; enmity; grudge: ～冰消。The ill feeling melted like ice. /他生性多疑，几乎和每个人都产生过～。Suspicious by nature he has borne grudges against almost everybody else.

嫌盐植物 xiányán zhíwù halophobe

嫌厌 xiányàn dislike; loathe: 她～油腻食物。She dislikes greasy food. /他好搬弄是非，遭人～。He is loathed as a terrible gossip-monger.

嫌疑 xiányí suspicion: 排除～ dispel (*or* remove) suspicion /他有偷盗的～。He was suspected of theft. /这篇文章有抄袭的～。This article is suspected to be a plagiarism.

嫌疑犯 xiányífàn (now 嫌疑人) suspect: 间谍～ suspected spy /谋杀～ suspect in a murder /他被当作杀人～拘留了。He was held in custody under suspicion of murder.

嫌疑分子 xiányífènzǐ suspect: 许多～被拘留了。Many marked men (*or* suspects) were detained.

嫌氧细菌 xiányǎng xìjūn *also* "嫌气细菌" anaerobic bacteria; anaerobe; anaerobium

嫌雨植物 xiányǔ zhíwù ombrophobe; ombrophoolus plant

嫌怨 xiányuàn grudge; ill will; resentment; enmity: 多年～顿时烟消云散。The long-standing resentment immediately dissolved like mist (*or* smoke).

嫌憎 xiánzēng dislike; detest; loathe: 他不仅未得谅解，反而更遭～。Instead of being understood, he was detested all the more.

贤(賢) xián

❶ virtuous; worthy; able: ～臣辅佐 assisted by virtuous and able ministers ❷ able and virtuous person; wise man: 前～ wise men of an older generation; wise men of a previous age /时～ great scholar of the period; wise man of the time /礼～下士 be courteous to the wise and the scholarly; go out of one's way to enlist the services of the talented and the learned /选～举能 recommend and appoint virtuous and able men to office /见～思齐 try to emulate a wise, virtuous man when one sees one ❸〈敬词〉(referring to people of the same or younger generation) worthy: ～昆仲 your worthy brothers

贤才 xiáncái virtuous talent; man of great capability: 难得的～ rare talent

贤达 xiándá prominent personage; worthy: 社会～ prominent public figures (*or* personage)

贤德 xiándé ❶ virtue; benevolence: 不忘恩师的～ never forget the benevolence of one's kind teacher /天生～，宽厚待人。Born a person of virtue, he was generous to people. ❷ virtuous and kind: ～女子 virtuous, kind woman

贤弟 xiándì (a term of respect for one's younger brother or man younger than oneself) my worthy brother

贤惠 xiánhuì *also* "贤慧" (of a woman) virtuous and kind; kind-hearted: 为人～ being kind and understanding /他妻子十分～，里里外外的事都帮他管了。He had a good and able wife, who helped him with the work both inside and outside the house.

贤慧 xiánhuì *see* "贤惠"

贤劳 xiánláo 〈书面〉work industriously (for the public): ～一生，廉以奉公 work industriously for the public and remain incorruptible all one's life

贤良 xiánliáng 〈书面〉❶ (of a man) virtuous and able ❷ virtuous and talented persons: 任用～ employ men of virtue and talent

贤路 xiánlù 〈书面〉channel through which worthy men of ability can attain officialdom: 广开～ open wide the channel through which worthy men of ability can become officials

贤妹 xiánmèi (a term of respect for one's younger sister or woman younger than oneself) my worthy sister

贤明 xiánmíng ❶ wise and able; capable and intelligent; sagacious: 他以～知人而名重一时。He was famous far and wide for being wise, able and good at judging people. ❷ wise and able man; sage: 另聘～ employ (*or* engage) sb. else who is wise and able

贤内助 xiánnèizhù good wife; understanding wife: 他有个～，得以专心搞科研。As he had an understanding wife, he could devote himself totally to scientific research.

贤能 xiánnéng ❶ able and virtuous ❷ able and virtuous persons: 任用～ employ (*or* recruit) people of virtue and talent

贤妻 xiánqī ❶ virtuous wife; good wife; understanding wife ❷〈敬词〉my wife

贤妻良母 xiánqī-liángmǔ (traditional ideal of womanhood) understanding wife and loving mother; virtuous wife and worthy mother

贤契 xiánqì 〈书面〉polite term for addressing one's student or the son of one's friend: ～见信如面。(formula for beginning a letter addressed to one's student or the son of one's friend) When you read this letter, it is just as if you saw me in person.

贤人 xiánrén person of virtue; wise man: 举用～ recruit persons of virtue /庸才易得，～难求。Whereas mediocrities are easy to come by, it's difficult to find virtuous persons.

贤士 xiánshì 〈书面〉person of virtue; wise men

贤淑 xiánshū 〈书面〉(of a woman) virtuous and kind; kind-hearted: ～夫人 virtuous and understanding wife /她～温良，深得婆母喜爱。Virtuous and good-natured, she was very much in favour with her mother-in-law.

贤哲 xiánzhé person outstanding in virtue and learning; wise man: 旷代～ person whose virtue and learning unsurpassed for generations

贤侄 xiánzhí (a polite term for one's nephew or the son of one's friend) my worthy nephew

咸[1] xián

❶〈书面〉all: 老少～宜 good for old and young alike /～称其德。Everybody praises his virtues. ❷ (Xián) a surname

咸[2](鹹) xián

salted; salty: 菜有点不够～。The dish lacks a pinch of salt. /吃太～的东西不利身体健康。It is harmful to one's health to eat too much salt.

咸不唧儿 xiánbujīr *also* "咸不滋儿" saltish: 这菜～的。The dish is saltish.

咸菜 xiáncài salted vegetables; pickles: 就～吃馒头 have steamed bread with pickles

咸淡 xiándàn degree of saltiness: 尝～ taste whether sth. is too salty

咸丰 Xiánfēng Xianfeng, title of the reign (1851-1861) of Aisin Gioro Yizhu (爱新觉罗·奕詝), 7th emperor of the Qing Dynasty, called reverently Qing Wenzong (清文宗) after death

咸海 Xiánhǎi Aral Sea, inland sea east of the Caspian Sea between Kazakhstan and Uzbekistan

咸津津 xiánjīnjīn somewhat salty; brackish: 这汤～的，挺有味道。The soup is somewhat salty and very tasty.

咸肉 xiánròu salted meat; bacon: ～煎鸡蛋 fried eggs with bacon

咸涩 xiánsè salty and bitter: 味道～，难以下咽 too salty and puckery to swallow /她低下头，吞咽着～的泪水。Lowering her head, she swallowed the salty and bitter tears.

咸水 xiánshuǐ salt water; brackish water

咸水歌 xiánshuǐgē song of boat dwellers
咸水湖 xiánshuǐhú saltwater lake
咸水虾 xiánshuǐxiā brine shrimp (*Artemia*)
咸水鱼 xiánshuǐyú saltwater fish
咸丝丝 xiánsīsī slightly salty; brackish:海边的空气～儿的。The air on the beach smells brackish.
咸盐 xiányán 〈方言〉 salt

涎 xián saliva:口角流～ saliva drools from the corner of one's mouth /垂～三尺 slaver so much that the saliva drools a metre from the mouth; have one's mouth watering; lick one's chops; smack one's lips /催～剂 sialagogue
涎分泌不足 xiánfēnmì bùzú 〈医学〉 sialaporia; sialoporia
涎沫 xiánmò 〈方言〉 saliva
涎皮赖脸 xiánpí-làiliǎn brazenfaced; shameless and loathsome; cheeky:一副～的无赖相 (behave) in a brazen-faced, rascally manner /不要～的! None of your cheek! /一天大似一天,还这么～的,连个理也不知道。You're not a child any more, yet you still carry on in this cheeky way. Can't you ever behave yourself?
涎石 xiánshí 〈医学〉 sialolith:～病 sialovolithiasis
涎水 xiánshuǐ 〈方言〉 saliva:流～ slobber; drool
涎腺 xiánxiàn 〈生理〉 salivary gland(s)
涎腺管炎 xiánxiànguǎnyán 〈医学〉 sialo-angitis
涎腺瘘 xiánxiànlòu 〈医学〉 sialosyrinx
涎腺炎 xiánxiànyán 〈医学〉 sialoadenitis
涎液素 xiányèsù 〈生化〉 salivin
涎溢 xiányì 〈医学〉 sialorrhoea
涎着脸 xiánzheliǎn 〈方言〉 behave in shameless or brazen-faced way:事已如此,你还～装做不知道,行吗? With things as they are, how can you brazen it out by pretending ignorance?

衔[1]**(啣)** xián ❶ hold in the mouth:春燕～泥 spring swallows carrying bits of earth in their bills /黑豹～着兔子奔向后山。The black panther ran into the mountain, carrying a rabbit in its mouth. ❷ cherish; harbour; bear:～恩 cherish a kindness ❸〈书面〉 accept (instructions or orders):～诏讨逆 launch an expedition against the rebels on imperial instructions ❹ connect; link:首尾相～。The beginning and the end are connected.

衔[2] xián rank; title:官～ official rank /学～ academic title /公使～参赞 counsellor with the rank of minister (*or* with ministerial rank) /拥有上校军～ hold the rank of colonel
衔恨 xiánhèn nurse hatred; harbour resentment; bear a grudge:～终生 bear a grudge all one's life /他～在心,伺机报复。Harbouring resentment, he waited for an opportunity to take revenge.
衔环结草 xiánhuán-jiécǎo do all one can to repay a kindness:～,以报救命之恩 do all one can to repay sb. for saving one's life
衔接 xiánjiē link up; connect; join:不相～ do not link up (*or* connect) properly /互相～ dovetail /～紧凑 tightly joined /把竹管～起来,引泉水到家门前。Have those bamboo pipes joined to each other so as to carry spring water to the house.
衔枚 xiánméi 〈书面〉 ancient custom of making soldiers bite a piece of wood in the mouth (while marching at night), to prevent making noise:～夜行 march at night biting a piece of wood in the mouth /～疾走 march swiftly and silently
衔命 xiánmìng 〈书面〉 carry out an order:～组阁 be authorized to form a government /～出使 go on a foreign mission
衔铁 xiántiě 〈电工〉 armature:～继电器 armature relay
衔头 xiántóu title:他是什么～的军官? What is his official title in the army?
衔尾 xiánwěi (as of animals) go in single file with one animal's snout touching the tail of the one in front; go in serried file:～相随 walking in Indian file; one closely behind another
衔冤 xiányuān nurse a bitter sense of injustice; suffer a wrong or miscarriage of justice:～多年 suffer a miscarriage of justice for years; have no chance to air one's grievance for years /～而死 die nursing a bitter sense of wrong; die with one's name uncleared

鰔 xián 〈动物〉 dragonet

挦(撏) xián tear; pull:～鸡毛 pull (*or* pluck) chicken feathers /～扯 pull and tear

xiǎn

幰 xiǎn 〈书面〉 curtain of a carriage

燹 xiǎn 〈书面〉 wild fire:兵～ ravages of war

显(顯) xiǎn ❶ apparent; evident; obvious; noticeable:明～ clear; obvious; conspicuous ❷ show; reveal; display; manifest:～威风 show off one's power or prestige; throw one's weight about /～身扬名 show one's mettle and make a name ❸ illustrious and influential:～职 influential post (*or* position)
显摆 xiǎnbai *also* "显白"〈方言〉 show off; boast:他总爱～自己。He is fond of showing off. /别臭～! Quit making a spectacle of yourself!
显鼻子显眼 xiǎnbízi-xiǎnyǎn 〈口语〉 too conspicuous; ostentatious:婚礼别搞得那么～的。There is no need for an ostentatious wedding.
显妣 xiǎnbǐ 〈书面〉 my late mother
显程序 xiǎnchéngxù 〈信息〉 explicit program
显出 xiǎnchū present; reveal; display:～一脸的不高兴 look displeased /～原形 reveal one's true colours /这虽是件小事,却～了这孩子的机灵。Though it is just a trifle, it shows how smart the child is.
显达 xiǎndá (usu. of an official) illustrious and influential; famous and powerful:一生～,权倾当朝 be so illustrious and influential throughout one's life that one wields greater power than anyone else at court /～之日,不忘旧友。I will never forget old friends when I achieve power and fame.
显得 xiǎnde look; seem; appear:初次登场,她～有点紧张。As it was her maiden appearance on the stage, she seemed a bit jittery. /理完发,他～年轻了些。He looked somewhat younger after the haircut.
显而易见 xiǎn'éryìjiàn obviously; clearly; as plain as daylight; as clear as day:～,这个问题的严重性应该引起我们的重视。Obviously, the seriousness of the problem should arouse our attention. /在这样的性格冲突中,结局是～的。The consequences are writ large in such a clash of personalities.
显光管 xiǎnguāngguǎn 〈电子〉 arcotron
显贵 xiǎnguì ❶ of high position; influential ❷ eminent personage; bigwig:朝中～ high officials in the (imperial) court /巴结～ curry favour with the powers that be
显函数 xiǎnhánshù 〈数学〉 explicit function
显赫 xiǎnhè eminent; illustrious; outstanding; influential:～的功绩 outstanding contribution /地位～ occupy an eminent position /声势～ have powerful prestige and influence /他出身于官宦之家,祖上也曾～一时。He was born into a family of officials, whose ancestors were once high and mighty.
显花植物 xiǎnhuā zhíwù phanerogam (*Phanerogamia*)
显怀 xiǎnhuái (of a woman) reveal one's pregnancy through one's figure:她还没～呢,才三个月。She has been pregnant for only three months, and so is not showing it yet.
显宦 xiǎnhuàn 〈旧语〉 ranking or high official:达官～ high officials
显豁 xiǎnhuò bright and clear; evident; conspicuous:内容～,文笔生动 clear in content and vivid in style
显见 xiǎnjiàn obvious; plain; self-evident; apparent:鉴于上述～的原因,我不得不提出辞呈。In view of the above-mentioned obvious reasons, I had to tender my resignation. /如此～的问题,你居然视而不见! How could you turn a blind eye to such conspicuous problems!
显考 xiǎnkǎo 〈书面〉 my late father
显灵 xiǎnlíng 〈迷信〉 (of a ghost or spirit) make a supernatural appearance or otherwise make its presence or power felt:诸路神明～赐福。All deities, please manifest your power and bestow blessings.
显亮 xiǎnliàng bright; conspicuous; striking:这房子又干净,又～。The room is clean and bright. /纪念碑立在最～的地方。The monument stands at the most conspicuous spot.
显露 xiǎnlù become visible; appear; reveal; show:～头角 make one's mark; show promise /他不愿～自己的身份。He did not want to reveal his identity. /母亲摸着孩子的头发,脸上～出慈爱的笑容。A loving smile appeared on the mother's face as she stroked her child's

hair.

显明 xiǎnmíng obvious; apparent; distinct; marked: ~的特点 distinct (*or* marked) characteristic /这样~的道理,恐怕用不着我多费口舌。The truth is too obvious, I trust, to need much explanation on my part. /全书前后文风~不同,很可能出自两个人的手笔。The first part of the book differs so strikingly in style from the second part that they were probably written by different people.

显目 xiǎnmù eye-catching; conspicuous: 分外~ extremely manifest (*or* striking) /把花束放在~的地方。Set the bunch of flowers in a conspicuous place.

显能 xiǎnnéng show off one's ability: 在人前~ try to show off in public /你在行家面前显什么能! Why, you are flaunting your ability in front of experts!

显派 xiǎnpai 〈方言〉 show off: 她穿件新衣服也要在人前~~。She would show off every new dress of hers in company.

显亲扬名 xiǎnqīn-yángmíng make one's family illustrious by achieving fame; make one's name and glorify one's family: 倘得一官半职,~,光耀门闾,乃儿之志也。If I manage to get an official post, it will bring me fame and credit to our family and the community. Such is my ambition as your son.

显然 xiǎnrán obvious; manifest; evident; clear: 这~是意外事故。This is obviously an accident. /~是她回答错了。Evidently she gave the wrong answer. /这~是为了蒙蔽公众。This is clearly designed to befuddle the public.

显荣 xiǎnróng 〈书面〉 conspicuous glory or fame: 生前坎坷,死后~,这样的例子历史上不是没有。It is not without precedent in history that one is beset with frustrations and setbacks during one's lifetime but crowned with fame and glory after one's death.

显色剂 xiǎnsèjì 〈化学〉 developer

显色染料 xiǎnsè rǎnliào 〈化工〉 developing dye

显山露水 xiǎnshān-lùshuǐ 〈方言〉 (used usu. in the negative) attract attention by displaying one's talent or skill: 他虽然有点儿文化和技术,可是在村里从来不~。Though he has some education and skill, he never tries to show off and attract attention in the village. /你看人家,不显山、不露水地就把这么件大事给办成了。Look at him! He got such a big job done without making the least fuss about it.

显身手 xiǎn shēnshǒu display one's talent or skill; distinguish oneself: 大~ display one's talent to the full; cut a brilliant figure

显圣 xiǎnshèng 〈迷信〉 (of a ghost or a saintly person) make its presence or power felt: 昨晚先帝~,托梦给了游方和尚。The late emperor appeared in the mendicant monk's dream last night.

显示 xiǎnshì show; display; demonstrate; manifest: 石油~ oil shows /地面~ surface indications /~管 display tube /~系统 display system /~终端 video terminal /新的经济政策~了它的巨大威力。The new economic policy has displayed (*or* demonstrated) its great power. /作品~了作者对生活的热爱和独特的感受能力。The work shows (*or* reveals) the author's love of life as well as his unique sensibilities.

显示剂 xiǎnshìjì 〈化学〉 developer

显示器 xiǎnshìqì 〈电子〉 monitor

显微光度计 xiǎnwēi guāngdùjì microphotometer

显微光谱图 xiǎnwēi guāngpǔtú 〈化学〉 microphotogram

显微胶片 xiǎnwēi jiāopiàn *also* "缩微胶卷" suōwēi jiāojuǎn microfilm; microfiche; (US) bibliofilm

显微解剖 xiǎnwēi jiěpōu 〈医学〉 microdissection

显微镜 xiǎnwēijìng microscope: 红外线~ infrared microscope /~载片 microslide /~检查 micrography

显微镜学 xiǎnwēijìngxué microscopy

显微摄像机 xiǎnwēi shèxiàngjī microfilmer

显微蚀刻 xiǎnwēi shíkè microectch

显微手术 xiǎnwēi shǒushù *see* "显微外科"

显微术 xiǎnwēishù microscopy

显微图 xiǎnwēitú micrograph

显微图像 xiǎnwēi túxiàng microimage

显微外科 xiǎnwēi wàikē 〈医学〉 microsurgery: ~手术 microsurgical operation

显微阅读机 xiǎnwēi yuèdújī *also* "缩微阅读机" suōwēi yuèdújī microfilm reader or viewer; microreader

显微照片 xiǎnwēi zhàopiàn microphotograph

显微照相术 xiǎnwēi zhàoxiàngshù microphotography

显现 xiǎnxiàn manifest or reveal oneself; appear; emerge; show: 晨雾渐消,燕山山脉~出它雄伟的轮廓。As the morning mist lifted, the Yanshan Mountains revealed their grand outlines. /穿上这件衣服更~出她的美貌。This dress would show her beauty to advantage.

显像管 xiǎnxiàngguǎn 〈电子〉 kinescope; picture tube

显像密度计 xiǎnxiàng mìdùjì densitometer

显效 xiǎnxiào ❶ show or produce an effect: 这种农药~快,毒性低。This pesticide produces quick results (*or* effects) and is low in toxicity. /合理施肥,才能使肥料充分~。The fertilizer will be most effective only when applied rationally. ❷ conspicuous result or effect: 未见~。There have been no conspicuous results.

显形 xiǎnxíng show one's (true) colours; reveal or betray oneself: 幕后人物终于~。The backstage manipulator revealed himself at last.

显性 xiǎnxìng dominance: ~因子 dominant factor (*or* gene) /~性状 dominant character

显学 xiǎnxué 〈书面〉 famous theory or school of thought: 孔、墨~ renowned schools of Confucius and Mozi

显眼 xiǎnyǎn eye-catching; conspicuous; showy: 样书展示在橱窗中最~的地方。The sample book is on display in a conspicuous spot in the shop window. /我这一身打扮是不是太~了! Am I too loudly dressed? *or* Am I overdressed?

显扬 xiǎnyáng ❶ 〈书面〉 make known; recommend; acclaim: 先生提携在先,诸多朋友~在后,拙作才为世人赏识。It was first due to your help and then the recommendation of many friends who wrote reviews that my work came to be appreciated by the public. ❷ widely-known; famous: 此人名声~,四海皆知。He has a reputation that is known far and wide.

显要 xiǎnyào ❶ powerful and influential; high and mighty: ~人物 influential figure; VIP ❷ powerful and influential people: 政界~ bigwigs in the political arena

显耀 xiǎnyào ❶ wield power and prestige; be powerful and influential: ~一时 enjoy power and prestige for a time /权势日盛,声名~。As one becomes increasingly powerful, one's fame and prestige spread. ❷ vaunt; show off: 小有得意,多方~,如此行为恐为世人所不齿。If you show off at every turn the little achievement you have made, you might be held in contempt by the public.

显影 xiǎnyǐng 〈摄影〉 develop: ~不足 underdeveloped /~过度 overdeveloped

显影机 xiǎnyǐngjī developing machine

显影剂 xiǎnyǐngjì developing agent; developer

显影盘 xiǎnyǐngpán developing dish

显影纸 xiǎnyǐngzhǐ *also* "相纸" xiàngzhǐ developing-out paper

显证 xiǎnzhèng 〈书面〉 clear proof: 这一事例是中国女子坚韧、刻苦品德的~。This story is a clear proof of the tenacity and industry of Chinese women.

显著 xiǎnzhù conspicuous; marked; striking; prominent: 这种新药疗效~。The new medicine has produced conspicuous (*or* notable) results. /新学期,他有了~的进步。He has made marked progress in the new term. /同一本书,两篇文章的评价却有~的不同。The two reviews offered clearly different evaluations of the same book.

显字管 xiǎnzìguǎn 〈电子〉 charactron

㬎

xiǎn *see* "显" xiǎn

蚬

xiǎn 〈动物〉 *Corbicula leana*, a fresh-water variety of bivalves

洗

Xiǎn a surname

see also xǐ

冼

Xiǎn a surname

跣

xiǎn 〈书面〉 bare-footed: ~足 with one's feet bare; barefooted

筅(箲)

xiǎn

筅帚 xiǎnzhǒu 〈方言〉 scraper (for cleaning pots and cauldrons)

铣

xiǎn

see also xǐ

铣铁 xiǎntiě cast iron

毨(毨)

xiǎn 〈书面〉 (of new-grown hairs or feathers)

X

neat; uniform

鲜(尟、尠) xiǎn little; rare: ～见 rarely seen; rare / ～有 rarely available; rare /～为人知 be little known *see also* xiān

藓 xiǎn 〈植物〉moss

崄(嶮) xiǎn

崄巇 xiǎnxī *see* "险巇" xiǎnxī

狝(獫) xiǎn 〈书面〉dog with a long snout and muzzle

狝狁 Xiǎnyǔn *also* "猃狁" Xiǎnyǔn ancient nomadic people inhabiting present north Shaanxi, northern Gansu, and western Inner Mongolia, later known as *Rong* (戎) or *Di* (狄)

险(險) xiǎn ❶ (of terrain, etc.) dangerous; perilous; difficult of access: 浪急滩～ with swift rapids and perilous shoals ❷ place difficult of access (such as a narrow pass or a swift river): 无～可守 have no advantageous terrain for defence; have no tenable defence position /凭～固守 put up a stout defence by making full use of the inaccessible terrain /长江天～ natural barrier of the Yangtze ❸ danger; peril; risk: 遇～ meet with danger; have an accident /历～ go through dangers and hardships; have adventures /风～ risk; hazard /艰～ hardships and dangers /化～为夷 turn danger into safety /北极探～ explore the North Pole /好～! What a narrow escape! *or* What a near thing! *or* What a close shave! ❹ sinister; perfidious; vicious; venomous: 阴～ sinister /奸～ treacherous ❺ by a hair's breadth; by inches; almost nearly: ～遭毒手 nearly fall a victim to sb.'s treachery; escape sb.'s plot by a hair's breadth /～些误车 nearly miss the train (*or* bus)

险隘 xiǎn'ài strategic pass; defile: 扼守～ hold a strategic pass

险地 xiǎndì ❶ strategic position; easily defended terrain: 城外还有几处～可以屯兵防守。There are several strategic positions outside the city wall, where troops can be stationed for defence. ❷ dangerous situation; perilous plight: 兵临～ lead one's troops into a dangerous situation; land in a perilous plight with one's army

险毒 xiǎndú treacherous and vicious: 用心～ have a sinister and venomous intention

险厄 xiǎn'è 〈书面〉❶ place difficult of access; easily defended position: 据此～, 可进可退。If we hold this strategic place, we can easily advance or evacuate. ❷ dangerous; perilous; hazardous: ～的境地 dangerous situation; perilous plight

险恶 xiǎn'è ❶ dangerous; treacherous; perilous; ominous: ～的暗礁 treacherous submerged reefs /处境～ find oneself (*or* be) in a perilous position /山势～ difficult mountain terrain ❷ sinister; venomous; vicious; malicious: ～的谣言 malicious rumour /居心～ harbour evil intentions

险峰 xiǎnfēng perilous peak (of a mountain): 攀登～ climb a precipitous summit /天生一个仙人洞, 无限风光在～。Nature has excelled herself in the Fairy Cave, On perilous peaks dwells beauty in her infinite variety.

险工 xiǎngōng perilous construction or engineering project: 这段～不断发生重大事故。Serious accidents have frequently occurred during this dangerous section (of the construction project).

险固 xiǎngù 〈书面〉difficult of access and easily defended: 地势～, 易守难攻。The topography is such as to make the place easy to hold but difficult to attack.

险关 xiǎnguān pass which is strategically located and difficult of access: 挑重担, 闯～ (be brave enough to) shoulder a heavy burden and surmount impossible obstacles

险乎 xiǎnhu (usu. of sth. undesirable) nearly; almost: ～跌倒 almost fall down /堤防～被洪水冲塌。The dykes were nearly breached by the flood.

险急 xiǎnjí critical; extremely urgent: 灾情～ dire disaster that demands urgent measures

险境 xiǎnjìng dangerous situation; perilous plight: 濒临～ find oneself in a dangerous situation (*or* perilous plight)

险绝 xiǎnjué extremely difficult of access: 山势～ mountain extremely difficult of access

险峻 xiǎnjùn ❶ dangerously steep; precipitous: ～的高山 dangerously steep high mountain /山崖～ precipitous cliff ❷ dangerous; severe: 形势异常～。The situation was fraught with danger. *or* It was a critical situation.

险僻 xiǎnpì dangerous and out-of-the-way: ～的山路 dangerous, out-of-the-way mountain path

险峭 xiǎnqiào dangerously steep: ～的山峰 dangerously steep mountain peak; giddy peak

险情 xiǎnqíng dangerous situation; danger: 一夜之中出现了数次～。Danger occurred several times during one night. /～发生之时, 几位主治大夫正好在场。Several physicians-in-charge happened to be on hand when the case turned critical.

险球 xiǎnqiú (mostly in football) near miss: 救出～ make a save

险区 xiǎnqū danger zone: 误入～ enter a danger zone by mistake

险胜 xiǎnshèng win by a narrow margin: 中国队以 70 比 69～客队。The Chinese team defeated the visiting team by a narrow margin of 70 to 69.

险滩 xiǎntān dangerous shoals; rapids: 船行～ sail the rapids

险巇 xiǎnxī *also* "崄巇" xiǎnxī 〈书面〉(as of a mountain path) dangerous; (of a road, journey, etc.) difficult: 山路蜿蜒曲折, ～异常。The tortuous mountain path is extremely difficult and dangerous to travel. /此生经历, ～坎坷, 难以尽言。My life has been so full of difficulties, dangers and setbacks that it is really beyond words.

险象 xiǎnxiàng dangerous sign or symptom: 病人出现～。The patient shows signs of danger.

险象环生 xiǎnxiàng-huánshēng dangerous symptoms appear one after another; be exposed to danger on all sides: 该国经济～。The economy of the country was fraught (*or* beset) with perils.

险些 xiǎnxiē narrowly (escaping from sth. untoward); nearly: 她骑车经过运河时, ～掉进河里。When cycling across the canal, she nearly fell in. /他～在飞机失事中遇难。He narrowly escaped from the air crash.

险性 xiǎnxìng dangerous; perilous: ～事故 dangerous accident

险要 xiǎnyào strategically located and difficult to approach: 地处～ be strategically located and difficult of access /～之地 location of strategic importance and easy defence

险语 xiǎnyǔ startling remarks; (of classical poetry) difficult and rare words

险韵 xiǎnyùn (of classical poetry) difficult rhyming (i.e. rhyming with difficult and rare words): 诗人自恃才高, 好用～。Vaunting his superb talent, the poet was fond of rhyming with difficult, rare words in his poems.

险遭不测 xiǎnzāo-bùcè have a narrow or near escape; barely escape an accident or trap; come within an ace of death

险诈 xiǎnzhà sinister and sly: 为人～ sinister and crafty by nature

险兆 xiǎnzhào harbinger of danger; dangerous omen: ～已经出现, 再不采取措施就晚了。There are signs of danger already. It will be too late if we don't take measures immediately. /病人亡故之前, 已有～。Dangerous omens had presented themselves before the invalid died.

险症 xiǎnzhèng dangerous illness or disease: 专治急症、～和疑难病症 specialize in treating acute, dangerous and various difficult illnesses

险阻 xiǎnzǔ (of roads) dangerous and difficult: 进了山口, 眼前是一条崎岖～的山路。Entering the pass, he found a dangerous and difficult mountain path in front of him. /谨以此书献给不畏艰难～, 奋力攀登科学高峰的勇士。This book is dedicated to those who defy dangers and difficulties and bravely scale the summits of science.

猕(獮) xiǎn (ancient custom of emperors) autumn hunting

猃(玁) xiǎn

猃狁 Xiǎnyǔn *see* "狝狁" Xiǎnyǔn

xiàn

宪(憲) xiàn ❶ 〈书面〉statute; law ❷ constitution: 立～ draw up a constitution /违～ violate a constitution; be unconstitutional /修～ revise a constitution /立～会议 constitutional assembly (*or* convention)

宪兵 xiànbīng military police; gendarme: ~队 military police corps; gendarmerie /国际~ international gendarme

宪法 xiànfǎ constitution; charter: ~草案 draft constitution /~修正案 amendment to a constitution /~条文 articles of a constitution /~权利 constitutional right

宪警 xiànjǐng gendarmes and police

宪令 xiànlìng 〈书面〉laws and ordinances

宪书 xiànshū 〈旧语〉almanac

宪章 xiànzhāng ❶〈书面〉take as one's model; follow; imitate: ~名家,多年苦练,这才有所成就。His achievement was due to years of unyielding practice with the masters as his models. ❷〈书面〉laws and institutions: 朝廷草创,~未立。As the dynasty had just been established, it did not yet have its laws and institutions in place. ❸ charter: 联合国~ United Nations Charter /~运动 (in British history) Chartist movement; Chartism (1837-1884) /太平洋~ Pacific Charter

宪政 xiànzhèng constitutional government; constitutionalism: 维护~和法统 defend constitutional government and legally constituted authority

羡(羨)

xiàn ❶ admire; envy; covet: 欣~ *also* "歆~" admire (with pleasure) /乡人无不称~ be the admiration of the whole village /临渊~鱼,不如退而结网。Sooner than stand by the pond coveting the fish, one should go home to weave a net. ❷〈书面〉plentiful; surplus: ~财 surplus money /~力 spare energy ❸ (Xiàn) a surname

羡妒 xiàndù *also* "羡嫉" admire and envy: 令人~ arouse both admiration and envy

羡慕 xiànmù admire; envy: 大家都~她的一头秀发。Everyone envied her her beautiful hair.

羡叹 xiàntàn admiring exclamation: ~之余,我们还要深刻反省,看看自己的不足。After exclaiming our admiration, we need to examine ourselves deeply to find out our own weaknesses.

羡余 xiànyú 〈旧语〉extra or additional taxes collected by local officials on behalf of the emperor

霰

xiàn *also* "雪子" xuězǐ; "雪糁" xuěshēn 〈气象〉graupel

霰弹 xiàndàn *also* "榴霰弹" liúxiàndàn shrapnel; canister (shot); case shot

献(獻)

xiàn ❶ offer; present; dedicate; donate: ~酒 offer wine or liquor; present wine or liquor /~俘 (in ancient times) present prisoners of war (to emperor as a token of victory) /~花圈 lay a wreath /捐~ donate /贡~ contribute /此书~给我的战友们。This book is dedicated to my comrades-in-arms. /为了和平,她~出了年轻的生命。She gave (*or* laid down) her young life for the cause of peace. ❷ show; display: ~歌一首 sing a song

献宝 xiànbǎo ❶ present a treasure: 这位老收藏家已多次向家乡博物馆~。The old collector has presented many treasures to the museum of his hometown. ❷ offer a valuable piece of advice or experience: 职工们纷纷~,提出了许多改造工厂的意见。All the workers and staff contributed their valuable advice and suggestions for the renovation of the factory. ❸ display what one treasures: 祖传的鼻烟壶,在他看来异常的珍贵,只有亲朋好友来时,他才肯~。The snuff bottle handed down from his ancestors was so precious to him that he would only show it to visiting relatives and friends.

献策 xiàncè give advice; make suggestions: 为家乡建设~出力 offer advice and help for the development of one's hometown

献丑 xiànchǒu 〈谦词〉show one's incompetence or inadequacy; make a fool of oneself: 既然人人都得画一幅,我也只好~了。Since everyone is required to paint a picture, I'll make a fool of myself by painting one. /~,~! (After giving a performance or showing one's work to others) There! I've made an exhibition of myself.

献词 xiàncí congratulatory message (on a particular occasion): 校庆一百周年~ address (*or* message) on the centenary (anniversary of the founding) of a school

献花 xiànhuā present flowers or bouquets: 儿童们向贵宾~。Children presented bouquets to the honoured guests.

献计 xiànjì give advice; offer suggestions: 近日来,到总经理办公室~献策的人络绎不绝。Recently, people have come in an endless stream to the president's office to offer advice or suggestions.

献技 xiànjì *also* "献艺" show one's skill; perform: 这次新年宴会,我们特请著名粤菜厨师王师傅为各位~。For this New Year banquet, we have invited Mr. Wang the famous chef of Guangdong cuisine to show you his culinary skill. /他在街头~多年,练了一手绝活。Having performed in the streets for years, he acquired certain unique skills.

献捷 xiànjié 〈书面〉announce a victory (to higher authorities)

献礼 xiànlǐ present a gift; offer a present: 以优异的成绩向祖国~ present one's outstanding success as a gift to the motherland /谨以本书作为国庆五十周年~。This book is humbly presented as a gift for the 50th anniversary of the founding of the People's Republic of China.

献媚 xiànmèi try to ingratiate oneself (with sb.); fawn; toady; truckle: 无耻~ shameless fawning /~的丑态 disgusting ingratiation /向敌人~ truckle (*or* make up) to the enemy /我认为他们是在向上级~取宠。I think they are trying to curry favour with their superiors.

献纳 xiànnà 〈书面〉❶ offer opinion or advice ❷ offer as a tribute; present: ~土仪 present local produce; make a gift of local produce

献旗 xiànqí present a banner: 病人病愈之后向高医生~,表示对他的感谢。The cured invalids presented a banner to Dr. Gao to express their thanks.

献芹 xiànqín *also* "芹献"〈书面〉〈谦词〉offer my humble gift

献勤 xiànqín curry favour; ingratiate oneself: 这个人能说会道,又会~。He not only has the gift of the gab but also knows how to ingratiate himself. /他不务正业,时间都花在向女同学~上去了。Instead of devoting himself to his studies, he spends his time running after girls.

献身 xiànshēn devote oneself to; lay down one's life for: ~教育事业 devote (*or* dedicate) oneself to the cause of education /准备为真理而~ be ready to give one's life for truth /~精神 spirit of selfless devotion

献演 xiànyǎn perform (on stage): 今晚~的节目有《天鹅湖》片段。The performance tonight includes scenes from *Swan Lake*.

献疑 xiànyí 〈书面〉raise doubts or suspicions: 这篇文章有许多读者投书~。Many readers wrote to raise their doubts about the article.

献艺 xiànyì display one's feat or skill; perform: 登台~ display one's skill on the stage /二十年前,她曾在伦敦~,获得好评。She performed in London and won acclaim 20 years ago.

献议 xiànyì 〈书面〉offer advice or suggestions: 强敌压境,却无人献退敌之议。With the powerful enemy massing his troops on the border, no one came forth with means or ways to repulse them.

献殷勤 xiàn yīnqín curry favour; ingratiate oneself; pay one's addresses (to): 当面~ fawn upon sb. to his face /他对漂亮的女演员大~。He showered attentions on the beautiful actress.

献拙 xiànzhuō 〈书面〉〈谦词〉show my incompetence; show my poor skill: 现在我就当场~,以博诸君一笑。Now allow me to try to amuse you by showing my poor skill.

县(縣)

xiàn county; (Japan) prefecture: 密云~ Miyun County (of Beijing) /长崎~ Nagasaki prefecture (of Japan) /~政府 county government /~委 county Party committee

县城 xiànchéng county seat; county town

县份 xiànfèn (never used with proper noun) county: 西部偏远~,这几年也有了很大变化。Great changes have taken place also in the remote western counties.

县令 xiànlìng *also* "县官"〈旧语〉county magistrate: 晚清时,他祖父当过~。His grandfather served as a county magistrate towards the end of the Qing Dynasty.

县太爷 xiàntàiyé 〈旧语〉popular term for county magistrate

县长 xiànzhǎng head of a county; county magistrate

县知事 xiànzhīshì ❶ (used in early Republican days) magistrate of a county ❷ (Japan) prefect

县志 xiànzhì general history of a county; county annals or records: 编写~ compile the history of a county /据~所记 according to the county annals

县治 xiànzhì 〈旧语〉county seat: 这个镇子有几千户人家,乃是~所在。The town, with its thousands of households, serves as the county seat.

粯

xiàn 〈书面〉broken rice

粯子 xiànzi 〈方言〉wholewheat; wholemeal

X

现(❺见) xiàn ❶ present; present-day; current; existing: ～况 present (*or* current) state of affairs /临安即～杭州。Lin An is present-day Hangzhou. /～派李同志前往你处学习取经。We are sending Comrade Li along to learn from your valuable experiences. /本餐厅～聘请广东名厨为顾客献艺。This restaurant has engaged famous chefs from Guangdong to cook for our customers. ❷ as the occasion arises; impromptu; extempore: ～宰的大活鱼 big live fish that has just been killed (for the occasion) /小时候没上过学,这点文化是在工作中～学的。I missed school when I was young. What little I know about reading and writing has been picked up on the job. /既然你们坚持要我唱,我就～编～唱吧。Since you insist, I'll improvise a song and sing it. ❸ on hand; ready; available: *see* "～货"; "～钞" ❹ cash; ready money: 付～ pay cash /兑～ pay cash on a check (*or* for a purchase); cash a check /贴～ (pay a) discount on the rate of exchange, etc. ❺ show; reveal; appear: 他终于～了原形。He showed his true colours at last. /她脸上～出傲慢的神情。A haughty expression appeared on her face.

现案 xiàn'àn (in contrast with 积案) current or active case: 这些时候局里忙,有几桩～急着要办。These days, we have been busy with several urgent cases in the bureau.

现报 xiànbào *see* "现世报"

现场 xiànchǎng ❶ scene (of an accident or crime): 勘验～ inspect the scene of a crime (*or* accident) /保护～ keep the scene of the crime (*or* accident) intact /此人有不在～的证据。He has proof of his absence from the scene of the accident (*or* crime). *or* He has an alibi. ❷ site; spot: ～教学 on-the-spot teaching /～培训 on-the-job training; shop-floor training /～维修人员 field maintenance personnel /～抽查 spot check /进行～采访的记者有多位。A number of reporters were covering the news on the spot. /我们明天在工作～开个碰头会。We'll have a brief meeting on the worksite tomorrow.

现场办公 xiànchǎng bàngōng handle official business on the spot: 市领导曾几次上门～,当场拍板帮助解决问题。The leaders of the municipality have been to the worksite several times and helped solve problems by making relevant decisions right on the spot.

现场会 xiànchǎnghuì on-the-spot meeting; on-site meeting

现场图 xiànchǎngtú sketch or picture of the scene of a crime or accident

现场直播 xiànchǎng zhíbō live broadcast; live

现钞 xiànchāo cash

现炒现卖 xiànchǎo-xiànmài sell what one has just made ready; use what one has just learned

现成 xiànchéng ready-made: 等～儿的 expect to have sth. without working for it /穿的吃的,现如今都有～儿的可买。People are able to purchase ready-made clothes and food nowadays.

现成饭 xiànchéngfàn food ready for the table; unearned gain: 男人也应干家务活,不能专吃～。Men should also do household chores, and not expect just to eat food ready for the table. /凡事自己多动脑子,别总想吃～。Use your brains in all matters and never expect unearned gain.

现成话 xiànchénghuà onlooker's unsolicited (usu. general and useless) remarks; kibitzer's comments: ～谁不会说? Who on earth is not able to give a kibitzer's comments? *or* How easy it is to peddle truisms! /你光会说～,有本事你来试试! You are good at kibitzing all right. Why don't you have a go at it for a change if you are really capable?

现丑 xiànchǒu make a fool of oneself; make an exhibition of oneself; bring shame on oneself: 当众～ make an exhibition of oneself in public /你这不是成心让我～吗? Aren't you trying to make a fool of me by this?

现存 xiàncún extant; on hand; in stock: 清点～设备物资。Make an inventory of the equipment and materials in stock. /这是～的原版本。This is the extant original edition.

现大洋 xiàndàyáng 〈口语〉 silver dollar

现代 xiàndài ❶ modern times; contemporary age: 从古代直至～ from the ancient times up to the contemporary age /在中国历史上,"～"多指五四运动到现在的时期。In Chinese historiography, "the modern times" usually refer to the period from the May Fourth Movement of 1919 to the present. ❷ modern; present-day; contemporary: ～交通工具和通讯手段 modern means of transport and communication /～新闻工具 modern information media /～作家 contemporary writer /～教育 modern education /～文学 present-day literature /～语言 modern language /～韵律体操 modern rhythmic gymnastics

现代化 xiàndàihuà modernize: 四个～ four modernizations (of agriculture, industry, national defence, and science and technology) /～管理 modern management /～办公设备 modernized office equipment; sophisticated office equipment

现代集团 Xiàndài Jítuán (ROK) Hyundai Group

现代派 xiàndàipài modernist (school); avant-garde

现代史 xiàndàishǐ modern history

现代舞 xiàndàiwǔ modern dance

现代戏 xiàndàixì modern opera; modern drama: 京剧～ Beijing opera on modern themes; modern Beijing opera /～剧目 repertoire of modern drama (*or* opera)

现代修正主义 xiàndài xiūzhèngzhǔyì modern revisionism

现代艺术 xiàndài yìshù modern art

现代主义 xiàndàizhǔyì modernism: ～作家 modernist writer /～作品 modernist work

现地 xiàndì 〈军事〉 site; terrain: ～备课 prepare a lesson on the site

现地勘察 xiàndì kānchá terrain survey

现地作业 xiàndì zuòyè terrain exercise

现而今 xiàn'érjīn 〈方言〉 nowadays; these days: ～年轻人都变了。Nowadays, youngsters are different. /～咱们农民日子好过多了。We farmers are much better off these days.

现饭 xiànfàn 〈方言〉 leftover rice; leftovers: 吃～ eat leftovers /炒～ heat leftover rice

现话 xiànhuà 〈方言〉 same old story; old hat: 长达两小时的报告毫无新意,尽是～。The lecture which lasted two hours offered nothing new; it was just a rehash of clichés.

现汇 xiànhuì spot exchange: ～汇率 spot exchange rate /～市场 spot exchange market

现汇结算 xiànhuì jiésuàn cash settlement

现货 xiànhuò 〈商业〉 merchandise or stock on hand; spot commodity; spots: ～价格 spot price /～交易 spot transaction; over-the-counter trading /～市场 spot market /～交易掮客 spot broker /买进一百包～棉花 purchase one hundred bales of spot cotton

现浇 xiànjiāo 〈建筑〉 cast-in-place; cast-in-situ: ～混凝土结构 cast-in-place (*or* cast-in-situ) concrete structure

现今 xiànjīn nowadays; at present; these days: ～世道大变了。The manners and morals of these days have greatly changed. /～年轻人审美观念与我们当年大不相同。Young people nowadays have a very different concept of beauty (*or* aesthetic concept) from what we had when we were young.

现金 xiànjīn ❶ ready money; cash: ～柜 cash box /～折扣 cash discount /～支付 payment in cash; cash payment /～回笼 cause banknotes to return to the bank of issue /～交易 cash transaction ❷ cash reserve in a bank: 库存～ cash holdings; cash in treasury

现金出纳机 xiànjīn chūnàjī *also* "现金进出记录机" cash register

现金流量 xiànjīn liúliàng cash flow: ～表 cash flow statement

现金收支表 xiànjīn shōuzhībiǎo 〈会计〉 receipts and payments account

现金账 xiànjīnzhàng cash account; cash book: 总经理要看一下～。The president wants to have a look at the cash book.

现局 xiànjú present situation; current state of affairs: ～动乱,人心不稳。The present turbulent situation has made the people jittery.

现刻 xiànkè 〈方言〉 right now; at the present moment; for the time being: 这东西～还存在他手里。It is still in his hands right now. /～是什么时候了? What time is it now?

现款 xiànkuǎn ready money; cash: 支付～ pay cash; cash down /应付～ should be paid in cash; cash due /收到～三十元 receive thirty *yuan* in cash

现蕾 xiànlěi 〈农业〉 bud: 棉花～期 squaring stage (*or* period) of the cotton plant /今年天冷,果树到现在还未～。Due to the cold weather this year, the fruit trees are not yet in bud.

现露 xiànlù show; reveal; come into view: 远处的村落模糊地～在眼前。The dim outline of a distant village came into view.

现年 xiànnián present age: 他～二十五岁。He is now twenty-five years old.

现期 xiànqī current: ～成本 current cost

现钱 xiànqián 〈口语〉 ready money; cash: 本店概不赊账,只收～。This shop doesn't give credit; only cash is accepted.

现任 xiànrèn ❶ hold the office of: 他～工会副主席。He is vice-

chairman of the trade union. ❷ currently in office; present; incumbent:～校长原来是英文教师。The present headmaster used to be a teacher of English.

现如今 xiànrújīn 〈方言〉 nowadays; at present; now:～他是县委书记。He is now secretary of the county Party committee.

现身说法 xiànshēn-shuōfǎ draw a moral from one's own experience; use one's own experience as an object lesson:报告人～,非常生动,引起了大家的感情共鸣。Using his own experience as an example, the speaker made his speech very vivid and drew a sympathetic response from the audience.

现时 xiànshí now; nowadays; at present:～旗袍又走俏,颇受中年女性的青睐。*Qipao* or cheongsam, a close-fitting woman's dress with a high neck and slit skirt, is in fashion again, especially among women in their 30's or 40's.

现实 xiànshí ❶ reality; actuality:逃避～ escape from reality /面对～ face the facts; be realistic /客观～ objective reality /理想变成了～,昔日的荒山秃岭如今已是绿树成林了。Our dream has come true: the once-barren hills and mountains have now turned into a green forest. ❷ real; realistic; factual; actual:～政治 politics as it is; actual politics; realpolitik /双方采取～、克制的态度,将有利于问题的解决。If both sides adopt a realistic, restrained attitude, it will facilitate the solution of the problem.

现实主义 xiànshízhǔyì *also* "写实主义" xiěshízhǔyì realism:～文学 realistic literature /批判～ critical realism /～者 realist

现世 xiànshì ❶ this life; this world:～与彼世〈宗教〉this life and the other life; this world and the other world ❷ lose face; be disgraceful; be discredited; bring shame on oneself:活～ living disgrace; very picture of disgrace /丢人～ lose face; be disgraced

现世报 xiànshìbào retribution in this life; timely punishment (for past wrongdoing, etc.);〈迷信〉temporal punishment

现世主义 xiànshìzhǔyì *also* "世俗主义" shìsúzhǔyì secularism

现势 xiànshì present or current situation:政局不定,～难料。The present situation is unpredictable due to political instability.

现下 xiànxià 〈口语〉right now; at present:～有些企业缺少资金和技术。At present, some enterprises are short of funding and technology.

现…现… xiàn…xiàn… (现 is sometimes pronounced as 旋 xuàn) (do sth.) as the need arises; extemporize:现想现说 speak extempore /现挣现吃 live from hand to mouth /现买现卖 *also* "现趸现卖" sell sth. immediately after it is bought

现象 xiànxiàng appearance (of things); phenomenon:暂时～ something transient; transient phenomenon /透过～看实质 grasp the essence through the appearance /种种不良～,应该引起我们的重视。All such unhealthy phenomena should engage our attention.

现象学 xiǎnxiàngxué phenomenology

现象主义 xiǎnxiàngzhǔyì phenomenalism

现行 xiànxíng ❶ currently in effect; in force; in operation:～价格 current price /～体制 present system (*or* regime) /～规章制度 rules and regulations in force /～规则 standing rules ❷ (of a criminal) active:～犯罪活动 active criminal offence

现行重置成本 xiànxíng chóngzhì chéngběn 〈经济〉current replacement cost (CRC)

现行法 xiànxíngfǎ law in effect

现行犯 xiànxíngfàn 〈法律〉criminal caught in, before or immediately after the act; active criminal

现形 xiànxíng reveal one's true nature or form; show one's true colours; betray oneself:《官场～记》*Officials Revealing Their True Features* (a popular satirical novel published at the end of the Qing Dynasty) /白蛇精酒醉后现了形。The drunken White Serpent revealed her true form.

现眼 xiànyǎn 〈方言〉make a spectacle or fool of oneself; be disgraced:好啦,别在大伙儿面前～啦! Enough! Don't make a fool of yourself in front of everyone.

现洋 xiànyáng *also* "现大洋" silver dollar

现役 xiànyì active service; active duty:～与后备役军官 officers on the active and reserve lists /服～ be on active service /儿子去年入伍,服完～就二十四、五了。My son enlisted last year and will be 24 or so when he completes his term of service.

现役军人 xiànyì jūnrén member of the armed forces in active service; serviceman:～与后备军人 serviceman and reservists

现役劳动军 xiànyì láodòngjūn 〈经济〉present labour force; active labour force

现银 xiànyín 〈旧语〉silver dollar

现有 xiànyǒu available; existing; on hand:～人力 available manpower /～建筑材料 building materials on hand /～设备 existing equipment

现在 xiànzài now; at present; today; for the time being:到～为止 up to now; up to the present /从～开始 from now on /我～不需要这本字典。I don't need the dictionary for the time being. /～这种时候还搞迷信,真是太愚蠢了。It's silly to be superstitious in this day and age. /～的情况已经够糟的了。The situation is bad enough as it is.

现职 xiànzhí present job; current post or position:～官员 official currently in office; incumbent official /胜任～工作 be competent for one's present job (*or* post)

现状 xiànzhuàng current situation; status quo; present state of affairs:恢复～ restore the status quo /打破～ break (*or* upset) the status quo /我们想对这个问题的历史和～进行研究。We want to study both the past and the present of this problem. /青年人不要安于～,要有敢于创新的进取心。Instead of being contented with things as they are, young people should have an enterprising spirit and dare to do new things.

苋

xiàn 〈植物〉amaranth

苋菜 xiàncài three-coloured amaranth (*Amaranthus tricolor*)

晛

xiàn 〈书面〉appearance of the sun; sunrise

岘

xiàn

岘港 Xiàngǎng Da Nang, port and city in central Viet Nam (used as a major US military base in the Viet Nam war)

锓

xiàn metal wire:漆包～ enamel-isulated wire /裸～ bare (metal) wire

腺

xiàn 〈解剖〉gland; aden:汗～ perspiratory (*or* sweat) gland /泪～ lachrymal (*or* tear) gland /唾～ salivary gland /甲状～ thyroid (gland) /淋巴～ lymphatic gland /肾上～ adrenal gland /前列～ prostate (gland) /小～ glandule /～热 glandular fever

腺癌 xiàn'ái 〈医学〉adenocarcinoma

腺病 xiànbìng 〈医学〉andenopathy:～毒 adenovirus

腺垂体 xiànchuítǐ 〈生理〉adenohypophysis

腺肌瘤 xiànjīliú 〈医学〉adenomyoma

腺淋巴瘤 xiànlínbāliú 〈医学〉adenolymphoma

腺瘤 xiànliú 〈医学〉adenoma

腺囊肿 xiànnángzhǒng 〈医学〉adenocele

腺嘌呤 xiànpiàolìng 〈药学〉adenine

腺体 xiàntǐ gland; aden

腺细胞 xiànxìbāo 〈生理〉glandcell

腺炎 xiànyán 〈医学〉adenitis

腺疫 xiànyì strangles (of horses)

腺脂瘤 xiànzhīliú 〈医学〉adenolipoma

腺周炎 xiànzhōuyán 〈医学〉periadenitis

线

xiàn ❶ *see* "线" xiàn ❷ (Xiàn) a surname

馅

xiàn filling; stuffing:羊肉～儿 mutton filling (*or* stuffing) /饺子～儿 stuffing for *jiaozi* (*or* dumplings) /菜～儿包子 steamed bun with vegetable stuffing /什锦～儿 mixed stuffing /三鲜～儿 filling with three delicious ingredients

馅儿饼 xiànrbǐng meat pie

馅子 xiànzi 〈方言〉❶ stuffing; filling:拌～ prepare filling (*or* stuffing) ❷ sth. hidden inside; catch:我听出他这句话里有～,只拿眼睛瞪了他一下。Sensing a catch in his words, I gave him a stare.

陷

xiàn ❶ pitfall; snare; trap:设～ lay a trap ❷ get stuck or bogged down; sink into:她一只脚～进了泥里。She got one foot stuck in the mud. /汽车在雪地里越～越深。The car sank deeper and deeper in the snow. /上任以来,他～进事务堆里,忙得不可开交。He has been bogged down in everyday routine since he took office. *or* He has been up to his neck with everyday routine since he came into office. /你这样作只能使自己～于孤立。You are only isolating yourself by doing this. ❸ sink; cave in:塌～ cave in; collapse /一夜未睡,她的眼睛～进去了。Her eyes were sunken after a sleepless night. /路基开

始下～了。The road bed began to sink (*or* cave in). ❹ frame (up); set up:诬～ make a false charge (against sb.); frame (sb.) ❺ (of a town, etc.) be captured; be taken; fall:攻～ capture; take by storm /失～ (of cities, territory, etc.) fall into enemy hands ❻ defect; flaw; deficiency:缺～ deficiency; flaw; shortcoming

陷波电路 xiànbō diànlù 〈电子〉 trap; trap circuit; wave trap

陷波滤波器 xiànbō lǜbōqì 〈电子〉 notch filter; notching filter

陷波器 xiànbōqì 〈电子〉 wave trap; trap

陷害 xiànhài frame (up); set up; make a false charge against:政治～ political frame-up /遭人～ be framed /他声称有人阴谋～他。He asserted that he had been set up.

陷阱 xiànjǐng pitfall; trap; snare:落入～ fall into a trap /他身陷仇家设下的～,命在旦夕。His life is hanging by a thread, as he has fallen into the snare laid by his enemy.

陷坑 xiànkēng pitfall; pit:在野兽出没的山道上挖了几个～。Some pits were dug in the mountain path frequented by wild animals.

陷落 xiànluò ❶ subside; sink; cave in:地基已～三英寸。The foundations have sunk three inches. /由于地壳～,这里出现了盆地。The basin here came into being through the subsidence of the earth's crust. ❷ sink into; land (oneself) in; be caught in:她害怕自己会～在同样的境地里。She was afraid that she would land herself in the same predicament. ❸ (of territory) fall (into enemy hands); be captured (by the enemy):～敌手 fall into enemy hands /该城不幸于昨天～。The city unfortunately fell yesterday.

陷落地震 xiànluò dìzhèn depression earthquake

陷没 xiànmò ❶ sink; be submerged; be lost:～在淤泥里 be submerged in the sludge; get caught in the silt /他～在沉思中。He is lost in deep thought. ❷ (of territory) fall (into enemy hands); be captured (by the enemy)

陷溺 xiànnì 〈书面〉 ❶ be submerged; be drowned:疏通河道,使百姓无～之患 dredge river courses so that the people will not worry about floods ❷ be lost; be immersed:他～在个人的哀愁里。He is lost in his personal sorrows.

陷入 xiànrù ❶ sink into; land (oneself) in; come to; get bogged down in:～绝境 land in a desperate predicament; be up a gum tree; find oneself (*or* be) at bay /～混乱状态 get into a mess /～危险 fall into danger /～法网 be caught in the meshes of the law /～魔掌 fall into the devil's hands; find oneself at the mercy of the devil ❷ be immersed in; be lost in; be deep in:～对往事的追忆 be immersed in reveries of the past /～苦闷 be in a state of depression /～绝望 sink into despair

陷入僵局 xiànrù jiāngjú come to a deadlock; land in an impasse; end in a stalemate:谈判～。The talks are deadlocked.

陷身 xiànshēn land oneself in; be caught in; get bogged down in:～泥潭 be bogged down in the mire

陷身囹圄 xiànshēn-língyǔ find oneself in prison; be put in jail

陷型模 xiànxíngmú *also* "冲模" chòngmú 〈机械〉 swage

陷于 xiànyú sink into; fall into; be bogged down in:～瘫痪 be paralyzed (*or* stymied); be at a standstill /～孤立 find oneself isolated /～被动 fall into a passive position; be put on the defensive

陷阵 xiànzhèn break into enemy ranks:冲锋～ charge on the enemy and break into enemy ranks; make a frontal attack /～杀敌 assault the enemy by breaking into his ranks

限

xiàn ❶ limits; bounds; confines:界～ demarcation line; boundary; bounds /权～ limits of one's authority; terms of reference; jurisdiction /期～ time limit /以 1997 年 6 月为～ with June, 1997 as the deadline /以财政问题为～ be confined to financial questions ❷ restrict; limit; prescribe; allow:厂房改建工程～三个月完成。Three months are allowed for the reconstruction of the factory buildings. /春运期间,每人～购两张火车票。During the busy Spring Festival period, each customer is limited to two train tickets. /有些规定～得太死。Some rules and regulations are too rigid. ❸ 〈书面〉 threshold:门～ threshold

限定 xiàndìng prescribe or set a limit to; limit; confine; restrict:在～的时间内 within the prescribed time (limit) /讨论的范围不作～。There is no restriction on the scope of discussion.

限产 xiànchǎn cut or limit production:～压库促销 cut production and stockpile and promote marketing

限度 xiàndù limit; limitation:超出正常的～ overstep the normal limit /最大～地发挥有利因素 exploit one's advantages to the full /把差错降低到最低～ reduce errors to a minimum /做什么事情都得有一个～。There is a limit to everything.

限额 xiàn'é norm; limit; quota:超过～ exceed the norm (*or* quota) /达到～ reach the full quota /货币～ currency restrictions /移民～ immigration quota /最高～ maximum limit; ceiling /最低～ minimum limit; floor

限幅 xiànfú 〈电子〉 limiting; clipping:～电子管 limiter valve /～信号 limited signal

限幅器 xiànfúqì 〈无线电〉 limiter; peak limiter; amplitude limiter:接收机～ receiver limiter

限价 xiànjià set or prescribe a price:采取统一调拨、～供给的办法 adopt the method of unified allocation and supply at set prices /规定商品的最高、最低～ set the ceiling and floor prices for a commodity

限界 xiànjiè limits; bounds; boundary:浅水区以浮在水面的浮标为～。The buoys floating on the water indicate the bounds of shallow water.

限量 xiànliàng ❶ limit the quantity; set the bounds:～供应 limit the quantity of supply; supply in limited quantities /令郎天资聪颖,前途不可～。Your son is so gifted that he has boundless (*or* unlimited) prospects. ❷ *see* "限度"

限令 xiànlìng ❶ order sb. to do sth. within a time limit:～二十四小时内离境 order sb. to leave the country within twenty-four hours; give sb. 24 hours' notice to leave the country /～三日内拆除违章建筑。A three-day limit is set for the demolition of the illegal buildings. ❷ orders to be executed within a time limit:放宽～ extend the time limit (*or* deadline)

限流继电器 xiànliú jìdiànqì 〈电工〉 current limit relay

限流器 xiànliúqì 〈电工〉 current limiter

限期 xiànqī ❶ set a definite time limit; prescribe or set a deadline:～报到 report for duty (*or* register) by the specified time /～离境 order sb. to leave the country within a time limit /双方～撤退,脱离接触。The two sides are to withdraw within a prescribed (*or* stated) time so as to disengage from each other. ❷ time limit; deadline:～一过,我们将不得不赔偿对方损失。When the deadline is over, we'll have to compensate for the loss of the other side. /延长～恐怕他也完不成这项任务。I'm afraid he won't be able to finish the task even if he is given more time.

限速 xiànsù speed limit:～每小时八十公里 speed limit of eighty kilometres per hour

限位 xiànwèi 〈机械〉 spacing:～套筒 spacing collar /～开关 〈电工〉 limit switch

限性遗传 xiànxìng yíchuán 〈生物〉 one-sided inheritance; sex-limited inheritance

限于 xiànyú be confined to; be restricted to; be limited to:～时间 as time is limited; owing to the limitation of time; for lack of time /～个人水平,书中错误一定不少,敬请读者指正。Due to my limited knowledge, there are bound to be mistakes in the book and I humbly request the readers' corrections. /此次讨论只～一些理论问题。The discussion was confined only to some theoretical problems. /此次申请只～本院教职工。This time, only staff members of the college can apply.

限止 xiànzhǐ limit; restriction:入选的人员和作品没有～。There is no limit on the number of people and works to be included.

限制 xiànzhì restrict; confine; limit:时速～ speed limit /年龄～ age limit /～对外贸易 impose restrictions on foreign trade /由于篇幅的～ owing to the limitation of space (*or* limited space) /他的行动受到严格～。His actions were severely restricted. /晚年,由于身体状况的～,他已很少动笔。Handicapped by poor health, he seldom took up the pen in old age.

限制器 xiànzhìqì limiter

限制性 xiànzhìxìng restricted; restrictive:～措施 restrictive measures / ～契约 restrictive covenant (in negotiation)

限制性从句 xiànzhìxìng cóngjù 〈语言〉 restrictive clause

限制性定语 xiànzhìxìng dìngyǔ 〈语言〉 restrictive attribute

限制性内切酶 xiànzhìxìng nèiqiēméi 〈生化〉 restriction enzyme

限制战略武器会谈 xiànzhì zhànlüè wǔqì huìtán strategic arms limitation talks (SALT)

线(綫)

xiàn ❶ thread; string; wire:棉～ cotton thread /毛～ knitting wool /～衣裤 cotton knitwear /～手套 knit cotton gloves /针～包 sewing kit /地～ ground (*or* earth) wire /天～ aerial; antenna /热～ hot line /输电～ transmission line /导～ lead; conducting wire ❷ 〈数学〉 line:直～ straight line /曲～ curve /垂～

perpendicular line; vertical line /平行～ parallel lines ❸ sth. shaped like a line or thread; ray:视～ line of vision; view /光～ ray /X光～ X-ray /放射～ radioactive ray /宇宙～ cosmic ray ❹ route; line:路～ route /公共汽车～ bus route /干～ main line /支～ branch line /航～ air line /补给～ line of supply /京广～ Beijing-Guangzhou Railway (line) ❺ (political) line:上纲上～ raise to a higher plane of principle and political line ❻ demarcation line; dividing line; boundary:分水～ watershed /海岸～ coastal line /国界～ demarcation line between two countries /防火～ fire line ❼ brink; verge; line:生命～ life line /贫困～ poverty line /在死亡～上挣扎 struggle on the verge of death ❽ clue; lead; thread:眼～ informer; spy /没想到案子的～儿断了。Unexpectedly, the clue was lost in the case. ❾〈量词〉*used after* 一 *to indicate a tiny amount*:一～光明 a gleam of light /一～生路 a slim chance of life /一～希望 a ray of hope

线板 xiànbǎn board around which thread is wound; thread-wound board:接～ socket board

线飑 xiànbiāo 〈气象〉line squall

线材 xiàncái 〈冶金〉wire rod:～滚轧机 looping mill /～坯 wire bars /～轧机 rod-rolling mill; wire mill

线虫 xiànchóng nematode

线虫病 xiànchóngbìng nematodiasis

线春 xiànchūn *also*"春绸" chūnchóu (famous product of Hangzhou, Zhejiang Province) silk fabric with a geometric design (usu. for spring wear)

线电压 xiàndiànyā *also*"线间电压" line voltage

线锭 xiàndìng ❶〈纺织〉spindle for thread ❷〈冶金〉wire-bar

线段 xiànduàn 〈数学〉line segment

线桄子 xiànguàngzi *also*"线桄儿"〈纺织〉reel for thread; bobbin

线规 xiànguī 〈机械〉wire gauge

线画 xiànhuà line drawing

线积分 xiànjīfēn 〈数学〉line integral

线间 xiànjiān 〈音乐〉space

线脚 xiànjiǎo 〈方言〉stitches (in sewing):～很密 close stitches /看～手工不错。Judging by the stitches, it is good handwork.

线粒体 xiànlìtǐ 〈生物〉mitochondrion; chondriosome:～基因 chondriogene

线路 xiànlù line; route; circuit:电话～ telephone line /公共汽车～ bus line (*or* route) /地铁～ subway line /～变压器 line transformer /～容量 circuit capacity /～通过能力 rail capacity

线路放大器 xiànlù fàngdàqì line amplifier

线路工 xiànlùgōng wireman; lineman

线路图 xiànlùtú circuit diagram;〈无线电〉plan or scheme of wiring

线路租费 xiànlù zūfèi line rental

线麻 xiànmá hemp

线描 xiànmiáo line drawing

线呢 xiànní cotton suitings

线膨胀 xiànpéngzhàng 〈物理〉linear expansion

线坯子 xiànpīzi coarse cotton yarn; semi-finished cotton thread

线圈 xiànquān coil:初级～ primary coil /～架 bobbin /～天线 coil antenna

X

线绕电位器 xiànrào diànwèiqì 〈电工〉wire-wound potentiometer

线人 xiànrén inner connection; informer; spy

线上项目 xiànshàng xiàngmù〈经济〉above-the-line item; above-the-line

线绳 xiànshéng cotton rope

线速度 xiànsùdù 〈物理〉linear velocity

线穗子 xiànsuìzi spindle (of yarn)

线索 xiànsuǒ clue; lead; thread:为破案提供了重要～ supply (*or* provide) an important clue for solving the case /故事的～有两条,一明一暗。The story has got two threads, one obvious, one hidden.

线毯 xiàntǎn cotton blanket

线膛 xiàntáng rifled bore:～炮 cannon with a rifled bore

线条 xiàntiáo ❶〈美术〉line:用～和色彩描写生命 translate life into line and colour /整幅画～粗犷,风格古朴。The picture is drawn in bold lines and a simple, unsophisticated style. ❷ lines; figure; outline:奔马造型奇特,～优美。The galloping horse (statue) is cast in an extraordinary mold and has graceful lines. /这位姑娘～不错,个头也合适。The girl has a good figure and suitable height.

线头 xiàntóu ❶ end of a thread:针眼太细,把～捻捻才穿得过去。The eye of the needle is so small that you have to twist the end of the thread to put it through. ❷ *also*"线头子" odd piece of thread:把两根～接在一起 tie (*or* join) two pieces of thread together

线下项目 xiànxià xiàngmù 〈经济〉below-the-line item; below-the-line

线香 xiànxiāng slender stick of incense

线心 xiànxīn 〈电工〉wire core:～线圈 wire-core coil

线形 xiànxíng linear

线形动物 xiànxíng dòngwù *also*"圆形动物" yuánxíng dòngwù round worm

线形叶 xiànxíngyè 〈植物〉linear leaf

线性 xiànxìng 〈数学〉linear:～代数 linear algebra /～组合 linear combination /～不等式组 linear inequations /～集成电路 linear integrated circuit

线性电动机 xiànxìng diàndòngjī linear motor

线性电容器 xiànxìng diànróngqì straight-line capacitor

线性方程 xiànxìng fāngchéng *also* "一次方程" yīcì fāngchéng linear equation

线性规划 xiànxìng guīhuà linear programming

线性函数 xiànxìng hánshù 〈数学〉linear function

线性控制 xiànxìng kòngzhì 〈电子〉linear control; linearity control; distribution control:～系统 linear control system

线衣 xiànyī cotton knitwear; cotton-knit sweater

线影法 xiànyǐngfǎ hatching

线闸 xiànzhá cable brake (of a bicycle); calipers brake

线胀系数 xiànzhàng xìshù coefficient of linear expansion

线轴儿 xiànzhóur reel (of thread); spool (of thread); bobbin

线装 xiànzhuāng traditional thread binding (of Chinese books):～本 thread-bound edition /～书 thread-bound Chinese book

线子 xiànzi 〈方言〉❶ cotton yarn:姑娘纺出来的～又细又牢。The cotton yarn spun by the girl is both thin and sturdy. ❷ spy; enemy agent:昨夜抓了一个～。An enemy agent was caught last night.

xiāng

襄 xiāng ❶〈书面〉assist; aid; help:～办 help manage; act as assistant or deputy /共～大事 join in a common effort to promote a great undertaking ❷ (Xiāng) a surname

襄礼 xiānglǐ *also*"相礼" xiānglǐ ❶ help in presiding over a wedding, funeral, etc. ❷ assistant to a Master of Ceremonies

襄理 xiānglǐ (used in banks, enterprises, etc.) assistant manager:他父亲曾在银行里任～,后来改行教书。His father was an assistant manager of a bank before becoming a teacher.

襄赞 xiāngzàn 〈书面〉support; assist in; sponsor

襄助 xiāngzhù 〈书面〉assist; aid; help:鼎力～ (usu. in complimentary reference to sb. else's help) do one's best to help; spare no effort to help

瓖 xiāng *see*"镶" xiāng

镶 xiāng ❶ inlay; set; mount:金戒指上～了一颗绿宝石。The gold ring was inlaid with an emerald. *or* An emerald was mounted (*or* set) in the gold ring. ❷ rim; edge; border:～花边的晚礼服 evening dress edged with lace

镶板 xiāngbǎn 〈建筑〉panel

镶边 xiāngbiān rim; edge; border:烫金～的书 book with gilt edges

镶嵌 xiāngqiàn inlay; set; mount:～餐具 inlaid tableware /～细工 inlaid work; marquetry; mosaic /～金丝象牙宝塔 gold-inlaid ivory pagoda /～在银托上的钻石胸针 brooch of diamonds mounted in silver

镶嵌玻璃 xiāngqiàn bōli mosaic glass

镶嵌画 xiāngqiànhuà mosaic; tesselated picture or design

镶牙 xiāngyá put in a false tooth; insert an artificial tooth:满口～ have a full mouth (*or* set) of false teeth

骧 xiāng 〈书面〉❶ (of a horse) prance; gallop:万马齐～。Thousands of horses galloped together. ❷ raise (one's head); hold aloft:蛟龙～首。The dragon raised its head.

相[1] xiāng ❶ each other; one another; reciprocally; mutually:～争 argue or wrangle with each other /～抱而哭 weep in each other's arms /～与愕然 stare at each other astounded /～忍为

安。When you bear with each other you'll have peace. *or* Peace means live and let-live. ❷ *used to indicate an action one side does to the other*：好言～劝 offer well-meant advice /有事～告 have sth. to tell (sb.) /～较见长 gain by contrast (*or* comparison) ❸ (Xiāng) a surname

相[2] xiāng see and evaluate in person; choose for oneself or for sb. close to oneself：～女婿 take a look at a prospective son-in-law (to see if he is to one's liking) /这件上衣我根本～不中。This jacket is not at all to my liking.
see also xiàng

相爱 xiāng'ài love each other; be in love with each other：～日深 become increasingly affectionate to each other /想不到这两个人会～。Nobody would expect these two people to fall in love.

相安 xiāng'ān live in peace with each other：彼此～ get along in peace; be on good enough terms with each other

相安无事 xiāng'ān-wúshì coexist without trouble; live in peace with each other：婆媳俩虽算不上亲热，倒也～。The woman and her daughter-in-law, though not on intimate terms, lived in peace with each other.

相帮 xiāngbāng help; aid：有朋友～，这事才办成功。I managed to do this only with the help of friends.

相悖 xiāngbèi be at variance or odds with：她身上有许多和我的旧道德观念～的东西。There was so much about her that ran counter to my old moral standards.

相比 xiāngbǐ compare; contrast：～之下 compared with sb. (*or* sth.); in contrast with sb. (*or* sth.) /～之下方见其长 gain by contrast /这个篮球队可以跟世界上最好的篮球队～。This basketball team compares favourably with the best in the world.

相差 xiāngchà differ：～悬殊 widely different; poles apart /～无几 not very different; about the same /冬天的室内和室外温度～二十多度。In winter there is a difference of over twenty degrees between the indoor and outdoor temperatures. /我们所作的努力距离观众的期望～还很远。What we have done is still far below the expectations of the audience. *or* What we have done still falls far short of what the viewers expect of us.

相称 xiāngchèn match; suit; fit：家具的颜色和地板不～。The colour of the furniture does not match (*or* go well with) that of the floor. /这件衣服同你的年龄有点不～。This dress doesn't suit (*or* become) a person of your age very well. /你这种做法和你的身份很不～。Your way of doing it is not worthy of your status.

相称 xiāngchēng call each other：以兄弟～ address each other as brothers

相成 xiāngchéng complement (each other)

相承 xiāngchéng pass on; inherit：世代～ pass (*or* be handed down) from generation to generation /一脉～ come down in one continuous line; can be traced to the same origin

相持 xiāngchí confront each other with neither side yielding; be locked in a stalemate：隔江～ confront each other across the river /两人你一言我一语，～了半天，谁也不让谁。The two talked back and forth locked in a stalemate, as neither would give in.

相持不下 xiāngchí-bùxià neither side yields to the other; be locked in a stalemate：两队龙争虎斗，～。The two well-matched teams were locked in a drawn game.

相处 xiāngchǔ get along (with one another)：和睦～ live in peace and harmony (with each other); get along well /不易～ not easy to get along with; hard to get on with /～甚欢 get on famously (*or* brilliantly); hit it off /尽管我们～时间不长，但你的为人给我留下了深刻的印象。Though we have not been together long, I'm deeply impressed by the way you conduct yourself.

相传 xiāngchuán ❶ tradition or legend has it; long been current among the people：～这个故事发生在几百年前。Tradition has it that the story took place hundreds of years ago. ❷ hand down or pass on from one to another：世代～ hand down from generation to generation /一脉～ pass on in one continuous line

相待 xiāngdài treat：以礼～ treat sb. with courtesy (*or* due respect) /～似亲兄弟 treat sb. as one's own brother

相当 xiāngdāng ❶ match; balance; correspond to; be equal to：实力～ matched in power (*or* strength) /输赢～ the gains balance the losses; break even /年龄～ about the same age; well matched in age /美国的国会～于英国的议会。The US Congress corresponds to the British parliament. /运动员从～于一百多层楼高的悬崖上纵身跳入水中。The sportsman dived into the water from a steep cliff as high as a building of more than a hundred storeys. ❷ suitable; proper; fit; becoming：这项工作最好交给一个条件～的人。It is better to entrust the work to an appropriate person. /他当队长倒是很～。He is the right man to be the team leader. ❸ quite; fairly; rather：～冷 rather cold /～多的人 quite a lot of people /～数量的资金 considerable funds; fairly large amounts of money

相得 xiāngdé get on well (with each other); be on harmonious or friendly terms：他们几个在一处颇为～。They get on well with each other.

相得益彰 xiāngdé-yìzhāng each shines more brilliantly in the other's company; each improves by association with the other; each supplements and enriches the other：花卉盆景配上淡绿色的窗帘真是～，恰到好处。The light green curtain matches the potted flowers and miniature trees so well that they form a perfect picture.

相等 xiāngděng be equal：价值～ equal in value; of equal value /两间办公室面积～。The two offices are equal in floor space.

相抵 xiāngdǐ ❶ offset; balance; counterbalance：收支～ be balanced in expenditure and revenue; make both ends meet; break even /收支～，略有亏欠。The accounts show a slight deficit. ❷ conflict with each other; go against each other：大家看法不一，意见～，这是正常的现象。It is normal to have different viewpoints and conflicting opinions.

相对 xiāngduì ❶〈书面〉opposite; face to face：～无言 face each other in silence /～而泣 look into each other's eyes and weep; mingle (their) tears /两座大厦～矗立。The two skyscrapers stand opposite to each other. ❷ opposed to each other：针锋～ be diametrically opposed (to each other); stand in sharp opposition (to sb.); give tit for tat："大"和"小"、"好"和"坏"，这些意义～或相反的词，叫"反义词"。The words "big" and "small", "good" and "bad" oppose or are contrary to each other in meaning and are called antonyms. ❸ relative：～贫困化 relative pauperization /静止是～的，运动是绝对的。Stillness is relative, while motion is absolute. ❹ relatively; comparatively：～而言 relatively speaking; comparatively speaking /这个时期的物价～稳定。Prices are comparatively stable during this period.

相对电容率 xiāngduì diànrónglǜ 〈物理〉dielectric constant

相对多数选举制 xiāngduì duōshù xuǎnjǔzhì plurality system; first-past-the-post system

相对高度 xiāngduì gāodù 〈测绘〉relative altitude; relative height

相对孔径 xiāngduì kǒngjìng relative aperture

相对论 xiāngduìlùn 〈物理〉theory of relativity; relativity：广义～ general theory of relativity /狭义～ special (*or* restricted) theory of relativity /～力学 relativistic mechanics

相对论性 xiāngduìlùnxìng 〈物理〉relativistic：～量子理论 relativistic quantum theory /～电子 relativistic electron

相对湿度 xiāngduì shīdù 〈气象〉relative humidity

相对速度 xiāngduì sùdù 〈物理〉relative velocity

相对误差 xiāngduì wùchā 〈数学〉relative error

相对性 xiāngduìxìng relativity：认识的～ relativity of knowledge

相对运动 xiāngduì yùndòng 〈物理〉relative motion

相对真理 xiāngduì zhēnlǐ 〈哲学〉relative truth

相对值 xiāngduìzhí relative value

相对主义 xiāngduìzhǔyì 〈哲学〉relativism

相度 xiāngduó 〈书面〉observe and survey; observe and measure：～地形 survey the topography /～堤防 inspect and survey the dikes

相烦 xiāngfán 〈套语〉trouble you; bother you：有一事～。May I bother you for something? *or* May I ask you to do me a favour?

相反 xiāngfǎn ❶ opposite; opposed; contrary：～命题 contrary proposition /～的意见 opposite (*or* contrary) view /汽车朝～的方向急驰而去。The car sped off in the opposite direction. /除非有～的证据，不然他将判为有罪。He is going to be judged guilty unless there is evidence to the contrary. ❷ on the contrary; just the opposite：入秋以后，不仅未见天气凉爽，～，更显得炎热了。These was no sign of cool weather in the early autumn. On the contrary, it seemed even hotter.

相反相成 xiāngfǎn-xiāngchéng (of two things) be both opposite and complementary to each other; oppose and yet complement each other：在一定条件下，失败与成功是～。Under certain circumstances, success and failure are complementary to each other.

相仿 xiāngfǎng similar; more or less the same：颜色～ similar in colour; of about the same colour /能力～ more or less equal in ability

相逢 xiāngféng meet (by chance); run into; come across: 萍水~ meet by mere chance; strike up a chance acquaintance /异地~ meet in a strange land /弦语愿~,知有几否? The strings bespeak a happy meeting, but would it come true?

相符 xiāngfú conform to; agree with; correspond to: 与事实~ conform to the facts; tally with the facts /名实~,言行一致。As the name should conform to the reality, one's deeds should match one's words.

相辅而行 xiāngfǔ'érxíng complement each other; go together: 只有使批发和零售二者~,才能提高公司的销售额。Only when we coordinate both wholesale and retail business well, can we raise the total sales of the company.

相辅相成 xiāngfǔ-xiāngchéng supplement each other; complement each other: 解决人民内部矛盾时,行政命令和说服教育是~的两个方面。Administrative orders and education by persuasion complement each other in handling contradictions among the people.

相干 xiānggān ❶ (often used in negative or interrogative sentences) have to do with; be concerned with: 这件事与她毫不~。This has absolutely nothing to do with her. *or* This is no concern of hers. /这件事与我有何~? What have I to do with this? *or* What concern is it of mine? ❷〈物理〉coherent: ~效应 coherence effect /~散射 coherent scattering /~信号 coherent signal

相干性 xiānggānxìng 〈物理〉coherence

相告 xiānggào tell; inform: 请稍候,我有一事~。Please wait a minute. I have something to tell you. /如有消息,务望~。Do let me know if you have some information.

相隔 xiānggé be separated; be apart; be at a distance: 前后~不过数月,想不到有了这么大的变化。I was surprised to see that such great changes had taken place during an interval of only a few months. /我与他~不过两条街,却很少相见。I seldom see him, though we live only two blocks apart.

相跟 xiānggēn 〈方言〉follow; accompany: 我就~上张医生进城,把这批药买下了。Following Dr. Zhang to the town, I bought this lot of medicine. *or* I went to town in Dr. Zhang's company and bought this medicine.

相顾 xiānggù look at each other; face each other: ~失色 look at each other in dismay; stare at each other in terror /~无言,惟有泪千行。We looked at each other in silence and melted into tears.

相关 xiāngguān ❶ related; interrelated; concerned: ~资料 related data /~课程 related courses /~学科 allied disciplines; allied subjects /毫不~ have nothing to do (with sth. or sb.); be not related at all /战场上的形势与我们的讨论密切~。The military situation has a direct bearing on our discussion. ❷〈数学〉correlation: ~比 correlation ratio /~系数 correlation coefficient /~分析 correlation analysis /~计算 calculation of correlation /~图 correlation diagram; correlogram

相关检索 xiāngguān jiǎnsuǒ correlative indexing

相关群体 xiāngguān qúntǐ 〈信息〉reference group

相关资料 xiāngguān zīliào 〈信息〉relevance feedback

相好 xiānghǎo ❶ be friends; be on intimate terms: 他们几个十分~,俨然成了一个"帮"。They were very close to each other and behaved like a "gang". ❷ intimate friend; close friend: 生活中谁没有几个~? How could one get along in the world without having close friends? ❸ have an illicit love affair ❹ lover: 打从她的~远走他乡,她神经就有些不正常了。Ever since her lover went off to distant parts, she has been suffering from a certain mental disorder.

相互 xiānghù mutual; reciprocal; each other: ~为用 reinforce each other /~包庇 shelter each other; one hand washes the other /~尊敬 mutual respect; reciprocal respect /~威慑 mutual deterrence /~关系 interrelationship; mutual relations /~渗透 mutual infiltration /~学习 learn from each other /~抵消 offset (*or* cancel out) each other

相互参股 xiānghù cāngǔ purchase each other's shares

相互代词 xiānghù dàicí 〈语言〉reciprocal pronoun

相互依存 xiānghù yīcún interdependence

相会 xiānghuì meet each other; meet; rendezvous: 夫妻~ reunion of husband and wife /鹊桥~ reunion (of lovers or husband and wife) after a long separation /他们约好在公园~。They made an appointment to meet (*or* a rendezvous) in the park.

相继 xiāngjì in succession; one after another: ~发生 happen in succession /~去世 die one after another

相煎何急 xiāngjiān-héjí *also* "相煎太急" (of brothers) fight each other with mortal hatred: 同室操戈,~! Why should brothers draw swords and fight each other with such hatred! /本是同根生,相煎何太急! Oh why, since we sprang from the selfsame root, Should you kill me with anger hot?

相见 xiāngjiàn meet; see each other: ~无日 will not be able to meet again /他们已有好几年未~了。It was several years since they had last seen each other.

相见恨晚 xiāngjiàn-hènwǎn feel regret for not being able to meet sb. sooner or earlier: 二人情投意合,~。The two of them loved each other so deeply that they regretted not having met earlier.

相间 xiāngjiàn alternate with: 沿岸桃柳~。Peach trees alternate with willows all along the bank. *or* The bank is planted with alternating peach trees and willows.

相将 xiāngjiāng 〈书面〉❶ in each other's company; together: 两人~回国。The two returned to their country together. ❷ be going to; be about to: 明日此时,友人~远去,从此天各一方,音讯难通。By this time tomorrow, my friend will have left for a distant place, and we shall be far apart, hearing little from each other.

相交 xiāngjiāo ❶ cross; intersect: 两线~于一点。The two lines intersect at a point. /两条山路在半山腰~,由此西行,可直抵山顶。The two paths cross half way up the mountain and you can go directly to the summit by taking the westward path. ❷ be friends; make friends: 朋友~,赤诚相待。When making friends, people should treat each other with absolute sincerity. /我们是~多年的老朋友。We are old friends of many years standing.

相较 xiāngjiào compare: 两国~,经济实力相去不远。By comparison the two countries are more or less equal in economic strength.

相接 xiāngjiē connect; intersect: 两条公路在此点~。The two highways intersect at this point.

相近 xiāngjìn ❶ similar: 他们俩声音~。Their voices are similar. /夫妻俩性格~,都挺随和的。The couple are similar in character and are both easy of approach. ❷ close; close by; near: 两座院校地点~,中间只隔了百十来米。The two colleges are close to each other, only a hundred metres or so apart.

相敬如宾 xiāngjìng-rúbīn (of husband and wife) treat each other with respect due to a guest; be courteous to each other as to a guest: 情深爱笃,~ love each other dearly and treat each other with impeccable respect /老两口多年来~,从未红过脸。The old couple were always courteous to each other during their long years of married life and had never quarrelled.

相救 xiāngjiù come to sb.'s help; try to save sb.; rescue sb. from danger

相距 xiāngjù apart; at a distance of; away from: ~不过五十米 only about fifty metres apart (*or* away from each other) /~咫尺 be but a step to sth. (*or* each other); be close by

相看 xiāngkàn ❶ look at each other: 脉脉两~。The two looked at each other affectionately. /执手~泪眼。Hand in hand we look at each other with tears in our eyes. ❷ regard; treat: 另眼~ regard sb. with special consideration /这孩子托付你了,你要好生~。I'll entrust this child to your care. Please treat him well. ❸ (xiāngkan) look at and appraise (for marriage, etc.): 明天我把姑娘带来,您老人家好好~~。I'll bring the girl tomorrow so that you can have a good look at her in person. /也~过了,就等着男家下聘礼了。Both the boy and the girl were appraised (by each other's parents), and all that was left was for the boy's family to send betrothal presents.

相克 xiāngkè 〈迷信〉be ill-matched (in horoscope, etc.): 算命的说他俩的命~,不能成婚。The fortune-teller said that they were ill-matched in horoscope and couldn't marry.

相类 xiānglèi similar; alike: ~的事件 similar episode (*or* incident)

相礼 xiānglǐ *also* "襄礼" xiānglǐ ❶ help in presiding over a wed-ding, funeral, etc. ❷ assistant to a Master of Ceremonies

相连 xiānglián connected; joined; linked: 前后~ front and back being connected; (of an article, etc.) beginning and ending being coherent /山水~ be joined by common mountains and rivers /血肉~ be linked like flesh and blood /心心~ hearts beating in harmony /地道户户~,村村相通。Houses and even villages were linked up by tunnels.

相联 xiānglián 〈计算机〉associative: ~陈列处理机 associative array processor /~存储器 associative memory /~数据处理 associative data processing

相邻 xiānglín adjoin; border on: ~的两户人家 two adjoining families (*or* houses) /两国~,只隔着一条江。The two countries border on

each other, with only a river separating them.

相邻沿海国 xiānglín yánhǎiguó adjoining coastal state

相骂 xiāngmà call each other names; abuse each other; trade insults

相骂无好言,相打无好拳 xiāngmà wú hǎoyán, xiāngdǎ wú hǎoquán 〈俗语〉there are no nice words in quarrels and no weak blows in fights

相瞒 xiāngmán hide sth. from sb.:实不～ to tell you the truth / 好朋友无事～。Good friends hide nothing from each other.

相门户 xiāng ménhù (usu. of a boy or girl's parents) visit the family of the prospective in-laws:亲家后晌来～,老两口里里外外紧收拾。As prospective in-laws were coming to visit in the afternoon, the old couple were busy tidying the house inside out.

相能 xiāngnéng 〈书面〉(usu. used in the negative) get along; be on good terms:积不～ have never got along; have been at odds for a long time

相陪 xiāngpéi accompany; keep company; be a companion to:闲暇之时总有好书～。Good books are my faithful companions in my spare time. / 为另有约会,不～了。I'm afraid I must leave now, as I have another appointment.

相配 xiāngpèi be well matched (as in a marriage); match each other:一个太高,一个太矮,不～ not match each other, as one is too tall and the other too short / 他们两个很～。They are well matched.

相偏 xiāngpiān 〈方言〉〈套语〉have already had one's meal or tea

相扑 xiāngpū 〈体育〉❶ (ancient game of) wrestling ❷ Japanese sumo wrestling:～运动员 sumo wrestler; sumoist

相期 xiāngqī expect (of each other); look forward:～来年相见 expect to see each other next year

相契 xiāngqì 〈书面〉be in accord; be good friends:二人～有年。The two of them have been on friendly terms for years.

相强 xiāngqiǎng force; compel; impose:他既然不愿意去,我也不便于～。Since he didn't want to go, I could not very well impose upon him.

相切 xiāngqiē 〈数学〉be tangent to; touch; abut; contact

相亲 xiāngqīn (of a boy or girl) see and size up a prospective mate (usu. at an arranged meeting); (of parents) see and size up a prospective mate for one's boy or girl (usu. at an arranged meeting):择日～ set a date for meeting the prospective mate / 姑娘长得很俊,这几年断不了常有人来～。The girl was so beautiful that for the past few years people kept coming to her house to propose marriage.

相亲相爱 xiāngqīn-xiāng'ài be affectionate to each other; love each other:两口子～,和和美美。The couple lived in love and harmony.

相去 xiāngqù be apart; differ:～甚远 be poles apart; differ widely; fall far short (of expectations, requirements, etc.) / 两地～几十里。There is a distance of dozens of *li* between the two places. / 他们两家～不远。The two families are not far from each other.

相去无几 xiāngqù-wújǐ not differ much; be about the same:两家公司实力～,谁也兼并不了谁。The two companies are more or less equal in strength, and so neither can annex the other.

相劝 xiāngquàn try to bring round; offer advice:苦口～ try in every way to convince sb.; talk oneself hoarse trying to persuade sb. / 我这是好意～,听不听全在你。I'm only offering well-meaning advice and it's all up to you to take it or not.

相让 xiāngràng ❶ exercise forbearance; make concessions; give in:不肯～ would not make any concessions / 各不～。Neither would give in. ❷ defer politely; yield modestly:礼貌～ defer to each other politely; yield to each other modestly

相扰 xiāngrǎo ❶ disturb; interfere:各不～ neither side interfering with the other ❷〈套语〉trouble you; bother you:无事不敢～。Never would I dare to trouble you for nothing. *or* I wouldn't dare to trouble you if I did not have something important. / 有一事～。Excuse me, but I have something to bother you about.

相忍为国 xiāngrěn-wèiguó 〈书面〉show tolerance in the national interests; exercise forbearance for the sake of the nation; put up with hardships and humiliations for the sake of the country:此次谈判,凡事～,不可意气用事。During this negotiation, you should exercise forbearance for the national interests and must never be swayed by emotion.

相认 xiāngrèn ❶ be acquainted (with each other); know:我和他从来不～。I don't know him at all. *or* I've never known him. ❷ recognize; identify:六亲不～ would not even recognize one's kith and kin; deny one's kith and kin / 夫妻～ husband and wife identifying (*or* recognizing) each other (after a long separation)

相容 xiāngróng ❶ be compatible with each other; tolerate each other:这两种思想是水火不～的。These two ideas are as imcompatible as fire and water. ❷〈数学〉consistent:～方程 consistent equation

相濡以沫 xiāngrúyǐmò help and comfort each other in time of adversity or crisis:老夫妻生活虽然清贫,却能～,知足长乐。The old couple helped and comforted each other in their poverty, content with what they had.

相若 xiāngruò 〈书面〉similar; alike:两人年貌～。They are similar in age and looks.

相商 xiāngshāng consult:既有要事～,我们另找个地方坐下来谈。Since you have something important to discuss with me, let's find another place to sit down and talk.

相涉 xiāngshè have to do with; be concerned with:这两件事毫不～。These two events are not at all related to each other.

相生相克 xiāngshēng-xiāngkè each produces and is overcome by the other (said of the five elements, a concept held by the ancients to explain natural phenomena and later used in traditional Chinese medicine, etc.); promote and restrain each other:若以五行～之理论之,须是以水克火。On the principle of the five elements producing and overcoming each other we'll have to overcome "fire" with "water".

相识 xiāngshí ❶ be acquainted with each other:素不～ have never met; be not acquainted with each other / 似曾～ (sth. or sb.) seems familiar / 不打不～ no discord, no concord; friendship begins after a fight / 相逢何必曾～。Now that destiny has brought us together, it matters little that we have never met before. ❷ acquaintance:旧～ old friend; former acquaintance / 我们是多年老～了,何必这般客气。We have known each other for many years. What's the point of being so ceremonious?

相视 xiāngshì look at each other:～而笑 look at each other and smile; smile into each other's eyes / ～无言 look at each other in silence

相熟 xiāngshú 〈方言〉be acquainted:两人一天一天地～起来。The two men got more and more chummy with each other day by day.

相率 xiāngshuài one after another; in succession:杂技演员～登场献艺。The acrobats came on the stage one after another to perform.

相思 xiāngsī yearning between lovers; lovesickness:单～ one-sided love; unrequited love / ～入骨 be hopelessly lovesick; languish for (sb.'s) love / 两地～ lovers far apart yearning for (*or* missing) each other / 只愿君心似我心,定不负～意。If only your heart be like mine, My love for you will not be in vain.

相思病 xiāngsībìng lovesickness:这姑娘害上了～。The girl is lovesick.

相思鸟 xiāngsīniǎo red-billed leiothrix

相思子 xiāngsīzǐ 〈植物〉❶ jequirity bean; Indian liquorice; rosary pea ❷ *also* "红豆" hóngdòu ormosia seed; love pea

相似 xiāngsì resemble; parallel; be similar; be alike:外表与性格都～ be similar both in appearance and character; resemble each other in both appearance and character / 两人十分～。The two are as like as two peas. / 何其～乃尔! What a striking similarity (*or* resemblance)! / 他的经历多与你～。His experiences parallel yours in many ways. / 与此～的例子很多,在此不一一列举。Similar examples are too numerous to mention here one by one.

相似三角形 xiāngsì sānjiǎoxíng 〈数学〉similar triangles

相似系数 xiāngsì xìshù 〈数学〉similarity coefficient

相似形 xiāngsìxíng 〈数学〉similar figures

相送 xiāngsòng see out; see part of the way:客人走时,起身～ get up when the guest is leaving and see him (*or* her) out

相随 xiāngsuí follow at sb.'s heels; follow; accompany:执手～ follow sb. by holding his (*or* her) hand; go hand in hand with sb. / 他们～着老师进了书店。They followed their teacher into the bookstore.

相提并论 xiāngtí-bìnglùn (often used in the negative) mention in the same breath; group together; place on a par:不能～ cannot be mentioned in the same breath; cannot be placed on a par / 怎能不顾它们的本质区别,笼统地～? How can one overlook their essential differences and lump them together?

相通 xiāngtōng communicate with each other; be connected or linked:～的房间 communicating rooms / 两家的院子～,只隔着一道柴

门。The courtyards of the two families (*or* houses) communicated with each other with only a rough wood-bar door between them. /我们的思想感情是～的。Our thoughts and feelings are interlinked. /虽然远隔千山万水,但我们的心是～的。Though we are separated by numerous mountains and rivers, our hearts are in communion.

相同 xiāngtóng identical; same; in common:在一些问题上持～的观点 hold identical views on some questions; share the same views on some questions /虽说是同胞兄弟,竟毫无～之处。Brothers by blood, they have nothing in common at all.

相投 xiāngtóu be congenial or compatible; agree with each other:气味～ be birds of a feather; be two of a kind /情趣～ be temperamentally compatible; have congenial (*or* similar) tastes and interests

相托 xiāngtuō entrust:有事～ entrust sb. with sth. /以性命～ place one's life in sb.'s hands; place oneself under sb.'s protection

相违 xiāngwéi disagree; go against; contradict:这和我本意～,我不能不另作考虑。As this goes against my original intention, I'll have to reconsider the whole thing.

相闻 xiāngwén be able to hear each other; be within earshot:鸡犬之声～,老死不相往来 (said of the Taoist ideal of a utopian society) never did they meet each other in their lifetime, though the crowing of their cocks and the barking of their dogs were well within hearing

相向 xiāngxiàng ❶ towards each other; facing each other:～而行 walk towards each other; come from opposite directions /～运输 transport (of the same goods) from opposite directions; redundant back-and-forth transport (of the same goods) ❷ targeted at the other party:武力～ ready to use force against (one's opponents)

相向国家 xiāngxiàng guójiā opposite states

相像 xiāngxiàng resemble; be much the same; be similar; be alike:与…有～的地方 bear some resemblance to sth.; look somewhat like sth. /事情虽然发生在两地,但案情颇为～。Though they occurred in different places, the cases were quite similar (*or* very much alike).

相偕 xiāngxié 〈书面〉together; in each other's company:～出游 go on a tour together

相信 xiāngxìn believe; trust; be convinced; have faith:～真理 believe in truth /～自己一定会取得成功 be convinced of one's success /别～他的话。Don't trust him. /～还是不～,随你的便! Believe it or not, do as you please! /经过多次失望后,他难以～医生了。After so many disappointments, he found it hard to have faith in doctors.

相形 xiāngxíng by contrast; by comparison: ～之下 by comparison

相形见绌 xiāngxíng-jiànchù prove inferior by contrast; not sustain comparison (with sth.); pale (into insignificance) by comparison; be outshone:与人民无限丰富的实践相比,理论总是～的。All theories pale by comparison with the infinitely rich practice of the people. /这本新手册的出版使旧作～。The publication of the new handbook throws the old one into the shade.

相形失色 xiāngxíng-shīsè seem pallid by comparison; compare unfavourably; pale into insignificance:与我们的产品比较,他们的产品就～了。Their product compares unfavourably with ours.

X

相沿 xiāngyán through long usage; following the old tradition

相沿成习 xiāngyán-chéngxí *also* "相沿成俗" become a custom through long usage:这种做法在当地～。Through long usage, this has become a common practice in this place.

相依 xiāngyī depending on each other; mutually dependent; interdependent:唇齿～ be as close as lips and teeth; be closely related and mutually dependent /两人～为伴,共度艰辛。They had only each other for company and shared the hardships together.

相依为命 xiāngyī-wéimìng depend on each other for survival:从此,母女俩～。From then on mother and daughter depended on each other to eke out a living.

相宜 xiāngyí suitable; fitting; advisable; appropriate:在这种场合,作为主人你一言不发是不～的。It is not appropriate for you as the host to remain silent under such circumstances. /清明前后栽秧是最～的。It is the best time to transplant rice seedlings around Pure Brightness.

相异 xiāngyì differ; be dissimilar:语言不同,肤色～ differ in languages and skin colour (*or* complexion)

相应 xiāngyīng 〈旧语〉(formula for official documents) should; must:～函达 should be conveyed in an official letter /～咨复 must reply after consultations

相迎 xiāngyíng welcome; meet:降阶～ walk all the way down the doorsteps to meet sb.; give sb. a respectful welcome /笑脸～ give sb. a smiling welcome

相应 xiāngyìng corresponding; relevant; pertinent; appropriate:文章前后不～。The beginning and ending of the article do not correspond to each other. /工作环境变了,我们工作方法也要～地变化。With the change of circumstances we should change our working methods accordingly. /会议改组了公司领导班子并通过了～的决议。The meeting reorganized the leadership of the corporation and passed relevant resolutions. /工厂对污水处理采取了～的措施。The factory took appropriate measures concerning sewage disposal.

相应 xiāngying 〈方言〉cheap; inexpensive

相映 xiāngyìng set each other off; form a contrast:～生辉 set each other off wonderfully; gain by contrast

相映成趣 xiāngyìng-chéngqù set each other off and form a pleasant contrast:湖光山色,～。The lakes and mountains form a delightful contrast. *or* The lakes and mountains contrast beautifully with each other.

相与 xiāngyǔ ❶ get along with (sb.); get on with (sb.):此人生性孤僻,极难～。As he is unsociable and eccentric, it is extremely difficult to get along with him. ❷ with each other; mutually; together:～谈笑 talk and laugh together /疑义～析 clear up a doubt together ❸〈旧语〉close friend:我有几个旧时～,你这次去有事可找他们帮忙。I have some old friends there. You can ask them for help if necessary.

相遇 xiāngyù meet; come across:真巧,分别多年的老朋友在列车上～了。It so happened that the old friends who had not seen each other for years met by chance on the train.

相约 xiāngyuē agree (on sth.); make an appointment:彼此～,三年后旧地再聚。They agreed (*or* made an appointment) to meet again at the same place three years later.

相悦 xiāngyuè love each other; be happy with each other:男女～ love between man and woman /相亲～的友情 congenial, affectionate friendship

相杂 xiāngzá mix together; mingle with each other:花坛上种着红白～的牡丹。The terrace is planted with red and white peonies in a mixed pattern.

相赠 xiāngzèng present to sb.; give as a gift:他临行以手表～。Before departure he gave me his watch as a souvenir.

相知 xiāngzhī ❶ be well acquainted with each other; be on intimate terms:～多年 have known each other long /～无疑。Suspicion will not prevail when people know each other well. ❷ bosom friend; great friend:清明那天,他约了几个～游西湖。He went with several bosom friends by appointment to tour the West Lake together on Pure Brightness day.

相知恨晚 xiāngzhī-hènwǎn *also* "恨相知晚" regret not having got to know each other earlier:二人彻夜畅谈,～。The two of them talked from dusk to dawn, regretting that they had not known each other earlier.

相值 xiāngzhí 〈书面〉❶ meet; come across; encounter:不知道我到上海的时候能否跟他～。I don't know whether I will come across him when I arrive in Shanghai. ❷ correspond; be in accordance:马克思在纽约《每日论坛报》发表有关中国问题论文的年代正与我国太平天国的年代～。The years when Marx published articles on China in the New York *Daily Tribune* corresponded to the period of the Taiping Revolution in China.

相中 xiāngzhòng take a fancy to; settle on; choose:对象是他自己～的。He chose his own fiancée. /这几件瓷器质地不好,我没有～。I didn't take a fancy to any of these porcelain wares since they were of inferior quality.

相助 xiāngzhù help; assist:彼此～ help each other /～一臂之力 lend a helping hand

相撞 xiāngzhuàng collide; crash:火车与卡车～。The train collided with a truck.

相左 xiāngzuǒ 〈书面〉❶ fail to meet each other:道中～,失之交臂。We failed to meet on the way and missed each other narrowly. ❷ fail to agree; disagree; come into conflict; be at odds:意见～ fail to agree; fail to see eye to eye /同事多年,议论每每～。Though they had worked together for years, they were often at odds with each other whenever there was any argument.

湘 Xiāng ❶ (short for 湘江) Xiangjiang River (in Hunan

Province) ❷ another name for Hunan Province
湘菜 xiāngcài Hunan cuisine; Hunanese food: ～馆 restaurant where Hunanese food is served; Hunan restaurant
湘妃竹 xiāngfēizhú *also* "湘竹" mottled bamboo; speckled bamboo
湘江 Xiāngjiāng major river in Hunan, originating in Guangxi and flowing into the Dongting Lake (洞庭湖)
湘剧 xiāngjù Hunan opera: ～团 Hunan opera troupe /～演员 Hunan opera singer
湘帘 xiānglián curtain made of split mottled bamboo
湘莲 xiānglián lotus seeds produced in Hunan
湘绣 xiāngxiù Hunan embroidery
湘语 xiāngyǔ Hunan dialect
湘竹 xiāngzhú *also* "湘妃竹" speckled bamboo

葙 xiāng *see* "青葙" qīngxiāng

厢(廂) xiāng

❶ (usu. of a one-storeyed house) wing; wing-room: 东～ eastern wing /一正两～ central room with two wing-rooms ❷ compartment; box: 包～ (private) box (in a theatre) /大车车～ box of a (horse-drawn) carriage /车～里挤满了人,连站脚的地儿都没有。The (railway) carriage was so packed with passengers that there was hardly any room for standing. ❸ areas just outside a city gate: 学校在城～,出了城门不远就是。The school is situated just outside the city, not far from the city gate. ❹ (often used in the early vernacular) side: 这～ this side /一～情愿 one-sided wish; wishful thinking /只见知府大人坐堂上,两～有衙役侍候。The prefect was seen sitting up straight in the hall with *yamen* runners standing on both sides waiting upon him.
厢房 xiāngfáng (usu. of a one-storeyed house) wing; wing-room: 东～住着姓刘的人家。The Lius live in the east wing-room.

箱 xiāng

❶ box; case; chest; trunk: 衣～ suitcase /柳条～ wicker case (*or* box, *or* hamper) /保险～ safety box; safe /集装～ container (box) /弹药～ ammunition chest /木～ wooden trunk; wooden chest ❷ box-like thing: 蜂～ beehive /邮～ mailbox /冰～ refrigerator; fridge; freezer
箱底 xiāngdǐ ❶ bottom of a chest or case: 多年压～的衣服 clothes that have been stowed away at the bottom of a chest for years ❷ valuables stowed away at the bottom of the chest; one's store of valuables; nest-egg: 她娘家有钱,陪嫁多,～儿自然厚。As her parents were rich, she had been given a huge dowry, and naturally had a large store of valuables.
箱龟 xiāngguī box turtle; box tortoise; terrapin (*Terrapene*)
箱笼 xiānglǒng (traveller's) boxes and baskets; luggage; baggage: 他此次出门行装简便,只带了两个～。As he intended to travel light this time, he took only two pieces of luggage with him.
箱渗碳 xiāngshèntàn 〈冶金〉 box hardening
箱式货车 xiāngshì huòchē boxcar; box van; commercial van
箱式炉 xiāngshìlú 〈冶金〉 batch-type furnace
箱式载重汽车 xiāngshì zàizhòng qìchē box van truck; boxcar; wagon truck
箱鲀 xiāngtún 〈动物〉 boxfish; trunkfish; cowfish
箱形 xiāngxíng box-type: ～百叶窗 box shutter; folding shutter /～泵 box pump /～电动机 box-frame motor /～天线 box antenna
箱型照相机 xiāngxíng zhàoxiàngjī box camera
箱子 xiāngzi box; case; chest; trunk

缃 xiāng 〈书面〉 light-yellow: ～素 light-yellow silk

香 xiāng

❶ fragrant; scented; sweet-smelling; aromatic: 幽～ delicate fragrance (*or* scent) /芳～ aroma /鸟语花～ twitter of birds and fragrance of flowers /～风习习 caressed by a scented wind; with a scented wind gently blowing ❷ savoury; palatable; appetizing; delicious: ～醪佳酿 delicious (*or* mellow) vintage wine /中国饭菜很～。Chinese food is appetizing. /好～的菜呀! 你是怎么做的? What a delicious dish! How did you cook it? /～饵之下,必有死鱼。Fish die in pursuit of savoury bait. *or* There must be fish that will rise to the bait and be caught. ❸ with relish; with good appetite: 这几天她胃口不好,吃饭不～。She has no appetite these days and doesn't enjoy her food. /肚子饿时吃什么都～。Hunger is the best sauce (*or* relish). ❹ (sleep) soundly: 小宝宝睡得正～呢! The baby is sleeping soundly. ❺ in vogue; popular; welcome: 这种电脑现在很吃～。This kind of computer is very popular nowadays. /科技人员在我们村里～着呢。Scientists and technicians are most welcome and respected in our village. ❻ perfume; scent; spice: 五～ "five spices" (prickly ash, star aniseed, cinnamon, clove and fennel) /麝～ musk /沉～ agalloch; eaglewood /龙脑～ Borneo camphor; borneol ❼ incense; joss stick: 烧～ burn incense; burn joss sticks /盘～ incense coil /蚊～ mosquito-repellent incense /进～ go and offer joss sticks; go on a pilgrimage ❽ 〈方言〉 kiss: ～面孔 kiss sb.'s face ❾ *used as a complimentary attribute, esp. of women in traditional literature*: ～柬 woman's letter /～魂 woman's departed soul or ghost /怜～惜玉 be tender towards women /偷～窃玉 have illicit relations with women ❿ (Xiāng) a surname
香案 xiāng'àn long table for incense burners; incense altar: ～接旨 get out the incense altar so as to receive the imperial edict (hand-carried by an imperial envoy) /堂屋中间是～,上面放着一个香炉。In the middle of the central room, there was a long table with an incense burner on it.
香柏 xiāngbǎi 〈植物〉 arbor vitae (*Arbor vitae*)
香槟酒 xiāngbīnjiǔ champagne, a white sparkling wine from Champagne, France
香波 xiāngbō (transliteration) shampoo: 去头屑～ anti-dandruff shampoo
香饽饽 xiāngbōbo 〈口语〉 sweet-smelling pie — popular or much desired person or thing; sweetie-pie: 别以为自己是～,离了你就不成! Don't think you are everybody's sweetheart as if nothing could be done without you! /他总觉得只有自己是～,别人都是臭狗屎。He thought he was the only sweetie-pie while everybody else was just dog-shit.
香菜 xiāngcài *also* "芫荽" yánsui coriander; cilantro
香草 xiāngcǎo (popular term for 香子兰) 〈植物〉 sweetgrass; vanilla: ～冰激淋 vanilla ice-cream
香草美人 xiāngcǎo-měirén 〈比喻〉 loyal and virtuous person; patriot
香草醛 xiāngcǎoquán *also* "香兰素"; "香草" vanillin; vanilline
香肠 xiāngcháng sausage
香车宝马 xiāngchē-bǎomǎ fragrant carriage and treasured horse (used by a beautiful woman)
香橙 xiāngchéng orange
香臭不分 xiāng-chòu bùfēn cannot tell stench from perfume; do not know good from bad
香椿 xiāngchūn 〈植物〉 Chinese toon (*Toona sinensis*): ～炒鸡蛋 tender leaves of Chinese toon stir-fried with eggs
香醇 xiāngchún *also* "香纯" fragrant and mellow; rich; pure: ～的美酒 delicious mellow wine /这种烤烟气味～。This flue-cured tobacco is rich in taste.
香袋 xiāngdài sachet (for perfume, etc.)
香肚 xiāngdǔ spiced meat-filled pig bladder (eaten as a delicacy with wine)
香榧 xiāngfěi 〈植物〉 Chinese torreya (*Torreya grandis*): ～子 Chinese torreya nut
香粉 xiāngfěn face powder: ～盒 powder box /～之资 (women's) pin money
香馥馥 xiāngfùfù strongly scented: 花室～的,沁人心脾。The fragrance of the flower house was intoxicating.
香附子 xiāngfùzǐ 〈中药〉 rhizome of nutgrass flatsedge (*Cyperus rotundus*)
香干 xiānggān smoked bean curd: ～炒油菜 greens stir-fried with smoked bean curd
香港 Xiānggǎng ❶ Hong Kong Island; Xianggang Island ❷ entire Hong Kong or Xianggang region, including Hong Kong Island, Kowloon and the "New Territories"
香港大学 Xiānggǎng Dàxué Hong Kong University
香港虎报 Xiānggǎng Hǔbào *Hong Kong Standard*, an English newspaper in Hong Kong
香港脚 xiāng gǎngjiǎo 〈医学〉 Hong Kong foot; athlete's foot
香港贸易发展局 Xiānggǎng Màoyì Fāzhǎnjú HK Trade Development Council
香港特别行政区 Xiānggǎng Tèbié Xíngzhèngqū Hong Kong Special Administrative Region (HKSAR): ～基本法 Basic Law of the Hong Kong Special Administrative Region /～行政长官 Chief

Executive of the HKSAR /～立法会 Legislative Council of the HKSAR
香港中文大学 Xiānggǎng Zhōngwén Dàxué Hong Kong Chinese University
香菇 xiānggū *also* "香菰"; "香蕈" *Xianggu* mushroom
香瓜 xiāngguā *also* "甜瓜" tiánguā muskmelon
香闺 xiāngguī (used in traditional literature) private room of a girl; boudoir
香蒿 xiānghāo *also* "青蒿" qīnghāo sweet wormwood (*Apiaceae hance*)
香花 xiānghuā ❶ fragrant flower: ～异草 fragrant flowers and exotic plants ❷ writings, artistic works, etc. that are regarded as wholesome or beneficial: 有些好作品实为～, 却被无端地斥为"毒草"。Works that were actually "fragrant flowers" were groundlessly denounced as "poisonous weeds".
香花木 xiānghuāmù *Tsoongiodendron odorum*
香桦 xiānghuà sweet birch; black birch; cherry birch; red birch (*Betula lenta*)
香灰 xiānghuī incense ash: 用～作药〈迷信〉use incense ash as medicine
香会 xiānghuì pilgrimage mission; group or party of pilgrims
香火 xiānghuǒ ❶ joss sticks and candles burning at a temple — devotees of a temple: ～日盛 (of a temple) attract an ever-increasing number of worshippers and pilgrims; attract a daily increasing following ❷ person who looks after incense and candles at a temple; temple attendant: 庙中的～是一位六十多岁的老人。The temple attendant was an old man over sixty. ❸ ceremony to burn incense for one's ancestors — continuance of a family line: 断了～ be unable to continue the ceremony to burn incense for one's ancestors; have one's family line discontinued (*or* cut short); have no male heir ❹ burning joss stick; burning incense: 用～点爆竹 light a firecracker with a burning joss stick /～兄弟 sworn brothers /早晨醒来, 点了一夜的～还没有灭。When I woke up in the morning, I found the incense which had been burning throughout the night was still on.
香几 xiāngjī 〈方言〉long table for incense burners; incense altar: 堂屋中间摆上了～, 我们小孩子们都等着磕头。The incense altar had been set in the middle of the hall with us children waiting for the time to kowtow.
香蕉 xiāngjiāo *also* "甘蕉" gānjiāo banana: ～皮 skin of a banana; banana peel /～共和国 banana republic /～座 banana-shaped seat
香蕉瓜 xiāngjiāoguā cassabanana; curuba (*Sicana Odorifera*)
香蕉苹果 xiāngjiāo-píngguǒ (of apples) Delicious: 红～ Red Delicious
香蕉水 xiāngjiāoshuǐ 〈化工〉banana oil
香精 xiāngjīng essence: 人造～ artificial essence /复合～ compound essence /食用～ flavouring essence /果香～ fruit essence /～油 essential oil
香客 xiāngkè pilgrim: 我们同几个朝山的～结伴, 一路同行。On the way, we kept company with some pilgrims who were going to a temple on the mountain.
香兰素 xiānglánsù *also* "香草醛" vanillin; vanilline
香料 xiāngliào ❶ perfume: ～厂 perfumery ❷ spice
香炉 xiānglú incense burner; censer
香茅 xiāngmáo 〈植物〉lemon grass (*Cymbopogon citratus*): 亚～〈植物〉citronella
香茅醛 xiāngmáoquán 〈化学〉citronellal
香茅油 xiāngmáoyóu citronella oil
香囊 xiāngnáng *also* "香袋"; "香荷包" perfume pouch; sachet; incense bag: 姑娘送给他一只～作为信物。The girl gave him a perfume pouch as a sign of her love.
香柠檬 xiāngníngméng bergamot
香喷喷 xiāngpēnpēn ❶ sweet-smelling; fragrant: 抹得～的 powdered and sweet-smelling ❷ delicious; savoury; appetizing: ～的海鲜汤 delicious (*or* appetizing) sea-food soup
香片 xiāngpiàn scented tea
香蒲 xiāngpú 〈植物〉cattail: ～菌 cattail fungus
香气 xiāngqì sweet smell; pleasant scent; fragrance; aroma: ～四溢 spreading an exquisite fragrance all around /～馥郁 rich in fragrance /～扑鼻。An aroma assails one's nostrils. *or* A sweet smell greets one. /厨房里飘出一股诱人的～。Appetizing fragrances came from the kitchen.
香钱 xiāngqian incense money — gift to a temple and its monks; donation to a temple
香芹 xiāngqín 〈植物〉*Petroselinum crispum*, a kind of parsley
香薷 xiāngrú 〈植物〉*Elsholtzia ciliata*
香色 xiāngsè ❶ fragrance and colour: ～鲜浓 be of strong fragrance and bright colour ❷ dark brown: ～礼帽 dark-brown hat
香山 Xiāngshān Fragrant Hill, west of Beijing
香石竹 xiāngshízhú *also* "康乃馨" kāngnǎixīn 〈植物〉carnation
香水 xiāngshuǐ perfume; scent
香水梨 xiāngshuǐlí a kind of sweet, juicy pear
香水浴 xiāngshuǐyù 〈中医〉bathing in water containing such herbal medicines as jasmine, rose tulip, lily, etc. as therapy for skin diseases, rheumatism, etc.; scented herb bath
香酥鸡 xiāngsūjī crisp-fried chicken
香梭鱼 xiāngsuōyú red barracuda
香桃木 xiāngtáomù 〈植物〉myrtle
香甜 xiāngtián ❶ fragrant and sweet: ～的瓜果 sweet melons and fruits /～的奶汁 sweet milk ❷ (sleep) soundly: 睡得～ sleep soundly
香豌豆 xiāngwāndòu sweet pea (*Lathyrus odoratus*)
香味 xiāngwèi sweet smell; fragrance; scent
香消玉减 xiāngxiāo-yùjiǎn (woman's attractions) lose their magic; (woman) become emaciated: ～为相思。She was emaciated by lovesickness.
香消玉殒 xiāngxiāo-yùyǔn (hackneyed euphemism of traditional literature) the fragrance vanishes and the jade perishes; the aroma disappears and the jade perishes — a beauty passes away
香雪球 xiāngxuěqiú 〈植物〉sweet alyssum; sweet alison (*Lobularia maritima*)
香蕈 xiāngxùn mushroom
香烟 xiāngyān ❶ *also* "香火" incense smoke: ～缭绕 smoke of incense rises in coils (*or* on all sides) /庙中～袅袅, 别有一番风味。Wisps of incense smoke curling up in the air lent the temple an exquisite touch. ❷ *also* "香火" ceremony to burn incense for one's ancestors: 断了～ be unable to continue the ceremony to burn incense for one's ancestors; have one's family line discontinued (*or* cut short); have no male heir ❸ *also* "纸烟" zhǐyān; "卷烟" juǎnyān; "烟卷儿" yānjuǎnr cigarette: ～盒 cigarette case /～头 cigarette butt (*or* end); fag-end /一条～ a carton of cigarettes
香艳 xiāngyàn (of poetry or other writing) flowery; sensual; voluptuous; sexy: 他的词格调～, 脂粉气甚浓。His poetry is flowery in style and voluptuous in taste. /这种小说内容～粗俗, 毫无文学价值可言。Such novels are just coarse pornography and have no literary merit whatsoever.
香羊肚 xiāngyángdǔ haggis, a Scottish dish consisting of a sheep's or calf's offal mixed with suet, oatmeal, etc., and boiled in a bag made from the animal's stomach
香胰子 xiāngyízi 〈方言〉perfumed soap; scented soap
香油 xiāngyóu sesame oil
香鼬 xiāngyòu alpine weasel
香鱼 xiāngyú sweetfish; ayu (*Plecoglossus altivelis*)
香橼 xiāngyuán *also* "枸橼" jǔyuán 〈植物〉citron
香云纱 xiāngyúnshā *also* "薯莨绸" shǔliángchóu; "拷纱" kǎoshā gambiered Guangdong gauze
香皂 xiāngzào perfumed soap; scented soap; toilet soap
香泽 xiāngzé 〈书面〉❶ hair ointment; pomade ❷ fragrance (esp. of a woman); scent
香獐子 xiāngzhāngzi 〈动物〉musk-deer
香樟 xiāngzhāng 〈植物〉camphor tree
香脂 xiāngzhī ❶ balm; balsam: 冷杉的～可治外伤。Fir balm can be used as medicine for injuries. ❷ face cream
香纸 xiāngzhǐ incense and paper (resembling coins or banknotes) burnt as offerings to the dead: 清明上坟, 烧～的满山都是。On the Pure Brightness day, the mountain was filled with people who visited graves and burned incense and paper coins as offerings to the dead.
香烛 xiāngzhú joss sticks and candles (burned when offering sacrifices to gods or ancestors): ～纸马 joss sticks, candles and paper horses
香资 xiāngzī incense money; donation to a temple
香子兰 xiāngzǐlán (popularly known as 香草) vanilla

乡(鄉)

xiāng ❶ country; countryside; rural area; vil-

lage：水～ area (*or* region) of rivers and lakes /城～一片繁荣 prosperity in town and country alike /入～随俗。When in Rome, do as the Romans do. ❷ native place; home village or town; birthplace：故～ native place; birthplace /异～ place other than one's native place; strange land /同～ *also* "老～" person from the same village, district or province /思～ homesick /离～背井 leave one's native place (*or* district); flee one's home and live as a vagabond /回～务农 return to one's native place to do farming ❸ township — rural administrative unit under county or district：～政府 township government /～公所〈旧语〉township office

乡巴佬儿 xiāngbalǎor *also* "乡下佬"〈贬义〉country bumpkin; hayseed; rube：没见过世面的～ country bumpkin who has not seen the world

乡愁 xiāngchóu nostalgia; homesickness：～难解 difficult to rid oneself of nostalgia

乡村 xiāngcūn village; country; countryside; rural area：～学校 village school; rural school /～生活 rural life

乡党 xiāngdǎng 〈书面〉❶ home village or town ❷ fellow villager or townsman

乡丁 xiāngdīng 〈旧语〉gatekeeper or runner for a township office

乡关 xiāngguān 〈书面〉native place; native village; hometown：日暮～何处是，烟波江上使人愁。The sun is setting, but what can I call home? The river's mists and billows make my heart forlorn.

乡贯 xiāngguàn place of one's origin; native place

乡规民约 xiāngguī-mínyuē written pledges or common pledges drawn up by farmers; village regulations and folk conventions; written rules drawn up by villagers for self-regulation

乡宦 xiānghuàn 〈旧语〉rural gentry who used to hold official positions

乡间 xiāngjiān village; country：～小道 country path /～小贩 village pedlar

乡井 xiāngjǐng 〈书面〉native place; home village; hometown：远离～ be far away from one's home village

乡佬儿 xiānglǎor *also* "乡下佬儿" country bumpkin

乡里 xiānglǐ ❶ village or small town (where one's family have long lived)：荣归～ return in glory to one's native place after becoming famous or rich /出身～，没见过什么大世面。Born and bred in a village, he had not seen much of the world. ❷ fellow villager or townsman：同行有几位～，一路上倒也热闹。Accompanied by several fellow townsmen, I had a good time on the way.

乡邻 xiānglín villager; fellow townsman：～们议论纷纷。The villagers were all talking about the matter.

乡民 xiāngmín 〈旧语〉country folk

乡僻 xiāngpì remote; far from town; out-of-the-way：地处～，十分安静，全无都市的繁杂纷乱。It was an out-of-the-way place, extremely quiet and away from the clamour and turmoil of the city.

乡气 xiāngqi rustic; uncouth; rude：这件衣服太～。The dress looks rustic in style.

乡亲 xiāngqīn ❶ person from one's native village or town; fellow villager or townsman：几个～来游北京，借住在我家。Some fellow villagers who came to visit Beijing were staying in my home. ❷ local people; villagers; folks：～们，给你们添麻烦了！Folks, I am afraid we have given you a lot of trouble. /～们现今的日子好过多了。The villagers are much better off these days.

乡情 xiāngqíng affection for one's hometown or village：割不断的～ be unable to get rid of one's homesickness; can't help missing one's hometown (*or* village)

乡曲 xiāngqū 〈书面〉❶ village：横行～ act like an overlord in the village; bully one's fellow villagers ❷ out-of-the-way rural place：身在～，却也心安 be contented to live in a remote, rural place

乡人 xiāngrén ❶ country folk; villagers：天还没大亮，卖菜的～便陆续挑担进城。Before it was quite light, villagers carried vegetables on shoulder-poles to the market in town one after another. ❷ person from the same village, town, or province; fellow countryman：他家里常有～来，谈些家乡的事情。Fellow villagers would often come to visit him and tell him about things back home.

乡绅 xiāngshēn country gentleman; squire：他父亲是方圆数十里闻名的～。His father was a squire who was known for tens of *li* around.

乡试 xiāngshì (during the Ming and Qing dynasties) civil service examination held once every three years at a provincial capital：～夺魁 come out first in the provincial civil service examinations /～中举 pass the provincial civil service examinations and become a *juren* (scholarly degree at the provincial level)

乡事委员会 xiāngshì wěiyuánhuì (HK) rural committee

乡塾 xiāngshú private school in a village; private rural school：～先生 master of a private village school

乡思 xiāngsī homesickness; nostalgia：～之情 homesickness; nostalgia /抒写～ describe one's yearnings for one's native place

乡俗 xiāngsú folk custom; rural custom; folkway：～人情 customs and human relationships in the country

乡谈 xiāngtán dialect of one's native place; local dialect：在异地他乡能听到～，怎能不兴奋！How can one help being excited to hear one's native dialect spoken in a strange land!

乡土 xiāngtǔ native land; native soil; home village：～气息 local colour; local flavour /～教材 teaching material reflecting local conditions and suited to local needs; local teaching material

乡土观念 xiāngtǔ guānniàn provincialism

乡土文学 xiāngtǔ wénxué local-colour literature; native literature

乡土志 xiāngtǔzhì local records; local annals

乡下 xiāngxia 〈口头〉village; country; countryside：每年夏天她都到～姥姥家过假期。Every summer she would go to her granny's house in the country for her vacation.

乡下人 xiāngxiarén country folk; villager; country cousin

乡贤 xiāngxián village sage or worthy

乡议局 Xiāngyìjú (HK) Heuong Yee Kuk

乡谊 xiāngyì 〈书面〉friendship between fellow villagers or townsmen

乡音 xiāngyīn accent of one's native place; local dialect：～未改 with one's local accent unchanged

乡邮 xiāngyóu rural postal service：～员 rural postman /50年代初，～始通，山村才算与外界有了联系。In the early 50's, rural postal service was first established, and the mountain village at last came into contact with the outside world.

乡友 xiāngyǒu fellow villager or townsman; friend from the same village or area

乡愿 xiāngyuàn 〈书面〉conformist hypocrite

乡约 xiāngyuē rules and regulations for an entire township

乡长 xiāngzhǎng head of a township or village

乡镇 xiāngzhèn ❶ villages and towns ❷ small towns

乡镇企业 xiāngzhèn qǐyè township enterprise; rural enterprise：随着～的诞生和发展，不少农村劳动力得到了就业的机会。With the inception and development of township enterprises, much of the rural labour force found opportunities for employment.

乡梓 xiāngzǐ 〈书面〉native place; hometown; home village

芗(薌)

xiāng ❶〈古语〉aromatic herbs mentioned in ancient books as a condiment ❷〈书面〉*see* "香" xiāng

芗剧 xiāngjù *xiangju* opera (named after the river Xiang and popular in Taiwan and southern Fujian)

xiáng

庠

xiáng 〈旧语〉school

庠生 xiángshēng 〈旧语〉student of a county or prefectural school

庠序 xiángxù 〈书面〉school; educational undertaking

详

xiáng ❶ detailed; minute：周～ comprehensive; complete /～征博引 quote extensively and at (great) length /不厌其～ never tire of the details; seek every detail /～见后文。For full particulars, see the chapters to come. *or* More of that later. ❷ explain in detail; elaborate：另～ to be explained elsewhere /内～。(written on an envelope) For further information, see inside. ❸ clear：不～ unknown

详备 xiángbèi detailed and complete; exhaustive：例证～ with exhaustive evidence and illustrations /注释～ with detailed, full annotations; with copious notes; exhaustively annotated

详尽 xiángjìn detailed; exhaustive; thorough：制定～的计划 make an elaborate plan /沿途风土人情，作者均有～的记载。The author made a detailed record of the local conditions and customs he observed on the way. /记者对此作了～深入的调查。The reporter made a thoroughgoing investigation (*or* study) of the matter. /他对情况的了解极其～。He knew the situation inside out.

详略 xiáng-lüè whether sth. should be detailed or brief; how detailed sth. should be; where sth. should be detailed and where brief:注释正确,～得当。The annotations are correct and of appropriate detail. /作者对剧情的～处理恰到好处。The writer was just right in his handling of the details of the plot.
详梦 xiángmèng 〈迷信〉interpret or explain a dream as an omen
详密 xiángmì elaborate; scrupulous; meticulous:～的安排 elaborate (*or* methodical) arrangements /他们制定了～的施工方案。They worked out a meticulous plan for the construction project.
详明 xiángmíng full and clear:记叙～ make detailed and clear records
详情 xiángqíng detailed information; details; specifics; particulars:～面谈。I will give you the details when we meet in person. /～请向经办人员具体了解。Please apply to the person in charge for particulars. /此中～她都告诉了我。She told me the ins and outs of the matter.
详实 xiángshí *also* "翔实" xiángshí detailed and accurate:叙事～ give a full and accurate account of the matter
详图 xiángtú detail (drawing):发动机～ engine detail /春季战局形势～ detailed map of the war in spring
详文 xiángwén 〈旧语〉official document or report to one's superiors
详悉 xiángxī ❶ know in detail; know clearly:前信所述,谅已～。I suppose you know already what was conveyed in the previous letter. ❷ detailed and exhaustive:内容～、笔调生动的调查报告 investigative report that is detailed and thorough in content and vivid in style
详细 xiángxì detailed; exhaustive; minute:～讨论某事 discuss sth. in detail; discuss sth. at length /我以后一定详详细细地告诉你。I'll tell you about it in full detail later. /现将～报告附上,请阅。Enclosed herewith is an exhaustive report for your information. /他要求将其发言做～记录。He requested that his statement be recorded *in extenso*.
详细流程图 xiángxì liúchéngtú detail chart
详注 xiángzhù annotate fully; provide full notes or detailed annotations

祥 xiáng ❶ auspicious; propitious; promising; lucky:吉～ lucky; auspicious; propitious /不～之兆 ominous sign; ill omen ❷ (Xiáng) a surname
祥和 xiánghé ❶ auspicious and peaceful:～之气 auspicious and peaceful ethos (*or* atmosphere) /过一个～的春节 enjoy a happy and peaceful Spring Festival ❷ kind; gentle; benign:老太太神情～。The old lady wore a benign expression.
祥瑞 xiángruì auspicious sign; propitious omen:天降～ heaven-sent auspicious sign /～之兆 good omen; propitious omen
祥云 xiángyún (as in mythology) auspicious cloud (ridden by a deity):一时只见～密布,众仙子飘然而临。In a minute the sky was covered with auspicious clouds, on which deities came flying.
祥兆 xiángzhào good omen:丰收的～ omen for a bumper harvest

X

翔 xiáng circle in the air; fly:翱～太空 soar across space /飞～ fly /滑～ glide /回～ wheel; circle round
翔贵 xiángguì 〈书面〉(of prices) soar:物价～。Prices soar.
翔实 xiángshí *also* "详实" xiángshí full and accurate; detailed and thorough:～可信 full, accurate and reliable /这本教材内容～。The textbook provides detailed and accurate materials.
翔舞 xiángwǔ circle and dance in the air; soar:白鹤～。White cranes soared in the air.

降 xiáng ❶ surrender; capitulate; show the white flag:受～ accept a surrender /请～ beg to surrender (*or* capitulate) /劝～ induce sb. to lay down arms /诱～ lure sb. to capitulate /招～ summon (*or* call on) sb. to surrender ❷ subdue; conquer; vanquish; tame:一物～一物〈俗语〉there is always one thing to conquer another; everything has its vanquisher
see also jiàng
降表 xiángbiǎo 〈书面〉petition for surrender; letter of capitulation
降敌 xiángdí ❶ surrender to the enemy ❷ conquer the enemy:～三十万众 conquer an enemy of 300,000 men
降伏 xiángfú subdue; overpower; vanquish; tame:～旱魔 vanquish drought; bring drought under control /～劣马 break in an intractable horse
降服 xiángfú yield; surrender:举国～ the whole nation surrenders
降将 xiángjiàng general who has capitulated
降龙伏虎 xiánglóng-fúhǔ subdue the dragon and tame the tiger — conquer natural forces; overcome powerful adversaries:战天斗地,～ fight against heaven and earth, subdue the dragon and tame the tiger; combat nature and surmount great obstacles
降旗 xiángqí white flag; flag of capitulation
降顺 xiángshùn 〈书面〉yield and pledge allegiance:内怀～之心 have the intention to surrender and pledge allegiance

xiǎng

享 xiǎng ❶ enjoy; share:共～富贵 enjoy wealth and honour together; share wealth and honour /以～天年 enjoy one's remaining years in peace; live out one's life in peace /坐～其成 sit idle and enjoy the fruits of others' work; reap where one has not sown /～国二十一年 (of a sovereign, etc.) enjoy a reign of 21 years; reign for 21 years /有福同～,有难同当 share joys and troubles alike ❷〈书面〉*see* "飨" xiǎng
享福 xiǎngfú enjoy a happy life; be in clover; live in ease and comfort:老来～ enjoy a happy life in old age /丈夫家务活儿十分能干,她可～了。As her husband is good at housework, she has an easy time of it at home.
享乐 xiǎnglè enjoy a life of pleasure; indulge in creature comforts:尽情～ indulge in creature comforts to one's heart's content; abandon oneself totally to creature comforts /～思想 preoccupation with pleasure-seeking
享乐主义 xiǎnglèzhǔyì hedonism; pleasure-seeking:～者 hedonist /～哲学 hedonist philosophy
享年 xiǎngnián 〈敬词〉die at or live to the age of:～八十四岁 die at the age of 84
享受 xiǎngshòu enjoy; treat:～别人的款待 enjoy sb.'s entertainment; be entertained by sb. /～局级待遇 enjoy the rights and perquisites of a bureau head; be treated as a bureau head /～递减律 law of diminishing enjoyment /吃苦在前,～在后 be the first to bear hardships and the last to enjoy comforts /贪图～,不思进取 abandon oneself to ease and comfort and not think of achieving anything /看她的舞蹈表演,无疑是一种难得的艺术～。Her dancing is undoubtedly a rare artistic treat.
享用 xiǎngyòng enjoy the use of; enjoy:心安理得地～自己的劳动果实 have an easy conscience in enjoying the fruits of one's own labour
享有 xiǎngyǒu enjoy (rights, fame, prestige, etc.):～盛名 enjoy (*or* have) great renown; be renowned /～崇高的威望 enjoy high prestige; be held in high esteem /在我国男女～同等的权利。In our country men and women enjoy equal rights.
享誉 xiǎngyù enjoy fame; be renowned:～海内外 be renowned at home and abroad; be famous worldwide

鲞(鮝) xiǎng dried fish:白～ dried croaker
鲞鱼 xiǎngyú dried fish

想 xiǎng ❶ think; reflect; mull over:～啥说啥 say what one thinks; speak straight from the heart /～困难 think of difficulties; anticipate difficulties /～一～ mull it over /往好里～ think of sb. (*or* sth.) in a better light; look at the bright side of things; give sb. the benefit of the doubt /～出路 try to find a way out /浮～ have thoughts (*or* recollections) cropping up in one's mind /遐～ reverie; day-dreaming /畅～ give free rein to one's thoughts /～得出神 muse; be lost in thought (*or* reverie) ❷ suppose; consider; think; reckon:我～他现在已经到家了。I suppose (*or* reckon) he has arrived home by now. ❸ want; would like; feel like (doing sth.); intend to:你～要哪件上衣? Which jacket do you want? /我今天下午～打篮球。I'd like to play basketball this afternoon. /看完电影后她直～哭。She felt like crying after the movie. ❹ remember with longing; pine for; miss:你可把我们～苦了! How we missed you! /我孤身一人在外,有时难免～家。I can't help yearning for (*or* missing) my family sometimes, as I'm away from home on my own.

想必 xiǎngbì presumably; most probably; most likely：我看见他在打行李，～是快走了。I saw him packing. He must be leaving soon. / 他信中只字未提此事，～没有看到我的去信。He didn't mention this in his letter. Presumably he hadn't received mine.

想不到 xiǎngbudào do not expect; fancy：～他会被公司录用。We didn't expect that he would be employed by the company. /～你居然会说这样的话! Fancy your saying such things!

想不开 xiǎngbukāi take things too seriously; take a matter to heart：她对下岗怎么也～。She simply could not stop fretting over her being laid off. /他一时～，寻了短见。Taking things too hard, he committed suicide.

想出 xiǎngchu think out; think up：～许多鬼点子坑人 think up a lot of tricks to cheat people /我可是一点办法也想不出了。I am at a loss what to do.

想出来 xiǎngchulai think up; work out; devise：一个好的计划终于～了。A good plan was worked out at last.

想当然 xiǎngdāngrán assume as a matter of course; take for granted：不要～地认为他会帮忙。Don't take his help for granted. *or* Don't take it for granted that he'll help us. /每个细节都要认真检查和核对，不要～。All particulars should be carefully checked and verified; nothing should be taken for granted.

想到 xiǎngdào think of; call to mind; (idea, etc.) occur to one：～远方的朋友 think of one's friend who is far away /～一个主意 hit upon an idea /她忽然～她也许不该来。It suddenly occurred to her that perhaps she shouldn't have come. /我们没～会下雨。We didn't think it would rain. *or* We didn't expect it to rain. /他从来没～她会说谎。It never crossed his mind to suspect her of lying.

想得到 xiǎngdedào (often used in a rhetorical question) think; guess; imagine; expect：谁～他会那么年轻就死去? Who would have imagined (*or* thought) that he would have died that young?

想得开 xiǎngdekāi not take to heart; take things easy; try to look on the bright side of things：～的人 one who takes things philosophically; one who always looks on the bright side of things /凡事还是～的好，人不能自己跟自己过不去。It's better not to take any misfortune to heart, or else you would just be too hard on yourself.

想法 xiǎngfǎ think of a way; try：～弄点吃的来。Try and get something to eat. /咱们得～救他。Let's think of a way to rescue him.

想法 xiǎngfa idea; opinion; view：按他的～ in his view; to his mind /各有各的～。Each has his own opinion. *or* Opinions differ. /你这个～不错，可以试试。This idea of yours is not bad. Let's give it a try. /把你的～说说，大伙儿看怎么办合适。Tell us what you have in mind, and we'll see what's the best way to go about it.

想方设法 xiǎngfāng-shèfǎ do everything possible; use all means; move heaven and earth; try by hook or by crook：～克服工作中的困难 do everything possible to overcome the difficulties in one's work

想家 xiǎngjiā be homesick

想见 xiǎngjiàn see; infer; gather：由此可以～当时是何等艰难。Form this we can see how hard things were at the time. /从他的表情难以～他是否满意。It was hard to tell from his expression whether he was satisfied or not.

想开 xiǎngkāi take things easy; not take sth. to heart; not take things too hard：这种事要～点儿。Don't take such things to heart.

想来 xiǎnglái it may be assumed that; presumably; supposedly：她是他的妹妹，～他不会骗她。As she is his own sister, presumably he would not lie to her. /他既然说了，～不会不做的。Since he has promised, I suppose he will do it.

想来想去 xiǎnglái-xiǎngqù give sth. a good deal of thought; turn sth. over and over in one's mind：我～，觉得还是去的好。I have thought it over and still believe that I should go.

想念 xiǎngniàn recall with longing; long to see again; yearn for; miss：～故乡和亲人 miss one's hometown and family /～死去的战友 cherish the memory of one's deceased comrades-in-arms

想起 xiǎngqǐ recall; remember; think of; call to mind：他出了门才～来那天是妻子的生日。It did not occur to him until he left home that it was his wife's birthday. /这情景使老人～了自己的童年。The sight recalled his childhood to the old man. *or* The sight reminded the old man of his own childhood. /我想不起来以前见过她。I can't recall having met her before.

想儿 xiǎngr 〈方言〉hope：有～ hopeful /没～ without hope; hopeless

想入非非 xiǎngrùfēifēi indulge in fantasy; allow one's fancy to run wild; entertain a wild hope; have maggots in one's head：读到这里，他不由得～起来。Reading this, he couldn't help indulging in fantasy. /金钱使她～。Money put maggots in her head.

想通 xiǎngtōng straighten out one's thinking; think through; think out; become convinced：～一个问题 think a problem through; clarify a question in one's mind /他终于～了。He finally came round to the idea. /对他的自杀，我怎么也想不通。I can't figure out why he committed suicide.

想头 xiǎngtou 〈口语〉❶ idea; notion：多怪的～啊! What a strange notion! /老人的这个～也不是一天两天了，只是没有说出来。The old man had the idea for a long time but did not have a chance to talk about it. ❷ hope：这事看来没什么～了。This appears to be quite hopeless now.

想望 xiǎngwàng ❶ hope; long; desire：他在学生时代就～着当律师。When he was a pupil he longed to be a lawyer. ❷〈书面〉admire; adore：～风采，思之若渴。I have always admired your graceful bearing and longed to make your acquaintance.

想像 xiǎngxiàng *also* "想象" ❶〈心理〉imagination ❷ imagine; envisage; fancy; visualize：不难～ not hard to imagine (*or* visualize) /不可～的痛苦 unimaginable pain (*or* suffering) /～不到的问题 unexpected problems

想像力 xiǎngxiànglì imaginative power; imaginative faculty; imagination：毫无～ having no imaginative power; without imagination /充分发挥～ give free rein to one's imagination

想着 xiǎngzhe bear in mind; not forget：心里～点儿。Keep it in mind. /你可～把书寄回来。Don't forget to send the book back.

响(響) xiǎng

❶ echo; resound：回～ echo; resound /反～ echo; repercussion /影～ impact; influence /如～斯应 respond like an echo; be quick in one's response ❷ sound; ring; beat; fire：一声炮～ report of a cannon /两～的爆竹 double-bang fire-cracker /～枪 fire a gun /～锣 beat (*or* sound) a gong /门铃～了。The door bell rang. /爆竹砰的一声～了。The fire-cracker went off with a bang. /大厅里～起一阵欢呼声。Cheers broke out in the hall. /教堂的钟～了八下。The church clock struck eight. ❸ loud; noisy：好的冰箱不太～。A good refrigerator doesn't make much noise. /口哨声真～。The sound of the whistle is loud. /～鼓还得重锤敲〈俗语〉a loud drum takes a heavy stick to beat it — even talented people require meticulous (*or* intensive) training ❹ sound; noise：声～ sound; noise /音～ sound; noise

响板 xiǎngbǎn 〈乐器〉castanets

响鼻 xiǎngbí (of a mule, horse, etc.) snort：这马连打～儿。The horse snorted again and again.

响鞭 xiǎngbiān ❶ crack a whip：赶车人抽了一～，马跑得更欢了。As the coachman cracked his whip, the horses pulled at a faster trot. ❷〈方言〉firecracker

响彻 xiǎngchè resound; reverberate：震耳的雷声～大地。The deafening thunder resounded all over the earth. /礼炮声～了整个广场。Salvoes of the salute reverberated throughout the square.

响彻云霄 xiǎngchè-yúnxiāo resound or reverberate through the skies; echo to the clouds; make the welkin ring：锣鼓声～。The beating of gongs and drums resounded through the skies. /观众的欢呼声～。The spectators made the welkin ring with their cheers.

响脆 xiǎngcuì loud and crisp：～的嗓音 loud and crisp voice

响当当 xiǎngdāngdāng ❶ ring loudly; clang：急骤的、～的锤打声 rapid, clangorous hammering sounds ❷ so good as to pass the stiffest test; worthy of the name; outstanding; thoroughbred：～的人物 outstanding personage; quite a figure /～的好汉 hero second to none; hundred percent brave man /～的汉子 true man worth his salt

响动 xiǎngdong sound of sth. astir; noise：夜里我睡得死，没听见有～。I was sound asleep last night and did not hear anything astir. /他蹑手蹑脚地走进院子，一点～也没有。He tiptoed into the courtyard without making the slightest noise.

响度 xiǎngdù *also* "音量" yīnliàng loudness; volume

响遏行云 xiǎng'èxíngyún (of singing) be so sonorous as to stop the passing clouds; pierce the clouds：雄浑、激越的歌声～。The vigorous, vehement song resounded through the nine Heavens.

响箭 xiǎngjiàn sounding or ringing arrow (used in old days as a signal)：林中～ whistling arrow in the woods

响雷 xiǎngléi ❶ thunder:～了,雨快来了。It thunders. The rain is coming. ❷ thunderclap:声如～ as loud as thunder /一个～,震耳欲聋。There was a deafening thunderclap.
响亮 xiǎngliàng loud and clear; ringing; resonant; sonorous:～的歌声 loud and clear song /给了一记～的耳光 give sb. a heavy slap in the face; give sb. a smart box on the ear /他说起话来声音～,底气十足。He spoke in a resounding voice, full of vitality.
响铃 xiǎnglíng jingle bell; cascabel:老远就听见马队的～声。The jingle bells of the caravan can be heard in the distance.
响马 xiǎngmǎ 〈旧语〉(used esp. in north China) highwayman; bandit:这条路不安全,常有～出没。The road is not safe, for it is often haunted by bandits.
响排 xiǎngpái 〈戏剧〉rehearsal with musical accompaniment (but without make-up and costume)
响器 xiǎngqì 〈乐器〉Chinese percussion instruments
响晴 xiǎngqíng (of sky) clear and cloudless:～的空中没有一丝游云。Not a speck of cloud is seen drifting in the clear sky.
响儿 xiǎngr 〈方言〉sound; noise:钱扔在水里还能听一声～! Even if I threw a coin into the water, I could yet hear a sound! (Why should I waste the money on you?)
响声 xiǎngsheng sound; noise:咯吱咯吱的～ creaking (sound) /半天听不见一点儿～。Not a single sound was heard for a long time.
响头 xiǎngtóu kowtow (with one's forehead knocking against the ground and thus making a sound):连磕三个～ kowtow three times, each with a dull sound
响尾蛇 xiǎngwěishé rattlesnake
响尾蛇导弹 xiǎngwěishé dǎodàn 〈军事〉(US) sidewinder
响岩 xiǎngyán 〈地理〉phonolite
响杨 xiǎngyáng 〈植物〉Chinese white poplar
响音 xiǎngyīn 〈语言〉resonant, i. e. vowels such as a, e, o or sonorants such as m, n, l; (somtimes) sonorant
响应 xiǎngyìng respond; reply; answer:～号召 answer a call; respond to a call /群起～ rise in response (to a call, etc.) /这个提议得到多数代表的～。The proposal was supported by a majority of representatives.
响应器 xiǎngyìngqì 〈自控〉responder; responser
响应性 xiǎngyìngxìng 〈物理〉responsiveness; responsibility
响指 xiǎngzhǐ sound made by snapping the fingers:打～ snap the fingers

蚼 xiǎng

蚼虫 xiǎngchóng 〈方言〉paddy insects such as leafhoppers

饷 xiǎng ❶〈书面〉entertain (with food and drink):～宾 entertain guests ❷〈旧语〉(usu. of soldiers, policemen, etc.) pay:月～ monthly pay /关～ (of a soldier, policeman, etc.) get one's pay /发～ issue pay /军～ soldier's pay and provisions /薪～ soldier's pay and rations
饷遗 xiǎngwèi 〈书面〉present (a gift); offer (a present)
饷银 xiǎngyín 〈旧语〉serviceman's pay:克扣～ shortchange soldiers' pay and keep it for oneself

曏(曏) xiǎng 〈书面〉previously; formerly; in the past

飨(饗) xiǎng 〈书面〉treat to food and drink; entertain:～客 entertain a guest /将其诗词辑为一集,以～读者 collect sb.'s poetry in one volume for the benefit of the reader /～以闭门羹 shut the door in sb.'s face; refuse sb. entrance
飨宴 xiǎngyàn 〈书面〉entertain by giving a banquet

xiàng

项[1] xiàng ❶ nape (of the neck):颈～ neck /～上枷锁 chain round one's neck ❷ (Xiàng) a surname

项[2] xiàng ❶〈量词〉*used of itemized things*:三～规定 three regulations /逐～讨论 discuss sth. item by item /单～运动 individual event /按合同第四条第二款第五～规定 according to article 4, clause 2, item 5 of the contract /这是一～十分重要的工作。This is a job (*or* task) of great importance. ❷ sum (of money):用～ *also* "出～" item of expenditure (*or* expense) /进～ income; revenue /存～ credit balance; balance /欠～ liability; debit ❸〈数学〉term:同类～ like term /后～ second term; last term /内～ inner term /常数～ constant term
项背 xiàngbèi one's back:不可望其～ not fit to hold a candle to sb.; be a far cry from sb.
项背相望 xiàngbèi-xiāngwàng walk one after another in close succession; walk in Indian file:游人如云,～。Tourists swarmed and followed on each other's heels.
项链 xiàngliàn *also* "项练" necklace
项目 xiàngmù item; project:经营～ item of business /议程上的重要～ important item on the agenda /出口～ export items; goods for export /重点建设～ key construction project /科研～ scientific research project /训练～ training course /游泳～ swimming event /～经理 project manager /～成本 project cost
项目融资 xiàngmù róngzī project financing
项圈 xiàngquān choker; neckband:狗～ dog collar
项羽 Xiàng Yǔ Xiang Yu (formerly translated as Hsiang Yu, 232-202 BC), leader of the uprising that overthrew the Qin Dynasty
项庄舞剑,意在沛公 Xiàng Zhuāng wǔ jiàn, yì zài Pèigōng Xiang Zhuang performed the sword dance as a cover for his attempt on Liu Bang's life; when Xiang Zhuang drew his sword to dance, he was actually attempting to kill Liu Bang — act with a hidden or ulterior motive:他的话里含有骨头,～,是攻击我们的。There is a sting in his words; it is a covert attack on us.

衖 xiàng *see* "巷" xiàng

巷 xiàng narrow street; lane; alley:陋～ mean alley /街头～尾 streets and lanes /深深的小～ long, narrow lane
see also hàng
巷口 xiàngkǒu entrance to a lane; either end of a lane
巷陌 xiàngmò streets and lanes:～人家 inhabitants of the streets and lanes; common townspeople
巷尾 xiàngwěi end of a lane
巷议 xiàngyì street gossip; talk of the town
巷战 xiàngzhàn street fighting; house-to-house fighting
巷子 xiàngzi 〈方言〉lane; alley:～口 entrance to a lane; either end of a lane /这条～里住着六户人家。There are six families living in this lane.

相[1] xiàng ❶ looks; countenance; appearance:可怜～ pitiful looks /凶～ fierce appearance /狼狈～ (cut a) sorry figure /扮～俊美 (of an actor or actress) look handsome (*or* pretty) in costume and make-up /奴才～ behave servily /出洋～ make a show of oneself /老～ look old for one's age /少～ look young for one's age /姑娘长～儿挺俊。The girl is pretty. ❷ appearance of things; facies:海～ marine facies /陆～ land facies /浅海～ neritic facies ❸ bearing; carriage; posture:站有站～,坐有坐～ how to stand or sit properly /睡～不好 sprawl all over the bed whiie asleep /他吃～难看。He ate ravenously. ❹ phase position: *see* "～位" ❺ phase:三～电动机 three-phase motor /单～ single phase ❻ form; image; picture:照～ take a photo /无～ formless; without form ❼ state of element; phase state:水蒸气、水和冰是氧化二氢的三个～。Steam, water and ice are the three states of H_2O. ❽ look at and appraise; examine the physiognomy of:～货 examine the goods (before payment is made) /～马 look at a horse to judge its worth /人不可貌～,海不可斗量。As the sea can't be measured by a bushel, so a man can't be known (*or* judged) by his looks. ❾ (Xiàng) a surname

相[2] xiàng ❶ assist; help:～夫教子 assist one's husband and bring up the children /吉人天～。God help the kind-hearted. ❷ chief minister; prime minister; chancellor:丞～ *also* "宰～" prime minister /～印 chief minister's seal of office /出将入～ have both civil and military abilities ❸ minister (in some countries):外～ (Japan) foreign minister ❹ minister, one of the pieces in Chinese chess ❺〈旧语〉attendant; usher:傧～ best man; bridesmaid; attendant
see also xiāng
相变 xiàngbiàn 〈物理〉phase change; phase transition; phase transformation:～位错 phase transformation dislocation /～滞后

hysteresis of phase transformation

相册 xiàngcè photo album

相衬 xiàngchèn 〈物理〉phase contrast: ~显微镜 phase-contrast microscope

相电流 xiàngdiànliú phase current

相电压 xiàngdiànyā phase voltage; star voltage

相电阻 xiàngdiànzǔ phase resistance

相府 xiàngfǔ 〈旧语〉residence of a prime minister

相公 xiànggong 〈旧语〉❶ respectful form of address for one's husband ❷ (often used in traditional drama or fiction) form of address for a young gentleman: ~此去何时可归? When will you be back, sir? ❸ male prostitute; pansy

相国 xiàngguó 〈旧语〉〈敬词〉prime minister; grand secretary

相机 xiàngjī ❶ watch for an opportunity; bide one's time: ~而动 wait for an opportune moment to act ❷ camera: 单镜头反光~ single lens reflex camera / 一次成相~ instant camera / 全景~ panoramic camera

相机行事 xiàngjī-xíngshì act according to circumstances; act as the occasion demands; do as one sees fit: 你要~, 不可莽撞。You must act according to circumstances and avoid anything rash. / 他奉命打入匪穴, ~。He was ordered to work his way into the bandits' den and do as he saw fit.

相继电器 xiàngjìdiànqì 〈电工〉phase relay

相角 xiàngjiǎo ❶ photo corner ❷ 〈数学〉phase angle

相控阵 xiàngkòngzhèn 〈无线电〉phased array: ~雷达〈军事〉phased-array radar

相里 Xiànglǐ a surname

相貌 xiàngmào facial features; looks; bearing; appearance: ~堂堂 have a dignified (*or* commanding) appearance; have a majestic bearing / ~平平 bland in appearance; plain looking / ~猥琐 be of a wretched appearance / 这小伙子个头不矮, ~也还端正。The young man is quite tall and has fairly regular features.

相面 xiàngmiàn practise physiognomy; read one's fortune in one's face

相敏探测 xiàngmǐn tàncè 〈电工〉phase sensitive detection

相片儿 xiàngpiānr 〈口语〉photograph; photo

相片 xiàngpiàn photograph; photo: ~放大机 enlarger; photoenlarger / ~上光 glazing / ~镶嵌 photograph montage (*or* mosaic)

相平衡 xiàngpínghéng 〈物理〉phase balance

相绕组 xiàngràozǔ 〈电工〉phase winding

相声 xiàngsheng 〈戏曲〉comic dialogue; crosstalk: ~表演 comic dialogue performance / ~艺术 art of crosstalk / 听~ enjoy a comic dialogue

相时而动 xiàngshí'érdòng wait for the right time or opportunity to take action; act when the right opportunity or moment offers itself; adapt oneself to circumstances

相时而退 xiàngshí'értuì withdraw at the right moment; beat a graceful retreat

相士 xiàngshì fortune-teller; physiognomist

相手 xiàngshǒu tell sb.'s future by reading the lines on the palm of his or her hand: ~的 palmist / ~术 palmistry / 给人~ read sb.'s palmistry for him (*or* her)

相书 xiàngshū ❶ 〈方言〉vocal mimicry; vocal imitation: 四川~ Sichuan vocal imitation / ~表演 performance of vocal mimicry ❷ book on physiognomy

相术 xiàngshù physiognomy: ~甚精 be well versed in physiognomy

相态 xiàngtài 〈物理〉phase state

相体裁衣 xiàngtǐ-cáiyī cut the garment according to the figure; make a garment fitting to sb.'s measurements

see also "量体裁衣" liàngtǐ-cáiyī

相图 xiàngtú 〈冶金〉equilibrium diagram; constitution diagram; phasigram

相位 xiàngwèi 〈物理〉〈电工〉phase; phase position: ~表 phase meter / ~跟踪 phase tracking / ~失真〈通信〉phase distortion / ~调制 phase modulation / ~控制 phase control / ~调整 phase adjustment / ~选择器 phase selector

相序 xiàngxù 〈电工〉phase sequence: ~继电器 phase-reversal relay; phase sequence relay

相移 xiàngyí 〈物理〉phase shift

相纸 xiàngzhǐ (photographic) printing paper; photographic paper: 黑白~ black-and-white printing paper / 彩色~ colour printing paper / ~曝光量范围 exposure scale

缿(銗) xiàng 〈古语〉❶ earthenware money box; piggy bank ❷ cylindrical vessel serving as a letter box

向[1] (❶❷❸嚮) xiàng ❶ direction; orientation; trend: 航~ direction of navigation / 趋~ tendency; trend; propensity / 人心所~ (the trend of) popular sentiment / 风~偏南,有小雨。Southerly wind with slight rain (*or* drizzle). / 此人去~不明。His whereabouts are unknown. ❷ face; turn towards: ~着观众 facing the audience / 心~北京 yearning for Beijing / 两人相~而行。The two moved towards each other. / ~阳的小屋是他的书房。The small room facing south is his study. ❸ 〈书面〉approaching; near; close to: *see* "~晓"; "~晚" ❹ take sb.'s part; side with; favour; be partial to: 我这人~理不~人,谁对我就支持谁。I stand by what is right, not by a particular person. I'll side with whoever is right. / 她~她小女儿。She favours (*or* is partial to) her younger daughter. ❺ 〈介词〉to; towards; against: ~劳动模范学习 learn from model workers / ~荒原进军 march towards the wilderness / 从胜利走~胜利 march from victory to victory / ~敌人发起了总攻 launch a general offensive against the enemy / ~东走大约十公里,有一条小河。Some ten miles eastwards is a stream. / 他~上级打报告,申请调动工作。He sent a report to his superior, applying for a transfer. ❻ (Xiàng) a surname

向[2] xiàng always; all along: 对此~有研究 have been doing research in this field all along / 我们这里~无此人。We've never seen this man here before.

向背 xiàng-bèi be for or against; support or oppose: 人心~不可违抗。We mustn't go against the will of the people.

向壁虚构 xiàngbì-xūgòu *also* "向壁虚造" make up out of one's head; create out of the void; fabricate: ~的故事 fabricated account; fabrication / ~的友谊 unreal friendship / 那全是~的。That is sheer imagination.

向晨 xiàngchén towards dawn; near daybreak: ~之时,天降小雪。A light snow fell before dawn.

向导 xiàngdǎo ❶ act as a guide; show sb. the way: 他会~你们进山的。He'll act as a guide for you in the mountain. ❷ guide: 清晨,我们随~出发,往山顶走去。Led by the guide, we set out early in the morning for the summit.

向导周报 Xiàngdǎo Zhōubào *Guide Weekly*, the first organ of the Communist Party of China which started circulation in Sept. 1922 in Shanghai

向迩 xiàng'ěr 〈书面〉approach: 不可~ unapproachable; inaccessible

向风群岛 Xiàngfēng Qúndǎo Windward Islands, a group of islands in the Eastern Caribbean Sea constituting the southern part of the Lesser Antilles

向光性 xiàngguāngxìng 〈生物〉phototropism

向后 xiànghòu towards the back; with the back first; backwards: ~倾斜 tip back / ~跳水 backward dive / ~转! (word of command) About face! *or* About turn! / ~转走! (word of command) To the rear, march!

向火 xiànghuǒ 〈方言〉warm oneself by a fire: 夜里冷,我们围着炉子~,一边聊天,一边喝茶。Surrounding a stove in the cold evening, we warmed ourselves by the fire, chatting and drinking tea.

向来 xiànglái always; all along; invariably: ~守时 have always been punctual / ~不守信 have never kept one's promise / 我~知道他有病。I knew all along that he was ill.

向例 xiànglì convention; usual practice: 打破~ break free from conventions / 山村的~,睡得早,起得也早。It is common for mountain villagers to go to bed early and rise early.

向量 xiàngliàng 〈数学〉vector: 活动~ activity vector / 不变~ invariant vector / ~分析 vector analysis / ~之和 vector sum / ~函数 vector function

向暮 xiàngmù at dusk; towards evening; early twilight; at nightfall: ~投宿 seek lodging before dark / ~时分,芦苇荡里摇出一只小船。A small boat darted out of the reed marshes at dusk.

向慕 xiàngmù admire; esteem; yearn for: 一片~之情 be all admiration / ~日久,无缘得见。If only I had the honour to meet him whom I have long held in esteem.

向年 xiàngnián 〈书面〉in previous years; in those years

向盘 xiàngpán 〈旧语〉compass

向前 xiàngqián towards the front; forward; onward; ahead:奋勇～ forge ahead /～推进 press forward /再～走五十米就到邮局了。Walk straight ahead for another fifty metres and you'll see the post-office. /～看,不要向后看。Look ahead of you, not behind. /～看!(word of command) Eyes front! *or* Ready, front!

向钱看 xiàngqiánkàn putting money above all else; money-oriented; lucrative-minded; money-grubbing:一切～是一种不良倾向。It's an unhealthy tendency to place money above all else (*or* to set one's sights on nothing but money).

向日 xiàngrì 〈书面〉(in) former days; (in) bygone days:～荣耀 former glory /～在京之时,承蒙厚遇,常记在心。I always remember the generosity and kindness you accorded me in those old days in Beijing.

向日葵 xiàngrìkuí *also* "朝阳花" cháoyánghuā; "葵花" kuíhuā 〈植物〉sunflower:～属 *Helianthus*

向日面 xiàngrìmiàn sunside:果子的～是红的。The sunside of the fruit is red.

向日性 xiàngrìxìng 〈植物〉heliotropism

向日仪 xiàngrìyí sunseeker

向善 xiàngshàn do good deeds:存心～ be bent on doing good; be philanthropic /吃斋念佛,一心～ observe a fast, pray to Buddha and devote oneself to good works

向上 xiàngshàng ❶ upward; up:～的趋势 upward trend /～举 lift up /飞机迅速～爬升。The plane climbed quickly. /公路顺着山势～延伸,直插白云深处。The highway wound up the mountain slope, into the depths of the white clouds. ❷ move forward; advance; improve:努力～的热情 zeal for improvement /好好学习,天天～。Study well and make progress everyday.

向上爬 xiàngshàngpá ❶ climb up:他们一个接一个,沿着峭壁～。They climbed up the cliff one by one. ❷〈比喻〉be intent on personal advancement; climb up the social ladder:结交权贵,一心～的人 social climber who fawns on the bigwigs

向使 xiàngshǐ 〈书面〉if; in case:～当年身便死 had he died then

向水性 xiàngshuǐxìng 〈生物〉hydrotropism

向酸性 xiàngsuānxìng 〈生物〉oxytropism

向晚 xiàngwǎn at dusk; at nightfall:～的草原万籁无声。Tranquillity reigned on the grassland at nightfall. /～风雨大作。A heavy storm raged at dusk.

向往 xiàngwǎng yearn or long for; look forward to:～大学校园生活 yearn for campus life /她怎么也压抑不住心中～之情。Somehow, she could not hold back her yearning.

向午 xiàngwǔ towards noon; close to noon; about noontime

向下 xiàngxià downward; down:～滑坡 downward slide /脸～躺着 lie with the face downward; lie on one's stomach

向晓 xiàngxiǎo at daybreak; at dawn:～雪止。The snow stopped when it was near dawn.

向斜 xiàngxié 〈地质〉syncline

向斜层 xiàngxiécéng 〈地质〉synclinal stratum

向斜谷 xiàngxiégǔ 〈地质〉synclinal valley

向斜轴 xiàngxiézhóu 〈地质〉synclinal axis

向心 xiàngxīn centripetal; towards the centre:～攻击 converging attack /四面一齐开火,组成～火网。Open fire from all sides to form a network of fire aiming at the centre.

向心泵 xiàngxīnbèng centripetal pump

向心加速度 xiàngxīn jiāsùdù centripetal acceleration

向心力 xiàngxīnlì 〈物理〉centripetal force

向心性 xiàngxīnxìng centrality

向性 xiàngxìng 〈生物〉tropism:～运动 tropic movement

向学 xiàngxué be resolved to pursue one's studies:～之心 be bent on seeking knowledge /一心～ be engrossed in academic pursuits; devote oneself to learning

向阳 xiàngyáng be exposed to the sun; face the sun; face south:近水楼台先得月,～花木早逢春。A waterfront pavillion gets the moonlight first, While the flowers exposed to the sun greet spring earlier. /～的屋子住着老人。The old couple live in the room having a southern exposure. /～的窗户上贴着两个斗大的"囍"字。Two big characters meaning "double happiness" were posted on the windows facing south.

向阳花 xiàngyánghuā (often used in literary works) sunflower

向右 xiàngyòu towards the right:～转!(word of command) Right face! *or* Right turn! /～看齐!(word of command) Eyes right! /～转走!(word of command) By the right flank, march! /先向左,后～,再往左。Turn left first, then right, and then left again. /〈比喻〉该政府的政策在～转。That government's policy is swinging (*or* turning) to the right.

向隅 xiàngyú 〈书面〉face a corner in a hall or room — feel very isolated or disappointed for lack of opportunity:～而坐 sit in a corner /以免～ not to miss the chance /～终日,愁思万千 always feel left out in the cold and be weighed down with anxiety

向隅而泣 xiàngyú'érqì weep all alone in a corner; be left to grieve in the cold:被人民抛弃,变为～的可怜虫 be spurned by the people and left to grieve out in the cold

向着 xiàngzhe ❶ turn towards; face:部队～桥头急速挺进。The troops pushed ahead towards the bridge at a high speed. /这一带的房子都～渡口。Houses here all face the ferry crossing. ❷〈口语〉take sb.'s part; side with; favour:办事要公正,不要～任何人。You should be fair in dealings and partial to no one. /妈妈凡事总是～弟弟。Mother always favours my younger brother.

向左 xiàngzuǒ towards the left:～转!(word of command) Left face! *or* Left turn! /～转走!(word of command) By the left flank, march! /顺着河道～,不远处有一处村镇。Turn left along the river and there is a village not far ahead.

象[1]

xiàng ❶ elephant:毛～ mammoth ❷ elephant, one of the pieces in Chinese chess

象[2]

xiàng ❶ appearance; look; shape; image:景～ scene; sight; view /天～ astronomical phenomena; celestial phenomena /印～ impression /气～ weather; meteorology /万～更新。Everything takes on a new look. *or* Everything looks new and fresh. ❷ imitate; mimic: *see* "～声"; "～形文字"

象鼻 xiàngbí trunk; proboscis

象鼻虫 xiàngbíchóng weevil; snout beetle:豌豆～ pea weevil /有～害的 weevilled

象鼻式软导管 xiàngbíshì ruǎndǎoguǎn flexible hose

象海豹 xiànghǎibào elephant seal; sea elephant

象脚鼓 xiàngjiǎogǔ 〈乐器〉drum on a pedestal shaped like an elephant's leg, popular among several minority nationalities in Yunnan Province

象皮病 xiàngpíbìng 〈医学〉〈方言〉elephantiasis

象皮鱼 xiàngpíyú *also* "马面鲀" mǎmiàntún black scraper

象棋 xiàngqí chess:国际～ chess /中国～ Chinese chess /～手 chess player /下～ play (a game of) chess /～子 chessman; piece /～盘 chessboard

象声 xiàngshēng 〈语言〉onomatopoeia

象声词 xiàngshēngcí 〈语言〉mimetic word; onomatope

象事 xiàngshì *also* "指事" zhǐshì one of the six categories (六书) of Chinese characters

象素 xiàngsù picture element; pixel

象限 xiàngxiàn 〈数学〉quadrant:～乘法器 quadrant multiplier /～角 quadrant(al) angle /～偏差 quadrantal deviation

象限仪 xiàngxiànyí 〈天文〉quadrant

象形 xiàngxíng 〈语言〉pictographic characters or pictographs, one of the six categories (六书) of Chinese characters:～符号 glyph

象形文字 xiàngxíng wénzì pictograph; hieroglyph; glyph

象形文字论 xiàngxíng wénzìlùn 〈哲学〉semiotics *see also* "符号论" fúhàolùn

象形字 xiàngxíngzì pictographic character

象牙 xiàngyá elephant's tusk; ivory:～艺术雕刻 artistic ivory carving (*or* sculpture) /～雕像 ivory statue /～扇 ivory fan /～球 ivory ball /～白 ivory white

象牙海岸 Xiàngyá Hǎi'àn Ivory Coast, former name of Côté d'Ivoire (科特迪瓦)

象牙色 xiàngyásè ivory tint

象牙之塔 xiàngyázhītǎ *also* "象牙塔" ivory tower — aloofness from practical life; separation from the harsh realities of ordinary life:生活在～里的大学教授们 university professors in their ivory tower

象牙质 xiàngyázhì ❶ (made of) ivory:～刀把 ivory handle of a knife ❷〈生理〉dentine

象牙棕榈 xiàngyá zōnglǘ 〈植物〉corozo ivory palm; ivory-nut palm:～果 corozo nut

X

象眼儿 xiàngyǎnr 〈方言〉rhombus; lozenge: ～的木格子 rhomboid wood lattices

象征 xiàngzhēng ❶ symbolize; signalize; signify; stand for: 火炬～光明。The torch symbolizes a bright future. /白色～纯洁。White stands for purity. /那些～着昔日辉煌的事物,都已荡然无存了。There is not a trace left of those things which were symbols of former grandeur. ❷ symbol; sign; emblem; token: 友谊的～ emblem (*or* token) of friendship /鸽子是和平的～。The dove is the symbol (*or* emblem) of peace.

象征性 xiàngzhēngxìng symbolic; emblematic: ～支付 token payment /～交货 symbolic delivery /北京－东京～长跑 symbolic Beijing-Tokyo long distance run /他来这里植树只是～的。That he came to plant trees was more of a symbolic gesture.

象箸玉杯 xiàngzhù-yùbēi ivory chopsticks and jade cups — living a luxurious life

橡 xiàng ❶ oak ❷ rubber tree

橡虫 xiàngchóng oak worm

橡浆 xiàngjiāng rubber latex

橡胶 xiàngjiāo rubber: 天然～ natural rubber; gum rubber /合成～ synthetic rubber /生～ raw rubber; caoutchouc /硫化～ vulcanized rubber /海绵～ foam rubber /～植物 rubber bearing plant; rubber plant /～种植园 rubber estate; rubber plantation /～刀 rubber tapping knife /～厂 rubber plant /～制品 rubber goods; rubberwear; rubber /～布 rubberized fabric; rubbered cloth /～轮胎 rubber tyre /～绝缘线〈电工〉india rubber wire /～基涂料 rubber-base paint

橡胶草 xiàngjiāocǎo 〈植物〉Russian dandelion; kok-saghyz

橡胶榕 xiàngjiāoróng *also* "印度橡胶" Yìndù xiàngjiāo rubber plant (*Ficus elastica*)

橡胶树 xiàngjiāoshù rubber tree

橡皮 xiàngpí ❶ rubber: ～子弹 rubber bullet /～胶水 rubber cement /～真空吸盘 rubber vacuum cup /～手套 rubber (operating) gloves ❷ eraser; rubber

橡皮版 xiàngpíbǎn rubber plate (in printing): ～印刷 flexographic printing

橡皮船 xiàngpíchuán rubber boat

橡皮底 xiàngpídǐ rubber sole: ～帆布鞋 plimsoll

橡皮膏 xiàngpígāo *also* "胶布" jiāobù adhesive plaster

橡皮筋 xiàngpíjīn rubber band

see also "猴皮筋儿" hóupíjīnr

橡皮泥 xiàngpíní plasticine

橡皮圈 xiàngpíquān ❶ rubber life ring or preserver; inflatable swimming aid ❷ rubber band (for tying things together)

橡皮树 xiàngpíshù *also* "印度橡皮树" Yìndù xiàngpíshù india rubber tree or plant

橡皮艇 xiàngpítǐng pneumatic boat; rubber dinghy; inflatable rubber boat

橡皮图章 xiàngpí túzhāng rubber stamp: ～式的立法机关 rubber-stamp legislative body

橡皮线 xiàngpíxiàn *also* "皮线" rubber-sheathed wire

橡实 xiàngshí *also* "橡子"; "橡碗子" acorn: ～电池 acorn cell

橡实病 xiàngshíbìng 〈植物〉acorn disease

橡实管 xiàngshíguǎn 〈电子〉acorn tube

橡树 xiàngshù oak: ～介壳虫 oak scale insect /～苗 oakling; oaklet

橡苔 xiàngtái 〈植物〉oakmoss

橡苔树脂 xiàngtái shùzhī 〈化工〉oakmoss resin

橡子 xiàngzǐ acorn: ～仁 acorn-nut

像 xiàng ❶ likeness (of sb.); portrait; statue; picture: 自画～ self-portrait /半身铜～ bronze bust /塑～ sculpture /蜡～ waxworks /录～带 video tape /遗～ portrait of the deceased /标准～ official portrait /石膏～ plastic statue /自由女神～ Statue of Liberty ❷ 〈物理〉image: 虚～ virtual image / 实～ real image ❸ be alike; resemble; take after; look like: 父子俩长得～极了。The father and the son are very much alike. /他～他父亲。He takes after his father. *or* He is a chip off the old block. /怪不得她俩这么～,原来是亲姐妹。No wonder there's strong resemblance between them. They are blood sisters. ❹ look as if; appear; seem: 屋里～是有人来过。It seems that someone has been in the room. /听声音～是个老头儿。He sounds like an old man. /那屋子～是没人住。The house appeared to be deserted. /他连声喊叫,～在发怒。He shouted again and again as if in a rage. ❺ such as; for example; like: ～他这一类的人 people like him; he and his kind /～爱因斯坦这样的科学家,人们永远不会忘记他们。People will never forget scientists like Einstein.

像差 xiàngchā 〈物理〉aberration

像个人样儿 xiàng ge rényàngr like a decent person; decent: 活得～ live a decent life /被折磨得不～了 be tortured beyond recognition

像话 xiànghuà (usu. used in the negative or in a rhetorical question) reasonable; appropriate; proper; right: 你这样瞎编乱造的,～吗? Aren't you ashamed of yourself making up stories out of thin air? /有这样求人的吗? 真不～! Is that the way to ask for help? It's simply outrageous!

像回事儿 xiànghuíshìr just like the real thing; in a decent manner; for real: 把婚礼办得～ have a grand wedding /他唱得还真～。He sang like a professional singer.

像框 xiàngkuàng frame

像录制 xiànglùzhì 〈电子〉image transcription

像模像样 xiàngmó-xiàngyàng up to the mark; respectable; proper: 他人虽小,做起事来挺～的。Young as he is, he is quite neat in getting things done. /这户人家日子还过得～。This family is comfortably off.

像频 xiàngpín 〈电子〉picture frequency: ～调制 image modulation /～抑制 image suppression

像散 xiàngsàn 〈物理〉astigmatism: ～镜 astigmatoscope /～透镜 astigmatic lens

像煞有介事 xiàng shà yǒu jiè shì *also* "煞有介事" make a show of being earnest; pretend to be serious; act as if one's going to handle a big deal; be affectatious or pretentious: 风传要任命他为主任,他便～似的,说话拿腔拿调起来。Getting wind of his possible appointment as dean, he began to act as if he was already a real one, talking haughtily.

像生 xiàngshēng ❶ handicrafts modelled on natural products; imitation: 这些花果都是～的。These flowers and fruits are all imitations. ❷ woman ballad singer (in the Song and Yuan dynasties)

像生磁器 xiàngshēng cíqì porcelain figure

像素 xiàngsù element of picture; picture element; pixel

像样 xiàngyàng *also* "像样子" up to the mark; not bad; presentable; decent: ～的饭菜 decent meal /～的针线活 presentable needlework /～的理由 sound excuse /不～的理由 lame excuse /他字写得挺～。He writes a good hand. /你做得太不～了! Your behavior (*or* conduct) was reprehensible!

像意 xiàngyì (often used in the early vernacular) to one's taste or liking; to one's satisfaction

像赞 xiàngzàn inscription on a portrait

像章 xiàngzhāng badge or button with sb.'s likeness on it: 毛主席～ Chairman Mao badge

xiāo

哓(嘵) xiāo

哓哓 xiāoxiāo 〈书面〉❶ (arguing) noisily ❷ frightened cries (of birds)

哓哓不休 xiāoxiāo-bùxiū argue endlessly: 整日～,成何体统? How unseemly it is to keep arguing all day long!

骁(驍) xiāo 〈书面〉valiant; valorous; brave: ～卫 imperial guards

骁悍 xiāohàn 〈书面〉brave and fierce; valiant and strong: ～善战 valorous and skilful in battle

骁健 xiāojiàn 〈书面〉valiant and robust: ～的武士 valiant fighter

骁将 xiāojiàng 〈书面〉valiant general: 一员～ valiant general /他们不仅是球场上的～,而且还是生产上的能手。They are not only good ball players but also good workers.

骁骑 xiāoqí 〈书面〉valiant cavalryman: 三百～ three hundred dashing cavalrymen

骁勇 xiāoyǒng 〈书面〉brave; courageous; valiant: ～善战 brave and skilful in battle /～无敌 valiant and unmatched; matchlessly brave

肖 Xiāo a surname

see also xiào

肖邦 Xiāobāng Frederic Chopin (1810-1849), Polish composer

and pianist

肖氏硬度 Xiāoshì yìngdù 〈物理〉 Shore hardness: ～计 Shore scleroscope / ～试验 drop hardness test

消 xiāo ❶ disappear; vanish; melt: 烟～云散 vanish like mist and smoke; vanish into thin air / 冰～瓦解 melt like ice and break like tiles; disintegrate / 患处已经～肿了。The swelling of the wound has gone down. / 他酒气未～就来了。He came when still under the influence of alcohol. ❷ eliminate; dispel; reduce; remove: 抵～ offset; counterbalance / 对～ offset; cancel each other out / 你最好早点打～这个念头。You'd better give up that idea as soon as possible. ❸ pass the time in a leisurely way; idle away (the time): 对弈～永夜 pass the long night by playing chess ❹ (after 不, 只, 何 etc.) need; require; take: 不～说 needless to say; it goes without saying; no doubt; undoubtedly / 打一套家具只～两三天。It takes only two or three days to carpenter a set of furniture.

消沉 xiāochén in low spirits; downhearted; dejected; depressed: 意气～ in poor (*or* low) spirits; downcast / 意志～ downhearted; demoralized; despondent / 因失恋而情绪～ feel down after being disappointed in love

消愁 xiāochóu allay cares; dispel worries; divert oneself from care: 以酒～愁更愁 try to drown one's sorrow in alcohol only to sink in deeper sorrow

消愁解闷 xiāochóu-jiěmèn divert oneself from boredom; dispel melancholia or ennui: 听听音乐, 看看电视, 借以～ try to dispel one's depression by listening to some music and watching TV

消除 xiāochú eliminate; dispel; get rid of; ease: ～分歧 eliminate (*or* iron out) differences / ～疑虑 clear one's mind of doubt; dispel misgivings / ～疾病 eliminate diseases / ～隔阂 clear up a misunderstanding / ～紧张局势 defuse (*or* ease) tension / ～薄弱环节 cut out weak links / ～祸根 eradicate (*or* remove) the root of trouble / ～赤字 erase a budget deficit / ～异己 liquidate those not of one's own kind (*or* ilk) / ～隐患 obviate a hidden danger

消除信号 xiāochú xìnhào erase signal; erasure signal

消磁 xiāocí degaussing; demagnetization; field discharge: ～绕组 degaussing belt / ～船 demagnetizing ship / ～器 magnetic eraser

消导 xiāodǎo 〈中医〉 cure indigestion: ～药 digestant

消电离 xiāodiànlí 〈电工〉 deionization; deion: ～箱 deionized chamber

消毒 xiāodú ❶ disinfect; sterilize; pasteurize: ～水 antiseptive solution / ～剂量 sterilization doze / ～牛奶 sterilized (*or* pasteurized) milk / 打针前用酒精～ sterilize (the needle) in alcohol before injection / 这些东西事先都用漂白粉消过毒。These things have all been disinfected with bleaching powder in advance. ❷ decontaminate; dispel pernicious influence: 尽管当局采取了种种～措施, 但效果并不显著。Despite the various measures taken by the authorities to counteract these pernicious influences, not much has come out of it.

消毒剂 xiāodújì disinfectant

消毒器 xiāodúqì sterilizer; sterilizing equipment

消毒药 xiāodúyào disinfectant; antiseptic

消乏 xiāofá ❶ deplete; expend; use up: ～了本钱 lose all the capital ❷ be impoverished; decline (in wealth and position): 家道～。The family declined. ❸ exhausted; tired out: 他跑了一天, 有些～了。He felt a bit tired, having being busy all day.

消法 xiāofǎ 〈中医〉 resolution — dispersing inflammatory or other lesions

消防 xiāofáng fire fighting; fire control; fire prevention: ～演习 fire drill / ～人员 fire fighter; fireman / ～署 fire department / ～安全检查员 fire runner / 本店专营～设备。We sell fire-fighting apparatus.

消防报警器 xiāofáng bàojǐngqì fire alarm

消防泵 xiāofángbèng fire pump

消防车 xiāofángchē fire engine or truck

消防队 xiāofángduì fire brigade

消防钩 xiāofánggōu fire hook

消防龙头 xiāofáng lóngtóu fire cock

消防事务处 Xiāofáng Shìwùchù (HK) Fire Services Department

消防栓 xiāofángshuān fire hydrant; fire plug

消防水龙 xiāofáng shuǐlóng fire hose

消防塔 xiāofángtǎ fire tower

消防梯 xiāofángtī fire escape

消防艇 xiāofángtǐng fireboat

消防站 xiāofángzhàn fire station

消费 xiāofèi consume: ～不足 underconsumption; inadequate consumption / ～高涨 spending boom; consumption boom / ～需求 consumer demand; demands of consumption / ～方式 pattern of consumption / ～失调 imbalance of consumption / 高～经济 high consumption economy / 家庭～ household consumption / 人均～量 per capita consumption / ～倾向 propensity to consume; trend of consumption

消费城市 xiāofèi chéngshì consumer city

消费函数 xiāofèi hánshù consumption function

消费合作社 xiāofèi hézuòshè consumers' cooperative; consumers' cooperative society

消费基金 xiāofèi jījīn fund for consumption; consumption fund

消费结构 xiāofèi jiégòu consumption pattern

消费经济学 xiāofèi jīngjìxué consumer economics

消费膨胀 xiāofèi péngzhàng inflation of consumption levels

消费品 xiāofèipǐn consumer goods; expendable materials: 日常生活中的～ daily commodities; consumer goods in everyday life / ～销售 consumer sales / ～购买 consumer purchases / ～需求结构 composition of consumer goods / ～工业 consumer goods industry / 耐用～ durable consumer goods; consumer durables / ～价格指数 consumer price index

消费水平 xiāofèi shuǐpíng consumption level; standard of consumption

消费税 xiāofèishuì consumption tax

消费心理学 xiāofèi xīnlǐxué consumer psychology

消费信贷 xiāofèi xìndài consumer credit: ～公司 consumer finance company

消费者 xiāofèizhě consumer: ～保障 consumer protection / ～倒账 consumer bad debt / ～动机 consumer motivation / ～风险 consumer's risk / ～联盟 consumer union / ～偏好 consumer preference / ～行为 consumer behaviour / ～主权 consumers' sovereignty / ～权益 consumer rights and interests / ～支出税 expenditure tax / ～至上 consumer-oriented / ～形象描述 consumer profile

消费者协会 xiāofèizhě xiéhuì consumers' association

消费主义 xiāofèizhǔyì consumerism

消费资料 xiāofèi zīliào *also* "生活资料" shēnghuó zīliào means of subsistence

消光 xiāoguāng ❶ 〈物理〉 extinction; matting; defrosting: ～系数 extinction coefficient / ～比 extinction ratio / ～灯泡 defrosted bulb / 这个镜框是经过～的。The frame has been matted. ❷ 〈纺织〉 deluster: ～纤维 delustered fibre

消光剂 xiāoguāngjì 〈纺织〉 delusterant; delustrant; dulling agent

消耗 xiāohào ❶ consume; use up: 高产、优质、低～ high productivity, good quality and low consumption (of raw material) / 这几天精力～太大。I've been consuming too much of my energy these days. ❷ expend; deplete; wear down: ～体力 wear sb. down; tire sb. / 低效益给企业人力物力带来的～, 已经引起了大家的重视。The drain on manpower and material resources resulting from low efficiency has attracted widespread attention. ❸ (often used in the early vernacular) news; mail; message: 他走后～全无。Nothing has been heard of him since he left.

消耗功 xiāohàogōng consumed work

消耗热 xiāohàorè 〈医学〉 hectic fever

消耗性材料 xiāohàoxìng cáiliào consumable material

消耗战 xiāohàozhàn war of attrition

消弧 xiāohú 〈物理〉 extinction of arc; extinction

消化 xiāohuà ❶ digest: 不易～ indigestible / 肠胃不好, 你多吃些好～的东西。You'd better take something easy to digest since you have a weak stomach. ❷ 〈比喻〉 digest; absorb; take in: 课上讲的东西太多, 一时～不了。The students found it hard to digest the abundance of materials they were taught in class. / 机关改革后, 多余的劳动力主要靠办公司企业来～吸收。The surplus manpower after the reform of government departments was mainly absorbed into various companies and businesses.

消化不良 xiāohuà bùliáng indigestion; dyspepsia: ～病人 dyspeptic / ～症状 dyspeptic symptom

消化道 xiāohuàdào alimentary canal; digestive tract: ～出血 bleeding in the digestive tract

消化率 xiāohuàlǜ digestibility

消化酶 xiāohuàméi digestive ferment; digestive enzyme

消化器官 xiāohuà qìguān digestive organ

消化系统 xiāohuà xìtǒng digestive system

消化腺 xiāohuàxiàn digestive gland
消化性溃疡 xiāohuàxìng kuìyáng 〈医学〉 peptic ulcer
消化药 xiāohuàyào digestant; digestive
消化液 xiāohuàyè digestive juice: ～缺乏〈医学〉achylia gastrica
消魂 xiāohún be overwhelmed with joy or sorrow
see also "销魂" xiāohún
消火器 xiāohuǒqì fire extinguisher
消火栓 xiāohuǒshuān fire hydrant; fire cock
消极 xiāojí ❶ negative: 起～作用 exert a negative influence; play a negative role / 化～因素为积极因素 turn negative factors into positive ones / ～言论 disheartening remarks / ～影响 harmful (*or* undesirable) impact ❷ passive; inactive; lethargic: ～抵抗 passive resistance / 采取～等待和观望的态度 adopt a passive wait-and-see attitude / ～旁观 look on passively / ～情绪 inactivity; lethargy; low spirits / ～怠工 be slack in work; go slow
消极干扰 xiāojí gānrǎo passive jamming
消极平衡 xiāojí pínghéng negative approach to the question of equilibrium; negative equilibrium
消极优生学 xiāojí yōushēngxué negative eugenics
消减 xiāojiǎn decrease; lessen; abate; reduce: 食欲～ diminished (*or* reduced) appetite
消解 xiāojiě get rid of; clear up; dispel; remove: 原先的猜疑、误会，顷刻之间全部～了。All former doubts and misunderstandings were gone instantly.
消渴病 xiāokěbìng 〈中医〉 ❶ diabetes ❷ any disease with the symptom of frequent drinking and urination
消弭 xiāomǐ put an end to; avert; prevent: ～灾祸 avert a disaster / 大坝一旦建成，便可～水患，造福于民。The dam, once finished, will prevent floods and bring benefit to the people.
消灭 xiāomiè ❶ perish; die out; become extinct: 许多古生物种早已经～了。Many Paleozoic species have long since died out. ❷ exterminate; annihilate; eradicate; wipe out: ～霍乱 eradicate cholera / ～苍蝇 wipe out flies / ～来犯之敌 annihilate the invaders / ～一切错误 eliminate all mistakes / ～病虫害 exterminate insect pests and plant diseases / ～贫困 root out poverty / ～文盲 put an end to illiteracy
消泯 xiāomǐn perish; die out; become extinct; erode: 意志～。One's willpower has eroded.
消磨 xiāomó ❶ wear down; fritter away; blunt: ～锐气 wear down one's drive; blunt one's enthusiasm / 琐碎的家务活儿～了人的精力。Household chores have frittered away one's energy. ❷ while away; fool away; idle away: 他喜欢用小说来～时间。He likes to kill time by reading novels. / 你不能再这样～岁月了。You can't go on whiling away the time like this.
消没 xiāomò disappear; vanish: 看着他渐渐远去，直至身影～在人流中。I saw him going farther and farther away until he disappeared into the crowd.
消纳 xiāonà store up for later disposal: 全市设立渣土～场七处，以解决渣土处理的问题。Seven garbage dumps have been set up in the city to dispose of waste.
消痞化积 xiāopǐ-huàjī 〈中药〉 relieve retained food and improve digestion: ～剂 retained food relieving prescription
消气 xiāoqì cool down; calm down; be mollified: 自己～ cool oneself down / 给父母认个错，让大人消消气。Make an apology to your parents to mollify them.
消遣 xiāoqiǎn ❶ relax oneself; while away the time: 几个小伙子正在下棋～。Some young men are playing chess to pass the time. / 带几本杂志路上～。Take some magazines with you so as to divert yourself from the boredom on the journey. / 他们一路上打扑克～。They beguiled the journey by playing cards. / 紧张的工作之后要～～。Have a little relaxation after hard work. ❷ pastime; distraction; diversion: 母亲最大的～是打麻将。My mother's favorite pastime is playing mah-jong. / 写信成了他唯一的～。Writing letters became his only distraction.
消去 xiāoqù 〈数学〉 cancellation; elimination: ～法 elimination method / ～三个零 cross out (*or* eliminate) three "0"s
消溶 xiāoróng *see* "消融"
消融 xiāoróng *also* "消溶" thaw; melt; ablate: ～面 ablating surface / 冰雪～，大地回春。Spring comes with the thawing of ice and snow.
消散 xiāosàn scatter and disappear; dissipate; vanish: 晨雾渐渐～，青山露出倩影。The beautiful mountain peaks emerged from behind the vanishing morning mist. / 听了这话，他一脸的愁容～了。When he heard these words his worried expression disappeared. / 一夜好睡，疲劳完全～了。My fatigue was gone after a night's sound sleep.
消散剂 xiāosànjì 〈药学〉 discussive; discutient
消色 xiāosè achromatism; decoloration: ～指示器 achromatic indicator / ～电路 colour killer circuit
消色差 xiāosèchā 〈物理〉 achromatism: ～度 achromaticity
消色差透镜 xiāosèchā tòujìng 〈物理〉 achromatic lens; achromat
消色目镜 xiāosè mùjìng achromatic eyepiece
消声 xiāoshēng noise elimination
消声管 xiāoshēngguǎn hush tube
消声器 xiāoshēngqì silencer; muffler; dissipative muffler
消声室 xiāoshēngshì anechoic chamber (of a recording studio)
消失 xiāoshī pass out of sight; disappear; vanish; fade away: 在远方～ disappear in the distance / 她朝我挥了挥手，～在人群中。She waved her hand at me and was then lost in the crowd. / 她脸上的笑容顿时～了。The smile on her face at once vanished.
消石灰 xiāoshíhuī hydrated lime
消食 xiāoshí digest; help digestion: ～化痰 help digestion and eliminate phlegm / ～导滞 eliminate indigestion
消蚀 xiāoshí corrode; wear away: 由于流水的～，巨石的底部有许多细小的空洞。The bottom of the giant rock is porous as a result of water corrosion.
消逝 xiāoshì die away; fade away; vanish; elapse: 随着时间的～ with the passage (*or* lapse) of time / 一抹残霞在天边～。The evening glow faded away on the horizon.
消释 xiāoshì ❶〈书面〉melt; thaw: 湖面上的冰～了。The ice on the lake is thawing. ❷ clear up; remove; dispel: ～前嫌，重归于好 remove ill will (*or* settle a grudge) and be friends again / 疑虑一旦～，他心里松快多了。Misgivings dispelled, he felt quite at ease (*or* much better).
消受 xiāoshòu ❶ (often used in the negative) enjoy: 无福～ not have the luck to enjoy / 礼物你请带回去，我～不起。Please take back the gift. It's more than I deserve. ❷ endure; bear; sustain; stand: 我再也～不了啦。I could no longer put up with it.
消瘦 xiāoshòu become thin; become emaciated: ～的面容 emaciated look / 日渐～ get thinner each day / 这失恋的人一天天地～下去。Day after day the disappointed lover peaked and pined.
消瘦症 xiāoshòuzhèng 〈医学〉 marasmus
消暑 xiāoshǔ ❶ take a summer holiday: 这几年，到海滨～的游客越来越多。In recent years, there has been an increasing number of visitors at the beach to spend the summer holiday. ❷ relieve summer heat; drive away summer heat: 来，喝一碗冰镇绿豆汤消消暑。Come on, have a drink of iced mung bean juice to drive away summer heat.
消损 xiāosǔn ❶ wear and tear: 严重～ heavy wear and tear / 检查设备～的程度 check (*or* examine) the wear and tear condition of the equipment ❷ erode; wear away; fritter away; decrease: ～岁月 fritter time away / 他的锐气～殆尽。His dashing spirit has flagged.
消索 xiāosuǒ ❶ decline; wane: 家道～。The family declined. ❷ vanish; scatter and disappear; dissipate: 神魂～ spiritless; distracted; out of one's wits
消停 xiāoting 〈方言〉 ❶ quiet; peaceful; stable; steady: 过上了～日子 live a peaceful life / 还没住～就走了。He went away before he had time to settle down. ❷ pause; stop; have a rest: 姐妹俩日夜纺线，从不～。The two sisters spin day and night without a rest.
消退 xiāotuì decrease; fade away; disappear bit by bit; gradually vanish: 永不～的笑容 smile that stays / 几天后炎症就会～。The inflammation will disappear in a few days. / 夕阳西下，暑热略略～。With the setting sun the summer heat abated.
消亡 xiāowáng wither away; die out; be extinct: 国家～ withering away of states / 旧习惯一定会～。Old customs are bound to die out. / 这件事永远也不会在我的记忆中～。It will never fade out of my memories.
消息 xiāoxi ❶ news; information; report: ～报道 news story; news report / 传播～ spread (*or* disseminate) the news / 发布～ news briefing / 封锁～ news blackout / 本地～ local news / 据可靠～ according to reliable sources / 内部～ inside story; internal information / 耸人听闻的～ sensational news (*or* story) / 头版头条～ front-page headline story / 透露～ disclose (*or* reveal) the news / 最新～ latest news; breaking news; last-minute news (*or* report) / ～来源 source of information / ～灵通人士 well-informed source / ～不灵通 ill-informed;

X

have no (*or* little) access to information ❷ tidings; news:他有～吗? Any news about him? /他这一去,十年间杳无～。I have not heard from him since he left ten years ago.

消息报 Xiāoxībào *Izvestia* (started in 1917 as organ of the former Soviet Union, now an independent newspaper in Russia)

消息儿 xiāoxir 〈方言〉hidden mechanical starter; contraption:地道暗藏着机关,只要触动～,就会射出冷箭。There were hidden mechanical starters in the tunnel. If you happened to touch them, they would trigger fatal arrows.

消夏 xiāoxià relieve summer heat; take a summer holiday; spend the summer at leisure: ～音乐会 summer holiday concert /～舞会 summer evening dance

消闲 xiāoxián ❶ kill leisure time; idle away the hours:～解闷 relieve boredom; distract the mind ❷ at leisure; carefree:别人忙得要命,他可真～,看戏去了。He even had the leisure to go to the theatre when others were up to their necks in work.

消歇 xiāoxiē *also* "销歇" xiāoxiē 〈书面〉stop; disappear; die away; subside:风雨～。The storm subsided. /狂风～,皓月当空。A bright moon hung in the sky when the fierce wind was over.

消协 xiāoxié (short for 消费者协会) consumers' association

消旋 xiāoxuán 〈化学〉racemize: ～化合物 racemic compound; racemoid /～体 racemic modification /～酶〈生化〉racemase

消炎 xiāoyán 〈医学〉diminish or allay inflammation: ～止痛 diminish inflammation and kill (*or* relieve) pain

消炎粉 xiāoyánfěn sulfadiazine powder; anti-inflammation powder

消炎剂 xiāoyánjì *also* "消炎药" antiphlogistic

消炎片 xiāoyánpiàn sulfaguanidine tablet; anti-inflammation pill

消夜 xiāoyè 〈方言〉❶ midnight snack:准备了几色瓜果点心当～。Some fruits and refreshments were prepared as midnight snack. ❷ have a midnight snack

消音 xiāoyīn *also* "消声" noise elimination or reduction: ～设施 equipment for noise elimination; noise eliminating equipment

消音磁头 xiāoyīn cítóu erase head; erasing head; magnetic tape erasure

消音器 xiāoyīnqì muffler; silencer:装～的手枪 handgun with silencer /汽车～ car muffler

消音效果 xiāoyīn xiàoguǒ 〈电子〉erasure effect

消隐 xiāoyǐn ❶ disappear; hide:此人～多时,今又见报。The man reappeared (*or* surfaced again) in today's newspaper after hiding from public view (*or* keeping himself out of sight) for quite some time. ❷〈电学〉blank; blackout: ～部件 blackout unit /～电平 blanking level; blackout level /～信号 blanking (*or* blackout) signal

消忧解愁 xiāoyōu-jiěchóu allay grief or sorrow; relieve sb. from worry (*or* anxiety)

消灾 xiāozāi avert calamities; stave off disasters:破财～ give some money in order to forestall misfortune

消灾降福 xiāozāi-jiàngfú ward off disasters and bring good luck; avert calamities and bring blessings

消灾免祸 xiāozāi-miǎnhuò avert calamities; avoid disasters

消长 xiāo-zhǎng growth and decline; rise and fall; wax and wane:敌我力量的～ growth and decline of the relative strength of ourselves and the enemy /资金的～ increase and decrease of funds

消痔术 xiāozhìshù 〈医学〉hemorrhoidolysis

消肿 xiāozhǒng 〈医学〉subsidence of a swelling; detumescence; reducing or removing a swelling:热敷～ remove a swelling by hot compress /用药物～ use medicine to cure a swelling /～止痛 subside (*or* reduce) a swelling and relieve pain /机关～是个大问题。Trimming is a major task for government organizations. *or* Trimming government agencies is a big problem.

消字灵 xiāozìlíng eraser; eradicator; ink eradicator

宵

xiāo night:通～ all night; throughout the night /良～ lovely night; happy night /春～ spring night /元～之夜 night of the Lantern Festival /今～酒醒何处? Where shall I be when I sober up tonight?

宵遁 xiāodùn 〈书面〉flee under the cover of night:～而去 flee under the cover of night /黄洋界上炮声隆,报道敌军～。From Huangyangjie roars the thunder of guns, Word comes the enemy has fled into the night.

宵旰 xiāogàn 〈书面〉*see* "宵衣旰食"

宵禁 xiāojìn curfew:～令 curfew decree /实行～ impose a curfew /解除～ lift (*or* end) a curfew

宵小 xiāoxiǎo 〈书面〉bandit; highwayman; gangster; bad people:～行径 gangster's conduct /沿途山高林深,～出没无常。The road runs through thickly forested mountains which were haunted by bandits.

宵行 xiāoxíng 〈书面〉go out at night; make a night journey:～之人 night owl; night roamer /秉烛～ take an evening stroll with a lantern /某些国家严禁～夜游。Roaming about at night is strictly forbidden in some countries.

宵夜 xiāoyè *see* "消夜 ❶" xiāoyè

宵衣旰食 xiāoyī-gànshí rise before dawn and eat after dusk — busy with state affairs; diligent in discharging official duties: ～,日夜操劳 rise early, eat late and work hard day and night; be up to one's neck in work day and night /～,日理万机 work conscientiously and be occupied with a myriad of state affairs

逍

xiāo

逍遥 xiāoyáo free and unfettered; carefree: ～一生 saunter through life /男女老少乐～。Men and women, old and young, all are happy.

逍遥法外 xiāoyáo-fǎwài go unpunished (by law); go scot-free; be or remain at large:罪犯仍～。The criminal is still at large. /我们不能让他们～。We cannot let them go unpunished (*or* with impunity). /他之所以能～,是因为他有很硬的靠山。He was able to get away with it only because he has very strong backing.

逍遥派 xiāoyáopài people who avoid getting involved (in the Cultural Revolution); people who stand aloof from political infighting:他们在"文革"中是～。They stayed away from all political factions during the Cultural Revolution.

逍遥自在 xiāoyáo-zìzài take life easy; be leisurely and carefree: 他活得～。He led a free and easy sort of life. /我们这里远离市声,水秀山青,～。Far from the clamour of the city, we are much better off living free among our clear waters and blue hills.

霄

xiāo clouds; sky; heaven:高耸入云～ towering into the sky; reach (*or* rise towards) the clouds /九～云外 beyond the highest heavens

霄汉 xiāohàn 〈书面〉sky; firmament:气冲～ spirit soaring to the firmament; be in a towering rage /万木霜天红烂漫,天兵怒气冲～。Forests blaze red beneath the frosty sky, The wrath of Heaven's armies soars to the clouds.

霄壤 xiāorǎng heaven and earth:由此看来,二人品格的高下,何啻～。It is thus clear that the two are as far apart in moral character as heaven and earth.

霄壤之别 xiāorǎngzhībié as far apart as heaven and earth; poles apart; world of difference:两者相比,有～。The two are poles apart. *or* There is a world of difference between the two.

硝

xiāo ❶ nitre; saltpetre: 大～ nitre; saltpetre /皮～ mirabi /硭～ mirabilite; Glauber's salt /墙～ wall saltpetre /炸～ blasting saltpetre ❷ taw; tan:皮硝可以～皮革。Mirabi can be used to taw (*or* tan) hide.

硝氨基 xiāo'ānjī nitramino

硝胺炸药 xiāo'àn zhàyào nitroamine (compound) explosive

硝化 xiāohuà 〈化工〉nitrify:～棉 nitrocotton /～纤维素 nitrocellulose /～反应 nitration reaction

硝化甘油 xiāohuà gānyóu 〈化工〉nitroglycerine:～火药 nitroglycerine powder /～炸药 nitroglycerine explosive

硝化火药 xiāohuà huǒyào 〈化工〉nitro-powder; nitro-explosive

硝化器 xiāohuàqì nitrator; nitration kettle

硝基 xiāojī *also* "硝铣基"〈化学〉nitro-: ～苯 nitrobenzene /～烷 nitroalkane /～胺 nitramine /亚～胺 nitrosamine /～苯胺 nitroaniline /～清漆 zapon /～磁漆 nitroenamel /～染料 nitro dye /～衍生物 nitro derivatives /～炸药 nitro-explosive

硝基安定 xiāojī āndìng 〈药学〉nitrazepam

硝基甲烷 xiāojī jiǎwán 〈化工〉nitromethane

硝镪水 xiāoqiāngshuǐ 〈化工〉nitric acid

硝石 xiāoshí *also* "火硝" huǒxiāo nitre; saltpetre:智利～ Chile nitre (*or* saltpetre); sodium nitre

硝酸 xiāosuān *also* "硝镪水"〈化工〉hydrogen nitrate; nitric acid: 亚～ nitrous acid

X

硝酸铵 xiāosuān'ǎn ammonium nitrate
硝酸钙 xiāosuāngài nitrate of lime
硝酸甘油片 xiāosuān-gānyóupiàn 〈药学〉 nitroglycerine tablet
硝酸根 xiāosuāngēn nitrate radical
硝酸钾 xiāosuānjiǎ *also* "火硝" huǒxiāo potassium nitrate; nitrate of potash
硝酸钠 xiāosuānnà *also* "智利硝石" Zhìlì xiāoshí sodium nitrate
硝酸纤维素 xiāosuān xiānwéisù cellulose nitrate
硝酸盐 xiāosuānyán nitrate: 亚～ nitrite
硝酸银 xiāosuānyín nitrate of silver; silver nitrate
硝酰基 xiāoxiānjī 〈化学〉 nitroxyl: 亚～ nitrosyl
硝烟 xiāoyān smoke of gunpowder: ～弥漫 be smoke-laden; be enveloped in smoke; a cloud of smoke floats over; be under a blanket of smoke / 一场大雨过后, ～散尽。The smoke of gunpowder dispersed after a heavy rain.
硝盐 xiāoyán earth salt
硝制 xiāozhì taw; tan

削

xiāo ❶ pare or peel with a knife; scrape; whittle: ～梨 peel a pear / ～竹片 whittle a piece of bamboo / ～铅笔 sharpen a pencil / 这种金属容易切～。This metal cuts easily. ❷ 〈体育〉 cut; chop: *see* "～球"
see also xuē
削笔刀 xiāobǐdāo penknife
削尖脑袋 xiāojiān-nǎodai 〈贬义〉 try hard to squeeze in; worm one's way in: ～往里钻 try by hook or by crook to worm one's way in
削面 xiāomiàn *also* "刀削面" dāoxiāomiàn noodles made by shaving strips of dough with a knife; shaved noodles
削皮刀 xiāopídāo paring knife
削皮器 xiāopíqì parer; peeler
削球 xiāoqiú (in pingpong) chop; cut: 她擅长～, 是有名的～手。She is good at cutting and is a well-known cutter.

蛸

xiāo *see* "螵蛸" piāoxiāo
see also shāo

销[1]

xiāo ❶ melt (metal): ～银 melt silver / ～兵 destroy arms ❷ cancel; annul; cross out: 注～ write off; cancel / 撤～ repeal; cancel; rescind / 核～ cancel after verification / 勾～ liquidate; write off; cross out / 吊～ revoke; withdraw ❸ put on sale; sell; market: 外～ sell abroad / 倾～ dumping / 定～ fix sales quotas / 购～ buy and sell / 推～ promote sales / 展～ exhibit for sale / 试～ (place goods on) trial sale / 畅～国内外 find a ready market both in and out of the country / 滞～商品 commodities in oversupply / 自产自～ sell the products produced by oneself / 产～平衡 balance between production and sales ❹ pay out; expend; spend: 花～ cost; expense / 不必要的开～ unnecessary expenditure

销[2]

xiāo ❶ pin: 摆～ 〈机械〉 balance pin / 开尾～ 〈机械〉 cotter pin; split pin / 锁～ locking pin / 螺栓～ bolt pin ❷ fasten with a latch: ～上销子 put on the latch; keep the pin on / 门已～好。The door is on the latch. *or* The door is latched.
销案 xiāo'àn close a case
销差 xiāochāi report to one's superior upon the end of a mission: 事情已办完, 回去～。Task fulfilled, I returned to report to my boss.
销场 xiāochǎng 〈方言〉 sale; market: 打开商品～ open up a new market for the commodities / ～很好 be salable; sell well; have a good (*or* ready) market
销钉 xiāodīng *see* "销子"
销户口 xiāo hùkǒu cancel one's residence registration
销毁 xiāohuǐ destroy by melting or burning; destroy: 彻底～核武器 thorough destruction of nuclear weapons / ～文件 burn up documents / ～尸体 cremate a dead body / 罪犯～罪证时被当场抓获。The criminal was caught red-handed when he was destroying incriminating evidence.
销魂 xiāohún *also* "消魂" xiāohún be overwhelmed with sorrow or joy; feel transported; be extremely happy and satisfied: ～夺魄 overwhelmed by sb.'s beauty or love
销货 xiāohuò sales: ～单 sales slip / ～合同 sales contract / ～限额 sales quotas / ～退回 sales returns / ～簿 record of sales / ～发票 sales invoice / ～与管理费用 selling and administrative expenses / ～定单 sales order / ～款 money for sold commodities / ～收益 sales revenue (*or* income) / ～凭证 sales voucher / ～折扣 (sales) discount and rebate / ～总额 gross sales
销价 xiāojià selling price; market value; sale price: 降低～ lower a selling price / 规定合理的～ set a reasonable selling price / 正常～和周末～ regular price and weekend sale price
销假 xiāojià report back after leave of absence: 探亲归来, 尽早～。Report back as soon as possible after returning from home leave.
销金 xiāojīn ❶ melt metal ❷ lavish wealth; squander money ❸ decorated with gold; gilt: ～纸 gilt paper / ～帐 gilt curtain
销金窟 xiāojīnkū money-squandering den — cabaret, brothel, etc., where money is spent freely for sensual pleasures
销量 xiāoliàng sales (volume): ～锐减 sharp decrease in sales / ～逐月递增。The sales volume increased progressively month after month.
销路 xiāolù sale; market; outlet: ～很广 find an extensive market; have a good sale; be in great demand / ～不佳 sell poorly; have a dull market; have poor sales / 打开商品～ find new markets for commodity / 新产品～很好, 行情一直看涨。The new product sells like hot cakes and the price has kept rising. / 只要质量好, 价格合理, 就不愁没有～。So long as the quality is guaranteed and the price reasonable, there will be a ready market (*or* sure demand) for it.
销密 xiāomì declassify: 文件的～制度 rules for the declassification of documents
销纳 xiāonà destroy and hold; dispose of: 新建城市要解决好垃圾的清运和～问题。A newly built city must solve the problem of garbage (*or* waste) disposal.
销声匿迹 xiāoshēng-nìjì keep silent and lie low; disappear from the scene; stay in oblivion: 从此～ disappear from the scene from then on / ～, 潜伏待命 lie low and await orders
销蚀 xiāoshí corrode; wear away: 追求物质享受的社会的～作用 corrosive influence of a materialist society
销蚀剂 xiāoshíjì corrodent; corrosive
销势 xiāoshì selling tendency; sales trend: ～很好。The sales trend is good (*or* favourable).
销售 xiāoshòu market; sales: ～成本 selling cost; cost of sales / ～导向 sales orientation / ～方针 marketing strategy / ～分析 sales analysis / ～概念 marketing concept / ～计划 sales plan / ～价格 selling price; retail price / ～收入 sales income / ～量 sales volume / ～金额 total (*or* aggregate) sales / ～经理 sales manager / ～代理商 sales agent / ～代表 sales representative / ～部门 sales department / ～淡季 period of slack sales; slack season / ～调查 marketing research / ～合同应收账款 sales contract receivable / ～后技术服务 after-sale service / ～后市场 after market / ～与固定资产比率 sales-fixed assets ratio / ～与净值比率 sales-net worth ratio / ～商品盘存比率 sales-inventory ratio / ～与应收账款比率 sales-receivable ratio / ～组合计划 marketing-mix programme / ～最大化 sales maximization
销售领域 xiāoshòu lǐngyù sales territory
销售疲软 xiāoshòu píruǎn sluggish market; dull sales
销售渠道 xiāoshòu qúdào channel of distribution: ～组合 distribution mix
销售税 xiāoshòushuì sales tax
销售网点 xiāoshòu wǎngdiǎn commercial network
销售危机 xiāoshòu wēijī sales crisis
销售学 xiāoshòuxué marketing science
销售佣金 xiāoshòu yòngjīn selling commission
销售预测 xiāoshòu yùcè sales forecast
销售者市场 xiāoshòuzhě shìchǎng seller's market: ～指的是商品短缺、物价昂贵、消费者选择余地较少的状况; 而消费者市场则情况相反。As opposed to the buyer's market, the seller's market denotes a state of affairs in which goods are scarce, prices are high and buyers have little choice.
销售组合 xiāoshòu zǔhé sales mix
销铄 xiāoshuò 〈书面〉 ❶ melt; eliminate; remove: ～金石 melt metals and rocks / ～芥蒂 remove grudges; eliminate differences ❷ thin and frail (as from long illness); emaciated: 形容～ wear an emaciated look; look emaciated
销歇 xiāoxiē *also* "消歇" xiāoxiē vanish; subside; die away
销行 xiāoxíng sell; be on sale: ～海内外 be sold both at home and overseas / 此书多次重印, ～达三百万册。This book has been reprinted many times, and three million copies have been sold.

销赃 xiāozāng 〈法律〉❶ disposal of stolen goods or spoils：参与盗窃、～的人有十多个。Over a dozen people got involved in the stealing and disposal of these stolen goods. ❷ destroy the stolen goods：～灭迹 destroy evidence by getting rid of stolen goods
销账 xiāozhàng cancel or remove from an account; write or cross off an account; cancel debts：补上欠款，请予～。Please cancel the debts since the arrears have now been paid off.
销子 xiāozi *also*"销钉" pin; peg; dowel：～锁 pinlock
销座 xiāozuò key seat

魈

xiāo *see*"山魈" shānxiāo

绡

xiāo 〈书面〉❶ raw silk ❷ fabric made of unprocessed or raw silk
绡头 xiāotóu silk ribbon for binding the hair; silk hair-ribbon

虓

xiāo 〈书面〉(of a tiger) roar

猇

xiāo ❶ *see*"虓" xiāo ❷ Xiāoting 猇亭, ancient name of the present area north of Yidu (宜都) County, Hubei Province

枵

xiāo 〈书面〉empty; hollow：～肠辘辘 have an empty stomach; be starving
枵腹从公 xiāofù-cónggōng attend to official duties on an empty stomach; do work without pay：～，十余年如一日 be selflessly devoted to one's official duties for more than ten years running

鸮

xiāo *also*"猫头鹰" māotóuyīng owl
鸮鹦鹉 xiāoyīngwǔ owl parrot; kakapo
鸮卣 xiāoyǒu 〈考古〉owl-shaped bronze wine jar

嚣(嚻)

xiāo clamour; hubbub; din：叫～ clamour /～尘 noise and dust; noisy world /烦～ noisy and annoying /喧～ din; clamour; hullabaloo
嚣闹 xiāonào noisy; clamorous：～声顿时平息下来。The commotion quieted down immediately (*or* abruptly).
嚣杂 xiāozá noisy confusion; commotion：远处传来～的人声。The babel of a crowd was heard from far away.
嚣张 xiāozhāng rampant; arrogant; insolent; aggressive：～一时 run rampant (*or* wild) for a time; be high and mighty for a while /气焰～ be swollen (*or* puffed up) with arrogance /真是太～了! What audacity!

翛

xiāo 〈书面〉unrestrained; carefree
翛然 xiāorán 〈书面〉free; unrestrained
翛翛 xiāoxiāo 〈书面〉(of feathers) broken

枭(梟)

xiāo ❶ owl; legendary bird said to eat its own mother：～鸟 owl /～獍 mother-eater and father-eater — unfilial child; ungrateful person ❷ 〈书面〉fierce and brave：～骑 elite cavalry unit ❸ chief; chieftain; ringleader：毒～ drug pusher; drug king ❹ 〈旧语〉salt smuggler：私～ smuggler ❺ 〈书面〉hang (severed heads)：～示 hang (sb.'s decapitated head) as a warning (for others)

X

枭将 xiāojiàng 〈书面〉brave general
枭首 xiāoshǒu 〈旧语〉decapitate a person and hang up his head, a kind of capital punishment in former times
枭首示众 xiāoshǒu-shìzhòng cut off sb.'s head and hang it up as a warning to all
枭雄 xiāoxióng 〈书面〉fierce and ambitious person; person who is capable but unscrupulous：一代～ fierce and ambitious person of the time (*or* age)

潇(瀟)

xiāo ❶ 〈书面〉(of water) deep and clear ❷ (of wind and rain) beating; driving ❸ Xiao River (tributary of the Xiang River 湘江 or 湘水)
潇洒 xiāosǎ *also*"萧洒" xiāosǎ natural and elegant; free and unconventional：～自如 free and elegant; with easy grace /神情～ with a debonair air (*or* manner) /笔法～ in a natural and graceful hand
潇湘 Xiāoxiāng ❶ poetic name for the Xiang River (湘江) ❷ poetic name for Hunan Province
潇潇 xiāoxiāo ❶ whistling and pattering：风雨～ whistling of wind and pattering of rain /～暮雨洒江天。At evening a driving rain swept over the river and the skies. ❷ drizzly：春雨～ drizzling spring rain

萧(蕭)

xiāo ❶ deserted and miserable; desolate; dreary ❷ (Xiāo) a surname
萧伯纳 Xiāobónà George Bernard Shaw (1856-1950), British-Irish playwright and novelist, winner of Nobel Prize for literature (1925)
萧规曹随 xiāoguī-cáosuí Cao Can (曹参 a Han Dynasty prime minister) followed the rules set by Xiao He (萧何 his predecessor) — follow in sb.'s footsteps; act according to established rules：新局长到来之后，～，不改旧章。After assuming office, the new director followed in his predecessor's footsteps without making any changes in the established rules.
萧何 Xiāo Hé Xiao He (?-193 BC), prime minister of the early Han Dynasty
萧墙 xiāoqiáng 〈书面〉screen wall inside the gate of a Chinese house：祸起～。Trouble starts at home.
萧墙之祸 xiāoqiángzhīhuò *also*"祸起萧墙" huòqǐ-xiāoqiáng trouble behind the screen wall — trouble arising at home; affliction from within; internal strife
萧然 xiāorán 〈书面〉❶ desolate; lonely：气氛～ desolate atmosphere ❷ empty; vacant：四壁～ have nothing but bare walls in one's house; be utterly destitute /囊橐～ have empty pocket ❸ unrestrained; detached; unhampered：～物外 (man's spirit) untrammeled by worldly affairs
萧洒 xiāosǎ *see*"潇洒" xiāosǎ
萧飒 xiāosà 〈书面〉desolate; bleak：北风凛烈，满山～ bleak hillside struck by the full force of the north wind /飓风一过，众多沿海城镇一片～。Many coastal towns lay desolate after the hurricane.
萧骚 xiāosāo 〈书面〉❶ howl (in the trees); whistle：朔风～。The north wind was howling. ❷ bleak; desolate：农庄位于荒凉～的山谷。The farm lies in a lonely desolate valley.
萧瑟 xiāosè ❶ rustle in the air; sough：～秋风今又是，换了人间。Today the autumn wind still sighs, But the world has changed! ❷ bleak; melancholy; desolate：秋景～ bleak autumn scene /落拓一生最～ be lonely and desolate all one's life
萧森 xiāosēn 〈书面〉❶ withered; wizened; bleak：秋树～。Trees are wizened in autumn. ❷ dreary and desolate：巫山巫峡气～。Dreary and desolate is the atmosphere around Wushan Mountain and Wuxia Gorge.
萧疏 xiāoshū ❶ desolate; bleak：千村薜荔人遗矢，万户～鬼唱歌。Hundreds of villages choked with weeds, men wasted away; Thousands of homes deserted, ghosts chanted mournfully. ❷ sparse; thinly scattered：欢笑情如旧，～鬓已秋。They laughed as heartily as before when they met again, but sadly they have gone grey at the temples.
萧索 xiāosuǒ bleak and chilly; desolate：晚秋气象～。It is a bleak and chilly late autumn scene.
萧条 xiāotiáo ❶ desolate; bleak：断墙老树，景象～。It was a desolate scene of dilapidated walls and old trees. ❷ 〈经济〉slump; depression：经济～ economic depression; slump /近来生意～，店面上冷冷清清的。Business has been slack recently with few shoppers.
萧闲 xiāoxián 〈书面〉❶ leisurely and at ease：他萧萧闲闲地走了进来。He came in unhurriedly. ❷ lonely and silent：～的古寺 quiet (*or* secluded) old temple
萧萧 xiāoxiāo ❶ 〈书面〉〈象声〉sound of wind soughing or of horses neighing：马鸣～。Horses are whinnying and neighing. /风～兮易水寒。The wind soughs and sighs, and cold is the water of the Yi River. ❷ (of hair) white and sparse：白发～。The hair is white and thinning.

蟏(蠨)

xiāo
蟏蛸 xiāoshāo *also*"喜蛛" xǐzhū；"蟢子" xǐzi Teraguatha, a kind of spider with long legs

箫(簫)

xiāo *xiao*, a vertical bamboo flute

xiáo

筊 xiáo 〈书面〉bamboo rope

淆 xiáo confuse; mix:混～ mix up; confuse; obscure

淆惑 xiáohuò 〈书面〉confuse; befuddle; bewilder:～视听 befuddle (*or* confuse) the minds of the public

淆乱 xiáoluàn ❶ confuse; befuddle:～事态 muddy up matters /～人言 confuse what others say ❷ disturb; confound:～社会秩序 create confusion in society; disrupt public order /～是非，颠倒黑白 confound right and wrong and call black white

淆杂 xiáozá mix; mingle:人言～，莫衷一是。There are a great many diverse opinions, and it is impossible to tell which is right.

崤 xiáo

崤山 Xiáoshān mountain in Henan Province

殽 xiáo ❶ *see* "淆" xiáo ❷ *see* "崤" xiáo

殽函 Xiáo-Hán short for 崤山(殽山) and 函谷关, two places in Henan Province, which are strategically located and difficult of access:～之固 impregnable as Xiao-Han; strongly fortified

xiǎo

小 xiǎo ❶ small; little; tiny; minor:～树 sapling /～地方 small (*or* little) place; one-horse town /～山 little hill; hillock /～毛病 minor problem; petty flaw /大街～巷 streets and lanes /大材～用 waste one's talent on a petty job /作些～改动 make some minor changes /声音太～ speak in a low voice; speak under one's breath /雨～些了。The rain has abated (*or* subsided). /这双鞋～了点儿。This pair of shoes is a bit too tight. /我比他～三岁。I'm three years younger than he is. ❷ for a short while; for a little time:～别重逢 meet again after a short interval /～坐片刻 sit for a little while /他每来北京，必来我家～住。Whenever he came to Beijing, he would come to stay in my house for a few days. ❸ a little; a bit; slightly:牛刀～试 first small display by a master /～有才干 of some ability ❹ a little less than; almost:～一百 a little less than a hundred /他都是～三十的人了。He is just a little under thirty. /此处离县城有～二十里。It is almost 20 *li* from the county seat. ❺ youngest:～儿子 youngest son /～孙子 youngest grandson ❻ young children; little ones:上有老下有～ have both aged parents and young children to provide for /两～无猜 two innocent children together — innocent childhood relationship (usu. between a boy and a girl) /我妈在农村养了许多～鸡、～狗、～猫、～牛。My mother raised a lot of chicks, puppies, kittens and calves in our country home. ❼ lesser or minor wife; concubine:讨～ take a concubine /做～ be a concubine ❽〈谦词〉I; me; my:～店 my store (*or* shop) /～儿 my son /～的不胜感激。I'm deeply grateful. ❾ *used before a surname to refer to a young person, or before a given name to refer to a child*:～马 Xiao Ma; Young Ma /～军 Xiao Jun; Little Jun

小矮凳 xiǎo'ǎidèng low stool

小八路 xiǎo Bālù little 8th Route Army man — under-age person who joined the Communist Army before Liberation (1949)

小巴 xiǎobā minibus

小把戏 xiǎobǎxì 〈方言〉child:这～会干活了。The child can do some work now.

小白菜 xiǎobáicài *also* "青菜" qīngcài variety of Chinese cabbage; bokchoi

小白菊 xiǎobáijú 〈中药〉feverfew (small, white chrysanthemum, used as a febrifuge)

小白脸儿 xiǎobáiliǎnr 〈贬义〉handsome young man (usu. with effeminate features)

小百货 xiǎobǎihuò small light-industrial or handicraft products used in everyday life; small articles of daily use; sundries

小百科全书 xiǎobǎikē quánshū micropaedia

小摆设 xiǎobǎishe bric-a-brac; knick-knack

小班 xiǎobān ❶ small class (of 15 students or less):英语练习课以～为宜。It's best to have English language drills in a small class. ❷ bottom class in a kindergarten:我女儿刚上～。My daughter has just been admitted to the bottom class of her kindergarten.

小半 xiǎobàn less than half; lesser or smaller part:～时间用来学习 spend less than half the time on study /缺席者差不多有一～。Almost half of the people (required to be present) were absent.

小半活 xiǎobànhuó 〈方言〉teenage farmhand; child labourer:十岁那年，他就当了～，给人放牛。He had to work as a cowherd when he was ten.

小包工 xiǎobāogōng contract for some part of a job or project

小包装 xiǎobāozhuāng small packages; pouch pack:～食品 small packages of food; pouch-packed food

小宝贝 xiǎobǎobèi little darling; baby; babe

小保姆 xiǎobǎomǔ young housemaid

小报 xiǎobào tabloid; tab:通俗～ popular tabloid

小报告 xiǎobàogào 〈贬义〉backbiting report; malicious hearsay information; complaint behind sb.'s back:打～ tell tales (on sb.); inform (on sb.); snitch (on sb.) /爱听～ gorge oneself on hearsay information or gossip /专打～的人 telltale; snitch

小辈 xiǎobèi younger member (of a family, profession, etc.); junior:我们作为～应尊敬老人。As juniors, we should respect our seniors. /别看不起后生～! 他们已经是教学骨干了。Don't look down upon these young people! They're already mainstays in teaching.

小本经营 xiǎoběn jīngyíng run a small business; do business in a small way:本店是～，经不起大风险。Ours is a small business and can't take great risks. /他们从～做起，没几年就发展成为一家大公司了。Starting business on a shoestring, they had become a big company within a few years.

小臂 xiǎobì forearm

小扁豆 xiǎobiǎndòu lentil

小便 xiǎobiàn ❶ urinate; pass water; pee; piss ❷ urine; urination:化验～ have a urine test /～不利 difficult urination /～淋沥 dribbling urination /～频繁 frequent urination /～疼痛 painful urination /～灼热 burning sensation during urination /～失禁 urinary incontinence; aconuresis /～不通 urinary obstruction /～赤黄 dark urine /～短赤 scanty dark urine ❸ penis; vulva

小便池 xiǎobiànchí urinal

小辫儿 xiǎobiànr short braid; pigtail:梳着两条～的姑娘 girl wearing her hair in two braids

小辫子 xiǎobiànzi ❶ short braid; pigtail ❷ mistake or shortcoming that may be exploited by others; vulnerable point; handle:抓～ exploit sb.'s mistakes or shortcomings; capitalize on sb.'s vulnerabilities /她打算抓住老杨的～狠狠地整他一下。She wanted to get a handle on Lao Yang so as to give him a hard time.

小标题 xiǎobiāotí subheading; subhead; subtitle

小冰川 xiǎobīngchuān glacieret

小冰期 Xiǎobīngqī Little Ice Age

小病大养 xiǎobìng-dàyǎng ask for or take a long recuperation leave with only a minor illness; make much ado with a minor indisposition

小不忍则乱大谋 xiǎo bù rěn zé luàn dàmóu lack of forbearance in small matters upsets or spoils great plans

小不点儿 xiǎobudiǎnr 〈方言〉❶ very small; tiny:一间～的屋子 tiny room ❷ tiny tot; brat:怀里抱着个～ hold a tiny tot in one's arms /你这个～，懂什么? What do you know, little brat?

小布 xiǎobù narrow home-spun cloth

小步 xiǎobù 〈军事〉half-step march:～前进 progress (*or* march) in measured steps

小步舞 xiǎobùwǔ 〈舞蹈〉minuet:～曲〈音乐〉minuet

小材大用 xiǎocái-dàyòng man of little ability in a high position:避免～ avoid giving great responsibilities to men of little abilities

小菜 xiǎocài ❶ side dish (such as pickles, fried peanuts, cold meats, etc. usu. to go with wine); hors d'oeuvres:几碟儿下酒的～ some side dishes to go with the wine ❷ easy job; no big deal:种这点地，还不是～儿一碟。Tilling that small plot of land is as easy as pie. ❸〈方言〉meat, fish or vegetable dishes as distinguished from rice, or other staples:买～ buy greengroceries; buy food /今天有客人来，准备些好～。As we have company today, we must prepare some delicious dishes.

小册子 xiǎocèzi pamphlet; booklet; brochure:编写出版～ compile and publish pamphlets /介绍我们学院的～ brochure about our college

小差 xiǎochāi (used in 开小差) ❶ (of soldiers) desert; AWOL:他

X

是开～回来的。He came back on AWOL. ❷ absent-minded; wool-gathering:你是不是思想开～了! Penny for your thoughts.

小产 xiǎochǎn miscarriage; abortion; (of animals) slink:先兆～ threatened abortion

小肠 xiǎocháng 〈生理〉small intestine:～痈 small intestinal abscess /～激素 intestine hormone

小肠串气 xiǎocháng chuànqì *also*"小肠疝气"〈口语〉hernia

小肠结肠炎 xiǎocháng jiéchángyán 〈医学〉enterocolitis

小抄儿 xiǎochāor 〈口语〉note brought in stealthily at examination; crib:传～ pass on a crib

小朝廷 xiǎocháotíng dynasty or imperial government retaining sovereignty over a small part of the country:南宋～ crippled Southern Song court

小潮 xiǎocháo neap (tide):～潮差 (mean) neap range /～流速 neap rate

小炒 xiǎochǎo individually stir-fried dish (cooked usually in a small wok as against food prepared in a big pot); à la carte dish:要一瓶啤酒和几个～ order some à la carte dishes with a bottle of beer

小车 xiǎochē ❶ wheelbarrow; handbarrow; handcart; pushcart ❷ sedan (car)

小车舞 xiǎochēwǔ wheelbarrow dance (a kind of folk dancing usu. with one actor or actress playing a woman sitting on a wheelbarrow and another playing her lover)

小乘 xiǎochéng 〈佛教〉Little Vehicle; Hinayana; Theravada:～佛教 Hinayana Buddhism /～教徒 Hinayanist; Theravadin

小吃 xiǎochī ❶ small and cheap dishes (in a restaurant):经济～ cheap simple dishes; cheap food ❷ snacks; refreshments:风味～ specialty snacks ❸ cold dish; hors d'oeuvre

小吃部 xiǎochībù snack counter; refreshment room; buffet

小吃店 xiǎochīdiàn snack bar

小吃街 xiǎochījiē snack street — street lined with snack bars

小丑 xiǎochǒu ❶ clown; buffoon:马戏团～ circus clown /扮～ act the clown; play the buffoon ❷ person who likes to poke fun at others; sport ❸ villain; mean person:政治～ political villain /文坛～ mean person in literary circles

小丑跳梁 xiǎochǒu-tiàoliáng contemptible wretch busy stirring up trouble

小除夕 xiǎochúxī *see*"小年夜"

小处落笔 xiǎochù-luòbǐ start from triviality; start with daily routine:大处着眼,～ keep the overall picture in mind but start with the daily routine

小春 xiǎochūn 〈方言〉❶ *also*"小阳春" tenth lunar month (when there is often a spell of warm weather); Indian summer; late autumn ❷ *also*"小春作物" crop planted in late autumn, such as wheat or pea

小春耕 xiǎochūngēng supplementary spring ploughing and sowing (planting in scattered pieces of land or uncultivated hillsides in addition to the spring sowing of major crops)

小疵 xiǎocī minor mistake; trivial defect or flaw:大醇～ sound on the whole despite some minor defects; more merits than faults

小词 xiǎocí 〈逻辑〉minor term

小葱 xiǎocōng ❶ shallot; scallion; spring onion:～拌豆腐 — 一清二白 as plain as a dish of white beancurd and green scallions; as clear as daylight ❷ young onion; tender shallot (for transplanting or as food)

小聪明 xiǎocōngming 〈贬义〉cleverness in trivial matters; petty shrewdness; petty trick:耍～ play petty tricks /办大事不能靠～取巧。One can never achieve great things through petty shrewdness. /他有点儿～,但很不踏实。He is smart in his own way but never thorough or conscientious.

小打扮儿 xiǎodǎbànr 〈方言〉(dressed in) tight-fitting clothes

小打小闹 xiǎodǎ-xiǎonào (do sth.) in dribs and drabs; on a small scale; in a piecemeal manner:他～,也赚了不少钱。He made quite a lot of money in bits and pieces.

小大姐 xiǎodàjiě 〈方言〉"young miss" — term of address for a young maid

小大人儿 xiǎodàrénr child behaving like an adult; demure child

小袋鼠 xiǎodàishǔ pademelon; wallaby

小旦 xiǎodàn 〈戏曲〉young female character

小刀 xiǎodāo ❶ small sword or knife ❷ pocket knife

小刀会起义 Xiǎodāohuì Qǐyì Xiaodaohui Uprising (After the Taiping Heavenly Kingdom had made Nanjing its capital, Xiaodaohui, or Small Sword Association, a branch of the Heaven and Earth Association, led by Huang Wei and Liu Lichuan, started an armed uprising in Xiamen and Shanghai in 1853. The Uprising was later suppressed by the Qing government assisted by British and French troops.)

小岛 xiǎodǎo small island; islet

小道 xiǎodào ❶ path; trail:羊肠～ winding trail /山间～ mountain path /走～儿近些,但不甚安全。The branch road is shorter but not quite safe. ❷ unorthodox; heterodox; lowly:在旧社会戏曲和小说始终还是～,不能跟诗文并列为正宗。In traditional Chinese culture, operas and novels were always regarded as something unorthodox or trivial, not to be ranked together with poetry and prose as mainstream literature. ❸ grapevine; bush telegraph:我是从～听来的。I heard it on (*or* through) the grapevine.

小道理 xiǎodàoli minor or petty principle:由于～可能损害长远和全面利益,因此～必须服从大道理。As they may run counter to the long-term and overall interests, minor principles must be subordinated to major ones.

小道儿消息 xiǎodàor xiāoxi grapevine (news); back-alley news; hearsay; rumour:这个～一度广为流传。This rumour was once widespread. /他喜欢散布～。He is fond of spreading hearsay news (*or* rumours).

小的 xiǎode ❶ little ones; young children:家里老的～无人照管。There is no one to take care of the old and the young at home. ❷ 〈旧语〉(used by commoners or *yamen* runners when speaking to officials) I; me; my:这是～错! It's my fault, sir.

小弟 xiǎodì ❶ youngest brother; little brother; kid brother:前日收到～来信。I received a letter from my youngest brother the day before yesterday. ❷ 〈谦词〉(used among friends) I; me:～不才,愿当此任。Though not gifted, I am ready to take the job.

小调 xiǎodiào ❶ popular tune; ditty:民间～ folk ditty; folk tune /江南～ tune popular south of the Yangtze River ❷ 〈音乐〉minor:C～协奏曲 concerto in C minor /～式 minor mode /～音阶 minor scale

小动脉 xiǎodòngmài arteriole; arteriola:～瘤 microaneurysm /～硬化 arteriosclerosis

小动作 xiǎodòngzuò petty action; little trick; manoeuvre:有的小学生上课时常好搞点～。Some pupils often engage in petty actions (*or* get fidgety) in class. /要光明磊落,不要搞～。Be open and aboveboard and play no petty tricks.

小洞不补,大洞吃苦 xiǎodòng bù bǔ, dàdòng chīkǔ 〈俗语〉a small leak will sink a great ship; a small neglect may breed great mischief; a stitch in time saves nine

小豆 xiǎodòu *also*"赤小豆" chìxiǎodòu red bean:～粥 red bean porridge

小豆蔻 xiǎodòukòu 〈植物〉cardamom; cardamon

小肚儿 xiǎodǔr ball-shaped preserved food made of pig bladder stuffed with starch and minced meat

小肚鸡肠 xiǎodù-jīcháng *also*"鼠肚鸡肠" shǔdù-jīcháng petty-minded; narrow-minded:几个～的妇女正在说三道四。Some petty-minded women were making irresponsible remarks. /没见过他这样～的人! I've never seen anyone as narrow-minded as he is!

小肚子 xiǎodùzi 〈口语〉region below the navel; underbelly; lower abdomen

小短片 xiǎoduǎnpiàn 〈影视〉film insert

小队 xiǎoduì team; squad; group:生产～ production team /飞行～ flying squad /按～分配任务 assign tasks among the groups /每个～五个人。Each team (*or* group) has five persons.

小额 xiǎo'é small sum or amount:～存款 small savings account

小额补贴 xiǎo'é bǔtiē fringe benefit

小恩小惠 xiǎo'ēn-xiǎohuì petty favours; small favours; sops:利用～笼络人心 try to win support by giving petty favours /这个人贪图小便宜,什么～都要。The man is so greedy that he will swallow any sops.

小儿 xiǎo'ér ❶ child; infant:黄毛～ chit of a child /～脑素麻痹 cerebral infantile paralysis /～食积 infantile indigestion with food retention /～杂病 miscellaneous infantile diseases ❷ 〈谦词〉my son:～不敏,请多指教。As my son is inexperienced, I would appreciate it if you'd kindly give him guidance.

see also xiǎor

小儿疾病 xiǎo'ér jíbìng children's disease; pediatric disease

小儿科 xiǎo'érkē ❶ 〈医学〉(department of) pediatrics:～医生 pediatrician ❷ kid's stuff; easy mark; petty stuff:我干这点事,还不是

~! Why, that's just as easy as pie for me. /把儿童文学称为文学界的"~",这是大错特错的。It is absolutely wrong to regard children's literature as kids' stuff in literature.

小儿连衫裤 xiǎo'ér liánshānkù creepers

小儿麻痹症 xiǎo'ér mábìzhèng 〈医学〉 infantile paralysis; poliomyelitis; polio

小儿糖尿病 xiǎo'ér tángniàobìng 〈医学〉 juvenile-onset diabetes

小二 xiǎo'èr *also* "小二哥" 〈旧语〉 young waiter (in wineshop); boy

小贩 xiǎofàn pedlar; vendor; hawker; badger: 小商~ small tradespeople and pedlars

小房 xiǎofáng lesser wife; concubine

小纺 xiǎofǎng thin, soft, plain-weave silk fabric: 苏、杭~,名扬天下。The plain-weave silk of Suzhou and Hangzhou is known all over the country.

小费 xiǎofèi *also* "小账" tip; gratuity: 收~ accept tips /付~ give a tip /去美国之前,最好先了解一下美国人付~的办法。Before going to the United States, one had better find out how the Americans tip.

小分队 xiǎofēnduì squad; detachment; contingent: 敌后~ detachment sent into the enemy's rear (*or* areas behind the enemy lines) /民兵~ militia detachment /文艺~ performing squad /支农~ aid-agriculture contingent

小粉 xiǎofěn starch; amylum

小服务程序 xiǎofúwù chéngxù 〈信息〉 servelet

小斧 xiǎofǔ hatchet: 单刃~ half hatchet

小腹 xiǎofù *also* "小肚子" underbelly; lower abdomen: ~痛 pain in the lower abdomen /~胀满 distension of the lower abdomen /踢了他的~一脚 kick him in the underbelly

小嘎 xiǎogǎ *also* "小尕" 〈方言〉 child; kid

小钢炮 xiǎogāngpào ❶ small calibre gun or cannon ❷ 〈比喻〉 outspoken person

小个子 xiǎogèzi little chap; small fellow

小工 xiǎogōng unskilled labourer: 打~ do odd jobs; work as an unskilled labourer

小公共汽车 xiǎogōnggòng qìchē minibus

小功率 xiǎogōnglǜ low power; miniwatt: ~电动机 fractional (*or* low-power) electric motor /~负载 low-power load /~晶体管 low-power transistor /~继电器 low-power relay /~电路 low-power circuit

小恭 xiǎogōng 〈书面〉 urinate; pass water; make water: 出~ go to the lavatory

小姑儿 xiǎogūr ❶ husband's younger sister; sister-in-law ❷ one's youngest paternal aunt

小姑独处 xiǎogū-dúchù young woman living on her own; girl not yet married; single young woman

小姑子 xiǎogūzi *also* "小姑儿" 〈口语〉 husband's younger sister; sister-in-law

小鼓 xiǎogǔ 〈乐器〉 side drum; snare drum

小褂 xiǎoguà (Chinese style) shirt: 中式~儿 Chinese-style shirt

小馆儿 xiǎoguǎnr small restaurant; cheap restaurant; pub: 下~ eat in a small restaurant /找个~随便吃点儿。Let's have something at a pub.

小广播 xiǎoguǎngbō gossip; rumour; grapevine; hearsay information: 这人可爱"~"了。He's keen on spreading rumours. *or* He's a terrible gossip. /有些人专爱听"~"。Some people indulge in gossip. *or* Some people gorge themselves on rumours.

小鬼 xiǎoguǐ ❶ 〈迷信〉 little devil that runs errands for the King of Hell; imp; goblin: ~勾魂 with one's soul taken away by the King of Hell's little devil /~作祟 haunted by goblins /阎王好见,~难缠。〈俗语〉 It is more difficult to dispose of the little devils than to see the King of Hell himself. ❷ (term of endearment in addressing a child) "little devil"; mischievous boy: 这几个~真不听话! These children are just mischievous! /这~真淘气! What a naughty boy!

小鬼头 xiǎoguǐtou 〈方言〉 "little devil"; mischievous child: 你这~,竟敢戏弄我! You mischievous monkey, how dare you make fun of me!

小孩儿 xiǎoháir 〈口语〉 ❶ *also* "小孩子" child; kid: ~鞋 shoes for children; children's shoes /~床 cot; crib /耍~脾气 behave childishly; be pettish ❷ sons and daughters (usu. those who have not yet grown up); children: 你有几个~? How many children do you have?

小寒 Xiǎohán ❶ Slight Cold, 23rd seasonal division point, marking the sun's position at 285° on the ecliptic ❷ day marking such a seasonal division point, usu. falling on the 5th or 6th of January ❸ period lasting from such a seasonal division point till the next one (Great Cold 大寒)

see also "节气" jiéqì; "二十四节气" èrshísì jiéqì

小号 xiǎohào ❶ small-size (as distinct from medium and large sizes): ~服装 small-size clothes /~字 〈印刷〉 fine print (*or* type) ❷ 〈旧语〉〈谦词〉 my store; our store: 您要的这批货,~三日内可备齐。Your order will be ready at this store within three days. ❸ 〈乐器〉 trumpet; clarion: 尖音~ clarion ❹ 〈方言〉 single-person prison cell; single cell

小黑麦 xiǎohēimài triticale: 异源八倍体~ allooctoploid triticale

小红书 xiǎohóngshū "little red book" (of Mao Zedong's quotations)

小红细胞 xiǎohóngxìbāo 〈生理〉 microcyte: ~症 microcytosis

小猴子 xiǎohóuzi (playful term for a naughty boy) little monkey

小胡桃 xiǎohútáo 〈方言〉 hickory

小户 xiǎohù ❶ family of limited means and without powerful connections; ordinary family: 穷苦无告的~ ordinary family that has no money or powerful friends ❷ small family: 几代单传的~ small family having only one son for several generations in succession

小花脸 xiǎohuāliǎn 〈戏曲〉 clown; buffoon

小话儿 xiǎohuàr 〈方言〉 ❶ gossip: 背后说~ gossip behind another's back /喜欢听~ greedy for gossip ❷ words of intercession: 你为什么老为别人传~? Why are you always taking up for others?

小环境 xiǎohuánjìng microenvironment; subenvironment

小鬟 xiǎohuán 〈旧语〉 ❶ little girl ❷ young maid (servant)

小皇帝 xiǎohuángdì ❶ child emperor: ~只是太后手中的傀儡而已。The child emperor was merely a puppet controlled by the empress dowager. ❷ "little king" — spoiled child: "~"一词指的是那些被宠坏了的独生子女。The term "little king" is used for pampered only sons.

小黄鱼 xiǎohuángyú little yellow croaker

小汇报 xiǎohuìbào backbiting gossip; malicious report; complaint behind sb.'s back: 打~ make a malicious report about sb.; snitch on sb. /主任从不听信~。The director never believes malicious backbiting (against his subordinates).

小惠 xiǎohuì small or petty favour; sop: 略施~ throw a few sops

小活儿 xiǎohuór odd job; miscellaneous work: 做~ do odd jobs

小火车 xiǎohuǒchē narrow gauge train; puddle jumper

小伙子 xiǎohuǒzi 〈口语〉 young man; lad; young fellow; youngster: 十几岁的~ lad in his teens /有趣的~ funny young chap /天不怕、地不怕的~ daredevil young man

小鸡儿 xiǎojīr *also* "小鸡鸡" 〈戏谑〉 little cock (referring to a small boy's penis)

小集体 xiǎojítǐ small collective; small group: 不能只考虑~的利益。We should not only consider the interests of our small group.

小集团 xiǎojítuán clique; coterie; faction: 搞~ set up a faction; form a clique /~活动 factional activities /~主义 small groupism — putting the interests of one's clique above all else

小计 xiǎojì subtotal: 以上各项~一百元。The above items add up to 100 *yuan*.

小蓟 xiǎojì 〈中药〉 field thistle (*Cephalanoplos segetum*)

小家碧玉 xiǎojiā-bìyù pretty girl of humble birth; daughter of a humble family: 她虽不是大家闺秀,也称得上~了。She was from a family of moderate means, though not actually rich.

小家电 xiǎojiādiàn small or minor electric appliance (such as electric irons, razors, cleaners, etc.)

小家伙 xiǎojiāhuo little thing; kiddy; toddler; baby: 可爱的~! What a lovely little thing!

小家鼠 xiǎojiāshǔ *also* "鼷鼠" xīshǔ house mouse (*Mus musculus*)

小家庭 xiǎojiātíng small family; nuclear family: 建立自己的~ start a family on one's own

小家子 xiǎojiāzi person of humble birth; humble or lowly family: 别看咱是~生长的,也看不惯这个! Though of humble birth, I can't bear that!

小家子气 xiǎojiāziqì *also* "小家子相" unease or nervousness (in public) typical of people of low birth; petty or vulgar behaviour; narrow-mindedness: 此人言谈举止有点~。There is something petty (*or* vulgar) about his speech and behaviour. /他太~,真让人扫兴! He was such a spoilsport with his petty ways! /若题目过于新巧,韵过于险,再不得好诗,倒~。Such far-fetched subjects and freakish

rhymes do not make for good poetry and seem rather low-class.

小件 xiǎojiàn small article; small item:～行李 small pieces of luggage /～寄存处 parcel checkroom

小建 xiǎojiàn *also* "小尽" lunar month of 29 days

小将 xiǎojiàng ❶ young general:一员白袍～ young general in a white robe ❷〈比喻〉young militant; young pathbreaker:革命～ young revolutionary /红卫兵～ (used in the Cultural Revolution) militant Red Guard

小脚 xiǎojiǎo bound feet (of women in former times):裹～ having one's feet bound; foot-binding

小脚女人 xiǎojiǎo-nǚrén woman with bound feet — not able to make big steps:他干起工作像个～。At work, he is just like a woman with bound feet — too cautious to make big strides.

小轿车 xiǎojiàochē sedan (car); car

小教堂 xiǎojiàotáng chapel

小节 xiǎojié ❶ small matter; trifle:生活～ matters concerning one's personal life only /拘泥～ be punctilious /他为人素来大大咧咧,不拘～。He is a happy-go-lucky sort of person and never bothers about trivial matters. ❷〈音乐〉bar; measure:～线 bar line; bar

小劫 xiǎojié minor suffering; small disaster; minor misfortune:他似乎命中注定有此～。It seemed that he was fated to suffer this small misfortune.

小结 xiǎojié ❶ brief sum-up; preliminary summary; summary:做课文～ make a summary of the text /他这个～写得很有水平。His summary is well-written. ❷ make a summary; summarize:～一周工作 summarize (*or* sum up) the week's work ❸〈医学〉nodule

小解 xiǎojiě urinate; pass water; make water

小姐 xiǎojie ❶〈旧语〉young lady:她可是～的身子丫环的命。Frail as a lady, she was destined to suffer like a common housemaid. ❷ (respectful term of address for a young woman) miss:导游～ miss guide; tourist guide /～请结账。Waitress, bill, please.

小金库 xiǎojīnkù "small exchequer" — funds or accounts owned by a subsidiary unit in violation of fiscal regulations

小襟 xiǎojīn smaller or inner piece on the right side of a Chinese garment which buttons on the right

小尽 xiǎojìn *see* "小建"

小径 xiǎojìng ❶ pathway; small path; trail:林间～ trail in the woods /～通幽。A narrow path leads to a secluded retreat. ❷ (of a log) small in diameter:～木材 timber of small diameter

小九九 xiǎojiǔjiǔ ❶ *also* "九九歌" jiǔjiǔgē multiplication table for the abacus ❷〈比喻〉calculation; scheming:谁心里没个～? Who doesn't have his own calculations or plans? /事到临头,你心里总该有个～吧。Now that things have come to a head, you must have a solution up your sleeve.

小舅子 xiǎojiùzi 〈口语〉wife's younger brother; brother-in-law

小开 xiǎokāi 〈方言〉❶ son of a boss; son of a capitalist:他是这家杂货店的～。He was the son of the grocer. ❷ rich young boy or man; rich young dandy:打扮得像个上海滩的～ dress up like a rich young dandy of the Shanghai Bund

小楷 xiǎokǎi ❶ regular script in small characters (as used in Chinese calligraphy exercises):蝇头～ neat small characters of regular script ❷〈印刷〉lowercase (letter)

小看 xiǎokàn look down upon; underrate; slight; belittle:你凭什么～人! What makes you look down upon others! /此人不可～。He is not to be slighted. /别～这个问题。Don't take the problem lightly.

小康 xiǎokāng comfortably off; comparatively well-off; moderately well-off:～水平 comparatively well-off standard of living; comfortable life /从温饱型向～型过渡 proceed from being adequately fed and clad to a comfortable life

小康之家 xiǎokāng zhī jiā family of moderate means; comfortably-off family; moderately well-off family

小考 xiǎokǎo minor examination; quiz:每周～ weekly quiz

小可 xiǎokě ❶ (often used in the early vernacular)〈谦词〉I; me:急煞了～。I am worried to death. /～无能,连累大家。Because of my incompetence, I got all of you into trouble. ❷ unimportant; trivial:非同～ not at all unimportant; no trivial matter

小客车 xiǎokèchē passenger car; minivan; minibus

小口径 xiǎokǒujìng small-calibre; small-bore:～步枪 small-bore rifle /～火箭 small-calibre rocket /～钻进 slim hole drilling

小老婆 xiǎolǎopo *also* "小婆儿" concubine

小老树 xiǎolǎoshù small but old tree; dwarf tree; stunted tree

小老头儿 xiǎolǎotóur prematurely old man

小礼拜 xiǎolǐbài ❶ one of the two Sundays of a fourteen-day work period on which one does not rest; working Sunday ❷ short weekend (consisting of one day off in contrast with the two-day weekend)

小礼拜堂 xiǎolǐbàitáng chapel

小礼服 xiǎolǐfú black tie; tuxedo; dinner jacket

小力笨儿 xiǎolìbenr 〈方言〉apprentice in a shop:～的苦处实在难当。The life of an apprentice is really hard.

小两口 xiǎoliǎngkǒu 〈口语〉young couple:～你敬我爱。The young couple showed mutual affection and respect.

小量 xiǎoliàng a little amount; small dose:～用药 take a small dose (of medicine) /～进食 eat a little for each meal /～成批生产 small lot production /据说每天～饮酒利多弊少。It is said that a little wine every day does you more good than harm.

小灵猫 xiǎolíngmāo rasse; small civet

小令 xiǎolìng ❶ shorter tonal pattern and rhyme scheme of *ci* poetry; short tonal poem:善作～ good at writing short tonal poems /《卜算子》是一种～。"Busuanzi" is a form of short tonal poetry. ❷ shorter form of *sanqu* (散曲) poetry

小瘤 xiǎoliú 〈植物〉tubercle; tubercule

小绺 xiǎoliǔ 〈方言〉pickpocket

小龙 xiǎolóng 〈方言〉(one of the twelve animal-symbols) snake:他是属～的,今年二十八岁。Born in the year of the snake, he is now twenty-eight years old.

小龙虾 xiǎolóngxiā *also* "淡水螯虾" dànshuǐ áoxiā crayfish; crawfish

小炉儿匠 xiǎolúrjiàng *also* "小炉匠儿" tinker

小萝卜 xiǎoluóbo radish

小萝卜头儿 xiǎoluóbotóur 〈方言〉❶ kid; child; small boy:一群～在草地上玩耍。Some kids are playing on the lawn. ❷ person of no importance; nobody; small potato; small fry:他自以为是个"大人物",其实和我们一样也是个～。Although he regards himself as a "big shot", he is actually a small potato like us.

小锣 xiǎoluó *also* "手锣" shǒuluó small gong

小骂大帮忙 xiǎomà dà bāngmáng criticize on minor aspects while helping on major issues; mix substantial support with non-essential criticism

小买卖 xiǎomǎimai small business

小麦 xiǎomài wheat:冬～ winter wheat /～草 wheat straw /～穗 ear of wheat /～粉 wheat-meal /～片 wheat groats

小麦赤霉病 xiǎomài chìméibìng wheat scab

小麦黑穗病 xiǎomài hēisuìbìng wheat smut

小麦吸浆虫 xiǎomài xījiāngchóng wheat midge

小麦线虫 xiǎomài xiànchóng wheat nematode:～病 nematode disease of wheat (*Anguina tritici*)

小麦腥黑穗病 xiǎomài xīnghēisuìbìng bunt of wheat

小麦锈病 xiǎomài xiùbìng wheat rust

小卖 xiǎomài ❶ (as in a restaurant) ready food; small dish:应时～ food for immediate service; food in season /柜台内摆放着各色风味～。There are various speciality dishes in the counter. ❷ do small business

小卖部 xiǎomàibù ❶ small shop attached to a hotel, school, factory, theatre, etc. (selling cigarettes, confectionery, etc.); retail section or department; store ❷ buffet; snack counter

小满 Xiǎomǎn ❶ Grain budding, 8th seasonal division point, marking the sun's position at 60° on the ecliptic ❷ day marking such a seasonal division point, usu. falling on the 21st or 22nd of May ❸ period lasting from such a seasonal division point till the next one (Grain in Ear 芒种)

see also "节气" jiéqì; "二十四节气" èrshísì jiéqì

小猫熊 xiǎomāoxióng *also* "小熊猫" lesser panda

小毛 xiǎomáo short-haired fur or pelt:灰鼠皮、银鼠皮是～中的上品。Squirrel and snow weasel furs are among top-grade short-haired pelts.

小毛头 xiǎomáotóu 〈方言〉infant; baby; child

小帽 xiǎomào skullcap:瓜皮～ skullcap /黑缎～ black satin skullcap

小门小户 xiǎomén-xiǎohù poor humble family

小米 xiǎomǐ millet:黏～ glutinous millet /～粥 millet gruel /～饭 cooked millet /～病 millet disease

小米草 xiǎomǐcǎo 〈植物〉eyebright

小米面 xiǎomǐmiàn ❶ millet flour ❷〈方言〉mixture of the flour

of broom corn millet, soybean and white maize
小名 xiǎomíng *also* "乳名" rǔmíng pet name (for a child); childhood name
小命儿 xiǎomìngr 〈戏谑〉 life:保住～ save one's own neck / 万一再搭上～,就更不上算了。It will be worse if you get killed.
小拇哥儿 xiǎomugēr 〈方言〉 little finger
小拇指 xiǎomuzhǐ 〈口语〉 little finger
小脑 xiǎonǎo 〈生理〉 cerebellum:～核 cerebellar nuclei / ～室 ventriculus cerebelli / ～髓质 cerebellar medulla / ～炎 cerebellitis / ～皮质 cerebellar cortex / ～垂体 cerebellar hypophysis
小鲵 xiǎoní 〈动物〉 *Hynobius chinensis*:～科 *Hynobiidae*
小年 xiǎonián ❶ lunar year of which the last month has 29 days ❷ Preliminary Eve — (holiday which falls on the 23rd or 24th of the 12th month of the lunar year when people offer sacrifices to the kitchen god) ❸ 〈农业〉 off-year
小年轻儿 xiǎoniánqīngr youngster; stripling
小年夜 xiǎoniányè ❶ night before the Eve of the Lunar New Year ❷ 23rd or 24th of the 12th month of the lunar year
小娘 xiǎoniáng 〈旧语〉 ❶ concubine or father's concubine ❷ (usu. used in the early vernacular) prostitute
小娘儿们 xiǎoniángrmen 〈贬义〉 young women
小娘子 xiǎoniángzǐ 〈旧语〉 young lady; young woman
小鸟依人 xiǎoniǎo-yīrén endearing little bird (used of a lovely child or girl endearing itself or herself to one)
小妞儿 xiǎoniūr *also* "小妞子" 〈口语〉 little girl; young girl:挺可爱的～ cute little girl
小牛 xiǎoniú calf; veal:～排 club steak / ～皮 calfskin
小牛肉 xiǎoniúròu veal; baby beef:～卷 veal bird
小农 xiǎonóng small peasant or farmer:～思想 mentality of a small peasant; small peasant's way of thinking; small-peasant mentality
小农经济 xiǎonóng jīngjì small-scale peasant economy; autarkical small-scale farming
小农业 xiǎonóngyè agriculture in the narrow sense; farming (as distinguished from livestock breeding, fishery, etc.)
小女 xiǎonǚ 〈谦词〉 my daughter:～初学钢琴,弹得不好。My daughter has just begun to learn to play the piano, so she doesn't play it well.
小爬虫 xiǎopáchóng 〈贬义〉 "little reptile" — a mean person who apes an evildoer at every step; vermin:欺世盗名的～ mean fellow who gains notoriety by deceiving the public
小跑 xiǎopǎo 〈口语〉 trot; jog; run:一溜儿～ at a trot (*or* jog) / 老孙一路～赶到车站。Lao Sun hurried to the station at (*or* on) the double.
小朋友 xiǎopéngyǒu ❶ children:～乐园 children's playground / 公园里到处都是～。Children are seen everywhere in the park. ❷ (term of address used by an adult to a child):～,几岁了? How old are you, kiddie?
小便宜 xiǎopiányi trivial gain; petty advantage:占～ gain trivial advantages / 他贪～,结果吃了大亏。Going after small gains, he eventually suffered big losses.
小票儿 xiǎopiàor bank notes of small denominations
小品 xiǎopǐn short, simple literary or artistic creation; essay; skit; sketch:时事～ essay on current affairs / 相声～ short crosstalk / 音乐～ musical sketch / 广播～ radio skit / 他善于演～。He is good at performing skits.
小品词 xiǎopǐncí 〈语言〉 particle
小品文 xiǎopǐnwén familiar essay; essay:优秀～集 collection of excellent essays / ～作者 essayist
小评论 xiǎopínglùn short comment (usu. on daily-life topics)
小婆 xiǎopó 〈方言〉 *also* "小婆子" concubine
小铺儿 xiǎopùr small store
小瀑布 xiǎopùbù cascade
小妻 xiǎoqī 〈书面〉 concubine
小气候 xiǎoqìhòu ❶ microclimate:田间～ microclimate in the fields / 大面积植树可以改变～。Large-scale tree-planting can change the microclimate. ❷ 〈比喻〉 specific political or economic climate:政治～ internal political climate
小气候学 xiǎoqìhòuxué microclimatology
小气旋 xiǎoqìxuán microcyclone
小气 xiǎoqi ❶ stingy; miserly; niggardly; mean:小里～ niggardly; mean / ～的人 stingy (*or* tight-fisted) person; miser ❷ 〈方言〉 narrow-minded; petty:别那么～,计较她那句话。Don't be so narrow-minded as to take what she said to heart. / 他生性～,容不下人。He is petty by nature and can never get along with people.
小气鬼 xiǎoqiguǐ miser; niggard; skinflint; penny pincher
小器 xiǎoqì small household utensil:盘盂～ utensils like plates and spittoons
小器 xiǎoqi *also* "小气" stingy; mean; niggardly; narrow-minded
小器易盈 xiǎoqì-yìyíng a small vessel is easily filled — he who is narrow-minded easily feels self-complacent
小器作 xiǎoqìzuō workshop which makes and repairs hardwood furniture or fine wooden articles; joinery
小憩 xiǎoqì rest for a little while:在树阴下～片刻。Have a little rest in the shade of the trees.
小前提 xiǎoqiántí 〈逻辑〉 minor premise
小钱 xiǎoqián ❶ inferior copper coin; coin ❷ small sum of money; petty cash:说大话,使～ talk big but spend little / ～不去,大钱不来 big money comes in only after petty cash goes out — there is no big gain without a little cost ❸ 〈旧语〉 small bribe
小钱柜 xiǎoqiánguì *see* "小金库"
小瞧 xiǎoqiáo 〈方言〉 look down upon; slight; belittle:别～人! Don't look down upon (*or* belittle) others! / 他爱～人,尤其是女人。He has a disdain for people in general, and women in particular.
小巧 xiǎoqiǎo small and nimble; small and skilful; small and ingenious:身材～的南方姑娘 southern girl with a small, slim figure; petite southern girl / 一本印得～精美的书 exquisitely-printed small book / ～的公文包 handy briefcase / 他家的客厅很～,没有什么装饰。Their sitting room was small and cozy, with few decorations.
小巧玲珑 xiǎoqiǎo-línglóng small and exquisite:～的座钟 small and exquisite table clock / ～的收音机 small and beautifully designed radio set
小青年 xiǎoqīngnián young people around twenty; youngsters; youth:这些～是国家队的希望。These youngsters are the promise of the national team.
小青瓦 xiǎoqīngwǎ *also* "蝴蝶瓦" húdiéwǎ Chinese-style tile
小丘 xiǎoqiū hillock; mound
小秋 xiǎoqiū ❶ 〈书面〉 early autumn ❷ minor autumn harvest or crop
小秋收 xiǎoqiūshōu minor autumn harvest, such as collecting edible wild plants; minor autumn crop:农家女子忙着～。Women in the villages were busy gathering in minor autumn crops.
小球 xiǎoqiú 〈体育〉 sports using smaller balls, such as table tennis, badminton, etc.
小球藻 xiǎoqiúzǎo 〈植物〉 chlorella
小区 xiǎoqū plot; estate:住宅～ housing estate / 工业～ industrial estate / ～建设 housing estate development / ～试验 〈农业〉 plot experimentation
小曲儿 xiǎoqǔr ditty; popular tune:哼～ hum a popular tune (*or* ditty) / 伤感的～ plaintive ditty
小觑 xiǎoqù despise; slight:～他人的神色 contemptuous look
小圈子 xiǎoquānzi ❶ small circle or set of people; narrow confining environment or surroundings:走出家庭～ step out of the narrow confines of family ❷ small coterie; clique:搞～ form a small coterie (*or* clique); engage in factional activities / ～主义 "small circle" mentality; small groupism / 这里的文艺界有好几个～。There are several cliques (*or* factions) in the community of art and literature here.

小犬 xiǎoquǎn 〈书面〉〈谦词〉 my son
小犬座 Xiǎoquǎnzuò 〈天文〉 Canis Minor
小儿 xiǎor 〈方言〉 ❶ babyhood; childhood:从～ from childhood; since childhood ❷ infant boy; baby boy:胖～ plump infant boy
see also xiǎo'ér
小人 xiǎorén ❶ 〈旧语〉 person of low position; (used by such a person to refer to himself) your humble servant — I or me:～听候吩咐。I'm humbly at your service. ❷ base or vile person; mean person; villain:卑鄙～ vile knave; dirty rat / 以～之心度君子之腹 gauge the heart of a gentleman with one's own mean measure / ～无大志。Little things amuse little minds. / ～当道。Vile characters are holding sway. *or* Villains are in power. / ～喻于利。The mind of the mean man is conversant with gain. ❸ 〈方言〉 son or daughter; child; kid:提倡只养一个～。Each couple is encouraged to have only one child. ❹ 〈方言〉 boy; kid; child:这个～可了不得! What a terrific kid!

小人得志 xiǎorén-dézhì small man swelled with success; villains holding sway
小人儿 xiǎorénr 〈方言〉(as a loving term of addressing a minor) lad; lass; laddie:怪招人疼的～ lovely lass /挺懂事的～ sensible lad (*or* laddie)
小人儿书 xiǎorénrshū 〈口语〉picture-story book; comics
小人物 xiǎorénwù nobody; cipher; nonentity; small potato:小说写的虽然是～,却反映了广阔的社会生活。The novel, though depicting unimportant persons, reflects a vast spectrum of social life.
小人家 xiǎorenjia *also* "小人儿家" youngster:你这～,敢和我比试比试? Dare you compete against me, youngster?
小日月 xiǎorìyuè 〈方言〉(of crops) fast-growing:～玉米 fast-growing corn
小日子 xiǎorìzi easy life of a small family; married life (usu. of a young couple):甜蜜的～ sweet happy life of a young couple /他们凑合买了点锅碗瓢盆,过起了～。They managed to buy some daily utensils and started their married life.
小容量存储器 xiǎoróngliàng cúnchǔqì 〈计算机〉small or modest capacity memory; small or modest capacity storage
小嗓儿 xiǎosǎngr 〈戏曲〉falsetto
小商品 xiǎoshāngpǐn small commodity:～市场 small commodities market /～批发商 small commodities wholesaler
小商品经济 xiǎoshāngpǐn jīngjì small commodity economy
小商品生产 xiǎoshāngpǐn shēngchǎn small commodity production:～者 small commodity producer
小商小贩 xiǎoshāng-xiǎofàn small tradespeople and pedlars
小晌午 xiǎoshǎngwu 〈方言〉close to noon; towards noon:时近～,天气越热了。It got even warmer towards noon.
小舌 xiǎoshé 〈生理〉uvula; tonguelet:～音 uvular
小婶儿 xiǎoshěnr ❶ wife of father's youngest brother; aunt ❷ *also* "小婶子"〈方言〉wife of a younger brother of one's husband; sister-in-law
小生 xiǎoshēng ❶〈戏曲〉young man's role:越剧中多由女演员来唱～。The young man's role in *yueju* opera is often played by an actress. ❷〈旧语〉〈谦词〉(used by a young scholar to refer to himself) I or me:～这厢有礼了。Allow me to pay you my respects.
小生产 xiǎoshēngchǎn small production; small-scale production:～观念 small-producer mentality /～所有者 ownership by small producers
小生产者 xiǎoshēngchǎnzhě small producer:～的狭隘眼界 narrow-mindedness of the small producer
小生态学 xiǎoshēngtàixué microecology
小狮座 Xiǎoshīzuò 〈天文〉Leo Minor
小时 xiǎoshí hour:～定额 hourly quota /～工资 hourly pay; hourly wage /按～付工资 pay by the hour /八～工作制 eight-hour working day
小时工 xiǎoshígōng ❶ worker paid by the hour ❷ maid or laborer paid by the hour:他家请了个～,周末打扫一次卫生。They have engaged a maid paid by the hour, to come and clean up the apartment once a week.
小时候 xiǎoshíhou 〈口语〉childhood; early youth:～的照片 childhood photo /游泳是～学的。I learned swimming as a boy. /我和他～就是好朋友。He and I have been good friends since childhood. /～,我家住在海边。My family was living on the seashore when I was a child.
小食 xiǎoshí 〈方言〉❶ snack:～铺 small restaurant; eatery; snack bar /卖～ sell snacks ❷ between-meal nibbles:爱吃～ fond of between-meal nibbles
小食蚁兽 xiǎoshíyǐshòu 〈动物〉tamandua; tamandu
小使 xiǎoshǐ 〈旧语〉young servant
小市 xiǎoshì bazaar or marketplace for second-hand or small articles:街头～ a small bazaar or market along the street /家庭～ tag sale; yard sale; garage sale
小市民 xiǎoshìmín ❶ urban petty bourgeois:高尔基笔下的～形象 urban petty bourgeois characters depicted by Gorky ❷ philistine:～意识 outlook (*or* mentality) of the philistine /～作风 philistinism
小视 xiǎoshì look down upon; slight; belittle:不可～对手的实力。Don't belittle your opponent's strength. /这些困难虽不严重,但也不可～。Though not very serious, these difficulties are not to be ignored.
小事 xiǎoshì small or petty thing; trifle; minor matter:从～做起 start from small things /计较～ fuss over trifles /～聪明,大事糊涂 penny-wise and pound-foolish /大事化小,～化了 turn serious problems into small ones, and small ones into nothing /～一桩,不足挂齿。This is a trivial matter not worth mentioning. /～注意,大事自成。Take care of the pence, and the pounds will take care of themselves. /我这个人大事办不了,只能做点～。Unequal to major assignments, I settle for minor ones.
小试锋芒 xiǎoshì-fēngmáng display only a small part of one's talent; manifest a little of one's skill; show the tip of the iceberg:他在第一轮比赛中的胜利,只不过是～。His victory in the first round was merely an initial indication of his skill.
小手工业者 xiǎoshǒugōngyèzhě small handicraftsman
小手鼓 xiǎoshǒugǔ 〈乐器〉tambourine; tabor; timbrel
小手小脚 xiǎoshǒu-xiǎojiǎo ❶ stingy; mean; niggardly:大手大脚固然不好,～也让人讨厌。Extravagance is bad, but miserliness is equally disgusting. ❷ lacking boldness; timid; cowardly:新上任的处长办事～,丝毫没有魄力。The new section chief is timid and indecisive.
小书 xiǎoshū ❶ picture-story book; comics ❷〈旧语〉children's primer ❸〈方言〉storytelling to the accompaniment of stringed instruments ❹ booklet
小叔子 xiǎoshūzi 〈口语〉husband's younger brother; brother-in-law
小暑 Xiǎoshǔ ❶ Slight Heat, 11th seasonal division point, marking the sun's position at 105° on the ecliptic ❷ day marking such a seasonal division point, usu. falling on the 7th or 8th of July ❸ period lasting from such a seasonal division point till the next one (Great Heat 大暑)
see also "节气" jiéqì;"二十四节气" èrshísì jiéqì
小数 xiǎoshù ❶〈数学〉decimal number; decimal fraction; decimal:～部分 decimal part /～位 decimal place /～表示法 fractional representation /～运算 fractional arithmetic ❷ small (in) number; small sum:三千万可不是～啊! Thirty million is by no means a small sum.
小数点 xiǎoshùdiǎn decimal point; radix point:～对位 decimal point alignment /～运算部件 fractional arithmetic unit
小水 xiǎoshuǐ 〈中医〉urine:～不利 difficult urination /车前子利～。Plantago seed is good for urination.
小水电 xiǎoshuǐdiàn small-scale hydroelectric power plant:发展～ promote the establishment of small-scale hydroelectric power plants
小睡 xiǎoshuì catnap; nap; doze:～片刻 have a catnap; doze for a while /她在赴宴前～了一会儿。She took her beauty sleep before the party.
小说 xiǎoshuō novel; fiction; story:长篇～ novel /中篇～ medium-length novel; novelette /短篇～ short story /武侠～ kung fu story /侦探～ detective story; mystery /科幻～ science fiction /文言～ novel in classical Chinese /白话～ novel written in the vernacular /历史～ historical novel /～连载 serial (of a novel)
小说家 xiǎoshuōjiā novelist; fiction-writer; storywriter
小私有者 xiǎosīyǒuzhě petty or small private owner; small proprietor
小厮 xiǎosī 〈旧语〉boy servant; page (boy):贴身～ valet /打发～去沽酒 send a page for some wine
小溲 xiǎosōu 〈书面〉urinate
小苏打 xiǎosūdá 〈化学〉sodium bicarbonate; bicarb; baking soda
小算盘 xiǎosuànpan selfish calculations; petty niggling:打～ think of one's selfish interests; be calculating
小摊贩 xiǎotānfàn street pedlar; vendor
小摊儿 xiǎotānr vendor's booth; stall; stand:摆～ set up a stall
小提琴 xiǎotíqín violin; fiddle:第一～ first violin; first fiddle /担任第二～ play second violin; play second fiddle
小提琴手 xiǎotíqínshǒu violinist:首席～ concertmaster; concertmeister
小题大作 xiǎotí-dàzuò make a fuss over a trifle; make a mountain out of a molehill; use a hammer to swat a fly; have a tempest in a teacup:何必～? Why fuss? /你们是不是有点～呢? Aren't you making a mountain out of a molehill?
小蹄子 xiǎotízi 〈旧语〉(abusive term for a girl) hussy; bitch
小天地 xiǎotiāndì little world; small world:个人的～ one's own little world /斗大的囚室,犯人们只能在这片～里轮流踱步。The prisoners could only take turns pacing to and fro within the confinement of the small cell.
小天使 xiǎotiānshǐ cherub; little angel

小帖儿 xiǎotiěr 〈方言〉card with the horoscope of a boy or girl sent as a proposal for betrothal
小艇 xiǎotǐng small boat; skiff; dinghy
小同乡 xiǎotóngxiāng person from the same village or county
小偷 xiǎotōu petty thief; sneak thief; pilferer; pickpocket
小偷小摸 xiǎotōu-xiǎomō petty theft; pilfering: 有～的毛病 have the habit of pilfering
小土地出租者 xiǎotǔdì chūzūzhě lessor or renter of small plots; petty lessor (of land)
小团体主义 xiǎotuántǐzhǔyì cliquism; small groupism; small-group mentality; factionalism
小腿 xiǎotuǐ *also* "胫" jìng shank: ～肚 calf /～肚围 calf circumference /～抽筋 spasm of calf; systremma
小娃娃 xiǎowáwa kid; baby; toddler
小玩意儿 xiǎowányìr ❶ knickknack; trinket; bauble: 你房里的～真可爱! What lovely knickknacks you've got in your room! ❷ petty skill: 我就靠这点～过活。I live by these petty skills.
小我 xiǎowǒ individual; ego; self: 牺牲～ sacrifice oneself (for a group or cause); self-sacrifice /不能只想～而不顾大局。One should not think only of oneself, and neglect the interests of the whole.
小巫见大巫 xiǎowū jiàn dàwū be like a small sorcerer in the presence of a great one — feel dwarfed; pale into insignificance by comparison; the moon is not seen when the sun shines: 这山与泰山相比,真是～,山势的奇伟险峻差远了。Compared with Mount Tai this mountain is nothing, being far less magnificent and precipitous. /就侵吞公款而论,同他的上级比,他还是～。So far as embezzlement is concerned, he is a mere pygmy while his superior is a real giant.
小屋 xiǎowū cottage; cabin; lodge
小五金 xiǎowǔjīn metal fittings (e.g. nails, wires, hinges, bolts, locks, etc.); (small) hardware: ～商店 hardware shop /批发～ metal fittings wholesale
小媳妇 xiǎoxífu ❶ young (married) woman: 村里的大姑娘、～都在这河里洗澡、洗衣服。The young women of the village, married or not, all came to bathe or wash clothes in the river. ❷ person whom anyone can vent his spite upon; one who always takes the rap; whipping boy: 在他手下工作,谁都会像～一样缩手缩脚。Anyone working under him would feel timid as a whipping boy, always ready to take the rap.
小戏 xiǎoxì operetta; short item of performance: 剧团下乡前新排了几出～。The troupe rehearsed some new operettas before going down to the countryside.
小先生 xiǎoxiānsheng little teacher (said of a student who plays the role of an assistant teacher): 家里请了一个～,辅导孩子做作业。The family has hired a young student tutor to help the children with their homework.
小线儿 xiǎoxiànr 〈方言〉thin cotton rope
小巷 xiǎoxiàng by-lane; alley
小像 xiǎoxiàng *also* "肖像" xiàoxiàng small likeness — portrait or miniature
小橡树 xiǎoxiàngshù 〈植物〉*Quercus glandulifera*
小小不言 xiǎoxiǎo-bùyán 〈口语〉too insignificant to mention; too trivial to talk about: ～的事,何必计较? Why fuss over such trivialities? /有件～的事想拜托你。I've a small favour to ask of you. *or* I'd like to ask you for a small favour.
小小说 xiǎoxiǎoshuō miniature story (usu. about 1,000 words long)
小小子 xiǎoxiǎozi kid; baby boy; little chap: 刘家的～长得十分可爱。The Lius' little boy looks cute.
小鞋 xiǎoxié 〈口语〉〈比喻〉tight shoes — unjustifiable, difficult situation deliberately created to bring pressure on or persecute one; restrictions or constraints imposed on one: 给人穿～儿 deliberately create a difficult situation to make sb. suffer; put sb. on a hot spot
小写 xiǎoxiě ❶ ordinary form of a Chinese numeral (e.g. 一,二,三 as against 壹,贰,叁): ～金额 amount in ordinary figures ❷ small letter: ～体〈印刷〉lower case /～字母 small letter
小心 xiǎoxīn watch out for; take care; be careful; be cautious: ～为妙 one cannot be too careful /～着凉。Be careful to avoid catching cold. /～,别弄坏了。Take care not to damage it. /易碎物品,～轻放! Fragile. Handle with care! /～脚下! Watch your step! /～危险! Watch out! Danger! /～,油漆未干! Mind the wet paint! /夜里值班,特别要～火灾。When on night duty, be on guard against fire especially.
小心谨慎 xiǎoxīn-jǐnshèn be careful; be cautious; mind one's p's and q's
小心眼儿 xiǎoxīnyǎnr ❶ narrow-minded; petty: 别太～了! Don't be petty! /像她这么～的人不多。There aren't many people as narrow-minded as she is. ❷ petty calculation; petty scheming: 要～ exercise one's wits in a petty manner; be calculating
小心翼翼 xiǎoxīn-yìyì with utmost care; with extreme caution; gingerly; on tiptoe: 把仪器～地搬下来 unload the instruments with the utmost care /黑暗中,车夫～地把马车赶出了院子。Cautiously the driver drove the carriage out of the yard in the dark.
小星 xiǎoxīng 〈婉词〉little star — concubine (usu. referring to another man's)
小行星 xiǎoxíngxīng 〈天文〉asteroid; minor planet; planetoid: ～流 asteroid stream /～带 asteroid belt
小型 xiǎoxíng small; small-scale; miniature: ～发电厂 small power plant /～出租汽车 minicab /～公共汽车 minibus /～打印机 miniprinter /～核武器 miniature nuclear weapon; mininuke; minuke /～潜艇 mini-sub; miniature submarine /～电池 compact battery /～最高级会议 mini-summit
小型化 xiǎoxínghuà miniaturization: 核武器～ miniaturization of nuclear weapons
小型计算机 xiǎoxíng jìsuànjī (shortened as 小型机) minicomputer; midget computer: ～系统接口 small computer system interface (SCSI)
小型联大 xiǎoxíng Liándà Little Assembly — Interim Committee of the UN General Assembly
小性儿 xiǎoxìngr 〈方言〉petty anger; childish temper; petulance: 使～ get angry at petty things; lose one's temper like a child; throw a tantrum; be petulant
小兄弟 xiǎoxiōngdì little brother; young member of a group, faction or gang: 每天晚上他都和几个～一起搓麻将。He played mahjong with some of his young cronies every night.
小熊猫 xiǎoxióngmāo *also* "小猫熊" lesser panda
小熊座 Xiǎoxióngzuò 〈天文〉Ursa Minor; Little Bear; Little Dipper
小修 xiǎoxiū minor repair: 汽车～ minor repairs on a car
小修小补 xiǎoxiū-xiǎobǔ tinker: 对经济进行～ tinker with the economy
小婿 xiǎoxù 〈谦词〉❶ my son-in-law ❷ I or me (when addressing one's own parent-in-law)
小学 xiǎoxué ❶ primary school; elementary school: 六岁儿童可以上～。Children can go to primary school when they are six years old. ❷ Little Learning (the study of the etymology, semantics and phonology of classical Chinese); philological studies
小学生 xiǎoxuéshēng (primary school) pupil; schoolboy or schoolgirl: 这家电影院每周都有～专场。This cinema provides special shows for school children every week. /要当好领导,首先要当好广大群众的～。To be a good leader one must first of all be a good pupil of the people.
小学生 xiǎoxuésheng ❶ student younger in age (than others of his class) ❷〈方言〉little boy
小雪 Xiǎoxuě ❶ Slight Snow, 20th seasonal division point, marking the sun's position at 240° on the ecliptic ❷ day marking such a seasonal division point, usu. falling on the 22nd or 23rd of November ❸ period lasting from such a seasonal division point till the next one (Great Snow 大雪) ❹ (xiǎoxuě) light snow: 昨晚儿下了场～。There was a light snow last night.
see also "节气" jiéqi; "二十四节气" èrshísì jiéqì
小循环 xiǎoxúnhuán 〈生理〉pulmonary circulation
小亚细亚 Xiǎoyàxìyà Asia Minor (the Turkish peninsula of West Asia with the Mediterranean on the south, the Aegean Sea on the west and the Black Sea to the north); Anatolia
小盐 xiǎoyán granulated salt
小扬琴 xiǎoyángqín cimbalom
小阳春 xiǎoyángchūn balmy weather characteristic of the tenth lunar month; mild warm weather in late autumn or early winter; Indian summer: 十月～ fine warm weather in the tenth lunar month
小洋 xiǎoyáng 〈旧语〉ten-cent or twenty-cent silver coin
小样 xiǎoyàng ❶〈印刷〉galley proof: 校对～ read galley proofs; proofread ❷〈方言〉model; sample (product): ～产品 sample product ❸〈方言〉small-minded; petty; stingy
小幺儿 xiǎoyāor (often used in the early vernacular) young ser-

vant; page boy
小咬 xiǎoyǎo 〈方言〉gnat
小业主 xiǎoyèzhǔ small proprietor; petty proprietor; small entrepreneur
小叶 xiǎoyè leaflet; lobule:～茶 young tea-leaves /～性肺炎 lobular pneumonia
小叶白蜡树 xiǎoyè báilàshù Chinese ash
小叶杨 xiǎoyèyáng poplar (*Populus simonii*)
小叶植物 xiǎoyè zhíwù microphyll
小夜班 xiǎoyèbān evening shift (usu. from 4 to 12 p.m.)
小夜曲 xiǎoyèqǔ 〈音乐〉serenade
小衣 xiǎoyī 〈方言〉underpants; drawers
小衣裳 xiǎoyīshang ❶ underwear; underclothing ❷ children's clothes
小姨儿 xiǎoyír ❶ wife's younger sister; sister-in-law ❷ youngest of maternal aunts
小姨子 xiǎoyízi 〈口语〉wife's younger sister; sister-in-law
小意思 xiǎoyìsi ❶〈谦词〉small token (of kindly feelings); small gift; souvenir; keepsake:这是一点～,送给你权作生日礼物。This is just a little keepsake for your birthday. ❷ not worth mentioning; insignificant; negligible:敌人只来了一个排,～。Only a platoon of enemy soldiers came. That was nothing. /花点儿钱～,问题是事情不该这么办。Money is but secondary; the thing is that it was not proper to do it that way.
小阴唇 xiǎoyīnchún 〈生理〉labium minus; labia minora; nymphae:～炎 nymphitis /～肿 nymphoncus
小音阶 xiǎoyīnjiē 〈音乐〉minor scale; minor
小引 xiǎoyǐn introductory note; foreword
小影 xiǎoyǐng (usu. one's own) small photo:庐山～ snapshots taken at Lushan /寄赠～二张,留作纪念。I'm sending you two photographs to remember me by.
小应用程序 xiǎoyìngyòng chéngxù 〈信息〉applet
小雨 xiǎoyǔ light rain; drizzle:一阵～过后 after a sprinkle of rain /黄梅时节,～连绵。There was an incessant drizzle during the rainy season.
小语种 xiǎoyǔzhǒng minor language; ethnic minority language
小渊惠三 Xiǎoyuānhuìsān Keizo Obuchi (1937-), president of the Liberal Democratic Party and Prime Minister of Japan (1998-)
小月 xiǎoyuè ❶ solar month of 30 days ❷ lunar month of 29 days
小月 xiǎoyue *also* "小月子" miscarriage; abortion:她前后坐过三次～,身体一直不好。She had three abortions altogether and was in poor health.
小灶 xiǎozào ❶ special mess (as for high-ranking officials):吃～ have special mess ❷ special treatment or privilege:给困难学生开～ give extra tuition to problem students
小泽征尔 Xiǎozézhēng'ěr Seiji Ozawa (1935-), Japanese conductor
小斋 xiǎozhāi 〈宗教〉abstinence
小站练兵 Xiǎozhàn Liànbīng training of the New Army by Yuan Shikai (袁士凯) at Xiaozhan near Tianjin during the Sino-Japanese War of 1894-1895
小账 xiǎozhàng tip; gratuity:付～ pay a tip; give a tip
小照 xiǎozhào (usu. one's own) small photograph
小折刀 xiǎozhédāo penknife
小侄 xiǎozhí 〈谦词〉❶ my nephew (used when speaking to others) ❷ your nephew—I or me (used when speaking to people of one's father's generation)
小指 xiǎozhǐ little finger; little toe; *digitus minimus*
小趾 xiǎozhǐ little toe; digitus minimus
小仲马 Xiǎozhòngmǎ Alexandre Dumas fils (1824-1859), French novelist and dramatist
小株密植 xiǎozhū mìzhí 〈农业〉close planting with fewer seedlings in each cluster; close planting in small clusters
小住 xiǎozhù stay for a short while:我打算在这里～数日。I'm going to stay here for a few days.
小注 xiǎozhù fine notes between vertical lines of a book (usu. written in two lines)
小传 xiǎozhuàn brief biography; biographical sketch; profile:作者～ biographical sketch of the author
小篆 xiǎozhuàn *also* "秦篆" Qínzhuàn *xiaozhuan*, an ancient style of calligraphy, adopted in the Qin Dynasty for the purpose of standardizing the Chinese script
小酌 xiǎozhuó 〈书面〉drinks with snacks
小资产阶级 xiǎozīchǎnjiējí petty bourgeoisie:～狂热 petty bourgeois fever (*or* fanaticism)
小资产者 xiǎozīchǎnzhě petty bourgeois; small proprietor
小子 xiǎozǐ 〈书面〉❶ youngster; teenager:后生～ younger generation ❷〈旧语〉term of address used by seniors to juniors:～识之。Be advised, young fellows. ❸〈旧语〉〈谦词〉I or me (used in the presence of elders or betters):～不敏,有一事请教。Your humble junior here begs to ask a question.
小子 xiǎozi 〈口语〉❶ boy:她生了个胖～。She gave birth to a plump baby boy. /这是他家的大～。This is the eldest boy of the family. ❷〈贬义〉bloke; fellow; chap; guy:这～真不是东西! What a despicable fellow! /好～,敢跟我使坏,看我怎么收拾你! You worthless trash, how dare you play such dirty tricks on me? See how I'll punish you!
小字 xiǎozì ❶ small character:～报 small-character poster /～笔 brush for writing small characters ❷ childhood name
小字辈 xiǎozìbèi youngsters; younger generation:别小瞧～,他们有的已经在挑大梁了。Don't look down upon youngsters; some of them are already mainstays in our work.
小宗 xiǎozōng ❶ small in number; small in quantity:～商品 small quantities of commodities /～债务 petty debt; small debt ❷ minor lineage; minor line
小卒 xiǎozú ❶ private:他在军中只是～一个。He is only a private in the army. ❷ nobody; cipher; man of no consequence:无名～ mere nobody; cipher ❸ (in chess) pawn:～过河赛只车。Once across the "river", a pawn may be as good as a chariot.
小组 xiǎozǔ group:～会 group meeting /学习～ study group /工作～ working group /领导～ leading group /党～ Party group /～作业 group work /～委员会 subcommittee /～循环赛 group round robin /～前二名 top two group finishers /按年龄段把孩子分成～ group the children according to their age /各队分～进行预赛。The teams will divide into groups for the preliminary contest.
小坐 xiǎozuò sit for a short while

谀

xiǎo 〈书面〉small:～闻 enjoy some reputation

晓(曉)

xiǎo ❶ dawn; daybreak:破～ daybreak; dawn /拂～ foredawn /～霞 morning glow /鸡鸣报～ cock proclaiming the dawn /残月脸边明,别泪临清～。The sinking moon still shines on the faces of the lovers, Who are shedding tears at parting in the early morning. /绿杨烟外～寒轻。Beside the misty green willows the morning chill is light. ❷ know:家喻户～ be known to all (*or* every family); widely known; be a household word ❸ let sb. know; inform; tell:～以大义 impress sb. with the rightness of sth.; enlighten sb. on what is right /～之以理 try to persuade sb. with reason; reason things out with sb.
晓畅 xiǎochàng ❶ be well versed in; have a good command of:～军事 be expert at military affairs /兵法韬略,无不～ be knowledgeable about military strategy and tactics ❷ (of writings) clear and fluent; readable:行文～ read smoothly and clearly /文字～ lucid writing; clear and smooth wording
晓得 xiǎode know; be aware of:天～! God knows! *or* Who knows! /此事我早已～了。I've long been aware of this. *or* I've known it for a long time. /我一点都不～。I'm entirely in the dark. *or* I know nothing about it.
晓风残月 xiǎofēng-cányuè morning breeze and waning moon:杨柳岸,～ under the willow trees by the riverside in the morning breeze and beneath the waning moon
晓岚 xiǎolán morning mist
晓示 xiǎoshì tell explicitly; announce; notify:～民众 announce to the public /～是非曲直 tell sb. of the rights and wrongs of a case /此中道理,早以～。The reason for this has long been made explicit.
晓市 xiǎoshì morning market
晓事 xiǎoshì sensible; intelligent; understanding:这人好不～! How thoughtless this man is!
晓悟 xiǎowù 〈书面〉❶ understand; realize:此事原委,她终于渐有～。It slowly dawned upon her why all this had happened. ❷ clever; bright:他天生～,聪明过人。He is born clever and surpasses all others in intelligence.
晓星残月 xiǎoxīng-cányuè faint morning stars and lingering moon

晓行夜宿 xiǎoxíng-yèsù start off at dawn and lodge for the night; travel by day and rest by night: 饥餐渴饮，～ travel all day, stopping only to refresh oneself when hungry and thirsty

晓以利害 xiǎoyǐlìhài explain to sb. where his or her interests lie; warn sb. of the possible consequences

晓谕 xiǎoyù 〈书面〉give explicit instructions or directions: ～天下 proclaim throughout the country

筱(篠) xiǎo ❶〈书面〉thin bamboo ❷ (usu. used in a person's name) substitute for 小

xiào

敩(斆) xiào 〈书面〉teach; instruct

see also xué

校[1] xiào school: 高～ college or university; institution of higher learning / 夜～ night school / 技～ technical school / 母～ one's former school; Alma Mater / 离～ leave school / 返～ return to school

校[2] xiào field officer: 少～ major / 中～ lieutenant colonel / 上～ colonel / 大～ senior colonel / 将～ high-ranking military officers

see also jiào

校办工厂 xiàobàn gōngchǎng factory attached to a school; school-run factory

校办农场 xiàobàn nóngchǎng farm attached to a school; school-run farm

校车 xiàochē school bus: 搭～回家 go home by school bus

校董 xiàodǒng trustee of a school: ～会 board of trustees of a school

校风 xiàofēng ethos of a school; school spirit: 优良～ excellent school spirit / ～不正 uncongenial school spirit / 新学校应有新的～。A new school should have a new spirit.

校服 xiàofú school uniform: 穿着～的学生 students in school uniforms

校歌 xiàogē school song; college song; Alma Mater

校工 xiàogōng school worker: 本校共有～十五名。There are altogether 15 workers on the school's payroll.

校官 xiàoguān field officer

校规 xiàoguī school regulations; school rules: 遵守～ obey school regulations / 违反～ violate school rules

校花 xiàohuā 〈旧语〉campus queen; school belle

校徽 xiàohuī school badge: 佩戴～ wear a school badge

校际 xiàojì interschool; intercollegiate: ～交流 interschool exchange / ～运动会 intercollegiate sports meet

校刊 xiàokān college journal; school magazine: 本期～目录 contents of the current issue of the school journal / ～合订本 bound volume of (the various issues of) the school magazine

校历 xiàolì school calendar: 按～，明天放暑假。Summer vacation begins tomorrow according to the school calendar.

校旗 xiàoqí school flag

校庆 xiàoqìng anniversary of the founding of a school or college: ～日 school day / 一百周年～ hundredth anniversary of the founding of a school / 邀请校友参加～活动。Alumni are invited to participate in the celebrations of the founding of the school.

校容 xiàoróng appearance or look of a school: ～整洁。The campus is clean and neat.

校舍 xiàoshè schoolhouse; school building: 修缮后的～焕然一新。The school buildings took on a new look after renovation.

校外 xiàowài outside school; after school; extramural; extracurricular: ～进修 extramural studies

校外辅导员 xiàowài fǔdǎoyuán guest counsellor for school children's activities

校外活动 xiàowài huódòng after-school activities; extracurricular activities: ～站 after-school activities club

校外评审员 xiàowài píngshěnyuán external examiner; external assessor

校务 xiàowù affairs of a school: 忙于～ busy with school affairs / ～会议 school (*or* college) administration meeting

校训 xiàoxùn school motto: 这所重点中学的～是"严谨、求实、进步"。The motto of this key secondary school is "strict, realistic and progressive".

校衣 xiàoyī school uniform

校医 xiàoyī school doctor

校役 xiàoyì 〈旧语〉school worker; school menial

校友 xiàoyǒu alumnus; alumna: 男～ alumnus (-ni) / 女～ alumna (-nae) / ～会 alumni association / ～录 alumni record / ～通讯录 address book of alumni; alumni address book

校园 xiàoyuán campus; school yard: ～政治 campus politics / ～生活 campus life; life on campus / ～音乐 campus music / ～文化 campus culture

校园歌曲 xiàoyuán gēqǔ campus song

校长 xiàozhǎng (primary or secondary school) schoolmaster; headmaster; principal; (university or college) president; chancellor: ～办公室 principal's office; president's office; chancellor's office / 副～ vice-president; vice-chancellor / ～助理 assistant president / ～负责制 principal accountability system

校址 xiàozhǐ location of a school or college: 新～ new location (*or* address) of a school / ～不详。The location of the school is not known.

效[1] xiào effect; result; efficiency: 肥～ fertilizer efficiency / 疗～ curative effect / 失～ cease to be effective / 见～ produce an effect; produce results / 行之有～ effective; effectual / 卓有成～ highly effective; fruitful / 以观后～ see how the offender behaves / 法令自通过之日起生～。The law will come into effect (*or* force) from the date of its adoption.

效[2](傚) xiào imitate; follow the example of; follow suit: 东施～颦 behave like an ugly woman imitating the frown of a famous beauty; blindly copy others and make oneself look foolish / 上行下～。Subordinates follow the example set by their superiors.

效[3](効) xiào devote (one's energy or life); dedicate (oneself); render (a service): 回国报～ return to one's homeland to offer one's service / ～犬马之劳 serve sb. faithfully

效法 xiàofǎ follow the example of; pattern or model oneself on; learn from; emulate: 这个厂的改革值得我们～。The reform of this factory is worthy of our emulation. / ～他人不能代替自己的创造。Following the example of others cannot replace one's own creation.

效仿 xiàofǎng imitate; copy; follow: ～先贤 follow the example of the sages of the past / 我们不能一味～别人的教学方法。We mustn't blindly copy others' teaching methods.

效果 xiàoguǒ ❶ effect; result: ～显著 bring about a striking effect; produce marked results; prove highly effective / ～不好 produce little effect; produce no good results / 动机和～的统一 unity of motive and effect ❷〈戏剧〉sound and lighting effects: 音响～ sound effects; acoustics / 灯光～ light effects

效劳 xiàoláo work for; serve: 为祖国～ serve one's own country; serve one's motherland / 请你告诉他，我愿为他～。Please tell him I'd be glad to offer him my service.

效力 xiàolì ❶ render one's service to; serve: ～边疆建设 render one's service to the construction of border areas / 我目前正～于国家足球队。At present I am serving (*or* playing) on the national football team. ❷ effect; force; avail: 发挥～ produce effects; prove effective / 具有同等～的文本 texts of equal authenticity / 这个文件具有法律～。This document has legal force. / 药因受潮而失去～。The medicine has been exposed to moisture and lost its potency.

效力射 xiàolìshè 〈军事〉fire for effect: ～前的预射 preparatory fire

效率 xiàolǜ productivity; efficiency: ～高 efficient / ～低 inefficient / 提高工作～ raise (*or* promote) work efficiency / ～比 efficiency ratio / ～曲线 efficiency curve / ～试验 efficiency test / ～调剂 efficiency modulation / ～是企业的生命。Efficiency is the lifeline of any enterprise.

效命 xiàomìng go all out to serve (one's country, etc.); be ready to die for (a cause, etc.): 军人～沙场，义无反顾。A soldier is duty-bound to be ready to die in battle.

效能 xiàonéng efficacy; usefulness; potency: 充分发挥计算机的～ make the best possible use of computers / 这种化学制品的防腐～很强。

These chemical products have a strong antiseptic efficacy.

效颦 xiàopín copy blindly; imitate servilely; play the ape
see also "东施效颦" Dōngshī-xiàopín

效死 xiàosǐ be ready to give one's life (for a cause); render service at the cost of one's life: ~图报 be ready to die for sb. to pay a debt of gratitude; pledge one's life to repay sb. / ~不恤 never hesitate to give one's life (for sb. or sth.) / ~疆场 be ready to lay down one's life on the battlefield

效验 xiàoyàn intended effect; desired result: 大见~ prove very effective; act like magic / 毫无~ prove totally ineffective; fall flat

效益 xiàoyì result; benefit: 社会~ social benefits / 经济~ economic results (*or* returns) / 改进技术,扩大~ improve techniques and increase efficacy

效益工资 xiàoyì gōngzī efficiency-related wages

效应 xiàoyìng ❶ (physical or chemical) effect: 热~ heat effect; thermal results / 化学~ chemical effect / 陀螺~ gyroscopic effect / 微观~ microeffect / 光电~ photoelectric effect ❷ effect; result: 风险~ risk effect / 补贴~ effect of the subsidy / 引起了轰动~ cause a great sensation

效应器 xiàoyìngqì 〈生理〉 effector

效用 xiàoyòng effectiveness; utility; usefulness: ~递减律 law of diminishing returns (*or* utility) / ~等高线 equal-utility contour / ~论 utility theory; theory of effectiveness / ~模型 utility model / 充分发挥~ make full use of sth.

效尤 xiàoyóu knowingly follow the example of a wrongdoer: 以儆~ warn others against following a bad example

效忠 xiàozhōng pledge loyalty to; dedicate oneself to: ~信 letter pledging one's allegiance; letter of fealty / ~宣誓 loyalty oath / ~于祖国 devote oneself heart and soul to the motherland

孝

xiào ❶ filial piety: 尽~ do one's filial duties (to one's parents); treat one's parents with filial piety / 古人云: ~当竭力,忠则尽命。As the ancients put it, "The filial son must do his utmost to wait on his parents, the loyal minister must stake his life to serve his country". / 不~有三,无后为大〈旧语〉 of the three kinds of unfilial conduct, the greatest is to have no male descendant; there are three major offences against filial piety, of which the worst is to have no male heir ❷ mourning period: 守~ observe mourning / 满~ go out of mourning; the mourning period is over / 吊~ pay a condolence call ❸ mourning dress: 带~ be in mourning dress / 重~ deep mourning ❹ (Xiào) a surname

孝道 xiàodào code of supporting and waiting on one's parents; filial piety: 尽~ do one's filial duty (to one's parents); treat one's parents with filial piety; provide for and wait on one's parents

孝道 xiàodao 〈口语〉 show filial obedience to one's parents; be filial and loving: 儿子、儿媳都很~。Both their son and daughter-in-law are filial and loving.

孝服 xiàofú ❶ mourning dress or garment: 穿~ in mourning dress ❷〈旧语〉 mourning period: ~已满。The mourning period is over. *or* One is out of mourning.

X

孝经 Xiàojīng *The Book of Filial Piety*, one of the Confucian classic works written towards the end of the 3rd century BC by anonymous Confucianists

孝敬 xiàojìng ❶ be obedient and respectful to: ~父母 treat one's parents with filial respect ❷ give presents (to one's elders or superiors): 他经常买些东西~母亲。He often buys presents for his mother. / 没有什么~您的,这是自家园子里的一点苹果。I have nothing better for you than these apples from my own orchard.

孝廉 xiàolián ❶ filial piety and clean record — criteria for selecting officials in the Han Dynasty: 举~ recommend people noted for their filial piety and moral records (for official positions) ❷ holder of second-degree scholarly title (successful candidate of provincial civil examinations in the Ming and Qing dynasties)

孝幔 xiàomàn curtain hung before the coffin (of one's parent)

孝男 xiàonán 〈旧语〉 bereaved son (term used in an obituary or on a tombstone)

孝女 xiàonǚ ❶〈旧语〉 bereaved daughter (term used in an obituary or on a tombstone) ❷ filial daughter; dutiful daughter

孝顺 xiàoshùn show filial obedience; show filial piety: ~的女儿 filial daughter

孝顺竹 xiàoshùnzhú *also* "孝子竹" "bamboo of filial piety" — a kind of bamboo

孝堂 xiàotáng hall or parlour in which the coffin (of one's parent) is laid

孝悌 xiàotì filial piety and fraternal duty: ~忠信 filiality, fraternity, loyalty and faithfulness; loyalty and filial piety

孝心 xiàoxīn love for and devotion to one's parents; filial love: 尽~ do one's filial duties (to one's parents); show one's filial love

孝行 xiàoxíng filial behaviour or conduct

孝养 xiàoyǎng provide and show filial respect for: ~父母 provide for one's parents with filial devotion

孝衣 xiàoyī mourning garment or apparel; mourning dress

孝子 xiàozǐ ❶ filial or dutiful son: ~节妇 filial sons and chaste widows / 他是有名的~,从来没干过让老人不满意的事。Well-known for his filial devotion, he never did anything against the wishes of his parents. ❷ bereaved son; son in mourning

孝子贤孙 xiàozǐ-xiánsūn worthy progeny; true son: 有志气的青年人绝不做旧制度的殉葬品,没落阶级的~。Young people with lofty ideals would hate to be sacrificial objects of an old regime and filial progeny of decadent classes.

哮

xiào ❶ heavy breathing; wheeze; cough ❷ roar; howl; yell: 咆~ roar; thunder / ~吼 yell and scream / ~声如雷 thunderous howl

哮喘 xiàochuǎn *also* "气喘" qìchuǎn have (a fit of) asthma; cough and gasp for breath

肖

xiào resemble; be similar; be like: 维妙维~ resemble to the last detail; be as like as two peas; be absolutely lifelike / 不~子孙 unworthy descendants (*or* progeny) / 这对孪生兄弟长相酷~。The twin brothers bear a striking resemblance to each other.
see also Xiāo

肖像 xiàoxiàng portrait; portraiture: ~权 portraiture right / ~雕塑 portrait sculpture / 给某人画~ paint a portrait of sb. / 让人给自己画~ have one's portrait painted; sit for one's portrait

肖像画 xiàoxiànghuà portrait-painting; portrait: ~法 iconography; portraiture / ~家 portraitist; portrait painter

肖像学 xiàoxiàngxué iconography

咲

xiào 〈书面〉 *see* "笑" xiào

笑

xiào ❶ smile; laugh: 大~ laugh heartily; roar with laughter; guffaw / 微~ smile / 苦~ laugh bitterly / 傻~ laugh (*or* smile) foolishly; giggle / 窃~ laugh up one's sleeve; snicker; snigger / 格格地~ cackle / ~断肚肠 split one's sides with laughter / ~岔了气 choke with laughter / ~得合不上嘴 grin from ear to ear / ~得直不起腰 laugh so much that one can't stand up; double up with laughter / 一~了之 laugh sth. away / 破涕为~ smile through tears / 眉开眼~ be all smiles / 微~表示感谢 smile one's thanks / 谁~在最后,谁~得最好。He laughs best who laughs last. ❷ ridicule; laugh at; deride: ~她那身打扮 laugh at her make-up / 贻~大方 make a laughing stock of oneself before experts; turn oneself into a laughing stock before experts / 五十步~百步 one who retreats fifty paces mocks one who retreats a hundred — the pot calls the kettle black

笑傲风月 xiào'ào-fēngyuè revel in the breezy moonlight; enjoy the breeze and moonlight; lead an easy, leisured life (in the country)

笑比河清 xiàobǐhéqīng be an upright official and enforce the law strictly and impartially

笑柄 xiàobǐng laughing stock; butt; joke: 成为~ turn oneself into a laughing stock; lay oneself open to ridicule / 传为~ become a standing joke; spread far and wide as a joke

笑不合口 xiàobùhékǒu laugh so much that one cannot close the mouth; keep on laughing: 他们都~。They couldn't stop laughing.

笑不可仰 xiàobùkěyǎng double up with laughter; split one's sides

笑不唧儿 xiàobujīr *also* "笑不唧唧" 〈方言〉 smiling; all smiles: 他老那么~的,平易近人。He is always smiling, amiable and easy of approach.

笑场 xiàochǎng (actor's or entertainer's) undue laughter during performance

笑翠鸟 xiàocuìniǎo 〈动物〉 (laughing) kookaburra; laughing jackass (*Dacelo gigas*)

笑掉大牙 xiàodiào-dàyá (make people) laugh their heads off; be utterly ridiculous
笑哈哈 xiàohāhā laugh heartily：他把孩子们逗得～。He set the children laughing. /听到好消息，乐得三个老汉～。The three old men laughed heartily upon hearing the good news.
笑呵呵 xiàohēhē all smiles; laughing heartily; happy and gay：日子越过越好，一家人成天～的。As their life improved day by day, the house was full of mirth all day long. /她既不还嘴，也不生气，就那么～地听着。She was just listening smiling, neither talking back nor getting angry.
笑话 xiàohua ❶ joke; jest; pleasantry：说～ tell (*or* crack) a joke / 闹～ make a fool (*or* exhibition) of oneself; make a laughing stock of oneself; make a ridiculous mistake ❷ laugh at; deride; ridicule：不懂可以学嘛，你别～人。Don't laugh at me. I can learn what I don't understand. /～人的人，反倒让人～了。The laugh is on those who laugh at others. ❸ deserving to be laughed at; ridiculous; absurd：一个编辑连这么两个常见的字都分不清，太～了。It's ridiculous to think that an editor cannot even differentiate between these two common words.
笑话百出 xiàohua-bǎichū make all kinds of foolish or stupid mistakes
笑剧 xiàojù *also* "闹剧" nàojù farce
笑噱 xiàojué 〈书面〉loud laughter; laughter：仰天～ turn one's face skyward and laugh uproariously
笑乐 xiàolè happy and cheerful：逗人～ make people happy and cheerful; amuse people
笑里藏刀 xiàolǐ-cángdāo hide a dagger in a smile — with murderous intent behind one's smiles; smile of treachery; iron hand in a velvet glove：她表面上和蔼可亲，实际上～。Seemingly kind, she hides her murderous intent behind her smiles. /他～，言清行浊。He has a dagger behind his smiles, noble in words but dirty in deeds.
笑脸 xiàoliǎn smiling face; beaming face：～相迎 greet with a (broad) smile /赔～ meet rudeness with a flattering smile; force a smile /只要她～一开，他就会把忧愁丢到脑后。Whenever she smiled, he would forget all about his worries.
笑料 xiàoliào laughing stock：把…当作～ regard as a laughing stock; take as a joke /她的笨拙成了邻居的～。Her clumsiness became a neighbourhood joke.
笑咧咧 xiàoliēliē grin; smile broadly：他～地张开嘴，露出整齐洁白的牙齿。He grinned, showing his regular and white teeth.
笑林 xiàolín collection of popular jokes
笑骂 xiàomà ❶ deride and taunt：～由他～，好官我自为之。(said ironically of a thick-skinned corrupt official) Let them ridicule and taunt as they like; I'll be an official in my own good way. /伽利略不顾他人的～，继续自己的科学试验。Undaunted by sneers and abuses, Galileo went on with his scientific experiments. ❷ twit teasingly; rally：她红着脸～道："你这个缺德鬼，就会开玩笑!" Flushing, she cursed teasingly: "You are mean and good at nothing but cracking jokes!"
笑貌 xiàomào smiling expression：虽然分别多年，但他的音容～仍然浮现在我的脑海。Though he has been away for years, his voice and smiling expressions appear fresh and vivid in my mind's eye.
笑眯眯 xiàomīmī smilingly; with a smile on one's face：～地望着孩子 watch a child with a smile on one's face /他一天到晚～的。He has a smile on his face from morning till night. *or* He is smiling all the time.
笑面虎 xiàomiànhǔ smiling tiger — an outwardly kind but inwardly cruel person; wicked person wearing a hypocritical smile; wolf at heart but lamb in appearance：人称"～" known as the "smiling tiger" /他那副～的神情，越发使她生气。It made her more furious than ever to see him putting on a wolf-in-sheep's-clothing manner.
笑纳 xiàonà 〈套语〉kindly accept (what is offered as a gift)：区区薄礼，不成敬意，请～。Kindly accept this small gift as a token of my respect.
笑气 xiàoqì 〈化学〉laughing gas; nitrous oxide
笑容 xiàoróng smiling expression; smile：满面～ be all smiles; smile all over one's face; have a broad smile on one's face /父亲严厉的脸上露出了一丝～。A faint smile crept over father's stern face. /老人脸上浮现出慈祥的～。A kindly smile appeared on the old man's face.
笑容可掬 xiàoróng-kějū be radiant with smiles; wear a charming or captivating smile：他～地走到我身边坐下来。Radiant with smiles, he came over and sat down beside me. /在县长面前，她变得～了。She smiled charmingly in front of the county magistrate.
笑声 xiàoshēng laugh; laughter：听到远处的～ hear sounds of laughter from afar /～不绝于耳。Bursts of laughter kept ringing in one's ear.
笑谈 xiàotán ❶ object of ridicule; laughing stock; butt：传为～ be the butt of everyone's jokes; become a standing joke ❷ joke; jest：关于他的～越来越多。There were more and more jokes about him.
笑微微 xiàowēiwēi smiling：脸上～的 with a smiling face; with a smile on one's face
笑纹 xiàowén laugh lines：眼角的～ laugh lines around one's eyes
笑窝 xiàowō *also* "笑涡" dimple
笑嘻嘻 xiàoxīxī smile：她抿着小嘴～的。She was smiling with her small lips closed.
笑星 xiàoxīng laughing star — well-known comedian or cross-talker
笑谑 xiàoxuè 〈书面〉tease; banter jokingly; make fun of：寓规劝于～ combine advice with fun
笑颜 xiàoyán smiling face：～常开 often wear a smile on one's face /他近来心事颇重，整日不见～。Anxiety-laden, he looked gloomy all the time.
笑靥 xiàoyè 〈书面〉❶ dimple：她微微一笑，脸上露出两个美丽的～。She smiled slightly, revealing two beautiful dimples on her cheeks. ❷ smiling face：服务员们面带～地接待我们。The attendants greeted us with smiling faces.
笑一笑，十年少 xiào yī xiào, shínián shào 〈俗语〉smiles make one young：～；愁一愁，白了头。Smiles make one young; worries make one old. *or* An ounce of mirth is worth a pound of sorrow.
笑吟吟 xiàoyīnyīn smiling happily：～的女孩 smiling girl /他说起话来总是～的。He always smiles when he speaks.
笑盈盈 xiàoyíngyíng smiling：她圆圆的脸上～地现出两个酒窝。Two smiling dimples appeared on her round face.
笑影 xiàoyǐng smiling expression; smiling look：父亲的言谈～常常浮现在眼前。Often would I see in my mind's eye father's smiling expression as he spoke.
笑语 xiàoyǔ talk and smile; talk and laugh：～欢歌 merry laughter and song /～声喧 confusing din of laughter and talk /姑娘们划着小船，～连天地向荷花荡驶去。Talking and laughing merrily, the girls paddled the boat towards the lotus pond.
笑逐颜开 xiàozhú-yánkāi beam with smiles; be wreathed in smiles：老人双喜临门，不由得～。As the double blessing descended upon him, the old man beamed (*or* the old man's face was wreathed in smiles).

啸(嘯、歗) xiào ❶ (of people) whistle：仰天长～ gaze into the sky and let out a long whistle (*or* sigh) ❷ (of birds or animals) scream; roar; howl：虎～ roar of a tiger ❸ sound of some natural phenomena：风～ whistling wind; howling wind /海～ tidal wave; tsunami ❹ whirring; buzzing; hissing; whizzing：飞机尖～着掠过。A plane buzzed over. /炮弹呼～而过。Artillery shells whistled past.
啸傲 xiào'ào 〈书面〉be leisurely and carefree：～林泉 enjoy one's country life in total freedom; live in leisure and freedom in the country /～风月的隐士 carefree hermit /～烟霞，放荡不羁 live a totally unconventional and unrestrained life in nature
啸歌 xiàogē keep whistling and singing; keep whistling songs
啸呼 xiàohū keep whistling and shouting
啸叫 xiàojiào scream; whistle：～的寒风 howling (*or* whistling) cold wind /战场上弹片～。Shrapnel whistled over the battlefield.
啸聚 xiàojù 〈书面〉band together; gang up：转相～ pass the news to one another and gather together
啸聚山林 xiàojù-shānlín (of bandits, etc.) form a band and take to the greenwood; go to the greenwood
啸鸣 xiàomíng ❶ whistle; scream; whizz：～林间 whistle in the woods /百鸟～。All kinds of birds are chirping and calling. ❷ roaring; howling：鸟兽凄厉的～ shrill cries of wild birds and beasts
啸声 xiàoshēng whistle; hiss：～流星 whistling meteor /～干扰 whistling interference; whistler /～电弧 hissing arc

xiē

楔 xiē ❶ wedge; peg ❷ drive (a wedge, etc.)：～钉子 drive

a nail (into a wall, board, etc.)
楔规 xiēguī 〈机械〉wedge gauge
楔形板 xiēxíngbǎn 〈建筑〉clapboard
楔形文字 xiēxíng wénzì cuneiform; sphenogram: ～学 sphenography
楔子 xiēzi ❶ wedge ❷ (wooden or bamboo) peg ❸ prologue or interlude in Yuan Dynasty drama ❹ prologue or prelude in a novel

揳 xiē 〈方言〉drive (a wedge, etc.): 榫眼开大了,得～个楔子。As the mortise is too wide, a wedge has to be driven into it to make it fast.

些 xiē ❶ (used to indicate an indefinite quantity) a few; some: 这～ this; these /那～ that; those /一～ some; certain /前～年 several years ago /买～水果 buy some fruit /有～积蓄 have laid aside some money; have some savings ❷ (used after an adjective as a modifier of degree) a little; a bit; rather; somewhat: 简单～ a little simpler; a bit easier /小声～ speak in a lower tone; speak more softly /好～ many; lots of /他比我略微高～。He's somewhat taller than I am.
些个 xiēge some; a little; a few: 他是弟弟,你应该让他～。Since he is your younger brother, you should try and humour him a bit. /这～东西你都拿走。Take all these things with you.
些微 xiēwēi slightly; a trifle; a little; a bit: 海风～有点儿凉意。The sea breeze was a little chilly. /他拿不出～的勇气来。He didn't show the least courage. /这菜～淡了点。This dish needs a bit more salt. /肚子～有点儿痛。My stomach aches slightly.
些小 xiēxiǎo ❶ a little; a bit: ～牢骚 grouse a little ❷ small amount; small: ～事情 trifling matter
些须 xiēxū (often used in the early vernacular) a few; a little: ～小事,何足挂齿? Such a trifling matter is not worth mentioning. /一家六口靠～薪水,如何度日? How could a family of six live on such a paltry salary?
些许 xiēxǔ a little; a bit: 此事我略知～。I know a little about this. /取得～成绩就沾沾自喜,你真没出息。What a good-for-nothing you are to gloat over such small achievement.
些子 xiēzǐ 〈方言〉a little; a few

蝎(蠍) xiē scorpion: ～毒 scorpion venom; buthotoxin /天～座〈天文〉Scorpion
蝎虎 xiēhǔ *also* "蝎虎子"; "壁虎" bìhǔ gecko; house lizard: ～座〈天文〉Lacerta
蝎子 xiēzi scorpion

歇 xiē ❶ rest; take a rest: ～一会儿 take (*or* have) a breather; take a break /～病假 be on sick leave /您～着吧,这事我来办。Please take a rest and leave this to me. /我现在已～过来了。I'm now fully rested. ❷ stop (work, etc.); knock off; quit: 这两个月他从未～过工。He's never asked for leave (from his work) during these two months. ❸〈方言〉go to bed: 白天累了一天,天刚黑他就～了。After a day's hard work, he went to bed as soon as it was dark. ❹〈方言〉a short time; a little while; a moment: 我现在正忙,过一～儿你再来,好吗? I am busy right now. Could you come back in a while?
歇鞍 xiē'ān 〈方言〉knock off; stop work; take a rest: 队长说了,这几天～。The team leader says we'll knock off for a few days.
歇班 xiēbān be off duty; have time off: 我下周～。I'll be off duty next week.
歇泊 xiēbó cast anchor; lie at anchor; put up (for the night): 运河沿岸,船～之处甚多。There are many anchorages along the canal. /他们一路上晓行夜宿,均在山村小店～。Setting off at dawn and stopping at dusk, they would put up at mountain village inns throughout their journey.
歇顶 xiēdǐng thin on top; becoming bald: 他不到三十岁,就～了。His hair is thinning on top though he is under thirty.
歇乏 xiēfá take a rest or break: 歇歇乏再干吧! Let's take a break before we start again.
歇伏 xiēfú stop or suspend work during the dog days: 这几天村里人～,地里看不见人。You can't find anybody in the fields, as the villagers have stopped work during the height of summer.
歇工 xiēgōng ❶ quit or stop work; knock off: 她趁这几天～串串亲戚。As she had a few days off, she spent the time visiting relatives. ❷ (of an enterprise) close down; (of a project) be suspended: 建楼工程因经费不足而～。The construction of the building was suspended due to shortage of funding.
歇后语 xiēhòuyǔ two-part allegorical saying (of which the first part, always stated, is descriptive, while the second part, often unstated, carries the message, e.g. 狗逮耗子 — 多管闲事 dog trying to catch mice — meddling in other people's business)
歇火 xiēhuǒ 〈航天〉burn-out
歇肩 xiējiān take the load off one's shoulder for a rest; have a short break: 山路又长又陡,途中他歇了好几次肩。He took quite a few breaks as he carried the load over the long and steep mountain trail.
歇脚 xiējiǎo *also* "歇腿" take a load off one's feet — take a break while walking; stop on the way for a rest: 走累了,坐下来歇歇脚吧。Sit down and have a rest since you are tired with walking.
歇凉 xiēliáng 〈方言〉relax in a cool place; enjoy the cool: 晚饭后,大人小孩都爱到院子里的大树下～。After supper, both adults and children loved to sit in the shade of the huge tree in the courtyard and relax themselves.
歇气 xiēqì stop for a breather; take a break: 别太累了,歇歇气再干吧。Come and take a breather. Don't tire yourself out. /他一直跑到学校,路上也没停下来歇口气。He ran all the way to the school without stopping to catch his breath.
歇憩 xiēqì have a rest: 他斜仰在靠背椅上～片刻。He was taking a little rest reclining on the high-backed chair.
歇晌 xiēshǎng take a midday nap or rest; have a doze at noon: 干完这点活儿咱们再～。Let's finish the job before we take the midday break.
歇梢 xiēshāo 〈方言〉take a rest: 来往行人常在这里～。Travellers often take a rest here. /歇一下梢,他觉得好些了。He felt much better after a short rest.
歇手 xiēshǒu stop doing sth.; stop working; break off: 忽然停电,我们只得～。We had to stop working as there was a sudden blackout. /趁地里活儿～的功夫,她打了些猪草。She spent the short break in the field cutting some green feed for the pigs.
歇斯底里 xiēsīdǐlǐ ❶〈医学〉(transliteration) hysteria ❷ morbidly emotional; hysterical: ～地嚎叫 scream hysterically (*or* wildly) /～大发作 go into hysterics; become hysterical /他突然爆发出一阵～的狂笑。All of a sudden, he burst into hysterical (*or* frenzied) laughter.
歇宿 xiēsù put up for the night; make an overnight stop; stay the night: 昨晚我在一个老乡家～。Last night I put up at a villager's cottage.
歇腿 xiētuǐ *see* "歇脚"
歇窝 xiēwō 〈方言〉(as of hens, ducks, etc.) stop laying eggs (due to hot or cold weather): 三伏天蛋少,鸡～了。There are fewer eggs during the dog days as most hens have stopped laying.
歇息 xiēxi ❶ have a rest; rest for a while: 活儿忙得连～的时间都没有。We were too busy to have a rest. ❷ go to sleep; put up for the night: 鸡犬无声,村里人都～了。Silence reigned in the village, as all the villagers had gone to bed.
歇夏 xiēxià *see* "歇伏"
歇闲 xiēxián 〈方言〉take a break from work; have a rest: 母亲一天到晚不～地操劳。Mother works from morning till night without a rest. /～的时候,咱们到林子里去转转。Let's go around the woods during the break.
歇心 xiēxīn ❶ set one's mind at rest; be relaxed in one's mind; be free from care and worry: 一天到晚没个～的时候 never have a moment's peace and relaxation the whole day ❷ give up trying; drop an idea: 别人回绝了好几次他也不～。He did not give up trying even though he had been refused several times.
歇业 xiēyè go out of business; close a business; close down: 这家商店因经营不当,两年前就～了。The shop went out of business two years ago as a result of poor management.
歇夜 xiēyè put up for the night; stay overnight: 今天就在这里～吧。Let's put up for the night here.
歇阴 xiēyīn 〈方言〉enjoy the cool in some shade; relax in a cool place: 几个老头儿在地头的树下～。A few old men were enjoying the cool shade under a tree at the edge of the field.
歇枝 xiēzhī (as of fruit trees) bear less fruit; have a lean year: 明年苹果树～,果农的收入怕要受影响。As it will be a lean year for the apple trees next year, the farmers' income may be adversely affect-

ed.

歇止 xiēzhǐ stop; halt:永不～的喷泉 ever-gushing fountain

xié

絜 xié 〈书面〉❶ measure the circumference of:树高数丈,～之十围。The tree was over a dozen metres tall and took almost ten people to link their arms around it. ❷ measure:度长～大 measure the height and size of sth.
see also jié

鞋 xié shoes:球～ *also* "运动～" sneakers; gym shoes /网球～ tennis shoes /布～ cloth shoes /棉～ cotton-padded shoes /拖～ slippers /草～ straw sandals /胶～ rubber overshoes; rubbers /雨～ rubber boots; galoshes /高跟～ high-heeled shoes; high heels

鞋拔子 xiébázi shoehorn

鞋帮 xiébāng upper (of a shoe)

鞋带 xiédài shoelace; shoestring:～包头 tag (of a shoelace)

鞋底 xiédǐ *also* "鞋底子" sole (of a shoe):～夹层 midsole /～前掌 half sole

鞋垫 xiédiàn shoe-pad; insole

鞋钉 xiédīng spike (as of a track shoe); hobnail (for mending a shoe)

鞋粉 xiéfěn shoe powder

鞋跟 xiégēn heel (of a shoe)

鞋匠 xiéjiang shoemaker; cobbler

鞋扣 xiékòu shoe buckle

鞋里 xiélǐ shoe lining

鞋脸 xiéliǎn front uppers (of shoes); vamp; instep:他走出林子,～上沾满了泥。He walked out of the woods, with the front uppers of his shoes covered with mud.

鞋面 xiémiàn *see* "鞋脸"

鞋刷 xiéshuā shoe brush

鞋趿拉 xiétāla 〈方言〉 *also* "鞋塌拉" slippers

鞋楦 xiéxuàn *also* "鞋楦头";"鞋楦子" last (for shaping a shoe); shoe tree

鞋眼 xiéyǎn eyelet (of a shoe)

鞋样 xiéyàng shoe pattern; outline of a shoe's upper and sole

鞋油 xiéyóu shoe polish or cream

鞋子 xiézi 〈方言〉 shoe

鲑 xié 〈古语〉 fish as food; fish dish
see also guī

挟(挾) xié ❶ hold under the arm:～伞外出 go out with an umbrella under one's arm ❷ coerce; compel; force sb. to submit or yield:要～ threaten; coerce /以性命相～ threaten sb. with death /～势弄权 abuse one's position and power ❸ bear; harbour (resentment, etc.): *see* "～怨"; "～恨"

挟持 xiéchí ❶ seize sb. (on both sides) by the arms:两个暴徒～着老人上了汽车。Two thugs got in the car, holding the old man by the arms on both sides. ❷ hold under duress; abduct; kidnap:他在匪徒的～下打开了钱柜。He opened the safe under the gangster's threats.

挟仇 xiéchóu harbour a grudge or rancour:～陷害 frame sb. because of a grudge one bears against him

挟带 xiédài carry or bring along forcibly:风～着沙砾袭击岩石和断崖。The wind was lashing hard at the rocks and cliffs with the sand and grit it was carrying along.

挟恨 xiéhèn nurse intense hatred

挟山超海 xiéshān-chāohǎi *also* "挟泰山以超北海" leap across the north sea with Mount Tai under one's arm — an impossible task; an impossibility:要我一时办成这么多的事,无异于～。It would simply be out of the question for me to accomplish so much in so short a time.

挟天子以令诸侯 xié tiānzǐ yǐ lìng zhūhóu have the emperor under one's thumb and order the dukes about in his name

挟细拿粗 xiéxì-nácū *also* "拿粗挟细" find fault; deliberately make things difficult (for sb.); nit-pick

挟嫌 xiéxián 〈书面〉 harbour or bear a grudge:～诬告 bring false charges against sb. out of resentment /～报复 retaliate against sb.; settle an old score (with sb.)

挟怨 xiéyuàn nurse a grudge; bear ill will:～生事 stir up trouble to vent one's resentment

挟制 xiézhì take advantage of sb.'s weakness to enforce obedience; force sb. to do one's bidding; have sb. under one's thumb:为人～ be under sb.'s thumb; be under sb.'s control

颉 xié ❶〈书面〉(of birds) fly upwards; soar ❷ (Xié) a surname

颉颃 xiéháng 〈书面〉❶ (of birds) fly up and down:飞鸟鼓翼,交颈～。Flapping their wings, the birds were flying up and down, neck to neck. ❷ compare; rival:与…相～ compare with; rank with

襭 xié 〈书面〉 carry with the front of one's garment

撷 xié ❶〈书面〉 pick; pluck:采～ gather; collect ❷ *see* "襭" xié

撷取 xiéqǔ pick; pluck; select:～精华 skim the cream; select the best

撷英 xiéyīng 〈书面〉 select the very best

缬 xié 〈书面〉 patterned silk fabric

缬草 xiécǎo 〈植物〉 garden heliotrope (*Valeriana officinalis*):～油 valerian oil

谐 xié ❶ harmony; accord:调～ harmonize; synchronize; 〈物理〉 tune ❷ come to an agreement; agree with; settle:事～之后,当即电告。I will send you a telegram as soon as the matter is settled. /如事不～,即刻离开。Leave immediately if the matter falls through. ❸ humorous:亦庄亦～ both serious and humorous

谐波 xiébō 〈物理〉 harmonic wave; harmonic component:～场 harmonic field /～干扰 harmonic interference /～失真 harmonic distortion /～天线 harmonic antenna /～电压 harmonic voltage /～检波器〈电子〉 harmonic detector

谐和 xiéhé harmonious; congenial; concordant:～的邻里关系 harmonious neighbourly relations /上下～ harmony between superiors and subordinates

谐剧 xiéjù ❶ another name for comedy ❷ *xieju*, one-man comic show combining storytelling, singing and acting, popular in Sichuan Province

谐美 xiéměi (of words, etc.) concordant and melodious:音律～ concordant prosody /语言～ melodious diction

谐频 xiépín 〈电子〉 harmonic frequency

谐趣 xiéqù ❶ humorous delight:～横生 be fraught with humour ❷ harmonious and interesting:～园 Garden of Harmonious Interest (situated in the Summer Palace outside the city of Beijing)

谐声 xiéshēng *also* "形声" xíngshēng pictophonetic character

谐谈 xiétán humorous talk or conversation:此人每多～。He is sparkling with wit.

谐调 xiétiáo harmonious; well-balanced:旋律～ harmonious melody /色彩～ well-matched colours /游览区周围的建筑物要跟名胜古迹～。Buildings around the tourist resort should be in harmony with its historical sites.

谐婉 xiéwǎn harmonious and gentle:歌曲音调～。The tune is harmonious and gentle.

谐戏 xiéxì 〈书面〉 make a humorous joke; poke fun (at sb.) in a humorous way:善谈吐,好～ good at conversation and fond of pleasantries /他缄口不语,任人～。He kept silent, not retorting to humorous jokes at his expense.

谐谑 xiéxuè poke fun; banter:好～ fond of jesting /夫妻～,不可认真。You mustn't take banter between husband and wife seriously.

谐谑曲 xiéxuèqǔ 〈音乐〉 scherzo

谐音 xiéyīn ❶ homophonic; homonymic:～现象 homophony /人们常用～使语言更加生动。People often use homophones to make their language vivid. ❷ enphony; harmony of sound

谐振 xiézhèn 〈物理〉 resonance; syntony:～瓶 syntonic jar /空腔～ cavity resonance

谐振腔 xiézhènqiāng resonant cavity

偕 xié together with; accompanied by; in the company of:相～出游 go on a tour together /～夫人抵京 arrive at the capital ac-

X

companied by his wife
偕老 xiélǎo (of husband and wife) grow old together:白头～ live to ripe old age in conjugal bliss; remain a devoted couple to the end of their lives
偕乐 xiélè 〈书面〉enjoy together:与民～ enjoy (a happy occasion, etc.) with the common people
偕同 xiétóng accompanied by; together with; along with:～前往 accompany sb. on a tour; go in sb.'s entourage /～外宾参观 accompany foreign guests on a visit
偕行 xiéxíng ❶〈书面〉walk together:携手～ walk together hand in hand ❷ coexist; stand together

邪

xié ❶ evil; heresy:奸～ crafty and crook /不信～ not believe in evil; refuse to be taken in by heresy (*or* fallacy, *or* superstition) /不搞歪的～的 not engage in irregularities and violations of law (*or* ethics) ❷ irregular; abnormal; strange:这可～了。This is most strange. /这两天热得～了。It has been abnormally hot these days. ❸〈中医〉unhealthy environmental influence that causes disease; miasma:风～ chilly draught (as a cause of disease) ❹〈迷信〉evil spirits that bring disasters:驱～ exorcise evil spirits /中～ be possessed by evil spirits
see also yé
邪不胜正 xiébùshèngzhèng *also* "邪不敌正" the evil will not prevail over the good:这个单位风气好,历来～。Evil has no place in this unit, as it is pervaded by a righteous spirit.
邪财 xiécái 〈方言〉ill-gotten gains:不取～ not accept (*or* seek) ill-gotten gains /早取～,晚必致祸。Ill-gotten wealth leads to disaster.
邪道 xiédào evil ways; depraved life:走～ take to evil ways; lead a depraved life; abandon oneself to vice /引上～ lead astray /歪门～ unethical practices; illegal activities
邪恶 xié'è evil; wicked; sinister; vicious:～势力 evil forces /～的念头 wicked ideas /正义必将战胜～。Justice (*or* Virtue) will triumph over evil.
邪乎 xiéhu *also* "邪活"〈口语〉❶ abnormal; extraordinary; extreme:闹腾得～ make a terrible row /他病得～。He is seriously ill. ❷ excessive; strange; fantastic:说得～ give an excessively exaggerated version (of sth.); spin a fantastic yarn
邪教 xiéjiào (evil) cult; heretic sect:以～煽聚亡命 incite and rally the desperate through evil preaching
邪路 xiélù *see* "邪道"
邪门儿 xiéménr 〈方言〉❶ abnormal; weird; strange; odd:我这病有点儿～,几家医院都诊断不出结果。It's a weird disease I've got, as several hospitals have failed to offer a proper diagnosis. /真～,人们竟然听信这种谎言! How odd people should swallow such lies! ❷ evil ways; crooked practices; vice
邪门歪道 xiémén-wāidào crooked ways or means; dishonest practices or methods; evil or illegal doings:专搞～ be given to dishonest practices /～的事情一定不能干。One must not get involved in evildoings. /他是靠～才进到我们单位来的。It was through devious ways that he got a job in our department.
邪魔 xiémó evil spirit; devil; demon:中了～ be possessed with evil spirits; be obsessed
邪魔外道 xiémó-wàidào ❶〈佛教〉demons and heretics ❷ unorthodox ways; crooked or devious means
邪念 xiéniàn evil thought or idea; wicked or lascivious intention:萌发～ conceive an evil idea /顿生～ a wicked (*or* evil) thought suddenly occurs to one; be seized with an evil (*or* lascivious) idea /他对这个漂亮而单纯的姑娘怀有～。He harboured evil intentions (*or* designs) on the pretty, simple girl.
邪僻 xiépì 〈书面〉evil; perverse:～之行 evil act
邪气 xiéqì ❶ perverse trend; evil influence; bad practice:歪风～ perverse trends and evil influences /正气压倒～ healthy trends prevail upon unhealthy ones /这人透着一股～。The man was exuding evil all over. ❷〈中医〉evil *qi* that causes various diseases
邪曲 xiéqū 〈书面〉perverted; crooked:为人～ be crooked by nature
邪术 xiéshù witchcraft; black magic; sorcery
邪说 xiéshuō heresy; fallacy:异端～ heretical belief; unorthodox opinion; heresy
邪祟 xiésuì evil spirit:驱除～ exorcise evil spirits
邪心 xiéxīn *see* "邪念"
邪行 xiéxíng wicked act; evil deed:他在外数年,多有～。He committed quite a few evil deeds over the years when he was away from home.
邪行 xiéxing 〈方言〉〈贬义〉abnormal; extraordinary; extreme:冷得～ abnormally cold /他的脾气可～啦,动不动就发火。He's got a most erratic temper and would flare up at the least provocation.

携(攜、擕)

xié ❶ carry; take or bring along:～酒助兴 bring wine to make the party merrier /～杖登山 climb a mountain with the help of a walking stick /～眷归国 return to one's native country with wife and children /～款外逃 flee abroad with funds /扶老～幼 help the old and lead the young (as on a journey); bring along the old and the young ❷ take or hold by the hand:相～而行 walk hand in hand
携带 xiédài ❶ carry; take; bring along:随身～ carry on one's person; carry about /～家属 bring one's family along /～方便 easy to carry about; handy ❷ guide and support:多承～。Thank you very much for your help and support.
携带式生命维持系统 xiédàishì shēngmìng wéichí xìtǒng portable life support system (PLSS)
携贰 xié'èr 〈书面〉harbour treason; be disloyal:四方臣服,不敢～。All the provinces declared their allegiance with none harbouring disloyalty.
携家带口 xiéjiā-dàikǒu *also* "携家带眷";"拉家带口" lājiā-dàikǒu bring all one's family; be burdened by one's family:～,出外逃荒 flee from famine with all one's family /我～的,不像你们单身汉,说走就能走。Burdened with a family, I can't just pull up stakes and leave like you bachelors.
携离 xiélí 〈书面〉betray; rebel:天下～,战祸又起。With the people rising up in rebellion, war broke out again.
携手 xiéshǒu ❶ hand in hand:～同行 walk hand in hand; go together ❷ cooperate; work together:～合作 work together; cooperate /～打击敌人 join hands in fighting the enemy

叶

xié rhyme; concordance
see also yè
叶韵 xiéyùn *also* "协句" xiéjù (in ancient prosody) varying the pronunciation of words in classic poetry to make them rhyme; varying rhyme

斜

xié oblique; slanting; tilted; askew:～航〈航海〉oblique sailing /～金顶 slanting roof /比萨～塔 Leaning Tower of Pisa /～躺着 lie in a reclining position /～眼一瞟 cast a sidelong glance; look askance (at sb.) /这根电线杆子有点～。The wire post is a little tilted. /一条小路～穿过公园。There is a cater-cornered path across the park.
斜边 xiébiān ❶〈数学〉hypotenuse ❷〈机械〉bevel edge:～凿 bevel chisel
斜长石 xiéchángshí 〈矿业〉plagioclase
斜长岩 xiéchángyán 〈地质〉anorthosite
斜齿轮 xiéchǐlún 〈机械〉bevel gear; skew gear; skew wheel
斜刺里 xiécìli diagonally; cater-cornered:从～跑出一个人来。A man ran out on a slant.
斜度 xiédù degree of inclination; gradient; slope
斜度标 xiédùbiāo gradient sign
斜对面 xiéduìmiàn *also* "斜对过" diagonally from; across from:杂货店就在饭馆～。The grocery is across from the restaurant.
斜方肌 xiéfāngjī 〈生理〉trapezius
斜风细雨 xiéfēng-xìyǔ gentle breeze and drizzling rain:～满江天。The sky over the river looks hazy in gentle breeze and light rain.
斜高 xiégāo 〈数学〉slant height
斜缓 xiéhuǎn (of topography) sloping gradually:山坡～。The mountain slope is gentle.
斜晖 xiéhuī 〈书面〉sun rays at dusk; slanting rays of the sun:落日～ slanting rays of the setting sun
斜角 xiéjiǎo ❶〈数学〉oblique angle:～坐标 oblique coordinate ❷〈机械〉bevel angle
斜角规 xiéjiǎoguī bevel square
斜井 xiéjǐng ❶〈矿业〉inclined shaft; slope ❷〈石油〉inclined well; slant hole
斜拉桥 xiélāqiáo stayed-cable bridge
斜楞 xiéleng 〈口语〉slanting; tilted:凳子一～,他就摔下来了。He

X

fell to the floor as the stool slipped to one side.
斜楞眼 xiélengyǎn squint eyes; cross eyes
斜路 xiélù wrong path:走上～ take the wrong path; go astray /他在～上越走越远。He has gone farther and farther down the wrong road.
斜率 xiélǜ 〈数学〉slope
斜面 xiémiàn ❶〈数学〉inclined plane ❷〈机械〉oblique plane; bevel (face)
斜乜 xiémie look sideways; squint:他～着眼睛偷看同座儿的答卷。He squinted at the paper of the student sitting beside him.
斜乜阡儿 xiémieqiānr 〈方言〉slanting slightly:由这儿～往北,就是市场。Go slantwise to the north and you'll find the market.
斜睨 xiénì squint; look sideways:他～了我一眼。He squinted at me.
斜盘电机 xiépán diànjī 〈电工〉swashplate motor
斜坡 xiépō slope:汽车拐过弯道,又驶下一段～,才到了江边。The car rounded a bend and descended a slope before it came to the bank of the river.
斜切面 xiéqiēmiàn 〈数学〉oblique section
斜射 xiéshè ❶ shine sideways or slantwise:～的日光 slanting sun rays /阳光透过窗子～到室内。Sunlight slanted across the room through the window. ❷〈军事〉oblique fire
斜视 xiéshì ❶ *also* "斜眼"〈医学〉strabismus:～计 strabismometer ❷ look sideways; cast a sidelong glance; look askance:目不～ not look sideways; look neither right nor left; refuse to be distracted /小姑娘被他看得头不敢抬,眼睛也不敢～。Under his stare, the little girl dared not lift her head or look sideways.
斜视图 xiéshìtú 〈机械〉oblique drawing
斜体字 xiétǐzì *also* "斜体"〈印刷〉italics
斜透视 xiétòushì 〈机械〉oblique perspective
斜纹 xiéwén twill (weave); drill
斜纹布 xiéwénbù twill; drill
斜线 xiéxiàn oblique line
斜线号 xiéxiànhào slant (/); slash (mark)
斜象眼儿 xiéxiangyǎnr 〈方言〉rhombus; lozenge:书房里铺了～的地板砖。The floor of the study was paved with rhomboid tiles.
斜眼 xiéyǎn ❶〈医学〉strabismus ❷ squint-eye; cross-eye:这个人五官不甚端正,长了一对～。The man has got squint eyes and is not exactly handsome. ❸ squint-eyed or cross-eyed person:客人中有一个～,穿戴倒也整齐。Among the guests was a squint eye, who was fairly well-dressed.
斜眼治疗手术 xiéyǎn zhìliáo shǒushù strabotomy
斜阳 xiéyáng setting sun:雨后复～,关山阵阵苍。The sun returns slanting after the rain And hill and pass grow a deeper blue.
斜域 xiéyù 〈数学〉skew field
斜轧 xiézhá 〈冶金〉skew rolling:～机 skew-rolling mill /～式轧机 skew mill
斜照 xiézhào ❶ shine slantwise:夕阳～,宝塔显得分外肃穆。With the setting sun shining slantwise, the pagoda looked all the more solemn. ❷ setting sun
斜轴线 xiézhóuxiàn 〈数学〉oblique axis

协(協) xié

❶ harmony; concord; coordination:正副主任不～调。The director and his deputy are out of harmony (*or* don't get on with each other). ❷ joint; concerted; common:齐心～力 join in a common effort; make a concerted effort ❸ aid; assist:～捕 assist in catching (*or* capturing) a criminal
协办 xiébàn cooperate in doing sth.; help sb. do sth.; assist:大奖赛由中央电视台主办,若干厂矿企业～。The grand prix was sponsored by CCTV with the cooperation (*or* assistance) of several industrial and mining enterprises.
协比 xiébǐ 〈书面〉act hand in glove; work in collusion:～为奸 work in collusion (with sb.); associate for conspiratorial purposes
协定 xiédìng ❶ agreement; convention; accord:边界～ boundary agreement /停战～ truce (agreement) /民用航空运输～ agreement on civil air transport /～法 conventional law ❷ reach an agreement (on sth.); agree on:～配额 bilateral quota /会议～了一项共同行动纲领。A programme of joint action was agreed on at the conference.
协定边界 xiédìng biānjiè conventional boundary
协定关税 xiédìng guānshuì conventional tariff or duty
协和 xiéhé harmonize; be consonant with; concert:～各方,共同努力 harmonize all the parties concerned in a joint effort /～万邦 make all nations coexist peacefully /北京～医院 Beijing Union Hospital
协和式飞机 Xiéhéshì fēijī Concorde (European supersonic jet)
协和音 xiéhéyīn 〈音乐〉consonance:不～ dissonance
协会 xiéhuì association; society:作家～ writers' association /消费者～ consumers' association
协理 xiélǐ ❶ assist in the management (of an enterprise, etc.); assist:校长委派张先生来～财务工作。The president has appointed Mr. Zhang to assist in financial administration. ❷ assistant manager
协理员 xiélǐyuán 〈军事〉political assistant (of the PLA):政治～ political assistant
协力 xiélì combine efforts; join in a common effort:同心～ work together with one heart; make concerted efforts /此项任务需各方～完成。It requires the joint efforts of all parties concerned to accomplish the task.
协领 xiélǐng (during the Qing Dynasty) brigade commander
协商 xiéshāng consult; discuss; talk things over:与有关人员～ consult with the people concerned /通过～取得共识 achieve consensus through consultation /友好～ friendly consultation
协商会议 xiéshāng huìyì consultative conference
协商委员会 xiéshāng wěiyuánhuì consultative committee or commission
协商一致 xiéshāng yīzhì (principle of) reaching unanimity through consultation
协调 xiétiáo coordinate; systematize; harmonize; be in tune with:～各政府机构的工作 coordinate the work of government agencies /动作～,舞姿优美 harmonious and graceful movements (of dancers) /～员 coordinator /～性机制 coordinative mechanism /发挥～作用 play a coordinating role; act (*or* serve) as coordinator /与环境不～ out of tune with one's surroundings; not in agreement with one's surroundings /必须使地方政府的投资计划与中央的产业政策～。The investment plans of local governments must be brought into line with the industrial policies of the central government.
协调委员会 xiétiáo wěiyuánhuì coordination committee
协同 xiétóng work in concert or coordination; cooperate:～作战 fight in coordination /～动作〈军事〉coordinated action /～器官〈生理〉synergistic organ /～作用〈物理〉synergism /～管理制 coordinative management /陆、海、空三军～实施突击。The army, navy and air force cooperated in the assault. /此事请～办理。Your cooperation is requested in handling this matter.
协同论 xiétónglùn synergetics
协心 xiéxīn to be of one mind; to be in accord
协议 xiéyì ❶ agree; consult:破坏～ break an agreement /书面～ written agreement /双方～成立一个联合小组。The two sides agreed to set up a joint group. /会议对具体意见没有达成～。No concrete proposals were agreed upon (*or* reached) at the conference. ❷〈信息〉protocol
协约 xiéyuē ❶ negotiate:就停战事宜三方共同～。The three parties negotiated a convention on an armistice. ❷ agreement; convention; entente:签订～ sign an convention /～期满 expiry of an agreement
协约国 Xiéyuēguó Entente countries (during World War I)
协约国际法 xiéyuē guójìfǎ conventional international law
协助 xiézhù assist; help:～校长处理日常工作 assist the president in his routine work /得到兄弟单位的大力～ be greatly assisted by fraternal units
协奏曲 xiézòuqǔ 〈音乐〉concerto:钢琴～ piano concerto
协作 xiézuò cooperation; collaboration:充分发扬～精神 give full play to the spirit of cooperation /实行学科间的大～ organize extensive cooperation (*or* collaboration) among different disciplines /经济～区 economic cooperation zone /有什么需要我们～的,你尽管说吧。Don't hesitate to tell us what you need from us. /这种名牌产品,有些零件是由乡镇企业～生产的。Some parts of this brand-name product are supplied by township enterprises.

胁(脅、脋) xié

❶ flank; side of the human body from the armpit to the waist:左～疼痛 have a pain in the left side ❷ compel; coerce; force:裹～ force to take part; coerce; abduct
胁逼 xiébī coerce; force; threaten:任凭他们怎么～,他也不肯吐露实情。However they threatened him, he refused to divulge the truth.
胁变 xiébiàn *also* "应变" yìngbiàn 〈物理〉strain:局部～ local strain /～规 strain gauge /～能 strain energy /～硬化 strain hardening

X

胁持 xiéchí *also* “挟持” xiéchí ❶ seize on both sides by the arms：她被匪徒～着上了一辆面包车。Seized on both sides by the thugs, she was forced into a minibus. ❷ hold under duress; abduct：这个人胆子小，干坏事可能是受人～。As he is timid by nature, he may have committed the wrong under duress.

胁从 xiécóng be an accomplice under duress：～分子 accomplice under duress; reluctant (*or* unwilling) follower /首恶必办，～不问。The ring leaders must be punished while accomplices under duress shall go free.

胁肩谄笑 xiéjiān-chǎnxiào cringe and smile obsequiously; behave in a servile manner：～，曲意逢迎 bow and scrape to curry favour with sb. /他一见李书记走进大厅，当即～地迎了上去。As soon as he saw Secretary Li enter the hall, he went up to greet him with a cringing smile.

胁肩累足 xiéjiān-lěizú 〈书面〉walk on tiptoe with bent shoulders — be fearful and nervous：此人每见长官，则～。The man became timid and nervous whenever he saw his superiors.

胁迫 xiépò intimidate; coerce; force：～某人服从 force sb. into submission /受坏人～ be coerced by bad guys

胁强 xiéqiáng *also* “应力” yìnglì 〈物理〉stress：外施～ applied stress

胁制 xiézhì hold under duress; abduct：总统已被政变者～。The President was abducted by those who had staged the coup.

勰 xié 〈书面〉harmony; concord (usu. used in personal names)

xiě

写(寫) xiě ❶ write：～白字 write the wrong word; write a word wrongly /～印刷体 write in block letters; print /这笔～起字来很流畅。This pen writes well. /请～下你的地址。Please write down your address. /标语牌上～着“不要大炮，要黄油”。The placard reads “We want butter, not guns”. ❷ compose; write：～一部交响乐 compose a symphony /～小说 write a novel /～日记 keep a diary; make an entry in one's diary /～初稿 write (*or* make) a draft; draft ❸ describe; portray; depict：把人物～活了 depict a character vividly; the character comes alive under one's pen /～农村生活 portray rural life /善于～人物性格 be good at characterization ❹ paint; sketch; draw：～生 paint from life; paint from nature /人物速～ sketch of a person

see also xiè

写本 xiěběn hand-written copy; manuscript; transcript：杜诗～ hand-copied collection of Du Fu's poems

写法 xiěfǎ ❶ method of writing：文章～ way of composition /独特的～ unique style of writing ❷ style of calligraphy：草书的～ style of cursive calligraphy

写稿 xiěgǎo write; contribute：为《中国日报》～ write for (*or* contribute to) *China Daily* /以～为生 live by one's pen; write for a living

X

写景 xiějǐng depict or describe scenery：这位作家善于～状物。This writer is good at depicting scenery.

写生 xiěshēng 〈美术〉paint or draw from life or nature：人物～ portrait from life /静物～ still-life painting

写生簿 xiěshēngbù sketch-block; sketch-book

写生画 xiěshēnghuà sketch

写实 xiěshí write or paint realistically：～的传统 realistic tradition of writing (*or* painting) /～的笔法 realistic way (*or* style) of writing /～文学 realistic literature

写实主义 xiěshízhǔyì (old name for 现实主义) realism

写头 xiětóu 〈计算机〉write head; writing head

写意 xiěyì 〈美术〉(in contrast with “工笔” in traditional Chinese painting) freehand brushwork aimed at catching the spirit of the object and expressing the author's impression or mood：这位画家长于～。The painter is good at freehand brushwork.

see also xièyì

写意画 xiěyìhuà freehand brushwork painting

写照 xiězhào ❶ portray; characterize：长于人物～ be good at characterization ❷ depiction; picture：栩栩如生的～ vivid, true-to-life portrayal (*or* picture) /昔日生活的真实～ authentic depiction (*or* picture) of past life

写真 xiězhēn ❶ paint or portray a person：工于～ be strong in portraying a person /这幅～很传神。The portrait is really true to life. ❷ describe sth. as it is：这篇小说是 30 年代知识分子心态的～。The novel faithfully describes the mentality of intellectuals in the 1930's.

写字间 xiězìjiān office; office space

写字楼 xiězìlóu office building; office

写字台 xiězìtái writing desk; desk

写作 xiězuò writing：为孩子们～ write for children /从事散文～ take up prose-writing /～技巧 writing technique

写作班子 xiězuò bānzi writing group

血 xiě colloquial variant of “血” (xuè)

see also xuè

血肠 xiěcháng blood sausage

血道子 xiědàozi welt; wale

血豆腐 xiědòufu (cooked as food) blood curd

血糊糊 xiěhūhū covered or smeared with blood; bloody：她脸上～的一片。Her face was covered with blood.

血淋淋 xiělīnlīn ❶ dripping with blood; bloody：断手～的，煞是吓人。What a frightful sight! The severed hand was dripping with blood. ❷ cruel; atrocious：～的教训 lesson paid for in blood /墨写的谎言掩盖不了～的事实。Lies penned in ink cannot cover up facts soaked in blood.

血丝 xiěsī trace of blood

血晕 xiěyùn bruise：这一跤摔得不重，腿上只有些～。The fall was not serious; only the legs were slightly bruised. /洗去沙土后，手掌上一层～。After the dirt was washed off, a bruise appeared on the palm.

see also xuèyùn

xiè

亵(褻) xiè ❶ treat with irreverence; slight; be disrespectful：～近 be intimate with (a woman); treat with familiarity ❷ lewd; obscene; indecent：猥～ be lewd (*or* salacious); act indecently towards (a woman); abuse sexually /～语 salacious language; dirty words; obscenities /～器 〈书面〉chamber pot

亵渎 xièdú blaspheme; desecrate; profane; pollute：～神明 blaspheme the gods /～神圣职责 profane one's sacred mission (*or* duty)

亵慢 xièmàn treat lightly; show disrespect：对工作、同事都不能有～之心。One should not treat one's work lightly or show disrespect for one's colleagues.

亵昵 xiènì be improperly familiar with：以～的口吻 in a tone of improper familiarity

亵玩 xièwán dally (with women)

亵衣 xièyī 〈书面〉underwear; underclothes

亵尊 xièzūn 〈书面〉lower oneself (to do sth.); condescend

燮(爕) xiè 〈书面〉regulate; harmonize; mediate; reconcile：～理阴阳 harmonize the *Yin* and the *Yang*; regulate affairs of the state /～和上下 harmonize the relationship between the superior and the subordinate

躞 xiè

躞蹀 xièdié *also* “蹀躞” walk in small steps; pace

灺(炧) xiè 〈书面〉remaining end of a candle

写(寫) xiè

see also xiě

写意 xièyì 〈方言〉comfortable; enjoyable：春风拂面，好不～ be exhilarated to breathe the spring breeze

see also xiěyì

泻(瀉) xiè ❶ flow swiftly; rush down; pour out：急流奔～而下。The torrents rush down. ❷ loose bowels; diarrhoea; (as in cattle) scour：止～药 antidiarrhoeal /上吐下～ suffer from vomiting and diarrhoea /我昨天～了一晚上，今儿一点劲儿也没了。I'm weak from having loose bowels throughout the night. ❸ 〈中医〉purge; quench：～肺 purge the lungs of pathogenic fire /～火 purge (the

body of) pathogenic fire; quench pathogenic fire
泻肚 xièdù loose bowels; diarrhoea
泻根属 xiègēnshǔ 〈植物〉bryony
泻湖 xièhú (old name for 潟湖)〈地理〉lagoon
泻盐 xièyán Epsom salts; salts
泻药 xièyào laxative; cathartic; purgative: 这水果有~的效用。This fruit has a purgative effect.

契(偰)

Xiè legendary ancestor of the Yin (殷) tribe who founded the Shang Dynasty
see also qì

械

xiè ❶ tool; device; instrument: 农~ farm implement / 器~不利 not have good tools ❷ weapon; arms: 枪~ arms; weapons; ordnance / 军~ tools of war; weapons / 缴~ lay down one's arms; surrender one's weapons; disarm ❸ 〈书面〉fetters; shackles: ~系 put fetters on sb.
械斗 xièdòu fight with weapons (as between groups of people): 聚众~ gang-fighting with weapons

泄(洩)

xiè ❶ let out; discharge; deflate; release: 水~不通 not even a drop of water could trickle through; be thoroughly blocked or packed / 气可鼓而不可~ morale should be boosted, not dampened ❷ divulge; let out; leak; disclose: 事以密成, 语以~败。When a secret is kept, it leads to success; when a secret is leaked, it results in failure. ❸ give vent to; vent: 发~怒气 give vent to one's anger
泄底 xièdǐ reveal or expose what is at the bottom of sth.; divulge the bottom line: 不小心泄了底 betray the bottom line out of carelessness; let the cat out of the bag
泄愤 xièfèn give vent to one's spite or resentment: 借端~ find an excuse to vent one's personal spite / 他这样说并非为了~。He said that not just to get it off his chest.
泄恨 xièhèn give vent to one's resentment or hatred: 他觉得这样做还不能~。He felt he hadn't done enough to vent his pent-up hatred.
泄洪 xièhóng 〈水利〉flood discharge: 开闸~ open a sluice to release (*or* discharge) floodwater / ~能力 flood carrying capacity
泄洪道 xièhóngdào flood-relief channel; floodway
泄洪隧道 xièhóng suìdào flood-discharge tunnel
泄洪闸门 xièhóng zhámén floodgate; sluicegate
泄劲 xièjìn lose heart; feel discouraged; lose momentum: 越说越~ become more dispirited as one goes on speaking / 遇到多大困难也不要~。Don't lose heart before any difficulty or hardship.
泄痢 xièlì *also* "泄利" diarrhoea
泄漏 xièlòu ❶ (of gases or liquids) leak; discharge: 这条管道不严紧, 常有煤气~出去, 很危险。The pipe is not airtight and often leaks gas. It is really dangerous. ❷ divulge; give away; let out: ~经济情报 give away (*or* leak) economic intelligence / 天机不可~。Secrets of the heaven must not be divulged. *or* This is a top secret that must be guarded at any cost. / 一语~天机。One single remark divulged the carefully-guarded secret. *or* One single remark gave away the whole show.
泄露 xièlòu *also* "泄漏" let out; disclose; reveal: ~秘密 let out (*or* disclose) a secret / ~心事 reveal what one is thinking (*or* worried) about / ~国家机密罪 (offence of) betrayal of state secrets
泄密 xièmì divulge or leak a secret; disclose confidential information: 严重的~事件 serious case of leakage of a state secret / 此次~事关重大, 务必追查清楚。Such leakage of confidential information is no small matter; it must be investigated thoroughly.
泄气 xièqì ❶ lose heart; feel frustrated; be disheartened: ~话 discouraging (*or* disheartening) remarks / 这事他听了准~。This is sure to dishearten him when he hears of it. ❷〈口语〉pathetic; piteous: 这么简单的题都做不出来, 你真~! How pathetic you couldn't even work out such simple problems!
泄水 xièshuǐ 〈水利〉sluicing: ~工程 outlet work
泄水道 xièshuǐdào sluiceway
泄水孔 xièshuǐkǒng outlet
泄水堰 xièshuǐyàn sluice weir
泄水闸 xièshuǐzhá sluicegate; sluice
泄泻 xièxiè 〈中医〉loose bowels; diarrhoea
泄殖道 xièzhídào 〈动物〉urodaeum
泄殖腔 xièzhíqiāng 〈动物〉cloacal chamber; cloaca: ~隔 cloacal septum / ~膜 cloacal membrane

绁(絏、緤)

xiè 〈书面〉❶ rope; bonds: 缧~ rope for tying up a criminal — jail / 身陷缧~ be in jail; be behind bars ❷ fasten; bind; tie: ~囚 tied-up criminal; prisoner behind bars

渫

xiè ❶〈书面〉remove; get rid of ❷〈书面〉discharge; dredge ❸ (Xiè) a surname

屟(屧)

xiè 〈书面〉wooden slippers

媟

xiè 〈书面〉dally (with a woman); be familiar: ~狎 behave in a licentious manner; philander / ~渎 blaspheme; profane / ~慢 treat cheaply or immodestly; dally with; take liberties with

瀣

xiè *see* "沆瀣" hàngxiè

薤

xiè *also* "藠头" jiàotou ❶ scallion ❷ scallion bulb

龂

xiè 〈书面〉❶(of teeth) grinding each other ❷ irregular (as of teeth)

卸

xiè ❶ unload; discharge: ~船 unload (*or* discharge) a ship / 从火车上~煤 unload coal from a train ❷ remove; take off: *see* "~装"; "~肩" ❸unhitch; unharness (draught animals, etc.): ~牲口 unhitch a draught animal / ~鞍 remove the saddle; unsaddle ❹ remove; strip; dismantle: ~车铃 remove a bell from a bicycle / 拆~机器 take apart a machine / ~螺丝 unscrew / 大~八块 cut up into small pieces ❺ lay down; shirk: ~过 shirk one's responsibility for an error
卸岸价格 xiè'àn jiàgé 〈外贸〉landed price (at a place of import or delivery)
卸包袱 xiè bāofu unload a parcel — be rid of one's burden: 卸掉思想包袱 take a load off sb.'s mind / 他的兼职过多, 你得给他卸卸包袱。Since he is charged with too many concurrent responsibilities, you should help remove some of his burdens.
卸车 xièchē unload (goods, etc.) from a vehicle: ~费 unloading charges
卸担子 xiè dànzi lay down a burden
卸货 xièhuò unload or discharge cargo; unload: 从卡车上~ unload a lorry (*or* truck) / ~站台 discharging platform / ~码头 discharging quay
卸货港 xièhuògǎng unloading port; discharge port
卸甲归田 xièjiǎ-guītián remove one's armour and go back to farm; be demobilized and return to civilian life
卸肩 xièjiān remove one's burden; shirk one's responsibility: 他总是碰上问题就~儿。He would invariably pass the buck to others whenever problems arose.
卸料 xièliào 〈化工〉blow down: ~导管 blowdown line / ~装置〈机械〉tripper
卸磨杀驴 xièmò-shālǘ kill the donkey the moment it leaves the millstone — give sb. the boot as soon as he has done his job: 这小子心狠手辣, 惯于~。Vicious and ruthless, he never hesitates to get rid of anyone who has outlived his usefulness to him.
卸任 xièrèn be relieved of one's office: 新校长上任不久就~了。The new school principal was relieved of his duties not long after he took office.
卸压 xièyā 〈机械〉pressure relief: ~阀 pressure relief valve / ~装置 pressure relief device
卸衣 xièyī undress
卸载 xièzài *also* "卸儎" unload cargo; lay down a burden: 好几条船等着~。There are quite a few ships waiting to be unloaded. / 孩子们都大了, 我也该~了。As all my children are grown up, it is time I had an easier life.
卸责 xièzé off-load responsibility (onto others); shirk responsibility; pass the buck: 作为第一把手, 出了问题你怎能~。As first-in-command, how could you shirk the responsibility when anything goes wrong?
卸职 xièzhí be relieved of one's post or office: 因与上级意见不合而

X

～ be relieved of one's office due to disagreement with one's superior

卸妆 xièzhuāng remove one's make-up; take off one's formal dress and ornaments:对镜～ remove one's make-up before a mirror

卸装 xièzhuāng remove stage make-up and costume:她一卸完装就回家了。She went home immediately after removing her stage make-up and costume.

谢

xiè ❶ thank:致～ express (*or* extend) one's thanks /酬～ thank sb. with a gift; repay sb.'s kindness /答～ return thanks ❷ make an apology; apologize:～过 apologize for having done sth. wrong; apologize for one's mistake (*or* error) ❸ decline; refuse:婉～ decline politely (*or* tactfully) /敬～不敏 beg to be excused; excuse oneself; beg off ❹ (of flowers, leaves, etc.) wither:四季不～ not wither the whole year; be in bloom throughout the year /凋～ wither and fade ❺ (Xiè) a surname

谢安 Xiè Ān Xie An(320-385), statesman and strategist of the Eastern Jin Dynasty

谢表 xièbiǎo 〈旧语〉letter of thanks (usu. to the emperor) for appointment to post or some other favour

谢病 xièbìng 〈书面〉excuse oneself on grounds of illness; beg off or decline on health grounds:～不出〈旧语〉decline an office on grounds of illness; decline to serve in public capacity on health grounds

谢步 xièbù 〈旧语〉pay a return call of thanks (on those who attended a wedding, funeral, etc. in one's family)

谢忱 xièchén gratitude; gratefulness; thankfulness:谨备薄礼,以表～。This humble gift is a token of our gratitude.

谢词 xiècí *also* "谢辞" thank-you speech:主宾致～。The guest of honour made a thank-you speech.

谢顶 xièdǐng get thin on top; be balding:他年轻时就～了。He began to go bald when he was still young.

谢恩 xiè'ēn thank (an emperor, a monarch, etc.) for a favour:领旨～ accept the imperial edict with thanks /磕头～ kowtow (to sb.) to express one's gratitude

谢候 xièhou extend thanks; render thanks

谢绝 xièjué refuse or decline with thanks:～一切馈赠 decline all gifts /难以～ find it hard to refuse /～参观 not open to visitors

谢客 xièkè ❶ decline to receive visitors; close one's door to guests:从此,他闭门～,不问世事。From then on he closed his door to all visitors and refused to get involved in public affairs. ❷ thank visitors or guests for their company:主人亲送大门之外,再三～。The host saw the guests beyond the gate, saying "thank you for coming" repeatedly.

谢礼 xièlǐ *also* "谢仪" gift in token of one's gratitude; gift of thanks:备了一份厚厚的～ make an expensive gift to express one's thanks

谢落 xièluò wither and fall:百花～。All the flowers began to wither.

谢媒 xièméi (of newlyweds right after the wedding ceremony) extend thanks to the matchmaker

谢幕 xièmù answer or respond to a curtain call:观众掌声不断,演员们不得不多次～。The actors had to respond to the curtain call repeatedly, as the audience went on applauding. /她～七次之多。She took as many as seven curtain calls. /剧作者和导演出场～。The playwright and the director were called before the curtain.

谢却 xièquè decline or refuse politely:他～了朋友的邀请。He politely declined his friends' invitation.

谢世 xièshì 〈书面〉depart this life; pass away; die:先父～之后,家道中落,度日艰难。After father passed away, the family fortune declined and life became extremely difficult.

谢事 xièshì 〈书面〉resign from office:～之后,返归故里 return to one's hometown after resigning from office

谢天谢地 xiètiān-xièdì thank God; thank heaven; count oneself lucky:～,地震中你竟然安然无恙! Thank God (*or* Heaven) you escaped unscathed from the earthquake! /只要你少给我添麻烦,我就～了! I'd count myself lucky if only you did not bring me more trouble.

谢帖 xiètiě note of thanks; thank-you note:差人送去～。A note of thanks was dispatched.

谢孝 xièxiào 〈旧语〉(of the deceased's children) visit and thank relatives and friends who attended the funeral

谢谢 xièxie thanks; thank you:他连一句～都没说。He didn't even say "Thank you".

谢仪 xièyí gift conveying one's gratitude; gift of thanks

谢意 xièyì gratitude; thankfulness:预致～ thank you in advance /聊表～ as a token of my gratitude

谢罪 xièzuì apologize for an offence; offer an apology:登门～ call at sb.'s house to offer an apology

墈

xiè 〈方言〉compost made from decomposed animal manure

榭

xiè pavilion or house on a terrace:水～ waterside pavilion /歌台舞～ halls for the performance of songs and dances

猲

xiè 〈书面〉dog with a short snout

see also hè

解[1]

xiè get the point; get wise to (sth.); be clear about; see:终于～开了这里的奥妙 get wise to the secret at last

解[2]

xiè 〈旧语〉acrobatic performance, especially on horseback:跑马卖～ earn a living by performing acrobatics on horseback

解[3]

Xiè ❶ Lake Xie, in Shanxi Province ❷ a surname

see also jiě; jiè

解数 xièshù movement of *wushu* or of the martial arts; skill; ability:使出浑身～ use all one's skills; do all one is capable of

澥[1]

xiè ❶ (of plaster, glue, porridge, etc.) become thinner:昨天剩的粥都～了。The porridge left over from yesterday has become watery. ❷〈方言〉dilute:糨糊太稠,加点水～一～。The paste is too thick. Dilute it with a bit of water.

澥[2]

xiè *also* "渤澥" Bóxiè ancient name for the Bohai Sea

廨

xiè 〈书面〉office of an official

廨舍 xièshè 〈书面〉office-cum-residence of an official

懈

xiè slack; lax; remiss:坚持不～ persist in (doing sth.); keep at (sth.) tenaciously /常备不～ be always ready; be ever on the alert /夙夜匪～〈书面〉without relaxing day and night

懈场 xièchǎng (as of actors) be inattentive or careless on the stage:演员上场要始终入戏,不可～。An actor should be entirely absorbed in the acting without relaxing a moment on the stage.

懈弛 xièchí slack; lax:纪律～ lax discipline /～无备 be lax and unprepared; be off one's guard

懈怠 xièdài slack; sluggish; careless:从不～ never slacken one's effort; be always diligent and attentive /工作～,玩忽职守 be careless in one's work and guilty of malfeasance

懈惰 xièduò lax and idle; sluggish:如此～,怎能把工作搞好! Being so sluggish, how can you do the job well!

懈劲 xièjìn slacken one's efforts; slack off; be disheartened:别～,下次再干。Don't lose heart! Try again next time.

懈慢 xièmàn 〈书面〉sluggish and impudent; devil-may-care:～无礼 impudent and impolite

懈气 xièqì relax one's efforts; slacken off:在这关键时刻,你可千万不能～。At this critical juncture, you must not slacken your efforts in the least.

懈意 xièyì sign of laxness; sign of slackening:示以～ pretend lack of alertness; pretend laxness /他虽然已连续工作了十个小时,却仍然毫无～。He showed no sign of slackening although he had worked for ten hours on end.

邂

xiè

邂逅 xièhòu 〈书面〉meet by chance; run into:久闻阁下大名,不期今日～。I have heard much about you, but didn't expect to have the pleasure of meeting.

邂逅相遇 xièhòu-xiāngyù unexpected encounter; chance meeting:老友～,乐何如之! It is most pleasant to run into an old friend!

蟹(蠏) xiè crab:河～ freshwater crab /寄居～ hermit crab /梭子～ swimming crab /虾兵～将 shrimp soldiers and crab generals — numerous underlings; ineffective forces

蟹簖 xièduàn *also* "蟹断" crab-weir (usu. made of bamboo sticks)

蟹粉 xièfěn 〈方言〉crab meat (eaten as food)

蟹黄 xièhuáng ovary and digestive glands of a crab (eaten as a delicacy)

蟹獴 xièměng 〈动物〉*also* "猸子" méizi crab-eating mongoose

蟹钳 xièqián crab claws

蟹青 xièqīng greenish-grey

蟹蛛 xièzhū 〈动物〉crab spider

蟹状星云 Xièzhuàng Xīngyún 〈天文〉Crab Nebula

嶰 xiè 〈书面〉ravine; gully:～壑 deep ravine /幽～ quiet gully

獬 xiè

獬豸 xièzhì legendary animal credited with ability to distinguish between right and wrong, virtue and evil:～冠〈历史〉hat worn by a judge, symbolizing justice

屑 xiè ❶ bits; scraps; fragments; crumbs:铁～ bits of iron /煤～ (coal) slack /木头～ bits of wood; filings /糕点～ crumbs of cake /头～ dandruff; scurf ❷ trifling; trivial:琐～ trifling; petty ❸ (mostly used in the negative)deign; consider worthwhile:不～一顾 disdain to take a look; refuse to look (at sth.) /不～于做某事 consider it beneath one to do sth.; not deign to do sth.

屑屑 xièxiè trifling; trivial; of little value:～小事 petty matter

屑意 xièyì mind; care:毫不～ not mind (sth.) at all; not care in the least; take no offence

屑子 xièzi bits; crumbs:饼～ crumbs of cake /细～ little bits

榍 xiè

榍石 xièshí sphene; titanite

xīn

心 xīn ❶ *also* "心脏" heart:～痛 cardialgia; cardiodynia /～输出量〈生理〉cardiac output /～输入量〈生理〉cardiac input ❷ heart; mind; feeling; moral nature or character; intention:～好 have a good (*or* great) heart; be kind-hearted; kind /好～ have a good intention; mean well /爱～ love for others /恻隐之～ compassion /～如火焚 with one's heart afire; burning with anxiety /～如蛇蝎 with one's heart as poisonous as a viper or scorpion; having the heart of the devil /～往一处想,劲往一处使 think with one mind and work with one heart /人在～不在 one's thoughts are elsewhere though one is physically present; be absent-minded; be woolgathering /留得住人,留不住～ even though you can keep sb. physically, you can't retain his or her allegiance /～之系之,口则含之。〈书面〉What the mind thinks, the tongue speaks. ❸ heart; centre; core:菜～ heart of a cabbage /重～ centre of gravity /圆～ centre of a circle /江～ middle of a river /轴～ axle centre; axis ❹ fifth of the 28 constellations in ancient Chinese astronomy

心爱 xīn'ài love; treasure; cherish:～的人 one's beloved; loved one /～的玩具 treasured (*or* prized) toy /他把一生奉献给～的教育事业。He dedicated his whole life to his beloved (*or* cherished) career as a teacher.

心安 xīn'ān feel at ease; have a good or easy conscience:～意适 with one's heart at rest and one's mood relaxed /～无梦 a heart at rest has no dreams to disturb it; sleep the sleep of the just /～即福。Peace of mind is a blessing.

心安理得 xīn'ān-lǐdé feel at ease and justified; have a good or easy conscience; have no qualms of conscience:凡事讲个实理儿,自己也就～了。One will always have a good conscience if one is honest and sincere in everything one does. /把孩子抚养成人,作母亲的也就～了。The mother can now put her heart at rest since her children have grown up under her care.

心瓣膜 xīnbànmó 〈生理〉heart valve; cardiac valve:～病 VDH (valvular disease of the heart) /～分离术 cardiovalvulotomy; valvulotomy

心包 xīnbāo 〈生理〉pericardium:～穿刺术〈医学〉pericardiocentesis /～切除术 pericardiectomy

心包炎 xīnbāoyán pericarditis:癌性～ carcinomatous pericarditis

心病 xīnbìng ❶ mental anguish; worry; anxiety:～还得心药治。Mental anguish can only be cured by heartening news. *or* A secret concern can only be relieved by psychological treatment. *or* The cure of a broken heart is happiness. ❷ secret cause of remorse; sore point; hang-up:年轻时的那段风流韵事成了她终生的一块～。The romance she had in her girlhood became a secret cause of remorse for the rest of her life.

心搏 xīnbó 〈生理〉heartbeat:～率 heart rate /～周期 cardiac cycle /～过速 tachycardia /～徐缓 bradycardia /～停止 cardiac arrest

心不在焉 xīnbùzàiyān absent-minded; inattentive; woolgathering:～地点着头 nod absent-mindedly /他整天～的,好像有什么心事。He was inattentive all day, as if there were something on his mind. /老先生在院子里～地踱来踱去。The old gentleman paced up and down the courtyard in a brown study. /我跟你说话呢,你怎么～! Penny for your thoughts! I'm speaking to you.

心材 xīncái 〈林业〉heartwood

心裁 xīncái mental plan; conception; notion:别出～ try to be different (*or* out-of-the-ordinary) /独出～ show originality; be original (*or* unique)

心肠 xīncháng ❶ intention; mind; heart:～狠毒 be evil-minded (*or* evil-hearted); be vicious by nature; harbour evil intentions (*or* designs) /你事事作梗,到底安的是什么～? What are you up to, creating obstacles right and left? ❷ feeling; emotion; heart:菩萨～ have as kind a heart as that of Buddha; have a heart of gold; be benevolent and merciful /铁石～ be dead to all feelings; have a heart of stone; be ruthless /～软 have a soft heart; be susceptible to emotions /我的邻居是个热～,肯帮别人的忙。My neighbour is a warm-hearted person, always ready to help others. ❸ state of mind; mood; inclination:没有～去郊游 be in no mood for an outing

心潮 xīncháo surge of emotion; surging thoughts and emotions:～涌动 thoughts surge through one's mind like the tides; thoughts and emotions churn in one's mind; one's mind is in a tumult /～起伏 one's thoughts and emotions seem to rise and fall like the waves; thoughts and emotions surge over one's mind /把酒酹滔滔,～逐浪高! I pledge my wine to the surging torrent, The tide of my heart swells with the waves.

心潮澎湃 xīncháo-péngpài one's emotions and thoughts surge like the tide; one's mind is flooded with emotions and thoughts; feel an upsurge of emotions:读了他的信,我～,彻夜难眠。I was so agitated after reading his letter that my emotions and thoughts surged like the tide and I remained sleepless the whole night.

心程 xīnchéng 〈方言〉state of mind; mood:她累极了,根本没有～去跳舞。She was so tired that she was in no mood for dancing.

心驰神往 xīnchí-shénwǎng yearn after (a place) as if one's mind were already there; be so excited by sth. as to take mental possession of it:那就是他日夜思念、～的地方。That was the place he had long been thinking about and yearning after. /听到故乡近年来的变化,他不禁～,恨不能插翅飞回去。He was so excited to hear about the changes which had taken place in his hometown in recent years that he wished he had wings and could fly back immediately.

心传 xīnchuán ❶〈宗教〉(in contrast with any written form of teaching by means of Sutras or commentaries) mental teaching:中国佛教的禅宗最讲究～。Chinese Zen Buddhism attaches great importance to teaching by intuition. ❷ doctrine or tenet handed down from generation to generation

心慈面软 xīncí-miànruǎn soft of heart and considerate of "face"; soft-hearted and lenient:众人都为小李说情,老太太～,也就宽恕了他。As everybody pleaded for Xiao Li, the old lady, who was soft-hearted and lenient, pardoned him.

心慈手软 xīncí-shǒuruǎn soft-hearted and merciful:我们对违法行为决不能～。We cannot afford to be soft-hearted and merciful towards violations of law.

心粗 xīncū careless; thoughtless:～胆大 careless and bold; thoughtless and rash

心粗气浮 xīncū-qìfú thoughtless and flighty:～的小伙子 thoughtless and impetuous young man

心存芥蒂 xīncúnjièdì nurse a grievance; bear a grudge

X

心胆 xīndǎn ❶ heart and gall ❷ guts; courage
心胆俱裂 xīndǎn-jùliè be frightened or scared out of one's wits; be thrown into a panic; be panic-stricken: 杀得敌军～。Our attack scared the hell out of the enemy.
心荡神驰 xīndàng-shénchí be thrilled;; be distracted (with rapture, excitement, etc.); go into ecstasies or raptures: 他猛然一见那女郎,不觉～。He was thrilled to every nerve at the sight of the girl.
心得 xīndé what one has learned from work, study, etc.: 学习～ what one learns from one's studies / 参观～ thoughts after a study tour / 交流～体会 compare notes on what one has learned
心底 xīndǐ ❶ bottom of the heart; heart of hearts: 从～里感到高兴 feel delighted from the bottom of one's heart / 从～里喜欢这个城市 love the city with all one's heart ❷ 〈方言〉 intention; intent: 这个人～不坏。This guy means no evil. *or* He means well.
心地 xīndì ❶ mind; character; nature: ～狭窄 narrow-minded / ～单纯 pure-hearted; simple-minded / ～正直的人 man of integrity; upright man ❷ state of mind; mood: 弹了一会钢琴后,他感到～轻松多了。Having played the piano for a while, he felt much of his tension had gone. *or* He felt much more relaxed after playing the piano for a while.
心电描记器 xīndiàn miáojìqì 〈医学〉 electrocardiograph
心电图 xīndiàntú 〈医学〉 electrocardiogram: ～学 electrocardiology
心动 xīndòng ❶ heartbeat: ～过缓 *also* "～徐缓" 〈医学〉 bradycardia / ～过速 〈医学〉 tachycardia / ～周期 〈生理〉 cardiac cycle ❷ have one's mind perturbed; have one's desire or enthusiasm aroused; be tempted; be stirred: 看见别人纷纷买股票,他也颇为～。Seeing others scrambling to buy stocks, he was sorely tempted.
心窦 xīndòu 〈生理〉 cardiac sinus
心毒 xīndú with poison in one's heart; callous-hearted; evil-minded; malicious: ～手辣 with a poisonous heart and relentless hand; callous and cruel; vicious and ruthless / ～如蛇蝎 with a heart as venomous as a viper or scorpion
心耳 xīn'ěr 〈生理〉 auricle
心烦 xīnfán troubled; vexed; perturbed: 我一听到这噪音就～。When I heard the noise, I went hot and cold.
心烦意乱 xīnfán-yìluàn be confused and worried; be terribly upset; be restless and disquieted: 这些琐事搅得我～。These trivial matters have upset me.
心房 xīnfáng ❶ 〈生理〉 atrium (of the heart) ❷ heart; mind: 一股暖流涌进我的～。I felt as if a warm current surged into my heart.
心房间隔缺损 xīnfáng jiàngé quēsǔn 〈生理〉 interatrial septal defect
心房纤颤 xīnfáng xiānchàn (short for 心房纤维性颤动) auricular fibrillation
心扉 xīnfēi 〈书面〉 door of one's heart — heart; mind; thought: 敞开～ open up one's heart (*or* mind) / 悲凉的笛声撞击着我的～。The sorrowful notes from a piccolo made a great impact upon my heart.
心肥大 xīnféidà 〈医学〉 cardiomegaly
心服 xīnfú be genuinely convinced; acknowledge sincerely; admire from the bottom of one's heart: 他做事向来干练、周到,不由人不～。He was so competent and considerate in everything he did that you could not help admiring him from the bottom of your heart.
心服口服 xīnfú-kǒufú be wholly convinced; be won round completely: 我被他说得～。I was sincerely convinced by his arguments.
心浮 xīnfú flighty and impatient; restless: 小伙子有点～,总也坐不下来。Being a bit flighty and impatient, the lad could not sit down to his work.
心浮气躁 xīnfú-qìzào be restless and fretful; be unsettled and short-tempered: 在这种关键时刻,切忌～。Don't get short-tempered at such a critical moment.
心腐病 xīnfǔbìng 〈农业〉 heart rot
心腹 xīnfù ❶ trusted; reliable: ～人 trusted person / ～之交 bosom friend ❷ trusted subordinate or follower; henchman: 手下有几个～ have under one a few trusted followers / 在关键岗位安插～ place one's henchmen in key positions ❸ secret; confidential: 说～话 confide in sb.; tell sb. sth. in strict confidence; exchange confidences / ～事 secret in the depth of one's heart
心腹之患 xīnfùzhīhuàn disease in one's vital organs — grave hidden trouble or danger: 视为～ regard (sb. or sth.) as a cancer in one's vital organs; consider as mortal enemy (*or* danger)
心甘 xīngān willing; ready: 只要能救孩子,母亲死也～。The mother was willing to die if that could save her child.
心甘情愿 xīngān-qíngyuàn be most willing to; do sth. gladly; be perfectly happy to: ～地做劳苦大众的老黄牛 be a willing horse for the toiling masses / 几十年来,他兢兢业业地工作,～地演好配角。For decades, he was conscientious at his work and perfectly happy to play supporting roles.
心肝 xīngān ❶ sense of right and wrong; conscience: 毫无～ be heartless; be dead to all feelings / 你这个没有～、不顾廉耻的畜牲! You heartless beast without any sense of shame! ❷ darling; deary: 你是妈妈的～宝贝儿! You're mom's darling baby (*or* darling child).
心高 xīngāo have high aspirations; cherish great ambitions; be lofty-minded: ～才拙 one's talents fall short of one's ambitions; one's eyes are bigger than one's stomach / 心比天高,命如纸薄。One's aspirations soar as high as the sky whereas one's fate is as hapless as a broken kite.
心高气傲 xīngāo-qì'ào *also* "心高气盛" ambitious and aggressive; proud and arrogant: 这人～,往往出言不逊。The man is proud and overbearing and often makes impertinent remarks.
心广体胖 xīnguǎng-tǐpán *also* "心宽体胖" when the mind is at ease, the body grows healthy; be carefree and well-nourished; be fit and happy: 李先生乐观豁达,～。Always optimistic, Mr. Li is fit and happy.
心寒 xīnhán 〈方言〉 be bitterly disappointed; be disenchanted: 他受恩不报,反而倒打一耙,实在令人～。It is bitterly disappointing that he should repay kindness with recrimination.
心黑 xīnhēi ❶ evil; venomous: 他图财害命,～手毒。He murdered people for their money in cold blood. ❷ greedy; predatory: 这老板宰起人来真～! The grasping boss stops at nothing to fleece his customers.
心狠 xīnhěn ruthless; merciless: 他为人～,一点儿同情心都没有。Cruel and merciless, he doesn't care about other people's sensibilities at all.
心狠手辣 xīnhěn-shǒulà cruel and evil; vicious and merciless
心花 xīnhuā ❶ happy mood ❷ 〈方言〉 state of mind; mood: 人老了,再没那个～了。As I am getting old, I am not in that sort of mood any longer.
心花怒放 xīnhuā-nùfàng burst with joy; be ecstatic; be elated: 喜讯从天而降,他不禁～。He was wild with joy to hear the happy tidings which had come as if from nowhere. / 人人～,个个手舞足蹈。Everybody was bursting with delight and dancing for joy.
心怀 xīnhuái ❶ harbour; cherish; bear; entertain: ～不轨 harbour evil designs; cherish treacherous intents ❷ feeling; mood; intention: 抒写～ write of one's feelings / 正中某人的～ play right into sb.'s hands ❸ nature; state of mind: ～坦白 candid by nature / 具有光明磊落的～ be open and above-board
心怀鬼胎 xīnhuáiguǐtāi cherish sinister motives; have evil designs
心怀叵测 xīnhuáipǒcè *also* "居心叵测" jūxīn-pǒcè harbour sinister or malicious motives; cherish evil designs; have some dirty trick up one's sleeve: 这个人～,不可轻信。Don't trust him. He is full of evil designs.
心慌 xīnhuāng ❶ be flustered; be jittery; get nervous: 这是她第一次打靶,不免有些～。She was somewhat nervous as it was her first target practice. ❷ 〈方言〉 (of the heart) palpitate: 老人～气紧。With his heart beating fast, the old man was gasping for breath.
心慌意乱 xīnhuāng-yìluàn be fidgety and flustered; be alarmed and confused; be all in a flutter: 他总也克服不了临考～的毛病。He never could avoid getting nervous and flustered whenever he had an examination.
心灰意懒 xīnhuī-yìlǎn *also* "心灰意冷" be disheartened or downhearted; be dispirited; lose heart completely: 丈夫故去后,她～,索性连门也不出了。She was so dispirited after her husband's death that she simply shut herself up.
心魂 xīnhún mind; state of mind; composure: 安定～ compose one's mind; reassure oneself (*or* sb.) / ～宁静 enjoy peace of mind / ～摇荡 have one's composure shaken
心活 xīnhuó be indecisive; be easily led; be pliable: 耳软～ credulous and pliable / 让人把他说得～了。He became hesitant after listening to the views of others.
心火 xīnhuǒ ❶ 〈中医〉 internal heat (symptoms of which include mental uneasiness, thirst, rapid pulse, etc.): ～盛 intensive internal heat ❷ hidden anger; pent-up fury: 几句好言相劝,他～全消。A few

soothing words relieved him of his pent-up fury.

心机 xīnjī thinking; calculating; scheming: 枉费～ rack (*or* cudgel) one's brains in vain; scheme to no avail; make futile efforts /费尽～ try one's utmost; spare no pains; leave no stone unturned /他为人颇有～。He is quite a calculating person.

心肌 xīnjī 〈生理〉cardiac muscle; myocardium: ～运动图 myocardiogram

心肌梗塞 xīnjī gěngsè 〈医学〉myocardial infarction; heart attack (esp. coronary thrombosis)

心肌心包炎 xīnjī xīnbāoyán 〈医学〉myopericarditis

心肌炎 xīnjīyán 〈医学〉myocarditis

心急 xīnjí impatient; anxious; short-tempered: ～如焚 be nervous with worry; be burning with impatience; be consumed by anxiety /～腿慢。The more impatient one is, the slower one finds one's legs. *or* More impatience makes slower movement. /～水不沸。A watched pot never boils.

心急火燎 xīnjí-huǒliǎo *also* "心急如焚";"心急如火" be burning with impatience or anxiety; get the jitters: 戏都要开演了,这位主要演员还未到,怎不叫人～! How agonizing it is to have the star actor absent when it is almost time for the performance to begin!

心计 xīnjì calculation; cunning; scheming; planning: 工于～ adept at scheming; very calculating /他是个有～的人。He is a calculating sort.

心迹 xīnjì true state of mind; true motives or feelings; heart: 剖白～ lay bare one's true feelings; bare one's heart

心悸 xīnjì ❶〈医学〉palpitation ❷〈书面〉fright; fear; dread: 这部电影中的恐怖情节,实在令人～。The scenes of terror in this movie are truly blood curdling.

心尖 xīnjiān ❶〈生理〉apex of the heart; apex cordis: ～搏动 apex beat; apex impulse /～搏动图 apex cardiography ❷ in the recess of one's mind; heart of hearts: 孩子总在母亲的～上。Mothers always have their children in their heart of hearts. ❸ *also* "心尖子"〈方言〉best-loved one; darling; dearie (usu. one's son or daughter): 小女儿是她的～儿。Her little daughter is the apple of her eye.

心间 xīnjiān in mind; at heart: 您托付的事我一定牢记～。I will bear in mind what you have entrusted to me.

心坚石穿 xīnjiān-shíchuān when one's heart is firm, even rocks are riven; an iron will wears through a rock; nothing is impossible for an indomitable will: 他相信"～",只要功夫到了,没有不成功的事情。He believes in the power of an indomitable will — if only you work at it hard enough, there is nothing you cannot achieve.

心焦 xīnjiāo anxious; troubled; worried: 等得～ wait (*or* await) anxiously /播种季节都快过了,天还不下雨,真叫人～。The sowing season is almost over but it has not rained yet. This is really worrying.

心绞痛 xīnjiǎotòng *also* "狭心症" xiáxīnzhèng 〈医学〉angina pectoris

心劲 xīnjìn ❶ thought; idea; mind: 我们都是一个～儿把工作干好。We are all of one mind: do our jobs well. /大家的～儿都一样,都希望你好。We all wish you well. ❷ mental capabilities; brains: 别看他人小,他很有～。Young as he is, he is really smart. ❸ spirit; zeal; drive: 搞科学种田,他的～可足啦! He is full of drive for scientific farming!

心旌 xīnjīng 〈书面〉have one's heart all aflutter; have a disturbed mind: ～摇曳 with one's mind torn between confused emotions; unable to maintain self-control

心惊胆战 xīnjīng-dǎnzhàn *also* "胆战心惊" tremble with fear; shake with fright; be panic-stricken: 他吓得～,浑身直打哆嗦。Badly scared, he was shaking from head to toe. /从这么高的地方往下望,真叫人～。It is frightening to look down from such a giddy height.

心惊肉跳 xīnjīng-ròutiào palpitate with anxiety and fear; feel nervous and jumpy; be filled with apprehension; shake in one's boots: 他整天～,连大门都不敢出。Shaking in his boots all day, he dared not even venture out of doors.

心净 xīnjìng free from worries; be completely at ease: 随便他去,我们图个～。Let him go and have his way. Out of sight, out of mind.

心境 xīnjìng state or frame of mind; mental state; mood: 平静的～ peace of mind /～苦闷 be in a gloomy mood; feel low /～闲适 be in a relaxed, tranquil mood /对诗的感受,往往取决于读者的～。The interpretation of a poem often depends on the reader's frame of mind.

心静 xīnjìng calm; composed: ～如水 one's heart is as calm as still water /～自然凉。If your heart is at peace, you can remain cool in the heat.

心疚 xīnjiù 〈书面〉compunction; guilty conscience: 你干了这种缺德事,难道不感到～? Don't you have a guilty conscience for doing something so unethical?

心坎 xīnkǎn ❶ pit of the stomach ❷ bottoms of one's heart: 这种赞美发自人们的～。Such praises came from the bottoms of people's hearts. /你的话说到了他的～儿上。Your words struck a chord in his heart. *or* Your words touched him to the quick.

心窠 xīnkē pit of the stomach: 一股凉气直透～。A chill draught assailed one right in the pit of one's stomach. /坦克支队插进了敌人的～。The tank detachment fought its way into the heart of the enemy encampment.

心肯 xīnkěn be willing at heart: 对此,他嘴上没说什么,其实早已～了。He agreed in his heart though he didn't utter a word about it.

心孔 xīnkǒng aperture of the heart considered as an organ for thinking; capacity for (clear) thinking

心口 xīnkǒu pit of the stomach; 〈生理〉precordium: ～痛 pain in the pit of the stomach; heartburn /感到～堵得慌 feel suffocated; feel a tightness in the chest

心口不一 xīnkǒu-bùyī say one thing and mean another; say what one does not think; be hypocritical: 这个人物是个城府极深、～的伪君子。The man is an unfathomable hypocrite who never says what he means.

心口如一 xīnkǒu-rúyī say what one thinks; be frank and unreserved; speak one's mind: 刘先生是个～、说话算数的君子,你尽管放心。You may rest assured, for Mr. Liu is a gentleman who says what he means and means what he says.

心宽 xīnkuān be broad-minded; take things easy: ～体泰 broad-mindedness brings health; be carefree and healthy; be fit and happy /既然事情已经发生,你还是～一些,听其自然吧。Now that the fat is in the fire, you might as well take things easy and let them run their course.

心宽体胖 xīnkuān-tǐpán *see* "心广体胖"

心旷神怡 xīnkuàng-shényí relaxed and happy; carefree and joyous; refreshed in mind and heart: 令人～的疗养胜地 most refreshing health resort /我觉得自己简直步入了仙境,顿时～。I felt as if I had stepped into a fairyland, instantly relaxed and happy.

心扩张 xīnkuòzhāng 〈医学〉cardiectasis

心劳 xīnláo mental effort; laboured thought

心劳计绌 xīnláo-jìchù cudgel or rack one's brains to no avail

心劳日拙 xīnláo-rìzhuō fare worse and worse for all one's scheming; get nothing for all one's pains: 他处处算计别人,到头来只能是～,自食苦果。Although he schemes against others at every turn, he will surely get nothing for all his pains in the end and be hoist with his own petard.

心理 xīnlǐ psychology; mentality: ～冲突 mental (*or* psychological) conflict /～压力 psychological (*or* mental) pressure /～因素 psychological factor /～障碍 psychological obstruction /儿童～ child psychology /青春期～ psychology of the adolescent /崇洋～ mentality of worshipping everything foreign /这位售货员很懂得顾客～。The shop assistant understands the wishes of his clients very well. /这是人们常有的～。This is how ordinary people feel about it. /我揣摩他的～,就是不愿老让别人照顾自己。As I see it, he just doesn't want others to take care of him on everything.

心理保健 xīnlǐ bǎojiàn mental health

心理病理学 xīnlǐ bìnglǐxué psychopathology

心理病态 xīnlǐ bìngtài morbid mentality or state of mind

心理测验 xīnlǐ cèyàn mental test: ～学 psychometry

心理定价法 xīnlǐ dìngjiàfǎ psychological pricing

心理分析 xīnlǐ fēnxī psychoanalysis: ～学家 psychoanalyst

心理概率 xīnlǐ gàilǜ 〈统计〉psychological probability

心理技术学 xīnlǐ jìshùxué psychotechnology

心理经济学 xīnlǐ jīngjìxué psychological economics

心理疗法 xīnlǐ liáofǎ psychotherapy: ～专家 psychotherapist

心理美学 xīnlǐ měixué psychoaesthetics

心理年龄 xīnlǐ niánlíng mental age

心理社会学 xīnlǐ shèhuìxué psychosociology: ～家 psychosociologist

心理生理学 xīnlǐ shēnglǐxué psychophysiology

心理生物学 xīnlǐ shēngwùxué psychobiology; biopsychology

心理声学 xīnlǐ shēngxué psychoacoustics

心理卫生学 xīnlǐ wèishēngxué mental hygiene

心理物理学 xīnlǐ wùlǐxué psychophysics

X

心理玄学 xīnlǐ xuánxué metapsychology; parapsychology
心理学 xīnlǐxué psychology: ～家 psychologist
心理医学 xīnlǐ yīxué psychological medicine
心理语言学 xīnlǐ yǔyánxué psycholinguistics
心理战 xīnlǐzhàn psychological warfare
心理治疗 xīnlǐ zhìliáo psychotherapy
心理咨询 xīnlǐ zīxún psychological consultation: ～专家 psychological consultant
心力 xīnlì mental and physical efforts: 竭尽～ make strenuous efforts; do one's level best
心力交瘁 xīnlì-jiāocuì be exhausted both mentally and physically: 这项工程使他～，完工后他卧床不起几达半年之久。He was so exhausted by the project, both mentally and physically, that he was confined to bed for almost six months after its completion.
心力衰竭 xīnlì shuāijié 〈医学〉 heart failure
心里 xīnli ❶ in the heart: ～发疼 feel pain in the chest / 他感到～不舒服，要上医院去查一查。As he felt there was something the matter with his heart, he decided to go to the hospital for a check-up. ❷ in (the) mind; at heart: ～打鼓 feel uneasy / 把老师的话记在～ bear the teacher's words in mind / ～想着人民的利益 have the people's interests at heart / ～有话说出来就痛快了。You'll feel much better when you speak out what is on your mind (*or* when you get it off your chest).
心里话 xīnlihuà what is on one's mind; one's innermost thoughts and feelings: 要他说出～可不容易。It is no easy matter to persuade him to come out with what's on his mind. / 说～，我不赞成你的意见。To be honest, I don't agree with your idea.
心里美 xīnlimĕi a kind of turnip with green skin and sweet purplish-red flesh
心连心 xīnliánxīn heart linked to heart: 全世界人民～。The hearts of the peoples of the world are linked to each other.
心灵 xīnlíng ❶ clever; astute; intelligent; quick-witted: ～手巧 have a lively mind and a quick hand; be clever and deft / 这孩子～，一点就通。The child is so intelligent that he picks up the cue at the slightest hint. ❷ heart; soul; mind: 纯洁的～ pure mind / 震撼～ be greatly shaken / ～深处 in the innermost depths of one's heart; deep in one's heart / ～之窗 (as of the eyes) window of the soul / 具有高雅情操的作品才能陶冶～。Only works of noble sentiments can refine the mind.
心灵感应 xīnlíng gǎnyìng telepathy
心灵美 xīnlíngmĕi noble character; high integrity
心灵学 xīnlíngxué parapsychology; psychics
心灵治疗 xīnlíng zhìliáo mind cure
心领 xīnlǐng ❶ understand; comprehend: 他那番话的意思我已～。I see the point of his remarks. ❷ 〈套语〉 (used to express one's thanks): 你的好意，我～了，但礼物不能收。I appreciate your kindness but must decline the gift.
心领神会 xīnlǐng-shénhuì understand tacitly; readily take a hint or cue: 小吴点点头，表示～，便走开了。Xiao Wu nodded his understanding and went away. / 他这个人呀，只要你递个眼神，他就能～。He is so smart that if only you cast him a glance, he'll know what you mean.
心路 xīnlù ❶ wit; intelligence; scheming: 颇有～ quite intelligent / 斗～ fight a battle of wits ❷ breadth of mind; tolerance: 他～宽，对这些小事不会介意的。He is broad-minded and will not bother about such trifles. ❸ intention; design; motive: ～不正 be ill-intentioned; have ulterior motives / 他话说得重了点儿，但～不坏。He meant well though his words were a bit strong. ❹ way of thinking; state of mind: 他的～我知道。I know his state of mind. / 这话正对他的～。These words are very much to his taste.
心律 xīnlǜ 〈医学〉 rhythm of the heart
心律不齐 xīnlǜ bùqí 〈医学〉 arrhythmia
心率 xīnlǜ 〈医学〉 heart rate
心乱如麻 xīnluàn-rúmá have one's mind as confused as a tangled skein; be utterly confused and disconcerted; have one's mind in a tangle: 这几件事搞得他～，坐卧不安。Utterly confused and disconcerted by such developments, he felt as if he was sitting on pins and needles.
心满意足 xīnmǎn-yìzú be perfectly content; be completely satisfied: 我在有生之年能看到这部著作出版，也就～了。I would be perfectly contented if I could live to see the work published.
心明眼亮 xīnmíng-yǎnliàng be sharp-eyed and clear-headed; be discerning; can tell right from wrong
心目 xīnmù ❶ vision (mental or physical); mind's eye: 养花育草，以娱～ amuse oneself by growing flowers and other plants / 那惨相犹在～。The horrifying scene remains fresh in one's mind's eye (*or* memory). ❷ mind; view: 在你们～中，什么才是生活中最重要的东西呢? What, to your mind (*or* in your view), is the most important thing in life? / 他是年轻一代～中的英雄。He is a hero in the eyes of the younger generation.
心内膜 xīnnèimó 〈生理〉 endocardium: ～病 〈医学〉 endocardiopathy / ～炎 endocarditis
心念 xīnniàn cherished wish; aspiration; idea: 这几句话说出了人民的～。These words expressed the people's cherished wish.
心皮 xīnpí 〈植物〉 carpel
心平气和 xīnpíng-qìhé even-tempered and good-humoured; unruffled; calm: ～地谈 talk calmly / ～，遇事不怒 be even-tempered and good-humoured without flaring up at provocations / 这人很顽固，跟他～地谈起不了什么作用。He's a stubborn man; soft words cut no butter with him.
心魄 xīnpò heart; soul; mind: 动人～ touch one's heart / 夺人～ thrilling; enthralling
心气 xīnqì ❶ motive; intention: 都是老朋友了，我的～你还不知道? As an old friend of mine, how could you fail to understand my intention? ❷ ambition; aspiration: ～高，干劲大 with high aspirations and full of vigor ❸ mood; state of mind: 这几天他有些～不顺。He has been in a bad mood these days. ❹ breadth of mind; tolerance: 女孩儿～窄，怕一时想不通。The girl is narrow-minded. I am afraid she won't get over it for the time being.
心窍 xīnqiào aperture of the heart as a thinking organ; capacity for clear thinking: 财迷～ be possessed (*or* obsessed) by a lust for money / 此话令我～大开。That cleared up my thinking.
心切 xīnqiè anxiety (to do sth.); over-eagerness: 求胜～ be anxious to win; be impatient for success / 治病～ be eager to find a cure
心怯 xīnqiè one's heart sinks; be timid or cowardly: 他一个人在山里走，有些～。Walking in the hills all alone, he felt a sinking of the heart. *or* He was somewhat afraid to walk in the hills all alone.
心情 xīnqíng frame or state of mind; mood; spirit: ～不佳 be in a bad mood; be in low spirits / 喜悦的～ be in a joyful frame (*or* state) of mind; be in a good (*or* happy) mood; be in high spirits; have a light heart / ～沉重 one's mind is weighed down (with sorrow, etc.); have a heavy heart / ～很矛盾 have mixed feelings / ～极不平静 be in a turbulent mood
心曲 xīnqū 〈书面〉 ❶ innermost being; mind: 诸多杂务，乱我～。There were so many distractions that I was unable to keep my mind unruffled. ❷ what is on one's mind: 畅叙～ pour out one's secret concerns (*or* pent-up feelings); give vent to one's grievances / 她整天愁眉紧锁，又有谁了解她的～? Her brows were knit in sorrow all day, but who actually knew what was on her mind?
心如刀割 xīnrúdāogē one's heart contracts in pain as if stabbed by a knife; one feels as if a knife were piercing one's heart; be cut to the quick: 妻子惨死的消息令他～。News of his wife's tragic death stabbed him to the heart. *or* It rent his heart to hear of his wife's tragic death.
心如死灰 xīnrúsǐhuī one's heart is as dead as ashes — completely disheartened; hopelessly apathetic: 他纵然～，也难把往事轻易忘记。He can hardly forget the past for all his apathy.
心如铁石 xīnrútiěshí have a heart of stone; be firm; be determined: 此人～，没有什么力量能动摇他的决心。The man is as firm as a rock, and nothing can shake his determination.
心软 xīnruǎn soft-hearted; tender-hearted; lenient: 口硬～ tough in words but soft at heart; tough-spoken but soft-hearted / 母亲见孩子一哭，也就～了。Mother instantly relented when her child broke into tears. / 对坏人坏事，处理要果断，决不能～。We mustn't be over-lenient towards evildoers and evil deeds but should deal with them resolutely.
心伤 xīnshāng sad; grieved; broken-hearted
心上人 xīnshàngrén person of one's heart; lover: 听说你有了～? I hear you've found a person of your heart. *or* I hear you've fallen in love.
心上 xīnshang in one's heart; at heart: 这些事他从不放在～。These matters don't bother him at all. *or* He doesn't care a damn about these matters.
心身 xīnshēn ❶ mind and body: ～舒泰 relaxed and comfortable

in body and mind /投入整个～ plunge (into sth.) heart and soul ❷〈医学〉psychosomatic:～病态 psychosomatic illness /患～疾病者 psychosomatic /～医学 psychosomatic medicine; psychosomatics

心神 xīnshén ❶ thought and energy:久病之后,他的～大不如前了。After a long illness, he was not so energetic as before both mentally and physically. ❷ state of mind; mind:～恍惚 be absent-minded; be distrait /～不安 be disturbed in mind; be restless and worried; have (*or* get) the fidgets

心神不定 xīnshén-bùdìng anxious and distracted:你好像～,有什么心事? You look anxious and preoccupied, what's troubling you?

心声 xīnshēng inner voice; heartfelt wish; aspiration:言为～。Words are the voice of the mind. *or* One's words are the reflection of one's thinking. *or* What the heart thinks the tongue says. /这篇文章写出了广大农民的愿望和～。This article voices the heartfelt wishes of the broad masses of farmers.

心盛 xīnshèng be in high spirits; be full of energy:我们大家越干越～。Our spirits soared as we worked. /众人～,活也干得快。As everybody was in high spirits, the work proceeded speedily.

心事 xīnshì sth. weighing on one's mind; load on one's mind; preoccupation; worry:～重重 laden with anxiety; weighed down with care; preoccupied with worry /了结一桩～ fulfil a long-cherished wish; take a load off one's mind /坐在一边想～ sit aside lost in thought /满腹～向谁诉? To whom shall I speak my mind?

心室 xīnshì 〈生理〉ventricle:～肥大 ventricular hypertrophy /～间隔缺损 interventricular septal defect /～内传导阻滞 intraventricular heart block /～纤颤〈医学〉ventricular fibrillation

心手相应 xīnshǒu-xiāngyìng what the mind wishes the hands are able to do; have everything under perfect control; do (*or* achieve) with facility:他雕刻起来,～,宛如天成。He sculpts with such facility that his work seems made by nature.

心输出量 xīnshūchūliàng 〈生理〉cardiac output

心术 xīnshù ❶〈贬义〉intention; design:～不正 harbour evil intentions (*or* designs) ❷ calculation; scheming:很有～的人 very calculating man /你少跟我要～! Don't you try to be smart with me!

心数 xīnshù calculation; scheming; shrewdness:颇有～ rather shrewd /他虽年轻,做事却很有～。Young as he is, he shows great intelligence in what he does.

心顺 xīnshùn in a good mood; pleased

心死 xīnsǐ totally demoralized; despondent; dead or indifferent to the world:哀莫大于～。The most saddening thing is to fall into despondency.

心思 xīnsi ❶ idea; thought; mind:坏～ wicked idea /想～ be lost in thought; ponder; contemplate /他的～谁也猜不透。Nobody can read his mind. *or* Nobody can figure out what's on his mind. ❷ thinking:颇费～ take a lot of hard thinking /挖空～ rack one's brains; try in every way; leave no stones unturned ❸ state of mind or mood for doing sth.:干什么都没～ be in no mood for anything

心酸 xīnsuān be sorrowful; feel sad:～落泪 shed tears in grief

心算 xīnsuàn mental arithmetic; mental calculation; doing sums in one's head:善于～ good at mental arithmetic

心髓 xīnsuǐ innermost being; heart of hearts:痛彻～ hurt one to one's innermost being; suffer excruciating pain

心碎 xīnsuì heartbroken:令人～的往事 heartbreaking past event

心态 xīntài psychology; mentality; mental attitude:顾客～ psychology of clients /国民～ national mentality /文化～ cultural mentality

心膛 xīntáng 〈方言〉breadth of mind; view of life:你还是把～放宽点儿,别急坏了身体。You might as well take things easy. Don't worry yourself sick.

心疼 xīnténg ❶ love dearly; love:他最～小儿子。He loves his youngest son best. ❷ feel painful; be tormented; be distressed:你别～,弄坏了我赔你个新的。Don't be distressed. I'll get you a new one if this one is damaged. /我不是小气,我是看着这些浪费～。I am not niggardly but it makes my heart ache to see such waste.

心田 xīntián ❶ heart:这些话像一股暖流注入了他的～。His heart was warmed by these words. ❷〈方言〉intention; motive:好～ good intention

心跳 xīntiào palpitation:刚上五楼,他就有点～。His heart palpitated just when he came up to the fifth floor.

心痛 xīntòng painful; distressed:令人～之极 cause great sorrow (*or* distress); be extremely painful

心头 xīntóu mind; heart:涌上～ surge to one's mind; occur to one /牢记～ bear (*or* keep) firmly in mind /压在～ prey (*or* weigh) on one's mind /～之恨 rankling hatred; deep-seated hatred /～火起 be inflamed with passion; flare up

心头肉 xīntóuròu darling of one's heart; best loved one; most treasured possession:孩子都是妈妈的～。All children are the darlings of their mothers' hearts. /他把珍藏的古董当作～。He regarded all the antiques he had collected as his most treasured possessions (*or* as the apple of his eye).

心投意合 xīntóu-yìhé *also* "情投意合" qíngtóu-yìhé find each other congenial; be perfectly suited to each other; hit it off perfectly; have mutual affection and affinity:两人～,结成终身伴侣。They found each other congenial and became life-long companions. *or* They fell in love with each other and got married.

心土 xīntǔ 〈农业〉subsoil

心外膜 xīnwàimó 〈生理〉epicardium

心窝儿 xīnwōr 〈口语〉pit of the stomach; heart of hearts:年轻人照着他的～打了一拳。The young man struck him a blow in the pit of his stomach. /他的话说进了我的～里。His words struck a chord in my heart.

心无二用 xīnwú'èryòng one cannot keep one's mind on two things at the same time; the mind cannot be devoted to two things at one time; he who pursues two hares catches neither:俗话说"～",不专心能学好技术吗? As the saying goes, "One cannot keep one's mind on two things at the same time"; how could one learn one's trade well without concentrating on it?

心细 xīnxì careful; meticulous:～如发 with a meticulous mind /姑娘胆大～,遇事不慌。Bold but cautious, the girl never panics in a crisis.

心下 xīnxia in the mind; in the heart:听了你的这番话,我～明白了。Your words have cleared my mind.

心弦 xīnxián heartstrings:动人～ pulling (*or* tugging) at one's heartstrings; soul-stirring; touching (*or* moving) /扣人～ suspenseful; exciting; thrilling

心羡 xīnxiàn admire at heart; envy

心想 xīnxiǎng think:祝你～事成。I hope you will get what you long for.

心向往之 xīnxiàngwǎngzhī long for; yearn for

心相 xīnxiàng 〈方言〉state of mind; mood:我哪有游玩的～啊! I'm not in a mood for sightseeing.

心象 xīnxiàng 〈心理〉mental image

心心念念 xīnxīn-niànniàn keep thinking of or about; long for:她～地想当电影明星。She has been longing to become a movie star.

心心相印 xīnxīn-xiāngyìn have heart-to-heart communion with each other; share the same feeling; have mutual love and affinity; show mutual understanding and attraction:夫妻俩～、恩恩爱爱,一起生活了四十多年。Closely attached to each other, the couple lived in a perfect communion of affection and thought for over forty years. /一路上,两人默默无语,却又～。Though they remained silent the whole way, their hearts spoke to each other.

心性 xīnxìng disposition; temper or temperament; nature:他们相识不久,彼此的～还不了解。As they haven't known each other for long, they are not certain of each other's temper.

心胸 xīnxiōng ❶ deep in one's heart; at heart; in one's mind:抑制不住～的怒火 unable to repress one's anger ❷ breadth of mind:～豁达 have a generous (*or* great) heart; be broad-minded /～狭窄 be narrow-minded; be parochial; be petty /～开朗 be cheerful and open by nature ❸ aspiration; ambition:小伙子有～,有气魄。The young fellow has great aspirations and boldness of vision.

心秀 xīnxiù be intelligent without seeming so:你别错看了这姑娘,她可～了。Don't get the girl wrong; she's actually very intelligent.

心虚 xīnxū ❶ afraid of being found out; with a guilty conscience; nervous:做贼～ a thief is bound to be nervous; a thief has a guilty conscience; a guilty conscience is a self-accuser /你既然没做亏心事,又何必～? Why should you feel nervous if you had done nothing wrong? ❷ lacking in self-confidence; timorous; diffident:这一类工作过去没干过,刚接手时还真有些～。When I took over the job, I really felt diffident for I had never done anything like it before.

心许 xīnxǔ ❶ consent tacitly; acquiesce:我的婚事父母已经～。My parents have acquiesced in my marriage. ❷ approve (of sth.); commend:他的学位论文深得导师～。His dissertation was highly commended by his tutor.

心绪 xīnxù (usu. in a negative sense) state of mind; mood:～不佳

in a bad mood; in low spirits /～烦乱 emotionally disturbed (*or* distressed); in a state of agitation

心绪不宁 xīnxù-bùníng in a disturbed state of mind; flustered:这消息让他～。The news put him in a flutter.

心血 xīnxuè painstaking care or effort:毕生的～ whole lifetime's work; one's entire life /费尽～ spare no pains; exert one's utmost; do one's level best /培育这个新品种,花费了他十几年的～。The breeding of this new strain took him over a dozen years of painstaking work.

心血管 xīnxuèguǎn 〈医学〉heart and blood vessels:～疾病 cardiovascular disease /～药 cardiovascular drug

心血管监护病房 xīnxuèguǎn jiānhù bìngfáng cardiovascular care unit

心血管系统 xīnxuèguǎn xìtǒng cardiovascular system

心血管学 xīnxuèguǎnxué cardioangiology; cardiovasology

心血管造影 xīnxuèguǎn zàoyǐng angiocardiography

心血来潮 xīnxuè-láicháo be prompted by a sudden impulse; be carried away by a whim; have a brainstorm:～,忘乎所以 forget oneself in an impulsive moment; be carried away by one's whims; lose one's head in a moment of excitement /他突然～,深更半夜跑到大街上看星星。Prompted by a sudden impulse, he ran into the street to look at the stars in the middle of the night.

心眼儿 xīnyǎnr ❶ heart; mind:打～里热爱自己的工作 love one's new job with all one's heart /一个～干活儿 devote oneself heart and soul to work; be heart and soul in work /看到改革开放以后的巨大成就,大家从～里感到高兴。It warms the cockles of all our hearts to see the great achievements scored since the implementation of the policy of reform and opening to the outside world. ❷ intention; heart: ～好 have a heart of gold; be kind-hearted /他看起来严厉,但～不坏。Though he looks stern, he has his heart in the right place. /我就知道这小子没安好～! I knew this fellow was up to no good! ❸ intelligence; wit:有～ be intelligent (*or* smart); be alert /缺～ be slow-witted /这孩子净长～不长个儿! Why, the child never seems to grow taller but gets smarter all the time! /长点～,别上当受骗。Smarten up (*or* Get smart) and don't get hoodwinked. /对这号人得留个～。We must be on our guard against such people. ❹ baseless doubts; unfounded misgivings:他这个人的毛病就是～太多。He's oversensitive — that's the trouble with him. ❺ breadth or narrowness of mind; (lack of) tolerance:～小 have a petty (*or* little) mind; be narrow-minded; be oversensitive /她～窄,受不了委屈。She has a one-track mind and cannot bear being wronged.

心痒 xīnyǎng itch for; have an itch for:见人下棋他就～。He is itching to have a game whenever he sees others playing chess.

心仪 xīnyí 〈书面〉admire in one's heart:对先生的道德文章,我～已久。I have long admired your moral integrity and literary work, sir.

心疑 xīnyí become suspicious; harbour a suspicion:他今天温和得叫人～。He is suspiciously gentle today.

心异位 xīnyìwèi 〈医学〉ectopia cordis

心意 xīnyì ❶ regard; kindly feelings; gratitude or hospitality:大家吃吧,不要辜负了杨大妈的～。Please help yourselves or you'll hurt Aunt Yang's feelings. /这点礼物实在难以表达我们的～。The humble gift can not really convey our gratitude. ❷ meaning; aim; intention:按自己的～来安排生活 live as one wishes /你的～虽好,但办法不对。Though you meant well, you went about it in the wrong way.

心意拳 xīnyìquán *also* "形意拳" xíngyìquán shadow boxing that imitates the movements of animals and birds of various kinds

心音 xīnyīn ❶〈生理〉heart sounds; cardiac sounds:第一～ first heart sound /～图 cardiophonogram ❷ *see* "心声"

心影 xīnyǐng impression

心硬 xīnyìng hard-hearted; heartless; callous; unfeeling:都说他～,轻易不流露感情。Everybody says he is so hard-hearted that he does not easily betray his emotions.

心有灵犀一点通 xīn yǒu língxī yī diǎn tōng hearts which beat in unison are linked; lovers' hearts are closely linked; strike a chord in sb.'s heart:身无彩凤双飞翼,～。I am not a phoenix with colourful wings, But our hearts have a common beat and are linked together.

心有余而力不足 xīn yǒuyú ér lì bùzú be more than willing, but lack the power (to do sth.); be unable to do what one wants very much to; one's ability falls short of one's wish; the spirits is willing, but the flesh is weak:不是我们不肯相助,实在是～。It's not that we don't want to help you, but our ability indeed falls short of our wish. /他近年来体弱多病,教书已是～了。As he was in poor health over the last couple of years, he has been unable to teach as he would have liked to.

心有余悸 xīnyǒuyújì one's heart still flutters with fear; have a lingering fear; the memory (of sth. etc.) still haunts one:想起昨天晚上那场车祸,她仍然～。Her heart still palpitated with fear when she recalled the traffic accident of the night before. *or* She shuddered at the thought of the traffic accident of the night before.

心余力绌 xīnyú-lìchù 〈书面〉be more than willing, but lack the ability (to do sth.); one's ability falls short of one's wish:我年事已高,常有～之感。I often feel I am not quite up to my tasks because of my age.

心源性休克 xīnyuánxìng xiūkè 〈医学〉cardiogenic shock

心猿意马 xīnyuán-yìmǎ restless and whimsical; fanciful and fickle; unsettled in mind; in several minds:你这样～,哪能读得进书去? How could you concentrate on your reading when you're so unsettled in mind?

心愿 xīnyuàn cherished desire; wish or dream:了却平生～ have one's lifelong wish fulfilled /姑娘的～难以启齿,只能深深埋在心里。Unable to bring herself to speak about it, the girl could only hide her cherished desire deep in her heart.

心悦诚服 xīnyuè-chéngfú admire from the bottom of one's heart; be completely convinced; submit willingly:对某人的才干～ admire sb.'s talents wholeheartedly (*or* sincerely) /他分析透彻,使我～。I am completely convinced by his penetrating analysis. /我输得～。I admit my defeat unreservedly.

心杂音 xīnzáyīn 〈医学〉heart murmur

心脏 xīnzàng 〈生理〉❶ heart:～畸形 heart malformation /～停跳 cardiac arrest ❷ centre; heart:北京—祖国的～ Beijing — heart of our motherland

心脏病 xīnzàngbìng heart disease; cardiopathy:风湿性～ rheumatic heart disease /先天性～ congenital heart disease /～患者 cardiopath; cardiac /～发作 heart attack /他有～。He has a heart condition.

心脏病学 xīnzàngbìngxué 〈医学〉cardiology:～家 cardiologist

心脏导管 xīnzàng dǎoguǎn cardiac catheter

心脏地带 xīnzàng dìdài 〈比喻〉heartland

心脏二尖瓣 xīnzàng èrjiānbàn 〈生理〉mitral valve

心脏肥大 xīnzàng féidà 〈医学〉cardiomegalia

心脏镜 xīnzàngjìng cardioscope

心脏控制论 xīnzàng kòngzhìlùn cardiocybernetics

心脏起搏器 xīnzàng qǐbóqì (cardiac) pacemaker

心脏水肿 xīnzàng shuǐzhǒng cardiac edema

心脏线 xīnzàngxiàn 〈数学〉cardioid

心脏炎 xīnzàngyán carditis

心脏移植 xīnzàng yízhí heart transplant:接受～ receive a heart transplant

心窄 xīnzhǎi have a one-track mind; be narrow-minded:她～,遇事容易想不开,你要多开导她。She has a one-track mind and tends to take things too hard. Please help her as much as you can.

心照 xīnzhào understand each other without speaking a word; have a tacit understanding; have quick or keen apprehension:这件事我们彼此～,不用多说。We have a tacit understanding on this and needn't say anything more.

心照不宣 xīnzhào-bùxuān understand each other without speaking a word; have a tacit mutual understanding; consider it unnecessary to say any more

心折 xīnzhé admire from the bottom of one's heart; be thoroughly convinced:他的一席话使人～。His talk was thoroughly convincing.

心之官则思 xīn zhī guān zé sī the office of the mind is to think; it is the function of the mind to think

心直口快 xīnzhí-kǒukuài *also* "心直嘴快" be frank and outspoken; speak one's mind without any hesitation; be plain-spoken and straightforward:他为人～,有一说一,有二说二。He is frank and outspoken, and always calls a spade a spade.

心志 xīnzhì will; meaning; resolve; determination:挂官而去,以明～ resign one's office to show one's determination

心智 xīnzhì intelligence; wisdom:献出自己全部～和力量 devote all one's wisdom and energy

心中 xīnzhōng at heart; in one's heart; on one's mind:～有难言之隐 have a painful secret at heart /深深埋在～ bury sth. (deep) in

X

one's heart /～有事 have sth. on one's mind /～暗喜 rejoice at heart; be secretly delighted (*or* pleased) /～有鬼 have a bellyful of tricks; be up to some mischief; have sth. unseemly to hide /～有愧 have a guilty conscience

心中无数 xīnzhōng-wúshù have no clear idea (of the situation, etc.); not know one's own mind; not know what's what:姑娘～,开不出价钱。As the girl did not know what was what, she could not quote a price. /这件事我心中全然无数。I'm wide at sea on this matter.

心中有数 xīnzhōng-yǒushù have a clear idea (of the situation, etc.); know one's own mind; know what's what:如不进行认真的调查研究,怎么能做到～呢? How could one get a clear idea of the situation without earnest investigation and study? /这些事该怎么办,他～。He knows exactly how to go about it.

心重 xīnzhòng take things too hard; be oversensitive:这孩子～,你不要责备他。This child is very sensitive; please do not scold him.

心轴 xīnzhóu 〈机械〉mandrel; arbor:花键～ splined mandrel /～印刷机 arbor press; mandrel press

心拙口笨 xīnzhuō-kǒubèn dull-witted and slow tongued:我这个人～,不会应酬。I'm rather clumsy in social functions.

心子 xīnzi ❶ (of things) centre; heart; core:这个菠萝的～都烂了。The heart of this pineapple is rotten. ❷〈方言〉heart of a pig, sheep, etc. as food:猪～ heart of a pig /牛～ heart of a cow

心醉 xīnzuì charmed; enchanted; bewitched; fascinated:令人～的表演 charming (*or* enchanting) performance

心醉魂迷 xīnzuì-húnmí be overwhelmed with admiration

芯

xīn rush pith:灯～ wick (for a lamp)

see also xìn

芯片 xīnpiàn *also* "集成电路块" jíchéng diànlùkuài 〈电子〉microchip; chip: 主副～ major-minor chip /电子表～ watch chip /～制造商 chip manufacturer

馨

xīn 〈书面〉strong and pervasive fragrance:如兰之～ as fragrant as an orchid

馨香 xīnxiāng 〈书面〉❶ fragrance; aroma:花繁叶茂,满院～。The courtyard is filled with the fragrance from lush leafage and blooming flowers. ❷ smell of burning incense:庙里经声不断,～扑鼻。Echoing with ceaseless recitation of Sutras, the temple greeted people with a strong smell of burning incense.

馨香祷祝 xīnxiāng-dǎozhù 〈书面〉burn incense and pray to the gods; earnestly pray for sth.:世界和平,这是各国人民所～的。The peoples of all countries earnestly pray for peace in the world.

鑫

xīn (usu. used in personal or shop names) financial prosperity

辛[1]

xīn ❶ (as in flavour) hot; pungent:此药味～。This medicine has a pungent flavour. ❷ hard; difficult; laborious:旅途艰～ difficult trip /千～万苦 untold hardships; endless trials and tribulations ❸ bitter; distressing; painful:悲～ pain and grief ❹ (Xīn) a surname

辛[2]

xīn eighth of the ten Heavenly Stems

see also "干支" gānzhī

辛楚 xīnchǔ 〈书面〉suffering; hardship; misery:百姓～,每念不忘。I will never forget the sufferings and hardships of the common people.

辛醇 xīnchún 〈化学〉octyl alcohol

辛丑条约 Xīnchǒu Tiáoyuē (unequal) Treaty of 1901 (signed between the Qing Government and the Eight Powers i. e. Britain, United States, Russia, Germany, Japan, Austria, France and Italy, plus Spain, Holland, and Belgium)

see also "八国联军" Bāguó Liánjūn

辛迪加 xīndíjiā 〈经济〉(transliteration) syndicate

辛亥革命 Xīnhài Gémìng Revolution of 1911 (led by Dr. Sun Yat-sen, which overthrew the Qing Dynasty)

辛基化合物 xīnjī huàhéwù 〈化学〉capryl compounds

辛苦 xīnkǔ ❶ hard; toilsome; laborious:～而有意思的工作 hard but interesting work /辛辛苦苦的官僚主义 painstaking but bureaucratic style of work /临终时,他把自己多年～搜集的字画都献给了故乡的博物馆。Before he died, he donated all the calligraphies and paintings he had taken great pains to collect over the years to the museum of his hometown. /同志们～了。You comrades have been working hard. *or* How are you, comrades! /大家一路上～了。Did you all have a good trip? /她辛辛苦苦地做了一桌小菜,可惜儿子一口也吃不下。Although she went to the trouble of preparing a sumptuous dinner, her son could not even take a mouthful. ❷ (formula for asking sb. to do sth.) go to trouble; take pains:您就代劳～一趟吧! I'm afraid you'll have to take the trouble of going there on our behalf! /这事又得～您了,别人怕是干不了。I'm afraid we'll have to trouble you again; no one else could really do it.

辛苦费 xīnkǔfèi "reward for help"— (lobbying) commission; service charge

辛辣 xīnlà pungent; bitter; incisive:～的食物 pungent (*or* hot, spicy) food /～的语言 sharp language; incisive remarks /～的讽刺 bitter irony; biting sarcasm; scathing (*or* caustic) satire

辛劳 xīnláo toil; pains:终年～ toil (*or* work hard) all the year round /不辞～ spare no pains; make painstaking efforts; take all the trouble (to do sth.)

辛普朗隧道 Xīnpǔlǎng Suìdào Simplon Tunnel, longest main-line railway tunnel in the world (about 20km) connecting Switzerland and Italy

辛弃疾 Xīn Qìjí Xin Qiji (formerly translated as Hsin Ch'i-chi, 1140-1207), patriotic general and *ci* poet of the Southern Song Dynasty

辛勤 xīnqín industrious; assiduous; hardworking:～工作 work hard; work assiduously /这位年近九旬的老人仍然每日～作画。This old man of almost ninety still works hard at painting every day.

辛醛 xīnquán 〈化学〉octyl aldehyde

辛酸 xīnsuān ❶ sad; bitter; painful; miserable:～的回忆 sad (*or* poignant) memories /饱尝亡国奴的～和屈辱 taste to the full the miseries and humiliations of one without a country ❷〈化学〉caprylic acid

辛糖 xīntáng 〈化学〉octose

辛烷 xīnwán 〈化学〉octane:～值 octane number (*or* value)

辛夷 xīnyí *also* "木兰" mùlán 〈中药〉flower bud of lily magnolia

锌

xīn 〈化学〉zinc (Zn)

锌白 xīnbái 〈化学〉zinc white

锌版 xīnbǎn 〈印刷〉zinc plate; zincograph

锌版印刷术 xīnbǎn yìnshuāshù zincography

锌钡白 xīnbèibái *also* "立德粉" lìdéfěn 〈化学〉lithopone

锌锭 xīndìng 〈冶金〉zinc pig

锌粉 xīnfěn 〈化学〉zinc powder; zinc dust:～蒸馏 zinc dust distillation

锌硅玻璃 xīnguī bōli zinc-silicate glass

锌极 xīnjí 〈电工〉zincode

锌钎料 xīnqiānliào 〈冶金〉spelter solder; brazing brass

锌酸盐 xīnsuānyán 〈化学〉zincate

锌阳极板 xīnyángjíbǎn ZAP (zinc anode plate)

新[1]

xīn ❶ occurring for the first time; new; fresh; modern:～品种 new variety (*or* strain) /～消息 new (*or* up-to-date) information; news /～风尚 new custom (*or* habit) /～气象 new atmosphere; new look /～女性 new woman; modern woman ❷ renewed; improved; new; neo-:面目一～ assume a new aspect; present a completely new appearance; take on an entirely new look; have a face-lift /一～耳目 find everything fresh and different /改过自～ turn over a new leaf /～古典主义 neoclassicism ❸ just begun; unused; new:～被子 new quilt /～钢笔 new pen ❹ sth. new; new things; new people:尝～ taste a fresh delicacy /推陈出～ weed through the old to bring forth the new /吐故纳～ exhale stale air and inhale fresh air; get rid of the stale and take in the fresh ❺ newly or recently married:～女婿 one who has just married a daughter of the family; newly-wed husband of one's daughter ❻ newly; just:～来的炊事员 new cook /～任命的大使 newly-appointed ambassador /～粉刷的墙 freshly whitewashed wall /这些书是～买的。These books were bought recently.

新[2]

Xīn ❶ name of dynasty founded by Wang Mang (王莽), AD 8-23 ❷ (short for 新疆维吾尔自治区) Xinjiang Uygur Au-

tonomous Region ❸ (short for 新加坡) Singapore:~、马、泰 Singapore, Malaysia and Thailand ❹ a surname

新兵 xīnbīng new recruit; recruit:征募~处 recruiting centre (*or* depot)

新柏拉图主义 Xīnbólātúzhǔyì 〈哲学〉Neoplatonism

新不列颠岛 Xīn-Bùlièdiāndǎo New Britain, an island of Papua New Guinea

新茶 xīnchá newly-picked tea; fresh tea

新长征 xīnchángzhēng New Long March — metaphor for the modernization drive:~突击手 pace-setter in the New Long March — title of honour for one who has made outstanding contributions to the modernization drive

新潮 xīncháo ❶ new trend or tendency:社会~ new social trend / 文艺~ new trends in art and literature ❷ modish; fashionable; avant-garde:~发型 new hair style; modish hairdo / ~服装 latest fashions; fashionable clothes / ~诗 avant-garde poetry

新陈代谢 xīnchén-dàixiè ❶〈生物〉metabolism:~是生物的基本特征之一。Metabolism is a fundamental characteristic of living organisms. ❷ the new superseding the old:干部的~ replacement of old officials with new ones

新成土 xīnchéngtǔ 〈地理〉Entisol

新仇旧恨 xīnchóu-jiùhèn new hatred piled on old; scores both old and new:~,一齐涌上心头。Scores both old and new surged to his mind.

新春 xīnchūn 10 or 20 days following the Lunar New Year's Day:~佳节 (on the) happy occasion of the Spring Festival / ~喜雨 auspicious rain after the Lunar New Year's Day

新词 xīncí new word; new expression; neologism:~,新义,新用法 new words, meanings and usages

新村 xīncūn new residential quarters; new housing development or estate; new settlement:渔民~ new housing estate for fishermen /往日的荒原,今日~星罗棋布。The former wasteland is now dotted with new settlements.

新大陆 Xīndàlù New World — the Americas

新东宝影片公司 Xīndōngbǎo Yǐngpiàn Gōngsī Shintoho Motion Picture Company, major movie producer of Japan

新法 xīnfǎ ❶ new law:推行~ implement a new law ❷ new method:~治疗 new therapy

新房 xīnfáng bridal chamber; wedding chamber:布置~ decorate the wedding chamber /闹~ "roughhouse in the wedding chamber", a custom of teasing the bride into laughter or playing tricks on the newlyweds on the wedding night

新芬党 Xīnfēndǎng ❶ Sinn Fein, nationalist political party of Ireland (1905-1927) ❷ Sinn Fein, political arm of the Irish Republican Army working for incorporation of Northern Ireland into the Irish Republic

新风 xīnfēng new trend or tendency:校园~,new trend on the campus /破旧俗,树~ break down old conventions and foster a new spirit

新弗洛伊德主义 Xīnfúluòyīdézhǔyì 〈哲学〉Neo-Freudianism

新妇 xīnfù ❶ bride ❷〈方言〉daughter-in-law

新干线 Xīngànxiàn Shinkansen Line, Japanese high-speed railway line connecting Tokyo and Fukuoka

新姑爷 xīngūye 〈口语〉bridegroom as an in-law of the bride's family (usu. used by its senior members to address the bridegroom)

新寡 xīnguǎ ❶ just widowed:文君~,尚未再醮。Wen Jun had just been widowed and was not remarried yet. ❷ new widow

新官上任三把火 xīnguān shàngrèn sān bǎ huǒ a new official introduces a rash of changes; a new broom sweeps clean:俗话说~,新来的主任决心干几件事,使车间改变面貌。As the old saying goes, "a new broom sweeps clean", the newly-appointed manager is determined to adopt several measures and give the workshop a new look.

新贵 xīnguì person newly appointed to a high post; the newly powerful:元老~ elderly statesmen and the newly powerful /每次大选都要产生一批~。Each presidential election brings a group of new people into power.

新赫布里底 Xīn-Hèbùlǐdǐ New Hebrides, now renamed Vanuatu (瓦努阿图), an island nation in the Southwest Pacific

新黑格尔主义 Xīnhēigé'ěrzhǔyì 〈哲学〉Neo-Hegelianism

新华门 Xīnhuámén Xin Hua Men, gate of the former Imperial Palace leading into *Zhongnanhai*, seat of the headquarters of the Communist Party of China and the central government

新华日报 Xīnhuá Rìbào ❶ *Xinhua Ribao* or *New China Daily*, organ of the Communist Party of China published in KMT-controlled areas during the War of Resistance Against Japan ❷ newspaper published in Nanjing

新华通讯社 Xīnhuá Tōngxùnshè (shortened as 新华社) Xinhua News Agency, first established in 1931 as Red China News Agency (红色中华通讯社), changed to present name (first translated as New China News Agency) in 1937, official news agency of the People's Republic of China since 1949

新欢 xīnhuān new sweetheart:另结~ acquire a new sweetheart

新婚 xīnhūn newly-married:~夫妇 newly-married couple; newlyweds /~之夜 wedding night /~燕尔 just happily married /~不如久别。Reunion after a long separation is even sweeter than a wedding. *or* A night after a long absence is better than a wedding night.

新几内亚 Xīn-Jīnèiyà New Guinea, second largest island of the world and part of Papua New Guinea, an island nation in the Southwest Pacific

新记录 xīnjìlù new record:女子跳高的世界~ new world record in the women's high jump /月营业额的~ new record in monthly sales (*or* turnover)

新纪元 xīnjìyuán new era; new epoch:开创了历史的~ usher in a new historical epoch; open a new chapter in history

新霁 xīnjì fine weather right after rain or snow:苦雨~ fine weather after prolonged rainfall /雪后~。It clears up after a snow.

新加坡 Xīnjiāpō Singapore:~人 Singaporean

新嫁娘 xīnjiàniáng newly-married woman; bride

新疆 Xīnjiāng (formerly a province) Xinjiang:~生产建设兵团 Xinjiang Production and Construction Corps

新疆维吾尔自治区 Xīnjiāng Wéiwú'ěr Zìzhìqū Xinjiang Uygur Autonomous Region, established in 1955

新交 xīnjiāo ❶ just get acquainted:他俩虽是~,却一见如故,相知颇深。Though they had become acquainted only recently, the two of them had a profound mutual understanding and treated each other like old friends. ❷ new friend or acquaintance:旧友~,欢聚一堂。Friends, old and new, were happily gathered under the same roof.

新教 Xīnjiào 〈基督教〉Protestantism:~徒 Protestant /~教派 Protestant sect (*or* denomination)

新界 Xīnjiè "New Territories", that part of Hong Kong south of the Shenzhen River and north of the Jiexian Street seized by the British in 1898, and returned to Chinese sovereignty in 1997

新近 xīnjìn recently; of late:~发生的事情 recent event (*or* development)

新进 xīnjìn 〈旧语〉those who have just passed the imperial civil examination or who have just started their official careers:提拔~ (as of a senior official) promote those who have just passed the imperial civil examination or who have just started their official careers

新旧约全书 Xīn-Jiùyuē Quánshū 〈基督教〉*Old and New Testaments*

新居 xīnjū new home; new residence; new housing:迁入~ move into a new apartment /~落成 completion of one's new house (*or* residence)

新剧 xīnjù 〈旧语〉modern drama; stage play

新喀里多尼亚 Xīn-Kālǐduōníyà New Caledonia, island in the Southwest Pacific and French overseas territory since 1946

新凯恩斯主义 Xīnkǎi'ēnsīzhǔyì 〈经济〉Neo-Keynesianism

新康德主义 Xīnkāngdézhǔyì 〈哲学〉Neo-Kantianism:~者 Neo-Kantian

新来乍到 xīnlái-zhàdào newly arrived:他~,你给他介绍一下学校的情况,好吗? He is a newcomer here. Why don't you give him a briefing about our school?

新郎 xīnláng bridegroom

新郎官 xīnlángguān 〈口语〉bridegroom

新浪潮 xīnlàngcháo new wave

新老交替 xīnlǎo-jiāotì succession of the older by the younger generation; replacement of the old by the new

新历 xīnlì solar calendar (in contrast with the lunar calendar); Gregorian calendar (in contrast with the Julian calendar)

新凉 xīnliáng fresh cool of early autumn:初秋~,繁星闪烁,清风宜人。It was a fresh cool night in early autumn, with twinkling stars and a gentle breeze.

新绿 xīnlǜ fresh green of early spring:五月的西山,一片~。May

X

saw the Western Hills covered with a fresh verdure.
新马尔萨斯主义 Xīnmǎ'ěrsàsīzhǔyì Neo-Malthusianism
新霉素 xīnméisù 〈药学〉neomycin
新民主主义 xīnmínzhǔzhǔyì new democracy:《~论》*On New Democracy* (by Mao Zedong, Jan. 1940) /~青年团 New Democratic Youth League
新民主主义革命 xīnmínzhǔzhǔyì gémìng new-democratic revolution
新名词 xīnmíngcí new term; new expression; neologism; vogue word:这篇文章用了许多~。This article is riddled with newfangled expressions.
新墨西哥 Xīn-Mòxīgē New Mexico, state in southwestern United States
新年 xīnnián New Year:~献词 New Year message /~健康! Good health in the New Year! /祝大家~好! I wish you all a happy New Year!
新娘 xīnniáng *also* "新娘子" bride
新女性 xīnnǚxìng 〈旧语〉new woman (a term used in the earlier years of the Chinese Republic for a woman with progressive ideas)
新派 xīnpài new style; modern style:~人家 modern families; people who follow the current trends /~作风 new style (of life, work, etc.)
新篇章 xīnpiānzhāng new page; new chapter:改革开放,揭开了中国历史上的~。The policy of carrying out reforms and opening to the outside world opened a new chapter in the history of China.
新瓶装旧酒 xīnpíng zhuāng jiùjiǔ old wine in a new bottle — same old stuff with a new label:他的讲话纯属~,没有什么新东西。His speech contained nothing new; it merely repeated the same old stuff with a new label.
新奇 xīnqí new and strange; novel:~而神秘的感觉 novel and mysterious feeling /~的环境 strange, new environment /他初到中国,处处觉得~。As it was his first visit to China, everything there struck him as novel.
新巧 xīnqiǎo new and ingenious:设计~,使用方便 ingeniously designed and easy to use
新青年 Xīnqīngnián *New Youth*, influential monthly journal edited by Chen Duxiu (陈独秀, 1879-1942), first published in 1915 in Shanghai under the name of *Youth* (青年), soon changed to *New Youth*, moved to Beijing in 1917, and suspended in 1922
新秋 xīnqiū early autumn:~之夜,月色皎洁,金风送爽。It was a moonlit night in early autumn with a refreshing gentle breeze.
新区 xīnqū ❶ newly developed area; newly added district:上海的浦东~ Shanghai's new Pudong district ❷ newly liberated area (during the Third Revolutionary Civil War, 1946-1949):在~进行土改 carry out land reform in the newly liberated areas
新人 xīnrén ❶ people of a new type:培养一代~ foster a generation of people of a new type ❷ new personality; new talent:这届政府~不多。There are few new faces in this administration. ❸ new recruit:我单位里增加了几位~。Our unit has recently recruited some staff members. ❹ reformed person:把失足青年改造成~ reform young delinquents and make them new members of society ❺ newlywed, esp. the bride:孙小宝今天结婚,听说~是他中学时的同学。Sun Xiaobao is getting married today. It is said that his bride was a classmate of his at middle school.
新人新事 xīnrén-xīnshì new people and new things:大力宣传~ give wide publicity to new people and new things
新任 xīnrèn ❶ newly-appointed:~的副校长 newly-appointed vice-principal ❷ new appointment; new post:他已有~。He has got a new post (*or* appointment).
新儒家 Xīnrújiā 〈哲学〉❶ Neo-Confucianism (as advocated by Zhu Xi 朱熹, 1130-1200) ❷ Neo-Confucian
新生 xīnshēng ❶ newborn; newly born:~国家 newly-established state ❷ new life; rebirth:古城重获~。The ancient city received a new lease of life. ❸ new student; freshman:招收~ enrol new students /~注册 registration of freshmen
新生代 xīnshēngdài ❶ (Xīnshēngdài)〈地质〉Cainozoic or Cenozoic Era ❷〈比喻〉younger generation; new generation:~领导人 younger-generation leaders; new generation of leaders
新生儿 xīnshēng'ér newborn (baby); neonate:~科学 neonatology /~呼吸窘迫综合征 RDS (respiratory distress syndrome of newborn) /~流行性腹泻 epidemic diarrhea of the newborn /~破伤风 trismus nascentium; trismus neonatorum /~眼炎 ophthalmia neonatorum
新生界 Xīnshēngjiè 〈地质〉Cainozoic Erathem; Cenozoic Erathem
新生力量 xīnshēng lìliàng newly emerging force; new force; new blood:协会吸收了一批新会员,增加了~。The association has admitted a number of new members, and thus become much strengthened.
新生霉素 xīnshēngméisù 〈药学〉albamycin
新生事物 xīnshēng shìwù newly emerging thing; new thing:~层出不穷。New things are emerging one after another.
新诗 xīnshī (in contrast with classical poetry) verse written in the vernacular; new poetry:这些都是~中的名篇。All these are famous specimens of vernacular verse.
新石器时代 Xīnshíqì Shídài Neolithic Age; New Stone Age:~文化 Neolithic culture
新实在论 xīnshízàilùn 〈哲学〉New Realism
新式 xīnshì new type; new-style; modern; up-to-date:~家具 new types of furniture /~服装 clothing of the latest fashion; fashionable clothes /最~的小轿车 sedan car of the latest model /~婚礼 new-style wedding
新手 xīnshǒu new hand; raw recruit; novice; rookie:干这种活儿他是个~。He is a new hand at this job.
新书 xīnshū ❶ new book:别把~给弄脏了。Don't soil the new book. ❷ book to be published or just off the press:~预告 advertisement of books to be published /本月~ books just off the press in the past month
新斯的明 xīnsīdìmíng 〈药学〉neostigmine
新四军 Xīnsìjūn New Fourth Army (Led by the Chinese Communist Party during the War of Resistance Against Japan, 1937-1945)
新岁 xīnsuì New Year:~伊始,村子里一派喜气洋洋的气象。The new year brought an atmosphere of jubilation to the village.
新台币 xīntáibì New Taiwan currency; NT $
新唐书 Xīn-Tángshū *Xin Tang Shu* or *New History of Tang*, one of *The Twenty-Four Histories* covering the Tang Dynasty
新特 xīntè new and peculiar; novel:此种产品并无~之处。There is nothing new or unique about this kind of product.
新体 xīntǐ (as of literature) new-style; modern; vernacular:他擅长旧体诗,很少写~诗。Master of classical poetry, he almost never wrote any vernacular verse.
新亭对泣 Xīntíng-duìqì 〈书面〉weeping together at Xinting (south of present Nanjing) over enemy-occupied native land (anecdote of late Jin Dynasty when the land north of the Yangtze was under the rule of nomadic tribes) — grief and indignation of patriots at lost territory
新钍 xīntǔ 〈化学〉mesothorium (MsTh)
新文化运动 Xīnwénhuà Yùndòng New Culture Movement (1915-1919)
新文学 xīnwénxué (in contrast with classical literature) vernacular literature; modern literature (promoted during the New Culture Movement)
新闻 xīnwén ❶ news:采访~ cover (*or* report) news /封锁~ suppress news /国际~ world (*or* international) news /国内~ domestic (*or* home) news /~阅读器 news reader /~自由 freedom of information; freedom of the press /~图片橱窗 newsphoto display case /~学院 school of journalism /从事~工作 devote oneself to journalism; pursue a journalistic career ❷ sth. new; hearsay; rumour:马路~ hearsay; rumour /你刚从乡下回来,有什么~给大家说说。You've just returned from the countryside. Please tell us about anything new there.
新闻处 xīnwénchù information office or service
新闻发布会 xīnwén fābùhuì news briefing
新闻稿 xīnwéngǎo press or news release
新闻工作者 xīnwén gōngzuòzhě journalist
新闻公报 xīnwén gōngbào press communiqué
新闻广播 xīnwén guǎngbō newscast
新闻记者 xīnwén jìzhě newsman; reporter; newspaperman; journalist
新闻检查 xīnwén jiǎnchá press censorship
新闻简报 xīnwén jiǎnbào news summary; news in brief
新闻界 xīnwénjiè press circles; the press
新闻联播 xīnwén liánbō news hook-up
新闻片 xīnwénpiàn newsreel; news film
新闻司 xīnwénsī department of information (of the Foreign Ministry)

新闻通讯 xīnwén tōngxùn newsletter
新闻学 xīnwénxué journalism
新闻纸 xīnwénzhǐ ❶〈旧语〉newspaper ❷ newsprint:去年~的供应十分紧张。There was a serious shortage of newsprint last year.
新闻周刊 Xīnwén Zhōukān *Newsweek*, US weekly published since 1933
新西伯利亚 Xīn-Xībólìyà New Siberia or Novosibirsk, major city in West Siberia, Russia
新西兰 Xīnxīlán New Zealand:~人 New Zealander
新西兰麻 xīnxīlánmá 〈植物〉phormium
新希伯来语 Xīn-Xībóláiyǔ New Hebrew
新媳妇儿 xīnxífur 〈口语〉bride
新禧 xīnxǐ new year greetings:恭贺~。Wish you a happy New Year. *or* Happy New Year to you!
新鲜 xīnxian ❶ fresh:~的鱼虾 fresh fish and shrimps /~的水果 fresh fruit /一束~的玫瑰花 a bunch of fresh roses /呼吸~空气 breathe in fresh air /黄油有点儿不~了。The butter is a bit off. ❷ new; original; novel; strange:~事物 something new; novelty /我想换个环境,~~。I want to have a change of air and get some new stimulus. /这个提法很~。The formulation is really novel.
新兴 xīnxīng new and developing; newly emerging; rising; burgeoning:~行业 emergent industry / ~的港口 new and developing port /~力量 newly-emerging forces; rising forces; forces in the ascendant /~的边缘科学 burgeoning frontier science
新星 xīnxīng ❶〈天文〉nova:~爆发 nova outburst /超~ supernova ❷〈比喻〉new star; rising star:足坛~ new football star /歌坛~ new singing star /政坛上一颗冉冉上升的~ rising star in the political arena
新型 xīnxíng new style; new type:~发式 new hair style /~农民 farmers of a new type
新修本草 Xīnxiū Běncǎo *also*"唐本草"Tángběncǎo *Revised Materia Medica*, China's first medical code completed in 53 volumes in 659 AD
新秀 xīnxiù rising star:羽坛~ rising badminton star /文坛~ promising young writer
新学 xīnxué 〈旧语〉(in contrast with classical Chinese learning) new learning; Western learning
see also"西学"xīxué
新雅 xīnyǎ fresh and elegant:诗句~ fresh and elegant lines
新药 xīnyào ❶ newly developed medicine ❷ Western medicine
新医 xīnyī 〈旧语〉(in contrast with traditional Chinese medicine) Western medicine
新义 xīnyì derivative meaning of a word or phrase
新异 xīnyì novel; strange:~的服装款式 novel fashion /大胆而~的见解 original and bold assertion
新意 xīnyì new idea or meaning; originality:这篇文章颇富~。The article is full of new ideas.
新英格兰 Xīn-Yīnggélán New England, northeastern part of the United States:~人 New Englander /~口音 New England accent
新颖 xīnyǐng new; original; novel:风格~ new (*or* novel) style /构思~ original conception /~独特的见解 original and unique view /~廉价的小玩意儿 novel but cheap trinket
新雨 xīnyǔ ❶ early spring rain; rain which has just fallen:春苗遇~,一日长三寸。Spring sprouts grow apace after each rain. ❷〈书面〉new friend:旧知~ friends, old and new
新约 Xīnyuē 〈基督教〉*The New Testament*
新月 xīnyuè ❶ crescent:一弯~ crescent moon /~旗 crescent ❷〈天文〉*also*"朔月"shuòyuè new moon
新月形沙丘 xīnyuèxíng shāqiū 〈地理〉barchan
新造 xīnzào newly-built; recently constructed
新泽西 Xīnzéxī New Jersey, a state of the United States bordering on the Atlantic
新崭崭 xīnzhǎnzhǎn 〈方言〉completely new; brand new; spick-and-span:~的票子 brand-new banknote /~的制服 spick-and-span uniform
新张 xīnzhāng (as of a new shop, etc.) open; begin doing business:~志喜 congratulations on the opening of a shop
新针疗法 xīnzhēnliáofǎ 〈中医〉new acupuncture (therapy)
新正 xīnzhēng first month of the lunar year:~一过,农民就下地干活儿了。As soon as the first lunar month was over, farmers began working in the fields.
新政 xīnzhèng ❶ new political measures; new policies ❷ New Deal, policies introduced by President Franklin D. Roosevelt of the United States in 1933 to deal with the Great Depression
新知 xīnzhī new-found friend
新殖民主义 xīnzhímínzhǔyì neocolonialism; new colonialism:~者 neocolonialist
新址 xīnzhǐ new address; new site; new location:这个工厂的~在东郊。The new location of the factory is in the eastern suburb of the city.
新制 xīnzhì new system
新妆 xīnzhuāng ❶ (of women) new look after make-up;〈比喻〉new appearance ❷ (women's) new style; new fashion
新装 xīnzhuāng new clothes:姑娘们穿着节日的~,且歌且舞。Girls were singing and dancing in their holiday best. /植树造林给荒山披上了绿色的~。Reafforestation has clothed the barren hills in lush green.
新作 xīnzuò new literary or artistic work:名家~ new works by famous authors

薪

xīn ❶ firewood; fuel; faggot:积~ piles of faggots /釜底抽~ take away the firewood from under the cauldron — take a drastic measure to deal with a situation; cut the ground from under sb.'s feet ❷ salary:加~ increase (*or* raise) sb.'s salary /月~一千元 monthly salary of 1,000 *yuan* /发~日 pay day
薪传 xīnchuán 〈书面〉(short for 薪尽火传) carry or pass on the torch of learning from teacher to student:~不息 the torch of learning is passed on generation to generation
薪俸 xīnfèng salary; pay; remuneration:~优厚 handsome salary; generous pay
薪桂米珠 xīnguì-mǐzhū *also*"米珠薪桂" fuel is as expensive as cinnamon and rice as pearls — exorbitant food prices:灾荒之年,~,百姓度日艰难。As food prices soared in a year of famine, the common people had a really hard time.
薪给 xīnjǐ salary; pay:~微薄 meagre salary (*or* pay)
薪金 xīnjīn salary; pay:~加奖金 salary plus bonus /~级差表 pay scale
薪尽火传 xīnjìn-huǒchuán as soon as one piece of fuel is consumed, another piece is set alight — the torch of learning is passed on from teacher to student and from generation to generation
see also"薪传"
薪水 xīnshui salary; pay
薪炭材 xīntàncái ❶ firewood ❷ fuel tree
薪炭林 xīntànlín 〈林业〉fuel forest
薪饷 xīnxiǎng pay (to the military and police) and supply (such as clothing, boots, etc.):克扣士兵的~ take a cut in soldiers' pay
薪资 xīnzī salary; pay; wages:~不丰 modest pay

忻

xīn ❶ *see*"欣"xīn ❷ (Xīn) a surname

炘

xīn 〈书面〉intense heat

昕

xīn 〈书面〉time just before the sun rises; dawn

欣(訢)

xīn glad; happy; elated; joyful:欢~鼓舞 be filled with joy; be elated /~逢盛世 happy to live in a prosperous (*or* flourishing) age /~生恶死 covet life and fear death; be afraid of death and cling to life
欣忭 xīnbiàn 〈书面〉happy; joyous
欣快 xīnkuài happy; blissful; euphoric:他完成了父亲的嘱托,感到无比~。He was most happy to have done what his father had asked him to.
欣快剂 xīnkuàijì euphoriant
欣快症 xīnkuàizhèng euphoria
欣慕 xīnmù admire; adore:~不已 be filled with admiration
欣企 xīnqǐ 〈书面〉happily look forward (to sth.); eagerly expect
欣庆 xīnqìng be glad and thankful; congratulate oneself:他~自己脱离了险境。He congratulated himself for escaping from danger.
欣然 xīnrán 〈书面〉joyfully; gladly; with pleasure:~允诺 gladly consent; readily agree /~采纳 accept with pleasure; happily adopt /~命笔 be happy to set pen to paper; start writing
欣赏 xīnshǎng ❶ enjoy; admire:~名家手笔 admire the work of

masters /～大自然的美景 enjoy (*or* admire) the beauty of nature ❷ appreciate; like: 自我～ self-appreciation; self-glorification /我非常～他的坦诚态度。I appreciate his candour and sincerity very much.
欣慰 xīnwèi gratified; satisfied: 幸福、～的泪水 tears of happiness and satisfaction /儿子有了好工作,她感到～。She was gratified that her son had found a good job.
欣悉 xīnxī 〈书面〉 be glad to learn or hear: ～试验获得成功,特表祝贺。On the happy occasion of the success of the experiment, we wish to express our congratulations to you.
欣喜 xīnxǐ glad; elated; joyful; happy: ～若狂 be wild with joy; be in an ecstasy of joy; go into raptures /～雀跃 dance (*or* jump) with joy
欣羡 xīnxiàn 〈书面〉 admire: 拜读大作,～不已。I was filled with admiration after reading your (magnificent) work.
欣欣 xīnxīn ❶ happily; gladly: ～自得 happy and complacent; pleased with oneself /～然有喜色 wear a happy expression ❷ luxuriant; exuberant; flourishing: 春草～绿。The grass in spring is a luxuriant green.
欣欣向荣 xīnxīn-xiàngróng thriving; flourishing; affluent; prosperous: 百花争妍、～的花园 flourishing garden with a hundred flowers contending in beauty /～的现代化城市 prosperous (*or* thriving) modern city /各行各业～。Every trade is thriving.
欣幸 xīnxìng be glad and thankful: 企业顺利渡过难关,大家都感到～。Everyone was glad and thankful that the enterprise had successfully tided over its difficulties.
欣愉 xīnyú joy; delight; happiness
欣悦 xīnyuè delight; pleasure; joy: ～的神情 joyful expression /新的生活使他感到～。He was delighted with his new life.
欣跃 xīnyuè dance or jump for joy

歆 xīn 〈书面〉 envy; admire; adore
歆慕 xīnmù 〈书面〉 admire; envy
歆羡 xīnxiàn 〈书面〉 envy; admire; long for: 他学术上的成就,令人～。He is admired for his academic achievement.

xín

镡 xín ❶ 〈古语〉 end of the handle of a sword ❷ ancient weapon which resembles a sword but is smaller

xǐn

伈 xǐn
伈伈 xǐnxǐn 〈书面〉 frightened; scared

xìn

芯(信) xìn core: 矿～ core /烛～ wick (of a candle)
see also xīn
芯子 xìnzi ❶ fuse; wick: 爆竹～ fuse of a firecracker ❷ forked tongue (of a snake): 蛇吐～。The snake stretched out its forked tongue.

信[1] xìn ❶ true; truthful: ～言不美,美言不～。Truthful words are not pleasant to the ear, while pleasant words are not truthful. ❷ faith; trust; confidence; reputation: 守～ keep one's promise (*or* word) /失～ break faith; go back on one's promise /～及豚鱼 one's sincerity (*or* truthfulness) extends even to the lowest creatures /～孚中外 have the confidence of foreigners and Chinese alike; enjoy a good reputation both at home and abroad ❸ believe; trust: ～而不疑 believe without the slightest doubt /偏听偏～ heed only one side; be biased /～以为真 accept sth. as true /～则全～,否则不～ trust sb. completely or not at all ❹ profess faith in; embrace; believe in: ～伊斯兰教 embrace (*or* profess, *or* believe in) Islam /改～天主教 be converted to Catholicism ❺ at will; at random; casually; without plan: *see* "～口"; "～步" ❻ pledge; token; sign; evidence: 凭～ evidence; pledge /印～ official seal ❼ letter; mail: 送～ deliver a letter /介绍～ letter of introduction /推荐～ letter of recommendation /快～ express letter (*or* mail) /挂号～ registered letter (*or* mail) ❽ message; news; word: 口～儿 oral (*or* verbal) message /帮人递个～儿 carry a message for sb. /通风报～ furnish secret information (to sb.); tip (sb.) off /音～全无。There's been no news (*or* word). *or* Nothing has been heard (from sb. *or* about sth.). ❾ fuse: 地雷引～ fuse of a land mine ❿ *see* "芯" xìn ⓫ (Xìn) a surname

信[2] xìn arsenic: 红～ red arsenic /白～ white arsenic
信笔 xìnbǐ write at random; scribble along: ～涂鸦 (usu. used in self-depreciating reference to one's work) scribble along; write at random /～写来,直抒胸臆 write as dictated by the surge of one's feelings
信标 xìnbiāo 〈航空〉〈航海〉 beacon: ～灯 beacon light /～接收机 beacon receiver /～应答机 beacon transponder
信步 xìnbù walk in a leisurely and aimless manner; stroll; roam: ～闲踱 walk about aimlessly; take a leisurely walk /～走来 stroll up aimlessly /～走到池边 roam casually to a pond /不管风吹浪打,胜似闲庭～。Let the wind blow and waves beat, Better far than idly strolling in a courtyard.
信不过 xìnbuguò not trust; distrust: 难道你连自己的爹娘都～吗? Don't you even trust your own parents? /人们对这家银行可是有些～。People think this bank is somewhat unreliable.
信不及 xìnbují distrust; not believe: 你信不过那些年轻人,连我这老头都～啦? I know you distrust those young fellows, but don't you even have confidence in an old man like me?
信不住 xìnbuzhù not trust; distrust: 我根本～他们。I don't trust them at all.
信插 xìnchā mail holder made of wooden board or cloth, usually nailed to a wall; mail rack
信差 xìnchāi 〈旧语〉 ❶ messenger or courier for official documents and mail ❷ postman
信从 xìncóng believe, trust, or follow without doubt: 盲目～ trust (*or* follow) blindly /对某些言论,不可一味～。Certain arguments are not to be taken for granted. *or* They should not be trusted unquestioningly.
信达雅 xìn-dá-yǎ (traditionally used as criteria for translation) fidelity, fluency and elegance; faithfulness, expressiveness and taste
信贷 xìndài credit: 短期～ short-term credit /～额度 line of credit /～最高额 credit ceiling /～机构 credit institution /～便利 credit facility /～保证 credit guarantee /～成本 〈商业〉 cost of credit /紧缩～ squeeze credit; contract credit /提供～ provide (*or* grant) credit /扩大～ expand credit
信贷安全系数 xìndài ānquán xìshù 〈金融〉 (credit) safety factor
信贷紧缩 xìndài jǐnsuō credit crunch or squeeze
信贷银行 xìndài yínháng credit bank
信贷资金 xìndài zījīn credit funds
信道 xìndào 〈电信〉 channel: ～选择器 channel selector /～组 〈电子〉 channel bank
信得过 xìndeguò have faith or confidence in; trust: ～商店 reliable shop /我们～你。We have confidence (*or* faith) in you. /他们的服务是～的。Their service is dependable.
信得及 xìndejí trust; have confidence or faith in: 你～他吗? Do you trust him? *or* Do you consider him reliable?
信得住 xìndezhù trust; have confidence or faith in: 他办事可靠,我们大家都～他。He is reliable in everything he does. We all have confidence in him.
信而有征 xìn'éryǒuzhēng reliable and borne out by evidence: ～的事实 proven fact /其说～,何谈虚妄。What he says is quite trustworthy. It is no sheer fancy.
信访 xìnfǎng letters and visits (by the people, usually airing complaints or making suggestions); correspondence and visitation (by the public): ～部门 correspondence and visitation departments (set up by government or Party institutions to handle letters and visits from the people) /搞好～工作 do a good job of handling the people's letters and visits
信风 xìnfēng *also* "贸易风" màoyìfēng 〈气象〉 trade (wind): 反～ antitrade wind; antitrades
信风带 xìnfēngdài trade wind zone
信封 xìnfēng envelope
信奉 xìnfèng believe in; profess: ～基督教 profess Christianity; be a Christian /～上帝 have faith and trust in God /～实用主义哲学 believe in pragmatism

信服 xìnfú have implicit faith in; accept completely; be convinced:令人～ be convincing /这种解释不能使人～。The explanation carries no conviction. /对于这位医生,我们是～的。We have faith in the doctor. /李逵虽然脾气暴躁,却最～宋江。Hot-tempered as Li Kui was, he admired Song Jiang wholeheartedly.

信鸽 xìngē carrier pigeon; homing pigeon; homer

信管 xìnguǎn fuse:触发～ contact fuse /近炸～ proximity fuse /延期～ delayed-action fuse /～电路 detonator circuit

信函 xìnhán letter; mail; correspondence:私人～ personal letter /～订单〈商业〉letter order /～档案〈审计〉correspondence file

信号 xìnhào ❶ sign; signal:联络～ liaison signal /灯光～ light signal /识别～ identification signal /臂板～〈铁路〉semaphore /遇难～ distress signal /起义开始的～ signal for starting an insurrection /这是暴风雨欲来的～。This is a harbinger of the oncoming storm. ❷〈电学〉signal:杂乱～〈无线电〉hash /～失真 signal distortion /～波 signal wave /～发生器 signal generator

信号板 xìnhàobǎn signal plate or panel

信号兵 xìnhàobīng signalman

信号刺激 xìnhào cìjī 〈心理〉signal stimulus

信号弹 xìnhàodàn signal flare

信号灯 xìnhàodēng signal lamp

信号机 xìnhàojī annunciator; teleseme

信号旗 xìnhàoqí signal flag; semaphore

信号枪 xìnhàoqiāng 〈军事〉flare (*or* signal) pistol; pyrotechnic pistol

信汇 xìnhuì 〈金融〉mail transfer (M/T); postal money order; letter transfer:～汇率 rate of mail transfer /～通知书 mail transfer advice

信笺 xìnjiān letter paper; writing paper

信件 xìnjiàn letter; mail:私人～ private (*or* personal) letter /往来～ outgoing and incoming mail; correspondence

信教 xìnjiào profess or believe in a religion; be religious:据我所知,她从不～。She has never professed a religion, so far as I know. /他一家人都～。All his family are religious. /公民有～自由。Citizens enjoy freedom of religion (*or* conscience).

信据 xìnjù convincing or reliable evidence:论文通篇引用的都是～,可见作者下了大功夫。The treatise cites nothing but convincing evidence throughout, which shows that the author took great pains. /仅有犯人的口供不能算是～。The prisoner's testimony alone cannot be regarded as conclusive (*or* authentic) evidence.

信口 xìnkǒu blurt out one's thoughts:～说出 blurt it out /～哼起了小曲 hum a melody

信口雌黄 xìnkǒu-cíhuáng wag one's tongue at random; make irresponsible remarks; talk sheer nonsense:你不能这样～,诬陷好人! You must not slander an honest man by making such irresponsible remarks. /通篇～,一派胡言。The article is filled with lies and nonsense from beginning to end.

信口开河 xìnkǒu-kāihé *also*"信口开合" talk off the top of one's head; let one's tongue run away with one; shoot one's mouth off; talk irresponsibly:不顾场合,～ talk off the top of one's head (*or* shoot one's mouth off) regardless of the occasion /他会上的发言纯属～,不可听信。What he said at the meeting was totally irresponsible and must not be taken seriously.

信赖 xìnlài trust; believe in; have faith in:有负人民的～ be unworthy of the people's trust; not live up to the people's expectations /老师赢得了全体学生的～和尊敬。The teacher won the trust and respect of all his students.

信马由缰 xìnmǎ-yóujiāng ride (a horse) with lax reins (to let it go where it pleases); amble or stroll aimlessly; let things take their own course:你都这么大了,为什么还是～地到处乱跑? Now that you are a big boy, why are you still rushing here and there aimlessly?

信念 xìnniàn faith; belief; conviction:毕生的～ life-long faith (*or* conviction) /～坚,南山移。Faith will even move the mountains.

信女 xìnnǚ woman believer; dévotée:善男～ devout men and women; dévotées to Buddhism

信皮儿 xìnpír 〈口语〉envelope

信然 xìnrán 〈书面〉indeed so:古诗曰:蜀道难,难于上青天。而今～。Classical poems described the passage to Sichuan as more difficult than going up to the sky. Now that I am here, I see it is indeed so.

信瓤儿 xìnrángr 〈方言〉written letter enclosed in an envelope

信任 xìnrèn trust; confidence:她用花言巧语骗取了老人的～。She cajoled the old man into trusting her. /他这个人疑心太重,对谁都不～。He was so suspicious that he never confided in anyone.

信任投票 xìnrèn tóupiào vote of confidence

信赏必罚 xìnshǎng-bìfá rewards and punishments are rigorously carried out; rewards and punishments are meted out without fail:他带兵几十年,一向～,号令严明。A commander for several decades, he has always been meticulous in meting out rewards and punishments and strict in implementing discipline and orders.

信石 xìnshí white arsenic produced in Xinzhou

信实 xìnshí ❶ trustworthy; honest; dependable:为人～ be trustworthy /他待人～、宽厚,车间里的人没有不夸他的。All the workers in the workshop admire him for his honesty and generosity towards others. ❷ reliable; authentic:史料～ reliable historical data

信史 xìnshǐ true or authentic history; reliable historical account:《左传》历来被称作～。*Zuo Zhuan*, or *Zuoqiu Ming's Chronicles*, has always been regarded as an authentic historical record.

信使 xìnshǐ courier; messenger; emissary:～证书 courier's credentials /外交～ diplomatic courier /～队 courier corps /～往返 exchange of correspondence and emissaries /～往来,络绎不绝。Messengers shuttled to and fro in a constant stream.

信士 xìnshì ❶ man who believes in Buddhism; Buddhist dévotée ❷〈书面〉trustworthy or honest person

信誓旦旦 xìnshì-dàndàn pledge or promise in all sincerity and seriousness; vow solemnly:想当初你～,好话说尽,为什么如今却抛弃我? In the beginning you used all the sweet words you could think of and vowed your love solemnly. How come you want to jilt me today?

信手 xìnshǒu at random; at will; wilfully:～写来 write at random; write effortlessly /～挥霍 squander money at will; spend money like water /他～从书架上取下一本书来翻阅。He took a book from the shelf at random and glanced over it.

信手拈来 xìnshǒu-niānlái have (words, material, etc.) at one's fingertips and write with facility:～,皆成文章 whatever comes to one's pen becomes fine writing; have great facility in writing about whatever comes to one's mind

信守 xìnshǒu keep faith; abide by; stick to:～协议 abide (*or* stand) by an agreement /～合同条款 stick to (*or* abide by) the terms of a contract /～誓约 keep one's pledge

信守不渝 xìnshǒu-bùyú be unswervingly faithful (to one's promise, etc.); abide by consistently:对这个条约,我方历来～。We have faithfully abided by the treaty.

信水 xìnshuǐ 〈书面〉menstruation; menses

信宿 xìnsù 〈书面〉two nights in succession:～可至 will arrive in two days' time /流连～,乐而忘返 stay two nights in succession and be reluctant to leave

信天翁 xìntiānwēng 〈动物〉albatross

信天游 xìntiānyóu *xintianyou* or *Ramble in the Sky*, one of the major folk tunes popular in northern Shaanxi:离开延安已有多年,直到今天,～的豪放歌声仍在我耳边萦绕。It is years since I left Yan'an, but to this day, I still seem to be hearing the lofty tunes of *xintianyou* around me.

信条 xìntiáo article of creed or faith; precept; tenet:触犯～ violate one's creed; run foul of a tenet (*or* precept) /恪守～ adhere to one's creed or tenets /"顾客就是上帝",这是本店的～。"The customer is God" — that is the creed of this shop.

信筒 xìntǒng *also*"邮筒" yóutǒng pillar-box; mailbox

信徒 xìntú believer; disciple; follower; devotee:基督的虔诚～ devout Christian /此人是利己主义的～,于己无利的事他是从来不干的。He was a faithful believer of egotism and never did anything that was of no benefit to him.

信托 xìntuō ❶ trust; entrust:我们是多年的老朋友,把事情～给他是情理之中的事。It was only natural for me to entrust him with the matter since we had been friends of long standing. ❷〈经济〉trust:～财产 trust estate

信托法 xìntuōfǎ law of trust

信托公司 xìntuō gōngsī trust company

信托基金 xìntuō jījīn trust fund

信托商店 xìntuō shāngdiàn commission shop; second-hand goods shop

信托投资公司 xìntuō tóuzī gōngsī trust and investment corporation

信望 xìnwàng prestige and reputation:颇有～ enjoy rather high prestige

信物 xìnwù authenticating object; token of pledge; keepsake: 定情的～ object pledging one's love or confirming one's engagement; token of love (such as a ring) /作为授权的～ as a token of empowerment /这孩子是他的遗腹子,有他留下的～为证。The boy is his son born after his death, with a keepsake left by him as proof.

信息 xìnxī ❶ message; news; word: 替人传递～ carry a message for sb.; pass on word for sb. /他三十年前离开家乡后,一直没有～。He has never been heard from since he left his home town thirty years ago. ❷ information: ～系统 information system /～管理 information management /～传递 information transmission /～量 volume of information /～中心 information centre

信息爆炸 xìnxī bàozhà information explosion

信息编码 xìnxī biānmǎ 〈计算机〉 information encoding

信息产业 xìnxī chǎnyè information industry

信息产业部 xìnxī chǎnyèbù Ministry of Information Industry

信息处理 xìnxī chǔlǐ information processing

信息存储器 xìnxī cúnchǔqì 〈计算机〉 information storage or memory

信息港 xìnxīgǎng cyber port

信息高速公路 xìnxī gāosù gōnglù information superhighway; digital superhighway

信息革命 xìnxī gémìng information revolution

信息工程学 xìnxī gōngchéngxué information engineering

信息检索 xìnxī jiǎnsuǒ information retrieval: ～系统 IR system; information retrieval system

信息经济 xìnxī jīngjì information economy

信息科学 xìnxī kēxué *see* "信息学"

信息库 xìnxīkù information base

信息论 xìnxīlùn information theory

信息社会 xìnxī shèhuì *also* "信息化社会" information society

信息市场 xìnxī shìchǎng information market

信息体 xìnxītǐ 〈生化〉 informosome

信息污染 xìnxī wūrǎn 〈计算机〉 information pollution

信息学 xìnxīxué information science; informatics

信息远距离传送学 xìnxī yuǎnjùlí chuánsòngxué telematics

信息娱乐 xìnxī yúlè infotainment

信息载体 xìnxī zàitǐ information carrier

信息战 xìnxīzhàn information warfare

信息中介商 xìnxī zhōngjièshāng intermediary on line that links buyers and sellers by efficiently distributing market information

信息子 xìnxīzǐ 〈生化〉 informofer

信箱 xìnxiāng ❶ post box; mail box ❷ post-office box (POB) ❸ letter box

信邪 xìnxié 〈口语〉 (usu. used in the negative) believe in heresy or fallacy; bow to evil: 不～的硬汉子 dauntless man who refuses to bow to evil; tough guy who won't be taken in by fallacies /我才不信那个邪。I don't believe that trash at all. *or* That trash won't scare me at all.

信心 xìnxīn confidence; faith: 充满～ brim with confidence /丧失～ lose confidence (*or* faith) /有～实现自己的目标 be confident of accomplishing one's goal

信仰 xìnyǎng belief; faith; conviction: 宗教～权利 right to religious belief; right to worship /具有坚定政治～的人 man of firm political conviction (*or* faith) /～自由 freedom of conscience /不同政治～的人 people of different political persuasions

信仰危机 xìnyǎng wēijī crisis in belief or conviction; credibility crisis

信仰主义 xìnyǎngzhǔyì 〈哲学〉 *also* "僧侣主义" sēnglǚzhǔyì fideism

信以为真 xìnyǐwéizhēn take as valid; accept as true

信义 xìnyì good faith; honour: 讲～的人 man of good faith; man of honour /重～ stand upon one's honour; act in good faith /为人不讲～ be a perfidious man; act in bad faith

信意 xìnyì wilfully; deliberately: ～胡闹 be wilfully mischievous /我不能看着她～把自己给毁了! I will not see her ruin herself at will.

信用 xìnyòng ❶ credibility; credit; honour: 建立～ establish one's credibility (*or* credit) /～差距 credibility gap /讲～的人 man of his word; man of honour /这事能否办成,就全看你在他们中有无～了。The success or failure of this depends entirely upon your credibility with them. ❷ credit: ～贷款 loan on credit; unsecured loan; fiduciary loan /～紧缩 credit squeeze /～销售 credit selling ❸ 〈书面〉 trust and appoint: ～奸臣 trust a treacherous court official and assign him to an important post

信用保险 xìnyòng bǎoxiǎn 〈保险〉 credit insurance

信用保证书 xìnyòng bǎozhèngshū 〈会计〉 letter of guarantee (L/G)

信用等级 xìnyòng děngjí 〈金融〉 credit rating or standing: 将该公司的～由 AAA 改为 AAA⁻ change the company's credit rating from AAA to AAA⁻

信用合作社 xìnyòng hézuòshè credit cooperative; credit union

信用卡 xìnyòngkǎ credit card

信用评估 xìnyòng pínggū *also* "信用评级" 〈金融〉 credit rating: 对该银行进行～ assess the bank's credit rating; rate the bank's credit standing

信用债券 xìnyòng zhàiquàn 〈金融〉 debenture

信用证 xìnyòngzhèng letter of credit (L/C)

信誉 xìnyù prestige; credit; reputation: 商业～ business reputation /国际～ international prestige (*or* reputation) /～卓著 with an outstanding reputation /～第一。Reputation first.

信约 xìnyuē covenant; pledge

信札 xìnzhá letters

信真 xìnzhēn take sth. as true: 他是说着玩儿的,你别～。Don't take him seriously. He was just joking.

信纸 xìnzhǐ letter paper; writing paper

信子 xìnzi *see* "芯子" xìnzi

焮 xìn ❶ burn; scorch: 为火所～ be burnt by fire ❷ 〈方言〉 (of skin, etc.) be inflamed and swollen: 痒也别挠,回头～了。Don't scratch the skin, even though it itches, or you may get it inflamed and swollen.

舋 xìn 〈书面〉 *see* "衅" xìn

衅(釁) xìn quarrel; row; dispute: 启～ start a quarrel (*or* fight); kick up a row /寻～闹事 seek a pretext for a fight; pick a quarrel

衅端 xìnduān 〈书面〉 cause for a quarrel or dispute: 挑起～ provoke a quarrel or dispute; start trouble /内乱未已,边陲又启～。Border disputes had arisen before internal turmoil was put to rest.

衅起萧墙 xìnqǐ-xiāoqiáng internal strife

see also "祸起萧墙" huòqǐ-xiāoqiáng

囟(顖) xìn *same as* "囟门"

囟门 xìnmén *also* "囟脑门儿" fontanelle (boneless area in a baby's skull)

xīng

兴(興) xīng ❶ rise; flourish; prevail; become popular: 新～力量 newly emergent forces /国运～则文艺～。Art and literature flourish with the rise of a nation. /现在不～这种款式了。This fashion (*or* style) is no longer in vogue. *or* It is out of date. ❷ encourage; foster; promote: 大～调查研究之风 energetically encourage the practice of investigation and study /多难～邦。Many trials rejuvenate a nation. ❸ begin; start; found: 大～土木 start building on a large scale /百废俱～ all neglected tasks are being undertaken; all things that had fallen into disrepair are reconstructed ❹ get up; rise: 晨～ get up in the morning /夙～夜寐 rise early and retire late ❺ 〈方言〉 (usually used in the negative) allow; let; permit: 要讲道理,不～打人。You must reason things out, not rough people up. /难道就～你说谎话,不～我揭穿你? How come I am not allowed to expose you while you have the cheek to tell lies? ❻ 〈方言〉 probably; maybe; perhaps: 明天去开会的事我还定不下来,也～去,也～不去。I haven't made up my mind about the meeting tomorrow; I may or may not attend it. ❼ (Xīng) a surname

see also xìng

兴安岭 Xīng'ānlǐng Xing'an Mountains, mountain ranges in the east of the Inner Mongolian Autonomous Region and north of Heilongjiang Province: 大～ the Greater Xing'an Mountains

兴办 xīngbàn set up; start; initiate: ～学校 set up a school /～第三产业 found establishments in the tertiary industry /这条商业街是由中外合资～的。This shopping street was built with joint Chinese-

foreign capital.

兴兵 xīngbīng initiate military operations; commit troops to action; dispatch troops: ~讨伐叛逆 send (*or* dispatch) an army to quell a rebellion /敌国~犯境。An enemy nation sent troops across the border.

兴废 xīng-fèi 〈书面〉 rise and fall; wax and wane: ~存亡 rise and fall (of a nation)

兴奋 xīngfèn ❶ excited; elated: 因某事而~ excited about (*or* over) sth. /~得又唱又跳 sing and dance with excitement /使人~的消息 exciting news /掩饰不住内心的~ could hardly conceal one's elation ❷〈生理〉 excitation: 不要让大脑皮层长期处于~状态。Do not keep your cerebral cortex in prolonged excitation.

兴奋剂 xīngfènjì stimulant; excitant; dope; upper: ~检查呈阳性反应 test positive for doping /这一消息好像给他打了一针~似的。The news gave him a shot in the arm.

兴奋剂检测中心 xīngfènjì jiǎncè zhōngxīn doping control centre

兴奋性 xīngfènxìng excitability

兴风作浪 xīngfēng-zuòlàng stir up or make trouble; fan the flames of disorder: 乘机~ seize an opportunity to create disturbances /警惕有人背后~,制造纠纷。Be on guard against anybody stirring up trouble and sowing seeds of discord behind the scenes.

兴复 xīngfù revive; rejuvenate: ~故国 revive (*or* rejuvenate) one's native country; make one's native country prosper again

兴革 xīnggé 〈书面〉 initiation (of the new) and abolition (of the old); reform: 他到任后,一改旧习,多有~,受到大家的称许。Upon taking office, he abolished outdated practices and instituted reforms, thus winning extensive acclaim.

兴工 xīnggōng commence work; begin building; start construction: 破土~ break the ground to start construction

兴国 xīngguó make a country prosperous; rejuvenate a nation: 科学~ invigorate a country through science; make a country strong by relying on science

兴建 xīngjiàn erect; build; construct: ~纪念碑 erect a monument /集资~铁路 raise funds to build (*or* construct) a railway /三峡工程正在~之中。The Three Gorges Project is under way.

兴利除弊 xīnglì-chúbì promote what is beneficial and abolish what is harmful; start good practices and weed out corrupt ones: 县长到任时间不长,大刀阔斧,~,干了几件大事。Though new on the job, the county magistrate had quite a few significant achievements to his credit by instituting bold reforms to initiate good practices and weed out corrupt ones.

兴隆 xīnglóng prosperous; thriving; flourishing; brisk: 生意~通四海,财源茂盛达三江。〈套语〉 May (your) brisk business extend to the four seas and (your) resources of fortune cover the three rivers. /他为人精明,几年之间买卖越做越~,赚了大钱。An astute businessman, he managed his business so well that it flourished during the past few years and made his fortune.

兴起 xīngqǐ ❶ rise; spring up; be on the upsurge: 突然~一股呼啦圈热。A hula hoop fever sprang up. /改革之风正在全球~。The current of reform is sweeping the world. /电脑的开发和利用,在我国是二十世纪八九十年代才~的。China began to develop and use computers in the last two decades of the 20th century. ❷〈书面〉 spring to action (on stimulus): 闻风~ spring to action upon hearing the news

兴荣 xīngróng prosperous; flourishing: 从街市的繁华景象可以看出整个城市的~。The brisk business and bustle of the streets bears testimony to the prosperity of the city.

兴设 xīngshè set up; establish; found: ~学校 found a school

兴盛 xīngshèng prosperous; thriving; flourishing; in the ascendant: 民族~ flourishing of a nation /事业~ success in one's career or business /本市旅游事业十分~。This city's tourist industry is thriving.

兴师 xīngshī 〈书面〉 raise, mobilize or send an army: 奉命~,千里赴难。He was ordered to mobilize his troops and lead them over a thousand *li* to save his country (from being subjugated by foreign aggressors).

兴师动众 xīngshī-dòngzhòng mobilize an army and rally the people — drag in a great number of people (to do sth.): 这点活儿我们几个干就行了,用不着~。It takes only a few of us to do this job; there's no need to drag in a lot of people.

兴师问罪 xīngshī-wènzuì make or send a punitive expedition; bring or lead an army to punish sb. (for his crime); bring a great number of people to denounce sb. (for his wrongdoing): 他们哪里是来拜望我啊,他们是来~的。They did not come to inquire after my health; they are here to denounce me in public. /你全家人打上门来~,也不怕人家笑话。Aren't you afraid of making a spectacle of yourselves by getting your whole family here to settle old scores?

兴时 xīngshí fashionable; in vogue; all the rage: 这种服装现在不那么~了。This kind of garment is no longer so fashionable.

兴衰 xīng-shuāi prosperity and adversity; rise and fall: 读史可知历代~,增长政治才干。The study of history enables one to learn about the rise and fall of previous dynasties and add to one's political wisdom.

兴叹 xīngtàn 〈书面〉 lament (one's inadequacy, etc.): 望洋~ lament one's insignificance before the vast ocean; gaze at the vast ocean with despair

兴腾 xīngténg prosperous; thriving; flourishing: 市区熙熙攘攘,一片~的景象。Bustling with activity, the city presents a picture of prosperity.

兴替 xīng-tì 〈书面〉 rise and fall: 世事~ vicissitudes of life

兴亡 xīng-wáng rise and fall (of a nation): 国家~,匹夫有责。The rise and fall of a nation is the concern of every one of its citizens. *or* Every citizen has a share of responsibility for the fate of his nation.

兴旺 xīngwàng prosperous; flourishing; thriving; on the upgrade: 住宅建设的~时期 in the heyday of house building /乡镇企业越办越~。The township enterprises are becoming more and more thriving. /这个城市到处是一派蒸蒸日上的~景象。The city is a scene of steadily growing affluence. /政通人和,百业~。With an efficient government and harmony among the people, there is general prosperity in all walks of life.

兴修 xīngxiū start construction (on a large project); build: 这里正在~一条高速公路。An expressway is under construction here. /二环路上~了许多立交桥。Many overpasses were built across the Second Ring Road.

兴许 xīngxǔ 〈方言〉 maybe; probably; perhaps: ~他还不知道我来了。Maybe, he doesn't yet know that I am here. /~会下雨的。It looks like rain.

兴学 xīngxué set up schools (to promote education): 他在乡间~数十年,名闻海内。He was well known all over the country as he had been setting up schools to promote education in the rural areas for decades.

兴妖作怪 xīngyāo-zuòguài conjure up demons to wreak havoc; raise the devil; stir up trouble: 有人~,大家千万不可上当受骗。Somebody has taken advantage of the confusion to raise the devil; we must all be on our guard. /照这样看起来,准是许忠那小子在~啦。Judging by this evidence, it must be that rascal Xu Zhong who stirred up all the trouble.

兴中会 Xīngzhōnghuì Revive China Society, revolutionary organization set up by Dr. Sun Yat-sen in 1894 in Honolulu, and precursor of the Kuomintang

星 xīng ❶ star: 月明~稀。Few stars are seen when the moon is shining brightly. /~月无光。Both the moon and the stars were dim. *or* The moon and the stars lost their brightness. ❷ any heavenly body: 恒~ fixed star /行~ planet /彗~ comet /卫~ satellite /流~ shooting star; meteor; meteorite /白矮~ white dwarf /北斗~ Big Dipper; Plough /北极~ North Star; Polestar ❸ bit; piece; particle: 零~ tiny bit /火~儿 spark ❹ marks (resembling asterisks) on the arm of a steelyard indicating *jin* and its fractions: 定盘~ marks of weight on a steelyard ❺ famous performer; star: 影~ film (*or* movie) star /笑~ famous comedian /通俗歌~ pop star ❻ twenty-fifth of the 28 constellations in ancient astronomy ❼ (Xīng) a surname

星表 xīngbiǎo 〈天文〉 star catalogue; star chart

星辰 xīngchén stars; constellations: 日月~ sun, moon and stars

星驰 xīngchí ❶ rapidly; quickly: ~电走 quick as a shooting star or a flash of lightning /~前往 go to a place in great haste ❷ journey night and day

星虫 xīngchóng *also* "沙虫" shāchóng 〈动物〉 siphon-worm; sipunculid; peanutworm

星传感器 xīngchuángǎnqì 〈航天〉 star sensor

星岛日报 Xīngdǎo Rìbào *Sing Tao Jih Pao*, a Chinese language newspaper in Hong Kong

星等 xīngděng 〈天文〉 (stellar) magnitude: 这颗星属于什么~? Of what magnitude is the star?

星点 xīngdiǎn 〈方言〉little bit; tiny bit:县长为人和气,没~官架子。The county magistrate was an amiable man and had no airs at all. /这盘菜~滋味也没有。This dish was completely tasteless. /人走了几十年了,~消息也没有。Nothing whatever has been heard of him since he left home decades ago.
星斗 xīngdǒu stars:满天~ star studded sky
星跟踪仪 xīnggēnzōngyí 〈航天〉star tracker
星光 xīngguāng starlight:~闪烁 twinkling (*or* sparkling) stars /昨夜~灿烂。The stars were shining bright last night. *or* The sky was spangled with stars last night.
星汉 xīnghàn 〈书面〉Milky Way:~西流夜未央。Night deepened in early autumn as the Milky Way shifted westward.
星号 xīnghào asterisk (*)
星河 xīnghé Milky Way
星火 xīnghuǒ ❶ spark:点点~ tiny sparks /~闪烁 scintillating sparks ❷ shooting star; meteor:急如~ requiring lightning action; extremely pressing; most urgent
星火计划 Xīnghuǒ Jìhuà Spark Programme (popular name for the Programme for the Promotion of Technological Development in Local Economies, initiated by the State Science and Technology Commission in 1985):~大大加速了乡镇企业的发展。The Spark Programme greatly accelerated the development of township enterprises.
星火燎原 xīnghuǒ-liáoyuán *also*"星星之火,可以燎原" a single spark can start a prairie fire
星级 xīngjí star (used in the ranking of hotels):~饭店 high-class hotel (ranked by stars) /这是一家五~宾馆。This is a five-star hotel.
星际 xīngjì interplanetary; interstellar:~通信 interplanetary (*or* interstellar) communication
星际大战 xīngjì dàzhàn interplanetary warfare; star war
星际分子 xīngjì fēnzǐ interstellar molecule
星际旅行 xīngjì lǚxíng interplanetary flight or travel; interstellar flight or travel; space flight or travel
星际探测器 xīngjì tàncèqì interstellar probe
星际物质 xīngjì wùzhì interstellar matter
星际云 xīngjìyún 〈天文〉interstellar cloud
星空 xīngkōng starlit night sky; starry sky:遥望~ gaze into the starlit sky
星离雨散 xīnglí-yǔsàn *also*"星离云散"(of relatives, friends, followers, etc.) scatter; disperse:昔日同窗如今~,天各一方。My former classmates are all far apart from each other now.
星历表 xīnglìbiǎo 〈天文〉ephemeris
星罗棋布 xīngluó-qíbù be scattered all over like stars in the sky or pieces on the chessboard; be scattered all over the place:入夜的海湾,渔火点点,~。The lights of fishing boats twinkled here and there on the bay at night, dotting it like stars in the sky or pieces on the chessboard. /农民新盖的小楼~地点缀在乡镇工厂的周围。Scattered around the township factory are farmers' newly-built houses.
星命 xīngmìng 〈迷信〉star under which one was born
星盘 xīngpán astrolabe
星期 xīngqī ❶ week:每个~ every (*or* each) week /每~工作五天 work five days a week /这~ this week /上~ last week /下~ next week ❷ *used in combinations with* 日,一,二,三,四,五,六 *to denote day of the week*:~日 Sunday (Sun.) /~一 Monday (Mon.) /~二 Tuesday (Tues.) /~三 Wednesday (Wed.) /~四 Thursday (Thur.) /~五 Friday (Fri.) /~六 Saturday (Sat.) /今天~几? What day (of the week) is today? ❸ Sunday:他是每逢~必钓鱼。He goes fishing (*or* angling) every Sunday.
星期天 xīngqītiān *also*"星期日" Sunday (Sun.)
星球 xīngqiú celestial or heavenly body:人类已登上了月球,将来还将飞往其他~。Man has been to the moon and will travel to other planets in the future.
星球大战 xīngqiú dàzhàn *also*"星球大战计划"〈军事〉Star Wars — alternative name for Strategic Defense Initiative (SDI) initiated by US President Ronald Reagan (in office 1981-1989)
星球风 xīngqiúfēng stellar wind (streams of charged particles generated by stars other than the sun)
星散 xīngsàn 〈书面〉(of one's family, friends, etc.) scatter about like stars in the sky; be scattered far and wide:故人~。My old acquaintances are now scattered far and wide.
星鲨 xīngshā 〈动物〉gummy shark
星术 xīngshù *also*"占星术" zhānxīngshù astrology
星速 xīngsù with meteoric speed; in the greatest hurry:~北上 go north with maximum speed; press northward as fast as possible
星体 xīngtǐ 〈天文〉celestial or heavenly body
星条旗 Xīngtiáoqí ❶ Stars and Stripes, US national flag ❷ Star-Spangled Banner, US national anthem
星图 xīngtú 〈天文〉star chart; star map; star atlas
星团 xīngtuán 〈天文〉(star) cluster
星系 xīngxì 〈天文〉galaxy:~分类法 classification of galaxies /~团 cluster of galaxies /总~ metagalaxy
星系场 xīngxìchǎng galactic field
星系核 xīngxìhé 〈天文〉galactic nucleus; nucleus of galaxy
星系天文学 xīngxì tiānwénxué extragalactic astronomy
星系晕 xīngxìyùn galactic halo
星相 xīngxiàng 〈迷信〉horoscope; fortune-telling by stargazing and analysis of physical features (of a person)
星象 xīngxiàng configuration and movement of the stars as basis for astrology:夜观~ observe the movement of stars at night
星协 xīngxié 〈天文〉stellar association
星星 xīngxīng tiny spot; a bit:家里一~盐都没有了,快去买吧。Go and buy some salt; there isn't a bit left in the house. /~鬼火在坟地上闪动。Will-o'-the-wisps were twinkling over the graveyard.
星星 xīngxing 〈口语〉star:孩子们坐在树下数~。The children sat under the tree, counting the stars in the sky.
星星点点 xīngxīng-diǎndiǎn tiny spots; bits and pieces; fragments:这些遥远的往事,我只是~地记得一些。All I could recall were fragments of these events of the remote past. /路旁~地开着一些小黄花。Blooming little yellow flowers were seen here and there on either side of the road.
星星之火,可以燎原 xīngxīng zhī huǒ, kěyǐ liáoyuán *see*"星火燎原"
星形接线 xīngxíng jiēxiàn 〈电工〉star connection
星形三角开关 xīngxíng sānjiǎo kāiguān 〈电工〉star-delta switch
星宿 xīngxiù 〈天文〉constellation
星眼 xīngyǎn (usu. of women) bright, beautiful eyes
星夜 xīngyè on a starlit night; by night:~奔忙 be busy even at night /~行军 march on a starlit night /~兼程 hurry day and night
星移斗转 xīngyí-dǒuzhuǎn *also*"星转斗移" the stars change their positions in the sky; the seasons change; time passes:完稿之时,已是~,残夜将尽了。Time flew past, and night was almost over when I finished writing. /~又一年。Another year has passed without our noticing it.
星移物换 xīngyí-wùhuàn *also*"物换星移" the stars move and things change — change of the seasons; lapse of time
星云 xīngyún 〈天文〉nebula:旋涡~ spiral nebula /银河~ galactic nebula /蟹状~ Crab Nebula /网状~ network nebula /~团 nebulous cluster /~假说 nebular hypothesis
星占 xīngzhān divine by astrology; cast a horoscope
星占术 xīngzhānshù astrology
星震 xīngzhèn 〈天文学〉starquake
星子 xīngzi ❶ bits; pieces:吐沫~ spittle; flying bits of saliva /肉末~ tiny bits of minced meat ❷〈方言〉star:满天的~ star-studded sky
星族 xīngzú 〈天文〉stellar population
星座 xīngzuò 〈天文〉constellation
星座图 xīngzuòtú 〈天文〉planisphere

惺

xīng 〈书面〉❶ intelligent; clever ❷ come to one's senses; be sober
惺忪 xīngsōng *also*"惺松"(of eyes) not yet fully open (as on waking up); bleary-eyed:睡眼~ eyes still heavy with sleep; bleary-eyed from sleep; sleepy eyes /醉眼~ eyes heavy from the aftereffect of drinking; drunken eyes
惺惺 xīngxīng ❶〈书面〉wide awake; sober:愁绝始~。Sobriety begins where grief ends. /只为太~,惹尽闲烦恼。One suffers no end of unnecessary worry just because one is too sober. ❷ clever; intelligent:此人半是~半是愚。He is half clever and half stupid. ❸ *also*"假惺惺" jiǎxīngxīng hypocritical; unctuous
惺惺惜惺惺 xīngxīng xī xīngxīng intelligent people like intelligence in others; the clever appreciate each other; like attracts like:他们一见如故,真可谓~。Like attracts like. Though it was the first time they had met, they treated each other as old friends.
惺惺作态 xīngxīng-zuòtài be affected; pretend; simulate (friend-

ship, innocence, etc.)：～，遮遮掩掩，说话一点儿也不老实。There was not a grain of truth in his words. He was merely acting and being evasive.

腥 xīng ❶ raw meat or fish (as food)：荤～ dishes of meat or fish ❷ having the smell of fish, seafood, etc.; rank：做鱼时加点醋可去～。If you use some vinegar in cooking fish, it helps to remove its smell. /～味太重！What a strong smell of fish! *or* What a rank smell!

腥臭 xīngchòu stinking smell as of rotten fish; reek; stench：～扑鼻。A stinking smell assails one's nostrils. /有股子～味。There is a rancid (*or* rank) smell.

腥风血雨 xīngfēng-xuèyǔ *also* "血雨腥风" foul wind and rain of blood — scene of ruthless massacre; reign of terror：那是～的 1937 年，日本侵略军在中国制造了震惊世界的南京大屠杀。The year 1937 saw the bloody atrocities of the Japanese aggressor troops in China, who launched the Nanjing massacre that shocked the world.

腥黑穗病 xīnghēisuìbìng 〈农业〉bunt (a disease of wheat)

腥秽 xīnghuì foul and filthy; smelly and dirty：这东西～难闻。This is unbearably foul and filthy.

腥气 xīngqi smell of fish, seafood, etc.; rank smell：这条鱼不新鲜了，有一股子～。This fish is not fresh; it stinks. /海风吹来，带来一阵～。As the sea breeze blows inland, it carries with it a rank smell of seafood.

腥臊 xīngsāo smell of fish and urine; stench; rancid, foul smell：屋子里有一股～味。There is a rancid, foul smell in the room.

腥膻 xīngshān smell of fish or mutton：许多人不服羊肉的～。Many people are not accustomed to the strong smell of mutton.

腥味儿 xīngwèir strong smell of fish; rank smell：这鱼肉倒挺嫩的，就是～太大。This fish has tender flesh but a strong smell.

猩 xīng orangutan

猩红 xīnghóng scarlet; bloodred：远远就看见了屋前一片～的石榴花。From a distance, one could see a patch of flaming pomegranate flowers in front of the house.

猩红热 xīnghóngrè 〈医学〉scarlet fever; scarlatina

猩红蛇 xīnghóngshé scarlet snake (*Cemophora coccinea*)

猩猩 xīngxing 〈动物〉orangutan; orang; *Pongo pygmaeus*：大～ gorilla /黑～ chimpanzee

猩猩草 xīngxingcǎo 〈植物〉painted euphorbia (*Euphorbia heterophylla*)

箵 xīng *see* "笭箵" língxīng

狌 xīng *see* "猩" xīng
see also shēng

骍 xīng 〈书面〉(of horse or cattle) red

xíng

刑 xíng ❶ punishment; sentence：徒～ prison term; imprisonment /死～ capital punishment; death sentence (*or* penalty) /缓～ suspension of a sentence; reprieve; probation /判～ sentence; pass a sentence /服～ serve one's term or time (in prison) /量～ penal discretion /减～ commute a sentence; reduce punishment /～满释放 be released upon completion of a sentence /～在禁恶。Punishment is aimed at deterring wrongdoing. /～不上大夫，礼不下庶人。〈旧语〉"Punishment according to the law" does not apply to the nobility, while etiquette is not meant for the commoners. ❷ torture; corporal punishment：动～ resort to torture; put (sb.) to torture /受～ suffer torture; be tortured ❸ (Xíng) a surname

刑部 Xíngbù 〈历史〉Ministry or Board of Punishments：～尚书 Minister of Punishments /～侍郎 Deputy Minister of Punishments /～大堂 court of trial at the Ministry of Punishments /提交～审决 refer a case to the Ministry of Punishments for trial and judgement

刑场 xíngchǎng execution ground

刑典 xíngdiǎn 〈法律〉penal code

刑鼎 xíngdǐng 〈历史〉tripod inscribed with the penal code

刑罚 xíngfá penalty; punishment：根据罪犯的犯罪事实和认罪态度来确定对罪犯的～ mete out punishment in accordance with the criminal's crime and the degree of his repentance

刑罚学 xíngfáxué 〈法律〉penology：～家 penologist

刑法 xíngfǎ penal code; criminal law：触犯～ breach the penal code; violate the criminal law /修改～ amend the penal code (*or* criminal law) /～典 criminal code

刑法 xíngfa corporal punishment; torture：动～ administer corporal punishment; resort to torture /这种～太厉害了！What a cruel torture!

刑法学 xíngfǎxué criminal jurisprudence; penal jurisprudence; science of criminal law：～家 criminal law expert; penal jurist

刑房 xíngfáng ❶ 〈旧语〉official in charge of criminal prosecution and its files：～小吏 petty official in charge of criminal prosecution ❷ torture chamber：私设～ set up a torture chamber illegally

刑警 xíngjǐng (short for 刑事警察) criminal police：～队 criminal police (force) /他从小就想当一名～。He has wanted to become a criminal policeman since he was a child.

刑具 xíngjù instruments of torture or punishment; handcuffs and fetters：犯人带着～。The prisoner was wearing handcuffs and fetters.

刑戮 xínglù 〈书面〉be or put to death：免于～ escape from imprisonment and death /横遭～ be arbitrarily tortured and executed

刑律 xínglǜ criminal law：触犯～ breach (*or* violate) criminal law

刑名 xíngmíng ❶ 〈历史〉law; especially criminal law：～之学 philosophy of the legalist school ❷ kinds of punishments or penalties, such as death penalty, life imprisonment, etc. ❸ (in the Qing Dynasty) secretary or official in charge of criminal prosecution：～师爷 secretary (to a government magistrate) specialized in law and in charge of criminal prosecution

刑期 xíngqī 〈法律〉term of imprisonment; prison term：～三年 three-year prison term /他服刑九年，～快满了。Having been in prison for nine years, he had almost completed his term.

刑辱 xíngrǔ 〈书面〉humiliating torture：在狱中，他受尽了～。When in prison, he was subjected to a full measure of humiliating torture.

刑事 xíngshì 〈法律〉criminal; penal：～案件 criminal case

刑事处分 xíngshì chǔfèn criminal sanction：免于～ be exempted from criminal sanction

刑事法庭 xíngshì fǎtíng criminal court or tribunal

刑事犯 xíngshìfàn criminal offender; criminal

刑事犯罪 xíngshì fànzuì criminal offence; criminal act

刑事管辖权 xíngshì guǎnxiáquán criminal jurisdiction

刑事检控专员 Xíngshì Jiǎnkòng Zhuānyuán (HK before 1 July 1997) Crown Prosecutor

刑事警察 xíngshì jǐngchá criminal police

刑事拘留 xíngshì jūliú criminal detention or custody

刑事判决 xíngshì pànjué verdict in a criminal case; sentence on a criminal

刑事诉讼 xíngshì sùsòng criminal suit; criminal proceedings; criminal procedure：～法 code of criminal procedure; criminal procedure law

刑事责任 xíngshì zérèn responsibility for a crime; criminal responsibility

刑事侦察 xíngshì zhēnchá criminal investigation

刑事罪 xíngshìzuì 〈法律〉criminal charge; penal offence

刑释 xíngshì be released after serving one's sentence：～分子 ex-convict

刑堂 xíngtáng 〈旧语〉torture chamber

刑庭 xíngtíng (short for 刑事法庭) criminal court or tribunal

刑网 xíngwǎng net of criminal law; long arm of the (criminal) law：陷入～ get caught in the net of criminal law; get into trouble through violating criminal law

刑讯 xíngxùn 〈法律〉question or interrogate by torture：～逼供 extort a confession by torture; subject (sb.) to torture to obtain a confession /在～之下，他只好承认自己犯了杀人罪。When subjected to torture, he had no choice but to plead guilty to manslaughter.

刑余 xíngyú 〈旧语〉❶ *also* "刑余之人" survivor of torture, punishment or prison term; ex-convict ❷ castrated man; eunuch

刑杖 xíngzhàng rod or bunch of sticks used in ancient times as instrument of torture：毙于～之下 die of torture

刑侦 xíngzhēn (short for 刑事侦察) criminal investigation

刑种 xíngzhǒng forms of penalty

型 xíng ❶ mould:砂～ sand mould ❷ model; type; variety; pattern:句～ sentence pattern /新～飞机 new-model plane /重～卡车 heavy-duty truck (*or* lorry) /小～水库 small reservoir /中～企业 medium-size enterprise /血～ blood group /脸～ cast of one's features (*or* face) /流线～ streamline

型板 xíngbǎn 〈机械〉template; templet

型棒 xíngbàng 〈冶金〉shaped rod

型材 xíngcái 〈冶金〉bar section; section material; sections:～矫直机 section-straightening machine

型锻 xíngduàn 〈冶金〉swaged forging; swaging; swage process: ～机 swaging machine /～模 swaging die; swage

型钢 xínggāng 〈冶金〉section (steel); shape (steel):～轧辊 shape roll

型钢矫形机 xínggāng jiǎoxíngjī shape straightener

型钢轧机 xínggāng zhájī section mill; shape (rolling) mill

型号 xínghào model; type:多种～的钢材 various types of steel

型砂 xíngshā 〈机械〉moulding sand:～控制 sand control /～挤压机 squeezer

型铁 xíngtiě 〈冶金〉sectional iron

型心 xíngxīn 〈冶金〉core:干砂～ baked core /湿砂～ green sand core /～砂 core sand; foundry core sand /～车床 core turning lathe /～烘干炉 core-baking oven /～机 core machine

型压铸造 xíngyā zhùzào 〈冶金〉squeeze casting; liquid forging

硎 xíng 〈书面〉❶ grinding stone; whetstone ❷ grind; polish

铏 xíng 〈古语〉tripod with two ears for holding vegetable custard

钘 xíng ❶ wine container used in ancient times ❷ *see* "铏" xíng

形 xíng ❶ form; appearance; shape:方～ square /圆～ round; circular /三角～ triangular /图～ map; plan; figure /地～ topography; terrain /～丑心善 look ugly but be kind at heart /～似实非 similar in appearance but different in essence /水无常～。Water has no constant form. *or* Water is formless. ❷ body; entity:有～ tangible; visible /无～ intangible; invisible ❸ appear; seem; look: 喜怒不～于色 able to conceal one's pleasure or anger; not to wear one's joy and displeasure on the face /～诸笔墨 put down in black and white ❹ compare; contrast:相～见绌 prove inferior by comparison; pale into insignificance (by contrast); be outshone

形变 xíngbiàn 〈物理〉deformation:长程～ long-range deformation /纵向～ longitudinal deformation /弹性～ elastic deformation / ～带 deformation band /～效应 deformation effect /～张量 deformation tensor

形成 xíngchéng form; take shape; shape up:～强烈反差 form a sharp contrast /～多极化的局面 take the form of multipolarity /石灰岩经地下水长期侵蚀～了这种岩洞。Such caves came into being after prolonged erosion of limestone by underground water. /这是他多年来～的习惯。This is one of the habits he developed (*or* formed) over the years. /安定团结的局面已经～。A situation of stability and unity has taken shape.

形成层 xíngchéngcéng 〈植物〉cambium

形单影只 xíngdān-yǐngzhī *also* "形只影单" solitary form, single shadow — extremely lonely; all on one's own; solitary:丈夫去世后, 她～,孤独地生活了十几年。After her husband's death, she was all on her own and lived on for a dozen of years or so in solitude. /每当夜幕降临,他感到～,心情郁闷。When night fell, he would feel extremely lonely and depressed.

形而上学 xíng'érshàngxué *also* "玄学" xuánxué 〈哲学〉❶ metaphysics ❷ world outlook or methodology opposed to dialectic materialism; static, isolated and one-sided approach to things of the world

形格势禁 xínggé-shìjìn 〈书面〉prohibited or impeded by circumstances:此书成稿后,由于～,一直未能问世。Due to the constraint of circumstances, the book was not published after the completion of the manuscripts.

形骸 xínghái 〈书面〉human body:放浪～ indulge in bodily (*or* sensual) pleasures; take to debauchery

形迹 xíngjì ❶ (a person's) movements and look:不露～ betray nothing in one's expression or behaviour /他康复得很快,已经没有一点病人的～了。He has recovered so fast that he does not look like a patient at all. ❷ sign (left behind); trace; mark:不留～ leave no trace /有～可寻 have some traces to follow ❸ etiquette; formality: 不拘～ without formality; not standing on ceremony

形迹可疑 xíngjì-kěyí suspicious in appearance; suspicious-looking:几个～的人受到了盘查。Several suspicious-looking people were interrogated.

形景 xíngjǐng condition; situation:～可怜 be in a sorry state (of affairs); be in a pitiable plight

形貌 xíngmào form and appearance; look:他的衣着～与当地人一样。He was dressed and behaved in the same way as the local people.

形旁 xíngpáng *see* "形声"

形容 xíngróng ❶〈书面〉look; appearance; countenance:～枯槁 look wizened /～憔悴 wan-looking; thin and pallid; gaunt; haggard /尸体已经腐烂,～难辨。As the corpse had decomposed, it was hard to recognize its features. ❷ describe:难以～ hard to describe; beyond description; beyond words /我简直无法～当时的心情。I can hardly describe my feelings at the time. /你把她～得太美了。You've painted too beautiful a picture of her. *or* You've made her out to be more beautiful than she is.

形容词 xíngróngcí 〈语言〉adjective

形色 xíngsè ❶ appearance and expression; look:～焦灼 look (*or* appear) worried ❷ image and colour:～鲜明 vivid image and bright colour

形声 xíngshēng *also* "谐声" xiéshēng 〈语言〉pictophonetic method of word-formation in Chinese (one of six major methods but accounting for 80% of all characters), with one element of a character indicating meaning and the other sound, e.g. in the character 秧 (seedling), the left-hand element (*or* radical) 禾 indicates meaning (grass), while the right-hand element 央 denotes pronunciation

形胜 xíngshèng 〈书面〉advantageous or favourable terrain; magnificent geographical situation:～之地 land (*or* place) of strategic terrain /山川～ magnificent mountains and rivers

形式 xíngshì form; mode; shape:从内容到～ both in content and in form /组织～ form of organization /表现～ mode of expression /不拘～ not stand on formality; be flexible /以书面～提出建议 put forward suggestions in writing /～上的夫妻关系 nominal ties of marriage; man and wife only in a legal (*or* nominal) sense /～上的一致 formal unity; unity in appearance only

形式逻辑 xíngshì luójí 〈逻辑〉formal logic

形式系统 xíngshì xìtǒng formal system

形式主义 xíngshìzhǔyì formalism:～法学 formalist jurisprudence

形势 xíngshì ❶ terrain; topography:～险要 strategically advantageous terrain /山川～ topographical features of mountains and rivers ❷ state of affairs; situation; circumstances:政治～ political situation /生产～ situation in production; how things are going in production /～严峻 grim situation; trying circumstances /目前～ current situation; as things now stand /实事求是地估计～ appraise (*or* estimate) the situation realistically; see things as they are

形势逼人 xíngshì-bīrén the situation is critical or pressing; the situation calls for prompt action

形似 xíngsì be similar (*or* resemble) in form or appearance:～不如神似。Formal resemblance is not as good as similarity in spirit. /两者～,只是大小不同。The two look similar and differ only in size.

形态 xíngtài ❶ form; shape; state; pattern:意识～ ideology /观念～ concept /～万千 multifarious in form; myriads of forms; multiform /～各异 all different in shape (*or* form) /人的～美 beauty of the human figure /水有三种～:液态、固态、气态。Water has three states: liquid, solid and gaseous. /小鸭的～活泼可爱。The duckling looks lovely. ❷〈语言〉〈生物〉morphology:生物的～ morphology of organisms

形态学 xíngtàixué 〈语言〉〈生物〉morphology

形态音位学 xíngtài yīnwèixué 〈语言〉morphophonemics

形体 xíngtǐ ❶ shape (of a person's body); figure; physique; body:北京猿人的～模型 model of the body of a Peking man /舞蹈演员的优美～ graceful figure of a dancer ❷ form and structure:汉字的～特点 features (*or* characteristics) of the form and structure of

X

Chinese characters

形同虚设 xíngtóngxūshè exist in name only:执法不严,法律岂不~? Without vigorous enforcement, laws will just be so much waste paper.

形稳性 xíngwěnxìng 〈纺织〉 dimensional stability

形相 xíngxiàng form and shape; appearance:看人不能只看~ cannot judge a person by his appearance alone /我们只见过一面,对他的~只有一个模糊的印象。I have only a vague impression of what he looks like as I met him only once.

形象 xíngxiàng ❶ image; figure; object; form:孩子的天真~ innocent image of a child /儿童通过实物~来识字。Children learn Chinese characters by observing objects. /这个国家有个~的问题。The country has an image problem. ❷ literary or artistic image; imagery:艺术~ artistic image /人物~的创造 creation of figures; characterization /文学通过~来反映社会生活。Literary works reflect social life through images. ❸ vivid; graphic; expressive:~的比喻 vivid figure of speech /童话~地讽刺了富人的贪婪。The fairy tale satirizes the greed of the rich in a graphic manner.

形象思维 xíngxiàng sīwéi *also* "艺术思维" yìshù sīwéi thinking in (terms of) images:文艺创作主要靠~。Literary and artistic creation depends mainly upon images.

形销骨立 xíngxiāo-gǔlì be reduced to a mere bag of bones; be emaciated:对丈夫的思念,使她~。Missing her husband, she was a shadow of her former self.

形肖神似 xíngxiào-shénsì be alike both in appearance and in spirit:他画的奔马,可以说是~。His paintings of galloping horses are true to life, both in appearance and in spirit.

形形色色 xíngxíng-sèsè of every colour and hue; of many varieties; of all shades; of all forms:~的人物 people of every description /~的刑事案件 various kinds of criminal cases /~的官僚主义 bureaucratism in its myriad forms

形意拳 xíngyìquán *also* "心意拳" xīnyìquán, shadow boxing that imitates the movements of animals or birds of various kinds (e.g. the dragon, tiger, monkey, horse, bear, cock, swallow, or eagle) and integrates physical motions with concentration of the mind

形影 xíngyǐng ❶ body and shadow; object and reflection:~相追 like body and shadow chasing each other; cheek by jowl /~孑立 live with only one's shadow for companion; live all alone ❷ shadow:窗子上映出了女主人的~。The shadow of the mistress was reflected on the window.

形影不离 xíngyǐng-bùlí inseparable as body and shadow; in each other's company all the time; always together:新婚夫妇如胶似漆,~。The newly-wed couple stuck to each other like glue and were always together. /这把剑久已和我~。This sword has long been with me like a shadow following its body.

形影相吊 xíngyǐng-xiāngdiào body and shadow comforting each other — accompanied only by one's shadow; extremely lonely; sad and solitary:从此以后,他只能~,暗自伤神。From then on, he would only have his own shadow to keep him company and bemoan his miserable solitude to himself.

形影相随 xíngyǐng-xiāngsuí always together as body and shadow; inseparable:~的好朋友 close friends who are always together

形于辞色 xíngyúcísè show in one's words and look:他一向感情外露,喜怒~。He is a person who is always loath to hide his feelings.

形制 xíngzhì (as of objects or buildings) shape and structure:这一对花瓶的~别具特色。The shape of this pair of vases is quite unique. /博物馆的~颇具民族特色。The structure of the museum presents distinct national characteristics.

形诸笔墨 xíngzhūbǐmò put in black and white; commit to writing:愤怒之情不免~ show one's indignation in one's writing

形状 xíngzhuàng shape; form; countenance; appearance:~丑陋 ugly in shape; ugly-looking /别具一格的~ unique form /这两种产品的~差不多。The two products look quite similar.

形左实右 xíngzuǒ-shíyòu Left in form but Right in essence

邢 Xíng a surname

荥(滎) xíng

荥阳 Xíngyáng county in Henan Province

行 xíng

❶ go; walk; travel:出~ go out; be out /步~ go on foot; walk /人~道 pavement; sidewalk /日~夜宿 travel by day and sleep by night /~不更名,坐不改姓。Whether I travel or stay at home, I never change my name. ❷ 〈古语〉 journey; road:千里之~,始于足下。A thousand-*li* road (*or* journey) begins with the first step. ❸ travel:欧洲之~ trip to Europe /送~ see sb. off; give sb. a send-off /辞~ take leave; say goodbye /此~何处?〈书面〉 Where are you bound for this time? ❹ temporary; makeshift:~灶 makeshift (*or* portable) cooking stove ❺ be current; prevail; circulate:施~ execute; implement /雷厉风~ carry out a policy vigorously and speedily /发~期刊 publish periodicals ❻ do; act; practise; implement:试~ implement on a trial basis; try out /量力而~ do what is within one's means (*or* capability); act according to one's ability /~得通 will do; will work /~不开 won't work; will get nowhere ❼ *used before a two-character verb to express the performance of the action*:即~查复 check and reply promptly /另~通知 till further notice ❽ (formerly pronounced xìng) behaviour; conduct; deeds:操~ character; conduct /善~ virtuous conduct; philanthropic deeds /言~ words and deeds /兽~ bestial act; atrocity /~不逾方 never exceed what is proper in one's behaviour; behave in a fit and proper way ❾ will do; be all right:你不来可不~。It won't do if you stay away. /走着去也~。It's all right if we walk there. /炖肉~了,可以出锅了。The stewed meat is okay and ready for the dinner-table. /你替我将这封信寄了,~吗? Will you please post this letter for me? ❿ able; capable; competent:他干活~,当车间主任就不~了。He is a good worker all right but doesn't make a competent floor manager. /我笔杆子不~。I'm no good at writing. *or* I'm not much of a writer. /你演老太太真~啊! You are terrific (*or* just great) at acting an old lady. ⓫ 〈书面〉 presently; shortly; soon:~将毕业 will graduate shortly (*or* soon) /~将灭亡 will soon perish; be on one's last legs ⓬ (of medicine) take effect ⓭ (Xíng) a surname

see also háng; hàng; héng

行百里者半九十 xíngbǎilǐzhě bàn jiǔshí ninety *li* is only half of a hundred-*li* journey — the nearer the end of a journey the tougher the going; one must not relax one's effort when a task is nearing completion

行板 xíngbǎn 〈乐器〉 andante

行波 xíngbō 〈无线电〉 travelling wave:~管 travelling wave tube /~加速器 travelling-wave accelerator /~放大器 travelling-wave amplifier /~天线 (travelling-)wave antenna

行不通 xíngbutōng unworkable; impracticable:这种办法~。This method won't work.

行藏 xíngcáng 〈书面〉 ❶ conduct; one's attitude towards an official career (e.g. appointment, promotion, demotion, dismissal, retirement, etc.) *see also* "用行舍藏" yòngxíng-shěcáng ❷ whereabouts; traces:问其~ inquire about sb.'s whereabouts /不露~ not disclose (*or* reveal) one's whereabouts (*or* traces) /看破~ see through sb.'s deeds

行草 xíngcǎo (of Chinese calligraphy) style of handwriting between the running hand and the cursive hand

行车 xíngchē drive (a vehicle):~速度 driving speed /~里程 distance travelled by a vehicle; mileage /~执照 driver's (*or* driving) license /安全~ safe driving /~十万公里无事故 have driven over 100,000 kilometres without an accident

see also hángchē

行成 xíngchéng 〈书面〉 seek a peaceful solution (to a dispute); seek or negotiate peace

行成于思 xíngchéngyúsī a deed is accomplished through taking thought; success depends on careful thought or planning:~而毁于随。Success comes from forethought, while thoughtlessness leads to failure.

行程 xíngchéng ❶ distance of travel; travel route:~万里 10,000 *li* journey; extremely long journey /去那里乘火车需两日~。It takes two days to go there by train. /不到长城非好汉,屈指~二万。If we fail to reach the Great Wall we are not men, We who have already measured twenty thousand *li*. ❷ course; process:历史发展的~ course of historical development ❸ *also* "冲程" chōngchéng 〈机械〉 stroke; throw; travel:滑枕~ ram stroke /偏心轮~ throw of an eccentric (wheel)/活塞~ pistol travel /~线 throw line

行驰 xíngchí drive; run:吉普车~在山间小路上。The jeep was running on a mountain road.

行船 xíngchuán sail; navigate:顺水~ sail with the waves (*or* current) /逆水~ navigate a ship against the waves; sail against the

current

行刺 xíngcì assassinate:～仇人 (try to) assassinate one's enemy / ～不成 fail in one's attempt to assassinate; attempt an assassination (without success)

行道 xíngdào 〈旧语〉 implement or carry out one's (political) ideas or ideals:志在～ determined to implement one's ideas /替天～ (formerly a favorite slogan adopted by rebels, etc. to justify their own actions) implement political ideals in the name of Heaven; do Heaven's bidding

see also hángdao

行道树 xíngdàoshù roadside or sidewalk trees

行得通 xíngdetōng workable; practicable:这个计划未必～。This plan may not work.

行动 xíngdòng ❶ move or get about:～不便 have difficulty getting about /他病好多了,可以下床稍微～了。He is much better and can move about a bit. /老人躺在床上不能～。The old man is confined to bed. ❷ act; operate; move:下一步～ next move; what to do next /按计划～ act according to plan; proceed as planned /法律～ legal action /军事～ military operation /～纲领 programme of action /～反常 act (*or* behave) abnormally /～起来,搞好环境保护。Go into action and do a good job of environmental protection.

行都 xíngdū provisional capital

行方便 xíng fāngbian make things easy (for sb.); be accommodating; do a favour:求您行个方便。Please do me a favour.

行房 xíngfáng 〈婉词〉 (as between husband and wife) sexual intercourse; sex; love-making

行歌坐月 xínggē-zuòyuè *also* "行歌坐夜" singing folk songs while walking and courting under the moon — a traditional way of communication and courting among the young men and women of the Dong nationality in southwest China

行宫 xínggōng imperial palace or temporary dwelling place for (the emperor's) short stays when away from the capital

行贾 xínggǔ 〈书面〉 ❶ itinerant trader; pedlar ❷ travel for business purposes; do business away from home

行好 xínghǎo act charitably; be merciful; do a favour; forgive:您老行行好,给点钱吧。Sir, please be merciful and give me some money! /求您行行好,别把这事告诉别人。Please do me a favour by keeping this a secret.

行贿 xínghuì offer a bribe; resort to bribery; grease sb.'s palm:～受贿 offer and accept bribes /四处～ bribe one's way through; grease everybody's palm /用～的手段拉人下水 corrupt sb. through bribery

行贿受贿分子 xínghuì-shòuhuìfènzǐ corruptionist

行贿受贿罪 xínghuì-shòuhuìzuì offence of bribery

行贿者 xínghuìzhě briber

行迹 xíngjì movements; whereabouts; tracks; traces:～可疑 suspicious (*or* dubious) movements /他～不定,四海为家。His whereabouts were uncertain as he roamed all over the country.

行奸 xíngjiān commit adultery

行检 xíngjiǎn ❶〈书面〉moral conduct or character:不修～ not cultivate one's moral character /无～ without character ❷ (short for 行李检查) luggage inspection; baggage check

行间 xíngjiàn (attempt to) sow discord among one's enemies:此次～不成,只好另谋他策。Failure to sow discord among their enemies forced them to think up another course of action.

行将 xíngjiāng 〈书面〉 soon; about to; on the point of:～就绪 about to be ready /～落成 (as of construction) nearing completion /由于生态环境遭到破坏,许多动植物～绝种。Many species of animals and plants are on the verge of extinction due to the destruction of ecosystems.

行将就木 xíngjiāng-jiùmù be drawing near the coffin — be fast approaching death; be near one's death; have one foot in the grave; one's days are numbered:我年届八十,已是～之人,但也要为国家、为民族做点事情。Although I am already eighty and have one foot in the grave, I should also do my bit for my country and nation.

行脚 xíngjiǎo (of a monk) travel far and wide

行脚僧 xíngjiǎosēng itinerant monk

行劫 xíngjié commit robbery:白日～ commit robbery in broad daylight /结伙～ gang up to rob /～杀人 kill to rob

行进 xíngjìn advance; march:队伍在大雨中～。The procession (*or* troops) marched through the heavy rain. /车队沿着新修的高速公路～。The motorcade was driving along the new expressway.

行经 xíngjīng ❶〈生理〉menstruate ❷ go by or through:此次列车～郑州、西安,直达成都。This train goes to Chengdu via Zhengzhou and Xi'an.

行径 xíngjìng 〈贬义〉 act; move:掠夺～ act of plunder /无耻～ despicable (*or* shameful) act /愚蠢～ foolish move (*or* conduct)

行酒 xíngjiǔ serve a round of drinks:主人起身～。The host stood up and served a round of drinks to the guests.

行军 xíngjūn (of troops) march:夜～ night march; march by night /急～ forced march; rapid march /～警戒 security on the march /部队经过长途～到达这个小镇待命。The troops stopped at the small town after a prolonged march to wait for further orders.

行军虫 xíngjūnchóng *also* "黏虫" niánchóng 〈方言〉 armyworm

行军床 xíngjūnchuáng *also* "帆布床" fānbùchuáng camp bed; camp cot

行军锅 xíngjūnguō field cauldron

行军壶 xíngjūnhú canteen

行军灶 xíngjūnzào field kitchen

行楷 xíngkǎi (of Chinese calligraphy) style of handwriting between the running hand and the regular script

行客 xíngkè passers-by; traveller:～拜坐客。It is up to the traveller to call on his (*or* her) friends in town.

行乐 xínglè 〈书面〉amuse oneself; indulge in merry making:及时～ enjoy the pleasures of life here and now; make merry (*or* enjoy life) while one can /虽然他每晚都到舞厅去～,其实并不幸福。Though he sought amusement in dancing halls every evening, he was not happy.

行礼 xínglǐ ❶ salute; greet:举手～ raise one's hand in salute /行注目礼 salute with one's eyes /相见之时,他们一一躬身～。They bowed to each other one by one when they met. ❷〈方言〉give a present:派人～ send sb. to present a gift

行李 xíngli luggage; baggage:托运两件～ check two pieces of luggage /～超重 excess luggage (*or* baggage) /随身～ hand-luggage; carry-on baggage /～标签 luggage label; baggage tag /～提取处 baggage claim

行李车 xínglichē luggage van; baggage car

行李寄存处 xíngli jìcúnchù left-luggage office; checkroom

行李架 xínglijià luggage or baggage rack

行李卷儿 xínglijuǎnr bedroll; bedding roll; bedding pack

行李票 xínglipiào luggage or baggage check

行猎 xíngliè 〈书面〉 hunt; go hunting:秋日～ go hunting in autumn /～图 (of a painting) hunting scene

行令 xínglìng play drinkers' wager game:猜拳～ play the drinkers' finger-guessing and wager games (in either case, the loser takes a drink)

行旅 xínglǚ traveller; wayfarer:剽劫～ waylay (*or* rob) travellers /～往来,络绎不绝。There is an unending stream of travellers to and fro. /交通闭塞,～甚感不便。Due to lack of transport services, people find it inconvenient to travel.

行门户 xíng ménhù 〈方言〉 present or give gifts

行囊 xíngnáng 〈书面〉travelling bag:他收拾好～,匆匆赶往火车站。He packed a bag and hurried to the railway station.

行骗 xíngpiàn practise deception; swindle; cheat:此人经常装扮港商～。This man often disguises himself as a Hong Kong businessman in his swindles.

行聘 xíngpìn 〈旧语〉present gifts to consummate a betrothal

行期 xíngqī date of departure:～在即,诸事尚未就绪。Although the date of departure is drawing near, everything is not yet in order.

行乞 xíngqǐ go begging; beg one's bread; beg:挨门～ beg from door to door /以～为生 beg for a living

行气 xíngqì 〈中医〉promote and normalize the flow of vital energy (in curing indispositions such as constriction in the chest and abdominal distension)

行腔 xíngqiāng 〈戏曲〉sing a tune:～咬字 sing (tunes) and declaim (lines)

行窃 xíngqiè commit theft; steal:～失手,被人抓住 be caught while stealing

行箧 xíngqiè 〈书面〉travelling suitcase:～已备,即可启程。As the luggage is packed, we can set out right away.

行取 xíngqǔ 〈旧语〉send an official order to have a local official transferred to a post in the capital

行人 xíngrén pedestrian:～走便道。Pedestrians must keep to the sidewalk (*or* footpath). /～过马路,要走人行横道。Pedestrians must

cross the streets by the zebra crossing.

行人情 xíng rénqíng 〈旧语〉present a gift or visit in person to express one's congratulations or condolences; do a favour:他儿子结婚,来~的亲友真不少。Numerous friends and relatives came to offer gifts and congratulations on the occasion of his son's wedding. /他从未为~而违犯制度。He never did personal favours in violation of rules and regulations.

行若狗彘 xíngruògǒuzhì *also* "行同狗彘" behave like curs and swine — act abominably:这家伙无恶不作,~,乡里人恨之入骨。People in the town hated the guts of this fellow, as he stopped at nothing in his evildoings.

行若无事 xíngruòwúshì behave as if nothing had happened; behave with perfect composure or total indifference:在这样非常严重的局势中,他~,表现得异常镇定。Even in such a grave situation, he remained cool and collected, as if nothing out of the ordinary were happening.

行色 xíngsè state of mind at departure; circumstances or style of departure:以壮~ (by giving a grand send-off, etc.) give (sb.) a boost before his (*or* her) departure; enable sb. to depart in style

行色匆匆 xíngsè-cōngcōng set out on one's journey in a great hurry

行善 xíngshàn do good deeds or works; be charitable:~修好 do good (*or* philanthropic) deeds /乐于~ take pleasure in doing good /~不图报 not expect a reward for one's good works

行商 xíngshāng travelling merchant; itinerant trader:~坐贾 itinerant traders and resident merchants

行赏 xíngshǎng present awards; bestow rewards or honours:论功~ give awards according to contributions

行尸走肉 xíngshī-zǒuròu walking corpse; zombies; utterly worthless person:如同~ be no different from a walking corpse; be as good as dead; be all but dead /饱食终日,无所事事,岂不成了~? If one eats three square meals a day without doing a stick of work, isn't one an utterly worthless person?

行时 xíngshí (of a thing) be fashionable; be in vogue; (of a person) be in the ascendant:此物必当~于世。This will surely be all the rage some day. /今夏超短裙颇为~。Miniskirts are much in vogue this summer. /他现在春风得意,颇为~。Now that he is in the ascendant, luck goes his way.

行实 xíngshí 〈书面〉❶ one's accomplishments in life ❷ write-up of one's career or accomplishments; résumé

行食 xíngshí ❶〈书面〉loaf about:~之徒 loafer; ne'er-do-well ❷ (often used in the early vernacular) walk after a meal to help digestion

行使 xíngshǐ exercise; perform; use:对香港恢复~主权 resume the exercise of sovereignty over Hong Kong /~职权 perform one's official functions

行驶 xíngshǐ (of a vehicle, ship, etc.) go; drive; ply; travel:飞速~ speedy or rapid travel /安全~ safe driving /公共汽车向北~。The bus is going north. /三峡工程完成后,长江中游将可以~万吨轮船。The completion of the Three-Gorges Project will render the middle reaches of the Yangtze River navigable by 10,000-ton steamers.

行世 xíngshì see the world; become popular:这篇著作就要出版~了。This work will soon be published.

行事 xíngshì ❶ behave or conduct oneself:他为人~,一向得体。He always conducts himself with impeccable propriety. ❷ do things; act:不会~ not good at doing things; no good as a man of action /看人~ act differently with different people /见机~ act as the occasion requires; act according to circumstances; do as one sees fit

行书 xíngshū (of Chinese calligraphy) running script; running hand

行署 xíngshǔ *see* "行政公署"

行述 xíngshù *see* "行状"

行水 xíngshuǐ 〈书面〉❶ flowing water:~畅通。The water flows smoothly. ❷ (of boats and ships) ply the waters; sail; navigate ❸ work in flood control ❹ inspect the waters; inspect a flood:~人员 flood inspectors

行所无事 xíngsuǒwúshì *see* "行若无事"

行头 xíngtou ❶ actor's costumes and paraphernalia:公司派了辆车替剧团运~。The corporation assigned a truck to carry the costumes and paraphernalia of the theatrical troupe. /演员们已穿戴好~,准备上场。The cast are all dressed up for the stage. ❷〈戏谑〉clothing:不瞒诸位,我只有这一身~,弄脏了我怎么出门? To tell you the truth, this is the only suit I have. What shall I go out in if it gets soiled?

行为 xíngwéi behaviour; conduct; act:不检点的~ indiscreet (*or* improper) behaviour, conduct or act; indiscretion /合理~ reasonable (*or* legitimate) act (*or* conduct) /~不轨 conspiratorial act /~模式 behaviour pattern /~良好 be well behaved

行为规范 xíngwéi guīfàn code of conduct

行为经济学 xíngwéi jīngjìxué behavioural economics

行为科学 xíngwéi kēxué behavioural science

行为能力 xíngwéi nénglì 〈法律〉disposing capacity; capacity

行为心理学 xíngwéi xīnlǐxué behavioural psychology

行为学 xíngwéixué ethology

行为遗传学 xíngwéi yíchuánxué behavioural genetics

行为主义 xíngwéizhǔyì 〈心理〉behaviourism

行文 xíngwén ❶ style or manner of writing:~尖刻 (of an author) wield a caustic pen; (of writing) be sharply-worded /~流畅 (of an author) write fluently; (of an article) read smoothly /这篇文章思路清晰,~简洁。This article is clearly thought out and succinctly written. ❷ (of a government office) send an official communication (to other organizations):~呈报 submit an official report to higher authorities /向下属单位~ send an official communication to subordinate organizations

行息 xíngxī pay interest at a given rate:牲畜、车辆折价,按一分五~。The draft animals and vehicles shall be evaluated and interest paid at a rate of 15%.

行销 xíngxiāo be on sale:~各地 be marketed (*or* on sale) in various places

行星 xíngxīng 〈天文〉planet:内~ inferior (*or* interior) planet /外~ superior (*or* outer) planet /大~ major planet /小~ minor planet; planetoid

行星齿轮 xíngxīng chǐlún 〈机械〉epicyclic gear; planetary gear:~系 planetary gear train

行星际 xíngxīngjì 〈航天〉interplanetary:自动~站 automatic interplanetary station /~飞船 interplanetary spacecraft /~探测器 interplanetary probe /~磁场 interplanetary magnetic field /~监测平台 interplanetary monitoring platform /~介质 interplanetary medium /~物质 interplanetary matter

行星卫星 xíngxīng wèixīng other-than-earth satellite

行星学 xíngxīngxué planetology

行刑 xíngxíng carry out a death sentence; execute:~人员 executioner /~队 execution (*or* firing) squad

行凶 xíngxiōng commit physical assault or murder; commit acts of violence:~杀人 commit murder (*or* manslaughter) /~打人 commit physical assault; assault sb. /~作恶 resort to physical violence and evildoing

行医 xíngyī practise medicine (usu. on one's own):~执照 permit to practise medicine; medical practitioner's license /无照~ practise medicine without a license

行吟 xíngyín recite poems while walking:~泽畔 recite (*or* chant) poems as one walks by a pond

行营 xíngyíng 〈旧语〉field headquarters:大元帅~ generalissimo's field headquarters

行辕 xíngyuán *see* "行营"

行远自迩 xíngyuǎn-zì'ěr a long journey starts with the first step; things must be done step by step; one must start with easy things before one proceeds to tackle difficult subjects

行云流水 xíngyún-liúshuǐ (of style of writing) like floating clouds and running streams — (write) with natural grace:这部小说的结构犹如~,层次分明、流畅自如。The novel is well-organized; like floating clouds and running streams, it is coherent in its development of plot and characterized by natural fluency and grace.

行在 xíngzài 〈旧语〉emperor's temporary abode on tour of inspection

行灶 xíngzào portable cooking stove

行者 xíngzhě ❶〈书面〉traveller:负者歌于途,~休于树。As porters were singing on their way, travellers were resting under the trees. /~络绎,游人不绝。There was an uninterrupted stream of travellers and tourists. ❷〈佛教〉unshaven monk

行针 xíngzhēn 〈中医〉manipulate the needle (in acupuncture)

行政 xíngzhèng administration; the executive:~区划 administrative division /~部门 administrative department; (in contrast with the legislative or judiciary) the executive branch; administration /~委员会 administrative council /~机构 administrative organ (*or*

agency）/～能力 administrative ability /～助理 administrative assistant /～纠纷 administrative dispute /～协定 administrative agreement /～费用 expenses of administration
行政处分 xíngzhèng chǔfèn administrative sanction; disciplinary sanction
行政村 xíngzhèngcūn administrative village (grass-roots administrative unit in rural areas, consisting of one or more hamlets)
行政当局 xíngzhèng dāngjú administrative authorities; executive authorities
行政法 xíngzhèngfǎ 〈法律〉administrative law
行政法规 xíngzhèng fǎguī administrative statute
行政法院 xíngzhèng fǎyuàn administrative court
行政干预 xíngzhèng gānyù administrative intervention
行政公署 xíngzhèng gōngshǔ *also* "行署" administrative office — local organ of power established under the provincial government to govern a number of counties; prefectural government
行政管理 xíngzhèng guǎnlǐ administration
行政管辖权 xíngzhèng guǎnxiáquán 〈法律〉administrative jurisdiction
行政会议 Xíngzhèng Huìyì (HK) Executive Council
行政机关 xíngzhèng jīguān administrative organ; administration
行政拘留 xíngzhèng jūliú 〈法律〉administrative detention; administrative attachment
行政立法 xíngzhèng lìfǎ administrative legislation
行政命令 xíngzhèng mìnglìng administrative decree or order
行政区 xíngzhèngqū ❶ administrative area or region: 香港特别～ Hong Kong Special Administrative Region ❷ administrative division
行政人员 xíngzhèng rényuán administrative personnel or staff
行政事业单位 xíngzhèng shìyè dānwèi government departments and state institutions
行政司 Xíngzhèngsī (HK before 1 July 1997) Secretary for Administrative Services and Information
行政诉讼 xíngzhèng sùsòng administrative lawsuit
行政诉讼法 xíngzhèng sùsòngfǎ administrative procedural law
行政预算 xíngzhèng yùsuàn administrative budget
行政院 Xíngzhèngyuàn Executive *Yuan* (China before 1949): ～院长 premier of the Executive *Yuan*
行政长官 Xíngzhèng Zhǎngguān (HK) Chief Executive
行政职务 xíngzhèng zhíwù administrative function or post
行政制度 xíngzhèng zhìdù administrative system
行之有效 xíngzhī-yǒuxiào effective; effectual: 这些措施，经过试行，证明都是～的。These measures have proved to be effectual through trial implementation.
行止 xíngzhǐ 〈书面〉❶ whereabouts: 问到此后～，他避而不答。He evaded questions concerning his whereabouts afterwards. /此人～不定。There is no telling where he is. ❷ moral conduct; behaviour: 不可污人～ must not smear (sb.'s) moral character /～欠佳 (one's) conduct leaves much to be desired
行舟 xíngzhōu sail (a boat): 学习如逆水～，不进则退。Study is like sailing against the current: you either forge ahead or fall back.
行装 xíngzhuāng outfit for a journey; travelling gear; luggage: 收拾～ pack (for a journey) /～从简 travel light; take as little luggage as possible
行状 xíngzhuàng *also* "行述" 〈书面〉brief biography of a deceased person (usu. accompanying an obituary notice): 代书～ write a brief biography of a deceased person on behalf of his family
行踪 xíngzōng whereabouts; track; trace: ～诡秘 be of mysterious (*or* uncertain) whereabouts /～难觅 hard to discover sb.'s traces /巡逻队发现了走私犯的～。The patrol found tracks of the smugglers.
行走 xíngzǒu ❶ walk: ～如飞 walk as if winged /沿着马路慢慢～ stroll along a street ❷ 〈旧语〉be appointed to a government department with all the privileges but no specific duties of the post

饧(餳) xíng ❶ 〈书面〉treacle made from malt ❷ (of candy, dough, etc.) become sticky and soft: 面～了。The dough is sticky now. ❸ be in low spirits or half asleep with one's eyes about to close: 眼睛发～。One's eyes are drowsy.
see also táng

陉(陘) xíng 〈书面〉defile; mountain pass: 井～ Jingxing (name of a county, Hebei Province)

xǐng

醒 xǐng ❶ regain consciousness; sober up; come round: 他酒～后给她道了歉。He apologized to her when he sobered up. /病人手术后就一直没有～过来。The patient has failed to regain consciousness after the operation. /在他脸上洒些凉水，他很快就会～过来。Splash some cold water on his face and he'll soon come to. ❷ wake up; awaken; be awake: 如梦初～ like awakening from a dream /惊～ wake up with a start /孩子还没睡～。The baby is still asleep. /他在床上翻来覆去，折腾到半夜还～着。He lay wide awake till midnight, tossing from side to side in bed. ❸ keep dough (after mixing it) till water and flour are well mixed: 等面～一～再做馒头。Wait till the dough becomes soft and even before making buns. ❹ clear in mind; alert; aware: 猛然～悟 become sober and alert all at once /提～ remind; warn ❺ striking to the eye; eye-catching; conspicuous: 用一句话把意思点～ make the meaning clear with a single remark
醒盹儿 xǐngdǔnr 〈方言〉wake up from a nap; become awake
醒豁 xǐnghuò obvious; clear; explicit: 寓意～。The moral (*or* message) is clear.
醒酒 xǐngjiǔ dispel or counter the effect of alcohol; sober up: ～汤 broth or liquid used to neutralize the intoxicating effect of alcohol; sobering broth /让他喝点儿醋，醒醒酒。Get him to take vinegar; it may sober him up.
醒觉 xǐngjué become aware of; come to realize: 老师指出他的错误后，他才～过来。He didn't come to realize his mistake before his teacher pointed it out to him.
醒木 xǐngmù small wooden block used by a storyteller to strike the table before him to draw the audience's attention
醒目 xǐngmù eye-catching; striking; conspicuous: ～的大字标题 bold headline /文章的题目不够～。The title of the article is not striking enough. /把奖状挂在～的地方。Hang the reward certificate in a conspicuous spot.
醒脾 xǐngpí 〈方言〉❶ while away one's time; divert oneself from boredom: 听段儿相声醒醒脾 kill time by listening to a comic dialogue ❷ make fun of others; crack jokes at others' expense: 你别拿他～啦! Stop pulling his leg!
醒腔 xǐngqiāng 〈方言〉wake (up) to reality; come to see the truth: 说了半天，他才醒过腔来。It took much persuasion to wake him up to the truth.
醒世 xǐngshì arouse the public; rock the world: ～良言 aphorisms to awaken the public
醒睡 xǐngshuì sleep lightly and keep alert: 今晚要小心～。We must keep alert tonight. Don't sleep like a log.
醒悟 xǐngwù come to oneself; come to see the truth; wake up to reality: 翻然～ wake up to reality quickly (*or* promptly) /他终于～过来了! He has finally come to his senses!
醒眼 xǐngyǎn 〈方言〉❶ eye-catching; conspicuous; striking: 这块布料看起来更～。This piece of cloth looks brighter in colour. ❷ perceptive; sagacious: 你怎么不～，如何能得罪此等人啊! What stupidity! How can you afford to offend people like him!

擤(揩) xǐng blow (one's nose): ～鼻涕 clear one's nose of mucus by breathing out hard; blow one's nose

省 xǐng ❶ examine oneself critically; introspect: 反～ examine oneself critically; make self-scrutiny; introspect /内～ mental self-examination; introspection /吾日三～吾身。Every day I examine myself in three respects. *or* I examine my own words and deeds three times a day. ❷ visit (esp. one's parents or elders): 归～ go home to pay respects to one's parents ❸ come to realize; become conscious or aware: 猛～ suddenly realize /不～人事 lose consciousness; become insensible /发人深～ provide much food for thought
see also shěng
省察 xǐngchá examine oneself critically; examine one's thoughts and conduct; make self-scrutiny
省墓 xǐngmù 〈书面〉pay homage at one's parents' or elders' tombs: 回乡～ go back to one's native place to pay homage at one's parents' tombs
省亲 xǐngqīn pay a visit to one's parents or elders (living elsewhere): 他长年在外，久未～。He has been away from home for years

and has not been able to visit his parents. /春节里海外侨胞纷纷回国～。Overseas compatriots flock back to visit their relatives during the Spring Festival.

省视 xǐngshì call upon; pay a visit to:部长曾几次到医院～病中的刘先生。The minister has visited Mr. Liu in the hospital quite a few times.

省事 xǐngshì be sagacious; be perceptive:你真不～! You are so thick-headed!

省悟 xǐngwù 〈书面〉come to realize the truth, one's error, etc.; wake up to reality

xìng

兴(興) xìng passion or appetite for sth.; mood or desire to do sth.; interest; excitement:游～ mood for sightseeing; interest in going on an excursion /酒～ fondness for drinking; excitement due to drinking /雅～ aesthetic or refined mood; interest /败～ spoil the fun; be dampened (*or* frustrated) /乘～ do sth. while one is in high spirits (*or* good mood) /即～ impromptu /余～ lingering excitement /助～ liven things up
see also xīng

兴冲冲 xìngchōngchōng in high spirits; with joy and excitement; excitedly:～地去赶集 go to a fair in high spirits /看你们一个个～的,有什么喜事? What are you all so excited about?

兴高采烈 xìnggāo-cǎiliè with great joy; in high spirits; in great delight; jubilant:孩子们～地在车里唱啊,笑啊。On the bus the kids are singing and laughing in high glee. /尽管我看不见,但我可以感到她那～的心情。Though I can't see, I can feel her immense joy.

兴会 xìnghuì sudden flash of inspiration; brain wave:乘一时的～,他一口气写了这首长诗。With a sudden rush of inspiration he wrote this long poem at one go.

兴趣 xìngqù interest:引起～ arouse (*or* induce, *or* kindle) interest /一时的～ ephemeral interest /他的一番话使我对这本书～索然。What he said blunted my interest in the book. /他对漫画发生了很大的～。He was very keen on cartoons. /我对金钱、名誉和社会地位不感～。I am not interested in money, fame or social position. *or* Money, fame and social status hold little interest for me.

兴头儿上 xìngtóurshang at the height of one's enthusiasm:不见人家正在～? 咱们别去打扰了。Can't you see that they are at the height of their enthusiasm? We'd better not disturb them. /他玩得正在～,不会回家的。He was carried away with the game and had no thought of going home.

兴头 xìngtou ❶ enthusiasm; zest; keen interest:～正足 be overflowing with enthusiasm at the moment ❷〈方言〉be delighted; be elated:衣锦还乡,好不～。He was filled with elation to return to his hometown in all his elegance and glory.

兴味 xìngwèi interest; relish:～十足 be full of interest; be greatly interested /虽然已经上了年纪,但他还是饶有～地跟年轻人一起玩儿。Though advanced in years, he enjoys playing with young people immensely.

兴味索然 xìngwèi-suǒrán be fed up; have lost all interest:他对这一类电视剧～。He is bored stiff with this kind of TV drama.

兴致 xìngzhì interest; agreeable mood:～索然 have lost all interest; be bored stiff; be totally uninterested /颇有～ be quite eager (*or* enthusiastic) /他对足球的～不减当年。He is as keen on football as before.

兴致勃勃 xìngzhì-bóbó full of enthusiasm; in high spirits; elated:这活儿一天干下来虽然累,却是～的。Tired as we are after a day's work, we are in high spirits.

幸(❺倖) xìng ❶ good fortune; happiness:万～ be very fortunate (*or* lucky) /荣～ be honoured; have the honour (to do sth.) /平生之～ one's good fortune; luck of a lifetime ❷ rejoice; be happy:喜～ rejoice /欣～ be pleased and happy ❸〈书面〉I hope; I trust:～勿推却。I hope that you will not decline my offer. *or* Pray do not refuse. ❹ fortuitously; fortunately; luckily:～得一物 get sth. by luck /不～而言中。Unfortunately the prediction came true. ❺〈书面〉favour:得～ win favour /爱～ loving care (*or* favour) ❻〈旧语〉(of a monarch) come; arrive:巡～江南 go south of the Yangtze on an imperial tour of inspection ❼ (Xìng) a surname

幸臣 xìngchén 〈贬义〉favourite at court; favoured court official

幸存 xìngcún (fortunately) survive:～者 survivor

幸而 xìng'ér luckily; fortunately:形势紧急,～他及时赶到。The situation was most pressing; fortunately, he came at the right moment.

幸福 xìngfú ❶ happiness; welfare; well-being:时时为人民～着想 always have the well-being of the people in mind ❷ happy; blissful:～的童年 happy childhood

幸好 xìnghǎo *see*"幸亏"

幸会 xìnghuì 〈套语〉be lucky enough to meet; have the honour to meet:心仪已久,今日～。Though I admired you so long, I never had the good fortune to meet you until today. /久闻这位作家大名,可惜无缘～。I've heard a lot about the writer, but haven't had the pleasure (*or* honour) of making his acquaintance.

幸进 xìngjìn 〈书面〉lucky or fortunate promotion:今获～,实赖天恩。I owe my chance of promotion entirely to Your Majesty's kindness and favour.

幸亏 xìngkuī 〈副词〉fortunately; luckily:～火车晚点了,要不我们都赶不上车。Fortunately, the train was delayed; otherwise, we would have missed it. /开始下雨了,～我们带了雨具。It is beginning to rain. It is just as well we've brought umbrellas with us. /晚会真没意思,～你没去。You didn't miss anything, for the party was a bore.

幸免 xìngmiǎn escape by sheer luck; have a narrow escape; be a close call or shave:～于难 survive a disaster (*or* holocaust); escape death by sheer chance /这次飞机失事,机组人员和乘客全部遇难,无一～。The crew and all the passengers died in the air crash. No one survived. *or* None of the crew or passengers survived the crash.

幸巧 xìngqiǎo luckily; fortunately; just as well:～我随身带着钱,才没出丑。Luckily I had some money on me and was not nonplussed.

幸甚 xìngshèn 〈书面〉❶ most fortunate; immensely blessed:剪除奸佞,国家～。It was a great blessing to the country that those crafty sycophants were got rid of. ❷ (usu. used in letter-writing) greatly honoured:承不吝赐教,～,～。I shall feel very much honoured if you are so kind as to point out my defects.

幸事 xìngshì good fortune; blessing:你没有跟着那伙人胡闹,实为～,否则你会跟着倒霉。Luckily, you didn't get mixed up with that bunch, or you would have been dragged down in the mud.

幸喜 xìngxǐ *see*"幸亏"

幸运 xìngyùn ❶ good fortune; unexpected luck ❷ fortunate; very gratifying:几百人应试而能被选中,他感到很～。He felt he was quite lucky that he had been chosen out of several hundred candidates.

幸运儿 xìngyùn'ér fortune's favourite; lucky fellow; lucky dog

幸灾乐祸 xìngzāi-lèhuò take pleasure in or gloat over others' misfortune; revel in sb.'s discomfiture; lick one's chops; show malicious joy:他觉得满屋子投向他的都是～的眼光。It seemed to him that the house was full of leering eyes glorying in his misfortune. /朋友破产,他却～。He relishes the bankruptcy of his friend.

悻 xìng

悻然 xìngrán disgruntled; piqued; put out; enraged:～拂袖而去 go away angrily; leave in a huff

悻悻 xìngxìng angry; enraged; resentful:他～地切齿摔杯。Gnashing his teeth in rage, he threw the glass onto the ground.

婞 xìng 〈书面〉stubborn; obstinate:～直 obstinate and unbending

荇(莕) xìng

荇菜 xìngcài 〈植物〉banana-plant (*Nymphoides peltatum*)

杏 xìng 〈植物〉apricot; almond (*Prunus amygdalus*)

杏脯 xìngfǔ sun-dried or preserved sweetened apricot

杏红 xìnghóng apricot pink

杏核儿 xìnghúr apricot stone

杏黄 xìnghuáng apricot yellow; apricot (colour)

杏仁 xìngrén apricot kernel; almond:～茶 almond tea /～露 drink with almond flavour; almond drink /～软糖 marzipan

杏仁油 xìngrényóu 〈化工〉persic oil; apricot kernel oil; peach kernel oil; almond oil

杏眼 xìngyǎn (of a woman) almond eyes; pretty eyes:柳眉～ arched eyebrows and almond eyes /～圆睁 pretty eyes staring (in anger)

杏子 xìngzi 〈方言〉apricot：～熟了。The apricot is ripe.

性 xìng ❶ nature; character; inclination; disposition：秉～ nature; personality; individuality /癖～ natural inclination (*or* propensity); idiosyncracy /习～ habit /劣根～ deep-rooted bad habit /共～ common characteristics; generality /慢～子 person of phlegmatic temperament /急～子 person of quick temper /血～ courage and uprightness /本～ inherent character; nature /烈～女子 woman of strong character; spirited woman /～好清高 be of exalted and proud nature ❷ property; quality; characteristic：属～ attribute; property /药～ medicinal properties /毒～ toxicity /磁～ magnetism /弹～ elasticity /黏～ viscosity; stickiness /碱～土壤 alkaline soil /金刚水柔，～之别也。Metal and water differ in their properties — that is why the former is firm and the latter soft. ❸ *noun-forming suffix used to express ideology, emotion, etc.*：党～ party spirit /阶级～ class nature (*or* character) /纪律～ sense of discipline /斗争～ fighting spirit ❹ *noun-forming suffix used to denote a category*：可塑～ plasticity /必然～ inevitability /排他～ exclusiveness /局限～ limitation /优越～ superiority; advantage /正确～ correctness /可能～ possibility /灵活～ flexibility /全国～ nationwide; national ❺sex：～生活 sexual life /～观念 concept of sex /～奴役 sexual enslavement /～糜乱 sexual promiscuity ❻ sexual distinction; gender：男～ masculine; male /女～ feminine; female /雄～ male /雌～ female /同～恋 homosexuality /两～关系 sexual (*or* gender) relationship ❼〈语言〉gender：阳～名词 masculine noun /阴～名词 feminine noun /中～名词 neutral noun

性爱 xìng'ài sexual love

性本能 xìngběnnéng sexual instinct

性变态 xìngbiàntài (sexual) perversion：～者 perverted person; pervert

性别 xìngbié sexual distinction; sex

性别比 xìngbiébǐ gender ratio; sex ratio

性别平等 xìngbié píngděng gender equality

性别歧视 xìngbié qíshì sexism; sexual discrimination

性病 xìngbìng 〈医学〉venereal disease or VD; cypridopathy：～学 cypridology; venereology /～学家 venereologist

性传播疾病 xìngchuánbō jíbìng STD (sexually transmitted disease)

性动机 xìngdòngjī sexual motivation; libido; sex drive

性度 xìngdù 〈心理〉sex distinction scale

性恶 xìng'è 〈哲学〉evil by nature; born evil;〈宗教〉inherent depravity

性分 xìngfen 〈方言〉personality; nature, character：你别生气，他就那个～。Please don't take offence. He is just that sort of a man.

性感 xìnggǎn sex appeal; sexiness

性高潮 xìnggāocháo 〈生理〉orgasm

性格 xìnggé nature; disposition; character; temperament：随和的～ easy-going (*or* genial) disposition /～柔顺 of pliant disposition /～孤僻 of retiring (*or* unsociable, *or* uncommunicative) disposition /～活泼开朗 have a bright and cheerful disposition /摸不透的～ unfathomable personality /容易激动的～ excitable temperament /陶冶～ build (*or* cultivate) one's character /～开放 be of liberal disposition; be large-minded /集中体现出中国人民的民族～ epitomize the national character of the Chinese people /我一眼就能看出她的～。I can read her character at first glance.

性根 xìnggēn true nature; innate quality

性功能障碍 xìnggōngnéng zhàng'ài 〈医学〉sexual dysfunction

性饥渴 xìngjīkě sex-starved

性激素 xìngjīsù 〈生化〉sex hormone：～疗法〈医学〉gonadotherapy

性急 xìngjí impatient; impetuous; short-tempered：你现在就去，恐怕太～了。It's rather rash of you to go just now. /她人很好，很爽直，只是有点儿性子急。She's a very nice person, very straightforward, though a bit hot-headed.

性交 xìngjiāo sexual intercourse; coitus; sex; love-making：含蓄～ coitus reservatus /不完全～ coitus interruptus /～行为 sex act /与人～ have sex with sb.; make love with sb.

性教育 xìngjiàoyù sex education

性解放 xìngjiěfàng sexual liberation

性角色 xìngjuésè *also* "性别角色"〈心理〉sex role

性灵 xìnglíng ❶〈书面〉soul; personality：陶冶～ cultivate one's personality ❷ clever; intelligent：这孩子～，学什么都快。An intelligent child, he learns everything fast.

性命 xìngmìng life：事关～。It is matter of life and death. /他～难保。His life is in danger. /要是我坐上那架飞机，早没了～。Had I taken that flight, I would have long left this world.

性命交关 xìngmìng-jiāoguān *also* "性命攸关" (matter) of life and death; of crucial importance：～，刻不容缓。It's a matter of vital importance and brooks no delay.

性能 xìngnéng function (of a machine, etc.); performance; property：～试验 performance test /阻冻～ antifreezing property /客户对这种机器的良好～十分满意。The customer was very satisfied with the machine's performance.

性气 xìngqì temper; temperament：一起生活了几十年，她摸透了丈夫的～。Having lived with her husband for decades, she knew his temperament inside out.

性器官 xìngqìguān 〈生理〉sexual organs; genitals

性情 xìngqíng disposition; temperament; temper：～温和 have a mild (*or* gentle) disposition /～固执 have an obstinate temperament; be bigoted

性染色体 xìngrǎnsètǐ 〈生物〉sex chromosome; idiochromosome; allosome：～遗传 allosomal inheritance

性骚扰 xìngsāorǎo sex harassment

性善 xìngshàn 〈哲学〉good by nature; born good

性体 xìngtǐ 〈方言〉temper; nature; temperament：他是个炮筒子～。He is a man of hot (*or* irascible) temper.

性卫生 xìngwèishēng sex hygiene

性腺 xìngxiàn 〈医学〉gonad; sexual or sex gland：～病 gonadopathy

性心理学 xìngxīnlǐxué sex psychology

性行 xìngxíng personality and conduct; character and behaviour：他的～你又不是不知道，跟他吵有什么用? You know his character very well, don't you? No use arguing with him.

性行为 xìngxíngwéi sex act; sexual behaviour or activity

性学 xìngxué sexology

性欲 xìngyù sexual desire or urge

性欲狂 xìngyùkuáng sex mania; sex maniac

性征 xìngzhēng sex character or characteristic

性知识 xìngzhīshi sex knowledge

性质 xìngzhì quality; nature; property; character：水的～ properties of water /这是两个～不同的问题。They are issues of different nature. /他的问题～很严重。His case is pretty serious. *or* His is a grave case.

性状 xìngzhuàng shape and properties; properties; character：土壤的理化～ physiochemical properties of soil /显性～〈生物〉dominant character /～进化 character phylogenesis /～分歧〈生物〉character divergence /～连锁 linkage of characters

性自由 xìngzìyóu sexual freedom

性子 xìngzi ❶ temper：～急 hot-tempered; impetuous / ～慢 placid; phlegmatic /使～ fly into a rage /捺住～ hold (*or* keep, *or* control) one's temper /～暴躁 have a fiery temper; be irascible ❷ strength; potency：这药的～真厉害。The medicine is very powerful. /他喜欢喝烈～的酒。He likes strong liquors.

姓 xìng family or clan name; surname：单～ single-character surname /复～ two-character surname; compound surname /她～丁。She is surnamed Ding. *or* Her surname is Ding. /你贵～? What's your surname? *or* May I know your name? /～"社"还是～"资"? Is it pertaining to socialism or capitalism? *or* Is it socialist or capitalist?

姓名 xìngmíng surname and given name; full name：通报～。Tell us your (full) name.

姓名权 xìngmíngquán 〈法律〉right to one's name

姓甚名谁 xìngshèn-míngshéi what one's (full) name is：不知这人～。We don't know his name. *or* We don't know who he is.

姓氏 xìngshì surname：以～笔划为序 in the order of the number of strokes of surnames

xiōng

芎 xiōng

芎䓖 xiōngqióng *also* "川芎" chuānxiōng rhizome of *chuanxiong* (*Liguoticum wallichii*)

兄 xiōng ❶ elder brother:胞～ elder brother of the same parents /长～ eldest brother /父～ father and elder brothers /尊～大作读毕,获益甚多。I've benefited immensely from reading your brother's great work. ❷ elder male relative of one's own generation:堂～ elder male cousin (on the paternal side) /表～ elder male cousin (on the maternal side) /内～ wife's elder brother; elder brother-in-law ❸ courteous form of address between men:老～ (familiar form of address between male friends) brother; man /仁～〈敬词〉my dear friend (between male friends)

兄弟 xiōngdì ❶ brothers; brethren:～失和 disunity (*or* disharmony) among brothers /～公司 company owned by brothers; brothers' company /～二人结伴同行。The two brothers travelled together. ❷ fraternal; brotherly:～民族 brotherly nationalities /～单位 brother units /～般的情谊 fraternal (*or* brotherly) sentiments

兄弟 xiōngdi ❶ younger brother:这是我～。This is my younger brother. ❷ familiar form of address for a man younger than oneself:～,快帮我一把。Young man, please give me a hand. ❸〈谦词〉your humble servant:～我向大伙儿道谢啦! Now, I would like to express my thanks to all of you.

兄弟阋墙 xiōngdì-xìqiáng quarrel between brothers; internecine strife; internal dispute:兄弟阋于墙,外御其侮。Brothers quarrelling at home join forces against attacks from without. *or* Internal disunity dissolves at the threat of external invasion.

兄嫂 xiōngsǎo elder brother and his wife; elder brother and elder sister-in-law

兄长 xiōngzhǎng ❶ elder brother ❷ respectful form of address for an elder brother or a male friend older than oneself:请～多指教。Kindly give us your advice.

凶(❸❹❺❻❼兇) xiōng ❶ inauspicious; unlucky; ominous:吉～ good or ill luck ❷ crop failure; famine: *see* "～年" ❸ fierce; menacing; ferocious:穷～极恶 extremely vicious; utterly evil; atrocious; diabolical /板着一副～面孔 wear a fierce look /他老婆很～。He has a termagant wife. ❹ terrible; violent; fearful:两个人打得很～。The two had a terrible fight. /蚊子咬得真～。The mosquitoes were biting mercilessly. /这场山洪来得很～。The mountain torrents came down with a vengeance. ❺ act of violence; murder:行～ commit physical assault or murder ❻ evildoer; criminal; murderer:元～ chief culprit; arch-criminal /帮～ accomplice; accessory ❼〈方言〉efficient; effective; tough:我们那个新的总经理很～,一来就把整个班子给换了。Our new general manager is really tough. He thoroughly reshuffled the management shortly after he took office. /这药可～了。This is a very strong medicine.

凶案 xiōng'àn murder (case); homicide

凶暴 xiōngbào brutally fierce; ferocious:性情～ brutal and fierce by nature; of ferocious and bestial temper

凶残 xiōngcán ❶ savage and cruel; brutal and ruthless:虎狼般～ tigerlike ferocity /～成性 be steeped in savagery and cruelty /他长期参与贩毒活动,性格也变得～起来。His long involvement in drug dealing brutalized him. /他们犯下了极其～的罪行。They committed the most atrocious (*or* heinous) crimes. ❷〈书面〉savage and cruel person

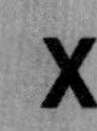

凶毒 xiōngdú ferocious and brutal; vicious:采取～的手段 do sth. in a most venomous and ruthless way

凶多吉少 xiōngduō-jíshǎo bode ill rather than well; be faced with a precarious situation; be fraught with grim possibilities:我们只好听天由命了,反正～。We have to resign ourselves to fate since things bode ill rather than well. /现在看来,形势～,我们得赶快做好准备。It's clear now that the situation is ominous (*or* fraught with danger). We must prepare for it.

凶恶 xiōng'è fierce; vicious; ferocious; fiendish:～的敌人 ferocious enemy /样子十分～ look vicious

凶犯 xiōngfàn one who has committed homicide; killer; murderer:杀人～ murderer /惩治～ bring murderers to justice

凶服 xiōngfú 〈书面〉mourning garb:～在身 wear a mourning cloak; be in mourning

凶悍 xiōnghàn ferocious and tough:目光～ have a fierce and ruthless look in one's eyes

凶耗 xiōnghào news of sb.'s death:她闻此～,痛不欲生。Upon hearing the news of his passing away, she was grieved to the marrow.

凶狠 xiōnghěn ❶ fierce and malicious; ferocious and ruthless:对人～,不讲道理 fierce and ruthless towards others and impervious to reason ❷ forceful; vigorous:扣球～ smash forcefully

凶横 xiōnghèng fierce and despotic:～不讲理 fierce, arrogant and not amenable to reason

凶荒 xiōnghuāng complete crop failure; famine:～年月 years of famine

凶具 xiōngjù coffin

凶狂 xiōngkuáng fierce and frenzied:逞～ play the bully; ride roughshod over

凶戾 xiōnglì ruthless and tyrannical; cruel and fierce:蛮横～的气焰 air of arrogance and ruthlessness

凶猛 xiōngměng fierce; violent; ferocious:～的野兽 ferocious wild animals /寒潮来势～。The cold front came with overwhelming force.

凶年 xiōngnián year of crop failure; year of famine

凶虐 xiōngnüè tyrannical and cruel:～无道的昏君 cruel and unprincipled ruler /婆母～,她度日如年。Under a tyrannical and cruel mother-in-law, she found time passing slowly for her.

凶殴 xiōng'ōu assault or beat ruthlessly:他～路人,引起民愤。His vicious assault on innocent passers-by aroused the wrath of the people.

凶气 xiōngqì ferocious appearance; fierce feature:满脸～ have a ferocious look on one's face

凶器 xiōngqì tool or weapon for criminal purposes; lethal weapon:杀人～ weapon used in a murder or homicide /警察迅速夺过～,制服了罪犯。The policeman swiftly disarmed the criminal and overpowered him.

凶杀 xiōngshā homicide; murder:～案 case of murder /他惨遭～。He was murdered in cold blood.

凶煞煞 xiōngshāshā ferocious; fierce; menacing:目光～的 look ferocious; have fierce-looking eyes

凶煞 xiōngshà *see* "凶神"

凶身 xiōngshēn 〈书面〉murderer; killer

凶神 xiōngshén demon; monster; fiend:瞧你那～样,谁还怕你不成! Don't think anyone would be afraid of your fiendish glare!

凶神恶煞 xiōngshén-èshà evil spirit; devil; fiend:他故意做出～的样子,想吓唬吓唬人。He was playing the devil just to scare people.

凶事 xiōngshì unlucky events such as death, burial, etc.:家有～,一门不安。The whole household was upset by unpropitious events. /兵者,～也。Fighting involves death and destruction.

凶手 xiōngshǒu murderer; killer; assassin; assailant (who has caused injury to sb.):杀人～ murderer; killer /～在逃。The killer (*or* murderer) is still at large.

凶死 xiōngsǐ die by violence; meet a violent death

凶岁 xiōngsuì *see* "凶年"

凶徒 xiōngtú cut-throat; ruffian; thug

凶顽 xiōngwán fierce and stubborn:～的敌人 wilful and ruthless enemy

凶险 xiōngxiǎn ❶ in a very dangerous state; precarious; critical:病情～ dangerously ill; critically ill; terminally ill; in a critical condition /地势～ perilous place; dangerous path /此为魔杖,可避～。This is a magic stick that can ward off dangers. ❷ ferocious and sinister; fiendish and insidious:～的敌人 treacherous enemy

凶相 xiōngxiàng ferocious features; fierce look:一脸～ ferocious look

凶相毕露 xiōngxiàng-bìlù look thoroughly ferocious; be ferocity itself:恶狼～,龇着牙向小羊扑来。Baring its fangs in all its savagery, the heinous wolf pounced on the lamb.

凶信 xiōngxìn news of sb.'s death:一听到父亲的～,他简直呆了。He was stunned by (*or* He stood transfixed to the spot at) the news of his father's death.

凶焰 xiōngyàn savage ferocity; aggressive arrogance:～万丈 extremely ferocious /煞一煞敌人的～ puncture the enemy's arrogance

凶宅 xiōngzhái haunted house; unlucky abode:据说那房子里闹过鬼,是所～,没人敢住。It's said that this is a haunted house and that no one dares to live in.

凶兆 xiōngzhào ill omen; evil boding:临出门时听见老鸹叫,他认为是个～。When he was going out he heard the crowing of a crow, which he believed to be an ill omen.

汹(洶) xiōng rush of water; tumult

汹汹 xiōngxiōng 〈书面〉❶ sound of roaring waves: 听涛声之～ listen to the roaring of the waves ❷ violent; fierce; truculent: 气势～ blustering and truculent /沙暴来势～ onslaught of a sandstorm ❸ 〈书面〉 *also* "讻讻" xiōngxiōng turbulent; tumultuous: 议论～ agitated debate; heated argument /天下～, 干戈四起。Fighting broke out all over the country, plunging the country into chaos.

汹涌 xiōngyǒng surging; tempestuous; turbulent: 巨浪～而来。Mountains of waves crashed against the shore. /改革洪流～向前。The raging tide of reform surges forward.

汹涌澎湃 xiōngyǒng-péngpài raging; turbulent; tempestuous: 黄河的浪涛～。The turbulent waves of the Yellow River keep surging ahead. /争取民族独立的斗争～。The struggle for national independence was on the upsurge (*or* rising high).

讻(詾、哅) xiōng

讻讻 xiōngxiōng *see* "汹汹❸" xiōngxiōng

匈 xiōng 〈书面〉 *see* "胸" xiōng

匈奴 Xiōngnú Xiongnu or Hun, ancient nomadic people living in the north of China

匈牙利 Xiōngyálì Hungary: ～人 Hungarian /～语 Hungarian (language)

恟(忷) xiōng 〈书面〉 in terror; panic-stricken

胸(胷) xiōng ❶ chest; breast; bosom; thorax: 挺～ throw out one's chest /护～ chest protector /齐～高 breast-high /鸡～〈生理〉 pectus carinatum; chicken (*or* pigeon) breast /一枪击中前～。A bullet hit him in the chest. ❷ mind; heart: 心～ breadth of mind; ambition; aspiration

胸靶 xiōngbǎ 〈军事〉 chest silhouette

胸壁炎 xiōngbìyán 〈医学〉 parapleuritis

胸部 xiōngbù chest; thorax: ～疼痛 pain in the chest /～手术 thoracic operation

胸部连胎 xiōngbù liántāi 〈生理〉 thoracopagus

胸次 xiōngcì 〈书面〉❶ mood: ～舒畅 feel happy /喜怒哀乐不入于～ not affected by strong emotions; remain impervious to deep feelings ❷ mind; heart: ～宽广 broad-minded

胸大肌 xiōngdàjī 〈生理〉 pectoris or pectoralis major; greater pectoral muscle

胸骨 xiōnggǔ 〈生理〉 breastbone; sternum

胸花 xiōnghuā corsage; chest pin

胸怀 xiōnghuái ❶ have in mind; cherish: ～天下 have the entire world in mind; be deeply concerned about international developments /～祖国 bear the interest of one's country in mind; be full of patriotic fervour ❷ heart; mind: ～坦荡 openhearted; frank; candid /革命者的伟大～ revolutionary's breadth of vision ❸ chest; bosom; thorax: 敞开～ bare one's chest /偎依在妈妈的～ nestle in mom's bosom

胸肌 xiōngjī pectoral muscle: ～痉挛 stethospasm /～痛 pectoralgia /～炎 stethomyositis (*or* stethomyitis)

胸甲 xiōngjiǎ breastplate; cuirass

胸襟 xiōngjīn ❶ mind; breadth of mind: ～开阔 broad-minded; open-minded; large-minded /～狭窄 narrow-minded; small-minded; parochial /伟大的～ great vision ❷ mood; state of mind: 抒写～ describe one's feelings /对事业的乐观～ be optimistic about one's cause ❸ upper front part of a jacket: ～上别着一朵小花。A small flower was pinned on the chest.

胸径 xiōngjìng 〈林业〉 diameter of a tree trunk taken at 1.3 metres above the ground

胸卡 xiōngkǎ name tag; identification badge

胸坎 xiōngkǎn *also* "胸坎子" pit of the stomach

胸口 xiōngkǒu pit of the stomach; chest: ～疼 pain at the pit of the stomach; chest pain

胸廓 xiōngkuò 〈生理〉 thorax: ～切开术 thoracotomy /～成形术 thoracoplasty

胸膜 xiōngmó *also* "肋膜" lèimó 〈生理〉 pleura; *membrana pleuralis*: ～壁层 pleura parietalis

胸膜穿刺术 xiōngmó chuāncìshù 〈医学〉 pleurocentesis

胸膜肺炎 xiōngmó fèiyán pleuropneumonia

胸膜积水 xiōngmó jīshuǐ hydrothorax

胸膜痛 xiōngmótòng pleuralgia

胸膜炎 xiōngmóyán pleuritis; pleurisy: 化脓性～ suppurative pleurisy /结核性～ tuberculous pleurisy

胸脯 xiōngpú *also* "胸脯子" chest; bust; breast: 宽阔结实的～ broad and sturdy chest /丰满的～ full bust; large breasts /拍着～儿打保票 strike one's chest as a gesture of guarantee or assurance /～丰满的女人 buxom woman

胸鳍 xiōngqí 〈动物〉 pectoral fin

胸腔 xiōngqiāng thoracic cavity; pectoral cavity: ～穿刺术 pleuracentesis; pleurocentesis; thoracocentesis /～镜 thoracoscope /～镜检查 thoracoscopy

胸墙 xiōngqiáng ❶ low wall up to the breast; chest-high wall ❷ 〈军事〉 breastwork; parapet

胸膛 xiōngtáng chest: 挺起～ throw out one's chest

胸痛 xiōngtòng 〈医学〉 thoracodynia; pain in the chest

胸围 xiōngwéi ❶ (of human body) chest measurement; bust ❷ 〈林业〉 circumference of a tree trunk taken at 1.3 metres above the ground

胸无城府 xiōngwúchéngfǔ simple and candid; of no sophistication; artless: 见义勇为, ～ help a lame dog over a stile (*or* do the right thing) without any thought of oneself

胸无点墨 xiōngwúdiǎnmò completely illiterate; uneducated; unlearned; unlettered: 这样～的人, 怎能指导他人? How could such an ignoramus give guidance to others?

胸无宿物 xiōngwúsùwù with nothing concealed in one's mind — straightforward; candid; frank: 为人坦直, ～ candid person who bears no grudges against others

胸腺 xiōngxiàn 〈生理〉 thymus: 副～ accessory thymus /～核酸 〈生化〉 thymus nucleic acid; thymonucleic acid /～激素 thymin /～瘤 〈医学〉 thymoma /～炎 thymitis

胸像 xiōngxiàng (sculptured) bust

胸小肌 xiōngxiǎojī 〈生理〉 pectoralis minor

胸臆 xiōngyì feelings; sentiments: 直抒～ express one's feelings in a straightforward manner

胸有成竹 xiōngyǒuchéngzhú *also* "成竹在胸" chéngzhúzàixiōng have a well-thought-out plan, stratagem, etc. in mind: 解决问题的办法他早已～。He has already in mind a detailed plan for solving the problems.

胸章 xiōngzhāng badge

胸罩 xiōngzhào brassiere; bra

胸针 xiōngzhēn brooch

胸中甲兵 xiōngzhōng-jiǎbīng be versed in military strategy: 他虽出身行伍, 但～, 人不能及。Though he rose from the ranks, he is a seasoned strategist that no one can compare with.

胸中无数 xiōngzhōng-wúshù *also* "心中无数" xīnzhōng-wúshù not know for certain; have little confidence; be not at all sure: 这计划是否可行, 我～。I'm not too sure whether this plan will work or not.

胸中有数 xiōngzhōng-yǒushù *also* "心中有数" xīnzhōng-yǒushù have a good idea of how things stand; have full confidence; know what's what: 对手下每个人的工作能力、性格特点, 他都～。He knows full well the capabilities and personal traits of everybody working under him.

胸椎 xiōngzhuī 〈生理〉 thoracic vertebra

xióng

雄 xióng ❶ male: 雌～ male and female; victory and defeat /～鸭 drake ❷ grand; imposing; commanding; majestic: ～姿 heroic carriage (*or* demeanour) ❸ virile; powerful; mighty: *see* "～壮" ❹ person or state having great power and influence: 英～ hero /称～ rule a district by force or power; hold sway over a region /奸～ master of political intrigues /群～逐鹿 powerful states locked in rivalry

雄辩 xióngbiàn ❶ convincing argument; eloquence: 事实胜于～。Facts speak louder than words. /我佩服他的～。I admire his eloquence. ❷ eloquently; convincingly: ～家 eloquent speaker; orator /事实～地证明, 这项改革是必要的。Facts have incontrovertibly proved that the reform is necessary.

X

雄兵 xióngbīng powerful army:胸中自有～百万 have in mind stratagems comparable to the strength of an army of million men
雄才大略 xióngcái-dàlüè (man) of great talent and bold vision; (statesman or general) of rare gifts and grand strategy:具有～的统帅 talented and far-sighted commander-in-chief
雄大 xióngdà full of power and grandeur:这位冠军的棋势～。This chess champion plays with impelling drive.
雄飞 xióngfēi strive for a higher level of achievement
雄风 xióngfēng ❶〈书面〉strong wind; gale ❷ heroic carriage; bold or gallant appearance:老将～犹在。The old general has lost none of his former gallantry.
雄蜂 xióngfēng 〈动物〉male bee; drone
雄关 xióngguān impregnable pass:～漫道真如铁,而今迈步从头越。Idle boast the strong pass is a wall of iron, With firm strides we are crossing its summit.
雄豪 xióngháo ❶ talented person; hero ❷ sublime; magnificent:潮水奔腾,势极～。The roaring tidal bore presents a magnificent scene.
雄厚 xiónghòu rich; huge; solid; abundant:～的资本 abundant capital /实力～ ample strength /～的群众基础 have the strong backing of the people /技术力量～ huge technical force (*or* staff)
雄花 xiónghuā 〈植物〉male flower; staminate flower
雄黄 xiónghuáng *also* "鸡冠石" jīguānshí; "雄精" realgar; red orpiment; arsenic disulfide
雄黄酒 xiónghuángjiǔ realgar wine, Chinese liquor seasoned with realgar to be drunk at the Dragon Boat Festival, the fifth day of the fifth lunar month
雄浑 xiónghún vigorous and firm; powerful; forceful:挥毫～苍劲 bold and vigorous brush work /这部交响乐～高亢。The symphony is powerful and resounding.
雄鸡 xióngjī cock; rooster
雄激素 xióngjīsù *also* "雄性激素"〈生化〉androgenic hormone; androgen
雄健 xióngjiàn robust; virile; vigorous; powerful:笔力～ vigorous strokes in calligraphy or painting /～的身姿 robust and martial figure /～有力的利爪 sharp and powerful claws
雄杰 xióngjié ❶ talented; gifted:～之士 man of outstanding talent ❷ outstanding talent; person of great ability:一代～ great talent of the time
雄精 xióngjīng 〈中药〉realgar; orpiment; arsenic disulfide
雄劲 xióngjìng powerful; robust; sturdy; brawny
雄赳赳 xióngjiūjiū valiantly; gallantly:～,气昂昂 valorously and spiritedly; full of mettle /卫兵～地立在旗杆之下。The guards are gallantly standing by the flagpole.
雄踞 xióngjù be positioned majestically:龟山和蛇山～长江之畔。The Turtle Hill and the Snake Hill sit majestically on the banks of the Yangtze.
雄俊 xióngjùn ❶ gallant and handsome; talented ❷ *also* "雄骏" outstanding talent
雄峻 xióngjùn magnificent and steep:山势～ towering mountain /挺拔～的山峰 mighty and imposing peaks

雄丽 xiónglì imposing and beautiful; sublime:江山～ landscape of overpowering beauty
雄奇 xióngqí imposing and extraordinary:华山巍峨～。Mount Hua towers majestically.
雄强 xióngqiáng robust; powerful; strong:笔势～ vigorous strokes
雄蕊 xióngruǐ 〈植物〉stamen; androecium:～柄 androphore /退化～ staminode
雄师 xióngshī powerful army:百万～过大江。Our mighty army, a million strong, has crossed the Great River. /～挥戈下江南。The powerful army, in full battle readiness, was sweeping ahead south of the Yangtze.
雄狮 xióngshī male lion
雄视 xióngshì watch with pride or dignity:～百代 tower over others for generations on end
雄肆 xióngsì (of calligraphy) powerful and unconstrained:笔力～ bold and vigorous strokes
雄素 xióngsù 〈生化〉androsin
雄酮 xióngtóng 〈生化〉androsterone
雄图 xióngtú lofty aspiration; great ambition; grand design:～大略 grand design and bold strategy /一展～ strive to realize one's great ambition
雄烷 xióngwán 〈生化〉androstane
雄威 xióngwēi valour; bravery; courage:一展我军的～ display the valour of our army
雄伟 xióngwěi ❶ grand; imposing; magnificent:～的殿堂 grand palace (*or* temple building) /～壮丽的景色 magnificent and enchanting scenery ❷ tall and strong; stalwart:身材～ of great stature; tall and sturdy
雄文 xióngwén powerful writing; great works; masterpiece:～数篇,垂名后世 great works which earn the author a lasting reputation
雄武 xióngwǔ martial; valiant; valorous; gallant:刚毅～的气质 staunch and gallant disposition
雄细胞 xióngxìbāo 〈植物〉androcyte
雄心 xióngxīn noble ambition; lofty aspiration:树～,立壮志。Cherish lofty ideals and set high aims. /他是个有～、有抱负的青年。He is a young man of (*or* imbued with) lofty aspirations.
雄心勃勃 xióngxīn-bóbó extremely ambitious:～的计划 very ambitious plan
雄心壮志 xióngxīn-zhuàngzhì lofty ideals and great aspiration:树立～ set one's sights high; aim high /年轻时,他也曾有过～。He, too, had his dreams when he was young.
雄性 xióngxìng male; masculine
雄性不育 xióngxìng bùyù 〈生理〉male sterility:～系 male-sterile line; A-line /～保持系 male-sterile maintenance line; B-line /～恢复系 male-sterile restorer line; R-line /～基因 male sterility gene
雄蚁 xióngyǐ 〈动物〉male ant
雄长 xióngzhǎng 〈书面〉predominance; supremacy; ascendancy:互争～ vie (*or* contend) with each other for supremacy /～一方 lord it over a region
雄主 xióngzhǔ ambitious and talented sovereign:一代～ great monarch of his time
雄壮 xióngzhuàng ❶ full of power and grandeur; imposing; magnificent; majestic:威武～之师 mighty army ❷ stalwart; robust:身材～ of sturdy build
雄姿 xióngzī majestic appearance; valiant carriage; heroic posture:女民兵的～ bright and brave look of the militia women /坦克部队的～ magnificent formation of the tank force
雄姿英发 xióngzī-yīngfā valiant and ambitious; majestic and full of vigour

熊[1]

xióng ❶ bear:北极～ polar bear /狗～ Asiatic black bear /棕～ brown bear /灰～ grizzly bear /树袋～ koala (bear) ❷ (Xióng) a surname

熊[2]

xióng 〈方言〉❶ rebuke; upbraid; abuse; scold:他为人粗暴,成天～人。Rude and ruthless, he is given to bullying others. ❷ impotent; timid; faint-hearted:兵～～一个,将～～一窝。A timid soldier would only keep his timidity to himself, but a faint-hearted general would demoralize the entire army under his command.
熊白 xióngbái white fat inside a bear's back, considered to be a delicacy
熊包 xióngbāo *also* "熊蛋包"〈方言〉useless person; chicken-heart; good-for-nothing; worthless wretch
熊胆 xióngdǎn gall of bear used as medicine
熊蹯 xióngfán *see* "熊掌"
熊蜂 xióngfēng bumblebee; humble-bee
熊果 xióngguǒ bearberry (*Arctostaphylos uva-ursi*)
熊猴 xiónghóu 〈动物〉Assamese macaque
熊据虎峙 xióngjù-hǔzhì *also* "熊据虎跱"〈书面〉(of a general, warlord, etc.) entrench oneself in a locality or region
熊狸 xiónglí 〈动物〉binturong (*Arctictis binturong*)
熊猫 xióngmāo *also* "猫熊"〈动物〉panda:大～ giant panda /小～ lesser panda
熊罴 xióngpí bears; ferocious animals (used sometimes figuratively to refer to brave warriors):～之士 courageous soldiers /独有英雄驱虎豹,更无豪杰怕～。Only heroes can quell tigers and leopards, And wild bears never daunt the brave.
熊市 xióngshì bear market, (stock) market with falling prices
熊瞎子 xióngxiāzi 〈方言〉bear
熊心豹胆 xióngxīn-bàodǎn heart of a bear and gall of a leopard — very bold

熊熊 xióngxióng flaming; ablaze; raging: ～烈火 raging flames; conflagration

熊样 xióngyàng 〈方言〉 cowardly look; unseemly bearing; unsightly appearance: 一副～ ne'er-do-well look; very image of cowardice /就他那～,还能入选? You think he could be selected with that unseemly look of his?

熊腰虎背 xióngyāo-hǔbèi *also* "虎背熊腰" bear's waist and tiger's back — (person) of sturdy build

熊鱼 xióngyú 〈书面〉 bear paws and fish — two rare delicacies (from a saying by Mencius: "Fish is what I desire, and so is bear paw. However, I cannot have both at once.")

熊掌 xióngzhǎng bear's paw (as a rare delicacy)

xiòng

诇 xiòng 〈书面〉 detect; spy on: ～察 probe into sth.; spy out sth.

敻 xiòng 〈书面〉 ❶ remote; distant: ～若千里。It's such a long distance, as if you were a thousand *li* away. ❷ far back; long long ago: ～古 in remote antiquity

xiū

羞[1] xiū ❶ shy; coy; bashful: 含～ bashfully /害～ feel bashful /怕～ be shy /～得面红耳赤 blush from (with) shyness ❷ embarrass; shame: 人们～得他一言不发。They shamed him into silence. ❸ shame; mortification; disgrace: 遮～ cover up one's embarrassment; conceal (*or* hide) one's disgrace /不知～ be shameless; shame on you ❹ feel ashamed: ～与为友 feel ashamed to have such a friend

羞[2] xiū *see* "馐" xiū

羞惭 xiūcán be ashamed; feel ill at ease from shame: 内心深感～ feel deeply ashamed /因～而低头 hang one's head in shame /他们的慷慨大方令我～。Their generosity put me to shame.

羞耻 xiūchǐ sense of shame; shame: 不知～ have no sense of shame; be impervious to shame; be lost to shame /引为～ consider sth. a disgrace

羞答答 xiūdādā *also* "羞羞答答" coy; shy; bashful; diffident: 少女～的样子 maidenly coyness /说话羞羞答答,很不自在 speak with uneasy bashfulness /她～的,不好意思讲她的爱情故事。She is coy about her love affairs.

羞愤 xiūfèn ashamed and indignant: ～异常 feel extremely ashamed and resentful

羞口 xiūkǒu feel embarrassed to say; feel it hard to speak up: 他想说,可又感到～。Though he had meant to come clean about it, yet he felt too embarrassed to do so.

羞愧 xiūkuì ashamed; discomfited; abashed: 我没有什么可以～的。There is nothing I should be ashamed of. /没能为国家作出什么贡献,我感到～。I feel ashamed at having done so little for my country. /很～,我没有尽全力帮忙。To my shame, I must confess that I didn't do my best to help you.

羞明 xiūmíng 〈医学〉 photophobia

羞赧 xiūnǎn 〈书面〉 blush: 使人感到～ cause sb. to blush

羞恼 xiūnǎo be annoyed or angry from shame: ～成怒 fly into a rage from shame

羞怩 xiūní coy; shy; embarrassed: 她脸上泛红,有些～。She felt somewhat shy, blushing all over.

羞恧 xiūnǜ 〈书面〉 be ashamed

羞怯 xiūqiè shy; coy; timid; sheepish: 小姑娘～地低下了头,躲到母亲身后。The little girl hung her head timidly and ran to hide behind her mother.

羞人 xiūrén feel embarrassed or awkward: 羞死人了! Oh, what embarrassment! *or* I'll die of shame! /她怕这些～的事情讲出去,被人耻笑。She was afraid of having such shameful stories made public and being laughed at.

羞人答答 xiūrén-dādā shy; embarrassed: 在那么多人面前讲话,小姑娘感到～的。The little girl felt quite shy to speak before such a big audience.

羞辱 xiūrǔ ❶ shame; dishonour; disgrace; humiliation: 他还是头一次受到这样的～。It was the first time that he had been subjected to such humiliation. /你的行为使双亲蒙受～。Your action brought disgrace upon your parents. ❷ make people feel ashamed; humiliate: 我狠狠地～了他一顿。I put him to shame with a vengeance.

羞臊 xiūsào ashamed; shameful: 你这么大的人欺负一个小孩儿,真是不知～。It's shameful of such a big boy like you to bully a small child.

羞涩 xiūsè shy; bashful; diffident; embarrassed: 她～地转过身去。She turned round shyly.

羞恶 xiūwù 〈书面〉 feel ashamed of and disgusted at sth. or sb.: ～之心 sense of shame or disgust

羞与为伍 xiūyǔ-wéiwǔ be ashamed to be seen with sb. or in sb.'s company; consider it beneath one to associate with sb.: 此人道德败坏,人人～。This man is morally corrupt. Everybody considered it a shame to have anything to do with him.

馐 xiū 〈书面〉 delicacy; choice food; dainty: 珍～ rare delicacy

休[1] xiū ❶ stop; end; cease: 吵个不～ quarrel endlessly /喋喋不～ talk garrulously /善罢甘～ leave the matter at that; be willing to give up ❷ rest; repose: ～病假 on sick leave /退～ retirement /轮～ rest in turn /午～ lunch break; nap after lunch; siesta /我今儿～礼拜。Today I am off. ❸ 〈旧语〉 divorce one's wife and send her home: ～妻 divorce and send one's wife away ❹ (often used in the early vernacular) don't: ～得多问。Don't ask too many questions. /闲话～提,言归正传。Chit-chat aside (*or* No more of this digression), let's come to the point.

休[2] xiū 〈书面〉 good fortune; rejoicing: ～征 auspicious omen

休班 xiūbān 〈方言〉 have a day off: 您明天不是～吗? Are you to have a day off tomorrow?

休兵 xiūbīng 〈书面〉 ❶ stop fighting; end hostilities: 从中斡旋,使两国～ use one's good offices to bring about an end to hostilities between the two countries ❷ well-rested and reorganized troops

休怪 xiūguài don't blame: ～我不讲情面。Don't blame me for not sparing your sensibilities.

休会 xiūhuì adjourn; recess: 暂时～ adjourn the meeting for the time being /无限期～ adjourn indefinitely (*or sine die*) /宣布～一小时 announce a one-hour recess /下午～,明天继续讨论。The meeting is adjourned in the afternoon, and we will resume discussions tomorrow.

休火山 xiūhuǒshān dormant volcano

休假 xiūjià (of workers, students, etc.) have or take a holiday or vacation; (of soldiers, personnel working abroad, etc.) be on leave or furlough: 回国～ go home on furlough /带薪～ holiday with pay; paid vacation /我们一年有二十天的～。We have an annual leave of twenty days.

休咎 xiūjiù 〈书面〉 good and ill luck; weal and woe

休刊 xiūkān (of newspapers or magazines) cease to publish; suspend publication

休克 xiūkè 〈医学〉 (transliteration) shock: 过敏性～ allergic or anaphylactic shock /心原性～ cardiogenic shock /中毒性～ toxic shock /冷～ cold shock /电～ electroconvulsive shock; galvanic shock; electric shock /由于青霉素过敏,他差点儿～。He nearly lost consciousness due to penicillin allergy.

休克疗法 xiūkè liáofǎ shock treatment; shock therapy: 美国某些经济学家建议一些东欧国家对它们的经济实行～。Some US economists suggested that East European countries should apply shock therapy to their economies.

休伦湖 Xiūlúnhú Lake Huron, one of the five Great Lakes of North America

休眠 xiūmián 〈生物〉 dormancy

休眠孢子 xiūmián bāozǐ hypnospore; resting spore

休眠火山 xiūmián huǒshān *also* "休火山" dormant volcano

休眠卵 xiūmiánluǎn resting egg

休眠期 xiūmiánqī period of dormancy; dormancy stage; rest period

休眠素 xiūmiánsù 〈生化〉 dormin

休眠体 xiūmiántǐ *also* "休眠幼虫" 〈生物〉 hypopus

X

休眠芽 xiūmiányá 〈植物〉resting or dormant bud; latent bud; statoblast
休眠账户 xiūmián zhànghù 〈经济〉dormant account
休眠状态 xiūmián zhuàngtài dormant state; (state of) dormancy
休沐 xiūmù 〈旧语〉rest and bath — regular leave or furlough for officials
休戚 xiūqī fortune and misfortune; weal and woe; joys and sorrows:与民共~ share weal and woe with the people
休戚相关 xiūqī-xiāngguān be bound together by common interests:~、生死与共的战友 comrades-in-arms bound by a common cause and sticking together in life and death
休戚与共 xiūqī-yǔgòng share weal and woe; stay together through thick and thin:~,生死相依 share weal and woe and stay together till death do them apart
休弃 xiūqì 〈旧语〉divorce one's wife and send her home
休憩 xiūqì have or take a rest; repose:稍事~ have a short break; rest for a while /鸟群在湖边~。A flock of birds were taking a rest by the lake.
休书 xiūshū 〈旧语〉letter by a husband unilaterally announcing his decision to divorce his wife
休息 xiūxi have or take a rest; rest:幕间~ intermission; interval /课间~ break (between classes) /~日 day off /找个地方~~。Let's find a place to take a rest. /邮局星期天不~。The post office is open on Sunday. /我明天~。I'm off tomorrow.
休息室 xiūxishì lounge; lobby; anteroom
休闲 xiūxián ❶ be not working; have leisure; spend or beguile one's leisure:假期里过一过~的日子 enjoy one's leisure during the vacation /~时光 leisure time /~娱乐 entertainment; relaxation /~场所 place to spend one's leisure; holiday resort ❷〈农业〉lie fallow:~地 fallow land /~作物 fallow crops
休闲服 xiūxiánfú leisure clothing; leisure wear
休闲鞋 xiūxiánxié leisure shoe
休想 xiūxiǎng don't think (you can do sth., etc.); don't imagine (that it's possible); stop dreaming (that things will come out as you wish):你~得逞。Don't imagine that you'll get it your way! /他要搞垮我的公司,~! It is mere daydreaming for him to try to ruin my company. *or* If he wants to ruin my company, he'll have to whistle for it!
休歇 xiūxiē rest; stop to rest:在树阴下~ rest in the shade of a tree /他一干起活来就不知道~。He never takes a breather once he begins working.
休学 xiūxué suspend one's schooling without losing one's status as a student; be temporarily absent from school; suspend schooling
休养 xiūyǎng ❶ recuperate; convalesce:她在海边~了三个月。She spent three months at the beach (*or* seaside) convalescing. ❷ (of economy) recover; rehabilitate; revitalize:~民力 give the people time to rest and recuperate; reinvigorate the people's (economic) strength
休养生息 xiūyǎng-shēngxī (of a nation) recuperate and multiply; rest and regenerate; rehabilitate:~的政策 rehabilitation policy /经过几十年~,国力大增。The national strength was greatly augmented through recuperation and rehabilitation over several decades.
休养所 xiūyǎngsuǒ rest home; sanatorium
休业 xiūyè ❶ suspend or close business:盘点货物,~一天。The shop is closed today for stock-taking (*or* taking inventory). ❷ (of a short-term course, etc.) end; wind up
休战 xiūzhàn truce; ceasefire; armistice:双方处于~状态。The two sides are under ceasefire. /两国~,重修旧好。Having concluded a truce agreement, the two countries patched up their differences and were on good terms again.
休整 xiūzhěng (of troops) rest and reorganize:部队利用战斗空隙进行~。The troops seized a lull in the fighting to rest and consolidate. /部队经过~后,士气大振。The army's morale was given a great boost by the rest and reorganization.
休止 xiūzhǐ end; stop; cease:无~地争论 no end of arguing /宇宙间的运动,永无~。The universe is in perpetual motion.
休止符 xiūzhǐfú 〈音乐〉rest

庥 xiū 〈书面〉shield (sb.); shelter; protect

髹(髤) xiū paint (furniture, etc.)

咻 xiū 〈书面〉make a din
咻咻 xiūxiū 〈象声〉❶ *used for the sound of breathing*:发出~的鼻息 breathe noisily ❷ *used to describe the cry of some birds and animals*:小鸭~。The ducklings were cheeping.

貅 xiū *see* "貔貅" píxiū

鸺 xiū
鸺鹠 xiūliú *also* "枭" xiāo 〈动物〉owl

脩[1] xiū 〈旧语〉dried meat or ham presented by pupils as tuition to their teachers at their first meeting:束~ tuition fee

脩[2] xiū *see* "修" xiū

蓨 xiū *also* "竹节虫" zhújiéchóng stick insect; walking stick

修[1] xiū ❶ embellish; decorate; adorn:装~ paint and decorate; fit up (a house, apartment, etc.) /不~边幅 pay no heed to one's appearance; be slovenly ❷ repair; mend; fix; overhaul:~电视机 repair a TV set /台灯坏了,找人来~一下。The lamp is broken. Get somebody to fix it. /这所房子长年失~。The house has been in bad repair for years. ❸ write; compile:~地方志 write annals of local history ❹ study; learn; cultivate:自~ study by oneself; teach oneself /进~ pursue further studies /必~课 required (*or* mandatory, *or* compulsory) course /主~ specialize (in a subject); major ❺〈迷信〉try to attain immortality through self-cultivation, etc.: *see* "~仙" ❻ build; construct:~路 build a road /~坝 build a dam /~仓库 construct a warehouse /~梯田 build terraced fields ❼ trim; pare; prune:~指甲 trim (*or* pare, *or* manicure) one's fingernails /~树枝 prune a tree /把后面的头发~一~ trim the hair in the back ❽ (short for 修正主义) revisionism:变~ turn revisionist ❾ (Xiū) a surname

修[2] xiū 〈书面〉long; tall and slim:~竹 tall bamboo
修补 xiūbǔ ❶ mend; patch up; repair; revamp:~自行车 repair (*or* mend) a bicycle /~衣裳 patch clothes /~轮胎 mend a tyre /房顶损坏得没法~了。The roof was damaged beyond repair. /这里的墙面需要~一下。The wall here needs to be replastered. /这壶不值得再~了,扔了吧。The kettle is not worth tinkering with. Throw it away. ❷〈医学〉repair:~合成 repair synthesis
修长 xiūcháng tall and slim; slender:身材~ tall and slender (*or* slim) /山间翠竹,~而又挺拔。The green bamboos on the hills are tall and sturdy.
修饬 xiūchì 〈书面〉prune; trim; repair and maintain
修船厂 xiūchuánchǎng shipyard; dockyard
修辞 xiūcí 〈语言〉rhetoric
修辞格 xiūcígé 〈语言〉figures of speech
修辞学 xiūcíxué 〈语言〉rhetoric
修道 xiūdào 〈宗教〉cultivate oneself according to a religious doctrine:深山~ cultivate oneself in a religious doctrine at a mountain retreat
修道士 xiūdàoshì *also* "修士"〈宗教〉monk
修道院 xiūdàoyuàn 〈宗教〉monastery (for men); convent (for women)
修道长 xiūdàozhǎng 〈宗教〉prior; abbot
修订 xiūdìng revise:~合同 revise a contract /重新~后,这本书又发行了一万册。Another 10,000 copies of this book were printed after its revision.
修订本 xiūdìngběn revised edition:《现代汉语词典》~ revised edition of *A Dictionary of Modern Chinese Language*
修短 xiūduǎn 〈书面〉length:这件衣服~适度,肥瘦合体。Neither too long nor too short, this jacket fits me perfectly.
修复 xiūfù ❶ restore; renovate; recondition; repair:~珍贵的古画 renovate a precious ancient painting /水灾后~河堤 repair the river embankments in the aftermath of flooding /~的发动机 reconditioned engine /古庙的~花了足足一年的时间。The restoration of the ancient temple took a full year. ❷〈医学〉repair:~机理 repair

X

mechanism

修复外科 xiūfù wàikē reconstructive surgery

修复牙科学 xiūfù yákēxué prosthodontics

修改 xiūgǎi revise; amend; modify; alter:~章程 revise a charter (*or* articles of association) /~宪法 amend (*or* revise) a constitution /文章要不厌其烦地~。One must take great pains to polish one's writing. /导师对我的论文提出三点~意见。My superviser recommended three modifications in my thesis.

修盖 xiūgài build (houses):~住宅楼 put up (*or* build) residential apartments

修函 xiūhán 〈书面〉 write a letter

修好 xiūhǎo ❶〈书面〉promote friendly relations (between states):遣使~ dispatch envoys to cultivate good relations (with another country) /两国政府捐弃前嫌,重修旧好。Putting aside all their previous differences, the governments of the two countries began to restore cordial relations between them. ❷〈方言〉do good; do good deeds:~积德 do good deeds to win Heaven's favour

修剪 xiūjiǎn ❶ trim; prune; clip; manicure:~葡萄藤 prune the grapevines /~指甲 pare one's fingernails; manicure /~工 trimmer ❷ film editing; montage

修建 xiūjiàn build; construct; erect; put up:~一座公寓楼 erect an apartment building /~立交桥 construct an overpass (*or* flyover) /~铁路新线 build a new railway line /~一座纪念碑 put up a memorial / 签署一项~、经营、移交协定 sign a "build-operate-transfer" (BOT) agreement

修脚 xiūjiǎo pedicure

修脚师 xiūjiǎoshī *also* "修脚工" pedicurist

修旧利废 xiūjiù-lìfèi repair and utilize old or discarded things:上半年,车间~,节约资金达三万元。In the first half of the year, the workshop saved as much as 30,000 *yuan* by repairing old (*or* discarded) articles and putting them to good use.

修浚 xiūjùn dredge:~港口 dredge a harbour /~护城河 dredge a moat

修理 xiūlǐ ❶ repair; mend; overhaul; fix:我的手表需要~。My watch needs fixing. /仪器正在~中。The apparatus is under repair. /收音机已无法~。The radio is beyond repair. ❷ prune; trim; pare:~花枝 trim the flowers ❸〈方言〉punish:把他~一顿。He was taken to task.

修理厂 xiūlǐchǎng repair shop; fix-it shop

修理行业 xiūlǐ hángyè repair trade

修炼 xiūliàn 〈宗教〉give oneself up to austere religious discipline (in order to achieve *nirvana* or immortality); go into religious self-discipline, especially Buddhist or Taoist control of mind and body

修面 xiūmiàn 〈方言〉shave; have a shave:需要~ need a shave

修面膏 xiūmiàngāo shaving cream

修面刷 xiūmiànshuā shaving brush

修明 xiūmíng 〈书面〉(of government, politics, etc.) honest and enlightened; clean

修女 xiūnǚ 〈宗教〉(of the Roman Catholic and Greek Orthodox churches) nun; sister:当~ become a nun; enter a convent /安妮~ Sister Anne /~院 nunnery; convent

修配 xiūpèi make repairs and supply replacements; repair:~车间 repair and spare parts shop /汽车~ auto repairs /~工 repairman; mechanic

修葺 xiūqì fix; repair; renovate:~一新 have a face-lift; take on a new look after renovation; be completely renovated /此房亟待~。The house badly needs repair.

修桥补路 xiūqiáo-bǔlù build bridges and repair roads (as a traditional way of doing good works):他们做了许多~的好事。They have done a lot of good works such as building bridges and mending roads.

修润 xiūrùn (of writings) polish; touch up:这些文章在选进课本之前还需略加~。These articles need some touching up before they are incorporated into the textbook.

修缮 xiūshàn repair; refurbish; renovate:房屋~队 house repairing team /~工程 renovation project /~、改建城市危房 repair or renovate dilapidated urban housing

修身 xiūshēn cultivate one's mind or moral character:~养性 cultivate one's mind and develop one's character /~、齐家、治国、平天下。(Confucian motto) Cultivate yourself, put your family in order, run the local government well, and bring peace to the entire country.

修史 xiūshǐ 〈书面〉write or compile history:直笔~ give a truthful account of history

修士 xiūshì 〈宗教〉(of the Roman Catholic and Greek Orthodox churches) monk; brother:托钵~ friar

修饰 xiūshì ❶ decorate; adorn; ornament; embellish:这间房一经~,满屋增辉。The chamber radiates after decoration. ❷ make up and dress up:出门前,她~打扮了一番。She spent quite a while making up and dressing before leaving home. ❸〈语言〉polish (a piece of writing); modify; qualify:文章~过度,反而损害了原有的朴素美。An over-embellished piece of writing would lose its beauty of simplicity.

修饰剂 xiūshìjì 〈皮革〉dressing agent

修饰语 xiūshìyǔ 〈语言〉modifier

修书 xiūshū 〈书面〉❶ compile a book:~多年,著作等身。After years of compilation, the works he has published measured up to his height when piled up. ❷ write or compose a letter

修伟 xiūwěi 〈书面〉tall and strong:身材~ be tall and powerfully built

修习 xiūxí practise; learn:~战备 practise skills useful in times of war; get prepared for war

修仙 xiūxiān 〈迷信〉cultivate oneself rigorously to become an immortal (often by taking "pills of immortality" prepared through alchemy):年老昏聩,笃于~ indulge in aspiring to be immortal in one's dotage

修心养性 xiūxīn-yǎngxìng cultivate one's mind and improve one's character; cultivate one's original nature

修行 xiūxíng practise Buddhism or Taoism:出家~ become a Buddhist or Taoist monk or nun /他一生~,乐善好施。He has practised Buddhism all his life and taken great delight in doing good and contributing to charity.

修省 xiūxǐng 〈书面〉self-cultivation and self-reflection:静坐~ sit quietly meditating and reflecting on one's own conduct /斋戒~ conduct self-scrutiny during a fast

修学 xiūxué study; research:~三年 study for three years

修养 xiūyǎng ❶ accomplishment; understanding; mastery:在艺术方面很有~ be of high artistic accomplishment /理论~甚高 have a good mastery of theories /文学~不够 lack in literary taste /有~的艺术家 accomplished artist ❷ self-cultivation:大学生应该有~,讲文明。University students should be cultured and well-behaved. /这人太没~了! This chap is really boorish!

修业 xiūyè study at school:~年限 length of schooling /王东先生于1995年2月至1996年2月在本校英语班学习,完成~,特此证明。This is to certify that Mr. Wang Dong studied in the English class of this school from February 1995 to February 1996 and completed all the required courses.

修业证书 xiūyè zhèngshū course transcript; transcript of course work; certificate showing courses taken

修造 xiūzào ❶ build as well as repair:~汽车 make and repair automobiles /~车间 building and repairing shop /~各类农业机械 build and repair all kinds of farm machinery ❷ construct; build:~厂房 construct factory workshops /~花园 build a garden

修整 xiūzhěng ❶ repair and maintain; recondition:~一新的教学楼 newly renovated teaching building /限日~完好 complete the repair within the given time /这些旧卡车需要~了。These old trucks need to be reconditioned. ❷ prune; trim:~花园树木 trim the garden plants /~小松树 prune a young pine tree ❸〈机械〉trim; dress; shave; true:~机 dressing machine /~剪切机 trimming shears /~压力机 trimming press

修正 xiūzhèng ❶ modify; revise; amend; correct:~错误 rectify (*or* correct) one's errors /~统计数字 revise statistical figures /~看法 modify one's views /对宪法提出~意见 put forward amendments to the constitution /我对自己前次发言作一些补充~。I have revised the speech I made last time. ❷ adulterate (Marxism-Leninism); revise

修正案 xiūzhèng'àn amendment

修正角 xiūzhèngjiǎo 〈航空〉correction angle

修正主义 xiūzhèngzhǔyì revisionism:~分子 revisionist (element) /~思潮 revisionist trend /现代~ modern revisionism /~者 revisionist

修枝 xiūzhī 〈农业〉prune:~剪枝 pruning and trimming /这几棵树该~了。These trees need pruning.

修枝剪 xiūzhījiǎn pruning scissors or shears

修治 xiūzhì repair and regulate; dredge:~河道 dredge a river

course
修竹 xiūzhú tall and slender bamboos：茂林～ thick forest and slender bamboos
修筑 xiūzhù build；construct；erect；put up：～铁路 build a railway /～机场 construct an airport /～防御工事 construct defences；build fortifications (*or* defence works) /～新屋 put up a new house
修纂 xiūzuǎn 〈书面〉compile：～方志 compile local chronicles (*or* gazetteers)

xiǔ

宿 xiǔ 〈量词〉*used to count nights*：在旅店里住了一～ stay in a hotel for one night /今晚你可以在我这儿住一～。I can put you up for the night. /他们路上走了三天三～。They spent three days and nights on the way here.
see also sù；xiù

朽 xiǔ ❶ (mostly of wood) rotten；decayed：枯～ withered and rotten /永垂不～ be immortal；live for ever ❷ senile：老～ old and useless；senile /衰～ feeble and decaying；decrepit
朽败 xiǔbài rotten；decayed：门窗～ decayed doors and broken windows
朽腐 xiǔfǔ rotten：棺椁～。The coffin is rotten.
朽坏 xiǔhuài decayed；decrepit；rotten：梁柱俱已～。The beams and pillars were all rotten.
朽烂 xiǔlàn rotten；decayed：几根～的木头 several decayed logs
朽迈 xiǔmài 〈书面〉old and weak；senile；decrepit：～无能 senile and worthless
朽木 xiǔmù rotten wood or tree；useless person：～不可雕也。As decayed wood cannot be carved so you can never help a good-for-nothing fellow.
朽木粪土 xiǔmù-fèntǔ *also*"朽木粪墙" rotten wood and dirt；worthless person；useless stuff：谁愿意被人视为～？谁不愿成为栋梁之材？Who on earth would like to be treated like dirt instead of a pillar of the community?
朽木菌 xiǔmùjùn house fungus
朽木死灰 xiǔmù-sǐhuī rotten wood and dead ashes — lifeless：心同～ one's heart is like rotten wood and dead ashes — utterly apathetic；hopelessly lifeless
朽索驭马 xiǔsuǒ-yùmǎ ride a horse with decayed leashes — be extremely precarious：工作多年，常怀～之惧。I often feel on the brink of an abyss, working here all these years.

滫 xiǔ 〈书面〉stinking pigwash

xiù

宿 xiù 〈古语〉constellation：二十八～ twenty-eight constellations /星～ star constellation
see also sù；xiǔ

褎(褏) xiù 〈书面〉*see*"袖" xiù

袖 xiù ❶ sleeve：长～ long sleeves /衣～ sleeves /套～ oversleeve /拂～而去 leave with a flick of one's sleeves — depart in a huff /长～善舞 those with long sleeves are good at dancing — success is easy for those with rich resources ❷ tuck or hide inside the sleeve：～手而立 stand there, tucking one's hands in one's sleeves
袖标 xiùbiāo badge worn on the sleeve；armband：有两个人带着～，在交叉路口指挥交通。Wearing badges on their sleeves, two men were directing the traffic at the crossroads.
袖狗 xiùgǒu *also*"袖珍狗"；"神笼小狗" shénlóng xiǎogǒu (as a pet) sleeve dog
袖箍 xiùgū armband
袖管 xiùguǎn ❶ sleeve：～破了。The sleeves are worn out. ❷〈方言〉cuff (of a sleeve)；wristband
袖箭 xiùjiàn arrows hidden in the sleeve and launched by springs therefrom
袖口 xiùkǒu cuff (of a sleeve)；wristband
袖扣 xiùkòu cuff links；sleeve buttons
袖笼 xiùlóng muffs
袖手旁观 xiùshǒu-pángguān look on with folded arms；stand by unconcerned；remain an indifferent spectator：朋友有难，他怎能～？How could he stand idly by when his friend was in trouble?
袖套 xiùtào oversleeve
袖筒 xiùtǒng sleeve
袖头 xiùtóu 〈方言〉cuff
袖章 xiùzhāng sleeve badge；brassard；armband
袖珍 xiùzhēn pocket-size；pocket；miniature：～字典 pocket dictionary /～书籍 miniature book
袖珍本 xiùzhēnběn pocket edition
袖珍电视机 xiùzhēn diànshìjī minitelevision (set)
袖珍计算器 xiùzhēn jìsuànqì vest-pocket calculator；pocket calculator
袖珍潜艇 xiùzhēn qiántǐng midget submarine
袖珍收录机 xiùzhēn shōulùjī miniradio-recorder
袖珍收音机 xiùzhēn shōuyīnjī pocket radio set；vest-pocket receiver
袖珍手枪 xiùzhēn shǒuqiāng pocket pistol；hideout gun
袖子 xiùzi sleeve：卷起～准备大干一场 roll up one's sleeves to go at sth.

岫 xiù 〈书面〉❶ cave；cavern：古之隐士，伏于重～之内。In ancient times, hermits lived hidden in deep (*or* remote) caves. ❷ mountain；mountain peak：远～ distant mountain peak /岩～ rocky mountain

秀[1] xiù (of grain crops) put forth flowers or ears：～穗 put forth ears /六月六，看谷～。The sixth day of the sixth (lunar) month sees millet putting forth ears.

秀[2] xiù ❶ elegant；beautiful；pretty and delicate：俊～ handsome；good-looking；personable /眉清目～ having well-chiselled features；good-looking /山清水～ beautiful hills and waters；lovely scenery ❷ clever；smart；intelligent：内～ intelligent (*or* clever) without showing it；inwardly smart /心～ bright without seemingly so ❸ excellent；superb：优～ excellent；first-rate ❹ excellent person；outstanding talent：新～ newly-emerged talent；new talent /后起之～ promising young person
秀拔 xiùbá beautiful and powerful：书法～ (write) a beautiful and forceful hand；beautiful and forceful calligraphy /文辞～ elegant and powerful diction
秀才 xiùcai ❶ *xiucai*, who passed the imperial examination at the county level in the Ming and Qing dynasties ❷ scholar；skilful writer：～造反，三年不成〈俗语〉three whole years won't be enough for genteel scholars to start a rebellion — a cause without any hope of success /张家小子考上大学，咱山沟里也出了个～。With the young man from the Zhang's enrolled in the university, we have finally got a scholar in this mountain recess. /～遇见兵，有理讲不清。〈俗语〉Even when right a man with the pen never can win an argument with a man with the gun.
秀才不出门，能知天下事 xiùcai bù chūmén, néng zhī tiānxià shì the scholar knows all the wide world's affairs without having to step outside his gate
秀才人情 xiùcai-rénqíng 〈谦词〉scholar's gift (usu. books, painting, calligraphy, etc.)；inexpensive gift：我这是～，非薄得很，请笑纳。Mine is a scholars' gift. Please accept this awfully modest present.
秀才人情纸半张 xiùcai rénqíng zhǐ bàn zhāng *also*"秀才人情半张纸"〈俗语〉a scholars' gift is a half sheet of paper — modest gift
秀出班行 xiùchū-bānháng *also*"班行秀出" head and shoulders above others；of superior talent or outstanding ability
秀顶 xiùdǐng bald head
秀而不实 xiù'érbùshí flowering but bearing no fruit — outwardly beautiful but inwardly empty
秀发 xiùfà beautiful hair：～垂肩 beautiful hair hanging about the shoulders
秀慧 xiùhuì elegant and intelligent：透着～的眼睛 eyes exuding elegance and intelligence
秀劲 xiùjìn (of calligraphy) elegant and powerful：字体～ elegant and powerful strokes

X

秀俊 xiùjùn beautiful; handsome; personable: 仪容～ handsome features (*or* appearance)

秀丽 xiùlì beautiful; pretty: 山川～ beautiful rivers and mountains / 故乡～的山水 lovely scenery in one's native land

秀流 xiùliu 〈方言〉 pretty: 这个小女孩长得真～! How pretty the girl is!

秀美 xiùměi graceful; delicate; elegant: ～的瘦西湖 graceful Slim West Lake / 这姑娘身材苗条，面庞～，谁见了谁喜欢。Slender in figure and elegant in features, the girl is most lovely.

秀媚 xiùmèi pretty and charming; pretty and lovely: ～的女子 pretty and charming girl / 她小时候就长得～，几年不见出落得更迷人了。Pretty and lovely when a child, she has grown into an enchanting beauty over the past few years since I last saw her.

秀气 xiùqi ❶ delicate; graceful; elegant; fine: 眉眼长得～ have graceful (*or* beautiful) eyes and brows / 写得一手～的好字 write a beautiful hand ❷ (of speech and manners) refined; gentle; urbane: 谈吐～ speak in a refined manner / 你也太～了，走路都怕踩死蚂蚁似的。Look at that finicky manner of yours! You are scared of tramping an ant to death when walking, aren't you? ❸ (of articles of use) delicate and well-made; superb; exquisite: 这种小刀做工精细，样子也～。The knife is both well-made and exquisite in form.

秀润 xiùrùn beautiful and sleek: 雨后荷花，清新～。The lotus blooms were fresh and beautiful after the rain.

秀色 xiùsè prettiness; beauty: 丽姿～ beautiful looks / ～迷人 enchanting (*or* ravishing) beauty

秀色可餐 xiùsè-kěcān (of attractive woman or beautiful scenery) feast to the eye; beauty to feast one's eyes on: 桂林山水真可谓～，百看不厌了。Guilin scenery is truly a feast for the eyes; one never tires of looking at it.

秀士 xiùshì 〈书面〉 person of outstanding talent and ability: 楚地多～。The land of Chu (now Hubei and northern Hunan) abounded in outstanding talents.

秀挺 xiùtǐng outstanding; out of the common run; beautiful and forceful: 草书～ beautiful and forceful cursive hand (in calligraphy)

秀外慧中 xiùwài-huìzhōng *also* "秀外惠中" (of women) be beautiful without and intelligent within; be endowed with both beauty and intelligence; be both pretty and bright

秀雅 xiùyǎ beautiful and gracious; graceful; elegant: ～的闺房，纤尘不染。The young lady's chamber is tastefully furnished and immaculately clean.

秀异 xiùyì distinguished; outstanding: 才智～ outstanding talent

秀逸 xiùyì elegant and free; handsome and liberal: 风姿～ elegant and free demeanour

秀油 xiùyóu tung oil produced in Xiushan (秀山) County, Sichuan Province

琇

xiù 〈书面〉 jade-like stone

锈(鏽)

xiù ❶ rust: 不生～ not rust; be rustless / 不～钢 stainless steel / 机器生～了。The machine is rusty. / 铁锅上长了一层～。The iron pan is coated with rust. ❷ become rusty: 这颗螺丝～住了，拔不出来。This screw is rusted in. I can't get it out. / 锁都～烂了，门一推就开了。As the lock had completely rusted away, the door opened at the slightest push. ❸ 〈农业〉 rust (disease)

锈斑 xiùbān ❶ (of metals) rust spot; rust stain: 刀上生～了。Rust spots have appeared on the knife. / 把铜盘上的～擦了。Scour the rust stains off the copper plate. ❷ (of crops) rust spots; russet: 叶子上～很多。There are many rust spots on the leaves. / 这些苹果有～和节疤。These apples are rusty and knotty.

锈斑驳病 xiùbānbóbìng 〈农业〉 rusty mottle

锈病 xiùbìng 〈农业〉 rust; rust disease: 小麦～ wheat rust / 抗～小麦 rust-resistant wheat

锈菌 xiùjūn rust fungus: 小麦秆～ wheat stem rust fungus

锈色 xiùsè rust; rusty colour: 深～ deep rust / ～的头发 rusty hair

锈蚀 xiùshí (of metals) rust out; be corroded by rust; be rust-eaten: 铁容易～。Iron corrodes easily. / 古钟上的文字清晰，没有～。The characters on the ancient bell are easily distinguishable, not in the least rust-corroded.

绣(繡)

xiù ❶ embroider: 刺～ embroider / ～手绢儿 embroider flowers on a hankerchief / 被面上～了一朵牡丹花。A peony flower was embroidered on the quilt cover. ❷ embroidery: 苏～ Suzhou embroidery / 湘～ Hunan embroidery

绣墩 xiùdūn ceramic stool with an embroidered cover

绣墩草 xiùdūncǎo dwarf lilyturf

绣房 xiùfáng 〈旧语〉 young lady's bedchamber; boudoir: 这是小姐的～。This was the young lady's bedroom.

绣阁 xiùgé 〈旧语〉 lady's private quarters; boudoir

绣工 xiùgōng ❶ embroidery worker ❷ embroidery (work)

绣花 xiùhuā embroider; do embroidery: ～被面 embroidered quilt cover / ～床罩 embroidered bed cover / 这位姑娘绣得一手好花。This girl is very good at embroidery.

绣花箍 xiùhuāgū embroidery hoop

绣花丝绒 xiùhuā sīróng embroidery silk; floss silk

绣花丝线 xiùhuā sīxiàn embroidery silk thread

绣花鞋 xiùhuāxié *also* "绣鞋" embroidered shoes: 一双～ a pair of embroidered shoes

绣花针 xiùhuāzhēn embroidery needle

绣花枕头 xiùhuā zhěntou ❶ pillow with an embroidered case: 一对～ a pair of embroidered pillows ❷ outwardly attractive but worthless person: ～，虚有其表 be like an embroidered pillow which has no substance / 这小伙子看着不错，其实是个～。The young man looks quite impressive but is actually a good-for-nothing.

绣画 xiùhuà embroidered picture

绣货 xiùhuò embroidered works; embroideries

绣球 xiùqiú ball made of rolled coloured silk: 抛～ (of a young girl) toss a coloured silk ball (to the man she likes as a pledge of love) / 狮子耍～ lion playing with a coloured silk ball — a folk dance

绣球风 xiùqiúfēng 〈中医〉 skin disease of the scrotum

绣球花 xiùqiúhuā 〈植物〉 big-leaf hydrangea (*Hydrangea macrophylla*)

绣线菊 xiùxiànjú meadowsweet; spiraea

绣像 xiùxiàng ❶ tapestry or embroidered portrait: 工艺品部出售各种人物～。The handicraft department sells embroidered portraits of public figures. ❷ exquisitely drawn portrait: ～小说 (popular) novel with illustrated portraits of heroes

绣鞋 xiùxié embroidered shoes (for women)

绣眼鸟 xiùyǎnniǎo 〈动物〉 silver-eye; white-eye (*Zosteropidae*)

臭

xiù ❶ odour; smell: 乳～ smell of milk — be childish / 无声无～ obscure; unknown / 铜～ stink of money — the mentality of "money is everything" ❷ *see* "嗅" xiù

see also chòu

溴

xiù 〈化学〉 bromine (Br)

溴胺酸 xiù'ànsuān bromamine acid

溴胺 T xiù'àn tì bromamine T

溴苯 xiùběn bromobenzene

溴化 xiùhuà bromination

溴化氢 xiùhuàqīng hydrogen bromide (HBr)

溴化物 xiùhuàwù bromide

溴化银 xiùhuàyín silver bromide

溴水 xiùshuǐ bromine water

溴酸 xiùsuān bromic acid

溴钨灯 xiùwūdēng bromine tungsten filament lamp

嗅

xiù scent; smell; sniff: ～来～去 scent (*or* sniff) about / 什么怪味儿？让我来～一～。What an odd smell? Let me take a sniff. / 猎犬～不到狐狸的味儿，停止了追踪。The hound had to give up its pursuit when it had lost scent of the fox.

嗅管 xiùguǎn 〈生理〉 olfactory duct (*Ductus olfactorius*)

嗅觉 xiùjué sense of smell; scent; olfaction: ～很灵 have an acute sense of smell / ～迟钝 be insensitive to smell; have a dull sense of smell / ～分析 olfactory analysis / ～器官 olfactory organ (*Organon olfactus*) / 政治～不灵 be politically dull (*or* insensitive)

嗅觉电子学 xiùjué diànzǐxué 〈电子〉 olfactronics

嗅觉减退 xiùjué jiǎntuì 〈医学〉 hyposmia

嗅觉丧失 xiùjué sàngshī 〈医学〉 anosmia

嗅神经 xiùshénjīng 〈生理〉 olfactory nerve (*Nervus olfactorius*)

xū

需

xū ❶ need; want; demand; require: 急～ need badly; re-

quire urgently /所～之物 things wanted; required goods /生活必～品 necessaries of life; daily necessities /按～分配 to each according to his need ❷ necessities; needs:军～ military supplies (*or* provisions)
需量 xūliàng demand (as a quantity):大蒜的～太大,无法满足。The demand for garlic is too big to meet.
需求 xūqiú requirement; demand; need:市场～ market demand /人的基本～ man's basic requirements /人们对精神生活的～ people's needs for intellectual life
需求律 xūqiúlǜ law of demand
需求论 xūqiúlùn *also* "需求理论" theory of demand; needs theory
需求曲线 xūqiú qūxiàn demand curve
需求弹性 xūqiú tánxìng demand elasticity
需索 xūsuǒ demand; exact; extort (money and material):他大肆挥霍,～无厌。He is a terrible spendthrift and has an insatiable demand for money.
需要 xūyào ❶ require; call for; want; demand:这件衬衣～洗洗。This shirt wants washing. /这个问题～立即加以解决。The problem calls for (*or* demands) prompt solution. /要开办一所学校,～政府的批准。Government approval is required to open a school. /这些食品要发放给最～的人。The food should be distributed among the most needy. ❷ needs:教学应从学生的～出发。Teachers should teach with the students' needs in mind. /我们的任务是要尽量满足人民的～。It is our task to meet the needs of the people as best as we can.
需要功率 xūyào gōnglǜ 〈电学〉 required power; power requirement

繻 xū ❶〈书面〉coloured silk fabric ❷〈古语〉permit made of silk for leaving and entering a country:弃～而去 leave without one's silk permit

欻(歘) xū 〈书面〉suddenly:风雨～至。Suddenly, a storm came up.
see also chuā

砉 xū 〈书面〉sound of the skin torn from the bone
see also huā

讦 xū 〈书面〉❶ brag; boast; exaggerate ❷ huge; big:～谟 grand plan

圩(墟) xū 〈方言〉country fair:赶～ go to a fair
see also wéi
圩场 xūchǎng 〈方言〉country fair; market:这个镇子是个大～。The town is a big marketplace.
圩日 xūrì *also* "圩期"〈方言〉market day
圩市 xūshì 〈方言〉country fair; market
圩镇 xūzhèn 〈方言〉market town

吁 xū 〈书面〉❶ sigh:长～一声 utter (*or* heave) a long sigh ❷〈叹词〉(expressing surprise) why; oh:～,可乎? Why, can this be allowed?
see also yū; yù
吁吁 xūxū 〈象声〉*used to describe sound of breathing*:～直喘 be breathing heavily; pant

盱 xū 〈书面〉look up with eyes wide open; stare upwards:～～然 glowering
盱衡 xūhéng 〈书面〉❶ stare; glower; glare:～厉色 stare sternly ❷ view from an overall perspective; survey:～大局 take stock of the overall situation

顼 Xū a surname

须[1] xū ❶ must; have to:～认真做好准备。Preparations have to be made in real earnest. /必～按时完成任务。We must accomplish these tasks as planned. ❷ (Xū) a surname

须[2] xū 〈书面〉wait; await:卬～我友。I am waiting for my friend.

须[3](鬚) xū ❶ beard; mustache:蓄发留～ wear one's hair long and grow a beard ❷〈动物〉palpus; feeler;〈植物〉tassel:触～ cirrus /花～ stamen; pistil
须疮 xūchuāng 〈医学〉sycosis; barber's itch
须发 xūfà beard and hair:～浓密 thick beard and hair /一夜之间,～尽白。His beard and hair turned grey overnight (because of anxiety).
须根 xūgēn 〈植物〉fibrous root
须鲸 xūjīng 〈动物〉fin whale (*Balaenoptera physalus*); finback; baleen whale; bone whale; whalebone whale
须眉 xūméi 〈书面〉❶ beard and eyebrows:～斑白 greying beard and eyebrows ❷ man:巾帼不让～。Women are in no way inferior to men. *or* Women are equal with men.
须弥座 xūmízuò ❶ pedestal of Buddha's statue ❷ base of a Buddhist temple or pagoda
须生 xūshēng *also* "老生" lǎoshēng elderly and upright male character in traditional Chinese opera
须虾 xūxiā mustache shrimp
须要 xūyào must; have to:这个花瓶易碎,～小心轻放。The vase is fragile and must be handled with care. /教育儿童～耐心。The education of children requires patience.
须臾 xūyú 〈书面〉moment; minute; instant:～不可或缺 cannot dispense with even for one minute /～转晴,又是丽日当空。The rain stopped instantly and the bright sun was overhead. /吾尝终日而思矣,不如～之所学也。Judging by my experience, a moment's study enriches the mind much more than thinking hard all day long.
须知 xūzhī ❶ points for attention; guide; notice:游览～ tourist guide; information for tourists /观众～ notice to audience /考试～ information for examinees ❷ one should know that; it must be understood (*or* borne in mind) that:～一粥一饭来之不易。One must know (*or* bear in mind) that every single grain is the fruit of hard work.
须子 xūzi ❶〈动物〉palpus; feeler:虾～ feelers of a shrimp ❷〈植物〉tassel:玉米～ tassels of maize

媭 xū 〈古语〉(in the ancient state of Chu) elder sister:女～ elder sister of Qu Yuan (屈原)

戌 xū eleventh of the twelve Earthly Branches
see also qu
戌时 xūshí period of the day from 7 p.m. to 9 p.m.

魆 xū *see* "黑魆魆" hēixūxū

虚 xū ❶ void; emptiness:避实就～ avoid essential questions by taking up non-essential ones; keep clear of the enemy's main force and strike at his weak points /国库空～。The national treasury is depleted. ❷ empty; void; vacant; unoccupied: *see* "～位以待" ❸ diffident; timid; cowardly:心～ feel diffident; have a guilty conscience /胆～ cowardly; lily-livered; faint-hearted ❹ in vain; futile:不～此行 have not made the trip in vain; have had a rewarding journey /弹无～发。All bullets hit the target. ❺ false; deceitful; nominal:～职 nominal position /～不掩实 false appearance can never cover up reality /弄～作假 resort to deceit; play tricks /名不～传 have a well-deserved reputation ❻ humble; unassuming; modest:谦～ modest ❼ weak; feeble; in poor health:气～ lacking vital energy; sapless /血～ deficiency of blood; blood insufficiency /体～ have a fragile constitution; be weak physically ❽ guiding principles; theory:务～ discuss principles (*or* ideological guidelines) /～实并举 pay attention to both theory and practical work ❾ eleventh of the twenty-eight constellations in ancient astronomy
虚报 xūbào make a false report:～产量 report the output untruthfully/ ～年龄 lie about one's age /～成绩 cook one's achievements /～冒领 make a fraudulent claim /～开支 padding /～价 sham offer
虚词 xūcí ❶〈语言〉function word; form word:汉语的～包括副词、介词、连词、助词、叹词、象声词六类。Chinese function words consist of the adverb, preposition, conjunction, adjunct, exclamatory word, and onomatopeia. ❷〈书面〉*see* "虚辞"
虚辞 xūcí 〈书面〉exaggeration; empty words:这个调查报告语多～,华而不实。This survey, full of overblown verbiage, is long on high-sounding words, but short on substance.
虚诞 xūdàn absurd; bizzare; fantastic; preposterous

虚度 xūdù spend (time) in vain; idle away; waste:～青春年华 let one's youth slip idly by; idle away one's precious youth /她为自己～一生而叹息。She sighed over her wasted life.

虚度光阴 xūdù-guāngyīn fritter away one's time; loaf about doing nothing:人生当有所作为,不可～。One should make one's life worthwhile instead of frittering it away.

虚度韶华 xūdù-sháohuá *also* "虚度年华" vainly live through one's prime; waste one's glorious youth:～,老大徒悲。An idle youth, a needy age. *or* They must hunger in frost that will not work in heat.

虚分类账 xūfēnlèizhàng 〈会计〉nominal ledger

虚浮 xūfú impractical; shallow; superficial:作风～ have a superficial style of work /此人好说大话,～不实,不可大用。This man should not be trusted with important tasks, for he is given to bragging, and is shallow and impractical.

虚根 xūgēn 〈数学〉imaginary root

虚构 xūgòu fabricate; concoct; make up:～之事 made-up (*or* trumped-up) story /艺术～ artistic fabrication; fiction /凭空～ out-and-out fabrication; sheer myth /故事中的人物并非～。The characters in the story are by no means fictional.

虚汗 xūhàn abnormal sweating due to general debility; deficiency sweat

虚华 xūhuá empty show; false embellishment; ostentation:讲求实际,不尚～。Be practical (*or* down-to-earth), and shun ostentation.

虚话 xūhuà empty talk; false allegation; uninformed statement:我说的都是实情,没有半句～。What I said was completely true, without an iota of falsehood.

虚怀若谷 xūhuái-ruògǔ have a mind as open as a valley; be of a receptive mind; be extremely open-minded; be very modest:刘先生一生～,敏而好学,品德、学问堪为人师。Throughout his life, Mr. Liu has been a keen and modest scholar, rightly regarded as a teacher to others in both character and erudition.

虚幻 xūhuàn unreal; illusory; imaginary:～的感觉 hallucination /生活中要有切实的追求,不要被～的东西所迷惑。In one's life, one should pursue solid goals, not illusions.

虚晃 xūhuǎng feint; deceptive movement

虚晃一枪 xūhuǎng-yīqiāng feint a thrust with one's spear; feint an attack; make a feint:我军摆开进攻架势,～,却向西北方向挺进。Our army feinted an attack and then turned round and marched northwest.

虚谎 xūhuǎng false; unreal; untrue

虚火 xūhuǒ 〈中医〉fire of deficiency type; deficiency of fire

虚己 xūjǐ 〈书面〉modest; humble; open-minded:～以受人 be open-minded; be receptive to others' advice

虚己纳物 xūjǐ-nàwù *also* "虚己以听" listen modestly to what others have to say; take others' advice with an open mind; earnestly heed others' criticism

虚假 xūjiǎ false; sham; hypocritical:～繁荣 false prosperity /～的同情心 spurious sympathy /～的友谊 hypocritical friendship /待人～ insincere to people /他对她的爱情是～的。His love for her was a mere sham. /科学来不得半点～。No sophistry is allowed in science. *or* There is no room for falsehood in science.

虚价 xūjià 〈经济〉nominal price

虚骄 xūjiāo superficial and conceited

虚焦点 xūjiāodiǎn 〈物理〉virtual focus

虚矫 xūjiǎo false and affected

虚惊 xūjīng false alarm:～之后,大家不禁相视大笑。After the false alarm, we looked at each other and burst out laughing.

虚空 xūkōng empty; hollow; void:内心～ feel empty and purposeless

虚夸 xūkuā exaggerative; pompous; bombastic; boastful:～成风。The unhealthy tendency of bragging has run rampant. /此人言谈～,让人难以相信。One finds it hard to believe what the man says because he likes to blow his own horn.

虚诳 xūkuáng falsehood; deceit:～之言 deceitful statement

虚痨 xūláo 〈中医〉consumptive disease; consumption

虚礼 xūlǐ matter of formalities; routine ceremonies; mere rituals; conventional courtesies:你我知交,何必讲此～? As bosom friends, we can well dispense with routine ceremonies. /众人相见,不免一番～,然后各自落座,谈正经事儿。When they met, they had to exchange the usual pleasantries before they sat down and began to talk business.

虚脉 xūmài 〈中医〉feeble pulse

虚名 xūmíng undeserved reputation; false fame:徒有～ not measure up to one's reputation /图～而招实祸 seek false reputation only to court real trouble

虚拟 xūnǐ ❶ suppositional; hypothetical; subjunctive ❷ invented; assumed; fictitious:小说中～的这几个人物,在生活中到处都有。These fictitious figures in the novel can be found everywhere in real life.

虚拟内存 xūnǐ nèicún 〈信息〉virtual memory

虚拟现实 xūnǐ xiànshí 〈信息〉virtual reality

虚拟语气 xūnǐ yǔqì 〈语言〉subjunctive mood

虚拟专用网 xūnǐ zhuānyòngwǎng 〈信息〉virtual private network (VPN)

虚胖 xūpàng puffiness

虚飘飘 xūpiāopiāo fluffy; unsteady:他这几天头晕,～的打不起精神来。He has been feeling dizzy and unsteady lately, unable to pull himself together. /措施不落实,心里～的。I am ill at ease about the lack of practicable measures of implementation.

虚怯 xūqiè ❶ have a guilty conscience; be ashamed and afraid at heart:吓人的大话后面往往隐藏着～。One often finds cowardice behind blustering rhetoric. ❷ weak; feeble:他大病初愈,身子还～。Recovering from a severe illness he is still rather frail.

虚情假意 xūqíng-jiǎyì false display of affection; hypocritical show of friendship; pretence of friendship; insincerity

虚荣 xūróng vanity:讲排场,图～ go in for ostentation and extravagance out of vanity

虚荣心 xūróngxīn vanity; vainglory:她的～特别强。She is extremely vain. /她好胜,但也不能说没有一点～。She wants to excel others, though not without a taint of vainglory.

虚弱 xūruò ❶ in poor health; frail; debilitated:～的体质 weak constitution /手术后身体很～ suffer from general debility after an operation; be very weak after an operation /病体～不堪 be seriously enfeebled by an ailment; be as weak as water from an illness ❷ (of national strength, military force, etc.) weak; debilitated; feeble:～的表现 sign of weakness /侵略者的～本质 inherent (*or* intrinsic) weakness of the aggressors /战争使国力～。The war has sapped the nation's strength.

虚设 xūshè existing in name only; nominal; titular:这个处形同～。The division is but an empty shell.

虚生浪死 xūshēng-làngsǐ *also* "浪死虚生" live a meaningless life and die a worthless death; waste one's life

虚声 xūshēng ❶ undeserved reputation ❷ false show of strength:～恫吓 make an empty show of force to intimidate others; bluff and bluster

虚实 xūshí false or true — actual situation (as of the opposing side); things as they are:派人去探听～ send people to scout the place; dispatch people to ascertain the strength (of one's opponent) /我俩不知～,如何能匆匆作出决定? How can we two make a decision without finding out how things stand? /两军对垒,阵中～,必须严加保密。Our actual deployments must be strictly kept secret when we are face to face with enemy troops.

虚饰 xūshì ❶ whitewash; falsify:～历史 falsify history ❷ flashy but without substance:～的文辞 superficial writing

虚数 xūshù ❶〈数学〉imaginary number ❷ unreliable figure or statistics

虚岁 xūsuì nominal age (age of a person reckoned by the traditional method, who is considered one year old at birth and adds a year each lunar new year)

虚堂悬镜 xūtáng-xuánjìng mirror hanging in an empty hall — impartial in administering justice:～的好法官 upright and impartial judge

虚套子 xūtàozi *also* "虚套" mere formalities; conventionalities:老朋友之间,就不讲这些～了。We are old friends. Let's forget about those formalities. *or* There is no need to stand on ceremony between old friends.

虚土 xūtǔ 〈方言〉turned-up soft soil:春雨过后,双脚踩在松软的～上,有一种说不出的舒适感觉。One experiences a sensation of indescribable comfort when treading on the loosened soil after the spring rain.

虚脱 xūtuō 〈医学〉collapse; prostration:她极度疲乏,一下子就～了。She collapsed as a result of exhaustion.

虚妄 xūwàng unfounded; fabricated; concocted; invented:～的幻想 sheer imagination; hallucination

虚伪 xūwěi sham; false; deceitful; hypocritical:～的小人 mean

hypocrite /～的民主 sham democracy /他看惯了官场的～和欺诈。In his lifetime he had seen enough of the hypocrisy and deception of officialdom.
虚位移 xūwèiyí 〈物理〉virtual displacement
虚位以待 xūwèiyǐdài *also* "虚席以待" leave a seat vacant for sb.; reserve a seat for sb.:公司经理一职～,希望你尽早回来。The corporation will keep the position of the manager vacant for you. We hope you'll be back soon.
虚温 xūwēn 〈气象〉virtual temperature
虚文 xūwén ❶ rules and regulations that people no longer observe; dead letter:交通规章大家都应遵守,不然就成了一纸～。Traffic regulations would become a dead letter in the absence of general observance. ❷ empty form:～浮礼 mere rituals; sheer formalities; conventionalities
虚无 xūwú nihility; emptiness; nothingness:道家以～为本。Taoism takes nothingness as the essence of its doctrine.
虚无缥缈 xūwú-piāomiǎo purely imaginary; ethereal; fanciful; illusory:～的海市蜃楼 mirage; delusion /～的故事 fantastic story /～的幻想成不了现实。Illusory ideals can never become reality.
虚无主义 xūwúzhǔyì nihilism:～者 nihilist
虚线 xūxiàn ❶ dotted line; line of dashes ❷〈数学〉imaginary line
虚像 xūxiàng 〈物理〉virtual image
虚心 xūxīn open-minded; humble; unassuming; modest:你能不能～点,听我把话说完? Could you be a little more open-minded and let me finish what I have to say? /～使人进步,骄傲使人落后。Modesty helps one move forward, whereas conceit makes one lag behind.
虚虚实实 xūxū-shíshí (of military tactics, etc.) combination of the true and the false; feints and ambushes:用兵之道,～。The art of war is to alternate the true with the false.
虚悬 xūxuán ❶ outstanding; unsettled:总工程师一职～已久。The post of the chief engineer has been vacant for a long time. ❷ purely made up; entirely concocted:此等～之事怎可轻信? How could such a cock-and-bull story be taken at face value?
虚言 xūyán empty words or talk; false statement; unfounded remarks
虚言妄语 xūyán-wàngyǔ unfounded statement; fairy tale; lies and falsehoods
虚掩 xūyǎn (of doors, gates, windows, etc.) unlocked or unlatched; (of jackets, shirts, etc.) open; not buttoned up:他见门～着,就推开进了屋。The door was left unlocked, so he pushed it open and walked in.
虚应故事 xūyìng-gùshì do sth. perfunctorily as a mere matter of form or as a routine practice; go through the motions:他每天到公司去一次,～,走走形式,其实心早不在此了。He put in an appearance in the company every day as a routine practice, but in reality his loyalty had already shifted somewhere else.
虚有其表 xūyǒuqíbiǎo look impressive but lack real worth; be striking only in appearance:真没想到他这么笨,真是～! I didn't realize that he is so dumb. His smart appearance is so misleading!
虚与委蛇 xūyǔwēiyí treat courteously but insincerely; feign politeness and compliance:他一边与来客～,一边想着脱身之计。Pretending to be talking courteously with the visitor, he was figuring how to get away.
虚誉 xūyù sham fame; false reputation
虚造 xūzào fabricate or invent out of thin air; forge:向壁～ make up sth. out of one's head while facing the wall — fabricate out of thin air
虚诈 xūzhà hypocritical and cunning; false and foxy
虚张声势 xūzhāng-shēngshì make an empty show of strength; make false pretences; bluff and bluster; be swashbuckling:明眼人一看就知道,他们不过在～而已。Anyone with discerning eyes could see immediately that they were just bluffing. /那不过是～而已,不用理它。That was mere puffery (*or* bombast). We needn't pay any attention to it. /你难道看不出来他这是～,给自己壮壮胆而已? Can't you see that he was merely whistling in the dark?
虚症 xūzhèng 〈中医〉chronic disease marked by deficiency of vital energy and diminishing body resistance
虚掷 xūzhì throw away; waste:～光阴 idle away one's time /多年的心血没有～。His painstaking efforts over the years paid off.
虚字 xūzì *also* "虚字眼儿" empty word; function word; form word
虚左 xūzuǒ 〈书面〉reserve the place of honour for a distinguished guest:～以待 leave the seat of honour open

墟

xū ❶ ruins:废～ ruins /殷～ ruins of the Imperial Palace of the Yin Dynasty ❷ *see* "圩" xū
墟落 xūluò 〈书面〉village
墟墓 xūmù 〈书面〉tomb; grave overgrown with wild grass
墟日 xūrì 〈方言〉fair day; market day

嘘

xū ❶ breathe out slowly:～气 exhale slowly ❷ utter a sigh; sigh:仰天而～ look up at the sky and give out a long sigh /长长地～了一口气 heave a deep sigh ❸ (of cooking fire, steam, etc.) come into contact with; scald; sear; burn:把冷饭在火上～一～ put the cold rice on the fire for a while (to heat it up) /不要让蒸锅～了手。Take care not to get your hands scalded by the steamer. ❹〈方言〉〈叹词〉sh; hush:～! 小声点,小孩儿睡了。Sh! Lower your voice. The child is asleep. ❺〈方言〉hiss; boo; give a Bronx cheer:他被观众～下了台。The audience hissed (*or* booed) him off the stage.
see also shī
嘘寒问暖 xūhán-wènnuǎn inquire after sb.'s well-being; be solicitous about sb.'s health; give sb. one's thoughtful attention; show great concern for sb.
嘘枯吹生 xūkū-chuīshēng revive the withered and scythe the living — great eloquence; having a silver tongue
嘘唏 xūxī *also* "歔欷" xūxī 〈书面〉sob

歔

xū
歔欷 xūxī *also* "嘘唏" xūxī 〈书面〉sob:～不已 keep on sobbing /无不为之～。Everyone shed tears for him.

胥[1]

xū ❶〈书面〉petty official:老～ old petty official ❷ (Xū) a surname

胥[2]

xū 〈书面〉all; each and every:万人～效。Everybody follows the example he sets.
胥吏 xūlì 〈书面〉petty official

谞

xū 〈书面〉❶ talent and wisdom ❷ scheme; stratagem

xú

徐

xú ❶〈书面〉slowly; gently:清风～来,水波不兴。A refreshing breeze is blowing gently over the calm river. ❷ (Xú) a surname
徐悲鸿 Xú Bēihóng Xu Beihong (formerly translated as Hsu Peihung, 1895-1953), Chinese painter
徐步 xúbù 〈书面〉walk slowly or leisurely; stroll:～而行 walk leisurely
徐大椿 Xú Dàchūn Xu Dachun (1693-1772), medical scientist of the Qing Dynasty
徐光启 Xú Guāngqǐ Xu Guangqi (formerly translated as Hsu Kuang-ch'i, 1562-1633), official and scientist of the Ming Dynasty
徐缓 xúhuǎn slowly; gradually:水流～。The water flows slowly.
徐娘半老 Xúniáng-bànlǎo *also* "半老徐娘" Xuniang, beautiful lady past her prime; middle-aged woman:～,风韵犹存。A beautiful woman in her middle age still retains her charm. *or* A woman has lost her youth but not all her beauty and attractiveness.
徐图 xútú 〈书面〉seek to achieve sth. gradually; make a gradual plan:～克之 plan to capture the fortress step by step /～后举 bide one's time for a future uprising
徐渭 Xú Wèi Xu Wei (formerly translated as Hsu Wei, 1521-1593), usually known as Xu Wenchang (徐文长), writer, painter and calligrapher of the Ming Dynasty
徐霞客 Xú Xiákè Xu Xiake (formerly translated as Hsu Hsia-k'eh, 1586-1641), Chinese traveller and geographer of the Ming Dynasty:《～游记》*Xu Xiake's Travel Notes* (known for its detailed and accurate information on geography as well as local customs and habits)
徐徐 xúxú 〈书面〉slowly; gently:帷幕～落下。The curtain slowly came down. /火车～开离车站。The train began to pull out of the station gradually.

X

xǔ

许[1] xǔ ❶ praise; commend: 称～ praise; speak favourably of sb. /推～ recommend ❷ make a promise; promise: 姐姐～过我一本日文字典。My elder sister has promised me a Japanese dictionary. /他～下今天陪我去游泳。He promised to go swimming with me today. ❸ betroth; be betrothed to: 他把女儿～给了一个银行家。He betrothed his daughter to a banker. /姑娘年方十八,尚未～人。The girl is aged 18 and is not yet engaged. ❹ allow; permit; consent: 特～ special permission /默～ acquiesce in /这桩婚事父亲没有应～。Father didn't give consent to this marriage. /只～成功,不～失败。There must be success. It allows of no failure. ❺ perhaps; probably; maybe: 云这么低,～是要下雨吧。The clouds are so low. It's probably going to rain. /她话里或～没有这个意思。Maybe she didn't mean this.

许[2] xǔ ❶ *expressing extent or amount*: 些～ a little; somewhat /少～ a little; somewhat /几～ how much; how many ❷〈书面〉about; approximately: 年二十～ about twenty years old /从者百～ approximately one hundred followers

许[3] xǔ 〈书面〉place: 何～人? Where is the person from? *or* Who is this man (*or* woman)?

许[4] Xǔ ❶ Xu, a principality of the Zhou Dynasty, to the east of today's Xuchang (许昌), Henan Province ❷ a surname

许道宁 Xǔ Dàoníng Xu Daoning (formerly translated as Hsu Taoning, dates unknown), painter of the Northern Song Dynasty

许多 xǔduō many; much; great deal of; lots of; large numbers of: 有～想法 rich in ideas /他教过～学生。He has taught many students. /她有～钱。She has heaps of money. /这样做会引起许许多多的麻烦。This will cause an awful lot of troubles.

许国 xǔguó 〈书面〉pledge to serve one's country; dedicate oneself to the nation: 丈夫誓～。Men vow to serve their country.

许婚 xǔhūn (of a girl's parents or the girl herself) agree to marry: 在他的一再恳求下,女方才～。The girl's parents finally agreed to accept the proposal for marriage upon his repeated pleading.

许久 xǔjiǔ for a long time; for ages: 对不起,让你等了～。Sorry to have kept you waiting for so long. /他们～未见面了。They have not seen each other for ages.

许可 xǔkě permit; allow; approve: 只要条件～,我们一定去。We will certainly go whenever conditions permit. /未经～,不得擅自入内。No admittance unless upon (*or* except with) permission.

许可费 xǔkěfèi licence fee

许可条件 xǔkě tiáojiàn licence conditions

许可证 xǔkězhèng licence; permit: 进口～ import licence /工作～ work permit /出入～ pass

许可证贸易 xǔkězhèng màoyì licensing trade

许诺 xǔnuò make a promise; promise; pledge: ～过的事一定要办。We must carry out what we promise. /他们～支持我们。They made a pledge to support us. /这样做事先已得到双方的～。Both parties have made a commitment to the deal.

许配 xǔpèi (of an arranged marriage) betroth a girl: 我自幼儿～赵家。I was betrothed to the Zhao family's son when I was a little girl.

许亲 xǔqīn accept a proposal of marriage

许身 xǔshēn 〈书面〉resolve to do sth.; dedicate oneself to: ～报国 dedicate oneself to one's country /～一何愚。What a foolish resolve!

许愿 xǔyuàn ❶ make a vow (to a god); make a resolution (to oneself): 烧香～ burn incense and offer a vow to a god /在生日会上许个愿 make a wish (*or* resolution) at one's birthday party /她在菩萨面前许了愿。She made a vow before the Buddha. ❷ promise sb. a reward: 封官～ promise to reward sb. with promotion /这件事你许过愿,答应帮人家忙。You've promised to help him out on this matter.

许字 xǔzì 〈书面〉(of a girl) agree to give one's hand to a man; be betrothed to sb.; plight one's troth

诩 xǔ 〈书面〉brag; boast; blow one's own horn: 自～ brag; boast; praise oneself /以专家自～ style oneself an expert

栩 xǔ

栩栩 xǔxǔ vivid; lively; lifelike: ～欲活 to the life; lifelike; vivid

栩栩如生 xǔxǔ-rúshēng lifelike; lively; spirited; vivid: 图成,～,不知画是我,我是画也。When done, the portrait was so true to life that I couldn't tell whether the portrait was me or I was the portrait.

湑 xǔ 〈书面〉❶ clear: 酒～ clear wine ❷ luxuriant: 枝繁叶～ luxuriant foliage and spreading branches; leafy profusion

糈 xǔ 〈书面〉grain

醑 xǔ ❶〈书面〉mellow wine ❷〈药学〉spirit; essence: 樟脑～ camphor essence (*or* spirit) /氯仿～ chloroform spirit

醑剂 xǔjì 〈药学〉spirit; essence

姁 xǔ 〈书面〉

姁姁 xǔxǔ 〈书面〉peaceful and happy; gentle; mild: 言语～ speak gently /母子～相乐。The mother and son enjoyed each other's company in peaceful harmony.

盨 xǔ bronze food container with two handles and a lid used in ancient China

xù

畜 xù raise (domestic animals); breed; rear: 牧～ rear livestock or poultry

see also chù

畜产 xùchǎn livestock or animal products: ～丰富 abundant animal products /～进出口 import and export of livestock products

畜产品 xùchǎnpǐn animal product; livestock products

畜牧 xùmù raising or rearing livestock or poultry; animal husbandry; stock farming: 以～为生 live on animal husbandry

畜牧场 xùmùchǎng animal farm; livestock or stock farm

畜牧经济学 xùmù jīngjìxué economics of animal husbandry

畜牧区 xùmùqū pastoral area

畜牧时代 xùmù shídài pastoral age

畜牧业 xùmùyè animal husbandry; livestock husbandry; livestock farming: 发展～ develop animal husbandry

畜养 xùyǎng raise (domestic animals): ～牲口 raise livestock

蓄 xù ❶ store up; save up: 储～ savings /私～ private savings /缸里～满了水。The vat is filled with water. ❷ cause to grow; grow: ～须 grow a beard /～发明志 wear one's hair long to show one's resolve ❸ harbour; cherish; entertain (ideas): 素～异志 have long harboured sinister intentions (*or* treacherous designs)

蓄藏 xùcáng save and store; lay up; lay in

蓄电池 xùdiànchí *also* "电瓶" diànpíng storage battery; accumulator

蓄电池车 xùdiànchíchē battery car; accumulator vehicle

蓄电池充电器 xùdiànchí chōngdiànqì accumulator or battery charger

蓄电瓶 xùdiànpíng accumulator jar

蓄洪 xùhóng 〈水利〉store floodwater: ～区 area for storing floodwater; flood storage area /～量 water storage capacity /～坝 flood dam /～工程必须于雨季到来之前完工。The flood storage project must be completed before the rainy season sets in.

蓄积 xùjī store up; save up: 水库～了大量雨水。The reservoir has stored up a lot of rainwater. /他工作多年,稍有～。He has saved a little money over many years of work.

蓄谋 xùmóu plan in advance; premeditate: ～反叛 harbour plans for an insurrection /这是一桩～已久的谋杀案。This is a long-premeditated murder.

蓄能 xùnéng energy storage

蓄念 xùniàn harbour or entertain ideas: ～已久 have long harboured the idea

蓄热 xùrè thermal storage; accumulation of heat

蓄墒 xùshāng preserve the moisture in the soil: 储水～ store up water to keep the soil moist

蓄水 xùshuǐ retain or store water：水池～不多。The pond does not hold much water. /水库～量不足，不能满足下游农田灌溉的需要。The reservoir doesn't store enough water to meet the needs of field irrigation downstream.
蓄水池 xùshuǐchí cistern; reservoir; catch basin
蓄水工程 xùshuǐ gōngchéng water storage project
蓄养 xùyǎng store up; build up; accumulate：～力量 accumulate strength /～精力 build up energy
蓄意 xùyì premeditated; calculated; deliberate：～攻击 calculated attack /～谋杀 premeditated murder; deliberate attempt to kill /～伤害 injure sb. with intent /～寻衅 pick a fight with sb.
蓄志 xùzhì have long cherished an ambition; have long harboured or entertained a resolve：～报国 have made up one's mind to dedicate oneself to the service of the country /他～改变家乡落后的面貌。He has long harboured a firm resolve to rid his native village of its backwardness.

酗

xù
酗酒 xùjiǔ be given to heavy drinking; indulge in excessive drinking; be alcoholic：～成性 become alcoholic; be given to alcoholism /～滋事 create a disturbance under the influence of liquor; get drunk and kick up a row

勖（勗）

xù 〈书面〉encourage
勖励 xùlì 〈书面〉encourage; inspire：～后进 encourage those lagging behind to catch up with others
勖勉 xùmiǎn 〈书面〉encourage; inspire：～有加 give repeated encouragement

昫

xù *also* "煦" xù 〈书面〉mostly used in the names of persons

煦

xù 〈书面〉warm; balmy：拂～（of wind）be blowing warmly /春风和～，游人如云。The spring breeze is balmy, and people go for outings in droves.
煦暖 xùnuǎn warm：～的春风 warm and gentle spring breeze
煦煦 xùxù ❶ warm：～的阳光 warm sunshine ❷〈书面〉happy and harmonious

叙（敍、敘）

xù ❶ talk; chitchat; chat：畅～旧事 chitchat cheerfully about old times /有空请来～～。Please drop in for a chat when you are free. ❷ give an account of; narrate; recount; relate：自～ account of oneself; autobiographic note (*or* statement) /～多论少 more narrating than theorizing ❸ assess; evaluate; appraise：～奖 appraise sb.'s service and reward it ❹ *see* "序[1]❶❷❹" xù
叙别 xùbié have a farewell talk; bid farewell to sb.
叙次 xùcì *also* "序次" xùcì 〈书面〉order; order of priority
叙道 xùdao 〈口语〉tell; recount：别着急，听我慢慢地给你～～。Be patient, and let me tell you all about it.
叙功 xùgōng 〈书面〉rate or assess sb.'s services：～行赏 decide awards on the basis of services rendered
叙话 xùhuà chat; talk：围炉～ chat round the stove
叙旧 xùjiù talk about the old days; reminisce about the past：昨晚老朋友聚在一起～，一直聊到深夜。The old friends stayed up late last night, reminiscing about the good old days.
叙利亚 Xùlìyà Syria：～人 Syrian
叙录 xùlù brief introduction (including collation and etymology) to a book
叙亲 xùqīn talk about or look into one's relationship with sb. else：要是～，我们是表兄妹关系。If you look at the family tree, we are first cousins.
叙事 xùshì narrate; relate; recount：这部小说～生动，笔法细腻。The narration in the novel is graphic and the characterization superb in every detail.
叙事歌剧 xùshì gējù ballad opera
叙事剧 xùshìjù epic theatre
叙事曲 xùshìqǔ 〈音乐〉ballade
叙事诗 xùshìshī narrative poem; ballade
叙事文 xùshìwén narration; narrative (prose)
叙述 xùshù narrate; recount; relate：小说～了一个真实而生动的故事。The novel recounts a true and moving story. /他把事情的前因后果又～了一遍。He narrated the story once again from beginning to end.
叙说 xùshuō tell; relate; narrate：他～了自己的悲惨遭遇。He gave an account of his miserable experiences.
叙谈 xùtán chat; chitchat
叙文 xùwén *also* "序文" xùwén preface; foreword
叙言 xùyán *also* "序言" xùyán foreword; introduction
叙用 xùyòng (of an official) appoint; employ：按才～ employ people according to their capabilities /天下英才，咸加～ recruit all the talents of the country

溆

xù 〈书面〉waterside

洫

xù 〈书面〉water duct in a field; ditch：沟～ field ditch (for irrigation or drainage)

恤（卹、賉）

xù ❶〈书面〉worry; misgiving; apprehension：殒身不～ lay down one's life without any misgivings; not hesitate to die for a cause ❷ pity; sympathize; commiserate：体～ show solicitude for /怜～ commiserate; be sympathetic to ❸ give relief; compensate：抚～ comfort and compensate a disabled person or a bereaved family
恤金 xùjīn *also* "抚恤金" fǔxùjīn pension for a disabled person or the family of the deceased
恤衫 xùshān 〈方言〉shirt

旭

xù ❶〈书面〉brilliance of the rising sun：朝～ brilliance of the morning sun ❷（Xù）a surname
旭日 xùrì rising sun
旭日东升 xùrì-dōngshēng sun rising in the eastern sky — symbol of youth and vigour：他的事业犹如～，蒸蒸日上。He has a rising career like the morning sun.

鲊（鱮）

xù silver carp

序[1]

xù ❶ order; sequence：顺～ sequence; order /程～ procedure /井然有～ in apple-pie order /工～ work process /维持秩～ keep (*or* maintain) order /以字母为～ in alphabetical order (*or* sequence) /以年代为～ in chronological order ❷〈书面〉arrange in order; order：～齿不～官 (arrange seats) according to age, not official rank ❸ initial; opening introductory: *see* "～幕"; "～论" ❹ preface：作～ write a preface for a work /赠～ offer to write a preface

序[2]

xù 〈古语〉❶ wing-room：东～ east wing ❷ type of local school：庠～之教 general education; primary education
序跋 xùbá preface and postscript
序齿 xùchǐ 〈旧语〉〈书面〉(seating arranged) in order of seniority：众人来到大堂之上，～入座。All of them went into the hall and sat down in order of seniority.
序次 xùcì ❶ order; sequence ❷〈书面〉(of books) arrange in serial order
序号 xùhào serial number; sequence number
序列 xùliè ❶ order; alignment; array：战斗～ battle array; battle order ❷〈数学〉sequence：～分析 sequence analysis; sequential analysis /～解码 sequential decoding ❸〈音乐〉serial：～技巧 serial technique /～音乐 serialism
序列主义 xùlièzhǔyì 〈音乐〉serialism
序论 xùlùn (of works) introductory chapter; introduction
序目 xùmù (of books) preface and table of contents：看过～之后，我对这本书有了一个大概的了解。I had a rough idea of the book after going over the preface and the table of contents.
序幕 xùmù ❶〈戏剧〉opening scene in a play; prologue; prelude ❷〈比喻〉prologue or prelude to major events：边境挑衅是大规模入侵的～。The border provocation proved to be the prologue to large-scale invasion.
序曲 xùqǔ ❶〈音乐〉overture：乐队奏起了～。The band began to play the overture. ❷ prelude (to an event, action, etc.)：大学期间的投稿，是我写作生涯的～。The contributions I made to magazines in my university years were the prelude to my writing career.

序时账 xùshízhàng 〈会计〉journal
序数 xùshù ordinal number; ordinal: ～和 ordinal sum / ～积 ordinal product / ～词 ordinal number
序文 xùwén also "叙文" xùwén preface; foreword: 这篇～对当前文艺思潮的剖析十分深刻。The analysis in the preface of the prevailing trends of literary thinking was very penetrating.
序言 xùyán also "叙言" xùyán preface; foreword
序战 xùzhàn also "初战" chūzhàn initial battle
序传 xùzhuàn also "叙传" xùzhuàn autobiography

埣 xù 〈古语〉east or west wall of a house (now used usually in personal names)

芧 xù 〈古语〉acorn
see also zhù

絮[1] xù ❶ (cotton) wadding; padding: 棉～ wadding for a quilt ❷〈古语〉coarse silk floss ❸ sth. resembling cotton: 柳～ willow catkins / 芦～ reed catkins ❹ wad or pad (as with cotton): ～丝棉被 wad a quilt with silk floss / ～棉衣 line (or wad) one's clothes with cotton

絮[2] xù ❶ long-winded; loquacious; talkative; garrulous ❷〈方言〉bored; fed up: 这话我听～了。I'm fed up with (or of) listening to all this.
絮被 xùbèi 〈方言〉quilt wadded with cotton; wadded quilt
絮叨 xùdao long-winded; garrulous; windy; wordy: ～的老太婆 garrulous old woman / 絮絮叨叨地谈自己的经历 talk tediously about one's experience / 你少～! No more of your nagging!
絮烦 xùfan be tired or bored (by monotonous repetition of sth.): 她老重复那几句话,大家都听～了。All of us became tired of listening to her repeating the same old story.
絮聒 xùguō ❶ long-winded; garrulous; chattery ❷ trouble (other people); bother: 别拿这些小事来～别人。Don't bother people with your trifles.
絮棉 xùmián cotton for wadding
絮凝 xùníng 〈化学〉flocculation: ～剂 flocculant
絮说 xùshuō talk garrulously; chatter; nag: ～个没完 keep on nagging; chatter away
絮窝 xùwō (of birds and animals) line a nest with dry grass or feathers; make a nest
絮絮 xùxù be garrulous; talk endlessly
絮语 xùyǔ 〈书面〉❶ prattle on and on: 我一进家门,妈妈就没断了～。Mother prattled endlessly ever after I got home. ❷ garrulous talk; endless chatter: 春夜柔柔的细雨就像那情人甜美的～。The soft drizzles of the spring night were like sweet words falling from the lips of lovers.
絮嘴 xùzuǐ nag; be chatty; talk garrulously: 这事用不着你～,我知道怎么做。I know how to go about the matter, so stop nagging at me.

婿(壻) xù ❶ son-in-law: 翁～ father-in-law and son-in-law ❷ husband: 夫～ husband / 姨～ aunt's husband; uncle-in-law

绪 xù ❶ beginning of a matter: 头～ main threads (of a complicated affair) / 千头万～ thousands of strands and loose ends (to tie up) / 一切就～ have straightened out all the threads of a matter; everything is in its proper place; all is set ❷〈书面〉remnants: ～风 remnants of a social trend ❸ mental or emotional state; mood: 情～ mood / 思～万千。A myriad thoughts crowded into one's mind. or One's mind is in a whirl. ❹〈书面〉task; cause; enterprise; undertaking: 续先辈之遗～ carry on an unfinished task left over by the older generation; take up where the older generation left off ❺ (Xù) a surname
绪论 xùlùn (of works) introduction
绪言 xùyán see "绪论"
绪余 xùyú 〈书面〉remainder: 门人数十,皆得其～。The several scores of his disciples only learned some of his lesser skills.

续(續) xù ❶ continuous; successive; one after another: 陆～ one after another; in succession / 继～ continue; carry on / 连～ (do sth.) continuously / 时断时～ on and off ❷ continue; resume; extend: ～会 resume a meeting / 后来～有所闻。More was heard of it later on. ❸ add; increase; supply more: ～茶 add more tea / 给火～煤 add coal to the fire ❹ (Xù) a surname
续编 xùbiān continuation (of a book); sequel: 杂文～ sequel to a collection of short essays
续貂 xùdiāo (short for 狗尾续貂)〈谦词〉join a dog tail to a sable — make an unworthy continuation of a great work; write a wretched sequel to a fine work: 先生去世后,该书由我～。I wrote a rather unworthy sequel to the book after the author passed away.
续订 xùdìng renew one's subscription (to a newspaper or magazine)
续断 xùduàn 〈中药〉teasel root
续航 xùháng (of airplanes and ships) continue a journey without refuelling: 这种客机～时间比一般客机长。This type of passenger aircraft flies longer than an ordinary one.
续航力 xùhánglì endurance (of flight); flying range (of an airplane); cruising radius (of a ship)
续集 xùjí continuation (of a book); sequel: 这部小说的～预计明年出版。A sequel to the novel is expected to come off the press next year.
续假 xùjià extend one's leave of absence; extend leave: 该生未曾～,逾期不归。The said student overstayed his leave without asking for prior permission to extend it.
续借 xùjiè renew (a library book): ～一周 be renewed for a week
续命汤 xùmìngtāng decoction to stimulate a dying person; lifesaver
续篇 xùpiān continuation or sequel (to a book or story)
续聘 xùpìn continue to engage sb.; continue the employment of sb.: 聘期满后可以～。The term of engagement (or service) may be extended upon expiration.
续娶 xùqǔ also "续亲" see "续弦❶"
续弦 xùxián ❶ remarry after the death of one's wife: 他六十岁～,找了个老伴儿。At 60, he was remarried to an elderly woman to keep him company. ❷ second wife (after the death of one's first wife)
续约 xùyuē renew a treaty or contract

xu

蓿 xu see "苜蓿" mùxu

xuān

宣 xuān ❶ announce; declare; proclaim; promulgate: ～赦 proclaim a general amnesty / 照本～科 echo what the books say; read a text item by item / 心照不～ have a tacit understanding; be understood but not expressed ❷ summon into the presence of the emperor by an imperial edict: see "～召" ❸ drain; lead off (liquids): see "～泄" ❹ (Xuān) referring to Xuancheng (宣城) in Anhui Province or Xuanwei (宣威) in Yunnan Province ❺ Xuan paper, a high quality rice paper made in Xuancheng or Jingxian (泾县): 玉版～ white tough rice paper / 虎皮～ coloured rice-paper with light stripes ❻ (Xuān) a surname
宣笔 xuānbǐ exquisite writing brush made in Xuancheng or Jingxian in Anhui Province
宣布 xuānbù announce; pronounce; declare; proclaim: ～无效 declare sth. invalid (or null and void); nullify sth. / ～会议结束 declare a meeting closed / ～政见 make political pronouncements / ～投票结果 announce the votes / ～公共假日 proclaim a public holiday / ～原判无效 quash an original judgment / 文件一经～即具有法律效力。The document becomes legal upon proclamation.
宣称 xuānchēng assert; declare; claim; profess: 自豪地～ proudly assert / 口头上～公正,实际上偏袒一方 profess to be fair, but actually be partial to one party / 他当众～自己在这桩贿赂案中是清白的。He publicly declared his innocence in the bribery case.
宣传 xuānchuán promote; publicize; disseminate; propagate: ～计划生育政策 publicize family planning / 为本公司的产品作～ promote the products of the company / 大力～ actively propagate / 广为～ give a great deal of publicity (to sth.) / 意识形态的～ ideological dissemi-

nation /新闻～ press publicity /～运动 publicity drive / ～办公室 information office /尽是一些～ nothing but propaganda /大肆～报道 media hype /向群众～ make known (a policy, etc.) among the masses /安全驾驶～月 month for safe driving /自我～ blow one's own trumpet (*or* horn); sell oneself

宣传部 xuānchuánbù information department; publicity ministry

宣传弹 xuānchuándàn shell or bomb containing information material fired for publicity or propaganda purposes

宣传队 xuānchuánduì publicity team; propaganda team: 文艺～ performing arts troupe engaged in publicity work /毛泽东思想～ Mao Zedong Thought propaganda team (in the Cultural Revolution)

宣传工具 xuānchuán gōngjù instrument or means of publicity; vehicle of propaganda; mass media

宣传工作者 xuānchuán gōngzuòzhě one who is engaged in publicity or propaganda work; publicist; propagandist

宣传画 xuānchuánhuà *also* "招贴画" zhāotiēhuà picture poster; poster: 街头～ street picture poster /张贴～ put up (*or* display) picture poster

宣传机构 xuānchuán jīgòu organ in charge of publicity or information; media

宣传机器 xuānchuán jīqì 〈贬义〉 propaganda machine

宣传品 xuānchuánpǐn publicity or propaganda material; promotion material: 散发～ distribute publicity materials /这些都是违禁的～。All these propaganda materials are contraband.

宣传网 xuānchuánwǎng publicity or propaganda network

宣传员 xuānchuányuán publicist; propagandist

宣德 Xuāndé Xuande, title of the reign (1426-1435) of Zhu Zhanji (朱瞻基), 5th emperor of the Ming Dynasty, called reverently Ming Xuanzong (明宣宗) after death

宣读 xuāndú read out (in public); announce: 当众～嘉奖令 read out a citation in public

宣告 xuāngào declare; proclaim; announce: 庄严～ solemnly proclaim /郑重～ declare in all seriousness /～破产 declare bankruptcy; go bankrupt /～停战 announce armistice /中华人民共和国～成立。The founding of the People's Republic of China was proclaimed.

宣和 Xuānhé Xuanhe, title of the reign (1119-1125) of Zhao Ji (赵佶), 8th emperor of the Northern Song Dynasty, called reverently Song Huizong (宋徽宗) after death

宣讲 xuānjiǎng explain and publicize; preach: 先进事迹～会 meeting to publicize meritorious deeds /～福音 preach the gospel

宣教 xuānjiào publicity and education: ～工作 publicity and education

宣劳 xuānláo 〈书面〉 ❶ serve; render a service to: 为国～ serve one's country ❷ issue an imperial edict in recognition of services rendered; (of an emperor or on behalf of him) extend greetings

宣明 xuānmíng proclaim or declare clearly; announce explicitly: ～观点 make known one's viewpoint /～谈判解决争端的主张 state (*or* announce) in explicit terms that one is for settling disputes through negotiations

宣判 xuānpàn 〈法律〉 pronounce judgment; deliver judgment: ～有罪 pronounce sb. guilty /～无罪 pronounce sb. not guilty; acquit sb. of a charge /对犯人作出～ pass judgment on a prisoner /～某人二年徒刑 pronounce a sentence of two years on sb. /～原告败诉 pronounce a judgment against the plaintiff

宣示 xuānshì express in public; make known publicly: 他向报界～，此次隐退皆因身体有病，决无他意。He declared to the press that his retirement from office was purely for reasons of health.

宣誓 xuānshì take or swear an oath; make a vow; make a pledge: 举手～ raise one's hand to make a vow /在国旗下～ take an oath in front of the national flag /～就任总统 take one's oath of office (*or* be sworn in) as president /～效忠政府 swear an oath of allegiance to a government

宣统 Xuāntǒng Xuantong, title of the reign (1909-1911) of Aisin Gioro Puyi (爱新觉罗·溥仪), 10th and last emperor of the Qing Dynasty

宣腿 xuāntuǐ ham produced in Xuanwei (宣威), Yunnan Province

宣泄 xuānxiè ❶ drain off; lead off (liquids): 连日暴雨，洪水不能及时～，可能会危及庄稼。The flood water resulting from successive days of rainstorm couldn't drain off, and the crops might be endangered. ❷ get sth. off one's chest; unbosom oneself; reveal: ～不满情绪 give vent to one's dissatisfaction /只有在母亲面前，她才能痛快地～自己的委屈。Only before her mother could she unbosom herself, pouring out her grievances. ❸ 〈书面〉 reveal; let out: 事关机密，不得～。This is confidential. Don't let it out.

宣叙调 xuānxùdiào 〈戏剧〉 recitative

宣言 xuānyán ❶ declaration; proclamation; manifesto: 《共产党～》 *Communist Manifesto* /世界人权～ The Universal Declaration of Human Rights (1948) /开罗～ Cairo Declaration (1943) /波茨坦～ Potsdam Proclamation (1945) /中立～ declaration of neutrality ❷ proclaim; declare; state: 中国政府对这一问题的立场，新华社昨已受权郑重～。Xinhua News Agency was authorized to solemnly declare the Chinese government's position on the question yesterday.

宣扬 xuānyáng publicize; propagate; advocate; advertise: 大肆～ make (*or* raise) a big fanfare /四处～ spread everywhere /～佛教 preach Buddhism /～气功的作用 advocate *qigong* /～改革开放的成就 publicize the achievements scored under the policy of reform and opening to the outside world

宣战 xuānzhàn ❶ declare or proclaim war: 这一步骤，无疑是向该国～。This is nothing short of declaring war against that country. ❷ battle; fight a battle; wage a struggle against: 向荒山进军，向干旱～ march on the barren hill and battle against the drought /向旧世界～ declare war on the old world

宣战书 xuānzhànshū declaration of war

宣召 xuānzhào summon sb. into the presence of the emperor by an imperial edict; summon to court

宣旨 xuānzhǐ 〈书面〉 issue or publicly read an imperial edict; announce an imperial edict

宣纸 xuānzhǐ *Xuan* paper, a high quality rice paper made in Xuancheng (宣城) or Jingxian (泾县) of Anhui Province, esp. good for traditional Chinese painting and calligraphy

煊

xuān 〈书面〉 *see* "喧[1]" xuān

煊赫 xuānhè illustrious; celebrated: 声名～ of great renown /名声～的人 celebrity; luminary

瑄

xuān round flat piece of jade with a hole in its centre (used as offering to heaven in ancient times)

萱(蘐)

xuān ❶ tawny day lily ❷ 〈书面〉〈敬词〉(your) mother: 椿～ parents

萱草 xuāncǎo ❶ *also* "黄花菜" huánghuācài yellow or tawny day lily ❷ a kind of herb or grass supposed by ancients to be capable of relieving one of sorrow (*or* anxiety)

萱椿 xuānchūn *also* "椿萱" 〈书面〉 parents: ～并茂。Both father and mother are in good health.

萱堂 xuāntáng 〈书面〉〈敬词〉 mother; your mother

揎

xuān ❶ roll up sleeves: ～拳捋袖 roll up one's sleeves and raise one's fists (to fight) ❷ 〈方言〉 push: ～开大门 push the gate open; open the gate at one push ❸ hit; strike: ～了他一拳 hit him with one's fist

喧(諠)

xuān noisy; clamorous; uproarious

喧宾夺主 xuānbīn-duózhǔ a presumptuous guest usurps the host's role; the secondary supercedes the primary; a noisy guest steals the host's thunder: 招待会上，来宾中几个小伙子异常活跃，大有～之势。At the reception a few young fellows among the guests were exceedingly active, stealing the show from the guest of honour.

喧传 xuānchuán be extensively circulated; be widely rumoured: 说他要回来的消息～了一阵，但不久又沉寂了。The news that he would soon come back had been going the rounds for some time before it died down.

喧呼 xuānhū shout loudly; call out loudly; clamour; shout at the top of one's voice

喧哗 xuānhuá ❶ noisy; full of confused noise; uproarious: 村子里鸡啼狗吠，孩子喊叫，一片～。The village was in a hubbub of cocks crowing, dogs barking and children shouting. ❷ uproar; hubbub: 请勿在病房～! Please keep quiet in the ward.

喧豗 xuānhuī 〈书面〉 (of water or wind) roaring; thundering: 飞瀑～。The waterfall splashes and roars.

喧叫 xuānjiào cry out loudly; shout; yell

喧呶 xuānnáo 〈书面〉 din; hubbub; uproar; confused noise

X

喧闹 xuānnào noise and excitement; din; bustle; racket:车辆的～声 roar of the traffic /城市街道的～ hubbub of city streets /～的市场 bustling market /除夕晚上的～ joyous din on New Year's eve /何人在外面如此～? Who's raising such a racket outside?

喧嚷 xuānrǎng clamour; hubbub; din; racket:一片～ hullabaloo /～起来 raise a clamour; kick up a rumpus /工人们～着要罢工。The workers clamoured for a strike. /这不过是愚蠢而徒劳的～。This is but foolish and futile clamour.

喧扰 xuānrǎo noise and disturbance; racket; tumult:身居闹市,日日～,苦不堪言。Living in a busy quarter, he was tortured by the hustle and bustle of the street day and night.

喧声 xuānshēng hubbub of voices; confused and loud talking; uproar:～阵阵 bursts of uproar

喧腾 xuānténg noise and excitement; uproar:锣鼓～ deafening sound of gongs and drums /万人～,喊声震天。The air was reverberating with the cries and shouts of the multitude.

喧天 xuāntiān fill the air with resounding noise:鼓乐～。The air is filled with crescendos of music accompanied by drumbeats.

喧阗 xuāntián 〈书面〉noise and crowdedness; hustle and bustle; clamour; racket:车马～ heavy traffic; clamour of the traffic /热闹～ scene of hustle and bustle

喧嚣 xuānxiāo ❶ noisy; clamorous:～的人声 hubbub of voices /这是一座繁华～的城市。It's a flourishing, bustling city. ❷ noise; din; clamour:震耳欲聋的～声 deafening uproar /远离城市的～ away from the din and bustle of the city /入夜,～了一天的工地平静了。Night fell and the worksite which had been filled with din during the day quieted down.

喧笑 xuānxiào chatting and laughing loudly:隔壁房间传来阵阵～声。Fits of laughter amid talking were heard from the next room.

喧啸 xuānxiào whistle violently; boom; thunder:～的海涛 roaring sea waves

喧杂 xuānzá (of noise) loud and confused:～的说笑声 loud and confused talking and laughing

喧噪 xuānzào loud shout; commotion:外面的～声把我吵醒了。The commotion outside woke me up.

暄[1]

xuān 〈书面〉warmth (of the sun); genial warmth:寒～ exchange of (conventional) greetings /负～ bask in the sunshine

暄[2]

xuān 〈方言〉fluffy; soft:～土 soft soil /新鲜面包很～。The fresh bread is very fluffy.

暄乎 xuānhu also "暄乎" 〈方言〉fluffy; soft; spongy:这馒头够～的。What fluffy steamed buns!

暄风 xuānfēng warm, gentle wind; spring breeze

暄和 xuānhuo soft; downy; loose:晒过的被褥～着呢。The quilt has just been sunned and is very fluffy.

暄暖 xuānnuǎn 〈书面〉warm:三月天气,阳光～。The sun in March is gentle and warm. or March is full of warm sunshine.

暄气 xuānqì summer heat; sweltering heat:～初收,金风送凉。The autumn breeze was pleasantly cool after the summer heat.

暄腾 xuānteng 〈方言〉fluffy; soft:这几屉馒头蒸得又大又～。These trayfuls of steamed buns (or bread) are big and fluffy.

轩[1]

xuān ❶〈书面〉high; lofty; dignified: see "～昂"; "～敞" ❷ (Xuān) a surname

轩[2]

xuān ❶ small room or veranda with windows; open corridor or pavilion:东～ east veranda /茶～ tea room /书～ study; studio ❷〈古语〉high-fronted, curtained carriage:乘～ ride in a curtained carriage /～车 carriage used by senior officials in dynastic China ❸〈书面〉window or door:雕～ carved window (or door) /～帘 curtain; door drape

轩昂 xuān'áng ❶ dignified; impressive; imposing:器宇～ present an imposing appearance; have an impressive presence /志气～ aim high in life; aspire to great success ❷〈书面〉tall and big:佛殿～ tall, grand temple

轩敞 xuānchǎng spacious and bright:这几间北屋虽说旧点儿,但住着又～又豁亮。Old as they are, the rooms facing south (or with a southern exposure) are spacious and bright.

轩豁 xuānhuò ❶ bright and airy; open and spacious:客厅十分～。The sitting-room is bright and spacious. ❷ optimistic; sanguine; hopeful:～的性格 be of a sanguine disposition

轩朗 xuānlǎng 〈书面〉❶ bright and airy; open and clear; sunny:屋宇～。The house is spacious. ❷ merry; sanguine; optimistic; cheerful:性格～ be always cheerful; be of a sanguine disposition

轩眉 xuānméi 〈书面〉raised eyebrows:～怒目 raise one's eyebrows and glare angrily

轩然 xuānrán ❶ (of laughter) loud and uncontrolled:～大笑 laugh a hearty laugh; burst out laughing ❷ rising high; towering:园中阁楼～。There are tall buildings and pavilions in the garden.

轩然大波 xuānrán-dàbō big, crushing wave; great disturbance; mighty uproar; crisis:这桩桃色事件在国内掀起了～。The sex scandal caused a great uproar in the country. /搞不好又是一场～。It may well turn into a stormy issue.

轩尾 xuānwěi cock the tail; strut like a rooster

轩轩自得 xuānxuān-zìdé self-satisfied; complacent; perked up:老汉～而去。The old man left, puffed up.

轩辕 Xuānyuán ❶ surname of the Yellow Emperor, legendary first Chinese ancestor:我以我血荐～。I will shed my blood for my motherland. ❷ also "狮子座" Shīzizuò 〈天文〉Regulus

轩轾 xuānzhì 〈书面〉high or low; good or bad:难分～ difficult to tell who or which is superior; about equal

愃

xuān 〈书面〉impetuous; irascible

谖

xuān 〈书面〉wisdom

儇

xuān 〈书面〉❶ frivolous; flighty; light:～子 frivolous person ❷ crafty; cunning; sly

儇薄 xuānbó 〈书面〉frivolous:～之徒 frivolous person /举止～ behave frivolously

儇佻 xuāntiāo 〈书面〉frivolous; flighty:为人～ be frivolous

翾

xuān 〈书面〉fly

禤

Xuān a surname

煖

xuān 〈书面〉warm

谖

xuān 〈书面〉❶ forget:永矢勿～ pledge never to forget; should always remember ❷ cheat; swindle; trick:诈～之辞 deceptive words; lie

xuán

旋

xuán ❶ revolve; circle; spin; wheel:上～ topspin /下～ underspin; back spin /侧～ sidespin /天～地转 feel as if heaven and earth were spinning round; feel one's head swim /与某人周～ deal with sb. /风吹得枯叶四处飞～。The wind whirled the dead leaves about. /海鸥在海上盘～。The sea-gulls were wheeling above the sea. /风向标在寒风中飞快地打着～儿。The weather vane turns swiftly in the cold wind. ❷ return; go back; come back:凯～ return in triumph ❸ part of the scalp where the hair is whorled:他头顶上有两个～儿。There are two parts in his scalp where the hair is whorled. ❹〈书面〉soon; quickly:～悔 regret it soon after /其病～愈。He got well presently. ❺ (Xuán) a surname

see also xuàn

旋板换热器 xuánbǎn huànrèqì 〈化工〉spiral plate exchanger

旋背 xuánbèi 〈书面〉turn round; face about:～即变 change as soon as one turns one's back; change instantly

旋臂起重机 xuánbì qǐzhòngjī also "旋臂吊机" jib crane; swing or turning crane

旋笛 xuándí siren

旋锻机 xuánduànjī rotary swaging machine; swager

旋耕 xuángēng rotary tillage

旋耕机 xuángēngjī 〈农业〉rotary cultivator; rotocultivator; rototiller

旋管 xuánguǎn coiled pipe; coil; coiler

旋光性 xuánguāngxìng 〈物理〉optical rotation; optical activity:～物质 optically active substance

旋归 xuánguī 〈书面〉return home:携手～ return home together /

客行虽云乐，不如早～。Though travel is most enjoyable, it's always best to return home as early as possible.
旋回 xuánhuí ❶ hover; circle: 直升飞机在空中～。The helicopter was hovering above. ❷〈地质〉cycle: 造山～ orogenic cycle /～构造 tectonic cycle
旋回层 xuánhuícéng 〈地质〉cyclothem
旋即 xuánjí shortly; soon afterwards; immediately: 彩票～售光。All the lottery tickets were speedily sold out. /他见事情已了结，～转身离去。Seeing that the business was over, he left at once.
旋卷 xuánjuǎn whirl round; hover over: 在着火的村庄上空～着大团大团的黑烟。Whirling over the burning village were volumes of black smoke.
旋里 xuánlǐ 〈书面〉return to one's hometown: 久在异地，常有～之念。I have lived in an alien land for so long that I often think of returning home.
旋量 xuánliàng 〈数学〉curl; spinor: ～场 spinor field /～统一场论 spinor unified field theory /～收缩 spinor contraction /～空间 spin space
旋流器 xuánliúqì 〈化工〉cyclone; swirler; mixer
旋流筛 xuánliúshāi whirl screen; whirl sieve
旋律 xuánlǜ 〈音乐〉melody: 优美的～ beautiful melody; melodious tune /欢快的～ cheerful melody /主～ keynote; theme; main theme
旋马 xuánmǎ 〈书面〉❶ turn the horse round; wheel the horse about: ～回阵 head the horse towards the camp /～而归 turn the horse homewards ❷ *see* "旋转木马"
旋毛虫 xuánmáochóng trichina (*Trichinella spiralis*)
旋木雀 xuánmùquè tree creeper
旋钮 xuánniǔ knob: 双套筒～ dual knobs /调谐～ tuning knob /卷片～ film winder /将～朝顺时针方向转 turn the knob clockwise
旋桥 xuánqiáo 〈建筑〉swing bridge
旋绕 xuánrào curl up; wind around: 炊烟～。Smoke is curling up from the kitchen chimney. /乐声～，余音徐歇。The reverberating sound of music died down gradually.
旋绕机 xuánràojī 〈电工〉spinning machine
旋塞 xuánsāi 〈机械〉cock: 放水～ drain cock /三通～ three-way cock
旋梯 xuántī winding stairs
旋涡 xuánwō *also* "漩涡" xuánwō whirlpool; eddy; vortex; maelstrom: 水面有几个～。There are some whirlpools in the water. /水中的一个～卷没了我的小纸船。An eddy sucked down my little paper boat. /他是无意中被卷进斗争～的。He was involuntarily drawn into the vortex of struggle.
旋涡星云 xuánwō xīngyún 〈天文〉spiral nebula
旋舞 xuánwǔ dance round; hover: 彩蝶在花丛中～。Colourful butterflies are dancing round among the flowers.
旋压 xuányā 〈机械〉rotary extrusion; spinning: ～成形铣床 spin forming machine /～机床 spinning lathe /～模 spinning block; spinning chuck
旋翼 xuányì 〈航空〉rotor (wing): 主～ main rotor /尾～ tail rotor /可折～ folding rotor /反扭矩～ anti-torque rotor /～支架 rotor pylon /～旋转面 rotor disc

旋翼机 xuányìjī 〈航空〉rotary-wing aircraft; rotorcraft; autogyro: ～驾驶员 rotorman
旋凿 xuánzáo 〈方言〉screw driver
旋踵 xuánzhǒng 〈书面〉❶ turn round on one's heel: 战不～ fight without turn back; fight courageously ❷ in the brief time it takes to turn round on one's heel; in an instant; immediately: ～之间 in a flash; in a twinkle /～而至 arrive immediately afterwards /～即逝 vanish before one can say Jack Robinson; disappear in a split second
旋转 xuánzhuǎn revolve; rotate; whirl; spin: 向右～ right-handed rotation /逆时针方向～ counterclockwise rotation /单人～ solo spin /每秒钟～六十圈 make sixty rotations in a second /～式玩具 whirligig /～式跳水 screw dive /～塔式起重机 rotary tower crane /～装置 swivelling mechanism /投手使球～。The pitcher gave (a) spin to the ball. /屋子好像在～。The room seems to spin round. /滑冰运动员做了一个漂亮的～动作。The skater made a beautiful whirl. /这对舞伴在舞池中～起舞。The couple whirled round the dance floor.
旋转餐厅 xuánzhuǎn cāntīng revolving restaurant
旋转窗 xuánzhuǎnchuāng pivoted casement
旋转磁场 xuánzhuǎn cíchǎng 〈物理〉rotating field; revolving magnetic field: ～发电机 revolving field alternator
旋转木马 xuánzhuǎn mùmǎ merry-go-round
旋转乾坤 xuánzhuǎn-qiánkūn *also* "旋乾转坤" effect a drastic change in nature or the established order of a country; be earthshaking or earthshattering: ～的气魄和胆略 have the daring and resourcefulness to reverse the course of events
旋转舞台 xuánzhuǎn wǔtái revolving stage
旋转钻井 xuánzhuǎn zuànjǐng 〈石油〉rotary drilling
旋子 xuánzi circle; whirl: 鸟儿见了火光惊飞起来，打了几个～，消失在黑暗中。The bird took off at the sight of light, and flew away after whirling round a few times.
see also xuànzi

漩 xuán whirlpool; eddy

漩涡 xuánwō *see* "旋涡" xuánwō

璇(璿) xuán 〈书面〉fine jade

璇玑 xuánjī 〈天文〉❶ armillary sphere ❷ ancient name for the first four stars in the Big Dipper

玄 xuán ❶ black; dark: ～鹤 black crane /～服 black gown ❷ profound; subtle; abstruse: ～略 subtle strategy /这个学派的理论深～，不好懂。The theory of this school is too abstruse to understand. ❸ mysterious; far-fetched; unreliable; incredible: 你说得也太～了。What you said is a pretty tall story.

玄奥 xuán'ào abstruse; profound; recondite: 学识～ great erudition /～的学术领域 recondite area of abstruse learning
玄根 xuángēn ❶〈道教〉mysterious root of all things ❷〈佛教〉natural endowment
玄狐 xuánhú *also* "银狐" yínhú 〈动物〉black fox
玄乎 xuánhu 〈口语〉inscrutable; mysterious; subtle: 你说的这事也太～了。What you talked about is incredible.
玄黄 xuánhuáng 〈书面〉black and yellow; heaven and earth: ～未判 before heaven and earth were separated; before creation
玄机 xuánjī ❶〈道教〉mysteries of the universe ❷ abstruse plot; profound secret; ingenious principle of action: 不露～ not reveal the secrets of one's plan (*or* design)
玄教 xuánjiào Taoism
玄驹 xuánjū 〈古语〉ants
玄览 xuánlǎn insight into the way the universe works; in-depth study of ancient books or classics
玄理 xuánlǐ ❶ abstruse principles; profound theories: 中医的～不是一下子就能讲清的。It's no easy matter to explain the abstruse theory of Chinese medicine. ❷ theories advocated by a philosophical sect in the Wei and Jin dynasties
玄秘 xuánmì mystery; occult: 不要把事情搞得这么～。Don't make a mystery of things. /整个大殿笼罩在一种～的气氛中。The entire hall is shrouded in mystery.
玄妙 xuánmiào mysteriously wonderful; abstruse: ～莫测 too mysterious to comprehend; inscrutable /～不可言也! It's wonderous beyond words!
玄明粉 xuánmíngfěn 〈中药〉compound of glaubersalt and liquorice
玄女 Xuánnǚ goddess who assisted the Yellow Emperor to subdue Chiyou (蚩尤, mythological warrior and enemy of the Yellow Emperor)
玄青 xuánqīng deep black: ～色的大褂 deep black long gown
玄穹 xuánqióng profound vastness beyond the skies; boundless universe
玄参 xuánshēn 〈中药〉root of Zhejiang figwort
玄室 xuánshì tomb vault; dark chamber
玄孙 xuánsūn great-great-grandson
玄武 xuánwǔ ❶ turtle; tortoise ❷ seven northern constellations of the 28 lunar mansions ❸〈道教〉god of the northern sky
玄武玻璃 xuánwǔ bōli tachylite; basalt glass
玄武湖 Xuánwǔhú Xuanwu Lake (in Nanjing)
玄武岩 xuánwǔyán 〈地质〉basalt
玄想 xuánxiǎng fantasy; fancy; illusion: 闭目～ indulge in fantasy with one's eyes closed
玄虚 xuánxū deceitful trick; occult; mystery: 故弄～ make a mystery of simple things; be deliberately mystifying; purposely turn simple things into mysteries
玄学 xuánxué ❶ *Xuanxue* or Dark Learning, a metaphysical sect in the Wei and Jin dynasties that tried to integrate Taoism with

Confucian doctrine：崇尚～ uphold the Dark Learning in the Wei and Jin dynasties ❷ *also*“形而上学”xíng'érshàngxué metaphysics
玄玉 xuányù black jade
玄远 xuányuǎn 〈书面〉profound and far-reaching：谈旨～，深不可测。The talk is too deep to be fathomable.
玄奘 Xuánzàng Xuanzang (formerly translated as Hsuan-tsang, 602-664), Buddhist scholar, translator and traveller of the Tang Dynasty, whose journey to India became the theme of the novel *Pilgrimage to the West* (西游记)
玄之又玄 xuánzhīyòuxuán mystery of mysteries; extremely abstruse; unfathomable：言者～，听者无动于衷。The speaker talked too abstrusely to interest the audience. /～，众妙之门。Mystery of mysteries is the gate to all wonders.

痃

xuán *see*“横痃”héngxuán

悬[1]（懸）

xuán ❶ hang; suspend; fly：倒～ hang by the feet; hang upside down /～在半空中的彩色气球 colourful balloons suspended in midair /大红灯笼高～拱门。Red lanterns are hanging high on the arched gate. ❷ announce openly; make known to the public：*see*“～赏” ❸ raise; lift：*see*“～腕” ❹ unresolved; unsettled; outstanding：一笔～账 unsettled account /此案还～着呢。The law case remains unsettled. *or* It's a pending lawsuit. /他的调动问题一直～在人事部门。His transfer is still under study in the personnel department. ❺ feel worried or anxious; be solicitous：心～两处 with one's heart in two places ❻ imagine：*see*“～拟” ❼ far apart：*see*“～隔”；“～殊”

悬[2]（懸）

xuán 〈方言〉dangerous; precarious; perilous：摸黑从独木桥上走过，真够～的！Walking on the one-log bridge in the dark is really dangerous. /刚才我差点给汽车撞了，真～哪！I was nearly run over by the car. What a narrow escape (*or* close shave)!
悬案 xuán'àn ❶ unsettled law case; pending lawsuit：这桩人命案三年未破，成了谁见谁棘手的～。The case of homicide remains unsettled for three years and has become a thorn for everybody. ❷ outstanding issue：这项工作归谁管，至今仍是～。It's still undecided who will take charge of the work.
悬臂 xuánbì 〈机械〉cantilever; overarm：～弹簧 cantilever spring
悬臂梁 xuánbìliáng 〈建筑〉cantilever beam; over-hanging beam
悬臂起重机 xuánbì qǐzhòngjī cantilever crane
悬臂桥 xuánbìqiáo cantilever bridge
悬臂式楼梯 xuánbìshì lóutī bracketed stairs
悬肠挂肚 xuáncháng-guàdù *also*“牵肠挂肚”qiāncháng-guàdù be very worried about; feel deep anxiety about; be deeply concerned：让人～ keep sb. in an awful suspense; give sb. a great deal of anxiety; cause terrible worry to sb.
悬揣 xuánchuǎi guess; conjecture; surmise：私下～ surmise in private /此事内中曲折甚多，不便～。The matter is very complicated, and it's not for me to speculate.
悬垂 xuánchuí (of objects) hang down：天车的挂钩在空中～着。The hook of the derrick was hanging down in midair.
悬胆 xuándǎn 〈比喻〉(long and straight as a) hanging bile：鼻如～，目似明星 have a (handsome) straight nose and bright eyes
悬灯结彩 xuándēng-jiécǎi hang up lanterns and festoons; decorate with lanterns and coloured streamers：春节临近，到处～。As the Spring Festival is approaching, lanterns and streamers are seen everywhere.
悬吊 xuándiào suspend; dangle; hang in midair; be held in midair：彩灯从天花板上～下来。Colourful lanterns lights suspended from the ceiling. /屋檐下～着一串串红辣椒。Bunches of red chil-lies were dangling from the eaves of the house.
悬动钻床 xuándòng zuànchuáng 〈机械〉overhead travelling drilling machine
悬断 xuánduàn deduce without foundation; conjecture; speculate：无从～ cannot deduce anything out of void
悬而未决 xuán'érwèijué outstanding; unsettled：～的议案 outstanding bill
悬浮 xuánfú ❶〈化学〉suspension：～染色 suspension dyeing /～剂 suspending agent /～搬运 suspension transport /～能力 suspending power /～液 suspension ❷ float：气球～在半空中。The balloon is floating in the air.
悬浮固体 xuánfú gùtǐ 〈环保〉suspended solid
悬浮火车 xuánfú huǒchē aerotrain
悬浮颗粒物质 xuánfú kēlì wùzhì suspended particulate matter
悬浮粒子 xuánfú lìzǐ *also*“悬浮颗粒”suspended particle
悬浮体 xuánfútǐ 〈环保〉suspended substance
悬隔 xuángé far apart; be widely separated：～重洋 be separated by a vast ocean /两地～千里，来往交通不便。As the two places were a thousand *li* apart, it was difficult to travel to and fro.
悬钩子 xuángōuzǐ *also*“覆盆子”fùpénzǐ 〈植物〉raspberry：～灌木 raspberrycane
悬谷 xuángǔ 〈地质〉hanging valley; suspended valley
悬挂 xuánguà ❶ hang; suspend; fly：半个月亮～在静静的夜空。A crescent (moon) was hanging in the quiet night sky. /军舰上～着中国国旗。The warship was flying the Chinese national flag. /半空的大气球上～着长幅标语。Long streamers trailed from huge balloons in midair. ❷ (of a motor vehicle) suspension：前～ front suspension /～线夹 suspension clamp
悬挂犁 xuánguàlí mounted plough
悬挂式传送器 xuánguàshì chuánsòngqì 〈机械〉overhead trolley conveyer
悬挂式滑翔 xuánguàshì huáxiáng 〈体育〉hang gliding：～者 hang glider
悬挂式滑翔机 xuánguàshì huáxiángjī hang glider
悬棺葬 xuánguānzàng *also*“崖葬”yázàng 〈考古〉custom of burying a dead person, prevalent among certain minority nationalities in ancient China, whereby the coffin was placed in a cave or crevice in a cliff
悬河 xuánhé ❶ hanging river (where the riverbed is higher than the land protected by the banks, e.g. the lower reaches of the Yellow River) ❷〈书面〉waterfall; cascade ❸ exceptional eloquence：口若～ have a great flow of speech; be very eloquent; talk glibly; utter a torrent of words
悬河泻水 xuánhé-xièshuǐ one's speech flows like a cataract; have the gift of the gab：说起话来如～ be very eloquent /文思如～。One's ideas in writing flow like a cataract.
悬壶 xuánhú 〈书面〉practise medicine (by hanging a gourd or bottle as the sign of a medicine shop)：～行医 practise medicine; be a doctor
悬乎 xuánhu 〈方言〉dangerous; perilous; unsafe：在这条河里游泳太～了。It's extremely dangerous to swim in this river. /真～！他差点被暗害。That was a close shave (*or* call) indeed! He nearly got assassinated.
悬涧飞瀑 xuánjiàn-fēipù deep ravine and flying cataract
悬胶 xuánjiāo 〈化学〉suspensoid：～态 suspensoid state /～催化裂化过程 suspensoid catalytic cracking process
悬空 xuánkōng ❶ hang in the air; suspend in midair：两脚～ leave one's feet dangling without support /～作业 work in midair /～脚手架 hanging scaffolding /～楼梯 hanging stairs ❷ divorced from reality; uncertain; unsettled：资金大半～，扩建工程从何谈起！The extension project is far from certain since more than half of the funding is still up in the air.
悬空寺 Xuánkōngsì Hanging Temple (propped up on wooden stilts on the precipice of a mountain in Shanxi Province)
悬跨 xuánkuà 〈建筑〉suspended span
悬梁 xuánliáng hang oneself from a beam：～自尽 commit suicide by hanging oneself from a beam; kill oneself by hanging
悬梁刺股 xuánliáng-cìgǔ tie one's hair on the house beam and jab one's side with an awl to keep oneself awake — take great pains with one's study; grind away at one's studies
悬料 xuánliào *also*“挂料”guàliào 〈冶金〉hanging
悬铃木 xuánlíngmù *also*“法国梧桐”Fǎguó wútóng 〈植物〉plane-tree; plane
悬虑 xuánlǜ worry; care; miss：不必～。There is no need to worry. *or* Don't worry.
悬拟 xuánnǐ conjecture; imagine; invent：小说情节纯系～。The plot of the novel was purely fictitious. /～之说却被别人当真了。A mere surmise was taken by others as a positive statement.
悬念 xuánniàn ❶〈书面〉be concerned or worried about (sb. who is elsewhere); think of (sb. in absence)：日日～ be worried day after day /游子去乡，家中父母甚为～。The parents are very much concerned about their son who resides far away from home. ❷ audience involvement in a film or play; reader involvement in a piece of

literature; suspense:～大师 master of suspense /～惊险故事 suspense thriller /制造～ create suspense
悬旗法 xuánqífǎ flags law
悬赏 xuánshǎng offer a reward; post a reward:～缉拿凶手 offer a reward for the capture of a murderer; set a price on a murderer's head /～三十万元 post a reward of 300,000 *yuan* (for finding sth. or sb.)
悬式经纬仪 xuánshì jīngwěiyí hanging theodolite
悬饰 xuánshì pendant
悬首 xuánshǒu 〈旧语〉display a chopped-off head (of a criminal or rebel) usually over the city gate:～示众 display a chopped-off head to scare the public
悬殊 xuánshū vast difference; great disparity; wide gap:敌我力量～。There is a great disparity in strength between ourselves and the enemy. /贫富差距日益～。The gap between the rich and the poor is widening. *or* There is a growing polarization between the rich and the poor. /两地生活条件～。The living conditions of the two areas are worlds apart.
悬水 xuánshuǐ 〈书面〉waterfall; cascade
悬索结构 xuánsuǒ jiégòu 〈建筑〉suspended-cable structure
悬索桥 xuánsuǒqiáo suspension bridge:～跨度 suspended span
悬索铁路 xuánsuǒ tiělù (suspension) cable railway
悬梯 xuántī hanging ladder
悬停 xuántíng (of helicopters, etc.) hover; stay still in midair
悬腕 xuánwàn (when writing with a brush pen) with the wrist raised, i.e. not touching the desk:他在笔杆上吊一重物,练～功夫。He hangs a weight to the shaft of his writing brush to practise the skill of writing Chinese characters with raised wrist.
悬望 xuánwàng think of longingly; hope for anxiously; be anxious for:家中妻儿～已久。His wife and children have been anxiously expecting his return for quite a long time.
悬系 xuánxì feel anxious about; be worried about:～家人 miss one's family
悬想 xuánxiǎng imagine; conjecture; fancy:闭室～,空生奇念 shut oneself up and indulge in wild flights of fancy /～不能替代现实。Imagination is after all not reality.
悬心 xuánxīn feel anxious; worry; be consumed by worry and anxiety:她近来一直为母亲的手术～。She has been filled with anxiety about her mother's pending operation.
悬心吊胆 xuánxīn-diàodǎn *also* "提心吊胆" tíxīn-diàodǎn be filled with anxiety or fear; be on tenterhooks:这～的日子我再也过不下去了。I have had enough of living constantly in fear.
悬悬 xuánxuán 〈书面〉❶ worry about (sb. who is absent); miss:日夜～ miss sb. day and night ❷ remote; faraway; distant:～南海 distant south seas
悬崖 xuányá overhanging or steep cliff; precipice:～绝壁 sheer precipices and overhanging rocks; cliffs and precipices /跌下～ fall off a precipice /已是～百丈冰,犹有花枝俏。On the ice-clad rock rising high and sheer, A flower blooms sweet and fair.
悬崖勒马 xuányá-lèmǎ rein in at the brink of the precipice; wake up to and escape disaster at the last moment; pull back before it is too late:奉劝某些人及早～,不要在错误的道路上走得太远。We would like to advise some people to rein in before they have gone too far down the wrong path.
悬崖峭壁 xuányá-qiàobì sheer precipices and overhanging rocks; perilous cliffs; precipices:四面尽是高山,左右是～。All around were high trackless mountains and steep pathless cliffs.
悬岩 xuányán steep rocks; precipice; overhanging or steep cliff:～峭壁 sheer precipices and steep rocks
悬雍垂 xuányōngchuí *also* "小舌" xiǎoshé 〈生理〉uvula
悬肘 xuánzhǒu *see* "悬腕"
悬质流 xuánzhìliú 〈地质〉turbidity current
悬浊液 xuánzhuóyè *also* "悬浮液" turbid liquid

xuǎn

烜 xuǎn *also* xuān 〈书面〉grand; magnificent
烜赫 xuǎnhè famous and influential:声威～ great renown and high prestige /声势～ tremendous influence (*or* power)
烜赫一时 xuǎnhè-yīshí have great renown and influence for a time:他在黑社会曾是～的人物。He was once very influential in the underworld.

晅 xuǎn 〈书面〉❶ bright; brilliant; promising ❷ dry in the sun; dry:日以～之 dry it in the sun

癣 xuǎn tinea; ringworm:体～ tinea corporis /脚～ tinea pedis; athlete's foot; ringworm of the foot /手～ tinea mamnum; fungal infection of the hand /颜面～ tinea barbae (*or* sycosis); barber's itch /股～ tinea cruris; tinea of the leg /发～ tinea capitis (*or* tonsurans); ringworm of the scalp /甲～ onychomycosis; ringworm of the nails /黄～ tinea interdigitalis /花斑～ tinea versicolour /疥～ mange /牛皮～ psoriasis /顽～ stubborn dermatitis
癣疥之疾 xuǎnjièzhījí only a skin complaint; some slight ailment:～,不足忧虑。It's only a trifling ailment. There is no need to worry.

选(選) xuǎn ❶ choose; select; pick:评～ choose or select through public appraisal /筛～ screen; sieve /遴～ select sb. for a post or job /精～材料 carefully chosen material /随意挑～ pick (out) at random /两者中任～一个 have one's choice between the two /礼品～得很合适。The gifts are a good selection. /～个吉日,铺子正式开张。We decided on an auspicious day to formally open the shop. ❷ elect:自下而上的普～ general election from the lower level upwards /落～ fail in an election /～他当班长 elect him monitor /总统竞～ presidential election /初～ primary election /大～ general election /补～ by-election ❸ those who are elected or chosen:最佳人～ best candidate; pick of the bunch /经投票当～ be elected by ballot ❹ selections; anthology:诗～ anthology of poems /民歌～ selections of folk songs /作品～ selected works
选拔 xuǎnbá select; choose; scout:～干部 select cadres /～科技人材 hunt (*or* scout) for qualified scientists and technicians /～小组 selection panel
选拔赛 xuǎnbásài 〈体育〉(selective) trials
选拔委员会 xuǎnbá wěiyuánhuì selection board
选本 xuǎnběn anthology; selected works:这个～,最足以反映作者的艺术风格。The author's artistic style finds its best expression in this selected works.
选编 xuǎnbiān ❶ compile:～一本宋代诗集 compile an anthology of poems written in the Song Dynasty ❷ selected works; anthology; collection:广告～ selected advertisements
选播 xuǎnbō selective broadcast; broadcast of selected items:小说～ broadcast of selected novels
选材 xuǎncái ❶ choose qualified personnel:为少年足球队～ scout promising boys for the youth football team ❷ select (suitable) material:精心～ make careful selection of material
选场 xuǎnchǎng selected scene (from an opera, a play, etc.)
选调 xuǎndiào select and transfer; transfer selected people (usu. for promotion):～技术骨干 select a core of technical personnel and transfer them (to more suitable posts, etc.)
选定 xuǎndìng make a decision after careful selection; make a choice of sth.:～题目 have chosen the subject /～接班人 the successor has been selected
选读 xuǎndú ❶ read selectively ❷ selected readings:报刊～ selected readings in newspapers and periodicals /～本 selected works /《古代诗歌～》*A Reader of Ancient Poetry*
选段 xuǎnduàn selected passages or parts:京剧～ selected passages (*or* arias) of Beijing opera
选购 xuǎngòu pick out and buy; choose:～生活用品 purchase articles for daily use /新到各种玩具,欢迎～。A new variety of toys awaits your choice. /大商店有更多种类的商品供顾客～。Big department stores offer a more varied choice of goods.
选集 xuǎnjí selected works or writings; selections; anthology:《周恩来选集》*Selected Works of Zhou Enlai* /十八世纪英国诗歌～ selections from 18th-century English poetry /当代获奖短篇小说～ anthology of contemporary prize-winning short stories
选辑 xuǎnjí ❶ select and edit:这是作者～的部分资料。These are parts of the data selected by the author. ❷ selected edition:《文史资料～》*Selected Edition of Historical Accounts of Past Events*
选举 xuǎnjǔ elect:无记名投票～ elect by secret ballot /直接～ direct election /间接～ indirect election /等额～ one-candidate election /差额～ competitive election; multiple choice election /中期～ midterm election /无效～ election invalid /～单位 electoral unit /

～出来的官员 elective official /～程序 electoral procedure (*or* proceedings) /～结果 election results (*or* returns) /举行～ hold an election /操纵～ rig an election /缺席～ absentee voting /缺席～人 absent (*or* absentee) voter

选举地理学 xuǎnjǔ dìlǐxué electoral geography

选举法 xuǎnjǔfǎ electoral law

选举权 xuǎnjǔquán right to vote; franchise: 有～和被～ have the right to vote and to stand for election /每一个公民都应充分行使自己的～。Every citizen should fully use his voting franchise.

选举人 xuǎnjǔrén voter; elector; electorate

选举日 xuǎnjǔrì polling day

选举团 xuǎnjǔtuán electoral college

选举学 xuǎnjǔxué psephology

选刊 xuǎnkān ❶ select and publish: 编者～的这三篇小说,是近年来作者的新作。The three novels selected and put into print by the editor are the latest works of the author. ❷ edition of selected articles; selections:《民间故事～》*Book of Selected Folk Stories*

选矿 xuǎnkuàng 〈矿业〉ore dressing; mineral separation; beneficiation: ～厂 ore dressing plant; concentration plant

选留 xuǎnliú select and retain: 从毕业生中～五名品学兼优的留校,充实教师队伍。We chose from among the graduates five people who excelled in both academic performance and moral calibre to reinforce the faculty.

选录 xuǎnlù select and include: 这本集子～了作者近十年来发表的论文共三十篇。Thirty of the writer's articles published in recent years were selected and included in the anthology.

选煤 xuǎnméi *also* "洗煤" xǐméi 〈矿业〉coal washing

选美比赛 xuǎnměi bǐsài beauty contest

选民 xuǎnmín (individually) voter; elector; (collectively) constituency; electorate: ～登记 registration of voters /～名册 voting register; roll of voters /合格～ qualified voter /对～负责 accountable to one's constituency

选民榜 xuǎnmínbǎng list of eligible voters

选民证 xuǎnmínzhèng elector's certificate; voter registration card

选派 xuǎnpài select and send; detail: ～代表参加会议 select sb. as representative to a meeting; depute sb. to attend a conference /～五名技工出国培训 select five technicians for overseas training /十名身强力壮的战士被～去护送文物。Ten hefty soldiers were detailed to escort the transport of ancient relics.

选配 xuǎnpèi ❶ select and provide; match: ～最合适的衣服和首饰 make the best match of clothing and jewelry /精心～的花束 well selected bunch of flowers /公司将负责为办公室～家具。The company will provide matching furniture for the office. ❷ cross-breeding: 这个牧场的～率很高。This stud farm has a high rate of cross-breeding.

选票 xuǎnpiào vote; ballot: 填写～ fill in a ballot /有效～ valid ballot /无效～ invalid ballot /收买～ buy a vote /核对～ check the votes cast /～作废 spoil a ballot /在选区获得压倒多数的～ sweep a constituency; win a landslide victory

选频 xuǎnpín frequency selection: ～系统 frequency-selective system

选聘 xuǎnpìn select and employ: ～干部 recruit cadres (*or* functionaries) /～工作将于月底截止。The selection and employment of personnel will terminate by the end of the month.

选区 xuǎnqū electoral or election district; electoral ward; constituency: 东城区～ Eastern District electoral ward /增设一个新～ establish a new constituency /在～做竞选演说 stump the constituency

选曲 xuǎnqǔ selected songs or tunes: 舞剧《红楼梦》～ selected tunes from the dance drama *A Dream of Red Mansions* /演奏几首～ play a few pieces from the selections

选取 xuǎnqǔ select; choose: 本校将从应考人员中～三十名学员。The school will admit thirty of those who have taken the examination.

选任 xuǎnrèn select and appoint: 大胆～中青年干部 be bold to appoint young and middle-aged cardres (to leading posts)

选任领事 xuǎnrèn lǐngshì *also* "名誉领事" míngyù lǐngshì honorary consul

选侍 xuǎnshì palace maid (in the Ming Dynasty)

选手 xuǎnshǒu athlete selected for a sports meet; player; contestant: 青年～ young player /种子～ seeded player /优秀～ top-notch player; ace athlete; top-ranking athlete

选送 xuǎnsòng select and recommend: ～新学员 select and recommend new students /～代表去开会 depute sb. to attend a conference /～运动员参加集训 choose players for training

选题 xuǎntí ❶ select or choose a topic; choose a subject: 可以自己～ can have a subject of one's own choice /最后两道是～。The last two problems are optional. ❷ chosen or selected subject: 根据～制定写作计划 draw (*or* work out) a writing plan according to the chosen subject /科研～ scientific research topic

选通 xuǎntōng 〈电学〉gating: ～电路 gate circuit /～电子束管 gate beam tube /～管 gate tube /～脉冲 strobe pulse; gating pulse; gating signal /～器 gate /～装置 strobe unit

选贤任能 xuǎnxián-rènnéng *also* "选贤举能" select the virtuous and employ the able; appoint people on their merits

选型 xuǎnxíng *also* "选模式" lectotype

选修 xuǎnxiū take as an elective course: ～中文 take Chinese as an elective (course)

选修课 xuǎnxiūkè elective course; optional course; elective

选样 xuǎnyàng sampling; sample: 请速寄～。Please mail us the sample soon.

选用 xuǎnyòng select and use; choose and apply: ～上等原料精制而成 be meticulously made of choice materials (*or* ingredients) /应试合格者,将分别量才～。Those candidates who have succeeded in the examination will be given work suited to their abilities.

选育 xuǎnyù 〈农业〉seed selection; breeding: ～良种水稻 develop high-quality rice strain by selection /～良种绵羊 evolve sheep of fine breed by selection

选择 xuǎnzé select; choose; pick; opt: ～佳期 choose a wedding day /～合适候选人 opt for a proper candidate /不能自由～ not free to make a choice /没有～的余地 have no alternative; be left with no choice /自然～〈生物〉natural selection

选择场地 xuǎnzé chǎngdì 〈体育〉choice of ends

选择题 xuǎnzétí multiple-choice test

选择问句 xuǎnzé wènjù alternative question

选择性 xuǎnzéxìng 〈电子〉selectivity: ～信息 selective information /～标记 selected marker

选种 xuǎnzhǒng 〈农业〉seed selection: ～育苗 select seeds and grow seedlings /人工～ manual seed selection

选中 xuǎnzhòng select; choose; decide on: 刘教授～我给他当助教。Professor Liu chose me to be his teaching assistant.

选准 xuǎnzhǔn make the right choice: ～体操苗子进行培养 choose the most promising gymnasts for further training

xuàn

渲

xuàn wash (a piece of drawing paper) with watercolours

渲染 xuànrǎn ❶ apply colours to a drawing: 这位画师善于使用～的方法。The painter excels in the technique of applying colours to a drawing. ❷ play up; exaggerate; overdo; pile it on: 大肆～他的新作 hype his latest work with a lot of publicity /～形势的严重性 exaggerate the seriousness (*or* gravity) of the situation /这些细腻的描写,有力地～了人物的心理活动。The minute description brings out the characters' mental activities in bold relief.

楦(楥)

xuàn ❶ (shoe) last; (hat) block: 鞋～ last; shoe last /帽～ hat block ❷ shape with a last or block: ～帽 block a hat /这些新做的鞋太紧,要～一～。These newly-made shoes are so tight that they need to be lasted. ❸〈方言〉stuff; fill up: 瓷器装好后,请把纸箱子～好。Please stuff the carton well after the porcelain is packed in it.

楦子 xuànzi *also* "楦头" ❶ shoe last; shoe tree ❷ hat block

碹(礦)

xuàn ❶ arching part of a bridge, culvert, etc. ❷ build arches with bricks or stones

旋[1](❷❸❹鏇)

xuàn ❶ whirl: *see* "～风" ❷ turn on a lathe; lathe; pare: ～根车轴 lathe an axle /把土豆皮～掉 peel a potato /你脚趾上这个鸡眼得～了。The corn on your toe must be pared. ❸ copper plate (for making sheets of bean-starch jelly) ❹ hot water container for warming wine

旋[2]

xuàn at the time when sth. is needed; at the last moment: ～用～买 buy sth. when you need it; buy for immediate use /～做饭怎么来得及! There is not time to prepare a meal now!

see also xuán
旋板机床 xuànbǎn jīchuáng 〈建筑〉rotary veneer lathe
旋床 xuànchuáng *also*“车床”chēchuáng 〈机械〉(turning) lathe
旋风 xuànfēng whirl; whirlwind; cyclone: 警车载着他们～般地开往作案现场。The police car whirled them off to the scene of the crime.
旋风计算机 xuànfēng jìsuànjī whirlwind computer
旋风炉 xuànfēnglú cyclone furnace
旋风滤器 xuànfēng lǜqì cyclone filter
旋风喷淋塔 xuànfēng pēnlíntǎ cyclone spray tower
旋风器 xuànfēngqì cyclone
旋风撒播机 xuànfēng sǎbōjī whirlwind seeder
旋风收尘器 xuànfēng shōuchénqì rotoclone collector
旋工 xuàngōng turner
旋子 xuànzi ❶ copper plate (for making sheets of been-starch jelly) ❷ hot water container for warming wine ❸ whirlwind somersault — a kind of movement in *wushu* or martial arts
see also xuánzi

泫 xuàn 〈书面〉fall in drops; drip; trickle: 花上露犹～。The flowers were still dripping dew drops. *or* Dew was trickling down the flower petals.
泫然 xuànrán 〈书面〉(usu. of tears) fall; trickle: ～泪下 tears trickling down the cheeks

炫(❷衒) xuàn 〈书面〉❶ daze; dazzle; blaze ❷ show off; display: 自～其能 show off one's talent; flaunt one's ability
炫惑 xuànhuò 〈书面〉mislead people by exaggeration or ostentation: 有着～作用的广告 alluring (*or* misleading) advertisement / 受到国外生活方式的～而出国 be beguiled by foreign life styles into leaving the country
炫目 xuànmù dazzling: 华丽～ brilliant splendour / 阳光～ dazzling sunlight
炫弄 xuànnòng show off; parade; flaunt; vaunt: ～技巧 show off one's skill (*or* craftsmanship); flaunt one's technique
炫示 xuànshì make a show of; show off; display: ～其能 show off one's ability
炫耀 xuànyào ❶ shine; illuminate ❷ make a display of; flaunt; vaunt: 自我～ show oneself off; indulge in self-glorification / ～财富 brag about one's wealth (*or* riches) / ～武力 make a show of force; flaunt one's military strength / ～自己的成就 make a parade of one's achievement; vaunt (of) one's achievement
炫玉贾石 xuànyù-gǔshí sell stone under the label of jade; try to fob or palm off sth. inferior: 此人～,小心上当。Beware! That man is trying to take you in.
炫鬻 xuànyù 〈书面〉brag about; show off; boast of; flaunt

铉 xuàn hook-like instrument to carry an ancient tripod by catching its rings or ears

眩 xuàn 〈书面〉sunshine; sunlight

眩 xuàn ❶ dizzy; giddy; vertiginous: 她感到有些晕～。She feels a little dizzy. / 阳光下的雪山令人目～。The snow mountain under the sunshine was dazzling. ❷〈书面〉dazzled; bewildered: ～于名实 confuse the real and unreal
眩惑 xuànhuò be misled; be bewildered; indulge in: ～于物质享受 obsessed with a desire for material comforts and pleasure; indulge in worldly pleasures
眩目 xuànmù dazzle; blind; daze: ～的火花 dazzling sparks
眩晕 xuànyùn ❶ dizziness; giddiness: 从令人～的高处向下望 look down from a giddy height ❷〈医学〉vertigo
眩晕症 xuànyùnzhèng 〈医学〉vertigo: 内耳～ auditory vertigo; aural vertigo

券 xuàn *also*“拱券”gǒngxuàn arch
see also quàn
券门 xuànmén arch entrance

绚 xuàn gorgeous; (of colour) prismatic
绚烂 xuànlàn brilliant; splendid; gorgeous: ～的刺绣 gorgeous embroidery / ～多彩 bright and colourful; riot of colour; gorgeous
绚丽 xuànlì bright and colourful; gorgeous; magnificent: 文采～ sparkling writing / 满山的红杜鹃,多么～,多么壮美! What a splendid blaze of red azaleas on the hills!

xuē

靴(鞾) xuē boots: 马～ riding boots / 皮～ leather boots / 长统～ high boots / 短统～ ankle boots / 毡～ felt boots / 橡胶～ wellington (boots); galoshes
靴筒 xuētǒng bootleg
靴靿 xuēyào neck of boot where it bends near the ankle; upper part of boot; leg of boot
靴子 xuēzi boots

薛 Xuē a surname
薛稷 Xuē Jì Xue Ji (formerly translated as Hsueh Chi, 649-713), calligrapher of the Tang Dynasty

削 xuē (used only in compound words) scrape; pare; whittle; cut: 剥～ exploit / 瘦～ lean; gaunt; very thin
see also xiāo
削壁 xuēbì precipice; cliff: 悬崖～ sheer precipice; steep cliff
削波 xuēbō 〈电子〉clipping: ～器 clipper / ～电路 clipping circuit / ～电平 clipping level
削葱 xuēcōng 〈书面〉slender fingers (of a lady): 十指如～ ten slender fingers
削牍 xuēdú *also*“削简”〈书面〉writing on bamboo strips in ancient times: ～为疏 write a memorial to the throne on bamboo strips
削发 xuēfà shave one's head (to become a monk or nun); take the tonsure: ～为僧 shave one's head to become a monk
削籍 xuējí 〈书面〉be struck off the official roll; be dismissed from office: ～为民 be dismissed from office and become a commoner
削价 xuējià cut prices; lower the price; reduce the price: ～出售 reduction sale / ～处理 be disposed of at reduced price / 这些产品多次～,还是销不动。These products are still dull of sale in spite of repeated reductions of price. / 他买了一件～衬衣。He bought a shirt on sale.
削肩 xuējiān drooping or sloping shoulders
削减 xuējiǎn cut (down); reduce; slash; whittle down: ～不必要的开支 cut unnecessary expenditure / ～军费 cut down on (*or* reduce) military spending / ～预算 slash the budget / 教育经费被～到了最低程度。Expenditure on education has been pared to the bone.
削木为兵 xuēmù-wéibīng sharpen wooden poles and use them as weapons; use sharpened wooden poles as weapons
削平 xuēpíng 〈书面〉suppress; wipe out; eliminate; put down: ～山头 pull down mountain strongholds; disband faction / ～叛乱,安定天下 put down the rebellion and restore peace and order to the whole country
削弱 xuēruò weaken; sap; enfeeble; undermine: ～某人的权力 weaken (*or* undercut) sb.'s power / 实力有所～。The strength has been sapped.
削瘦 xuēshòu very thin; gaunt; lank: 双颊～ gaunt cheeks; sunken cheeks / 身材颀长～ have a lanky figure
削铁如泥 xuētiě-rúní (of a knife, sword, etc.) cut through iron as though it were mud — extremely sharp: ～的宝刀 extremely sharp sword
削正 xuēzhèng *also*“削政”〈书面〉〈套语〉point out mistakes (in poems or writings) so that they can be corrected: 附上拙作,敬请～。Enclosed herewith is my humble work. Be kind enough to honour me with your opinion. / 请大笔～。You are kindly requested to prune. *or* Please oblige me with your valuable comments.
削职 xuēzhí be dismissed from office
削足适履 xuēzú-shìlǚ cut the feet to fit the shoes; mechanically copy regardless of specific conditions

xué

学(學、斈) xué ❶ study; learn: ～手艺 learn a trade; acquire a skill / ～知识 acquire knowledge / ～中文 study (*or*

learn) Chinese /自~ study by oneself; self-study; be self-taught /~先进 emulate the advanced /~好一种技术 master a skill /~得快,忘得快。Soon learnt, soon forgotten. /活到老,~到老。Live and learn. *or* One is never too old to learn. /~而不思则罔,思而不~则殆。Learning without thinking will give rise to confusion; thinking without learning will lead people astray. ❷ imitate; mimic; copy: ~狗叫 mimic the barking of a dog /他喜欢~他父亲的举止。He likes to imitate his father's manner. /他~青蛙叫,~得像极了。He can give a good imitation of a frog's croaking. ❸ learning; knowledge; scholarship:博~多才 be of great learning and remarkable talent /博~者 erudite scholar /治~ pursue one's studies; do scholarly research ❹ subject of study; field or branch of learning:汉~ Chinese studies; Sinology /哲~ philosophy /化~ chemistry /物理~ physics /逻辑~ logic ❺ school; college:小~ primary school /第五中~ No.5 secondary school /北京大~ Beijing University /上~ go to school /退~ leave school; drop out of school /休~ temporarily suspend one's schooling /转~ transfer to another school

学报 xuébào learned journal; university journal:~编辑部 editorial department of a learned journal /投书~ write a letter to the school journal

学步 xuébù ❶ (usu. of babies) learn to walk:刚刚~的孩子 toddler ❷ grope forward; feel one's way along:这是一件陌生的工作,我们必须在不断摸索中~前进。As the job is entirely new to us, we'll have to feel our way forward.

学步邯郸 xuébù-Hándān imitate others slavishly and lose one's own individuality; to walk like a swan, the crow loses its own gait *see also* "邯郸学步"

学部 xuébù ❶ ministry of education of the Qing Dynasty ❷ academic committee (sometimes translated as scientific division) of the Chinese Academy of Sciences

学潮 xuécháo student strike; campus upheaval: ~迭起 one student strike after another

学而不厌 xué'érbùyàn have an unquenchable desire to learn; be insatiable in learning:~,诲人不倦 be insatiable in learning and tireless in teaching

学而优则仕 xué ér yōu zé shì (a Confucian slogan for education) a good scholar can become an official; he who excels in study can follow an official career

学阀 xuéfá scholar-tyrant:~习气 scholastic despotism (*or* tyranny)

学房 xuéfáng old-style private school

学非所用 xuéfēisuǒyòng one's job is not in line with one's training; one's education does not meet the needs of one's job

学费 xuéfèi ❶ tuition fee; tuition ❷ education expenses:你出国留学的~从何而来? Where will you get the money for furthering your studies abroad?

学分 xuéfēn credit:~制 credit system

学风 xuéfēng style of study; academic atmosphere:树立良好的~ foster a good style of study /~严谨 meticulous and rigorous academic discipline /提倡理论联系实际的~ advocate the style of integrating theory with practice

学府 xuéfǔ institution of higher learning; seat of learning:高等~ institution of tertiary education; institution of higher learning

学富五车 xuéfù-wǔchē read enough books to fill five wagons; be erudite in learning:这位老教授称得上~。The old professor is truly an erudite scholar.

学工 xuégōng *also* "学徒工" apprentice

学贯古今 xuéguàn-gǔjīn well versed in the learning of both ancient and modern times

学棍 xuégùn tyrant in the field of education:此人名为学者,实为~,霸道极了。Scholar in name and despot in essence, the man is extremely overbearing and domineering.

学海 xuéhǎi ❶ persevere in one's studies ❷ sea of learning; academic studies:~无涯苦作舟。On the boundless sea of learning, diligence is one's own vehicle of passage.

学海波澜 xuéhǎi-bōlán (of a scholar) play an outstanding role in the literary or academic world

学好 xuéhǎo learn from good examples; emulate good:临行时,他嘱咐孩子,一定要~,要上进。Before his departure he told his children to behave well and strive to make progress.

学坏 xuéhuài follow bad examples; succumb to evil; pick up bad habits

学会 xuéhuì ❶ learn; grasp; master:~一种新技术 master a new skill /孩子应该~尊重别人。Children should learn how to respect others. /你慢慢就~了。You'll gradually get the hang of it. ❷ learned or professional society; institute:国际法~ international law society

学级 xuéjí 〈旧语〉classes and grades in school

学籍 xuéjí one's status as a student; one's name on the school roll:保留~ keep (sb.) on the school roll; retain one's status as a student /取消~ be struck off the school roll /开除~ throw (sb.) out of school; expel sb. from school /~管理 administration of student records; registrar's work

学监 xuéjiān 〈旧语〉school inspector

学界 xuéjiè educational circles: ~名人 eminent figure (*or* celebrity) in the educational circles

学究 xuéjiū ❶ scholar ❷ pedant:老~ pedantic schoolmaster; old pedant /~气 pedantry; academicism /~式的人物 pedantic person; bookworm

学科 xuékē ❶ branch of learning; field of study:~带头人 leading scholar in a branch of learning ❷ course; subject; discipline:基础~ basic course /专业~ specialized course /拓宽~ expand a discipline (to include more subjects) /跨~组织 interdisciplinary academic organization /边缘~ fringe discipline /前沿~ frontier (*or* pioneering) discipline /计算机是一个热门~。Computer science is a hot subject. ❸〈军事〉knowledge course

学理 xuélǐ scientific law or principle; theory:先生知识渊博,精于~。The master is an erudite scholar, good at academic reasoning.

学力 xuélì knowledge; educational level; academic attainments:具有同等~ with the same educational level (as school graduates) /论~和才华,他都在我们之上。He is head and shoulders above us in academic attainments and literary talent.

学历 xuélì record of formal schooling; record of education:具有大学~ be a university graduate /他没上过学,没有什么~。He had no academic credentials since he had never been to school.

学联 xuélián federation of students' unions

学龄 xuélíng school age:~儿童 children of school age; school age children; school-agers /~前儿童 pre-school children; pre-schoolers

学路 xuélù ❶ ways of education:广开~ encourage all means of education; broaden the channels of learning ❷ range of study:他的知识扎实,~宽广,很有发展前途。He has a bright future before him, for he has solid and extensive knowledge.

学名 xuémíng ❶ one's registered name at school; formal name used at school (as distinguished from pet name at home):他的小名叫狗儿,~叫刘铁宝。His pet name is Gou'er but his school name is Liu Tiebao. ❷ scientific name (e.g. Latin name for plants, etc.):食盐的~是氯化钠。The scientific name of salt is sodium chloride.

学年 xuénián academic or school year:新~开学典礼 opening ceremony of a new academic year /~考试 year-end examination

学派 xuépài school of thought; school:紫阳~ Zhu Xi's (朱熹) school of Confucian thought (which advocated upholding heavenly principles and overcoming human desires) /我们应该克服~之间的门户之见。We should try to overcome sectarian bias among different schools of thought.

学期 xuéqī school term; term; semester

学前班 xuéqiánbān preschool (education) class

学前教育 xuéqián jiàoyù preschool education

学前期 xuéqiánqī pre-school age: ~儿童的智力开发 intellectual development of pre-school children

学区 xuéqū school district

学然后知不足 xué ránhòu zhī bùzú the more one learns, the more one sees the need to learn; only through learning can one realize one's inadequacy

学人 xuérén scholar; learned person

学舌 xuéshé ❶ mechanically repeat other people's words; parrot:鹦鹉~ parrot; imitate mechanically /文章毫无新意,不过是跟在别人后面~。Devoid of anything new, the article is little more than a parrot cry. ❷〈口语〉loose-tongued; gossipy

学生会 xuéshēnghuì student union; student council; student association

学生运动 xuéshēng yùndòng student movement

学生 xuésheng ❶ student; pupil:小~ primary school pupil /中~ secondary school pupil (*or* student) /大~ college (*or* university) student; undergraduate /法科~ law student /~权利 student's right /~腔 student talk; student jargon ❷ disciple; follower:孔夫子

的～ disciples of Confucius /甘当群众的小～ be willing to be pupils of the masses ❸〈方言〉male child; boy

学生票 xuéshengpiào ticket at student discount

学生证 xuéshengzhèng student's identity card; student card

学生装 xuéshengzhuāng ❶ a kind of suit, with a stand-up collar and three pockets in the jacket (worn by students before World War II) ❷ student uniform

学生子 xuéshengzi 〈方言〉student; pupil

学识 xuéshí learning; knowledge; erudition; scholarly attainments: 渊博的～ immense (*or* profound) knowledge; vast (*or* great) learning /博大精深的～ extensive knowledge and profound scholarship /～浅陋 shallow in knowledge; little learning /～过人 surpass others in knowledge

学时 xuéshí class hour; period

学士 xuéshì ❶ scholar: 文人～ scholars; men of letters /翰林～ member of the imperial academy ❷ bachelor: 理～ Bachelor of Science (BS) /文～ Bachelor of Arts (BA) /法～ Bachelor of Laws (LLB)

学塾 xuéshú old-style private school

学术 xuéshù learning; science: ～领域 sphere (*or* realm) of learning /～交流 academic exchanges /～报告 learned report; academic report; academic lecture /～论文 research paper; scientific paper; thesis /～讨论会 academic discussion; scientific conference; symposium /～团体 learned society /～研究 academic research /～思想 academic thinking /～刊物 learned journal; academic publication /～自由 academic freedom

学术界 xuéshùjiè academic community; academic circles; academic world; academia

学说 xuéshuō theory; doctrine; teachings: 马克思主义～ theory of Marxism /爱因斯坦的相对论～ Einstein's theory of relativity /新创立的～ newly founded theory /弗洛伊德～ Freudian doctrines /共产主义～ communist teachings /～上的争论 doctrinal dispute

学堂 xuétáng 〈方言〉school

学田 xuétián 〈旧语〉community farm allocated to a school, the profit from which was used as school fund: 侵吞、霸占～ appropriation and seizure of public school farm

学童 xuétóng young pupil; school child

学徒 xuétú ❶ serve one's apprenticeship: 在工厂～ be an apprentice in a factory; serve one's apprenticeship at a factory /～期间 during one's apprenticeship /他学了二年徒。He apprenticed himself for two years. ❷ apprentice; trainee: 当老张的～ be apprentice to Old Zhang

学徒工 xuétúgōng *also* "徒工" apprentice (in a factory)

学位 xuéwèi degree; academic degree: 学士～ bachelor's degree; baccalaureate /硕士～ master's degree /博士～ Ph. D. degree; doctor's degree; doctorate /名誉～ honorary degree /攻读～ study for a degree; do a degree /取得～ take (*or* receive, *or* acquire) a degree /攻读～的学生 degree student /～课程 degree course

学位评定委员会 xuéwèi píngdìng wěiyuánhuì academic degree evaluation committee

学问 xuéwen ❶ branch of learning: 新兴的～ new branch of learning ❷ learning; knowledge; scholarship; scholarly attainments: 大～家 man of great learning /做～ engage in scholarship; do research /卖弄～ flaunt (*or* show off) one's knowledge /他的～过于专业化。His knowledge is over-specialized. /搞好企业管理,这里面大有～。Enterprise management requires a lot of knowledge and expertise.

学无常师 xuéwúchángshī a scholar has no permanent teacher; learn from anybody who has a speciality

学无坦途 xuéwútǎntú there is no royal road to learning; there is no smooth sailing in one's study

学无止境 xuéwúzhǐjìng knowledge knows no bounds; there is no limit to knowledge: ～,学海无涯,最要不得的是浅尝辄止。As there is no limit to learning and scholarship is boundless, the thing one must guard against most is to feel satisfied with a smattering of knowledge.

学习 xuéxí ❶ study; learn: ～文化 learn to read and write /～成绩 academic record; school record; school performance /～态度 attitude of study /～风气 style of study /～方法 study method ❷ learn from; follow the example of; emulate: 向某人～ learn from sb. /～别人的好榜样 follow sb.'s example; model oneself on sb.

学衔 xuéxián academic rank or title

学校 xuéxiào school; educational institution: 师范～ teachers' school; normal school /职业～ vocational school /专业～ specialized school /高等～ institution of higher learning; colleges and universities /补习～ continuation school /函授～ correspondence school /业余～ spare-time school /聋哑～ school for deaf-mutes

学行 xuéxíng scholarly attainments and moral conduct

学行车 xuéxíngchē *also* "学步车" walker (for a baby or invalid learning to walk); walking frame

学兄 xuéxiōng 〈敬词〉one's former schoolmate

学养 xuéyǎng 〈书面〉learning and cultivation: 刘老是一位学贯中西,～渊深的学者。The venerable Liu is an erudite scholar, well versed in both Chinese and western knowledge.

学业 xuéyè one's studies; school work: ～平平 of average school achievement /～有成 be academically accomplished /～未竟 unfinished studies

学以致用 xuéyǐzhìyòng study for the purpose of application; study sth. in order to apply it; put what one has learned into practice

学艺 xuéyì ❶ learn a trade; learn a skill: 孩子在戏校～。The child is learning performing arts in a theatrical school. ❷ knowledge and expertise; learning and skill: 经过刻苦钻研,他在～上有了明显提高。Through painstaking effort, he has made obvious progress in his knowledge and skill.

学友 xuéyǒu classmate; schoolmate; fellow alumnus or alumna: 他是我的复旦～。He was my schoolmate in Fudan University.

学员 xuéyuán (college) student; trainee

学院 xuéyuàn college; academy; institute: 师范～ teachers' college /军事～ military academy /工业～ technical college /理工～ institute of technology; polytechnic /美术～ school of art /音乐～ conservatory (*or* academy) of music /女子～ women's college /文～ liberal arts college /工商管理～ school of business

学运 xuéyùn (short for 学生运动) student movement

学长 xuézhǎng ❶〈敬词〉one's former schoolmate ❷〈旧语〉head of a branch of learning in college: 文科～ head of liberal arts

学者 xuézhě scholar; learned man; man of learning: 大～ eminent (*or* renowned) scholar; man of great learning /～风度 style of a scholar; scholar's elegant carriage /访问～ visiting scholar

学制 xuézhì educational system; school system: ～改革 reform in the school system /～四年 4-year's schooling

学子 xuézǐ 〈书面〉student; scholar: 莘莘～ great number of disciples; lot of students /海外～ students studying overseas

学租 xuézū 〈旧语〉rent paid to a school for using the land belonging to it

敩(斆) xué 〈书面〉*see* "学" xué

see also xiào

穴 xué ❶ cave; hole: 洞～ cave /孔～ hole /空～来风。An empty hole invites the wind — weakness lends wing to rumour. ❷ den; lair; nest: 虎～ tiger's lair /匪～ bandits' den /巢～ nest; hideout ❸ grave; tomb: 墓～ coffin pit ❹〈中医〉acupuncture point; acupoint: 太阳～ temple acupoint /耳～ ear acupuncture point /人中～ *Renzhong* point (between mouth and nose) ❺ (Xué) a surname

穴播 xuébō 〈农业〉bunch planting; dibble seeding; dibbling: ～机 hole sowing machine /～器 dibble; dibbler

穴处 xuéchǔ 〈书面〉❶ live in caves: 巢居知风,～知雨 those who perch in trees know about wind and those who dwell in caves know about rain — knowledge comes from experience ❷ shallow or superficial learning: 群居～之徒 mediocrity; those of the common run

穴道 xuédào *see* "穴位"

穴见 xuéjiàn 〈书面〉superficial viewpoint; desultory opinion: 临事战惧,不敢以～妄为。When faced with trouble, one gets cold feet and dare not proffer any idea.

穴居 xuéjū live in caves: ～人 cave dweller; troglodyte

穴居野处 xuéjū-yěchǔ live a primitive life: 上古之人,穴居而野处。Prehistoric (*or* Primitive) men dwelt in caves and lived in the wild.

穴施 xuéshī *also* "点施" diǎnshī 〈农业〉apply manure in small holes near the plant; hole application of manure (*or* fertilizer)

穴头 xuétóu illicit broker (who organizes or induces actors or actresses from the state-owned troupes to perform on their own for extra money)

穴位 xuéwèi ❶ acupuncture point; acupoint: ～埋线疗法 surgical

suture embedding therapy; catgut embedding therapy /～注射疗法 point-injection therapy ❷ location of a coffin pit
穴隙 xuéxì hole; cavity
穴植法 xuézhífǎ 〈农业〉hole planting

茓

xué store grain by enclosing it with coarse mat
茓子 xuézi *also* "踅子" xuézi coarse mat

踅

xué pace up and down; walk to and fro; turn back half way:～来～去 walk back and forth
踅摸 xuémo 〈口语〉look for:～半天,什么也没找到。I've been looking for it for some time, but have found nothing.
踅子 xuézi *see* "茓子" xuézi

噱

xué 〈方言〉laugh:发～ make one laugh; excite laughter; raise a laugh
see also jué
噱头 xuétóu 〈方言〉❶ words or acts meant to amuse people or to elicit laughter:靠～迎合观众 please the audience with amusing tricks; play to the gallery /～多 full of amusing tricks; no end of buffoonery ❷ tricks; gimmicks:摆～ try (*or* play) tricks ❸ funny; farcical:这段相声～极了。This comic dialogue is very funny.

xuě

雪[1]

xuě ❶ snow:初～ first snow /冰～ ice and snow /大～ heavy snow /瑞～ auspicious (*or* timely) snow /多～天气 snowy weather /雨夹～ sleet /暴风～ snowstorm /鹅毛～ fluffy snow /飞～ swirling snow /为～所阻 be snowed up; be snowed in /下～了。It's snowing. ❷ snow-like: *see* "～亮" ❸ (Xuě) a surname

雪[2]

xuě wipe out (a humiliation, disgrace, etc.); avenge (a wrong):洗～ right (*or* redress) a wrong; clear (sb.) of an unjust or false charge; vindicate sb. who has been wronged
雪白 xuěbái as white as snow; snow-white:～的纱巾 pure white silk scarf /～的头发 snowy hair; snows /～的肌肤 fair skin; fair complexion /～的梨花纷纷落入池水中。The pear blossom snows its petals on the pond.
雪板 xuěbǎn 〈体育〉ski:一副～ a pair of skis
雪豹 xuěbào 〈动物〉snow leopard (*Panthera uncia*); ounce
雪暴 xuěbào snowstorm; blizzard:他途中遇上了～。He was caught in a snowstorm on his way here.
雪崩 xuěbēng ❶ (snow) avalanche; snowslide:～气浪 avalanche wind ❷ 〈电子〉(Townsend) avalanche:～光电二极管 avalanche photodiode /～击穿 avalanche breakdown /～晶体管 avalanche transistor
雪崩效应 xuěbēng xiàoyìng 〈物理〉avalanche effect
雪铲 xuěchǎn snow-shovel
雪车 xuěchē *see* "雪橇"
雪耻 xuěchǐ wipe out a humiliation; avenge an insult:报仇～ take revenge and wipe out a humiliation /若不～,誓不为人! I wouldn't be a man if I couldn't avenge the insult!
雪地鞋 xuědìxié snow boots
雪貂 xuědiāo 〈动物〉ferret; fitchet
雪豆 xuědòu 〈植物〉sieva bean (*Phaseolus lunatus*)
雪堆 xuěduī snow drift; snowbank
雪顿节 Xuědùnjié Sour Milk Drinking Festival (in China's Tibet)
雪纺绸 xuěfǎngchóu 〈纺织〉chiffon
雪腐病 xuěfǔbìng snow mold
雪糕 xuěgāo ❶ ice lolly; popsicle ❷ ice cream
雪柜 xuěguì refrigerator
雪果 xuěguǒ snowberry
雪恨 xuěhèn wreak vengeance; revenge; avenge:申冤～ redress wrong and avenge oneself /感谢你为我雪了杀兄之恨。I'm grateful to you for revenging my brother's murder.
雪花 xuěhuā snowflake:～纷飞 snowflakes flying hither and thither /漫天～ swirling snowflakes
雪花膏 xuěhuāgāo vanishing cream
雪花莲 xuěhuālián 〈植物〉snowdrop (*Galanthus*)
雪花石膏 xuěhuā shígāo alabaster
雪鸡 xuějī 〈动物〉snow cock
雪茄 xuějiā *also* "卷烟" juǎnyān cigar
雪窖冰天 xuějiào-bīngtiān *also* "冰天雪窖" all covered with snow and ice; exceedingly cold place; icebound area; icy place
雪晶 xuějīng 〈气象〉snow crystal
雪莱 Xuělái Percy Bysshe Shelley (1792-1822), English poet
雪梨 xuělí snow pear (*Pyrus nivalis*)
雪犁 xuělí 〈体育〉skibob:～运动 skibobbing /～运动员 skibobber
雪里红 xuělǐhóng *also* "雪里蕻" 〈植物〉potherb mustard (*Brassica cernua*)
雪里蕻 xuělǐhóng *see* "雪里红"
雪里送炭 xuělǐ-sòngtàn *see* "雪中送炭"
雪利酒 xuělìjiǔ sherry
雪连纸 xuěliánzhǐ a kind of writing paper smooth on one side
雪莲 xuělián 〈植物〉snow lotus (*Saussurea involucrata*)
雪亮 xuěliàng bright as snow; shiny; sharp:地板擦得～ polish the floor till it has a good shine /日光灯把教室照得～。The dazzling fluorescent lamp lit up the classroom. /群众的眼睛是～的。The eyes of the masses are discerning.
雪量 xuěliàng 〈气象〉snowfall:～计 snow gauge
雪柳 xuěliǔ ❶ *also* "过街柳" guòjiēliǔ; "稻柳" dàoliǔ 〈植物〉fontanesia (*Fontanesia fortunei*) ❷ 〈迷信〉wand or staff wrapped with sliced white paper held by a mourner at the head of a funeral procession
雪盲 xuěmáng 〈医学〉snow blindness
雪泥鸿爪 xuění-hóngzhǎo swan's claw prints on the mud wetted by melting snow — traces of bygone days:往事点点滴滴,如同～,却难忘怀。Memories of past events keep coming to my mind.
雪虐风饕 xuěnüè-fēngtāo raging snowstorm; severely cold weather:他们乘雪橇昼夜赶路,不惧～。They defied the icy and inclement weather, pressing forward in a sled day and night.
雪片 xuěpiàn snowflake:冬日的夜空,～翻飞。Snowflakes were swirling in the wintry night sky. /各方唁电如～飞来。Messages of condolence from different places kept pouring in. /院长收到的申请书,有如～。The president of the university was swamped by an avalanche of applications.
雪橇 xuěqiāo sled; sledge; sleigh
雪青 xuěqīng lilac (colour):～马 lilac horse /～的毛衣 lilac woolen sweater
雪球 xuěqiú snowball
雪雀 xuěquè 〈动物〉snow finch
雪人 xuěrén ❶ human-like figure made of snow; snowman:孩子们在院子里堆～。The children were making a snowman in the yard. ❷ human-like primate believed to live in Tibet or other frigid areas in China; abominable snowman; Yeti; Bigfoot
雪山 xuěshān snow-capped mountains:千里～ snow-capped mountain range stretching a thousand *li* /翻～,过草地 cross the snow-capped mountains and plod through grassy swamps
雪上加霜 xuěshàng-jiāshuāng snow plus frost — add to the miseries of sb. who is already unfortunate enough; rub salt into sb.'s wounds:丈夫新故,爱子又遇车祸重伤,这真是～。One after another disasters befell her — her husband died recently, and then her darling son was seriously injured in a car accident.
雪上汽车 xuěshàng qìchē snowmobile:～运动〈体育〉snowmobiling
雪糁 xuěshēn *also* "雪糁子" 〈方言〉snow pellets; graupel:午后天气骤寒,天上落下～。It turned cold abruptly in the afternoon and snow pellets began to fall.
雪水 xuěshuǐ newly-melted snow; snow-broth
雪松 xuěsōng 〈植物〉cedar; deodar; white pine (*Cedrus deodara*)
雪条 xuětiáo 〈方言〉ice lolly; frozen sucker; popsicle
雪铁龙 Xuětiělóng Citroen, French car manufacturer and brand name
雪兔 xuětù 〈动物〉snow hare; snowshoe rabbit; varying hare (*Lepus timidus*)
雪线 xuěxiàn 〈地理〉snow line
雪压 xuěyā snow pressure
雪雁 xuěyàn snow goose; wavey
雪野 xuěyě *see* "雪原"
雪冤 xuěyuān clear (sb.) of a false charge; redress a wrong; be rehabilitated:他被整多年,临终时才得以～。He had been persecuted

for years only to be cleared of the frame-up before his death.
雪原 xuěyuán snowfield：骏马在～上奔驰。Horses were galloping in the snowfield.
雪杖 xuězhàng 〈体育〉ski pole；ski stick
雪中送炭 xuězhōng-sòngtàn *also*"雪里送炭" send charcoal in snowy weather — provide timely help；bring comfort to those in trouble
雪子 xuězǐ 〈方言〉graupel

鳕 xuě 〈动物〉cod
鳕鲸 xuějīng sei whale；Rudolphi's rorqual (*Balaenoptera borealis*)
鳕鱼 xuěyú cod：～肝油 cod-liver oil／～卵 cod roe／～圈网 cod purse seine

xuè

谑 xuè 〈书面〉joke；banter；tease；jest：戏～ banter；tease／谐～ humorous joke；wisecrack；pleasantry
谑而不虐 xuè'érbùnüè tease without embarrassing

血 xuè ❶ blood：鲜～ fresh blood／流～ shed blood／出～ bleed；haemorrhage／止～ stop bleeding；stanch bleeding／补～ enrich the blood／放～ bloodletting／活～ invigorate the circulation of blood／贫～ anaemia／充～ hyperaemia／吐～ blood spitting／潜～ occult blood／～的教训 lesson paid for with blood；lesson written in blood ❷ related by blood：*see*"～亲" ❸ zeal；ardour；courage：热～青年 courageous and upright young people ❹ menstruation；period
see also xiě
血癌 xuè'ái blood cancer；leukemia；leukocythemia
see also"白血病" báixuèbìng
血案 xuè'àn homicide or murder case：调查～ investigate a homicide or murder case
血斑 xuèbān bloodstain：他的外衣上有些～。There is some caked blood on his jacket.
血本 xuèběn principal；original capital：不恤～ not afraid of losing one's principal；willing to do sth. at any cost／亏了～ lose one's original capital／～无归 cannot even recover one's capital；lose every cent invested
血崩 xuèbēng *also*"崩症" bēngzhèng 〈中医〉flooding；metrorrhagia
血崩症 xuèbēngzhèng metrorrhagia
血沉 xuèchén 〈医学〉erythrocyte sedimentation rate (ESR)：～试验 sedimentation test／～素 sedimentin／～淀素 hematoprecipitin
血仇 xuèchóu debt of blood；blood feud；vendetta：报～ avenge a blood feud；settle (*or* square) a debt of flood／结下～ start a blood feud
血滴石 xuèdīshí bloodstone；heliotrope
血防 xuèfáng 〈医学〉prevention of snail fever：这一地区～工作搞得好，血吸虫病得到了有效控制。A good job was done in bringing schistosomiasis under effective control in the area.
血粉 xuèfěn blood powder (made of the blood of such animals as cows, goats and hogs and used as feed or fertilizer)
血管 xuèguǎn 〈生理〉blood vessel；vascellum；vessel：～紧张 vasotonia
血管病 xuèguǎnbìng angiopathy；vascular disease
血管梗阻 xuèguǎn gěngzǔ 〈医学〉angiemphraxis
血管痉挛 xuèguǎn jìngluán vasospasm
血管扩张 xuèguǎn kuòzhāng 〈医学〉angiectasis；blood distention
血管瘤 xuèguǎnliú 〈医学〉angioma；haemangioma
血管膜 xuèguǎnmó 〈生理〉tunica vasculosa
血管破裂 xuèguǎn pòliè angiorrhexis
血管切除术 xuèguǎn qiēchúshù 〈医学〉angiectomy
血管收缩 xuèguǎn shōusuō vasoconstriction
血管舒张 xuèguǎn shūzhāng vasodilatation
血管炎 xuèguǎnyán 〈医学〉angeitis
血管硬化 xuèguǎn yìnghuà 〈医学〉angiosclerosis；sclerosis vascularis；vascularis sclerosis
血管再造 xuèguǎn zàizào 〈医学〉revascularization
血管造影 xuèguǎn zàoyǐng 〈医学〉angiography
血光之灾 xuèguāngzhīzāi 〈迷信〉(omen of) mortal danger
血海 xuèhǎi sea of blood：大屠杀把村庄变成了一片～。The massacre turned the village into a bloodbath.
血海深仇 xuèhǎi-shēnchóu huge debt of blood；intense and inveterate hatred
血汗 xuèhàn blood and sweat；sweat of one's brow：～钱 money earned by onerous toil／粒粒粮食都是农民用～换来的，要十分珍惜。We must cherish every grain of rice because it is raised by farmers in the sweat of their brows.
血汗工厂 xuèhàn gōngchǎng sweat shop
血红 xuèhóng blood red：～的军旗 blood-red army flag
血红蛋白 xuèhóng dànbái *also*"血红素"；"血色素"〈生化〉haemoglobin (Hb)：～尿 hemoglobinuria；haemoglobinuria
血花 xuèhuā splattering blood
血迹 xuèjì bloodstain：～斑斑 be bloodstained／他企图擦掉地板上的～。He tried to efface the bloodstains from the floor.
血祭 xuèjì sacrificial offering of animal blood：以～祭社稷 consecrate sacrificial animal blood to the God of Earth and the God of Grains
血痂 xuèjiā blood scab or crust around a wound
血浆 xuèjiāng 〈生理〉(blood) plasma：～疗法 plasmatherapy
血浆蛋白 xuèjiāng dànbái plasma protein
血竭 xuèjié *also*"麒麟竭" qílínjié 〈中药〉dragon's blood (dried resin of *Daemonorops draco*)
血口 xuèkǒu blood-dripping mouth：张开～ (of a beast of prey) open its blood-dripping mouth／要用～把整个国家吞掉 try to gobble up the whole country
血口喷人 xuèkǒu-pēnrén maliciously attack；venomously slander：他～，全是一派谎言！It's a pack of lies! He is trying to smear my reputation.
血枯病 xuèkūbìng 〈中医〉blood exhaustion (referring to cessation of menstruation caused by wasting diseases)；serious anaemia
血库 xuèkù 〈医学〉blood bank
血块 xuèkuài half-solid lump formed from blood；blood clot
血亏 xuèkuī 〈中医〉severe deficiency of blood；anaemia
血泪 xuèlèi blood and tears；tears of blood：充满～的人生经历 life written in blood and tears
血泪斑斑 xuèlèi-bānbān be filled with blood and tears：～话童年 speak of childhood full of blood and tears
血痢 xuèlì 〈医学〉hematodiarrhoea
血流 xuèliú blood flow：～受阻 blood flow being blocked
血流成河 xuèliú-chénghé river of blood；bloodbath：战场上尸横遍野，～。The battlefield was drenched in blood with dead bodies scattered all over.
血流动力学 xuèliú dònglìxué 〈医学〉haemodynamics
血流漂杵 xuèliú-piāochǔ so much blood was shed that wooden pestles could float on it — mass killing in war；massacre
血流如注 xuèliú-rúzhù blood gushing forth；spouting blood
血路 xuèlù path crimson with blood：杀出一条～ break through an encirclement after bloody fighting
血脉 xuèmài ❶〈中医〉blood circulation：～不畅。The blood doesn't circulate smoothly. ❷ blood relationship：～相通 be related by blood
血尿 xuèniào 〈医学〉blood urine；haematuria；hematuresis：～素 blood urea
血凝固 xuènínggù 〈医学〉blood coagulation；hematopexis
血浓于水 xuènóngyúshuǐ blood is thicker than water — people of the same blood are naturally bound together；family relationships are stronger and more important than other ties
血泊 xuèpō pool of blood；bloodbath：躺在～中 welter in blood／把伤者从～中救起 rescue the wounded from the bloodbath
血气 xuèqì ❶ animal spirits；sap；vitality；vigour：～已衰。One's vitality has sagged. ❷ courage and rectitude
血气方刚 xuèqì-fānggāng full of sap or mettle；of hot blood：～的青年 youths of hot blood；young people full of vim and vigour
血气之勇 xuèqìzhīyǒng animal or reckless courage：不逞～ not let one's animal courage get the better of oneself
血亲 xuèqīn blood relations；consanguinity：他们二人有～关系。The two of them are related by blood.／我们是～。We are of the same blood.
血亲关系 xuèqīn guānxi blood ties；relation by blood；relationship by consanguinity

血亲婚配 xuèqīn hūnpèi marriage between people of the same blood; consanguineous marriage
血清 xuèqīng 〈生理〉serum：抗毒～ antitoxic serum /马～ horse serum
血清白蛋白 xuèqīng báidànbái serum albumin
血清病 xuèqīngbìng serum sickness or disease
血清肝炎抗原 xuèqīng gānyán kàngyuán serum hepatitis antigen (SHA)
血清疗法 xuèqīng liáofǎ serotherapy
血清酶 xuèqīngméi 〈生化〉seroenzyme：～反应 seroenzyme reaction
血清素 xuèqīngsù 〈生化〉serotonin
血清型 xuèqīngxíng serotype
血清性肝炎 xuèqīngxìng gānyán serum hepatitis
血球 xuèqiú 〈生理〉blood cell; blood corpuscle
血球计数器 xuèqiú jìshùqì 〈医学〉haemacytometer
血染沙场 xuèrǎnshāchǎng shed one's blood on the battlefield; lay down one's life in battle
血刃 xuèrèn bloodstained blade of knife：兵不～ win victory without fighting
血肉 xuèròu ❶ blood and muscle ❷ extremely close relationship
血肉横飞 xuèròu-héngfēi blood and flesh flying in all directions：把他们炸得～ blow them into a disorderly pile of dead bodies
血肉模糊 xuèròu-móhu badly mauled：被打得～ be mangled almost out of recognition
血肉相连 xuèròu-xiānglián *also* "血肉相联" as close as flesh and blood：劳动人民～。We working people are as close as flesh and blood.
血肉之躯 xuèròuzhīqū human body; flesh and blood; mortal flesh：为国雪耻，何惜～！I'm ready to sacrifice my life to wipe out the national humiliation.
血色 xuèsè redness of the skin; colour：面无～ have little colour in the cheeks; look pale (*or* pallid) /他病后失去了平日的～。He is off colour after the illness.
血色素 xuèsèsù 〈生理〉haemochrome：～沉着 haemochromatosis
血色原 xuèsèyuán hemochromogen
血书 xuèshū letter (expressing one's determination, last wish, etc.) written in one's own blood：为了表示决心，他写了一封～。He wrote a letter in his own blood to show his determination.
血栓 xuèshuān 〈医学〉thrombus
血栓脉管炎 xuèshuān màiguǎnyán thromboangiitis
血栓栓塞 xuèshuān shuānsè thromboembolism
血栓心内膜炎 xuèshuān xīnnèimóyán thromboendocarditis
血栓形成 xuèshuān xíngchéng thrombosis：脑～ cerebral thrombosis /冠状动脉～ coronary thrombosis
血水 xuèshuǐ thin and watery blood：伤口上渗出了～。Watery blood oozed out of the wound.
血丝虫病 xuèsīchóngbìng 〈医学〉filariasis
血糖 xuètáng 〈医学〉blood sugar：～高 hyperglycemia /～低 hypoglycemia
血统 xuètǒng blood relationship; blood lineage; extraction：中国～的外国人 foreign nationals of Chinese descent (*or* origin) /意大利～的美国人 Americans of Italian stock (*or* extraction) /他们是犹太]～。They have Jewish blood in their veins.
血统工人 xuètǒng gōngrén (industrial) worker of working class parentage
血污 xuèwū bloodstain：抹去脸上的～ wipe the bloodstains off one's face
血吸虫 xuèxīchóng blood fluke; schistosome：～病 snail fever; schistosomiasis
血洗 xuèxǐ drench in bloodbath：侵略军～山城。The aggressor troops massacred the inhabitants of the mountain city.
血细胞 xuèxìbāo *also* "血球" blood cell：～计数 blood count
血象 xuèxiàng 〈医学〉blood picture; hemogram
血小板 xuèxiǎobǎn 〈生理〉(blood) platelet：～病 thrombocytopathy /～机能不全 thrombasthenia /～增多 thrombocythaemia /～减少 thrombocytopenia
血腥 xuèxīng reeking of blood; bloody; bloodthirsty; sanguinary：～味 smell of blood /～统治 sanguinary (*or* bloodthirsty) rule /～镇压 bloody suppression /～屠杀 cold-blooded massacre /那是充满～味儿的昧心钱。That's blood and guilt money.
血型 xuèxíng 〈生理〉blood group; blood type：～分类 blood grouping
血性 xuèxìng upright and courageous：～男儿 brave and righteous man
血胸 xuèxiōng 〈医学〉haemothorax
血虚 xuèxū 〈中医〉blood deficiency and its resultant pathological changes
血循环 xuèxúnhuán 〈生理〉blood circulation
血压 xuèyā 〈生理〉blood pressure：～正常 normal blood pressure /高～ high blood pressure; hypertension /低～ low blood pressure; hypotension
血压计 xuèyājì 〈医学〉sphygmomanometer
血样 xuèyàng blood sample or specimen
血液 xuèyè ❶〈生理〉blood：～循环 blood circulation /～体外循环 extracorporeal circulation ❷ fresh blood; lifeline; backbone force：为部队输送新鲜～。Infuse fresh blood (*or* new blood) into the army. /水是农业的～。Water is the lifeblood of agriculture.
血液病 xuèyèbìng blood disease
血液动力学 xuèyè dònglìxué haematodynamics
血液透析 xuèyè tòuxī haemodialysis：～器 haemodialyster
血液学 xuèyèxué haematology
血衣 xuèyī bloodstained garment; clothes covered with gore; blood-shirt：有～为证 use the gore-covered clothes as evidence
血印 xuèyìn bloodstain：在嫌疑犯的长袖上，找到了几点～。Several bloodstains were found on the suspect's sleeves.
血勇 xuèyǒng animal courage or spirits：～之人 hot blood
血友病 xuèyǒubìng 〈医学〉haemophilia：～患者 haemophiliac
血雨腥风 xuèyǔ-xīngfēng *also* "腥风血雨" foul wind and rain of blood — reactionary reign of terror：难忘那反动统治～的年代。It's difficult to forget those years of the reactionary reign of terror.
血郁 xuèyù 〈中医〉a kind of circulatory disorder with symptoms such as enfeeblement of the limbs and having blood in the stool; blood stasis
血原虫 xuèyuánchóng 〈医学〉haematozoon
血缘 xuèyuán ties of blood; consanguinity; relationship by birth：～关系 of blood relationship; related by blood /～关系太近的人不得结婚。People are not allowed to marry within certain degrees of consanguinity.
血缘婚 xuèyuánhūn consanguineous marriage
血缘家庭 xuèyuán jiātíng consanguineous family
血晕 xuèyùn 〈中医〉coma due to excessive loss of blood during childbirth
see also xiěyùn
血债 xuèzhài debt of blood：有～ have blood on one's hands /～要用血来还。Debts of blood must be paid in blood.
血债累累 xuèzhài-lěilěi have heavy blood debts; have a mountain of blood debts; commit a string of murders
血战 xuèzhàn ❶ bloody battle; extremely fierce battle：两军展开～。The two armies were locked in a bloody battle. ❷ wage desperate struggle：～到底 fight to the bitter end; fight to the last drop of one's blood; fight to the last man
血账 xuèzhàng *see* "血债"
血证 xuèzhèng bloodstained evidence (such as clothes and articles stained with the blood of the murdered person)
血脂 xuèzhī blood fat：～过多 hyperlipidemia /～蛋白过少 hypolipoproteinemia
血肿 xuèzhǒng 〈医学〉haematoma
血中毒 xuèzhòngdú 〈医学〉haematotoxicosis
血渍 xuèzì bloodstain：洗去衣服上的～ wash the bloodstains off one's clothes

xūn

窨 xūn *also* "熏" xūn add aroma to tea by mixing it with jasmine
see also yìn

荤 xūn
see also hūn

荤粥 Xūnyù *see* "獯鬻" Xūnyù

埙(壎) xūn ancient Chinese wind instrument, made of

X

porcelain with one to six holes and shaped like an egg

勋(勳) xūn ❶ meritorious service; exploit; merit; achievement:功～ exploit; meritorious service; contribution /殊～ outstanding merit; meritorious service /元～ man of great merit; founding father /屡建奇～ render outstanding service time and again; perform many renowned exploits ❷ medal; decoration:授～ confer orders or medals; award a decoration

勋臣 xūnchén official who has rendered meritorious service

勋绩 xūnjì meritorious service; outstanding contribution; remarkable achievements:盖世～ unparalleled meritorious service /彪炳史册的～ achievements shining through the ages /他的～将与山河永在,和日月同辉。His outstanding exploits will outlast the mountains and rivers, and shine forever like the sun and the moon.

勋爵 xūnjué ❶ feudal title of nobility conferred for meritorious service ❷ (UK) Lord

勋劳 xūnláo meritorious service; exploit:屡建～ make repeated contributions /这位将军在战场上～卓著,为人民所崇敬。The general won respect from the people for his valiant exploits in the battlefield.

勋业 xūnyè 〈书面〉meritorious service; great achievement:不朽的～ immortal meritorious deeds; lasting achievement; monumental service

勋章 xūnzhāng medal; decoration:荣誉～ honorary decoration /军功～ medal for meritorious military service /红旗～ red flag decoration /授予某人～ award sb. with a medal; confer a medal on sb.

熏(❶❷燻) xūn ❶ smoke; fumigate:把野兽～出窝来 smoke an animal from its lair /墙壁给烟～黑了。The wall was blackened by smoke. /用醋～一～屋子,防止感冒。Fumigate the room with vinegar to prevent catching cold. /这屋里消毒水的味儿真～人。The smell of the disinfectant in the house is suffocating. /他的手指都让烟头～黄了。His fingers were yellowed by the cigarette smoke. ❷ treat (meat, fish, etc.) with smoke; smoke:～牛肉 smoked beef /～茶叶 add aroma to tea leaves by mixing them with jasmine /把鸡～一下。Cure the chicken in smoke. ❸ pleasantly warm; genial: *see* "～风"

see also xùn

熏风 xūnfēng 〈书面〉warm southerly breeze:～自南至,吹我池上林。A warm southerly breeze blew through the woods round the pond.

熏干 xūngān dry smoked beancurd

熏鸡 xūnjī smoked chicken

熏笼 xūnlóng bamboo or wire net over a brazier for scenting clothing or drying laundry

熏炉 xūnlú brazier used for scenting clothing or warming oneself; censer

熏沐 xūnmù 〈迷信〉burn incense and take a bath — a ritual for showing respect for the supernatural forces

熏染 xūnrǎn exert a gradual, corrupting influence on; be corrupted by:受不良环境的～ be gradually influenced by a bad environment /受到金钱名利思想的～ become corrupted by a craving for money and fame

熏肉 xūnròu smoked meat or pork

熏陶 xūntáo exert a gradual, uplifting influence on; foster; nurture; cultivate:受到爱国主义思想的～ nurtured in the spirit of patriotism /在父兄的～下长大成人 be brought up under the influence of one's father and elder brothers /由于先生的悉心指教,他受到了良好的艺术～,画技日进。The tender guidance of his teacher imbued him with fine artistic taste, and his skill in painting improved with each passing day.

熏天 xūntiān overwhelming:热气～ overwhelming heat /气焰～ overweening arrogance; overbearing conceit /这里的下水道臭气～。This place stinks of the sewage. *or* The sewage has stunk the place out.

熏衣草 xūnyīcǎo lavender (*Lavandula angustifolia*)

熏鱼 xūnyú smoked fish

熏蒸 xūnzhēng ❶ stifling; suffocating:暑气～,令人难熬 suffer from steamy heat in the summer; be suffocated in the sweltering weather ❷〈中医〉fuming or steaming — treating diseases with fumes as in moxibustion or with steam generated by boiling medicinal herbs ❸ fumigate:～消毒 disinfect by fumigation /～消毒器 fumigator /～剂〈农业〉fumigant

熏制 xūnzhì smoke; fumigate (sth. with jasmine, etc.); cure (meat, etc.) by smoke:～食品 smoked food /～腊肉 cured pork

薰[1] xūn 〈书面〉a kind of sweet grass; fragrance (of flowers, etc.):陌上草～ fragrance of wild flowers in the field /花～ jade vessel for perfuming; jade perfumer

薰[2] xūn *see* "熏" xūn

薰草 xūncǎo *Loumarouna odorata*, a medical herb with a strong smell

薰衣草 xūnyīcǎo *also* "熏衣草" xūnyīcǎo lavender:～油 lavender oil

薰莸不同器 xūn-yóu bù tóng qì *also* "薰莸异器" fragrant herbs and stinking weeds must not be kept in the same vessel — the good and the bad don't mix

醺 xūn drunk:醉～～ dead drunk; tight; as drunk as a fiddler /三杯过后,他已微～,话也多起来了。He was tipsy after drinking his third cup and became loquacious.

曛 xūn 〈书面〉❶ dim glow of the setting sun:夕～ dim glow at sunset ❷ dusk; nightfall:～黄 dusk /～暮 dusk; nightfall

獯 xūn

獯鬻 Xūnyù *also* "荤粥" Xūnyù 〈古语〉ethnic group in the north of China

纁 xūn 〈书面〉light red

xún

纠 xún 〈书面〉silk ribbon; silk braid

循 xún follow; abide by; act in accordance with:遵～ follow; adhere to; abide by; conform with /因～守旧 move in a rut; follow the convention /～流而下 sail down the river /～阶而上 go up by the steps /～途守辙 follow the track and keep to the rut

循道公会 Xúndào Gōnghuì 〈基督教〉Methodist Church

循道宗 Xúndàozōng 〈基督教〉Methodism:～信徒 Methodist

循分 xúnfèn 〈书面〉act according to one's duties:～守理 do one's duties and abide by reason

循规蹈矩 xúnguī-dǎojǔ observe rules and follow orders docilely; follow accepted customs and practices; conform to convention; toe the line:他向来～,工作稳妥可靠,领导很放心。Having always followed rules and been reliable in work, he has won the thorough trust of the leaders. /她们是干了二十来年的老保姆,最是～的。They're the steadiest, most reliable old nannies with over twenty years' experience.

循环 xúnhuán circulate; cycle:～期 cycle period /～群 cyclic group /～效应 cyclical effect /～作业 cycle operation /～流动 circular flow /恶性～ vicious circle /良性～ virtuous circle /体外～ extracorporeal circulation /血液～ blood circulation /～水 circulating water /心脏使血液在全身～。The heart circulates blood round the body.

循环基金 xúnhuán jījīn revolving fund

循环进位 xúnhuán jìnwèi 〈数学〉end-around carry

循环论 xúnhuánlùn 〈哲学〉theory of cycles; cyclicism

循环论证 xúnhuán lùnzhèng 〈逻辑〉arguing in a circle; circular argument

循环赛 xúnhuánsài 〈体育〉round robin

循环水泵 xúnhuán shuǐbèng water circulation pump

循环往复 xúnhuán-wǎngfù move in cycles

循环系统 xúnhuán xìtǒng 〈生理〉circulatory system

循环小数 xúnhuán xiǎoshù 〈数学〉recurring decimal

循环信用证 xúnhuán xìnyòngzhèng revolving letter of credit

循理守分 xúnlǐ-shǒufèn abide by the law and behave oneself; be law-abiding and conscientious

循吏 xúnlì 〈书面〉honest or upright official

循例 xúnlì follow the usual practice; follow a precedent; act in ac-

cordance with precedents：类似情况，可以～办理。Follow the usual practice in dealing with cases like this.

循良 xúnliáng 〈书面〉upright；honest and law-abiding

循名责实 xúnmíng-zéshí expect the reality to correspond to the name；see that the reality matches the name：你身为主任，大家自然可以～，用主任的标准来要求你的工作。Since you are the director, people will naturally set the demands of a director on your work.

循序 xúnxù in proper order or sequence：新任大使们～向驻在国总统递交国书。The newly-appointed ambassadors successively presented their credentials to the president of the country to which they were accredited.

循序渐进 xúnxù-jiànjìn follow in order and advance step by step；proceed in an orderly and gradual way：～的教学法 progressive teaching method / 学习应该～，日有所获。In our study, we must proceed in a systematic way and make steady progress every day.

循循善诱 xúnxún-shànyòu be good at giving systematic guidance；be methodical in imparting knowledge；teach with skill and patience：教育孩子要～，不能急躁。Teaching children needs skill and patience and admits of no impetuosity. / 我的导师对我～，使我获益不少。I benefited a great deal from the systematic and patient guidance of my supervisor.

旬 xún ❶ period of ten days：上～ first ten days of a month / 七月下～ last ten-day period of July ❷ period of ten years in an old person's age：年届七～的老人 old man of seventy / 老父已近九～。My father is approaching ninety.

旬刊 xúnkān publication appearing once every ten days

旬日 xúnrì 〈书面〉ten days：～可至 arrive in ten days / ～为期 with a time limit of ten days

洵 xún 〈书面〉really；truly；indeed：～属可贵 truly precious；indeed praiseworthy；really valuable / ～美且仁 truly handsome and kind / ～不诬也。Indeed it's true and not hearsay.

恂 xún 〈书面〉❶ honest；respectful：～谨 respectful and circumspect ❷ fear；dread：～然 in fear

询 xún ask；inquire；consult：征～ seek (*or* solicit) the opinion of；hold consultations with / 质～ ask for an explanation；interpellate；question / 咨～ seek advice from；consult / 探～ make cautious inquiries；try to sound out (sb.'s view) / ～明原委 ascertain the cause by inquiry

询查 xúnchá make inquiries：～电话号码 inquire about the telephone numbers

询问 xúnwèn ask；inquire：～道路 ask the way / ～处 inquiry office；inquiries / ～系统〈电子〉inquiry system / ～显示终端〈电子〉inquiry display terminal / 请入内～。Inquire within. / 她用～的目光望着他。She gave him an inquiring look. / 经向有关方面～，我们弄清了这个组织的背景。We are now clear about the background of the organization after making inquiries of the people concerned. / 经～，我得知她已经回国了。I learned upon inquiry that she had already gone back to her country.

珣 xún 〈书面〉name of a kind of jade

荀 Xún a surname

荀子 Xúnzǐ ❶ *also* "荀况" Xunzi (formerly translated as Hsuntzu, c.313-238 BC), philosopher and educationist of the late Warring States Period ❷ *Book of Xunzi*

栒 xún

栒子木 xúnzimù 〈植物〉cotoneaster

峋 xún *see* "嶙峋" línxún

郇 Xún a surname

see also Huán

巡(廵) xún ❶ patrol；inspect；make one's rounds：出～ go out on an inspection tour / 南～ inspection tour to the south ❷ 〈量词〉round of drinks：斟一～酒 serve out a round of wine / 酒过三～，主人起立致辞。When the wine had gone round three times, the host stood up to make a speech.

巡边员 xúnbiānyuán 〈体育〉linesman

巡捕 xúnbǔ ❶ retinue of a provincial governor in the Qing Dynasty：带着多名随身～ have a large retinue ❷ police or policeman (in former foreign concessions)

巡捕房 xúnbǔfáng *also* "捕房" police station (in former foreign concessions)

巡查 xúnchá go on a tour of inspection；make one's rounds：维修人员定期～电话线路。The maintenance personnel make an inspection of the telephone line regularly. / 火是在他～工厂时发现的。The fire was discovered when he was doing the rounds of the factory.

巡察 xúnchá make an inspection tour：省长到各县～春耕情况。The provincial governor is touring the counties to see how spring ploughing is getting on.

巡风 xúnfēng keep watch；watch：派人到村口～ send sb. to keep watch at the village gate

巡抚 xúnfǔ 〈历史〉(Qing Dynasty) provincial governor for military and civil affairs；(Ming Dynasty) imperial inspector；roving minister

巡更 xúngēng 〈旧语〉keep night watch；go on night patrol：～守夜 keep night watch

巡官 xúnguān police inspector

巡航 xúnháng cruise：～半径 cruising radius / ～速度 cruising speed / 巡逻艇在海疆～。The patrol boat was cruising offshore. / ～归来，初次出海的战士异常兴奋。Back from a first-ever cruise on the sea, the new recruits were elated.

巡航导弹 xúnháng dǎodàn cruise missile：～运载工具 cruise missile carrier / "战斧"式～ Tomahawk cruise missile

巡回 xúnhuí tour；go the rounds；make a circuit of：～辅导 mobile coaching / ～讲学 lecturing tour

巡回大使 xúnhuí dàshǐ roving ambassador

巡回法官 xúnhuí fǎguān 〈法律〉circuit judge；circuit justice；itinerant judge；justice in eyre

巡回法庭 xúnhuí fǎtíng 〈法律〉circuit court；circuit tribunal

巡回法院 xúnhuí fǎyuàn 〈法律〉court in eyre；circuit court

巡回放映队 xúnhuí fàngyìngduì mobile film projection unit

巡回检查制 xúnhuí jiǎncházhì circular inspection

巡回剧团 xúnhuí jùtuán itinerant theatrical troupe

巡回审判 xúnhuí shěnpàn 〈法律〉circuit justice；itinerate

巡回图书馆 xúnhuí túshūguǎn mobile library；circulating library

巡回学校 xúnhuí xuéxiào circuit school；mobile school

巡回演出 xúnhuí yǎnchū performing tour

巡回医疗队 xúnhuí yīliáoduì mobile medical team

巡警 xúnjǐng ❶〈旧语〉policeman ❷ patrolling police or policeman

巡礼 xúnlǐ ❶ visit a sacred land；make a pilgrimage：每年去麦加～的人络绎不绝。Each year, people go on a pilgrimage to Mecca in an endless stream. ❷ visit；tour；sightseeing (usu. used as title of book, etc.)：《泉城～》*Fountain City Visited* / 市场～ visit the market

巡逻 xúnluó go on patrol；patrol：海空～ sea and air patrol / 民兵在战时担负着～放哨的任务。Militiamen are entrusted with the task of patrol and sentry in times of war. / 警察在街上～。The police are patrolling the streets. / 晚间在营房四周布置了～。Night patrol is maintained round the barracks.

巡逻队 xúnluóduì patrol party；patrol

巡逻护卫舰 xúnluó hùwèijiàn patrol escort；patrol craft

巡逻警车 xúnluó jǐngchē patrol car

巡逻路线 xúnluó lùxiàn patrol route；beat

巡逻哨 xúnluóshào person on patrol duties；patrol

巡逻艇 xúnluótǐng patrol boat

巡哨 xúnshào (of a small security detachment) go on patrol

巡视 xúnshì ❶ make an inspection tour；tour：～员 inspector / ～大江南北 make an inspection tour of the vast areas along the Yangtze Valley ❷ look around：用望远镜～远处的海滩 survey a distant beach through a telescope / 他的眼睛来回～着整个教室。His eyes roved about the classroom.

巡视官 xúnshìguān ombudsman

巡天 xúntiān tour the heavens：古人～的梦想，今日已经实现。The dream of the ancient people to tour the heavens has come true. / 坐地日行八万里，～遥看一千河。Motionless, by earth I travel eighty

thousand *li* a day, Surveying the sky I see a myriad Milky Ways from afar.

巡行 xúnxíng go on a circuit; make one's rounds; patrol: ~市区 make one's rounds in the urban district

巡幸 xúnxìng 〈书面〉(of a monarch) go on an inspection tour; tour

巡洋舰 xúnyángjiàn 〈军事〉cruiser: 导弹~ guided missile cruiser

巡夜 xúnyè make night patrol: 春节期间,学院有专人~。During the Spring Festival, people were assigned to make night patrol of the college campus.

巡弋 xúnyì (of warships) cruise; ply the waters: 舰队在南海~。The fleet cruised in the South China Sea.

巡游 xúnyóu ❶ saunter; stroll: 闲暇无事,我就在大街上~。When I was free, I liked to wander about the street. /他无所事事,到处~。He is idle and always on the gad. ❷ patrol: 警察在广场四周~。Policemen are patrolling around the square.

巡阅 xúnyuè make inspection tours of different places

巡展 xúnzhǎn exhibition tour; roving exhibition

巡诊 xúnzhěn (of a doctor) make a round of visits: 医生们定期下乡~,工作很辛苦。These doctors worked very hard making round of visits regularly to the countryside.

寻[1](尋)

xún ❶ ancient measure of length, equal to about eight *chi* (尺): 高可百~。It is about 800 *chi* tall. ❷ (Xún) a surname

寻[2](尋)

xún try to find; look for; search; seek: ~人启事 notice for looking for sb. /~亲访友 call on relatives and friends /自~烦恼 bring vexation on oneself; ask for trouble

寻查 xúnchá look for: 四处~走失的孩子 search high and low for the missing child

寻常 xúncháng ordinary; common; normal; usual: ~老百姓 common folk; man in the street /这件事异乎~。This case is out of the ordinary. /乘飞机旅行已是~的事了。Air travel is now a commonplace.

寻趁 xúnchèn 〈方言〉❶ look for: 往来~ look for (sth. or sb.) here and there ❷ find fault with; reprimand: 也不知道他为了什么,跑到这里~我。I don't know why he came to pick on me.

寻的 xúndì 〈军事〉target-seeking; homing: 自动~导弹 automatic homing missile

寻的雷达 xúndì léidá target-seeking radar

寻短见 xún duǎnjiàn *also* "寻短路" try to commit suicide: 她一时想不开,竟寻了短见。She took things too hard and went so far as to take her own life.

寻访 xúnfǎng look for (sb. whose whereabouts is unknown); try to find; inquire about: ~故友 try to find an old friend /我~此书,已有整整十年。I have been looking for this book for ten whole years.

寻根 xúngēn ❶ trace sth. to its source; get to the bottom of things: 这类小事似无~的必要。I don't think it's necessary to get to the bottom of such a trivial matter. ❷ find the roots of one's family

寻根究底 xúngēn-jiūdǐ *also* "寻根问底" trace sth. to its root; get to the bottom of things; inquire deeply into; investigate thoroughly: 这人好认死理,凡事总爱~。The man takes everything seriously and is always trying to get to the root of a matter. /让你去就去,何必~? You simply go when you are asked. Stop asking why.

寻行数墨 xúnháng-shǔmò keep on reading while paying no attention to the meaning; read without understanding

寻呼 xúnhū beep-page; bleep: 他~伙伴多次,未有回音。He beep-paged his partener several times, but has got no reply.

寻呼机 xúnhūjī beep pager; pager; beeper; bleeper

寻花问柳 xúnhuā-wènliǔ *also* "问柳寻花" ❶ enjoy the spring scenery: 他一路~,饱览山色之美。He had a good time on the way, enjoying the beautiful mountains and the spring scenery. ❷ frequent houses of ill fame (*or* prostitution); visit brothels; go whoring

寻欢作乐 xúnhuān-zuòlè seek pleasure and make merry; indulge in sensual pleasures; sow one's wild oats: 她的丈夫经常和一些不三不四的女人~,这就是她和他离婚的原因。Her husband was often fooling around with some loose women. That's why she divorced him.

寻机 xúnjī 〈书面〉look for an opening or opportunity: 他平日里总要~跟经理搭搭腔。He grabs every opportunity to talk with the manager.

寻究 xúnjiū probe into; investigate thoroughly; pursue: ~来历 probe into the origin; investigate the background

寻开心 xún kāixīn 〈方言〉make fun of; joke: 你少同我~! Stop making fun of me!

寻觅 xúnmì try to find; seek; look for: 这几味中药极难配齐,你要耐心~。These medical herbs are extremely difficult to come by, so you must be patient in looking for them.

寻摸 xúnmo 〈口语〉grope for; look for; seek: 她在黑暗中~她的大衣。She groped for her coat in the dark.

寻求 xúnqiú seek; pursue; search for; go in quest of: ~真理 seek after the truth /~政治庇护 seek political asylum /~政治解决的办法 search for a political solution (of a problem) /~成功的途径 explore the path to success /~知识 go in quest of knowledge /~合作伙伴 seek (out) partners for cooperation

寻声 xúnshēng try to locate (sth. or sb.) by following the sound: ~查找 look for sth. by following the sound

寻事 xúnshì seek a quarrel; pick a fight: 他是上门~来的。He has come to pick a quarrel.

寻事生非 xúnshì-shēngfēi seek a quarrel; stir up trouble: 出门人要处处小心,不可~。When you are away from home, you must be cautious and avoid provoking a row. /请别在这件事上~! Don't kick up a rumpus about this matter!

寻死 xúnsǐ commit suicide; try to kill oneself

寻死觅活 xúnsǐ-mìhuó threaten to commit suicide: 你一天到晚~的,心里究竟有何冤屈? You threaten all the time to kill yourself. What wrong has been done to you?

寻思 xúnsi ❶ meditate; ponder; reflect; contemplate: 你好好~~吧,你这样做对得起谁? Turn it over in your mind carefully. Is your behaviour up to people's expectations? ❷ 〈方言〉plan; think of: 我~着今年夏天去一次北京。I'm thinking of making a trip to Beijing this summer.

寻索 xúnsuǒ ❶ look for; pursue; seek: ~他的踪迹 look for his whereabouts ❷ probe into; explore: ~解决方案 explore a solution

寻味 xúnwèi chew sth. over; ruminate; mull over; think over: 耐人~ provide much food for thought /他反复~她信中意味深长的话语。He was chewing over the meaningful wording of her letter.

寻问 xúnwèn seek; explore; look for; inquire: 今天不断有人来打听消息,~情况。People keep coming to inquire about the matter today.

寻隙 xúnxì ❶ find fault with sb. (to provoke an argument): ~闹事 kick up a row by nitpicking ❷ seek an opportunity; try to find a loophole: ~行窃 take advantage of an opportunity to steal

寻衅 xúnxìn pick a quarrel; provoke: ~打架 provoke a fight /以武力~ provoke by force; resort to armed (*or* military) provocation /~找茬儿 find quarrel in a straw; fasten (*or* fix) a quarrel on sb. /他们想~滋事。They wanted to kick up a row and make trouble.

寻绎 xúnyì 〈书面〉probe and explore; unravel; inquire into; seek out: ~哲理 probe into the philosophical theory or principles

寻幽访胜 xúnyōu-fǎngshèng search for and visit secluded places of quiet beauty

寻章摘句 xúnzhāng-zhāijù cull phrases and cite passages from other's writings; write in clichés without originality; load one's writings with hackneyed phrases: 丝毫不见~的痕迹 without the least sign of hackneyed writing /不效书生一味~。He is no pedant seeking remarkable passages and culling model sentences.

寻找 xúnzhǎo seek; pursue; look for: ~借口 seek an excuse /~真理 seeking truth; in quest of truth /~失散的亲人 look for separated relatives /~新的水源 search for new water sources /~失物 try to find sth. lost /~出路 find a way out /~油田 hunt for oilfields /~新的线索 cast about for fresh clues

寻枝摘叶 xúnzhī-zhāiyè look for and pick the branches and leaves — pay attention to unimportant and non-essential things; stress side issues; treasure trifles

浔[1](潯)

xún ❶ 〈书面〉waterside; water margin: 江~ river bank ❷ (Xún) another name for Jiujiang (九江), Jiangxi Province

浔[2](潯)

xún *also* hǎixún (old name for 海寻) nautical fathom

珣(璕)

xún 〈书面〉a kind of beautiful stone

荨(蕁、䔿) xún
see also qián

荨麻疹 xúnmázhěn also "风疹块" fēngzhěnkuài nettle rash; urticaria

咰 xún also yīngxún (old name for 英寻) fathom (6 feet for depth of water)

鲟(鱘、鱏) xún 〈动物〉sturgeon:(中华)白～ Chinese paddlefish

xùn

蕈 xùn 〈植物〉gill fungus:香～ chamignon /松～ pine mushroom /羊肚～ morel

训 xùn ❶ lecture; instruct; teach:教～ lesson; moral /他常常板起面孔～人。He often puts on a stern expression and lectures people. /我昨天被他～了一通。He gave me a good dressing-down (*or* talking-to) yesterday. ❷ teachings; precept; maxim:家～ parental precept /遗～ teachings of the deceased /古～ ancient maxim /校～ school motto ❸ train; drill:军～ military training /培～ train; cultivate /整～ train and consolidate (troops) ❹ standard; model; paragon; example:不足为后人～ not fit to serve as a model for later generations ❺ explanation of words:实词易～,虚词难释。Notional words are easy to explain, functional words are not.

训斥 xùnchì reprimand; rebuke; scold; dress down:他不止一次受到老板的～。He was reprimanded by his boss on several occasions. /父亲～了半天,他只当没有听见。His father took him to task for quite some time, but he simply turned a deaf ear to all that.

训词 xùncí admonition; instructions:我已听惯了他的这种～。I am used to hearing such speechifying (*or* admonitions) from him.

训导 xùndǎo admonish; advise; guide; teach:～晚辈 guide (*or* teach) the younger generation

训导长 xùndǎozhǎng 〈旧语〉person appointed to watch over the conduct of college students; student counsellor

训迪 xùndí 〈书面〉teach (the young); instruct; enlighten:牢记前辈～之言 bear in mind the teachings from the elders

训诂 xùngǔ explanations of words in ancient books; gloss; textual exegesis:文字～ written explanations; exegetics of words in ancient books

训诂学 xùngǔxué critical interpretation of ancient texts; studies of exegesis; scholium

训话 xùnhuà (give) an admonitory talk to subordinates:教官～时,大家屏息静听。When the instructor was giving an admonitory talk, everyone listened with bated breath.

训诲 xùnhuì 〈书面〉instruction; teaching:父亲的～我一直记在心里。I always bear in mind father's admonition.

训教 xùnjiào teach; admonish; advise:他是名师～出来的高徒。He is an accomplished disciple of a great master.

训诫 xùnjiè also "训戒" ❶ admonish; advise:～部下 admonish one's subordinates ❷〈法律〉rebuke; reprimand

训练 xùnliàn train; drill:专业～ professional training /适应性～ acclimatization training /在职～ on-the-job training /军事～ military training /消防～ fire drill /外语强化～ intensified foreign language training /实战～ exercises under battle conditions /这所学校很重视对学生基本技能的～。This school lays great emphasis on training the basic skills of the students.

训练班 xùnliànbān training class; training course:短期～ short course /英语～ English training course /我正在一个微机～学习。I am now going through a training course in personal computer.

训练有素 xùnliàn-yǒusù well-trained:一支纪律严明、～的军队 well-disciplined and well-trained army

训令 xùnlìng instructions; orders; directive:总统～ presidential instructions

训蒙 xùnméng 〈旧语〉teach children; tutor teenagers

训勉 xùnmiǎn instruct and encourage:导师对我多有～。My supervisor gave me a lot of guidance and encouragement.

训示 xùnshì instructions; orders:上级对此有过多次～。The higher authorities have given instructions on the matter several times.

训释 xùnshì explain; interpret:～字义 explain the meaning of words

训诱 xùnyòu 〈书面〉instruct and guide:对孩子要善于～。Children need to be instructed and guided with patience.

训育 xùnyù 〈旧语〉moral instruction

训喻 xùnyù also "训谕"〈书面〉instruct; teach

训责 xùnzé admonish and reprimand:他因品行不端而屡受～。He got a rap on the knuckles several times for not behaving himself.

汛 xùn ❶ seasonal flood or high water:桃花～ spring flood /伏～ summer flood /秋～ autumn flood /凌～ winter flood; ice run /潮～ high tide /防～ flood control; flood prevention ❷ season when fish schools emerge; fishing season:黄鱼～ yellow croaker season

汛期 xùnqī 〈水利〉flood season; high-water season:～警报 warning for the flood season /今年～提前到来了。Flood season came earlier this year.

汛情 xùnqíng flood situation; water level in flood season:通报～ circulate a notice of the flood situation

讯 xùn ❶ ask; inquire:问～ ask after; inquire about; send one's regards to /～之四方 inquire about sth. everywhere ❷ interrogate; question:传～ summon for interrogation /候～ await court trial; await cross-examination /提～ bring (a prisoner) before the court /审～ interrogate /刑～ try by torture ❸ message; dispatch; news:简～ news in brief /新华社～ dispatch from Xihua News Agency /通～设备 communication apparatus /喜～迅速传遍了大街小巷。The good news spread to every street and lane like wildfire. /亲友闻～而至。On hearing the news, friends and relatives all came over.

讯号 xùnhào ❶ signal sent by electro-magnetic wave ❷ signal

讯实 xùnshí confirm through interrogation:以上犯罪事实～,罪犯供认不讳。The truth of the above criminal fact has been established through interrogation and the criminal has also confessed to the crime.

讯问 xùnwèn ❶ ask about; inquire:医生一边按脉,一边向我～病情。While taking my pulse, the doctor inquired about my illness. ❷〈法律〉interrogate; question:～同案犯 interrogate an accomplice /法官详细～证人。The judge questioned the witness at length.

讯息 xùnxī message; wire signal

迅 xùn fast; swift:～若流矢 fast as a flying arrow /～逝如飞 vanish rapidly into thin air

迅步 xùnbù 〈书面〉walk fast; hurry:～赶到 hurry to the scene /～追踪 in hot pursuit

迅风 xùnfēng swift wind; gale

迅即 xùnjí immediately; speedily; at once:～行动 take prompt action /望接信后～启程。I hope you will set out immediately after receiving this letter.

迅急 xùnjí very fast; at high speed; in a flash:有关案情请～报告。Please report the particulars of the case at once. /情况～发生变化。The situation has changed abruptly. *or* There has been a sudden turn of events.

X

迅疾 xùnjí swiftly; rapidly:～前往 rush to a place /他身子～一转,噌地一下跑了。He turned abruptly and took to his heels.

迅捷 xùnjié fast; rapid; agile; quick:他们用简报的形式,～地反映市场动态。They use news bulletins to inform people promptly of the latest developments in the market. /小张动作～,投篮命中率高。Xiao Zhang is agile in movement and good at shooting, with a high percentage of hits.

迅雷不及掩耳 xùnléi bùjí yǎn ěr a sudden peal of thunder leaves no time for covering the ears; be as sudden as a flash of lightning; be as quick as a flash:公安人员以～之势捣毁匪巢。The police destroyed the bandits' den with the suddenness of a thunderbolt. *or* The police swooped on the bandits in the den before they could react.

迅猛 xùnměng sudden and violent:暴风雨来势～。The thunderstorm came bucketing down. /形势急转直下,～发展。The situation took a sudden turn and developed rapidly. /他以～有力的一记重拳把对手击倒在地。He knocked his opponent down with a swift and powerful blow.

迅速 xùnsù rapid; swift; quick; fast:～反应 quick response /～赶到门前 rush to the gate /发展～ develop rapidly; grow by leaps and bounds /～南下 march speedily towards the south /我们应～采取有力措施。We must take prompt and effective measures.

熏 xùn 〈方言〉be poisoned or suffocated by coal gas:被煤气～倒了 be poisoned by coal gas /要是安上烟筒,就不至于～着了。If they had a stovepipe, they wouldn't have been suffocated in the room.
see also xūn

殉(❷徇) xùn ❶ be buried alive with the dead ❷ sacrifice one's life for; die for: *see* "～职"; "～国"

殉道 xùndào die for a just cause or one's ideals; die a martyr:～者 martyr

殉国 xùnguó die for one's country; give one's life for the country: 以身～ lay down one's life for one's country

殉教 xùnjiào sacrifice one's life for a religious cause

殉节 xùnjié ❶ die in loyalty to one's country:重义轻生,亡身～,此乃志士之本色。Valuing cause above one's life and dying in loyalty to one's country is the distinctive character of a man of integrity. ❷ 〈旧语〉(of a woman) commit suicide after her husband's death ❸ 〈旧语〉(of a woman) commit suicide to defend her chastity:～自尽 kill oneself in defence of one's chastity

殉难 xùnnàn die for a just cause; die a martyr:～的烈士仁人 martyrs and public-spirited people who laid down their lives for a just cause

殉情 xùnqíng die or commit suicide for love:双双～。Both of them committed suicide for their love.

殉死 xùnsǐ ❶ be buried alive with the dead ❷ commit suicide in order to follow the deceased to the grave

殉葬 xùnzàng be buried alive with the dead:～制度 institution of burying the living with the dead /这座商代坟墓中的～奴隶多达四百人。There are more than four hundred immolated slaves buried in this Shang Dynasty grave.

殉葬品 xùnzàngpǐn funerary object; sacrificial object; sacrifice:封建礼教的～ victim to the feudal ethical code

殉职 xùnzhí die at one's post; die in line of duty; die in the course of performing one's duty:白求恩大夫是为抢救伤员而～的。Dr. Norman Bethune died at his post for saving wounded soldiers.

徇(狥) xùn ❶ comply with; give in to; submit to; yield to:不～私情 not practise favouritism; act impartially /～从人意 act in compliance with popular wishes or feelings ❷ 〈书面〉declare to the public; announce publicly:以～三军 announce it to the armed forces; make it known to the armed forces ❸ 〈书面〉*see* "殉 ❷" xùn

徇情 xùnqíng 〈书面〉act dishonestly out of personal considerations; practise favouritism:～偏袒 practise favouritism and be partial

徇情枉法 xùnqíng-wǎngfǎ bend the law for the benefit of one's relatives or friends:国家工作人员决不能～。Government functionaries must in no case bend the law to benefit their relatives or friends.

徇私 xùnsī act wrongly out of consideration for one's personal interests:背公～ go against the interests of the public out of personal considerations; be swayed by selfish motives

徇私舞弊 xùnsī-wǔbì practise favouritism and engage in irregularities; resort to fraudulent practices for personal gain:有些干部因贪污受贿、～而被撤职法办。Some cadres are discharged from their posts and prosecuted for embezzlement and malpractices.

驯 xùn ❶ tame and docile; gentle; obedient:温～ tame and docile /桀骜不～ stubborn and intractable; obstinate and unruly /这小媳妇～如羔羊。The young daughter-in-law is as gentle as a lamb. ❷ tame; domesticate:～兽 tame animals /～一匹小野马 break in a wild colt /马戏团里有一位～虎女郎。The circus has got a female tamer of tigers.

驯服 xùnfú ❶ docile; meek; tame; tractable:～如羊,任人宰割 like a docile (*or* meek) lamb under a butcher's knife /马戏团的狮虎熊豹,样子很凶猛,其实都是很～的。The animals of the circus, such as lions, tigers, bears and leopards, look fierce but are all very tame. ❷ tame; subdue; break in; domesticate:～野兽 domesticate wild animals /～黄河 harness the Yellow River /谁也～不了这匹野马。No one has been able to break in this wild horse. /经过几天的奋战,咆哮的洪水终于被英雄的人们～了。After days of arduous struggle, the heroic people at last brought the roaring flood under control.

驯鸽 xùngē domestic pigeon (*Columba livia*)

驯化 xùnhuà domestication; taming:野稻的～过程 domestication of the wild paddy /经过～的大象可以学会表演节目。A domesticated elephant can be trained to perform in front of an audience.

驯良 xùnliáng tractable; docile; tame:她骑术不高,只能骑这匹性情～的马。Poor in horsemanship, she can only ride on this tame and gentle mare.

驯鹿 xùnlù *also* "四不象" sìbùxiàng reindeer

驯扰 xùnrǎo 〈书面〉meek; docile; tame

驯善 xùnshàn tractable; docile; tame and gentle:～的羔羊 tame and gentle lamb

驯熟 xùnshú ❶ docile; tame and gentle:～的绵羊 tame and docile sheep ❷ experienced; skilful:技艺～ very skilful

驯顺 xùnshùn submissive; tame and docile:这匹深棕色的马,比过去～多了。This dark brown horse is tamer and more gentle than before.

驯养 xùnyǎng raise and train (animals); domesticate:他在动物园干过多年～鸟兽的工作。He has worked in the zoo for years, raising and training birds and animals.

逊(遜) xùn ❶ abdicate: *see* "～位" ❷ unassuming; modest:～言恭色 be modest in language and respectful and submissive in manner /傲慢不～ rude and arrogant /出言不～ utter impudent remarks ❸ 〈书面〉inferior:稍～一筹 a shade inferior

逊尼派 Xùnnípài Sunni, one of the two main branches of Islam regarding Sunna (圣训) as equal in authority to the Koran:～教徒 Sunnite

逊色 xùnsè inferior; disappointing:毫无～ be in no way inferior /相比之下,大为～ pale by comparison /比起某些老演员来,她的表演并不～。Her performance is not at all disappointing compared with some experienced actresses.

逊顺 xùnshùn self-effacing; unassuming; modest and docile

逊位 xùnwèi 〈书面〉abdicate (one's throne):他最后被迫～。He was at last forced to abdicate.

巽 xùn one of the Eight Trigrams (formerly used in divination), representing the wind

噀(潠) xùn 〈书面〉keep in the mouth so as to spurt:～水 spurt water

X

yā

丫 yā ❶ bifurcation (at top end); fork: 枝～ branch; twig ❷〈方言〉little girl: 小～ little girl

丫巴儿 yābar 〈方言〉❶ foot: 不小心,脚～拉了个大口子。Carelessly, I got a bad cut on my foot. ❷ bifurcation; fork; crotch: 这个鸟窝正好搭在树～上。The bird's nest was built just in the fork of a branch.

丫杈 yāchà see "桠杈" yāchà

丫鬟 yāhuan also "丫环" slave girl; servant girl; maid: 贴身～ chamber maid /粗使～ servant girl who does heavy manual work; girl of all work

丫髻 yājì double-looped coiffure, worn by some young girls

丫角 yājiǎo upturned plaits worn by a girl

丫头 yātou ❶ girl: 她是个招人喜欢的～。She is a cute girl. /我一共生了三个～。I have given birth to three daughters altogether. ❷ slave girl; servant girl: 她从小就在地主家当～。She had worked as a servant girl in the landlord's house ever since her childhood.

垭(埡) yā 〈方言〉(mainly used in place names) strip of land or pass between hills: 马头～ Matouya, place in Hubei Province

垭口 yākǒu 〈方言〉entrance to a strip of land between hills; pass

桠(椏、枒) yā fork (of a tree)

桠杈 yāchà also "丫杈" yāchà ❶ fork (of a tree); branch; crotch: 修剪～ prune a tree /这棵小树已分出几个～了。The little tree has already sent out several branches. ❷ forked; crotched; ramified: 这树长得桠桠杈杈的。The tree has many forks. *or* The tree is branchy.

桠枫 yāfēng also "三角枫" sānjiǎofēng trident maple

桠枝 yāzhī branch; twig

桠子 yāzi 〈方言〉branch; twig

哑(啞) yā see "呀" yā

see also yǎ

哑哑 yāyā 〈象声〉❶ croak; caw (of a crow): 一群乌鸦～地叫着飞过去了。A flock of crows flew past croaking (*or* cawing). ❷ sound of a baby learning to speak; babble

压(壓) yā ❶ press; crush; hold down; weigh down: 挤～ press /～碎 crush (to pieces) /～塌了 collapse under pressure /把像片～在玻璃板下面 place the photo under a glassplate /用镇纸把卡片～住 put the cards under a paperweight /泰山～顶 bear down on one with the weight of Mount Tai; exert extremely great pressure on one /被流言飞语～得抬不起头来 unable to hold up one's head in face of rumours and slanders /这皮箱怕不怕～? Will this leather suitcase stand the strain? /那个问题沉重地～在他心上。The problem weighed heavily on his mind. /大雪～青松,青松挺且直。Under the weight of heavy snow the pine tree stood straight and proud. ❷ surpass; exceed: 技～群芳 have incomparable skills /才不～众 of mediocre talent ❸ keep under control; hold down or back; keep (sb. or sth.) still or calm; repress: ～住阵脚 hold the line /～住咳嗽 hold back a cough /～住气 control one's anger; repress one's rage /～住敌人的火力 stifle (*or* still) the enemy's fire /要不是我在那儿～着,他俩早打起来了。If I hadn't weighed in to stop them, they'd have come to blows. /她的精彩表演肯定～得住台。Her excellent performance will surely delight the audience (*or* keep the audience spellbound). ❹ bring pressure to bear on; force; awe; intimidate: 镇～暴乱 suppress (*or* put down) a riot /困难～不倒我们。We will not be cowed by difficulty. /我可不想以势～人。I don't want to coerce people with my power. ❺ approach; get closer; near: 太阳～树梢。The setting sun was touching the treetops. ❻ pigeonhole; shelve; set aside; defer: 积～资金 let funds stay idle /新买来的设备还～在码头上。The newly-bought equipment is still held up on the wharf. /你的申请被～下来了。Your application has been pigeonholed. /人手少,活儿～得太多。Too much work remains to be done because of short of hands. ❼ take a risk on sth.; stake: 在这种股票上～十万元 stake 100,000 *yuan* on the stock /这个楼我～一百万元。I'll put (*or* invest) one million *yuan* into the building. ❽ pressure: 血～ blood pressure /高～锅 pressure cooker /水～ hydraulic pressure /高～ high pressure

see also yà

压宝 yābǎo also "押宝" yābǎo gambling game, played with dice under a bowl; stake; wager

压编 yābiān reduce or cut staff

压扁 yābiǎn 〈冶金〉press flat; flatten: ～机 flattening mill

压不住 yābuzhù be unable to hold back or down; lose control of: ～火 be unable to hold back one's anger; lose control of one's temper /～场 unable to keep the situation under control

压不住台 yābuzhù tái unable to hold the audience; unable to keep the situation under control: 我年纪轻,去那里怕～。I'm too young to keep the situation there under control.

压舱物 yācāngwù 〈航海〉ballast

压差 yāchā 〈物理〉differential pressure: ～传感器〈电工〉differential pressure pickup /～换能器 pressure-gradient transducer

压场 yāchǎng ❶ have the situation under control: 完全压得住场 be fully able to keep the situation well in hand /他说话没人听,压不住场。He was unable to keep the situation under control for nobody took what he said seriously. ❷ serve as the last item and usually the climax of a theatrical programme; serve as the grand finale: ～戏 grand finale of a theatrical performance /以千人大合唱～ put the thousand-strong chorus at the very last as the grand finale

压车 yāchē also "押车" yāchē escort goods on a train, truck, etc.

压秤 yāchèng ❶ be relatively heavy per unit volume: 这东西看起来不大,可真～。It looks fairly small but is rather heavy. /棉花蓬蓬松松的,不～。Cotton is fluffy and doesn't weigh much. ❷ deliberately under-weigh sth. (in order to underpay the seller): 收购粮食严禁～、压级。It is strictly forbidden to under-weigh and downgrade the grain farmers sell to the state.

压出 yāchū extrusion: ～机 extruder

压船 yāchuán hold up cargo ships in harbour because of delay in loading and unloading or because of bad weather: 这个港口迅速改变了～的被动局面。The situation in which a long line of cargo ships were held up at the harbour has quickly changed for the better.

压床 yāchuáng 〈机械〉press (machine)

压倒 yādǎo overwhelm; overpower; overcome; subdue: 与我们意见一致的人占～多数。Those who agree with us constitute an overwhelming majority. /当前～一切的任务是搞好春耕生产。The overriding task at present is to do a good job of spring ploughing. /在这轮辩论中,我们～了对方。We gained the upper hand over our opponents in this round of debate.

压得住 yādezhù able to keep (sth. or sb.) under control; able to

Y

have the situation well in hand:～火 able to hold one's temper
压低 yādī lower; force down:～粮价 force down the price of grain /他怕别人听见,便～声音说话。He lowered his voice for fear that others might hear him.
压底 yādǐ be at the bottom of (the list, etc.); serve as the last resort
压电 yādiàn 〈物理〉piezoelectricity:～材料 piezoelectric
压电晶体 yādiàn jīngtǐ piezoelectric crystal; piezocrystal
压电拾音器 yādiàn shíyīnqì piezoelectric pickup
压电陶瓷 yādiàn táocí piezoelectric ceramic
压电效应 yādiàn xiàoyìng piezoelectric effect; piezoeffect; piezoelectricity
压顶 yādǐng (figuratively) press down from above:乌云～ dark clouds were bearing down; threatening clouds were gathering /形成～之势 become an overwhelming force /泰山～志不移 not change one's mind even if Mount Tai topples overhead; not give in to any pressure or difficulty
压锻 yāduàn 〈冶金〉press forging
压队 yāduì *also* "押队" yāduì bring up the rear:那次撤退,由我们连～。In that withdrawl our company was to bring up the rear.
压风机 yāfēngjī 〈矿业〉pressure fan; forcing fan; blowing fan
压服 yāfú *also* "压伏" force to submit; coerce into submission:～解决不了思想问题。Ideological problems cannot be solved by coercion. /不能靠～树立威信。Prestige cannot be established by force. /～的结果总是压而不服。The harder one tries to bring people to their knees, the more unyielding they will be.
压盖 yāgài 〈机械〉gland
压盖填料 yāgài tiánliào gland packing
压港 yāgǎng cargoes held up or backlogged on the wharf:这个码头～严重。A lot of cargo has been held up on this wharf. /大力开展内河航运,缓解～现象。Great efforts should be made to develop inland water transport so as to reduce the backlog of cargoes on wharfs.
压光 yāguāng finishing:～机 calender
压焊 yāhàn 〈冶金〉push welding; pressure welding:～机 pressure welder; pressure welding machine
压痕 yāhén impression; indentation:～深度 depth of indentation (*or* impression) /～硬度 indentation hardness; penetration hardness /～试验 indentation test
压痕性水肿 yāhénxìng shuǐzhǒng 〈医学〉pitting edema:非～ non-pitting edema
压花 yāhuā emboss:凸印～名片 business card with embossed name and address
压花玻璃 yāhuā bōli pattern glass; figured sheet glass
压花布 yāhuābù dacian cloth
压花长毛绒 yāhuā chángmáoróng stamped plush; peluche gaufrée
压货 yāhuò cargo held up on a wharf or at a railway station
压挤 yājǐ 〈机械〉extrusion
压挤成形 yājǐ chéngxíng extrusion moulding
压价 yājià force prices down; demand price reduction:～收购 purchase at a reduced price; offer low payment for sth. /他们一再～,这买卖无法做。There is no way we can strike a deal with them. They have tried repeatedly to force down our price.
压惊 yājīng help sb. get over a shock (by entertaining him, etc.):母亲备些酒菜为我～。Mother prepared some drink and food for me to help me get over the shock.
压井 yājǐng 〈石油〉kill the well
压境 yājìng press on to the border:强敌～。Massed enemy troops are bearing down on the border. *or* Enemy troops are massed threateningly on the border.
压卷 yājuàn best of all one's works; one's masterpiece:这小说是王先生的～之作。This is the best novel Mr. Wang has ever written.
压库 yākù ❶ overstock:这种电风扇～严重。There is an excessive stock of such electrical fans. ❷ reduce stocks:限产～ limit production and reduce stocks
压垮 yākuǎ collapse under pressure:人们没有被水灾～。People were undaunted by the flood. /沉重的精神负担把他～了。He broke down under great mental strain.
压块 yākuài 〈冶金〉briquetting:～机 briquette press
压力 yālì ❶〈物理〉pressure:大气～ atmospheric pressure /～加工 pressed work /～容器 pressure vessel /～送风 forced-draft ❷ pressure; strain:舆论～ pressure of public opinion /人口～ population pressure /社会～ social pressure /施加～ put pressure on; bring pressure to bear on /在极大的～下 under tremendous strain /在～下供认 confess under coercion /减轻～ ease (*or* lighten) the pressure (*or* strain)
压力泵 yālìbèng force-pump; forcing pump; pressure pump
压力传感器 yālì chuángǎnqì pressure transducer; pressure capsule; pressure probe
压力管反应堆 yālìguǎn fǎnyìngduī 〈核物理〉pressure-tube reactor
压力锅 yālìguō pressure cooker
压力机 yālìjī press
压力集团 yālì jítuán pressure group
压力计 yālìjì *also* "压力表" pressure gauge; manometer
压力送风机 yālì sòngfēngjī forced draft fan
压力铸造 yālì zhùzào pressure casting; pressure diecasting
压裂 yāliè 〈石油〉fracture:水力～ hydraulic fracture
压裂车 yālièchē fracturing unit truck
压路机 yālùjī steamroller; roller
压滤作用 yālǜ zuòyòng filter-pressing
压铆机 yāmǎojī 〈机械〉riveting squeezer (RVSZ)
压敏 yāmǐn pressure-sensitive:～半导体 pressure-sensitive semiconductor /～电阻 piezo-resistance; voltage dependent resistor (VDR)
压模机 yāmójī 〈冶金〉molding press
压坯 yāpī pressed compact; pressed green compact; pressed shape
压平 yāpíng flatten; flattenout:～机 flatter
压迫 yāpò ❶ oppress; repress:～弱小民族 oppress small and weak nations /被～者站起来了。The oppressed people have stood up. /这是一场反对～的伟大斗争。This is a great struggle against oppression. ❷ constrict:有～感 feel a constriction (in the chest, etc.) /睡觉时～心脏,就容易做噩梦。One is likely to have a nightmare when his heart is constricted in sleep. /腿被～得麻木了。My leg is asleep (*or* goes numb) because of constriction.
压迫者 yāpòzhě oppressor:～阶级 oppressor class
压气 yāqì ❶ calm sb.'s anger; placate:我劝了许久,她才压下气去。It was after my repeated efforts to pacify her that she eventually got over her anger. ❷ compress or inject air:～爆破 compressed air blasting
压气机 yāqìjī compressor machine; compressor
压强 yāqiáng 〈物理〉intensity of pressure; pressure
压强计 yāqiángjì pressure gauge
压青 yāqīng 〈农业〉green manuring or dressing
压热效应 yārè xiàoyìng 〈物理〉piezocaloric effect
压舌板 yāshébǎn 〈医学〉(tongue) depressor
压实 yāshí compaction; ramming:～器 compactor /～修整机 compacting and finishing machine
压岁钱 yāsuìqián money given to children as a lunar New Year gift:每当除夕,爷爷都要给孙子一些～。Every New Year's Eve grandpa would give some money to his grandson as a gift. /今年春节她得了许多～。This Spring Festival she got a lot of gift money.
压碎 yāsuì 〈矿业〉crush:～机 crusher /回转式～机 gyrating crusher /盘式～机 disc crusher /棍式～机 roller-crusher
压缩 yāsuō ❶ compress; compact; condense:～比 compression ratio /～冲程 compression stroke /～点火 compression ignition ❷ reduce; condense; cut down on:～开支 pare down expenses /～机关团体购买力 reduce (*or* limit) government institutions' purchase of consumer goods /我们单位的编制已大大～了。The staff in our unit has been greatly reduced. /这篇文章太长,要～一下。The article is too long and needs condensing (*or* trimming).
压缩饼干 yāsuō bǐnggān ship biscuit or bread; hard tack; pilot biscuit or bread
压缩光盘只读存储器 yāsuō guāngpán zhǐdú cúnchǔqì 〈信息〉compact disk read-only memory (CD-ROM)
压缩机 yāsuōjī compressor:空气～ air compressor
压缩空气 yāsuō kōngqì compressed air:～瓶 compressed air bottle
压缩疗法 yāsuō liáofǎ 〈医学〉collapse therapy
压缩食品 yāsuō shípǐn compressed food
压台 yātái *see* "压场"
压台戏 yātáixì grand finale of a theatrical performance; last but most important item

压条 yātiáo *also* "压枝"〈农业〉〈林业〉layer; layering:～区 layering plot /～法 layerage /环剥～法 layerage by girdling /连续～法 continuous layering /扭枝～ layerage by twisting /切伤～ layerage by notching
压痛 yātòng 〈医学〉tender; sore to the touch:仍有～ still sore to the touch; still tender
压头 yātóu 〈水利〉pressure head:有效～ effective head
压弯 yāwān bend (with the weight of sth.); weigh down
压蔓 yāwàn 〈农业〉cover the vines of plants (e.g. melon, gourd, etc.) with earth at intervals to protect them from strong wind and animals
压尾 yāwěi bring up the rear:他带着几个战士在后～。He brought up the rear with several soldiers.
压误 yāwù pigeonhole and delay:处理公文要及时,不要～。Documents must be attended to without delay.
压线球 yāxiànqiú 〈体育〉line ball
压心电缆 yāxīn diànlǎn 〈电工〉pressed-core cable
压延 yāyán 〈冶金〉roll; calender; malleate:～能力 rolling capacity /～玻璃 rolled glass /可～性 malleableness /～机 calenderstack (*or* calender); rolling machine
压抑 yāyì constrain; inhibit; restrain; contain:～群众的积极性 restrain (*or* dampen) the enthusiasm of the people /～新生力量 inhibit the newly emerging force /～不住心头的哀思 unable to contain one's grief /胸口感到～ feel tight in the chest /这种精神上的～使人无法忍受。One cannot bear such mental constraint. /那～在她内心多年的痛苦第一次倾吐出来。For the first time she gave vent to the agony she had suppressed inside her over the years.
压印 yāyìn 〈印刷〉stamp; impression
压应力 yāyìnglì 〈物理〉compressive stress; pressure stress
压油机 yāyóujī grease press
压韵 yāyùn *also* "押韵" yāyùn rhyme:讲究～ be strict in rhyme schemes /这首诗不～。This poem does not rhyme. *or* This poem has no rhyme.
压载舱 yāzàicāng ballast tank
压载物 yāzàiwù *also* "压舱物"〈航海〉ballast
压皂机 yāzàojī soap stamping press:自动～ automatic soap press
压榨 yāzhà ❶ press; squeeze:～柑桔,制成桔汁 squeeze juice from oranges /用甘蔗制糖,要经过～这道工序。Pressing is a necessary process in obtaining sugar from sugar cane. ❷ exploit; fleece; bleed white:地主把农民的血汗都～干了。The landlords bled the peasants white. /我们不能忍受这种残酷的～。We cannot stand such ruthless exploitation.
压寨夫人 yāzhài fūren 〈旧语〉wife of a bandit chieftain who entrenched himself in a mountain fortress
压蔗机 yāzhèjī 〈农业〉sugar cane mill
压阵 yāzhèn ❶ bring up the rear:他～掩护大家脱险。He brought up the rear to cover the others' escape from danger. ❷ keep order; keep under control:压不住阵 unable to keep the situation under control /上自习时,老师在教室～。When the pupils were studying in the classroom, the teacher was present to keep order.
压枝 yāzhī 〈植物〉*see* "压条"
压纸型机 yāzhǐxíngjī 〈印刷〉stereotype press
压制 yāzhì ❶ suppress; stifle; repress; hold back or down:～人才 suppress talented people /～群众 keep the masses down /～民主 put a lid on the demand for democracy; stifle democracy /～批评 gag (*or* muzzle, *or* smother) criticism /～改革 hold back reform /～怒火 repress (*or* hold back) one's indignation /对思想问题,采取粗暴的办法,～的办法,那是有害无益的。It will do harm rather than good to tackle ideological problems by coercion or suppression. ❷〈机械〉pressing:～砖坯 pressed unfired brick; adobe /～纤维板 pressed fibreboard /采用～的方法制作工具 make the tool by pressing /老师傅在花瓶的瓷坯上～出别致的图案。The old master worker pressed a unique pattern on the porcelain base of a flower vase.
压制板 yāzhìbǎn pressboard
压制茶 yāzhìchá broken tea leaves pressed into various shapes without losing their original flavour; pressed tea
压轴戏 yāzhòuxì last and best item on a theatrical programme; grand finale
压轴子 yāzhòuzi ❶ present a theatrical performance as the last but one item on a programme or the second major item for a performance ❷ last item but one on a theatrical programme.
压铸 yāzhù 〈冶金〉die-casting; die-cast:～件 die casting /～模 compression mold

呀

yā ❶〈叹词〉(indicating surprise) ah; oh:～,屋子里怎么这么多烟气! Oh, how come the room is full of smoke? ❷〈象声〉creak:～的一声殿门开了。The gate of the hall squeaked open. *or* The gate of the hall opened with a creak.
see also ya

雅

yā
see also yǎ
雅片 yāpiàn *see* "鸦片" yāpiàn

鸦(鵶)

yā crow
鸦胆子 yādǎnzǐ 〈中药〉Java brucea (*Brucea Javanica*)
鸦飞鹊乱 yāfēi-quèluàn *also* "鸦飞雀乱" crows and sparrows fly in all directions — utter disorder
鸦鸣鹊噪 yāmíng-quèzào crows cry and magpies chirp — confused voices; cacophony
鸦默雀静 yāmò-quèjìng even crows and sparrows are quiet — utter silence:会场上～,气氛异常严肃。Silence reigned in the meeting room, and the atmostphere was heavy and solemn.
鸦片 yāpiàn *also* "雅片" yāpiàn opium:吸～ smoke opium /戒～ give up opium-smoking /～鬼 opium addict /～馆 opium den
鸦片战争 Yāpiàn Zhànzhēng Opium War (Britain's war of aggression against China, 1840-1842):第二次～ Second Opium War (launched by Britain and France against China, 1856-1860)
鸦雀无声 yāquè-wúshēng not even a crow or sparrow can be heard — silence reigns:他一开口,会场上立刻～。The audience became quiet the moment he began to speak.
鸦头 yātou *see* "丫头" yātou

押[1]

yā ❶ give as security; mortgage; pawn; pledge:抵～ mortgage /典～ pawn /我把那只古瓶～给他,他才借给我点儿钱。He lent me some money only after I had given him an ancient vase as security. /你得～点儿东西,他才相信你呀。He won't trust you unless you leave something as a pledge. /把我那金项圈拿去,暂且～些钱。Take my gold necklace and pawn it for some money. ❷ detain; take away; take into custody:拘～ take sb. into custody /在～犯 criminal in custody /把他～下去! Take him away (*or* to prison)! /他被警察～起来了。He has been detained by the police. ❸ accompany as an escort; escort:老杨～着粮食车进城。Lao Yang escorted the grain truck to the town. /他和班长～着俘虏走了许多天才到目的地。It took him and his squad leader many days to escort their captives to the destination. ❹ *see* "压" yā (used only in 押宝, 押队, 押韵, etc.) ❺ (Yā) a surname

押[2]

yā ❶ sign a written statement; put one's mark on:知县在文书上亲～。The county magistrate signed the document in person. ❷ signature; mark made on a written statement in place of signature:他在地契上画了～。He signed the title deed for land. *or* He marked the title deed for land in lieu of signature.
押板 yābǎn 〈方言〉rent deposit:～金 rent deposit
押宝 yābǎo *see* "压宝" yābǎo
押差 yāchāi ❶ take on the task of escort ❷ person entrusted with the task of escort
押车 yāchē *also* "压车" yāchē escort a vehicle (in transport)
押当 yādàng ❶ pawn sth. ❷ small pawnshop
押队 yāduì *also* "压队" yāduì bring up the rear
押汇 yāhuì loan secured from a bank by an exporter with the waybill of the export as mortgage
押解 yājiè ❶ lead or take (a criminal or captive) away under escort; escort:～出境 deport under escort /他奉命～两个犯人到河南。He was ordered to escort two prisoners to Henan. ❷ *see* "押运"
押金 yājīn ❶ deposit; security:每个瓶子要五角～ five *jiao* for each bottle as a deposit /退还～ return the deposit ❷ *see* "押款❷"
押禁 yājìn take into custody
押款 yākuǎn 〈商业〉❶ borrow money on security ❷ secured loan; loan on security
押契 yāqì ❶ contract of mortgage ❷ mortgage:～地 mortgaged land
押送 yāsòng ❶ take (a prisoner of captive to a place) under es-

cort; escort ❷ escort (goods) in transport
押头 yātou 〈方言〉pledge; security; pawn; collateral
押尾 yāwěi sign or mark in place of signature at the end of a written statement
押运 yāyùn escort (goods) in transport: ～货物 transport goods under escort
押韵 yāyùn *also* "压韵" yāyùn rhyme
押账 yāzhàng leave or offer sth. as security for a loan
押租 yāzū rent deposit

鸭 yā duck: 公～ drake / 母～ duck / 子～ duckling / 戏水的～群 flock of ducks splashing in the water / 填～ force-fed duck / 板～ pressed salted duck / 烤～ roast duck / 盐水～ salted duck / 香酥～ crispy duck / 这些野～真漂亮。These wild ducks are very beautiful.
鸭步鹅行 yābù-éxíng *see* "鸭行鹅步"
鸭蛋 yādàn ❶ duck's egg: 腌～ preserve duck's eggs in salt / 咸～ salted duck's eggs ❷〈口语〉(as a score, etc.) duck's egg; goose egg; zero
鸭蛋脸 yādànliǎn oval face
鸭蛋青 yādànqīng pale blue
鸭蛋圆 yādànyuán 〈方言〉egg-shaped; oval: ～的脸型 oval face
鸭黄 yāhuáng ❶ tender yellow ❷〈方言〉duckling
鸭脚铲 yājiǎochǎn 〈农业〉duckfoot sweep
鸭绿江 Yālùjiāng Yalu River, rising in the mountains of Jilin Province of northeast China and forming part of the border between China and the Democratic People's Republic of Korea
鸭茅 yāmáo orchard grass
鸭苗 yāmiáo newborn duckling
鸭农 yānóng duck raiser
鸭儿梨 yārlí a kind of crisp, juicy pear grown in Hebei Province
鸭绒 yāróng duck's down; eiderdown: ～被 eiderdown quilt; duck's down quilt / ～睡袋 down sleeping-bag / ～背心 eiderdown waistcoat / ～枕心 down pillow (without pillow case)
鸭舌帽 yāshémào peaked cap
鸭式飞机 yāshì fēijī 〈航空〉canard; tail-first aircraft or aeroplane
鸭喜 yāxǐ 〈方言〉duck's egg which is being hatched
鸭行鹅步 yāxíng-ébù *also* "鸭步鹅行" walk slowly and unsteadily like a duck or goose; waddle
鸭翼 yāyì 〈航天〉canard (a short stubby wing-like horizontal extension affixed to the spacecraft to provide better stability)
鸭掌 yāzhǎng duck's foot or web
鸭掌铲式中耕机 yāzhǎngchǎnshì zhōnggēngjī 〈农业〉duckfoot cultivator
鸭胗儿 yāzhēnr duck's gizzard
鸭跖草 yāzhícǎo 〈中药〉dayflower (*Commelina communis*)
鸭子儿 yāzǐr duck's egg
鸭子 yāzi 〈口语〉duck: 放～ tend ducks / ～的叫声 quack
鸭嘴笔 yāzuǐbǐ drawing pen; ruling pen
鸭嘴龙 yāzuǐlóng duck-billed dinosaur; hydrosaur
鸭嘴式装载机 yāzuǐshì zhuāngzàijī 〈机械〉duckbill loader; duckbill
鸭嘴兽 yāzuǐshòu platypus; duckbill; duckmole

yá

涯 yá ❶ shore; bank ❷ margin; bound; limit: 无边无～ boundless / 天～海角 remotest corners of the earth; end of the earth
涯岸 yá'àn embankment
涯际 yájì limit; bound; boundary: 漫无～的海洋 boundless sea; vast expanse of water / 茫无～的宇宙 boundless universe
涯涘 yásì 〈书面〉❶ waterside ❷ limit; margin; boundary

睚 yá 〈书面〉corner of the eye
睚眦 yázì 〈书面〉❶ angry stare ❷ petty grievance: ～之怨 enmity arising from tiny grievance
睚眦必报 yázì-bìbào seek revenge for the smallest grievance — be utterly narrow-minded and revengeful

崖(厓、崕) yá ❶ precipice; cliff; crag: 山～ cliff / 悬～ steep cliff; precipice ❷ limit; bound; boundary: *see* "～略"
崖岸 yá'àn ❶ high and steep cliff or embankment ❷〈书面〉〈比喻〉(of a person) supercilious and difficult of approach
崖壁 yábì precipice; cliff; escarpment
崖柏 yábǎi arborvitae
崖谷 yágǔ valley between precipices; canyon
崖壑 yáhè *see* "崖谷"
崖画 yáhuà *also* "岩画" yánhuà; "崖壁画" rock painting
崖刻 yákè inscriptions (engraved) on a cliff
崖略 yálüè 〈书面〉general sketch; rough idea; outline
崖墓 yámù grave which is dug in a cliff
崖山之战 Yáshān Zhī Zhàn Battle of Yashan (1279), which marked the fall of the Southern Song Dynasty
崖头 yátóu clifftop or protruding brow of a cliff
崖盐 yáyán rocksalt; halite
崖葬 yázàng *also* "悬棺葬" xuánguānzàng form of burial whereby coffins are placed in niches dug in cliffs
崖子 yázi 〈方言〉cliff

牙[1] yá ❶ tooth: 整齐的～ regular teeth / 乳～ milk tooth / 虫～ decayed tooth / 虎～ pointed tooth / 洗～ have one's teeth cleaned (by a dentist) / 补～ have a tooth filled / 拔～ have a tooth out (*or* pulled); extract a tooth / 镶～ have a denture made; fix a false (*or* artificial) tooth / 剔～ pick one's teeth / 刷～ brush one's teeth / 这孩子的～还没出齐。The kid's incisors are yet to appear. / 你儿子开始换～了吗? Has your son begun to grow permanent teeth? / 他不在，看～去了。He is not in. He's gone to the dentist. ❷ ivory: ～筷 ivory chopsticks / ～骨扇 ivory fan ❸ sth. shaped like a tooth: 檐～ eaves / ～边儿 tooth-like lace ❹ (Yá) a surname

牙[2] yá broker; middleman
牙巴骨 yábagǔ 〈方言〉upper and lower jaws; mandibular joint: 咬紧～ clench (*or* grit) one's teeth
牙白 yábái creamy white; ivory: ～的窗帘儿 ivory window curtain
牙白口清 yábái-kǒuqīng articulate: 他～地说出了生产责任制的优越性。He spoke articulately about the advantages of the production responsibility system.
牙本质 yáběnzhì 〈生理〉dentine
牙病 yábìng 〈医学〉odontopathy; tooth disease
牙槽 yácáo 〈生理〉socket of the tooth; odontobothrion: ～脓肿 alveolar abscess
牙槽骨髓炎 yácáo gǔsuǐyán alveolar osteomyelitis
牙槽炎 yácáoyán alveolitis odontobothritis; dentoalveolitis
牙碜 yáchen ❶ (of food) gritty: 菜没洗干净，有点儿～。The vegetable hasn't been washed clean. It tastes a bit gritty. ❷ (of language) vulgar; coarse: 他说话总带脏字，也不嫌～。He is always swearing. Isn't he ashamed of himself? / 这话我听着就～。This remark jars on my nerves.
牙齿 yáchǐ tooth: 齐而细小的～ tiny and even teeth / ～打战。One's teeth chatter. / 贪吃甜食坏～。Weakness for sweets may lead to decayed teeth.
牙床 yáchuáng ❶〈生理〉gum ❷ ivory-inlaid bed
牙雕 yádiāo ivory carving
牙粉 yáfěn tooth powder
牙缝 yáfèng slit between the teeth; slit between two rows of teeth: 剔～ pick one's teeth / 从～里省下一点钱买书 squeeze a little money out of one's tight food budget to buy books / 他恶狠狠地从～里挤出一句话。He blurted it out of his teeth fiercely.
牙疳 yágān 〈医学〉noma; cancrum oris
牙缸 yágāng *also* "牙缸子" glass or mug for teeth-cleaning; tooth glass
牙膏 yágāo toothpaste
牙根 yágēn gum: ～疼 have a pain in one's gum / 咬定～不说 set one's teeth and refuse to talk
牙狗 yágǒu 〈方言〉male dog
牙垢 yágòu *also* "牙花" dental calculus; tartar
牙骨质 yágǔzhì 〈生理〉cementum; cement
牙关 yáguān mandibular joint: 咬紧～ grit one's teeth / ～紧闭〈医学〉lockjaw
牙冠 yáguān 〈生理〉crown (of a tooth)
牙行 yáháng 〈旧语〉❶ middleman ❷ brokerage
牙花 yáhuā *also* "牙花子"〈方言〉❶ tartar; dental calculus ❷ gum

牙慧 yáhuì remarks made by others：拾人～ pick up remarks made by other people and pass them off as a sample of one's own wit；repeat what sb. else has said；parrot sb. else
牙纪 yájì *see* "牙行"
牙祭 yájì good meal with meat dishes：打～ have a special treat
牙具 yájù things for teeth-cleaning and mouth-rinsing
牙科 yákē 〈医学〉(department of) dentistry：～诊所 dental clinic / ～综合治疗台 dental unit；universal dental (treatment) machine
牙科技师 yákē jìshī dental technician
牙科全息照相术 yákē quánxī zhàoxiàngshù 〈医学〉holodontography
牙科学 yákēxué dentistry
牙科医生 yákē yīshēng *also* "牙科大夫" dentist；dental surgeon
牙口 yákou ❶ age of a draught animal as shown by the number of its teeth：这匹马～太老。Just look at the number of its teeth. This horse is too old. ❷ condition of an old person's teeth：奶奶的～还好。Granny's teeth are still in good condition. /人老了，～不济了。I'm getting old and my teeth are no good.
牙侩 yákuài 〈书面〉broker；middleman
牙瘤 yáliú 〈医学〉odontoma
牙轮 yálún gear wheel；gear
牙买加 Yámǎijiā Jamaica：～人 Jamaican
牙牌 yápái *also* "骨牌" gǔpái domino
牙鲆 yápíng 〈动物〉lefteye flounder (*Paralichthys*)
牙婆 yápó 〈旧语〉middle-woman in human trafficking
牙签 yáqiān ❶ toothpick：～筒 toothpick-holder ❷〈书面〉ivory bookmark
牙色 yásè light yellow similar to ivory；creamy white
牙商 yáshāng middleman who brings the buyer and the seller together to make a deal and collects a commission from the two parties
牙石 yáshí ❶ *see* "牙垢" ❷ *also* "缘石" yuánshí traffic spacer
牙刷 yáshuā toothbrush
牙髓 yásuǐ 〈生理〉dental pulp
牙髓炎 yásuǐyán pulpitis
牙痛 yátòng toothache
牙推 yátuī *see* "衙推" yátuī
牙线 yáxiàn dental floss
牙鳕 yáxuě whiting (*Gadus merlangus*)
牙牙 yáyá 〈象声〉babble：～学语 babble out first speech sounds；learn to speak
牙医 yáyī dentist
牙龈 yáyín 〈生理〉gum：～脓肿 parulis；gumboil
牙龈炎 yáyínyán gingivitis
牙釉质 yáyòuzhì enamel；substantia admantina
牙獐 yázhāng *also* "獐子" zhāngzi river deer
牙质 yázhì ❶ made of ivory：～的饰物 ivory ornament ❷〈生理〉dentine
牙质瘤 yázhìliú 〈医学〉dentinoma
牙周 yázhōu 〈生理〉periodontal：～溃坏 periodontoclasia /～浓溢 peripyema
牙周病 yázhōubìng 〈医学〉periodontosis；periodontopathy：～学 periodontics
牙周炎 yázhōuyán periodontitis
牙子 yázi ❶〈口语〉serrated edge ❷〈旧语〉middleman

芽

yá ❶ bud；sprout；shoot：麦～ malt /豆～ bean sprout /幼～ young shoot /抽～ put forth buds /菜地上长出一片嫩～。The vegetable field is grown with tender sprouts. ❷ sth. resembling a bud or sprout：肉～〈医学〉granulation
芽孢 yábāo 〈生物〉gemma (of a fungus)；spore
芽变 yábiàn 〈植物〉bud mutation
芽茶 yáchá young tea leaves；bud-tea
芽豆 yádòu sprouted broad bean
芽接 yájiē 〈植物〉bud grafting；budding
芽鳞 yálín 〈植物〉bud scale
芽体 yátǐ 〈生物〉gem；sprout；bud；gemmule
芽眼 yáyǎn 〈植物〉eye (of a potato)

蚜

yá aphid；aphis；plant louse
蚜虫 yáchóng plant louse；aphid；aphis：棉～ cotton aphid /～采集器 aphidozer /～专家 aphidologist
蚜黄素 yáhuángsù aphideine

伢

yá 〈方言〉child；kid
伢崽 yázǎi 〈方言〉child；kid
伢子 yázi 〈方言〉child；kid

衙

yá *yamen*
衙门 yámen *yamen*，government office in feudal China
衙门作风 yámen zuòfēng bureaucratic style of work
衙内 yánèi ❶ imperial bodyguard ❷〈旧语〉children of high officials
衙署 yáshǔ *see* "衙门"
衙推 yátuī *also* "牙推" yátuī (usu. used in the early vernacular) person engaged in medicine, fortune-telling or astrology
衙役 yáyi *yamen* runner

yǎ

痖(瘂)

yǎ *see* "哑" yǎ

哑(啞)

yǎ ❶ incapable of speech；mute；dumb：先天性聋～ congenitally deaf-mute；deaf and dumb from birth /他因病致～。He became mute after the illness. ❷ (of voice) hoarse；husky：嗓音沙～ have a husky voice /把嗓子喊～了 shout oneself hoarse ❸ (of artillery shell or bullet) ineffective；dud：*see* "～弹"
see also yā
哑巴 yǎba dumb person；mute：你怎么不说话！～啦？Why don't you talk? Are you dumb?
哑巴吃黄连，有苦说不出 yǎba chī huánglián, yǒu kǔ shuōbuchū unable to express his discomfort like a dumb person tasting bitter herbs；have to suffer in silence
哑巴亏 yǎbakuī loss which has to be suffered in silence：吃～ swallow one's grievances in silence；be compelled to keep one's grievances to oneself
哑场 yǎchǎng period of silence during a meeting or discussion：一阵～使会议主持者感到很难堪。The chairman felt rather embarrassed by the silence that descended upon the meeting.
哑弹 yǎdàn undetonated (artillery) shell；dud
哑号儿 yǎhàor 〈方言〉secret signal or sign：打～ give a secret signal /拍三下儿做～ make (*or* send) a secret signal by clapping the hands three times
哑火 yǎhuǒ ❶ dud ❷ (of a person) quiet：那么爱说话的人，今天怎么～了？How come a talkative person like you is so quiet today?
哑酒 yǎjiǔ drink without playing the finger-guessing game
哑剧 yǎjù dumb show；mime
哑口 yǎkǒu stop talking；become quiet：她们正说笑得起劲，见来了客人，便立即～了。They were talking and laughing away but they stopped as soon as a visitor appeared.
哑口无言 yǎkǒu-wúyán be left without an argument；be tongue-tied；be rendered speechless：被质问得～ become completely tongue-tied under questioning /他知道自己错了，一时～。He lost his tongue for a while when he realized he was wrong.
哑铃 yǎlíng 〈体育〉dumbbell
哑谜 yǎmí puzzling remark；enigma；riddle：猜～ solve a riddle /你这人就爱打～。You are always keeping us guessing.
哑默 yǎmò silent：大家～了好一阵子，谁也不愿先开口。Everybody remained silent for some time and no one wanted to break the ice.
哑默悄声 yǎmò-qiāoshēng 〈方言〉❶ quiet；still；silent：厅内～地一个人也没有。The hall was quiet without a single soul. ❷ whisper：他附在耳边～地告诉了我这个消息。He whispered the news in my ear.
哑炮 yǎpào *also* "瞎炮" xiāpào dud
哑然 yǎrán ❶〈书面〉quiet；still；silent：全场～。There is utter silence in the hall. *or* Silence reigns in the hall. ❷ be struck dumb with amazement：这消息使她～失惊。The news silenced the words in her mouth. *or* The news left her dumbfounded. ❸ sound of laughing；laugh：～失笑 be unable to suppress a laugh；cannot help laughing
哑涩 yǎsè hoarse；husky：～的嗓子 hoarse voice；husky voice
哑笑 yǎxiào quiet laugh
哑语 yǎyǔ sign language；dactylology：打～ communicate with the

aid of dactylology /～动作 dactylological gesticulations

哑子 yǎzi 〈方言〉mute

雅[1] yǎ ❶〈书面〉standard; orthodox; proper; correct: ～音 refined music; standard pronunciation /～儒 orthodox Confucian scholar ❷ refined; polished; elegant: 古～ of classic elegance /文～ cultured; polished; refined /温文尔～ gentle and cultivated /无伤大～ not deviating much from propriety; harmless /俗中见～ the elegant perceived in the commonplace /房间布置得很～。The room is tastefully furnished. ❸ court hymns of Western Zhou, one of the three genres of *The Book of Songs* (the other two being 风 and 颂) ❹〈敬词〉your: see "～教"

雅[2] yǎ 〈书面〉❶ acquaintance; friendship: 一日之～ casual acquaintance ❷ usually; customarily; often: ～善鼓琴 usually play the harp well ❸ very; extremely: ～以为美 consider sth. very beautiful

see also yā

雅爱 yǎ'ài be fond of; have a liking for: ～丹青 take to painting; be keen on painting

雅饬 yǎchì 〈书面〉refined and well-organized: 文辞～ refined diction; elegant language

雅淡 yǎdàn simple and in good taste; quietly elegant: 装束～ be quietly and tastefully dressed /～的色调 quiet and delicate colour

雅典 Yǎdiǎn Athens, capital of Greece: ～人 Athenian

雅典娜 Yǎdiǎnnà Athena, Greek goddess of wisdom, learning and war

雅尔塔 Yǎ'ěrtǎ Yalta, port city on the Black Sea in the Ukraine: ～会议 Yalta Conference, held in February 1945 between the allied leaders Churchill, Roosevelt and Stalin who met to plan the final stages of the Second World War and the post-war world order /～协定 Yalta Agreement (1945)

雅歌 Yǎgē *The Song of Solomon*, love poems ascribed to Solomon, King of Israel (c. 970-930 BC)

雅观 yǎguān (often used in the negative) refined (in manner, etc.); tasteful: 很不～ unseemly; unsightly; boorish

雅号 yǎhào ❶ elegant name (often used to refer to other people's names deferentially) ❷ (humorously) nickname: 我倒不晓得他还有这么一个～呢! I didn't know he had such a nickname.

雅怀 yǎhuái 〈书面〉refined sentiments

雅集 yǎjí 〈书面〉gathering of literati

雅加达 Yǎjiādá Djakarta, capital of Indonesia

雅教 yǎjiào your esteemed advice

雅洁 yǎjié elegant and neat: 端庄～的山茶花 dignified and elegant camellia /客厅的布置相当～。The drawing room is neat and tastefully furnished.

雅静 yǎjìng ❶ tasteful and quiet: ～的房间 unostentatious room ❷ gentle and quiet: ～的姑娘 gentle girl

雅克萨之战 Yǎkèsà Zhī Zhàn Battle of Yakesa(1685), in which the army of the Qing government defeated and drove away the aggressor troops of Tsarist Russia

雅丽 yǎlì elegant and beautiful: 这布花型新颖, 色彩～。The cloth is new in design and elegant in colour.

雅量 yǎliàng ❶ large-mindedness; magnanimity; generosity: 倾听批评的～ be magnanimous (*or* broad-minded) enough to listen to criticisms ❷ great capacity for liquor

雅鲁藏布江 Yǎlǔzàngbùjiāng Yarlung Zangbo or Yalu Tsangpo River in the Tibet Autonomous Region, which flows into the Bramaputra River in India

雅皮士 yǎpíshì Yuppie, acronym for young urban (*or* upwardly-mobile) professional

雅气 yǎqì ❶ refined atmosphere or bearing: 这套茶具不失～。This tea set looks quite elegant. ❷〈书面〉healthy or moral trend

雅趣 yǎqù good taste: 这篇散文～盎然。The prose has a delightful flavour (*or* is in delightful taste).

雅人 yǎrén scholar who considers himself above politics and material pursuits; person of refinement

雅人深致 yǎrén-shēnzhì a refined scholar has profound thoughts

雅什 yǎshí 〈书面〉refined poetry and prose

雅士 yǎshì refined scholar; person of refined taste: 文人～ refined men of letters

雅司病 yǎsībìng yaws, a tropical skin disease

雅俗共赏 yǎsú-gòngshǎng (of a work of art or literature) be enjoyed by both highbrows and lowbrows; suit both refined and popular tastes: 这可是一本～的好书。This is a good book to the taste of both intellectuals and ordinary readers.

雅玩 yǎwán ❶ refined object for amusement: 这花瓶玲珑可爱, 堪作案头～。This delicate and lovely vase can be placed on the desk as a curio. ❷ (polite expression used when one gives sb. a work of art as a gift) for your amusement or enjoyment

雅兴 yǎxìng aesthetic mood; aesthetic pretensions: 他每日寄情书画, 颇有～。He has some pretension to good taste and does painting and calligraphy every day. /围棋我是下不来的, 实在无此～。I don't know how to play *weiqi* (*or* go). I do not really take to it.

雅相 yǎxiàng (mainly used in the negative) decent; graceful: 快别胡说, 叫人听见多不～。You must stop talking like that. How unseemly it would be if you were overheard.

雅驯 yǎxùn 〈书面〉(of diction) refined; elegant

雅言 yǎyán 〈书面〉❶ standard language ❷ worthy opinion; good advice: 察纳～ take good counsel

雅意 yǎyì ❶ noble sentiments: 高情～ lofty and noble sentiments ❷〈敬词〉your kindness; your opinion

雅乐 yǎyuè imperial ceremonial music in ancient China

雅贼 yǎzéi one who steals only books and works of art; plagiarizer

雅正 yǎzhèng ❶〈书面〉standard; correct; appropriate ❷ upright; honest; virtuous ❸ (a polite expression used when giving one's works as a gift) kindly remedy any errors in my work

雅致 yǎzhi refined; elegant; tasteful: 室内陈设十分～。The room is furnished in good taste. /她的衣着显得庄重～。She is dressed in a sober and elegant style.

雅座 yǎzuò private room (in a restaurant, etc.): 楼上设有～。Private rooms available upstairs.

疋 yǎ see "雅" yǎ

yà

亚[1](亞) yà ❶ of lower quality; inferior; second: 这种自行车的质量不～于名牌车。The quality of this bicycle is as good as that of famous brands. /他的才学不～于你。He is by no means inferior to you in intelligence and learning. ❷ sub-: ～科 subfamily /～原子学 subatomics ❸ of lower (atomic) valence: 硫酸～铁 ferrisulphas; ferrous sulphate /～氨基 imino group

亚[2](亞) Yà (short for 亚洲) Asia: 东～ East Asia

亚矮星 yà'ǎixīng 〈天文〉subdwarf (star that is smaller and about 1.5-2 magnitudes fainter than normal dwarf stars of the same spectral type)

亚表土 yàbiǎotǔ 〈农业〉subsurface soil: ～施肥机 subsurface applicator /～中耕机 subsurface cultivator

亚当 Yàdāng Adam, the first man in the Biblical and Koranic traditions

亚当斯 Yàdāngsī ❶ John Adams (1735-1826), 2nd President of the United States (1797-1801) ❷ John Quincy Adams (1767-1848), 6th President of the United States (1825-1829) and son of John Adams

亚的斯亚贝巴 Yàdìsī Yàbèibā Addis Ababa, capital of Ethiopia

亚丁 Yàdīng Aden, port of Yemen commanding the entrance to the Red Sea

亚丁湾 Yàdīngwān Gulf of Aden, between the Red Sea and the Arabian Sea

亚得里亚海 Yàdélǐyàhǎi Adriatic Sea, an arm of the Mediterranian Sea lying between Italy and the Balkan Peninsula

亚非会议 Yà-Fēi Huìyì *also* "万隆会议" Wànlóng Huìyì Asian-African Conference held at Bandung, Indonesia, 18-24 April 1955, by over 20 Asian and African countries and regions including China and India

亚非拉 Yà-Fēi-Lā Asia, Africa and Latin America

亚分子 yàfēnzǐ 〈物理〉submolecule

亚砜 yàfēng 〈化学〉sulphoxide

亚高山带 yàgāoshāndài 〈地理〉subalpine belt

亚铬酸盐 yàgèsuānyán 〈化学〉chromite
亚共晶 yàgòngjīng 〈冶金〉hypoeutectic:～合金 hypoeutectic alloy /～铸铁 hypoeutectic cast iron
亚共析 yàgòngxī 〈冶金〉hypoeutectoid:～钢 hypoeutectoid steel; hyposteel
亚光速 yàguāngsù 〈物理〉subvelocity of light
亚光子 yàguāngzǐ 〈物理〉tardyon
亚行 Yàháng (short for 亚洲开发银行) Asian Development Bank (ADB)
亚磺酸 yàhuángsuān 〈化学〉sulfinic acid:～盐 sulfinate
亚基因 yàjīyīn 〈生物〉sub-gene
亚急性 yàjíxìng 〈医学〉subacute:～病 subacute disease
亚巨星 yàjùxīng 〈天文〉subgiant (of smaller size and lower luminosity than normal giants of the same spectral type)
亚军 yàjūn second place (in a sports contest); runner-up:我们班在拔河比赛中得了～。Our class won second place in the tug-of-war. *or* Our class came second in the tug-of-war.
亚喀巴 Yàkābā Aquaba, Jordan's only port at the head of the Gulf of Aquaba
亚喀巴湾 Yàkābāwān Gulf of Aquaba, northeastern arm of the Red Sea
亚拉巴马 Yàlābāmǎ Alabama, state in southern United States
亚里士多德 Yàlǐshìduōdé Aristotle (384-322 BC), Greek philosopher and scientist
亚里士多德主义 Yàlǐshìduōdézhǔyì Aristotelianism
亚利桑那 Yàlìsāngnà Arizona, state in southwestern United States
亚磷酸 yàlínsuān 〈化学〉phosphorous acid:～盐 phosphite
亚硫酸 yàliúsuān 〈化学〉sulphurous acid
亚氯酸 yàlǜsuān 〈化学〉chlorous acid:～盐 chlorite
亚麻 yàmá 〈植物〉flax (*Linum usitatissimum*)
亚麻布 yàmábù linen (cloth)
亚麻醇 yàmáchún 〈化学〉linolenyl alcohol; octadecatrienol
亚麻画 yàmáhuà toiles peintes
亚麻精纺机 yàmá jīngfǎngjī flax spinning frame
亚麻揉碎机 yàmá róusuìjī flax brake; flax breaker
亚麻酸 yàmásuān 〈化学〉linolenic acid
亚麻籽 yàmázǐ linseed; flaxseed
亚麻籽油 yàmázǐyóu linseed oil
亚马孙河 Yàmǎsūnhé Amazon River, situated in South America and largest river in terms of waterflow in the world:～流域 Amazon River Basin
亚马孙雨林 Yàmǎsūn yǔlín Amazon Rain Forest
亚美尼亚 Yàměiníyà Armenia:～人 Armenian /～语 Armenian (language)
亚平宁山脉 Yàpíngníng Shānmài Apennines, range of mountains forming the spine of the Italian peninsula
亚热带 yàrèdài 〈地理〉subtropical zone; subtropics; semitropics:～雨林 subtropical rain forest;warm temperate rain forest
亚赛 yàsài *also* "亚似" can be compared to; like; as:这姑娘很能干,～当年的穆桂英。The girl is as capable as Mu Guiying, the legendary heroine.
亚筛 yàshāi 〈冶金〉subsieve:～粉末 subsieve powder /～粒度 subsieve size
亚圣 yàshèng lesser sage — Mencius (孟子, as lesser to the sage 至圣 — Confucius 孔子)
亚视 Yàshì (short for 亚洲电视台) Asia Television Ltd. (ATV) of Hong Kong
亚述 Yàshù Assyria, ancient Kingdom in what is now northern Iraq:～人 Assyrian
亚速尔群岛 Yàsù'ěr Qúndǎo the Azores, a group of volcanic islands in the North Atlantic, west of Spain
亚速海 Yàsùhǎi Sea of Azov, inland sea in southern Russia
亚太 Yà-Tài Asia-Pacific:～地区 Asia-Pacific region /～经济合作会议 Asia-Pacific Economic Cooperation (APEC)
亚特兰大 Yàtèlándà Atlanta, capital and largest city of Georgia, United States, where the centenary Olympic Games (1996) were held
亚铁 yàtiě 〈化学〉ferrous:氧化～ ferrous oxide /氮化～ ferrous chloride /硝酸～ ferrous nitrate /硫酸～ ferrous sulphate
亚土 yàtǔ subsoil
亚稳态 yàwěntài 〈物理〉metastable state
亚硒酸 yàxīsuān 〈化学〉selenous acid; selenious acid:～盐 selenite
亚细亚 Yàxìyà *also* "亚洲" Asia
亚硝酸 yàxiāosuān 〈化学〉nitrous acid:～盐 nitrite
亚烟煤 yàyānméi subbituminous coal
亚音频 yàyīnpín 〈物理〉subaudio frequency
亚音速 yàyīnsù 〈物理〉subsonic speed:～飞机 subsonic aircraft
亚音速空气动力学 yàyīnsù kōngqì dònglìxué subsonic aerodynamics
亚油酸 yàyóusuān 〈化学〉linoleic acid; linolic acid:～盐 linoleate
亚原子 yàyuánzǐ 〈物理〉subatom:～粒子 subatomic particle
亚运村 Yàyùncūn Asian Games Village, now a housing neighbourhood in Beijing
亚运会 Yàyùnhuì Asian Games
亚种 yàzhǒng subspecies
亚洲 Yàzhōu Asia:～人 Asian
亚洲基金会 Yàzhōu Jījīnhuì (US) Asia Foundation
亚洲开发银行 Yàzhōu Kāifā Yínháng Asian Development Bank (ADB)
亚洲四小龙 Yàzhōu sìxiǎolóng four little dragons of Asia, referring to Singapore, Republic of Korea, and China's Hong Kong and Taiwan
亚洲卫星 Yàzhōu wèixīng Asiasat

挜(掗) yà 〈方言〉insist on giving as a gift or selling to the buyer

氩(氬) yà 〈化学〉argon (Ar)

氩弧 yàhú 〈物理〉argon arc:～焊 〈冶金〉argon-arc welding /～切割 argon-arc cutting
氩激光器 yàjīguāngqì 〈光电〉argon laser

娅(婭) yà *see* "姻娅" yīnyà

压(壓) yà

see also yā

压板 yàbǎn 〈方言〉*also* "跷跷板" qiāoqiāobǎn seesaw; teeter board; teeter-totter
压根儿 yàgēnr (mainly used in the negative) from the start; in the first place; simply; altogether:～没这回事。It's sheer fabrication. /我～就没见过他。I've never seen him before. /这一夜他～就没睡。He didn't go to sleep at all the whole night.

揠 yà 〈书面〉pull up; tug upward

揠苗助长 yàmiáo-zhùzhǎng *also* "拔苗助长" bámiáo-zhùzhǎng try to help the shoots grow by pulling them upward — spoil things by excessive enthusiasm; haste makes waste

轧[1] yà ❶ flatten with a roller; roll; run over:～棉花 gin cotton /～路 roll a road /被车～伤 get run over and injured by a car /他的手指被机器～断了。He got his fingers crushed when his hand was caught in the machine. ❷ squeeze out; push out:倾～ engage in internal strife ❸ 〈方言〉jostle; push against ❹ (Yà) a surname

轧[2] yà 〈象声〉(of a machine) click:他被机器～～的嘈杂声吵醒。He was woken up by the clicking machine.

see also gá; zhá

轧板机 yàbǎnjī 〈冶金〉mangle; rolling machine
轧布机 yàbùjī 〈纺织〉mangle (for ironing or pressing cloth)
轧场 yàcháng level a threshing ground or the grain on it with a stone roller
轧道车 yàdàochē line inspection trolley or car; track-testing trolley
轧道机 yàdàojī road-roller
轧光 yàguāng 〈纺织〉calendering:～机 calender
轧花 yàhuā 〈纺织〉cotton ginning:～厂 cotton ginning mill
轧花机 yàhuājī cotton gin
轧轹 yàlì ❶ roll to crush ❷ 〈书面〉squeeze out; oust:纷争～ quarrel and try to push each other out

讶 yà 〈书面〉be surprised; be astonished; be amazed:惊～

shocked; stunned
讶然 yàrán be astonished：不觉～失色 turn ashen with fright
讶异 yàyì be surprised; be astonished; be shocked：面露～之色 show surprise; look astonished

迓 yà 〈书面〉welcome; greet; meet：迎～ welcome; greet

砑 yà press and smooth (leather, cloth, etc.); calender
砑光 yàguāng 〈印刷〉calender;〈纺织〉calendering：～工 calenderer /～滚 calender bowl
砑光机 yàguāngjī 〈纺织〉〈造纸〉calender; calenderstack; mangle

ya

呀 ya 〈助词〉*variant of* 啊 *used after a word ending phonetically in* a, e, i, o *or* ü：他搞了这么多发明，真了不起～。What a terrific man he is with so many inventions to his credit. /事情都过去了，还提它干什么～！Don't mention it any more. Let bygones be bygones. /你怎么回来得这么快～？How did you manage to come back so quickly? /他～，真勤快。He is really diligent.
see also yā

yān

阏 yān
see also è
阏氏 yānzhī 〈古语〉main wife of a Hun or Xiongnu monarch; queen

恹（懨、懕） yān
恹恹 yānyān 〈书面〉weak and weary through illness; tired and ill; run-down：～欲睡 feel sleepy from infirmity; be weak and drowsy /她病～的，走路都困难。She was too ill to walk.

焉 yān 〈书面〉❶ here; this：心不在～ with one's attention elsewhere; absent-minded /乐莫大～。There's no greater happiness than this. *or* How happy it is! /率乡人来此，不复出～。He brought his fellow villagers here and they never left the place ever after. ❷ (often used in a rhetorical question) how; why：如无老师栽培，～有今日？How could I fare so well without your help as my teacher? /不入虎穴，～得虎子？How can you catch tiger cubs without entering the tiger's lair? /割鸡～用牛刀？Why kill a chicken with an ox cleaver? ❸ (used in the main clause of a complex sentence to indicate the condition stated in the subordinate clause as a prerequisite) only then：必知乱之所自起，～能治之。You have to know the cause of the trouble before you can deal with it. ❹〈助词〉：吾行将就木～。I already have one foot in the grave. /君为政～，勿卤莽；治民～，勿灭裂！You should not be rash as long as you govern the country. You should not be rude as long as you rule the people.

鄢 Yān a surname

嫣 yān 〈书面〉pretty; beautiful; handsome
嫣红 yānhóng bright red：姹紫～ riot of colour; beautiful flowers
嫣然 yānrán beautiful; lovely; charming：～一笑 give a charming (*or* sweet) smile /～含笑 with a winsome smile

燕 Yān ❶ one of the warring states of the Eastern Zhou dynasty ❷ northern Hebei Province ❸ a surname
see also yàn
燕京 Yānjīng old name for Beijing
燕山 Yānshān Yanshan Mountains, mountain range in the north of Hebei Province

淹（❶渰） yān ❶ cover with a flood; flood; inundate; submerge：洪水～了许多村庄。The flood inundated many villages. /他被～死了。He was drowned. ❷ be tingling or smarting from sweat：他的胳肢窝被汗～了。His armpits are tingling from sweat. ❸〈书面〉wide; extensive：～究史学 make a comprehensive study of history /～通古今 be thoroughly acquainted with the ancient and the modern ❹〈书面〉delay; tarry：～思 be slow in thinking /勿在山中久～。Do not stay long in the mountains.
淹博 yānbó 〈书面〉well-read; of great learning：学问～ erudite; very learned
淹缠 yānchan 〈方言〉❶ suffer from a lingering disease ❷ procrastinate
淹贯 yānguàn 〈书面〉erudite; learned：～群书 be well read
淹灌 yānguàn 〈农业〉basin irrigation
淹蹇 yānjiǎn ❶〈书面〉be thwarted; be frustrated; be disappointed：宦途～ have a disappointing official career ❷ delay; detain; hold up：他老不回来，不知道什么事情～住了。He has been away for some time. I wonder what has held him up.
淹践 yānjian 〈方言〉*see* "淹浸" yānjin
淹浸 yānjìn submerge; flood; inundate：洪水～了农田。The fields were flooded.
淹浸 yānjin 〈方言〉waste; ruin; spoil：加工时当心点儿，别把这么好的材料～了。Do it carefully. Don't spoil such good material.
淹留 yānliú 〈书面〉stay long：～他乡 have been away from one's hometown for a long time
淹埋 yānmái cover up; bury：铁路被淤泥～了。The railway was buried in silt. /从北面沙漠里刮来的沙土慢慢地把森林～了。The sand blown from the desert in the north gradually covered up the forest.
淹灭 yānmiè *also* "埋没" máimò bury; cover up; stifle
淹没 yānmò submerge; flood; inundate; drown：洪水～了庄稼。The flood inundated the crops. /小草屋被流沙～。The thatched cottage was submerged by drift sand. /拉拉队的欢呼声～了一切。The rooters' cheers drowned out everything.
淹没式水力发电机组 yānmòshì shuǐlì fādiàn jīzǔ submerged hydroelectric unit

阉 yān ❶ castrate; spay：～鸡 capon /～猪 castrated boar or spayed sow; hog; barrow /～牛 bullock; steer/～羊 wether /～马 gelding ❷〈书面〉eunuch
阉党 yāndǎng 〈历史〉faction of eunuchs and their followers
阉割 yāngē ❶ castrate; spay; neuter ❷ deprive a theory, etc. of its essence; emasculate：这一理论的实质被～了。The theory has been stripped of its essence.
阉宦 yānhuàn eunuch
阉人 yānrén castrated man; eunuch
阉寺 yānsì 〈书面〉eunuch

崦 yān
崦嵫 Yānzī ❶ name of a mountain in Gansu Province ❷〈古语〉where the sun sets：日薄～。The sun was setting over the horizon.

腌（醃） yān preserve in salt, sugar, etc.; salt; pickle; cure：～肉 salted meat; bacon /～鱼 salted fish; cured fish /～黄瓜 pickled cucumber /把西红柿用糖～一下再吃。Put sugar on the tomato slices before eating them. /她每年冬天都～点儿菜。Every winter she pickles some vegetables.
see also ā
腌货 yānhuò salted food
腌泡 yānpào marinade; marinate：～过的猪肉 marinated pork
腌制 yānzhì make by preserving in salt：～咸菜 make pickles
腌渍 yānzì preserve in salt, sugar, etc.; salt; pickle; cure：～蔬菜 pickle vegetables /跑了一天的路，汗～得身上难受。I've been walking all day. I'm soaked with sweat and feel rather uncomfortable.

湮 yān 〈书面〉❶ sink into oblivion; bury in obscurity：这个家族渐渐～微。The family gradually declined. ❷ silt up
湮灭 yānmiè bury in oblivion; disappear
湮没 yānmò ❶ be consigned to oblivion; be neglected; be drowned; be forgotten：许多古籍久已～。Many ancient books have long been consigned to (*or* buried in) oblivion. /远远看去，水和天空的界线～了。The dividing line between the sky and the water disappeared into obscurity in the distance. ❷〈物理〉annihilation：～反应 annihilation reaction /～辐射 annihilation radiation /～质子 annihilation proton /～光子 annihilation photon
湮没无闻 yānmò-wúwén fall into oblivion; drift into obscurity;

pass into extinction：其人其事早已～。The man and his deed are long since forgotten.

烟（煙、❹菸） yān ❶ smoke：缕缕炊～ wisps of smoke from kitchen chimneys /浓～滚滚 billows of smoke /煤～呛鼻子。The smoke irritated my nose. ❷ mist; thin fog; vapour：袅袅轻～在山巅缭绕。Mist is curling around the summit. ❸ (of eyes) be irritated by smoke：～了我的眼睛了。My eyes have been irritated by the smoke. ❹ tobacco; cigarette：烤～ flue-cured tobacco /香～ cigarette /鼻～ snuff /卷～ cigarette; cigar /雪茄～ cigar /纸～ cigarette /一条～ a carton of cigarettes /一盒～ a pack of cigarettes /一听～ a tin of cigarettes /一袋～ a pipeful of tobacco /点～ light up a cigarette /戒～ give up smoking; swear off tobacco /～酒不分 smoke and drink together; hobnob; hang together /请勿吸～！No smoking! ❺ opium：禁～ ban opium /抽大～ smoke opium ❻ soot：松～ pine soot
see also yīn

烟霭 yān'ǎi 〈书面〉mist and clouds：远处是淡蓝色的～。There is a light blue mist in the distance.

烟标 yānbiāo cigarette label：收集～ collect cigarette labels

烟波 yānbō mist-covered waters：～浩瀚 vast expanse of misty waters /一片片帆影出现在远接天际的～之上。Sail after sail appeared above the mist-covered waters on the horizon.

烟波浩淼 yānbō-hàomiǎo *also* "烟波浩渺" vast expanse of mist-covered waters：莽莽大江，～，流水滔滔。The great river flows on, carrying with it a vast expanse of misty, rolling waters.

烟草 yāncǎo 〈农业〉tobacco (*Nicotinana tabacum*)：～行业 tobacco industry /～制品 tobacco product /～花叶病 tobacco common mosaic (*Nicotiana virus*) /～环叶病 tobacco ring spot virus (*Nicotiana virus*) /～中毒 〈医学〉tabagism; tabacosis

烟尘 yānchén ❶ smoke and dust：～弥漫 (of a place) be enveloped in smoke and dust ❷ 〈旧语〉beacon-fire and dust in the battlefield; war：宇内太平，无～之惊。Peace prevails and the whole world is free from war. ❸ 〈书面〉densely populated area

烟尘肺 yānchénfèi 〈医学〉tabacosis

烟尘探测器 yānchén tàncèqì 〈环保〉smoke detector

烟囱 yāncōng chimney; smoke stack; funnel; stovepipe：～喷吐着黑烟。The chimneys are belching (out) dark smoke.

烟村 yāncūn village enveloped in mist

烟袋 yāndài small-bowled, long-stemmed (tobacco) pipe：旱～ long-stemmed Chinese pipe /水～ water pipe; hooka(h)

烟袋杆儿 yāndàigǎnr *also* "烟杆儿" stem of a pipe

烟袋锅 yāndàiguō *also* "烟袋锅子" pipebowl

烟袋荷包 yāndài hébao tobacco pouch (often attached to a pipe)

烟袋嘴儿 yāndàizuǐr stem or mouthpiece of a pipe

烟道 yāndào flue; chimney; stack：～气 flue gas /～工 flueman /～灰 〈冶金〉flue dust /～闸 stack damper; flue damper /～孔 〈冶金〉floss hole

烟灯 yāndēng lamp for cooking opium (to prepare it for smoking)

烟蒂 yāndì cigarette end, butt or stub

烟斗 yāndǒu ❶ (tobacco) pipe：吸～ smoke a pipe /衔着～ hold a pipe in one's mouth; have a pipe between one's teeth ❷ pottery bowl or mouthpiece of an opium pipe

烟斗架 yāndǒujià pipe rack

烟斗丝 yāndǒusī *also* "斗烟丝" pipe tobacco

烟斗嘴 yāndǒuzuǐ bit (of a smoking pipe); mouthpiece

烟缸 yāngāng ashtray

烟膏 yāngāo opium paste

烟垢 yāngòu soot：～吹净装置 soot blowing equipment

烟馆 yānguǎn opium den

烟鬼 yānguǐ ❶ opium addict：那些～们整日吞云吐雾。The opium addicts passed all their time in smoking. ❷ heavy smoker; chain smoker

烟锅儿 yānguōr bowl of a long-stemmed pipe; pipe bowl

烟海 yānhǎi vast sea of fog — huge and voluminous：浩如～ tremendous amount of (data, etc.); voluminous /如堕～ as if lost in an immense fog; wide (*or* lost) at sea

烟害 yānhài 〈环保〉smoke-injury; smoke nuisance

烟盒 yānhé cigarette case

烟黑 yānhēi soot

烟花 yānhuā ❶ 〈书面〉beautiful scenery in spring：～三月下扬州 go to Yangzhou in the misty month of flowers ❷ 〈旧语〉prostitute; prostitution：～女 streetwalker; prostitute /～巷 red-light lane (*or* district) ❸ fireworks：大放～ put on a wonderful display of fireworks /～品种丰富。There is a great variety of fireworks.

烟花爆竹 yānhuā-bàozhú fireworks：市区禁放～。It is prohibited to let off fireworks in the city.

烟灰 yānhuī ❶ tobacco or cigarette ash：轻轻弹掉～ flick the ash off one's cigarette /他穿着一身儿～色的中山服。He was in ash-grey tunic and trousers. ❷ soot：～吹除机 soot blower (SB)

烟灰缸 yānhuīgāng ashtray

烟火 yānhuǒ ❶ smoke and fire：建筑工地严禁～。Smoking and fire are strickly forbidden on a construction site. ❷ cooked food：不食人间～ not eat anything of this world; not belong to this world ❸ 〈书面〉beacon fire; flames of war：百年不见～ not know war for a century ❹ 〈旧语〉incense for worshipping one's ancestors; 〈比喻〉progeny; offspring：绝了～ (of a family line) have no male offspring

烟火 yānhuo fireworks

烟火食 yānhuǒshí cooked food

烟火探测器 yānhuǒ tàncèqì smoke detector

烟碱 yānjiǎn 〈化学〉nicotine：～中毒 nicotinism

烟晶 yānjīng 〈地质〉smoky quartz; smoky topaz

烟景 yānjǐng beautiful scenery; misty scenery：阳春的～ misty spring scenery

烟具 yānjù smoking paraphernalia; smoking set

烟卷儿 yānjuǎnr 〈口语〉(UK) fag; (US) butt; cigarette

烟客 yānkè smoker

烟岚 yānlán 〈书面〉mists in the mountains

烟煤 yānméi bituminous coal; soft coal

烟民 yānmín smoker

烟幕 yānmù smokescreen：放～ put up (*or* throw up) a smokescreen /在民主的～下干涉别国内政 interfere in the internal affairs of other countries on the pretext of democracy /他这招儿不过是遮人耳目的～罢了。This stroke of his is nothing but a smokescreen.

烟幕弹 yānmùdàn ❶ smoke shell; smoke bomb ❷ smokescreen

烟农 yānnóng tobacco grower

烟泡儿 yānpàor cooked opium

烟癖 yānpǐ be addicted to smoking

烟屁股 yānpìgu 〈口语〉fag-end; cigarette end, butt or stub

烟气 yānqì flue gas; stack gas：～分析器 flue gas analyzer /～脱硫 flue gas desulfurization (FGD) /～洗涤器 smoke washer

烟枪 yānqiāng opium pipe

烟曲霉 yānqūméi 〈微生物〉Aspergillus fumigatus：～素 fumagillin

烟圈 yānquān smoke ring：喷～ blow smoke rings

烟容 yānróng (of opium addict) wan and sallow

烟色 yānsè dark brown：一套～西服 dark brown western-style suit

烟丝 yānsī cut tobacco; pipe tobacco

烟酸 yānsuān 〈化学〉nicotinic acid; niacin

烟酸缺乏症 yānsuān quēfázhèng 〈医学〉pellagra

烟筒 yāntong chimney; funnel; stovepipe：三节～ three sections of stovepipe

烟头 yāntóu cigarette butt, end or stub

烟突 yāntū 〈书面〉chimney; funnel; stack

烟突污染物 yāntū wūrǎnwù 〈环保〉stack pollutant

烟土 yāntǔ raw or crude opium

烟雾 yānwù smoke; mist; vapour; smog：～弥漫 full of smoke; covered by smoke /四下升起的～把村庄笼罩起来。The village was enveloped in the rising mist. /会议室里～腾腾。The meeting-room was filled with smoke. /浓厚的～低低地笼罩在这个工业城市的上空。A heavy smog was hanging low over the industrial city.

烟霞 yānxiá 〈书面〉mist and clouds

烟霞癖 yānxiápǐ 〈书面〉❶ fondness for sightseeing ❷ be addicted to opium

烟消云散 yānxiāo-yúnsàn *also* "云消雾散" yúnxiāo-wùsàn vanish like smoke; melt into thin air：经他一番劝说，我的气才～。My anger melted away thanks to his persuasion. /他大笑，仿佛这一天来的不快已经全部～。He laughed as if all the displeasures of the day had competely vanished. /这位部长辞职后其影响力也～了。The minister's influence was all lost after his resignation.

烟硝 yānxiāo *also* "硝烟" smoke of gunpowder

烟熏火燎 yānxūn-huǒliǎo smoke and burn：厨房的墙壁长年～，已经变成黑色。The walls of the kitchen have turned black after years of cooking. /我嗓子～地难受，快给我点水喝。My throat is burning. Get

me some water please.

烟熏室 yānxūnshì house for smoking fish, meat, etc.; smokehouse

烟蚜 yānyá tobacco budworm

烟焰 yānyàn smoke and flame:～涨天 be full of smoke and flame

烟叶 yānyè tobacco leaf; leaf tobacco

烟夜蛾 yānyè'é tobacco budworm

烟瘾 yānyǐn craving for tobacco:他～大,一天抽两、三包烟。He was a heavy smoker, smoking two or three packets a day./～一上来,他就哈欠连连。He couldn't help yawning when he was craving for a smoke.

烟油子 yānyóuzi ❶ tobacco tar ❷ greasy dirt in a chimney

烟雨 yānyǔ misty rain:远远望去,满湖～,一片迷蒙。With a misty rain falling steadily, the lake was only a blur in the distance.

烟云 yānyún smoke and clouds:～缭绕。Smoke and clouds are curling round.

烟瘴 yānzhàng miasma

烟柱 yānzhù column of smoke

烟子 yānzi soot

烟嘴儿 yānzuǐr cigarette holder

咽 yān 〈生理〉pharynx

see also yàn; yè

咽鼓管 yāngǔguǎn 〈生理〉Eustachian tube

咽喉 yānhóu ❶〈生理〉pharynx and larynx; throat ❷ vital passage; key point:～要道 junction of strategic importance; key junction/这里就是被称为"川鄂～"的宜昌港。The port of Yichang is known as "the throat of Sichuan and Hubei".

咽喉炎 yānhóuyán 〈医学〉pharyngolaryngitis

咽喉要地 yānhóu-yàodì junction of strategic importance; key junction; vital passage:兵家必争的～ junction of strategic importance in any war/山海关是连接东北和华北的～。The Shanhaiguan Pass is the vital passage joining northeastern China and north China.

咽镜 yānjìng 〈医学〉pharyngoscope:～检查 pharyngoscopy

咽麻痹 yānmábì 〈医学〉pharyngolysis

咽门 yānmén 〈生理〉fauces:～炎〈医学〉faucitis

咽痛 yāntòng 〈医学〉pharyngalgia; sore throat

咽头 yāntóu 〈生理〉pharynx

咽峡炎 yānxiáyán angina

咽炎 yānyán pharyngitis

胭(臙) yān rouge

胭粉 yānfěn rouge and powder; cosmetics

胭红 yānhóng carmine; rouge:～的野百合 carmine flowers of the wild lily

胭脂 yānzhi ❶ rouge:往脸上擦～ rouge ones cheeks ❷ kermes; cochineal

胭脂红 yānzhihóng ❶ carmine; rouge ❷ (of porcelain) famille rose

胭脂花 yānzhihuā 〈植物〉four-o'clock (*Mirabilis jalapa*)

胭脂树 yānzhishù 〈植物〉annatto; arnotta; arrotto (*Bixa orellana*)

胭脂鱼 yānzhiyú mullet (*Myxocyprinus asiaticus*)

殷 yān 〈书面〉blackish red

see also yīn; yǐn

殷红 yānhóng blackish red; dark red:～的血迹 dark red bloodstain

Y

yán

颜 yán ❶ face; look; countenance:笑逐～开 face wreathed in smiles/喜闻丰收尽欢～。Everybody was overjoyed to hear about the bumper harvest./他待人总是温～逊辞。He is always kind and modest. ❷ decency; face:无～见人 feel too ashamed to see anyone; not have the face to appear in public/厚～无耻 brazen and shameless ❸ dye; colour:五～六色 of various colours; multi-coloured; colourful ❹ (Yán) a surname

颜厚 yánhòu brazen; barefaced; shameless

颜料 yánliào pigment; colour; dyestuff:人造～ artificial pigment/～箱 paintbox

颜面 yánmiàn ❶ face:～神经麻痹 facial paralysis ❷ decency; face:不顾～ have no concern for face (*or* sensibility)/～扫地 lose face completely; be throughly discredited

颜容 yánróng countenance; complexion; (facial) expression; look:～枯槁 wear a withered look

颜色 yánsè ❶ colour; hue:～单调 dull in colour/～失真〈电子〉cross-colour ❷〈书面〉countenance; look:～憔悴 haggard look ❸ facial expression:他的脸上带着惭愧的～。He blushed with shame. ❹ look worn or action taken to warn or punish sb.:要给他们一点～看。We must teach them a lesson.

颜色 yánshai pigment; dyestuff

颜氏家训 Yánshì Jiāxùn *Admonitions of the Yan Family*, written by Yan Zhitui (颜之推,531-c. 590) of the Northern Qi Dynasty of the Northern Dynasties

颜体 Yántǐ (of calligraphy) the Yan style (modelled after 颜真卿 Yan Zhenqing of the Tang Dynasty):他能写一手好～。He writes a beautiful Yan style.

颜真卿 Yán Zhēnqīng Yan Zhenqing (formerly translated as Yen Chen-ch'ing) (709-784), calligrapher of the Tang Dynasty

言 yán ❶ speech; remark; word:空～ empty words/格～ maxim/诺～ promise; pledge/发～ make a speech; take the floor/闲～碎语 gossip/有～在先 let it be clearly understood beforehand/我有一～相劝。I have a piece of advice to offer. ❷ say; talk; speak:知无不～ say whatever one thinks (*or* knows)/不～而喻 it goes without saying/自～自语 talk to oneself; think aloud/妙不可～ too wonderful for words; beyond words (*or* description)/生性不好～ be quiet (*or* taciturn) by nature/换～之 in other words/不幸而～中。One's prediction unfortunately proved true. ❸ character; word:五～诗 poem with five characters in a line/万～书 letter of ten thousand characters/下笔千～ write a thousand words at a stroke; wield a facile pen ❹ (Yán) a surname

言必信,行必果 yán bì xìn, xíng bì guǒ promises must be kept and action must be resolute; be true in word and resolute in deed:当领导,只有～才能有威信。One must be true in word and resolute in deed to be a credible leader.

言必有中 yánbìyǒuzhòng make remarks that are very much to the point:他不言则已,～。He says nothing unless he is sure to hit the nail on the head.

言不及义 yánbùjíyì never talk about anything serious; talk trivialities:此人群居终日,～。The man mixes with one crowd after another, making nothing but facetious remarks.

言不尽意 yánbùjìnyì I should like to say more (but I have to conclude this letter now):～,就此搁笔,盼来日相聚,畅谈胸怀。I have to end my letter here though I should like to say more. I hope to meet you soon and talk to our hearts' content.

言不由衷 yánbùyóuzhōng speak insincerely:在这种会上发言,常常是人云亦云,～。At this kind of meeting people often repeat what others say and speak tongue in cheek.

言差语错 yánchà-yǔcuò erroneous utterances:偶尔有个～,谁也不会责怪。Nobody will mind if you make a slip of the tongue occasionally.

言出必行 yánchūbìxíng be as good as one's word; keep faith; keep one's promise:他素重然诺,～。He never commits himself without being ready to carry out what he says.

言出法随 yánchū-fǎsuí upon its promulgation the law shall be enforced to the letter:～,勿谓言之不预。The order, once given, will be strictly enforced. Don't say this point has not been made clear in advance.

言传 yánchuán express or explain in words:难以～的痛苦 indescribable suffering (*or* pain)/只可意会,不可～ only to be sensed, not explained

言传身教 yánchuán-shēnjiào teach by personal example as well as verbal instruction; set an example to others in whatever one says or does; teach by precept and example

言喘 yánchuǎn 〈方言〉utter a sound or word

言辞 yáncí *also* "言词" words; remarks; speech:不善～ not good at expressing oneself/～恳切 be sincere in what one says; speak earnestly/～锋利 speak daggers; use sharp words/～明确的声明 explicit statement/～激烈往往使人难以接受。Caustic remarks are often

unacceptable to others.

言次 yáncì 〈书面〉the way one talks:～有归田之意。From the way he talks he seems to have the desire to leave his office and go back to his hometown (*or* have the intention of retiring).

言道 yándào say:他～他和老张是同学。He said he and Lao Zhang were fellow students.

言定 yándìng settle; agree on; come to an agreement:他们在会上～三天后签合同。They settled at the meeting that they would sign a contract in three days.

言多语失 yánduō-yǔshī *also*"言多必失" he who talks much is bound to err

言而无信 yán'érwúxìn fail to keep faith; break one's word

言而有信 yán'éryǒuxìn keep one's promise; be true to one's word; be as good as one's word:与朋友交,～。One should always make good what one promises to one's friend.

言官 yánguān counsellor at the Chinese imperial court whose job was to admonish the emperor

言归于好 yánguīyúhǎo become reconciled; restore to friendship; make it up with sb.:他以为钱先生会拒绝与他～的。He thought Mr. Qian would refuse to make friends with him again. /他俩～之后,相处得更亲密了。After their reconciliation they got along even better.

言归正传 yánguīzhèngzhuàn to come back to our story; to return to the subject:大家说了几句闲话,方才～。After some gossip, we returned to the topic under discussion.

言过其实 yánguòqíshí overstate; blow up; make a mountain out of a molehill:他的话显然～,不可全信。We mustn't believe his words completely; he obviously overstated the case.

言和 yánhé make peace; bury the hatchet:握手～ shake hands in reconciliation; shake hands and make it up

言欢 yánhuān chat amiably; talk and laugh:杯酒～ talk merrily over a cup of wine

言简意赅 yánjiǎn-yìgāi brief and to the point; concise and thorough; compendious:～的发言 compendious speech (*or* statement) /文章写得～。The article is concise and to the point.

言讲 yánjiǎng say:听人～,他昨天就走了。It is said that he left yesterday.

言教 yánjiào teach by word of mouth; give verbal instruction:不仅要～,更要身教。Example is more important than precept. *or* Deeds speak louder than words.

言近旨远 yánjìn-zhǐyuǎn simple words but with deep meaning; plain remarks of profound significance:其书～,文简义明。Written in simple and succinct language, the book is explicit but profound in its meaning.

言路 yánlù channels through which criticisms and suggestions may be conveyed to the authorities:广开～ provide more and better means for people to air their views /～不畅。Channels for criticisms and suggestions are restricted (*or* obstructed).

言论 yánlùn opinion on public affairs:～自由 freedom of speech /散布错误～ spread wrong opinions (*or* erroneous views) /～与行动不一致 words at variance with deeds

言情 yánqíng (of works) romantic; sentimental:～作品 romantic work

言情片儿 yánqíngpiānr film with a romantic story; sentimental movie

言情小说 yánqíng xiǎoshuō romantic fiction; sentimental novel:～作家 writer of sentimental fiction

言筌 yánquán *also*"言诠"〈书面〉traces of one's words:不落～ leave no written traces

言人人殊 yánrénrénshū different people give different views; each person offers a different version; opinions are varied

言三语四 yánsān-yǔsì gossip:她有话不明说,背地里却～。Instead of airing her views in the open she gossiped behind people's backs.

言声儿 yánshēngr utter a sound:不～ stand mute; remain silent /你缺什么,只管～。Just let me know what you need.

言说 yánshuō say; speak; talk:不可～ cannot be conveyed in words /听了这个好消息真有难以～的痛快。Words could hardly express my happiness at the news. *or* My happiness at the news was beyond description.

言谈 yántán the way one speaks; what one says:～举止 speech and bearing /～之间流露出抱怨的情绪 betray one's grievance by the way one speaks

言听计从 yántīng-jìcóng act upon whatever sb. says; always follow sb.'s advice; have implicit faith in sb.:他对哥哥的话是～的。He does whatever his elder brother tells him. *or* He hangs on his elder brother's every word.

言外之意 yánwàizhīyì *also*"言下之意" meaning behind what is openly said or stated; what is actually meant; implication:领会～ read between the lines /听你这话,～好像是我惹他生气似的。From what you are saying it seems that I am to blame for his loss of temper.

言为心声 yánwéixīnshēng words are the voice of the mind; words express one's inner thoughts; what the heart thinks the tongue speaks:～,书为心画。As words are the voice of the mind, so calligraphy gives its image.

言笑 yánxiào speak and laugh; talk animatedly:不苟～ be serious in speech and manner /～自若 be at ease in one's deportment

言行 yán-xíng words and deeds; speech and action:～不一 one's deeds do not match (*or* square with) one's words /～一致 suit one's actions to one's words; be as good as one's word /每人要对自己的～负责。Everybody must be responsible for what he says and does.

言行录 yánxínglù record of the words and deeds (of a famous or notorious person):《朱子～》*Sayings and Deeds of Master Zhu Xi*

言议 yányì 〈书面〉comment; talk; discuss

言犹在耳 yányóuzài'ěr the words are still ringing in one's ears:老师十年前的这些教诲,至今～。The words my teacher said to me ten years ago still ring clear and true in my ears.

言有尽而意无穷 yán yǒu jìn ér yì wúqióng there is an end to the words but not to their message

言语 yányǔ spoken language; speech:他逐渐昏迷,～不清了。He gradually lost consciousness and mumbled indistinctly.

言语 yányu 〈方言〉speak; answer; reply:你要走的时候～一声儿。Let me know when you wish to leave. /我们对面坐着,谁都不～。Sitting face to face, neither of us said anything. /我问她许久,她没～。I had been questioning her for quite a long time but she made no reply.

言语合成器 yányǔ héchéngqì speech synthesizer

言语生理学 yányǔ shēnglǐxué physiology of speech

言语障碍麻痹 yányǔ zhàng'ài mábì 〈医学〉laloplegia

言喻 yányù 〈书面〉(mainly used in the negative) explain in words:不可～ cannot be explained in words; inexplicable /难以～ beyond words

言责 yánzé ❶〈旧语〉responsibility of an official to advise and admonish his monarch ❷ responsibility for what one says or writes:～自负。Each should be responsible for the opinion they express.

言者无心,听者有意 yánzhě wúxīn, tīngzhě yǒuyì while the speaker is careless, the hearer is attentive; a casual remark may sound significant to a suspicious listener

言者无罪,闻者足戒 yánzhě wú zuì, wénzhě zú jiè blame not the speaker but be warned by his words

言者谆谆,听者藐藐 yánzhě zhūnzhūn, tīngzhě miǎomiǎo while the speaker is earnest, the listener is inattentive; earnest words fall on deaf ears

言之不预 yánzhī-bùyù 〈书面〉(often used in the negative) fail to make it clear in advance:对于贪污腐化者,我们一定严惩不贷,勿谓～。We will punish all grafters and corrupt officials with severity. Don't say you're not warned in advance (*or* forewarned)!

言之成理 yánzhī-chénglǐ *also*"言之有理" sound reasonable; speak in a convincing way

言之无物 yánzhī-wúwù (of speech or writing) lacking in substance; devoid of content; hollow:空话连篇,～的讲演 speech that is full of hot air but totally devoid of substance

言之有据 yánzhī-yǒujù speak on good grounds or with convincing proof:～的观点 well-grounded view

言之凿凿 yánzhī-záozáo say with certainty or conviction:他这话～,令人不能不信。He spoke with such certainty that we all believed his words.

言重 yánzhòng overstate:他不过是个孩子,不懂事,您～了。I'm afraid you've overstated the case, for he is only a child, unfamiliar with the way of the world.

言状 yánzhuàng (often used in the negative) describe; explain:不可～ beyond description (*or* words)

阎(❷閆)

yán ❶〈书面〉gate of a lane ❷ (Yán) a surname

Y

阎立本 Yán Lìběn Yan Liben (?-673), painter of the Tang Dynasty

阎罗 Yánluó *also* "阎罗王";"阎王";"阎王爷" 〈宗教〉 Yama

阎王 Yánwang ❶ Yama; King of Hell: 活～ living King of Hell; devil incarnate / 见～ kick the bucket; die / ～好见, 小鬼难当。〈俗语〉 It's easier to deal with the King of Hell than his underlings — the lackeys are worse than their master. ❷ extremely cruel person, usu. referring to a local tyrant in the old society

阎王殿 Yánwangdiàn *also* "阎罗殿" Palace of Hell

阎王账 yánwangzhàng 〈口语〉 usury; shark's loan: 还不清的～ shark's loans that can never be paid off entirely; be buried in usury

炎

yán ❶ scorching; extremely hot: 此山高且寒, 五月不觉～。 The mountain is high and cold; one doesn't feel hot even in summer. ❷ inflammation: 发～ inflammation / 消～ counteract (*or* allay) inflammation / 皮～ dermatitis ❸ 〈比喻〉 power; infuence: 趋～附势 toady to the powers that be; be snobbish ❹ (Yán) Yandi or Red Emperor

炎帝 Yándì Yandi or Red Emperor, one of the original five legendary rulers, also known as 神农 Shen Nong

see also "炎黄"

炎旱 yánhàn extremely hot and dry: ～的夏季 hot and dry summer

炎黄 Yán-Huáng Yandi and Huangdi, usu. used together to refer to the ancestors of the Chinese nation: ～子孙 descendants of Yandi and Huangdi; the Chinese nation

炎凉 yánliáng hot and cold, meaning different attitudes towards people of different fortunes: 世态～ the world as it is, fawning on the influential and snubbing the less fortunate; snobberies of the world

炎热 yánrè (of weather) scorching; blazing; sweltering; burning hot: 这里十分～。It's sweltering in here! / 在～的太阳下, 他的衬衣被汗水浸湿了。His shirt was wet with sweat in the scorching sun.

炎日 yánrì blazing or broiling sun; scorching sun: ～当空 with a blazing sun overhead

炎暑 yánshǔ ❶ hot summer; sultry summer; dog days: 时值～。It was in the height of summer. ❷ summer heat: ～逼人。The summer heat was oppressive (*or* stifling).

炎天 yántiān ❶ hot weather; summer: ～烈日 sweltering day ❷ 〈书面〉 southern part of the country

炎威 yánwēi oppressive heat: 虽然已是秋天, 太阳的～依然没有减退。Although it was autumn, the heat of the sun remained quite oppressive.

炎夏 yánxià hot summer; sultry summer days: ～盛暑 dog days

炎性癌 yánxìng'ái 〈医学〉 inflammatory carcinoma

炎炎 yányán ❶ (of the summer sun) scorching; blazing; burning: ～酷日 scorching sun ❷ (of fire) flaming; ablaze; raging: ～烈火 raging flames

炎焰 yányàn flame: 红彤彤的～ red flames

炎阳 yányáng blazing or broiling sun; burning sun

炎症 yánzhèng inflammation

炎症细胞 yánzhèng xìbāo inflammatory cell

研(硏)

yán ❶ grind; rub; pestle: ～药 grind medicine / ～墨 rub an ink stick on an inkslab (to make ink for writing with a brush) / ～成粉末 grind into fine powder; pulverize by grinding ❷ study; research: 科～ scientific research / 钻～ study assiduously; probe into

see also yàn

研钵 yánbō mortar

研杵 yánchǔ pestle; pounder

研床 yánchuáng 〈机械〉 lapper; lapping machine

研读 yándú read intensively; study assiduously: ～剧本 study the playscript assiduously / 他正在认真～这部史学专著。He is making an intensive study of this monograph on historical science.

研究 yánjiū ❶ study; research: 学术～ academic study; scholarly research / 基础～ basic research / 语言学～ linguistic studies / 专题～ case study / ～项目 research project (*or* item) / ～人员 research fellows; people engaged in research / ～成果 fruit of one's study / ～范围 range (*or* field) of one's study / 从事理论～ be engaged in theoretical studies; pursue theoretical studies / 值得～ warrant (*or* be worthy of) study; merit research / 治疗这种病的特效药正在～之中。A specific drug for this disease is under study. / 他提交了一份有关这个项目的可行性～报告。He submitted a feasibility study of the project. ❷ consider; study; discuss; deliberate on (problems, suggestions, applications, etc.): ～提高经济效益的问题 discuss how to enhance economic returns (*or* improve economic performance) / 下次会议～环境保护的问题。We'll take up the problem of environmental protection at the next meeting. / 对于你的要求, 我们认真～后再作答复。We'll give you a reply after careful consideration.

研究生 yánjiūshēng postgraduate (student); graduate student: 硕士～ MA (*or* MS) candidate / 博士～ doctoral candidate

研究生院 yánjiūshēngyuàn graduate school

研究室 yánjiūshì research room; laboratory

研究所 yánjiūsuǒ research institute

研究员 yánjiūyuán research fellow; researcher

研究院 yánjiūyuàn ❶ research institute; academy: 煤矿～ research institute of the coal-mining industry ❷ graduate school

研具 yánjù lapper; lap tool

研磨 yánmó 〈机械〉 ❶ grind; pestle: 细加～ grind sth. finely ❷ abrade; polish; lap: 无心～法 centreless lapping / ～粉 abrasive powder / ～机 abrader; grinding miller; lapper / ～剂 abrasive (*or* abraser) / ～加工 abrasive machining / ～液 lapping liquid; grinding fluid

研拟 yánnǐ discuss and work out: ～有关法规 discuss and formulate the relevant laws and regulations

研求 yánqiú study carefully: 演员反复～台词。The actor studied his lines again and again.

研碎 yánsuì pestle

研索 yánsuǒ *see* "研求"

研讨 yántǎo deliberate; discuss: ～持续发展经济的途径 explore ways to promote sustained development of the economy

研讨会 yántǎohuì workshop; seminar; symposium

研习 yánxí study: ～各科知识 study various subjects

研修 yánxiū engage in research and advanced studies: 出国～ pursue one's studies abroad

研修生 yánxiūshēng advanced student

研制 yánzhì research and manufacture; research and develop (R and D); develop: 急需～一种新型设备 urgent need for developing a new type of equipment

揅

yán 〈书面〉 *see* "研" yán

妍(姸)

yán 〈书面〉 beautiful; enchanting: 百花争～。A hundred flowers vie with each other in beauty.

妍媸 yán-chī *also* "妍蚩" beautiful and ugly: 不辨～ unable to tell what is beautiful and what is ugly

妍丽 yánlì beautiful: 色彩～ beautiful colours

妍雅 yányǎ beautiful and elegant

妍艳 yányàn bright-coloured and beautiful; gorgeous: 花朵～ gorgeous flowers

盐(鹽)

yán salt: 粗～ crude salt / 精～ refined salt / 食～ table salt / 正～ normal salt / 海～ sea salt / 岩～ rock salt / 井～ well salt / 酸式～ acid salt / 碱式～ basic salt / 碘～ iodate / 大雪后主要马路上都撒了～。After the heavy snow all the main streets have been salted.

盐巴 yánbā 〈方言〉 salt; table salt: 鱼很咸, 怕是～放多了。The fish is salty. I'm afraid you've put too much salt in it.

盐层 yáncéng salt deposit; salt bed

盐场 yánchǎng saltern; saltworks

盐池 yánchí salt pond

盐度 yándù salinity: ～测量 salinity measurement / ～表 salinograph / ～计 salinometer

盐分 yánfèn salt content; salinity; salt: ～移动 salt movement

盐肤木 yánfūmù 〈植物〉 Chinese sumac

盐肤木根皮 yánfūmù gēnpí 〈中药〉 root bark of Chinese sumac

盐罐 yánguàn saltcellar; saltshaker

盐湖 yánhú salt lake

盐花 yánhuā ❶ a little salt; pinch of salt: 吃凉拌黄瓜要搁点儿～。Before you eat sliced cucumber raw, mix it with just a little salt. ❷ 〈方言〉 salt frosting; salticing: 咸鱼透着～。The salted fish was covered with frosting.

盐化 yánhuà salinization: ～土 salinized soil

盐基 yánjī old name for alkali

盐碱地 yánjiǎndì saline-alkali land
盐碱化 yánjiǎnhuà salinization or alkalinization (of soil)
盐碱滩 yánjiǎntān 〈地质〉salt marsh
盐碱土 yánjiǎntǔ 〈农业〉saline-sodic soil; saline-alkali soil: ～改良 saline-sodic soil amelioration; saline-alkali soil amelioration
盐浸处理 yánjìn chǔlǐ 〈农业〉brining
盐井 yánjǐng salt well
盐矿 yánkuàng salt mine
盐卤 yánlǔ bittern
盐民 yánmín 〈旧语〉person engaged in salt production; salter
盐木 yánmù *also* "鹾树" cuóshù; "琐琐树" suǒsuǒshù *Haloxylon ammodendron*
盐浓度 yánnóngdù salinity
盐瓶 yánpíng saltcellar; saltshaker
盐汽水 yánqìshuǐ salt soda water
盐丘 yánqiū 〈地质〉salt dome
盐泉 yánquán brine or salt spring
盐霜 yánshuāng salt efflorescene; salt frosting or icing
盐水 yánshuǐ salt solution; brine: ～电解 saline electrolysis
盐水输液 yánshuǐ shūyè saline solution for medical infusion; saline infusion
盐水选种 yánshuǐ xuǎnzhǒng seed sorting by salt water
盐水鸭 yánshuǐyā salted duck
盐酸 yánsuān 〈化学〉hydrochloric acid: ～橡胶 hydrochlorinated rubber /～盐 hydrochloride
盐滩 yántān ❶ beach for making sea salt ❷ salt marsh; salina
盐田 yántián square shallow pit for making sea salt by evaporation; salt pan
盐土 yántǔ 〈农业〉solonchak; saline soil
盐坨子 yántuózi pile of salt (in the open air)
盐析 yánxī 〈化学〉salt out or salting-out: ～剂 salting-out agent /～蒸化器 salting-out evaporator
盐枭 yánxiāo 〈旧语〉armed salt smuggler
盐业 yányè salt industry
盐液 yányè saline solution (medical)
盐液比重计 yányè bǐzhòngjì salinometer; salimeter
盐浴 yányù 〈冶金〉salt bath: ～电炉 salt-bath electric furnace /～淬火 salt-bath hardening; salt-bath quenching /～热处理 salt-bath heat treatment
盐沼 yánzhǎo salt marsh; salina
盐渍化 yánzìhuà salinization (of soil)
盐渍土 yánzìtǔ 〈农业〉salinized soil

严(嚴)

yán ❶ tight: 关～ shut (*or* close) tight /治学谨～ adopt a rigorous approach to one's studies /做西红柿酱，需要把瓶口封～。The bottle must be sealed up when you make tomato sauce. /他嘴很～，从不乱传话。He is too tight-lipped to pass on messages without permission. ❷ strict; stern; exacting; rigorous: 规矩～ rigorous rules; strict discipline /～加管束 bring under stern discipline /～而不苛 exacting but not harsh /～以律己，宽以待人 be strict with oneself and lenient with others /坦白从宽，抗拒从～ leniency to those who confess their crimes and severity to those who refuse to (do so) /～防死守 exert one's utmost to ensure the safety (of a dyke, embankments, or one's goal) ❸ heavy; severe; acute; extreme: ～寒 severe cold ❹ used to refer to one's father: 家～ my father ❺ (Yán) a surname
严办 yánbàn deal with strictly; punish with severity: 依法～ punish strictly according to law
严惩 yánchéng mete out severe punishment; punish severely: ～凶犯 punish the criminal (*or* felon) severely /～不贷 punish without mercy
严饬 yánchì 〈书面〉❶ issue strict orders: ～部下。Strict orders are given to all the troops under his command. ❷ careful and precise; meticulous: 治家～。One has to be exact in managing a household.
严处 yánchǔ severely punish
严词 yáncí in strong terms; in stern words: ～驳斥 sternly refute; repudiate in strong terms /～拒绝 sternly rebuff; categorically reject
严慈 yáncí be both strict and kind: 他自幼受父母～的管教。His parents have brought him up with firmness tempered with love.
严打 yándǎ crack down on crime; take severe measures against illegal and criminal activities: ～斗争 campaign to crack down on crime /对重大刑事犯实行～方针 carry out the policy of severely punishing those who commit serious crimes
严冬 yándōng severe winter
严防 yánfáng be on full alert for; take strict precautions against: ～偷税漏税 take strict precautions against tax evasion
严父 yánfù stern father: ～慈母 stern father and loving mother
严复 Yán Fù Yan Fu (1854-1921), enlightenment scholar and translator of the late Qing Dynasty and early Republic Period
严格 yángé ❶ strict; stiff; rigorous; stringent: ～的训练 rigorous training; strict discipline /～的考试 rigorous (*or* stiff) examination /制订～的学习制度 establish stringent study regulations /～要求自己 be strict with oneself /～说来 strictly speaking; in a strict sense /～执行规章制度 enforce rules and regulations to the letter /产品质量标准很～。The qualitative standards of the products are very demanding. ❷ rigorously enforce; regulate strictly: ～物价管理 strictly regulate commodity prices /～组织纪律 rigidly enforce the discipline of the organization
严固 yángù tight and consolidated: 防守～ have a solid and impregnable defence
严寒 yánhán icy cold; bitter cold: ～的北极 severe frigidity of the North Pole /抵御冬季～ withstand the severity of winter /该城市遭到～的袭击。The city was in the grip of a severe freeze.
严紧 yánjǐn ❶ strict; stern: 对孩子管得～才好。It is better to be strict with children. ❷ tight; close: 保卫～ closely guarded /无论把门关得怎样～，他们也会闯进来。No matter how tight you shut the door, they will break in.
严谨 yánjǐn ❶ careful and prudent; circumspect; scrupulous: 为人～ careful and prudent by nature /治学～ be scrupulous (*or* exact) in one's scholarly work ❷ strict; meticulous; precise and exact: ～的学者 meticulous scholar /措词～ precise and measured wording /说话～ be exact in one's words /文章结构～。The article is well organized.
严禁 yánjìn strictly forbid or prohibit: ～烟火。Smoking and fire are strictly forbidden.
严峻 yánjùn ❶ stern; rigorous; grim: 露出～的神情 look stern; wear a stern expression /执法～ enforce the law mercilessly /成功之路是艰苦～的。The way to success is hard and harsh. /历史是～无情的。History is inexorable. ❷ grave; serious; severe: ～的形势 grave situation /面临～的挑战 be confronted with a severe challenge
严苛 yánkē stern and harsh: 待人～ be hard upon others /条件～ rigid and harsh terms
严刻 yánkè severe and caustic: 措辞～ couched in severe and biting terms
严酷 yánkù ❶ harsh; bitter; grim: ～的考验 grim test /～的现实 hard (*or* cold) fact; harsh reality ❷ cruel; merciless; ruthless: ～压迫 ruthless oppression /～的战斗岁月 grim years of struggle
严冷 yánlěng ❶ stern; severe: 他板着～的面孔，一言不发。With a stern expression (*or* frigid countenance) he remained silent. ❷ bitter cold: ～的天气 extremely cold weather
严厉 yánlì stern; harsh; severe: 目光～ stern look /～的统治 severe rule /～批评 harsh criticism /～的处罚 heavy penalty /～的制裁 drastic sanction /～打击经济犯罪活动 ruthlessly crack down on economic crimes /他说话的口气十分～。He spoke in a stern voice.
严烈 yánliè stern; strict: 他对学生虽～，却能得到学生的敬爱。He was respected by his students despite his strictness with them.
严令 yánlìng rigorously order: ～禁止贩毒、吸毒 issue strict orders to prohibit drug traffic and use
严密 yánmì ❶ compact; well-knit: ～的囚室 compact cell /这种冰箱的构造～。This kind of refrigerator is compact in construction. /这篇小说的结构十分～。The novel is well-knit. ❷ tight; close; meticulous: ～的搜查 close search /～的封锁 tight blockade /管理～ meticulous management /～的逻辑推理 unassailable logic /～监视他的行动 keep close watch on him; put him under close surveillance /～注视市场动态 closely follow developments in the market /准确而～地表达自己的意思 express oneself in accurate and well-defined terms /由于我队～防守，对方的进攻没有成功。The other team's attack failed due to our tight defence. ❸ make compact; tighten: ～规章制度 tighten up the rules and regulations
严明 yánmíng ❶ strict and impartial: 执法～ be strict and impartial in law enforcement /纪律～ enforce (*or* maintain) rigorous discipline /治军～ enforce strict discipline in the army ❷ rigorously enforce: ～纪律，制止不正之风。We must strictly enforce discipline and check unhealthy tendencies.

严命 yánmìng 〈书面〉❶ strictly order: ～缉查 give strict orders to apprehend the criminal and bring him to justice. ❷ one's father's order
严判 yánpàn stiff sentence
严声 yánshēng (say) in a stern voice: ～厉色 stern in voice and countenance /～喝问 shout a question in a stern voice
严师 yánshī teacher who is strict with his students; exacting master
严师出高徒 yánshī chū gāotú a strict teacher produces outstanding students; capable pupils are trained by exacting masters
严师诤友 yánshī-zhèngyǒu teacher who is exacting in demand and friend who gives forthright admonition; strict teacher and outspoken friend
严实 yánshi 〈方言〉❶ tight; close: 把药瓶盖～。Cap the medicine bottle tight. /湖面冻～了。The surface of the lake is completely frozen. /穿～些，天气冷。Cover yourself up. It's cold. ❷ (hide) in safety: 他把钱藏得严严实实的。He hid his money in a safe place.
严守 yánshǒu ❶ strictly observe: ～军纪 strictly abide by the discipline of the army /～中立 observe strict neutrality ❷ guard closely; maintain strictly: ～国家机密 closely keep state secrets
严霜 yánshuāng heavy frost
严丝合缝 yánsī-héfèng fit together perfectly; dovetail: 门窗都～，寒气一点儿也进不来。The door and window fit so well as to keep out any cold draught.
严肃 yánsù ❶ (of expression, atmosphere, etc.) serious; solemn; stern; grave: 神情～ look serious (*or* grave, *or* stern) /会场气氛～。The atmosphere in the assembly hall is rather solemn. /他是个～的人。He is grave by nature. ❷ (of style, manner, etc.) strict; exacting; earnest; severe: ～的批评 severe criticism /对他的错误要～处理。His mistake must be dealt with strictly. /我们不得不～地思考这个问题。We have to ponder over the problem in real earnest. ❸ tighten up; enforce strictly: ～法纪 strictly enforce law and discipline
严细 yánxì meticulous: 做事～认真 work with meticulous care
严刑 yánxíng cruel or harsh punishment; torture: ～拷打 cruelly beat up; subject sb. to torture
严刑峻法 yánxíng-jùnfǎ stern laws and severe punishments; draconian law: 非～，无以治乱世。Nothing but draconian legal measures can bring order out of social chaos.
严讯 yánxùn sternly interrogate; question harshly
严阵以待 yánzhènyǐdài be fully prepared for any eventuality: ～的战士们 soldiers in combat readiness /我军～。Our army was drawn up in full battle array.
严整 yánzhěng ❶ in neat formation; under strict discipline: 军容～。The troops are in gallant array. /军纪十分～。Military discipline is much in evidence. ❷ meticulous; scrupulous: 治家～ manage the family in a meticulous manner /文章布局～。The article is well organized.
严正 yánzhèng solemn and just; stern and principled: ～声明 issue a solemn statement; solemnly state or declare /～抗议 lodge a stern protest (with sb. against sth.) /～指出 point out in all seriousness /表明我国的～立场 state the solemn and just position of our country
严重 yánzhòng serious; grave; severe; critical: ～问题 serious problem /～关头 critical moment (*or* juncture) /～的事件 grave event /～教训 bitter lesson /～错误 grievous mistake; blunder /～事故 major accident /～的损失 severe loss /～障碍 formidable obstacle /～影响 profound impact (*or* influence) /感到～不安 be deeply disturbed /亏损～ great deficit /病情～ be critically ill /交通堵塞～ acute traffic jam /～破坏社会治安 grave disruptions of public order /～伤害了中国人民的感情 greatly hurt the national pride of the Chinese people

严妆 yánzhuāng 〈书面〉(of woman) be dressed up
严装 yánzhuāng (of troops) be ready; be fully prepared: ～待发 ready for setting out

芫 yán

see also yuán
芫荽 yánsui 〈植物〉coriander; cilantro (*Coriandrum sativum*): ～油 coriander oil

檐(簷) yán

❶ eaves: 房～ eaves of a house /廊～ eaves of a veranda /～下 under the eaves ❷ ledge; brim: 帽～ visor of a cap; brim of a hat
檐板 yánbǎn eaves board
檐沟 yángōu 〈建筑〉eaves gutter
檐口 yánkǒu end sprout of eaves gutter
檐溜 yánliù rainwater or snowmelt that flows along the eaves
檐马 yánmǎ aeolian bells hung under the eaves of a house; wind chimes
檐头 yántóu edge of eaves
檐瓦 yánwǎ verge tile
檐牙 yányá indentations on the eaves of a house; projecting tiles at a roof edge
檐子 yánzi eaves

岩(巖、嵒) yán

❶ rock: 花岗～ granite ❷ cliff; crag
岩岸 yán'àn 〈地质〉rocky coast
岩崩 yánbēng 〈地质〉rock-fall
岩壁 yánbì perpendicular rock; palisades
岩层 yáncéng rock stratum; rock formation
岩床 yánchuáng 〈地质〉rock bed
岩顶圆顶寺 Yándǐng Yuándǐngsì *also* "麦尔清真寺" Mài'ěr Qīngzhēnsì Dome of the Rock, Islamic shrine in Jerusalem surrounding the sacred rock
岩洞 yándòng grotto
岩蜂 yánfēng 〈动物〉rock bee
岩高兰 yángāolán 〈植物〉crowberry
岩鸽 yángē rock pigeon; rock dove
岩壑 yánhè rocky ravine; mountain valley
岩化作用 yánhuà zuòyòng lithification
岩画 yánhuà cliff carving; rock painting
岩浆 yánjiāng 〈地质〉magma: ～发育 magmatic development /～分异作用 magmatic differentiation /～作用 magmatism
岩浆岩 yánjiāngyán magmatic rock
岩居穴处 yánjū-xuéchǔ dwell in mountain caves; live in cliff dwelling
岩羚 yánlíng *also* "岩羚羊"〈动物〉chamois (*Rupicapra rupicapra*)
岩漠 yánmò 〈地质〉rock desert; hammada
岩溶 yánróng 〈地质〉karst: ～湖 karst lake /～现象 karst phenomenon
岩溶地貌 yánróng dìmào karst feature or topography
岩石 yánshí rock: ～风化 rock decay /～冰川 rock glacier /～强度 rock strength /～突出〈矿业〉rock bust
岩石力学 yánshí lìxué rock mechanics
岩石圈 yánshíquān lithosphere
岩石学 yánshíxué petrology
岩石钻 yánshízuàn 〈机械〉rock borer: ～头 rock drill bit
岩相 yánxiàng 〈地质〉lithofacies: ～图 lithofacies map
岩心 yánxīn 〈地质〉(drill) core: ～断面 core intersection; core interval /～回收率 core recovery /～提取器 core lifter; corer /～筒 core barrel /～样品 core sample /～管钻头〈矿业〉biscuit cutter /～钻机 core drill machine
岩性学 yánxìngxué 〈地质〉lithology
岩穴 yánxué cave; cavern
岩崖 yányá cliff
岩盐 yányán rock salt; halite
岩羊 yányáng blue sheep; bharal; burhel (*Pseudois nayaur*)
岩样 yányàng ❶〈地质〉rock specimen ❷〈矿业〉core sample

延 yán

❶ prolong; extend; lengthen: 绵～ extend; stretch; spread /～首远望 stretch one's neck and look far ahead /苟～残喘 be at one's last gasp; be on one's last legs ❷ postpone; put off: 迁～时日 cause a long delay /运动会遇雨顺～。In case of rain the sports meet will be postponed till the first fine day. ❸〈书面〉engage; employ: ～师 hire a teacher /～医 send for a doctor ❹ (Yán) a surname
延挨 yán'ái delay; put off: ～时日 play for time
延安 Yán'ān Yan'an, seat of the Central Committee of the Communist Party of China in 1936-1947
延安精神 Yán'ān Jīngshén Yan'an spirit — the spirit of self-reliance and hard struggle fostered by the army and the people of Yan'an and the Shaanxi-Gansu-Ningxia Border Region during 1936-1948

延安整风运动 Yán'ān Zhěngfēng Yùndòng Yan'an Rectification Movement, a movement carried out in Yan'an by the Chinese Communist Party during the War of Resistance Against Japanese Aggression to rectify the style of the Party from 1942 to 1944
延安作风 Yán'ān zuòfēng Yan'an style
see also "延安精神"
延爆炸弹 yánbào zhàdàn delayed action bomb
延长 yáncháng lengthen; prolong; renew; extend: 假期～ extension of holiday /～期限 extend the deadline /～有效期三个月 validity renewed for another 3 months /～寿命 prolong one's life /截稿日期～到下星期一。The closing date for contributions is postponed to next Monday. /路基将向南～三十公里。The roadbed will extend 30 kilometres towards the south.
延长号 yánchánghào 〈音乐〉 pause
延长线 yánchángxiàn extension line
延迟 yánchí ❶ delay; postpone; defer: 开会时间～了。The meeting has been put off (*or* deferred). ❷〈电子〉time delay; delay: ～式荧光屏 delay screen /～线 delay line; artificial delay line /～信道 delayed-channel
延宕 yándàng delay; put off; procrastinate: 他～到九点方出去。He kept putting off his departure till 9 o'clock.
延发 yánfā 〈军事〉 delayed action: ～爆破 delayed blasting (*or* explosion)
延发引信 yánfā yǐnxìn delayed action or delay fuse
延搁 yángē delay; postpone; procrastinate
延胡索 yánhúsuǒ 〈中药〉 *yanhusuo* (*Corydalis yanhusuo*)
延缓 yánhuǎn postpone; put off: ～建设速度 retard the progress (*or* pace) of construction /～行期 delay the journey /手术不能再～了。The operation can no longer be put off.
延会 yánhuì postponement of a meeting
延见 yánjiàn 〈书面〉 ❶ introduce ❷ receive; grant an audience or interview
延接 yánjiē 〈书面〉 receive (a guest): ～贵宾 receive distinguished guests
延颈企踵 yánjǐng-qǐzhǒng *also* "延颈举踵" anxiously anticipate; eagerly look forward to: ～盼郎归。She fervently wished that her lover would soon return.
延揽 yánlǎn 〈书面〉 scout around for; recruit: ～人才 scout around for talent
延蔓 yánmàn spread; extend
延袤 yánmào 〈书面〉 continuous; unbroken; uninterrupted: ～不绝 extend continuously /～千里 stretch for a thousand *li*
延绵 yánmián be continuous; stretch long and unbroken
延纳 yánnà 〈书面〉 receive; admit; recruit
延年益寿 yánnián-yìshòu (of tonics, etc.) prolong life; conduce to longevity: 积极参加体育锻炼是～的好办法。The best bet to prolong one's life is to go in for sports.
延聘 yánpìn ❶〈书面〉 engage; employ: ～知名学者任教 engage well-known scholars to teach ❷ prolong or extend the employment of: ～一年 be employed for another year (beyond one's retirement)
延期 yánqī extend; postpone; defer; put off: 办理签证～手续 have one's visa extended; extend one's visa /同意再次～ grant a further extension /～付款 defer payment /～偿付 moratorium /～交货 back order /～装船 delay shipment /讲座因故～举办。The lecture was put off for some reason.
延企 yánqǐ 〈书面〉 look forward to earnestly: 对您的来访，我们正～以待。We are eagerly looking forward to your visit.
延请 yánqǐng engage; employ: 我们特地～王教授前来指导。We've specially invited Prof. Wang to give us the benefit of his advice.
延烧 yánshāo (of fire) spread: 大火～，数千英亩森林被焚。As the fire spread, thousands of acres of forests were destroyed.
延伸 yánshēn stretch; extend; lengthen; elongate: ～航道 extend a river channel /大路～到深山。The road stretches far into the mountains. /波罗的海是北海的～部分。The Baltic Sea is a continuation of the North Sea.
延伸火力 yánshēn huǒlì 〈军事〉 creeping or lift fire
延伸率 yánshēnlǜ 〈冶金〉 percentage elongation
延绳钓 yánshéngdiào longline fishing; long-lining
延时 yánshí 〈电子〉 delay: ～电路 delay circuit; time-delay circuit /～扫描 delayed sweep /～伺服系统 time-delay servo
延时器 yánshíqì delayed action; selftimer
延时摄影 yánshí shèyǐng time-lapse photography
延寿 yánshòu prolong life
延髓 yánsuǐ 〈生理〉 medulla oblongata: ～性麻痹 bulbar paralysis /～炎 bulbar myelitis
延误 yánwù incur loss through delay; miss: ～时机 miss an opportunity because of delay /～出版日期 miss the deadline for the publication of a book /～病情 delay in medical treatment /～工程进度。The project is behind schedule.
延祥纳福 yánxiáng-nàfú induce good luck
延性 yánxìng 〈物理〉 ductility: ～试验机 ductility (testing) machine; ductilimeter /～铸铁 ductalloy
延续 yánxù continue; prolong; last: ～生命 prolong life /这种杂乱无章的情况不能再～下去了。This chaotic situation must not be allowed to continue. /封建统治在我国～了几千年。Feudal rule lasted for thousands of years in China. /这个美丽的传说一直～至今。The beautiful legend has come down to us from ancient times.
延续性 yánxùxìng continuity
延音 yányīn 〈音乐〉 tenuto
延誉 yányù 〈书面〉 speak highly of sth. to make it known far and wide; spread the fame of
延展 yánzhǎn stretch; extend: 公路穿过沙漠～到很远的地方。The road stretched (out) across the desert into the distance.
延展性 yánzhǎnxìng 〈物理〉 ductility; malleability
延滞 yánzhì delay; stagnate: ～岁月 idle time away

蜒

yán ❶ *see* "蜒蚰" ❷ *see* "蚰蜒" yóuyan; "海蜒" hǎiyán
蜒蚰 yányóu 〈方言〉 slug

筵

yán ❶〈古语〉 bamboo mat spread on the floor for people to sit on ❷ banquet; feast: 寿～ birthday feast (usu. for an elderly person)
筵席 yánxí ❶ seats arranged around a table at a banquet ❷ banquet; feast

沿(沿)

yán ❶ along: ～着河边走 walk along the river /～着烈士的足迹前进 follow in the footsteps of the martyrs; advance along the tracks of the martyrs /～街栽着一排梧桐。Chinese parasol trees line the street. /他～着西湖散步。He took a stroll around the West Lake. ❷ follow or conform to (a tradition, pattern, etc.): 相～成习 become common practice through long usage /世代相～ be handed down from generation to generation /～老章程办事 do according to convention; follow the beaten track ❸ trim (with tape, ribbon, etc.): 在衬衫袖口上～一道边 trim the wristband ❹ edge; brim; border: 炕～儿 edge of a *kang* /缸～儿 edge of a jar
沿岸 yán'àn along the bank or coast; littoral or riparian: 长江～城市 cities along the Yangtze River /湄公河～国家 riparian states along the Mekong /波罗的海～国家 littoral countries of the Baltic
沿边儿 yánbiānr trim (with tape, ribbon, etc.); braid: 用花边给裙子～ trim the skirt with lace
沿波讨源 yánbō-tǎoyuán go along the river to trace its source — get down to the bottom of the matter
沿革 yángé course of change and development; evolution: 历史～地图 map of historical changes and developments
沿海 yánhǎi along the coast; coastal: ～地区 coastal area /～领地 coastal domain /～岛屿 offshore island /～国家 coastal state; littoral country /～航行 coastal navigation; cabotage /～航船 coaster /～贸易 cabotage; coastal trade; coasting trade /～航运权 cabotage /～渔业 coast fisheries; inshore fishing /～自然资源 natural resources of coastal waters /～石油 offshore oil /～海床区 coastal seabed area /～经济开放区 open coastal economic area /～地区经济发展战略 coastal economic development strategy
沿洄 yánhuí 〈书面〉 go downstream and upstream
沿江 yánjiāng along the river (usu. the Yangtze)
沿阶草 yánjiēcǎo 〈植物〉 dwarf lilyturf
沿街 yánjiē along the street: ～叫卖 peddle; hawk /～乞讨 go begging along the street
沿例 yánlì following the precedents; according to established practice: ～办理 act according to precedent
沿流水 yánliúshuǐ 〈方言〉 meltwater on the surface of a frozen river before it thaws
沿路 yánlù along the road; on the way: ～全是高高的杨树。All along the road are tall poplars. /乘火车旅游，～可以观风景。If you

Y

travel by train you can enjoy the scenery on the way.
沿门托钵 yánmén-tuōbō (of Buddhist monks or Taoist priests) beg food or collect alms from door to door; go begging from place to place
沿条儿 yántiáor silk trimming ribbon or tape; welt
沿途 yántú along the road; on the way: ～受到热情接待 be warmly received throughout the journey / 这是直达快车，～不能上下车。This is an express. You cannot get on or off it on the way. / ～风景极好。The scenery along the road is very beautiful.
沿途贸易 yántú màoyì way-port trade
沿袭 yánxí carry on as before; continue; follow: ～陈规 keep to the beaten track; follow convention / 这种习俗一直～下来。The custom has lasted to this day.
沿线 yánxiàn along the line: 铁路～ along the railway line / 公路～有许多工厂。There are many factories along the highway.
沿用 yányòng continue to use or employ (an old method, etc.): ～旧的规章制度 follow old rules and regulations / ～原来的名称 keep the old name / 这种做法一直～下来。This old practice is still in use.

阽 yán *see* "阽" diàn

yǎn

演 yǎn ❶ develop; evolve: 一种风俗习惯之～成，与社会有密切关系。The evolution of a custom is closely related to the conditions of society. ❷ elaborate; deduce: 推～ deduce ❸ drill, practise or calculate according to a set pattern, formula or style: 操～ drill; exercise / ～兵场 parade ground ❹ perform; play; act; stage: 公～ put on a public performance / ～杂技 perform acrobatics / ～电影 show a film / 他～过李大钊。He once played the part of Li Dazhao. / 这出戏共～十场。This play is to be staged ten times.
演变 yǎnbiàn change; develop; evolve: 宇宙间一切事物都是不断～的。Everything in the universe changes constantly. / 我们时刻注意局势的～。We keep close watch on the development of the situation (*or* trend of events). / 谁料到事情会～成这个样子。None of us expected that things would have turned out like this.
演播 yǎnbō televise or broadcast performances: ～设施 broadcast facilities
演播室 yǎnbōshì television studio; studio
演草 yǎncǎo calculating draft: ～本 pad for calculating drafts
演唱 yǎnchàng sing (in a performance); act a part in Beijing or provincial opera: ～通俗歌曲 sing pop songs / ～京剧 act in Beijing opera / 他的～获得了热烈的掌声。His singing won warm applause.
演唱会 yǎnchànghuì concert (for singing or Chinese opera)
演出 yǎnchū perform; show; put on (a show): 专业～ professional performance / 业余～ amateur performance / 流动～队 mobile troupe / 巡回～ performance tour / 首场～ first performance; first show; première (of a play, film, etc.) / 观看～ watch a performance / 为炼钢工人～节目 give performances to steel workers / ～开始。The performance begins. / ～成功。It is a successful show.
演出本 yǎnchūběn acting version; playscript; script
演出单位 yǎnchū dānwèi producer
演词 yǎncí speech; address
演化 yǎnhuà develop; evolve: 从猿到人，经历了一个～过程。Man has evolved from the ape.
演技 yǎnjì acting: ～精湛 excellent acting
演讲 yǎnjiǎng give a lecture; make or deliver a speech: 参加～比赛 take part in a speech contest / 讲究～技巧 pay attention to speech-making technique / ～人 speaker; lecturer / ～术 elocution / ～家 elocutionist
演进 yǎnjìn gradual progress; evolution: 语言在不断～。Language is constantly evolving.
演剧 yǎnjù act a part in a play or an opera; put on a play
演练 yǎnliàn drill; practise: ～规定动作 practise the compulsories / 地面～〈航空〉ground drill / ～场 drill ground
演示 yǎnshì demonstrate: 运用～的方法进行教学 teach through demonstration
演说 yǎnshuō give a speech; make an address: 深刻动人的～ profound and moving speech / 发表竞选～ deliver a campaign speech; make a stump speech / 他很会～。He is an eloquent speaker. / 这人～时东拉西扯。The man wandered in his speech.
演说词 yǎnshuōcí text of a speech
演说术 yǎnshuōshù oratory; elocution
演算 yǎnsuàn make or perform mathematical calculations: ～习题 do sums
演替 yǎntì (of vegetation) be replaced as a result of change: 植树的～ succession of plants / 这里原是松树林，现在～成以桦、杨为主的次生林。It used to be a pine forest here but has now been replaced by a secondary forest of birch and poplar trees.
演武 yǎnwǔ practise *wushu* or traditional martial arts: ～所 hall for practising *wushu*
演习 yǎnxí manoeuvre; exercise; drill; practice: 海军～ naval exercise (*or* manoeuvre) / 实弹～ live ammunition manoeuvre / 消防～ fire drill / ～拼刺刀 bayonet exercise (*or* drill) / 举行大规模的～ carry out a large-scale manoeuvre
演戏 yǎnxì put on a play; act in a play: 学～ learn the art of acting / 别再～了! Stop play-acting.
演义 yǎnyì ❶〈书面〉extend the meaning on the basis of the text: 这出戏根据《红楼梦》的一段情节～而成。The play is based on an episode in *A Dream of Red Mansions*. ❷ historical novel; historical romance: 《隋唐～》*Romance of the Sui and Tang Dynasties*
演艺 yǎnyì performing arts such as drama, acrobatics, *quyi*, etc.
演绎 yǎnyì 〈逻辑〉deduction; a priori: ～推理 apriorism / ～性 apriority
演绎法 yǎnyìfǎ deductive method; deduction
演绎主义 yǎnyìzhǔyì 〈哲学〉deductivism
演员 yǎnyuán actor or actress; performer; player: 电影～ film (*or* movie) actor or actress / 相声～ cross-talk performer (*or* artist) / 喜剧～ comedian / 舞蹈～ dancer / 杂技～ acrobat / 色艺双绝的～ actress of unique beauty and unrivalled skill / 他是个戏路很宽的～。He is a versatile actor.
演奏 yǎnzòu play a musical instrument in a performance: ～二胡 play the *erhu*, a Chinese two-stringed instrument / ～钢琴 play the piano / 精湛的～ excellent performance / 扣人心弦的～ thrilling performance
演奏家 yǎnzòujiā accomplished performer (of a musical instrument)

缜 yǎn 〈书面〉extend; prolong

兖 yǎn
兖州 Yǎnzhōu name of a county, in Shandong Province

扊 yǎn
扊扅 yǎnyí 〈书面〉(door) bolt; (door) bar

琰 yǎn 〈书面〉a kind of jade

剡 yǎn 〈书面〉❶ sharpen ❷ sharp; sharp-pointed

蝘 yǎn 〈古语〉cicada

偃 yǎn 〈书面〉❶ fall on one's back; lie down: 大风过后，秧苗尽～。After a strong wind all the seedlings were strewn flat on the ground. / 草上之风必～。The grass must bend when the wind blows. *or* The weak must yield to the strong. ❷ desist; stop; cease: 谁家能驻西山日？谁家能～东流水？Who could keep the sun from setting? Who could prevent the river from running east? *or* Time and tide wait for no man.
偃蹇 yǎnjiǎn 〈书面〉❶ stand tall and erect; tower ❷ proud; arrogant; conceited ❸ exhausted; tired out
偃仆 yǎnpū 〈书面〉(of body) fall down
偃旗息鼓 yǎnqí-xīgǔ ❶ lower the banners and silence the drums — stop fighting; cease to criticize or attack others: 敌人当晚就～，逃得无影无踪了。That night the enemy gave up fighting and ran away. / 这个问题双方争论了一段时间，也就～了。The two sides stopped arguing over the issue after a while. ❷ be on a secret (and silent) march: 我部队～，插入敌人背部。Our troops made their way secretly into areas behind the enemy lines.
偃师戏 yǎnshīxì 〈书面〉puppet show
偃卧 yǎnwò 〈书面〉lie supine; lie on one's back
偃武修文 yǎnwǔ-xiūwén cease military activities and encourage

culture and education
偃息 yǎnxī 〈书面〉❶ rest ❷ stop; cease
偃仰 yǎnyǎng 〈书面〉bend or lift one's head (as the occasion requires); comply with convention: 与世～ do as everybody else does
偃月 yǎnyuè ❶ crescent-moon ❷ crescent-moon shape: ～刀 crescent-moon-shaped sword

奄

yǎn 〈书面〉❶ cover; overspread: 万物至众，而知不足以～之。The universe is so vast that human wisdom is not enough to cover everything in it. ❷ suddenly; all of a sudden: ～闻敌军来犯。Suddenly it was reported that the enemy had begun to invade our territory.
奄忽 yǎnhū 〈书面〉suddenly; quickly: 火苗～熄灭。The flame suddenly died out.
奄然 yǎnrán 〈书面〉suddenly; unexpectedly: 山洪～而至。All of a sudden torrents of water rushed down the mountain.
奄奄 yǎnyǎn feeble breathing: 气息～ breathe feebly; be sinking fast; be dying /～待毙 life hanging by a thread; on the point of dying
奄奄一息 yǎnyǎn-yīxī at one's last gasp; on one's last leg: 只见他～，话也说不出来了。He could hardly talk, as he was on the verge of death.

掩(揜)

yǎn ❶ cover; conceal; hide: 迅雷不及～耳 as swift as a sudden clap of thunder (which leaves no time for covering one's ears) /他们忙～了口，不提此事。They immediately stopped talking about it. ❷ close; shut: ～门 shut the door ❸〈方言〉get squeezed when closing a door, lid, etc.: 给门～了手 get one's fingers caught in the door ❹〈书面〉launch a surprise attack: 义军自后～之，杀得官军大败。The rebels suddenly attacked from behind and routed the government army.
掩鼻 yǎnbí hold one's nose: ～而过 pass by (sth. nauseating) holding one's nose /令人～ nauseating; disgusting
掩闭 yǎnbì close; shut: 门～着，大概人都出去了。As the door was shut, they might have all gone out.
掩蔽 yǎnbì ❶ cover; camouflage; hide: ～物 cover; screen /我们的工事～得十分巧妙。Our works were ingeniously covered (*or* camouflaged). /听到警报，大家纷纷找地方～起来。Upon hearing the alarm everybody took shelter. ❷ cover; screen: 这片茂盛的高粱地正好成为我们的～。This field of thriving sorgum provided us with cover (*or* a screen).
掩蔽部 yǎnbìbù shelter
掩蔽阵地 yǎnbì zhèndì covered position
掩藏 yǎncáng cover up; hide; conceal: 敌人就要来搜查，快把同志们～好。The enemy will soon come to search. Hide the comrades in a safe place at once. /不要～工作中的缺点与错误。Do not conceal the shortcomings and errors in one's work.
掩耳 yǎn'ěr plug one's ears: ～却步 plug the ears and step back /～不闻 turn a deaf ear
掩耳盗铃 yǎn'ěr-dàolíng plug one's ears while stealing a bell; bury one's head in the sand like an ostrich; practise self-deception
掩覆 yǎnfù cover; conceal: 乌云～了山巅。Dark clouds covered the summit.
掩盖 yǎngài ❶ cover; overspread: 积雪～了大地。The ground is covered with a thick layer of snow. ❷ hide; conceal; cover up: ～真相 conceal facts /～罪行 cover up a crime /～着内心的喜悦 disguise one's happiness /极力～内心的恐惧 try hard to keep back one's fears
掩护 yǎnhù screen; shield; shelter; cover: ～主力突围 cover the main force's breaking out of the encirclement /他在公司工作只是为间谍活动作～。His job at the firm was just a sceen for his life as a spy. /为使她免受不公正的惩罚，我只好替她打～。I had to shield her so as to keep her from unjust punishment. /这个小山包成了我们的～。We used the little hill as cover.
掩护部队 yǎnhù bùduì covering force
掩护火力 yǎnhù huǒlì covering fire
掩襟 yǎnjīn bottom part of the front of a garment
掩卷 yǎnjuàn 〈书面〉close a book: ～长叹 close a book and heave a deep sigh
掩埋 yǎnmái bury
掩泣 yǎnqì weep with one's face covered by one's hand
掩青 yǎnqīng green manuring or dressing
掩人耳目 yǎnrén'ěrmù deceive the public; fool people
掩杀 yǎnshā 〈书面〉attack by surprise; pounce on
掩食 yǎnshí (of one celestial body) occulting (another)
掩始 yǎnshǐ 〈天文〉immersion (entry of a celestial body into a state of invisibility during an eclipse or occultation)
掩饰 yǎnshì cover up; gloss over; hide; conceal: ～罪行 cover up one's crime /～缺点 gloss over one's shortcoming /～窘态 smooth over one's embarrassment /～内心的痛苦 conceal one's agony /毫不～地吐露自己的心里话 bare one's heart; make no secret of one's feelings /她毫不～对他的反感。She has taken an undisguised dislike to him.
掩体 yǎntǐ 〈军事〉blindage; bunker; emplacement: 机枪～ machine gun emplacement
掩袭 yǎnxí make a surprise attack
掩星 yǎnxīng 〈天文〉occultation: 月～ lunar occultation
掩眼法 yǎnyǎnfǎ cover-up; camouflage
掩隐 yǎnyǐn cover; screen
掩映 yǎnyìng set off (one another): 桃红柳绿相互～。The red peach blossoms and the green willows set each other off.

晻

yǎn 〈书面〉gloomy; dim
see also àn

罨

yǎn ❶〈书面〉net for catching birds or fish ❷ cover; apply: 热～ hot compress (therapy) /拿湿冷毛巾～在烫伤处 cover the burn with a cold wet towel

黡(黶)

yǎn 〈书面〉black mole (on skin)

厣(厴)

yǎn ❶ operculum ❷ opercular

魇(魘)

yǎn ❶ have a nightmare ❷〈方言〉talk in one's sleep; somniloquy
see also "梦魇" mèngyǎn

甗

yǎn ancient cooking utensil with a grid

巘(巘)

yǎn 〈书面〉mountain peak; summit: 绝～ summit

眼

yǎn ❶ eye: 大而亮的杏核～ big, bright, almond eyes /不怀好意的三角～ ill-intentioned triangular eyes /瞅了一～ take a look (*or* glance) at /一～认出 recognize at first glance /～冒金星 see stars /～里有活 see what needs to be done; be quick to spot work /这可是我亲～所见。This is what I've seen with my own eyes. /他那人～里没人。He looks down upon everyone else. ❷ small hole: 泉～ mouth of a spring /针～ eye of a needle /炮～ muzzle of a gun /网～ mesh (of a net) /在纸板儿上扎个～儿 punch a hole in the cardboard ❸ key point; crux: 节骨～儿 at a critical juncture ❹ (in *weiqi* or go) trap ❺ unaccented beat in traditional Chinese music: 一板三～ one accented beat and three unaccented beats in a bar ❻〈量词〉*used of a well or cave-dwelling*: 打一～井 sink a well /三～砖窑 three brick-lined cave-dwellings
眼巴巴 yǎnbābā ❶ (of expectation) eager; anxious: 母亲～地盼着离家十年的女儿回来。The mother was eagerly looking forward to the return of her daughter who had been away for ten years. ❷ unable to do anything to help; helpless (as when watching sth. unpleasant happen): 老人～地看着他们把东西抢走却动弹不得。The old man helplessly watched them take away his belongings, unable to make a move.
眼巴眼 yǎnbāyǎn 〈方言〉*see* "眼巴巴"
眼白 yǎnbái 〈方言〉white of the eye
眼斑病 yǎnbānbìng eye spot
眼保健操 yǎnbǎojiàncāo ocular exercises
眼病 yǎnbìng 〈医学〉oculopathy; eye trouble: 垂体性～ pituitarigenic oculopathy
眼波 yǎnbō (usu. of a woman) look; glance: 她递给他一个迷人的～。She gave him an enchanting (*or* a bewitching) look.
眼不见为净 yǎn bù jiàn wéi jìng 〈俗语〉❶ what the eye doesn't see is clean enough ❷ what the eye doesn't see, the heart doesn't worry about; out of sight, out of mind
眼不见，心不烦 yǎn bù jiàn, xīn bù fán what the eye doesn't see,

the heart doesn't grieve over
眼岔 yǎnchà 〈方言〉mistake one for another:原来前面那个人不是我老师,是我~了。The man in front turns out to be someone else. I mistook him for my teacher.
眼馋 yǎnchán eye covetously; covet; envy:这些画册真让人~。These picture albums are everyone's envy. /小时候看人家穿新衣,就~得慌。I always envied other children for their new clothes when I was a little child.
眼眵 yǎnchī gum (in the eyes)
眼虫 yǎnchóng *also* "眼虫藻" euglena
眼瞅着 yǎnchǒuzhe 〈方言〉❶ see sth. happen:~老鹰把小鸡抓走了。I saw with my own eyes a hawk snatch the chick away. ❷ soon; quickly; in no time:~春节又到了。The Spring Festival is drawing close again.
眼袋 yǎndài eye-bag
眼底 yǎndǐ ❶〈生理〉eyeground; fundus oculi:~出血 bleeding of the eyeground ❷ before one's eyes; in sight:登楼眺望,全城景色尽收~。When I went upstairs and looked around, the whole city came into sight.
眼底检查 yǎndǐ jiǎnchá examination of the eyeground; fundus-copy; fundus examination
眼底镜 yǎndǐjìng 〈医学〉ophthalmoscope; funduscope
眼底下 yǎndǐxia *also* "眼皮底下" ❶ right before one's eyes:跟紧他,别让他从你~溜了。Follow him closely and don't let him slip away right before your eyes. ❷ at present:先办~的事吧。Let's settle the business on hand first.
眼点 yǎndiǎn eyespot (of a protozoan); stigma
眼电图 yǎndiàntú 〈医学〉electro-oculogram
眼蝶 yǎndié satyr butterfly; satyrid
眼毒 yǎndú 〈方言〉sharp-eyed:他~,见过一次面,隔那么久还能认出来。He really has sharp eyes. He still can recognize me though we met only once a long time ago.
眼风 yǎnfēng hint given with the eyes; meaningful glance:他向小王丢了个~。He tipped Xiao Wang the wink. *or* He cast a hint to Xiao Wang.
眼锋 yǎnfēng sharp gaze:她不敢看他,怕他那冷酷的~。She didn't dare to look at him, afraid of meeting his icy gaze.
眼福 yǎnfú fortunate enough to see sth. rare or beautiful:有~ be lucky enough to enjoy a wonderful view (*or* to see sth. rare) /饱~ feast one's eyes on sth.; have (*or* get) an eyeful of sth.
眼干症 yǎngānzhèng 〈医学〉xerophthalmia
眼高手低 yǎngāo-shǒudī have high standards but little ability; be fastidious but incompetent; be exacting but incapable:~,志大才疏 have great ambition but little talent
眼膏 yǎngāo 〈药学〉eye ointment
眼格 yǎngé 〈方言〉field of view; outlook; perspective
眼观六路,耳听八方 yǎn guān liùlù, ěr tīng bāfāng have sharp eyes and keen ears; be all eyes and ears; be on the alert
眼光 yǎnguāng ❶ eye:大家都用期待的~望着他。Everyone eyed him with expectation. ❷ sight; foresight; insight; vision:~远大的政治家 farsighted statesman /~短浅的政客 shortsighted politician /用挑剔的~看待这件事 look at the matter with critical eyes /他办事有~。He is a man of vision. ❸ viewpoint; standpoint; outlook:用新~看待这个问题 adopt a new (*or* different) approach towards the problem; see the problem in a new light /把~放远点 see things in a broader perspective
眼黑 yǎnhēi 〈方言〉pupil; black centre of the iris; aperture at the centre of the eye
眼红 yǎnhóng ❶ covetous; envious; jealous:看着别人成功了,他真~。He is really jealous of others' success. ❷ with flaming eyes; furious:仇人见面,分外~。When two foes meet, their eyes flash fire.
眼花 yǎnhuā have dim eyesight; have blurred vision:头昏~ feel dizzy; one's head swims /太阳照得人~。The sunlight is dazzling. /老人耳不聋,眼不花。The old man is neither hard of hearing nor dim-sighted.
眼花缭乱 yǎnhuā-liáoluàn dazed; dazzled:海滩上的贝壳那么多,令人~。Numerous shells on the beach are dazzling. /街上车水马龙,他看得~。He was dazed by the sea of vehicles in the street.
眼机 yǎnjī eyephone, a headset with telescreens
眼肌 yǎnjī 〈生理〉eye muscles
眼肌瘫痪 yǎnjī tānhuàn 〈医学〉ophthalmoplegia
眼犄角儿 yǎnjījiǎor 〈方言〉corner of the eye; canthus
眼疾 yǎnjí eye ailment; eye trouble
眼疾手快 yǎnjí-shǒukuài *see* "手疾眼快" quick of eye and deft of hand; agile
眼尖 yǎnjiān be sharp-eyed; have sharp eyes:他眼真尖,从那么多人中间一眼就看出你了。His eyes are so sharp that he spotted you immediately in the crowd.
眼睑 yǎnjiǎn eyelid:下垂的~ drooped eyelid
眼睑下垂 yǎnjiǎn xiàchuí 〈医学〉ptosis
眼见 yǎnjiàn soon; in a moment:~就要立冬了,棉衣还没做好。Winter is fast approaching but the padded clothes haven't been made yet.
眼见得 yǎnjiànde 〈方言〉(of sth. unpleasant) evident; obvious:这么一折腾,~我就要倾家荡产了。After such a sharp turn for the worse I was obviously about to lose my family fortune. /她~支持不住了。She evidently can't hold on much longer.
眼见为实 yǎnjiàn-wéishí seeing is believing
眼角 yǎnjiǎo corner of the eye; canthus:她从~斜瞥了说话人一眼。She glanced at the speaker out of the corner of her eye.
眼睫毛 yǎnjiémáo eyelash:~膏 mascara
眼界 yǎnjiè field of vision or view; outlook:开扩~ widen one's field of vision; broaden one's horizons /~狭小 with limited perspective /这次出国考察,真是大开~。This study tour abroad is really an eyeopener.
眼镜 yǎnjìng glasses; spectacles:一副~ pair of glasses /~盒 glasses case /~链 spectacle-string /~架 *also* "~框" spectacle-frame; bow /~腿 earpiece /~店 optician's /老花~ presbyopic glasses /近视~ near-sighted glasses /隐形~ contact lenses /变色~ chameleon /戴~ wear glasses /配~ have one's glasses made
眼镜豆 yǎnjìngdòu *also* "榼藤子" kēténgzǐ 〈植物〉*Entada phaseoloides*
眼镜猴 yǎnjìnghóu tarsier (*Tarsius spectrum*)
眼镜蛇 yǎnjìngshé cobra:~毒 cobra venom
眼镜王蛇 yǎnjìngwángshé 〈动物〉king cobra (*Naja hannah*)
眼镜熊 yǎnjìngxióng spectacled bear; andean bear (*Tremarctors ornatus*)
眼睛 yǎnjing eye:张开~ open one's eyes /闭上~ close one's eyes /眨~ blink one's eyes /眯起~ narrow one's eyes /淡蓝色的~ azure-blue eyes /熠熠生辉的~ shining eyes /~里揉不进沙子 not to put up with a mote in one's eye — not to tolerate blemishes or deceptions /他简直不敢相信自己的~。He can hardly believe his own eyes.
眼看 yǎnkàn ❶ soon; in no time:~就要上课了,你别走远了。It's almost time for class. Don't go far away. /洪水~就要过来了。The flood is coming soon (*or* will be here any moment). ❷ watch helplessly; look on indifferently:他有困难,我们怎能~着不管呢? How can we just stand by and look on passively when he is in trouble?
眼科 yǎnkē (department of) ophthalmology
眼科学 yǎnkēxué ophthalmology
眼科医生 yǎnkē yīshēng oculist; ophthalmologist; eye-doctor
眼孔 yǎnkǒng 〈方言〉field of vision; horizon; outlook:~小,没见识 be short-sighted and inexperienced; have a narrow outlook and little sense
眼库 yǎnkù eye bank
眼快 yǎnkuài be sharp-sighted; have keen eyes
眼眶 yǎnkuàng *also* "眼眶子" ❶ eye socket; orbit:伤心的泪水涌出她的~。Sad tears well up in her eyes. /他深陷的~里布满了血丝。His sunken eyes were bloodshot. ❷ rim of the eye:他一拳把对手的~打青了。He gave his opponent a black eye with one blow.
眼蓝 yǎnlán 〈方言〉be worried; be anxious
眼泪 yǎnlèi tears:擦干~ wipe off tears; dry one's eyes /忍住~ hold back tears /~夺眶而出。Tears welled up from one's eyes. /激动的~顺着她脸颊流下来。Joyful tears were running down her cheeks.
眼泪汪汪 yǎnlèi-wāngwāng full of tears; with tears in one's eyes:她气得~。She was so angry that tears filled her eyes.
眼离 yǎnlí 〈方言〉have blurred vision; be seeing things:是我一时~,看错了人。At the time my eyes failed me and I mistook you for someone else.
眼力 yǎnlì ❶ eyesight; vision; perception:~差 have poor eyesight /~减弱 one's eyesight is weakening (*or* failing) ❷ judgment; discrimination; perceptiveness:王教授有~,推荐的学生都非常出色。Prof. Wang is a good judge of people. The students he recommends are all outstanding. /她挺有~,买来的东西都让人满意。She has an

Y

eye for nice things. What she buys is always satisfactory.
眼力见儿 yǎnlìjiànr 〈方言〉quick to see what needs doing; resourceful; clever:这孩子真有～，看见我扫地，就把簸箕拿过来了。The child was smart. He brought me the dustpan as soon as he saw me sweeping the floor.
眼帘 yǎnlián eye:映入～ come into view; meet (*or* greet) the eye
眼眉 yǎnméi 〈方言〉eyebrow
眼面前 yǎnmiànqián 〈方言〉❶ before one's eyes; at the moment: ～就是你要找的地址。The address you're asking for is right under your eyes. /～我还有许多事要做，不能休息。I have so many things to attend to that I cannot rest now. /～该办的事先办，其他留待以后再说。Let's deal with what is on hand first and leave the rest till some other time. ❷ common; everyday:虽说他文化低，～的字倒也认识不少。He knows quite a few common words though he hasn't received much schooling.
眼明手快 yǎnmíng-shǒukuài sharp-eyed and fast-moving; quick of eye and deft of hand
眼明心亮 yǎnmíng-xīnliàng have sharp eyes and a clear mind; be sharp-sighted and clear-headed
眼目 yǎnmù ❶ eye:强烈的灯光，眩人～。The brilliant light (*or* glare) dazzled the eyes. ❷ one who spies for sb. else; spy:你的行动要当心，这里可能有敌人的～。Be careful. There may be enemy spies around.
眼目前 yǎnmùqián *see* "眼面前"
眼目下 yǎnmùxià 〈方言〉at present; at the moment:我不问她的婚事了，反正～时兴自由了。I won't bother about her marriage. Anyway, it's the practice now to marry a person of one's own choice.
眼内渗血 yǎnnèi shènxuè 〈医学〉helmalopia
眼内压 yǎnnèiyā 〈生理〉intraocular pressure
眼泡 yǎnpāo upper eyelid:～浮肿 swollen eyes
眼皮 yǎnpí eyelid:双～ double-edged eyelid /单～ single-edged eyelid /她垂下～，显得很害羞、拘谨。She dropped her eyelids, shy and reserved.
眼皮底下 yǎnpí dǐxia right before one's eyes; under one's nose: ～的事你都不知道。You should have known what happened right under your nose. /这孩子是在我～长大的。I saw this child grow up with my own eyes.
眼皮子 yǎnpízi ❶ eyelid:困得～都睁不开了 too drowsy to open one's eyes ❷ outlook; view; experience
眼皮子高 yǎnpízi gāo *also* "眼皮儿高" ambitious; conceited; haughty:他～，看不起咱。He thinks much of himself and turns up his nose at me.
眼皮子浅 yǎnpízi qiǎn superficial; easily pleased; shallow
眼气 yǎnqì 〈方言〉eye covetously; covet; envy:看人家日子过好了，你别～。Don't be green with envy when you see others getting prosperous.
眼前 yǎnqián ❶ before one's eyes:～是一片繁荣景象。Before our eyes is a scene of prosperity. /颐和园就在～。The Summer Palace is in view. /胜利就在～。Success is at hand (*or* just round the corner). ❷ at the present time; at the moment; now:～利益服从长远利益 place long-term interests above immediate interests /只顾～是不行的。We shouldn't think only of the present. /～没什么问题，以后怎样很难说。Everything is all right now, but it's hard to predict the future.
眼前欢 yǎnqiánhuān pleasure of the moment; fleeting pleasure:只图～，会造成终身遗憾。You'll regret for the rest of your life if you seek only transient pleasure.
眼前亏 yǎnqiánkuī immediate humiliation:好汉不吃～。A sensible man would avoid present humiliation at any cost (*or* avoid fighting at a disadvantage).
眼浅 yǎnqiǎn short-sighted; with very limited outlook
眼球 yǎnqiú eyeball; bulbus oculi:～突出 exophthalmos; ocular protosis; ophthalmoptosis
眼球炎 yǎnqiúyán 〈医学〉ophthalmitis
眼屈光计 yǎnqūguāngjì 〈医学〉ophthalmometer
眼圈 yǎnquān *also* "眼圈子" rim of the eye; eye socket; orbit:～红肿 with swollen eyes /～红了 be about to cry; be on the verge of tears /他睡眠不足，～发黑。Because of lack of sleep he had livid rings round his eyes.
眼热 yǎnrè covet; envy:他们公司福利好，我们都～。We all envy them for their fringe benefits provided by their company.
眼仁 yǎnrén 〈方言〉black eyeball
眼色 yǎnsè ❶ meaningful glance; wink:使～ wink at sb.; tip sb. the wink /递了个～ give sb. a wink /到时候看我的～行事。Take your cue from me when it is time. ❷ ability to act according to circumstances:他是个没长～的糊涂虫。He is so dumb that he has never learned to act as befits the occasion.
眼色素 yǎnsèsù 〈生理〉ommochrome:～层 uvea
眼梢 yǎnshāo 〈方言〉corner of the eye close to the temple:他的～已经有了鱼尾纹。He's got wrinkles (*or* crow's feet) at the corners of his eyes.
眼神 yǎnshén ❶ expression in one's eyes:温柔的～ tender eyes /痛苦不堪的～ painful eyes ❷〈方言〉eyesight; sight:～不济 failing eyesight; poor sight /我～不好，连针都穿不上。My eyesight is so poor that I can't even thread the needle.
眼神 yǎnshen 〈方言〉meaningful glance; wink:他使了个～儿让大家避开。He winked at us to step back.
眼神经 yǎnshénjīng 〈生理〉ophthalmic nerve
眼生 yǎnshēng look unfamiliar:这地方变化真大，看着都～了。The place has greatly changed so it looks unfamiliar to me. /这人看着～。It seems that I've never seen the man before.
眼时 yǎnshí 〈方言〉at the present time; nowadays
眼屎 yǎnshǐ 〈方言〉gum (in the eyes)
眼熟 yǎnshú look familiar:这字儿看着～，就是想不起意思了。This word looks familiar but I can't remember its meaning.
眼跳 yǎntiào twitching of the eyelid; tic in the eyelid
眼窝 yǎnwō eye socket; eyehole
眼下 yǎnxià at present; right now:～正是试验的关键时刻，我怎么能离开呢? We are right at the crucial moment of the experiment. How can I leave now? /～什么事都让他不顺心。Now everything seems to work against him.
眼弦赤烂 yǎnxián chìlàn 〈中医〉blepharitis
眼线 yǎnxiàn ❶ eye-line:描～ paint eye-lines; line one's eyes ❷ scout, who also acts as a guide if required; informer; snitch:充当～ be a scout
眼线笔 yǎnxiànbǐ (of cosmetics) eye-liner
眼压 yǎnyā 〈生理〉intraocular tension or pressure:正常～ normal intraocular tension /～计 tonometer; electronic tonometer; ophthalmotonometer
眼炎 yǎnyán 〈医学〉ophthalmia; ophthalmitis:感光～ photophthalmia /卡他性～ catarrhal ophthalmia; mucous ophthalmia /脓性～ purulent ophthalmia; ophthalmoblennorrhea
眼药 yǎnyào medication for the eye; eyedrops; eye-ointment:～膏 eye ointment /点～ put drops in the eyes /上～ apply eye ointment to the eyes
眼药水 yǎnyàoshuǐ eyedrops
眼翳 yǎnyì 〈医学〉mist
眼影 yǎnyǐng eye shadow
眼影粉 yǎnyǐngfěn eye shadow powder; eye shadow
眼晕 yǎnyùn feel dizzy (owing to faulty vision):我觉着～，站不稳。I felt dizzy and couldn't stand firm.
眼摘除术 yǎnzhāichúshù 〈医学〉ophthalmectomy
眼罩儿 yǎnzhàor ❶ blinders (for horses); blindfold; blinkers ❷ eyeshade; eye patch ❸ shade one's eyes:他站在阳光下，打着～眺望。Standing in the sun, he looked in the distance with one hand across his forehead.
眼睁睁 yǎnzhēngzhēng (looking on) helplessly or indifferently:我们怎能～地看着这些孩子因贫困而失学呢? How can we just sit here and watch these children drop out of school because of poverty?
眼中钉 yǎnzhōngdīng thorn in one's flesh or side:他讨厌我，把我看成～。He dislikes me, looking on me as a thorn in his flesh.
眼中钉，肉中刺 yǎnzhōngdīng, ròuzhōngcì thorn in the flesh and sting in the eye; eyesore
眼中无人 yǎnzhōng-wúrén look down upon others; be arrogant or supercilious
眼珠子 yǎnzhūzi ❶ eyeball ❷ apple of one's eye
眼拙 yǎnzhuō 〈套语〉*used to indicate that the speaker forgets whether he has met the other before*:恕我～，您贵姓? Please forgive me for my poor memory. May I know your name?
眼子菜 yǎnzǐcài a kind of weeds in the paddy field

弇 yǎn 〈书面〉cover
弇陋 yǎnlòu 〈书面〉(of knowledge) meagre; shallow

Y

俨(儼) yǎn 〈书面〉❶ majestic; serious; dignified ❷ just as; like

俨然 yǎnrán 〈书面〉❶ solemn; majestic; dignified: 神色～ dignified air / 他～正容地说:"决不允许这样干!" He said solemnly: "I'll never allow anything like this." ❷ neatly arranged; in apple-pie order: 会场布置就绪,望之～。The assembly hall has been set out in neat order. ❸ just as; like: 他那神情～是位古董行家。He behaves like an expert in antiques. / 以往的许多情景～像昨天刚发生的一样。The past is still fresh in my memory as if it had just happened yesterday.

俨如 yǎnrú just like: 他俩～同胞兄弟。They are like brothers.

鼹(鼴) yǎn mole

鼹鼠 yǎnshǔ mole

衍[1] yǎn 〈书面〉❶ spread out; develop; enfold: 推～ elaborate; develop ❷ redundant; superfluous; tautological

衍[2] yǎn 〈书面〉❶ low-lying flatland: 广～沃野 vast stretch of fertile flatland ❷ marsh; swamp; bog

衍变 yǎnbiàn develop; evolve

衍传 yǎnchuán propagate

衍化 yǎnhuà evolve; develop

衍射 yǎnshè 〈物理〉diffraction: ～角 diffraction angle / ～波 defracted wave / ～线 diffracted ray

衍生 yǎnshēng ❶ derive: ～蛋白质 derived protein ❷ evolve; produce

衍生金融工具 yǎnshēng jīnróng gōngjù financial derivatives

衍生物 yǎnshēngwù 〈化学〉derivative: 纤维素～〈纺织〉cellulose derivative

衍文 yǎnwén redundancy or tautology due to misprinting or miscopying

衍续 yǎnxù flourish and continue: 让各国人民的友谊～和发展下去。Let the friendship between the people of all countries flourish and continue.

衍绎 yǎnyì 〈书面〉deduce; infer

yàn

堰 yàn weir; dam; barrage

堰坝式水电站 yànbàshì shuǐdiànzhàn barrage power station

堰塞湖 yànsèhú barrier lake

堰式罐 yànshìguàn 〈石油〉weir tank

堰式溢洪道 yànshì yìhóngdào 〈水利〉barrage-type spillway

彦 yàn 〈书面〉man of virtue and ability

彦士 yànshì man of virtue and talent

谚 yàn proverb; saying; saw: 农～ peasants' proverb; farmers' saying / 民～ common adage

谚语 yànyǔ proverb; saying; adage

喭 yàn 〈书面〉❶ rude; boorish ❷ condolence

唁 yàn extend condolences

唁电 yàndiàn telegram or cable of condolence; message of condolence

唁函 yànhán letter or message of condolence

焱 yàn 〈书面〉spark; flame

谳(讞) yàn 〈书面〉decide a law case; sentence: 定～ pronounce a sentence

艳(艷、豔) yàn ❶ bright; fresh and attractive; gorgeous: 娇～ pretty and charming / 争芳斗～ contend in beauty and fragrance / 浓妆～抹 heavily made up / 百花吐～ flowers blossom in a riot of colour / 这件衣服太～。The dress is too gaudy. ❷ amorous; romantic: ～事 love affair; romance ❸ 〈书面〉admire; envy: 新歌一曲令人～。The new song is highly popular.

艳称 yànchēng 〈书面〉praise; speak highly of; acclaim: 李白、杜甫之间的真挚友情为后世所～。The sincere friendship between Li Bai and Du Fu has won the acclaim of later generations.

艳服 yànfú gorgeous dress

艳福 yànfú (of man) lucky to win the favour of a beauty: ～不浅 lucky in love

艳歌 yàngē 〈旧语〉love song

艳红 yànhóng bright red; scarlet: ～的花朵 bright red flowers

艳丽 yànlì bright-coloured; gorgeous: ～迷人 of ravishing beauty / 色彩～ gaily coloured / 用词～ use flowery diction / 身着～服装的妇女们 gorgeously dressed women

艳绿 yànlǜ bright green

艳美 yànměi beautiful and attractive: ～的玫瑰花 charming rose

艳情 yànqíng amorous; erotic: ～小说 love novel; erotica / 书中有许多～描写。There are many descriptions of love affairs in the book.

艳如桃李 yànrútáolǐ (of a woman) as beautiful as peach and plum blossoms — very beautiful: ～,冷若冰霜 (of a woman) as beautiful as peach and plum blossoms, but as cold as frost and ice

艳色 yànsè beauty; voluptuousness: ～动人。Her voluptuousness excited men.

艳诗 yànshī love poem in a flowery style

艳史 yànshǐ love story; amorous adventures

艳羡 yànxiàn 〈书面〉admire; envy: 她～富贵人家。She regarded the rich family with great envy.

艳阳 yànyáng ❶ radiant sun: ～高照。The sun rides high in the sky. ❷ bright sunny skies; bright spring day: 好一派～景色! What lovely spring scenery!

艳阳天 yànyángtiān bright spring day; bright sunny skies

艳冶 yànyě 〈书面〉pretty and coquettish; sexy; seductive

艳装 yànzhuāng *also* "艳妆" gaily dressed

滟(灩) yàn *see* "潋滟" liànyàn

燕[1](鷰) yàn swallow: 家～ house swallow

燕[2](讌、❶醼) yàn ❶ *see* "宴❶❷" yàn ❷ *see* "宴❸" yàn

see also Yān

燕菜 yàncài food made of edible bird's nest

燕巢幕上 yàncháo-mùshàng a swallow nests on the screen — in a precarious situation; at great peril

燕尔 yàn'ěr *see* "宴尔" yàn'ěr

燕尔新婚 yàn'ěr-xīnhūn *see* "宴尔新婚" yàn'ěr-xīnhūn

燕颔虎颈 yànhàn-hǔjǐng look sturdy and powerful

燕好 yànhǎo 〈书面〉family harmony; connubial bliss: 夫妇～ conjugal harmony / 百年～ lifelong harmony

燕鸻 yànhéng 〈动物〉pratincole

燕乐 yànlè *also* "宴乐" yànlè 〈书面〉ease and comfort
see also yànyuè

燕侣 yànlǚ swallows perching in pair; couple living in harmony: ～莺俦 happily married couple

燕麦 yànmài oats: ～片 oatmeal

燕麦草 yànmàicǎo 〈植物〉oatgrass (*Arrhenatherum*)

燕鸥 yàn'ōu 〈动物〉tern

燕雀 yànquè ❶ brambling; bramble finch ❷ swallows and sparrows

燕雀安知鸿鹄之志 yànquè ān zhī hónghú zhī zhì how could a sparrow understand the ambitions of the swan — how can a common fellow read the mind of a great man

燕雀处堂 yànquè-chǔtáng swallows and sparrows nesting in the hall, unmindful of the spreading blaze — be unaware of imminent danger

燕式跳水 yànshì tiàoshuǐ swallow dive; swan dive

燕隼 yànsǔn 〈动物〉hobby

燕婉之欢 yànwǎnzhīhuān domestic harmony; conjugal felicity

燕尾服 yànwěifú swallow-tailed coat; swallowtail; tails

燕窝 yànwō edible bird's nest

燕饮 yànyǐn 〈书面〉*see* "宴饮" yànyǐn

燕鱼 yànyú 〈动物〉Spanish mackerel

燕语莺声 yànyǔ-yīngshēng *also* "燕语莺啼" scene of spring with birds chirping cheerfully — now used to describe the soft and charming voices of girls
燕乐 yànyuè *also* "宴乐" yànyuè music played at a court banquet
see also yànlè
燕子 yànzi swallow

嬿
yàn 〈书面〉lovely; charming

酽(釅)
yàn (of tea, etc.) thick; strong: ～茶 strong tea /墨磨得～～的。The ink is thick.

厌(厭)
yàn ❶ be satisfied or satiated: 学而不～ have an insatiable desire to learn /多方努力，以～民心 try all possible means to meet the wishes of the people ❷ be sick of; be bored with: 我吃～了方便面。I am fed up with instant noodles. /这部侦探小说他百读不～。He never tires of reading this detective story. ❸ be disgusted with; dislike intensely; detest: 人皆～之。Everybody hates it (*or* him). /他的谈话真令人生～。I've had enough of his talk.
厌薄 yànbó 〈书面〉detest; abhor; loathe: ～名利之争 be disgusted with the scramble for fame and gain
厌烦 yànfán be sick of; be bored with: ～的心情 boredom /对任何事都～ be tired of everything /他对那些人很～。These people are a dreadful bore to him.
厌恨 yànhèn bitterly detest; loathe; abhor: 他～那些溜须拍马的人。He had a loathing for shameless bootlickers.
厌倦 yànjuàn be weary of; be tired of: ～的眼神 weary look /～的情绪 feeling of tiredness and boredom; ennui /～频繁的交际 be sick of frequent social engagements /对单调刻板的生活感到～ be tired of a dull and monotonous life
厌腻 yànnì be fed up with; be sick of; be disgusted with: 这些作品单调乏味，使人～。These works are dull and boring.
厌弃 yànqì detest and avoid or spurn
厌气 yànqi 〈方言〉❶ be tired of; be fed up with ❷ lonely
厌食 yànshí ❶ inappentence; loss of appetite: 暑天容易～。People are prone to lose their appetite in hot weather. ❷ anorexia
厌食症 yànshízhèng anorexia (nervosa)
厌世 yànshì be sick of life; be world-weary; be pessimistic
厌恶 yànwù detest; abhor; abominate; loathe: ～虚伪 be sickened by hypocrisy /～人类者 misanthrope /～婚姻者 misogamist /我～这种寄生生活。I loathe this kind of parasitical life. /他对腐朽的旧制度充满～和憎恨。He regarded the decayed old system with disgust and hatred.
厌恶疗法 yànwù liáofǎ aversion therapy
厌氧 yànyǎng 〈微生物〉anaerobic: ～代谢 anaerobic metabolism /～菌 anaerobion; anaerobe /～细菌 anaerobic bacteria
厌氧微生物 yànyǎng wēishēngwù anaerobion; anaerobe
厌战 yànzhàn be weary of war; be war-weary: ～情绪 war-weariness
厌足 yànzú *see* "餍足" yànzú

餍(饜)
yàn 〈书面〉❶ have enough food; be satiated ❷ satisfy; gratify
餍足 yànzú 〈书面〉(of personal desire) be satisfied

雁(鴈)
yàn wild goose
雁过拔毛 yànguò-bámáo pluck feathers off a passing wild goose — catch every chance to seek personal gain; fleece people wherever possible
雁行 yànháng orderly ranks of wild geese in flight, used to refer to brothers
雁来红 yànláihóng 〈植物〉tricolour amaranth (*Amaranthus tricolour*)
雁门关 Yànménguān Yanmenguan Pass, one of the major passes of the Great Wall in Shanxi Province
雁杳鱼沉 yànyǎo-yúchén not receive any news or letters
雁序 yànxù 〈书面〉*see* "雁行"
雁阵 yànzhèn formation of wild geese in flight

赝(贗)
yàn 〈书面〉counterfeit; spurious; fake; pseudo-: ～真难辨 hard to distinguish the false from the true (*or* the fake from the authentic)
赝本 yànběn spurious edition or copy
赝币 yànbì 〈书面〉counterfeit coin or money
赝标量 yànbiāoliàng 〈物理〉pseudoscalar
赝电介质 yàndiàn jièzhì 〈物理〉pseudodielectric
赝鼎 yàndǐng 〈书面〉counterfeit tripod; art forgery in general
赝晶体 yànjīngtǐ 〈物理〉pseudocrystal
赝品 yànpǐn art forgery; fake relic
赝矢量 yànshǐliàng 〈物理〉pseudovector
赝张量 yànzhāngliàng 〈物理〉pseudotensor

宴
yàn ❶ entertain to dinner; fete: ～客 entertain guests with a feast; host a dinner in honour of visitors /欢～ gather happily at a banquet ❷ feast; banquet; spread: 设～ give a banquet; serve (*or* hold) a banquet /赴～ attend a banquet /盛～ grand banquet; sumptuous dinner; magnificent spread /国～ state banquet /午～ midday banquet; luncheon ❸ ease and comfort
宴安 yàn'ān ease and comfort: 以～为戒。One shouldn't indulge oneself in physical (*or* sensual) pleasures.
宴安鸩毒 yàn'ān-zhèndú seeking sensual pleasure is like drinking poisoned wine
宴尔 yàn'ěr *also* "燕尔" yàn'ěr 〈书面〉❶ peace and comfort ❷ newly-married: ～之乐 marital happiness
宴尔新婚 yàn'ěr-xīnhūn *also* "燕尔新婚" yàn'ěr-xīnhūn newly married
宴会 yànhuì banquet; feast; dinner party: 举行～ hold (*or* throw) a banquet /答谢～ reciprocal banquet /告别～ farewell banquet
宴会厅 yànhuìtīng banquet hall
宴集 yànjí have a big dinner together: 上月他约数位朋友～了一次。Last month he invited several friends to dinner.
宴客 yànkè entertain guests at a banquet; host a dinner in honour of the guests
宴乐 yànlè *also* "燕乐" yànlè 〈书面〉ease and comfort; pleasure
see also yànyuè
宴请 yànqǐng entertain at a banquet; fete: ～宾客 entertain guests (with dinner); give a banquet in honour of guests
宴席 yànxí banquet; feast: 丰盛的～ sumptuous banquet /～上山珍海味俱全。Delicacies of every kind were served at the feast.
宴饮 yànyǐn enjoy drinking together at a banquet; wine and dine
宴乐 yànyuè *also* "燕乐" yànyuè music played at a court banquet
see also yànlè

晏
yàn ❶ behind time; late: ～起 get up late ❷ ease and comfort ❸ (Yàn) a surname
晏驾 yànjià 〈旧语〉(of an emperor) pass away
晏子春秋 Yànzǐ Chūnqiū *Yanzi's Spring and Autumn Annals*, supposed to be written by Yan Ying (晏婴 ?-500 BC), minister of the State of Qi during the Spring and Autumn Period

鷃(鴳)
yàn
鷃雀 yànquè 〈古语〉〈动物〉quail

咽(嚥)
yàn swallow; devour: 一口～下去 swallow sth. at one gulp /狼吞虎～ wolf down one's food; devour ravenously /～不下这口气 unable to swallow (*or* stomach, *or* take) an insult /他连嚼也不嚼，就往下吞～。He swallowed it whole (*or* without chewing). /见有人来，他赶紧把话～了回去。He quickly checked himself when he heard someone coming.
see also yān; yè
咽气 yànqì breathe one's last; die

砚
yàn ❶ inkstone; inkslab ❷ 〈旧语〉fellow student; classmate: 同～ fellow student; classmate
砚池 yànchí inkstone; inkslab
砚滴 yàndī *also* "水注" shuǐzhù small receptacle for holding water for use on an inkslab
砚弟 yàndì 〈旧语〉junior fellow student
砚耕 yàngēng make a living by writing
砚石 yànshí ❶ stone suitable for making an inkslab ❷ inkstone;

inkslab
砚台 yàntai inkstone; inkslab
砚田 yàntián 〈旧语〉inkstone; inkslab
砚兄 yànxiōng 〈旧语〉senior fellow student
砚友 yànyǒu 〈旧语〉fellow student; classmate

研 yàn *see*“砚”yàn
see also yán

焰(燄) yàn flame; blaze:熊熊烈～ blazing (*or* raging) flames
焰火 yànhuǒ *also*“烟火”yānhuo fireworks:放～ display fireworks; let off fireworks
焰口 yànkou 〈佛教〉hungry ghosts who spit fire:放～ (at a Buddhist service) feed hungry ghosts
焰色反应 yànsè fǎnyìng flame reaction
焰色试验 yànsè shìyàn 〈化学〉flame (colour) test
焰心 yànxīn flame core

墕 yàn ❶〈方言〉land between two mountains ❷ weir; dam; barrage

验(驗、騐) yàn ❶ examine; check; verify; test:～单据 check receipts and invoices /～尿 test the urine /～护照 examine (*or* check) a passport /试～ experiment ❷ prove effective; produce the expected result:灵～ effective /应～ (of prediction) come true /屡试屡～ prove effective in every test ❸ intended effect; desired result
验潮器 yàncháoqì 〈气象〉tide gauge
验电器 yàndiànqì electroscope
验方 yànfāng 〈中医〉proved recipe; ready prescription
验关 yànguān customs examination or inspection
验光 yànguāng optometry:～技师 optometrist
验核 yànhé examine; check; inspect
验看 yànkàn examine; check:～指纹 examine the fingerprint /～护照 check a passport
验明正身 yànmíng-zhèngshēn make a positive identification of a criminal before execution; identify the criminal
验讫 yànqì checked; examined
验枪 yànqiāng 〈军事〉inspect arms
验墒 yànshāng 〈农业〉examine and determine the moisture of the soil
验尸 yànshī 〈法律〉postmortem; autopsy
验尸官 yànshīguān coroner:～证书 coroner's certificate (of a death)
验尸所 yànshīsuǒ mortuary
验湿器 yànshīqì hygroscope
验收 yànshōu accept sth. as up to standard after a check; check and accept:工程正在～。The completed project is being checked upon delivery. /这座新宿舍大楼尚未～。The newly-built apartment building hasn't been checked and accepted yet.
验收单 yànshōudān receipt (issued upon acceptance of goods)
验收合格证 yànshōu hégézhèng acceptance certificate
验收试验 yànshōu shìyàn acceptance test
验算 yànsuàn 〈数学〉check computations:～公式 check formula
验血 yànxiě blood test
验证 yànzhèng test and verify:这条原理已得到科学的～。This principle has been scientifically verified.
验证载荷 yànzhèng zàihè 〈航空〉proof load

yāng

央[1] yāng entreat; beg; earnestly ask:～人说情 ask sb. to put in a good word for one /我～了他许久，他才答应给我一幅画儿。He didn't agree to give me a painting until I'd begged him for some time.

央[2] yāng centre:中～ centre; in the middle

央[3] yāng 〈书面〉end; finish:国家安宁乐无～。Peace in the country brings infinite happiness. /夜未～而客至。The night was not yet spent when the guests arrived.
央告 yānggao beg; implore:我～爸爸饶恕我。I implored dad to forgive me.
央及 yāngji *see*“央求”
央恳 yāngken beg; plead; entreat; implore:我～她给我们当顾问。I begged her to be our adviser.
央浼 yāngměi (mainly used in the early vernacular) request; entrust
央戗 yāngqiang 〈方言〉manage or maintain with difficulty:他的病也不过～一天是一天罢了。His condition was so critical that the best he could hope for was to survive a few more days.
央求 yāngqiú beg; entreat; implore:苦苦～ entreat (*or* beg) piteously /～宽恕 beg for forgiveness /我苦苦～，他都无动于衷。I desperately pleaded with him but he remained indifferent.
央托 yāngtuō request; entrust; ask:我～李先生帮我找点资料。I've asked Mr. Li to get some data for me.
央中 yāngzhōng (document language used in old times) request sb. to be a middleman

泱 yāng
泱泱 yāngyāng 〈书面〉❶ (of waters) vast:湖水～ vast lake; vast expanse of water in the lake ❷ great; magnificent:～大国 great country

鞅 yāng leather harness used in ancient times
see also yàng
鞅掌 yāngzhǎng 〈书面〉be busy with business:国事～ be fully occupied with state affairs

殃 yāng ❶ scourge; disaster; calamity; misfortune:祸～ calamity; disaster /遭～ meet with (*or* suffer) disaster ❷ bring disaster to; spell calamity for:祸国～民 bring calamity to the country and the people
殃榜 yāngbǎng 〈旧语〉obituary notice of the dead's name, age, the return of his spirit, etc., written on white paper and put up beside the front door
殃及 yāngjí bring calamity to; (of a calamity, etc.) affect; involve:～无辜 involve innocent people /这次大火，～许多住户。Many households were affected by the fire.
殃及池鱼 yāngjí-chíyú misfortune befalls the fish in the moat:城门失火，～ when the city gate catches fire, the fish in the moat are made victims — innocent people nearby get hurt when there is trouble

秧 yāng ❶ seedling; sprout:白菜～儿 cabbage sprout /树～儿 tree seedling ❷ rice seedling:插～ transplant rice seedlings /育～ raise rice seedlings /～畦 rice seedling bed ❸ vine; stem:豆～ bean vines /瓜～ melon vines ❹ (of some domestic animals) young; fry:鱼～ young fish; fry ❺〈方言〉cultivate; raise:～瓜 grow melons /～了一池鱼 raise a pond of fish
秧歌 yāngge *yangge* (dance), a popular rural folk dance:扭～ do the *yangge* dance
秧歌剧 yānggejù *yangge* opera
秧鸡 yāngjī water rail
秧脚 yāngjiǎo root of rice seedling
秧龄 yānglíng growing period of seedlings in seedling beds
秧苗 yāngmiáo rice shoot; rice seedling:～长得十分茁壮。The rice seedlings have grown very sturdy.
秧田 yāngtián rice seedling bed
秧子 yāngzi ❶ *see*“秧❶”:树～ tree seedling ❷ *see*“秧❸”:花生～ peanut vine ❸ *see*“秧❹”:猪～ piglet ❹〈方言〉〈贬义〉type or sort of person:病～ sickman; valetudinarian /奴才～ flunkey; lackey

鸯 yāng *see*“鸳鸯”yuānyang

yáng

羊 yáng ❶ sheep; goat:绵～ sheep /山～ goat /羚～ antelope /黄～ Mongolian gazelle /公～ ram /母～ ewe /小～ lamb /种～

Y

stud ram /奶～ milch goat /头～ bellwether /养一群～ keep a flock of sheep /～叫 baa; bleat /放～ graze sheep /牧～犬 sheep dog ❷ (Yáng) a surname
羊草 yángcǎo *also* "碱草" jiǎncǎo *Aneurolepidium chinense*
羊肠 yángcháng sheep's intestine or gut
羊肠线 yángchángxiàn 〈医学〉catgut (suture)
羊肠小道 yángcháng-xiǎodào narrow winding trail; meandering footpath: 通往后山的一条～ narrow footpath leading to the hills behind (a village, etc.) /我们沿着崎岖的～爬上山顶。We climbed up the hilltop along the rugged winding trail.
羊齿 yángchǐ 〈植物〉fern; bracken
羊痘 yángdòu 〈畜牧〉sheep pox
羊肚儿手巾 yángdǔr shǒujin 〈方言〉towel
羊肚蕈 yángdǔxùn 〈植物〉morel
羊羔 yánggāo ❶ lamb ❷ famous wine brewed in ancient Fenzhou (in today's Shanxi Province)
羊羹 yánggēng a kind of pastry made of red bean powder, agar and sugar
羊工 yánggōng sheepman; shepherd
羊倌 yángguān shepherd
羊毫 yángháo writing brush made of goat's hair
羊狠狼贪 yánghěn-lángtān as bellicose as a goat and as greedy as a wolf — ruthless exploitation by corrupt officials: 这群人～，没有一点人性。Ruthlessly greedy and totally corrupt, this pack of people are just inhuman.
羊胡子草 yánghúzicǎo cotton grass
羊角 yángjiǎo ❶〈书面〉whirlwind (shaped like a ram's horn); tornado; cyclone: 鲲鹏展翅，九万里，翻动扶摇～。The roc wings fanwise, Soaring ninety thousand *li* And rousing a raging cyclone. ❷ ram's horn
羊角锤 yángjiǎochuí claw hammer
羊角风 yángjiǎofēng (popular term for 癫痫) epilepsy
羊脚碾 yángjiǎoniǎn 〈建筑〉sheepfoot roller
羊疥 yángjiè sheep mange
羊圈 yángjuàn sheepfold; sheep pen; sheepcot
羊栏 yánglán sheepfold
羊痢疾 yánglìji sheep dysentery
羊落虎口 yángluòhǔkǒu lamb falls into a tiger's mouth — certain death or ruin: 此一去有如～，有死无生。There is no hope of his return alive, just like a lamb falling into a tiger's mouth.
羊毛 yángmáo sheep's wool; fleece: 纯～的 of pure wool /纯～标志 pure woolmark /剪～ shear a sheep /～剪 clippers /～开衫 cardigan /～毯 woollen blanket /～商 wool stapler; wool merchant; woolman
羊毛出在羊身上 yángmáo chū zài yáng shēnshang after all, the wool still comes from the sheep's back; you pay for what you get; there is no such thing as a free lunch: 商店里大搞有奖销售之类的花样，都是～的事儿。There's no free lunch. "Win a prize" is just one of many tricks played by storekeepers to promote sales.
羊毛衫 yángmáoshān woollen sweater
羊毛袜 yángmáowà woollen socks; woollen stockings
羊毛脂 yángmáozhī wool oil; wool fat; lanolin
羊茅 yángmáo 〈植物〉(sheep) fescue
羊膜 yángmó 〈生理〉amnion: ～穿刺术 amniocentesis /～炎 amnionitis
羊排 yángpái mutton chop; lamb chop
羊皮 yángpí sheepskin: ～袄 sheepskin jacket /～手套 sheepskin glove /～筏子 sheepskin raft /披着～的狼 wolf in sheep's clothing
羊皮纸 yángpízhǐ parchment
羊栖菜 yángqīcài ❶ *also* "发菜" fàcài flagelliform nostoc (*Nostoc eommune*) ❷ a kind of seaweed
羊群里头出骆驼 yángqún lǐtou chū luòtuo stand out like a camel in a flock of sheep; Triton among the minnows: 真是～，想不到咱山沟沟儿里也出了个研究生。It's nothing short of a miracle that this small mountain village boasts a graduate student.
羊绒 yángróng cashmere
羊绒衫 yángróngshān cashmere sweater
羊肉 yángròu mutton: 涮～ boiled mutton in a Mongolian hotpot /烤～ roast lamb (*or* mutton)
羊肉不曾吃，空惹一身膻 yángròu bùcéng chī, kōng rě yīshēn shān miss the mutton and just get its odour; bring trouble upon oneself without any compensating reward; go for wool and come back shorn: 同他合伙做生意，到头来定是～，你这又何苦！Why hook up with him? He will bring you nothing but trouble.
羊肉串 yángròuchuàn mutton cubes roasted on a skewer; shashlik; shish kebab
羊入狼群 yángrùlángqún sheep in a pack of wolves — in a perilous situation; utterly helpless: 这个弱女子落到他们手中，无异于～。The poor girl will be like a sheep in a pack of wolves if she falls into their hands.
羊水 yángshuǐ 〈生理〉aminiotic fluid: ～过多 polyhydramnios; hydramnios /～过少 oligohydramnios
羊桃 yángtáo 〈植物〉carambola
羊驼 yángtuó 〈动物〉alpaca (*Lama alpacos*)
羊驼毛 yángtuómáo alpaca wool
羊莴苣 yángwōjù corn salad; lamb's lettuce (*Valerianella olitoria*)
羊痫风 yángxiánfēng epilepsy
羊眼 yángyǎn screw eye
羊靥 yángyè 〈中药〉goat's or sheep's thyroid gland used to cure goitre
羊脂 yángzhī suet: ～玉 white jade
羊踯躅 yángzhízhú 〈植物〉Chinese azalea
羊质虎皮 yángzhì-hǔpí sheep in a tiger's skin — outwardly strong but inwardly weak: ～的新老军阀 old and new warlords who look strong but are actually weak

洋

yáng ❶ vast; abundant: 汪～大海 boundless sea ❷ ocean: 太平～ Pacific Ocean /漂～过海 sail across the ocean ❸ foreign; imported: ～腔怪调 exotic accent; outlandish way of talking /出～ go abroad /留～ study abroad /～文 foreign language ❹ modern: ～办法 modern methods /土～结合 combine the old-fashioned and the modern ❺〈旧语〉silver dollar: 大～ silver dollar /小～ silver coin /罚～一百元 fine 100 silver dollars
洋八股 yángbāgǔ foreign stereotyped writing; foreign stereotypes
洋白菜 yángbáicài (popular term for 结球甘蓝) cabbage
洋博士 yángbóshì foreign-trained Ph. D.; doctor educated abroad
洋布 yángbù 〈旧语〉plain cloth woven by machine
洋财 yángcái big fortune; windfall: 他两年前去的澳大利亚，听说发了～。He went to Australia two years ago and is said to have made a big fortune.
洋菜 yángcài agar
洋插队 yángchāduì (borrowed from the term referring to young Chinese students sent to the countryside during the Cultural Revolution of 1966-1976) work or study in a foreign country under straitened circumstances: 他大学没毕业，就凭着海外关系"～"去了。With the help of overseas relatives, he left China for further studies abroad before graduating from college.
洋场 yángchǎng metropolis infested with foreign adventurers (usu. referring to pre-liberation Shanghai in a derogatory sense): ～恶少 rich urban young bully /十里～ (nickname for old Shanghai) paradise for foreign adventurers
洋车 yángchē 〈口语〉rickshaw: 拉～的 rickshaw boy
洋瓷 yángcí enamel: ～碗儿 enamel bowl
洋葱 yángcōng *also* "葱头" cōngtóu onion: ～头 onion bulb
洋地黄 yángdìhuáng digitalis: ～苷〈药学〉digitalin /～中毒 digitalism
洋缎 yángduàn satin-like cloth, mainly used for trimming the brim of a hat or used as the lining of a garment
洋房 yángfáng Western-style house
洋粉 yángfěn see "洋菜"
洋服 yángfú Western-style clothes; occidental dress
洋橄榄 yánggǎnlǎn 〈植物〉*also* "橄榄"; "油橄榄" yóugǎnlǎn olive
洋镐 yánggǎo pickax
洋狗 yánggǒu dog of foreign breed
洋鬼子 yángguǐzi 〈旧语〉foreign devil (derogatory term for foreigners regarded as aggressors and oppressors)
洋行 yángháng 〈旧语〉foreign company (in pre-liberation China)
洋红 yánghóng ❶ pink pigment ❷ darkish pink; carmine
洋红霉素 yánghóngméisù 〈医学〉carminomycin
洋槐 yánghuái *also* "刺槐" cìhuái locust (tree)
洋灰 yánghuī (popular term for 水泥) cement
洋火 yánghuǒ (popular term for 火柴) matches
洋货 yánghuò imported goods

洋脊 yángjǐ oceanic ridge:～地震带 oceanic ridge seismic belt
洋蓟 yángjì (French) artichoke; globe artichoke (*Cynara Scolymus*)
洋碱 yángjiǎn 〈方言〉soap
洋姜 yángjiāng Jerusalem artichoke; artichoke
洋金花 yángjīnhuā 〈中药〉datura flower (*Datura metel*)
洋泾浜 yángjīngbāng pidgin (English)
洋井 yángjǐng 〈旧语〉motor-pumped well; tube well
洋框框 yángkuàngkuang restrictive foreign conventions:打破～ break with foreign conventions
洋里洋气 yánglìyángqì 〈贬义〉in a flashy foreign style:一身～的打扮 exotically dressed; in foreign-style clothes
洋流 yángliú 〈地质〉ocean current
洋楼 yánglóu Western-style building of two stories or more
洋码子 yángmǎzi 〈方言〉Arabic numerals
洋妞 yángniū young non-Chinese woman or girl
洋奴 yángnú 〈比喻〉slave of a foreign master; flunkey of imperialism; worshipper of everything foreign:～买办 lackeys and compradors at the beck and call of foreign bosses /～思想 slavish mentality towards foreigners and foreign things /～哲学 slavish comprador philosophy; fetish of everything foreign
洋盘 yángpán 〈方言〉inexperienced and easily deceived person in a metropolis; sucker
洋盆 yángpén *also* "海盆" hǎipén 〈地质〉ocean basin
洋气 yángqi ❶ foreign flavour; Western style ❷ foreign; outlandish; stylish:这身衣服挺～。This suit looks quite stylish.
洋钱 yángqián silver dollar
洋琴 yángqín dulcimer
洋枪队 Yángqiāngduì Foreign Musketeers, organized by the Qing government in collusion with US, British and French aggressors to suppress the Taiping Rebellion in the middle of the 19th century
洋取灯儿 yángqǔdēngr 〈方言〉matches
洋人 yángrén foreigner (usu. Westerner)
洋伞 yángsǎn umbrella
洋嗓子 yángsǎngzi voice trained in the Western style of singing
洋纱 yángshā 〈旧语〉❶ cotton yarn woven by machine ❷ a kind of thin, plain cloth used for making handkerchiefs, mosquito nets and summer clothes
洋柿子 yángshìzi 〈方言〉tomato
洋苏木 yángsūmù logwood (*Haematoxylon campechianum*)
洋钿 yángtián 〈方言〉silver dollar
洋铁 yángtiě 〈旧语〉tinplate
洋铁皮 yángtiěpí tinplate; galvanized iron; tin
洋娃娃 yángwáwa doll
洋为中用 yángwéi-zhōngyòng make foreign things serve China; adapt foreign things to Chinese use:吸收外国先进的技术,做到～。Absorb advanced technology from abroad to make foreign things serve China.
洋文 yángwén foreign (usu. Western) language
洋务 yángwù ❶ management of foreign affairs in the late Qing Dynasty ❷ foreign-oriented service industry in Hong Kong
洋务运动 Yángwù Yùndòng Westernization Movement (initiated mainly by Qing bureaucrats in the latter half of the 19th century to introduce techniques of capitalist production for the purpose of propping up the tottering Qing government)
洋相 yángxiàng *usu. used in the set phrase* 出洋相:他想出我的～。He wanted to make a spectacle of me. /你今天大出～。You cut a sorry figure today.
洋绣球 yángxiùqiú *also* "天竺葵" tiānzhúkuí fish pelargonium (*Pelargonium hortorum*)
洋烟 yángyān imported cigarettes
洋洋 yángyáng ❶ abundant; copious:～万言 run to ten thousand words; be very lengthy ❷ *also* "扬扬" yángyáng complacent; self-satisfied
洋洋大观 yángyáng-dàguān of great variety and richness; spectacular; magnificent:从一条简单的新闻演绎成一篇～的文章 make an impressive article out of a brief news item
洋洋得意 yángyáng-déyì proud and happy; as pleased or proud as Punch:领导夸奖了他几句,他便～起来。A little praise from the boss made him as proud as a peacock.
洋洋洒洒 yángyáng-sǎsǎ ❶ (of an article or a talk) fluent; voluminous; of great length:～地写了好几页 write on and on for quite a few pages ❷ great or grand in scale or momentum:大湖如镜,岛上红绿掩映,～,如入画中。Surrounded by the shimmering lake, the island with its red houses contrasting with the green vegetation presents a view of picturesque grandeur.
洋洋自得 yángyáng-zìdé be self-satisfied; be complacent:有一点成绩就～ feel conceited at the slightest achievement
洋溢 yángyì be full of; brim with:豪情～ full of lofty sentiments /热情～的讲话 speech brimming with warm feeling /到处～着欢乐的气氛。It was permeated with a joyous atmosphere everywhere. /她眼里～着欣喜的神采。Her eyes glistened with delight.
洋油 yángyóu ❶〈方言〉kerosene ❷ imported crude oil or oil product
洋芋 yángyù 〈方言〉potato
洋装 yángzhuāng ❶ Western-style clothes ❷ Western way of bookbinding:～书 book bound in the Western way

烊

yáng 〈方言〉melt; dissolve:冰棍～了。The popsicle is melting. /这种巧克力拿在手里勿～。This chocolate doesn't go soft in the hand.
see also yàng

垟

yáng 〈方言〉(mainly used in names of places) field:黄～ Huangyang (a place in Zhejiang Province)

蛘

yáng 〈方言〉insects such as the rice weevil

佯

yáng pretend; feign; fake; sham:～死 play dead; feign death; play possum /～羞 pretend to be shy
佯嗔 yángchēn pretend to be angry or displeased:～薄怒 put on a displeased look
佯称 yángchēng claim or allege falsely; lie; feign:～有病 claim falsely that one is ill; pretend to be ill; feign illness
佯动 yángdòng 〈军事〉feint; false move
佯攻 yánggōng 〈军事〉feign or simulate an attack; make a feint:一连主攻,二连～。Company I will attack with Company II making a feint.
佯狂 yángkuáng *also* "阳狂" yángkuáng 〈书面〉pretend to be mad:～以逃避审判 feign madness to avoid a trial
佯言 yángyán 〈书面〉claim falsely; prevaricate; lie:～粮断以迷惑敌人 feign food shortages to deceive the enemy
佯装 yángzhuāng pretend; feign; sham:～不知 pretend not to know; feign ignorance

徉

yáng *see* "徜徉" chángyáng

阳(陽)

yáng ❶ (in Chinese philosophy, medicine, etc.) *yang*, the masculine or positive principle in nature:阴盛～衰 too much *yin* and too little *yang*; more women than men (in a group) ❷ sun:灿烂的朝～ bright rising sun /殷红的夕～ red setting sun /向～的屋子 room with a sunny exposure ❸ south of a hill or north of a river:衡～ Hengyang (city situated on the south side of Hengshan Mountain) /洛～ Luoyang (city situated on the north side of the Luohe River) ❹ in relief; convex: *see* "～文" ❺ open; overt; outward:～为镇静,实则胆怯 outwardly calm but inwardly timid ❻ of this world; of this life; concerned with living beings:还～ come to life again ❼〈物理〉positive:～电荷 positive charges ❽ male genitals ❾ (Yáng) a surname
阳春 yángchūn spring (season):～三月 third lunar month in (late) spring /十月小～。The lunar 10th month may be as warm and lovely as spring.
阳春白雪 yángchūn-báixuě ❶ Spring Snow (a melody of the élite in the State of Chu) ❷ highbrow art and literature:"～"与"下里巴人"的统一 strike a balance between "Spring Snow" and "the Song of the Rustic Poor", i. e. between higher standards and popularization /～,曲高和寡。A highbrow tune is never popular. *or* Highbrow art and literature are caviar to the general.
阳春面 yángchūnmiàn 〈方言〉noodles in plain sauce
阳地植物 yángdì zhíwù sun plant
阳电 yángdiàn positive electricity
阳电子 yángdiànzǐ positive electron; positron
阳奉阴违 yángfèng-yīnwéi agree in public but oppose in private;

Y

feign compliance：人们憎恨他～的作法。People detest his double-faced tactics.
阳刚 yánggāng masculine qualities; masculinity; virility：～之美 beauty of masculine vigour or manly virility /字体充满了～之气。The calligraphy is full of manliness and virility.
阳沟 yánggōu open drain; ditch
阳关道 yángguāndào *also* "阳关大道" broad road; thoroughfare：走上了繁荣富强的～ embark on the road to prosperity /你走你的～，我过我的独木桥。You take the wide and easy road; I'll cross the narrow log bridge. *or* You go your way; I'll go mine.
阳光 yángguāng sunlight; sunshine：明媚的～ bright sunshine /灿烂的～ brilliant sunshine /金色的～ golden sunlight /耀眼的～ glaring sunlight /一线～ ray of sunshine /沐浴着～ bathe in the sun; sunbathe /反射～ flash back (*or* reflect) the sunlight /遮挡～ keep off the sun /在～下闪烁 glitter in the sun /这间屋子终日不见～。The room never gets any sun at all.
阳和 yánghé 〈书面〉warm：春日～。It's a warm spring.
阳极 yángjí ❶〈电学〉positive pole ❷〈电子〉positive electrode; anode：～保护〈冶金〉anodic protection /～炉 anode furnace /～氧化 anode oxidation /～镀层〈化工〉anode coating
阳极板 yángjíbǎn 〈电工〉positive plate
阳极栅 yángjíshān 〈电工〉anode grid
阳极射线 yángjí shèxiàn 〈电子〉positive ray
阳间 yángjiān in this (human) world
阳狂 yángkuáng *also* "佯狂" yángkuáng pretend to be mad
阳离子 yánglízǐ 〈物理〉cation; positive ion：～层 cationic layer /～交换〈化学〉cation exchange /～交换树脂 cation exchange resin
阳离子表面活性剂 yánglízǐ biǎomiàn huóxìngjì cationic surfactant
阳离子电泳 yánglízǐ diànyǒng cataphoresis
阳历 yánglì ❶ *also* "太阳历" tàiyánglì solar calendric system; solar calendar ❷ Gregorian calendar
阳面 yángmiàn south or sunny side of a building：楼房～的房间冬天很暖和。Rooms on the sunny side of a building are warm in winter.
阳明山 Yángmíngshān Mount Yangming, well-known hill in Taiwan, China
阳谋 yángmóu do openly, not engaging in conspiracy
阳模 yángmú 〈冶金〉force plug; force piston; force plunger
阳平 yángpíng 〈语言〉rising tone, second of the four tones in modern standard Chinese pronunciation
阳坡 yángpō hillside exposed to the sun
阳婆 yángpó 〈方言〉sun
阳畦 yángqí 〈农业〉seed bed with windbreaks; cold bed; cold-frame
阳起石 yángqǐshí 〈矿业〉actinolite
阳伞 yángsǎn parasol; sunshade
阳世 yángshì human world; this world
阳寿 yángshòu lifespan; life
阳燧 yángsuì brass mirror-like implement used to get fire from the sun in ancient times
阳台 yángtái balcony; sun porch
阳痿 yángwěi 〈医学〉erectile disfunction (ED); sexual impotence
阳文 yángwén character cut in relief：～图章 seal in relief; relief seal
阳性 yángxìng ❶〈医学〉positive：～反应 positive reaction /化验呈～。The test was positive. *or* He tested positive (for sth.). ❷〈语言〉masculine gender
阳性植物 yángxìng zhíwù sun-loving plant; heliophilous plant
阳虚 yángxū 〈中医〉deficiency of *yang*; lack of vital energy
阳一套，阴一套 yáng yī tào, yīn yī tào *see* "阴一套，阳一套"
阳韵 yángyùn 〈语言〉words with m, n, ng as the terminal sounds
阳宅 yángzhái residence; dwelling

疡(瘍) yáng ❶〈书面〉sore ❷ ulcer：胃溃～ ulcer in the stomach

炀(煬) yáng 〈书面〉❶ melt (metal) ❷ roaring fire

玚(瑒) yáng 〈古语〉a kind of jade
see also chàng

杨(楊) yáng ❶ poplar ❷ (Yáng) a surname

杨广 Yáng Guǎng Yang Guang(569-618), last emperor of the Sui Dynasty
杨贵妃 Yáng Guìfēi *also* "杨玉环" Yáng Yùhuán Yang Guifei (719-755), favourite concubine of Emperor Xuanzong of the Tang Dynasty, famous for her beauty
杨辉三角 Yáng Huī sānjiǎo *also* "贾宪三角" Jiǎ Xiàn sānjiǎo Yang Hui's triangle — binomial array (known in the West as Pascal's triangle)
杨柳 yángliǔ ❶ poplar and willow ❷ willow
杨梅 yángméi 〈植物〉❶ red bayberry (*Myrica rubra*) ❷ fruit of red bayberry ❸〈方言〉strawberry ❹〈方言〉syphilis
杨梅疮 yángméichuāng 〈方言〉syphilis
杨树 yángshù poplar：亭亭玉立的～ tall and erect poplar
杨桃 yángtáo 〈植物〉*also* "羊桃" yángtáo parambola
杨万里 Yáng Wànlǐ Yang Wanli (1127-1206), poet of the Southern Song Dynasty
杨无咎 Yáng Wújiù Yang Wujiu (formerly translated as Yang Wu-chiu) (1097-1169), painter of the Southern Song Dynasty
杨幺 Yáng Yāo Yang Yao (?-1135), leader of a peasant uprising in the early Southern Song Dynasty
杨振宁 Yáng Zhènníng Yang Chen Ning *or* Frank C. N. Yang (1922-), Chinese-American physicist and Nobel Prize winner of 1957
杨枝鱼 yángzhīyú pipefish

扬[1](揚、敭) yáng ❶ raise; hoist：～起风帆 hoist a sail; lift a sail /尘土飞～ raise a cloud of dust /趾高气～ self-complacent and arrogant /他～着小旗，疏散车辆。He waved the flag to disperse the traffic. ❷ throw up and scatter; winnow：～谷 winnow the chaff from the grain ❸ spread; publicize; make known：宣～ propagate; publicize /发～ develop; carry on (*or* forward) /名～世界 be known throughout the world; be of world renown /隐恶～善 cover up sb.'s faults and make known his merits ❹ good-looking; be of distinguished appearance：其貌不～ look quite plain; be unprepossessing in appearance; have undistinguished features

扬[2](揚) Yáng ❶ Yangzhou (city) in Jiangsu Province ❷ a surname

扬波 yángbō swelling of waves：海水～ rolling up of waves in the sea; raging sea waves
扬长 yángcháng swaggeringly; in a stalking manner：～离开 leave with a swagger; stalk away
扬长避短 yángcháng-bìduǎn avoid one's weaknesses while exploiting one's strengths; make the best use of advantages and fight shy of disadvantages：知人善任，～ be good at judging people and know how to use their strengths while avoiding their weaknesses
扬长补短 yángcháng-bǔduǎn foster strengths to make up for weaknesses：大家要团结一致，～，共同提高。We should unite as one so as to achieve common progress by exploiting our advantages to make up for our disadvantages.
扬长而去 yángcháng'érqù swagger off; stalk off; stride off：他带了几个人来把店里洗劫一空后～。He took several men to the shop, looted it and swaggered off.
扬场 yángcháng 〈农业〉winnowing
扬场机 yángchángjī winnowing machine; winnower
扬程 yángchéng (of a pump) lift：低～水泵 low-lift pump /高～抽水站 high-lift pumping station
扬帆 yángfān 〈书面〉hoist the sails; set sail：～远航 set sail for a long voyage
扬幡招魂 yángfān-zhāohún fly a funeral streamer to summon the spirit of the dead — now used figuratively to refer to attempts at reviving what is obsolete or dead：这篇文章是为封建思想～的。This article attempts at resurrecting feudal ideas.
扬风 yángfēng ❶ blow：～飘雪 blowing and snowing ❷〈方言〉spread news：外面都～说你要提升了。The news was going around that you were about to get a promotion.
扬花 yánghuā 〈农业〉flowering (of cereal crops)
扬基债券 yángjī zhàiquàn 〈金融〉Yankee bond
扬剧 yángjù local opera popular in Yangzhou, Jiangsu Province
扬厉 yánglì 〈书面〉carry forward; develop：铺张～ extremely extravagant /好传统要加以～。Good traditions should be carried for-

ward.

扬眉吐气 yángméi-tǔqì hold one's head high; feel happy and proud:新中国建立后,中国人民才得以～。With the founding of the People's Republic of China, the Chinese people began to hold their heads high.

扬名 yángmíng make a name for oneself; win renown:～天下 become famous throughout the land; become world-famous /～于世 achieve a high reputation in the world

扬旗 yángqí 〈铁路〉semaphore

扬弃 yángqì ❶〈哲学〉sublate; develop what is useful and discard what is not ❷ abandon; discard:文化遗产中的封建糟粕必须～。The feudal trash in our cultural heritage must be discarded.

扬气 yángqi 〈方言〉arrogant; haughty:别有了几个钱就～。Don't get high-and-mighty because you've a fat purse.

扬琴 yángqín dulcimer

扬清激浊 yángqīng-jīzhuó *also* "激浊扬清" bring in fresh water and drain away the mud — eradicate evil and usher in good

扬榷 yángquè 〈书面〉discuss briefly:～古今 succinct review of modern and ancient events

扬声 yángshēng ❶ raise the voice:～争论 argue loudly ❷ make known; disclose:他这人很可靠,不会把这事往外～的。He is reliable and won't breathe a word of it. ❸ *see* "扬名"

扬声器 yángshēngqì loudspeaker:低频～ woofer /高频～ tweeter

扬手 yángshǒu wave one's hand:～告别 wave goodbye

扬水 yángshuǐ pump up water:～浇地 pump up water to irrigate land

扬水泵 yángshuǐbèng lift pump

扬水站 yángshuǐzhàn pumping station

扬汤止沸 yángtāng-zhǐfèi try to stop water from boiling by scooping it up and pouring it back — halfway solution; ineffective measure; palliative:与其～,不如釜底抽薪。The best way to stop water from boiling is to withdraw the burning firewood. *or* Take away fuel, take away flame.

扬威 yángwēi make a show of one's might:耀武～ bluff and bluster /～海外 show one's might overseas

扬言 yángyán prate; boast; threaten (to take action):～要进行报复 threaten to retaliate /～冠军非他莫属。He boasted that no one except him would be the champion.

扬扬 yángyáng *also* "洋洋" yángyáng with great self-satisfaction; complacently; triumphantly:身居高位,意气～ feel complacent because of one's high office

扬扬得意 yángyáng-déyì *also* "洋洋得意" yángyáng-déyì look immensely complacent

扬扬自得 yángyáng-zìdé *also* "洋洋自得" yángyáng-zìdé be pleased with oneself; feel smug; be complacent

扬州 Yángzhōu city in Jiangsu Province, north of the Yangtze

扬州八怪 Yángzhōu Bāguài Eight Eccentrics of Yangzhou, so called because they broke with traditions of Chinese painting and blazed new, unconventional trails in integrating painting with poetry and calligraphy, the eight being Wang Shishen (汪士慎), Huang Shen (黄慎), Jin Nong (金农), Gao Xiang (高翔), Li Shan (李鱓), Zheng Xie (郑燮), Li Fangying (李方膺) and Luo Pin (罗聘), all living and working in Yangzhou during the reign of Emperor Qianlong of the Qing Dynasty

扬子鳄 yángzǐ'è 〈动物〉Chinese alligator

旸(暘) yáng 〈书面〉❶ sunrise ❷ fine; sunny

旸谷 yánggǔ 〈书面〉place where the sun was said to rise in ancient books

钖(鍚) yáng ornament on the forehead of a horse

飏(颺) yáng fly upward; flutter:杨柳轻～直上重霄九。Poplar and Willow soar to the Ninth Heaven (*or* the heaven of heavens).

yǎng

痒(癢) yǎng itch; tickle:浑身发～ feel itchy all over; itch all over /怕～ ticklish /搔～ scratch an itch /搔小孩的胳肢窝呵～ tickle a child in the armpits /搔到～处 scratch where it itches; find out where the shoe pinches /无关痛～ irrelevant; of no consequence

痒痒 yǎngyang 〈口语〉itch; tickle:脚心～。The arch (of a foot) itches.

痒痒挠儿 yǎngyangnáor 〈方言〉itch scratcher

痒疹 yǎngzhěn 〈医学〉prurigo

养(養) yǎng ❶ support; keep; provide for:赡～ support; provide for /哺～ feed; rear /收～ adopt /娇生惯～ pampered since childhood ❷ raise; keep; grow; rear:驯～ raise and train; domesticate /～猪 raise pigs /～花 grow flowers /～蜂 keep bees /～鱼 breed fish /笼～鸟 keep caged birds ❸ give birth to:这对夫妇只～了一个孩子。The couple have one child only. ❹ adoptive; foster: *see* "～父" ❺ form; acquire; contract:～成不良习惯 contract bad habits /姑息～奸。To tolerate evil is to abet it. ❻ nourish; rest; convalesce; recuperate:～伤 take rest and nourishment to heal a wound /保～ conserve (*or* take good care of) one's health /疗～ recuperate; convalesce /调～ be nursed back to health; keep fit by resting, taking nourishing food and exercise, etc. ❼ cultivate; refine:素～ accomplishment /涵～ self-restraint ❽ maintain; keep in good repair: *see* "～路" ❾ (of hair) grow long:把头发～起来 grow long hair ❿ foster; support:以工～农 foster agriculture by industry

养兵 yǎngbīng maintain or keep an army:～自守 keep an army for self-defence /维护主权则不可不～。Armed forces are indispensable for safeguarding national sovereignty.

养兵千日,用兵一时 yǎngbīng qiānrì, yòngbīng yīshí maintain an army for a thousand days to use it for a moment; soldiers are trained for years on end for the sake of a few days of battle

养病 yǎngbìng recover from illness and regain one's health by rest and nourishment; rest and recuperate:别人都在忙,我哪有心思在家～。How could I possibly rest and recuperate at home while everybody is busy?

养蚕 yǎngcán raise silkworms; engage in sericulture:～业 sericulture /～人 silkworm grower

养成工 yǎngchénggōng 〈旧语〉apprentice; trainee (in a textile mill)

养地 yǎngdì enrich the soil by application of fertilizer and crop rotation

养儿防老 yǎng'ér-fánglǎo bring up children to provide against old age:积谷防饥,～ just as one stores up grain against lean years, one rears children against old age

养分 yǎngfèn nutrient:土壤～ soil nutrient /这些蔬菜～充足。The vegetables are full of nutrients.

养蜂 yǎngfēng bee-keeping; apiculture:～人 bee-keeper; apiarist

养蜂场 yǎngfēngchǎng apiary; bee yard

养蜂业 yǎngfēngyè apiculture; bee-keeping

养父 yǎngfù foster father; adoptive father

养汉 yǎnghàn (of woman) commit adultery; have an affair with a man

养虎遗患 yǎnghǔ-yíhuàn to rear a tiger is to court calamity; to appease an enemy is to invite disaster:此非善类,留下来岂不是～? They are an evil sort, and to keep them is to bring trouble on oneself.

养护 yǎnghù ❶ maintain; conserve:～公路 maintain public highways /设备～ equipment maintenance /～植被 conservation of vegetation ❷ take care of one's health; nurse:他刚做了手术,还需特别～。He's just had an operation and needs special care. ❸ curing:～石料 stone curing /混凝土～ concrete curing /～剂 curing agent

养晦待时 yǎnghuì-dàishí dwell in retirement awaiting opportunity; bide one's time in obscurity:此人非池中物,如今不过是～罢了。He is no ordinary person and is just biding time in reclusion.

养活 yǎnghuo ❶ support; keep; feed:～一大家子人 support a big family /他小小年纪便赚钱～母亲。Young as he was, he started to provide for his mother. ❷ raise (animals); rear:她～了一只波斯猫。She raises a Persian cat. ❸〈方言〉give birth to:前不久,她又～了一个孩子。A few days ago she gave birth to another baby.

养鸡场 yǎngjīchǎng chicken run; chicken farm

养家 yǎngjiā keep a family; bring home the bacon:～餬口 support a family; have a family to provide for:挣钱～ earn bread for the family

养家活口 yǎngjiā-huókǒu *also* "养家餬口" support one's family:我挣的这点工资仅够～。The little money I earn is barely enough to feed my family.

养精蓄锐 yǎngjīng-xùruì conserve energy and build up strength; store up (one's) energy:指挥员让大家～,准备打一场硬仗。The commander told us to build up strength for a tough battle ahead.
养疴 yǎngkē 〈书面〉 *see* "养病"
养口 yǎngkǒu eke out a living; support a family
养老 yǎnglǎo ❶ provide for the aged (usu. one's parents):这个村子现在无儿无女的老人再也不担心无人～了。Nowadays childless old people in this village no longer worry that their old age won't be provided for. ❷ live out one's life in retirement:退休后他想回老家～。He wanted to go and live in his hometown for the rest of his life after retirement.
养老保险 yǎnglǎo bǎoxiǎn endowment insurance
养老基金 yǎnglǎo jījīn pension fund
养老金 yǎnglǎojīn old-age pension:靠～过活 live on one's old-age pension /领～ draw one's old-age pension /退休后享受～ retire with a pension
养老送终 yǎnglǎo-sòngzhōng look after one's parents in the sunset of their lives and give them a proper burial after they die
养老院 yǎnglǎoyuàn *also* "敬老院" jìnglǎoyuàn house of respect for the aged; home for the old:在～里安度晚年 spend one's remaining years in a home for the aged
养廉 yǎnglián 〈书面〉 cultivate honesty and integrity:俭以～ cultivate personal integrity through a simple life
养料 yǎngliào nourishment; nutriment:从生活中吸取～ draw nourishment from life /植物可以从腐殖质中吸取～。Plants can draw nutrients from humus.
养路 yǎnglù maintain a road or railway:～工 path master; section hand /～队 section gang /～道班 road maintenance crew
养路费 yǎnglùfèi road toll
养马场 yǎngmǎchǎng (horse) ranch
养母 yǎngmǔ foster mother; adoptive mother
养目镜 yǎngmùjìng sunglasses
养女 yǎngnǚ adopted daughter; foster daughter
养气 yǎngqì 〈书面〉 ❶ cultivate one's moral character; exercise self-control ❷ way of cultivation in Taoism
养人 yǎngrén nutritious:小米～。Millet is very nutritious.
养伤 yǎngshāng take rest and nourishment to heal one's wound
养神 yǎngshén rest to attain mental tranquility; repose:闭目～ sit in repose with one's eyes closed; relax in meditation /你休息一下,养养神。Please have a rest to restore yourself.
养生 yǎngshēng preserve one's health; keep in good health:～要素 essential elements (*or* quintessence) of life
养生学 yǎngshēngxué (science of) health preservation
养生之道 yǎngshēngzhīdào way to stay healthy:这位老人自有一套～。The old man has a way to keep in good health.
养兔场 yǎngtùchǎng rabbit farm
养息 yǎngxī rest and recuperate
养媳妇 yǎngxífù 〈方言〉 child daughter-in-law
养心 yǎngxīn cultivate mental tranquility:～殿 Hall of Mental Cultivation (in Beijing)
养性 yǎngxìng cultivate one's nature (*or* natural character):修真～ cultivate one's true nature /～殿 Hall of Character Cultivation in the Palace Museum, Beijing
养血 yǎngxuè 〈中医〉 nourish the blood:～剂 blood-nourishing prescription
养痈成患 yǎngyōng-chénghuàn *also* "养痈遗患" a boil neglected becomes the bane of one's life; leaving evil unchecked spells ruin; appeasement means no end of trouble
养鱼 yǎngyú fish-farming:～场 fish farm /～池 fishpond /～业 fish raising industry
养育 yǎngyù bring up; rear:～子女 bring up children /报答父母～之恩 repay one's parents for their loving care /雄伟的黄河～了祖辈先人。Our ancestors were reared by the great Yellow River.
养殖 yǎngzhí breed or cultivate (aquatics):～淡水鱼 cultivate fresh-water fish /海水～ sea-farming; marine culture; sea water aquiculture /淡水～ freshwater aquiculture
养殖场 yǎngzhíchǎng (breeding) farm:水产～ aquatic farm
养殖业 yǎngzhíyè breeding industry; fish breeding or poultry raising; aquiculture:这个村的～很发达。The breeding industry in this village is highly developed.
养殖珍珠 yǎngzhí zhēnzhū cultured pearl
养猪场 yǎngzhūchǎng pig farm; piggery
养子 yǎngzǐ adopted son; foster son
养尊处优 yǎngzūn-chǔyōu enjoy a high position and a life of ease and comfort; live in clover:这些皇亲国戚～,哪里知道百姓的苦处。Leading a life of ease and comfort these imperial family members know nothing about the miseries of the common people. /他是个～的豪门子弟。Born into a rich and powerful family, he is in clover.

氧 yǎng 〈化学〉 oxygen (O):液态～ liquid oxygen /缺～ lack oxygen /含～酸 oxygen acid; oxyacid
氧吧 yǎngbā oxygen bar (for oxygen therapy)
氧丙烷切割 yǎngbǐngwán qiēgē 〈冶金〉 oxy-propane cutting
氧不足 yǎngbùzú 〈医学〉 hypoxia
氧割 yǎnggē *also* "氧炔切割" 〈机械〉 oxyacetylene metal-cutting
氧合 yǎnghé 〈生化〉 oxygenate:～器 oxygenator /～酶 oxygenase /～血红蛋白 oxyhemoglobin
氧合作用 yǎnghé zuòyòng 〈生理〉 oxygenation
氧化 yǎnghuà 〈化学〉 oxidize; oxidate:～层 oxidizing layer; oxidizing zone /～反应 oxidizing reaction /～催化剂 oxycatalyst /～分解 oxygenolysis /～裂解 oxicracking /～酶 oxidase /～纤维素 oxycellulose /～抑制 oxidation retarder (*or* inhibitor) /～作用 oxidation
氧化法 yǎnghuàfǎ oxidizing process; oxo-process
氧化还原 yǎnghuà huányuán redox; oxidation-reduction:～酶 oxidation-reductase /～剂 REDOX; reductant-oxidant
氧化剂 yǎnghuàjì oxygenant; oxidizer; oxidant
氧化铝 yǎnghuàlǚ aluminum oxide:～陶瓷 aluminum oxide ceramics
氧化镁 yǎnghuàměi megnesium oxide
氧化膜 yǎnghuàmó oxidation film; oxidic film; oxide film:～避雷器 oxide film arrester
氧化皮 yǎnghuàpí 〈冶金〉 scale cinder; scale:清除～ scale-handling /～清除器 scale breaker
氧化数 yǎnghuàshù oxidation number
氧化态 yǎnghuàtài oxidation state
氧化铁 yǎnghuàtiě ferric oxide
氧化土 yǎnghuàtǔ oxisol
氧化物 yǎnghuàwù oxide:～陶瓷 oxide ceramics
氧化锌 yǎnghuàxīn zinc oxide (ZnO)
氧化焰 yǎnghuàyàn oxidizing flame
氧化抑制剂 yǎnghuà yìzhìjì oxidation retarder or inhibitor
氧基化合物 yǎngjī huàhéwù 〈化学〉 oxo-compound
氧激光器 yǎngjīguāngqì oxygen laser
氧硫化物 yǎngliúhuàwù 〈化学〉 oxysulphide
氧矛切割 yǎngmáo qiēgē 〈冶金〉 oxygen lancing; oxygen lance cutting
氧气 yǎngqì oxygen gas:～设备 oxygen apparatus /～站 oxygen station /～转炉 oxygen converter /～炼钢 oxygen steelmaking /～焊接 oxygen weld /～切割 oxygen cutting; oxygen lancing /～熔炼 oxygen smelting
氧气袋 yǎngqìdài oxygen bag
氧气顶吹转炉 yǎngqì dǐngchuī zhuànlú oxygen top-blown converter
氧气面具 yǎngqì miànjù oxygen mask
氧气瓶 yǎngqìpíng oxygen cylinder:手提式～ oxygen walker
氧气枪 yǎngqìqiāng 〈冶金〉 oxygen lance
氧气帐 yǎngqìzhàng 〈医学〉 oxygen tent
氧气罩 yǎngqìzhào oxygen mask
氧炔 yǎngquē *also* "氧乙炔" oxyacetylene:～焊接 oxyacetylene welding /～切割 oxyacetylene cutting
氧炔吹管 yǎngquē chuīguǎn 〈机械〉 oxyacetylene blowpipe
氧熔剂切割 yǎngróngjì qiēgē 〈冶金〉 powder oxygen cutting (POC)
氧循环 yǎngxúnhuán oxygen cycle
氧债 yǎngzhài 〈生理〉 oxygen debt
氧族元素 yǎngzú yuánsù oxygen group element:～化合物 oxygen group compounds

仰 yǎng ❶ look up; face upward:～起头 raise one's head /俯～ bending forward and backward; bending and lifting of the head /～见群峰突兀 look up and see the peaks towering towards the sky ❷ admire; revere; look up to:敬～ revere; venerate /瞻～ pay one's respects to /信～ believe in /～其为人 admire his integrity ❸ rely on; depend on:解愁～酒浆 drink to drown one's worries /五谷

Y

粮食乃民之所～。People live on grain. ❹〈旧语〉(usu. used in official letters) respectfully:～请即示 looking forward to your prompt instructions /～即遵照 please comply immediately with this ❺ (Yǎng) a surname
仰八叉 yǎngbachā also "仰八脚儿" (fall) flat on one's back
仰尘 yǎngchén 〈书面〉ceiling
仰承 yǎngchéng ❶〈书面〉rely on; depend on:～前辈栽培 depend on one's seniors for help (or advance) in one's career ❷〈敬词〉comply with:～尊意 comply with your wish
仰毒 yǎngdú 〈书面〉take poison:～自尽 commit suicide (or kill oneself) by taking poison
仰俯之间 yǎngfǔzhījiān between the lifting and bending of the head — in an instant; in a flash
仰攻 yǎnggōng attack a higher position from a lower position
仰光 Yǎngguāng Yangon (formerly Rangoon), capital of Myanmar (formerly Burma)
仰给 yǎngjǐ depend on others (for a living, etc.):～于人 depend on others for support
仰角 yǎngjiǎo 〈数学〉angle of elevation
仰壳 yǎngké also "后仰壳" hòuyǎngké 〈方言〉be on one's back:摔了个大～儿 fall flat on one's back
仰赖 yǎnglài rely on; depend on:衣食～父母 rely on one's parents for a living
仰面 yǎngmiàn face upwards:～倒下 fall down, face upwards /～朝天 flat on one's back
仰面求人 yǎngmiàn-qiúrén implore others for help:不屑于～ disdain to ask for help /不得不～ have to ask humbly for help
仰慕 yǎngmù admire; hold in high esteem:～英雄 admire heroes /他的人品令人～。His character commands admiration. /人们对他非常～。People hold him in high esteem.
仰攀 yǎngpān 〈书面〉❶ climb up; clamber up ❷ make friends or forge ties of kinship with someone of a higher social position:～权贵 attach oneself to bigwigs
仰人鼻息 yǎngrénbíxī be slavishly dependent on others; be at sb.'s beck and call:他可不是那种～的人。He is no yesman. /寄人篱下,不得不～。A poor dependent, I had no choice but to be at others' beck and call.
仰韶文化 Yǎngsháo wénhuà 〈考古〉Yangshao culture, prototypical Chinese culture of the Neolithic period, relics of which were first unearthed in Yangshao Village, Mianchi (渑池) County, Henan Province in 1921
仰射 yǎngshè fire upwards
仰食 yǎngshí 〈书面〉rely on others for a living:～父兄 sponge on one's father and brother
仰视 yǎngshì raise one's eyes; look up:～繁星 look up at the stars
仰视图 yǎngshìtú upward view
仰首 yǎngshǒu raise one's head:～望明月 look up at the bright moon
仰首伸眉 yǎngshǒu-shēnméi raise one's head and smooth out one's eyebrows — look high-spirited:少年得志,～。Achieving success when young, he felt quite elated.
仰天 yǎngtiān look up at the sky; throw up one's head:～长叹 throw up one's head and sigh deeply; lament loudly /～长啸 utter cries that rend the air /～大笑 laugh sardonically (or boisterously)
仰望 yǎngwàng ❶ look up:翘首～ look up /～长空 look up at the sky ❷ respectfully seek guidance or advice from; look up to:～前贤 look up to and seek advice from one's seniors
仰卧 yǎngwò lie on one's back; lie supine:她～在床上,望着天花板出神。Lying in bed, with her eyes fixed on the ceiling, she was lost in thought.
仰卧起坐 yǎngwò qǐzuò 〈体育〉sit-ups
仰屋兴叹 yǎngwū-xīngtàn also "仰屋窃叹" look up at the ceiling and lament — be at one's wits' end:遇上这样的事,他只是～而已。Fate being so, he felt totally helpless.
仰屋著书 yǎngwū-zhùshū experience hardship in writing a book:张先生二十年来～,成果不菲。Totally immersed in writing for 20 hard years, Mr. Zhang accomplished quite a lot.
仰息 yǎngxī see "仰人鼻息"
仰药 yǎngyào 〈书面〉take poison
仰泳 yǎngyǒng 〈体育〉backstroke:游～ do the backstroke
仰仗 yǎngzhàng count on; look to sb. for support:人民的军队～人民的支持。The people's army depends on the people's support. /那个国家的粮食～进口。That country lives on imported grain.

yàng

漾 yàng ❶ ripple:湖面上～起了层层波纹。The surface of the lake rippled. or There were ripples on the lake. /这想法在她的脑海里～起了微波。The thought sent ripples through her mind. ❷ brim over; overflow:杯里的茶水太满,都～出来了。The tea in the glass is brimming over. /盆里的水直往外～。The water in the basin is full to overflowing. /她脸上～着天真的笑容。Her face was brimming with an innocent smile. ❸〈方言〉small lake; lakelet
漾奶 yàngnǎi (of a baby) throw up or spit up milk; vomit milk from repletion
漾漾 yàngyàng rippling; full of ripples:湖面～,十分恬静。The lake looked quiet and peaceful with gentle ripples.

烊 yàng see "打烊" dǎyàng
see also yáng

恙 yàng 〈书面〉ailment; illness; indisposition:染～卧床 sick in bed /安然无～ safe and sound /别来无～乎? How have you been since we last saw each other?
恙虫 yàngchóng tsutsugamushi mite
恙虫病 yàngchóngbìng scrub typhus; mite-borne typhus; tropical typhus; flood fever; inundation fever
恙虫热 yàngchóngrè tsutsugamushi disease; scrub typhus
恙螨 yàngmǎn chigger; scrub mite; harvest mite; rete rouge; chigger mite

样(樣) yàng ❶ shape; pattern:花～ pattern /式～ style; design /时装日日翻新～儿。New fashions keep coming out. or New designs of clothes appear every day. ❷appearance; expression:她长得跟她母亲一个～儿。She takes after her mother. /几年没见,他可是大变～儿了。It's years since I last saw him. He's a different person now. /站有站～儿,坐有坐～儿。Stand up straight and sit up straight. ❸ sample; model; pattern:榜～ model /取～ take a sample /看～订货 have a look at a sample before placing an order /校～ proof sheet ❹〈量词〉kind; type; variety:几～儿风味菜 a few local delicacies /两～儿点心 two kinds of cakes /你替我带这两～东西。Please take these two things for me. ❺ trend; situation:看～儿这一场他能赢。It seems he will win this game.
样板 yàngbǎn ❶ sample plate ❷ templet; template ❸ model; example:树～ set an example /学～ follow the example /～县 model county
样板田 yàngbǎntián demonstration field; model plot
样板戏 yàngbǎnxì model Beijing opera, term used during the Cultural Revolution (1966-1976) to refer to Beijing operas with a modern, revolutionary theme
样本 yàngběn ❶ sample book ❷ sample; specimen:字体～ type specimen book /家具～ furniture designs book /服装～ dress pattern book
样稿 yànggǎo sample manuscript or typescript
样机 yàngjī ❶〈航空〉prototype (aeroplane) ❷ prototype machine
样件 yàngjiàn sample spare part
样款 yàngkuǎn pattern; style; sample
样片 yàngpiàn (of film) rushes; work print; (of TV programme) pilot film; sample film or telefilm:审看～ preview the sample of a film for examination
样品 yàngpǐn sample (product); specimen:试验～ pilot sample; test specimen /取～ take samples /免费赠送的～ free sample /符合～规格 come (or be) up to sample; comply with sample /～展示会 sample products show /你们批量生产的鞋不如～。Your mass-produced shoes are below sample.
样式 yàngshì pattern; type; style; fashion:各种～的电风扇 electric fans in all types /不同的文学～ different genres of literature /～典雅 in an elegant style /最流行～的服装 clothes of the latest fashion /这衣服～太旧。The dress is old-fashioned. or The dress is out of style. /请照这个～裁。Please pattern the dress on this model.
样书 yàngshū sample book; specimen book
样图 yàngtú master drawing

样样 yàngyàng each and every; everything; all: 她做的菜大家～都爱吃。We like everything she cooks. /这孩子在学校里～功课都好。This child is good at each and every course he takes at school. /本体育中心各种健身器械～俱全。Every kind of body-building apparatus is available at this sports centre.
样张 yàngzhāng ❶〈印刷〉specimen page ❷ pattern sheet
样子 yàngzi ❶ appearance; look; shape: 这件衣服～不好。The dress is poorly cut. /你的手包是什么～的? What does your handbag look like? /我不喜欢这种～和颜色。I don't like its look and colour. ❷ manner; air; expression: 显出不高兴的～ look unhappy /装出爱理不理的～ assume an air of aloofness (*or* indifference) /瞧他那～,像是有什么心事。Judging by his behaviour, he seems to have something on his mind. ❸ sample; model; pattern: 时装～ fashion pattern /争口气,做出个～来给大家看看。Work hard and set us an example to win honour for yourself. ❹ tendency; inclination; likelihood: 我觉得不舒服,像是要生病的～。I'm not feeling well. I'm likely to be sick. /看～就要下雨了。It looks like rain.

怏 yàng

怏然 yàngrán 〈书面〉❶ unhappy; displeased: ～不悦 displeased; annoyed ❷ arrogant; self-important: ～自足 arrogant and self-satisfied
怏怏 yàngyàng disgruntled; morose: ～不乐 disgruntled; depressed; morose /～不得志 sullen with failure (*or* frustration)

鞅 yàng *see* "牛鞅" niúyàng

see also yāng

yāo

要 yāo ❶ demand; claim; ask ❷ force; compel; coerce ❸ *see* "邀" yāo ❹ (Yāo) a surname

see also yào

要功 yāogōng *see* "邀功" yāogōng
要击 yāojī *see* "邀击" yāojī
要买 yāomǎi *see* "邀买" yāomǎi
要求 yāoqiú ❶ ask for; claim; demand; request: ～发言 ask to be heard; ask for the floor /～赔偿损失 claim compensation for one's loss /～某人出席 request sb.'s presence /～对方道歉 demand an apology from the other party /严格～自己 be strict with oneself; set high standards for oneself /～大家遵守纪律 call on everybody to observe discipline /～立即撤出外国军队 call for the immediate withdrawal of foreign troops ❷ demand; claim; requirement; request: 明确的～ clear requirement /合理的～ reasonable request /过分的～ excessive demand /领土～ territorial claims /提出～ make a demand; present a request /满足～ satisfy one's demand; fulfil one's requirement /符合～ conform to the reqirements /答应～ grant a demand (*or* request)
要挟 yāoxié coerce or threaten (sb.) by taking advantage of sb.'s weakness; put pressure on; blackmail: ～政府 blackmail the government; put pressure on the government /～群众就范 coerce the people into submission /受到绑架者的～ be blackmailed by the kidnappers

喓 yāo

喓喓 yāoyāo 〈书面〉(of insects) chirr; chirp: ～草虫 chirping grasshoppers

腰 yāo ❶ waist; small of the back: 细～ small (*or* slender) waist /～粗 be round at the waist /～越来越粗 get fatter round the middle (*or* waist) /扭～ wriggle one's waist /弯～ bend down; stoop /伸懒～ stretch oneself /叉～ with one's hands on one's hips; arms akimbo /闪了～ sprain one's back (muscles) /膀阔～圆 broad-shouldered and solidly-built /拦～抱住 seize sb. round the middle /站在齐～深的水中 be waist-deep in water /不为五斗米折～ not bend down for five *dou* of rice ❷ waist (of a garment): 高～裙 high-waisted skirt /裤～做肥了。The waist of the trousers is too big. ❸ pocket; purse; wallet: ～里无钱 have no money in one's purse /手绢装在～里。The handkerchief is in my pocket. ❹ middle: 半山～ halfway up a hill /拦～切一刀 cut sth. in half; cut sth. in the middle ❺ waist-like terrain: 海～ strait ❻ (Yāo) a surname

腰板儿 yāobǎnr ❶ waist and back: 挺着～ straighten one's back ❷ physique; build: 我爷爷都八十多岁了,～还挺硬朗。My grandpa is over eighty now and still going strong (*or* is still hale and hearty).
腰板脖硬 yāobǎn-bóyìng stiff and rigid in movements
腰包 yāobāo purse; pocket; wallet: 肥了老板的～ line the boss's pocket /他的～鼓起来了。His purse is bulging with money. /大家赚来的钱都让他装了～。He pocketed all the money we earned. /谁来掏～? Who is going to pay?
腰部 yāobù waist; small of the back: 使～变细 slim the waist /～结肠造口术〈医学〉lumbocolostomy
腰缠 yāochán 〈旧语〉things one carries; personal effects
腰缠万贯 yāochán-wànguàn very rich: 他经营有方,没过两年,便已～。Good at business, he became very rich in the short space of two years.
腰带 yāodài waistband; belt; girdle: 系着～ wear a waistband /松～ loosen one's waistband (*or* belt) /束紧～ tighten one's belt
腰刀 yāodāo dagger; knife worn at the waist
腰肥 yāoféi waistline; waist size
腰杆子 yāogǎnzi *also* "腰杆儿" ❶ waist; back: ～挺得老直 stand as straight as a stick /挺起～ straighten one's back — be confident and unafraid ❷ backing; support: 他是总部派来的,～硬。He is from the headquarters with strong backing.
腰鼓 yāogǔ ❶ waist drum ❷ waist-drum dance
腰锅 yāoguō gourd-shaped pot, used by ethnic minorities in Yunnan Province
腰果 yāoguǒ cashew: ～仁 cashew nut /～树 cashew (tree)
腰花 yāohuā scalloped pork or lamb kidneys: 炒～ stir-fried kidneys
腰黄 yāohuáng 〈中药〉a kind of realigar; red orpiment
腰肌 yāojī 〈生理〉psoas; lumbar muscles: ～炎 psoitis
腰肌劳损 yāojī láosǔn strain of lumbar muscles; psoatic strain
腰扭伤 yāoniǔshāng lumbar sprain
腰牌 yāopái ❶ plate hung on the side of a bus or trolley bus to show the bus number and destination ❷〈旧语〉pass worn in the waist which showed that one was permitted to enter the court or barracks
腰身 yāoshen waistline; waist; waist measurement; girth: 收～ take in the waist of a dress /～细 have a slender (*or* slim) waist /我这两年胖了许多,连～也没了。I've put on a lot of weight these two years and no longer have any waist. /他喜欢穿～肥大的衣服。He likes clothes with a large (*or* loose) waist.
腰酸背痛 yāosuān-bèitòng with a sore waist and an aching back — aching all over
腰痛 yāotòng 〈医学〉lumbago
腰腿 yāotuǐ waist and legs, used to refer to the physical mobility of aged people: 别看张大爷七十多岁了,～倒还挺灵便。Grandpa Zhang is well over seventy but he is still quite nimble.
腰围 yāowéi ❶ waistline: ～细 have a slim (*or* slender) waistline /他的～为七十九公分。His waist measures seventy-nine cm. around. ❷ waistband
腰窝 yāowō 〈方言〉either side of the small of the back
腰眼 yāoyǎn ❶ either side of the small of the back ❷ key; crux: 您这话算是点到～上了。What you said is very much to the point.
腰斩 yāozhǎn ❶ cut a person in half at the waist, cruel way of execution in ancient times ❷ cut sth. in half: 这项工程只进行了一年便给～了。The project was discontinued (half way through) after a year's work.
腰肢 yāozhī *also* "腰支" waist; figure
腰椎 yāozhuī 〈生理〉lumbar vertebra; abdominal vertebra
腰椎穿刺 yāozhuī chuāncì lumbar puncture; rachicentesis; Corning's anaesthesia puncture
腰子 yāozi (popular term for 肾) kidney

夭[1](殀) yāo die young: 寿～ long life or early death; live long or die young

夭[2] yāo 〈书面〉luxuriant; exuberant

夭阏 yāo'è *also* "夭遏"〈书面〉check; stop
夭矫 yāojiǎo 〈书面〉twisted and robust: ～婆娑的古柏 twisted and robust ancient cypress

夭疽 yāojū 〈中医〉malignant sore on the left side of the back of the ear

夭殇 yāoshāng 〈书面〉die young

夭寿 yāoshòu 〈方言〉die young; be short-lived

夭桃秾李 yāotáo-nónglǐ beautiful peach and plum blossoms — beautiful young girl

夭亡 yāowáng die young

夭折 yāozhé ❶ die young ❷ come to a premature end; stop halfway: 改革～了。The reform has miscarried. /影片资金不足拍了一半便～了。The shooting of the movie stopped halfway due to lack of funding. /由于条件不具备，这项试验～了。The experiment came to an early end for lack of the required conditions.

妖 yāo

❶ monster; demon; evil spirit: 照～镜 monster-revealing mirror /兴～作怪 stir up trouble ❷ evil and bewitching: *see* "～术" ❸ (of a woman) coquettish; seductive: 这女人挺～气。She is a coquettish woman. ❹〈书面〉beautiful; charming: *see* "～娆"

妖道 yāodào Taoist priest who practises black art; Taoist sorcerer

妖氛 yāofēn ominous atmosphere (often portending disaster); evil trend: 扫荡一切～ eliminate all evil tendencies

妖风 yāofēng evil wind; noxious trend: 刮～ stir up an evil trend

妖怪 yāoguai monster; devil; evil spirit; demon

妖精 yāojing ❶ bogey; demon ❷ alluring woman; seductress; fairy fox: 我饶不了那个小～! I shall not let that foxy woman get away with it.

妖里妖气 yāoliyāoqì coquettish; bewitching; sexy in an evil way: 我就看不惯她那个～的样儿。I'm sick of her coquettish manner.

妖媚 yāomèi seductively charming; bewitching: ～的年轻女子 bewitching young girl

妖魔 yāomó evil spirit; devil; demon

妖魔鬼怪 yāomó-guǐguài demons and ghosts; monsters of every description

妖孽 yāoniè 〈书面〉❶ thing or event associated with evil or misfortune ❷ evil spirit; demon ❸ evildoer

妖娆 yāoráo 〈书面〉enchanting; fascinating: 这小女子出落得百般～。The girl has grown into a most charming young lady. /须晴日，看红装素裹，分外～。On a fine day, the land, Clad in white, adorned in red, Grows more enchanting.

妖人 yāorén enchanter; sorcerer

妖声怪气 yāoshēng-guàiqì *also* "妖声妖气" speak flirtatiously: 她～地叫了他一声。She called him coquettishly.

妖术 yāoshù black magic; black art; witchcraft; sorcery: 玩弄～ resort to black magic

妖妄 yāowàng weird; fantastic: ～之说 fallacy; heresy

妖物 yāowù demon; monster; evil spirit; fiend

妖言 yāoyán bewitching heresy or fallacy: ～惑众 spread fallacies to hoodwink the public; stir up public feeling by sophistry

妖艳 yāoyàn pretty and flirtatious

妖冶 yāoyě pretty and coquettish

邀 yāo

❶ invite; ask; request: 特～代表 specially invited delegate /应～赴宴 go to a banquet on invitation /～游 invite to an excursion ❷〈书面〉gain; receive; seek: 他想请假半日而未能～准。He wished to take half a day off but failed to get permission. /谅～同意。This will probably meet with your approval. ❸ intercept: 举兵～讨 send troops on an intercept mission

邀宠 yāochǒng curry favour with; ingratiate oneself with: 向皇帝～ try to win the emperor's favour

邀功 yāogōng *also* "要功" yāogōng claim credit for someone else's achievements: 虚报成绩以～请赏 make a false report of one's successes in order to seek rewards /他为了～，不惜打击别人。In order to get credit for himself he went so far as to harm others.

邀击 yāojī *also* "要击" yāojī intercept (the enemy); ambush; waylay: ～逃犯 intercept the flight of a criminal

邀集 yāojí invite or ask a group of people to meet; call together: 他～了几个朋友在他家小聚。He invited several friends to have a get-together in his house.

邀买 yāomǎi *also* "要买" yāomǎi buy over; bribe: ～选票 buy votes

邀买人心 yāomǎi-rénxīn seek or court popularity; buy popular support

邀请 yāoqǐng invite (usu. for certain specific purposes): ～入内 invite (sb.) in /～赴宴 ask (sb.) to dinner /发～ issue an invitation; send (*or* extend) an invitation /～各界人士参加我们的座谈会 invite people from all walks of life to (attend) our symposium /被正式～出席开幕式 be formally invited for (*or* to) the opening ceremony /应教育部～访问中国 visit China at the invitation of the Ministry of Education

邀请国 yāoqǐngguó host country

邀请赛 yāoqǐngsài invitational tournament: 乒乓球～ invitational table-tennis tournament

邀请书 yāoqǐngshū invitation

邀请信 yāoqǐngxìn (letter of) invitation

邀赏 yāoshǎng seek rewards: 报功～ report one's success (*or* achievement) in order to seek rewards

邀约 yāoyuē invite: 盛情～ warmly invite

幺(么) yāo

❶ one (used orally for the numeral "一") ❷〈方言〉youngest: ～妹 youngest sister /～叔 youngest uncle ❸〈书面〉small; thin: ～小 petite; small ❹ (Yāo) a surname

幺蛾子 yāo'ézi 〈方言〉trick; mischief; wicked idea: 这小子又在出什么～? What tricks has he got up his sleeve? *or* What mischief is he up to now?

幺麽 yāomó 〈书面〉small; little; petty: ～小丑 insignificant wretch

幺豚 yāotún runt of the litter (smallest and last of a litter of pigs)

吆(吆) yāo

bawl; shout; cry out: ～牲口 loudly urge on a draught animal

吆喊 yāohǎn shout; cry out; call: 他～了几声，也没人回答。He shouted several times but got no response.

吆喝 yāohe ❶ shout; cry out; call; hawk (wares): 他一～，大家都出来了。Everybody came out at his call. /小贩卖力地～，想招徕更多的顾客。The pedlar was shouting at the top of his voice for more customers. ❷ loudly urge (on) an animal: 他～着把牲口赶进了圈。He urged his cattle loudly into the fold.

吆呼 yāohu shout; cry out; call: 售票员～乘客赶紧上车。The conductor urged the passengers onto the bus in a loud voice.

吆唤 yāohuan call: 你～几个人把这些椅子搬走。Please call some men to move these chairs away.

吆五喝六 yāowǔ-hèliù *also* "吆三喝四" ❶ calls made when playing dice; noise in a gambling house: 屋里一群男人正在～地豪赌。A group of men were gambling in the room, making a terrible din. ❷〈方言〉domineering; arrogant; overbearing: 他整天～地抖威风。He is always bossing people about self-importantly. /谁敢在这里～! Who has the impudence to swagger about here!

约 yāo

weigh: 请～三斤葡萄。Please weigh out three *jin* of grapes for me. /～～这个西瓜有多重。See how much the watermelon weighs. /～～够不够分量。See if it gives short measure.

see also yuē

yáo

垚 yáo

〈书面〉(usu. used in personal names) high mountain

尧(堯) Yáo

❶ Yao, legendary monarch and model for all rulers in ancient China ❷ a surname

尧舜 Yáo-Shùn Yao and Shun, legendary model monarchs in ancient China; ancient sages: 人皆可为～ everybody can become a Yao or Shun — human nature is virtuous

尧天舜日 yáotiān-shùnrì days of Yao and Shun — the golden age of remote antiquity; times of peace and prosperity; good old days

峣(嶢) yáo

〈书面〉high and steep

侥(僥) yáo

see "僬侥" jiāoyáo

see also jiǎo

珧 yáo

shell of clam

铫 yáo ❶ big hoe used in ancient times ❷（Yáo）a surname
see also diào

姚 Yáo a surname

姚黄魏紫 yáohuáng-wèizǐ *also*"魏紫姚黄" rare peonies：牡丹花会上，～，争奇斗艳。At the Peony Festival, one can see a variety of rare peonies in brilliant colours.

姚剧 yáojù local opera in Zhejiang Province

肴（餚） yáo meat and fish dishes：菜～ vegetable and meat dishes / 酒～ wine and dishes

肴肉 yáoròu salted meat；cured pork

肴馔 yáozhuàn 〈书面〉courses at a banquet；sumptuous dishes：备办～ prepare dishes

爻 yáo whole and broken lines which form the eight trigrams in *The Book of Changes*（易经）：阳～ whole line（"—"）/ 阴～ broke line（"--"）

窑（窰、窯） yáo ❶ kiln：砖瓦～ brickkiln / 石灰～ lime pit；limekiln ❷（usu. small and manually operated）pit：煤～ coal pit ❸ cave dwelling ❹〈方言〉brothel

窑变 yáobiàn flambé, a process in which a special glaze is formed in making pottery owing to the unexpected mingling of pigments：古代～花瓶 ancient flambé vase

窑洞 yáodòng cave dwelling：依山开凿了十眼～ dig ten cave dwellings at the foot of a hill

窑灰钾肥 yáohuī jiǎféi flue ash potash

窑姐儿 yáojiěr 〈方言〉whore；prostitute

窑坑 yáokēng kiln；pit

窑葬 yáozàng cave-burial

窑子 yáozi 〈方言〉brothel；bawdy house：逛～ go to the brothel；go whoring

谣 yáo ❶ ballad；rhyme：民～ ballad；popular verse / 童～ children's rhyme / 古代统治者常常听～观政。Ancient rulers often sized up the political situation by listening to ballads（*or* the stories that were making the rounds among the people）. ❷ rumour；hearsay：造～ start a rumour；cook up a story / 造～者 rumour-monger / 传～ pass on a rumour（after hearing it）；spread a rumour / 辟～ refute a rumour / 不信～ disbelieve a rumour

谣传 yáochuán ❶ as it is rumoured；according to hearsay：～她后来嫁了一位巨贾。Rumour has it that she later married a rich businessman. ❷ rumours that go about：最近有涨价的～。It is rumoured that there will be a price hike.

谣风 yáofēng unhealthy tendency to spread rumours：刹住～ check the tendency to spread rumours；stop rumour-mongering

谣俗 yáosú 〈书面〉social customs；folkways

谣言 yáoyán rumour；hearsay；gossip：制造～ start a rumour；cook up a story / 散布～ spread rumours；circulate rumours / 发动～攻势 launch a rumour-mongering campaign；attack by spreading rumours / 追查～ trace a rumour to its source / 制止～的扩散 stop the spread of a rumour / ～对社会有极大的破坏性。Rumour does great damage to society.

谣谚 yáoyàn ballads and popular sayings；folksongs and folk adages

谣诼 yáozhuó 〈书面〉slander；calumny；vilification

遥 yáo distant；remote；faraway：路～难行。The journey is long and difficult. / ～祝平安。Wish you to be safe and sound from afar.

遥测 yáocè remote monitoring；telemetering；remote metering：空间～ space telemetry / ～发射机 telemetering transmitter / ～接收机 telemetering receiver / ～控制装置 telemetering control assembly / ～仪 telegauge；telemeter / ～装置 telemetry；telequipment

遥测地震学 yáocè dìzhènxué 〈地质〉teleseismology

遥测计 yáocèjì telemeter

遥测气象计 yáocè qìxiàngjì 〈气象〉telemeteorograph

遥测器 yáocèqì remote detector

遥测术 yáocèshù *also*"遥测学" telemetry

遥测温度计 yáocè wēndùjì telethermometer

遥测心电图 yáocè xīndiàntú telemetric radio cardiogram

遥导 yáodǎo teleguide

遥感 yáogǎn 〈电子〉remote sensing：红外～ infrared remote sensing / ～仪器 remote sensing instrument / ～技术 remote sensing technique / ～器 remote sensor

遥感卫星 yáogǎn wèixīng remote sensing satellite

遥见 yáojiàn see from a distance：在香山上可以～北京城。Standing on the top of Fragrant Hill, one can see the city of Beijing in the distance.

遥控 yáokòng 〈自控〉remote control；telecontrol；distance control：～板 remote control hand unit / ～机器人 teleoperator / ～系统 telechirics；remote control system / ～配电盘〈电工〉power remote control panel（PRCP）/ ～飞行器〈航空〉remotely piloted vehicle / ～采煤法 remote control coal mining；push button coal mining / ～轰炸机 robot bomber；bomber drone / ～艇 distance controlled boat / ～诊疗术〈医学〉telemedography

遥控开关 yáokòng kāiguān teleswitch

遥控力学 yáokòng lìxué telemechanics

遥示 yáoshì remote-indicating：～器 remote indicator / 数据～器 remote-data indicator

遥望 yáowàng look into the distance；look far ahead：～故乡 look in the direction of one's hometown / 凝神～ gaze into the distance / 极目～ look as far as the eye can reach / 他站在山顶，～大海。He stood on the peak and gazed out to sea.

遥相呼应 yáoxiāng-hūyìng echo each other at a distance；coordinate with each other from afar：他们一伙人，里外勾结，～，做尽了坏事。They colluded with each other from within and without by coordinating their efforts, and did all kinds of evil to the people.

遥想 yáoxiǎng ❶ think back；recollect；recall：～往昔岁月，感慨良多。Recalling his past years, he sighed with deep emotion. ❷ think of the future；envisage：～21 世纪科技发展的前景 envisage the prospect of the development of science and technology in the 21st century

遥信 yáoxìn 〈电子〉remote signalling：～装置 remote signalling plant

遥遥 yáoyáo ❶ far distant；far away；remote：路途～ long way to go / 两地～（of a couple, etc.）live far apart / 山东半岛和辽东半岛～相对。Shandong peninsula and Liaodong peninsula face each other across the sea. ❷ long time ago or off；far into the future；remote：～华胄 offspring of ancient sages or distinguished families of remote past

遥遥领先 yáoyáo-lǐngxiān be far ahead：这场球赛，甲队的比分～。During the match, team A scored far more than the other team.

遥遥无期 yáoyáo-wúqī not in the foreseeable future：大楼竣工还～。It will take an unconscionable time to complete the building.

遥夜 yáoyè 〈书面〉eternal night；long night：～深思 spend the whole night meditating

遥远 yáoyuǎn distant；remote：～的地方 distant place；place at the back of beyond / ～的距离 long distance / ～的天空 far away in the sky / ～的年代 remote past / ～的往事 time-honoured events；far-back memories / 两岸相距～。There is quite a distance between the two banks. *or* The two banks are far apart from each other.

遥瞻 yáozhān 〈书面〉look far：～未来 look far into the future；look far ahead / ～故乡 look in the direction of one's native place

遥指 yáozhǐ point to the distance

遥瞩 yáozhǔ look into the distance：凝眸～ gaze into the distance

瑶 yáo 〈书面〉❶ precious jade：琼～ fine jade ❷ precious；wonderful：～浆 good wine

瑶池 Yáochí Jasper Lake, a legendary place where a fairy queen（i.e. Mother of the West）lives

瑶琴 yáoqín fiddle inlaid with jade

瑶章 yáozhāng good poetry：欣读～ read your fine poems with great pleasure

瑶族 Yáozú Yao nationality, distributed over Guangxi, Yunnan, Guangdong and Guizhou

摇 yáo shake；wave；wag；rock：～旗 wave a flag / ～一～药瓶 shake up a bottle of medicine / ～纺车 turn a spinning wheel / ～船 row a boat；scull a boat / ～着他的肩膀 shake him by the shoulder / 别～这小船，我会头晕的。Please don't rock the boat or I'll

feel dizzy. /小狗～着尾巴跑了过来。The puppy came wagging its tail. /他大～大摆地走进来。He swaggered into the room. /树上的黄叶飘～落地。Golden leaves fluttered to the ground.
摇把 yáobà 〈机械〉cranking bar
摇摆 yáobǎi sway; swing; rock; waver: 小树迎风～。Young trees swayed in the breeze. /船身～得利害。The ship rocked a great deal. /几只鸭子一摇一摆地走了过去。A few ducks went wobbling by. /我们的政策不会左右～。Our policies will not swing back and forth. /他立场坚定，从不～。He is steadfast in his stand and never wavers.
摇摆不定 yáobǎi-bùdìng swing to and fro; chop and change; vacillate; waver: ～的人 waverer; wobbler /他对这个问题的态度总是～。He always wavers (*or* vacillates) on the question.
摇摆舞 yáobǎiwǔ rock and roll; rock'n'roll
摇摆乐 yáobǎiyuè swing; swing music
摇板式进料器 yáobǎnshì jìnliàoqì 〈机械〉wobble plate feeder
摇臂 yáobì rocker or rocking arm; swinging arm: ～轴 rocker shaft /～吊车 swinging crane /～钻床 radial drilling machine
摇颤 yáochàn shake; quiver: 她越想越害怕，心不由自主地～起来。The more she thought about it the more she was frightened. Her heart beat violently (*or* throbbed) with fear.
摇车 yáochē 〈方言〉❶ cradle ❷ spinning wheel
摇床 yáochuáng 〈矿业〉table: 粗选～ roughing table /选矿～ cleaning table /～造矿法 tabling
摇唇鼓舌 yáochún-gǔshé flap one's lips and wag one's tongue; engage in loose talk: 他们～，到处煽动。They tried to stir up trouble by gossiping everywhere.
摇荡 yáodàng shake; rock; sway: 荷花在晚风中～。Lotuses swayed in the evening breeze. /军心～。The morale of the army has been shaken.
摇动 yáodòng ❶ wave; shake: ～彩旗 wave coloured flags /使用前请～瓶子。Shake the bottle before use. ❷ rock; sway: 地震时，吊灯猛烈地～起来。During the earthquake the chandelier began to sway wildly. /婴儿～着四肢，大声哭叫。The baby flailed its limbs, crying loudly. ❸ waver; vacillate; shake: 信念～ waver in one's faith /人心～。The morale of the people is low.
摇动机 yáodòngjī 〈化工〉shakeout machine
摇动流槽 yáodòng liúcáo shaking chute; shake chute
摇动筛 yáodòngshāi shaking screen; shaker
摇动输送机 yáodòng shūsòngjī shaker conveyer
摇鹅毛扇 yáo émáoshàn wave a goose-feather fan (stereotypical of an adviser in old novels or operas) — give counsel behind the scenes; mastermind: ～的 man waving a feather fan — mastermind behind a scheme; moving force /这个人才真正是在这伙人背后～的。He is the man who is pulling the strings behind the bunch.
摇杆 yáogǎn 〈机械〉rocker; rocker-bar; rocker lever; sway rod: ～机构 rocker gear; rocker mechanism /～轴 rocker shaft
摇滚乐 yáogǔnyuè big beat; rock'n'roll
摇撼 yáohan rock or shake violently; shake to the root or foundation: 过路的坦克～着房子。The passing tanks shook the house to its foundation. /风怒吼着，猛烈地～着窗户。The roaring wind rattled the window violently.
摇晃 yáohuang shake; sway; rock: ～的桌子 shaky (*or* rickety, *or* wobbly) table /树影～ swaying shadow of trees /轮船在大浪里～着。The ship was rocking in the rough sea. /铁索桥被狂风吹得直～。The chain bridge swung wildly in the gale. /他骑上自行车，摇摇晃晃地顶风向前。He got on the bike and wobbled forward against the wind. /病人摇摇晃晃地站起身来。The patient staggered to his feet.
摇惑 yáohuò confuse; perplex: ～人心 confuse the people
摇奖 yáojiǎng lottery
摇篮 yáolán cradle: 摇～ rock a cradle /摇着～哄孩子睡觉 cradle a baby to sleep /扼杀在～中 strangle sth. in the cradle /东方文化的～ cradle of Eastern culture
摇篮曲 yáolánqǔ lullaby; cradlesong; *berceuse*
摇耧 yáolóu rock a drill barrow in planting; plant with a drill barrow
摇蜜 yáomì extract honey: ～机 honey extractor
摇旗呐喊 yáoqí-nàhǎn wave flags and shout battle cries; raise a hue and cry; drum up support: 一队人马，～，冲了上去。A troop of soldiers and horses charged forward, waving flags and shouting battle cries. /他们还在为旧制度～。They still tried to drum up support for the old system.
摇钱树 yáoqiánshù legendary tree that sheds coins when shaken; money tree; milch cow; cash cow; ready source of money: 他把女儿当成～。He looked on his daughter as his source of income.
摇纱 yáoshā 〈纺织〉reeling: ～工 reeler /～机 reeling machine; reeling frame
摇摄 yáoshè *also* "摇镜头"〈摄影〉pan: ～全景 pan the camera across the scene
摇身一变 yáoshēn-yībiàn give oneself a shake and change into another form; metamorphose at an instant: 他这个大汉奸，～竟成了"爱国人士"。This rank traitor, changing like a chameleon, had suddenly become a "patriot".
摇式卸车机 yáoshì xièchējī rocker unloader
摇手 yáoshǒu ❶ gesture with one's hand in admonition or disapproval: 让她给大家唱个歌，她直～。She refused by waving her hand when she was invited to sing us a song. /他偷偷地冲我～，叫我不要签合同。He beckoned me in secret not to sign the contract. ❷ cranking bar
摇头 yáotóu shake one's head: 我跟父亲谈了我的想法，他～反对。My father shook his head at my idea when I told him all about it.
摇头摆尾 yáotóu-bǎiwěi shake the head and wag the tail — assume an air of complacency; strut; swagger: 他～地走来，人们侧目而视。People looked askance at him as he strutted along with an air of complacency.
摇头晃脑 yáotóu-huàngnǎo wag one's head — look very much pleased with oneself; assume an air of self-conceit or self-satisfaction: 他听京戏听到得意处，便～起来。He enjoyed his favourite Beijing opera so much that he began to wag his head.
摇头丸 yáotóuwán Ecstasy, a narcotic
摇尾乞怜 yáowěi-qǐlián wag one's tail ingratiatingly; beg like a dog for mercy: 这种人只会向主子～，毫无出息。A man of this sort could do nothing but fawn on his master.
摇蚊 yáowén midge; chironomid
摇窝 yáowō 〈方言〉cradle
摇漾 yáoyàng shake; rock; sway; swing: 小船在湖心～。The small boat rocked gently in the middle of the lake.
摇摇欲坠 yáoyáo-yùzhuì tottering; crumbling; falling apart; teetering on the verge of collapse: ～的古塔 tottering ancient tower /～的统治 crumbling rule (*or* regime) /那座小楼，满身弹痕，有点～的样子。That small building, covered all over with bullet holes, was nodding to its fall.
摇曳 yáoyè flicker; sway; flirt: 他踏着斑驳～的月光树影。He walked along the road covered with flickering dots of moonlight and shadows of trees. /夜风～着柳枝。The branches of willow swayed in the night breeze. /她的长裙～着。Her long skirt flirted.
摇椅 yáoyǐ rocking chair
摇钻 yáozuàn brace; bit-stock

徭(傜) yáo forced labour; compulsory service; corvée
徭役 yáoyì corvée: 沉重的～ heavy corvée
徭役地租 yáoyì dìzū labour rent

鳐 yáo ray; skate

猺 yáo *see* "黄猺" huángyáo; "青猺" qīngyáo

飖 yáo *see* "飘飖" piāoyáo

繇 yáo 〈书面〉❶ *see* "徭" yáo ❷ *see* "谣" yáo
see also yóu; zhòu

轺 yáo
轺车 yáochē light vehicle in ancient times

yǎo

窅 yǎo 〈书面〉deep and remote: 下临深渊，～然无底。The valley below is too deep to fathom.
窅冥 yǎomíng 〈书面〉❶ dim; dusky ❷ deep; profound; abstruse
窅然 yǎorán 〈书面〉remote: 桃花流水～去。The water carried peach blossoms far away into the distance.

Y

窈 yǎo 〈书面〉❶ deep; profound ❷ dim

窈冥 yǎomíng *also* “窅冥” yǎomíng; “杳冥” yǎomíng ❶ dim; dusky ❷ deep; profound

窈窕 yǎotiǎo 〈书面〉❶ (of a girl or woman) gentle and graceful: ～淑女 graceful fair maiden /身材～ have a graceful figure ❷ (of a palace or landscape) deep and quiet; secluded: 山涧～ deep mountain stream /～九重闱 secluded boudoir

杳 yǎo 〈书面〉too far away to be readily accessible: 归路～漫 long, long way from home /此处～无人烟。This is a desolate place, where not a single soul can be seen. *or* The place is completely deserted.

杳渺 yǎomiǎo *also* “杳眇”〈书面〉remote; deep: ～的天际 distant horizon /沉入那～的海底 sink to the deep bottom of the sea

杳冥 yǎomíng *see* “窈冥” yǎomíng

杳然 yǎorán 〈书面〉totally silent or still; without a trace: 信息～ be heard of no more

杳如黄鹤 yǎorúhuánghè disappear like the yellow crane — gone for ever; nowhere to be found: 那信发出去以后，～，我一直没收到回信。Like the yellow crane that is gone never to return, my letter hasn't got any reply. /他离家已有五年，～。He's been away from home for five years and nobody knows his whereabouts.

杳无音信 yǎowúyīnxìn have absolutely no news about sb.; disappear for good and all: 这些年来他到处打听哥哥的下落，却都～。He's been trying to locate his brother these years but has got no news at all about him. /她日夜思念着～的丈夫。Day and night she missed her husband whom she had never heard of ever since his departure.

杳无踪迹 yǎowúzōngjì disappear without a trace; vanish into thin air

咬(齩、鼩) yǎo ❶ bite; gnaw; snap at: ～嘴唇 bite one's lip /～了一大口苹果 take a good bite of the apple /～不动 too hard to bite (*or* chew) /用嘴～绳子 snap at a rope /小心，狗～人。Be careful. The dog bites. /老鼠在箱子上～了个洞。Rats have gnawed a hole in the trunk. /蚊子在我腿上～了几个包。There are some mosquito bites in my leg. ❷ grip; bite: 大吊钳～住钻杆。The suspension pincers grips the drillrod. /齿轮～死了，转不动。The gear has got stuck. ❸ (of a dog) bark: 昨天半夜狗～得厉害。The dog barked fiercely last midnight. ❹ incriminate another person (usu. innocent); implicate: 乱～好人 implicate innocent people indiscriminately/反～一口 make a false countercharge against one's accuser ❺ 〈方言〉(of paint, etc.) cause a swelling or itch; irritate; corrode: 我最怕漆～。I am dreadfully allergic to paint. /碱水把铝锅～坏了。The aluminium pot was corroded by alkaline water. ❻ pronounce; enunciate; articulate: 字音～得准 pronounce words accurately /她声音很低，但字眼～得很清楚。Although in a low voice, she enunciated every word clearly. ❼ be fastidious or nit-picking (about the use of words): *see* “～字眼儿” ❽ follow closely; close in; advance on: 双方比分～得很紧。It's a close game. /他见后面～得不紧，步子就慢了下来。He slowed down as he saw he was not closely followed.

咬定 yǎodìng insist; assert: 他～完工的日子不能变。He insisted that the deadline of the work be not changed. /这孩子一口～他是凶手。This child said definitely that he was the murderer.

咬耳朵 yǎo ěrduo 〈口语〉whisper in sb.'s ear; whisper: 你们有什么事就公开说出来，别～啦! Whatever is on your mind, speak out. Stop whispering, please.

咬合 yǎohé occlude; interlock; mesh: ～纸〈医学〉occluding paper /～器 occluder /错位～〈医学〉malocclusion /齿轮～〈机械〉meshing (*or* engaging) of gear wheels

咬肌 yǎojī 〈生理〉great masticatory

咬架 yǎojià (of animals) fight with each other: 两只狗为抢骨头～。Two dogs fought for a bone.

咬嚼 yǎojiáo chew; ruminate over; mull over: 他反复～着这句话的意义。He was ruminating on the meaning of the sentence.

咬紧牙关 yǎojǐn yáguān grit or clench one's teeth; bite the bullet; endure with dogged will

咬啮 yǎoniè nibble at; bite: 痛苦正～着他的心。Agony was gnawing at his heart.

咬群 yǎoqún 〈口语〉❶ (of a domestic animal) be liable to fight within the herd ❷ (of a person) apt to pick a quarrel within a group; fractious: 他太爱～，与谁都处不好。He is apt to pick a fight with people, and never gets along with anybody.

咬舌儿 yǎoshér *also* “咬舌子” ❶ lisp ❷ lisper

咬噬 yǎoshì bite

咬手 yǎoshǒu 〈方言〉❶ (of hand) swell or itch (because of frostbite, or irritation of paint or acid): 寒冬腊月冷得～。Hands get frostbitten in severe winter. ❷ (of price) cannot afford: 我喜欢这种音响，可价钱太～。I like this kind of hi-fi system but it's too expensive for me. ❸ difficult; hard; troublesome: 这事还真～。It's really a hard nut to crack.

咬文嚼字 yǎowén-jiáozì juggle with words like a pedant; be fastidious about the use of language: 读这篇文章要抓实质，不要～。You should grasp the gist of the article instead of paying too much attention to its wording.

咬牙 yǎoyá ❶ clench or gnash one's teeth (out of indignition or in agony): 恨得直～ gnash one's teeth with hatred /～忍痛 grit one's teeth in pain ❷ grind one's teeth in sleep

咬牙切齿 yǎoyá-qièchǐ gnash or clench one's teeth: 那男人～地骂着。That man cursed through clenched teeth. /只要一提起那个恶棍，没有一个人不恨得～。Everybody would gnash his teeth with hatred at the mere mention of that scoundrel.

咬住 yǎozhù ❶ bite into; grip with one's teeth: 那狗突然蹿了上来，～我的腿。That dog jumped at me suddenly and bit me in the leg. ❷ grip; get on; take firm hold of; refuse to let go of: 你们团必须紧紧地～敌人。Your regiment must follow closely on the heels of the enemy. /他迅速～了敌机并将其击落。He got on the tail of the enemy plane immediately and brought it down. /这件事跟我没关系，你干吗总～我? It has nothing to do with me. Why do you keep nagging me about it?

咬字儿 yǎozìr pronounce; enunciate; articulate: ～清楚 have clear pronunciation; be articulate

咬字眼儿 yǎo zìyǎnr nit-picking about words; fastidious about diction: 你们当心点儿，他可是专爱～。You must be careful with your words, for he is there to nit-pick.

咬嘴 yǎozuǐ difficult to articulate; hard to pronounce: 这几句诗真～，不好念。These lines are too difficult to read, just like a tongue-twister.

舀 yǎo ladle out; spoon up; scoop up: ～水 ladle out water

舀子 yǎozi dipper; ladle; scoop

yào

疟(瘧) yào
see also nüè

疟子 yàozi malaria: 发～ have got malaria; catch malaria

袎 yào 〈书面〉*see* “靿” yào

靿 yào leg of a boot or stocking: 高～儿袜子 stocking; panty-hose /靴～儿 bootleg

靿子 yàozi 〈方言〉*see* “靿”

爇 yào ❶ *see* “药” yào ❷ (Yào) a surname

药(藥) yào ❶ medicine; drug; remedy: 西～ western medicine /中～ traditional Chinese medicine /草～ herbal medicine /避孕～ contraceptive drugs /感冒～ medicine for colds /抗癌～ anti-cancer drugs /特效～ specific medicine; specific /预防～ preventive medicine; prophylactic /丸～ pill (*or* bolus) of Chinese medicine /汤～ decoction of medicinal ingredients /膏～ plaster /补～ tonic /安眠～ sleeping pill /止痛～ pain killer /止泻～ antidiarrhea /止血～ haemostatic /退热～ antipyretic /镇静～ sedative /内服～ for oral administration /外用～ for external use /服～ take medicine /换～ change dressings /煎～ decoct herbal medicine /开～ prescribe a medicine; write out a prescription /配～ (of a pharmacist) make up a prescription /上～ apply ointment to /抓～ have a prescription filled /用草～治病 use herbal remedies ❷ certain chemicals: 火～ gun-powder /炸～ explosive; dynamite /农～ farm chemical; pesticide /杀虫～ insecticide /耗子～ rat-poison; ratsbane ❸ 〈书面〉cure

with medicine: 不可救～ incurable; beyond cure; incorrigible ❹ kill with poison: ～蟑螂 poison cockroaches /～死人 kill a man with poison

药补 yàobǔ improve one's health by taking tonics: ～不如食补。Nourishing food is better than a tonic to one's health. *or* Food cures better than medicine.

药材 yàocái medicinal material; crude drug; medicinal herb: 名贵～ rare medicinal herb

药草 yàocǎo medicinal herb

药叉 yàochā *also* "夜叉" yècha ❶〈佛教〉yaksha, an evil spirit ❷ hideous, ruthless person

药厂 yàochǎng pharmaceutical factory or plant

药单 yàodān prescription

药典 yàodiǎn pharmacopoeia

药店 yàodiàn ❶ drugstore; chemist's shop; pharmacy ❷〈方言〉herbal medicine shop

药饵 yào'ěr *see* "药物"

药方 yàofāng prescription: 开～ write out a prescription /抄～ copy a prescription /这～治病挺管用。This prescription works well.

药房 yàofáng ❶ drugstore; chemist's shop; pharmacy ❷ hospital pharmacy; dispensary: 中～ dispensary for Chinese medicine

药费 yàofèi expenses or charges for medicine: 报销～ be reimbursed for medical expenses

药粉 yàofěn medicinal powder

药膏 yàogāo ointment; salve; plaster: 上～ apply a plaster to; put a salve on

药罐子 yàoguànzi ❶ pot for decocting herbal medicine ❷〈比喻〉chronic patient; perennial invalid: 我都记不清吃了多少药，我简直是个～。I can't remember how many medicines I've taken. I'm simply a herbal medicine pot.

药害 yàohài damage to crops caused by improper use of farm chemicals

药衡 yàohéng apothecaries' measure or weight

药剂 yàojì medicament; drug

药剂拌种 yàojì bànzhǒng 〈农业〉seeds treated with insecticides

药剂师 yàojìshī pharmacist; druggist; chemist

药剂士 yàojìshì asistant pharmacist or chemist

药剂天平 yàojì tiānpíng dispensing balance

药剂学 yàojìxué pharmaceutics; pharmacy

药检 yàojiǎn drug test: 通过～ pass a drug test /这些运动员经过～，都呈阴性。These athletes all showed negative reaction to the drug test.

药箭 yàojiàn poisonous arrow; poisoned arrow

药劲儿 yàojìnr efficacy of a drug

药酒 yàojiǔ medicinal liquor

药具 yàojù medical instrument

药理 yàolǐ ❶ pharmacodynamics ❷ pharmacology

药理学 yàolǐxué pharmacology

药力 yàolì efficacy of a drug or medicine: 充分发挥～ make the most of a drug /～就要发作了。The drug is going to take effect.

药料 yàoliào medicinal material; crude drug

药麻 yàomá *also* "麻药" anesthetic; drug used as an anesthetic

药棉 yàomián absorbent cotton

药面 yàomiàn medicinal powder

药捻儿 yàoniǎnr ❶ fuse (for explosives) ❷ *see* "药捻子"

药捻子 yàoniǎnzi 〈中医〉slender roll of medicated paper or gauze (to be inserted into wounds, boils, etc.); medicated wick

药碾子 yàoniǎnzi 〈中医〉metal roller used for grinding medicine

药农 yàonóng farmer who cultivates or collects medicinal herbs; medicinal herb grower or collector; herbalist

药片 yàopiàn (medicinal) tablet: 糖衣～ sugar-coated tablet

药品 yàopǐn medicines and chemical reagents: ～监督 drug control /家庭备用～ family pharmacy /把～及时送到灾区 send medicine to the afflicted (*or* disaster) area in time

药瓶 yàopíng medicine bottle

药铺 yàopù herbal medicine shop

药签 yàoqiān swab; antiseptic wipe

药球 yàoqiú medicine ball

药膳 yàoshàn medicated diet; food cooked with medicinal herbs

药石 yàoshí medicines and stone needles for acupuncture — remedies: ～罔效。All medical treatment has been in vain.

药石之言 yàoshízhīyán words that work like medicine — unpalatable but wholesome exhortation; salutary advice: 他这是～，你要认真考虑。You should seriously consider his sincere advice.

药室爆破 yàoshì bàopò 〈矿业〉coyote blasting; coyote-hole blasting; gopherhole blasting

药水 yàoshuǐ liquid medicine; medicinal liquid: 眼～ eyedrop /红～ mercurochrome /紫～ gentian violet

药筒 yàotǒng shell case; cartridge case

药丸 yàowán *also* "药丸子" pill; bolus

药味 yàowèi ❶ herbal medicines in a prescription ❷ flavour of a drug

药物 yàowù medicines; pharmaceuticals; medicaments: ～副作用 side effect of medicine /～治疗 pharmacotherapy

药物过敏 yàowù guòmǐn drug allergy

药物化学 yàowù huàxué pharmaceutical chemistry

药物学 yàowùxué *materia medica*; pharmacology

药物牙膏 yàowù yágāo medicated toothpaste

药物中毒 yàowù zhòngdú drug poisoning

药箱 yàoxiāng medical kit; medicine chest: 急救～ first-aid kit

药效 yàoxiào effectiveness of a medicine: 这药～特别好。The medicine is very effective.

药械 yàoxiè implements for applying farm chemicals; sprayer; duster

药性 yàoxìng property of a medicine: ～平和 mild medicine /～猛 strong medicine

药性气 yàoxìngqi flavour of a drug

药学 yàoxué pharmacy: ～家 pharmacist

药学院 yàoxuéyuàn pharmaceutical college

药言 yàoyán 〈书面〉advice; admonition; exhortation: 金石～ sincere, wholesome advice

药引子 yàoyǐnzi 〈中医〉ingredient added to enhance the efficacy of a dose of medicine

药用 yàoyòng used as medicine; medicinal

药用炭 yàoyòngtàn medical charcoal

药用植物 yàoyòng zhíwù medicinal plant: ～学 medical botany /～园 medicinal garden

药浴 yàoyù ❶〈畜牧〉dipping: 羊～ sheep dipping / ～池 dipping tank or vat ❷ medicated bath

药皂 yàozào medicated soap

药渣 yàozhā dregs of a decoction

药疹 yàozhěn 〈医学〉drug rash or eruption

药政 yàozhèng drug administration: ～法 drug administration law /～机构 drug administration organ

要[1]

yào ❶ important; significant: 主～ principal; prime /首～ first and foremost /紧～ imperative; urgent /险～ of strategic importance /文件精神希迅速传达为～。It is imperative that the gist of the document be conveyed (*or* relayed) immediately. ❷ important substance; essentials: 摘～ abstract /纲～ outline /纪～ summary of minutes

要[2]

yào ❶ want; desire; need; like to keep: ～钱不～命 want money more than one's own life /这本词典我还～，那本我不～了，你拿去吧。I still need this dictionary but I don't need that one any more, so you can have it. ❷ ask for; demand: ～债 demand payment of a debt /我跟老张～了两张票。I asked Lao Zhang for two tickets. /我～了两菜一汤。I ordered two dishes and a bowl of soup. /喂！我～公关部。Hello, will you put me through to the PR department, please. ❸ ask sb. to do sth.; request: 她～系主任给她开个介绍信。She asked the dean to write a letter of recommendation for her. /是你～我留下的。It's you who asked me to stay. /他～我们明早结账。He told us to check out tomorrow morning. ❹ want to; desire: 他～学游泳。He wants to learn swimming. /就这个问题我还～再说几句。I'd like to say a few more words on this matter. /他～找那个骗他的人算账。He has an account to settle with the man who cheated him. /我～做的事太多了。I've got too many irons in the fire. ❺ must; should; have to: 写文章～简明扼要。An article must be brief and to the point. /年轻人～尊重老年人。The young should show respect for the old. /这自行车～修修才行。This bike needs repairing. /咱们～多学点，努力适应新形势的需要。We have to learn more to adjust ourselves to the new situation. ❻ require; need; take: 从这儿到机场乘出租车～用一个半小时。It takes an hour and a

half to get to the airport by taxi from here. /你～几个人帮忙? How many people do you need? ❼ be going to; be about to: ～下雨了, 咱们快跑回家吧。It's going to rain. Let's run back home. /她～发脾气了, 咱们别说了。She is just about to fly into a temper. Let's stop talking. /中秋节～到了。The Mid-Autumn Festival is drawing near. /他快～大学毕业了。He'll graduate from the university soon. ❽ *used to indicate an estimation in comparisons*: 对这件事你～比我了解得清楚些。You must have known more than I did about it. /屋子里太热, 树荫底下～凉快得多。It's too hot in here. It'll be much cooler in the shade outside. /我认为第二个方案～切实可行些。I reckon the second plan is more practicable.

要[3] yào ❶ if; suppose; in case: 你～见着小王的话, 替我问个好。If you see Xiao Wang give my best regards to him, please. /我～赶不回来, 你们就先开始。In case I can't get back in time, please start without me. /他～不同意怎么办? What if he doesn't agree? *or* Suppose he doesn't agree? ❷ either... or...: ～就去看电影, ～就去溜冰, 别再犹豫了。We either go to a film or go skating. Don't hesitate any more.

see also yāo

要隘 yào'ài strategic pass: 扼守～ hold (*or* defend) a strategic pass

要案 yào'àn major case: 查处～ investigate and try major cases

要不 yàobù *also* "要不然" ❶ otherwise; or else; or: 咱们该动身了, ～就赶不上这班车了。We have to leave now, or we'll miss the bus. /你应该抓紧时间学习, ～就应付不了工作。You should study harder, otherwise you can't do a good job. ❷ either...or...: ～去看戏, ～去听音乐。Either go to a play or to a concert.

要不得 yàobude no good; of no use; intolerable: 他当经理可～。He'd be no good as manager. /考试作弊～。Cheating in examination is not to be tolerated.

要不是 yàobushì if it were not for; but for; without: ～你及时帮助, 我们就成功不了啦。If it hadn't been for your timely help, we wouldn't have succeeded. /～这场大雾, 飞机就按时起飞了。But for the heavy fog, the plane would have taken off on time.

要冲 yàochōng communications centre or hub: 军事～ strategic military post /郑州是中原地区的交通～。Zhengzhou is the communications centre of the Central Plains.

要道 yàodào ❶ main artery; arterial highway; thoroughfare: 交通～ important line of communications /这里是通向军事基地的～。This is the vital road (leading) to the military base. ❷ major principle: 此乃治学之～。This is the cardinal principle of learning (*or* scholarly research).

要得 yàodé 〈方言〉 good; fine; okay: 我看让这个小伙子替你～。I think it's alright to let this young man take your place. /"你看这样好不好?" "～, ～!" "How do you like it?" "That's fine."

要地 yàodì ❶ important place; strategic point: 徐州是历史上的军事～。Xuzhou was a place of strategic importance in history. ❷〈书面〉 important position: 身处～ hold an important position

要点 yàodiǎn ❶ main points; essentials; gist: 抓住～ grasp the essence /写出文章的～ write an outline of the article ❷ key stronghold: 军事～ key military stronghold /战略～ strategic position

要端 yàoduān main points; essentials; gist: 举其～ give the main points (of an article, speech, etc.)

要短儿 yàoduǎnr 〈方言〉 disclose sb.'s faults; make a fool of sb. before others: 让我这破锣嗓子唱个歌? 别当大伙儿的面儿要我的短儿了! Invite me to sing in my hoarse voice? Don't try to make a fool of me before you all!

要厄 yào'è *also* "要扼" 〈书面〉 narrow pass; strategic pass; defile: 此地乃川陕之交通～。This is the vital pass joining Sichuan and Shaanxi provinces.

要犯 yàofàn important or principal criminal

要饭 yàofàn beg (for food or money): 沿街～ go begging in the streets /～的 beggar

要公 yàogōng 〈旧语〉 urgent official business

要害 yàohài ❶ (of one's body) vital part: 那一枪没打中～。That shot missed his vital organs. /这篇文章切中～。This article has hit the nail on the head. ❷〈比喻〉 crucial or strategic point: ～部门 key department /此村地处～。The village is located at a point of strategic importance. /我们要设法解决～问题而不是回避它。We should do everything possible to settle crucial issues instead of evading them.

要好 yàohǎo ❶ be on good terms; be friends: 她们～得难舍难分。They are such close friends that they are almost inseparable. ❷ be eager to improve oneself; want to do well: 这孩子很～, 学习成绩总在前几名。This child always wants to do well in his studies and is one of the top students in his class.

要好看 yào hǎokàn make a fool of sb. in the presence of others: 你要再捣乱, 我就要你的好看! If you make trouble again, I'll teach you a lesson you won't forget.

要谎 yàohuǎng overcharge: 早市上的东西常常～。If you shop at the morning fair, more often than not you'll be overcharged.

要价 yàojià ❶ ask a price; charge: 漫天～ demand an exorbitant price /他～太高的话, 咱们就到别处去买。We'll buy it somewhere else if he asks too much. ❷ attach conditions; ask terms: 在谈判中他们～过高, 我方无法接受。The terms they asked in the negotiation are too high for us to accept.

要价还价 yàojià-huánjià *also* "讨价还价" tǎojià-huánjià bargain; haggle; dicker

要件 yàojiàn ❶ important document ❷ essential condition

要津 yàojīn ❶ ferry of strategic importance; important communication hub ❷〈比喻〉important post: 位居～ occupy a key post

要紧 yàojǐn ❶ vital; important; essential: ～的事 urgent thing; matter of vital importance /信誉～ good faith is all important /救人～。It's most urgent to rescue people. /做这种工作, ～的是细心。This job requires absolute care. ❷ serious; critical: 他的病～吗? Is he very ill? /就是有点儿头疼, 不～。I've only got a slight headache, nothing serious. /没带介绍信不～, 带身份证了就行。It doesn't matter if you haven't got a letter of introduction. Your ID card will do. ❸〈方言〉 be in a hurry to do sth.: 我～去看戏, 得马上走。I'm in a hurry to go to the theatre, so I must be off now.

要诀 yàojué essential secret of success; key trick of trade; knack: 读书的～ secret of learning /做官的～ knack of moving up in officialdom

要脸 yàoliǎn have a sense of shame: 不～ shameless; impudent /他这个人很～, 不会做这种事的。He's a man of honour. He couldn't have done it.

要领 yàolǐng ❶ main points; gist: 读书时记笔记要学会抓～。When reading one should learn to take down the gist of a book. /我给他讲了好几遍, 他就是不得～。I explained the matter to him many times but he just couldn't get it right. ❷ basic requirements (of an exercise or skill); knack; essentials: 操作～ essentials of operation /掌握～ get the knack (*or* hang) of sth.

要路 yàolù ❶ major road; major artery; arterial highway ❷〈比喻〉 key position; key post

要略 yàolüè outline; summary; synopsis: 《修辞～》 *Essentials of Rhetoric*

要么 yàome *also* "要末" or; either... or...: 电话里说不清楚, ～你亲自去一趟。You can't explain it clearly on the phone. How about going there yourself? /船票没买到, ～就改坐火车吧。We haven't got ship tickets. Let's go by train instead. /～加班干完它, ～拖到明天再说。你们说吧。We either work overtime to finish it or leave it till tomorrow. It's up to you.

要面子 yào miànzi be keen on face-saving; be anxious to preserve one's reputation: 他太～, 不讲究实际。He worries so much about keeping up appearances that he fails to get down to brass tacks.

要命 yàomìng ❶ cost one one's life; drive one to one's death; kill: 癌症要了他的命。He died of cancer. *or* Cancer killed him. /这是～的病。It's a fatal disease. ❷ to an extreme degree; extremely; terribly: 吵得～ terribly noisy /好得～ extremely good /急得～ worried to death /挤得～ packed like sardines /胆小得～ timid as a rabbit ❸ nuisance: 真～, 我的表又慢了。What a nuisance! My watch is slow again.

要目 yàomù important items; major entries: 阅读～ go over the important titles (*or* headlines) /把～列出来 make a list of all the important entries

要强 yàoqiáng be eager to excel in whatever one does; be anxious to outdo others: 他事事～。He is eager to outdo others in whatever he undertakes. /他虽年纪大了, 可仍像当年一样好胜～。Old as he is, he's still as eager to excel as he used to be.

要人 yàorén very important person (VIP); important personage; bigwig: 政界～ important political figure /这是一个商界～的聚会。This is a party for business magnates.

要塞 yàosài fort; fortress; fortification: 海军～ naval fortress /～区 garrison area /～炮兵 garrison artillery

Y

要事 yàoshì important matter or business:有～相商。I have something important to discuss with you.
要是 yàoshi if; suppose; in case:～明天下雨，你还去不去看足球赛? In case it rains tomorrow, will you still go to the football match? /～你有兴趣的话，咱们一起去。We can go together if you're interested.
要枢 yàoshū important hub; key position:交通～ important hub of communications
要死 yàosǐ to an extreme degree; terribly; awfully:疼得～ terribly hurt; awfully painful /吓得～ be scared out of one's wits; be scared to death /气得～ be furious
要死不活 yàosǐ-bùhuó more dead than alive:这病把他拖得～。The illness has worn him out.
要素 yàosù essential factor; crucial component; key element:构成汉字的～ key elements in the formation of Chinese characters
要素成本 yàosù chéngběn 〈经济〉factor cost
要图 yàotú important plan:城市建设～ master plan of the city
要闻 yàowén important news; front-page story:国际～ major international news /每日～ (news) headlines of the day
要务 yàowù important affairs:此次前来是有～在身。This time I come here to do some important business.
要项 yàoxiàng important matter or point
要言不烦 yàoyán-bùfán concise and succinct in speech or in writing; terse:这篇文章～，值得一读。This article is worth reading as it is succinct and to the point.
要样儿 yàoyàngr strive to reach a certain standard; be particular about form or appearance:这孩子有上进心，干什么都要个样儿。The child is eager to make progress. He strives to do well in whatever he does.
要义 yàoyì main points or ideas; essentials:认真领会文件～。Grasp the essence of a document. /作人～不可不懂。One must know the essentials of how to behave (in society).
要员 yàoyuán important official:政府～ high government official
要之 yàozhī 〈书面〉in a word; in short:～，倘若没有可以师法的东西，就只好自己来开创。In short, if we have no example to follow, we shall have to blaze a trail ourselves.
要职 yàozhí key post:身居～ hold a key post
要旨 yàozhǐ main idea or point; gist:讲话～ gist of a speech
要子 yàozi ❶ rope made of wheat or rice straw, used to bundle up wheat or rice:草～ straw rope ❷ string used to tie up goods or to bale:铁～ iron string

鹞

yào ❶ harrier ❷ *also* "雀鹰" quèyīng sparrow hawk
鹞鹰 yàoyīng sparrow hawk
鹞子 yàozi ❶ sparrow hawk ❷〈方言〉kite:放～ fly a kite
鹞子翻身 yàozi fānshēn do a somersault; tumble:一个漂亮的～ beautiful somersault

钥(鑰)

yào
see also yuè
钥匙 yàoshi key:一串～ a bunch of keys /万能～ master key /保险柜的～ key to a safe /配～ have a key made to fit a lock /一把～开一把锁。Each lock has its own key. *or* Different problems must be solved with different methods.
钥匙包 yàoshibāo key case
钥匙环 yàoshihuán key ring
钥匙孔 yàoshikǒng keyhole:从～里偷看 peep through a keyhole
钥匙链 yàoshiliàn key chain

燿

yào *see* "耀" yào

耀

yào ❶ shine; radiate; illuminate; dazzle:照～ shine on; illuminate /闪～ glitter /焰火把人们的眼都～花了。Fireworks dazzled people's eyes. ❷ vaunt; show off; boast of:炫～ vaunt; make a show of /显～ show off ❸ brilliance; glow:光～ brilliance ❹ glory; honour; credit:荣～ honour
耀斑 yàobān 〈天文〉solar flare
耀武扬威 yàowǔ-yángwēi make a show of one's strength; show off one's prowess; swagger about:这帮贪官污吏骑在老百姓头上为非作歹，～。These corrupt officials were high and mighty, riding roughshod over ordinary people. /别看他们现在～，迟早他们是要垮台的。They were swaggering around now, but they would surely come to grief sooner or later.
耀星 yàoxīng flare star
耀眼 yàoyǎn (of light) dazzling; blinding:～的阳光 dazzling sunshine /闪光太～。The flashlight was blinding. /美丽的红旗映着蓝天，显得格外～。The beautiful red flag looked especially bright against the blue sky.

曜

yào 〈书面〉❶ sunlight ❷ shine; radiate; illuminate ❸ *used to refer to the sun, the moon and the stars*:日～日 Sunday /月～日 Monday

yē

耶

yē
see also yé
耶和华 Yēhéhuá 〈宗教〉Jehovah, name of God in the *Old Testament*
耶鲁大学 Yēlǔ Dàxué Yale University, founded in 1701 at Killingworth and Saybrook, now located at New Haven, Connecticut, the United States
耶路撒冷 Yēlùsālěng Jerusalem, holy city for both Islam and Judaism, now capital claimed by both Israel and Palestine
耶稣 Yēsū 〈基督教〉Jesus:～受难 Passion (of Jesus)
耶稣诞辰 Yēsū Dànchén *also* "圣诞节" Shèngdànjié Christmas; Xmas
耶稣会 Yēsūhuì (Catholic) Society of Jesus; Jesuits:～传教士 Jesuit missionary
耶稣基督 Yēsū Jīdū Jesus Christ
耶稣教 Yēsūjiào Protestantism

椰

yē 〈植物〉coconut palm; coconut tree; coco
椰雕 yēdiāo coconut carving
椰干 yēgān *also* "椰仁干" copra
椰胡 yēhú a kind of two-stringed *huqin* (胡琴), whose box-type music body is made of half a coconut shell faced with paulownia wood
椰壳 yēké coconut shell or husk:～纤维 coir fibre; coir
椰奶 yēnǎi *see* "椰汁"
椰仁 yērén coconut kernel; coconut meat
椰仁干 yēréngān copra
椰蓉 yēróng coconut mash (used as stuffing for mooncakes, etc.)
椰丝 yēsī shredded coconut
椰油 yēyóu coconut oil; coconut butter
椰枣 yēzǎo ❶ date palm ❷ palm date
椰汁 yēzhī *also* "椰子汁";"椰奶" coconut milk
椰子 yēzi ❶ coconut palm; coconut tree; coco ❷ coconut
椰子肉 yēziròu coconut meat
椰子树 yēzishù coconut palm (*Cocos nucifera*)
椰子糖 yēzitáng coconut candy
椰子蟹 yēzixiè robber crab; coconut crab (*Birgus latro*)
椰子油 yēziyóu coconut oil
椰子汁 yēzizhī coconut milk

倻

yē *see* "伽倻琴" jiāyēqín

掖

yē tuck in or up; thrust in between:把手绢～在兜里 tuck a handkerchief into the pocket /腰里～着把砍刀 with a chopper in one's belt /她给病人～好被子才离开。She tucked the patient up before leaving. /虎妞背地里～给他两块钱。Huniu slipped him two *yuan*.
see also yè
掖咕 yēgu 〈方言〉leave about; stow away carelessly:你把我的手套～在哪儿了? Where did you put my gloves?

噎

yē ❶ choke:因～废食 give up eating for fear of choking /快给我点水喝，我～着了。Get me some water quickly, please. I've choked over my food. /别吃那么快，会～着的。Don't eat too fast or you may choke. ❷ be choked by wind ❸〈方言〉render sb. speechless by saying sth. blunt or rude; interrupt rudely; choke off:我刚

一开口就被他～了回去。No sooner did I begin to speak than he choked me off. /他这个人不好相处，平时讲话太～人。He's difficult to get along with, for he's always contradicting people.

噎嗝 yēgé 〈中医〉cancer of the esophagus

暍

yē 〈书面〉suffer sunstroke; be affected by the heat

yé

耶

yé 〈书面〉〈助词〉*used to indicate the interrogative*：将军怯～? Are you scared, General? /何为以死相惧～? Are you threatening me with death?

see also yē

揶

yé

揶揄 yéyú 〈书面〉mock; ridicule; deride：我～他数语，责其幼稚。I derided him as childish. /他以～的口吻谈论其事。He talked about the matter in a tone of mockery.

邪

yé ❶ *see* "莫邪" mòyé ❷ *see* "耶" yé

see also xié

铘

yé *see* "镆铘" mòyé

爷(爺)

yé ❶〈方言〉father：～娘 father and mother ❷〈方言〉grandfather：姥～ (maternal) grandfather /太～ great grandfather ❸ respectful form of address for a man of the older generation：大～ uncle /张～ Uncle Zhang ❹〈旧语〉form of address for an official or rich man：老～ lord; master; sir /少～ young master (of the house) ❺ form of address for god, used by superstitious people：阎王～ Yama; King of Hell /土地～ village god

爷们 yémen 〈方言〉❶ man; menfolk：～家敢做敢当。A man should have the courage to take the responsibility for what he does. ❷ husband

爷们儿 yémenr 〈方言〉❶ *see* "爷儿们" ❷ familiar form of address between men：～，今儿钓鱼去不? Hey, man! Are you going fishing today?

爷儿 yér 〈口语〉*used of an elder man and his juniors often followed by numerals*：～俩全到了。Both father and son have come.

爷儿们 yérmen 〈口语〉men of two or more generations：老少～ all the men, both old and young

爷爷 yéye ❶ (paternal) grandfather; grandpa ❷ *used as a respectful form of address for an old man*：老～ grandpa

yě

冶[1]

yě ❶ smelt (metal) ❷ (Yě) a surname

冶[2]

yě 〈书面〉(of a woman) be coquettishly or seductively dressed：妖～ coquettish; seductive

冶荡 yědàng skittish and dissolute; lewd; lascivious

冶金 yějīn metallurgy

冶金粉尘 yějīn fěnchén metallurgical dust

冶金工程学 yějīn gōngchéngxué metallurgical engineering

冶金工业 yějīn gōngyè metallurgical industry：国家～局 State Bureau of Metallurgical Industry

冶金焦炭 yějīn jiāotàn smelter coke

冶金学 yějīnxué metallurgy

冶炼 yěliàn smelt：～设备 smelting equipment /～操作 smelting operation /～工 smelter /～时间 duration of heat

冶炼厂 yěliànchǎng smeltery

冶炼炉 yěliànlú smelting furnace; smelter

冶容 yěróng ❶ be seductively dressed or made up：～诲淫 seductive dress or make-up invites adultery ❷ bewitching or seductive appearance

冶笑 yěxiào coquettish smile

冶艳 yěyàn 〈书面〉pretty and coquettish：装束～ be coquettishly dressed

冶游 yěyóu visit prostitutes; go whoring

冶铸 yězhù smelting and casting

野(埜)

yě ❶ open country; wild land：四～ vast expanse of open country /旷～ in the open /荒～ the wilds; wilderness /沃～ fertile land /漫山遍～ all over the hills and plains ❷ limit; boundary：分～ line of demarcation; watershed /视～ field of vision ❸ not in power; out of office：在～ out of office; not in power /下～ retire from office; be out of power ❹ wild; uncultivated; undomesticated：～狗 stray dog; wild dog /～果 wild fruit ❺ rude; rough; wild：撒～ behave rudely /举止～ boorish manner ❻ unrestrained; unruly; undisciplined：这孩子玩电子游戏机把心都玩～了。The child is so crazy about electronic games that he just can't take his mind off them. /他在外头～惯了，在家呆不住。Accustomed to rushing about outside, he's reluctant to stay at home.

野菜 yěcài edible wild herbs：靠～充饥 allay one's hunger with wild herbs; live on wild herbs

野餐 yěcān picnic：～会 picnic party /～者 picnicker /中午在外～ have a picnic lunch /到香山去～ go on (*or* for) a picnic at Fragrant Hill

野蚕 yěcán wild silkworm

野草 yěcǎo weeds：～丛生 be overgrown (*or* choked) with weeds; weeds run riot /拔～pull up weeds

野草闲花 yěcǎo-xiánhuā *also* "野花闲草" ❶ weeds and wild flowers ❷〈旧语〉women other than one's spouse, with whom one has an affair; women of easy virtue; prostitutes

野传 yěchuán (of baseball or softball) wild throw：～球 passed ball

野炊 yěchuī cook in the open; cook out

野地 yědì wild country; wilderness; the wilds：荒郊～ wild country; the wilds

野调无腔 yědiào-wúqiāng rude; audacious：这孩子总是～的，让人看不惯。This child is a nuisance, for he has no manners.

野鸽 yěgē *also* "原鸽" yuángē wild pigeon

野葛 yěgé *also* "钩吻" gōuwěn elegant jessamine

野果 yěguǒ wild fruit

野汉子 yěhànzi lover：养～ (usu. of a married woman) support a man with whom she carries on an affair; commit adultery

野合 yěhé 〈书面〉❶ inappropriate marriage ❷ illicit sexual relations

野鹤闲云 yěhè-xiányún *also* "闲云野鹤" be completely free as cloud or wild crane

野黑麦 yěhēimài wild rye; lyme grass

野狐禅 yěhúchán 〈佛教〉heterodoxy; heresy

野胡萝卜 yěhúluóbo Queen Anne's lace; wild carrot (*Daucus carota*)

野花生 yěhuāshēng *also* "决明" juémíng *Cassia obtusifolia*

野火 yěhuǒ wildfire; prairie fire; bush fire：～烧不尽，春风吹又生。Not even a prairie fire can destroy green grass, It grows again when the spring breeze blows. *or* Burnt by flames yet unsubdued, The grass surges back in the spring winds.

野鸡 yějī ❶ (popular term for 雉) pheasant ❷ street girl; streetwalker ❸ unlicensed：～公司 unlicensed company

野鸡大学 yějī dàxué unlicensed university; diploma mill

野景 yějǐng wild scenery; country view

野菊花 yějúhuā mother chrysanthemum

野苣 yějù 〈植物〉corn-salad (*Valerianella olitoria*)

野驴 yělǘ Asiatic wild ass; kiang

野萝卜 yěluóbu wild radish; jointed charlock (*Raphanus raphanistrum*)

野麻 yěmá wild hemp

野马 yěmǎ wild horse; mustang; bronco

野麦 yěmài 〈植物〉wild rye (*Elymus*)

野蛮 yěmán ❶ uncivilized; barbarian; savage：～人 savage; barbarian /～的习俗 savage customs /这里还处于～状态。The place remains in a primitive state. ❷ atrocious; barbarous; brutal：举止～ be barbaric; be ill-mannered /～的行径 barbarous act /～的统治 brutal rule /～的挑衅 atrocious provocation /这帮土匪手段极其～。The bandit gang was extremely ruthless. /严禁～装卸。No savage loading and unloading.

野猫 yěmāo ❶ wildcat ❷ stray cat ❸〈方言〉hare

野牛 yěniú wild ox; buffalo：美洲～ bison; American buffalo

野牛草 yěniúcǎo buffalo grass (*Buchloe dactyloides*)

野炮 yěpào field gun; field artillery
野蔷薇 yěqiángwēi multiflora rose
野禽 yěqín wild fowl
野趣 yěqù idyllic taste; pastoral appeal:这园子虽然荒凉，却富有～。The garden was a bit bleak, but it was full of idyllic appeal.
野人 yěrén ❶〈古语〉country bumpkin; peasant; commoner:～献曝 country bumpkin presenting sunshine (to the monarch) — a respectful gesture ❷ uncivilized man; savage; barbarian ❸ rough fellow
野山参 yěshānshēn wild ginseng
野烧 yěshāo prairie fire
野生 yěshēng wild; uncultivated:～生物研究 wildlife research /～生物保护区 wildlife sanctuary; wildlife preserve /处于～状态 in a wild state
野生动物 yěshēng dòngwù wild animal; wildlife:～管理 wildlife management /～资源保护 wildlife conservation /～园 wildlife park; safari park
野生植物 yěshēng zhíwù wild plant:～资源保护法 law on the protection of wild plant resources
野乘 yěshèng〈书面〉unofficial history
野食儿 yěshír ❶ food found in the fields by domestic animals:这鸡常在外头吃～。This chicken often gets something to eat in the fields. ❷〈比喻〉extra irregular income; earnings from moonlighting:打～ make extra money outside one's regular job; indulge in extra-marital affairs
野史 yěshǐ unofficial history
野兽 yěshòu wild beast; wild animal
野鼠 yěshǔ field rat
野台子戏 yětáizixì performance given by itinerant entertainers, usu. in the open air
野兔 yětù hare
野外 yěwài open country; field:～作业 field operation /～活动 outdoor activities; the outdoors /～运动 fieldsports (i.e. hunting, fishing, etc.) /～标志 field mark /～试验 field trial
野外工作 yěwài gōngzuò fieldwork:做～ do fieldwork
野外露营汽车 yěwài lùyíng qìchē camping wagon; campmobile; camper
野豌豆 yěwāndòu vetch (*Vicia sativa*)
野味 yěwèi game (as food):打～ go to hunt wild game /猎到的～当场烤着吃 barbecue the hunted game on the spot
野物 yěwù wild animal and fowl; game
野心 yěxīn audacious ambition; wild ambition; careerism:篡权的～ ambition for usurping power /识破他的～ see through his ambitious designs /极力掩盖自己妄想称霸世界的～ spare no effort to cover up one's wanton ambition for world domination /侵略～ aggressive ambitions
野心勃勃 yěxīn-bóbó be overweeningly ambitious; burn with wild or insensate ambition; be thirsty for power
野心家 yěxīnjiā careerist
野心狼 yěxīnláng vicious wolf — person of evil ambition
野性 yěxìng wild nature; unruliness:～十足 be not tamed at all; be untamed /这匹马已经没了～。This horse has been broken in. /他的言谈举止总透着股～。There is always something wild about him.
野鸭 yěyā wild duck
野宴 yěyàn picnic
野燕麦 yěyànmài wild oat
野意 yěyì rustic or idyllic appeal; call of the wild
野营 yěyíng camp; bivouac:～训练 camp and field training /喜欢～ be fond of camping
野游 yěyóu go for an outing; go on a country excursion:带孩子去～ take one's children on an outing
野战 yězhàn〈军事〉field operations:～电台 field station /～仓库 field depot /～电话机 camp telephone /～工事 fieldwork /～轻便电话机 field telephone (*or* walkie-talkie); buzzerphone
野战军 yězhànjūn field army
野战炮 yězhànpào fieldpiece; field gun or artillery
野战医院 yězhàn yīyuàn field hospital
野种 yězhǒng bastard
野猪 yězhū wild boar

也[1]

yě〈书面〉〈助词〉❶ *used to indicate judgement or explanation*:荀况者，赵人～。Xun Kuang was a native of the State of Zhao. /师者，所以传道受业解惑～。A teacher is one who propagates the doctrines of ancient sages, passes on knowledge and helps to clear up doubts. ❷ *used to pose a question or counter question*:来何疾～? How come it arrived so quickly? ❸ *used to indicate a pause in a sentence*:是日～，天朗气清，惠风和畅。It was a bright sunny day with gentle breeze.

也[2]

yě〈副词〉❶ also; too; as well; either:他工作认真，学习～很努力。He works hard and also studies conscientiously. /你不开口，我～不开口。If you don't speak, I shan't speak either. /这么说你是个记者，我～是。You're a reporter? So am I! /等我长大了～去参军。When I'm grown up, I'll join the army too. /风停了，雨～住了。It stopped both blowing and raining. / ❷ (used in pairs) both... and...; as well as:我们～划船，～游泳。We'll go boating as well as swimming. /他的个儿～高，力气～大。He's both tall and strong. ❸ (used in pairs) either... or...; whether... or...; no matter whether:这～不是，那～不是，到底该怎么办? What is to be done if neither this nor that is right? /你付现款～行，付支票～行。You can pay either in cash or by cheque. /没关系，你～可以给我打电话，～可以写信。It doesn't matter whether you call me up or write to me. ❹ *used to indicate concession*:宁可牺牲，～绝不向敌人投降。We'd rather die than surrender to the enemy. /即使以前没学过游泳，～不妨试一试。You can still have a try even if you haven't learned to swim before. ❺ *used to indicate resignation*:我看～只好如此了。I'm afraid we'll have to leave it at that. /他显得瘦了些，但～还结实。He's quite strong though he looks a bit thin. ❻ *often used together with* 一点，连，*etc. to indicate emphasis*:这话一点～不错。There's nothing at all wrong with this remark. /只要有决心，什么困难～不怕。There is no insurmountable difficulty before a determined mind. /天空连一丝云～没有。There's not even a single trace of a cloud in the sky. /小武乐得嘴～合不拢了。Xiao Wu was so happy that he smiled like a Cheshire cat.
也罢 yěbà ❶ *indicating tolerance or resignation*:他不同意～，不必勉强。It's alright if he doesn't agree. Don't force him. /你工作忙，不去～，我自己去吧。All right, I'll go by myself since you're too busy to go. ❷〈助词〉whether... or...; no matter whether:说～，不说～，反正你的想法大家都知道。It doesn't matter whether you tell us or not, since we all know what's in your mind. /花～，鸟～，什么都引不起他的兴趣。Nothing can arouse his interest no matter whether it's a flower or a bird.
也好 yěhǎo〈助词〉❶ *used to indicate tolerance or resignation*:～，你一定要请我去讲，我也就不推辞了。All right. If you insist on inviting me to give a talk, I won't refuse. /你讲一讲～，免得大家发生误会。To avoid any misunderstanding, you'd better give them an explanation. /让他们去打打工～，他们可以了解了解社会。We might as well let them work part-time since they can get to know about society from their own experience. ❷ (reduplicated) whether... or...; no matter whether:你～，我～，咱们都不了解这里的情况。Neither you nor I know what is happening here.
也门 Yěmén Yemen:～共和国 Republic of Yemen /～人 Yemeni; Yemenite
也许 yěxǔ〈副词〉perhaps; maybe; probably:这书～是他的。Perhaps it's his book. /她～没赶上车。She might have missed the bus. /"今晚上有电影吧?""～，我不清楚。""Is there going to be a film tonight?" "Maybe. I've no idea."
也…也… yě…yě… ❶ both...and...; either...or...:钱也花了，工也费了，房子就是修不成。Though we've spent both the money and the time, the house is still unfinished. /你也不发火，我也不生气，咱们好好商量。Neither of us should get angry, we should talk it over in a friendly manner. ❷ no matter (whether; who, etc.):这话听也由你，不听也由你。It is up to you whether you listen to me or not.

yè

夜(亱)

yè ❶ night; evening:～里 at night /入～ at nightfall /熬～ stay up late; burn the midnight oil /巡～ go on night patrol /守～ keep watch at night; keep vigil /新婚之～ wedding night; bridal evening /昼～兼程 travel by night and day /一～成名 become famous overnight /晓行～宿 set off at dawn and stop at dusk /～静更深 in the still of night; in the dead of night /～深了。The night grows late. ❷〈方言〉get or grow dark; evening falls:天

快～了。It's getting dark.
夜暗 yè'àn night:～时间 night time
夜班 yèbān night shift:上～ on night duty; on night shift /～车 night bus /～编辑 night editor /～护士 night nurse /今晚我值～。I am on night shift (*or* duty) tonight. *or* It's my turn to be on night duty today.
夜半 yèbàn middle of the night; midnight:～歌声 singing late at night /他到家已经是～了。It was already midnight when he got home.
夜不安枕 yèbù'ānzhěn toss and turn all night:这件事愁得他～。He was so worried about it that he hardly slept a wink at night.
夜不闭户 yèbùbìhù leave the door open at night — not have to worry about being burglarized:社会安宁,～。It's unnecessary to bolt the door at night thanks to social stability and the prevalence of law and order. *or* You can leave your door open at night thanks to the excellent law and order situation.
夜餐 yècān midnight snack
夜叉 yècha *also* "药叉" yàochā ❶〈佛教〉yaksha (an evil spirit) ❷ hideous and ferocious person:母～ hideous woman; termagant (woman)
夜长梦多 yècháng-mèngduō when night is long, dreams are many; a long delay may mean trouble:这事要快点办成,免得～。Please get it done without delay, otherwise something untoward may happen.
夜场 yèchǎng evening show
夜车 yèchē ❶ night train ❷〈比喻〉*used in* "开夜车" kāi yèchē
夜出动物 yèchū dòngwù nocturnal animal
夜大学 yèdàxué evening college or university
夜盗 yèdào burglar
夜蛾 yè'é noctuid
夜饭 yèfàn 〈方言〉supper; dinner:～准备好了。Supper is ready.
夜分 yèfēn 〈书面〉midnight
夜工 yègōng night work; night job:做～ do a night job /打～ work at night
夜光杯 yèguāngbēi luminous wine glass:葡萄美酒～ fine grape wine in the evening-radiant cup
夜光表 yèguāngbiǎo luminous watch
夜光虫 yèguāngchóng noctiluca
夜光螺 yèguāngluó green snail
夜光云 yèguāngyún noctilucent cloud
夜航 yèháng night flight or voyage
夜合 yèhé ❶ silktree ❷〈方言〉tuber of multi-flower knotweed (*Polygonum multiflorum*)
夜黑 yèhēi night darkness; dark night:～迷路 get lost in a dark night
夜壶 yèhú chamber pot
夜话 yèhuà evening talk, mainly used in the title of a book:《燕山～》*Evening Chats in Beijing* (collection of essays published in the 1960's)
夜活 yèhuó night work; night job:做～ work at night
夜间 yèjiān at night:～行车 drive at night /～飞行 night flying /～磨牙〈医学〉bruxism /～遗精 nocturnal (seminal) emission /～照明 night illumination /～门诊 night clinic
夜交藤 yèjiāoténg 〈中医〉vine of multi-flower knotweed (*Polygonum multiflorum*)
夜禁 yèjìn night curfew
夜景 yèjǐng night scene; nocturnal sight:华灯满街的～ illuminated street scene at night /雄伟的人民大会堂～ magnificent night view of the Great Hall of the People
夜课 yèkè evening course or class
夜空 yèkōng evening sky; night sky:沉寂的～ quiet night sky /一道闪电划破～。A flash of lightning streaked across the evening sky.
夜来 yèlái 〈书面〉❶ yesterday ❷ at night:～风雨声,花落知多少? The tumult of wind and rain had filled the night, How many blossoms fell during the raging storm?
夜来香 yèláixiāng 〈植物〉cordate telosma
夜阑 yèlán 〈书面〉late at night
夜阑人静 yèlán-rénjìng in the depths of night; in the still of the night:一到～时,他就感到分外孤独。In the quiet of the night he felt all the more lonely. /～,只有淅沥的雨声。It was deep night. The world was still except for the patter of the rain.
夜郎自大 Yèláng-zìdà conceit stemming from pure ignorance; parochial arrogance:我们不能固步自封,～,有了一点成绩就沾沾自喜。We shouldn't feel conceited and self-satisfied and rest on our laurels because of some success.
夜礼服 yèlǐfú evening dress
夜里 yèli at night:～单独出门要多加小心。Be careful when you go out alone at night.
夜盲 yèmáng *also* "夜盲症" nyctalopia; night blindness
夜猫子 yèmāozi 〈方言〉❶ owl:～是捕捉老鼠的能手。Owls are good at catching mice. /～进宅,无事不来。When an owl (*or* weasel) comes visiting, he is sure to have his eyes on something. ❷ person who likes staying up late:这人是个～,越到晚上越精神。This man is a night owl who becomes increasingly spirited with the deepening of the night.
夜明珠 yèmíngzhū legendary luminous pearl
夜幕 yèmù gathering darkness; night:在～中消失 disappear into the darkness /～沉沉 night is falling /～笼罩着大地。The darkness of night settled over the land.
夜尿症 yèniàozhèng enuresis; bed-wetting
夜勤 yèqín night duty:出～ be on duty at night
夜曲 yèqǔ nocturne:小～ serenade
夜儿个 yèrge 〈方言〉yesterday
夜入私宅罪 yèrù-sīzháizuì 〈法律〉burglary
夜色 yèsè night scene; darkness; dusk:趁着～ under cover of night; by moonlight (*or* starlight) /～苍茫 gathering dusk /浓郁的～ thick darkness /朦胧的～ dim view (*or* light) of night /在茫茫～中 in the darkness of night /天将晚,～渐浓。As it's getting late, darkness is gathering around us.
夜生活 yèshēnghuó night life:过～ enjoy oneself at night /这个城市的～非常乏味。Night life was rather dull in the city.
夜市 yèshì ❶ night fair or market:逛～ go to the night fair /～非常热闹。The night market is bustling with activity. ❷ business at night:上月的～收入可不少。The earnings from the business at night for the last month were quite substantial.
夜视 yèshì night vision:～距离 night vision range
夜视瞄准器 yèshì miáozhǔnqì 〈军事〉sniperscope
夜视望远镜 yèshì wàngyuǎnjìng night-vision telescope
夜视仪 yèshìyí 〈军事〉night vision device or instrument
夜谈 yètán night talk
夜啼 yètí (of babies) cry aloud at night
夜头 yètóu 〈方言〉at night
夜晚 yèwǎn night:寂静的～ still night; silent night /月色清朗的～ moonlit night
夜望镜 yèwàngjìng 〈军事〉snooperscope
夜未央 yèwèiyāng 〈书面〉in the small hours
夜袭 yèxí night attack or raid
夜戏 yèxì night (opera) performance:听～ go to the theatre at night
夜宵 yèxiāo *also* "夜消" food or refreshments taken late at night:吃～ have some midnight snacks
夜校 yèxiào night or evening school:上～ go to night school
夜行 yèxíng ❶ walk at night:～者 night traveller ❷ night flight; night navigation:～航标 night navigation mark
夜行军 yèxíngjūn night march
夜学 yèxué ❶ night school ❷ night course
夜眼 yèyǎn eye able to see clearly at night
夜宴 yèyàn evening banquet
夜夜 yèyè every night or evening:夏天,他和祖母～在这里纳凉。He and his grandma enjoyed the cool here every summer night.
夜以继日 yèyǐjìrì day and night; round the clock:为加快工程进度,许多人～地苦干。In order to speed up the project, many people were working hard day and night.
夜莺 yèyīng nightingale:～在树上千鸣百啭。Nightingales sing beautifully in the trees.
夜鹰 yèyīng nighthawk; nightjar; goatsucker
夜游神 yèyóushén legendary god on patrol at night; person who is up and about most of the night; night owl:他每天晚上一出去就是半宿,真是个～。He's really a night owl, for he seldom returns home before midnight.
夜游症 yèyóuzhèng sleep-walking; somnambulism:～患者 sleep-walker; somnambulist
夜游子 yèyóuzi person who is up and about at night
夜战 yèzhàn ❶ night fighting ❷ work at night:挑灯～ work by

lamplight /打两个～，保证完成任务。We can guarantee to fulfil the task by working overtime for two nights.

夜总会 yèzǒnghuì nightclub

夜作 yèzuò night work：打～ work at night

液 yè liquid; fluid; juice：废～ waste liquid /体～ body fluid /胃～ gastric juice /唾～ saliva; spittle /血～ blood /溶～ solution

液泵 yèbèng liquid pump

液氮 yèdàn 〈化学〉liquid nitrogen：～冷却系统 liquid nitrogen cooling system

液肥 yèféi liquid manure or fertilizer：～喷洒机 liquid manure spreader

液封 yèfēng 〈机械〉liquid seal

液固火箭发动机 yè-gù huǒjiàn fādòngjī 〈航天〉liquid-solid rocket engine

液果 yèguǒ juicy or pulpy fruit

液化 yèhuà liquate; liquefy：～空气 liquified air /～沼气 liquid marsh gas /病变部分已发生～。The dead tissue has liquified.

液化器 yèhuàqì liquefier

液化热 yèhuàrè liquefaction heat

液化石油气 yèhuà shíyóuqì liquefied petroleum gas (LPG)

液化天然气 yèhuà tiānránqì liquefied natural gas (LNG)

液晶 yèjīng 〈物理〉liquid crystal：～显示 liquid crystal display (LCD) /～显示器〈信息〉liquid crystal display device

液晶成像系统 yèjīng chéngxiàng xìtǒng 〈电子〉liquid crystal imaging system

液晶电视 yèjīng diànshì liquid crystal TV

液冷 yèlěng 〈机械〉liquid cooled or cooling：～喷管 liquid-cooled nozzle /～式发动机 liquid-cooled engine

液力 yèlì hydraulic：～传动 hydraulic transmission

液力变速箱 yèlì biànsùxiāng hydraulic transmission box

液力传动柴油机车 yèlì chuándòng cháiyóu jīchē diesel-hydraulic locomotive

液力制动器 yèlì zhìdòngqì hydraulic brake

液流 yèliú liquid flow; liquor stream：～式播种机 liquid drill

液面 yèmiàn 〈物理〉liquid level：～计 liquid indicator; liquid level meter

液膜 yèmó liquid film; liquid membrane

液泡 yèpào 〈生理〉vacuole

液氢 yèqīng liquid hydrogen：～泵 liquid-hydrogen pump /～火箭发动机 liquid-hydrogen rocket engine

液态 yètài 〈物理〉liquid condition; liquid state; liquidness：～合金〈冶金〉liquid alloy /～金属 liquid metal /～空气 liquid air /～空气发动机 liquid-air engine /～逻辑电路〈电子〉liquid logic circuit /～金属冷却反应堆 liquid-metal cooled reactor /～金属燃料反应堆 liquid-metal-fueled reactor (LMFR)

液体 yètǐ liquid：～冷却 liquid cooling /～退火 liquid annealing /～电容 liquid condenser; liquid capacitor /～混合燃料 liquid combination (fuel)

液体比重计 yètǐ bǐzhòngjì hydrometer

液体电极 yètǐ diànjí 〈电工〉liquid electrode

液体激光器 yètǐ jīguāngqì liquid-dye laser; liquid laser

液体绝缘体 yètǐ juéyuántǐ 〈电工〉liquid insulator

液体燃料 yètǐ ránliào liquid fuel; liquid power：～火箭 liquid-fuel rocket

液体渗碳 yètǐ shèntàn liquid carbonization

液体研磨机 yètǐ yánmójī liquid honing machine

液相 yèxiàng liquid state：～色谱法 liquid chromatography /～线 liquidus

液芯光纤 yèxìn guāngxiān liquid-core fibre

液压 yèyā 〈机械〉hydraulic pressure：～阀 hydraulic valve /～缸 hydro-cylinder; hydraulic cylinder /～机构 hydraulic unit; hydraulic gear /～控制 hydraulic control /～千斤顶 hydraulic jack /～升降机 hydraulic lift /～马达 hydromotor (*or* hydraulic motor); hydraulic slave motor /～伺服机构 hydraulic servo system; hydraulic servo

液压泵 yèyābèng hydraulic pump

液压表 yèyābiǎo hydraulic pressure gauge

液压成形 yèyā chéngxíng hydroforming

液压传动 yèyā chuándòng hydraulic transmission or drive：～装置 hydraulic transmission gear

液压机 yèyājī hydraulic press

液压技术 yèyā jìshù hydraulic pressure technique

液压起重机 yèyā qǐzhòngjī hydraulic crane; hydrocrane

液压制动器 yèyā zhìdòngqì hydraulic brake

液氧 yèyǎng liquid oxygen：～泵 liquid oxygen pump /～火箭发动机 liquid-oxygen rocket engine /～汽油发动机 liquid-oxygen-gasoline unit /～炸药 oxygen explosive

掖 yè support sb. by the arm; support; assist; promote：扶～ help; support /奖～ reward and promote

see also yē

掖庭 yètíng residences of concubines in the imperial palace

腋 yè ❶〈生理〉axilla; armpit ❷〈植物〉axil

腋臭 yèchòu bromhidrosis; underarm odour

腋毛 yèmáo armpit hair; hircus

腋气 yèqì underarm odour

腋生 yèshēng poverty weed (*Iva axillaris*)

腋窝 yèwō armpit

腋芽 yèyá 〈植物〉axillary bud

谒 yè 〈书面〉call on (a superior or an elder person); pay homage to; pay one's respects to：进～ call on (a superior)

谒拜 yèbài pay a formal visit; call to pay respects：～陵墓 pay homage at a mausoleum

谒见 yèjiàn pay a call on (a superior or senior person)：have an audience with

谒陵 yèlíng pay homage at sb.'s mausoleum

靥(靨) yè dimple：酒～ dimple /笑～ dimple; smiling face

页(頁、葉、篥) yè ❶ leaf; sheet：散～ loose leaf /增～ supplementary sheet /活～本 loose leaf notebook ❷ page：扉～ title page /插～ inset; insert /我的课本缺一～。There is one page missing in my textbook. /永远牢记中国历史上这光辉的一～。Never forget this glorious page in Chinese history.

页边 yèbiān margin

页理 yèlǐ leaf-structure of shale

页码 yèmǎ page number

页心 yèxīn 〈印刷〉type page

页岩 yèyán 〈地质〉shale

页岩油 yèyányóu shale oil

业[1](業) yè ❶ trade; industry; business：保险～ insurance business /旅游～ tourism; tourist industry (*or* trade) /美容～ beauty industry /饮食～ catering trade (*or* industry) /畜牧～ livestock industry/工农～ industry and agriculture ❷ occupation; profession; employment：就～ employment /失～ unemployed; be out of a job; be made redundant /转～ (of an armyman) be transferred to civilian work; be demobilized /安居乐～ live in peace and work contentedly ❸ course of study; course：修～ study in a school /毕～ graduate; finish school /结～ complete a course of study /肄～ study in school or at college (without graduation) ❹ cause; enterprise; undertaking：伟～ great cause; exploit /基～ foundation; base /守～ maintain what has been achieved by one's forefathers or predecessors ❺ estate; property：家～ family property /祖～ ancestral property ❻〈佛教〉karma; (usu. evil or sinful) deed; action ❼ engage in; go in for：～商 engage in commerce; be in business ❽ (Yè) a surname

业[2](業) yè already; before now：肇事者～已查处。The delinquent has already been investigated and dealt with accordingly.

业报 yèbào 〈佛教〉karma; retribution; judgment

业海 yèhǎi 〈佛教〉sea of sin; iniquity

业绩 yèjì outstanding achievement; exemplary accomplishment：不朽的～ monumental exploit /创建～ have achievements to one's credit

业界 yèjiè 〈方言〉business circles; trade：该公司正占据～头把交椅。The company is holding the lead in business circles.

业经 yèjīng already：～核准 have been approved /～呈报备案 have already submitted a report for the record

业精于勤 yèjīngyúqín scholarship comes from diligence; mastery

of a subject results from diligent study：～，荒于嬉。Progress in studies comes from diligence and is retarded by indolence.

业师 yèshī 〈旧语〉my former teacher

业务 yèwù vocational work；professional work；business：～娴熟 be adept in one's profession /～差 be incompetent for one's job /懂～ know the business；know the ropes /钻研～ study one's profession diligently /～范围 business scope /～能力 professional competence（*or* ability）/～水平 professional skill；vocational level /～素质 professional quality /～学习 study of one's profession；vocational study /～知识 professional knowledge；expertise /～专长 specialized skill；speciality

业务班子 yèwù bānzi professional team；business team

业务代理人 yèwù dàilǐrén business agent

业务挂帅 yèwù guàshuài （formerly used for denunciation） put professional work in command；professional work comes first

业务尖子 yèwù jiānzi top-notch professional

业已 yèyǐ （usu. used in officialese） already：～准备就绪 be prepared；be ready /工程～完竣。The project has already been completed.

业余 yèyú ❶ sparetime；leisure：～时间 sparetime；leisure /～爱好 hobby /～进修班 after-hours class /～消遣 sparetime occupation ❷ amateur；dabbler；nonprofessional：～剧团 amateur troupe /～演员 amateur actor or actress /～作家 amateur writer /～无线电爱好者 radio amateur

业余补习学校 yèyú bǔxí xuéxiào sparetime continuation school

业余教育 yèyú jiàoyù sparetime education

业余学校 yèyú xuéxiào sparetime school

业障 yèzhàng ❶〈佛教〉sin that detracts from one's good works ❷（a term of abuse formerly used by the elders of a clan cursing their juniors） evil creature；vile spawn；medium of retribution

业种 yèzhǒng ❶ *also*"孽种" nièzhǒng bastard；vile spawn ❷（often used in the early vernacular） term of endearment for sb. one loves dearly

业主 yèzhǔ owner of （an enterprise or estate）；proprietor

叶[1]（葉）

yè ❶ leaf；blade；foliage：红似火焰的枫～ flaming maple leaves /枯黄的残枝败～ yellow dead twigs and withered leaves /树～纷纷飘落。Leaves begin to fall off trees. ❷ leaf-like thing：百～窗 shutter；blind /肺～ lobe of the lung ❸ page；leaf ❹（Yè） a surname

叶[2]（葉）

yè part of a historical period：中～ middle period /末～ end （of a century or dynasty）/19世纪初～ early in the 19th century；early 1900's

see also xié

叶斑病 yèbānbìng leaf spot

叶柄 yèbǐng petiole；leafstalk

叶蝉 yèchán leafhopper

叶蜂 yèfēng sawfly

叶公好龙 Yègōng-hàolóng Lord Ye's love of dragons — professed love of what one does not really understand or even fears

叶红素 yèhóngsù *also* "胡萝卜素" húluóbosù phylloerythrin；carotene

叶猴 yèhóu leaf monkey

叶黄素 yèhuángsù xanthophyll

叶尖 yèjiān apex

叶枯病 yèkūbìng leaf blight

叶蜡石 yèlàshí pyrophyllite

叶利钦 Yèlìqīn Boris Yeltsin （1931- ），President of the Russian Federation from 1990 to 1999

叶龄 yèlíng age of a leaf

叶绿素 yèlǜsù chlorophyll

叶绿体 yèlǜtǐ chloroplast

叶轮 yèlún impeller；vane wheel：～泵 vane pump /～式破碎器 impeller breaker /～液压马达 vane motor

叶落归根 yèluò-guīgēn falling leaves settle on their roots；a person residing away from his ancestral home eventually returns to it：树高千丈，～，我们都要有个归宿才好呀。No matter how tall a tree is, its fallen leaves will gather round its roots. Likewise we should also have somewhere to return to in the future. /老人侨居海外多年，终于～，返回故乡。Like fallen leaves that return to their roots, the old man finally went back and settled down in his home town after many years spent overseas.

叶脉 yèmài （leaf） vein

叶霉病 yèméibìng 〈植物〉leaf mould：番茄～ leaf mould of tomato （*Cladosporium fulvum*）

叶霉素 yèméisù phyllomycin

叶面施肥 yèmiàn shīféi *also* "根外施肥" gēnwài shīféi foliage dressing or spray

叶疱病 yèpàobìng leaf blister；leaf curl

叶片 yèpiàn ❶〈植物〉（leaf） blade ❷〈机械〉vane：～泵 sliding gate pump；vane pump /～式风速计 vane anemometer /～式压缩机 vane compressor /～式油马达 vane motor /～式弹簧 leaf spring

叶鞘 yèqiào leaf sheath

叶肉 yèròu mesophyll

叶酸 yèsuān folic acid；folacin

叶苔 yètái leafy liverwort

叶甜菜 yètiáncài leaf beet （*Belacicla*）

叶纤维 yèxiānwéi leaf fibre

叶䗛 yèxiū *also* "竹节虫" zhújiéchóng stick insect；walking stick

叶锈病 yèxiùbìng leaf rust （*Puccinia triticina*）：小麦～ leaf rust of wheat （*Puccinia rubigovera*）

叶序 yèxù phyllotaxy；leaf arrangement

叶芽 yèyá leaf bud

叶腋 yèyè leaf axil

叶栅 yèzhà 〈机械〉vane cascade

叶针 yèzhēn leaf thorn

叶枝 yèzhī leaf branch

叶子 yèzi ❶ leaf ❷〈方言〉playing cards ❸〈方言〉tea leaves；tea

叶子烟 yèziyān dry tobacco leaf

曳（拽、抴）

yè drag；haul；tug；pull：衣长～地 dress long enough to drag along the ground /弃甲～兵 cast off one's armour and drag one's weapon behind one；be routed

曳白 yèbái 〈书面〉❶ hand in a blank examination paper in the imperial examination ❷ page of examination paper unintentionally left blank while making a clean copy

曳冰床 yèbīngchuáng ice-sled

曳扯 yèche 〈方言〉bring up；raise：这孩子是他姑姑～大的。The child was brought up by his aunt.

曳光穿甲弹 yèguāng chuānjiǎdàn 〈军事〉armour-piercing tracer

曳光弹 yèguāngdàn 〈军事〉tracer bullet or shell；tracer：～头 tracer bullet

曳力 yèlì 〈物理〉drag force

曳炮车 yèpàochē 〈军事〉ordnance tractor；vehicle for towing artillery pieces

曳绳钓 yèshéngdiào trolling

曳引 yèyǐn drag；pull；draw；tow：木船由一只汽艇～着，在江上缓缓行驶。Towed （*or* Pulled） by a tug, the boat was moving slowly in the river.

咽

yè （of sound） obstructed and therefore low：哽～ choke with sobs /喇叭声～ muffled sound of a horn

see also yān；yàn

咽泣 yèqì choke with sobs

咽哑 yèyǎ hoarse：声音～ have a hoarse voice

烨（燁、爗）

yè 〈书面〉❶ firelight；sunlight ❷（of light） brilliant；bright：～～震电 blasting thunder and glaring lightning

晔（曄）

yè 〈书面〉（of light） bright

馌

yè 〈书面〉deliver a meal to the field

yī

衣

yī ❶ clothing；clothes；garment；dress：内～ underclothes；underwear /寒～ winter clothes /毛～ sweater；woollen sweater /成～ ready-made clothes /大～ overcoat；topcoat /风雨～

raincoat; mackintosh (*or* mac) /更～ change clothes /节～缩食 economize on food and clothing; live frugally /量体裁～ cut the garment according to the figure — act according to actual circumstances ❷ coating; covering: 糖～ sugar coating /琴～ piano cover ❸ afterbirth: 胞～ (human) afterbirth ❹ (Yī) a surname
see also yì

衣摆 yībǎi lower hem of a gown, jacket or skirt: 把～改短 take in the hem (of a skirt)

衣包 yībāo paper bag containing paper garment and paper money burned as offerings to the dead

衣胞 yībao (human) afterbirth

衣钵 yībō Buddhist monk's mantle and alms bowl which he hands down to his disciple; legacy: ～相传 hand down the cassock and bowl — pass on to a successor (authority or symbol of office); hand down the legacy /继承了祖上的～ inherit the mantle of one's ancestors

衣不蔽体 yībùbìtǐ be dressed in rags: ～的难民 refugee dressed in rags

衣不解带 yībùjiědài cannot take off one's clothes and have a proper sleep because of pressure of work: 老父病重, 小陆日夜守候, 五日～。When his father was seriously ill, Xiao Lu waited on him day and night, having hardly a wink of sleep for five days.

衣不如新, 人不如旧 yī bùrú xīn, rén bùrú jiù 〈谚语〉 while new clothes are better than old ones, old friends are better than new ones; new clothes are best, and so are old friends

衣橱 yīchú wardrobe

衣兜 yīdōu *also* "衣袋" pocket

衣蛾 yī'é (casemaking) clothes moth

衣分 yīfēn 〈农业〉 ginning outturn; gin turnout

衣服 yīfu clothing; clothes; garment; dress: 打了补丁的～ clothes with patches /朴素～ plain clothes /他穿～从不讲究。He's never fastidious about his clothing. /这身～很值钱。It's an expensive suit.

衣钩 yīgōu clothes hook

衣冠 yīguān hat and clothes; dress; attire: ～整齐 be neatly attired /～褴褛 be shabbily dressed /～云集 gathering of respectably dressed people (*or* of luminaries)

衣冠楚楚 yīguān-chǔchǔ immaculately dressed: 进来的是一个～, 很有几分学者风度的男子。In came an impeccably dressed, scholarly mannered gentleman.

衣冠禽兽 yīguān-qínshòu beast in human attire; brute: 我原以为他是个品格高尚的正人君子, 不料想是个～。I had thought that he was a noble gentleman, but he turned out a brute.

衣冠冢 yīguānzhǒng *also* "衣冠墓" tomb containing hat, clothes, or other personal effects of the deceased, whose remains are either missing or buried elsewhere: 北京西山有孙中山先生的～。There is a tomb containing the personal effects of Dr. Sun Yat-sen in West Mountain, Beijing.

衣柜 yīguì wardrobe

衣架 yījià ❶ coat hanger; clothes-rack ❷ clothes tree; clothes stand ❸ *also* "衣架子" stature; figure: 他的～好, 穿什么衣服都精神。He has such a good figure that he looks smart no matter how he is dressed.

衣架饭囊 yījià-fànnáng clothes-horse and food-bag — worthless person; good-for-nothing

衣角 yījiǎo end-ridge of the lower hem of a gown, jacket or skirt

衣襟 yījīn one or two pieces making up the front of a Chinese jacket or gown

衣锦还乡 yījǐn-huánxiāng *also* "衣锦荣归" return to one's home town in silken robes — return home after making good: 他希望有一天～, 也好让父母高兴。He hoped that one day he would return home with fame and fortune and make his parents happy and proud.

衣锦夜行 yījǐn-yèxíng walk out in silken robes during the night — one's illustriousness remains unknown to others: 富贵不归故乡, 如～。It's like walking in silken robes in the dark if one doesn't return home after acquiring wealth and power.

衣裾 yījū 〈书面〉 one or two pieces making up the front and back of a Chinese jacket

衣料 yīliào material for clothing; dress material: ～考究 choice materials

衣领 yīlǐng collar

衣履 yīlǚ clothes and shoes — attire: ～不整 be sloppily dressed

衣帽架 yīmàojià clothes rack; clothes tree

衣帽间 yīmàojiān cloakroom

衣纽 yīniǔ button

衣衾 yīqīn clothes and quilts (esp. used for burying the dead)

衣衫 yīshān clothes; dress

衣衫褴褛 yīshān-lánlǚ shabbily dressed; dressed in rags: 此人虽然～, 但气度与常人不同。Though shabbily dressed, he was a man out of the ordinary run.

衣裳 yīshang clothing; clothes: 洗～ wash clothes /缝补～ mend clothes

衣食 yīshí food and clothing: ～之谋 plan of earning a living /～不周 be short of food and clothing; live in straitened circumstances /～足而知荣辱。Only when one is adequately fed and clad can one have a sense of honour and shame.

衣食父母 yīshí-fùmǔ people on whom one relies for living: 顾客是我们的～。Our business relies on customers for success.

衣食住行 yī-shí-zhù-xíng food, clothing, shelter and transport — basic necessities of life: 市长要关心市民们的～。The mayor should concern himself with the daily life of the people in his city.

衣饰 yīshì clothing and ornaments: 她很朴实, 从不在～上用心思。She is an unaffected woman and never gives much thought to clothing and ornaments.

衣物 yīwù clothing and other articles of daily use; personal effects

衣箱 yīxiāng suitcase; trunk

衣鱼 yīyú *also* "蠹鱼" dùyú; "纸鱼" zhǐyú silverfish; fish moth; bookworm

衣装 yīzhuāng ❶ clothes; dress; attire ❷ clothes and luggage: 他已把～收拾停当。He has packed up his belongings.

衣着 yīzhuó clothing, headgear and footwear: ～朴素 be plainly dressed /～华丽 be gorgeously dressed

柃

yī *see* "移柃" yíyī

铱

yī 〈化学〉 iridium (Ir)

铱金笔 yījīnbǐ iridium-point pen

依

yī ❶ depend on; rely on; count on; look to: 无～无靠 have nobody to depend on; be totally helpless /唇齿相～ (of two interdependent things) share a common lot ❷ obey; comply with; yield to: 百～百顺 be docile and obedient; be all obedience /你就～了我吧! Please be so kind as to comply with my wish. /你要是再这样, 我可不～你。If you do this again, I won't let you off so easily. /我们劝他休息, 他怎么也不～。We advised him to have a rest, but he simply wouldn't hear of it. ❸ according to; in the light of; judging by; on the basis of: ～着图样剪裁 cut according to the design /有法必～。If there is a law, we must abide by it. /～你说该怎么办? What shall we do in your view? ❹ (Yī) a surname

依傍 yībàng ❶ look to; count on; depend on: 互相～ depend on each other /无可～ have nobody (*or* nothing) to fall back on /他小时候～兄嫂过日子。He relied on his brother and sister-in-law for a living when he was young. /我忽然有一种无所～的孤单空落感。I suddenly felt helpless and lonely. ❷ imitate; copy: 一味～前人的艺术家是没有出息的。Any artist who blindly copies his predecessors has no future.

依草附木 yīcǎo-fùmù depend on others; cannot act on one's own: 这些人不过是～之辈。These people are mere yesmen.

依此类推 yīcǐ-lèituī the rest may be inferred; infer by analogy

依次 yīcì in proper order; one after another; successively: ～进入会场 enter the meeting hall one after another /～递补 fill vacancies in order of precedence /～说明下列问题 illustrate the following points in their given order /菜一道一道地～上来, 摆了满满的一桌。Dishes were served successively and spread all over the table.

依从 yīcóng obey; comply with; yield to: ～上级 obey one's superior /～长辈 comply with one's senior /当时～他的主张, 便断不会有今天这种被动的局面。We wouldn't have got ourselves in such a predicament if we had done as he said.

依存 yīcún depend on sb. or sth. for existence: 要了解世界和中国的相互～关系 get to know the interdependence between China and the rest of the world

依法 yīfǎ ❶ according to fixed rule: ～炮制 prepare herbal medicine by the prescribed method — follow a set pattern; follow suit ❷ according to law: ～惩办 punish according to law; mete out

punishment in accordance with the law

依附 yīfù ❶ be attached to:爬山虎～在山崖上。The ivy spread over the cliff. ❷ depend on; rely on; become an appendage to:～豪门 attach oneself to powers that be /～别人者决不能自由。He who depends on others will never be free. /她准备退休后也不～儿子。She has made up her mind that she won't be a burden on her son even after her retirement.

依归 yīguī ❶ home to return to; be-all and end-all; guide:以人民的利益为～ regard the people's interests as the end-all ❷ reliance; dependence:孤身海外,无所～ live abroad alone and helpless

依旧 yījiù as before; as usual; as of old; still:这东西他用了半年,～和新的一样。It remains as good as a new one though he has used it for half a year. /别人都已就寝,独有他～在灯下看书。Others had already gone to bed; only he was still reading by the light. /古今兴亡多少事,江水～向东流。The river water keeps running eastwards as always, despite so many great changes throughout history.

依据 yījù ❶ basis; grounds; foundation:科学的论断须以客观事实为～。Scientific judgments should be formed on the basis of facts. /你说这话的～是什么? What grounds do you have for saying so? ❷ according to; on the basis of; judging by; in line with:～先例 act in the light of the precedents; go by the precedents /我们是～文件的精神办事的。We act in the spirit of the document.

依靠 yīkào ❶ rely on; depend on; count on:可以～的人,在他心目中只有两个。In his eyes there are only two people that he may count on. /他是一位～战功而获得威望的将军。He is a general whose prestige is built on his war exploits. ❷ sb. or sth. to fall back on; support; backing:如果他出来主持工作,那我们就有了～。We will have strong backing if he takes charge of the work. /爸爸去世后,我们全家失去了生活的～。Our family lost means of livelihood after father died.

依赖 yīlài ❶ rely on; depend on:～性 dependence /这个国家的粮食主要～进口。This country relies on imports for most of its grain. /她不想～任何人。She does not want to be dependent on anybody. ❷ be interdependent:世界上的事物都是相互～、相互制约的。All matters in the world are interdependent and act on each other.

依兰香 yīlánxiāng 〈植物〉 ilang-ilang; ylang-ylang (*Canangium odoratum*):～油 ilang-ilang oil

依恋 yīliàn be reluctant to leave; feel regret at separation:在即将分别的时刻,我们相互～地拉着手。Hand in hand, we were reluctant to part from each other at the time of saying goodbye. /离开故乡几十年了,但心中总有一种～之情。Though I have been away from my hometown for dozens of years, I am still sentimentally attached to it.

依凭 yīpíng ❶ rely on; depend on:～险隘,坚守待援 take advantage of a strategic pass to hold on and wait for relief ❷ grounds; evidence:我的推断自有～。I do have evidence for my inference.

依然 yīrán still; as before; as usual:风景～。The scenery remains the same. /这～是一本不可不读的好书。It's still a good book that everyone should read.

依然故我 yīrán-gùwǒ remain one's same old self; stay just the same as before:任凭父母如何苦口婆心地教育,他～,坏习惯一点也没改变。Despite his parents' repeated admonitions, he remained unrepentant and refused to mend his ways.

依然如故 yīrán-rúgù remain as before; stay unchanged:他吃、喝、玩耍,～。He indulges in eating, drinking and playing as he did before. /别处都在日新月异地变化,唯独这里～。Changes are taking place with each passing day almost everywhere, and this is the only place that remains stagnant.

依山傍水 yīshān-bàngshuǐ be situated at the foot of a hill and beside a stream:山海关～,形势险要。Situated at the foot of Mount Jiao and beside the Bohai Sea, the Shanhai Pass is a strategic point.

依实 yīshí ❶ comply with; approve; consent:他见说得有理,也就～了。Since the statement was quite reasonable, he made no objection. ❷ strictly according to the facts; as things really are:要～说,不要说谎。Report what happened accurately. Don't tell lies. *or* Tell the truth; no lies.

依恃 yīshì rely on; count on; depend on:～权势 rely on one's power and position

依顺 yīshùn comply with; be obedient:～丈夫的愿望 comply with her husband's wishes /千依百顺 be all obedience

依随 yīsuí submit to; yield to:孩子说什么她都～。She yields to her child's every request.

依贴 yītiē snuggle up to; lean close to:孩子怕羞地～在母亲身旁。Being shy, the child snuggled up to his mother's side.

依托 yītuō ❶ rely on; count on; depend on:无～射击 fire without prop /～权贵 count on one's powerful connections /他们以岩石、树林为～,边退边射击。Under cover of the rocks and woods, they fired back while retreating. ❷ pretext; excuse:"健康欠佳"只不过是他闭门谢客的～而已。"Not feeling well" is simply his pretext for refusing to receive guests.

依偎 yīwēi snuggle up to; nestle up against; lean close to:一条小狗～在她脚边。A little dog nestled up at her feet. /树下,一对情人互相～着。A pair of lovers were snuggling up to each other under the trees.

依违 yīwéi 〈书面〉 comply with or go against — be equivocal or ambiguous; remain undecided:～不决 remain hesitant /～两可 be ambiguous; equivocate

依稀 yīxī vaguely; faintly; dimly:童年的有些事情我还～记得。I still vaguely remember some of the things that happened in my childhood. /远处人家的灯火～可辨。The twinkling lights in the distance were faintly visible. /我借着～星光,踏上田间的石板路。I walked on the stone path of the fields in the dim starlight.

依循 yīxún accord with; abide by; adhere to:制定一个章程,使大家有所～ work out a set of rules so that people will have something to go by

依样 yīyàng in the same old way; all the same; as before:湖山～妩媚多姿。The lake and the mountain remain as lovely as ever.

依样葫芦 yīyàng-húlu *also* "依样画葫芦" draw a gourd according to the model — copy mechanically:～地做些应时的公文 write some official documents perfunctorily according to a model

依依 yīyī ❶〈书面〉(of branch or twig) frail and gentle, swaying in the wind:杨柳～。The tender branches of the willow trees are swaying in the breeze. ❷ reluctant to part:～惜别 be reluctant to say goodbye

依依不舍 yīyī-bùshě be reluctant to part; cannot bear to leave:～地告别亲友 be reluctant to bid farewell to one's relatives and friends /我们～地挥手告别。We were loath to wave goodbye.

依约 yīyuē 〈书面〉 indistinct; faint:碑上的字迹～可辨。The inscription on the tablet is faintly recognizable.

依允 yīyǔn comply with; approve; assent; consent:他点头～了孩子的要求。He nodded assent (*or* approval) to the child's request.

依仗 yīzhàng count on; rely on; depend on:～人多 count on the advantage of having more people; rely on one's numerical superiority

依照 yīzhào according to; in the light of; on the basis of:～上级指示执行 act in accordance with the directives of higher authorities /会议～预定程序进行。The meeting was held according to the set procedure. /你可～他的办法去试试看。You may try his method.

祎(禕)

yī 〈书面〉(usu. used in personal names) glorious; fine

一[1]

yī ❶ one:一个 one; a; an /～种办法 a method /万无～失 no risk at all; perfectly safe /孤身～人 all by oneself /他连～口饭也吃不进。He couldn't even eat a mouthful. /～针～线都来之不易。Not even a single needle and thread comes easily. /～个和尚挑水吃,两个和尚担水吃,三个和尚没水吃。One monk will carry two buckets of water; two monks will share the load; when there're three monks, no one will want to fetch the water. *or* One boy is a boy, two boys half a boy, three boys no boy. ❷ same:大小不～ different in size /千篇～律 following the same pattern; stereotyped /你们～路走。You go the same way. /我们是～家人。We're of one family. /各家的说法不～。Different people had different stories. ❸ another; also; otherwise:汞溴红～名红汞。Another name for merbromin is mercurochrome. *or* Merbromin is also known as mercurochrome. ❹ whole; entire; all:～身的汗 wet through with sweat /焕然～新 take on an entirely new look (*or* aspect); look brand-new /～天到晚 from dawn to dusk; the whole day; all day long /～冬没下雪。It didn't snow the whole winter. ❺ concentrated; wholehearted:专心～意 heart and soul; wholeheartedly ❻ *indicating that the action is just for once, or of short duration, or that the action is an experimental one* (a) *used between reduplicated (often monosyllabic) verbs*:看～看 take a look /闻～闻 have a smell /唱～唱 sing /歇～歇

have a rest /让我听~听。Let me listen. /每天早晨我也跟着他跑~跑。I do some running with him every morning. (b) *used after a verb and before a verbial classifier*:哭~场 have a cry /白跑~趟 make a fruitless trip /大吵~通 have a big row /重读~遍 reread; read it again /头上挨了~扁担 be hit by a carrying pole on the head /快来帮我~把 come here quickly to give me a hand /他来过~次。He has been here once. ❼ *used before either a verb or a verbial classifier to indicate that the action leads to the following consequence*:~脚把它踢开 force it open with a kick /~到冬天,这里满山遍野都是冰雪。When winter comes, all the mountains and fields here are covered with snow. /~听说哥哥得了冠军,全家高兴极了。On hearing that the elder son won the championship, the whole family were overjoyed. ❽ once; now that:此鸟不飞则已,~飞冲天。This bird usually does not fly; but once it does, it goes soaring into the sky. ❾〈书面〉〈助词〉*used for emphasis*:~何速也! How fast it is! /洪水为害之甚,~至于此! To think that the flood should have wreaked such great havoc!

Note: When used alone or at the end of an expression or sentence, 一 is pronounced in high-level tone; when used before a word that is in falling tone, it is pronounced in rising tone, e.g. 一去 yíqù, 一旦 yídàn; when used before a word in either high-level, rising or falling-rising tone, it is pronounced in falling tone, e.g. 一边 yìbiān, 一人 yìrén, 一马 yìmǎ. For the sake of convenience, 一 in all the entries of this dictionary is marked in high-level tone.

一[2] yī 〈音乐〉a note of the scale in *gongchepu* (工尺谱), corresponding to 7 in numbered musical notation

一把好手 yībǎ hǎoshǒu good hand; past master:做针线活儿,她可是~。She is adept at needlework.

一把手 yībǎshǒu ❶ (a) party to an undertaking; member; hand:咱们搭伙干,你也算~。We're going to pool our efforts and we'll count you in. ❷ *also* "一把好手" good hand; past master; able person:她可是里里外外~。She is adept at everything she does, both inside and outside the house. ❸ *also* "第一把手" leading official in a unit; number one; first-in-command:我们厂的~到省里开会去了。The first-in-command of our factory has gone to the capital of our province to attend a meeting.

一把死拿 yībǎsǐná 〈方言〉stubborn; headstrong; inflexible:这是个~的人,谁的话他都不听。This bigoted person won't listen to anybody else's advice.

一把钥匙开一把锁 yī bǎ yàoshi kāi yī bǎ suǒ use different keys to open different locks; solve different problems with different methods:~,她最听你的,只有你去才说得通。A lock can be opened only by the right key. As she listens only to you, you are exactly the person to bring her round.

一把抓 yībǎzhuā ❶ take everything into one's own hands; attend to every thing oneself:要调动组长们的积极性分头管,不能什么事情都由你~。Encourage the team leaders to take their respective responsibilities. You just can't attend to everything by yourself. ❷ grasp all indiscriminately; try to tackle all problems at once regardless of their relative importance:他干事样样都没计划,人称~。He never gets his priorities right and is nicknamed "Mr Grasp-All".

一百八十度 yībǎi bāshí dù (make or represent a) 180-degree turn; (do an) about-turn or about-face; (do a) U-turn; (turn into the) opposite direction:昨天他积极赞成,今天突然来了个~的大转变,热情全没了。Only yesterday he was in favour of it, but today he made a volte face and his enthusiasm was nowhere to be found.

一百一 yībǎiyī 〈方言〉excellent; perfect; flawless:~的老师 excellent (*or* perfect) teacher /他待我真是~,我可忘不了他。He treated me very well. How could I ever forget him?

一败如水 yībài-rúshuǐ fall to the ground like spilt water; meet with utter defeat; be routed:在赌场上~ suffer an overwhelming loss in gambling

一败涂地 yībài-túdì fall to the ground; suffer a crushing defeat; be ruined completely; be completely wiped out:我队在联赛中~。Our team was thoroughly defeated in the league matches. /这样一来,他的信誉就~了。In this way he was discredited completely.

一班人 yībānrén members of a squad — a small body of people working together:党委~ all the members of the Party Committee /厂领导~ entire factory leadership

一般 yībān ❶ same as; just like; as... as...:钢铁~的意志 iron will /两个物件~重。The two objects are of the same weight. /五个指头不能~齐。The five fingers can't be of the same length. *or* It takes all sorts to make the world. /眼睛像秋水~明亮。The eyes are as clear as autumn waters. ❷ one kind:别有~滋味在心头 a kind of indescribable taste in the heart /这里的一切对他都是那样陌生,如同来到另~的天地。Everything here was so strange to him as if he had come into a completely new world. ❸ general; usual; ordinary; common:~性 generality /~情况 ordinary circumstances /~用法 common usage /~性辩论 general debate /~等价物 universal equivalent /这篇文章的内容很~。There's nothing striking about this article. *or* The article is quite mediocre. /这次的任务非同~。This is an extraordinary mission. /下午我~在家写作。I usually stay at home writing in the afternoon. /~地说,这种可能性不大。Generally speaking, it is improbable.

一般规律 yībān guīlǜ universal law; general rule

一般化 yībānhuà generalization:~的读物 generalized reading material /他的讲话太~。His speech is full of generalities.

一般见识 yībān jiànshi lower oneself or bring oneself down to the same level as sb.:何必跟这种人~! Don't stoop to (*or* debase yourself by) arguing with such people. /你都大人了,不必跟小孩子~。You're an adult. Don't behave like a child.

一斑 yībān one spot on a leopard — a small but typical part of the whole, or of many similar things:管中窥豹,可见~。Look at one spot on a leopard and you can visualize the whole animal. *or* You can conjure up the whole thing through seeing a part of it.

一板一眼 yībǎn-yīyǎn following a prescribed pattern in speech or action; meticulous and methodical:他~地说明了如何改进经营方法的意见。He explained the ideas for improving business management in scrupulous detail.

一板正经 yībǎn-zhèngjīng in all seriousness; in dead earnest

一半 yībàn one half; half; in part:不到~ less than half /~以上的人 more than half of the people; majority /你不能一人独占,我们各分~。You can't keep it all to yourself, we should go halves. /利润~用于扩大再生产,~用于改善工人生活。The profit is used in part for extended reproduction and in part for improving the workers' life.

一…半… yī…bàn… *used separately before synonyms or related words, meaning not many (or much) or very soon*:就凭我这点手艺,一时半会儿还饿不死。My skills will enable me to keep the wolf from the door for some time. /她至今也没生下一男半女。She hasn't given birth to any child yet. /这事不是一言半语能说清楚的。It cannot be explained in a few words.

一半天 yībàntiān in a day or two:这商场~就开张。The department store is to open for business in a day or two. /这任务~完不成。The work can't be done overnight. /事情~就会有结果。The result will come out soon. *or* Things will work out in a day or so.

一帮 yībāng *also* "一帮子" a group; a band; a crowd:~人 a group of people

一包在内 yībāozàinèi all included; altogether:车钱、店钱、饭钱、~,花了二百块钱。It cost 200 *yuan*, including fares, boarding fees and meals.

一报还一报 yī bào huán yī bào one turn deserving another; retribution in kind; an eye for an eye and a tooth for a tooth

一辈子 yībèizi all one's life; throughout one's life; as long as one lives; one's entire life:享了~的福 live in lifelong ease and comfort /辛劳~ work hard all one's life /他~见过好多事情。He has witnessed many events throughout his life. /学习是~的事。One should keep on learning as long as one lives. *or* Live and learn.

一本万利 yīběn-wànlì a small investment brings a ten thousand-fold profit; make big profits out of a small capital:~是商人的最大愿望。The biggest wish of businessmen is to make big profits with a small capital.

一本正经 yīběn-zhèngjīng in all seriousness; in real earnest:~地坐着不动 sit still in dead earnest /她那小小的年纪和她这~的神态不相称。Her serious manner doesn't match her age.

一鼻孔出气 yī bíkǒng chūqì breathe through the same nostrils; sing the same tune; collude with one another; be cheek by jowl (with):他们俩一个腔调,完全是~。The two of them sang the same tune and acted in collusion with each other.

一笔不苟 yībǐ-bùgǒu (in writing, drawing, etc.) be scrupulous about every stroke; be conscientious and meticulous; not be the least bit negligent:老人~地写下了自己的名字。The old man wrote his name in an extremely careful way.

一笔带过 yībǐ-dàiguò touch upon lightly; mention in passing:这

Y

个问题不是本文的重点，可～。As this is not a key point in the article, we may just mention it in passing.

一笔勾销 yībǐ-gōuxiāo write off at one stroke; cancel: 前账～ cancel all debts /他所有的抱负、志向、希望、前程，全被～了。All his ambition, hopes, and future were written off. /只要你认错，我们过去的事情就算～了。So long as you admit your mistakes, we'll let bygones be bygones.

一笔抹杀 yībǐ-mǒshā dismiss sth. with a wave of the hand; blot out at one stroke; totally negate; flatly deny: 这个人物在历史上的地位不能～。This personage's role in history shouldn't be dismissed out of hand. /为什么要把前人的业绩～呢? Why should one totally negate (*or* deny) the achievements of one's predecessors?

一碧 yībì stretch of greenness: ～如洗 so green as to seem freshly washed by rain; fresh green /湖面～万顷。The lake is a vast expanse of green.

一壁 yībì *also* "一壁厢" at the same time; simultaneously; while: 她～哭，～骂。She is both crying and cursing.

一臂之力 yībìzhīlì helping hand: 我愿助你～，将这件事办成。I'm willing to help you get it done. /希望你助我～。I hope you will lend me a hand.

一边 yībiān ❶ one side: 这苹果只有～儿红。Only one side of the apple is red. /两方面争论，往往总有～儿理屈。There is usually one side in the wrong when an argument arises. ❷ by the side of: 书柜～儿是书桌。The desk is at the side of the bookcase. /小韩～儿站着，什么话也没说。Standing to one side, Xiao Han didn't say a word. /我们玩儿的时候，他在～儿坐着。He sat nearby while we were playing. ❸ *indicating two actions taking place at the same time*: 孩子们～唱，～跳。The children sang as they were dancing. /他～翻阅着资料，～随手摘录在笔记本上。He made notes in the notebook while looking through the materials. ❹〈方言〉same; equal: 他俩～高。The two are of the same height. /天下乌鸦～黑。Crows are black the world over. *or* In every country dogs bite.

一边倒 yībiāndǎo ❶ lean to one side; side with sb. without reservation; be partial to: 在处理两个局的争论时，老袁明显地～，站在工业局一方。In dealing with the quarrel between the two bureaus, Lao Yuan was apparently on the side of the Industry Bureau. ❷ be far superior; enjoy overwhelming superiority: 这是一场～的比赛。This is an unequal match.

一表非凡 yībiǎo-fēifán be handsome and poised; have an impressive or striking appearance: 这人生得～，而且声音洪亮，谈吐大方。The man looks not only impressively handsome, but has also a sonorous voice and speaks with ease and confidence.

一表人才 yībiǎo-réncái *also* "一表人物" (of appearance) handsome: 他生得浓眉大眼，～。He is a handsome man with thick eyebrows and big eyes.

一表堂堂 yībiǎo-tángtáng noble and dignified; impressive-looking

一并 yībìng 〈副词〉along with all the others; together with sb. or sth. else; in the lump: ～考虑 be considered together with sth. else / ～告知 inform sb. of sth. along with other matters /读者提出的几个疑问，现在～答复如下。The following is a comprehensive reply to questions put forward by readers.

一病不起 yībìng-bùqǐ take to one's bed and never leave it again; fall ill and fail to recover: 他妻子得了肝炎，～。His wife caught hepatitis and never recovered.

一拨儿 yībōr *also* "一拨子" a group; a band; a batch: ～打手 a bunch of thugs /他住院时，学生们～、～地去看他。While he was in hospital, his students visited him in one group after another.

一波三折 yībō-sānzhé (of strokes of a Chinese character) be tortuous and unrestrained; strike one snag after another; be full of twists and turns or ups and downs: 笔势飘逸，～ free and elegant calligraphy /想不到这个问题会如此～，复杂多变! We hadn't thought that the matter would turn out to be so complicated and elusive.

一波未平，一波又起 yī bō wèi píng, yī bō yòu qǐ hardly has one wave subsided when another rises — one trouble follows another; have troubles galore: 今年对他来说是多事之秋，母亲刚去世，孩子又住进了医院，真是～。This year is really hard for him with one trouble coming on the heels of another; shortly after his mother died, his child was sent to hospital.

一…不… yī…bù… ❶ *used respectively before two verbs meaning that the action or condition is unchangeable once it takes place or is established*: 一借不还 borrow sth. but never return it /一蹶不振 never be able to recover after a setback ❷ *used respectively before a noun and a verb for emphasis or as a hyperbole*: 一介不取 refuse to take anything undeserving /一丁不识 not know a single word /一动不动 not move an inch; not stir; be perfectly still /一文不花 spend not a single penny /一事不晓 be completely ignorant

一不怕苦，二不怕死 yī bù pà kǔ, èr bù pà sǐ fear neither hardship nor death

一不做，二不休 yī bù zuò, èr bù xiū carry sth. through at all cost once you've started it; in for a penny, in for a pound: 留下哪个都是病，干脆，～，一遭都卖了，免除后患。Keeping any one of them is asking for trouble, so we may as well make a clean sweep and sell the whole lot.

一步登天 yībù-dēngtiān reach heaven in a single bound — attain the highest level in one step; have a meteoric rise; be rapidly successful: 女子一旦成了皇后或妃子，她的家族便～，十分显赫富贵。Once a woman was made empress or imperial concubine, her family would have a meteoric rise in position and wealth.

一步一个脚印儿 yī bù yīgè jiǎoyìnr every step leaves its print — work steadily and make solid progress; do solid work: 老徐自从参加工作以来，做事总是～。Lao Xu has always done his job in a down-to-earth manner ever since he began his career.

一差二错 yīchā-èrcuò possible mistake or mishap; unexpected accident: 万一有个～ just in case there is a slip somewhere; just in case of accident /人有失足，马有失蹄，谁办事也难保不出个～。As people may lose their footing and horses may slip, nobody can be entirely free from making mistakes.

一刹 yīchà in an instant; in a flash; in a split second; in the twinkling of an eye: 地震来时，～间地动山摇，房倒屋塌。When the earthquake occurred, mountains moved and buildings collapsed in a split second.

一刹那 yīchànà in an instant; in a flash; in the twinkling of an eye: 在枪响前的～，他闪到了树后。The moment the gun was fired, he dodged nimbly behind a tree.

一划 yīchàn ❶〈方言〉one and all; without exception; totally: 这些家具是～儿新。All the furniture is brand-new. ❷ (usu. used in the early vernacular) always; consistently: ～地陷害忠良 spare no effort to frame up faithful and upright people

一长两短 yīcháng-liǎngduǎn *also* "三长两短" sāncháng-liǎngduǎn unexpected misfortune; sth. unfortunate, esp. death: 他万一有个～，叫我们怎么活! If anything should happen to him, how could we live on?

一场春梦 yīcháng-chūnmèng fond dream in spring — evanescent happiness; daydream

一场空 yīchángkōng all in vain; futile; to no avail: 竹篮打水～ as futile as drawing water with a bamboo basket /都是你出的主意，现在落得～! It was all your idea. Now we've ended up with nothing.

一场秋雨一场寒 yī cháng qiūyǔ yī cháng hán *also* "一场秋雨一场凉" a spell of autumn rain, a spell of cold; the weather gets colder with each autumn rain

一倡百和 yīchàng-bǎihè *also* "一唱百和" when one starts singing, all the others join in; one sings, all follow; one person proposes and a hundred others respond; (of a suggestion, etc.) meet with general approval: 不料此种似是而非的说法，正迎合许多人的心理，竟收到了～的效果。Unexpectedly this specious argument met with general approval, as it catered to popular feeling.

一倡三叹 yīchàng-sāntàn *also* "一唱三叹" one sings, and three others join in; (of poems and articles) be beautiful and emotionally appealing

一唱一和 yīchàng-yīhè 〈贬义〉sing a duet with sb.; sing the same tune; echo each other; chime in with each other: 你们俩可不能这样～地欺骗他这个老实人。You two shouldn't collude with each other to cheat a simple person like him.

一朝天子一朝臣 yī cháo tiānzǐ yī cháo chén every new sovereign brings his own courtiers; when a new king is crowned, he fills the court with his own favourites; a new chief brings in his own aides: 真是～，总统下台，百官也跟着卷铺盖。New governments have new ministers, and when the president steps down, his officials have to pack up and leave with him.

一尘不染 yīchén-bùrǎn ❶ (of person) pure-minded; pure-hearted: 他做了几十年的官，依然是两袖清风，～。He remained honest and clean-handed, even after being an official for dozens of years. ❷ (of environment) not soiled or stained by a speck of dust; spotlessly clean: 海滩～。The beach was spotlessly clean.

一成不变 yīchéng-bùbiàn fixed and immutable; unalterable; stick in a rut: 任何事物都不可能是～的。Nothing is unchangedable (*or* remains fixed). /天底下没有～之法。Nowhere is there any hard and fast rule.

一程子 yīchéngzi 〈方言〉for some days; for some time: 我到上海去了～。I've been to Shanghai for a few days.

一宠性儿 yīchǒngxìngr *also* "一宠性子";"一铳子性儿" wilful; self-willed; wayward; headstrong: 凡事要三思,不能只顾当时～。Look before you leap, and don't do anything on an impulse.

一筹 yīchóu a chip; a counter; a move (as in chess); a shade: 略逊～ be slightly inferior /计高～ have a better stratagem; be a cut above (sb.)

一筹莫展 yīchóu-mòzhǎn can find no way out; be at a loss; be at one's wits' end; be at the end of one's tether: 面对这么多困难, 她～。She was at a loss what to do in the face of so many difficulties.

一触即发 yīchù-jífā may be triggered at any moment; be on the verge of breaking out; be explosive: 敌对双方面对面地摆好了阵势, 大有～之势。The opposing sides had deployed their troops in battle array, and the situation was explosive. /这两人水火不容, 冲突～。The two of them were totally incompatible and might come into conflict at any moment.

一触即溃 yīchù-jíkuì be routed or crumble at the first encounter: 这支队伍本是乌合之众, ～。Being a disorderly band, it collapsed at the first encounter with the enemy.

一传十,十传百 yī chuán shí, shí chuán bǎi one person tells ten, who tell a hundred; (of news) spread far and wide or quickly; flit from mouth to mouth: 这消息～, 很快便全城皆知。The news spread like wildfire, and soon everyone in town knew about it.

一串红 yīchuànhóng 〈植物〉scarlet sage (*Salvia splendens*)

一锤定音 yīchuí-dìngyīn *also* "一槌定音" set the tune with one beat of the gong — say the last word; make the final decision: 最后还是厂长～, 把事情定了下来。It was the director of the factory who gave the final word and made the decision.

一锤子买卖 yī chuízi mǎimai "once-for-all" deal (by which a customer is fleeced so much that he won't come a second time): ～干不得。It is not at all wise to do anything for maximum temporary advantage without consideration of the consequences. /这种不讲信誉的～, 肯定会砸了他的招牌。Such a dishonest, once-for-all deal would completely tarnish his reputation as a businessman.

一词多义 yīcí-duōyì polysemy; one word with many meanings: 汉语里～的现象较普遍。Polysemy is quite common in the Chinese language.

一次 yīcì once; one: 缺了～课 miss one class /不只～ more than once /今年这次灯会是最热闹的～。This year's lantern fair is the most lively one. /客轮～试航成功。The passenger ship ran successfully on its first trial voyage.

一次方程 yīcì fāngchéng 〈数学〉linear equation

一次函数 yīcì hánshù 〈数学〉linear function

一次能源 yīcì néngyuán primary energy (resources)

一次性 yīcìxìng only once: ～使用针管 hypodermic syringes that are used only once; disposable syringes /～削价处理 sale at a just-for-once discounted price /～补贴 subsidy paid in one lump sum /～用品 throwaways /～筷子 throwaway chopsticks

一从 yīcóng ever since; since: ～别后, 音信不通。I havn't heard from you since we departed. /～大地起风雷, 便有精生白骨堆。A thunderstorm burst over the earth, So a devil rose from a heap of white bones.

一蹴而就 yīcù'érjiù accomplish in one move; reach the goal with one leap; succeed overnight: 发明创造并非～。No invention can be accomplished by one single effort.

一寸丹心 yīcùn-dānxīn *also* "一片丹心" one's heart remains true to the end; be thoroughly faithful and reliable; be true as steel: ～报效祖国 devote one's whole self to serving the country

一寸光阴一寸金 yī cùn guāngyīn yī cùn jīn an inch of time is an inch of gold; time is money: ～, 寸金难买寸光阴。An inch of time is an inch of gold, but even gold cannot buy time.

一搭 yīdā 〈方言〉together; at the same place: 大家在～儿混熟了。We got to know each other fairly well after having been together for some time.

一搭两用儿 yīdā-liǎngyòngr one thing with two uses; dual-purpose article: 这件旧大衣白天能挡风, 晚上当被子, ～。This old coat serves two purposes as a windbreaker during the day and as a quilt at night.

一打一拉 yīdǎ-yīlā use the stick and the carrot; strike and stroke alternately; hit and wheedle by turns; employ both hard and soft tactics

一大二公 yīdà-èrgōng (of people's communes) large in size and collective in nature; larger in size and having a higher degree of public ownership (than the cooperatives)

一大早儿 yīdàzǎor daybreak; dawn: 他～就遛弯儿去了。He went out for a walk as soon as day broke.

一代 yīdài ❶ dynasty: 有清～ during (*or* throughout) the Qing Dynasty ❷ era; epoch; present age; contemporary era: ～英豪 heroes of the times /～天骄 proud son of Heaven for his time ❸ lifetime; generation: 年轻的～ younger generation /我们的祖先在这块土地上, ～～地辛勤劳动, 创造出灿烂的文化。Our ancestors worked hard on this land from generation to generation and created a brilliant civilization.

一带 yīdài surrounding area: 北京～ Beijing and the surrounding (*or* nearby) area /江南～雨量充足。There is plenty of rain in areas south of the Yangtze River. /他是这～出名的歌手。He is a well known singer around here.

一旦 yīdàn ❶ in one day; in a single day; in a very short time: 毁于～ be destroyed in one day ❷ some day; once: 相处三年, ～离别, 怎么能不想念呢? Having been together for three years, we couldn't help missing each other once (*or* after) we were separated. /孩子～上床, 很快就会入睡。Once in bed, the children will soon fall asleep.

一担儿挑 yīdànrtiāo 〈方言〉husbands of sisters

一氮化物 yīdànhuàwù 〈化学〉mononitride

一刀两断 yīdāo-liǎngduàn sever at one blow; make a clean break: 他和那伙人早就～了。He made a clean break with that group of people a long time ago.

一刀切 yīdāoqiē *also* "一刀齐" cut it even at one stroke — make it rigidly uniform; impose uniformity (in all cases); find a single solution (for all problems); allow no flexibility: 全国的改革不能～。We should not try to use a single model for reform all over the country.

一道 yīdào together; side by side; along with: 你下次就把笔、墨、纸～带来吧! You may as well bring the pen, ink and paper with you when you come next time. /你何不跟他～去? Why don't you two go together? /我们应当～分担家务劳动。We should share the home-work.

一得之功 yīdézhīgōng occasional, minor success: 我们不能因～而忘乎所以。We shouldn't be swollen-headed just because of a minor success.

一得之见 yīdézhījiàn 〈谦词〉point of view; opinion; understanding: 我希望自己的～不致贻误读者。I hope my own views won't mislead the readers.

一得之愚 yīdézhīyú 〈谦词〉my humble opinion: 试伸～。Let me state my humble view.

一等 yīděng first-class; first-rate; top-notch: ～奖 first prize /～舱 first-class cabin /～品 first-rate (*or* top-quality) product

一等兵 yīděngbīng (US Army) private first class; (US Navy) seaman first class; (US Air Force) airman first class; (US Marine Corps) marine first class; (UK Army) lance corporal; (UK Navy) leading seaman; (UK Air Force) senior aircrafts man (UK Marine Corps) marine first class

一等功 yīděnggōng merit citation class I; first-class merit

一等秘书 yīděng mìshū 〈外交〉first secretary

一等一 yīděngyī 〈方言〉A1; superior; best: ～的武林高手 great master of martial arts

一点就透 yīdiǎnjiùtòu take the hint quickly: 他的脑子好使, 什么事～。He has a quick mind and takes the hint swiftly in everything he does.

一点论 yīdiǎnlùn doctrine that everything has only one aspect; doctrine affirming only one aspect

一点儿 yīdiǎnr ❶ a bit; a little: 再给你添～吧。I'll give you a little more. /要把工作做得好～。You must do a better job. /我～也不知道。I didn't have the faintest idea. /还有～希望。There is still a gleam of hope. /这是我们的～心意。This is just a small token of our appreciation. /桌子没有～灰尘。There isn't a speck of dust on the desk. *or* The desk is spotlessly clean. ❷ (sometimes used after 这么 or 那么) very small; very little: 我～意见也没有。I have no objection at all. /冰箱里找不到～吃的。No food can be found in the refrig-

erator. /那么～活儿,一天就可以干完了。We can finish that little bit of work in a day.

一点一滴 yīdiǎn-yīdī every little bit:从～的小事做起 start from working on small matters /～地积累资本 accumulate capital bit by bit

一碘化物 yīdiǎnhuàwù 〈化学〉monoiodide

一丁点儿 yīdīngdiǎnr 〈方言〉a wee bit; a tiny bit:这样做,对你～好处也没有。You will not benefit a tiny bit by doing so. /食物就剩～了。Only a little bit of food was left.

一定 yīdìng ❶ fixed; specified; definite; regular:在～的时间内完成此项任务 complete the task in a fixed time /按照～的要求进行操作 operate according to specifications /那个博物馆开馆时间不～。That museum doesn't have regular hours. ❷ definitely; inevitably; necessarily:文章的好坏跟篇幅的长短,并没有～的关系。The quality of an article is not necessarily related to its length. /这东西很大,可是不～很重。It is large, but it is by no means heavy. /他～是记错了。He must have got it wrong. /有你的帮助,～没问题。There surely won't be any problem with your help. /这些书他不～都读过。He might not have read all these books. ❸ be bound to; be sure to; resolutely; firmly:他～会照办。He is sure to comply (with your request). /他～要走,就让他走吧。If he is determined to leave, just let him go. /这种新产品～受欢迎。This new product is bound to become popular in the market. /这封信～要在今天发出。The letter must be sent out today. /我们～会赢。We are certain to win. /你～别忘了。Make sure that you don't forget it. ❹ given; particular; certain:在～程度上 to a certain degree /在～条件下 under given circumstances /从～意义上说,这次会议还是成功的。In a sense, the meeting was a success. /人类社会发展到～阶段,就产生了私有制。Private ownership came into being when human society reached a particular stage of its development. ❺ fair; proper; considerable; due:达到～水平 reach a fairly high level /有～的工作经验 have a good deal of work experience /给以～的重视 attach due importance /双方的立场尚有～距离。There is still a considerable gap between the positions of the two sides. /这个意见,我准备在～场合发表。I'm going to air this view when the proper occasion arises. /老王的看法也有～的道理。Lao Wang has (got) a point there.

一定之规 yīdìngzhīguī ❶ fixed pattern; set rule:历史的发展,有它新陈代谢的～。The supersession of the old by the new is a fixed law of the evolution of history. ❷ fixed idea or way of doing things; one's own way:你有千言万语,我有～。No matter what you may say, I will act in my own way.

一丢点儿 yīdiūdiǎnr 〈方言〉very small; very little

一动 yīdòng easily; often; at every turn:这天儿～就出汗。People were apt to sweat in such sweltering weather. /他～就骂人。He swears at people easily. /在大城市里生活,～就得花钱。You have to spend money at every turn if you live in a big city.

一动不如一静 yī dòng bùrú yī jìng better be still than stir; better stay put than move; taking no action is better than taking any action:～,看看事态的发展再说。It's better to stay put than to move. Let's just watch how things develop before making any decision.

一肚子 yīdùzi filled with; full of:～坏水 plenty of sinister ideas /～牢骚 full of complaint

一度 yīdù ❶ period of time; spell:经过～紧张的抢修,高炉又恢复了生产。After a spell of emergency repairs, the blast furnace resumed working. ❷ once; for a time:物价～失控。Prices were once out of control. /奶粉～脱销。Milk powder was out of stock for some time.

一端 yīduān ❶ one end (of sth.):绳子的～拴在树上。One end of the rope was tied on the tree. ❷ one point or aspect (of a matter):仅此～ this point alone; only this point /各执～ each sticking to his own argument (*or* his guns)

一堆儿 yīduīr together; in company:我们小时常～玩。We used to play together when we were kids.

一多半 yīduōbàn more than half; greater part:领导班子里～是专业技术人员。More than half of the leaders are professionals.

一…而… yī…ér… *used respectively before a verb, meaning the result comes immediately after the action*:一望而知 get to know at a glance /一战而溃 be routed at the first battle /一跃而下 jump down at one bound /一闪而过 pass in a flash; flash past /一轰而上 rush into mass action; jump on the bandwagon in a swarm

一而再,再而三 yī ér zài, zài ér sān again and again; time and again; repeatedly:～地失利 repeated reverses (*or* setbacks) /～地找茬儿 keep on finding fault (*or* nitpicking)/我～地叮嘱他,他还是忘了。He forgot all about it though I had reminded him for God knows how many times.

一二 yī'èr one or two; some; just a few; just a little:内情我略知～。I know a little inside information. /在可能的范围内,请方便～。Please do me a favour or two if possible. /这个方案也有～可取之处。This plan also has something to recommend it.

一…二… yī…èr… *each used before a morpheme of some disyllabic adjectives, verbs, etc., for emphasis*:如有一差二错 if there should be an error (*or* mishap) /一来二去地两人成了好朋友。They met each other several times and became close friends. /我一老二实地全都说了。I made a clean breast of everything.

一二报数 yī-èr bàoshù (word of command) by twos, number; by twos, count off

一二·九运动 Yī'èr-Jiǔ Yùndòng December 9th Movement, a demonstration staged on 9 December 1935 by Beijing students under the leadership of the Chinese Communist Party, calling for resistance to Japanese aggression and for national salvation, turning eventually into a nation-wide movement

一发 yīfā ❶ more; still more; even more:如果处理不当,就～不可收拾了。The matter may become even more unmanageable if it is handled improperly. ❷ along with; together:他这匹马和我家的牲口～喂养。His horse was fed together with our draught animals.

一乏子 yīfázi 〈方言〉*also*"一乏儿" some days; period of time; spell:这～患流感的很多。Many people have got flu recently.

一发千钧 yīfà-qiānjūn *also*"千钧一发" a hundredweight hangs by a hair — be in imminent danger; hang by a thread:在这～之际 at this critical juncture

一帆风顺 yīfān-fēngshùn plain or smooth sailing; successful career:生活道路不都是～的。Life is not always plain sailing. /谨祝～,旅途平安。Wish you a smooth and safe journey. *or* Bon voyage.

一反常态 yīfǎn-chángtài depart from one's normal behaviour; be not one's usual self; act out of character:从此,她～,见了我爱理不理。Ever after, she changed her attitude and became cold and indifferent to me.

一方困难,八方支援 yīfāng kùnnan, bāfāng zhīyuán when one place is in trouble, assistance comes from all quarters

一方面 yīfāngmiàn ❶ one side; one aspect:不能只看问题的～。We shouldn't only look at one side of the matter. ❷ on the one hand..., on the other hand...; for one thing..., for another...:～增加生产,～厉行节约。It is necessary to increase production on the one hand and practise strict economy on the other.

一飞冲天 yīfēi-chōngtiān soar into the sky; make astonishing achievements; do sth. amazing:立下了～的志气 have lofty aspirations (*or* ambition) /他常想～。He is always thinking of achieving amazing successes.

一分耕耘,一分收获 yī fēn gēngyún, yī fēn shōuhuò the more ploughing and weeding, the better the crop; one reaps no more than what one has sown; no pain, no gain

一分钱掰两半用 yī fēn qián bāi liǎngbàn yòng make a little money go a long way; live a frugal life:庄稼人恨不得把一分钱掰成两半使唤。The peasants tried to make every cent do the work of two.

一分钱,一分货 yī fēn qián, yī fēn huò the higher the price, the better the quality of the goods; get what one pays for:～,就看你出多大价钱了。What you can buy depends on how much you pay; the higher the price, the better the quality.

一分为二 yīfēnwéi'èr 〈哲学〉one divides into two; there are two sides to everything:～,这是普遍的现象。It's a general phenomenon that everything divides into two.

一风吹 yīfēngchuī scatter to the winds; dismiss (charges, etc.) altogether; write off:宣布债务～ declare the cancellation of all debts; announce that all debts be written off/咱们往日的交情就这么～了? Are we going to allow our friendship to end in such an abrupt way?

一佛出世,二佛涅槃 yī fó chūshì, èr fó nièpán *also*"一佛出世,二佛升天" suffer extreme hardship:打得他～。He was beaten half to death.

一夫当关,万夫莫开 yī fū dāng guān, wàn fū mò kāi with one man guarding the pass, ten thousand men cannot break it open; one man can hold out against ten thousand at a strategic pass:这里是～的地方,轻易攻不下来。This is a pass where one man can hold out against ten thousand. It's very hard to capture.

一夫多妻制 yīfū-duōqīzhì polygyny; polygamy

一夫一妻制 yīfū-yīqīzhì monogyny; monogamy

一氟化物 yīfúhuàwù 〈化学〉monofluoride

一概 yīgài 〈副词〉one and all; without exception; totally; altogether: ～没收 confiscate everything /对那些攻击～置之不理 pay no attention whatsoever to any of those attacks /单据未经盖章,～无效。All the invoices that don't bear official seals are invalid. /未经允许,～不得入内。No entry without permission. *or* Authorized person only.

一概而论 yīgài'érlùn (often used in the negative) treat (different matters) all alike; lump together: 不能～ not to be lumped together; must not generalize about sth. /各国情况不一样,～就要犯错误。Every country has specific conditions, and it would be wrong to treat them all alike.

一干 yīgān all that is related to sth. (esp. a case): ～人犯 all the suspects and prisoners involved

一干二净 yīgān-èrjìng wholly; thoroughly; completely: 打扫得～ sweep spotlessly clean /推脱得～ try to absolve oneself of all wrongdoings; shove off all the blame /她早就把这件事忘得～了。She has forgotten all about it.

一竿子到底 yī gānzi dào dǐ *also* "一竿子插到底" carry sth. down to the grass-roots level; carry through to the end: 这些政策要～,让每个农民都知道。These policies should be relayed to the grass roots and made known to every farmer.

一个巴掌拍不响 yīge bāzhang pāibuxiǎng you can't clap with one hand; it takes two to make a quarrel; it takes two to tango: ～,你不打他,他能打你? It takes two to make a fight. How could he have beaten you if you had not hit him first?

一个鼻孔出气 yīge bíkǒng chūqì *see* "一鼻孔出气"

一个好汉三个帮 yīge hǎohàn sān gè bāng even an able fellow needs the help of three other people: 一个篱笆三个桩,～,你可不要把别人的作用看轻了。A fence needs the support of stakes and an able fellow needs the help of other people. You shouldn't belittle the roles played by others.

一个将军一个令 yīge jiāngjūn yīge lìng every change of command brings a new set of orders; new lords, new laws: ～,叫我们下面怎么工作? There're so many different orders. What shall we subordinates do?

一个劲儿 yīgejìnr without stopping; continuously; persistently: 小孩～地哭。The child kept on crying. /风～地吹。The wind persisted. /她～地干工作。She devotes all her energy to work.

一个萝卜一个坑 yīge luóbo yīge kēng ❶ one radish to every hole (in planting); with everyone kept busy and no one remaining idle: 我们这个部门人手有限,～。Our department has a limited staff, everyone has his own job and no one is dispensable (*or* redundant). ❷ be steadfast in one's work: 他是～的人,不至于有什么闪失。He's a steady worker and there won't be anything amiss.

一个心眼儿 yīge xīnyǎnr ❶ with one's heart set on sth.; devotedly; of one mind: ～为集体 work wholeheartedly for the collective /大家～奔小康。We are all determined to work for a comfortable life. ❷ stubborn; obstinate: 你这个人就～,不会变个法子办吗? What an obstinate person you are! Can't you think of other ways to do it?

一根藤上的瓜 yī gēn téngshangde guā melons growing on the same vine; people who share weal and woe: 咱们是～,就不要说那些外道话了。Don't talk as if we were strangers. We're two gourds from the same vine.

一共 yīgòng altogether; in all; all told: 每月～收入多少? How much do you earn a month in all? /三个小组～是十七个人。There are seventeen people all told in the three groups.

一股劲儿 yīgǔjìnr at a stretch; at one go; not relaxing one's efforts from beginning to end: ～地干 work hard without a break

一股拢总 yīgǔ-lǒngzǒng 〈方言〉all; completely: 他把错误～都归罪在别人身上。He put all the blame on others.

一股脑儿 yīgǔnǎor *also* "一古脑儿"〈方言〉all; completely; lock, stock and barrel; root and branch: 他把揪心事儿～都忘掉了。He forgot all about his worries and anxieties. /我们不得不把家产～变卖出去。We had to sell our family possessions, lock, stock and barrel.

一鼓作气 yīgǔ-zuòqì do sth. at one go; press on to the finish without letup; get sth. done in one vigorous effort: 他从床上爬起来,～地把信写完。He got up from the bed and finished the letter at one go.

一官半职 yīguān-bànzhí some (official) position or other; minor official post: 他们这几个人都想捞个～。They all wanted to become some kind of officials.

一贯 yīguàn consistently; persistently; steadily; all along: ～努力工作 work hard unfailingly /～工作作风 consistent working style /～支持你们的正义斗争 have supported your just struggle all along

一贯道 Yīguàndào *Yiguandao*, a reactionary secret society which, under the cover of religious activities, served the Japanese aggressors and Kuomintang reactionaries successively

一棍子打死 yī gùnzi dǎsǐ finish off with one blow; knock down at one stroke; deal one fatal blow; completely negate: 我们反对采取"一棍子把人打死"的办法。We are against (*or* opposed to) the method of "finishing people off with a single blow". /他工作中有过失,但不能～。It is true that he has made some errors in his work, but we must not write him off as totally worthless.

一锅端 yīguōduān eliminate or wipe out completely; give all one has: 这回咱们要给敌人来个～。This time we will wipe out the enemy completely. /各式各样的意见,大的小的,对的和不对的,～地往外倒。All kinds of views, important or otherwise, right or wrong, were poured out.

一锅粥 yīguōzhōu pot of porridge — a shambles; complete mess; all in a muddle: 乱成～ be all muddled up; in total confusion / 她在这里胡搅～。She was making a complete mess of the matter here.

一锅煮 yīguōzhǔ *also* "一锅烩";"一勺烩" cook everything in one pot — treat indiscriminately; deal with (different matters) in one and the same way; provide a uniform solution (for diverse problems): 这些问题情况各异,不能～。These are quite different issues and cannot be handled in the same way.

一国两制 yīguó-liǎngzhì one country, two systems: 是邓小平提出了"～"的设想。It was Deng Xiaoping who put forward the concept of "one country, two systems".

一国三公 yīguó-sāngōng state with three rulers — divided leadership: ～,吾谁适从? The state has three leaders. Which one of them should I obey?

一裹圆儿 yīguǒyuánr 〈旧语〉cape; cloak

一寒如此 yīhán-rúcǐ poverty-stricken: 万没料到,老丘竟～! No one had ever expected to find Lao Qiu living in such straitened circumstances.

一黑早儿 yīhēizǎor 〈方言〉as soon as day breaks; at daybreak; at dawn: 他～起来到集市上去了。He got up at daybreak and went to the market.

一哄而起 yīhōng'érqǐ rush headlong into mass action; be brought about in a rush; mushroom: 那阵子,争着办各种公司的人～。Many people then rushed headlong into setting up all kinds of corporations.

一哄而散 yīhòng'érsàn break up in a hubbub; scatter in a rush; disperse helter-skelter: 听说今晚的戏不演了,人们～。Hearing that tonight's play was cancelled, people dispersed helter-skelter (*or* scattered in no time).

一呼百诺 yīhū-bǎinuò when a (wealthy and powerful) man gives a call, a hundred people say aye; have hundreds at one's beck and call: 他如今当上了总经理,真是令出如山,～。Now that he is general manager, he gives stringent orders and has many subordinates at his beck and call.

一呼百应 yīhū-bǎiyìng hundreds respond to a single call; receive warm response: 这个动议立刻得到与会者～的赞同。This motion met with wide and instant approval of those who attended the meeting.

一忽儿 yīhūr 〈方言〉a little while: 午饭～就得。Lunch will be ready in a moment.

一环扣一环 yī huán kòu yī huán one ring linked with another — closely linked: 工作安排得～。The work is arranged in apple-pie order. /故事情节～。The plot of the story is very compact.

一晃 yīhuǎng in a flash: 那人在人群中～就不见了。The man disappeared quickly in the crowd.

一晃 yīhuàng (of time) pass in a flash; fly: 你我～快三十年没见面了。Nearly 30 years have passed in a flash since we met last time.

一挥而就 yīhuī'érjiù flourish the pen and it's done; finish a piece of writing or a painting at one go: ～,文不加点 finish a piece of writing with a facile pen

一回生,二回熟 yī huí shēng, èr huí shú ❶ first time strangers, second time acquaintances; ill at ease the first time, at home the second; getting to know in no time: ～,不出一个月,他俩便成了好朋友。As first time strangers, the two of them became good friends within a month. ❷ first time clumsy, second time skilful; difficult

at first, but easy afterwards; green the first time, experienced the second:～,多干干就行了。Though this may seem difficult at first, you'll get the knack through more practice.

一回事 yīhuíshì ❶ one and the same (thing); same:他俩说的不是～。The two of them were talking at cross-purposes. ❷ one thing:嘴上说说是～,动手去做又是～。While talking is one thing, getting things done is quite another.

一会儿 yīhuìr ❶ a little while:我们在这里等～。Let's wait here for a while. ❷ in a moment; in a minute; presently:我～再告诉你。I'll tell you in a jiffy. /～就准备好。I won't be a minute. ❸ *used before each of a pair of antonyms, indicating alternating circumstances*:你是怎么回事,～哭～笑的。How come you cry one moment and laugh the next? /她～进,～出,忙个不停。She was very busy, now going in, now coming out.

一级方程式赛车 yījí fāngchéngshì sàichē *also* "F-1 方程式赛车"〈体育〉Formula One (car racing); F-1

一级风 yījífēng 〈气象〉force 1 wind; light air

一级交易商 yījí jiāoyìshāng primary dealer

一级品 yījípǐn first-class product; primes

一级市场 yījí shìchǎng primary market

一级战备 yījí zhànbèi first-degree combat readiness

一级准尉 yījí zhǔnwèi (US Army and Air Force) chief warrant officer; (US Navy and Marine Corps) commissioned warrant officer; (UK Army, Navy, Air Force and Marine Corps) warrant officer (Class I)

一己 yījǐ oneself:～之见 personal point of view

一技之长 yījìzhīcháng proficiency in a particular line or field; professional skill; useful trade; speciality:用其～ make use of his particular skills /他无～,但人很勤劳。Although he has no speciality, he's hard-working.

一家伙 yījiāhuo *also* "一傢伙"〈方言〉in a short while; soon; all of a sudden:他喝酒喝得太多,～就醉了。He drank so much that he soon got drunk.

一家人 yījiārén members of a family; people on one's own side; one of us:～人不说两家话。As friends we don't need to stand on ceremony.

一家之言 yījiāzhīyán distinctive point of view or theory; particular school of thought; style of one's own:成～ establish one's own school, theory, or style /～,仅供参考。As one theory (*or* view), this is only for your information.

一家子 yījiāzi ❶ family:这～是新搬来的。The family has just moved in here. ❷ whole family:～都非常高兴。All the family are very happy.

一价 yījià 〈化学〉univalent; monavalent; monacid; monatomic:～碱 monacid base; monatomic base /～染色体 univalent chromosome /～酸 monatomic acid

一价元素 yījià yuánsù monad

一见倾心 yījiàn-qīngxīn love at first sight

一见如故 yījiàn-rúgù feel like old friends at the first meeting; take to each other immediately:我们真是～。We took to each other the moment we met.

一见喜 yījiànxǐ *also* "穿心莲" chuānxīnlián 〈中药〉creat

一见钟情 yījiàn-zhōngqíng fall in love or become captivated at first sight

一箭双雕 yījiàn-shuāngdiāo shoot two hawks with one arrow; kill two birds with one stone:此举会使他名利兼收,～。This move would help him gain fame and fortune. It was to kill two birds with one stone.

一箭之仇 yījiànzhīchóu wrong of an arrow shot — loss or defeat to be avenged:她一直在设法报这～。She has been trying to avenge the wrong she suffered.

一箭之地 yījiànzhīdì stone's throw; not far:他家离渡口不过是～。It's only a stone's throw from his home to the ferry.

一劲儿 yījìnr continuously; persistently:他～地往前跑。He kept on running forward.

一经 yījīng as soon as; the moment; once:～解释,他就恍然大悟。He came to his senses as soon as the matter was explained to him.

一径 yījìng ❶ directly; straight; straightaway:他没和别人打招呼,～走进屋里。He went straight into the room without greeting anyone. ❷〈方言〉continuously; always:她～在微笑。She kept smiling.

一将功成万骨枯 yī jiàng gōng chéng wàngǔ kū *also* "功成骨枯" ten thousand deaths make a single general famous; what millions died that Caesar might be great

一…就… yī…jiù… (of two things closely linked in sequence of time) no sooner... than...; hardly... when...; the moment...; as soon as; once:一请就来 come as soon as one is invited /门一推就开了。The door opened at a push. /他一接到信就作了答复。He wrote a reply the moment he received the letter. /我一到家,天就下起雨来了。Just as I returned home, than it began to rain.

一举 yījǔ with one action; at one stroke; at one (fell) swoop; at the first try:成败在此～。This very action will decide our success or failure. /登山队员～登上地球之巅。The mountain climbers reached the roof of the world on their first attempt.

一举成名 yījǔ-chéngmíng make a name for oneself at the first try; become famous overnight; achieve instant fame:她以演唱流行歌曲～。She achieved instant fame as a pop singer.

一举两得 yījǔ-liǎngdé serve two purposes at once; kill two birds with one stone:屋里养几盆花,既能美化居室,又能清洁空气,真是～的事。Potted flowers can beautify the house and purify the air inside — they serve two purposes at the same time.

一举手之劳 yī jǔshǒu zhī láo hand's turn; just to lift a hand:不必感谢,这不过是～。You don't have to thank me, for it's just a hand's turn (*or* no effort at all).

一举一动 yījǔ-yīdòng every single action:这几天,他们很注意我的～。Recently they've paid close attention to my every move.

一句话 yījùhuà ❶ in a word; in short; in a nutshell ❷ easily done:这是～的事儿,你不必感谢我。No need to thank me for it. That was an easy job.

一决雌雄 yījué-cíxióng fight it out; fight to see who is the stronger; wage a decisive battle:两名围棋顶尖高手将在周末～。The two master go players will play a decisive match this weekend.

一蹶不振 yījué-bùzhèn collapse after one setback; be unable to recover after one defeat or failure:这家公司在股票生意中伤了元气,从此～。This company was never able to recover its vitality after suffering a serious setback in the stock market.

一俊遮百丑 yī jùn zhē bǎi chǒu a beautiful appearance covers up many defects and deficiencies

一看二帮 yīkàn-èrbāng watch and help:他是初次犯错误,对他要～。It's the first time he committed an error. We should not only see how he will behave but also help him to improve.

一刻 yīkè a moment; a little while:再忙也不在乎这一时～。You can surely spare this little time even though you are a busy person.

一刻千金 yīkè-qiānjīn every minute or moment is precious; time is precious; value every minute:花烛之夜,～。Every minute of the bridal night is precious.

一客不烦二主 yī kè bù fán èr zhǔ *also* "一客不烦二家" (said when asking sb. for more favours) a guest should not trouble two hosts; one shouldn't impose on two patrons

一空 yīkōng with nothing left:把银行抢劫～ ransack a bank /销售～ all sold out

一孔之见 yīkǒngzhījiàn peephole view; limited or one-sided view:不要囿于～。One should not be limited by one's personal narrow view.

一口 yīkǒu ❶ (of accent and intonation) pure:说～标准的普通话 speak pure standard Chinese ❷ with certainty; readily; outright:～应允 readily agree; promise right away /～否认 categorically deny /～拒绝 flatly reject

一口吃不成个胖子 yī kǒu chībuchéng ge pàngzi no one grows fat on just one mouthful; you can't build up your constitution on one mouthful; nothing can be accomplished with one single effort

一口两匙 yīkǒu-liǎngchí two spoons in one mouth — be greedy

一口气 yīkǒuqì ❶ one breath:只要还有～,我就要干下去。As long as there's breath left in me, I'll keep on working. ❷ in one breath; without a break; at one go:～写成初稿 finish the first draft at a stretch /～爬到山顶 climb to the top of the mountain without pausing to rest

一口咬定 yīkǒu-yǎodìng assert emphatically; state categorically; insist:他～不认识被告。He insisted that he didn't know the defendant.

一口钟 yīkǒuzhōng 〈方言〉cape; cloak; mantle

一匡天下 yīkuāng-tiānxià bring order and peace back to the country

一块堆儿 yīkuàiduīr 〈方言〉together; in company:大伙坐～聊聊。Let's sit down together and have a chat.

一块儿 yīkuàir ❶ at the same place：我和他～办公。He and I work in the same office. ❷ together; in company：我不跟他～走。I won't go together with him.

一块石头落地 yī kuài shítou luò dì have a load (taken) off one's mind; set one's mind at rest; feel relieved：听到他平安无事的消息，大家心里才～。Hearing that he was safe, we all felt greatly relieved.

一揆 yīkuí 〈书面〉same reason：古今～。The same principle applies to both modern and ancient times.

一拉溜 yīlāliù 〈方言〉*see* "一溜儿"

一来 yīlái first of all; first; on the one hand：我业余种点花，～为了调剂生活，二来可以美化环境。I plant flowers in my spare time because first, it can enliven my life, and second, it helps beautify the surroundings.

一来二去 yīlái-èrqù in the course of contacts：两人在一个办公室里工作，～就产生了感情。As the two of them worked in the same office, they grew attached to each other over time.

一览 yīlǎn general survey; bird's-eye view; overview：《北京旅游宾馆～》*A Guide to Beijing's Tourist Hotels*

一览表 yīlǎnbiǎo chart; table; schedule; checklist：航班时刻～ flight timetable

一览无余 yīlǎn-wúyú take in everything at a glance：登临崖顶，海景尽收眼底，～。The seascape could be taken in at a glance from the top of the cliff.

一揽子 yīlǎnzi wholesale; package：～建议 package proposal /～交易 package deal /～免责〈外贸〉"catch-all" exceptions /～裁军措施 package of disarmament measures /他们下了很大决心，才提出了"～解决"的设想。It required firm resolve for them to propose the package solution.

一浪接一浪 yī làng jiē yī làng wave upon wave：观众席上呐喊助威声～。Cheer after cheer kept coming from the audience.

一劳永逸 yīláo-yǒngyì gain lasting repose by one supreme effort; have or get sth. done once and for all; achieve a permanent solution (to a problem)：世界上～的事是极少的。Few things in the world can be settled once and for all.

一力 yīlì make every effort; do one's best; do all one can：～承当 do one's best to assume the responsibility /～举荐 do all one can to recommend sb.

一例 yīlì same; alike; uniform：～看待 treat alike (*or* equally)

一粒老鼠屎，坏了一锅汤 yī lì lǎoshǔ shǐ, huàile yī guō tāng 〈俗语〉one bit of rat's dung in the soup spoils the whole pot; be a fly in the ointment：这帮小青年都是他一个人带坏的，～。It's his bad example that has led all these young people astray; he's really a fly in the ointment

一连 yīlián in a row; successively; running：～三次夺冠 win championships three times in a row /今天～来了四批参观的人。Four batches of visitors came today one after another. /雨淅淅沥沥地～下了七天。It rained for seven days running.

一连串 yīliánchuàn succession of; series of; string of; chain of：～的事故 a succession of accidents /～的失败 a series of failures

一连气儿 yīliánqìr 〈方言〉in a row; in one go; running：他～喝了四瓶啤酒。He drank four bottles of beer in one go.

一了百了 yīliǎo-bǎiliǎo all troubles end when the main trouble ends; death ends all one's troubles; death pays all debts：一去世，他的苦恼就～了。Death ended all his sorrows.

一鳞半爪 yīlín-bànzhǎo *also* "东鳞西爪" dōnglín-xīzhǎo odd bits; scraps; fragments：～的知识 fragmentary knowledge; smattering of knowledge /这件事我也知道个～。I also have an inkling of the matter.

一零儿 yīlíngr a little; a fraction：我的学习连人家的～都够不上。My knowledge isn't even a fraction of his.

一流 yīliú ❶ of the same kind; of the kind or sort：他是属于大款～人物。He is one of the nouveaux riches. ❷ first-rate; top-grade; first-class：～文学作品 first-rate literary works

一溜风 yīliùfēng (run) very quickly：他～地从山上跑下来。He ran down the hill rapidly like a gust of wind.

一溜儿 yīliùr 〈方言〉❶ row：～十间瓦房 a row of ten tile-roofed houses ❷ nearby area; neighbourhood; vicinity：以前这～住的都是工人。This place used to be the living quarters for working people. ❸ in a burst or fit：～小跑进了屋 come running into the house

一溜歪斜 yīliù-wāixié 〈方言〉(walk, etc.) unsteadily in a zigzag; staggering：他喝得醉醺醺的，～地就进来了。He staggered into the room, drunk.

一溜烟 yīliùyān (run away) swiftly：那车向西～驶去。The car sped off towards the west. /他骑上车，～进村去了。He got on his bicycle and rushed into the village.

一路 yīlù ❶ all the way; throughout the journey：～领先 take the lead all the way /～风尘 have endured the hardships of a long journey; be travel-worn /～欣赏四周的景色 enjoy the scenery along the way ❷ of the same kind; of like kind：他们两个不是～人。The two of them are not of the same sort. ❸ go the same way; take the same road：我是跟他们～来的。I came the same way with them. ❹〈方言〉continuously; always：今年国际市场铜价～上扬。The copper price has kept going up on the world market.

一路货色 yīlù huòsè *also* "一路货" same stuff; one of a kind; birds of a feather：她们俩完全是～，俗不可耐。The two women were birds of a feather, vulgar in the extreme.

一路平安 yīlù píng'ān have a pleasant journey; have a nice trip; bon voyage

一路顺风 yīlù shùnfēng plain sailing; pleasant journey; good trip：大船～地驶进了洞庭湖。The big ship sailed smoothly into the Dongting Lake. /这次总算～地平安抵家。This time I arrived home safe and sound. /他在车下向我挥手："～，一年后再见。" He waved to me outside the bus, saying, "Have a good trip and see you next year."

一律 yīlǜ ❶ same; alike; identical; uniform：千篇～ stereotyped; all following the same pattern /强求～ seek (*or* impose) rigid uniformity /式样相同，规格～ be uniform in design and specification ❷ all; each and all; without exception：公民在法律面前～平等。All (citizens) are equal before the law. /此项规定，全校师生应～遵守。All the teachers and students in the school should abide by this rule without exception.

一落千丈 yīluò-qiānzhàng drop a thousand *zhang* in one fall — experience a disastrous decline or drastic fall; have a big comedown：信誉～ disastrous decline of one's reputation /情绪～ be in low spirits; be dispirited /对外贸易～ drastic drop in foreign trade

一抹平 yīmāpíng ❶ same; equally matched; uniform：要按质论价，不能～。Prices should be set according to qualities; they shouldn't be uniform. ❷ even; level; smooth：路修得～。The road is very even.

一麻黑 yīmāhēi *also* "一抹黑" completely dark; pitch-dark：山洞内～，什么也看不见。It was pitch-dark inside the cave and nothing was visible. /人生地不熟，两眼～。Being a stranger, I am wide at sea here.

一马当先 yīmǎ-dāngxiān gallop at the head — take the lead; be in the forefront or foremost position：他～，率领战士奋勇突围。Fighting in the forefront himself, he led the soldiers out of the encirclement.

一马平川 yīmǎ-píngchuān wide expanse of flat land; flat country：小镇周围，～，无险可守。It was all flat country around the small town. There was no tenable defence position.

一脉相承 yīmài-xiāngchéng *also* "一脉相传" come down in one continuous line; can be traced to the same origin; be in the same strain：这几位作家～，所以风格相近。Being in the same tradition, these writers were close in their styles.

一满 yīmǎn 〈方言〉❶ always：这话我～没说过。I have never said this. ❷ completely; entirely：他的积蓄～输光了。He lost all his savings in gambling. ❸ very; extremely：这孩子～不听话。This child is very obstreperous. ❹ altogether：全村～百十号人。There are altogether about a hundred people in the village.

一毛不拔 yīmáo-bùbá unwilling to give up even a hair — very stingy; miserly; close-fisted：这样～的吝啬鬼世上少见。Such close-fisted misers are rare.

一门心思 yīmén-xīnsi be lost (in doing sth.); be engrossed：他～搞技术革新。He devotes himself heart and soul to technological renovation.

一秘 yīmì 〈外交〉(short for 一等秘书) first secretary

一面 yīmiàn ❶ one side：这种纸～光～毛。This kind of paper is smooth on one side and coarse on the other. ❷ one aspect; one field：独当～ take charge of a department or locality ❸ at the same time; simultaneously：～听～作笔记 take notes while listening /他～检查我的身分证，～问我各种问题。He inspected my ID card, asking me all kinds of questions. ❹〈书面〉have met once：～之识 have met just once /～如旧 feel like old friends at the first meeting

一面儿官司 yīmiànr guānsi law case in which one party is in the disadvantageous position

一面儿理 yīmiànrlǐ reason given by one party only; one-sided or lopsided argument:他说的尽是~。The reasons he gave were one-sided.

一面之词 yīmiànzhīcí statement of only one of the parties; one side of the story:听信了他的~ believe his version of the story

一面之交 yīmiànzhījiāo *also* "一面之雅" have met only once; be casually acquainted:我与他有~。I have a nodding acquaintance with him. *or* I have met him only once.

一面之缘 yīmiànzhīyuán chance of meeting only once:我和他就只有这么~。He and I met each other only once.

一抿子 yīmǐnzi 〈方言〉❶ little; few:省不下~钱 can hardly save any money ❷ piece; single item:事儿~接着~。Incidents occurred one after another.

一鸣惊人 yīmíng-jīngrén (of an obscure person) amaze the world with a single brilliant feat; set the Thames on fire:五年来,他朝思暮想着~。Over the past five years he has dreamed day and night of amazing the world with a tour de force.

一瞑不视 yīmíng-bùshì close one's eyes and never open them again — die:可惜他已~,永远不能再看到这个美丽的城市和学校了。It's a pity that he has passed away and can never see the beautiful city and school again.

一命归阴 yīmìng-guīyīn *also* "一命归天" die; go west; go the way of all flesh

一命呜呼 yīmìng-wūhū die; kick the bucket; bite the dust; give up the ghost:老太爷~之后,儿女们争着分遗产。After the old man died, his children began to scramble for the legacy.

一模活脱 yīmú-huótuō 〈方言〉exactly alike; very image; as like as two peas:他俩长得~儿。The two of them were as like as two peas.

一模一样 yīmú-yīyàng exactly alike; as like as two peas:他跟他父亲长得~。He takes after his father. *or* He is a chip off the old block. /这两块宝石颜色、花纹~。The colour and veins of these two precious stones are exactly the same. *or* These two precious stones are exactly alike in colour and veins.

一木难支 yīmù-nánzhī *also* "独木难支" dúmù-nánzhī one pillar alone can not prop up a building; a difficult task cannot be accomplished by a single person:大厦将倾,~。One pole cannot shore up a falling building.

一目了然 yīmù-liǎorán see clearly at a glance; be as plain as the nose on sb.'s face:眼前这几位实业家的资力和才干,他是~的。He knew only too well about the financial standing and abilities of the businessmen before him.

一目十行 yīmù-shíháng take in ten lines at a glance — read very rapidly:此人读书~,过目不忘。He reads rapidly and memorizes everything he reads.

一纳头 yīnàtóu 〈方言〉❶ be determined; resolve:他横下一条心,~地跟一伙人跑买卖。He made up his mind to join a group of commercial travellers. ❷ immerse oneself in; devote oneself to:每天晚上他都~钻研学问。He devoted himself to his studies every evening.

一奶同胞 yīnǎi-tóngbāo (brothers or sisters) of one mother:你们是~的兄妹,应该互相体贴。You should take care of each other as you're brothers and sisters of one mother.

一男半女 yīnán-bànnǚ a child or two (usu. used in the negative):膝下并无~ have no children at all; be childless

一年半载 yīnián-bànzǎi in a year or so; in about a year:再有~,他就回来了。He will be back in about a year.

一年到头 yīnián-dàotóu throughout the year; all (the) year round:他~总是忙。He is busy all year round.

一年生 yīniánshēng 〈植物〉annual:~植物 annual plant; annual /~作物 annual crop

一年四季 yīnián-sìjì during the four seasons of the year; throughout the year; all the year round:这里~被冰雪覆盖着。The ground here is covered with snow all the year round.

一年一度 yīnián-yīdù once a year; annually:~的春节晚会 annual party on the eve of the Chinese New Year

一年之计在于春 yī nián zhī jì zàiyú chūn the whole year's work depends on a good start in spring; the work for the year has to be planned well in the spring:~,一日之计在于晨。The work for the year is best begun in the spring and the day's work in the morning.

一念之差 yīniànzhīchā wrong decision made in a moment of weakness (with serious consequences); momentary slip:不要因~而悔恨终生。Avoid making a wrong decision that you'll regret all your life.

一诺千金 yīnuò-qiānjīn promise that is worth a thousand pieces of gold; solemn promise:他出言不苟,是个~的人。He is a man of his word.

一拍即合 yīpāi-jíhé hit it off readily; chime in easily:双方在这件事上有共同利益,所以~。Having interests in common on this matter, they fit in easily with each other.

一盘棋 yīpánqí layout of a game of chess; situation as a whole:全国~ take into consideration the overall situation of the country

一盘散沙 yīpán-sǎnshā (like) a sheet or heap of loose sand — in a state of disunity or disarray:中国人~的日子已一去不复返了。Gone are the days when the Chinese people were disunited like a heap of loose sand.

一盘死棋 yīpán-sǐqí (like) dead pieces in a game of chess — hopeless case; no way out:再不走这一步,我们县的生产还是~。The production of our county will remain hopeless if we don't take this measure.

一旁 yīpáng one side:站在~看热闹的人不少。Quite a few people stood by watching the fun.

一炮打响 yīpào-dǎxiǎng become an instant success:他的小说~,在文学界引起了巨大反响。His novel was an instant hit, making a great impact on the literary world.

一偏 yīpiān one-sided; biased:~之见 one-sided view /~之论 biased argument

一片 yīpiàn ❶〈量词〉*used to describe object, landscape, sound, feeling or mood, etc.*:~废墟 all in ruins /~汪洋 a vast sheet (*or* expanse) of water /窗外~雨声 a patter of rain outside the window /~丹心 a loyal heart /~碧绿 a scene of greenness ❷ whole; entirety:军民打成~。The army and the people are at one with each other.

一片冰心 yīpiàn-bīngxīn purity and integrity:~在玉壶 chasteness of soul

一瞥 yīpiē ❶ quick glance:她向我投来忧郁的~。She cast me a melancholy glance. ❷ (often used as a title) glimpse; brief survey:《史海~》*A Brief Survey of History* /《美国~》*A Glimpse of the United States*

一撇子 yīpiězi 〈方言〉slap (in the face); blow:他打我~。He slapped me in the face.

一贫如洗 yīpín-rúxǐ penniless; in utter destitution; as poor as a church mouse:这场大火烧得他~。The big fire left him utterly destitute.

一品 yīpǐn ❶ (of officials in feudal times) highest in rank; first-class; first-rate; top-grade:~官 top-rank official ❷〈书面〉one kind:此~樱花,系近年由日本引进。This kind of cherry blossom has been introduced from Japan recently.

一品锅 yīpǐnguō ❶ pot with a stand holding a fire underneath it; a kind of chafing dish ❷ name of a dish that is cooked with chicken, duck, ham, pork and mushrooms in such a pot

一品红 yīpǐnhóng 〈植物〉Christmas flower; poinsettia (*Euphorbia pulcherrima*)

一平二调 yīpíng-èrdiào equalitarianism and indiscriminate transfer of resources (esp. between units of the people's commune, or between the state and state-owned enterprises)

一瓶子不响,半瓶子晃荡 yī píngzi bù xiǎng, bàn píngzi huàngdang the half-filled bottle sloshes, but the full bottle makes no sound — the dabbler in knowledge chatters away, whereas the wise man remains silent; empty vessels make the most sound; he who knows least boasts most

一抔黄土 yīpóu-huángtǔ ❶〈书面〉a handful of yellow earth — a grave ❷ sth. utterly insignificant

一扑纳心 yīpū-nàxīn *also* "一扑心"〈方言〉wholeheartedly; heart and soul:~地过日子 be intent on getting along well in life

一暴十寒 yīpù-shíhán work hard for one day and do nothing for ten — work by fits and starts; lack in perseverance:~是什么事也做不好的。Nothing can be done without perseverance.

一妻多夫制 yīqī-duōfūzhì polyandry

一齐 yīqí at the same time; simultaneously; one and all; in unison:~动手 go into action one and all /~高呼 shout in unison /~努力 make a concerted effort /几盆水仙几乎~开花了。These pots of narcissus have flowered almost simultaneously.

一起 yīqǐ ❶ in the same place:他们俩在~工作。The two of them work in the same place. ❷ together; in company:我不跟他~走。I won't go with him. /这几个问题~讨论。Discuss these matters con-

Y

currently. ❸〈方言〉altogether; in all; all inclusive: 我们这个班~二十八个人。There are altogether 28 people in our class. ❹〈方言〉(in) the same group or gang: 他们是~的。They are in the same group.

一气 yīqì ❶ at one go; without a break; at a stretch: ~儿喝了三大碗粥 have three bowls of porridge without a break / ~儿走上十八层 walk to the 18th floor without stopping / 他~写了两天。He continued to write for two days. ❷〈贬义〉cheek by jowl; hand in glove: 串通~ work hand in glove; collude ❸〈贬义〉spell; fit: 胡侃~ tell tall tales; tell cock-and-bull stories / 瞎画~ scrawl; chicken tracks; graffiti

一气呵成 yīqì-hēchéng ❶ (of an essay) form a coherent whole; make smooth reading ❷ accomplish sth. at one go; carry sth. through without stopping or interruption: 该队奋战三昼夜, ~地完成了任务。Working very hard for three days and nights, the team completed the task at one go.

一气之下 yīqìzhīxià in a fit of pique; in an outburst of anger

一汽 Yīqì (short for 长春第一汽车制造厂) No. 1 Motor Vehicle Plant in Changchun, Jilin Province

一千零一夜 Yīqiān Líng Yī Yè *The Thousand and One Nights* or *Arabian Nights Entertainments*, a collection of fairy stories and romances originally written in Arabic

一钱不值 yīqián-bùzhí *also* "一文不值"; "不值一钱" not worth a penny; utterly worthless; load of rubbish; mere trash: 把那本书贬得~ condemn the book as not worth the paper it is printed on

一钱如命 yīqián-rúmìng regard a penny as precious as life — extremely stingy; niggardly; miserly: 此人吝啬非常, ~。The man is such a miser that he would rather part with his life than a single penny.

一腔 yīqiāng *also* "一腔子" have one's heart filled with: ~热情 be filled with enthusiasm / 甘洒~热血 be willing to sacrifice one's life

一窍不通 yīqiào-bùtōng know nothing about; have no knowledge of; be completely ignorant of: 我对建筑艺术是~的。I don't know anything about architecture.

一切 yīqiè all; every: 采取~措施 take every measure / 想~办法 try every means possible / ~手续都办好了 have got through all the formalities / 把~献给现代化建设事业 give one's all to the cause of modernization / 这里~都好。Everything is fine here.

一切向钱看 yīqiè xiàng qián kàn put money above all else; be money-oriented

一清二白 yīqīng-èrbái ❶ perfectly clear: 案情已调查得~。The case is perfectly clear after investigation. ❷ clean; blameless: 此人素来~。He's always been squeaky clean.

一清二楚 yīqīng-èrchǔ very clear; distinct; as clear as day: 把要办的几件事交代得~ clearly explain the jobs to be done

一清如水 yīqīng-rúshuǐ as clear as water — (of officials) honest and upright; free from corruption: 谁不知道他是个~的好官。Everybody knew that he was an honest official.

一清早 yīqīngzǎo in early morning: 每天~儿起来跑步 go out jogging early in the morning every day

一穷二白 yīqióng-èrbái poor and blank: 我的家乡是个偏僻的山庄, ~。My home is in a remote mountain village steeped in poverty. / 我们要共同努力改变这里~的面貌。We must work together to lift the area from the state of poverty and ignorance.

一丘之貉 yīqiūzhīhé 〈贬义〉jackals from the same lair; birds of a feather; tarred with the same brush: 我发现你的堂兄和他父亲是~。I find that your cousin and his father are birds of a feather.

一去不复返 yī qù bù fù fǎn gone for ever; gone never to return; never to be found again: 旧时代已经~了。The old days have gone for ever.

一犬吠影,百犬吠声 yī quǎn fèi yǐng, bǎi quǎn fèi shēng one dog barks at a shadow, and a hundred dogs join in — blindly follow suit

一人得道,鸡犬升天 yī rén dédào, jī-quǎn shēngtiān when a man attains the Tao (enlightenment and immortality), even his pets ascend to heaven — when a man gets to the top, all his friends and relations get there with him; when one man is promoted, all those connected with him benefit; nepotism is rampant

一人做事一人当 yī rén zuòshì yī rén dāng a man should be responsible for his actions; a man must bear the consequences of his own acts: 我~, 怎敢连累诸位! I will take full responsibility for what I have done and will not get any of you implicated.

一任 yīrèn 〈书面〉allow: 我们所有人~你调遣。Everyone of us is at your service. / 岂能~他如此为所欲为? How can we let him get away with it?

一仍旧贯 yīréng-jiùguàn stick to the old practice; be in a rut: 我们厂正处在深化改革之中, 怎能~呢? How can we go on in the same old rut while the reform in our factory is well under way?

一日夫妻百日恩 yī rì fūqī bǎi rì ēn *also* "一夜夫妻百日恩" one night of love is worth a hundred days of affection; a day together as husband and wife means devotion for the rest of their life

一日千里 yīrì-qiānlǐ a thousand *li* a day — at a tremendous pace; with giant strides; by leaps and bounds: 工农业生产的发展~。Both industry and agriculture are developing apace.

一日三秋 yīrì-sānqiū *also* "一日不见,如隔三秋" a day's separation seems as long as three years; miss sb. very much: 新婚乍别, 不免有~之感。To the newly-weds, one day of separation is as long as three years.

一日为师,终身为父 yī rì wéi shī, zhōngshēn wéi fù a tutor for a day is a father for a lifetime; if a man has been your teacher for a day, you should treat him as your father for the rest of his life

一日游 yīrìyóu one-day tour: 长城、十三陵~ one day tour of the Great Wall and Ming Tombs

一日之长 yīrìzhīcháng slight superiority or advantage: 不跟他们争~。Don't compete with them for temporary advantages (*or* gains). / 在这方面, 与你相比, 我似有~。I seem to have an edge over you in this respect.

一日之雅 yīrìzhīyǎ a day's acquaintance — not on intimate terms: 这位先生我久闻大名, 可惜无~。Though I've heard of him for a long time, I haven't the pleasure of his acquaintance.

一日之长 yīrìzhīzhǎng a little older; somewhat senior in age: 我虽有~, 但见识并不比在座诸位强。Although senior in age, I am not necessarily as knowledgeable as those present here.

一如 yīrú just as; as: ~所见 just as what is seen / 情况~所述。The situation is as described.

一如既往 yīrú-jìwǎng just as in the past; as usual; as before; as always: 我们将~为和平而奋斗。We will, as always, work for peace. / 我们对这件事的态度~。Our attitude towards this matter remains unchanged.

一若以往 yīruò-yǐwǎng as usual; as before: 家中安好, 情况~, 请勿挂念。Everything at home is fine as usual. Please don't worry.

一扫而光 yīsǎo'érguāng make a clean sweep of; wipe out completely; finish off; get rid of lock, stock and barrel: 心中的顾虑~ rid oneself of all trace of worry / 桌上的饭菜被他~。He ate up (*or* finished off) all the dishes on the table.

一色 yīsè ❶ of the same colour: 海天~。The sea and the sky are of one hue. ❷ of the same type; unmixed; uniform: ~的小洋楼 all Western-style storeyed-houses / 全身~新 be dressed in new clothes

一霎 yīshà twinkling or blink of an eye; very short time: ~时 all of a sudden / ~间乌云密布。Instantly, dark clouds closed in.

一山难容二虎 yī shān nán róng èr hǔ no two rival tigers can exist in the same mountain; when Greek meets Greek, then comes the tug of war: 剧团~, 看来我最好离开。Since the troupe can't have two best actors at the same time, it seems that I'd better leave.

一闪念 yīshǎnniàn fleeting thought; passing idea

一善掩百恶 yī shàn yǎn bǎi è one good deed may cover up a hundred ill deeds

一晌 yīshǎng ❶ short time: 忙得~也没歇 be too busy to rest even for a little while ❷ all along; always: 他就是我们~背后常夸奖的那个人。He is the man whom we've often praised among ourselves. ❸ period of time: 我前~身体不适。I wasn't feeling well for some time.

一上来 yīshànglai at the beginning; from the start: 他~就指责我。The first thing he did was to denounce me. *or* He immediately started accusing me.

一勺烩 yīsháohuì *see* "一锅煮"

一身 yīshēn ❶ whole body; all over the body: ~是债 be head over heels in debt; be up to one's neck in debt / ~臭味 be smelling all over / ~是劲 be full of energy; have no end of strength ❷ suit (of clothes): ~灰色的西装 a grey suit / ~休闲服 be casually dressed ❸ by oneself; alone: 孑然~ solitary; all alone

一身两役 yīshēn-liǎngyì *also* "一身二任" hold two jobs concurrently; serve in a dual capacity: ~, 无乃劳乎? Isn't it too much of a burden to hold two jobs at the same time? / 一身而二任焉, 虽圣者不可能也。Even a sage can not serve in a dual capacity.

一身是胆 yīshēn-shìdǎn know no fear; be absolutely dauntless; to be every inch a hero: 他果然名不虚传, 是一位~的英雄。He is in-

trepid and lives up to the name of a fearless hero.

一神教 yīshénjiào monotheism

一审 yīshěn 〈法律〉 first instance:～法庭 court of first instance

一生 yīshēng all one's life; in one's lifetime:光辉的～ glorious life/在饥寒交迫中度过～ live in hunger and cold throughout one's life

一生一世 yīshēng-yīshì all one's life; in one's lifetime:～也不和他来往了。I won't have anything to do with him for the rest of my life.

一声不响 yīshēng-bùxiǎng keep quiet; not utter a sound:他一切都看到了,却～。He saw everything but remained silent.

一失足成千古恨 yī shīzú chéng qiāngǔ hèn one false move brings everlasting grief; a single slip may cause eternal sorrow; the error of a moment becomes the regret of a lifetime

一石二鸟 yīshí-èrniǎo kill two birds with one stone

一石激起千层浪 yī shí jīqǐ qiān céng làng a stone tossed into the water raises a thousand ripples; a slight hint or small action causes a big stir

一时 yīshí ❶ period of time:～无出其右。For some time, nobody could surpass him./此～彼～。Times have changed. ❷ ephemeral; temporary; momentary:风行～ be popular for a while; be all the rage/～的表面现象 transient (*or* ephemeral) phenomenon/～冲动 (act) on the spur of the moment/～还离不开 can not leave yet/～想不通 remain unconvinced (right now)/这几本我～还不需要,你先留着吧。I don't need these books for the time being. You may keep them. ❸ offhand; by chance:他的名字我～想不起来。I can't recall his name offhand (*or* for the moment)./他～高兴,送了我一个古花瓶。He happened to be in a good mood, and gave me an ancient vase. ❹ now..., now...; one moment..., the next...:天气变化无常,～晴,～雨。The weather is unpredictable: one moment it's clear, the next it rains./她的情绪～好,～坏。She has got a very mercurial temperament.

一时半会儿 yīshí-bànhuìr a short time; a little while:他～还回不来。He won't be back for a little while yet.

一时三刻 yīshí-sānkè *also* "一时半刻";"一时片刻" a short time; a little while:这件事～办不成。This cannot be done in a short time.

一时一刻 yīshí-yīkè (usu. used in the negative) for a single moment:我～也不会忘记这个教训。Never for a single moment will I forget the lesson.

一世 yīshì ❶ all one's life; throughout one's life:他～没做过亏心事。He has never done anything that pricks his conscience all his life. ❷ times; age; era ❸ period of time

一世界 yīshìjie 〈方言〉 everywhere; all over:你怎么把瓜子皮扔了～? Just look at the melon seed shells that you have thrown all over the place!

一世之雄 yīshìzhīxióng hero of the times; great man of an era:这几位政治家足称～。These statesmen were worthy of the name of great men of their times.

一式 yīshì same form:文件～三份 document in triplicate

一事 yīshì 〈方言〉 be related organizationally or professionally; belong to the same group or organization:这两家商店是～,都是他开的。These two shops are one and the same outfit, both owned by him.

一事无成 yīshì-wúchéng accomplish nothing; have no achievement to one's credit; get nowhere:风尘碌碌,～。He accomplished nothing in his bustling, hard-working life.

一视同仁 yīshì-tóngrén treat all alike without discrimination; regard all as equals:法律对每个公民都～。Everyone is equal in the eyes of the law./教师对学生应～。A teacher should extend the same treatment to all his students.

一是一,二是二 yī shì yī, èr shì èr one is one, and two is two; call a spade a spade; be unequivocal:他说话从来～,毫不含糊。He never equivocates but is always clearcut in what he says.

一手 yīshǒu ❶ proficiency; skill; expertise:留～ hold back a trick or two/技术上有～ be proficient in one's own line; know the ropes/他写得～好字。He writes a good hand./他一有机会就想露～。He tries to show off his skill whenever there is a chance./这位医生在治癌方面有～。This doctor is good at treating cancer. ❷ trick; gimmick; move:我真没想到他会跟我来这～儿。I really hadn't thought that he would play such tricks on me. ❸ single-handed; all by oneself; all alone:这僵局是他～造成的。The stalemate was all his doing./我是我姑姑～拉扯大的。I was brought up single-handed by my aunt.

一手包办 yīshǒu-bāobàn keep everything in one's own hands; take sole control of; monopolize:局里的大事都是他～的。He monopolized all the important affairs in the bureau.

一手交钱,一手交货 yī shǒu jiāo qián, yī shǒu jiāo huò give me the cash, and I'll give you the goods; COD (cash on delivery)

一手一足 yīshǒu-yīzú a hand and a foot — a single person; a single effort:这件事要办好,不是～所能奏效的。To succeed in this job requires far more than the effort of any single person.

一手遮天 yīshǒu-zhētiān shut out the heavens with one palm — abuse one's power to hide the truth; hoodwink the public:人家～,在这个单位实际上是他说了算。He has the last say in this unit, for he is, so to speak, powerful enough to block out the sun.

一水儿 yīshuǐr 〈方言〉(of clothes, furniture, etc.) of the same colour and type; unmixed; uniform:那套家具～都是棕色的。That set of furniture is all brown in colour.

一水之隔 yīshuǐzhīgé separated by a strip of water

一顺儿 yīshùnr in the same direction or sequence:靠墙～摆着八张椅子。Eight chairs were lined along the wall.

一瞬 yīshùn an instant; a flash; twinkling of an eye:～即逝 vanish in a flash; be transitory; be transient or fleeting/火箭飞行,～千里。The rocket flies a thousand *li* in the twinkling of an eye.

一丝 yīsī a tiny bit; a trace:她脸上露出～笑容。There is a faint smile on her face.

一丝不苟 yīsī-bùgǒu scrupulous about every detail; conscientious and meticulous; with meticulous care; in a careful and serious manner:编纂字典需要～。Meticulous care is required in compiling a dictionary.

一丝不挂 yīsī-bùguà not have a stitch on; be stark-naked; be in one's birthday suit:～地在街上跑 streak (along a street)

一丝一毫 yīsī-yīháo one jot or tittle; an iota; a trace; a tiny bit:没有～的好处 without the least benefit/再没有比恋爱中的青年人更敏感的了,对方～的变化,他们都能感觉出来。Nobody is more sensitive than young people in love. They can sense the slightest flicker of a change in their beloved.

一死儿 yīsǐr 〈方言〉 stubbornly; obstinately:要她出个节目,她～不肯。We want her to do one show but she firmly refused.

一似 yīsì 〈书面〉 same as; like:光阴～流水。Time flows away like water.

一塌刮子 yītāguāzi 〈方言〉 ❶ all; entirely; lock, stock and barrel:把东西～搬走。Remove the whole lot. *or* Remove them all. ❷ altogether:观众～才五六十人。There were only fifty to sixty people altogether in the audience.

一塌糊涂 yītāhútú in an awful or terrible state; in a muddle; messy:争吵得～ kick up a terrible row/球队输得～。The ball team suffered an overwhelming defeat./事情已经糟得～了。Things had come to a horrid pass.

一胎率 yītāilǜ proportion of families with one child; one-child family ratio

一潭死水 yītán-sǐshuǐ pool of stagnant water; lethargic or lifeless situation:外面到处在搞改革,这里却是～。Reform is going on everywhere, but this place remains a pool of stagnant water.

一碳化物 yītànhuàwù 〈化学〉 monocarbide

一体 yītǐ ❶ organic or integral whole; one:融成～ merge into an organic whole/军民同心～。The army and the people are of one mind. ❷ all people concerned; everyone:～周知 it is hereby notified to all concerned that/上述各项望～遵照。It is expected that the above stipulations will be observed by all.

一体化 yītǐhuà integration:欧洲～ European integration/～区域合作 integrated regional cooperation

一天 yītiān ❶ one day:～工作八小时 work eight hours a day ❷ daytime:他整整写了～一夜。He kept writing throughout the day and the night. ❸ one day (in the past):～,他把事情的经过都告诉了我。One day he told me all about it. ❹〈方言〉 whole day; all (the) day; from morning till night:～也没闲一会儿 have been busy all day

一天到晚 yītiān-dàowǎn from morning till night; from dawn to dusk; all day long; whole day:这里～嘈杂异常。It is frightfully noisy here all day long.

一条鞭 yītiáobiān ❶〈历史〉 integrated cash tax (during the late Ming Dynasty) ❷ integrated management; integration (of various aspects of business, etc.)

一条道跑到黑 yī tiáo dào pǎo dào hēi follow one road until it's dark — cling stubbornly to one course; be pigheaded:这小子认死理,

～。He's a stubborn guy with a fixed idea. *or* The guy is as stubborn as a mule.

一条龙 yītiáolóng ❶ one continuous line:等待加油的车辆排成～。There was a long line of cars waiting for refuelling. ❷ coordinated process of work; connected sequence:产运销～ coordinated process of production, transport and marketing

一条藤儿 yītiáoténgr 〈方言〉collusive gang:你们俩～,变着法儿气我。You two are ganging up on me and are trying every means to make me unhappy.

一条线儿拴两个蚂蚱 yī tiáo xiànr shuān liǎngge màzha be like two grasshoppers tied to one cord — to stick together (come) rain or shine:咱们俩是～,飞不了我也跑不了你! We're like two grasshoppers tied to one cord; neither can get away!

一条心 yītiáoxīn be of one heart and one mind; be at one:全厂上下～。Both the management and the workers of the factory are of one mind.

一通 yītōng ❶ a copy:～文书 a document ❷ once; for a time:他和我吵过～。He quarrelled with me once.

一通百通 yītōng-bǎitōng master one and you'll master a hundred; sort this one thing out and you'll sort out all the rest

一同 yītóng together; in company; at the same time and place:～欢度新年 celebrate the New Year together

一统 yītǒng unify (a country):大～ unified domain; whole empire under one ruler

一统天下 yītǒng-tiānxià unify the whole country; dominate the whole world:那个国家总想把世界变成它的～。That country always attempts to dominate the whole world. /这个公司简直成了他的～。The company has literally become his fief.

一头 yītóu ❶ *of several things happening at the same time*:他～走,～说。He talked as he walked. ❷ directly; straightaway:打开车门,他～钻了进来。As soon as I opened the door, he climbed into the car. ❸ suddenly; all of a sudden:冷不防～碰见他 run into him all at once ❹ headlong:～扎进水里 plunge headlong into the water /～倒在床上 collapse in one's bed ❺ one end; one side; one aspect:顾了这～,顾不上那～ cannot attend to both sides (*or* all aspects) at once /桌子的～靠床,～挨着书柜。One end of the desk is next to the bed and the other to a bookshelf. ❻ a head:他高我～。He is a head taller than I am. /白马领先～获胜。The white horse won by a head. /你的点子比我高～。Your idea is superior to mine. ❼ be on the same side; belong to the same group:昨晚我们玩牌,我和小王～。We played cards last night. Xiao Wang and I were partners. ❽〈方言〉together; with each other:他们是～来的。They came here together.

一头儿沉 yītóurchén 〈方言〉❶ heavy-at-one-end — a desk with a cupboard or drawers at one end ❷ be partial (in mediation); be biased against:要是他～,我是绝不会答应的。If he is partial to one party, I will never let him have his way.

一吐为快 yītǔ-wéikuài have to get it off one's chest; have a view one must air; find it necessary to speak up

一团和气 yītuán-héqì keep on good terms with everybody at the expense of principle; keep on the right side of everyone; curry favour with people all round:姚经理待人接物～。Manager Yao is ingratiating himself with everyone he meets. /他俩表面上～,其实内心里意见大得很。They look as though they're on good terms but are actually at loggerheads with each other.

一团火 yītuánhuǒ like a roaring fire; enthusiastic (towards people):待人像～ be warm and enthusiastic towards others /发扬"～"精神,站好柜台。When tending the counter, be keen on helping the customers.

一团乱麻 yītuán-luànmá like a mass of tangled flax — totally confused; in a complete mess; in a turmoil:我脑子里～,写什么文章哟! How can I write in such a confused state of mind? /她心里像～,不知怎么办好。Her mind being in a turmoil, she did not know what to do.

一团漆黑 yītuán-qīhēi *also*"漆黑一团" pitch-dark; utterly hopeless:四周～,什么也看不见。Nothing was visible in the pitch dark. /不能把我们的教育事业说得～。We must not paint a black picture of our educational work.

一团糟 yītuánzāo complete or sorry mess; chaos; muddle:家里乱成～。The family was in chaos (*or* a shambles).

一退六二五 yī tuì liù èr wǔ *also*"一推六二五" evade or deny all responsibility; pass the buck:这个人什么事都～。This man has always been a buck-passer. /你为何事到临头～? Why do you step back at the critical moment?

一碗水端平 yī wǎn shuǐ duānpíng when the cup is full, carry it even — treat everyone equally; be impartial:处理问题要～,不能有偏向。One must be free from bias and should be impartial in dealing with matters in hand.

一汪水儿 yīwāngshuǐr ❶ pretty and vivacious:这姑娘长得～似的。The girl looks pretty and lively. ❷ juicy:～的大蜜桃 big juicy peach

一网打尽 yīwǎng-dǎjìn catch the whole lot in a dragnet; net the whole lot; round up the whole gang at one fell swoop; make a clean sweep:不如此,不能把这伙歹徒～。Only in this way can we net the whole bunch of scoundrels.

一往情深 yīwǎng-qíngshēn be passionately devoted; be deeply attached; be full of affection for; be head over heels in love:他们相处时间不长,但已经～了。They have not been together long, but are already deeply in love. /他读完这封～的信,非常激动。He was greatly moved after reading the passionate letter.

一往无前 yīwǎng-wúqián press forward with indomitable will; forge ahead relentlessly:他具有～的献身精神。He has an indomitable spirit of dedication.

一望无际 yīwàng-wújì stretch as far as the eye can see; stretch to the horizon; there is a boundless stretch before one:～的原野 vast expanse of open country

一位论 yīwèilùn *also*"上帝一位论" Shàngdì yīwèilùn 〈基督教〉Unitarianism:～派 Unitarian

一味 yīwèi purely; stubbornly; persistently; blindly:～追求名利 persistently hanker after fame and gain; seek nothing but fame and wealth /～强调客观条件 put unjustified emphasis on (*or* unduly stress) objective conditions /～推脱责任 try in every way to evade responsibility

一文不名 yīwén-bùmíng penniless:走出商店,他已是～了。His pocket was empty when he went out of the store.

一文不值 yīwén-bùzhí *also*"一钱不值" not worth a penny; worthless

一文钱难倒英雄汉 yī wén qián nándǎo yīngxiónghàn without money, even a hero will be driven to the wall:短五角钱,这张火车票就是买不了,真是～啦! I won't be able to buy the train ticket because I'm short of 50 cents. I'm really cornered.

一问三不知 yī wèn sān bù zhī say "I don't know" to every question — not know a thing; be completely in the dark:对于工作中的许多实际问题,他常常是～。He was often ignorant of many practical matters in his work.

一窝蜂 yīwōfēng (of a crowd of people) like a swarm of bees:这些人～地嚷起来,表示不同意。These people cried out their disagreement like a swarm of bees. /观众～拥向出口处。The audience swarmed towards the exit. /一个人搞装修赚了,大家～地都去搞。When one man made money in interior decoration, everyone else made rush for it.

一窝子 yīwōzi whole bunch or band; many; lots:想不到竟惹出～是非 unexpectedly cause a whole series of disputes /这里有～赌徒。There is a den of gamblers here.

一无 yīwú not in the least; not at all:～所求 require nothing at all /～所好 have no hobby whatsoever /～所能 without a single skill; good for nothing

一无长物 yīwú-chángwù have nothing on one — be very poor; be poverty-stricken:他平生～。He lived in poverty all life long.

一无可取 yīwú-kěqǔ have nothing to recommend one; be without a single merit:此人所作所为～。There is nothing positive in whatever the man does.

一无是处 yīwú-shìchù without a single redeeming virtue or quality; devoid of any merit:你们谁也不要把对方说得～。No one should talk as if the other side had no saving graces at all.

一无所长 yīwú-suǒcháng have no special skill; be Jack of all trades but master of none:他虽本事不大,但也并非～。Though he is not a very capable person, he is by no means without merit.

一无所成 yīwú-suǒchéng without any accomplishment:回首这几年,竟是～。Looking back at the last few years, he was surprised to find that he had little achievement to his credit.

一无所得 yīwú-suǒdé gain nothing; be fruitless:他钓了几天鱼,结果是～地回家来了。He came back empty-handed after fishing for several days.

一无所有 yīwú-suǒyǒu not own a thing in the world; not have a thing to one's name; be stony broke:我除了影子以外～。I have noth-

Y

ing to my name in the world except my own shadow.

一无所知 yīwú-suǒzhī be completely in the dark; not have the least inkling of; be absolutely ignorant of:我对电子技术~。I know nothing about electronic technology.

一五一十 yīwǔ-yīshí (narrate) systematically and in full detail; from first to last:他把昨天的事~地告诉了老师。He told his teacher all about what happened yesterday. /请你把出事经过~地讲出来。Would you give us a detailed account of the accident?

一物降一物 yī wù xiáng yī wù there is always one thing to conquer another; every force has a counterforce; everything has its nemesis:这老家伙谁见了都怕,可他就怕他的女儿。真是~。To everyone else, the old man was a holy terror, but as everything has its nemesis, his daughter could wrap him around her little finger(*or* could make him dance to her tune).

一误再误 yīwù-zàiwù ❶ commit one error after another; make no end of mistakes:这件事我们已经处理错了,现在不能知错不改,~。We've already mishandled the matter, and we must make amends and not go on making more mistakes ❷ make things worse by repeated delays:他这病~,怕是难治了。His illness has been delayed far too long, and he has very little hope of recovery now.

一息尚存 yīxī-shàngcún as long as one still has breath left; so long as one remains alive; till one breathes one's last:~,当努力不懈。One should keep on striving as long as one lives.

一席话 yīxíhuà what one says during a conversation:你的~对我很有启发。What you've said is quite enlightening. /听君~,胜读十年书。I profit more from one conversation with you than from ten years of reading.

一席之地 yīxízhīdì area covered by a sitting mat — a small place or position:我只需要~,将就过一夜。I only need a very small place to pass the night. /这部小说将在世界文学史上占~。This novel will have a niche in the history of world literature.

一系列 yīxìliè a series of:~重大问题 a whole series of major issues /~的想法 a whole train of thought /采取~的有力措施 take a set of effective measures

一下 yīxià *also* "一下子" ❶ *used after a verb, indicating an act or an attempt*:看~ have a look /打听~ make an inquiry /商量~ have a consultation /再试~ have another try /让我们研究~。Let us mull it over. /请等~。Please wait a minute (*or* moment). /叫车在学校门前停~。Ask the car to stop over at the school gate. ❷ in a short while; all at once; suddenly:气温~降低了十度。Suddenly, the temperature dropped by 10°C. /谈话~就转到国际问题上去了。The topic of conversation was soon changed to international issues. /他的病~好,~坏,不大稳定。Being in an unsteady condition, he gets better for a while and then has a relapse. /贪污腐化不可能~都清除掉。Graft and corruption cannot be eradicated overnight.

一线 yīxiàn ❶ war front; front line:~战场 front line battlefield /~工人 worker at the production line /他被调到~作战。He was sent to fight at the front line. ❷ a ray of; a gleam of:~阳光 a ray of sunlight /~希望 a gleam of hope /生死系于~。Life now hangs by a thread (*or* in the balance).

一线生机 yīxiàn-shēngjī a gleam of hope in despair; a slim chance of survival:他的生意似乎还有~。It seemed that there was still a gleam of hope for his business.

一相情愿 yīxiāng-qíngyuàn *also* "一厢情愿" wishful thinking:不能把计划建立在~的基础上。One should not base one's plans on wishful thinking.

一向 yīxiàng ❶ earlier on; of late:前~工程的进度很快。There was rapid progress in the project earlier on. /这~他学习很努力。He has worked fairly hard lately. ❷ consistently; all along; always:你~好吗? How have you been (since I saw you last)? /他~冷静。He always keeps his head. /我~不喜欢逛商店。I've never liked going shopping. /小陆~爱好音乐。Xiao Lu has been a music lover all along.

一小撮 yīxiǎocuō handful:~破坏分子 a handful of saboteurs

一小儿 yīxiǎor 〈方言〉 from childhood; as a child:这孩子~就很聪明。The boy has been clever ever since he was a child.

一笑千金 yīxiào-qiānjīn One smile is worth a thousand pieces of gold; the smile of a beauty is very precious indeed

一笑置之 yīxiào-zhìzhī dismiss with a laugh or smile; laugh off:对这类事,他总是~,从不把它们放在心上。He always laughs off such things and never takes them seriously.

一些 yīxiē ❶ a number or amount of; certain; some:~水 a little water /有~人就是不明白这个道理。Some people just wouldn't understand this. /有~情况还不清楚。The matter is not completely clear yet. ❷ tiny bit; few; little:就这么~钱了。This is all the money left. ❸ more than once; more than one:他去过~地方,有过~经历。He's been to quite a few places and has some experience. /他曾担任过~重要职务。He used to hold certain important positions. ❹ *placed after an adjective, a verb or a verbal phrase to indicate a slight change in degree*:小声~! Lower your voice. /快~! Faster! /多装~。Put more in.

一泻千里 yīxiè-qiānlǐ ❶ (of a river) rush down a thousand *li* — flow down vigorously:长江~,东流入海。The Yangtze River rushes down for thousands of *li* towards the ocean in the east. ❷ (of a writer's style) unrestrained and fluent; bold and flowing:他写起诗来,热情奔放,~。His poems are bold and flowing, full of spirit.

一蟹不如一蟹 yī xiè bùrú yī xiè each crab is smaller than the one before — each one is worse than the last; get worse and worse

一心 yīxīn ❶ wholeheartedly; earnestly; heart and soul:~为公 serve the public heart and soul /~扑在工作上 devote oneself wholeheartedly to work /~想进大学学习 be bent on studying in a university ❷ of one mind; with one heart:万众~。Millions of people are all of one mind. /只要你我~,不愁工作搞不好。As long as you and I work with one mind, we will make a success of the job.

一心不能二用 yī xīn bùnéng èr yòng one cannot apply oneself to two jobs at once; one cannot spin and reel at the same time:你看我哪里有功夫? 俗话说:~。Where would I get the time? As the old saying goes: you can't do two things at one time.

一心一德 yīxīn-yīdé *also* "一德一心" be of one heart and one mind:只要我们~,什么事情都能办到。Nothing is impossible so long as we are of one heart and one mind.

一心一意 yīxīn-yīyì heart and soul; wholeheartedly; with undivided attention:他~想把工作做好。He is fully devoted to his work. /她低着头,~地在抄写。She was copying something with great concentration.

一新 yīxīn completely new; brand new:房屋整修~。The house looks completely new after repairs.

一星半点儿 yīxīng-bàndiǎnr tiny bit; very small amount:~的知识(have) a smattering of knowledge /不能有~的马虎。There mustn't be the slightest carelessness.

一星儿 yīxīngr tiny bit; very small amount; shred:~活也不干 not do a slightest bit of work /衣服上没~污渍。There is not a speck of dirt on the clothes. /四下里没~灯光。Not a ray of light was visible around.

一行 yīxíng ❶ people travelling together; party; team:大使及其~受到了当地人们的欢迎。The ambassador and his party were welcomed by the local people. /体操队~今晨离京去香港。The gym team left Beijing for Hong Kong this morning. ❷ *indicate two actions taking place simultaneously*:她~哭着,~诉说她的遭遇。She was crying while recounting her ordeal. ❸ (Yīxíng) Yixing (formerly translated as I-Hsing, 683-727), astronomer and Buddhist philosopher of the Tang Dynasty

一行作吏 yīxíng-zuòlì 〈书面〉 once one becomes an official

一宿 yīxiǔ 〈口语〉 one night:~没睡好 didn't sleep well the whole night

一薰一莸 yīxūn-yīyóu when a fragrant herb is placed besides a blade of stinking grass, you smell nothing but the latter; when the evil is placed besides the good, the former overshadows the latter

一言半语 yīyán-bànyǔ a word or two; very few words:他很少说话,时常只有~。He is a man of few words.

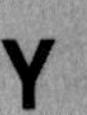

一言不发 yīyán-bùfā not say a word; remain silent:他~,坐在那里生闷气。He sat there sulking without a word. /在今天的会上,你为何~? Why didn't you speak out at today's meeting?

一言抄百总 yī yán chāo bǎi zǒng all in all; in a word; in a nutshell

一言既出,驷马难追 yī yán jì chū, sìmǎ nán zhuī a word once spoken cannot be overtaken even by a team of four horses — what is said cannot be unsaid:大丈夫做事,~。A real man never goes back on his words.

一言九鼎 yīyán-jiǔdǐng decisive word:她最佩服你,你的话对她~。You are her idol. Your words carry great weight with her.

一言难尽 yīyán-nánjìn you cannot explain the matter in a few words; it is a long story:他叹口气道:"~。"就不往下说了。He sighed and said, "It is difficult to explain." Then he fell silent.

一言堂 yīyántáng ❶〈旧语〉(sign hung in a shop) fixed prices; no bargaining ❷ what I say goes; one person alone has the say; person who won't tolerate dissenting views:～作风 dictatorial style of work /要搞"群言堂",不搞"～"。Let all have a say, not just one.

一言为定 yīyán-wéidìng that's settled then; keep one's word:你我～,决不反悔。You and I will keep our word and never go back on it. /好! ～,我们都按新方案办! Well, that's settled then. Let's act according to the new plan. /那你～,我就指望着你了。Now that I have your word, I'll count on you.

一言一行 yīyán-yīxíng every word and every deed:他的～都给我们留下了深刻的印象。We are deeply impressed by what he says and does.

一言以蔽之 yī yán yǐ bì zhī to sum up in a word; in short:我要说的,～,就是要实行计划生育,控制人口的过快增长。In short, all I want to say is that we should carry out family planning to check the undue growth of population.

一氧化碳 yīyǎnghuàtàn carbon monoxide

一氧化物 yīyǎnghuàwù monoxide

一样 yīyàng same; equally; alike; as... as...:～能干 be equally capable /像白昼～明亮 as bright as day /他们俩性格～。The two of them are of the same temperament. /他们吃的穿的都～。They eat and dress alike. /他们俩都是～的货色。The two of them are birds of a feather. /她把我们看做自己的亲儿女～。She treats us as if we were her own children.

一叶蔽目,不见泰山 yī yè bì mù, bù jiàn Tàishān *also* "一叶障目,不见泰山" a leaf before the eye shuts out Mount Tai — partial or superficial phenomenon interferes with one's understanding of the essence of things:别～,让眼前的一点挫折影响了长远的计划。Don't you be short-sighted and let the temporary setback block your long-term strategy.

一叶萩碱 yīyèqiūjiǎn 〈药学〉securinine

一叶知秋 yīyè-zhīqiū the falling of one leaf heralds the coming of autumn; a straw shows which way the wind blows; a small sign can point to a great trend:只有高瞻远瞩的人才能具有～的洞察力。Only those who have great foresight can see great trends through small signs.

一夜夫妻百夜恩 yī yè fūqī bǎi yè ēn *see* "一日夫妻百日恩"

一一 yīyī one by one; one after another:～解释 explain one by one /～记在心里 remember everything (*or* every detail) /～告别 say goodbye to everyone (*or* one after another); bid farewell to all /恕不～答复。Sorry for not being able to reply to the questions one by one. *or* Sorry for not replying to each and every of the questions.

一…一… yī…yī… ❶ *used before two nouns of similar kind* (a) *indicating the whole*:一街一巷 whole street (b) *indicating a very small amount of sth.*:一草一木 every tree and grass /一分一秒 every minute; every second /一兵一卒 every soldier; a single soldier ❷ *used before two nouns of different kinds* (a) *indicating contrast*:一龙一猪 dragon and pig — two persons between whom there is a great disparity (b) *indicating relationship between them*:一本一利 capital and profit; profit proportionate to the capital ❸ *used before two verbs, indicating the continuance of the action*:一摇一晃 sway and stagger /一惊一乍 fuss and fluster ❹ *used before two related verbs, indicating the coordination or alternation of actions*:一起一落 rising one moment and falling down the other; rise and fall in turn /一推一拉 pull and drag /一亮一灭 flicker on and off ❺ *used before two opposite nouns of direction or two opposite adjectives, indicating contrary positions or situations*:一上一下 one above, one below /一前一后 one in front, one following /一高一矮 one tall, one short

一衣带水 yīyīdàishuǐ narrow strip of water:两国是～的邻邦。The two countries are close neighbours separated only by a strip of water.

一以当十 yīyǐdāngshí *also* "以一当十" pit one against ten

一以贯之 yīyǐguànzhī run through sth. with a single thought or theory:吾道～。A basic idea (i. e. loyalty and forbearance) runs through the entire Confucian teachings.

一意 yīyì heart and soul; wholeheartedly:我知道,他是～想要帮助我。I know he's quite sincere in trying to help me.

一意孤行 yīyì-gūxíng cling obstinately to one's course; act wilfully:他不顾大家的劝告,公然～。He insists on acting arbitrarily in disregard of other people's advice.

一应 yīyīng all; every:～花销 all the expenses /～事务统由该员管理。This person is in charge of all the matters here.

一应俱全 yīyīng-jùquán everything needed is there or available:家用电器,本店～。This store supplies all kinds of electrical appliances.

一拥而上 yīyōng'érshàng ❶ rush up in a crowd; gather round at once:大家～,争着和他握手。People crowded round him immediately, trying to shake hands with him. ❷ *also* "一轰而上" rush at sth. in confusion; make no distinction between the important and the trivial:我们要加快建设进度,但不能～。We should speed up our project, but not without an order of priority.

一隅 yīyú 〈书面〉❶ corner:偏安～ seek temporary security in reduced territory under enemy threat ❷ one-sided; narrow; limited:～之见 one-sided view

一隅三反 yīyú-sānfǎn *also* "举一反三" jǔyī-fǎnsān draw inferences (about other cases) from one instance

一语道破 yīyǔ-dàopò lay bare the truth with one penetrating remark:你～他的真实意图。You hit the nail on the head when you pointed out what he was really after.

一语破的 yīyǔ-pòdì hit the mark with a single comment:你真是～,事情的奥妙就在这里。You've grasped the essence of the matter with a single comment.

一语双关 yīyǔ-shuāngguān phrase with a double meaning; pun

一元方程 yīyuán fāngchéng 〈数学〉first-order equation; equation of the first order

一元化 yīyuánhuà ❶ integrated; centralized ❷ unified:～领导 unified leadership /～管理 unified management

一元论 yīyuánlùn 〈哲学〉monism

一元酸 yīyuánsuān 〈化学〉monoacid; monoatomic acid

一院制 yīyuànzhì unicameral or one-chamber legislature

一月 yīyuè January

一再 yīzài time and again; again and again; repeatedly:～声明 state repeatedly /～表示歉意 apologize again and again

一…再… yī…zài… *used before the same replicated verb, indicating the repetition of the action*:一误再误 make repeated delays (*or* mistakes) /一等再等 wait and wait; wait unconscionably long /一忍再忍 hold one's temper again and again; try hard to keep one's temper

一早 yīzǎo ❶ early in the morning:明天～first thing tomorrow morning ❷〈方言〉at first; in the beginning:他是现在这样待你,还是～就如此呢? Has he always treated you like this or differently at first?

一眨巴眼 yīzhǎbayǎn *also* "一眨眼" instant; flash; twinkling of an eye:这孩子～就不见了。In a jiffy, the child was nowhere to be found.

一张一弛 yīzhāng-yīchí tension alternating with relaxation; ruling the country with flexible measures:文武之道,～。The principle of kings Wen and Wu was to alternate tension with relaxation.

一长制 yīzhǎngzhì system of one-man leadership

一着不慎,满盘皆输 yī zhāo bù shèn, mǎn pán jiē shū one careless move and the whole game is lost; one wrong move spoils the entire game

一朝 yīzhāo once; in one day:～之忿 momentary anger /～事露,惟有一死而已。There will be no choice but death once the secret is out.

一朝被蛇咬,十年怕井绳 yīzhāo bèi shé yǎo, shí nián pà jǐngshéng once bitten by a snake, one shies at a coiled rope for the next ten years — once bitten, twice shy; a burnt child dreads the fire:真是～,有了这回经历,我再也不敢与陌生人同行了。Once bitten, twice shy. Having had this awful experience, I never dare to travel with a stranger again.

一朝权在手,便把令来行 yīzhāo quán zài shǒu, biàn bǎ lìng lái xíng start to issue orders as soon as one comes to power

一朝一夕 yīzhāo-yīxī in one morning or evening; in a single day:练就如此高超的本领,恐非～之功。This superb skill is not the work of a single day. /这不是～的工程。It's not a project that can be accomplished overnight.

一针见血 yīzhēn-jiànxiě draw blood with the first prick of a needle — get to the truth with a single pertinent remark; hit the nail on the head:～地指出了问题的症结所在 point out sharply where the shoe pinches /这些批评～。The criticism hit home.

一枕黄粱 yīzhěn-huángliáng Golden Millet Dream — a brief dream of grandeur; delusory fame and power

一阵 yīzhèn a burst; a fit; a peal:～鞭炮声 a burst of firecrack-

ers /～狂风 a violent gust of wind; a squall /～咳嗽 a fit (*or* spasm) of coughing /一阵阵笑声 peals of laughter /～又～的掌声 rounds of applause /感到～轻松 sudden feeling of relaxation / 他耳边传来～轻柔的音乐。Some soft music came to his ears. /这鬼天气, ～风～雨的。The weather is terrible, now the wind blowing hard, now the rain pouring down.

一阵风 yīzhènfēng ❶ like a whirlwind; very quickly:战士们～地冲了上去。The soldiers rushed forward like a whirlwind. ❷ transient; brief; of short duration:落实党的政策,不能～。The implementation of Party policies must not be a flash in the pan.

一阵子 yīzhènzi period of time; spell:这～天气不好。We've had a spell of bad weather recently. /他这～工作很忙。He has been busy with his work these days.

一之谓甚 yīzhīwèishèn even once is more than enough:～,其可再乎? Once is already too much; how can it be allowed to happen again?

一知半解 yīzhī-bànjiě have a smattering of knowledge; have scanty or half-baked knowledge:对这些事情,我也只是～。I only have a smattering of knowledge of these things. /不能满足于～。We shouldn't feel satisfied with a little learning.

一直 yīzhí ❶ straight:～走 go straight ahead; keep (*or* move) straight on ❷ continuously; always; without intermission:雨～下了三天三夜。It had been raining for three days and nights running. /我们～是好朋友。We've been good friends all along. /这个讲座打算～办到年底。It is planned that the lectures will go on right up to the end of the year. ❸ all the way:从老人～到小孩,没有不喜欢他的。Everyone likes him, old and young. /从东头～到西头,路两边摆满了鲜花。The whole street, from east to west, is decorated with flowers.

一纸空文 yīzhǐ-kōngwén a mere scrap of paper:这个协定不过是～。This agreement is nothing but a scrap of paper (*or* is not worth the paper it is written on).

一至于此 yīzhìyúcǐ should have come to such an extent:吸毒之危害～! To think that the harm of taking drugs should have been so devastating!

一致 yīzhì ❶ showing consensus; identical; unanimous; consistent:言行～ be as good as one's word /步调～ march in step; act in unison /见解～ hold identical views; be of the same opinion /官兵～ unity between officers and men /根本利益～ identity of fundamental interests /提案～通过了。The resolution was adopted (*or* carried) unanimously. *or* The vote for the resolution was unanimous. /他的说法前后不～。What he said is not consistent. /双方达到了完全的～。The two parties reached a consensus. ❷ work together; act in unison:共赴国难,～对外 unite all forces to fight foreign aggressors and meet national crisis.

一掷千金 yīzhì-qiānjīn ❶ stake a thousand pieces of gold on one throw (of the dice, etc.) ❷ spend one's money wastefully and extravagantly; throw away money like dirt; spend money like water

一柱擎天 yīzhù-qíngtiān one pillar holding up or supporting the sky; (of person) shoulder great responsibilities; be charged with important tasks:在公司的对外业务中,他起到～的作用。He is the mainstay of the company's overseas business.

一专多能 yīzhuān-duōnéng specialize in one thing and be good at many

一准 yīzhǔn sure; surely; certainly:你这个计划,领导～同意。The leadership will certainly approve your plan. /他说去就～会去。If he says yes, he will surely go.

一字褒贬 yīzì-bāobiǎn one word clearly expressing praise or censure — exact and precise wording; strict choice of words

一字长蛇阵 yīzì chángshézhèn single-line battle array:摆开～ string out in a long line:选民们在门口排成～。The voters are queuing up at the gate.

一字千金 yīzì-qiānjīn one word is worth a thousand pieces of gold — excellent literary work or calligraphy

一字儿 yīzìr in a row; in a line:桌上～摆着五只茶杯。Five teacups were lined up on the table.

一字一板 yīzì-yībǎn (speak) unhurriedly and clearly:～地向她解释 give her an unhurried and clear explanation /他开始～地讲起话来。He began to speak deliberately.

一字一珠 yīzì-yīzhū each word worth a pearl; (of article) well-written

一字之师 yīzìzhīshī one who corrects a word in a poem or essay is regarded by the author as his teacher; one-word teacher

一自 yīzì since; ever since:～他走后,再无音信。We've never heard from him ever since he left.

一总 yīzǒng ❶ altogether; in sum total; in all:～来了百来个人。There came about a hundred people altogether. /我们欠他的钱～一千元。We owe him one thousand *yuan* in all. ❷ all:把这些工作～交给我去干吧。Leave all the work to me.

壹(弌)

yī one (used for the numeral 一 on cheques, banknotes, etc. to prevent mistakes or alterations)

椅

yī *also*“山桐子” shāntóngzǐ idesia

see also yǐ

猗

yī 〈书面〉❶〈助词〉*often used at the end of a sentence with similar function as* 啊:河水清且涟～。The river is clear and rippling. ❷〈叹词〉*used for praise*:～欤盛哉! Magnificent! *or* Superb! /～嗟昌兮! What a strong and healthy body!

猗猗 yīyī 〈书面〉beautiful and flourishing:绿竹～ luxuriant green bamboo

漪

yī 〈书面〉ripples:清～ clear ripples

漪澜 yīlán 〈书面〉ripples and billows

漪涟 yīlián 〈书面〉ripples

欹

yī *see*“猗❷” yī

see also qī

医(醫、毉)

yī ❶ doctor (of medicine); medical practitioner:西～ doctor trained in Western medicine /中～ doctor of traditional Chinese medicine; practitioner of Chinese medicine /牙～ dentist /兽～ veterinarian; vet /军～ medical officer; army surgeon/法～ legal medical expert /神～ highly skilled doctor; miracle-working doctor /庸～ quack; chalatan /延～诊治 call in a doctor for treatment ❷ medical science; medical service; medicine:行～ practise medicine /中西～结合 combine traditional Chinese and Western medicine /他是学～的。He majors in medicine. ❸ treat; cure; heal:有病早～ get timely medical treatment /讳疾忌～ hide one's sickness for fear of treatment /他把我的病～好了。He cured me of my illness.

医案 yī'àn record of treatment of patients in traditional Chinese medicine

医道 yīdào (esp. of traditional Chinese medicine) art of healing; medical expertise; physician's skill:～高明 well versed in the art of healing; of high medical expertise

医德 yīdé medical ethics:～高尚 exemplary medical ethics

医方 yīfāng ❶ medical skill; art of healing; ❷ prescription

医护 yīhù cure and nurse; provide medical service: ～人员 doctors and nurses; medical staff /精心～ give careful medical treatment

医家 yījiā (mainly) doctor of traditional Chinese:收集各地～祖传秘方 collect traditional secret recipes of Chinese medicine

医经 yījīng ancient Chinese medical classics

医科 yīkē medical education in general; medicine:～大学 medical university /报考～ apply for medical school

医理 yīlǐ principles of medical science; medical knowledge

医疗 yīliáo medical treatment: ～卫生工作 medical and health work /～事故 unskilful and faulty medical or surgical treatment; malpractice /公费～ public health services; free medical care /合作～ cooperative medicare or medicine

医疗保险 yīliáo bǎoxiǎn medical insurance

医疗队 yīliáoduì medical team:流动～ mobile medical team

医疗辐射学 yīliáo fúshèxué atomic or radiological medicine

医疗器械 yīliáo qìxiè medical apparatus and instruments

医疗体育 yīliáo tǐyù medico-athletics

医疗站 yīliáozhàn medical station; health centre

医生 yīshēng doctor; medical man: 内科～ doctor of internal medicine; physician /外科～ surgeon /儿科～ paediatrician /产科～ obstetrician /妇科～ gynaecologist /牙科～ dentist /眼科～ oculist /耳鼻喉科～ ENT (ear-nose-throat) doctor /皮肤科～ dermatologist /泌尿科～ urologist /结核病～ doctor for tuberculosis /传染病～ doctor for infectious diseases /肿瘤科～ oncologist /整形外科～ plastic surgeon /骨科～ orthopedist /值班～ doctor on duty /实习～ intern /

住院～ resident physician /赤脚～ barefoot doctor

医圣 yīshèng (in ancient times) sage in medicine — doctor of great accomplishments

医师 yīshī (qualified) doctor：主任～ chief physician /主治～ physician (*or* surgeon) in charge; attending doctor /放射科～ radiologist

医士 yīshì practitioner with secondary medical school education; feldscher; medical assistant

医书 yīshū (esp. of traditional Chinese medicine) medical book

医术 yīshù medical skill; art of healing：～精湛 consummate medical skill

医坛 yītán medical circles

医务 yīwù medical matters：～部门 medical department /～工作 medical work /～工作者 medical worker /～人员 medical personnel (*or* staff, *or* workers); public health worker

医务所 yīwùsuǒ clinic

医学 yīxué medical science; medicine：～硕士 master of medicine /～博士 medical doctor; MD/～文献 medical literature /～遗产 medical heritage /～界 medical circles

医学科学院 yīxué kēxuéyuàn academy of medical sciences

医药 yīyào medicine：～费 medical expenses (*or* costs) /～常识 general medical knowledge /～公司 medical company

医院 yīyuàn hospital：妇产～ maternity hospital /儿童～ children's hospital /牙科～ dental hospital /口腔～ stomatology hospital /肿瘤～ tumour hospital /结核～ tuberculosis hospital /整形外科～ plastic surgery hospital /专科～ specialized hospital /综合～ general hospital /中医～ hospital of Chinese medicine /附属～ affiliated (*or* attached) hospital /陆军～ army hospital /野战～ field hospital /红十字会～ Red Cross hospital

医治 yīzhì cure; treat; heal：及时～ give (*or* get) timely treatment /～无效 fail to respond to medical treatment; be unable to restore to health /住院～ be hospitalized /受到精心的护理和～ receive careful nursing and medical treatment/～精神创伤 heal mental wound (*or* emotional trauma) /你这个病应该赶快～一下。Your disease needs immediate medical attention.

医嘱 yīzhǔ doctor's advice or orders：遵～用药 take medicine as advised by the doctor (*or* as prescribed)

医助 yīzhù ❶ assistant doctor (in the army) ❷ paramedic

医宗金鉴 Yīzōng Jīnjiàn *Golden Book of Medicine*, classic work of Chinese medicine completed in 1742 during the Qing Dynasty

鹥

yī 〈古语〉 gull

婴

yī

婴妮 yīní 〈书面〉 newly-born baby; infant

繄

yī 〈书面〉 ❶ only; alone：～我独无! Only I have none. /一雨三日，～谁之力? Whose force alone can make it rain for three days? ❷ be tantamount to：君王之于越也，～起死人而肉白骨也。To the people of Yue, Your Majesty is a benefactor who has brought the dead back to life.

揖

yī 〈书面〉 (make a) bow with hands clasped

揖别 yībié 〈书面〉 bid farewell by bowing with hands clasped

揖让 yīràng 〈书面〉 (an etiquette of ancient times between the guest and the host) bow and yield (to each other) — formalities of courtesy; standing on ceremony

噫

yī 〈叹词〉 ❶ 〈书面〉 alas ❷ why; how come：～，他今天怎么来了? How come he came here today?

噫嘻 yīxī 〈书面〉〈叹词〉 alas

伊[1]

yī ❶ 〈书面〉〈助词〉 *used to introduce a phrase or sentence*：～故乡之可怀。I miss my homeland very much. ❷ (Yī) a surname

伊[2]

yī he; she

伊甸园 Yīdiànyuán 〈基督教〉 Garden of Eden; Paradise

伊尔库茨克 Yī'ěrkùcíkè Irkutsk, chief city of Siberia on the western shore of Lake Baikal in Russia

伊瓜苏河 Yīguāsūhé Iguacu River, river in southern Brazil, famous for the Iguacu Falls, close to the frontier with Argentina

伊克度 yīkèdù 〈药学〉 ichthyol; ichthammol

伊拉克 Yīlākè Iraq：～人 Iraqi

伊兰伊兰 yīlányīlán *also* "芳香树" fāngxiāngshù Ylang-ylang; perfume tree; Canadian odorata

伊朗 Yīlǎng Iran：～人 Iranian

伊犁河 Yīlíhé Ili River, a river about 1, 500 km long with its source in the Xinjiang Uygur Autonomous Region

伊犁条约 Yīlí Tiáoyuē Treaty of Kuldja, unequal treaty imposed on the Qing Government by Tsarist Russia in 1881

伊丽莎白二世 Yīlìshābái Èrshì Elizabeth II (1926-), queen of the United Kingdom from 1952

伊丽莎白一世 Yīlìshābái Yīshì Elizabeth I (1533-1603), famous queen of England whose reign (1558-1603) saw one of its greatest eras, and was known as the Elizebethan age

伊利诺伊 Yīlìnuòyī Illinois, a state in the Middle West of the United States

伊人 yīrén 〈书面〉 that person (esp. woman)：所谓～，在水一方。The girl I miss lives on the other side of the river.

伊始 yīshǐ 〈书面〉 beginning：上任～ upon assuming office /新春～ at the beginning of the new year /下车～ as soon as one alights from the official carriage — on arrival at a new post

伊斯兰堡 Yīsīlánbǎo Islamabad, capital of Pakistan

伊斯兰教 Yīsīlánjiào Islam; Islamism：～国家 Islamic country /～教徒 Moslem; Muslim /～教规 Islamic law; Moslem (*or* Muslim) law /～教义 Moslem (*or* Muslim) doctrine

伊斯兰教历 Yīsīlánjiàolì Moslem calendar, a kind of lunar calendar dating back to 16 July 622 AD

伊斯曼-柯达公司 Yīsīmàn-Kēdá Gōngsī (US) Eastman Kodak Company, a major manufacturer of film, cameras and photographic equipment

伊斯坦布尔 Yīsītǎnbù'ěr Istanbul, port and former capital (until 1923) of Turkey, situated on the Bosporus, partly in Europe and partly in Asia

伊藤博文 Yīténgbówén Ito Hirabumi (1841-1909), Japanese statesman and first Prime Minister (1885-1888)

伊蚊 yīwén *also* "黑斑蚊" hēibānwén 〈动物〉 aedes; yellow-fever mosquito

伊于胡底 yīyú-húdǐ 〈书面〉 where will it all end：长此以往，不知～。If things go on like this, we don't know where it will all end.

咿

yī

咿唔 yīwú 〈象声〉 sound of reading aloud：南窗之下，书声～。There was sound of reading aloud coming out of the window facing the south.

咿呀 yīyā ❶ 〈象声〉 squeak; creak：桨声～ squeak of oars in oarlocks ❷ prattle; babble：小儿～学语 babbling baby

yí

沂

Yí (short for 沂河) Yihe River (in Shangdong and Jiangsu provinces)

宜

yí ❶ suitable; appropriate; desirable; fitting：适～ appropriate; fitting and proper /不合时～ be out of keeping with the times /少儿不～ not suitable for children /因地制～ suit measures to local conditions /老少皆～ good for both young and old ❷ should; ought to (esp. used in the negative)：事不～迟。No more delays. *or* No further delay is called for. *or* The matter needs immediate attention. /不～操之过急。You should not act in haste. *or* You should avoid undue haste. ❸ 〈书面〉 of course; certainly; with no doubt：～其无往而不利。Without any doubt they will meet success wherever they go. ❹ (Yí) a surname

宜昌 Yíchāng Yichang, industrial city and port in the middle reaches of the Yangtze River

宜林 yílín (area) suitable for planting trees

宜人 yírén pleasant; delightful; attractive：景色～ attractive (*or* charming) scenery /气候～ pleasant (*or* delightful) weather /这种房子冬暖夏凉，舒适～。This type of house is very pleasant to live in, warm in winter and cool in summer.

宜室宜家 yíshì-yíjiā conjugal bliss or harmony
宜兴壶 yíxīnghú teapot made in Yixing county, Jiangsu Province
宜于 yíyú good for; suitable to:此地～度假 This is a nice place for holiday.

一 yí see "一" yī

圯 yí 〈书面〉bridge

夷[1] yí 〈书面〉❶ level; smooth; safe:化险为～ turn danger into safety; head off a disaster /履险如～ cross a dangerous pass as easily as walking on level ground; handle a crisis without difficulty ❷ raze; level (to the ground):～为平地 level to the ground; raze ❸ exterminate; wipe out: see "～族"

夷[2] yí ❶ ancient name for tribes in the east of China; barbarians:东～ East *Yi* /四～ all the ethnic minorities around China (in ancient times) ❷〈旧语〉foreign country; foreigner:华～杂处地区 area inhabited by both Chinese and foreigners
夷旷 yíkuàng 〈书面〉amiable and sanguine:襟怀～ be affable and sanguine
夷戮 yílù 〈书面〉kill:遭敌寇～者不可胜数。Countless people were slaughtered by the enemy.
夷灭 yímiè 〈书面〉annihilate; exterminate:全家惨遭～。Everyone in the family was killed.
夷平 yípíng level to the ground; raze:村庄被炮火～。The village was razed to the ground by artillery fire.
夷然 yírán 〈书面〉calm and confident; completely at ease:～不以为忤 take no offence at all
夷犹 yíyóu 〈书面〉❶ *also* "夷由" hesitate to go forward:君不进兮～。Hesitant you are to take any steps. ❷ calmly; unhurriedly:小船～而去。The small boat sailed off slowly.
夷州 Yízhōu ancient name for Taiwan Province
夷族 yízú exterminate an entire family (a punishment in ancient times)

痍 yí 〈书面〉wound; trauma:满目疮～。Everywhere a scene of desolation meets the eye. /～伤者未瘳。The wounded have not been cured yet.

荑 yí 〈书面〉clear the fields of weeds; weed
see also tí

咦 yí 〈叹词〉(indicating surprise) well; why:～! 你还在这儿! Well, so you are still here! /～,他怎么一下子没了? Why, he's suddenly nowhere to be found!

胰 yí *also* "胰腺";"胰脏"〈生理〉pancreas
胰病 yíbìng pancreatopathy
胰蛋白酶 yídànbáiméi 〈生化〉trypsin
胰岛 yídǎo 〈生理〉Langerhans' islet; pancreas islet:～机能亢进 insulism
胰岛瘤 yídǎoliú insulinoma; insuloma
胰岛素 yídǎosù 〈药学〉insulin:人～ human insulin / 猪～ pork insulin /完全人工合成结晶牛～ total synthetic crystalline bovine insulin
胰岛素过多症 yídǎosù guòduōzhèng 〈医学〉hyperinsulinism
胰岛素过少症 yídǎosù guòshǎozhèng 〈医学〉hypoinsulinism
胰岛素疗法 yídǎosù liáofǎ 〈医学〉insulinization; insulinotherapy
胰岛炎 yídǎoyán insulitis
胰淀粉酶 yídiànfěnméi 〈生化〉amylopsin
胰瘤 yíliú 〈医学〉pancreatoncus
胰酶 yíméi 〈药学〉pancreatin
胰切除术 yíqiēchúshù 〈医学〉pancreatectomy
胰石 yíshí 〈医学〉pancreatolith:～病 pancreatolithiasis /～切除术 pancreatolithectomy; pancreatolithotomy
胰腺 yíxiàn 〈生理〉pancreas:～癌 cancer of the pancreas; pancreatic cancer /～机能异常〈医学〉heteropancreatism
胰腺炎 yíxiànyán pancreatitis
胰液 yíyè 〈生理〉pancreatic juice
胰皂 yízào 〈方言〉soap
胰脂酶 yízhīméi 〈生化〉pancreatic lipase; steapsin
胰子 yízi ❶ pancreas (of pigs, sheep, etc.); sweetbreads ❷〈方言〉soap:香～ perfumed (*or* scented) soap; toilet soap

姨 yí ❶ one's mother's sister; aunt ❷ one's wife's sister; sister-in-law:大～子 one's wife's elder sister /小～子 one's wife's younger sister
姨表 yíbiǎo maternal cousin:～兄弟 male maternal cousins /～姐妹 female maternal cousins /我们是～亲。We are maternal relatives.
姨夫 yífu *also* "姨父" husband of one's maternal aunt; uncle
姨姐 yíjiě wife's elder sister
姨姥姥 yílǎolao sister of one's maternal grandmother
姨妈 yímā (married) maternal aunt; aunt
姨妹 yímèi wife's younger sister
姨母 yímǔ maternal aunt; aunt
姨奶奶 yínǎinai ❶ sister of one's grandmother ❷ concubine
姨娘 yíniang ❶〈旧语〉one's father's concubine ❷〈方言〉maternal aunt; aunt
姨婆 yípó sister of one's maternal grandmother
姨儿 yír 〈方言〉maternal aunt; aunt
姨太太 yítàitai 〈口语〉concubine
姨兄弟 yíxiōngdì son of one's maternal aunt
姨姨 yíyi 〈方言〉aunt
姨丈 yízhàng husband of one's maternal aunt; uncle
姨姊妹 yízǐmèi *also* "姨姐妹" daughter of one's maternal aunt

宧 yí 〈古语〉northeast corner of a room

颐[1] yí 〈书面〉cheek:支～ cheek in palm /解～ (of a face) smile

颐[2] yí 〈书面〉keep fit; take care of; preserve:～神养性 preserve one's vital energy /～年堂 Hall of (preserving) Health and Longevity (in Beijing)
颐和园 Yíhéyuán Summer Palace (in Beijing)
颐养 yíyǎng 〈书面〉keep fit; take care of oneself:～天年 take care of oneself so as to enjoy one's natural span of life
颐指气使 yízhǐ-qìshǐ order people about by facial expressions; be extremely arrogant:他～,心狠手辣。He is not only insufferably arrogant, but also cruel and evil.

蛇 yí see "委蛇" wēiyí
see also shé

遗 yí ❶ lose: see "～失" ❷ sth. lost:路不拾～。No one pockets anything found on the road. ❸ omit; forget:拾～补阙 make good omissions and deficiencies /补～ addendum ❹ leave behind; keep back; stint:不～余力 spare no efforts /养虎～患 to rear a tiger is to court calamity; appeasement brings disaster ❺ leave to others at one's death; bequeath: see "～作";"～骨" ❻ involuntary discharge (of urine, etc.):小～ urinate; pass (*or* make) water; empty one's bladder /梦～ nocturnal emission; wet dream
see also wèi
遗案 yí'àn unsolved case
遗笔 yíbǐ posthumous writings; writings of one immediately before death
遗产 yíchǎn ❶ inheritance; legacy:继承父母的～ inherit the legacy of one's parents /留下大笔～ bequeath a huge legacy /～继承法 inheritance law /～纠纷 legacy dispute /～管理人 administrator (of an estate) /～管理书 letter of administration ❷ legacy; heritage:丰富的文化～ rich cultural heritage /优秀的文学～ splendid literary heritage /历史～ legacy of history
遗产承受人 yíchǎn chéngshòurén legatee; inheritor
遗产税 yíchǎnshuì estate tax; succession duty; inheritance tax
遗臭万年 yíchòu-wànnián leave a stink for ten thousand years — go down in history as a byword of infamy; earn eternal notoriety:这个卖国贼的累累罪行,载于史书,～。The numerous crimes of the traitor have been recorded in history and will be held up to infamy for ever.
遗传 yíchuán 〈生理〉heredity; inheritance:交叉～ crisscross inher-

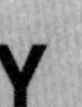

itance /从性～ sex-influenced inheritance /限性～ sex-limited inheritance /显性～ dominant inheritance /隐性～ recessive inheritance / ～梅毒 heredoleus /～性皮肤病 genodermatosis /～畸形 genetic freak /～选型交配〈生物〉genetic assortative mating /～移植技术 genetic transplantation technique /～特征 hereditary feature; heredity /这种病有～性。This disease is hereditary. /她原本就有一副爸爸～下来的好嗓子。She was born with a good voice inherited from her father.

遗传变异 yíchuán biànyì hereditary variation

遗传病 yíchuánbìng hereditary disease

遗传工程 yíchuán gōngchéng *also*“基因工程”jīyīn gōngchéng genetic engineering /～学 genetic engineering

遗传基因 yíchuán jīyīn hereditary gene

遗传密码 yíchuán mìmǎ genetic code

遗传免疫 yíchuán miǎnyì heredoimmunity

遗传信息 yíchuán xìnxī hereditary or genetic information

遗传学 yíchuánxué genetics: ～家 geneticist

遗传因子 yíchuán yīnzǐ genetic factor

遗存 yícún ❶ leave over; hand down: 这些石刻～至今已有千年。These carved stones have existed for over a thousand years. ❷ things left over from ancient times; remains; legacy: 古代文化～ cultural remains from ancient times

遗大投艰 yídà-tóujiān entrust sb. with an important and arduous task: 此人久经历练, 可～。The man has rich experience and can therefore be entrusted with important tasks.

遗毒 yídú baneful legacy; harmful tradition; pernicious influence: 封建等级观念的～ evil legacy of the feudal concept of social hierachy

遗范 yífàn model of one's predecessors: ～犹存 the predecessors' model still survives

遗风 yífēng tradition or influence left over from the past: ～余烈 customs and achievements left over by one's forefathers /这个偏远的山村还保留着古代的～。The ancient tradition and practice are still well preserved (*or* observed) in this remote village.

遗腹子 yífùzǐ posthumous child

遗稿 yígǎo manuscript left unpublished by the author at his death; posthumous manuscript: 他的～已经友人整理出版。His posthumous manuscript was published after it was collated by his friends.

遗孤 yígū orphan: 抚育烈士的～ foster a martyr's child (*or* children)

遗骨 yígǔ skeleton: 烈士～ remains of a martyr /猿人～化石 fossile of the ape-man

遗骸 yíhái remains (of the dead): 生物～ remains of creatures

遗害 yíhài leave harm behind: ～后人 do harm to later generations

遗憾 yíhàn ❶ deep regret; remorse: 这是他终生的～。This is his lifelong regret. ❷ regret; deplore: 令人～的事 matter of regret /对于武装干涉某国的内政深表～ deeply regret the armed intervention in the internal affairs of a country /对会议仍未取得进展深表～ deplore the continued lack of progress in the meeting /很～, 我不能去。I'm very sorry I won't be able to go. /你不能来, 实在～。It's really a pity that you can't come.

遗痕 yíhén mark or trace left over by sth.: ～犹存。The trace is clearly discernible.

遗恨 yíhèn eternal regret; remorse: ～千古 eternal remorse or regret /终生～ lifelong regret

遗患 yíhuàn cause evil consequences: 养痈～ a boil neglected becomes the bane of one's life

遗祸 yíhuò leave harm behind; do harm to sb.: 兹事体大, 须考虑周全, 以免～子孙。To avoid harming later generations, we must take care in handling this matter of great importance.

遗迹 yíjì historical ruins; remains; vestiges; traces: 古代文明的～ vestiges (*or* traces) of an ancient civilization /他考察过许多历史～。He has investigated and studied many historical ruins. /这里有汉唐两代宫殿的～。Here are the sites of the palaces of both the Han and Tang dynasties.

遗教 yíjiào teachings and works left behind by one after one's death

遗精 yíjīng 〈生理〉(seminal) emission

遗老 yílǎo ❶ surviving adherent of an overthrown dynasty; old fogy; old diehard: 封建～ old feudal diehard /～遗少 old fogies and young diehards /早年这里住着一位前清～。An old adherent of the Qing Dynasty used to live here. ❷〈书面〉old people who have experienced or witnessed important social changes: 欲知其事, 最好去访问一下当地～。If you want to know what happened, you'd better go and visit some of the old local witnesses of history.

遗烈 yíliè achievements of one's predecessors: 仰其～ admire the exploits of one's predecessors

遗留 yíliú leave behind; hand down: 历史上～下来的问题 issue left over by history; question left over from the past; legacy from the past /多年～下来的弊病 long-standing abuse; age-old malpractice/ 你还有什么～的事情需要我办理? Is there any remaining matter that you would like me to settle for you? /这古关隘～下来许多历史踪迹。Many historical traces of the ancient pass can still be seen.

遗漏 yílòu fail to do sth.; omit; leave out: 所引数据有重大～。The quoted data has important omissions. /名册上把他的名字给～了。His name was missing from the list. /他回答得很完全, 没有～。He made a complete answer without leaving out anything.

遗落 yíluò ❶ lose: 他～了一个笔记本。He has lost a notebook. ❷〈书面〉discard; throw aside; get rid of: ～世事 ignore worldly affairs; put worldly cares aside

遗民 yímín ❶ adherent of an overthrown dynasty; survivor of a former age: 此书为明末～所作。This book was written by a survivor of the Ming Dynasty. ❷ survivor of a great upheaval: 劫后～ survivors of disaster

遗命 yímìng testament; will; dying words

遗墨 yímò letters, manuscripts, scrolls of painting, calligraphy, etc. left behind by the deceased: 这幅山水画是我父亲的～。This landscape painting was done by my late father.

遗尿 yíniào *also*“夜尿症”yèniàozhèng 〈医学〉enuresis; bedwetting

遗篇 yípiān poem or essay left behind by the deceased: 吟诵前人歌咏西湖的～ recite verses written by the ancients in praise of the West Lake

遗弃 yíqì ❶ abandon; forsake; cast aside: 一座～的城堡 abandoned fortress ❷ abandon, forsake, or desert one's relatives that one should support or foster: ～妻儿 forsake one's wife and children /她抱回一个被～的女婴。She took back an abandoned baby girl.

遗缺 yíquē vacancy (made available because of the death or departure of the person holding the position): 由他顶替副院长的～。He'll move up to fill the vacancy for vice president.

遗容 yíróng ❶ looks of the deceased; remains: 瞻仰～ pay one's respects to the remains of sb. /老人的～像生前那样慈祥。The dead old man wore the same kindly look as when he was alive. ❷ portrait of the deceased: 向～默哀 stand in silent tribute in front of the portrait of the deceased

遗少 yíshào young adherent of an overthrown dynasty; young man with the mentality of an old fogy; young diehard: 封建阶级的遗老～ diehards of the feudal class, old and young

遗失 yíshī lose: ～钱包 lose one's wallet /～启事 lost property notice /我可能把手提箱～在出租车上了。I probably left my briefcase on the taxi.

遗矢 yíshǐ 〈书面〉empty one's bowels; defecate

遗世独立 yíshì-dúlì separate oneself from the rest of the world; live in seclusion; lead a carefree life: 现在, 像他这种～的人难见了。Persons like him who cuts himself off from the rest of the world are rare nowadays.

遗事 yíshì ❶ incident of the past: 这个剧本写的是前代～。This play is about some of the incidents of past ages. ❷ deeds of those now dead: 革命烈士的～ deeds of revolutionary martyrs

遗书 yíshū ❶ (usu. used as book titles) posthumous papers; writings of an author now dead:《章氏～》*Posthumous Writings of Mr. Zhang* ❷ letter or note left by one immediately before death: 他自杀前留下了一封～。He wrote a letter before committing suicide. *or* He left a suicidal note. ❸〈书面〉books that have been lost; books that are no longer extant or available (in market or library): 朝廷令人求～于天下。The court ordered people to look for lost books throughout the country.

遗属 yíshǔ family dependants of the deceased

遗孀 yíshuāng widow; relict

遗俗 yísú ❶ custom left over from ancient times ❷〈书面〉be rejected by common customs

遗体 yítǐ remains (of the dead): 向～告别 pay one's last respects to the remains of the deceased

遗蜕 yítuì 〈书面〉remains (of the dead, usu. of Taoist priests)

Y

遗忘 yíwàng slip one's memory; forget:被～的角落 forgotten corner /我永远不会～他。I will never forget him. /童年的生活,至今尚未～。I still remember my childhood life.
遗忘性失语症 yíwàngxìng shīyǔzhèng 〈医学〉amnesia aphasia
遗忘症 yíwàngzhèng 〈医学〉amnesia:～患者 amnesiac; amnesic
遗文 yíwén writings left behind by the deceased; posthumous papers
遗闻 yíwén tales of old times:访求～ search for old-time tales /这本笔记收集了许多近代政坛～。Many modern political anecdotes were collected in this notebook.
遗物 yíwù thing left behind by the deceased; relic:被害者的～ personal effects of the victim
遗像 yíxiàng portrait or photo of the deceased
遗绪 yíxù 〈书面〉*see*“遗业❶”
遗训 yíxùn teachings of the deceased:～可秉 act on (*or* follow) the teachings of the deceased
遗言 yíyán (a person's) last words; last testament; words of the deceased:这是烈士在他生命的最后时刻留下的～。They are the last words of the martyr as he died.
遗业 yíyè ❶ cause or enterprise left over by one's predecessors ❷ property left by the deceased; legacy
遗愿 yíyuàn unfulfilled wish of the deceased; last wish:实现先烈的～ realise (*or* fulfil) the last wish of the martyr /我从来没有忘记过母亲的～。I've never forgotten the behests of my late mother.
遗泽 yízé bounty or estate left behind by the deceased:斯人已逝,～在民。The people continued to benefit by his work, although he was dead.
遗赠 yízèng give (one's belongings or property to designated persons or institutions) upon one's death; bequeath
遗诏 yízhào imperial edict left behind by an emperor upon his death
遗照 yízhào photos of the deceased before his death
遗址 yízhǐ ruins; relics:凭吊古战场～ pay a visit to the ruins of ancient battle fields
遗志 yízhì unfulfilled wish; work leftover by the deceased:实现先辈的～ carry out the behests of our predecessors
遗珠 yízhū lost pearl — lost treasure or unrecognized talent
遗嘱 yízhǔ ❶ make a will; leave one's last words:他～将其骨灰抛洒于大海。He said in his will that he wanted his ashes to be scattered in the ocean. ❷ will; testament; dying words:立～ make (*or* draw up) a will /未立～ intestate; will-less /～检验 probate (a will)/～赠与 gift by will /～公证 notarization of a will /～执行人 executor (of a will)
遗著 yízhù posthumous work (of an author)
遗踪 yízōng leftover traces; trail; track:追寻～ pursue sb. or sth. by following the traces left behind
遗族 yízú family of the deceased
遗作 yízuò unpublished work of a deceased person; posthumous work:老画家～展 exhibition of a deceased old painter's works

仪[1](儀) yí

❶ appearance; bearing; looks:威～ dignified bearing ❷ ceremony; rite; protocol:礼～ courtesy; protocol /司～ master of ceremonies (MC) ❸ present; gift:菲～ little present; small gift /谢～ present for expressing one's gratitude; thank-you gift ❹ 〈书面〉admire; yearn for; look forward to:心～已久 have long admired sb. ❺ (Yí) a surname

仪[2](儀) yí

apparatus; instrument:地球～ (terrestrial) globe /地震～ seismograph /水准～ surveyor's level; levelling instrument
仪表 yíbiǎo ❶ appearance; looks; bearing:～不凡 striking appearance /美于～ have handsome looks /注意自己的～ be careful about one's manners (*or* deportment) ❷ meter:飞机～ aeroplane meters /～厂 instrument and meter plant /～板 instrument panel; meterboard; (of car, plane) dashboard
仪表堂堂 yíbiǎo-tángtáng dignified in appearance; impressive-looking; imposing:～,名震四海。Noble and dignified, he was a man of great renown.
仪表着陆系统 yíbiǎo zhuólù xìtǒng 〈航空〉instrument landing system (ILS)
仪观 yíguān 〈书面〉appearance; demeanour
仪节 yíjié protocol; etiquette
仪门 yímén 〈旧语〉ceremonial gate (of a magistrate's office)
仪器 yíqì instrument; apparatus:精密～ precision instrument /光学～ optical instrument /电子～ electronic instrument /～厂 instrument plant /～制造业 instrument-making industry
仪容 yíróng looks; appearance:～俊秀 handsome appearance
仪式 yíshì ceremony; rite; function:奠基～ foundation stone laying ceremony /开幕～ opening (*or* inaugural) ceremony /剪彩～ cut the ribbon at an opening ceremony /签字～ ceremony for signing; signing ceremony /宗教～ religious rites /追悼～ funeral service (*or* ceremony) /不拘～ do not stand on ceremony
仪态 yítài 〈书面〉bearing; deportment; carriage; posture:这姑娘～大方,倒是个好人选。The girl has easy and unaffected manners and should be the ideal choice. /演讲时还要注意声调、～。One should take tones and bearing into consideration when making a speech.
仪态万方 yítài-wànfāng *also*“仪态万千”(of a beauty) appear in all her glory or splendour
仪刑 yíxíng *also*“仪型”〈书面〉example; model:人皆景慕而～之。Everyone admire him and holds him up as a model.
仪仗 yízhàng ❶ flags, weapons, etc. carried by the guards when the emperor or high officials went out in ancient times ❷ weapons carried by guards of honour at state ceremonies or welcoming ceremony for foreign guests; flags, slogans, models, etc. carried in the front of a procession
仪仗队 yízhàngduì guard of honour; honour guard:陆海空三军～ guard of honour of the three services /检阅～ review the guard of honour /～的分列式 marching-past of the guard of honour
仪注 yízhù 〈书面〉protocol; etiquette:撰立～ write rules of protocol

迻 yí

〈书面〉*see*“移”yí
迻录 yílù 〈书面〉write down; transcribe:请将此段～另纸。Please transcribe this paragraph on a separate sheet.
迻译 yíyì *also*“移译”yíyì 〈书面〉translate:我拟将此书的主要部分～为法文。I intend to translate the main part of the book into French.

扅 yí

see“扊扅”yǎnyí

栘 yí

栘椛 yíyī 〈植物〉*Docynia delavayi*

移 yí

❶ move; remove; divert; shift:转～ shift; transfer; divert /迁～ remove; migrate; relocate /把菊花～到花盆里去 move the chrysanthemum into the flowerpot /售票处～往别处了。The booking office has moved elsewhere. ❷ change; alter; transform:坚定不～ firm and unshakable; unswerving; unflinching:潜～默化 imperceptibly influence
移调 yídiào 〈音乐〉transposition:～乐器 transposing instrument
移东补西 yídōng-bǔxī resort to a makeshift solution
移动 yídòng ❶ move; shift:～脚步 shift one's feet /敌军正在向西北～。The enemy troops were moving towards the northwest. /他一边说,一边在椅子里～了一下。He said this, shifting in his chair. /有人把公共汽车站牌～了。The bus stop post has been moved. ❷〈机械〉move; travel; shift:～催化裂化 moving-bed catalytic cracking /～电动机 travel motor /～器 shifter /～装置 shifting unit; shifter/～式计算机 movable computer /～喷灌机 travelling sprinkler /～式起重机 mobile hoist (*or* crane); travelling crane; run-about crane /～式输送带 movable apron /～式遥控机械装置 MOBOT (*or* mobile remote-controlled robot)
移动电话 yídòng diànhuà cellular phone; mobile phone
移动电台 yídòng diàntái mobile station:海上无线电导航～ maritime radio navigation mobile station /～通信 mobile service
移动交换中心 yídòng jiāohuàn zhōngxīn 〈通信〉mobile switching centre (MSC)
移防 yífáng (of troops) be moved or shifted elsewhere for garrison duty:这支部队最近已经～。The army unit has taken up garrison duty elsewhere.
移风易俗 yífēng-yìsú transform established social traditions; change prevailing customs and habits:提倡～ advocate the changing of the established social traditions to improve public morals

Y

移晷 yíguǐ move of sunshine (on the sundial) — passage of time: 伏案攻读，～忘倦 not feel tired after bending over one's desk reading for a long time

移行 yíháng (of alphabetical language) divide (a word) with a hyphen at the end of a line and continue at the beginning of the next one

移花接木 yíhuā-jiēmù ❶ graft one twig on another; graft ❷ stealthily substitute one thing for another; surreptitiously replace: 他用～的手段，把王后刚生下的小女孩换了宰相家初生的男孩。He replaced in secret the queen's new-born girl with the new-born boy of the prime minister.

移交 yíjiāo ❶ turn over; transfer; hand over: 这个案件应该～中级法院审理。This case should be transferred to an intermediate court. /英语系把一批国外赠书～给图书馆。The English Department has turned over to the library a number of books presented by foreign institutions. ❷ hand over one's job to a successor: 我退休前还有些工作须～一下。I have some work to hand over before I retire.

移解 yíjiè escort (a prisoner) from one place to another for imprisonment

移居 yíjū move or change one's residence; migrate: 他五十年前～国外。He emigrated abroad 50 years ago.

移苗 yímiáo transplant seedlings

移民 yímín ❶ migrate; emigrate; immigrate; relocate: 向边远地区～ emigrate to remote areas; relocate people (from densely populated areas) in remote areas /三峡～工程 relocation projects of the Three Gorges area ❷ emigrant; immigrant: 申请成为永久性～ apply for permanent immigrant status /这里有一批从内地来的～。There are a group of immigrants here who came from the interior of the country.

移民点 yímíndiǎn settlement; relocation point

移民法 yímínfǎ immigration law

移民局 yímínjú immigration service or office

移民签证 yímín qiānzhèng immigrant visa

移频 yípín 〈通信〉 frequency shift: ～调制器 frequency-shift modulator /～制 frequency-shift system /～制通信 frequency-shift communication/ ～通信系统 frequency-shift communication system

移情 yíqíng ❶ change one's interest or affection: ～山水 become interested in mountains and rivers (*or* scenery) /～别恋 shift one's affection to another person ❷ 〈心理〉 empathize; transfer: ～作用 empathy /～抵抗 transference resistance

移让 yíràng transfer: ～权利 transfer of rights

移山倒海 yíshān-dǎohǎi remove mountains and drain seas; transform nature; make tremendous effort to conquer nature: 我们要以～的精神，完成这项巨大的水利工程。We should complete this giant water conservancy project in the dauntless spirit of conquering nature.

移摄 yíshè 〈摄影〉 moving shot; tracking

移师 yíshī move or shift the troops: ～北上 move the troops northward

移时 yíshí 〈书面〉 after some time; after a while: ～醒来，已是傍晚。It was already dusk when he woke up some time later.

移天易日 yítiān-yìrì *also* "移天换日" shift the heaven and replace the sun — carry out an audacious scheme of deception; deceive one's superiors and subordinates by resorting to intrigues

移位 yíwèi 〈计算机〉 shift: ～计数器 shift (*or* shifting) counter /～寄存器 shift register /～装置 shifter

移徙 yíxǐ move; migrate; change one's residence: 牧民随牲畜～。The herdsmen move along with their cattle.

移项 yíxiàng 〈数学〉 removal of a term to the other side of the equal-sign in solving an equation; transposition

移相 yíxiàng 〈电学〉 phaseshift: ～变压器 phasing transformer; phase-shifting transformer /～器 phaser; phase shifter

移像管 yíxiàngguǎn 〈电子〉 image tube; image converter: 电子～ electron image tube

移译 yíyì *see* "迻译" yíyì

移易 yíyì 〈书面〉 change; alter: 一字不可～。Not a word can be altered (*or* changed). /此乃不可～之法则。This is a hard-and-fast rule.

移用 yíyòng use methods or materials for purposes other than their original ones: 这笔专款不能～。This special fund must not be used for other purposes. /在国外，有人把孙子的用兵之道～于经营管理。Some foreigners have applied Sun-tzu's art of war in business management.

移玉 yíyù 〈书面〉〈敬词〉 please move your footsteps; please come over

移栽 yízāi 〈农业〉 transplant: ～机 transplanter /～机具 transplanting equipment

移植 yízhí ❶ transplant: 这些樱花树是从日本～来的。These cherry blossom trees were transplanted from Japan. ❷ 〈医学〉 transplant; graft: ～手术 transplanting operation /心脏～ heart transplanting /皮肤～ skin graft

移转 yízhuǎn shift; transfer; divert; change: ～视线 divert sb.'s attention /～念头 change one's mind

移樽就教 yízūn-jiùjiào take one's wine cup to another person's table to seek his advice — go to sb. for advice; consult others modestly: 新校长一上任，就向几位老教授～。As soon as he assumed his post, the new president went to several old professors for advice.

簃

yí 〈书面〉 small cabin or hut beside a storeyed building or a pavilion (usu. used in naming a study)

彝[1]（彛）

yí 〈考古〉 ❶ wine vessel: ～器 sacrificial vessel/ 鼎～ wine vessel with two loop handles and three legs ❷ 〈书面〉 law; rule: ～典 common code /～准 common law

彝[2]（彛）

Yí Yi nationality, distributed over Yunnan, Sichuan, and Guizhou provinces

彝剧 Yíjù Yi opera

彝陵之战 Yílíng Zhī Zhàn *also* "猇亭之战" Xiāotíng Zhī Zhàn Battle of Yilin, famous battle in which the weak army of the Kingdom of Wu defeated the strong army of the Kingdom of Shu in 222 during the Three Kingdoms Period

彝族 Yízú Yi nationality

疑

yí ❶ doubt; disbelieve; suspect: 半信半～ half-believing, half-doubting; not quite convinced /形迹可～ of suspicious appearance; suspicious-looking /无可置～ beyond doubt; undoubtedly /迟～ hesitant ❷ doubtful; suspicious; uncertain: ～事 suspicious matter /析～ explain doubtful points /存～ leave the question open /质～问难 call in question; raise doubts; put forward difficult questions for discussion

疑案 yí'àn ❶ doubtful or disputed case: 因为证据不足，这个案子至今还是～。The case still remains a disputed one for lack of evidence. ❷ open question; mystery: 这位皇帝的死因是千古～。The death of the emperor is an eternal mystery.

疑兵 yíbīng troops deployed to mislead the enemy; deceptive deployment: 巧布～，大溃敌军。We routed the enemy troops by (using) deceptive deployment.

疑病 yíbìng 〈医学〉 hypochondria; hypochondriasis: ～患者 hypochondriac

疑猜 yícāi harbour suspicions; be distrustful; have misgivings: 引起～ arouse suspicions

疑点 yídiǎn doubtful or questionable point: 消除～ clear up doubtful points /这件事的～甚多。There are quite a few questionable points about the matter. /听了他的解释，我仍有一些～。In spite of his explanation, I still have doubts about certain points.

疑窦 yídòu 〈书面〉 cause for suspicion; doubtful point: ～丛生 full of suspicions /这篇文章虽有可取之处，但～百出，不足以使人信服。Although the article has some merits, it is not convincing because there are many points that raise suspicion.

疑端 yíduān doubtful or questionable point; doubt; suspicion: ～顿生 suddenly become suspicious /多有～ have quite a few doubtful points

疑怪 yíguài feel puzzled and suspicious

疑惑 yíhuò feel puzzled; be doubtful: 经他这么一说，我心里也～起来。I myself began to feel puzzled after hearing what he had said. /我们现在对这消息不再有～了。We have no more doubts about the news now.

疑忌 yíjì be suspicious; distrust: 心怀～ feel suspicious /～功臣 distrust and have misgivings about ministers and generals who performed outstanding service

疑惧 yíjù apprehensions; misgivings: 我心中～不安。I was assailed with misgivings. /她用～的眼光看着那个人。She looked at the man, her eyes filled with apprehensions.

疑虑 yílǜ misgivings; doubts; uncertainties: 心存～ have doubts in one's mind /解除～ clear one's mind of doubt; free sb. from doubts and misgivings

疑谜 yímí mystery; enigma; riddle: 这案子还是一团～。The case is still a mystery.

疑难 yínán difficult; thorny; knotty: 解决～问题 solve a knotty problem /～病症 difficult and complicated cases (of illness)

疑难杂症 yínán zázhèng cases (of illness) that are both hard to diagnose and to cure; difficult and complicated problems: 这个医院有几位老中医, 专门诊断～。Some old doctors of traditional Chinese medicine in the hospital specialize in diagnosing all kinds of difficult and complicated cases.

疑念 yíniàn doubts; misgivings: 他心中顿生～。He was suddenly gripped by misgivings.

疑人勿使,使人勿疑 yí rén wù shǐ, shǐ rén wù yí *also* "疑人不用, 用人不疑" if you suspect a man, don't employ him; if you employ a man, don't suspect him — trust people who work for you

疑神疑鬼 yíshén-yíguǐ be even afraid of one's own shadow; be unreasonably suspicious: 要大刀阔斧地去干, 别那么～的。Go ahead with boldness and resolution. Don't be so timid and suspicious.

疑似 yísì partly certain and partly uncertain: ～之词 ambiguous remarks

疑团 yítuán doubts and suspicions: 虽经他反复说明, 仍然排解不开我心中的～。Even his repeated explanations could not free my mind of all the doubts and suspicions.

疑问 yíwèn query; question; doubt: 毫无～, 这件事是他干的。He did it; that's beyond any doubt.

疑问句 yíwènjù 〈语言〉interrogative sentence

疑心 yíxīn ❶ suspicion: 起～ become suspicious of or about sb. or sth. /这件事引起他的～。This aroused his suspicion. ❷ suspect; wonder: 我～他另有企图。I suspect that he has ulterior motives. /她～自己搞错了。She was afraid that she might be mistaken. /他～自己没有痊愈的希望了。He wondered if he had any chance of recovery.

疑心病 yíxīnbìng suspicious frame of mind; paranoia: 这人～太重。He is over-suspicious (*or* paranoiac).

疑心生暗鬼 yíxīn shēng ànguǐ suspicions create grotesque fears: 他是～, 把我的话尽往坏处想了。He was so suspicious that he thought I had ulterior motives for saying this.

疑讶 yíyà feel puzzled and surprised; be both confused and astonished: 她～地看着他, 半天说不出话来。Looking at him in confusion and astonishment, she was speechless for a long time.

疑义 yíyì doubt; doubtful point: 毫无～, 这是他的笔迹。It is his hand, beyond a shadow of doubt. /大家对他的能力没有～。No one doubted his ability.

疑狱 yíyù 〈书面〉lawsuit in which it is difficult to pronounce a judgment: 善断～ good at cracking complex cases

疑云 yíyún suspicion clouding one's mind; doubt: 驱散～ dispel suspicion /～难消。Misgivings are hard to dispel (*or* clear up).

疑阵 yízhèn deceptive battle array to confuse the enemy; stratagem: 布下～ display a misleading array; lay a deceptive trap

嶷

yí *used in place names*: 九～ Jiuyi, name of a mountain in Hunan Province

see also nì

嶷

yí

嶷嶷 yíyí (of an animal horn) sharp and pointed

怡

yí 〈书面〉be happy or joyful: 心旷神～ feel relaxed and happy; be in a cheerful frame of mind /～声下气 speak with a pleasing voice and in a respectful and submissive manner

怡和 yíhé 〈书面〉amiable; genial; happy: 神情～ look amiable; be happy

怡和洋行 Yíhé Yánghóng (HK) Jardin Matheson (Holdings) Ltd.

怡乐 yílè happy; cheerful; joyful

怡情悦性 yíqíng-yuèxìng *also* "怡情理性" feel happy and free from all worries; feel cheerful and relaxed: 闲来也看看电视, 听听音乐, 以～。I watch TV and listen to music after work, just to relax.

怡然 yírán happy; contented; satisfied: 神情～ looking happy and relaxed

怡然自得 yírán-zìdé be happy and satisfied; feel a glow of happiness: 居室虽小, 他生活在里面却～。Small as the room was, he felt happy and contented living in it.

怡神 yíshén 〈书面〉become relaxed and happy: ～养性 cultivate one's temperament and feel relaxed

怡悦 yíyuè happy; joyous: 心情～ with a feeling of joy /～自得 feel happy and contented

诒

yí 〈书面〉*see* "贻" yí

贻

yí 〈书面〉❶ send sb. a gift; make sb. a present of sth.: 馈～ present a gift /花～专家学者 present specialists and scholars with flowers /～我诗帕。A handkerchief inscribed with a poem was given to me as a gift. ❷ bequeath; leave behind: 将其杰作～于国家博物馆 bequeath his masterpiece to the national museum /～范古今 leave a good example to later generations /无数珍宝, ～于后人。Countless treasures were passed on to later generations.

贻贝 yíbèi *also* "壳菜" qiàocài; "淡菜" dàncài 〈动物〉mussel

贻臭万年 yíchòu-wànnián *see* "遗臭万年" yíchòu-wànnián

贻害 yíhài leave a legacy of trouble to: ～将来 leave trouble to the future

贻害无穷 yíhài-wúqióng cause no end of trouble; entail untold harm: 此风不纠, 必将～。If this practice is left unchecked, there will be endless trouble in the future.

贻患 yíhuàn leave trouble; sow seeds of disaster: ～后代 leave endless trouble to posterity

贻人口实 yírén-kǒushí give occasion for ridicule; provide one's critic with a handle: 偶一不慎, ～。An accidental imprudence gives people grounds for ridicule.

贻误 yíwù adversely affect; miss; bungle: ～战机 bungle (*or* miss) the chance of winning a battle; forfeit a chance for combat /～农时 miss the farming season /～终身 bring ruin upon one's whole life /～后学 mislead the young students /把～的时间夺回来 make up for lost time

贻笑大方 yíxiào-dàfāng make a laughing stock of oneself before connoisseurs; incur the ridicule of experts: 班门弄斧, ～ display one's incompetence before an expert and make a fool of oneself

贻训 yíxùn *also* "遗训" yíxùn teachings of the deceased

饴

yí maltose: 甘之如～ enjoy sth. bitter as if it were sweet as malt sugar; gladly endure hardships/高粱～ sorghum candy

饴糖 yítáng maltose; malt sugar

诡（訑、詑）

yí 〈书面〉be pleased with oneself

诡诡 yíyí 〈书面〉self-complacent; conceited: ～之声音颜色, 拒人于千里之外。Complacency, either in expression or in voice, serves to keep people at a distance.

迤（迆）

yí *see* "逶迤" wēiyí

see also yǐ

椸（杝）

yí 〈古语〉tree similar to white poplar

see also duò

椸（箷）

yí 〈书面〉coat hanger; clothes-rack; clothes tree

匜

yí 〈考古〉ladle shaped like a gourd; gourd-shaped ladle

眙

yí 〈书面〉move; shift

see also yì

yǐ

扆

yǐ ❶〈古语〉a kind of screen ❷ (Yǐ) a surname

旖

yǐ

旖旎 yǐnǐ 〈书面〉charming and gentle; enchanting: 春色～ charming scenery of spring /五光十色、万般～的花丛 colourful and attrac-

tive flower clusters /湖山交辉，风光～ enchanting scene with splendid lakes and mountains

椅 yǐ chair：～垫 chair cushion /藤～ cane chair；rattan chair/竹～ bamboo chair /躺～ deck chair；sling chair /转～ swivel chair；revolving chair /轮～ wheelchair /桌～板凳 desks，chairs and benches
see also yī

椅背 yǐbèi back of a chair

椅披 yǐpī decorative chair cover，usu. made of red silk and satin or cotton cloth，forming a complete set with chair cushions and table-enclosing cloth，still used in traditional Chinese operas

椅套 yǐtào slipcover for a chair

椅子 yǐzi chair

椅子顶 yǐzidǐng 〈杂技〉balancing on a pyramid of chairs

齮 yǐ 〈书面〉bite；snap at

齮龁 yǐhé 〈书面〉❶ bite；gnaw；nibble ❷ hate out of envy；engage in internal strife

踦 yǐ 〈书面〉prop up；sustain；support；withstand

倚 yǐ ❶ lean on or against；rest on or against：～门而望 lean on the door and gaze into the distance /～树而立 stand leaning against a tree ❷ rely on；depend on；count on：～官仗势 take advantage of one's power and position；count on one's powerful connections /～财仗势 exploit one's wealth and power ❸〈书面〉biased；prejudiced；partial：中立而不～ remain neutral；be unbiased；stay impartial

倚傍 yǐbàng ❶ rely on；depend on ❷（mostly of arts and learning）imitate；copy；model oneself on

倚伏 yǐfú 〈书面〉interdependence and mutual transformation：祸福～ ill luck and good fortune depend on and transform into each other

倚酒三分醉 yǐ jiǔ sān fēn zuì （after drinking some wine）behave with impropriety as if one were drunk：～地大喊大叫 cry loudly though only half drunk；yell like a drunkard

倚靠 yǐkào ❶ lean on or against；rest on or against：～着桥上的石栏杆 lean on the stone balustrade of the bridge /她紧紧地～着我。She nestled（up）to me. ❷ rely on；depend on；count on：我们有许多事情要～他。We have to depend on him for help in many things.

倚赖 yǐlài rely on；be dependent on：以不～别人为荣 take pride in being independent of others（*or* in one's independence）/作出这样的结论，必须完全～事实。To draw such a conclusion one must completely rely on facts.

倚老卖老 yǐlǎo-màilǎo show self-importance for being aged；flaunt one's seniority：他～，不把我们放在眼里。Flaunting his seniority he regarded us as beneath his notice.

倚马可待 yǐmǎ-kědài *also*"倚马千言" have a ready pen；write quickly：此人年少博学，下笔千言，～。Young but erudite，he had a facile pen.

倚门倚闾 yǐmén-yǐlǘ （of parents）wait eagerly for their children to come home：学成早归，以免父母～。One should return home upon completing his studies，so as to free his parents from anxious waiting.

倚强凌弱 yǐqiáng-língruò *see*"以强凌弱" yǐqiáng-língruò

倚声 yǐshēng *also*"填词" tiáncí compose a poem to a given tune of *ci*

倚势 yǐshì take advantage of power and position（to do evil）：～凌人 use one's power and influence to bully others

倚恃 yǐshì rely on；count on：～权势 rely on one's power and position /光～一点小聪明是不可能成功的。One cannot possibly succeed by resorting to petty tricks.

倚托 yǐtuō rely on；depend on：～祖上的基业 depend on one's family inheritance

倚偎 yǐwēi lean on or against affectionately；nestle against：孩子紧紧～在母亲身边。The child nestled against her mother.

倚音 yǐyīn 〈音乐〉appoggiatura

倚仗 yǐzhàng bank on；count on：～人多势众 count on one's numerical strength；exploiting one's numerical advantage /～有人撑腰 bank on someone's backing

倚重 yǐzhòng value and trust：他是一位为大家所～的老前辈。People respected and trusted him as their senior. /他～几个得力的助手。He leaned heavily on several competent assistants. /他的小说过于～技巧。He attached too much importance to technique in his novel.

目 yǐ 〈书面〉*see*"以" yǐ

苢 yǐ *see*"芣苢" fúyǐ

颉（顗） yǐ 〈书面〉quiet；tranquil

蛾 yǐ 〈书面〉*see*"蚁" yǐ
see also é

蚁（蟻、❶螘） yǐ ❶ ant：兵～ soldier ant；dinergate/工～ ergate；worker ant /雄～ aner /雌～ gyne /白～ termite；white ant /食～兽 ant eater /蝼～ mole cricket and ant；tiny organism；〈比喻〉those of humble background ❷（Yǐ）a surname

蚁蚕 yǐcán 〈动物〉newly-hatched silkworm

蚁巢 yǐcháo ant nest

蚁垤 yǐdié 〈书面〉*see*"蚁封"

蚁封 yǐfēng mound of earth heaped by ants outside their nest；ant hill

蚁后 yǐhòu gyne；ant queen

蚁䴕 yǐliè 〈动物〉wryneck

蚁蛉虫 yǐlíngchóng doodlebug，nickname for V-rocket in World War II

蚁民 yǐmín 〈旧语〉term mostly used by common people to refer to themselves in a petition to the authorities

蚁命 yǐmìng humble life

蚁丘 yǐqiū ant hill

蚁醛 yǐquán *also*"甲醛" jiǎquán formaldehyde

蚁狮 yǐshī ant lion

蚁酸 yǐsuān *also*"甲酸" jiǎsuān formic acid；methanoic acid

蚁冢 yǐzhǒng ant hill

舣（艤、檥） yǐ 〈书面〉pull in a boat to shore

乙[1] yǐ ❶ second of the ten Heavenly Stems ❷ second：～等 second grade；grade B ❸（Yǐ）a surname

乙[2] yǐ 〈音乐〉note of the scale in *gongchepu*（工尺谱），corresponding to 7 in numbered musical notation

乙[3] yǐ often a mark or sign（ㄥ）formerly used in reading unpunctuated classical Chinese to show where one stops，or the end of a paragraph，or in writing to correct an omission or to indicate a transposition

乙胺 yǐ'àn 〈化学〉ethylamine；aminoethane

乙苯 yǐběn 〈化学〉ethylbenzene；phenylethane

乙部 yǐbù *also*"史部" shǐbù division of history，second of the four categories of Chinese bibliography
see also"四部" sìbù

乙叉 yǐchā 〈化学〉ethidene；ethylidene

乙醇 yǐchún *also*"酒精" jiǔjīng 〈化学〉ethanol；alcohol

乙醇中毒 yǐchún zhòngdú ethylism

乙肝 yǐgān （short for 乙型肝炎）hepatitis B

乙基 yǐjī 〈化学〉ethyl：～化 ethylation；ethylization /～化物 ethylate /～氯 ethyl chloride；chloroethane /～汽油 ethylated gasoline；ethyl gasoline /～纤维素 ethyl cellulose

乙级股 yǐjígǔ 〈金融〉beta

乙阶酚醛树脂 yǐjiē fēnquán shùzhī 〈化工〉resitol B-stage resin

乙腈 yǐjīng 〈化学〉acetonitrile；ethane nitrile；methyl cyanide

乙醚 yǐmí 〈化学〉ether

乙脑 yǐnǎo （short for 乙型脑炎）〈医学〉meningitis B

乙醛 yǐquán 〈化学〉acetic aldehyde；acetaldehyde

乙炔 yǐquē 〈化学〉acetylene；ethyne：～焊 acetylene welding/～发生器 acetylene generator/～灯 acetylene burner

乙酸 yǐsuān 〈化学〉acetic acid；acetidin；ethanoic acid：～纤维 acetate fibre/～纤维素 cellulose acetate / ～铵 ammonium acetate

乙烷 yǐwán 〈化学〉 ethane
乙烯 yǐxī 〈化学〉 ethylene; ethene
乙烯醇 yǐxīchún vinyl alcohol; ethenol
乙烯基 yǐxījī vinyl
乙烯醚 yǐxīmí vinyl ether
乙烯树脂 yǐxī shùzhī ethenoid resin; ethylene resin; polyethylene; polyethylene resin
乙烯塑料 yǐxī sùliào vinyl group of plastics
乙酰 yǐxiān *also* "乙酰基"〈化学〉 acethyl
乙酰胆硷 yǐxiān dǎnjiǎn acetylcholine
乙酰基 yǐxiānjī *see* "乙酰"
乙酰水杨酸 yǐxiān shuǐyángsuān ❶〈化学〉 acetylsalicylic acid ❷〈药学〉 aspirin
乙酰唑胺 yǐxiān zuò'àn 〈药学〉 acetazolamide; diamox
乙型超声波 yǐxíng chāoshēngbō *also* "B超" B-mode ultrasound
乙型肝炎 yǐxíng gānyán *also* "乙肝" serum hepatitis; hepatitis B
乙型脑炎 yǐxíng nǎoyán *also* "乙脑" meningitis B (*meningitis cerebrospinalis epidemica*)
乙夜 yǐyè second watch at around 10 o'clock at night
乙种粒子 yǐzhǒng lìzǐ 〈物理〉 beta particle
乙种射线 yǐzhǒng shèxiàn 〈物理〉 beta ray
乙状结肠 yǐzhuàng jiécháng 〈生理〉 sigmoid; sigmoid colon: ~镜 sigmoidoscope / ~镜检查 sigmoidoscopy / ~炎 sigmoiditis

钇

yǐ yttrium (Y)

以[1]

yǐ ❶ use; take: ~农业为基础 take agriculture as the foundation / ~丰补歉 store up in fat years to make up for lean ones; have high yield areas help low yield areas / ~工补农 use industry to supplement (*or* subsidize) agriculture; have industry help agriculture/晓之~利害 enable sb. to see the advantages and disadvantages / ~诚相待 treat people with sincerity / ~大局为重 set store by the overall situation (*or* interests) / ~实际工作经验而论，我不如他。In terms of practical work experience, I am no match for him. /这块地~种大豆为宜。This plot is suitable for growing soybeans. ❷ according to; in order of: 平均每户~四口计算 according to an average of four people per household / ~姓氏笔画为序 in order of the number of strokes of a person's surname /物~类聚 birds of a feather flock together ❸ because of; for; by: 不~言举人 not promote (*or* recommend) a person by what he says (only)/长城~其雄伟而闻名于世。The Great Wall is known to the world for its magnificent grandeur. /何~为由? What is the reason? ❹ in order to; so as to; for: ~博一笑 in order to elicit a smile; so as to amuse sb. /坐~待旦 sit to wait for daybreak /降格~求 settle for second best /发展轻工业，~满足人民日益增长的需要 develop light industry to meet the growing needs of the people ❺〈书面〉 at (a certain time); on (a fixed date): ~公元一九五六年三月五日生于西安 born in Xi'an on 5 March 1956 / 今年暑假~七月十五日始，八月三十一日终。The summer vacation this year will start on July the fifteenth and end on August the thirty-first. ❻〈书面〉〈连词〉(used in the same way as 而) and; as well as: 水阔~深。The river is wide and deep. /其责己也重~周，其待人也轻~约。They were strict with themselves but lenient to others. /木欣欣~向荣。The trees were thriving.

以[2]

yǐ *used before words of locality to indicate the limits of time, place, direction or number*: 有生~来 ever since one was born /三日~后 in three days; three days later /长此~往 continue like this for a long time /处级~上 above the department level /长江~南 south of the Yangtze River /三十岁~下 below thirty years of age /三日~内完成任务 accomplish the task within three days
以暴易暴 yǐbào-yìbào replace one tyranny or despotic rule by another: 一家失势，他家代之，~而已矣。When one family lost power, another family took its place, thus merely replacing one tyranny by another.
以备不虞 yǐbèi-bùyú be prepared for all possible contingencies: 我们要多准备几手，~。Various options should be prepared for unforeseen circumstances.
以便 yǐbiàn so that; in order to; with a view to; for the purpose of: 你把材料准备好，~开会研究。Get the reference material ready so that it may be discussed at the meeting. /本社今年起设立邮购部，~更好地为读者服务。Beginning from this year, this publishing house will start a mail-order department so as to better serve our readers.
以不变应万变 yǐ bùbiàn yìng wànbiàn cope with all changes by remaining unchanged — deal with a volatile situation by adhering to a fixed principle: 有了这几套方案，工作中就能~，始终处于主动。With these options to choose from, we can cope with any contingency unperturbed, and keep the initiative in our own hands.
以词害意 yǐcí-hàiyì the words interfere with the sense; sacrifice the meaning for the sake of words: 写作中不可~。One should not embellish the words at the expense of the sense in writing.
以此类推 yǐcǐ-lèituī deduce the rest from this; infer on the analogy of this; the rest can be done in the same manner
以此为戒 yǐcǐ-wéijiè take this as a lesson; take warning from this: 不遵守规定者，应~。Those who defy the regulations must take this as a warning.
以次 yǐcì ❶ in proper order; in sequence: ~购票 book tickets one by one / ~通报姓名 announce the names in order ❷ the following: ~各项还应重新商定。The following items will have to be reconsidered.
以德报德 yǐdé-bàodé return or repay good for good; one good turn deserves another: 这个厂以前帮助过我们，我们要~，帮他们渡过这次难关。This factory helped us before. As one good turn deserves another, we should help them tide over the present crisis.
以德报怨 yǐdé-bàoyuàn return good for evil; repay ingratitude with kindness: 君子不念旧恶，~。A gentleman gives no thought to old grievances and requites ingratitude with kindness (*or* repays good for evil).
以点带面 yǐdiǎn-dàimiàn fan out from a point to an area; spread the experience gained at selected units to an entire area: 做工作要善于~，在一个地区取得经验后，再推广开去。In our work, we should be good at popularizing our successful experience by applying what we have achieved at selected units to the work in the entire area.
以毒攻毒 yǐdú-gōngdú combat poison with poison; use poison as an antidote to poison; set a thief to catch a thief: 据说以蛇毒为成分的药物治麻风病，可以收到~的效果。It is said that a medicine made of snake poison can cure leprosy, for it has the effect of combating poison with poison.
以讹传讹 yǐ'é-chuán'é circulate or spread an erroneous message; pass on a rumour or an erroneous story; propagate an error or falsehood: 这件事~，完全走了样。Having been wrongly relayed the matter was totally distorted.
以耳代目 yǐ'ěr-dàimù rely on hearsay instead of seeing for oneself; hear and believe: 官僚主义的特征之一就是~，脱离实际。One of the characteristics of bureaucratism is to rely on reports instead of on-the-spot investigation, thus divorcing themselves from reality.
以防万一 yǐfáng-wànyī ready for any eventuality; prepared for all contingencies; (just) in case: 从目前情况看，这次洪峰对我县的威胁不大，但也要做好准备，~。At the moment the flood peak does not pose a great threat to our county. However, we should be prepared just in case.
以工代赈 yǐgōng-dàizhèn give relief to people by employing them to build public utility works; provide jobs as a form of relief; provide work-relief: 在灾区修复堤坝，~。Dams and dikes were repaired in disaster areas to provide work-relief for the victims.
以功补过 yǐgōng-bǔguò make up for one's mistake by rendering meritorious service
以攻为守 yǐgōng-wéishǒu use offence as a means of defence; attack in order to defend: 采取~的策略 employ the tactics of mounting attack as a means of defence
以古非今 yǐgǔ-fēijīn use the past to attack the present; disparage the present by extolling the past
以寡敌众 yǐguǎ-dízhòng pit the few against the many; fight against all the odds: 敌军~，势难持久。The enemy troops cannot hope to last long when fighting against such overwhelming odds.
以观后效 yǐguān-hòuxiào (lighten a punishment and) see if the offender mends his ways: 给他一段改正错误的时间，~。Give him some time to correct his mistakes and see how he will behave.
以管窥天 yǐguǎn-kuītiān look at the sky through a tube; have a narrow and biased view: ~，妄加评语 take a narrow-minded view and make improper comments
以广招徕 yǐguǎng-zhāolái so as to attract more customers; with a view to promoting sales; for promotional purpose: 树立产品形象，~

establish the reputation of a product and promote its sales

以后 yǐhòu after; afterwards; later; since: 从今～ from now on / 从那～,我再也没见过他。I've never seen him again since then. /毕业～ after graduation /十年～ ten years later /我们不能只顾眼前利益,要多为～想想。We should not think of immediate interests only but must take the future into consideration. /那是很久～的事情,现在谁也无法预料。That will be a matter for the distant future. No one can predict it now.

以还 yǐhuán 〈书面〉since; after: 隋唐～,方兴科举。The imperial examination system was not established until the Sui and Tang dynasties.

以火救火 yǐhuǒ-jiùhuǒ try to extinguish fire with fire — a wrong method of handling affairs; aggravate the situation; worsen the matter: 用你这种办法去调解他们的纠纷,无异于～。Your way of mediating between them is no different from trying to pour oil on the flames.

以及 yǐjí 〈连词〉as well as; along with; in addition: 中国～全世界 China as well as the rest of the world /亚洲～太平洋地区 Asia and the Pacific region /本店经销录像机、电视机、收录机,～其他音响设备。This shop deals in video-recorders, television sets, radio cassette players and other acoustic equipments.

以己度人 yǐjǐ-duórén judge others by oneself; put oneself in sb. else's shoes; measure others' corn by one's own bushel: 你如有～之心,这件事就好办多了。If you could put yourself in other people's shoes, things would be much better.

以假乱真 yǐjiǎ-luànzhēn mix the spurious with the genuine; create confusion by passing off the fake as the real thing: 他仿齐白石的画达到了～的程度。His imitation of Qi Baishi's drawings was so good that it was difficult to tell the fake from the real thing.

以解倒悬 yǐjiě-dàoxuán free sb. from distress: 备受战火煎熬的各国人民,盼望早日停战,～。People in the war-devastated countries desired an early armistice so as to relieve their sufferings.

以近 yǐjìn 〈交通〉up to: 今天只出售武汉～的车票。Tickets only up to Wuhan are sold today.

以儆效尤 yǐjǐng-xiàoyóu punish sb. as a warning to others; make an example of sb.: 对这几个欺行霸市的人要从严处理,～。Those who rig (*or* corner) the market must be severely punished to serve as a warning to others.

以来 yǐlái since: 近一个时期～ in recent years; of late /改革开放十五年～,我们取得了巨大成就。We have scored great achievements over the last fifteen years since the implementation of the policy of reform and opening to the outside world.

以泪洗面 yǐlèi-xǐmiàn have a tearful face; swim with tears: 丈夫去世以后,她悲痛欲绝,整日～。She's been wearing a woebegone look ever since her husband's death.

以蠡测海 yǐlí-cèhǎi measure the sea with a ladle; have a very superficial view: ～之论 narrow view; shallow argument

以礼相待 yǐlǐ-xiāngdài treat sb. with due respect; be polite to people: 对外国友人要～。Treat foreign friends with courtesy.

以理服人 yǐlǐ-fúrén convince people by reasoning: 对于错误的意见,不是压服,而是说服,～。We should argue things out with those who hold wrong opinions so as to convince them by reasoning instead of by coercion.

以力服人 yǐlì-fúrén resort to coercive measures to force sb. to submit: 压服的结果总是压而不服,～是不行的。Coercion always results in defiance. Forcing people to submit will not work.

以邻为壑 yǐlín-wéihè use one's neighbour's field as a drain — shift one's troubles onto others; benefit oneself at the expense of others: 这家工厂～,把污水排到我们这里来了。The factory is shifting its problem onto us by draining polluted water to our side.

以卵投石 yǐluǎn-tóushí *also* "以卵击石" throw an egg against a rock — overrate oneself and court defeat by fighting sb. far stronger: 我们仅有三千人,去和几十万的秦兵死拼,实在是～。We only had three thousand men. If we pitted ourselves against several hundred thousand Qin troops, we would be courting certain defeat.

以貌取人 yǐmào-qǔrén judge people by appearances: ～就难免会看错人,把有真才实学的人冷落了。If we judge people solely by their appearance, we would go badly awry and leave talented people out in the cold.

以免 yǐmiǎn 〈连词〉in order to avoid or prevent; lest: 应该总结一下教训,～再发生类似事件。We should draw a lesson from this in order to avoid the recurrence of similar incidents. /要做好防汛工作,～临时措手不及。We must do a good job of flood prevention so as not to be caught unprepared.

以沫相濡 yǐmò-xiāngrú *also* "相濡以沫" (of stranded fish) moisten each other with spit — render mutual help and relief in time of difficulty: ～的知己 bosom friends who give each other whatever help they can in time of difficulty /患难之中,～,使他们建立了真挚的爱情。Their mutual support in time of adversity helped to develop genuine love between them.

以内 yǐnèi inside; within; less than: 会场～inside the meeting hall/千字～的文章 article not exceeding one thousand words /三小时～ within three hours /这是你们权限～的事情,不必请示。This matter falls within your competence, so you do not need to ask for instructions. /这项工程在计划～。This project is included in the plan. /随身行李限制在二十公斤～。No more than 20 kilos of hand-carried luggage is allowed.

以偏概全 yǐpiān-gàiquán regard the part as the whole; be lopsided: 要全面看问题,不能～。We should avoid a one-sided approach and look at problems all-sidedly.

以期 yǐqī so as to: 反复核对,～准确无误。Check and cross-check to avoid mistakes. /再接再励,～全胜。Make persistent efforts for a complete victory.

以其昏昏,使人昭昭 yǐ qí hūnhūn, shǐ rén zhāozhāo try to enlighten others while one remains in darkness oneself: ～,真是可笑! It is ridiculous trying to enlighten others while in darkness oneself!

以其人之道,还治其人之身 yǐ qí rén zhī dào, huán zhì qí rén zhī shēn pay sb. back in his own coin; repay in kind; give sb. a dose of his own medicine; do unto him as he does unto others

以前 yǐqián before; ago; formerly; previously: ～我们并不认识。We didn't know each other before. /十年～,这里还是一片荒地。Ten years ago, this place was a wasteland. /很久～,有这么一个美丽的传说。Once upon a time there was a beautiful legend. /这个地方跟～大不一样了。This place is very different from what it used to be.

以强凌弱 yǐqiáng-língruò the strong bullying the weak: 在国际关系中,我们反对以大欺小,～。In international relations we are opposed to the big coercing the small and the strong bullying the weak.

以求 yǐqiú in order to; in an attempt to: ～一逞 in an attempt to fulfil one's ambition; in a bid for success /～自保 in the hope of protecting oneself /～相安无事 in order to live in peace with each other

以屈求伸 yǐqū-qiúshēn bend in order to straighten up; fall back so as to leap better: 在古代,有的小国用～的策略,灭掉了强大的邻国。In ancient times a small country sometimes managed to destroy its powerful neighbour by employing the tactics of "retreating in order to attack".

以权谋私 yǐquán-móusī abuse one's power for personal gains; seek personal benefit by taking advantage of one's power and position: 当干部的不能～。Those who serve as cadres should not abuse their power for personal gains.

以人废言 yǐrén-fèiyán reject an opinion because the speaker is in disgrace or not to one's liking: 不以言为罪,不～。Punish no one for what he says and reject no opinion because the speaker is out of favour.

以人为镜 yǐrén-wéijìng *also* "以人为鉴" benefit from others' advice or experience: ～可以明得失。To listen to others' advice will enable one to see clearly one's own strengths and weaknesses.

以色列 Yǐsèliè Israel: ～人 Israeli; Israelite

以色列议会 Yǐsèliè Yìhuì Knesset (Israeli parliament)

以上 yǐshàng ❶ more than; exceeding; over; above: 半山～,终年积雪。The mountain is snow-covered half way up. /这件事三十岁～的可能还记得。People above thirty may still remember this incident. /今年的产量比去年增加一成～。The output this year has increased more than 10% over that of last year. ❷ above; foregoing; above-mentioned: ～几点请立即传达到基层。The above-mentioned points should be communicated (*or* relayed) to the grass roots level immediately. /我对你～所谈的观点不完全同意。I do not entirely agree with what you have said.

以身试法 yǐshēn-shìfǎ defy or challenge the law personally: 这是一起监守自盗,～的案件。This is a case involving someone who, in defiance of the law, stole what was entrusted to his care.

以身相许 yǐshēn-xiāngxǔ (of a girl) pledge to marry sb.: 姑娘被小伙子的诚心所打动,遂～。Touched by the young man's sincere love, the girl decided to marry him.

以身殉国 yǐshēn-xùnguó lay down one's life for one's country;

die a martyr in the service of one's country：他祖父是一位抗日将领，在战场上～。His grandfather was a general during the anti-Japanese war who died in battle for his country.

以身殉职 yǐshēn-xùnzhí die at one's post; die in harness：这位仓库保管员，在与歹徒搏斗中～。The warehouseman died at his post while fighting the thugs.

以身作则 yǐshēn-zuòzé set an example with one's own conduct; set a personal example：领导干部更应～，严守法令。Leading cadres in particular should set an example in strictly abiding by the laws and decrees.

以手加额 yǐshǒu-jiā'é put one's hand on one's forehead to show respect, rejoicing or gratitude：此公复出，人们无不～，同庆国家有救。When that respected man was rehabilitated, people all felt elated, hailing him as a saviour of the country.

以守为攻 yǐshǒu-wéigōng use defence as a means of offence：我军决定暂时～，消耗敌人的兵力。Our army decided to use defence as a means of offence so as to wear down the enemy troops.

以售其奸 yǐshòu-qíjiān so as to pursue one's evil plot; in order to achieve one's treacherous purpose：利用某些人的无知～ achieve one's evil purposes by explorting the ignorance of some people

以税代利 yǐshuì-dàilì (of a state-owned enterprise) pay tax in lieu of handing over profits; substitute taxation for profit delivery to the state

以太 yǐtài 〈物理〉ether

以太网 yǐtàiwǎng 〈信息〉ethernet

以汤沃雪 yǐtāng-wòxuě melt snow with hot water — work that requires little effort：以他的才干，办这件事自然是～，马到功成。For a person of his ability, it is no doubt an easy job and promises instant success.

以汤止沸 yǐtāng-zhǐfèi add boiling water to stop the pot from boiling — adopt a wrong method of doing things; be of no avail：你这种～的办法只会使情况更混乱。The erroneous method you adopted could only add to the confusion.

以天下为己任 yǐ tiānxià wéi jǐ rèn take the destiny of one's country as one's own; regard the future of one's country as one's own responsibility

以退为进 yǐtuì-wéijìn retreat in order to advance; fall back so as to move forward; make concessions to gain advantages

以外 yǐwài beyond; outside; other or more than; except：山海关～ beyond Shanhaiguan Pass (i.e. in northeast China) /课堂～ outside the classroom /不觉已走出十里～ have covered more than ten *li* without realizing it /除小张～，所有的人都通知到了。Everyone has been notified except Xiao Zhang. /正文～还有两个附录。There are two appendices to the main body of the text. /他已是五十岁～了。He is already over fifty.

以往 yǐwǎng before; formerly; previously; in the past：～的生活经历 one's previous life experience /足球队改变了～的战术。The football team has changed the tactics it formerly used. /在～，这事就会说成是政治路线错误。In the past, this would have been described as an error of the political line. /～，他常来我家。He used to come to my home very often.

以为 yǐwéi think; believe; consider：我原～这样是正确的。I believed this to be true. /他们～当务之急是提高教学质量。They consider it a task of top priority to improve the quality of teaching. /大家的意见，他不～然。He took exception to our opinions. /我总～人的一生应该是有意义的一生。I'm of the opinion (*or* It is my view) that a man should lead a meaningful life.

以…为… yǐ…wéi… take... as...; regard... as...; consider... to be...：以雷锋为榜样 take Lei Feng as one's role model; model oneself upon Lei Feng /以助人为乐 regard it as a pleasure to help others /不以人的意志为转移的客观规律 objective laws independent of man's will /以自力更生为主 depend mainly on self-reliance/以和为贵。The best policy is to work for peace.

以文会友 yǐwén-huìyǒu make friends through the exchange of writings：这个笔会的宗旨是～，推动文学创作的繁荣。The aim of the Pen Association is to make friends through the exchange of writings so as to help promote the flowering of literary works.

以下 yǐxià ❶ below; under：二十五岁～的青年 young people under 25 years of age /摄氏二十度～ below 20 degrees C /团～的干部 cadres from regiment commanders down /膝关节～ from the knees downward /沙子口村～水位猛涨。The water level suddenly rose from Shazi Village on down (stream). ❷ the following：～是详细的行动计划。The following is a detailed plan of action. /我就谈这些，～由老张来谈。I'll stop here and leave the rest to Lao Zhang.

以销定产 yǐxiāo-dìngchǎn plan production according to sales：～，压低库存 gear production to sales and reduce the inventory

以小见大 yǐxiǎo-jiàndà be able to discern a question of major principle from minor issues or petty matters

以小人之心，度君子之腹 yǐ xiǎorén zhī xīn, duó jūnzǐ zhī fù a mean man always uses his own yardstick to measure the mind of the great; gauge the heart of a gentleman with one's own mean measure：不料你～，完全误解了我们的好意。To our regret you misunderstood our good intention like a little fellow trying to gauge the heart of the great.

以眼还眼，以牙还牙 yǐ yǎn huán yǎn, yǐ yá huán yá an eye for an eye and a tooth for a tooth; paying sb. back in his own coin：他竟然下此毒手，我也要来个～。He went so far as to stab people in the back, so I'm determind to pay him back in his own coin.

以一当十 yǐyī-dāngshí pit one against ten; fight courageously; work efficiently：我们的战士打起仗来，个个～。In fighting, every one of our soldiers is worth ten. /在工作中，他往往能起～的作用，是难得的干才。He is one of the few capable people who can do the work of ten.

以夷伐夷 yǐyí-fáyí *also* "以夷攻夷"；"以夷制夷" play off one barbarian state against another; play off one foreign power against another; play both ends against the middle

以逸待劳 yǐyì-dàiláo be rested and ready to meet a tired-out enemy or opponent; wait at one's ease for an exhausted enemy or opponent：这场球的安排对我不利，我队连续作战，对方则～。The arrangement of this football match is to our disadvantage because our team has been playing one match after another while our opponents will be fresh and wait for us at their ease.

以远 yǐyuǎn beyond：今天出售武汉～的车票。Tickets for Wuhan and beyond are available today.

以远权 yǐyuǎnquán 〈交通〉right to extend a flying route (beyond one's destination); right to fly beyond designated points

以怨报德 yǐyuàn-bàodé return evil for good; repay good with evil; requite kindness with ingratitude：你自己想一想，你们做的事合理不合理？是不是～？Don't you think what you have done is unreasonable? Aren't you repaying good with evil?

以战去战 yǐzhàn-qùzhàn fight a war to end war

以昭信守 yǐzhāo-xìnshǒu in faith whereof; in witness whereof

以正视听 yǐzhèng-shìtīng in order to ensure a correct understanding of the facts：说明真相，～ present the facts as they are to ensure a correct understanding of them

以直报怨 yǐzhí-bàoyuàn requite injustice with justice; meet ill will with fair play：以前我是主张"以德报怨"，现在"～"。I used to advocate requiting ingratitude with kindness. Now I believe in meeting ingratitude with a principled stand.

以至 yǐzhì *also* "以至于"〈连词〉❶ down to; up to：从沿海城市～内地农村 from coastal cities to inland rural areas /生产效率提高几倍～十几倍。Productivity has grown by several times and even by over a dozen times. /省市～全国都出现这种现象。Such phenomenon appeared in cities, provinces, and indeed throughout the country. ❷ to such an extent as to...; so... that...; even：他专心看书，～有人喊他也没听到。He was so engrossed in his reading that he didn't even hear that someone was calling him.

以致 yǐzhì 〈连词〉so that; consequently; as a consequence; as a result：由于疏忽大意～出了严重事故。A serious accident happened as a result of carelessness (*or* negligence). /由于我过分激动，～把要讲的话丢掉了一大半。I was so excited that I forgot more than half of what I intended to say. /你们事先没有充分调查研究，～作出了错误的结论。You didn't conduct adequate research and investigation beforehand; consequently, you came to the wrong conclusion.

以资 yǐzī as a means of; as：～证明 in testimony thereof; this is to certify that /～参考 as a reference /献上一面锦旗，～感谢 present a silk banner to sb. as a token of appreciation

以子之矛，攻子之盾 yǐ zǐ zhī máo, gōng zǐ zhī dùn set your own spear against your own shield; refute sb. with his own argument; place sb. in a self-contradictory position or dilemma：在辩论中，她善于～，使对手处于被动尴尬的境地。She is good at putting her adversary in a predicament in the debate by turning his own argument against him.

苡 yǐ 〈植物〉Job's tears

苡米 yǐmǐ *also*"薏米"yìmǐ;"苡仁" seed of Job's tears

苡仁 yǐrén *see*"苡米"

矣 yǐ 〈古语〉〈助词〉❶ *used at the end of a sentence like* 了:由来久～。It dated way back. /俱往～。All is over now. ❷ *used in exclamation*:难～哉! How difficult! /甚～,汝之不惠! How stupid you are!

已 yǐ ❶ stop; halt; cease; end:冲突不～ endless conflict /感叹不～ keep sighing /死而后～ until one's dying day; to the end of one's life /旱情有增无～。The drought continued to worsen. /学不可以～。Learning should be pursued without intermission. ❷ already:他～走了。He's already gone. /早～如此。It has long been so (*or* the case). /天色～晚。It's getting late. /早～过开放时间。It long past closing time. ❸〈书面〉thereafter; later on; afterwards:～忽不见 disappear afterwards /～而悔之 regret later on /他体力不支,～又昏迷。He was so weak that he fainted again after a short while. ❹〈书面〉too; excessively:待身～廉,责人～详 be lenient with oneself but strict with others; be far more demanding with others than with oneself

已而 yǐ'ér 〈书面〉❶ soon; before long; then; afterwards:突然雷电大作,～大雨倾盆。Suddenly there were lightning and peals of thunder soon accompained by a heavy downpour. ❷ let it be; let it pass:～,～! 今之从政者殆而! Now, now, aren't those in power imperiling themselves?

已故 yǐgù deceased; late:～京剧大师梅兰芳先生 late master of Beijing opera, Mr. Mei Lanfang

已极 yǐjí extremely; to the nth degree:糟糕～ too bad; can't be worse/糊涂～ what an idiot; height of folly

已经 yǐjing already:孩子～大了。The child has already grown up. /风～停了。The wind has stopped. /天气～不热了。It's no longer hot. /火车～开了,他才急急忙忙赶到。The train had left when he hurriedly arrived.

已决犯 yǐjuéfàn 〈法律〉convicted prisoner; convict

已然 yǐrán ❶ already:事情～过去,何必为此烦恼? It is all over already, why feel so upset? ❷ be already so; have long been the case:自古～。It has been so since ancient times. /我能知～,不能知未然。I can see what has already happened but not what is going to happen.

已甚 yǐshèn 〈书面〉excessive; undue:不为～ not go too far; not overdo sth. /过为～ overdo a thing; overstep the limits

已往 yǐwǎng before; previously; in the past:～的事情不必说了。Let bygones be bygones. /现在的生活条件比～好多了。Living conditions are much better than before. /～的繁华烟消云散。The former prosperity has vanished like mist and smoke.

已知领域 yǐzhī lǐngyù *terra cognita*

已知数 yǐzhīshù 〈数学〉known number

尾 yǐ ❶ hairs on a horsetail:马～ hairs on a horsetail ❷ spikelets on a cricket's tail:三～儿 female cricket (with three spikelets on its tail)

see also wěi

酏 yǐ 〈药学〉elixir:芳香～ aromatic elixir

酏剂 yǐjì 〈药学〉elixir

迤(迆) yǐ stretch or extend towards:天安门～东是劳动人民文化宫。To the east of Tian An Men is the Working People's Palace of Culture.

see also yí

迤逦 yǐlǐ winding; circuitous; tortuous; meandering:队伍沿着山道～而行。The troops meandered along the mountain path. /小河从这里～向东。From here the small river followed a winding course to the east.

yì

意[1] yì ❶ meaning; idea:说明来～ explain why one is here; explain the intention of one's coming /～简言赅 simple ideas expressed succinctly /言不尽～ words cannot fully express what one means to say /虚情假～ pretended cordiality; insincere warmth ❷ wish; desire; intention:随～ as one pleases /任～ wilfully /称心如～ to one's heart's content; after one's own heart /怀有恶～ harbour evil intentions ❸ believe what is going to happen; anticipate; expect:出其不～ catch sb. unprepared; take sb. by surprise /我们不～中途迷路。Unexpectedly, we got lost in the middle of our journey. ❹ suggestion; conception; hint; trace: 醉～ feeling of getting drunk; tipsy /笔～ artistic conception of an author in painting, calligraphy or poetry /春～盎然。Spring is in the air.

意[2] Yì (short for 意大利) Italy:～军 Italian army

意表 yìbiǎo beyond one's expectation; unexpected:每有新议,出人～。Every new idea came as a surprise.

意大利 Yìdàlì Italy:～人 Italian /～语 Italian (language)

意大利半岛 Yìdàlì Bàndǎo Italian Peninsula

意大利肉饼 Yìdàlì ròubǐng *also*"比萨饼"bǐsàbǐng pizza

意会 yìhuì understand what's implied; sense:只可～,不可言传 can be sensed, but not explained in words

意见 yìjian ❶ idea; view; opinion; suggestion:建设性～ constructive ideas /充分交换～ full exchange of views /征求～ seek (*or* solicit) opinions; ask for criticisms /提出有益的～ put forward some useful suggestions /双方对所讨论的问题达成一致～。Both parties reached a consensus on the issues discussed. /在这个问题上,彼此的～很不一致。The two parties do not see eye to eye on this question. ❷ differing opinion; objection; criticism; complaint:他对你～很大。He has a lot of complaints against you. /有～当面提。Those who have differing opinions should air their views openly. /他俩正在闹～。They have been quarrelling with each other. /群众对以权谋私的做法很有～。The people take strong exception to the practice of abusing one's power for personal gain.

意见簿 yìjianbù visitors' book; customers' book

意见箱 yìjianxiāng suggestion box

意匠 yìjiàng artistic conception (of a poem, painting, etc.):别具～ have a distinctive artistic conception; be original in artistic conception

意境 yìjìng artistic mood or conception:～恢弘的作品 magnificently conceived work /用朴素的语言表现出清新的～ use simple language to produce a fresh artistic conception /作者在小说中营造了一种高远的～。The author has created a lofty artistic ambience in his novel.

意料 yìliào anticipate; expect:～之中 as expected /天地间出乎～的事太多了! The world is full of surprises. /他们暗中干着人们～不到的事情。Secretly, they were doing something which no one would have foreseen.

意马心猿 yìmǎ-xīnyuán *also*"心猿意马" restless; fidgety

意念 yìniàn idea; thought:脑子里深藏着一个～ have an idea deep down in one's mind /他那时心中压倒一切的～,就是救起那个快淹死的男孩。At the moment, the thought uppermost in his mind was saving the drowning boy.

意气 yìqì ❶ will and spirit; how one feels and looks:～轩昂 have an imposing appearance and brim with vigour and vitality /～自得 look arrogant and pleased with oneself /～自若 appear calm and composed; look unperturbed ❷ temperament:二人～不合。The two were incompatible in temperament. ❸ personal feelings or prejudice:闹～ give vent to personal feelings /不能凭一时的～ not to be swayed by whimsical feelings

意气风发 yìqì-fēngfā high-spirited and vigorous; full of daring and vigour:～,斗志昂扬 be high-spirited and ready for action; be full of militancy and drive

意气相投 yìqì-xiāngtóu be congenial in temperament; see eye to eye:他俩萍水相逢,却也～。The two of them met by chance, yet they hit it off with each other.

意气扬扬 yìqì-yángyáng *also*"意气洋洋" put on grand airs and look immensely proud; look arrogant and pleased with oneself:他见别人惧怕,便～,自以为得计。Seeing that others were scared of him, he looked extremely proud, thinking himself very smart.

意气用事 yìqì-yòngshì act on impulse or whim; be swayed by personal feelings:这场争论实在属于～。The debate was indeed swayed by personal feelings. /～是最容易坏事的。Impulsive acts most easily lead to ruin.

意趣 yìqù temperament and taste; flavour and interest:～盎然 full of interest /彼此～不同 be different from each other in temperament and taste

意识 yìshi ❶〈哲学〉consciousness:思想～ ideology /爱国～ patriotism; patriotic feelings /封建～ feudal ideas /存在决定～。One's social being determines one's consciousness. ❷ (often used together with 到) be conscious or aware of; awake to; realize:～到情况的严重 come to realize the seriousness of the situation /我充分～到这个任务的危险性。I'm fully aware of the danger involved in the task.

意识流 yìshiliú 〈文学〉stream of consciousness

意识形态 yìshi xíngtài 〈哲学〉ideology:社会～ social ideology

意识域 yìshiyù 〈心理〉sphere of consciousness

意思 yìsi ❶ meaning; idea; implication:这个词的～不好懂。The meaning of the word is difficult to grasp. /你说的是什么～? What point are you trying to make? *or* What are you driving at? /这段的中心～很明白。The central idea of the paragraph is very clear. /我不太明白她的～。I don't quite get what she meant. /她脸上没有一丝嘲弄的～。There was no trace of mockery in her expression. /点点头,是表示同意的～。Nodding means consent. /这个词丝毫没有轻蔑的～。The word does not in the least imply contempt. ❷ opinion; view; wish; desire:我的～是今天去。In my opinion we should go today. /我想去看望老齐,你有没有这个～? I want to go to visit Lao Qi. Do you wish to go? / 他还没有要走的～。He was not ready to leave yet. ❸ token of affection, appreciation, gratitude, etc.:这微薄的礼品却也是朋友们的一片～。Modest as it is, the gift is a token of the warm sentiments of all your friends. ❹ express appreciation, gratitude, etc.:大家辛苦了,得买些东西～一下。Everybody has worked hard, we'd better buy something for them, to express our appreciation. /他认为还得给对方～～,不然,事情怕办不好。He thought we should make some gifts to the other party, otherwise things may not get done properly. ❺ suggestion; hint; trace:这几天天气有点转暖的～了。It looks as if the weather is getting warmer these days. /他们两个是不是有点什么～? Do they two take a fancy to each other? ❻ interest; fun:他是个怪有～的人物。He is an interesting fellow. /这部电影没～。The movie is boring. /这玩意儿倒挺有～。This gadget is great fun. ❼ *used together with* 好 *or* 不好:你这样做好～吗? Don't you feel a bit ashamed of what you have done? /大伙儿笑得我怪不好～的。Everybody laughed and I felt rather embarrassed. /有个事儿我想求你帮忙,可是不好～说。I want to ask your help on something, but I find it a bit awkward to bring it up.

意态 yìtài demeaner; bearing; mien; attitude:～自若 appear cool; look calm and collected

意图 yìtú intention; intent:领会领导的～ understand the intentions of the leaders /摸清他的～ find out what he is after /作者写这篇文章的～是什么? What is the purpose of the author in writing this article?

意外 yìwài ❶ unexpected; unanticipated; unforeseen:感到～ feel surprised; be taken unawares /事出～。It came as a surprise. /他这才知道局势是～的严重。Only then did he realize that the situation was unusually serious. ❷ accident; mishap; bad luck:怕发生～ fear that something untoward may happen /要是没有什么～,我们就这样做下去了。If nothing goes wrong we will continue our work along these lines. /为了防止～,我们研究了三套方案。In order to prevent any accident we have worked out three sets of plans.

意外风险 yìwài fēngxiǎn emergency risk

意味 yìwèi ❶ meaning; sense; significance; implication:你这番话很有～。Your remarks were quite meaningful. /他含笑点头,听出了这里的～。Having understood the implications, he nodded smiling. ❷ interest; overtone; flavour:威胁～ threatening overtones /这篇散文,大有诗的～。This prose has much poetic flavour.

意味深长 yìwèi-shēncháng profound in significance; pregnant with meaning; highly significant:书中所述的人生哲理,～。The philosophy of life expounded in the book is profound in meaning. /读之愈久,愈觉～。The more one reads, the more one feels the profundity of the work.

意味着 yìwèizhe signify; mean; intimate; imply:柳梢吐绿,～春天来了。It heralds the coming of spring when the tips of the willow branches begin to turn green.

意下 yìxià ❶ in mind; to heart:他全不把别人的议论放在～。He doesn't heed others' comments in the least. ❷ view; idea; thought:我们现在就去,你～如何? We are going there right now. What do you think (*or* What about you)?

意想 yìxiǎng imagine; expect; anticipate:演出获得～不到的成功。The performance was unexpectedly successful. /得分之高,出于我们的～。The high score was beyond our expectation.

意向 yìxiàng intention; purpose:这是大家共同的～。This is the intention of us all. /对方提出这个问题的～何在? What has the other party in mind in raising such an issue?

意向书 yìxiàngshū letter of intent:双方签订了共同投资建厂的～。The two parties signed a letter of intent on joint investment in constructing a factory.

意向性 yìxiàngxìng intentionality; intention

意象 yìxiàng image; imagery:这首民歌～新颖。The folk song is conceived with originality.

意兴 yìxìng interest; eagerness; enthusiasm:这几个人对游泳始终～勃勃。These people have always been keen on swimming. /这电影令人～索然。The movie was boring.

意绪 yìxù mood; spirit; state of mind:～低沉 be in the doldrums

意义 yìyì ❶ meaning; sense:这篇文章的～不明确。The meaning of the article is not clear. /成语所表示的～,有时候不能照字面理解。Sometimes, the sense of an idiom cannot be understood from the actual words. ❷ meaning; significance: 积极～ positive meaning; significance /有教育～ instructive; educational / 过一个有～的暑假 spend a meaningful summer vacation /这次大会具有深远的历史～。The meeting is of historic and far-reaching importance.

意译 yìyì ❶ free translation (as distinguished from literal translation) ❷ semantic translation (as distinguished from transliteration)

意意思思 yìyì-sīsī *also* "疑疑思思" yíyí-sīsī hesitant; indecisive:真说要走,她又～地有些舍不得。She became rather hesitant and reluctant when it came to leaving the place.

意欲 yìyù intend; plan:他～独自前去。He intends to go there by himself.

意愿 yìyuàn wish; longing; desire; aspiration:尊重老人的～ respect the wishes of the elderly /统一祖国是全中国人民的共同～。The reunification of the motherland is the common aspiration of the Chinese people.

意蕴 yìyùn inner meaning; implication:反复琢磨才能领会这首诗的～。Only by pondering over it again and again can you grasp the inner meaning of the poem.

意在笔先 yìzàibǐxiān (in writing, painting, etc.) think or compose carefully before putting it down on paper:其诗～,力透纸背。His poems were powerful and penetrating, for he had always thought out the lines before putting them down on paper.

意在言外 yìzàiyánwài the meaning is implied; there is more than meets the eye:这首小诗,～,耐人寻味。The short poem has more than meets the eye and provides much food for thought.

意旨 yìzhǐ intention; wish; will:秉承上级～行事 act in deference to the wishes of the higher-ups

意志 yìzhì will:坚强的～ strong will; iron determination /～消沉 be in broken (*or* low, *or* poor) spirits; be depressed or demoralized /艰苦生活锻炼了他的～。Hard life tempered his willpower. /～薄弱者经受不起这种物质诱惑。Those of flabby will are unable to withstand such material temptation.

意致 yìzhì 〈书面〉spirit and pose

意中 yìzhōng ❶ in one's heart; after one's heart ❷ as expected:他一向骄傲自满,这次犯错误本是～的事。As he has always been conceited, it came as no surprise that he had made this mistake.

意中人 yìzhōngrén person one is in love with; person of one's heart:朝思暮想的～ beloved person constantly in one's mind, whether dreaming or awake; sweetheart one pines for day and night

意中事 yìzhōngshì sth. to be expected:从他们目前的精神状态看,这场球失利是～。Judging by their present state of mind, that they lost the game was to be expected.

癔 yì

癔病 yìbìng *also* "歇斯底里" xiēsīdǐlǐ 〈医学〉hysteria:～患者 hysteriac

薏 yì

薏米 yìmǐ *also* "薏仁米";"苡仁" yǐrén ;"苡米" yǐmǐ seed of Job's tears

薏仁米 yìrénmǐ *see* "薏米"

薏苡 yìyǐ 〈植物〉Job's tears

镱 yì 〈化学〉ytterbium (Yb)

臆(肊) yì ❶ chest: 胸～ chest ❷ subjectively: *see* "～断"

臆测 yìcè conjecture; surmise; speculation: 只凭～,不作调查,结论难免有错。One cannot help drawing wrong conclusions by relying merely on surmise without investigation.

臆断 yìduàn assume; suppose, speculate: 在科学研究中要严防～。We must strictly guard against speculation in scientific research. /事不目见耳闻,而～其有无,可乎? How can one assume that something exists without seeing or hearing about it?

臆度 yìduó 〈书面〉conjecture; surmise; speculation; supposition: 这都是你的～,并非事实。It is all your conjecture, not real facts.

臆见 yìjiàn subjective opinion; personal view: 他说得头头是道,其实是一种经不起实践检验的～。Although he sounded quite plausible, it was in fact only his personal assumption and could not stand the test of practice.

臆说 yìshuō assumption; supposition: 说话要有根据,防止～。One should base one's statements on facts and avoid guesswork.

臆想 yìxiǎng imagination; supposition; assumption: 你这全是靠不住的～。That's entirely your imagination.

臆造 yìzào fabricate (a story, reason, etc.); invent; concoct: 作品的情节颇多～,缺乏生活实感。The plot of the book was full of artificiality and not true to life.

癔 yì *also* "呓" yì talk in one's sleep

瘗(瘞) yì 〈书面〉bury; inter: ～之路侧 bury the dead at the roadside /～玉埋香。A beautiful woman was dead.

亦 yì ❶〈书面〉also; too; as well as: ～无不可。Why not? /～复如是。It's also the same. /此文结构严密,文字～好。The article was well organized and the language was good too. ❷(Yì) a surname

亦步亦趋 yìbù-yìqū ape sb. at every step; imitate sb.'s every move; blindly follow suit; follow slavishly: 中国的事情要按照中国的情况来办,不能跟在别人后面～。China should manage its affairs in the light of its own conditions and must not copy others mechanically. /如果只是跟着别人～,是不会有什么成就的。One cannot accomplish anything by blindly aping others.

亦即 yìjí that is; i. e.; namely; viz.: 扬子江～长江。The Yangtze River, that is, the Changjiang River.

亦且 yìqiě 〈书面〉and; also; as well as: 此物有色有光～有声。The material has sound as well as colour and lustre.

亦然 yìrán also; too: 反之～ and the reverse is also true; and vice versa

亦庄亦谐 yìzhuāng-yìxié solemn and witty; serious and comical at the same time; serio-comic: 这篇杂文寓劝戒于讽刺之中,～,值得一读。This essay is worth reading, for it gives admonition by way of satire and is both serious and witty.

奕 yì ❶〈书面〉grand; magnificent ❷(Yì) a surname

奕奕 yìyì ❶ great; magnificent ❷ radiating power and vitality: 神采～ glowing with health and vitality /～传神 vivid and vigorous /～的眼神 clear and sparkling eyes ❸ feel restless; be distracted: 忧心～ sense of great anxiety

弈 yì 〈书面〉❶ *weiqi*, a game played with black and white pieces on a board of 361 intersections; go ❷ play chess: 对～ play chess against each other /～者举棋不定。The chess-player hesitated over the next move.

弈林 yìlín community of chess players; place where chess players gather together; chess circles: ～高手 a master (*or* ace) chess player

弈棋 yìqí play chess

衣 yì 〈书面〉wear; put on; be dressed in: ～布衣 put on cotton clothes

see also yī

裔 yì ❶〈书面〉descendants; posterity: 孙中山的后～ descendants of Dr. Sun Yat-sen /华～美国人 American of Chinese descent (*or* origin, *or* extraction); Chinese American ❷〈书面〉distant land: 四～ far distant land in all directions ❸(Yì) a surname

裔孙 yìsūn 〈书面〉remote or distant decendants; remote posterity

益[1] yì ❶ good; benefit; profit; advantage: 有～无害 do good rather than harm; be harmless /受～不浅 derive much benefit from; benefit a lot from /无～之举 useless act /开卷有～。It's always rewarding to start reading. ❷ beneficial; helpful: 良师～友 good teacher and helpful friend ❸(Yì)a surname

益[2] yì ❶ increase; add to: ～智 enhance intelligence /～兵 reinforce the troops /延年～寿 prolong life ❷ all the more; still more; increasingly: 精～求精 strive for perfection; always endeavour to do better / 须发～白。The beard and hair are turning greyer.

益虫 yìchóng beneficial or useful insect

益处 yìchu benefit; profit; advantage: 适当喝点茶对身体有～。Moderate tea drinking is good to health.

益发 yìfā all the more; even more; further: 雨雪交加,气候～寒冷了。With the fall of sleet the weather was getting even colder.

益加 yìjiā more; increasingly; to a greater extent: 情绪～激昂。Feelings are running higher than ever.

益母草 yìmǔcǎo 〈中药〉motherwort (*Leonurus heterophyllus*)

益鸟 yìniǎo beneficial or useful bird

益气生津 yìqì-shēngjīn 〈中医〉supplementing *qi* (energy) and helping the production of body fluid

益友 yìyǒu friend and mentor; helpful friend: 能对我的缺点直言不讳者,都是我的～。Those who point out my shortcomings without mincing words are all my friends and mentors.

溢 yì ❶ overflow; spill: 洪水暴～ overflow of the rapidly rising flood /喜悦心情～于言表 beam with joy in one's speech /～彩流光的桃花 colourful and lustrous peach flowers /花香四～。The fragrance of flowers permeated the air. ❷ excessive; exaggerated: 美声～誉,言过其实。His high reputation falls short of reality.

溢出 yìchū spill over; overflow: 湖水～堤岸。The lake overflowed its embankment.

溢洪坝 yìhóngbà *also* "溢流坝"〈水利〉overfall dam; spillway dam

溢洪道 yìhóngdào 〈水利〉spillway

溢洪闸 yìhóngzhá 〈水利〉spillway gate

溢价 yìjià premium pricing

溢流 yìliú flood; spill; spill-out; spillover: ～阀 spillover valve; spill valve /～管 flooding pipe; overflow pipe; spillway /船舶装运油类或有毒货物,必须采取防止～和渗漏的措施。Measures against spill or leakage should be adopted when vessels are carrying oils or toxic substance.

溢流坝 yìliúbà *see* "溢洪坝"

溢美 yìměi overpraise; laud to the sky: ～之词 excessive praise /对文艺作品的评价要实事求是,不可～。We must base ourselves on facts and avoid too much eulogy in literary criticism.

溢目 yìmù 〈书面〉too many things for the eye to take in: 珍宝～。The eye cannot take in all these treasures. *or* There are too many treasures for the eye to take in.

溢水 yìshuǐ spillwater; spilling water: ～道 spillway /～管 spillway conduit

溢于言表 yìyú-yánbiǎo show in one's words and expression; come through in overtones: 愤激之情～。His indignation came through in overtones. /一片热诚,～。He exudes warmth and sincerity.

嗌 yì 〈书面〉throat

螠 yì 〈动物〉echiuroid

镒 yì ancient unit of weight (equal to 20 *liang*)

鹢 yì 〈古语〉a kind of water bird

缢 yì 〈书面〉hang: 自～ hang oneself /～杀 strangle to death;

kill by strangling

谊 yì ❶ friendship:友~ friendship /情~ friendly feelings; friendly sentiment /师生之~ friendly relationship between teacher and student ❷〈书面〉see "义" yì

一 yì see "一" yī

懿 yì 〈书面〉exemplary:嘉言~行 helpful remarks and noble conduct

懿德 yìdé 〈书面〉virtue:嘉行~ praiseworthy conduct and virtue

懿亲 yìqīn 〈书面〉close kin; very close relative

懿旨 yìzhǐ 〈书面〉edict of an empress or empress dowager

殪 yì 〈书面〉❶ die ❷ kill

曀 yì 〈书面〉overcast; cloudy

饐 yì 〈书面〉(of food) decompose; rot

蓺 yì 〈书面〉grow; plant; cultivate:~菊 plant chrysanthemums /树~五谷 grow all food crops

勚 yì ❶〈书面〉toil; hard work:莫知我~。No one realized my toil. ❷ wear and tear:螺丝扣~了。The thread of the screw was worn out.

鹝 yì see "鹢" yì

虉 yì see "虉草"

虉草 yìcǎo *Phalaris arundinacea* — a kind of perennial reed grass

栧(栧) yì 〈书面〉oar

瞖 yì 〈书面〉see "翳" yì

翳 yì ❶〈书面〉hide from view; cover; screen:荫~ be shaded (*or* hidden) by foliage ❷〈中医〉slight corneal opacity; nebula

翳然 yìrán 〈书面〉❶ wild; desolute:榛莽~ wild hazelnut bushes; wild and lush vegetation ❷ covert; hidden; shaded

翳翳 yìyì 〈书面〉❶ dark; dim; hazy:日光~ dim day ❷ obscure; vague:文理~ obscure writing

翳障 yìzhàng ❶ screen; conceal:日光为浮云所~。The sun was concealed by floating clouds. ❷ concealment; obscurity:这条线索揭开了案子的一层~。The clue helped peel one layer of obscurity off the criminal case.

嫕 yì 〈书面〉affable; amiable:婉~ pliant and amiable

弋 yì ❶〈书面〉shoot with a retrievable arrow with a string attached to it ❷〈书面〉such retrievable arrow ❸ (Yì) a surname

弋获 yìhuò 〈书面〉❶ hit (birds) ❷ arrest, or take (escaped convicts, bandits or robbers)

弋取 yìqǔ 〈书面〉hunt; hunt for; seek; pursue

弋阳腔 yìyángqiāng *also* "弋腔"〈戏曲〉Yiyang tune, opera style from Yiyang in Jiangxi Province

杙 yì 〈书面〉small wooden stake

抑[1] yì press down; suppress; restrain; curb:~恶扬善 suppress the bad and commend the good /感到压~ feel depressed /高者~之,下者举之 lower the high and raise the low

抑[2] yì 〈书面〉〈连词〉❶ or:官之命,宜以材耶? ~以姓乎? Should the appointment of a government official be based on one's ability or on family background? ❷ yet; but:多则多矣,~君似鼠。The monarch had accomplished much, yet he acted as timidly as a mouse. ❸ besides; moreover:非惟天时,~亦人谋也。It was not only because of a good opportunity but also because of skilful planning and preparation.

抑遏 yì'è restrain; control; check:不可~的悲痛 irrepressible grief

抑或 yìhuò 〈书面〉〈连词〉or:不知他们是赞成,~是反对。It is not clear whether they are for or against it.

抑菌作用 yìjūn zuòyòng 〈医学〉bacteriostasis

抑强扶弱 yìqiáng-fúruò restrain the powerful and help the weak; curb the strong and assist the weak:~,乃英雄本色。It is in the nature of a true hero to support the weak against the strong.

抑且 yìqiě 〈书面〉(but) also; moreover:此种行为不但有损于个人名誉,~有害于公共利益。Such conduct not only discredits the individual, it also hurts public interest.

抑屈 yìqū 〈书面〉swallow the humiliation:不堪~ can't swallow the humiliation

抑塞 yìsè 〈书面〉constrain; depress; hold back:他感到一种被~的苦闷。He felt depressed (*or* frustrated).

抑压 yìyā constrain; depress; inhibit; hold back

抑扬 yìyáng (of sound) rise and fall; modulate:声调~。The tone rises and falls. /舞厅里爵士音乐~缓疾地响起来。In the ball room, Jazz music started in changing rhythms, fast and slow.

抑扬顿挫 yìyáng-dùncuò with a rising and falling rhythm; in measured tones; in cadence:他便~地背诵起来。He then began reciting in cadence.

抑郁 yìyù dejected; depressed; despondent; gloomy:心情~ be depressed /他用~的眼光看着我。He looked at me with gloomy eyes. /忧愁~严重地损害了她的健康。Worry and dejection seriously affected her health.

抑郁症 yìyùzhèng 〈医学〉depression

抑止 yìzhǐ restrain; check; hold back:~着眼泪 hold back one's tears /~不住心里的怒火 unable to restrain one's fury /他感到忿懑,却又强行~着。He felt indignant but repressed his feelings.

抑制 yìzhì ❶〈生理〉inhibition:睡眠是大脑皮层全部处于~的现象。Sleep is the phenomenon of complete inhibition of the cerebral cortex. ❷ restrain; curb; control; check:~怒火 restrain (*or* hold) one's temper /~内心的激动 control one's excitement /~豪强势力 curb despotic power /~群众积极性 check (*or* dampen) the enthusiasm of the masses

抑制剂 yìzhìjì 〈化学〉inhibitor

抑制神经 yìzhì shénjīng 〈生理〉inhibitory nerve

易[1] yì ❶ easy:来之不~ has not come easily; be hard earned /简便~行 be simple, convenient and easy to apply /显而~见 obviously; evidently /他~晕船。He is liable to seasickness. ❷ amiable:平~近人 be amiable and easy of approach ❸〈书面〉despise; look down upon; underestimate:素~众人 always look down upon everybody /国无小,不可~也。Small and weak as it may be, a country should not be despised.

易[2] yì ❶ change; alter:改名~姓 change one's name /~地而处 if one were in someone else's position /不~之论 irrefutable argument ❷ exchange:贸~ trade /交~ transaction; deal /以暴~暴 substitute violence for violence ❸(Yì) a surname

易爆物 yìbàowù explosive substance or material

易北河 Yìběihé Elbe River, one of major rivers of Europe:~会师 meeting of Allied and Soviet forces on the Elbe (28 April 1945)

易卜生 Yìbǔshēng Henrik Ibsen (1828-1906), Norwegian dramatist and founder of modern prose drama

易感者 yìgǎnzhě 〈医学〉susceptible person; susceptible

易构化 yìgòuhuà 〈化学〉isomerization:~橡胶 isomerized rubber

易货贸易 yìhuò màoyì barter (trade)

易货协定 yìhuò xiédìng barter agreement; agreement on the exchange of commodities

易经 Yìjīng *Yi Jing* (formerly spelt *I-Ching*) or *The Book of Changes*, one of Confucian classics
see also "五经" Wǔjīng

易拉罐 yìlāguàn pop-top or ring-pull can

易洛魁人 Yìluòkuírén Iroquois, one of the native peoples of eastern North America

易切削金属 yìqiēxiāo jīnshǔ 〈冶金〉free cutting metal

易燃物 yìránwù combustible; inflammable; flamable

Y

易熔 yìróng fusible:～金属 fusible metal /～塞 fusible plug

易熔合金 yìróng héjīn 〈冶金〉fusible alloy

易如反掌 yìrúfǎnzhǎng as easy as turning one's hand over; as easy as falling off a log; duck soup; piece of cake:你办成此事,～。You can accomplish this hands down.

易手 yìshǒu (of land, political power, etc.) change of holders; change hands:江山～ dynastic change /他童年时代的住宅已经～好几次了。The house where he spent his childhood has had several different owners since.

易性癖 yìxìngpǐ transsexualism: ～者 transsexual; trannie

易于 yìyú be easy to:这个办法～实行。This method is easy to carry out.

易箦 yìzé 〈书面〉change of bed mat — dying: ～之际 just before death; at one's dying moment

易辙 yìzhé (of a cart) depart from its rut — change the course of action; go off track

易帜 yìzhì change the flag of an army or country — shift one's allegiance; effect a change of regime

易子而食 yìzǐ'érshí exchange children and eat them to allay hunger (as in years of severe famine or a prolonged siege in the past)

埸

yì 〈书面〉❶ low bank of earth between fields; ridge ❷ boundary; border:疆～ border

晹

yì 〈书面〉the sun appears and vanishes among floating cloud

蜴

yì *see* "蜥蜴" xīyì

邑

yì ❶ city:都～ capital city /通都大～ big city; metropolis ❷〈古语〉county: ～宰 county magistrate

浥

yì 〈书面〉wet; soak

悒

yì 〈书面〉sad; worried; in low spirits: 郁～ depressed; dejected

悒闷 yìmèn distress; anxiety:喜讯传来,驱散了我心中的～。The happy news dispelled all my anxiety.

悒悒 yìyì look worried or depressed: ～不乐 feel depressed; mope

悒郁 yìyù depressed; heavyhearted:神情～ look disheartened

悒郁寡欢 yìyù-guǎhuān disturbed and downhearted:他的病与长期～不无关系。His ailment was not unconnected with his dejection over a long time.

挹

yì 〈书面〉❶ scoop up; ladle out ❷ pull:奖～ award and promote

挹彼注兹 yìbǐ-zhùzī scoop up from there to pour in here:国家～,利用东部的部分财力,来加速西部的发展。To make up for deficency in one locality by drawing from the surplus of another, the state uses some of the capital in the east for the accelerated development of the west.

挹取 yìqǔ 〈书面〉ladle out; spoon up; scoop up

挹注 yìzhù 〈书面〉pour

唈

yì 〈书面〉*see* "悒" yì

貤

yì 〈书面〉repetition; duplication

see also yí

乂

yì 〈书面〉administer; govern; stabilize; pacify: ～安 peace and stability

义[1](義)

yì ❶ justice; righteousness:仗～疏财 distribute wealth for a just cause; be generous in aiding needy people /仁至～尽 have done one's best to help /见利忘～ forget all moral principles at the sight of personal gain /背信弃～ break faith; commit perfidy /多行不～必自毙。Those who indulge in evildoing are bound to come to no good end. ❷ righteous; equitable; fair: *see* "～举";"～演" ❸ friendly feeling or affection involved in human ties or relationship:无情无～ cold and ungrateful /忘恩负～ ingratitude ❹ adopted; adoptive: ～父 adoptive father /～子 adopted son /结～ become sworn brothers or sisters ❺ artificial; false: ～手 artificial hand /～发 wig ❻ (Yì) a surname

义[2](義)

yì meaning; sense; significance:释～ interpret the meaning of a word or a text /断章取～ quote out of context

义兵 yìbīng righteous army:起～ rise in rebellion to uphold a just cause

义不容辞 yìbùróngcí be duty-bound; have an bounden duty; be incumbent on: ～的责任 unshirkable (*or* bounden) duty /做好这个工作,是文化部门和出版部门～的责任。It is incumbent on the cultural and publishing departments to do the job well.

义仓 yìcāng 〈旧语〉public granary set up to provide against famine years

义齿 yìchǐ 〈医学〉false tooth; denture

义胆 yìdǎn (of a person) loyal and righteous:忠肝～ loyalty and devotion

义地 yìdì 〈旧语〉public graveyard for poor people; potter's field

义方 yìfāng 〈书面〉right course to follow in life; correct attitude to adopt towards life; rules to abide by; code of conduct:勉之以～ exhort sb. to follow the right path in life

义愤 yìfèn righteous indignation; moral indignation:激起～ rouse righteous indignation /满腔～ filled with righteous anger

义愤填膺 yìfèn-tiányīng be filled with (righteous) indignation:战士们听到这消息,一个个～,怒火万丈。On hearing the news every soldier was filled with fury and indignation.

义和团运动 Yìhétuán Yùndòng Yihetuan Movement (Known in the West as the Boxer Uprising), an anti-imperialist armed struggle waged by north China peasants and handicraftsmen in 1900

义举 yìjǔ magnanimous act undertaken for the public good; righteous deed:赈灾济民的～ righteous deed of relieving the people in stricken areas /他的～受到了赞扬。He was acclaimed for his righteous conduct.

义捐 yìjuān donate money or things for a just cause or the public good: ～门诊 benefit outpatient service /～古画 donation of ancient paintings

义军 yìjūn righteous army:兴举～,讨平叛贼 raise a righteous army to quell a rebellion

义理 yìlǐ ❶ meaning and significance; argumentation (of a speech or essay):剖析～ in-depth analysis of the argumentation ❷〈哲学〉universal truth: ～之学 study of universal truths contained in Confucian classics

义例 yìlì theme and style of a work; main purpose and style of writings

义烈 yìliè 〈书面〉fiery and upright

义卖 yìmài sale of goods (usu. at high prices) for charity or other worthy causes; charity bazaar:为赈灾而举行～ organize charity sales for disaster relief

义旗 yìqí banner of an army fighting a just war; banner of justice:高举～,号召天下 hold aloft the banner of righteousness to rally the people all over the country against injustice

义气 yìqi ❶ code of brotherhood; personal loyalty:讲～ be loyal (to one's friends) /重～ set store by personal loyalty /哥们儿～ code of brotherhood; chumminess ❷ quality or sentiment of being loyal to one's friends:你看他多么慷慨,多么～! Look, how loyal and generous he is!

义犬 yìquǎn faithful dog

义师 yìshī army fighting a just war; righteous army:兴～ mobilize (*or* raise) a righteous army

义士 yìshì noble-minded or chivalrous person; person who upholds the cause of justice; generous and upright man

义疏 yìshū detailed annotations of classics or classical literary works

义塾 yìshú 〈旧语〉private or community-run schools charging no tuition; free schools

义无反顾 yìwúfǎngù *also* "义无返顾" honour permits no turning back; be duty-bound not to retreat:勇往直前,～ march bravely ahead without any thought of turning back /以身许国,～ dedicate oneself to one's country without the least reservation

义务 yìwù ❶ duty; obligation:履行公民的权利和～ fulfil the rights and duties of a citizen /没有非去不可的～ be under no obligation to

go /公民有～维护社会治安。Citizens have the duty to maintain public order. /这篇稿子,我有～帮他改一改。I feel duty-bound to help him with the revision of the draft. ❷ volunteer; be voluntary: ～演出 voluntary performance /为民办小学～承担教学任务 teach for free at a primary school run by local inhabitants

义务兵 yìwùbīng compulsory serviceman; conscript

义务兵役制 yìwù bīngyìzhì compulsory military service; conscription

义务教育 yìwù jiàoyù compulsory education

义务劳动 yìwù láodòng voluntary labour

义侠 yìxiá ❶ chivalrous: ～之举 chivalrous act ❷ righteous and gallant person; person skilled in martial arts and given to chivalrous conduct

义项 yìxiàng item of an entry (in a dictionary)

义形于色 yìxíngyúsè with indignation written on one's face; filled with righteous anger: ～地猛击桌子 pound the table indignantly /他慷慨陈词,～。Indignant at the injustice, he made a rousing speech.

义学 yìxué 〈旧语〉tuition-free private or community-run school; free school

义演 yìyǎn benefit or charity performance: 文艺界积极参加～。People from art and literary circles actively participated in the benefit performance.

义勇 yìyǒng brave in fighting for a just cause; righteous and courageous: ～之气 bravery in fighting for a just cause /～冠三军 distinguish oneself by peerless valour in battle

义勇军 yìyǒngjūn army of volunteers; volunteers: 抗日～ army of volunteers in the War of Resistance Against Japan

义勇军进行曲 Yìyǒngjūn Jìnxíngqǔ *March of the Volunteers* (written in 1935 with words by Tian Han 田汉 and music by Nie Er 聂耳, now national anthem of China)

义园 yìyuán *see* "义地"

义蕴 yìyùn nuance: 琢磨每个词的～ dwell on (*or* explore) the nuances of each word

义战 yìzhàn war of justice; just war: 反抗外来侵略的～ war of justice against foreign aggression /春秋无～。There was no just war during the Spring and Autumn Period.

义诊 yìzhěn ❶ medical consultation to benefit some worthy cause ❷ free medical consultation

义正词严 yìzhèng-cíyán speak sternly out of a sense of justice; speak in all seriousness: ～地驳斥对方的谬论 sternly (*or* solemnly) refute the fallacies of the other party /～地告诫对方不要轻举妄动 warn the other side in all seriousness not to act rashly

义肢 yìzhī 〈医学〉artificial limb

义旨 yìzhǐ 〈书面〉gist; significance

义冢 yìzhǒng 〈旧语〉burial ground for the destitute; potter's field

义庄 yìzhuāng 〈旧语〉country estate bought by individuals to support their destitute clanspeople

议(議) yì

❶ opinion; view; proposal: 建～ suggestion; proposition /协～ agreement /抗～ protest /倡～ proposal; move /此～不妥。This idea (*or* view) is not quite right. ❷ discuss; deliberate; exchange views on; talk over: 此事另～ discuss (*or* deliberate on) the matter at another time /从长计～ take one's time in coming to a decision; think sth. over carefully /自报公～ make a self-assessment and put it to the public for discussion; self-assessment and public discussion ❸ comment; remark; debate: 物～ public comment; public criticism or censure /无可非～ indisputable; irreproachable

议案 yì'àn proposal; motion; bill

议程 yìchéng agenda; order of business; order of the day: 公布会议的～ announce the agenda of a conference /列入～ place on (*or* include in) the agenda /上午的会议有两项～。There are two items on the agenda for the meeting this morning.

议处 yìchǔ examine and punish: 从严～ punish severely

议定 yìdìng reach a decision after discussion; agree upon: ～条款 agreed provisions /～价款 negotiated (*or* agreed) price

议定书 yìdìngshū protocol: 经济合作～ protocol of economic cooperation /互换条约批准书的～ exchange protocols of instruments of ratification of an agreement

议而不决 yì'érbùjué discuss sth. without reaching a decision; hold inconclusive discussions: 此事总是～。The discussion on the matter has always been inconclusive. /～,决而不行。The discussion is fruitless; the decision, if any, remains on paper.

议购 yìgòu buy at negotiated prices: ～合同 contract of purchase at a negotiated price

议和 yìhé negotiate peace: 交战双方派人～。The two belligerent parties sent envoys to negotiate peace. /～未成,战端又起。War broke out again after the peace negotiations failed.

议合 yìhe 〈方言〉consult; discuss: 这事我们三个人～了一下。We three had a discussion on this matter.

议会 yìhuì *also* "国会" guóhuì (UK) Parliament; (US) Congress; (France) National Assembly; (Japan) Diet; (Germany) Reichstag; (Russia) Duma; (Israel) Knesset: ～会议 parliamentary session /～民主 parliamentary democracy /～大厦 parliamentary house /召开或解散～ convene or dissolve a parliament /在～中占有多数席位 be (*or* hold) a majority in the parliament (*or* legislative assembly) /～迷 parliamentary cretinism

议会党团 yìhuì dǎngtuán parliamentary group

议会制 yìhuìzhì parliamentarism
see also "代议制" dàiyìzhì

议价 yìjià ❶ negotiate a price: ～不成 fail to negotiate a price ❷ negotiated price: ～粮 grain at a negotiated price /这种豆制品是～的。This kind of bean product is sold at a negotiated price.

议决 yìjué resolve after deliberation; adopt a resolution: 经过会议～的事情,我们个人无权改变。As individuals we have no right to change what has been resolved at the meeting.

议论 yìlùn talk; deliberate; discuss; comment: ～时政 talk about the current political situation /～不休 carry on endless discussions /大发～ speak at great length; hold forth /～他的最近表现 comment on his recent behaviour /他从不乱发～。He never makes any irresponsible comment (*or* remarks). /这个问题要认真～一下。The matter requires careful deliberation.

议论纷纷 yìlùn-fēnfēn give rise to much discussion; be widely discussed: 这次事件引得众人～。The incident gave rise to a flurry of discussion.

议论文 yìlùnwén argumentative writing; argumentation

议事 yìshì discuss official business: ～所 meeting hall; meeting room /～日程 agenda; order of the day /～规则 rules of procedures or debate /学院领导班子每周～一次。The leadership of the college meets to discuss official business once a week.

议事先决 yìshì xiānjué heads of agenda

议题 yìtí subject under discussion; topic for discussion: 本次会议有两个～。There are two topics for discussion at the present meeting.

议席 yìxí seat in a legislative assembly or parliament

议销 yìxiāo sell at negotiated price

议员 yìyuán member of a legislative assmebly; (UK) Member of Parliament (MP); (US) Congressman or Congresswoman; (Japan) Dietman: 前座～ frontbencher /后座～ backbencher /当选为～ be elected an MP; be returned to parliament .

议院 yìyuàn legislative assembly; parliament; congress: 上～ House of Lords /下～ House of Commons /众～ House of Representatives /参～ Senate

议长 yìzhǎng Speaker (of a legislative body); president

议政 yìzhèng deliberate on political and governmental affairs: 参政～ participate in the discussion and administration of political and government affairs

艾 yì

❶ *see* "乂" yì ❷ punish; penalize: 惩～ mete out punishment
see also ài

刈 yì

〈书面〉mow; cut down: ～草 mow grass /～麦 cut wheat

刈草机 yìcǎojī mowing machine; mower

刈除 yìchú weed out; exterminate: ～杂草 root out weeds

苅(刈) yì

see "刈" yì

泆 yì

〈书面〉❶ indulgence: 骄奢淫～ arrogant, extravagant and dissipated ❷ *see* "溢" yì

轶 yì

see "逸 ❹❺" yì

轶材 yìcái 〈书面〉outstanding talent
轶出 yìchū 〈书面〉exceed: ~前人的范围 go beyond the limits set by predecessors
轶伦 yìlún 〈书面〉tower over one's peers; surpass one's contemporaries
轶事 yìshì anecdote: 名人~ celebraties and their anecdotes

昳 yì

see also dié

昳丽 yìlì 〈书面〉beautiful; pretty

佚 yì *see* "逸" yì

佚失 yìshī scattered and lost: 这部书久已~。The book was lost long ago.
佚游 yìyóu 〈书面〉ramble without restraint

屹 yì 〈书面〉towering like a mountain peak: 烽台~~。The beacon tower stood high like a mountain peak.

see also gē

屹立 yìlì stand towering like a giant: 雄峰~, 刺破青天。An imposing mountain peak soars to the sky. /天安门城楼在广场上巍然~。The rostrum of Tian An Men stands lofty and majestic on the square. /新中国~在世界的东方。New China stands like a giant in the eastern world. /那灯塔~在波涛汹涌的海面。The lighthouse towered aloft above the roaring sea.
屹然 yìrán towering; majestic: 雪野中, 那高松古柏披着银装~挺立。In the white wilderness there stood imposing tall pines and aged cypresses coated with snow.

仡 yì

see also gē

仡仡 yìyì 〈书面〉❶ strong and brave: ~勇夫 strong and bold man ❷ tall; high

佾 yì ranks of ancient dance accompanied by music, one *yi* being one rank consisting of eight people: 天子八~。The emperor was entitled to eight *yi* of dancers.

劓 yì cruel torture by cutting off the nose as a punishment in ancient times

鹝(鶂) yì 〈书面〉*see* "鹢" yì

鹝鹝 yìyì 〈书面〉(of a goose) honk

鮨 yì 〈动物〉cabrilla

诣 yì 〈书面〉❶ call on (sb. one respects); visit: ~前请教 call on sb. for advice /~烈士墓致祭 go to the tomb of martyrs to pay one's respects ❷ (academic or technical) attainments: 造~很深 high scholarly attainments

逸 yì ❶ ease; leisure; rest: 好~恶劳 love ease and hate work /闲情~致 leisurely and carefree mood /劳~结合 strike a proper balance between work and rest; alternate work with rest and recreation /一劳永~ get sth. done once and for all ❷ escape; flee; run away: 逃~ escape /奔~ gallop away ❸ live in seclusion or solitude: 隐~ lead the life of a hermit ❹ be lost: ~文 ancient essay no longer extant ❺ surpass; excel: 少有~群之才 one whose talent excel all others in one's youth

逸才 yìcái person of exceptional ability and talent: 旷世~ person of unparalleled ability and talent in his or her time
逸荡 yìdàng *also* "逸宕" 〈书面〉dissolute; dissipated: 风流~ dissolute and unrestrained
逸乐 yìlè comfort and pleasure; leisure and joy
逸民 yìmín hermit; recluse: 古之~ recluse in ancient times
逸趣 yìqù easy and unaffected interest; unconventional and original charm: ~横生 replete with humour; replete with refined interest
逸群 yìqún be preeminent; excel all others
逸散 yìsàn (of gas, liquid, etc.) be lost; evaporate; dissipate: 天气炎热, 地里的水分很快就~了。The weather being so hot, the soil moisture in the fields soon evaporated. /石英粉新产品必须用纸袋包装, 防止粉尘~。Products of arenaceous quartz must be packed in paper bags in order to prevent any loss of quartz dust.
逸史 yìshǐ historical records not included in official history; unofficial history
逸事 yìshì anecdote (esp. about a famous person and not to be found in official records): 名人~ celebrities and their anecdotes
逸闻 yìwén anecdote (not to be found in official records); hearsay: ~趣事 anecdotes and interesting episodes /搜集前代作家的~ collect the anecdotes of writers of former generations
逸豫 yìyù 〈书面〉leisure and pleasure; ease and comfort: ~可以亡身。Leisure and sensual pleasure may lead to self-destruction. /吾惟日孜孜, 无敢~。I work hard day and night, not daring to play and enjoy.
逸韵 yìyùn unconventional charm or appeal: 画面上寥寥几笔, ~无穷。With just a few strokes, the drawing strikes the eye as unusually appealing.
逸致 yìzhì unconventional and original interest: 闲情~ leisurely and carefree mood; free and unconventional frame of mind

肄 yì study

肄业 yìyè study in school or at college: 大学~ study at college (without graduating)

狭 yì *see* "林狭" línyì

毅 yì firm; resolute; steadfast: 坚~ firm and staunch /刚~不拔 resolution and fortitude

毅力 yìlì willpower; will; tenacity; stamina: 锻炼~ temper one's willpower /具有异常顽强的~ have great tenacity /以惊人的~与病魔作顽强的斗争 carry on a tenacious struggle against a disease with amazing stamina
毅然 yìrán resolutely; firmly: ~辞职 be set on resigning /他~表示, 毕业后到边疆去参加建设。He resolved that upon graduation he would go to the border areas and throw himself into the development work there.
毅然决然 yìrán-juérán determinedly; resolutely; with a will: 当年, 她~抛弃了优裕的生活, 奔赴延安, 投身革命。In those years she resolutely gave up an easy life and went to Yan'an in pursuit of the revolutionary cause.
毅勇 yìyǒng staunch and courageous: 小说塑造了一个朴实~的农民形象。The novel gives a vivid portrayal of a simple and dauntless peasant.

疫 yì epidemic disease; pestilence: 瘟~ plague /鼠~ bubonic plague /防~ epidemic prevention; prophylaxis /免~ immunity (from disease) /检~ quarantine

疫病 yìbìng epidemic disease: 防止~蔓延 prevent an epidemic disease from spreading
疫疠 yìlì epidemic disease; pestilence
疫苗 yìmiáo 〈医学〉vaccine
疫情 yìqíng information about and appraisal of an epidemic; epidemic situation: 控制~ keep the epidemic under control /~报告站 station for reporting epidemic diseases
疫区 yìqū epidemic-stricken area

役 yì ❶ labour: 劳~ corvée; forced labour /徭~ corvée /赋~ taxes and corvée ❷ military service: 现~ active service; active duty /服~ serve in the army /退~ retire from military service /免~ exempt from service ❸ work; use: 使~ work (livestock) /奴~ enslave ❹ 〈旧语〉servant: 仆~ servant; flunkey /差~ runner or bailiff in a feudal *yamen* /杂~ odd-jobs man (in office, school, etc.) /夫~ (forced) labourer; hard labourer /衙~ *yamen* runner ❺ battle; campaign: 平津之~ Beiping-Tianjin campaign /台儿庄之~ battle of Tai'erzhuang /毕其功于一~ win victory in a single battle; accomplish the whole task at one stroke

役畜 yìchù draught animal; beast of burden
役龄 yìlíng ❶ enlistment age; conscription age: ~青年 enlistment ager (person whose age falls within the span suitable or authorized for military service) ❷ years of military service: 他有五年~。He served in the army for five years.

役使 yìshǐ work (domestic animals); use: ～耕牛犁地 plough the fields with farm oxen / 反动统治阶级无情地～百姓。The reactionary ruling class mercilessly worked the common people as if they were beasts of burden.

役用 yìyòng work (domestic animals): ～牛 draught ox

忆(憶) yì

recall; recollect: 回～往事 recall the past / 记～犹新 remain fresh in one's memory

忆苦 yìkǔ recall one's sufferings in the old society: 吃一顿～饭 have a poor meal specially prepared to remind people of past sufferings

忆苦会 yìkǔhuì meeting to recall past sufferings

忆苦思甜 yìkǔ-sītián recall past sorrows and savour present joys; tell of one's sufferings in the old society and one's happiness in the new; contrast past misery with present happiness

忆念 yìniàn miss; think of; cherish the memory of: ～战友 cherish the memory of (*or* miss) one's comrades-in-arms

忆述 yìshù recall and relate: ～往事 recount past events

忆昔抚今 yìxī-fǔjīn take a look at the present while recollecting the past; relate the present to the past: ～, 心潮澎湃 be seized with an upsurge of emotion when contrast the present with the past

忆想 yìxiǎng think back; recall; recollect: ～往事 recollect past events / ～当年话别的情景 recall the scene of parting

亿(億) yì

❶ hundred million ❷〈古语〉hundred thousand

亿万 yìwàn hundreds of millions; millions upon millions: 以～计 (in) hundreds of millions; millions upon millions / ～电视观众收看了这场足球赛。Hundreds of millions of TV viewers watched the football match.

亿万富翁 yìwàn fùwēng billionaire; multi-millionaire

亿万斯年 yìwàn-sīnián billions of years; time without end; aeons; infinity: 从此以后, 人类将～长享其利。Thereafter and for all time, mankind will always enjoy the benefits.

艺(藝) yì

❶ skill; technique: 手～ craftsmanship; workmanship / 园～ horticulture; gardening / 农～ agronomy / 多才多～ be of many gifts; be talented ❷ art: 文～ art and literature ❸〈书面〉norm; criterion; limit: 用人无～ choose people without criteria / 贪贿无～ be insatiably greedy for bribes

艺高人胆大 yì gāo rén dǎn dà *also* "艺高胆大" boldness of execution stems from superb skill; great skill engenders bravery

艺妓 yìjì (Japan) geisha

艺林 yìlín ❶ places where collections of classic books are stored ❷ art circles; art world

艺龄 yìlíng length of one's artistic career: 他们的～都在十年以上。They have all been performing artists for over ten years.

艺名 yìmíng stage name (of an actor or actress): 京剧艺术家周信芳先生的～是麒麟童。The famous Beijing opera actor Mr. Zhou Xinfang is known by the stage name Qilintong.

艺能 yìnéng artistic skill; art; skill

艺人 yìrén ❶ actor or artist (in traditional Chinese opera, storytelling, acrobatics, etc.): 京剧～ Beijing opera actor / 相声～ comic dialogue (*or* crosstalk) performer / 杂技～ acrobat / 说书～ storyteller ❷ artisan; handicraftsman: 绣花～ embroiderer / 牙雕～ ivory carver

艺术 yìshù ❶ art: 民间～ folk art / 语言～ linguistic art / ～标准 artistic standard / ～风格 artistic style / ～技巧 artistry; craftsmanship / ～珍品 art treasure / ～水平 artistic level / ～形式 artistic form; forms of art / ～价值 artistic value / ～魅力 artistic attraction / ～天才 artistic talent; artistic gift / 很深的～造诣 profound artistic attainments / 为～而～ art for art's sake / ～至上 art is supreme; art above all else / ～是生活的反映。Art is the reflection of life. ❷ skill; art; craft: 教学～ teaching skills; art of teaching / 管理是一门～。Management is an art. ❸ artistic; tasteful; stylish: 这种服装样式挺～。The style of this kind of dress is in very good taste. / 这幅招贴画很～。This poster is very artistic.

艺术家 yìshùjiā artist: ～协会 artists' association

艺术界 yìshùjiè art world; art circles: ～联合会 federation of art circles

艺术品 yìshùpǐn work of art: 精美的～ elegant work of art / 这件～价值连城。This work of art is priceless.

艺术思维 yìshù sīwéi *also* "形象思维" xíngxiàng sīwéi thinking in terms of images

艺术体操 yìshù tǐcāo *also* "韵律体操" yùnlǜ tǐcāo artistic or rhythmic gymnastics

艺术团 yìshùtuán art troupe; art ensemble

艺术性 yìshùxìng artistic quality; artistry: 思想性和～的统一 unity of ideological content and artistic quality

艺术指导 yìshù zhǐdǎo art director

艺坛 yìtán art circles: ～新秀 new star in the art circles; promising young artist / ～大师 great master of the arts; master artist; great artist

艺徒 yìtú〈方言〉apprentice; trainee

艺文 yìwén ❶ (general term for) books: *see* "～志" ❷ art and literature: 希腊罗马科学之盛殊不逊于～。In Greece and Rome science flourished no less than art and literature.

艺文类聚 Yìwén Lèijù *Collection of Books*, encyclopaedic work compiled by Ouyang Xun (欧阳询, 557-641) et al. of the Tang Dynasty

艺文志 yìwénzhì ❶ catalogue of biographical history, political literature and local records; bibliography ❷ poems and essays collected in local records

艺苑 yìyuàn realm of art and literature; art and literary circles: ～奇葩 superb work of art

艺苑卮言 Yìyuàn Zhīyán *Observations on Literature*, work by Wang Shizhen (王世贞, 1526-1590) of the Ming Dynasty

呓(囈、讛) yì

talk in one's sleep: 梦～ talk in one's sleep; somniloquy

呓语 yìyǔ ❶ talk in one's sleep: 他夜里～不断。He kept talking in his sleep during the night. ❷ delirious utterances; crazy talk; ravings: 此文连篇～, 不知所云。The article was full of crazy talk. No one knew what it was driving at.

呓怔 yìzheng *also* "呓挣" panic in one's sleep; struggle in one's sleep

怿(懌) yì

〈书面〉rejoice; be happy: 不～ not happy

译(譯) yì

translate; interpret: 口～ oral interpretation / 笔～ written translation / 直～ literal translation / 意～ liberal (*or* free) translation / 摘～ translate extracts / ～成密码 encipher; encode / 破～密码 crack a code / 古文今～ translate ancient Chinese prose into contemporary Chinese / 把讲话～成英语 translate the speech into English

译本 yìběn translation; version: 《红楼梦》的最早英～ earliest English version of *A Dream of Red Mansions* / 他的著作有多种文字～。His works have been translated into many languages.

译笔 yìbǐ quality or style of a translation: ～传神 vivid translation / ～生硬 awkward translation / ～流畅。The translation reads well (*or* smoothly).

译电 yìdiàn ❶ encode; encipher ❷ decode; decipher: ～费 coding fee

译电员 yìdiànyuán decoder; code clerk; cryptographer

译电组 yìdiànzǔ code and cipher section

译稿 yìgǎo translated manuscript; script of a translation

译介 yìjiè translate and introduce; translate with introductory notes

译码 yìmǎ decode; decipher

译码器 yìmǎqì decoder; decipherer

译名 yìmíng translated term or name

译述 yìshù translate and narrate; render freely

译文 yìwén translated text; translation: ～与原文 translation and the original / 非正式～ tentative (*or* unofficial) translation

译意风 yìyìfēng simultaneous interpretation installation

译音 yìyīn transliteration: 这个汉语词是英文的～。This Chinese word is a transliteration from the English.

译员 yìyuán interpreter

译载 yìzǎi translate (an article, etc.) and carry it in the paper

译者 yìzhě translator

译制 yìzhì dub: ～导演 dubbing director

译制片 yìzhìpiàn dubbed film

译注 yìzhù translate and annotate: ～古籍 translate classics with

annotations
译著 yìzhù works of translation
译作 yìzuò translated works (essays, books, etc.)

驿(驛) yì 〈旧语〉post station (now usu. used in place names): 龙泉～ Longquanyi or Dragon Spring Station, a place in Sichuan Province
驿丞 yìchéng official in charge of the post
驿道 yìdào post road
驿馆 yìguǎn *also* "驿舍" posthouse
驿吏 yìlì posthouse officer
驿路 yìlù post road
驿马 yìmǎ posthorse
驿舍 yìshè posthouse (where formerly couriers changed horses or rested)
驿使 yìshǐ courier (travelling on a post road)
驿站 yìzhàn *see* "驿舍"
驿卒 yìzú runner at a post

绎(繹) yì 〈书面〉unravel; sort out: 抽～ sort things out; get things into shape / 演～ deduction

斁(斁) yì 〈书面〉loathe; be tired of
see also dù

翌 yì 〈书面〉immediately following in time; next: ～年 next year / ～晨 next morning
翌日 yìrì next day

翊 yì 〈书面〉assist (a ruler): ～卫 assist in safeguarding sth. / ～戴 assist and support (a ruler)
翊赞 yìzàn 〈书面〉assist (a monarch, etc.)

熠 yì 〈书面〉brilliant light; brilliance; brightness
熠耀 yìyào 〈书面〉brilliant; dazzling
熠熠 yìyì 〈书面〉radiant; brilliant: 光彩～ brilliant splendour / 霓虹灯～闪光。The neon light flashed brilliantly.

羿 Yì ❶ name of a hero in ancient Chinese legend who was good at archery ❷ a surname

异(異) yì ❶ not the same; different; dissimilar: 同母～父 uterine; born of the same mother but not the same father / 求同存～ seek common ground while reserving differences / 标新立～ flaunt sth. new in order to be different; do sth. unconventional or unorthodox / 同中有～。There is difference in identity. ❷ strange; bizarre; unusual; extraordinary: 优～ excellent; outstanding / 特～功能 extrasensory function (of certain organs) / 奇装～服 exotic costume; bizarre dress ❸ surprising; astonishing; odd: 诧～ be surprised; be astonished / 骇～ be appalled; be shocked / 深以为～ it strikes one as very odd / 观此奇景，余甚～之。Seeing the wonderful view I was greatly impressed. ❹ other; another: 见～思迁 change one's mind the moment one sees sth. new / 党同伐～ defend those who belong to one's own faction and attack those who don't ❺ separate; part; divide: 离～ divorce
异邦 yìbāng alien land; foreign country: 漂泊～ wander in an alien land
异步 yìbù 〈物理〉asynchronous: ～发电机 asynchronous generator / ～计算机 asynchronous computer / ～操作 asynchronous operation / ～振子 nonsynchronous vibrator
异才 yìcái outstanding ability or talent
异彩 yìcǎi extraordinary splendour; radiant brilliance: 大放～ blossom in radiant brilliance / ～纷呈 in varied colourful splendour / 这部巨著在文学史上永放～。The monumental work will always shine with extraordinary splendour in the history of literature. / 阳光下，宫殿的琉璃瓦放射出光辉灿烂的～。In the sunshine the glazed tiles of the palace radiated with dazzling splendour.
异常 yìcháng ❶ unusual; abnormal; odd: 举动～ act strangely / 感觉～ not feel one's usual self / 出现了某种～的情况。Something unusual has happened. / 心肺未见～。Nothing abnormal about the heart and lungs has been observed. / 眼神里有一种～的表情。There was an odd expression in the eyes. ❷ extremely; exceedingly; particularly: ～凶猛 extremely ferocious / 天气～炎热。It is exceedingly hot. / 这青年～朴实可爱。The youth was exceptionally simple and lovable. / 这个问题～重要。The matter was particularly important.
异常蛋白 yìcháng dànbái 〈生化〉paraprotein
异常期 yìchángqī anomalistic period
异词 yìcí dissenting words; disagreement; objection: 会上颇有～。Many people raised objections at the meeting.
异地 yìdì place far away from home; alien land: 在～经商 engage in trade far from home / 父子～相逢。The father and son met in an alien land.
异动 yìdòng ❶ unusual step or move: 军队～ unusual movement of troops ❷ sudden change: 人事～ sudden personnel reshuffle
异读 yìdú variant pronunciation
异端 yìduān unorthodox belief; heterodoxy; heresy: ～思想 unorthodox idea (*or* thinking) / ～教义 heretical religious doctrine / 视为～ regard as heterodoxy
异端邪说 yìduān-xiéshuō heretical beliefs; unorthodox opinions: 这种学说刚刚提出时，被人视为～。When first expounded the theory was regarded as a heresy.
异构 yìgòu 〈化学〉isomerism: ～体 isomer / ～现象 isomerism / ～化 isomerization
异构裂化 yìgòu lièhuà 〈化工〉isocracking: ～物 isocrackate
异构酶 yìgòuméi 〈生物〉isomerase
异国 yìguó foreign country or land: ～他乡 alien land / 流落～ wander destitute in a foreign country / 远适～ go to a far away foreign country / ～情调 exotic flavour; the exotic / ～风光 scene of a distant land
异核体 yìhétǐ 〈生物〉heterocaryon
异乎 yìhū different from; not the same as: 其言行～往昔。The way he spoke and behaved was not the same as before.
异乎寻常 yìhū-xúncháng out of the ordinary; unusual; extraordinary: ～地紧张 be extraordinarily nervous / ～地兴奋 be unusually excited
异花传粉 yìhuā chuánfěn 〈植物〉cross-pollination
异花受精 yìhuā shòujīng 〈植物〉allogamy; cross-fertilization
异化 yìhuà ❶ alienate: 同一稻种，种在不同地区，会发生～。Alienation may occur if the same strain of rice is planted in a different area. ❷〈哲学〉alienation: 劳动的～ alienation of labour ❸〈语言〉dissimilation
异化作用 yìhuà zuòyòng 〈生物〉dissimilation
异基因 yìjīyīn 〈生物〉heterogen
异己 yìjǐ dissident; alien: ～分子 dissident; alien element / 排除～ exclude those who hold different views; shut out dissidents
异教 yìjiào paganism; heathenism: ～徒 pagan; heathen
异军突起 yìjūn-tūqǐ a new force emerges all of a sudden: 80 年代，通俗音乐在我国～。In the eighties pop music became all the rage in our country.
异口同声 yìkǒu-tóngshēng with one voice; in unison: 大家～表示赞成。Everyone consented with one voice. / 人们～地称赞他是一名好教员。People all (*or* unanimously) praised him as a good teacher.
异喹啉 yìkuílín 〈化工〉isoquinoline
异类 yìlèi ❶〈旧语〉people not of the same ethnic group ❷ (of birds, animals, grass, trees, ghosts, etc.) different from humans
异能 yìnéng ❶ different in function ❷ outstanding talent
异配生殖 yìpèi shēngzhí 〈生物〉heterogamy; anisogamy
异氰酸 yìqíngsuān 〈化学〉isocyanic acid
异曲同工 yìqǔ-tónggōng *also* "同工异曲" sing different tunes with equal skill; be different in approach but equally satisfactory in result; achieve the same goal through different means: 这两种做法～。Though different, the two methods are equally satisfactory. / 两部小说～，各有千秋。The two novels are equally good and have merits of their own despite their different approaches.
异趣 yìqù ❶ different in taste and interest ❷ peculiar taste: 这个画家运笔着色多有～。The painter exhibited an unconventional taste in the delineation and colouration of his paintings.
异染色体 yìrǎnsètǐ 〈生物〉heterochromosome; allosome
异人 yìrén ❶〈旧语〉unusual person; immortal ❷ other people
异日 yìrì 〈书面〉❶ some other day; future days: 待诸～ wait till some other day / ～必将报答 will surely repay (sb.'s kindness, etc.) in future ❷ (in) former days; (in) bygone times: ～情怀，萦绕心头。Memories of former days lingered in the mind.

Y

异生长素 yìshēngzhǎngsù 〈植物〉heteroauxin
异兽 yìshòu strange animal：珍禽～ rare birds and animals
异数 yìshù 〈书面〉special courtesy or hospitality
异说 yìshuō ❶ differing views：百家～ differing views of myriad schools；hundred schools of thought ❷ absurd remarks；absurdity
异酞酸 yìtàisuān 〈化工〉isophthalic acid
异体 yìtǐ ❶ variant (as of a word) ❷ not belonging to the same body or individual：～组织移植 alien tissue transplant
异体受精 yìtǐ shòujīng 〈动物〉allogamy；cross-fertilization
异体字 yìtǐzì variant form of a Chinese character
异同 yìtóng ❶ similarities and dissimilarities：试比较一下二者的～。Try to compare the similarities and differences between the two. ❷ 〈书面〉objection；dissent：会上既已决定，不宜再有～。Once decided at the meeting, it is no longer appropriate to raise objections before others.
异图 yìtú plot；intention to rebel
异途 yìtú ❶ different road ❷ unusual path or way：解决这个难题，他别有～。He adopted an unusual way to solve the difficult problem.
异途同归 yìtú-tóngguī *also*"殊途同归"shūtú-tóngguī different roads lead to the same destination；all roads lead to Rome：他们的试验取得了～的效果。Their experiments, though different in approach, produced the same results.
异外 yìwài extraordinarily；extremely；exceptionally：～舒畅 extremely happy
异位妊娠 yìwèi rènshēn 〈医学〉heterotopic pregnancy
异位素 yìwèisù 〈化学〉heterotope
异味 yìwèi ❶ rare delicacy：今日得以品尝～。I was able to taste a rare delicacy today. ❷ peculiar smell；strange odour：打开门就闻到一股～。There was a whiff of a peculiar smell when the door was opened.
异文 yìwén ❶ variant (of a character) ❷ variations (about sth.) in different editions of the same book；different versions (about the same event, etc.)
异戊基 yìwùjī 〈化学〉isoamyl：～氯 isoamyl chloride
异物 yìwù ❶ foreign matter；foreign body：气管～ foreign body in the trachea ❷ 〈书面〉dead person：化为～ turn into a dead body；die ❸ 〈书面〉queer articles；bizarre goods
异乡 yìxiāng foreign land；strange land：～人 person from elsewhere；stranger；alien／身居～ live in a foreign land／独在～为异客，每逢佳节倍思亲。As an alien visitor in a strange land all by oneself, One thinks all the more of one's dear relatives on festive occasions.
异香 yìxiāng peculiar fragrance：～满室。The room is permeated with a peculiar fragrance.
异想天开 yìxiǎng-tiānkāi indulge in the wildest fantasy；have a most bizarre idea：休要～。Don't indulge in fantasies.
异心 yìxīn apostasy；infidelity；disloyalty：怀有～ harbour disloyalty／上下～。The leadership and the rank and file are not of one mind.
异行 yìxíng 〈书面〉excellent deed；exemplary conduct
异形钢材 yìxíng gāngcái 〈冶金〉special-shaped steel
异形管 yìxíngguǎn 〈冶金〉special pipe
异形细胞 yìxíng xìbāo 〈生物〉heterocyst
异型 yìxíng irregular shape；special type：～钢管 special-shaped steel pipe
异性 yìxìng ❶ opposite sex：～间的往来 contacts between the (opposite) sexes ❷ different or dissimilar in nature：～的电互相吸引，同性的电互相排斥。Unlike electric charges attract each other, while like ones repel each other.
异姓 yìxìng not have the same surname：同名～ have the same first name but different surnames／～结亲 marriage between people of different surnames
异烟肼 yìyānjǐng 〈药学〉isoniazid；rimifon
异言 yìyán 〈书面〉dissenting words；objection：毫无～ no objection whatsoever
异样 yìyàng ❶ different：没有太大～ be not much different／她看上去与两年前没有～。She looks the same as she did two years ago. ❷ unusual；peculiar；odd：衣着～ wear peculiar dress (*or* outlandish clothes)／～的沉着 unusually calm／这几天他有些～。He has been a bit odd these days.／村民们用～的眼光看着来客。Villagers looked at the visitor with curious eyes.
异议 yìyì disagreement；objection；dissent：持～ dissent；have objections／～蜂起 outburst of dissenting voices／对这个方案没有～。There is no opposition to the plan.／我们对这种做法提出～。We took exception to this approach.
异域 yìyù ❶ foreign country：身在～，心怀祖国 have one's native land in mind while residing in a foreign country ❷ other than one's native place：兄弟均在～打工。Both brothers are working away from home.
异源多倍体 yìyuán duōbèitǐ 〈生物〉allopolyploid
异质嫁接 yìzhì jiàjiē 〈生物〉heteroplastic graft
异质组织 yìzhì zǔzhī 〈生物〉heterogeneous tissue
异种移植 yìzhǒng yízhí 〈医学〉heterograft；heteroplasty；heterotransplantation：～物 heteroplastid
异重流 yìzhòngliú 〈水利〉density current
异状 yìzhuàng ❶ strange shape ❷ unusual condition
异族 yìzú different race or nation：～通婚 mixed marriage／不适应～的生活习惯 be not used to the way of life of a different race

翼

翼 yì ❶ wing of a bird, etc.：蝉～ cicada's wings／如虎添～ like a tiger that has grown wings — with might redoubled／不～而飞 disappear without a trace；vanish into thin air／比～双飞 pair off wing to wing；fly side by side ❷ wing of an aeroplane：机～ wing of an aeroplane／副～ aileron／尾～ tail surface；empennage ❸ side；flank：左～ left side／右～ right side／两～阵地 both flanks of the front ❹ one of the twenty-eight constellations in ancient astronomy ❺ 〈书面〉assist (a ruler)；aid：扶～ render assistance (to a ruler) ❻ 〈书面〉*see*"翌"yì ❼ (Yì) a surname
翼蔽 yìbì 〈书面〉cover；conceal
翼侧 yìcè *also*"侧翼"〈军事〉flank：～迂回 outflank／从～向敌发起攻击 launch a flank attack／～的兵力已掩蔽在丛林中。The flank forces have already been deployed under the cover of the forest.
翼翅 yìchì wing
翼护 yìhù shield someone with one's body
翼手龙 yìshǒulóng 〈生物〉pterodactyl (*Pterodactylus*)
翼手目 yìshǒumù 〈动物〉*Chiroptera*：～动物 chiropter；chiropteran
翼型 yìxíng 〈航空〉wing section；aerofoil
翼翼 yìyì ❶ in a grave and cautious manner；cautiously：小心～ with exceptional caution；very carefully ❷ in neat formation；in good order：商邑～ as neat and tidy as the capital city of the Shang (Dynasty) ❸ thriving；flourishing；multitudinous；numerous：草花～。The grass and flowers were flourishing.
翼展 yìzhǎn horizontal length between the tips of the two wings of a monoplane；span of wings：这种鹰的～可达三米。When the eagle spreads its wing, it spans 3 metres from tip to tip.
翼指龙 yìzhǐlóng *see*"翼手龙"
翼状胬肉 yìzhuàng nǔròu 〈生理〉pterygium

廙

廙 yì 〈书面〉respect；reverence

yīn

音

音 yīn ❶ sound；voice：杂～ sound interference／录～ sound-recording／乡～未改 not change one's home accent／口～太重 speak with a strong accent ❷ news：静候佳～ wait patiently for the good news (*or* glad tidings) ❸ syllable：双～词 disyllabic word ❹ pronounce："区"字作姓时～"欧"。The character "区"(qū) is pronounced as "欧"(Ōu) when used as a family name. ❺ tone：纯～ pure or simple tone／重～ complex tone
音爆 yīnbào 〈航空〉sonic boom
音爆风洞 yīnbào fēngdòng sonic boom wind tunnel
音标 yīnbiāo 〈语言〉phonetic symbol；phonetic transcription：国际～ International Phonetic Symbols／给这些单词注上～。Give phonetic transcriptions to these words.
音波 yīnbō sound wave
音波发光机 yīnbō fāguāngjī 〈物理〉phonophote
音叉 yīnchā tuning fork：～断路器〈电工〉tuning-fork circuit breaker／～控制〈通信〉tuning fork control
音叉手表 yīnchā shǒubiǎo Accutron or electronic watch
音叉钟 yīnchāzhōng electronic clock
音长 yīncháng sound length

音尘 yīnchén 〈书面〉information; message; news
音程 yīnchéng (musical) interval
音带 yīndài magnetic tape; cassette (tape)
音调 yīndiào tone; pitch: ～深沉 (speak) with a full and deep voice /轻柔的～ soft tone /降低～ lower one's pitch /改变～ modulate the pitch /说话的～ tone of one's voice /这歌儿的～太高。This song is too high-pitched. /这种乐器的～太沉闷。The sound of this instrument is too mournful. /朗诵诗应注意～的变化。Attention should be paid to cadence when one recites a poem.
音调计 yīndiàojì tonemeter
音调失真 yīndiào shīzhēn tonal distortion
音读 yīndú pronunciation (of a Chinese character)
音符 yīnfú 〈音乐〉(musical) note: 全～ semi-breve /二分～ half note; minim /四分～ quarter note; crotchet /八分～ eighth note; quaver /十六分～ sixteenth note; semi-quaver /三连～ triplet
音高 yīngāo 〈音乐〉pitch
音鼓 yīngǔ sound drum
音耗 yīnhào 〈书面〉news: 久无～ have not heard from sb. for a long time
音级 yīnjí sound level
音阶 yīnjiē 〈音乐〉scale
音节 yīnjié *also* "音缀"〈语言〉syllable: 单～的词 single syllable word; monosyllablic word /多～字 polysyllable /重音在第三个～上。The accent is on the third syllable.
音节表 yīnjiébiǎo syllabary
音节文字 yīnjié wénzì syllabic language
音控开关 yīnkòng kāiguān voice-operated switch
音量 yīnliàng sound volume: ～控制 volume control /最大～ maximum volume /最小～ minimum volume
音律 yīnlǜ *also* "乐律" yuèlǜ 〈音乐〉temperament
音名 yīnmíng 〈音乐〉musical alphabet
音频 yīnpín audio frequency: ～系统 audio system /～信号 sound signal /～电波 voice-frequency electric waves /～振荡器 audio-frequency oscillator
音频调制 yīnpín tiáozhì 〈无线电〉voice or tone modulation
音品 yīnpǐn *see* "音色"
音强 yīnqiáng *see* "音势"
音区 yīnqū section of the sound range; register: 高～ upper register /低～ lower register /中～ medium register
音儿 yīnr 〈方言〉❶ voice: 气得他连～都变了。His voice changed with anger. ❷ implication: 听话听～ listen for the meaning behind sb.'s words /他觉出她的话～带着刺儿。He sensed a sarcastic tone in her voice.
音容 yīnróng 〈书面〉voice and look of sb.; likeness of sb.: ～笑貌, 历历在目 sb.'s look and voice still fresh in one's memory /这幅肖像画画出了他的～神韵。The portrait is a good likeness of him.
音容宛在 yīnróng-wǎnzài one could recall sb.'s voice and look as if sb. were still alive
音色 yīnsè *also* "音品"; "音质" tone colour; timbre: 这个女演员的～不错。This woman singer has good timbre. /这把小提琴～欠佳。This violin doesn't have the best tone colour.
音诗 yīnshī 〈音乐〉tone poem
音势 yīnshì 〈语言〉intensity of sound
音素 yīnsù 〈语言〉phoneme
音素文字 yīnsù wénzì *see* "音位文字"
音速 yīnsù 〈物理〉speed of sound; sound velocity: 亚～ subsonic /超～ supersonic /高超～ hypersonic
音位 yīnwèi 〈语言〉phoneme
音位文字 yīnwèi wénzì *also* "音素文字"〈语言〉phonemic language
音位学 yīnwèixué phonemics
音问 yīnwèn news; word: ～断绝。All channels of communication have been severed.
音息 yīnxī message; news; word: 互通～ communicate with each other; stay in touch with one another /渺无～ have no news whatsoever of sb.; have not heard from sb.
音系学 yīnxìxué 〈语言〉phonology
音箱 yīnxiāng sound box; speaker
音响 yīnxiǎng ❶ sound; acoustics: ～效果 sound effects; acoustics /～设备 sound (*or* acoustic) equipment /～导航 acoustic navigation /～鱼雷〈军事〉acoustic torpedo ❷ (short for 组合音响) hi-fi stereo component system; hi-fi system
音像 yīnxiàng audio and video: ～制品 audio and video products /～器材 audio and video equipment /～出版社 audio-video publishing house /～市场 audio-video tape market
音信 yīnxìn *also* "音讯" news; mail: ～杳无 no news (about sb.) whatsoever /～不断 keep in communication (with each other) /常有～来往 be in frequent correspondence
音型 yīnxíng 〈音乐〉figure (a characteristic pattern of sounds that gives expression to certain emotions or artistic conceptions)
音讯 yīnxùn *see* "音信"
音义 yīnyì ❶ pronunciation and meaning of a word: ～不同 different both in pronunciation and meaning ❷ (often used in book titles) annotations on questions of pronunciation and semantics in a book
音译 yīnyì *also* "译音" translate words of one language into another by similar sounds; transliterate
音域 yīnyù 〈音乐〉range; compass; gamut
音乐 yīnyuè music: ～中心 music centre /～效果 musical effect /爱听～ be fond of music; love music /～欣赏 enjoyment (*or* appreciation) of music /古典～ classical music /现代～ modern music /流行～ popular music; pop /民间～ folk music /乡村～ country music /～指挥 (concert) conductor /无标题～ absolute music /标题～ programme music
音乐电视 yīnyuè diànshì music TV (MTV)
音乐会 yīnyuèhuì concert: 独奏～ (instrumental) recital
音乐家 yīnyuèjiā musician
音乐节 yīnyuèjié musical festival
音乐剧 yīnyuèjù musical comedy
音乐美学 yīnyuè měixué music aesthetics
音乐片 yīnyuèpiàn musical film; musical
音乐社会学 yīnyuè shèhuìxué music sociology
音乐厅 yīnyuètīng concert hall: 北京～ Beijing Concert Hall
音乐学 yīnyuèxué musicology
音乐学院 yīnyuè xuéyuàn conservatory of music; music school
音韵 yīnyùn ❶ harmonious sounds; meter and rhyme of poems and other literary writings: ～悠扬 melodious sounds; rhythmical sounds ❷ sound, rhyme and tone of Chinese characters
音韵学 yīnyùnxué 〈语言〉phonology: ～家 phonologist /～专著 treatise on phonology
音障 yīnzhàng sound barrier; sonic barrier
音值 yīnzhí 〈语言〉value
音质 yīnzhì ❶ tone colour ❷ tone quality (of musical instrument) ❸ acoustic fidelity (of radio, recording, etc.)
音专 yīnzhuān (short for 音乐专科学校) school of music (at the polytechnical level)
音缀 yīnzhuì *see* "音节"
音准 yīnzhǔn 〈音乐〉tone accuracy

愔 yīn

愔愔 yīnyīn quiet; silent

喑(瘖) yīn

〈书面〉❶ hoarse, husky: ～不能言 have lost one's voice ❷ silent; mute: 万马齐～ ten thousand horses stand mute — an apathetic atmosphere
喑哑 yīnyǎ (of voice) hoarse; husky: 嗓音～低沉 with a hoarse, muffled voice /一排子弹射去, 敌人的机枪～了。A volley of bullets silenced the enemy machine-gun.

闉 yīn

❶〈古语〉gate of a barbican outside a walled city ❷〈书面〉block up

禋 yīn

❶〈古语〉name of the rites of offering a sacrifice to heaven ❷ offer a sacrifice to gods or ancestors

堙 yīn

〈书面〉❶ mound ❷ block up; stop up

因 yīn

❶〈书面〉follow; carry on: 陈陈相～ follow a set routine; stay in the same old groove ❷〈书面〉on the basis of; in accordance with; in the light of: ～病下药 prescribe for a patient according to the symptoms /～利乘便 take advantage of the opening; exploit the opportunity ❸ cause; reason; grounds: 前～后果 cause and effect; whys and hows; ins and outs /内～ internal fac-

Y

tor /外～ external factor /事出有～。There is good reason for it. *or* It's by no means accidental. ❹ because; due to; as a result of:～病未能出席会议 be absent from a meeting because of one's health (*or* illness) /～公负伤 getting injured while on duty; work-related injury /这次春游～故取消了。The spring trip was cancelled for some reason. /～天气不好,飞机不能按时起飞。The departure of the flight has been delayed due to bad weather.

因变数 yīnbiànshù 〈数学〉dependent variable; function

因材施教 yīncái-shījiào teach a person in accordance with his (*or* her) aptitude; suit the instruction to the student's level

因此 yīncǐ therefore; consequently; for this reason; as a result:我们事先作了充分准备,～会议开得很成功。The conference was a big success as a result of our meticulous preparations. /我俩同窗四年,～结下深厚友谊。We were in the same class for four years and became very good friends.

因次 yīncì 〈物理〉dimension:～分析 dimensional analysis /～公式 dimensional formula /～单位 dimensional unit

因地制宜 yīndì-zhìyí do what is appropriate in the light of local circumstances; act according to circumstances; suit measures to local conditions:在山区普及小学教育要～。To popularize education at the primary school level in remote mountainous areas, we must take flexible measures in line with local conditions. /我们可以～,办一个水果罐头厂。We can set up a fruit-canning factory to make full use of the fruits grown in the locality.

因而 yīn'ér therefore; thus; as a result; with the result that:雪融化时要吸收热量,气温～会下降。The snow absorbs heat when melting, and the temperature would drop as a result.

因钢 yīngāng 〈冶金〉invar

因果 yīnguǒ ❶ cause and effect:颠倒～ invert cause and effect; put the cart before the horse /互为～ interact as both cause and effect ❷〈佛教〉karma; destiny; preordained fate

因果报应 yīnguǒ-bàoying retribution for sin

因果律 yīnguǒlǜ law of causality; law of causation

因果论 yīnguǒlùn theory of causation; causationism

因祸得福 yīnhuò-défú profit by adversity:你可以说是～。Yours is a case where good comes out of misfortune.

因陋就简 yīnlòu-jiùjiǎn make do with whatever is available; do things as simply and thriftily as possible:他们十个人～,挤在一个小房间里办公。The ten of them made do with a small room and used it as their office.

因明 yīnmíng science of argumentation and refutation in ancient India; classical Indian logic

因人成事 yīnrén-chéngshì achieve sth. with the help of others; rely on others for success:我哪里有多大功劳,不过是～罢了。The credit is not really mine. My success would have been impossible without the support of others.

因人而异 yīnrén'éryì *also* "因人而施" differ from person to person; vary with each individual:下药～ prescribe different medicine for different people /教练～地制定了训练方案。The coach drew up a training plan which catered to the needs of each of the athletes.

因人设事 yīnrén-shèshì create a job to accommodate a person:～是造成机构臃肿,人浮于事的主要原因之一。Creating unnecessary jobs is one of the main causes for overstaffing and bloated bureaucracy.

因人制宜 yīnrén-zhìyí make arrangements for individuals according to their specific conditions; do what is suited to each person; vary from one person to another:确定研究生的研究课题,要～。The research topics should vary with each individual graduate student.

因仍 yīnréng 〈书面〉pursue as before; carry on; follow:转相～ follow sb. else by carrying on as before /～旧贯 follow an old routine

因时制宜 yīnshí-zhìyí suit measures to the changing circumstances; do what is suited to the occasion

因式 yīnshì *also* "因子"〈数学〉factor:～分解 factoring; factor analysis

因势利导 yīnshì-lìdǎo make the best use of the situation and guide sth. along in the light of its general trend; adroitly guide action according to circumstances; take the tide at the flood:～,争取胜利 make the best use of the situation and seize victory

因数 yīnshù 〈数学〉factor; divisor:～分解 resolution into factors; factorization

因素 yīnsù ❶ element (of the essence of sth.); component:英语词汇中的拉丁～ Latin element in English vocabulary ❷ cause or circumstance that brings about success or failure; factor:重要～ important factor /心理～ psychological factor /社会～ social factor /积极～ positive factor /未知～ unknown factor /决定性～ determinant /～论〈哲学〉theory of factors

因素分析法 yīnsù fēnxīfǎ 〈经济〉factor analysis

因特网 yīntèwǎng *also* "国际互联网" guójì hùliánwǎng (formerly ARPAnet) Internet:～服务提供者 ISP (Internet service provider) /～接入提供者 IAP (Internet access provider) /～内容经营商 ICP (Internet content provider) /～查询服务 Internet search service /上～ access the Internet; get on line /下～ exit the Internet; get off line /浏览～ surf the Internet; browse the Internet

因头 yīntóu 〈方言〉❶ pretext; excuse:这出戏他实在不想看,就借个～出去了。As he didn't want to watch the opera at all, he left on an excuse. ❷ reason; cause:事体总有个～,不会无中生有。Things must have a cause and can't come from nowhere. *or* There is no smoke without fire.

因为 yīnwei because; for; as; on account of:昨天没来看你,是～我有急事要办。I did not come to see you yesterday because I had some urgent matters to attend to. /～治疗及时,他的病好得很快。He recovered speedily thanks to timely treatment.

因袭 yīnxí follow (old customs, rules, methods, etc.); copy:～古制 copy the ancient system /～陈规 stick to outmoded rules

因小见大 yīnxiǎo-jiàndà from small things one can see important issues

因小失大 yīnxiǎo-shīdà try to save a little only to lose a lot; be penny wise and pound foolish; be wise or careful in small matters but not in important ones:我们不能鲁莽行事,～。We mustn't make any rash move, or else we'll be paying too big a price for a little gain.

因循 yīnxún ❶ continue to follow (old customs, rules, etc.); stay in the same rut:～旧例 follow the old rules ❷ procrastinate; delay:～延误 procrastinate until it is too late

因循守旧 yīnxún-shǒujiù stay in the old rut; stick to old ways; follow the beaten track

因噎废食 yīnyē-fèishí give up eating for fear of choking — refrain from doing sth. necessary for fear of a slight risk; throw out the baby with the bathwater:在教育改革中,不能因为出了点问题就～。In educational reform, we should not abandon our efforts simply because of a few minor setbacks.

因应 yīnyìng cope with; deal with:研议～之道 study and discuss ways to cope with the situation /销路不好,以减产～ have to deal with slack business by cutting down on production /～经济形势而调整利率 adjust the interest rate in accordance with the changing economy

因由 yīnyóu reason; cause:不同～ regardless of the cause /事情的～ the whys and wherefores of the matter

因缘 yīnyuán ❶〈佛教〉principal and subsidiary causes; cause ❷ predestined relationship:有～ be predestined /这也是我们前世结下的～。This relationship between us is ordained by fate.

因之 yīnzhī therefore; hence; consequently; thus:风势愈大,海浪～愈加汹涌。The stronger the wind, the more rough the seas.

因子 yīnzǐ 〈数学〉factor; divisor

see also "因数";"因式"

洇(湮) yīn

(of ink) spread and sink in; run:～色 diffusion (*or* running) of colouring matter / 这种纸写字～得厉害。Ink blots this paper. *or* Ink runs on this paper.

烟 yīn

see also yān

烟煴 yīnyūn *see* "氤氲" yīnyūn

茵(裀) yīn

mattress:在绿～场上驰骋 run freely on the green (*or* grass-covered) playground /芳草如～ carpet of green grass; sweet meadow

茵陈 yīnchén 〈中药〉capillary artemisia (*Artemisia capillaris*)

茵褥 yīnrù mattress

茵茵 yīnyīn (of plants, grass, etc.) lush and thick:芳草～ lush growth of fragrant grass /一片～嫩绿的麦苗 patch of lush green wheat seedlings

铟 yīn 〈化学〉indium (In)

氤 yīn

氤氲 yīnyūn *also* "烟煴" yīnyūn; "细缊" yīnyūn 〈书面〉(of smoke, mist, etc.) dense; thick: 云烟～ enshrouding mist / 灵山多秀色, 空水共～。What splendid beauty the Lingshan Mountains have, The air, the water, all enshrouded in mist.

姻(婣) yīn ❶ marriage: 联～ connect by marriage / 婚～ marriage ❷ relation by marriage: ～兄 brother-in-law

姻伯 yīnbó brother's or sister's father-in-law

姻亲 yīnqīn relation by marriage: 结为～ become relatives through marriage / 这两家有～关系。The two families are related by marriage.

姻娅 yīnyà *also* "姻亚" 〈书面〉relatives by marriage; in-laws

姻缘 yīnyuán predestined marital relationship; match made by Heaven: 美满～ happy marriage; conjugal felicity (*or* bliss) / 千里～一线牵。The happy fate brings together lovers a thousand *li* apart.

骃 yīn 〈古语〉black horse with streaks of white hair

细 yīn

细缊 yīnyūn *see* "氤氲" yīnyūn

殷[1] yīn 〈书面〉❶ rich; plentiful; abundant: 海内～商 well-known rich merchant ❷ eager; ardent: 国家对诸位期望甚～。The country cherishes high hopes of you. ❸ hospitable; cordial: 情意甚～ sincere hospitality; deep affection

殷[2] Yīn ❶ Yin Dynasty, the later period of the Shang (商) Dynasty ❷ a surname

see also yān; yǐn

殷富 yīnfù rich; wealthy: ～之国 rich and prosperous country

殷钢 yīngāng 〈冶金〉invar

殷鉴 yīnjiàn 〈书面〉bitter lesson; example of past setback as a warning

殷鉴不远 yīnjiàn-bùyuǎn the lessons of history are close at hand; one need not look far back for a lesson; the setbacks of one's predecessors should be taken as a warning

殷切 yīnqiè earnest; ardent; eager: ～的期望 ardent expectations / ～的教诲 sincere (*or* earnest) teaching

殷勤 yīnqín *also* "慇懃" yīnqín keen to please; eagerly attentive; solicitous: ～接待 show solicitous hospitality / ～地马上端茶倒水 bring in tea immediately with eager attentiveness / 一个劲儿地向她献～ do everything to please her; shower attentions upon her

殷实 yīnshí well-to-do; well-off; substantial: ～之家 well-off family / 家道～ family of substance

殷墟 Yīnxū 〈考古〉Yin ruins, ruins of the capital city of the late Shang Dynasty near Xiaotun Village (小屯村), Anyang (安阳) City, Henan Province, where inscriptions on bones and tortoise shells were discovered in 1899

殷殷 yīnyīn ❶ ardent; eager: ～嘱咐 exhort again and again ❷ sad; distressed: 忧心～ be extremely worried and sad

殷忧 yīnyōu deep worries; profound anxiety: 内怀～ anxiety gnawing at the heart; have gnawing pains of anxiety

慇 yīn

慇懃 yīnqín *see* "殷勤" yīnqín

阴(陰、隂) yīn ❶ principle of *Yin* (as opposed to 阳 *Yang* in Chinese philosophy); feminine or negative principle in nature: ～阳交错。The *Yin* and *Yang* forces are opposing but complementary to each other. ❷ moon: 太～ moon ❸ (of weather) overcast; cloudy; gloomy: ～转晴 (of the weather) become sunny; clear up / 这些日子天气又～又晦。It's been gloomy and miserable these days. ❹ shade: 背～儿的地方 shady spot / 树～ shade of a tree ❺ north of a hill or south of a river: 淮～ Huaiyin (county south of the Huaihe River) / 泰山之～ north side of Mount Tai ❻ back: 碑～ back of a stone tablet ❼ in intaglio: *see* "～文" ❽ hidden; secret; underhand: 阳奉～违 say nice things to a person's face but play tricks behind his back; overtly agree but covertly oppose; double-deal ❾ sinister; perfidious; foul: ～笑 sinister smile (*or* laughter) / 此人很～, 你要小心。He is a treacherous person. You've got to be careful with him. ❿ of the nether world: *see* "～司" ⓫ 〈物理〉negative: ～射线 negative ray ⓬ private parts (esp. of the female) ⓭ (Yīn) a surname

阴暗 yīn'àn dim; dark; gloomy: ～的色调 gloomy colour; depressing colour / ～的房间 dingy (*or* dim) room / 他的脸色～。He wore a glum face. / 她的心情随着暮色的～也～起来。She fell prey to melancholy as dusk sank into murky night. / 这个消息使整个村子笼罩在一种～的气氛之中。The news cast a gloom over the village.

阴暗面 yīn'ànmiàn 〈比喻〉dark or seamy side of things; unhealthy things in life: 社会的～ seamy side of society / 揭露～ expose unhealthy things (*or* malpractices)

阴病 yīnbìng 〈中医〉disease of deficiency

阴部 yīnbù 〈生理〉private parts; pudenda

阴惨 yīncǎn ❶ (of weather) overcast; gloomy; dismal: 天色～ gloomy, dismal day ❷ wretched; miserable; tragic: 神色～ look wretched; look miserable / ～的叫声 agonized cries / 庙中空无一人, 野草丛生, 一副～的样子。It was a desolate-looking temple, deserted and overgrown with weeds.

阴曹 yīncáo *also* "阴曹地府" Hades; nether world

阴沉 yīnchén overcast; gloomy; sombre; dismal: 暮色～ gloomy dusk / 脸色～ be grim-faced; look glum / 天色越变越～了。The sky was getting heavier with dark clouds. / 他的面色很快地～下来。His face darkened instantly.

阴沉沉 yīnchénchén sombre; overcast; gloomy: 天色～的 gloomy sky / 脸色～ have a sombre expression on one's face; look glum

阴沉木 yīnchénmù *also* "阴杪" a kind of hard, fine-grained wood (usu. cypress), long buried underground due to movement of the earth's crust, formerly regarded as best material for making coffins

阴唇 yīnchún 〈生理〉labia (of the vulva)

阴错阳差 yīncuò-yángchā *also* "阴差阳错" mistake or error due to a strange combination of circumstances; accidental mistake or error: 我们～地把这份通知落下了。Quite accidentally, we forgot to send out this notice.

阴丹士林 yīndānshìlín ❶ 〈化学〉indanthrene ❷ cotton fabric dyed with indanthrene

阴道 yīndào 〈生理〉vagina: ～出血 vaginal haemorrhage / ～镜 colposcope / ～牵开器 vaginal retractor / ～闭塞 elytroclesis

阴道缝合术 yīndào fénghéshù 〈医学〉colporrhaphy

阴道切开术 yīndào qiēkāishù 〈医学〉vaginotomy

阴道炎 yīndàoyán vaginitis

阴德 yīndé good deed to the credit of the doer in the next world: ～不小 accumulate much credit for good work (e.g. kindness and generosity to the poor, sick, etc.) / 你就积点～不好吗? Why don't you do some good deeds which will exempt you from sufferings when you get to the nether world?

阴地 yīndì shaded place or land; shade

阴地植物 yīndì zhíwù shade plant

阴蒂 yīndì 〈生理〉clitoris: ～头 glans clitoridis / ～体 corpus clitoridis / ～系带 frenulum clitoridis

阴电 yīndiàn negative electricity; negative charge: ～子 negatron / ～势 electronegative potential

阴毒 yīndú treacherous and vicious; sinister; insidious: ～的心肠 vicious by nature / 手段～ insidious means

阴风 yīnfēng ❶ chill winds: 他来到园中, 突然～四起, 不觉打了一个寒颤。As he went into the garden, chill winds began to sweep in, sending a cold shiver down his spine. ❷ evil or ill wind: 扇～, 点鬼火 fan the winds of evil and spread the fires of turmoil; stir up (*or* foment) trouble

阴符经 Yīnfújīng *also* "黄帝阴符经" Huángdì Yīnfújīng *Yin Fu Jing* or *Classic of Secret Revelation*, a Taoist classical work

阴阜 yīnfù 〈生理〉mons veneris; mons pubis

阴干 yīngān dry in the shade: 这件纯毛毛衣洗了要～。This pure wool sweater should be dried in the shade.

阴功 yīngōng ❶ *see* "阴德" ❷ sinister energy

阴沟 yīngōu sewer; covered drain; sewerage: 挖～ dig a sewer / ～里翻船 capsize in a drain — fail where failure is least expected / ～堵了。The sewer is blocked up. *or* The drains are stopped up. / 那个小村庄哪有什么～? That village is too small to have a sewerage system.

阴河 yīnhé underground river

阴黑 yīnhēi dark; dusky; gloomy:脸色～ look glum; be grim-faced /天色～。It is dark and gloomy.
阴狠 yīnhěn sly and vicious; sinister; ruthless:～的敌人 cunning and ruthless enemy
阴户 yīnhù *see* "阴门"
阴晦 yīnhuì dark; gloomy:脸色～ have a sombre countenance /天色～,说不定会下雨。The sky is so dark; it'll probably rain.
阴魂 yīnhún 〈迷信〉soul; spirit; ghost
阴魂不散 yīnhún-bùsàn one's spirit refuses to leave; the ghost lingers on; the evil influence remains:在这些地方,浮夸风仍然～。In these places, exaggeration and boasting remain a problem.
阴极 yīnjí ❶〈电学〉negative electrode ❷〈电子〉negative pole; cathode:～棒 cathode bar /～板 negative plate /～块 cathode block /～区 negative polarity zone /～效率 cathode efficiency /～端子 cathode terminal /～调制 cathode modulation /～极化 cathodic polarization /～耦合 cathode coupling /～电容 cathode capacitance /冷～ cold cathode
阴极保护 yīnjí bǎohù 〈冶金〉cathodic protection; electrolytic protection
阴极射线 yīnjí shèxiàn 〈物理〉cathode ray:～炉 cathode-ray furnace /～管 cathode-ray tube /～输出 cathode-ray output /～磁控管 cathode-ray magnetron /～加速器 cathode-ray accelerator /～录波器 cathode-ray oscillograph
阴间 yīnjiān *also* "阴曹";"阴司" nether world; Hades
阴茎 yīnjīng 〈生理〉penis; phallus:～根 radix penis; root of penis /～囊 cirrus penis /～骨 baculum; os penis /～套 condom /～包皮 prepuce of penis; praeputium penis /～海绵体 corpus spongiosum /～炎〈医学〉penitis /～异常勃起〈医学〉priapism
阴刻 yīnkè intaglio
阴冷 yīnlěng ❶ (of weather) cold and gloomy:～的早晨 freezing and gloomy morning /屋里～～的,使人觉得寒气袭骨。It's so cold in the room that the chill goes into the bones. ❷ sombre; cold; glum:脸色～ be grim-faced; look sombre /～的性格 of a cold and glum nature
阴离子 yīnlízǐ 〈物理〉negative ion; anion:～交换 anion exchange
阴历 yīnlì lunar calendar; traditional Chinese calendar:～腊月初八 eighth day of the twelfth month of the lunar year
阴凉 yīnliáng ❶ shady and cool:那棵大树底下很～。It's nice and cool under that big tree. /找一个～的地方坐一坐。Let's go and find a shady and cool spot for a rest. ❷ (usu. followed by 儿) cool shade:那儿有个～儿,咱们去歇歇。Let's go and have a rest in the shade over there.
阴灵 yīnlíng soul; spirit
阴霾 yīnmái haze:秋日的清晨,远处的群山透过一层～,依稀可见。The mountain ranges in the distance are vaguely visible through the early morning haze of the autumn day. /他们在战争的～下生活。They lived under the shadow of war.
阴毛 yīnmáo 〈生理〉pubic hair; pubes; pubisure
阴门 yīnmén *also* "阴户"〈生理〉vagina; vaginal orifice; vulva
阴面 yīnmiàn (of buildings, etc.) northern or shady side
阴谋 yīnmóu conspiracy; plot; underhand scheme:～活动 conspiracy /～诡计 conspiracy; schemes and intrigues /～手段 conspiratorial means /～陷害某人 plot (*or* conspire) to frame sb. /～政变 scheme to stage a *coup d'état* /不让他们的～得逞 not let them succeed in their evil design /粉碎他们的～ shatter their machination (*or* scheme)
阴谋集团 yīnmóu jítuán conspiratorial clique
阴谋家 yīnmóujiā conspirator; intriguer; schemer
阴模 yīnmú 〈冶金〉matrix
阴囊 yīnnáng 〈生理〉scrotum; oscheo:～瘤 oscheocele; oscheoma /～石 oscheolith /～炎 oscheitis (*or* oschitis); scrotitis /～水肿 hydrocele; scrotal hydrocele
阴匿 yīnnì *also* "阴蚀";"阴痒"〈中医〉vulvitis
阴平 yīnpíng high and level tone (first of the four tones in modern standard Chinese pronunciation)
阴坡 yīnpō northern or shady slope of a hill
阴凄 yīnqī ❶ gloomy; dark and miserable:～的牢房 dark and miserable prison cell ❷ gruesome; ghastly:深夜山上传来豺狼～的嚎叫声。In the dead of night there came from the hills the gruesome howls of wolves.
阴器 yīnqì private parts; genital organ
阴燃 yīnrán burn without flame; smoulder
阴森 yīnsēn gloomy and horrid; ghastly; gruesome:～的古庙 gruesome looking old temple /～的树林 deep, dark wood /洞里阴森森的,寒气逼人。It was ghastly in the cave and there was a forbidding chill.
阴山 Yīnshān Yinshan Mountains, lying along the northern periphery of North China Plain, and natural border between Hans and minority nomads in ancient time
阴山背后 yīnshān-bèihòu 〈口语〉remote and secluded place:你躲在那～干吗呢? What on earth are you doing hidden out there?
阴生植物 yīnshēng zhíwù *see* "阴地植物"
阴盛 yīnshèng predominance of *Yin*
阴盛阳衰 yīnshèng-yángshuāi ❶〈中医〉*Yin* rises while *Yang* declines; the preponderance of *Yin* impairs *Yang* ❷ the *Yang* forces recede in favour of the *Yin* forces (the female being stronger and more powerful, or more numerous than the male)
阴虱 yīnshī crab louse; phthirus pubis
阴湿 yīnshī dark and damp:～的夹道 dark and damp passage
阴事 yīnshì 〈书面〉secret doings not known to others
阴寿 yīnshòu ❶ (old custom of) celebration of every tenth anniversary of the birthday of a late elder member of the family:为某人做～ celebrate the birthday of a dead person ❷〈迷信〉life span of dead person's ghost in the nether world
阴司 yīnsī nether world; Hades
阴私 yīnsī secret not to be divulged; shameful secret; skeleton in the cupboard:揭穿～ expose a shameful secret /不可告人的～ sinister secret; skeleton in the cupboard
阴燧 yīnsuì ancient utensil made of bronze and tin used to collect dew drops on moonlit nights
阴损 yīnsǔn ❶ insidious and acrimonious; sly and sarcastic:这人说话～。This person speaks with vicious and biting sarcasm. ❷ harm on the sly; secretly do harm to:当面装笑脸,背后～人。All smiles to your face, he will stab you in the back.
阴桫 yīnsuō *see* "阴沉木"
阴天 yīntiān overcast sky; cloudy sky
阴文 yīnwén characters cut in intaglio
阴险 yīnxiǎn sinister; insidious; sly and crafty; treacherous:～毒辣 sinister and vicious; insidious and ruthless /居心～ have (*or* harbour) a sinister motive /为人～狡猾 be crafty and treacherous /～的敌人 insidious foe
阴笑 yīnxiào sinister smile or grin:他脸上露出一丝～。The shadow of a sinister smile flickered over his face.
阴性 yīnxìng ❶〈医学〉negative:～反应 negative reaction /他的类固醇化验结果为～。He tested negative for steroid. ❷〈语言〉feminine gender:"火车"这个词在法文里是～还是阳性? What gender is "train" in French, feminine or masculine?
阴性植物 yīnxìng zhíwù 〈植物〉sciophyte
阴虚 yīnxū 〈中医〉deficiency of *Yin* (insufficiency of body fluid or of vital essence of internal organs):～宜补 make up for the deficiency of *Yin* (usu. by taking more nutritious food) /～肺燥 dryness of the lung due to deficiency of *Yin*, with symptoms such as dry cough, sore throat, and thready and rapid pulse, seen in pulmonary tuberculosis or chronic bronchiectasis /～阳亢 deficiency of *Yin* brings on pathological hyperactivity of *Yang*, symptoms of which are tidal fever, flushed cheeks, night sweating, insomnia, etc.
阴阳 yīnyáng ❶ (in ancient Chinese philosophy) *Yin* and *Yang*, opposite principles or forces existing in nature and human affairs ❷ ancient theory on the rules governing the functioning of celestial bodies such as the sun and the moon ❸ astrology, divination, geomancy, etc.; astrologer, geomancer, sorcerer, etc.
阴阳怪气 yīnyáng-guàiqì ❶ eccentric; queer; cynical; abnormal:这人～的。This is a queer chap. *or* He is eccentric. /这些日子天气老是～的,不晴也不雨。The weather has been abnormal these days, neither clear nor rainy. ❷ (usu. purposefully) mystifying; equivocal; enigmatic; ambiguous:他这个人净说些～的话,肚子里不知画的是啥道道。He always speaks enigmatically. Nobody knows what he has up his sleeve.
阴阳家 yīnyángjiā ❶ (Yīnyángjiā) *Yin-Yang* School; School of Positive and Negative Forces (in the Warring States Period) ❷ *see* "阴阳生"
阴阳历 yīnyánglì lunisolar calendar:农历是一种～。The traditional Chinese calender is a kind of lunisolar calendar.

阴阳人 yīnyángrén ❶ bisexual person; hermaphrodite ❷ *yin-yang* adept; geomancer

阴阳生 yīnyángshēng *also* "阴阳先生" geomancer (usu. employed as adviser on selection of a grave site, housesite or propitious day for doing sth.)

阴阳水 yīnyángshuǐ 〈中医〉 mixed drink of cold and boiling water, or of river and well water usu. to go with medicine or be mixed with it

阴阳头 yīnyángtóu head half shaved (as a sign of humiliation, esp. during the Cultural Revolution, 1966-1976)

阴一套,阳一套 yīn yī tào, yáng yī tào *also* "阳一套,阴一套" act one way in public and another in private; be engaged in double-dealing: 我发现这个人～。I found him Janus-faced. /这个人～,很难对付。The man is a double-dealer, very hard to deal with.

阴翳 yīnyì *see* "荫翳" yīnyì

阴影 yīnyǐng shadow; shade: 树的～ shade of a tree /高楼的～ shadow (*or* shade) of a tall building /他做过肺部透视,发现～。He had an X-ray, and a shadow was found on his lungs. /一场悲剧的～正笼罩着这座深宅大院。The shadow of a tragedy is hanging over the mansion. /他脸上现出失望的～。A faint expression of disappointment appeared on his face. /这件丑闻给他的名誉投下一层～。This scandal has cast a slur on his reputation.

阴雨 yīnyǔ overcast and rainy: 连日的～使她心情郁闷。An unbroken spell of wet and miserable weather plunged her into a deep gloom. /碰上～天,这路就不成路了。Whenever it rains, the road simply becomes a muddy ditch.

阴郁 yīnyù gloomy; miserable; dismal; depressed: ～的天色 gloomy sky /～的眼睛 sad eyes /脸色～ look depressed; have a face shaded with melancholy /她总是那么～。She always looks sad and miserable.

阴云 yīnyún dark clouds: ～密布。The sky is overcast. /～四合。Dark clouds are gathering.

阴韵 yīnyùn 〈语言〉 category of all classical Chinese *yunmu* (韵母) except those belonging to *rusheng* (入声), i.e. those ending in b, d and g, and *yangyun* (阳韵), i.e. those ending in m, n and ng

see also "阳韵" yángyùn

阴贼 yīnzéi 〈书面〉 sinister and sly; crafty and vicious

阴宅 yīnzhái 〈迷信〉 residence in the nether world; graveyard

阴着儿 yīnzhāor 〈方言〉 treacherous act; insidious trick: 使～ play a treacherous trick

阴鸷 yīnzhì 〈书面〉 crafty and ruthless

阴骘 yīnzhì *also* "阴德" good deed to the credit of the doer in the next world

荫(蔭) yīn

shade (of a tree): 在凉爽的树～下 under the cool shade of the trees /大树成～。Big trees give shade. *or* Leafy trees make shade. /她喜欢在湖畔柳～里散步。She enjoys strolling in the shadow of willow trees along the lake.

see also yìn

荫蔽 yīnbì ❶ shade; cover: 在树丛的～之中 within the shadow of the grove /到了炎热的夏天,这些树木～住灼热的阳光。When summer comes, these trees give shade from the scorching sun. ❷ be shaded or hidden as by foliage: 在灌木丛里～起来 hide out in the bushes; hide among the bushes /小屋～在丛林之中。The shed lies hidden among the trees. /他已经～两个月了。He has remained in hiding for two months.

荫凉 yīnliáng *see* "阴凉" yīnliáng

荫棚 yīnpéng ❶ shed over saplings, etc. ❷ shed that provides shade (in hot days)

荫翳 yīnyì ❶ 〈中医〉 corneal opacity; nebula ❷ shade; shadow (of trees): 树木～的河边 river banks shaded by trees ❸ rich foliage: 桃李～ peach and plums trees with rich foliage

荫影 yīnyǐng *also* "阴影" yīnyǐng shade of a tree: 房子正好处在树的～里。The house is shaded nicely by the trees.

yín

淫(❸❹婬) yín

❶ excessive; extreme: *see* "～雨"; "～威" ❷ indulge; wallow: 乐而不～ enjoy oneself without indulging in sensual pleasures ❸ adulterous; promiscuous; dissolute: 卖～ prostitution /奸～ rape; ravish ❹ lewd; obscene; pornographic: ～笑 lewd (*or* lustful) smile /～话 obscene language; dirty remark

淫奔 yínbēn 〈旧语〉 (of women) elope

淫辞 yíncí *also* "淫词" ❶ 〈书面〉 exaggeration: ～滥调 unbridled talk ❷ obscene language; obscenity: ～浪语 obscene language; dirty talk /～秽语 bawdy language; obscene remarks

淫荡 yíndàng loose (in morals); licentious; lascivious; lewd: ～不羁 lascivious and unbridled

淫风 yínfēng licentious habits; wanton customs; lax sex morals: 此种～不可长。This licentious custom must be checked.

淫妇 yínfù wanton woman; adulteress; scarlet woman

淫棍 yíngùn satyr; womanizer; rake

淫画 yínhuà pornographic or obscene pictures

淫秽 yínhuì obscene; pornographic; salacious; bawdy: ～书刊 pornographic books and magzines /～录像带 pornographic videotapes

淫贱 yínjiàn morally loose; lewd and low; lascivious and mean

淫乐 yínlè indulging in carnal pleasures; sexual indulgence

see also yínyuè

淫乱 yínluàn sexually promiscuous; licentious; loose in sexual relations: ～的行为 licentious conduct; promiscuous sex

淫靡 yínmǐ ❶ obscene and decadent; immoral: ～的歌曲 obscene and decadent songs ❷ extravagant; showy and luxurious: 风俗～ wasteful and extravagant custom (*or* way of life)

淫书 yínshū pornographic book; pornography

淫威 yínwēi abuse of power; despotic power: 慑于权贵的～ be cowed by the despotic power of bigwigs (*or* the establishment) /施～ abuse one's power; ride roughshod over others

淫猥 yínwěi obscene; salacious: ～的话语 obscene remarks /～的画面 salacious scene

淫邪 yínxié obscene and wicked; lewd and vicious

淫亵 yínxiè obscene; salacious; sexually harassing: ～的行为 salacious conduct /语言～。The language is obscene.

淫刑 yínxíng 〈书面〉 ❶ abuse power of punishment; mete out punishment freely ❷ excessive punishment

淫羊藿 yínyánghuò 〈中药〉 longspur epimedium (*Epimedium macranthum*)

淫逸 yínyì *also* "淫佚"; "淫泆" loose; licentious; given to ease and luxury

淫雨 yínyǔ *also* "霪雨" yínyǔ too much rain; excessive rain: 这些天～霏霏,庄稼可倒了霉了。The crops have been suffering from excessive rain these days.

淫欲 yínyù sexual desire; lust

淫乐 yínyuè 〈书面〉 obscene and decadent music

see also yínlè

霪 yín

霪雨 yínyǔ *see* "淫雨" yínyǔ

寅 yín

third of the twelve Earthly Branches

see also "干支" gānzhī

寅吃卯粮 yínchī-mǎoliáng *also* "寅支卯粮" eat next year's food; eat one's corn in the blade; anticipate one's income; spend on deficit: 公司近年不景气,常常是～。In recent years, the company has been doing poorly and often has to operate on borrowed money.

寅时 yínshí period of the day from 3 a.m. to 5 a.m.

夤 yín

〈书面〉 ❶ hold in respectful awe: ～畏 hold sb. in respect and awe ❷ deep: *see* "～夜"

夤夜 yínyè 〈书面〉 late at night; in the depths of the night; in the dead of night; in the small hours of the morning: ～出击 attack (the enemy) in the middle of the night /～来访,必有要事。You wouldn't call on me so late at night if you didn't have some important business.

夤缘 yínyuán 〈书面〉 make use of one's connections to climb up the social ladder; try to advance one's career by fawning on bigwigs: ～得官 use one's connections (*or* networking) to get an official position

訚 yín

訚訚 yínyín 〈书面〉 have proper manners in debate

狺 yín

狺狺 yínyín 〈书面〉yap; yelp:猛犬~。A fierce dog was barking furiously.

蟫

yín 〈古语〉silverfish; fish moth

嚚

yín 〈书面〉❶ stupid and stubborn:愚~ stupid and stubborn ❷ sly and vicious

吟(唫)

yín ❶ intone; recite; chant:~诗作画 recite (*or* compose) poetry and do brush-work /仰天长~ chant loud and long to the sky /缓行低~ walk slowly and chant to oneself ❷〈书面〉groan; lament; sigh:昼~宵哭 groan in the day and weep at night ❸ song (as a type of classical poetry):李白的《江上~》Li Bai's *Song on the River* ❹ cry of certain animals (usu. used in poetry):猿~ cry of monkeys /蝉~ cicada's song /龙~虎啸 roar of dragons and tigers

吟唱 yínchàng sing; chant; recite:~流行歌曲 sing pop songs /低声~ sing (*or* chant) in a low voice

吟哦 yín'é *see* "吟咏"

吟风弄月 yínfēng-nòngyuè *also* "吟风咏月" sing of the moon and the wind — write sentimental verse; write pastoral poetry:写的无非是些~的文章。His writings are simply devoted to praising the wind and the moon. *or* He writes nothing but sentimental prose.

吟诵 yínsòng chant; recite:~古诗 chant (*or* recite) a classic verse

吟味 yínwèi hum or recite with appreciation; intone with relish:仔细~ recite with deep appreciation /~再三 recite again and again in appreciation

吟咏 yínyǒng recite with a cadence; intone; chant:高声~诗词 recite (*or* intone) poems loudly

崟(崯)

yín *see* "嵚崟" qīnyín

圻

yín 〈书面〉*see* "垠" yín

see also qí

龂

yín 〈书面〉❶ *see* "龈" yín ❷ *see* "龂龂" yínyín

龂龂 yínyín 〈书面〉argue

垠

yín 〈书面〉boundary; limit:平沙无~ boundless desert; vast expanse of desert /一望无~ stretch beyond the horizon; stretch far into the distance; stretch as far as the eye can see

龈

yín gum; gingiva:牙~ gum /~出血 ulorrhagia; oulorrhagia /~袋 gingival pocket /牙~炎 gingivitis

龈瘤 yínliú 〈医学〉epulis

龈脓肿 yínnóngzhǒng 〈医学〉gum-boil; parulis

龈炎 yínyán 〈医学〉gingivitis:疱肿性~ herpetic gingivitis

银

yín ❶ silver (Ag):~项链 silver necklace /~线 silver thread /~质奖章 silver medal /包~戒指 silvered ring /镀了~ be coated with silver; be silver-coated ❷ relating to money:收~台 cashier's desk /~箱 cash box /库中已无~。No money is left in the bank. ❸ silver-coloured:~灰色 silver grey; silvery /~色的月光 silvery moon; silver moon; silvern moon ❹ (Yín) a surname

银白 yínbái silvery white:~色的窗纱 silvery white inner curtain /月光把池塘照得一片~。Moonlight silvered the pond.

银白杨 yínbáiyáng white poplar

银杯 yínbēi silver cup:他们捧回了大赛的~。They won a silver cup at the game. *or* They brought home a silver cup from the contest.

银本位 yínběnwèi 〈经济〉silver standard

银币 yínbì silver coin:~收藏家 silver coin collector

银箔 yínbó silver foil; silver paper

银柴胡 yínchaíhú *also* "银胡";"土参" tǔshēn 〈中药〉*Stellaria sophiloides*

银鲳 yínchāng 〈动物〉silver pomfret (*Stromateoides argenteus*)

银川 Yínchuān Yinchuan, capital city of the Ningxia Hui Autonomous Region

银大麻哈鱼 yíndàmáhǎyú coho; silver salmon (*Oncorhynchus kisutch*)

银弹外交 yíndàn wàijiāo "silver bullet" diplomacy; dollar diplomacy

银锭 yíndìng ❶ silver ingot ❷〈迷信〉ingot made of silvery paper used as offering to ghosts and spirits

银耳 yín'ěr *also* "白木耳" báimù'ěr tremella (*Tremella fuciformis*):~汤 tremella soup

银发 yínfà white hair; silver hair:她上了年岁,已是满头~。Age silvered her hair.

银粉 yínfěn (popular term for 铝粉) aluminium powder

银根 yíngēn 〈经济〉supply in money market; money supply:~紧 tight money /~松 easy money /收紧~政策 tight money policy /~吃紧。The money market is tight.

银光霜 yínguāngshuāng 〈气象〉silver frost; silver thaw

银汉 Yínhàn 〈书面〉Milky Way

银汉鱼 yínhànyú silverside

银焊料 yínhànliào silver solder

银行 yínháng bank:~户头 bank account /~存款 bank deposit /~存折 bankbook /~贷款 bank advance; bank loan /~票据 bank bill /~汇票 bank draft /~倒闭 bank failure /~融资 bank financing /~担保 bank(er's) guarantee /~透支 bank overdraft /~利率 bank rate /~报表 bank return /~支付 bank payment /~职员 bank clerk /~公会 bankers' association /中国人民~ People's Bank of China /中国~ Bank of China /中国工商~ Industrial and Commercial Bank of China /中国农业~ Agricultural Bank of China /建设~ Construction Bank /开发~ Development Bank /联邦储备~ (US) Federal Reserve Bank /美洲~ (US) Bank of America /第一花旗~ (US) Citibank /运通~ (US) American Express Bank /大通~ (US) Chase Manhatten Bank /大陆~ (US) Continental Illinois Bank /英格兰~ Bank of England /巴克莱~ (UK) Barclays Bank /汇丰~ Hongkong and Shanghai Banking Corporation /渣打~ (HK) Charter Bank /恒生~ (HK) Hang Seng Bank /欧洲投资~ European Investment Bank /东京~ Bank of Tokyo /第一劝业~ (Japan) Dai-Ichi Kangyo Bank /法兰西~ Banque de France /世界~ World Bank

银行承兑汇票 yínháng chéngduì huìpiào banker's acceptance

银行法 yínhángfǎ banking law

银行家 yínhángjiā banker

银行团 yínhángtuán (bank) consortium

银行信贷 yínháng xìndài bank credit:~额度 credit line

银毫 yínháo *also* "银毫子" silver coin (of small denominations)

银号 yínhào *also* "钱庄" qiánzhuāng 〈旧语〉banking house

银河 Yínhé 〈天文〉Milky Way:~星云 galactic nebula

银河-III巨型计算机 Yínhé-sān Jùxíng Jìsuànjī Galaxy III Supercomputer

银河系 Yínhéxì Milky Way system; the Galaxy

银河星团 Yínhé xīngtuán 〈天文〉galactic cluster

银红 yínhóng silver pink

银狐 yínhú silver fox

银胡 yínhú *see* "银柴胡"

银桦 yínhuà 〈植物〉silver birch

银环蛇 yínhuánshé silver-ringed snake

银晃晃 yínhuānghuāng silvery:一对~的镯子 pair of silvery bracelets

银灰 yínhuī silver grey:~漆 aluminium paste

银辉 yínhuī silvery rays; white rays:机身在阳光下闪着~。The plane shone silvery in the sun.

银婚 yínhūn silver wedding; 25th wedding anniversary:~纪念 silver wedding anniversary

银匠 yínjiàng silversmith

银胶菊 yínjiāojú 〈植物〉guayule (*Parthenium argentatum*)

银角子 yínjiǎozi *see* "银毫"

银金矿 yínjīnkuàng electrum

银菊胶 yínjújiāo guayule (rubber)

银冷杉 yínlěngshān 〈林业〉silver fir (*Abies alba*)

银莲花 yínliánhuā anemone; pasqueflower; windflower

银两 yínliǎng silver (as currency)

银亮 yínliàng bright and shiny like silver:~的枪尖 flashing bayonet /太阳照得湖面一片~。The lake shone like silver under the bright sun.

银铃 yínlíng silver bell:悦耳的~声 beautiful chime of a silver bell /~般的嗓音 ringing voice /她~般的笑声依然在我耳边回旋。Her peals of laughter seem to be still ringing in my ears.

银楼 yínlóu silverware shop; jewellery or jeweller's shop

银鲈 yínlú 〈动物〉silver perch; white perch; mojarra

银幕 yínmù (motion-picture) screen; silver screen:宽~ wide

Y

screen /这部小说被搬上了～。The novel has been made into a film (*or* movie). /他不适合上～。He doesn't screen well.

银镍合金 yínniè héjīn 〈冶金〉silver-nickel

银鸥 yín'ōu 〈动物〉herring gull (*Larus argentatus vegae*)

银牌 yínpái silver medal:得了一块～ win a silver medal

银票 yínpiào 〈旧语〉paper money (with amount stated in taels of silver)

银屏 yínpíng silver screen (of motion picture or television):～歌声 songs made for the screen /～之花 film (*or* TV) star /重上～ return to the screen

银槭 yínqì 〈植物〉silver maple

银器 yínqì silverware; silver; silver work

银钎焊 yínqiānhàn 〈冶金〉silver brazing

银钎料 yínqiānliào 〈冶金〉silver solder; silver-brazing alloy

银钱 yínqián money:～短缺 short of money

银杉 yínshān 〈植物〉*Cathaya argyrophylla*

银鼠 yínshǔ snow weasel

银树 yínshù 〈植物〉silver tree (*Leucadendron argenteum*)

银丝工艺 yínsī gōngyì silver filament work (such as vases, fruit trays, tea sets, etc., made of silver filament)

银条 yíntiáo silver bar; silver ingot

银团 yíntuán bank consortium; bank syndicate; bank association

银屑病 yínxièbìng psoriasis

银心 yínxīn 〈天文〉galactic centre

银星石 yínxīngshí wavellite

银杏 yínxìng ginkgo; maidenhair:～树 ginkgo tree; ginkgo /～叶 ginkgo leaf

银盐 yínyán 〈化学〉silver salt:～溶液 silver bath

银燕 yínyàn (affectionate term for airplanes) silver bird:十多架～展翅飞翔。There were a dozen or so planes soaring into the sky.

银洋 yínyáng see "银圆"

银样镴枪头 yínyàng làqiāngtóu pewter spearhead that shines like silver; lead counterfeit of a silver spearhead; a good-for-nothing with an impressive appearance; fine feathers but no fine birds:你原来苗而不秀,是个～。So you are really useless like a stalk of grain that bears no ears, a spearhead made of solder!

银鹰 yínyīng (affectionate term for fighter planes) silver eagle

银鱼 yínyú whitebait; salangid; icicle fish; icefish

银元 yínyuán *see* "银圆"

银圆 yínyuán *also* "银元"; "银洋" silver dollar used in the old days

银圆券 yínyuánquàn paper money issued by the Kuomintang government in Guangzhou, Chongqing and other places in July 1949

银晕 yínyùn 〈天文〉galactic halo

银针 yínzhēn silver acupuncture needle

银纸 yínzhǐ paper money; note; bill

银质奖 yínzhìjiǎng silver medal

银钟花 yínzhōnghuā 〈植物〉silver bell

银朱 yínzhū vermilion:～涂料 vermilion paint

银子 yínzi silver

银座 Yínzuò Ginza, fashionable downtown area of Tokyo

yǐn

饮 yǐn ❶ drink; drink wine or other liquor:～酒 drink wine; have a drink /善～ have a great capacity for liquor; be given to drink /痛～ drink to one's heart's content /牛～ drink like a fish /一～而尽 gulp down; drink off (a flagon of wine, etc.) ❷ sth. to drink; drink:冷～ cold drink; ice drink /热～ hot drink ❸〈中药〉decoction of Chinese medicine to be taken cold ❹〈中医〉watery sputum ❺ keep in the heart; nurse; bottle up; bite down hard (usu. of hatred):～辱 nurse humiliation; bury one's humiliation deep

see also yìn

饮冰茹檗 yǐnbīng-rúbò drink ice and eat the tiller — endure the hardest life:此人～数十年而不改其志。The harshest circumstances over the decades did not change the man's high resolve.

饮弹 yǐndàn 〈书面〉be hit or killed by a bullet

饮恨 yǐnhèn 〈书面〉nurse a grievance; bury one's hatred deep in one's heart:～终身 die with a deep grievance in one's heart

饮恨吞声 yǐnhèn-tūnshēng swallow one's hatred and choke back one's sobs; endure insults and humiliations:为报大仇而～ put up with insults and humiliations for the sake of revenge

饮灰洗胃 yǐnhuī-xǐwèi drink lime in order to cleanse the stomach — repent and reform:我当～,痛改前过。I will purge myself of my sins and turn over a new leaf.

饮料 yǐnliào drink; beverage:天然～ natural beverage /软～ soft drink /果汁～ fruit juice

饮片 yǐnpiàn 〈中药〉herbal medicine in small pieces ready for decoction

饮泣 yǐnqì 〈书面〉weep in silence; weep silent tears:～吞声 swallow one's tears; choke back one's sobs

饮刃 yǐnrèn kill or be killed by a knife or sword:～而死 take one's own life by means of a sword; commit suicide by stabbing oneself /～沙场 die by the enemy sword on the battleground

饮食 yǐnshí ❶ food and drink; diet:～卫生 dietetic hygiene; healthful food and drink; healthy diet /～失调 have improper (*or* unbalanced) diet /～结构 diet; pattern of one's diet /调整～ rearrange one's diet /～性肥胖 alimentary obesity /限制～ put sb. on a diet ❷ drink and eat:～不溽 eat a simple diet /～节制 be abstemious in eating and drinking

饮食店 yǐnshídiàn eating house; snack bar; cafe; eatery

饮食工业 yǐnshí gōngyè food and beverage industry

饮食疗法 yǐnshí liáofǎ dietotherapy; sitology; dietetic treatment

饮食男女 yǐnshí-nánnǚ food, drink and sex — man's major desires

饮食学 yǐnshíxué dietetics; sitology

饮食业 yǐnshíyè catering trade

饮水 yǐnshuǐ drinking water; potable water; water for cooking:～卫生 hygiene of drinking water /～短缺 shortage of drinking water

饮水不忘掘井人 yǐn shuǐ bù wàng juéjǐngrén 〈比喻〉when you drink water remember the well digger

饮水器 yǐnshuǐqì 〈畜牧〉drinking bowl; drinker

饮水思源 yǐnshuǐ-sīyuán when you drink water, think of its source — never forget where one's happiness comes from; feel grateful:～当报答,受恩深处岂能忘。I will always bear in mind the kindness I receive and try to repay it.

饮宴 yǐnyàn *also* "饮燕" feast

饮用水 yǐnyòngshuǐ drinking water; potable water

饮誉 yǐnyù enjoy fame; be acclaimed; win praise:～海内外 win worldwide fame /他的作品～文坛。His works are highly acclaimed in literary circles.

饮鸩止渴 yǐnzhèn-zhǐkě drink poison to quench thirst — seek temporary relief regardless of the consequences:运动员靠兴奋剂提高成绩,无异于～。For an athlete, depending on stimulant drugs to improve his (*or* her) performance is just like drinking poison to quench thirst.

饮子 yǐnzi decoction of Chinese medicine to be taken cold

歆 yǐn *see* "饮" yǐn

尹 yǐn ❶ ancient official title:府～ prefect /道～ prefect /京兆～ magistrate of the capital city ❷ (Yǐn) a surname

引 yǐn ❶ draw; pull; stretch:～弓 draw a bow /～车卖浆 sell drinks from a barrow ❷ draw; lead; guide:～路人 guide /～兵南下 lead the army southwards /～滦入津 divert water from the Luan River to Tianjin /～水灌田 draw water to irrigate the fields /一阵浓郁的丁香花的芳香把我们～入园内。A breeze of lilac fragrance drew us into the garden. ❸ leave: *see* "～退"; "～避" ❹ stretch; crane; extend: *see* "～颈"; "～领" ❺ attract; draw; induce:用纸～火 light a piece of paper to start a fire /勾～ lure; seduce /抛砖～玉 cast a brick to attract jade; say a few opening words to induce others to come up with valuable opinions /～燃物 tinder /～蛇出洞 lure the snake out of the hole /栽得梧桐树,～来金凤凰。Plant plane trees to attract the golden pheonix (Opportunity knocks only where conditions are favourable). ❻ cause; arouse; trigger; set off: *see* "～起"; "～人注目" ❼ quote; cite:旁征博～ quote copiously from all available sources /援～名言警句 quote well-known proverbs and adages /～以为耻 regard as a shame ❽ white cloth used to drape over the coffin in a funeral procession ❾〈旧语〉unit of length (= 33⅓ metres)

引爆 yǐnbào ignite; detonate:～装置 igniter; detonator; detonat-

ing device /～雷管 detonating primer; detonator /～速度 detonating rate /～键 firing key /～剂 flashing composition

引避 yǐnbì ❶ make way (for sb.); try to avoid (sb.) ❷ resign one's position (to avoid suspicion or implicity):～去位 resign in order to avoid suspicion

引柴 yǐnchái *also* "引火柴" kindling

引产 yǐnchǎn induced labour:～术 induction of labour

引出 yǐnchū draw forth; lead to; result in:～意想不到的结果 lead to unexpected results /这个偶然的事件～一场大辩论。This accidental event gave rise to a major debate.

引导 yǐndǎo ❶ lead; pilot; show round:你愿意～客人们参观我们农场吗? Would you like to show the guests around our farm? ❷ guide:不要简单地批评学生,要正确地～他们。Instead of rash criticism, we should give the students proper guidance. / 对孩子的学习要善于～。We must learn to guide the children in their study.

引导机车 yǐndǎo jīchē pilot engine

引导脉冲 yǐndǎo màichōng pilot pulse

引导驱动器 yǐndǎo qūdòngqì bootstrap driver

引导信号 yǐndǎo xìnhào pilot signal

引得 yǐndé *also* "索引" suǒyǐn (transliteration) index

引动 yǐndòng touch off; arouse (emotions, moods, etc.):～乡愁 touch off a tinge of nostalgia /这哭声～了他的怜悯心。The weeping aroused sympathy in him.

引逗 yǐndòu tease; tantalize; lure; entice:用一根骨头～小狗 tease a puppy with a bone /她的允诺～得他终日心神不宁。He was tantalized by her promise, feeling restless all day. /他经不起她的～。He was too weak to resist her lure.

引渡 yǐndù ❶ lead across (a river, etc.); guide:～迷津 lead sb. out of confusion ❷〈法律〉extradite:～程序 extradition proceedings/～法 extradition act (*or* law) /～条约 extradition treaty /～方式 form of extradition /可～的人 extraditable person /～罪犯 extradition of criminal /～请求书 demandant of extradition /欧洲～公约 European Convention on Extradition (13 Dec. 1957)

引而不发 yǐn'érbùfā draw the bow but not discharge the arrow — enlighten people through guidance; be skilful at guidance or control; bide one's time fully prepared:～,跃如也。Draw the bow without shooting, just indicate the motions.

引发 yǐnfā initiate; set off; give rise to; arouse:～炸药的导火线 fuse for explosive /天象表演～了大家对天文学的浓厚兴趣。The show of the celestial bodies aroused the audience's keen interest in astronomy.

引发剂 yǐnfājì 〈化学〉initiator

引发价格 yǐnfā jiàgé 〈经济〉trigger price

引港 yǐngǎng *also* "领港" lǐnggǎng ❶ pilot a ship (into or out of a harbour) ❷ pilot

引吭高歌 yǐnháng-gāogē sing at the top of one's voice; sing joyfully in a loud voice; sing heartily:他一时心潮澎湃,不禁～。He was gripped by a sudden surge of emotion and found himself singing loudly. /忽听得江上有人～。Suddenly, someone was heard belting out a song on the river.

引航 yǐnháng *also* "引水" pilotage

引航员 yǐnhángyuán pilot

引号 yǐnhào quotation mark; quote:滥用～ abuse quotation marks /双～ double quotation marks /单～ single quotation marks

引河 yǐnhé ❶ irrigation channel ❷ diversion canal

引火 yǐnhuǒ kindle fire; ignite; light (fire, etc.):引个火 strike a fire /连～的木片也找不到。Not even a thin piece of wood could be found to start (*or* kindle) a fire.

引火烧身 yǐnhuǒ-shāoshēn ❶ *also* "惹火烧身" rěhuǒ-shāoshēn draw fire on oneself — bring trouble on oneself ❷ draw fire against oneself — make self-criticism to encourage criticism from others:我就是要暴露自己的真实思想,～。I've revealed my real thoughts in order to encourage others to comment on them.

引火线 yǐnhuǒxiàn (blasting) fuse

引疾 yǐnjí resign one's official post on ground of ill health

引见 yǐnjiàn introduce; present:承蒙尊夫人～,我结识了这位有名的画家。I was graced by your wife with an introduction to this famous artist. /此人我早已闻名,不知能否～～? I've heard about him so much. I wonder if you could introduce me to him?

引荐 yǐnjiàn recommend:极力～ recommend with enthusiasm; recommend without qualification /我很乐意～他到贵公司任职。I'm pleased to recommend him to your company for a post.

引酵 yǐnjiào ferment; leaven; yeast

引进 yǐnjìn ❶ recommend ❷ introduce from elsewhere; import; absorb:～技术 import (*or* introduce) technology /～外资 absorb foreign funds (*or* investment) /～新品种 introduce new varieties of products /智力～ bring in talents (usu. from abroad) /这是从荷兰～的生产线。This production line was imported from Holland.

引经据典 yǐnjīng-jùdiǎn quote the classics or authoritative works:李教授讲课惯于～。Professor Li often makes copious references to the classics in his lectures.

引颈 yǐnjǐng stretch or crane one's neck:～就戮 stretch one's neck for the execution; wait idly for one's death (*or* defeat) /～企待 eagerly wait for sth. or sb. /他～向窗外张望。He craned his neck to look out of the window.

引咎 yǐnjiù 〈书面〉acknowledge one's mistake; take the blame:～自责 take the blame and reproach oneself /～辞职 admit one's mistake and resign

引据 yǐnjù cite (facts) or quote (from books) as evidence or argument: ～经典著作 quote authoritative works or classics (as argument)

引决 yǐnjué *also* "引诀"〈书面〉commit suicide:～自裁 commit suicide; punish oneself by suicide

引狼入室 yǐnlángrùshì bring the wolf into the house — open the door to a dangerous foe:你这种行为无异于～,难道不该受到谴责吗? What you have done is as condemnable as letting a wolf into the fold, is it not?

引理 yǐnlǐ 〈数学〉lemma

引力 yǐnlì 〈物理〉gravitation; gravitational force; attraction:万有～ universal gravitation /地心～ earth gravitation /核～ nuclear attraction /～场 gravitational field /～波 gravitational wave /～带 girdle /～势 gravitational potential /～子 graviton /～层 gravisphere /～常数 gravitational constant

引例 yǐnlì ❶ quote; cite:文中～过多。There are too many quoted examples in the article. ❷ quotation:这些～颇有说服力。These quotations are quite convincing.

引领 yǐnlǐng ❶ guide; lead; take:当地老乡～勘探队员进山探宝。The local people led the prospecting team deep into the mountains to explore precious mineral deposits. ❷〈书面〉crane one's neck to look afar — eagerly await

引领而望 yǐnlǐng'érwàng stretch one's neck to look ahead; eagerly look forward to:我们都～祖国统一。All of us are eagerly looking forward to the reunification of the motherland.

引流 yǐnliú 〈医学〉drainage:～物 drain /～术 drainage /十二指肠～ duodenal drainage /作～ have (*or* conduct) drainage

引流管 yǐnliúguǎn drainage tube; drain

引路 yǐnlù guide; lead (the way):你给我们～好吗? Would you lead us there? /在这里无人～是要迷失方向的。You'll lose your bearings (*or* go astray) without a guide in this place.

引起 yǐnqǐ set off; touch off; bring about; generate:～争论 set off a debate /～反感 arouse antipathy /～麻烦 give rise to trouble /～一阵骚动 cause a commotion /～连锁反应 touch off a chain reaction /她的话～了我的思索。Her words set me thinking. /这场事故是由管理人员玩忽职守～的。The accident was the result of negligence on the part of the management.

引桥 yǐnqiáo 〈交通〉bridge approach

引擎 yǐnqíng engine:汽车～ automobile engine /～盖 hood; bonnet

引燃管 yǐnránguǎn ignitron

引人入胜 yǐnrénrùshèng thrilling; fascinating; enchanting; bewitching:这部侦探小说故事情节～。The detective story has a thrilling plot. /风景优美,～。The beauty of the scene is enchanting.

引人注目 yǐnrénzhùmù eye-catching; noticeable; conspicuous:～的成就 noticeable success /她不想太～。She doesn't like to be in the limelight. *or* She doesn't want to be too conspicuous. /街头有一所十分～的西式小楼。There is an eye-catching western style building round the corner of the street. /这里的变化十分～。Spectacular changes have taken place here. /他的新作在京城书市颇为～。His new book made quite a splash in the capital's book market. /她在舞会上很～。She cut a fine figure at the ball.

引入歧途 yǐnrù-qítú lead astray; mislead:被拜金思想～ be led astray by money-worshipping ideas

引商刻羽 yǐnshāng-kèyǔ high-brow music; excellent music (商,羽: two of the five notes in the ancient Chinese musical scale):真乃穿云裂石之声,～之奏! It was such wonderful music, penetrating and

reverberating!

引蛇出洞 yǐnshé-chūdòng draw a snake out of its hole — induce sb. to reveal his true colours:他们采取了~的办法,一网打尽了一个抢劫团伙。They netted an entire gang of robbers at one go by luring them into the open.

引申 yǐnshēn extend (the meaning of a word or a phrase):~义 extended meaning /词义的比喻~ figurative extension of the meaning of words /该词的~义为"…"。The word means "..." by extension.

引首 yǐnshǒu lift up one's head; crane one's neck:~向港口望去。He craned his neck, looking eagerly towards the port.

引述 yǐnshù quote:~权威人士的评论 quote authoritative commentators

引水 yǐnshuǐ ❶ draw water; channel water:~浇地 channel water to irrigate the fields /~上山 draw (*or* pump) water up a hill /~渠道 diversion channel ❷ pilot a ship into harbour

引水工程 yǐnshuǐ gōngchéng flood diversion works or project

引水员 yǐnshuǐyuán pilot

引头 yǐntóu take the lead; be the first to do sth.:只要你引个头,这件事就办起来了。You have only to kick off and the ball will start rolling.

引退 yǐntuì quit or leave office; resign:自动~ retire from office on one's own initiative (*or* of one's own accord); resign /被迫~ be forced to resign; resign under pressure

引文 yǐnwén quoted passage; quotation:~恰到好处 quotation that fits in aptly; apt quotation /~要忠实于原文。When you quote, you must quote faithfully.

引线 yǐnxiàn ❶ fuse; detonator ❷〈电工〉lead; lead-in (wire); leg wire:~潮湿了。The lead has got damp. ❸ go-between; catalyst ❹〈方言〉sewing needle:我年纪大了,~也看不清了。I'm getting old, and can not see the needle clearly.

引信 yǐnxìn *also* "信管" xìnguǎn detonator; fuse:定时~ time-fuse /触发~ contact fuse /延期~ delay fuse /给一枚炸弹装上~ set a fuse to a bomb /~头部 fusehead /~保险隔板 interrupter

引言 yǐnyán foreword; introduction; opening remarks:王教授为该书写了一篇很有分量的~。Professor Wang wrote a very substantial introduction for the book. /他在书的~中提到你的名字。Your name is mentioned in the foreword of his book.

引以为戒 yǐnyǐwéijiè *also* "引为鉴戒" learn a lesson from a previous error; learn from sb.'s mistake; take warning:这个事故你要~,不能再犯。You should take warning from the accident and do not let it happen again.

引以为荣 yǐnyǐwéiróng take or regard as an honour:这并不是丢脸的事。相反,你应该~。This is no shame. Instead, you should take it as an honour. /孩子出息了,父母也~。The success of a child brings credit to his (*or* her) parents.

引用 yǐnyòng ❶ quote; cite; invoke:~某个案例来证明自己的论点 cite a certain case to support one's argument /~古人的话 quote the classics; quote an ancient saying; quote an ancient master /李主任在讲话中~了恩格斯著作里的一句话。In his speech Director Li quoted a sentence from Engels. ❷ recommend; employ; appoint:~贤能 appoint virtuous and talented people /~私人 employ one's own people

引诱 yǐnyòu lead astray; lure; entice; seduce:~青少年犯罪 entice youngsters into crime /~良家妇女从娼 seduce innocent women into prostitution /经不起甜言蜜语的~ submit to (*or* fall victim to) cajolery /经不起广告花言巧语的~ fall into the trap of slick advertising

Y

引玉之砖 yǐnyùzhīzhuān〈谦词〉brick cast to attract jade — brief commonplace remarks offered to stimulate and bring forth valuable opinions:我先说两点意见,算是~。I'd like to make two points first, so as to draw out more valuable comments.

引针 yǐnzhēn *also* "出针" chūzhēn〈中医〉withdraw an acupuncture needle

引枕 yǐnzhěn a kind of pillow which has a square hole in the middle to hold the ear when one is lying on his side

引证 yǐnzhèng quote or cite as evidence:多方~ quote extensively to support one's argument /~词典 cite a dictionary /权威性的~ authoritative citation (*or* quotation)

引致 yǐnzhì cause; lead to; give rise to:经济过热将会~通货膨胀。An overheated economy will lead to inflation.

引种 yǐnzhǒng bring in or introduce a new breed or strain:这种高产小麦要由外省~。The seed for this high-yield wheat has to be brought from another province.

引种 yǐnzhòng〈农业〉plant an introduced variety

引子 yǐnzi ❶〈戏曲〉first piece in the musical compositions of *nanqu* (南曲) and *beiqu* (北曲); prelude ❷〈戏曲〉opening lines of an actor or actress ❸ introductory part of some music ❹ (of speech or writing) introductory remarks:这段话是下文的~。This paragraph is introductory to what follows in the statement. ❺〈中药〉ingredient added to enhance the efficacy of medicine

吲 yǐn

吲哚 yǐnduǒ (transliteration)〈生化〉indole:~胺 indoleamine /~丁酸 indolebutyric acid (IBA)

蚓 yǐn *also* "蚯蚓" qiūyǐn earthworm

蚓体 yǐntǐ〈生理〉vermis

蚓突 yǐntū *also* "阑尾" lánwěi〈生理〉appendix

螾 yǐn *see* "蚓" yǐn

隐(隱) yǐn

❶ hide (from view); conceal:~入树丛 hide in the woods; hide in the bushes /~在屏风后面 concealed behind the screen /时~时现 now visible, now hidden; flickering /山峰~入云中。The peak is hidden in the clouds. ❷ latent; dormant; lurking:~欲 latent desire /~恨 lurking resentment (*or* hatred) /~才 dormant talent ❸ privacy; secret:难言之~ sth. embarrassing to mention; unspeakable personal secret

隐白血病 yǐnbáixuèbìng〈医学〉cryptoleukemia

隐蔽 yǐnbì ❶ take cover; conceal; hide:~在干草垛后面 take cover behind a hay stack /~阵地 covered position /以~的方式进行 do sth. under cover /~的敌人 hidden enemies /~了自己的真实身份 conceal one's true identity /~得十分巧妙 well-concealed; under ingenious concealment ❷ serving for concealment; cryptic; hidden:~地形 hidden terrain

隐蔽抗原 yǐnbì kàngyuán〈医学〉inaccessible antigen

隐蔽色 yǐnbìsè〈生物〉cryptic colour or coloration

隐避 yǐnbì hide; conceal; go under cover:风声太紧,我得到乡下去~一阵。As the situation is getting tense, I have to hide out in the country for some time.

隐藏 yǐncáng hide; conceal; remain under cover:~的敌人 hidden enemy /~证据 conceal evidence /~罪犯 screen offenders /~在暗处 lurk in the shadows /她把这件事~在自己心中已有多年。She has kept this to herself for years. /把这些东西转移到一个安全的地方~起来。Move these things to a safe hideout.

隐遁 yǐndùn ❶ hide; conceal:阳光~。The sun is hidden from sight. /狗獾~在洞穴里。The badger hid itself in the cave. ❷ live in seclusion; withdraw from society and live in solitude; be a hermit:~田园 live in the country as a hermit

隐恶扬善 yǐn'è-yángshàn cover up evil and publicize virtue; overlook sb.'s faults and praise his merits; conceal faults of others and praise their good deeds:这是一篇~的悼词。This was a funeral oration that sang praises of the deceased while whitewashing his demerits.

隐伏 yǐnfú lie hidden; lie low; lurk:~着的危险 lurking danger /兔子~在草丛中。The rabbit hid in the grass. /这个间谍在国防部竟然~了二十年之久! The mole has hidden in the defence ministry for as long as 20 years! /解放以后,他改名换姓,~了下来。After liberation, he changed his name and lay low.

隐睾 yǐngāo〈生理〉cryptorchid:~症〈医学〉cryptorchidism

隐含 yǐnhán imply; contain vaguely:他的眼神里~着失望。There was a vague look of disappointment in his eyes. /她的心中~着无限羞愧。Deep down in her heart she was haunted by a gnawing shame.

隐函数 yǐnhánshù〈数学〉implicit function

隐花植物 yǐnhuā zhíwù〈植物〉cryptogam

隐患 yǐnhuàn hidden trouble; lurking danger; snake in the grass:留下了~ leave behind a hidden danger; leave a landmine /彻底消除~ remove a hidden peril for good /这个暴露的电源是个~,早晚会引起火灾的。The exposed mains are a source of trouble and will cause a fire sooner or later.

隐讳 yǐnhuì cover up; (of mistakes, opinions, etc.) hide; avoid mentioning:~自己的缺点 gloss over one's shortcomings /~自己的错误 cover up one's mistakes /我有什么可~的? I have nothing to hide!

隐晦 yǐnhuì obscure; veiled; indistinct; ambiguous: 语意～ be couched in ambiguous terms /这篇文章写得太～。This article is written with deliberate vagueness. *or* This article is full of obscurities. /他也在会上发了言，不过话说得比较～。He, too, spoke up at the meeting. But his remarks were rather obscure.

隐晦曲折 yǐnhuì-qūzhé (of statements) obscure and roundabout: 他的诗过于～，一般人看不懂。An ordinary reader could hardly understand his vague and involved poetry.

隐疾 yǐnjí shameful disease (such as VD): 他患了～，搬到乡下去住了。Having contracted a disease of which he was ashamed, he moved away to live in the country.

隐经 yǐnjīng 〈医学〉cryptomenorrhoea

隐居 yǐnjū withdraw from society and live in solitude; live in seclusion; live in the shadow; be a hermit: ～田园 dwell in seclusion in the countryside; retire to country hermitage /～生活 secluded life; hermetic life /～者 hermit /战后他离开京都，到一个僻静的小渔村～起来。After the war, he left the capital and lived in seclusion in a quiet small fishing village.

隐君子 yǐnjūnzǐ *also* "瘾君子" yǐnjūnzǐ dope addict; dope; doper

隐括 yǐnkuò *see* "檃栝" yǐnkuò

隐沦 yǐnlún 〈书面〉❶ bury; cover up (with earth, snow, etc.); pass unnoticed by public ❷ live in seclusion; be a hermit

隐瞒 yǐnmán hide; conceal; hold back: ～身份 conceal one's (true) identity /～事实 cover up the truth; hold back facts /～财产 hide one's property /～真相 withhold the truth; suppress the truth; keep the lid over sth. /～工作中的失误 gloss over mistakes in one's work /她好像对我有什么～。She seems to be holding something back from me. /我什么都知道，你～不了。I know everything, and it's no use for you to try to pass it over.

隐秘 yǐnmì ❶ hidden; concealed: ～的山洞 hidden cave /～之事 secret /这地方非常～。This is a well-concealed place. /他是个十分～的人，从不向人交心。He is very much a private man and confides in no one. ❷ secret: 内心的～ bosom secret; inner secret /探听某人的～ try to find out sb.'s secret; pry (*or* worm) a secret out of sb. /我对你没有任何～。I have absolutely no secrets from you.

隐灭 yǐnmiè disappear; be lost from sight: 东方露白，繁星～。As day broke, the stars faded away.

隐没 yǐnmò hide behind; disappear; be concealed: 他的身影渐渐～在人群中。He slowly disappeared in the crowds. /月亮羞涩地～在云后。The moon veiled itself shyly behind the clouds.

隐匿 yǐnnì 〈书面〉hide; conceal; lie low: ～逃犯 hide an escaped convict /暗地～起来 lie low; go into hiding /～行为 act of concealment /～证据 suppress the evidence

隐匿罪 yǐnnìzuì 〈法律〉misprision

隐僻 yǐnpì ❶ remote: ～的角落 faraway corner ❷ obscure and rare: 用典～ quote from obscure sources

隐情 yǐnqíng fact or reason one wishes to hide; unmentionable secret: 他有难言的～。He's got something embarrassing to mention. /这些话触动了她的～。These words touched upon a painful topic that she did not wish to discuss. /他这段～只有妈妈一人知道。No one else except his mother knows about this awkward experience of his.

隐球菌 yǐnqiújūn *also* "隐球酵母" cryptococcus: ～病 cryptococcosis

隐然 yǐnrán indistinctly; faintly; implicitly: ～可见 faintly visible /～可闻 barely audible

隐忍 yǐnrěn bear patiently; endure silently; forbear: ～不语 bite one's tongue; forbear from speaking /为了孩子，她只得～苟活下来。It was only for the sake of her children that she swallowed the humiliation and lived on.

隐射 yǐnshè insinuate; hint; imply: 她话里带刺，句句都在～他。Her words carry stings, all innuendoes about him. /他用这个寓言来～、攻击当今的政府。He attacked the present government by insinuation with this fable.

隐身草 yǐnshēncǎo 〈比喻〉person or thing that serves as cover (for one's activity); blind; cover: 以小买卖为～ use a small shop as his cover

隐身术 yǐnshēnshù disappearing act; vanishing act: 变了一个～ do a disappearing act

隐士 yǐnshì hermit; recluse

隐事 yǐnshì private matter one does not want to make public; secrets

隐饰 yǐnshì cover up; conceal; gloss over: 如实陈述，毫无～。This is a statement of facts without the slightest attempt at covering up anything.

隐私 yǐnsī private matter one wants to keep to oneself; personal secret; privacy: 他专爱去揭人～。He is fond of poking his nose into others' private affairs. /要尊重个人～。Privacy should be respected. /这是他的～，我怎么好去打听？This is his personal secret. Why should I pry into his private business?

隐私权 yǐnsīquán privacy rights; privacy

隐慝 yǐntè 〈书面〉hidden wickedness or evil: 展氏有～焉。Alas, Mr. Zhan has concealed evils.

隐痛 yǐntòng ❶ pain endured silently; secret anguish: 多年来这事给他造成的～终于消散了。The pain he has been suffering all these years in the aftermath of the incident has at last gone. /心中的～在煎熬着他。He was tormented by the secret anguish in his heart. ❷ dull pain: 我觉得肚子有些～。There is a dull pain in my abdomen.

隐头花序 yǐntóu huāxù 〈植物〉hypanthium

隐退 yǐntuì ❶ recede; fade away; disappear: 黑夜渐渐地～，东方透出一片鱼肚白。The dark night had gradually gone, and in the east the sky was brightening up. ❷ live in seclusion; retire from political life: 因病～。He retired from political life for reasons of health.

隐微 yǐnwēi ❶ implicit and delicate; subtle: 这部书通过爱情故事～曲折地表现了当时的政治斗争。By telling a love story, the book indirectly depicted the political struggle of the time. ❷ well-concealed; hidden; latent: ～的悲哀 well-hidden sadness /～的痛苦 well-concealed anguish

隐位 yǐnwèi 〈医学〉cryptotope

隐显墨水 yǐnxiǎn mòshuǐ invisible ink

隐现 yǐnxiàn be now clear, now vague; appear vaguely; flicker: 远处灯光～。Lights were flickering in the distance. /水天相接，岛屿～。As the sky joins the water, a few islets on the horizon are barely visible. /林木深处，～一座古庙。The outline of an ancient temple can be seen in the dense woods.

隐斜视矫正镜 yǐnxiéshì jiǎozhèngjìng 〈医学〉phoriascope

隐斜眼 yǐnxiéyǎn 〈医学〉heterophoria; phoria

隐形飞机 yǐnxíng fēijī stealth aircraft

隐形轰炸机 yǐnxíng hōngzhàjī stealth bomber: "幽灵"～ B2-A Spirit stealth bomber

隐形收入 yǐnxíng shōurù invisible income; off-payroll income

隐形眼镜 yǐnxíng yǎnjìng *also* "接触眼镜" jiēchùyǎnjìng contact lens

隐形战斗机 yǐnxíng zhàndòujī stealth fighter: "夜鹰"～ F117A Nighthawk stealth fighter

隐性 yǐnxìng 〈生物〉recessive: ～基因 recessive gene /～性状 recessive character /～突发 recessive mutation /～遗传 recessive inheritance /～遗传病 recessive hereditary disease /～遗传学 cryptogenetics /～脑积水 occult hydrocephaly

隐性调查 yǐnxìng diàochá 〈商业〉blind test

隐性失业 yǐnxìng shīyè recessive unemployment

隐姓埋名 yǐnxìng-máimíng conceal or hide one's identity; live incognito: 他到了乡下，～地生活了二十年。He changed his name and lived in the country for twenty years. /老人情愿～，作个农夫，也不愿攀附权贵。The old man would rather live incognito as a farmer than rise in the world under the patronage of bigwigs.

隐血 yǐnxuè *also* "潜血" qiánxuè occult blood

隐逸 yǐnyì 〈书面〉❶ live in seclusion; live in solitude: ～之士 recluse; hermit /～林壑 retire to a life of solitude among woods and streams ❷ hermit; recluse

隐隐 yǐnyǐn faint; indistinct; dull: 下腹～作痛 feel a dull pain in the lower abdomen /浓雾中青山～可见。Green mountains are faintly visible in the fog. /～的歌声从远处传来。The sound of distant singing can be heard.

隐隐绰绰 yǐnyǐn-chuòchuò vague; dim; indistinct: 远处～有个人影在移动。There was the indistinct shadow of a man moving about in the distance.

隐映 yǐnyìng 〈书面〉set off (one another): 奇花异卉互相～。Exotic flowers and rare grass set each other off.

隐忧 yǐnyōu secret worry or anxiety: 心怀～ be secretly worried about sth. /耿耿不寐，如有～。As if weighed down with anxiety, he tossed over in bed, unable to sleep.

隐语 yǐnyǔ ❶ insinuating language; enigmatic language; deliberately vague remarks: 善用～ be skilled at using insinuations ❷ argot; cant

隐喻 yǐnyù *also*"暗喻"ànyù 〈语言〉metaphor:混杂～ mixed metaphor /以荷花～人之清廉。A lotus flower is metaphorically used to describe a man's incorruptibility.

隐约 yǐnyuē indistinct; faint; dim; vague:淡淡的月光下～可见对岸的山峰。The mountain peaks rose silhouetted across the river under the faint moonlight. /暮霭中一座古寺～可见。An ancient temple was dimly visible in the evening mist.

隐约其词 yǐnyuē-qící use ambiguous language; speak or write in equivocal terms; be evasive; equivocate:看他～的样子,好像有什么顾虑。He was hedging as if apprehensive of something.

隐衷 yǐnzhōng feelings one wishes to keep to oneself; inner feelings:他俩各有～。They each have some inner thoughts that they do not want to disclose.

瘾(癮) yǐn ❶ addiction; habitual craving:吸毒成～ be addicted to drugs /打牌上～了 become addicted to card playing; have formed a habit of playing cards /有酒～ have a craving for alcoholic drink; be addicted to alcohol; have a special affinity for booze /犯烟～ have an urge to smoke; crave a cigarette ❷ strong interest; passion:我父亲年轻时跳舞的～还真不小! My father had indeed a passion for dancing when he was young. /这孩子看电视看上～了。The kid is crazy about TV.

瘾君子 yǐnjūnzǐ ❶ dope addict; doper ❷ heavy smoker; chain smoker

瘾头 yǐntóu addiction; obsession; strong interest:哥儿几个钓鱼的～儿挺大。These guys were very keen on fishing.

讔(讔) yǐn 〈书面〉cant; insinuating remarks; riddle

檃(㯗、檼) yǐn

檃栝 yǐnkuò *also*"隐括"yǐnkuò 〈书面〉❶ tool used to bend warped wooden planks back to shape ❷ adapt (a piece of writing)

缊 yǐn 〈方言〉sew with long stitches; baste

殷 yǐn 〈书面〉〈象声〉sound of thunder; thundering:～其雷 loud crashes of thunder

see also yān; yīn

yìn

垽 yìn 〈书面〉sediment; precipitate

窨 yìn cell; cellar; basement

see also xūn

窨井 yìnjǐng 〈建筑〉inspection well or shaft

慭(憖) yìn 〈书面〉❶ wish; would rather:～使君安。I wish you safe and sound. ❷ damage; loss:两军之士皆未～也。Neither side incurred (*or* suffered) any casualties.

慭慭 yìnyìn 〈书面〉careful; cautious; circumspect:虎近驴,～然莫相知。The tiger cautiously approached the donkey, wondering what it could be.

荫(蔭、❷❸廕) yìn ❶ shady and damp:这里太～,外边坐吧。Let's sit outside as it's too dark and damp here. ❷〈书面〉shelter; protect ❸〈旧语〉privileges given to one's descendants because of one's meritorious service

see also yīn

荫庇 yìnbì 〈旧语〉protection by one's elders or ancestors

荫凉 yìnliáng shady and cool:找个～的地方歇会儿。Let's go and find a shady and cool spot for a rest.

荫生 yìnshēng student admitted to the Imperial College (国子监) in recognition of the distinguished services of his deceased father or ancestors during the Ming and Qing dynasties

印 yìn ❶ seal; chop:用～ stamp a seal; affix one's seal /钢～ embossing seal; steel seal /官～ official seal /私～ personal seal ❷ print; mark:指～ fingerprint /脚～ footprint /烙～ brand ❸ print; engrave:～名片 print name cards /～照片 print a photo; have a print made /～报 print newspapers /复～几份文件 photocopy a few documents /油～ mimeograph /排～ typeset /打～ cut a stencil and mimeograph /深深地～在记忆中 one's mind is deeply imprinted with sth.; sth. has left a deep impression on one's mind ❹ tally; conform; accord with:心心相～ have mutual affinity; be mutually attracted ❺ (Yìn) a surname

印把子 yìnbàzi seal of authority; power:那就要看～在谁手里了。It will depend on who wields political power. /人民掌握着～,怕他什么! The power is in the hands of the people, why fear him?

印版 yìnbǎn printing plate; form; forme:～滚筒 plate cylinder /～墨辊 forme rollers

印本 yìnběn printed book:～的质量 quality of the print (of a book) /～的数量 number of printed copies /一个二次大战以前的～ edition (of a book) printed before World War II

印鼻 yìnbí *see*"印纽"

印次 yìncì 〈印刷〉impression:此书的～已达二十。This book has had twenty impressions so far.

印地语 Yìndìyǔ Hindi

印第安纳 Yìndì'ānnà Indiana, state in the Middle West of the United States

印第安人 Yìndì'ānrén American Indian; Native American; Red Indian; Indian

印度 Yìndù India:～人 Indian /～共和国 Republic of India (from 1 Jan. 1948)

印度报业托拉斯 Yìndù Bàoyè Tuōlāsī Press Trust of India (PTI)

印度大麻 Yìndù dàmá hashish; *Cannabis indica*

印度国大党 Yìndù Guódàdǎng Indian Congress Party

印度河 Yìndùhé Indus River, a river of southern Asia about 2,900 km in length

印度红木 Yìndù hóngmù 〈林业〉Indian mahogany (*Soymida febrifuga*)

印度教 Yìndùjiào Hinduism:～徒 Hindu /～寺庙 mandir

印度历 Yìndùlì Hindu calendar

印度萝芙木 Yìndù luófúmù 〈植物〉rauwolfia

印度棉 yìndùmián Indian cotton

印度尼西亚 Yìndùníxīyà Indonesia:～人 Indonesian /～语 Indonesian

印度牛 yìndùniú gayal; mithan (*Bos frontalis*)

印度人民党 Yìdù Rénmíndǎng (India) *Bharatiya Janata* Party

印度橡胶树 Yìndù xiàngjiāoshù India rubber plant; India rubber tree (*Ficus elastica*)

印度新闻社 Yìndù Xīnwénshè India Press Agency (IPA)

印度洋 Yìndùyáng Indian Ocean

印度野牛 Yìndù yěniú gaur (*Bos gaurus*)

印度支那 Yìndù-Zhīnà Indo-China, consisting of Laos, Cambodia and Vietnam:～半岛 Indo-China Peninsula; Indo-Chinese Peninsula

印发 yìnfā print and distribute; issue and circulate:～传单 print and distribute leaflets (*or* fliers) /文件～单位 unit responsible for the circulation of a document /这份文件是由国务院～的。This document is printed and distributed by the State Council. *or* This document is issued and circulated by the State Council.

印格 yìngé grid printing

印盒 yìnhé seal box:景泰蓝～ cloisonné seal box /红漆～ red lacquer seal box

印痕 yìnhén mark of print

印花 yìnhuā ❶〈纺织〉printing:～布 printed calico; printed cotton fabric; cotton print; prints /～真丝绸 printed silk /～床单 printed bed sheet /～厂 printworks /～机 printing machine /～技术 printing technique /～工人 textile printer ❷ revenue stamp; stamp:贴～ pay stamp tax

印花税 yìnhuāshuì stamp tax; stamp duty

印花税票 yìnhuā shuìpiào revenue stamp; fiscal stamp

印记 yìnjì ❶〈旧语〉seal; chop; stamp ❷ mark; print; trace:文书上留有公章鲜红的～。On the document is the bright red print of an official seal. /这篇作品带有鲜明的时代～。This piece of work is marked clearly with the characteristics of the times. ❸ impress or stamp on one's mind; keep the impression of sth.:她要把这些话牢牢地～在心里。She will lock these words fast in her mind.

印迹 yìnjì mark; stain:衬衣上有血的～。The shirt has blood stains on it. /他脸上有口红的～。There is a lipstick mark on his face.

印加 Yìnjiā Inca：～人 Inca /～帝国 Inca Empire (c. 1200-1537)
印鉴 yìnjiàn specimen seal impression for checking when making payments：私人～ personal seal /以～为凭 have a seal impression as evidence (*or* guarantee)
印模 yìnmó stamp; die
印模电路 yìnmó diànlù 〈电子〉die-stamped circuit
印泥 yìnní red ink paste used for seals
印纽 yìnniǔ *also* "印鼻"；"印钮" seal top engraved in the likeness of animals, with a hole for a tassel
印欧语系 Yìn-Ōu Yǔxì Indo-European Languages
印谱 yìnpǔ book of ancient seals; collection of impressions of seals by famous seal-engravers
印染 yìnrǎn 〈纺织〉printing and dyeing：～厂 printing and dyeing mill /～业 printing and dyeing industry /～技术 printing and dyeing technique
印色 yìnsè *see* "印泥"
印绶 yìnshòu 〈旧语〉(usu. rather large) seal and the silk tassel on it
印数 yìnshù printing; impression：～太少 rather limited impression (*or* printing) /～很大 very big printing /这一版～为六万册。This edition has an impression of 60,000 copies.
印刷 yìnshuā printing：彩色～ coloured printing /立体～ stereoscopic printing; three-dimensional printing /三色版～ three-colour halftone /第一次～ first impression (*or* printing) /～线路板 printed substrate /～纸令 printer's ream /～油墨 printing ink /今天的报纸已～完毕。Today's newspaper was just off the press. /这本书的～不清楚。The printing in this book is not clear.
印刷厂 yìnshuāchǎng printing house; print shop; press
印刷错误 yìnshuā cuòwù printing mistake; misprint; typographic error
印刷电路 yìnshuā diànlù printed circuit：～板 printed circuit board
印刷工人 yìnshuā gōngrén printer; printing worker
印刷合金 yìnshuā héjīn type metal
印刷机 yìnshuājī printing machine; press：滚筒～ cylinder press /轮转～ rotary press /双面～ perfecting press; perfector
印刷品 yìnshuāpǐn printed matter：请在邮件上标明"～"。Please mark your mail with "Printed Matter".
印刷术 yìnshuāshù act of printing; printing
印刷体 yìnshuātǐ block letter; print hand：整齐的～ neat print hand /表上请用～填写姓名。Please enter your name in block letters. *or* Please print your name on the form. /他的～写得很漂亮。His print hand is beautiful.
印刷业 yìnshuāyè print
印刷纸 yìnshuāzhǐ printing paper
印台 yìntái *also* "打印台" dǎyìntái ink pad; stamp pad
印堂 yìntáng part of the forehead between two eyebrows
印堂穴 yìntángxué 〈中医〉*yintang* point; ophryon
印铁 yìntiě tin-printing; aluminium printing：～油墨 tin-printing ink
印纹陶文化 yìnwéntáo wénhuà 〈考古〉Stamped Pottery Culture
印玺 yìnxǐ imperial seal
印相纸 yìnxiàngzhǐ 〈摄影〉photographic paper
印象 yìnxiàng impression：～模糊 vague impression /她见了一面后，对他产生了良好的～。She had a good impression of him after the first meeting. /这次访问给我留下了不可磨灭的～。The visit has left an indelible impression on me.
印象派 yìnxiàngpài impressionist school; impressionist
印象主义 yìnxiàngzhǔyì impressionism：～油画 impressionistic oil painting
印信 yìnxìn official seal
印行 yìnxíng print and distribute; publish：本词典将由商务印书馆～。This dictionary is to be published by The Commercial Press.
印油 yìnyóu stamp-pad ink
印张 yìnzhāng 〈印刷〉printed sheet (equal to half a sheet of printing paper or newsprint)
印章 yìnzhāng seal; stamp; chop; signet：刻～ engrave a seal
印章学 yìnzhāngxué sigillography; sphragistics
印证 yìnzhèng ❶ confirm; verify; corroborate; substantiate：他的交待经～属实。His confessions were verified. /这些话还有待～。The statement is yet to be confirmed. *or* The statement needs corroboration. /这件事～了我对她的怀疑。This confirmed my suspicion of her. ❷ sth. that confirms, verifies, or corroborates
印制 yìnzhì print (plates, illustrations, forms, etc.)
印子 yìnzi ❶ mark; print; trace：两个很深的脚～ two deep footprints /墙上有几个小孩的手～。There are some children's handprints on the wall. /他的脸给打出几道血～。His face was bloodied in the fight. ❷ *see* "印子钱"
印子钱 yìnziqián *also* "印子" loan at exorbitant interest, to be repaid (both in terms of principal and interest) in predetermined instalments; usury：借～ borrow from a usurer /放～ practise usury

茚

yìn 〈化学〉(transliteration) indene

鮣

yìn 〈动物〉remora; shark sucker

胤

yìn 〈书面〉offspring; posterity：～嗣 offspring

饮

yìn water (an animal)：～牲口 water draught animals /这马～过了。The horse has been watered.
see also yǐn

饮场 yìnchǎng 〈旧语〉(of opera singer) drink water to moisten throat on stage
饮马投钱 yìnmǎ-tóuqián pay for a horse's drink (from a river) — be extremely honest
饮人以和 yìnrényǐhé treat others with kindness

yīng

应[1]（應）

yīng ❶ answer; reply; respond：我喊了他几声他都不～。I called him several times, but he didn't answer. /叫天天不～。My appeal to heaven elicited no reply. ❷ promise; agree; accept：这事是他～下来的，他不管谁管？It was he who promised to look into the matter; who else would attend to it if he didn't? ❸ (Yīng) a surname

应[2]（應）

yīng should; ought to：理～如此 this is as it should be /～尽的义务 duty incumbent on one; one's bounden duty /～给予奖励 deserve (*or* merit) a reward /～谦虚谨慎。One should be modest and prudent. /赡养老人是子女～尽的责任。It is the children's obligation to support their parents.
see also yìng

应当 yīngdāng should; ought to：同学之间～坦诚相待。As classmates, we ought to be sincere and frank with each other. /不必客气，这是我们～做的。Don't feel obliged. This is really what we should do.
应得 yīngdé deserve; merit; be due (to sb.)：～的荣誉 well-deserved honour /～的奖赏 due reward /他罪有～。He deserves the punishment.
应分 yīngfèn what one should do; part of one's job：救死扶伤，是我们医务工作者～的事。It is what we should do as medical workers to treat the wounded and rescue the dying.
应付 yīngfù payable; due：～票据 bill (*or* note) payable /～债券 bond payable /～账款 account payable /～利息 interest due; interest in the red /～未付费用 accrued expenses
see also yìngfu
应该 yīnggāi should; ought to; must：学生～努力学习。Students should study hard. /领导干部～与群众打成一片。Leading cadres ought to identify themselves with the people. /我们不～做这种事。We shouldn't (*or* mustn't) do anything like this.
应工 yīnggōng 〈戏曲〉role that suits one
应届毕业生 yīngjiè bìyèshēng graduating students; this year's graduates：她是北大的～。She is among the graduating students of Peking University this year. /今年～的分配工作由他负责。He is responsible for the job assignments for this year's graduates.
应名儿 yīngmíngr ❶ serve as titular head; lend one's name (to sth.)：成立这个学会，他只是应个名儿，不管实际工作。He serves as titular head of the society, but is not actually involved. ❷ only in name; nominally：他们～是夫妻，实际上已分居多年了。Though they are still nominally man and wife, they have been separated for a number of years. /他是个～的董事长。He is president of the company in name only.
应声 yīngshēng answer; reply; respond：他一连问了几遍都没人～

儿。Nobody responded even though he asked several times.
see also yìngshēng

应收 yīngshōu 〈会计〉receivable:～票据 bill (*or* note) receivable / ～利息 interest receivable; interest in the black / ～账款 account receivable / ～未收收益 accrued income

应税商品 yīngshuì shāngpǐn taxable good; dutiable commodity

应税收益 yīngshuì shōuyì taxable income

应许 yīngxǔ ❶ agree to do sth.; promise: 他～的事一定会办。He will certainly do whatever he promises to. ❷ allow; permit; assent: 不得领导的～,谁也不能离开。Nobody may leave without the leaders' permission.

应有 yīngyǒu due; deserved; appropriate; proper: 保持～的尊严 maintain a proper (*or* befitting) dignity / 受到～的谴责 receive due condemnation; be duly censured / ～的地位 position appropriate for sb.

应有尽有 yīngyǒu-jìnyǒu have everything that one expects to find: 这家百货商店真是个"大世界",商品～。This department store was indeed worthy of the name of "Great World", with everything one could wish for.

应允 yīngyǔn agree; assent; permit; approve: 点头～ nod one's assent (*or* agreement, *or* approval) / 父母～了他的要求。His parents consented to (*or* approved) his request.

譍

yīng 〈书面〉*see* "应" yīng
see also yìng

膺[1]

yīng 〈书面〉chest; breast: 抚～长叹 heave a long sigh with one's hand on one's chest / 义愤填～ be filled with righteous indignation

膺[2]

yīng 〈书面〉❶ bear; shoulder; receive: 荣～要职 be honoured to assume a post of great responsibility / 荣～劳动模范的光荣称号 be awarded the honourable title of a model worker ❷ send a punitive expedition against; attack; smite

膺惩 yīngchéng 〈书面〉attack and punish; send a punitive expedition against: ～国贼 punish the traitors of the nation / ～叛逆 launch a punitive attack on the rebels

膺赏 yīngshǎng be rewarded; be awarded a prize

膺受 yīngshòu receive: ～恩典 receive an imperial favour

膺选 yīngxuǎn 〈书面〉be elected; be selected: 他以德高望重而～为理事长。He was elected chairman of the board of directors because of his seniority and prestige.

鹰

yīng hawk; eagle: 飞～ flying eagle / 雄～展翅 powerful hawk spreading its wings

鹰鼻鹞眼 yīngbí-yàoyǎn hawk-nosed and eagle-eyed; sinister- and fierce-looking: 此人长得～,十分凶恶。Hawk-nosed and eagle-eyed, this fellow looks extremely ferocious.

鹰钩鼻子 yīnggōubízi aquiline nose

鹰猎 yīngliè falconry

鹰派 yīngpài 〈政治〉hawk: 他是该国政府中有名的～。He is known as a hawk in that government.

鹰犬 yīngquǎn falcons and hounds — lackeys; running dogs; hired thugs: 宁死也不作帝国主义的～ would rather die than to be lackeys of (*or* running dogs for) imperialism / 无恶不作的～ hired thugs who will stop at no atrocities

鹰隼 yīngsǔn 〈书面〉hawks and falcons — fierce or doughty people: 猛如～ as fierce as a hawk or falcon

鹰洋 yīngyáng Mexican silver dollar, which used to be in circulation in old China

鹰爪花 yīngzhǎohuā *also* "鹰爪";"莺爪" yīngzhǎo 〈植物〉*Artabotrys hexapetalus*

鹰爪毛儿 yīngzhǎomáor "eagle's claws", a kind of sheep's fur with short curly wool

英[1]

yīng ❶〈书面〉blossom; bloom; petal: 遍地落～ fallen petals everywhere ❷ hero; man of valour; outstanding person: 群～毕集 galaxy of talented people / 精～ people with distinguished (*or* remarkable) accomplishments; elite ❸ (Yīng) a surname

英[2]

Yīng Britain; England: 大～帝国 British Empire / ～女王 English Queen

英镑 yīngbàng pound sterling: ～汇票 sterling bill / ～结存 sterling balance / ～集团 sterling bloc (before 1939) / 这台机器约值三千～。This machine is worth about 3,000 pounds.

英镑区 yīngbàngqū sterling area (established in 1939)

英才 yīngcái ❶ (usu. of sb. young) talented person; person of outstanding ability: 敬重～ respect and care for talented people ❷ talent; wisdom: ～盖世 matchless talent; exceptional wisdom

英尺 yīngchǐ (formerly also 呎) foot: 一～等于 0.9144 市尺或 0.3048 米。One foot equals 0.9144 Chinese *chi* or 0.3048 metre.

英寸 yīngcùn (formerly also 吋) inch: 十二～为一英尺。There are twelve inches in a foot. *or* Twelve inches makes a foot.

英断 yīngduàn wise decision: 这个决定实为有胆识之～。This is indeed a wise and far-sighted decision.

英吨 yīngdūn long ton (2,240 pounds): 这种卡车可载重十～。This kind of lorry can carry as much as ten long tons.

英发 yīngfā 〈书面〉shine; radiate: 豪气～ radiating with heroism; dashing and spirited / 雄姿～ brilliant display of one's gallantry

英风 yīngfēng heroic spirit; lofty quality; brilliance (of talent, etc.): 仰其～ admire sb. for his brilliance

英格兰 Yīnggélán England, a part of the United Kingdom: ～人 Englishman; the English

英格兰银行 Yīnggélán Yínháng Bank of England

英国 Yīngguó Britain; England: ～公民 British citizen / ～国民 British national / ～臣民 British subject / ～海外公民 British overseas citizen / ～属土公民 British dependent territories citizen (BDTC) / ～文学家 British man of letters / 去～留学 study in Britain

英国管 yīngguóguǎn 〈音乐〉English horn

英国广播公司 Yīngguó Guǎngbō Gōngsī British Broadcasting Corporation (BBC)

英国人 Yīngguórén Briton; Englishman or Englishwoman; the British: 三个瘦长的～ three lanky Britons / 两个～的故事 tale of two Britishers

英国圣公会 Yīngguó Shènggōnghuì Church of England

英国石油公司 Yīngguó Shíyóu Gōngsī British Petroleum Company (BP)

英豪 yīngháo heroes; men of great bravery; outstanding figures: 当今～ heroes (*or* great men) of our time / ～辈出。Outstanding figures come to the fore in large numbers.

英荷壳牌石油公司 Yīng-Hé Qiàopái Shíyóu Gōngsī Royal Dutch Shell Group (RD/SG)

英华 yīnghuá outstanding figures; extraordinary things; essence; cream

英魂 yīnghún spirit of those departed which still commands our respect: 烈士～永存。The martyrs are immortal.

英吉利海峡 Yīngjílì Hǎixiá English Channel

英杰 yīngjié *see* "英豪"

英俊 yīngjùn ❶ eminently talented; outstanding; brilliant: ～有为 brilliant and promising ❷ handsome and spirited; good-looking and bright; smart: ～少年 handsome young man / 长相～ handsome appearance; good looks

英里 yīnglǐ (formerly also 哩) mile (5,280 feet or 1,760 yards): 一英里为 1.609 公里。There are 1.609 kilometres to a mile.

英联邦 Yīngliánbāng British Commonwealth (of Nations): 退出～ withdraw from the British Commonwealth (of Nations) / ～成员国 member state of the British Commonwealth / ～总理会议 Conference of Commonwealth Prime Ministers

英两 yīngliǎng (formerly also 唡, now 盎司) ounce

英烈 yīngliè ❶ courageous and unyielding; indomitable: ～女子 courageous and virtuous woman ❷ martyrs who died heroically: 学习～的革命精神 learn from the revolutionary spirit of the martyrs ❸ 〈书面〉outstanding exploits: ～永存。Their heroic exploits will always live with us.

英灵 yīnglíng *also* "英魂" ❶ spirit of the brave departed; spirit of a martyr: 求～保佑 pray to the spirit of the departed for blessing / 告慰～ console the spirit of the martyr ❷ 〈书面〉person of outstanding talent and ability: 女中～ exceptionally talented woman

英伦三岛 Yīnglún Sāndǎo British Isles

英名 yīngmíng illustrious name: 有损～ detrimental to one's illustrious name / ～扬天下 heroic name known to the whole nation

英明 yīngmíng wise; sagacious; brilliant: 决策～ wise decision / ～的领导 brilliant leadership / ～果断 sagacious and decisive (*or* reso-

lute)
英模 yīngmó heroes and model workers: ～事迹 exemplary deeds of the heroes and model workers
英亩 yīngmǔ (formerly also 畝) acre: 这块地约有三～。This plot measures about three acres in area.
英年 yīngnián prime of life; youthful years; youth: ～早逝 die in one's prime
英气 yīngqì dashing spirit; heroic spirit: ～勃勃 be filled with heroic spirit
英石 yīngshí stone quarried at Yingde (英德) County, Guangdong Province, used in building rockeries for Chinese gardens and parks
英爽 yīngshuǎng dashing; handsome; smart: 他身穿戎装, 显得更加～。He looked even more handsome and smart in uniform.
英特尔公司 Yīngtè'ěr Gōngsī Intel
英特耐雄纳尔 Yīngtènàixióngnà'ěr (transliteration) Internationale — International Working Men's Association (1864-1876); ideal of international communism
英挺 yīngtǐng tall and handsome
英王制诰 Yīngwáng Zhìgào Letters Patent, the Charter of Hong Kong promulgated by the British Queen in 1843 and in effect until 1 July 1997
英伟 yīngwěi handsome and stalwart: ～的战士 big and handsome soldier
英文 Yīngwén English (language): 学～ learn English / ～课本 English textbook / ～系学生 students of the English department
英武 yīngwǔ 〈书面〉 of soldierly or martial bearing
英仙座 Yīngxiānzuò 〈天文〉 Perseus
英雄 yīngxióng hero: 女～ heroine / 战斗～ combat hero / 无名～ unknown heroes / 盖世～ matchless (*or* peerless) hero / 民族～ national heroes / ～气概 heroic spirit; intrepidity
英雄本色 yīngxióng běnsè action or conduct befitting a hero
英雄气短 yīngxióngqìduǎn the spirit of a hero proves feeble (before hardships or in conflict with love); the heroic spirit is fleeting or brief: 儿女情长, ～。The spirit of a hero is overshadowed by the love between man and woman.
英雄所见略同 yīngxióng suǒjiàn lüè tóng heroes share the same thought; great minds think alike
英雄无用武之地 yīngxióng wú yòngwǔ zhī dì hero with no place to display his prowess — have no chance to put one's abilities to good use: 只要自己努力, 英雄岂无用武之地? With sustained efforts one is sure to find an opportunity to exercise one's abilities.
英雄造时势 yīngxióng zào shíshì heroes create their times: ～, 还是时势造英雄? Do heroes create their times or times create their heroes? *or* Do events make men or men shape events?
英秀 yīngxiù ❶ handsome; pretty; smart: 眉目～ with delicate features; have well-chiselled features / ～的男孩 handsome lad ❷ talented people
英寻 yīngxún (formerly also 㖠) fathom (6 feet)
英勇 yīngyǒng heroic; brave; valiant; gallant: ～无比 with unparalleled heroism / ～善战 valiant and skilful in battle / 作战异常～ fight with great bravery
英语 Yīngyǔ English (language): 英国～ British English / 美国～ American English / 纯正～ pure English; king's (*or* queen's) English / 洋泾浜～ pidgin English / ～角 English corner
英语系 Yīngyǔxì English department; department of English
英制 yīngzhì British system of weights and measures
英主 yīngzhǔ wise sovereign or monarch
英姿 yīngzī heroic bearing
英姿焕发 yīngzī-huànfā audacious and spirited; dashing: 好一个～的少年英雄! What a gallant young hero!
英姿飒爽 yīngzī-sàshuǎng valorous and heroic in bearing; bright and brave: ～的女兵 bold and brave women soliders

霙 yīng 〈旧语〉 snow flakes

瑛 yīng 〈书面〉 ❶ beautiful jade: 琼～ translucent jade ❷ lustre of jade

锳 yīng 〈书面〉 tinkling of bells

媖 yīng 〈书面〉〈褒义〉 woman; girl

嘤 yīngmǔ *also* mǔ (now 英亩) old translation for acre

吋 yīngcùn *also* cùn (now 英寸) old translation for inch

哃(哃) yīngliǎng *also* liǎng (now 盎司) old translation for ounce

哩 yīnglǐ *also* lǐ (now 英里) old translation for mile
see also lī; li

呎 yīngchǐ *also* chǐ (now 英尺) old translation for foot

㖠 yīngxún *also* xún (now 英寻) old translation for fathom

䓨(罃) yīng *see* "罂" yīng

莺(鶯、鸎) yīng warbler; oriole: 飞～ flying oriole / 黄～ yellow warbler / ～簧婉转 talk as glibly and eloquently as a chirping oriole
莺歌燕舞 yīnggē-yànwǔ orioles sing and swallows dart — joy of spring; scene of prosperity; excellent situation: ～的升平景象 scene of peace and prosperity / 到处～, 更有潺潺流水, 高路入云端。Everywhere orioles sing, swallows dart, Streams babble, And the road mounts skyward.
莺声燕语 yīngshēng-yànyǔ *also* "燕语莺声" like the trill of an oriole and the song of a swallow — sweet, delicate voice of a woman
莺爪 yīngzhǎo *see* "鹰爪花" yīngzhǎohuā

罂(罌) yīng 〈书面〉 small-mouthed jar
罂粟 yīngsù 〈植物〉 poppy: ～花 poppy flower / ～籽 poppy seed / ～科 Papaveraceae
罂粟碱 yīngsùjiǎn 〈药学〉 papaverine
罂粟壳 yīngsùké 〈中药〉 poppy capsule or shell
罂子桐 yīngzitóng *also* "油桐" yóutóng tung oil tree

婴[1] yīng baby; infant: 妇～ mother and baby / 产一女～ give birth to a baby girl

婴[2] yīng 〈书面〉 touch; contract; surround; entangle: ～疾 contract a disease / ～城固守 fortify the city to beef up its defence / 世网～我身。I got entangled in complicated and complex worldly affairs.
婴儿 yīng'ér baby; infant: ～食品 baby food
婴儿车 yīng'érchē pram; baby carriage; stroller; pushchair
婴儿床 yīng'érchuáng crib; cot; cradle
婴儿湿疹 yīng'ér shīzhěn 〈医学〉 eczema infantum
婴儿死亡率 yīng'ér sǐwánglǜ infant mortality
婴孩 yīnghái baby; infant: 不满半岁的～ baby under six months / ～用品 articles for baby use
婴幼儿 yīng-yòu'ér infants and pre-school children

璎 yīng jade-like stone
璎珞 yīngluò 〈古语〉 necklace made of pearls and jade: 这位公主佩带的那串珠宝～价值连城。The necklace of pearls and jade the princess was wearing was priceless.

蘡 yīng
蘡薁 yīngyù 〈植物〉 *Vitis adstricta*

樱 yīng ❶ cherry: ～颗 cherry fruit ❷ oriental cherry (*Prunus serrulate*)
樱草 yīngcǎo 〈植物〉 primrose
樱唇 yīngchún cherry lips (ruby lips of a pretty woman)
樱花 yīnghuā 〈植物〉 oriental cherry; cherry blossom: 日本～ Japanese flowering cherry / ～盛开的季节 time when (oriental) cherry trees are in full blossom
樱桃 yīngtáo cherry: ～树 cherry tree / ～园 cherry orchard / ～沟 Cherry Vale (in Beijing) / ～好吃树难栽。Cherries taste delicious, but what backbreaking work it is to grow them!

Y

撄 yīng 〈书面〉❶ butt against; arouse; oppose; challenge:～怒 arouse one's anger /不敢～其锋 dare not challenge (*or* meet head-on) the spearhead of the attack ❷ disturb; harass

嘤 yīng 〈书面〉〈象声〉chirp

嘤鸣 yīngmíng ❶ (of birds) chirp; sing:树上的小鸟在婉转～。The little birds are singing melodiously in the tree. ❷〈书面〉empathy between friends

嘤鸣求友 yīngmíng-qiúyǒu *also* "嘤其鸣矣,求其友声" a bird sings to seek a mate — try to find a true friend:～之心,人皆有之。Everyone wants to find a bosom friend.

嘤泣 yīngqì sob quietly

嘤嘤 yīngyīng 〈象声〉chirp; low and soft sound: 鸟鸣～ birds chirping continuously /～啜泣 sob quietly

鹦 yīng

鹦哥 yīngge 〈动物〉parrot:巧嘴儿～ eloquent parrot — glib talker

鹦哥绿 yīnggelǜ parrot green:她身着一件～的长裙。She was wearing a long parrot-green skirt.

鹦鹉 yīngwǔ parrot:能言～ talking parrot /长尾～ parakeet /虎皮～ budgerigar

鹦鹉螺 yīngwǔluó nautilus

鹦鹉热 yīngwǔrè 〈医学〉psittacosis; parrot fever

鹦鹉学舌 yīngwǔ-xuéshé repeat the words of others like a parrot; parrot:你自己不会讲,难道非要～不可吗? Why parrot others? Don't you know how to speak your own mind?

鹦嘴鱼 yīngzuǐyú parrot fish

缨 yīng ❶ ribbon or band used to fasten the hat in ancient times:仰天大笑,冠～索绝。The hat ribbon snapped when he guffawed with his head thrown back. ❷ tassel:红～枪 red-tasselled spear ❸ sth. shaped like a tassel:芥菜～儿 mustard leaves

缨络 yīngluò ❶ *see* "璎珞" yīngluò ❷ tassel ❸〈书面〉entangle; bind

缨帽 yīngmào red-tasselled hat worn by court officials of the Qing Dynasty

缨穗 yīngsuì ear-shaped ornaments tied on to clothes or utensils

缨子 yīngzi ❶ tassel; tassel-shaped ornament:帽～ hat tassel ❷ sth. shaped like a tassel:萝卜～ radish leaves

yíng

赢 yíng ❶ win; beat; defeat:这场比赛我们队准～。Our team will surely win the match. /这盘棋他～了我三子。He beat me at this game of *weiqi* by three pieces. ❷ gain or obtain (profit):有亏有～ sometimes gain and sometimes lose

赢得 yíngdé win; gain; earn:～胜利 achieve (*or* score) a victory /～利润 gain profit /～世界冠军 win world championship /～观众的喝彩 draw applause from the audience /～用户的信任 obtain consumers' confidence

赢家 yíngjia winner:核战争没有～。There will be no winner in a nuclear war.

赢利 yínglì *also* "盈利" yínglì ❶ profit:他把这一季度的～全部用于职工的福利。He committed all the profit of this quarter to the employees' welfare. ❷ gain profit:这场买卖～五千元。This business deal brought in a profit of 5,000 *yuan*.

赢余 yíngyú *also* "盈余" yíngyú surplus; profit; (favourable) balance:有～ have a favourable balance; be in the black /～颇丰 have a big surplus

嬴 Yíng a surname

瀛 yíng ❶〈书面〉sea; ocean:东～ East Sea; Japan /～台 Yingtai or Sea Terrace Islet (in Beijing) ❷ (Yíng) a surname

瀛海 yínghǎi 〈书面〉vast sea or ocean

瀛寰 yínghuán 〈书面〉whole world; the globe:誉满～ gain worldwide fame

瀛洲 Yíngzhōu Yingzhou — fabled abode of immortals

籝(籯) yíng 〈书面〉❶ basket-shaped container ❷ chopstick holder

莹(瑩) yíng 〈书面〉❶ jade-like stone ❷ lustrous and transparent:晶～ as clear as crystal; sparkling

莹白 yíngbái bright and clean; shining white:～的月色 gleaming moonlight

莹澈 yíngchè lustrous and transparent:荷叶上托着～的露珠。There were sparkling dewdrops on the lotus leaves.

莹洁 yíngjié shiny; bright and clean:～的沙石 glistening sand and pebbles

莹然 yíngrán crystal-clear; shiny:泪珠～ sparkling tears

莹润 yíngrùn smooth and lustrous:砚石～ smooth and lustrous inkstone

莹莹 yíngyíng sparkling; glittering:泪水～ glittering tear

滢(瀅) yíng 〈书面〉crystal-clear:湖水汀～ limpid lake water

茔(塋) yíng 〈书面〉grave; cemetery:～地 graveyard /坟～ grave /祖～ ancestral cemetery (*or* grave)

荧(熒) yíng 〈书面〉❶ glimmering; gleaming; dim (light):～烛 dim candle light ❷ (of one's glance or eyes) dazzled; perplexed

荧光 yíngguāng 〈物理〉fluorescence; fluorescent light:～染料〈化工〉fluorescent dye; fluorochrome /～增白剂〈化工〉fluorescent whitening agents; fluorescer /～透视检查 fluoroscopy /～探伤〈冶金〉zyglo; zyglo inspection

荧光灯 yíngguāngdēng fluorescent lamp

荧光粉 yíngguāngfěn fluorescent powder; phosphor particles

荧光管 yíngguāngguǎn fluorescent tube

荧光计 yíngguāngjì fluorimeter; fluorometer

荧光镜 yíngguāngjìng fluorescope; fluoroscope:透视～ transmission fluoroscope /～检查 fluoroscopy

荧光屏 yíngguāngpíng fluorescent screen; screen (of a television, monitor, etc.):～显示出清晰的图像。Sharp images appear on the screen.

荧光摄影 yíngguāng shèyǐng fluorescence photography

荧光素 yíngguāngsù fluorescein; luciferin

荧惑 yínghuò ❶〈书面〉perplex; bewilder:～人心 confuse people's minds /～观众 bewilder the audience ❷〈古语〉Mars

荧屏 yíngpíng ❶ fluorescent screen; screen (of a television, monitor, etc.) ❷ television:十名民歌手今晚将亮相～。Ten folksong singers will appear on television tonight.

荧石 yíngshí *also* "萤石" yíngshí fluorite; fluorspar

荧荧 yíngyíng gleaming or glimmering starlight or candlelight:众星～ sparkling stars /孤灯～ glimmering lone lamp

萤(螢) yíng *also* "萤火虫" firefly; glowworm:流～ flying glowworms

萤火 yínghuǒ glowworm's light

萤火虫 yínghuǒchóng firefly; glowworm; lightning bug

萤石 yíngshí *also* "氟石" fúshí 〈矿业〉fluorite; fluorspar

营[1](營) yíng ❶ seek; pursue:～福 pursue happiness /无求无～ seek nothing for oneself ❷ operate; manage; run:私～ privately-run; privately owned /合～ jointly-run; jointly operated ❸ (Yíng) a surname

营[2](營) yíng ❶ camp; barracks:军～ army barracks /安～扎寨 pitch a camp; camp ❷ battalion:一～ First Battalion

营办 yíngbàn run; manage:他把店铺交给儿子～。He let his son run the shop.

营巢 yíngcháo (of birds) build a nest; nest

营地 yíngdì campsite; camping ground:视察～ inspect a camping ground /～周围遍布哨兵。Sentinels were posted around the campsite.

营房 yíngfáng barracks:整洁的～ neat and clean barracks /一排排

Y

~ rows upon rows of barracks
营工 yínggōng 〈旧语〉sell one's labour: ~度日 earn a living by selling one's labour
营混子 yínghùnzi 〈旧语〉army riffraff
营火 yínghuǒ campfire: 点起~ light a campfire
营火会 yínghuǒhuì campfire party: ~在小河边草地举行。The campfire party was held on the meadow near a stream.
营建 yíngjiàn construct; build: ~校舍 construct a school building /~了三间砖房 build a three-chamber brick house
营救 yíngjiù rescue; save; succour: 千方百计地~事故的幸存者 try by every means to rescue survivors of the accident
营垒 yínglěi ❶ barracks and the enclosing walls: 构筑~ construct barracks and the enclosing walls ❷ camp; bloc: 两个对立的~ two opposing blocs /同一~的战友 comrades-in-arms in the same camp
营利 yínglì seek or pursue profit: 不择手段地~ seek profit by hook (*or* by crook)
营林 yínglín afforest: 加强~更新工作 step up reforestation
营盘 yíngpán 〈旧语〉barracks: ~四周都有持枪的军人守卫。The barracks were guarded by armed soldiers on all sides.
营求 yíngqiú ❶ seek; pursue; go after: ~私利 hanker after personal gain ❷ seek out; look for
营区 yíngqū area where barracks are located; barracks site
营舍 yíngshè barracks
营生 yíngshēng make or eke out a living: 靠打零工~ eke out a living by doing odd jobs /靠打鱼~ earn a living as a fisherman
营生 yíngsheng 〈方言〉line of business; occupation; job: 什么~他都干过。He has done all kinds of jobs. /打铁这~他干了很久了。He has been an ironsmith (*or* a blacksmith) for a long time.
营私 yíngsī seek private gain; pursue selfish ends; feather one's nest: 结党~ form a clique (*or* band together) for selfish purposes
营私舞弊 yíngsī-wǔbì engage in malpractices for selfish ends; practise graft: 利用职权, ~ abuse one's power for personal gains
营销 yíngxiāo marketing: ~员 salesman
营销管理 yíngxiāo guǎnlǐ marketing management
营销学 yíngxiāoxué marketing
营养 yíngyǎng nutrition; nourishment; aliment: 富于~ nourishing; nutritious; nutritive /~水平 nutritional level /~状况 nutritional condition /~平衡 nutritional equilibrium /~不良 malnutrition; undernourishment /~不良性水肿 alimentary oedema; nutritional oedema; hunger oedema /蔬菜富有~。Vegetables are very nutritious (*or* highly nourishing).
营养钵 yíngyǎngbō 〈农业〉feeding block; nutritive bowl
营养级 yíngyǎngjí trophic level
营养价值 yíngyǎng jiàzhí nutritive or nutritional value
营养链 yíngyǎngliàn food chain
营养面包 yíngyǎng miànbāo enriched bread
营养品 yíngyǎngpǐn nutriment; nutrient
营养缺乏症 yíngyǎng quēfázhèng deficiency disease; deprivation disease
营养师 yíngyǎngshī nutritionist; dietitian
营养霜 yíngyǎngshuāng nourishing cream
营养素 yíngyǎngsù nutrient
营养型 yíngyǎngxíng nutritional type
营养性贫血 yíngyǎngxìng pínxuè nutritional anemia; deficiency anemia
营养学 yíngyǎngxué nutriology
营养元素 yíngyǎng yuánsù 〈化学〉nutritive element
营业 yíngyè do business: 节日照常~ business as usual during the festival /暂停~ business suspended for the time being (*or* temporarily) /扩大~ expand business operation /~收入 business income (*or* receipts, *or* earnings) /~范围 scope of business operation /~方式 mode of business operation /~利润 operating profit
营业部 yíngyèbù business department
营业额 yíngyè'é turnover; volume of business
营业时间 yíngyè shíjiān business hours
营业税 yíngyèshuì business tax; turnover tax; transactions tax: 交纳~ pay business tax /征收~ collect business tax
营业员 yíngyèyuán shop employee; shop assistant; buyer (for a shop): 她是百货公司的~。She is a shop assistant in a department store.
营营 yíngyíng be busy making a living: 他毕生~, 追逐名利。He has been busy all his life chasing fame and gain.
营运 yíngyùn ❶ (of trains, trucks and ships) operate; be put into operation; be commissioned: 这条新船即将投入~。This new ship will soon be commissioned. ❷ (often used in the early vernacular) manage; operate; do business
营运资本 yíngyùn zīběn working capital
营葬 yíngzàng arrange funeral affairs: 代办~ make funeral arrangements on behalf of the family of the deceased
营造 yíngzào ❶ build; construct: ~住宅 housing construction /~一个舒适的安乐窝 build a comfortable safe haven for oneself ❷ plant trees; afforest: ~防护林 plant windbreak forests /大规模地~ large-scale reforestation
营造尺 yíngzàochǐ standard *chi* (equal to 0.32 metre) of the Qing Dynasty
营造法式 Yíngzào Fǎshì *A Treatise on Architectural Methods*, work of ancient Chinese architecture compiled in 1091 during the Northern Song Dynasty
营造商 yíngzàoshāng builder (as a businessman)
营造业 yíngzàoyè building industry
营寨 yíngzhài 〈旧语〉barracks
营长 yíngzhǎng battalion commander
营帐 yíngzhàng tent: 支起~ pitch a tent

萦(縈)

yíng 〈书面〉entwine; entangle; encompass: 公务~身 be preoccupied with official business
萦怀 yínghuái occupy one's mind; absorb one's attention: 梦寐~ can not keep one's mind away from sth. day and night /家事~。Family matters keep him occupied.
萦回 yínghuí go round and round; hover; linger: 绿水~ winding river /临别情景常在脑际~。The parting scene lingered on in his mind. /耳边经常~老师的谆谆教诲。The teacher's sincere admonitions kept ringing in my ears.
萦念 yíngniàn think of; be concerned about; miss: 回到~已久的祖国 return to the native land which one has been missing so much
萦绕 yíngrào go round and round; hang about; linger: 云雾~ hovering clouds /~于心 linger in one's mind /~耳际 keep ringing in one's ears
萦系 yíngxì be concerned about; miss: 思乡之念~心头。Homesickness gnawed at my heart.
萦纡 yíngyū winding; meandering: 山径~ winding mountain trail (*or* path)

潆(瀠)

yíng
潆洄 yínghuí swirl: 江水~ swirling river water
潆绕 yíngrào go round and round; wind: 清溪~ winding clear brook

蝇(蠅)

yíng housefly; fly: 灭~ wipe out flies /蚊~ mosquitoes and flies
蝇粪点玉 yíngfèn-diǎnyù flyspeck on a piece of jade — fly in the ointment
蝇虎 yínghǔ a kind of spider that feeds on flies
蝇拍 yíngpāi flyswatter; flyflap: 塑料~ plastic flyswatter
蝇蛆病 yíngqūbìng myiasis
蝇甩儿 yíngshuǎir 〈方言〉horsetail whisk
蝇头 yíngtóu small as the head of a fly; tiny: 他能写一手漂亮的~小楷。He can write very small characters beautifully.
蝇头微利 yíngtóu wēilì petty profits: 靠小本生意赚点~ make petty profits by doing some small business
蝇营狗苟 yíngyíng-gǒugǒu *also* "狗苟蝇营" drag out an ignoble existence; shamelessly seek personal gain: 不屑与~之辈为伍 be loath to be seen in the company of those who are shamelessly self-seeking
蝇蛹 yíngyǒng fly pupa
蝇子 yíngzi 〈口语〉fly

盈

yíng ❶ fill; pack; throng: 车马~门 one's gateway is thronged with horses and carriages — the house is honoured with rich and distinguished guests /恶贯满~ one's sum of iniquity is made up — face retribution for a life of crime /物资充~ abundance of goods ❷ surplus; gain: 年终总计, 有亏有~。On the year's balance sheet, one can find both losses and gains.
盈亏 yíngkuī ❶ waxing and waning of the moon ❷ profit and

loss：自负～ (of an enterprise) assume sole responsibility for its own profits and losses /～统筹 exercise overall control over profits and losses

盈利 yínglì *also* "赢利" yínglì make a profit

盈利能力 yínglì nénglì profitability

盈利收益率 yínglì shōuyìlǜ earning yield

盈满 yíngmǎn ❶ be full of; be filled with：老人高兴得眼里～了泪水。The old man's eyes were brimming with joyous tears. ❷ (of power, sin and crime, etc.) at the zenith; in full measure：罪孽～ have committed one's full share of sins and crimes

盈千累万 yíngqiān-lěiwàn thousands upon thousands; myriad; numerous：参观展览的人～。Thousands upon thousands (of people) visited the exhibition.

盈溢 yíngyì be full of; be brimming with：热情～ be filled with enthusiasm /眼里～着晶莹的泪花 eyes brimming with sparkling tears

盈盈 yíngyíng ❶ clear; translucent：春水～ sparkling spring water /荷叶上露珠～。On the lotus leaves are translucent dewdrops. ❷ (of carriage, demeanour, etc.) engaging; enchanting：～顾盼 enchanting gaze ❸ full display (of sentiments, etc.)：喜气～ visible delight /笑脸～ broadly smiling faces ❹ agile; nimble; lithe：～起舞 dance lithely /她～地走了过来，默然无声。She came over sprightly, without making a sound.

盈余 yíngyú *also* "赢余" yíngyú surplus; gain; profit：可～三百元 have a surplus of 300 *yuan* /略有～ make a small profit /全年的～数目可观。The year's balance was quite impressive.

楹

yíng ❶ principal column of a hall; pillar：以巨木为～ use huge logs as columns ❷〈书面〉〈量词〉room (in a house)：园内有小舍三～。There is a small three-roomed house in the garden.

楹联 yínglián couplet written on a scroll and hung on a pillar of a hall：撰写～ write a couplet to hang on the pillars

迎

yíng ❶ meet; greet; welcome; receive：热烈欢～ warmly welcome /远～ go over a long distance to meet sb. /喜～嘉宾 joyously greet distinguished guests /～来送往 receive and see off guests /～新年 sing (*or* usher) in the new year ❷ go or move towards; meet face to face; face：～着风浪前进 forge ahead in the teeth of winds and waves /～着黎明 go towards the dawn /～上前去，抽了他一个耳光 step forward and slap him across the face

迎宾 yíngbīn meet or welcome a guest; receive a visitor：在大门口列队～ line up in front of the gate to welcome guests /乐队高奏～曲。The band was striking up a tune of welcome.

迎春 yíngchūn 〈植物〉winter jasmine (*Jasminum nudiflorum*)

迎风 yíngfēng ❶ facing the wind; against the wind：～而立 stand against the wind /村口正～，特别凉快。With a breeze blowing, it is quite cool at the approach to the village. ❷ down the wind; with the wind：五星红旗～招展。The Five-Star Red Flag was fluttering in the wind.

迎风面 yíngfēngmiàn windward side

迎合 yínghé make a special effort to please; cater to; pander to：～上级的心意 go along with the wishes of one's superior /～低级趣味 cater to vulgar (*or* base) tastes and interest; play to the gallery /专会～ be good at pleasing

迎候 yínghòu await the arrival of：专程前往广州～贵宾 make a special trip to Guangzhou to await the arrival of the distinguished guests

迎击 yíngjī meet (an approaching enemy) head-on; attack head on：奋勇～ bravely meet sb. head-on

迎接 yíngjiē receive; meet; welcome; greet：热情地～外宾 warmly welcome foreign guests /高兴地～好友 be happy to meet one's bosom friends /用浴血奋战来～一个新国家的诞生 be ready to fight and shed one's blood to usher in a new country

迎客松 Yíngkèsōng Guest-Welcoming Pine (of Huangshan Mountain in Anhui Province)

迎面 yíngmiàn head-on; face to face; in one's face：～坐着 sit face to face /西北风～刮来。A northwest wind blew in one's face. /只见弟弟～走来。I saw my younger brother coming up to me.

迎亲 yíngqīn 〈旧语〉send a sedan chair over to the bride's home to bring her over：～的队伍 wedding procession

迎娶 yíngqǔ marry a woman

迎刃而解 yíngrèn'érjiě (of a bamboo) split all the way down as it meets the edge of a knife — (of a problem) be readily solved; be readily done or resolved：只要他到场，难题自可～。Once he is present, the difficult problem can be readily solved.

迎头 yíngtóu head-on; straight; directly：～相撞 head-on collision

迎头赶上 yíngtóu-gǎnshàng strive to catch up with the foremost; try hard to catch up：～时代的潮流 strive to keep pace with the trend of the times

迎头痛击 yíngtóu-tòngjī deal a head-on blow; attack head-on：敌军业已发动进攻，我军准备予以～。Now that the enemy is attacking, we'll deal him a head-on blow.

迎新 yíngxīn ❶ see the New Year in：辞旧～ ring out the old year and ring in the new ❷ welcome new arrivals：～送旧 welcome the new arrivals and send off the retirees /～晚会 welcoming party in honour of the newcomers

迎迓 yíngyà 〈书面〉meet; greet; welcome：亲临大门～ go in person to welcome sb. at the entrance

迎战 yíngzhàn meet (an approaching enemy) head-on：～强敌 take on a powerful enemy directly and resolutely

yǐng

瘿

yǐng ❶〈中医〉goitre ❷ gall

瘿虫 yǐngchóng 〈动物〉gall insect

影

yǐng ❶ shadow：阴～ shadow /举杯邀明月，对～成三人。I hold up my cup to invite the bright moon to join me, And then we'll have a company of three including my own shadow. ❷ reflection; image：倒～ inverted image ❸ trace; vestige; vague impression：消失得无～无踪 vanish without a trace /那件事我连点～儿也记不清了。I cannot even vaguely remember what it is all about. *or* I have not even the vaguest idea of the matter. /这件事他忘得没～儿了。He has clean forgotten it. ❹ photograph; picture：全家合～ group photograph (*or* picture) of the whole family /摄～ photograph; take pictures /留～ take a photo as a reminder of one's visit to a place ❺〈旧语〉portrait of one's ancestor ❻ motion picture; film; movie：她十五岁开始从～。She began her career as a film actress at 15. ❼ leather silhouette show; shadow play; galanty show ❽〈方言〉hide; cover; conceal：草丛里～着一只野兔。Concealed in the grass was a wild hare. /他把木棍～在背后。He hid the wooden stick behind his back. ❾ trace; copy：～宋本 traced copy of the Song Dynasty

影壁 yǐngbì ❶ screen wall (facing the gate inside a traditional Chinese courtyard)：北边立着一个粉油大～。Standing in the north was a huge painted screen wall. ❷ outside screen wall facing the gate of a house：～上的字迹已经模糊不清了。The characters on the screen wall facing the gate of the house were already blurred. ❸ wall with carved murals

影抄 yǐngchāo *also* "影写" copy in the style or format of Song and Yuan books

影带 yǐngdài videotape of a TV programme, film, etc.; MTV tape：这支流行歌已拍成～。This pop song has been made into MTV.

影帝 yǐngdì king of the silver screen — most popular male movie star

影调剧 yǐngdiàojù new type of local opera based on the tunes of the Tangshan leather-silhouette show and quite popular in and around Tangshan City, Hebei Province

影碟 yǐngdié 〈方言〉VCR disk; video disc

影戤 yǐnggài (of enterpreneurs and businessmen) pirate brand names

影格儿 yǐnggér checkered paper with Chinese characters to be put under a thin sheet so that small children using the brush can write properly by tracing them

影后 yǐnghòu cinema queen or movie queen; most popular female movie star

影集 yǐngjí photograph or picture album; photo album：他送我一本漂亮的～。He gave me a beautiful photo album.

影迹 yǐngjì trace; shadow：又一天过去了，哪里都没有他的～。Another day has passed, yet no trace of him has been found.

影剧界 yǐngjùjiè film and theatrical circles

影剧院 yǐngjùyuàn cinemas, theatres, opera-houses, etc.

影迷 yǐngmí film or movie fan

影片儿 yǐngpiānr 〈口语〉film; movie; picture：国产～ home-made

film /外国～ foreign film
影片 yǐngpiàn film; picture:故事～ feature film /喜剧～ comedy film
影评 yǐngpíng film review:～家 film reviewer /这些～的内容大同小异。These film reviews are very much the same.
影青瓷 yǐngqīngcí shadowy blue porcelain
影射 yǐngshè allude to; suggest indirectly; hint obliquely at; insinuate:应该正面批评,不要～攻击。We should criticize openly, and not attack by innuendo.
影视 yǐngshì film and television:～演员 film and TV actors and actresses /～文化 film and TV culture
影视界 yǐngshìjiè *also* "影视圈" film and TV circles
影坛 yǐngtán film circles; filmdom:～生涯 career in film circles /退出～ withdraw from filmland
影堂 yǐngtáng 〈旧语〉hall where the portraits of one's gods or ancestors were displayed and worshipped
影条 yǐngtiáo 〈纺织〉shadow stripes:～巴里纱 shadow-striped voile
影戏 yǐngxì ❶ leather-silhouette show; shadow play; galanty show ❷〈方言〉film; motion picture; movie:爱看～ love watching movies /迷上了～ be fascinated by films
影响 yǐngxiǎng ❶ affect; influence:～儿童的成长 adversely affect children's growth /～生产进度 hold up production /～领导的威望 impair (*or* harm) the leadership's prestige /～工作 interfere with one's work /～情绪 dampen one's spirits (*or* enthusiasm) /政治和贸易是互相～的。Politics and trade interact on each other. ❷ influence; effect; impact:产生了重大～ exert a significant influence; produce a great impact /受到了良好～ be (*or* come) under very good influence /消除坏的～ eliminate (*or* remove) bad effects ❸ hearsay; rumour:模糊～之谈 talk based on vague hearsay
影像 yǐngxiàng ❶ portrait; picture:室内挂有他父母的～。A portrait of his parents hung in the room. ❷ figure; features:他的～经常在我的眼前浮动。His features often floated before my eyes. ❸ image:～清晰 clear (*or* sharp) image /～模糊 blurred image /荧光屏上出现了色彩鲜明的～。Bright and colourful images have appeared on the screen.
影像编码 yǐngxiàng biānmǎ 〈电子〉image coding
影像传感 yǐngxiàng chuángǎn 〈电子〉image sensing
影协 yǐngxié (short for 电影家协会) association of film artists
影写 yǐngxiě ❶ facsimile copy, made by placing thin and transparent paper over the original and tracing it; tracing ❷ *see* "影抄"
影星 yǐngxīng film star; movie star
影业 yǐngyè film-making industry:～公司 film-making company
影印 yǐngyìn 〈印刷〉photomechanical printing; photoprinting; photo-offset process:～本 photo-offset copy; facsimile /～法 photolithography /～术 autotype /～件 photocopy /～书籍 photocopied books /～照像机 process camera /～制版 photomechanical process /～珍本书籍 photolithograph rare books
影影绰绰 yǐngyǐng-chuòchuò vaguely; dimly; indistinctly:那儿～地有几个人影儿。A few people could be vaguely seen over there.
影影糊糊 yǐngyǐng-hūhū *also* "影影忽忽" *see* "影影绰绰"
影院 yǐngyuàn cinema; movie theatre:首都～ Capital Cinema /现代化～ modern movie theatre
影展 yǐngzhǎn ❶ photograph exhibition ❷ film exhibition
影子 yǐngzi ❶ shadow:树～ shadow of a tree ❷ reflection; image:他在镜中看到了自己的～。He saw his own image in the mirror. ❸ trace; vestige; vague impression:关于他我连点～都没有了。My mind is a blank on him.
影子价格 yǐngzi jiàgé shadow price
影子内阁 yǐngzi nèigé shadow cabinet:～成员 members of the shadow cabinet
影踪 yǐngzōng *also* "踪影" trace; sign; vestige

郢

Yǐng capital of the State of Chu (楚) in the Zhou Dynasty, located in the present Hubei Province:～爰 gold coin of Chu
郢书燕说 yǐngshū-yānshuō a letter from the State of Chu was explained by the people in the State of Yan — distorted interpretation of the original

颖

yǐng 〈书面〉❶ glume; grain husk: *see* "～果" ❷ tip (of a writing brush, etc.); point:锋～ sharp tip /脱～而出 an awl-point sticks out through a bag — talent shows itself ❸ clever; bright:聪～ clever
颖果 yǐngguǒ 〈植物〉caryopsis
颖慧 yǐnghuì 〈书面〉(usu. of a teenager) clever; intelligent:年少～,为时人所称。Young and bright, he was highly commended by his contemporaries.
颖悟 yǐngwù 〈书面〉(usu. of a teenager) clever; bright; smart:～无比 exceptionally bright
颖异 yǐngyì 〈书面〉❶ exceptionally clever:天资～ born with uncommon intelligence ❷ new and unique:构思～ new and original thinking

yìng

应(應)

yìng ❶ answer; reply; respond; echo:彼此互～ act in concert with each other; support each other /轻轻地～了一声 give a quiet answer ❷ comply with; grant; concede:有求必～ grant every request; respond favourably to every plea /～观众要求 at the request of the audience /～邀访问中国 visit China on invitation ❸ suit; conform to; accord with: *see* "～景"; "～手"; "～时" ❹ deal with; cope with; meet:从容以～ deal with sth. calmly
see also yīng
应变 yìngbiàn ❶ meet an emergency or contingency:～措施 emergency measure /随机～ act according to circumstances; suit one's actions to changing conditions; be flexible /他善于～。He is capable of rising to the occasion. ❷〈物理〉strain:～硬化 strain hardening
应变规 yìngbiànguī strain gauge
应变计 yìngbiànjì strainmeter
应变率 yìngbiànlǜ 〈物理〉strain rate
应差 yìngchāi accept an assignment; do as one is ordered to
应承 yìngchéng agree (to do sth.); consent; accept (an order, etc.):～得很痛快 agree promptly to do sth. /她一口把这事～下来。She consented to it without a moment's hesitation. *or* She accepted the task promptly.
应酬 yìngchou ❶ socialize; entertain; treat with courtesy:～不开 have too many social engagements on one's hands; be bogged down in a lot of social functions /写几封～信 write a few courtesy letters /说几句～话 say a few polite words /她作为公关经理,～很多。She has a lot of entertaining to do as public relations manager. ❷ dinner party:晚上母亲有个～,我得陪她。My mother is going to a dinner party this evening, and I will have to go along with her.
应从 yìngcóng agree to; assent; consent:他点头～了大家的意见。He nodded his agreement with the opinions of others.
应答 yìngdá ❶ reply; answer:从容～ answer calmly (*or* with composure) /～如流 answer readily and fluently ❷〈电子〉answer; answer-back; respond:～机 responder; responser /～器 responder; responser /～设备 answering machine; answering equipment /～台 answering board
应敌 yìngdí deal with one's enemy or opponent; meet an enemy in battle:仓促～ meet the enemy (*or* opponent) in haste /采取～的紧急措施 adopt emergency measures to repel the enemy
应典 yìngdiǎn *also* "应点"〈方言〉practise what one preaches; do what one promises
应电流 yìngdiànliú 〈电学〉induced current
应对 yìngduì reply; answer:善于～ always have a ready answer; be good at repartee
应对如流 yìngduì-rúliú respond readily and promptly:辩论会上,甲方女辩手～。In the debating contest, the girl debator of Team A responded quickly and fluently.
应付 yìngfu ❶ deal with; cope with; treat; handle:准备～可能发生的意外事件 get prepared against possible contingencies /～复杂情况 cope with a complicated situation /此人很难～。He is really very difficult to deal with. ❷ do (sth.) perfunctorily; do (sth.) after a fashion; go through the motions:这样的事怎能采取～的态度? How could you take such a perfunctory attitude towards this matter? ❸ make do; serve as a makeshift:这件大衣我想今年冬天还可以～得过去。I think I can make do with this coat for the winter. /这工作我一个人还可以～。I can somehow manage (the job) by myself.
see also yīngfù
应付裕如 yìngfu-yùrú *also* "应付自如" cope with or handle a situation with ease; be equal to the occasion:他这方面经验丰富,再复杂的

Y

情况也能～。As he is very experienced in this regard, he can manage it, however complicated the case may be.

应和 yìnghè respond to; echo:众人群起～。People rose en masse to respond to the call.

应机 yìngjī suit the occasion; seize an opportunity that rises:～立断 promptly decide at the right moment; make a prompt decision as the occasion requires

应激 yìngjī 〈心理〉stress:～激素 stress hormone

应急 yìngjí meet an urgent need; meet an emergency or contingency:采取～措施 adopt an emergency measure /～计划 exigency plan; crash programme /～拨款 contingency fund /～储备金 contingency reserve /～流动资金 emergency liquidity funds /供～使用 for emergency use

应接 yìngjiē ❶ receive:我到达后受到主人的热情～。I was warmly received by the host when I arrived. ❷ cope with; deal with:～从容 deal with sth. or sb. calmly ❸ correspond:书法家讲究字的点画要互相～。Calligraphers are quite particular about the correspondence between the dots and strokes in writing Chinese characters.

应接不暇 yìngjiē-bùxiá have not a moment's leisure in (handling) one's work; have more visitors or business than one can attend to:前来咨询的人很多,我们实在～。We could hardly attend to so many people coming to consult us. /最近公务繁忙,他大有～之势。Recently he has almost been overwhelmed by the flood of official business.

应节 yìngjié ❶ sing to the beat:歌声婉转～。The singing is both melodious and well keyed. ❷ suit the season; be in season

应景 yìngjǐng ❶ do sth. after a fashion; act for the sake of politeness, formality, expediency, etc.; go through the motions:他本不会唱歌,但在联欢会上也不得不应个景儿。Though he did not sing well, he had to go through the motions at the get-together. ❷ do sth. for the occasions:～果品 seasonal fruit /中秋节吃月饼是～。Some people eat moon cakes at the Mid-Autumn Festival just for the occasion.

应举 yìngjǔ sit for the imperial examination:到京中～去 go to the capital for the imperial examinations

应考 yìngkǎo take or sit for an examination:～的人 examinee /～者不下千人。No less than a thousand people sat for the examination.

应口 yìngkǒu answer; consent; agree:凭你怎么说,他就是不～。No matter how hard I tried to persuade him, he just refused to open his mouth.

应力 yìnglì 〈物理〉stress; tension:正～ direct stress /内～ internal stress /预～ prestress /～分析 stress analysis /～画 stress diagram /～分布 stress distribution /～张量 stress tensor

应力波 yìnglìbō 〈物理〉stress wave

应力性骨折 yìnglìxìng gǔzhé 〈医学〉stress fracture

应卯 yìngmǎo sign in between 5 and 7 a.m. (in the dynastic times); answer the roll call; put in a routine appearance:你总得应个卯吧。You should at least put in an appearance at the roll call.

应门 yìngmén open and close the door:内无～五尺之童。There was not even a boy in the house to answer the door.

应募 yìngmù respond to the call for recruits; enlist; enrol; join up:他们中有两人～。Two of them joined up.

应诺 yìngnuò give assent to; agree to do sth.; promise; undertake:大声～ agree loudly /凡～之事,无不照办。He never fails to do what he promises to.

应聘 yìngpìn accept an offer or invitation:他～到广州教书。He accepted an offer to teach in Guangzhou. *or* He was invited to teach in Guangzhou.

应声 yìngshēng appear right away when called; happen right at the sound of sth.:小姑娘～而至。The little girl appeared right on call. /枪声一响,野兔～倒地。The hare dropped to the ground at the report of the shotgun.

see also yīngshēng

应声虫 yìngshēngchóng yesman; echo:智囊团里怎么可以有～! How can the brain trust include yesmen? /她是丈夫的～。She always echoes whatever her husband says.

应时 yìngshí ❶ seasonable; in season:～菜蔬 seasonable vegetables /～瓜果 fruits of the season ❷〈方言〉at the appointed time:他一连几天没吃上一顿～饭。He has not had a meal at regular hours for days on end. ❸ at once; promptly; immediately:绿灯亮,车子～开动。The car began moving as soon as the green light was on.

应市 yìngshì make sth. available on the market; market sth.:新产品即将～。The new products will soon be marketed.

应试 yìngshì sit for or take an examination:应乡试〈旧语〉sit for the county examination

应试教育 yìngshì jiàoyù examination-oriented education:反对～,提倡素质教育。We should oppose schooling that is merely geared to examinations, and advocate education aimed at improving the all-round qualities of the students.

应手 yìngshǒu ❶ immediate; prompt:～奏效 take immediate effect ❷〈方言〉(of tool, weapon, etc.) handy; convenient:得心～ with facility (*or* proficiency); handy /使别人的笔不～。It's inconvenient to use another's pen.

应诉 yìngsù 〈法律〉self-defence by the accused; respond to charges:～人 respondent

应选 yìngxuǎn ❶ (of a candidate) participate in an election ❷〈旧语〉put oneself up for selection by the monarch or ministers

应验 yìngyàn come true; be confirmed; be fulfilled:他的预言～了。His predictions have been confirmed by later developments (*or* have come true).

应邀 yìngyāo at sb.'s invitation; on invitation; (be) invited:～来我国访问 come to visit China on invitation /～出席大会 be invited to the congress

应用 yìngyòng ❶ use; employ; apply:～新技术 apply new technology /～先进方法 employ advanced methods /～计算机 use a computer /这种工艺～得很普遍。This technology is in wide use. ❷ applied:～物理 applied physics

应用程序 yìngyòng chéngxù application

应用科学 yìngyòng kēxué applied sciences

应用逻辑 yìngyòng luójí applied logic

应用软件 yìngyòng ruǎnjiàn application software

应用卫星 yìngyòng wèixīng applications satellite:应用技术卫星 applications technology satellite

应用文 yìngyòngwén practical writing (as in official documents, notices, receipts, advertisements, etc.):重视～的写作 lay stress on practical writing

应用心理学 yìngyòng xīnlǐxué applied psychology

应用语言学 yìngyòng yǔyánxué applied linguistics

应援 yìngyuán 〈军事〉come to the relief of an ally

应运 yìngyùn in conformity with the times:他那个冷门专业如今～了。His speciality which used to receive little attention is now much in demand as times change.

应运而生 yìngyùn'érshēng arise at the right moment; emerge as the times require:在市场经济的大潮中,一批新兴行业～。In the great tide of market economy, a number of new trades have cropped up.

应战 yìngzhàn ❶ meet an invading enemy:沉着～ remain calm (*or* collected) in meeting the invading enemy /仓促～ meet the enemy attack in a hurry ❷ accept or take up a challenge:坚决～ resolutely take up (*or* accept) a challenge; pick up the gauntlet

应战书 yìngzhànshū letter accepting a challenge

应招 yìngzhāo enlist; join up

应召 yìngzhào 〈书面〉respond to a call:～晋见总统 be granted an audience by the president

应召女郎 yìngzhào nǚláng call girl; prostitute

应诏 yìngzhào accept an imperial edict

应诊 yìngzhěn (of a doctor) see patients:随时～ be always ready to see (*or* treat) patients

应征 yìngzhēng ❶ be recruited; enlist; join up:广大青年踊跃～入伍。Large numbers of youths enthusiastically joined the army (*or* joined up). ❷ respond to a call for contribution:～稿件 contribution to a periodical, etc., at the editor's public invitation /～的对联 contributed couplet

应制 yìngzhì 〈旧语〉write articles or poems on the order of the emperor:～诗 poem written for the emperor

膺

yìng *see* "应" yìng

see also yīng

硬

yìng ❶ hard; solid; stiff; tough:坚～ solid /僵～ rigid; inflexible /～领 stiff collar ❷ strong; firm; tough; rigid:口气非常～ in a very tough tone /生搬～套 copy mechanically /欺软怕～ bully the weak and fear the strong /不许他干,他～要干。He insisted on doing it even without permission. ❸ manage to do sth. with effort:～充大方 feign generosity /～充内行 deck oneself out as an expert /带病～挺着上班 force oneself to work despite one's illness ❹ good; able; capable:笔头儿～ write a powerful hand /功夫～ masterly skill

硬癌 yìng'ái *also* "慢性癌" mànxìng'ái 〈医学〉 scirrhoma; scirrhus; scirrhous carcinoma

硬板 yìngbǎn ❶ rigid; harsh:你这话太～,怕他难以接受。Your criticism is a bit too harsh. I'm afraid it may be difficult for him to take it. ❷〈方言〉 solid; firm; rigorous:没有几年～工夫,是练不出这一手的。It would require a few years of rigorous training before one could acquire such skill.

硬邦邦 yìngbāngbāng very hard; stiff; clumsy:话说得～ express one's ideas clumsily /动作～的,真难看。His stiff movements are quite ungainly.

硬棒 yìngbang 〈方言〉 strong; hale and hearty:祖父八十多了,身体还挺～。Though eighty years old, Grandpa is still hale and hearty.

硬包装 yìngbāozhuāng ❶ hard packaging: ～的奶粉 hard-packaged milk powder ❷ hard packaging materials such as tinplate can, glass bottle, etc.

硬绷绷 yìngbēngbēng very hard; stiff; rigid:这豆儿～,嚼不动。The beans are too tough to chew.

硬笔 yìngbǐ hard-tipped pen (such as a fountain pen, pencil, or ball pen): ～书法 calligraphical works by hard-tipped pens

硬币 yìngbì ❶ hard cash; coin; specie:用～支付 pay in specie /他喜爱收藏各种～。He is fond of collecting various kinds of coins. ❷ hard currency

硬变 yìngbiàn 〈医学〉 cirrhosis:肺～ cirrhosis of lung; pulmonary cirrhosis /肝～ cirrhosis (of liver) /肾～ cirrhosis of kidney /胃～ cirrhosis of stomach

硬玻璃 yìngbōli 〈化工〉 hardglass

硬材 yìngcái 〈林业〉 hardwood

硬撑 yìngchēng manage to do sth. with difficulty; force oneself to do sth.:有病不要～着。Don't force yourself to work when you are not feeling well.

硬磁材料 yìngcí cáiliào 〈电工〉 hard-magnetic material

硬磁盘 yìngcípán *also* "硬盘" hard magnetic disk

硬蛋白 yìngdànbái scleroprotein

硬道理 yìngdàoli inescapable truth; established truth:发展是～。Development is top priority.

硬顶 yìngdǐng ❶ retort or talk back rudely:对长辈你怎能～? How could you be so rude as to talk back to your elders? ❷ strongly oppose; stand firmly (against sth. or sb.):对不合理的做法就得～。One must stand firmly against unreasonable practices.

硬度 yìngdù ❶〈物理〉 hardness:布氏～ Brinell hardness /维氏～ Vickers hardness (*or* Vickers diamond hardness); diamond penetrator hardness /～试验 hardness testing /～试验机 hardness testing machine; hardness tester ❷ hardness of water

硬度计 yìngdùjì sclerometer; hardmeter

硬腭 yìng'è 〈生理〉 hard palate

硬钢 yìnggāng 〈冶金〉 hard steel

硬弓 yìnggōng very strong bow

硬功 yìnggōng *also* "硬功夫" high proficiency; great skill:他的成名,全靠一手～。His masterly skill has won him fame and recognition.

硬骨头 yìnggǔtou ❶ hard bone; person of indomitable will:咱们村的小伙子都是～。The young men in our village are all people of great daring. ❷ hard nut; difficult task:啃～ crack a hard nut; work at a difficult task

硬骨鱼 yìnggǔyú bony fish

硬光漆 yìngguāngqī 〈化工〉 hard-gloss paint

硬汉 yìnghàn *also* "硬汉子" dauntless, unyielding man; man of iron will; macho man:他是一条宁死不屈的～。He is a dauntless man who would rather die than submit.

硬焊 yìnghàn 〈冶金〉 hard-soldering:～料 hard solder

硬化 yìnghuà ❶〈医学〉 sclerosis; hardening:动脉～ arteriosclerosis /血管～ vascular sclerosis ❷〈机械〉 harden:时效～ age hardening /冷加工～ cold hardening ❸ (of ideas) rigid; ossified:思想～ rigid mind; petrified thinking

硬话 yìnghuà strong words; harsh utterances:拿～压人 try to silence others with threats

硬环境 yìnghuánjìng infrastructure

硬货 yìnghuò specie; hard currency

硬货币 yìnghuòbì hard currency

硬件 yìngjiàn ❶〈计算机〉 hardware ❷ machinery and other equipment used in production, scientific research or business operations:这个旅游点～是上去了,但软件还差得远啊。Though all the physical equipment is in place, the tourist resort still leaves much to be desired in terms of management and service.

硬结 yìngjié ❶ indurate; harden ❷〈医学〉 scleroma

硬撅撅 yìngjuējuē 〈方言〉 ❶ very hard; stiff:被子浆得～的,盖着不舒服。The quilt was starched too hard to sleep comfortably under it. ❷ (of statement) harsh; stiff; rigid:他说话～的,让人不痛快。His words are harsh and sound unpleasant to others.

硬拷贝 yìngkǎobèi hard-copy:～外围设备 hard-copy peripherals

硬科学 yìngkēxué hard science

硬朗 yìnglang ❶ hale and hearty; sturdy:老人身子骨挺～。The old man is still going strong. ❷ (of statements) forceful:在这一问题上,他讲话～,其他人就不再多言了。His strong and forceful remarks on this issue quietened all other participants.

硬铝 yìnglǚ 〈航空〉 dural; duralumin:～板 duralumin sheet /～型合金 duralumin type alloy

硬铝线 yìnglǚxiàn 〈电工〉 hard-drawn aluminium wire

硬煤 yìngméi hard coal; anthracite

硬锰矿 yìngměngkuàng psilomelane

硬面 yìngmiàn unleavened dough; stiff dough:～馒头 steamed bread made of unyeasted (*or* unleavened) dough

硬模 yìngmú die:～铸造 die-casting

硬木 yìngmù hardwood:～家具 hardwood furniture

硬盘 yìngpán 〈计算机〉(short for 硬磁盘) hard magnetic disk

硬磐 yìngpán 〈地质〉 hardpan; caliche; duricrust

硬碰硬 yìngpèngyìng ❶ meet force with force; match strength with strength; confront the tough with toughness:今天比赛的两对真可谓～。The pair of teams for today's match is really a case of diamond cutting diamond. ❷ (of a job) demanding solid, painstaking work or real skill:翻译是～的工作。Translation is painstaking and exacting work.

硬皮病 yìngpíbìng 〈医学〉 scleroderma; dermatosclerosis:局限性～ localized scleroderma /全身性～ systemic scleroderma; diffuse scleroderma; generalized scleroderma

硬皮树 yìngpíshù hard-bark tree

硬片 yìngpiàn *also* "干板"〈摄影〉 photographic plate

硬拼 yìngpīn fight recklessly; act in a foolhardy manner:踢球也得动脑子,不能一味地～。Playing football also requires using the brains, not foolhardiness.

硬气功 yìngqìgōng "hard *qigong*", the kind of traditional breathing exercise that is supposed to enable a person to break stone slabs or piles of bricks with bare hands, etc.

硬气水 yìngqìshuǐ Alcopop

硬气 yìngqi 〈方言〉 ❶ tough; unyielding:为人～ unyielding by nature ❷ feel justified; have no qualms about sth.:她觉得用自己劳动挣的钱～。She felt no qualms about spending the money she had earned by the sweat of her brow.

硬钎焊 yìngqiānhàn 〈冶金〉 solder brazing

硬钎料 yìngqiānliào 〈冶金〉 hard solder; brazing alloy

硬任务 yìngrènwù task that must be carried out to the letter; exacting task

硬砂岩 yìngshāyán 〈地质〉 greywacke

硬设备 yìngshèbèi (of a computer) hardware

硬生生 yìngshēngshēng tough; obstinate; obdurate:他还要争,被人～地拉走,才算没吵起来。He wanted to go on arguing. A quarrel was prevented only when he was drawn away from the spot against his will.

硬石膏 yìngshígāo anhydrite

硬是 yìngshì ❶〈方言〉 actually; just:～不怕死 actually not afraid to die; simply fearless of death /～要得。Just wonderful! *or* Terrific! ❷ despite all (difficulties, etc.); still:工作十分困难,可我们～按时完成了任务。We fulfilled the task on schedule despite great difficulties. /他已经连续工作了十多个小时,～不肯休息。Even though he had worked for over ten hours on end, he refused to stop for a rest.

硬实 yìngshi 〈方言〉 strong and sturdy

硬手 yìngshǒu past master; tough nut:干这一行,他可是个～儿。He is quite an expert in this line of business. /今天的球赛他们碰到了～。They have encountered tough opponents (*or* met their match) in today's games.

硬水 yìngshuǐ hard water

硬说 yìngshuō insist; assert; allege:他～自己没病,非要坚持上班。He insisted that he was not ill and that he be allowed to go to

work. /她～那篇文章不是她写的。She asserted stubbornly that she did not write the article.

硬挺 yìngtǐng endure with all one's will; hold out with all one's might; stick it out: 有病就该早点儿就医，这样～会使病情恶化。You should immediately go and see a doctor when you fall ill. If you stick it out, your condition will get worse.

硬通货 yìngtōnghuò hard currency

硬铜 yìngtóng 〈电工〉hard copper: ～线 hard-drawn wire

硬头黄 yìngtóuhuáng 〈植物〉a kind of tall, strong bamboo

硬土层 yìngtǔcéng 〈地质〉hardpan

硬卧 yìngwò (short for 硬席卧铺) sleeping carriage with hard berths; hard sleeping berth: 买两张～ buy two tickets for hard sleeping berths

硬武器 yìngwǔqì 〈军事〉lethal or destructive weapons

硬席 yìngxí 〈交通〉hard seats (on a train): ～车厢 hard seater (compartment) /～卧铺 hard sleeping berth /～卧铺车厢 hard sleeper; sleeping carriage with hard berths

硬橡胶 yìngxiàngjiāo 〈化工〉hard rubber; ebonite; vulcanite

硬性 yìngxìng rigid; stiff; hard; inflexible: ～摊派 mandatory apportionment /具体执行办法由各单位自行决定，不作～规定。The actual methods of implementation shall be left to the various units to decide, and no hard and fast rules will be laid down.

硬岩 yìngyán 〈地质〉hard rock: ～矿 hard-rock mine /～开采〈矿业〉hard-rock mining

硬玉 yìngyù jadeite

硬皂 yìngzào hard soap

硬扎 yìngzha 〈方言〉❶ strong; sturdy: 身子挺～ be sturdy; be in very good health ❷ firm; resolute; tough: 对他要说得～一些。You must be tough when talking to him.

硬仗 yìngzhàng tough battle; formidable task: 这队专打～。The team is especially strong in tackling formidable tasks.

硬着头皮 yìngzhe tóupí toughen one's scalp; brace oneself; force oneself to do sth. against one's will: ～顶住 grin and bear it; bite the bullet; tough it out; stick it out /他觉得只能～做下去。He felt that the only thing to do was to toughen his scalp and bear it. /他～走下去。He steeled himself to go on.

硬着心肠 yìngzhe xīncháng toughen one's heart; force oneself to discard tender feelings; steel oneself: 当时他正在病中，我能～丢下他不管吗? At the time, he was down with a serious illness. How could I have brought myself to leave him to his own devices?

硬正 yìngzheng upright; strong-willed: 人穷不要紧，但不能不～。It doesn't matter much if one is poor, but the important thing is to maintain one's uprightness and dignity.

硬挣 yìngzheng 〈方言〉❶ hard but elastic: 这纸～，包东西好使。This kind of paper is tough but elastic, and it can be used as good wrappers. ❷ strong; tough; powerful: 找个～的伙计 find a strong partner

硬脂 yìngzhī 〈化学〉tristearin; stearin

硬脂醇 yìngzhīchún stearyl alcohol

硬脂酸 yìngzhīsuān 〈化学〉stearic acid

硬脂酸盐 yìngzhīsuānyán stearate

硬脂油 yìngzhīyóu stearine oil

硬纸板 yìngzhǐbǎn hardboard; cardboard: 这种～用途很广。This kind of cardboard has many uses.

硬指标 yìngzhǐbiāo inflexible target, goal or requirement; mandatory quota or criterion: 优质服务是这家百货公司的～。To provide high quality service is the first priority of this department store.

硬质合金 yìngzhì héjīn 〈冶金〉hard alloy; carbide alloy; hard carbide; hard metal: ～刀具〈机械〉carbide cutter; carbide-tipped (cutting) tool; carbide tool; hard alloy cutter; hard metal tool /～钢 hard alloy steel /～工具磨床 carbide-tip tool grinding machine; carbide tool grinder /～钻头 carbide drill

硬质塑料 yìngzhì sùliào 〈化学〉rigid plastics: 半～ semi-rigid plastics /～制品 rigid plastic products

硬着陆 yìngzhuólù ❶〈航天〉hard-land ❷〈经济〉hard landing

硬座 yìngzuò (of trains) hard seat: ～车厢 hard seater

映

yìng reflect; mirror; image; shine: 反～ reflect /垂柳倒～在水里。The weeping willow was mirrored on the water. /夕阳把湖水～得通红。The setting sun crimsoned the lake (*or* turned the lake to crimson).

映衬 yìngchèn ❷ set off: 山光水色互相～。The beautiful hills and the gleaming lake match each other well. ❷〈修辞〉contrast one thing sharply against another; use antithesis: 为人民而死，就比泰山还重；替法西斯卖力，就比鸿毛还轻。这两句话互相～，对比鲜明。To die for the people is weightier than Mount Tai, while to work for the fascists is lighter than a feather. There is a sharp contrast in the antithetical sentence.

映带 yìngdài 〈书面〉set off; add to: 湖光山色，～左右。The colourful hills and gleaming lakes set each other off in complete harmony.

映山红 yìngshānhóng 〈植物〉azalea: 这儿，满山遍野盛开着～。Here azaleas are in full blossom all over the hills and fields.

映射 yìngshè shine upon; shed light on: 月光～在湖面上。The moon was shining on the lake.

映托 yìngtuō set off: 蔚蓝色的天空把云朵般的降落伞～得分外鲜明。The cloud-like parachutes looked extremely beautiful against the blue sky.

映现 yìngxiàn come into view: 轮船驶向海岸，热带岛国的景色～眼前。As the steamer was sailing towards the shore, the beautiful scenery of the tropical island country came into view. /一幕难忘的情景又～在脑际。An unforgettable scene once again came to my memory.

映照 yìngzhào shine upon; cast light on: 骄阳～着沙滩。The scorching sun was shining upon the beach. /月光～着小溪。The moon was casting light on the brook.

暎

yìng *see* "映" yìng

媵

yìng 〈书面〉❶ accompany a bride to her new home ❷ servants accompanying a bride to her new home: ～臣 minister sent together with the bride (normally a princess) to her new country of residence ❸ concubine

yō

育

yō *see* "杭育" hángyō

see also yù

唷

yō *see* "哼唷" hēngyō

哟

yō 〈叹词〉*used to express slight astonishment or surprise, sometimes with a tone of light-hearted joking*: ～，几天不见你又瘦了。Oh! You've become even thinner since we met a few days ago.

see also yo

yo

哟

yo ❶〈助词〉*used at the end of a sentence to urge sb. on*: 快点来～! Come over here, quick! /使劲拉～! Heave ho! ❷ *used in songs as a fill-in word*: 呼儿嗨～! Hu-er-hai-yo!

see also yō

yōng

庸[1]

yōng ❶ commonplace; ordinary; mediocre: 凡～ ordinary; dull /平～之辈 person of mediocre calibre; mediocrity ❷ inferior; second-rate; incompetent: 昏～ fatuous; muddle-headed

庸[2]

yōng 〈书面〉❶ (used in the negative) need: 毋～讳言 without mincing matters /无～细述 no need to go into details (*or* give full particulars) ❷ (used in a rhetorical question) how could: ～有济乎? How could this be of any help?

庸暗 yōng'àn 〈书面〉ignorant; benighted

庸才 yōngcái 〈书面〉mediocre person; mediocrity: ～难当重任。A mediocre person is not equal to such important tasks.

庸常 yōngcháng ordinary; commonplace; mediocre: ～之才 one of the ordinary run of people

庸夫 yōngfū person of average ability; mediocrity: ～俗子 philis-

tine
庸劣 yōngliè commonplace and inferior
庸陋 yōnglòu mediocre; ignorant; superficial: 见解～ superficial view
庸碌 yōnglù mediocre and unambitious: ～之辈 mediocre and incompetent person / 庸庸碌碌, 无所作为 be inept and accomplish nothing
庸懦 yōngnuò mediocre and weak: ～无能 weak and incompetent
庸人 yōngrén mediocre person: 罪至重而刑至轻, ～不知恶矣, 乱莫大焉。The lightest penalty for the most hideous crime would fail to deter the common run of people from doing evil and would lead to social chaos.
庸人自扰 yōngrén-zìrǎo worry about imagined troubles; fuss or worry unnecessarily; be much ado about nothing: 天下本无事, ～之。There is nothing wrong with the world; only the ignorant fuss over trifles. *or* All is well with the world; only the naive make a fuss over nothing.
庸俗 yōngsú vulgar; coarse; philistine; low: ～化 vulgarize; debase / 趣味～ low tastes and base interests / 作风～ vulgar style of work / ～不堪 philistine / ～进化论〈哲学〉vulgar evolutionism / ～唯物主义〈哲学〉vulgar materialism
庸医 yōngyī quack; charlatan: ～司性命, 俗子议文章。Quacks monopolize the medical profession, and mediocre critics nit-pick the works of men of letters.
庸中佼佼 yōngzhōng-jiǎojiǎo Triton of the minnows; giant among dwarfs; big frog in a little pond: 他才华出众, 绝非～。He is by no means overrated, for he is remarkably talented.

慵

yōng 〈书面〉weary; lethargic; languid: 晚节～转剧。During the evening of my life, physical exhaustion aggravated.
慵惰 yōngduò 〈书面〉lazy; languid
慵倦 yōngjuàn *also* "慵困" tired and drowsy
慵懒 yōnglǎn *see* "慵惰"

墉(牅)

yōng 〈书面〉city wall; high wall: 谁谓鼠无牙, 何以穿我～? Who said that rats had no teeth? If so, how could they have drilled through my wall?

镛

yōng big bell used in ancient China to keep other musical instruments in tune

鳙

yōng *see* "鳙鱼"
鳙鱼 yōngyú *also* "胖头鱼" pàngtóuyú variegated carp; bighead (*Aristichthys nobli*)

雍

yōng ❶〈书面〉harmony ❷ (Yōng) a surname
雍和 yōnghé harmony and peace
雍和宫 Yōnghégōng Yonghegong Lamasery or Lamasery of Harmony and Peace, Beijing
雍睦 yōngmù *also* "雍穆"〈书面〉friendly; harmonious: 家门～ harmonious family
雍容 yōngróng natural; graceful and poised: 进止～ remain graceful and poised whether promoted or demoted / 仪态～ graceful demeanour
雍容大雅 yōngróng-dàyǎ display poise and refinement: 一派～的文坛巨子作风 refined and cultivated style of a literary giant
雍容华贵 yōngróng-huáguì elegant and poised; stately; distingué: ～的世家少妇 elegant and graceful young lady of a distinguished family
雍正 Yōngzhèng Yongzheng, title of the reign (1723-1735) of Aisin Gioro Yinzhen (爱新觉罗·胤禛), 3rd emperor of the Qing Dynasty, called reverently Qing Shizong (清世宗) after death

壅

yōng ❶〈书面〉stop up; bar; obstruct: 且奸人在上, 则～遏贤者而不进。With evil people holding the top posts, the talented and the virtuous were prevented from moving up. ❷ heap soil or fertilizer over and around the roots (of plants and trees): ～肥 apply fertilizer around the roots
壅蔽 yōngbì 〈书面〉cover up; deceive
壅塞 yōngsè clog up; jam; congest: ～言路 clog up the channel of communication from below; stifle criticisms and suggestions / 泥沙～河道。The course of the river is blocked up by silt.
壅水 yōngshuǐ 〈水利〉dammed water; damming
壅土 yōngtǔ ❶ heap up (with earth); earth up: 给棉苗～ heap soil around the roots of young cotton shoots; earth (*or* hill) up young cotton shoots ❷ earth collected on the ploughshares when ploughing or levelling newly-turned soil
壅滞 yōngzhì 〈书面〉clogged up; jammed; blocked up: 神思～ dull and lethargic; listless (state of mind)

饔

yōng 〈书面〉cooked food; breakfast
饔飧 yōngsūn breakfast and supper
饔飧不继 yōngsūn-bùjì 〈书面〉cannot afford three square meals a day: 虽终身勤劳, 却无所积累, 暮年, 竟然～。Having laid up very little, though he had worked hard all his life, he could hardly keep the wolf from the door in his old age.

臃

yōng 〈书面〉swollen
臃肿 yōngzhǒng ❶ too fat to move freely: 棉衣太大, 穿着显得～。He looks cumbersomely dressed in his loose padded overcoat. ❷ overstaffed; bloated: 机构～ overstaffed organization; bloated bureaucracy

痈(癰)

yōng 〈医学〉carbuncle; large boil: 背～ carbuncle on the back / 养～遗患 neglecting a carbuncle will cause trouble; leaving evil unchecked spells ruin
痈疽 yōngjū ulcer: 是～, 就得割除。An ulcer must be removed if found.

拥(擁)

yōng ❶ clasp or hold in one's arms; embrace; hug: 她把妹妹紧紧地～在怀里。She held her sister tightly in her arms. ❷ surround; gather around: 前呼后～ with large numbers of attendants crowding around / 人们簇～他走进大厅。He came into the hall surrounded by a crowd of people. ❸ crowd; throng; flock; swarm: 一～而上 throng forward / 人们拼命地向车站～去。People were surging towards the station. ❹ support; uphold: *see* "～军优属" "～政爱民" ❺〈书面〉have; possess; boast: ～兵自重 build up one's power by dint of one's army; assume importance by raising an army
拥抱 yōngbào embrace; hug: 久别重逢的姐弟俩热烈～, 互诉离情别绪。Sister and brother warmly embraced each other at the reunion, each telling the other the sorrows they felt about their long separation.
拥脖 yōngbó 〈方言〉collar for a horse
拥簇 yōngcù cluster round; crowd round: 大家都～在作家周围。We all clustered round the writer.
拥戴 yōngdài support; hold in esteem: 这位县长受到全县人民的～。The county head enjoyed the support of the people in the whole county.
拥护 yōnghù support; back; uphold; be for: 群众热烈～改革。The people warmly support the reforms. / 大家～现行政策。We all endorse the current policies. / 要自觉～四项基本原则。We must conscientiously uphold the four cardinal principles.
拥挤 yōngjǐ crowd; push and squeeze: 巷小人流～。A crowd of people swarmed through the narrow lane. / 候车室里～着许多旅客。A great many passengers were crowded in the waiting room. / 顺序上车不要～! Don't push! Get on the bus one by one.
拥进 yōngjìn (of people) crowd into: 他俩在屋里谈得起劲, 忽然吵吵嚷嚷地～一群人来。The two of them were engaged in earnest talk when a group of people crowded into the room shouting and quarrelling.
拥聚 yōngjù gather together; crowd together: 场院上～了一些人。A number of people gathered on the threshing ground.
拥军优属 yōngjūn-yōushǔ (of civilians) support the army and give preferential treatment to families of armymen and martyrs: 每逢节日, 都要开展～活动。We conduct activities of supporting the army and giving preferential treatment to their dependents during every festival.
拥塞 yōngsè jam; congest; crowd: 疏导～路口的车辆 help direct vehicles out of a jam at an intersection / 道路～。Roads are congested.
拥有 yōngyǒu own; have; possess: ～强大的武装力量 have power-

ful armed forces /～枪支弹药 possess firearms and ammunition /这个工厂～现代化设备。The factory boasts state-of-the-art equipment. /我国是世界上～人口最多的国家。China is the most populous country in the world. /第三世界～丰富资源。The third world countries abound in national resources.

拥政爱民 yōngzhèng-àimín (of the army) support the government and cherish the people:春节期间～的活动搞得热火朝天。During the Spring Festival, activities of supporting the government and cherishing the people were in full swing.

佣(傭) yōng ❶ hire; employ:雇～ hire (a labourer) /他少时,尝为人～耕。He worked as a hired hand on a farm when young. ❷ servant:女～ maid; woman servant

see also yòng

佣保 yōngbǎo 〈书面〉 *see* "佣工"

佣妇 yōngfù maidservant; maid

佣工 yōnggōng *also* "佣保" hired labourer; servant:他在张家做～。He worked as a hired labourer at the Zhangs'.

佣人 yōngrén servant; maid

邕 Yōng ❶ Yong Jiang, river in the Guangxi Zhuang Autonomous Region ❷ another name for Nanning (南宁)

邕剧 yōngjù one of the local operas popular in the Yue-dialect-speaking areas in the Guangxi Zhuang Autonomous Region

喁(噰) yōng

喁喁 yōngyōng 〈书面〉〈象声〉 birds cry: 雁鸣～ honking of wild geese

雝 yōng *see* "雍" yōng

yóng

颙 yóng 〈书面〉 ❶ big; huge; large ❷ look up to; respect; revere:～望 look up to /苍生～然,莫不欣戴。The entire populace looked up to you with wholehearted reverence and trust.

喁 yóng 〈书面〉 fish sticking its mouth out of the water

see also yú

喁喁 yóngyóng 〈书面〉〈比喻〉 everyone looking up to sb.:天下英雄～,冀有所望。Valiant men all over the country are looking up to you, placing their hope in your able leadership and guidance.

see also yúyú

yǒng

永 yǒng perpetually; forever; for all time: ～不反悔 will never go back on one's word /一劳～逸 (solve a problem) once and for all /隽～ meaningful

永辈子 yǒngbèizi forever; always; ever:咱们～也不能忘记这个教训。We will never forget this lesson.

永别 yǒngbié part never to meet again; be separated by death; part forever:他们谁也没料到这次分别竟成了～。None of them had expected that the parting would turn out to be the last.

永垂不朽 yǒngchuí-bùxiǔ be immortal; live forever:人民英雄～! Eternal glory to the people's heroes! /革命精神～! The revolutionary spirit lives forever!

永垂青史 yǒngchuí-qīngshǐ go down in history; have a niche in history

永磁 yǒngcí 〈物理〉 permanent magnet; permanent magnetism:～电机〈电工〉 permanent-magnet machine /～抹音头〈电子〉 permanent-magnet erasing head

永磁发电机 yǒngcí fādiànjī permanent-magnet alternator; permanent-magnet-field generator; permanent-magnet generator; magneto

永磁体 yǒngcítǐ permanent magnet

永存 yǒngcún everlasting;evergreen:友谊～ everlasting friendship

永定门 Yǒngdìngmén Yongdingmen or Gate of Everlasting Stability, Beijing

永动 yǒngdòng 〈物理〉 perpetual motion: ～机 perpetual motion machine

永冻 yǒngdòng permafrost:～气候 eternal frost climate

永冻层 yǒngdòngcéng permafrost

永恒 yǒnghéng eternal; perpetual; everlasting; permanent:～的爱情 eternal love /～的真理 everlasting truth /～的友情 permanent friendship /～的追求 endless pursuit /～的主题 timeless theme

永恒运动 yǒnghéng yùndòng 〈物理〉 perpetual motion

永嘉 Yǒngjiā Yongjia, title of the reign (307-313) of Sima Chi (司马炽), 3rd emperor of the West Jin Dynasty, called reverently Jin Huaidi (晋怀帝) after death

永久 yǒngjiǔ permanent; everlasting; forever; eternal: ～主权 permanent sovereignty /～中立 permanent neutrality /～的住所 permanent abode /企图～霸占 attempt to perpetuate the occupation of /革命热情应该～地保持下去 always keep up the revolutionary spirit /～积雪原〈地理〉 firn field /～牧场 permanent pasture /～性草地 permanent grass land /～植被 permanent vegetation cover /～变形〈物理〉 permanent deformation; permanent extension; permanent strain /～铸模〈冶金〉 permanent mould

永久磁铁 yǒngjiǔ cítiě permanent magnet

永久存储器 yǒngjiǔ cúnchǔqì non-volatile storage; permanent memory

永久冻土 yǒngjiǔ dòngtǔ permafrost

永久居留证 yǒngjiǔ jūliúzhèng permanent residence card

永久雪线 yǒngjiǔ xuěxiàn firn (snow) line

永诀 yǒngjué 〈书面〉 part forever; be separated by death:临穴～,抚榇尽哀。Paying my last respects at the tomb of the deceased, I gave full vent to my grief in bereavement by the coffin.

永乐 Yǒnglè Yongle, title of the reign (1403-1424) of Zhu Di (朱棣), 3rd emperor of the Ming Dynasty, called reverently Ming Chengzu (明成祖) after death

永乐大典 Yǒnglè Dàdiǎn *Yong Le Da Dian* or *Great Encyclopaedia of Yongle* of the Ming Dynasty, completed in 1408

永眠 yǒngmián 〈婉词〉 eternal sleep — death

永年 yǒngnián ❶ all the year round; year long:松柏～长青。Pine and cypress trees are green all the year round. ❷ long life; longevity

永生 yǒngshēng ❶ eternal life; immortality:灵魂～ immortality of souls /为争取民族解放而牺牲的烈士们～! The martyrs who laid down their lives for national liberation will live forever! ❷ throughout one's life; lifelong:～难忘 will not forget as long as one lives /～的追求 life-long pursuit

永生永世 yǒngshēng-yǒngshì all one's life; for ever and ever:你的恩情,我～铭记心中。I will forever bear in mind your great kindness.

永世 yǒngshì forever; always:～不忘 will never forget /～牢记 will remember for the rest of one's life /～长存 live for ever and ever; be everlasting

永逝 yǒngshì ❶ lose forever:韶华～ one's youthful years are gone forever ❷ death

永续 yǒngxù continuous; continued; sustained:～前进 continuous advance /保护森林资源,使青山常在,～利用。Protecting forest resources ensures that our mountains will always remain green and there will be a sustained supply of timber.

永夜 yǒngyè long night; throughout the night

永远 yǒngyuǎn 〈副词〉 always; forever; once and for all:～忠于自己的祖国 be forever loyal to one's own country /～记住自己的根 will always remember one's roots /～结束战争 end a war once and for all

永志不忘 yǒngzhì-bùwàng will forever be imprinted on one's mind; will always cherish the memory of sb. or sth.:先生之教诲,我将～。I will always bear in mind your kind admonitions.

永昼 yǒngzhòu 〈书面〉 long dreary day:对弈消～ while away a dreary day by playing chess

泳 yǒng swim:蝶～ butterfly /仰～ backstroke /自由～ free style; free stroke /蛙～ breaststroke /侧～ sidestroke /潜～ underwater swimming /冬～ winter swimming

泳程 yǒngchéng swimming distance

泳道 yǒngdào (swimming) lane

泳坛 yǒngtán swimming circles:世界～ world swimming circles /～名将 star swimmer

咏(詠) yǒng ❶ chant; recite; intone: 吟～ recite (a poem) /歌～ sing ❷ express or narrate in poetic form: 《～雪》*Ode to the Snow* /歌以～志 chant a poem to express one's aspirations
咏唱 yǒngchàng chant (a poem)
咏怀 yǒnghuái express one's sentiments and aspirations in poetic form: ～诗 poem expressing one's aspirations
咏史 yǒngshǐ compose poems in memory of historical personages or events
咏叹 yǒngtàn sing; intone; chant: 反复～ sing sth. repeatedly
咏叹调 yǒngtàndiào 〈音乐〉aria; operatic solo
咏赞 yǒngzàn sing in praise of; praise: ～松柏 sing in praise of pine and cypress

甬 Yǒng ❶ Yong Jiang, river in Zhejiang Province flowing through Ningbo ❷ another name for Ningbo (宁波)
甬道 yǒngdào ❶ *also* "甬路" paved path leading to a main hall or a tomb: 一条青石～ path paved with grey stones ❷ corridor; passageway: 狭窄的～ narrow passageway /～里空无一人。There was not even a soul in the corridor.
甬剧 yǒngjù one of the local operas in Zhejiang Province, popular in and around Ningbo

涌 yǒng ❶ gush; well; pour; surge: 风起云～ wind rising and clouds scudding — press ahead vigorously /泪如泉～ tears welling up in one's eyes /清泉喷～而出。Clear water gushes out of the spring. ❷ rise; surge; emerge: 一轮明月从东山之巅～出。A brilliant moon rose from behind the mountain peak in the east. /历历往事～上心头。Memories of the past rushed through my mind. ❸ mountainous wave: 大浪～滚而来。A mountainous wave washed over.
see also chōng
涌潮 yǒngcháo *also* "暴涨潮" bàozhǎngcháo; "怒潮" nùcháo strong tide; raging tide; tidal bore
涌动 yǒngdòng roll; stream; surge: 心潮～ surging emotions /人们像潮水般地～。People were moving forward like waves.
涌进 yǒngjìn pour or swarm into; forge ahead; surge forward: 人们从四面八方～会场。People were streaming (*or* swarming) into the auditorium from all directions. /革命运动不断～。The revolutionary movement surged ahead ceaselessly.
涌浪 yǒnglàng surging waves
涌流 yǒngliú (of liquid) gush; pour; surge: 石油从管道中～出来。Oil gushed out of the pipe.
涌上 yǒngshang surge through; well up: 一股暖流～他的心头。His heart was filled with warmth.
涌现 yǒngxiàn emerge in large numbers; come to the fore; come forth: 好人好事大批～。Good people and good deeds came to the fore in large numbers. /东方～一轮鲜红夺目的太阳。A dazzlingly red sun arose in the east.
涌溢 yǒngyì overflow; gush out: 泉水～。The spring gushed out.

恿(慂) yǒng *see* "怂恿" sǒngyǒng

蛹 yǒng pupa; chrysalis: 蚕～ silkworm chrysalis /蝶～ chrysalis

踊(踴) yǒng leap up; jump up: 跛者不～。A cripple cannot leap.
踊跃 yǒngyuè ❶ leap; jump: ～欢呼 leap and cheer ❷ falling over each other (to do sth.); keenly; enthusiastically: 座谈会上发言～ eager to speak at the seminar /～参加 participate enthusiastically /青年参军相当～。Youths fall over each other to join the army.

俑 yǒng wooden or earthen human figurine buried with the dead in ancient times; tomb figure; figurine: 女～ female burial figurine /木～ wooden figurine /兵马～ terracotta warriors and horses

鲬 yǒng flathead; sand gurnard

勇 yǒng ❶ brave; valiant; courageous; dauntless: 奋～杀敌 fight the enemy bravely /骁～无比 exceptionally valiant /智～双全 have both wisdom and courage ❷ temporary recruits in times of war during the Qing Dynasty: 散兵游～ stragglers and disbanded soldiers ❸ (Yǒng) a surname
勇敢 yǒnggǎn brave; courageous; valorous: 机智～ resourceful and brave /中国人民勤劳～。The Chinese people are both industrious and courageous.
勇冠三军 yǒngguànsānjūn bravest of the brave in the whole army; of peerless valour: ～的青年将领 most courageous young general
勇悍 yǒnghàn bold and fierce
勇健 yǒngjiàn valiant and strong
勇决 yǒngjué 〈书面〉brave and resolute; courageous and firm
勇力 yǒnglì courage and strength: ～过人 with exceptional courage and might
勇略 yǒnglüè 〈书面〉courageous and resourceful; brave and tactful
勇猛 yǒngměng courageous and powerful; full of valour and vigour: ～果敢 courageous and resolute /战士们作战～无比。The soldiers were fighting with matchless daring and vigour.
勇气 yǒngqì nerve; courage; mettle: 鼓起～ pick up (*or* screw up, *or* muster) one's courage /失去～ lose one's nerve /承认和改正错误需要很大的～。It requires a great deal of guts to own up to one's mistakes and correct them.
勇士 yǒngshì person of great courage and strength; warrior: 抢渡大渡河的十八～ eighteen brave fighters who forced their way across the Dadu River
勇往直前 yǒngwǎng-zhíqián march forward courageously; advance bravely: 面对困难人人～。Every member of the team was pressing forward, braving great difficulties.
勇武 yǒngwǔ valiant; valorous: ～过人 surpass others in valour; be singularly valorous
勇毅 yǒngyì brave and strong-willed; courageous and resolute
勇于 yǒngyú dare to; be brave or bold in; have the courage to: ～承担重任 be bold in shouldering heavy responsibilities /～发表不同意见 dare to air differing views /～批评与自我批评 have the courage to criticize others as well as oneself; be brave in conducting criticism and self-criticism
勇鸷 yǒngzhì 〈书面〉bold and vigorous; brave and powerful; fierce: 其人～有智谋。The man is dauntless and resourceful.
勇壮 yǒngzhuàng valiant; gallant: ～的行为 valorous acts

湧 yǒng ❶ *see* "涌" yǒng ❷ (Yǒng) a surname

yòng

用 yòng ❶ use; utilize; employ; apply: 大材小～ large material put to small use — talent wasted on a petty job /公～ for public (*or* official) use /～毛笔写字 write with a brush /～手推～脚踢 push and kick /～高标准要求自己 demand highly of oneself ❷ expense; spending; outlay: 家～ family expenses /零～ pocket money; spending money /强本而节～ strengthen the economic foundation and cut back on expenses ❸ use; usefulness; utility: 功～ function /作～ part; role /这本书很有～。This book is quite useful. /天生我材必有～。Since I have been born, I must be of some use to society. /没～的东西! You good-for-nothing! ❹ (mostly used in the negative) need; have to: 不～麻烦他。You needn't trouble him. *or* There is no need to trouble him. /不～惦记我。You needn't (*or* don't have to) worry about me. *or* Don't worry about me. /不～客气。Don't stand on ceremony. /不～费心。Don't bother, please. ❺ 〈敬词〉eat; drink; have: 请～茶。Won't you have some tea, please. /请～点儿饭。Please have some rice. ❻ 〈书面〉hence; therefore: ～特函达。Hence the present letter.
用兵 yòngbīng employ military forces; resort to arms: 不善于在沼泽地带～ be inept in fighting in marshes /连年～ fight wars for years on end
用兵如神 yòngbīng-rúshén direct military operations with miraculous skill; be a past master in the art of war
用不了 yòngbuliǎo ❶ have or be more than is needed: 把～的衣物捐献出来 donate one's spare clothes and articles /这么多钱我一下子～。I can't spend so much money all at once. ❷ less than: ～两个钟头，他就能写出一篇文章。It took him less than two hours to write an

article./别看他们现在吵得厉害，～一会儿就和好了。They may be quarrelling furiously with each other, but they will make up in no time.

用不着 yòngbuzháo ❶ not need; have no use for:这些茶具暂时～，可以先收起来。Put this teaset away if you don't need it for the time being. ❷ need not; it is not worthwhile to: ～为他担心。You needn't worry about him. *or* There is no need for you to worry about him. /～跟他生气。It is not worthwhile to be angry with him.

用材林 yòngcáilín 〈林业〉commercial forest; timber forest

用场 yòngchǎng use; application:这些资料大有～。These data can be put to good use. /这批复员兵回乡后都派上了大～。These demobilized soldiers have all been assigned important jobs since their return.

用处 yòngchu use; utility; good:这里的每一件东西都有特殊的～。Each of these articles here has its own specific use. /光说不做有什么～? What's the use (*or* good) of talking without doing? /信用卡外出度假时会有～。The credit card may come in handy when you're away holidaying.

用得了 yòngdeliǎo need all that; need that much or many:这个小项目～那么多人吗? Does this small project require all that many people? /这么多稿纸，你～吗? Do you really need so much writing paper?

用得着 yòngdezháo ❶ need; require; find sth. useful:只要～我，一定随叫随到。I will surely make myself available any time you need me. /有～我帮忙的地方，千万别客气。Please don't hesitate to ask if you need my help. /别看这些旧资料，搞科研可是～! Although these reference materials are no longer new, they may be quite useful in scientific research! ❷ there is need to; it is necessary or worthwhile to:这样的小事，～你亲自处理吗? Is it really necessary for you to attend to such trivial matters in person?

用度 yòngdù expense; spending; outlay: 尽量减少家里的～ try one's best to reduce one's family expenses

用法 yòngfǎ use; usage; application:～说明 directions for use /淋浴器使用之前，要了解～。One must get to know how to use a shower set before operating it. /开处方时一定要写明～与用量。Explain the usage (*or* application) and dosage clearly when writing out a prescription.

用饭 yòngfàn 〈敬词〉eat; have a meal:请您～。Please have your meal.

用非所长 yòngfēisuǒcháng fail to make use of sb.'s strengths:避免～的现象。Do not fail to put a person's forte to good use.

用非所学 yòngfēisuǒxué not do what one is trained to do:大学毕业生常有～的情况。It often happens that a college graduate may be assigned to a job he (*or* she) is not trained for in school.

用费 yòngfèi expense; charge; cost:节约～ cut down expenses

用工 yònggōng recruit and use workers:改革～制度 reform the recruitment system

用工夫 yòng gōngfu make every effort; exert oneself; work hard:他对气功很～。He worked very hard at practising *qigong* (breathing exercise). /他在宋词的研究上用过不少工夫。He devoted much time and energy to studying the *ci* poetry of the Song Dynasty.

用功 yònggōng hardworking; industrious; diligent; studious:～的学生 hardworking (*or* diligent) student /这孩子从小就很～。The boy has been studious since childhood.

用户 yònghù user; consumer:终极～ end-user /电话～ telephone subscriber /受到～的好评 be commended by users /采纳～的意见 adopt consumers' (*or* customers') advice

用户电报 yònghù diànbào telex

用户终端 yònghù zhōngduān user terminal

Y

用进废退说 yòngjìn-fèituìshuō 〈生物〉theory of use and disuse

用劲 yòngjìn exert oneself; make one's effort:一个人～没用，大家～，力量就大了。It won't be of much use if only one man exerts himself, but if all of us put our efforts together, there will be a tremendous force.

用具 yòngjù utensil; implement; appliance:学习～ student (*or* learning) utensils /园艺～ gardening utensils /厨房～ kitchen (*or* cooking) utensils /生产～ production implements /钓鱼～ fishing gear /救生～ lifesaving equipment

用力 yònglì use one's strength; exert oneself; put one's shoulder to the wheel:全身～ use one's entire strength; go all out /手腕～ use one's wrist power /～地呼喊 shout at the top of one's voice /他～过猛，险些摔倒。He pushed too hard and almost fell on his face.

用命 yòngmìng 〈书面〉follow instructions; obey orders; serve:将士～。Officers and men serve wholeheartedly.

用品 yòngpǐn articles for use:日常～ articles for daily use; daily necessities /办公～ things for office use; stationery /劳保～ labour protection articles

用人 yòngrén ❶ employ people; make use of personnel:～单位 employing unit; employer /～不当 fail to choose the right person for a job; employ (*or* use) people inappropriately /领导应善于～。The leadership must be good at making proper use of its personnel. ❷ need hands:正当～之际。Now there is a growing need for qualified personnel.

用人 yòngren 〈旧语〉servant:他家有一个男～，两个女～。His family employs a male servant and two maidservants.

用舍行藏 yòngshě-xíngcáng *also* "用行舍藏" enter officialdom when one is needed and go into retreat when not:其为道也，～，进退可度。His philosophy is to enter officialdom when needed and withdraw from it when not needed, so that he knows when to advance and when to retreat.

用世 yòngshì 〈书面〉serve the state; take official posts

用事 yòngshì ❶〈书面〉be in power:奸臣～。Treacherous officials were in power. ❷ act; conduct oneself:意气～ be swayed by one's feelings and act rashly /感情～ act impetuously (*or* impulsively) ❸〈书面〉quote classical allusions

用途 yòngtú use; application; purpose:多～蓝图 multi-purpose blueprint /这种仪器的～很广。This kind of apparatus has many uses.

用武 yòngwǔ ❶ use military force; resort to arms:这类事只可用谋，不可～。You can solve such matters only by stratagem, not by force. ❷ prove oneself; display one's abilities or talents:英雄无～之地 have no scope for displaying one's abilities

用项 yòngxiàng item of expenditure; expenditure:减少不必要的～ reduce unnecessary expenditure

用心 yòngxīn ❶ diligently; attentively; with concentration: ～学习 concentrate on one's studies /办事不够～ not take enough care in handling matters /～听他讲话 listen to him attentively /～竭力 exert oneself to the utmost /～思考 think hard; mull over ❷ motive; purpose; intention: ～歹毒 harbour a sinister intention /～良苦 have thought over the matter really hard /他这样干完全是别有～。He did this with ulterior motives.

用刑 yòngxíng torture; put sb. to torture

用以 yòngyǐ in order to; so as to; for the purpose of:他举出大量事例，～说明现行的办法是行之有效的。He cited numerous examples to show that the method in use was practical and effective.

用意 yòngyì intention; aim; purpose:他讲这番话的～，只是为了提醒大家注意危险。The purpose of his statement was to remind others of the dangers./你的～何在? What are you up to?

用印 yòngyìn affix an official seal; seal:这个证明需要人事部门～后才能生效。This letter of certification will not take effect until the personnel department affixes its official seal to it.

用语 yòngyǔ ❶ choice of words; wording; diction: ～委婉含蓄。The wording was tactful and implicit. /～精当。The choice of words is exact and concise. ❷ phraseology; terminology; term:外交～ diplomatic language /技术～ technical terms /商业～ commercial vocabulary /法律～ legal parlance

佣 yòng commission
see also yōng

佣金 yòngjīn commission; brokerage; middleman's fee: ～优厚 handsome commission /支付了一大笔～ pay a large brokerage fee

佣钱 yòngqian *see* "佣金"

yōu

耰 yōu ❶ a kind of rake in ancient China ❷ turn over the soil and cover up the seeds with soil

忧(憂) yōu ❶ worried; sad; depressed:担～ worry about /排～解难 free sb. of his (*or* her) worries and distress ❷ sorrow; anxiety; concern; care:高枕无～ shake up the pillow and have a carefree sleep /人无远虑，必有近～。Sorrow will come knocking at your door if you have no long-term plans. ❸ worry; concern oneself (about sb. or sth.): *see* "～国～民" ❹〈书面〉funeral of one's parent:丁～ in mourning for one's deceased parent

忧愁 yōuchóu sad; worried; depressed:满怀～ be seized with sad-

ness /忘却～ forget all about one's worries
忧烦 yōufán dejected; troubled: 满心的～无法排遣 not know how to rid oneself of vexations and anxieties /她感到异常～。She felt unusually dejected.
忧愤 yōufèn worried and indignant: 她为这场争执处理不公而感到～。She felt worried and indignant over the injustice of the settlement.
忧国忘家 yōuguó-wàngjiā be concerned about the fate of one's country to the neglect of one's family
忧国忧民 yōuguó-yōumín concern oneself with one's country and one's people
忧患 yōuhuàn suffering; misery; privations: 饱经～ have gone through a great deal of hardship /～意识 sense of anxiety (*or* urgency) about lagging behind
忧患余生 yōuhuàn-yúshēng one who has survived great adversity and misfortunes
忧惶 yōuhuáng worry and fear; dread: 神色～ look worried and afraid
忧急 yōují worried and anxious
忧煎 yōujiān have gnawing worries or anxiety: 我心中～, 夜不成寐。I could not fall asleep with great worries gnawing away at my heart.
忧惧 yōujù worried and afraid: 对眼前的处境, 他感到十分～。He felt greatly worried and apprehensive about his present predicament.
忧恐 yōukǒng worried and scared: ～万状 be overwhelmed with fears and worries
忧苦 yōukǔ anxiety and distress: 你究竟有什么～的事, 能跟我谈谈吗? What on earth is tormenting you? Can you tell me about it?
忧劳 yōuláo worries and toil
忧虑 yōulǜ worried; anxious; concerned: 他最近的言行引起了家人深深的～。His recent words and deeds have caused great worries to his family.
忧闷 yōumèn depressed; dejected; feeling low; weighed down with cares: 心情～ feel depressed /内心的～使他的性格都变了。His pent-up cares and worries have changed his temperament.
忧念 yōuniàn be worried about; be concerned about: ～家事 be worried about one's family matters
忧戚 yōuqī 〈书面〉 worried; depressed; apprehensive: 面容～ look depressed
忧容 yōuróng troubled or distressed appearance: 面带～ look anxious (*or* worried)
忧色 yōusè *see* "忧容"
忧伤 yōushāng distressed; upset; laden with grief: ～的面孔 grief-stricken face /～的少妇 distressed young woman
忧思 yōusī ❶ concern and care; worry: 日夜～ feel worried day and night ❷ moodiness; feelings of anxiety
忧心 yōuxīn ❶ worried; concerned: 大家都替他的身体～。Everybody was worried about his health. ❷ 〈书面〉 worry; anxiety: ～忡忡 heavy-hearted; care-laden; laden with anxieties
忧心如焚 yōuxīn-rúfén burning with anxiety; extremely worried
忧悒 yōuyì 〈书面〉 feel worried and disturbed
忧郁 yōuyù melancholy; heavy-hearted; dejected: 性格～ be of a melancholy disposition /内心～ heavy-hearted
忧郁症 yōuyùzhèng 〈医学〉 melancholia: ～患者 melancholic

优[1] (優)

yōu ❶ good; excellent: 品学兼～ excel in both scholarship and moral fibre /～胜劣败 the good prevailing over the bad /择～录取 enrol the cream of the candidate students ❷ 〈书面〉 adequate; plentiful; affluent: *see* "～渥"; "～裕" ❸ give preferential treatment; favour: 拥军～属 support the army and give preferential treatment to army dependants

优[2] (優)

yōu 〈旧语〉 actor or actress: 一代名～ actor (*or* actress) famous in his (*or* her) own time /俳～ comedian
优待 yōudài give special or preferential treatment: ～侨胞 give favoured treatment to overseas Chinese compatriots (*or* nationals) /～军烈属 give preferential treatment to the families of servicemen and martyrs /种种～ perks and privileges /学生半价～票 special half-price tickets for students
优待券 yōudàiquàn complimentary ticket
优等 yōuděng top-notch; first-rate; excellent: ～品 quality (*or* first-rate) product /～生 top-notch student /～质量 high quality /学习成绩～ excellent academic record /名列～ rank among the best
优点 yōudiǎn merit; strong point; forte; virtue: 发扬～ give play (*or* scope) to one's strengths /学习别人的～ learn from the strong points of other people /国家不论大小, 都有自己的～。Each nation, big or small, has its own merits. /谦虚是他的突出的～。Modesty is his outstanding virtue. /这个计划的～很多。The plan has many advantages.
优抚 yōufǔ give special care and preferential treatment (as to disabled servicemen and family members of revolutionary martyrs and servicemen): 烈属～金 allowances to family members of revolutionary martyrs
优厚 yōuhòu munificent; generous; liberal; favourable: 酬金～ emolument /条件～ liberal terms /福利～ favourable fringe benefits /收入～ handsome income
优弧 yōuhú 〈数学〉 major arc
优化 yōuhuà optimize: ～产品结构 optimize the product mix /～组合 optimization (*or* optimal) grouping (*or* regrouping) /～编程 optimum programming
优惠 yōuhuì 〈经济〉 preferential; favourable: ～贷款 loan on favourable (*or* liberal) terms; soft loan; concessional loan /实行～政策 follow (*or* adopt) a preferential policy /全部都买了, 还可以～点。If you buy all of them, I'll give you a discount.
优惠待遇 yōuhuì dàiyù preferential or favoured treatment: 享受～ enjoy preferential treatment /给予～ grant preferential treatment (*or* preferences)
优惠关税协定 yōuhuì guānshuì xiédìng preferential tariff agreement
优惠国 yōuhuìguó favoured nation
优惠权 yōuhuìquán preferential right
优惠券 yōuhuìquàn coupon
优惠条件 yōuhuì tiáojiàn favourable terms; concessional terms
优惠条款 yōuhuì tiáokuǎn preferential clause
优价 yōujià ❶ preferential price; low price: ～出售 sell at a low price ❷ good price: 这衣服虽然贵点儿, 但优质～, 还是买吧。This jacket may be a little bit expensive, but good money for good quality, you'd better take it.
优卡仿 yōukǎfǎng 〈药学〉 eucaform (a kind of antiseptic)
优卡因 yōukǎyīn 〈药学〉 eucaine
优礼 yōulǐ treat with courtesy: ～教师 treat teachers with due respect and courtesy /对远方来客～有加 receive visitors from afar with great courtesy
优良 yōuliáng fine; good; superior: 继承我军的～传统 carry on the fine traditions of our army /发扬勤俭节约的～作风 develop the fine style of industry and frugality /培育小麦的～品种 cultivate a superior strain of wheat /学业～ do well in one's school work
优劣 yōu-liè good and bad: ～不分 not discriminate (*or* distinguish) between good and bad; treat good and bad alike /两本书一比, 就分出～了。If you compare the two books, you can see which is better.
优伶 yōulíng 〈旧语〉 actor or actress
优霉素 yōuméisù 〈生化〉 eumycin
优美 yōuměi graceful; elegant; fine; exquisite: 环境～ fine environment (*or* surroundings) /姿态～ graceful carriage; fine posture /～的剪纸艺术 exquisite paper-cutting art /音色～ melodious tune /这儿的风景～极了。The scenery over here is most beautiful.
优美露 yōuměilù 〈药学〉 eumenol
优孟衣冠 Yōumèng-yīguān imitate others; perform on the stage (During the Spring and Autumn Period, after the death of Premier Sun Shu'ao, his son became impoverished. Actor Meng decked himself up as Sun Shu'ao and persuaded the King of Chu to confer favours on the late premier's son.)
优俳 yōupái 〈古语〉 comedy; farce
优球蛋白 yōuqiúdànbái 〈生化〉 euglobulin
优人 yōurén 〈旧语〉 opera actor or actress
优容 yōuróng 〈书面〉 treat leniently
优柔 yōuróu ❶ 〈书面〉 with composure; at ease: ～不迫 (do sth.) in a leisurely and unhurried manner ❷ 〈书面〉 placid; gentle ❸ irresolute; hesitant: ～的性格 irresolute character
优柔寡断 yōuróu-guǎduàn irresolute and hesitant; irresolute; indecisive: 他做事一向～, 没有主见。He always hesitates and has no opinion of his own.

优生 yōushēng giving birth to healthy babies; healthy birth; aristogenesis:提倡少生、～。It is urged that there should be fewer but healthier births.

优生学 yōushēngxué eugenics:～家 eugenist

优生优育 yōushēng-yōuyù giving birth to healthy babies and bringing them up in a sound way; healthy birth and sound care

优胜 yōushèng winning; superior; excellent:～红旗 championship red banner /～奖 winning award; excellent award /～班组 prize-winning team

优胜劣败 yōushèng-lièbài *also* "优胜劣汰" survival of the fittest: 物竞天择,～。Nature selects and the fittest survive.

优势 yōushì superiority; advantage; dominant position:局部～ partial superiority /空中～ air supremacy /集中～兵力,各个歼灭敌人 concentrate a superior force to destroy the enemy forces one by one /保持～ maintain one's dominant position /扩大～ press one's advantage; increase one's superiority /占～ gain the upper hand /占压倒～ predominate; be overwhelmingly superior /使某人占～ tip the scale in sb.'s favour /在实力上他们占有绝对～。They have an absolute preponderance in terms of strength.

优势种 yōushìzhǒng dominant species

优渥 yōuwò 〈书面〉favourable; munificent; generous; liberal:馈遗～ munificent bequeathal

优先 yōuxiān have priority; take precedence; have precedence:～发展农业 give priority to the development of agriculture /～次序 order of precedence; priorities /上车时老人、孕妇～。Old people and pregnant women should precede all others when boarding a bus.

优先购买权 yōuxiān gòumǎiquán 〈金融〉pre-emption rights

优先股 yōuxiāngǔ preference shares; preferred shares

优先权 yōuxiānquán priority; preference

优先债权人 yōuxiān zhàiquánrén 〈金融〉preferential creditor

优闲 yōuxián easy; leisurely; carefree:生活～ live an easy life /～自在 relaxed and at ease

优型树 yōuxíngshù 〈林业〉specimen tree

优型学 yōuxíngxué 〈医学〉euphenics

优秀 yōuxiù excellent; fine; worthy; outstanding:成绩～ excellent academic results /才干～ outstanding talent /～的中华儿女 fine (*or* worthy) sons and daughters of the Chinese nation /～的文化遗产 splendid cultural heritage /～手工艺品 superb arts and crafts works /～作曲家 top-notch composer

优叙 yōuxù 〈书面〉enumerate sb.'s meritorious services; reward sb. for his or her outstanding service

优选 yōuxuǎn optimize; select the best:对各种方案进行～,确定出最佳方案 decide upon the best of all the programmes available through optimization

优选法 yōuxuǎnfǎ optimum seeking method; optimization:～得到了普遍推广。The optimum-seeking method has been extensively applied.

优雅 yōuyǎ elegant; graceful; exquisite; in good taste:唱词～ elegant lyrics /举止～ elegant manners; graceful manners /～宽敞的客厅 exquisite and spacious lounge

优异 yōuyì exceedingly good; superb; excellent; outstanding:初赛战绩～ do very well in the preliminary (contest)/她在工作中做出了～的成绩。She has made outstanding contributions in her work.

优游 yōuyóu 〈书面〉❶ live a leisurely and carefree life:～自得 leisurely and contented /～岁月 spend one's time in carefree leisure ❷ have leisurely fun; amuse oneself in a leisurely way:～林下 enjoy oneself among the trees in a leisurely manner

优育 yōuyù provide children with the best possible health care and education

优裕 yōuyù well-off; affluent; abundant:生活～ be well-off; be well-to-do; live in affluence /家境～ come from a wealthy family

优遇 yōuyù give special treatment; treat well:以示～ so as to show special consideration for sb. /～有加 give sb. exceedingly good treatment

优越 yōuyuè superior; favourable; advantageous:～制度 superior system /～的地形 favourable terrain /～条件 excellent conditions /位置～ advantageous location

优越感 yōuyuègǎn sense of superiority;〈心理〉superiority complex:他的～很强。He has a strong sense of superiority. /～往往与自卑感同在。Superiority complex often goes together with inferiority complex.

优越性 yōuyuèxìng superiority; advantage:社会主义制度的～在中国越来越明显。The superiority of the socialist system has been increasingly evident in China. /充分发挥集体经济的～。Give full play to the advantages of the collective economy.

优哉游哉 yōuzāi-yóuzāi 〈书面〉living a life of ease and leisure; leisurely and carefree; leisurely and unhurried:这个人终日～,好不自在! The man is without a worry in the world and lives a life of ease and leisure.

优质 yōuzhì high quality; high grade; top-notch:～产品 quality product /～材料 high-grade materials /～服务 top-notch service

优种化 yōuzhǒnghuà ❶〈植物〉popularization of good strains ❷〈动物〉select a fine breed of animal

优种学 yōuzhǒngxué 〈生物〉euphenics

呦

yōu 〈叹词〉*used to express surprise, astonishment, etc.*:～! 电视机怎么坏了? Why, the television no longer works.

呦呦 yōuyōu 〈书面〉cry of a deer

麀

yōu 〈古语〉female deer; doe

幽[1]

yōu ❶ deep and remote; out-of-the-way; secluded; dim:清～ quiet and remote /～远 deep and distant (*or* far away) ❷ secret; hidden; covert: *see* "～居"; "～会"; "～怨" ❸ quiet; tranquil; serene: *see* "～思" ❹ imprison; place in confinement:深～囹圄之中 be securely locked up in prison (*or* behind bars) ❺ nether world: *see* "～灵"

幽[2]

Yōu ❶ name of an ancient prefecture covering present northern Hebei and southern Liaoning provinces:～州 Youzhou Prefecture ❷ a surname

幽暗 yōu'àn dim; shadowy; gloomy:～的灯光 dim light /～的角落 shadowy corner /～的山谷 darkened valley

幽闭 yōubì ❶ incarcerate; put under house arrest:这种生活与～何异? This kind of life is in no way different from incarceration. ❷ shut oneself up; confine oneself indoors:她断绝了一切交往,把自己～在家中。She has cut all communication with the outside world and confined herself indoors.

幽沉 yōuchén ❶ (of voice) low and husky ❷ gloomy and depressing:阴森～的景象 depressing and bloodcurdling sight

幽愤 yōufèn hidden grief; pent-up resentment:我内心的～何时才能发泄? When shall I be able to give vent to all my pent-up resentment?

幽谷 yōugǔ deep and secluded valley:密林～ dense forest and deep valley

幽光 yōuguāng dim light:窗外照进来路灯的～。The dim light of a street lamp shone into the room through the window.

幽篁 yōuhuáng secluded bamboo grove

幽会 yōuhuì secret meeting of lovers; lovers' rendezvous; tryst:两人多次在公园里～。The two of them had several rendezvous in a park.

幽魂 yōuhún ghost; spectre

幽寂 yōujì quiet and secluded; lonely:他习惯了山村的～,不适应城里的环境。He is yet to get accustomed to the urban environment because he was used to the quiet and secluded life in his mountain village.

幽禁 yōujìn incarcerate; put under house arrest; imprison:～犯人 imprison criminals /～生活 life in jail; life under house arrest

幽景 yōujǐng quiet and tranquil scene:月光如水,～绝胜。With the moon shedding silvery light overhead, the scene of quietude and tranquility was supreme.

幽径 yōujìng secluded path

幽静 yōujìng quiet and secluded; tranquil; peaceful:校园很～。The campus is quiet and peaceful. /妈妈厌烦城市的嘈杂,留恋乡村的～。Fed up with the noise of the city, mother misses a great deal the quiet and tranquil life in the country.

幽居 yōujū ❶ live as a hermit; live in seclusion ❷ quiet and tranquil abode

幽兰 yōulán 〈书面〉orchid

幽蓝 yōulán dark blue:坚硬的冰面上反射出～的光。A dark blue light was projected from the hard surface of the ice.

幽丽 yōulì quiet and beautiful:景色～ scene of quietude and beauty

幽灵 yōulíng ghost; spectre; spirit:他整天～似地游来逛去,不知是怎么了? He has been loafing around like a spectre the whole day. What has come over him?
幽美 yōuměi *see* "幽丽"
幽门 yōumén 〈生理〉pylorus
幽门梗阻 yōumén gěngzǔ 〈医学〉pyloric stenosis
幽眇 yōumiǎo 〈书面〉meticulous; elaborate; profound and subtle
幽明 yōumíng 〈书面〉the living and the dead; world of the dead and world of the living:～异路 the living and the dead never meet / ～永隔 be separated forever by death
幽冥 yōumíng ❶ dim; dark; gloomy ❷ nether world
幽默 yōumò (transliteration) humour:～感 sense of humour / 缺少～感 lack humour / ～作家 humorous writer; humorist / ～大师 great master of humour / 冷酷的～ grim humour / 黑色～ black humour / 不动声色的～ dry humour / 他显得非常～。He seemed to be a great wit.
幽默曲 yōumòqǔ 〈音乐〉humoresque
幽僻 yōupì quiet and remote:～的小山村 distant and tranquil mountain village
幽期 yōuqī *see* "幽会"
幽情 yōuqíng profound and undefinable sentiments; exquisite feelings:发思古之～ muse over things of the remote past / 别有～暗恨生,此时无声胜有声。Furthermore, unspoken emotions welled up in my bosom, But silence was more in tune with the occasion than was speech.
幽囚 yōuqiú imprison; incarcerate
幽趣 yōuqù elegant taste (as of a hermit); delightful serenity of seclusion:此间富有～。The place here is fraught with delights of seclusion.
幽人 yōurén 〈书面〉recluse; hermit
幽深 yōushēn (of forests, palaces, etc.) deep and serene; deep and tranquil:庭院～ deep and quiet courtyard / ～的竹林 deep and serene bamboo grove / 她有一对～而明亮的眼睛。She has bright and deep-set eyes.
幽思 yōusī ❶ be lost in reverie; ponder; meditate:屈原因忧愁～而作《离骚》。Qu Yuan wrote the poem *Li Sao* out of rumination over and worries about the fate of his country. ❷ innermost thoughts and feelings; hidden sentiments
幽邃 yōusuì 〈书面〉deep and serene; deep and quiet:峡谷～ deep and quiet gorge
幽婉 yōuwǎn *also* "幽宛" (of literary works, voice, tone, etc.) profound and elegant; deep and graceful:～的诗篇 profound and elegant poems / 故事～感人。The story is profoundly moving.
幽微 yōuwēi ❶ (of sound, smell, etc.) faint; weak; feeble:～的香味 faint fragrance (*or* aroma) / 声音～ weak sound ❷ 〈书面〉deep; profound; subtle:涵义～ with deep meanings (*or* implications)
幽闲 yōuxián ❶ *see* "幽娴" ❷ *also* "悠闲" yōuxián leisurely and carefree
幽娴 yōuxián (of a woman) gentle and serene:～的少女 gentle and serene young maiden / 姑娘端庄～。The girl is dignified and serene.
幽香 yōuxiāng delicate or faint fragrance:兰花～四溢。The delicate fragrance of the orchid permeates everywhere. / 飘来阵阵～。Gusts of faint fragrance were wafted over on the wind.
幽敻 yōuxiòng 〈书面〉far-reaching; profound
幽雅 yōuyǎ tranquil and elegant; (of a place) quiet and tastefully laid out:环境～ fine (*or* elegant) surroundings / 房间陈设～。The room is tastefully furnished.
幽咽 yōuyè 〈书面〉❶ whimpering; sobbing:有妇夜～。A woman was sobbing at night. ❷ murmuring; gurgling:山泉～ murmuring mountain spring / 小溪～ gurgling brook
幽隐 yōuyǐn ❶ deep and obscure; abstruse:洞察～ discern hidden and obscure meanings ❷ recluse:寻访～ seek out and visit a recluse
幽忧 yōuyōu 〈书面〉overcome with grief; grief-stricken:～过度 overwhelmed with sorrow
幽幽 yōuyōu ❶ (of sound, light, etc.) faint; feeble; weak:气息～ feeble breath / ～饮泣 sob quietly / 露出一线～的亮光。A faint ray of light came in sight. ❷ 〈书面〉looming in the distance:～南山。The southern mountain looms indistinctly in the distance.
幽远 yōuyuǎn deep and serene; profound; remote:～的夜空 remote and tranquil night sky / 意境～ of profound implications
幽怨 yōuyuàn hidden bitterness (as of a young woman thwarted or disappointed in love):深闺～。Alone in her chamber, a young woman was nursing her sorrow for want of love.
幽韵 yōuyùn melodious tunes

攸 yōu 〈书面〉*used like* 所 *in certain combinations*:利害～关 with one's interests at stake / 责有～归。The responsibility should lie where it belongs.

悠[1] yōu ❶ remote in time or space; long; far:亲朋～隔 be separated from one's friends and relatives for a long time ❷ leisurely; with ease; unhurried: *see* "～闲"; "～然"

悠[2] yōu 〈口语〉swing; sway:他在秋千上～来～去。He was swaying back and forth on the swing.
悠长 yōucháng long; long-drawn-out; protracted:～的旅途 long journey / 发出一声～的叹息 breathe a long sigh
悠打 yōuda *also* "悠搭"; "悠跶" 〈方言〉rock or swing to and fro; sway back and forth:悠打打地走着 walk in an unhurried manner; loiter along / 两条小辫子直～。The two little pigtails kept swaying back and forth.
悠荡 yōudàng swing to and fro; sway back and forth:秋千在空中来回～。The swing was going back and forth in mid air.
悠忽 yōuhū 〈书面〉lazy and idle; leisurely and languid
悠缓 yōuhuǎn leisurely and gentle; slow and unhurried:声音～ in a slow and unhurried voice / 雪花～地落着。Snow flakes were falling gently.
悠久 yōujiǔ long; long-standing; age-old:年代～ of the remote past; age-old / 影响～ long-lasting influence / 文化传统～ cultural tradition of long standing / 两国人民～友谊的象征 symbol of the time-honoured friendship between the two peoples
悠邈 yōumiǎo 〈书面〉remote in time and space; of remote antiquity; far distant:年代～ in the remote past
悠谬 yōumiù *also* "悠缪" 〈书面〉absurd; preposterous:～至极 absurd to the extreme; height of absurdity
悠然 yōurán easy and carefree:神态～ look carefree and at ease / ～神往 (one's thoughts) be carried away (to things in the remote past or far distance)
悠然自得 yōurán-zìdé at leisure; carefree and content:几个老人在公园里～地漫步。A few old people are strolling leisurely in the park.
悠停 yōuting 〈方言〉take one's time; do sth. slowly and unhurriedly:喝酒要～着点儿,别喝过量。You must drink slowly, and don't overdo it.
悠闲 yōuxián leisurely and carefree:～的退休生活 leisurely and carefree life in retirement
悠徐 yōuxú *see* "悠缓"
悠扬 yōuyáng (of music, etc.) rising and falling; in harmony; melodious:～的歌声 melodious song (*or* singing) / ～的钢琴声 sweet piano music
悠悠 yōuyōu ❶ long; remote; infinite:～岁月 long years / ～山川 remote mountains and rivers / 念天地之～,独怆然而涕下。Thinking of this infinite universe, Alone, in my sorrow, I shed tears. ❷ 〈书面〉numerous; myriad; a multitude of:～万事 myriads of events / 恨～ unending hatred ❸ leisurely; unhurriedly:慢～地走着 be walking at a leisurely pace ❹ 〈书面〉absurd; senseless; preposterous:～之谈 absurd remarks
悠游 yōuyóu ❶ move with ease and leisure:小艇在荡漾的春波中～。The small boat was floating leisurely on the rippling lake in spring. ❷ *see* "悠闲"
悠远 yōuyuǎn ❶ long time ago; long ago; of the remote or distant past:～的童年 childhood of the remote past / ～往事 events of the distant past ❷ far; distant; remote:故乡离他是那么～。His native country seemed so far away.
悠着 yōuzhe 〈方言〉take it easy; take things easy:～着点儿,别累病了。Take it easy. Don't overwork yourself and fall ill with fatigue.

yóu

斿 yóu 〈书面〉❶ streamers or ribbons of a flag ❷ *see* "游"

Y

yóu

游 yóu ❶ swim:鱼在水中～来～去。The fish was swimming to and fro in the water. /江河边上的孩子个个会～泳。Every child living near rivers can swim. ❷ stroll or rove about; travel; tour:闲～ rove about; wander /周～全国 travel all over the country; go on a country-wide tour /北京七日～ seven-day tour of Beijing /黄山之～给我留下了美好的印象。The tour to Huangshan made a fine impression on me. ❸〈书面〉associate with:交～颇广 have a wide range of acquaintances /与英俊并～ associate oneself with the best and the brightest ❹ roving; migrating; unsettled: *see* "～牧"; "～击"; "～资" ❺ part of a river; reach:长江中下～ middle and lower reaches of the Yangtze River ❻ (Yóu) a surname

游遨 yóu'áo roam; travel:～千里 travel a thousand *li*

游伴 yóubàn travel companion:结成～ travel in company /理想的～ ideal travel companion

游标 yóubiāo 〈机械〉vernier:～千分尺 vernier micrometer

游标卡尺 yóubiāo kǎchǐ vernier calliper

游程 yóuchéng ❶ swimming distance:比赛的～是一千米。The swimming distance for the contest is one thousand metres. ❷ trip; journey:一日～ one-day trip /～三千里 tour (*or* travel) three thousand *li* ❸ travel programme; itinerary:时间有限,把～排得紧一点儿。As time is limited, we will have a tight (*or* full) tour schedule.

游船 yóuchuán pleasure boat:租了一只～ hire a pleasure boat

游串 yóuchuàn roam; wander:四处～ roam about

游春 yóuchūn go on an outing in spring

游春戏 yóuchūnxì one of the local operas in northern Fujian Province

游词 yóucí *also* "游辞"〈书面〉❶ unfounded statement; groundless remarks ❷ joke; kidding

游荡 yóudàng ❶ loaf about; idle; loiter; wander:整天～ idle all day long ❷ stroll; saunter:独自一人在公园里～ stroll alone in the park ❸ float:船在湖上～。A boat is floating on the lake.

游动 yóudòng ❶ rove around; move about:鲤鱼在水里～得挺欢。The carp was briskly swimming to and fro in the water. ❷ moving or going from place to place; mobile; roving:～目标 moving target

游动哨 yóudòngshào roving sentry; patrol

游斗 yóudòu parade sb. in the street (as a form of punishment)

游惰 yóuduò given to loafing around; idle:～成性 be a loafer by nature

游泛 yóufàn float leisurely:几只小鸭在池塘里悠闲地～着。A few ducklings are floating leisurely on the pond.

游方 yóufāng ❶ rove about; roam:～和尚 roving (*or* itinerant) monk ❷ social gathering of boys and girls of the Miao nationality during festivals or the slack season, where they sing songs, exchange gifts and make advances to each other

游舫 yóufǎng pleasure boat

游逛 yóuguàng go sightseeing; stroll about:在公园里～ saunter around the park

游宦 yóuhuàn 〈书面〉hold an official post away from home

游魂 yóuhún ❶〈迷信〉wandering homeless spirit; hovering spectre ❷〈比喻〉remnant influence of old forces or customs

游混 yóuhùn loaf around; fritter away time:你成天价～,多无聊!You loaf about all day long. How silly!

游击 yóujī guerrilla warfare:在敌后打～ wage guerrilla warfare behind enemy lines

游击队 yóujīduì guerrilla forces; guerrilla detachment:～队员 guerrilla; partisan /～队长 commander of guerrilla forces; leader of a guerrilla detachment

游击区 yóujīqū guerrilla area or zone

游击战 yóujīzhàn guerrilla war or warfare:抗日～ anti-Japanese guerrilla war

游记 yóujì travel notes; travels:读～ read travel notes

游街 yóujiē ❶ parade sb. through the streets:～示众 parade sb. through the streets to expose him to the public ❷ walk through the streets at the head of a parade (as an honour):披红～ have red silk draped over sb.'s shoulders and parade with him at the head of a public procession (in order to honour him)

游客 yóukè visitor (to a park, etc.); tourist; excursionist; sightseer:中外～ Chinese and foreign tourists

游览 yóulǎn go sightseeing; tour; visit:～路线 itinerary for a tour /～泰山 tour Mount Tai /～故宫 visit the Imperial Palace Museum

游览车 yóulǎnchē tour bus; tourist coach; tourist bus

游览地 yóulǎndì tourist resort; place for sightseeing; excursion centre

游览区 yóulǎnqū tourist area

游览图 yóulǎntú tourist map; tourist guide

游廊 yóuláng covered corridor (linking two or more buildings); veranda

游乐 yóulè amusement; recreation:～场 recreational park; amusement park /供儿童～之用 for children to play in

游乐车 yóulèchē fun vehicle; ride (in an amusement park)

游乐园 yóulèyuán amusement park; pleasure ground; recreational garden

游离 yóulí ❶〈化学〉free:～酸 free acid ❷ dissociate; drift away:～于集体之外 be aloof from the collective; be detached from the group

游离电子 yóulí diànzǐ *also* "自由电子" zìyóu diànzǐ free electron

游离基 yóulíjī *also* "自由基" zìyóujī free radical

游离基因 yóulí jīyīn episome

游离碱 yóulíjiǎn free base; free alkali

游离金 yóulíjīn free gold

游离生长素 yóulí shēngzhǎngsù free auxin

游离态 yóulítài free state

游离碳 yóulítàn free carbon

游历 yóulì travel for pleasure; tour; travel:他盼望有朝一日去塞外～。He looks forward to touring the country north of the Great Wall.

游猎 yóuliè go hunting

游轮 yóulún ❶〈机械〉loose pulley ❷ pleasure boat

游民 yóumín hobo; tramp; vagrant; vagabond:无业～ vagrant; vagabond /季节～ seasonal migrants

游民无产者 yóumín wúchǎnzhě *also* "流氓无产者" liúmáng wúchǎnzhě lumpenproletariat

游目 yóumù 〈书面〉raise one's eyes to see; glance at:～纵览 take a full view of sth.

游目骋怀 yóumù-chěnghuái look far and broaden one's horizons

游牧 yóumù move about in quest of pasture; rove about as a nomad:～部落 nomadic tribe /～生活 nomadic life; nomadism /以～为生 live as a nomad

游骑 yóuqí 〈旧语〉cavalrymen who served as a patrol or task force

游气 yóuqì ❶ feeble breathing:病人只剩一丝～了。The patient was breathing his last. ❷〈书面〉thin floating clouds

游憩 yóuqì stroll about or have a rest

游禽 yóuqín natatorial bird; swimming bird; waterfowl

游人 yóurén visitor (to a park, etc.); sightseer; tourist:公园里到处都是～。The park was crowded (*or* thronged) with visitors.

游刃有余 yóurèn-yǒuyú handle a butcher's cleaver skilfully — do a job with skill and ease; accomplish sth. effortlessly; be more than equal to a task:他自信干这种工作～。He is confident that he can do the job perfectly well.

游散 yóusàn go for a leisurely walk; take a stroll:晚饭后,他们到湖边～了一会儿。After supper, they went to the lakeside for a leisurely walk.

游山玩水 yóushān-wánshuǐ *also* "游山玩景";"游山逛景" tour mountains and rivers to enjoy the beauty of nature; travel from one scenic spot to another

游僧 yóusēng travelling Buddhist monk

游赏 yóushǎng go sightseeing:我们缓步～,时行时息。We walked slowly to enjoy the beautiful scenery, now resting and now moving on.

游士 yóushì 〈书面〉lobbyist

游手 yóushǒu ❶ loafer ❷〈书面〉empty-handed

游手好闲 yóushǒu-hàoxián idle about; loaf:～,无所事事 lounge about and do no work /经过教育,村里～的人明显减少。After education, the number of loafers in the village was markedly reduced.

游耍 yóushuǎ play around; fool around

游水 yóushuǐ swim

游说 yóushuì go about selling an idea; go about drumming up support; go canvassing; lobby:为他人～ go about canvassing for others /为减少国防开支而四处～ lobby hard for a reduction in defence spending

游丝 yóusī ❶ gossamer:细若～ as slender as gossamer ❷〈机械〉balance spring; hairspring

Y

游丝测微器 yóusī cèwēiqì 〈机械〉filar micrometer
游艇 yóutǐng yacht; pleasure boat: 油饰一新的～ newly painted pleasure boat
游玩 yóuwán ❶ amuse oneself; have fun; play: 小孩常在院子里～。The children often play in the courtyard. ❷ go sightseeing; visit: 动物园是孩子们最喜欢～的地方。The zoo is the place children like to visit most.
游息 yóuxī ❶ enjoy oneself and rest; play and rest: 公园是人们～的地方。Parks are the places where people enjoy and rest themselves. ❷ (of fish, birds, etc.) move about and rest: 这里水草茂盛，最适于水鸟～。This is the best dwelling place for water birds, for there is an abundance of waterweeds.
游嬉 yóuxī frolic; play: 孩子们在海滩上尽情～。The children were frolicking with abandon on the beach.
游戏 yóuxì ❶ pastime; game: 做～ play games / 竞技性～ competitive games / ～规则 rules of the game ❷ play; have fun: 他们从小就爱在一起～。They loved to play together from childhood.
游戏机 yóuxìjī (short for 电子游戏机) video game player
游戏理论 yóuxì lǐlùn game theory
游侠 yóuxiá 〈旧语〉roving brave; knight-errant
游仙诗 yóuxiānshī poetry about immortals
游乡 yóuxiāng ❶ parade sb. through a village as a form of punishment ❷ peddle from village to village: ～郎中 roving country doctor / ～货郎 itinerant pedlar
游心 yóuxīn 〈书面〉have an interest in; be interested in: ～于文学艺术 be interested in art and literature
游行 yóuxíng ❶ wander about; roam; rove: ～四方 roam about ❷ parade; march; demonstration: ～队伍 (contingent of) paraders / 抗议～ protest march (*or* demonstration) / ～路线 route of the demonstration / 国庆～ National Day parade
游兴 yóuxìng interest in going on an excursion or sightseeing: ～大发 be seized with the desire to go sightseeing; be full of interest in an excursion (*or* trip)
游幸 yóuxìng (of emperors and kings) imperial tour or visit
游学 yóuxué 〈旧语〉study away from one's home; study abroad: ～东瀛 study in Japan / ～国外 study abroad
游医 yóuyī itinerant doctor
游移 yóuyí ❶ move back and forth: 浮云在空中～。Clouds are floating in the sky. ❷ (of attitude, policy, etc.) waver; hesitate; vacillate; wobble: 不容～ allow no vacillation / 没有丝毫～的余地。There is no room whatsoever for shilly-shallying. / 这个小党经常在两大党之间～。This small party often wavers between the two major parties.
游弋 yóuyì ❶ cruise; patrol: 美国舰艇在地中海～。American warships were plying the waters of the Mediterranean Sea. ❷ move on water: 几只小鸭在湖里～。Several ducklings are moving about on the lake.
游艺 yóuyì entertainment; recreation: ～节目 programme of theatrical and other performances / 举办～活动 organize recreational activities
游艺会 yóuyìhuì cultural get-together: 在～上演了京剧。Beijing opera was performed at the entertainment gathering.
游泳 yóuyǒng ❶ swim: 江河湖海都是～的好地方。Rivers, lakes and seas are all nice places to swim in. ❷ 〈体育〉swimming: ～比赛 swimming contest / ～健将 first-rate (*or* ace) swimmer / ～队 swimming team / ～教练 swimming coach
游泳池 yóuyǒngchí swimming pool
游泳馆 yóuyǒngguǎn natatorium; enclosed swimming pool
游泳裤 yóuyǒngkù bathing or swimming trunks
游泳帽 yóuyǒngmào bathing or swimming cap
游泳衣 yóuyǒngyī swimsuit; swimming suit or costume; bathing suit or costume: 三点式～ bikini
游勇 yóuyǒng stragglers and disbanded soldiers
游游磨磨 yóuyou-mōmō 〈方言〉idle about; loaf: 他一天到晚～的没点事干，总不是长事。He idles about all day long without doing any work. It simply won't do for him to drag on and on like this.
游园 yóuyuán ❶ visit a park or garden: 带领外宾～ show foreign guests around a park ❷ mass celebrations in parks: 全班同学一起参加国庆节的～联欢活动。The entire class joined in the National Day celebrations in a park.
游园会 yóuyuánhuì garden party: 丰富多彩的～ interesting and colourful garden party
游转 yóuzhuàn roam about; stroll about aimlessly: 他每天晚饭后都要出去～一会儿。After supper every evening, he would go out for a short leisurely stroll.
游资 yóuzī idle money; floating capital: 利用～ make use of (*or* utilize) idle funds
游子 yóuzǐ 〈书面〉person who has been away from his home or country for a long time: 漂泊异乡的～ people who have wandered in a foreign land / 海外～ overseas Chinese
游子 yóuzi decoy
游踪 yóuzōng traveller's whereabouts
游走 yóuzǒu 〈医学〉(of an organ or pain) moving; migrating; unfixed: ～肾 movable kidney; wandering kidney / ～脾 movable spleen; wandering spleen; floating spleen

遊

yóu *see* "游 ❷❸❹" yóu

蝣

yóu *see* "蜉蝣" fúyóu

猷

yóu 〈书面〉plan; design: 新～ new plan / 宏～ grand design

楢

yóu 〈古语〉kind of tree with soft timber

輶

yóu ❶ 〈古语〉light carriage ❷ 〈书面〉light

蝤

yóu
see also qiú
蝤蛑 yóumóu 〈动物〉swimming crab

莜

yóu
莜麦 yóumài *also* "油麦" yóumài 〈植物〉naked or raw oats: ～面 naked oat flour

尤[1](尢)

yóu ❶ remarkable; conspicuous; outstanding: 无耻之～ shameless in the extreme / 人，动物之～也。Man is the most outstanding of all animals. ❷ particularly; especially; in particular: ～妙 even better; all the better / 他酷嗜游泳，～以蛙泳为最。He loves swimming, especially the breaststroke. ❸ (Yóu) a surname

尤[2](尢)

yóu ❶ fault; error; wrongdoing: 以儆效～ so as to warn others not to follow the example of the wrongdoer / 莫知其～ not know one's own fault ❷ have a grudge against; resent; blame: 怨天～人 blame everyone and everything but oneself
尤里卡 Yóulǐkǎ EUREKA (European Research Coordination Agency)
尤其 yóuqí 〈副词〉especially; particularly: 他喜欢体育，～喜欢游泳。He likes sports, and swimming in particular. / 北方的风沙很大，～是在春天。In the north it is often windy and dusty, especially in spring.
尤甚 yóushèn more so; especially: 本城市民多是足球迷，而青年人～。Most of the people in this city are football fans, particularly the youngsters.
尤为 yóuwéi 〈副词〉particularly; especially: ～不满 particularly dissatisfied
尤物 yóuwù 〈书面〉extraordinary or outstanding thing or people; rarity; beauty: 人们都说她是天生的～。Everybody says she is a rare beauty.
尤异 yóuyì 〈书面〉uncommon; exceptional; excellent: 政绩～ outstanding achievements in performing one's official duties

疣(肬)

yóu *also* "肉赘" ròuzhuì; "瘊子" hóuzi 〈医学〉wart: 扁平～ flat wart / 传染性软～ contagious soft wart
疣猴 yóuhóu 〈动物〉guereza
疣猪 yóuzhū 〈动物〉warthog (*Phacochoerus aethiopicus*)
疣赘 yóuzhuì *also* "赘疣" ❶ wart ❷ sth. unnecessary or superfluous

鱿

yóu
鱿鱼 yóuyú squid

犹(猶) yóu 〈书面〉❶ just as; like: ~鱼得水 like a stranded fish put back into water /过~不及。Going too far is like falling short. ❷ still; even: 言~在耳 sb.'s words still ringing in one's ears /困兽~斗。Even a cornered animal will fight on.

犹大 Yóudà 〈基督教〉Judas Iscariot (? -c. 30) one of the 12 Apostles, who betrayed Christ for 30 pieces of silver

犹且 yóuqiě 〈书面〉still; yet: 他~不能,而况我。Even he cannot do it, let alone me.

犹然 yóurán still; as usual: 虽然时隔多年,那事他~记得很清楚。Although many years have passed, he still vividly remembers what happened.

犹如 yóurú just as; like; as if: 二人~兄弟一般。The two of them treat each other like brothers.

犹他 Yóutā Utah, a western state of the United States

犹太复国主义 Yóutài fùguózhǔyì Zionism

犹太教 Yóutàijiào Judaism; Hebraism zion: ~教士 rabbi /~教堂 synagogue

犹太人 Yóutàirén Jewish people; Jew: 他是~。He is Jewish.

犹疑 yóuyí waver; hesitate: ~不定 hesitate; be of two minds /小王~地瞥了他一眼。Xiao Wang looked at him uncertainly.

犹豫 yóuyù hesitate; vacillate; be irresolute: 态度~ vacillating attitude /~观望 watch in hesitation

犹豫不决 yóuyù-bùjué hesitate; remain undecided; waver: 因~而痛失良机。The golden opportunity slipped through his fingers as he hesitated.

犹之乎 yóuzhīhū 〈书面〉just as; like: 人离不开土地,~鱼离不开水。Man cannot live without land just as fish cannot leave the water.

犹子 yóuzǐ 〈书面〉nephew; brother's son

犹自 yóuzì still; even: 现在提起那件事儿,~叫人心惊肉跳。Even today, the mere mention of that incident leaves people shaking with horror.

莸(蕕) yóu ❶ common bluebeard (*Caryopteris incana*) ❷〈古语〉stinking grass; 〈比喻〉stinking personality: 薰~不同器。The good and bad do not mix.

由 yóu ❶ cause; reason; grounds: 事~ cause /理~ reason; grounds /来~ cause; origin ❷ because of; owing to; due to: ~管理不善造成的经济损失 economic losses due to (*or* resulting from) mismanagement ❸ pass by or through: 必~之路 path (*or* road) one must follow; only way /~民主协商选出代表 deputies elected through democratic consultation ❹ follow; obey: 只好~着她 cannot but allow her to do as she pleases /身不~己 do sth. in spite of oneself; lose control over oneself /信不信~你 believe it or not /品种繁多,~顾客挑选。There is a large variety of goods for customers to choose from. ❺〈介词〉to or for (sb.); by (sb.): 这顿饭~我作东。The dinner is on me. /会议~你主持。We leave it to you to chair the meeting. /班长~她担任。It is for her to be the monitor. ❻〈介词〉by means of: ~此可知 know from this; tell by it /人体是~各种细胞组成的。The human body is composed of various kinds of cells. ❼〈介词〉(starting) from: ~南到北 from north to south /~上海出发 set out from Shanghai /~简及繁 from the simple to the complex /~近及远 from the near to the distant ❽ (Yóu) a surname

由表及里 yóubiǎo-jílǐ from the surface to the centre; from the outside to the inside; from the exterior to the interior: ~地进行分析 proceed from the outside to the inside in analyzing sth.; analyze methodically

由不得 yóubude ❶ not be up to sb.; not admit of; be beyond the control of: 这事可~你了。This matter is not up to you (to decide). /事关重大,~意气用事。It's a matter of great importance which allows of no whim (*or* caprice). ❷ cannot help; cannot but: 他态度那么诚恳,~你不信。He was so sincere in his attitude that you could not help believing what he said.

由此 yóucǐ from this; therefrom; as a result: ~而引起的矛盾 resulting contradictions /~入内。This way in. *or* Entrance. /~看来,这个问题的确很复杂。We can thus see the complexity of the problem. /对方要承当~而产生的一切后果。The other side will be held responsible for all the consequences arising therefrom.

由此及彼 yóucǐ-jíbǐ from this to that; from one to the other: ~地联系起来看问题 look at the issues by examining their interrelationships

由此可见 yóucǐ-kějiàn thus it can be seen; it is therefore clear; this shows; that proves: ~,谈判破裂的责任全在你方。This shows (*or* It's thus clear) that your side is entirely responsible for the failure of the negotiation.

由打 yóudǎ 〈方言〉❶ since; from: ~家乡来 come from one's hometown /~入冬以来,这里没下过雪。It has not snowed here since the beginning of winter. ❷ past; via; through; by way of: 黄河水~这儿往北,再向东入海。The Yellow River bends from here to the north, then turns to the east, and finally empties itself into the sea.

由得 yóude be up to; allow; permit: 辛辛苦苦种出的粮食,~你作践糟蹋吗? How could you be allowed to waste the grain the farmers produced by the sweat of their brows?

由来 yóulái ❶ evolution from the inception; duration up to now ❷ cause; source; reason: 此事的~一言难尽。The cause of the incident could not be explained in a few words.

由来已久 yóulái-yǐjiǔ long-standing; of long duration; time-honoured: 两人的观点分歧~。The differences between the two men's views have existed for a long time. /过春节的习惯~。Celebrating the Spring Festival is a time-honoured custom.

由浅入深 yóuqiǎn-rùshēn from the easy to the difficult; from the shallow to the deep; from the elementary to the profound: 老师的讲解~,使我们一步步了解问题的实质。The teacher's explanation proceeded from the easy to the difficult, thus enabling us to grasp the essence of the issue step by step.

由头 yóutou pretext; excuse: 拿不出~ fail to find a pretext

由性 yóuxìng wilful; bent on having one's own way: 放了假也得读点书,不能~儿玩。You have to read some books during the vacation and must not play as much as you please.

由于 yóuyú owing to; thanks to; on grounds of; because of: ~健康原因 on health grounds /~众所周知的原因 owing to causes known to all /~种种原因,施工计划未能按时完成。The project has not been completed as scheduled due to all sorts of reasons.

由衷 yóuzhōng from the bottom of one's heart; earnest; heartfelt: 言不~ insincere words /感到~的高兴 heartily rejoice /表示~的赞美 express heartfelt admiration

由衷之言 yóuzhōngzhīyán words from the bottom of one's heart: 他这番话,看来是~。His words sound sincere.

由子 yóuzi 〈方言〉excuse; pretext: 借~整人 find an excuse to fix sb.

油 yóu ❶ oil; fat; grease: 花生~ groundnut (*or* peanut) oil /菜籽~ rapeseed oil /猪~ pork fat; lard /石~ petroleum /汽~ petrol; gasoline; gas /煤~ kerosene /炼~厂 oil refinery /加~站 petrol filling station; gas station /~枯灯灭 when the oil gives out, the lamp expires — (of a person) die ❷ apply tung oil or varnish; paint: ~家具 paint furniture /这扇窗子该~一~了。This window needs painting. ❸ be stained with oil or grease: 衣服~了一大块。The dress has got a big oil stain on it. ❹ oily; slick; glib: 别看他人小,可~得很哩。Though rather young, he is extremely slick.

油泵 yóubèng 〈机械〉oil pump: ~坏了,必须马上修理。The oil pump is out of order and must be repaired at once.

油比重计 yóubǐzhòngjì oleometer

油饼 yóubǐng ❶ *also* "油枯"; "枯饼" kūbǐng soya bean or groundnut dregs after oil been extracted; oil cakes: 他终于买到了~做猪饲料。He has at last bought soya bean cakes as pig feed. ❷ oil-fried dough cake: 炸~ fried cakes

油驳 yóubó oil barge: ~船〈石油〉oil hulk; tank barge

油布 yóubù oilcloth; oilskin; tarpaulin: 用~把水泥盖上 cover the cement up with tarpaulin

油彩 yóucǎi greasepaint; paint: 洗净脸上的~ wash the greasepaint off one's face /~太厚 be too thickly painted

油菜 yóucài ❶ *also* "芸薹" yúntái rape (*Brassica juncea* or *B. napus*): ~籽 rapeseed /今年的~可望丰收。A good harvest of rape is expected this year. ❷ green rape (*Brassica chinensis* or *B. campestris*): 炒~ fry green rape

油藏 yóucáng 〈石油〉oil deposit; oil pool: 地层~ stratigraphic oil pool /构造~ structural oil pool /岩性~ lithogical oil pool

油槽 yóucáo 〈石油〉oil reservoir; oil bath; oil trough; oil duct: ~车 petrol tanker /~汽车 tank car; tank truck /~拖车 tank trailer

油层 yóucéng 〈石油〉oil reservoir; oil layer; oil horizon: ~压力 reservoir pressure /~动态 reservoir behaviour (*or* performance) /

Y

～很厚 thick layer of oil /发现～ find (*or* locate) an oil horizon
油茶 yóuchá ❶〈植物〉tea-oil tree; oil-tea camellia:种植～ plant tea-oil trees ❷ gruel of sweetened, fried flour:端上一碗～ bring in a bowlful of sweetened fried flour gruel
油茶面儿 yóuchámiànr flour fried in beef fat with sugar and sesame
油船 yóuchuán (oil) tanker; oil carrier
油床 yóuchuáng 〈石油〉oil pool; oil accumulation; oil reservoir
油淬 yóucuì 〈冶金〉oil hardening or quenching:～钢 oil-hardening steel
油淬火 yóucuìhuǒ 〈机械〉oil hardening or quenching
油灯 yóudēng oil lamp:暗淡的～ dim oil lamp /点燃～ light an oil lamp
油底子 yóudǐzi *also* "油脚"〈口语〉oil dregs
油地毡 yóudìzhān linoleum
油豆腐 yóudòufu fried bean curd (cube)
油断路 yóuduànlù 〈电工〉oil-break:～器 oil circuit breaker; oil-break switch
油坊 yóufáng oil mill:老式～ old type oil mill
油风 yóufēng 〈中医〉alopecia
油封 yóufēng 〈机械〉oil seal
油橄榄 yóugǎnlǎn *also* "齐墩果" qídūnguǒ 〈植物〉olive
油膏 yóugāo 〈医学〉ointment
油垢 yóugòu greasy filth; grease:满手～ greasy hands
油瓜 yóuguā *also* "油渣果"〈植物〉large-fruited hodgsonia (*Hodgsonia macrocarpa*)
油管 yóuguǎn 〈石油〉❶ oil pipe:铺设～ lay oil pipes ❷ oil tube:～深度 tubing depth /～头 tubing head
油罐 yóuguàn 〈石油〉oil tank; storage tank:～车 fuel tank truck; fuel tanker; tank-car; tank wagon
油光 yóuguāng glossy; shiny; varnished: ～碧绿的树叶 shiny green leaves /把桌子擦得～闪亮 clear the table until it shines
油光水滑 yóuguāng-shuǐhuá extremely shiny and smooth:他把头发梳得～的。He combed his hair shiny and smooth.
油鬼 yóuguǐ 〈方言〉deep-fried dough stick
油果 yóuguǒ 〈方言〉*also* "油果子" deep-fried twisted dough stick
油耗 yóuhào (of vehicles, machines, etc.) consumption of petrol, engine oil, diesel oil, etc.:降低～ bring down (*or* reduce, *or* cut) oil consumption
油耗子 yóuhàozi illegal dealer in petrol and diesel oil:不能让～钻空子。There should be no loophole for the illegal oil dealer to take advantage of.
油黑 yóuhēi jet black; shiny black:～的脸儿 shiny black face /她的两条辫子～发亮。Her pigtails are glossy black and shiny.
油乎乎 yóuhūhū oily; greasy:～的糕点 oily pastries /工作服～的。The working overalls were greasy.
油壶 yóuhú oilcan; oiler
油葫芦 yóuhulǔ 〈动物〉a kind of large cricket (*Gryllus testaceus*)
油花 yóuhuā drops of oil on the surface of soup; blobs of oil
油滑 yóuhuá slick; slippery; foxy:这人～得很。This fellow is quite wily.
油画 yóuhuà oil painting:～家 oil painter /候机室里有一幅巨型～。There is a huge oil painting on the wall of the passenger lounge.
油画颜料 yóuhuà yánliào oil colours; oils
油灰 yóuhuī 〈建筑〉putty:抹上一点～ apply some putty
油回火 yóuhuíhuǒ oil tempering
油鸡 yóujī 〈动物〉cochin:又肥又大的～ large and fat cochin
油迹 yóujì oil stains; grease spots:衣服上有几处～。There are a few oil stains on the clothes. /～可用洗涤液除去。Grease marks can be removed with liquid detergent.
油煎火燎 yóujiān-huǒliǎo with burning anxiety; on pins and needles:孩子病得很重,母亲心里～的。With her child seriously ill, the mother was on pins and needles.
油减震柱 yóujiǎnzhènzhù oil strut (for an aeroplane, etc.)
油匠 yóujiàng *see* "油漆匠"
油脚 yóujiǎo *see* "油底子"
油浸 yóujìn oil-immersed:～变压器〈电工〉oil-immersed transformer /～电缆 oil-impregnated cable /～电容器 oil condenser /～法 oil-immersion method
油精 yóujīng 〈化学〉olein
油井 yóujǐng oil well:高产～ high-yield oil well; highly-productive oil well /钻一口～ drill (*or* bore) an oil well

油锯 yóujù 〈林业〉chain saw:～手 chain saw operator
油绝缘 yóujuéyuán 〈电工〉oil-insulated:～子 oil insulator
油枯 yóukū *see* "油饼"
油库 yóukù oil depot; oil house; oil tankage; tank farm:地下～ oil cellar /转运～ oil terminal
油矿 yóukuàng ❶ oil deposit:发现了新的～ find a new oil deposit ❷ oilfield:～工人 oilfield worker /他到这个～工作好几年了。He has been working in this oilfield for quite a few years.
油老虎 yóulǎohǔ "oil tiger" — oil or gas guzzler
油冷却 yóulěngquè 〈机械〉oil cooling
油梨 yóulí *also* "鳄梨" èlí 〈植物〉avocado
油量计 yóuliángjì 〈机械〉oil gauge
油亮 yóuliàng shiny; glossy:他把皮鞋擦得～～的。He polished his shoes till they took on a shiny gloss.
油料 yóuliào oil-bearing seed; oilseed
油料作物 yóuliào zuòwù oil bearing crop; oil crop:今年全国的～普遍丰收。The whole country reaped a bumper harvest of oil crops this year.
油裂化 yóulièhuà *also* "油裂解"〈石油〉oil-breaking; oil-cracking:～器 oil cracker /～塔 cracking tower
油篓 yóulǒu small-mouthed and big-bellied basket made of wicker chips or bamboo chips and lined with oil paper used to contain oil
油炉 yóulú oil furnace; oil stove
油绿 yóulǜ glossy dark green:～色的地毯 glossy dark green carpet
油轮 yóulún *also* "油船" (oil) tanker:超级～ super tanker /地中海上的～ oil tankers on the Mediterranean Sea
油马达 yóumǎdá 〈机械〉oil motor
油码头 yóumǎtou oil jetty; oil wharf; tanker (loading) terminal
油麦 yóumài *also* "莜麦" yóumài 〈植物〉naked or raw oats
油毛 yóumáo raw or untreated wool, rabbit hair, etc.
油毛毡 yóumáozhān 〈建筑〉asphalt felt
油门 yóumén 〈机械〉❶ throttle:开大～ turn the throttle up /关上～ turn off the throttle ❷〈口语〉accelerator:踩～ step on the accelerator
油焖 yóumèn braise:～大虾 braised prawns
油苗 yóumiáo 〈石油〉oil seepage:勘探队发现了～。The prospecting team discovered oil seepage.
油膜 yóumó oil slick
油膜轴承 yóumó zhóuchéng 〈机械〉filmatic bearing; Kelmet
油墨 yóumò printing ink:满手～ hands stained with printing ink /快干～ quicksetting ink
油母岩质 yóumǔ yánzhì kerogen
油母页岩 yóumǔ yèyán oil shale; kerogen shale
油泥 yóuní greasy filth; grease:擦～ remove the grease /把表的～擦一下 clean and oil the watch
油腻 yóunì ❶ oily; greasy:菜的味道不错,就是太～了。The dish tastes all right, but it is a bit too oily. ❷ greasy food:有病的人不宜多吃～。Patients should not eat greasy food.
油盘 yóupán lacquer tray; wooden food tray
油皮 yóupí 〈方言〉❶ outermost layer of skin:只是擦破了点～儿。It's only a scratch. ❷ skin of soya-bean milk
油票儿 yóupiàor ❶ coupon for edible oil ❷ petrol coupon
油漆 yóuqī ❶ paint; varnish:～商店 paint shop /一层～ a coat of paint ❷ cover with paint; paint:把书桌～一下 give the desk a coat of paint /当心,～未干! Be careful! Wet paint!
油漆匠 yóuqījiàng *also* "油匠" painter (for painting buildings, walls, etc.):他是本地最好的～。He is the best painter in this locality.
油气 yóuqì 〈石油〉(short for 油田伴生气) associated gas
油气比 yóuqìbǐ oil-gas ratio
油气界面 yóuqì jièmiàn 〈石油〉oil-gas interface
油气田 yóuqìtián oil and gas field
油气显示 yóuqì xiǎnshì oil-gas showing; oil-gas indications
油枪 yóuqiāng 〈机械〉oil gun
油腔滑调 yóuqiāng-huádiào glib; unctuous:他说话总是～的,没正经。He always talks unctuously (*or* glibly) and is never serious.
油区 yóuqū oil-producing area
油泉 yóuquán oil spring
油裙 yóuqun cooking apron:她系着一条花布～。She wore a coloured cloth apron.
油然 yóurán ❶ spontaneously; unwittingly:～萌发出报国之志 have a natural desire to serve the country ❷ densely; profusely:～

作云 gathering clouds
油然而生 yóurán'érshēng (of a feeling) rise of itself:一种~的敬意 uprush of respect /爱慕之情~。Love and admiration welled up in one's heart.
油溶剂 yóuróngjì oil solvent
油溶性染料 yóuróngxìng rǎnliào oil-soluble dye
油鞣 yóuróu 〈皮革〉oil tanning
油润 yóurùn shiny and smooth; glossy:烟叶~ shiny and smooth tobacco leaves
油色 yóusè painting oils; oil paints
油砂 yóushā 〈石油〉oil sand:稠~ heavy oil sand /~层 pay sand
油杉 yóushān *also* "杜松" dùsōng keteleeria (*Keteleeria fortunei*)
油石 yóushí 〈机械〉oilstone
油饰 yóushì paint; varnish:门窗~一新。The doors and windows have been freshly painted.
油柿 yóushì 〈植物〉wild kaki persimmon (*Diospyros kaki* var. *silvestris*)
油树脂 yóushùzhī 〈化学〉oleoresin
油刷 yóushuā cover with paint:~门面 paint the front of sth.
油水 yóushui ❶ grease; oil:由于胃病,他很久不沾~了。He has not had oily food for quite a long time because of stomach trouble. ❷ profit; gain:捞~ make some gain; pick up a few crumbs /这活儿的~大。This is a lucrative job.
油松 yóusōng 〈植物〉Chinese pine (*Pinus tabulaeformis*)
油酥 yóusū short; crisp; flaky:~火烧 crisp baked cake
油酸 yóusuān 〈化学〉oleic acid:~盐 oleate /~酯 oleate /~酯酶 olease
油桃 yóutáo nectarine (*Prunus persica* var. *nectarina*)
油提 yóutí oil-dipper
油田 yóutián oilfield:大庆~ Daqing Oilfield /多层~ multi-pay oilfield /~注水 oilfield flooding
油田伴生气 yóutián bànshēngqì *also* "油田气";"油气" associated gas
油条 yóutiáo ❶ deep-fried twisted dough stick ❷ sly person; foxy old hand:他是有名的老~。Everybody knows he is an old fox.
油桐 yóutóng 〈植物〉tung oil tree; tung tree (*Aleurites fordii*):此地盛产~。This place is rich in tung trees.
油桶 yóutǒng oil drum
油头粉面 yóutóu-fěnmiàn sleek-haired and creamy-faced — coquettish or dandified in appearance:~的年轻人 dandified young man /~的妇女 heavily made-up woman
油头滑脑 yóutóu-huánǎo slick; glib; flippant:此人~很不实在。The man looked slick and dishonest.
油汪汪 yóuwāngwāng ❶ dripping with oil; greasy:这菜炒得~的,一看就腻了。A mere look at this greasy dish would spoil one's appetite. ❷ glossy; shiny:~的麦苗儿 shiny green wheat seedlings
油位 yóuwèi 〈机械〉oil level
油位表 yóuwèibiǎo oil (level) gauge
油污 yóuwū greasy dirt or filth:满身~ with greasy dirt all over the person
油箱 yóuxiāng fuel tank:~爆炸 fuel tank explosion /副~ auxiliary fuel tank; auxiliary tank
油香 yóuxiang cakes made of mixed flour, water and salt fried in sesame oil for Moslems
油鞋 yóuxié old fashioned galoshes (for use in wet weather)
油星 yóuxīng *also* "油星子" oil blobs:菜里一点~都没有。There is not even a single drop of oil in the dish.
油性 yóuxìng containing much oil or grease:这东西~太大。It's too fatty.
油靴 yóuxuē *see* "油鞋"
油压 yóuyā 〈机械〉oil pressure
油压泵 yóuyābèng oil pressure pump
油压表 yóuyābiǎo oil pressure gauge
油压传动 yóuyā chuándòng hydraulic transmission
油压机 yóuyājī hydraulic (oil) press
油压计 yóuyājì fuel pressure gauge
油压减震器 yóuyā jiǎnzhènqì oleo-gear
油压千斤顶 yóuyā qiānjīndǐng hydraulic or oil jack
油烟 yóuyān ❶ *also* "油烟子" soot ❷ lampblack
油椰子 yóuyēzi *see* "油棕"
油页岩 yóuyèyán oil shale
油衣 yóuyī 〈方言〉raincoat made of oilcloth; oilskins; slicker
油印 yóuyìn mimeograph:~的材料 mimeographed materials /~五十份 mimeograph 50 copies
油印机 yóuyìnjī mimeograph
油印蜡纸 yóuyìn làzhǐ stencil; stencil paper
油油 yóuyóu 〈书面〉❶ sleek; glossy; shiny:禾黍~ shiny green crops ❷ floating; moving:江水~ flowing water in the river ❸ luxuriant; natural:~然充满生机 luxuriant and vigorous
油浴 yóuyù 〈化学〉oil bath
油渣 yóuzhā ❶ dregs of fat ❷ 〈石油〉oil residue
油渣果 yóuzhāguǒ *see* "油瓜"
油炸 yóuzhá deep-fry:~土豆片 French fries; chips
油炸鬼 yóuzhágui deep-fried dough stick or doughnut
油毡 yóuzhān *also* "油毛毡"〈建筑〉asphalt felt
油盏 yóuzhǎn 〈方言〉oil lamp
油樟 yóuzhāng *also* "香樟" xiāngzhāng camphor tree
油脂 yóuzhī oil; fat:植物~ vegetable fat (*or* oil) /动物~ animal fat (*or* oil); tallow; grease
油脂麻花 yóuzhi-máhuā *also* "油渍麻花"〈方言〉be covered with oil stains; greasy:看你的衣服~的,也该洗一洗了。You should wash your jacket. It's covered all over with grease stains.
油纸 yóuzhǐ oilpaper:破旧的~伞 worn-out oilpaper umbrella
油籽 yóuzǐ oilseed
油渍 yóuzì greasy filth; oily dirt
油子 yóuzi ❶ black sticky substance; gunk:烟袋~ tar inside a tobacco pipe ❷ foxy old hand:老~ foxy old fellow /他是一个有名的京~。He is a wily old Beijinger known to all.
油棕 yóuzōng 〈植物〉oil palm (*Elaeis guineensis*)
油嘴 yóuzuǐ ❶ glib; sleek; unctuous:这小子生就一张~。This young man was born with a glib tongue. ❷ glib talker ❸ spray nozzle; spray head
油嘴滑舌 yóuzuǐ-huáshé glib-tongued; slick:~的推销员 slick salesman

柚 yóu

see also yòu
柚木 yóumù 〈植物〉teak:上好的~家具 high quality teak furniture /~贴面的写字台 teak-faced desk

蚰 yóu

蚰蜒 yóuyan 〈动物〉common house centipede
蚰蜒草 yóuyancǎo alpine yarrow (*Achillea alpina*)

铀 yóu

〈化学〉uranium (U):天然~ native uranium /~矿石 uranium ore /浓缩~ enriched uranium /低浓缩~ low-enrichment uranium
铀棒 yóubàng uranium bar
铀玻璃 yóubōli uranium glass
铀弹 yóudàn 〈军事〉U-bomb
铀反应堆 yóufǎnyìngduī uranium reactor
铀钙石 yóugàishí uranothallite
铀后元素 yóuhòu yuánsù 〈化学〉transuranium element; transuranium
铀沥青 yóulìqīng pitch uranium
铀浓缩 yóunóngsuō uranium enrichment
铀前元素 yóuqián yuánsù 〈化学〉cis-uranium element
铀石 yóushí coffinite
铀试剂 yóushìjì uranol
铀酸 yóusuān 〈化学〉uranic acid:~盐 uranate
铀添加合金 yóutiānjiā héjīn uranium additive alloy
铀钍反应堆 yóutǔ fǎnyìngduī uranium-thorium reactor
铀系 yóuxì 〈化学〉uranides; uranium series:~元素 uranide
铀云母 yóuyúnmǔ uranite

鲉 yóu

〈动物〉scorpionfish

邮(郵) yóu

❶ post; mail:~一封信 post a letter /~五十元钱 send a 50 *yuan* postal order /包裹~了吗? Have you mailed the parcel? ❷ postal; mail: *see* "~局";"~票" ❸ stamps:集~ collect stamps; go in for philately
邮包 yóubāo postal parcel; parcel:~保险 parcel post insurance /

Y

他给家里寄去了一个～。He posted a parcel home.
邮编 yóubiān (short for 邮政编码) postcode; zip code
邮差 yóuchāi 〈旧语〉postman
邮车 yóuchē postal or mail car:快把邮件装上～。Come on, load the mails onto the postal car.
邮传 yóuchuán 〈书面〉postal or mail delivery
邮船 yóuchuán (ocean) liner; packet ship:一艘直达大连的～ packet ship headed direct for Dalian
邮戳 yóuchuō postmark:盖～ put a postmark on; postmark /盖有东京～的信 letter postmarked Tokyo /征文截稿日期为四月三日,以当地～为准。The deadline for the submission of requested articles is April 3, judging by the date of the postmark by the sending post office.
邮袋 yóudài postbag; mailbag; (mail) pouch:外交～ diplomatic pouch
邮递 yóudì ❶ send by post or mail ❷ postal or mail delivery:～路线 mail route /～工作亟待改进。Postal delivery must be improved as soon as possible.
邮递员 yóudìyuán postman; mailman
邮电 yóudiàn post and telecommunications:～业务 postal and telecommunication service /～部门 department of posts and telecommunications /～学校 post and telecommunication school
邮电部 yóudiànbù Ministry of Post and Telecommunications
邮电局 yóudiànjú post and telecommunication office:～局长 post and telecommunication master; director of a post and telecommunication office
邮费 yóufèi postage:调整～ adjust postage /～免收 post-free
邮封纸 yóufēngzhǐ a kind of packaging paper, one side of which is smooth
邮购 yóugòu buy or purchase by mail or postal order:～英语教学磁带五盘 buy five English-teaching tapes by mail order /～部 mail order department
邮花 yóuhuā 〈方言〉stamp
邮汇 yóuhuì remit by post:货款直接～到商店。The money for the purchase will be remitted direct to the department store by post.
邮集 yóují stamp-album
邮寄 yóujì send by post; post:这批资料一律～,不必随身携带。You may send the whole lot of materials by post and don't have to take them along with you.
邮件 yóujiàn postal matter; post; mail:快递～ express mail /航空～ air mail /普通～ ordinary mail /挂号～ registered mail /小包～ postal packet
邮件服务器 yóujiàn fúwùqì 〈信息〉mail server
邮件网关 yóujiàn wǎngguān 〈信息〉mail gateway
邮局 yóujú post office:全市～共有几百所。There are several hundred post offices in the city.
邮路 yóulù postal or mail route:不通～ not served by a mail route /几年前～已通到这个小山村。Postal service for this small mountain village started a few years ago.
邮轮 yóulún *see* "邮船"
邮票 yóupiào postage stamp; stamp:纪念～ commemorative stamp /特种～ special stamp /无齿孔～ imperforate (stamp) /欠资～ postage-due stamp
邮区 yóuqū postal district; postal zone:～号码 postal zone number; postal code
邮售 yóushòu sell by mail order
邮坛 yóután philately community or circles:世界～ world philatelic community
邮亭 yóutíng postal kiosk:～附设报刊销售处。There are newspapers and periodicals for sale in the postal kiosk.
邮筒 yóutǒng pillar box; postbox; mailbox:把信投入～ put a letter into the pillar box
邮务 yóuwù postal service
邮箱 yóuxiāng postbox; mailbox:为了方便居民,他们添置了两个～。For the convenience of the residents, two more mailboxes were installed.
邮展 yóuzhǎn philatelic exhibition; stamp show:国际～ international stamp exhibition
邮政 yóuzhèng postal service:～业务 postal operations /～规程 postal regulations
邮政包裹 yóuzhèng bāoguǒ postal parcel
邮政编码 yóuzhèng biānmǎ postcode; zip code; zip
邮政车 yóuzhèngchē post truck; post office vehicle; mail bus; mail car; mail motor truck:厢式～ mail van; mail wagon
邮政储蓄 yóuzhèng chǔxù postal savings (deposit)
邮政代办所 yóuzhèng dàibànsuǒ postal agency
邮政汇票 yóuzhèng huìpiào postal (money) order
邮政局 yóuzhèngjú post office:～局长 postmaster
邮政网 yóuzhèngwǎng postal network
邮政信箱 yóuzhèng xìnxiāng post-office box (POB)
邮资 yóuzī postage:～总付 postage prepaid /～不足 postage underpaid; postage due /～已付 postage paid; postpaid /包括～在内共二十元 twenty *yuan* altogether including postage

繇

yóu 〈书面〉*see* "由 ❻❼" yóu
see also yáo; zhòu

圝

yóu
圝子 yóuzi *also* "游子" yóuzi decoy

yǒu

莠

yǒu ❶ *also* "狗尾草" gǒuwěicǎo green bristlegrass ❷ 〈书面〉bad (people):不分良～ not distinguishing between the bad and the good /良～不齐。The good and the bad are intermingled.

酉

yǒu tenth of the twelve Earthly Branches
see also "干支" gānzhī
酉时 yǒushí 〈旧语〉period of the day from 5 p.m. to 7 p.m.:他是五月初六～生人。He was born between 5 p.m. and 7 p.m. on the sixth of the fifth lunar month.

槱

yǒu 〈书面〉gather wood for a fire

有

yǒu ❶ have; own; possess:你～没有《石头记》? Do you have a copy of *The Story of the Stone*? /这家小工厂只～一台新式机床。The small factory possesses (*or* boasts) only one modern lathe. /他既～热情,又～干劲儿。He is full of enthusiasm and drive. /这份遗产归他所～。This portion of the legacy belongs to him. /你真～两下子! You really are smart! ❷ there is; exist:事情大～改进的余地。There is plenty of room for improvement. /天气预报说,明天～大雨。The weather forecast says that we are going to have heavy rain tomorrow. ❸ *used for estimation or comparison*:你～一米八吧? You are about 1.80 metres tall, aren't you? /你弟弟～你高吗? Is your brother as tall as you are? /她～那么聪明吗? Is she that intelligent? /这条鱼大概～三斤重。The fish weighs approximately 1.5 kilos. ❹ *used to indicate that sth. takes place or appears*:情况～了新的变化。There was a new change in the situation. /事情忽然～了转机。The matter suddenly took a turn for the better. /～了病就该去找医生。One should go and see a doctor as soon as one is ill. /最近小王各方面都～进步。Recently Xiao Wang has made progress in every respect. ❺ *used to indicate ample amount*:他管理很～经验。He is very experienced in management. /她富～才华。She is a woman of great talent. /～了年纪的人要注意保养。Those who are getting on in years should take good care of their health. ❻ *used in a general sense, similar to the meaning of* 某:～些事还需要从长计议。Certain things need to be given further thought and deliberation. /～一天我去看过他。I went to see him the other day. /～一个下午他来得特别晚。He came especially late one afternoon. /～人这样告诉我。Someone told me so. ❼ *used before people, time, or place to indicate a part*:～人赞成,～人反对。Some are for it, others are against it. /这里～时候很热,～时候又很冷。It is sometimes very hot and sometimes very cold here. /这个办法在～的地方适用,～的地方却行不通。This method is applicable in some places but not in others. ❽ *used before certain verbs to form polite formulae*: *see* "～劳"; "～请" ❾ 〈书面〉*prefix used before the names of dynasties*:～宋一代 Song Dynasty
see also yòu
有碍 yǒu'ài hinder; obstruct; affect (adversely):～生产 hinder production /～风化 adversely affect morals and manners /于面子～ hurt one's feelings (*or* sensibilities) /～卫生 be bad for public sanitation

有碍观瞻 yǒu'ài guānzhān offend the eye; be unpleasant to look at; be an eyesore:校园里乱扔字纸,~。It's unsightly to leave scrap paper scattered all over the campus.

有案可稽 yǒu'àn-kějī *also* "有案可查" be on record; be documented:这是~的事情。This matter has been documented. /这一系列的侵略活动都~。There are records about these acts of aggression.

有板有眼 yǒubǎn-yǒuyǎn rhythmical; measured; orderly; systematic:他发言的时候,态度不慌不忙,语句~。When he spoke, he was unhurried and his words were well measured. /他说得~,叫人没法不信。What he said was well argued. People could not but believe him.

有备无患 yǒubèi-wúhuàn where there is precaution, there is no danger; preparedness averts peril; be prepared; get ready:老人早就在准备过冬的柴火,为的是~,免得临时抓瞎。The old man started to collect firewood for the winter very early so that he would get prepared and would not be in a rush when winter came.

有鼻子有眼儿 yǒubízi-yǒuyǎnr with every detail vividly described; show or portray sth. or sb. to the life:她把这事儿说得~的,谁还怀疑呢? Who could have doubted it since she described the whole thing in such vivid detail?

有差 yǒuchā 〈书面〉differentiate; distinguish:赏罚~ be discriminating in rewards and punishments

有产阶级 yǒuchǎnjiējí propertied class

有产者 yǒuchǎnzhě man of property

有偿 yǒucháng compensated with payment:~服务 paid service

有成 yǒuchéng 〈书面〉score success; succeed:三年~ achieve success in three years /计划可望~ can expect the plan to succeed

有酬劳动 yǒuchóu láodòng *also* "有偿劳动"〈经济〉paid labour

有错必纠 yǒucuò-bìjiū a wrong must be righted when done:~,这是我们的一条方针。It is our policy to correct mistakes wherever made.

有待 yǒudài remain (to be done); be pending; await:事故如何处理~上级决定。The handling of the accident remains to be decided upon by the higher authorities. /论点正确与否还~证明。The correctness of the argument has yet to be proved. /问题~进一步研究。The matter awaits further consideration.

有袋动物 yǒudài dòngwù marsupial

有担保贷款 yǒudānbǎo dàikuǎn secured loan

有道 yǒudào have attained the Way; uphold truth and principle; be just and sagacious:~明君 sagacious ruler /国~。The country has a wise and clean government.

有得 yǒudé what one has learned from work, study, etc.:钻研~ have obtained understanding through assiduous study /读书~ have gained sth. from reading

有的 yǒude some:这些办法~大家同意,~没有同意。Some of these methods have been approved while others have been rejected.

有的是 yǒudeshì have plenty of; be in abundance; there is no lack of:办法~。There is no lack of methods. /这种人我们单位~。We have plenty of such people in our unit. /退休后她~时间。She had all the time in the world after retirement.

有底 yǒudǐ know what's what; be fully prepared for what is coming:经你这么一说,我心里就~了。After your explanation I now know how things stand and feel confident.

有的放矢 yǒudì-fàngshǐ shoot one's arrow at the target — have a definite object in view; do sth. with a definite purpose in mind:写文章要~。When writing an article, one must have something to write about.

Y

有点 yǒudiǎn ❶ some; small amount; a little:口袋里还~钱。There is still some money in my pocket. /这幅漫画很~意思。This caricature is quite meaningful. ❷〈副词〉(usu. used of sth. unfavourable) somewhat; rather; a bit:我~不舒服。I am a bit under the weather. /她~骄傲自满。She is somewhat arrogant and complacent. /他~生你气了。He is rather angry with you.

有毒 yǒudú poisonous; toxic:~废料 toxic wastes /~排放物 toxic discharge /~鱼类 ichthyotoxic fishes /~植物 poisonous plant

有法必依 yǒufǎ-bìyī ensure that laws be observed:~,执法必严,违法必究。Laws must be observed and strictly enforced and violators must be brought to justice.

有法可依 yǒufǎ-kěyī there are laws to go by:~,有法必依。There are laws to go by and they must be obeyed.

有方 yǒufāng with the proper method; in the right way; methodically:指导~ give proper guidance /布局~ be becomingly laid out

有分量 yǒu fènliang weighty; significant:~的讲话 weighty remarks; statement that carries weight /~的国家 country of consequence (*or* importance)

有份儿 yǒufènr take a part in; have a share:功劳~,责任无干 take a share of the credit but none of the responsibility /奖金不该人人~。Not everyone should have a share of bonus.

有福同享,有祸同当 yǒu fú tóng xiǎng, yǒu huò tóng dāng share happiness and suffering; share weal and woe; stick together through thick and thin:咱穷人家一向都是~。Well, we poor folk share joys and sorrows together. /我们一定要~。Let us share good luck as well as bad luck.

有感 yǒugǎn thoughts or reflections on sth.:读书~ thoughts on a book /观光~ reflections on a sightseeing trip

有感地震 yǒugǎn dìzhèn 〈地质〉felt earthquake

有根 yǒugēn ❶ *see* "有底" ❷ with reason; well-grounded:姑娘听他说得~,也就信了。The girl believed what he said, for he sounded quite reasonable. ❸ have powerful backing:这个人~,不可小看他。Don't underrate him. He has all the right connections (*or* He is well connected).

有功 yǒugōng ❶ have made great contribution; have performed meritorious service:~之臣 official who has done meritorious service /~人员 people with a fine record of service /他对革命~,对这个家也~。He contributed to the revolution as well as to the family. ❷〈电工〉active:~电流 active current /~电压 active voltage /~功率 active power

有功不赏,有罪不罚 yǒugōng bù shǎng, yǒuzuì bù fá merit is not rewarded, while crime is not punished:如果~,这个国家的事情就麻烦了。A nation will get into trouble if virtue is not rewarded and vice not punished.

有骨头 yǒu gǔtou ❶ have strength of character; have backbone:~的人 man of integrity ❷〈方言〉carry a sting (in one's words):他的话里~。There is a catch (*or* sting) in his remarks.

有关 yǒuguān ❶ have sth. to do with; bear on; relate to; concern:~当局 authorities concerned; competent (*or* relevant) authorities /~方面 the parties concerned /~机构 related organizations (*or* institutions) /此事跟领导~。The matter concerned the leadership. /这几个问题都和经费~。All these problems are related to funds. /这件事与人民群众的生活水平直接~。The matter has a direct bearing on the people's living standards. ❷ concerning; regarding; as to; relevant to:~提高产品质量的问题必须尽快解决。The matter concerning the improvement of product quality must be dealt with immediately. /~人的处理理应慎重。As to (*or* for) the handling of people, it ought to be done with great care. *or* People should be handled with great care.

有光 yǒuguāng ❶ glazed ❷〈纺织〉bright:~人造丝 bright rayon

有光纸 yǒuguāngzhǐ (machine glazed) cap paper; glazed paper

有轨电车 yǒuguǐ diànchē tramcar; streetcar:那时北京只有~。At that time there were only tramcars in Beijing.

有鬼 yǒuguǐ there is sth. fishy; smell a rat; have a guilty conscience:他这样做是因为心中~。He did so because he had a guilty conscience. /此事一定~。There must be something fishy about the matter. /我一听说这事便感到其中~。I smelt a rat the moment I heard of this.

有过之无不及 yǒu guò zhī wú bùjí (mostly used in a bad sense) go even farther than; outdo:在欺压讹诈方面,他比其前任~。He outdid his predecessor in bullying and blackmailing.

有害 yǒuhài harmful; injurious; pernicious; detrimental:对青少年十分~ be very harmful to teenagers /~于两国的友好关系 be detrimental to the friendly relations between the two countries /对健康~ hazardous (*or* injurious) to health /产生~结果 produce (*or* cause) damaging results /这种做法对安定团结~无利。This practice undermines unity and stability.

有行无市 yǒuháng-wúshì (of a market) have only quotations but no actual trading

有核国家 yǒuhé guójiā nuclear state or power

有恒 yǒuhéng persevering:治学贵在~。Perseverance is essential to study.

有会子 yǒuhuìzi *also* "有会儿" quite a while; quite some time:可~没见你啦! Haven't seen you for quite a while.

有机 yǒujī ❶〈化学〉organic:~半导体 organic semiconductor /~氮 organonitrogen /~硅 organosilicon /~金属化合物 organometallic compound; pantamethide /~可变电容器 polymer-variable condenser

/～磷 organophosphorus /～卤素 organic-halogens /～膨润土 organobentonite /～盐 organic salt ❷〈比喻〉organic; intrinsic:～的整体 organic whole /事物之间的～关系 intrinsic relationships between things /～组成部分 component part

有机玻璃 yǒujī bōli organic glass; polymethyl methacrylate; plexiglass; perspex

有机肥料 yǒujī féiliào organic fertilizer; manure

有机耕作 yǒujī gēngzuò organic farming; organic gardening

有机合成 yǒujī héchéng organic synthesis

有机化合物 yǒujī huàhéwù organic chemical compound

有机化学 yǒujī huàxué organic chemistry

有机界 yǒujījiè bios

有机进化 yǒujī jìnhuà organic evolution

有机可乘 yǒujī-kěchéng opportunity to take advantage of; loophole that can be exploited:他以为～,想敲我们的竹杠。Thinking that he had found a loophole, he tried to fleece us.

有机染料 yǒujī rǎnliào organic dyestuff

有机溶胶 yǒujī róngjiāo organosol

有机酸 yǒujīsuān *also*"羧酸" suōsuān organic acid:～症〈医学〉organacidia

有机体 yǒujītǐ organism

有机土 yǒujītǔ histosol

有机物 yǒujīwù organic matter:～冷却堆 organic-cooled reactor /～慢化反应堆 organic-moderated reactor

有机质 yǒujīzhì organic substance

有奇 yǒujī 〈书面〉(used after round numbers) odd:年八十～ over eighty years old

有计划 yǒu jìhuà have a plan; do sth. in a planned way:～地发展经济 develop the economy in a planned way

有加利 yǒujiālì *also*"桉" ān 〈植物〉(transliteration) eucalyptus

有加无已 yǒujiā-wúyǐ increasingly; in an ever increasing degree:她的病情～。Her illness has got increasingly worse. /捐税～。Taxes are getting heavier.

有价证券 yǒujià zhèngquàn negotiable securities; securities:～交易所 securities exchange

有奸 yǒujiān commit adultery

有间 yǒujiàn 〈书面〉❶ in a while; in a moment:～,大雨如注。Presently, it began to pour with rain. ❷ (of illness) get slightly better; be improving ❸ grudge; feeling of animosity:二人素～。There was no love lost between them.

有奖储蓄 yǒujiǎng chǔxù lottery-attached deposit

有奖债券 yǒujiǎng zhàiquàn premium bond

有教无类 yǒujiào-wúlèi (a saying of Confucius) in education, there should be no distinction of social status

有节 yǒujié with restraint; having a sense of proportion

有劲 yǒujìn ❶ have great physical strength ❷ with keen interest:他越讲越～。The more he talked the more enthusiastic he became.

有旧 yǒujiù 〈书面〉had been on good terms; be of long-standing friendship:我和他～,我去求他也许行。We are old friends. Maybe I can get him to help.

有救 yǒujiù can be saved, cured, or remedied:孩子终于～了! The child could be saved at last!

有孔虫 yǒukǒngchóng foraminifer

有空儿 yǒukòngr have time; be free:～请来我这里一趟。Please drop in when you have time.

有口皆碑 yǒukǒu-jiēbēi be praised by everyone; win universal commendation; be universally acclaimed:他舍身救人的英雄行为,广泛传播,～。The news of his heroic conduct of saving others at the cost of his own life spread from mouth to mouth, and won universal acclaim.

有口难分 yǒukǒu-nánfēn *also*"有口难辩" find it difficult to defend or vindicate oneself:面对假证,她～,只一个劲儿地流眼泪。Confronted with false evidence she found it impossible to vindicate herself, and her tears kept rolling down.

有口难言 yǒukǒu-nányán cannot bring oneself to mention sth.; find it hard or embarrassing to bring up a matter; be unable to speak out:官吏们无心正法,使百姓～。When the officials show no justice, the people dare not speak their mind.

有口无心 yǒukǒu-wúxīn be sharp-tongued but mean no malice:她这人性子直,一向是～,你可别和她计较。She is blunt and sharp-tongued but not malicious (*or* Her bark is worse than her bite), so don't take her words too seriously.

有愧 yǒukuì feel guilty or qualms about sth.:问心～ have a guilty conscience

有来有往 yǒulái-yǒuwǎng give and take; be reciprocal:两家～,关系密切。The two families are on good terms, often visiting each other.

有赖 yǒulài rely on; rest on:如期完成任务,～于大家的共同努力。Whether or not the task can be accomplished as scheduled depends on the concerted efforts of all of us.

有劳 yǒuláo polite formula used to ask others to do sth. or thank others for having done sth.:～您代我发一封电报。Would you be so kind as to (*or* May I trouble you) to send a telegram for me? /这件事实在～您了。I deeply appreciate what you have done on this matter.

有劳有逸 yǒuláo-yǒuyì work and rest:工作要～。We must alternate work with rest.

有落儿 yǒulàor 〈方言〉have assured source of income:她母女俩的生活总算～了。At last, mother and daughter were financially provided for.

有了 yǒule ❶ (as an exclamation) I've got it! ❷〈婉词〉be pregnant:听说她～。It's said that she is in an interesting condition.

有理 yǒulǐ reasonable; in the right; (have) justice on one's side:～、有利、有节 on just grounds, to our advantage, with restraint /他说得～。What he said was reasonable. /我们～,不怕他胡闹。We are in the right and not afraid of his kicking up a row.

有理方程 yǒulǐ fāngchéng rational equation

有理分式 yǒulǐ fēnshì (shortened as 分式) rational fraction

有理函数 yǒulǐ hánshù rational function

有理式 yǒulǐshì rational expression

有理数 yǒulǐshù rational number

有理无情 yǒulǐ-wúqíng ❶ not spare sb.'s personal feelings (*or* sensibilities) ❷ for no apparent reason:～地白跑了一趟 have made a futile trip

有理走遍天下,无理寸步难行 yǒulǐ zǒubiàn tiānxià, wúlǐ cùn bù nán xíng with justice on your side, you can go anywhere; without it, you can't take a step

有力 yǒulì strong; mighty; powerful; vigorous:给予～的支持 give strong (*or* effective) support /进行～的回击 give a powerful rebuff /提出～的论据 advance convincing argument /简短～ terse and forceful /～地进行针锋相对的斗争 wage a vigorous tit-for-tat struggle /～无处使 have little room for exercising one's abilities

有利 yǒulì advantageous; conducive; beneficial; favourable:～地形 favourable terrain /～时机 opportune time /既～于国家,又～于个人 be of benefit not only to the state but also to the individual /～于改善干群关系 be conducive to the improvement of relations between cadres and the masses /～于提高领导的威信 help enhance the prestige of the leaders /国际舆论对我们～。World opinion is to our advantage (*or* is favourable to us).

有利可图 yǒulì-kětú have good prospects of gain; stand to profit; be profitable:他这样拼命干,是因为～。He is working for all he is worth because there is profit to be reaped.

有利无弊 yǒulì-wúbì have all the advantages and not a single disadvantage

有利有弊 yǒulì-yǒubì have both merits and demerits; have advantages as well as disadvantages:天下事有利必有弊。Everything has its drawbacks as well as benefits.

有脸 yǒuliǎn have prestige; have face:孩子们有成绩,做父母的也～。The achievement of the children do credit to their parents. /你也～去见他? So you have the cheek to see him!

有两下子 yǒu liǎngxiàzi have real skill; be quite skilful; know one's stuff:想不到他还真～,很快就把饭菜烧好了。He really knows the ropes. To our surprise he had the meal ready in a jiffy.

有零 yǒulíng odd:四十～ forty odd /一百～ just over a hundred

有令不行,有禁不止 yǒu lìng bù xíng, yǒu jìn bù zhǐ disobey orders and defy prohibitions:～,各行其事 go one's own way in disregard of orders and prohibitions

有眉目 yǒu méimu begin to take shape; begin to see light:建宿舍楼的事儿～了。It's more or less definite that they are going to put up a residence building.

有门儿 yǒuménr ❶ begin to find a solution; be hopeful (of success):看样子,这事～了! It looks as if there is hope of getting it started (*or* done). /你想改变她的看法,我看不大～。I don't believe it's possible for you to change her view. ❷ get the hang:他在计算机室泡了半个多月,才算有点门儿。He buried himself in the computer

room for more than two weeks before he began to get the hang of it.

有名 yǒumíng well-known; noted; famous; celebrated: ～的古诗 well-known classic poem /～的地方 noted place /他是～的京剧表演艺术家。He is a celebrated Beijing opera performer. /她是～的跳水运动员。She is a renowned diver. /四川的小吃很～。Sichuan snacks are famous.

有名无实 yǒumíng-wúshí in name but not in reality; in name only; merely nominal; titular: ～的冒牌货 mere imitation /协会下面的几个委员会都是～。The committees under the association exist only in name.

有名有姓 yǒumíng-yǒuxìng identifiable by both name and surname — of established identity; of some repute: 你可别小看他，他也是～的人物。Don't you underestimate him. He is a somebody.

有目共睹 yǒumù-gòngdǔ be there for all to see; be obvious to all; be as clear as day: 改革开放以来取得的成绩是～的。The achievements since the implementation of the policy of reform and opening to the outside world are there for all to see.

有目共赏 yǒumù-gòngshǎng have a universal appeal: 北海的灯会，千姿百态，～。The Lantern Festival in Beihai Park, with lanterns of all shapes and designs, appealed to all alike.

有奶便是娘 yǒu nǎi biànshì niáng 〈俗语〉 whoever suckles me is my mother; submit oneself to anyone who feeds one; dance to the tune of those who pay one: 他这人～，哪管什么原则、交情等等。He would lick the hand of anyone who threw him a few crumbs, caring nothing about principles or friendship.

有你的 yǒunǐde ❶ good for you: 事儿办得漂亮，真～! It's beautifully done! You're really something! ❷ you'll suffer for it: ～，咱们走着瞧! Well, let's wait and see. You will get your come-uppance!

有年 yǒunián 〈书面〉 for years: 习艺～，技巧纯熟。Having been practising the art for many years he is highly skilled.

有盼儿 yǒupànr 〈方言〉 have hope for; become hopeful: 眼看孩子一天天长大，她觉得未来的日子～了。Seeing the child grow up day by day she felt hopeful about the future.

有偏 yǒupiān 〈套语〉 have already had one's meal

有凭有据 yǒupíng-yǒujù fully substantiated; well-grounded: 他说得～，人人信以为真。Everybody believed him since his statement seemed to be well-founded.

有谱儿 yǒupǔr 〈方言〉 know what's what: 该怎么办，我心里～。I know very well what to do and how.

有期徒刑 yǒuqī túxíng 〈法律〉 set term of imprisonment: 被判～三年 be sentenced to three years' imprisonment

有其父，必有其子 yǒu qí fù, bì yǒu qí zǐ like father, like son: ～，这孩子将来准是个人物。As is the father, so is the son. The child is sure to take the world by storm in the future.

有气 yǒuqì get angry; take offence; be in a fit of pique: 我一见到他就～。I get angry at the sight of him.

有气儿 yǒuqìr be breathing: 快救救他吧，他还～。Please help him and be quick. He's still breathing!

有气无力 yǒuqì-wúlì listless; feeble; faint and weak: 两天粒米未进，他饿得～了。Not having had any food for two days he became very weak from starvation.

有钱 yǒuqián rich; affluent; wealthy: ～的大少爷 eldest son of a rich family /他家很～。His family is wealthy.

有钱买马，无钱置鞍 yǒuqián mǎi mǎ, wúqián zhì ān 〈俗语〉 have money to buy a horse but no money to buy a saddle — be ready to spend a large sum on sth. but not a little extra to make it work; be penny-wise and pound-foolish

有钱能使鬼推磨 yǒuqián néng shǐ guǐ tuīmò with money you can make the devil turn the millstone; money makes the mare go; money talks

有钱有势 yǒuqián-yǒushì have money and power; be wealthy and influential

有腔有调 yǒuqiāng-yǒudiào in a singsong voice; sonorous and rhythmic: 马先生把这几个字念得～的。Mr. Ma chanted these words in a musical voice.

有情 yǒuqíng ❶ be in love; be feeling: 他俩是男～，女有意。The love between the man and the woman is reciprocal. /天若～天亦老。Were Nature sentient, she too would pass from youth to age. ❷ 〈书面〉 interesting; appealing: 画外～。The painting has appealing implications.

有情人 yǒuqíngrén lovers; sweethearts

有情人终成眷属 yǒuqíngrén zhōng chéng juànshǔ 〈俗语〉 lovers are destined to be married; Jack shall have Jill, all shall be well

有情有义 yǒuqíng-yǒuyì affectionate and true; true and loyal

有顷 yǒuqǐng 〈书面〉 after a while; sometime later

有请 yǒuqǐng polite formula used to express the host's desire to see the guest: 老爷～先生书房相见。Would you please go to the study where the master is waiting?

有求必应 yǒuqiú-bìyìng respond to every plea; comply with every request: 我向他请教，他总是～。Every time I ask him for advice he is always ready to help.

有求于人 yǒuqiúyúrén ask a favour of sb.; need sb.'s help: 我们～，只好忍着点儿。Since we look to him for help, we have to put up with him.

有去无还 yǒuqù-wúhuán gone never to return: 他这次恐怕是～了。I'm afraid this time he will be gone forever.

有趣 yǒuqù interesting; amusing; fascinating; absorbing: 这故事很～。The story is quite interesting. /这次短期旅行非常～。The recent trip has been very exciting indeed. /他觉得生活变得越来越～。He feels that life is getting increasingly fascinating.

有染 yǒurǎn have illicit sexual relations; have an affair

有扰 yǒurǎo 〈套语〉 thanks for your hospitality: 今日多蒙款待，～了。Thank you very much for your warm reception.

有人家儿 yǒu rénjiār (of a woman) be engaged: 她早就～了。She's already engaged.

有日 yǒurì 〈书面〉 see "有日子"

有日子 yǒu rìzi ❶ for quite a few days; for some time: 咱俩～没闲聊了。We haven't had a chat for quite some time. /他出差已经～了。He's been away on business for days. ❷ have set a date: 这次会议～了没有? Has the date for the meeting been fixed?

有容乃大，无欲则刚 yǒuróng nǎi dà, wúyù zé gāng whoever is tolerant is great; whoever is unselfish is strong

有如 yǒurú just as; be like; as if: 他们侍奉这位孤寡老人～亲生父母。They waited on (*or* tended to) the old childless widower as if he'd been their own parent. /他俩好得～同胞兄弟。The two of them were as intimate as brothers.

有辱 yǒurǔ be a discredit or disgrace (to sb.): ～门楣 be a discredit to one's family /～斯文 be a disgrace to the educated

有色 yǒusè coloured: ～玻璃 coloured glass /～灯泡 coloured bulb

有色金属 yǒusè jīnshǔ nonferrous metal: ～研究所 institute of nonferrous metal

有色人种 yǒusè rénzhǒng coloured race or people: 不准歧视～。There must be no prejudice (*or* discrimination) against coloured people.

有色眼镜 yǒusè yǎnjìng coloured spectacles: 戴着～看人 look at people through coloured spectacles — be biased against sb.

有伤 yǒushāng be destructive or harmful to; offend against: ～风化 be harmful (*or* destructive) to the morals; offend against decency

有商量儿 yǒu shāngliangr can be discussed: 这事还能～。There is still room for discussion on the matter.

有身 yǒushēn *also* "有娠" 〈书面〉 be pregnant; be expecting; be with child

有身子 yǒushēnzi *see* "有身"

有神 yǒushén ❶ be miraculous: 下笔若～ write as if (endowed) with magic power ❷ full of vigour: 她的眼睛大而～。She has big, sparkling eyes.

有神论 yǒushénlùn theism: ～者 theist

有生 yǒushēng ❶ ever since one's birth: 他是～第一次坐飞机。This is the first time he has ever travelled by airplane. ❷ while still alive: ～之时一件未了的大事 important thing one wishes to do while still alive

有生力量 yǒushēng lìliàng ❶ effective troop strength; effectives: 这个机关编制虽大，～不多。Though it has a big payroll, the institution has very few effectives. ❷ troops; army: 保存我军实力，尽量消灭敌人的～。Preserve the strength of our own forces and wipe out as many enemy troops as possible.

有生以来 yǒushēng-yǐlái ever since one's birth: ～头一遭 first time in one's life (*or* in all one's born days) /～他还从未看见过海洋。He's never seen an ocean in all his life.

有生之年 yǒushēngzhīnián in one's remaining years: ～一定要完成这部书稿。I hope I shall live to finish the book.

有声 yǒushēng ❶ having sound: ～图书馆 audio-library ❷ 〈书面〉

have a good reputation

有声片儿 yǒushēngpiānr see "有声片"

有声片 yǒushēngpiàn sound film; phonofilm; talkie

有声有色 yǒushēng-yǒusè full of sound and colour; vivid and dramatic; spirited: 导演出许多～、威武雄壮的戏剧 direct the performance of many a drama, full of sound and colour, power and grandeur / 他把事情的经过讲述得～。He gave a spirited (*or* vivid, *or* graphic) description of how it happened.

有失身份 yǒushī shēnfèn beneath one's dignity: 大使参加这样的活动，～。It is beneath the dignity of an ambassador to attend such activities.

有识 yǒushí 〈书面〉 have vision; be far-sighted

有识之士 yǒushízhīshì person with breadth of vision; person of great discernment; man of insight: 世间不乏～。There is no lack of insightful people in this world.

有时 yǒushí sometimes; at times; from time to time: 最近天气变化无常，～冷，～热。The weather has been changeable (*or* fickle) recently; sometimes cold, sometimes hot. / 他～喜欢哼几句京剧。He likes to hum a few lines of Beijing opera now and then.

有史以来 yǒushǐ-yǐlái since the beginning or dawn of history; throughout history: ～最大的骗局 biggest fraud ever / 他种的小麦，创造了当地～的最高产量。The yield of wheat he grew set the highest record in history in the locality.

有始无终 yǒushǐ-wúzhōng start sth. but fail to carry it through to the end: 做事～，是他最大的毛病。His biggest defect was the failure to carry through what he had started. / 他没想到，这工作就这样～地收了场。He never thought that the work would tail off like this.

有始有终 yǒushǐ-yǒuzhōng manage sth. from beginning to end; carry sth. through: 不管干什么都应该持之以恒，～。One must have perseverance and stick it out in whatever one does.

有事 yǒushì ❶ have a job; be employed: 他现在～，每月有固定的收入。Now he has a job with a regular income. / 毕业不久他就～了。He got employment not long after graduation. ❷ be engaged; be occupied; be busy: 星期天我～，不能进城了。I will not be able to go to town on Sunday as I am occupied. / 明天你～吗? Have you anything on tomorrow? *or* Are you free tomorrow? ❸ when sth. untoward happens; get into trouble; meet with an accident: 我看不会～，你放心去吧。I don't think anything would happen, so don't worry and just go. / 一旦～，大家都会来帮忙。Should there be an accident, we'll all come to your help. ❹ have sth. on one's mind; worry: 看他这样子，心里一定～。The look on his face tells deep worry.

有恃无恐 yǒushì-wúkǒng secure in the knowledge that one has strong backing; emboldened by sb.'s support; fear nothing with sb. at one's back: 有金融界的支持，难怪他那么～! No wonder he feared nothing because he enjoyed strong support from the financial world.

有数 yǒushù ❶ know exactly how things stand; know the score: 他心里早已～，只是没说出来。He already knew exactly how things stood. Only he didn't speak out. / 凡事都要做到心中～，切忌盲目乱来。One should have a definite idea of what one's doing and must not act recklessly and blindly. ❷ not many; only a few: 离交稿的日期只剩下～的几天了，不加把劲儿怎么成呢? There are only a few days left before the deadline for handing in the draft. How can you make it if you do not put in more effort?

有说有笑 yǒushuō-yǒuxiào talk and laugh: 几个人～地在聊天。Several people were chatting and laughing merrily together.

有司 yǒusī 〈书面〉 government official: 不敢得罪～ dare not offend the authorities

有丝分裂 yǒusī fēnliè 〈生物〉 mitosis: ～因子 mitogenic factor

有素 yǒusù ❶ be constantly engaged in: 训练～ be well trained ❷ 〈书面〉 have known sb. for a long time: 与某人～ have long been friends with sb.

有所 yǒusuǒ to some extent; some; somewhat: ～保留 have reservations / ～减少 have somewhat reduced (*or* decreased) / ～增加 increased to some extent / 你～不知。There are some things you don't know. / 谈判～进展。There has been some progress in the negotiations (*or* talks).

有所不为而后可以有所为 yǒusuǒ bù wéi érhòu kěyǐ yǒusuǒ wéi leave some things undone in order to do other things

有蹄动物 yǒutí dòngwù ungulate (animal)

有蹄类 yǒutílèi ungulate class (of animals)

有天无日 yǒutiān-wúrì *also* "有天没日" ❶ wanton; unbridled; impudent: 你可别听他那些～的话。Pay no attention to his outrageous remarks. ❷ utter darkness — absence of justice

有条不紊 yǒutiáo-bùwěn in apple-pie order; methodically; systematically: 他把屋子收拾得整整齐齐，～。He tidied up the room, putting everything in good order. / 文章层次分明，～。The article is well organized and systematically argued.

有条有理 yǒutiáo-yǒulǐ methodical; orderly: 他事事都～。He is methodical in everything he does.

有头无尾 yǒutóu-wúwěi have a beginning but no end; give up sth. halfway: 做事不可～。One mustn't leave anything unfinished.

有头有脸 yǒutóu-yǒuliǎn have fame or a good reputation; enjoy prestige: 他是县里～的人物，谁都敬畏他三分。He was quite a personage in the county and was held in awe and veneration.

有头有脑 yǒutóu-yǒunǎo be well organized; be methodical: 他办事～，你就放心吧。He does things in a methodical way. You needn't worry. / 她说起话来～。She is a well-organized speaker.

有头有尾 yǒutóu-yǒuwěi have a beginning and an end: 把事情～地说一遍 tell the story from beginning to end

有望 yǒuwàng hopeful: ～调职 be hopeful of being transferred to another post / 提级～。There is hope of a promotion.

有为 yǒuwéi full of promise; promising: 奋发～ be industrious and promising / ～的年轻一代 bright younger generation

有味 yǒuwèi *also* "有味儿" ❶ (of food) palatable; tasty; delicious: 他炒的菜挺～的。The dish he cooked is delicious. ❷ (of food) smell bad; be off: 这剩菜～了。The left-over dish has gone off (*or* bad). ❸ meaningful; entertaining; interesting: 你还别说，这电视剧还挺～。Actually, the TV play is quite interesting.

有闻必录 yǒuwén-bìlù record whatever one hears: 报告文学可不是～。You don't record whatever you hear in a piece of reportage.

有…无… yǒu…wú… ❶ *used to indicate that there is the former but not the latter*: 有勇无谋 have courage but no tactics; be more brave than wise / 有职无权 hold the post but not the power; be a figurehead / 有损无益 have all harm but no benefit ❷ *used to emphasize that there is only the former*: 有加无已 be ever-increasing; get increasingly formidable / 有来无回 only take, not give; not be reciprocal; one-way traffic / 有我无他，有他无我。It's either me or him. We two cannot coexist. ❸ *used to indicate that with the former there is no need for the latter*: 有恃无恐 have strong backing and fear nothing / 有备无患。Preparedness averts peril. ❹ *used to mean that something may or may not exist*: 有意无意 wittingly or unwittingly; consciously or unconsciously; by accident or design

有息 yǒuxī interest-bearing: ～账户 interest-bearing account

有喜 yǒuxǐ be pregnant; be expecting: 她知道这是～的反应。She knew this was a sign of pregnancy.

有戏 yǒuxì 〈方言〉 hopeful; likely: 你的工作～了。There is hope that you may get the job. *or* You're likely to get the job now.

有隙 yǒuxì ❶ 〈书面〉 bear a grudge: 他俩～。The two of them harbour a grudge against each other. ❷ loophole

有隙可乘 yǒuxì-kěchéng there is a crack to squeeze through — there is a loophole to exploit; take advantage of a rift (between people): 加强财务管理，不要让某些人～。Tighten financial management so as not to leave any loophole for anyone to exploit.

有闲 yǒuxián have leisure: ～阶级 idle rich

有限 yǒuxiàn ❶ limited; finite: 授权～ have limited authority (over sth.) / ～主权论 theory of limited sovereignty / ～战争 limited war ❷ not many; not high in degree: 资金～ have limited funds / 学识～ have little learning / 工作能力～ be not equal to the task / 生命～，艺术无穷。Life is short; art is long.

有限公司 yǒuxiàn gōngsī limited company; limited-liability company: 殿扬广告～ Dianyang Advertising Company Limited

有限花序 yǒuxiàn huāxù 〈植物〉 definite inflorescence

有限级数 yǒuxiàn jíshù 〈数学〉 finite progression; finite series

有限论 yǒuxiànlùn *also* "有穷论" finitism

有限小数 yǒuxiàn xiǎoshù 〈数学〉 finite fraction

有限元法 yǒuxiànyuánfǎ 〈数学〉 finite element method

有限责任 yǒuxiàn zérèn 〈经济〉 limited liability

有限准入 yǒuxiàn zhǔnrù 〈经济〉 managed access

有线 yǒuxiàn wired

有线传真 yǒuxiàn chuánzhēn wirephoto

有线电报 yǒuxiàn diànbào line telegraphy; cablegram: ～学 wire telegraphy

有线电话 yǒuxiàn diànhuà electrophone; line telephony; wire

Y

telephony:安装～ install a wire telephone
有线电视 yǒuxiàn diànshì closed-circuit television; wired television; cable TV
有线广播 yǒuxiàn guǎngbō wire or wired broadcasting; rediffusion on wire:～网 wire-broadcasting network; wired broadcast network /～站 wired boradcast station; rediffusion station
有线通信 yǒuxiàn tōngxìn wire communication
有线制导导弹 yǒuxiàn zhìdǎo dǎodàn wire-guided missile
有向线段 yǒuxiàng xiànduàn directed line segment
有向直线 yǒuxiàng zhíxiàn directed line
有效 yǒuxiào efficacious; effective; authentic; valid:～时间 effective time; net time /～方法 effective method /此证明一周内～。This certificate is only valid (*or* good) within a week of its issuance. /两种文本同样～。Both texts are equally authentic. /这项规定仍然～。This regulation still holds good. /这药治疗肝炎十分～。It is a very efficacious drug for hepatitis.
有效分蘖 yǒuxiào fēnniè 〈农业〉effective tillering
有效供给 yǒuxiào gōngjǐ effective supply
有效荷载 yǒuxiào hèzài useful load; payload
有效积温 yǒuxiào jīwēn effective accumulated temperature
有效库容 yǒuxiào kùróng 〈水利〉effective storage
有效票 yǒuxiàopiào valid ballot paper
有效期 yǒuxiàoqī term or period of validity; time of efficacy:药品的～已过,不能再用了。The medicine cannot be used because it has passed its expiry (*or* expiration) date. /合同的～为一年。The contract is valid for a year. /两国商定正式延长条约的～。After consultation the two countries agreed to officially extend the period of validity of the treaty.
有效射程 yǒuxiào shèchéng effective range
有效数字 yǒuxiào shùzì significant digits or figures
有效温度 yǒuxiào wēndù effective temperature
有些 yǒuxiē ❶ some; part:听众中,～人激动不已,～人却无动于衷。Among the audience, some were very excited but some were indifferent. ❷ some; not much; not many:她把～旧衣服捐献给灾区人民了。She donated some of her old clothes to the people in the disaster areas. ❸ to some extent; somewhat; rather:心情～沉重 with rather a heavy heart /灯光～昏暗。The light was rather dim. /我觉得～累。I felt a bit tired.
有心 yǒuxīn ❶ have a mind to; be bent on:他～帮助她,又怕她拒绝。He would like to help her but was afraid that she might reject it. /她早就～成全他和妹妹的婚事。She long had a mind to facilitate his marriage with her younger sister. ❷ intentionally; purposely; by design:你这是～气人。You are annoying me on purpose. /他是～这样做的! He did it by design.
有心人 yǒuxīnrén person who is resolved to do sth. useful; person with high aspirations and determination; observant and conscientious person:世上无难事,只怕～。Nothing in the world is difficult for one who sets his mind on it. /功夫不负～。Hard work never fails a determined person. /他从小就是个～。He was observant and conscientious even when he was a little boy.
有形 yǒuxíng tangible; visible:～损害 physical harm (*or* damage)
有形贸易 yǒuxíng màoyì visible trade
有形损耗 yǒuxíng sǔnhào *also* "物质损耗" wùzhì sǔnhào material loss
有形资本 yǒuxíng zīběn physical capital; material capital
有形资产 yǒuxíng zīchǎn tangible assets; tangibles
有幸 yǒuxìng have the luck or pleasure; be fortunate:我～游览过天池。I have had the pleasure of visiting Lake Tianchi.
有性 yǒuxìng 〈生物〉sexual:～世代 sexual generation
有性生殖 yǒuxìng shēngzhí zoogamy; sexual reproduction
有性杂交 yǒuxìng zájiāo sexual hybridization
有血有肉 yǒuxuè-yǒuròu (of descriptions in literary works, etc.) true to life; vivid:这篇通讯生动具体,～。The news report was graphic and true to life. /小说中的英雄人物～。The characterization of the hero in the novel was lifelike.
有言在先 yǒuyán-zàixiān make it clear beforehand; caution in advance; forewarn:谁也不准反悔,这是～,大家都同意的。No one was allowed to go back on his word as it had been made clear beforehand and agreed upon.
有眼不识泰山 yǒu yǎn bù shí Tàishān have eyes but fail to see Mount Tai — fail to recognize a person of eminence in his presence; entertain an angel unawares:原来你就是鼎鼎大名的大作家,我真是～了。So you are the famous great writer. I'm sorry for failing to recognize your eminence.
有眼无珠 yǒuyǎn-wúzhū have eyes but no pupils — have eyes but see not; undiscerning:他～,不识好歹。He is so dense that he fails to see what is good for him.
有焰燃烧 yǒuyàn ránshāo flaming combustion
有要没紧 yǒuyào-méijǐn unimportant; indifferent:他在局里谋了个闲差,管些～的事儿。He held an unimportant position in the bureau looking after some trivial matters.
有一搭没一搭 yǒu yīdā méi yīdā ❶ try to strike up a conversation; engage sb. in a small talk:～地闲扯 chat at random ❷ of little significance; not essential:～地找点零活儿干 get oneself an odd job only occasionally
有一得一 yǒuyī-déyī neither more nor less; as much as actually is:她把事儿～地全对他说了。She told him about the matter exactly as it has happened.
有一分热,发一分光 yǒu yī fēn rè, fā yī fēn guāng give as much light as the fuel can produce — do all one can, however little it may be
有一手儿 yǒu yīshǒur ❶ have special skill:修理家电他可～。He is good at repairing electric appliances. ❷ have an illicit love affair:他俩儿～。They two are having an affair.
有益 yǒuyì profitable; beneficial; valuable; useful:做一个～于人民、～于国家的人 be a person who is of value to the people and the country /经常锻炼身体～于健康。Regular physical exercise is good for health. /凡是～的话都要听,～的事都要做,～的东西都要学。Listen to whatever is beneficial, do whatever is useful and learn whatever is valuable.
有意 yǒuyì ❶ have the intention (to do sth.); have a mind; be inclined or disposed:～帮忙 be ready (*or* disposed) to help /他～和你交朋友。He would like to make friends with you. /主席～要在下午开会。The chairman intended to hold the meeting in the afternoon. /～栽花花不发,无心插柳柳成荫。When you grow flowers on purpose, they fail to bloom; when you plant willows at random, they grow into a shady grove. *or* Follow love, and it will flee; flee love, and it will follow thee. ❷ be attracted sexually; take a fancy:她对你～,你没看出来? Don't you see that she is attracted to you? ❸ intentionally; deliberately; purposely:～造谣生事 start a rumour to create trouble on purpose /～歪曲事实真相 intentionally distort the actual state of affairs /他这是～刁难你。He was deliberately making things difficult for you.
有意识 yǒu yìshi consciously:～地改正缺点 make conscious efforts to overcome one's weaknesses /他这样做完全是～的。He was fully conscious of what he was doing.
有意思 yǒu yìsi ❶ significant; meaningful:这个剧本～。The scenario was meaningful. /他讲得～。What he said was significant. ❷ interesting; amusing; enjoyable:今天的聚会很～。The party today was most enjoyable. /他这人真～! What an amusing fellow he is. /他感到这样的生活～极了。He found this kind of life extremely interesting. ❸ be attracted sexually; take a fancy:我不管他是不是对我～,我对他没意思。I don't care if he takes a fancy to me or not. He is certainly not the man of my heart.
有意无意 yǒuyì-wúyì intentionally or unintentionally; consciously or unconsciously; wittingly or unwittingly; by accident or design:她便～地卖弄她的率真。Knowingly or not, she capitalized on her brashness.
有影没影 yǒuyǐng-méiyǐng groundless; baseless; unfounded:她爱散布些～的小道消息。She enjoys spreading rumours through the grapevine.
有勇无谋 yǒuyǒng-wúmóu have valour but lack tactics; be brave but not resourceful; be more brave than wise; be foolhardy:他～,所以经常吃亏。He had all courage but no resourcefulness, so he often came to grief. /打仗需要智勇双全的战将,不需要～的莽夫! Battles need generals who are both intelligent and courageous, not rash men who are more brave than wise.
有用功 yǒuyònggōng 〈物理〉useful work
有…有… yǒu…yǒu… ❶ *used separately before two nouns or verbs opposite or contrastive in meaning to indicate that both are present*:有始有终 from beginning to end; carry sth. through to the end /有利有弊 have both advantages and disadvantages /有职有权 hold both the post and the power; have the authority that goes with one's post /有借有还 borrow and return /有得有失 gains as well

as losses ❷ *used separately before two nouns or verbs with the same or similar meaning for the sake of emphasis*：有吃有喝 eat and drink; have ample food /有商有量 hold discussions /有声有色 full of sound and colour; vivid and dramatic /有情有理 be reasonable /有棱有角 have both edges and corners; have pointedness /有鼻子有眼儿 with every detail vividly described

有余 yǒuyú ❶ have a surplus; be more than enough：绰绰～ more than enough; enough and to spare /她聪明～，温厚不足。She was more intelligent than gentle and kind. ❷ odd：他年已三十～。He was over thirty.

有源 yǒuyuán 〈电学〉active：～电路 active circuit /～器件 active device; active parts /～卫星 active satellite

有缘 yǒuyuán (usu. used in a good sense) be predestined; be fated; be bonded with; have an affinity for：看来你我～，在这个地方相遇。Well, it seems to be our happy fate to meet each other here. /如果跟你～，我们会再相见的。We shall meet again if we're destined to.

有缘千里来相会 yǒuyuán qiānlǐ lái xiānghuì people living far apart will meet if they are destined to：～，无缘对面不相逢。If fated (*or* destined), people come together though a thousand *li* apart. If not, they miss each other though they meet face to face.

有则改之，无则加勉 yǒu zé gǎi zhī, wú zé jiā miǎn correct mistakes if you have made any, and guard against them if you have not：我们应该实行"知无不言，言无不尽"，"言者无罪，闻者足戒"，"～"这些中国人民的有益的格言。We should apply such good popular Chinese maxims as "say all you know and say it without reserve", "blame not the speaker but be warned by this words" and "correct mistakes if you have committed them and guard against them if you have not".

有增无已 yǒuzēng-wúyǐ ever-growing; ever-expanding; ever-increasing：险情～。It's becoming increasingly dangerous. /危机～。The crisis is deepening.

有章可循 yǒuzhāng-kěxún there are rules and regulations to go by：～的事不要随意改变。On matters governed by existing rules and regulations, don't change the rules at will.

有朝一日 yǒuzhāo-yīrì some day; one day：他坚信，这些恬不知耻的家伙～终会受到历史的审判。He was convinced that these shameless scoundrels would be tried by history some day.

有着 yǒuzhe there is; exist; have：两国人民之间～深厚的友谊。The people of the two countries enjoy profound friendship. /这次会议对我国的建设事业～巨大的意义。The conference is of tremendous significance to the cause of our national construction.

有枝添叶儿 yǒuzhī-tiānyèr *also* "添枝加叶" tiānzhī-jiāyè embellish a story：这事儿让她～地一说性质全变了。After her embellishment the nature of the matter completely changed.

有志者事竟成 yǒuzhìzhě shì jìng chéng where there's a will there is a way：常言道：～，只要有决心，有志气，哪有办不到的事！As the old saying goes, where there's a will there is a way. With determination and aspiration one can accomplish anything.

有志之士 yǒuzhìzhīshì person of noble aspirations; person with lofty ideals

有致 yǒuzhì of taste; appealing; interesting：错落～ in picturesque disorder (*or* charming disarray)

有种 yǒuzhǒng have guts; be plucky; have courage：～的出来跟我掰腕子！Who has the guts to hand-wrestle with me!

有助于 yǒuzhùyú contribute to; be conducive to; help：这次谈话～消除彼此的隔阂，增进团结。The talk helped to clear up misunderstanding and enhance unity. /两国领导人保持经常接触，～增进相互间的了解。Frequent contacts between the leaders of the two countries are conducive to better mutual understanding.

有滋有味 yǒuzī-yǒuwèi ❶ tasty; delicious：菜炒得～。The dish is delicious. ❷ with relish or enjoyment：活得～ enjoy life /这电视剧她看得～。She is absorbed in the TV series.

有嘴无心 yǒuzuǐ-wúxīn be sharp-tongued but mean no malice; be tactless：她可是个～的人。She has a sharp tongue but no bad intention.

有罪 yǒuzuì be guilty of a crime; be guilty

铕

yǒu 〈化学〉europium (Eu)

友

yǒu ❶ friend：知心好～ intimate (*or* bosom) friend /战～ comrade-in-arms /交～之道 way to make friends ❷ be on intimate terms; be close to：他二人相～甚笃。They two are very close. ❸ friendly：*see* "～邦"；"～军"

友爱 yǒu'ài friendly affection; fraternal love：团结～ unity and fraternity; fraternal unity /兄弟二人甚是～。The two brothers loved each other affectionately.

友伴 yǒubàn friend; companion

友邦 yǒubāng friendly nation or country：他是来自～的使者。He was an envoy from a friendly nation.

友道 yǒudào 〈书面〉moral norms governing friendly contacts

友好 yǒuhǎo ❶ close friend; friend：相约二三～至湖边垂钓 invite two or three friends to go fishing at the lake side ❷ friendly; amiable; amicable：～人士 friendly personage /～使者 envoy of friendship /～条约 treaty of friendship /在诚挚～的气氛中举行会谈 hold a talk in a sincere and amicable atmosphere /各国均应～相处。All nations should coexist in amity. /几家人相处得十分～。Several families got along fine with one another.

友好城市 yǒuhǎo chéngshì cities of friendship; sister cities; twin cities

友好代表团 yǒuhǎo dàibiǎotuán goodwill mission

友好协会 yǒuhǎo xiéhuì friendship association

友好邀请赛 yǒuhǎo yāoqǐngsài friendship invitational tournament

友军 yǒujūn friendly forces：在～的配合下打了一个漂亮仗 fight a successful battle in coordination with friendly forces

友军炮火 yǒujūn pàohuǒ *also* "己方炮火" jǐfāng pàohuǒ friendly fire：为～所击毙 killed by friendly fire

友邻 yǒulín ❶ friendly neighbour：告别了～ bid farewell to one's neighbours ❷ friendly and neighbouring

友朋 yǒupéng 〈书面〉friend

友情 yǒuqíng friendly sentiments; friendship：建立了深厚的～ have built (*or* forged) ties of profound friendship /珍惜他们之间纯真的～ set store by the sincere friendly sentiments between them

友人 yǒurén friend：国际～ foreign friend

友善 yǒushàn 〈书面〉friendly; genial; amicable：素相～ have been on friendly terms all along

友谊 yǒuyì friendship：革命～ revolutionary friendship /牢不可破的～ unbreakable friendship /建立了深厚的～ have built profound friendly ties /～的纽带 ties of friendship /～的沃土 fertile soil of friendship

友谊赛 yǒuyìsài friendly match or contest; friendly：职工排球～ friendly volleyball match by workers and staff members /举行象棋～ hold a friendly match of Chinese chess

友谊商店 yǒuyì shāngdiàn friendship store (chiefly catering to foreign visitors)

卣

yǒu 〈古语〉small-mouthed wine vessel

黝

yǒu black; dark

黝黯 yǒu'àn *also* "黝暗" dim; dark：～的墙角 dark corner

黝黑 yǒuhēi dark; swarthy：皮肤～ dark skin /胳膊和大腿都晒得～ with sun-tanned arms and thighs /她面孔～，但很俊美。She had a swarthy complexion but was very pretty.

黝黝 yǒuyǒu dim; shadowy：～的山影 indistinct (*or* faint) mountain shadows

牖

yǒu 〈书面〉window

yòu

又

yòu 〈副词〉❶ *used to indicate repetition or continuation*：看了～看 look at sth. again and again /说了～说 speak repeatedly; keep on speaking /洗了～洗 continue washing /过了一天～一天 day after day /野火烧不尽，春风吹～生。No prairie can be burnt out utterly; The spring wind blows it back to life again. ❷ *used to indicate that several conditions or qualities exist at the same time*：～说～笑 talk and laugh at the same time /～聪明～能干 be intelligent as well as capable /～方便～安全 be both convenient and safe /他是劳动模范，～是人民代表。He was a model worker and also a deputy to the people's congress. /这项革新提高了产品质量，～可以节约成本。The innovation improved the quality of the products and reduced

the cost. ❸ furthermore; in addition; moreover: 山高路滑,～是夜间,困难真不小。The journey was really difficult, the mountain being tall and the road slippery. In addition, it was a dark night. /他很聪明,～肯努力,所以一学就会了。On top of his intelligence he worked hard and soon learned how to do it. ❹ besides; apart from: 除了教课以外,她～担任了工会主席的工作。Apart from her teaching she also shouldered the responsibility of a trade-union chairwoman. ❺ *used to indicate that an odd number is added to a whole number*: 三～二分之一 three and a half /两小时～十分 two hours and ten minutes ❻ *used often in parallel to indicate two contradictory things*: 今晚这场电影,她～想看,～不想看,一时还拿不定主意。She couldn't make up her mind whether or not to see the film tonight. ❼ but; yet; however: 她想吃冰淇淋,可～怕发胖。She loves ice cream but is afraid of getting fat. /他心里有千言万语,嘴里～说不出来。Though he has a lot to say, he doesn't know how to put it into words. ❽ *used for emphasis in negative sentences or rhetorical questions*: 你～不是第一次上台,紧张什么? Why so nervous? This is not the first time you've appeared on the stage. /他～不是什么了不起的大人物,你怕什么呢? What is there to be afraid of? He isn't a big shot.

又红又专 yòuhóng-yòuzhuān both red and expert; both socialist-minded and vocationally proficient: 成为～的无产阶级知识分子 become proletarian intellectuals with both political consciousness and professional competence

又及 yòují postscript (PS): 大哥～ postscript of the elder brother

又惊又喜 yòujīng-yòuxǐ be both startled and delighted; be pleasantly surprised: 这消息让我～。The news was a pleasant surprise to me.

又拉又打 yòulā-yòudǎ *also* "又打又拉" strike and stroke alternately; employ a carrot-and-stick policy; combine reward and threat: 为了逼那个小国就范,他们～。They used both carrot and stick to compel that small country to submit.

又名 yòumíng alias; assumed name

又想当婊子,又想立牌坊 yòu xiǎng dāng biǎozi, yòu xiǎng lì páifang lead the life of a whore and want a monument put up to one's chastity

又要马儿好,又要马儿不吃草 yòuyào mǎr hǎo, yòuyào mǎr bù chī cǎo 〈俗语〉 expect the horse to run fast but not let it graze; try to eat one's cake and have it: ～,天底下没有这样的便宜事。There is no such thing as reaping only the advantages of something without the disadvantages that go with it. *or* There is no gains without pains.

右

yòu ❶ right side; right: 靠～行驶 drive on the right side of the road /向～拐 turn right ❷ west: 山～ areas west of the Taihang Mountains, specifically Shanxi Province /陇～ areas west of the Longshan Mountains in Shaanxi Province ❸ right side as the side of precedence: 位在某人之～ hold a post higher than (*or* superior to) that of sb. /无出其～ second to none ❹ 〈书面〉 uphold; advocate: ～武 advocate a military (*or* martial) spirit ❺ conservative; the Right: 此人太～。This man was too far to the Right. /极～分子 ultra-rightist ❻ 〈书面〉 *see* "佑" yòu

右边锋 yòubiānfēng 〈体育〉 outside right; right wing: 他是我们国家足球队著名的～。He was a famous right wing of our national football team.

右边 yòubian right or right-hand side; right: 邮局在工厂的～。The post office was to the right of the factory.

右侧 yòucè right side

右舵 yòuduò right standard rudder; right rudder

右锋 yòufēng 〈体育〉 right forward

右后卫 yòuhòuwèi 〈体育〉 right back

右面 yòumiàn right or right-hand side: 马路～是一片树林。To the right of the road was a tract of woods.

右内锋 yòunèifēng 〈体育〉 inside right

右派 yòupài ❶ the Right; right wing: ～组织 right-wing organization /～人士 right-wingers ❷ (short for 资产阶级右派) bourgeois rightist: ～分子 rightist

右前轮 yòuqiánlún 〈汽车〉 off-front wheel

右前卫 yòuqiánwèi 〈体育〉 right halfback; right half

右倾 yòuqīng Right deviation: 批判他的～思想 criticize his Right-deviationist thinking /他一贯被认为～保守。He was always regarded as a Right-deviationist conservative.

右倾机会主义 yòuqīng jīhuìzhǔyì Right opportunism

右手 yòushǒu ❶ right hand: ～拿笔 hold a pen in one's right hand ❷ right-hand side; right: ～拐弯 turn right

右手定则 yòushǒu dìngzé 〈电学〉 right-hand rule

右首 yòushǒu *also* "右手" right-hand side; right: 老人坐在～。The old man was seated on the right.

右袒 yòutǎn be partial (to one side)

右文 yòuwén stress culture and learning; value cultural and educational undertakings

右舷 yòuxián 〈航海〉 starboard

右旋 yòuxuán 〈化学〉 dextrorotation: ～糖酐〈药学〉 dextran /～物质 dextrorotatory substance

右旋球 yòuxuánqiú 〈体育〉 right spin

右旋糖 yòuxuántáng *also* "葡萄糖" pútaotáng grape sugar; glucose

右翼 yòuyì ❶ 〈军事〉 right wing; right flank: 向我～进攻 attack us on the right flank ❷ Right; right-wing: ～分子 right-winger; member of the Right

佑(祐)

yòu help; protect; defend; bless: ～贤辅德 help the virtuous /上天～我。Heaven bless me!

佑护 yòuhù protect; defend

佑助 yòuzhù aid; assist; foster: ～幼主 assist the young emperor /暗中～ secretly aid sb.

有

yòu 〈书面〉 *used to add an odd number to a whole number*: 他今年三十～二。He is thirty-two this year.

see also yǒu

宥

yòu 〈书面〉 excuse; forgive: 原～ excuse; condone /宽～ forgive /务祈见～。Please accept my sincere apologies.

囿

yòu 〈书面〉 ❶ animal farm; enclosure; park: 园～ animal farm /鹿～ deer farm; deer park ❷ limited; constrained; hampered: ～于传统陋习 constrained by corrupt traditional customs

囿于成见 yòuyú chéngjiàn be blinded by prejudice; be biased: ～而不能自拔 be hopelessly blinded by prejudice

侑

yòu 〈书面〉 press (sb. to eat or drink); press: ～食 urge sb. to have food /～饮 press sb. to drink

柚

yòu ❶ Rangoon teak; Burma teak: ～树 Rangoon teak; Burma teak ❷ fruit of Rangoon teak commonly known as shaddock or pomelo: ～汁儿 shaddock juice /葡萄～ grapefruit /沙田～驰名中外。Shaddocks from Shatian are famous both in China and abroad.

see also yóu

柚木 yòumù Rangoon teak; Burma teak

柚子 yòuzi shaddock; pomelo: 广西今年～丰收。There is a bumper harvest of shaddocks in Guangxi this year.

釉

yòu glaze: 白～瓷器 white glazed porcelain

釉彩玻璃 yòucǎi bōli enamelled glass

釉工 yòugōng glazer

釉里红 yòulǐhóng red within the glaze or underglaze red, a kind of traditional Chinese porcelain

釉料 yòuliào 〈化工〉 frit; glaze

釉面砖 yòumiànzhuān 〈建筑〉 glazed tile

釉上彩 yòushàngcǎi overglaze colour

釉陶 yòutáo glazed pottery

釉下彩 yòuxiàcǎi underglaze colour

釉窑 yòuyáo 〈化工〉 enamel kiln

釉质 yòuzhì *also* "珐琅质" fàlángzhì 〈生理〉 enamel: ～龋 enamel caries /～冠 enamel cap /～发育不全 hypoplasia of enamel

釉子 yòuzi glaze

鼬

yòu 〈动物〉 weasel: 黄～ yellow weasel /白～ stoat

鼬獾 yòuhuān ferret badger

狖

yòu 〈古语〉 a kind of monkey

幼

yòu ❶ young; minor; under age: 有一子,尚～ have one son who is still young /年～无知 young and ignorant ❷ children;

the young：尊老爱～ respect the old and care for the young / 扶老携～ bring along the old and the young
幼辈 yòubèi younger generation
幼冲 yòuchōng 〈书面〉young in age
幼虫 yòuchóng 〈动物〉larva：苍蝇的～ larvae of flies
幼雏 yòuchú young bird；nestling
幼儿 yòu'ér child；infant：婴～ babies / ～师范 school for teachers of preschool children
幼儿急疹 yòu'ér jízhěn 〈医学〉exanthema subitum
幼儿教育 yòu'ér jiàoyù preschool education：她从事～多年。She has been engaged in preschool education for years.
幼儿园 yòu'éryuán kindergarten；nursery school；infant school：北海～ Beihai Kindergarten / 一个设备良好的～ nursery school with good facilities
幼发拉底河 Yòufālādǐhé Euphrates，a river of southwest Asia that rises in eastern Turkey and flows to join the Tigris
幼功 yògōng skills (of acrobats，martial artist，etc.) acquired during childhood
幼果 yòuguǒ young fruit
幼教 yòujiào (short for 幼儿教育) pre-school education
幼驹 yòujū pony
幼林 yòulín forest of young trees：保护～ protect forests of young trees
幼龄林 yòulínglín 〈林业〉young growth
幼苗 yòumiáo seedling：嫩绿的蔬菜～ green and tender seedlings of vegetables / 茁壮的～ sturdy seedlings / 桑树的～ mulcherry saplings
幼嫩 yòunèn ❶ small and young：～的禾苗 tender seedlings of cereal crops ❷ naive；not mature：思想～ be naive / 他还～了点。He's a little immature.
幼年 yòunián childhood；infancy：他是我～时代的朋友。He was my friend from childhood.
幼女 yòunǚ little girl
幼弱 yòuruò ❶ young in years；of tender years ❷ small and weak：照料～儿童 look after small and frail children
幼时 yòushí early childhood：～的伙伴 childhood mate
幼树 yòushù sapling
幼体 yòutǐ 〈生物〉the young；larva
幼童 yòutóng young child
幼小 yòuxiǎo immature：～的年纪 immature age / ～的心灵 immature mind
幼学琼林 Yòuxué Qiónglín *You Xue Qiong Lin*，old-time primer for children written by Cheng Yunsheng (程允升) of the Qing Dynasty
幼芽 yòuyá young shoot；bud：蔬菜的～ young shoots of vegetables / 小草长出了～。Buds of little grass appeared. / 种子发出了～。The seeds sprouted.
幼稚 yòuzhì ❶ young；juvenile；infantile：～无知 young and ignorant ❷ childish；puerile；immature；naive：思想～ naive thinking / 谈吐～ talk childishly / ～的行为 puerile act / ～的看法 immature viewpoint
幼稚病 yòuzhìbìng ❶〈心理〉infantilism ❷ infantile disorder
幼稚工业 yòuzhì gōngyè infant industry
幼稚细胞 yòuzhì xìbāo 〈医学〉juvenile cell
幼稚型 yòuzhìxíng 〈医学〉infantilism：垂体性～ hypophyseal infantilism；pituitary infantilism
幼稚园 yòuzhìyuán 〈旧语〉kindergarten
幼株 yòuzhū young plant；seed plant
幼子 yòuzǐ youngest son；baby son：弱妻～ frail wife and little children / ～是她的掌上珠。The youngest son was the pearl in her palm (*or* the apple of her eye).

蚴

yòu 〈动物〉larva of a tapeworm or cercaria of a schistosome：毛～ miracidium / 尾～ cercaria

诱

yòu ❶ guide；direct；lead；induce：劝～ induce；try to convince ❷ lure；tempt；seduce；entice：不为威胁，不为利～ not submit to threat or enticement / ～他上钩 lay (*or* set) a trap for him
诱逼 yòubī *also* "诱迫" cajole and coerce；entice and threat
诱变 yòubiàn 〈生物〉mutagenesis；mutagenicity
诱变基因 yòubiàn jīyīn mutator；mutator gene
诱变因子 yòubiàn yīnzǐ *also* "诱变剂"〈生物〉mutagen；mutagenic agent
诱捕 yòubǔ trap (animals)：～害虫 trap injurious insects (*or* pests)
诱虫灯 yòuchóngdēng *also* "诱蛾灯" moth-killing lamp
诱导 yòudǎo ❶ guide；lead；induce：善于～学生进行学习 be good at guiding students in their studies / 接受～ accept guidance ❷〈物理〉〈生理〉induction：～说 induction theory / ～系统 inducible system / ～效应 inductive effect
诱导反应 yòudǎo fǎnyìng induced reaction
诱敌深入 yòudí-shēnrù lure the enemy in deep
诱饵 yòu'ěr ❶ ledger-bail ❷ bait：企图以她作～让那人上钩 attempt to use her as a bait to hook him
诱发 yòufā ❶ guide and inspire；induce：～联想 inspire association ❷ bring out (sth. potential or latent)；cause to happen：～癌症 induce cancer / 稍一不慎，会～气管炎。A little carelessness may precipitate bronchitis.
诱供 yòugòng trap a person into confession；coax a person into making a confession：利用～的方法 try to induce a person to make a confession / 不准～。No trickery to secure confessions is permitted.
诱拐 yòuguǎi abduct；carry off (a woman) by force or fraud；kidnap (a child)：～儿童 kidnap children / 他们把这些年轻的妇女～出来，然后卖到边远地区。They abducted these young women from their homes and then sold them to remote areas.
诱惑 yòuhuò ❶ entice；seduce；tempt；lure：用名利思想～青年 tempt young people with promise of personal fame and gain ❷ attract；captivate；allure：眼前是一片迷人的景色，谁见了谁都会受到～。No one could help being fascinated by the enchanting scene before his eyes.
诱集 yòují attract (to gather around sth.)：用灯光～飞蛾 use lights to attract moths
诱奸 yòujiān tempt sb. to have unlawful sexual intercourse；seduce
诱骗 yòupiàn inveigle；cajole；trap；ensnare：用～的方法让人说出秘密 cajole sb. into divulging a secret
诱迫 yòupò cajole and coerce：～妇女卖淫 cajole women into prostitution
诱取 yòuqǔ trap and obtain：～猎物 trap animals
诱劝 yòuquàn inveigle；lure：多方～ try every way to lure sb. into (doing) sth.
诱人 yòurén captivating；enchanting；bewitching：景色～。The scenery is enchanting.
诱杀 yòushā trap and kill；lure to destruction：用灯光～棉铃虫 lure bollworms to their death with lamp light
诱使 yòushǐ trick into；ensnare：～上当 entrap
诱降 yòuxiáng lure into capitulation：实行～敌人的办法 adopt the practice of luring the enemy into surrender
诱胁 yòuxié cajole and coerce：他们对她～威逼，无所不至。They tried on her cajolery，coercion and what not.
诱掖 yòuyè 〈书面〉guide and foster：～后进 guide and encourage the younger generation
诱因 yòuyīn immediate cause；cause (of a disease)：受凉感冒是这类疾病突发的一个重要～。Cold is an important cause of the sudden outbreak of this disease.
诱引 yòuyǐn lure；entice；seduce：～少女 entice a young girl / 受到～ be seduced
诱致 yòuzhì lead to；result in；cause：～违法乱纪 lead to the violation of law and discipline

yū

於

Yū a surname
see also wū

淤（❹瘀）

yū ❶ silt up：雨后，院子里～了一层泥。There was a layer of silt in the courtyard after the rain. ❷ silted (up)：*see* "～泥"；"～地" ❸ silt；sediment；mud：河～ river mud；alluvium / 沟～ drainage silt / 清～之后的昆明湖 Kunming Lake after being cleared of its silt ❹ stasis：散～ treatment of stasis / 活血化～ improve blood circulation and dissolve stasis ❺〈方言〉spill；overflow：米汤～了一锅台。The boiling rice spilt all over the cooker range.
淤斑 yūbān 〈医学〉hemorrhage spot；ecchymosis；petechia：他的胳臂上出现～。Petechiae have appeared on his arms.

淤地 yūdì silted-up land; silt land; alluvial land
淤地坝 yūdìbà 〈水利〉silt arrester; silt dam
淤点 yūdiǎn 〈医学〉petechia：他腿上～不少。There are quite a few petechiae on his legs.
淤淀 yūdiàn silt; sedimentation; deposition：河身～。The river silts up.
淤灌 yūguàn 〈农业〉warping：用～法改善土质 improve the soil by warping
淤积 yūjī silt up; deposit：河口泥沙～很厉害。The river mouth was very much silted up. /愤怒～在心头。Anger was pent up in his heart.
淤埋 yūmái be buried in silt：洪水过后，河泥～了许多农田。The floods over, large tracts of cultivated land were covered with (*or* buried in) silt.
淤泥 yūní silt; sediment; sludge; ooze：河底的～足有一米深。The riverbed silt is a good metre in depth. /塘里尽是～。The pond is just like a mire.
淤浅 yūqiǎn become shallow with silt：河槽逐年～。The river shallows with silt year after year.
淤塞 yūsè silt up; be blocked or choked with silt：河道～。The river was blocked with silt. /泥沙～了湖泊。The lake has silted up.
淤血 yūxuè extravasated blood：颈部的～几天不散。The extravasated blood stayed for several days in the neck. /伤口周围出现～。Blood extravasated around the wound.
淤滞 yūzhì ❶ be retarded with silt; silt up：疏通～的航道 dredge the sluggish channel ❷〈中医〉blood stasis in the circulatory channels：肠～ colon stasis

迂 yū ❶ go round; take a detour; wind one's way：～路出关 go round the pass /舍近而就～ give up the shortcut and take a detour ❷ given to outworn rules and ideas; pedantic; impractical：他太～了。He is very pedantic.
迂夫子 yūfūzǐ pedant
迂腐 yūfǔ stubborn adherence to outworn rules and ideas; pedantry：～之论 pedantic views /～无用 doltish and useless /～的老头 impractical old man /～的老学究 old pedant
迂缓 yūhuǎn (of movement) sluggish; dilatory; slow-moving：行动～ slow in movement; sluggish
迂回 yūhuí ❶ circuitous; devious; tortuous; roundabout：～的小巷 tortuous lane (*or* alley) /～而进 advance in a roundabout way ❷〈军事〉outflank：巧妙地～到敌人后方 outflank the enemy tactfully /向右侧～ attempt to outflank sb. on the right
迂回曲折 yūhuí-qūzhé circuitous; tortuous; full of twists and turns：山路～ zigzags of the mountain path /故事情节～。The plot of the story was devious.
迂回战术 yūhuí zhànshù outflanking tactics
迂见 yūjiàn foolish ideas; impractical or pedantic views
迂拘 yūjū 〈书面〉stay in a rut; get into a rut; go by the book：此公一向～陈规，无首创精神可言。He goes by outmoded conventions all the time and never shows any initiative.
迂阔 yūkuò high-sounding and impractical：我看他～得很。I think he is too impractical.
迂论 yūlùn impractical or pedantic view
迂磨 yūmo 〈方言〉slow in words and action; dilatory：他以前干活挺麻利的，怎么会变得这么～呢？He used to be rather quick and neat. How come he has (*or* Why has he) become so dilatory?
迂气 yūqi foolish and impractical behaviour; pedantic airs
迂曲 yūqū tortuous; winding; circuitous：～的小径 tortuous (*or* winding) path
迂儒 yūrú pedant
迂远 yūyuǎn impractical and high-sounding
迂执 yūzhí impractical and stubborn：～不化 incurably impractical and bigoted
迂拙 yūzhuō impractical and foolish：～之举 impractical and foolish act

吁 yū 〈象声〉call to an animal to halt; whoa
see also xū; yù

纡 yū ❶ tortuous; circuitous; winding：萦～ hover; linger /山险路～。A narrow path zigzags down the perilous peak. ❷〈书面〉tie; bind：～金佩紫 wear a gold ornament and a purple gown (symbolic of high official rank)
纡回 yūhuí 〈书面〉*see* "迂回❶" yūhuí
纡徐 yūxú 〈书面〉slow in action; dilatory：行步～ walk slowly
纡尊降贵 yūzūn-jiàngguì condescend; stoop：他～，结交下层。He condescends to befriend his inferiors.

yú

于[1]（於） yú ❶〈介词〉(a) in; at; on：黄河发源～青海。The Yellow River originates in Qinghai. /火车～六时三十分到达。The train arrived at 6:30. /来信～四月十八日收到。I got the letter on 18 April. /爱因斯坦以相对论而闻名～世。Einstein is known all over the world for his theories of relativity. (b) towards; to：问道～盲 ask a blind man about the way /求救～人 ask people for help (c) to; onto：嫁祸～人 shift the blame onto others /让位～人 give place to others; make room for others (d) for; to：忠～人民 be loyal to the people /习惯～这种生活 be used to this kind of life (e) from; out of：出～好心 out of good will /出～自愿 of one's own free will; of one's own accord /青出～蓝而胜于蓝。Blue comes from the indigo plant but is bluer than the plant itself. (f) than：出发时间不能晚～上午八点。The start-off time should not be later than eight o'clock in the morning. /参加者不得多～二十。The number of attendants should not exceed twenty. /为人民而死，重～泰山。It is weightier than Mount Tai to die for the people. (g) (used in the passive voice) by：见笑～人 be laughed at by others /限～水平 be restricted by one's ability ❷ *used as a suffix* (a) *after a verb*：属～ belong to /在～ lie in /至～ as for (b) *after an adjective*：敢～斗争 dare to fight /善～斗争 be good at fighting

于[2] Yú a surname
于飞 yúfēi 〈书面〉〈比喻〉harmonious relationship between husband and wife; conjugal harmony：凤凰～。The male and female phoenixes always fly together — husband and wife live in harmony.
于归 yúguī 〈书面〉(of women) get married; marry
于今 yújīn ❶ up to the present; by now; since：重庆一别，～八年。It is eight years since we parted in Chongqing. ❷ nowadays; today; now：家乡发展迅速，～已是旧貌换新颜了。My native place has developed rapidly and taken on an entirely new look.
于今为烈 yújīn-wéiliè be stronger or more prevalent than before：这种做法古已有之，～。This long-standing practice has now become more widespread than ever.
于谦 Yú Qiān Yu Qian (1398-1457), minister of war and patriot of the Ming Dynasty
于思 yúsāi 〈书面〉heavily bearded：～者如故。He is as heavily bearded as before.
于是 yúshì *also* "于是乎" thereupon; hence; therefore; consequently; as a result：在大伙儿的热情鼓励下，他～又恢复了信心。With our warm-hearted encouragement, he regained his confidence.
于心不忍 yúxīn-bùrěn not have the heart to; cannot bear to：我想不管他，可是又～。I had intended to leave him to himself, but I did not have the heart to.
于心无愧 yúxīn-wúkuì have a clear conscience; feel no prick of conscience
于心有愧 yúxīn-yǒukuì have something on one's conscience; feel guilty：工作出了差错，自感～。I felt guilty when something went wrong in my work.

盂 yú broad-mouthed receptacle; jar：水～ water basin /痰～ spittoon
盂兰盆会 Yúlánpénhuì 〈佛教〉Ullambana, a Buddhist ceremony held on the 15th of the 7th lunar month to redeem the souls of one's deceased ancestors

竽 yú *yu*, ancient Chinese windpipe (made of a number of reed pipes blown through a single mouth piece)：吹～ blow *yu* /滥～充数 pretend to play the *yu* in order to make up the number; be there just to make up the number; put in an appearance just to swell the total; hold an office though unequal to the task

Y

雩 yú 〈古语〉sacrificial rites in quest of rain

与(與) yú see "欤" yú
see also yǔ; yù

旟(旟) yú 〈古语〉army standard

玙(璵) yú 〈书面〉beautiful jade

欤(歟) yú 〈书面〉〈助词〉❶ *expressing doubt or used in rhetorical questions*: 子非三闾大夫～? Aren't you the cabinet minister Qu Yuan? ❷ *used in an exclamation*: 论者之言,一似管窥虎～! Indeed, the speaker's argument was as one-sided as looking at a tiger through a bamboo tube!

舆[1] yú 〈书面〉❶ cart; coach; carriage: ～马 coach horse / 弃～登舟 change from coach to ship / 出则同～,坐则同席 travel in the same coach and sit on the same mat — be on intimate terms ❷ coach body ❸ palanquin; palankeen; sedan chair

舆[2] yú land; area; territory: see "～地"

舆[3] yú public; popular: ～人 the populace; the public / 公共～论 public opinion

舆地 yúdì 〈书面〉earth; land; territory

舆论 yúlùn public opinion: 世界～ world opinion / 左右～ manipulate public opinion / 迫于～ under the pressure of public opinion / 蒙蔽～ hoodwink (*or* befuddle) the public / 制造～ create public opinion

舆论工具 yúlùn gōngjù mass media; the media

舆论界 yúlùnjiè the media; press circles

舆情 yúqíng public sentiment; popular feeling: ～激昂 seething public sentiment / 了解～ understand popular feeling

舆台 yútái lower-class people; people of humble status; lowly people

舆图 yútú 〈书面〉territorial map

虞[1] yú ❶ speculate; suppose; expect; predict: 以防不～ just in case of an (unforeseen) emergency / 不～有此变故。I did not expect this should happen. ❷ anxiety; misgiving; worry: 无饥寒冻馁之～ not have to worry about food and clothes / 大兴水利,可保旱涝无～。Large-scale water conservancy projects are guarantees against both droughts and floods. ❸ deceive; cheat; dupe: 尔～我诈 each trying to cheat the other / 无贰无～ with neither disloyalty nor deceit

虞[2] Yú ❶ Yu Kingdom, legendarily established by Shun (舜) ❷ kingdom during the Zhou Dynasty, situated northwest of what is now Pinglu (平陆) County, Shanxi Province ❸ a surname

虞美人 yúměirén 〈植物〉corn poppy; field poppy

娱 yú ❶ give pleasure to; entertain; amuse: 以～宾客 entertain the guests ❷ joy; pleasure; amusement: 耳目之～ entertainment; public amusement; pleasures of the senses / 甚觉欢～ be filled with joy; take great pleasure; rejoice

娱老 yúlǎo live through one's remaining years happily; live happily in one's old age

娱乐 yúlè ❶ amusement; pleasure; entertainment; recreation: ～场所 public place of entertainment / 节日期间要好好地～～。We should enjoy ourselves on holidays. ❷ recreational activity; hobby: 晚会上有各种～。There are lots of recreational activities at the evening party. / 他惟一的～便是种花。His only hobby is growing flowers.

娱乐场 yúlèchǎng amusement park

娱乐室 yúlèshì recreation room

娱心 yúxīn 〈书面〉pleasant; joyous; enjoyable: ～适意 feel pleased and joyful / ～悦耳 be pleasant (*or* pleasing) to the ear

娱悦 yúyuè please; make happy; give pleasure: ～其心 please sb.; make sb. happy

禺 yú 〈古语〉a kind of monkey

喁 yú 〈书面〉echo
see also yóng

喁喁 yúyú 〈书面〉❶ echo; parrot ❷ talk in an undertone; whisper: ～私语 talk privately in low voice
see also yóngyóng

愚 yú ❶ foolish; doltish; stupid: 大智若～。A man of great wisdom often appears slow-witted. ❷ make a fool of; fool: 为人所～ be strung along; be made a monkey (*or* fool) of ❸ 〈谦词〉humble: 以～兄之见 in my humble opinion / ～兄××× (used at the end of a letter) Humbly yours, (signature) / ～见所及 as far as I can see

愚騃 yú'ái 〈书面〉stupid; foolish; silly

愚暗 yú'àn unreasonable; ignorant

愚笨 yúbèn foolish; stupid; slow-witted: ～呆滞 stupid and dumb / 生性～ slow-witted by nature

愚不可及 yúbùkějí stupid in the extreme; hopelessly stupid; impossibly dim-witted: 办了蠢事还自我欣赏,真是～! It's indeed the height of folly to gloat over one's own stupidity!

愚痴 yúchī stupid; muddle-headed; foolish

愚蠢 yúchǔn stupid; foolish; silly: ～无知 stupid and ignorant / ～的想法 silly idea / ～的举动 foolish act / 他的～使我们脸面丧尽。His stupidity brought utter disgrace on us.

愚钝 yúdùn slow-witted; dull; stupid: 脑子～ slow-witted; dull in mind

愚公移山 Yúgōng-yíshān Foolish Old Man who removed the mountains — spirit of perseverance: 在现代化建设中,也要发挥～的精神。The spirit of the Foolish Old Man who removed the mountains should be encouraged in the modernization drive.

愚见 yújiàn *also* "愚意"〈谦词〉in my opinion; to my mind

愚陋 yúlòu ignorant and shallow: 乡俗～ stupid provincial ways

愚鲁 yúlǔ stupid; foolish; slow-witted: 不揣～,斗胆陈言 venture one's opinion, foolish as it may be

愚昧 yúmèi ignorant; foolish: ～落后 ignorant and backward / ～未开的小镇 provincial town enveloped in ignorance

愚昧无知 yúmèi-wúzhī foolish and ignorant; benighted; unenlightened: ～是农村治穷致富的极大障碍。Ignorance is the greatest obstacle to eradicating poverty in the countryside.

愚氓 yúméng stupid person; dolt; fool: 一个十足的～! An out and out fool! / 僧是～犹可训,妖为鬼蜮必成灾。The deluded monk was not beyond the light, But the malignant demon must wreak havoc.

愚蒙 yúméng stupid; ignorant: ～之至 ignorant in the extreme

愚民 yúmín ❶ ignorant people ❷ keep the people in ignorance; practise obscurantism

愚民政策 yúmín zhèngcè policy of keeping the people in ignorance; obscurantist policy; obscurantism

愚弄 yúnòng dupe; make a fool of; deceive: ～人民 dupe the people / 受到～ be hoodwinked; be made a fool of / 多次被人～ be taken in time and again

愚懦 yúnuò stupid and timid; ignorant and timid

愚人 yúrén foolish or stupid man; fool; dunderhead; dolt

愚人节 Yúrénjié All Fools' Day; April Fools' Day (April 1)

愚傻 yúshǎ foolish; stupid; muddle-headed

愚顽 yúwán stupid and stubborn; foolish and headstrong; mulish: ～不灵 incorrigibly obstinate

愚妄 yúwàng ignorant but arrogant; stupid but conceited: ～之论 foolish and senseless argument

愚者千虑,必有一得 yúzhě qiān lǜ, bì yǒu yī dé even an ignorant person occasionally hits on a good idea

愚忠 yúzhōng blind loyalty (to a master, ruler, etc.): 回师京都以尽～ withdraw one's army to the capital in blind loyalty to the emperor

愚拙 yúzhuō foolish; stupid; clumsy: ～的乡巴佬〈贬义〉clumsy country bumpkin; rube; oaf

髃 yú 〈中医〉front of the shoulder

嵎 yú ❶ mountain curve ❷ see "隅" yú

隅 yú ❶ corner; nook: 墙～ (in the) corner / 屋～ corner of a

room /向～而泣 weep all alone in a corner ❷ outlying area; border: 海～ seaboard

俞 yú ❶〈叹词〉*used in classical Chinese to indicate permission* ❷ (Yú) a surname

俞允 yúyǔn 〈书面〉permit; allow: ～与否, 尚在两可。It is equally possible whether or not permission will be given.

渝[1] yú change (of faith, oath, etc.): 忠贞不～ remain loyal to (a cause) /至死不～ be staunch till one's death /舍命不～ remain unswerving at the risk of one's life; would rather die to keep one's promise

渝[2] Yú (another name for 重庆) Chongqing, fourth municipality directly under the State Council: 成～铁路 Chengdu-Chongqing Railway

窬(踰) yú 〈书面〉climb over a wall: 穿～ get over a wall

愉 yú pleased; happy; delighted; overjoyed: 面露不～ look displeased; have an annoyed look on one's face /欢～之时 at the time of great rejoicing

愉快 yúkuài happy; glad; joyful; cheerful: ～的姑娘们 joyful girls /～的心情 with a merry heart /～的回忆 happy memories /工作很～ work cheerfully /过得非常～ have a very good time /令人～的天气 pleasant weather

愉乐 yúlè happy; delightful; cheerful: ～的表情 happy expression; cheerful countenance /家庭融和～ family harmony and happiness

愉悦 yúyuè joyful; cheerful; delighted; in high spirits: 心情～ (with) a joyful heart; be delighted (*or* cheerful) /～的微笑 happy smile

逾(❶踰) yú ❶ surpass; exceed; go beyond: 年～花甲 be over 60 years of age /饮酒～量 drink to excess /～墙而走 jump over the wall ❷ even more: 悲痛～甚 even more grieved

逾常 yúcháng out of the ordinary; extraordinary: 欣喜～ particularly overjoyed /悲感～ specially sad

逾分 yúfèn beyond the limit; excessive: 这种要求实已～。These are truly excessive demands. /此乃～之举。This is going too far. *or* You've overdone it.

逾恒 yúhéng 〈书面〉extraordinary; unusual; special: 勤奋～ unusually diligent

逾期 yúqī exceed the time limit; be overdue: ～不归 fail to return after one's leave is up /借书～不还, 每书罚款一元。For each book overdue, one will have to pay a one-*yuan* fine.

逾限 yúxiàn beyond the time limit; behind time; overdue

逾越 yúyuè exceed; go beyond; surmount: 不可～的障碍 insurmountable obstacle (*or* barrier) /不可～的界限 limit that one can not go beyond /～常规 depart from the usual practice /～权限 overstep one's authority (*or* power); go (*or* get) beyond one's competence /～界限 go beyond the limits; go out of bounds

逾越节 Yúyuèjié 〈宗教〉Passover, a holiday in memory of the escape of the Jews from Egypt

褕 yú *see* "襜褕" chānyú

瑜 yú 〈书面〉❶ beautiful jade: 佩～ wear a jade ornament ❷ splendour or lustre of jade; 〈比喻〉virtues; strong points: 瑕不掩～。One flaw cannot obscure the splendour of the jade. *or* The defects cannot obscure the virtues.

瑜伽 yújiā *also* "瑜珈" yoga

榆 yú elm

榆荚 yújiá elm fruit

榆木脑袋 yúmù-nǎodai blockhead; foolish, brainless person

榆钱 yúqián 〈口语〉elm fruit

榆树 yúshù elm tree

榆叶梅 yúyèméi flowering plum (*Prunus triloba*)

揄 yú 〈书面〉raise; tow; draw

揄扬 yúyáng 〈书面〉❶ praise: 极口～ praise (*or* extol) to the sky; speak highly of ❷ propagate; publicize; advocate; advertise: ～大义 publicize the significance of

蝓 yú *see* "蛞蝓" kuòyú

觎 yú *see* "觊觎" jìyú

歈 yú 〈书面〉❶ song ❷ pleased: 色～ look pleased

骗 yú 〈书面〉purple horse

余[1] yú ❶〈书面〉I; me; my: ～老矣。I am old (*or* aged). /～弟尚幼。My younger brother is still in his childhood. ❷ (Yú) a surname

余[2]**(餘)** yú ❶ surplus; spare; left; remaining: ～粮 surplus grain /自给有～ more than self-supporting /收支相抵, 尚有盈～ make both ends meet and have some to spare /～下的钱不多 not much money left /落日～辉 afterglow of a setting sun; twilight at sunset ❷ more than; odd; over: 一百～人 more than one hundred people /二十～天 over twenty days /三十～里 some thirty odd *li* ❸ after; later than; beyond: 学习之～ after class; during a student's spare time /悲痛之～ when sobered down after sorrow /业～爱好 hobby

余波 yúbō repercussions; aftermath: ～未平。The repercussions of the event are still felt.

余存 yúcún balance; remainder: 略有～ with a slight balance /把～的钱存入银行 deposit the remainder in the bank /取出一千元, ～三千元。The balance is 3,000 *yuan* after the withdrawal of 1,000.

余党 yúdǎng remnants of an overthrown clique; remaining cohorts: 他们是匪帮～。They are the remnants of the bandit gang.

余地 yúdì leeway; room; latitude; margin: 说话要留有～ allow some leeway in speech /大有商量的～ much room for discussion /没有回旋～ no space for manoeuvre /没有思考的～。There is no latitude for giving the matter further consideration.

余毒 yúdú residual poison; pernicious vestige; evil influence: 肃清无政府主义思潮的～ eliminate the pernicious influence of anarchism /伤口虽经冲洗, 但～未尽。There is some residual poison in the bite despite the cleansing.

余对数 yúduìshù 〈数学〉cologarithm

余额 yú'é ❶ vacancy yet to be filled; opening: 后备队员还有三个～。There are three replacement vacancies to be filled up. ❷ balance; remaining sum: ～表 balance sheet /本月有三千元～。There is a balance of 3,000 *yuan* for this month.

余额递减折旧法 yú'é dìjiǎn zhéjiùfǎ 〈经济〉reducing balance depreciation

余风 yúfēng lingering old practice; leftover practice: ～未改。The old practice still lingered.

余甘子 yúgānzi (another name for 油柑)〈植物〉emblic (*Phyllanthus emblica*); Indian gooseberry

余割 yúgē 〈数学〉cosecant

余晷 yúguǐ spare time

余函数 yúhánshù 〈数学〉complementary function

余痕 yúhén remaining trace or sign; vestige

余晖 yúhuī *also* "余辉" last rays of the setting sun; afterglow; evening glow: 夕阳的～ last rays of the setting sun /晚霞的～ last glow of sunset clouds; sunset glow

余悸 yújì lingering fear: 心有～ have a lingering fear /～未消 one's heart is still throbbing with fear

余角 yújiǎo 〈数学〉complementary angle

余烬 yújìn ❶ ashes; embers: 篝火～ burning ashes of a camp fire ❷〈比喻〉ruins; wreckage: 劫后～ devastated waste of smoldering embers after a war; war ruins

余可类推 yúkělèituī the rest may be inferred by analogy

余款 yúkuǎn remaining money; money left; balance

余力 yúlì remaining strength, vigour, etc.: 不遗～ spare no pains (*or* efforts); do one's utmost

余沥 yúlì ❶〈书面〉leftover alcohol; heeltap ❷〈比喻〉meagre fringe benefits

余利 yúlì profit of business: ～微薄 meagre profit /～颇丰 fairly fat

profit
余粮 yúliáng surplus grain: ~户 household with grain to spare; grain-surplus household /无~户 household without grain reserves
余量 yúliàng 〈机械〉allowance: 留~ make allowance /加工~ metal (machining) allowance /机械加工~ machining allowance; allowance for machining
余留 yúliú left over; left; remaining: 一场大火，烧得什么也未~下来。There was nothing left after the big fire.
余流 yúliú (of seas or oceans) residual current
余年 yúnián remaining years: ~之乐 live a happy life during one's remaining years /~可数 one's failing years are numbered
余孽 yúniè remnant evil force; remaining evil element; leftover evil; surviving supporter of an evil cause: 封建~ dregs of feudalism /奸党~ remnants of the evil party (*or* clique)
余怒 yúnù lingering anger: ~未消 one's anger lingers on
余钱 yúqián money left over; surplus money: 把~存入银行 deposit one's surplus money in the bank
余切 yúqiē 〈数学〉cotangent (ctg): ~向量 cotangent vector
余曲面 yúqūmiàn complementary surface
余缺 yú-quē surplus and shortage: ~互补 mutually supplementary in each other's needs /调剂~ each making up the other's deficiency; help supply each other's needs
余热 yúrè ❶ surplus heat; waste heat; delayed heat; residual heat: ~锅炉 waste heat boiler /~发电 power generation by waste heat; electricity-generation from residual heat /利用~取暖 keep warm with residual heat ❷〈比喻〉energy of retirees: 为国为民献~ make continued contributions to the country and people in one's retirement
余三角函数 yúsānjiǎo hánshù complementary trigonometric function
余色 yúsè complementary colour
余生 yúshēng ❶ one's remaining years; remainder of one's life: 安度~ live through one's remaining years in peace /~不幸 be unhappy in the remainder of one's life ❷ survival: 劫后~ survive a holocaust; survive a disaster
余剩 yúshèng surplus; remainder: 她勤俭持家，钱粮每年都有~。She was industrious and thrifty in managing the household and had grain and money to spare by the end of each year.
余矢 yúshǐ 〈数学〉coversed sine
余数 yúshù 〈数学〉remainder: 九减四，~为五。Nine minus four is five. /八除以三得二，~为二。Eight divided by three makes two, with a remainder of two.
余头 yútou change: 别把~忘在柜台上! Don't leave your change on the shop counter!
余唾 yútuò *also* "唾余" idle talk
余外 yúwài 〈方言〉except; apart from: 这屋里只有你我二人，~无人。There was no one in the room except us two.
余威 yúwēi fame that still remains; remaining prestige or influence: ~尚在 one's influence remains /老将军~不减当年。The aged general was as prestigious as ever.
余味 yúwèi agreeable aftertaste; pleasant impression: ~无穷 leave a lasting and pleasant impression (*or* aftertaste) /犹有~ have an agreeable aftertaste
余隙 yúxì ❶ remaining space or room; gap: 衣箱里满满的，一点~都没有。There's no room left in the suitcase. ❷〈机械〉clearance: 切屑~ chip clearance
余暇 yúxiá spare time; leisure time; leisure: 他把很少的一点儿~都用在孩子身上了。He devoted the little spare time he had to the child.
余下 yúxià remaining; leftover: 手中~的钱不多了。I didn't have much money left. /~的事以后再说。The rest shall be dealt with later.
余闲 yúxián *also* "余暇" spare time; leisure (time): 少有~ have little leisure /他~时听听音乐，看看电视。He would listen to music or watch television in his spare time.
余弦 yúxián 〈数学〉cosine: ~定律 cosine law /~加权 cosine weighting
余香 yúxiāng lingering fragrance
余项 yúxiàng 〈数学〉remainder term; remainder; residue
余兴 yúxìng ❶ lingering interest: 犹有~ have a lingering interest ❷ entertainment after a meeting or a dinner party: 会议到此结束，~表演现在开始。It's the end of the meeting, and the performances shall begin now.
余蓄 yúxù savings; money saved: 手中~殆尽 have spent all one's savings
余因子 yúyīnzǐ 〈数学〉complementary divisor
余音 yúyīn lingering sound: ~袅袅。The air echoed with the lingering sound.
余音绕梁 yúyīn-ràoliáng the sound lingers in the air; the voice keeps reverberating in the air even after the vocalist has stopped singing; the music lingers in the air long after the performance: ~，三日不绝。The echoes of songs lingered about the roof for three days.
余荫 yúyìn 〈书面〉shield or protection one receives from one's elders or ancestors
余勇可贾 yúyǒng-kěgǔ still have plenty of mettle to show; have strength yet to spare: 吾虽老迈，然尚有~。Although I am quite old, I still have plenty of fight in me.
余裕 yúyù surplus; ample; having enough and to spare: 绰有~ more than sufficient; more than enough; have enough and to spare /~的时间不多了。There isn't much time left.
余韵 yúyùn remaining grace: ~不减当年 as graceful as before
余震 yúzhèn 〈地质〉aftershock: 这次大震后，还发生过多次~。Several aftershocks occurred following the strong earthquake.

畲

yú 〈书面〉land that has been cultivated for two years
see also shē

艅

yú
艅艎 yúhuáng 〈古语〉wooden boat

狳

yú *see* "犰狳" qiúyú

馀

yú ❶ *see* "余²" yú ❷ (Yú) a surname

舁

yú 〈书面〉raise or lift together: 市门石鼓，十人~，弗能举。Ten people tried but failed to lift the stone drum at the city gate.

臾

yú *see* "须臾" xūyú

谀

yú 〈书面〉fawn on; curry favour; flatter: 阿~奉承 flatter and toady
谀辞 yúcí *also* "谀词" flattering remarks; flattery: 这篇评论颇有~。This commentary is full of flattery.
谀言 yúyán flattery; sycophantic words: ~邀宠 curry favour with sb. by flattery

萸

yú *see* "茱萸" zhūyú

腴

yú ❶ fat; plump; rounded out: 体态丰~ fat; plump ❷ fertile: 膏~之地 fertile land
腴润 yúrùn 〈书面〉❶ fat; rounded out; plump: 肌肤~ plump and smooth-skinned ❷ fertile: 土地~，宜于农业。The land is fertile and good for farming.

鱼(魚)

yú ❶ fish: 黄花~ yellow croaker /鲤~ common carp /鲫~ crucian carp /白鲢~ silver carp /青~ black carp /草~ grass carp; Chinese ide /胖头~ *also* "花鲢" spotted silver carp; big head /鲳~ pomfret /石斑~ roach /大麻哈~ salmon /鳐~ skate /鲥~ shad /小口鳕~ haddock /武昌~(团头鲂) blunt-snout /鲟~ sturgeon /桂~ mandarin fish /鲽~ flounder /凤尾~ long tailed anchovy /鲈~ perch /鳗~ sea eel /鲇~ catfish /鲆~ left-eyed flounder /鲭~ mackerel /鳝~ fresh-water eel /梭子~ pike /银~ whitebait; salangid /河豚~ globefish /鱿~ squid /墨~ cuttlefish /章~ octopus /比目~ turbot; flat fish /带~ hairtail; cutlass fish /金枪~ tuna /沙丁~ sardine /鲨~ shark /鼋~ *also* "甲~" turtle /三条~ three fish /两条鲤~ two carp /钓~ go fishing /养~场 fish farm /年捕~量 annual catch /养~ fish-culture; pisciculture /淡水养~ freshwater fish-culture /葬身~腹 feed the fishes /缘木求~ fish in the air — futile attempt ❷ (Yú) a surname
鱼白 yúbái ❶ fish sperm; milt ❷〈方言〉*see* "~鳔" ❸ whitish: 东方一线~，黎明已经到来。The first whitish ray appeared and the

dawn broke.
鱼鳔 yúbiào air bladder; fish-sound
鱼舱 yúcāng fish hold (in a ship)
鱼叉 yúchā *also*“渔叉”yúchā fish spear; fishgig; fish fork:投掷～ throw a fish spear
鱼沉雁杳 yúchén-yànyǎo be heard of no more; lose contact
鱼池 yúchí fish pond
鱼翅 yúchì *also*“翅”;“翅子”shark's fin
鱼虫 yúchóng water flea (used as fish feed):捞～ scoop up (*or* catch) water fleas
鱼唇 yúchún shark's lip
鱼刺 yúcì fishbone:剔～ bone a fish /被～卡住了 have a fish bone in one's throat
鱼大水小 yúdà-shuǐxiǎo big fish in shallow water — ponderous apparatus without adequate resources for maintenance:这个厂～,坐办公室的比工人还多。With more staff than floor (*or* line) workers, the factory is absolutely bloated.
鱼打挺儿 yúdǎtǐngr jump like a fish:他一个～翻身下了床。He jumped out of his bed in a flash.
鱼道 yúdào *also*“鱼梯”fishway; fish ladder
鱼灯舞 yúdēngwǔ fish-lantern dance
鱼肚 yúdǔ fish maw:红烧～ fish maw stewed in soybean sauce
鱼肚白 yúdùbái whitish colour of a fish's belly; pale; greyish white:天边泛出～。The first thin pale light was seen over the horizon.
鱼饵 yú'ěr bait:上～ bait (with) /投下～ cast bait /吞掉～ swallow a bait /咬～ take bait /用假苍蝇作～钓鱼 fish with artificial flies as bait
鱼贩子 yúfànzi fishmonger
鱼粉 yúfěn fish meal
鱼腹式大梁 yúfùshì dàliáng 〈建筑〉inverted bow and chain girder; fish-bellied girder
鱼肝油 yúgānyóu cod-liver oil
鱼竿 yúgān fishing rod:～式天线 fish pole antenna
鱼缸 yúgāng goldfish bowl; fish jar
鱼钩 yúgōu *also*“渔钩”yúgōu fishhook; hook
鱼狗 yúgǒu kingfisher
鱼骨形天线 yúgǔxíng tiānxiàn fishbone (type) antenna; fishbone aerial
鱼鼓 yúgǔ *see*“渔鼓”yúgǔ
鱼鼓道情 yúgǔ dàoqíng *see*“渔鼓道情”yúgǔ dàoqíng
鱼贯 yúguàn one following the other; in single file:～而行 move in single file
鱼贯而入 yúguàn'érrù enter in single file; file in:客人～,主人在大厅与他们一一握手。The host shook hands with the guests as they filed into the hall.
鱼花 yúhuā *also*“鱼苗”fish fry
鱼际 yújì interface between the dark- and light-coloured parts either on the back of the hand or on the instep of the foot
鱼酱油 yújiàngyóu fish sauce
鱼胶 yújiāo ❶ fish glue; isinglass ❷〈方言〉air bladder (esp. of the yellow croaker)
鱼精蛋白 yújīng dànbái protamine
鱼具 yújù *also*“渔具”yújù fishing gear or tackle:～商店 fishing tackle store
鱼口 yúkǒu *also*“鱼口疗”〈中医〉lymphogranuloma inguinale; climatic or tropical bubo
鱼雷 yúléi 〈军事〉torpedo:发射～ launch a torpedo /空投～ aircraft torpedo /人控～ hunter torpedo /寻的～ target-seeking torpedo; homing torpedo /自潜～ diving torpedo /～兵 torpedoman /～发射管 torpedo tube /～轰炸机 torpedo bomber (TB) /～舰 motor torpedo boat; mosquito boat /～轰炸侦察机 torpedo bomber reconnaissance aircraft (TBR)
鱼雷艇 yúléitǐng *also*“鱼雷快艇”torpedo boat; patrol torpedo boat (PT boat)
鱼类学 yúlèixué ichthyology
鱼类养殖 yúlèi yǎngzhí fish farming; fish-rearing
鱼类制品厂 yúlèi zhìpǐnchǎng fishworks
鱼鳞 yúlín fish scale; scale:刮～ scale a fish; scrape the scales off a fish
鱼鳞板 yúlínbǎn 〈建筑〉gills; overlapping board
鱼鳞病 yúlínbìng *also*“鱼鳞癣”ichthyosis; fishskin disease
鱼鳞坑 yúlínkēng pits arranged like fish scales, dug on mountain slopes for holding water or planting trees; fish-scale pits:按规定每人每天挖两个～。Each person is required to dig two fish-scale pits every day.
鱼龙 yúlóng 〈考古〉ichthyosaur
鱼龙混杂 yúlóng-hùnzá dragons and fish jumbled together; the genuine being mixed with the false; thread and thrum:因而未免泥沙俱下,～。So inevitably the waters were muddied, and the bad became mixed with the good.
鱼笼 yúlóng fishpot
鱼篓 yúlǒu bamboo fish hamper; creel
鱼露 yúlù fish sauce
鱼卵 yúluǎn roe
鱼螨 yúmǎn fish mite
鱼米之乡 yúmǐzhīxiāng land of fish and rice; land of milk and honey; land of abundance
鱼苗 yúmiáo fish fry:投放三万尾～ throw in 30,000 fries
鱼目混珠 yúmù-hùnzhū pass off fish eyes as pearls; palm off the bad as the good; pass off the sham as the genuine:他们～,自称为爱国之士。They posed as patriots, in order to confuse the public.
鱼片 yúpiàn sliced fish meat; fish meat slice
鱼漂 yúpiāo cork on a fishing line; bob; float:～晃动。The float shook. /～下沉。The bob dipped.
鱼鳍 yúqí fin
鱼情 yúqíng traces of a fish shoal
鱼群 yúqún shoal of fish
鱼群探测 yúqún tàncè fish detection:～装置 fish detector
鱼肉 yúròu ❶ flesh of fish; fish and meat:～丸子 fishball /人为刀俎,我为～ be meat on sb.'s chopping block; be at sb.'s mercy ❷ oppress; victimize:～乡里 cruelly oppress the people in the locality
鱼生 yúshēng finely sliced raw fish
鱼生粥 yúshēngzhōu rice gruel with fish slices
鱼虱 yúshī fish louse; carp louse
鱼石螈 yúshíyuán *Ichthyostegalia*
鱼石脂 yúshízhī 〈药学〉ichthammol; ichthyol
鱼市 yúshì fish market
鱼水 yúshuǐ fish and water; intimacy; interdependence:～和谐 harmony between husband and wife; marital harmony
鱼水情 yúshuǐqíng close relationship between fish and water; fish-and-water relationship:谱写了一曲军民～的新歌 compose a new song in praise of the close relations between the army and the people
鱼水情深 yúshuǐ-qíngshēn as close as fish and water; of profound friendship
鱼死网破 yúsǐ-wǎngpò 〈比喻〉the fish dies and the net gets torn — perish together; fight like the Kilkenny cats; end up in common ruin:拼个～ fight at the risk of mutual destruction
鱼松 yúsōng *also*“鱼肉松”dried fish floss:优质～ quality fish floss
鱼塘 yútáng fish pond
鱼藤 yúténg 〈植物〉trifoliate jewelvine
鱼藤精 yúténgjīng 〈农业〉derris extract
鱼藤酮 yúténgtóng 〈农业〉rotenone
鱼梯 yútī *also*“鱼道”(of a dam, etc.) fish ladder; fishway
鱼丸子 yúwánzi fish ball
鱼网 yúwǎng *also*“渔网”yúwǎng fishnet; fishing net:织～ weave a fishnet /补～ mend (*or* repair) a fishnet /晒～ air a fishnet; spread a fishnet in the sun
鱼尾 yúwěi fishtail:～螺栓 fish bolt /～铣刀 fish tail cutter /～锥 fishtail drill
鱼尾板 yúwěibǎn 〈铁路〉fish-plate
鱼尾号 yúwěihào boldface square brackets (〖〗;【】)
鱼尾纹 yúwěiwén crow's feet:不到三十,她的眼角上已出现了～。Crow's feet had appeared round the corners of her eyes before she was thirty.
鱼鲜 yúxiān fish and shellfish as food; seafood:～市场 fish market; seafood market /尝遍了各种～ have tasted all kinds of seafood
鱼香肉丝 yúxiāng ròusī fish-flavoured shredded pork
鱼腥草 yúxīngcǎo 〈植物〉cordate houttuynia:～既可食用,又可用来治疗肝病。Cordate houttuynia is not only edible but also good for curing liver trouble.

Y

鱼汛 yúxùn *also*"渔汛"yúxùn fishing season:今年～期早。This year's fishing season arrived earlier than usual.
鱼眼石 yúyǎnshí apophyllite
鱼雁 yúyàn 〈书面〉〈比喻〉epistolary correspondence:频通～ have (*or* keep) constant correspondence
鱼雁往来 yúyàn-wǎnglái incoming and outgoing of epistolary correspondence:他们偶有～。They occasionally write to each other.
鱼秧子 yúyāngzi fingerling:这批～长势好。These fingerlings look fine and healthy.
鱼鹰 yúyīng ❶ osprey; fish hawk; sea eagle; erne ❷ cormorant
鱼油 yúyóu fish oil
鱼游釜中 yúyóufǔzhōng like fish swimming in a cooking pot — in imminent danger; in a perilous situation:若～,喘息须臾间耳。He will soon breathe his last, just like a fish swimming in a cooking pot.
鱼圆 yúyuán 〈方言〉fish-ball
鱼跃 yúyuè ❶ jump or leap of a fish:海阔从～,天空任鸟飞。The fish swims merrily in the vast sea; the bird soars freely in the broad sky. *or* There is broad scope for one's talent. ❷〈体育〉fish dive (as in volleyball):～救球 diving save / 只见他一个漂亮的～,竟把球救了起来。He saved the ball by a beautiful fish dive.
鱼闸 yúzhá water or sluice gate of a fish pond; fish lock
鱼找鱼,虾找虾 yú zhǎo yú, xiā zhǎo xiā fish draws to fish and shrimp to shrimp — like attracts like; birds of a feather flock together:～,周末他俩总是在一起的。As the saying goes, like attracts like, they are always found together at weekends.
鱼种 yúzhǒng fish breed:挑选优良～ select good fish breeds
鱼子 yúzǐ roe; fish eggs
鱼子酱 yúzǐjiàng caviar(e)

渔(漁)

yú ❶ fishing:竭泽而～ dry up the pond to catch all the fish therein — exhaust the source of revenue; kill the goose that lays the golden eggs ❷ take sth. one has no right to: *see* "～利"
渔霸 yúbà fish tyrant:坚决打击～控制鱼市 deal resolute blows at the fish tyrants who dominate the fishmarket
渔叉 yúchā *also*"鱼叉"yúchā fish spear; fishgig; fish fork
渔产 yúchǎn aquatic products:今年～可获丰收。A rich harvest of aquatic products is expected this year.
渔场 yúchǎng fishing ground; fishery:近海～ in-shore fishery / 远洋～ deep-sea fishery
渔船 yúchuán fishing vessel; fishing boat:拖网～ trawler / 围网～ purse seiner; seine-boat / 机动～ motorized fishing junk / ～出海。The fishing boat puts out (*or* goes) to sea.
渔村 yúcūn fishing village
渔貂 yúdiāo fisher; fisher marten; fisher cat
渔夫 yúfū fisherman
渔父 yúfǔ 〈书面〉old fisherman
渔妇 yúfù fisherwoman
渔港 yúgǎng fishing harbour or port
渔歌 yúgē fisherman's song:～唱和 one fisherman singing and others joining in
渔工 yúgōng fisher; fisherman
渔钩 yúgōu *also*"鱼钩"yúgōu fishhook; hook
渔鼓 yúgǔ *also*"鱼鼓"yúgǔ ❶ percussion instrument made of bamboo and leather; fisherman's drum ❷〈戏曲〉folk tales sung to the accompaniment of a fisherman's drum
see also"道情"dàoqíng
渔鼓道情 yúgǔ dàoqíng *also*"道情"dàoqíng;"鱼鼓道情"yúgǔ dàoqíng folk tales sung to the accompaniment of simple percussion instruments
渔户 yúhù fishing household
渔火 yúhuǒ lights on fishing boats:点点～ scattered lights (on the sea) / 岸边的～,明灭可见。Lights on the fishing boats at anchor are clearly visible.
渔获量 yúhuòliàng catch:～限额 catch quota / ～限制 catch limit
渔家 yújiā fishing household:～女 fisherman's daughter
渔具 yújù *also*"鱼具"yújù fishing tackle or gear
渔捞 yúlāo mass fishing
渔利 yúlì ❶ reap unfair gains; profit at others' expense:从中～ exploit a situation to benefit oneself; cash in on other people's efforts / 从中～三千元 cash in 3,000 *yuan* from it ❷ easy gains; spoils
渔猎 yúliè ❶ fishing and hunting:从事～ go in for fishing and hunting ❷〈书面〉plunder; grab:～百姓 rob the ordinary folks ❸〈书面〉hanker after; pursue:～女色 seek carnal pleasure; womanize
渔猎标枪 yúliè biāoqiāng harpoon
渔轮 yúlún fishing ship; fishing vessel
渔民 yúmín fisherman; fishing population:～俱乐部 fishermen's club
渔民结 yúmínjié fisherman's bend
渔婆 yúpó fisherwoman; fishwife
渔区 yúqū fishing zone; area where people depend mainly on fishery for their living
渔人 yúrén fisherman
渔人之利 yúrénzhīlì fisherman's gains — profit seized by a third party:坐收～ quietly wait to benefit from a fight between others
see also"鹬蚌相争,渔人得利"yù-bàng xiāng zhēng, yúrén dé lì
渔色 yúsè 〈书面〉hunt for women; sex-hunt; on the prowl for sex:～之徒 rake; satyr; wolf
渔网 yúwǎng *see*"鱼网"yúwǎng
渔翁 yúwēng elderly fisherman
渔线 yúxiàn fish-line; fishing line
渔汛 yúxùn *see*"鱼汛"yúxùn
渔业 yúyè fishery:～权 fishery (*or* fishing) right / ～地段 fishery servitude / ～封闭线 fishery closing line / ～控制区 fishery control zone / ～毗连区 fishery contiguous zone / ～分布情况 fisheries distribution / ～管理机构 regulatory fishery body / 发展～生产 develop fisheries (*or* fishing industries)
渔业公约 yúyè gōngyuē fishery convention:欧洲～ European Fishery Convention (9 March 1964)
渔业区 yúyèqū fishing zone; fishery limits
渔业协定 yúyè xiédìng fisheries agreement
渔业资源 yúyè zīyuán fishery or fishing resources:～保护区 fishery conservation zone
渔舟 yúzhōu 〈书面〉fishing boat; fisher:～唱晚 chant on a returning fishing boat at dusk

予

yú 〈书面〉I; me:予之才,～所不及也。I cannot equal you in intellect.
see also yǔ
予取予求 yúqǔ-yúqiú take whatever one wants — take freely; make unlimited demands:官吏～,百姓怒不敢言。Officials extorted freely from the ordinary folk, who dared not show their anger.

伃

yú *see*"倢伃"jiéyú

妤

yú *see*"婕妤"jiéyú

yǔ

宇

yǔ ❶ eaves; house:屋～ house; building / 御～ imperial house; imperial palace / 庙～ temple ❷ space; universe; world:声震寰～ world renowned / 名扬～内 be famous the world over ❸ manner; bearing; temperament:眉～〈书面〉manner; features / 器～不凡 have extraordinary poise ❹ (Yǔ) a surname
宇称 yǔchēng 〈物理〉parity:～定律 parity law / ～守恒 conservation of parity; parity conservation / ～不守恒 parity nonconservation / 奇～ *also*"负～性" odd parity / 偶～ *also*"正～性" even parity
宇航 yǔháng ❶ space navigation; astronavigation ❷ astronavigation-related:～学校 school for space navigation / ～基地 base of space navigation
宇航病 yǔhángbìng space sickness
宇航服 yǔhángfú space suit
宇航学 yǔhángxué astronautics
宇航员 yǔhángyuán astronaut; spaceman; cosmonaut
宇航站 yǔhángzhàn space station
宇文 Yǔwén a surname
宇宙 yǔzhòu ❶ universe; space; cosmos:～站 space station / ～辐射 cosmic radiation ❷ world
宇宙尘 yǔzhòuchén cosmic dust; meteoroid
宇宙成因 yǔzhòu chéngyīn cosmogenesis
宇宙传播学 yǔzhòu chuánbōxué cosmography
宇宙飞船 yǔzhòu fēichuán spaceship; spacecraft:无人驾驶～ pilot-

less spaceship /有人驾驶～ manned spaceship /载人～ man-carrying spaceship /发射～ launch a spaceship
宇宙飞行 yǔzhòu fēixíng space flight
宇宙飞行器 yǔzhòu fēixíngqì spacecraft
宇宙飞行员 yǔzhòu fēixíngyuán spaceman; (US) astronaut; (Russian) cosmonaut
宇宙服 yǔzhòufú *see*“宇航服”
宇宙观 yǔzhòuguān *also*“世界观” shìjièguān world view; world outlook:树立正确的～ have a correct world outlook
宇宙航行 yǔzhòu hángxíng space navigation; astronavigation
宇宙航行学 yǔzhòu hángxíngxué astronautics; cosmonautics
宇宙航行员 yǔzhòu hángxíngyuán *see*“宇航员”
宇宙火箭 yǔzhòu huǒjiàn space rocket; cosmic rocket:发射～ launch a space rocket
宇宙空间 yǔzhòu kōngjiān cosmic or outer space:～站 space station
宇宙论 yǔzhòulùn cosmology:～者 cosmologist
宇宙年 yǔzhòunián 〈天文〉cosmic year; galactic year (the period of revolution of the sun round the centre of the galaxy, equal to about 220 million years)
宇宙射线 yǔzhòu shèxiàn *also*“宇宙线” cosmic rays:～爆发 cosmic ray burst
宇宙生物学 yǔzhòu shēngwùxué cosmobiology
宇宙速度 yǔzhòu sùdù 〈航天〉cosmic speed; cosmic or astronautical velocity:第一～ first cosmic velocity; circular speed (*or* velocity) /第二～ second cosmic velocity; earth escape speed (*or* velocity); parabolic speed (*or* velocity) /第三～ third cosmic velocity; solar escape speed (*or* velocity); hyperbolic speed (*or* velocity)
宇宙物理学 yǔzhòu wùlǐxué cosmophysics
宇宙线 yǔzhòuxiàn *see*“宇宙射线”
宇宙相对论 yǔzhòu xiāngduìlùn astrorelativity
宇宙学 yǔzhòuxué 〈天文〉cosmology:克莱因－阿尔芬～ Klein Alven cosmology
宇宙演化论 yǔzhòu yǎnhuàlùn cosmogony
宇宙云 yǔzhòuyún cosmic cloud
宇宙噪声 yǔzhòu zàoshēng cosmic noise
宇宙站 yǔzhòuzhàn space station
宇宙志 yǔzhòuzhì cosmography:～学者 cosmographer

窳

yǔ 〈书面〉(of things) bad; evil; disgusting:良～ good or bad
窳败 yǔbài 〈书面〉degenerate; corrupt
窳惰 yǔduò 〈书面〉indolent; lazy
窳劣 yǔliè 〈书面〉inferior; bad; of poor quality:器具～ tools and equipment of inferior quality

语

yǔ ❶ language; tongue; words:英～ English (language) /阿姆哈拉～ Amharic /班图～ Bantu /豪萨～ Hausa /斯瓦希里～ Swahili /俗～ (common) saying; folk adage /成～ idiom; set phrase /谚～ proverb /古～ classic (*or* ancient) language /千言万～ (have) innumerable words (to say) /甜言蜜～ fine-sounding words; honey (*or* oily) tongue /冷言冷～ ironical remark(s); sarcastic comment(s) ❷ speak; say:低声细～ speak in a low voice; whisper /默默不～ speak nothing; keep quiet; be speechless; remain silent ❸ adage; proverb; saying; idiom:～曰:"唇亡则齿寒。"As the saying goes, "If the lips are gone, the teeth will be cold." ❹ nonlinguistic means of communicating ideas; sign; signal:旗～ semaphore; flagsignal /手势～ dactylology; sign language
see also yù
语病 yǔbìng faulty wording:这话有～。There's something wrong in the wording.
语不惊人死不休 yǔ bù jīngrén sǐ bù xiū not cease racking one's brains until one finds some words and phrases that can cause a great sensation; never rest until one finds the most catching turn of phrase
语词 yǔcí words and phrases
语次 yǔcì ❶〈书面〉in the course of conversation ❷ arrangement of ideas in speech:～凌乱 confused argument
语调 yǔdiào 〈语言〉intonation; voice:温柔的～ (in) a soft voice /～深沉 (in) a deep voice /～是英语的重要组成部分。Intonation is an important component of the English language.
语法 yǔfǎ grammar:传统～ traditional grammar /结构～ structural grammar /生成－转换～ generative-transformational grammar /比较～ comparative grammar /实用～ applied grammar /系统～ systemic grammar /英语～ English grammar /～课 class on grammar; grammar class /造句要注意～。Pay attention to grammar when you are making a sentence.
语法学 yǔfǎxué grammar:～家 grammarian
语锋 yǔfēng thread of discourse; topic of conversation:～一转 change the topic of conversation (*or* one's talk)
语符学 yǔfúxué glossematics
语感 yǔgǎn (instinctive) feel for the language
语汇 yǔhuì vocabulary:～丰富 have a rich (*or* an extensive) vocabulary /～贫乏 have a limited vocabulary
语句 yǔjù sentence:～欠通 faulty sentence /～通顺 clear and smooth sentence /～分析 sentence analysis; analysis of sentences
语库 yǔkù language data bank
语料 yǔliào language data or material
语料库 yǔliàokù *see*“语库”
语录 yǔlù recorded utterance; quotation:马恩～ quotations from Marx and Engels
语妙天下 yǔmiàotiānxià speak or write with sparkling wit:这位语言大师的散文往往～。This master of language often writes with inimitable wit.
语气 yǔqì ❶ tone; manner of speaking:～冷淡 in cold tone /～委婉 speak politely (*or* tactfully) /用友好的～说 speak in a friendly tone ❷〈语言〉mood:陈述～ indicative mood /祈使～ imperative mood /疑问～ interrogative mood /虚拟～ subjunctive mood
语气助词 yǔqì zhùcí modal particle
语塞 yǔsè tongue-tied; speechless:悲愤之下，一时～ speechless with grief
语声 yǔshēng voice; tone:～未断泪自流。Tears rolled down one's cheeks before one finished speaking.
语失 yǔshī make an indiscreet remark; make an erroneous utterance; make a slip of the tongue:言多～ too much talk breeds indiscretion; talk much and err much
语素 yǔsù morpheme
语态 yǔtài 〈语言〉voice:被动～ passive voice /主动～ active voice
语体 yǔtǐ 〈语言〉type of writing; variety of language; style:口语～ colloquial style; colloquialism /～风格 style of language /书面～ written language
语体文 yǔtǐwén prose written in the vernacular:～小说 fiction in vernacular; vernacular fiction
语文 yǔwén ❶ language:～水平 language proficiency /～造诣很深 be well-versed in a language /～课 Chinese (as a course) ❷ language and literature
语文学 yǔwénxué philology
语无伦次 yǔwúlúncì speak incoherently or illogically; talk in a confused manner:他因着急而～，请你谅解。He is too worried to talk coherently. Please forgive him.
语系 yǔxì 〈语言〉family of languages; language family:拉丁～ Latin family of languages /汉藏～ Han-Tibetan language family /印欧～ Indo-European languages
语序 yǔxù 〈语言〉word order:严格的～是汉语语法特点之一。Strict word order is a characteristic of the Chinese grammar.
语焉不详 yǔyānbùxiáng not go into detail; not elaborate; not be clear:书上对这件事的记载～。There is no detailed historical record of the event.
语言 yǔyán ❶ language:～规范化 standardization of speech /～科学 linguistic science /～的变化 evolution of language /～的运用 use of language /～著作 works on languages; linguistic writings /～无味 insipid speech or writing /～简炼 in concise language /～粗野 in coarse language /古代～ ancient (*or* classic) language /文学～ literary language /外交～ diplomatic language /～与文字 spoken and written language /工作～ working language /正式～ official language /生动的～ graphic expression /～是人们交流思想的工具。Language is a tool for communication. ❷ discourse; language
语言美 yǔyánměi beauty of one's verbal expressions
语言年代学 yǔyán niándàixué glottochronology
语言实验室 yǔyán shíyànshì language lab
语言心理学 yǔyán xīnlǐxué linguistic psychology
语言学 yǔyánxué linguistics; philology:～家 linguist; philologist /～专著 works on linguistics; philologic writings /工程～ engineering linguistics /宏观～ macrolinguistics /微观～ microlinguistics /计算～

computational linguistics /理论～ theoretical linguistics /应用～ applied linguistics /比较～ comparative philology /对比～ contrastive linguistics /共时～ synchronic linguistics /历时～ diachronic linguistics /历史～ historical linguistics /普通～ general linguistics /社会～ sociolinguistics /心理～ psycholinguistics
语义 yǔyì meaning of a word; semantic meaning: ～扩展 semantic extension /～缩合 semantic condensation /～要素 semantic feature
语义学 yǔyìxué semantics: ～家 semanticist /结构～ structural semantics /解释～ interpretative semantics
语意 yǔyì meaning of a remark: ～深长 (of one's remarks) very meaningful
语音 yǔyīn speech sounds; pronunciation: ～课 phonetics class /～教材 teaching materials (*or* textbook) on phonetics /她的～很标准。Her pronunciation is standard.
语音识别 yǔyīn shíbié 〈通信〉voice recognition
语音信号编码器 yǔyīn xìnhào biānmǎqì VODER; Voice coder
语音信息 yǔyīn xìnxī 〈通信〉audiotext
语音信箱 yǔyīn xìnxiāng 〈通信〉voice mail
语音学 yǔyīnxué phonetics: ～家 phonetician /实用～ practical phonetics /有关～的著作 works on phonetics
语用学 yǔyòngxué pragmatics
语源学 yǔyuánxué etymology
语种 yǔzhǒng kind of language; language variety
语重心长 yǔzhòng-xīncháng sincere words and earnest wishes; (say sth.) in all earnestness: 我们永远不忘老师～的教导。We shall never forget our teachers' sincere instructions. /他～地询问道:"你这次真的有办法吗?" He asked with great concern, "Are you sure you can manage this time?"
语助词 yǔzhùcí *also* "语气助词" 〈语言〉auxiliary word that is used at the end of a sentence or during a pause to indicate one's tone or manner of speaking; tonal adjunct
语族 yǔzú *see* "语系"

龉

yǔ *see* "龃龉" jǔyǔ

圄

yǔ *see* "囹圄" língyǔ

铻

yǔ *see* "钼铻" jǔyǔ
see also wú

敔

yǔ ancient percussion musical instrument

雨

yǔ rain: 春～ spring rain /小～ slight (*or* gentle) rain /大～ heavy (*or* pluvial) rain /～夹雪 sleet /倾盆大～ pouring rain; raining cats and dogs; rain coming down in buckets; torrential rain /暴～ torrential rain; downpour; cloudburst /暴风～ storm; tempest /雷～ thunderstorm /黄梅～ plum rains /细～ drizzle /阵～ shower /热带季～ monsoon rain /人工降～ rainmaking /～淋日晒 wetted by the rain and dried by the sun; long exposure to the sun and rain /大～瓢泼而下。The rain was coming down in sheets. *or* The rain fell in torrents. /狂风急～吹打着窗户。The driving wind and slanting rain beat (*or* pelted) against the windows.
see also yù
雨暴 yǔbào rainstorm
雨布 yǔbù waterproof cloth; waterproof; rainwear: 披着一块～ have a piece of waterproof cloth draped over one's shoulders
雨层云 yǔcéngyún 〈气象〉nimbostratus
雨带 yǔdài rain belt
雨滴 yǔdī raindrop
雨点 yǔdiǎn raindrop: 豆大的～ big raindrop(s) /密集的～ thick and fast raindrops
雨刮器 yǔguāqì *also* "雨刷" windscreen or windshield wiper (of a car)
雨过地皮湿 yǔ guò dìpí shī the ground is hardly wet after the rain — do sth. perfunctorily or superficially; do sth. as a mere formality: 这次检查只怕又是～,走走形式。The inspection this time will be no more than a mere formality, I'm afraid.
雨过天晴 yǔguò-tiānqíng the sun shines again after the rain; the rain passes off and the sky clears up; after gloom comes brighteness
雨果 Yǔguǒ Victor-Marie Hugo (1802-1885), French poet, novelist, dramatist and central figure of the Romantic Movement in France
雨后春笋 yǔhòu-chūnsǔn spring up like bamboo shoots after a spring rain; grow or shoot up like mushrooms: 随着旅游业的繁荣,旅行社像～般地发展起来。As tourist industry flourishes, travel agencies are mushrooming.
雨后送伞 yǔhòu-sòngsǎn send sb. an umbrella when the rain is over; offer help when the work is all done; after meat, mustard; after death, doctor: 他此举不过～,做做表面人情。His help came only when it was no longer needed. It was just for show.
雨花石 yǔhuāshí colourful pebbles (found in the Yuhuatai area in Nanjing)
雨花台 Yǔhuātái Yuhuatai, or Terrace of Raining Flowers, in Nanjing, Jiangsu Province
雨季 yǔjì rainy season; monsoon (season); rains (in tropical areas): 这里只有～和旱季之分。Here we have only two seasons — the rainy season and dry season. /今年～来得比较早。The rains have started early this year.
雨脚 yǔjiǎo thick and fast raindrops: 床头屋漏无干处,～如麻未断绝。Above every bed, the roof leaked; nowhere could one find a dry spot. Down it poured without stop (*or* Water continuously fell in drops).
雨具 yǔjù rain gear: 这是专卖～的商店。This is a rain-gear store.
雨涝 yǔlào rain-caused flooding or waterlogging
雨帘 yǔlián *also* "雨帘子" *see* "雨幕"
雨量 yǔliàng 〈气象〉rainfall; precipitation: ～强度 rainfall density /～过多 excess rain /～稀少 little rain /～丰富 adequate (*or* abundant) rainfall /年降～不足 40 毫米 with an annual precipitation of less than 40 mm
雨量分布图 yǔliàng fēnbùtú hyetograph
雨量计 yǔliàngjì rain gauge; hyetometer; udometer
雨量学 yǔliàngxué hyetology
雨量站 yǔliàngzhàn precipitation station; rainfall station
雨林 yǔlín rainforest: 热带～ tropical rainforest /～气候 rainforest climate
雨露 yǔlù ❶ rain and dew: ～滋润禾苗壮。Crops grow luxuriant with life-giving rain. ❷ favour; bounty; grace: 普施～ show kindness and generosity to everyone
雨帽 yǔmào rain cap or hat
雨幕 yǔmù curtain of rain; rain streak; blinding rain: 西湖笼罩在灰白色的～之中,平添了一种情趣。The West Lake, blurred in the greyish veil of rain, took on an added appeal.
雨棚 yǔpéng 〈建筑〉canopy
雨披 yǔpī 〈方言〉raincape
雨前 yǔqián *Yuqian*, a green tea, picked before Grain Rain (谷雨, about mid-April)
雨情 yǔqíng rainfall (in a designated area): 密切注视～的变化 keep a close watch on the rainfall
雨区 yǔqū rainfield; rain area
雨日 yǔrì rainy day
雨伞 yǔsǎn umbrella: 塑料～ plastic umbrella /打～ put up (*or* open) an umbrella
雨师 Yǔshī rain god
雨势 yǔshì force or intensity of the rain: ～平稳 steady rain /～渐弱。The rain abated.
雨刷 yǔshuā *see* "雨刮器"
雨水 yǔshuǐ ❶ rainwater; rainfall; rain: 今年～充足,庄稼可望丰收。As there has been abundant rainfall, a good harvest is expected this year. /～冲茶最好不过。Tea made with rain water is superb. ❷ (Yǔshuǐ) Rain Water, 2nd seasonal division point, marking the sun's position at 330° on the ecliptic ❸ (Yǔshuǐ) day marking such a seasonal division point, usu. falling on the 19th or 20th of February ❹ (Yǔshuǐ) period lasting from such a seasonal division point till the next one (Waking of Insects 惊蛰)
see also "节气" jiéqì; "二十四节气" èrshísì jiéqì
雨水管 yǔshuǐguǎn *also* "水落管" shuǐluòguǎn 〈建筑〉rain pipe; rain downpipe; rainspout
雨水口 yǔshuǐkǒu gully (with grating and leading to sewer)
雨丝 yǔsī drizzle: ～风片 fine rain and light wind
雨凇 yǔsōng *also* "冰挂" bīngguà glazed ice; verglas; silver frost
雨蛙 yǔwā 〈动物〉tree frog; tree toad
雨雾 yǔwù misty rain: ～茫茫 vast blur in the misty rain
雨鞋 yǔxié rainshoes; rubber boots; rubbers; galoshes: 她脚上穿一

Y

双蓝色～。She was in blue rainshoes.
雨靴 yǔxuē rainboots; rubber boots; rubbers
雨烟 yǔyān misty rain:远处的村寨和树林都笼罩在朦胧的～之中。Distant villages and woods lay in the blue haze of the mist and rain.
雨燕 yǔyàn 〈动物〉swift
雨衣 yǔyī raincoat; raincape; waterproof:特大号塑料～ extra large (*or* XL) plastic raincoat /带雨帽的～ hooded raincoat
雨意 yǔyì signs of approaching rain:天空阴云密布,～甚浓。Dark clouds are gathering and threaten rain.
雨云 yǔyún 〈气象〉nimbus; rain cloud:～渐散,太阳复出。The rain clouds dispersed and the sun shone again.
雨珠 yǔzhū raindrop

与[1](與) yǔ ❶ give; offer; grant:她赠～他一本相册。She gave him an album. ❷ associate with; be in friendly contact with:不欺其～ not bully one's friend(s) /二人相～甚厚。They are on very good terms with each other. ❸ praise; commend; support; assist:朝过夕改,君子～之。A gentleman commends one who corrects one's error as soon as it is discovered. ❹〈书面〉wait for; await:岁不我～。Time doesn't await me.

与[2](與) yǔ ❶ with; against:～他交友 make friends with him /～人民为敌 set oneself against the people /～日月同辉 shine as long and brightly as the sun and moon; shine forever ❷ and; together with:老师～学生 teachers and students /成功～失败,在此一举。Success or failure depends on this single act.
see also yú; yù
与夺 yǔ-duó *see* "予夺" yǔ-duó
与共 yǔgòng together:生死～ share a common destiny; go through thick and thin together /朝夕～ be together from morning till night; be closely associated /荣辱～ share (in) honour or disgrace
与虎谋皮 yǔhǔ-móupí ask a tiger for its skin; expect sb. to act against his or her own interests; attempt the impossible:向他求助,不啻～。To ask him for help is like crying for the moon.
与民更始 yǔmín-gēngshǐ begin a new era or phase together with the people;〈比喻〉carry out political reforms
与民休息 yǔmín-xiūxī rehabilatate (the country) with the people — reduce taxes and levies so that the people can rest and rehabilitate
与其 yǔqí (used. usu. with 毋宁 or 不如) (would rather...) than; rather than:～临渊羡鱼,毋宁退而结网。Better go back and make a net than stand by the lake longing for fish. /～说是鼓励,还不如说是批评。It is more criticism than praise. *or* It's not so much praise as criticism. /～多而杂,不如少而精。Less but better rather than more but inferior. / ～补救于已然,不如防患于未然。Prevention is better than cure.
与人方便,自己方便 yǔ rén fāngbiàn, zìjǐ fāngbiàn 〈俗语〉things would be easy for you if you make things easy for others; he who helps others helps himself
与人为善 yǔrén-wéishàn have good intentions towards; be friendly or kind to:～是团结的前提条件。Goodwill is a prerequisite to unity.
与日俱增 yǔrì-jùzēng grow with each passing day; increase daily:声望～ one's reputation rises with each passing day /～的产量 output being steadily on the increase; speedily increasing production
与世长辞 yǔshì-chángcí 〈书面〉depart from the world for ever; pass away; die:老人家三年前就～了。The old man departed this life three years ago.
与世沉浮 yǔshì-chénfú *also* "与世俯仰" drift with the tide; follow the general trend; go with the flow:他可不是个屈己从俗,～的人。He is not one of those who bow to conventions and drift with the tide.
与世无争 yǔshì-wúzhēng hold oneself aloof from the world; stand aloof from worldly strife:在这个竞争日益剧烈的社会里,想～是办不到的。It is out of the question for one not to vie with others in this increasingly competitive world.
与众不同 yǔzhòng-bùtóng out of the ordinary; different from the common run; unconventional:他做事从来～。He has his own way of doing things. /她的想法～。She has an original idea.

屿(嶼) yǔ small island; islet:岛～ island and islets; islands

圄 yǔ 〈书面〉stable:～人 stable boy (*or* lad)

俣 yǔ
俣俣 yǔyǔ 〈书面〉of large stature

伛(傴) yǔ 〈书面〉❶ hunchback ❷ bow to show respect
伛拊 yǔfǔ 〈书面〉love and rear
伛偻 yǔlǚ 〈书面〉❶ be hunchbacked:～的老者 hunchbacked old man; old hunchback ❷ bow to show respect

庾 yǔ ❶〈书面〉open-air barn:～积 store grain outdoors ❷ (Yǔ) a surname

瘐 yǔ
瘐毙 yǔbì *see* "瘐死"
瘐死 yǔsǐ 〈书面〉die of cold and hunger in jail; die of illness in jail:～狱中 die of illness in prison

禹 Yǔ ❶ legendary leader who led the people in conquering floods and succeeded Shun (舜) as ruler:夏～ Yu of the Xia Dynasty (as his son founded the Xia Dynasty) ❷ a surname
禹贡 Yǔgòng *Yugong*, classic work of Chinese geography completed in the Warring States Period
禹域 yǔyù 〈书面〉territories of China

瑀 yǔ 〈书面〉jade-like stone

偊 yǔ 〈书面〉walk alone

羽[1] yǔ ❶ feather; plume:鸟～ bird feather /～翎 plume ❷ (of birds, etc.) wing:振～ flap the wings /如虎添～ like a tiger with wings ❸〈量词〉*used of birds*:一～信鸽 a carrier pigeon

羽[2] yǔ (of classical Chinese 5-tone scale) tone similar to 6 of the numbered musical notation
see also "五音" wǔyīn
羽葆 yǔbǎo feathered canopy
羽翅 yǔchì wing:扇动～ flap the wings
羽缎 yǔduàn *also* "羽毛缎" sateen
羽冠 yǔguān crest (of a bird)
羽管笔 yǔguǎnbǐ quill
羽化 yǔhuà ❶ ascend to heaven and become immortal:人称山上遍长不老药,服之能～登天。It is said that longevity herbs grew everywhere in the mountains and those who ate them would become immortal. ❷〈婉词〉(Taoist term for) death ❸ (of insects) eclosion; emergence
羽客 yǔkè Taoist priest
羽林 yǔlín (another name for 禁军) imperial guards
羽毛 yǔmáo ❶ feather; plume ❷〈比喻〉reputation:爱惜～ cherish one's reputation
羽毛缎 yǔmáoduàn *also* "羽缎" sateen
羽毛丰满 yǔmáo-fēngmǎn full-fledged; mature:我们不能坐看对手～。We must not sit back and wait till our adversary grows powerful.
羽毛画 yǔmáohuà feather patch-work; feather picture
羽毛球 yǔmáoqiú ❶ badminton:～网 badminton net /～拍 racket /～赛 badminton match /～场 badminton court /打～ play badminton ❷ shuttlecock:～很容易打坏。Shuttlecocks get damaged easily.
羽毛扇 yǔmáoshàn feather fan:如今市场上不易买到～了。Feather fans are not easy to find on sale nowadays. /他是这帮家伙里摇～的。He is the mastermind of these thugs.
羽毛未丰 yǔmáo-wèifēng with one's feathers not yet fully grown — young and immature; unfledged; inexperienced:他眼下规规矩矩,是因为他～啊! He is deferential now just because he is not yet full-fledged!
羽毛状晶体 yǔmáozhuàng jīngtǐ feather crystal
羽人 yǔrén ❶ flying god or goddess ❷ Taoist priest

Y

羽绒 yǔróng eiderdown; down: ～衣 down-padded anorak /～被 down quilt
羽纱 yǔshā camlet: ～常用作大衣里子。Camlet is often used to line a heavy overcoat.
羽扇 yǔshàn feather fan: ～纶巾 feather fan and head scarf — the image of a wise counsellor or strategist
羽虱 yǔshī *also* "鸟虱" niǎoshī bird louse
羽士 yǔshì Taoist priest
羽书 yǔshū urgent military document; urgent dispatch
羽坛 yǔtán badminton circles
羽檄 yǔxí urgent military document; urgent dispatch
羽衣 yǔyī ❶ plumage ❷〈书面〉feather clothing ❸ Taoist robe; Taoist priest
羽翼 yǔyì ❶ wing ❷ assistant; supporter; support: ～未成 without assistance /～渐成 have enough trustworthy assistants
羽族 yǔzú feathered tribe; birds

予 yǔ give; grant; bestow; award: 授～战斗英雄的光荣称号 award sb. the honourable title of combat hero /不～批准 not endorse; reject; turn down /免～起诉 exempt sb. from indictment
see also yú
予夺 yǔ-duó *also* "与夺" yǔ-duó〈书面〉❶ give or strip off; bestow or deprive of: 生杀～ hold absolute power over sb.'s life; have sb. completely under one's thumb ❷ commend or disparage; laud or belittle: 褒贬～ extol or deprecate; praise or belittle
予人口实 yǔrén-kǒushí give sb. a handle; give cause for gossip: 你这样做是～啊! You are just giving others a handle against you.
予以 yǔyǐ give; grant; bestow: ～鼓励 give encouragement /～批评 subject (sb.) to criticism /～警告 sound (*or* serve) a warning /～便利 provide facilities (for sb.) /～解释 throw some light on /～通报表扬 circulate a notice of commendation

yù

育 yù ❶ give birth to; bear: 节～ birth control /生儿～女 bear children ❷ rear; raise; bring up; grow: ～婴 raise babies ❸ educate; cultivate: 德～ moral education /智～ intellectual education /体～ physical culture /美～ aesthetic education /教书～人 impart knowledge and educate students in an all-round way
see also yō
育才 yùcái cultivate talent; train people: ～工作 personnel training; development of human resources
育草 yùcǎo cultivate forage or lawn grass: 封滩～ close the flood land (to livestock grazing) for grass cultivation
育成品种 yùchéng pǐnzhǒng cultivated breed; improved variety
育雏 yùchú〈畜牧〉brood
育雏器 yùchúqì brooder
育雏室 yùchúshì brooder house
育儿袋 yù'érdài〈动物〉brood pouch; marsupium: 母袋鼠下腹部长有携带幼兽的～。The female kangaroo has a pouch in the lower half of her body, in which to carry her young.
育肥 yùféi〈畜牧〉fatten: 这种鸭子用填食的办法在很短时间内～。These ducks are to be fattened in a short time by forced feeding.
育空河 Yùkōnghé Yukon River, one of the major rivers of North America
育林 yùlín afforestation; tree-planting: 封山～ close a hill or mountainous area (to livestock grazing, fuel gathering, etc.) to facilitate afforestation
育龄 yùlíng childbearing age: ～妇女 women of childbearing age
育苗 yùmiáo〈农业〉〈林业〉grow seedlings: ～区 nursery garden /～技术 seedling technique /科学～ scientific seedling
育性 yùxìng〈农业〉fertility: ～恢复系 fertility restorer line
育秧 yùyāng〈农业〉raise rice seedlings: 新法～ raise (*or* cultivate) rice seedlings by a new method
育养 yùyǎng ❶ bring up; rear: 是奶奶把他～成人的。It is his grandma that brought him up. ❷ breed: ～鱼虾 breed fish and prawns
育婴堂 yùyīngtáng orphanage; foundling hospital: 从～领养一个女孩 adopt a baby girl from an orphanage
育种 yùzhǒng〈农业〉breeding: ～家 breeder /～方法 breeding method /杂交～ crossbreeding; hybridization /激光～ breeding by laser /太空～ space breeding /单倍体～ haploid breeding /多倍体～ polyploid breeding
育珠 yùzhū cultivate pearls: 人工～ (artificial) pearl cultivation /河蚌～ freshwater mussel cultivation of pearls

堉 yù〈书面〉rich or fertile soil

语 yù〈书面〉tell; inform; let sb. know: 不以～人 not tell others about sth.; keep sth. from others /吾～汝。Let me tell you.
see also yǔ

玉 yù ❶ jade; jade-like stone: 白～ white jade /碧～ jasper /墨～ jet /黄～ topaz /绿～ emerald /青～ sapphire /纹～ veined jade /岫～ soapstone /紫翠～ alexandrite /汉白～ white marble /金～良缘 happy marriage (*or* union) /抛砖引～ cast a brick to attract jade — throw out a few tentative comments to elicit valuable opinions ❷ pure; fair; handsome; beautiful: ～颜 beautiful features /～容 fair looks ❸〈敬词〉your: *see* "～体"; "～音" ❹ (Yù) a surname
玉版宣 yùbǎnxuān quality white *Xuan* paper for calligraphy or painting
玉版纸 yùbǎnzhǐ a kind of writing paper produced in Hunan
玉帛 yùbó〈书面〉jade objects and silk fabrics (used as state gifts in ancient China): 化干戈为～ turn hostility into friendship
玉不琢,不成器 yù bù zhuó, bù chéng qì jade cannot be made into anything without being cut and polished — one can not be useful without being educated; the best horse needs breaking in and the aptest child needs teaching
玉成 yùchéng〈敬词〉kindly help make a success of; assist sb. in accomplishing a task or attaining a goal: 深望～此事,本人将感激不尽。It is my earnest hope that you will kindly help to make it a success, and I shall be very grateful for this.
玉成其事 yùchéng-qíshì kindly help make it a success
玉带 yùdài jade belt (worn by officials in ancient times): 腰围～ wear a jade belt round the waist
玉雕 yùdiāo jade carving; jade sculpture: ～工人 jade carver /～技艺 art of jade carving /～作品 jade work (*or* article)
玉佛 yùfó jade statue of Buddha: ～寺 Jade Buddha Temple (in Shanghai)
玉钩 yùgōu ❶ jade hook ❷〈比喻〉crescent moon
玉皇大帝 Yùhuáng Dàdì *also* "玉帝" Jade Emperor of Heaven, the supreme deity of Taoism
玉茭 yùjiāo *also* "玉茭子"〈方言〉maize; Indian corn; corn: ～面儿 corn flour
玉骨冰肌 yùgǔ-bīngjī (usu. of women) of fair and smooth complexion: ～的傲寒梅花 pure and noble plum blossom in the snow
玉洁 yùjié as pure and clean as jade: ～的月亮 bright moon
玉洁冰清 yùjié-bīngqīng *also* "冰清玉洁" as pure as jade and as chaste as ice; pure and virtuous: 其人～,为世仰慕。He was held in great esteem for his spotless noble character.
玉筋鱼 yùjīnyú sand lance
玉兰 yùlán〈植物〉*yulan* magnolia (*Magnolia denudata*): 院子里长着两棵～。There are two magnolia trees in the courtyard.
玉兰片 yùlánpiàn hydrated dried slices of tender bamboo shoots: 四川优质～ quality hydrated dried bamboo-shoot slices from Sichuan
玉立 yùlì ❶ graceful (carriage): 亭亭～ have a graceful carriage; be fair, slim and graceful /眉清目秀,长身～。He is tall and has handsome features. ❷〈书面〉moral integrity
玉麦 yùmài〈方言〉maize; corn; Indian corn
玉米 yùmǐ *also* "玉蜀黍" maize; Indian corn; corn: ～秆 cornstalk /～糠秕 corn-chop /～播种机 corn drill; corn planter /～割捆机 corn binder; maize binder /煮几个老～吃 boil a few ears of tender maize for food
玉米楂 yùmǐchá hominy grits
玉米大斑病 yùmǐ dàbānbìng leaf blight of corn (*Helminthosporium twicicum*)
玉米粉 yùmǐfěn cornmeal; cornflour
玉米根芽 yùmǐ gēnyá corn root aphid (*Anuroophis maidiradicis*)
玉米黑粉病 yùmǐ hēifěnbìng corn smut (*Ustilogo maydis*)
玉米花儿 yùmǐhuār popcorn
玉米粒儿 yùmǐlìr kernel of corn; grain of corn

玉米面 yùmǐmiàn maize flour; maize meal; cornmeal: ～窝窝头 steamed cornbread
玉米螟 yùmǐmíng corn borer
玉米朊 yùmǐruǎn zein
玉米脱粒机 yùmǐ tuōlìjī maize sheller; corn cribbler
玉米象虫 yùmǐ xiàngchóng maize billbug (*Calendra maidis*)
玉米小斑病 yùmǐ xiǎobānbìng leaf spot of corn (*Helminthosporium maydis*)
玉米心 yùmǐxīn corncob; cob
玉米叶蚜 yùmǐ yèyá corn-leaf aphid (*Aphis madis*)
玉米油 yùmǐyóu corn oil
玉米粥 yùmǐzhōu maize gruel; corn porridge
玉面狸 yùmiànlí 〈动物〉 masked civet; gem-faced civet
玉茗 yùmíng 〈植物〉 white camellia
玉女 yùnǚ Jade Maiden: 金童～ Golden Boy and Jade Maiden — attendants of the Taoist immortals
玉盘 yùpán ❶ jade plate, tray, etc. ❷ 〈比喻〉 moon
玉佩 yùpèi jade pendant
玉器 yùqì jade article or object; jadeware: ～工厂 jade workshop / 制作～ make jadeware / 收藏～ collect jadeware
玉泉山 Yùquánshān Jade Spring Hill (in Beijing)
玉人 yùrén ❶ 〈书面〉 jade sculptor or carver ❷ carved jade figurine ❸ 〈书面〉 beautiful woman
玉容 yùróng 〈书面〉 (of women) beautiful features; fair complexion
玉润 yùrùn smooth and fair as jade: 光泽～ lustrous and smooth / 珠圆～ round (as pearls) and smooth (as jade); sweet and mellow (voice); polished (writing)
玉搔头 yùsāotóu jade hairpin: 碧～ emerald hairpin
玉色 yùshai 〈方言〉 jade green; light bluish green
玉石 yùshí jade: 这座雕像是～的。This sculpture is carved out of jade.
玉石俱焚 yù-shí jùfén jade and stone burned together; everything destroyed, be it jade or stone; destruction of good and bad alike: 奉劝及早投降，免得城破之日，～。The sooner you surrender, the better, or else when your city falls under our attack, you will all be destroyed and no life spared.
玉食锦衣 yùshí-jǐnyī eat delicacies and wear gorgeous clothes; live luxuriously
玉手 yùshǒu jade hands — slender white hands (of a beauty)
玉蜀黍 yùshǔshǔ see "玉米"
玉树 yùshù also "桉" ān eucalyptus: ～青葱 thicket of green eucalyptus
玉髓 yùsuǐ also "石髓" shísuǐ chalcedony: 绿～ chrysoprase / 肉红～ cornelian
玉碎 yùsuì broken piece of jade — heroic death: 宁为～，不为瓦全。I would rather die than surrender (*or* live in humiliation). / 玉可碎而不可改其白，竹可焚而不可毁其节。Jade may be shattered but its whiteness cannot be changed; bamboo may be burned, but its integrity remains.
玉台新咏 Yùtái Xīnyǒng *Yu Tai Xin Yong*, anthology of ancient Chinese songs and poems compiled by Chen Xuling (陈徐陵) of the Liang Dynasty (502-557) of the Southern Dynasties
玉体 yùtǐ ❶ 〈敬词〉 your (his, her, etc.) health: ～欠安 be unwell; be ill ❷ beautiful, full body of a woman
玉兔 yùtù 〈书面〉 Jade Hare — moon: ～东升。The moon was rising in the east.
玉玺 yùxǐ imperial jade seal
玉言 yùyán 〈敬词〉 your (his, her, etc.) remarks
玉颜 yùyán ❶ fair complexion ❷ beautiful woman
玉叶金枝 yùyè-jīnzhī also "金枝玉叶" jade leaves and golden branches — people of imperial or royal lineage
玉液 yùyè 〈比喻〉 good wine: ～琼浆 top-quality wine
玉衣 yùyī jade burial suit
玉音 yùyīn 〈敬词〉〈书面〉 reply or answer from sb.: 伫候～ look forward to a (*or* your) reply
玉宇 yùyǔ ❶ beautiful palace for God: ～琼楼 magnificent buildings ❷ universe
玉簪 yùzān ❶ also "玉搔头" jade hairpin ❷ 〈植物〉 fragrant plantain lily (*Hosta plantaginea*)
玉札 yùzhá ❶ 〈中药〉 garden burnet root ❷ 〈敬词〉 your letter
玉照 yùzhào 〈敬词〉 (your, his, her, their) photo: 蒙赐签名～，不胜感谢。I deeply appreciate the gift of your signed photo.
玉质金相 yùzhì-jīnxiàng (of writing) superb in form and content; (of persons) handsome and talented: ～内外俱美 be of both excellent appearance and noble character

钰 yù 〈书面〉 treasure

芋 yù ❶ 〈植物〉 taro; dasheen: 煮～子 boiled taro / ～头白菜 cabbage and taro ❷ similar tuber crop: 洋～ potato / 山～ sweet potato
芋螺 yùluó 〈动物〉 cone shell
芋艿 yùnǎi 〈植物〉 taro
芋泥 yùní poi
芋头 yùtou 〈植物〉 ❶ taro: ～当饭 live on taro ❷ 〈方言〉 sweet potato

吁（籲） yù appeal; plead; call on: 呼～全国团结一致 call on the nation to unite
see also xū; yū
吁请 yùqǐng appeal and request; petition: ～当局采取有效措施保障社会秩序 appeal to the authorities for effective measures to ensure public order (*or* law and order) / ～警方调查这桩案件 appeal to the police to investigate the case
吁求 yùqiú appeal earnestly for: ～各界人士捐助救灾 appeal earnestly to all quarters for disaster relief

菀 yù 〈书面〉 flourishing; luxuriant
see also wǎn

雨 yù 〈书面〉 (of rain, snow, etc.) fall: ～雪不止。The snow falls continuously.
see also yǔ

阈 yù 〈书面〉 doorsill; threshold; limits; confines: 听～ audibility (*or* aural) threshold / 视～ visual range; visual threshold / 痛～ 〈心理〉 pain threshold / ～电流 threshold current / ～调整 threshold adjustment
阈限 yùxiàn 〈心理〉 threshold: 差别～ 〈心理〉 difference threshold
阈限值 yùxiànzhí 〈医学〉 threshold limit value (TLV)
阈值 yùzhí threshold value; threshold: 生态～ ecological threshold

域 yù ❶ land within certain boundaries; territory; area; region: 绝～ inaccessible (*or* unreachable) remote area / 身处异～ on foreign lands / 亚太区～ Asia-Pacific region / 地～辽阔 vast territory ❷ domain; sphere; range: 境～ situation; circumstances; plight / 音～ range; register / 广～信息服务系统 WAIS; wide area information server
域名 yùmíng 〈信息〉 DN; domain name
域外 yùwài outside the country: ～庇护 extraterritorial asylum
域中 yùzhōng inside the country

棫 yù 〈古语〉 a kind of plant

蜮（魊） yù legendary demon hidden in water to harm people; water demon

罭 yù 〈书面〉 fine fishing net

彧 yù 〈书面〉 literary grace; literary talent

郁[1] yù ❶ of powerful or strong fragrance; strongly fragrant: 浓～的香气 rich fragrance ❷ (Yù) a surname

郁[2]（鬱） yù ❶ (of plants) teeming; luxuriant; lush: 林木蓊～ dense wood ❷ (of sorrow, anger, etc.) pent-up; gloomy; depressed: 抑～不乐 be depressed; be in low spirits / 神情忧～ look gloomy
郁闭 yùbì 〈林业〉 closing; closure: 林冠～ canopy closure / ～度 canopy density / 十年前栽的树木已经～成林。The trees planted ten years ago have grown into dense woods.

Y

郁葱 yùcōng ❶ exuberant; luxuriant; lush; verdant: ～的树林 exuberant woods ❷〈书面〉profuse: 佳气～ enjoy profuse good luck
郁愤 yùfèn sorrow and indignation: 满腔～ full of sorrow and indignation
郁馥 yùfù 〈书面〉rich fragrance; intense perfume: 香气～ heavy perfume; strong scent
郁积 yùjī smouldering; pent-up: ～在心头的烦恼 pent-up vexation / 愤怒～在胸膛。He was smouldering with anger.
郁结 yùjié see "郁积"
郁金 yùjīn 〈中药〉root-tuber of aromatic turmeric (*Curcuma aromatica*)
郁金香 yùjīnxiāng 〈植物〉tulip
郁李仁 yùlǐrén 〈中药〉brush-cherry seed
郁烈 yùliè strong scent: 花香～。The air was strongly scented with flowers. *or* There was an overpowering fragrance of flowers.
郁闷 yùmèn gloomy; depressed: 心情～ feel depressed / ～无聊 be depressed and cheerless; have a thin time / 有～之感 have a feeling of oppression
郁怒 yùnù full of pent-up indignation; gloomy and exasperated; sulky: 一腔～ full of pent-up indignation
郁气 yùqì the sulks: 心存～ sulk; be sulky; be sullen; be in a fit of the sulks
郁然 yùrán ❶ gloomy; sorrowful; worried: ～成疾 become ill from worries ❷〈书面〉(of trees, etc.) profuse; luxuriant; lush: 竹树～。The bamboos and trees grew luxuriantly.
郁热 yùrè sultry; stuffy; sweltering: 天气～。It was hot and stuffy.
郁血 yùxuè 〈医学〉stagnation of the blood; venous stasis
郁抑 yùyì constrained; depressed; gloomy: 他满布皱纹的脸上现出～的神情。There was a depressed look on his heavily wrinkled face.
郁悒 yùyì 〈书面〉dejected; depressed: ～不乐 feeling low; downhearted / 神情～ look gloomy
郁郁 yùyù 〈书面〉❶ high literary grace; great literary talent: 文采～ overflowing with literary elegance ❷ strongly fragrant: 花香～。The flowers are emitting strong fragrance. ❸ (of plants) lush and green; luxuriant; verdant: ～园中柳 dense green willows in the garden ❹ gloomy; depressed: ～而亡 die from sorrow
郁郁不乐 yùyù-bùlè depressed; melancholy; sad
郁郁葱葱 yùyù-cōngcōng *also* "郁郁苍苍" (of plants) lush and green: ～的密林 lush and green forest / 战士指看南粤，更加～。Our soldiers point southward to Guangdong Looming lusher and greener in the distance.
郁郁寡欢 yùyù-guǎhuān joyless and melancholy; depressed and unhappy: 诸事不遂，他～。Everything has gone wrong, and he feels much depressed.
郁蒸 yùzhēng 〈书面〉sultry; hot and close: 酷暑～。It is suffocatingly hot in the intense heat of summer.
郁滞 yùzhì 〈中医〉stasis

与(與)

yù join in; participate in: 参～ participate in; take part in; join in / 干～ intervene in; get involved in
see also yú; yǔ
与会 yùhuì participate in a conference; attend a meeting: ～国 participating country (*or* state); country (*or* state) represented at a conference / ～者 participant; conferee / ～单位 participating unit; unit represented at a conference
与闻 yùwén *also* "预闻" yùwén have the knowledge of an insider; be let into (a secret, etc.): ～其事 have a participant's knowledge of a matter; be in the know / ～有关机密 have an insider's knowledge of related secrets

誉(譽)

yù ❶ reputation; renown; fame: 荣～ glory / 美～ good reputation / ～满宇内 be famed all over the world / 载～而归 return home with honour ❷ praise; commend; extol: 毁～参半 get both praise (*or* commendation) and censure / 毁～不一 opinion varies; find a mixed reception / ～不绝口 be full of praise; praise (*or* extol) to the skies / ～为国画大师 be acclaimed as master of traditional Chinese painting
誉满全球 yùmǎnquánqiú *also* "誉满天下" of world renown; world-famous: 我们的产品～。Our products enjoy a high reputation all over the world. *or* Our products are world-famous.

昱

yù 〈书面〉❶ sunshine; sunlight; daylight ❷ shine: 日以～乎昼，月以～乎夜。The sun shines by day and the moon by night.

煜

yù 〈书面〉shine; illuminate
煜煜 yùyù bright; shining: 湖水在阳光照射下～闪光。The lake shimmered under the sunlight.

寓(庽)

yù ❶ inhabit; reside; live: ～于上海 live in Shanghai ❷ residence; dwelling; abode: 客～ guest house / 公～大楼 apartment building / 住公～ live in a flat ❸ imply; place; contain: ～教于乐 education through entertainment / ～庄于谐 seriousness (*or* serious intent) contained in humour (*or* facetious remarks) / 责任～于权利之中。Rights imply duties.
寓处 yùchù residence; abode; house; dwelling place
寓邸 yùdǐ residence or mansion (of a high official): 部长～ minister's residence
寓公 yùgōng official or landlord or capitalist in exile; unemployed politician or gentleman away from home: 他厌倦了～的生活。He was fed up with his life in exile.
寓居 yùjū live or make one's home in: 他早年～纽约。He lived in New York in his early years.
寓目 yùmù look over or check for approval: 陈列之展品，我已～。I have looked carefully over all the exhibits. / 请君～。Please check.
寓舍 yùshè dwelling place; house one lives in
寓所 yùsuǒ residence; abode; dwelling: 宽敞、豪华的～ spacious and luxurious residence / 这是他在天津求学时的～。This was where he lived in Tianjin when he was at high school.
寓言 yùyán ❶ parable; allegory: ～诗 allegorical poem ❷ fable: 《伊索～》*Aesop's Fables*
寓意 yùyì implied meaning; moral; message; import: 明显的～ clear message / ～十分深刻 have a profound moral / 领会其中的～ grasp the implication
寓于 yùyú reside; lie; be contained or embodied: 矛盾的普遍性～矛盾的特殊性之中。The universality of contradictions resides in their particularity.
寓斋 yùzhāi 〈书面〉dwelling place; residence

遇

yù ❶ meet; encounter: 巧～ meet by chance; come across / 他乡～故知 meet one's friend in an alien (*or* foreign) land / ～到劲敌 encounter a powerful rival; catch a Tartar / 途中～雨 be caught in the rain halfway ❷ treat; receive: 待～ treatment; remuneration; pay / 他～我甚厚。He treats me very generously. ❸ chance; opportunity: 难得的机～ rare opportunity ❹ (Yù) a surname
遇便 yùbiàn at sb.'s (earliest) convenience; when it is convenient for sb.: ～请回个电话。Please give me a call when it is convenient.
遇刺 yùcì be attacked by an assassin: 在住所～身亡 be assassinated at home / ～身负重伤 be badly wounded by an assassin / 他改变了行车路线，幸免～。He changed his driving route and escaped an attempt on his life.
遇到 yùdào meet; run into; come across: ～麻烦 get into trouble / ～困难 come up against difficulties / ～意外 have an accident / ～风暴 be caught in a storm / ～一位老乡 run into one's fellow townsman / 路上～一个多年不见的朋友 come across a friend one has not seen for many years
遇害 yùhài be murdered: 他三年前在国外～。He was murdered in a foreign country three years ago.

遇合 yùhé ❶ meet and hit it off: 他们～有年。They met and fell in with each other many years ago. ❷ come across; run into: 我和他碰巧在街上～。We bumped into each other in the street.
遇见 yùjiàn meet; run into; come across: 他在上班的路上～一位熟人。He ran into an old acquaintance on his way to work. / 他们虽在同一公司供职，但很少～过。They seldom see each other although they are with the same company.
遇救 yùjiù be rescued; be saved
遇难 yùnàn ❶ be killed in an accident; be murdered: 他在飞机失事中～。He died (*or* got killed) in an air crash. / 烈士～时刚二十三岁。The martyr was only 23 years old when he was murdered. ❷ be in trouble; face danger: ～成祥 misfortune turned into good luck
遇事 yùshì when anything crops up; when confronted with a problem: ～同群众商量 consult the masses when anything crops up /

～谨慎 be prudent when confronted with a problem /～不惊 be calm in times of difficulties

遇事生风 yùshì-shēngfēng make trouble at every opportunity; sow discord wherever possible:此人惯于～,不可不防。He is a seasoned trouble-maker, and you must be on your guard.

遇险 yùxiǎn meet with a mishap; be in danger; be in distress:～登山队员 mountaineers in distress /海上～ meet with a mishap at sea

遇险信号 yùxiǎn xìnhào distress signal; GMDSS; SOS

遇缘 yùyuán by chance; as luck world have it:你我～而会,实在不易。That we could meet each other is rare luck.

谷

yù *see* "吐谷浑" Tǔyùhún

see also gǔ

浴

yù have a bath; bathe:沐～ take a bath /淋～ shower /沙～ sand bath /泥～ mud bath /日光～ sunbath /海水～ sea bathing /桑那～ sauna; Finnish hot-air bath; vapour bath /冷水～ cold bath /土耳其蒸汽～ Turkish bath

浴场 yùchǎng outdoor bathing place:天然～ natural bathing place /海滨～ bathing beach

浴池 yùchí ❶ common bathing pool:这是个能容几十人同时洗澡的～。This is a bathing pool for dozens of people. ❷ public bathhouse; public bath:～的设备不错。The bathhouse is well equipped.

浴凳 yùdèng bathroom stool

浴缸 yùgāng bathtub; bath:标准～ full-length bath

浴巾 yùjīn bath towel

浴具 yùjù bathroom facilities

浴炉 yùlú 〈冶金〉 liquid furnace

浴盆 yùpén bathtub:老式木制～ old-type wooden bathtub /搪瓷～ enamel bathtub (*or* bath)

浴室 yùshì bathroom; shower room:男～ men's bathroom /女～ women's bathroom /公共～ bathhouse /～磅秤 bathroom scale; personal weighing machine

浴堂 yùtáng bathroom; bathhouse; shower room

浴血 yùxuè bathed in blood; bloody; sanguinary:～沙场 fight in a sanguinary battle /多年～奋战 fight a bloody war for many years

浴衣 yùyī bathrobe; bathing-wrap; bathing-gown:清洁舒适的～ clean and comfortable bathrobe

浴皂 yùzào toilet soap

浴罩 yùzhào bath hood (used to cover a bath and keep the water warm)

裕

yù ❶ abundant; plentiful; ample:富～ abundant; affluent; well-to-do; well-off /充～ plentiful; ample /宽～ ample; comfortably off ❷ 〈书面〉 enrich; make affluent:新油田的开发,可富国～民。The discovery and opening-up of new oilfields will enrich the nation. ❸ (Yù) a surname

裕固族 Yùgùzú Yugur nationality (inhabiting Gansu Province):～姑娘 Yugur girl /～的风俗习惯 customs and habits of the Yugur nationality (*or* ethnic group)

裕仁天皇 Yùrén Tiānhuáng Hirohito (1901-1989), 124th emperor of Japan (1926-1989)

裕廊 Yùláng Jurong, an industrial district of Singapore

裕如 yùrú ❶ needing little effort; effortlessly; with ease:应付～ handle with ease ❷ plentiful; abundant; affluent:生活～ well-to-do life

Y

峪

yù (often used in place names) ravine; valley:嘉～关 Jiayuguan (a pass of the Great Wall) /慕田～长城 the Mutianyu section of the Great Wall

鹆

yù *see* "鸲鹆" qúyù

欲(❶慾)

yù ❶ desire; longing; yearning; wish:名利～ desire for fame and wealth /性～ sexual desire (*or* urge) /贪～ greed /情～ lust; erotic feeling; sexual passion /食～ appetite (for food) /求知～ thirst for knowledge ❷ wish; want; yearn; desire:～益反损 good intentions end up in harm /从心所～ get what one wants; do what one pleases /～哭无泪 with no tears to shed even though one is in deep sorrow /跃跃～试 itch to have a try /～穷千里目,更上一层楼 ascend another storey to see a thousand *li* ahead ❸ need; should:胆～大而心～细 one should be both bold and prudent ❹ about to; just going to; on the point of:摇摇～坠 on the verge of collapse; about to totter; tottering; crumbling /山雨～来风满楼。The rising wind forebodes the coming storm.

欲罢不能 yùbà-bùnéng try to stop but cannot; be unable to rein in even though one wants to:事已至此,～。Under the present circumstances, we cannot stop even if we wish to.

欲盖弥彰 yùgài-mízhāng the more one tries to hide, the more one is exposed; the harder one tries to conceal a thing, the more it attracts attention; try to cover up a misdeed, only to make it more conspicuous

欲海 yùhǎi 〈佛教〉 ocean of desire

欲壑难填 yùhè-nántián greed is like a valley that can never be filled; the covetous are never satisfied; avarice knows no bounds:此人贪赃枉法,只因～。The man took bribes and violated the laws all because of his insatiable greed.

欲火 yùhuǒ 〈比喻〉 strong desire (usu. sexual); carnal lust:～中烧 be hot with sexual desire /～难熬 lust for sex

欲加之罪,何患无辞 yù jiā zhī zuì, hé huàn wú cí if you are out to condemn sb., you can always trump up a charge; if a charge is to be laid, why worry how it is made; give a dog a bad name and hang him:～。既要搞掉他,罗织罪名还不是易如反掌? He who has a mind to beat his dog will easily find his stick. Now that they have decided to get rid of him, charges can easily be framed.

欲念 yùniàn desire; wish:无法满足的～ insatiable desire /个人～ personal wants

欲擒故纵 yùqín-gùzòng leave sb. at large the better to apprehend him; give sb. enough line or rope; play cat and mouse with sb.:他们放了他,无非是～,想进一步从他身上发现线索。They released him, only to give him enough line for more clues.

欲求 yùqiú desires and requests:没有止境的～ insatiate desire

欲取姑与 yùqǔ-gūyǔ give in order to take; concede so as to gain; make concessions for the sake of future advantages:他们使的是～的手段。They are using the strategy of conceding so as better to win.

欲速则不达 yù sù zé bù dá more haste, less speed; haste makes waste:～,还是稳妥些为好。Haste does not bring success. Better play safe.

欲望 yùwàng wish; desire; lust:满足个人～ satisfy (*or* gratify) one's wish /受～驱驶 be driven by desire /对财富的～ lust for wealth

谕

yù (used by superior to subordinate or senior to junior) decree; instruct; order:面～ give orders personally; instruct face to face /圣～ *also* "上～" imperial edict /总统手～ presidential order in his own hand /晓～部下 give instructions to one's subordinates

谕告 yùgào 〈书面〉 announce by edict; notify in a decree:～天下 announce (sth.) to the entire country

谕令 yùlìng 〈书面〉 order

谕示 yùshì 〈书面〉 instruction; order

谕旨 yùzhǐ imperial decree or edict:奉皇上～ by imperial decree

愈[1](❶瘉、癒)

yù ❶ be cured; heal; recover:痊～ fully recover from an illness; be fully recovered /病～出院 leave hospital after recovery /伤口已～。The wound has healed. ❷ be better than; overtake; surpass:彼～于此。That is better than this.

愈[2]

yù (used in duplicates) the more... the more; more and more:～早～好。The sooner the better. /风～刮～大。The wind grew stronger and stronger. /表扬～多,～应谦虚谨慎。The more you are praised, the more modest you should be. /事情～闹～大。The situation is worsening. *or* The matter is snowballing.

愈创醇 yùchuàngchún *also* "愈疮醇" 〈化学〉 guaiol

愈创树脂 yùchuāng shùzhī *also* "愈疮树脂" 〈化学〉 guaiac (resin); guaiacum

愈疮木 yùchuāngmù 〈植物〉 guaiacum

愈发 yùfā more; all the more; even more:她出挑得～美丽了。As she grew, she became even more beautiful.

愈合 yùhé 〈医学〉 heal up:手术后一周,伤口就～了。The wound healed up only one week after the operation.

愈加 yùjiā increasingly; even more; all the more:生活条件比以前～好了。Living conditions are even better than before. /问题变得～

麻烦了。Things have become increasingly troublesome.
愈演愈烈 yùyǎn-yùliè become increasingly fierce or intense; grow even more violent; go from bad to worse:战争～。The war is escalating. /矛盾～。The contradictions are sharpening. /赌博之风～。Gambling has run rampant.
愈益 yùyì increasingly; even more; all the more:人们对未来的信心～增强了。People are becoming increasingly confident of the future.

喻 yù ❶ explain; tell; inform:晓～ enlighten; persuade /不可理～ won't listen to reason; be perverse ❷ understand; know; be aware of:家～户晓 known to every family; widely known; known to all /不言而～ it goes without saying ❸ analogy; figure of speech:比～ analogy /明～ simile /暗～ metaphor /讽～ parable; allegory ❹ (Yù) a surname
喻皓 Yù Hào Yu Hao, famous architect of the early Northern Song Dynasty
喻世 yùshì admonish the people
喻义 yùyì allegorical or metaphorical meaning

毓 yù ❶〈书面〉rear; raise; bring up:丰圃草以～兽 grow grass in the garden to rear animals ❷ (Yù) a surname

燠 yù 〈书面〉warm; hot:寒～失时 unseasonable weather
燠热 yùrè 〈书面〉sultry; close and hot:天气～。It is sweltering.

蓣 yù *see* "蘡薁" yīngyù

噢 yù 〈书面〉*see* "燠" yù

隩 yù 〈书面〉bend of a river

御[1] yù ❶ drive; ride:～者 carriage driver /～马 ride a horse /～风 ride on the wind and fly ❷〈旧语〉control; dominate:～下 control one's subordinates /～众 govern one's subjects (*or* the masses, populace, etc.) /～世 rule the country /～事 manage affairs ❸ related to the emperor or king; imperial:～旨 imperial decree (*or* edict) /～前 in his majesty's presence

御[2]（禦） yù defend (against sb.); resist; keep out:防～ defend /抵～ resist; ward off
御宝 yùbǎo imperial seal
御笔 yùbǐ emperor's handwriting
御赐 yùcì bestowed by the emperor
御道 yùdào imperial road; road for the emperor only
御敌 yùdí resist the enemy:起兵～ send troops to resist the enemy /～于国门之外 keep the enemy beyond the border of the country
御夫座 Yùfūzuò 〈天文〉Auriga
御寒 yùhán keep out the cold; keep warm:～用品 things (*or* articles) used to keep out the cold /饮酒～ drink wine (*or* alcohol) to keep warm
御花园 yùhuāyuán imperial garden
御极 yùjí 〈书面〉ascend the throne; be enthroned
御驾 yùjià his majesty's carriage:～亲征 expedition directly (*or* personally) commanded by his majesty
御览 yùlǎn seen or read by the emperor
御林军 yùlínjūn palace guards; imperial guards; 〈比喻〉elite armed forces
御路 yùlù road for exclusive use by the emperor in a palace or imperial mausoleum
御膳 yùshàn food for the emperor
御膳房 yùshànfáng imperial kitchen
御膳橘 yùshànjú bunch berry; dwarf cornel (*Cornus canadensis*)
御手 yùshǒu *also* "驭手" yùshǒu soldier in charge of pack animals; warrior driving a chariot
御侮 yùwǔ resist invasion:一致～ resist foreign aggression as one (*or* in unison)
御玺 yùxǐ imperial seal; (UK) privy seal
御医 yùyī imperial physician
御用 yùyòng ❶ employed by the emperor; for the use of an emperor:～药品 medicine for the use of his majesty ❷ hired; in the pay of:～报刊 hired (*or* paid) press /～学者 hired scholar
御用文人 yùyòng wénrén scribbler hired by the imperial court; hack writer
御苑 yùyuàn imperial garden
御仗 yùzhàng emperor's insignia
御制 yùzhì made by order of his majesty

䮾 yù 〈书面〉(of birds) fly fast

狱（獄） yù ❶ prison; jail:牢～ jail /地～ hell /下～ be put in prison (*or* behind bars); be jailed /越～ escape from prison; make a jailbreak ❷ lawsuit; case:文字～ literary inquisition; persecution of authors for writing something considered offensive by the imperial court /冤～ unjust charge; unjust verdict
狱警 yùjǐng prison guard
狱吏 yùlì prison warder or wardress; prison warden; jailer; goaler
狱室 yùshì (prison) cell
狱政 yùzhèng management of a prison; control and education of prisoners
狱卒 yùzú prison guard

饫 yù 〈书面〉be full:饱～ be well fed

豫[1] yù 〈书面〉❶ pleased; happy; glad:心中不～ be displeased ❷ comfort; contentment:逸～亡身。Over indulgence spells ruin.

豫[2] yù *see* "预[1]" yù

豫[3] Yù (another name for 河南) Henan
豫剧 yùjù *also* "河南梆子" Hénán bāngzi Henan opera (a local opera popular in Henan and parts of Shaanxi and Shanxi):～演员 Henan opera singer /～剧目 repertoire of Henan opera /河南～院 Henan Opera House

预[1] yù in advance; beforehand:报费请～交。Please pay for the subscriptions in advance. /勿谓言之不～。Do not say that you have not been forewarned. *or* Do not blame us for not having forewarned you.

预[2] yù *see* "与" yù
预案 yù'àn plan or option against a possible development; contingency or emergency plan
预报 yùbào forecast; prediction:天气～ weather forecast /地震～ earthquake forecast; earthquake prediction /洪水～ flood forecasting /航空～ aviation forecast /一般～ general forecast /长期～ long-range forecast /短期～ short-range forecast /无线电～ radio forecast
预备 yùbèi prepare; get ready:～发言提纲 prepare a speech outline /～两个房间 get two rooms ready /～参赛 prepare for the race /各就各位! ～! 跑! On your mark! Get set! Go! /这件事你～怎么办? What do you plan to do about this?
预备党员 yùbèi dǎngyuán probationary Party member
预备队 yùbèiduì reserve force; reserves
预备会议 yùbèi huìyì preparatory meeting
预备金 yùbèijīn reserve fund
预备军 yùbèijūn reserve army; reserves
预备期 yùbèiqī probationary period
预备役 yùbèiyì 〈军事〉reserve duty:～士兵 reservist /～军官 officer in the reserve /征召～部队 call out the reserve(s) /～部队 reserve units
预编译程序 yùbiānyì chéngxù 〈计算机〉precompiler program
预卜 yùbǔ augur; foretell; predict:～吉凶 foretell one's good or ill luck (*or* one's fate) /比赛成绩尚难～。It is difficult to predict who will win the race.
预测 yùcè predict; foresee; forecast:～龙卷风 detect a tornado /～气象 forecast the weather /～局势的发展 foresee the future changes (*or* developments) in the situation /～比赛结果 predict the outcome of the match /市场～ market prediction (*or* forecasting)
预产期 yùchǎnqī 〈医学〉expected date of childbirth:准确地计算～ accurately calculate the expected date of childbirth

Y

预成型 yùchéngxíng 〈冶金〉preforming:～钢缆 preformed steel cable

预处理 yùchǔlǐ prehandle; pretreat:对伤口进行～ pretreat the wound

预淬火 yùcuìhuǒ 〈冶金〉prequenching:～部件 prequenched part

预订 yùdìng reserve (in advance); place an order for; subscribe; book:～饭桌 reserve a table /～旅馆 make hotel reservations /～机票 book an air ticket /～报刊杂志 subscribe to a magazine or newspaper /～三箱啤酒 place an order for three cases of beer /这场音乐会的坐位早已～一空。The seats have long been booked up for the concert.

预定 yùdìng fix or arrange in advance; predetermine; schedule:～产值 fix the output value in advance /～的行动方针 predetermined course of action /在～的时间和地点 at the fixed time and place /会议将按～的计划进行。The meeting will take place (*or* proceed) as planned (*or* scheduled). /这项工作达到了～的目标。The work has met its expected goal.

预断 yùduàn predict; anticipate; prejudge:难以～ hard to predict (*or* prejudge) /事实证明,他的～是正确的。Facts proved that his prediction was correct.

预防 yùfáng take precautions against; guard against; prevent:冬季流感之～ prevention of influenza in winter /采取～措施 take preventive measures /～水灾 take precautions against floods /～性战争 preventive (*or* preemptive) war /～天花接种证书 certificate of vaccination against smallpox /～胜于治疗。Prevention is better than cure.

预防免疫接种 yùfáng miǎnyì jiēzhòng 〈医学〉prophylactic immunization

预防性拘留 yùfángxìng jūliú preventive detention; take into preventive custody

预防医学 yùfáng yīxué preventive medicine

预防注射 yùfáng zhùshè *also* "预防接种" vaccination; preventive or prophylactic inoculation:坚持定期～ persist in regular preventive inoculations

预分 yùfēn ❶ initial distribution:社员在麦收后进行了～。After the harvest the members of the cooperative made an initial distribution of the wheat. ❷ initial plan of distribution:住房～方案 plan for house distribution

预付 yùfù payment in advance:～费用 advance charge /～汇款 advance remittance /～贷款 cash before delivery (CBD) /～三个月房租 pay three months' rent in advance; pay a deposit of three months' rent

预付款项 yùfù kuǎnxiàng prepayments

预感 yùgǎn have a premonition or presentiment:他～到情况不妙。He has a premonition that things will not go well. /对这次灾祸,她早有～。She had an ominous presentiment of the disaster.

预告 yùgào ❶ announce in advance; herald:燕子呢喃,～着春天的到来。The chirps of the swallows herald the coming of spring. ❷ (of theatrical announcements, publications, etc.) advance notice:电影～ movie announcements /新书～ notice of new publications; prepublication notice

预购 yùgòu purchase in advance:～合同 forward purchasing contract /～农产品 purchase agricultural produce in advance:～机票 buy an air ticket in advance

预烘干 yùhōnggān prebake

预后 yùhòu 〈医学〉prognosis:～良好 favourable prognosis /～不良 unfavourable prognosis

预会 yùhuì *see also* "与会" yùhuì attend or take part in a meeting

预计 yùjì calculate in advance; estimate; anticipate: ～产量 estimated output /～收入 anticipated revenue /～成本 predicted cost /～数据 scheduled data /～到达时间〈航海〉estimated time of arrival (ETA)/～下月初可完成内部装修工作。It is estimated that internal repairs will finish early next month.

预加工 yùjiāgōng 〈机械〉pre-process

预见 yùjiàn ❶ foresee; foretell; predict:在可以～的将来 in the foreseeable future /只有深入调查,全面分析,才能正确地～事物的发展。Only through in-depth investigation and all-round analysis can one correctly predict the future trends of things. ❷ foresight; prevision:～性 foresight; farsightedness /科学的～ scientific prevision /他对这种变化早有～。He foresaw the change long ago.

预警 yùjǐng forewarning; early waring: ～卫星 early warning satellite /～雷达 early warning radar /～系统 early-warning system /机载～与控制系统飞机 airborne warning and control system (*or* AWACS) plane

预聚合 yùjùhé 〈化工〉prepolymerization:～物 prepolymer

预决算制度 yùjuésuàn zhìdù budget and final account system

预科 yùkē preparatory course:大学～ preparatory school; prep school

预扣 yùkòu withhold:～所得税表 income tax withholding table

预扣税 yùkòushuì withholding tax

预拉伸 yùlāshēn pretensioning; Hoyer method of prestressing; pre-drawing

预料 yùliào expect; predict; anticipate:如所～ as expected /出乎～ beyond expectation (*or* all expectations) /大大超出～ in excess of one's wildest expectations /事态的发展很难～。It is hard to predict the developments. /今年的秋粮～可获丰收。It is anticipated that we shall have a bumper autumn harvest.

预埋件 yùmáijiàn 〈电工〉built-in fitting

预谋 yùmóu premeditate; plan beforehand; prearrange:～杀人 premeditated murder; murder with malice prepense (*or* aforethought) /有～的行为 deliberate (*or* predesigned) action

预期 yùqī expect; envision; anticipate:比～的要好 better than expected /收到～的效果 achieve the desired results /达到～的目的 attain the anticipated objective(s)

预燃 yùrán 〈机械〉precombustion; preignition:～式柴油机 prechamber diesel engine; precombustion diesel; precombustion engine

预燃室 yùránshì precombustion chamber; prechamber; antechamber

预热 yùrè 〈机械〉preheat:～锅炉 preboiler /～器 preheater /蓄热式空气～器 regenerative air preheater

预赛 yùsài 〈体育〉preliminary contest; preliminary heat; preliminary; trial match:～成绩 preliminary results /排球～ volley-ball preliminary contest /在～中被淘汰 be eliminated in the trial match

预审 yùshěn ❶ antecedent trial; preliminary hearing:～程序 inquisitional procedure /～法官 investigating magistrate /～审判员 preliminary judge /～庭 preliminary hearing court ❷ questioning during investigation; inquiry

预示 yùshì betoken; foretell; presage; forebode:狂风大作,乌云满天,～着暴风雨即将来临。The wind rose suddenly and dark clouds gathered in the sky. It foreboded a big storm.

预收 yùshōu collect or take advance payment:～定金 take bargain (*or* earnest) money /～保险金 collect premium

预售 yùshòu open to or for booking; advance booking:本站～三日内火车票。Train tickets are open to booking two days ahead of schedule at this station.

预算 yùsuàn budget:国家～ state budget /地方～ local government budget /～赤字 budget deficit /～结余 budget surplus /～年度 budget year /～收入 budgetary receipts /～项目 budget items /～程序 budget process /～法案 budget act /～拨款 budget allocations; budget appropriations /～收支 budgetary revenues and expenditures /～外投资 extra-budgetary investment /～外支出 off-budget expenditure /～执行 budget execution /～执行情况 budget performance /～咨文 budget message /行政和～问题咨询委员会(UN) Advisory Committee on Administrative Budgetary Questions (ACABQ) /财政～ financial budgeting /编制～ work out a budget /他的责任是平衡～。His job is to balance the budget.

预填骨料混凝土 yùtián gǔliào hùnníngtǔ 〈建筑〉prepack concrete

预闻 yùwén *also* "与闻" yùwén participate and get to know

预习 yùxí prepare lessons before class; preview

预先 yùxiān beforehand; in advance; pre-:～准备 prepare in advance /～布置 prearrange /～通知 notify in advance; give an advance notice /～断定 prejudge /～声明 state beforehand; make a statement in advance /～装配的 pre-assembled; prefabricated

预想 yùxiǎng anticipate; envisage; expect:达到～目标 hit a set target; reach an objective one has in mind /～未来 envisage the future /～不到的后果 unexpected consequences /事情不像～的那样简单。Things are not as simple as anticipated.

预行 yùxíng do sth. in advance; take measures beforehand:～警报 forewarning

预选 yùxuǎn ❶ proceedings of selecting candidates before election; primaries; straw vote ❷〈体育〉preliminary:世界杯足球～赛 preliminary contests (*or* preliminaries) for the soccer world cup championships

预压机 yùyājī 〈机械〉preformer

Y

预言 yùyán prophesy; predict; foretell：如他所～的那样（things turn out）as he predicted / 他的～证实了。His prophecy was later fulfilled.
预言家 yùyánjiā prophet
预演 yùyǎn （of a show）preview：该剧正式演出前要～一场。A preview of the play should be given before its premiere.
预氧化 yùyǎnghuà 〈化工〉preoxidation
预印 yùyìn 〈印刷〉preprint：～本 preprint
预应力 yùyìnglì 〈物理〉prestressing force：～构件 prestressed component / ～梁 prestressed beam
预应力混凝土 yùyìnglì hùnníngtǔ prestressed concrete
预约 yùyuē make an appointment：门诊～挂号 make an appointment with a doctor / 牙科～号 have a dental appointment / ～会见某人 meet sb. by appointment; make（*or* fix）an appointment to see sb.
预早 yùzǎo 〈方言〉in advance; beforehand：～做个安排 make preparations in advance
预展 yùzhǎn （of an exhibition）preview：产品～ preview of exhibits
预兆 yùzhào omen; portent; sign; harbinger：不祥的～ bad omen / 心悸是心脏病的～。Palpitation is a warning of heart trouble. / 政变前必有～。There must be signs before a coup. / 瑞雪～来年丰收。An auspicious snow foretells a good harvest in the coming year.
预征 yùzhēng collect（a tax or levy）in advance
预支 yùzhī pay or get in advance：～费用 prepaid expenses / 申请～三个月工资 ask for an advance of three months' salary
预知 yùzhī know in advance; foresee
预制 yùzhì prefabricate; precast：～板 precast slab / ～房屋 prefabricated house / ～（钢筋）混凝土 precast（reinforced）concrete / ～拼装结构 section（al）construction / ～装配式房屋 prefabricated house; prefab
预制构件 yùzhì gòujiàn precast unit; prefabricated components or parts
预祝 yùzhù wish：～成功！Wish you success!
预装配 yùzhuāngpèi 〈机械〉preframe; preassemble

蓣

yù *see*“薯蓣”shǔyù

矞

yù 〈书面〉auspicious colourful clouds

澦

yù 〈书面〉（of water）gush

燏

yù 〈书面〉flame; blaze

遹

yù 〈书面〉in accordance with

鹬

yù 〈动物〉sandpiper; snipe
鹬蚌相争，渔人得利 yù-bàng xiāng zhēng, yúrén dé lì when the snipe and the clam grapple, it's the fisherman who stands to benefit; two dogs strive for a bone, and a third runs away with it
鹬鸵 yùtuó *also*“几维鸟”jīwéiniǎo；“无翼鸟”wúyìniǎo kiwi

尉

yù
see also wèi
尉迟 Yùchí a surname

熨

yù
see also yùn
熨帖 yùtiē ❶（of wording）appropriate; fitting; proper：文中成语、典故准确～，恰到好处。The idioms and allusions in the writing are appropriate and to the point, fitting the context nicely. ❷ calm; peaceful; quiet：听了老人的一番话，他心里感到十分～。Having heard the old man's words, he felt very much at ease. ❸〈方言〉comfortable; well：他身上不～。He's not feeling well. ❹〈方言〉settled; well done：这事办得真～！You did a good job!

粥

yù ❶〈书面〉give birth to（a child）; bear ❷ *see*“鬻”yù
see also zhōu

鬻

yù 〈书面〉sell：～歌 make a living with singing / ～画为生 sell（one's）paintings for a living / 卖儿～女 sell one's children for survival

妪（嫗）

yù 〈书面〉old woman; old lady：翁～ old couple / 老～力虽衰，请从吏夜归。The crone, though decrepit and frail, Would follow the official that very night.

驭

yù ❶ drive：驾～马车 drive a coach（*or* a horse-drawn vehicle）❷〈书面〉command; master：驾～自然 control nature
驭手 yùshǒu *also*“御手”yùshǒu soldier in charge of pack animals; driver of a military pack train：～班 driving squad / 炮车～ gun-carriage driver

yuān

渊（淵）

yuān ❶ deep pool：为～驱鱼 drive the fish into deep waters; play into rival's hands / 天～之别 as far apart as heaven from earth; worlds apart / 积水成～。Water accumulates to become a pool. ❷ deep：～泉 deep spring / ～识博学 profound knowledge and extensive learning ❸（Yuān）a surname
渊博 yuānbó broad and profound; scholarly; erudite：学问～ erudite; learned; scholarly / ～的学者 erudite scholar
渊海 yuānhǎi deep pool and vast sea —（of content）wide in range and great in depth：笔墨～ of great literary talent
渊默 yuānmò 〈书面〉profound and taciturn
渊深 yuānshēn profound; deep; erudite：学识～ be erudite; be profound in learning
渊薮 yuānsǒu 〈比喻〉gathering place of fish or beasts; haunt; den; lair：盗贼的～ den（*or* haunt, *or* lair）of bandits and thieves / 罪恶的～ hotbed（*or* breeding ground）of crime; sink of iniquity / 宛为大都，士之～也。Wan was a big city, where scholars gathered.
渊源 yuānyuán origin; source：探寻～ find the origins; trace the beginnings of sth. / 家学～ long tradition of family learning / ～极深 be closely connected

冤（寃）

yuān ❶ wrong; grievance; injustice：含～负枉 be wronged; be treated with injustice / 伸～ redress a grievance; right a wrong / 喊～ call for redressing a grievance; complain of injustice / 沉～ long-standing injustice / 含～而死 die of unjust treatment / 不白之～ be wrongly accused ❷ hatred; enmity; feud：结～ become enemies; incur hatred of; start a feud ❸ not commensurate with the effort or money; not worthwhile; in vain; for nothing：跑～路 run all the way for nothing / 这些钱花得太～。The money was spent in vain. ❹〈方言〉kid; fool; pull sb.'s leg：别～人！Don't kid me! / 放心吧，我决不会～你！You can breathe easy（*or* easily）. I won't pull your leg.
冤案 yuān'àn wrong verdict; unjust case; injustice; wrong：平反～ overturn a wrong verdict; redress injustice; put right a wrong（done to sb.）
冤沉海底 yuānchénhǎidǐ the injustice will remain unredressed for ever
冤仇 yuānchóu enmity; rancour; feud：几代～ enmity（*or* feud）for generations / 你和他真有那么大的～吗？Do you really feel such rancour against him?
冤仇宜解不宜结 yuānchóu yí jiě bùyí jié 〈俗语〉the knot of hatred should be untied, not tightened; it's always better to lose an enemy than to make one
冤大头 yuāndàtóu blockhead in money matters; foolish spender; sucker：他当了回～，心里挺别扭。He felt quite upset at being a sucker.
冤愤 yuānfèn indignation at injustice：满腔～ be filled with indignation at injustice; one's blood boils with indignation at unjust treatment
冤魂 yuānhún 〈迷信〉wronged person's ghost; spirit of someone who died of injustice：～不散。The wronged man's spirit lingered.
冤家对头 yuānjiā-duìtou opponent and foe; enemy：也不知为什么，他总把我看成～。Strangely, he always took me as his enemy.
冤家路窄 yuānjiā-lùzhǎi foes are fated to meet on a narrow road：咱们可真是～呀，没想到又碰面了。It's a small world, and we run（*or* come）across each other again.

冤家宜解不宜结 yuānjiā yí jiě bùyí jié *see* "冤仇宜解不宜结"

冤家 yuānjia ❶ enemy; foe: 这两个人是生死～。They are deadly enemies. ❷ one's destined love; sweetheart or lover in a love-hate relationship: 不是～不聚头。Enemies and lovers are destined to meet.

冤假错案 yuān-jiǎ-cuò'àn cases in which people were unjustly, falsely, or wrongly charged or sentenced: 平反～ redress the wrongs done to people who were unjustly, falsely, or wrongfully accused and sentenced

冤结 yuānjié unredressed injustice; long-standing injustice: 几十年的～，一时难解。A decades-long injustice can not be redressed overnight.

冤苦 yuānkǔ ❶ injustice and suffering: 饱尝～ experience a great deal of injustice and distress ❷ wrong; do sb. an injustice: 我们说他叛国实在～了他。We did him a great injustice by calling him a traitor.

冤孽 yuānniè enmity and sin: ～深重 steeped in enmity and sin

冤气 yuānqì resentment at being wronged; indignation about unjust treatment; feeling against injustice: 一肚子～ feel strongly about the injustice; resent one's wrong deeply

冤钱 yuānqián *also* "冤枉钱" money paid for nothing; money spent in vain: 我可不花这～。I won't throw away my money on this.

冤情 yuānqíng true state or facts of an injustice: ～大白。The truth of the injustice has become known to all. *or* Murder is out.

冤屈 yuānqū ❶ wrong; treat unjustly: ～好人 wrong a good person ❷ wrongful treatment; injustice: 洗雪～ redress (*or* remedy) injustice

冤死 yuānsǐ die from injustice: 替～的人昭雪 rehabilitate those who died from injustice

冤头 yuāntóu enemy; foe: 他是全村人的大～。He is the worst enemy of the whole village.

冤枉 yuānwang ❶ unfair; unjust; wrong: ～官司 unjust verdict; uncalled-for lawsuit / 这样批评我，真～。It was so unfair to criticize me like this. ❷ wrong; treat unjustly or unfairly: 别～好人。Don't wrong an innocent person. / 我觉得没有～他。I think we've done him no wrong. ❸ not worthwhile; not repaying the effort; in vain: 花～时间 spend time in vain / 这个钱花得～！I did not get my money's worth.

冤枉路 yuānwanglù vain trip; lengthy route; the long way: 跑了半天～ walk on and on only to find it was a vain trip / 今天进城走了不少～。We went the long way to town today.

冤枉气 yuānwangqì unfair criticism; undeserved spite; uncalled-for maltreatment: 他那些年受了不少～。He was treated unjustly in those years. / 为他我可受了许多～。I was the target of much unfair criticism for his sake.

冤枉钱 yuānwangqián *also* "冤钱" money spent in vain; wasted money: 买这种华而不实的物件，实在是花～。It's a sheer waste of money to buy such showy trinkets. / 这个精明人这回可花了～了。This time the smart guy did not get his money's worth.

冤诬 yuānwū bring a false charge (against sb.); frame up

冤抑 yuānyì unredressed injustice; unrighted wrong

冤有头，债有主 yuān yǒu tóu, zhài yǒu zhǔ every injustice has its perpetrator and every debt its debtor: ～，跟我们过不去又有何用。You should go after the one who wronged you. It's useless to be hard on us.

冤狱 yuānyù unjust charge or verdict; miscarriage of justice; failure to administer justice properly: 制造～ bring in an unjust verdict; frame (sth.) up; frame (sb.) / 平反～ reverse an unjust verdict

冤冤相报 yuānyuān-xiāngbào reprisal breeds reprisal: ～，何时可了？你们还是和解了吧！Injury for injury, and there would be no end of reprisals. You'd better make peace.

鸢

yuān 〈动物〉kite; hawk: ～飞鱼跃 (with) kites hovering and fish diving

鸢尾 yuānwěi 〈植物〉iris

痯

yuān 〈书面〉❶ ache ❷ melancholy

蜎

yuān 〈书面〉wiggler; wriggler

蜎蜎 yuānyuān 〈书面〉(of a worm) twistingly: ～而行 twist along

箢

yuān

箢篼 yuāndōu 〈方言〉*see* "箢箕"

箢箕 yuānjī 〈方言〉*also* "箢篼" bamboo basket

鹓

yuān

鹓鶵 yuānchú 〈古语〉legendary bird like the phoenix

眢

yuān 〈书面〉❶ (of eyes) dry and sunken ❷ drained dry: *see* "～井"

眢井 yuānjǐng 〈书面〉dry well

帘

yuān *see* "缗帘" fányuān

鸳

yuān mandarin duck: ～侣 husband and wife / ～衾 quilt shared by husband and wife

鸳鸯 yuānyang ❶ mandarin duck: ～戏水 mandarin ducks playing on water ❷ loving couple: 人们称他们是一对好～。People praised them as an affectionate couple.

鸳鸯座 yuānyangzuò love seat (in a cinema, etc.)

yuán

元¹

yuán ❶ first; initial; primary: 纪～ beginning of an era, epoch, etc. ❷ arch; chief; principal: *see* "～首"; "～凶" ❸ basic; essential; fundamental: *see* "～音"; "～素" ❹ element: 一～论 monism / 二～论 dualism ❺ unit; component: 单～ unit; section; apartment / 一～化领导 unified (*or* centralized) leadership

元²

yuán unit of money: 两～五角 two *yuan* and fifty *fen* / 一百日～ one hundred Japanese yen / 三美～ three US dollars

元³

Yuán ❶ Yuan Dynasty (1271-1368) ❷ a surname

元宝 yuánbǎo shoe-shaped gold or silver ingot used as money in feudal China: 金～ gold ingot

元宝枫 yuánbǎofēng *also* "柜柳" jǔliǔ; "枫杨" fēngyáng 〈植物〉Chinese ash; *Pterocarya stenoptera*

元宝铁 yuánbǎotiě 〈机械〉V-block

元程序 yuánchéngxù 〈计算机〉metaprogram

元大都 Yuán Dàdū Yuan capital Dadu, located in today's Beijing area

元旦 Yuándàn New Year's Day: 欢庆～ celebrate New Year's Day joyously / ～联欢会 New Year's Day party (*or* get-together)

元恶 yuán'è 〈书面〉arch criminal; principal culprit: 铲除～ eliminate a principal culprit

元古代 Yuángǔdài 〈地质〉Proterozoic Era

元古界 Yuángǔjiè 〈地质〉Proterozoic Erathem

元件 yuánjiàn element; component; cell: 仪表～ elements of meters and instrument / 电路～ circuit component (*or* element) / 敏感～ sensor / 双向～ bilateral element / 光敏～ light-sensitive cell / 延时～ delay cell / 电光～ electrooptic cell / 平衡～ balancing (*or* equalizing) component / 分立～ discrete component / 设备～ equipment component / 混合～ hybrid component / 红外～ IR component / 无源～ passive component / 发光～ light-emitting component / 制导系统～ elements of the guidance system

元件寿命 yuánjiàn shòumìng component life

元件误差 yuánjiàn wùchā component error

元老 yuánlǎo senior or elder statesman; founding member: 三朝～ minister to three emperors; official who stays in power under different regimes / 政界～ senior politician

元伦理学 yuánlúnlǐxué 〈哲学〉meta-ethics

元逻辑 yuánluóji metalogic

元麦 yuánmài *also* "青稞" qīngkē highland barley

元煤 yuánméi *also* "原煤" yuánméi raw coal

元谋猿人 Yuánmóu yuánrén *also* "元谋人" Yuanmou Man (*Homo erectus Yuanmouensis*), whose fossil remains, about 1, 700, 000 years old, were found in Yuanmou, Yunnan Province in 1965

元年 yuánnián first year (of an era or of an emperor's reign)

元配 yuánpèi *also* "原配" yuánpèi first wife: ～夫人 (sb.'s) first wife

元气 yuánqì vitality; vigour: ～大伤 one's constitution being undermined; one's vitality being sapped / 恢复～ regain one's health;

recuperate one's strength /～旺盛 full of vim and vigour /～不足 lack vitality
元器件 yuán-qìjiàn elements and parts
元青 yuánqīng deep black
元曲 yuánqǔ 〈戏曲〉Yuan opera, popular during the Yuan Dynasty:～作家 playwright of Yuan opera /《～选》*Selected Pieces of Yuan Opera*
元日 yuánrì first day of the lunar year
元戎 yuánróng 〈书面〉chief or supreme commander; commanding general:一代～ outstanding commanding general of his time
元首 yuánshǒu ❶〈书面〉monarch ❷ head of state; chief executive:中国的国家～是国家主席。China's head of state is the president.
元书纸 yuánshūzhǐ a kind of writing paper, produced in Zhejiang Province
元数学 yuánshùxué metamathematics
元帅 yuánshuài 〈军事〉❶ marshal:人民解放军十大～ PLA's ten great marshals /陆军～(UK, Germany, etc.) field marshal /英国皇家空军～ Marshal of the Royal Air Force /英国海军～ Admiral of the Fleet /大～ generalissimo ❷〈古语〉supreme commander:授～印 assume one's duties as supreme commander
元素 yuánsù ❶ element; essential factor ❷〈化学〉〈数学〉element:稀有～ rare element /～成分 elementary composition /～分析 ultimate analysis
元素符号 yuánsù fúhào element symbol
元素起源 yuánsù qǐyuán origin of elements
元素周期表 yuánsù zhōuqībiǎo periodic table of elements
元宵 yuánxiāo ❶ 15th night of the 1st lunar month:～佳节 Lantern Festival /～晚会 evening party on the Lantern Festival /正月十五闹～ have festive celebrations on the 15th night of the 1st lunar month ❷ (glutinous) rice dumpling:什锦～ assorted rice dumplings /包～ make rice dumplings /煮～ boil rice dumplings
元宵节 Yuánxiāojié *also* "灯节" Dēngjié; "上元节" Shàngyuánjié Lantern Festival
元凶 yuánxiōng prime culprit; archcriminal:他是这次劫机事件的～。He was the prime culprit in the hijacking.
元勋 yuánxūn man of outstanding merit; founding father:劳苦功高的开国～ state founder of great merit
元夜 yuányè 〈书面〉15th night of the 1st lunar month; night of the Lantern Festival:～观灯 watch lanterns during the Lantern Festival night
元音 yuányīn 〈语言〉vowel:～字母 vowel letter /～发音 vowel sound
元鱼 yuányú *also* "鼋鱼" yuányú soft-shelled turtle
元语言 yuányǔyán metalanguage
元元 yuányuán 〈书面〉the populace; the people
元元本本 yuányuán-běnběn *also* "原原本本" yuányuán-běnběn from beginning to end
元月 yuányuè first lunar month; January:～十五日 15th of the 1st lunar month; January 15th
元稹 Yuán Zhěn Yuan Zhen (779-831), poet of the Tang Dynasty

沅

Yuán Yuanjiang River which originates in Guizhou Province and flows into Hunan Province

芫

yuán
see also yán
芫花 yuánhuā 〈植物〉lilac daphne
芫菁 yuánjīng blister beetle

园(園)

yuán ❶ garden; plot; plantation:花～ flower garden /菜～ vegetable garden (*or* plot) /种植～ plantation /竹～ bamboo plantation (*or* land) /桃～ peach garden (*or* orchard) /果～ orchard /葡萄～ vineyard ❷ place of recreation; park; garden:公～ park /动物～ zoological garden; zoo /植物～ botanical garden /梨～ theatre/游乐～ amusement park /儿童乐～ children's playground /颐和～ Summer Palace /迪斯尼乐～ Disneyland
园地 yuándì ❶ garden plot; plot:这是学生们的小麦实验～。This is the students' experimental wheat plot. ❷ field; scope:文学创作～ scope of literary creation /艺术探讨的～ field of artistic exploration
园丁 yuándīng ❶ gardener:辛勤的～ hard-working gardener ❷〈比喻〉(usu. primary school) teacher
园林 yuánlín garden; park:～艺术 gardening; horticulture /～工人 gardener /～建筑 garden architecture /～绿化 landscaping /～设计 landscape design /～化的城市 city green with parks and trees; garden city
园陵 yuánlíng cemetery; mausoleum:烈士～ cemetery of revolutionary martyrs /帝王～ imperial mausoleum
园圃 yuánpǔ garden; plot for growing vegetables, fruits or flowers:扩建～ extend the vegetable (*or* fruit, *or* flower) plot
园容 yuánróng look or layout of a park, garden, etc.:清新整洁的～ fresh and tidy look of the park
园田 yuántián vegetable garden:耕作～化 garden-style cultivation of farmland
园艺 yuányì horticulture; gardening
园艺家 yuányìjiā *also* "园艺师" horticulturist
园艺学 yuányìxué horticulture; gardening
园囿 yuányòu 〈书面〉❶ public garden ❷ zoo
园子 yuánzi ❶ garden; plot; plantation:菜～ vegetable garden (*or* plot) /果～ orchard ❷ theatre

鼋(黿)

yuán 〈动物〉soft-shelled turtle
鼋头渚 Yuántóuzhǔ Tortoise Head Garden in Wuxi, Jiangsu Province
鼋鱼 yuányú *also* "元鱼" yuányú soft-shelled turtle:～汤 turtle soup /清炖～ stewed turtle

袁

Yuán a surname
袁世凯 Yuán Shìkǎi Yuan Shikai (1859-1916), President of the Republic of China (1912-1916), and chieftain of the Northern Warlords
袁头 yuántóu *also* "大头" dàtóu; "袁大头" Chinese silver dollar (bearing Yuan Shikai's head, issued from 1914)

辕

yuán ❶ shafts (of a cart, palanquin, etc.):驾～ pull a cart; be harnessed in the shafts ❷〈旧语〉outer gate of a government office or barracks;〈比喻〉government office; *yamen*:行～ field headquarters
辕骡 yuánluó shaft-mule; mule in the shafts
辕马 yuánmǎ shaft-horse; horse in the shafts
辕门 yuánmén outer gate of a government office or barracks:大开～ open the outer gate wide
辕子 yuánzi shafts of a cart or palanquin:车～ shafts of a cart; shafts

猿(猨)

yuán ape:长臂～ gibbon /类人～ anthropoid ape /从～到人 from ape to man
猿猴 yuánhóu apes and monkeys
猿人 yuánrén ape-man:北京～ Beijing (Peking) Man /兰田～ Lantian (Lantien) Man

垣

yuán 〈书面〉❶ wall:短～ low wall /城～ city wall /断～残壁 debris; ruins ❷ town; city:省～ provincial capital ❸ (Yuán) a surname
垣墙 yuánqiáng wall:翻过～ get over a wall
垣墉 yuányōng 〈书面〉wall

原[1]

yuán ❶ primary; initial; inceptive: *see* "～始"; "～人"; "～生动物" ❷ original; former:～作者 original writer /～有人数 former number of persons /～地不动 remain where one is; stay put ❸ unprocessed; crude; raw: *see* "～油"; "～木"; "～煤" ❹ (Yuán) a surname

原[2]

yuán excuse; forgive; pardon:情有可～ excusable; pardonable

原[3]

yuán ❶ plain; level; open country:平～ plain /高～ plateau /雪～ snow-clad plain /大草～ prairie; grassland ❷ terrace; tableland
原班人马 yuánbān rénmǎ old cast; original team:这部词典的修订人员已非～。The editing staff for the revision of the dictionary is no longer the former one.

原版 yuánbǎn original edition; in the original: ~片 film in the original /~书 original edition of the book
原本 yuánběn ❶ original manuscript; master copy: 这本书的~现存北京图书馆。The original manuscript of the book is now kept in the Beijing Library. ❷ first edition ❸ original edition; the original: 这本书是根据俄语~翻译的。This book was translated from the Russian original. ❹ originally; formerly: 他~是个商人。He was formerly a businessman.
原病毒 yuánbìngdú protovirus: ~学 protovirus theory
原材料 yuán-cáiliào raw and processed materials: ~奇缺 raw and processed materials being in extremely short supply /~工业 raw and semifinished materials industries
原蚕 yuáncán 〈书面〉 second hatch of silkworms in a year
原产地 yuánchǎndì country or place of origin: ~证明书 certificate of origin
原肠 yuáncháng 〈动物〉 primitive gut; archenteron
原虫 yuánchóng protozoan: ~病 protozoiasis /~感染 protozoan infection /杀~药 protozoacide
原初 yuánchū at first; in the beginning; originally: 他~不是这个样子。He used to be quite different.
原初宇宙线 yuánchū yǔzhòuxiàn primary cosmic ray
原抵押 yuándǐyā 〈法律〉 original mortgage
原地 yuándì (in) the same place: ~踏步 mark time; make no headway /停止前进,~休息! Stop and relax!
原电池 yuándiànchí 〈电工〉 primary cell; galvanic cell
原定 yuándìng originally decided; original: ~计划 original plan / ~日程 original schedule
原动机 yuándòngjī 〈机械〉 prime mover; prime motor
原动力 yuándònglì motive power or force; motivity
原腭 yuán'è 〈生理〉 primary palate
原发价 yuánfājià original offer (of price)
原发性癌 yuánfāxìng'ái primary cancer
原防 yuánfáng original encampment or station: 撤回~ withdraw to the original garrison
原封 yuánfēng intact; with the seal unbroken: ~陈酒 distilled liquor /~退回 return sth. unopened
原封不动 yuánfēng-bùdòng be left intact; remain untouched: 信件被~地退回。The letter was returned to the sender unopened.
原辅料 yuán-fǔliào raw and supplementary materials
原稿 yuángǎo original manuscript; master copy: ~一律不退。The manuscript shall not be returned as a rule.
原稿纸 yuángǎozhǐ drafting paper; writing paper
原告 yuángào 〈法律〉 plaintiff (for civil cases); prosecutor (for criminal cases): ~证人 evidence for the prosecution /~律师 lawyer for the plaintiff /~不服上诉。The plaintiff appealed (against) the unfavourable ruling.
原鸽 yuángē wild pigeon; dove
原故 yuángù *see also* "缘故" yuángù reason; cause
原国籍 yuánguójí nationality of origin
原猴 yuánhóu 〈动物〉 prosimian
原鸡 yuánjī jungle fowl; jungle cock or hen
原级 yuánjí 〈语言〉 positive degree
原籍 yuánjí ancestral home; native place; native home; domicile of origin: 发回~ send sb. back to his native place (as a punishment) /此人~湖北,寄籍北京。He is from Hubei and now lives in Beijing.
原价 yuánjià original price: 按~打七折 give a 30% discount on the marked price
原件 yuánjiàn script; master copy; original copy or document: 清理~ sort out the manuscripts /退回~ return the master copy /这不是~。This is not the original document.
原教旨主义 yuánjiàozhǐzhǔyì fundamentalism: ~者 fundamentalist /基督教~ Christian fundamentalism
原旧 yuánjiù 〈方言〉 ❶ original; former: 他~住在这里。He used to live here. ❷ remain: 他的计划~不变。His plan remained unchanged.
原口动物 yuánkǒu dòngwù 〈生物〉 protostomia
原矿 yuánkuàng *also* "原矿石" 〈矿业〉 run-of-mine ore; crude ore; raw ore
原来 yuánlái ❶ original; former: 他~学法律,后改学历史。He was formerly a law student and shifted to history later. /这才是他~的样子。That's his former self. /她~住这里,最近才搬走。She lived here until recently. ❷ so; as it turns out to be: ~是他在捣鬼。It turned out that he was behind the plot. /我说他今天为何不来,~他是病了。So he is ill! I was just wondering why he was absent today.
原来如此 yuánlái rúcǐ so, that's how it is; I see: 事情的真相~! So, this is the fact of the matter! *or* So, that's how it all happened!
原理 yuánlǐ principle; theory; tenet: 马克思主义的基本~ fundamental tenets of Marxism /普遍~ universally applicable principle
原粮 yuánliáng unhusked grain; unprocessed grain
原谅 yuánliàng excuse; forgive; pardon: 请~我的过错。Please forgive my mistakes. /我迟到了,请~。Excuse my being late, please. /这种行为简直不能~! Such behaviour is just unpardonable.
原料 yuánliào raw material: ~消耗 material consumption /~加工 processing of raw material /~生产国 raw material producing country /讨论~和发展问题的联大特别会议 Special Session of the UN General Assembly on the Problems of Raw Materials and Development
原羚 yuánlíng 〈动物〉 goa, a gazelle of the Tibetan Plateau
原麻 yuánmá hemp
原毛 yuánmáo *also* "油毛" yóumáo raw wool or hair
原貌 yuánmào original look; original state: 保持~ keep (*or* leave) sth. in its original state
原煤 yuánméi raw coal: 高质~ high-quality raw coal
原蜜 yuánmì unprocessed honey; raw honey
原棉 yuánmián raw cotton: ~等级 grades of raw cotton /收购~ purchase raw cotton
原木 yuánmù log: ~小屋 log house /调拨~三十立方 allocate thirty cubic metres of logs
原判 yuánpàn 〈法律〉 original judgment; original sentence
原配 yuánpèi *also* "元配" yuánpèi first wife; wife by first marriage
原人 yuánrén ape-man
原任 yuánrèn ❶ predecessor ❷ formerly hold the post of: 他~科长,现任副处长。Formerly section chief, he is now deputy division chief.
原色 yuánsè *also* "基色" jīsè primary colour
原设计 yuánshèjì original design
原审 yuánshěn 〈法律〉 first trial: 维持~判决 uphold the judgment of the lower court /推翻~判决 reverse (*or* overrule) the judgment of the lower court
原肾 yuánshèn 〈生理〉 archinephros
原生 yuánshēng primordial; proto-: ~蜂群 prime swarm (of bees) /~物质 primordial matter
原生动物 yuánshēng dòngwù protozoan: ~学 protozoology
原生矿物 yuánshēng kuàngwù primary mineral
原生林 yuánshēnglín *also* "原始林" primeval forest; virgin forest
原生生物 yuánshēng shēngwù protist; primitive organism: ~学 protobiology
原生土 yuánshēngtǔ primary soil; protosoil
原生植物 yuánshēng zhíwù protophyte
原生质 yuánshēngzhì 〈生物〉 protoplasm
原声带 yuánshēngdài original sound tape; master tape (as made by an orchestra)
原始 yuánshǐ ❶ primary; original; firsthand: ~材料 firsthand material (*or* information); primary data /~凭证 original certificate / ~证据 original (*or* primary) evidence ❷ primeval; primitive: ~文化 primitive culture; protoculture /~部落 primitive tribe /~状态 state of nature /~人 primitive man
原始公社 yuánshǐ gōngshè primitive society; primitive commune
原始积累 yuánshǐ jīlěi primitive accumulation
原始基督教 yuánshǐ Jīdūjiào primitive Christianity
原始记录 yuánshǐ jìlù original record
原始林 yuánshǐlín *also* "原生林";"原始森林" primeval or virgin forest
原始群 yuánshǐqún primitive herd or horde
原始社会 yuánshǐ shèhuì primitive society
原始石器 yuánshǐ shíqì 〈考古〉 eolith
原始主义 yuánshǐzhǔyì primitivism
原始宗教 yuánshǐ zōngjiào primitive religion
原诉 yuánsù 〈法律〉 original suit: 撤回~ withdraw an original suit
原索动物 yuánsuǒ dòngwù protochordate; prochordate
原汤 yuántāng original soup or juice; stock
原糖 yuántáng raw sugar

原田 yuántián 〈方言〉plateau fields：开发～ open up plateau fields
原委 yuánwěi also "源委" yuánwěi whole story; all the details：诉述～ give a full account of sth. /不明～，不便妄加评论。I am in no position to make any comment without knowing the whys and the wherefores.
原尾虫 yuánwěichóng proturan
原位癌 yuánwèi'ái 〈医学〉carcinoma in situ; preinvasive carcinoma
原文 yuánwén ❶ original：读～ read in the original /译文应忠实于～。The translation should be faithful to the original. ❷ original text; master copy：篡改～ tamper with the original text /核对～ check with the original text /～如此 *sic*; *ipsissima verba*; *sic in originali*
原物 yuánwù original：这是赝品，～早已丢失。This is an imitation; the original has long been missing.
原先 yuánxiān former; original：～的计划 former plan /～的想法 original idea /他～是工人，现在成了工程师。He used to be a worker, but now he's become an engineer.
原线圈 yuánxiànquān primary coil
原薪 yuánxīn original salary, wage or pay
原行星 yuánxíngxīng protoplanet
原形 yuánxíng original shape; true features; true shape beneath the disguise：温度变化，～仍能保持不变。It stays in the original shape (*or* keeps its original shape) despite changes in temperature.
原形毕露 yuánxíng-bìlù be revealed for what one is; show one's true colours or features：几个月的调查取证，使这个大贪污分子～。Evidence gathered through several months of investigation enabled people to see the big embezzler in his true colours.
原型 yuánxíng prototype：～反应堆 prototype reactor /～快中子反应堆 prototype fast reactor (PFR) /～导弹 prototype missile (PM) /～战略导弹 prototype strategic missile (PSM) /据说故事主人公的～是一位著名火箭专家。It is said that the prototype of the hero in the story is a well-known rocket expert.
原盐 yuányán crude salt
原样 yuányàng original look or state：你还是～，一点不见老。You look just as young as ever.
原野 yuányě open country; champaign：辽阔的～ vast open country /丰饶的～ fertile champaign
原义 yuányì primary meaning; original meaning：词的～ primary meaning of a word
原意 yuányì meaning; original meaning or intention：曲解～ distort the meaning /此话不是我的～。This is not what I mean. /～虽好，方法却是糟糕的。The method is poor despite the good intentions.
原因 yuányīn cause; grounds; reason：主要～ main reason; basic cause /追究～ find out the reason (*or* cause) for /～和结果分析 cause-and-effect analysis /由于这个～ on this account
原由 yuányóu cause; reason
原油 yuányóu crude oil; crude：含硫～ sour crude /低硫～ sweet crude /多蜡～ waxy crude /无蜡～ wax-free crude /优质～ high quality crude /～库 crude oil storage /～脱水 dehydration of crude oil /～分馏塔 crude fractionating tower /～裂化设备 crude cracker
原宥 yuányòu 〈书面〉forgive; pardon：不当之处，敬请～。I wish to ask your pardon for any improprieties on my part.
原原本本 yuányuán-běnběn also "元元本本" yuányuán-běnběn whole story; everything：我把这件事～向领导作了汇报。I reported everything to the boss. /请把事情经过～叙述一遍。Please tell the whole story exactly as it happened.
原韵 yuányùn rhyme sequence of a poem, used in reply：步～和诗一首 write a poem in reply to someone else's, using the same rhyme sequence
原早 yuánzǎo 〈方言〉in the past; before; originally：我～也是农民。I used to be a farmer, too.
原则 yuánzé ❶ principle：坚持～ stick (*or* adhere) to principle; live up to one's principle(s) /不讲～ in disregard of principle(s) /符合～ accord with (*or* conform to) principle /拿～作交易 barter away principles; trade in principles /和平共处五项～ the Five Principles of Peaceful Coexistence ❷ in principle; in general：～上同意 agree (*or* accept) in principle /～指示 policy directive /～协议 agreement in principle /～性错误 mistake (in matters) of principle /～立场 principled stand (*or* position)
原职 yuánzhí former post or job：官复～ be rehabilitated in one's former post
原址 yuánzhǐ former address; original site：八·七会议～ site of the August 7th Meeting /来信仍写～。Address the letter as before.
原纸 yuánzhǐ body paper; body stock; base paper; raw stock
原种 yuánzhǒng protospecies; stock：～场 seed stock station
原种种子 yuánzhǒng zhǒngzi original seed
原主 yuánzhǔ original owner：物归～ return sth. to its owner
原注 yuánzhù original note or footnote
原著 yuánzhù original work; original：读莎士比亚的～ read Shakespeare in the original
原装 yuánzhuāng ❶ factory-packed (in the country of origin)：～家用电器 factory-packed electrical (*or* home) appliances ❷ original packing：～名酒 liquor in the original packing
原状 yuánzhuàng original state; previous condition; status quo ante：保持～ remain in the original state; leave sth. in the original state; leave sth. intact /恢复～ restore the status quo ante; return to the former state
原子 yuánzǐ atom：α-碳～ alpha-carbon atom /束缚～ bound atom /复合～ compound atom; complex atom /自由～ free atom /电离～ ionized atom /示踪～ tracer atom /收定～ stationary atom /标记～ labelled atom /～讹诈 atomic blackmail /～弹头 atomic warhead /～辐射 atomic radiation /～结构 atomic structure /～动力 atomic power /～防护 atomic protection /～装置 atomic device
原子笔 yuánzǐbǐ also "圆珠笔" yuánzhūbǐ ball-point pen
原子尘 yuánzǐchén atomic fallout
原子弹 yuánzǐdàn A-bomb; atom bomb; atomic bomb：投～ drop an atomic bomb
原子弹头导弹 yuánzǐ dàntóu dǎodàn atomic warhead missile
原子动力船 yuánzǐ dònglìchuán atomic-powered ship
原子反应堆 yuánzǐ fǎnyìngduī atomic reactor; atomic pile
原子光谱 yuánzǐ guāngpǔ atomic spectrum
原子核 yuánzǐhé atomic nucleus
原子核物理学 yuánzǐhé wùlǐxué nuclear physics; nucleonics
原子价 yuánzǐjià also "化合价" huàhéjià valence; atomicity
原子键 yuánzǐjiàn atomic bond
原子结构化学 yuánzǐ jiégòu huàxué metachemistry
原子量 yuánzǐliàng atomic weight
原子论 yuánzǐlùn atomic theory; atomism
原子能 yuánzǐnéng atomic energy：～发电站 atomic power station /和平利用～ peaceful utilization of atomic energy; atomic energy for peaceful purposes /国际～机构 International Atomic Energy Agency (IAEA)
原子炮 yuánzǐpào atomic cannon or artillery
原子时 yuánzǐshí atomic time
原子团 yuánzǐtuán 〈化学〉atomic group
原子武器 yuánzǐ wǔqì atomic weapon
原子物理学 yuánzǐ wùlǐxué atomic physics
原子序数 yuánzǐ xùshù atomic number
原子战争 yuánzǐ zhànzhēng atomic war or warfare
原子质量 yuánzǐ zhìliàng atomic mass
原子钟 yuánzǐzhōng atomic clock
原罪 yuánzuì 〈宗教〉original sin
原作 yuánzuò ❶ master or primary copy：步～和诗二首。The two poems were written in reply to the primary one. ❷ original text or book; original：剧本改编较好地保持了～的风格。The stage version reproduces the style of the original.

源

yuán ❶ water source; fountainhead：泉～ fountainhead /大江之～ source of a big river /～清水清 clear source, clear stream /饮水思～ when drinking water think of its source — never forget where one's happiness comes from /水有～，树有根。Every river has its source and every tree has its roots. *or* Everything has its origin. ❷ source; cause; root：货～ source of supplies /资～ resources /财～ source of income /电～ power supply /病～ cause of a disease /根～ root ❸ (Yuán) a surname
源程序 yuánchéngxù 〈计算机〉source program：～库 source library /～模块 source module
源代码 yuándàimǎ 〈信息〉source code
源流 yuánliú source and course; origin and development：追溯～ trace sth. back to its source (*or* origin)
源泉 yuánquán well-spring; fountainhead：知识是力量的～。Knowledge is the source of strength.
源头 yuántóu fountainhead; source：～活水 with running water from one's source — ever-fresh inspiration /寻找大江的～ trace the

source of a big river
源委 yuánwěi *see*"原委"yuánwěi
源语言 yuányǔyán 〈计算机〉source language
源源 yuányuán in a steady stream; steadily; continuously:山西的煤炭~不断地运往祖国各地。An unfailing (*or* uninterrupted) supply of coal from Shanxi is transported to every corner of the country.
源源本本 yuányuán-běnběn *also*"原原本本"yuányuán-běnběn from beginning to end; exactly as it is:请将事情~地告诉我。Please tell me exactly as it is.
源源不绝 yuányuán-bùjué in an endless flow; continuously; incessantly:满载的卡车~。Heavily loaded trucks rolled on in an endless stream.
源源而来 yuányuán'érlái come in a steady or an endless stream:慰问信~。Letters of sympathy kept pouring in.
源远流长 yuányuǎn-liúcháng ❶ distant source and long stream:伟大的长江~。The great Yangtze River is long and has a distant source. ❷〈比喻〉of long standing; having a long history:我国的书法艺术~。Chinese calligraphy traces its history back to ancient times.

羱

yuán 〈动物〉ibex
羱羊 yuányáng *also*"北山羊"běishānyáng ibex

塬

yuán 〈地理〉tableland; terrace

螈

yuán *see*"蝾螈"róngyuán

员

yuán ❶ person engaged in a certain field of activity:职~ clerk; staff member /演~ actor; actress /教~ teacher /学~ student; trainee /人~ personnel /船~ seaman; sailor; crew member /汽车售票~ bus conductor /售货~ shop assistant; shop girl; sales clerk /销售~ salesman /炊事~ cook /战斗~ combatant /驾驶~ driver; pilot ❷ member (of an organization):成~ member /少先队~ member of the Chinese Young Pioneers; Young Pioneer /共青团~ member of the Communist Youth League of China; League member /中共党~ member of the Chinese Communist Party; Party member /会~证 membership card ❸〈量词〉:一~猛将 a valiant general; a vigorous man
see also yún; Yùn
员额 yuán'é specified number of personnel:招工~已满 no vacancies left; fully staffed
员工 yuángōng staff; personnel:师生~ teachers, students, administrative personnel and workers; staff and student; all members of a school /铁路~ railway workers and staff; railway employees
员司 yuánsī 〈旧语〉junior government officials; junior functionary
员外 yuánwài ❶ *also*"员外郎"〈古语〉ministry counsellor ❷ (often used in the early vernacular) rich landowner; landlord; squire:本地富绅王~ Mr. Wang, a local wealthy gentleman

圆

yuán ❶ round; circular; spherical:~桌 round table /~领衬衫 collarless shirt /~脸小姑娘 round-faced little girl /~月东升。A full moon is rising in the east. ❷〈数学〉circle:半~ semicircle /椭~ ellipse; oval /同心~ concentric circle /内切~ inscribed circle /外接~ circumscribed circle; circumcircle ❸ ball-shaped:滚~ round as a ball ❹ tactful; satisfactory:他话说得很~。He was very tactful in his remarks. ❺ justify; make perfect or complete:自~其说 make one's statement consistent; justify oneself /破镜重~ reunion of husband and wife after separation /好梦难~。Good dreams seldom come true. ❻ *also*"元"yuán (a unit of currency):定价五十~ priced at 50 *yuan* /三张十~钞票 three 10-*yuan* notes ❼ *also*"元"yuán coin:银~ silver dollar /铜~ copper coin ❽ (Yuán) a surname
圆白菜 yuánbáicài cabbage
圆刨 yuánbào 〈机械〉circular plane; rounding plane
圆编织机 yuánbiānzhījī 〈纺织〉circular knitting machine
圆材 yuáncái 〈林业〉roundwood; log
圆场 yuánchǎng ❶ mediate; smooth things over; help to effect a compromise:他俩为区区小事闹翻了,我出来打~才算了事。They fell out over some trivial matter and did not make peace until I mediated. ❷ (of traditional opera singers or actors) walk in circles on the stage at a heel-and-toe pace — a gesture of travelling a long distance in haste:她的~走得帅极了。She did exceedingly well in the round-the-stage walk.
圆成 yuánchéng help sb. to achieve sth.:如能~此事,将十分感激。I shall be very grateful if you can help me out in this matter.
圆唇元音 yuánchún yuányīn 〈语言〉round vowel
圆锉刀 yuáncuòdāo 〈机械〉round file; circular file
圆到 yuándào perfect; satisfactory:面面~ attentive and thoughtful in every aspect
圆雕 yuándiāo sculpture-in-the-round
圆顶 yuándǐng dome:一座~宫廷式建筑 domed palatial building /大楼白色的~映衬着蓝色的天空,显得分外耀眼。The white dome of the building stood sharply against the blue sky.
圆嘟嘟 yuándūdū *also*"圆敦敦"full and round; plump:~的小脸 chubby face /~的手 plump hands
圆度 yuándù circular degree; roundness:~盘 circular dial /~仪 roundness measuring equipment (*or* instrument)
圆范 yuánfan 〈方言〉appropriate; satisfactory:连话都说不~ not even able to speak properly
圆房 yuánfáng consummate a marriage (when a child daughter-in-law and her husband reached adulthood)
圆坟 yuánfén 〈旧语〉add fresh soil onto the grave three days after the burial
圆钢 yuángāng 〈冶金〉round steel; round bar; round rod:~轧制 round steel rolling
圆工 yuángōng *also*"圆功"complete; finish; wind up:务必在两日内~。It must be completed within two days.
圆骨碌 yuángūlu round; ball-like:~的大脑袋上长着一对滴溜圆的小眼睛 big round head with a pair of small round eyes
圆鼓鼓 yuángǔgǔ bulging; sticking out round; rotund:挺着~的肚子 with one's belly sticking out
圆光 yuánguāng 〈迷信〉round light image (image is supposed to appear on a mirror or piece of white paper after incantations are chanted, and supposed to indicate a clue for lost property or tell one's fortune)
圆规 yuánguī compasses:一副~ a pair of compasses /制图~ drawing compasses /长杆~ beam compasses
圆滚滚 yuángǔngǔn very round; plump:~的小石子儿 small round stone /~的小肥猪 plump piglet
圆函数 yuánhánshù 〈数学〉circular function
圆焊缝 yuánhànfèng 〈机械〉circular joint; circular seam
圆号 yuánhào 〈音乐〉French horn; horn:~独奏 (French) horn solo /吹~ blow a horn
圆和 yuánhe ❶ mediate; help to bring about a reconciliation:从中~ try to mediate ❷ flexible; accomodating:办事~ be flexible in handling business ❸ mellow and full:他有一副~的中音嗓子。He has the mellow and full voice of a baritone.
圆乎乎 yuánhūhū rather round; plump:~的脸颊 round face /~的手 plump hand
圆乎 yuánhu roundish:~脸 roundish face
圆弧 yuánhú 〈数学〉circular arc:~齿轮〈机械〉circular tooth gear
圆滑 yuánhuá smooth and wily; slick and sly; tactful:他为人世故~。He is quite a smooth character. /这是个处事~的家伙。He is a sly old fox.
圆滑线 yuánhuáxiàn 〈音乐〉slur
圆谎 yuánhuǎng make a lie sound plausible:我看你怎么圆这个谎。I would like to know how you are going to explain the lie away.
圆浑 yuánhún 〈书面〉❶ (as of voice) rich; round:唱腔流畅而~ sing in a smooth and rich voice /~而深沉的音调 deep and round mellow voice ❷ (as of poetry and essays) smooth:语言生动~。The language is natural, vivid, and smooth.
圆活 yuánhuo ❶ flexible; not dull:说话~ flexible in speech ❷ mellow and full:声音~ mellow and full voice
圆寂 yuánjì 〈佛教〉Parinirvana; passing away
圆角 yuánjiǎo 〈机械〉circular bead; fillet
圆径概率误差 yuánjìng gàilǜ wùchā 〈物理〉circular error probable; circle of equal probability; circle of probable error; measure of the accuracy of a missile (the radius of a circle around a target area within which a missile has a 50% probability of landing)
圆锯 yuánjù circular or disk saw; annular saw; rim saw; ring saw:横割~ circular cross cut saw /双盘~ double-circular saw /升降~机 jump saw
圆孔 yuánkǒng circular aperture:~拉刀 round broach /~筛 circular screen

Y

圆括号 yuánkuòhào parenthesis; curve
圆溜溜 yuánliūliū round:～的腮颊 round cheeks
圆笼 yuánlóng large, round food basket:饭菜装了满满一～ basketful of dishes
圆颅方趾 yuánlú-fāngzhǐ human race; *Homo sapiens*:同是～,为何自相残杀? Why do humans always engage in fratricide?
圆满 yuánmǎn satisfactory; perfect:～的方案 flawless plan /给以～答复 give a satisfactory reply /访问～结束。The visit came to a successful conclusion. /祝大会～成功! We wish the conference complete success!
圆梦 yuánmèng ❶〈迷信〉oneiromancy; divination by interpretation of one's dream; have one's dream expounded or read ❷ have one's dream fulfilled or realized:圆了上大学的梦 realize one's long-cherished desire to go to college
圆梦术 yuánmèngshù oneirocriticism; oneiromancy
圆明园 Yuánmíngyuán Yuanmingyuan, or the old Summer Palace, imperial garden in the northwest of Beijing, built from 1709 onwards and burned down by the British and French aggressor troops in 1860
圆盘 yuánpán disc; disk:～除草机 disk weeder /～开沟器 disk boot; disk coulter /～磨床 disk grinder /～平地机 disk planer /～形电容器 discap /～机关枪 drum-fed gun /～剪床 circular shears
圆盘耙 yuánpánbà disc harrow
圆盘播种机 yuánpán bōzhǒngjī disk drill; disk seeder
圆盘锯 yuánpánjù disk saw; circular saw
圆盘犁 yuánpánlí disc plough
圆球 yuánqiú ball; globe
圆球体 yuánqiútǐ sphere; globe
圆圈 yuánquān circle; ring:画～儿 draw a circle /他用铁丝做个～儿。He made a ring with iron wire.
圆全 yuánquan〈方言〉satisfactory; thoughtful:这事儿办得很～。The work was well done. /您想得真～。You are so thoughtful (*or* considerate).
圆润 yuánrùn ❶ mellow and full:～的嗓子 sweet, melodious voice /～白皙的肌肤 smooth and fair skin ❷ (of handwriting, etc.) fluent; smooth:他的书法～有力。He writes a smooth, vigorous hand.
圆鲹 yuánshēn〈动物〉round scad
圆石 yuánshí cobble; cobble boulder; cobblestone
圆实 yuánshi round and solid; round and compact:～而红润的脸膛 round rosy cheeks /～饱满的籽粒 round and solid seeds
圆熟 yuánshú ❶ skilful; proficient:手法～灵巧 resort to (*or* employ, *or* adopt) skilful and clever tactic ❷ astute; tactful; flexible:处事～ be astute in one's behaviour /她～地应酬着客人。She handled her guests tactfully.
圆说 yuánshuō explain; justify:不要为他的缺点和错误～了。Don't try to justify his shortcomings and mistakes.
圆台 yuántái ❶ *also* "圆锥台"〈数学〉frustum of a cone; truncated cone ❷〈建筑〉section or drum of a stone pillar or column
圆通 yuántōng flexible; conciliatory; accomodating:他办事灵活～。He is flexible and accomodating in whatever he does.
圆筒 yuántǒng〈机械〉circular cylinder; drum:～铆机 cylinder riveting machine /～筛 cylindrical-shaped screen; cylindrical trommel; drum sieve; drum sifter /～形球磨机 cylindrical ball mill /～洗矿机 drum washer /～选矿机 drum cobber
圆头 yuántóu〈机械〉round head:～刨 rounding plane /～车刀 round-nose tool /～螺钉 round (head) screw; round head carriage bolt /～铆钉 round headed rivet
圆舞曲 yuánwǔqǔ〈音乐〉waltz
圆铣 yuánxǐ〈机械〉circular milling:～装置 circular milling device
圆心 yuánxīn centre of a circle
圆心角 yuánxīnjiǎo〈数学〉central angle
圆形 yuánxíng circular; round:～大厅 round hall
圆形建筑 yuánxíng jiànzhù round building; tholos; rotunda
圆形剧场 yuánxíng jùchǎng amphitheatre
圆凿方枘 yuánzáo-fāngruì *also* "方枘圆凿" like a square tenon for a round mortise — a square peg in a round hole; not in agreement with each other; imcompatible:这二人～,如何在一起共事? In view of their utter imcompatibility, how can they be partners?
圆周 yuánzhōu circumference; periphery:～磨削 peripheral grinding /～铣削 peripheral milling
圆周角 yuánzhōujiǎo〈数学〉circumferential angle
圆周接缝 yuánzhōu jiēfèng〈机械〉circumferential seam; transverse seam
圆周率 yuánzhōulǜ〈数学〉ratio of the circumference of a circle to its diameter; *pi* (π)
圆周运动 yuánzhōu yùndòng〈物理〉circular motion
圆珠笔 yuánzhūbǐ ball-point pen; ball-pen
圆柱 yuánzhù ❶〈数学〉cylinder ❷ column; round post or pillar
圆柱根 yuánzhùgēn〈植物〉cylindrical root
圆柱体 yuánzhùtǐ cylinder:正～ right cylinder
圆柱坐标 yuánzhù zuòbiāo circular cylindrical coordinates:～机器人 cylindrical coordinates robot
圆锥 yuánzhuī circular cone; taper:～投影 conical projection
圆锥根 yuánzhuīgēn〈植物〉conical root
圆锥花序 yuánzhuī huāxù〈植物〉panicle
圆锥曲线 yuánzhuī qūxiàn conic; conic section; parabola
圆锥台 yuánzhuītái〈数学〉*also* "圆台" frustum of a cone
圆桌 yuánzhuō round table:一张大理石～ a round marble table
圆桌会议 yuánzhuō huìyì round-table conference:举行～ hold a round-table conference
圆桌面 yuánzhuōmiàn round table-top:特制大号～ specially-made super-sized round table-top
圆子 yuánzi ❶ dumpling made of glutinous rice flour:芝麻～ sweet sesame dumpling ❷〈方言〉ball:鱼～ fish ball

圜

yuán *see* "圆" yuán
see also huán
圜丘 Yuánqiū Circular Mound Altar (in the Temple of Heaven, Beijing)

爰

yuán〈书面〉❶ where:～其适归? Where to? ❷ thus; then; accordingly:～书其事以告 write a report accordingly

湲

yuán *see* "潺湲" chányuán

援

yuán ❶ pull by hand; hold:攀～而上 climb up ❷ quote; cite:可～旧例 may cite a precedent /～经引典 quote from classics and canons ❸ help; aid; assist; rescue:救～ come to sb.'s rescue /增～ reinforce /求～ ask for help; appeal for aid /孤立无～ isolated and cut off from outside help
援笔 yuánbǐ〈书面〉take up a pen (to write):～立就 take up a pen and finish it in no time
援兵 yuánbīng reinforcements; relief troops
援建 yuánjiàn provide aid in construction:中国～工程 construction project with Chinese aid
援救 yuánjiù rescue; help; save; deliver from danger:～溺水儿童 rescue a child from drowning
援军 yuánjūn reinforcements; relief troops:派出～ dispatch reinforcements
援款 yuánkuǎn relief money or fund; financial assistance or aid
援例 yuánlì cite a precedent:～处理 follow (the) precedent /一律援先例 act according to precedent without exception
援手 yuánshǒu〈书面〉helping hand; help; assistance:给予～ lend sb. a helping hand
援外 yuánwài aid a foreign country; give aid to a foreign country:～物资 materials in aid of a foreign country /～项目 foreign aid project /～医疗队 medical team to assist a foreign country
援引 yuányǐn ❶ cite; invoke; quote:～经典 quote from classics /～条款 quote an article /～国际惯例 cite an international precedent /～法律规定 invoke a legal provision ❷ recommend or appoint sb. out of favouritism:～旧部 recommend one's former subordinates
援用 yuányòng ❶ quote; cite; invoke:～惯例 cite a precedent /～条约 invoke a treaty /～代表人物的言论 quote representative figures (*or* leading exponents) ❷ recommend for appointment:～贤能 recommend the able and virtuous
援助 yuánzhù help; support; aid; assist:～灾区 assist disaster areas /～受难者 help victims /～弱小民族 support small and weak nations /经济～ economic aid /无私的～ selfless assistance /接受国际～ accept foreign aid /在力所能及的范围内予以～ render assistance within one's means; give what one can afford /不附带条件的～ aid with no strings attached /道义～ moral support

媛

yuán *see* "婵媛" chányuán

see also yuàn

缘 yuán ❶ reason：无～无故 without rhyme or reason；for no reason at all ❷ because；for：*see* "～何" ❸ predestined relationship or affinity；happy fate or chance：姻～（predestined）marriage／今朝相识，算是有～。Our meeting today is written in the stars.／她人～不错。She is liked by everybody.／运动与我无～。Sports do not agree with me. ❹ along：～溪行，忘路之远近。He walked along the stream，forgetting how far he had gone. ❺ rim；brink；edge；fringe：边～ rim；edge／地处古城北～ be located on the northern fringe of the old city

缘簿 yuánbù 〈宗教〉donation book

缘法 yuánfǎ *see* "缘分"

缘分 yuánfèn fate or chance that brings people together；predestined affinity or relationship：你俩真是有～。You two are brought together by fate.／我们的～已尽。Our relationship has come to an end. *or* It's time for us to part.

缘故 yuángù *also* "原故" yuángù cause；reason；motive：探明～ discover (*or* find，*or* seek) the cause of／不解其中～ do not know the whys and the wherefors of／瞧他一副紧张的样子，我猜想一定有什么～。He looked very nervous and I guess there must be something behind it.

缘何 yuánhé 〈书面〉why：你～发怒？What's the reason for your anger?

缘木求鱼 yuánmù-qiúyú climb a tree to catch fish — wrong and fruitless approach：向他告贷无异于～。Asking him for a loan is no different from trying to get blood out of a stone.

缘起 yuánqǐ ❶ cause；origin：争执～何在？What's the origin of the dispute? ❷ exposition of the cause or origin of：成立学会的～ account of the founding of the Association

缘悭一面 yuánqiān-yīmiàn never have the luck to meet sb.：久仰阁下大名，然～。Your name resounds far and wide，yet I have never had the pleasure of meeting you before.

缘石 yuánshí *also* "牙石" yáshí guiding kerb

缘饰 yuánshì ❶ lace trimmings ❷ polish：文贵自然，何须～？The merit of an article lies in its naturalness，and there is no need to gild the lily.

缘由 yuányóu *also* "原由" yuányóu reason；cause：他这样做必有～。There must be a reason for his action.

橼 yuán *see* "香橼" xiāngyuán

yuǎn

远(遠) yuǎn ❶ (of time and space) far；distant；remote：遥～ far，far away；far off；remote／～山 distant mountain／～离家乡 far away from one's home village (*or* homeland，*or* native country) ❷ (of blood relationship) distant：～房表亲 distant cousin ❸ (of differences) by far：～～超过 far exceed／～非我能力所及 far beyond my ability／我比他差～了。I am simply no match for him. ❹ not intimate：敬而～之 stay at a respectable distance from sb.／疏～ drift apart；become estranged ❺ (Yuǎn) a surname

远痹 yuǎnbì 〈中医〉chronic numbness caused by rheumatism，etc.

远程 yuǎnchéng long-range；long-distance：～运输 long-distance transport／～控制 long-range control／～导航 long-range navigation／～炮兵 long-range artillery／～航行 long voyage

远程登录 yuǎnchéng dēnglù 〈信息〉telenet；remote login

远程访问 yuǎnchéng fǎngwèn 〈信息〉remote access

远程工作者 yuǎnchéng gōngzuòzhě 〈信息〉teleworker

远程轰炸机 yuǎnchéng hōngzhàjī long-range bomber

远程计算系统 yuǎnchéng jìsuàn xìtǒng 〈信息〉remote computing system：～交换器 remote computing system exchange／～语言 remote computing system language

远程教育 yuǎnchéng jiàoyù distance learning

远程显示 yuǎnchéng xiǎnshì 〈信息〉remote indication

远程信息传送 yuǎnchéng xìnxī chuánsòng 〈信息〉telematic

远程巡航导弹 yuǎnchéng xúnháng dǎodàn long-range cruise missile

远程医学 yuǎnchéng yīxué telemedicine

远处 yuǎnchù (in the) distance；at a distant point or place：～的枪声接连不断。Firing was heard constantly in the distance.

远大 yuǎndà long-range；broad；lofty；ambitious：～前程 (have a) bright future；(person of) great promise／～理想 lofty aims；high aspirations／目光～ be farsighted；have a broad vision／～的目标 grand objective；great aim／～的规划 ambitious plan

远道 yuǎndào long way：～而来的好友 good friend who has come a long way (*or* come from afar)

远地点 yuǎndìdiǎn 〈天文〉apogee

远东 Yuǎndōng Far East：～地区 Far Eastern region／亚洲及～经济委员会(亚远经委会) Economic Commission for Asia and the Far East (ECAFE)

远东经济评论 Yuǎndōng Jīngjì Pínglùn *Far Eastern Economic Review*，weekly magazine of Asian business and news published in Hong Kong since 1946

远动学 yuǎndòngxué 〈自控〉telemechanics；telemechanism

远渡 yuǎndù cross vast seas or oceans：～重洋，来到中国 come to China from across the vast ocean

远方 yuǎnfāng distant place：～的亲人 one's family members (*or* dear ones) who live in distant places／～的山峰 mountain peak standing in the distance／有朋自～来，不亦乐乎？Isn't it a pleasure to have friends from afar?

远房 yuǎnfáng distantly related：～亲戚 distant relative；remote kinfolk／～伯父 distant uncle

远隔 yuǎngé far apart：～千山万水 separated by numerous mountains and rivers；far，far apart

远隔重洋 yuǎngé-chóngyáng separated by vast oceans：两国～，但往来不断。Though separated by vast expanses of water，the two countries have maintained close ties.

远古 yuǎngǔ remote antiquity：～时代 remote antiquity／～以来 from time immemorial／有关～的传说 legend related to the antediluvian age；antediluvian legend；legend from ancient times (*or* from before the Flood)

远海 yuǎnhǎi high or open seas

远航 yuǎnháng long voyage：～南极洲 long voyage to Antarctica

远话 yuǎnhuà sth. said as if by an outsider：近人不说～。A close friend should not talk like an outsider.

远见 yuǎnjiàn foresight；far-sightedness；vision：政治～ political foresight (*or* vision)／有～的人 person of foresight (*or* forward-looking vision)；far-sighted person

远见卓识 yuǎnjiàn-zhuōshí foresight and sagacity；far-sightedness：具有～的政治家 statesman with breadth of vision

远交近攻 yuǎnjiāo-jìngōng befriend distant states while attacking those nearby：采取～的策略 adopt the strategy of uniting those far away against those next door

远郊 yuǎnjiāo outer suburbs；exurbs：～区县 counties and districts in the outer suburbs／家住～ live in the far outskirts

远近 yuǎnjìn ❶ distance：不论～我们都要去参观。We must go for a visit despite the distance. ❷ far and near；far and wide；everywhere：他们的产品～驰名。Their products are known far and wide.

远井不解近渴 yuǎnjǐng bù jiě jìnkě *see* "远水解不了近渴"

远景 yuǎnjǐng ❶ distant view：眺望西山的～ take a distant view of the Western Hills ❷ long-range perspective；prospect：～规划 long-range plan／展望家乡的～ take a long-range look at one's home village ❸ 〈影视〉long shot

远距离操纵 yuǎnjùlí cāozòng remote control；telecontrol

远距离操作 yuǎnjùlí cāozuò remote-controlled operation

远距离控制 yuǎnjùlí kòngzhì remote control；telecontrol：～起重机 remote-control rack／～仪器 tele-gauge

远距离射击 yuǎnjùlí shèjī long-range shooting

远距离投篮 yuǎnjùlí tóulán 〈体育〉long shot

远客 yuǎnkè guest or visitor from afar：难得来的～ rare visitor from afar

远路 yuǎnlù long journey；long way；detour：走～ take a long journey

远路无轻担 yuǎnlù wú qīngdàn light burdens，long borne，grow heavy

远虑 yuǎnlǜ foresight；long view：深谋～ think deeply and plan carefully；be circumspect and far-sighted／人无～，必有近忧。A person without foresight will soon find himself in trouble.

远略 yuǎnlüè long-term strategy

远门 yuǎnmén ❶ go on a distant journey：他打算出～。He plans to

Y

make a long journey. ❷ (of family relationship) distant：～表亲 distant cousin
远谋 yuǎnmóu long-term plans：～深算 circumspect and far-seeing
远年 yuǎnnián many years：～陈酒 wine kept for a long time; mellow wine
远僻 yuǎnpì remote; farway; out-of-the-way：～的地方 out-of-the-way place
远期 yuǎnqī at a specified future date; relating to the future; forward：～汇价 forward rate /～外汇 forward exchange /～合同 forward contract /～汇票 time bill
远亲 yuǎnqīn distant relative; remote kinfolk：他是我的一位～。He is a distant relation of mine.
远亲不如近邻 yuǎnqīn bùrú jìnlín a close neighbour means more than a distant relative; a distant relative is not as helpful as a near neighbour
远人 yuǎnrén ❶ people who live far away ❷ individual of distant relationship; nodding acquaintance
远日点 yuǎnrìdiǎn 〈天文〉aphelion
远涉 yuǎnshè cover a vast distance：～重洋 come (*or* go) across a vast ocean; travel across the high seas
远射程 yuǎnshèchéng long range：～炮 long-range gun /～喷灌机 long-range sprinkler
远射武器 yuǎnshè wǔqì 〈军事〉standoff weapon
远摄镜头 yuǎnshè jìngtóu ❶〈影视〉long shot ❷〈摄影〉telephoto lens
远识 yuǎnshí foresight; far-sightedness; vision：极富～ be of great vision / 求近利，无～ seek immediate profit but lack foresight
远视 yuǎnshì ❶ long sight; long-sightedness; hyperopia; hypermetropia：～眼镜 spectacles for long sight; spectacles for the long-sighted (*or* far-sighted) /我～越来越厉害了。My long-sightedness is getting worse. ❷ far-sight; far-sightedness
远水解不了近渴 yuǎnshuǐ jiěbuliǎo jìnkě *also*“远水不解近渴” distant water cannot quench present thirst; a far-off well is no help to a thirsty man：你这个办法虽然稳妥，但～。Your suggestion is quite prudent but won't solve our immediate problem.
远水救不了近火 yuǎnshuǐ jiùbuliǎo jìnhuǒ *also*“远水不救近火” distant water won't put out a fire nearby; while the grass grows, the horse starves; a slow remedy cannot meet an emergency：目下只有这一条路子，其他都是～。At present, this is the only way out and the rest are all too slow to meet the urgent need.
远台 yuǎntái 〈体育〉(of pingpong) far from the table：～防守 long defence; far-from-table defence /～削球 off-table chop /～长抽 off-table long drive /～对攻 off-table mutual long attacks
远天 yuǎntiān remote sky; lofty sky：遥望～ look into the lofty sky
远眺 yuǎntiào look into the distance：登高～ ascend a height to enjoy (*or* take) a distant view
远图 yuǎntú foresight; long-range planning
远系繁殖 yuǎnxì fánzhí 〈生物〉outbreeding
远销 yuǎnxiāo sell to faraway places：～海外 sell sth. overseas (*or* abroad)
远行 yuǎnxíng go on a long journey：出门～，一切都需格外小心。Extra caution should be exercised while on a long journey.
远扬 yuǎnyáng become known far and wide：臭名～ be notorious / 声威～ be widely famous; enjoy great prestige far and near
远飏 yuǎnyáng 〈书面〉flee far away：凶犯闻风～。The convict fled far away at the tip (*or* news).
远洋 yuǎnyáng of an ocean; oceanic：～航行 oceangoing voyage /～货轮 oceangoing freighter /～渔业 deep-sea fishing; pelagic fishing /～捕鲸 pelagic whaling /～船队 oceangoing fleet /～客轮 ocean liner /～通信 transoceanic communication
远洋海军 yuǎnyáng hǎijūn blue-sea navy
远因 yuǎnyīn remote cause; distant cause
远游 yuǎnyóu travel far away; be on a distant journey：他～在外，已数月不归。He has been away for months on a distant journey.
远缘 yuǎnyuán 〈生物〉distant：～类型 distant form /～杂种 distant hybrid
远缘嫁接 yuǎnyuán jiàjiē distant grafting
远缘杂交 yuǎnyuán zájiāo distant hybridization
远月点 yuǎnyuèdiǎn 〈天文〉apocynthion
远在天边，近在眼前 yuǎn zài tiānbiān, jìn zài yǎnqián close at hand though seemingly far away (used to emphasize that sth. or sb. is right in front of a person)：你所说的人～，不才便是。The person you mentioned is right here before your eyes, and that's me.
远征 yuǎnzhēng expedition：～军 expeditionary army (*or* force) / 红军不怕～难，万水千山只等闲。The Red Army fears not the trials of the Long March, Holding light ten thousand crags and torrents.
远支 yuǎnzhī distant branch (of a clan)
远志 yuǎnzhì ❶ lofty ideals; high aspirations：胸怀～ cherish noble aspriations ❷ Chinese narrow-leaved polygala; polygala-root (*Polygaya terrinfolia*)
远走高飞 yuǎnzǒu-gāofēi soar high and fly far; flee to faraway places：与其坐以待毙，不如～。I'd rather flee for life than wait for death.
远足 yuǎnzú excursion; hike; pleasure trip on foot; walking tour：到郊外去～ go on an outing
远祖 yuǎnzǔ remote ancestor

yuàn

垸 yuàn 〈方言〉protective embankment in a riverside or lakeside area; levee：堤～ dyke; embankment /～田 field protected by embankments
垸子 yuànzi (used in Hunan and Hubei provinces, etc.) protective embankments around houses and fields

院 yuàn ❶ yard; courtyard; compound：四合～儿 compound with houses around a courtyard; quadrangle /后～儿 backyard /～里～外都收拾得干干净净。The courtyard is spotless in and out. ❷ designation for certain government institutions and public places：国务～ State Council /检察～ procuratorate /医～ hospital /博物～ museum /戏～ theatre ❸ institute of higher learning; college：全～师生员工 all the staff and students of the college (*or* institute) ❹ hospital：住～ be hospitalized /出～ be discharged from hospital ❺ (Yuàn) a surname
院坝 yuànbà 〈方言〉yard behind or in front of a house; courtyard
院本 yuànběn ❶ drama script in the Jin and Yuan dynasties ❷ drama or romance in the Ming and Qing dynasties
院画 yuànhuà *see*“院体画”
院落 yuànluò courtyard; yard; compound：很大的～ large compound /这房子共有三重～。The house has three courtyards.
院墙 yuànqiáng wall surrounding a house; courtyard wall
院士 yuànshì academician：通讯～ corresponding academician /中国科学院～ member of the Chinese Academy of Sciences
院试 yuànshì 〈旧语〉imperial civil service examinations at the provincial level during the Ming and Qing dynasties
院套 yuàntào 〈方言〉courtyard; yard; compound
院体画 yuàntǐhuà *also*“院画” imperial-court decorative painting, usually of flowers and birds or landscapes, or concerning religious topics
院外活动 yuànwài huódòng lobbying
院校 yuànxiào colleges and universities：高等～ institutions of higher learning /本地有十几所～。There are more than a dozen colleges and universities locally.
院子 yuànzi courtyard; yard; compound：～里种有各种各样的花卉。There are all kinds of flowers in the courtyard. *or* The courtyard is planted with all kinds of flowers.

衏 yuàn *see*“衏衏” hángyuàn

愿[1] yuàn 〈书面〉honest and prudent：诚～ honest and sincere /幼～ naive and honest /～，吾爱之。I like honesty and cautiousness.

愿[2]**(願)** yuàn ❶ wish; hope; desire：夙～ long-cherished wish /事与～违 things go against what one desires /一切如～。Everything has been as wished. /但～如此。If only it were true. *or* Let's hope so. /～天下有情人终成眷属。May all lovers unite in marriage! ❷ be willing; be ready; be glad：心甘情～ be most willing; be perfectly happy /自觉自～ of one's own free will; voluntarily /～供差遣 willingly put oneself at sb.'s disposal /～侍箕帚〈旧语〉be glad to be sb.'s wife /～效犬马之劳〈书面〉be willing to do what little one

can; wish to render one's service / 我～为祖国的建设事业添砖加瓦。I am ready to do all I can in the construction of our motherland. ❸ vow; declare solemnly: 许～ make a vow

愿望 yuànwàng wish; hope; desire; intention: 主观～ subjective desire; wishful thinking / 良好的～ best of wishes; good intention / 从团结的～出发 proceed from the desire for unity; start with the intention of unity

愿心 yuànxīn ❶ vow (made before Buddha or a god): 许下～ make a vow / 偿还～ redeem a vow ❷ wish; desire; hope: 他这份报国～早就有了。He has long wished to serve his country.

愿意 yuànyì ❶ be willing; be ready: 他～帮助你。He is ready (*or* willing) to help you. / 我～接受他的批评。I will readily (*or* happily) accept his criticism. / 你～出席这次座谈会吗? Would you like to attend the symposium? ❷ wish; want; hope (for sth. in the future): 全家人都～我学医。The whole family want (*or* wish) me to study medicine. / 外面太吵, 我～在这儿安静一会儿。It is too noisy outside. I prefer to have some quietness in here.

掾

yuàn 〈书面〉 subordinate; petty official; clerk (working in a government institution)

瑗

yuàn 〈书面〉 round flat piece of jade with a large hole in the centre (used for ceremonial purposes in ancient China): 问士以璧, 召人以～。When consulting sb. on state affairs one should use the jade with a small hole; when summoning an envoy one should use the jade with a large hole.

媛

yuàn 〈书面〉 beautiful woman

see also yuán

怨

yuàn ❶ resentment; hatred; grudge: 抱～ complain / 结～ incur sb.'s hatred (*or* enmity) / 面有～色 wear an expression of resentment (*or* discontent) / 不计个人恩～ give no thought to personal feelings; not allow oneself to be swayed by personal feelings ❷ blame: 埋～ blame (sb. for sth.); complain / 任劳任～ work hard and not be upset by criticisms; willingly bear the burden of office / 这事不～别人, 只～我自己。There is nobody else but myself to blame for this. *or* I have only myself to blame for what has happened.

怨不得 yuànbude ❶ cannot blame: 刚才的事～小王, 是我脾气不好。Xiao Wang is not to blame for what has happened; it was just my bad temper. ❷ no wonder: 大雪阻塞道路, ～他们没来呢。The road was blocked by snow. No wonder they didn't turn up.

怨仇 yuànchóu resentment; enmity; hatred; rancour

怨敌 yuàndí enemy; foe

怨毒 yuàndú 〈书面〉 hatred; enmity; venom: ～太深 deep-seated hatred; profound hatred / ～之于人甚矣哉! Nothing warps a man like venomous spite!

怨怼 yuànduì 〈书面〉 resentment; enmity; hatred: 心存～ bear (*or* have) a grudge; be resentful

怨愤 yuànfèn discontent; indignation: ～难平 can hardly restrain one's indignation (*or* suppress one's discontent)

怨府 yuànfǔ 〈书面〉 object or target of common hatred: 毋为～, 毋为祸梯。Be not the target of common hatred, or the cause of trouble.

怨怪 yuànguài blame: ～别人多嘴 blame sb. for not keeping his mouth shut (when he should) / ～自己事先考虑不周 blame oneself for not having given adequate consideration to the matter in advance

怨恨 yuànhèn ❶ have a grudge against; resent; hate: ～战争 hate war / ～官僚主义 resent bureaucratism ❷ hatred; resentment: 满心的～ be full of hatred / ～的语气 tone of discontent (*or* resentment, *or* hatred) / 这种不负责任的作风引起了无比的～。Such an irresponsible style of work aroused intense dissatisfaction (*or* resentment).

怨悔 yuànhuǐ regret remorsefully; repent: ～无济于事, 重要的是如何弥补失误。It is useless crying over spilt milk; what's important is how to make amends for it.

怨嗟 yuànjiē 〈书面〉 sigh in resentment or anger: 遭此灾难, 他～不已。He complained bitterly about what he had suffered.

怨苦 yuànkǔ hatred and anguish; painful resentment

怨詈 yuànlì abuse with hatred; rail (at sb.) fretfully

怨懑 yuànmèn discontented and angry; hostile and resentful: ～之情, 跃然纸上。One's discontent and anger are clearly discernible on the paper.

怨怒 yuànnù resentful and indignant

怨女 yuànnǚ 〈书面〉 girl pining for a husband; single woman long overdue for marriage: 帮助怨男～寻偶 help bachelors and spinsters to find appropriate mates

怨偶 yuàn'ǒu 〈书面〉 unhappy couple

怨气 yuànqì grievance; complaint; resentment: ～冲天 towering resentment / 充满～ be full of grievances (*or* complaints) / 发泄心头的～ air (*or* vent) one's grievances

怨声载道 yuànshēng-zàidào complaints (of the people) fill the streets; complaints are heard everywhere: 旧社会, 民不聊生, ～。Cries of discontent rose all round in the old society as people had no means of livelihood.

怨天尤人 yuàntiān-yóurén blame God and man; find fault with everyone and everything: 你成天这样～, 有什么用呢? What is the use of querulously blaming God and man, as you always do? / 有些人稍遇困难就牢骚满腹, ～。Whenever difficulties pop up, some people just grumble and blame everyone and everything but themselves.

怨天怨地 yuàntiān-yuàndì blame heaven and earth; curse fate: 球输了, 不要～, 还是认真研究一下如何改进我们的训练为好。We should earnestly look into our own training programme to see how we can improve it, instead of cursing fate for losing the game.

怨望 yuànwàng 〈书面〉 grudge; resentment; enmity: ～日深 deepen a grudge with each passing day

怨言 yuànyán complaint; grumble: 满口～ spout complaints; grumble ceaselessly / 从无～ have no complaint for anybody or anything / ～四起 grumbles are heard all round / 少发～, 多提建议 fewer complaints, more suggestions

怨艾 yuànyì 〈书面〉 hatred; resentment; enmity: ～之心 feeling of resentment (*or* enmity)

怨尤 yuànyóu hatred; resentment; enmity: 心怀～ harbour enmity; nurse a hatred; feel resentful

苑

yuàn ❶〈书面〉 enclosed ground for growing trees, keeping animals, etc.; imperial garden; park: 林～ hunting park for the emperor; imperial garden / 鹿～ deer park ❷〈书面〉 centre (of art and literature, etc.): 文～ centre of literature; literary world ❸ (Yuàn) a surname

苑囿 yuànyòu animal farm or park

yuē

矱

yuē 〈书面〉 measurement; scale; yardstick

蠖(蠖)

yuē 〈书面〉 ❶ measurement; scale; yardstick ❷ measure; weigh

曰

yuē 〈书面〉 ❶ say: 子～: "学而时习之。" The Master (i.e. Confucius) said, "Review what you learn from time to time." / 孙子～: "兵者, 国之大事。" Sun-tzu said, "Military affairs are a major concern of a state." ❷ call; name: 名之～文化社团 name it a cultural society / 美其名～ describe sth. euphemistically as; give sth. the fine-sounding name of / 一～水, 二～火, 三～木, 四～金, 五～土。The first is called water, the second fire, the third wood, the fourth metal, and the fifth earth.

约

yuē ❶ make an appointment; agree; arrange: 预～ make an appointment (in advance); book reserve / 我们～好在校门口见面。We agreed to meet at the school gate. ❷ ask or invite (in advance); engage: ～王小姐吃晚饭 invite (*or* ask) Miss Wang to dinner / 特～有经验的厨师当场献艺。An experienced chef has been specially engaged to demonstrate his skills on the spot. ❸ pact; treaty; agreement; appointment: 践～ keep an appointment; keep one's word / 订～ make a pact; come to an agreement / 毁～ break an appointment (*or* agreement); abrogate a treaty (*or* pact) / 和～ peace treaty / 盟～ treaty of alliance / 契～ contract; deed; charter / 我们是有～在先。We have had a prior agreement. ❹ check; restrict; restrain: 互相制～ check (*or* restrain) each other; mutually restrict; check and balance (each other) ❺ economical; thrifty; frugal: 节～

Y

economize / ～食蓄谷 store up grain by economizing on food ❻ simple; brief; succinct: ～而详 succinct but full / 由博返～ return to simplicity from complexity; arrive at succinctness through exhaustiveness ❼ about; around; or so; approximately: 大～ about / 年～十五 around the age of fifteen / ～有七八辆车 seven cars or so ❽ reduction of a fraction: 九分之六可以～成三分之二。Six over nine can be reduced to two over three. *or* Six ninths can be reduced to two thirds.
see also yāo

约旦 Yuēdàn Jordan: ～人 Jordanian / ～河 Jordan River / 外～ (former name for Jordan) Transjordan

约定 yuēdìng agree; appoint; arrange: 事先～ arrange or agree in advance / ～的地点 appointed place / ～的事项 items agreed on / ～在车站碰头 agree to meet at the station

约定俗成 yuēdìng-súchéng established by popular usage; approved by the people; accepted through common practice: 语言是～的，新词一旦为群众认可，也就通用了。As language is shaped by common practice, new words and expressions will come to be accepted once they are approved by the people.

约法 yuēfǎ provisional constitution: 《中华民国临时～》 *Provisional Constitution of the Republic of China* (March 1912)

约法三章 yuēfǎ-sānzhāng agree on a three-point decree; make or agree on a few simple rules to be observed by all concerned: 两人事先～: 决不为上学之事影响其他工作。The two of them both agreed that going to school should in no way affect their work.

约分 yuēfēn 〈数学〉 reduction of a fraction: 八分之四可～成二分之一。Four over eight can be reduced to one over two. *or* Four eighths can be reduced to one half.

约翰内斯堡 Yuēhànnèisībǎo Johannesburg, largest city of South Africa

约翰牛 Yuēhànniú John Bull (nickname for England or the English)

约翰斯顿岛 Yuēhànsīdùndǎo Johnston Island, south of Hawaii

约翰逊 Yuēhànxùn ❶ Andrew Johnson (1805-1875), 17th President of the United States (1865-1869) ❷ Lyndon Baines Johnson (1908-1973), 36th President of the United States (1963-1968)

约合 yuēhé call together; invite to meet: ～几个人玩桥牌 invite some people to meet for a bridge game

约会儿 yuēhuìr appointment; engagement; date; rendezvous: 这几天～太多。There have been too many engagements these days. / 晚上我要去赴～。I have a date (*or* appointment, *or* engagement) this evening.

约会 yuēhui make an appointment; make an arrangement to meet: ～在公园碰头 arrange to meet in the park / 同学们～好一同返校。The students made an appointment to go back to school together.

约集 yuējí call together; invite to meet; gather: ～全班一起过除夕 gather the whole class to spend the (lunar) New Year's Eve together / 请你把大家～到这里来。Would you please call everybody to come here?

约计 yuējì count roughly; come approximately to: 这次展销会～赢利一百万元。The profit from this commodity fair came approximately to one million *yuan*. / 他家的书～三千册。He has roughly three thousand books at home (*or* in his house).

约见 yuējiàn (usu. used for diplomatic occasions) make an appointment: 要求～助理国务卿 ask for (*or* request) an appointment with the assistant secretary of state / 该国外交部紧急～美国大使。The foreign ministry of the country urgently summoned the American ambassador.

约据 yuējù (general term for 合同, 契约) contracts and deeds

约克夏猪 yuēkèxiàzhū 〈畜牧〉 Yorkshire (hog), a fine strain of pig originally bred in Yorkshire, England

约略 yuēlüè ❶ rough; approximate: ～知道一些 have a rough idea (of sth. etc.); know a bit (about sth.) / 据～的估计，村民们的人均收入已超过五千元了。According to approximate estimates, the per capita annual income of the villagers is over five thousand *yuan*. ❷ vaguely; dimly: ～听见有人在隔壁房间里谈话。I dimly heard some people talking in the next room. / 远处山影～可见。One could see the vague outline of a mountain in the distance.

约莫 yuēmo *also* "约摸" about; roughly; or so: 高镇距这儿～有五里路。Gao Town is about five *li* from here. / 现在离开车～还有一刻钟。There are fifteen minutes or so to go before the train sets off.

约期 yuēqī ❶ agree on a date or time; fix or set a date; appoint a time: ～会晤 fix a date to meet ❷ fixed date; time of appointment: ～到了，他人没有来。He did not turn up for the appointment. / 小心别误了～。Take care not to miss the appointed time. ❸ term or duration of a contract or agreement: ～订为三年。It is a three-year contract. / ～未满。The contract has not yet expired.

约期买卖权 yuēqī mǎimàiquán option

约请 yuēqǐng invite; ask: ～专家会诊 ask (medical) experts for a group consultation / ～著名诗人来作报告 invite a well-known poet to come and give a speech

约束 yuēshù keep within bounds; restrain; constrain; bind: ～不了别人 cannot restrain others / 受条约的～ be bound by a treaty / 自我～ self-discipline / 感到舆论的～ feel the restraint of public opinion / 用校规～不守规矩的学生 take unruly students in hand by means of school regulations / 他觉得在这里受～。He felt he was under constraint here. / 对孩子应加以适当的～。Children should be kept within certain bounds of discipline.

约束力 yuēshùlì binding force: 对签字方具有法律～ be legally binding on the signatory parties

约数 yuēshù ❶ approximate number ❷ divisor: 公～ common divisor

约谈 yuētán make an appointment to talk over sth.; arrange talks or discussions: 许多客商～进出口业务。Many clients made appointments to discuss import-export business (with a company).

约同 yuētóng 〈书面〉 invite sb. to go somewhere together: ～好友前往济南 ask a good friend to go to Jinan together; ask a good friend to join one on a trip to Jinan

约言 yuēyán promise; word; pledge: 信守～ abide by one's promise (*or* word) / 违反～ break one's promise; go back on one's word; break one's pledge / 实践～ redeem one's pledge; fulfil one's promise

约制 yuēzhì restrain; check; bind; keep within bounds: ～属下 restrain one's subordinates (*or* followers)

yuě

哕(噦) yuě ❶ 〈象声〉 sound of vomiting ❷ 〈口语〉 vomit; throw up: 干～ retch / 心里只想～ feel like vomiting; feel sick / 吃的药全都～出来了。All the medicine taken was thrown up.
see also huì

yuè

悦 yuè ❶ happy; glad; pleased; delighted: 心情不～ unhappy; displeased / 心～诚服 feel admiration for sb.; be utterly convinced ❷ please; delight: 取～于上司 ingratiate oneself with one's superior / 不以佞言～人。Do not please people with flattery. *or* Do not flatter people in order to please them. ❸ (Yuè) a surname

悦耳 yuè'ěr pleasing to the ear; sweet: ～的歌声 melodious song / ～的嗓音 sweet voice

悦服 yuèfú enthusiastically agree or assent; heartily admire: 他的论点令人～。His argument won our hearty acclaim. *or* His argument was thoroughly convincing.

悦目 yuèmù pleasing to the eye; attractive; good-looking: 赏心～ pleasing to both the eye and the mind / 鲜艳～ bright-coloured and attractive

悦怿 yuèyì 〈书面〉 delighted; happy; joyful

悦意 yuèyì 〈方言〉 pleased; glad; happy

悦豫 yuèyù 〈书面〉 pleased; delighted

阅 yuè ❶ read; go over; scan; peruse: 翻～报纸 go (*or* glance) over newspapers / 查～期刊 look up periodicals / 此件送吴经理～。Please send this document for Manager Wu's reading. *or* Have Manager Wu read this document. ❷ review; inspect: 检～部队 review troops ❸ experience; undergo; pass through: 历尽沧桑，～人多矣 have had a great deal of experience with men after going through the vicissitudes of life / 他来此任职，已～三年。It is three years since he took up his post here.

阅兵 yuèbīng review or inspect troops: ～场 parade ground / ～典礼 dress parade / ～台 (grand) stand for reviewing a military parade /

Y

举行盛大的～式 hold a massive military parade
阅操 yuècāo inspect or watch a military drill; review troops at drill
阅读 yuèdú read: 仔细地～ go over carefully; read intensively /泛泛地～ read extensively; browse; skim /～书报 read books and newspapers /～材料 reading material (*or* matter) /～机 reading machine; reader /～技巧 reading skill /～理解力 reading comprehension /他的英语～能力很强,但是说得不好。He reads English perfectly but doesn't speak it well.
阅卷 yuèjuàn read and score (examination) papers; grade (examination) papers
阅览 yuèlǎn read
阅览室 yuèlǎnshì reading room: 报纸～ newspaper reading room /期刊～ periodical reading room
阅历 yuèlì ❶ see, hear or do for oneself: 一生～过很多事情 have gone through a lot in life /出去～一番 go out and experience life ❷ experience: ～有限 limited experience /～丰富 rich experience /增长～ enrich one's experience; gain experience /他学贯中西, ～深广。Well versed in both Chinese and Western learning, he was a man of much experience.
阅年 yuènián *also* "阅岁" 〈书面〉 with the passage of a year; after a year
阅世 yuèshì 〈书面〉 see the world: ～很深 have seen a great deal of life; have seen much of the world

说 yuè *see* "悦" yuè
see also shuì; shuō

越[1] yuè ❶ get over; jump over; cross: 偷～国境 illegally cross the border /～窗而出 jump out of the window ❷exceed; pass; overstep: 李翁年～八十。Old man Li is over eighty. ❸ (of voice or emotion) be at a high pitch; vigorous: 情绪激～ be excited /清～的二胡声 clear and far-reaching sound of the *erhu* ❹ 〈书面〉 loot: 杀人～货 kill a person and seize his belongings; rob and kill

越[2] yuè ❶ *used in duplicates* "越…越…": 技艺～练～好。The more one practises, the more skilful one becomes. /～多～好。The more, the better. /雨～下～大。The rain is getting heavier. /真理～辩～明。Truth becomes all the clearer after debate. ❷ *used in* "越来越…": 他的进步～来～大。He is making greater and greater progress. /形势～来～好。The situation is better and better. /事情～来～有希望。Things have become increasingly hopeful.

越[3] Yuè ❶ name of a state in the Zhou Dynasty, covering east Zhejiang Province and later extending to Jiangsu and Shandong provinces ❷ eastern part of Zhejiang Province ❸ a surname
越次 yuècì 〈书面〉 transcend the normal order: ～而进 overtake others in forward movement
越冬 yuèdōng live through the winter: 有些昆虫的卵潜伏在土内～。Eggs of certain insects hide under the earth to survive the winter.
越冬作物 yuèdōng zuòwù winter crop; overwintering crop
越发 yuèfā ❶ even more; still more; all the more: 小姑娘长得～漂亮了。The little girl is getting even prettier than before. ❷ (placed after 越 or 越是) the more... the more...: 越是艰苦的地方, ～需要我们去工作。The harder the life in the locality, the greater the need for us to go and work there.
越分 yuèfèn exceed certain confines or limits (in speech or action); presumptuous: 在这种场合, 说话不可～。On such occasions, one must be careful not to speak out of turn.
越瓜 yuèguā *also* "菜瓜" càiguā snake melon
越轨 yuèguǐ go beyond the limits; exceed the bounds; transgress: 他从未有过～的行为。He has never committed an act of indiscretion (*or* transgression).
越过 yuèguò cross; traverse; surmount; negotiate: ～边境 cross the border; overstep the boundary /～高山大河 negotiate high mountains and big rivers /～艰难险阻 surmount hardships and obstacles; overcome difficulties and hindrances
越级 yuèjí ❶ skip a rank or grade: ～提拔 promote sb. more than one grade (*or* rank) at one time ❷ bypass the immediate leadership: ～上告 bypass the immediate leadership and submit one's complaints to a higher level; go over sb.'s head to the higher-ups with one's complaints
越加 yuèjiā even more; still more; all the more: 她越想, 心里就～发慌。The more she thought, the more worried she became.
越界 yuèjiè overstep the boundary; cross the border: ～筑路 build roads across the border
越境 yuèjìng cross the boundary line illegally; sneak in or out of a country: ～的走私分子 smuggler who sneaks in and out of a country /～污染 trans-frontier pollution
越橘 yuèjú 〈植物〉 cowberry
越剧 yuèjù Shaoxing opera: ～演员 Shaoxing opera actor (*or* actress) /～的保留剧目 repertoire of Shaoxing opera
越礼 yuèlǐ ❶ unprescribed courtesy; unwanted etiquette ❷ not abide by the protocol; be improper; be indecorous
越理 yuèlǐ (of one's behaviour) abnormal; unreasonable
越南 Yuènán Vietnam: ～人 Vietnamese /～语 Vietnamese (language)
越南战争 Yuènán Zhànzhēng Vietnam War (1955-1975)
越权 yuèquán exceed one's powers; overstep one's authority; *ultra vires*: ～处理 go beyond one's powers in handling a problem /～行为 act in excess of one's authority; overstepping one's authority
越位 yuèwèi 〈体育〉 (of football, ice hockey, etc.) offside
越席 yuèxí leave one's seat
越洋 yuèyáng transoceanic: ～电缆 transoceanic cable
越野 yuèyě cross-country: ～滑雪 cross-country skiing /～赛车 offroad racing /～识途比赛 orienteering /～行驶 cross-country run /～载重车 cross-country truck; cross-country cargo carrier
越野汽车 yuèyě qìchē cross-country vehicle
越野赛 yuèyěsài (of vehicles) cross-country race
越野赛跑 yuèyě sàipǎo cross-country race
越铀元素 yuèyóu yuánsù 〈化学〉 transuranic element
越狱 yuèyù escape from prison; break jail: 制止～行动 stop prison-breaking /追捕～逃犯 chase after a prison escapee
越狱犯 yuèyùfàn prison breaker; escaped convict
越障 yuèzhàng 〈军事〉 steeplechase; obstacle race
越俎代庖 yuèzǔ-dàipáo do things outside one's area of responsibility; exceed one's mandate and meddle in other people's affairs; take sb. else's job into one's own hands: 这事应由工会管, 行政部门不要～。This is the trade union's responsibility. The administrative department must not meddle in it.

樾 yuè 〈书面〉 shade of a tree

钺(戉) yuè ancient weapon made of bronze or iron and shaped like a broad axe; ancient battle-axe

黦 yuè 〈书面〉 yellowish-black

跃(躍) yuè jump; leap; spring: 飞～ leap /腾～ jump /欢呼雀～ leap to one's feet and cheer /～居先进行列 leap to the forefront; rise to become one of the best
跃动 yuèdòng jump; spring; leap: 夜幕下, 长长的火苗在噼噼啪啪声中～飞舞。The elongated flames leaped and crackled, dancing in the darkness of the night.
跃进 yuèjìn ❶ take or make a leap: 向右侧～ make a leap to your right ❷ leap forward; jump: 这个厂的产品质量～到全国同行业首位。The quality of this factory's products has jumped to first among their kind in the country. /今年的工农业生产呈现出～的局面。This year's industrial and agricultural production has made big strides (*or* has increased by leaps and bounds).
跃居 yuèjū leap or jump to: ～世界首位 leap to first in the world; leap to lead the world (in)
跃马 yuèmǎ spur the horse on
跃迁 yuèqiān 〈物理〉 transition: 自发～ spontaneous transition /俘获～ capture transition /～能 transition energy
跃迁概率 yuèqiān gàilǜ transition probability
跃然 yuèrán appear vividly: 忧愁之色～ sadness is clearly written on his face
跃然纸上 yuèrán-zhǐshàng show graphically in one's writing: 欣喜之情～。The great rejoicings of the writer are clearly reflected in his writing.
跃跃欲试 yuèyuè-yùshì be eager to have a go; be anxious to have

Y

a try; itch for action:看着大家翩翩起舞,我也有点~了。Seeing others all dancing trippingly, I was eager to have a try (*or* a go).

龠[1] yuè ancient unit of capacity that equals 0.05 litre

龠[2](**籥**) yuè ancient flute-shaped musical instrument

瀹 yuè 〈书面〉❶ boil; cook:~茗 boil (*or* make) tea ❷ dredge (a river)

爚 yuè 〈书面〉flame

篗 yuè *see* "籰" yuè

籰(**篗**) yuè 〈书面〉reel; spool

岳(❶**嶽**) yuè ❶ high mountain:五~ famous Five Mountains in China /东~泰山 Mount Tai in East China ❷ wife's parents and paternal uncles:叔~ wife's uncle; uncle-in-law ❸ (Yuè) a surname

岳飞 Yuè Fēi Yue Fei (formerly translated as Yueh Fei, 1103-1142), patriotic military commander of the Southern Song Dynasty

岳父 yuèfù *also* "岳丈" wife's father; father-in-law:~待他甚好。His father-in-law treats him quite well.

岳家 yuèjiā home of one's wife's parents:他目前正住在~。He is now staying at his wife's parents'.

岳家军 Yuèjiājūn General Yue's Army, troops led by General Yue Fei against Jin invaders in the early Southern Song Dynasty:撼山易,撼~难。It was easier to shake the mountain than General Yue's Army.

岳母 yuèmǔ wife's mother; mother-in-law:他一直在照顾卧病的~。He has been looking after his bedridden mother-in-law all the time.

岳丈 yuèzhàng *see* "岳父"

粤 Yuè ❶ Guangdong (广东) and Guangxi (广西):两~ Guangdong and Guangxi ❷ another name for Guangdong

粤菜 yuècài Guangdong dishes; Guangdong food; Cantonese cuisine

粤剧 yuèjù Guangdong opera:著名~演员红线女 Hongxiannü, a well-known actress of Guangdong opera

粤绣 yuèxiù *also* "广绣" guǎngxiù Guangdong embroidery

粤语 Yuèyǔ Chinese dialect, common to central and south-western Guangdong and south-eastern Guangxi

月 yuè ❶ moon:新~ crescent /~上柳梢头。The moon has climbed up over the tip of the willow. /~圆则亏,水满则盈。The full moon wanes; full water overflows. ❷ month:二~上旬 first ten days of February /八~十五日 15th of August; August 15 ❸ monthly:~刊 monthly (magazine) /~报表 monthly report ❹ full-moon shaped; round

月白 yuèbái bluish white; pale blue:~色的衬衫 bluish-white shirt

月白风清 yuèbái-fēngqīng bright moon and gentle breeze — a quiet and beautiful night

月半 yuèbàn 15th day of a month:七~ 15th of July; July 15

月报 yuèbào ❶ monthly (magazine):《新华~》*Xinhua Monthly* ❷ monthly report:~统计表 monthly statistical report

月表土 yuèbiǎotǔ lunar regolith

月饼 yuèbing moon cake:中秋~ moon cakes for the Mid-Autumn Festival

月长石 yuèchángshí 〈矿业〉moonstone

月尘 yuèchén moon dust

月城 yuèchéng 〈书面〉outer walled city

月池 yuèchí moon pool

月初 yuèchū beginning of a month; early in a month:三~ beginning of March; early in March; early days of March; early March

月底 yuèdǐ end of a month; late in a month:~盘点 take stock at the end of the month

月地 yuèdì surface of the moon; lunar surface

月洞门 yuèdòngmén 〈建筑〉moon gate; lunar gate

月度 yuèdù monthly:制定~计划 make a monthly plan /完成~生产指标 reach the monthly production target

月房 yuèfáng 〈方言〉lying-in woman's bedroom

月份 yuèfèn month:出生的~ month in which one is born /他五~要去上海出差。He is going to Shanghai on business in May.

月份牌 yuèfènpái 〈口语〉calendar:她仍保存着 1960 年的~。She still keeps the calendar of 1960.

月俸 yuèfèng monthly salary or pay

月工 yuègōng worker employed by the month; monthly worker:当~ be a monthly worker /雇用~ employ a monthly helper

月宫 yuègōng ❶ legendary palace on the moon ❷ moon

月光 yuèguāng ❶ moonlight; moonshine; moonbeam:暗淡的~ pale moonlight ❷〈方言〉moon

月光花 yuèguānghuā moonflower

月规钱 yuèguīqián 〈旧语〉monthly pocket money (for an apprentice)

月桂 yuèguì 〈植物〉laurel; bay tree (*Laurus nobilis*):~树〈植物〉laurel; bay tree /~醇〈化学〉lauryl alcohol /~醛 lauryl aldehyde /~酸 lauric acid

月海 yuèhǎi sea on the moon; mare

月核 yuèhé lunar core

月黑天 yuèhēitiān *also* "月黑夜" moonless night; first and last days of the lunar month:风高~ on a windy moonless night

月黑头 yuèhēitóu 〈方言〉moonless night; dark night

月黑夜 yuèhēiyè *see* "月黑天"

月华 yuèhuá ❶〈书面〉moonlight:~如水 watery moon; flood of translucent moonlight ❷〈气象〉lunar corona

月极 yuèjí lunar pole

月季 yuèjì *also* "月月红"〈植物〉Chinese rose:盆栽~ potted Chinese rose /盛开的~散发出阵阵清香。The Chinese rose in bloom sent forth a delicate fragrance.

月家疾 yuèjiājí 〈方言〉delivery-caused illness; puerperal fever

月建 yuèjiàn month

月经 yuèjīng menstruation; menses; menstrual flow; (monthly) period:~不调 menoxenia; irregular (*or* abnormal) menstruation /~停止 cessation of menstruation; menopause /~周期 menstrual cycle /~过多 menorrhagia; excessive menstruation (*or* menstrual flow) /~过少 hypomenorrhea

月经带 yuèjīngdài sanitary belt; sanitary napkin

月刊 yuèkān monthly (magazine):文学~ literary monthly

月窠 yuèkē *also* "月窝"〈方言〉(of a baby) month after birth:出~ one month old /~儿 one-month-old baby

月蓝 yuèlán light-blue:~的围巾 light-blue scarf

月老 yuèlǎo *also* "月下老人" god who unites man and woman in marriage; matchmaker; go-between

月历 yuèlì monthly calendar

月利 yuèlì monthly interest:~高达八厘。The monthly interest is as high as 0.8%.

月例 yuèlì ❶ monthly payment; monthly allowance ❷〈婉词〉menstruation

月亮 yuèliang moon:多圆的~啊! What a full moon!

月亮地儿 yuèliangdìr moonlit place

月亮门儿 yuèliangménr moon gate:穿过~,里边又是一番景象。Entering the moon gate, you will find a different world inside.

月令 yuèlìng weather and phenology in a certain lunar month

月轮 yuèlún full moon

月幔 yuèmàn lunar mantle

月门 yuèmén moon gate; lunar gate

月面测量学 yuèmiàn cèliángxué selenodesy

月面发射 yuèmiàn fāshè 〈航天〉lunar departure; lift-off from the moon

月面旅行车 yuèmiàn lǚxíngchē lunar rover; lunar roving vehicle

月面图 yuèmiàntú selenograph

月面行走 yuèmiàn xíngzǒu moonwalk

月面学 yuèmiànxué 〈天文〉selenography (the study of the physical features of the moon's surface)

月杪 yuèmiǎo 〈书面〉end of a month

月末 yuèmò end of a month:上~他住进医院。He was hospitalized at the end of last month.

月偏食 yuèpiānshí partial lunar eclipse

月票 yuèpiào monthly ticket:通用~ monthly ticket for all urban and suburban lines /市区~ monthly ticket for urban lines only /专线~ monthly ticket for all urban lines plus one chosen suburban line /

学生～ monthly ticket (at half price) for students
月婆子 yuèpózi 〈方言〉lying-in woman
月钱 yuèqian monthly pocket money (given to one's family members, apprentices, etc.):本月的～还没领到。I have not yet received this month's pocket money.
月琴 yuèqín four-stringed moon-shaped Chinese mandolin; *yueqin*:他弹得一手好～。He is an excellent *yueqin* player.
月球 yuèqiú 〈天文〉moon:～背面 far side of the moon /～内部 lunar interior /～土壤 lunar soil /～车 moonbuggy /～地球通信线路 lunar communication back line /～飞船 mooncraft; moonship; lunar spacecraft /～轨道宇宙飞行器 lunar orbit spacecraft /～火箭发射站 moonport /～考察船 lunar exploration module /～舱 lunar module
月球地理学 yuèqiú dìlǐxué *also* "月面学" selenography
月球探测 yuèqiú tàncè moon exploration:～器 lunar probe /～飞船 lunar excursion module
月球学 yuèqiúxué selenology
月球仪 yuèqiúyí lunar globe or sphere
月全食 yuèquánshí total lunar eclipse
月入 yuèrù monthly income:～甚丰 handsome monthly income
月色 yuèsè moonlight:～中的海面显得更美了。The moonlight on the sea added to the beauty of the scene.
月石 yuèshí 〈中药〉borax
月食 yuèshí *also* "月蚀"〈天文〉lunar eclipse:前年七月十五日发生过～。A lunar eclipse took place on 15 July two years ago.
月事 yuèshì 〈书面〉menstrual period; menstruation
月台 yuètái ❶〈旧语〉platform where people could stay and enjoy the moon ❷ platform built before the main hall of a palace, with a flight of steps on each of the other three sides ❸ *also* "站台" zhàntái railway platform
月台票 yuètáipiào *also* "站台票" zhàntáipiào platform ticket
月坛 Yuètán Altar of the Moon, Beijing
月头儿 yuètóur 〈口语〉❶ time for monthly payment:到～了,该付水电费了。It is time to pay this month's electricity and water bills. ❷ beginning of a month:上月的地铁月票还可以用到这～。Last month's underground (*or* subway) ticket is still valid for the beginning of this month.
月外 yuèwài 〈天文〉translunar; beyond the orbit of the moon:～空间 translunar space
月尾 yuèwěi (at the) end of the month; (at the) month's end
月窝 yuèwō *see* "月窠"
月夕 yuèxī 〈书面〉❶ moonlight night; moonlit night ❷ end of a month; month's end
月息 yuèxī monthly interest:～降到四厘。The monthly interest has dropped to 0.4%.
月下老人 yuèxià lǎorén *see* "月老"
月相 yuèxiàng 〈天文〉phases of the moon (the chief of which are 朔 new moon, 上弦 first quarter, 望 full moon and 下弦 last quarter)
月薪 yuèxīn monthly pay or salary:他终于找到了工作,～一百块大洋。He eventually found himself a job, with a monthly pay of 100 silver dollars.
月信 yuèxìn menstrual period
月行车 yuèxíngchē 〈航天〉lunokhod (an eight-wheeled Soviet unmanned lunar roving vehicle softlanded on the moon by Lunar 17 and 21)
月牙 yuèyá *also* "月芽" crescent (moon); new moon
月岩 yuèyán 〈天文〉lunabase; lunar rock; marebase:～球 lunar nodule
月夜 yuèyè moonlit night; moonlight night:这是一个多么美好的～啊! What a beautiful moonlight night!
月月红 yuèyuèhóng *see* "月季"
月晕 yuèyùn *also* "风圈" fēngquān lunar halo
月晕而风,础润而雨 yuè yùn ér fēng, chǔ rùn ér yǔ a halo round the moon means wind; a damp plinth means rain — coming events cast their shadows before them
月震 yuèzhèn moonquake
月氏 Yuèzhī name of a state in the Western Regions during the Han Dynasty
月中 yuèzhōng middle of a month
月终 yuèzhōng end of a month; month-end:～结算 settle accounts at the end of the month
月子 yuèzi ❶ month of confinement after childbirth:坐～ be in confinement /你～里要好好休息。You should take a good rest while in confinement. ❷ time of childbirth; confinement:她的～是五月中。She expects to be confined in the middle of May.
月子病 yuèzibìng puerperal fever

玥 yuè legendary magic pearl

抈 yuè 〈书面〉❶ shake ❷ break

刖(跀) yuè form of cruel punishment in ancient times by chopping a person's foot off

钥(鑰) yuè key:北门锁～ key town in the north; city of strategic importance in the north
see also yào

鸑(鸑) yuè
鸑鷟 yuèzhuó 〈古语〉aquatic or water bird

乐(樂) yuè ❶ music:声～ vocal music /器～ instrumental music /打击～ percussion music /吹奏～band music; wind music /管～ wind instrument music /管弦～ orchestral music /交响～ symphonic music; symphony /古典音～ classical music /民间音～ folk music /流行音～ pop music /～感 music aptitude; sense of music /奏～ play music /配～朗诵 poem recitation with musical accompaniment ❷ (Yuè) a surname
see also lè
乐池 yuèchí orchestra pit; orchestra
乐段 yuèduàn 〈音乐〉period
乐队 yuèduì band; orchestra:民～ ethnic instruments orchestra /铜管～ brass band /管弦～ orchestra /军～ military band /交响～ symphony orchestra
乐队指挥 yuèduì zhǐhuī conductor; bandmaster
乐府 yuèfǔ ❶ official conservatory set up in the Han Dynasty for the collection of folk songs and ballads:～官员 official collector of folk songs and ballads in the Han Dynasty ❷ folk songs or ballads in the Han style:～民歌 folk songs in the Han style; Han-styled folk songs
乐府诗集 Yuèfǔ Shījí *General Anthology of Yuefu Poems*, compiled by Guo Maoqian (郭茂倩) of the Song Dynasty
乐歌 yuègē ❶ music and songs ❷ song set for accompaniment (with musical instruments)
乐工 yuègōng *see* "乐师"
乐户 yuèhù 〈历史〉❶ woman criminal or suspect who was forced to serve as music player and prostitute; singsong girl ❷ brothel
乐籍 yuèjí 〈历史〉❶ list of government prostitutes, music players, etc. ❷ status as a prostitute or music player
乐句 yuèjù 〈音乐〉phrase
乐理 yuèlǐ 〈音乐〉music theory:～知识 knowledge of music theory
乐律 yuèlǜ 〈音乐〉temperament
乐迷 yuèmí music aficionado; music devotee
乐谱 yuèpǔ music score; sheet music; music:他不识～。He cannot read a music score.
乐谱架 yuèpǔjià music stand
乐器 yuèqì musical instrument; instrument:管弦～ wind and stringed instruments /打击～ percussion instrument /铜管～ brass instrument /弦～和铜管～ the strings and brass
乐曲 yuèqǔ (musical) composition; (a piece of) music:～作者 music composer /～的旋律 melody of the music /优美的～ melodious music /新创作的～ new composition /极为流行的～ very popular piece of music
乐师 yuèshī music player; musician
乐坛 yuètán musical circles:誉满～ enjoy high prestige in the musical world
乐团 yuètuán ❶ philharmonic society ❷ philharmonic orchestra:军～ brass band /北京交响～ Beijing Symphony Orchestra /中央～ Central Phiharmonic Orchestra
乐舞 yuèwǔ dance with music accompaniment
乐音 yuèyīn musical sound; tone
乐章 yuèzhāng 〈音乐〉movement

yūn

赟 yūn 〈书面〉fine; glorious

晕 yūn ❶ dizzy; giddy; faint: 她经常头～。She often feels faint (*or* dizzy, *or* giddy). /他忽然感到～得厉害。He was suddenly struck with a dizzy spell. *or* He suddenly felt his head spinning (*or* swimming). ❷ swoon; faint; lose consciousness; pass out: 他～过去了。He went off in a faint. *or* He lost consciousness.
see also yùn

晕倒 yūndǎo fall (down) in a faint; faint; pass out: 她气得一下就～了。She was in such a fit of anger that she fainted right away.

晕得忽儿的 yūndehūrde 〈方言〉dizzy; giddy: 我这几天高血压, 脑袋有点～。My high blood pressure has made me feel rather dizzy these days.

晕动 yūndòng motion sickness (e.g. sea sickness, car sickness, etc.)

晕糊 yūnhu *also* "晕乎" dizzy; giddy; reeling: 才喝了一杯酒就～了 feel dizzy after the first drink

晕厥 yūnjué 〈医学〉syncope; faint

晕头晕脑 yūntóu-yūnnǎo *also* "晕头打脑" dizzy; giddy; muddle-headed: 他把我气得～的。He made me angry that I couldn't think clearly. /我～地没听得太明白。I was in a daze and so did not quite catch the meaning.

晕头转向 yūntóu-zhuànxiàng muddled; confused and disorientated: 这几天忙得我～。I am so busy these days that I am just about to go crazy.

晕眩 yūnxuàn feel dizzy or giddy

晕晕忽忽 yūnyun-hūhū ❶ dizzy; giddy: 喝到第二杯时, 他已经有点～。He found his head swimming slightly after his second drink. ❷ muddle-headed; in a daze: 脑子～的, 不知该想啥。I was in a daze. *or* I was dazed.

煴 yūn 〈书面〉slow fire
see also yùn

氲 yūn *see* "氤氲" yīnyūn

缊 yūn *see* "细缊" yīnyūn
see also yùn

yún

云[1] yún ❶ say; utter: 古人～ as the ancients said /不知所～ not understand what sb. means (*or* says, *or* utters); find (sth.) unintelligible /人～亦～ repeat what others say; parrot ❷ *auxiliary word in classical Chinese*: ～谁之思? Whose idea is it? /岁～暮矣。It is late in the year.

云[2]**(雲)** yún cloud: 乌～滚滚 dark rolling clouds

云[3]**(雲)** Yún ❶ Yunnan (Province): ～烟 cigarettes made in Yunnan ❷ a surname

云霭 yún'ǎi thin, floating clouds: 远处的山峦蒙上一层薄薄的～。The hills in the distance appear behind a thin veil of floating clouds.

云板 yúnbǎn *also* "云版" a kind of percussion instrument, made of long strips of iron sheet and used in the old times to give the correct time or announce an event in government offices or influential families

云豹 yúnbào *also* "猫豹" māobào clouded leopard; clouded tiger

云表 yúnbiǎo 〈书面〉beyond the clouds: 山峰耸入～。The mountain peak towered into the clouds.

云鬓 yúnbìn 〈书面〉thick, beautiful hair (of women): 梳理～ comb her hair

云彩 yúncai cloud: 满天～ clouds all over the sky; cloudy sky

云层 yúncéng cloud layer: 飞机终于冲出～。The plane eventually broke through the clouds.

云催化剂 yúncuīhuàjì 〈气象〉cloud-seeding agent

云带 yúndài *also* "云条" 〈气象〉cloud bar

云滴 yúndī 〈气象〉cloud drop; droplet

云底 yúndǐ 〈气象〉cloud base

云顶 yúndǐng 〈气象〉cloud top

云豆 yúndòu *also* "芸豆" yúndòu kidney bean

云端 yúnduān high in the clouds: 高耸的山峰直插～。The peak of the mountain pierced through the clouds.

云朵 yúnduǒ mass of clouds; cloud

云缝 yúnfèng clearing (in the clouds); clearance

云冈石窟 Yúngāng Shíkū Yungang Grottoes, near Datong (大同), Shanxi Province

云贵 Yún-Guì Yunnan and Guizhou (provinces): ～两省的交界处 border (land) between Yunnan and Guizhou provinces

云贵高原 Yún-Guì Gāoyuán Yunnan-Guizhou Plateau

云海 yúnhǎi sea of clouds: ～茫茫 boundless sea of clouds

云汉 yúnhàn 〈书面〉❶ Milky Way ❷ high sky: 飞机直插～。The airplane soared into the sky.

云鬟 yúnhuán (of woman's hair) bun

云集 yúnjí come together from various places; gather; converge: 各地劳模～首都。Model workers of the entire country gathered in the capital city.

云际 yúnjì 〈书面〉high in the clouds: 天地～ high in the clouds over the horizon

云锦 yúnjǐn cloud-pattern brocade; silk Jacquard — de luxe silk with a long history in China: 斑斓绚丽的～ bright and colourful silk Jacquard

云谲波诡 yúnjué-bōguǐ *also* "波诡云谲" 〈比喻〉(of the development of events) volatile and unpredictable; bewilderingly changeable

云开见日 yúnkāi-jiànrì *also* "开云见日" the clouds disperse and the sun shines — darkness recedes and light dawns; all misunderstanding is dispelled: 我相信我们的误会定有～之时。I believe that the day will come when we shall be able to clear up all our misunderstandings.

云量 yúnliàng 〈气象〉cloud amount; cloudiness: 总～ total cloud cover /天空～增多。The clouds are gathering.

云林 yúnlín cloud forest; montane rain forest

云锣 yúnluó 〈乐器〉Chinese gong chimes

云幕 yúnmì 〈气象〉ceiling; height of cloud base

云幂灯 yúnmìdēng ceilometer

云幂高度 yúnmì gāodù ceiling height

云幂气球 yúnmì qìqiú ceiling balloon

云母 yúnmǔ 〈矿业〉mica: ～铁矿 micaceous iron-ore

云母板 yúnmǔbǎn micarex

云母板岩 yúnmǔ bǎnyán mica-slate

云母电容器 yúnmǔ diànróngqì mica condenser

云母片 yúnmǔpiàn mica sheet; sheet mica: ～岩 〈地质〉mica schist; micacite

云南 Yúnnán Yunnan (Province)

云泥之别 yúnnízhībié 〈比喻〉(of social status) as far apart as cloud and mud; worlds or poles apart: 这两兄弟如今的境况已然是～。There is now a world of difference between the lives of the two brothers.

云霓 yúnní cloud and secondary rainbow

云片 yúnpiàn 〈气象〉cloud-sheet

云片糕 yúnpiàngāo a kind of rice wafers mixed with walnut

云起龙骧 yúnqǐ-lóngxiāng *also* "云起龙襄" heroes come forth along with the times; the times produce their heroes

云气 yúnqì thin, floating clouds

云区 yúnqū 〈气象〉cloud-land

云雀 yúnquè 〈动物〉skylark

云扰 yúnrǎo 〈书面〉confusion; turmoil: 四方～。There is turmoil all over the country.

云散 yúnsàn ❶ disperse; scatter: 旧友～。Old friends were dispersed. *or* Old friends all went away to different places. ❷ die away; disappear; vanish: 烟消～ disappear like smoke and cloud; vanish

云山雾罩 yúnshān-wùzhào ❶ enveloped in (cloud and) mist; heavy with mist ❷ discursive; rambling; confusing: 他们～地闲聊了整整一上午。They were shooting the bull (*or* breeze) the whole

morning. *or* They were chatting all morning of this and that. /这人说话~的,难捉摸。The man speaks evasively and it's very hard to get at what he means.
云杉 yúnshān 〈植物〉dragon spruce (*Picea asperata*)
云上轰炸 yúnshàng hōngzhà 〈军事〉overcast bombing
云室 yúnshì 〈物理〉cloud chamber:威尔逊~ Wilson (cloud) chamber
云涛 yúntāo billowing or rolling clouds:滚滚的~ rolling clouds; billowing clouds
云梯 yúntī scaling ladder:架设~ erect (*or* fix, *or* set up) a scaling ladder
云天 yúntiān sky:高耸~ tower into the sky; reach towards the sky
云头 yúntóu cluster of clouds:看这~的样子,天很快就要下雨了。The heavy clouds show that it is going to rain soon.
云头儿 yúntóur design or pattern based on cloudscape
云图 yúntú 〈气象〉cloud atlas; cloud chart:~分析 nephanalysis (study of the form and structure of clouds, particularly on meteorological satellite imagery)
云土 yúntǔ 〈旧语〉opium produced in Yunnan
云团 yúntuán cloud cluster
云腿 yúntuǐ ham produced in Yunnan
云屯 yúntún 〈书面〉gather together; assemble:万骑~。Thousands upon thousands of cavalrymen were assembled.
云雾 yúnwù cloud and mist; mist:浓浓的~ heavy mist /~笼罩着山头 mountain top enveloped in mist and clouds /拨开~见青天 see the sky again after the clouds are dispelled — restore justice /他俩昨儿还在吵,今儿满天~全散了。They were quarrelling only yesterday and today the clouds are all dispelled.
云雾天 yúnwùtiān soupy weather
云系 yúnxì 〈气象〉cloud system
云霞 yúnxiá rosy or pink clouds; rose-tinted clouds:~似锦 pink clouds as beautiful as brocade /~满天 rose-tinted clouds covering the sky
云消雾散 yúnxiāo-wùsàn *also* "烟消云散" yānxiāo-yúnsàn the clouds melt and the mists disperse — cease to exist; vanish into thin air; pass off:别看他俩现在闹得这么厉害,待到~,又不知好得什么样子哩! They are kicking up a terrible row now, but when the storm is over, they will be pally with each other as ever.
云霄 yúnxiāo sky:直上~ rise (*or* fly) right towards the sky /口号声响彻~。The shouting of slogans resounded to the skies.
云崖 yúnyá cliff towering into the clouds
云烟 yúnyān cloud and smoke; mist and smoke:犹如过眼~ like a fleeting cloud; passing quickly; transient
云阳 Yúnyáng name of a county in the Qin Dynasty, where criminals were imprisoned and executed; (in traditional operas) execution ground
云翳 yúnyì ❶ grey clouds:清澄的蓝天上没有一点~。The sky was azure (*or* blue) without a speck of cloud. /他脸上总罩着一层忧郁的~。He always looks gloomy. ❷〈医学〉nebula
云涌 yúnyǒng ❶ clouds scud:风起~。The wind rises and clouds scud. ❷ emerge in large numbers; spring up; come to the fore:才思~ be bursting with creative ideas
云游 yúnyóu (of a Buddhist monk or Taoist priest) roam; wander:~四方 roam from place to place /~天下 wander about the world over /有一高僧~到此。An eminent monk once visited here.
云雨 yúnyǔ (usu. used in traditional fiction) sexual intercourse; love-making
云云 yúnyún 〈书面〉and so on; and so on and so forth; etc.:他们所谓"和平"、"友谊"~,纯粹是空谈。What they call "peace", "friendship" and so on is just so much empty talk.
云遮雾障 yúnzhē-wùzhàng heavy with cloud and mist; mist-laden; be enveloped in mist
云蒸霞蔚 yúnzhēng-xiáwèi *also* "云兴霞蔚" (of scenery) splendid; gorgeous; magnificent:远山在阳光下~,颇为壮观。The mountains bathed in the sun look magnificent.
云中白鹤 yúnzhōng-báihè white crane amid the clouds — person of refined taste and moral integrity, aloof from the vulgar
云子 yúnzi 〈方言〉designs based on patterns of clouds:描花绣~ trace (*or* copy) designs of flowers and embroider patterns of clouds /她脚上穿着双鞋帮上纳~的黑布鞋。She wore a pair of black cloth shoes with cloud designs on the uppers.

沄[1]
yún *see* "沄沄"

沄[2](澐)
yún 〈书面〉great waves
沄沄 yúnyún 〈书面〉(of water) flowing:流水兮~。The river is flowing (on).

耘
yún weed:春耕夏~,秋收冬藏。Plough in spring, weed in summer, harvest in autumn and store in winter.
耘锄 yúnchú 〈农业〉hoe
耘稻 yúndào loosen the soil and weed in paddy fields
耘耥 yúntāng weed and loosen the soil in paddy fields
耘田 yúntián weed the fields

芸[1]
yún *also* "芸香"〈植物〉rue

芸[2](蕓)
yún *see* "芸薹"
芸豆 yúndòu *also* "云豆" yúndòu kidney bean
芸薹 yúntái 〈植物〉rape
芸香 yúnxiāng 〈植物〉rue
芸芸 yúnyún 〈书面〉many; large amounts of; numerous:万物~ myriads of things
芸芸众生 yúnyún-zhòngshēng 〈佛教〉all living things; all mortal beings:我等~,管不了这些事。These things are beyond us mortal beings.

纭
yún
纭纭 yúnyún numerous and disorderly; myriad and confused

员
yún personal name:伍~ Wu Yun (who lived during the Spring and Autumn Period)
see also yuán; Yùn

筼
yún
筼筜 yúndāng 〈书面〉big bamboo that grows by the waterside

匀
yún ❶ even; equitable:食品分配不~,他们有意见。They resented the uneven distribution of food. ❷ even up; divide evenly:这两份苹果多少不等,应该再~一~。The two portions of apples are not equal and need evening up. ❸ take from sth. and give to sb.; take from sth. for some other purpose; spare:工作太忙,~不出时间来读小说 be too busy with one's work to spare any time for reading fiction /把药品~一点给他们吧。Let's give them some of our medicine.
匀称 yúnchen well-proportioned; well-balanced; even:~的体形 well-proportioned figure /五官~ regular features /排列得十分~ in even arrangement; well-balanced in arrangement /粗细~ of uniform thickness /他身材长得很~。He is of proportional build.
匀度 yúndù evenness
匀兑 yúndui take from sth. and give to sb.; take from sth. for some other purpose; spare:最终他们设法给马戏团~了两间大屋子。Finally they managed to give two big rooms for the circus troupe.
匀和 yúnhuo *also* "匀乎" ❶ even; steady:呼吸~ steady breathing /针脚~。The stitches are even (*or* neat). ❷ even up; equalize:这桃儿的大小不一,先~~再分。There are big and small peaches. Mix them first and then divide them evenly.
匀加速度 yúnjiāsùdù 〈物理〉uniform acceleration
匀加速运动 yúnjiāsù yùndòng uniformly accelerated motion
匀减速运动 yúnjiǎnsù yùndòng uniformly retarded motion
匀净 yúnjing even; in proportion; uniform:颜色涂得十分~。The colour is evenly spread.
匀脸 yúnliǎn rub powder and paint evenly on one's face; paint rouge and powder evenly on one's face
匀溜 yúnliu of uniform size, thickness, or density:面条切得真~。The noodles were cut so neatly, all of the same thickness!
匀染 yúnrǎn 〈纺织〉level dyeing
匀染剂 yúnrǎnjì levelling agent
匀实 yúnshi 〈口语〉even; uniform; neat:这布又细密又~。The cloth is of close and even texture. /棉苗出得很~。The cotton seedlings come out in uniform density.

匀速运动 yúnsù yùndòng 〈物理〉 uniform motion
匀调 yúntiɑo even; regular; in proportion: 气息～ breathe evenly / 她眉眼长得很～。She has very regular features.
匀停 yúnting 〈方言〉 be moderate: 吃东西要～。One should be moderate in eating.
匀妥 yúntuǒ even and proper; equitable; fair: 分配应当～。Everyone must have a fair share.
匀细 yúnxì neat; even: ～洁白的牙齿 neat white teeth / ～的鼾声 snoring evenly; stertorous breathing at an even pace
匀圆 yúnyuán smooth and round: 颗颗樱桃～饱满。Smooth and round, every one of the cherries appears so plump.
匀整 yúnzheng neat and well spaced; tidy, even and orderly: 他的作业写得十分～。His papers are so neat and tidy.

昀 yún 〈书面〉 sunlight; sunshine

畇 yún

畇畇 yúnyún 〈书面〉 (of fields) well-arranged; neat; tidy

鋆 yún (also pronounced jūn when used in personal names) 〈书面〉 gold

筠 yún 〈书面〉 ❶ green bamboo skin ❷ bamboo

yǔn

殒 yǔn perish; die; pass away

殒灭 yǔnmiè 〈书面〉 die; perish; be killed; meet one's death
殒命 yǔnmìng 〈书面〉 die; expire; meet one's death
殒殁 yǔnmò 〈书面〉 (of human beings) die; pass away
殒身 yǔnshēn 〈书面〉 die; perish; be killed; meet one's death: ～亡国 die and lose one's country
殒阵 yǔnzhèn 〈书面〉 be killed in action; fall in battle

陨 yǔn fall from the sky or outer space

陨落 yǔnluò (of a heavenly body, meteorite, etc.) fall from the sky or outer space: 巨星～。A giant star fell from the sky. *or* A great man passed away.
陨灭 yǔnmiè ❶ fall from the sky or outer space and burn up ❷ *also* "殒灭" yǔnmiè die; be killed; perish
陨石 yǔnshí 〈天文〉 aerolite; stony meteorite
陨石雨 yǔnshíyǔ 〈天文〉 meteorite shower
陨铁 yǔntiě 〈天文〉 siderite; meteorite iron; iron meteorite
陨星 yǔnxīng 〈天文〉 meteorite: 石～ aerolite; stony meteorite / 铁～ siderite; iron meteorite / 石铁～ siderolite; stony iron meteorite / ～坑 metorite orater
陨星学 yǔnxīngxué meteoritics
陨越 yǔnyuè 〈书面〉 fail; neglect one's duty: 幸免～ barely avoid the neglect of duty

允[1] yǔn consent; grant; allow; permit: 满口应～ consent readily; readily promise / 坚决不～ flatly refuse to give consent (*or* permission) / 不～其请 not grant his request

允[2] yǔn just; fair; impartial: 貌似公～ seem to be fair; be fair in appearance

允承 yǔnchéng consent (to); undertake; promise; commit oneself to: 他～了这个任务。He has promised to do the job.
允从 yǔncóng consent to; agree to: 他的要求我已～。I have already given my consent to his request.
允当 yǔndàng proper; suitable; appropriate: 难易～ just the right degree of difficulty
允诺 yǔnnuò commit oneself (to); promise; consent; undertake: 勉强～ reluctantly (*or* unwillingly) promise / 被迫～ be compelled (*or* forced) to commit oneself / 欣然～ readily consent / 如蒙～，请即赐复为盼。Your early consent in writing will be highly appreciated.
允许 yǔnxǔ allow; permit; agree to: 情况～的话 when circumstances permit; circumstances permitting / 你应事先得到家长的～。You ought to have gained permission from your parents beforehand. / 学术上的不同意见，应该～存在。All opinions should be allowed to exist in academic studies.
允许误差 yǔnxǔ wùchā 〈机械〉 allowable error; permissible error
允许载荷 yǔnxǔ zàihè allowable load
允准 yǔnzhǔn permit; give permission: 商店被～十月一日开业。The shop has received permission to open business on October the first.

狁 yǔn *see* "猃狁" Xiǎnyǔn

yùn

恽 Yùn a surname

晕 yùn ❶ dizzy; giddy; faint; sick: 发～ feel dizzy / 头～目眩 have a giddy spell; be afflicted with vertigo / 他刚上船就觉得～。No sooner had he embarked on the ship than he felt faint. ❷ halo: 日～ solar halo / 月～ lunar halo ❸ haze or halo round some colour or light: 墨～ running ink / 脸上的红～ blush on one's face / 彩虹的光～笼罩着瀑布。Rainbows haloed the waterfalls.
see also yūn

晕舱 yùncāng 〈航天〉 space sickness; motion sickness
晕场 yùnchǎng (of students taking an exam or an actor giving a performance) be so nervous as to faint; have stage fright
晕车 yùnchē be carsick: 我女儿好～。My daughter is susceptible (*or* liable) to carsickness.
晕池 yùnchí *also* "晕堂" faint in a bathhouse; be bathsick
晕船 yùnchuán be seasick: 海上风浪大，～的人很多。High winds and waves at sea made many people seasick.
晕房 yùnfáng feel dizzy or giddy high up in a skyscraper; be seized with vertigo
晕高儿 yùngāor 〈方言〉 feel dizzy when climbing high
晕机 yùnjī be airsick
晕机袋 yùnjīdài airsickness bag
晕针 yùnzhēn be afflicted with vertigo when being given an injection or under acupuncture

运[1]**（運）** yùn ❶ motion; movement: *see* "～行" ❷ transport; haul; carry: 客～ passenger transport / 货～ freight transport / 水～ water transport / 空～ air transport; airlift / 往山区～煤 haul (*or* carry) coal to the mountain area ❸ use; wield; utilize: ～笔如神 wield a pen with miraculous skill ❹ (Yùn) a surname

运[2]**（運）** yùn luck; fortune; destiny; fate: 幸～ be lucky; be fortunate / 交好～ have a stroke of luck; be in luck (*or* lucky) / 这一周来他都不走～。He has had bad luck all week. *or* He has been out of luck (*or* unlucky) all week.

运笔 yùnbǐ wield a pen; write or paint with a brush: 他时而搁笔沉思，时而～如飞。Sometimes he stopped writing, lost in thought, sometimes he wrote furiously fast.
运程 yùnchéng 〈交通〉 haul: ～达两千余里。It was a haul of over 2,000 *li*.
运筹 yùnchóu devise strategies; plan: 这个会议开得成功，全亏他～。The meeting would not have been a success without his careful planning.
运筹管理 yùnchóu guǎnlǐ operations management
运筹帷幄 yùnchóu-wéiwò devise strategies in a tent: ～之中，决胜千里之外 plan strategies within a command tent and ensure victory on the battle front a thousand *li* away
运筹学 yùnchóuxué operational research; operations research: 他专攻～。He majors in operational research.
运单 yùndān booking note or list
运道 yùndao 〈方言〉 luck; fortune: 她虽努力，但～坏极了。She has done her bit, but she has just been unlucky.
运动 yùndòng ❶ motion; movement: 物质～ motion of matter / 思维～ motion of thought / ～的方式 mode of motion / 正常～ regular movement / 波浪形～ undulating movement / 曲线～ curvilinear motion / 机械～ mechanical movement / ～群众 (often used in the Cultural Revolution) manipulate the masses / 宇宙无时无刻不在～。The universe is in constant motion. / 部队隐蔽地向前～。The troops were moving forward secretly. ❷ sports; exercise; athletics: ～项目

Y

(sports) events and games /田径～ track and field sports; athletics /室内～ indoor sports /户外～ outdoor sports /登山是一种很好的～。Mountain-climbing (*or* Mountaineering) is a very good sport. ❸ (political) movement; campaign; drive: ～的声势 momentum of a campaign /现代化～ drive for modernization /开展扫盲～ launch an anti-illiteracy campaign /声援学生的爱国～ support the students' patriotic movement

运动 yùndong arrange things through pull; canvas: ～官府 canvas (*or* drum up) support from the authorities /暗中～ make secret arrangements

运动场 yùndòngchǎng sports ground; playground; stadium: 校内建有一个很大的～。There is a very big playground on the campus.

运动服装 yùndòng fúzhuāng sportswear

运动负荷 yùndòng fùhè *see* "运动量"

运动会 yùndònghuì sports meet; games; athletic meet: 全国大学生～ National University Games /他是这次～的组织者之一。He is one of the organizers of the sports meet.

运动健将 yùndòng jiànjiàng 〈体育〉 master of sports; sportsmaster

运动量 yùndòngliàng amount of (physical) exercises

运动疗法 yùndòng liáofǎ 〈医学〉 kinesitherapy; kinesiotherapy; kinesiatrics

运动衫 yùndòngshān sports shirt

运动神经 yùndòng shénjīng *also* "传出神经" chuánchū shénjīng motor nerve: ～束 motor tract /～元 motor neuron /～末梢 motor nerve ending /～纤维 motor fibre

运动学 yùndòngxué 〈物理〉 kinematics

运动医学 yùndòng yīxué sports medicine

运动员 yùndòngyuán sportsman; sportswoman; athlete; player: 一级～ class one sportsman /游泳～ swimmer /体操～ gymnast /优秀少年～ excellent juvenile athlete /职业～ professional player (*or* sportsman)

运动战 yùndòngzhàn mobile war or warfare

运动知觉 yùndòng zhījué 〈心理〉 consciousness of motion

运费 yùnfèi transport expenses; freight; carriage; freightage: ～待收 freight to be collected /～免付 carriage free /～已付 freight paid /～预付 freight prepaid; advanced freight /～到付 freight forward

运费表 yùnfèibiǎo freight list

运费单 yùnfèidān freight note

运费吨 yùnfèidūn freight ton

运费率 yùnfèilǜ freight rate

运费条款 yùnfèi tiáokuǎn freight clause

运河 yùnhé canal: 大～ Grand Canal /巴拿马～ Panama Canal /苏伊士～ Suez Canal /疏通～ dredge a canal

运河税 yùnhéshuì canal fees or tolls

运货车 yùnhuòchē wagon; wagonage: 有篷～ wagon truck

运货列车 yùnhuò lièchē wagon train

运价 yùnjià *see* "运费"

运脚 yùnjiǎo 〈方言〉 transport charge or fee; traffic expense; freight; carriage: 用船运货～比较便宜。Transport by boat is much cheaper.

运斤成风 yùnjīn-chéngfēng 〈比喻〉 wield one's hatchet like magic; have superb skill; be extremely skilful: 只见他～, 雕刻的人物个个栩栩如生。He wielded his chisel like magic, and all the carved figures were vivid and true to life.

运力 yùnlì means of transport: 优先安排～, 运送外调物资。Priority must be given to the arrangement of means of transporting materials allocated for transfer to other places.

运量 yùnliàng *see* "运输量"

运煤船 yùnméichuán coal carrier; collier

运命 yùnmìng *also* "命运" fate; luck; fortune

运能 yùnnéng transport capacity: 解决～与运量的矛盾 resolve the contradiction between transport capacity and freight volume

运气 yùnqì (the art of) directing one's strength, through concentration, to a part of the body: 他运了运气, 然后猛地抓起杠铃。He took a deep breath and, through an exertion of strength, grasped the weight and lifted it high above his head.

运气 yùnqi ❶ fate; lot: 他～不好, 好事总与他没缘。His lot has been a hard one, and no good fortune has ever come his way. ❷ luck; fortune: 他今天真～, 买奖券中了奖。He is lucky today, drawing a prizewinning ticket in the lottery.

运球 yùnqiú dribble (in basketball or field hockey)

运神 yùnshén 〈方言〉 mull over; ponder; contemplate

运输 yùnshū transport; carriage; conveyance: ～队 transport team /～方式 mode of transport /～工具 means of transport; conveyance /～公司 transport company /～网 transport network /水果的冷藏～ refrigerated carriage of fruit /～旅客到各地 transport passengers to all parts of the country/水路～受阻就改从陆上～。We shall resort to land transport if water transport becomes impossible.

运输部队 yùnshū bùduì 〈军事〉 transport troops

运输船 yùnshūchuán cargo ship; transport ship

运输机 yùnshūjī ❶〈航空〉 transport plane; airfreighter ❷〈矿业〉 conveyor

运输舰 yùnshūjiàn naval or military cargo ship; naval transport

运输里程 yùnshū lǐchéng transport mileage

运输量 yùnshūliàng freight volume

运输能力 yùnshū nénglì transport capacity

运输司 Yùnshūsī (HK before 1 July 1997) Secretary for Transport

运输业 yùnshūyè transport service; carrying trade; transportation

运数 yùnshù 〈书面〉 fortune; destiny; lot: 他～已尽。His days are numbered.

运思 yùnsī put one's thoughts into words (esp. in poetry): ～敏捷 quick at writing /～精细 meticulous writing /～灵巧 ingenious wording

运送 yùnsòng transport; carry; ship; convey: ～的地点 shipping destination /把救济品～到灾区 transport (*or* carry) relief to the disaster area

运算 yùnsuàn 〈数学〉 operation; calculation: ～能力 operation capacity; calculating ability /每秒钟～次数 calculations per second /四则～ four fundamental operations of arithmetic /快速～ fast calculating

运算分析 yùnsuàn fēnxi operational analysis

运算器 yùnsuànqì arithmetic unit

运算微积分 yùnsuàn wēijīfēn operational calculus

运算误差 yùnsuàn wùchā arithmetic error

运土 yùntǔ earthmoving: ～刮土机 earthmoving scraper /～机械 earthmoving machinery

运腕 yùnwàn use one's wrist (so as to control the tip of a writing brush)

运销 yùnxiāo transport and sale (of commodities): 公司还开展了～业务。The company is now also engaged in the transport and sale of commodities.

运行 yùnxíng move; be in motion; be in action; be in operation: 列车～表 train schedule /人造卫星的～轨道 orbit of a man-made satellite /火车现在正在～。The train is in motion right now. /这辆机车已～了三天三夜。The engine has been in operation for three days and nights.

运移 yùnyí (of fluids such as water, magma, petroleum, natural gas, etc.) move; shift; flow

运营 yùnyíng ❶ (of vehicles or ships) open to service; put into operation: 投入～ put into commission (*or* operation) /～范围 range of service /～期限 service time /增加山货的～ extend service regarding mountain products ❷ operate; run; be in operation: 有些矿井没能正常～。Some mining pits are not yet in normal operation.

运用 yùnyòng utilize; apply; use; put into practice; wield: 灵活～新技术 flexible utilization of new technologies /普遍～科研成果 widespread application of scientific achievements /巧妙～手中的权力 cleverly wield (*or* exercise) one's power /把这一理论～于实践中 put this theory into practice

运用之妙, 存乎一心 yùnyòng zhī miào, cún hū yī xīn ingenuity in varying tactics depends on mother wit; tactics depend on how they are used

运用自如 yùnyòng-zìrú use or handle with skill; have a perfect command: 成语典故, 在他笔下～。He is expert at putting proverbs and allusions to good use.

运载 yùnzài conveyance; shipment; loading and delivery

运载工具 yùnzài gōngjù means of delivery; carrier: 增加～ increase means of delivery /战略～ strategic vehicles

运载火箭 yùnzài huǒjiàn carrier rocket: 发射～ launch a carrier rocket

运载技术 yùnzài jìshù delivery technology

运针 yùnzhēn 〈中医〉 apply or handle the needle

运转 yùnzhuǎn ❶ move in a circular orbit; revolve; turn round: 人造卫星正沿着轨道正常～。The man-made satellite is revolving regu-

larly in its orbit. /日月～,桑田变迁。The world is always in a flux. ❷ operate; run; work:车轮～轻快。The wheels run light. /发动机～正常。The motor is operating regularly. /新成立的公司开始～。The new company has started its operation.
运转阻力 yùnzhuǎn zǔlì 〈物理〉running resistance
运作 yùnzuò implement; operate; carry through: ～方式 way to implement (*or* operate); mode of implementation (*or* operation) / 具体如何～还要仔细商量。Detailed discussions will be held on how to carry the plan through.
运祚 yùnzuò (usu. of a dynasty) fate; destiny; fortunes

酝(醖) yùn 〈书面〉❶ make wine; brew beer ❷ wine: 佳～ good wine
酝酿 yùnniàng brew; ferment; deliberate (upon): ～小组长人选 consider and discuss the candidate(s) for group leadership /经过多次～,终于统一了看法。They reached consensus after repeated deliberations. /一场暴风雨正在～着。A storm is brewing.

愠 yùn 〈书面〉angry; annoyed; irritated:微～ look a little irritated
愠恼 yùnnǎo angry; irritated; annoyed
愠怒 yùnnù angry; indignant; furious: ～的神气 angry look /他～地瞪了她一眼。He gave her a furious stare.
愠容 yùnróng 〈书面〉angry look; irritated countenance
愠色 yùnsè 〈书面〉angry look:面带～ appear angry; look irritated

煴 yùn *see* "熨" yùn
see also yūn

韫(韞) yùn 〈书面〉include; contain: ～椟 hidden in a box — unrecognized talents

缊 yùn 〈书面〉❶ bits of hemp, flax, jute, etc. ❷ silk wadding: ～袍 silk-padded robe
see also yūn

蕴 yùn 〈书面〉❶ contain; hold in store ❷ profoundness: 底～ depth (of sth.); profundity; hidden strength
蕴藏 yùncáng contain; store; hold in store:我国～的煤矿很丰富。Our country is rich in coal resources. /青年一代中～了极大的聪明才智。There is a galaxy of talents among the young people. /书里～着丰富的知识。Books are a vast reservoir of knowledge.
蕴含 yùnhán contain; embrace; hold in store
蕴涵 yùnhán ❶〈书面〉contain; entail: 这篇文章～极深。The article has a profound message. ❷〈逻辑〉implication
蕴结 yùnjié pent-up; smouldering: ～心头的愤懑 pent-up indignation
蕴藉 yùnjiè 〈书面〉(of people, their words, etc.) restrained; well-controlled; temperate; refined: ～的笑容 modest smile /～的语言 polite words; refined language /风流～ urbanely charming
蕴聚 yùnjù gather; accumulate:他身上～着极大的创造力。He is remarkably creative (*or* ingenious).
蕴蓄 yùnxù latent; implicit; hidden and undeveloped:新事物～着强大的生命力。New things have great inborn vitality.

员 Yùn a surname
see also yuán; yún

韵(韻) yùn ❶ beautiful or sweet sound; sound pleasant to the ear: 松声竹～ melodious sound of the wind blowing through the pines and bamboos ❷ simple or compound vowel (of a Chinese syllable): 押～ rhyme (with); be in rhyme /叠～ rhyming couplet ❸ appeal; charm: 她风～犹存。She is still as charming (*or* graceful) as ever. ❹ (Yùn) a surname
韵白 yùnbái ❶ spoken parts in Beijing opera to be pronounced according to the opera's tradition rather than Beijing dialect ❷ rhyming spoken parts in traditional opera
韵调 yùndiào tone; tune: ～优美 lovely tone /～悠扬 sweet tune
韵腹 yùnfù 〈语言〉essential vowel in a compound vowel in Chinese (e.g. a in ua, ao, or iang), or simple vowel (e.g. a, e, i, o, u, or ü) by itself
韵脚 yùnjiǎo rhyming word that ends a line of verse; rhyme
韵律 yùnlǜ metre and rhyme scheme in verse; prosody:古诗很讲究～。Ancient poetry is quite particular about metre and rhyme scheme.
韵律体操 yùnlǜ tǐcāo *also* "韵律操" rhythmic gymnastics
韵律学 yùnlǜxué prosody
韵母 yùnmǔ 〈语言〉simple or compound vowel (of a Chinese syllable), consisting of a *yunfu*(韵腹) with or without a *yuntou*(韵头) or a *yunwei*(韵尾):～相同的字 rhyming words
韵目 yùnmù catalogue in a dictionary of rhyming words
韵事 yùnshì romantic or anecdotic event; love affair:文坛～ romantic literary or artistic pursuits /风流～ love affairs
韵书 yùnshū dictionary of rhyming words
韵头 yùntóu head vowel (usu. i, u, or ü) in a compound vowel (e.g. i in iang)
韵尾 yùnwěi tail vowel or a terminal nasal consonant in a compound vowel or syllable (e.g. i in ei; ng in ang)
韵味 yùnwèi ❶ meaning implied by sound and rhythm; implicit richness:颇有～的唱腔 tune impregnated with meaning /她唱得～十足。She sang in a voice of enormous implicit richness. ❷ charm; interest; appeal:古塔古树相互映衬,为山村增添了无穷的～。The ancient pagoda and old trees, which set off each other so harmoniously, lent an implicit charm to the mountainous village. /他的散文有一种质朴的～。His prose has a kind of simple, natural appeal.
韵文 yùnwén verse
韵语 yùnyǔ rhyme (such as poetry, *ci* poetry, song, etc.)
韵致 yùnzhì graceful bearing; charm; taste: ～淡雅 natural and graceful bearing /别有一番～ unique poise and charm

孕 yùn pregnant:怀～ be pregnant; be in the family way; be conceived /避～ contraception /她有身～。She is pregnant. *or* She is big with child. /她多年不～。She has not conceived for years.
孕产妇死亡率 yùnchǎnfù sǐwánglǜ maternal mortality rate
孕畜 yùnchù pregnant domestic animal;精心饲养～ feed the pregnant animal with particular care
孕妇 yùnfù pregnant woman:汽车上设有～专座。On buses there are seats reserved for the pregnant.
孕激素 yùnjīsù 〈生化〉progestational hormone; progestin
孕期 yùnqī 〈医学〉pregnancy; gestation
孕穗 yùnsuì 〈农业〉booting:～期 boot stage
孕酮 yùntóng 〈生化〉luteal hormone; progesterone; corporin:类～ progesteroid
孕吐 yùntù 〈医学〉vomiting during pregnancy; morning sickness
孕育 yùnyù be pregnant with; breed:～着危机 be fraught with crises /我们的祖国～着无限生机。Our motherland is full of vigour. /新时代～着新作家。A new age gives birth to a new generation of writers. /黄河～了中国的文化。The Yellow River has bred the Chinese culture. /在封建社会内部,～着资本主义生产关系的萌芽。The feudal society carried within itself the seeds of capitalist relations of production.
孕震构造 yùnzhèn gòuzào seismic structure; earthquake-prone structure

熨 yùn iron; press:请把这条裤子给～一下。Please iron this pair of trousers. /这衬衣～得真平。The shirt has been pressed so well.
see also yù
熨斗 yùndǒu flatiron; iron:电～ electric iron /蒸汽～ steam iron
熨衣板 yùnyībǎn ironing board

Z

zā

扎(紮、紥) zā ❶ tie; bind; fasten:用缎带～一个蝴蝶结 tie the ribbon in a bow /皮带～得很紧。The leather belt is fastened tight. /那女孩子～小辫儿。The little girl wore plaits. ❷〈方言〉〈量词〉bundle:一～钞票 a bundle of banknotes
see also zhā; zhá

扎把子 zābǎzi 〈方言〉❶ tie in a bundle ❷ unite as one:大家～跟自然灾害作斗争。Let's unite to fight natural calamity. *or* We made a united effort to combat natural disaster.

扎彩 zācǎi hang up festoons or streamers

扎筏子 zāfázi 〈方言〉vent one's spleen or spite on; give vent to one's anger:你哪来的气，拿我～呀! What on earth made you vent your anger on me? *or* Why pick on me? What the hell irritated you?

扎染 zārǎn 〈纺织〉tie-dye:～上衣 tie-dyed jacket

拶 zā 〈书面〉force; coerce:逼～ force; compel
see also zǎn

匝(帀) zā ❶〈书面〉circle; circumference:绕树两～ circle a tree twice ❷ surround; encircle:杂树～清池。A limpid pond is surrounded by sundry trees. ❸ whole; full

匝道 zādào 〈书面〉ring road

匝地 zādì 〈书面〉all around; everywhere

匝月 zāyuè 〈书面〉full month:瞬已～。In the tinkling of an eye, a full month has elapsed.

咂 zā ❶ sip; suck:～一口茶 take a sip of tea /～手指头 suck one's thumb (*or* finger) ❷ smack one's lips (in admiration, praise, etc.) ❸ taste or savour carefully:我一直在细～你这话的滋味儿。I have been turning your words over in my mind and trying to figure out what they mean.

咂摸 zāmo 〈方言〉savour; taste:～不透 beyond one's comprehension (*or* understanding); fail to grasp the meaning of sth. /他站在窗边，细细～她临别时的话。He stood by the window, savouring the words she said at parting.

咂嘴 zāzuǐ smack one's lips (in admiration, praise, agreement, etc.):大家聚精会神地听着酋长的话，不时地点头～，表示赞许。Everyone listened intently to the chieftain, nodding and clicking their tongues in agreement now and then.

咂嘴弄舌 zāzuǐ-nòngshé ❶ greedy; envious ❷ self-satisfied

臜 zā *see* "腌臜" āza

zá

Z

砸 zá ❶ pound; crush; tamp:～石头 crush stones or rocks /～地基 tamp the foundations solid /搬起石头～自己的脚 pick up a rock only to drop it on one's own feet /掉下来的石头把他腿～伤了。He was injured in the leg by a falling rock. /他的头部被～了。His head was smashed. /这些核桃很好～。The walnuts crack easily. ❷ break; shatter; smash:盘子～了。The plate is broken. /玻璃～得粉碎。The glass was shattered to pieces. /他差点儿把镜子～了。He just missed breaking the mirror. ❸〈方言〉fail; fall through; foul up; be bungled:考～了 blow an exam /幸亏没听他的，听他的准～。Thank God, I didn't heed his advice. If I had, I would certainly have come to grief. /由于行动过急，他把事情办～了。He bungled the business by overhasty action.

砸巴 zába 〈方言〉pound; tamp; ram

砸饭碗 zá fànwǎn be fired; lose one's work; get the sack:弄不好～，我一家人就要喝西北风。My family would have nothing to live on if I should get the sack.

砸锅 záguō 〈方言〉fail; fall through; come a cropper:这次演出彻底～了。The performance was a total failure (*or* a complete flop). /这件事千万不能～。We simply can't afford to fail in this.

砸锅卖铁 záguō-màitiě spend one's entire fortune; give away all one has:为供弟弟上大学，他不惜～，倾其所有。He didn't hesitate to spend all he had to see his brother through university. /就是～，村里人也决心把这座水库建起来。The villagers were determined to have the reservoir built even if they had to spend their last penny on the project.

砸明火 zá mínghuǒ 〈方言〉rob; loot; plunder

砸牌子 zá páizi smash the signboard — mar the reputation of a firm:这个厂以自己的劣质产品砸了自己的牌子。This factory has ruined its own reputation with its inferior products.

咱(喒、偺) zá (often used in the early vernacular) I
see also zán; zan

咱家 zájiā (often used in the early vernacular) I

杂(雜、雜、襍) zá ❶ varied; diverse; mixed; sundry:复～ complicated; complex / 公务冗～ miscellaneous official duties ❷ extra; irregular: *see* "～费"; "～牌" ❸ mix; combine; mingle:混～ mix; mingle /树丛中～有一些青翠的毛竹。There is a scattering of green bamboo in the grove. /他们～在人丛中。They mingled with the crowd.

杂八凑儿 zábacòur 〈方言〉knock together:这些杯儿、碟儿不成套，是～。The cups and saucers do not make a set; they are just a motley collection.

杂拌儿 zábànr ❶ mixed sweetmeats; assorted preserved fruits:～糖 assorted candies ❷ miscellany; mixture; medley; hotchpotch or hodgepodge:这个集子是个大～，有诗、有杂文、有游记，还有短篇小说。The collection is a miscellany of poems, essays, travel notes and stories.

杂病 zábìng *also* "杂症"〈中医〉diseases of internal organs other than those caused by such external factors as cold, heat, dampness, etc.

杂波 zábō 〈无线电〉clutter:～滤波器 clutter filter /～噪声 clutter noise

杂草 zácǎo weeds; rank grass:～丛生 be overgrown with weeds; grass running riot /清除～ remove weeds; weed

杂处 záchǔ (of people from different areas) live in one place:五方～。People from different localities live in the area.

杂凑 zácòu put together at random; jumble up; knock together:这台节目是临时～起来的，质量不高。The performance was far from perfect, consisting merely of random items hurriedly put together.

杂芳族化合物 záfāngzú huàhéwù 〈化学〉heteroaromatics

杂肥 záféi subsidiary fertilizers, such as refuse from a city, etc.

杂费 záfèi ❶ miscellaneous expenses; incidental expenses; incidentals:节约～的开支 cut down miscellaneous expenses ❷ sundry fees or charges; extras:学～ tuition fee and extras /滥收～ make a

variety of excessive charges /～名目繁多。There is a multitude (*or* multiplicity) of sundry fees.

杂酚 záfēn 〈化工〉creosote:～油 creosote oil

杂感 zágǎn ❶ sundry impressions; random thoughts:谈几点～ make a few random remarks ❷ literary genre that records such thoughts:～集 collection of random thoughts

杂环 záhuán 〈化学〉heterocycle; heterocyde ring

杂环化合物 záhuán huàhéwù heterocyclic compound

杂环硝基化合物炸药 záhuán xiāojī huàhéwù zhàyào heteronitrocompound explosive

杂烩 záhuì ❶ dish of various ingredients; mixed stew; hotchpotch or hodgepodge:荤～ assorted meat delicacies /素～ assorted vegetarian delicacies /炒～ stir-fried mixed delicacies /～汤 hotchpotch ❷ mixture; miscellany; olio; medley:这是一篇道地的东拼西凑的大～。The article is nothing but a scissors-and-paste job.

杂活儿 záhuór odd jobs; sundry duties

杂货 záhuò sundry goods; groceries; general merchandise:～摊儿 grocer's stall (*or* stand) /日用～ various household supplies; groceries

杂货船 záhuòchuán break-bulk ship or carrier

杂货店 záhuòdiàn *also* "杂货铺" grocery; the grocer's; sundry or general store

杂货商 záhuòshāng grocer

杂和菜 záhuocài mixed stew (of leftovers); hotchpotch or hodgepodge

杂和面儿 záhuomiànr maize flour mixed with a little soya bean flour:～窝窝头 steamed bun made of maize flour mixed with soya bean flour

杂记 zájì ❶ miscellanies (as a type of literature); olio ❷ jottings; notes:旅行～ notes of a journey /～簿 notebook

杂技 zájì acrobatics:观看～表演 watch acrobatics (*or* an acrobatic show) /表演～ perform acrobatics

杂技团 zájìtuán acrobatic troupe

杂技演员 zájì yǎnyuán acrobat

杂家 zájiā ❶ (Zájiā) Eclectics, a school of thought flourishing at the end of the Warring States Period and the beginning of the Han Dynasty ❷ eclectic; jack-of-all-trades:我没有什么专长,充其量是个～而已。I'm just a jack-of-all-trades without any speciality to speak of. /他的确是一位知识渊博的大～。He is indeed a Renaissance man.

杂件 zájiàn odds and ends; sundry goods:日用小～ small articles of daily use

杂交 zájiāo 〈生物〉hybridize; crossbreed; cross:无性～ vegetative (*or* asexual) hybridization /有性～ sexual hybridization /通过～改良品种 improve crop varieties through hybridization /交叉～ crisscrossing /种内～ intraspecific cross (*or* hybridization) /～繁育 crossing; cross-breeding

杂交后代 zájiāo hòudài 〈生物〉filial generation

杂交水稻 zájiāo shuǐdào hybrid rice

杂交优势 zájiāo yōushì hybrid vigour; hybrid heterosis

杂交玉米 zájiāo yùmǐ hybrid or crossbred maize

杂交育种 zájiāo yùzhǒng crossbreeding

杂居 zájū (of two or more nationalities or ethnic groups) live together:多民族～地 areas inhabited by many nationalities or ethnic groups

杂剧 zájù *zaju*, poetic drama set to music, flourishing in the Yuan Dynasty, usu. consisting of four acts called *zhe* (折), with one character having the singing role throughout:宋元～ *zaju* of the Song and Yuan dynasties /著名的～家如关汉卿、王实甫等 well-known *zaju* playwrights such as Guan Hanqing and Wang Shifu

杂聚合 zájùhé 〈化学〉heteropolymerization:～物 heteropolymer

杂粮 záliáng coarse cereals; coarse food grains (e. g. maize, sorghum, barley, oat, millet, etc. as distinct from wheat and rice):多食～有益健康。Eating more coarse grains is good for your health.

杂乱 záluàn untidy; chaotic; confused; in a jumble:一片～ in (a state of) chaos /～的思绪 confused train of thought (*or* state of mind) /～的脚步声 confused footsteps /～而尘封的案卷 untidy and dusty files /桌上～地摆着纸、笔和书。Paper, pens and books were all jumbled up on the desk.

杂乱无章 záluàn-wúzhāng disorderly and unsystematic; jumbled; incoherent:房间里堆满了东西,显得～。The room was packed with articles and looked disorderly. /这篇文章写得～,重点不突出。The article lacks unity and coherence, and has no focus to speak of.

杂乱信号 záluàn xìnhào (of radio, radar or TV reception) random signal; hash

杂络物 záluòwù 〈化学〉heterocomplex

杂面 zámiàn *also* "杂合面" ❶ flour made from various coarse cereals and beans:～饼 pancake made of flour of coarse cereals and beans ❷ noodles made from such flour

杂木 zámù 〈林业〉weed tree:～林 weed tree forest

杂念 zániàn distracting thoughts; selfish considerations:私心～太重 be too calculating /走钢丝表演时,思想必须高度集中,容不得半点～。When performing, a tightrope walker needs a high degree of concentration and must not allow any thought to distract his attention. /干什么都不能掺杂个人私心～。One should not let personal considerations interfere with one's work.

杂牌 zápái less known or inferior brand:这台微机是～儿。This computer is of inferior quality.

杂牌货 zápáihuò goods of inferior brand

杂牌军 zápáijūn miscellaneous troops; troops of miscellaneous allegiances

杂品 zápǐn odds and ends; sundry goods; groceries:～柜 cupboard; cabinet /清理～ sort out the odds and ends /收集～ collect sundry articles

杂七杂八 záqī-zábā mixed; motley; assorted:～的东西 odds and ends; medley /～的思想 eclectic ideas /～的人 all sorts of people; people of different backgrounds /～的声音 babble of voices /屋里～堆得满满的,实在没地方了。The room is crammed with junk, and there is absolutely no space left. /～的事儿太多。There are too many things to attend to.

杂糅 záróu (of different things) mix; mingle; combine; blend:古今～ blending of the ancient and the modern /新旧～ combination (*or* blending) of the new and the old /精粗～ mixture of the fine and the coarse

杂散 zásǎn 〈物理〉stray:～磁场 stray magnetic field /～辐射 stray radiation /～电流 stray current

杂色 zásè ❶ variegated; varicoloured; particoloured; motley:～布料 varicoloured (*or* multicoloured) cloth; cloth of various colours /～服饰 particoloured (*or* motley) garments /～图形 mottled patterns ❷ less known or inferior brand

杂生 záshēng 〈植物〉intergrowth

杂食 záshí eating all kinds of things; omnivorous:～性 omnivory /～性寄生物 omnivorous parasite /～性昆虫 omnivorous insect

杂食动物 záshí dòngwù omnivorous animal; omnivore

杂史 záshǐ ❶ history book recording only one event from beginning to end or giving an eye-witness account of an affair ❷ private record of anecdotes

杂事 záshì trivial matters; sundry matters of daily life

杂书 záshū ❶ non-essential books (not directly related to the subjects of the imperial examination) ❷ books not directly pertaining to one's field of studies:浏览～ browse through miscellaneous books

杂耍 záshuǎ 〈旧语〉variety show; vaudeville

杂税 záshuì miscellaneous levies; sundry taxes:苛捐～ exorbitant taxes and levies

杂说 záshuō ❶ different versions or views; different opinions:对此事～不一。People have different views of the incident. *or* Opinions differ on the matter. ❷〈书面〉miscellaneous writings of argumentation:文史～ miscellaneous writings on literary and historical topics ❸〈书面〉unorthodox theories:封建时代视儒家经典以外的各家学说为～。In feudal China, all schools of thought but the Confucian classics were regarded as unorthodox.

杂酸 zásuān 〈化学〉heteroacid

杂碎 zásui ❶ chopped cooked entrails of sheep, oxen, etc. ❷ chop suey

杂沓 zátà *also* "杂遝" disorderly:马蹄～ clatter of horses' hoofs

杂遝 zátà *see* "杂沓"

杂文 záwén essay; satirical essay:～家 essayist /～集 collection of essays

杂务 záwù odd jobs; sundry duties:～繁多 have a host of (*or* too many) miscellaneous things to attend to

杂物 záwù odds and ends

杂烯系 záxīxì 〈化学〉heteroenoid system

杂项 záxiàng sundry items; miscellaneous items (in an account):～开支 miscellaneous expenses

杂役 záyì *also*“打杂的”dǎzáde〈旧语〉odd-job man; odd-jobber

杂音 záyīn ❶ noise ❷〈电学〉static:～干扰 noise interference /这收音机～很大。There is much static in the radio. ❸〈医学〉souffle; murmur; bruit:心脏～ heart murmur; cardiac souffle /心肺～ cardiopulmonary murmur; cardiorespiratory murmur /风箱状～ bellows murmur /脾～ splenic souffle

杂院儿 záyuànr *also*“大杂院儿”dàzáyuànr compound occupied by many households

杂症 zázhèng *see*“杂病”

杂脂 zázhī〈化学〉heterolipid

杂志 zázhì ❶ magazine:订～ subscribe to a magazine /过期～ back numbers ❷ (usu. used as titles of books) records; notes

杂志架 zázhìjià magazine rack

杂质 zázhì ❶ impurities of a material:将水过滤除去其中～ filter the water to remove its impurities ❷〈化学〉foreign matter or substance

杂种 zázhǒng ❶〈生物〉hybrid; crossbreed:～羊 crossbred sheep ❷〈粗话〉bastard; son of a bitch

杂种不育性 zázhǒng bùyùxìng〈生物〉hybrid sterility

杂种优势 zázhǒng yōushì〈生物〉hybrid vigour; heterosis

杂字 zázì collection of words in common use (usu. appearing in the form of rhyming verses):《农村四言～》*Book of Four-Character Rhyming Verses for Rural Usage*

zǎ

咋(嚓) zǎ〈方言〉what; how; why:这事～办? What should we do about it? *or* What's to be done? /你～不去开会? Why didn't you go to the meeting? /他～样了? How is he now? /你～搞的? See what you've done!
see also zé; zhā

咋个 zǎge〈方言〉how; why:我～晓得? How could I know?

zāi

灾(災) zāi ❶ calamity; disaster; catastrophe:天～ natural disaster /风～ cyclone disaster /水～ flood /虫～ plague of insects /防～ take precautions against natural calamities /救～ provide relief for a disaster area; help the people tide over a natural disaster /赈～ relieve the people in disaster-stricken areas /旱～受～面积达三十万平方公里。The drought hit an area of 300,000 square kilometres. ❷ personal misfortune; ill luck; mishap:招～惹祸 court (*or* invite) trouble /三～八难 suffer one misfortune or ailment after another /多～多难 be dogged by misfortunes and mishaps; be ill-starred

灾变 zāibiàn〈书面〉natural calamities

灾变说 zāibiànshuō〈地质〉catastrophism

灾病 zāibìng misfortune and diseases; pestilence; epidemic

灾厄 zāi'è〈书面〉suffering; disaster; catastrophe

灾害 zāihài disaster; calamity; misfortune:自然～ natural calamity /严重的社会～ tremendous social misfortune /遭受地震～ hit by the earthquake /～并不可怕,可怕的是失去战胜～的信心。It is not the disaster that is fearful but the loss of confidence to conquer it.

灾患 zāihuàn〈书面〉disaster; calamity:屡经～ suffer repeated calamities /～频仍。Disasters came in quick succession.

灾荒 zāihuāng famine due to crop failure; famine:躲避～ flee from famine; stay away from a famine-stricken area /那时此地水旱连年,～不断。Stricken either by drought or flood for years running, it used to be a famine-ridden area.

灾祸 zāihuò disaster; calamity; adversity:历史上罕见的～ disaster seldom seen (*or* heard of) in history /～临头。A catastrophe is imminent (*or* hanging over us).

灾梨祸枣 zāilí-huòzǎo printing of useless or unworthy books

灾民 zāimín victims of a natural calamity; afflicted people:～人数众多。A great many people fell victim to the disaster. /～得到救济。The afflicted people have been provided with relief.

灾难 zāinàn suffering; disaster; catastrophe:战争～ scourge of war /一场大～ catastrophe /～后果 devastating consequences /地震给人民带来了巨大的～。The earthquake brought intense sufferings to the people.

灾难深重 zāinàn shēnzhòng disaster-ridden; long suffering:～的中国人民终于解放了。The Chinese people who had experienced untold sufferings won liberation at long last.

灾年 zāinián famine year

灾歉 zāiqiàn crop failures due to natural calamity

灾情 zāiqíng damage caused by a disaster:了解～ find out about the damage inflicted by a disaster /雨后～有所减轻。The effects of the drought have been mitigated by the rain.

灾区 zāiqū disaster area; afflicted area:水旱～ flooded (*or* inundated) and drought-stricken area /支援～ aid a disaster area /～人民努力生产自救。The people in the afflicted area helped save themselves through production.

灾星 zāixīng〈迷信〉ill luck; misfortune:他今年遇到～了。He is out of luck this year.

灾殃 zāiyāng suffering; misfortune; disaster; calamity

灾异 zāiyì natural calamities and unusual natural phenomena (such as flood, earthquake, landslide, solar and lunar eclipses, etc.)

烖 zāi〈书面〉*see*“灾”zāi

栽[1] zāi ❶ plant; grow:～玫瑰 grow roses /他们～了几十棵树苗。They've planted dozens of saplings. /马路两边～满了树。The street is lined with trees on both sides. ❷ insert; erect; plant:～汽车站牌 erect a sign for the bus stop ❸ impose sth. on sb.:～罪名 trump up a charge against sb.; frame sb. /想不到他会把事故的责任～到我头上。I never imagined that he would shift the blame for the accident onto me. ❹ young plant; seedling:桃～ peach seedlings

栽[2] zāi ❶ tumble; topple; fall:～了一跤 trip and fall /头上～了个大包 fall down and get a bump on one's head /他～得鼻青脸肿。He had a bad fall and his nose was bloody and face swollen. ❷〈方言〉setback; frustration:今儿我算～到他手里了。I've suffered defeat at his hands this time.

栽插 zāichā put in the ground to grow; plant; transplant:～树苗 transplant saplings / 早先～的柳树都长大了。The willows planted in those days have all grown up.

栽盹 zāidǔn〈方言〉doze off; nod off:闭目～ doze off

栽跟头 zāi gēntou ❶ go head over heels; tumble; fall:道路泥泞,小心～。The road is muddy. You must be careful or you'll slip and fall. /昨晚夜行军,他一连栽了好几个跟头。He tripped and fell several times during the march last night. ❷ suffer a setback; come a cropper:我从来没有栽过这么大的跟头。I have never suffered such serious setbacks. /他这么胡来,早晚要～的。If he keeps on acting recklessly like this, he'll come to grief (*or* land himself in trouble) sooner or later. /有些人不栽几次跟头,总是不明事理。Some people won't see sense unless they fall flat on their faces a couple of times.

栽跤 zāijiāo ❶ fall:他走路心不在焉,栽了一跤。Walking absent-mindedly, he tripped and fell. ❷ suffer a setback; come to grief:在政治上搞投机,迟早要～的。A political opportunist is bound to come a cropper sooner or later.

栽培 zāipéi ❶ cultivate; tend; grow:～花卉 cultivate (*or* grow) flowers /～谷物 grow cereals /～异国树木 domesticate foreign trees /积累棉花～经验 accumulate experience in cotton culture /人工～ artificial cultivation ❷ foster; train; instruct; educate:～科技人才 train competent scientific and technological personnel ❸ help advance sb.'s career; support and encourage; patronize:那时,没有权贵～很难得到提升。It was then difficult for anyone to get promotion without patronage of influential people.

栽培品种 zāipéi pǐnzhǒng cultivar

栽培植物 zāipéi zhíwù cultivated plant

栽绒 zāiróng〈纺织〉tufted fabric:～机 tufting machine

栽诬 zāiwū fabricate a charge against sb.; frame sb.:恶毒～好人 viciously trump up a charge against an innocent person

栽秧 zāiyāng (of tomatoes, eggplant, etc.) transplant seedlings

栽赃 zāizāng plant stolen or contraband goods on sb.; fabricate a charge against sb.; frame sb.:～陷害 plant a stolen article on sb. in order to frame him /采用～的手法 resort to frame-up

栽植 zāizhí plant; grow; transplant:～树苗 plant saplings /～葡萄 grow grapes /～机 planting machine /先进的～技术应加以推广。Advanced planting techniques should be popularized.

栽种 zāizhòng plant; grow: ～花木 grow flowers and plant trees / ～观赏植物 grow ornamental (*or* decorative) plants / 这里不宜～西瓜。Watermelons won't grow well here.

栽子 zāizi young plant; seedling: 树～ seedlings / 柳树～ willow slips / 培植梨树～ cultivate pear seedlings

哉 zāi 〈书面〉❶ *indicating exclamation*: 呜呼哀～! Alas! / 燕雀安知鸿鹄之志～! Alas! How could a sparrow know the aspirations of a swan? — How could a common fellow read the mind of a great man? ❷ *used together with an interrogative to express doubt or form a rhetorical question*: 如此而已, 岂有他～! That's all there is to it! / 何足道～! It is really not worth mentioning!

甾 zāi *also* "类固醇" lèigùchún 〈生化〉 steroid

zǎi

宰[1] zǎi ❶ be in charge of; head: 主～ dominate; be in actual control of; have the final say in ❷ government official (in ancient China)

宰[2] zǎi ❶ slaughter; butcher: 屠～ slaughter / 杀猪～羊 butcher (*or* slaughter) pigs and sheep / 杀鸡～鸭 kill chickens and ducks ❷ force to pay through the nose; overcharge; fleece: 挨～ be made to pay much more for what one gets; be fleeced

宰割 zǎigē invade; persecute; oppress and exploit: 任人～ allow oneself to be trampled upon / 殖民主义者任意～弱小民族。Colonialists rode roughshod over small and weak nations at will.

宰人 zǎirén fleece; soak; overcharge; rip off: 那家餐馆宰起人来心可黑啦! They really rip people off (*or* soak people) at that restaurant!

宰杀 zǎishā slaughter; butcher: ～牲畜 slaughter domestic animals

宰牲节 Zǎishēngjié *also* "古尔邦节" Gǔ'ěrbāngjié 〈伊斯兰〉 *'Id al-Adha*; *'Id al-Kurban*

宰相 zǎixiàng prime minister (in feudal China); chancellor: 担任～之职 hold the position (*or* post) of prime minister

宰相肚里能撑船 zǎixiàng dùli néng chēng chuán a prime minister's heart is big enough to pole a boat in — be large-minded; be broad-minded: 您大人大量, ～, 哪会和这帮孩子一般见识。As a man of the older generation, you are of course broad-minded and above arguing with these youngsters.

宰制 zǎizhì rule; control; dominate: ～万物 dominate over everything on earth

载[1] zǎi year: 三年五～ three to five years / 千～难逢 occurring only once in a thousand years; once in a blue moon; very rare

载[2] zǎi put down in writing; enter (in a register); record: 登～ publish (in the press); carry / 《人民日报》转～ be reprinted in the *People's Daily* / ～入记录 place on record; record in the minutes / 据《中国日报》～ according to the *China Daily* / 史～ as history records; according to historical records / 契约～明 be clearly stated in the contract
see also zài

载籍 zǎijí 〈书面〉 books

载入史册 zǎirù shǐcè go down in the annals of history: 长征将士的英雄业绩已～。The heroic exploits of the Long Marchers have been written into the annals of history.

崽 zǎi 〈方言〉❶ son: 张老汉的～如今上了大学。The son of old man Zhang is now a university student. ❷ young man: 打工～ young manual worker ❸ young animal; whelp: 生了一窝猪～ give birth to a litter of piglets

崽子 zǎizi 〈粗话〉 whelp; brat; bastard: 你这个小兔～! You brat! / 狗～! Son of a bitch!

仔 zǎi *see* "崽" zǎi
see also zī; zǐ

zài

载[1] zài ❶ carry; bring; be loaded with: 搭～ carry (on the side) / 满～而归 return fully loaded; come back with fruitful results; return from a rewarding journey; be much profited by one's trip / 医疗队满～着非洲人民的友谊回国。The medical team returned home, bringing with it (*or* bearing) the friendship of the African people. ❷ (the road) be filled with: 风雪～途。The snowstorm has blocked the road. / 怨声～道。Popular grievances are openly voiced. *or* Voices of public discontent are heard everywhere. *or* Public dissatisfaction is open and widespread. ❸ (Zài) a surname

载[2] zài 〈书面〉 and; moreover; at the same time: ～笑～言 talking and laughing at the same time / ～欣～奔 run about joyfully
see also zǎi

载波 zàibō carrier wave; carrier: 三路～ three-channel carrier / ～电报 carrier telegraphy / ～电话机 carrier telephone / ～电源 carrier current / ～电压 carrier voltage / ～传输 carrier transmission

载驳船 zàibóchuán ❶ *also* "载驳货船" barges on board; barge carrying vessel; barge carrier; barge carrier ship ❷ *also* "载驳母船" lighter aboard ship (LASH)

载畜 zàichù (of pasture or grasslands) capacity for feeding farm animals; feeding capacity

载畜量 zàichùliàng *also* "载牧量" 〈畜牧〉 carrying capacity (of a pasture)

载歌载舞 zàigē-zàiwǔ singing and dancing joyously: 全城市民～, 热烈欢迎嘉宾。Singing and dancing, the whole town turned out to greet the honoured guests warmly.

载荷 zàihè load: ～变化 load fluctuation / ～装置 load device / ～能力 loadability

载荷子 zàihèzǐ charge carrier

载货 zàihuò carry cargo or freight: ～吨位 cargo tonnage / ～甲板 cargo deck / ～卡车 truck; lorry / ～船只 freighter

载货容积 zàihuò róngjī cargo carrying capacity

载客 zàikè carry passengers

载客量 zàikèliàng (carrying) capacity; busload

载流子 zàiliúzǐ carrier; charge carrier; current carrier

载牧量 zàimùliàng *see* "载畜量"

载频 zàipín 〈无线电〉 carrier frequency: ～波 carrier wave / ～放大器 carrier amplifier / ～全息图 carrier-frequency hologram

载热体 zàirètǐ 〈物理〉 heat carrier

载人 zàirén 〈航天〉 manned: ～的宇宙飞行 manned space flight

载人飞行器 zàirén fēixíngqì manned craft; manned vehicle

载人罐笼 zàirén guànlóng 〈矿业〉 man cage

载人轨道空间站 zàirén guǐdào kōngjiānzhàn manned orbital space station (MOSS)

载人轨道实验室 zàirén guǐdào shíyànshì manned orbital laboratory (MOL)

载人轨道研究站 zàirén guǐdào yánjiūzhàn manned orbital development station (MODS)

载体 zàitǐ carrier: 催化剂～ 〈化学〉 catalyst carrier / 数据～ data carrier / 语言文字是信息的～。Languages are the carriers of information.

载途 zàitú ❶ (of means of transport) passage; transit: 提高运输效率, 缩短～时间 increase transport efficiency to shorten the transit ❷ 〈书面〉 (the road) be filled with: 荆棘～ path overgrown with brambles — path beset with difficulties

载氧体 zàiyǎngtǐ 〈化学〉 oxygen carrier

载誉 zàiyù win great honour; be highly acclaimed: ～而去 leave (*or* depart) with great honour / 女排～归来。The women's volleyball team came back with flying colours.

载运 zàiyùn transport; ship; carry: 用卡车～大白菜 transport Chinese cabbages by truck / 用轮船～救灾物资 ship disaster relief to; transport disaster relief by ship / 本市公共汽车每天～乘客十万左右。The city buses carry about 100,000 passengers a day.

载重 zàizhòng load; carrying capacity: ～轮胎 high-capacity tyre

载重表尺 zàizhòng biǎochǐ deadweight scale

载重吨位 zàizhòng dūnwèi deadweight tonnage

载重降落伞 zàizhòng jiàngluòsǎn cargo parachute

载重量 zàizhòngliàng (of a ship, etc.) loading capacity or deadweight capacity:这辆汽车的~是多少? What's the carrying capacity of the lorry?
载重马车 zàizhòng mǎchē wagon
载重汽车 zàizhòng qìchē heavyduty truck; truck; lorry
载重线 zàizhòngxiàn load line:~标志 load line mark; freeboard mark; Plimsoll line (*or* mark)
载舟覆舟 zàizhōu-fùzhōu the water that carries the boat can also overturn it — a warning to the ruler that he should heed the voice of the people

傤

zài ❶ cargo; load:卸~ unload; land a cargo /过~ be overloaded ❷〈方言〉cargo carried by a ship

再

zài ❶ again; once more; another time:学习,学习,~学习。Study, study, and study again. /一而~,~而三 again and again; time and again; over and over again; repeatedly /~破世界记录 break another world record /我不能~喝了。I can't drink any more. /这篇文章还得~改一次。The essay needs further polishing. /~来一个! Encore! *or* Bring us another! ❷ to a greater extent or degree:音量~大点儿 turn it up a little louder, please /这事~糟不过了。It couldn't be worse. /问题~严重,也得设法解决。However serious the problem is, we have to try to solve it. /~苦~累我都不怕。I am not afraid of hardship, nor of any physical or mental exertion that may be required. ❸ *indicating what will happen if things are allowed to continue*:~不快点,我们上课就要迟到了。We'll be late for class if we don't hurry up. /~这样胡闹下去,你会闯祸的。If you continue behaving like this, you'll get into trouble. /~过几年,你或许就认不出这个地方了。A few more years and you probably will not be able to recognize the place. ❹ *indicating that one action takes place after the completion of another*:先到重庆,~去成都 first go to Chongqing and then Chengdu /把情况了解清楚之后~下结论 find out all about the matter before drawing conclusions ❺ *indicating additional information*:花园里种满了月季、牡丹、茉莉,~就是石榴和海棠。The garden is planted with Chinese roses, peonies and jasmine as well as pomegranates and crab apple trees. /参加会议的有编辑、记者,~就是学生代表。Present at the meeting were editors, reporters and also representatives of the students. ❻ *often followed by* 也 *for emphasis*:~贵也得买。We'll have to buy it no matter how expensive it is. /一个人~有本领也办不成这件事。Nobody can accomplish it single-handedly however capable he is. ❼〈书面〉continue; return:青春不~。One's youth never returns. *or* Youth's a stuff (that) will not endure. /良机难~。Opportunity knocks but once.
再版 zàibǎn ❶ second edition:此书 1983 年初版,1986 年~。The first edition of this book came out in 1983, and the second in 1986. ❷ (sometimes also) second impression or printing
再保险 zàibǎoxiǎn reinsurance:~公司 reinsurance company
再不 zàibu〈口语〉if not; or else; or:让老周去参加会议,~叫小黄去也行。Ask Lao Zhou to attend the meeting, or else Xiao Huang.
再不然 zàiburán or else; otherwise:只有一张票,要么你去,要么我去,~就都不去。There is only one ticket. Either you or I go to the cinema — or else neither of us.
再出口 zàichūkǒu〈商业〉re-export
再创造 zàichuàngzào recreation
再次 zàicì once more; once again; one more time:~说明了一个真理 demonstrate (*or* prove) a truth once again /避免类似事故的~发生 prevent the recurrence of similar accidents /~当选劳模 be reelected a model worker /外交部~就此事发表声明。The Ministry of Foreign Affairs issued another statement on this matter.
再度 zàidù once more; once again; second time:~访华 visit China a second time; pay another visit to China; revisit China /计划~修改 revise the plan once again /~改组内阁 reshuffle the cabinet once more /~判刑 reconvicted after discharge
再犯 zàifàn ❶ repeat an offence ❷ repeated or old offender
再分配 zàifēnpèi redistribution
再分 zàifen〈方言〉as long as; provided:他~有一点儿办法,也决不向别人开口。As long as he can think of a way out himself, he won't ask others for help.
再感染 zàigǎnrǎn〈医学〉reinfection
再固化 zàigùhuà〈物理〉resolidification
再合成 zàihéchéng〈化工〉resynthesis
再会 zàihuì good-bye; see you again; au revoir
再婚 zàihūn remarry; marry again:他~后,又生了一个小孩。He had another child in his second marriage (*or* after he remarried).
再加 zàijiā in addition; moreover; on top of that:她本来就聪明,~学习刻苦,所以进步很快。She made rapid progress as she was intelligent and also very hard-working. /路滑,~天黑,所以他没能准时赶到那里。The road was slippery; besides, it was dark, so he failed to get there in time.
再加工 zàijiāgōng reprocessing
再嫁 zàijià (of a woman) remarry:有些边远地区仍然存在着反对寡妇~的现象。In some remote areas there is still opposition to widows' getting married.
再见 zàijiàn good-bye; farewell; so long; I'll be seeing you
再教育 zàijiàoyù re-education (a practice adopted in the latter stage of the Cultural Revolution when young students were sent to the army, the countryside or the factories to be re-educated):进行~ re-educate /接受~ be re-educated
再醮 zàijiào〈旧语〉(of a widow) remarry
再接再励 zàijiē-zàilì make persistent efforts; work ceaselessly and unremittingly; advance from strength to strength:望你们不吃老本,~,把工作做得更好。I hope you won't rest on your laurels, but will make redoubled efforts so as to achieve still better results in your work.
再结晶 zàijiéjīng〈冶金〉recrystal; recrystallization:~热处理 recrystallizing heat treatment /~退火 recrystallization annealing
再进口 zàijìnkǒu〈商业〉reimport
再就业 zàijiùyè (of laid off wokers, etc.) find jobs again; be re-employed:~工程 re-employment project (*or* programme)
再裂化 zàilièhuà〈化工〉recracking
再硫化 zàiliúhuà〈化工〉resulphurize
再起 zàiqǐ recurrence; resurgence; return; revival:防止事端~ avert the recurrence of disturbances /两族冲突~。The two ethnic groups have clashed again.
再热 zàirè〈冶金〉reheat:~炉 reheating furnace /~器 reheater
再熔 zàiróng〈冶金〉resmelt
再熔技术 zàiróng jìshù resmelt technique
再熔炉 zàiróngIú resmelting furnace
再融资 zàiróngzī〈金融〉refinancing
再入效应 zàirù xiàoyìng〈航天〉re-entry effect
再入制导 zàirù zhìdǎo〈航天〉re-entry guidance
再三 zàisān over and over again; time and again; repeatedly:~挽留 press sb. to stay on; repeatedly urge sb. not to quit /~请求 insistently request /~道谢 thank over and over again
再烧结 zàishāojié〈冶金〉resinter
再审 zàishěn ❶ review; examine again:要求~ call for re-examination of ❷〈法律〉retrial; reopening of a case; fresh trial:法庭对该案进行了~。The court granted a retrial of the case. *or* The court retried the case.
再生 zàishēng ❶ revive; rise again:即使华陀~,亦无能为力。Even if Hua Tuo (legendary Chinese physician) came to life, he could do nothing about it. ❷〈生物〉regenerate:毛发~精 hair restorer /蚯蚓有~的机能。Earthworms have regenerative capacity. *or* The earthworm is regenerative. ❸ reprocess; recycle; regenerate:~纤维素 regenerated cellulose /~纸 recycled paper
再生产 zàishēngchǎn〈经济〉reproduction:进行~ reproduce /扩大~ extended (*or* expanded) reproduction; reproduction on an extended scale
再生父母 zàishēng fùmǔ one's second parent (said with gratitude to a person who has saved one's life); one's great benefactor:他们真是我的~啊。They have given me a second life.
再生检波器 zàishēng jiǎnbōqì〈无线电〉regenerative detector
再生林 zàishēnglín regenerated or regrown forest
再生能源 zàishēng néngyuán renewable source of energy
再生塑料 zàishēng sùliào regenerated plastics
再生现象 zàishēng xiànxiàng orthogenesis
再生橡胶 zàishēng xiàngjiāo reclaimed or regenerated rubber
再生障碍性贫血 zàishēng zhàng'àixìng pínxuè〈医学〉aplastic anemia; refractory anemia; regenerative anemia
再世 zàishì ❶ next life:~再图报答 repay sb.'s kindness in one's next life ❷〈书面〉reappearance in the world; reincarnation:华陀~ Hua Tuo reincarnated
再衰三竭 zàishuāi-sānjié the fighting spirit aroused by the first roll of drums is depleted by the second and exhausted by the third

— be nearing exhaustion; be dispirited:敌军已呈～之势。The enemy troops are exhausted and demoralized.

再说 zàishuō ❶ talk about sth. later; not consider or tackle a problem until some other time:这事儿先搁一搁,过几天～。Let's put the matter aside for a few days. /先集中精力讨论主要问题吧,这事儿待会儿～。Let's leave this for the moment and concentrate on the major problem. ❷ besides; moreover:现在去找他来不及了,～他也不一定在家。It's too late to go and see him now; besides, he may not be at home. /我没接到邀请,～我对这样的晚会一点儿不感兴趣,所以没去。I didn't go to the party as I hadn't received an invitation; what's more, I am not at all interested in such parties.

再碳化 zàitànhuà 〈冶金〉 recarbonize

再提纯 zàitíchún 〈化工〉 repurification:～器 repurifier

再贴现 zàitiēxiàn 〈金融〉 rediscount:～率 rediscount rate

再投资 zàitóuzī reinvest; plough back:将利润～于原工厂 plough profits back into the plant (as investment)

再吸收 zàixīshōu reabsorption

再现 zàixiàn (of a past event) reappear; be reproduced:银幕上生动地～了那次战斗的情景。The scenes of the battle are vividly reproduced on the screen. /离别时的情景清晰地～在她眼前。The parting scene reappeared clearly before her eyes.

再循环 zàixúnhuán 〈化工〉 recycle:～物料 recycle stock /～加热系统〈机械〉 recirculation heating system

再造 zàizào give sb. a new lease of life:恩同～ favour tantamount to giving sb. a new lease of life

再则 zàizé in addition; furthermore; besides:我今天没空,～事情也不急,改日再谈吧。I'm busy today; besides, the matter isn't urgent, so let's talk it over some other time. /婚事从简,一则可以节省开支,～可以免去许多麻烦。A simple wedding saves not only expenses but a lot of trouble as well.

再者 zàizhě 〈书面〉 what is more; furthermore; besides:我们无法接受这个任务,一来条件不具备,～时间也来不及。We can't possibly accept the task. The conditions necessary for its accomplishment do not exist; besides, there is not enough time for it either.

再蒸馏 zàizhēngliú 〈化工〉 rerunning; redistilling:～锅 rerunning still /～设备 redistilling unit

再植 zàizhí reattaching; rejoining; replantation:断肢～ reattaching a severed limb; replantation of a limb

再置成本 zàizhì chéngběn 〈经济〉 replacement cost

在

zài ❶ exist; be living:他父母都健～。His parents are both living and in robust health. /这问题还～,并没有解决。The problem still remains to be solved. /留得青山～,不怕没柴烧。As long as the green mountains are there, there'll be no shortage of firewood. *or* While there is life, there is hope. ❷ *indicating where a person or thing is*:我今晚不～家。I won't be in this evening. /信～桌子上。The letter is on the desk. ❸ remain:～校学生 in-school student; student /～职员工 staff and workers on the regular payroll ❹ join or belong to an organization:她～东方歌舞团。She works with the Oriental Song and Dance Ensemble. ❺ consist in; rest with; rely on:事～人为。Human effort is the decisive factor. /贵～坚持。The most important thing is perseverance. /谋事～人,成事～天。Man proposes, God disposes. ❻ *used together with* 所 *and often followed by* 不 *to indicate emphasis*:成败～所不计。I don't care whether this will lead to success or end up in failure. ❼ *indicating time, place, condition, scope, etc.*:～光天化日之下 in broad daylight /～最后时刻 at the eleventh hour; at the last moment /～他看来 in his opinion; as he sees it /～此期间 during this period /～学习方面 in terms of studies /开会时间是～星期一上午八点。The meeting is scheduled (*or* fixed) for 8:00 a.m. Monday morning. /事故发生～三个月以前。The accident occurred three months ago. /孩子～地上乱爬。The child crawled around the floor on all fours. /这事～处理方式上值得斟酌。The way in which the matter has been handled is open to question. ❽ *indicating an action in progress*:～任期间 while in office /风～吼,马～叫,黄河～咆哮! The wind is howling, the horses are neighing, and the Yellow River is roaring. /父子关系～好转。The relationship between the father and son is on the mend.

在案 zài'àn be on record:一一记录～ be put (*or* placed) on record one by one

在版编目 zàibǎn biānmù cataloguing in publication (CIP)

在帮 zàibāng 〈旧语〉 be a member of a secret society or an underworld gang, such as the Qing Bang(青帮) or the Hong Bang (洪帮)

在编 zàibiān (of personnel) be on the permanent staff:这几个人已退休,不～了。These people have retired and are no longer on the regular payroll.

在编人员 zàibiān rényuán those on the regular payroll; permanent staff:全院～共有两千多。The institute has a permanent staff of more than two thousand. /除～之外,还有不少临时工。Besides those on the regular payroll, there are also quite a few temperary employees.

在册 zàicè registered; on the namelist

在场 zàichǎng on the scene; on the spot; present:事故发生时他～。He was there when the accident happened. /因为有父亲～,他感觉拘束。He felt ill at ease in the presence of his father.

在场权 zàichǎngquán right of presence; right to be present

在朝 zàicháo hold office in court; be in power; be in office:～官宦 imperial court officials /两个政党,一个～,一个在野。There are two political parties; one is in power while the other is in opposition.

在朝党 zàicháodǎng party in power or office; ruling party

在此一举 zàicǐyījǔ everything depends on the action one is taking; prompt decision is needed in matters of importance:成败～。Success or failure hinges on this one action.

在党 zàidǎng be a member of a political party (esp. the Communist Party of China):此人～不～? Is he a Party member?

在岗 zàigǎng at one's post; employed:～职工 employed workers and staff

在官言官 zàiguān-yánguān speak what befits one's position

在行 zàiháng be a professional; be expert at sth.; know the ropes:做针线活她很～。She is handy with her needle. /裁剪衣服她十分～。Tailoring is very much in her line. /烹调我可不大～。I am not much of a cook. /他对电器很～。He knows a lot about electric appliances.

在乎 zàihu ❶ lie in; rest with:事情要办好,不～人多,而～心齐。Success depends not on the number of people but unity of purpose. /诗之所以为诗,～意境,并不～堆砌词藻。Poems are admired not because they are loaded with ornate diction, but because they are artistically conceived. ❷ (often used in the negative) care about; bother about; mind; take to heart:满不～ couldn't care less; not care a bit/人家取笑你,你～不～? Do you mind others' joking about you? /他不～别人的态度。He doesn't care what other people think. /山里人一天走一百里路毫不～。People living in mountainous areas think nothing of walking a hundred *li* a day.

在即 zàijí near at hand; before long; shortly; soon:暑假～。The summer vacation is drawing near (*or* is near at hand). /亚运会开幕～。The Asian Games will be held shortly. /厂房竣工～。The factory building will soon be completed.

在家 zàijiā ❶ be at home; be in:明晚我～。I'll be in tomorrow evening. /春节他们一家人～团聚。They all came home for a family reunion at the Spring Festival. /～靠父母,在外靠朋友。At home you count on your parents, outside on your friends. ❷〈宗教〉 remain a layman:～人 layman

在家千日好,出门一时难 zàijiā qiānrì hǎo, chūmén yīshí nán at home you may feel quite comfortable all the time, away from home you may be in instant trouble; there's always comfort at home but endless hardship abroad

在建 zàijiàn under construction:清理～工程 screen the projects under construction

在教 zàijiào ❶ believe in a religion ❷ believe in Islam

在劫难逃 zàijié-nántáo it is impossible to escape one's doom; what is destined cannot be avoided:挨一天是一天呗,～,有什么法儿? What else can we do but let the days drag on? There is no escape from fate. /看来你我真是～了! It seems that we are both doomed.

在理 zàilǐ stand to reason; be reasonable; be sensible:这话说得～。That's a sensible comment. /他不～。He is in the wrong.

在理会 Zàilǐhuì Righteous Society, an anti-Manchu secret society established in the late 17th century, later turned a superstitious sect

在内 zàinèi including:所有人,连我～,都要参加植树活动。All people, including me, will take part in tree planting.

在谱 zàipǔ conform to the general norm; be to the point:他懂行,说话～。As he knows his trade, he always speaks to the point.

在旗 zàiqí be a member of the "Eight Banners" in the Qing Dynasty

在前 zàiqián formerly; in the past; before:～他在家乡务农。He

used to be a farmer in his native place.

在世 zàishì be living; be above ground:父亲～的时候 when father was alive /他父母都不～了。Both his parents are dead. /人生～应有一番作为。One should accomplish something worthwhile in one's lifetime.

在数 zàishù ❶〈迷信〉doomed:～难逃。One's doom is sealed. ❷ included in a number, sum, etc.:参加晚会的有十人,你也～。Ten people are invited to the soirée, including you.

在所不辞 zàisuǒbùcí will not decline under any circumstances:为保护国家财产,虽赴汤蹈火也～。I wouldn't hesitate to go through fire and water to protect state property.

在所不计 zàisuǒbùjì regardless of the risk; whatever the cost:为了国家的振兴,即使献出生命,他也～。He would risk even his own life for the sake of national rejuvenation.

在所不惜 zàisuǒbùxī be regardless of the cost or sacrifice; will not grudge:只要有利于人民的事业,我肝脑涂地,～。I will balk at nothing, not even the loss of my life, for the cause of the people.

在所难免 zàisuǒnánmiǎn can hardly avoid; be unavoidable:仓促成篇,错误草率之处,～。There are bound to be errors and inadequacies in the essay, which I wrote in a great hurry. /回到久别的故乡,亲友间的应酬总是～的。When you return to your hometown after years of absence, it is unavoidable that you should have an exchange of visits, or even dinner parties, with your friends and relatives.

在逃 zàitáo〈法律〉has escaped; be at large; be on the run:～被告 absconding defendant /～期间 while the criminal is at large /搜捕～凶犯 track down and arrest the murderer on the run

在逃犯 zàitáofàn〈法律〉fugitive; escaped convict; criminal at large

在天之灵 zàitiānzhīlíng soul of the deceased resting in heaven:聊以告慰先生～ just to give consolation to my master's soul in heaven

在途 zàitú en route; on the way:通火车以后,鲜菜～时间比过去缩短了一天左右。After the construction of the railway, the time it takes to transport fresh vegetables has been reduced by about one day.

在外 zàiwài ❶ be away; be out:出门～ be away from home ❷ apart from; excluding; not including:这批货物包装、运费花了三百元,捐税～。The packing and transport expenses of the goods amounted to 300 *yuan*, apart from taxes.

在望 zàiwàng ❶ be visible; be in sight; come in view:宝塔山隐隐～。The Pagoda Hill is dimly visible. /雪峰遥遥～。Snow-clad peaks are discernible in the distance. ❷ will soon materialize; be in the offing; be round the corner:夏粮丰收～。Summer crops promise a good harvest. *or* A bumper summer harvest is in the offing. /胜利～。Victory is near at hand. *or* Success is round the corner.

在位 zàiwèi ❶ be on the throne; reign:康熙皇帝～时间很长。Emperor Kangxi reigned for a long time. ❷ be at one's post; be on the job

在握 zàiwò be in one's hands; be within one's grasp; be quite certain:大权～ be in the saddle; with power in one's hands /金牌～ be certain to win the gold medal /胜利～。Victory is in the bag.

在昔 zàixī〈书面〉in the past:～原始之民,茹毛饮血,穴居野处。The early primitive people lived in the wild and dwelt in caves, ate animal flesh raw and drank its blood.

在下 zàixià〈旧语〉I:容～申述理由。Please allow me to give an explanation.

在先 zàixiān ❶ formerly; before:～我对事实真相一无所知。I had not the slightest knowledge of the facts before. ❷ in advance; beforehand:此事利害,～已反复讲明,不能反悔。You've been told repeatedly of the gains and losses involved beforehand, so you can't back out now.

在先权 zàixiānquán right of precedence

在线 zàixiàn〈信息〉on-line:～存储器 on-line memory; on-line storage /～模型 on-line model /～数据处理 on-line data reduction /～计算机 on-line computer / ～公共存取目录 On-line Public Access Catalogue (OPAC)

Z

在心 zàixīn feel concerned; care about:他一心扑在事业上,别的什么都不～。His heart is in nothing but his work. /年纪这么大了,这婚姻的事儿,你为什么还是不～? You are old enough to get married. Why don't you give the matter some thought? /这事你该在点儿心了。You should keep an eye on the matter.

在学 zàixué be studying at a school:～人员 students

在押 zàiyā〈法律〉under detention; in custody:～期间 while in custody

在押犯 zàiyāfàn criminal in custody; prisoner

在野 zàiyě out of office; in opposition

在野党 zàiyědǎng party not in office; opposition party

在业 zàiyè be employed; be on the job:～人口 working population /～人员 people in employment

在意 zàiyì (usu. used in the negative) pay attention to; care about; mind:没～ not take notice of; not notice /生活小事,他从不～。He never minds trifling matters in everyday life.

在于 zàiyú ❶ lie in; rest with:他们以往的失败往往～轻敌。Their past failures often resulted from an underestimate of the enemy's strength. /这批小戏的特点就～生活气息浓。These short plays are characterized by a rich flavour of life. /这个工程的关键不～进度,而～质量。The crux of the project lies not in the rate of progress but in quality. ❷ be determined by; depend on:一年之计～春。The whole year's work depends on a good start in spring. /去不去～你自己。It's up to you to decide whether you'll go or not.

在运品 zàiyùnpǐn goods in transit

在在 zàizài〈书面〉everywhere; all over:那时,城里乞丐～皆是。Beggars could be found everywhere in the city in those days.

在早 zàizǎo〈方言〉formerly; in the past:～他俩上中学时,就很要好。They were already close friends in their school days.

在职 zàizhí be on the job; be employed; be at one's post:～人员 people in employment /～培训 in-service training; on-the-job training /～期间 during one's tenure of office

在职干部 zàizhí gànbù cadre at his or her post

在职研究生 zàizhí yánjiūshēng one who is enrolled in an in-service postgraduate programme; on-the-job postgraduate:～计划 in-service training postgraduate programme

在职总统 zàizhí zǒngtǒng sitting president; incumbent president

在制品 zàizhìpǐn products being made; unfinished products

在座 zàizuò be present (at a meeting, banquet, etc.); participate in:～的贵宾 distinguished guests present here /～有文有武。Among those present were both military and civilian personnel. /有长辈～,他不便多言。He felt it was inappropriate to make comments in the presence of the elders. /请～的各位谈谈自己对此的见解。We hope everyone here will tell us their own ideas on the subject.

zān

糌 zān

糌粑 zānba *zanba*, roasted *qingke* barley (青稞) flour, a staple of the Zang nationality

簪 zān ❶ hairpin:玉～ jade hairpin /扁～ flat hairpin ❷ wear in one's hair:～花 wear flowers in one's hair

簪缨 zānyīng〈书面〉❶ ornamental hairpins and tassels on the hats of the nobility and influential people (in ancient China) ❷〈比喻〉high-ranking official:～之家 family of a high official

簪子 zānzi hair clasp; hairpin

篸(篸) zān〈书面〉*see* "簪" zān

see also cǎn

zán

咱(喒、偺) zán ❶ we (including both the speaker and the person or persons spoken to):～大伙儿一条心。We are all of one heart and one mind. /他们不干,～干! They won't do it, but we will! ❷〈方言〉I:～不懂他的话。I don't understand his words. /～斗不过他。I am not his match.

see also zá; zan

咱们 zánmen ❶ we (including both the speaker and the person or persons spoken to):～厂 our factory /～工人有力量。We workers are powerful. /他们来～这里两次了,～也得去回拜一下。We have to repay their visits since they have come to see us twice. ❷ *used to mean oneself or the person addressed*:～乡下人,喜欢直来直往。I am from the country and like to be straightforward. /谁欺负～了? 找他说理去。Who bullied you? Let's go and reason things out with him. /小明,～乖,～不哭。There, there! Xiaoming, be a good boy, don't cry.

zǎn

喒 zǎn 〈书面〉❶ hold in the mouth：～味含甘 taste sweet ❷ sting；bite：蚊虻～肤 mosquitoes and gadflies bite and sting

趱 zǎn ❶ (often used in the early vernacular) hurry or rush through：～赶 push on (with one's journey) ❷ urge；press：～马向前 spur a horse on

攒(儹) zǎn accumulate；collect；save：积～ save (*or* collect) bit by bit /光～不用 saving without spending /～粮食 hoard (up) food /～钱买书 save up to buy books；save up for books /她～的钱都买衣服了。She spent all her savings on clothing.
see also cuán

拶(桚) zǎn press hard；squeeze forcibly
see also zā

拶指 zǎnzhǐ squeeze a person's fingers between sticks (a torture in old China)

拶子 zǎnzi sticks for squeezing a person's fingers (as a torture in old China)

zàn

暂 zàn ❶ of short duration；transient；brief：人生是短～的。Life is short (*or* fleeting). ❷ for the time being；for the moment；momentarily：～住在一位朋友处 stay with a friend for the time being /～停营业 business suspended /会议～告结束。The meeting is adjourned. *or* The meeting is called to a temporary halt.

暂存器 zàncúnqì 〈计算机〉temporary memory or storage

暂定 zàndìng temporary；tentative；provisional：～合同 temporary contract /这次会议～五月中旬召开。The meeting is tentatively set for mid May. /试用期限～半年。The trial-use time is fixed at six months for the time being.

暂短 zànduǎn short；brief：～的旅程 brief journey；short trip

暂缓 zànhuǎn put off；postpone；suspend；defer：～执行命令 put off (*or* defer) carrying out an order /这事可以～几天。This can be postponed for a few days.

暂记账 zànjìzhàng suspense account

暂且 zànqiě temporarily；for the time being；for the moment：这话，～不提。Let's not talk about it for the moment. /这事～搁一搁，以后再议。For the time being, let's put the matter aside for further consideration. /你感冒了，～休息几天。You are having a cold. You'd better take a few days off.

暂缺 zànquē ❶ (of a post) be left temporarily vacant：主任的人选～。The position of the director will remain vacant for the time being. ❷ (of a commodity) be out of stock at the moment

暂时 zànshí temporary；transient；for the time being：～的工作 temporary work /～的幸福 transient happiness /～代理 acting /这本书可否～借我一阅？Could you let me have the book for a few days? /你～得和别人合住一间屋。You'll have to share the room with someone else for the time being. /他～还不能给你明确的答复。He is not able to give you a definite answer right now.

暂时磁铁 zànshí cítiě 〈物理〉temporary magnet

暂停 zàntíng ❶ suspend；discontinue：～交货 suspend delivery /车辆～通行。The road is temporarily closed to traffic. ❷〈体育〉time-out：教练要求～。The coach asked for time-out.

暂星 zànxīng nova (as called in ancient China)

暂行 zànxíng provisional；temporary：～法规 provisional rules and decrees /～办法 temporary measures /～条例 interim regulations

蹔 zàn 〈书面〉*see* "暂" zàn

錾 zàn ❶ engrave on gold or silver；carve；incise；chisel：～花 carve flowers or patterns /～金 engrave on gold ❷ engraving tool；chisel；graver

錾刀 zàndāo (engraver's) burin；graver

錾子 zànzi cold chisel；chisel (for cutting stone)：石～ chisel for cutting stone

赞(賛、❷❸讚) zàn ❶ support；aid；assist：乡人共～ fellow townsmen all extend support and assistance to /此人能～大事。This man is able to assist you in your important undertaking. ❷ praise；laud；commend：盛～ extol /～长城之壮观 admire the magnificence of the Great Wall /～声四起。Praises are heard from all around. ❸ eulogy：像～ inscription eulogizing the subject of a portrait /《樱花～》*Ode to Cherry Blossoms*

赞比西河 Zànbǐxīhé Zambezi River, an African river flowing through Angola, Zambia and Mozambique to the Indian Ocean

赞比亚 Zànbǐyà Zambia：～人 Zambian

赞不绝口 zànbùjuékǒu be full of praise；praise unceasingly：游客们对这美丽的景色～。The tourists showered praises on the beautiful scenery.

赞成 zànchéng ❶ approve of；agree with；assent；favour：她不～我的意见。She doesn't agree with me. /五票～，四票反对。Five votes for and four against. /全班投票～他的提议。The class voted assent to (*or* in favour of) his proposal. /我不～你让孩子自行其是。I don't approve of your letting the child have his own way. /选他当组长，你～吗？How about electing him group leader? ❷〈书面〉help accomplish：～其事 help accomplish the task

赞成票 zànchéngpiào affirmative vote；vote of assent：投～的占多数。The ayes have it. /我们都投了～。We all voted in the affirmative.

赞词 zàncí *also* "赞辞" eulogy；word of praise

赞服 zànfú esteem；admire：我对那些克己奉公的领导干部深为～。I have great esteem and admiration for those leading cadres who work selflessly for the interests of the people.

赞歌 zàngē song of praise；paean；hymn：唱～ sing the praises of /一曲和平、友谊的～ paean of peace and friendship

赞和 zànhè approve of；agree with

赞画 zànhuà *also* "赞划"〈书面〉assist in planning：～军务 help manage military affairs；assist in handling military affairs

赞礼 zànlǐ ❶ perform the duty of master of ceremonies at a wedding, funeral, or sacrificial rites：～毕 ceremony being over；end (*or* conclusion) of the ceremony ❷ master of ceremonies at a wedding, funeral, or sacrificial rites

赞理 zànlǐ 〈书面〉assistant

赞美 zànměi eulogize；extol；praise：人们作诗～桂林山水。Many people have written poems in admiration (*or* praise) of Guilin's landscape. /这有关大自然的描写是对生命的～。This description of nature is a eulogy to life.

赞美诗 zànměishī 〈基督教〉hymn；psalm；canticle；chant

赞慕 zànmù admire：投以～的眼光 look at admiringly；cast an admiring glance at；give an admiring look

赞佩 zànpèi hold in esteem；esteem；admire：邻居们都～他助人为乐的精神。His neighbours all admired him for his generosity in giving help to others.

赞赏 zànshǎng think highly of；appreciate；admire：以～的语气说 say with a tone of admiration /他这种实事求是的工作态度值得～。His practical and realistic style of work deserves commendation (*or* is worthy of praise). /我们对贵国政府这一公正立场表示～。We express our appreciation for the just stand taken by your government.

赞颂 zànsòng laud；eulogize；sing the praises of：～老一辈的功勋 eulogize the older generation for the great contributions they have made；sing the praises of the great contributions of the veterans. /他被～为佛罗伦萨画派的鼻祖。He was extolled as the founder of the Florentine school.

赞叹 zàntàn highly praise；marvel at；gasp in admiration：厨师们的高超技艺令人～不已。The spectators all marvelled at the superb skill of the cooks. /他们对职业的忠心，使我不禁为之～。Their devotion to their profession filled me with admiration.

赞同 zàntóng approve of；agree；accept；endorse：他不～这次军事行动。He doesn't approve of the military operation. /我不～钱能使人幸福的观点。I don't subscribe to the idea that money brings happiness. /全厂上下一致～精简机构。The whole factory unanimously endorsed streamlining the administrative structure. /在这点上我～你的意见。I'll go along with you on this point.

赞羡 zànxiàn admire：人们～他的才气。People admire his talent. /他话里含有～的口气。There was a note of admiration in what he said.

赞襄 zànxiāng 〈书面〉support；assist：～政务 assist in government

administration /～和议 support the negotiations to end the war and restore peace

赞许 zànxǔ praise; commend; approve of: ～的微笑 approving smile /厂长对小王的工作态度表示～。The director of the factory commended Xiao Wang for his attitude towards work. /他勇于承认错误,因而得到人们的～。He was praised for his courage to admit his own mistakes.

赞扬 zànyáng speak highly of; pay tribute to; praise; commend: ～孩子的进步 praise the children for the progress they have made /巴金的成就使他赢得了整个文学界的～。Ba Jin's achievements earned him the acclaim of the entire literary world. /他高度～了两国之间的文化交流。He paid high tribute to the cultural exchanges between the two countries. /他的工作值得～。His work merits (*or* deserves) commendation. /演出博得了人们的普遍～。The performance won universal applause. /同她接触过的人都～她。Those who are acquainted with her all speak highly of her.

赞仰 zànyǎng admire

赞语 zànyǔ words of praise; praise: 热情的～ enthusiastic praises

赞誉 zànyù praise; commend; approve; acclaim: ～之辞不绝于耳。People are profuse in their praises. /饭店的优良服务受到外宾的～。The hotel's fine service has won the commendation of foreign guests.

赞助 zànzhù support; assistance; aid: 来自海外华人的～ help and assistance from overseas Chinese /本节目得到好几个单位的～。This programme has the financial support of several units. /这部电视连续剧由几家公司共同～。This TV series is jointly sponsored by several companies. /这台音乐会是在音乐家协会的～下安排的。The concert has been arranged under the auspices of the Union of Musicians.

濽 zàn 〈方言〉 splash; spatter: 开过去的车～了我一身泥。A passing car spattered me with mud (*or* splashed mud over me).

瓒 zàn jade spoon used at sacrificial rites (in ancient China)

zan

咱(喒、偺) zan 〈方言〉 *used in* 这咱, 那咱 *and* 多咱, *as a combined pronunciation of* 早 *and* 晚: 他多～来的? When did he come? /你多～走? When are you leaving?

see also zá; zán

zāng

赃(贜、臟) zāng ❶ stolen goods; booty; loot; spoils: 追～ recover stolen money or goods /退～ disgorge the spoils; return one's booty; surrender ill-gotten gains /分～不均 share the loot (*or* divide the spoils) unequally /栽～ plant stolen goods on sb. ❷ embezzled money or goods; bribes: 贪～枉法 take bribes (*or* practise graft) and bend the law

赃官 zāngguān corrupt official; dishonest official

赃款 zāngkuǎn stolen money; accepted bribes; illicit money: 收受～二十万元 take (*or* accept) a bribe of ¥200,000 /退还全部～ return all the bribes (*or* money embezzled)

赃物 zāngwù ❶ stolen goods; booty; loot; spoils: 窝藏～ harbour stolen goods /查获～两箱 discover and seize two boxes of stolen goods ❷ embezzled money or goods; bribes

赃证 zāngzhèng evidence of bribery, embezzlement, theft or robbery

脏(髒) zāng dirty; filthy; unclean: ～活儿 dirty work /把手上的～东西洗掉 wash the dirt off one's hands /她鞋上的泥把地毯弄～了。She soiled the carpet with her muddy shoes. /白手套易～。White gloves soil easily. /别把新帽子弄～了。Don't dirty your new hat. /这里到处是垃圾和其他～东西。The place was littered with garbage and other filth.

see also zàng

脏病 zāngbìng VD (venereal disease)

脏话 zānghuà dirty word; obscene language; swearword; four-letter word: 说～ talk dirt; use filthy and dirty words /他常常是满口～。He is often foul-mouthed. /他对邻居嚷了许多～。He shouted a lot of filth at his neighbour.

脏乱 zāngluàn dirty and disorderly; untidy: 他们的住处环境～,卫生很差。They lived in filthy and disorderly surroundings with poor sanitation.

脏钱 zāngqián 〈口语〉 illegal or immoral earnings; filthy money

脏水 zāngshuǐ filthy water; slops; sewage

脏土 zāngtǔ dust; dirt; rubbish; garbage: 倒～ tip (*or* dump) rubbish

脏污 zāngwū ❶ filthy; dirty: ～的衣裳 soiled clothes; dirty linen ❷ dirt; filth: 车身擦得很亮,没有半点～。The car was polished spotlessly clean.

脏症 zāngzhèng *see* "脏病"

脏字 zāngzì four-letter word; rude word: 话里带～ speak in abusive terms; use dirty words; be foul-mouthed

牂 zāng ewe

牂牂 zāngzāng 〈书面〉 (of grass and trees) luxuriant; lush

臧 zāng ❶ 〈书面〉 good; right ❷ (Zāng) a surname

臧否 zāngpǐ 〈书面〉 pass judgment on; appraise: ～是非 judge between right and wrong; decide which side is right /～功过 make an appraisal of one's achievements and errors

臧否人物 zāngpǐ-rénwù comment on the merits and demerits of people; pass judgment on people

zǎng

驵 zǎng 〈书面〉 fine horse; steed

驵侩 zǎngkuài 〈书面〉 middleman in horse trade; middleman; broker; agent

zàng

葬 zàng consign to the grave; bury; inter: 安～ bury (the dead) /火～ cremation /海～ burial at sea; sea-burial /天～ celestial burial (by which bodies are exposed to birds of prey)

葬地 zàngdì burial ground; grave

葬礼 zànglǐ funeral rites; funeral: 参加他的～ attend his funeral /举行～ hold a funeral

葬埋 zàngmái bury (the dead); entomb: ～烈士的遗骨 bury the remains of the martyrs

葬身 zàngshēn be buried: ～火海 perish in the flames; be engulfed in a sea of flames /～海底 get drowned in the sea; be swallowed up by the waves of the sea /死无～之地 die without a burial place — come to a bad end

葬身鱼腹 zàngshēn-yúfù become food for the fish; be drowned: 船遇风浪,全家～。The ship wrecked in the storm and all the family were drowned.

葬送 zàngsòng ruin; wreck: ～了前程 ruin one's future (*or* prospects, *or* career) /罪恶的封建礼教不知～了多少青年的爱情和性命。The evil feudal ethics robbed many young people of both their love and their lives.

葬仪 zàngyí funeral rites; funeral

藏[1] zàng ❶ storage; depository: 宝～ hidden treasures; valuable (mineral) deposits /府～ (in ancient China) storage for national treasures and documents ❷ Buddhist or Taoist scriptures: 道～ Taoist scriptures /大～经 Tripitaka; whole collection of Buddhist texts

藏[2] Zàng ❶ (short for 西藏自治区) Xizang (*or* Tibet) Autonomous Region: ～南地区 southern Tibet ❷ Zang or Tibetan nationality

see also cáng

藏刀 zàngdāo *also* "折刀" zhédāo clasp knife

藏旱獭 zànghàntǎ 〈动物〉 Himalayan marmot

藏红花 zànghónghuā ❶ 〈植物〉 saffron crocus (*Crocus sativus*): 西藏盛产～。Tibet abounds in saffron crocuses. ❷ 〈中药〉 saffron: ～

Z

是治疗妇科病的良药。Saffron is a good (*or* an effective) remedy for gynecological diseases.

藏剧 zàngjù Zang or Tibetan opera:演出～《文成公主》 stage the Zang opera *Princess Wencheng*

藏蓝 zànglán purplish blue:身着～色西服 be (dressed) in a purplish blue suit

藏历 Zànglì lunar calendar used by the Tibetan nationality:藏族牧民习用～。The Tibetan herdsmen use the Tibetan lunar calendar.

藏历新年 Zànglì xīnnián Tibetan New Year Festival, the greatest festival of the Tibetan nationality which lasts the entire first month of the Tibetan lunar calendar

藏青 zàngqīng dark blue:着一身～色中山装 be in dark blue tunic and trousers

藏青果 zàngqīngguǒ myrobalan (*Terminalia chebula*)

藏戏 zàngxì Zang or Tibetan opera

藏香 zàngxiāng joss stick produced in Tibet and used by the Tibetans

藏医 zàngyī ❶ traditional Tibetan medical science; traditional Tibetan medicine ❷ doctor or practitioner of traditional Tibetan medicine

藏语 Zàngyǔ language of the Zang nationality; Tibetan language

藏族 Zàngzú Zang or Tibetan nationality, distributed over the Tibet Autonomous region, Qinghai, Sichuan, Gansu and Yunnan; Tibetan ethnic group:～人民能歌善舞。The Tibetan people are good at singing and dancing. /～文化源远流长。The Tibetan culture has a long history behind it.

脏(臟)

zàng internal organs of the body, such as the heart, liver, spleen, lungs and kidneys; viscera:心～ heart /肾～ kidneys /肝～ liver /脾～ spleen /五～六腑 internal organs of the body; viscera
see also zāng

脏腑 zàngfǔ 〈中医〉internal organs consisting of the heart, liver, spleen, lungs, and kidneys as well as stomach, gall, three visceral cavities, small and large intestines, and bladder; viscera

脏器 zàngqì internal organs of the body; viscera

脏象 zàngxiàng 〈中医〉state of internal organs; visceral manifestations indicating physiological function as well as pathological changes of the internal organs

脏躁症 zàngzàozhèng *also* "癔病" yìbìng hysteria

奘

zàng ❶〈书面〉(often used in human names) strong; robust ❷〈方言〉rough; boorish in manner and speech
see also zhuǎng

zāo

糟

zāo ❶ distillers' grains; brewers' grains; grains:酒～ distillers' grains; grains ❷ be pickled with grains or in wine:～鱼 pickled fish ❸ rotten; worn out:房梁～了。The roof beam is rotton. ❹ in a wretched state; in a mess:你把这事办得～透了。You've made a pretty bad (*or* terrible) mess of the matter. /别把邻里关系搞～了。Don't mess up your relations with your neighbours. /这孩子身体～得很。He is a very frail child. /～了! 赶不上火车了! Oh, blast! We'll miss the train!

糟床 zāochuáng press for distillers' grains

糟蛋 zāodàn ❶ egg (usu. duck's egg) pickled with grains, salt and in vinegar; pickled egg ❷〈比喻〉idiot; good-for-nothing; sth. bad:这群～ that pack of idiots /净说些～话 talk nothing but nonsense

糟坊 zāofáng *see* "糟行"

糟改 zāogǎi 〈方言〉make caustic and ironical remarks; ridicule:这也算创作? 别～人啦! Can this be called creative work? God forbid it! (*or* Don't be so sarcastic!)

糟糕 zāogāo what bad luck; too bad; in a terrible mess:～, 我把开会的事忘了! My goodness! I forgot all about the meeting. /～, 自行车钥匙丢了! What bad luck! I've lost the key to my bicycle. /没有比这再～的事儿了。Nothing could be worse! /这地方实在～。The place is in a terrible mess. /幸好他不知道, 否则宣扬出去就更～了。Fortunately, he didn't know about that, otherwise he might spread it around and the fat would really be in the fire.

糟疙瘩 zāogēda (popular term for 痤疮) acne

糟害 zāohai 〈方言〉(of birds or beasts) damage; ruin; make havoc of:麻雀～庄稼。Sparrows damage crops. /老鼠～粮食。Rats nibbled away the grains. /这些无赖尽～人。Those scoundrels are always making trouble for others. *or* Those rascals are always trying to get people into trouble.

糟行 zāoháng *also* "糟坊" distiller's; brewer's

糟毁 zāohuì ruin; spoil:这座古庙竟～成这样, 真可惜。What a pity that the old temple should have fallen into such disrepair.

糟践 zāojian 〈方言〉❶ waste; damage; ruin; spoil:～东西 waste useful things /～庄稼 damage (*or* ruin) a standing crop ❷ insult; trample on:～人 insult sb. ❸ ravage; violate (a woman); rape:～良家女子 ravage women of respectable families

糟糠 zāokāng distillers' grains, husks, chaff, etc. — things used by the poor to allay hunger:权且以～糊口 live on chaff for the time being

糟糠之妻 zāokāng zhī qī wife of one's "chaff and husks" days; woman married to a man before he became prosperous; wife who shared her husband's hard lot:他发财以后便遗弃了～。After he became rich, he forsook his wife who had gone through the difficult times with him.

糟糠之妻不下堂 zāokāng zhī qī bù xiàtáng wife of one's "chaff and husks" days shall never go down from the hall; one should not abandon one's wife who has shared the hard lot with one:贫贱之交不可忘, ～。One must not forget those who befriended one in poverty and obscurity, nor should one forsake the wife who accompanied one in times of difficulty and hardship.

糟烂 zāolàn rotten; decayed; worn out:这大衣已穿得～不堪了。The overcoat is worn to rags.

糟粕 zāopò waste or useless matter; dross; dregs:弃其～, 取其精华 discard (*or* reject) the dross and assimilate (*or* select) the essence

糟踏 zāota *see* "糟蹋"

糟蹋 zāota *also* "糟踏" ❶ waste; ruin; damage:白～了光阴 idle away one's time /～人才 stifle real talents /不应该～一粒粮食。You shouldn't waste a single grain. /这山上的林子被～光了。The mountain was denuded of trees. /你这样下去, 只会～自己的身子。You will ruin your health if you go on like this. ❷ insult; trample on; ride roughshod over:这城市屡遭敌人～。The city has been repeatedly ravaged by the enemy. /你怎么随便～人? How can you talk about others in such dreadful terms? /这简直是～知识分子! This is simply an insult to the intellectuals. ❸ violate (a woman); ravish; rape:匪徒离村前～了很多妇女。The bandits raped many women before they left the village.

糟心 zāoxīn vexed; annoyed; depressed:这结果令人～。The result was very disappointing. /这些天尽碰上～的事。I've had nothing but vexations these days.

糟朽 zāoxiǔ rotten; decayed:木料～, 不能再用。The timber has rotted and cannot be used.

糟鸭片 zāoyāpiàn duck slices in wine sauce

糟渣类饲料 zāozhālèi sìliào pomace and dreg fodder

遭[1]

zāo meet with (disaster, misfortune, etc.); sustain; suffer:～险 run into (*or* meet with) danger /屡～失败 suffer repeated failures /惨～毒手 be killed in cold blood /险～不测 come within an ace of death; have a near (*or* narrow) escape

遭[2]

zāo 〈量词〉❶ time; turn:来回走了好几～ walk back and forth several times /他病后公开露面, 这还是头一～。This is the first time he has made a public appearance since he fell ill. /一～生, 两～熟。Strangers at the first meeting, friends at the second. *or* Green the first time, experienced the second. *or* Ill at ease the first time, at home the second. ❷ round:沿城墙跑了两～ run round the city wall twice

遭报 zāobào suffer a retribution:恶人迟早要～。Evil will sooner or later be repaid with evil. *or* Retribution will overtake evildoers one day.

遭到 zāodào suffer; meet with; sustain; encounter:～天灾人祸 suffer both natural and man-made disasters /～不幸 meet with misfortune /～损失 sustain losses /～冷落 be left out in the cold; be

Z

given the cold shoulder /提案～否决。The motion was turned down (*or* rejected). /这个地区～台风的严重破坏。The area was devastated by a typhoon.

遭逢 zāoféng suffer; come across; encounter: ～盛世 live in an age of prosperity /～意外变故 sth. quite unforeseen happened (*or* cropped up) /～巨大困难 encounter formidable (*or* tremendous) difficulties

遭际 zāojì 〈书面〉❶ circumstances; experience; lot: 他这些年～很不好。He has had a hard time these years. /你听到自己亲人的不幸～，能不动心么? Can you remain unmoved when you hear about your dear one's hard lot? ❷ meet with; come across; encounter: ～危难 be in danger

遭劫 zāojié come face to face with calamity: 屡次～ one terrible blow after another

遭罹 zāolí 〈书面〉suffer; be subjected to; meet with: ～疾病 suffer from (*or* be attacked by, *or* contract) a disease; be taken ill /～文网 be caught in the meshes of the law; be brought to justice

遭难 zāonán 〈方言〉meet with difficulties: 孩子淘气，您带着少不了～费心。The children are naughty, and you'll have a hard time taking them in hand.

遭难 zāonàn ❶ suffer misfortune or disaster ❷ be killed in an accident; be murdered

遭年成 zāo niáncheng *also* "遭年景"〈方言〉have a bad or lean year for crops

遭孽 zāoniè endure hardships, tortures, rough conditions, etc.; have a hard time

遭扰 zāorao 〈方言〉〈婉词〉disturb or trouble (used after being entertained by sb. at his house as a guest): ～了人家一星期 put them to much trouble for a week /～您了，多谢! Thank you very much for your hospitality.

遭事 zāoshì 〈方言〉meet with misfortune

遭受 zāoshòu suffer; be subjected to; undergo; sustain: ～折磨 suffer torments; undergo torture /～经济损失 sustain financial losses; suffer both money and material losses /～战争的破坏 be damaged (*or* devastated) by war /～台风袭击 be hit (*or* struck) by a typhoon /尽管～许多挫折，但他并没有放弃自己的计划。Despite many setbacks, he did not give up his plan.

遭瘟 zāowēn 〈方言〉❶ be smitten with a plague; suffer from pestilence ❷ (as a curse) bring misfortune or disaster to: 这个～的天气，立秋后还这么热! What wretched weather! It's still so hot now autumn has set in!

遭殃 zāoyāng suffer disaster or calamity; suffer: 森林火灾使那一带的野生动物～了。The forest fire was a disaster for the wildlife of the area. /他不愿因为自己的缘故让大家～。He didn't want the others to suffer on his account. /你如果得罪他，你早晚得～。You will get into trouble sooner or later if you offend him.

遭遇 zāoyù ❶ come across; encounter; run into: ～挫折 suffer (*or* meet with) setbacks /～车祸 have a traffic accident /～不幸 have bad luck; meet with adversity /我突击部队和敌人的巡逻队～上了。Our shock troops encountered (*or* ran into) the enemy patrol. ❷ (bitter) experience; (hapless) fate; (hard) lot: 我们同情她的不幸～。We have sympathy for her misfortune. /他童年的～催人泪下。His bitter childhood experiences brought tears to our eyes. /但愿今后不再有这样的～。Let's hope that such things will never happen again.

遭遇战 zāoyùzhàn 〈军事〉encounter; meeting engagement; contact battle

遭灾 zāozāi suffer disaster; be hit by a natural calamity

遭罪 zāozuì suffer hardships, tortures, etc.; suffer: 给他打一针吧，别让他～了。Please give him an injection to relieve his pain. /看他～的样子，真受不了。I can't bear to see him suffer like this.

záo

凿[1]（鑿） záo ❶ chisel: 平～ broad chisel /扁～ flat chisal; plain chisel /槽～ groove chisel; framing (*or* heading) chisel ❷ bore a hole; chisel; dig: ～冰 cut (*or* make) a hole in the ice /在门上～个窟窿 bore a hole in the door /～地道 dig a tunnel /用大理石～一尊雕像 chisel a statue out of (*or* from) the marble /～一条隧道穿过这岩石 tunnel through the rock

凿[2]（鑿） záo 〈书面〉mortise; hole: 方枘圆～ square peg in a round hole — incompatible

凿[3]（鑿） záo 〈书面〉certain; sure; authentic; irrefutable: 证据确～ the evidence is conclusive; (sth.) be proved beyond doubt

凿槽机 záocáojī 〈机械〉mortising slot machine

凿定 záodìng 〈方言〉certainly; surely: 我明天～要回家去。I must go home tomorrow.

凿工 záogōng chiseller

凿沟机 záogōujī 〈机械〉channeller; channelling machine

凿井 záojǐng ❶ dig (*or* sink, *or* bore) a well ❷ 〈矿业〉shaft sinking; pit sinking: 冻结法～ freeze sinking /～工 shaftman

凿空 záokōng 〈书面〉forced; farfetched; implausible: ～之谈 irrelevant talk

凿孔机 záokǒngjī puncher; perferator; mortising machine

凿密 záomì 〈机械〉caulking

凿枘 záoruì *also* "枘凿"〈书面〉❶ mortise and tenon — compatible; in harmony ❷ (short for 圆凿方枘) square tenon for a round mortise — incompatible; square peg in a round hole; at variance with each other

凿死理儿 záo sǐlǐr 〈方言〉obstinate; bigoted; dogged: 他这人爱～。He is as stubborn as a mule.

凿榫 záosǔn mortise: ～机 mortiser; mortising machine

凿形犁 záoxínglí 〈农业〉chisel plough

凿岩 záoyán 〈矿业〉(rock) drilling

凿岩机 záoyánjī rock drill

凿凿 záozáo 〈书面〉true; certain; positive: 言之～ speak with assurance /～有据 with indisputable evidence (*or* proof)

凿子 záozi chisel

zǎo

枣（棗） zǎo jujube; (Chinese) date: 红～ dried jujube (*or* date) /～林 jujube grove /黑～ dateplum persimmon

枣脯 zǎofǔ dried dates preserved in honey

枣糕 zǎogāo cake made of wheat flour and dates

枣圪针 zǎogēzhen *also* "枣针" thorns on the jujube tree

枣红 zǎohóng purplish red; claret

枣骝马 zǎoliúmǎ purplish red horse

枣泥 zǎoní jujube paste: ～月饼 moon cake with jujube paste filling

枣泥酥 zǎonísū shortbread with jujube paste filling

枣树 zǎoshù jujube tree: 满山坡都是～。The slope is covered with jujube trees.

枣椰 zǎoyē date palm

枣子 zǎozi jujube; date

早 zǎo ❶ morning: 清～ early morning /从～到晚 from morning to night; from dawn till dusk /～出晚归 leave early in the morning and return late at night /一大～就出发 set out before dawn ❷ long time ago; as early as: 他～就毕业了。It has been a long time since he graduated. *or* He graduated long ago. /～在两年前他们就搬走了。They moved out as early as two years ago. /我～就想和你聊聊了。I have been wanting to have a chat with you. ❸ (as in a time sequence) former; previous; early: *see* "～先"; "～年"; "～稻" ❹ earlier (than scheduled or expected); beforehand; in advance; early: ～睡～起 go to bed early and get up early; early to bed and early to rise /小车～开了十分钟。The car left ten minutes in advance. /你～来两天就好了。If only you had come two days earlier. /别着急，离火车开动还～着呢。Take your time. It's still quite a while before the train leaves. /请尽～答复。Please reply at your earliest convenience. *or* An early reply would be appreciated. ❺ (word of greeting) good morning: 先生～! Good morning, sir!

早安 zǎo'ān good morning: 互道～ greet each other by saying "good morning"; say "good morning" to each other

早白垩纪 Zǎobái'èjì 〈地质〉Early Cretaceous Epoch

早班 zǎobān ❶ morning shift: 上～ be on morning shift ❷ 〈方言〉(rise, come, etc.) early: 您二位真～呀，离开会还有一小时呢。You are

early birds. It's still an hour before the meeting starts.
早半天儿 zǎobàntiānr *also* "早半晌儿"〈口语〉in the morning; before noon:这～我什么活儿也没干。I have done nothing the whole morning.
早搏 zǎobó 〈医学〉premature beat; extrasystole
早餐 zǎocān breakfast:我今天～吃咸肉煎蛋。I had bacon and eggs for breakfast today.
早操 zǎocāo morning exercises:做～ do morning exercises
早茶 zǎochá morning tea:粤式～ Guangdong-style breakfast
早产 zǎochǎn 〈医学〉premature delivery or birth:孩子～了一个月。The baby was born a month before it was due.
早产儿 zǎochǎn'ér premature baby
早产儿保育箱 zǎochǎn'ér bǎoyùxiāng infant incubator
早场 zǎochǎng morning show (at a cinema, theatre, etc.):～票 ticket for the morning show
早车 zǎochē morning train or bus:搭～进城 go to town on the morning bus
早晨 zǎochen (early) morning
早春 zǎochūn early spring:～时节 in early spring
早稻 zǎodào early (season) rice:播种～ sow early rice /～丰收 fine crop (*or* good harvest) of early rice
早稻田大学 Zǎodàotián Dàxué (Japan) Waseda University
早点 zǎodiǎn (light) breakfast:匆匆吃些～ eat a light breakfast hurriedly; hurry through a light breakfast; snatch a hasty breakfast
早饭 zǎofàn breakfast:没吃～就上班 go to work without breakfast /～一定要吃饱。One should have a substantial breakfast.
早古生代 Zǎogǔshēngdài 〈地质〉Lower Paleozoic Era
早禾树 zǎohéshù coral tree
早花 zǎohuā 〈农业〉early blossoming
早慧 zǎohuì precocious:～神童 child prodigy
早婚 zǎohūn marrying too early; early marriage:在某些农村地区,～相当普遍。It is fairly common for people in some Chinese villages to get married at an early age. *or* Early marriage is still fairly common in some villages.
早经 zǎojīng already:他每日清晨跑步,～习以为常。He is already accustomed to going for a jog every morning.
早课 zǎokè (of a Buddhist monk) chant scriptures or sutra in the morning
早恋 zǎoliàn puppy love; calf love
早年 zǎonián ❶ many years ago; in the past:～这里不通汽车。There was no bus service here in the past. ❷ in one's early years:他～在上海居住。He lived in Shanghai in his early years.
早期 zǎoqī early stage; early phase:他被确诊为～胃癌。His case was diagnosed as early stage gastric cancer (*or* carcinoma). *or* The diagnosis revealed that he was in the early stage of gastric cancer.
早期白话 zǎoqī báihuà writings in the vernacular between the Tang and Song dynasties and the May 4th Movement of 1919; early writings in the vernacular:这些小说是用～写的。These novels were written in the early vernacular.
早期报警卫星 zǎoqī bàojǐng wèixīng early-warning satellite
早期电影放映机 zǎoqī diànyǐng fàngyìngjī biograph
早期症状 zǎoqī zhèngzhuàng 〈医学〉incipient or early symptom(s)
早起 zǎoqi 〈方言〉(early) morning:今儿～ early this morning
早前 zǎoqián 〈方言〉previously; in the past:他～教过法语。He taught French in the past.
早清儿 zǎoqīngr 〈方言〉(early) morning:我从～转到过午,也没找到他。I looked for him from morning till afternoon, but all in vain (*or* but he was nowhere to be found).
早秋 zǎoqiū early autumn
早日 zǎorì ❶ at an early date; early; soon:～归来 return as soon as possible /争取～建交 work for the establishment of diplomatic relations at an early date /希望～读到你的大作。I hope to have the pleasure of reading your work soon. ❷ in the past:这古庙失去了～的光彩。The ancient temple has lost its past lustre.
早晌 zǎoshǎng 〈方言〉morning
早上 zǎoshang (early) morning
早生品种 zǎoshēng pǐnzhǒng early maturing variety
早市 zǎoshì ❶ morning fair; morning market ❷ morning business transactions; morning business:本店～供应各种早点。Our restaurant offers a variety of foods for breakfast in the morning.
早是 zǎoshì ❶〈书面〉already:～离人伤感,况值暮秋时候。Parting is already sorrowful enough, All the more so in late autumn. ❷ (often used in the early vernacular) luckily; fortunately
早逝 zǎoshì 〈婉词〉die an early (*or* an untimely, *or* a premature) death; die young
早熟 zǎoshú ❶〈生理〉precocity:如今的孩子一般都～。Children on the average mature early nowadays. ❷ early-ripe; early-maturing:～玉米 early-maturing maize
早熟禾 zǎoshúhé bluegrass
早熟品种 zǎoshú pǐnzhǒng early-maturing variety; early variety
早熟栽培 zǎoshú zāipéi early-maturing culture
早熟作物 zǎoshú zuòwù early-maturing crop; early crop
早衰 zǎoshuāi 〈医学〉premature senility or decrepitude; early ageing:记忆力～ early declining (*or* failing) of one's memory
早霜 zǎoshuāng early frost:普降～。Early frost occurred in large areas.
早岁 zǎosuì one's early years
早退 zǎotuì leave earlier than is allowed according to the regulations; leave early:迟到～ arrive late and leave early
早晚 zǎowǎn ❶ morning and evening:～散步都可以。You can go for a walk either in the morning or in the evening. ❷ sooner or later; one of these days:～你会引以为憾的。You will regret it sooner or later. ❸ time:这～他许是到上海了。He may have arrived in Shanghai by this time. ❹〈方言〉some time in the future; some future time; some day:我～有空就来看你。I will drop in on you if I have time.
早晚服务部 zǎowǎn fúwùbù before-and-after hours shop; department for after-hours service
早午餐 zǎowǔcān brunch
早先 zǎoxiān formerly; previously; before:你比～高多了。You've grown much taller than before. /～的荒山坡,现在是果树林了。The barren hillside has now become a grove of fruit trees.
早泄 zǎoxiè 〈医学〉premature ejaculation
早已 zǎoyǐ ❶ for a long period of time; long ago:此事～决定。This was decided long ago. /这使他想起了～忘却的往事。It reminded him of things he had long forgotten. ❷〈方言〉in the past:现在人们大都用钢笔写字,～都用毛笔。Nowadays most people write with pens while in the past they used writing brushes.
早育 zǎoyù early child-bearing:不提倡早婚～。Early marriage and child-birth is discouraged.
早早儿 zǎozǎor as soon as possible; well in advance:她～地就来了。She came well ahead of time. /这项工程最好～就开工。This project should be started as early as possible.
早造 zǎozào early (season) crops:夺回～受灾的损失 make up the early crop losses caused by the natural disaster
早知 zǎozhī precognition; foreknowledge
早知今日,悔不当初 zǎo zhī jīnrì, huǐ bù dāngchū *also* "早知如此,悔不当初" had I known it, I wouldn't have done it; if only I knew

澡

zǎo bath:洗个凉水～ take a cold bath /搓～ give sb. a rubdown with a wet towel /擦～ rub oneself down with a damp towel; take a sponge bath /给婴儿洗～ give the baby a bath
澡帕 zǎopà 〈方言〉bath towel
澡盆 zǎopén bathtub:木制～ wooden bath
澡身浴德 zǎoshēn-yùdé keep one's moral integrity through self-cultivation
澡堂 zǎotáng public baths; bathhouse:男～ public baths for men; men's bathhouse
澡塘 zǎotáng ❶ common bathing pool (in a bathhouse) ❷ *see* "澡堂"
澡雪精神 zǎoxuě-jīngshén 〈书面〉purify one's spirit by cleansing; rid people of philistime ideas

璪

zǎo silk tassels threaded with jades hanging from a crown

藻

zǎo ❶ algae:水～ algae /小球～ chlorella /螺旋～ *Spirulina platensis* ❷ aquatic plants ❸ literary adornment:辞～ ornate diction
藻绘 zǎohuì embellishment; flowery description
藻井 zǎojǐng 〈建筑〉coffer; sunk panel; caisson ceiling
藻类学 zǎolèixué algology:～家 algologist
藻类植物 zǎolèi zhíwù algae
藻丽 zǎolì 〈书面〉(language) flowery

藻煤 zǎoméi boghead coal
藻饰 zǎoshì 〈书面〉embellishments in writing：忌～ avoid flowery language
藻虾 zǎoxiā grass shrimp

蚤

zǎo flea：水～ water flea /沙～ beach flea；sand hopper
蚤草 zǎocǎo fleabane；fleawort
蚤蝼 zǎolóu pygmy sand cricket；pygmy mole cricket
蚤蝇 zǎoyíng humpbacked fly；coffin fly

zào

灶（竈）

zào ❶ kitchen range；cooking stove：煤气～ gas stove（*or* range）/土～ kitchen range made of adobe /另起炉～ set up（*or* start）a new stove（*or* kitchen）— make a fresh start ❷ kitchen；mess；canteen；cafeteria：开小～ dine in a special mess；have special mess /学生～ students' cafeteria or canteen /教工～ teachers' dining room；cafeteria for the staff（in a school）❸ kitchen god：祭～ offer sacrifices to the kitchen god
灶房 zàofáng *also* "灶屋"〈方言〉kitchen
灶火 zàohuo 〈方言〉❶ kitchen ❷ kitchen range；cooking stove：～上烧着一壶水。A kettle is boiling on the stove.
灶间 zàojiān kitchen
灶具 zàojù 〈方言〉cooking utensils
灶君 Zàojūn *see* "灶神"
灶马 zàomǎ camel cricket；cave cricket
灶鸟 zàoniǎo ovenbird
灶披间 zàopījiān 〈方言〉kitchen
灶神 Zàoshén *also* "灶王爷"；"灶君" kitchen god；god of the hearth：供奉～ enshrine and worship the kitchen god
灶神星 Zàoshénxīng 〈天文〉Vesta
灶台 zàotái top of a kitchen range
灶膛 zàotáng chamber of a stove or a kitchen range
灶糖 zàotáng malt sugar；maltose
灶头 zàotou 〈方言〉kitchen range；cooking stove：锅碗都放在～上。The pots, pans and bowls were all put on top of the kitchen range.
灶突 zàotū 〈书面〉stovepipe；chimney；flue
灶王爷 Zàowangyé *see* "灶神"
灶屋 zàowū 〈方言〉*see* "灶房"

燥

zào dry：干～ dry；arid
燥火 zàohuǒ *see* "燥热❷"
燥裂 zàoliè dry and chapped：皮肤～ chapped skin
燥热 zàorè ❶ hot and dry：这里冬季干冷，夏季～。It's cold and dry here in winter and hot and dry in summer. ❷〈中医〉suffer from loss of body fluid（with such symptoms as toothache, tinnitus, dry cough, etc.）
燥湿 zàoshī 〈中医〉using bitter medicine of a dry or cold nature for the treatment of excessive internal humidness

噪（❷譟）

zào ❶（of birds, insects, etc.）chirp：群鸦乱～。Numerous crows are cawing. ❷ make an uproar；clamour：聒～ make an uproar ❸ become well known：声名大～ gain great fame /名～一时 be enormously popular for a time
噪聒 zàoguō 〈方言〉be noisy；be clamorous；make an uproar：乌鸦～，令人心烦意乱。The caw of the crows is getting on my nerves.
噪叫 zàojiào （of birds or insects）chirp
噪鹃 zàojuān Chinese koel or cuckoo
噪鹛 zàoméi laughing thrush
噪嚷 zàorǎng clamour；hubbub；din：别～了！Stop that noise！/门外一阵～，惊醒了他的午睡。The din outside woke him up from his afternoon nap.
噪声 zàoshēng *also* "噪音" noise；din：～扰人。The noise is disturbing（*or* annoying）.
噪声监测 zàoshēng jiāncè noise monitoring
噪声治理 zàoshēng zhìlǐ noise abatement
噪音 zàoyīn ❶ discordant（as distinct from musical 乐音）❷ *also* "噪声" noise：降低～ reduce noise /～测试 noise testing /低～马达 low-noise motor
噪音防护器 zàoyīn fánghùqì noise protector
噪音干扰 zàoyīn gānrǎo noise jamming
噪音驱鸟器 zàoyīn qūniǎoqì bird rattle
噪音污染 zàoyīn wūrǎn 〈环保〉noise pollution
噪音抑制 zàoyīn yìzhì 〈无线电〉noise suppression
噪杂 zàozá （of voices）loud and confused：街头人声～ hubbub of the streets
噪钟鹊 zàozhōngquè currawong；piping-crow；crow-shrike

躁

zào rash；impetuous；impulsive：烦～ irritable；agitated；restless /急～ impetuous；rash；impatient /戒骄戒～ guard against arrogance（*or* conceit）and rashness（*or* impetuosity）/他的脾气太～。He is too hot-tempered（*or* quick-tempered）.
躁动 zàodòng ❶ move agitatedly；be jittery：～不安的婴孩 fretful baby /用大红气球拖着的巨幅标语，像是一条条～的玉龙，挣扎着要往东飞去。The giant slogans hoisted by red balloons look like restless jade dragons, struggling to fly eastward. ❷ keep moving up and down；beat；pulsate；throb：～于母腹中的快要成熟了的婴儿 child about to be born moving restlessly in its mother's womb
躁汗 zàohàn sweat（as with anxiety, agitation, etc.）：他急出了一身～。He sweated all over with anxiety.
躁急 zàojí irritable；rash；impetuous；restless：他生性～。He has a hot temperament.
躁进 zàojìn 〈书面〉be overanxious；be impatient（usu. for fame and position）：此人性褊而～。The man is narrow-minded and craves impatiently for fame and position.
躁狂 zàokuáng 〈医学〉mania：～者 maniac

造[1]

zào ❶ make；build；construct；create：创～ invent；create /建～ build；construct /～机器 make（*or* manufacture）machines/～花名册 compile a register（of names）/～预算 draw up（*or* make）a budget /通过传媒大～舆论 whip up public opinion through mass media /生～词语 coin words and expressions /这楼是用钢筋水泥～的。The building was constructed of reinforced concrete. ❷ fabricate；cook up；concoct：～假象 create a false image；put up a facade /～谣言 start a rumour；cook up a story /捏～罪名 trump up charges against sb.

造[2]

zào ❶ one of the two parties to a legal agreement or in a lawsuit：两～具备 both parties are present /甲～ first party ❷〈方言〉crop：早～ early crops /一年三～皆丰收。We reaped three bumper crops this year.

造[3]

zào ❶〈书面〉go to；arrive at；reach：～门迎宾 meet the guest at the door /登峰～极 reach great heights；reach the peak of perfection ❷ achievements；accomplishments；success：～诣 academic or artistic attainments ❸ train；educate；cultivate：可～之才 person of promise；hopeful（*or* promising）young person /深～ pursue advanced studies；have further specialized training
造币厂 zàobìchǎng mint
造册 zàocè tabulation
造成 zàochéng cause；give rise to；bring about；result in：～被动局面 land sb.（*or* oneself）in a passive position /～不可弥补的损失 cause irreparable losses /～失误 make an error /～严重后果 entail（*or* have, *or* lead to）serious consequences /～思想混乱 create ideological confusion /～灾难 bring about a disaster /经济萧条～了广大的失业群。The depression gave rise to widespread unemployment.
造船 zàochuán shipbuilding：～工人 shipbuilder
造船厂 zàochuánchǎng shipyard；dockyard
造船工业 zàochuán gōngyè shipbuilding industry
造次 zàocì 〈书面〉❶ hurried；hasty：～之间 in a hurry；in a moment of haste ❷ rash；imprudent；impetuous：不可～。Don't be impetuous（*or* rash）. /这样做过于～。This is a reckless move indeed.
造端 zàoduān 〈书面〉begin；start；originate
造反 zàofǎn rise in rebellion；rebel；mutiny；revolt
造反派 zàofǎnpài rebel faction（a term for those who rose against the "capitalist and reactionary line" and "capitalist roaders" during the Cultural Revolution in China, 1966-1976）
造饭 zàofàn （often used in the early vernacular）prepare a meal：埋锅～ set the pot to prepare a meal
造访 zàofǎng 〈书面〉pay a visit（at sb.'s house）；call on
造福 zàofú bring benefit to；do good for：～后代 benefit posterity

(*or* future generations) /为人民～ work for the well-being of the people
造府 zàofǔ 〈书面〉call at your house: ～拜访 call at sb.'s house; call on sb. at his house /～求教 call on sb. for counsel; come to seek advice
造管术 zàoguǎnshù 〈医学〉canalization
造化 zàohuà 〈书面〉❶ the Creator; Nature: ～是公正的,只要你勤劳,她总会给你报偿。Nature is fair; she'll reward you if you work hard. /～予人,可谓多矣! How generous Nature is towards man! ❷ create; nurture: 如此胜景,只能由天地～。Only Mother Nature can create such scenic beauty.
造化 zàohua smile of fortune; good luck: 这可是我的～了! It's just my luck! /是否成功,这要看他有没有～了。It is a matter of luck whether he is successful or not.
造化小儿 zàohuà-xiǎo'ér god of destiny; god of fate
造话 zàohuà 〈方言〉lie; untruth
造激素系统 zàojīsù xìtǒng 〈生理〉hormonopoietic system; hormone production system
造价 zàojià cost (of construction or manufacture): 这座大厦～太高。It costs too much to build the mansion. /这种机床质量好,～低。This kind of machine tool is of good quality and low cost.
造就 zàojiù ❶ create; train; bring up: ～人才 train competent personnel /～了新一代知识分子 bring up a new generation of intellectuals /时代～英雄。The times produce (*or* create) their heroes. ❷ (usu. of young people) achievements; attainments: 学术上的～ scholarly (*or* scholastic) attainments /他在专业上的～很深。He is a man of great accomplishments in his field.
造句 zàojù sentence-making: 学习～ learn to make (*or* construct) sentences
造口术 zàokǒushù 〈医学〉ostomy
造块 zàokuài 〈冶金〉agglomeration
造林 zàolín afforestation: ～成活率 survival rate of afforestation /在大片荒地上～ forest a wide stretch of wasteland /～面积 area under afforestation; afforested area
造林学 zàolínxué silviculture; sylviculture
造陆运动 zàolù yùndòng 〈地质〉epeirogenic or epeirogenetic movement; epeirogeny; epeirogenesis
造魔 zàomo *also* "造模"〈方言〉tell a lie; start a rumour: 别听他瞎～。Don't listen to him. He is telling the wildest of stories.
造孽 zàoniè *also* "作孽" zuòniè ❶〈宗教〉do evil; commit a sin: 这简直是～。This is downright sinning. ❷〈方言〉pitiful; pitiable; poor: 这孩子没爹没娘,多～啊! What a poor orphan!
造山带 zàoshāndài 〈地质〉orogenic zone
造山运动 zàoshān yùndòng 〈地质〉orogenic movement; orogeny; orogenesis
造始 zàoshǐ 〈书面〉begin; come into being: 此事～于两年之前。It all began two years ago.
造微入妙 zàowēi-rùmiào (of painting, etc.) reach the acme of perfection; be superb
造物 zàowù divine force that created the universe; Nature
造物主 Zàowùzhǔ 〈宗教〉God; the Creator
造像 zàoxiàng 〈美术〉statue: ～生动 lifelike statue
造心机 zàoxīnjī 〈冶金〉core machine
造型 zàoxíng ❶ modelling; mould-making ❷ model; mould; form: ～独特 unique in shape /纪念碑上的浮雕,～栩栩如生。The carvings in relief on the monument are true to life. /泥塑的～富有新意。The shapes of the clay figures are quite original. ❸〈机械〉moulding: ～车间 moulding workshop /干砂～ dry sand moulding /潮砂～ green sand moulding /开砂～ open sand moulding
造型板 zàoxíngbǎn mould board
造型艺术 zàoxíng yìshù plastic arts
造血 zàoxuè ❶ hematopoiesis; hemopoiesis: ～器官 blood forming organ /～系统 hemopoietic system /～障碍性贫血 hypoproliferative anemia ❷〈比喻〉internal functions (of a department, district, etc. in solving its own problems or promoting its own development): 坚持科技扶贫就是增强贫穷地区的～机能。To give persistent scientific and technological aid to backward areas is to strengthen their internal functions.
造谣 zàoyáo cook up a story; spread a rumour: ～可耻。It's shameful to spread rumours. /他们以～来混淆视听。They misled the public by rumourmongering.
造谣惑众 zàoyáo-huòzhòng *also* "造言惑众" spread rumours to confuse the people
造谣生事 zàoyáo-shēngshì start a rumour to create disturbances; stir up trouble by rumourmongering
造谣诬蔑 zàoyáo-wūmiè spread rumours and sling mud at: 极尽～之能事 stop at nothing to spread rumours and sling mud (at sb.); have no scruples at all about rumourmongering and mudslinging
造谣者 zàoyáozhě rumourmonger
造谣中伤 zàoyáo-zhòngshāng circulate calumnious rumours
造诣 zàoyì (academic) achievments; (artistic) attainments: 文学～高深 of high literary attainments /有～的作家 accomplished writer /在明史研究方面,他是一个极有～的学者。He is a distinguished scholar of the history of the Ming Dynasty.
造意 zàoyì 〈书面〉initiate; start
造影 zàoyǐng 〈医学〉radiography: 支气管～ brochography /钡餐～检查 barium meal examination
造园鸟 zàoyuánniǎo bowerbird
造渣 zàozhā 〈冶金〉slag making; slag formation
造纸 zàozhǐ papermaking: ～工业 papermaking industry
造纸厂 zàozhǐchǎng paper mill
造纸机 zàozhǐjī paper machine
造纸术 zàozhǐshù papermaking technology
造作 zàozuò make; manufacture: ～飞机模型 make a model plane /～小型照相机 manufacture miniature cameras
造作 zàozuo affected; unnatural; artificial: 举止矫揉～ be affected in manner

慥 zào

慥慥 zàozào 〈书面〉honest and sincere

簉 zào 〈书面〉secondary; subsidiary

簉室 zàoshì 〈旧语〉concubine

皂(阜) zào ❶ black: ～衣 black coat ❷〈旧语〉office boy; *yamen* runner ❸ soap: 香～ toilet soap /药～ medicated soap /婴儿～ baby toilet soap

皂白 zàobái black and white — right and wrong: 青红不分,～莫辨 not distinguish black from white — make no distinction between (*or* confound) right and wrong
皂泵 zàobèng 〈机械〉soap pump
皂苷 zàogān saponin
皂化 zàohuà 〈化工〉saponification: ～剂 saponifier /～乳化剂 saponified emulsifier /～石油 saponated petroleum
皂荚 zàojiá *also* "皂角"〈植物〉Chinese honey locust
皂角苷 zàojiǎogān 〈化工〉saponin
皂隶 zàolì *yamen* runner
皂片 zàopiàn soap flakes
皂石 zàoshí 〈矿业〉saponite; soaprock; soapstone
皂素 zàosù saponin
皂洗机 zàoxǐjī 〈纺织〉soaper: 平幅～ open soaper

埠 zào 〈方言〉col

唣(啅) zào *see* "罗唣" luózào

zé

责 zé ❶ duty; obligation; responsibility: 专～ specific responsibility /尽～ do one's duty /为国效劳,人人有～。Everyone has a duty to his country. ❷ demand; exact; require: ～人宽,～己严 be strict with oneself and generous towards others /循名～实 see that the reality matches the name ❸ interrogate; question closely; call sb. to account ❹ criticize; reproach; blame; reprove: 斥～ denounce; reprimand; rebuke /指～ criticize; censure /谴～ condemn /苛～ excoriate; criticize severely /自～ reprove (*or* blame) oneself /痛～ castigate; rebuke severely ❺ punish: 笞～ punish by flogging

责备 zébèi reproach; blame; reprimand; give sb. a (good) wigging: ～的话 word of reproach /狠狠地～他忘恩负义 rebuke him bitterly for ingratitude /受到良心的～ feel a prick of conscience; be conscience-stricken /求全～ demand perfection; nitpick /那是他自己

Z

的过错，～不着别人。He can't blame anybody else for his own fault. / 上级～下来，我们怎么交代? How can we clear ourselves if the boss lays the blame on us?

责编 zébiān (short for 责任编辑) editor in charge (in a publishing house for the finishing work of a text, manuscript, etc.); editor

责成 zéchéng instruct (a person or an organization to fulfil a task); order (sb. to do sth.):经理～他监督新来的雇员。The manager instructed him to oversee the new employees.

责斥 zéchì reprimand; rebuke:厉声～ reprimand severely; excoriate /警察～司机开车太鲁莽。The policeman bawled at the driver for reckless driving.

责打 zédǎ punish by beating

责罚 zéfá punish; penalize:严加～ punish severely; mete out a severe punishment /因违反操作规程受到～ be punished for violation of the operating rules and regulations

责怪 zéguài blame; reproach:投以～的目光 cast a look of reproach (on) /不要一味地～孩子。Don't blame everything (*or* lay all the blame) on the child. /计划行不通，不能全～他。It is not all his fault that the plan didn't work. *or* He is not solely responsible for the failure of the plan.

责令 zélìng order; instruct; enjoin; charge:～有关部门采取措施防止此类事件再次发生 instruct the department concerned to take measures to prevent the recurrence of similar incidents

责骂 zémà scold; reprove; rebuke; dress down:挨了一顿～ get a good scolding (*or* dressing-down) /经理～他无礼。The manager told him off for his insolence.

责难 zénàn censure; reproach; blame:受到公开～ receive a public censure /备受～ be blamed in every possible way

责任 zérèn ❶ duty; obligation; responsibility:明确～ clearly define one's responsibilities /尽～ do one's duty; fulfil one's obligation / 他没有尽到做父亲的～。He neglected (*or* failed to perform) his paternal duties. /帮助贫困者和残疾人是我们的～。We are duty-bound to help the needy and handicapped. /他有～赡养父母。It is incumbent upon him to provide for his parents. ❷ responsibility for a wrong or failing to do what one should; blame:推卸～ shirk responsibility; shift the blame onto others; pass the buck /对由此而产生的一切严重后果承担全部～ bear full responsibility for all the serious consequences arising therefrom /此事必须由他负法律～。He must be held legally responsible for this. /我愿承担这起事故的～。I am ready to take the blame for the accident. *or* I admit my liability for the accident.

责任保险 zérèn bǎoxiǎn liability insurance

责任编辑 zérèn biānjí *see* "责编"

责任感 zérèngǎn *also* "责任心" sense of responsibility; sense of duty

责任事故 zérèn shìgù accident due to dereliction of duty; accident involving criminal or civil liability

责任田 zérèntián responsibility field (a term for the land which a production team contracts out, in accordance with relevant regulations, to a production group, household, or individual to cultivate)

责任制 zérènzhì responsibility system; system of job responsibility:实行岗位～ adopt the system of job responsibility /多种形式的生产～ diverse forms of responsibility system for production /家庭联产承包～ system of contracted responsibilities on the household basis with remuneration linked to output; contractual household responsibility system linking remuneration to output

责任状 zérènzhuàng responsibility pledge (a pledge to have a job done, failing which the pledger would be ready to accept penalty)

责望 zéwàng 〈书面〉 blame; censure; complain:因职责不明而相～ blame each other due to lack of clear definition of responsibilities

责问 zéwèn ask reprovingly; call sb. to account:我有件事要～他。I have a bone to pick with him. /出纳因现金丢失而受到～。The cashier was called to account over some missing cash.

Z

责无旁贷 zéwúpángdài be one's unshirkable responsibility; be duty-bound:为祖国的现代化作贡献，我们～。It is incumbent upon us (*or* our unshirkable responsibility) to contribute to the modernization of our country. /她觉得照顾这两个孤儿自己～。She considered it her duty to look after the two orphans.

责有攸归 zéyǒuyōuguī responsibility rests where it belongs:因循坐误，～。The responsibility will fall squarely on those who procrastinate and allow the situation to deteriorate. *or* Those who procrastinate accept full responsibility for the worsening situation.

责怨 zéyuàn censure; blame; complain

赜

zé 〈书面〉 subtle; profound; abstruse:探～索隐 search for hidden meanings; investigate and trace what is hidden

啧

zé ❶〈书面〉 subtle; abstruse ❷ dispute; compete for a chance to speak ❸ click of the tongue

啧有烦言 zéyǒu-fányán there are complaints all around; there are a lot of complaints:此事给大家造成很多不便，因而～。The matter that caused much inconvenience to people has given rise to widespread complaints.

啧啧 zézé ❶ click of the tongue:～赞叹 be profuse in one's praise / 人言～。There is a good deal of public criticism. ❷〈书面〉 chirping:雀声～。Sparrows are chirping.

啧啧称羡 zézé-chēngxiàn *also* "啧啧称赞" click the tongue in admiration; highly praise:她的演技令同行们～。Her acting is greatly admired by her colleagues.

帻

zé man's headdress used in ancient China

箦

zé bed mat made of woven strips of bamboo:易～ change the mat (of a dying person)

齰(齚)

zé 〈书面〉 bite

则[1]

zé ❶ standard; gauge; norm; criterion:准～ criterion; standard /以身作～ set an example by one's own conduct ❷ rule; decree; regulation:总～ general rules; general principles /细～ detailed rules and regulations /法～ law; rule /章～ rules and regulations /小学生守～ rules of conduct for primary school pupils ❸〈书面〉 take as a model; imitate; follow:～先烈之言行 follow the example of the martyrs in word and deed ❹〈量词〉 item (of news); paragraph or piece (of writing):一～新闻 an item of news /寓言两～ two fables /笑话一～ a joke /试题四～ four examination questions

则[2]

zé ❶〈书面〉〈连词〉 (a) *indicating that one action follows another*:每首歌曲唱完，～掌声四起。Each song was greeted by loud applause. (b) *indicating cause and effect, condition, etc.*:欲速～不达。More haste, less speed. *or* Haste makes waste. /唇亡～齿寒。If the lips are gone, the teeth will be cold. /兼听～明，偏听～暗 listen to both sides and you will be enlightened; heed only one side and you will be benighted (c) *indicating contrast*:其事虽易为，其理～难明。While the work is easy to do, the reason is hard to explain. /夜深了，人们都已入睡，而他～在紧张备课。It was late at night, and everyone was asleep, but he was still busy preparing his lessons. (d) *used between two identical words to indicate concession*:你的方法好～好，却不易学会。Though your method is good, it is difficult to learn. ❷ *used together with* 一，二，三 *to enumerate causes or reasons*:他没有考上大学，一～基础差，二～复习时间短，三～临考时发高烧。He failed the matriculation (*or* college entrance) examination because, first, he lacked a good grounding in the subjects; second, he didn't have enough time for revision; and third, he was running a high fever when the examination was close at hand. ❸〈书面〉 be:此～意料中之事也! That's to be expected! /此～众人之力，非我一人之功。The credit should go to the collective, not to me alone.

则个 zégè (often used in the early vernacular) *placed at the end of a sentence to indicate hope or wish or for emphasis, balance or euphony*:你要仔细～。You must be careful.

则例 zélì 〈书面〉 set rules; regulations

则甚 zéshèn (often used in the early vernacular) what for:你理他～? Why pay attention to him?

则声 zéshēng make a sound; speak:他只好不～。He could only keep silent. /此事真叫我～不得。I'd better refrain from making any comment on this matter.

迮

zé ❶〈书面〉 narrow ❷ (Zé) a surname

咋

zé 〈书面〉 bite

see also zǎ; zhā

咋舌 zéshé 〈书面〉bite into one's tongue or refrain from speech (as a result of bitter remorse or great fear)

舴 zé

舴艋 zéměng 〈书面〉small boat

泽(澤) zé ❶ pool; pond; swamp:沼～ swamp; marsh /湖～ lakes /深山大～ remote mountains and large rivers and lakes ❷ wet; moist; damp:润～肌肤 wet one's skin ❸ lustre (of metals, pearls, etc.):光～ lustre; gloss; sheen /色～鲜明 bright colour and lustre ❹〈书面〉favour; largesse; beneficence:恩～ favour; beneficence /名闻天下,～流后世。His name spreads far and wide, and his benevolence reaches down to later generations.

泽国 zéguó 〈书面〉❶ land that abounds in rivers and lakes:我们这里是有名的水乡～。Our region is famous for its rivers and lakes. ❷ flooded area:连降暴雨,此地沦为～。The area became submerged due to the continual storms.

泽鸡 zéjī moorhen; common gallinule

泽兰 zélán ❶ boneset (*Eupatorium perfoliatum*) ❷ Japanese Eupatorium (*Eupatorium japonicum*)

泽鹿 zélù *also* "坡鹿" pōlù 〈动物〉slope deer (*Cervus eldi*)

泽漆 zéqī wartwort (*Euphorbia helioscopia*)

泽润 zérùn moist; wet

泽泻 zéxiè 〈中药〉rhizome of oriental water plantain (*Alisma plantago-aquatica* var. *orientale*)

泽西牛 zéxīniú *also* "娟姗牛" juānshānniú Jersey (cow)

泽鹰 zéyīng marsh hawk

择(擇) zé select; choose; opt for; pick:～日动工 fix a date to begin construction /～婿嫁女 choose a worthy husband for one's daughter /不～手段 by hook or by crook; unscrupulously /饥不～食 hunger finds no fault with the cooking; hungry dogs will eat dirty pudding; beggers can't be choosers /无选～余地。This is Hobson's choice.
see also zhái

择伐 zéfá 〈林业〉selective cutting or felling:～矮林作业 selective coppice system /～作业 selective system

择肥而噬 zéféi'érshì pick out the rich as one's target of blackmail:这些差役们个个摩拳擦掌,～。The bailiffs all rolled up their sleeves, ready to squeeze a fortune out of the rich.

择吉 zéjí select an auspicious day (for a marriage, funeral, etc.):～开张 choose an anspicious (*or* lucky) day to start a business

择交 zéjiāo choose friends:～而友 be cautious in choosing one's friends

择偶 zé'ǒu choose one's spouse:～不可片面地追求外貌美。One should not choose one's spouse by mere appearances.

择期 zéqī choose or fix a date:～完婚 select a day for the marriage

择取 zéqǔ select; choose; pick:～数篇,作为范文 select a few essays as models

择善而从 zéshàn'ércóng choose and embrace what is good:我们应当～。We should accept what is sound and reasonable.

择选 zéxuǎn select; choose:～良种 selection of improved varieties

择业 zéyè select a job; choose an occupation:～权 right to choose one's calling

择优 zéyōu select the superior or the best:～录取 enrol (*or* admit, *or* employ) on the basis of competitive selection; enrol only those who are outstanding /～招工 employ workers on their merits

择主而事 zézhǔ'érshì choose and serve a wise master:良禽择木而栖,贤臣～。The prudent bird selects its perch and the wise man his master.

择捉岛 Zézhuōdǎo Etorofu islands, one of the four northern islands claimed by Japan but now under Russian jurisdiction

zè

仄[1] zè ❶ narrow:逼～ narrow; cramped ❷ uneasy; sorry:歉～ feel sorry (*or* apologetic)

仄[2] zè 〈语言〉oblique tones:古诗的平～ tone patterns in classical Chinese poetry

仄声 zèshēng 〈语言〉oblique tones, i.e. the falling-rising tone (上声), the falling tone (去声), and the entering tone (入声), as distinct from the level tones (平声) in classical Chinese pronunciation

昃 zè 〈书面〉sun inclining to the west:日中则～。The sun will incline towards the west after midday.

侧 zè *see* "仄[2]" zè
see also cè; zhāi

zéi

贼[1] zéi ❶ thief; burglar:盗～ robber; bandit /窃～ thief; burglar /擒～先擒王。To capture bandits, first catch the ringleader. ❷ traitor; enemy:奸～ conspirator; traitor /工～ scab; blackleg /独夫民～ autocrat and traitor to the people /卖国～ traitor (to one's country) ❸ wicked; crooked; evil:～相 thievish-looking ❹ wily; sly; cunning:那小子～得厉害,一肚子鬼心眼儿。That guy is very crafty and full of tricks. /瞧,他那个～样儿! Doesn't he look like a sly old fox? ❺〈书面〉injure; harm; maim:戕～ harm; injure

贼[2] zéi 〈方言〉(often used to indicate disapproval or abnormality) extremely; exceedingly; disagreeably:～冷 terribly cold /此人～坏。That man is a thorough rascal. /这灯～亮。The light is uncomfortably dazzling. /他长得～胖。He is really fat.

贼巢 zéicháo thieves' den

贼船 zéichuán pirate ship:上～ board the pirate ship — join a criminal gang or become a member of a reactionary faction

贼风 zéifēng wind that blows in through the cracks in the door or window

贼骨头 zéigǔtou 〈方言〉thief; burglar

贼鬼溜滑 zéigui-liūhuá 〈方言〉crafty; cunning; sly

贼喊捉贼 zéihǎnzhuōzéi a thief crying "Stop thief":识破了他～的把戏 see through his trick of a thief crying "Stop thief" /这强盗居然～,指控起别人来。The robber went so far as to act like a cop and bring accusations against others.

贼横 zéihèng 〈方言〉very rude and unreasonable; arbitrary; peremptory:耍～ be rude and unreasonable

贼话儿 zéihuàr 〈方言〉what one hears by eavesdropping:听～ eavesdrop

贼寇 zéikòu ❶ bandit ❷ invader; aggressor:痛歼入侵的～ wipe out the aggressors

贼溜溜 zéiliūliū shifty-eyed; thievish-looking; furtive:～的眼睛 shifty eyes /～地进了屋 steal into the room

贼眉鼠眼 zéiméi-shǔyǎn wear a thievish expression; look like a sly old fox:～地到处看 cast furtive glances around /此人～,怕不是好人。I am afraid he is not a decent man, for his eyes are shifty and his expression is thievish.

贼鸥 zéi'ōu skua

贼去关门 zéiqù-guānmén *see* "贼走关门"

贼人 zéirén ❶ thief; burglar ❷ evildoer:这伙～无恶不作。This gang of evildoers is capable of anything.

贼人胆虚 zéirén dǎnxū guilty conscience needs no accuser

贼死 zéisǐ 〈方言〉extremely; exceedingly:累了个～ be tired out; be dog-tired; be totally exhausted /气了个～ be exceedingly angry; be beside oneself with fury

贼头贼脑 zéitóu-zéinǎo thievish; stealthy; furtive:匪徒们～地互相使眼色。The bandits winked stealthily at one another.

贼窝 zéiwō thieves' den; family of thieves

贼心 zéixīn evil designs or intentions:他见钱眼红,顿起～。He was wide-eyed at the sight of the money and an evil thought came over him.

贼心不死 zéixīn-bùsǐ still harbour evil intentions; cannot suppress evil thoughts; refuse to give up one's sinister designs

贼星 zéixīng (popular name for 流星) meteor

贼眼 zéiyǎn shifty eyes; furtive glance

贼赃 zéizāng stolen goods; loot; booty; spoils

贼着 zéizhe 〈方言〉keep watch on; keep an eye on:我老～他,看他

到底要干什么。I'll keep an eye on him and see what he is up to.
贼子 zéizǐ 〈书面〉 person who harms the country and oppresses the people; traitor：乱臣～ rebellious subjects and undutiful sons; traitors and usurpers
贼走关门 zéizǒu-guānmén *also* "贼去关门" lock the door after the thief has gone; take action only after the harm is done：你们这是～，放放马后炮而已。What you are doing is like locking the stable door after the horse has been stolen. It's like firing belated shots (*or* all too late).

鲗 zéi *see* "乌鲗" wūzéi

zěn

怎 zěn 〈方言〉 why; what; how：试验成功了，大家～能不高兴呢? How can we refrain from rejoicing over the success of the experiment? /这事如此重要，你～早不告诉我呀? Why didn't you tell me sooner about such an important matter? /这事该～办? What's to be done about it?
怎地 zěndi *see* "怎的"
怎的 zěndi *also* "怎地" 〈方言〉 what; why; how：他～还未来? Why hasn't he turned up yet? /我就是不答应，你能把我～? I just won't agree. What can you do with me?
怎么 zěnme ❶ *used to inquire about nature, condition, cause, etc.*：水～不热? Why isn't the water hot enough? /你是～学会跳舞的? How did you learn to dance? /她～会对此一无所知? How come she knows nothing about it? /这是～回事儿? What's all this about? /你这是～啦? What's the matter with you? *or* Why, is there anything wrong? /他究竟是～一个人? What kind of a person is he? /你～搞的! See what you've done! ❷ *used to indicate nature, condition or manner in general*：这事该～处理就～处理。Handle the matter the way it should be handled. /你愿意～干就～干吧。Do as you please. /不管你～说，他也不会让步。Whatever you say, he won't give in. /这上衣的几处油垢～洗也洗不掉。No matter how I tried, I couldn't get the stains off the coat. /老太太脾气怪，～说也不行。The old lady is eccentric and insusceptible to persuasion. ❸ *used in the negative to indicate inadequacy*：我不～了解他。I don't know him well enough. /我对木匠活儿不～在行。I am not much of a carpenter. ❹ *used at the beginning of a sentence to indicate surprise, usu. followed by a pause*：～，他又病了? So he's ill again? /～，你想不认账? What? You want to deny your debt?
怎么得了 zěnme déliǎo where will it all end; what a terrible mess it is：如果这些谣言传到他的耳朵里，～! What a terrible thing it would be if these rumours reached his ears! /如果他们继续争吵下去，～? If they keep on quarrelling, where will it all end?
怎么样 zěnmeyàng ❶ *see* "怎样" ❷ *euphemistic formula used in the negative*：这幅画画得不～。This is not a particularly good painting. /她跳舞跳得不～。She is not much of a dancer. /这人实在不～，但经理信任他。The man is not really up to much, but the manager trusts him. /他后台硬，我们也不好把他～。We can do nothing about him since he has got strong backing.
怎么着 zěnmezhe ❶ *used to inquire about an action or state*：今晚干什么? 是看电视还是～? What are we going to do tonight? Watch TV or what? /我们假期去南方旅游，你～? We are going on a trip to the south for the holidays. What about you? ❷ *indicating an action or state of affairs in general*：我愿意～就～，你管不着。I'll do as I please, and that is none of your business. /我没什么意见，～都可以。Whatever you decide will be fine with me. /～也得把任务完成。The task must be accomplished no matter what happens. ❸ *see* "怎么❶"
怎奈 zěnnài (often used in the early vernacular) but; however：那时候他想上学，～家里太穷，上不起。He wanted to go to school, but his family couldn't afford it.
怎生 zěnshēng (interrogative pronoun often used in poetry or writings in the early vernacular) what; why：此事～是好? What's to be done about it? /他们～不见来? Why haven't they turned up yet?
怎样 zěnyàng *also* "怎么样" ❶ *used in an interrogative sentence inquiring about nature, condition, manner, volition, etc.*：你是～劝他改变主意的? How did you talk him round (*or* into changing his mind)? /情况进展～? How is everything? /再来杯咖啡～? How about another cup of coffee? /你看这条连衣裙～? How do you like the dress? /那老人后来～了? What became of the old man? /那又～? So what? ❷ *indicating nature, condition or manner in general*：他根本不了解穷人生活是～的。He has no idea at all what life is like for the poor. /别人～看待这事，我不在乎。I don't care how other people may look at the problem.

zèn

谮 zèn 〈书面〉 falsely charge; defame; slander; calumniate：～言 calumny; defamation

zēng

曾 zēng ❶ relationship between great-grandchildren and great-grandparents：那位老太太是我的～祖辈了。The old lady is of (*or* belongs to) my great-grandparents' generation. ❷ (Zēng) a surname
see also céng
曾国藩 Zēng Guófān Zeng Guofan (1811-1872), founder of the Hunan Army (湘军), who helped the Qing government suppress the Taiping Revolution (1851-1864)
曾鲸 Zēng Jīng Zeng Jing (formerly translated as Tseng Ching, 1564-1647), painter of the late Ming Dynasty
曾母暗沙 Zēngmǔ Ànshā Zengmu Shoal, southernmost part of Chinese territory
曾孙 zēngsūn great-grandson
曾孙女 zēngsūnnü great-granddaughter
曾祖 zēngzǔ (paternal) great-grandfather
曾祖母 zēngzǔmǔ (paternal) great-grandmother

憎 zēng hate; loathe; abhor：可～ repulsive; repellent /爱～分明 be clear about what to love and what to hate
憎称 zēngchēng derogatory name for sb. one hates or detests; term of condemnation
憎恨 zēnghèn hate; loathe; detest：～官僚主义 detest (*or* hate) bureaucratism /怀有强烈的～ harbour bitter hatred for; bear deep hatred against /他用～的目光看着我。He looked at me with hate in his eyes.
憎恶 zēngwù detest; abhor; loathe; abominate：我～伪君子。I detest hypocrites. /他对于拍马逢迎极为～。Flattery is detestably abhorrent to him.
憎嫌 zēngxián loathe; abhor; detest
憎厌 zēngyàn detest; abhor; abominate; be disgusted with

增 zēng increase; enhance; grow; gain：与日俱～ grow with each passing day /～调消防车去救火 dispatch more fire engines to combat the blaze /信心倍～ with redoubled confidence /产量一直有～无减。The output has been on the increase all the time. /来京旅游人数猛～。The number of tourists to Beijing increased sharply.
增白剂 zēngbáijì 〈化学〉 brightening agent; brightener
增白霜 zēngbáishuāng fair complexion cream
增编 zēngbiān ❶ (short for 增加编制) enlarge an establishment; expand the size of staff or a unit ❷ addendum
增补 zēngbǔ increase; supplement; augment：科室人员略有～。The administrative staff has slightly expanded. /该书插图～不少。The book has been supplemented with quite a few illustrations. /货物品种有所～。There is a greater variety of goods now.
增补本 zēngbǔběn enlarged edition
增产 zēngchǎn increase production：～节约运动 campaign (*or* drive) to increase production and practise economy /棉花～百分之五。Cotton production increased by 5%. *or* There was an increase of 5% in cotton production.
增充剂 zēngchōngjì 〈化学〉 extender
增稠 zēngchóu 〈化工〉 thickening：～器 thickener
增大 zēngdà enlarge; amplify; magnify：效益～ increased benefits /取胜的可能性～。There is a greater possibility for success.
增订 zēngdìng ❶ revise and enlarge (a book); expand and improve：本书此次再版，内容有所～。There are revisions and supplements in this new edition of the book. ❷ subscribe to (more newspapers, magazines, etc.)：～许多期刊 subscribe to many more peri-

odicals

增订本 zēngdìngběn revised and enlarged edition

增多 zēngduō increase; become larger or more numerous: 回大陆探亲的台胞日益~。More and more compatriots from Taiwan come to the mainland to visit their families and relatives. /新型建筑明显~。There was a marked increase in buildings of modern designs.

增防 zēngfáng fortify the defences; strengthen the garrison

增幅 zēngfú increasing range; growing rate: 在出口商品中,纺织品增长最快,~为百分之三十。Among the export commodities, textiles have been growing most rapidly at a rate of 30%.

增高 zēnggāo ❶ increase in height; become higher; heighten: 厂房比原设计~了。The factory building was higher than originally designed. ❷ raise: ~室温 raise the temperature of the room

增股 zēnggǔ 〈金融〉rights issue

增光 zēngguāng add lustre to; do credit to; bring glory on: 为国~ do credit (*or* add glory) to one's country /他的英雄行为给他的家庭增了光。His heroic deeds added lustre to his family.

增广 zēngguǎng broaden; expand; enlarge: ~见闻 add to one's knowledge

增辉 zēnghuī add lustre to

增加 zēngjiā increase; augment; add; raise: ~工资 get a raise (*or* rise) in pay /~速度 gather (*or* pick up) speed; accelerate /~报纸发行量 promote (*or* increase) the circulation of a newspaper /~财富 multiply (*or* augment) one's wealth /~花色品种 increase the variety of colours and designs /大大~工作难度 add greatly to the difficulty of the work /~信心 heighten one's confidence; gain fresh confidence /~体重 put on weight; grow heavier /~抵抗力 build up one's resistance to disease /~造林面积 extend (*or* enlarge) the afforested areas /~两口人吃饭 have two more people to feed /利润比去年同期~了百分之二十。The profit is 20% higher than that of the same period last year. /该地区人口过去十年中~近一倍。The population of the area has almost doubled in the past ten years. /工人由五百~到八百。The number of workers has gone up from 500 to 800.

增减 zēngjiǎn increase and decrease; fluctuate: 根据市场的需要,产品的数量有所~。There are both increase and decrease in the number of the products, depending on the demand of the market.

增进 zēngjìn enhance; improve; promote; further: ~食欲 sharpen (*or* whet) one's appetite /~学术交流 promote academic exchanges /~市场繁荣 reinvigorate (*or* enliven, *or* activate) the market /~相互了解 further (*or* strengthen) mutual understanding /~两国人民之间的友谊 enhance the friendship between the two peoples

增剧 zēngjù exacerbate; aggravate; intensify: 病情~。The patient's condition has worsened (*or* taken a turn for the worse).

增刊 zēngkān supplement (to a newspaper or periodical); supplementary issue: 《人民日报》~ supplement to the *People's Daily*; *People's Daily* supplement /文学~ literary supplement

增量 zēngliàng 〈数学〉increment: ~电感 incremental induction /~计算机 incremental computer /~数字记录器 incremental digital recorder /~法 reinforcement method

增黏剂 zēngniánjì tackifier

增强 zēngqiáng make strong or stronger; strengthen; heighten; enhance: ~团结 strengthen unity; close one's ranks /~体质 build up one's health /~责任感 deepen one's sense of duty (*or* responsibility) /~凝聚力 enhance the cohesion (of an organization, community, etc.) /~企业活动 revitalize (*or* invigorate) an enterprise /~法制观念 enhance one's awareness of law /~保安措施 beef up security /~产品的竞争能力 make the product more competitive; increase the competitiveness of the product /~诗歌的艺术感染力 add to the artistic appeal of poems

增强塑料 zēngqiáng sùliào reinforced plastic

增色 zēngsè add lustre to: 他的表演给晚会~不少。His performance made the evening party much more entertaining.

增删 zēngshān additions and deletions; alterations: 该书再版时内容有所~。Some modifications were made in the second edition of the book.

增设 zēngshè add; set up more (departments, etc.): ~门市部 set up an additional retail (*or* sales) department /本校近几年~了许多新专业。In recent years our school has added new specialities and disciplines to its curriculum.

增生 zēngshēng 〈医学〉hyperplasia; proliferation; multiplication: 骨质~ calcium deposits; condensing osteitis; osteitis ossificans

增饰 zēngshì give additional polish to (a piece of writing, etc.)

增收 zēngshōu increase one's income; increase revenue: ~计划 plan to increase the revenue /我们不能靠歪门邪道来~。We cannot increase our income by dishonest means.

增收节支 zēngshōu-jiézhī increase revenue and reduce (*or* cut) expenditure

增速 zēngsù 〈机械〉increase of speed; speed increase: ~器 speed increaser; speed increasing gear /~装置 increase gear; increasing gear; speed increase unit; speeder

增塑 zēngsù 〈化工〉plasticize: ~油 plasticizing oil

增塑剂 zēngsùjì 〈化学〉plasticizer; plastifier

增碳 zēngtàn 〈冶金〉recarburize: ~器 carburetor /~作用 carburetion /~水煤气 〈化工〉carburated water gas

增添 zēngtiān add; increase; augment: ~娱乐设施 increase recreational facilities; offer additional facilities for recreation /~麻烦 put sb. to much trouble (*or* inconvenience) /彩旗给会场~了节日欢乐的气氛。Coloured flags added to the festivity of the occasion. /锻炼使他浑身~了活力。Exercises infused fresh vigour into his whole being. /艰难的岁月使她的额上~了几抹皱纹。Hard times left more wrinkles on her forehead. /人人都该为祖国建设~砖瓦。Everybody should do his bit in building up his country.

增效 zēngxiào synergy; synergism: ~剂 〈化学〉synergist

增修 zēngxiū *see* "增订❶"

增选 zēngxuǎn election of additional members; election

增压 zēngyā ❶〈机械〉supercharge; pressure boost: 涡轮~ turbocharge /涡轮~器 turbocharger /~泵 force lift pump; booster pump /~发动机 supercharger engine /~器 supercharger ❷〈电工〉boost; boosting: ~变压器 booster transformer /~器 booster /~机组 booster set

增压服 zēngyāfú pressurized suit

增氧健身法 zēngyǎng jiànshēnfǎ aerobics; aerobic exercise

增益 zēngyì ❶ increase; add: ~减损 increase profit and reduce cost /翻译这一句时须有所~。Amplification is needed in translating this sentence. ❷〈电学〉gain: 高~ high gain /分贝~ decibel gain /控制~ gain control /~测量 gain measurement

增音机 zēngyīnjī 〈通信〉repeater

增盈 zēngyíng increase profits: 扭亏~ eliminate losses and increase profits

增援 zēngyuán reinforce: ~前线 send (*or* dispatch) reinforcements to the battlefront /派技术力量去~ provide technical assistance

增长 zēngzhǎng increase; enhance; rise; grow: ~见识 enrich (*or* broaden) one's knowledge and experience /在实践中~才干 develop (*or* enhance) one's abilities in practice /经济~ economic growth /~潜力 growth potential /下游水位急骤~。The water rose sharply at the lower reaches of the river. /人民收入成倍~。The income of the people has doubled and redoubled. /工业产值平均~百分之十。Industrial output value has registered an average increase of 10%. /家电产品的生产~速度太快。The production of electric appliances is expanding too fast.

增长分析 zēngzhǎng fēnxī incremental analysis

增长率 zēngzhǎnglǜ rate of growth or increase; growth rate

增值 zēngzhí 〈经济〉rise or increase in value; appreciation; increment; value added: 日元~ revaluation of Japanese yen /(土地的)自然~ unearned increment /年~量 annual (*or* yearly) increment

增值税 zēngzhíshuì value added tax (VAT)

增殖 zēngzhí ❶〈医学〉hyperplasia; proliferation; multiplication: 细胞~ proliferation of cells ❷ breed; reproduce; multiply; propagate: ~耕牛 propagate oxen

增殖反应堆 zēngzhí fǎnyìngduī breeder reactor

增殖率 zēngzhílǜ 〈畜牧〉rate of propagation; rate of increase

增殖腺 zēngzhíxiàn adenoids: ~炎 adenoiditis /~切除术 adenoidectomy

增殖腺学 zēngzhíxiànxué adenology

罾 zēng square-shaped fishing net with poles as supports: 扳~ use such a fishing net

熷 zēng arrow with a string, used to shoot birds (in ancient China)

缯 zēng 〈古语〉silk fabrics

see also zèng

Z

zèng

甑 zèng ❶ ancient earthen utensil for steaming rice ❷ rice steamer：木～ wooden rice steamer ❸ utensil for distilling water, etc.：曲颈～ retort

甑子 zèngzi rice steamer shaped somewhat like a wooden bucket

赠 zèng send as a gift; give as a present：互～礼品 exchange (*or* present each other with) gifts /～给学校五千册图书 present the school with 5,000 books /学生小玉敬～ with the compliments of your student Xiaoyu

赠别 zèngbié 〈书面〉present gifts or poems to a friend who is going on a long journey; see a friend off：折柳～ give a friend a willow branch as a parting present; bid sb. farewell

赠答 zèngdá present each other with gifts, poems, etc.：诗文～ present each other with poems

赠礼 zènglǐ gifts; presents

赠票 zèngpiào ❶ complimentary ticket ❷ give sb. a complimentary ticket

赠品 zèngpǐn (complimentary) gifts; giveaway

赠书 zèngshū ❶ present sb. with a book; donate books ❷ complimentary copy

赠送 zèngsòng present as a gift; give as a present：～锦旗 present sb. with a silk banner /～粮食和医药 donate food and medicine

赠送仪式 zèngsòng yíshì presentation ceremony

赠言 zèngyán words of advice or encouragement offered to a friend at parting：临别～ parting advice

赠与 zèngyǔ *also* "赠予" present; donate：他～该校巨款，修建新的图书馆。He donated a huge sum of money to this school for the building of a new library.

赠与国 zèngyǔguó donor country

赠与税 zèngyǔshuì gift tax; donation tax

赠予 zèngyǔ *see* "赠与"

赠阅 zèngyuè (of a book, periodical, etc.) given free by the publisher

赠阅本 zèngyuèběn complimentary copy; presentation copy

缯 zèng 〈方言〉bind; tie：竹竿儿裂了，用绳子把它～起来。The bamboo pole is cracked. Please bind it with a piece of string.
see also zēng

锃 zèng (of utensils, etc.) polished：～光 shiny

锃光瓦亮 zèngguāng-wǎliàng shiny：玻璃窗～。The windows are bright and shiny.

锃亮 zèngliàng (of utensils, etc.) polished：他把家具擦得～。He polished up the furniture.

综 zèng 〈纺织〉heddle; heald：～框 heald frame
see also zōng

zhā

查(査) zhā ❶ *see* "山查" shānzhā ❷ (Zhā) a surname
see also chá

渣 zhā ❶ dregs; slag; sediment; residue：沉～ sediment /煤～ coal cinder /残～ dregs /油～ scraps /豆～ soya-bean residue (after making bean curd) /炉～ slag; cinder /蔗～ bagasse /中药～ dregs of Chinese medicine ❷ broken bits：面包～ crumbs /碎玻璃～ bits of broken glass

渣比 zhābǐ 〈冶金〉slag ratio

渣车 zhāchē slag car; slag wagon

渣沟 zhāgōu 〈冶金〉slag runner

渣罐 zhāguàn 〈冶金〉slag pot; slag basin; slag ladle; slag pan：～车 slag car; slag ladle and carriage

渣坑 zhākēng 〈冶金〉hunch pit

渣口 zhākǒu 〈冶金〉cinder notch; cinder monkey slag hole; slag eye

渣块 zhākuài 〈冶金〉slag block

渣瘤 zhāliú 〈冶金〉slag nodule

渣炉 zhālú 〈冶金〉slag hearth

渣煤 zhāméi 〈矿业〉dross coal

渣土 zhātǔ dirt with waste residue

渣眼 zhāyǎn 〈冶金〉slag blister

渣油 zhāyóu 〈石油〉residuum; residual oil：～路 residual-oil road

渣子 zhāzi 〈口语〉dregs; sediment; residue：点心～ crumbs; scraps of pastry /涮干净茶壶里的～ rinse the dregs out of the teapot

渣滓 zhāzi ❶ dregs; sediment; residue：炼猪油的～ residue (*or* dregs) of pig fat with lard boiled out; pork scraps; cracklings ❷ dregs; riffraff：人类的～ dregs of humanity /盗贼、骗子、流氓等都是社会～。Robbers, swindlers and hooligans are all scum of society.

楂(樝) zhā *see* "山楂" shānzhā
see also chá

揸(摣、叡) zhā 〈方言〉❶ pick up sth. with the fingers：～一点盐 take a pinch of salt ❷ spread one's fingers

喳 zhā ❶〈旧语〉yes, sir — a response from an inferior to a superior ❷〈象声〉chatter：麻雀叽叽～～叫个不停。Sparrow are twittering nonstop.
see also chā

齄(皻) zhā red blotch (on nose)：酒～鼻 acne rosacea

扎(❸紮、紥) zhā ❶ prick; needle into：～得相当疼 prick rather badly /背后被～了一刀 be stabbed in the back /在纸板上～洞 punch holes in the cardboard /我手指～流血了。I pricked my finger and it started to bleed. ❷〈方言〉plunge into; dive into; get into：树根深深地～在泥土里。The tree has taken root deeply in the earth. /他整天～在图纸设计中。He buried (*or* immersed) himself in piles of blueprints. /一转眼，他就～到人堆里去不见了。He pushed his way into the crowd and disappeared in a twinkling of an eye. ❸ (of troops) be stationed; be quartered：安营～寨 pitch a camp
see also zā; zhá

扎除 zhāchú 〈医学〉removal by ligature

扎堆 zhāduī gather around：干活～儿聊天 chat in groups while at work

扎耳朵 zhā ěrduo 〈口语〉grate or jar on the ear; be earpiercing：这话听着～。Such words grate on my ears. /这刮擦声真～。The scratch was really earpiercing.

扎耳朵眼儿 zhā ěrduoyǎnr pierce the earlobe for earrings

扎根 zhāgēn take root; strike root：～于群众之中 take (*or* strike) root among the masses /～边疆的青年人 young people who settled in the border areas /这种思想已在青年人心中深深地扎下了根。This idea is deeply rooted in the minds of the young people.

扎工 zhāgōng form of mutual aid by exchange of work or labour in farming

扎咕 zhāgu 〈方言〉treat; cure：他的眼病，医生给～好了。The doctor cured him of his eye ailment.

扎裹 zhāguo 〈方言〉dress up; deck out：～一新 be freshly decked out; be dressed up in new clothes

扎花 zhāhuā 〈方言〉embroider：她静静地坐着～。She sat quietly at her embroidery.

扎猛子 zhā měngzi 〈方言〉dive：她从跳板上一个猛子扎到游泳池里，姿势很优美。From the spring-board, she made a graceful dive into the swimming pool.

扎枪 zhāqiāng 〈方言〉spear; red-tasselled spear：把～刺入敌人的心脏 thrust a spear into the enemy's breast

扎煞 zhāsha *also* "挓挲" zhāsha 〈方言〉(of hands, branches, etc.) spread; stretch out; (of hair, etc.) stand on end

扎什伦布寺 Zhāshílúnbùsì Tashilhunpo or Tashi Lhunpo, a monastery of the Yellow sect of Lamaism in the Tibet Autonomous Region

扎实 zhāshi ❶ sturdy; strong; robust：身板儿～ be physically strong ❷ solid; firm; sound; down-to-earth：工作很～ do a solid piece of work; do a solid job /～的理论基础 firm grounding in theory /～地做几件事 do a few things in real earnest /打下～的英语基础 lay a good foundation in English /他的学问很～。He has sound schol-

arship. /运动员们的基本功训练得很～。The sportsmen have gained mastery of basic skills through hard training.

扎手 zhāshǒu ❶ prick the hand：玫瑰花有刺，留神～。Take care lest the roses prick your hands. ❷ difficult to handle; thorny; ticklish：～的局面 ticklish situation /～的问题 thorny problem /解决民族冲突问题是件～的事。The question of ethnic conflict is a hard nut to crack.

扎眼 zhāyǎn ❶ dazzling; loud; garish：～的颜色 garish colour; colour unpleasant to the eye /一望无际的原野上覆盖着白雪，阳光一照，很～。The sun was dazzling on the vast expanse of snow. ❷ offensively conspicuous; very showy：这件衣服过于～，不宜穿着去参加招待会。The dress is too gaudy to wear at a reception.

扎伊尔 Zhāyī'ěr (now called Congo again) Zaire：～人 Zairian

扎营 zhāyíng pitch a camp; camp：～过夜 set up camp for the night /部队在山下～。The troops encamped at the foot of the mountain.

扎寨 zhāzhài pitch a camp; camp：在荒野安营～ pitch a camp in the wilderness

扎针 zhāzhēn 〈中医〉give or have an acupuncture treatment：～技术好 be skilful at treating patients with acupuncture needles /她害怕～。She is afraid of having an acupuncture treatment.

哳 zhā *see* "啁哳" zhāozhā

咋 zhā
see also zǎ; zé

咋呼 zhāhu *also* "咋唬"〈方言〉❶ cry out loudly; shout blusteringly：大声～ shout at the top of one's voice /你～个啥? What are you shouting about! ❷ show off; make a display (of one's authority or ability)：到处～ try to show off everywhere /这姑娘有点～。The girl is rather noisy. /他整天咋咋呼呼，自以为了不起。He talks big all the time, thinking himself terrific.

咋喇 zhāla *also* "咋啦"〈方言〉talk too much and in a loud voice：大清早，他就～起来了。It is still early morning, and he has already started loudmouthing.

劄 zhā *see* "扎❶❸" zhā
see also zhá

挓 zhā

挓挲 zhāsha *also* "扎煞" zhāsha〈方言〉(of hands, branches, etc.) spread; stretch out; (of hair, etc.) stand on end：吓得他毛发直～。His hair stood on end with fright. /孩子～起胳膊要我抱。The child spread out his arms for me to take him in my arms.

吒 zhā *used as a personal name in myths and fables*

zhá

闸(牐) zhá ❶ floodgate; sluice; sluice gate：开～放水 open (*or* let loose) the sluices ❷ dam up water：溪流被坝～住。A stream was dammed up. ❸ brake：气～ air (*or* pneumatic) brake /紧急～ emergency brake /制动～ damper brake /脚～ foot brake /真空～ vacuum brake /踩～ step on the brake /捏～ apply the hand brake /松～ take off the brake /自行车的～坏了。The brake (of the bicycle) is not working properly (*or* out of order). ❹〈口语〉electric switch：总～ main switch /合～ close a switch /扳～ operate a switch; switch on or off /拉～限电 switch off as a constraint on electricity consumption (*or* to control the use of electricity)

闸盒 zháhé fuse box：打开～看看，保险丝坏了没有? Open the fuse box and see if the fuse has blown out or not.

闸口 zhákǒu sluiceway

闸流管 zháliúguǎn 〈电子〉thyratron

闸门 zhámén ❶ water gate; sluice gate; lock gate; gate：打开～放船。Open the lock gate to let the ships pass. /～大开让洪峰通过。The sluice gate is wide open for the oncoming flood crest. /我们要打开思想的～，让思绪自由翱翔。We must open our mind to independent thinking. ❷〈机械〉throttle valve

闸门开度 zhámén kāidù gatage

闸门启闭机 zhámén qǐbìjī gate hoist

闸瓦 zháwǎ 〈机械〉brake shoe

喋 zhá *see* "唼喋" shàzhá
see also dié

劄 zhá *see* "劄子"
see also zhā

劄记 zhájì reading notes：旅途～ notes made on a tour; travel notes

劄子 zházi 〈旧语〉official documents in the Tang and Song dynasties, later restricted to documents dispatched to official subordinates

铡 zhá ❶ hand hay cutter; fodder chopper：磨～ sharpen a hand hay cutter /使～ use a fodder chopper ❷ cut up with a hay cutter：～草 chop hay

铡草机 zhácǎojī hay cutter; chaff cutter; chaff slicer; straw breaker：小型～ small hay cutter

铡刀 zhádāo hand hay cutter; fodder chopper; straw chopper：锋利的～ sharp hay cutter /～太笨重。The fodder chopper is rather cumbersome.

炸(煠) zhá ❶ fry in deep fat or oil; deep-fry：～鸡蛋 fried egg /～油饼 deep-fried dough cake /～油条 deep-fried twisted dough sticks /～肉丸子 fried meat balls /软～鱼 soft-fried fish /～烹大虾 grilled prawns in sauce ❷〈方言〉dip in boiling water; scald (as a way of cooking)：把菠菜放在开水里～一下。Scald the spinach in boiling water.
see also zhà

炸酱 zhájiàng fried bean sauce：肉末～ minced meat with fried bean sauce

炸酱面 zhájiàngmiàn noodles served with fried bean sauce

炸土豆条 zhátǔdòutiáo French fried potatoes; French fries; chips

炸虾 zháxiā fried shrimps

扎 zhá
see also zā; zhā

扎挣 zházheng 〈方言〉move with difficulty (because of physical weakness); struggle to maintain：病人～着从椅子上站起来。The patient struggled to his feet from the chair.

札 zhá ❶ thin pieces of wood used for writing on in ancient China ❷〈书面〉letter：大～ your letter /信～ letter /简～ short note /手～ personal letter

札幌 Zháhuǎng Sapporo, a city in northern Japan and capital of Hokkaido

札记 zhájì *also* "劄记" zhájì reading notes or commentary：旅行～ travel notes /凡读书必作～。I always make notes when I read.

札木聂 zhámùniè *Zhamunie*, a plucked six-stringed Tibetan instrument

轧 zhá roll (steel)：～钢板 roll out in plates
see also gá; yà

轧钢 zhágāng steel rolling：～工人 steel rolling worker; roller

轧钢厂 zhágāngchǎng steel rolling mill：大型～ heavy rolling mill /小型～ small-sized rolling mill

轧钢机 zhágāngjī rolling mill：国产～ Chinese-built rolling mill /进口～ imported rolling mill

轧辊 zhágǔn 〈冶金〉roll; roller：～调整装置 roll adjusting device /～车床 roll lathe /～电热炉 electric roll heater

轧机 zhájī 〈冶金〉rolling mill：二辊式～ two-high mill /可逆式～ reversing mill /连续式～ continuous mill /型钢～ shape rolling mill

轧件 zhájiàn rolled piece

轧屑 zháxiè mill scale

轧制 zházhì 〈冶金〉rolling：～钢 rolled steel /～公差 rolling tolerance /～钢轨 roll out steel rail

zhǎ

眨 zhǎ blink; wink; bat (the eyes)：眼睛也不～一～ without

Z

even batting an eyelid /～了一眼 give a wink /星星～着眼。The stars are twinkling.

眨巴 zhǎba 〈方言〉blink：这男孩有些吃惊地～眼睛看着我。The boy blinked at me in surprise.

眨眼 zhǎyǎn ❶ wink; blink：杀人不～ kill a man without batting an eyelid; not blink at killing a man ❷ very short time; wink; twinkling：一～就不见人影 disappear in a twinkling

苲 zhǎ

苲草 zhǎcǎo waterweed; water plant：在河里捞～ dredge up water plants from the river

砟 zhǎ tiny fragments of stone, coal, etc.：焦～（coking）cinder /道～ small stone; cobblestone /炉灰～儿 cinder

砟子 zhǎzi fragments of stone, coal, etc.：煤～ coal cinder /石头～ small stones /煤烧成了～。The coal was burnt to cinders.

拃（搩） zhǎ ❶ measure by stretching one's hand across in one span; span：我来～一～有多宽。Let me measure its width by spans. ❷〈量词〉span：这块布有三～宽。This cloth is three spans wide. /她比她妈妈矮一～。She is even shorter than her mother by a hand's span.

鲊 zhǎ 〈书面〉❶ salted fish ❷ vegetables seasoned with salted ground rice and other condiments：茄子～ eggplants in salted ground rice and other condiments

鲊肉 zhǎròu 〈方言〉pork steamed with ground glutinous rice：四川人善制～。The people from Sichuan are good at steaming pork with ground glutinous rice. /酸～独具风味。Sour pork steamed with ground rice is unique in flavour.

鲝 zhǎ ❶ *see*“鲊”zhǎ ❷ *see*“苲”zhǎ

zhà

咤（吒） zhà *see*“叱咤”chìzhà

蚱 zhà 〈方言〉jellyfish

栅（柵） zhà railings; palisade; paling; bars：木～ paling; palisade /铁～ iron railings; metal rails; iron bars /拦鱼～ fish screen /木～门 wooden fence gate /炉～ grate

see also shān

栅栏 zhàlan ❶ railings; paling; bars; fence rails：用～围住 fence in with palings; rail in /用～隔开 fence off /工地被～围着。The construction site is surrounded by fences. ❷〈军事〉boom：～网 boom nets /～防御 boom defence

栅子 zhàzi 〈方言〉enclosure fenced by bamboo, reeds, etc. for keeping poultry

奓 zhà 〈方言〉open; spread; extend：～翅 open out the wings /衣服的下摆太～了。The hem of the dress is too outspread.

奓刺儿 zhàcìr 〈方言〉make trouble and foment discord

奓毛 zhàmáo 〈方言〉lose one's temper; get angry：～变色 turn pale with anger /万一这家伙奓了毛，那就麻烦了。There will be real trouble if he flies into a rage.

奓着胆子 zhàzhe dǎnzi 〈方言〉pluck up one's courage; summon up one's courage：小男孩～摸黑上了楼。The small boy screwed up his courage and went upstairs in the dark. /他～走进了山洞。He plucked up his courage and went into the cave.

Z

蜡（褚） zhà a kind of sacrifice offered at the end of a year (in ancient China)

see also là

乍 zhà ❶ first; at first; for the first time：～一看 at first glance /初来～到 be a newcomer; be a new arrival /～看起来，像是个好主意，但实际上行不通。It seemed a good idea at first, but it really wouldn't work. ❷ all of a sudden; suddenly; abruptly：风～起，吹皱了平静的河水。A sudden breeze rippled the quiet lake. ❸ open out; spread; extend：～翅 stretch wings ❹（Zhà）a surname

乍得 Zhàdé Chad：～人 Chadian

乍得湖 Zhàdéhú Lake Chad, biggest lake in West Africa

乍猛的 zhàměngde 〈方言〉suddenly; abruptly：他～一问我，我倒想不起来了。I could not call it to mind when he asked me abruptly.

乍暖还寒 zhànuǎn-huánhán after a short warm spell, the weather has turned cold again：天气～，最容易生病。It is easy to fall ill when the weather turns cold again after getting warmer suddenly.

乍然 zhàrán suddenly; unexpectedly：狂风～而起。A fierce wind rose all of a sudden.

乍着胆子 zhàzhe dǎnzi *see*“奓着胆子”zhàzhe dǎnzi

痄 zhà

痄腮 zhàsai 〈医学〉mumps

炸 zhà ❶ explode; break; burst：～得粉碎 explode into pieces /爆竹在他手里～响了。The firecrackers went off in his hands. /气球～了。The balloon has burst. /后胎～了。The rear tyre blew out. ❷ blow up; blast; bomb：～碉堡 blow up the blockhouse /狂轰滥～ indiscriminate bombing; wanton bombing and bombardment /在墙上～出了一个洞 blow a hole through the wall /从山中～出一条隧道 blast a tunnel through a mountain /桥～断了。The bridge was blown away. /他的一条腿被～飞了。He had his leg blown off. ❸〈口语〉fly into a rage; explode with anger; flare up：他一听这话就～了。He flew into a towering rage when he heard it. ❹〈方言〉scamper; scurry away; flee in terror：鸡～了窝了。The chickens have all fled from their coop.

see also zhá

炸刺儿 zhàcìr *also*“奓刺儿”zhàcìr〈方言〉sow discord; foment trouble

炸弹 zhàdàn bomb：埋下一颗定时～ place a time bomb /投下大批～ drop (*or* release) a large quantity of bombs /爆破～ demolition bomb /杀伤～ antipersonnel bomb /常规～ conventional bomb /催泪～ tear bomb /毒气～ gas bomb /燃烧～ incendiary bomb /高爆～ high capacity bomb /热核～ thermonuclear bomb /深水～ diving torpedo; depth charge /塑料～ plastic bomb /未爆～ unexploded bomb; dud /细菌～ germ bomb /液体～ liquid bomb /传单～ leaflet bomb /～坑 bomb-crater; crater

炸锅 zhàguō 〈方言〉get excited and angry; lose one's temper：顿时，全场炸了锅。Instantly, the whole place was in an uproar. /听到比赛失利的消息，球迷们就炸了锅。The fans flared up on hearing the loss of the match.

炸胶 zhàjiāo 〈化学〉blasting gelatine

炸雷 zhàléi 〈方言〉clap of thunder：像～一样响 (of sound) as loud as thunder

炸毛 zhàmáo *also*“奓毛”zhàmáo 〈方言〉flare up; fly into a temper

炸群 zhàqún (of horses, mules, etc.) scamper; flee in terror; stampede：一声惊雷使牲畜炸了群。A sudden clap of thunder stampeded the animals.

炸市 zhàshì (of a crowd in busy streets) flee in terror; ran away in all directions

炸窝 zhàwō 〈方言〉❶ (of birds, bees, etc.) flee in fright：枪声一响，鸟儿都炸了窝。The birds have all fled from their nests at the report of a gun. ❷ (of a crowd of people) be thrown into confusion; be in disarray：敌人一下子炸了窝。Instantly, the enemy was thrown into great confusion.

炸响 zhàxiǎng 〈方言〉(of thunder, etc.) loud and clear：鞭子甩得～。The whip cracked.

炸药 zhàyào explosive (charges); dynamite; TNT：烈性～ high explosive /甘油～ dynamite /可塑性～ plastic explosive /引爆～ ignite the explosive /装填～ charge with dynamite

炸药包 zhàyàobāo pack or satchel of dynamite; explosive package; satchel charges

炸营 zhàyíng be thrown into confusion; be in disarray：这一回全村都炸了营。This time, the whole village was thrown into panic and confusion.

炸子 zhàzǐ dumdum bullet

诈 zhà ❶ cheat; swindle; deceive：欺～ cheat; swindle /讹

～ blackmail / 敲～ extort; racketeer; blackmail / ～人钱财 cheat (*or* swindle) people out of their money; get money by fraud / 尔虞我～ each trying to cheat or outwit the other / 到处行～ practise extortion everywhere ❷ pretend; feign; fake: ～死 feign death; play possum / ～病 feign illness; pretend sickness; malinger / 兵不厌～。All is fair in war. ❸ bluff sb. into giving information; feel out: 你不要拿话来～我。Don't try to draw me out. / 他是拿话～我，我一听就知道。I knew from the beginning that what he said was all bluff.

诈称 zhàchēng falsely claim

诈唬 zhàhu bluff; bluster: 你别拿大帽子～人。Don't try to bluff people by pinning political labels on them.

诈冒 zhàmào falsely claim as one's own: ～他人财物 falsely claim other's money and property as one's own

诈骗 zhàpiàn defraud; swindle; trick into: 进行～活动 practise fraud / ～别人钱财 swindle sb. out of his money and property; defraud sb. of his money and property

诈骗犯 zhàpiànfàn swindler

诈骗罪 zhàpiànzuì crime of fraud: 犯有～ be guilty of fraud

诈尸 zhàshī ❶〈迷信〉(of a corpse) suddenly rise before being interred ❷〈方言〉〈贬义〉run or scream as if being chased by a corpse come to life: 他大清早就在院儿里～，喊起来没个完。He has been screaming like mad in the yard since early morning.

诈降 zhàxiáng pretend to capitulate; feign surrender

诈语 zhàyǔ lie; deceit; falsehood; fabrication: ～诓人 trick sb. into doing sth. with false stories; hoax sb. with a falsehood

榨(❶搾) zhà

❶ press; extract; squeeze out: ～桔子汁 squeeze juice from an orange / ～出水分 squeeze the water out / ～干血汗 bleed sb. white; wring every ounce of sweat and blood out of sb. ❷ press for extracting oil, juice, etc.: 酒～ wine press

榨菜 zhàcài ❶ mustard tuber (*Brassica juncea* var. *tsatsai*) ❷ hot pickled mustard tuber: ～肉丝汤 soup with shredded pork and hot pickled mustard tuber

榨果汁机 zhàguǒzhījī juice extractor

榨寮 zhàliáo 〈方言〉sugar refinery; sugar refining house

榨取 zhàqǔ ❶ press; extract; squeeze: ～豆油 press oil from soya beans / ～柠檬汁 squeeze juice from a lemon ❷ extort; squeeze: ～高额利润 gain extortionate profits / ～钱财 squeeze money out of sb. / ～民脂民膏 feed on the flesh and blood of the people

榨油 zhàyóu extract oil

榨油机 zhàyóujī oil press

榨汁机 zhàzhījī juicer

醡 zhà

press for extracting oil, etc.

蚱 zhà

蚱蝉 zhàchán *also* "知了" zhīliǎo cicada

蚱蜢 zhàměng grasshopper: 捉～ catch grasshoppers

zha

馇 zha

see "饹馇" gēzha

see also chā

zhāi

斋[1](齋) zhāi

❶ abstain from meat, wine, etc. (when offering sacrifices to gods or ancestors); fast: ～祭 offer sacrifices to gods or ancestors while refraining from wine and meat ❷ vegetarian diet adopted by Buddhists and Taoists: 吃～ be on a vegetarian diet as religious observances; be a vegetarian for religious reasons / 清～ abstinence from meat; fast / 长～ permanent abstention from meat, fish, etc. / 化～ (of Buddhist monks or Taoist priests) beg a vegetarian meal ❸ give alms (to a monk): ～僧 give alms to monks

斋[2](齋) zhāi

room or building: 书～ study / 我住在三～二层。My apartment is on the first floor of Building No.3.

斋饭 zhāifàn ❶ food that monks obtained by begging: 向店主讨点～ beg some food from the owner / 给行脚僧人布施～ give food to itinerant monks ❷ vegetarian meal in a monastery

斋公 zhāigōng ❶ person responsible for joss sticks and candle burning at a temple ❷ vegetarian

斋果 zhāiguǒ 〈方言〉sacrificial offering; oblation: 佛座前供着～。Offerings are presented in front of the statue of Buddha.

斋会 zhāihuì Buddhist gathering: 庙里举行盛大～。A great Buddhist gathering was held at the temple.

斋醮 zhāijiào (Buddhist and Taoist priests) set up an altar for prayer rites

斋戒 zhāijiè ❶ wear clean clothes and abstain from meat, wine, etc. to show one's piety (when offering sacrifices to gods or ancestors); fast: 进行十天的～ perform a fast of ten days / ～日 fast day / 他们在某些天～。They fast on certain days. ❷ day of fasting

斋戒节 Zhāijièjié Ramadan; fast of Ramadan

斋戒沐浴 zhāijiè-mùyù fast and ablution; fasting and taking a bath before a religious observance: ～，以示虔诚 fast and bathe to show one's piety towards God

斋期 zhāiqī fast days; fast; Lent: 长达一个月的～ fast of a month's duration

斋日 zhāirì fast day

斋舍 zhāishè ❶ room for observing religious abstinence before worship ❷ study: ～幽静 quiet and secluded study

斋坛 zhāitán sacrificial altar

斋堂 zhāitáng dining room at a temple

斋月 Zhāiyuè 〈伊斯兰〉Ramadan; 9th month of the Muslim year, during which no food or drink may be taken between sunrise and sunset; month of fast

斋月战争 Zhāiyuè Zhànzhēng Yom Kippur War (Egypt-Israel War of October 1973)

摘 zhāi

❶ pick; pluck; remove; take off: ～葡萄 pick grapes / ～花 pluck flowers / 第一批采～的桃子 first pick of peaches / ～眼镜 take off one's glasses / 把墙上的画儿～下来 remove the picture on the wall / ～掉贫穷的帽子 cast off the label of poverty; eliminate poverty / ～下面具 tear off the mask; unmask / 他们把梨全～了。They have picked off all the pears. ❷ select; pick out; make extracts from: ～喜欢的段落朗读 read aloud excerpts one likes best ❸ borrow money when in urgent need: ～几个钱救急 borrow some money to meet an urgent need

摘编 zhāibiān ❶ select and edit; extract and compile: ～报刊 compile extracts from newspapers and magazines ❷ extracts: 文件～ extracts from documents

摘抄 zhāichāo ❶ take passages; make extracts; extract; cull: ～书中要点 extract main points from the book / 从语法书中～例子 cull examples from grammar books ❷ extracts; excerpts: 日记～ pages from a diary / 《古今笑话》～ excerpts from *Ancient and Present Humours*

摘除 zhāichú 〈医学〉remove; excise: ～肿瘤 excise a tumour / 白内障～术 cataract extraction / ～子宫 have an uterectomy / ～阑尾 have one's appendix removed / 大夫说她的扁桃腺应该～。The doctor says her tonsils ought to come out.

摘登 zhāidēng publish excerpts of sth. in newspapers or magazines: 在报上～代表发言 publish excerpts of speeches by the delegates in the newspaper

摘兑 zhāidui 〈口语〉borrow money when in urgent need: 我去～五百块钱做盘费。I'll go and borrow 500 *yuan* to cover my travel expenses.

摘发 zhāifā ❶ publish excerpts of sth.: 本刊最近一期～了他的讲话。The latest issue of the magazine carried excerpts of his speech. ❷〈书面〉make charges or accusations ❸〈书面〉reveal; bring to light: ～新理 expound the new theory

摘记 zhāijì ❶ take notes: ～讲话要点 take down the gist of a speech / 他讲得很快，连～都来不及。He spoke so fast that nobody could even jot down the main points. ❷ extracts; excerpts: 善于～ be good at making extracts

摘借 zhāijiè borrow money when in urgent need: 向邻居～ borrow money from a neighbour to meet an urgent need

摘录 zhāilù ❶ take passages; make extracts; extract: 把文章中的几段～下来 take a few passages from the article / ～文件重点 extract main points from a document ❷ extracts; excerpts; summary: 报刊～ excerpts from newspaper articles

摘帽子 zhāi màozi remove the label of: 摘掉右派帽子 have the

rightist label removed
摘棉铃机 zhāimiánlíngjī 〈农业〉cotton stripper
摘评 zhāipíng review of selected passages
摘取 zhāiqǔ ❶ pick; pluck: ～蔷薇 pick roses ❷ select; choose: ～自己需要的资料 select materials one wants /这戏是～小说的精彩部分改编的。The play is adapted from the most interesting parts of the novel.
摘心 zhāixīn ❶〈农业〉topping; pitching ❷ painful; heart-breaking: 要她不见女儿就像摘她的心一样。It's heartrending for her to stay away from her daughter.
摘要 zhāiyào ❶ make a summary; make an abstract: ～刊登 carry a summary in a newspaper or magazine /～记录 jot down the main points ❷ brief; summary; abstract; précis: 文章～ précis of an article /一本书的～ résumé of a book /统计～ statistical summary
摘译 zhāiyì select (passages) and translate (them); translate selected passages: 外论～ abridged translation of views and editorials from foreign press
摘引 zhāiyǐn quote: ～名人语录 cite quotations from a celebrity /～文件内容 quote from a document /～自《鲁迅全集》quotations from *The Complete Works of Lu Xun*
摘由 zhāiyóu key extracts (of a document); résumé: 文件～ key extracts of a document /公函～ résumé of an official letter
摘载 zhāizǎi publish excerpts from sth.

侧 zhāi 〈方言〉tilt; incline; slant
see also cè; zè
侧棱 zhāileng 〈方言〉lean; slant; incline: ～着耳朵听 prick up one's ears
侧歪 zhāiwai 〈方言〉oblique; slant; tilt: 她写的字向一边儿～。Her handwriting slanted to one side. /车在山坡上～着开。The car was tilted while moving forward on a hillside.

zhái

宅 zhái residence; dwelling; house: 住～ residence; dwelling /深～大院 imposing dwellings and spacious courtyard /无～容身 without shelter; shelterless /王～ the Wangs' residence
宅第 zháidì 〈书面〉mansion: ～大门外有一对石狮子。There is a pair of stone lions standing on either side of the entrance to the mansion.
宅基 zháijī foundations of a house; house site
宅门 zháimén ❶ gate of a mansion or an old-style big house: ～紧闭。The gate of the big house is tightly closed. ❷ family living in such a mansion: 这条胡同里有好几个～儿。There are several big families living in the lane.
宅舍 zháishè residence; dwelling: 私人～ private residence
宅院 zháiyuàn house with a courtyard; house: 宽大的～ mansion with a spacious courtyard /一所富人家的～ rich family's house
宅子 zháizi 〈口语〉residence; house

择(擇) zhái select; choose; pick: ～鸡毛 pick a chicken
see also zé
择不开 zháibukāi ❶ unable to disentangle or undo; impossible to unravel; past disentanglement: 一团～的乱麻线 a skein of tangled linen thread ❷ cannot tear oneself away from: 忙得一点工夫也～ be fully occupied; not have a moment to spare
择菜 zháicài trim vegetables for cooking: 孩子们学会了～。The children have learned how to trim vegetables.
择床 zháichuáng 〈方言〉*see* "择席"
择铺 zháipù 〈方言〉*see* "择席"
择食 zháishí be choosy about one's food: 他从不～。He is never choosy about his food.
择席 zháixí unable to sleep well in a new place: 因为～, 昨晚未睡好。Being in a new place, I did not sleep well last night.

翟 Zhái a surname
see also dí

zhǎi

窄 zhǎi ❶ narrow: 道儿～。The road is narrow. /此处河面变～。The river narrows at this point. ❷ petty; small-minded: 心眼儿～ narrow-minded ❸ hard up; badly off; on the rocks: 他日子过得挺～。He lives in straitened circumstances.
窄巴 zhǎiba 〈方言〉❶ narrow and small; narrow: 屋子太～。The room is rather small. ❷ hard up; badly off: 手头～ be short of money; be hard up /～着勉强度日 live from hand to mouth; barely make ends meet
窄憋 zhǎibie 〈方言〉❶ narrow and small: 屋里多～, 连个书桌也放不下。The room is too small even for a writing desk. ❷ feel oppressed; be depressed: 近来心里怪～的。I feel rather depressed lately. ❸ hard up; badly off: 这几年的生活好多了, 不像从前那么～了。Life has much improved these years; we are no longer so badly off.
窄带 zhǎidài 〈无线电〉narrow band: ～调频 narrow-band frequency modulation /～通路 narrow-band path
窄导轨 zhǎidǎoguǐ narrow guide or track
窄幅联合收获机 zhǎifú liánhé shōuhuòjī 〈农业〉narrow combine
窄轨 zhǎiguǐ narrow gauge
窄轨铁路 zhǎiguǐ tiělù narrow-gauge railway
窄行 zhǎiháng narrow-row: ～播种 narrow-row drilling /～播种机 narrow-row seeder /～中耕机 narrow-row cultivator
窄间隙焊 zhǎijiànxìhàn 〈冶金〉narrow gap welding
窄片 zhǎipiàn 〈影视〉narrow gauge film; substandard film stock
窄头眼镜蛇 zhǎitóu yǎnjìngshé mamba
窄狭 zhǎixiá narrow; cramped: ～的山沟 narrow valley
窄小 zhǎixiǎo narrow and small; narrow: ～的阁楼 tiny attic /～的堑壕 narrow trench

鉙 zhǎi 〈方言〉flaw; blemish: 没～儿的苹果 apples without any blemish /茶杯上有点～儿。The cup had a flaw in it.

zhài

寨 zhài ❶ stockade; fence ❷ camp: 安营扎～ pitch a camp; encamp /偷营劫～ raid an enemy camp ❸ mountain stronghold: ～中兵丁近千人。There were nearly a thousand soldiers in the mountain stronghold. ❹ stockaded village; fenced hamlet: 本村本～ home village /村村～～ all the villages
寨主 zhàizhǔ 〈旧语〉brigand chief
寨子 zhàizi ❶ stockade; enclosure: ～坚固 strongly built stockade ❷ stockaded village: 潜入～ steal into the stockaded village

摖 zhài 〈方言〉sew: ～花边 trim a dress with lace /替他～上领章 sew collar badges onto his uniform

砦 zhài ❶ stockade; enclosure: 鹿～ enclosures for deer ❷ (Zhài) a surname

债 zhài debt: 负～ be in debt; get into debt /借～ borrow money /内～ internal debt /外～ external debt /举～ raise a loan /公～ government bonds /三角～ debt chains /还～ pay (*or* repay, *or* pay back) one's debt /讨～ press for payment of debt /血～要用血来还。Debts of blood must be paid in blood. /～多不愁。When there are too many debts, one stops worrying about them. *or* Too many obligations will numb a person's sense of responsibility. /有了这个头衔, 就有扯不完的皮, 开不完的会, 还不完的～。With this title came endless wranglings, incessant meetings, and unrequited kindnesses and obligations.
债户 zhàihù debtor: 无偿付能力的～ insolvent debtors
债家 zhàijia creditor
债款 zhàikuǎn loan; debt: 偿还～ repay a loan /过期～ debt overdue /～收入 revenue from loans /～支出 expenditure for loan payments /应付～账户 debts payable account
债利 zhàilì interest on a loan
债权 zhàiquán 〈法律〉creditor's rights; obligatory right: ～投资人 credit-investor /～保险 credit insurance
债权国 zhàiquánguó creditor nation
债权人 zhàiquánrén creditor; lender: ～违约 default of creditor /～账户 creditor's account /～权益 creditor's claim /～损失 creditor's damage /～产权 creditor's equity /判定～ judgment creditor
债权证书 zhàiquán zhèngshū document of obligation

债券 zhàiquàn bond; debenture:金融～ financial bonds /国库～ treasury bonds /短期～ short-term liabilities /储蓄～ savings debenture /产业～ industrial bonds /附息票～ coupon bonds /购买政府～ buy government bonds /偿还到期～ redeem bonds for payment /发行建设～ issue construction bonds /把钱投资于～ invest one's money in debentures /持有大量～ hold a large amount of bonds /认购～ bond subscription /～持有者 bond holder /～折价 bond discount /～股息 bond dividends /～保险 bond insurance /～兑换 bond conversion /～计价 bond pricing /～溢价 bond premium /～债务 bonded debts /～值 bond value

债券市场 zhàiquàn shìchǎng bond market

债台高筑 zhàitái-gāozhù be heavily in debt; be up to one's ears in debt; be head over heels in debt; be debt-ridden:他结婚讲排场,致使～。He got heavily into debt as a result of his extravagant wedding.

债务 zhàiwù debt; liabilities; amount due:清理～ clear one's debts /偿还～ pay back the debt; meet one's debt /取消～ debt cancellation /～缠身 be involved in debt; be up to one's neck in debts /国际～问题 international debt issue /无息～ passive debt /战争～ war debts /私人～ private debt /～免除 debt relief /～限额 debt ceiling; debt limit /～折扣 debt discount /～清结 performance of debt /～纠纷 dispute over obligation /～额 amount of debt / ～期 debt duration

债务重整 zhàiwù chóngzhěng 〈金融〉rescheduling (of a debt)

债务国 zhàiwùguó debtor nation

债务人 zhàiwùrén debtor:已破产的～ bankrupt debtor

债息 zhàixī debt interest; bond interest

债务资本 zhàiwù zīběn debt capital

债主 zhàizhǔ creditor:避开～ stave off creditors

债转股 zhàizhuǎngǔ 〈经济〉transformation of debt into equity rights; debt-equity swap: ～协议 debt-equity agreement / 在这次～之后,该公司的资产负债率将降低百分之二十五左右。After the debt-equity swap, the liabilities-assets ratio of the company will drop by some 25%.

瘵

zhài 〈书面〉illness; ailment:痨～ tuberculosis

zhān

邅

zhān *see* "迍邅" zhūnzhān

饘(飦)

zhān 〈书面〉thick gruel

旃[1]

zhān 〈书面〉felt

旃[2]

zhān 〈书面〉auxiliary word (used as a contraction of 之 and 焉):勉～! Hope you'll do a good job of it!

旃檀 zhāntán 〈古语〉sandalwood; white sandalwood

栴

zhān

栴檀 zhāntán *see* "旃檀" zhāntán

占

zhān ❶ practise divination; divine: ～断吉凶 try to find out one's lot by divination; tell one's fortune ❷ (Zhān) a surname

see also zhàn

占卜 zhānbǔ practise divination; divine:用硬币～ divine by tossing coins

占卦 zhānguà divine by means of the Eight Trigrams (八卦): ～问卜 divine by means of the Eight Trigrams or by consulting oracle bones and shells

占课 zhānkè divine by tossing coins

占梦 zhānmèng divination by interpreting dreams; oneiromancy

占星 zhānxīng divine by astrology; cast a horoscope: ～术 astrology /～家 stargazer

沾(❶❷霑)

zhān ❶ moisten; wet; damp:被汗水～湿 dripping wet with sweat /～满泪痕 be blotted with tears ❷ be stained with; be soiled with: ～有油渍 stained with grease /～满了泥 covered with mud stains ❸ touch:脚不～地 one's feet do not touch the ground — walk very fast; run very fast; be extremely busy /他滴酒不～。He never touches any alcoholic drinks. *or* He is a teetotaller. ❹ gain by association with sb. or sth.; benefit from some sort of relationship:利益均～ have an equal share of the benefit; share the benefit equally /～点便宜 gain some advantages /有好处大家～。Everyone is entitled to whatever benefit there is. ❺〈方言〉all right; okay:这事可不～。This won't do!

沾包 zhānbāo 〈方言〉implicate; involve; get sb. into trouble:那会儿,大家真怕～。In those days, we were really afraid of getting involved in it. /他们因～被判有罪。They were pronounced guilty because of their implication in the matter.

沾边 zhānbiān ❶ touch on only lightly; have sth. to do with:此事与他毫不～。He had nothing at all to do with the matter. /这项工作,他只沾了点边儿。He is only involved in the work to a very small extent. *or* His involvement in the work is only minimal. /关键性问题你没～。You didn't touch upon the key issues. *or* You didn't hit the nail on the head. ❷ be close to what it should be; be relevant; be pertinent:你的批评根本不～。Your criticisms are completely off the mark. /我认为他的话与我们的议题不～。I don't think his remarks are pertinent to our discussion. /这几句话还算～。These words are somewhat to the point. *or* These words are not entirely irrelevant.

沾补 zhānbu 〈口语〉share the benefit:这钱你不能独吞,给大家都～点儿。You can't take all the money by yourself. Everyone should have a share.

沾溉 zhāngài 〈书面〉irrigate (fields) — enjoy the benefits of sth.; benefit people: ～后人 bring benefits to later generations

沾光 zhānguāng benefit from association with sb. or sth.; cash in on one's connection with sb.; gain from the support or influence of sb.:你干出了成绩,全科室都会～。Everyone in the office will share in the credit you may gain for your outstanding achievement. /如果那样,我也会沾点儿光。If that should happen, I for one would benefit from it.

沾花惹草 zhānhuā-rěcǎo womanize; be promiscuous in sex relations:他喜欢～。He is a womanizer.

沾亲 zhānqīn be somewhat related

沾亲带故 zhānqīn-dàigù have ties of kinship or friendship; be related somehow or other:村里人少,各家都有点～的关系。There aren't too many people in the village, and each family is related to the other one way or another. /我与他既不沾亲也不带故。I have no ties of kinship or friendship with him at all.

沾染 zhānrǎn contract; be infected with; be tainted with; be contaminated by: ～物 contaminant; contaminator /～事故 contamination accident /～了细菌的创口 open wound infected by germs /～恶习 contract bad habits /～了民族虚无主义的恶劣思想 be contaminated with the pernicious ideas of national nihilism

沾染区 zhānrǎnqū contaminated area

沾惹 zhānrě provoke; incur; invite:这样就会～是非。This is merely inviting trouble.

沾润 zhānrùn soak up some gains; derive benefits from:他们白忙了一天,一个钱也没～着。They toiled the whole day for nothing.

沾手 zhānshǒu ❶ touch with one's hand:这东西太脏,你别～。This stuff is dirty. Don't touch it. /花儿一～就容易蔫。Flowers are easily spoiled by touch. ❷ have a hand in; interfere:这事你不必～。You need not intervene in this matter. /这是他们的事,我沾不了手。This is their business, and I am not supposed to butt in.

沾污 zhānwū sully; smear; soil; taint: ～了手 soil one's hands /不要～墙壁。Don't smear the wall.

沾沾自喜 zhānzhān-zìxǐ feel complacent; be pleased with oneself; be self-satisfied:稍有点成绩,他就～。He easily hugged himself for joy at what little achievements he had made. /这不过是一得之功,而他却～。This success is purely accidental, and yet he looks on it with such complacency and satisfaction.

粘

zhān glue; stick; paste:把椅子腿～上 glue the leg on to the chair /～信封 seal up an envelope /这张邮票～不上。This stamp doesn't stick. /糖块～在一起了。The sweets got glued together. /她死～住他不放。She sticks to him like a leech.

see also nián

粘合 zhānhé *also* "粘结";"粘接" binding; bonding; splicing: ～剂 binder; bonding /～素 conglutinin

粘连 zhānlián ❶〈医学〉adhesion:肠～ intestinal adhesion /胸膜～ pleural adhesion /～现象 adhesion phenomenon /纤维性～ fibrous adhesion /瘢痕性～ cicatricial adhesion ❷ link; involvement:他与此

事无～。He has nothing to do with this matter.

粘贴 zhāntiē glue; paste; stick:～邮票 stick a stamp (on an envelope) /～布告 put up a notice /把相片～到硬衬纸上 paste a photograph on to a mount

毡(氈、氊) zhān felt:～靴 felt boots /油～ asphalt felt /～衬 packing felt

毡包 zhānbāo ❶ yurt:这个时候,一个牧民匆匆钻进～。At this moment, a herdsman hurried into the yurt. ❷ felt bag

毡垫 zhāndiàn felt pad:～圈〈机械〉felt washer

毡房 zhānfáng yurt:参观牧民的～ visit the herdsman's home

毡合织物 zhānhé zhīwù 〈纺织〉felt fabric

毡条 zhāntiáo 〈方言〉felt; felt rug

毡帐 zhānzhàng felt tent

毡子 zhānzi felt; felt rug; felt blanket:崭新的～ brand new felt blanket

詹 Zhān a surname

詹天佑 Zhān Tiānyòu Zhan Tianyou (1861-1919), pioneer of Chinese railway engineering

谵 zhān 〈书面〉rave; rant; be delirious:～言 delirious speech; ravings; wild talk

谵妄 zhānwàng 〈医学〉delirium:～性呓语 delirious ravings /陷入～状态 lapse into a delirious state /～者 deliriant /震颤性～ delirium tremens /高热使病人～烦乱。The patient's high fever made him delirious.

谵语 zhānyǔ 〈书面〉delirious speech; wild talk; ranting and raving:新纳粹分子的～激怒了很多人。The wild ravings of the neo-Nazis infuriated many people.

瞻 zhān ❶ look up; look forward:高～远瞩 look far ahead and aim high; be farsighted /观～ sight; view ❷ (Zhān) a surname

瞻拜 zhānbài look at with reverence; call to pay one's respects to:～圣地 pay homage at a sacred place /～遗像 pay one's respects to a portrait of the deceased

瞻顾 zhāngù 〈书面〉❶ look ahead and behind:～再三 think over again and again; take careful consideration ❷ look after; take care of:多承～。I am grateful to you for your kindness.

瞻礼 zhānlǐ ❶〈宗教〉religious holiday or festival ❷〈宗教〉day of a week (except Sunday):～二 Monday ❸〈书面〉worship; go to church:入寺～ conduct a church service

瞻念 zhānniàn look ahead; think of:～前途 look ahead to the future /～后代 think of the future generations

瞻前顾后 zhānqián-gùhòu ❶ look ahead and behind; consider carefully; weigh the pros and cons; take into account both past experience and possibilities:他做事总是～,考虑周密。Whatever he does, he is always circumspect and takes every possibility into account. ❷ be overcautious and hesitate:危急关头应当机立断,决不可～,犹豫不决。In crisis we've got to make a prompt decision and never be shilly-shally and indecisive.

瞻望 zhānwàng look forward; look far ahead:抬头～ look into the distance /～21世纪 look to the 21st century /放眼～ look far ahead

瞻仰 zhānyǎng look at with reverence; pay tribute to:～遗容 pay respects to someone's remains /～纪念碑 pay homage before the monument /能不能～您的墨宝? May I have the honour to see your treasured scrolls of calligraphy? /北京这个富丽堂皇的古都谁不想～～? Who on earth doesn't wish to visit such a magnificent ancient capital as Beijing?

瞻谒 zhānyè 〈书面〉pay a call on (a superior or a senior); have an audience with

zhǎn

戋(琖) zhǎn 〈书面〉see "盏" zhǎn

盏(琖) zhǎn ❶ small cup:杯盘碗～ tableware /茶～ tea cup /轮番把～ pour wine in turn ❷〈量词〉一～花灯 a festive lantern /两～电灯 two electric lamps

斩 zhǎn ❶ chop; cut; kill:～断魔爪 cut off the devil's talons /快刀～乱麻 cut the Gordian knot /披荆～棘 break through brambles and thorns /～头去尾 chop the head and tail off /～风劈浪 speed through wind and waves /立～不赦 excute immediately without mercy ❷〈方言〉fleece; blackmail

斩波 zhǎnbō 〈物理〉chopped wave:～器 chopper; clipper /～放大器 chopper amplifier

斩草除根 zhǎncǎo-chúgēn cut the weeds and dig up the roots — destroy root and branch; stamp out the source of trouble:～,杜绝后患 wipe out the whole family and leave no one to cause trouble later on /～,萌芽不发。If the roots are removed, the grass will not come up again. /斩草不除根,逢春又发青。If the weed is not uprooted, it will revive the next spring.

斩除 zhǎnchú root out; eradicate; wipe out:～荆棘 root out thorny undergrowth /～园中杂草 eradicate weeds from a garden /～干净 wipe out completely

斩钉截铁 zhǎndīng-jiétiě firm and decisive; categorical; final:～地表示 state in categorical terms; speak with finality /～地表态 take a resolute and decisive stand; maintain a firm stand /老板～地拒绝了。The boss flatly refused. /他说话～,办事干净利落。He speaks with decisiveness and acts with efficiency.

斩关夺隘 zhǎnguān-duó'ài take strategic points; take one stronghold after another; pierce through the enemy's lines

斩光盘 zhǎnguāngpán chopper disc

斩假石 zhǎnjiǎshí 〈建筑〉artificial stone; imitation stone

斩将搴旗 zhǎnjiàng-qiānqí kill enemy generals and capture their flags:有～之功 perform meritorious deeds in battle /乃～之士 be a daring soldier

斩截 zhǎnjié firm; irrevocable; resolute:他说得那么～,像是真的。He said this with an absolute certainty as if it were real. /他斩斩截截地拒绝了。He refused categorically.

斩尽杀绝 zhǎnjìn-shājué ❶ exterminate; wipe out:入侵者把这个村子的人～了。The invaders killed all the villagers. ❷ go to extremes; make no allowance:这件事要留有余地,不可～。We should leave some leeway and not go to extremes in handling this matter.

斩决 zhǎnjué execute (a criminal); behead; decapitate

斩齐 zhǎnqí also "崭齐" zhǎnqí neat; in good order

斩首 zhǎnshǒu behead; decapitate:～市曹 execute somebody in the marketplace /罪当～ capital offence

𣊬 zhǎn 〈方言〉blink; wink

崭 zhǎn ❶〈书面〉rise high; towering (over):～岩 (of peaks) steep and towering; (of rocks) overhanging ❷〈方言〉fine; superb; swell:滋味真～! It is delicious. *or* It tastes very nice indeed.

崭劲 zhǎnjìn 〈方言〉exert all one's strength; make great efforts; try hard:～把工作做好 strive to do one's work well /从今往后～干吧! Please work hard from now on.

崭亮 zhǎnliàng 〈方言〉bright; shiny:把铜器擦得～ put a good shine on the brasses /灯光～ dazzling lamplight /整个房间通明～。The whole room is brightly lit up.

崭露头角 zhǎnlù-tóujiǎo begin to distinguish oneself; display one's brilliant talents; stand out conspicuously; cut a striking figure:那位外科大夫才三十多岁,就在医学界～了。The surgeon had already made a name for himself in the medical circles in his early thirties.

崭齐 zhǎnqí also "斩齐" zhǎnqí neat; in good order:一排排～的居民住宅 well-laid-out blocks of residential quarters

崭晴 zhǎnqíng 〈方言〉fine; sunny:～天 bright sunny day

崭然 zhǎnrán 〈书面〉become eminent; be outstanding:那栋新楼～高耸。The new building towers conspicuously over the surrounding area.

崭新 zhǎnxīn brand new; wholly new:～的生活 completely new life /～的气象 entirely new scene /他买的那辆车是～的。The car he bought was brand new. /北京将以～的面貌迎接这次体育盛会。Beijing will greet the opening of the grand sports meet with a completely new look.

飐 zhǎn 〈书面〉quivering in the wind

黵 zhǎn 〈方言〉make dirty; dirty; smudge; soil: 黑布禁～。Black cloth does not show the dirt easily. /墨水把衣服～了。The dress is stained with ink.

展 zhǎn ❶ open up; spread out; stretch; unfold: 伸～ spread; stretch /～诵 open a book and read /愁眉不～ knit one's brows in anxiety; wear a worried frown /～眉舒目 stretch the eyes and relax the brows; beam with joy ❷ put to good use; give free play to; display: 大～身手 show one's capabilities /一筹莫～ be at one's wits' end /施～鸿才 give full play to one's talent; put one's talent to use ❸ put off; postpone; extend; prolong: ～期 extend a time limit ❹ exhibition; show: 花～ flower show /影～ film exhibition /书～ book fair; exhibit of books /巡回～出 travelling show /参～者 participants of the exhibition ❺ (Zhǎn) a surname

展播 zhǎnbō arrange and broadcast (television programmes): 举办春节文艺节目～ conduct broadcasts of the Spring Festival theatrical performances

展布 zhǎnbù ❶〈书面〉state (one's views); voice (one's opinions): 详情容日后～。With your permission, I will give the details later. ❷ unfold before one's eyes; emerge: 登高瞭望, 全城都～在眼前。The whole city unfolded before us as we ascended the height. ❸ put to good use; give free play to: ～经纶 put one's statecraft to full use

展翅 zhǎnchì unfold the wings; get ready for flight: ～高飞 soar to great heights /～飞翔 spread its wings to fly /大鹏～。The roc is getting ready for flight.

展出 zhǎnchū put on display; be on show or view; display; exhibit: 公开～ make a public exhibition; exhibit /正在～ on display; on view; on exhibition /～手工艺品 place handicrafts on exhibition /巡回～ itinerant exhibition /初次～ première show /许多重大科技成果在工业展览会上～。Many important scientific and technical achievements are on display at the industrial exhibition.

展读 zhǎndú open (a book or a letter) and read: ～家信 open and read a letter from home /～朋友的新作 read a new work by a friend

展缓 zhǎnhuǎn put off; postpone; extend: 婚期可以～。The wedding can be postponed. /交款限期不得～。The date for payment is not to be extended.

展卷 zhǎnjuàn 〈书面〉open a book or scroll

展开 zhǎnkāi ❶ spread out; roll out; open up; unfold: ～地形图 unfold the topographic map /～地毯 roll out the carpet /～科学新领域 open up a new field of study in science /眼前～了一片绿茵。A carpet of grass unfolded before us. /剧情自此逐渐～。The theme of the play evolves from this incident. /我～谈一谈这个问题。I'll elaborate on this question at some length. ❷ launch; unfold; set off; carry out: ～激烈的辩论 set off a heated debate /～竞争 launch an emulation drive /～批评与自我批评 practise (*or* carry out) criticism and self-criticism /～攻势 mount an offensive /～学术争鸣 conduct an academic debate /～坚决的斗争 wage a resolute struggle against /篮球场上～了一场龙争虎斗。A fierce contest was going on between the two basketball teams.

展宽 zhǎnkuān broaden; widen (road, riverbed, etc.): ～马路 widen the road

展览 zhǎnlǎn display; exhibit; show: 农业～ agricultural exhibition /花卉～ flower show /摄影～ photo exhibition /盆景～ bonsai (*or* potted landscape) show /时装～ fashion display /举办个人油画～ hold a one-man exhibition of oil paintings

展览馆 zhǎnlǎnguǎn exhibition centre; exhibition hall: 农业～ Agricultural Exhibition Hall

展览会 zhǎnlǎnhuì exhibition

展览品 zhǎnlǎnpǐn exhibit; item on display

展览室 zhǎnlǎnshì exhibition room; showroom

展露 zhǎnlù become visible; appear: ～才华 show one's talents /脸上～出亲切的笑容。A genial smile appeared on his face. /她拉开窗帘, 一座美丽的花园赫然～在眼前。She drew the curtains aside to reveal a beautiful garden.

展眉 zhǎnméi 〈书面〉relax the eyebrows to show pleasure

展品 zhǎnpǐn exhibit; item on display: ～丰富 great variety of exhibits /展出的～有五百件以上。There are over 500 items on display. /请勿触摸～。Please do not touch the exhibits. *or* Hands off the exhibits. /～概不出售。Display goods — not for sale.

展评 zhǎnpíng put on display and appraise through comparison: ～会 exhibition and appraisal meeting

展期 zhǎnqī ❶ extend a time limit; postpone: 大会～举行。The conference has been postponed (*or* put off). /应观众要求, 服装展览～三天闭幕。The fashion show will be extended for another three days at the request of the public. ❷ exhibition period: 缩短～ shorten the exhibition period /此次工业展览～定为一月。The industrial exhibition will last for a month. ❸〈金融〉roll-over

展示 zhǎnshì put on display; show; reveal; lay bare: ～样品 put sample products on display /～证据 show evidence /～真相 lay bare the truth /～了人物的崇高品质 reveal the character's noble quality /～历史的本来面目 present historical facts as they actually occurred /这些思想在当时的文学作品中得到了～。These ideas are reflected in the literature of the time.

展示会 zhǎnshìhuì exhibition; show

展室 zhǎnshì exhibition room; showroom

展台 zhǎntái showcase; booth; display counter

展望 zhǎnwàng ❶ look into the distance; look to the future; look ahead: 登高～ ascend a height to enjoy a distant view /忧心忡忡地～未来 look to the future with anxiety /怀着疑虑的心情～不断变化的局面 watch the changing situation with apprehension /～前程, 我们意识到一种强烈的责任感。Looking ahead, we feel a strong sense of responsibility. ❷ forecast; prospect; vista: 世界局势～ in anticipation of the world situation /90年代～ prospects for the 1990's /有关股票市场行情的～ forecasts about the stock market /21世纪～ 21st century in prospect

展现 zhǎnxiàn unfold before one's eyes; emerge; show; appear: ～才华 show one's talent; display one's abilities /这本书为读者～了美丽的前景。The book opens splendid vistas to readers. /美丽的乡村风光突然～在眼前。A scene of rustic beauty suddenly appeared before us. /那事件仍时时～在我脑海中。The event still flashes across my mind from time to time. /夜空中这房子～出清晰的轮廓。The outline of the building is discernible against the night sky.

展限 zhǎnxiàn extend a time limit; extend a deadline; (in law) grant a moratorium: ～一周 give a week's grace /答应再次～ grant a further extension /请～几天。Please extend the deadline a few days.

展销 zhǎnxiāo display and sell (goods and products): 冬季服装～ winter's clothes on display and sale /～部 exhibition and sales department

展销会 zhǎnxiāohuì commodities fair: 服装～ garment fair

展性 zhǎnxìng 〈物理〉malleability

展眼 zhǎnyǎn ❶ stretch or strain one's eyes to see far ahead: 他～远望, 只见万里长江, 奔腾东去。Looking ahead, he saw the mighty Yangtze River rolling and surging towards the east. ❷ in the twinkling of an eye; in a flash; in an instant: 一～工夫, 田野已被白雪覆盖。The fields were covered with a layer of snow in the twinkling of an eye. /～间, 一年已经过去。A year had passed before we knew it.

展眼舒眉 zhǎnyǎn-shūméi have ease of mind; feel very happy

展样 zhǎnyang 〈方言〉❶ natural in manner: 这姑娘又～, 又稳重。The girl is natural in manner and dignified in behaviour. ❷ in good taste; pleasing to the eye; beautiful: 屋里摆得挺～。The room is artistically furnished.

展转 zhǎnzhuǎn *see* "辗转" zhǎnzhuǎn

展子虔 Zhǎn Zǐqián Zhan Ziqian (formerly translated as Chan Tzu-ch'ien), painter of the Sui Dynasty

搌 zhǎn wipe or dab with a soft dry object to sop up liquid: 用吸墨纸把墨水～一～。Blot up the ink.

搌布 zhǎnbu dishcloth; dish towel

辗 zhǎn

辗转 zhǎnzhuǎn *also* "展转" zhǎnzhuǎn ❶ toss about (in bed); toss and turn: ～难眠 toss and turn (in bed); be unable to go to sleep; lie in bed wide awake /～难忘 turn a thing over and over in one's mind; keep thinking in one's mind; be unable to forget it ❷ pass through many hands or places: ～传抄 make private copies of a manuscript that has been passed from hand to hand /他吃尽苦头, ～来到延安。He endured untold sufferings on his roundabout trip to Yan'an. /这封信～到了我手里。The letter reached me eventually.

辗转不安 zhǎnzhuǎn-bù'ān 〈医学〉jactitation

辗转反侧 zhǎnzhuǎn-fǎncè toss about (in bed); toss and turn restlessly; turn over in bed: 他～, 彻夜不寐。He lay wide awake all night, turning restlessly.

辗转流传 zhǎnzhuǎn-liúchuán spread from place to place or hand to hand:这个故事已～了一千多年。The story has been told and retold for more than a thousand years.
辗转相除法 zhǎnzhuǎn-xiāngchúfǎ 〈数学〉division algorithm

zhàn

湛 zhàn ❶ profound; thorough; deep:精～ superb; consummate ❷ crystal clear; limpid:清～ limpid ❸ (Zhàn) a surname
湛碧 zhànbì dark green:～的湖水 green lake
湛蓝 zhànlán azure blue; azure:～的天空 clear blue sky; azure sky /～的海洋 blue sea /～色的湖泊 sapphire lake /湖水一片～。The lake is a vast expanse of azure blue.
湛清 zhànqīng crystal clear:河水～碧绿。The river water is limpid and green. /天空～如水。The sky is beautifully clear.
湛然 zhànrán tranquil; calm
湛深 zhànshēn profound and thorough:～的艺术功力 consummate artistic skill

颤 zhàn shake; tremble; shiver; shudder:浑身发～ tremble from head to foot /她打了个寒～。A cold shiver ran down her spine.
see also chàn
颤栗 zhànlì *also* "战栗" zhànlì shake; tremble; shiver; shudder

蘸 zhàn dip in (ink, sauce, etc.):～酱油 dip in soy sauce /饱～浓墨,挥笔而书。He dipped his brush heavily in Chinese ink and started to write.
蘸火 zhànhuǒ 〈冶金〉quenching
蘸水钢笔 zhànshuǐ gāngbǐ pen (with a nib fixed into a penholder); dip pen

栈(棧) zhàn ❶ shed; pen; fold:马～ stable /羊～ sheep pen; sheepfold /牛～ cattle shed ❷ *see* "栈道" ❸ warehouse:货～ warehouse; storehouse /客～ inn
栈道 zhàndào plank road built along the face of a cliff; viaduct:明修～,暗渡陈仓 pretend to prepare to advance along one path while secretly going along another — do one thing under cover of another; feign action in one place and make the real move in another
栈房 zhànfáng ❶ warehouse; storehouse:修建一间大的～ build a large storehouse /把货物存入～ store goods in a warehouse ❷ 〈方言〉inn
栈桥 zhànqiáo landing stage (at a port); loading bridge (at a railway station)

占(佔) zhàn ❶ take possession of; occupy; seize; take:～座位 occupy seats /强～别国领土 forcibly occupy the territory of another country /抢～有利地形 race to control a favourable terrain; occupy a vantage point /多吃多～ grab more than one's share; take more than one is entitled to /对不起,～用了您不少宝贵时间。Sorry to have taken up so much of your valuable time. ❷ constitute; form; hold; make up:在数量上～优势 be superior in numbers; enjoy numerical superiority /～绝对优势 hold an overwhelming advantage; hold all the trumps /～第一位 take the first place; rank first /～绝大多数 constitute an overwhelming (*or* absolute) majority /学生中女生～一半。Girls make up 50 per cent of the student population. *or* Half of the students are girls./农民～中国人口的百分之八十。Farmers account for 80 per cent of China's population. /公有制在我国～主导地位。Public ownership dominates in our national economy./教育费用将～国民总产值的百分之五。Expenditure on education will take about 5 per cent of the gross national product.
see also zhān
占鳌头 zhàn áotóu come out first; head the list of successful candidates; be the champion:全国男子篮球赛,辽宁队勇～。The Liaoning team captured the national men's basketball championship.
占地 zhàndì (of a garden, building, etc.) cover an area of:这座大楼～一万五千平方米。This building covers an area of 15,000 square metres.
占房 zhànfáng 〈方言〉childbirth
占居 zhànjū be (in a certain condition):～优势 have the advantage /～重要地位 hold an important position
占据 zhànjù occupy; seize; hold:～电台 seize the radio station /～领导位置 hold a leading position /～战略要地 occupy a position of strategic importance
占理 zhànlǐ make sense; be sensible; be reasonable:他说话～。He is reasonable in his argument.
占领 zhànlǐng capture; take; seize; occupy:～制高点 capture a commanding point /～敌人要塞 seize the enemy stronghold /～前沿阵地 occupy a forward position /军事～ military occupation
占领国 zhànlǐngguó occupation power
占领军 zhànlǐngjūn occupation army
占领区 zhànlǐngqū occupied area
占便宜 zhàn piányi ❶ take an undue advantage; profit at the expense of others:占了便宜卖乖 show off one's cleverness after gaining an advantage /他最大的毛病是处处想～。His greatest weakness is to try to get everything on the cheap. ❷ have the edge over; be advantageous; be favourable:他跑得快,肯定～。He certainly has an advantage over others as he runs fast.
占上风 zhàn shàngfēng get the upper hand; have the edge over; turn the tables on:他在第二局中占了上风。He turned the tables on his opponent in the second set.
占先 zhànxiān go before; take the lead; get ahead of:在前两局中～ take the lead in the first two games (*or* sets, etc.) /这次演讲比赛,甲队占了先。Team A is ahead of other teams in the speech contest.
占线 zhànxiàn 〈通信〉the line is busy or engaged:～音 busy-back tone; busy tone; busy signal /他家电话老是～,打不进去。His line was busy all the time, and I just couldn't get through.
占线通道 zhànxiàn tōngdào 〈通信〉active channel
占小便宜 zhàn xiǎopiányi gain petty advantages; make small gains at others' expense:爱～ be in the habit of gaining petty advantages /～吃大亏 suffer major losses in seeking petty gains
占压 zhànyā occupy and keep long in stock:不要～国家资金。Don't let state funds lie idle.
占用 zhànyòng occupy:～公房 occupy a public house /～某人时间 take up sb.'s time /～公款 use public money for one's own end /不能随便～耕地。Don't divert cultivated land to other uses. /保险公司～一幢坐落在市中心的二十层大楼。The insurance company occupies a 20-story building in the heart of the city. /这项工程～了本市不少资金。This project has consumed a lot of the municipal funds.
占有 zhànyǒu ❶ take possession of; possess; own; have:～第一手资料 have firsthand data /非法～财产 wrongful possession of property; illegal possession of property /～资金 own funds /～事实 have facts well in hand /～市场 capture a market /～权 right of possession /～物 possession /～者 possessor; holder /～期间 occupancy /～数 occupation number ❷ occupy; hold:在美国文学中～独特地位 occupy a unique place in American literature
占着茅坑不拉屎 zhànzhe máokēng bù lāshǐ sit on the toilet seat but not shit — hold on to a post without doing a stroke of work and refuse to let anyone else take over; be a dog in the manger:你如果觉得不胜任,就不要"～"。You mustn't be "the-dog-in-the-manger" if you feel not equal to the job.

站¹ zhàn stand; get up; be on one's feet:并排～着 stand side by side /～起来发言 rise to speak /～在一边袖手旁观 stand aside with folded arms /～在人民的立场上 uphold the stand of the people /我在试验室里整天～着。I'm on my feet all day long in the laboratory. /请～开,让车子通过。Please step aside (*or* stand clear) to let the car pass.

站² zhàn ❶ stop; come to a halt:车还没～稳。The bus has not come to a full stop yet. ❷ station; stop:长途汽车～ coach station /起点～ departing station /终点～ terminal; terminus /中继～ stop-over station /公共汽车～ bus stop /进～ pull into a station /出～ pull out of a station ❸ station or centre for rendering certain services:文化～ cultural centre /试验～ experiment station /保健～ health centre; clinic /粮～ grain supply centre /加油～ filling station; gas station /服务～ service station /急救～ first-aid station /儿童课外活动～ after-school activities centre for children
站班 zhànbān 〈旧语〉stand in line at attention

Z

站得高,看得远 zhàndegāo, kàndeyuǎn stand high and see far ahead; have foresight; be far-sighted
站队 zhànduì line up; fall in; stand in line:注意,准备~了。Attention please, get ready to line up. /请站好队。Stand in line please.
站岗 zhàngǎng stand or mount guard; stand sentinel; stand sentry:~放哨 stand sentinel /~的警察 police on sentry /在门口~守卫 sentry oneself at the gate /他正在~。He is on sentry duty now. /他站好了离职前的最后一班岗。He discharged his duties faithfully till he left his post.
站柜台 zhàn guìtái serve as a shop assistant; serve behind the counter (as a shop assistant):他在商店里~。He is a shop assistant.
站立 zhànlì stand; rise; be on one's feet:~姿势 standing posture /~在世界科学技术的顶峰 be at the pinnacle of world science and technology /他默默地~在烈士墓前。He stood in respectful silence before the martyr's tomb.
站笼 zhànlóng 〈旧语〉instrument of torture in the form of a cage, in which a criminal was to stand with his head sticking out; pillory cage
站票 zhànpiào ticket for standing room:出售~ sell tickets for standing room
站哨 zhànshào 〈方言〉stand guard; be on sentry duty; stand sentinel:在山头~ stand guard on a hilltop
站台 zhàntái *also* "月台" yuètái platform (in a railway station):走进第七号~ enter No.7 platform
站台票 zhàntáipiào platform ticket
站头 zhàntou 〈方言〉station; stop
站稳 zhànwěn ❶ come to a standstill:车~后再下。Don't get off until the bus has come to a stop. /冰冻路滑,很难~。It is difficult to keep one's footing on the slippery icy road. ❷ stand firm; take a firm stand:~立场 take a firm stand /~脚跟 gain a firm foothold
站长 zhànzhǎng head of a station, centre, etc.:他被任命为气象站~。He was appointed head of the meteorological station.
站住 zhànzhù ❶ come to a stop; stop; halt:~,否则我要开枪了。Halt, or I'll shoot. /这辆车子突然在路中央~不动。The car came to a dead stop (*or* a standstill) in the middle of the road. ❷ stand firmly on one's feet; keep one's footing:她病刚好,只能勉强~。She has just recovered from illness and can barely manage to keep her footing. /他腿发软,站不住。He felt weak in his legs and could hardly stand. ❸ stand or hold one's ground; consolidate one's position:他在这个单位总算~了。He finally obtained (*or* gained) a foothold in this unit. ❹ hold water; be valid; be tenable:这个说法能~。The statement holds water. /这种理论站不住。This theory is untenable. ❺〈方言〉(of colour, paint, etc.) remain fast:墙面太光,抹的灰站不住。The wall is too smooth to hold lime mortar.
站住脚 zhànzhùjiǎo ❶ stop moving; stop; halt:坡太陡,车不容易~。The slope was steep and we could hardly stop the car on it. /他刚~,后边的人就赶上来了。He had hardly stopped running when the people behind were catching up. ❷ stay put:她忙得很,根本站不住脚。She was in such a tearing hurry that he could not stay put at all. ❸ keep or hold one's ground; consolidate one's position:他终于在城里站住了脚。He finally gained a footing in the city. ❹ hold water; be valid; be tenable:站不住脚 (of opinions, actions, etc.) not have a leg to stand on; be untenable /他的论点能~。His argument is valid. /这种借口根本站不住脚。It's simply a flimsy excuse.

战[1](戰) zhàn

❶ war; warfare; combat; armed conflict:宣~ declare war /休~ truce /停~ armistice /挑~ challenge to fight /游击~ guerrilla warfare /正义之~ just war /遭遇~ encounter /防御~ defensive warfare /持久~ protracted war /运动~ mobile warfare /宣传~ propaganda war /贸易~ trade war /模拟~ sham battle /地道~ tunnel warfare /冷~ cold war /热~ shooting war /血~ bloody battle /心理~ psychological warfare /笔~ paper war; war of the pen /细菌~ bacteriological warfare ❷ fight; battle:为和平而~ fight for peace /~死沙场 die on the battlefield /为捍卫祖国的尊严而~ fight to defend the dignity of one's homeland /愈~愈勇 grow ever more courageous with fighting /百~百胜 win victory in every fight; come out victorious in every battle ❸ (Zhàn) a surname

战[2](戰) zhàn

tremble; shiver; shake; shudder:心惊胆~ tremble with fear; be scared out of one's wits /冷得打寒~ shiver with cold

战败 zhànbài ❶ suffer a defeat; be defeated; lose (a battle or war):在孤立无援的情况下,他的部队~了。Being isolated and cut off from any help, his troops were defeated. ❷ triumph over; vanquish; beat:他们~了敌人。They defeated the enemy.
战败国 zhànbàiguó conquered or vanquished nation; defeated country
战报 zhànbào war communiqué; battlefield report:发表~ issue a war communiqué
战备 zhànbèi war preparedness; combat readiness; war preparations:进入一级~ go (*or* enter) into first degree combat readiness /要有~意识 be mentally prepared against war /处于~状态 be in combat readiness; be on the alert /~工作 preparations against war
战备等级 zhànbèi děngjí degree of combat readiness
战备粮 zhànbèiliáng grain stockpiled in preparation for war
战备行军 zhànbèi xíngjūn tactical march; tactical movement
战备状态 zhànbèi zhuàngtài alert posture; combat readiness
战表 zhànbiǎo letter declaring war (as in a traditional novel or play); written challenge to a fight:下~ issue a declaration of war; throw down the gauntlet /甲队已经递去了~。Team A has already sent out a letter of challenge.
战场 zhànchǎng theatre of operation; battlefield; battleground; battlefront:古~ ancient battleground /欧洲~ European theatre /开辟第二~ open the second front /在谈判桌上取得~上所得不到的东西 gain at the negotiating table what one cannot achieve on the battlefield
战车 zhànchē (war) chariot; combat car:~百辆 hundreds of war chariots
战尘 zhànchén dust that settles on one in battle; dust of battle:布满~ (of soldiers) be covered with dust in combat
战船 zhànchuán warship; war vessel; man-of-war
战刀 zhàndāo sabre:挥舞~ wield a sabre /抡起~ brandish a sabre /锋利的~ sharp sabre
战地 zhàndì battlefield; battleground; combat zone:今又重阳,~黄花分外香。On this Double Ninth, The yellow blooms on the battlefield smell sweeter.
战地记者 zhàndì jìzhě war correspondent
战抖 zhàndǒu tremble; shake; shiver; shudder:~的身躯 shivering body /~的手 trembling hands /全身都在~ shudder all over /他的身子禁不住~起来。He could not help shaking like a leaf.
战斗 zhàndòu ❶ battle; combat; fight; hostilities:~部队 combat forces /~编组 combat grouping /~队 fighting force /~队形 battle formation /~命令 combat orders /~岗位 position in battle; fighting post /~任务 combat mission; fighting task /~序列 order of battle; battle array /~部署 tactical disposition /非~人员 noncombatant /~友谊 militant friendship; comradeship-in-arms /并肩~ fight shoulder to shoulder /进行~动员 give a pep talk before a battle /艰苦的~ hard-fought battle /作好~准备 get ready for action; be combat ready /在~中负伤 be wounded in action /进行短兵相接的~ fight at close quarters; engage in a hand-to-hand battle ❷ fight (in general); struggle:没有硝烟的~ fight (*or* struggle) without the smoke of gunpowder /经济战线的~ fight on the economic front /生命不息,~不止 keep on fighting as long as one lives; never cease fighting until one breathes one's last
战斗轰炸机 zhàndòu hōngzhàjī fighter-bomber
战斗机 zhàndòujī fighter plane; fighter:击落一架~ shoot down a fighter /护航~ escort fighter /第一线~ first-line fighter /喷气式~ jet fighter /远距离~ long-range fighter
战斗舰 zhàndòujiàn battleship; combat ship
战斗力 zhàndòulì combat effectiveness or capability; fighting capacity:~强 high combat effectiveness /提高部队的~ improve the fighting capacity of the armed forces /加强~ increase the combat strength /有~ combat-worthy
战斗性 zhàndòuxìng militancy:这篇文章很有~。This is a militant essay.
战斗英雄 zhàndòu yīngxióng combat hero
战斗员 zhàndòuyuán fighter:指挥员和~ commanders and fighters; officers and men
战端 zhànduān 〈书面〉beginning of a war:挑起~ provoke a war
战法 zhànfǎ (military) tactics; ways of operation
战犯 zhànfàn war criminal
战防炮 zhànfángpào 〈旧语〉antitank gun
战费 zhànfèi war expenses:要求赔偿~ demand reparations for

Z

war expenses

战氛 zhànfēn 〈书面〉war atmosphere

战俘 zhànfú prisoner of war; POW: 病伤～ sick and wounded prisoners of war /～的交接 delivery and reception of prisoners of war /～的处理 disposition of prisoners of war /关于～的安排 arrangements relating to prisoners of war /交换～ exchange POWs /～营 prisoner-of-war (POW) camp /～收容所 prisoner-of-war collecting post /～遣返委员会 Committee for Repatriation of Prisoners of War

战斧式巡航导弹 zhànfǔshì xúnháng dǎodàn (US) Tomahawk cruise missile

战歌 zhàngē battle song; fighting song: 一曲钢铁工人的～ battle song of the steel workers

战功 zhàngōng meritorious military service; great feats in war; outstanding military exploits: ～卓著 brilliant military exploits; illustrious battle achievements /屡立～ distinguish oneself time and again on the battlefield (*or* in action) /～赫赫 perform many meritorious deeds in war; win great distinction in war; achieve miraculous feats in battles

战鼓 zhàngǔ war drum; battle drum: 擂响～ beat the war drum /～动地。The roll of drums shook the earth.

战国 Zhànguó Warring States (475-221 BC): ～时代 period of the Warring States /～七雄 seven major powers during the period of the Warring States (Qi 齐, Chu 楚, Yan 燕, Zhao 赵, Han 韩, Wei 魏 and Qin 秦)

战国策 Zhànguócè *Strategies of the Warring States*, collection of strategies and remarks made by touring scholars of the Warring States Period, first compiled by Liu Xiang (刘向) of the Western Han Dynasty, and later revised and expanded by Zeng Gong (曾巩) of the Northern Song Dynasty

战果 zhànguǒ fruits of victory; results of battle; combat success: ～辉煌 brilliant combat performance; splendid results on the battlefield /取得初步～ achieve initial success on the battlefield

战壕 zhànháo trench; entrenchment: 挖掘～ dig a trench /加固～ fortify a trench /同一条～里的战友 comrades-in-arms fighting for the same cause; comrades-in-arms in the same trench

战后 zhànhòu postwar: ～余殃 aftermath of war /～的经济复苏 postwar economic recovery /这些大楼都是～重建的。These buildings were reconstructed after the war.

战火 zhànhuǒ flames of war: ～蔓延。The flames of war are spreading. /～连天。Gunfire licks the heavens. /许多名胜古迹毁于～。Many scenic spots and historical sites were destroyed in the war.

战火纷飞 zhànhuǒ-fēnfēi flames of war raging far and wide: ～的年代 war-ridden years; years of war

战祸 zhànhuò scourge of war: ～频仍 be subjected to repeated war disasters

战机 zhànjī ❶ opportunity for combat: 失去最好的～ lose the best opportunity to win a battle /捕捉～ seize the opportunity for battle; seize the right moment to strike ❷ secret information about military actions; military secret: 泄露～ leak military secrets ❸ fighter plane; fighter

战绩 zhànjì military successes or exploits; combat achievements: ～卓著 win great distinction in battle /取得辉煌的～ achieve splendid military successes /～平平 with mediocre military achievements

战舰 zhànjiàn war vessel; warship: 向地中海派遣～ dispatch warships to the Mediterranean Sea /超龄～ overage war vessels

战将 zhànjiàng skilful high-ranking military officer; able general

战兢兢 zhànjīngjīng 〈书面〉trembling with fear; shaking with terror; with fear and trepidation: 敌军官～地举起手来。The enemy officer raised his hands with fear.

战局 zhànjú war situation: 控制～ have the war situation under control /扭转～ turn the tables on the enemy /～严峻。The military situation is grim.

战具 zhànjù weapons; arms

战况 zhànkuàng situation on the battlefield; progress of a battle; battle situation: 了解～ find out the progress of the battle /～不明。The situation on the battlefield is murky.

战利品 zhànlìpǐn spoils of war; war trophies or booty: 缴获大批～ capture a large quantity of spoils of war

战例 zhànlì specific example of a battle (in military science); casebook or selected cases of battles: 一个著名的～ famous battle /以弱胜强的典型～ typical example of the weak defeating the strong in battle

战栗 zhànlì *also* "颤栗" zhànlì shake; tremble; shiver; shudder: 四肢～ tremble in every limb /他突然全身一阵～。A sudden shiver came upon him. /我一想到它就浑身～。I shuddered all over at the very thought.

战列舰 zhànlièjiàn ship-of-the-line; battleship

战列巡洋舰 zhànliè xúnyángjiàn battle cruiser

战乱 zhànluàn chaos caused by war; war turmoil: ～时期 chaotic years of war; in the turmoil of war /这对夫妻是在～中失散的。The husband and wife lost touch with each other in the turbulent years of the war.

战略 zhànlüè strategy: ～和战术 art of war; strategy and tactics /全球～ global strategy /～思想 strategic thinking /～部署 strategic plan (*or* deployment, *or* disposition) /～转移 strategic shift /～攻势 strategic offensive /～守势 strategic defence /～退却 strategic retreat /～要地 area (*or* place) of strategic importance; important strategic point /～方针 strategic principle /～决策 strategic policy decision /～储备 strategic reserves (*or* stockpiles) /～核武器 strategic nuclear weapons /～目标 strategic objective /～同盟 strategic alliance /～能力 strategic capability /～优势 strategic superiority /～重点 strategic priority /限制～武器会谈 Strategic Arms Limitation Talks (SALT) /消减～武器会谈 Strategic Arms Reduction Talks (START) /从～角度考虑问题 approach a problem from the strategic point of view /～上藐视敌人, 战术上重视敌人。Despise the enemy strategically and take full account of him tactically.

战略防御计划 Zhànlüè Fángyù Jìhuà (US) Strategic Defense Initiative (SDI); Star Wars

战略格局 zhànlüè géjú strategic setting or situation; strategic structure; strategic pattern

战略后方 zhànlüè hòufāng strategic rear

战略伙伴关系 zhànlüè huǒbàn guānxi strategic partnership

战略家 zhànlüèjiā strategist

战略物资 zhànlüè wùzī strategic goods and materials: 储备～ store up strategic goods and materials /抢运～ rush transport of strategic *matériel*

战略学 zhànlüèxué science of strategy

战马 zhànmǎ battle steed; war-horse: ～嘶鸣。The battle steeds are neighing.

战幕 zhànmù 〈比喻〉curtain on war, sport games, etc.: ～揭开了。The curtain rose on the war.

战袍 zhànpáo robes of ancient soldiers

战评 zhànpíng military appraisal of a battle or an action

战前 zhànqián prewar: ～准备工作 prewar preparations; preparations for a battle

战勤 zhànqín civilian war service: ～人员 personnel for civilian war service

战情 zhànqíng military or war situation

战区 zhànqū war zone; theatre of operations; theatre of war: 第一～ first theatre of war

战区导弹防御系统 Zhànqū Dǎodàn Fángyù Xìtǒng (US) Theater Missile Defense (TMD)

战裙 zhànqún pair of padded guards worn to protect the legs (shins) by ancient soldiers

战胜 zhànshèng triumph over; defeat; vanquish; conquer: ～顽敌 rout a tough enemy /～对方 defeat the opponents /～困难 overcome (*or* surmount) difficulties /～洪涝灾害 control the flood /～疾病 cure one's illness /善良～邪恶 triumph of good over evil /不可～ invincible /～恐惧心理 vanquish one's fears

战胜国 zhànshèngguó victorious nation; victor

战时 zhànshí wartime: ～配给 wartime rationing /～紧急动员 emergency mobilization during wartime /～的物资供应 wartime supplies of goods and materials /～编制 wartime establishment; troop establishment on a war footing /～内阁 wartime cabinet

战史 zhànshǐ war history; military history: 中国人民解放军～ military history of the People's Liberation Army

战士 zhànshì ❶ soldier; man: 武警～ armed policeman /公安～ public security officer (*or* man) /老～ veteran soldier ❷ champion; warrior; fighter: 伟大的国际主义～ great champion of internationalism /无产阶级～ proletarian fighter /白衣～ medical worker

战事 zhànshì war; battle; hostilities: ～起因 cause of hostilities /～消息 war news /～频起, 百姓逃亡。Battles erupted frequently and

people fled from home.

战书 zhànshū written challenge to war; letter of challenge: 下～ send out (*or* dispatch) a letter of challenge

战术 zhànshù (military) tactics: ～防御 tactical defence /～攻势 tactical offence /～思想 tactical thinking /闪电～ blitz tactics /游击～ partisan tactics /～指挥员 commander of a tactical operation /～预备队 tactical reserve /～电子系统 tactical electronic warfare system (TEW) /～核武器 tactical nuclear weapons /～轰炸机 tactical bomber /～航空导弹 tactical air missile /～空中导航设备 tactical air navigation (TACAN) /～空中突击部队 tactical air strike force /～强击战斗机 tactical strike fighter (TSF) /～演习 tactical manoeuvre; tactical exercise /～预警 tactical early warning /～侦察 tactical reconnaissance

战术家 zhànshùjiā tactician

战术学 zhànshùxué science of tactics

战术战斗机 zhànshù zhàndòujī tactical fighter: ～大队 tactical fighter group (TFGP) /～中队 tactical fighter squadron (TFS) /～联队 tactical fighter wing (TFW)

战死 zhànsǐ die in battle; be killed in action

战悚 zhànsǒng 〈书面〉 tremble; shiver; shudder

战天斗地 zhàntiān-dòudì fight heaven and earth; combat nature; brave the elements: 谱写一曲～的颂歌 score a resounding victory against nature /他们～，不避艰辛。They braved the elements and defied all hardships.

战位 zhànwèi action position: 进入～ get into the action position (*or* station) /各就～! Man your posts! *or* Action stations!

战无不胜 zhànwúbùshèng always triumphant; ever-victorious; all-conquering: 这支部队所向披靡，～。The troops swept forward from victory to victory and vanquished all enemies. /～，攻无不克。There is no battle it cannot win and no fortress it cannot capture. *or* It is an army that has never failed to win a battle or to take a city.

战线 zhànxiàn battle line; battlefront; front; action front: 缩短～ shorten the battle line /建立统一～ form (*or* establish) a united front /教育～ educational front /在各条～上 in every field of endeavour; on all fronts /前方～ fighting front /后方～ home front /思想～ ideological front /～太长。The battle fronts are too far-flung (*or* over-extended).

战衅 zhànxìn cause for war; incidents that lead to hostilities: 挑起～ provoke a war; provoke incidents that sparked a war

战役 zhànyì campaign; battle: 三大～ Three Great Campaigns (the Liaoxi-Shenyang Campaign 辽沈战役, the Huai-Hai Campaign 淮海战役 and the Beiping-Tianjin Campaign 平津战役 during 1948-1949) / 滑铁卢～ Battle of Waterloo /～指挥员 commander of a campaign

战役学 zhànyìxué science of campaign

战役战术导弹 zhànyì zhànshù dǎodàn tactical operational missiles

战鹰 zhànyīng fighting eagle (pet name for a fighter plane): ～直冲云霄。The fighting eagle (*or* fighter plane) soared into the sky.

战友 zhànyǒu comrade-in-arms; battle companion: 共生死的～ fellow soldiers through thick and thin /老～ old-time comrade-in-arms /～情谊comradeship-in-arms

战云 zhànyún war clouds: ～笼罩着整个地区。War clouds hang over the area.

战战兢兢 zhànzhàn-jīngjīng ❶ shivering with fear; with fear and trepidation: 他接过信，～地拆开来读。He took the letter, opening it with apprehension. /男女老少～地望着他。Men and women, young and old, watched him with fear. ❷ with caution; gingerly: 他做事～，极为小心。He was overcautious in his work.

战阵 zhànzhèn battle array or formation; disposition of combat forces; battlefield; battleground: 摆开～ deploy the ranks in battle array

战争 zhànzhēng war; warfare: 正义～ just war /非正义～ unjust war /侵略～ war of aggression /防止～ avert (*or* prevent) war /医治～创伤 heal the war wounds /反对～ oppose war /～的危险 danger of war /制约～的力量 forces deterring war /～双方 both belligerents; two sides in a war /～的爆发 outbreak of war /～的终止 termination of war /煽动～ foment (*or* stir up) war /～升级 war escalation /～罪行 war crime /～冒险 war venture; war gamble /～温床 hotbed of war /～阴影 shadow of war /～物资 war materiel /～目的 war aims /～法则 rules of warfare /～环境 wartime conditions /～赔偿 war indemnity; war reparations /～宣传 war propaganda

战争边缘政策 zhànzhēng biānyuán zhèngcè policy of brink-of-war; brink-of-war policy; brinkmanship

战争法 zhànzhēngfǎ laws of war

战争贩子 zhànzhēng fànzi warmonger: 狂热的～ hysterical warmonger

战争机器 zhànzhēng jīqì war machine; war apparatus

战争狂 zhànzhēngkuáng war mania; war hysteria: ～人 war maniac

战争学 zhànzhēngxué polemology

战争状态 zhànzhēng zhuàngtài state of war

绽 zhàn split; tear; burst: 破～ flaw; weak point /他的上衣～线了。His coat has split at the seams. /皮开肉～。The skin is torn and the flesh gapes open (*or* is gaping).

绽放 zhànfàng come into bloom; break out into blossom: 樱花～。The cherry-trees are in full bloom. /蓓蕾竞相～。The buds are all bursting. /红色的鲜花正在～。The red flowers are in blossom.

绽裂 zhànliè split; break; burst: 他被打得皮肉～。He was badly bruised by flogging. *or* He was beaten till his flesh was torn to shreds. /棉桃～，露出雪白的棉花。The cotton bolls have burst forth in a riot of white.

绽露 zhànlù appear; become visible: 他脸上～微笑。A smile crept across his face. /他的手背青筋～。Blue veins stood out on the backs of his hands.

组 zhàn 〈书面〉 mend by sewing; sew

zhāng

章[1] zhāng ❶ chapter; section; division: 第三乐～ third movement (of a symphony, etc.) /宏伟的篇～ magnificent writing /优美的诗～ exquisite poem /下笔成～ have a ready (*or* facile) pen /全书共计十二～。The whole book is divided into twelve chapters. ❷ clauses and subclauses: 约法三～ agree on a three-point law — make a few simple rules to be observed by all concerned /《土地法》第二～ second clause of the *Land Law* ❸ order; orderliness: 杂乱无～ disorderly and unsystematic ❹ rules; regulations; charter; constitution: 典～ institutions; decrees and regulations /党～ Party Constitution /大宪～ (UK) Magna Charta; Magna Carta /联合国宪～ United Nations Charter /规～制度 rules and regulations /招生简～ general regulations for enrolling new students ❺ memorial to the throne: 奏～ memorial to the throne ❻ (Zhāng) a surname

章[2] zhāng ❶ seal; signet; stamp: 私～ personal seal /公～ official seal /印～ seal; signet; stamp /盖～ affix a seal; seal; stamp /刻一枚图～ engrave a seal ❷ badge; insignia; medal: 徽～ badge /臂～ armband; armlet /领～ collar badge; insignia /肩～ epaulet /勋～ medal; decoration

章炳麟 Zhāng Bǐnglín Zhang Binglin (1869-1936), also known as Zhang Taiyan (章太炎), democratic thinker of modern China

章草 zhāngcǎo (in Chinese calligraphy) *zhangcao*, style of cursive hand which retains some techniques of *lishu* (*or* official script, often used in memorials): 善书法，尤工～。He is good at calligraphy, especially *zhangcao*.

章程 zhāngchéng rules; regulations; constitution: 必须按～办事 act according to rules /按一定程序修改～ amend the regulations in accordance with the procedure /学生会～ regulations of the students' union

章程 zhāngcheng 〈方言〉 solution; way: 事儿怎么办，心里得有个准～。One must be sure of what is the best way to go about it.

章动 zhāngdòng 〈天文〉 nutation: 黄经～ nutation in longitude /倾角～ nutation in obliquity /月球～ lunar nutation

章法 zhāngfǎ ❶ organization and structure of a piece of writing; art of composition: 讲究～ pay attention to the art of composition /不拘～ with no regard for the logical presentation of ideas /文章～严谨。The essay is well organized. /这篇文章结构混乱，毫无～。The essay is rather loose, lacking in unity and coherence. ❷ orderly; methodical: 此人精干老练，办事很有～。Capable and experienced, this chap is quite methodical in his work. /事起突然，他没了～。The

abrupt turn of events threw him off balance.

章回体 zhānghuítǐ *zhanghui* style — a type of traditional Chinese novel divided into several chapters with each chapter headed by a couplet giving the gist of its contents: 中国古典小说大多是~。Most Chinese classical novels are in *zhanghui* style.

章回小说 zhānghuí xiǎoshuō *also* "章回体小说" (traditional) novel in *zhanghui* style

章节 zhāngjié chapters and sections; chapters: 全书共有八个~。The whole book has eight chapters in all.

章句 zhāngjù ❶ chapters, sections, and sentences and phrases in ancient writings: 阅读典籍, 必须准确理解~。In reading ancient books one must try to understand essay phrases and sentence accurately. ❷ syntactic and semantic analysis of ancient writings; philological study: ~之学 analysis and interpretation of ancient writings

章学诚 Zhāng Xuéchéng Zhang Xuecheng (1738-1801), thinker and historian of the Qing Dynasty

章鱼 zhāngyú octopus

章则 zhāngzé rules and regulations: 严守~ strictly abide by rules and regulations

章子 zhāngzi 〈方言〉 seal; stamp: 刻~ engrave a seal

章奏 zhāngzòu memorial to the throne

漳 Zhāng

❶ Zhanghe River which originates in Shanxi Province and empties into River Wei ❷ Zhangjiang, name of a river in Fujian Province

漳绒 zhāngróng *Zhang* silk, a kind of silk produced in Zhangzhou, Fujian Province

璋 zhāng

jade tablet

樟 zhāng

also "香樟" xiāngzhāng camphor tree

樟蚕 zhāngcán camphor silkorm; *Eriogyna pyretorum*

樟茶鸭 zhāngcháyā camphorwood and tea smoked duck

樟木 zhāngmù camphorwood: ~箱 trunk (*or* chest) made of camphorwood / ~家具 camphorwood furniture

樟脑 zhāngnǎo *also* "潮脑" cháonǎo camphor

樟脑丸 zhāngnǎowán 〈方言〉 camphor ball; moth-ball

樟脑油 zhāngnǎoyóu camphor oil

樟树 zhāngshù camphor tree; camphor laurel (*Cinnamomum camphora*)

蟑 zhāng

蟑螂 zhāngláng *also* "蜚蠊" fěilián cockroach; roach

彰 zhāng

❶ obvious; evident; conspicuous: 欲盖弥~ try to hide a mistake, only to make it more conspicuous / 相得益~ each shining more brilliantly in the other's company; complement each other ❷ cite (in dispatches); commend: 不~其功, 不扬其名 neither commend his meritorious service nor extol his reputation ❸ (Zhāng) a surname

彰明较著 zhāngmíng-jiàozhù conspicuous; outstanding: 这个人物在历史上的作用~, 不容置疑。This personage undoubtedly played an outstanding role in history.

彰善瘅恶 zhāngshàn-dàn'è commend the good and denounce the evil: ~, 以为惩劝 praise the good and condemn the evil so as to teach people by example

彰彰 zhāngzhāng obvious to all; clear; evident: 其德~若斯。His virtue is obvious to all.

獐(麞) zhāng

river deer; Chinese water deer (*Hydropotes inermis*)

獐头鼠目 zhāngtóu-shǔmù with the head of a buck and the eyes of a rat — with hideous features and shifty eyes; repulsively ugly and sly-looking: 但见那人形容猥琐, ~。The man was wretched-looking and repulsively ugly.

獐牙菜 zhāngyácài *also* "当药" dāngyào swertia

獐子 zhāngzi *also* "牙獐" yázhāng river deer

嫜 zhāng

〈书面〉 husband's father; father-in-law: 姑~ husband's parents; parents-in-law

伥(餦) zhāng

伥馆 zhānghuáng 〈书面〉 ❶ malt sugar; maltose ❷ a kind of cooked wheaten food

张(張) zhāng

❶ open; spread; draw; stretch: ~开嘴 open one's mouth / ~网捕鱼 spread a net to catch fish / ~弓射箭 draw a bow to shoot / 一~一弛 tension alternates with relaxation / 纲举目~。Once the key link is grasped, everything falls into place. ❷ lay on; display: 铺~浪费 extravagant and wasteful ❸ magnify; amplify; exaggerate: 虚~声势 make a show of strength; bluff and bluster / 夸~事实 exaggerate (*or* overstate) the facts ❹ look; glance: 东~西望 glance (*or* peer) around; look this way and that; look around in all directions ❺ open a new shop: 开~ open a business / 择日开~ choose an auspicious day for the opening of the shop ❻ 〈量词〉 (a) *of paper, paintings, tickets, etc.*: 一~报纸 a piece of paper / 两~火车票 two train tickets (b) *of articles such as bed, table, etc.*: 一~写字台 a writing desk / 一~沙发 a sofa (c) *of human face, mouth, etc.*: 一~笑脸 a smiling face / 一~利嘴 a sharp tongue (d) *of bow, plough; etc.*: 一~弓 a bow / 一~犁 a plough ❼ one of the twenty-eight constellations ❽ (Zhāng) a surname

张榜 zhāngbǎng put up a proclamation: ~招贤 put up a proclamation to recruit talented people / 得奖者名单将~公布。The list of successful contestants will be made public in a bulletin.

张本 zhāngběn ❶ anticipatory action: 这一抗议是后来出兵的~。This protest was an anticipatory action for the subsequent dispatch of troops. ❷ sth. foreshadowing later developments in a story: 故事开头二人之间发生的误会是他们后来交恶的~。The misunderstanding that arises between them at the beginning of the story foreshadows the subsequent deterioration of their relations.

张伯伦 Zhāngbólún Arthur Neville Chamberlain (1869-1940), British Prime Minister in 1937-1940

张驰 zhāng-chí tension and relaxation: ~结合 combine tension with relaxation

张大 zhāngdà 〈书面〉 magnify; exaggerate; blow up: ~其词 overstate the case; exaggerate / 竭力~其事 the matter was blown up out of all proportion

张大千 Zhāng Dàqiān Zhang Daqian (formerly translated as Chang Ta-ch'ien, 1899-1983), Chinese painter

张道陵 Zhāng Dàolíng Zhang Daoling (34-156), founder of Taoism in the Eastern Han Dynasty

张道 zhāngdao *also* "张刀" 〈方言〉 ❶ meddle: 什么事他都~。He likes to have a finger in every pie. ❷ act impetuously; behave impulsively: 这个人太~, 一点儿准谱都没有。Rash and impulsive, this man is not in the least reliable.

张灯结彩 zhāngdēng-jiécǎi hang up lanterns and silk festoons; be decorated with lanterns and colourful streamers: ~迎亲人 bedecked with lanterns and colourful bunting to welcome the dear ones / 大厅上~, 金碧辉煌。The big hall, decked out with lanterns and colourful decorations, looked resplendent and magnificent.

张帆 zhāngfān set sails; hoist sail; make sail: ~远航 set sails for a long voyage

张飞 Zhāng Fēi Zhang Fei (formerly translated as Chang Fei, ?-221), general of Shu of the Three Kingdoms, known for his sometimes rash bravery: 这位营长是个猛~, 有时不够稳。The battalian commander is as brave as the proverbial Zhang Fei, but sometimes a bit rash.

张飞鸟 zhāngfēiniǎo 〈方言〉 wagtail

张公吃酒李公醉 Zhānggōng chījiǔ Lǐgōng zuì lay the blame on the wrong person (out of misunderstanding)

张挂 zhāngguà hang up (a picture, etc.): ~彩灯 hang colourful lanterns / 字画~在墙上。The scrolls and paintings were hung up on the wall.

张冠李戴 zhāngguān-lǐdài put Zhang's hat on Li's head — confuse one thing with another; attribute sth. to the wrong person; get things mixed up: 他的历史知识欠缺, 引用起来常常是~。As he had only a smattering knowledge of history, he often misquoted historical allusions.

张国焘 Zhāng Guótāo Zhang Guotao (formerly translated as Chang Kuo-tao, 1897-1979), one of the early leaders of the Communist Party of China who defected in 1938

张果老 Zhāng Guǒlǎo Zhang Guolao (formerly translated as

Chang Kuo-lao), one of the Eight Immortals in Taoist mythology

张衡 Zhāng Héng Zhang Heng (formerly translated as Chang Heng, 78-139), Chinese scientist and writer of the Eastern Han Dynasty

张皇 zhānghuáng 〈书面〉 alarmed; frightened; flurried; flustered: 举止～ have a flustered manner /神色～ look scared

张皇失措 zhānghuáng-shīcuò be in a flurry of alarm; lose one's nerve; be scared stiff: 临变～ lose one's nerve in the face of an abrupt change /吓得～ be scared out of one's wits

张家长,李家短 Zhāngjiā cháng, Lǐjiā duǎn the virtues of the Zhangs and the defects of the Lis — gossip; idle talk; tittle-tattle: 两个老太太坐在炕上,～地扯开闲篇了。The two old women started gossiping as soon as they sat down.

张角 Zhāng Jiǎo Zhang Jiao (?-186 BC), leader of the Yellow Turbans Uprising towards the end of the Eastern Han Dynasty

张居正 Zhāng Jūzhèng Zhang Juzheng (formerly translated as Chang Chu-cheng, 1525-1582), statesman of the Ming Dynasty

张口 zhāngkǒu ❶ open one's mouth (to say sth.): 气得他半天没～。He remained speechless with rage. /他一～讲的就是行话。Every time he opened his mouth, he talked shop. ❷ 〈方言〉 gape; yawn: 打～ give a yawn

张口结舌 zhāngkǒu-jiéshé be agape and tongue-tied; be at a loss for words; be unable to say anything: 谎言揭穿,他～,无话可说。As his lies were laid bare, he became tongue-tied, not knowing what to say.

张狂 zhāngkuáng rampant; insolent; arrogant; impudent: 这小子太～! This fellow is too impudent by half!

张力 zhānglì 〈物理〉 ❶ tension; tensile force: 表面～ surface tension ❷ pulling force

张力计 zhānglìjì tensiometer

张力学说 zhānglì xuéshuō strain theory

张良 Zhāng Liáng Zhang Liang (formerly translated as Chang Liang, ?-189 BC), statesman of the early Western Han Dynasty

张量 zhāngliàng 〈数学〉 tensor

张罗 zhāngluo ❶ take care of; get busy about; attend to: ～家务 manage household affairs /～老人的后事 make arrangements for the old man's funeral /此事必须有人～。There has to be somebody looking after the matter. /开会需要的东西应及早准备,不要临时才～。Get things ready for the meeting in good time so as to avoid a last-minute rush. ❷ raise (funds); collect (money, etc.): 为偿还债务,他四处～。He went everywhere trying to borrow money to pay his debt. ❸ greet and entertain (guests); wait on (customers, etc.): 客人太多,她简直～不过来。There were so many guests that she could hardly attend to all of them.

张目 zhāngmù ❶ open one's eyes wide: ～注视 gaze at sth. with wide-open eyes ❷ inflate sb.'s arrogance: 为坏人～ boost the arrogance of evildoers /为官僚主义～ encourage the practice of bureaucratism

张骞 Zhāng Qiān Zhang Qian (formerly translated as Chang Ch'ien, ?-114 BC), first envoy of the Western Han Dynasty to kingdoms in the Western Regions

张三李四 Zhāngsān-Lǐsì Zhang, Li or anybody; any Tom, Dick or Harry: 不管他～,我谁都不想见。Whoever it is, I don't want to see him.

张僧繇 Zhāng Sēngyóu Zhang Sengyou (formerly translated as Chang Seng-yu, 502-557), painter of the Southern Dynasties

张声 zhāngshēng 〈方言〉 make a sound (as when speaking, coughing, etc.): 他被人说得红着脸,不～了。Being taken to task for what he had done, he went red in the face and kept quiet.

张贴 zhāngtiē post (a notice, poster, etc.): ～广告 put up an advertisement /～寻人启事 post a notice to locate someone /此处禁止～。Post no bills here.

张望 zhāngwàng ❶ peep (through a crack, etc.); peer: 偷偷地从窗户向里～ peep inside through the window ❷ look around: 抬头～ raise one's head and look around

张献忠 Zhāng Xiànzhōng Zhang Xianzhong (formerly translated as Chang Hsien-chung, 1606-1646), leader of a peasant uprising in the late Ming Dynasty

张心 zhāngxīn 〈方言〉 bother; worry about; trouble about: 只要我有个地方暂住几天,您什么也不必～了。You don't have to worry about me as long as I have somewhere to stay for a couple of days.

张旭 Zhāng Xù calligrapher of the Tang Dynasty, esp. famous for cursive-hand calligraphy

张萱 Zhāng Xuān Zhang Xuan (formerly translated as Chang Hsuan, 618-907), painter of the Tang Dynasty

张学良 Zhāng Xuéliáng Zhang Xueliang (formerly translated as Chang Hsueh-liang, 1901-), commander of the Northeastern Army and organizer of the Xi'an Incident (西安事变) in 1936

张牙舞爪 zhāngyá-wǔzhǎo bare fangs and brandish claws — make threatening gestures; be arrogant and ferocious: 他～地在那里大闹起来。He was ferociously aggressive and made a dreadful scene then and there.

张扬 zhāngyáng come out into the open; make widely known; make public: 大肆～ give enormous publicity to /不必～ have no need to make sth. public /四处～ publicize everywhere; spread (a story) all over the place /此事若～出去,后果不堪设想。If the matter were made public, the consequences would be too ghastly to contemplate.

张仪 Zhāng Yí Zhang Yi (?-310 BC), politician sent by princes to drum up support during in the Warring States Period

张应力 zhāngyìnglì tensile stress

张载 Zhāng Zài Zhang Zai (formerly translated as Chang Tsai, 1020-1077), philosopher of the Northern Song Dynasty and advocate of Guan learning (关学) of Confucianism

张璪 Zhāng Zǎo Zhang Zao (formerly translated as Chang Tsao), painter of the Tang Dynasty

张择端 Zhāng Zéduān Zhang Zeduan (formerly translated as Chang Tseh-tuan), painter of the Northern Song Dynasty, known for his masterpiece *The Festival of Pure Brightness on the River* (清明上河图)

张致 zhāngzhì posture; manner; air (often used in the early vernacular): 他装出些～来恫吓人。He assumed an air of importance, trying to scare people off.

张仲景 Zhāng Zhòngjǐng Zhang Zhongjing (formerly translated as Chang Chung-ching, 150-219), medical scientist of the Eastern Han Dynasty

张嘴 zhāngzuǐ ❶ open one's mouth (to say sth.): 他只要一～,话就没完没了。Once he started talking, he would rattle on interminably. ❷ request a loan; ask for a favour: 他一～就是几百块钱。When he asked for a loan, he would ask for no less than several hundred *yuan*.

zhǎng

掌 zhǎng ❶ palm: 鼓～ clap one's hands; applaud /摩拳擦～ be eager for a fight; itch to have a go /易如反～ as easy as turning one's hand over; easy as pie ❷ strike with the palm of the hand; slap: ～颊 slap sb. on the face ❸ hold in one's hand; take charge of; control; wield: ～权 wield (*or* hold) power /分～人事 be put in charge of personnel affairs ❹ bottom of certain animals' feet; pad; sole: 脚～ sole (of a human foot) /鸭～ duck's web /熊～ bear's paw ❺ horseshoe: 给马钉～的叫蹄铁工。A man who shoes horses is called a farrier. ❻ shoe sole or heel: 钉鞋～ have a shoe soled /鞋后～ heel of a shoe ❼ 〈方言〉 mend the sole of a shoe: ～鞋 mend the sole of a shoe ❽ 〈方言〉 add; put in (cooking oil, salt, etc.): ～点醋 add a bit of vinegar /这菜太淡,还该～点盐。The dish is bland and needs a bit more salt. ❾ 〈方言〉〈介词〉 *used in the same way as* 把: ～门关上 close the door ❿ (Zhǎng) a surname

掌案儿的 zhǎng'ànrde 〈旧语〉 one who cuts the meat at the butcher's

掌班 zhǎngbān 〈旧语〉 one who manages a theatrical troupe or a brothel

掌鞭 zhǎngbiān *also* "掌鞭的" 〈方言〉 cart driver; carter

掌厨 zhǎngchú chef: 他在一家饭店里～。He is a chef at a restaurant.

掌灯 zhǎngdēng ❶ hold a lamp: 她给奶奶掌着灯。She was holding a lamp to light up the way for her grandma. ❷ light an oil lamp: 大约是～时分,他来了。He came when it was almost lighting-up time.

掌舵 zhǎngduò ❶ operate the rudder; steer a boat ❷ be at the helm: 这家公司缺少个有经验的人～。The company needs someone experienced to take charge. ❸ helmsman; steersman: 航船必须有个好～。There must be a good steersman to pilot a ship.

掌骨 zhǎnggǔ 〈生理〉 metacarpal bone

Z

掌故 zhǎnggù anecdotes; tales:历史～ historical anecdotes / 有趣的～ amusing tales

掌管 zhǎngguǎn take charge of; run; administer: ～两家大饭店 manage two big hotels / ～行政事务 be in charge of administrative affairs / ～人事工作 take charge of personnel matters / ～一家公司 run a company

掌柜 zhǎngguì *also* "掌柜的" ❶〈旧语〉shopkeeper; manager (of a shop): 粮店～ manager of a grain shop ❷〈方言〉〈旧语〉landlord: 给～交租子 pay rent to the landlord ❸〈方言〉husband: 你家～在吗? Is your husband at home?

掌锅 zhǎngguō do the cooking: 有老师傅～，这个菜味道错不了。With an experienced chef in the kitchen, the dish is sure to taste nice.

掌权 zhǎngquán hold power; exercise control: 他只是个挂名的头头儿，并不～。Being chief in name only, he wields no real power. / 这家公司实际上由他～。He is in actual control of this firm. *or* He calls the tune (*or* shots) in this firm.

掌扇 zhǎngshàn *also* "障扇" zhàngshàn long-handled fan made of thin, tough silk or birds' feather carried by a guard of honour in ancient times

掌上计算机 zhǎngshàng jìsuànjī palm computer

掌上明珠 zhǎngshàng-míngzhū *also* "掌珠"; "掌上珠"; "掌中珠" pearl in the palm — beloved daughter; apple of one's eye: 她是老人的～。She is the beloved daughter of the old man.

掌勺儿 zhǎngsháor prepare a banquet; do the cooking: ～的 chef / 本店美食节由一级厨师～。First-class chefs will be doing the cooking in our restaurant during the gourmet festival.

掌声 zhǎngshēng clapping; applause: ～雷动 burst into thunderous applause / 礼堂内～四起。A big round of applause was heard in the auditorium.

掌事 zhǎngshì 〈方言〉be in charge of the routine; manage general affairs

掌握 zhǎngwò ❶ grasp; master; learn thoroughly: ～技术 master techniques / ～规律 learn the rules thoroughly / ～市场经济的理论 grasp the theory of the market economy / ～商业信息 with business information at one's fingertips / 熟练～英语口语 have a perfect command of spoken English / ～国际局势新动态 keep abreast of new developments in the international situation ❷ have in hand; take charge of; control: ～方向盘 be at the wheel (*or* helm) / ～主动 take the initiative / ～政权 wield political power / 他～了这个部门的领导权。He is in charge of the department. / 军人集团～了政府大权。The junta took control of the government.

掌玺大臣 Zhǎngxǐ Dàchén (UK) Lord Privy Seal

掌心 zhǎngxīn ❶ centre or hollow of the palm ❷ sphere of control: 孙悟空跳不出如来佛的～。Monkey King cannot jump out of Buddha's palm — be unable to escape.

掌印 zhǎngyìn keep the seal — take control; be in power: 掌帅印 take overall command / 这个厂由他一人～。The factory is put entirely under his control.

掌灶 zhǎngzào cook; prepare (in a restaurant, canteen, or a family that is giving a feast): 这次宴会由特级厨师～。The banquet will be prepared by a special-class chef.

掌子 zhǎngzi ❶ *also* "礃子" zhǎngzi; "掌子面"〈矿业〉face; work area ❷ horseshoe: 他牵着马上铁匠炉钉个～。He led the horse to the blacksmith's to be shod. ❸ sole (of a shoe); heel: 给这双鞋打个～。Have these shoes resoled.

掌嘴 zhǎngzuǐ slap sb. on the face

礃 zhǎng

礃子 zhǎngzi *see* "掌子❶" zhǎngzi

长[1](長) zhǎng

❶ older; elder; senior: 年～ be a senior / 他～我几岁。He is a few years older than I am. *or* He is my senior by a few years. ❷ eldest; oldest: ～兄 eldest brother / ～房～孙 eldest son's eldest son ❸ older generation: 师～ teacher / 尊～ elders / 他们是尊敬的～辈。They are the elder generation esteemed by all. ❹ chief; head; leader: 处～ division chief / 首～ leading cadre; senior officer / 部～ minister; head of a department under the Central Committee of the CPC / 代表团团～ head (*or* leader) of a delegation

长[2](長) zhǎng

❶ come into being; spring up; form: 柳树～叶儿了。The willow leaves are coming out. / 庄稼开始～芽了。The crops are sprouting up. / 头上～了个大包。There is a boil on his head. / 地上～满了青草。The ground is overgrown with green grass. ❷ grow; develop: 麦苗～得很好。The wheat seedlings are growing well. / 孩子～得真胖。What a chubby child! / 他生～在一个工人家庭。He was born in a worker's family. ❸ boost; enhance; increase: ～信心 boost one's confidence / ～学问 increase one's learning (*or* knowledge) / ～才干 enhance one's abilities

see also cháng

长辈 zhǎngbèi senior member of a family; person of the elder generation: 这些孩子从来不听～的话。These children have never been good at listening to their elders.

长膘 zhǎngbiāo (of a domestic animal) get fat; fatten; put on flesh; flesh out

长大 zhǎngdà grow up; be brought up: 他已～成人，懂事多了。He is grown up and has become much more sensible than before. / 她在农民家庭～。She was brought up in a farmer's family.

长房 zhǎngfáng branch of the eldest son in a family or clan: 他是这个大家族的～长孙。He is the eldest grandson of the major lineage of the extended family.

长公主 zhǎnggōngzhǔ eldest princess; grand princess

长个儿 zhǎnggèr grow taller: 几个月不见，这孩子～了。The child has grown taller since I last saw him a few months ago.

长官 zhǎngguān ❶〈旧语〉senior officer or official; commanding officer ❷ (Japan) Director-General: 防卫厅～ Director-General of the Defence Agency ❸ (ROK) Minister: 经济企划院～ Minister of Economic Planning

长官意志 zhǎngguān yìzhì will of a senior official: 按～办事 act solely according to the instructions of the higher-ups

长机 zhǎngjī 〈军事〉lead aircraft; leader: 僚机要注意与～的配合。The wing planes should concentrate on coordination with the lead aircraft.

长进 zhǎngjìn progress; improvement: 弟弟的书法大有～。My brother's calligraphy has improved a lot. / 骄傲自满，妨碍了他学业的～。Complacency has hampered his progress in studies.

长老 zhǎnglǎo ❶〈书面〉elder people: 向地方的～了解过去的情况 learn about past events from the local elders ❷ (respectful form of address for an old monk) elder ❸ (of Judaism and Christianity) local religious leader; elder

长老会 Zhǎnglǎohuì 〈基督教〉Presbyterian Church

长脸 zhǎngliǎn do credit to: 他得了大奖，真为咱们～。He has won the first prize and is a credit to us all.

长毛 zhǎngmáo 〈方言〉become mildewed; be covered with mildews: 阴雨潮湿，东西容易～。Things easily get mouldy in rainy and damp climate.

see also chángmáo

长门 zhǎngmén *see* "长房"

长年 zhǎngnián 〈方言〉owner of a ship

see also chángnián

长亲 zhǎngqīn senior relatives

长肉 zhǎngròu put on flesh; fill out; get fatter: 不得了，最近又长了几斤肉。Dear me! I have put on quite some weight lately.

长上 zhǎngshàng ❶ elder member of a family; elder; senior ❷ superior; boss

长势 zhǎngshì the way a crop is growing; growth: 禾苗～旺盛。The seedlings of cereal crops are growing luxuriantly. / 蔬菜～喜人。The vegetables are coming along fine.

长孙 zhǎngsūn ❶ eldest son's eldest son; eldest grandson ❷ (Zhǎngsūn) a surname

长尾巴 zhǎng wěiba 〈俗语〉child's birthday: 这孩子今天～。Today is the boy's birthday.

长相 zhǎngxiàng 〈口语〉looks; features; appearance; countenance: 她俩的～几乎一模一样。They look as like as two peas. / 从～上看，她绝不像是三十岁的人。She looks much younger for a woman of thirty.

长者 zhǎngzhě ❶ man senior in the family hierarchy and advanced in age ❷ venerable elder

长子 zhǎngzǐ eldest son

长子继承权 zhǎngzǐ jìchéngquán (right of) primogeniture; birth right

涨(漲) zhǎng

(of water, prices, etc.) rise; go up;

Z

become higher：物价暴～。The prices skyrocketed. /水～船高。When the water rises, the boat rises with it.
see also zhàng

涨潮 zhǎngcháo rising tide; flood tide：～了。The tide is at the flood. *or* The tide is on the flow.

涨风 zhǎngfēng trend of price hikes

涨幅 zhǎngfú (of prices, etc.) range or rate of rise; rise：零售物价～回落了一个百分点。The rise of retail prices dropped by one percent.

涨价 zhǎngjià rise in price; hike a price：不少物品都已～。Many commodity prices have already gone up.

涨价风 zhǎngjiàfēng tendency of price hikes：采取坚决措施制止～ resolutely check the tendency of jacking up prices; take resolute measure to check price hikes

涨落 zhǎng-luò (of water, prices, etc.) rise and fall; ebb and flow; fluctuate：控制价格的～ control the fluctuations of prices /潮水～都有一定的时间。The ebb and flow of the tide abide by their own rhythm.

涨钱 zhǎngqián 〈口语〉❶ rise in price ❷ pay raise or rise：我们下月要～了。We will have a pay raise next month.

涨水 zhǎngshuǐ (of water) rise; go up：这条河的上游～，蹚水已经过不去了。The upper reaches of the river have gone up. It is now impossible to wade across it.

zhàng

瘴 zhàng miasma：～雨蛮烟 miasmatic rain and harmful fog

瘴疠 zhànglì communicable diseases in damp subtropical regions, such as pernicious malaria, etc.

瘴气 zhàngqì miasma

嶂 zhàng screen-like mountain peak：重岩叠～ cliffs rising one higher than another /千峰万～插云天。Peaks upon peaks point towards the blue sky.

幛 zhàng large, oblong sheet of silk with an inscription presented at a wedding, birthday or funeral：寿～ large sheet of silk inscribed with good wishes for a birthday /贺～ large silk sheet with an inscription of congratulations on it /挽～ large silk sheet with an inscription of condolences on it presented at a funeral

幛子 zhàngzi large, oblong sheet of silk with an appropriate message attached, presented at a wedding, birthday or funeral：给老人家送去一幅上好绸缎做的～，以示庆贺 have a sheet of quality silk inscribed with greetings and sent to grandpa as a token of congratulation

障 zhàng ❶ hinder; impede; obstruct：一叶～目。A leaf obstructed the view. ❷ screen; barrier; block：屏～ protective screen /路～ roadblock; barricade

障碍 zhàng'ài ❶ hinder; block; obstruct：～科学的发展 impede the development of science /～车辆的通行 block the traffic /～物 obstacle; hindrance; barrier; entanglement ❷ obstacle; obstruction; barrier; impediment：排除～ remove (*or* clear away) an impediment / 语言～ language barrier /成为两国关系发展的～ constitute an obstacle to the development of relations between the two countries

障碍船 zhàng'àichuán 〈军事〉 blockship

障碍赛跑 zhàng'ài sàipǎo steeplechase; obstacle race

障蔽 zhàngbì block; obstruct; shut out：月亮为乌云所～。The moon was blocked by dark clouds. /浓烟～了他们的视线。The dense smoke obstructed their view.

障谷 zhànggǔ V-shaped river valley with steep slopes

障扇 zhàngshàn see “掌扇” zhǎngshàn

障眼法 zhàngyǎnfǎ *also* “遮眼法” zhēyǎnfǎ; “掩眼法” yǎnyǎnfǎ cover-up; camouflage; disguise：他用～蒙我。He throw dust into my eye. *or* He pulled the wool over my eyes. /这是敌人惯用的～。This was the camouflage habitually employed by the enemy.

障翳 zhàngyì 〈书面〉 obstruct; block; cover; screen

障子 zhàngzi barrier made of reeds, sorghum stalks or closely planted shrubs; hedge; fence：树～ tree hedge /篱笆～ bamboo or twig fence

丈[1] zhàng ❶ *zhang*, a unit of length (＝3⅓ metres)：十尺为一～。Ten *chi* equals one *zhang*. ❷ measure (land)：清～ make an exact measurement of the land /这块土地已经～过。This piece of land has been measured.

丈[2] zhàng ❶ respectful form of address for an old man in ancient times：老～ venerable old man ❷ form of address for certain male relatives by marriage：姑～ husband of one's father's sister; uncle /岳～ wife's father; father-in-law /姐～ husband of one's sister; brother-in-law /姨～ husband of one's mother's sister; uncle

丈二和尚，摸不着头脑 zhàng èr héshang, mōbuzháo tóunǎo you cannot touch the head of a ten-foot monk — cannot make head or tail of it; completely fail to understand; be wide at sea：你这话从何说起？我真有点～了。I am all at sea about what you've just said.

丈夫 zhàngfū man：～气概 manliness /男子汉大～ true man

丈夫 zhàngfu husband：她有位能干的好～。She has a very able husband.

丈量 zhàngliáng measure (land)：～地亩 measure land in *mu*

丈母 zhàngmu *also* “丈母娘” wife's mother; mother-in-law：～疼女婿。The mother-in-law dotes on her son-in-law.

丈人 zhàngrén 〈古语〉 respectful form of address for an old man in ancient times

丈人 zhàngren wife's father; father-in-law

杖 zhàng ❶ cane; stick：拐～ walking stick /手～ (walking) stick /竹～ bamboo stick /拄～而立 stand with a cane under one's arm ❷ rod or staff used for a specific purpose：魔～ magic wand /禅～ Buhhdist monk's staff /擀面～ rolling pin

杖刑 zhàngxíng punishment by flogging with a stick in ancient China

杖头木偶 zhàngtóu mù'ǒu *also* “托偶” tuō'ǒu type of puppet show with actors holding puppets and operating their performance using wooden sticks

杖子 zhàngzi barrier made of weeds, sorghum stalks, etc. (usu. used in place names)：大～ Dazhangzi (in Hebei Province)

仗[1] zhàng ❶ 〈书面〉 weaponry; weapons; arms：仪～ flags, weapons, etc. carried by a guard of honour /明火执～ carry torches and weapons in a robbery — robbery in broad daylight ❷ hold (a weapon)：～剑 hold a sword ❸ rely on; depend on; on the strength of：仰～ rely on; look to sb. for backing (*or* support) /依～人数优势 by dint of numerical superiority

仗[2] zhàng fight; battle; war：胜～ win a battle; triumph over /再打一个漂亮～ score another brilliant victory /一定要打好财务检查这一～ make a success of the financial inspection

仗胆 zhàngdǎn by dint of one's courage：仗着胆子 pluck up one's courage

仗火 zhànghuǒ 〈方言〉 action; fighting; combat：没经过～的新兵 newly recruited soldiers who have not seen action

仗马寒蝉 zhàngmǎ-hánchán remain silent out of fear; dare not speak out

仗势 zhàngshì take advantage of one's own or other's power：～横行 ride roughshod over people by abusing one's power

仗势欺人 zhàngshì-qīrén abuse one's power and bully people; play the bully on the strength of one's powerful connections or position：他～，硬要人家转让铺面。He abused his power and browbeated the owner into yielding the shop to him.

仗恃 zhàngshì rely on; depend on：～权势 by dint of one's powerful connections

仗腰 zhàngyāo *also* “仗腰子”；“仗腰眼子” 〈口语〉 back up; support; bolster：怪不得他这样大胆，原来有人给他～。It turned out that he had someone backing him up. No wonder he was so reckless.

仗义 zhàngyì ❶ 〈书面〉 uphold justice：～而动 take action to uphold justice ❷ be loyal to (one's friends)：你们再胡闹，可别怪我不～！If you keep on making trouble, don't blame me for being unfriendly.

仗义疏财 zhàngyì-shūcái generous in helping the poor or needy：为人～ be generous to people /此人一向～。The man always helps

needy people without stinting.

仗义执言 zhàngyì-zhíyán speak out to uphold justice:挺身而出,～ step forward bravely and speak out from a sense of justice /他敢于～,不畏权势。He stood in no fear of power and influence and dared to speak boldly in defence of justice.

涨(漲) zhàng ❶ swell after absorbing water, etc.:发好的海参～了许多。Well soaked in water, the sea cucumbers swelled a lot. ❷ be swelled by a rush of blood; redden:脑子发～ feel one's head swimming /担子压得他～红了脸。His face went red under the weight of the load. ❸ (of weights and measures, etc.) be more, longer, etc. than expected:～出了二寸布。The cloth was 0.2 *chi* longer than expected. /上个月他钱花～了。Last month, he spent more than he got. *or* His expenditure exceeded his income last month.

see also zhǎng

帐(帳) zhàng ❶ curtain; tent; canopy:蚊～ mosquito net /锦～ brocade curtain /青纱～ green curtain of tall crops /～篷桩子 tent-peg ❷ *see* "账" zhàng

帐钩 zhànggōu bed-curtain hook; mosquito net hook:一副铜～ pair of brass mosquito net hooks

帐幔 zhàngmàn heavy curtain

帐幕 zhàngmù tent

帐篷 zhàngpeng tent:帆布～ canvas tent /尼龙～ nylon tent /搭起～ pitch a tent /拆除～ strike a tent

帐子 zhàngzi ❶ bed-curtain:床上挂着一顶印花～。Over the bed hangs a printed bed-curtain. ❷ mosquito net

账(賬) zhàng ❶ account:记～ keep accounts /查～ check (*or* audit, *or* examine) accounts /结～ settle (*or* square) the accounts /赊～ buy sth. on credit /报～ get refunded /记在我的～上 put it on my account; charge it to my account ❷ account book:一摞～ stack of account books ❸ debt; credit:欠～ owe a debt /还～ repay a debt /要～ demand payment of debt /赖～ repudiate a debt

账本 zhàngběn *also* "账簿" account book

账簿 zhàngbù account book

账册 zhàngcè account book:清点～ check account books

账单 zhàngdān bill; account; check:凭～报销 reimbursement may be claimed on handing in the bills /请将～送来。Send in your account, please.

账房 zhàngfáng 〈旧语〉❶ accountant's office ❷ accountant:他在财主家任～多年。He worked in a rich man's family as an accountant for many years.

账号 zhànghào account number

账户 zhànghù account:开立～ open an account with (*or* in) a bank /结清～ close an account with (*or* in) a bank /银行里有他的～。He has an account in the bank.

账款 zhàngkuǎn funds on account; credit:清理～ clear up funds on account /结算～ settle the credit /～亏空 overdraft

账面 zhàngmiàn items of an account:～利润 book profit /～损失 book loss /先把～弄清楚,再去核对库存 sort out the account before checking the stock

账面价值 zhàngmiàn jiàzhí 〈会计〉book value

账面净值 zhàngmiàn jìngzhí 〈会计〉net book value

账目 zhàngmù items of an account; accounts:清查～ check accounts /～公开 accounts open to public inspection /定期公布～ publish the accounts regularly /～混乱。The accounts (*or* books) are a confused mess.

账头 zhàngtou 〈方言〉❶ items of an account; accounts:～清楚。The accounts are in order. ❷ bills due; outstanding accounts:镇上的～去年只收起八成。Only eighty per cent of the bills due in the town were paid last year.

Z

账先儿 zhàngxiānr *also* "账先生"〈方言〉〈旧语〉someone who managed financial affairs for a landlord, capitalist, etc.

账主子 zhàngzhǔzi 〈方言〉creditor:～到我家追债。The creditor came to my home to press for repayment of debts.

胀(脹) zhàng ❶ grow in size; expand; distend:热～冷缩 expand when heated and contract when cooled ❷ swell; be bloated:～肚子 feel bloated in the stomach /眼睛～得酸疼。The eyes swelled so much that they ached.

胀库 zhàngkù stocked to the full:牛肉～ store houseful of beef

胀闸 zhàngzhá damper brake (of a bicycle); hub brake

zhāo

着(❶❷招) zhāo ❶ move in chess:一步高～儿 clever move /这一～确实不同凡响。This is really a splendid stroke (*or* move). /只因一～错,输却满盘棋。One wrong move and the whole game is lost. ❷ trick; device; tactic:别耍花～儿。Don't play tricks. *or* None of your petty tricks. /我实在没～儿了。I'm at my wits' end. /三十六～,走为上～。Moving away is the best of all choices. *or* Better make yourself scarce. ❸ 〈方言〉put in; add:～点儿醋 add a bit vinegar /～些糖 put in some sugar ❹ 〈方言〉all right; okay:～,你们就这么办吧! Okay, go ahead as (has been) agreed. /这话～哇! That says it all!

see also zháo; zhe; zhuó

着法 zhāofǎ *also* "招法" zhāofǎ ❶ move in a chess game ❷ movement in *wushu* (武术)

着数 zhāoshù *also* "招数" zhāoshù ❶ move in chess:计算～ count the moves in chess ❷ movement in *wushu* (武术):～利落 be nimble in *wushu* movements ❸ trick; device:使尽了～也不灵 have exhausted all the devices in vain

朝 zhāo ❶ early morning; dawn; morning:不是一～一夕可以办到的 cannot be achieved overnight ❷ day:今～ today /来～ some day in the future /明～ tomorrow /有一～一日 some day; one of these days /一～他得手 once he got his way; once he succeeds

see also cháo

朝不保夕 zhāobùbǎoxī *also* "朝不虑夕" not know in the morning what may happen in the evening; be in a critical condition:祖父已是～了。Grandpa's health is extremely precarious.

朝不谋夕 zhāobùmóuxī be unable to plan out one's day; be preoccupied with the current crisis:整个朝廷已经到了～、岌岌可危的地步了。The days of the imperial government were numbered. *or* The imperial court was teetering on collapse.

朝发夕至 zhāofā-xīzhì start at dawn and arrive at dusk — a short journey:由此地乘船去省城,～。By boat it is a day's journey from here to the provincial capital.

朝歌夜舞 zhāogē-yèwǔ sing and dance all day long; lead a life of dissipation

朝过夕改 zhāoguò-xīgǎi err in the morning and mend in the evening — correct one's mistakes in time

朝晖 zhāohuī morning sunlight:我欲因之梦寥廓,芙蓉国里尽～。And I am lost in dreams, untrammelled dreams Of the land of hibiscus glowing in the morning sun.

朝令夕改 zhāolìng-xīgǎi issue an order in the morning and rescind it in the evening; make changes in policy at will:政策不可～。Policies should not be subjected to frequent changes.

朝露 zhāolù 〈书面〉morning dew — short lived; ephemeral; transitory:譬如～,去日苦多。Life is like morning dew, and much of it has evaporated.

朝暮 zhāomù ❶ morning and evening ❷ all day long; often; constantly:～相处 be together all the time

朝气 zhāoqì youthful spirit; vim and vigour; vitality:充满～ be full of vitality /～焕发 radiate vigour /显然,他的～早已消失了。It was evident that he had long since lost the spark of youthful vigour.

朝气蓬勃 zhāoqì-péngbó be bursting with youthful spirit; brim over with vigour and vitality:一批～的年轻人 group of spirited young people /这是一个～和富有战斗精神的民族。This is a militant nation, full of vigour and vitality.

朝乾夕惕 zhāoqián-xītì exert oneself day and night:对于学业,他从来是～,不敢懈怠。He has devoted wholeheartedly to his studies, never relenting his efforts.

朝秦暮楚 zhāoqín-mùchǔ serve the State of Qin in the morning and the State of Chu in the evening — change one's loyalty frequently; inconstant:他岂～之辈! He is certainly not the type who quickly switches sides. /他一向～,反复无常。He has always been fickle and capricious.

朝日 zhāorì morning sun:却见东边海际,～已升起半轮。One saw the morning sun already rising halfway over the sea in the east.

朝日新闻 Zhāorì Xīnwén *Asahi Shimbun*, a Japanese daily newspaper first published in 1879
朝三暮四 zhāosān-mùsì blow hot and cold; play fast and loose; chop and change: 这种～的人,千万不要和他交往。Never associate with those who chop and change the moment they see something different.
朝思暮想 zhāosī-mùxiǎng long day and night; pine for sth.: 人民～的改革成了现实。The reform that people have been longing (*or* yearning) for has become a reality.
朝闻夕死 zhāowén-xīsǐ yearn for truth; thirst after knowledge
朝夕 zhāoxī ❶ morning and evening; day and night; every day; constantly: ～共处 be constantly together / ～思念 think about sb. day and night / 两人～相伴。The two are in each other's company every day. ❷ shortly; very short time: 只争～ seize the day, seize the hour; seize every minute / 这么多事情,～间怎能完成? How can we achieve so much overnight? / 水墨画达到这种境界,非～之功。Such a high level of wash painting cannot be attained in a short time.
朝霞 zhāoxiá morning glow; rosy dawn: ～满天。The sky is covered with the rosy clouds of dawn. / ～映红了广场。The morning glow dyed the square red.
朝阳 zhāoyáng rising sun; morning sun: 如～初升 like the rising sun / 一轮～冉冉升起。A morning sun rose slowly.
see also cháoyáng
朝阳工业 zhāoyáng gōngyè sunrise industries (e.g. microelectronics, information, new materials, automation, bioengineering, space navigation, ocean development, etc.)
朝夷暮跖 zhāoyí-mùzhí a virtuous man in the morning and an evildoer in the evening — people change, and a good man goes to the bad easily

嘲 zhāo

see also cháo
嘲哳 zhāozhā *see* "啁哳" zhāozhā

啁 zhāo

see also zhōu
啁哳 zhāozhā 〈书面〉 twitter

钊 zhāo 〈书面〉 encourage; urge; spur; exhort

招[1] zhāo

❶ beckon; gesture: ～之即来 come at sb.'s beck (*or* sb.'s beck and call) / 他一～手,大家都向他跑去。Everyone rushed over to him when he beckoned. ❷ recruit; engage; enlist; enrol: ～临时工 recruit temporary workers ❸ attract; invite; incur; court: ～蚊子 attract mosquitoes / ～人厌恶 incur displeasure; be offensive ❹ offend; provoke; tease: 这孩子脾气大,别～他。The child is hot-tempered. Don't tease him. ❺ draw; cause: ～人注意 draw people's attention / ～人忌恨 rouse envy and hatred ❻ 〈方言〉 infect; be catching: 小心点,这病～人。Be careful. The patient is contagious. ❼ (Zhāo) a surname

招[2] zhāo

confess; admit; own up: 不打自～ own up without being pressed / 面对人证物证,他不得不～。He had to confess when confronted with human testimony and material evidence.

招[3] zhāo trick; device; move

招安 zhāo'ān (of feudal rulers) offer amnesty to rebels and enlist their service: 接受～ (of former rebels) accept amnesty and pledge loyalty to the ruler / 反对朝廷～ be opposed to the royal government's amnesty to and enlistment of rebels
招标 zhāobiāo invite tenders (*or* bids, *or* public bidding): ～人 tenderer / 公开～ open tender; open bidding (for projects) / ～单位 tendering entity
招标承包 zhāobiāo chéngbāo make a contract through public bidding
招兵 zhāobīng enrol or draft new recruits
招兵买马 zhāobīng-mǎimǎ recruit men and buy horses — raise or enlarge an army; recruit personnel: 到处～ try to enlist followers everywhere
招财进宝 zhāocái-jìnbǎo "bring in money and treasure"— formula used to wish oneself or sb. else good fortune in business: 开张大吉,～。(used by a shop owner or his well-wisher) May the auspicious opening bring good fortune (to the shop)!
招潮 zhāocháo 〈动物〉 fiddler crab; calling crab
招待 zhāodài give reception; offer hospitality; entertain; serve (customers): ～客人 entertain guests / ～顾客 serve customers / 受到热情的～ be cordially received; be given warm reception / ～不周,务请原谅。Forgive me if I have offered inadequate hospitality.
招待费 zhāodàifèi entertainment allowance or expenses
招待会 zhāodàihuì reception: 冷餐～ buffet reception / 记者～ press conference / 参加～ attend a reception / 举行国庆～ give (*or* hold) a reception on National Day
招待券 zhāodàiquàn complimentary ticket
招待所 zhāodàisuǒ guesthouse; hostel: 扩建～ extend the guesthouse / 青年～ youth hostel
招待员 zhāodàiyuán attendant; service personnel
招法 zhāofǎ ❶ move in chess ❷ movement in *wushu* or martial arts
招风 zhāofēng catch the wind — attract too much attention and court trouble: 树大～ a tall tree catches the wind — a person in a high position is liable to be attacked / 这样做太～。This sort of action is too ostentatious.
招风耳 zhāofēng'ěr protruding ears
招风惹草 zhāofēng-rěcǎo *also* "招风惹雨"; "招风揽火" bring trouble on oneself; invite trouble: 你安稳一些吧,别这样不知深浅地～啦! Stop fooling around and getting yourself into trouble like that.
招蜂引蝶 zhāofēng-yǐndié attract bees and butterflies — flirt with men: 这姑娘不老实,在外面～。The girl is a coquette and likes to flirt with every young man.
招抚 zhāofǔ *see* "招安"
招柑 zhāogān *also* "蕉柑" jiāogān a kind of late-maturing orange
招工 zhāogōng recruit workers
招供 zhāogòng confess one's crime; confess: 被迫～ be forced to confess; confess under duress / 犯人～了。The prisoner has confessed his crime. / 他是在严刑之下～的。His confession was obtained under cruel torture.
招股 zhāogǔ raise capital by floating shares
招雇 zhāogù recruit and employ: ～工人 employ workers
招呼 zhāohu ❶ call; shout: ～小船靠岸 shout to the small boat to pull in to shore / ～同学们过来 call the students to come over / 外面好像有人在～我。It sounds as if somebody is calling me outside. ❷ hail; greet; say hello to: 亲切地跟他们打～ greet them cordially / 人太多,我真不知该～谁好。I really don't know whom I should say hello to since there are so many people around. ❸ ask; tell; notify: ～他快上车。Tell him to get on the bus at once. / 请～大家来开会。Please ask everyone to come to the meeting. ❹ take care of; look after; attend to: ～病人 take care of the patients / ～客人 look after the guests / ～牲口 mind draught animals / ～得很周到 attend to sth. carefully / 生病的祖母全靠他～。The ailing grandmother depended on him for care and attention. ❺ 〈方言〉 watch; mind; take care: 天气不好,～着凉了。Take care not to catch a cold; the weather is so bad.
招唤 zhāohuàn call: 把孩子们都～来 call the children to come over
招魂 zhāohún call back the spirit of the dead; revive: 为封建迷信～ resurrect feudalistic superstition
招集 zhāojí muster; convene; gather: ～组员们议一议。Call together the team members for a discussion.
招架 zhāojià ward off blows; hold one's own: 只有～之功,毫无还手之力 be able only to parry attacks with no strength left to hit back / 他们的势力太大,我们～不住。We could hardly hold our own in the face of our powerful opponents. / 打得敌军无法～。The enemies were sent reeling back under our fierce attack.
招聚 zhāojù call together; convene: ～工人 call the workers together
招考 zhāokǎo give public notice of entrance examination; employ by examination: ～新生 enrol students by examination / ～服务员 recruit attendants by examination
招徕 zhāolái solicit (customers or business); attract: ～顾客 appeal to customers / 旅行社把凡是能够～游客的点子都想到了。The travel agencies thought up all sorts of ways to attract tourists.
招揽 zhāolǎn solicit (customers or business); canvass: ～买卖 canvass business orders; drum up trade / ～顾客 attract customers
招领 zhāolǐng announce the finding of lost property: ～失物

Z

Found (as in notice) /～启事 notice of the finding of lost property / 拾物～处 Lost and Found; Lost Property Office
招骂 zhāomà ask for a scolding; invite censure: 你这些做法～。The way you do it is an open invitation to abuse.
招门纳婿 zhāomén-nàxù *see* "招女婿"
招募 zhāomù recruit; enrol; enlist: ～翻译 enrol interpreters (*or* translators) /～志愿人员 recruit volunteers
招纳 zhāonà 〈书面〉 seek and admit; scout about and recruit: ～专门人才 recruit professional talents
招女婿 zhāo nǚxu have the groom move into the bride's house after marriage
招牌 zhāopai shop sign; signboard: 金字～ gold-lettered signboard / 砸了老字号的～ defame a brand name /打着集资的～搞金融诈骗 engage in financial fraud under the pretence of raising funds /打着义演的～捞大钱 grab huge sum of money in the name of charity show
招盘 zhāopán put a business up for sale: 门上贴着～启事。A notice was put on the door announcing the sale of a business.
招聘 zhāopìn engage by public notice; invite applications for a job: 饭店～厨师。The hotel has advertised for cooks. /他们到全国各地～人员。They went all over the country to invite applications for jobs (*or* to seek prospective employees). *or* They went headhunting throughout the country.
招聘广告 zhāopìn guǎnggào job advertisement or ad
招亲 zhāoqīn ❶ *see* "招女婿" ❷ marry into and live with one's bride's family
招请 zhāoqǐng recruit and invite; take in: ～帮工 take in helpers
招权纳贿 zhāoquán-nàhuì arrogate power to oneself and take bribes
招惹 zhāore ❶ invite; incur; court: 到处～麻烦 court trouble everywhere ❷ 〈方言〉 (mostly used in the negative) tease; annoy; provoke: 千万别～这个人。Never provoke that fellow. *or* Don't rub him up the wrong way. /谁也不敢～他。No one dares to tease him. / 这个人脾气大，～不得。Leave that fellows alone; he is hot-tempered.
招惹是非 zhāore-shìfēi court trouble: 何必为这件小事～。Why invite trouble over such a trifle?
招认 zhāorèn make a confession of one's crime; plead guilty: 拒不～ refuse to confess one's crime /在事实面前，他只好～。He had to plead guilty in the face of facts.
招商 zhāoshāng invite outside investments: 开埠～ open the commercial city to outside investment
招商会 zhāoshānghuì meeting to invite investments
招商局 Zhāoshāngjú China Merchants Steam Navigation Co. Ltd. (China Merchants)
招商银行 Zhāoshāng Yínháng China Merchants Bank
招商引资 zhāoshāng-yǐnzī attract investments from overseas
招生 zhāoshēng enrol new students; recruit students: 改革～制度 reform the enrolment (*or* admission) system /～人数 number of students to be enrolled /～委员会 committee for enrolling students; admission committee /～简章 school admission brochure / ～办公室 admission office
招式 zhāoshì movement and posture in *wushu* or traditional opera performance
招事 zhāoshì bring trouble on oneself; court trouble: 他爱多嘴，好～。He is in the habit of shooting his mouth off and brings trouble on himself as a consequence.
招收 zhāoshōu enrol; recruit; take in: ～学员 enrol new students / ～服务员 recruit attendants
招手 zhāoshǒu move one's hand as a signal; beckon; wave: 他亲切地向我～。He cordially waved to me. /出租汽车，～即停。You have only to give a hand signal for a passing cab to stop.
招数 zhāoshù ❶ move in chess ❷ movement in *wushu* or martial arts ❸ trick; device
招贴 zhāotiē poster; placard; bill: 公园门口的大型～，引人注意。The huge poster in front of the park gate is eye-catching.
招贴画 zhāotiēhuà picture poster or placard: 墙上贴着～。There is a pictorial placard on the wall.
招贤 zhāoxián summon men of worth to serve their country; call talented people to service: 张榜～ put up posters recruiting talents / ～纳士 invite men of virtue and wisdom
招降 zhāoxiáng call on sb. to surrender: 采用～的手段来瓦解农民起义军 resort to summoning the peasant insurrectionary army to surrender so as to disintegrate it
招降纳叛 zhāoxiáng-nàpàn recruit turncoats and receive renegades; recruit deserters and mutineers: 搞拉帮结派，～的非法活动 go in for illegal activities of forming factions and recruiting turncoats and renegades /为了扩充实力，他们到处网罗人员，甚至～。To expand their forces they went everywhere to enlist people and even drew deserters and rebels into their ranks.
招笑儿 zhāoxiàor 〈方言〉 laughable; comical; funny: 小丑用些滑稽动作～。The clown performed some funny tricks to draw a laugh.
招延 zhāoyán recruit (followers); scout about for (talents, etc.): ～四方豪杰 recruit people of exceptional ability from all quarters
招眼 zhāoyǎn attract people's attention; be ostentatious: 她这身打扮很～。Her attire was far too ostentatious.
招摇 zhāoyáo act ostentatiously; show off: 事情是否能成功还没有把握，你何必如此～呢? Why trumpet the matter as we are not sure of the success yet?
招摇过市 zhāoyáo-guòshì swagger through the streets — blatantly seek the limelight; strive to court publicity: 他西装革履，在一群人的簇拥下～。Wearing a western suit and leather shoes, he swaggered through the streets escorted by a crowd of people.
招摇撞骗 zhāoyáo-zhuàngpiàn browbeat and swindle: 到处～ bluff and cheat everywhere /此人利用他爸爸在文艺界的地位～。Exploiting his father's position in the art and literary circles, this man swaggered about to beguile people.
招引 zhāoyǐn draw; attract; induce: ～了不少人围观 draw a crowd of onlookers /～顾客 attract customers
招诱 zhāoyòu attract; lure; induce: 商店粉饰一新，～行人。Having been newly whitewashed, the shop attracts passers-by.
招怨 zhāoyuàn spark resentment; give rise to grudges
招灾 zhāozāi bring about disaster; invite calamity
招灾惹祸 zhāozāi-rěhuò court disaster; bring trouble on oneself: 只要这孩子不～，我们就放心了。So long as the child does not get into trouble, we will feel reassured.
招展 zhāozhǎn move to and fro; flutter; wave: 随风～的彩旗 coloured flags flapping in the wind /花枝～的女郎 gorgeously dressed young woman /红旗迎风～。Red flags fluttered in the breeze.
招致 zhāozhì ❶ recruit; seek and employ: ～人才 scout for talents / ～了不少能工巧匠 have recruited many skilful craftsmen ❷ result in; bring about; lead to: ～灭亡 lead to destruction /～生命危险 put one's own life in jeopardy (*or* on the line)/～意外的麻烦 cause unexpected trouble
招赘 zhāozhuì have the groom move into the bride's house after marriage: ～了一个好女婿 marry one's daughter to a good husband and have him move into one's house after the marriage
招子 zhāozi ❶ poster; placard; bill ❷ flag with the shop's name on it hung at the doorway of a shop, or other signs for attracting customers ❸ device; move; means; stratagem: 别跟我玩儿心～! Don't you play tricks on me!
招租 zhāozū 〈旧语〉 ask for lodgers; attract lodgers; to let

昭 zhāo ❶ clear; evident; obvious: ～著 obvious; conspicuous; evident ❷ 〈书面〉 show; demonstrate: 以～信守 demonstrate one's good faith
昭布 zhāobù explicitly declare; clearly proclaim: ～天下 proclaim to the world
昭告 zhāogào publicly declare; proclaim: ～世人 proclaim to the public
昭然 zhāorán obvious; manifest; very clear: 事理～。The reason is obvious to all.
昭然若揭 zhāorán-ruòjiē all too obvious; clear as daylight: 侵略野心～。The aggressive designs are all too clear. /他的险恶用心～。His sinister intentions were absolutely unmistakable.
昭示 zhāoshì make clear to all; declare publicly; proclaim: ～全体军民 proclaim to the whole army and nation; declare to all soldiers and civilians /～后世 make it clear to the postesity
昭苏 zhāosū 〈书面〉 revitalize; revive: ～万物 revive all things on earth
昭雪 zhāoxuě exonerate; rehabilitate; redress: 平反～ redress and exonerate /十年沉冤得以～。The ten-year-old gross injustice was redressed.
昭彰 zhāozhāng clear; manifest; obvious; evident: 罪恶～ have

committed flagrant crimes /天理～，罪责难逃。Justice clearly demands that the culprit should not escape punishment.

昭昭 zhāozhāo 〈书面〉❶ bright; light; well-lit:日月～。The sun and the moon are shining brightly. ❷ clear; obvious; plain:以其昏昏，使人～，是不可能的。It is impossible (*or* won't do) for the ignorant to enlighten other people. *or* You cannot expect any enlightenment from an ignoramus.

昭著 zhāozhù clear; evident; manifest:军功～ have performed signal military exploits /臭名～ of ill repute; notorious

zháo

着 zháo ❶ touch; contact:说话不～边际 not speak to the point /前不～村，后不～店 can't find a decent place to have a rest in (*or* to spend the night in) ❷ feel; suffer: *see* "～凉"; "～风" ❸ burn:房子～火了! The house is on fire! /煤油灯点～了。The kerosene lamp has been lit. ❹ *used after a verb to indicate the result of the action*:谜语猜～了 have guessed a riddle right /我没见～他。I haven't seen him. ❺〈方言〉fall asleep:上床就～ fall asleep as soon as one lies down on one's bed
see also zhāo; zhe; zhuó

着边 zháobiān be close to what it should be; be relevant:他这些话乍听起来好像不～，仔细一想，却头头是道。These remarks of his may sound irrelevant at first, but they are actually very much to the point when you think carefully.

着风 zháofēng be chilled by the wind; become unwell through being in a draught:两腿疼痛，想必～了。My legs ache. I must have been chilled through being in the draught.

着慌 zháohuāng panic; feel alarmed; become flustered or jittery:没找到孩子，全家都～了。The whole family was thrown into a panic when they couldn't find the child.

着火 zháohuǒ catch fire; be in flames:库房～啦。The storehouse is on fire. /邻居家～，大家都急忙地跑去扑救。When a neighbour's house caught fire, everyone rushed to put it out.

着火点 zháohuǒdiǎn *also* "燃点" rándiǎn ignition point; burning or kindling point

着急 zháojí worry; feel anxious; have ants in one's pants:干～ be anxious but unable to do anything about it /瞎～ worry to no purpose /白～ get worried for nothing /你着什么急呢? There is nothing to worry about.

着紧 zháojǐn 〈方言〉❶ lose no time; hasten; hurry:他吃了饭还～去开会。He still has to hurry to the meeting after the meal. ❷ important; essential:不～的事。It doesn't matter. ❸ be close; be near in relationship:他们两家很～。The two families are on very good terms.

着凉 zháoliáng catch cold; catch a chill:我～发烧了。I've caught a cold and have a temperature.

着忙 zháománg ❶ be in a hurry or rush:旅行用的东西必须事先准备好，免得临时～。Get ready the things you will need for the trip so as to avoid a last-minute rush. ❷ worry; feel anxious; panic:听说家里失盗，他可着了忙了。He became panicky on learning that his house had been broken into. /别～，他说完了你再说。Take your time. You may speak when he has finished.

着迷 zháomí be fascinated; be enchanted:最近他对跳舞简直～了。He has been crazy about dancing recently. /大家听她唱歌都听得～了。Everyone became spellbound listening to her singing. /这孩子对电视～了。The child has been glued to the television.

着魔 zháomó be bewitched; be entranced; be possessed:他像着了魔似的迷上了气功。He was fascinated by *qigong* as if he were possessed. /他这些天练太极拳练得像～了似的。He has been practicing *taijiquan* (shadow boxing) like mad these days.

着恼 zháonǎo be angry; be vexed:他们拣老实的欺，叫人好不～。It is most vexing that they should always pick on simple-minded persons.

着三不着两 zháo sān bù zháo liǎng scatter-brained:这人办事经常是～的。This chap is always erratic in whatever he does.

zhǎo

沼 zhǎo natural pond:池～ pond; pool

沼地 zhǎodì marsh; swamp; bog

沼鹿 zhǎolù barasingha; swamp deer (*Cervus duvauceli*)

沼煤 zhǎoméi peat; moor coal

沼气 zhǎoqì marsh gas; bio-gas; methane:农民都爱用～。Peasants all like to use marsh gas.

沼气池 zhǎoqìchí methane-generating pit

沼气发电 zhǎoqì fādiàn marsh gas power generation

沼蝇 zhǎoyíng marsh fly

沼泽 zhǎozé marsh; swamp; bog:～土 bog soil /一眼望不到头的～地带 vast expanse of swamp land

沼泽地 zhǎozédì marshland; swamped land

找[1] zhǎo look for; hunt for; try to discover; want to see:～东西 look for sth. /～事故的原因 try to find out the cause of the accident /在边远山区～到了一座金矿 have discovered a gold mine in a remote mountain area /我在全镇到处～你。I have been hunting all over the town for you. /我下次来时一定再来～你。I'll surely call on you again when I come next time. /我来～你是关于下周郊游的事。I have come to see you about the excursion next week. /你如果需要有人给你出主意，你随时可以～他。You can always approach him for advice.

找[2] zhǎo give change:这是～给你的钱。Here is your change. /售货员～给我十元钱。The shop assistant gave me 10 *yuan* (in) change. /甭～了。(to a taxi driver, etc.) Keep the change. /你少～钱了。You have short-changed me. /我们谁也不～谁的钱。Now we are quits (*or* even).

找病 zhǎobìng bother one's head about:想开些吧，何必自己去～! Don't take things too seriously. There is no need to worry about it.

找不自在 zhǎo bùzìzài ask or look for trouble:你成心挤对我，是～。You'll be looking for trouble if you think you can browbeat me.

找不开 zhǎobukāi have no small change (for money of a higher denomination):没零钱，百元大钞～。I have no small change to break a 100-*yuan* note.

找补 zhǎobu make up a deficiency; add:你如果钱不够，我这里可以再～点儿。If you don't have enough money, I will make it up. /话还没说清楚，还得～几句。As I haven't made myself sufficiently clear, I would like to add a few more words. /这块墙抹得不太好，应该再～几下。This part of the wall that is not well plastered needs touching up. /他吃了两大碗面，还～了个花卷儿。He ate a steamed twisted roll in addition to two bowlfuls of noodles.

找茬儿 zhǎochár *also* "找碴儿" find fault; pick holes; nitpick:故意～ deliberately pick a quarrel /专找别人的茬儿 find fault with sb. on purpose

找岔子 zhǎo chàzi purposefully look for errors; find fault; pick holes; nitpick

找刺儿 zhǎocìr nitpick; be fastidious; pick faults and criticize:我怕说错了，别人又找我的刺儿。I'm afraid that I might say the wrong thing and others will pick on me.

找对象 zhǎo duìxiàng 〈方言〉seek a partner in marriage:他正在～。He is looking for someone to marry.

找缝子 zhǎo fèngzi *also* "找岔子" look for a flaw and use it as an excuse for attacks

找麻烦 zhǎo máfan look for trouble; cause sb. trouble:自～ ask for trouble; ask for it /他尽给家里～。All he did was to get his family into trouble.

找平 zhǎopíng level up or down:这边的墙只差两层砖了，先～了再往上砌吧。This side of the wall only needs two more layers of bricks. Let's make it level before we build it any higher.

找婆家 zhǎo pójia look for a husband:姑娘二十七八了，急着找个婆家。The girl is anxious to get married, as she is over twenty-seven years old.

找齐 zhǎoqí ❶ make uniform; even up; balance:篱笆顶上还要～。The top of the fence needs to be made even. ❷ make complete; make up a deficiency:今儿给你一部分，余下的明儿～。We'll pay you part of the money today and the balance will be made up tomorrow.

找钱 zhǎoqián give change:你还没有找他钱。You haven't yet given him the change.

找俏 zhǎoqiào 〈方言〉seek for ill-gotten gains

找事 zhǎoshì ❶ look or hunt for a job; seek employment ❷ kick

up a row：别惹这些人，他们是故意来～的。Don't provoke these people. They are here to pick a quarrel.
找死 zhǎosǐ court death：过马路不注意过往车辆，你～呀！Why don't you watch out for the passing vehicles when crossing the street. You are trying to kill yourself, aren't you?
找台阶儿 zhǎo táijiēr find a way out of the difficulties or predicament：咱们得赶紧找个台阶儿下，别再耽搁了。Let's find an excuse to get out of this predicament and not delay any longer.
找头 zhǎotou change (from money paid)：没有多少～。It's a small amount of change.
找寻 zhǎoxún try to find; look for; seek：耐心地～需要的资料 patiently search for the needed materials /失物无处～。The lost article is nowhere to be found.
找寻 zhǎoxun 〈方言〉 find fault; pick holes; embarrass：你怎么尽～人？Why are you always finding fault with others?
找辙 zhǎozhé 〈方言〉 ❶ find an excuse; use a pretext：我实在坐不住了，赶紧～告辞回家。I really could not sit there any longer, and I quickly found an excuse to leave. ❷ find a solution; seek a way out：下个月工资没着落，厂里正在～。The factory has no money to pay the workers next month and is busy trying to look for a way out.
找主 zhǎozhǔ 〈方言〉 look for a man for marriage：她都二十好几了，也该找个主儿啦。She is in her twenties and ought to find somebody and get married.

爪

zhǎo claw; talon：鹰～ hawk's talon /张牙舞～ bare fangs and brandish claws — make threatening gestures; engage in sabre rattling /乌龟趾间有蹼，趾端有～。A turtle has webs in between its toes and a talon at the tip of each toe.
see also zhuǎ
爪哇 Zhǎowā Java, the 4th largest island of Indonesia：～人 Javanese
爪哇海沟 Zhǎowā Hǎigōu Java Trench
爪哇猿人 Zhǎowā yuánrén Java man (a type of ape-man who lived during the Paleolithic Age, and whose fossil was discovered in 1891, the earliest discovery of its kind in the world, in Java, Indonesia)
爪蛙 zhǎowā clawed frog (*Xenopus*)
爪牙 zhǎoyá talons and fangs — flunkeys; underlings：忠实的～ faithful lackey /当权者的～ henchman for those in power

zhào

肇（肈）

zhào ❶ cause (trouble, etc.); lead to ❷ 〈书面〉 begin; commence; initiate：～开帝业。The great enterprise for an empire has begun. ❸ (Zhào) a surname
肇端 zhàoduān 〈书面〉 beginning; origin：此乃两国交兵之～。This was the beginning of hostilities between the two countries.
肇祸 zhàohuò bring trouble; cause an accident：他因酒后开车而～。The accident happened when he was driving a car under the influence of alcohol.
肇生 zhàoshēng 〈书面〉 begin to take place; start to happen：～万物。All things on earth begin to grow.
肇始 zhàoshǐ 〈书面〉 begin; start; commence; initiate：此事～于一年之前。The incident started a year ago.
肇事 zhàoshì make trouble; stir up a disturbance：聚众～ collect a gang of thugs to create disturbance /严惩～者 mete out severe punishment to troublemakers
肇因 zhàoyīn cause; origin

赵（趙）

Zhào ❶ one of the seven major powers of the Warring States Period in the western and southern parts of present-day Hebei Province and the northern and central parts of present-day Shanxi Province ❷ used in classical Chinese writings to refer to the southern part of present-day Hebei Province：燕～之士 people from Hebei ❸ a surname
赵匡胤 Zhào Kuāngyìn Zhao Kuangyin (927-976), first emperor of the Song Dynasty
赵孟頫 Zhào Mèngfǔ Zhao Mengfu (formerly translated as Chao Mengfu, 1254-1322), calligrapher and painter of the Yuan Dynasty
赵公元帅 Zhàogōng Yuánshuài Marshal Zhao, or Zhao Gongming, God of Wealth in Chinese folklore：过去老百姓对～礼拜最勤。The ordinary people used to worship most frequently Zhao Gongming, the God of Wealth in Chinese folklore.
赵体 Zhàotǐ Zhao style, a style of Chinese calligraphy created by Zhao Mengfu during the Yuan Dynasty：他工书法，尤其擅长～。He was well versed in calligraphy, especially Zhao style.
赵州桥 Zhàozhōuqiáo Zhaozhou Bridge, China's earliest stone arch bridge built in 591-599 in Hebei Province

棹（櫂、艄）

zhào 〈方言〉 ❶ oar：橹～ rudder and oar ❷ boat：归～ returning boat /～歌 boatmen's song /买～南归 return to the south by boat ❸ row：自～孤舟 row a boat all by oneself

罩

zhào ❶ cover; envelop; overspread; wrap：笼～ envelop; shroud /他毛衣外面～着一件旧西服。He wore an old western-style jacket over his sweater. /烟雾笼～着江面。The lake is shrouded in mist. /天空～满了乌云。The sky is covered with dark clouds. /山顶被～在浓雾中。The mountain top is wrapped in a thick fog. /夜的香气弥漫在空中，像一张柔软的网，把所有景物都～在里面。A fragrance spread from the night like a soft net, enveloping all in its folds. ❷ cover; shade; hood; casing：口～ gauze mask (worn over nose and mouth); surgical mask /纱～ gauze or screen covering over food /电视机～ TV cover /灯～ lampshade /防护～ protecting casing ❸ outer garment; dustcoat; overall：袍～儿 outer garment of a robe (*or* gown); dust-robe; dust-gown; overall ❹ small cage or coop for raising chickens ❺ bamboo fish trap
罩布 zhàobù antimacassar
罩盖 zhàogài cover cap
罩袍 zhàopáo outer garment; dust-robe; dust-gown; overall：棉袄外面套着一件蓝布～ wear a blue dust-robe over one's cotton-padded (*or* -quilted) jacket
罩棚 zhàopéng awning over a gateway or a courtyard：院子里搭了一个～。An awning was put up in the courtyard.
罩衫 zhàoshān 〈方言〉 overall; dustcoat：她新做了一件花布～。She has made a new overall of cotton print.
罩袖 zhàoxiù 〈方言〉 oversleeve; sleevelet：戴着～ wear oversleeves /一副的确良布的～ a pair of dacron sleevelets
罩衣 zhàoyī *also* "罩褂儿" overall; dustcoat：这件～很合身。This dustcoat fits perfectly. /棉袄的～太长了。The overall of the cotton-padded jacket is too long.
罩子 zhàozi cover; shade; hood; casing：玻璃～ glass cover

笊

zhào
笊篱 zhàoli bamboo, wicker or wire strainer：一个竹编的～ bamboo strainer /用～捞饺子 scoop up meat dumplings with a strainer

兆[1]

zhào ❶ sign; omen; foreboding：先～ omen; sign; portent; indication /前～ omen; forewarning; premonition /凶～ ill omen /吉～ good omen; propitious sign /不祥之～ ill (*or* evil) omen ❷ augur; portend; foretell：瑞雪～丰年。A timely snow promises a good harvest. ❸ (Zhào) a surname

兆[2]

zhào ❶ million; mega- ❷ million million; trillion
兆比特 zhàobǐtè 〈信息〉 megabit
兆伏安 zhàofú'ān 〈电工〉 megavolt-ampere
兆赫 zhàohè 〈电子〉 megahertz (MHz); megacycles per second
兆候 zhàohòu omen; presage; foreboding; harbinger：不吉的～ inauspicious omen
兆欧 zhào'ōu 〈电工〉 megohm：～表 megohmmeter
兆头 zhàotou sign; omen; foreboding; portent：暴风雨来临的～ sign of an impending storm /是一个好～！It is a good omen. *or* It augurs well.
兆瓦特 zhàowǎtè 〈电工〉 megw (megawatt)：～小时 megwh (megawatt-hour)
兆周 zhàozhōu 〈无线电〉 megacycle

旐

zhào type of flag in ancient times

鮡

zhào a kind of scaleless fish

召[1]

zhào ❶ call together; gather; convene; summon：请问，

Z

～我们来干什么? Excuse me, what do you want us to be here for? ❷ (Zhào) a surname of the Dai nationality

召[2] zhào (usu. used in place names) temple; monastery *see also* Shào

召唤 zhàohuàn call; summon:这是时代的～。This is the call of the times.

召回 zhàohuí recall:～外交代表 recall a diplomatic envoy /～国书〈外交〉letter of recall

召祸 zhàohuò 〈书面〉invite disaster:行不慎则常～。Failure to act prudently often courts disaster.

召集 zhàojí call together; convene; assemble:～学生开会 call the students together for a meeting /会议由部长～。The meeting was convened by the minister.

召集人 zhàojírén convener

召见 zhàojiàn ❶ call in (one's subordinates) officially ❷〈外交〉summon (envoy of a foreign country) to an interview:外交部～某国大使。The ambassador of a particular country was summoned to the Foreign Ministry.

召开 zhàokāi hold; convene; convoke:～学术会议 hold a symposium /庆祝全国英模大会的～ celebrate the convening (*or* opening) of the national conference of heroes and model workers /主席经安理会任何理事国的请求,应～安理会会议。The President shall call a meeting of the Security Council at the request of any of its members.

召之即来 zhàozhī-jílái be on call at any hour; be ready to assemble at the first call; report for duty at a moment's notice

炤 zhào *also* "照" zhào〈书面〉shine; illuminate; light up:列星随旋,日月递～。Numerous stars rotate, and the sun and moon alternate (each other) in illuminating the world.

诏 zhào ❶〈书面〉instruct; admonish; warn; exhort:若子不听父之～。This child does not follow the father's instructions. ❷ imperial edict:密～ confidential imperial edict /遗～ posthumous edict /皇帝手～ edict written by an emperor

诏令 zhàolìng order issued by an emperor; imperial edict

诏书 zhàoshū imperial edict:草拟～ draft an imperial edict /宣读～ read out an imperial edict

诏谕 zhàoyù order issued by an emperor:颁布～ publish an imperial edict

诏旨 zhàozhǐ imperial instruction

照 zhào ❶ shine; radiate; illuminate; light up:日～ sunshine /光～ illumination /往远处～ light the way far ahead /用手电筒～一～ light up with a torch /闪电把屋子都～亮了。The lightning lit up the whole room. /火光把他的脸～得通红。His face turned ruddy from the fire light. /阳光普～大地。The sunlight floods the earth. *or* The sun illuminates every corner of the land. ❷ reflect; mirror:～镜子 look in the mirror /湖面如镜,把岸上的树木～得清清楚楚。Like a mirror, the lake reflected clearly the trees on the banks. ❸ take a picture; photograph; shoot:这张相片～得真好。This picture is well taken. /她～了一张穿军装的像。She had a photo taken in an army uniform. ❹ photograph; picture:彩～ colour picture /半身～ half-length photo; portrait /剧～ stage photo; still ❺ licence; permit:车～ licence (of a car, bicycle, etc.) /牌～ licence plate; numberplate; licence tag /办理护～ go through the formalities (*or* procedure) for a passport /申请营业执～ apply for a business licence ❻ take care of; look after; attend to:～料家务 manage household affairs /～看老人 look after old people /请帮忙～顾一下孩子,我一会儿就回来。I'll be back in a minute. Please keep an eye on my child. ❼ inform; notify:～会 note /关～一声 notify sb.; let sb. know ❽ compare; contrast:对～ contrast; check (against sth. else) /查～ please note ❾ make out; understand:心～不宣 have a tacit understanding ❿ in the direction of; towards:～那边看 look in that direction /～着马路走。Go towards that road. ⓫according to; in conformity with:～此办理 handle it accordingly /～她的衣服样子做 tailor it according to the style of her dress /～大家的意见办 act upon what everyone thinks right /～我看,他的办法行不通。It seems to me that (*or* In my opinion) his method won't work.

照搬 zhàobān indiscriminately imitate; mechanically copy:～教条 mechanically repeat a dogma /盲目地～ follow sth. blindly /～别人的经验 copy indiscriminately the experience of others

照办 zhàobàn act in accordance with; act upon; conform to; comply with:一切照你的意见办。Everything will be done according to your ideas. /你们的要求都可以～。All your requests will be complied with. /这事无法～。The matter cannot be handled the way you have suggested.

照本宣科 zhàoběn-xuānkē read entirely from the text; echo what the book says:他的讲演,总是～,一点也不生动。His lectures are dull for he always reads from his prepared notes from beginning to end.

照壁 zhàobì *also* "照墙";"照壁墙" screen wall facing the gate of a house:大门开着,门外有一座灰砖砌的高大的～。The gate was open, and a tall screen wall of grey bricks stood outside facing the gate.

照补 zhàobǔ make up a deficiency:扣发的工资全部～。All the salary that has been docked will be made up.

照常 zhàocháng as usual:～工作 work as usual /～演出。The performance will be staged as planned.

照抄 zhàochāo ❶ copy word for word; copy verbatim:～不误 copy without fail /～两份 make two copies ❷ indiscriminately imitate; blindly copy:吸取经验要结合本地情况,不能～。One must not copy others' experience mechanically but should apply it in the light of local conditions.

照登 zhàodēng publish (manuscripts, letters, etc.) without alteration:来函～。All letters will be published verbatim.

照度 zhàodù 〈物理〉intensity of illumination; illuminance

照度计 zhàodùjì lumeter

照发 zhàofā ❶ approve for distribution:此件～。This document is approved for distribution. ❷ be paid as usual:节假日工资～。Salaries will be paid in full on festivals and holidays. /出差旅费～。Allowance for business trips will be granted as before.

照拂 zhàofú 〈书面〉take care of; look after; attend to:多方～ look after in many ways /承蒙～ be grateful for the care one has received /～病人 attend to patients

照改 zhàogǎi revise according to someone's suggestion; alter according to a certain model

照顾 zhàogu ❶ take into account; show consideration for; allow for:～周到 be thoughtful; be considerate /～幼儿心理 take child psychology into account /适当～他的困难 give due consideration to his difficulties /～到大多数人的意见 make allowances for the opinion of the majority /一时～不到,就要出问题。A momentary neglect will cause trouble. ❷ keep an eye on; look after:行李请您～一下,我去去就回。Please keep an eye on my luggage. I'll be back in a minute. ❸ look after; care for; attend to:～烈军属 look after families of martyrs and servicemen /～老人 take care of the old people /对残疾人加以特殊～ give special care to the handicapped /对旅客～得十分周到 give thoughtful attention to passengers ❹ (of a customer) patronize; shop at:他经常来～我们的生意。He is our regular customer. *or* He is our patron.

照管 zhàoguǎn look after; care for; be in charge of:～家务 take care of household chores /～小孩 look after children; be a babysitter /此事由他～。Let him take charge of the matter.

照葫芦画瓢 zhào húlu huà piáo draw a dipper with a gourd as a model — ape; repeat; mechanically imitate:学习先进经验不能～,不能搞"一刀切"。In learning from advanced experience, one should not mechanically copy it, nor apply it uniformly.

照护 zhàohù take care of (patients, the wounded, etc.):～伤员 look after the wounded /耐心地～孕妇 attend to the pregnant woman patiently

照会 zhàohuì ❶ present, deliver, or address a note to:就这个问题～美国驻华使馆 present a note to the US Embassy in China on this issue ❷ note:递交～ present a note /交换～ exchange notes /正式～ personal note; formal (*or* official) note /普通～ note verbale /抗议～ note of protest /答复～ note of reply; note in reply

照价 zhàojià according to the cost or set price:～赔偿 compensate according to the cost /～交付 pay according to the arranged price

照讲 zhàojiǎng 〈方言〉ordinarily; as a rule:～他这时该起床了。Ordinarily, he should be getting up now.

照镜子 zhào jìngzi look in the mirror — self examination:每个人都要～,找差距。Everyone should try to examine himself to find out where he falls short.

照旧 zhàojiù as before; as of old:～行事 act as usual /新版内容有所修改,体例～。The content of the new edition has been revised but the stylistic rules and layout remain unchanged.

照看 zhàokàn look after; care for; keep an eye on:～孩子 attend to the children /～电话 mind the telephone

照理 zhàolǐ ❶ in the ordinary course of events; normally:～他现在该来了。Normally, he would have been here. ❷〈方言〉look after; attend to:～家务 do household chores

照例 zhàolì as a rule; in general; as usual; usually:星期日他～要回家看父母。As a rule, he pays a visit to his parents on Sundays. /我们的党团活动～安排在星期五下午。Our Party and League activities are usually arranged on Friday afternoons.

照量 zhàoliang 〈方言〉❶ measure one's strength with; have a contest; have a trial or test of strength:你敢不敢跟我～～? Do you dare to try me? ❷ try; attempt:我来～～。Let me have a try. /不要太性急,要～着来。Don't be impatient. You have got to do it on a trial basis.

照料 zhàoliào care for; attend to:～弟妹 take care of one's brothers and sisters /～孤寡老人的生活 attend to the life of childless and single old people /孩子由奶奶～。The children are left in the care of the grandmother. /他年纪太小,连自己还不会～,哪能～别人。He is too young even to look after himself, let alone others. /别看她还是个小姑娘,但把家里～得挺好。Although only a little girl, she manages her house very well.

照临 zhàolín shine on; illuminate:月光～田野。The moonlight lit up the fields.

照猫画虎 zhàomāo-huàhǔ draw a tiger with a cat as a model — copy; imitate:只会～地模仿别人,是学不好绘画的。One cannot learn drawing well by copying others alone. /教孩子写字,开始就是根据字帖～,一笔一划地写。When teaching a child to write Chinese characters, one should let him imitate the copybook stroke by stroke at the beginning.

照面儿 zhàomiànr ❶ encounter; run into; come across:在路上和他打了个～ come face to face with him in the street; run into him on the way ❷ (mostly in the negative) put in an appearance; show up; turn up; meet:不敢～ dare not show up /他们彼此不～的原因谁也摸不透。No one knew why they avoided seeing each other.

照明 zhàomíng illumination; lighting:会场～ conference-room illumination /～设备 lighting equipment /～器材 lighting equipment (*or* material) /～装置 lighting installation /～电路 lighting circuit

照明弹 zhàomíngdàn flare; star shell:发射～ fire a flare /～光耀人眼目。The light of star shells dazzles one's eyes. /～把周围照得如同白昼一般。The illuminating shell lit up the surroundings as if it were daytime.

照明炮弹 zhàomíng pàodàn illuminating shell

照排 zhàopái phototype setting; photocomposition; filmsetting

照排机 zhàopáijī phototypesetter; filmsetter

照片儿 zhàopiānr 〈口语〉photo; picture:彩色～ colour photo /风景～ landscape photo (*or* picture)

照片子 zhào piānzi X-ray:他到医院照了个片子。He went to the hospital and had an X-ray.

照片 zhàopiàn photograph; picture:洗～ develop (a film) /印～ print off copies from a negative; make copies of a print /放大～ make enlargements of a photograph; have a photograph enlarged

照墙 zhàoqiáng *see*"照壁"

照射 zhàoshè shine; illuminate; irradiate:激光～ irradiate with laser rays /阳光～着大地。Sunlight illuminates the earth.

照实 zhàoshí according to facts:你～说吧! Tell me the plain, bare facts. *or* Tell me the truth.

照说 zhàoshuō ordinarily; generally; as a rule:现在才十月中旬,～天气不该这么冷。It is only mid-October. Normally, the weather shouldn't be that cold. /～这些数学题他应该能做出来。He should be able to work out these maths problems.

照相 zhàoxiàng *also*"照像" take a picture or photo; photograph:～的技术 photographic technique /她很喜欢～。She likes photography very much. /他最近学会了～。He has recently learned how to take pictures. /她穿旗袍照了一张相。She had a picture taken in a *qipao* (*or* cheongsam).

照相版 zhàoxiàngbǎn process plate

照相簿 zhàoxiàngbù photo album

照相弹 zhàoxiàngdàn 〈军事〉photoflash bomb; flash bomb

照相复制 zhàoxiàng fùzhì photocopy

照相馆 zhàoxiàngguǎn photo studio

照相机 zhàoxiàngjī *also*"摄影机" shèyǐngjī camera:反射式～ reflex camera /立体～ stereroscopic (*or* stereo) camera /全景～ panoramic camera /傻瓜式～ foolproof camera /小型～ miniature camera; minicamera; minicam /折叠式～ folding camera /制版～〈印刷〉process camera /～焦镜 focusing camera mirror /～快门 camera shutter; time /～架 camera mount /～附件 camera accessories

照相胶版印刷 zhàoxiàng jiāobǎn yìnshuā photo-offset process

照相排字 zhàoxiàng páizì *see*"照排"

照相平版印刷 zhàoxiàng píngbǎn yìnshuā photolithography

照相枪 zhàoxiàngqiāng 〈军事〉gun camera

照相凸版术 zhàoxiàng tūbǎnshù photoengraving

照相纸 zhàoxiàngzhǐ photographic paper

照相制版 zhàoxiàng zhìbǎn photomechanical process

照相制图 zhàoxiàng zhìtú photomap

照眼 zhàoyǎn bright; shining:家具都油漆得～。The furniture has a beautiful sheen after painting. /白塔的金顶发出～的金光。The golden top of the White Pagoda sends out dazzling golden light.

照样 zhàoyàng ❶ after a pattern or model:～儿复制一份 reproduce a copy from the original /别问,～儿做就是了。Don't ask question. Just do it the way I did it. ❷ in the same way; all the same; as before:～完成定额 accomplish the quota all the same /～坚持工作 persist in working as usual /～进行 proceed in the same way /尽管工作条件极差,小伙子们～情绪高昂,干劲十足。Despite the poor working conditions, the youngsters were full of vim and vigour just the same.

照妖镜 zhàoyāojìng mirror that shows up the monster for what it is; monster-detector:在检查部门的～下,伪劣产品纷纷现出原形。All the fake and shoddy commodities betrayed their true features under the sharp eyes of the inspectors.

照耀 zhàoyào shine; irradiate; illuminate:灿烂的阳光～着天安门广场。A bright sun is shining over Tian'anmen Square.

照应 zhàoyìng coordinate; correlate:前后～ be well organized /在工作上各部门应互相～。Different departments should coordinate their work.

照应 zhàoying look after; care for:民警热情地～过马路的小学生。The people's police warmly guided the pupils across the road. /空中小姐对旅客～很周到。The air hostesses attended thoughtfully to all passengers.

照映 zhàoyìng shine; illuminate; light up; irradiate:明亮的探照灯,～着节日里的城楼。The bright searchlight lit up the gate tower during the festival.

照章 zhàozhāng (act) according to the rules:～办事 act according to the rules /～罚款 fine according to the regulations

照直 zhàozhí ❶ (walk) straight ahead:～往东,就是菜市。Straight on to the east, and you'll find the food market. ❷ straightforward; blunt; point-blank:有话就～说,不要吞吞吐吐的。If you have anything to say, out with it. Don't hem and haw.

照准 zhàozhǔn ❶〈旧语〉(used in official documents) request granted ❷ aim at:～靶心射击。Shoot at the bull's-eye.

照准仪 zhàozhǔnyí 〈机械〉alidade

zhē

遮 zhē ❶ cover; conceal; hide; screen:货物给帆布～住了。The cargo was covered (over) with canvas. /树木～住了房子。The trees screen the house from view. /我的视线被高楼～住了。My view was blocked by the skyscraper. ❷ hinder; obstruct; impede:横～竖拦 impede in every possible way ❸ cover up; cloak:～不住真实感情 unable to conceal one's true feelings /～人耳目 throw dust in people's eyes; hoodwink (*or* fool) the public /一手～天 shut out the heavens with one palm — pull the wool over the eyes of the people (*or* public)

遮蔽 zhēbì ❶ conceal; cover; screen:～光线 shut out the light ❷ shelter; block; obstruct:～严寒 shelter from the severe cold /树木～了视线。The woods obstruct (*or* block) the view. ❸〈军事〉defilade

遮蔽物 zhēbìwù 〈军事〉defilade

遮蔽阵地 zhēbì zhèndì 〈军事〉defiladed position

遮藏 zhēcáng keep out of sight; hide; cover up; conceal:～在大树后面 hide behind a big tree /厚厚的脂粉～不住她那深深的皱纹。Even heavy cosmetics cannot cover up the deep wrinkles on her face.

遮丑 zhēchǒu hide one's shame; screen one's fault; gloss over one's blemishes; cover up one's defect or weakness:他总是千方百计地为自己～。He would try every means to whitewash himself. /他说

这些漂亮话，无非是想为自己～。Those high-sounding words of his are but meant to gloss over his mistakes.

遮挡 zhēdǎng ❶ keep out; shelter from; cover: ～风沙 keep out wind and dust /所有的窗子都用帘子～起来了。All the windows are covered with blinds. /他用自己的身体为她～寒风。He sheltered her from the cold wind with his own body. ❷ things used as a cover; shelter: 草原一望无际，没有什么～。The grassland extended as far as the eye could reach, and there was nothing to obstruct the view.

遮断 zhēduàn 〈军事〉 interdict: ～射击 interdiction fire

遮幅电影 zhēfú diànyǐng masked wide-screen film

遮盖 zhēgài ❶ cover; spread over: 井口被石板～住了。The mouth of the well is covered with a stone slab. /水泥上～着塑料布。A plastic sheet has been spread over the cement. ❷ conceal; hide; cover up; screen: ～矛盾 conceal contradictions /～罪行 cover up one's crime /～缺点 hide one's weaknesses /有了错误应该承认，而不应该～。One should acknowledge one's mistakes once they are made and should not try to gloss them over.

遮光板 zhēguāngbǎn gobo (a lens or microphone shield)

遮光玻璃 zhēguāng bōli shade glass

遮光框 zhēguāngkuàng 〈摄影〉 masking frame

遮光片 zhēguāngpiàn anti-dazzling screen

遮光漆 zhēguāngqī black-out paint

遮光罩 zhēguāngzhào 〈摄影〉 lens hood

遮护 zhēhù shield; protect: 墨镜有～眼睛的作用。Sunglasses can protect the eyes.

遮拦 zhēlán block; obstruct; hinder: 防风林可以～风沙。The windbreak serves to keep out wind and sand. /房子周围一片空旷，毫无～。Around the house there is a vast expanse of open country, with nothing to obstruct the view.

遮瞒 zhēmán cover up; hide; conceal: ～事实 hide the facts; withhold the truth /他直抒胸臆，毫无～。He poured himself out, with nothing held back.

遮没 zhēmò cover; envelop: 云雾～了山头。The mountaintop was shrouded in mist.

遮目鱼 zhēmùyú milkfish (*Chanos chanos*)

遮三掩四 zhēsān-yǎnsì cover sth. up; be not straightforward; dodge and dissemble: 你有什么错误就说什么，别这么～的。Tell us whatever mistakes you have made. Don't be so evasive and dissembling.

遮饰 zhēshì gloss over; hide; screen; whitewash: 他看～不住了，只好说了实话。He told the truth when he could no longer withhold it.

遮天蔽日 zhētiān-bìrì (of thick foliage) block the sunlight: 这里的森林枝叶茂密，～。Trees in the forest are thick with leaves, blocking the sunlight (*or* blotting out the sun).

遮天盖地 zhētiān-gàidì ❶ (of wind, rain, sand, etc.) blot out the sky and cover up the earth — be overwhelming: 大风沙～而来。A smothering sand-storm blew up with an overwhelming force. /蝗虫飞来，～。The locusts came in great swarms. *or* There is a cloud of locusts coming down in force. /～地下起鹅毛大雪。Heavy snow came down thick and fast. ❷ (of a group of people) be enormous in number: 几十万南下大军，～，纵横驰骋。Thousands upon thousands of PLA troops drove south, sweeping away all obstacles before them.

遮羞 zhēxiū ❶ cover one's private parts: 小小年纪，他居然也懂得～了。Little as he is, he knows what is indecent exposure. ❷ cover up one's embarrassment; hush up a scandal: ～解嘲 make excuses to get out of a scrape /他这么说是为了～。He said this to hush up the scandal.

遮羞布 zhēxiūbù ❶ loincloth; fig leaf ❷ 〈比喻〉 disguise; veil; cover-up: 这些冠冕堂皇的说法，只不过是掩盖其私心的～罢了。His high-sounding remarks are just a cover-up for his selfish motives.

遮掩 zhēyǎn ❶ cover; envelop; block: 月亮被云彩～。The moon was enveloped in the clouds. /雨雾～了视线。Rain obstructed our view. ❷ cover up; conceal; gloss over: ～错误的态度是不对的。It is wrong to gloss over one's mistakes.

遮眼法 zhēyǎnfǎ cover-up; camouflage

遮阳 zhēyáng sunshade: ～帽 sun helmet; topee /～伞 parasol

遮阳板 zhēyángbǎn 〈建筑〉 sunshading board; brise-soleil

遮阳篷 zhēyángpéng awning

遮阴 zhēyīn *also* "遮荫" shade: 院子里要多种几棵～的树。We should plant more trees in the courtyard to offer better shade.

遮荫 zhēyīn *see* "遮阴"

嗻 zhē *see* "唓嗻" chēzhē
see also zhè

折 zhē 〈口语〉 ❶ roll over; turn over and over: 天黑路滑，他～到坑里去了。As it was pitch-dark and the road was slippery, he fell into a pit. ❷ pour back and forth between two containers: 用两个碗把开水～一～就凉了。The water will soon be cool if you pour it back and forth from one bowl to another.
see also shé; zhé

折个儿 zhēgèr *also* "折过儿" 〈口语〉 turn over; roll over: 他在床上翻来覆去地～，好久才睡着。He had tossed and turned for quite some time before he fell asleep. /汽车折了个儿。The car overturned.

折跟头 zhē gēntou 〈口语〉 turn or throw a somersault; loop the loop

折过儿 zhēguòr *see* "折个儿"

折箩 zhēluó 〈方言〉 leftovers from a feast: 中午请客，晚上一家人吃～。We entertained friends to lunch and the family ate the leftovers in the evening.

折腾 zhēteng 〈口语〉 ❶ turn from side to side; toss and turn: 他～了一宿。He tossed about all night. /她几乎～到半夜才入睡。She tossed and turned restlessly, unable to fall asleep until midnight. ❷ do sth. again and again; fool around with; mess with: 他没事就～他的那些花。He spends nearly every minute of his spare time tending flowers. /这些机器可禁不起～。These machines are rather delicate and must not be tampered with. ❸ cause physical or mental suffering; torment: 慢性病真是～人。A chronic disease can be such a torment. /天气忽冷忽热的，多～人。This fickle weather is really getting me down.

蜇 zhē ❶ prick with a sting; sting: 他的脸被马蜂～了。A wasp stung him on the cheek. ❷ cause sharp pain; smart; sting: 切洋葱～眼睛。Your eyes will smart when you cut onions. /碘酒擦在伤口上～得慌。You feel a sharp sting when iodine is applied to the cut.
see also zhé

蜇针 zhēzhēn 〈动物〉 sting; stinger

zhé

谪(讁) zhé 〈书面〉 ❶ (as a punishment in feudal China) relegate a high official to a minor post in a remote border town; banish from the court; exile: 贬～ relegate; banish from the court ❷ (of an immortal, etc.) be banished from Heaven ❸ blame; rebuke; censure: 众口交～ be subject to public censure (*or* condemnation)

谪居 zhéjū 〈书面〉 (after being banished) settle or live in: ～边城 be exiled to a border town; live in a border town after being banished

谪迁 zhéqiān 〈书面〉 (as a punishment in feudal China) relegate a high official to a minor post in a remote region

谪戍 zhéshù 〈书面〉 (as a punishment in feudal China) be sent away to guard the borders

磔[1] zhé (as a punishment in ancient China) dismember the body; tear limb from limb; draw and quarter

磔[2] zhé 〈书面〉 right-falling stroke in Chinese characters

詟(讋) zhé 〈书面〉 fear; awe; apprehension; dread: ～服 surrender (*or* yield) in fear

折[1] zhé ❶ fracture; break; snap: 大腿骨～ have a fracture in the thigh; fracture one's thigh /～颈而死 break one's neck /把竹竿～成两截 snap the bamboo pole in half ❷ be deprived of; lose: 损兵～将 suffer heavy casualties ❸ bend; turn; twist: 曲～ twists and turns /百～不挠 be unbending; be undaunted by repeated setbacks /人生的道路是曲～的。Life is full of ups and downs (*or* vicissitudes). ❹ turn back; change direction: 转～ turn in the course of an event /我半路又～了回去。I turned back after I walked halfway. ❺ be filled

with admiration; be won over; be convinced:心～ come round willingly; be deeply convinced ❻ convert into; change into; amount to:～价 convert into money; evaluate in terms of money /一美元～成人民币是多少? How much does one US dollar amount to in *Renminbi*? *or* At what rate does the US dollar convert into *Renminbi*? ❼ discount; rebate:打七～ give 30% discount; charge 70% of the original (*or* full) price /不～不扣 without the slightest discount; one hundred per cent; out and out; to the letter /全部货物～价 20% 出售。We allow 20% discount off the prices of all our goods. ❽ (of a musical drama) act:清代杂剧不限四～。There are more than four acts in the musical drama of the Qing Dynasty. ❾ turning stroke (in Chinese characters)

折[2] zhé ❶ fold:～衬衣 fold a shirt /把信～起来装好。Fold the letter and put it into an envelope. ❷ book or booklet used for keeping accounts, etc.:存～ deposit book; bankbook /奏～ memorandum (presented to an emperor)
see also shé; zhē

折板结构 zhébǎn jiégòu 〈建筑〉folded plate structure
折半 zhébàn give 50% discount; discount 50% on; reduce (a price) by half:有的货物按定价～处理。Some commodities are sold at half price. *or* We give (*or* allow) 50% discount off the price of some goods.
折边机 zhébiānjī 〈机械〉hemmer; hemming machine; folding machine
折变 zhébiàn 〈方言〉sell off (one's property):他只得将田地都～了,投他岳父家去。He had to sell off his farmland and go to live with his father-in-law.
折布机 zhébùjī 〈纺织〉folding machine
折尺 zhéchǐ folding rule
折冲 zhéchōng 〈书面〉defeat or subdue an enemy:～千里之外 use stratagem or diplomacy to vanquish the enemy long before they get near
折冲厌难 zhéchōng-yānnàn overcome the danger by defeating the enemy
折冲御侮 zhéchōng-yùwǔ (of generals) repel foreign aggression
折冲樽俎 zhéchōng-zūnzǔ ❶ outmanoeuvre the enemy over glasses of wine; win by diplomacy:却敌于谈笑之际,～之间 outmanoeuvre the enemy over glasses of wine; win through diplomatic negotiations ❷ engage in diplomatic negotiations:他善于～。He is a good negotiator.
折刀 zhédāo ❶ pocketknife; jackknife ❷ Tibetan waist knife
折叠 zhédié fold:～衣服 fold the clothes /把被子～整齐 fold up a quilt /可～的小艇 collapsible skiff (*or* boat)
折叠床 zhédiéchuáng folding bed; foldaway bed
折叠剪 zhédiéjiǎn folding scissors
折叠伞 zhédiésǎn folding umbrella
折叠天线 zhédié tiānxiàn telescopic (*or* collapsible) antenna
折叠椅 zhédiéyǐ folding chair; foldaway chair; collapsible chair
折叠翼飞机 zhédiéyì fēijī folding-wing aircraft
折叠桌 zhédiézhuō folding table; foldaway table
折兑 zhéduì exchange (gold or silver) for money; convert (into)
折返 zhéfǎn turn back:他刚走出一里多路便～回来。He had only walked one *li* away when he turned back.
折服 zhéfú ❶ subdue; bring sb. to his knees:～对手 beat one's rival; subdue one's opponent /任何艰难困苦都～不了革命者。No hardship can break a revolutionary. ❷ win over; fill with admiration:使人～ be fully convinced; compel admiration /我们常为他的无私所～。We are often filled with great admiration for his selflessness.
折福 zhéfú 〈迷信〉ruin one's happy lot (either through the acquisition of an undeserved fortune or through enjoying comfort to excess)
折干 zhégān give money in place of a present; present sb. with money instead of a gift:人家送这送那,咱干脆送点钱～得了。Let others send gifts. We shall give money instead.
折骨器 zhégǔqì 〈医学〉osteoclast
折骨术 zhégǔshù 〈医学〉osteoclasis; osteoclasty
折光 zhéguāng ❶〈物理〉refract ❷〈比喻〉reflection (of the essence of things)
折光度 zhéguāngdù 〈物理〉dioptre
折光镜 zhéguāngjìng enoscope
折光透镜 zhéguāng tòujìng dioptric lense
折光仪 zhéguāngyí refractometer
折桂 zhéguì 〈比喻〉pass an imperial examination
折合 zhéhé ❶ convert into:把美元～成人民币 convert US dollars into *Renminbi* ❷ amount to; be equal to:苹果一筐六十市斤,～三十公斤。Each basket of apples weighs 60 *jin*, or 30 kilogrammes. /一吨原油通常～七点三桶。Generally, a ton of crude oil is equal to 7.3 barrels.
折合率 zhéhélǜ conversion rate; exchange rate
折回 zhéhuí turn back (halfway):她发现忘了带钱包,只好～。She found that she did not have her purse with her, so she had to turn back to get it.
折戟沉沙 zhéjǐ-chénshā broken halberds buried in sand turn into scrap iron — disastrous defeat:最阴险的阴谋家也没有逃脱～的命运。A most sinister schemer that he was, he did not escape the fate of utter defeat.
折价 zhéjià evaluate in terms of money:～赔偿 pay compensation at the market price /学校的旧家具要～处理了。The school's old furniture will be sold at reduced prices.
折节 zhéjié 〈书面〉❶ act beneath one's dignity; go out of the way to do sth.:～下士 be extremely courteous to people below oneself ❷ give up one's interest to do sth. else:～读书 pursue studies at the cost of one's other interests
折旧 zhéjiù 〈经济〉depreciation:机器～ depreciation of machinery
折旧费 zhéjiùfèi depreciation charge
折旧基金 zhéjiù jījīn depreciation fund
折旧率 zhéjiùlǜ rate of depreciation
折旧年限 zhéjiù niánxiàn depreciable life
折扣 zhékòu discount; rebate:这些书仍按定价出售,不打～。These books sell at fixed (*or* full) prices rather than at a discount. /他执行命令从来不打～。He always carries out orders to the letter.
折柳 zhéliǔ ❶〈比喻〉see sb. off:～赠别 bid sb. farewell ❷ ancient song
折门 zhémén 〈建筑〉folding door; accordion door
折磨 zhémo cause physical or mental suffering; torment; torture; harass:遭受～ be tortured; be in torment /～自己 torture oneself; make oneself suffer /他正忍受着嫉妒的～。He is suffering the anguish of jealousy. /贫困的～使他不得不整天拼命干活挣钱。Grinding poverty keeps him working all day long to eke out a living.
折辱 zhérǔ 〈书面〉humiliate; insult:他们千方百计地～这个青年。They tried to humiliate the young man by every possible means.
折杀 zhéshā 〈口语〉〈套语〉treat one better than one deserves; flatter:您这是～我。You flatter me. /您这么做实在～了我们。You have really shown us more kindness than we deserve.
折扇 zhéshàn folding fan:一把精美的～ an exquisite folding fan
折射 zhéshè ❶〈物理〉refraction ❷ reveal; reflect:这个顺口溜～出了某些青年职工的消极心态。The doggerel reveals the passive mentality of some young workers.
折射波 zhéshèbō refracted wave
折射计 zhéshèjì refractometer
折射角 zhéshèjiǎo angle of refraction; refraction angle
折射率 zhéshèlǜ index of refraction; refractive index; refracting power
折射望远镜 zhéshè wàngyuǎnjìng refracting telescope
折射线 zhéshèxiàn refracted ray
折实 zhéshí ❶ reckon the actual amount after allowing a discount ❷ adjust payment according to the price index of certain commodities
折寿 zhéshòu 〈迷信〉reduce one's lifetime (because of high living, etc.)
折受 zhéshou 〈方言〉〈套语〉treat one better than one deserves; flatter:您如此优待,未免太～我了。You have shown me more kindness than I deserve.
折算 zhésuàn convert:用外汇～ convert into foreign exchange
折算率 zhésuànlǜ conversion rate; rate of exchange
折头 zhétou 〈方言〉discount; rebate:打～ give a discount
折纹 zhéwén ❶ wrinkle line:眼角的～ crow's feet /满脸～ have a wrinkled face ❷ fold; crease:你衣服的左边下摆都是～。The left lower hem of your jacket is creased.
折息率 zhéxīlǜ 〈金融〉offer rate:银行～ interbank offer rate
折线 zhéxiàn 〈数学〉broken line
折线图 zhéxiàntú broken-line graph
折腰 zhéyāo 〈书面〉humble oneself; bow; cringe:不为五斗米～

will not bow for five *dou* (＝1 decalitre) of rice; not give up one's dignity for material gain

折页 zhéyè folding; dogear:～机 folding machine / 请别在书中～。Please make no dogears in the book.

折椅 zhéyǐ folding chair; foldaway chair

折狱 zhéyù 〈书面〉 settle a lawsuit; give a verdict

折账 zhézhàng pay a debt in kind:将房产～ pay a debt with one's house

折证 zhézhèng (often used in the early vernacular) verify; check

折证 zhézheng 〈方言〉 argue; reason; debate; dispute:你如果有理,就跟他～～去。If you think you are in the right, go and reason with him.

折纸 zhézhǐ paper-folding; origami:老师教孩子们～。The teacher taught the children how to do paper-folding.

折中 zhézhōng *also* "折衷" aim at the golden mean; compromise:～的办法 compromise solution / 采取～方针 take a middle course

折衷 zhézhōng *see* "折中"

折衷主义 zhézhōngzhǔyì eclecticism

折皱 zhézhòu *see* "折纹"

折转 zhézhuǎn turn back; turn round; change direction:听到喊声,他立即～身来。As soon as he heard the cry, he turned round. / 正往南走,他又突然～向西去了。While going south, he suddenly turned west.

折子 zhézi booklet in accordion form with a slipcase, used for keeping accounts, etc.:存款～ deposit book; bankbook

折子钱 zhéziqián 〈方言〉 usurious loan; usury

折子书 zhézishū 〈戏曲〉 highlight episode from a story (as told by a professional story-teller)

折子戏 zhézixì 〈戏曲〉 scene or excerpt from a traditional opera; highlight from an opera:今晚咱们看的差不多全是～。The programme for us tonight consists almost entirely of highlights from operas.

折罪 zhézuì expiate one's crime; atone for one's crime or misdeed; make amends for one's crime (*or* fault, *or* mistake):将功～ atone for one's crime by meritorious service (*or* good deeds) / 下回我一定推荐一个有真才实学的来～。I shall make amends and recommend a genuine talent next time.

摺 zhé *see* "折²" zhé

哲(喆) zhé ❶ intelligent; wise; sagacious:知人则～。One is wise who understands others. ❷ wise man; sage:贤～ great thinker; sage / 先～ great thinker of the past; sage of old

哲蚌寺 Zhébàngsì Drepung, biggest monastery of the Yellow sect of Lamaism built in Lhasa in 1416

哲理 zhélǐ philosophy; philosophical theory:富于～ teeming with philosophical wisdom / 这其中大有～。This is highly philosophical.

哲人 zhérén 〈书面〉 philosopher; sage:～辈出的时代 times marked by a galaxy of philosophers

哲学 zhéxué philosophy:～理论 philosophical theory; philosophical thinking

哲学家 zhéxuéjiā philosopher

哲言 zhéyán philosophical saying; wise remark; aphorism; maxim

晢(晣) zhé bright; shining:～～明星 bright stars; twinkling stars

蜇 zhé *see* "海蜇" hǎizhé

see also zhē

箝 zhé

箝子 zhézi 〈方言〉 a kind of bamboo mat

蛰(蟄) zhé 〈书面〉 hibernate:入～ start hibernation / 惊～ Waking of Insects (3rd solar term)

蛰藏 zhécáng hibernate; lie concealed

蛰虫 zhéchóng insect that lies dormant in the soil during winter

蛰伏 zhéfú ❶ (of animals) dormancy; hibernation:春天到了,～的动物开始苏醒。Spring is on the way, and hibernating animals are beginning to wake up. ❷ 〈比喻〉 live in seclusion or solitude:结束了～生活,他常常在公开场合露面。His secluded life came to an end, and he started to make frequent appearances in public.

蛰居 zhéjū 〈书面〉 live in seclusion or solitude:～乡里 live in seclusion in the country / ～斗室 cloister oneself in one's little room

辙 zhé ❶ track of a wheel; groove; rut:重蹈覆～ take the road where carts have overturned; repeat the same mistake / 如出一～ follow the same track; be exactly the same ❷ direction of traffic:顺～ go in the right direction; follow the track / 上下～ up the road, down the road ❸ rhyme (of a song, poetic drama, etc.):合～押韵 in rhyme ❹ 〈方言〉 way; idea; wit:我实在没～了。I am really at my wits' end. / 这方面他可有～了。He is very resourceful on matters like this.

辙叉 zhéchā 〈铁路〉 frog (a device to permit wheels to cross intersecting rails)

辙口 zhékǒu rhyme (of a song, poetic drama, etc.):这段词儿换换～就容易唱了。A change in the rhyme of these lines will certainly make singing easier.

辙乱旗靡 zhéluàn-qímǐ (of an army) crisscross chariot tracks and drooping banners — flee in disarray; be put to headlong flight:趁敌军～之际出击,必获全胜。If we attack the enemy when they are in disorderly retreat, we are certain to win a complete victory.

辄(輒) zhé 〈书面〉 ❶ always; often; regularly:逢人～问 ask whoever one happens to see / 动～得咎 be blamed for whatever one does ❷ as soon as; soon after:浅尝～止 stop studying soon after getting a smattering of a subject / 稍饮～醉 get drunk after a few drops

zhě

褶(襵) zhě pleat; crease; fold; wrinkle:百～裙 pleated skirt / 你衬衣上有一道～儿。You have got a crease in your shirt. / 这料子不起～。This material does not crease (*or* wrinkle). / 旗袍不用打～。A *qipao* (*or* cheongsam) does not have to have pleats (*or* folds).

褶曲 zhěqū 〈地质〉 fold

褶皱 zhězhòu ❶ 〈地质〉 fold:～作用 folding ❷ wrinkle (in the skin):一双满是～的手 a pair of wrinkled hands

褶皱山 zhězhòushān 〈地质〉 folded mountain

褶子 zhězi ❶ pleat:裙子上的～一定要匀称。Pleats in the skirt should be well spaced out. ❷ crease; fold:熨平衣服上的～ iron out the creases in the garment ❸ wrinkle (on the face):她眼角开始有～了。She is beginning to get crow's feet round her eyes. / 他满脸的～。He has got a wrinkled face.

者¹ zhě 〈助词〉 ❶ person or thing; -er; -or:蒙面～ masked person / 劳动～ labourer / 作～ writer; author / 读～ reader / 学～ scholar / 使～ messenger; envoy / 患～ patient; the sick / 强～ the strong; the top dog / 弱～ the weak; the underdog / 违反校规～ violator of the school regulations / 不符合要求～ those that fail to meet the requirements; what is below standard ❷ follower of a doctrine, etc.; -ist:唯物主义～ materialist / 社会主义～ socialist / 个人主义～ individualist; self-seeker / 独身主义～ celibate ❸ 〈书面〉 *used after such numerals as* 二, 三 *or* 数 *to refer to things mentioned above*: 两～必须并重。Both should be equally stressed. / 二～必居其一。It must be one or the other. ❹ 〈书面〉 *indicating a rhetorical pause*: 光阴～,百代之过客。Time is a passer-by that never stops for any generation. ❺ *often used in the early vernacular to give force to a command*:路上小心在意～! Do take care while on your way.

者² zhě (used mostly in the early vernacular) this:～边 (over) here; this side / ～番话 this talk; these remarks

赭 zhě burnt ochre; reddish brown

赭石 zhěshí 〈矿业〉 ochre

锗 zhě 〈化学〉germanium (Ge):氧化～ germanium oxide / ～酸盐 germanate / ～烷 germane

锗晶体管 zhějīngtǐguǎn 〈电子〉 germanium transistor

zhè

浙(淛) Zhè (short for 浙江) Zhejiang (Province)

浙江 Zhèjiāng Zhejiang (Province)

这(這) zhè ❶ this; these:～孩子真听话。This child does what he is told. /～两个杯子是刚买的。These two glasses are newly bought. /～叫什么? What is this called? /～有什么用? What is the use of this? ❷ now; then:她～去哪儿? Where is she going now? /他～才明白事情的真相。Only then did he realize the truth.
see also zhèi

这般 zhèbān so; such; like this:～认真 so serious /关心得～周到 take such good care (of) /他如此～地一说,大家都笑了。As he told us thus and thus (*or* so), everyone laughed.

这边 zhèbiān this side; here; this way:请～走。This way please. /到～坐。Come and sit here. /我们～占优势。Our side had the upper hand. /你们～人手太少。You are shorthanded here.

这程子 zhèchéngzi 〈方言〉these days; of late; recently:～他到哪儿去了? Where has he been these days? /～她学开法语了。She has recently begun to learn French.

这次 zhècì this time; present; current:～学习很重要。The current study is very important. /我们～的任务是很艰巨的。Our present task is arduous. /～他们赢了我们,下次我们一定要赢他们。They beat us this time, but next time we must trounce them.

这搭儿 zhèdar 〈方言〉here:请到～来看一下。Please come over here and have a look.

这等 zhèděng ❶ such; such kind of; like this:天下哪有～事? How can such thing happen? *or* Has anyone ever heard of such things? ❷ so; such:你为何～苛刻? Why are you so nit-picking?

这番 zhèfān ❶ this time:你～来京有何贵干? What have you come to Beijing for this time? ❷ this kind of; this sort of:你～心情我能理解。I understand how you feel.

这个 zhège ❶ this one:～人真怪。This man is really odd. /～箱子比那个轻。This trunk is lighter than that one. ❷ this:就因为～,我才来找你。I'm here just for this. ❸ (used in exclamations) what; how:这孩子小脸～红啊! What rosy cheeks the child has got! /晚会上我们～乐啊! How happy we were at the party!

这号人 zhèhàorén this kind of person; people of this sort:～得罪不得。You can't afford to offend people of this sort.

这会儿 zhèhuìr *also* "这会子"〈口语〉right now; just now; at the moment:～雨下得正大。It is pouring right now. /～他正在开会。He is having a meeting at the moment.

这里 zhèlǐ over here; here:把椅子放在～。Put the chair over here. /我们～交通方便。We have a good transport service here. *or* Our transport is convenient.

这么 zhème *also* "这末" so; such; like this; this way:～多人 so many people /他就是～个脾气。This is the way he is. /他们都～说。They all say so. *or* So they all say. /这件事本不该～办。It should not have been handled this way.

这么点儿 zhèmediǎnr such a tiny bit:～盐,还不够两天吃的。Such a little bit of salt will hardly last two days. /就～路,咱们走着去得了。It is so near; let's walk there.

这么些 zhèmexiē so much; that many:～糖 so much sugar /～苹果,你怎么能吃得完? How can you eat that many apples? /有～客人来,你该高兴了吧? You must be very happy to have so many guests, eh?

这么样 zhèmeyàng *also* "这样" this way; like this:我不喜欢～打扮。I do not like to dress up like this. /行,就～办吧! Well, go ahead!

这么着 zhèmezhe like this; this way:～不行。It will not do this way. /要是～,那我就答应来。In that case, I promise I will come.

这儿 zhèr 〈口语〉❶ here:你要找的人不在～。The man you are looking for is not here. ❷ then; now:从～以后他再也没来过。Since then he has never come again. /打～起,我再不抽烟了。From now on, I'll give up smoking.

这山望着那山高 zhè shān wàngzhe nà shān gāo it is always the other mountain that looks higher; the grass is greener on the other side of the fence; never feel satisfied with one's lot:就在这儿好好干吧,别老是～。You should stay on and do a good job of your present work instead of hankering for something better all the time.

这些 zhèxiē *also* "这些个" these:～日子老刮风。It is quite windy these days. /～人我都认识。I know all of them. /～东西请他拿走。Ask him to take these things away.

这样 zhèyàng *also* "这么样" such; so; of this kind; like this:～的问题 such (*or* these kinds of) problems /请跟着我～做。Please follow me. /事实就是～的。Such is the truth. /人们一般更喜欢～的文学作品。Literary works of this kind usually have greater appeal. /～一来,所有的问题都不存在了。This has solved all problems.

这样那样 zhèyàng-nàyàng this or that; one kind or another; all kinds of:～的意见 all sorts of complaints /由于～的原因 for one reason or another /可能还会有～的变化。There might be changes of various kinds.

这咱 zhèzan 〈方言〉now; at present; at the moment:～该动身了。It's time to leave. /～他还在书店呢。He is still in the bookstore now. /～哪还能找得到他? How can you find him at this moment?

这早晚儿 zhèzǎowǎnr ❶ now; at the moment; at present:你怎么～还没走呢? Why are you still here? /她～正在客厅里喝茶呢。She is having tea in the sitting-room now. ❷ so late:天已经～了,别出去了! Don't go out now. It is so late.

蔗 zhè sugarcane:～田 sugarcane field

蔗茅草 zhèmáocǎo plume grass

蔗螟 zhèmíng sugarcane borer

蔗农 zhènóng sugarcane grower

蔗鼠 zhèshǔ cane rat (*Thryonomys*)

蔗糖 zhètáng ❶〈化学〉sucrose:～酶 sucrase /～合物 sucrate ❷ cane sugar:～厂 cane mill /～蜜 sugar cane molasses; molasses

蔗渣 zhèzhā bagasse

嗻 zhè (usu. said by a servant in reply to the master's command) yes; alright; yeah:"滚出去,滚!" "～。" "Out, I said...out!" "Yes, sir."
see also zhē

䗪 zhè

䗪虫 zhèchóng *also* "地鳖" dìbiē ground beetle

鹧 zhè

鹧鸪 zhègū 〈动物〉francolin; partridge

鹧鸪菜 zhègūcài 〈中药〉*zhegucai* (*Caloglossa leprieurii*)

柘 zhè 〈植物〉three-bristle cudrania (*Cudrania tricuspidata*)

zhe

着 zhe 〈助词〉❶ be doing:他们正开～会呢。They are having a meeting. /坐～怎么也比站～好。Anyway, sitting is better than standing. ❷ *used to indicate a state*:所有的窗子都开～。All the windows are open. /桌上放～很多书。There are a lot of books on the desk. ❸ *used to give force to a verb or adjective*:你仔细听～。Just listen. /声音小～点儿。Lower your voice. /你快～点。Hurry up. *or* Be quick. ❹ *used in forming a preposition*:朝～ towards /顺～ along /为～ for (the sake of)
see also zhāo; zháo; zhuó

着哩 zheli 〈方言〉very; quite:他对我好～。He is very kind to me. /两人可亲～! They are quite thick with each other.

着呢 zhene 〈口语〉quite; very:我累～。I am dog-tired. /外面天气冷～。It's freezing cold outside. /那地方美～。That is a very beautiful place.

著 zhe *see* "着" zhe
see also zhù; zhuó

zhèi

这(這) zhèi (variant pronunciation for 这, used as a determiner) this; these:～封信 this letter /～几本书 these books /～三辆卡车 these three trucks

see also zhè

zhēn

蓁 zhēn
蓁蓁 zhēnzhēn 〈书面〉❶ luxuriant; exuberant; profuse: 其叶～ with luxuriant foliage; thick with leaves /草木～ exuberant vegetation ❷ growing thickly or densely; densely-wooded: 荆棘～ be overgrown with brambles

榛 zhēn 〈植物〉❶ hazel ❷ hazelnut; filbert
榛鸡 zhēnjī also "飞龙" fēilóng hazel grouse
榛莽 zhēnmǎng 〈书面〉luxuriant vegetation: 狼豺窜～。Wolves and jackals run about in the dense wood.
榛狉 zhēnpī also "獉狉" zhēnpī 〈书面〉densely wooded and frequented by wild animals
榛实 zhēnshí hazelnut
榛榛 zhēnzhēn 〈书面〉be overgrown with plants or trees: 草木～ overgrowth of vegetation
榛子 zhēnzi ❶ hazel ❷ hazelnut; filbert

臻 zhēn 〈书面〉❶ attain (a higher level); become (better): 他的思想益～成熟。He is becoming more and more mature in thinking. /市场日～繁荣。The market is booming day by day. /她的画渐～佳境。Her paintings are gradually attaining to perfection. ❷ arrive; come: 百福并～。May a hundred blessings descend on you!

獉 zhēn
獉狉 zhēnpī see "榛狉" zhēnpī

斟 zhēn pour (tea or wine): 互～ pour each other a glass of wine /自～自饮 help oneself to the wine
斟酌 zhēnzhuó turn over in one's mind; consider; deliberate: ～字句 weigh one's words /～损益 make alterations after due consideration /当初为给孩子起名,他们是费过一番～的。They pondered for quite some time as to what name to give their son. /经过再三～,他们决定会议延期。After much deliberation they decided to put off the meeting. /这件事你自己～处理吧。I'll leave the matter to you.

椹 zhēn see "砧" zhēn
see also shèn

砧(碪) zhēn hammering block; anvil: 台～ bench anvil /锻～ smith anvil
砧板 zhēnbǎn chopping block; chopping board
砧骨 zhēngǔ 〈生理〉incus; anvil
砧木 zhēnmù 〈农业〉stock
砧子 zhēnzi 〈口语〉hammering block; anvil

甄 zhēn ❶〈书面〉draw a distinction; distinguish; discriminate; examine: ～录 examine and employ ❷ (Zhēn) a surname
甄拔 zhēnbá select; choose: ～人才 select qualified people
甄别 zhēnbié ❶ distinguish; screen; discriminate; examine: ～积案 examine long-pending cases /～史料 identify historical data (*or* materials) ❷ test and assess: 进行～考试 give an assessment test /公司录用职员是经过严格～的。The company takes on employees through strict tests and assessments.
甄录 zhēnlù examine and then employ; test before taking on: 我们必需严格～。We must give every job applicant a rigorous test.
甄审 zhēnshěn examine and distinguish; screen; discriminate
甄选 zhēnxuǎn select: ～展览品 select exhibits

真 zhēn ❶ true; real; factual; genuine: ～丝头巾 genuine silk scarf /千～万确 absolutely true /～假难分 the true is mingled with the false; find it hard to tell truth from falsehood /是～发还是假发? Is it real hair or a wig? ❷ really; truly; indeed: 他～聪明。He is really bright. /～麻烦您了。Sorry to have put you to so much trouble. /音乐会～精彩。The concert was just wonderful. /窗外的景色～美。There was a truly beautiful view from the window. /这人～有两下子。The man is very smart indeed. ❸ clearly; distinctly; unmistakably: 布告上的字你看得～么? Can you see the words in the notice clearly? /他说英语时每个音都咬得～。He would pronounce every sound distinctly when he spoke English. ❹ (in Chinese calligraphy) regular script ❺ portrait; image: 写～ draw a portrait /传～ fax; facsimile (transmission) ❻〈书面〉nature; natural state: 返朴归～ recovering one's original simplicity; back to nature ❼ (Zhēn) a surname
真北 zhēnběi 〈地理〉true north
真才实学 zhēncái-shíxué real ability and learning; genuine knowledge or competence: 有～的老教师 senior teacher with great competence and learning /他们大多具有～。Most of them are persons of real learning. /这个厂拥有一批有～的青年技术员。There is a group of really talented young technicians in this factory.
真诚 zhēnchéng sincere; true; earnest; honest: ～的心意 sincerity /她对朋友～。She is true to her friends. /那男孩的样子显得非常～。The boy appeared extremely sincere and honest. /她的～感动了在场的每个人。Her earnestness touched everyone present.
真传 zhēnchuán essence of a craft or knowledge imparted by a master: 他的相声得到侯大师的～。He learned the art of comic dialogue under the tutelage of Master Hou.
真纯 zhēnchún pure; sincere; true: ～的爱情 sincere (*or* true) love /他的感情是那样～。He is all sincerity. *or* He is sincerity itself.
真刀真枪 zhēndāo-zhēnqiāng real swords and spears — the real thing; working in real earnest: 别空谈了,要～地干。Stop your empty talk and get down to brass tacks. /他这人工作中总是～的,从不来虚的。He is always serious with his work.
真地平 zhēndìpíng 〈天文〉true horizon
真谛 zhēndì true meaning; essence: 探求人生的～ seek (after) the true meaning of life /懂得生活的～ know the essence of life
真鲷 zhēndiāo also "加级鱼" jiājíyú genuine porgy; red porgy
真分式 zhēnfēnshì 〈数学〉proper fraction
真分数 zhēnfēnshù 〈数学〉proper fraction
真格的 zhēngéde 〈方言〉serious; real; true: 这次他可是动了～! He means business this time. /说～,我不想去。To tell the truth, I don't want to go. /～,你喜欢这姑娘? Seriously, do you like the girl?
真个 zhēngè 〈方言〉indeed; really; truly: 他～不简单。He is a remarkable man indeed. /这孩子～变了! The child has really changed.
真果 zhēnguǒ 〈植物〉true fruit
真核 zhēnhé 〈生物〉eukaryon: ～生物 eucaryote (*or* eukaryote) /～细胞 eucaryon
真话 zhēnhuà truth: 说～,办实事 speak the truth, do solid work
真际 zhēnjì 〈书面〉essence; nature; true meaning: 测其～ seek the truth (of it) /生命的～ true meaning of life
真迹 zhēnjì authentic work (of painting or calligraphy): 这幅画确实是齐白石的～。The painting is no doubt the authentic work of Qi Baishi.
真假 zhēn-jiǎ true and false; genuine and sham: 辨别～ distinguish between truth and falsehood; tell the real from the sham
真金不怕火炼 zhēnjīn bù pà huǒ liàn true gold fears no fire — a good anvil does not fear the hammer; a person of integrity can stand severe tests: ～,我才不怕这些谣言哩! An honest man has a clear conscience, so why should I worry about those rumours?
真菌 zhēnjūn eumycete; fungus: 皮肤～ cutaneous fungus /抗～素 eumycin /杀～剂 fungicide
真菌学 zhēnjūnxué mycology
真空 zhēnkōng vacuum; space with little or no air; situation characterized by emptiness: 完全～ perfect vacuum /未尽～ partial vacuum /～处理 vacuum treatment /～电容器〈电工〉vacuum capacitor /～继电器 vacuum relay /～开关 vacuum switch /～光电管〈电子〉vacuum phototube /～结晶器〈化工〉vacuum crystallizer /～蒸馏 vacuum distillation; reduced-pressure distillation /～电弧炉〈冶金〉vacuum arc furnace /～压铸 vacuum die casting /～吸尘器〈机械〉vacuum cleaner /～制动器 vacuum brake /他想填补权力～。He tried to fill the power vacuum.
真空包装 zhēnkōng bāozhuāng vacuum packing
真空泵 zhēnkōngbèng vacuum pump; pick-up pump
真空地带 zhēnkōng dìdài 〈军事〉no man's land
真空度 zhēnkōngdù vacuity; degree of vacuum
真空管 zhēnkōngguǎn vacuum tube; vacuum valve; valve
真空计 zhēnkōngjì vacuum gauge; vacuometer
真理 zhēnlǐ truth: 普遍～ universal truth /绝对～ absolute truth /相对～ relative truth /颠扑不破的～ irrefutable truth /捍卫～ uphold

the truth /追求～ seek (after) truth; pursue truth /实践是检验～的唯一标准。Practice is the sole criterion of truth.

真理报 Zhēnlǐbào *Pravda*, organ of the former Communist Party of the Soviet Union

真两性畸形 zhēnliǎngxìng jīxíng 〈医学〉true hermaphroditism; ovotesticular hermaphroditism

真亮 zhēnliang 〈方言〉clearly; distinctly:还没进屋,屋里人的交谈就听得很～。Even before entering the room, he could clearly hear the talk inside.

真面目 zhēnmiànmù true face; true features; true colours:不识庐山～,只缘身在此山中。I see not the true face of Lushan, Because I am in this very mountain. /这么多年下来,你仍不能认清他的～。After so many years, you still fail to see him in his true colours (*or* know him for what he is).

真名实姓 zhēnmíng-shíxìng real name:他常用的是化名,他的～是什么呢? He often uses an assumed name (*or* a pseudonym), but what is his real name?

真命 zhēnmìng 〈迷信〉sent by God or Heaven:～天子 Son of Heaven; emperor

真纳 Zhēnnà Mohammed Ali Jinnah (1876-1948), founder of Pakistan

真皮 zhēnpí ❶〈生理〉derma; corium ❷ real or genuine leather; true leather:～包 genuine leather bag

真品 zhēnpǐn genuine piece; authentic work:这古董是～。The antique is genuine. /这瓶茅台酒怕不是～。I'm afraid this bottle of Maotai spirit is fake.

真凭实据 zhēnpíng-shíjù hard or factual evidence; ironclad or conclusive proof:你必须提供～。You must provide us with factual evidence. /目前我们仍缺乏～。For the moment we still lack hard evidence.

真朴 zhēnpǔ simple and sincere; honest:她是个单纯～的女孩子。She is an innocent and honest girl.

真漆 zhēnqī lacquer

真枪实弹 zhēnqiāng-shídàn real guns and bullets; live ammunition:他们进行了一次～的演习。They conducted manoeuvres with live ammunition. /双方都动用了～。Both sides resorted to (*or* used) arms.

真切 zhēnqiè ❶ distinct; clear; graphic:听得很～ hear quite distinctly /有关细节,我记不～了。I cannot remember the details clearly. ❷ sincere; genuine:情意～ genuine feeling /他的讲话～动人。His speech was sincere and moving.

真情 zhēnqíng ❶ real or true situation; actual circumstances; facts; truth:全部～ whole story /说出了病人的～ tell the patient's real condition /了解车祸的～实况 find out all the facts of the car accident /不要再继续隐瞒～了。Don't try to conceal the truth any longer. ❷ genuine feelings; real sentiments:倾诉～ pour out (*or* open) one's heart /掩藏内心的～ hide one's innermost feelings /他深埋在心底的～终于表露出来了。He finally revealed his pent-up feelings.

真诠 zhēnquán 〈书面〉correct explanation; faithful interpretation

真确 zhēnquè ❶ authentic; true; genuine:千真万确 absolutely true /你对情况的了解并不～。What you've learned is not the real situation. /消息～可靠吗? Is the news reliable? ❷ plain; clear; distinct:我看得～,绝对没有错误。I saw it clearly and there was no question about it.

真人 zhēnrén ❶ true man (a man who has attained enlightenment or immortality through practising Taoism) ❷ real people:这是一个～的故事。This is a story about a real person.

真人真事 zhēnrén-zhēnshì real people and real events; real story:这篇小说是根据～写出来的。This novel is based on a real story (*or* on real people and real events).

真容 zhēnróng ❶ portrait:绣～ embroidered portrait; tapestry portrait ❷ true face; true features:撕去假面具,露出～ tear off the mask and lay bare one's true features

真溶液 zhēnróngyè *also* "分子溶液" fēnzǐ róngyè molecular solution

真鲨 zhēnshā carcharhinid

真善美 zhēn-shàn-měi the true, the good and the beautiful:达到～的境界 attain the realm (*or* ideal) of the true, the good and the beautiful /～与假恶丑总是对立的。Truth, good and beauty exist in contrast with falsehood, evil and ugliness.

真身 zhēnshēn 〈迷信〉body of a god or Buddha

真实 zhēnshí real; true; actual; authentic:～地址 real address /～消息 authentic news /感情～ true feelings /报道不～。The report is false. /小说～地反映了当时社会的情况。The novel depicts the society as it actually was at that time.

真实感 zhēnshígǎn sense of reality:剧情缺乏～。The plot of the play seems unreal.

真实性 zhēnshíxìng authenticity; verisimilitude; truthfulness; factuality:故事的～很强。The story is true to life.

真释 zhēnshì faithful and correct interpretation or explanation

真是 zhēnshi (used in a complaint) indeed; really:你～,也不快拿个主意! You are the limit! Can't you make your mind up! /～! 这雨老也不停! What a shame (*or* nuisance)! The rain just doesn't stop! /刚穿的新鞋已经弄脏了,～! Why, you have just put on your new shoes, and now they are soiled!

真书 zhēnshū regular script (of Chinese calligraphy)

真数 zhēnshù 〈数学〉logarithm

真率 zhēnshuài sincere; candid; unaffected; straightforward:感情～ be sincere /为人～ be straightforward

真丝 zhēnsī pure silk; 100% silk:～衬衫 shirt made of pure silk; silk shirt

真髓 zhēnsuǐ essence; quintessence:对其理论的～有所领略 have some idea about the quintessence of his theory

真伪莫辨 zhēnwěi-mòbiàn unable to distinguish between the true and the false

真武 Zhēnwǔ ❶ northern God in ancient Chinese mythology ❷ Taoist God

真藓 zhēnxiǎn 〈植物〉true moss (*Muscus*)

真相 zhēnxiàng *also* "真象" real situation; actual state of affairs; facts; truth:揭露～ reveal (*or* disclose) the truth /了解事情的～ find out the facts (*or* truth) /阴谋家总是给人一种假象,而将～隐蔽起来。The schemer always tries to assume (*or* put on) a false appearance and hide his true features.

真相大白 zhēnxiàng-dàbái the truth is out (*or* fully revealed); the facts are clear now:好在真相已经大白,我不再背黑锅了。Fortunately, now everything has come out into the open, and I've been exonerated.

真心 zhēnxīn heartfelt; wholehearted; true; sincere:～相爱 be truly in love (with each other) /～地帮助别人 help others wholeheartedly /他说的不是～话。He was not speaking his mind. /她请你去吃饭是出于一片～。She was quite sincere when she asked you to dinner.

真心实意 zhēnxīn-shíyì *also* "真心诚意" sincerely; genuinely; wholeheartedly; truly:～地为残疾人服务 serve the handicapped heart and soul /她对人一向是～的。She has always been sincere towards people. /他得到了群众～的拥护。He has gained genuine support from the masses.

真性 zhēnxìng ❶ true:～霍乱 cholera ❷〈书面〉nature; natural instincts

真性血友病 zhēnxìng xuèyǒubìng 〈医学〉haemophilia vera

真言 zhēnyán ❶ truth:酒后吐～。One usually tells the truth when drunk. ❷ incantation

真意 zhēnyì ❶ true meaning; essence:生命的～ true meaning of life ❷ heartfelt; sincere; genuine:你看不出他是真心～吗? Can't you see he is sincere?

真影 zhēnyǐng portrait of one's dead ancestors (hung during sacrificial rites)

真赃实犯 zhēnzāng-shífàn *also* "真赃实据" conclusive evidence; hard evidence; criminal evidence

真章儿 zhēnzhāngr 〈方言〉effective solution; real action:你这回要不拿出点～来,准出洋相。If you fail to come up with a feasible solution, you'll make a spectacle of yourself in time. /这事八字还没一撇,你怎么就急急忙忙地动～了呢? Nothing is definite yet and you have rushed into action! *or* How could you take such a rash action when virtually nothing has been decided on?

真着 zhēnzhe 〈方言〉clear; distinct:这本画册印得挺～。The picture album is well printed. /电话的声音太小,听不～。The phone call was hardly audible as the voice was too low.

真真假假 zhēnzhēn-jiǎjiǎ the true mingled with the false:～的一堆材料,叫人好生难辨。We have a pile of materials here, containing both true and fake data. It's so difficult to tell them apart.

真正 zhēnzhèng ❶ real; true; genuine:～的友谊 true friendship /～的人民公仆 faithful servant of the people /～的贵州茅台酒 genuine

(*or* real) Maotai from Guizhou / 群众是～的英雄。The masses are real heroes. ❷ really; truly; genuinely: 这个人～不简单。The man is truly remarkable. / 他～变了，几乎让人认不出来了。He has changed so much that one could hardly recognize him. / 直到最近，她才～理解了"老师"这个词的意义。Not until recently did she come to fully realize the meaning the word "teacher".

真知 zhēnzhī real knowledge; knowledge: 任何～都发源于实践。Practice is the only source of knowledge. *or* All knowledge comes from practice.

真知灼见 zhēnzhī-zhuójiàn correct and deep understanding; profound insight; penetrating judgment: 在他的著作中，有一些关于人生的～。His works showed his deep insights into the meaning of life.

真值 zhēnzhí 〈物理〉true value; truth value: ～函数 truth function

真值表 zhēnzhíbiǎo 〈物理〉truth table

真挚 zhēnzhì sincere; genuine; cordial: ～的话语 cordial remarks / ～的感情 genuine feelings / ～的态度 sincere (*or* earnest) attitude / 表达～的感谢 express one's heartfelt thanks

真珠 zhēnzhū *also* "珍珠" zhēnzhū pearl

真珠层 zhēnzhūcéng 〈生物〉pearly or nacreous layer

真主 Zhēnzhǔ 〈伊斯兰〉Allah

真主党 Zhēnzhǔdǎng Party of God; *Hizbollah*

真字 zhēnzì (in Chinese calligraphy) regular script

禎 zhēn happiness and luck (often used in personal names)

贞[1] zhēn ❶ loyal; staunch; faithful: 坚～ staunch / 忠～不二 unswerving in one's loyalty ❷ (of a woman in the feudal society) chastity or virginity: ～妇 chaste woman

贞[2] zhēn 〈书面〉divination

贞操 zhēncāo ❶ chastity; virginity: 严守～ strictly maintain one's virginity ❷ loyalty; moral integrity

贞观 Zhēnguān Zhenguan, title of the reign (627-649) of Li Shimin (李世民, 599-649), 2nd emperor of the Tang Dynasty, called reverently Tang Taizong (唐太宗) after death: ～之治 Golden Years of Zhenguan, marked by peace, prosperity, openness, and efficient government

贞节 zhēnjié ❶ moral integrity; loyalty: 其性温厚，有～。He is honest, kind, and a man of integrity. ❷ virginity (of an unmarried woman); chastity (of a widow): ～牌坊 chastity arch (erected as an honour to a woman who defended her chastity, or to a widow who remained faithful to her dead husband)

贞洁 zhēnjié (of a woman) chaste

贞静 zhēnjìng 〈书面〉(of a woman) chaste and quiet

贞烈 zhēnliè (of a woman) would rather die than lose one's chastity

贞女 zhēnnǚ virgin; chaste girl

贞淑 zhēnshū 〈书面〉(of a woman) chaste and kindhearted

祯 zhēn 〈书面〉auspicious

桢 zhēn terminal posts used in building a wall in ancient times

桢干 zhēngàn 〈书面〉backbone; mainstay; core; key member: 国家～ pillar of the state

桢木 zhēnmù Nüzhen (an ancient nationality in northeast China)

帧 zhēn 〈量词〉*of paintings and calligraphy, etc.*: 一～画 a painting

侦 zhēn investigate; explore; scout; detect: 警察只用了三天就～破了这个案子。It took the police only three days to break the case.

侦办 zhēnbàn investigate and handle (a case): 公安局正在努力～，以期尽快结案。The Public Security Bureau is busy making investigations so as to close the case as soon as possible.

侦查 zhēnchá investigate (a crime): 立案～ enter a case on file for investigation / ～走私活动 investigate a smuggling case / 他们正在～这一流氓团伙的犯罪事实。They were looking for evidence against this gang of hooligans.

侦察 zhēnchá 〈军事〉reconnoitre; scout: ～排 scout platoon / ～飞行 reconnaissance flight / 电信～ gather communications intelligence / 在敌前沿阵地～ scout the enemy's forward position / 到敌人后方～ make a reconnaissance behind the enemy lines / ～敌方的火力部署 reconnoitre the enemy's fire disposition / 进行政治～ throw out a political feeler

侦察兵 zhēnchábīng scout: 他童年时曾梦想当一名～。As a boy, he had dreamt of becoming a scout.

侦察部队 zhēnchá bùduì reconnaissance troops; scouting force

侦察机 zhēnchájī reconnaissance plane; scout: 我们发现了一架敌人的～。We have detected an enemy reconnaissance plane.

侦察接收机 zhēnchá jiēshōujī 〈军事〉melodeon; melodion

侦察卫星 zhēnchá wèixīng reconnaissance satellite

侦察员 zhēncháyuán scout

侦谍 zhēndié 〈书面〉investigate; scout; detect

侦获 zhēnhuò investigate and crack: ～一批赃物 hunt for and seize a batch of stolen goods

侦缉 zhēnjī track down and arrest: ～队 tracking team

侦破 zhēnpò investigate and crack; break (a criminal case): 这是个难于～的案子。This is a hard case to break (*or* solve).

侦伺 zhēnsì detect; spy upon; scout: ～他的下落 scout around for him

侦探 zhēntàn ❶ do detective work; spy: ～敌情 spy upon the enemy ❷ detective; spy: 私人～ private detective / 外国～ foreign spy

侦探小说 zhēntàn xiǎoshuō detective story

侦听 zhēntīng 〈军事〉intercept (enemy radio communications); monitor; tap

侦听器 zhēntīngqì detectaphone; detectagraph; monitor

侦听台 zhēntīngtái intercept station

侦讯 zhēnxùn investigate and interrogate

箴 zhēn 〈书面〉❶ advise; exhort; admonish ❷ didactic literary style

箴言 zhēnyán 〈书面〉admonition; exhortation; advice; maxim

鱵 zhēn 〈动物〉halfbeak

针(鍼) zhēn ❶ needle: 毛线～ knitting needle / 缝纫机～ needle for sewing machine / 穿～引线 thread a needle; 〈比喻〉act as a go-between / 铁杵磨成～ grind an iron pestle down to a needle — little strokes fell great oaks ❷ stitch: 在外衣上缝两～ sew (*or* put) a couple of stitches in one's jacket / 你手上的伤口要缝五～。The cut in your hand needs five stitches. / 一～不补，十～难缝。A stitch in time saves nine. ❸ anything like a needle: 指南～ compass; compass needle / 别～ safety pin / 撞～ firing pin / 时(分、秒)～ hour (minute, second) hand ❹ injection; inoculation; shot: 防疫～ inoculation / 退烧～ injection of antipyretic / 强心～ injection of cardiotonic / 打了一～ have (*or* give) an injection ❺ acupuncture: 大夫给他扎～。The doctor applied acupuncture to him.

针鼻儿 zhēnbír eye of a needle; needle's eye: 这根针的～太小。This needle's eye is much too small. / ～大的事儿，他也要大惊小怪。He likes to kick up a great fuss about trifles.

针砭 zhēnbiān ❶ ancient form of acupuncture ❷ criticise; refute: ～朝政 criticise the handling of state affairs / ～不正之风 condemn unhealthy tendencies

针布 zhēnbù 〈纺织〉card clothing

针插 zhēnchā pincushion

针插不进，水泼不进 zhēn chābujìn, shuǐ pōbujìn impenetrable and watertight — (of an organization, body, etc.) not allowing any outsider to look into its affairs: 这是一个～的独立王国。This is an independent kingdom that tightly closes its door to the outside.

针吹 zhēnchuī 〈化工〉needle blow

针刺画 zhēncìhuà pinpricked picture

针刺机 zhēncìjī 〈纺织〉needle machine

针刺疗法 zhēncì liáofǎ acupuncture treatment: 推广～ popularize (*or* universalize) acupuncture treatment

针刺麻醉 zhēncì mázuì acupuncture anaesthesia: 改药物麻醉为～ replace drug anaesthesia with acupuncture anaesthesia / ～镇痛 using acupuncture to stop pain / 用～进行大手术的事例已屡见不鲜。Acupuncture anaesthesia applied in major surgical operations is quite common now.

针垫掌 zhēndiànzhǎng 〈植物〉pincushion cactus

针对 zhēnduì be aimed at; be targeted on; be directed against; take into consideration:缺乏~性 without a clear aim /他的这番话绝不是~你的。His remarks are not in the least aimed at you. /这篇杂文是~那些见利忘义者的。The essay is directed against those who forget all moral principles at the sight of profits. /应~学生的思想感情对他们进行教育。We should educate the students by taking into consideration their views and feelings. /他们~现存的困难制定了一系列计划。They made a series of plans in dealing with the present difficulties.

针阀 zhēnfá 〈机械〉needle valve:~减震器 needle valve shock absorber

针锋相对 zhēnfēng-xiāngduì tit for tat; measure for measure; in direct opposition to:~的方针 tit-for-tat policy /~地和他斗争 give him tit for tat; wage a tit-for-tat struggle against him /两个人的观点~,谁也没法说服谁。Having diametrically opposed views, neither could convince the other.

针工 zhēngōng needlework; needlecraft:这条裙子的布料好,~也好。The skirt is made of excellent material, and the needlework is superb too.

针箍 zhēngū 〈方言〉thimble:请把~儿借我用用。May I use your thimble?

针管 zhēnguǎn needle tube

针剂 zhēnjì 〈药学〉injection:研制新的~ develop new injections /使用~比吃药见效快。Injections have faster effect than medicines.

针尖 zhēnjiān point of a needle; pinpoint

针尖大的窟窿,斗大的风 zhēnjiān dà de kūlong, dǒu dà de fēng 〈俗语〉big wind can flow through a small hole — a damage should be repaired in time lest it cause much worse harm in future; a little leak can sink a great ship

针尖儿对麦芒儿 zhēnjiānr duì màimángr a pin against an awn — confront eyeball to eyeball; diamond cut diamond:两个人~,谁也不让谁。Neither would budge. It was a case of diamond cutting diamond (*or* a standoff).

针脚 zhēnjiao ❶ line of stitches:还是用同色线好,你看,袖子上的那道~几乎看不见。It is better to use thread of the same colour. Just look, the line of stitches in the sleeve is hardly visible. ❷ stitch:~细密 short stitches /~太大。The stitches are too long (*or* loose). /~匀称。The stitches are neat.

针灸 zhēnjiǔ acupuncture and moxibustion:~是我国医学的宝贵遗产。Acupuncture and moxibustion are a valuable Chinese medical heritage.

针灸甲乙经 Zhēnjiǔ Jiǎyǐjīng *A Classic of Acupuncture and Moxibustion*, China's earliest extant classic on acupuncture and moxibustion completed in 215-282 of the Three Kingdoms Period

针灸疗法 zhēnjiǔ liáofǎ acupuncture and moxibustion treatment

针灸铜人 zhēnjiǔ tóngrén bronze human figure marked with acupuncture points

针刻 zhēnkè needle etching; drypoint

针孔 zhēnkǒng pinhole:~型浇注口〈化工〉pinpoint gate /~照相机 pinhole camera

针栎 zhēnlì pin oak

针麻 zhēnmá (short for 针刺麻醉) acupuncture anaesthesia

针码 zhēnmǎ stitch:这鞋上的~又密又匀。The stitches in the shoe are both short and neat.

针茅草 zhēnmáocǎo needlegrass

针梳机 zhēnshūjī 〈纺织〉gill box

针头 zhēntóu 〈医学〉syringe needle:~必须消毒。The syringe needles must be sterilized.

针头线脑 zhēntóu-xiànnǎo 〈口语〉odds and ends needed for sewing; needle, thread, etc.:他很勤俭,连一点~都舍不得扔。He is a thrifty man who hates to throw away even odds and ends.

针尾鸭 zhēnwěiyā 〈动物〉pintail

针线 zhēnxian needlework; needlecraft:学做~ learn to do needlework

针线包 zhēnxianbāo sewing kit

针线活儿 zhēnxianhuór needlework; sewing; stitching:做~累眼。Your eyes get easily tired from needlework.

针眼 zhēnyǎn ❶ eye of a needle; needle's eye:这绣花针的~太小。The eye of this embroidery needle is too small. ❷ pinprick:不露~ invisible pinpricks

针眼 zhēnyan 〈医学〉sty(e):害~ have a stye

针鼹 zhēnyǎn 〈动物〉echidna; spiny anteater:食蚁~ ant-eating echidna

针叶 zhēnyè 〈林业〉needle; acerose leaf:~灌木林 conifruticeta /~林 coniferous forest; aciculisilvae /~植被 aciculignosa

针叶树 zhēnyèshù conifer; coniferous tree; softwood:~材 coniferous wood

针织 zhēnzhī knitting:~围巾 knitted (*or* knit) scarf

针织厂 zhēnzhīchǎng knit goods mill; knitting mill

针织机 zhēnzhījī knitting machine

针织品 zhēnzhīpǐn knitting; knit goods; knitwear; hosiery:大量~ large quantity of knit goods /去年夏天~畅销。Knitwear sold well last summer.

针织衫 zhēnzhīshān sweater

针黹 zhēnzhǐ 〈书面〉needlework:~女工 needlewoman

针锥 zhēnzhuī *also* "针锥子"〈方言〉awl

珍(珎)

zhēn ❶ treasure; riches:山~海味 delicacies from land and sea; choice food of every kind /奇~异宝 rare treasures ❷ treasured; precious; rare; valuable: *see* "~禽" ❸ value highly; set great store by

珍爱 zhēn'ài love dearly; cherish; treasure:这是他最~的一本书。This is the book he loves most dearly. /战士们像~眼睛一样~他们的武器。The soldiers treasure their weapons as they do their eyes.

珍宝 zhēnbǎo jewellery; riches; treasure:寻找~ seek after treasures /罕见的~ rare jewellery /如获~ as if one had found stored riches /世代相传的~ family treasure; treasures that have passed from generation to generation

珍本 zhēnběn rare edition; rare book:难得的~ rare book /这是仅有的~。This is the only extant edition.

珍藏 zhēncáng ❶ collect (rare books, art curiosities, etc.); treasure up:~古画 collect ancient paintings /他至今~着父亲的手稿。He has kept his father's manuscripts to this day. /他把过去的所有事情都~在记忆里。He treasures up all past events in his memory. ❷ rare and valuable articles collected or treasured up:故宫博物馆的~ rare treasures kept in the Palace Museum

珍存 zhēncún treasure up; collect:~了不少纪念邮票 keep quite a few commemorative stamps

珍贵 zhēnguì precious; valuable; rare:~史料 prized historical materials /~药品 valuable medicine /~的古籍 rare ancient books /人才最~。Talents are most precious. /时间特别~。Time is priceless. /童年的生活对他来说无比~。His childhood life is invaluable to him.

珍眉 zhēnméi *zhenmei*, a kind of green tea

珍品 zhēnpǐn treasure; curiosity; curio:难得的艺术~ art treasures; art curiosities /这是国画中的~。It counts as a gem among traditional Chinese paintings.

珍奇 zhēnqí rare:~动物 rare animals

珍禽 zhēnqín rare bird:~异兽 rare birds and unusual animals; rare birds and animals

珍赏 zhēnshǎng treasure and appreciate

珍摄 zhēnshè 〈书面〉〈套语〉(esp. in letters) take care of yourself; look after yourself:至盼善自~。Sincerely hope that you will take good care of yourself.

珍视 zhēnshì treasure; prize; value; set store by:~今天的幸福生活 cherish today's happy life /~家庭的和睦 value family harmony /~两国间的传统友谊 set store by the traditional ties of friendship between the two countries /这是友谊的象征,是值得~的。This is a symbol of our friendship that ought to be treasured.

珍玩 zhēnwán (rare) curio(s); curiosity:他家里有几件无价的~。He has some priceless curios.

珍味 zhēnwèi delicacies; dainties

珍闻 zhēnwén news titbits; fillers:海外~ news titbits from overseas (*or* abroad) /文学~ literary briefs (*or* miscellany)

珍惜 zhēnxī treasure; cherish; value; prize:~友谊 treasure friendship /~人才 value talents /~名誉 cherish one's reputation (*or* fame) /~他人的信任 prize other's trust /~自己的健康 hold dear one's health /这种纯洁、真挚的感情是值得~的。This kind of pure, genuine feeling is invaluable.

珍稀 zhēnxī rare:大熊猫是一种~动物。The giant panda is a rare animal.

珍馐 zhēnxiū *also* "珍羞" delicacies; dainties:~美味 delicacies; dainties

珍异 zhēnyì rare:他养的花中有两种是~品种。Among the flowers he grows, two kinds are very rare.

珍重 zhēnzhòng ❶ prize; cherish; treasure; value highly: ～权利 value one's right /～家庭的和睦幸福 treasure family peace and happiness /我们非常～孩子们的进取心。We cherish very much our children's enterprising spirit. ❷ take care of yourself; look after yourself: 后会有期，多加～！We'll meet again. Please take good care of yourself!
珍珠 zhēnzhū *also* "真珠" zhēnzhū pearl: ～项链 pearl necklace /一串晶莹的～ a string of glittering pearls
珍珠贝 zhēnzhūbèi pearl shell; pearl oyster: 养殖～ raise pearl oysters
珍珠粉 zhēnzhūfěn pearl powder
珍珠港 Zhēnzhūgǎng Pearl Harbour: ～事件 Pearl Harbour Incident of 7 Dec. 1941
珍珠鸡 zhēnzhūjī 〈动物〉guinea fowl
珍珠梅 zhēnzhūméi 〈植物〉false spiraea
珍珠米 zhēnzhūmǐ 〈方言〉maize; (Indian) corn
珍珠霜 zhēnzhūshuāng pearl cream
珍珠岩 zhēnzhūyán pearlite
珍珠云母 zhēnzhū yúnmǔ margarite

胗

zhēn gizzard: 鸡～儿 chicken's gizzard /鸭～儿 duck's gizzard
胗肝儿 zhēngānr gizzard and liver (esp. chicken's or duck's)

zhěn

鬒(黰)

zhěn 〈书面〉(of hair) thick and black

缜(稹)

zhěn 〈书面〉careful; painstaking; meticulous
缜密 zhěnmì careful; deliberate; detailed; meticulous: 计划～ carefully planned /文思～ meticulously written /～的分析和讨论 detailed analysis and discussion

枕

zhěn ❶ pillow: 药～ medicinal pillow /凉～ summer pillow ❷ rest one's head on: 孩子～在妈妈的胳膊上入睡了。The child fell asleep in her mother's arm.
枕藏电话机 zhěncáng diànhuàjī pillowphone
枕戈待旦 zhěngē-dàidàn wait for daybreak with one's head pillowed on one's weapon; be on guard; be vigilant; be on the alert: ～，严守边防。Guarding the frontier, they are always on the alert.
枕骨 zhěngǔ 〈生理〉occipital bone
枕藉 zhěnjiè 〈书面〉(of a number of people) lie or fall down together higgledy-piggledy: 相与～乎舟中 lie higgledy-piggledy in the boat
枕巾 zhěnjīn towel used to cover a pillow
枕木 zhěnmù 〈铁路〉sleeper; tie: 更换～ replace the sleepers
枕套 zhěntào *also* "枕头套" pillowcase; pillow slip: 尼龙～ nylon pillowcase
枕头 zhěntou pillow: 一对鸭绒～ a pair of eiderdown pillows /绣花～ pillow with an embroidered case; 〈比喻〉good-for-nothing with an attractive appearance
枕头箱 zhěntouxiāng box in the bedroom used to keep valuables: 一个精致的～ exquisite bedroom box
枕席 zhěnxí ❶〈书面〉bed: ～边儿的话 bedside (*or* private) conversation; pillow talk ❷ *also* "枕头席儿" mat used to cover a pillow
枕心 zhěnxīn *also* "枕头心儿" pillow (without the pillowcase): 木棉～ kapok pillow

疹

zhěn bleb; rash: 疱～ herpes /麻～ measles /风～ urticaria; nettle-rash /斑～ macula /皮～ rash /热～ heat-rash /湿～ eczema /汗～ prickly heat
疹子 zhěnzi 〈口语〉(the) measles: 孩子正在出～。The child is having the measles.

诊

zhěn examine (a patient): 门～ outpatient service /出～ (of a doctor) visit a patient at home /医生巡回出～ doctor's round of visits /会～ group consultation of doctors /误～ erroneous diagnosis
诊病 zhěnbìng make a diagnosis; diagnose a disease: 给他～的是位老中医。It was an old doctor of traditional Chinese medicine who handled his case.
诊察 zhěnchá examine (a patient): 全面～ full medical check-up /进行必要的～ give a patient necessary examinations
诊断 zhěnduàn ❶〈医学〉diagnose: 临床～ clinical diagnosis /物理～ physical diagnosis /作出～ make a diagnosis /正确的～ correct diagnosis /大夫～他的病为肺炎。The doctor diagnosed his illness as pneumonia. ❷〈计算机〉diagnosis: ～程序 diagnotor; diagnostic routine
诊断书 zhěnduànshū medical certificate
诊断学 zhěnduànxué diagnostics
诊候 zhěnhòu 〈书面〉examine (a patient)
诊金 zhěnjīn medical expenses
诊例 zhěnlì case: 非典型～ borderline case
诊疗 zhěnliáo make a diagnosis and give treatment: ～时间 consulting hours
诊疗器械 zhěnliáo qìxiè medical instruments
诊疗室 zhěnliáoshì consulting room
诊疗所 zhěnliáosuǒ clinic; dispensary
诊脉 zhěnmài *also* "按脉" ànmài; "号脉" hàomài feel the pulse: 大夫仔细地为病人～。The doctor carefully felt the pulse of the patient.
诊视 zhěnshì examine (a patient)
诊室 zhěnshì consulting room
诊所 zhěnsuǒ ❶ clinic: 私人～ private clinic /～的设备良好。The clinic is well equipped. ❷ small hospital
诊治 zhěnzhì make a diagnosis and give treatment: 研究如何～ hold consultations of doctors /～疑难病症 treat difficult and complicated cases

袗

zhěn 〈书面〉❶ unlined garment ❷ (of clothes) gorgeous

轸[1]

zhěn ❶〈书面〉cross board at the rear of an ancient carriage; carriage ❷〈天文〉one of the 28 constellations

轸[2]

zhěn 〈书面〉sorrowful; grieved: ～悼 grieve (*or* mourn) over sb.'s death /～怀 sorrowfully cherish the memory of sb.
轸念 zhěnniàn 〈书面〉sorrowfully cherish the memory of: ～尤甚 express special solicitude for sb.

畛

zhěn 〈书面〉low bank of earth between fields
畛域 zhěnyù 〈书面〉boundary: 进入了文明的～ enter the realm of civilization /不分～ regardless of distinctions

紾

zhěn 〈书面〉twist; turn

zhèn

鸩(❷❸酖)

zhèn ❶ legendary bird with poisonous feathers ❷ poisoned wine: 饮～止渴 drink poisoned wine to quench thirst — seek immediate relief regardless of consequences /饮～而卒 be killed with poisoned wine ❸〈书面〉kill with poisoned wine
鸩毒 zhèndú 〈书面〉poisoned wine: 与～无异 be no different from poisoned wine /宴安～。Seeking pleasure is like drinking poisoned wine.
鸩酒 zhènjiǔ poisoned wine

震

zhèn ❶ shake; quake; shock: 地～ earthquake /威～四方 be renowned far and wide /玻璃器皿怕～。Glassware should be handled with care. ❷ be shocked; be greatly excited: 感到～惊 be astonished (*or* stunned); be taken aback ❸ one of the Eight Trigrams *see also* "八卦" bāguà
震波 zhènbō 〈地质〉seismic wave; earthquake wave: ～图 seismogram
震颤 zhènchàn tremble; quiver; vibrate: 浑身～ quiver (*or* tremble) all over /～心弦 tug at one's heartstrings /风刮起来，窗户便发出～声。The windows rattled in the wind. /他一走动，地板都会～。His heavy footsteps can make the floor vibrate.
震颤性麻痹 zhènchànxìng mábì paralysis agitans
震旦 Zhèndàn China (called by ancient Indians)
震旦纪 Zhèndànjì 〈地质〉Sinian Period
震荡 zhèndàng shake; quake; shock; reverberate: 社会～ social

Z

upheaval /火车的汽笛声在山谷里～。The sound of the train's steam whistle reverberated in the valleys. /四海翻腾云水怒,五洲～风雷激。The Four Seas are rising, clouds and waters raging, The Five Continents are rocking, wind and thunder roaring.

震悼 zhèndào be shocked at and grieve over sb.'s death: 举世～ shock and grief to the whole world

震动 zhèndòng ❶ shake; quake; tremble; quiver: 地面～起来。The ground began to quake. /船身突然～了一下。The ship gave a jerk. /炮声～了整个城市。The thunder of guns reverberated throughout the whole city. /炸弹受到～,有可能爆炸。A bomb is likely to burst when given a shake. ❷ shock (people); astonish; stir; excite: 这份战报～了全国。This battlefield report stunned the whole nation. /他逝世的噩耗～了海内外人士。The sad news of his death shocked people both at home and abroad. /他的讲话在工人当中引起强烈的～。His speech made a great impact on the workers.

震耳欲聋 zhèn'ěryùlóng deafening; thunderous: 鞭炮声～。The firecrackers were deafening. /礼堂里响起了～的掌声。The auditorium resounded with thunderous applause.

震感 zhèngǎn seismaesthesia: 百里之外亦有～。One can feel the earthquake (*or* tremor) a hundred *li* away.

震古烁今 zhèngǔ-shuòjīn surpassing the ancients as well as amazing the contemporaries; be earthshaking: 这项成就～。It is an earthshaking achievement.

震骇 zhènhài shock; stun; astound

震撼 zhènhàn shake; shock; stir; touch: ～全球的事件 earthshaking event /火车站送别的场面～了她。She was deeply touched by the parting scene at the railway station.

震撼人心 zhènhàn-rénxīn stirring; exciting: ～的事件 stirring events /～的社会变动 thrilling social changes

震级 zhènjí 〈地质〉(earthquake) magnitude: 地震～为 6.4 级。It reads 6.4 on the Richter scale.

震惊 zhènjīng stun; shock; amaze; astonish: ～世界的女作家 world-famous woman writer /小说一问世,立即～了文艺界。The novel amazed art and literary circles soon after it was published.

震恐 zhènkǒng panic; be stunned: 枪声一响,敌人～。The enemy soldiers panicked at the sound of the guns.

震例 zhènlì case of earthquake

震栗 zhènlì quiver; tremble: 全身～ quiver all over

震怒 zhènnù be furious; be enraged; be infuriated: 感到～ feel outraged /引起人们广泛～ lead to widespread resentment

震情 zhènqíng losses caused by an earthquake; condition of an earthquake: ～十分严重。The losses caused by the earthquake were very serious.

震区 zhènqū seismic zone

震慑 zhènshè frighten; awe; scare; intimidate: ～敌人 terrify the enemy /大小官员,莫不为之～。All officials, junior and senior, were frightened.

震烁 zhènshuò 〈书面〉shake and overwhelm; surpass and outshine: ～千古的诗篇 poems that shine throughout the ages

震悚 zhènsǒng 〈书面〉tremble or quiver with fear; make one's blood run cold: 内心～异常 be terror-stricken

震天动地 zhèntiān-dòngdì *also* "震天撼地" shaking heaven and earth; earthshaking; overwhelming; stupendous: 这喊声～。The thunderous roar shook the heavens. /群众的力量将会～,翻江倒海。The strength of the masses will be stupendous, overwhelming and carrying everything before it.

震响 zhènxiǎng ❶ give a deafening sound: 锣鼓～。Gongs and drums deafened the ears. ❷ deafening sound: 一声天崩地裂的～ earsplitting sound

震音 zhènyīn 〈音乐〉tremolo

震源 zhènyuán 〈地质〉focus (of an earthquake); seismic origin or focus

震灾 zhènzāi damages caused by an earthquake

震中 zhènzhōng 〈地质〉epicentre: ～距 epicentral distance /～烈度 epicentral intensity /～区 epicentral area

振

zhèn ❶ shake; flutter; flap: ～笔疾书 write with flying strokes; wield one's pen furiously /～翅高飞 flutter and soar high ❷ vibrate: 共～ resonance /谐～ resonance ❸ rise with force and spirit; brace up; boost: ～作起来 cheer (*or* brace) up /食欲不～ lose one's appetite; have a jaded (*or* poor) appetite /大～官兵的士气 greatly boost the morale of both officers and men /委靡不～ dispirited; dejected and apathetic /勉强～作起精神 pull oneself up with an effort

振拔 zhènbá 〈书面〉extricate oneself (from a predicament) and brace up: 难于～ find it hard to extricate oneself

振臂 zhènbì raise one's arm: ～一呼,万众云从。People followed in tens of thousands when he raised his arm and called for action.

振荡 zhèndàng ❶〈物理〉vibrate: 不停地～ be constantly vibrating ❷〈电学〉oscillate: ～放电 oscillatory discharge

振荡电路 zhèndàng diànlù 〈电学〉oscillatory circuit; oscillating circuit

振荡管 zhèndàngguǎn 〈电学〉oscillator valve

振荡器 zhèndàngqì 〈电学〉oscillator (OSC)

振捣混凝土 zhèndǎo hùnníngtǔ vibrated concrete

振捣器 zhèndǎoqì 〈建筑〉vibrator

振动 zhèndòng ❶〈物理〉vibration: 简谐～ simple harmonic vibration /等时～ isochronous vibration /～频率 vibration frequency ❷〈机械〉vibration; vibratory motion: ～筛 oscillating screen; vibrating screen; vibrating riddle /～台 vibro-bench; vibrating table; vibrating platform

振动计 zhèndòngjì 〈物理〉vibrometer; vibration meter

振动器 zhèndòngqì 〈机械〉vibrator

振动造型机 zhèndòng zàoxíngjī 〈冶金〉jolting or jolt molding machine; jarring molding machine

振发 zhènfā ❶ be inspired with enthusiasm; rouse oneself: 精神陡然～起来 sudden rise in spirit ❷ promote; develop; boost: ～家业 make family fortunes

振奋 zhènfèn ❶ rise with force and spirit; rouse oneself; be high-spirited: 精神～ be in high spirits /群情～。Everyone is exhilarated. /他显得十分～。He appeared full of enthusiasm and vigour. ❷ encourage; inspire; stimulate: ～精神 inspire sb. with enthusiasm /～士气 heighten (*or* boost) the morale (of the troops) /这好消息～了大家的情绪。The good news stimulated (*or* heartened) people all round.

振奋人心 zhènfèn-rénxīn inspiring; stimulating: ～的喜讯 good news that fires people with enthusiasm

振幅 zhènfú 〈物理〉amplitude (of vibration): 脉冲～ pulse amplitude /～畸变 amplitude distortion /～平衡 amplitude balance (*or* equilibrium)

振簧 zhènhuáng 〈电工〉vibrating reed: ～式继电器 vibrating relay /～仪表 vibrating-reed instrument /～整流器 vibrating-reed rectifier

振铃 zhènlíng 〈通信〉ringing: ～键 ringing key /～信号 ringing signal /～指示灯 ringing pilot lamp

振聋发聩 zhènlóng-fākuì rouse the deaf; awaken the muddle-headed; enlighten the benighted: 这种批评很尖锐,在当时能起到～的作用。The criticism was keen enough to awaken the muddle-headed at that time.

振实 zhènshí 〈机械〉jolt: ～式型芯机 core jolter machine /～造型机 jolting machine

振刷 zhènshuā 〈书面〉bestir oneself; brace up; take heart: ～精神 bestir oneself; brace (*or* cheer) up /～斗志 arouse one's fighting enthusiasm (*or* militant spirit)

振兴 zhènxīng promote; invigorate; vitalize: ～中华 achieve China's rejuvenation; rejuvenate China /大力～农业 vigorously develop agriculture /～社会主义道德 promote socialist morality /为～旅游事业创造条件 create conditions favourable to the promotion of tourism /为～地方经济,他付出了所有的精力。He devoted all his energy to the invigoration of local economy.

振压造型机 zhènyā zàoxíngjī *also* "振动压实造型机"〈冶金〉jolt squeeze (moulding) machine

振振有词 zhènzhèn-yǒucí speak glibly (to justify oneself): ～地为自己的行为辩护 speak in defence of one's own actions plausibly and at length

振子 zhènzǐ 〈电工〉vibrator; vibration generator; oscillator

振作 zhènzuò pull oneself together; bestir oneself; display vigour: ～情绪 cheer up; brace up; buoy up one's spirits /精神～ be in high spirits /她终于从悲痛中～起来了。She finally roused herself from her sorrow.

赈

zhèn bring relief to; relieve; aid: ～贫 aid the poor /以工代～ relieve disaster victims by providing them with work; provide work as a form of relief; provide work-relief

赈济 zhènjì relieve; aid: ～水灾灾民 relieve the flood victims /～灾

区的物资 relief to be sent to the disaster area
赈捐 zhènjuān relief donations
赈款 zhènkuǎn relief money or fund：五万元～ relief fund of 50,000 *yuan* /为难民筹集～ raise funds for refugees
赈恤 zhènxù 〈书面〉relieve; aid：～灾民 provide relief for the people in the disaster area; aid the victims of natural calamities
赈灾 zhènzāi relieve the people in a disaster area：参加～工作 join in the effort to relieve the victims in the disaster area

瑱 zhèn 〈书面〉jade earring

镇[1] zhèn ❶ press down; force down; ease：强～ suppress /～痛 ease pain ❷ calm; tranquil; stable; at ease：～定 calm; cool ❸ keep peace by force; garrison：坐～ assume personal command (of a garrison, etc.) /～国家，抚百姓 stabilize the country and comfort the people ❹ garrison post：边防重～ key frontier post ❺ township：～公所〈旧语〉seat of township administration /乡～企业 township and village enterprises ❻ relatively large town：景德～ town of Jingdezhen (famous for its ceramics) ❼ cool with cold water or ice; ice：冰～桔子汁 iced orange juice /～一～这瓶啤酒 ice the bottle of beer /在冷水里～一～。Put this in cold water to chill it. ❽ (Zhèn) a surname

镇[2] zhèn (often used in the early vernacular) ❶ often; time and again; frequently：十年～相随 frequently accompanying sb. for ten years ❷ (usu. used in the early vernacular) all the time：*see* "～日"
镇尺 zhènchǐ paperweight bar (usu. made of metal and shaped like a ruler or straightedge)
镇喘药 zhènchuǎnyào antiasthmatic
镇定 zhèndìng ❶ calm; collected; composed; unruffled：～自若 be perfectly calm and collected; be in possession of oneself /力求～ try to keep cool; strive to keep one's head /他的态度极为～。He behaved with great composure and presence of mind. ❷ calm down：竭力～自己 try hard to calm oneself down
镇反 zhènfǎn (short for 镇压反革命) suppress counterrevolutionaries：下达～的命令 issue an order to suppress counterrevolutionaries
镇反运动 Zhènfǎn Yùndòng Movement to Suppress Counterrevolutionaries (1950-1952)
镇服 zhènfú *also* "镇伏" force sb. to submit; bring sb. to his knees; intimidate sb. into surrender：～群雄 subdue all contenders for state power
镇河铁犀 Zhènhé Tiěxī Iron Rhinoceros Guarding the Dykes of the Yellow River (in Kaifeng, Henan Province)
镇唬 zhènhu 〈口语〉frighten; scare; intimidate：他想杀鸡给猴看，～～那家伙。He thought to make an example of someone just as a warning to that fellow.
镇痉 zhènjìng 〈医学〉antispasmodic
镇静 zhènjìng ❶ calm; cool; composed; collected：面容～ keep one's countenance /恢复～ resume one's composure /显得十分～ appear very calm and collected ❷ calm down：～些！不要慌乱。Keep calm! Don't get flustered.
镇静钢 zhènjìnggāng 〈冶金〉killed steel
镇静剂 zhènjìngjì sedative; tranquillizer：服用～ take tranquillizers
镇咳 zhènké antibechic：～药 antitussive
镇流管 zhènliúguǎn 〈电学〉ballast tube
镇流器 zhènliúqì 〈电学〉ballast
镇日 zhènrì (often used in the early vernacular) from morning till night; all day long：～闲逛 idle about all day long
镇慑 zhènshè subdue or cow sb. into submission; deter：～人心 fill people with awe /他的英雄气概～了歹徒。The hoodlum was completely overawed by his heroism.
镇市 zhènshi 〈方言〉country fair; market
镇守 zhènshǒu garrison or guard (a place of strategic importance)：～边关 guard a strategic pass on the frontier /长期～小城 garrison a town for years
镇痛 zhèntòng ❶ ease pain：起～作用 relieve the pain ❷〈医学〉analgesia：针刺～ acupuncture analgesia
镇痛剂 zhèntòngjì pain-killer; anodyne; analgesic
镇痛效果 zhèntòng xiàoguǒ 〈医学〉analgesic effect
镇物 zhènwù ❶〈书面〉stabilizer ❷〈迷信〉sth. used to repel evil spirits and avert misfortunes
镇星 Zhènxīng 〈天文〉〈古语〉Saturn; Quelling Star
镇压 zhènyā ❶ suppress; quell; put down：～暴乱 put down a riot /～叛乱 suppress a rebellion ❷ execute (a criminal)：～恶霸 put a local tyrant to death /公开～这个地头蛇 execute that local bully in public ❸〈农业〉rolling; compacting; tamping：播种后要及时～田地。We must tamp down the earth in the fields as soon as we finish sowing.
镇压器 zhènyāqì 〈农业〉roller
镇宅 zhènzhái (when building a house in old times) bury a stone tablet, etc. at the corners of a house (to expel evil spirits and bring good fortune)
镇长 zhènzhǎng town head
镇纸 zhènzhǐ paperweight
镇住 zhènzhù keep sb. under control; bring sb. to submission; subdue：几句话把他给～了。A few words put him in his place.
镇子 zhènzi 〈方言〉town; market town：这个～不大。It is a small town. /那个～相当繁荣。The market town is fairly prosperous.

圳(甽) zhèn 〈方言〉ditch (between fields)

揕 zhèn 〈书面〉stab：手～奸邪 personally stab the evildoer

朕[1] zhèn I, the sovereign; we (used by an emperor to refer to himself)：～为始皇帝。I, the sovereign, am the first emperor.

朕[2] zhèn 〈书面〉sign; omen
朕兆 zhènzhào 〈书面〉sign; omen：事先毫无～。There wasn't the slightest sign of it. *or* Nobody sensed it in advance.

阵[1] zhèn ❶ battle array; battle formation：严～以待 be ready in full battle array; remain in combat-readiness ❷ position; front lines; front：冲锋陷～ charge and shatter the enemy position; charge the enemy lines /临～脱逃 desert on the eve of a battle; sneak away at a critical juncture /赤膊上～ go into battle stripped to the waist; strip off all disguises and come to the fore

阵[2] zhèn ❶ period of time; some time：他走了有一～儿了。He has been away for some time. /那～儿他出差了。He was away on business at the time. /这～儿他迷上了桥牌。He is crazy about bridge these days. ❷〈量词〉：～～狂风 gusts of wind /一～雨 a spatter of rain /～～北风 blasts of the north wind /一～大笑 a fit (*or* burst) of laughter /一～欢呼 a burst of cheers /一～狂热 a furore /一～咳嗽 a fit (*or* spasm) of coughing /一～恶心 a spell (*or* fit) of vomiting; a vomiting spell /一～掌声 a shower of applause /心中一～～不安 be restless; suffer fits of anxiety
阵地 zhèndì position; front：坚守～ hold one's ground; hold fast to one's position /人在～在 fight to the death in defence of one's position; hold one's position at all costs /思想和文化～ ideological and cultural fronts /教育～ educational front
阵地战 zhèndìzhàn 〈军事〉positional warfare
阵发 zhènfā 〈医学〉paroxysm
阵发性 zhènfāxìng 〈医学〉paroxysmal：～心搏过速 paroxysmal tachycardia /～痉挛 clonic spasm; clonus
阵法 zhènfǎ tactical disposition or deployment of troops
阵风 zhènfēng gust (of wind)
阵脚 zhènjiǎo ❶ front line ❷ position; condition; situation; circumstances：压住～ secure one's position /～大乱 be thrown into confusion
阵垒 zhènlěi *also* "阵营" camp
阵挛 zhènluán 〈医学〉clonus：连续～ clonism /～状态 clonicity
阵容 zhènróng ❶ battle array; battle formation：排好～ be arrayed /改变原先的～ change the original battle formation ❷ lineup：～整齐 well-balanced cast /这个剧团～强大。The opera troupe has a strong lineup.
阵势 zhènshi ❶ battle array; battle formation; combat disposition：秘密的～ secret disposition of combat forces /扰乱敌人的～ undermine the disposition of enemy forces; break up the enemy formations ❷ circumstances; scene; condition; situation：谁见过这样惊

Z

人的～！This is a most amazing scene!

阵痛 zhèntòng ❶〈医学〉labour pains; birth pangs; throes (of childbirth): 感到～ be in the throes of childbirth / 逐渐加剧的～ ever intensifying labour pains ❷ throes of giving birth to a new thing; 〈比喻〉birth pangs: 改革过程中难免有～。The throes of reform are unavoidable.

阵头雨 zhèntóuyǔ 〈方言〉thunder shower

阵图 zhèntú battle array; battle formation: 八～ Eightfold Maze (a battle array deployed by Zhuge Liang, a noted strategist in Chinese history)

阵亡 zhènwáng fall in battle; be killed in action: ～将士 officers and men killed in action / 他在前线～了。He fell at the front.

阵线 zhènxiàn front; alignment: 民主～ alignment of democratic forces / 民族统一～ national united front

阵型 zhènxíng formation

阵雪 zhènxuě snow shower

阵营 zhènyíng camp: 民主～ democratic camp / 二次大战的反法西斯～ anti-fascist camp in the Second World War

阵雨 zhènyǔ shower: 遇到～ be caught in a shower / 昨晚下了～。It showered last night.

阵仗 zhènzhang ❶ battle; combat, action; fight: 咱见过大～，打过硬仗。I fought in important campaigns as well as tough battles. ❷〈方言〉scene; spectacle: 节日的～ scene of festivity / 丰收的～ spectacle of bumper harvest

阵子 zhènzi 〈方言〉period of time: 忙了一～ be busy for a few days / 那～他挺高兴。He was quite happy in those days.

纼 zhèn 〈方言〉*also* "纼子" tether for tying domestic animals

zhēng

正 zhēng first month of the lunar year; first moon: 新～ first month of the lunar new year
see also zhèng

正旦 zhēngdàn 〈书面〉first day of the first lunar month; lunar New Year's Day
see also zhèngdàn

正朔 zhēngshuò 〈书面〉❶ first day of the first lunar month ❷ new calendar issued by an emperor: 定～ establish the imperial calendar

正月 zhēngyuè first month of the lunar year; first moon: ～初二 second (day) of the first lunar month

症（癥） zhēng 〈中医〉lump in the abdomen; abdominal agglomerate or mass
see also zhèng

症瘕 zhēngjiǎ 〈中医〉lump in the abdomen; abdominal mass

症瘕积聚 zhēngjiǎ jījù 〈中医〉lump in the abdomen causing distension and pain

症结 zhēngjié crux; core; crucial cause: 究竟～何在? Where on earth does the crux of the matter lie? / 问题的～总算找到了。We eventually discovered the crucial cause of the problem.

怔 zhēng terror-stricken; panicked
see also zhèng

怔忡 zhēngchōng 〈书面〉palpitation

怔营 zhēngyíng 〈书面〉be terrified; be in terror and uncertainty; be seized with fear or terror: ～惶怖 be panic-stricken / ～怖悸 be seized with terror

怔忪 zhēngzhōng 〈书面〉be seized with terror; be scared; be panic-stricken: 百姓～。The people were thrown into a panic.

钲 zhēng bell-shaped percussion instrument with a handle, used in ancient times by troops on march

征[1] zhēng ❶ make a long journey: 长～ Long March ❷ go on an expedition: 出～ go out to battle / 举兵北～ make an expedition to the north / 南～北战 fight in both the north and south; campaign up and down the country

征[2]（徵） zhēng ❶ levy (troops); recruit; call up; draft: 应～服役 be drafted into the army ❷ levy (taxes); collect; extort; impose: ～税 impose a tax; make a levy / ～租 collect a land tax / 横～暴敛 levy exorbitant taxes; extort excessive taxes and levies ❸ solicit; ask for: ～文 solicit articles or essays (on a chosen subject)

征[3]（徵） zhēng ❶ evidence; proof: 信而有～ be borne out by evidence / 有文献可～。There are historical documents as proof. ❷ sign; portent; phenomenon: 特～ characteristics; features / 象～ symbol; emblem

征鞍 zhēng'ān 〈旧语〉horse used on a long journey

征辟 zhēngbì 〈书面〉appoint sb. to an office; recommend sb. for an official post

征兵 zhēngbīng conscription; draft; callup; recruitment: 今年的～工作已经结束。This year's recruitment of soldiers is now over.

征兵法 zhēngbīngfǎ conscription law; draft law

征兵年龄 zhēngbīng niánlíng conscription age; age for enlistment; draft-age

征兵站 zhēngbīngzhàn draft centre; recruiting station

征兵制 zhēngbīngzhì conscription system; universal military service; recruiting system

征尘 zhēngchén dust settling on one during an expedition: 拂去满身～ whisk the dust off oneself

征程 zhēngchéng journey: 踏上新的～ set off (*or* start) on another journey

征调 zhēngdiào requisition; draft; call up: ～一名厨师 draft a chef / ～救灾粮 call up relief grain / ～全市机动车辆 requisition all motor vehicles in the city

征订 zhēngdìng solicit subscriptions: ～单 subscription list

征发 zhēngfā 〈旧语〉(of a government) make a requisition for supplies and personnel: ～私家车马 requisition private carts and horses

征伐 zhēngfá go on a punitive expedition: ～叛逆 send (*or* dispatch) a punitive expedition against the rebels

征帆 zhēngfān 〈书面〉boat or ship on a long voyage: 伫立望～ stand still for a long while looking at the receding ship

征服 zhēngfú conquer; vanquish; subjugate: ～敌人 subjugate the enemy / ～大自然 conquer nature / ～江河 tame rivers / ～观众 captivate the audience / 我被他的才能所～。I was very much impressed by his talent.

征稿 zhēnggǎo solicit contributions (to a magazine, journal, etc.): ～启事 notice soliciting contributions

征购 zhēnggòu (of a state) requisition by purchase: ～棉花 cotton purchase by the state / 粮食～任务 state grain purchase quotas

征购派购 zhēnggòu-pàigòu purchase (grain or other agricultural products) by the state on fixed quota

征候 zhēnghòu sign; indication: 他的病情已有恶化的～。The patient's condition shows signs of worsening. / 看这～天气要变。There are portents of a change in the weather.

征婚 zhēnghūn marriage seeking: ～启事 lonely hearts ad

征集 zhēngjí ❶ solicit or seek publicly; gather or collect through public channels: ～读者意见 solicit readers' suggestions / ～文物 collect historical relics (through public channels) ❷ call up; draft; requisition: ～新兵 draft (*or* recruit) soldiers / ～民兵 call up militiamen / ～粮草 requisition grain and fodder (as for an army)

征君 zhēngjūn hermit who rejects any position offered by the imperial court

征粮 zhēngliáng impose grain levies; collect farm taxes in kind

征马 zhēngmǎ war horse; battle steed

征募 zhēngmù enlist; recruit: ～战地医疗队员 recruit people for the field medical team / ～空军飞行员 enlist pilots for the air force

征聘 zhēngpìn advertise a vacancy; invite applications for a job; give public notice of vacancies to be filled: ～公关人员 advertise for PR personnel / ～一位部门经理 wanted: a department manager

征求 zhēngqiú solicit; invite; seek; ask for: ～观众的意见 seek (*or* solicit) criticisms from the audience / ～顾客的反应 ask for customers' comments / ～专家的看法 consult the experts (*or* specialists) / ～订户 canvass for subscriptions

征求意见本 zhēngqiú yìjiànběn trial edition; edition for soliciting comments

征人 zhēngrén 〈书面〉traveller; man on a long journey; man out for battle
征实 zhēngshí levies in kind; grain levies; grain tax
征收 zhēngshōu levy; collect; charge; impose:～公粮 collect agricultural tax paid in grain /～营业税 levy business tax /～进口税 impose import duties /～烟酒税 charge (*or* impose) taxes on tobacco and wine
征戍 zhēngshù 〈书面〉enlist in the army to guard the frontier
征税 zhēngshuì levy taxes; collect taxes:～范围 range of taxation; range of dutiable goods /～的标准 standards for taxation
征税货物 zhēngshuì huòwù dutiable goods
征讨 zhēngtǎo go on a punitive expedition:～叛军 punitive expedition against rebel forces
征途 zhēngtú journey:～艰险 hard journey /踏上漫长的～ start (*or* set out on) a long journey
征文 zhēngwén solicit articles or essays on a chosen subject:国庆～ essays or articles written in honour of the National Day /"我的家乡"～ solicit essays on "My Home Town"
征文启事 zhēngwén qǐshì notice soliciting articles or essays on a chosen subject (for a special issue, etc.)
征象 zhēngxiàng symptom; sign; indication:病人出现药物过敏的～。The patient shows signs of drug allergy. /乌云常常是下雨的～。Very often dark clouds herald rain.
征询 zhēngxún consult; seek the opinion of:～乘客的意见 seek the opinion of the passengers /他向我投来～的目光。He looked at me inquiringly.
征衣 zhēngyī 〈书面〉clothes worn by people on an expedition or journey
征引 zhēngyǐn mention as an example; cite; quote:～名言警句 quote epigrams /～最新统计数字 cite the latest statistics /忠实地～原文 faithfully quote every word of the original passage
征用 zhēngyòng requisition; commandeer; take over for use:～农具 requisition farm tools /～他家的房子 commandeer his house /～补偿 compensation for requisitioned property
征战 zhēngzhàn go out to battle; go on an expedition or a campaign:到处～ campaign up and down the country /过惯了～和行军的生活 be used to a life of fighting and incessant marches
征召 zhēngzhào ❶ recruit; enlist; draft; call up:响应～ answer the call to enlist in the army /他是～入伍的新兵。He is a new recruit. ❷〈书面〉appoint sb. to an office; place sb. in an official position
征兆 zhēngzhào sign; omen; portent:好的～ good omen /地震前一般都有～。Usually there are portents of an earthquake beforehand.
征逐 zhēngzhú 〈书面〉❶ (of friends) frequently get together or invite each other to dinners:酒食相～ often invite each other to dinners ❷ chase; pursue

丁 zhēng

see also dīng

丁丁 zhēngzhēng 〈书面〉〈象声〉sound of chopping wood, playing a harmonica, etc.
see also dīngdīng

鲭 zhēng 〈书面〉fish cooked together with meat

see also qīng

争[1] zhēng

❶ contend; compete; vie; strive:～权 contend for power /～名誉 strive for fame /～地位 scramble (*or* jockey) for position /力～上游 aim high; aim for the best /群芳～艳 flowers vying with each other in beauty /明～暗斗 open quarrels and secret wrangles /与世无～ at peace with the world; content with life ❷ argue; dispute; wrangle:意气之～ dispute caused by personal grudges /据理力～ argue strongly on just grounds /你们不要再～了。You'd better stop bickering. ❸〈方言〉short of; shy; wanting:还～一块钱。You are one *yuan* shy. /还～多少才能还清那笔账? How much more is needed for us to pay off the debt?

争[2] zhēng

(poetic) how; why:～忍 how can one have the heart to /～奈 but; however; nevertheless
争霸 zhēngbà contend for hegemony; strive for supremacy:～世界 scramble for world supremacy; strive to dominate the world
争辩 zhēngbiàn argue, dispute; debate; contend:面对无可～的事实,他认输了。Faced with indisputable (*or* irrefutable) facts, he gave in. /两个人～得面红耳赤,互不相让。They had a heated argument, neither conceding an inch.
争长论短 zhēngcháng-lùnduǎn *also* "争长竞短" haggle over petty gains; argue over minor issues; fuss:对这些小事何必～? Why must we squabble over such trifles?
争吵 zhēngchǎo quarrel; bicker; wrangle; squabble:～不止 endless bickering /为一件小事而～ make a fuss over a trifle /结婚后夫妻俩一直～不休。The couple led a cat-and-dog life since the day they were married.
争持 zhēngchí refuse to yield; stick to one's guns:两方面～不下。Neither side was willing to give in (*or* back down).
争宠 zhēngchǒng vie (with each other) for sb.'s favour
争斗 zhēngdòu ❶ fight; struggle:～不停 fight endlessly /双方恶狠狠地～着,互不相让。The two contending sides were slugging it out ferociously, neither yielding an inch. ❷ contend; oppose:暗中和他～ oppose him secretly
争端 zhēngduān dispute; conflict; controversy; controversial issue:由来已久的～ long-standing feud /避免产权～ try to avoid controversy over property rights /引起领土～ give rise to territorial disputes; provoke territorial conflicts /调解两国间的贸易～ act as a mediator (*or* mediate) in a trade dispute between the two countries
争夺 zhēngduó struggle for; enter into rivalry with sb. over sth.:～遗产 contend for the legacy /～权力 vie for power /～市场 scramble for markets /双方激烈～合同 fierce rivalry between the two sides to get the contract /～山头阵地 fight for possession of a hilltop position /目前他们的～集中在中东这个具有重大战略意义的地区。At present, their contention centres upon the Middle East, an area of great strategic significance.
争分夺秒 zhēngfēn-duómiǎo make every minute and second count; seize every minute and second; race against time:他们～,力争提前完成生产任务。In order to fulfil their production quotas ahead of the schedule they are working against time.
争风吃醋 zhēngfēng-chīcù be jealous (of a rival in love):二人～,大打出手。Striving to win the affection of the same woman, the two men came to blows.
争锋 zhēngfēng fight to see who is the winner; carry out a decisive fight; fight for mastery:两军～。The two armies locked horns with each other for supremacy.
争购 zhēnggòu hectic buying
争光 zhēngguāng win honour for; do credit to:为祖国～ do credit to one's motherland /为中华民族～ win honour for the Chinese nation
争衡 zhēnghéng scramble for supremacy; have a trial of strength; be in rivalry with:今晚中国男排与日本队～。This evening the Chinese men's volleyball team will play a crucial match with the Japanese team.
争斤论两 zhēngjīn-lùnliǎng be particular about; haggle over; fuss about:我们不必在一些细节问题上～。We do not have to be so particular about the details.
争竞 zhēngjing 〈方言〉squabble; argue:我不愿和她～。I don't like to argue with her.
争脸 zhēngliǎn *also* "争面子" win honour (for); do credit (to):给父母～ do credit to one's parents /你得了金牌,这可是～的事! What an honour it is for you to have won a gold medal!
争论 zhēnglùn controversy; debate; dispute; contention:～的焦点 focus of a dispute; point at issue /没有结果的～ fruitless debate /毫无意义的～ meaningless contention /激烈的～ heated argument /他们为一件小事发生了～。They took issue with each other over trifles. /涨价问题引起了很多～。The price hike has evoked much controversy.
争面子 zhēng miànzi *see* "争脸"
争名夺利 zhēngmíng-duólì scramble or fight for fame and gain:～何时休? When will the struggle for fame and fortune end?
争鸣 zhēngmíng contend (over academic issues):诸子～ contention among the exponents of various schools of thought
争奈 zhēngnài (often used in the early vernacular) unfortunately; however:～他自己不争气,终日与底下人鬼混。Unfortunately he was not the aspiring sort, and spent his days hanging out with the servants.

争闹 zhēngnào quarrel; wrangle; row:为这事她和儿子~过好几次。She has had several rows with her son over the matter.
争奇斗艳 zhēngqí-dòuyàn compete with one another for beauty; contend for beauty and fascination:各种展品竞放异彩,~。The various exhibits appeared as if they were competing with one another for glamour. /各样品种的茶花~,美不胜收。Various strains of camellia seemed to vie with one another for beauty and fascination so one simply couldn't take them all in.
争强好胜 zhēngqiáng-hàoshèng be up on things; be emulative:我这一辈子~,到今天才明白有什么用啊! I've been up on things all my life only to realize today that it is all useless.
争气 zhēngqì try to make a good showing; try to bring credit to; try to win honour:给全家人~ bring (*or* win) credit to the whole family /为中国妇女~ win honour for Chinese women /这孩子一上学就很~。The child has been making a good showing ever since he went to school. /那样,在他们面前,也好争口气。Then we'll be able to hold our heads up before them.
争抢 zhēngqiǎng scramble or contend for; vie (with sb.) for:~食物 scramble for food
争取 zhēngqǔ make every effort to achieve; strive for; win over:~荣誉 try to win honours /~胜利 fight for victory /努力~多数 take pains to win over the majority /~主动 make efforts to seize the initiative /尽力~立功 do one's best to render meritorious service /~更好的经济效益 strive for better economic results /尽量~提前完成任务 spare no effort to accomplish the task ahead of schedule
争权夺利 zhēngquán-duólì scramble for power and wealth:为了~,他可以不顾一切。He stops at nothing to grab power and money. /那些~、唯利是图的人是为人所不齿的。Those who jockey for power and turn everything to their own advantage are always held in contempt.
争胜 zhēngshèng seek to surpass others; try to excel:好强~ seek to outdo others /~之心人皆有之。Everyone likes to do better than others.
争讼 zhēngsòng contest a lawsuit
争先 zhēngxiān try to get ahead of the others; strive to be the first to do sth.:同学们都~回答老师的提问。Every student tried to be the first to answer the teacher's questions. /人人努力,个个~。Everyone exerted themselves, each trying to outdo others.
争先恐后 zhēngxiān-kǒnghòu strive to be the first and fear to lag behind; vie with each other for the lead; fall over each other:他们个个~。They all strive to keep in the forefront of the fight. /大家~地奔向车站。People flocked to the station. /他们~地报名参军。They fell over each other to sign up for military service.
争闲气 zhēng xiánqì squabble; fuss over; haggle over:何必为这些小事~。There is no need to fuss over such trivialities.
争雄 zhēngxióng contend for hegemony:两强~ contention between two powers for hegemony
争议 zhēngyì dispute; debate; controversy:无可~ beyond dispute /有~的领土 disputed territory /有~的问题 controversial issue /对他的处分,群众间有不少~。There is still much disagreement among the rank and file over the disciplinary action taken against him.
争战 zhēngzhàn fight; go to war; make or wage war:两国长期~。The two countries were at war with each other for a long period of time.
争执 zhēngzhí take issue with; dispute; quarrel:~不休 endless dispute /对这个问题,父子间有过一次~。There has been a quarrel between the father and son over the issue.
争执不下 zhēngzhí-bùxià each holds on to his position; each sticks to his guns:二人各执己见,~。Equally self-opinionated, the two of them stood their own grounds.
争执点 zhēngzhídiǎn point of dispute
争嘴 zhēngzuǐ 〈方言〉❶ scramble for a bite to eat:这孩子吃什么都~,从不让人。When it comes to eating, the child will always try to have more without considering others. ❷ quarrel; row:你们俩怎么又~了? How come you two had a row again?

挣 zhēng

see also zhèng

挣扎 zhēngzhá struggle; battle:垂死~ last-ditch (*or* death-bed) struggle /~着立起来 struggle to one's feet /他~着到了窗前。He struggled his way to the window. /他在水中奋力~。He floundered desperately in the water. /世上仍有许多人在饥饿线上~。Many people in this world are still suffering from starvation (*or* struggling on the verge of starvation). /全家就靠一个女人在~。The family has to rely on a woman battling alone.

鬇 zhēng

鬇鬡 zhēngníng 〈书面〉(of hair) fluffy

睁 zhēng

open (the eyes):半~着眼 with one's eyes half open /眼睛~得大大的 with one's eyes wide open
睁眼瞎子 zhēngyǎn xiāzi *also* "睁眼瞎" illiterate person:他当了半辈子的~。He was an illiterate for the first half of his life.
睁着眼睛说瞎话 zhēngzhe yǎnjing shuō xiāhuà tell a bare-faced or whopping lie; lie in one's teeth or throat:他简直是~。He was telling a bare-faced lie. *or* He was simply talking through his hat.
睁只眼,闭只眼 zhēng zhī yǎn, bì zhī yǎn *also* "睁一眼,闭一眼" turn a blind eye to sth.; keep one eye closed; wink at sth.:对坏人坏事决不能采取~的态度,要与之作斗争。We must not turn a blind eye to evil people and evil deeds, but must combat them in earnest.

峥 zhēng

峥嵘 zhēngróng ❶ towering; soaring; lofty and steep:~的山峰 soaring (mountain) peaks /岩石~ lofty and steep rocks /挺拔~的劲松 straight and towering pines ❷ outstanding; remarkable; extraordinary:偶尔露~ reveal one's talent every now and then /初露~的文学青年 a literary youth beginning to show his natural gift
峥嵘岁月 zhēngróng-suìyuè eventful years; memorable times:回顾当年的~ recall those eventful years

筝 zhēng

❶ Chinese zither with 21 or 25 strings ❷ kite

铮 zhēng

see also zhèng

铮鏦 zhēngcōng 〈书面〉〈象声〉clank; clang
铮铮 zhēngzhēng 〈象声〉clang; clank:镣铐~作响 clank of chains /铁中~ remarkable person; outstanding (*or* extraordinary) person

狰 zhēng

狰狞 zhēngníng sinister; hideous, ferocious:~可怕的样子 repulsive appearance /他面孔上露出了~的笑容。A sinister smile appeared on his face.
狰狞面目 zhēngníng-miànmù hideous visage; ferocious features

烝 zhēng

great number of; large amounts of:~民 masses of people

蒸 zhēng

❶ evaporate:~气 vapour ❷ steam:~米饭 steam rice /把包子~一~ put the stuffed buns in the steamer
蒸饼 zhēngbǐng steamed cake:此店卖~。This restaurant serves steamed cake.
蒸发 zhēngfā evaporation:热使水~。Heat evaporates water.
蒸发计 zhēngfājì evaporimeter
蒸发镜 zhēngfājìng evaporoscope
蒸发冷却塔 zhēngfā lěngquètǎ wet cooling tower
蒸发器 zhēngfāqì 〈化工〉evaporator; vaporizer
蒸发热调 zhēngfā rètiáo 〈生理〉evaporative heat regulation
蒸发蒸腾 zhēngfā zhēngténg evapotranspiration
蒸锅 zhēngguō steamer; pot for steaming food:我刚买了一个大号~。I've just bought a large-sized steamer.
蒸饺 zhēngjiǎo steamed dumpling (with meat and vegetable stuffing):~比水饺好吃。Steamed dumplings taste better than boiled ones.
蒸馏 zhēngliú 〈物理〉distillation:分解~ destructive distillation /干~ dry distillation /拔顶~〈化学〉topping distillation /常压~〈化学〉atmospheric distillation /真空~〈化学〉vacuum distillation
蒸馏罐 zhēngliúguàn retort
蒸馏酒 zhēngliújiǔ distilled liquor
蒸馏器 zhēngliúqì distiller; distilling vessel; retort
蒸馏室 zhēngliúshì distillery
蒸馏水 zhēngliúshuǐ distilled water:优质~ distilled water of high quality
蒸馏塔 zhēngliútǎ distilling tower

蒸笼 zhēnglóng steamer (made of bamboo or wood):竹编的大～ big steamer made of bamboo /工艺粗糙的～ steamer of poor workmanship
蒸馍 zhēngmo 〈方言〉steamed bun:这些～真暄哪! Look at these wonderfully fluffy steamed buns!
蒸呢 zhēngní 〈纺织〉decatizing; decating
蒸气 zhēngqì vapour:汞～〈物理〉mercurial vapour /水～〈物理〉aqueous vapour /～烙术〈医学〉vapocauterization /～治疗〈医学〉vapotherapy
蒸气田 zhēngqìtián vaporous field
蒸气压 zhēngqìyā vapour pressure
蒸汽 zhēngqì steam:～发电厂〈电工〉steam electric generating station; steam power plant /～发电机组〈电工〉steam electric generating set /～干燥器〈化工〉steam drying apparatus /～精炼〈化工〉steam refining /～裂化〈化工〉steam cracking /～泵〈机械〉steam pump; vapour pump /～锅炉〈机械〉steam boiler (*or* steam heating boiler); steam raising unit /～轮机〈机械〉steam turbine /～机车〈交通〉steam locomotive /～供暖〈建筑〉steam heating /～重水反应堆〈原子能〉steam-generating heavy water reactor
蒸汽锤 zhēngqìchuí 〈机械〉steam hammer
蒸汽动力 zhēngqì dònglì steam power
蒸汽发生器 zhēngqì fāshēngqì steam generator
蒸汽机 zhēngqìjī steam engine
蒸汽机船 zhēngqì jīchuán steamboat
蒸汽灭火 zhēngqì mièhuǒ steam smothering
蒸汽浴 zhēngqìyù sauna; steam bath
蒸汽脱脂 zhēngqì tuōzhī vapour degreasing
蒸汽吸入器 zhēngqì xīrùqì thermohale
蒸汽学 zhēngqìxué atmology
蒸球 zhēngqiú (in papermaking) rotary spherical digester
蒸食 zhēngshi steamed wheaten foods (e.g. stuffed bun, twisted roll, etc.)
蒸腾 zhēngténg (of steam) rising:暑气～ heat of summer rising (from the ground, etc.) /热气～ steaming /水气～ vaporizing
蒸腾作用 zhēngténg zuòyòng 〈植物〉transpiration
蒸蒸日上 zhēngzhēng-rìshàng prosper day by day; make rapid progress; be developing fast; be thriving:近年他的声望～。In recent years, his fame has been rising with each passing day. /我们国家的经济建设～。The economy of our country is flourishing rapidly.
蒸煮器 zhēngzhǔqì (in papermaking) digester; boiler:连续～ continuous digester

zhěng

整 zhěng ❶ whole; complete; total; entire:～天 whole day; all day long /一～月 a full month /两年～ two solid years /八点～ eight o'clock sharp /～套卧室用家具 bedroom suite ❷ in good order; orderly; tidy; neat:齐齐～～ neat and orderly; in apple-pie order /～然有序 in an orderly manner; everything placed where it belongs /仪容不～ untidy in appearance ❸ put in order; straighten; rectify:～顿校纪 strengthen school discipline /去把你的床铺～一～。Go and tidy up your bed. ❹ repair; fix; mend; renovate:修～ fix; repair ❺ punish; castigate; make sb. suffer:挨～ be the target of attack; be made to suffer /他总觉得有人～他。He always felt being plotted against by someone. ❻〈方言〉make; do; work:他上衣～破了。He got his jacket torn. /她把线～断了。She snapped the thread in two. /把桌子～干净。Clear up the table.
整备 zhěngbèi reorganize and outfit (troops):这支部队已～完毕。This troop has been reorganized and is now well equipped.
整倍数 zhěngbèishù 〈数学〉integral multiple
整编 zhěngbiān reorganize (troops); restructure:～机构 restructure the institutions /他对手下的人马进行了～。He reorganized his troops.
整补 zhěngbǔ reorganize and reinforce:部队刚从前线下来,需要～。Back from the front, the army needs to be reinforced and reorganized.
整饬 zhěngchì ❶ put in order; rectify; strengthen:～军纪 strengthen military discipline /～军容 maintain required standards for a soldier's bearing and appearance ❷ orderly; neat; tidy:衣冠～ neatly dressed /仪容～ appear neat (*or* tidy)
整除 zhěngchú 〈数学〉be divided with no remainder; divide exactly
整党 zhěngdǎng consolidate the Party organization:学习～文件 read documents concerning the consolidation of the Party organization
整地 zhěngdì 〈农业〉soil preparation:抓紧～,准备播种。Seize the opportunity to prepare the soil for sowing (*or* planting).
整点 zhěngdiǎn ❶〈数学〉integral point ❷ on the hour
整锻 zhěngduàn 〈冶金〉monobloc forging:～转子 integral rotor
整队 zhěngduì dress the ranks; line up:赶快～ dress the ranks at once /～进入会场 file into the meeting hall
整顿 zhěngdùn strengthen; rectify; consolidate; reorganize:～经济秩序 rectify the economic order /～医疗秩序 address problems in the medical system /～音像工作 straighten out irregularities in the audio-visual industry /～市场 put the markets in order /～企业 check up on an enterprise; reorganize an enterprise /～基层组织 overhaul a grass-roots organization /～党风 rectify the working style of the Party /～物价 readjust prices /～规章制度 strengthen rules and regulations /～校风 improve the school spirit /公司需要好好～一下。The company needs a good shake-up.
整顿乾坤 zhěngdùn-qiánkūn create order out of chaos; run the country well
整风 zhěngfēng rectify incorrect styles of work or thinking:在党内开展～势在必行。It is imperative that we rectify incorrect styles of work in our Party.
整风运动 zhěngfēng yùndòng movement to rectify the styles of the Party; rectification movement
整复 zhěngfù renovate:脱臼～ replace dislocated joints
整改 zhěnggǎi reform and consolidate:～措施 measures for reform and consolidation
整个 zhěnggè whole; entire; full:～星期 full week /在中国革命的～过程中 throughout the period of the Chinese revolution /～来说,工作是成功的。Generally speaking (*or* By and large), the work was a success. /～广场挤得水泄不通。The entire square was packed with people. /他把事情的内幕～讲了出来。He told the whole story.
整股 zhěnggǔ 〈金融〉round lot
整合 zhěnghé ❶ integrate; consolidate; unify; unite:～学科专业 integrate academic disciplines /重新～趋于分裂的社会 reunify (*or* reunite) a disintegrating community ❷〈地质〉conformity
整合系统 zhěnghé xìtǒng 〈计算机〉integrated system
整纪 zhěngjì strengthen discipline
整洁 zhěngjié clean and tidy; orderly; neat; trim:～的街道 clean streets /～的病房 trim wards /他的办公室总是很～。He keeps his office neat. /教室里显得十分～。The classroom appeared very clean and tidy.
整经 zhěngjīng 〈纺织〉warping:分段～ sectional warping
整经机 zhěngjīngjī warping machine
整军经武 zhěngjūn-jīngwǔ outfit and reinforce an army; enhance military capabilities:～,巩固国防 build up the armed forces to strengthen national defence
整块 zhěngkuài monoblock:～铸造(件) monoblock casting
整理 zhěnglǐ straighten out; tidy up; sort out; arrange:～笔记 arrange one's notes /～抽屉 sort out things in the drawer /～屋子 tidy (up) a room /～思路 straighten out one's thinking /～材料出版 prepare materials for publication /赶快～行装 pack one's things straight away /着手～会议记录 set about sorting out the minutes of a meeting /～古代文物 sift archaeological relics /他的东西～得井然有序。He has everything placed where it belongs. /图书应分类进行～。The books should be catalogued.
整脸儿 zhěngliǎnr save one's face; save face for sb.:这样他就能落个～。In this way he was able to save his face. *or* That was face-saving to him.
整脸子 zhěngliǎnzi ❶〈方言〉straight face:他不爱说话,外带还是个～。Not only is he reserved, but he always keeps a straight face. ❷ (in theatrical circles) reference to those whose facial muscles are a bit stiff
整料 zhěngliào material all in one piece for a given job; whole piece of material:你把好好的一块～浪费了。The material could have been put to good use as a whole, but you've ruined it.
整流 zhěngliú 〈电学〉rectification
整流管 zhěngliúguǎn 〈电学〉rectifier tube
整流器 zhěngliúqì 〈电学〉rectifier:硅～ silicon rectifier /硅控～

silicon-controlled rectifier (SCR); thyristor /～电动机 commutator motor /～继电器 rectifier relay
整流子 zhěngliúzǐ 〈电学〉commutator
整年累月 zhěngnián-lěiyuè all the year round; year in and year out; from year to year; year after year:他～在田里干活。He toiled in the fields year after year.
整齐 zhěngqí ❶ orderly; neat; tidy:步调～ keep in step /着装～ neatly dressed /～的歌声 singing in unison /～的花园 trim garden /～的头发 well-groomed hair /货架上的东西摆得非常～。The goods are kept neat on the shelves. ❷ even; level; regular:～的稻田 even rice field /～的厂房 well-laid-out factory buildings /～的节奏 regular rhythms /～的字迹 neat handwriting /学生们的英语程度很～。The students are level in their English proficiency.
整齐划一 zhěngqí-huàyī uniform; alike:商场售货员的着装～。The shop assistants are dressed the same.
整儿 zhěngr 〈方言〉round number:凑个～ make up a round number; make up an even amount
整人 zhěngrén make sb. suffer; make things difficult for sb.; give sb. a hard time; fix:她喜欢～。She likes to make others suffer. /～要不得。It is wrong to persecute people.
整容 zhěngróng face-lift:经过～,她的面容恢复了原样。Her face was restored through face-lifting.
整容术 zhěngróngshù cosmetic operation (*or* surgery); cosmetology; face-lifting
整式 zhěngshì 〈数学〉integral expression
整饰 zhěngshì repair and decorate:房屋～一新 renovate the house
整数 zhěngshù ❶〈数学〉integer; whole number ❷ round number or figure:把～存进银行,零头留下。Deposit your money in a bank in round figures and keep the small amounts.
整肃 zhěngsù 〈书面〉❶ serious; solemn; earnest:法纪～ solemn law and discipline /军容～ serious appearance and bearing of the soldiers ❷ put in order; consolidate:～衣冠 tidy up one's dress /～军纪 strengthen army discipline ❸〈方言〉purge:～异己 purge those disloyal to oneself
整套 zhěngtào whole set of:～家具 whole set (*or* suite) of furniture /～安全装置 complete set of safety devices /他对这件事有一～处理意见。He puts foward a comprehensive proposal on how to handle the matter. /很快他就拿出了这个工程的一～设计图。Very quickly he came up with a whole set of designs for the project.
整体 zhěngtǐ whole; totality; entirety:进行～规划 make an overall plan /要有～观点 keep in mind the interests of the whole /凡事都必须以人民的～利益为出发点。We should proceed in all cases from the overall interests of the people.
整体吊装 zhěngtǐ diàozhuāng 〈建筑〉integral hoisting
整体观念 zhěngtǐ guānniàn concept of viewing the situation as a whole or in its totality:树立～ take the overall situation into consideration
整体化 zhěngtǐhuà integration
整天 zhěngtiān whole day; all day; all day long:～忙碌 be busy all day long /她花了两～才把屋子收拾干净。She spent two whole days cleaning up the house.
整形 zhěngxíng 〈医学〉plastic
整形手术 zhěngxíng shǒushù plastic operation
整形外科 zhěngxíng wàikē plastic surgery; plastics
整修 zhěngxiū rebuild; renovate; recondition:～水渠 rebuild a canal /～危房 renovate a dilapidated house /～河道 dredge a river /～堤坝 reinforce the dam
整训 zhěngxùn train and consolidate:～干部 train cadres /部队～ train and consolidate an army
整整 zhěngzhěng whole; full; solid:～两卡车货 two truckfuls of goods /他走了～两天。He has been away for two whole days. /我到北京已～三十年。I've been in Beijing for 30 solid years. /两地相距～二十公里。The two places are a good 20 kilometres apart.
整枝 zhěngzhī prune (off or down); train (a plant):该给这些树～了。It's time we pruned the branches of those trees. /她学会了～技术。She has learned the skill of pruning (*or* training).
整治 zhěngzhì ❶ renovate; repair; recondition:～农具 repair farm tools /～旧房 renovate old houses /已经开始～长江口的航道。Channels at the mouth of the Yangtze River are being dredged. ❷ punish; fix; make to suffer:～害群之马 fix the black sheep /～无照摊贩 punish the unlicensed vendors /那个流氓受到了应有的～。That hooligan was given due punishment. ❸ do; perform; work at:把库房～得有条有理 put the warehouse in order /她很快就～出好几样可口的菜肴。In no time she had prepared several delicious dishes.
整装 zhěngzhuāng pack one's things (for a journey); get one's things ready (for a journey)
整装待发 zhěngzhuāng-dàifā all packed up and ready to set out
整装待命 zhěngzhuāng-dàimìng in full battle array awaiting orders; ready for departure at short notice
整庄 zhěngzhuang 〈方言〉❶ whole; intact:屋里没有一件～家具。No piece of furniture in the room remains intact. ❷ in good order; tidy; neat:把这些东西放得～点。Put these things in an orderly way.

拯 zhěng save; rescue; free; deliver:～民于水深火热之中 save the people from untold miseries
拯救 zhěngjiù save; rescue; deliver; preserve:～病人 save a patient's life /～被奴役的人们 free the enslaved /把他从苦难的深渊中～出来 deliver him from the abyss of suffering

zhèng

郑(鄭) Zhèng ❶ name of a state in the Zhou Dynasty in the vicinity of today's Xinzheng (新郑) County, Henan Province ❷ a surname
郑板桥 Zhèng Bǎnqiáo Zheng Banqiao (formerly translated as Cheng Pan-ch'iao, 1693-1765), with Zheng Xie (郑燮) as his official name, poet, painter and calligrapher of the Qing Dynasty
郑成功 Zhèng Chénggōng Zheng Chenggong (formerly translated as Cheng Ch'eng-kung, 1624-1662), national hero known for his recovery of Taiwan from the Dutch colonialists during the late Ming and early Qing dynasties
郑和 Zhèng Hé Zheng He (formerly translated as Cheng Ho, 1371-1435), navigator and diplomat of the Ming Dynasty
郑樵 Zhèng Qiáo Zheng Qiao (formerly translated as Cheng Ch'iao, 1104-1162), historian of the Southern Song Dynasty
郑燮 Zhèng Xiè *see* "郑板桥"
郑重 zhèngzhòng serious; solemn; earnest; grave:语气～ in an earnest tone /～宣布 solemnly declare /说话时显得极为～ speak in all seriousness /外交部发表了～声明。The Foreign Ministry made a solemn statement.
郑重其事 zhèngzhòng-qíshì solemnly; seriously; in earnest:～地宣布 solemnly declare /～地告诫他 advise him in good earnest
郑州 Zhèngzhōu Zhengzhou, capital of Henan Province

正 zhèng ❶ straight, upright; perpendicular:～西 due west /在～前方 directly ahead /地图挂得不～。The map on the wall is not straight. ❷ situated in the middle; main:～门 main entrance /～院儿 main courtyard ❸ (of time) sharp; on time; punctually:六点～ at six o'clock sharp /～午时分 noon ❹ front; obverse; right (side):钱币的～面 obverse side of a coin /这种纸～反面都很光洁。Both the front and the back of this kind of paper are very smooth. /这料子质量真好,简直分不出～反。The material is of such good quality that one can hardly tell its right side from its wrong side (*or* tell which is the right side). ❺ upright; impartial; honest:公～无私 selfless and impartial /清～廉明 be clean and upright ❻ correct; right; proper:走～道儿 follow the correct path /此人作风不～。He is a man without moral integrity. ❼ (of colour and flavour) pure; right:～红 pure red /布的颜色不～。The colour of the cloth is not pure. /这菜的味儿～。The dish is of the right flavour. ❽ regular; normal:～楷 regular script /五官端～ have regular features ❾ chief; prime; principal:～副厂长 factory manager and deputy factory manager /～教授 full professor /～驾驶员 first pilot ❿ (of figures, designs, etc.) regular:～六边形 regular hexagon ⓫〈数学〉positive; plus:～号 positive sign; plus sign /负乘负得～。A negative multiplied by another negative is a positive. ⓬〈物理〉positive:～电 positive electricity ⓭ set right; put straight:把帽子～一～ put one's hat straight ⓮ set to rights; rectify:～人先～己。These who wish to make others upright must be upright themselves first. /政者,～也;己之不～,何以～人? Government means rectitude. If you are not a man of rectitude, how can you rectify others? ⓯ correct (mistakes):斧～ make corrections /请给他～一～音。Will you please correct his pronunciation? ⓰ just; right; exactly; precisely:～中下怀 precisely to one's liking /

～好赶上 arrive in the nick of time /这～合我意。That suits me fine. /你～中了他的圈套。You have fallen right into his trap. /这～是我需要的书。This is just the book I need. /时针～指在九点上。The hour hand was pointing exactly at 9. /他～是我所要找的人。He is the very person I'm looking for. ⓱ be doing：我～在听广播。I'm listening to the radio. /他～忙着做饭。He was busy preparing dinner. ⓲ (Zhèng) a surname
see also zhēng

正榜 zhèngbǎng published list of people who have passed the imperial examination：中～ have passed the imperial examination

正本 zhèngběn ❶ reserved copy (of a library book)：这是～，不外借。This is the reserved copy; it's not for lending. ❷ original (of a document, etc.)：经理在合同～上签了字。The manager signed (his name on) the original of the contract.

正本清源 zhèngběn-qīngyuán tackle a problem at its root; radically reform; thoroughly overhaul：只有～，才能使工厂面貌一新。Only by introducing a thoroughgoing reform can we give the factory a new look.

正比 zhèngbǐ ❶ direct proportion：速度不变，所走的路程与所用的时间成～。At a given speed, the time needed is directly proportional to the distance covered. ❷ direct ratio

正比例 zhèngbǐlì 〈数学〉 direct ratio

正步 zhèngbù 〈军事〉 parade step; goose step：练习走～ practise marching in goose step /～走! Parade step, march!

正餐 zhèngcān lunch or supper; dinner

正册 zhèngcè 〈旧语〉 regular register of residence (for listing honest households)

正茬 zhèngchá main crop (of a particular region)：～麦 main crop of wheat

正产 zhèngchǎn mature birth

正长石 zhèngchángshí orthoclase

正长岩 zhèngchángyán syenite

正常 zhèngcháng normal; usual; regular：～交往 regular contact /～情况 normal conditions /～的生活水平 average living standard /两国关系恢复～。The relations between the two countries have been normalized (*or* have returned to normal). /这两天气候不太～。The weather is rather unusual these days. /学术问题上的争论是～现象。Controversies over academic issues are quite normal.

正常化 zhèngchánghuà normalize

正常贸易关系 zhèngcháng màoyì guānxi (formerly 最惠国待遇) normal trade relations (NTR)：永久性～ permanent normal trade relations (PNTR)

正常性 zhèngchángxìng normality

正出 zhèngchū 〈旧语〉 be born of the legal wife

正大 zhèngdà (of words or deeds) fair and square; upright; honest; aboveboard

正大光明 zhèngdà-guāngmíng open and aboveboard; frank and honest：～地做人 be a just and honest person

正大集团 zhèngdà Jítuán (Thailand) Chai Tai Co. Ltd.; Charoen Pokphand; CP Group

正旦 zhèngdàn 〈戏曲〉 main female character
see also zhēngdàn

正当 zhèngdāng just when; just as; just the time for：～盛夏之时 just at the height of summer /～腹背受敌之际，增援部队赶来了。Just when they were being attacked front and rear, the reinforcements arrived.

正当年 zhèngdāngnián in the prime of life; in one's prime：二十七八～。A man is in the prime of life when in late twenties.

正当时 zhèngdāngshí just the right season or time：眼下插秧～。Now is the right time for rice transplantation.

正当中 zhèngdāngzhōng right in the middle or centre：一张圆桌摆在屋子的～。A round table was placed right in the middle of the room.

正当 zhèngdàng ❶ proper; appropriate; lawful; legitimate：～权益 legitimate (*or* lawful) rights and interests /～的要求 just (*or* rightful) claim (*or* demand) /～的方法 proper ways; suitable means /～的经营 legitimate business operation ❷ (of a person's character) upright; honest

正当防卫 zhèngdàng fángwèi justifiable defence

正道 zhèngdào ❶ right way or track; correct path; 引上～ lead sb. on to the right track /年轻人要走～。Young people should follow the right path. ❷ truth; law：人间～是沧桑。But Man's world is mutable, seas become mulberry fields. *or* It's the law of this world that all things are changing.

正德 Zhèngdé Zhengde, title of the reign (1506-1521) of Zhu Houzhao (朱厚照), 11th emperor of the Ming Dynasty, called reverently Ming Wuzong (明武宗) after death

正点 zhèngdiǎn (of trains, ships, planes, etc.) at the expected time; on time; on schedule; punctually：火车～到站。The train arrived on time. /机车～运行。The locomotive was running on schedule.

正电 zhèngdiàn *also* "阳电" yángdiàn positive electricity

正电荷 zhèngdiànhè positive charge

正电子 zhèngdiànzǐ *also* "阳电子" yángdiànzǐ positive electron; positron

正电子发射断层显像 zhèngdiànzǐ fāshè duàncéng xiǎnxiàng 〈医学〉 PET (Positron Emission Tomography)

正殿 zhèngdiàn main hall (in a palace or temple)：故宫有三大～。There are three main halls in the Imperial Palace.

正定霉素 zhèngdìngméisù 〈药学〉 daunomycin

正多边形 zhèngduōbiānxíng *also* "正多角形" 〈数学〉 regular polygon：花坛呈～。The flower bed was in the form of a regular polygon.

正多角形 zhèngduōjiǎoxíng *see* "正多边形"

正法 zhèngfǎ execute (a criminal)：立即～ execute the criminals immediately; carry out summary execution /就地～ execute the condemned right on the spot

正反 zhèng-fǎn positive and negative：听取～两方面的意见 listen to the pros and cons /吸取～两方面的经验教训 learn from both positive and negative experience

正反向比 zhèngfǎnxiàngbǐ 〈物理〉 front-to-back ratio

正反应 zhèngfǎnyìng positive reaction

正犯 zhèngfàn principal criminal; chief culprit

正方 zhèngfāng ❶ square：一张～桌子 a square table ❷ (of debaters) those holding affirmative or positive views：～占了上风。The positive side had the upper hand. /～的理由不够充足。Arguments for the affirmative view were inadequate.

正方体 zhèngfāngtǐ cube

正方形 zhèngfāngxíng square：一条～的头巾 a square scarf

正房 zhèngfáng ❶ principal or main rooms (in a courtyard, usu. facing south); northernmost rooms in a courtyard：父母住在～。The parents lived in the northernmost rooms. ❷ 〈旧语〉 legal wife (in contrast with concubines)

正负电子对撞机 zhèngfù diànzǐ duìzhuàngjī electron-positron collider

正告 zhènggào earnestly admonish; sternly warn：我们要～某些人，休要造谣生事。We want to warn certain people not to start a rumour and create trouble.

正割 zhènggē 〈数学〉 secant

正宫 zhènggōng ❶ empress' palace ❷ empress

正宫娘娘 zhènggōng niángniang empress consort; emperor's legal wife

正骨 zhènggǔ 〈中医〉 bonesetting：祖传～术 skill of bonesetting handed down in the family from generation to generation

正规 zhèngguī standard; regular; proper：～训练 regular training /操作方法不够～。The method of operation was not up to standard.

正规部队 zhèngguī bùduì regular troops; regulars

正规化 zhèngguīhuà regularize; standardize; be put on a regular basis

正规教育 zhèngguī jiàoyù proper education; regular education

正规军 zhèngguījūn regular army

正规学校 zhèngguī xuéxiào regular school：～教育 formal school education

正规战 zhèngguīzhàn regular warfare

正轨 zhèngguǐ right track; correct path：逐步走上～ gradually get on to the right track

正果 zhèngguǒ 〈佛教〉 attain consummation and become a Buddha：终成～ eventually attain consummation and become a Buddha

正好 zhènghǎo ❶ (of time, position, size, number, degree, etc.) just right：这支笔你用～。This is just the right pen for you. /我看你来得～。I guess you have come just in time. /这件衬衣他穿～。The shirt fits him nicely. /这一切～证明他受了冤屈。All this only proves that he has been woefully wronged. ❷ happen to; chance

to; as it happens; it (so) happens that: 那时我～出差在外。I happened to be away on business at the time. /下午开会～向老王请教。This afternoon's meeting will be a chance for you to ask advice from Lao Wang.

正号 zhènghào positive sign; plus sign: 他把～当成了负号。He mistook the positive sign for a negative one.

正话 zhènghuà ❶ serious talk: 他那人就是玩笑话多, ～少。He is kidding most of the time and is seldom serious. ❷ original meaning; real intention: 她正在气头上, 那话怕是～反说吧。In a fit of anger, she might say something she didn't really mean.

正火 zhènghuǒ 〈冶金〉 normalizing: ～钢 normalized steel /～炉 normalizing furnace

正畸学 zhèngjīxué orthodontics

正极 zhèngjí 〈电学〉 positive electrode; positive pole; anode

正极板 zhèngjíbǎn 〈电学〉 positive plate

正交 zhèngjiāo 〈数学〉 orthogonal: ～化 orthogonalization /～坐标 orthogonal coordinate

正交轨线 zhèngjiāo guǐxiàn 〈物理〉 orthogonal trajectory

正教 Zhèngjiào *also* "东正教" Dōngzhèngjiào Orthodox Church: 笃信～ be a devout believer in the Orthodox Church

正襟危坐 zhèngjīn-wēizuò 〈书面〉 straighten one's clothes and sit properly; sit bolt upright; be all seriousness: 我面前的这位老人～, 不苟言笑。In front of me sat an old man, solemn and serious.

正经 zhèngjīng 〈旧语〉 Confucian canon; 13 Confucian classics

正经 zhèngjing ❶ decent; honest; respectable: 正正经经的企业家 decent entrepreneur /他可是个～的买卖人。He is a respectable businessman. /你们都是～的好人。All of you are honest and kind people. ❷ serious; proper; right: 还是谈～事吧。Let's get down to brass tacks. /应当把精力花在～事上。We should devote our energy to weighty matters. /你老爱开玩笑, 人家在说～话。You are always joking, but I'm quite serious. ❸ formal; standard: ～货 standard goods ❹ 〈方言〉 truly; indeed; very much so: 这块料子～不错。The cloth is fine indeed. /那姑娘～长得漂亮。The girl is really attractive.

正经八百 zhèngjīng-bābǎi *also* "正经八摆" 〈方言〉 serious; earnest: 你没瞧见小男孩脸上那副～的神色? Didn't you notice the serious look on the boy's face? /两年之后, 他才开始～地念书。It was not until two years later that he started to study in real earnest.

正剧 zhèngjù serious play; serious drama

正角 zhèngjué leading role; lead; leading man (lady)

正楷 zhèngkǎi *also* "正书" regular script (in Chinese calligraphy): 练书法必须先练～。To practise Chinese calligraphy, one should begin with the regular script.

正课 zhèngkè ❶ 〈旧语〉 taxes ❷ subjects or courses in a school curriculum or military training programme: 要注意～, 但也不要忽略课外活动。We must pay attention to the subjects we study, but should by no means neglect extracurricular activities.

正离子 zhènglízǐ positive ion; cation or kation

正理 zhènglǐ correct principle; valid reason; truth: 这才是做人的～。This is the right way to conduct oneself. /这些都是～, 应该坚信不移。These are all correct principles and should be followed steadfastly.

正梁 zhèngliáng 〈建筑〉 ridge purlin

正磷酸 zhènglínsuān 〈化学〉 orthophosphoric acid: ～盐 orthophosphate

正六面体 zhèngliùmiàntǐ 〈数学〉 regular hexahedron

正路 zhènglù correct path; right way: 这才是～。This is the right path to follow.

正论 zhènglùn valid argument; right thing to say: 这才是治国安民的～啊! This is the right thing to say about running the state and reassuring the people.

正门 zhèngmén front door; main entrance: 从～进去, 可以看见一栋小楼。Go through the front gate and you will see a small building.

正面 zhèngmiàn ❶ front; frontage; face; facade: 大楼的～ facade (*or* front) of a building /～的火力 frontal fire /～突围 break out of an encirclement from the front ❷ obverse side; right side: 硬币的～ obverse side of a coin /绸子的～ right side of the silk /分不出～与反面 can not tell the right (*or* obverse) side from the wrong (*or* reverse) side ❸ positive: ～的意见要听, 反面的意见也要听。We must listen to criticisms as well as praises. ❹ straightforwardly; directly; openly: ～冲突 head-on conflict (*or* clash) /他从不～回答问题。He never answers your question directly. /有意见请～提。Please express your views openly.

正面教育 zhèngmiàn jiàoyù positive education; education by positive example

正面人物 zhèngmiàn rénwù positive character; hero: 他总是扮演～。He always plays the part of a hero. /他擅长塑造～。He is good at creating positive characters.

正面图 zhèngmiàntú front view

正面战场 zhèngmiàn zhànchǎng frontline battlefield

正牌 zhèngpái quality product: ～茅台酒 genuine Maotai /我看这富士胶卷不是～货。I believe this Fuji film is a fake.

正派 zhèngpài just; upright; honest; decent: ～人家 honest family /～的生意人 decent businessman /他为人～。He is an upright man.

正片儿 zhèngpiānr 〈口语〉 *see* "正片"

正片 zhèngpiàn ❶ 〈摄影〉 positive ❷ 〈影视〉 copy ❸ 〈影视〉 feature (film)

正品 zhèngpǐn quality products; certified goods: 这批货全是～。This batch of goods are all quality products.

正剖面 zhèngpōumiàn normal cross section

正气 zhèngqì ❶ healthy trend; healthy atmosphere; probity; moral spirit: 扶植～ foster healthy trends ❷ unyielding integrity; moral courage: ～凛然 awe-inspiring rectitude ❸ 〈中医〉 human resistance to diseases

正桥 zhèngqiáo bridge (as compared with bridge approach)

正巧 zhèngqiǎo ❶ happen to; have the luck to; as it happens: 他急着送病人上医院, ～有一辆出租车开过来。He was anxious to send the patient to hospital, and it so happened that a taxi came along. ❷ just in time; in the nick of time; just at the right moment: 你来得～, 我们正有事要问你。You have come just in time to answer our questions.

正切 zhèngqiē 〈数学〉 tangent

正取 zhèngqǔ be admitted or enrolled (in contrast with being on the waiting list)

正确 zhèngquè correct; sound; right; proper: ～的方针 sound policy /～的方向 right direction /～的判断 valid judgement /～的方法 correct method (*or* approach) /～地引导 guide properly /～地分析形势 accurately appraise (*or* assess, *or* analyze) the situation /～地对待群众 adopt a correct attitude towards the masses /你回答的不够～。Your answer is not quite accurate.

正确性 zhèngquèxìng correctness; soundness; validity

正儿八经 zhèngrbājīng 〈方言〉 serious; earnest: 一脸～的神色 looking earnest; with a serious look on one's face /～地向他们介绍计划生育的好处 tell them earnestly about the advantages of family planning

正人君子 zhèngrén-jūnzǐ gentleman; man of honour; man of high principle: 道貌岸然的～ man who puts on a sanctimonious air /有人力求把自己装扮成～。Some people go out of their way to pose as men of high morals.

正日 zhèngrì *also* "正日子" day proper for a ceremony: 今天是他们结婚的～。Today is the auspicious day for their wedding.

正三角形 zhèngsānjiǎoxíng 〈数学〉 equilateral triangle

正色 zhèngsè ❶ 〈书面〉 pure colours ❷ with a stern or severe countenance: ～批评 criticise sternly /她～地说: "我不同意。" "I don't agree," she said in a grave tone.

正色胶片 zhèngsè jiāopiàn 〈摄影〉 orthochromatic film

正身 zhèngshēn identity: 验明～ make a positive identification of a criminal before execution

正史 zhèngshǐ official history books written in biographical style: 据～记载 according to official history books

正式 zhèngshì formal; official; regular: ～职业 regular occupation /～警告 formal warning /～规格 regular specifications /～签署 official signature /～委托 official commission /～授权 duly authorized /会议～代表 full representative to a conference /达成～协议 reach a formal agreement /～通过决议 formally adopt (*or* pass) a resolution

正式党员 zhèngshì dǎngyuán full member of the Party; full Party member

正式访问 zhèngshì fǎngwèn official visit; formal visit

正式会谈 zhèngshì huìtán formal talks; formal negotiations

正式记录 zhèngshì jìlù official records; formal minutes (of a meeting)

正式声明 zhèngshì shēngmíng official statement

正式文本 zhèngshì wénběn official text

正式照会 zhèngshì zhàohuì formal or official note; personal note

正视 zhèngshì look in the face; look squarely at; face squarely; face up to:～现实 face reality /～自己的缺点 acknowledge one's shortcomings /～别人的批评 take others' criticisms seriously /～改革中的困难 face up to difficulties during reform
正视图 zhèngshìtú front view; elevation
正事 zhèngshì one's proper business:他整天游荡,不干～。He idles about all day long. /这不是玩笑,我谈的是～。It is no laughing matter. I'm quite serious.
正室 zhèngshì ❶〈旧语〉legal wife:立她为～ make her his legal wife ❷〈书面〉eldest son born by one's legal wife
正手 zhèngshǒu 〈体育〉forehand:～打法 forehand stroke /～抽球 forehand drive
正书 zhèngshū ❶ regular script (in Chinese calligraphy) ❷ subject matter of any Chinese folk art form
正数 zhèngshù 〈数学〉positive number
正税 zhèngshuì 〈旧语〉main taxes (e.g. land tax, poll tax, etc.)
正酸 zhèngsuān 〈化学〉ortho-acid
正态分布 zhèngtài fēnbù 〈统计〉normal distribution
正堂 zhèngtáng ❶ middle room that faces south ❷〈旧语〉hall where local authorities handle official business ❸ county or prefectural official in the Ming and Qing dynasties
正题 zhèngtí subject or topic of a talk or essay; main theme:不要离开～。Don't digress. /文章一开始就直入～。The article comes straight to the main theme at the very outset.
正体 zhèngtǐ ❶ standardized form of Chinese characters ❷ regular script (in Chinese calligraphy) ❸ block letter:请用～写姓名。Please print your name.
正厅 zhèngtīng ❶ main hall; central hall:咱们在～见面。We'll meet in the main hall. ❷ stalls (in a theatre):一个～的坐位 a stall seat
正统 zhèngtǒng ❶ legitimism:按～应由嫡长子继位。According to legitimism, it is the legal wife's eldest son who should succeed to the throne. ❷ orthodox:～思想 orthodox thinking /～人物 orthodox person ❸ (Zhèngtǒng) Zhengtong, title of the reign (1436-1449) of Zhu Qizhen (朱祁镇), 6th emperor of the Ming Dynasty, called reverently Ming Yingzong (明英宗) after death
正统派 zhèngtǒngpài orthodox school; orthodox party
正投影 zhèngtóuyǐng orthographic projection:～法 orthography /～图 orthograph
正头香主 zhèngtóu xiāngzhǔ ❶ lineal descendant ❷ master
正途 zhèngtú correct path; right way:走上～ be (*or* embark) on the right track /封建社会以科举出身做官为～。In the feudal society, the right thing to do was first pass the imperial examination and then hold an official position.
正文 zhèngwén main body (of a book, etc.); text:该书的～部分是由他亲自撰写的。He wrote the text of the book himself.
正屋 zhèngwū principal or main rooms (in a courtyard, usu. facing south); northernmost rooms in a courtyard
正午 zhèngwǔ high noon; midday:时值～ at high noon
正误 zhèngwù correct (typographical) errors
正误表 zhèngwùbiǎo errata; corrigenda
正弦 zhèngxián 〈数学〉sine
正弦波 zhèngxiánbō 〈电学〉sine wave
正项 zhèngxiàng main project; regular project
正薪 zhèngxīn 〈方言〉basic salary:房租就占了他～的大部分。The house rent takes up the major part of his basic salary.
正形 zhèngxíng 〈口语〉proper behaviour; good manners:他简直没一点儿～。He simply has no manners. /这么大的姑娘,该有点～了。You are no longer a little girl, so you should know how to behave yourself.
正凶 zhèngxiōng 〈法律〉principal murderer:捉拿～归案 bring the principal murderer to justice
正选 zhèngxuǎn (of sports) top player:他应召回国,再次成为国家队～。He was recalled from abroad and became one of the top players of the national team again.
正牙学 zhèngyáxué 〈医学〉orthodontology:～家 orthodontologist
正言厉色 zhèngyán-lìsè in a grave tone and with a severe look:她皱起眉头,～地斥责了那家伙。Frowning, she reprimanded the fellow severely.
正盐 zhèngyán 〈化学〉normal salt
正颜厉色 zhèngyán-lìsè put on a stern countenance; be serious and severe:继父见了她总是～。Her stepfather would put on a stern countenance whenever he saw her. /经理～地教训了年轻人一顿。With a severe look on his face, the manager gave the young man a good dressing-down.
正眼 zhèngyǎn look sb. or sth. in the face; look squarely at:她从来不敢～看她的老板。She never dares to look her boss squarely in the eye.
正阳门 Zhèngyángmén South-Facing Gate, Beijing
正业 zhèngyè regular occupation; decent work:他一向不务～。He has never engaged in honest work. *or* He never attends to his proper duties.
正一道 Zhèngyīdào Way of Orthodox Unity, one of the two major sects of Taoism which came into being in the 2nd century
正义 zhèngyì ❶ justice:伸张～ uphold justice; let justice prevail /～最终要战胜邪恶。Justice will eventually triumph over evil. ❷ just; righteous:～的斗争 just struggle /～的举动 just action /我们的事业是～的。Ours is a just cause. ❸ (of words) correct meaning; proper meaning
正义感 zhèngyìgǎn sense of justice; sense of what is right:他是一个很有～的青年人。He is a young man with a strong sense of justice.
正音 zhèngyīn 〈语言〉❶ correct one's pronunciation:帮他～ help him (to) improve his pronunciation ❷ standard pronunciation
正音法 zhèngyīnfǎ 〈语言〉orthoepy
正应力 zhèngyìnglì 〈物理〉direct stress
正用 zhèngyòng (put to) proper use:还是省了这笔钱作～吧。Let's reserve this sum of money for proper use.
正院儿 zhèngyuànr main courtyard
正在 zhèngzài in the process of; in the course of; be doing:～打电话 be making a phone call /前面～修路。The road ahead is under construction. /谈判～进行。Negotiations are well under way.
正直 zhèngzhí open and aboveboard; honest; upright; fair-minded:～的学者 honest scholar /为人～ upright person /大家信任他,因为他～。He is trusted because he is fair-minded.
正职 zhèngzhí ❶ (of a unit) principal; chief:他还从未任过～。he has never been a chief. ❷ main occupation or profession; full-time job:他的～是教师,也兼职当律师。He is a teacher by profession, but he is also a part-time lawyer.
正治 zhèngzhì 〈中医〉normal treatment (i.e. administer medicines of a cold nature to treat a febrile disease)
正中 zhèngzhōng *also* "正当中" middle; centre:桌子～放着一个花瓶。There is a vase in the middle of the table. /她站在大厅～。She stood in the centre of the hall.
正中下怀 zhèngzhòng-xiàhuái fit in exactly with one's wishes or desires; be just what one wants or wishes for; come up to one's expectation; be precisely to one's liking or taste:这话正中他的下怀,听了心中暗喜。Finding the remark precisely to his taste, he was gratified but without showing it.
正传 zhèngzhuàn main story; subject itself:闲话少说,言归～。We have had enough digression, now let's come back to our subject.
正庄 zhèngzhuāng 〈方言〉standard:～货 standard goods /咱可是～的庄稼人。I'm a farmer in the truest sense. *or* I'm a typical farmer.
正字 zhèngzì ❶ correct a wrongly written character or a misspelt word ❷ regular script (in Chinese calligraphy) ❸ standard form of Chinese characters; block letter
正字法 zhèngzìfǎ 〈语言〉orthography:学习～ learn orthography
正宗 zhèngzōng ❶ orthodox school ❷ authentic:～川菜 authentic Sichuan-style dishes
正座 zhèngzuò stalls (in a theatre)

症(證) zhèng

disease; malady; illness:病～ disease; illness /急～ acute disease /顽～ chronic and stubborn disease; persistent ailment /炎～ inflammation /对～下药 suit the medicine to the illness; suit the remedy to the case

see also zhēng

症候 zhènghou ❶ disease ❷ symptom:有肝炎的～ show symptoms of hepatitis
症候群 zhènghouqún *also* "综合征" zōnghézhēng 〈医学〉syndrome
症状 zhèngzhuàng symptom:临床～ clinical symptoms /肺结核的～ symptom of tuberculosis /早期～ early (*or* incipient) symptoms /晚期～ terminal symptoms
症状疗法 zhèngzhuàng liáofǎ symptomatic treatment
症状性贫血 zhèngzhuàngxìng pínxuè symptomatic anemia

症状学 zhèngzhuàngxué 〈医学〉semiology

怔 zhèng 〈方言〉stare blankly; be in a daze; be in a trance: 他还～在那儿。He was still in a daze.
see also zhēng

怔神儿 zhèngshénr 〈方言〉be in a daze; be in a trance: 他一～, 马跑了。While he was in a trance, the horse ran away.

怔怔 zhèngzhèng 〈方言〉in a stupefied state; in a daze; in a trance: 他～地站在那儿。He stood there staring blankly.

证(證) zhèng ❶ testify to; prove; demonstrate: 论～ demonstrate; expound and prove /求～ seek to prove /出庭作～ give evidence (*or* bear witness) in a law court; serve as a witness at court /人～ testimony of a witness /物～ material evidence; exhibit /旁～ circumstantial evidence; collateral evidence /确～ positive proof; conclusive evidence ❷ certificate; card: 出入～ pass /出生～ birth certificate /身份～ ID card; identity card /工作～ employee's ID card /许可～ permit; licence /拘留～ order for provisional apprehension

证词 zhèngcí *also* "证辞" testimony: 提供～ bear testimony

证果寺 Zhèngguǒsì Temple of Buddhahood, Beijing

证婚人 zhènghūnrén chief witness at a wedding ceremony: 我是他们的～。I was the chief witness at their wedding (ceremony).

证见 zhèngjiàn evidence; proof: 你把这封信带着, 也好做～。You'd better take this letter with you as proof.

证件 zhèngjiàn credentials; papers; certificate: 交出～ hand in one's credentials (*or* papers) /唯一的～ only (*or* sole) certificate /出行时要随身带着必要的～。When going long journey, you must take with you all the necessary certification papers.

证据 zhèngjù proof; evidence; testimony: 书面～ written (*or* documentary) evidence /口头～ oral (*or* parol) evidence /～充分 sufficient evidence /～确凿 irrefutable evidence; verified (*or* ironclad) proof /提供～ give evidence; offer testimony /收集～ collect evidence /掌握～ have evidence in one's hands

证明 zhèngmíng ❶ prove; uphold; testify; bear out: 实践～ verify through practice /有说服力地～ convincingly prove /事实～, 她是无辜的。Facts have testified to her innocence. /武力不能使我们屈服, 这早已为历史所～。It has long since been borne out by history that we will not yield (*or* submit) to force. ❷ certificate; identification; testimonial; papers: 开具～ write out a testimonial /伪造～ forge a certificate /记者～ press card /结婚～ marriage certificate (*or* lines)

证明书 zhèngmíngshū certificate; testimonial: 健康～ health certificate /家庭情况～ certificate of family background /开写～ write out a testimonial

证明文件 zhèngmíng wénjiàn certificate; testimonial; papers

证券 zhèngquàn bond; securities: 流通～ negotiable securities /～价格 prices of securities

证券持有人 zhèngquàn chíyǒurén securities holder; bill holder

证券代理 zhèngquàn dàilǐ securities business on commission

证券兑换 zhèngquàn duìhuàn exchange of securities

证券公司 zhèngquàn gōngsī securities company

证券行 zhèngquànháng securities house; bond house

证券化 zhèngquànhuà securitisation

证券监督管理委员会 Zhèngquàn Jiāndū Guǎnlǐ Wěiyuánhuì (shortened as 证监会) China Securities Regulatory Commission

证券交易 zhèngquàn jiāoyì securities trading; dealings in securities

证券交易法 zhèngquàn jiāoyìfǎ securities exchange act

证券交易税 zhèngquàn jiāoyìshuì securities transaction tax

证券交易所 zhèngquàn jiāoyìsuǒ stock exchange; securities exchange

证券交易委员会 zhèngquàn jiāoyì wěiyuánhuì (US) Securities Exchange Commission (SEC)

证券交易指数 zhèngquàn jiāoyì zhǐshù stock exchange index

证券经纪人 zhèngquàn jīngjìrén bill broker; stock broker

证券经纪业 zhèngquàn jīngjìyè stock brokerage

证券融资 zhèngquàn róngzī securities finance

证券商 zhèngquànshāng stockjobber; securities dealer

证券市场 zhèngquàn shìchǎng securities market; stock market

证券投机 zhèngquàn tóujī speculation in securities

证券投资 zhèngquàn tóuzī investment in securities; portfolio investment

证券信托 zhèngquàn xìntuō securities trust

证券业 zhèngquànyè securities business

证券转让 zhèngquàn zhuǎnràng transfer of portfolio; securities transfer

证人 zhèngren ❶ witness: 传讯～ summon the witness for interrogation at a trial /～的证词对被告不利。The evidence given by the witness testifies against the accused. ❷ authenticator

证人席 zhèngrenxí witness-box; witness stand

证认 zhèngrèn identify; verify

证实 zhèngshí confirm; verify; establish: 这一消息的可靠性还有待～。The news remains to be confirmed (*or* authenticated). /目前的事态恰好～了我过去的预言。The present situation is precisely a confirmation of my previous predictions. /只有通过实践, 才能～真理。Truth can only be verified through practice. /我们已经～他无罪。We have established his innocence.

证书 zhèngshū certificate; testimonial; credentials: 发给毕业～ grant sb. a diploma /领取合格～ receive a quality certificate (*or* certificate of inspection)

证书审查委员会 zhèngshū shěnchá wěiyuánhuì credentials committee

证物 zhèngwù 〈法律〉exhibit (produced in court as evidence): 唯一的～ only exhibit /寻觅有力的～ look for effective exhibits

证言 zhèngyán verbal evidence; (oral) testimony; deposition; witness

证验 zhèngyàn ❶ test and verify: ～书本知识 test and verify one's book knowledge (*or* learning) ❷ intended effect; desired result: 这种药没有～。The medicine is ineffective.

证章 zhèngzhāng badge: 佩戴～ wear a badge

政 zhèng ❶ politics; government; political affairs: 执～ be in power (*or* office) /从～ engage in politics /参～ participate in government administration /议～ discuss state affairs /军～领导 heads of government and army /精兵简～ better troops and simpler administration ❷ administrative affairs of certain government departments: 邮～ postal service /民～ civil administration /市～当局 municipal authorities /财～部长 Minister of Finance ❸ affairs of a family or an organization: 家～ household management /校～ school administration ❹ (Zhèng) a surname

政变 zhèngbiàn coup d'état; coup: 发动～ mount (*or* stage) a coup d'état /平息～ put down (*or* suppress) a coup d'état /阴谋策划～ hatch a coup plot

政柄 zhèngbǐng 〈书面〉political power: 这个家族三世执掌～。The family was in power for three generations.

政策 zhèngcè policy: 制定～ formulate a policy /落实～ implement (*or* apply) a policy /纠正执行～中的偏差 correct deviations made in carrying out a policy

政策性补贴 zhèngcèxìng bǔtiē subsidies granted for policy consideration

政策性亏损 zhèngcèxìng kuīsǔn policy-related losses

政策性银行 zhèngcèxìng yínháng policy bank

政潮 zhèngcháo political fluctuation: 股票行情随着～而涨落。The stock market rises and falls with the turn of the political tide.

政出多门 zhèngchūduōmén lack of unified authority; (confusing) multiple leadership; contradictory policies resulting from conflicting departmental interests

政党 zhèngdǎng political party; party: 组织～ organize a political party /～政治 party politics

政敌 zhèngdí political foe: 两个人是势不两立的～。As political opponents they are at loggerheads with each other.

政法 zhèngfǎ politics and law: ～人员 procurators and judicial and public security officers /～学院 institute of political science and law

政法机关 zhèngfǎ jīguān procuratorial, judicial and public security organs or organizations

政府 zhèngfǔ government: 各级地方～ governments at various levels /市～ municipal government /中央人民～ Central People's Government /美国～ US Administration /军～ military junta /流亡～ government-in-exile /～工作人员 public (*or* civil) servant; government personnel /～公债 government bonds; government securities

政府部门 zhèngfǔ bùmén government departments or authorities

政府代表 zhèngfǔ dàibiǎo government representative

政府发言人 zhèngfǔ fāyánrén government spokesperson

政府公文 zhèngfǔ gōngwén government documents

政府官员 zhèngfǔ guānyuán government official
政府机构 zhèngfǔ jīgòu government apparatus or structure
政府机关 zhèngfǔ jīguān government agencies or bodies; government organizations:～人数分流一半 transfer (*or* re-direct) half of the government functionaries to other posts
政府间组织 zhèngfǔjiān zǔzhī intergovernmental organizations
政府人士 zhèngfǔ rénshì government circles
政府首脑 zhèngfǔ shǒunǎo head of government
政府新闻处 Zhèngfǔ Xīnwénchù (HK) Information Services Department
政纲 zhènggāng (short for 政治纲领) political programme; platform:制定～ draw up a political programme /公布～ publish a platform
政工 zhènggōng (short for 政治工作) political work:～人员 political worker
政工师 zhènggōngshī (used in professional ranking) human relations coordinator
政工组 zhènggōngzǔ political work office or section
政躬 zhènggōng 〈书面〉〈敬词〉(used of a politician, esp. one's political boss or superior) your health:倾闻近日～违和。I learned that you have been indisposed lately.
政纪 zhèngjì government discipline:整肃～ straighten up government discipline
政绩 zhèngjì achievements in one's political career:～不佳 have little credit to claim in one's political career /颇有～ have many achievements to one's credit in one's political career
政简刑清 zhèngjiǎn-xíngqīng simple government that ensures social stability and popular content
政见 zhèngjiàn political view:～相同 share the same political view /～各异 (people) of different political persuasions /持不同～者 (political) dissidents
政教分离 zhèng-jiào fēnlí separation of church and state; separation of religion from politics
政教合一 zhèng-jiào héyī integration of church and state
政界 zhèngjiè political circles; government circles:～人士 political figures; government circles /～元老 political elders; elder statesmen
政局 zhèngjú political situation; political scene:～动荡 turbulent political scene /～不稳。The political situation was volatile.
政客 zhèngkè politician; demagogue:～作风 ways of a demagogue; demagoguery /玩弄～手腕 play politics
政历 zhènglì (short for 政治历史) political history; political record
政令 zhènglìng government decree or order:～严明 stern and impartial government decree:～不畅。Government orders are often blocked.
政论 zhènglùn political comment:发表～ make political comments /撰写～文 write a political essay /著名的～家 famous (*or* renowned) political essayist (*or* commentator)
政派 zhèngpài political grouping; faction:这个国家虽小,但～众多。Small as it is, the country has a great many political factions.
政企责任分开 zhèng-qǐ zérèn fēnkāi *also* "政企分开" separation of the functions or responsibilities of the enterprises from those of the government; detachment of enterprises from the government
政情 zhèngqíng political situation:观察～ follow the political developments
政权 zhèngquán ❶ political power; state power; regime:夺取～ seize state power /掌握～ be in power; be at the helm /巩固～ consolidate political power /丧失～ lose (*or* forfeit) political power ❷ organs of political power; state organs:建立各级～ establish organs of state power at various levels
政权机关 zhèngquán jīguān agencies or organs of political or state power; state agencies or organs
政权交接 zhèngquán jiāojiē transfer of government
政审 zhèngshěn (short for 政治审查) examine sb.'s political record; be vetted for one's political background
政声 zhèngshēng 〈旧语〉official's reputation for his or her administration:这个县长～甚佳。The county magistrate enjoys an excellent political reputation.
政事 zhèngshì government affairs:不亲～ do not manage (*or* attend to) government affairs personally
政书 zhèngshū books that record government decrees and regulations, etc.
政坛 zhèngtán political arena:～人物 political figure /～新星 rising star in the political arena
政体 zhèngtǐ system of government; form of government:这两国～不同。The two countries have different government systems.
政通人和 zhèngtōng-rénhé good government and harmonious people:现在中国是～,百废俱兴。At present, with a good government and a united people China is forging ahead in every field of endeavour.
政委 zhèngwěi (short for 政治委员) political commissar (of a PLA regiment and above); commissar:师～ division commissar /副～ vice commissar
政务 zhèngwù administrative affairs; government affairs or administration:总揽～ assume overall responsibility of government affairs /～参赞 counsellor for political affairs /～繁忙 be busy with administrative affairs
政务次长 zhèngwù cìzhǎng (Taiwan Province) political vice minister
政务官 zhèngwùguān (Taiwan Province) political appointee
政务科 Zhèngwùkē (HK) District Administration Branch
政务司司长 Zhèngwùsī sīzhǎng (HK) Chief Secretary for Administration:第一任～陈方安生 first Chief Secretary for Administration Anson Chan
政务院 zhèngwùyuàn Government Administrative Council (replaced by the State Council in 1954):～总理 premier of the Government Administrative Council
政务总署 Zhèngwù Zǒngshǔ (HK) Home Affairs Branch
政协 zhèngxié (short for 政治协商会议) political consultative conference
政争 zhèngzhēng political struggle:～幕后人物 string-puller of political struggles /～工具 cat's paw of political strife
政治 zhèngzhì politics; political affairs:～活动 political activities /～表现 political behaviour; political record /～态度 political attitude (*or* approach) /～团体 political organization /～任务 political task /～形势 political situation (*or* scene) /～运动 political movement (*or* campaign) /～阴谋 political intrigue (*or* plot, *or* scheme) /～气候 political climate /～基础 political basis /～生活 political life /～活动家 political activist /～责任感 sense of political responsibility /～思想教育 political and ideological education /～合格 be politically qualified
政治罢工 zhèngzhì bàgōng political strike
政治背景 zhèngzhì bèijǐng political background
政治庇护 zhèngzhì bìhù political asylum:寻求～ seek political asylum
政治避难 zhèngzhì bìnàn political refuge; political asylum
政治部 zhèngzhìbù political department
政治待遇 zhèngzhì dàiyù treatment due to political status; political seniority
政治独立 zhèngzhì dúlì political independence
政治多元化 zhèngzhì duōyuánhuà political pluralism
政治犯 zhèngzhìfàn political offender; political prisoner
政治纲领 zhèngzhì gānglǐng political programme; platform
政治工作 zhèngzhì gōngzuò political work
政治顾问处 Zhèngzhì Gùwènchù (HK) Political Adviser Office
政治挂帅 zhèngzhì guàshuài put politics in command
政治机器 zhèngzhì jīqì political machine
政治集团 zhèngzhì jítuán political group
政治纪律 zhèngzhì jìlǜ political discipline
政治家 zhèngzhìjiā statesman:受人爱戴的～ beloved statesman /富有远见卓识的～ statesman of foresight and sagacity
政治教导员 zhèngzhì jiàodǎoyuán *also* "教导员" political instructor (of a PLA battalion)
政治经济学 zhèngzhì jīngjìxué political economy
政治局 Zhèngzhìjú Political Bureau (of the CPC):～常委 member of the Standing Committee of the Political Bureau /～委员 member of the Political Bureau
政治觉悟 zhèngzhì juéwù political consciousness or awareness; political understanding
政治立场 zhèngzhì lìchǎng political stand
政治路线 zhèngzhì lùxiàn political line
政治面目 zhèngzhì miànmù political affiliation; political background:查一查～ check up on one's political affiliation (*or* background)
政治派别 zhèngzhì pàibié political grouping; faction

Z

政治权利 zhèngzhì quánlì political rights
政治实体 zhèngzhì shítǐ political entity
政治体制 zhèngzhì tǐzhì political structure：～改革 political restructuring
政治危机 zhèngzhì wēijī political crisis
政治委员 zhèngzhì wěiyuán *also* "政委" political commissar (of a PLA regiment and above)
政治文化 zhèngzhì wénhuà political culture
政治舞台 zhèngzhì wǔtái political arena or scene; political stage
政治协理员 zhèngzhì xiélǐyuán political assistant (of a PLA regiment and above)
政治协商会议 zhèngzhì xiéshāng huìyì *also* "政协" political consultative conference：四川省～ Sichuan Political Consultative Conference /第六届中国人民～第一次会议 First Session of the Sixth Chinese People's Political Consultative Conference
政治心理学 zhèngzhì xīnlǐxué political psychology
政治信仰 zhèngzhì xìnyǎng political conviction; political belief
政治性 zhèngzhìxìng political nature
政治嗅觉 zhèngzhì xiùjué political acumen or sensitiveness; political sense of smell：具有敏锐的～ have a keen political sense of smell
政治学 zhèngzhìxué political science; science of government
政治哲学 zhèngzhì zhéxué political philosophy
政治指导员 zhèngzhì zhǐdǎoyuán political instructor (of a PLA company)
政治制度 zhèngzhì zhìdù political system; system of government

阐

zhèng
阐闼 zhèngchuài *see* "挣揣" zhèngchuài

诤

zhèng 〈书面〉 criticise frankly; expostulate; remonstrate; admonish：苦～ earnestly admonish
诤谏 zhèngjiàn 〈书面〉 criticise frankly; remonstrate; admonish：我很感激他的直言～。I was grateful for his forthright remonstration with me.
诤言 zhèngyán 〈书面〉 frank criticism; forthright admonition or remonstration：好友的～ frank criticism offered by one's good friend
诤友 zhèngyǒu 〈书面〉 friend who will give forthright admonition or expostulation：你真是我的良师～。You are both a good teacher and a helpful friend to me.

挣[1]

zhèng struggle to get free; try to shake off：他把捆绑的绳子～开了。He broke loose the rope that bound him.

挣[2]

zhèng get by one's labour; earn; make：～生活费 earn money to cover one's living expenses /～碗饭吃 earn (*or* make) a living; make (*or* earn) one's bread /他这几年可是～了。These years he has made a lot of money.
see also zhēng
挣揣 zhèngchuài 〈书面〉 struggle; strive
挣命 zhèngmìng struggle to save one's life; work flat out：那人正在水里～。The man was floundering desperately in the water. /这么大岁数，别～了！At your age, you must not work flat out any more!
挣钱 zhèngqián earn or make money：～交学费 earn money to pay tuition fee /他要养家糊口，得拼命～。He has a family to support and must strive to make as much money as he can.
挣生 zhèngshēng 〈方言〉 make ends meet：在城里打工～也不易啊！It is by no means easy eking out a living by working in the city.
挣脱 zhèngtuō throw off; break away from：～枷锁 throw off shackles

铮

zhèng 〈方言〉 dazzling; shining：玻璃窗擦得～亮。The window panes are dazzling after cleaning.
see also zhēng

Z

zhī

汁

zhī juice：果～ fruit juice /柠檬～ lemon juice /番茄～ tomato juice /牛肉～ beef extract /豆～ fermented drink made from ground beans /乳～ milk /菠萝～ pineapple milk /墨～ prepared Chinese ink /胆～ bile /毒～ venom
汁水 zhīshui 〈方言〉 juice：这种橘子～很多。The orange is juicy.
汁液 zhīyè juice

之[1]

zhī 〈书面〉 go to：不知所～ not knowing where to go /由京～宁 leave Beijing for Nanjing /心之所～ where one longs to be

之[2]

zhī 〈书面〉 ❶ *used in place of a person or thing as an object*：言～无物 speech devoid of substance /学而时习～ learn and constantly review what one has learned /取而代～ replace (*or* supersede) someone /求～不得的好机会 most welcome opportunity /无不为～高兴。Everybody feels excited about it. /生活是文艺创作取～不尽，用～不竭的源泉。Life is the inexhaustible source of literary and artistic creation. ❷ *without actual reference*：总～ to sum up; in short; in a word /生死共～ live and die together /久而久～ with the passage of time /谚有～曰… As the saying goes... /我最喜欢喝茶，咖啡次～。I like tea best and coffee second best. ❸ this; that：～人也，～德也 this kind of man and this kind of behaviour /～二虫又何知? What can these two creatures understand?

之[3]

zhī 〈书面〉 ❶ *used to connect the modifier and the word modified*：赤子～心 pure heart of a newborn babe /大灾～年 year of a great natural calamity /以子～矛，攻子～盾 beat sb. with his own weapon /汝～过也。You are to blame. *or* This is your fault. /以其人～道，还治其人～身 pay somebody back in his own coin; do unto somebody as he does unto others /千岛～国 country of a thousand islands /光荣～家 honourable family /意料～中 as was expected /缓兵～计 stalling tactics /应享～权利，应尽～义务 the rights one is entitled to enjoy, the obligations one is bound to fulfil ❷ *placed between the subject and the predicate to express subordination*：皮～不存，毛将焉附? With the skin gone, to what can the hair attach itself? /世界～大，无奇不有。Nothing is too strange in this big world. /此次改革声势～大，范围～广，影响～深，都是前所未有的。This reform is unprecedented in momentum, in scope and in the profound influence it exerts.
之后 zhīhòu later; after; afterwards; thereafter：毕业～，她留校任教。She became a teacher in her alma mater after graduation. /～，他们的往来便密切起来了。They have been in close contact since then. /～我们在花园里吃午饭。Afterwards we had lunch in the garden. /两年～再会。See you again in two years.
之乎者也 zhī-hū-zhě-yě literary jargon; pedantic terms; pedantries; archaisms：他满口～，令人发笑。He mouthed so many pedantic terms that people could not help laughing.
之间 zhījiān between; among：我们～没有任何分歧。There is no divergence of views between us. /小镇坐落在群山～。The small town is located among the hills.
之类 zhīlèi or the like; and so on; and so forth：火车、公共汽车～的交通工具 trains, buses, or the like /他找了许多借口，房子太少，人太多～。He found many excuses: too few rooms, too many people, and what not.
之流 zhīliú 〈贬义〉 and his like：希特勒～ Hitler and his ilk
之内 zhīnèi in; within：在法律许可的范围～ within the limits permitted by law /三天～完成。Get the work done in three days.
之前 zhīqián ago; before; prior to：我是两年～认识她的。I came to know her two years ago. /看样子天黑～不会下雨。It seems that it won't rain before dark. /今天～她在巴黎。She was in Paris until today.
之上 zhīshàng over; above：在平均水平～ be above the average /一个自以为高踞于法律～的君主 a monarch who thought himself above the law
之死靡它 zhīsǐ-mǐtā be loyal or faithful to one's lover unto death
之外 zhīwài besides; except; beyond; outside：除月薪～，他还有奖金。Besides (*or* In addition to) the monthly salary he gets some bonus as well. *or* He gets some bonus over and above his monthly wage. /除了他最亲密的朋友～，没有人知道那件事。Nobody, except his most intimate friends, knows of it. /除天公不作美～，我们过得很愉快。We had a very pleasant time, except for the weather. /除指示我做的工作～，其他的我一概不干。I will do nothing beyond what I am told to do. /这在我计划～。That is outside my plan.
之下 zhīxià under; beneath：普天～ all under heaven /光天化日～ in broad daylight /上尉的军阶在少校～。A captain is beneath a major.

之无 zhīwú characters 之 and 无 — simplest and most common characters: 不识～ know not how to read and write; be illiterate

之中 zhīzhōng in; in the midst of; among: 生活在群众～ live among the masses /他是我们～的一员。He is one of us. /这在我们意料～。That's what we expected.

之字路 zhīzìlù zigzag course; S curve in a road

芝

zhī 〈古语〉❶ glossy ganoderma (*Ganoderma lucidum*) ❷ root of Dahurian angelica

芝艾俱焚 zhī'ài-jùfén iris and artemisia are burnt together — the honourable and lowly perished together; the good perishes with the bad

芝焚蕙叹 zhīfén-huìtàn the orchid sighs at the burning of the iris — sympathize with one's kind

芝加哥 Zhījiāgē Chicago, third largest city of the United States on Lake Michigan

芝加哥谷物交易所 Zhījiāgē Gǔwù Jiāoyìsuǒ Chicargo Board of Trade (CBOT)

芝加哥期权交易所 Zhījiāgē Qīquán Jiāoyìsuǒ Chicargo Board of Options Exchange (CBOE)

芝加哥商业交易所 Zhījiāgē Shāngyè Jiāoyìsuǒ Chicargo Mercantile Exchange (CME)

芝兰 zhīlán irises and orchids (used by ancients to symbolize noble character, true friendship, or beautiful surroundings): 如入～之室 like going into a room full of fragrant orchids — benefit from associating with people of a noble character

芝兰玉树 zhīlán-yùshù fine children; people of perfection

芝麻 zhīma *also* "脂麻" zhīma ❶ sesame ❷ sesame seed: 拣了～,丢了西瓜 pick up the sesame seeds but overlook the watermelons — concentrate on minor details to the neglect of major issues; penny wise and pound foolish

芝麻菜 zhīmacài roquette; rocket salad (*Eruca vesicaria sativa*)

芝麻官 zhīmaguān (used sarcastically) petty government official: 七品～ petty government official of the seventh rank (in dynastic times)

芝麻糊 zhīmahù sweetened sesame paste

芝麻酱 zhīmajiàng *also* "麻酱" sesame paste

芝麻街 Zhīmajiē Sesame Street, an educational TV series for preschool children, first screened in 1969 in the United States

芝麻开花节节高 zhīma kāihuā jiéjié gāo shoot up higher and higher like sesame flowers — (of living standards, etc.) rise steadily

芝麻糖 zhīmatáng sesame candy

芝麻油 zhīmayóu *also* "香油" xiāngyóu; "麻油" sesame oil

支[1]

zhī ❶ prop up; set up: 把布景～起来 prop the stage scenery /屋里临时～张床 set up a makeshift bed in the room /把病人的头用枕头～住 prop up the patient's head by putting pillows behind it ❷ protrude; raise; prick up: 两颗大牙朝外～着 with two protruding teeth ❸ sustain; stand; bear: 体力不～ too tired to go on doing sth.; too weak physically to stand it /乐不可～ overwhelmed with joy; overjoyed /吃这么一点怎么～得了一天? How can such a light meal sustain you through the day? /他牙疼得真有点～不住了。He could hardly bear the toothache any more. ❹ send away; put sb. off; order about: 他把记者～开。He put the reporters off (*or* sent the reporters away) with some excuses. /干吗老把别人～来～去的? Why always order people about? /他自己不动手,老是～别人。He always bosses others about instead of doing the work himself. ❺ pay out or draw (money): 预～两个月工资 get two months' pay in advance /开～ expenses /透～ overdraw; make an overdraft /超～ overspend /本月收～平衡。Revenue and expenditure are balanced this month. ❻ (Zhī) a surname

支[2]

zhī ❶ branch; offshoot: 分～机构 branch institutions /中国人民银行东单～行 Chinese People's Bank, Dongdan Sub-branch ❷ 〈量词〉(a) *of army units*: 一～军队 an army contingent (b) *of songs*: 唱一～民歌 sing a folk song /一～动人的乐曲 a melodious musical composition (c) *of watts*: 二十五～光的灯泡 a 25-watt bulb (d) *textile counts*: 一百～纱 100-count yarn /细～棉纱 fine count yarn (e) *for long, thin, inflexible objects*: 一～铅笔 a pencil

支[3]

zhī twelve earthly branches (used in combination with the heavenly stems to designate years, etc.)

支边 zhībiān support the border area; go and help with the development of the border regions: 大力～,开辟中西部和沿海地区交流的渠道 make great efforts to support the border areas by opening up channels for economic interchange between the middle-west and the coast

支部 zhībù ❶ branch of political parties or organizations: 民盟～ branch of the China Democratic League ❷ branch of the Chinese Communist Party or the Chinese Communist Youth League: 党～ Party branch / 团～ League branch /～大会 general membership meeting of the branch /～书记 branch secretary

支差 zhīchāi 〈旧语〉do enforced and unpaid work for the government or landlord

支撑 zhīchēng ❶ prop up; hold up; sustain; support: 这四根柱子～着整个建筑物。These four posts sustain the entire building. /这桥～得住载重卡车吗? Is the bridge strong enough to support heavy lorries? ❷ be barely able to; maintain; shore up: 全家人的生活由他一人～着。He is supporting the whole family all by himself. /他们力图～一个摇摇欲坠的政权。They strove to shore up a tottering regime. /他确实～不住了。He could hardly hold himself up. /老奶奶～着坐了起来。Old grandma propped herself up into a sitting position. ❸ 〈建筑〉strut; brace: ～系大梁 braced girder

支撑点 zhīchēngdiǎn 〈军事〉strong point; centre of resistance: ～式防御 defence by strong point

支承 zhīchéng 〈机械〉supporting; bearing; backup: ～点 bearing point /～力 supporting force /～圈 backup ring; support ring /～面积 area of bearing /大跨度屋顶结构,四面～的效果较好。The large-span-roof structure is well supported on all sides.

支持 zhīchí ❶ hold out; bear up; sustain: 我累得～不住了。I'm too tired to hold out any longer. /我今天不舒服,但还能～。I'm not feeling well today, but can manage to bear up. /这些食品可以～几天? How many days can the food sustain you? ❷ support; back; stand up for; be in favour of: ～各国人民的正义斗争 support the just struggles of the people of all countries /许多有权有势的人都大力～他。Many influential people gave him strong backing. /他认为正确的,他就～。He stands up for what he thinks is right. /议会中的自由党人～政府。The Liberals in Parliament came out in favour of the government. /我们～这种理论。We espouse (*or* are all for) this theory.

支持产业 zhīchí chǎnyè supporting industries (in an industry complex)

支出 zhīchū ❶ pay (money); spend; expend: ～七十元房租 pay 70 *yuan* for the room rent /他们已～一万美元的广告费。They have already spent $10,000 in advertising. ❷ expenses; expenditure; outlay; disbursement: 教育～ expenditure on education /追加～ supplementary expenditure /～超过自己的财力 overspending /～凭证检查 examination of disbursement vouchers /～大于收入。The expenses exceed the income.

支绌 zhīchù (of funds) not enough; inadequate; insufficient: 由于经费～,不得不压缩编制 have to reduce the staff due to shortage of funds

支词 zhīcí *also* "枝辞" zhīcí flowery words

支单 zhīdān certificate for drawing money; voucher

支点 zhīdiǎn ❶ 〈物理〉fulcrum ❷ strongpoint; fortified point; stronghold: 战略～ strategic strongpoint

支电缆 zhīdiànlǎn 〈电工〉branch cable

支队 zhīduì ❶ detachment (corresponding to a regiment or division): 独立～ independent detachment ❷ military unit organized temporarily for a certain purpose: 先遣～ advance military unit

支墩坝 zhīdūnbà 〈水利〉buttress dam

支付 zhīfù pay (money); defray: ～房租 pay rent /～旅行费用 defray the expenses of the trip /从福利费中～ be paid out of the welfare fund /立即～ immediate payment /现金～ payment in cash; cash payment /～能力 capacity to pay; payment capacity; paying ability /～手段 means of payment /～协定 payments agreement /～额 amount paid

支杆 zhīgān support bar

支工 zhīgōng support industry

支管 zhīguǎn branch; branch ducts; branch pipe

支行 zhīháng sub-branch (of a bank)

支护 zhīhù prop up (roof of a pit, pit shaft, etc.)

支唤 zhīhuàn 〈方言〉 order about or around:吃着人家的饭,就得听人家的~。He who accepts food from others must accept their orders (*or* dance to their tune). *or* He who pays the piper calls the tune.

支架 zhījià ❶ support; stand; trestle:自行车~ prop stand of a bicycle /照相机~ camera stand ❷ prop up; put up:~屋梁 prop up the roof beam /~帐篷 put up a tent ❸ ward off blows; withstand:寡不敌众,~不住 fight against hopeless odds ❹ 〈美术〉 armature

支教 zhījiào support educational undertakings; go to the rural or remote areas to help promote local education:去年我校有四名教师到西藏~。Four teachers from our college went to Tibet last year to help with the local educational undertakings.

支解 zhījiě *also* "肢解" zhījiě dismember:~遗骸 dismember the remains /这个国家被~。The country was dismembered.

支局 zhījú branch office;〈通信〉 satellite exchange

支矿脉 zhīkuàngmài 〈矿业〉 dropper; branched lode; feeder

支棱 zhīleng 〈方言〉 prick up (one's ears); stick up; bend upwards; turn upwards:听见人家说他,他~着耳朵听。He pricked up his ears when he heard some people talking about him. /他的头发都~着。His hair sticks straight up (*or* stands on end).

支离 zhīlí ❶ fragmented; broken; disconnected ❷ (of writing) wordy and jumbled; incoherent

支离破碎 zhīlí-pòsuì broken up; shattered; fragmented; (of argument) occupied with unimportant details:这个家早已~了。The family has been broken up. /单凭这些~的材料,很难下结论。It is difficult to reach a conclusion on such scrappy information alone.

支链 zhīliàn 〈化学〉 branch:~化合物 branched (chain) compound /~烃 branched bydrocarbon

支链反应 zhīliàn fǎnyìng *also* "链式反应" liànshì fǎnyìng 〈化学〉 chain reaction

支领 zhīlǐng receive; draw; get:~军粮 receive army provisions

支流 zhīliú ❶ tributary; branch:大河的主要~ main branch of a river /淮河的~ tributaries of the Huaihe River ❷ minor aspects; minor current; nonessentials:看问题时,要分清主流和~。In considering a problem, one must distinguish between the essentials and nonessentials.

支炉儿 zhīlúr earthern pan with holes, used over an oven for baking cakes

支路 zhīlù ❶ side road; byroad ❷ 〈电工〉 branch; branch circuit; branch line; branch path:~电流 branch current /~开关 branch switch

支脉 zhīmài offshoot (of a mountain range); branch range:昆仑山的~ branch range of the Kunlun Mountains

支蔓 zhīmàn *also* "枝蔓" zhīmàn complicated and jumbled

支那 Zhīnà *Zhina*, an ancient translation for 中国(China), later used by the Japanese as a derogatory term

支农 zhīnóng support agriculture; supply the needs of agriculture:下乡~ go to the countryside to aid agriculture /~工业 aid-agriculture industries /~产品 goods produced to support agriculture; products serving the needs of agriculture

支派 zhīpài ❶ branch; division; sect; offshoot ❷ order; send; dispatch:我们不受别人的~。We are not to be ordered about. /厂长~小王去采购钢板。The factory director sent Xiao Wang to purchase steel plates.

支配 zhīpèi ❶ allocate; arrange; dispose:善于~劳力 be good at allocating the work force /合理地~时间 arrange one's time properly; make good use of one's time /下午的时间由个人~。The afternoons will be free. /这笔贷款由地方政府~。The loan is at the disposition of the local authorities. ❷ control; determine; dominate; govern:他在偏见的~下做了蠢事。Swayed by prejudice, he did something foolish. /人体的活动受大脑~。Movements of the body are directed by the cerebrum. /思想~行动。Thinking determines action.

支配权 zhīpèiquán right of disposal; dominative power

支票 zhīpiào cheque; check:开一张两千元的~ write a cheque for 2,000 *yuan* /~兑现 cash a cheque /未兑现~ outstanding cheque /划线~ crossed cheque /空白~ blank cheque /空头~ rubber cheque; 〈比喻〉 empty promise /来人~ bearer cheque; cheque to bearer /保付~ certified cheque /不记名~ cheque payable to bearer /记名~ order cheque /转账~ cheque only for account; cheque for transfer /旅行~ traveller's cheque /~簿 chequebook /~票根 stub of a cheque; counterfoil

支票兑现机 zhīpiào duìxiànjī check-cashing machine

支票外交 zhīpiào wàijiāo checkbook diplomacy

支气管 zhīqìguǎn bronchus

支气管肺炎 zhīqìguǎn fèiyán branchopneumonia

支气管痉挛 zhīqìguǎn jìngluán bronchial spasm; bronchospasm

支气管镜检查 zhīqìguǎn jìngjiǎnchá bronchoscopy

支气管扩张 zhīqìguǎn kuòzhāng bronchiectasis

支气管腺瘤 zhīqìguǎn xiànliú bronchial adenoma

支气管性气喘 zhīqìguǎnxìng qìchuǎn bronchial asthma

支气管炎 zhīqìguǎnyán bronchitis

支气管周炎 zhīqìguǎn zhōuyán perikronchitis

支前 zhīqián support the front:~模范 model in supporting the front

支渠 zhīqú branch (irrigation) canal

支取 zhīqǔ draw (money); receive:~工资 draw one's pay /~经费 receive funds

支使 zhīshi ❶ order about; boss about:他特会~人。He is always ordering people about. ❷ send to another place; send away; put sb. off:把他~走。Send him away with an excuse.

支书 zhīshū secretary of a Party or League branch; branch secretary

支枢 zhīshū 〈机械〉 pivot

支数 zhīshù 〈纺织〉 number (of yarn); count:纱线~ yarn number; yarn size /~不均率 size variation

支腾 zhīteng 〈方言〉 ❶ sustain; keep up; last:这笔费用足够~到年底。This sum of money is enough to last (us) till the end of the year. ❷ delay; put off:这件事不能老~着不办。The matter should not be put off again and again.

支委 zhīwěi member of a Party or Youth League branch committee

支吾 zhīwu hedge; equivocate; prevaricate; hum and haw:一味~ be evasive throughout /别站在那儿支支吾吾的,快说出来。Don't stand humming and hawing, but speak out.

支吾其词 zhīwu-qící speak equivocally; be evasive in speech

支线 zhīxiàn branch line; feeder (line):铁路~ feeder railway /公路~ feeder highway /~运输港 feeder service ports /~运输系统 feeder system

支颐 zhīyí 〈书面〉 rest one's chin on one's hand (*or* in one's hands):~默想 be lost in deep thoughts with one's chin resting in one's hands /~养神 sit in repose, resting one's chin on one's hand

支应 zhīyìng ❶ manage; handle; deal with:~差事 do an errand /事太多,我~不过来。There is more work than I can cope with. ❷ supply:~粮草 supply rations and fodder ❸ care for; wait on; attend to:今天店里我来~。I shall attend to the customers in the shop today.

支原体 zhīyuántǐ mycoplasma:肺炎~ mycoplasma pneumoniae /~病 mycoplasmosis

支援 zhīyuán support; aid; assist; help:我们要互相~。We should help and support each other. /全国~灾区。People all over the country gave a helping hand to the disaster area. /感谢你们的大力~。Thank you for your generous assistance.

支援部队 zhīyuán bùduì support unit; supporting troops

支援系统 zhīyuán xìtǒng 〈计算机〉 support system

支着儿 zhīzhāor *also* "支招儿" (usu. in chess-playing) watch a game of chess and give advice to a chess player; kibbitz:这一着儿支得不错。That's a good piece of advice (to the chess player).

支柱 zhīzhù ❶ pillar; prop:这里要撑上一根~。There should be a prop here to hold it up. ❷ 〈比喻〉 pillar; mainstay:他是教会的~。He is the pillar of the church. /父亲过世后,长子成了这个家庭的~。After the father's death the eldest son became the mainstay of the family.

支柱产业 zhīzhù chǎnyè *also* "支柱行业" pillar industries (in an industry complex)

支柱根 zhīzhùgēn 〈植物〉 prop root

支子 zhīzi ❶ stand; support:自行车~ kickstand of a bicycle ❷ gridiron (as a cooking utensil)

支嘴儿 zhīzuǐr 〈方言〉 give advice; advise:让他自己想点子,我们别~。We should not make any suggestions; let him think out a plan by himself.

支左 zhīzuǒ support the Left wing; support the broad masses of the Left (a term frequently used during the Cultural Revolution)

枝 zhī ❶ branch; twig: 树~ branches of a tree; tree branches /果~ fruit-bearing shoot; fruit branch; (of a cotton plant) boll-bearing branch /疯~ branch that bears no fruit /歇~ (of fruit trees) bear less fruit the year after a big crop /徒长~ excessive growth of branches /插~ plant (willows, etc.) by sticking branches into the soil /~繁叶茂 (of trees) with luxuriant foliage and spreading branches ❷〈量词〉*for flowers with stems intact*: 一~樱花 a spray of cherry blossoms ❸〈量词〉*for stick-like things*: 一~步枪 a rifle /三~钢笔 three pens /一~鱼竿 a fishing rod

枝插 zhīchā 〈林业〉stem cutting

枝杈 zhīchà branch; twig

枝辞 zhīcí 〈书面〉*also* "枝词";"支词" zhīcí redundant or flowery words: ~蔓语 lengthy and confused talk

枝根 zhīgēn ramose root

枝接 zhījiē 〈农业〉scion grafting

枝节 zhījié ❶ branches and knots — side issue; minor aspect: ~问题 side issue; trifle; trivial matter /那些枝枝节节的事,留待下次解决。Let's put those minor issues aside for another time. /我们不能从~谈问题。We cannot discuss the problem in bits and pieces. ❷ unexpected complications: 横生~ deliberately complicate an issue; raise unexpected difficulties

枝解 zhījiě *also* "支解" zhījiě dismemberment

枝晶 zhījīng 〈物理〉dendrite; dendrite crystal: ~体 dendritic crystal

枝柯 zhīkē 〈书面〉branches of a tree

枝蔓 zhīmàn branches and tendrils — complicated and confused; involved and jumbled: 写文章要紧紧围绕主旨,不可~旁生。When writing, one should try to drive the main points home, leaving out unnecessary and confusing details.

枝条 zhītiáo branch; twig: 修剪~ prune the twigs off

枝头 zhītóu on a branch: 硕果满~。The branches are weighed down with fruit.

枝梧 zhīwú *also* "枝捂";"支吾" zhīwu 〈书面〉equivocate; hum and haw

枝桠 zhīyā *also* "枝丫" branch; twig

枝叶 zhīyè ❶ branches and leaves: 那大树~茂盛。The big tree is a mass of branches and leaves. ❷ nonessentials; trifles; minor details

枝状闪电 zhīzhuàng shǎndiàn streak lightning

枝子 zhīzi branch; twig

吱 zhī 〈象声〉creak: 嘎~作响的竹椅 creaky bamboo chair /楼梯的嘎~嘎~声 creak in the stairs /牛车~地一声停住了。The oxcart creaked to a stop.

see also zī

肢 zhī limb: 上~ upper limbs; arms /下~ lower limbs; legs /假~ artificial limb /前~ forelimbs (of an animal or insect) /后~ hind limbs (of an animal or insect)

肢端肥大症 zhīduān féidàzhèng acromegaly

肢端硬化病 zhīduān yìnghuàbìng acrosclerosis

肢解 zhījiě *also* "支解" zhījiě dismemberment

肢势 zhīshì 〈畜牧〉standing or erect posture (of domestic animals)

肢体 zhītǐ ❶ limbs ❷ limbs and trunk: ~健壮 healthy body

肢体语言 zhītǐ yǔyán 〈婉词〉come to blows; free fight

肢痛症 zhītòngzhèng acrodynia

榰 zhī 〈书面〉❶ stone or wooden base of a column ❷ prop up; strut

只(隻) zhī ❶ isolated; single; one only: 片纸~字 slip of paper with a few isolated words on it — just a brief note ❷〈量词〉(a) *for one of a pair*: 一~手套 one glove /一~鞋 one shoe /两~耳朵 two ears (b) *for certain animals, birds*: 一~猫 one cat /六~燕子 six swallows (c) *for certain containers*: 四~皮箱 four leather suitcases (*or* trunks) (d) *for certain boats*: 一~小船 a boat /一~橡皮筏 a rubber raft

see also zhǐ

只轮不返 zhīlún-bùfǎn not a single chariot wheel returns — destruction of the whole army; overwhelming defeat

只身 zhīshēn alone; solitarily; all by oneself: ~在外 be alone and far away from home /~幸免 be the sole survivor /~孤影 all alone; in solitude

只言片语 zhīyán-piànyǔ a word or two: 他离家时竟没留下~。He left home without leaving behind even a single line. /虽是~,却情深意长。Though written in a few words, the message conveys deep affection.

只字不提 zhīzì-bùtí not say a single word (about sth.); not breathe a word (about sth.): 对那件事他~。He did not mention it at all. /那本书对他的历史功绩~。His contributions in history have been completely ignored in that book.

织(織) zhī ❶ weave: 纺~ spinning and weaving /纺~品 textile; fabric /~地毯 weave rugs /~席编履 make mats and straw sandals ❷ knit: ~围巾 knit a scarf /钩~ crochet

织边 zhībiān 〈纺织〉selvage; selvedge

织补 zhībǔ darning; invisible mending: ~袜子 darn (holes in) socks /她善~。She darns well. /你能看得出我毛衣上~过的地方吗? Can you see the darn in my sweater?

织布 zhībù weave cloth; weave: 纺纱~ spin and weave /~工 weaver

织布鸟 zhībùniǎo weaverbird

织带机 zhīdàijī inkle loom; webbing loom

织花 zhīhuā woven pattern (in fabrics)

织机 zhījī loom: 多梭箱~ multiple box loom /自动~ automatic loom /自动换梭~ shuttleless loom /喷气~ jet loom /格子布~ check loom

织锦 zhījǐn ❶ brocade ❷ in silk: 一幅精美的~画 an elegant picture woven in silk

织锦厂 zhījǐnchǎng brocade mill

织锦缎 zhījǐnduàn tapestry satin

织女 zhīnǚ ❶ woman weaver ❷ (Zhīnǚ) Weaver Girl or Spinning Damsel in the legend "The Cowherd and the Weaver Girl"

织女星 Zhīnǚxīng 〈天文〉Vega (in the constellation Lyra)

织品 zhīpǐn textile; fabric

织袜机 zhīwàjī hosiery machine

织物 zhīwù fabric: 机织~ woven fabric /棉~ cotton fabrics /毛~ wollen fabrics /麻~ linen /混纺~ mixture fabric; blend fabric /黏合~ bonded fibre fabric /绣花~ embroidered fabric /~经纬密度 thread count /~耐磨试验 wear testing

织造 zhīzào (machine-)weaving

织造厂 zhīzàochǎng weaving mill

织针 zhīzhēn knitting needle

织轴 zhīzhóu 〈纺织〉beam (of a loom)

知 zhī ❶ know; be aware (of): 略~兵法 have some knowledge of the art of war /~之为~之,不~为不~,是~也。If you know a thing, say you know it; if you don't know the thing, say you don't; this is true knowledge. *or* It is wise not to pretend to know what you don't know. /得~你将赴前线,特来送行。I've learned that you are going to the front, and here I am to see you off. /不~不为过。Ignorance is a valid excuse. ❷ inform; notify; tell; learn: 告~ inform; notify; tell ❸ knowledge; learning: 求~ seek knowledge /实践出真~。Genuine knowledge comes from practice. ❹〈书面〉intimate friend: 新~ new friend ❺〈旧语〉administer; be in charge of: *see* "~县"

知彼知己,百战不殆 zhī bǐ zhī jǐ, bǎi zhàn bù dài *also* "知己知彼,百战百胜" know the enemy and know yourself, and you can fight a hundred battles with no danger of defeat (*or* and you can win every battle you fight)

知宾 zhībīn 〈方言〉*see* "知客 ❶"

知耻 zhīchǐ have a sense of shame: 恬不~ have no sense of shame; be shameless /~近乎勇。Having a sense of shame is akin to courage.

知单 zhīdān 〈旧语〉invitation

知道 zhīdao know; realize; be aware of; wise up (to): ~内情 be in the secret; be on the inside /~事情的窍门 know the ropes /这个银行家~其利益所在。The banker understood on which side his bread was buttered. /他不~自己做错了。He is not aware of having done anything wrong. /我们~事态的严重性。We realize how serious the situation is. /到时你会~这儿的情况的。You'll wise up to what's going on here in good time.

知底 zhīdǐ know the inside story; possess inside information:这笔交易他～。He was on the inside in that deal.

知法犯法 zhīfǎ-fànfǎ know the law but break it; deliberately flout the law; knowingly violate the law:你这样做,完全是～。By doing that you wilfully flouted the law.

知法守法 zhīfǎ-shǒufǎ know the laws and abide by them

知府 zhīfǔ 〈历史〉magistrate of a prefecture:他曾任杭州～。He was once the magistrate of Hangzhou Prefecture.

知高识低 zhīgāo-shídī speak and act within proper limits; have sense of proportion in words and deeds

知根知底 zhīgēn-zhīdǐ know (sb. or sth.) through and through:我们是老朋友啦,彼此都～。We are old friends and know each other exceedingly well.

知更鸟 zhīgēngniǎo robin; redbreast

知过必改 zhīguò-bìgǎi correct one's mistake without fail when one becomes aware of it

知会 zhīhui 〈口语〉notify orally:你去～他一下,让他下午开会。Go and tell him that he is to be at a meeting in the afternoon.

知几 zhījī *also*"知机"〈书面〉sense what is coming:～观变 sense what is coming and watch the development of events

知己 zhījǐ ❶ on intimate terms; understanding:说点～话 exchange a few intimate words; have a heart-to-heart talk /他俩很～。They hit it off very well with each other. ❷ bosom friend:海内存～,天涯若比邻。A bosom friend afar brings the distance near. /人生得一～足矣! One may be content with but one friend whose heart he knows. /他眉飞色舞,像是遇到了～。He beamed delightedly, as if he had found a man after his heart.

知交 zhījiāo bosom or intimate friend; alter ego; second self:二人结为～。They became intimate friends. /他是我的～,我们一起度过童年,现在又一起上学。He is my second self; we were childhood playmates together and now are at school together.

知近 zhījìn intimate:～的亲友 intimate relatives and friends

知觉 zhījué ❶〈心理〉perception:～异常 abnormal perception ❷ consciousness:失去～ lose consciousness; pass out; go into a coma /恢复～ recover consciousness; come to oneself

知觉常性 zhījué chángxìng 〈心理〉perceptual constancies

知客 zhīkè ❶〈旧语〉*also*"知宾" person in charge of reception at ceremonies ❷ *also*"知客僧"〈佛教〉monk in charge of monastery receptions

知冷知热 zhīlěng-zhīrè look after sb. with meticulous care; be very considerate; feel for another person as for oneself:人总得有个亲人,～的人。Everyone needs the love and special care of his or her dear ones.

知了 zhīliǎo 〈动物〉cicada

知名 zhīmíng famous; renowned; noted; celebrated:～作家 famous writer /～人士 well-known (*or* noted) personage; eminent person; public figure; celebrity /海内外～ be well-known at home and abroad; be of great renown

知名度 zhīmíngdù extent to which a person is known to the public:颇具～ quite well-known to the public /在学术界他～很高。He is a famous figure in academic circles.

知命 zhīmìng 〈书面〉❶ know the will of heaven:～安身 be contented with one's lot ❷ fifty years of age; fifty years old (from a statement by Confucius that at fifty he knew the will of heaven):～之年 50 years old /年逾～ over 50; on the wrong side of 50

知母 zhīmǔ 〈中药〉rhizome of wind-weed (*Anemarrhena asphodeloides*)

知难而进 zhīnán'érjìn press forward in the face of difficulties; keep advancing in defiance of difficulties; take or seize the bull by the horns

知难而退 zhīnán'értuì beat a retreat in the face of difficulties; shy away from difficulties

知其然,不知其所以然 zhī qí rán, bù zhī qí suǒyǐrán know the hows but not the whys; understand the superficial but not the essential

知其一,不知其二 zhī qí yī, bù zhī qí èr be aware of one aspect of a thing but ignorant of the other; see only one side of the picture; hold a one-sided view; have only a partial understanding of the situation:～;见其利,不睹其害 have a one-sided view of the thing; notice the advantages but overlook the disadvantages

知青 zhīqīng (short for 知识青年) educated youth (usu. referring to secondary school graduates who were unable to pursue their studies in institutions of higher learning during the Cultural Revolution):上山下乡～ educated youth sent to the countryside for reeducation (during the Cultural Revolution) /～小说 novel about such young people and their later experiences

知青点 zhīqīngdiǎn settlement of urban youth sent to the countryside in the Cultural Revolution

知情 zhīqíng ❶ know the inside story; have inside information:～不报〈法律〉misprision; failure to give to the proper authority information one has which may lead to the apprehension of a felon /～者交易〈金融〉insider dealing (*or* trading) ❷ feel grateful for sb.'s kindness:你为我做了这么多事,我很～。I feel much obliged to you for all that you've done. /你整天为这件事操心,谁知你的情! You're busy working on this all day long, but it's a thankless task!

知情达理 zhīqíng-dálǐ reasonable; sensible; fair:她～,一向为人称道。She is a reasonable woman and is highly spoken of by others.

知情人 zhīqíngrén insider; person in the know:～的证据 state's evidence

知趣 zhīqù *also*"识趣" shíqù behave properly in a delicate situation; show good sense; be tactful:这人一点也不～! This man has no idea how to behave! /见此光景,他～地悄悄离去了。Sensing the delicate situation, he was tactful enough to leave quietly.

知人论世 zhīrén-lùnshì make comments on public figures and state affairs

知人善任 zhīrén-shànrèn (of a leader) know one's subordinates well enough to assign them jobs commensurate with their abilities; know how to judge and use people:他～,深得部下的拥护。He won the esteem of his subordinates as he knew them well and always put them where they could give full play to their abilities.

知人之明 zhīrénzhīmíng ability to appreciate a person's talent and character; keen insight into a person's qualities:他既有自知之明,又有～。He knows how to take a proper measure of others as well as himself.

知人知面不知心 zhī rén zhī miàn bù zhī xīn 〈俗语〉you may know a person's face but not his heart; it's difficult to understand a person's true nature:画虎画皮难画骨,～。As a picture of a tiger shows its pelt but not its bones, you may know a person's face but not his heart.

知事 zhīshì ❶ *also*"县知事" xiànzhīshì 〈历史〉magistrate of a county ❷ (Japan) prefecture governor; prefect; (ROK) provincial governor

知识 zhīshi ❶ knowledge:～渊博 have encyclopedic knowledge; be knowledgeable; be learned; be erudite /～广泛 have a wide range of knowledge /技术～ technical know-how /书本～ book learning /他的管理～很丰富。He is an expert in management. ❷ pertaining to learning or culture; intellectual:他属于～阶层。He belongs to the intelligentsia.

知识爆炸 zhīshi bàozhà knowledge explosion (rapid growth of knowledge and intelligence):当今是～的时代。Today, we are in an era of knowledge explosion.

知识贬值 zhīshi biǎnzhí undervaluation of knowledge and intellectual pursuit

知识财产 zhīshi cáichǎn intellectual property

知识产权 zhīshi chǎnquán intellectual property right

知识产业 zhīshi chǎnyè *also*"智力产业" zhìlì chǎnyè knowledge industry (institutions of higher learning and research, etc.)

知识分子 zhīshifènzǐ educated person; intellectual; the intelligentsia:高级～ intellectuals; highbrow /～是工人阶级的一个重要组成部分。Educated people are an important component of the working class.

知识更新 zhīshi gēngxīn updating of one's knowledge

知识工厂 zhīshi gōngchǎng knowledge factory (referring to colleges and universities)

知识工程 zhīshi gōngchéng knowledge engineering

知识化 zhīshihuà become better educated; be knowledgeable:干部必须～才能适应四化建设的需要。Only when the cadres are better educated will they be able to meet the requirements of the four-modernization drive.

知识界 zhīshijiè intellectual circles; the intelligentsia

知识经济 zhīshi jīngjì knowledge economy; knowledge-based economy

知识就是力量 zhīshi jiù shì lìliàng knowledge is power

知识库 zhīshikù knowledge bank or base (a kind of data base that

Z

stores specialized knowledge)
知识老化 zhīshi lǎohuà outdating of one's knowledge
知识密集产业 zhīshi mìjí chǎnyè knowledge-intensive industry
知识青年 zhīshi qīngnián *see* "知青"
知书达理 zhīshū-dálǐ be well-educated and sensible：她是一个～的女子。She was a well-read, sensible young woman.
知疼着热 zhīténg-zháorè show consideration for; give every care to：大家都夸他是个～的好丈夫。Everybody says he is a very affectionate and considerate husband.
知无不言，言无不尽 zhī wú bù yán, yán wú bù jìn say all you know and say it without reserve：～；言者无罪，闻者足戒；有则改之，无则加勉。Say all you know and say it without reserve; blame not the speaker but be warned by his words; correct your mistakes if you have made any and guard against them if you have not.
知悉 zhīxī know; learn (of); be informed of：情况无从～ have no way to know what's going on / 详情～ be informed of the details of the matter
知县 zhīxiàn 〈历史〉magistrate of a county; county magistrate
知晓 zhīxiǎo know; be aware of：这事我完全～。I know all about it.
知心 zhīxīn heart-to-heart; intimate：～人 intimate friend; one who can confide in; confidant / ～话 words from the heart / ～换命 stick together through thick and thin
知行 zhī-xíng 〈哲学〉knowledge versus practice; knowing and doing：～统一观 theory of the unity of knowing and doing
知雄守雌 zhīxióng-shǒucí (according to Taoist teaching, one should) hide one's abilities and hold oneself aloof from the world
知音 zhīyīn person who is deeply appreciative of sb.'s talents; bosom friend; alter ego
知友 zhīyǒu close or intimate friends
知遇 zhīyù receive appreciation (of one's ability, etc.) and help (as from a higher-up)：～之感 gratitude for a superior who is appreciative of one's ability and has rendered help and encouragement / 王部长对他有～之恩。He owes Minister Wang a debt of gratitude for appreciation and recognition of his talents.
知照 zhīzhào send word to; inform; tell：你去～她一声，请她下午出席会议。Please go and tell her that she is to attend a meeting in the afternoon.
知州 zhīzhōu 〈历史〉magistrate of a prefecture; prefect
知子莫若父 zhī zǐ mòruò fù no one knows a son better than his father
知足 zhīzú be content with what one has：你怎么这样不～！Why! You're too greedy.
知足不辱 zhīzú-bùrǔ he who is contented has no fear of disgrace or humiliation
知足常乐 zhīzú-chánglè happy is he who is content; contentment is happiness

蜘 zhī

蜘蛛 zhīzhū spider：红～ red spider / 海～ sea spider / 幼～ spiderling / ～网 spiderweb; spider's web; cobweb
蜘蛛抱蛋 zhīzhū bàodàn 〈植物〉(common) aspidistra (*Aspidistra elatior*); cast-iron plant
蜘蛛蜂 zhīzhūfēng spider wasp
蜘蛛猴 zhīzhūhóu spider monkey
蜘蛛兰 zhīzhūlán spider orchid; spider orchis
蜘蛛丝 zhīzhūsī ❶ thread of a spiderweb; cobweb ❷ spider line (an optical instrument)
蜘蛛蟹 zhīzhūxiè spider crab
蜘蛛痣 zhīzhūzhì spider nevus

稙 zhī

(of crops) early-planting or early-maturing：～庄稼 early-planting crops / 白玉米～。White corn ripens early.

卮(巵) zhī

ancient wine vessel：赐之～酒 present a vessel of wine to sb. / 乃左手持～，右手画蛇。He was painting a snake with his right hand while holding a wine vessel in his left.

栀(梔) zhī

栀子 zhīzi 〈植物〉Cape jasmine
栀子花 zhīzihuā gardenia
栀子皮 zhīzipí bark of gardenia; gardenia bark

氏 zhī

see "阏氏" yānzhī; "月氏" Yuèzhī
see also shì

祇 zhī

〈书面〉venerate; esteem; respect：～候光临。We request the pleasure of your company.

跃 zhī

see "跰跃" piánzhī

胝 zhī

see "胼胝" piánzhī

脂 zhī

❶ fat; grease; tallow; resin：油～ fat; grease / 乳～ butterfat / 树～ resin / 松～ resin; pine resin / 防锈～ antirust grease / 脱～ de-fat; degrease ❷ rouge：胭～ rouge / 擦～抹粉 apply rouge and powder to the face — make up
脂沉积症 zhīchénjīzhèng 〈医学〉lipoidosis
脂醇 zhīchún 〈生化〉lipidol
脂蛋白 zhīdànbái 〈生化〉lipoprotein
脂肪 zhīfáng fat：动物～ animal fat / 植物～ vegetable fat / ～变性 〈医学〉fatty degeneration
脂肪肝 zhīfánggān 〈医学〉fatty liver
脂肪痢 zhīfánglì steatorrbea
脂肪酶 zhīfángméi 〈生化〉lipase
脂肪酸 zhīfángsuān *also* "脂酸" fatty acid
脂肪组织 zhīfáng zǔzhī 〈生理〉adipose tissue
脂粉 zhīfěn rouge and powder; cosmetics
脂粉气 zhīfěnqì womanlike ways; womanliness; femininity：眼下有些作家的作品～太浓。Nowadays the works of some writers are rather effeminate.
脂膏 zhīgāo ❶ fat; grease; blubber：鲸鱼的～可以炼油。Whale oil can be obtained from blubber. ❷〈比喻〉fruits of labour of the people; wealth of the people：榨取人民的～ extort fruits of labour from the people
脂膏不润 zhīgāo-bùrùn not get glossy after being put in the grease — incorruptible official
脂肌瘤 zhījīliú 〈医学〉lipomyoma
脂鲤 zhīlǐ characin
脂瘤 zhīliú *also* "脂肪瘤" lipoma：～病 lipomatosis
脂麻 zhīma *also* "芝麻" zhīma ❶ sesame ❷ sesame seed
脂酶 zhīméi lipase
脂膜炎 zhīmóyán panniculitis
脂尿 zhīniào lipuria：～症 pimeluria
脂性肾变病 zhīxìng shènbiànbìng 〈医学〉liponephrosis; renal lipoidosis
脂血症 zhīxuèzhèng 〈医学〉lipohemia; lipoidemia
脂眼鲱 zhīyǎnfēi Pacific round herring
脂溢性皮炎 zhīyìxìng píyán seborrheic dermatitis
脂油 zhīyóu 〈方言〉leaf fat or lard

zhí

摭 zhí

〈书面〉pick up; collect：～芳 collect the best (books, etc.) / 采经～传 gather classical works
摭拾 zhíshí 〈书面〉pick; gather; muster; collect：～故事 collect anecdotes of the past

蹠 zhí

❶〈生理〉metatarsus ❷〈书面〉sole of the foot：～穿膝暴。Shoes are worn out, revealing the soles. ❸〈书面〉tread; step on：眇不知其所～。I'm wandering about without aim, without hope.
蹠骨 zhígǔ 〈生理〉metatarsal bones

职(職) zhí

❶ duty; job：尽～尽责 carry out one's duties faithfully / 失～ neglect one's duty / 渎～ malfeasance; dereliction of duty / 天～ bounden duty / 称～ competent for one's job / 做好本～工作 do one's job well / 以身殉～ die on the job; die at one's post ❷ position; post; office：在～ be on the job; be at one's post / 就～ assume office; take office / 兼～ hold two or more posts concurrently / 辞～ resign / 撤～ be removed (*or* dismissed) from office / 停～ suspend sb. from his duties / 革～ be discharged from office; deprive

sb. of his post ❸〈旧语〉your subordinate:鄙～ your humble subordinate ❹ be in charge of; administer; manage ❺〈书面〉for:～是之故 for this reason /～此而已。It is only for this reason.

职别 zhíbié official rank

职称 zhíchēng professional title (such as engineer, professor, lecturer, etc.):高级～ senior professional titles (such as professor, associate professor and their equivalents) /技术～ technical titles /～评审委员会 committee for evaluation of professional titles; academic promotion committee

职大 zhídà (short for 职工大学) special university for adult job holders

职代会 zhídàihuì (short for 职工代表大会) employees' representatives conference:企业的重大问题,均由～讨论后决定。All the major questions of an enterprise were decided after discussion by the employees' representatives conference.

职分 zhífèn ❶ bounden duty:做好这些工作是我的～。It is my bounden duty to do the job well. ❷ official post; position

职高 zhígāo (short for 职业高中) vocational high school

职工 zhígōng ❶ workers and staff members:～参与企业经营管理。Workers and staff members participate in the management of the enterprise. ❷〈旧语〉workers:～运动 labour movement; trade union movement

职工保险基金 zhígōng bǎoxiǎn jījīn employees' insurance fund

职工代表大会制 zhígōng dàibiǎo dàhuìzhì system of conference of workers and administrative staff (in a factory, etc.)

职工股 zhígōnggǔ staff shares

职工考绩 zhígōng kǎojì merit rating; performance rating

职工入股计划 zhígōng rùgǔ jìhuà (US) employee stock ownership plan (ESOP)

职工手册 zhígōng shǒucè employees' handbook

职工证 zhígōngzhèng employee identification card

职官 zhíguān official of all ranks

职能 zhínéng function:政府的～ functions of a government /商品的～ functions of commodities /～部门 functional departments

职权 zhíquán powers or authority of office; functions and powers:行使～ exercise one's functions and powers /滥用～ abuse one's authority of office /利用～谋私 misuse one's powers for personal gain

职权范围 zhíquán fànwéi limits or scope of one's functions and powers; terms of reference:这是他～内的事。That's within his functions and powers. /此事不属该委员会的～。This problem is outside the committee's terms of reference.

职事 zhíshì ❶ post; job ❷〈旧语〉occupation; profession; calling

职守 zhíshǒu post; duty:擅离～ leave one's post without permission; be (*or* go) AWOL (absent without leave); take French leave /玩忽～ neglecting one's duties; dereliction of duty /坚持～ stand fast at one's post /忠于～ be faithful in the discharge of one's duties

职司 zhísī〈书面〉❶ duty; job; post:尽其～ fulfil one's duty ❷ be in charge of; take control of; administer:～教育的人有很大的责任。Those in charge of education have a grave responsibility. *or* Being in charge of education is a grave responsibility.

职位 zhíwèi position; post:他在公司谋得一个好～。He got a good position in the firm. /给了他一个总经理的～。He was given a post as general manager.

职务 zhíwù post; position; duty; job:他在空军担任重要～。He held an important post in the air force. /他履行了自己的～。He has done (*or* performed) his duties. /我们～不同,但都是为国效力。Our jobs may be different but we are all serving our country.

职务变更 zhíwù biàngēng reassignment

职务工资 zhíwù gōngzī pay according to one's post

职务分析 zhíwù fēnxī job analysis

职务津贴 zhíwù jīntiē duty allowance

职衔 zhíxián ❶ post and military rank (such as regiment commander with the rank of lieutenant colonel) ❷〈书面〉official title:外交～ diplomatic titles

Z

职业 zhíyè ❶ occupation; profession; vocation; calling:～教育 vocational education /～妇女 career girl (*or* woman) /～上的特权 professional privilege /～责任 professional responsibility /～安全法 job-safety law /请问你的～? Your occupation, please. /他是从事什么～的? What calling does he follow? ❷ professional:～军人 career officer /～进出口商 professional importer and exporter

职业病 zhíyèbìng occupational disease

职业道德 zhíyè dàodé professional ethics; work ethic

职业介绍所 zhíyè jièshàosuǒ hiring hall; job centre

职业疗法 zhíyè liáofǎ occupational therapy

职业团体 zhíyè tuántǐ professional organization

职业外交官 zhíyè wàijiāoguān career diplomat

职业性皮炎 zhíyèxìng píyán〈医学〉industrial dermatosis; industrial dermatitis; occupational dermatitis

职业学校 zhíyè xuéxiào vocational school

职业运动员 zhíyè yùndòngyuán professional athlete; professional

职员 zhíyuán clerk; office worker; staff member; functionary

职责 zhízé duty; obligation; responsibility:～范围 scope of official duty /为人父母者的～ obligations imposed by parenthood; parents' obligation /教育下一代是我们的～。It is our responsibility to educate the young.

职掌 zhízhǎng take charge of:～政务 be in charge of state affairs

职志 zhízhì〈书面〉lifework; mission; undertaking:以慈善事业为～ take philanthropy (*or* charities) as one's lifelong work

直

直 zhí ❶ straight:把椅子排成一～行 arrange the chairs in a straight line ❷ vertical; upright:～上云霄 soar straight up into the sky /笔～地站着 stand (*or* hold oneself) upright /这山坡看上去几乎是垂～的。The hillside looked almost vertical. ❸ perpendicular:形成直角的两线垂～。One line is perpendicular to another when it makes a square corner with another. /这个操场～里有五十米,横里有三十米。This playground is fifty metres in length and thirty metres in width (*or* thirty metres by fifty). ❹ straighten:从坐位上～起身来 straighten up from the seat /把铁丝拉～ straighten a piece of wire ❺ just; upright:正～ upright; fair-minded; just /是非曲～ rights and wrongs; truth and falsehood /举～错枉 appoint upright officials and remove the crooked ones — replace bad officials by good ones /宁在～中取,不向曲中求。I would rather get what I want by honest means than by crooked means. ❻ candid; frank; straightforward:心～口快 plain-spoken and straightforward; frank and outspoken /他说话太～,得罪了不少人。Being blunt and plain-spoken, he has offended many people. ❼ vertical stroke (in Chinese characters):"王"字的笔画是三横一～。The Chinese character "王" has three horizontal strokes and one vertical stroke. ❽ directly; direct; straight:～飞巴黎 fly nonstop to Paris /这条海底通道～通伦敦。The tunnel under the seabed leads directly to London. /这条铁路～贯南北。The railway links the south with the north. ❾ continuously; straight:伤口鲜血～流。Blood was (continuously) oozing out of the wound. /他热得～出汗。He was so hot that he kept perspiring. /雨一～下了四天。We have had four straight days of rain. *or* It has been raining four days on end. ❿ just; simply; exactly:疼得～像针扎似的 feel a piercing pain /老人待她～如亲闺女。The old man treated her just like his own daughter. ⓫ (Zhí) a surname

直白 zhíbái say plainly; tell straight:有话～说,别攥在手心让我猜。Speak your mind. Don't keep me guessing.

直笔 zhíbǐ record faithfully; give a faithful account:～不讳 give a faithful account of the event (without any intention to conceal the facts)

直拨 zhíbō〈通信〉direct dialing

直拨长途电话 zhíbō chángtú diànhuà direct distance dialing (DDD)

直播 zhíbō ❶〈农业〉direct seeding:～稻 direct seeding of rice /高空～树种 direct seeding of trees by airplane ❷ live broadcast by a TV or radio station:现场～开幕式 make a live broadcast of the opening ceremony /世界上大多数国家的广播电台都～新闻。Radio stations in most countries of the world make direct news broadcasts.

直布罗陀 Zhíbùluótuó Gibraltar, a fortified town at the southern tip of the Iberian peninsula on the Strait of Gibraltar

直布罗陀海峡 Zhíbùluótuó Hǎixiá Strait of Gibraltar, the only outlet of the Mediterranean Sea to the Atlantic Ocean between Spain and the northwest of Africa

直肠 zhícháng〈生理〉rectum

直肠癌 zhícháng'ái carcinoma of the rectum

直肠镜 zhíchángjìng *also* "直肠窥器"〈医学〉proctoscope; rectal speculum

直肠切除术 zhícháng qiēchúshù proctectomy

直肠脱垂 zhícháng tuōchuí prolapse of rectum

直肠炎 zhíchángyán proctitis; rectitis

直肠直肚 zhícháng-zhídù frank; forthright; straightforward:他是个～的人,没有学会嘴上一套,心里一套的本事。He is open and straightforward, never says one thing while meaning another.
直肠子 zhíchángzi ❶ frank; straightforward; forthright ❷ candid person:他是个～,心里有话存不住。He is such a straightforward person that he always speaks out his thought.
直陈 zhíchén state (one's views) frankly; make a straightforward statement
直诚 zhícheng honest and forthright:他是个～人,从来不会说假话。He is an honest man and never tells a lie.
直尺 zhíchǐ straightedge; ruler
直齿轮 zhíchǐlún 〈机械〉straight gear
直翅目昆虫 zhíchìmù kūnchóng orthopteran
直冲冲 zhíchōngchōng 〈方言〉in earnest; bluntly:～地说 speak frankly
直刺 zhícì ❶〈体育〉straight thrust (in fencing) ❷〈中医〉perpendicular inserting (in acupuncture)
直达 zhídá through; nonstop; direct:～车票 through ticket /～路线 through route /～船 direct steamer /～港 direct port /～货运 drop shipment; direct shipment /～货物 through cargo /～提单 direct B/L; through bill of lading / 列车由上海～北京。It's a through train from Shanghai to Beijing.
直达快车 zhídá kuàichē through express (train)
直打直 zhídǎzhí 〈口语〉directly; straight; bluntly:～往村里跑 run straight (*or* directly) to the village /有什么话,你就～地说吧。Tell me straight what you think.
直待 zhídài wait until:～所有的工人都下了班,车间主任才回家。The head of the workshop did not leave for home until all the workers knocked off.
直捣 zhídǎo press straight on to:～叛军巢穴 drive straight on to the rebels' lair
直捣黄龙 zhídǎo-Huánglóng storm the enemy's lair; follow in hot pursuit right up to the enemy's headquarters; press forward to the enemy's capital
直到 zhídào until; up to; up till:～二战结束后我才重返故土。I did not set foot in my native land again until after the Second World War. /～今天我一直认为他是个诚实的人。Up to now I always thought he was honest.
直道而行 zhídào'érxíng act impartially:忠诚职守,～ be devoted to one's duty and upright in one's behaviour
直瞪瞪 zhídēngdēng stare blankly:他～地望着地面,神色十分呆滞。He fixed his gaze on the ground, expressionless.
直盯盯 zhídīngdīng fix one's eyes on:她～地看着那个陌生人。She fixed her eyes on the stranger.
直读 zhídú direct reading; direct readout:～式电桥 direct reading bridge /～式仪表 direct reading instrument; direct reading meter /～装置 direct readout
直端 zhíduān 〈方言〉directly; straight:他俩～到学校去找老师。The two went straight to the school to see their teacher.
直裰 zhíduō monk's or Taoist priest's robe
直感 zhígǎn direct perception (through the senses); personal experience or instinct:我有～,此人不可信。My instinct tells me that this man is not to be trusted.
直根 zhígēn 〈植物〉taproot
直贡呢 zhígòngní 〈纺织〉venetian
直勾勾 zhígōugōu (look) straight (at sb.); (stare) fixedly:他～地望着我。He fixed his gaze on me.
直挂 zhíguà direct ties:产销～ direct link between production and marketing
直观 zhíguān directly perceived through the senses; audio-visual:～教育 audio-visual education /～教具 aids to object teaching; audio-visual aids /～教学 object teaching /～教学课 object lesson /～式存储管 direct-view storage tube /～文件 visible file /～追踪 direct visual tracing /～效果 visual effect
直航 zhíháng nonstop flight; direct route:～东京 straight flight to Tokyo
直和 zhíhé 〈数学〉direct sum:～分解 direct sum decomposition; decomposition into direct sum
直话 zhíhuà frank remarks:～直说 call a spade a spade /我说的是～。I've given you a bit of my mind.
直积 zhíjī 〈数学〉direct product:～表示 representation of direct product /～分解 direct product decomposition; decomposition into direct product /～码 direct-product code; direct-sum code
直谏 zhíjiàn admonish (one's superior or friend) frankly; remonstrate with the emperor:忠言～ admonish sb. in all sincerity
直僵僵 zhíjiāngjiāng stiff:他～地躺在床上。He lay stiff in bed.
直角 zhíjiǎo 〈数学〉right angle:～交会 right-angle intersection /～棱镜 right angle prism /～转弯梯台 quarter space stair
直角尺 zhíjiǎochǐ square
直角三角形 zhíjiǎo sānjiǎoxíng right or right-angled triangle
直角坐标 zhíjiǎo zuòbiāo rectangular coordinates
直接 zhíjiē direct; straight; immediate:～联系 direct contact /～后果 direct outcome; immediate consequence /～成本 direct cost /～损失 direct loss /～投资 direct investment /～责任 direct liability /～证据 direct evidence; positive evidence /～胁迫伤害 direct stress injury /～瞄准轰炸 direct bombing /～后方 immediate rear /～指挥官 immediate commander /你可～去找董事长。You may go straight to the chairman of the board (of directors). /双方代表将～会谈。Representatives of both parties will meet face to face to talk things over. *or* Representatives of both parties will negotiate directly with each other.
直接宾语 zhíjiē bīnyǔ 〈语言〉direct object
直接肥料 zhíjiē féiliào direct fertilizer
直接分裂 zhíjiē fēnliè *also* "无性分裂" wúxìng fēnliè 〈生物〉amitosis
直接借记 zhíjiē jièjì direct debit
直接经验 zhíjiē jīngyàn 〈哲学〉direct experience:一切真知都来自～。All genuine knowledge originates from direct experience.
直接贸易 zhíjiē màoyì direct trade
直接起飞 zhíjiē qǐfēi rolling take-off; rolling start
直接染料 zhíjiē rǎnliào direct dye
直接税 zhíjiēshuì direct tax
直接三通 zhíjiē sāntōng direct links in trade, mail and air and shipping services (between the two sides of the Taiwan Straits)
直接推理 zhíjiē tuīlǐ immediate reasoning
直接推论 zhíjiē tuīlùn eduction
直接选举 zhíjiē xuǎnjǔ direct election
直接着陆 zhíjiē zhuólù straight-in landing
直截 zhíjié *also* "直捷" straightforward; come straight to the point:～拒绝 flatly refuse (*or* turn down)
直截了当 zhíjié-liǎodàng blunt; point-blank; straightforward; flat and plain:～地提出要求 make demands in explicit terms /我只～地向你说句话。I will just say a few blunt words. /你说话能不能～一点? Please don't mince words. /我要的是对这个问题的～的答复。I want a straight answer to the question.
直劲儿 zhíjìnr 〈方言〉persistently; continuously:她急得～哭。She cried incessantly with anxiety.
直径 zhíjìng 〈数学〉diameter:～为三米 three metres in diameter /大～〈机械〉major diameter /小～〈机械〉minor diameter
直撅撅 zhíjuējuē 〈方言〉straight and stiff:你～地站在那儿干吗? Why the devil are you standing there straight and stiff?
直觉 zhíjué 〈心理〉intuition:凭～感到 feel (it) in one's bones /凭～得到的知识 intuitive knowledge /基于～的猜测 intuitive guess /～方法 intuitive approach /～能力 powers of intuition /～阶段〈心理〉intuitive stage
直觉主义 zhíjuézhǔyì 〈哲学〉intuitionism:～数学 intuitionistic mathematics
直快 zhíkuài (short for 直达快车) through express (train):京沪～列车 through express from Beijing to Shanghai
直来直去 zhílái-zhíqù ❶ go straight to and return directly:这次去广州是～,过不几天就回来了。This time they are going straight to Guangzhou and will return directly; so they'll be back in a few days. ❷ straightforward; frank; candid:他是个～的人,说话有口无心。He is outspoken and often appears sharp-tongued but cherishes no malice.
直愣愣 zhílēnglēng (stare) straight; fixedly; blankly:他两眼～地望着天空。He gazed blankly into the sky (as if in a daze). /那只狼两眼～瞪着羊群。The wolf riveted its eyes on the flock of sheep greedily.
直理 zhílǐ truth; justice:他是个敢说～的人。He is a man who dares to speak the truth. /他老人家直肠子认～。The revered old man has a strong sense of justice.
直立 zhílì stand erect; stand upright:两名警卫～在大门两侧。The two guards stand ramrod straight on the two sides of the gate.

Z

直立茎 zhílìjīng 〈植物〉erect stem
直立人 zhílìrén *Homo erectus*
直谅多闻 zhíliàng-duōwén upright and well-informed; honest and knowledgeable
直溜溜 zhíliūliū straight:～的一条大马路 a straight avenue
直溜 zhíliu straight:小树长得挺～。What a straight sapling!
直流 zhíliú ❶〈电学〉DC (direct current):～电源 direct current main; direct-current power supply /～输电 direct-current transmission ❷〈机械〉straight-through /～锅炉 once-through boiler /～电磁泵 conduction pump /～型联合收割机 straight-through combine
直流电 zhíliúdiàn direct current; DC
直馏 zhíliú 〈石油〉straight-run distillation:～汽油 distilled gasoline; direct gasoline
直落 zhíluò 〈体育〉win several games successively in a match:中国女排～三局获胜。The Chinese women's volleyball team won three games in a row.
直埋式光缆 zhímáishì guānglǎn plow-in optical cable
直眉瞪眼 zhíméi-dèngyǎn ❶ stare in anger; glare; fume:你干吗对我～的? Why are you glaring at me like that? ❷ in a trance; stupefied:他～地站在空荡荡的广场上。He stood in the deserted square staring blankly.
直面 zhímiàn face squarely; look squarely at:～现实 look at reality in the face; face reality
直木先伐 zhímù-xiānfá 〈谚语〉tall, straight trees are felled first; persons of talent first come under attack
直朴 zhípǔ upright and simple; honest and sincere:他为人～忠厚。He is open, sincere and kind-hearted.
直前 zhíqián go forward; march forward; forge ahead:勇往～ stride bravely forward; march courageously forward; forge ahead valiantly
直情径行 zhíqíng-jìngxíng go one's own way; act all on one's own:他是个～的人,不大在乎别人的议论。He is a man of strong will and doesn't really care what others think of him.
直熔锭 zhíróngdìng 〈冶金〉direct ingot; dingot:～块 dingot regulus
直熔矿石 zhíróng kuàngshí direct-smelting ore
直闪石 zhíshǎnshí anthophyllite
直上直下 zhíshàng-zhíxià vertical; steep:～的峭壁 steep cliff
直射距离 zhíshè jùlí 〈军事〉battle-sight range; point-blank range
直升飞机 zhíshēng fēijī helicopter; hoverplane; copter; chopper:～机场 heliport; helidrome /～降落场 helipad /～临时降落场 helispot /～母舰 helicopter carrier /～驾驶员 helicopterist /用～运送 helilift /乘～作短程旅行 helihop /用～把旅客载运到机场 chopper passengers to the airport
直生论 zhíshēnglùn 〈生物〉orthogenesis
直视 zhíshì look or gaze straight ahead:两眼～前方 look straight ahead /～人生 face life squarely; look life in the face
直书 zhíshū 〈书面〉write what has actually happened; give a truthful account of an event
直抒 zhíshū express freely; state frankly
直抒己见 zhíshū-jǐjiàn state one's views frankly; be plain-spoken
直抒胸臆 zhíshū-xiōngyì pour out one's heart; speak one's mind plainly
直属 zhíshǔ directly under; directly subordinate or affiliated:～外交部 be directly affiliated to the Foreign Ministry
直率 zhíshuài outspoken; candid; straightforward:～的批评 candid criticism /尽管他有不少缺点,他是～、诚实的。With all his faults he is frank and honest. /他～地谈了他对我的工作的意见。He gave me a piece of his mind about my work.
直爽 zhíshuǎng outspoken; forthright; frank; candid:性格～的人 frank person
直体 zhítǐ 〈体育〉stretched or straight body:～前空翻 forward fly-away; hollow forward somersault
直挺挺 zhítǐngtǐng straight and stiff; bolt upright:～地站着 stand ramrod straight /～地坐在椅子边上 sit bolt upright on the edge of the chair
直通 zhítōng 〈通信〉direct connection:～线 direct through line /～中继线 direct trunk
直通车 zhítōngchē through train
直通通 zhítōngtōng straightforward; blunt
直筒子 zhítǒngzi one who wears one's heart on one's sleeve:他是个～,说话做事从不会拐弯抹角。He is a straightforward person, never beating about the bush.
直系 zhíxì lineal:～后代 lineal descendant /～继承人 heir of line; heir of one's body
直系卑亲属 zhíxì bēiqīnshǔ 〈法律〉lineal descendents
直系亲属 zhíxì qīnshǔ 〈法律〉directly-related members of one's family such as parents, spouse or children
直系尊亲属 zhíxì zūnqīnshǔ 〈法律〉lineal ascendants
直辖 zhíxiá directly under the jurisdiction of:国务院的～机构 organizations directly under the State Council
直辖市 zhíxiáshì municipality directly under the Central Government
直线 zhíxiàn ❶ straight line:两市之间的～距离 crow-fly (*or* straight-line) distance between two cities /两点之间最短的距离是～。A straight line is the shortest distance between two points. ❷ linear; rectilinear; direct:～杆塔 straight line pole /～程 crow-flight path (*or* as the crow flies) /～飞行 rectilinear (*or* straight) flight /～爬高 rectilinear (*or* straight) climb ❸ steep; rising and falling sharply:产量～上升。The output has shot up. /物价～下降。Commodity prices have plummeted.
直线电话 zhíxiàn diànhuà direct-dial telephone
直线加速器 zhíxiàn jiāsùqì 〈物理〉linear accelerator
直线思维 zhíxiàn sīwéi linear thinking; linear thought
直线运动 zhíxiàn yùndòng 〈物理〉rectilinear motion
直线折旧法 zhíxiàn zhéjiùfǎ 〈经济〉straight-line depreciation
直心眼儿 zhíxīnyǎnr 〈口语〉❶open; frank; direct:我是～,有一句说一句。I'm direct and outspoken and never mince words. ❷ straightforward person
直心直肠 zhíxīn-zhícháng honest and straightforward:他是一位～的人。He is an honest and straightforward man.
直性 zhíxìng straightforward; frank; candid:～人 outspoken person
直性子 zhíxìngzi ❶ straightforward; downright; blunt ❷ straightforward person:他是个～,有什么说什么。He is a straight fellow, always ready to say what's on his mind.
直言 zhíyán speak bluntly; state candidly:～相劝 give frank advice
直言不讳 zhíyán-bùhuì call a spade a spade; speak bluntly; not mince words; talk straight:他是那种～的人。He is the kind of person who always calls a spade a spade. /真正的朋友应该～。A real friend should talk straight.
直言谠议 zhíyán-dǎngyì sincere advice and outspoken criticisms
直言贾祸 zhíyán-gǔhuò *also*"直言取祸" straight talk courts disaster:他果真～。As expected, he was persecuted for his frank criticism.
直言命题 zhíyán mìngtí 〈逻辑〉categorical proposition
直焰式锅炉 zhíyànshì guōlú direct-flame boiler
直译 zhíyì literal translation
直音 zhíyīn 〈语言〉traditional method of indicating the pronunciation of a Chinese character by citing another simpler character with the same pronunciation (e.g. "盅" pronounced as "古")
直泳类 zhíyǒnglèi 〈动物〉orthonectid
直展云 zhízhǎnyún 〈气象〉cloud with vertical development
直正 zhízheng 〈方言〉honest; just; fair-minded:这人心眼儿很～。He is fair and square.
直至 zhízhì till; until; up to; up till:他参加了这项工程的全过程,从开工～收尾。He was involved in the project from beginning to end. /～此时她还没有脱离危险。Up to now she is still not out of danger.
直戆 zhízhuàng upright and simple; simple and honest

埴

zhí 〈书面〉clay:垆～ dark clay
埴轮 zhílún (Japan) haniwa

植

zhí ❶ plant; grow:种～ plant; grow /移～ transplant /补～ replant /手～ plant (a tree, etc.) personally /密～ close planting /春～ plant in spring ❷ set up; build; establish:培～个人的势力 build up one's personal influence /扶～新生力量 foster new-emerging forces ❸ plant; flora ❹ (Zhí) a surname
植保 zhíbǎo (short of 植物保护) plant protection; crop protection:～机械 equipment for plant protection /～员 plant protector
植被 zhíbèi 〈植物〉vegetation:～类型 vegetation form /～圈 circle of vegetation /～地理学 vegetational plant geography
植成土 zhíchéngtǔ phytogenic soil

Z

植虫学 zhíchóngxué zoophytology; dermatoplasty
植醇 zhíchún 〈生化〉phytol
植党营私 zhídǎng-yíngsī form a clique to further one's own selfish interests
植根 zhígēn take or strike root (usu. used in a figurative sense):伟大的文学创作,总是～于人民生活中。Great literary works are always rooted in the life of the people.
植立 zhílì stand upright; stand:～不动 stand rooted to the ground
植苗 zhímiáo transplant saplings
植皮 zhípí skin-grafting:～刀 dermatome /～术 skin-grafting
植绒 zhíróng 〈纺织〉flocking
植入 zhírù 〈医学〉embedding; implantation:～法 implantation /～物 implant
植生素 zhíshēngsù phytamin
植食蝽 zhíshíchūn plant bug; leaf bug
植树 zhíshù tree planting:～造林 afforestation /～机 tree-planting machine; tree planter
植树节 Zhíshùjié Arbor Day (in China, March 12)
植酸 zhísuān 〈化学〉phytic acid:～酶 phytase
植物 zhíwù plant; vegetable; phyto-:～性蛋白 phytalbumin; textured vegetable protein /～羊皮纸 vegetable parchment /气生～ aerial plant /两栖～ amphibious plant /水生～ aquatic plant /芳香～ aromatic plant /雌雄同株～ monoecious plant /雌雄异株～ dioecious plant
植物保护 zhíwù bǎohù *see*"植保"
植物病害 zhíwù bìnghài plant disease
植物病理学 zhíwù bìnglǐxué phytopathology; plant pathology
植物地理学 zhíwù dìlǐxué phytogeography; plant geography
植物分布学 zhíwù fēnbùxué botanical geography
植物分类学 zhíwù fēnlèixué plant taxonomy:～家 plant taxonomist
植物化石 zhíwù huàshí phytolite; phytolith
植物化学 zhíwù huàxué phytochemistry; vegetable chemistry
植物检疫 zhíwù jiǎnyì plant quarantine
植物胶 zhíwùjiāo vegetable gum
植物解剖学 zhíwù jiěpōuxué phytotomy
植物界 zhíwùjiè plantage; flora; plant kingdom; vegetable plant
植物净化 zhíwù jìnghuà 〈环保〉plant purification
植物区系 zhíwù qūxì flora
植物群落 zhíwù qúnluò plant community; phytocoenosis; phytobiocenose
植物人 zhíwùrén person who is physically alive but mentally inert; vegetable
植物生态学 zhíwù shēngtàixué plant ecology; phytoecology
植物生长激素 zhíwù shēngzhǎng jīsù *also*"植物生长素" plant hormone; phytohormone; auxin
植物生长调节剂 zhíwù shēngzhǎng tiáojiéjì plant-growth regulator
植物纤维 zhíwù xiānwéi vegetable fibre
植物性神经 zhíwùxìng shénjīng 〈生理〉autonomic nerve:～紊乱 autonomic nerve disorder
植物学 zhíwùxué botany:～家 botanist
植物油 zhíwùyóu vegetable oil
植物育种 zhíwù yùzhǒng plant breeding
植物园 zhíwùyuán botanical garden
植物志 zhíwùzhì flora
植形动物学 zhíxíng dòngwùxué zoophytology
植株 zhízhū 〈农业〉plant:新种的小树～生长良好。The newly-planted saplings are growing well.

殖

zhí breed; multiply; propagate:繁～ reproduce; multiply; propagate /生～ breed; reproduce /养～ breed (aquatics) /增～ reproduce; multiply; propagate; 〈医学〉hyperplasia /垦～ reclaim wasteland and go in for production /万物蕃～。All things on earth flourish.
see also shi
殖民 zhímín colonize; establish a colony:～统治 colonial rule /非～化 decolonization /～国家 colonialist power /～扩张 colonial expansion/～战争 colonialist war
殖民部 Zhímínbù (UK) Colonial Office (before Aug. 1966)
殖民地 zhímíndì colony:～国家 colonial country /半～国家 semi-colonial country /～人民 people under colonial rule; colonial people /～总督 colonial governor /～开拓者 colonist /不列颠的～帝国 Britain's colonial empire /英国人在新英格兰开拓了～。The English colonized New England.
殖民地经验 zhímíndì jīngyàn (Australia) colonial experience (experience of farming, etc. gained by young Englishmen in colonial Australia)
殖民主义 zhímínzhǔyì colonialism:新～ new colonialism; neo-colonialism /～列强 colonial powers /～压迫 colonial oppression /～者 colonialist

值

zhí ❶ value:币～ currency value /贬～ devalue; devaluate; depreciate /升～ appreciate; rise or increase in value /增～ added value /增～税 value added tax (VAT) /绝对～ absolute value /相对～ relative value /总产～ total output value ❷ what a specified sum of money can buy:这古画～多少钱? How much is the ancient painting worth? /这画至少～十万美元。The painting is worth at least 100,000 US dollars. ❸ 〈数学〉value:数～ numerical value /近似～ approximate value /比～ specific value; ratio ❹ worth; worthwhile:这东西买得～。It is worth the price. /那玩意儿一钱不～。That's not worth a damn. /这不～一提。It's not worth mentioning. ❺ happen to; chance to:～此国家危急之秋 at this time of national crisis /我们到时适～秋收季节。We happened to arrive there in the autumn-harvest season. ❻ be on duty; take one's turn at sth.:轮～ work in shifts / 明天该你当～。It's your turn to be on duty tomorrow.
值班 zhíbān be on duty or shift:～员 person on duty /～经理 manager directly supervising the operation (in a shop, etc.) /～军官 duty officer; watch officer /～火器 firearms on duty /～战斗机 scramble fighters /节假日大家轮流～。People work in shifts during the holidays. /明天我值白班。I'll be on the day shift tomorrow.
值不当 zhíbudàng 〈方言〉not worthwhile; not worth it:为孩子～生这么大的气。Why get so angry with children? It isn't worth it. /为这点儿事吵架～。It's not worthwhile to squabble over such a trifle.
值乘 zhíchéng work on a train, ship, or plane in turns
值当 zhídàng 〈方言〉be worth (sb.'s) while; be worthwhile:这事～让你亲自跑一趟吗? Is it worth your while to go there in person?
值得 zhíde ❶ be worth the money:这房子～买。The house is worth buying. ❷ be of value; be worthwhile:这事～劳那么大的神吗? Is it worth all the trouble? /～试一试。It's worth trying. /他的建议～认真考虑。His proposal deserves serious consideration. /这种苗头～注意。The symptoms of the tendency merit attention. /这件事不～大惊小怪。The matter doesn't warrent such a hue and cry. /那确是件～他骄傲的事。That's a real feather in his cap.
值分布理论 zhífēnbù lǐlùn 〈数学〉value distribution theory
值个儿 zhígèr 〈方言〉be worthwhile:为孩子和邻居吵架,～吗? I don't think it worthwhile to pick quarrels with the neighbour because of the children.
值更 zhígēng 〈方言〉keep night watch
值过儿 zhíguòr 〈方言〉❶ be worth:多花点儿钱也～。It's worth it even if you have to pay more. ❷ be satisfactory:这件事办得总算落了～。We've done the job fairly well.
值价 zhíjià 〈方言〉valuable:他家最～的东西要算是那几件家具了。The few pieces of furniture can be counted as valuables in his house.
值年 zhínián take one's turn in a certain year to preside over (a symposium, a conference, etc.)
值钱 zhíqián worth much; of great value; valuable; expensive:这是古董,很～。This is an antique, which is worth a great deal. /她把～的衣物都带走了。She took with her all the expensive clothes and other articles of value.
值勤 zhíqín (of soldiers, policemen, etc.) be on duty; be on point duty:～交通警 policeman on point duty /晚上有警卫～巡逻。There are night patrols by the guards.
值勤簿 zhíqínbù duty roster
值日 zhírì be on duty for the day; be one's turn to be on duty:～表 rota; duty roster /～军官 officer on duty (for the day) /今天我～。I'm on duty today. /～生请擦黑板。Student on duty, please clean the blackboard.
值宿 zhísù take one's turn to spend the night in the office or at school, etc. to be on duty; be on night-duty
值星 zhíxīng (of army officers) be on duty for the week:～官 of-

ficer of the week
值夜 zhíyè on night-duty; on the night watch
值遇 zhíyù 〈书面〉 meet with; come across; chance on; encounter:～不幸 come upon misfortune
值重 zhízhòng 〈方言〉 be of value; be of importance:人不能把金钱看得那么～。One should not overvalue (*or* attach undue importance to) money.

执(執) zhí

❶ hold; grip; grasp:～手同行 walk together hand in hand /～干戈卫社稷 take up arms to defend the country ❷ take charge of; control; manage:～炊 cook; prepare meals ❸ stick to; adhere to; persist in:固～己见 stubbornly stick to one's own view; obstinately adhere to one's opinions /固～不允 resolutely object; put one's foot down /坚～不易 firmly persist in (sth.); refuse to budge an inch /各～一词。Different people tell different stories. *or* Different people hold different views. ❹ carry out; execute; observe:～弟子礼 treat sb. as one's teacher (*or* mentor) ❺ 〈书面〉 catch; seize; capture:小偷当场被～。The thief was caught on the spot (*or* red-handed). ❻ written acknowledgment:收～ receipt ❼ 〈书面〉 intimate friend:父～ intimate friend of one's father ❽ (Zhí) a surname

执傲 zhí'ào obstinate and haughty:性格～ obstinate and conceited in character
执笔 zhíbǐ do the actual writing; put on paper; write:请大家提建议,我来～。Please give us your suggestions; I shall put them down in writing.
执鞭 zhíbiān 〈书面〉 ❶ hold the horse whip — be sb.'s driver:～随镫 be willing to drive the horse for sb. and walk behind the stirrup of the saddle — be willing to be sb.'s devoted follower ❷ hold the (teacher's) pointer — be a teacher or coach:～教头 coach
执导 zhídǎo direct (a film, etc.):他～本片。He was the director of the film.
执法 zhífǎ enforce laws and decrees:～机关 law enforcement agency /～人员 law enforcement officials (*or* officers) /～者 law-executor; law enforcer /～相绳 observe the law and measure with a plumb line; strictly execute the law /～不阿 impartial in executing the law; uphold justice /～不公 denial of (*or* miscarriage) justice /有法必依,～必严,违法必究。We must abide by the law, enforce it strictly and punish all law-breakers.
执法犯法 zhífǎ-fànfǎ infringement of rules of law by law-executors:严处～行为 severely punish those law-executors who abuse their power
执法如山 zhífǎ-rúshān enforce the law strictly; uphold the law firmly
执绋 zhífú hold a long cord pulling the hearse — take part in a funeral procession:～送殡 attend a funeral
执管 zhíguǎn be in charge of; manage; administer:家里的产业一齐交给她～。She was put in charge of all the family property.
执教 zhíjiào teach; be a teacher:他在北大～多年。He taught in Beijing University for many years.
执经问难 zhíjīng-wènnàn (of a disciple) receive instruction from one's master
执柯 zhíkē *also* "伐柯" fákē be a matchmaker; be a go-between:～作伐 arrange a match
执礼 zhílǐ 〈书面〉 observe etiquette; treat people with courtesy:～甚恭 punctiliously observe etiquette; be extremely courteous
执迷不悟 zhímí-bùwù be perverse; persist in pursuing a wrong course; refuse to mend one's ways:他坚持作恶,至今～。He persists in his evil ways and refuses to come to his senses. /嗐,你真是～! Oh, you are really perverse!
执泥 zhíní be an obstinate stickler for (sth.); stubbornly and rigidly adhere to (sth.):～于古法 be an obstinate stickler for ancient notions (*or* ways)
执牛耳 zhí niú'ěr (of an ancient prince presiding over a ceremony marking the conclusion of an alliance) hold the plate on which lie the ears he cut off from a sacrificial bull — be the acknowledged leader; hold the leading position; rule the roost:由他执诗坛之牛耳。He rules the roost in the poetic circles.
执拗 zhíniù obstinate; pigheaded; self-willed:一位～的学者 a stubborn scholar /我看你是不必那么～的。I advise you to stop being so bigoted.
执票人债券 zhípiàorén zhàiquàn 〈金融〉 bearer bond
执勤 zhíqín (of soldiers, policemen, etc.) be on duty
执事 zhíshì 〈书面〉 ❶ attendant ❷ 〈敬词〉 (in letters) ask sb.'s attendant to convey what one wants to say
执事 zhíshi 〈旧语〉 flags, weapons, etc. carried by a guard of honour:打～的 guard of honour
执刑 zhíxíng execution of punishment (esp. of capital punishment)
执行 zhíxíng ❶ carry out; perform; execute; implement:～任务 perform a task /～指示 carry out an instruction /～计划 execute a plan; carry out (*or* fulfil) a plan /～纪律 enforce discipline /～政策 implement a policy /～独立自主的和平外交政策 pursue (*or* follow) an independent foreign policy of peace /公正地～法律 dispense the law justly /～判决 enforcement of judgement /～裁决 execution of a decision /遗嘱～人 executor ❷ 〈计算机〉 execute:～程序 executive routine; master routine; monitor routine /～模块 executive module /～指令 execute instructions
执行董事 zhíxíng dǒngshì executive director
执行机构 zhíxíng jīgòu executive body
执行机关 zhíxíng jīguān executive organ
执行秘书 zhíxíng mìshū executive secretary
执行委员会 zhíxíng wěiyuánhuì executive committee
执行系统 zhíxíng xìtǒng executive system; monitor system; operating system
执行员 zhíxíngyuán 〈法律〉 marshal (responsible for executing all civil case and criminal case decisions concerning questions of property)
执行主席 zhíxíng zhǔxí executive or presiding chairman
执性 zhíxìng wilful; self-willed; headstrong:这孩子一向是温顺的,怎么今天这样～起来。The child used to be quite meek. Why is he so self-willed today?
执意 zhíyì insist on; persist in; be bent on:～不肯 obstinately refuse /～不从 stubbornly refuse to comply with /他～要与我同行。He insisted on going together with me. /她～要当一名记者。She is determined to become a reporter.
执友 zhíyǒu 〈书面〉 close friend; bosom friend
执掌 zhízhǎng be in control of; control; wield:～财权 have control over financial matters /～人事大权 be in charge of personnel affairs /～政权 hold the reins of government; be at the helm of government; wield political power
执照 zhízhào licence; permit:驾驶～ driver's licence; driving permit /行医～ licence to practise as a doctor /营业～ business licence /施工～ builder's licence /～税 permit fee
执政 zhízhèng be in power; be in office; wield state power; be at the helm of state
执政党 zhízhèngdǎng party in power or office; ruling or governing party
执中 zhízhōng 〈书面〉 fair; unbiased; impartial:～之说 middle course; golden mean
执著 zhízhuó *also* "执着" ❶ inflexible; rigid:～的态度 inflexible attitude /对生活小事不宜过于～。It's no good to be too particular about trivials. ❷ work unflaggingly; be persevering:～地追求真理 persevere in the pursuit of truth

絷(縶) zhí

〈书面〉 ❶ bind; tie; bundle up ❷ take into custody:南冠而～者谁也? Who was the jailed man wearing a hat of the southern state (Chu)? ❸ reins; halter:言授之～,以絷其马 give him the reins to rein in his horse

踯(躑) zhí

踯躅 zhízhú 〈书面〉 walk to and fro; loiter about; tramp:在池边～ loiter around the pond

跖 zhí

also "蹠" zhí ❶ matatarsus ❷ 〈书面〉 sole of the foot ❸ 〈书面〉 tread

侄(姪) zhí

brother's son; nephew

侄妇 zhífù 〈书面〉 *see* "侄媳妇"
侄女婿 zhínǚxu husband of brother's daughter; niece's husband
侄女 zhínü brother's daughter; niece
侄孙 zhísūn brother's grandson; grandnephew; greatnephew
侄孙女 zhísūnnü brother's granddaughter; grandniece; greatniece

侄媳妇 zhíxífu wife of brother's son; nephew's wife
侄子 zhízi *also* "侄儿" brother's son; nephew

zhǐ

止 zhǐ ❶ stop; halt; cease; desist: 终～ cease; end /泪流不～。Tears keep rolling down. /令则行,禁则～。Act at once when you're ordered to act; stop immediately when you are told to stop (strict enforcement of orders and prohibitions). ❷ prohibit; check; hold back: 遏～ check; hold back; contain /劝～ dissuade sb. from doing sth.; advise sb. not to do sth. /吃个梨子～～渴。Have a pear to quench your thirst. ❸ to; till; until: 到目前为～ to date; up to now /从第二页起到第五页～ from page 2 to page 5 /老汉望着八路军的队伍离去,直到他们的身影在远方消失为～。The old man watched the Eighth Route Army soldiers leaving till they were out of sight. ❹ only; sole: 不～一次 not just once; more than once

止步 zhǐbù halt; stop; go no further: 游人～ no visitors; out of bounds; off limits /～不前 stand still; mark time; make no headway /请～。Please go no further. /这是关键时刻,千万不可就此～。We must under no circumstances stop where we are at this critical moment.
止喘药 zhǐchuǎnyào antasthmatic; antiasthmatic
止动杆 zhǐdònggǎn arresting lever; gag lever; stop arm
止动机制 zhǐdòng jīzhì 〈机械〉stop motion mechanism
止动键 zhǐdòngjiàn locking key
止付 zhǐfù 〈经济〉stoppayment: ～命令 stop-payment order /～通知书 stop-payment notice /～支票 stopped check; stop payment of a check
止戈为武 zhǐgē-wéiwǔ real military prowess is to ensure peace and prevent resort to arms
止汗药 zhǐhànyào *also* "止汗剂" antiperspirant; antihidrotic
止回阀 zhǐhuífá check valve; non-return valve
止境 zhǐjìng limit; boundary: 学无～。There is no end to learning. /人类对宇宙奥秘的探索是没有～的。The probe into the secret of the universe by mankind has no limit.
止咳 zhǐké relieve a cough
止咳合剂 zhǐké héjì cough mixture
止咳平喘药 zhǐké-píngchuǎnyào medicine for the treatment of cough and asthma
止咳糖浆 zhǐké tángjiāng cough syrup
止渴 zhǐkě quench or satisfy one's thirst: ～生津 slake thirst and help produce saliva /～消劳 relieve thirst and fatigue
止痢药 zhǐlìyào antidysenteric
止水 zhǐshuǐ stagnant water; still water: 心如～ mind as tranquil as still water
止宿 zhǐsù stop over for the night; get accommodation
止谈风月 zhǐtánfēngyuè talk only about the wind and moon — make no comments on state affairs so as to avoid political persecution
止痛 zhǐtòng relieve pain; stop pain: 针刺～ use acupuncture to stop pain; acupuncture analgesia
止痛药 zhǐtòngyào anodyne; analgesic; pain-killer
止吐药 zhǐtùyào antemetic
止推轴承 zhǐtuī zhóuchéng 〈机械〉thrust bearing; antithrust bearing
止息 zhǐxī cease; stop; subside: 那响声到深夜才～。The sound did not cease until late into the night. /大风一直刮到第二天早晨方～。The wind subsided the next morning. *or* Not until the next morning did the strong wind die down (*or* away). /对客观规律的认识永无～。There is no end to learning the objective laws.
止泻药 zhǐxièyào antidiarrheal
止血 zhǐxuè stop bleeding; stanch bleeding: ～棉 haemostatic cotton /～纱布 haemostatic gauze
止血带 zhǐxuèdài tourniquet
止血法 zhǐxuèfǎ haemostasis; haemostasia
止血器 zhǐxuèqì haemostat
止血散 zhǐxuèsǎn styptic powder
止血药 zhǐxuèyào haemostatic
止痒剂 zhǐyǎngjì antipruritic
止于至善 zhǐyú-zhìshàn consummate; make perfect; arrive at the supreme good

沚 zhǐ 〈书面〉islet; small piece of land in a pond: 宛在水中～ as if sb. (*or* sth.) were standing on a small piece of land in the water

祉 zhǐ 〈书面〉happiness; felicity; blessedness: 为人民谋福～ work for the well-being of the people

址(阯) zhǐ site; location; ground: 厂～ factory site /校～ location of a school or university /废～ abandoned site /旧～ site of a former organization, building, etc. /故～ site of an ancient monument, etc. /遗～ ruins; relics /住～ address /原～ former address /新～ new address

芷 zhǐ *see* "白芷" báizhǐ

趾 zhǐ ❶ toe: 脚～ toe /蹼～ webbed toe ❷ foot: 举～ raise one's feet

趾高气扬 zhǐgāo-qìyáng be haughty; be high and mighty; strut about and give oneself airs; be on one's high horse: 他～,目中无人。He was swollen with arrogance and looked down his nose at everybody. /他是那么～,因为他父亲有钱。He is on his high horse because he has a rich father. /他打胜了第一仗便～,气势汹汹。He only won the first battle, and he put on such an extremely haughty and arrogant air. /他那副～的样子我实在受不了。I simply cannot put up with his high and mighty airs.
趾骨 zhǐgǔ phalanx; matatarsus
趾关节 zhǐguānjié toe joint
趾甲 zhǐjiǎ toenail
趾头 zhǐtou toe
趾行动物 zhǐxíng dòngwù digitigrade

黹 zhǐ 〈书面〉needlework; embroidery: 针～ needlework

只(衹、秖) zhǐ ❶ only; merely: 我～去过巴黎,还没去过伦敦。I've been to Paris only, not to London yet. ❷ all that there is; only: 屋里～我一个人。I'm alone in the room. /～此一遭,下不为例。Only this time and no more. *or* No more exceptions after this.
see also zhī

只不过 zhǐbùguò only; just; nothing but: 别担心,他～是太累了,没别的。Don't worry. He's only very tired; that's all. /这～是我运气不好。It's just (*or* nothing but) my bad luck. /我相信她～是跟他开开玩笑。I believe that she was merely teasing him.
只此一家,别无分店 zhǐ cǐ yī jiā, bié wú fēndiàn the one and only store selling the goods — have a monopoly; be the only authentic one
只当 zhǐdang as if; (treat sth.) as: 我在后面连声唤他,他～没听见。I kept calling him from behind, but he ignored me as if he heard nothing at all.
只得 zhǐdé have no choice but to; be compelled to; have to: 天下大雨,比赛～延期举行。It is raining heavily; we have no alternative but to put the match off. /厂长已经批准了,我～同意。The factory director has approved it, so I have to agree.
只读存储器 zhǐdú cúnchǔqì 〈计算机〉ROM (read-only memory); read-only storage
只顾 zhǐgù ❶ be absorbed in: 他～工作,把开会的事全忘了。He was so engrossed in his work that he forgot all about the meeting. ❷ pay attention only to; care only for: 这人～他自己。He cares only for his own interests. /不能～数量,不顾质量。It won't do to pay attention to quantity at the expense of quality.
只管 zhǐguǎn ❶ by all means; feel free to: 你～把试验搞下去,经费的事我来管。You go ahead with the experiment by all means. I shall take care of the funding. /有什么问题～问。Please feel free to ask any question. ❷ just; merely: 整天雨～哗哗地下。It's been simply bucketing down all day.
只好 zhǐhǎo cannot but; have to; be forced to: ～另谋出路 cannot but find another way out /时间到了,这个问题～下次再谈。Time is up. We'll have to discuss it again next time. /大家都反对,他～作罢。As all the others are against it, he is forced to give up.
只见树木,不见森林 zhǐ jiàn shùmù, bù jiàn sēnlín be unable to

see the wood for the trees; note only the details, but not the overall picture

只今 zhǐjīn 〈书面〉now; nowadays:当初不听别人劝,～成了阶下囚。He refused to listen to others' advice then, and now has ended up in prison.

只可意会,不可言传 zhǐkě yìhuì, bùkě yánchuán to be felt, but beyond description; can be apprehended but not expressed:这音乐之妙,～。You can feel how wonderful the music is, but you can't put it into words.

只怕 zhǐpà be afraid:这倒是个好主意,～太晚了。That's a good idea, but I'm afraid it's too late.

只是 zhǐshì ❶ merely; only; just; nothing but:这～托词。It's merely a pretext. /这～个时间问题。It is only a question of time. /没什么,我～有点好奇而已。Oh, nothing particular. I was just being a little curious. ❷ simply:随你怎么问,他～摇头,不回答。For all your questioning he simply shook his head and refused to say a thing. ❸ but; however:这件大衣样式不错,～太贵了点。This coat is very stylish, only (*or* but) it's a little bit too expensive.

只说不做 zhǐshuō-bùzuò be all talk and no action or deed:我丈夫是个～的人,他的想法可多啦,却从不付诸实施。My husband's all talk and no action; he has plenty of ideas but never puts them into practice.

只索 zhǐsuǒ (often used in the early vernacular) have to; be obliged to

只听楼梯响,不见人下来 zhǐ tīng lóutī xiǎng, bù jiàn rén xiàlai one keeps hearing footsteps on the staircase, but does not see anyone coming down — much cry but little wool; like a hen that cackles often but never lays an egg; all talk and no action:提拔他当总经理的事,至今还是～。There is a lot of talk about his being promoted to general manager, but up to now that's just so many empty words.

只闻雷声,不见雨点 zhǐ wén léishēng, bù jiàn yǔdiǎn all empty thunder and no rain — much cry and little wool; feckless bombast

只消 zhǐxiāo 〈方言〉all one has to do is; you only need to; do no more than:欲知详情,～填这份表格。For more information just fill out this form. /现在有了复印机,你～按一下电钮,就可得到一份复印件。Now that we have the Xerox machine, all you have to do is to press a button in order to get a copy.

只许州官放火,不许百姓点灯 zhǐ xǔ zhōuguān fànghuǒ, bùxǔ bǎixìng diǎndēng giving officials complete licence to commit arson while forbidding ordinary people even to light their lamps; one man may steal a horse while another may not look over the hedge

只要 zhǐyào so long as; provided; if:～肯下功夫,哪儿有学不会的道理? Anyone can learn as long as he makes an effort. /～她朋友能去,她就去。She will go provided her friends can go too.

只要功夫深,铁杵磨成针 zhǐyào gōngfu shēn, tiěchǔ móchéng zhēn constant grinding can turn an iron rod into a needle — perseverance spells success; with time and patience the leaf of the mulberry becomes satin; many strokes fell great oaks

只有 zhǐyǒu only; alone:～他才能解决这个问题。Only he (*or* He alone) can solve the problem. /这样～好处,没有坏处。This is all to the good, and no harm can come of it. /～这一个办法了。There is no other alternative.

只争朝夕 zhǐzhēng-zhāoxī seize the day, seize the hour; seize every second; race against time:要以～的精神发展我国的科技事业。We must seize the day, seize the hour and develop our science and technology as fast as we can.

只知其一,不知其二 zhǐ zhī qí yī, bù zhī qí èr *also* "知其一,不知其二" know only one aspect of a matter, but be ignorant of the other; be one-sided:这事你是～。You only know part of it, but not the whole story.

只重衣衫不重人 zhǐ zhòng yīshān bù zhòng rén *also* "只敬衣衫不敬人" only value the clothes sb. wears, but not the man himself; attach more importance to wealth than virtue:岳父是个势利眼,～。My father-in-law is very snobbish, having eyes only for a person's riches but not his character.

枳

zhǐ *also* "枸橘" gōujú 〈植物〉trifoliate orange

枳机草 zhǐjīcǎo *also* "芨芨草" jījīcǎo splendid achnatherum

枳椇 zhǐjǔ raisin tree; honey tree; Japanese raisin tree (*Hovenia dulcis*)

枳壳 zhǐqiào 〈中药〉ripening fruit of citron or trifoliate orange

枳实 zhǐshí 〈中药〉unripe or green fruit of citron or trifoliate orange

轵

zhǐ 〈书面〉axletree terminal

咫

zhǐ ancient measure of length, equal to eight *cun* (寸)

咫尺 zhǐchǐ 〈书面〉very close or near:～之间 only a short distance; very close

咫尺山河 zhǐchǐ-shānhé physically very near, but separated as if by rivers and mountains — see little of each other though living very near

咫尺天涯 zhǐchǐ-tiānyá short distance away, and yet poles apart — see little of each other though living nearby:有～之感 feel that we are so far apart though we live so near

抵

zhǐ 〈书面〉flank attack with one's hand

抵掌 zhǐzhǎng 〈书面〉clap (one's hands to show pleasure):～而谈 talking while clapping one's hands rhythmically (a habit in ancient times); have a heart-to-heart chat

纸(帋)

zhǐ ❶ paper:草～ rough straw paper /道林～ glazed printing paper /牛皮～ kraft paper /绵～ tissue paper /宣～ Xuan paper (a high quality paper made in Xuancheng, Anhui Province) /皱纹～ crepe paper /砂～ abrasive paper /包装～ wrapping paper /打字～ typing paper /放大～ enlarging paper /复写～ carbon paper /绘图～ drawing paper /命薄如～ one's fate is as thin as paper — hapless fate ❷ 〈量词〉:一～空文 a mere scrap of paper /一～家书 a letter from home

纸板 zhǐbǎn ❶ paperboard; cardboard:波纹～ corrugated cardboard /～箱 cardboard case; cardboard box; carton ❷ 〈印刷〉paper mould; paper matrix

纸包不住火 zhǐ bāobuzhù huǒ you can't wrap fire in paper — there is no hiding the facts; truth will out:他知道纸是包不住火的,瞒过初一也瞒不过十五。He is aware that fire cannot be wrapped up in paper and that even if the truth can be concealed for a time it cannot be concealed all the time.

纸杯 zhǐbēi paper cup

纸币 zhǐbì paper money; paper currency; (bank) note:发行～ issue (bank) notes /～发行银行 bank of issue /～流通量 amount of paper money (*or* currency) in circulation /～投放量 amount of currency issued into circulation /～兑换成硬币 redeem notes /不兑现～ fiat money

纸餐巾 zhǐcānjīn paper napkin

纸带 zhǐdài paper tape:～机 paper-tape unit; paper-tape equipment /～阅读机 paper-tape reader; punched-tape reader; tape reader /～穿孔机 paper tape punch; tape punch /～打印机 bound printer /～发报机 tape transmitter /～校对机 paper tape verifier /～到卡片转换器 tape-to-card converter

纸锭 zhǐdìng shoe-shaped ingot made of tinfoil paper (burned as an offering to the dead)

纸贵洛阳 zhǐguì-Luòyáng wide circulation of a popular work makes paper expensive

see also "洛阳纸贵"

纸花 zhǐhuā paper flower

纸黄金 zhǐhuángjīn 〈经济〉paper gold

纸婚 zhǐhūn first wedding anniversary

纸浆 zhǐjiāng paper pulp; pulp:～板 pulp board /～泵 pulp pump /～回收机 pulp-saver /～筛滤器 pulp strainer /～浓缩机 pulp thickener /～制造机 macerator /～原料 pulpwood /～厂 pulp mill

纸介电容器 zhǐjiè diànróngqì 〈电工〉paper condenser

纸巾 zhǐjīn paper towel; kleenex

纸绝缘 zhǐjuéyuán 〈电工〉paper insulation:～电缆 paper cable; paper-insulated cable

纸拉花 zhǐlāhuā paper festoon

纸老虎 zhǐlǎohǔ paper tiger (used to refer to sth. or sb. that is outwardly strong but inwardly weak):帝国主义是～。The imperialists are paper tigers.

纸马 zhǐmǎ 〈迷信〉❶ paper printed with pictures of idols to be burned at the altar ❷ 〈方言〉paper horse, etc. (burned at a funeral, meant to be the horse, etc. of the deceased in the next world)

纸媒儿 zhǐméir *also* "纸媒儿" *see* "纸捻 ❶"
纸捻 zhǐniǎn ❶ spill of rolled paper used to light a pipe, etc.; (paper) spill:用～点烟 light a pipe (*or* cigarette) with a spill /搓～ twist a strip of paper to make a spill ❷ tough paper strips twisted into strings for binding thin books
纸尿片 zhǐniàopiàn paper diaper; nappy
纸牌 zhǐpái playing cards
纸坯 zhǐpī ground paper
纸皮桦 zhǐpíhuà paper birch; canoe birch; silver birch; white birch
纸片 zhǐpiàn scraps of paper
纸票 zhǐpiào *also* "纸票子" *see* "纸币"
纸钱 zhǐqián 〈迷信〉paper made in the form of a coin and burned as an offering to the dead
纸上谈兵 zhǐshàng-tánbīng talk about stratagems on paper; be an armchair strategist — indulge in empty talk; talk glibly about generalities without getting down to specific problems:真正能干的军事指挥员,必须在战争中学习,不是仅仅善在～。A genuine competent military commander must learn war from war. It simply won't do to engage in idle theorizing. /这些人只会～,一遇到实际问题就寸步难行了。Those people are giants when talking about generalities, but dwarfs when confronted with practical problems.
纸绳 zhǐshéng paper string
纸莎草 zhǐsuōcǎo papyrus
纸莎草形柱 zhǐsuōcǎoxíngzhù papyrus column
纸条 zhǐtiáo slip of paper
纸通货 zhǐtōnghuò paper currency
纸头 zhǐtóu 〈方言〉paper:到处都是～。Paper, and paper everywhere. *or* Paper lies all over the places.
纸型 zhǐxíng 〈印刷〉paper mould; paper matrix:～纸 matrix paper /～干燥机 scorcher
纸烟 zhǐyān cigarette
纸样 zhǐyàng paper pattern (for tailoring)
纸鹞 zhǐyào 〈方言〉kite:蓝天上飞着几只蝴蝶形的～。A few butterfly-shaped kites are flying in the blue sky.
纸叶子 zhǐyèzi 〈方言〉playing cards
纸鱼 zhǐyú silverfish; fish moth
纸鸢 zhǐyuān 〈书面〉kite
纸张 zhǐzhāng paper; sheets of paper:笔墨～ pen, ink and paper
纸醉金迷 zhǐzuì-jīnmí *also* "金迷纸醉" (a life of) luxury and dissipation:声色犬马,～ wallow in the fleshpots; lead a life of debauchery /他沉溺在五光十色、～的生活中。He indulged in worldly pleasures.

徵

zhǐ 〈音乐〉note of the ancient Chinese five-tone scale, corresponding to 5 in numbered musical notation

旨[1]

zhǐ 〈书面〉tasty; delicious; delectable:甘～ delicacies

旨[2] (❶恉)

zhǐ ❶ purport; purpose:主～ purport; main purpose /宗～ purpose; aim /会议通过了一项～在进一步加强各国科学技术合作的决议。The meeting adopted a resolution aimed at further strengthening international cooperation in the field of science and technology. ❷ intention; wish; decree:意～ intention, wish /法～ God's decree /圣～ imperial edict or decree
旨酒 zhǐjiǔ 〈书面〉excellent wine
旨令 zhǐlìng (imperial) order; edict; decree:下了一道～ issue an imperial decree
旨趣 zhǐqù 〈书面〉purport; objective; intent:本刊～在发刊词中业已言明。The purport of this publication has already been stated in the foreword.
旨要 zhǐyào *also* "指要" zhǐyào 〈书面〉main idea; gist
旨意 zhǐyì decree; order:秉承主人的～行事 act on the orders of one's master

酯

zhǐ 〈化学〉ester:聚～ polyester /醛～ aldehydoester /～交换 ester exchange /～解(作用) esterlysis /～缩合(作用) ester condensation
酯化 zhǐhuà 〈化学〉esterification:～催化剂 esterification catalyst /～反应 esterification /～剂 esterifying agent /～律 esterification law /～树脂 esterified resin
酯基转移作用 zhǐjī zhuǎnyí zuòyòng transesterification
酯键 zhǐjiàn ester bond
酯胶 zhǐjiāo ester gum
酯蜡 zhǐlà ester wax
酯酶 zhǐméi esterase
酯强混凝土 zhǐqiánghùnníngtǔ 〈建筑〉estercrete
酯树胶 zhǐshùjiāo 〈化工〉estergum or ester gum; rosin ester
酯油 zhǐyóu ester oil

指

zhǐ ❶ finger:大拇～ thumb /食～ index finger; forefinger /中～ middle finger /无名～ ring finger; third finger /小拇～ little finger /六～儿 six-finger hand; one whose hand has six fingers /～如玉葱 have slim, delicate fingers /兰花～ orchid-shaped fingers (a gesture in traditional Chinese operas) /屈～可数 can be counted on one's fingers — very few /首屈一～的当代作家 modern writer of the first (*or* purest) water /天黑得伸手不见五～。It was so dark that you couldn't see your own fingers (*or* couldn't see your hand in front of your face). ❷ fingerbreadth; digit:两～宽的贴边 hem (of a dress, etc.) two fingerbreadths wide /这双鞋大出一～。This pair of shoes is a digit larger (*or* one size larger) than your size. ❸ show the direction of; point to:手～着北方。The hand points north. /时针～着九点半。The hands of the clock point to half past nine. /千人所～,无病而死。When a thousand people point accusing fingers at a man he will die even without sickness (— it is dangerous to incur public wrath). ❹ (of hair) stand; bristle:其罪行令人发～。The crime makes one's blood boil (*or* makes one bristle with indignation). ❺ direct; point out:灯塔给航船～明了前进的方向。The lighthouse directs the ships on their way forward. /请～出我们的不足之处。Please point out our shortcomings. ❻ refer to:特～ refer in particular to /泛～ make a general reference; be used in a general sense /暗～ hint at /我说有些人真愚蠢,不是～你。When I said some people are stupid, I wasn't referring to you. ❼ depend on; rely on; count on:这个家就～望你了。We depend on you to support the family. /单～着一个人是不能把事情做好的。You cannot possibly do a job well by counting on the help of one person.
指北针 zhǐběizhēn compass
指标 zhǐbiāo target; quota; norm; index:制定生产～ set a norm for production /未完成去年的钢产～ miss (*or* fall short of) last year's steel production target /国家征购～ state purchase quota /质量～ quality index
指拨 zhǐbō appropriate or allocate (a sum of money) for a designated purpose:国家～巨款兴修水利。The state appropriated a huge sum of money for building water conservancy projects.
指拨 zhǐbo ❶ give directions; give advice:我工作上没有经验,您多～吧。I'm a novice at the job; your advice will be highly appreciated. ❷ order sb. to do sth.; dispatch:除非队长来,你甭想～我。I accept orders from nobody except the team leader.
指驳 zhǐbó criticize and refute; censure and retort:当面～ criticize and refute sb. to his face
指不胜屈 zhǐbùshèngqū *also* "指不胜数" too numerous to be counted on the fingers; great many:数十年来,这所大学培养的科学人才～。Over the decades, this university has turned out a great many qualified scientists.
指不定 zhǐbudìng not sure; perhaps; maybe:你甭等他了,他～来不来呢。You don't have to wait for him; maybe he won't come.
指陈 zhǐchén point out; state clearly:～利弊 point out the advantages and disadvantages
指斥 zhǐchì reprove; reprimand; condemn:舆论对该部长的不端行为多有～。The minister's irregular behaviour was much censured by the public.
指导 zhǐdǎo guide; direct; instruct:～思想 guiding principle /～价格 guided price /希望在工作上你多多～我们。I hope we shall always have the benefit of your guidance. /本学年张教授～两篇研究生论文。Professor Zhang is supervising two graduates in writing their MA theses this academic year.
指导性计划 zhǐdǎoxìng jìhuà guidance planning
指导员 zhǐdǎoyuán ❶ instructor ❷ political instructor (of a PLA company)
指点 zhǐdiǎn ❶ instruct; give directions or advice:老师耐心地～学生作业中的错误。The teacher is patiently pointing out the mistakes in his pupils' homework. /多亏你的～,使我顿开茅塞。I'm enlightened by your advice (*or* pointers). /这本书对攻读那门复杂的课程有～迷津

之效。This book may serve to throw light on the complicated subject. /请给我们～～。Please show us how to do it. ❷ point the (*or* one's) finger at; pick on:遭人～ be picked on /他自己不工作,却专门对别人的工作指指点点。He does no work but is always pointing an accusing finger at people who are working.

指定 zhǐdìng appoint; assign; name:～的停车场 assigned parking lot /～代理人 authorized agent /～管辖 designated jurisdiction; determination of jurisdiction /～继承人 designated heir /～监护人 designated guardian /～买主 nominee buyer /～一个日期 appoint a date /到～的地点集合 assemble at the appointed meeting place /～一位副厂长接待来宾 assign one of the deputy directors of the factory to receive the guests /他被～为会议召集人。He was named the convener.

指东说西 zhǐdōng-shuōxī *also* "指东话西";"指东画西" pointing to the east while speaking of the west — not to the point; irrelevant

指法 zhǐfǎ fingering:她每天练钢琴,现在懂得～了。She plays the piano every day. She knows the fingering now.

指腹为婚 zhǐfù-wéihūn proposing a future marriage between two unborn babies by pointing to the belly of their pregnant mothers; the two being engaged to each other before they were born; antenatal (*or* prenatal) betrothal

指供 zhǐgòng ❶ extract a confession by throwing out hints to the defendant ❷ expose the defendant (by the witness) during a trial:由于叛徒当面～,他的身份暴露了。His identity was revealed because the turncoat told everything at court.

指骨 zhǐgǔ 〈生理〉phalanx

指顾 zhǐgù 〈书面〉snap of the finger; twinkling of an eye; in a short while; instantly:～之间,勇怯立异。In the twinkling of an eye, each one showed his true colours — the brave ones as well as the cowards. /侵略者的崩溃是～间的事。The collapse of the aggressors is imminent.

指归 zhǐguī 〈书面〉aim; purpose; intention:辨其～ find out one's intention; identify one's purpose

指猴 zhǐhóu 〈动物〉aye-aye

指画 zhǐhuà ❶ point at; point to:老师边讲,边～着地图。The teacher, while speaking, pointed at the map. ❷ paint with the finger (in place of a brush) ❸ finger painting

指环 zhǐhuán (finger) ring

指挥 zhǐhuī ❶ command; direct; conduct:～千军万马 command a vast army of infantry and cavalry; have millions of troops under one's command /～一场战役 take command of a battle (*or* campaign) /～作战 direct operations /～交通 direct traffic /～乐队 conduct an orchestra /舰队的～舰 commanding ship of the fleet /军队由总统直接～。The army is under the president's direct command. /我～不动他们。I'm not in a position to call the tune (*or* shots) here. ❷ commander; director; conductor:新来的乐队～ new conductor of the orchestra /任命他为前线～。He was named the frontline commander.

指挥棒 zhǐhuībàng ❶ baton:交通～ traffic policeman's baton /乐队～ conductor's baton ❷〈贬义〉something that symbolizes authority:随着别人的～转 dance to someone else's baton (*or* tune)

指挥部 zhǐhuībù command; headquarters:防空～ air defence command /前沿～ forward command post /设立罢工～ establish strike headquarters

指挥舱 zhǐhuīcāng 〈航天〉command module

指挥车 zhǐhuīchē command car

指挥刀 zhǐhuīdāo officer's sword

指挥官 zhǐhuīguān commander; commanding officer

指挥控制与通讯自动化 zhǐhuī kòngzhì yǔ tōngxùn zìdònghuà C3A (command, control, and communications automation)

指挥若定 zhǐhuī-ruòdìng be perfectly calm and collected in directing a battle; direct (work, etc.) with perfect composure; give competent leadership

指挥所 zhǐhuīsuǒ command post

指挥塔台 zhǐhuī tǎtái 〈航空〉control tower

指挥系统 zhǐhuī xìtǒng command system

指挥员 zhǐhuīyuán ❶ commander (in the army) ❷ someone who is in charge (of a project, etc.)

指鸡骂狗 zhǐjī-màgǒu *also* "指桑骂槐" scold the dog while pointing at the chicken — point at one and abuse another; attack by innuendo

指甲 zhǐjia nail:手～ fingernail /脚～ toenail /灰～ ringworm of the nails; onychomycosis /修～ manicure

指甲锉刀 zhǐjia cuòdāo nail file

指甲刀 zhǐjiadāo nail clippers

指甲盖儿 zhǐjiagàir fingernail

指甲花 zhǐjiahuā garden balsam

指甲心儿 zhǐjiaxīnr nail

指甲油 zhǐjiayóu nail polish

指尖 zhǐjiān finger tip

指间襞 zhǐjiānbì interdigital fold

指教 zhǐjiào ❶ instruct; teach:在新教练的～下,他成绩提高很快。He is making rapid progress under the instruction of the new coach. ❷〈套语〉give advice or comments:望不吝～。Feel free to give your comments.

指节 zhǐjié ❶ phalangeal joints ❷〈动物〉dactylus

指痉病 zhǐjìngbìng athetosis

指疽草 zhǐjūcǎo whitlow grass

指靠 zhǐkào depend on; rely on; look to (for help):他的生计就～投资所得的一点点收入。He depends for his livelihood upon a small income from investments. /我～你的支持。I look to you for support.

指控 zhǐkòng accuse (sb. of); charge (sb. with):有人～他贪赃枉法。He's been accused of perverting the course of justice for a bribe. /～他犯盗窃罪。He is charged with larceny. /这些～纯属捏造,根本站不住脚。These charges are trumped up and simply cannot hold water.

指叩诊 zhǐkòuzhěn finger percussing; finger-tapping

指令 zhǐlìng ❶ instruct; order; direct:上级～迅速破案。The higher authorities ordered that the case be cracked as soon as possible. ❷〈旧语〉written instructions or directives:顷接上峰～ have just received written instructions from one's superior ❸〈计算机〉instruction; command; order:遥控～ remote control command /～处理机 instruction processor /～带 instruction tape /～发送器 command sender /～计数器 instruction counter /～寄存器 order register /～接收机 command receiver /～译码器 command decoder /～码 instruction code /～系统 instruction repertoire; instruction set

指令舱 zhǐlìngcāng 〈航天〉command module

指令性计划 zhǐlìngxìng jìhuà mandatory planning (state plans concerning important projects in the national economy which are sent down in the form of directives to administrative units at all levels)

指鹿为马 zhǐlùwéimǎ (said of the prime minister in the Qin Dynasty named Zhao Gao 赵高 who demanded absolute obedience by pointing at a stag and calling it a horse and killing everyone who disagreed) call a stag a horse — distort facts; confuse right and wrong:这种说法纯粹是～。It's sheer deliberate misrepresentation.

指路明灯 zhǐlù míngdēng bright lamp for one's journey;〈比喻〉beacon light:他的作品是许多爱国青年的～。His writings served to point up the road ahead for many young patriots.

指路牌 zhǐlùpái roadsign; signpost; fingerpost; guidepost

指名 zhǐmíng mention by name; name:不～地旁敲侧击 make innuendoes against sb. /会上～批评了我们班。Our class was criticized by name at the meeting. /老师～要你参加演讲比赛。The teacher named you to take part in the speech contest.

指名道姓 zhǐmíng-dàoxìng mention sb.'s full name; name names:人家又没有～,你干吗硬要往自己头上联系? They didn't mention your name. Why do you think they are targeting at you? /我不想～。I don't want to name names.

指明 zhǐmíng indicate clearly; point out:～事情的严重性 point out the serious nature of the matter /他的话给我～了努力方向。What he said showed me clearly the way forward.

指模 zhǐmó *also* "指摹"〈方言〉fingerprint; finger mark

指目 zhǐmù 〈书面〉look at and point at:路人～。All the men in the street were pointing their fingers at him.

指南 zhǐnán guide; guidebook:行动的～ guide to action /做为生活的～ serve as a guide in life /购物～ buying guide /大英博物馆参观～ guide to the British Museum /英语实用～ practical guide to English

指南车 zhǐnánchē ancient Chinese vehicle with a wooden figure always pointing to the south; compass vehicle

指南针 zhǐnánzhēn ❶ compass:～是中国四大发明之一。The compass is one of China's four great inventions. ❷〈比喻〉something that guides people along the right direction:马克思主义是引导中国革命走向胜利的～。Marxism is the guide that has led to victory in the Chinese revolution.

指派 zhǐpài appoint; assign; designate; name:～她当学习小组长

appoint her (to be) study group leader /～代表出席联合国裁军会议 name delegates to the UN Disarmament Conference /～他去领导这次起义。He was designated to lead the uprising.

指蹼 zhǐpǔ web

指趣 zhǐqù *also* "旨趣" zhǐqù aim; purport; objective

指认 zhǐrèn identify; recognize; point out and affirm:请受害人～作案嫌疑人。Ask the victim to identify the suspect.

指日可待 zhǐrì-kědài can be realized very soon; be just round the corner:工程的完成～。The project will soon be completed. /本地区的和平～。Peace in this region is just round the corner.

指桑骂槐 zhǐsāng-màhuái *also* "指鸡骂狗" abuse the locust when they mean mulberry — point at one but abuse another; attack by innuendo:他明明是冲着我在那里～。He is pretending to be telling another off while it's me he is having a dig at.

指山卖岭 zhǐshān-màilǐng *also* "指山卖磨" empty talk; idle talk; hollow words:他一味～应付着,一点实情也不露。He has been using evasive tactics, not breathing a single word of truth.

指山说磨 zhǐshān-shuōmò pointing at a mountain while talking about a grindstone — pointing at one thing but actually talking about another

指使 zhǐshǐ instigate; incite; stir up; put sb. up to sth.:～一群暴徒抢百货商店 incite a group of mobsters to plunder the department store /受别人～ act on sb.'s instigation; act as sb.'s cat's-paw /幕后～者是谁? Who is the person behind the scenes (*or* the hidden instigator)?

指示 zhǐshì ❶ indicate; show:箭头～着前进方向。The arrow indicates the direction of advance. /会有人给你～穿过森林的道路。Someone will show you the way through the forest. ❷ instruct; direct:～有关部门解决环境脏乱问题 instruct the departments concerned to clean up the area /～他们严格遵守协议 direct them to adhere strictly to the agreement ❸ instruction; directive; order:发出～ give (*or* issue) instructions /不折不扣地执行中央政府的～ carry out instructions of the central government to the letter /我们接到～,要严密监视敌人。We have received orders to keep close watch on the enemy. /事情怎么处理,他给了我们明确的～。He has given us precise directives about how to do it.

指示板 zhǐshìbǎn indicator board

指示代词 zhǐshì dàicí 〈语言〉demonstrative pronoun

指示灯 zhǐshìdēng pilot lamp

指示功率 zhǐshì gōnglǜ 〈机械〉indicated power

指示管 zhǐshìguǎn indicator tube

指示剂 zhǐshìjì 〈化学〉indicator

指示目标 zhǐshì mùbiāo 〈军事〉indication of target

指示旗 zhǐshìqí 〈军事〉guide flag

指示器 zhǐshìqì indicator:～开启(关闭) indicator ON (OFF) /～信号灯 indicator light /刻度盘～ dial indicator /液面～ level indicator

指示植物 zhǐshì zhíwù indicator plant

指事 zhǐshì 〈语言〉self-explanatory characters, one of the six categories of Chinese characters (六书), e.g. 上 (above), which was originally written as 二, and 下 (below), which was originally written as 亖

指手画脚 zhǐshǒu-huàjiǎo *also* "指手划脚" ❶ make animated gestures; gesticulate profusely:～地高谈阔论 talk volubly with dramatic gestures /他～,讲说着鲁智深拳打镇关西、景阳岗上武松打虎的故事。He gestured as he spoke, acting out Lu Zhishen's fight with a bully or Wu Song's killing of the tiger. ❷ issue orders right and left; criticize this and condemn that; carp and cavil:他不做任何调查,下车伊始就～。He did not bother to make any investigation and started issuing orders right and left as soon as he arrived. /他对年轻人不是帮助,总是～。He is always carping about the young people, instead of giving them any help.

指授 zhǐshòu 〈书面〉teach; instruct:～韬略 teach sb. military strategy

指书 zhǐshū ❶ write with the finger (in place of a brush) ❷ calligraphy done with the finger (in place of a brush)

指数 zhǐshù ❶〈数学〉exponent:～曲线 exponential curve /～因数 exponential factor /～值 exponential value /正～ positive exponent /负～ negative exponent ❷ index number; index:生活费～ cost of living index /物价～ price index /综合～ composite index /颅～〈生理〉cranial index /～化〈经济〉indexation

指数定律 zhǐshù dìnglǜ 〈数学〉exponential law; index law; law of indices

指数方程 zhǐshù fāngchéng 〈数学〉exponential equation; indicial equation

指数函数 zhǐshù hánshù 〈数学〉exponential function

指数律 zhǐshùlǜ 〈数学〉index law

指天画地 zhǐtiān-huàdì gesticulate while speaking; hold forth without restraint

指天椒 zhǐtiānjiāo tabasco

指天誓日 zhǐtiān-shìrì swear by the heaven and the sun; swear by God:他～,说一定讲真话。He swore by God to tell the truth.

指头 zhǐtou ❶ finger:手～ finger /小～ little finger ❷ toe:脚～ toe

指头肚儿 zhǐtoudùr 〈方言〉finger cushion

指头脓炎 zhǐtou nóngyán *also* "甲沟炎" jiǎgōuyán;"脓性指头炎" nóngxìng zhǐtouyán 〈医学〉felon; whitlow

指望 zhǐwang ❶ look forward to; count on; expect:～有一天我们这儿建一个水电站 look forward to the day when a hydropower station will be built here /这人～不住。You cannot rely on him for help. /我们～夏粮丰收。We expect a good harvest of the summer grain crops. ❷ hope:他这病已经没有～。He is beyond recovery (from his illness). /儿子在事故中丧生,老人觉得再也没什么～了。After the death of his son in an accident, the old man felt life was without hope.

指纹 zhǐwén ❶ loops and whorls on a finger ❷ fingerprint:取～ register (*or* take) sb.'s fingerprint /～鉴定 fingerprint identification /～档案 fingerprint file

指纹法 zhǐwénfǎ fingerprint method

指纹鉴定法 zhǐwén jiàndìngfǎ dactyloscopy

指纹学 zhǐwénxué dactylography

指向 zhǐxiàng ❶ directional:～天线 directional antenna /航空线～标志 directional airway marker /～植物 compass plant /～构造 directional structure /～聚焦 directional focusing ❷ point to:～天空 point to the sky ❸ direction that is being pointed to:我顺着他的～望去,只见桥洞里穿出一条小船来。I looked in the direction he was pointing to and saw a small boat coming out of the bridge opening.

指相化石 zhǐxiàng huàshí facies fossil

指雁为羹 zhǐyànwéigēng console oneself with a pie in the sky; feed on illusions

指要 zhǐyào *also* "旨要" zhǐyào 〈书面〉main idea; gist:得其～ get the main idea of it

指引 zhǐyǐn point (the way); lead; guide; show:～前进的道路 show (*or* point) the way forward /～航向 chart the course /～目标轰炸机 master (*or* lead) bomber /一位猎手～我们穿过了丛林。A hunter guided us through the jungle.

指印 zhǐyìn fingerprint; finger mark:取囚犯的～ take the prisoner's fingerprint

指责 zhǐzé censure; criticize; reproach:屡受～ be criticized repeatedly /他的行为受到了公众的～。He received a public censure for his behaviour. /我们的所作所为是无可～的。Our conduct is above reproach.

指摘 zhǐzhāi nitpick; pick faults and criticize

指战员 zhǐzhànyuán officers and men

指仗 zhǐzhàng 〈方言〉rely on; depend on:这里农民的一年生计就～地里的收成。The farmers here depend for their livelihood solely on the harvest from the fields.

指针 zhǐzhēn ❶ (needle) indicator; pointer:～平衡器 pointer counterbalance /～式温度计 dial thermometer ❷ guiding principle; guideline:这个文件是发展教育事业的～。This document serves to guide (*or* provides guidelines for) the development of education. ❸ 〈中医〉pressing with a finger (on an acupuncture point); finger-pressing

指诊 zhǐzhěn 〈医学〉touch; digital examination:肛门～ rectal touch /阴道～ vaginal touch

指正 zhǐzhèng ❶ point out and correct mistakes:王教授～了书中的几处错误。Professor Wang corrected a few mistakes in the book. ❷ 〈套语〉(invite people to) make comments or criticisms:不对之处务请～。Please don't hesitate to remedy our errors.

指指戳戳 zhǐzhǐ-chuōchuō gossip behind one's back

指重表 zhǐzhòngbiǎo 〈石油〉weight indicator

zhì

滞(滯) zhì stagnant; sluggish; be at a standstill:沉～

〈书面〉stagnate; cease to flow; lie still /凝～ remain motionless; be at a standstill /停～不前 stagnate; bog down; reach a stalemate /～水 stagnant water

滞碍 zhì'ài 〈书面〉obstruct; block; hinder: ～难行 be obstructed and difficult to get through

滞背 zhìbèi sell sluggishly; be in poor market demand: ～货 goods which sell sluggishly; slow-selling goods; drug on the market

滞尘 zhìchén retard the spread of the dust (by vegetation)

滞船费 zhìchuánfèi demurrage

滞呆 zhìdāi dull; dim-witted: 他两眼～地看着窗外。He looked out of the window, dull and spiritless.

滞钝 zhìdùn slow (in thought or action); thick; obtuse: 脑筋～ slow in thought; slow-witted

滞洪 zhìhóng 〈水利〉flood detention: ～区 detention basin; retarding basin /～水库 detention reservoir

滞后 zhìhòu lag behind: 改变交通运输～的状况 change the situation in which transport is unable to meet current needs /生产工艺～于科学技术的发展。Technical skills are lagging behind the development of science and technology.

滞后角 zhìhòujiǎo 〈物理〉lag angle

滞缓 zhìhuǎn slow; tardy; torpid; sluggish: 电视机需求增长～ sluggish growth in the demand for TV sets /迈着～的步子 walk with slow steps

滞留 zhìliú be detained; be held up; (of ship, vehicle, etc.) wait on demurrage: 我因公事在京～多日。I was detained in Beijing for quite a few days on business. /这场大雾使许多旅客～在机场。A great many travellers were held up at the airport by the bad fog. /有二百条船在港口外～，等待泊位。There were 200 ships waiting on demurrage outside the port for berths.

滞留费 zhìliúfèi demurrage; detention charge

滞纳金 zhìnàjīn fine for delaying payment; fine for paying late; overdue fine

滞纳税 zhìnàshuì tax in arrears

滞泥 zhìní ❶ be a stickler for (form, etc.); be punctilious: ～于章句之末。Pay too much attention to minor details (*or* nonessentials) in writing. ❷ languid and sloppy

滞碾 zhìnian *also* "滞粘"〈方言〉dilatory; sluggish; laggard: 这件事～半年也不办。This has been put off for half a year.

滞涩 zhìsè ❶ clumsy; awkward; blunt; dull: 举止～ clumsy (*or* awkward) manners /目光～ dull looks ❷ obscure; difficult; not fluent: 这篇文章有一些～的地方，要修改一下。The article needs polishing; some places make difficult reading.

滞塞 zhìsè obstructed; impeded; be held up: 航运～。Shipping is held up. /思路～。There is a lack of the flow of ideas.

滞销 zhìxiāo unsalable; unmarketable: ～商品 commodities which sell sluggishly; unsalable goods /～品资金融通 finance for dead stock /这种产品长期～。The product has been a drug on the market for a long time.

滞育 zhìyù (of insects, etc.) diapause

滞运 zhìyùn sluggish transport: 这里的煤炭堆积如山，～滞销。The coal here is piling up high because of deficient transport and poor market.

滞胀 zhìzhàng stagflation

寘

zhì 〈书面〉place; put: ～之于怀 keep in mind

治

zhì ❶ rule; govern; harness; control: ～校 run a school /自～ self-government; autonomy /法～ rule of law /辖～ rule; govern /分而～之 divide and rule /～淮 harness the Huai River /～土改水 bring the water under control and improve the soil /～山驯水 tame rivers and mountains /整～运河 dredge a canal ❷ stability; order; peace: 天下大～ great order across the land ❸ 〈旧语〉seat of a local government: 县～ county seat /省～ provincial capital ❹ treat (a disease); heal; cure: 医～ treat (a disease) /防～ prophylaxis and treatment /根～ cure once and for all /洁～ clean the teeth with instruments or specially made toothpaste /食～ food therapy /不～之症 incurable disease /～好伤 heal a wound /他的病～好了。He was cured of his illness. /这病不能再拖，得～啦！You can't let it go like that. You must see the doctor at once. ❺ eliminate; stamp out: ～虫子 eliminate harmful insects /～蟑螂 exterminate cockroaches ❻ punish: 处～ punish /惩～ punish; mete out punishment to /～～那坏蛋。Let's teach that skunk a lesson. ❼ pursue one's studies; study; research: ～经 study classics /～史 specialize in history ❽ (Zhì) a surname

治安 zhì'ān law and order; peace and security; public order: 维持～ maintain law and order /扰乱社会～ disturb peace and order /～机关 law enforcement office (*or* agency) /～官员 peace officer /～保卫人员 guardian of the peace; security personnel /～管理处罚条例 Security Administration Punishment Act

治安法院 zhì'ān fǎyuàn magistrates' court

治安官 zhì'ānguān justice of the peace

治安军 Zhì'ānjūn puppet army in northern China during the War of Resistance Against Japanese Aggression

治保 zhìbǎo public security work: 地方～组织 local public security organizations /～委员 public security commissioner

治本 zhìběn effect a permanent cure; tackle a problem, etc. at its root: 疏通河流要从～着眼。We must aim at a permanent control of the river when we dredge it.

治标 zhìbiāo effect a temporary cure; merely alleviate the symptoms of an illness: 只～不治本是不能解决问题的。You cannot solve the problem by taking only stopgap measures.

治病救人 zhìbìng-jiùrén cure the sickness to save the patient; help sb. mend his or her ways: 对犯错误的同志要抱着～的态度帮助他改正。To help erring comrades correct their mistakes we should adopt the approach of curing the sickness to save the patient.

治产 zhìchǎn manage property

治厂 zhìchǎng run a factory: 从严～ manage a factory with a firm hand

治喘灵 zhìchuǎnlíng isoprenaline; isoproterenol

治国 zhìguó govern a country; manage state affairs: ～安邦 administer the state well and ensure national security

治国安民 zhìguó-ānmín run the country well and ensure peace and security for the people: 各级领导都要懂得～的道理。Leading cadres at various levels should all understand the importance of ensuring good government and security for the people.

治蝗 zhìhuáng wipe out locusts

治绩 zhìjì (meritorious) performance of an official or government; achievements in office: 按～升迁官员 promote or demote officials according to their performance / 无～可言 have no achievements to speak of (as an official or government)

治家 zhìjiā run or manage a household

治碱 zhìjiǎn combat alkalinity

治理 zhìlǐ ❶ administer; rule; govern: ～国家 administer (*or* govern) a country; run a state /在英国，君主是国家元首，但不～国事。In Britain the monarch reigns but does not rule. ❷ (of nature) harness; tame; bring under control; put in order: ～黄河 harness the Yellow River; bring the Yellow River under control /重视沙漠的～ attach great importance to the transformation of desert /～环境污染 prevent and control environmental pollution

治理整顿 zhìlǐ-zhěngdùn improve the economic environment and rectify the economic order; make economic retrenchments: 停产～ suspend production to improve management and performance

治疗 zhìliáo treat; cure: ～疾病 treat a disease /～见效 respond well to treatment /住院～ be hospitalized /隔离～ treat sb. in quarantine /～效果 therapeutic effect /对癌症尚无绝对有效的～办法。There is no certain cure for cancer yet.

治疗学 zhìliáoxué therapeutics

治贫 zhìpín eliminate poverty; get rid of poverty; be lifted out of poverty: 把现代科技引向农村，是农村～的主要途径。To introduce modern science and technology into rural areas is an important way to help lift the countryside out of poverty.

治穷致富 zhìqióng-zhìfù get rid of poverty and bring about prosperity: 我们必须帮助贫困地区发展生产，～。We must help impoverished areas increase production in order to get rich.

治权 zhìquán administrative power; right of administration

治丧 zhìsāng arrange a funeral; make funeral arrangements: ～委员会 funeral committee

治沙 zhìshā sand control: ～造田 reclaim land by sand control

治山治水 zhìshān-zhìshuǐ green mountains and tame rivers

治生 zhìshēng earn or make a living: 他没有～的本领，终身穷困。He knew very little about earning a livelihood and remained poor all his life.

治世 zhìshì 〈书面〉❶ times of peace and prosperity: 生逢～ live in times of peace and prosperity ❷ run a state; govern a country: ～不

Z

一道。There are ways and ways to run a state. *or* Ways to run a state vary.

治水 zhìshuǐ harness rivers; bring the waters under control; prevent floods by water control: ～工程 water control project / 大禹～。Yu the Great (in ancient China) brought the waters under control.

治丝益棼 zhìsī-yìfén *also* "治丝而棼" try to sort out silk threads only to tangle them further — complicate matters by adopting wrong methods; make confusion worse confounded

治所 zhìsuǒ 〈旧语〉seat of local government

治外法权 zhìwài fǎquán extraterritoriality; exterritoriality; extrality

治污 zhìwū reduce and control pollution

治下 zhìxià 〈书面〉❶ under the rule of; under or within the jurisdiction of: 暴君～的人民纷纷起义。The people under the rule of the tyrant rose up in revolt one after another. ❷ rule the people: ～严酷 ride roughshod over the people under one's rule

治学 zhìxué pursue scholarly work; do scholarly research: ～的正确态度是实事求是。The correct approach to scholarly pursuits is seeking truth from facts. / 他严谨的～精神给我留下了深刻的印象。I was quite impressed by his rigorous scholarship.

治印 zhìyìn engrave a seal: ～艺术 art of seal engraving

治愚 zhìyú eliminate ignorance and backward state of mind: 治穷必先～。Improving people's minds is the first step in getting rid of poverty.

治愈率 zhìyùlǜ 〈医学〉cure rate; curative rate: ～达百分之九十 ninety percent cure rate / 提高～ improve the curative rate

治装 zhìzhuāng 〈书面〉purchase things (esp. clothes) necessary for a long journey: ～费 clothing allowance (for officials sent on a mission abroad, etc.) / 他将去法国，现正忙着～。He is busy purchasing clothes and other necessities for going to France.

治罪 zhìzuì bring to justice; punish: 凡触犯刑律的，都要～。Those who break the law will be brought to justice. / 此人罪大恶极，不～不足以平民愤。This man is guilty of the most heinous crimes and must be severely punished in order to redress the grievances of the people.

瘈

zhì 〈书面〉crazy; mad

see also chì

忮

zhì 〈书面〉jealousy: ～心 jealousy / 不～不求 be neither jealous of others nor avaricious

志[1]

zhì ❶ will; aspiration; ambition; ideal: 奇～ lofty aspiration / 夙～ long-cherished ambition / 有～于此 be bent upon this / 胸怀大～ cherish high ideals; have lofty aspirations / 少年得～ realize one's ambition (*or* have a successful career) in early youth / 不得～ under a cloud / 矢～不渝 swear that one will never change; swear that nothing can change one's mind / 人穷～不穷 be poor materially but not in will-power / 有～者事竟成。Where there is a will, there is a way. / 燕雀安知鸿鹄之～哉! How could the sparrow understand the ambition of the swan? — The mind of the great is beyond the comprehension of a common fellow. ❷ (Zhì) a surname

志[2]

zhì 〈方言〉ascertain the weight, length, size, etc.; weigh; measure: 用秤～～。Let's weigh it in the scale. / ～出两碗面粉。Measure out two bowls of flour.

志[3](誌)

zhì ❶ remember; keep in mind: 博闻强～ have wide learning and retentive memory; have extensive experience and a good memory / 永～不忘 forever bear in mind ❷ records; chronicles; annals: 碑～ inscriptions on a tablet recording an event / 墓～ inscriptions on the memorial tablet within a tomb / 地方～ local chronicles; annals of a locality / 乡土～ local records or annals / 县～ annals of a county / 动物～ fauna / 植物～ flora / 人物～ dictionary of biographies; biographical dictionary; who's who / 人种～ ethnography / 《三国～》*History of the Three Kingdoms* ❸ mark; sign: 标～ mark / 两国在边界上立碑为～。The two countries erected a tablet on their common border as a boundary marker.

志哀 zhì'āi express mourning: 鸣枪～ fire a gun as a signal of mourning / 下半旗～ fly a flag at half-mast as a sign of mourning

志大才疏 zhìdà-cáishū have lofty aspirations but little talent; be highly ambitious but mediocre in ability

志得意满 zhìdé-yìmǎn feel fully satisfied and contented when one's ambition is achieved; be complacent

志怪 zhìguài record of supernatural events or wierd things: ～小说 supernatural stories

志贺菌病 zhìhèjūnbìng shigellosis

志留纪 Zhìliújì 〈地质〉Silurian Period, the third period of the Palaeozoic Era (古生代), during which fish first appeared

志留系 Zhìliúxì 〈地质〉Silurian System; Silurian

志气 zhìqi aspiration; ambition; ideal: 长自己的～，灭敌人的威风 boost our own morale and puncture the arrogance of the enemy / 人贵有～。A man should have high aspirations. / 他～轩昂，不辱祖宗。He is a man of high principle, a credit to his ancestors.

志趣 zhìqù aspiration and interest; interest; inclination: ～广泛 have wide interests / 两人～相投。The two have similar inclinations.

志士 zhìshì person of ideals and integrity; person of firm resolve: ～惜时如宝。A man of resolve values his time as gems.

志士仁人 zhìshì-rénrén people with high aspirations

志书 zhìshū local, district or provincial histories, outlining topography, history, personages, products, custom, etc.; local chronicles; local annals

志同道合 zhìtóng-dàohé cherish the same ideals and take the same course; be devoted to a common cause; be of like mind: 他们是一对～的伴侣。The couple are of like mind. / 这些人～，决心为民族解放事业而奋斗。This group of people have a common goal, striving for the cause of national liberation.

志喜 zhìxǐ serve as celebration or congratulation: 新春～ (by way of) Spring Festival celebrations / 新婚～ (offer) congratulations on sb.'s wedding / 刘教授八十华诞～。(written on a gift, scroll, etc. for the occasion) Congratulations on Professor Liu's 80th Birthday.

志向 zhìxiang aspiration; ideal; dream; ambition: 立下救国图强的～ make up one's mind to struggle for the salvation and prosperity of one's motherland / 舒适的生活消磨了他的～。Ease and comfort have eaten away his ambition.

志行 zhì-xíng ideals and conduct

志学 zhìxué devote oneself to studies; set one's mind on learning or study: ～之年 at the age of fifteen (when one should set one's mind on study) according to Confucius

志愿 zhìyuàn ❶ aspiration; wish; ideal: 他的～是当一名工程师。He has aspirations to become an engineer. *or* His wish is to become an engineer. ❷ volunteer; do sth. of one's own accord: ～参军 volunteer to join the army / 她～参加这次危险的行动。She volunteered for the dangerous mission.

志愿兵 zhìyuànbīng volunteer (soldier)

志愿兵制 zhìyuànbīngzhì volunteering (system) (in contrast to conscription); volunteerism

志愿军 zhìyuànjūn people who volunteer to fight in another country; volunteers

志愿书 zhìyuànshū application form: 填写加入探险队的～ fill in the application form for joining the exploration party

志在必得 zhìzàibìdé be determined to win; be bent on winning: 这个队有备而来，对冠军～。This team comes well-prepared and is determined to win the championship.

志子 zhìzi 〈方言〉implement for measuring

痣

zhì nevus; mole: 色～ pigmented mole (*or* nevus) / 胎～ birthmark

痣癌 zhì'ái 〈医学〉nevocarcinoma

痣脂瘤 zhìzhīliú 〈医学〉nevolipoma

疐(疐)

zhì 〈书面〉❶ encounter or meet with obstruction ❷ fall: 跋前～后 equally difficult to go on or to retreat — between the devil and the deep sea; on the horns of a dilemma

庤

zhì 〈书面〉store up

痔

zhì haemorrhoids; piles: 内～ internal piles / 外～ external piles / 血～ bleeding piles

痔疮 zhìchuāng haemorrhoids; piles: ～挂线疗法 thread ligature therapy for piles and anal fistula

痔漏 zhìlòu 〈医学〉anal fistula

痔切除术 zhìqiēchúshù hemorrhoidectomy

畤 zhì 〈书面〉place where nature and ancient emperors were worshipped

峙 zhì 〈书面〉stand erect; rise aloft; tower:两军对～。Two opposing armies confront each other. /三国鼎～。Three antagonistic kingdoms (*or* countries) confronted one another (like the three legs of a tripod). /一山飞～大江边。Perching as after flight, the mountain towers over the Yangtze.

峙立 zhìlì stand towering; tower aloft:两山隔河～。The two mountains stand towering aloft with a river in between.

栉(櫛) zhì 〈书面〉❶ comb:手执巾～ have the towel and comb in hand ❷ comb (hair)

栉比 zhìbǐ 〈书面〉be placed closely side by side (like the teeth of a comb)

栉比鳞次 zhìbǐ-líncì *also* "鳞次栉比" (of buildings) be close together like comb teeth and fish scales:高楼～。There are row upon row of tall buildings.

栉风沐雨 zhìfēng-mùyǔ be combed by the wind and washed by the rain — travel or work braving the elements:这支勘探队,长年累月～地奋战在高山深谷之中。Year in and year out, the prospecting team travel and work on high mountains and in deep valleys braving wind and rain.

栉沐 zhìmù 〈书面〉comb and wash

栉水母 zhìshuǐmǔ comb jelly; ctenophore

至 zhì ❶ reaching; to; until:无远弗～ reach the remotest corners (of a country, etc.); go everywhere /从头～尾 from beginning to end /自夏～冬 from summer to winter /时～今日 at this late hour /截～今日为止 up to today /会议开～十二点半。The meeting lasted until 12:30. ❷ go so far as; go to the extent of:甚～ even /竟～ go so far as ❸ extremely; very; most:侍母～孝 practise deep filial piety towards one's mother /感人～深 extremely moving; deeply touching /～关重要 of utmost importance /仁～义尽 show extreme forbearance; do everything required by humanity and duty /不胜感激之～ be deeply grateful; be very much obliged

至宝 zhìbǎo priceless treasure:视为～ regard it as an invaluable treasure /如获～ feel as if one had found a most valuable treasure

至不济 zhìbùjì 〈口语〉at least:他们当中有的会三、四种外语,～也会说一种外语。Everyone of them speaks at least one foreign language, and some speak three or four.

至诚 zhìchéng with complete sincerity; in real earnest:一片～ in all sincerity; from the bottom of one's heart

至诚 zhìcheng honest; sincere; straightforward:为人～ be honest and sincere

至迟 zhìchí at (the) latest; no later than:大厦～九月落成。The building shall be completed in September at the latest. /我们～周六给你答复。We shall give you a reply no later than Saturday.

至此 zhìcǐ ❶ at this point; here and now; thus:会议～结束。The meeting thus ended. ❷ until now:～,大家明白了事情的全部真相。Nobody knew the actual state of affairs (*or* the whole truth) until now. ❸ to such an extent:事已～,无法挽回了。Things have gone too far to be remedied.

至当 zhìdàng 〈书面〉most proper; most suitable:～不易 most suitable and not to be altered /反复修改文稿,期于～。Revise (*or* Polish) the manuscript again and again till it's almost perfect.

至多 zhìduō 〈副词〉at (the) most; not more than:我～去两天。I'll be away two days at most. /你这汽车～卖五万元。You'll get fifty thousand *yuan*, at the most, for that car of yours. /这年轻人～二十岁。The young man can't be more than twenty.

至高无上 zhìgāo-wúshàng highest; supreme; paramount:～的权力 supreme authority; absolute power /～的领袖 paramount leader

至关紧要 zhìguān-jǐnyào most important; imperative:他强调的这一点～。What he has stressed is of vital importance.

至好 zhìhǎo most intimate friend; bosom friend:二人结为～。The two became the best of friends.

至极 zhìjí extremely; exceedingly:精巧～ extremely delicate /荒谬～ height of absurdity /可恶～! How very wicked!

至交 zhìjiāo most intimate friend; best friend:多年～ very good friend of long standing

至今 zhìjīn so far; up to now; to date:～他还没有来过信。I have heard nothing from him up to now. /这案子～没破。To date the case has not been cleared up. /此人～下落不明。His whereabouts are still unknown.

至理 zhìlǐ valid reason; irrefutable logic:团结御侮,天下之～。To unite against (*or* to resist) aggression is of course the right thing to do.

至理名言 zhìlǐ-míngyán famous dictum; maxim; golden saying; well-known truth:"血浓于水"是一～。"Blood is thicker than water" is an old adage.

至品 zhìpǐn very best work or thing

至亲 zhìqīn next of kin; closest relative; very close relative:骨肉～ kinfolk

至亲好友 zhìqīn-hǎoyǒu close relatives and good friends; kith and kin

至情 zhìqíng true feelings; heartfelt emotion:～的表白 sincere expression (*or* manifestation) of one's true feelings

至日 zhìrì day on which the winter solstice or summer solstice falls

至若 zhìruò 〈书面〉as for; as regards

至善至美 zhìshàn-zhìměi the best and the most beautiful; perfection incarnate

至上 zhìshàng supreme; highest:顾客～ customers (*or* patrons) first

至少 zhìshǎo 〈副词〉at (the) least:文章写完以后～看两遍。Read the article at least twice when you finish writing it. /～可以说,他没有把事情办好。He has not done a good job, to say the least. /这地方你没有来过,～听说过的吧。You haven't been to the place, but surely you must have heard of it.

至圣 zhìshèng greatest sage — Confucius

至圣先师 zhìshèng xiānshī greatest sage and teacher — Confucius

至死 zhìsǐ unto death; till death; to the end of one's life:～不渝 will never change until death /～不改 refuse to mend one's ways to the very end /～方休 persist in doing sth. to the end of one's life; be released only by death /我～都不会忘记那次经历。I shall remember that experience to my dying day.

至死不变 zhìsǐ-bùbiàn refuse to change even unto death:初衷～ stick to one's early decision until the end of one's days

至死不屈 zhìsǐ-bùqū not yield even unto death

至死不悟 zhìsǐ-bùwù refuse to come to one's senses to the very end; be incorrigibly stubborn:可惜这道理他～。It's a pity that he didn't understand this even on his death bed.

至性 zhìxìng 〈书面〉man's deepest instinct (e. g. love of parents and children); natural instincts

至言 zhìyán 〈书面〉profound truth

至友 zhìyǒu closest friend; best friend; bosom friend:～良朋 one's bosom friends /结为～ become closest friends

至于 zhìyú ❶ go as far as to; go to such an extent:他不～不辞而别吧? He wouldn't go so far as to leave without saying goodbye, would he? /他要是早点求医,何～病成这样子。He wouldn't be so seriously ill had he seen the doctor sooner. /他虽然亏了本,但还不～破产。He suffered a severe loss, but it wasn't so bad as to make him go bankrupt. ❷ as for; as to:～我,我不成功决不罢休。As for me, I will not stop until I succeed.

至嘱 zhìzhǔ 〈书面〉(often used in a letter) earnestly hope that you will act accordingly

至尊 zhìzūn ❶ most revered and respected; most distinguished ❷ emperor

窒 zhì 〈书面〉stop up; block; obstruct:气～ be suffocated; hiccup /～欲 suppress one's desire

窒碍 zhì'ài 〈书面〉have obstacles; be blocked:～难行 difficult to go ahead because of many obstacles on the way

窒闷 zhìmèn close; stuffy:屋子里～得很。It's very close in the room. *or* The room is very stuffy. /他感到唇干舌燥,呼吸～。He felt his lips were dry, tongue parched and breathing difficult.

窒塞 zhìsè stop up; block

窒息 zhìxī stifle; choke; suffocate:屋子里的空气叫人～。The air in the room is stifling. /浓烟几乎使消防队员～。The dense smoke al-

Z

most suffocated the firemen. /〈比喻〉他们企图～民主。They tried to strangle democracy.
窒息性毒气 zhìxīxìng dúqì asphyxiating gas; choking gas

桎

zhì 〈书面〉fetters
桎梏 zhìgù 〈书面〉fetters and handcuffs; chains; shackles: 打碎精神上的～ smash mental (*or* ideological) fetters /摆脱旧传统的～ free oneself from the shackles of old convention

轾

zhì *see* "轩轾" xuānzhì

蛭

zhì leech: 水～ leech
蛭石 zhìshí vermiculite

螲

zhì *see* "蝼螲" lóuzhì
see also dié

铚

zhì 〈书面〉❶ sickle; reaping hook; reap hook ❷ reap or cut (crops)

致[1]

zhì ❶ send; extend; make; deliver: ～书 send (sb.) a letter /～以热烈的祝贺 extend warm congratulations ❷ concentrate; devote: 专心～志 be wholeheartedly devoted to; be wholly absorbed in ❸ achieve; attain; apply: 学以～用 study sth. in order to apply it ❹ bring about; incur; result in; lead to: 导～失败 lead to (*or* end in) defeat /招～杀身大祸 incur a fatal disaster /他不听劝告，以～全军覆没。He refused to heed others' advice, which resulted in the annihilation of the entire army. /措词晦涩，～使人误解本意。The wording is so ambiguous that it causes misinterpretations.

致[2]

zhì manner or style that attracts attention or arouses interest; interest: 兴～ interest; mood to enjoy /情～ temperament and interest /雅～ elegant; refined /别～ original in style /故事曲折有～。The plot is intricate and full of interest.

致[3]（緻）

zhì fine; delicate; exquisite: 做工精～ of excellent workmanship /作风细～ be meticulous in one's work style
致哀 zhì'āi pay one's respects to the deceased: 向死难烈士～。Pay tribute to the martyrs.
致癌物质 zhì'ái wùzhì 〈医学〉carcinogen; carcinogenic substance
致病菌 zhìbìngjūn 〈医学〉pathogenic bacteria
致残 zhìcán cause disability; become disabled; be crippled: 他因车祸～。He became disabled after a car accident.
致辞 zhìcí *also* "致词" make an address; deliver a speech: 致答辞 make a speech in reply (to a speech of welcome, an address of congratulation, etc.) /致开幕辞 deliver an opening speech /新年～ New Year message /请大会主席～。Let's invite the chairman to address the conference.
致动 zhìdòng 〈自控〉actuate: ～凸轮 actuating cam /～器 actuator /液压～器 hydraulic actuator /线性～器 linear actuator
致富 zhìfù amass a fortune; acquire wealth; become rich: 发家～ build up family fortunes /增产～ become wealthy by increasing production /勤劳～ get rich by doing honest labour (*or* by the sweat of one's brow)
致公党 Zhìgōngdǎng Zhi Gong Dang of China, one of China's democratic parties mainly composed of returned overseas Chinese and relatives of Chinese nationals living abroad (set up in 1925)
致函 zhìhán send a letter to; write to: 正式～ write formally to /～总公司 write a letter to the head office of the company
致贺 zhìhè extend one's congratulations: 握手～ shake hands with sb. to express one's congratulations
致幻剂 zhìhuànjì hallucinogen
致敬 zhìjìng salute; pay homage to; pay tribute to: 鸣礼炮二十一响～ fire a 21-gun salute /向战斗英雄～! Salute the combat heroes!
致敬电 zhìjìngdiàn message of greetings
致冷 zhìlěng refrigeration: ～循环 refrigeration cycle
致冷剂 zhìlěngjì refrigerant; cryogen
致冷器 zhìlěngqì freezer
致力 zhìlì be devoted to: 他毕生～于世界和平事业。He dedicated himself to the cause of world peace all his life. /毕业后，她留校～于教学工作。After graduation, she stayed in the college and devoted herself to teaching.
致密 zhìmì fine and close; compact: ～的分析 careful (*or* close) analysis /结构～ fine and close in texture /～射电源 compact radio source /～天体 compact object; compact celestial body /～质 compact tissue
致密化动力学 zhìmìhuà dònglìxué densification kinetics
致密结构 zhìmì jiégòu 〈地质〉compact texture
致密星系 zhìmì xīngxì compact galaxy
致敏 zhìmǐn sensitization: ～物质 sensitizer /～细胞 sensitized cell
致敏源 zhìmǐnyuán 〈医学〉sensibiligen
致敏作用 zhìmǐn zuòyòng 〈医学〉sensitization
致命 zhìmìng lethal; fatal; deadly; mortal: ～的错误 fatal error /～的打击 deadly blow /～伤 mortal (*or* vital) wound /～凶器 lethal weapon /氰化钾一点儿即可～。A little potassium cyanide can cause death. /敌军的～弱点在于海港防御差。The enemy's Achilles' heel was his weak harbour defences.
致气 zhìqì take offence and get sulky: 别和这种人～。It's not worthwhile to get angry with such people.
致使 zhìshǐ cause; lead to; result in: 民族矛盾激化，～内战爆发。The sharpening of contradictions among different ethnic groups resulted in a civil war. /他没有及时就医，～病情恶化。His condition is worsening because he failed to see the doctor in time.
致仕 zhìshì 〈书面〉resign (from) one's official post
致死 zhìsǐ causing death; lethal; deadly: ～原因不明 cause of death unknown /煤气中毒～ die of gas poisoning /～量照射 radiation lethality /～中量（半数～量）lethal dose of 50% (LD50) /～中浓度（半数～浓度）lethal concentration of 50% (LC50) /～中时（半数～时间）lethal time of 50% (LT50)
致死基因 zhìsǐ jīyīn lethal gene
致死率 zhìsǐlǜ lethality
致死性毒剂 zhìsǐxìng dújì lethal agents
致死性毒气 zhìsǐxìng dúqì lethal gas
致谢 zhìxiè express one's thanks; show one's gratitude; extend thanks to: 登门～ call on sb. to express thanks
致意 zhìyì send one's regards; present one's compliments; extend one's greetings: 互相～ exchange greetings /他向我微笑～。He greeted me with a smile. /请向老朋友们代为～。Please give my best wishes to our old friends.
致知 zhìzhī 〈书面〉attain knowledge; acquire learning: 格物～ attain knowledge through studying the essence of things

膣

zhì 〈旧语〉vagina

郅

zhì ❶〈书面〉most; very: ～治 best administration; supreme order /～盛 great prosperity ❷ (Zhì) a surname

擿

zhì 〈书面〉*see* "掷" zhì
see also tī

掷（擲）

zhì throw; cast; fling; hurl: 投～ throw; fling /抛～ throw; cast /弃～ cast aside; throw away /～骰子 cast the dice; play dice /一～千金 throw money away like dirt; spend money like water /孤注一～ risk everything on a single throw; put all one's eggs in one basket /～杯为号 give a signal by throwing one's wine cup on the floor
掷币猜先 zhìbì cāixiān 〈体育〉toss
掷标枪 zhì biāoqiāng 〈体育〉javelin throw
掷弹兵 zhìdànbīng 〈军事〉grenadier
掷弹筒 zhìdàntǒng grenade discharger; grenade launcher
掷地有声 zhìdì-yǒushēng *also* "掷地金声" make a ringing sound when thrown to the ground — (of writings) sonorous and forceful language
掷果潘安 zhìguǒ-Pān'ān *also* "掷果盈车" handsome young man; Prince Charming
掷还 zhìhuán 〈套语〉please return (to the writer, etc.): 前寄之拙稿，如不蒙采用，请早日～。If you've decided not to publish the manuscript sent to you, please return it at your earliest convenience.
掷界外球 zhì jièwàiqiú 〈体育〉(of football) throw-in
掷铁饼 zhì tiěbǐng 〈体育〉discus throw

贽(贄) zhì 〈书面〉gift presented to a senior as a mark of esteem at one's first visit:以玉帛为～ present jade objects and silk fabrics as gifts

贽见 zhìjiàn call on sb. with gifts:～礼 gifts one presents to a senior when one calls on him for the first time

贽敬 zhìjìng 〈旧语〉gift presented to one's teacher (often as a way of paying tuition)

挚(摯) zhì 〈书面〉sincere; earnest; heartfelt:诚～ sincere /恳～ earnest and sincere /深～ profound and sincere /真～的友谊 true friendship

挚爱 zhì'ài sincere love:深情～ profound and sincere love /他的作品洋溢着对祖国的～之情。His works are brimming with heartfelt love for his motherland.

挚诚 zhìchéng earnest; heartfelt:他～的话语深深地感动了我。I was deeply moved by the sincerity of his remarks. *or* I was very touched by his sincerity.

挚切 zhìqiè earnest; sincere; wholehearted:情意～ be in all sincerity

挚情 zhìqíng true feelings

挚友 zhìyǒu close friend; bosom friend:～良朋 intimate friends and good companions

鸷(鷙) zhì 〈书面〉ferocious; fierce; violent:阴～ sinister and ruthless /～禽猛兽 vultures and beasts

鸷悍 zhìhàn ferocious and tough; fierce and tough

鸷鸟 zhìniǎo birds of prey:～不群。Birds of prey do not go in flocks.

识(識) zhì 〈书面〉❶ remember; bear in mind; commit to memory:博闻强～ have wide learning and a retentive memory; have encyclopaedic knowledge ❷ mark; sign; symbol:款～ inscriptions (on bronzes, etc.) /标～ sign

see also shí

帜(幟) zhì ❶ flag; streamer; banner:旗～ banner; flag; streamer; colours /独树一～ fly one's own colours — develop a school of one's own ❷〈书面〉sign; mark:标～ sign; symbol

置 zhì ❶ place; set; put:放～ put; place /搁～ put aside; shelve; pigeonhole /倒～ put upside down; invert /漠然～之 be indifferent to the matter /～之高阁 put sth. on the shelf; shelve ❷ set up; form; establish; install:设～新机构 establish new organs /设～障碍 set up (*or* place, *or* put) obstacles /装～避雷针 install a lightening rod /为办公室配～计算机 equip the office with computers ❸ buy; purchase:买房～地 buy land and houses; purchase real estate /添～些行头 buy actor's costumes and paraphernalia /～家立室 get married and set up a home

置办 zhìbàn buy; purchase:～嫁妆 buy a dowry /～课桌椅 purchase school desks and chairs

置备 zhìbèi purchase (equipment, implements, etc.):～办公用品 procure office equipment and stationary

置辩 zhìbiàn 〈书面〉(usu. used in the negative) argue; justify:不屑～ disdain to argue /不容～ indisputable /无须～。There's no need to debate the point.

置产 zhìchǎn purchase real estate; buy property

置放 zhìfàng place; put:把电视机～在五斗柜上。Place the TV set on the chest of drawers.

置换 zhìhuàn 〈化学〉displacement; replacement; substitution; 〈数学〉permutation:～比 replacement ratio /～反应 substitution reaction /锌～了稀酸中的氢。Zinc displaces the hydrogen of dilute acids.

置换 zhìhuan ❶ replace; substitute; switch (from sth. to sth. else):～天然气 switch to (use of) natural gas /这两组设备是不可～的。The two sets of devices are not mutually replaceable. ❷〈方言〉purchase; procure:～结婚用品 go shopping for a wedding

置喙 zhìhuì 〈书面〉(usu. used in the negative) interrupt; chip in; speak out of turn:不容～ brook no interruption (*or* interference)

置买 zhìmǎi buy; purchase:～家具 purchase pieces of furniture

置评 zhìpíng (usu. used in the negative) make comments; comment on; discuss:不予～ make no comment

置闰 zhìrùn establish intercalary or leap day or intercalary or leap month in the calendar

置若罔闻 zhìruòwǎngwén turn a deaf ear to; ignore:他对别人的忠告都～。He turned a deaf ear to all advice.

置身 zhìshēn place oneself; get involved; stay:～其间 put oneself in the midst of sth. — get involved /～险境 put one's head into the lion's mouth /～名流之列 rub shoulders with the celebrities

置身事外 zhìshēn-shìwài keep aloof from the affair; take no part in the business; refuse to get involved in the matter:对这场家庭纠纷,他想～。He wishes to keep out of the family wrangle.

置身无地 zhìshēn-wúdì have no place of shelter; have nowhere to go; be in a predicament

置信 zhìxìn (usu. used in the negative) believe; trust:令人难以～ hard to believe; unbelievable; incredible /谣传不可～。Don't trust rumours.

置疑 zhìyí (usu. used in the negative) doubt:不容～ allow of no doubt; beyond any doubt /这消息千真万确,无可～。The news is absolutely true. There is not a shadow of a doubt about it.

置于死地 zhìyú-sǐdì work for someone's destruction; expose someone to mortal danger:他心狠手毒,欲置他的竞争者于死地。Cruel and evilminded, he would stop at nothing to have his rival destroyed.

置之不顾 zhìzhī-bùgù leave out of account; pay no heed to; ignore:对群众的利益不能～。The interests of the people should not be disregarded.

置之不理 zhìzhī-bùlǐ close one's eyes to; brush aside; pay no heed to:对于这种霸权主义行动,我们不能～。We cannot shut our eyes to such hegemonist acts. /委员会对群众的建议～。The committee ignored suggestions of the people.

置之度外 zhìzhī-dùwài give no thought to; disregard:把个人利害得失～ think nothing of personal gain or loss /为了抢救地震中受难者,他把个人安危～。He risked his life to save the earthquake victims. *or* He went to rescue the earthquake victims regardless of personal danger.

置之脑后 zhìzhī-nǎohòu dismiss from one's mind; ignore and forget:把个人恩怨～ put aside personal grievances /他一心想把试验搞成功,早把度假的事～了。He was bent on carrying his experiment through to a successful conclusion and banished any idea of holiday from his mind. /此时他求胜心切,把别人的劝告全都～了。Right now he is so anxious to win that he clean forgets the advice given by others.

置之死地而后快 zhì zhī sǐdì érhòu kuài will not feel content unless the person one dislikes is got rid of:对敢于不同意他意见的人,他欲～。He will not be satisfied with anything less than the ruin of those people who dare to disagree with him.

置之死地而后生 zhì zhī sǐdì érhòu shēng deploy troops in such a way as to leave them no route for retreat so that they have to fight for their lives and win the battle as a result; one would fight to live when confronted with danger of death

豸 zhì 〈书面〉(as mentioned in ancient books) insect without feet or legs:虫～ insects

制(❶製) zhì ❶ make; manufacture:自～教具 make teaching aids oneself /缝～书包 sew a school satchel /机～ machine-made /粗～滥造 coarsely manufactured /监～ supervise the manufacture of /定～ have sth. made to order ❷ work out; draw up; formulate:创～ formulate; create /炮～ concoct; cook up /～礼作乐 set up rites and compose music (for the occasion) /编～年度计划 draw up (*or* compile) annual plans /因地～宜 work out measures to suit local conditions ❸ restrict; check; control:统～ govern; rule /限～ restrict /控～ control /扼～ keep under control by force /压～ suppress; quell /遏～ contain /受～于人 be under the control of someone; be under sb.'s thumb /先发～人 gain the initiative by striking first /～敌于死命 have the enemy by the throat; spell death to the enemy ❹ system:一国两～ one country, two systems /联邦～ federal system /两党～ two-party system /体～改革 structural reform /百分～ hundred-point marking system /五分～ five-grade marking system /公～ metric system /币～ currency (*or* monetary) system

制癌菌素 zhì'áijūnsù 〈生化〉carcinostatin

制版 zhìbǎn 〈印刷〉plate making:～车间 plateroom /平版～

Z

lithographic plate making
制版墨 zhìbǎnmò tusche
制备 zhìbèi 〈化学〉preparation：氢的～ preparation of hydrogen /～色谱法 preparative chromatography
制币 zhìbì standard national currency：～厂 mint
制表 zhìbiǎo 〈统计〉tabulation：～机 tabulator; tabulating machine
制裁 zhìcái impose sanction; punish：对侵略国实行～ apply (*or* establish) sanctions against the aggressor country /实行经济～ impose economic sanctions (against a country) /解除对某国的～ lift the sanctions against a country /给以严厉～ mete out severe punishment to sb.
制茶机械 zhìchá jīxiè tea manufacturing machine
制成品 zhìchéngpǐn end products; finished products; manufactured goods; manufactures
制导 zhìdǎo control and guide (a missile, etc.); guide：被动～ passive guidance /主动～ active guidance /雷达～ radar guidance /～发射机 guidance transmitter /～武器 guided weapon /～机器人 guided robot /～系统 guidance system /激光～炸弹 laser-guided bomb /～导弹防御系统 guided missile defence system
制导宇宙飞船 zhìdǎo yǔzhòu fēichuán guided space vehicle (GSV)
制订 zhìdìng work out; formulate：～第九个五年计划 draw up the Ninth Five-Year Plan
制定 zhìdìng lay down; draw up; enact; make：～章程 draw up rules and regulations; lay down rules /～法律 enact laws /～工作计划 make a work plan /～政策 formulate (*or* work out) a policy
制动 zhìdòng apply the brake; brake：火车司机看见前面的停车信号，立即采取紧急～措施。On seeing the signal for the train to halt, the engine driver applied the emergency brake at once.
制动测力计 zhìdòng cèlìjì brake dynamometer
制动阀 zhìdòngfá brake valve
制动杆 zhìdònggǎn brake lever
制动轨道 zhìdòng guǐdào braking orbit
制动火箭 zhìdòng huǒjiàn retro-rocket
制动距离 zhìdòng jùlí 〈交通〉braking or stopping distance
制动开关 zhìdòng kāiguān brake switch
制动器 zhìdòngqì brake
制动闸 zhìdòngzhá damper brake
制动装置 zhìdòng zhuāngzhì arrester; brake
制度 zhìdù ❶ rules; regulations：规章～ rules and regulations /遵守～ abide by the rules /作息～ work schedule; timetable /违反了财务～。It was a breach of the financial regulations. ❷ system; institution：社会～ social system; social order /资本主义～ capitalist system
制度化 zhìdùhuà institutionalization
制度经济学 zhìdù jīngjìxué institutional economics
制伏 zhìfú *also* "制服" check; subdue; overpower; bring under control：～风沙 check wind and sand /警察～了抢劫银行的匪徒。The police subdued the bank robbers. /轻而易举地～了窃贼。The burglar was easily overcome. /谁能～这匹烈马？Who can bring this fiery horse under control?
制服 zhìfú ❶ uniform ❷ *see* "制伏"
制服呢 zhìfúní uniform coating
制高点 zhìgāodiǎn 〈军事〉commanding elevation; commanding height or point; dominating terrain features
制诰 zhìgào proclamations and decrees issued by the emperor; imperial mandate; imperial decree
制革 zhìgé process hides; tan：～厂 tannery /～工人 tanner /～工业 leather industry
制海权 zhìhǎiquán 〈军事〉mastery of the seas; command of the seas
制剂 zhìjì 〈药学〉preparation：标准～ standard preparation /～机械 pharmaceutical machine
制件 zhìjiàn *also* "作件" zuòjiàn workpiece; work
制浆 zhìjiāng pulping：～车间 pulp making department
制空权 zhìkōngquán 〈军事〉control of the air; air domination; air supremacy
制冷 zhìlěng 〈机械〉refrigerate：～厂 refrigerating plant /～机 refrigerating machinery /～剂 refrigerant /～压气机 refrigeration compressor /～循环 refrigeration cycle
制粒机 zhìlìjī granulator
制霉菌素 zhìméijūnsù fungicidin; mycostatin; nystatin
制片厂 zhìpiànchǎng 〈影视〉film studio
制片人 zhìpiànrén 〈影视〉producer
制品 zhìpǐn products; wares; goods：乳～ dairy products /石油～ petroleum products /钢铁～ iron and steel products /木～ wood products /化学～ chemical products /黄麻～ jute goods /塑料～ plastic articles; plastic wares /竹～ articles made of bamboo; bamboo articles /搪瓷～ enamel goods; enamelware /手工～ hand-made articles /精～ refined products /粗糙的～ slovenly product /～成本 cost of goods manufactured
制钱 zhìqián copper coins manufactured in the Ming and Qing dynasties
制胜 zhìshèng get the upper hand of; best; defeat：～顽敌 bring the stubborn enemy to its knees /出奇～ defeat one's opponent by a surprise move /克敌～ gain mastery over the enemy; defeat the enemy and win victory
制式 zhìshì ❶ service-type; service pattern：～军服 prescribed uniform; regulation uniform /～服装用品 regulation clothing /～军用物品 military items /～装备 authorized equipment; standard equipment ❷ system; format：～转换 conversion of system /多～电视机 multi-system TV set
制式教练 zhìshì jiàoliàn 〈军事〉formation drill
制售 zhìshòu produce and sell：～假药 make and sell fake medicine
制台 zhìtái viceroy in the Ming and Qing dynasties
制糖 zhìtáng refine sugar：～厂 sugar refinery
制图 zhìtú ❶〈测绘〉charting; map-making：～测量 cartographic survey /～员 cartographer ❷〈机械〉〈建筑〉drafting; drawing：～仪器 drawing (*or* drafting) instrument /～员 draftsman
制图学 zhìtúxué cartography; graphics
制宪 zhìxiàn draw up a constitution：～会议 conference for drawing up a constitution
制销 zhìxiāo 〈机械〉cotter
制氧车间 zhìyǎng chējiān oxygen generating plant
制药 zhìyào pharmacy：～厂 pharmaceutical factory
制药学 zhìyàoxué pharmaceutics
制艺 zhìyì *also* "制义"〈旧语〉stereotyped writing
制音器 zhìyīnqì 〈音乐〉damper
制御 zhìyù *also* "制驭"〈书面〉control; master：～自然 tame nature
制约 zhìyuē restrict; restrain; limit; condition：受历史条件的～ be limited by historical conditions /相互～ condition (*or* restrain) each other; interact /～作用 restrictive function /～地区经济平衡 regulate local economic balance /～平衡制度 check-and-balance system; checks and balances /主要矛盾～着次要矛盾。Secondary contradictions are conditioned by the principal contradiction. /这个地区的发展受到交通条件的～。The development of this area has been held back by poor transport facilities.
制造 zhìzào ❶ make; manufacture; produce：～飞机 make aircraft /～机器 manufacture machines /中国～ made in China /手工～ hand-made /～成本 cost of manufacture; output cost; manufacturing cost /全部设备是我们自己～的。All equipment is of our own manufacture. ❷ create; foment; fabricate; engineer：～紧张气氛 create tension /～事端 engineer an incident /～分裂 foment splits /～矛盾 sow dissension /～骚乱 incite a riot /～谣言 concoct (*or* invent) rumours /～假象 put up a facade /～烟幕 throw up a smoke screen /～内乱 stir up internal strife /～舆论 shape (*or* mould) public opinion /～重重障碍 place one obstacle after another /在他们中间～不和 drive a wedge between them /～政治阴谋 hatch political plots
制造厂 zhìzàochǎng manufacturing plant; factory
制造商 zhìzàoshāng manufacturer
制造业 zhìzàoyè manufacturing industry
制止 zhìzhǐ check; ban; prevent; stop：～侵略战争 stop aggression /～通货膨胀 fight inflation /～黑市交易 ban the black market /～疾病的发展 stay the progress of the disease /～这类事件再次发生 prevent the recurrence of similar incidents /～不正之风 put an end to unhealthy tendencies /～一场群架 put a stop to the fighting between two groups of people /～令 inhibition
制砖 zhìzhuān 〈建筑〉brickmaking：～工 brickmaker /～机 brickmaking machine; brickmolding machine; brick press
制装费 zhìzhuāngfèi *also* "治装费" zhìzhuāngfèi clothing allowance for officials sent on missions abroad
制作 zhìzuò make; manufacture：～道具 make props (*or* stage property) /精心～ make with meticulous care (*or* elaborate work-

manship)

猘(猘) zhì 〈书面〉(of dog) mad; rabid

帙 zhì 〈书面〉❶ cloth slip-case for a book ❷〈量词〉slip-case of thread-bound Chinese books: 一～宋版书 a slip-case of thread-bound Chinese books published in the Song Dynasty / 此书凡五～，每～十卷。This set of books is in 5 cloth slip-cases, each containing 10 volumes.

秩[1] zhì 〈书面〉❶ order: 井然有～ orderly; in good order ❷ official salary; official rank: 厚～ high official salary / 加官进～ promotion and salary increase

秩[2] zhì 〈书面〉decade: 七～大寿 seventy years of age / 八～寿辰 eightieth birthday

秩序 zhìxù order; sequence: ～井然 in good order; in apple-pie order / 社会～ public order / 维持～ keep order / 建立世界新～ establish a new world order / 战争结束后～已经恢复。Law and order has been restored after the war.

秩序册 zhìxùcè 〈体育〉programme

紩 zhì 〈书面〉(of clothing) sew; mend

智 zhì ❶ wisdom; intelligence; resourcefulness: 明～ wise; sensible / 足～多谋 wise and resourceful / 斗～ battle of wits / 大～若愚。A man of great wisdom often appears slow-witted. / 吃一堑，长一～。A fall in the pit, a gain in your wit. / ～者通达愚者顽。A wise man changes his mind, a fool never. / ～者贵于乘时。The wise man takes the occasion when it serves. ❷ (Zhì) a surname

智残 zhìcán mentally-retarded

智齿 zhìchǐ *also* "智牙"〈生理〉wisdom tooth

智多星 zhìduōxīng ❶ nickname for Wu Yong (吴用), the resourceful strategist of the peasant army in *Water Margin* (水浒传) ❷ resourceful person; mastermind: 你是～，自然有办法。You're a real wizard, and you should be able to manage.

智慧 zhìhuì wisdom; sagacity; intelligence: 从别人的愚行中学到～。Learn from the follies of others. / 群众中蕴藏了无穷的～。Great wisdom lies latent among the masses. / 金字塔显示了古代埃及人民惊人的～。The pyramids demonstrate the remarkable intelligence of the ancient Egyptian people.

智力 zhìlì intelligence; intellect: ～不行 poor intelligence / ～缺陷 mental deficiency / ～衰退 intellectual deterioration / ～迟钝 slow-witted / ～工程 intelligence engineering / ～资源 intelligence resources / 此人～超群。He is a man of very high intelligence. *or* He excels in intellect.

智力测验 zhìlì cèyàn intelligence test

智力产业 zhìlì chǎnyè *also* "知识产业" zhīshi chǎnyè institutions such as universities, research institutes and information centres where there is a concentration of intellect

智力竞赛 zhìlì jìngsài quiz game; quiz

智力开发 zhìlì kāifā tap or develop intellectual resources: 发展教育事业是～的根本途径。Developing education is the best way for tapping intellectual resources.

智力库 zhìlìkù storehouse of intelligence — a unit or an organization where there is a big convergence of talented people of various professions: 人民政协汇集了社会各个层次、各个方面的代表人士，是一个高层次的～。The Chinese People's Political Consultative Conference with representative personages from various circles of society is a high-level storehouse of intelligence.

智力圈 zhìlìquān 〈生物〉noosphere

智力商数 zhìlì shāngshù intelligence quotient (IQ)

智力投资 zhìlì tóuzī investment in education; intellectual investment: 家长对子女都很注意～。Parents spare no expense in the education of their children.

智力学说 zhìlì xuéshuō theories of intelligence

智力引进 zhìlì yǐnjìn introduce into the country experts and technical know-how from abroad

智力障碍 zhìlì zhàng'ài 〈医学〉dysgnosia

智利 Zhìlì Chile: ～人 Chilean

智利硝石 Zhìlì xiāoshí *also* "硝酸纳" xiāosuānnà sodium nitrate

智龄 zhìlíng (short for 智力年龄) intelligence age (IA)

智略 zhìlüè wisdom and resourcefulness

智谋 zhìmóu wit; resourcefulness: 要战胜对手，不仅要靠勇敢，还要靠～。To beat your rival you need not only courage but also resourcefulness. / 此人很有～。The man is full of good ideas.

智囊 zhìnáng brain truster: 他是这个党的～人物之一。He is one of the back-room boys of the political party.

智囊团 zhìnángtuán think tank; brain trust

智能 zhìnéng ❶ intellect and ability; intellectual power: 培养～ foster intellect and ability ❷ things that have some intellect and ability of man: ～机器人 intelligent robot / ～终端〈计算机〉intelligent terminal; smart terminal / ～存储器〈计算机〉intelligent memory

智能大厦 zhìnéng dàshà intelligent building

智能电话 zhìnéng diànhuà smart phone

智能卡 zhìnéngkǎ 〈金融〉smart card

智能网 zhìnéngwǎng 〈信息〉intelligent net (IN)

智能炸弹 zhìnéng zhàdàn 〈军事〉intelligent bomb

智巧 zhìqiǎo wit and skill; brains and tact

智穷才尽 zhìqióng-cáijìn at one's wits' end; at the end of one's tether

智取 zhìqǔ capture (a fort, town, etc.) by stratagem: 敌人阵地只可～，不能强攻。The only way to take the enemy position is by stratagem, not by violent attack. / 只可～，不可力敌。It's brains, not brawn, that will do it.

智人 zhìrén *Homo sapiens*

智商 zhìshāng *also* "智力商数" intelligence quotient (IQ): 检测儿童～ test children's IQ / 他～很高。His IQ is very high.

智神星 Zhìshénxīng 〈天文〉Pallas

智术 zhìshù trickery; scheme; stratagem

智牙 zhìyá *see* "智齿"

智勇双全 zhìyǒng-shuāngquán be both brave and intelligent; combine wisdom and courage: ～的指挥员 brave and sagacious military commander

智育 zhìyù intellectual education; mental development: 必须使学生在德育、～、体育几方面都得到发展。It is imperative to help the students to develop morally, intellectually and physically.

智圆行方 zhìyuán-xíngfāng be round in tact but square in conduct — be resourceful and upright

智者千虑，必有一失 zhìzhě qiān lǜ, bì yǒu yī shī the ideas of a wise man may be amiss once every thousand times; even the wise are not always free from error; nobody is infallible; a good marksman may miss; even Homer sometimes nods

智珠在握 zhìzhū-zàiwò be endowed with high intelligence; be of great intellectual endowments

雉[1] zhì pheasant: ～尾扇 fan made of pheasant's tail feather

雉[2] zhì parapet section of a city wall (approximately 10 ft. high and 30 ft. long): 率寡弱之众，据十～之城 guard a city surrounded by a wall of ten parapets with a small weak army under one's command

雉堞 zhìdié crenelation; battlement

雉鸠 zhìjiū turtledove

稚(穉) zhì young; childish: 幼～ childish; naive / ～童 child

稚虫 zhìchóng 〈动物〉naiad

稚龄 zhìlíng very young age: 两个～女孩子 two little girls

稚嫩 zhìnèn ❶ young and delicate: ～的脸蛋儿 young and delicate face / ～的童音 child's tender voice ❷ immature; puerile: 这些青年人的作品还有些～。The works by these young writers are still not quite mature.

稚气 zhìqì childishness: 她言谈话语中仍显出一些～。The remarks she made revealed her naivety.

稚弱 zhìruò childish and frail: ～的心灵 childish and frail heart

稚鱼 zhìyú fingerling

稚拙 zhìzhuō (of art, architecture, etc.) simple and unsophisticated: ～的作品 simple and unsophisticated work / 这套泥人，～有味，别具一格。This set of clay figurines, simple and unadorned, has a unique style.

稚子 zhìzǐ 〈书面〉child

质[1]**(質)** zhì ❶ nature; character; essence: 性～ nature; character /实～ substance; essence /本～ innate character; essence; quintessence /音～ tone quality; acoustic fidelity /变～ go bad; deteriorate ❷ quality: 优～地毯 high-quality (*or* high-grade) carpet /劣～产品 low-quality goods; inferior goods /保～保量 guarantee both quality and quantity /按～定价 fix the price according to quality ❸ matter; substance: 釉～ enamel /铁～器皿 iron utensils /铝～壶 kettle made of aluminium /木～纤维 wood fibre /流～食物 liquid food /杂～ foreign matter (*or* substance) ❹ simple; natural; plain: 朴～ simple and honest /遗华反～ go back to the simple and plain by discarding embellishments

质[2]**(質)** zhì ask; question: 让两人对～ let the two confront each other /以时事～于当局 ask the government authorities to answer questions concerning current state affairs

质[3]**(質)** zhì 〈书面〉❶ pawn; pledge: 典～ pawn; mortgage /以衣物～钱 pawn one's clothes for money (*or* a loan) ❷ pledge; security: 以祖传珍宝为～ with the family heirloom as a pledge /人～ hostage

质变 zhìbiàn qualitative change: 量变引起～ quantitative change leading to qualitative change

质地 zhìdì ❶ quality of a material; texture; grain: ～精美 of superb (*or* exquisite) texture /～粗的石头 stone of coarse grain /生产不同～的产品 manufacture goods of various qualities /～等级 texture grade ❷ character; traits; disposition

质点 zhìdiǎn 〈物理〉particle: ～速度 particle velocity /～动力学 particle dynamics /～力学 particle mechanics

质对 zhìduì *also* "对质" confrontation (in court)

质感 zhìgǎn (of works of art) sense of reality: 这幅作品用多种绘画手段，表现了不同物体的～。Making use of several painting mediums, this work of art gives a life-like portrayal of various objects.

质检 zhìjiǎn quality testing; quality control: 为把好质量关，他们对每种产品都进行严格～。In order to guarantee the quality, they exercise strict control over the quality of products of every kind.

质粒 zhìlì 〈生物〉plasmid

质量 zhìliàng ❶〈物理〉mass: ～单位 mass unit /～重正化 mass renormalization /～的相对论性变化 relativistic change in mass /～倒逆不变性 mass reversal invariance; invariance under mass reversal /一克就是一立方厘米水的～。The gram is the mass of one cubic centimetre (cc) of water. /一块铅熔化时～不变。The mass of a piece of lead is not changed by melting. ❷ quality: ～好 of high quality; superior /～差 of poor quality; inferior /工程～ quality of project /教学～ quality of teaching /提高～ improve the quality /～鉴定 quality determination /～检查制度 rules for testing quality

质量比 zhìliàngbǐ 〈物理〉mass ratio

质量巅 zhìliàngdiān 〈物理〉mass peak

质量管理 zhìliàng guǎnlǐ quality management; quality control

质量经济学 zhìliàng jīngjìxué quality economics

质量守恒 zhìliàng shǒuhéng 〈物理〉conservation of mass: ～定律 law of conservation of mass

质量数 zhìliàngshù 〈物理〉mass number

质量作用定律 zhìliàng zuòyòng dìnglǜ 〈物理〉law of mass action

质料 zhìliào material: ～不佳 material of inferior quality; inferior material /～很好 quality material

质难 zhìnàn blame; reprove; reproach

质能关系式 zhì-néng guānxìshì 〈物理〉mass-energy relation

质能守恒 zhì-néng shǒuhéng 〈物理〉conservation of mass-energy

质朴 zhìpǔ simple and unadorned; natural; plain: 衣着～ simply dressed /感情～ sincere /为人忠厚～ be simple and kindhearted; be unsophisticated /文章写得很～。The article is written in a simple style.

质谱 zhìpǔ 〈物理〉mass spectra: ～分析 mass spectrographic analysis

质谱测定法 zhìpǔ cèdìngfǎ mass spectrometry

质谱仪 zhìpǔyí mass spectrometer; mass spectrograph

质铺 zhìpù *also* "当铺" dàngpù 〈书面〉pawnshop

质权 zhìquán mortgage: ～人 mortgagee

质数 zhìshù 〈数学〉prime number

质素 zhìsù ❶ *also* "素质" quality ❷ factor; element ❸ simple; unassuming; plain: 他穿着～的制服。He is in plain uniform.

质问 zhìwèn put questions to; question; interrogate: 你有什么权利～我? What right have you to question me?

质心 zhìxīn barycentre

质询 zhìxún inquire about; ask for an explanation: 与会代表就此事纷纷提出～。Deputies to the congress all addressed inquiries concerning the matter.

质言 zhìyán truthful words

质疑 zhìyí call in question; question: 当场～ confront sb. with a query; question sb. to his face

质疑问难 zhìyí-wènnàn raise doubts and difficult questions for discussion; seek solutions to thorny problems

质因数 zhìyīnshù prime number when it can be a submultiple of another number

质证 zhìzhèng question the witness (in court)

质直 zhìzhí 〈书面〉simple, honest and straightforward: 为人～ be upright and straightforward /文辞～简洁 concise and unadorned writing

质子 zhìzǐ ❶ proton: ～传递 proton transfer /～给予体 proton donor /～核磁共振 proton magnetic resonance /～接受体 proton acceptor /～加速器 proton accelerator /～同步加速器 proton synchrotron; synchrophasotron /～自旋共振 proton spin resonance /～轰击 proton bombardment ❷〈书面〉person sent to another state as hostage

质子层 zhìzǐcéng 〈物理〉protonosphere

质子素 zhìzǐsù 〈物理〉protonium

碛(礩) zhì 〈书面〉base stone of a pillar

踬(躓) zhì 〈书面〉❶ trip; fall; stumble: 颠～ trip over sth. ❷ suffer a setback and fall: 中年遭～ suffer a setback at middle age

锧(鑕) zhì 〈书面〉❶ chopping block ❷ executioner's block: 斧～ (executioner's) axe and block

炙 zhì ❶ broil; grill; roast: ～肉 broil meat; barbecue; barbeque ❷〈书面〉roast meat: 残杯冷～ leftovers of a dinner (*or* banquet)

炙烤 zhìkǎo broil; grill: 火辣辣的太阳～着人们。People are being broiled in the scorching sun.

炙热 zhìrè scorching hot; burning hot: ～的阳光 broiling sun; scorching sun

炙手可热 zhìshǒu-kěrè if you stretch out your hand you feel the heat — extreme arrogance of the very powerful people: 此人久握重权，～。That man, being long at the helm of the state, is very powerful and exceedingly arrogant.

觯(觶) zhì ancient drinking vessel

陟 zhì 〈书面〉climb; ascend a height: ～山 climb mountains /～黜 promotion and dismissal (of officials)

骘 zhì 〈书面〉fix; determine: 评～ pass judgment on; evaluate

彘 zhì 〈书面〉pig; swine: 牧～ tend pigs /～狗不如 worse than curs and swine

zhōng

忪(伀) zhōng *see* "怔忪" zhēngzhōng

see also sōng

中 zhōng ❶ centre; middle: 居～ in the centre /震～ epicentre /房间的正当～ right in the middle (*or* centre) of the room ❷ (Zhōng) China: 洋为～用 make foreign things serve China /～日邦交正常化 normalization of Sino-Japanese relations /古今～外 at all times and in all lands ❸ in; among; amid; amidst: 半空～ in

midair /铭记心~ keep firmly in mind /她在人群~消失。She was lost among the crowd. /他在一片掌声~走下讲台。He descended from the platform amidst applause. /在旅途~我们变成了好朋友。In the course of our travels we became good friends. ❹ middle; mid:八月~ in the middle of August /期~考试 mid-term exam /一位~年妇女 middle-aged woman ❺ medium; intermediate:~号 medium size /~硬钢 medium steel /~速行驶 travel at an intermediate speed ❻ impartial; mean; between two extremes:适~ moderate /折~ compromise ❼ intermediary:作~ act as an intermediary; be a middleman ❽ suitable for; fit for; good for:不~用 no good; good for nothing ❾〈方言〉all right; okay:~不~? Is it all right? /~! 就这样办。Okay! Let's do it this way. ❿ in the process of; in the course of:发展~国家 developing country /大坝正在修建~。The dam is under construction. *or* The dam is being built. /列车在运行~。The train is running.

see also zhòng

中巴 zhōngbā mini-bus; van

中班 zhōngbān ❶ middle class in a kindergarten ❷ middle shift; swing shift:我今天上~。I'm on the middle shift (*or* work the swing shift) today.

中板 zhōngbǎn ❶〈冶金〉medium plate ❷〈音乐〉moderato

中饱 zhōngbǎo batten on or profit from money entrusted to one's care; line one's pockets (*or* feather one's nest) with public funds or other people's money; misappropriate; embezzle:贪污~ embezzle /~私囊 divert public money to one's private purse

中保 zhōngbǎo middleman and guarantor:由村长作~。The village head acted as the middleman and guarantor.

中变 zhōngbiàn sudden change in the course of sth.

中表 zhōngbiǎo ❶ children of grandfather's sisters or grandmother's brothers and sisters; aunts and uncles ❷ children of father's sisters or mother's brothers and sisters; cousins

中波 zhōngbō medium wave:~天线 medium wave antenna

中部 zhōngbù central section; middle part:~非洲 central Africa /该国~是一片大沙漠。The central part of the country is a desert. /郑州是中国~的交通枢纽。Zhengzhou is a hub of communications in the middle of China.

中不溜儿 zhōngbuliūr *also* "中溜儿"〈方言〉medium; middling:那学生成绩~。The student's work is middling. /要不大不小,~的。We want neither big ones nor small ones, but those of medium size.

中材 zhōngcái person of average ability; ordinary talent; mediocrity

中餐 zhōngcān Chinese cuisine; Chinese food

中草药 zhōngcǎoyào Chinese herbal medicine

中策 zhōngcè second best plan:既无万全之策,只好采取~了。Since there is no surefire plan, we have to make do with the second best.

中层 zhōngcéng ❶ middle-level:~经理 middle manager /~管理人员 middle management /~干部 middle-level cadres /~鱼类 mid-water fishes /~拖网 middle layer trawl; mid-depth trawl; mid-water trawl ❷〈气象〉mesosphere

中产阶级 zhōngchǎnjiējí middle class; middle bourgeoisie:上层~ upper middle class /美国~ Middle America

中长大衣 zhōngcháng dàyī midi

中长石 zhōngchángshí andesine

中长铁路 Zhōngcháng Tiělù (short for 中国长春铁路) Chinese Changchun Railway, a railway in China's northeast under joint management of China and the USSR in 1946-1952

中长纤维 zhōngcháng xiānwéi medium-length fibres

中常 zhōngcháng middling; average; ordinary:~年景 average harvest /收成~的土地 moderately-productive lands /歌手是第一流的还是~的? Is the singer first-class or merely middling?

中场 zhōngchǎng 〈体育〉(of football) midfield

中成药 zhōngchéngyào prepared Chinese medicine (ready-made product of pharmaceutical factories through mass production according to scientific prescriptions)

中程 zhōngchéng intermediate range; medium range:~弹道导弹 medium-range ballistic missile; intermediate-range ballistic missile /~监视雷达 moderate-range surveillance radar /~轰炸机 medium bomber

中垂线 zhōngchuíxiàn 〈数学〉perpendicular bisector

中辍 zhōngchuò stop in the middle (of doing sth.); give up halfway:~学业 discontinue one's studies; drop out of school /事业~ give up an undertaking halfway

中词 zhōngcí 〈逻辑〉middle term

中档 zhōngdàng middling quality:~茶叶 tea of middling quality /~货 goods of middling grade

中导 zhōngdǎo (short for 中程导弹) medium-range missile (whose range of fire is about 500 to 5,000 km.)

中道 zhōngdào ❶ halfway; midway:事业~而废。The undertaking was abandoned halfway. /家庭~衰落。The family fortunes were on the decline. *or* The family had seen its best days. ❷〈书面〉doctrine of the golden mean ❸〈宗教〉Madhyama-pratipada

中稻 zhōngdào semilate rice; middle-season rice

中等 zhōngděng ❶ (of education) secondary ❷ medium; moderate; average; middling:~城市 medium-sized city /~身材 of medium height /~距离 moderate distance /这孩子在班上表现~。The pupil behaves fairly well in class.

中等技术学校 zhōngděng jìshù xuéxiào secondary technical school

中等教育 zhōngděng jiàoyù secondary school education; secondary education

中等师范学校 zhōngděng shīfàn xuéxiào secondary normal school

中等职业学校 zhōngděng zhíyè xuéxiào secondary vocational school

中等专科学校 zhōngděng zhuānkē xuéxiào polytechnic school

中低产田 zhōng-dīchǎntián farmland with low or medium yields

中点 zhōngdiǎn 〈数学〉midpoint; middle point

中东 Zhōngdōng Middle East:~条约组织 Middle East Treaty Organization /~经济委员会 (UN) Economic Commission for the Middle East (ECME)

中东欧 Zhōng-Dōng Ōu Central and Eastern Europe

中东战争 Zhōngdōng Zhànzhēng Middle East Wars (the four wars between Israel and Arab states)

中短波 zhōngduǎnbō intermediate waves; medium-short wave

中断 zhōngduàn suspend; break off; hold up; interrupt:~讨论 break off the discussion /两国关系~了好多年之后重新恢复。Relations between the two countries are back to normal after being suspended for many years. /交通因车祸~了一小时。Traffic was held up for an hour due to a car accident. /他~了学习。He discontinued his studies.

中队 zhōngduì ❶ detachment:交通~ detachment of traffic police ❷〈军事〉squadron:飞行~ air squadron /战斗机~ fighter squadron /轰炸机~ bomber squadron /导弹~ missile squadron

中俄瑷珲条约 Zhōng-É Àihuī Tiáoyuē Sino-Russian Treaty of Aigun (1858)

中俄北京条约 Zhōng-É Běijīng Tiáoyuē Sino-Russian Treaty of Peking (1860)

中俄布连斯奇条约 Zhōng-É Bùliánsīqí Tiáoyuē Sino-Russian Burinsky Treaty (1727)

中俄尼布楚条约 Zhōng-É Níbùchǔ Tiáoyuē Sino-Russian Treaty of Nipchu or Nerchinsk (1689)

中俄天津条约 Zhōng-É Tiānjīn Tiáoyuē Sino-Russian Treaty of Tientsin (1858)

中俄伊犁条约 Zhōng-É Yīlí Tiáoyuē Sino-Russian Ili Treaty (1881)

中耳 zhōng'ěr 〈生理〉auris media; middle ear:~气压损伤 otitic barotrauma; barotraumatic otitis

中耳腔 zhōng'ěrqiāng tympanum

中耳炎 zhōng'ěryán 〈医学〉otitis media; tympanitis; inflammation of the middle ear:化脓性~ supperative otitis media /卡他性~ catarrhal otitis media /粘连性~ adhesive otitis media /结核性~ tuberculosis otitis media

中耳炎性脑炎 zhōng'ěryánxìng nǎoyán 〈医学〉otocerebritis

中法战争 Zhōng-Fǎ Zhànzhēng Sino-French War (1884-1885); the Arrow War

中帆 zhōngfān 〈航海〉topsail

中饭 zhōngfàn midday meal; lunch

中幡 zhōngfan 〈杂技〉flagpole waving

中非 Zhōngfēi Central Africa:~共和国 Central African Republic

中沸石 zhōngfèishí mesolite

中分 zhōngfēn ❶ divide sth. into two halves ❷ part hair in the middle

中锋 zhōngfēng ❶〈体育〉(of football, etc.) centre forward ❷ (of basketball) centre

中缝 zhōngfèng ❶ column on the folding line of a newspaper (for advertisements and notices) ❷ line sewn down the back of a jacket in the middle
中伏 zhōngfú ❶ second of the three ten-day periods of the hot season (sometimes lasting twenty days instead of ten) ❷ first day of the second period of the hot season
中服 zhōngfú traditional Chinese garment
中腹部 zhōngfùbù 〈生理〉midabdomen
中高频 zhōnggāopín 〈无线电〉medium high frequency
中高压 zhōnggāoyā 〈气象〉mesohigh
中耕 zhōnggēng 〈农业〉intertill:～作物 intertilled crop /～机 cultivator /～间苗机 hoe-thinner /～培土机 cultivator-cumridger; cultivator-hiller /～追肥机 cultivator-fertilizer /～除草机 extirpator; trash cultivator /～拖拉机 row-crop tractor
中工 zhōnggōng 〈旧语〉common run of doctors
中共 Zhōng-Gòng (short for 中国共产党) Communist Party of China
中共中央 Zhōng-Gòng Zhōngyāng (short for 中国共产党中央委员会) Central Committee of the Communist Party of China:～政治局 Political Bureau of the Central Committee of the Communist Party of China /～军事委员会 Military Commission of the Central Committee of the Communist Party of China /～对外联络部 International Department of the CPC Central Committee /～纪律检查委员会 Central Commission for Discipline Inspection of the Communist Party of China
中古 zhōnggǔ ❶ middle ancient times (in Chinese history, from the 3rd to the 9th century) ❷ medieval times; Middle Ages (from the fall of the Roman Empire in the west in the 5th century to the fall of Constantinople in 1453):～史 medieval history
中观学派 Zhōngguān Xuépài 〈宗教〉Madhyamika
中官 zhōngguān 〈书面〉(court) eunuch
中贵 zhōngguì 〈书面〉celebrated and powerful eunuch
中国 Zhōngguó China:～人 Chinese /～版画 traditional Chinese print /～壁画 Chinese mural painting
中国板块 Zhōngguó bǎnkuài 〈地质〉China plate
中国残疾人福利基金会 Zhōngguó Cánjírén Fúlì Jījīnhuì China Welfare Fund for the Disabled
中国大百科全书 Zhōngguó Dàbǎikē Quánshū *Encyclopedia of China*, published since 1980 in 80 volumes with about 100 million words
中国地震局 Zhōngguó Dìzhènjú China Seismological Bureau
中国工程院 Zhōngguó Gōngchéngyuàn Chinese Academy of Engineering
中国工农红军 Zhōngguó Gōng-Nóng Hóngjūn Chinese Workers' and Peasants' Red Army (1928-1937)
中国工农民主政府 Zhōngguó Gōng-Nóng Mínzhǔ Zhèngfǔ Chinese Workers' and Peasants' Democratic Government (of the revolutionary base areas during the Second Revolutionary Civil War, 1927-1937)
中国公学 Zhōngguó Gōngxué China College, set up in Shanghai in 1906, moved to Chongqing in 1949, and later merged into Southeast China University of Finance and Economy
中国共产党 Zhōngguó Gòngchǎndǎng Communist Party of China; Chinese Communist Party; CPC:～全国代表大会 National Party Congress /～中央委员 member of the Central Committee of the CPC /～中央政治局常务委员会 Standing Committee of the Political Bureau of the Central Committee of the CPC /～中央书记处 Secretariat of the Central Committee of the CPC /～总书记 General Secretary of the CPC /～基层委员会 primary (*or* grass-roots) Party Committee
中国共产主义青年团 Zhōngguó Gòngchǎnzhǔyì Qīngniántuán Communist Youth League of China
中国馆 Zhōngguóguǎn China pavilion (as in an international exposition, etc.)
中国国际旅行社 Zhōngguó Guójì Lǚxíngshè China International Travel Service (CITS)
中国国民党 Zhōngguó Guómíndǎng Nationalist Party of China; the Kuomingtang
中国国民党革命委员会 Zhōngguó Guómíndǎng Gémìng Wěiyuánhuì Revolutionary Committee of the Kuomintang, one of China's democratic parties
中国化 Zhōngguóhuà Sinicize; Sinify:佛教的～ Sinicization of Buddhism
中国话 Zhōngguóhuà Chinese language; Chinese
中国画 zhōngguóhuà traditional Chinese painting
中国科学院 Zhōngguó Kēxuéyuàn Chinese Academy of Sciences
中国历 Zhōngguólì Chinese calendar
中国民用航空总局 Zhōngguó Mínyòng Hángkōng Zǒngjú Civil Aviation Administration of China (CAAC)
中国民主促进会 Zhōngguó Mínzhǔ Cùjìnhuì China Association for Promoting Democracy, one of China's democratic parties
中国民主建国会 Zhōngguó Mínzhǔ Jiànguóhuì China Democratic National Construction Association, one of China's democratic parties
中国民主同盟 Zhōngguó Mínzhǔ Tóngméng Democratic League of China, founded in 1941 and one of China's democratic parties
中国农工民主党 Zhōngguó Nóng-Gōng Mínzhǔdǎng Chinese Peasants' and Workers' Democratic Party, one of China's democratic parties
中国气象局 Zhōngguó Qìxiàngjú China Meteological Bureau
中国热 zhōngguórè China fever; China craze:～在降温。China fever is abating.
中国人民大学 Zhōngguó Rénmín Dàxué Renmin University of China
中国人民对外友好协会 Zhōngguó Rénmín Duìwài Yǒuhǎo Xiéhuì Chinese People's Association for Friendship with Foreign Countries
中国人民解放军 Zhōngguó Rénmín Jiěfàngjūn Chinese People's Liberation Army
中国人民银行 Zhōngguó Rénmín Yínháng People's Bank of China
中国人民政治协商会议 Zhōngguó Rénmín Zhèngzhì Xiéshāng Huìyì Chinese People's Political Consultative Conference
中国人民志愿军 Zhōngguó Rénmín Zhìyuànjūn Chinese People's Volunteers (who fought in the War to Resist US Aggression and Aid Korea, 1950-1953)
中国日报 Zhōngguó Rìbào *China Daily*, the first English newspaper of the PRC published since 1981
中国社会科学院 Zhōngguó Shèhuì Kēxuéyuàn Chinese Academy of Social Sciences (CASS)
中国时报 Zhōngguó Shíbào (Taiwan) *China Times*
中国通 zhōngguótōng China expert; Sinologist; China hand:这个外国人真是个～。This foreigner is truly an authority on China.
中国同盟会 Zhōngguó Tóngménghuì United League of China (organized by Dr. Sun Yat-sen in 1905, which became the Chinese Nationalist Party in 1912)
中国象棋 Zhōngguó xiàngqí Chinese Chess; *xiangqi*
中国学 Zhōngguóxué Sinology
中国银行 Zhōngguó Yínháng Bank of China
中国猿人 Zhōngguó yuánrén *also* "北京人" Běijīngrén Peking Man (*Sinanthropus Pekinensis*)
中国证券监督管理委员会 Zhōngguó Zhèngquàn Jiāndū Guǎnlǐ Wěiyuánhuì China Securities Regulatory Commission (CSRC)
中国致公党 Zhōngguó Zhìgōngdǎng China Zhi Gong Dang, one of China's democratic parties
中国字 zhōngguózì Chinese characters, written Chinese language
中果皮 zhōngguǒpí 〈植物〉mesocarp
中号 zhōnghào medium size; M:～夹克衫 jacket of medium size / 这大衣我要件～的。Give me an M of the coat, please.
中和 zhōnghé 〈化学〉neutralization:～反应 neutralization:～点 point of neutralization /～试验 neutralization test /～剂 neutralizer
中和殿 Zhōnghédiàn Hall of Central Harmony in the Palace Museum of Beijing
中红外 zhōnghóngwài middle infrared (Mid-IR):～光谱学 middle infrared spectroscopy
中华 Zhōnghuá China:振兴～ rejuvenate (*or* revitalize) China /爱我～ love my motherland — China
中华航空公司 Zhōnghuá Hángkōng Gōngsī (Taiwan) China Airlines
中华民国 Zhōnghuá Mínguó Republic of China (1912-1949)
中华民族 Zhōnghuá Mínzú Chinese nation
中华人民共和国 Zhōnghuá Rénmín Gònghéguó the People's Republic of China:～国务院 State Council of the People's Republic of China /～国家主席 President of the People's Republic of China
中级 zhōngjí middle rank; mid-level; intermediate:～人民法院 intermediate people's court /～班 class at the intermediate level /～职

称 academic (*or* professional) titles of middle rank /～会计员 middle-level accountant
中技 zhōngjì (short for 中等技术学校) secondary technical school
中继 zhōngjì relay:～电视 relay television
中继电缆 zhōngjì diànlǎn junction cable
中继发射机 zhōngjì fāshèjī retransmitter
中继发生器 zhōngjì fāshēngqì relaying sounder
中继镜 zhōngjìjìng relay lens
中继器 zhōngjìqì repeater
中继线 zhōngjìxiàn junction line; relay line; trunk line
中继站 zhōngjìzhàn relay point; relay station
中坚 zhōngjiān nucleus; backbone; mainstay; hard core:社会～ salt of the earth /～分子 backbone elements /他们是民族解放阵线的～力量。They made up the nucleus (*or* They were the mainstay) of the Front for National Liberation.
中间 zhōngjiān ❶ among:他几个孩子～二儿子最聪明。His second son is the brightest among his children. /小偷混在看热闹的人群～。The pickpocket hid in the crowd watching the fun. ❷ centre:广场～是个大花坛。A raised flower terrace lies at the centre of the square. /饺子皮要～厚,边上薄。Dumpling wrappers should be made thick in the middle and thin at the periphery. /两支箭稳稳地插在靶心～。Two arrows were shot right into the bull's eye. ❸ between; intermediate: ～剥削 middleman's exploitation /～道路 middle road /～地带 intermediate zone /～分子 middle (*or* intermediate) element; middle-of-the-roader /小孙孙坐在爷爷奶奶～。The little boy sits between his grandpa and grandma. /报告长达五小时,～休息两次。The talk lasted 5 hours, with 2 breaks in between.
中间层 zhōngjiāncéng mesosphere
中间产品 zhōngjiān chǎnpǐn intermediate product
中间带 zhōngjiāndài mesopelagic zone
中间价 zhōngjiānjià middle price
中间阶层 zhōngjiān jiēcéng intermediate strata
中间力量 zhōngjiān lìliàng middle-of-the-road forces; intermediate forces
中间路线 zhōngjiān lùxiàn middle road; middle-of-the-road line
中间派 zhōngjiānpài middle elements; middle-of-the-roaders; intermediate sections or forces:这次选举,～起了很大作用。The result of this election is largely due to the role played by the middle elements. /我是个～,不介入你们的斗争。I'm a middle-of-the-roader and don't want to get myself involved in your contention.
中间判决 zhōngjiān pànjué 〈法律〉 interlocutory decree
中间儿 zhōngjiānr 〈口语〉 *see* "中间"
中间人 zhōngjiānrén middleman; jobber; go-between:～的赢利 jobber's turn /他在调解劳资纠纷中充当～。He acted as a go-between in the dispute between the workers and the management.
中间税 zhōngjiānshuì intermediate tax
中间诉讼阶段 zhōngjiān sùsòng jiēduàn 〈法律〉 mesne process
中间宿主 zhōngjiān sùzhǔ 〈生物〉 intermediate host
中间体 zhōngjiāntǐ 〈化学〉 intermediate
中间线 zhōngjiānxiàn 〈机械〉 medium line
中将 zhōngjiàng 〈军事〉 (UK and US Army, US Air Force) lieutenant general; (UK Air Force) air marshal; (UK and US Navy) vice admiral
中焦 zhōngjiāo 〈中医〉 part of the body cavity between the diaphragm and the umbilicus housing the spleen, stomach, etc.
中觉 zhōngjiào nap:睡～ take a nap
中介 zhōngjiè intermediary; medium:起～作用 be an intermediary
中介离子 zhōngjiè lízǐ mesomeric ion
中介日冕 zhōngjiè rìmiǎn intermediate corona
中介效应 zhōngjiè xiàoyìng mesomeric effect
中介子 zhōngjièzǐ 〈物理〉 neutretto
中景 zhōngjǐng 〈影视〉 medium shot
中局 zhōngjú (of chess or other games) middle phase of a game
中距离 zhōngjùlí 〈体育〉 middle distance:～赛跑 middle-distance race (*or* running)
中楷 zhōngkǎi regular script in medium-sized characters, as used in Chinese calligraphy exercise
中看 zhōngkàn be pleasant to the eye; look nice:～不中用 be pleasant to the eye but of little use
中看不中吃 zhōngkàn bù zhōngchī look good but taste bad; be pleasant to the eye but not agreeable to the palate; (of a man) handsome but good for nothing:似这种～的人要他何用? What's the use of this kind of person, outwardly attractive but actually worthless?
中考 zhōngkǎo entrance examination for secondary school
中空 zhōngkōng midheaven:～导弹 medium-altitude missile
中馈 zhōngkuì 〈书面〉 ❶ cooking (as behooves the mistress of the house):主～ do cooking /～乏人 have no one to cook one's food — have no wife ❷ wife:～犹虚。The man is not married yet.
中栏 zhōnglán 〈体育〉 intermediate hurdles
中浪 zhōnglàng moderate sea
中立 zhōnglì neutrality:保持～ keep neutrality; remain neutral /恪守～ observe strict neutrality /破坏～ violate neutrality/永久～ permanent neutrality /善意～ benevolent neutrality /武装～ armed neutrality /～地位 neutral status /～港 neutral port (*or* harbour) /～水域 neutral waters /～护航 neutral convoy /～公约 neutrality pact /该国宣布～。That state declared neutrality.
中立法 zhōnglìfǎ law of neutrality; neutrality law
中立国 zhōnglìguó neutral state:～船舶 neutral vessel
中立化 zhōnglìhuà neutralization
中立主义 zhōnglìzhǔyì neutralism
中量级 zhōngliàngjí 〈体育〉 middleweight:～举重冠军 champion in middleweight lifting
中林 zhōnglín 〈林业〉 middle forest; coppice with standards; composite coppice:～作业 composite system; coppice with standards system
中流 zhōngliú ❶ midstream:泛舟～ sail in midstream /～击水 sail against waves in midstream ❷ middle reaches (of a river):长江～ middle reaches of the Yangtze River ❸ middle; middling:～社会 middle society /～水平 of middling level
中流砥柱 zhōngliú-dǐzhù firm rock in midstream; tower of strength; mainstay:我们时代的～ mainstay of our era /他是那个政党的～。He is a pillar of strength to that party.
中流击楫 zhōngliú-jījí will to recover lost territories; determination to rejuvenate the country
中路 zhōnglù ❶ (of goods) mediocre:～货 mediocre goods ❷ halfway; midway:徘徊～ hesitate midway
中路梆子 zhōnglù bāngzi *also* "晋剧" jìnjù Shanxi opera
中略 zhōnglüè part omitted or left out (used within brackets as an ellipsis mark in a quoted passage)
中落 zhōngluò (of family fortunes) decline; sink; ebb:家道～。The family is on the decline.
中美海沟 Zhōngměi Hǎigōu Middle America Trench, in the Pacific west of Central America
中美合作所 Zhōng-Měi Hézuòsuǒ (short for 中美特种技术合作所) Sino-American Cooperation Organization (SACO), an intelligence organization between the KMT government and the US, which ceased to exist in 1946
中美三个联合公报 Zhōng-Měi sān gè liánhé gōngbào three joint communiqués signed by China and the US (*Shanghai Joint Communiqué* of Feb. 1972, *Joint Communiqué on Establishment of Diplomatic Relations* of Dec. 1978 and *August 17 Joint Communiqué* of 1982 on reduction of US arms sales to Taiwan)
中美商约 Zhōng-Měi Shāngyuē (short for 中美友好通商航海条约) Sino-American Treaty of Friendship, Commerce and Navigation, signed between the KMT government and US in Nov. 1946
中美望厦条约 Zhōng-Měi Wàngxià Tiáoyuē Sino-American Treaty of Wangxia, signed at Wangxia village near Macao, July, 1844
中美洲 Zhōngměizhōu Central America
中美洲共同市场 Zhōngměizhōu Gòngtóng Shìchǎng Central American Common Market
中美洲国家组织 Zhōngměizhōu Guójiā Zǔzhī Organization of Central American States
中拇指 zhōngmuzhǐ *also* "中指" middle finger
中南海 Zhōngnánhǎi Zhongnanhai, former imperial compound in Beijing, now housing the headquarters of the CPC and the State Council
中脑 zhōngnǎo 〈生理〉 deutocerebrum; mesocerebrum; mesencephalon; midbrain:～顶盖 mesencephalic tectum /～盖 optic tectum /～节 antennal segment /～中枢 mesencephalic centre /～炎 mesencephalitis
中能 zhōngnéng 〈物理〉 moderate-energy:～中子 intermediate neutron /～(中子反应)堆 intermediate reactor

中年 zhōngnián middle age; middle life: ~教师 middle-aged teachers / 人到~ one who has reached middle age

中农 zhōngnóng middle peasant (a political term used in China's liberated areas and in the early days of the People's Republic of China, meaning self-sufficient farmers): 上~ upper-middle peasant / 下~ lower-middle peasant / 富裕~ well-to-do middle peasant

中欧 Zhōng Ōu Central Europe

中盘 zhōngpán (of chess) mid-game

中跑 zhōngpǎo 〈体育〉 middle-distance race (which is between a sprint and a long-distance race in length, e.g. 800 or 1,500 metres)

中胚层 zhōngpēicéng 〈生物〉 mesoblast; mesoderm

中篇小说 zhōngpiān xiǎoshuō medium-length novel; novelette; novella

中频 zhōngpín intermediate frequency; IF: ~波 intermediate wave / ~电波传播 propagation of IF radio wave / ~干扰 intermediate-frequency interference / ~信号 intermediate-frequency signal / ~增益 mid-frequency gain / ~调制 IF modulation / ~抑制 IF rejection

中频道 zhōngpíndào mid band

中平 zhōngpíng average; middling: 孩子考试成绩~。The children's grades were just so-so on the test.

中葡联合联络小组 Zhōng-Pú Liánhé Liánluò Xiǎozǔ Sino-Portuguese Joint Liaison Group (for the return of Macao to Chinese sovereignty)

中期 zhōngqī ❶ middle period; metaphase: 搞好棉田~管理 do a good job in cotton field management in the middle of the growth period / ~审查 mid-term review / ~选举 mid-term election / ~板 metaphase plate / ~分裂 metakinesis ❷ medium term: ~贷款 medium term loan / ~计划 medium term plan / ~预报 extended forecast; mid-range forecast

中期报告 zhōngqī bàogào interim report

中期股息 zhōngqī gǔxī interim dividend

中气 zhōngqì ❶ 〈天文〉 12 of the 24 divisions of the solar year in the traditional Chinese calendar; 12 of the 24 solar terms ❷ 〈中医〉 vitality or vital energy of the part of the body cavity between the diaphragm and the umbilicus housing the spleen, stomach, etc.: ~不足 lack of vitality; deficiency of vital energy ❸ volume of breath (when one sings): ~十足 have good lungs (*or* lung power)

中气候 zhōngqìhòu mesoclimate

中秋 Zhōngqiū Mid-Autumn Festival (15th day of the 8th lunar month); Moon Festival

中人 zhōngrén ❶ middleman; go-between; mediator; intermediary ❷ 〈书面〉 man of ordinary ability, bearing, etc.: 他智力不及~。His intelligence is below average.

中日甲午战争 Zhōng-Rì Jiǎwǔ Zhànzhēng Sino-Japanese War of 1894-1895

中日马关条约 Zhōng-Rì Mǎguān Tiáoyuē Sino-Japanese Treaty of Shimonoseki (1895)

中日友好二十一世纪委员会 Zhōng-Rì Yǒuhǎo Èrshíyī Shìjì Wěiyuánhuì 21st Century Committee for China-Japan Friendship

中沙群岛 Zhōngshā Qúndǎo Zhongsha Islands

中山狼 zhōngshānláng Zhongshan wolf in the fable — person who returns good with evil; perfidious person: 子系~,得志便猖狂。Perfidious person that he is, he became all the more ferocious when in power.

中山陵 Zhōngshānlíng Sun Yat-sen Mausoleum in Nanjing

中山装 zhōngshānzhuāng Chinese tunic suit: 身着~ be in tunic and trousers

中肾 zhōngshèn mesonephros

中生代 Zhōngshēngdài 〈地质〉 Mesozoic era; Mesozoic

中生动物 Zhōngshēng dòngwù Mesozoa

中生界 Zhōngshēngjiè 〈地质〉 Mesozoic Erathem

中生林 zhōngshēnglín mesophytic forest

中师 zhōngshī (short for 中等师范) secondary normal school: ~教育 secondary normal school education

中石器时代 zhōngshíqì shídài Mesolithic Period; Middle Stone Age

中士 zhōngshì 〈军事〉 (UK and US Army, UK Air Force) sergeant; (US Navy) petty officer second class; (UK Navy) petty officer first class; (US Air Force) staff sergeant

中世纪 zhōngshìjì Middle Ages

中式 zhōngshì Chinese style: ~烹饪 Chinese cuisine

see also zhòngshì

中式盐 zhōngshìyán also "中性盐" 〈化学〉 neutral salt

中枢 zhōngshū centre: 领导~ leading core / 交通~ communication hub / 电讯~ telecommunications centre / ~淋巴器官 central lymphoid organs / ~查询 hub polling / ~抑制 central inhibition

中枢神经 zhōngshū shénjīng nervous centralis: ~环路 central nervous circuitry / ~系统 central nervous system / ~末梢 central endings

中水期 zhōngshuǐqī also "平水期" píngshuǐqī period when the (river, etc.) water is at its normal level

中苏友好同盟互助条约 Zhōng-Sū Yǒuhǎo Tóngméng Hùzhù Tiáoyuē Sino-Soviet Treaty of Friendship, Alliance and Mutual Assistance, concluded between the governments of the PRC and the USSR in Moscow in 1950 and ceased to be in force in 1980

中苏友好同盟条约 Zhōng-Sū Yǒuhǎo Tóngméng Tiáoyuē Sino-Soviet Treaty of Friendship and Alliance, concluded between the KMT government and the Government of the USSR in Moscow in 1945 and nullified in 1950

中速 zhōngsù intermediate speed: ~齿轮 intermediate gear / ~扫描 medium-fast sweep; medium sweep

中碳钢 zhōngtàngāng 〈冶金〉 medium carbon steel

中堂 zhōngtáng ❶ central room; master room (of a one-storey Chinese traditional house) ❷ central scroll (hung in the middle of the wall of the main room) ❸ nave

中堂 zhōngtang form of address for a Grand Secretary in the Ming and Qing dynasties

中提琴 zhōngtíqín viola

中天 zhōngtiān ❶ in the air; in the sky: 一轮明月高悬~。The bright moon is hanging high above in the sky. ❷ 〈天文〉 culmination; meridian passage or transit: ~观测 meridian observation / ~射电望远镜 transit radio telescope

中听 zhōngtīng pleasant to the ear; to one's liking: 号声清远,悦耳~,声闻数里。The call of the bugle, clear and pleasant, could be heard miles and miles away. / 她觉得女儿的话句句~。She found every word her daughter said agreeable (*or* to her liking).

中统 Zhōngtǒng (short for 中国国民党中央执行委员会调查统计局) Bureau of Investigation and Statistics of the Central Executive Committee of the Kuomintang, an espionage organization

中途 zhōngtú halfway; midway: ~停顿 stop halfway / ~停业 terminate operations before scheduled expiration / 不要~换马 don't change (*or* swap) horses in midstream — never change the leader midway / 飞机~在东京停留两小时。The plane stops over in Tokyo for 2 hours. / 他们很气愤,~退出会场。They felt indignant and walked out before the meeting was over.

中途岛 Zhōngtúdǎo Midway Island: ~战役 Battle of Midway (in World War II, June 1942)

中途返航 zhōngtú fǎnháng 〈航空〉 abort

中途港 zhōngtúgǎng also "中途停泊港" port of call

中土 Zhōngtǔ 〈书面〉 ❶ Central Plains (comprising the middle and lower reaches of the Yellow River) ❷ China

中外 Zhōng-wài China and foreign countries; at home and abroad: 闻名~ well known both in China and in foreign countries / ~合资企业 Chinese-foreign joint venture / ~合作企业 Chinese-foreign cooperative venture / 产品深受~顾客的欢迎。The product is very popular among customers both at home and abroad.

中外比 zhōngwàibǐ extreme and mean ratio; golden section

中微子 zhōngwēizǐ 〈物理〉 neutrino: ~发光度 neutrino luminosity / ~天文学 neutrino astronomy

中纬度 zhōngwěidù middle latitude

中卫 zhōngwèi 〈体育〉 (of football) centre halfback

中位数 zhōngwèishù 〈统计〉 median

中尉 zhōngwèi 〈军事〉 (US Army and Air Force) first lieutenant; (US Navy) lieutenant junior grade; (UK Army) lieutenant; (UK Navy) sublieutenant; (UK Air Force) flying officer

中温回火 zhōngwēn huíhuǒ 〈冶金〉 medium tempering

中温细菌 zhōngwēn xìjūn mesophilic bacteria

中温植物 zhōngwēn zhíwù mesotherm

中文 Zhōngwén Chinese (written) language; Chinese: ~报刊 newspapers and magazines in Chinese / 学习~ learn Chinese

中午 zhōngwǔ noon; midday: 正~ high noon

中西 Zhōng-Xī Chinese and Western: ~合璧 Chinese and Western styles combined; fine points of Western art interwoven with tradi-

tional Chinese style /～医结合 combine traditional Chinese and Western medicine

中夏 Zhōngxià 〈古语〉China

中线 zhōngxiàn ❶〈数学〉central line ❷〈体育〉(of basketball and volleyball) centre line; (of football) halfway line

中项 zhōngxiàng 〈数学〉medium term; middle term

中宵 zhōngxiāo midnight

中小企业 zhōng-xiǎo qǐyè small and medium-sized enterprises (SME):外资～ foreign-owned SME; foreign-funded SME

中校 zhōngxiào (UK and US Army, US Air Force) lieutenant colonel; (UK and US Navy) commander; (UK Air Force) wing commander

中心 zhōngxīn ❶ middle; central position:小镇～有座花园。There is a garden in the centre of the small town. /广场～耸立着旗杆。A flagpost stands in the middle of the square. ❷ main; key:～工作 focus of work; central task /～思想 main idea; gist /问题的～ heart of the matter /～人物 key figure; central character ❸ centre; core:政治～ political centre /文化～ cultural centre /交通～ hub of communications ❹ unit or institution with adequate equipment and technical force; centre:培训～ training centre /研究～ research centre

中心规 zhōngxīnguī 〈机械〉centre gauge

中心角 zhōngxīnjiǎo *also* "圆心角" yuánxīnjiǎo 〈数学〉central angle

中心孔 zhōngxīnkǒng centre opening; centre hole:～机床 centre-hole machine /～磨床 centre-hole grinder /～研磨机 centre-hole lapping machine /～钻床 centre-drilling lathe

中心外圆磨削 zhōngxīn wàiyuán móxiāo 〈机械〉centre-type cylindrical grinding

中心线 zhōngxīnxiàn 〈医学〉centre line

中心项 zhōngxīnxiàng 〈哲学〉centre term

中新世 Zhōngxīnshì 〈地质〉Miocene Epoch

中兴 zhōngxīng resurgence (usu. of a nation):国运～ resurgence of the nation /家道～。The family prospered again.

中星仪 zhōngxīngyí 〈天文〉meridian instrument; transit instrument

中型 zhōngxíng medium; medium-duty; medium-scale; medium-type:～车床〈机械〉medium heavy lathe /～电动机 medium-sized motor /～计算机 medium-sized computer /～卡车 medium (type) truck /～反装甲武器〈军事〉medium antiarmour weapon /～轰炸机 medium bomber; medium bombardment aircraft /～炮 medium artillery /～坦克 medium tank /～原子弹 medium-calibre atomic bomb /～钢轧机〈冶金〉medium section mill

中性 zhōngxìng ❶ neutral:～反应 neutral reaction /～土〈农业〉neutral soil /～的一元论 neutral monism ❷〈语言〉neuter:～名词 neuter noun ❸ (of words) neither appreciative nor pejorative; neutral

中性花 zhōngxìnghuā 〈植物〉neuter flower

中性货币 zhōngxìng huòbì neutral money; neutral currency

中性粒子 zhōngxìng lìzǐ neutral particle

中性岩 zhōngxìngyán intermediate rock; neutral rock

中性盐 zhōngxìngyán neutral salt

中性原子 zhōngxìng yuánzǐ neutral atom

中性植物 zhōngxìng zhíwù indeterminate plant

中休 zhōngxiū break

中修 zhōngxiū 〈机械〉medium maintenance; medium repair

中学 zhōngxué ❶ secondary school; high school:初级～ junior secondary school /高级～ senior secondary school ❷ (Zhōngxué) late Qing Dynasty term for Chinese traditional learning; Chinese learning:～为体,西学为用。Chinese learning as the base, Western learning for application.

中学生 zhōngxuéshēng secondary school student; high school student

中雪 zhōngxuě 〈气象〉moderate snowfall (a snowfall of 2.5-5.0 mm in 24 hours)

中旬 zhōngxún middle ten days of a month:他将于本月～来京。He'll be coming to Beijing in the middle of this month.

中压 zhōngyā ❶〈机械〉medium-pressure:～泵 medium lift pump /～锅炉 medium-pressure boiler /～气流式输送机 medium-pressure pneumatic conveyer /～汽轮机 medium-pressure steam turbine ❷〈电工〉medium voltage:～供电网 medium voltage network

中压轮胎 zhōngyā lúntāi medium-pressure tyre

中亚 Zhōng Yà Central Asia

中央 zhōngyāng ❶ centre; middle:～航道 central waterway; central course /广场～有一座烈士纪念碑。A monument to the martyrs stands in the middle of the square. ❷ highest leading body (of a state, party, etc.):党～ Central Committee of the Party; Party's Central Committee /团～ Central Committee of the Communist Youth League /～政府 Central Government /～各部委 Ministries and Commissions under the State Council /～工作会议 Central Working Conference /～机构 central organs (*or* institutions) /～领导同志 leading comrades of the central authorities /发挥～和地方两个积极性。We should bring into play the initiative of both central and local authorities.

中央处理机 zhōngyāng chǔlǐjī 〈计算机〉central processor; central processing unit (CPU) /～复算 centre processing unit retry

中央电视台 Zhōngyāng Diànshìtái China Central Television Station (CCTV)

中央工农民主政府 Zhōngyāng Gōng-Nóng Mínzhǔ Zhèngfǔ Central Democratic Workers' and Peasants' Government, established in 1931 in Jiangxi Province

中央顾问委员会 Zhōngyāng Gùwèn Wěiyuánhuì Central Advisory Commission (1982-1992)

中央广播电台 Zhōngyāng Guǎngbō Diàntái Central Broadcasting Station

中央候补委员 zhōngyāng hòubǔ wěiyuán alternate member of the Central Committee (of the Communist Party of China)

中央集权 zhōngyāng jíquán centralization (of power or authority):～的国家 centralized state

中央纪律检查委员会 Zhōngyāng Jìlǜ Jiǎnchá Wěiyuánhuì Central Commission for Discipline Inspection

中央情报局 Zhōngyāng Qíngbàojú (US) Central Intelligence Agency (CIA)

中央全会 zhōngyāng quánhuì plenary session or plenum of a Party's Central Committee

中央日报 Zhōngyāng Rìbào *Central Daily News*, organ of the KMT since 1927

中央社 Zhōngyāngshè (Taiwan) Central News Agency (CNA)

中央数字计算机 zhōngyāng shùzì jìsuànjī central digital computer (CDC)

中央条约组织 Zhōngyāng Tiáoyuē Zǔzhī Central Treaty Organization (CENTO) (1959-1979, parties to the Treaty: Iran, Turkey, Pakistan, the UK)

中央委员 zhōngyāng wěiyuán member of the Central Committee (of the Communist Party of China)

中央银行 zhōngyāng yínháng central bank

中央终端 zhōngyāng zhōngduān 〈计算机〉central terminal:～装置 central terminal unit

中药 zhōngyào traditional Chinese medicine

中药铺 zhōngyàopù shop or store of traditional Chinese medicines; Chinese pharmacy

中药学 zhōngyàoxué traditional Chinese pharmacology

中叶 zhōngyè ❶ middle period:20世纪～ mid-twentieth century; middle of the 20th century /明代～ middle period of the Ming Dynasty ❷〈生物〉lobus centralis; lobus medius

中衣 zhōngyī 〈旧语〉underpants; pants

中医 zhōngyī ❶ traditional Chinese medical science ❷ doctor of traditional Chinese medicine; practitioner of Chinese medicine

中医学 zhōngyīxué traditional Chinese medicine

中医学院 zhōngyī xuéyuàn college of traditional Chinese medicine

中医研究院 zhōngyī yánjiūyuàn academy of traditional Chinese medicine

中音号 zhōngyīnhào 〈乐器〉alto horn; althorn

中英北京条约 Zhōng-Yīng Běijīng Tiáoyuē Sino-British Convention of Peking (1860)

中英联合联络小组 Zhōng-Yīng Liánhé Liánluò Xiǎozǔ Sino-British Joint Liaison Group

中庸 zhōngyōng ❶ golden mean (of the Confucian school) ❷ (Zhōngyōng) *The Doctrine of the Mean* see also "四书" Sìshū ❸〈书面〉mediocre; average; middling:他仅有～之资。He is a man of mediocre abilities. /他才能不及～。He is below average as far as his capability is concerned.

中庸之道 zhōngyōngzhīdào doctrine of the mean; golden mean

中用 zhōngyòng (often used in the negative) be of use; be helpful:我老了,不～了。I'm getting old and become quite useless. /

他家大儿子太不～。His eldest son is a good-for-nothing.
中游 zhōngyóu ❶ middle reaches (of a river):长江～ middle reaches of the Yangtze ❷ state of being middling; mediocre; so-so:不甘～ not resigned to the middling state; not content to stay middling /～思想 mentality of wishing to stay middling
中雨 zhōngyǔ 〈气象〉moderate rain
中元节 Zhōngyuánjié Zhongyuan Festival (15th of the seventh lunar month during which sacrifices are offered to the dead)
中原 Zhōngyuán Central Plains (i.e. the middle and lower reaches of the Yellow River, comprising most of Henan Province, the western part of Shandong Province, and the southern parts of Hebei and Shanxi provinces):地处～ be situated in the Central Plains /～板荡 social upheavals all over the country
中原逐鹿 Zhōngyuán-zhúlù fight (among rivals) for supremacy or the throne
中岳 Zhōngyuè Central Sacred Mountain (another name for 嵩山 Songshan Mountain in Henan Province)
see also "五岳" Wǔyuè
中云 zhōngyún 〈气象〉medium cloud
中允 zhōngyǔn 〈书面〉*also* "公允" gōngyǔn fair-minded; equitable; impartial
中灶 zhōngzào mess for medium ranking cadres; medium mess (between an ordinary mess and a special mess)
中曾根康弘 Zhōngzēnggēn Kānghóng Nakasone Yasuhiro (1918-), Japanese Prime Minister (1982-1987)
中正 zhōngzhèng 〈书面〉fair; just; impartial
中支 zhōngzhī 〈纺织〉medium-counts:～纱 medium-count yarn
中直 zhōngzhí departments under the Central Committee of the Chinese Communist Party
中值定理 zhōngzhí dìnglǐ 〈数学〉mean-value theorem
中止 zhōngzhǐ discontinue; suspend; cut short; break off:～学习 discontinue one's studies /～订货 suspend an order for goods /～付款 suspension of payment /～营业 wind up its operations /～上诉 discontinuance of appeal /～诉讼 abatement of action; stopping a case /～诉讼通知 notice of discontinuance /～谈判 cut short (*or* break off) negotiations /～会员资格 suspension of membership /～射击 lift fire
中指 zhōngzhǐ *also* "将指" jiàngzhǐ middle finger
中州 Zhōngzhōu 〈旧语〉middle of China (referring to Henan Province and the surrounding area)
中州韵 zhōngzhōuyùn Zhongzhou intonations (used in traditional opera)
中轴 zhōngzhóu 〈机械〉central line; centre shaft
中注管 zhōngzhùguǎn 〈冶金〉running-gate
中专 zhōngzhuān (short for 中等专科学校) secondary specialized or technical school; polytechnic school:美术～ secondary fine arts school /农艺～ agrotechnical school
中转 zhōngzhuǎn ❶〈交通〉change trains:～签字 sign a transfer /你到佳木斯得～一次。You have to change trains to get to Jiamusi. ❷〈经济〉entrepot; transit shipment:～货物 goods to be transhipped /～贸易 entrepot trade /～运输 traffic in transit /～局 intermediate office
中转港 zhōngzhuǎngǎng transhipment port; entrepot
中转站 zhōngzhuǎnzhàn tranfer station
中装 zhōngzhuāng traditional Chinese clothing
中子 zhōngzǐ neutron:快～ fast neutron /慢～ slow neutron /热～ thermal neutron /瞬发～ prompt neutron /～反应 neutron reaction /～俘获 neutron capture; neutron absorption /～辐照 neutron irradiation /～感生裂变 neutron-induced fission /～数 neutron number /～通量 neutron flux /～源 neutron source; neutron producer
中子弹 zhōngzǐdàn neutron bomb
中子发射器 zhōngzǐ fāshèqì neutron howitzer
中子发射体 zhōngzǐ fāshètǐ neutron emitter
中子光学 zhōngzǐ guāngxué neutron optics
中子态 zhōngzǐtài neutron state
中子物理学 zhōngzǐ wùlǐxué neutronics
中子显示器 zhōngzǐ xiǎnshìqì neutrovision
中子星 zhōngzǐxīng neutron star

衷 zhōng ❶ innermost feelings:无动于～ not be moved in the least; be apathetic /言不由～ speak insincerely /由～之言 words spoken from the bottom of one's heart ❷ (Zhōng) a surname
衷肠 zhōngcháng 〈书面〉heartfelt remarks:畅叙～ heart-to-heart talk
衷情 zhōngqíng 〈书面〉heartfelt feelings:她向他倾吐～。She opened her heart to him.
衷曲 zhōngqū 〈书面〉heartfelt emotion; inmost feelings:尽情地吐露～ bare one's heart; pour out one's soul
衷心 zhōngxīn heartfelt; wholehearted; cordial; from the bottom of one's heart:～拥护 give wholehearted support to /～祝愿 sincerely wish /～折服 admire sb. from the heart /表示～的祝贺 extend cordial greetings; congratulate sb. heartily /受到人民群众的～爱戴 be deeply loved and respected by the people /～感谢你们所作的努力。For your noble effort, I thank you from the bottom of my heart.

忠 zhōng loyal; staunch; faithful; devoted:～君 loyal to the throne (*or* sovereign) /～于其主 faithful to one's master /为国尽～ serve the country faithfully; die for the country /效～祖国 devote oneself heart and soul to one's motherland /～义之士 honest and righteous man
忠臣 zhōngchén loyal court official:～烈士 loyal and noble-hearted official /～孝子 loyal court official and dutiful son
忠忱 zhōngchén loyal; faithful; honest
忠诚 zhōngchéng loyal; faithful; sincere; staunch:～的爱国者 staunch patriot /～待人 treat people with warmth and sincerity /～党的教育事业 be devoted to the Party's educational cause (*or* undertaking) /对祖国无限～ be boundlessly loyal to one's motherland /这人～老实。He is honest and faithful. /他～地信守诺言。He is as good as his word.
忠肝义胆 zhōnggān-yìdǎn faithful and gallant; daring and patriotic
忠告 zhōnggào ❶ sincerely advise; exhort; admonish:我们曾～她不要仓促结婚。We have sincerely advised her against marrying in haste. /我～他饮酒过多有害。I admonished him of the harm of too much drinking. ❷ sincere advice; exhortation:他把大夫的～当作耳旁风。He turned a deaf ear to the advice of the doctor.
忠鲠 zhōnggěng loyal and outspoken; faithful and straight:～之臣 loyal and upright court official
忠骨 zhōnggǔ loyal bones; dead body of a martyr:青山处处埋～,何必马革裹尸还。There are green hills everywhere to bury loyal bones; Why wrap the corpse in horse hide and bring it back home?
忠厚 zhōnghòu honest and tolerant; sincere and kindhearted:为人～ be honest and kindhearted /他们都是～的乡下人。They are simple and kindly country folks. /他性子很～。He is of a sincere and kindly disposition.
忠魂 zhōnghún loyal soul; soul of a martyr:万里长空且为～舞 to dance for these loyal souls in infinite space /我今吟诗一首,以慰～。Let me chant a poem to console the soul of our martyr.
忠荩 zhōngjìn 〈书面〉devote oneself to the country
忠君爱国 zhōngjūn-àiguó be loyal to the sovereign and faithful to the country
忠良 zhōngliáng ❶ loyal and honest; faithful and staunch:～之士 loyal and upright person ❷ the loyal and virtuous:陷害～ plot a frame-up against a loyal and virtuous man
忠烈 zhōngliè ❶ lay down one's life out of boundless loyalty to the country:～之臣 loyal court official who remains faithful to the last ❷ martyr:缅怀～ cherish the memory of the martyrs
忠实 zhōngshí ❶ true; faithful; trustworthy:～于自己的理想 true to oneself (*or* to one's ideals) /～的朋友 devoted (*or* loyal) friend /～的信徒 faithful follower /～可靠 honest and reliable; trustworthy ❷ true; truthful; real:～报道事情的经过 give a truthful account of what has happened /这是现实生活的～写照。This is a true picture of real life.
忠恕 zhōngshù loyalty and forbearance
忠顺 zhōngshùn loyal and obedient:她对主人极为～。She is a loyal and willing servant of her master.
忠孝 zhōngxiào loyalty and filial piety:～难全。Loyalty and filial piety seldom go together.
忠心 zhōngxīn loyalty; dedication; devotion:赤胆～ ardent loyalty; wholehearted devotion; utter dedication /表～ pledge one's loyalty /～报国 work for the country heart and soul
忠心耿耿 zhōngxīn-gěnggěng loyal and devoted; most faithful and steadfast:～、勋劳卓著的老臣 most loyal court official who is noted for his meritorious service /对教育事业～ be dedicated to the

cause of education /～地为人民谋福利 work most faithfully for the well-being of the people
忠信 zhōngxìn faithful and true; loyal and honest
忠言 zhōngyán sincere advice; earnest exhortation: 进～ give sincere advice /～谠论 earnest advice and honest comment /～嘉谟 earnest exhortation and excellent plan (*or* strategy)
忠言逆耳 zhōngyán-nì'ěr candid advice grates on the ear; honest exhortations may be unpleasant to the ear; golden words offend the ear: ～利于行。Honest advice, though harsh to the ear, induces good conduct. /我劝他不要跟那些人来往, 可是～, 他哪里听得进! I admonished him to stay away from those people, but he refused to listen to me. Good advice often jars on the ear!
忠义 zhōngyì ❶ faithful and righteous; loyal and staunch: ～之士 man of loyalty and righteousness ❷〈旧语〉loyal and righteous court official: 表彰～ commend loyal and righteous official
忠勇 zhōngyǒng loyal and brave: ～的战士 loyal and brave fighters
忠于 zhōngyú steadfast in the performance of duty; true to; loyal to; devoted to: ～祖国 be loyal to one's country /～真理 abide by the truth /～诺言 true to one's promise; keep faith /～职守 be devoted to one's duty
忠贞 zhōngzhēn loyal and staunch: ～不二 be unswerving in one's allegiance
忠贞不渝 zhōngzhēn-bùyú unswervingly loyal; steadfast and unyielding: 对爱情～ be faithful to one's love /为了伟大的理想, 他～地奋斗了一生。He has devoted his whole life to the realization of this great ideal.
忠直 zhōngzhí faithful and honest; devoted and upright: ～的好朋友 devoted and honest friend

盅

zhōng handleless cup: 茶～ teacup /酒～ winecup /来喝几～。Let's have a few cups of wine.
盅子 zhōngzi 〈口语〉handleless cup

钟[1]（鐘）

zhōng ❶ bell: 洪～ large bell /撞～ toll (*or* ring) a bell /～鼓齐鸣。Bells and drums sound simultaneously. ❷ clock: 摆～ pendulum clock /电～ electric clock /挂～ wall clock /闹～ alarm clock /座～ desk clock /石英～ quartz clock /子母～ synchronized clocks /天文～ astronomical clock /原子～ atomichron; atomic clock ❸ time (as measured in hours and minutes): "几点～啦?" "八点～。" "What time is it?" "Eight o'clock." /离开车还有五分～。The train leaves in five minutes.

钟[2]（鍾）

zhōng ❶ concentrate (one's affections, etc.); focus on: 全部慈母之爱～于女儿一身。The loving mother dotes on her daughter. /泽, 水之～也。A pool is the concentration of water. ❷ (Zhōng) a surname

钟[3]（鍾）

zhōng *see* "盅" zhōng
钟爱 zhōng'ài love dearly; cherish: 所有的孩子中他最得父母～。Of all the children in the family, he is his parents' favourite.
钟摆 zhōngbǎi pendulum: ～轴承 pendulum bearing
钟表 zhōngbiǎo clocks and watches; timepiece: ～零部件 parts and accessories of clocks and watches /～店 watchmaker's shop /～油 watchmaker's oil; watch oil /～制造术 horology
钟锤 zhōngchuí clock weight
钟点 zhōngdiǎn 〈口语〉❶ time for sth. to be done or to happen; appointed time: 再等一会儿, 还不到～。Let's wait a few more minutes; it's not time yet. ❷ hour: 我们在这儿等了两个～了。We've been waiting here for two hours.
钟鼎文 zhōngdǐngwén *also* "金文" jīnwén inscriptions on ancient bronze objects
钟馗 Zhōng Kuí Zhong Kui (formerly translated as Chung K'uei), a deity who can drive away evil spirits in Chinese folklore
钟离 Zhōnglí a surname
钟离权 Zhōnglí Quán Zhongli Quan (formerly translated as Chung-li Ch'uan), one of the Eight Immortals in Taoist mythology
钟灵毓秀 zhōnglíng-yùxiù a fine environment or beautiful land nurtures talents
钟楼 zhōnglóu ❶ bell tower; belfry ❷ clock tower
钟鸣鼎食 zhōngmíng-dǐngshí dine at a meal with many cooking vessels of food and to the accompaniment of music — live an extravagant life; enjoy affluence: ～之家 very rich family
钟鸣漏尽 zhōngmíng-lòujìn the bell has rung and water in the clepsydra is exhausted — near (*or* approach) the end of one's life; one's days are numbered; be old and feeble
钟琴 zhōngqín *also* "颤音琴" chànyīnqín 〈乐器〉carillon; glockenspiel
钟情 zhōngqíng be deeply in love; be captivated: 一见～ (fall in) love at first sight /～于这位美丽的姑娘 fall for this beautiful girl
钟雀 zhōngquè bellbird
钟鹊 zhōngquè bell-magpie
钟乳石 zhōngrǔshí *also* "石钟乳" shízhōngrǔ stalactite
钟乳体 zhōngrǔtǐ 〈生物〉cystolith
钟塔 zhōngtǎ bell tower; campanile
钟铜 zhōngtóng bell metal (a bronze and tin alloy)
钟头 zhōngtóu 〈口语〉hour: 我们已干了三个～。We've been working for 3 hours.
钟相杨幺起义 Zhōng Xiàng Yáng Yāo Qǐyì Peasant Uprising led by Zhong Xiang (? -1130) and Yang Yao (? -1135) in the early Southern Song Dynasty
钟繇 Zhōng Yóu Zhong You (formerly translated as Chung Yu) (151-230), Chinese calligrapher of the Three Kingdoms Period

柊

zhōng
柊叶 zhōngyè *also* "棕叶" zōngyè 〈植物〉*Phrynimu capitatum*

螽

zhōng
螽斯 zhōngsī 〈动物〉katydid; long-horned grasshopper

终

zhōng ❶ end; close; finish: 年～总结 sum up one's work at the end of the year /自始至～ from beginning to end; from start to finish /有始有～ start well and end well; see sth. through /以失败告～ end up in failure /从一而～ faithful to one's husband to the very last ❷ death; end: 临～ on one's deathbed; when one is dying /善～ die a natural death /送～ wait upon a dying person (usu. one's parent); arrange the burial of one's parent /他年八十乃～。He died at the age of 80. ❸ eventually; ultimately; in the end; after all: 一对情人～成眷属。The two lovers got married eventually. /他～遂所愿。He had his wish fulfilled in the end. /持之以恒, ～必有成。Perseverance brings success. /此～非长久之计。It isn't a permanent solution after all. ❹ whole; full; entire; all: ～岁 whole year; throughout the year /～夜不眠 lie awake all night ❺ (Zhōng) a surname
终板电位 zhōngbǎn diànwèi end-plate potential (EPP)
终不成 zhōngbùchéng *also* "终不然" 〈副词〉(usu. used in the early vernacular) *giving emphasis to a rhetorical question*: 自小学成十八般武艺, ～只这般休了? I've learned all the skills of martial art since my youth. How can I give it up like this?
终场 zhōngchǎng ❶ end of a game, performance or show: ～前客队又投进一球。The visiting team shot one more basket just before the game ended. /当～落幕的时候, 观众发出了热烈的掌声。Warm applause rose from the audience as the curtain fell at the end of the show. ❷〈旧语〉final session in an examination
终底于成 zhōngdǐyúchéng succeed in the end; finally achieve one's aim
终点 zhōngdiǎn ❶ end point; terminal; destination: 旅途的～ end of a journey /列车到达～。The train has reached its destination. ❷〈体育〉finish: ～线 finishing line; finishing tape /～裁判 judge at the finish
终点站 zhōngdiǎnzhàn terminus; terminal: 公共汽车～ bus terminus /航空～ air terminal
终端 zhōngduān terminal: ～电缆 terminal cable /～绝缘子 end insulator; terminal insulator /～线路 terminal line /～塔架 terminal tower /～机室 terminal room /～适配器 terminal adapter /～控制系统 terminal control system (TCS) /智能～ intelligent terminal
终端局 zhōngduānjú 〈通信〉terminal office; terminal station; terminating office
终伐 zhōngfá 〈林业〉final cutting or felling
终伏 zhōngfú *also* "末伏" mòfú last ten days of the hottest period of the year
终古 zhōnggǔ 〈书面〉forever: 这虽是一句老话, 却令人感到～常新。This is an old saying, but it always sounds fresh to people.
终归 zhōngguī eventually; finally; in the end; after all: 她～会原谅

Z

她的儿子。She will forgive her son eventually. /这问题～会解决的。This problem will be solved in the end. /他～还是个孩子。He is still a kid after all.

终轨 zhōngguǐ final orbit

终极 zhōngjí final; ultimate: ～目标 final aim /达到～目的 attain the ultimate goal

终接器 zhōngjiēqì 〈通信〉 final selector

终结 zhōngjié ❶ end; final stage: 生命的～ end of one's life /～账簿 book of final entry /～参数 terminal parameter ❷ come to an end: 谈判突然～了。The negotiations suddenly came to an end. /事情远未～。The matter is far from being resolved.

终竟 zhōngjìng ❶ after all; all in all; in the final analysis: 有缺点的战士～是战士，完美的苍蝇也～不过是苍蝇。An imperfect fighter is a fighter, while a perfect fly is nothing but a fly. ❷ 〈书面〉 termination; end: 人类与大自然的斗争永无～。There is no end to man's struggle against nature.

终究 zhōngjiū eventually; all in all; after all: 他～会体会父母的苦心。He will eventually understand the pains taken by his parents for his sake. /这～是件小事，何必太认真。This is after all a trivial matter. Why take it so seriously? /他是有缺点，但～是个认真的人。He has his faults, but all in all he is a conscientious man.

终久 zhōngjiǔ *see* "终究"

终局 zhōngjú end; outcome; result: ～判决 final judgment /～性仲裁裁决 final award /这场球的～出乎人们的意料。The outcome of the match is most unexpected.

终老 zhōnglǎo spend the last years of one's life: 他～故乡。He spent his last years in his native village.

终了 zhōngliǎo end (of a period): 运动～ end of a political campaign

终南捷径 zhōngnán-jiéjìng shortcut to high office or success; royal road to fame: 他挖空心思，总想找到一条名利双收的～。He racked his brains, trying to find a royal road to fame and wealth.

终年 zhōngnián ❶ all the year round; throughout the year: ～积雪的高山 high mountains covered with snow all the year round /这儿山高林密，～难见人迹。No traces of human activity can be spotted anytime of the year in these high mountains and dense forests. ❷ age at which one dies: 他～八十岁。He died at the age of eighty.

终篇 zhōngpiān 〈书面〉 finish a piece of writing

终曲 zhōngqǔ 〈音乐〉 finale

终日 zhōngrì all day long; all day: ～闷闷不乐 be depressed all day long /饱食～，无所用心 eat three square meals a day without exercising one's mind; be sated with food and lead an idle life

终身 zhōngshēn lifelong; throughout one's life: ～残废 permanent disability /～监禁 life imprisonment /～人寿保险 whole life insurance /私定～ arrange one's own marriage (without asking for permission of one's parents) /那造成了他的～大恨。That cost him lifelong regret.

终身伴侣 zhōngshēn bànlǚ lifelong companion (referring to one's spouse): 结成～ get married

终身大事 zhōngshēn dàshì event of lifelong significance; important event in one's life (usu. meaning marriage): 婚姻乃～，岂可视为儿戏！Marriage is an event of lifelong significance and not to be trifled with.

终身监护制 zhōngshēn jiānhùzhì perpetual guardianship

终身教育 zhōngshēn jiàoyù lifelong education

终身制 zhōngshēnzhì lifelong tenure: 废除干部～ abolish lifelong tenure for cadres

终审 zhōngshěn 〈法律〉 last instance; final judgment: ～法院 court of last instance /～判决 final adjudication; final judgment; last judgment /～权 power of final adjudication

终生 zhōngshēng one's lifetime; all one's life: ～难忘的教训 will not forget the lesson to the end of one's days /～的事业 one's lifework /～与古籍为伴 be buried (*or* immersed) in classic works all one's life /那情景令我～难忘。I shall never forget that scene.

终始 zhōngshǐ from beginning to end; all along; throughout: 愿～以友谊为重。Let's value friendship from first to last.

终霜 zhōngshuāng 〈气象〉 latest frost

终速 zhōngsù final speed

终岁 zhōngsuì whole year; all the year round; throughout the year: 全家～平安。The whole family is well throughout the year. /祖辈们在这贫瘠的土地上～劳作。Year after year, our forefathers toiled on this impoverished land.

终天 zhōngtiān ❶ whole day; all day long: ～操劳家务 do household chores all day long ❷ 〈书面〉 lifelong; all one's life: 抱恨～ regret all one's life

终天之恨 zhōngtiānzhīhèn lifelong regret; eternal remorse: 壮志未酬，遂成～。Not having fulfilled his lofty aspirations, he was gnawed by eternal regret.

终席 zhōngxí end of a banquet or meeting: 没到～，他就起身回家了。He stood up and left for home before the banquet was over.

终宵 zhōngxiāo *also* "终夜" all night; whole night; throughout the night: ～不寐 did not sleep a wink all night

终须 zhōngxū have to do sth. in the end; be unavoidable in the long run

终于 zhōngyú at (long) last; in the end; finally; eventually: 经过多次失败，试验～成功。The experiment succeeded at last after repeated failures. /问题～解决了。The problem was solved finally.

终轧 zhōngzhá 〈冶金〉 finish to gauge: ～机 finishing mill

终朝 zhōngzhāo 〈书面〉 ❶ whole morning ❷ *see* "终日"

终止 zhōngzhǐ ❶ stop; put an end to; terminate: ～合同 terminate a contract /～日期 closing date; expiry date /～协议 terminate an agreement /～条约通知书 notice of termination of a treaty; notice of denunciation /这次谈判到此～。The negotiation stops here. ❷ 〈音乐〉 cadence

终止符 zhōngzhǐfú 〈音乐〉 full stop; period

zhǒng

冢(塚) zhǒng tomb; grave: 荒～ abandoned tomb /丛～ group of graves /义～ burial ground for the destitute /衣冠～ tomb containing personal effects of the deceased, whose remains are either missing or buried elsewhere /～中枯骨 rotten bones in the graveyard — good-for-nothing and incompetent people

种(種) zhǒng ❶ 〈生物〉 species: 绝～ (of a species) become extinct; die out ❷ race: 黄～人 yellow race /黑～人 black race ❸ seed; strain; breed: 稻～ rice seeds /菜～ vegetable seeds /选～ selecting seed; strain selection /劣～ inferior strain /杂交～ hybrid strain /纯～ pure breed /良～牛 good breed of cattle /配～ breed /同～繁殖 breed in and in /异～繁殖 breed out and out /鱼～ fingerling ❹ guts; grit; nerve; pluck: 真孬～！What a coward! /有～的站出来！Let anyone who has guts step forward! ❺ 〈量词〉 kind; style; sort; type: ～～不同的情况 all kinds of situations /两～不同的思想 two different ideas (*or* views) /这～人 this sort of people /十五～灯具 fifteen types of lights /连衣裙的样子有好多～。There are woman's dresses in different styles. ❻ (Zhǒng) a surname

see also Chóng; zhòng

种差 zhǒngchā intraspecific diversity

种畜 zhǒngchù breeding stock; stud stock

种蛋 zhǒngdàn breeding egg

种肥 zhǒngféi seed manure

种间杂交 zhǒngjiān zájiāo interspecific hybridization or crossing; cross-breeding

种类 zhǒnglèi kind; variety; category: 不同～的花卉 flowers of different kinds /～繁多的纺织品 great variety of textiles /属于同一～ come under the same category

种麻 zhǒngmá *also* "苴麻" jūmá female plant of the hemp

种马 zhǒngmǎ stallion kept for breeding; stud: ～场 stud farm; stud

种苗 zhǒngmiáo seedling: ～园艺 horticulture; nursery gardening

种内杂交 zhǒngnèi zájiāo intraspecific hybridization or crossing

种牛 zhǒngniú bull kept for covering; stud

种禽 zhǒngqín fowl kept for breeding

种群 zhǒngqún population: ～动态 population dynamics /～密度 population density /～平衡 population balance /～循环 population cycle /～生态学 genecology

种仁 zhǒngrén kernel

种条 zhǒngtiáo branch or twig for layering

种姓 zhǒngxìng caste (of India): ～制度 caste system (by which Indian society is divided up into different social classes according to the principles of Hinduism)

种鱼 zhǒngyú *also* "亲鱼" qīnyú parent fish

种种 zhǒngzhǒng all sorts or kinds of; variety of; various: 提出～

设想 put forward various proposals /克服了～困难 overcome all kinds of difficulties /采取～办法 resort to all sorts of measures; use every possible means /凡此～，不一而足。Such instances are legion.

种子 zhǒngzi ❶ seed:留下的玉米～ corn seeds reserved for planting /～处理 seed treatment /～测定 seed testing /～改良 seed amelioration /～清选机 seed cleaner; seed-cleaning apparatus /～植物 seed plant; spermatophyte /埋下了仇恨的～ have sown the seeds of hatred ❷〈体育〉seed:被列为～ be seeded

种子地 zhǒngzidì *see* "种子田"

种子队 zhǒngziduì 〈体育〉seed(ed) team

种子田 zhǒngzitián *also* "留种地" liúzhǒngdì seed-breeding field

种子选手 zhǒngzi xuǎnshǒu 〈体育〉seeded player; seed

种族 zhǒngzú race:～平等 racial equality /～偏见 racial prejudice /～特征 racial traits /～冲突 ethnic (*or* racial) conflict

种族隔离 zhǒngzú gélí racial segregation

种族隔离政策 zhǒngzú gélí zhèngcè apartheid, a policy of racial segregation enforced in South Africa until early 1990's

种族灭绝 zhǒngzú mièjué genocide

种族歧视 zhǒngzú qíshì racial discrimination

种族清洗 zhǒngzú qīngxǐ ethnic cleansing

种族主义 zhǒngzúzhǔyì racism; racialism:～者 racist

肿(腫)

zhǒng swell; be swollen:红～ red and swollen /脓～ abscess /浮～ edema; dropsy /囊～ cyst /消～ detumescence /你的脸怎么～了? Why? Your face is swollen! /～消了一点。The dropsy has gone down (*or* subsided).

肿大 zhǒngdà enlargement; tumefaction; swelling:肝～ enlargement of the liver; hepatomegaly /淋巴结～ enlargement of lymph nodes

肿骨鹿 zhǒnggǔlù thick-jawed deer

肿块 zhǒngkuài phyma; tumour; mass:腹内～ abdominal mass /～切开术〈医学〉oncotomy

肿瘤 zhǒngliú tumour:良性～ benign tumour /恶性～ malignant tumour; cancer /～医院 tumour hospital /～抗原 tumour antigen

肿瘤学 zhǒngliúxué oncology; phymatology

肿胀 zhǒngzhàng ❶ swelling ❷〈中医〉oedema and abdominal distension

踵

zhǒng 〈书面〉❶ heel:接～而至 follow on one's heels /比肩继～ (of people) stand shoulder to shoulder and follow close on one another's heels — overcrowded with people ❷ call in person:～门相告 call in person to pass the news ❸ follow on sb.'s heels; follow close behind

踵事增华 zhǒngshì-zēnghuá 〈书面〉undertake and further a predecessor's cause; take over and carry forward

踵武 zhǒngwǔ 〈书面〉follow suit; imitate; copy

踵趾相接 zhǒngzhǐ-xiāngjiē *also* "踵足相接" follow in sb.'s footsteps; come one after another; arrive in quick succession:送礼道喜者～。People came one after another with gifts to offer congratulations.

踵至 zhǒngzhì arrive on the heels of another; come close after another

zhòng

中

zhòng ❶ hit; fit exactly; be just right:命～ hit the target /没～ miss the target /击～要害 hit the most vulnerable point; hit home; hit where it hurts /正～下怀 fit in exactly with one's wishes; be just what one hopes for /猜～ guess right /我在商店里看～了一件大衣。I found in the shop a coat that I like. ❷ fall into; sustain; suffer:臂上～了一弹 be shot in the arm /～了圈套 walk into a trap /～埋伏 fall into an ambush /～煤气 be gassed

see also zhōng

中标 zhòngbiāo be chosen to be the tender (of a bid); get or win a bid:在投标竞争中，我公司夺魁～。In the competition among bidders, our company won the tender (*or* our company's tender has been accepted).

中彩 zhòngcǎi draw a prizewinning ticket in a lottery

中弹 zhòngdàn be struck by a bullet; get shot:～身亡 be shot dead

中的 zhòngdì hit the target; hit it:他的讲话一语～。His talk hit the nail squarely on the head.

中毒 zhòngdú poisoning; toxicosis; toxication:药物～ drug poisoning /铅～ lead poisoning /煤气～ gas poisoning /马钱子碱～ poisoning by strychnine /酒精～ alcoholism /～性疾病 toxicopathy /～量 dosis toxica

中毒性皮炎 zhòngdúxìng píyán toxicodermatitis

中毒性贫血 zhòngdúxìng pínxuè toxanemia

中风 zhòngfēng *also* "卒中" cùzhòng ❶ be seized with apoplexy; suffer from a stroke of apoplexy ❷ apoplexy; stroke

中计 zhòngjì be taken in; walk into a trap; be ensnared; play into the hands of:中了诡计 be taken in by a manoeuvre /我们～了。We've fallen into a trap. /我们不要中了敌人的计。Beware lest we play into the hands of the enemy.

中奖 zhòngjiǎng win a prize in a lottery; get the winning number in a lottery-attached deposit

中举 zhòngjǔ become a successful candidate in the imperial examinations at the provincial level in the Ming and Qing dynasties

中肯 zhòngkěn ❶ (of remarks) sincere and pertinent:～之论 pertinent comments /他的批评很～。His criticisms are sincere and to the point. ❷ *also* "临界" línjiè 〈物理〉critical:～大小 critical size /～电势 critical potential /～照度 critical illumination /～质量 critical mass

中魔 zhòngmó be bewitched; be possessed:她一瞬间像～似的，两眼直视，坐在那儿，一动也不动。For a moment she sat there still, looking straight forward blankly, as if bewitched.

中签 zhòngqiān be the lucky number (in drawing lots, etc.)

中伤 zhòngshāng slander; vilify; caluminate:造谣～ spread slanderous rumours /恶意～ slander (*or* malign) sb. viciously

中式 zhòngshì pass the imperial examination

see also zhōngshì

中试 zhòngshì pass the test:这项科研成果通过了～鉴定。The achievement in scientific research has passed appraisal.

中暑 zhòngshǔ ❶ suffer heatstroke or sunstroke; be affected by the heat ❷ fever, headache, etc. caused by exposure to strong sunlight; sunstroke; heatstroke

中邪 zhòngxié be bewitched

中选 zhòngxuǎn be chosen; be selected; be opted for:这三幅画～，将在画廊展出。These three paintings are selected to be exhibited in the art gallery.

中意 zhòngyì be to one's taste; catch the fancy of:这几个装饰图案我都不～。None of these ornamental designs is to my liking. /张家姑娘最中他的意。The daughter of Mr. Zhang has caught his fancy.

种(種)

zhòng sow; grow; plant; cultivate:～菜 grow vegetables /～果树 plant fruit trees /补～玉米 resow maize /～大片农田 cultivate vast tracts of farmland /这里每年可～三季水稻。The paddy fields here yield three crops a year.

see also Chóng; zhǒng

种地 zhòngdì till land for growing crops; go in for farming:他中学毕业后就回乡～。He returned to his hometown and took up farming after he graduated from secondary school.

种痘 zhòngdòu *also* "种牛痘" vaccination (against smallpox):医院明天给孩子们～。The hospital will give vaccination to the children tomorrow.

种瓜得瓜，种豆得豆 zhòng guā dé guā, zhòng dòu dé dòu plant melons and you get melons, sow beans and you get beans — as you sow, so will you reap; you must reap what you have sown:～，谁种下仇恨谁遭殃。As the saying goes, "As you make the bed, so you must lie on it", those who have sown the seed of hatred will have to reap its bitter fruits. /～，真正的幸福是用血汗创造出来的。As you sow, so will you reap; genuine happiness is the fruit of hard labour.

种花 zhònghuā ❶ cultivate or grow flowers ❷〈方言〉vaccination (against smallpox) ❸〈方言〉grow cotton

种牛痘 zhòngniúdòu *see* "种痘"

种田 zhòngtián till the land; do farm work; farm:～人 farmer; peasant /他白天～，晚上写作。He did farm work during the day and worked on his book at night.

种因 zhòngyīn 〈书面〉sow the seed (of later clash, suffering, etc.); do sth. that eventually leads to grave consequences:两国交恶，由此～。That led to the deterioration of relations between the two countries.

种植 zhòngzhí plant; grow; cultivate: 扩大棉花～面积 enlarge cotton-growing areas /～期 planting season /～深度 planting depth

种植园 zhòngzhíyuán plantation; hacienda: ～主 plantation owner; planter /香蕉～ banana plantation

仲 zhòng ❶ middle; intermediate ❷ (of the three months in a season) second:《～夏夜之梦》*Midsummer Night's Dream* ❸ (of brothers) second in order of birth: ～父 father's younger brother / 伯～叔季 eldest, second eldest, younger, and youngest brothers ❹ (Zhòng) a surname

仲裁 zhòngcái arbitrate: 国际～ international arbitration /海事～ marine arbitration /～法庭 court of arbitration; arbitration court; arbitral tribunal /～人 arbitrator /～委员会 arbitration commission; board of arbitration /～长 umpire /～协定 arbitration agreement; *compromis* /～条款 arbitration clause /～书 (arbitration) award /将争端付诸～ submit a dispute to arbitration /～裁决的不可撤回性和具有强制执行力 irrevocability and enforceability of the award

仲裁试验 zhòngcái shìyàn 〈石油〉referee test

仲春 zhòngchūn second month of spring; mid-spring: ～之月,雷始发生。Thunder starts in midspring.

仲冬 zhòngdōng second month of winter; midwinter: ～之日 day in midwinter

仲家 Zhòngjiā old name for Bouyei nationality (布依族), and part of the Zhuang nationality (壮族) in Yunnan Province

仲秋 zhòngqiū second month of autumn; mid-autumn: ～之月,雷始收声。Thunder stops in midautumn.

仲夏 zhòngxià second month of summer; midsummer: ～之夜 night in midsummer

众(衆) zhòng ❶ many; numerous; innumerable: 寡不敌～ be hopelessly outnumbered; fight against hopeless odds /敌～我寡。The enemy are many, we are few. ❷ large number of people; crowd; multitude: 民～ common people; the masses /公～ the public /观～ spectators; viewers; audience (watching a performance, TV show, etc.) /听～ audience; listeners /乌合之～ motley crowd; disorderly band /拿出示～ publicly expose sth.; put sth. before the public /当～宣布无效 declare sth. invalid in the presence of all (*or* in public)

众多 zhòngduō many; numerous; multitudinous: 人口～的城市 populous city /我国人口～。Our country has a large population. /在～的求职者中,她是幸运者。She was the lucky one among the numerous applicants for the job.

众寡悬殊 zhòngguǎ-xuánshū wide gap or great disparity in numerical strength: 双方的人数～。One side is numerically far superior to the other. /在～的形势下,他没有惊慌失措。He showed no sign of panic when he was outnumbered.

众口难调 zhòngkǒu-nántiáo it is difficult to cater to all tastes; one man's meat is another man's poison; it is difficult to please everybody; tastes differ: 单位人多,～,哪能每件事都能让个个满意? There are so many people in the unit; it is difficult to please everybody.

众口铄金 zhòngkǒu-shuòjīn public clamour can melt metals — public clamour can confound right and wrong; if you throw enough mud, some of it will stick: ～,积非成是。Public clamour can confound right and wrong. A falsehood repeated many times may be accepted as the truth.

众口一词 zhòngkǒu-yīcí unanimous in opinion; with one voice; all telling the same story: 其他人～,我不能只听你一个人的。All the others tell the same story; I cannot take your word against theirs. /人们～,我有口难辩。They spoke with one voice; I found it hard to vindicate myself.

众目睽睽 zhòngmù-kuíkuí under the watchful eyes of the people; with all eyes centred (*or* fixed) on sth. or sb.; in the public eye: 那里人多,～,料他不敢欺侮你。I bet he dare not bully you under the watchful eyes of so many people there.

众目昭彰 zhòngmù-zhāozhāng the masses are sharp-eyed; be seen clearly by the public; be glaring: 在这～的大街上,那人与他拉近乎的样子使他感到很难堪。Before so many people in the street he was rather embarrassed by the unwelcome familiarities of that fellow.

众怒 zhòngnù public wrath; popular anger: 犯了～ arouse public indignation

众怒难犯 zhòngnù-nánfàn you cannot afford to incur public wrath; it is dangerous to arouse people's anger: 厂主知道～,只好部分地答应了工人们提出的要求。Knowing that it is dangerous to incur public anger, the factory owner had to meet some of the workers' demands.

众叛亲离 zhòngpàn-qīnlí be opposed by the public and deserted by one's followers; face utter isolation: 他陷入了山穷水尽、～的困境。With the masses rising in rebellion and his followers deserting, he is now at the end of his rope.

众擎易举 zhòngqíng-yìjǔ if many people work together, even a difficult task can be accomplished; many hands make light work: ～,独力难支。Many hands make light work; a single hand cannot sustain heavy weight.

众人 zhòngrén everybody: ～一心,黄土成金。If all of us are of one mind, we can turn soil into gold. /～眼睛是杆秤。The eyes of the masses see best.

众人拾柴火焰高 zhòngrén shí chái huǒyàn gāo the fire burns high when everybody brings wood to it: ～。每人多出把力,任务就可以提前完成。When everybody adds fuel, the flames rise high. If everyone puts in a bit more effort, the job will be finished ahead of time.

众生 zhòngshēng all living creatures: 芸芸～ all living beings; all mortal beings /普救～ save all living beings from calamities

众生相 zhòngshēngxiàng panorama of faces and behaviour: 这部小说刻画了当今商界的～。This novel gives a vivid picture of all kinds of people in the business world today.

众矢之的 zhòngshǐzhīdì target of a thousand arrows; object of angry public criticism: 他成了～。He has become the object of public censure.

众庶 zhòngshù 〈书面〉common people

众数 zhòngshù 〈统计〉mode: ～指数 mode index

众说 zhòngshuō diverse views; public opinion: ～不一,无所适从。Opinions vary, and it's hard to make a decision.

众说纷纭 zhòngshuō-fēnyún opinions differ greatly: 事情的起因～。Everybody has his own story about the cause of the incident. /关于这个问题,～,一时尚难形成一致的看法。As opinions are quite divided on this question, it's difficult to reach a consensus for the moment.

众所周知 zhòngsuǒzhōuzhī as everyone knows; as is well known; it is common knowledge that: 由于～的原因 for reasons known to all /他的忠厚是～的。Everybody knows he is an honest and kind man. /～,地球绕着太阳转。It is common knowledge that the earth revolves round the sun.

众望 zhòngwàng people's expectations; popular trust: 不孚～ fall short of people's expectations

众望所归 zhòngwàng-suǒguī enjoy popular confidence or trust; command public respect and support: 他当医院的院长是～的事。That he has become the director of the hospital accords with the wishes of everyone.

众星捧月 zhòngxīng-pěngyuè *also* "众星托月" a myriad of stars surround the moon: 他被这么多人拥在中间,～似的,他高兴极了。It gave him much satisfaction, surrounded as he was by so many admirers, like stars crowding round the moon.

众议员 zhòngyìyuán representative (in a Congress); Congressman or Congresswoman; member of the House of Representatives

众议院 zhòngyìyuàn ❶ (US, Australia, Japan, etc.) House of Representatives; (Italy, Mexico, Chile, etc.) Chamber of Deputies — lower house or chamber of the bicameral system ❷ (Luxembourg) Chamber of Deputies — name of parliament of some monocameral countries

众志成城 zhòngzhì-chéngchéng the united will of the masses is like a fortress; unity is strength; unity is the path to victory: ～,无往不胜。We can vanquish all enemies by relying on the united will of the masses.

众醉独醒 zhòngzuì-dúxǐng all are besotted, except one is sober: 他总认为自己处于～之中。It is his belief that all the others are besotted and that he alone is sober.

重 zhòng ❶ weight: 举～ weight-lifting /毛～ gross weight /净～ net weight /超～信件 overweight letter /加～自行车 heavy duty bike /你有多～? How much do you weigh? /这孩子已有三十公斤～了。The child is already 30 kilos. ❷ heavy; weighty; considerable in amount or value: ～金购买 pay a high price for /任务很～ have an arduous task to perform /这包够～的! This bag is quite weighty. /

Z

这机器太～。The machine is too heavy. /话说得太～了。That's putting it too strongly. /我得把话说～一点。I won't mince words. ❸ deep; serious:案情很～ very serious case /灾情很～ be hard hit by natural calamities /口味～ have a heavily seasoned taste /四川口音很～ have a marked (*or* strong) Sichuan accent /礼轻情意～。A small gift carries with it deep affection. ❹ important:事情不要轻～倒置。We must not place trivial matters over important ones. /任～道远。The task is arduous and the road is long. ❺ lay stress on; set store by; attach importance to:～基础教育 lay stress on basic education /以友谊为～ set store by friendship; value friendship /把文凭看得太～ attach too much importance to diplomas /～义轻利 value justice more than material gains ❻ prudent; discreet:庄～ demure /慎～ careful; cautious; circumspect /稳～ steady; prudent; dignified /自～ self-respect /老成持～ experienced and prudent /郑～其事 in all seriousness

see also chóng

重办 zhòngbàn mete out severe punishment to (a criminal):对制造假药者必须～。Those who manufacture fake medicines should be severely punished.

重臂 zhòngbì (old name for 阻力臂)〈物理〉distance between the point of resistance and the fulcrum while using a lever

see also "阻力臂" zǔlìbì; "阻力点" zǔlìdiǎn

重冰 zhòngbīng heavy ice

重兵 zhòngbīng large number of troops; huge forces:派出～ dispatch massive forces /用～包围 surround a place with a large number of troops /～压境 be heavily pressed by the enemy forces on the border

重柄 zhòngbǐng 〈书面〉(hold) great power

重病 zhòngbìng serious disease:身染～ become seriously ill; be struck down by serious illness

重才轻德 zhòngcái-qīngdé value ability above integrity:用人要德才并重,不可～。When you recruit people, you should lay equal stress on ability and moral integrity and must not prefer ability to moral character.

重彩 zhòngcǎi strong colouring:浓墨～ (paint in) dark ink and rich colours

重差计 zhòngchājì gravity meter

重柴油 zhòngcháiyóu diesel fuel oil

重臣 zhòngchén 〈书面〉court officials charged with heavy responsibilities; high court officials:元老～ senior court officials charged with important tasks

重惩 zhòngchéng punish harshly:～不贷 punish severely without mercy; punish mercilessly

重酬 zhòngchóu ❶ generously or liberally reward ❷ handsome reward; high reward

重创 zhòngchuāng inflict grievous losses or casualties on; wound badly; maul (heavily):～敌军 inflict heavy casualties on the enemy

重大 zhòngdà great; major; significant; tremendous:具有～的价值 be of great value /～原则问题 problem of major principle /～成就 significant (*or* outstanding) achievements /～变化 tremendous change /～事故 serious (*or* big) accident /～损失 heavy (*or* grievous) losses /～嫌疑犯 main suspect /～刑事犯 principal criminal /～事件 matter of consequence /～违约 fundamental breach (of contract) /～责任 colossal responsibility /～牺牲策略 major sacrifice gambit

重担 zhòngdàn heavy burden; difficult task; great responsibility:丈夫去世后,她一人挑起了抚养两个孩子的～。She bore the sole burden of raising two children after her husband's death. /他在工作中敢挑～。He dares to shoulder great responsibilities in work.

重氮 zhòngdàn 〈化学〉diazonium:～甲烷 diazoimethane

重氮化合物 zhòngdàn huàhéwù diazo compound

重氮乙酰胺基酸 zhòngdàn yǐxiān ànjīsuān 〈医学〉azaserine

重地 zhòngdì place of importance which is out of bounds to the general public:军事～ important military area /机房～,严禁抽烟。Machine in operation. Smoking forbidden. /施工～,闲人免进。Construction Site. No Admittance.

重典 zhòngdiǎn 〈书面〉❶ severe law; draconian law:治乱国用～。Severe laws are needed to govern a country when it is in disorder. ❷ important books or codes of law and records

重点 zhòngdiǎn ❶ (old name for 阻力点)〈物理〉point of resistance (at which a lever is applied at a weight, etc.) *see also* "阻力点" zǔlìdiǎn; "阻力臂" zǔlìbì ❷ focal point; key; emphasis:～科研项目 key research project /～工程 major (*or* priority) project /～防御 defence of key points /～护理病房 intensive care unit (ICU) /我们要突出工作的～。We must make the focal (*or* key) points of our work stand out. /新计划要把～放在降低成本上。The emphasis of the new plan must be on cutting costs. ❸ give priority to; stress:有～地支持发展某些项目 give priority to the development of selected projects /今天～讨论中东形势。Our discussion today will centre on the situation in the Middle East. *or* We'll focus our discussion today on the situation in the Middle East.

重点学校 zhòngdiǎn xuéxiào key school; key university or institute

重电子 zhòngdiànzǐ 〈物理〉heavy electron

重读 zhòngdú 〈语言〉stress:～音节 stressed syllable /非～音节 unstressed syllable /动词要～。Stress the verbs.

see also chóngdú

重吨 zhòngdūn gross ton; long ton

重犯 zhòngfàn criminal or offender guilty of a serious crime

重负 zhòngfù heavy load; crushing burden:如释～ feel as if relieved of a heavy load /一家九口人生活的～,压得他喘不过气来。Supporting a family of nine people, he felt almost crushed under the heavy burden (*or* he was burning the candle at both ends).

重工业 zhònggōngyè heavy industry:～集约式发展 intensive (form of) development of heavy industry

重轨 zhòngguǐ heavy rail

重过磷酸钙 zhòngguòlínsuāngài double superphosphate

重荷 zhònghè heavy burden; grave responsibility:身负～ carry a heavy burden

重轰炸机 zhònghōngzhàjī heavy bomber

重话 zhònghuà biting remarks; harsh or sharp words:他俩结婚多年,互敬互爱,连句～都没有过。They have been married for many years; they respect and love each other, and have never exchanged any sharp words.

重活 zhònghuó heavy work

重机关枪 zhòngjīguānqiāng heavy machine gun

重寄 zhòngjì 〈书面〉great trust; be charged with an important task by the country:身膺～ be entrusted with heavy responsibilities by the state

重价 zhòngjià high price:不惜～ not hesitate to pay high prices for sth.

重剑 zhòngjiàn épée:～运动员 épée fencer; épéeist; duellist

重奖 zhòngjiǎng ❶ rich or ample rewards ❷ offer rich or ample rewards

重金 zhòngjīn huge sum of money:～收买 buy over sb. with a huge sum of money

重金属 zhòngjīnshǔ heavy metal:～染料 heavy-metal stain /～毒害作用 heavy metal toxicity /～元素污染 heavy metal contamination

重金主义 zhòngjīnzhǔyì bullionism

重晶石 zhòngjīngshí barite; heavy spar

重聚合物 zhòngjùhéwù 〈化学〉heavy polymer

重离子 zhònglízǐ heavy ion

重力 zhònglì 〈物理〉gravity; gravitational force:～加速度 acceleration of gravity /～异常 gravity anomaly

重力坝 zhònglìbà 〈水利〉gravity dam

重力场 zhònglìchǎng gravitational field

重力秤 zhònglìchèng gravity balance

重力除尘器 zhònglì chúchénqì gravitational precipitator

重力感受器 zhònglì gǎnshòuqì gravirecepter

重力流 zhònglìliú gravity current

重力势 zhònglìshì gravitational potential

重力水 zhònglìshuǐ 〈水利〉gravitational water; free water

重力选矿 zhònglì xuǎnkuàng 〈矿业〉gravity separation (*or* concentration)

重力仪 zhònglìyí gravity meter; gravimeter

重力值 zhònglìzhí gravity value

重利 zhònglì ❶ high or exorbitant interest:～盘剥 practise usury ❷ huge profit:牟取～ seek excessive profits ❸ 〈书面〉value material gains:～轻义 place material gains above what is right

重量 zhòngliàng weight:启运～ shipping weight /实际～ actual weight /～损失 loss in weight /～戳印 weight stamp /～单 weight list; weight memo; weight note /～证明书 weight certificate /～鉴定证明书 surveyor's report on weight

重量吨 zhòngliàngdūn weight ton; dead weight ton:～计算法

Z

weight ton method
重量级 zhòngliàngjí heavyweight：～拳王 heavyweight boxing champion
重名 zhòngmíng high prestige
重男轻女 zhòngnán-qīngnǚ value men and belittle women; regard men as superior to women
重农主义 zhòngnóngzhǔyì physiocracy：～者 physiocrat
重炮 zhòngpào heavy artillery; heavy artillery piece; heavy gun：～猛轰敌军阵地 loose a stonk on the enemy's positions; pound the enemy with heavy shelling
重器 zhòngqì 〈书面〉❶ valuable article; treasure ❷ great talent; great mind
重切削 zhòngqiēxiāo 〈机械〉heavy cut; deep cut
重氢 zhòngqīng heavy hydrogen; deuterium
重任 zhòngrèn important task; heavy responsibility：肩负～ hold a position of great responsibility /委以～ entrust sb. with important tasks
重伤 zhòngshāng serious wound; severe injury
重商主义 zhòngshāngzhǔyì mercantilism：～者 mercantilist
重赏 zhòngshǎng rich reward; handsome reward：～捉拿要犯 offer big reward for the capture of an important criminal
重赏之下，必有勇夫 zhòngshǎng zhī xià, bì yǒu yǒngfū a big reward will make the brave come forward
重身子 zhòngshēnzi ❶ pregnant; with child ❷ pregnant woman
重石脑油 zhòngshínǎoyóu heavy naphtha
重视 zhòngshì attach importance to; set store by; lay stress on; think highly of：～教育 attach importance to education /～妇女在社会中的作用 stress (*or* emphasize) the role of women in society /～对青少年的教育 give priority to the education of teenagers /我们很～他的意见。We set great store by his opinion. *or* We value his opinion greatly. /这个人很受领导～。His superior thinks highly of him.
重实 zhòngshi 〈方言〉heavy：这个提包挺～，不知里头装的是什么东西。The bag is rather heavy. I wonder what's in it.
重水 zhòngshuǐ 〈化学〉heavy water; deuterium oxide：～反应堆〈核物理〉heavy-water reactor
重水合物 zhòngshuǐhéwù deuterate
重税 zhòngshuì heavy duties; onerous taxes
重听 zhòngtīng hard of hearing
重同位素 zhòngtóngwèisù 〈化学〉heavy isotope
重头戏 zhòngtóuxì ❶ opera in which great exertion is needed to act or sing ❷ important part of an activity：这个～谁来唱？Who will take on this important task? /这可是个～，我怕是唱不了。I'm afraid that is too heavy a responsibility for me.
重托 zhòngtuō great trust：不负～ prove worthy of the great trust reposed in one
重望 zhòngwàng ❶ good reputation; great fame; high renown：身负～ enjoy high prestige ❷ great expectations：辜负了父老的～ did not live up to the great expectations of the elders
重武器 zhòngwǔqì heavy weapons
重孝 zhòngxiào in deep mourning：带～ be dressed in deep mourning
重心 zhòngxīn ❶〈物理〉barycentre; centre of gravity：～规则 centre-of-gravity rule ❷〈数学〉median point ❸ heart; crux; core; focus：问题的～ heart (*or* crux) of the matter /把工作的～转移到经济发展上来。Shift the focus of our work to economic development.
重刑 zhòngxíng severe punishment; heavy penalty; cruel corporal punishment
重型 zhòngxíng heavy-duty; heavy：～车床 heavy-duty lathe /～坦克 heavy tank /～飞机 heavy airplane /～飞机跑道 heavy-duty runway /～经济结构 heavy economic structure
重压 zhòngyā strong pressure; heavy load; heavy strain：树枝经不起雪堆的～，终于折断了。The tree branches broke under the weight of the snow. /生活的～使他变得沉默了。The heavy burden of life made him a reticent man.
重要 zhòngyào important; significant; essential; major：～标志 important sign (*or* hallmark) /～角色 major role /～人物 eminent person; prominent figure; VIP /～目标 major goal; key target /～任务 vital task; crucial mission /～的发现 significant discovery /～关头 critical juncture; moment of truth /～原则 cardinal principle /～政策 essential policy /～讲话 key speech /～防御地域 vital defense area /这次成功可能对你一生都是很～的。Your success this time may be significant for your whole future.
重音 zhòngyīn ❶〈语言〉stress; accent：句子～ sentence stress /单词～ word stress /次～ secondary accent /主～ primary accent ❷〈音乐〉accent：～记号 accent
重用 zhòngyòng assign sb. to a key post：要～有创新精神的人。Put people having creative minds (*or* with innovative ideas) in key positions. /他很受上级信任和～。He has the full trust of his superior and is put in an important position.
重油 zhòngyóu ❶ heavy oil; dead oil; mazut：～机 heavy oil engine ❷ naphtha residue; thick oil
重于泰山 zhòngyú-Tàishān weightier than Mount Tai — of great significance：为人民而死，死得～。Die for the people and the death is worth it.
重元素 zhòngyuánsù 〈化学〉heavy element
重载 zhòngzài heavy-duty; freight：几十辆～的大车 dozens of fully-loaded carts /～轮胎 heavy-duty tire /～吃水 loaded draught
重枣 zhòngzǎo brownish red (like the colour of dry dates)：面如～ have a brownish red face
重责 zhòngzé ❶ heavy responsibilities：身负～ be entrusted with heavy responsibilities ❷ severely reprimand：受到～ be severely rebuked
重镇 zhòngzhèn place of strategic importance：边防～ place of strategic importance at the border
重浊 zhòngzhuó ❶ (of voice) deep and thick：～的声调 in a deep and thick voice ❷ heavy and turbid; heavy and muddy：天色暗淡～。The sky's dim, heavy and turbid.
重资 zhòngzī colossal fund：投～办教育 make big investment in education /我将不惜～改进工厂的设备。I'm ready to invest as much as I can to reequip the factory.
重子 zhòngzǐ 〈物理〉baryon：～八重态 baryon octet /～波谱学 baryon spectroscopy /～共振子 baryon resonon /～规范 baryon gage /～夸克 baryon quark /～素 baryonium /～组元 baryon constituent
重罪 zhòngzuì 〈法律〉capital felony; felony; heavy offence：～犯 felonry; felon

zhōu

州 zhōu ❶〈历史〉administrative division (now still retained in names of some places, such as Suzhou, Dezhou, etc.)：跨～连郡 transprefectural ❷ (autonomous) prefecture：湘西土家族苗族自治～ Autonomous Prefecture of the Tujia and Miao Nationalities of Western Hunan ❸ (US) state

洲 zhōu ❶ continent：欧亚两大～ continents of Asia and Europe; Eurasia ❷ islet in a river; sandbar：沙～ sandbar; sandbank /绿～ oasis /关关雎鸠，在河之～。Water birds quacked on the island.
洲际 zhōujì intercontinental：～贸易 intercontinental trade
洲际导弹 zhōujì dǎodàn intercontinental missile
洲际弹道导弹 zhōujì dàndào dǎodàn intercontinental ballistic missile (ICBM)

喌 zhōu 〈象声〉call to attract chickens

诪(譸) zhōu 〈书面〉❶ curse; swear ❷ deceive; cheat
诪张 zhōuzhāng *also* "侜张" zhōuzhāng cheat; deceive; fake

诌(謅) zhōu spin (a yarn); cook up：瞎～ make up wild stories /别听他～。Don't believe (*or* listen to) his tall tales.

舟 zhōu 〈书面〉boat：一叶扁～ small boat /泛～湖上 go boating on the lake /龙～竞赛 dragon boat race
舟车 zhōuchē 〈书面〉❶ boat and carriage; vessel and vehicle：途中几易～ change coaches and boats several times on the way ❷ travel; journey：尽尝～之苦 have experienced all the hardships of an arduous journey
舟蛾 zhōu'é prominent moth
舟楫 zhōují 〈书面〉vessels：他借～之便，畅游了江南水乡。Taking advantage of its water transport, he toured southern Jiangsu, a region of rivers and lakes.
舟桥 zhōuqiáo pontoon; pontoon bridge; floating bridge
舟山群岛 Zhōushān Qúndǎo Zhoushan Archipelago, off the coast

of Zhejiang Province

舟中敌国 zhōuzhōng-díguó all people in the boat are enemies — be isolated and in a precarious situation

舟子 zhōuzi 〈书面〉boatman

辀 zhōu 〈书面〉shafts of a cart or carriage

侜 zhōu 〈书面〉deceive; cheat

侜张 zhōuzhāng *also* "诪张" zhōuzhāng 〈书面〉deceive; fake: ~为幻 mislead; deceive

周[1](週) zhōu ❶ circumference; perimeter; circuit; periphery: 圆~ circumference (of a circle) /绕城墙一~ make (*or* do) a circuit of the city wall /月亮绕地球一~大约为一个月。It takes the moon about one month to revolve around the earth. /飞机在空中盘旋了三~方才降落。The plane circled around in the sky three times before landing. /饲养场的四~筑起了一道篱笆。A fence was erected round the stock farm. ❷ circle; make a circuit; move in a circular course ❸ all; whole: 众所~知 as is known to all /~身温暖 be warm all over ❹ thoughtful; considerate; attentive: 考虑不~ not be thoughtful enough /招待不~,请多包涵。Please forgive us for any neglect on our part in attending to our guests. ❺ week: 下~ next week /上上~ week before last /两~ fortnight; two weeks ❻〈电学〉cycle: 兆~ megacycle /820 千~ 820 kc

周[2] zhōu help out (the needy); assist; relieve: ~济灾民 relieve the victims of the disaster; send relief to the people in the afflicted area

周[3] Zhōu ❶ Zhou Dynasty (c. 11th century - 256 BC) ❷ Northern Zhou of the Northern Dynasties (557-581) ❸ Later Zhou of the Five Dynasties (951-960) ❹ a surname

周邦彦 Zhōu Bāngyàn Zhou Bangyan (formerly translated as Chou Pang-yen, 1056-1121), *ci* poet of the Northern Song Dynasty

周报 zhōubào weekly publication; weekly: 《统计~》 *Statistics Weekly*

周备 zhōubèi thoughtful; considerate; attentive; well-prepared

周髀算经 Zhōubì Suànjīng *Zhoubi Suanjing*, classic work on astronomy and mathematics written in the first century BC during the Western Han Dynasty

周边 zhōubiān ❶ neighbouring; surrounding: ~地区 surrounding areas (*or* regions) /要搞好~国家的关系 maintain good relations with the neighbouring countries ❷〈机械〉periphery

周遍 zhōubiàn all round; all over

周波 zhōubō 〈电学〉❶ cycle ❷ SI unit of frequency, equal to one cycle per second; hertz

周布 zhōubù distribute; spread all over; be found everywhere: 血管~全身。Blood vessels distribute all over the body.

周长 zhōucháng circumference; perimeter; girth: 这广场~是多少? What is the perimeter of the square? /这棵树的~是两米。The tree has a girth of two metres. *or* The tree is two metres in girth. /颐和园昆明湖的~约三公里。Kunming Lake in the Summer Palace is about three kilometres in circumference.

周到 zhōudao thoughtful; considerate; solicitous; attentive: 照顾~ take very good care of; be very attentive to /服务~ offer excellent service /她为别人考虑十分~。She is very considerate (*or* thoughtful). /样样事情都安排得很~。Everything was carefully worked out. /他处理问题比我们更~。He handles problems more satisfactorily than we do.

周敦颐 Zhōu Dūnyí Zhou Dunyi (formerly translated as Chou Tun-i, 1017-1073), philosopher of the Northern Song Dynasty

周恩来 Zhōu Ēnlái Zhou Enlai (formerly translated as Chou En-lai, 1898-1976), one of the top leaders of the CPC and PRC and Premier of the PRC (1949-1976)

周而复始 zhōu'érfùshǐ go round and begin again; move in cycles: 随着季节的变换,天地万物,~,千姿百态。With the change of seasons, all living things on earth alternately take on different looks. /否极泰来,荣辱自古~。The extreme adversity is the beginning of prosperity, and vice versa; honour and disgrace follow each other in an unending cycle.

周昉 Zhōu Fǎng Zhou Fang (formerly translated as Chou Fang), traditional painter of the Tang Dynasty

周公 Zhōugōng Zhougong, or Duke of Zhou, born Ji Dan (姬旦), statesman and regent who consolidated the newly established Western Zhou Dynasty

周回 zhōuhuí 〈书面〉❶ around; all around: 故城~九里余。The old town is over 9 *li* in circumference. ❷ surround: 群山~ be surrounded by mountains

周忌 zhōujì first anniversary of sb.'s death

周济 zhōujì help out; assist; relieve: ~穷人 help out the poor /这孤儿寡母全靠张家~才渡过饥荒。It was the Zhangs who saw the widow and her children through the famine.

周角 zhōujiǎo perigon; round angle

周接 zhōujiē (often used in the early vernacular) relieve (the poor)

周刊 zhōukān weekly publication; weekly: 《新闻~》(US) *Newsweek*

周口店 Zhōukǒudiàn Zhoukoudian (formerly translated as Chou-Kou-tien), site of the fossils of Peking Man (北京人, about 0.5-1 million years old) and Upper Cave Man (over 10,000 years old), about 50 km from Beijing

周流 zhōuliú go round continuously; circulate

周率 zhōulǜ *also* "频率" pínlǜ 〈物理〉frequency

周密 zhōumì careful; thorough; well-conceived: 推理~ meticulous reasoning /进行~的调查和分析 carry out a thorough investigation and make a detailed analysis /方案不够~。The plan is not well-conceived. /敌军部署之~,出人意外。The enemy surprised us with circumspect deployment.

周末 zhōumò weekend: ~晚会 weekend party

周纳 zhōunà *also* "周内" zhōunà 〈书面〉trump up or cook up charges (against innocent people): 深文~ bring or make trumped-up charges against innocent people

周年 zhōunián anniversary: 建国四十二~ 42nd anniversary of the founding of the republic /五十~纪念 golden jubilee; jubilee /一百~纪念 centenary /结婚六十~纪念 diamond wedding

周期 zhōuqī ❶ cycle: 缩短资金周转的~ shorten the cycle of fund circulation /工作~〈机械〉action cycle ❷ period; cycle period; duration ❸ classification of elements (as in the periodic table)

周期表 zhōuqībiǎo 〈化学〉periodic table

周期律 zhōuqīlǜ 〈化学〉periodic law

周期性 zhōuqīxìng periodicity; cyclicity: ~波动 cyclical fluctuations /某些疾病发病存在~。Some diseases have the characteristic of periodic attacks.

周期性经济危机 zhōuqīxìng jīngjì wēijī periodic or cyclical economic crises

周期性通货膨胀 zhōuqīxìng tōnghuò péngzhàng cyclical inflation

周期性循环 zhōuqīxìng xúnhuán periodic return

周全 zhōuquán ❶ circumspect; thorough; comprehensive: 计划~ plan everything carefully; plan to the last detail ❷ help sb. attain his aim; assist: 我俩的婚事,全靠您~了。We count on you to help arrange our marriage.

周身 zhōushēn all over the body; whole body: ~不适 general malaise /~湿透 be wet all over /~打量 look sb. over from head to toe; eye sb. up and down /我感到~发冷。I felt a chill creep (*or* come) over me. *or* It sent shivers down my spine.

周岁 zhōusuì one full year of life; exactly one year: 今天是孩子的~。Today is the child's first birthday. /他已十八~了。He is already eighteen years old.

周天 zhōutiān ❶ great circle of the celestial sphere ❷ heaven and earth; universe

周围 zhōuwéi round; around; about: 坐在桌子~ sit round the table /大楼~ around the building /环视~ look about (*or* around) /~的居民 neighbourhood /~一个人也没有。Nobody was in sight. /小岛的~是茫茫大海。The islet is surrounded by the vast sea. /她使~充满了欢乐的气氛。She diffused cheerfulness around her.

周围神经 zhōuwéi shénjīng 〈生理〉peripheral nerve: ~系统 peripheral nervous system / ~损伤 peripheral nerve injury

周围神经炎 zhōuwéi shénjīngyán 〈医学〉peripheral neuritis

周围温度 zhōuwéi wēndù environment or ambient temperature

周文王 Zhōu Wénwáng Zhou Wenwang, or King Wen of Zhou, born Ji Chang (姬昌), ethnic leader in the late Shang Dynasty

周武王 Zhōu Wǔwáng Zhou Wuwang, or King Wu of Zhou, born Ji Fa (姬发), son of Zhou Wenwang and founder of the Western

Zhou Dynasty
周息 zhōuxī *also* "年息" niánxī annual interest
周详 zhōuxiáng careful; detailed; thorough; comprehensive: ～的报告 exhaustive report /论述得很～ discuss thoroughly
周恤 zhōuxù 〈书面〉 sympathize with and help out: ～贫病之人 give one's sympathy and help to the poor and the sick
周旋 zhōuxuán ❶ circle; wheel; spiral: 苍鹰在蓝天～。Goshawks were wheeling in the azure sky. /汽车顺着盘山公路～而上。The car wound up the mountain. ❷ mix with; fraternize; socialize: 善于与人～ be a good mixer /虚与～ deal with sb. courteously but without sincerity /宴席上的～ compliments exchanged at a banquet /～于客商之间 move in the business community ❸ engage; deal with; contend with: 机动灵活地与敌人～ fight with (*or* engage) the enemy with great tactical skill and flexibility
周延 zhōuyán 〈逻辑〉 distribution
周游 zhōuyóu travel or journey round: ～各地 travel to many places; travel far and wide /～西欧各国 tour Western Europe
周瑜打黄盖 Zhōu Yú dǎ Huáng Gài strategy adopted by Zhou Yu who flogged Huang Gai with the latter's consent — both parties are willing: 这桩买卖是～，一家愿打，一家愿挨，两相情愿。The deal is acceptable and satisfactory to both sides.
周缘 zhōuyuán periphery; rim; outer edge: 池塘的～布满水草。The pond is overgrown with waterweeds at its periphery.
周匝 zhōuzā 〈书面〉 ❶ make a circuit; circle: 其亭有水～。A stream runs round the pavilion. ❷ careful; thorough; complete: 思虑～ give careful consideration to
周遭 zhōuzāo around; round: ～阒寂无声。Everything around was quiet and still. *or* Silence reigned everywhere.
周章 zhōuzhāng 〈书面〉 ❶ scared; terrified: ～失措 be scared out of one's wits; be panic-stricken ❷ effort; trouble; pains: 煞费～ take great pains; go to a lot of trouble
周折 zhōuzhé twists and turns; trouble; setbacks: 几经～ after repeated setbacks /此事颇费～。This caused us a lot of trouble.
周正 zhōuzheng 〈方言〉 regular; proper; upright: 模样儿长得～ have regular features /把帽子戴～ wear (*or* put on) one's hat properly
周知 zhōuzhī be known to all; make sth. public: 特此通告～ it is hereby announced to the public that
周至 zhōuzhì thoughtful; considerate; attentive: 殷勤～ be very thoughtful and attentive
周转 zhōuzhuǎn ❶ 〈经济〉 turnover: 现金～ cash flow /资金～不灵 slow turnover of funds /加快资本～速度 speed up capital turnover /商店再次降价以加速资金～。The store reduced the prices again to make a quick turnover. /资金～越快，赢利越多。The faster the turnover, the greater the profit. ❷ be adequate to meet the need: 手头～不开 not have enough money to cover expenses; be hard up /班次太多，教室～不开。We are short of classrooms as there are too many classes now.
周转货币 zhōuzhuǎn huòbì vehicle currency
周转粮 zhōuzhuǎnliáng turnover grain
周转量 zhōuzhuǎnliàng volume of circular flow
周转率 zhōuzhuǎnlǜ turnover rate
周转税 zhōuzhuǎnshuì turnover tax
周转信贷 zhōuzhuǎn xìndài revolving credit
周转资金 zhōuzhuǎn zījīn working fund; circulating fund; revolving fund

调(搊) zhōu 〈方言〉 help lift (one side of) a heavy object: 老太太上车，劳驾～她一把。Please give the old lady a lift onto the bus. /帮我把这箱子～到肩膀上去。Lend me a hand and lift the case onto my shoulder, please.

啁 zhōu
see also zhāo
啁啾 zhōujiū 〈书面〉 〈象声〉 (of birds) chirp; twitter; warble: 鸟儿在林中～鸣唱。Birds are chirping (*or* twittering) in the woods.

赒 zhōu relieve; assist

粥 zhōu gruel; porridge; congee: 麦片～ oatmeal porridge /玉米～ corn gruel /莲子～ rice and lotus seed gruel
see also yù
粥少僧多 zhōushǎo-sēngduō *also* "僧多粥少" many monks, little porridge — not enough to go round: 招工中～的问题何时才能解决? When can you create enough jobs for all the applicants?

zhóu

碡 zhóu *see* "碌碡" liùzhou

轴 zhóu ❶ axle; shaft: 轮～ wheel axle /车～ car (*or* bicycle) axle; axle /前～ front axle /后～ rear axle /主～ 〈机械〉 main shaft /心～ 〈机械〉 mandrel; spindle /曲～ 〈机械〉 crank shaft ❷ axis; pivot: 地～ earth's axis /椭圆的长短～ major and minor axes of an ellipse ❸ spool; roller; rod: 线～ spool (for thread) /画～ roller for a scroll of Chinese painting ❹ 〈量词〉: 一～棉线 a spool of thread /几～字画 several scrolls of calligraphy
see also zhòu
轴测法 zhóucèfǎ 〈测绘〉 axonometry
轴测投影 zhóucè tóuyǐng 〈测绘〉 axonometric projection
轴测图 zhóucètú 〈测绘〉 axonometric(al) drawing
轴衬 zhóuchèn 〈机械〉 axle bush
轴承 zhóuchéng 〈机械〉 bearing: 滚动～ rolling bearing /滚珠～ ball bearing /滑动～ journal bearing; plain bearing; sliding bearing /含油～ self-oiling bearing /止推～ thrust bearing /～钢 bearing steel /～合金 bearing metal
轴对称 zhóuduìchèn 〈数学〉 axial symmetry
轴颈 zhóujǐng 〈机械〉 axle neck; bearing neck; journal: ～轴承 journal bearing /～磨床 axle journal grinder
轴距 zhóujù wheelbase (of a vehicle)
轴流 zhóuliú 〈机械〉 axial flow
轴流泵 zhóuliúbèng 〈机械〉 axial-flow pump; axial pump
轴流鼓风机 zhóuliú gǔfēngjī 〈机械〉 axial blower; axial flow blower
轴流式汽轮机 zhóuliúshì qìlúnjī axial flow steam turbine
轴流式燃气轮机 zhóuliúshì ránqìlúnjī axial flow gas turbine
轴流式水力发电机组 zhóuliúshì shuǐlì fādiàn jīzǔ axial flow hydroelectric unit
轴流压缩机 zhóuliú yāsuōjī axial flow compressor
轴套 zhóutào 〈机械〉 axle sleeve
轴突 zhóutū 〈生理〉 axon; nerve-fibre
轴瓦 zhóuwǎ 〈机械〉 *see* "轴衬"
轴线 zhóuxiàn ❶ 〈机械〉 axis: 垂直～ normal axis /～角 axis angle ❷ spool thread; spool cotton
轴箱 zhóuxiāng 〈机械〉 axle box; axle housing
轴向 zhóuxiàng 〈机械〉 axial: ～剖面 axial section /～运动 axial motion /～对称性 axial symmetry
轴心 zhóuxīn ❶ 〈机械〉 axle centre ❷ axis: 罗马柏林～ Rome-Berlin Axis (of World War II)
轴心国 Zhóuxīnguó Axis Powers (military alliance of Nazi Germany, Fascist Italy and militarist Japan during World War II); the Axis
轴子 zhóuzi ❶ roller (for a scroll of Chinese painting) ❷ turning peg; peg (of a stringed instrument)

妯 zhóu
妯娌 zhóuli wives of brothers; sisters-in-law: ～不和。The sisters-in-law are at loggerheads with each other.

zhǒu

肘 zhǒu ❶ elbow: 掣～ hold sb. back by the elbow; impede ❷ upper part of a leg of pork
肘杆 zhǒugǎn 〈机械〉 toggle link; toggle rod: ～传动 knuckle-lever drive /～式冲床 toggle press /～压力机 knuckle-lever press
肘关节 zhǒuguānjié 〈生理〉 elbow joint; articulatio cubiti: ～炎 〈医学〉 anconitis
肘管 zhǒuguǎn 〈机械〉 knee
肘接 zhǒujiē 〈机械〉 toggle or elbow joint
肘节 zhǒujié 〈机械〉 toggle: 制动～ brake toggle /～压力机 toggle press

肘窝 zhǒuwō crook of the arm; *fossa cubitalis*
肘腋 zhǒuyè 〈书面〉❶ elbow and armpit ❷〈比喻〉(of trouble, disaster, etc.) very close
肘腋之患 zhǒuyèzhīhuàn trouble coming from those closest to one
肘子 zhǒuzi ❶ upper part of a leg of pork: 酱～ pork joint simmered in marinated (*or* brown) sauce ❷ elbow

帚(箒) zhǒu broom: 扫～ broom /炊～ pot-scouring brush /敝～自珍 value one's own old broom — cherish sth. of little value simply because it is one's own
帚蕨 zhǒujué 〈植物〉whisk fern

zhòu

酎 zhòu 〈书面〉double-fermented wine
酎金 zhòujīn contributions of nobles to the emperor for sacrificial purposes

纣[1] zhòu 〈书面〉canvas or leather strap round the rump of a shaft-horse; crupper

纣[2] Zhòu last ruler of the Shang Dynasty, reputedly a tyrant: 助～为虐 help a tyrant do evil; abet the evildoer
纣棍 zhòugùn wooden bar fixed under the tail of a horse or a donkey and tied on both ends to the saddle to prevent it from sliding forward

荮 zhòu 〈方言〉❶ wrap sth. up with straw ❷〈量词〉a bundle (of bowls, dishes, etc. tied with straw rope)

咮 zhòu 〈书面〉beak; bill

宙 zhòu time (conceived as past, present and future): 宇～ universe; cosmos
宙克西斯 Zhòukèxīsī Zeuxis (later 5th century BC), Greek painter
宙斯 Zhòusī Zeus, supreme god in Greek mythology

轴 zhòu *see* "压轴子" yāzhòuzi
see also zhóu

胄[1] zhòu descendants; offspring (of feudal rulers or aristocrats in ancient China): 贵～ descendants of aristocrats /帝～ descendants of feudal rulers

胄[2] zhòu helmet: 甲～ armour and helmet

咒(呪) zhòu ❶ incantation: 念～ chant incantations /符～ Taoist magic figures or incantations ❷ curse; swear; damn: 你为什么～他? Why do you curse him? /他气起来，见人就诅～。In his anger, he damns everyone in sight.
咒骂 zhòumà utter curses against; curse; swear; abuse: 粗野下流的～ coarse invectives /他的话里充满了恶毒的～。His talk was full of vile curses. /你在～谁? Who are you swearing at?
咒语 zhòuyǔ incantation; spell
咒诅 zhòuzǔ curse

繇 zhòu oracle inscriptions of the Shang Dynasty on tortoise shells or animal bones
see also yáo; yóu

Z

籀 zhòu 〈书面〉❶ read aloud; chant; recite: 讽～ read with intonation and expression ❷ *see* "籀文"
籀文 zhòuwén style of calligraphy, current in the Zhou Dynasty

甃 zhòu 〈方言〉❶ wall of a well ❷ build (a well, pond, etc.) with bricks

㤘 zhòu *see* "㑳㤘" chánzhòu

㑇(㤘) zhòu 〈方言〉obstinate; opinionated; stubborn: 他脾气～得很。He is a very obstinate person.

㑳(㑳) zhòu (often used in the early vernacular) handsome; pretty; cute

皱(皺) zhòu wrinkle; crease: 眉头一～，计上心来。Knit the brows and a stratagem comes to one's mind. /小心，别把我的书弄～了。Take care not to crumple my book. /她刚做过平～整容术。She's just had her face lifted. /衣服～了。The dress is creased.
皱巴巴 zhòubābā full of wrinkles; crumpled; rumpled: ～的瘦脸 lean and wrinkled face /一张～的纸 a crumpled sheet of paper /总见他穿着那身～的衣服。He is always seen in that rumpled suit.
皱襞 zhòubì 〈书面〉fold; crease; wrinkle
皱痕 zhòuhén crease; wrinkle: 脸上满布～ face full of wrinkles; wrinkly face
皱眉头 zhòu méitóu knit or contract one's brows; frown: 她皱着眉头，深深地叹了口气。She heaved a long sigh, knitting her brows. /她皱着眉头看着自己的考卷。She looked at her exam paper with a frown. /他皱着眉头沉思。His brow furrowed in deep thought.
皱缩 zhòusuō shrivel: ～度 shrinkage
皱胃 zhòuwèi 〈动物〉abomasum
皱纹 zhòuwén wrinkles; lines: 布满～的前额 wrinkly forehead; furrowed brow /眼角～ crow's feet /除去～ remove one's wrinkles /他二十多岁时脸上就有～了。He got lines in his face when he was still in his twenties. /很多人过了四十岁眼角就出现～了。After forty, many people get wrinkles around their eyes.
皱纹法兰绒 zhòuwén fǎlánróng crepe flannel
皱纹革 zhòuwéngé shrink leather
皱纹棉府绸 zhòuwén miánfǔchóu crepenette
皱纹切除术 zhòuwén qiēchúshù 〈医学〉rhytidectomy
皱纹纸 zhòuwénzhǐ crepe paper; tissue paper
皱褶 zhòuzhé fold; rumple; wrinkle; crease: 烫平衬衣上的～ iron out (*or* press out, *or* smooth) the wrinkles (*or* creases) in the shirt /她的衣服平平整整，没有一个～。She was neatly dressed from head to toe without a crease or rumple anywhere. /把衣服挂起来，不然会起～。Hang up the dress so it won't wrinkle.
皱皱巴巴 zhòuzhou-bābā *see* "皱巴巴"

绉(縐) zhòu crape; crepe: 双～ crêpe de Chine
绉布 zhòubù cotton crepe; crepe
绉纱 zhòushā crape
绉纹针织品 zhòuwén zhēnzhīpǐn crepe knit
绉织物 zhòuzhīwù 〈纺织〉crepe

昼(晝) zhòu daylight; daytime; day: 月光照得旷野如同白～。In the brilliant moonlight, the wilderness looked as if it did in the daytime. /白～逐渐长(短)了。The days are drawing out (in). *or* The days are getting longer (shorter).
昼出动物 zhòuchū dòngwù diurnal animal
昼盲 zhòumáng day blindness; hemeralopia
昼夜 zhòuyè day and night; round the clock; all the time: ～兼程地赶路 press on day and night /工厂～不停地生产。The factory operated round the clock. /他已三～未合眼了。He hasn't got a wink of sleep for three days and nights.

骤 zhòu ❶ (of a horse) trot: 驰～ gallop ❷ rapid; hurried: 风狂雨～。The wind blew hard and the rain came down in torrents (*or* sheets). ❸ sudden; abrupt: ～不及防 be taken by surprise /气温～降。The temperature suddenly dropped. /敌军～至。The enemy troops appeared out of nowhere. /枪声～起。There was a burst of gunfire.
骤然 zhòurán all of a sudden; suddenly; abruptly: ～一惊 with a start /天气～冷了下来。There was a sharp drop in temperature. *or* The weather suddenly turned cold. /～响起一阵暴风雨般的掌声。A storm of applause burst (*or* broke) out.

zhū

朱(❷硃) zhū ❶ vermilion; bright red ❷ cinnabar;

vermilion:近～者赤 he who stays near vermilion gets stained red — one takes on the colour of one's company ❸ (Zhū) a surname
朱巴舞 zhūbāwǔ juba, a dance characteristic of plantation Negroes in America in the 18th-19th centuries before emancipation
朱笔 zhūbǐ writing brush dipped in red ink (formerly used in marking students' papers or writing comments on books and official documents as distinct from the original written or printed in black):～批点 comments or remarks written in red with a brush
朱唇皓齿 zhūchún-hàochǐ red lips and white teeth — pretty; handsome
朱耷 Zhū Dā Zhu Da (formerly translated as Chu Ta, 1624-1705), eminent monk and painter of the early Qing Dynasty, alias Badashanren (八大山人)
朱德 Zhū Dé Zhu De (formerly translated as Chu Teh, 1886-1976), one of the top leaders of the CPC and the PRC
朱棣 Zhū Dì Zhu Di (1360-1424), fourth son of Zhu Yuanzhang (朱元璋) founder of the Ming Dynasty, who as Prince of Yan (燕王) took the throne from his nephew Emperor Jianwen (建文帝) and became 3rd emperor of Ming (1403-1424), called reverently Ming Chengzu (明成祖) after death
朱顶 zhūdǐng *also* "朱顶雀"; "贮点红" zhùdiǎnhóng redpoll (linnet)
朱古力 zhūgǔlì chocolate
朱红 zhūhóng vermilion; bright red
朱鹮 zhūhuán 〈动物〉 red ibis
朱槿 zhūjǐn 〈植物〉 Chinese hibiscus
朱卷 zhūjuàn (of imperial examinations) examination papers copied in red ink by special copyists for the graders
朱鹭 zhūlù (crested) ibis
朱轮华毂 zhūlún-huágǔ luxury carriage with red wheels (used by nobles in ancient times)
朱门 zhūmén vermilion gates — red-lacquered gates of wealthy people's mansions:～酒肉臭,路有冻死骨。Behind the vermilion gates of the rich meat and wine are left to rot, While out on the road lie the bones of the poor who have frozen to death.
朱门绣户 zhūmén-xiùhù ❶ vermilion gate and richly ornamented chamber — mansion of the rich ❷ 〈比喻〉 wealthy family
朱墨 zhūmò ❶ red and black:～套印 printed in red and black ❷ ink made of cinnabar; vermilion ink
朱墨本 zhūmòběn ancient books printed in red and black
朱鸟 zhūniǎo *see* "朱雀 ❷❸"
朱批 zhūpī comments or remarks written in red with a brush
朱漆 zhūqī red paint; red lacquer:～家具 red-lacquered furniture /～大门 vermilion gate
朱雀 zhūquè ❶ *also* "红麻料儿" hóngmáliàor rosefinch ❷ term for the seven southern mansions of the 28 lunar mansions in ancient astronomy ❸ Southern God worshipped by Taoists
朱砂 zhūshā cinnabar
朱文 zhūwén characters on a seal carved in relief
朱熹 Zhū Xī Zhu Xi (formerly translated as Chu Hsi, 1130-1200), philosopher and scholar of the Southern Song Dynasty
朱颜 zhūyán ❶ peach and cream complexion; peach blossom face of a beauty ❷ youthful and healthy looks:～鹤发 hale aged man
朱元璋 Zhū Yuánzhāng Zhu Yuanzhang (1328-1398), leader of a peasant uprising which helped to overthrow the Yuan Dynasty, and founder of the Ming Dynasty, called reverently Ming Taizu (明太祖) after death
朱载堉 Zhū Zǎiyù Zhu Zaiyu (1536-c.1610), music theoretician of the Ming Dynasty

诛

zhū 〈书面〉❶ put (a criminal) to death; execute:罪不容～ even death cannot atone for the offence /天～地灭 be destroyed by heaven and earth /～杀无辜 kill the innocent /卖国贼人人得而～之。Everybody has the right to put traitors to death. ❷ condemn; punish:口～笔伐 denounce (*or* condemn) both in speech and in writing
诛除 zhūchú *see* "诛锄❷"
诛锄 zhūchú 〈书面〉❶ root up; extirpate (weeds, plants, etc.) ❷ wipe out; exterminate; massacre:～城中盗贼 rid the city of robbers
诛锄异己 zhūchú-yìjǐ finish off or destroy dissenters:不惜用卑劣的手段去～ not hesitate to use mean tricks to get rid of alien elements
诛戮 zhūlù 〈书面〉 kill; slaughter:悉遭～ be killed one and all
诛灭 zhūmiè 〈书面〉 kill; wipe out
诛求 zhūqiú 〈书面〉 extort; blackmail:～无厌 make incessant, inordinate demands
诛求无已 zhūqiú-wúyǐ make endless extortions:贪官污吏对百姓～。Corrupt officials made incessant exorbitant demands on the ordinary people.
诛杀 zhūshā kill; put to death
诛心之论 zhūxīnzhīlùn exposure of sb.'s ulterior motives; incisive criticism

珠

zhū ❶ pearl:夜明～ night-luminescent pearl /鱼目混～ pass off fish eyes as pearls — palm sth. off ❷ bead:汗～ beads of sweat /露～ dewdrops; beads of dew /泪～ teardrop /念～ beads; rosary /钢～ ball bearing; steel ball /有眼无～ eye without pupil — be as blind as a bat; fail to recognize a thing for what it is
珠蚌 zhūbàng mussel; pearl oyster; pearl shell; nacre
珠宝 zhūbǎo pearls and jewels; jewelry:珍奇～ rare jewelry /～店 jeweller's (shop) /～商 jeweller
珠茶 zhūchá bead tea, a kind of green tea with the tea leaves looking like beads
珠翠 zhūcuì pearls and jade; ornaments made with pearls and jade
珠光宝气 zhūguāng-bǎoqì be adorned with brilliant jewels and pearls; be richly bejewelled:满身～ (of a woman) richly bedecked with jewels
珠光漆 zhūguāngqī pearlescent lacquer
珠光体 zhūguāngtǐ 〈冶金〉 pearlite
珠花 zhūhuā flower-shaped hair decoration made with pearls
珠还合浦 zhūhuán-Hépǔ *also* "合浦珠还" pearls returned to Hepu — recovery of things lost; return of someone after a long absence
珠玑 zhūjī 〈书面〉❶ pearl; jewel; gem ❷ excellent writing; exquisite diction:字字～ each word a gem /满腹～ one's mind is full of valuable ideas — extensive knowledge
珠鸡 zhūjī 〈动物〉 guinea fowl (*Numida meleagris*)
珠江 Zhūjiāng Zhujiang River; Pearl River:～三角洲 Zhujiang Delta (in Guangdong)
珠兰 zhūlán *zhulan* tree
珠泪 zhūlèi teardrop:～纵横 cheeks bathed in tears
珠帘 zhūlián bead curtain
珠联璧合 zhūlián-bìhé strings of pearls and girdles of jade — an excellent combination; a perfect pair:两位歌唱家的同台演出,可谓～。The two singers performing on the same stage were a perfect duet, each shining brilliantly in the company of the other.
珠落玉盘 zhūluò-yùpán pearls falling on a jade dish — the clear, sweet notes of the *pipa* (琵琶)
珠母 zhūmǔ nacre; mother-of-pearl
珠母贝 zhūmǔbèi pearl shell; pearl oyster
珠穆朗玛峰 Zhūmùlǎngmǎfēng Mount Qomolangma (known in the West as Mt. Everest):攀登～ scale Mount Qomolangma
珠算 zhūsuàn calculation with an abacus; counting by the abacus
珠围翠绕 zhūwéi-cuìrào 〈旧语〉❶ be dressed up to the nines and richly ornamented:陈太太打扮得～的走出来。Mrs. Chen came out, richly dressed and bejewelled. ❷ be surrounded by ladies-in-waiting
珠芽 zhūyá bulbil; bulblet
珠圆玉润 zhūyuán-yùrùn round as pearls and smooth as jade — excellent singing or polished writing; elegance and polish:她那～的歌声,仍然萦绕在观众的耳边。Her sweet and beautiful singing is still lingering (*or* ringing) in the audience's ears.
珠子 zhūzi ❶ pearl ❷ bead:算盘～ beads on an abacus

茱

zhū
茱萸 zhūyú *also* "山茱萸" shānzhūyú; 吴茱萸 wúzhūyú; "食茱萸" shízhūyú cornel (*Cornus officinalis*)

株

zhū ❶ base of a tree; stump:枯木朽～ withered trees and rotten stumps ❷ individual plant; plant:幼～ sapling; young plant /母～ mother plant; maternal plant /病～ diseased plant ❸ 〈量词〉 *of plants and trees*:三～桃树 three peach trees
株距 zhūjù 〈农业〉 spacing in the rows:这几行稻秧～太密。These rows of rice seedlings are planted too close together.
株连 zhūlián involve; incriminate; implicate:他的伪供使几位同事受到～。His false confession implicated several of his colleagues. /一人

有罪,往往～亲友。When one is found guilty, one's relatives and friends often get involved.
株式会社 zhūshì huìshè (Japanese) *Kabuskiki Kaisha*; limited-liability company; limited company.
株守 zhūshǒu 〈书面〉hold on without letting go; cling stubbornly to:～陈规陋习 cling tightly to bad customs and habits
株选 zhūxuǎn select strong and fine grains in the fields and keep them for seed

蛛 zhū spider
蛛丝马迹 zhūsī-mǎjì thread of a spider and trail of a horse — clues; traces; tracks:露出～ disclose some traces /捕捉有关他行踪的～ try to find a clue to his whereabouts
蛛网 zhūwǎng spider web; cobweb
蛛形纲动物 zhūxínggāngdòngwù arachnid
蛛蛛 zhūzhu spider

铢 zhū ancient unit of weight, equal to $\frac{1}{24}$ *liang* (两)
铢积寸累 zhūjī-cùnlěi accumulate bit by bit or little by little; build up gradually:为学须～。Knowledge is accumulated little by little.
铢两悉称 zhūliǎng-xīchèn exactly equal in weight or quality; have the same weight:这两块金锭的成色～。The two gold ingots contain exactly the same percentage of gold.

侏 zhū 〈书面〉dwarf
侏罗纪 Zhūluójì 〈地质〉Jurassic Period (second period of the Mesozoic Era 中生代 with evidence of many large dinosaurs)
侏罗系 Zhūluóxì Jurassic system
侏儒 zhūrú dwarf; midget; pygmy:～症〈医学〉dwarfism /～观戏 a dwarf watches a show — echo the views of others; be without any definite views of one's own

诸[1] zhū ❶ all; numerous; various:～兵种 various arms of the services /～事顺遂。Everything went smoothly. ❷ (Zhū) a surname

诸[2] zhū 〈书面〉(mixed pronunciation of 之于 or 之乎):付～东流 throw into the eastward flowing stream — have all one's efforts wasted / 子闻～? Have you ever heard of such a thing, sir?
诸般 zhūbān various; all kinds of:～困难 all kinds of difficulties
诸病源候总论 Zhūbìng Yuánhòu Zǒnglùn *General Treatise on Diseases*, compiled by Chao Yuanfang (巢元方) and others, and printed in 610
诸多 zhūduō 〈书面〉(used with abstract things) plenty of; a good deal; lots of:～不便 great inconvenience; lots of trouble /～烦恼 many worries
诸葛 Zhūgě ❶ a surname ❷ *short for Zhuge Liang, esp. in certain combinations*:活～ Zhuge Liang incarnate; as resourceful as Zhuge Liang / 小～ latter-day Zhuge Liang; youthful Zhuge Liang / ～再世 Zhuge Liang born again (*or* incarnate)
诸葛亮 Zhūgě Liàng ❶ Zhuge Liang (formerly translated as Chu-Keh Liang, 181-234), statesman and strategist in the State of Shu during the period of the Three Kingdoms, who became an incarnation of wisdom and resourcefulness in Chinese folklore ❷ mastermind; person of great sagacity and resource:事后～ wiseacre after the event; Monday morning quarterback; belated wisdom /三个臭皮匠,顶个～ three cobblers with their wits combined equal Zhuge Liang the mastermind — two heads are better than one
诸葛亮会 zhūgěliànghuì meeting of Zhuge Liangs — a meeting to pool the wisdom of the collective
诸公 zhūgōng (used to address a group of men) gentlemen:衮衮～ high-ranking officials /～有何高见? What do you gentlemen think about it?
诸宫调 zhūgōngdiào ballad form of the Song, Jin and Yuan dynasties
诸侯 zhūhóu dukes or princes
诸君 zhūjūn 〈套语〉ladies and gentlemen...:～将来都是国之栋梁。All of you will be the pillars of the state one day.
诸亲好友 zhūqīn-hǎoyǒu relatives and friends
诸如 zhūrú such as; for example:他擅长好几种乐器,～钢琴、小提琴、双簧管等。He is good at playing a number of musical instruments, such as the piano, the violin, the oboe and so on.
诸如此类 zhūrúcǐlèi things like that; and all that; and what not; and so on and so forth:我们所说的谷类是指小麦、大麦、燕麦及～的粮食。By cereals we mean wheat, barley, oats, and all that. /～的日常用品你在街拐角的店里就能买到。You can get such daily necessities as these in the store at the street corner.
诸色 zhūsè 〈书面〉all kinds of:～人等 all kinds of people
诸事 zhūshì every thing; all matters:～如意。Wish you every success.
诸位 zhūwèi polite term for addressing a number of people:～女士先生 Ladies and Gentlemen /在座的～,谁有兴趣? Is there anyone here (*or* present) interested in this? /～好! Hi, everybody!
诸子百家 zhūzǐ-bǎijiā various schools of thought and their exponents during the period from pre-Qin times to the early Han Dynasty

槠 zhū 〈植物〉sweet oak

猪(豬) zhū pig; hog; swine; porker:乳～ suckling pig / 小～ piglet; shoat /母～ sow /公～ boar /野～ wild boar /豪～ porcupine /海～ dolphin /江～ black finless porpoise /蠢～ idiot /肥～ big porker /瘦肉型～ pork pig /一窝子～ litter of pigs /养～ keep (*or* raise) pigs
猪八戒倒打一耙 Zhūbājiè dào dǎ yī pá (in reference to the character Pig in *Pilgrimage to the West*《西游记》, who carries a rake as a weapon) make unfounded counter-charges; put the blame on one's victim
猪草 zhūcǎo greenfeed for pigs; hogweed
猪场 zhūchǎng pig farm; piggery
猪丹毒 zhūdāndú swine erysipelas; diamond-skin disease
猪肚 zhūdǔ pork tripe
猪肝 zhūgān pork liver:酱～ pork liver simmered in brown sauce
猪倌 zhūguān swineherd
猪獾 zhūhuān *also* "沙獾" shāhuān sand badger
猪圈 zhūjuàn pigsty; pigpen; hogpen; swinery
猪苓 zhūlíng 〈中药〉umbellate pore fungus (*Polyporus umbellata*)
猪笼草 zhūlóngcǎo 〈植物〉common nepenthes (*Nepenthes mirabilis*)
猪猡 zhūluó 〈方言〉pig; swine
猪苗 zhūmiáo piglet; shoat
猪囊虫病 zhūnángchóngbìng pork measles
猪排 zhūpái pork chop:红烧～ pork chop braised in brown sauce
猪皮 zhūpí pigskin; hogskin
猪婆龙 zhūpólóng common name for the Chinese alligator (鼍)
猪气喘病 zhūqìchuǎnbìng swine enzootic pneumonia
猪肉 zhūròu pork:瘦～ lean pork /～片 sliced pork /～末 minced pork
猪肉杠 zhūròugàng 〈方言〉〈旧语〉butcher's (shop)
猪舍 zhūshè pigpen; swinery; sty; pigsty
猪食 zhūshí pigwash; pig feed; swill:～缸 (pig) trough
猪蹄 zhūtí pig's foot; trotter
猪头 zhūtóu pig's head:～肉 meat slices cut from a cooked pig's head
猪腿 zhūtuǐ pig's leg; leg of pork; ham
猪娃 zhūwá 〈方言〉❶ piglet; shoat ❷ swineherd
猪瘟 zhūwēn swine fever; hog cholera:～流行。There is an epidemic of hog cholera.
猪窝 zhūwō pigsty
猪血 zhūxiě pig's blood; coagulated pig's blood (used as food)
猪榭 zhūxiè 〈方言〉pig wastes; hog dung
猪殃殃 zhūyāngyāng 〈植物〉goose-grass (*Galium aparine*)
猪腰子 zhūyāozi pork kidney
猪油 zhūyóu lard
猪油果 zhūyóuguǒ *also* "油瓜" yóuguā large-fruited hodgsonia
猪仔 zhūzǎi ❶〈方言〉piglet; shoat ❷〈旧语〉men shanghaied to work as coolies abroad:卖～ press-gang people and sell them as coolies abroad
猪只 zhūzhī pigs
猪鬃 zhūzōng (hog) bristles
猪鬃草 zhūzōngcǎo *also* "铁线蕨" tiěxiànjué 〈植物〉venushair fern

Z

潴(瀦) zhū 〈书面〉❶ (of water) gather; accumulate; store ❷ puddle; pool
潴留 zhūliú 〈医学〉retention:尿～ retention of urine
槠(櫧) zhū 〈书面〉wooden stake for tethering a domestic animal

zhú

烛(燭) zhú ❶ candle:香～ joss sticks and candles /蜡～ (wax) candle /火～ things that may cause a fire /秉～ hold a candle; carry a lamp ❷〈书面〉make bright with light; illuminate; light up:火光～天 night sky lit up with raging flames /洞～其奸 see through sb.'s tricks ❸ (common name for 瓦特) watt:四十～灯泡 40-watt bulb
烛光 zhúguāng ❶〈物理〉candlepower; candle ❷ candlelight
烛花 zhúhuā snuff:剪～ trim off the snuff; snuff /～报喜。The hopping wick announces happy news.
烛架 zhújià candlestand
烛剪 zhújiǎn snuffer
烛泪 zhúlèi melted wax running down the sides of a guttering candle; gutterings of a candle
烛煤 zhúméi cannel (coal)
烛台 zhútái candlestick; candleholder; candlestand
烛心 zhúxīn *also* "烛芯" candlewick:剪掉燃过的～ cut (*or* trim) the burnt wick; snuff
烛影斧声 zhúyǐng-fǔshēng *coup d'état*; palace coup
烛照 zhúzhào 〈书面〉shine; illuminate; light up:阳光～大地。The sun beams down upon (*or* shines over) the earth.
蠋 zhú larva of a butterfly or moth
躅(躅) zhú *see* "踯躅" zhízhú
术 zhú *see* "苍术" cāngzhú; "白术" báizhú
see also shù
瘃 zhú 〈书面〉chilblain
逐 zhú ❶ pursue; seek; chase:追～ pursue /争名～利 seek (*or* hanker after) personal fame and gain /随波～流 sail with the stream; drift with the tide /～水草而居 move from place to place in search of water and grass; migrate to wherever water and grass are available /笑～颜开 beam with smiles ❷ expel; oust; drive out:～出家门 be driven out of one's home /被～出境 be deported; be expelled from a country ❸ one by one; in turn:～条讲解 explain point by point /～段修改 revise (an essay, etc.) paragraph by paragraph /～月检查 examine every month /按情况～项处理 address each case on its merits
逐北 zhúběi 〈书面〉pursue routed enemy; pursue the enemy in flight:追奔～ chase the defeated enemy
逐步 zhúbù step by step; gradually; progressively:～养成节约的习惯 gradually form a habit of thrift /～解决争端 settle the disputes step by step /～消除贸易壁垒 phased removal of trade barriers /战争～升级 escalation of war /物价～回落。The prices are dropping steadily.
逐臣 zhúchén official banished by the imperial court
逐臭之夫 zhúchòuzhīfū person who runs after "stink" — one who has strange tastes or hankerings;〈比喻〉man hankering after money, rank, and fame; person of a worldly disposition
逐处 zhúchù everywhere; in all places:刚到这里,人地生疏,～都感不便。As a stranger here, I ran up against inconvenience everywhere.
逐个 zhúgè one by one; one after another:～解决问题 solve (*or* settle) the problems one by one /～征求同学意见 seek (*or* solicit) opinions from one student after another
逐渐 zhújiàn gradually; steadily; by degrees:～意识到自己的无知 gradually come to see one's own ignorance /人到老年,视力往往～衰退。There is often a progressive loss of sight in old age. /天气～转暖。It's getting warmer and warmer.
逐客令 zhúkèlìng order for guests to leave:下～ show sb. the door; ask an unwelcome guest or visitor to leave /他看出她已下～,心里十分不高兴地站起来。He saw that she had given her signal for him to leave, so he stood up, feeling quite upset.
逐鹿 zhúlù 〈书面〉chase the deer — fight for the crown; bid for state power:群雄～ feudal lords vying for the throne; influential politicians fighting for supremacy
逐鹿中原 zhúlù-Zhōngyuán fight for domination in the country; fight for the throne
逐年 zhúnián year by year; with every passing year:物价～上涨。Prices rise year by year. /生活水平～提高。The standard of living improves with each passing year.
逐日 zhúrì day by day; every day; daily:情况～好转。The situation is improving day by day. /废品率～下降。The reject rate is dropping every day.
逐水 zhúshuǐ 〈中医〉relieve oedema or abdominal distension through diuresis or purgation
逐条 zhútiáo article by article; point by point; item by item:～修订 revise article by article /～讲解 explain point by point
逐一 zhúyī one by one:他把客人～介绍给大家。He introduced the guests to us one by one.
逐字 zhúzì in exactly the same words; word for word; verbatim:～记录 verbatim record /～校对 proofread word by word
逐字逐句 zhúzì-zhújù word by word and sentence by sentence; word for word; literally:～地讲解 explain word by word and sentence by sentence /～地翻译 word-for-word (*or* literal) translation; translation *ad litteram*
竺 Zhú a surname
竹 zhú bamboo:毛～ *mao* bamboo /修～ tall bamboo; slender bamboo /紫～ black bamboo /斑～ *also* "湘妃～" mottled bamboo
竹板 zhúbǎn bamboo clappers (held in the hands like castanets)
竹板书 zhúbǎnshū singing and storytelling to the rhythm of bamboo clappers
竹报平安 zhúbào-píng'ān letter sent home to say all is well
竹箅子 zhúbìzi bamboo grid (used for steaming food)
竹编 zhúbiān handicraft articles made of thin bamboo strips
竹编织品 zhúbiānzhīpǐn bamboo basketwork
竹鞭 zhúbiān ❶ subterranean stem of bamboo ❷ whip with a bamboo whiphandle
竹帛 zhúbó bamboo slips and silk (used for writing on in ancient times); ancient books:功垂～ be recorded in history in letters of gold; be crowned with eternal glory
竹布 zhúbù light blue or white fine cotton cloth used for making summer wear
竹材 zhúcái bamboo used for building and making things
竹蛏 zhúchēng 〈动物〉razor clam; razor shell
竹筹 zhúchóu bamboo chip
竹刀鱼 zhúdāoyú saury
竹簟 zhúdiàn mat made of thin bamboo strips
竹雕 zhúdiāo bamboo engraving; bamboo carving
竹二青 zhú'èrqīng *see* "竹茹"
竹筏 zhúfá bamboo raft
竹竿 zhúgān bamboo pole; bamboo
竹竿舞 zhúgānwǔ tinikling — bamboo-pole dancing
竹工 zhúgōng bamboo working
竹黄 zhúhuáng *also* "竹簧" ❶ handicraft articles made from bamboo with its green covering removed ❷ tabasheer; tabashir
竹黄菌 zhúhuángjùn 〈中药〉bamboo parasitic fungus
竹鸡 zhújī bamboo partridge
竹筴鱼 zhújiāyú saurel; horse mackerel
竹简 zhújiǎn bamboo slip (used for writing on in ancient times)
竹浆 zhújiāng pulp made from bamboo
竹节 zhújié bamboo joint
竹节虫 zhújiéchóng stick insect; walking stick
竹节钢筋 zhújié gāngjīn corrugated bar
竹节石 zhújiéshí *Tentaculites*
竹刻 zhúkè bamboo carving; bamboo engraving
竹篮打水一场空 zhúlán dǎshuǐ yīchángkōng draw water with a bamboo basket (*or* a sieve) — achieving nothing; futile effort;

Z

fruitless labour：但现在他感到真是闹了个～。But now, he felt like he was drawing water with a bamboo basket; everything was falling through.

竹篱茅舍 zhúlí-máoshè thatched cottage enclosed with a bamboo fence — simple dwelling of a recluse

竹笠 zhúlì bamboo hat (with a conical crown and broad brim)

竹帘 zhúlián bamboo curtain; bamboo screen

竹帘画 zhúliánhuà painting on a bamboo curtain

竹林 zhúlín bamboo forest：～更新 bamboo-stand regeneration

竹笼 zhúlóng bamboo cage

竹楼 zhúlóu two-storied bamboo stilt houses of the Dai people in Yunnan, southwestern China (the upper floor of the house contains bedrooms, kitchens and balconies and the ground floor is used to house poultry and domestic animals)

竹篓 zhúlǒu bamboo crate; bamboo basket

竹马 zhúmǎ ❶ bamboo stick used as a toy horse：青梅～ friendship (between boys and girls) formed in childhood; playmates in childhood ❷ bamboo horse (used in a folk dance)

竹马灯 zhúmǎdēng folk dance in which the dancers have horses made of bamboo strips, paper and cloth fixed at the waist to look like riding on horses

竹马戏 zhúmǎxì local opera of Fujian Province, popular in such coastal areas as Zhangpu(漳浦), Longhai(龙海), Dongshan(东山) and Yunxiao(云霄)

竹马之交 zhúmǎzhījiāo playmates in childhood; friendship formed in childhood days：小王和她是～，关系很亲密。Xiao Wang was her playmate as a child, and they were on very intimate terms.

竹篾 zhúmiè bamboo strips (for weaving)

竹幕 zhúmù bamboo curtain or screen

竹排 zhúpái bamboo raft

竹牌 zhúpái 〈方言〉mah-jong

竹器 zhúqì articles made of bamboo：～商店 store selling articles made of bamboo

竹扦 zhúqiān bamboo spike

竹茹 zhúrú 〈中药〉slices of skinned bamboo stem (of *Phyllostachys nigra* var. *henonis* or *Bambusa breviflora*)

竹鼠 zhúshǔ bamboo rat

竹荪 zhúsūn *Dictyophora phalloidea* (a kind of edible fungus found in bamboo groves)

竹笋 zhúsǔn bamboo shoots

竹筒 zhútǒng thick bamboo tube

竹筒倒豆子 zhútǒng dào dòuzi empty the bamboo container of its beans — hold nothing back; make a clean breast of sth.：别吞吞吐吐的，来个～，全都撤出来。Don't hesitate and try to hold things back; tell us all about it.

竹头木屑 zhútóu-mùxiè bamboo ends and wood shavings — things of little value but of some use; odds and ends：～亦有以应吾之需者。Even bamboo ends and wood shavings may be useful to me.

竹席 zhúxí bamboo-strip mat

竹下登 Zhúxiàdēng Takeshita Noboru (1924-), Japanese Prime Minister (1987-1989)

竹叶青 zhúyèqīng ❶ poisonous green bamboo snake ❷ bamboo-leaf-green liqueur, a pale green *Fen* (汾) liquor ❸ light yellow Shaoxing (绍兴) wine

竹椅 zhúyǐ bamboo chair

竹芋 zhúyù 〈植物〉❶ arrowroot (*Maranta arundinacea*) ❷ subterranean stem of arrowroot

竹枝词 zhúzhīcí ❶ ancient folk songs with love as their main theme ❷ poems in the classical style portraying local conditions and custom

竹纸 zhúzhǐ paper made from young bamboo

竹制品 zhúzhìpǐn bamboo ware

竹子 zhúzi bamboo

Z

舳

zhú stern (of a ship, etc.)

舳舻 zhúlú 〈书面〉convoy of ships, stem touching stern：～千里 thousand-*li* convoy of ships; vast fleet

zhǔ

主

zhǔ ❶ host：宾～ host and guest /客随～便 the guest will do as the host wishes; the guest will go along with the host /～随客便 what the guest wishes, the host will oblige ❷ owner; lord; master：～仆 master and servant; master and man /当家作～ be master in one's own house /一家之～ head of a family /房～ landlord /地～ landowner; landlord /奴隶～ slave owner ❸ person or party concerned：买～ buyer /卖～ seller /失～ owner of lost property ❹〈基督教〉God; Lord; the Master：求～保佑! God bless me! ❺〈伊斯兰〉Allah ❻ principal; main：～教练 principal coach /先入为～ first impressions being strongest; prejudiced /预防为～ prevention first; prevention (is) better than cure /以自力更生为～ rely mainly on one's own efforts ❼ be in charge of; preside over; manage：～其事 be in charge of the business; manage the affairs ❽ advocate; favour：力～和议 strongly advocate peace negotiations ❾ foretell; indicate; signify：早霞～雨，晚霞～晴。Rosy morning clouds mean rain and a rosy sunset fine weather. ❿ hold a definite view about sth.：这事儿该怎么办，我实在没～。I have no idea at all how to deal with this matter. ⓫ be of one's own accord; take the initiative：*see* "～动" ⓬ memorial tablet：木～ wooden ancestral tablet /神～ spirit tablet ⓭ (Zhǔ) a surname

主板 zhǔbǎn 〈信息〉motherboard

主办 zhǔbàn sponsor; direct; be under the auspices of：～单位 sponsor /此次竞赛是由中央电视台～的。The contest was sponsored by the CCTV.

主笔 zhǔbǐ ❶ editor in chief ❷ chief commentator

主币 zhǔbì standard money

主编 zhǔbiān ❶ supervise the publication of (a newspaper, magazine, etc.); edit：这本词典由他～。He is the chief compiler of this dictionary. ❷ chief editor or compiler; editor in chief：他是《人民日报》的～。He is the editor in chief of the *People's Daily*.

主宾 zhǔbīn guest of honour：～席 head table (at a banquet, etc.); seat for the guest of honour

主操纵台 zhǔcāozòngtái 〈自控〉master operational console

主槽 zhǔcáo main river course

主场 zhǔchǎng 〈体育〉home：～比赛 home match /今天北京队～对大连队。The Beijing Team, as the home team, is going to meet the Dalian Team in today's match.

主持 zhǔchí ❶ preside over; chair; host：～宴会 host a banquet (*or* dinner party) /～会议 chair a meeting; preside over a meeting /本届大会在您的～下定能顺利完成它的使命。The current session will fulfil its mission successfully under your presidency. ❷ take charge of; be responsible for; direct：～日常工作 take care (*or* charge) of the day-to-day work (*or* routine matters) /～修改方案 be in charge of revising the plan /谁～考试? Who will be the chief examiner? ❸ uphold; champion; stand for：～公道 uphold justice; stand for fair play

主持人 zhǔchírén host or hostess; master of ceremonies：节目～ anchorperson

主厨 zhǔchú ❶ do the cooking ❷ person in charge of the cooking at a hotel, canteen, etc.; chief cook; chef

主传动 zhǔchuándòng main transmission

主词 zhǔcí 〈逻辑〉subject term; subject

主次 zhǔ-cì primary and secondary; major and minor：分清～ distinguish between the primary and the secondary; make a distinction between the major and the minor issues /～不分 confuse the principal with the secondary

主从 zhǔ-cóng principal and subordinate：～关系 relationship between the principal and the subordinate; subordination /这是一个～复合句。This is a complex sentence.

主从计算机 zhǔ-cóng jìsuànjī master-slave computer

主存储器 zhǔcúnchǔqì 〈计算机〉main memory or storage; primary store or storage

主单位 zhǔdānwèi primary unit

主刀 zhǔdāo operating surgeon; operator

主导 zhǔdǎo ❶ guiding; leading; ruling; dominant：国有经济的～地位 leading position of the state economy /～原则 guiding principle /～思想 ruling ideas; dominant ideology /以行政为～ executive-led (government) /这种看法在 19 世纪曾占～地位。The belief held sway during the 19th century. ❷ leading factor：以农业为基础，以工业为～ take agriculture as the foundation and industry as the leading factor

主导风 zhǔdǎofēng 〈建筑〉prevailing wind

主导主题 zhǔdǎo zhǔtí 〈音乐〉leitmotiv

主祷文 Zhǔdǎowén 〈基督教〉Lord's Prayer

主调 zhǔdiào ❶〈音乐〉homophony ❷ keynote; main or domi-

nant theme:大会的～是维护世界和平。Safeguarding world peace is the keynote of the conference.

主调音乐 zhǔdiào yīnyuè homophonic music; homophony

主动 zhǔdòng ❶ initiative:掌握或赢得～ seize or win the initiative /失去～ lose the initiative /争取更大的～权 try to gain more leverage /～、热情地待客 be attentive and hospitable to one's guests /他很腼腆,从不～交友。He is very shy and never takes the initiative in making acquaintances (*or* never makes acquaintances on his own initiative). /张先生～提出帮她找工作。Mr Zhang offered to find a job for her. /饭后她～洗了碗碟。After dinner, she did the dishes of her own accord. ❷〈机械〉driving:～齿轮 driving gear; power gear /～轮 action wheel; drive wheel; main drive wheel /～轴 main drive shaft; main axle; drive

主动出口限制 zhǔdòng chūkǒu xiànzhì voluntary export restraints

主动红外跟踪系统 zhǔdòng hóngwài gēnzōng xìtǒng 〈自控〉active infrared tracking system

主动激光跟踪系统 zhǔdòng jīguāng gēnzōng xìtǒng active laser tracking system

主动脉 zhǔdòngmài 〈生理〉aorta:～扩张〈医学〉aortectasia; aortectasis /～狭窄〈医学〉aortostenosis /～硬化〈医学〉aortosclerosis

主动脉弓 zhǔdòngmàigōng 〈生理〉arch of aorta

主动脉炎 zhǔdòngmàiyán 〈医学〉aortitis

主动声呐 zhǔdòng shēngnà active sonar

主动语态 zhǔdòng yǔtài 〈语言〉active voice

主读存储器 zhǔdú cúnchǔqì 〈计算机〉read-mostly memory (RMM)

主队 zhǔduì 〈体育〉home team; host team:～以三比一获胜。The home team won the match three to one.

主发电机 zhǔfādiànjī main-generator

主发动机 zhǔfādòngjī 〈航天〉sustainer

主伐 zhǔfá 〈林业〉final felling or cutting

主阀 zhǔfá 〈机械〉main valve

主犯 zhǔfàn 〈法律〉prime culprit; principal criminal or offender; principal:～和从犯应区别对待。We should treat the principal and accessories in a crime differently.

主峰 zhǔfēng highest peak in a mountain range

主父 Zhǔfǔ a surname

主妇 zhǔfù housewife; hostess

主干 zhǔgàn ❶〈植物〉trunk ❷ main force; mainstay; backbone:这个航校毕业的学员成了航空部队的～。Graduates from the aviation school became the mainstay of the air force.

主干家庭 zhǔgàn jiātíng main trunk family — a three-generational family composed of a married couple, their children and one set of grandparents; extended family

主缸 zhǔgāng 〈机械〉master cylinder

主稿 zhǔgǎo principal drafter of a document or work:我参加了这个文件的起草,但不～。I am on the drafters' team for this document, but not the principal drafter.

主格 zhǔgé 〈语言〉nominative case

主根 zhǔgēn ❶〈植物〉main root; taproot ❷〈数学〉principal root

主公 zhǔgōng title used by officials for addressing the feudal ruler

主攻 zhǔgōng 〈军事〉main attack:由二连担任～ second company assigned to launch the main attack /～部队 main attack force /～方向 main direction of attack /～方面 main phase of attack

主攻手 zhǔgōngshǒu 〈体育〉ace striker; spiker

主构件 zhǔgòujiàn 〈机械〉main member

主顾 zhǔgù customer; client; patron:招揽～ solicit customers /她是本店的老～了。She is a regular patron of our store.

主观 zhǔguān subjective:～臆断 subjective conjecture /～愿望 subjective desire; wishful thinking /～解释 arbitrary interpretation /～印象 personal impression /～性 subjectivity /他的判断非常～。His judgment is very subjective. /遇到挫折,要多找找～原因。When you suffer a setback, you should try to find the causes for which you yourself are responsible.

主观能动性 zhǔguān néngdòngxìng 〈哲学〉subjective initiative; dynamism

主观唯心主义 zhǔguān wéixīnzhǔyì 〈哲学〉subjective idealism

主观主义 zhǔguānzhǔyì subjectivism

主管 zhǔguǎn ❶ be in charge of; be responsible for:～外事工作 be in charge of external relations /～学生思想工作 look after the students' ideological education /～部门 department responsible for the work concerned /～机关 *also* "～当局" competent (*or* appropriate) authorities; responsible institutions ❷ person in charge:他是这个单位的行政～。He is the chief administrator of this organization.

主光轴 zhǔguāngzhóu primary optical axis; principal optic axis

主航道 zhǔhángdào central line of the main channel; thalweg:～中国一侧 on the Chinese side of the central line of the main channel (of a river)

主和 zhǔhé advocate peace; favour a peaceful settlement

主和派 zhǔhépài peace party; peace faction; dove:他是～的代表人物。He is the representative of the peace faction.

主河道 zhǔhédào main river course

主户 zhǔhù 〈旧语〉family that lived in a place and owned land there for generations

主婚 zhǔhūn preside over a wedding ceremony; officiate at a wedding:～人 master of ceremonies (MC) at a wedding

主机 zhǔjī ❶〈机械〉main engine; principal machine:～组 principal mechanical components; main set ❷〈计算机〉mainframe; host computer:～程序 mainframe program ❸〈军事〉lead plane; leader

主计算机 zhǔjìsuànjī host computer

主祭 zhǔjì officiate at funeral or sacrificial rites

主家 zhǔjiā ❶ home of one's master ❷ manage household affairs:在这个家庭里她～。She keeps house at home.

主见 zhǔjiàn one's own judgment; definite opinion:没～ have no definite views of one's own; be easily swayed /她很有～。She is her own mistress. *or* She knows her own mind.

主讲 zhǔjiǎng give lectures; lecture on:下学期李教授～英美文学。Professor Li will give lectures on English and American literature next term.

主将 zhǔjiàng ❶〈军事〉chief commander; commanding general ❷ backbone; mainstay; pillar:他是这个研究领域的～之一。He is one of the leading scholars in this field.

主焦点 zhǔjiāodiǎn prime focus; principal focus

主焦煤 zhǔjiāoméi *also* "焦煤" coking coal

主教 zhǔjiào 〈宗教〉bishop:大～ archbishop /红衣～ cardinal /坎特伯雷大～ Archbishop of Canterbury /～区 diocese /～座堂 cathedral

主教制 zhǔjiàozhì episcopacy

主茎 zhǔjīng 〈植物〉main shaft; main axis; main stem

主井 zhǔjǐng 〈矿业〉main shaft

主句 zhǔjù 〈语言〉main or principal clause

主角 zhǔjué leading role; star part; lead:男女～ leading actor and actress /这部电影由他演～。He starred (*or* had a starring role, *or* played the lead) in the film. /这个项目由总工程师唱～。The chief engineer takes charge of the project.

主开关 zhǔkāiguān 〈电工〉mainswitch

主考 zhǔkǎo ❶ be in charge of an examination ❷ chief examiner

主考官 zhǔkǎoguān ❶〈旧语〉official in charge of an imperial examination at the provincial or national level ❷ chief examiner

主客 zhǔkè ❶ host and guest ❷ guest of honour

主课 zhǔkè main subject; main course; major

主坑道 zhǔkēngdào 〈矿业〉gangway

主控 zhǔkòng 〈电工〉master control:～开关 master switch /～盘 master panel /～器 master controller; main controller /～制台 main control console

主理 zhǔlǐ take charge or care of; manage:～这个协会的日常事务 be in charge of the day-to-day work of this association

主力 zhǔlì main force; main body or strength of an army:科研～ leading researchers /～队员〈体育〉top players of a team /～兵团〈军事〉main formation /他们是厂里生产的～。They are the mainstay of the work force in the factory.

主力舰 zhǔlìjiàn 〈军事〉capital ship; battleship

主力军 zhǔlìjūn main or principal force

主链 zhǔliàn fundamental chain

主梁 zhǔliáng 〈建筑〉girder

主粮 zhǔliáng staple food grain

主林带 zhǔlíndài main forest belt

主流 zhǔliú ❶ main current; mother current; mainstream:长江的～和支流 mainstream and tributaries of the Yangtze River ❷ essential aspect; main trend:历史的～ mainstream of history /分清～和支流 distinguish between the principal and secondary aspects /共和党～派 mainstream Republican

主楼 zhǔlóu main building

主麻 zhǔmá 〈伊斯兰〉Djumah (in reference to Friday or the noon prayer on Friday)
主名 zhǔmíng 〈书面〉prime culprit; principal criminal; chief instigator; chief plotter
主谋 zhǔmóu ❶ head a conspiracy; be the chief plotter ❷ chief instigator; chief plotter:他是这次刺杀行动的～。He is the chief plotter of the assassination.
主母 zhǔmǔ 〈旧语〉title used by a servant for addressing his or her mistress
主脑 zhǔnǎo ❶ part that plays the central role; centre of operation:发动机是飞机的～。The engine is the control centre of a plane. ❷ head; chief; leader
主排水沟 zhǔpáishuǐgōu main drain
主炮 zhǔpào 〈军事〉main armament; main artillery
主气旋 zhǔqìxuán 〈气象〉primary cyclone; primary low
主汽轮机 zhǔqìlúnjī 〈电工〉main turbine
主权 zhǔquán sovereign rights; sovereignty:领土～ territorial sovereignty /～国家 sovereign state /～平等 sovereign equality /～行为 sovereign act /～豁免〈法律〉sovereign immunity /～范围内 within one's sovereign rights; within the sovereignty of /对香港恢复行使～ resume the exercise of sovereignty over Hong Kong /侵犯…的～ violate the sovereignty of /互相尊重～和领土完整是国际法的一项基本原则。Mutual respect of sovereignty and territorial integrity is a fundamental principle of international law.
主儿 zhǔr 〈方言〉❶ master; boss ❷ certain type of person:他是说到做到的～。He is the kind of person who does what he says. ❸ husband; husband's family
主人 zhǔrén ❶ host:我们受到～的殷勤款待。We were hospitably entertained by the host. ❷〈旧语〉master:女～对仆人很好。The mistress is very kind to the servants. ❸ owner:财产的～ owner of the property /国家的～ masters of the country
主人公 zhǔréngōng hero or heroine (in a literary work); protagonist:小说～是一个双目失明的姑娘。The heroine of the novel is a blind girl.
主人翁 zhǔrénwēng ❶ master (of one's own country, society, etc.):劳动人民成了国家的～。The working people have become the master of their own country. ❷ *see* "主人公"
主任 zhǔrèn director; chief; head; chairman:副～ deputy director (*or* chairman) /车间～ director of a workshop; workshop director /居委会～ head of the neighbourhood committee /班～ teacher in charge of a class /教研室～ chief of teaching and research section /英语系～ dean (*or* chair, *or* chairman) of the English Department /人大外事委员会～ Chairman of the Foreign Affairs Committee of the National People's Congress (NPC) /外交部翻译室～ Director General of the Department of Translation and Interpretation, Ministry of Foreign Affairs /国家发展计划委员会～ Minister in charge of the State Development Planning Commission
主日 zhǔrì 〈基督教〉Sunday; Lord's Day:～学校 Sunday school
主丧 zhǔsāng officiate at a funeral
主上 zhǔshàng title used by officials in addressing a feudal ruler
主食 zhǔshí staple food; principal food:今天的～是米饭。The principal (*or* main) food today is rice. /当地人的～是玉米面。Corn flour is the staple food for the local people.
主使 zhǔshǐ instigate; incite; stir up; abet:～某人犯罪 abet sb. in a crime /受人～ at sb.'s instigation
主视图 zhǔshìtú 〈机械〉front view; elevation
主事 zhǔshì be in charge of:～人 person in charge /你们家是你～，还是你妻子～? Who wears the trousers in your house, you or your wife? *or* Who calls the shots in your family, you or your wife?
主帅 zhǔshuài chief commander; commander in chief
主诉 zhǔsù (term used by a medical institution) patient's complaint:病人～呼吸困难。The patient complained of difficulty in breathing.
主题 zhǔtí theme; subject; motif:文章或谈话的～ subject of an essay or conversation /作品的～ motif of a literary work /演讲者的～是美国人的价值观。The speaker's theme is American values.
主题词 zhǔtící subject terms
主题歌 zhǔtígē theme song
主体 zhǔtǐ ❶ main body; main or principal part:以青年技术人员为～的队伍 team composed mainly of young technicians (*or* with young technicians as its main body) /～工程 principal part of a project /～思想 (DPRK) *Juche* Idea /新建校舍的～是图书馆。The library is the main structure of the new school buildings. ❷〈哲学〉subject:～和客体 subject and object; the perceiver and the world ❸〈法律〉subject:国际法的～ subject of international law
主体经济 zhǔtǐ jīngjì principal sector or mainstay of the economy
主位 zhǔwèi ❶ status of a sovereign ❷ seat of the host at the table
主谓词组 zhǔwèi cízǔ 〈语言〉subject-predicate word group
主谓句 zhǔwèijù 〈语言〉subject-predicate sentence
主文 zhǔwén 〈法律〉main body of a court verdict
主席 zhǔxí ❶ chairman (of a meeting):担任～ be in the chair; take the chair; chair (*or* preside over) a meeting ❷ chairperson or president (of an organization or state):学生会～ chairperson of the student union /中华人民共和国～ President of the People's Republic of China /联大～ President of the UN General Assembly
主席台 zhǔxítái rostrum; platform
主席团 zhǔxítuán presidium
主线 zhǔxiàn main threads of (a literary work, etc.); motif:这个爱情故事是全书的～。The love story is the motif through the book.
主心骨 zhǔxīngǔ ❶ backbone; mainstay; pillar; chief support:母亲是全家的～。Mother is the mainstay of the family. /没了他,大家就像没了～一样。We feel as if we've lost our bearings without him. ❷ one's own mind; ideas of one's own:她是个有～的女人。She is a woman who knows her mind. /他真是个没～的人! What an indecisive person he is!
主星 zhǔxīng 〈天文〉primary (component)
主星序 zhǔxīngxù 〈天文〉main sequence
主刑 zhǔxíng 〈法律〉principal penalty
主凶 zhǔxiōng archcriminal (in a murder case); principal murderer; principal assassin
主修 zhǔxiū ❶ specialize (in a particular field of study); major:～科目 major subject /他～英语,兼修德语。He majors in English and minors in German. /她是～化学的学生。She is a chemistry major. ❷ be in charge of the repair or overhaul (of a machine):这台机器由李师傅～。Master Worker Li is put in charge of the overhaul of the machine.
主旋律 zhǔxuánlǜ ❶〈音乐〉theme; principal melody ❷ theme; main idea; basic concept:时代的～ central theme of the era /报告的～ keynote of the report
主眼 zhǔyǎn key or important part (of a play, novel or other literary works):全篇的～ central part of the whole article
主演 zhǔyǎn play the leading role (in a film, etc.):领衔～ head the cast /她～了五部电视剧。She starred in five TV plays.
主要 zhǔyào main; major; primary; principal:～问题 central issue (*or* problem) /～矛盾 principal contradiction /～点 essentials; gist /～敌人 chief enemy /～方面 principal (*or* primary) aspect /～劳动 essential labour /～目标 major objective /～因素 primary factor /～街道 main street /会议～不是讨论这个问题。This is not the focus of the discussion at the meeting. /教科书仍是他们国家的～出版物。Textbooks remain the meat and potatoes of publishing in their country.
主业 zhǔyè main occupation; mainline
主页 zhǔyè 〈信息〉homepage
主义 zhǔyì doctrine; -ism:现实～与浪漫～ realism and romanticism /辩证唯物～ dialectical materialism /官僚～ bureaucratism /封建～ feudalism /地区霸权～ regional hegemonism /大国沙文～ great-power (*or* great-nation, *or* big-power) chauvinism /本位～ selfish departmentalism /自由～ liberalism; licence /大男子～ male chauvinism /个人～ individualism; egoism; self-seeking /门罗～ Monroe Doctrine
主意 zhǔyi ❶ decision; judgment; definite view:拿定～ make up one's mind; make a decision /拿不定～ be in two (*or* twenty) minds (about sth.); hesitate /没有～ be at a loss (what to do) /看来她很有～。It seems she knows her own mind. ❷ idea; way; plan:出～ give advice /想出个好～ hit upon a good idea
主因 zhǔyīn main reason
主音 zhǔyīn 〈音乐〉keynote; tonic
主语 zhǔyǔ 〈语言〉subject
主宰 zhǔzǎi dominate; govern; control:～自己的命运 decide one's own destiny; have one's fate in one's own hand /思想是人们行动的～。One's behaviour is governed by one's thinking. /在西方社会里,金钱～一切。Money holds sway in Western society. /世界不能由大国～。The world must not be dominated by a few big powers.

主战 zhǔzhàn favour the use of force; advocate settlement by war
主战派 zhǔzhànpài war faction; war party; war hawk
主张 zhǔzhāng ❶ hold; maintain; advocate; favour: ～对话,不～对抗 favour dialogue, not confrontation /～和平解决争端 advocate a peaceful settlement of the dispute /我们一贯～大小国家一律平等。We have always maintained that all nations, big or small, should be treated as equals. *or* We consistently stand for equality among all nations, big or small. /中国一贯～国与国之间要和平相处。It is China's consistent stand (*or* position) that countries should live in peace with each other. ❷ view; stand; proposition; position: 我赞成你的～。I am for your proposal. /这个～似乎行不通。The proposition seems infeasible.
主掌 zhǔzhǎng be in charge of; be responsible for; be in control of: ～财务 be in charge of financial affairs
主震 zhǔzhèn main shock of an earthquake
主枝 zhǔzhī limb (of a tree); bough
主旨 zhǔzhǐ purport; substance; gist: 社论的～ gist of the editorial
主治 zhǔzhì 〈医学〉 indications: 这种药～高血压。This medicine is mainly for hypertension. /～支气管炎、感冒、肺炎等病。(used on a label) Indications: bronchitis, colds, pneumonia, etc.
主治医生 zhǔzhì yīshēng physician-in-charge; doctor in charge of a case
主轴 zhǔzhóu 〈机械〉 principal axis; mainshaft; spindle: ～盖 mainshaft cap /～箱 spindle box
主子 zhǔzi master; boss: 为～效劳 serve one's master /看～的脸色行事 adjust one's behaviour to one's master's facial expression

拄 zhǔ lean on (a stick, etc.): ～杖而行 walk with a stick (*or* cane) /他年近九旬还不用～拐棍儿。He does not use a walking stick even though he is approaching ninety.

麈 zhǔ (in ancient books) animals such as deer whose tails can be used as whisks

讵(詝) zhǔ 〈书面〉 wisdom

煮 zhǔ boil; stew; cook: ～面条 cook noodles /别把水～干了。Don't let the kettle (*or* water) boil away (*or* boil dry). /水～开了。The water is boiling.
煮豆燃萁 zhǔdòu-ránqí make a fire of beanstalks for boiling beans — fraternal persecution; fratricidal strife: 煮豆燃豆萁,豆在釜中泣。本是同根生,相煎何太急? They were boiling beans on a beanstalk fire; There came a plaintive voice from the pot, O why, since we sprang from the self-same root, Should you kill me with anger hot? /你们兄弟之间有什么事不能商量解决? 为何要同室操戈, ～呢? Can't you brothers settle your differences through discussion? Why all this fratricidal strife?
煮鹤焚琴 zhǔhè-fénqín *also* "焚琴煮鹤" cook the crane for meat and burn a stringed instrument for fuel — destroy sth. valuable or fine; spoil the fun; throw a wet blanket on: 你为何要干这种～,大杀风景的事呢? Why (do you) spoil all the fun we are having?
煮茧 zhǔjiǎn 〈纺织〉 cocoon cooking: ～车间 cocoon cooking workshop
煮浆锅炉 zhǔjiāng guōlú revolving boiler
煮呢 zhǔní 〈纺织〉 potting /～机 decatizing machine; decating machine; decator; crabbing

渚 zhǔ 〈书面〉 small piece of land surrounded by water; islet: 江～ islet in a river /沙～ sandbar

褚 zhǔ 〈书面〉 ❶ silk floss ❷ pad with silk wadding ❸ bag; satchel; sack
see also Chǔ

属(屬) zhǔ 〈书面〉 ❶ join; connect; combine: 相～于道 flow of people on the road ❷ centre (one's attention, etc.) upon; concentrate on
see also shǔ
属草 zhǔcǎo 〈书面〉 make a draft of; draft; draw up
属目 zhǔmù *also* "瞩目" zhǔmù fix one's eyes on
属望 zhǔwàng 〈书面〉 hope; look forward to: 他～孩子们有美好的前程。He hopes the children will have a bright future.
属意 zhǔyì fix one's mind on; have the inclination to: 科长的人选,人人都～于老王。Everyone favours Lao Wang as candidate for the section chief.
属垣有耳 zhǔyuán-yǒu'ěr walls have ears; someone has his ear to the wall: 此事高度机密,谨防～。This is highly confidential, so beware of eavesdroppers.

劚(斸、斵) zhǔ 〈书面〉 cut; hack

嘱(囑) zhǔ exhort; advise; urge: 叮～ urge again and again; exhort /遗～ will; testament
嘱咐 zhǔfu urge; exhort; tell: 牢记师长的～ always bear in mind the teacher's exhortations /临别～ injunction before departure /～他必须节俭 impress on him the need for frugality /父亲～他注意身体。Father told him to pay attention to his health.
嘱告 zhǔgào enjoin; exhort
嘱托 zhǔtuō entrust; ask: 他～我替他还书。He asked me to return the books for him. /李太太～我帮她照看孩子。Mrs Li entrusted me with the care of her children. /我是受朋友的～来看你的。I've come to see you at the request of my friend.

瞩(矚) zhǔ fasten one's look on; look steadily; gaze: 凝神远～ look long and steadily into the distance /高瞻远～ stand high and see far; show foresight; be a person of vision
瞩目 zhǔmù fix one's eyes upon; rivet one's attention on: 万众～ be the focus of public attention /引人～的长篇小说 novel that arrests people's attention
瞩望 zhǔwàng 〈书面〉 ❶ *also* "属望" zhǔwàng look forward to; earnestly expect: 老人～着儿子重整家业。The old man cherished high hopes that his son would restore the family fortunes. ❷ have a steady look at; gaze at

zhù

苎(苧) zhù
苎麻 zhùmá 〈植物〉 ramie: ～布 cloth made from ramie; ramie cloth

贮(貯) zhù store; save; keep; lay aside: ～粮备荒 store up grain against a lean year; store away grain against famine /仓里～满了粮食。The granary is bursting with grain. /这个水库～水约3,000万立方米。The reservoir has in storage (*or* a storage capacity of) about 30 million cubic metres.
贮备 zhùbèi store; keep; have in reserve: ～粮草过冬 store (*or* reserve) grain and fodder against the winter /我们的～品已经不足了。Our stores have fallen short.
贮藏 zhùcáng store up; lay in: ～不少木柴 lay in a good supply of firewood /地窖里～了蔬菜 have a store of vegetables in the cellar /矿产～丰富 be rich in mineral resources
贮存 zhùcún keep in storage; keep; store: 物价稳定后,人民愿意～货币。When prices become stable, people are willing to keep their money. /她每年都要～一些腌菜。She puts up stores of preserved vegetables every year. /这些数字都～在他脑子里了。All these figures were stored in his memory.
贮存期 zhùcúnqī storage time
贮点红 zhùdiǎnhóng *also* "朱顶雀" zhūdǐngquè redpoll (linnet)
贮积 zhùjī keep in storage; store; stockpile
贮木场 zhùmùchǎng timber depot; timber yard; lumber yard
贮蓄 zhùxù ❶ store up; lay up: 土壤～养分的能力 capacity of soil to keep (*or* conserve) nutrients ❷ savings: 他一有钱就花,没有～。He is not a saving man and lives a hand-to-mouth life. *or* He spends every penny he earns and never saves up.
贮运 zhù-yùn storage and shipping: 这种水果耐～。This kind of fruit bears well both storage and transport (*or* keeps well and ships well).

伫(佇、竚) zhù 〈书面〉 stand for a long time: ～听风雨声 stand still listening to the wind and rain
伫候 zhùhòu 〈书面〉 stand waiting: ～大驾光临。Your presence is

requested.
伫立 zhùlì stand still for a long time:她呆痴痴地~着。She stood dumb.

纻(紵) zhù 〈书面〉 cloth made from ramie

注[1] zhù ❶ pour:往杯中~入清水 pour clear water into a glass / 血流如~。Blood gushed out (*or* streamed down). /大雨如~。The rain came down in torrents. *or* The rain was bucketing down. ❷ pay full attention; concentrate; fix:引人关~ attract (*or* arrest) one's attention /全神贯~ be absorbed (*or* engrossed) in; concentrate on ❸ stakes:下~ stake (*or* bet money or things); lay a stake / 孤~一掷 stake everything on a single throw; have all one's eggs in one basket; sink or swim; make a last desperate effort ❹ 〈量词〉 *often used of money or business transactions*:一~钱 a sum of money /两~买卖 two business transactions /一~交易 a deal

注[2](註) zhù ❶ make annotations; explain with notes; annotate:评~ make comments and annotations; annotate /此书引文未~出处。Sources of quotations (*or* References) are not given in this book. ❷ notes:脚~ footnote /尾~ endnote /附~ annotations ❸ put on record; record; register

注册 zhùcè register:~处 registrar's office; registration office /~商标 registered trademark /~护士 registered nurse (RN) /~会计师 certified public accountant /~资本 registered capital /~证书 registration certificate /新生九月一日开始报到~。Registration of new students begins on 1 September.

注带 zhùdài 〈纺织〉 casting

注定 zhùdìng be doomed; be fated; be destined:~要灭亡 be destined to destruction /~要遭厄运 be doomed to misfortune /正如命中~的那样 as fate would have it /婚姻是命中~的吗? Is marriage predestined?

注脚 zhùjiǎo footnote

注解 zhùjiě ❶ explain with notes; annotate:~古诗 annotate ancient poetry /~难点 explain the difficult points with notes ❷ (explanatory) note; annotation:第一卷的~ notes to Volume I /详细的~ copious notes

注明 zhùmíng give clear indication of; label:这封信未~日期。The letter bears no date (*or* is undated). /这个胶卷未~出厂日期和失效期。The dates of production and expiry (*or* expiration) are not given on this film. /瓶上~有毒。The bottle was labelled poisonous.

注模 zhùmú 〈化工〉 injection mode:~法 injection moulding /~机 injector

注目 zhùmù fix one's eyes on; have a steady look at:引人~ eye-catching; spectacular /四海~ attract attention from all over the world

注目礼 zhùmùlǐ salute with eyes:向国旗行~ salute the national flag with wrapt attention

注坯吹塑 zhùpī chuīsù 〈化工〉 injection blow molding

注气 zhùqì 〈石油〉 gas injection:~井 gas-injection well

注入 zhùrù pour into; empty into:把药水慢慢~口腔里 pour the liquid medicine slowly into the mouth /珠江~南海。The Pearl River empties into the South China Sea.

注入井 zhùrùjǐng 〈石油〉 injection well

注入式教学法 zhùrùshì jiàoxuéfǎ spoon-feeding way of teaching; cramming

注入式教育 zhùrùshì jiàoyù spoon-fed education

注射 zhùshè 〈医学〉 inject:肌肉~ intramuscular injection /静脉~ intravenous injection /皮下~ hypodermic injection /给病人~镇静剂 give the patient a tranquillizer injection /~葡萄糖 inject glucose into sb.; inject sb. with glucose

注射剂 zhùshèjì injection

注射器 zhùshèqì injector; syringe

注射针头 zhùshè zhēntóu syringe needle

注视 zhùshì look attentively at; gaze at; closely watch:凝神~着远方 stare fixedly into the distance /目不转睛地~着他的脸 look intently at his face /密切~这个地区局势的发展 closely follow the development of the situation in the region /密切~幼儿智力的发育 intently watch the development of the infant mind /在这么多人好奇的目光~下,她的脸红了。Her cheeks grew hot beneath the gaze of so many curious eyes. /小男孩坐在那儿,目不转睛地~着舞台。The little boy sat there with eyes glued to the stage.

注释 zhùshì explanatory note; annotation:为李白的诗作~ annotate Li Bai's poems /附有~的莎士比亚剧本 annotated plays of Shakespeare /这在~中加以说明了。This is explained in the notes.

注疏 zhùshū 〈书面〉 notes and commentaries

注水 zhùshuǐ 〈石油〉 water flooding:边缘~ edgewater flooding /~动态 flood performance /~泵站 water flooding pump station

注塑 zhùsù injection moulding

注塑成型 zhùsù chéngxíng 〈化工〉 injection moulding:~机 injection moulding machine; injection machine /塑料~机 injection mould

注文 zhùwén explanatory notes; annotation

注销 zhùxiāo cancel; annul; write off:~欠款 write off the debt /~户口 cancel sb.'s household registration /~登记 nullify the registration

注意 zhùyì pay attention to; take notice of; be careful about:~服务态度 pay attention to your attitude in serving the customers /~饮食 be careful in one's diet /~产品质量 look after the quality of the product /我没~他是否来开会了。I didn't notice whether he was at the meeting. /到姑姑家要~规矩。Mind your p's and q's when you are at your aunt's house. /~别让这种事再次发生。Make sure that this doesn't happen again. /~留有充分余地。See to it that there is enough leeway. /~,汽车来了! Watch out! There is a car coming. / 请大家~,会议就要开始了。Attention, please! The meeting is about to start.

注意广度 zhùyì guǎngdù 〈心理〉 attention span; degree of concentration

注意力 zhùyìlì attention

注意事项 zhùyì shìxiàng points for attention; matters needing attention

注音 zhùyīn 〈语言〉 phonetic notation:用汉语拼音给这一篇文章~ mark the article with Chinese phonetic alphabets /给外国留学生用的~课本 phonetically annotated textbooks for foreign students

注音字母 zhùyīn zìmǔ *also* "注音符号" national phonetic alphabet (in use before the publication of the Scheme for the Chinese Phonetic Alphabet)

注油 zhùyóu ❶ oiling; greasing ❷ fuel-injection

注油枪 zhùyóuqiāng grease gun; oil gun

注重 zhùzhòng lay stress on; stress; emphasize:~社会效益和经济效益 lay stress on social effects and economic performance /这本教科书特别~解释语法。The textbook places a special emphasis on explanation of the grammatical rules. /厂领导一向非常~产品质量。The leadership of the factory has always attached great importance to the quality of its products. /他这人的特点是~实际。He is pragmatic by nature.

注子 zhùzi 〈方言〉 wine pot; flagon:一~酒 a pot of wine

疰 zhù

疰夏 zhùxià ❶ 〈中医〉 summer disease, usu. contracted by children with symptoms of fever, loss of appetite, lassitude, etc.; summer infixation ❷ 〈方言〉 loss of appetite and weight in summer

炷 zhù 〈书面〉 ❶ wick (of an oil lamp):艾~ moxa cone ❷ burn:~香 burn a joss stick ❸ 〈量词〉:三~香 three burning joss sticks

柱 zhù ❶ post; pillar; column:支~ pillar; prop; mainstay / 顶梁~ pillar /房~ pillars of a house; upright /门~ doorposts /大理石圆~ marble column ❷ column-like thing:冰~ icicle /五月节花~ Maypole /水~ water column; pillar of water /水银~ mercury column ❸ 〈数学〉 cylinder

柱础 zhùchǔ stone under a pillar of a house; plinth

柱顶 zhùdǐng 〈建筑〉 capital

柱廊 zhùláng 〈建筑〉 colonnade

柱面 zhùmiàn 〈数学〉 cylindrical surface; cylinder:椭圆~ elliptic cylinder /~螺旋线 cylindrical helix

柱塞 zhùsāi 〈机械〉 plunger piston; plunger:~泵 plunger pump; plunger-type pump /~压力机 plunger press /~式马达 plunger motor

柱塞式热压铸机 zhùsāishì rèyāzhùjī 〈冶金〉 submerged plunger die-casting machine

柱身 zhùshēn 〈建筑〉 shaft

柱石 zhùshí pillar; mainstay; tower of strength: 国家的～ pillar (*or mainstay*) of the country

柱头 zhùtóu ❶〈建筑〉column cap; column head; capital ❷〈方言〉post; pillar ❸〈植物〉stigma

柱形浮标 zhùxíng fúbiāo 〈航海〉pillar buoy

柱状剖面 zhùzhuàng pōumiàn 〈地质〉columnar section; geologic column

柱子 zhùzi post; pillar

柱座 zhùzuò column base; plinth

蛀

zhù ❶ moth or any other insect that eats books, clothes, wood, etc. and makes holes in them ❷ (of moths, etc.) eat into; bore through: 木头已遭虫～。The wood was worm-eaten.

蛀齿 zhùchǐ dental caries; decayed tooth

蛀虫 zhùchóng insect that eats or feeds on books, clothes, wood, etc.; moth; borer: 米里出了～了。There are weevils in the rice. /贪污分子是社会主义事业的～。Embezzlers are vermin undermining the foundation of the socialist cause.

蛀蚀 zhùshí worm-eaten; eroded: ～的灵魂 eroded soul /毛衣被虫～了。The woolen sweater was moth-eaten.

蛀心虫 zhùxīnchóng borer

住

zhù ❶ live; stay; reside; dwell: ～乡下 live in the country /永久居～在纽约 reside permanently in New York /当晚～在朋友家 stayed overnight at a friend's house /～进新房 move into a new house /他们三人～一间屋。They three shared a room. /她设法为这两家人解决了吃、～问题。She managed to feed and house (*or* to accommodate) the two families. ❷ stop; end; cease: 风停雨～。The wind died down and the rain stopped. ❸ *used after some verbs as a complement indicating a halt, stillness, fastness, etc.*: 受不～这份儿气 cannot swallow the insult; cannot bear being bullied /支持不～ can no longer withstand /记～ remember; bear in mind /接～! Catch it! /站～! Halt! /拦～他! Stop him! /血止～了。It ceased bleeding. /她没被吓～。She was not intimidated.

住持 zhùchí 〈宗教〉(Buddhist or Taoist) abbot

住处 zhùchu residence; lodging; dwelling; accomodation: 肮脏的～ foul (*or* dirty) dwelling /临时～ temporary residence /固定～ fixed abode /你的～在哪儿? Where do you live? /我已找到～。I've found accommodation (*or* lodgings).

住地 zhùdì residence; dwelling place: 我的～离这儿不远。I live not far from here.

住读 zhùdú attend a boarding school: ～生 resident student

住房 zhùfáng housing; lodgings; accommodation: ～短缺 housing shortage /～分配 allocation of dwelling houses /～津贴 accommodation allowance; housing subsidy /农民～ peasant housing /她分到一套～。She was allotted an apartment.

住房制度改革 zhùfáng zhìdù gǎigé housing reform

住户 zhùhù household; resident: 这座楼有十八家～。There are eighteen households in the building. /他是新来的～。He's just moved in. /我找一位姓王的～。I am looking for a Wang living here.

住家 zhùjiā ❶ (of one's family) live; reside in: 他在城里～。He lives with his family in town. ❷ household: 这一带的～儿多是双职工。Those who live in this area are mostly working couples.

住居 zhùjū live; dwell; reside: 少数民族～的地区 areas inhabited by minority nationalities (*or* ethnic minorities)

住口 zhùkǒu stop talking; shut up; keep quiet: 你们太吵人了, 快～! You are making too much noise. Cut it out! /他不～地发牢骚。He kept grumbling. /你再不～, 我可就不客气了。If you don't shut up, don't say I haven't warned you (*or* I won't be so easy on you).

住声 zhùshēng stop talking, laughing, or crying; hold one's tongue: 他们有说有笑, 半天没～了。They have been talking and laughing without stopping for quite a while.

住室 zhùshì room where one lives; bedroom

住手 zhùshǒu stop (doing sth.); stay one's hand: 得～时且～ know when one should stop /～! 你不能这样打孩子! Stop! You cannot beat the child like this!

住宿 zhùsù stay; put up; accommodate: 安排～ find lodgings (*or* arrange accommodation) for sb. /今晚能让我们在这儿～吗? Can you put us up here for the night?

住所 zhùsuǒ dwelling place; residence; abode; domicile: 固定～ permanent dwelling place (*or* residence); domicile /临时～ temporary abode /我得找个～安顿下来。I have to find a place to settle down.

住闲 zhùxián have no occupation; out of work; unemployed

住校 zhùxiào be at a boarding school; live on campus (*or* in the students' dormitory): 现有约三百名学生～。There are now about 300 students in residence. /多数大学生～。Most college students are boarders.

住校生 zhùxiàoshēng resident student

住友化学工业公司 Zhùyǒu Huàxué Gōngyè Gōngsī Sumitomo Chemical Co. Ltd., a major Japanese chemical producer since 1913

住友银行 Zhùyǒu Yínháng Sumitomo Bank, one of Japan's major commercial banks established since 1895

住院 zhùyuàn be hospitalized; be in hospital: 因癌症而～治疗 be hospitalized by cancer

住院病人 zhùyuàn bìngrén in-patient

住院部 zhùyuànbù in-patient department

住院处 zhùyuànchù admission office (in a hospital)

住院费 zhùyuànfèi hospitalization expenses

住院医生 zhùyuàn yīshēng resident physician

住宅 zhùzhái residence; dwelling; abode: ～区 residential quarters (*or* district, *or* area) /～商品化 commercialize residential building /非法侵入公民～ unlawful intrusion into a citizen's home /周围的农田现已变成～区。The surrounding farmland has now turned residential.

住宅合作社 zhùzhái hézuòshè residential co-op (nonprofit-making and public-welfare organization formed by city residents who raise funds by themselves and work together in the construction of their new dwellings)

住址 zhùzhǐ address: 她已换了～。She's changed her address. /这封信～写错了。The letter is wrongly addressed.

住嘴 zhùzuǐ *see* "住口"

驻

zhù ❶ stop; halt; stay: ～足观赏 stop to enjoy (*or* admire) the beautiful sight ❷ be stationed; be posted: ～外工作 overseas postings /美国～华大使馆 US Embassy in China /我国～法大使 our ambassador to France /中华人民共和国常～联合国代表团 Permanent Mission of the People's Republic of China to the United Nations /常～代表 permanent representative /～京记者 resident correspondent in Beijing; journalist based in Beijing /福特公司～京办事处 Ford Company's Office in Beijing /镇上～有两个连。There are two companies stationed in town.

驻跸 zhùbì 〈书面〉(of a monarch on a tour) stay temporarily; stop over

驻波 zhùbō 〈物理〉standing wave; stationary wave: ～天线 standing wave antenna /～保护电路 stationary wave protecting circuit /～检测器 standing wave detector

驻地 zhùdì ❶ place where troops or fieldworkers are stationed: 石油勘探队～ encampment of a petroleum prospecting team /边防军～ frontier guard station ❷ seat (of a local administrative organ): 省人民政府～ seat of the provincial people's government; provincial capital

驻防 zhùfáng defend with or as a garrison; be on garrison duty; garrison: ～边疆 garrison the frontiers /～部队 garrison (troops)

驻节 zhùjié ❶〈旧语〉(of high officials) stay temporarily in other parts of the country on business ❷ resident; permanent seat

驻节公使 zhùjié gōngshǐ minister resident; resident minister

驻军 zhùjūn ❶ station troops; base troops: ～澳门 station troops in Macao ❷ troops stationed (at a place); garrison

驻守 zhùshǒu garrison; defend: ～海疆 garrison coastal areas and territorial seas /这个地区有一个师～。The area is garrisoned with a division.

驻屯 zhùtún *see* "驻扎"

驻颜 zhùyán remain youthful in appearance: ～有术 have a recipe for maintaining youthful appearance; be able to preserve one's youthful looks

驻在国 zhùzàiguó 〈外交〉country of residence; state to which a diplomatic envoy is accredited

驻扎 zhùzhā (of troops) be stationed; be quartered: 那里～着一支警备队。A garrison is stationed there.

驻足 zhùzú make a temporary stay; halt: ～观看 stop and watch

祝[1]

zhù ❶ offer good wishes; wish: ～你早日康复。I wish you

a speedy recovery. /～你生日快乐! Happy birthday to you! /～你一路顺风。Have a pleasant journey. *or* Bon voyage! /～你俩顺利。Good luck to you both. /～您长寿! (greeting on sb.'s birthday) Many happy returns (of the day)! /～贵国繁荣昌盛。May your country enjoy prosperity! ❷ (Zhù) a surname

祝[2] zhù 〈书面〉cut:～发为僧 cut off one's hair and become a monk

祝词 zhùcí *also* "祝辞" ❶ (in ancient times) prayers at sacrificial rites ❷ congratulatory speech; congratulations:元旦～ New Year's speech

祝辞 zhùcí *see* "祝词"

祝祷 zhùdǎo wish and pray: ～双亲安康 pray for the health of one's parents /～上苍 say one's prayers to God

祝福 zhùfú ❶ blessing; benediction; wish:带着亲朋好友的～启程了 depart with the benediction of one's relatives and close friends /请接受我最良好的～。Please accept my best wishes. ❷ new year's sacrifice (an old custom in certain parts of China):家中都一律忙,都在准备着～。Every family was busy preparing for "the sacrifice".

祝告 zhùgào *see* "祝祷"

祝贺 zhùhè congratulate; felicitate:致以节日的～ extend holiday greetings /我过三十岁生日时,他来信表示～。He sent me congratulations on my 30th birthday. /同事们衷心～他所取得的成就。His colleagues congratulated him most heartily on what he had achieved.

祝捷 zhùjié celebrate a victory; offer congratulations on winning a victory:～大会 victory celebration (meeting)

祝酒 zhùjiǔ drink a toast; toast:向贵宾～ toast the distinguished guests /致～词 propose a toast /答谢～ respond (*or* reply) to a toast /总理的～词 toast by the Prime Minister

祝融 Zhùróng legendary God of Fire

祝圣 zhùshèng 〈宗教〉consecration

祝寿 zhùshòu congratulate (an elderly person) on his or her birthday; offer birthday congratulations (to an elderly person)

祝颂 zhùsòng extend greetings; express good wishes:新年人们都要互相～。People exchange good wishes on New Year's Day.

祝由 zhùyóu (in ancient China) treat a disease by drawing magic figures and chanting incantations

祝愿 zhùyuàn wish:～贵国人民幸福。May your people enjoy happiness. *or* We wish your people well-being. /请接受我真诚的～,祝你事业成功,家庭幸福。Please accept my sincere wishes for success in your work and happiness of your family.

著 zhù ❶ marked; conspicuous; outstanding:政绩卓～ signal (*or* outstanding) achievements in one's official career /彰明较～ be crystal clear; be as plain as noonday /臭名昭～ notorious ❷ show; display; prove: *see* "～名" ❸ write; compose:编～ compile; write ❹ work; book:大～〈敬词〉your writing /译～ translation /巨～ monumental work; masterpiece /遗～ posthumous writings

see also zhe; zhuó

著称 zhùchēng 〈书面〉be celebrated for; be famous for; be noted for:此地以盛产稻米～。This area is a well-known rice-bowl.

著录 zhùlù put down in writing; write down; record

著名 zhùmíng famous; noted; well-known; celebrated:～诗人 celebrated poet /～学者 noted scholar /～的江西土产 famous native product of Jiangxi /～风景区 well-known scenic spot /～的作家 prominent (*or* renowned) writer; writer of distinction

著书立说 zhùshū-lìshuō write a book to expound a theory or doctrine; produce scholarly works

著述 zhùshù ❶ write; compile:埋头～ be engrossed in the writing and compilation of scholarly works ❷ writings; book; work:～颇丰 be a prolific author; write many books

著述等身 zhùshù-děngshēn *also* "著作等身" one's works are piled up to one's own height — write in great quantity; be a prolific writer:～的大学者 great scholar with extensive publications to his credit

著者 zhùzhě author; writer

著作 zhùzuò ❶ write:他晚年～甚多。He wrote many books in his later years. ❷ work; book; writings:鲁迅的～ works of Lu Xun /一部五卷的文学～ literary work of five volumes /关于这个题材的～相当多。A considerable literature exists on the subject.

著作权 zhùzuòquán copyright

著作人 zhùzuòrén author; writer

箸(筯) zhù 〈方言〉chopsticks:象牙～ ivory chopsticks

翥 zhù 〈书面〉(of birds) fly; soar:龙翔凤～ the dragon soars and the phoenix flies aloft

苎 zhù *also* "苧" zhù 〈书面〉ramie

see also xù

杼 zhù ❶〈纺织〉reed ❷ shuttle

杼轴 zhùzhóu 〈书面〉❶ two parts of an old-fashioned loom which control the warp and woof ❷〈比喻〉conception (of a piece of writing):该文别出～。The article is uniquely conceived. *or* The article is original in conception.

助 zhù give help to; help; assist; aid:互～ help each other /资～某人 aid someone with money /协～医生开刀 assist the doctor in performing the operation /～她一臂之力 lend (*or* give) her a (helping) hand /～人渡过难关 help sb. tide over difficulties; help a lame dog over a stile

助爆药 zhùbàoyào 〈军事〉booster charge; booster

助产 zhùchǎn midwifery

助产士 zhùchǎnshì midwife

助词 zhùcí 〈语言〉auxiliary word, an unstressed form word which performs the grammatical functions of structure (as 的, 地, 得, 所), of tense (as 了, 着, 过) or of mood (as 呢, 吗, 吧, 啊); function word; empty word

助催化剂 zhùcuīhuàjì 〈化学〉promoter; catalyst-accelerator

助动词 zhùdòngcí 〈语言〉auxiliary verb

助耕 zhùgēng help others till the land

助工 zhùgōng (short for 助理工程师) assistant engineer

助攻 zhùgōng 〈军事〉holding or secondary attack; 〈体育〉assist in attack (in basketball):～部队 holding element /上半场他～三次。He had three assists in the first half.

助剂 zhùjì 〈化学〉assistant; auxiliary

助祭 zhùjì 〈基督教〉deacon

助教 zhùjiào (of a college faculty) assistant; teaching assistant:历史～ assistant of history /～职务 assistantship

助桀为虐 zhùjié-wéinüè aid King Jie in his tyrannical rule; help a tyrant to do evil; hold a candle to the devil; abet an evildoer:你竭力袒护这么个恶棍,不是～吗? Aren't you holding a candle to the devil, trying to defend such a ruffian? /他们貌似公允,其实是在～。Seemingly evenhanded, they were actually helping the evildoer.

see also "助纣为虐" zhùzhòu-wéinüè

助理 zhùlǐ assistant:部长～ assistant minister /～国务卿 (US) assistant secretary of state

助力 zhùlì help; aid:在困难中,他曾给我很大的～。He offered (*or* rendered) me great help when I was in difficulties.

助磨剂 zhùmójì 〈机械〉grinding aid

助跑 zhùpǎo 〈体育〉run-up; approach

助燃 zhùrán 〈化学〉combustion-supporting:～气体 combustion-supporting gas

助燃物 zhùránwù comburant; comburent

助人为乐 zhùrén-wéilè find it a pleasure to help others; take delight in helping others:他一生以～。He was always ready to help others throughout his life.

助熔剂 zhùróngjì flux

助熔矿石 zhùróng kuàngshí 〈冶金〉fluxing ore

助色团 zhùsètuán 〈化学〉auxochrome

助手 zhùshǒu assistant; helper; aide:医生的～ assistant to a physician /你需要个～帮着干吗? Do you need a helper in doing the job?

助听器 zhùtīngqì audiphone; hearing aid; deaf-aid

助推 zhùtuī 〈航天〉boost

助推火箭 zhùtuī huǒjiàn 〈航天〉booster rocket; booster

助推级 zhùtuījí 〈航天〉booster

助推器 zhùtuīqì 〈航天〉boost motor; launch vehicle; auxiliary booster:～系统 booster system

助威 zhùwēi boost the morale of; cheer; root:为主队加油～ cheer (*or* root) for the home team

助兴 zhùxìng add to the fun; make things more lively; liven

things up:他们还请来了乐队为晚会～。They also invited a band to add to the fun of the party (*or* to liven up the party).
助学 zhùxué support and help the learner (usu. those who study on their own):开展～活动,鼓励自学成才。Let's give our help and encouragement to those who strive to become useful personnel through self-education.
助学金 zhùxuéjīn (student) grant; grant-in-aid; stipend:颁发～award a grant /领取～ receive a grant /领～的学生 grant-aided student
助研 zhùyán (short for 助理研究员) assistant research-fellow
助益 zhùyì help and benefit:你这样放纵孩子对他毫无～。You won't do the child any good by being so indulgent with him.
助战 zhùzhàn ❶ assist in fighting ❷ bolster sb.'s morale; cheer for sb.
助长 zhùzhǎng 〈贬义〉abet; foster; foment:这会～不正之风。This will put a premium on malpractices. /别总替孩子做事,～他的惰性。Don't encourage the child's laziness by doing everything for him. /这只能～她的傲气。That could only boost (*or* add to) her arrogance.
助阵 zhùzhèn *see*“助威”
助纣为虐 zhùzhòu-wéinüè aid King Zhou in his tyrannical rule; help a tyrant to do evil; aid and abet the evildoer
see also“助桀为虐” zhùjié-wéinüè

筑[1](築) zhù build; construct:构～工事 build defences (*or* fortifications) /修～公路 construct a road

筑[2] zhù *zhu*, an ancient 13-stringed instrument played by striking the strings with a light bamboo stick:击～ play the *zhu*

筑[3] Zhù another name for Guiyang (贵阳), capital of Guizhou Province
筑坝 zhùbà 〈水利〉damming:～排水 dam out
筑长城 zhù chángchéng 〈戏谑〉play mah-jong
筑巢引凤 zhùcháo-yǐnfèng build nests to attract phoenixes — make facilities available first to attract people of talent
筑堤 zhùdī ❶embankment; levee; dyke ❷ build a dyke: ～工人 dyke-builder /～机 dyke-building machinery
筑港工程 zhùgǎng gōngchéng harbour work(s)
筑埂机 zhùgěngjī 〈农业〉ridger
筑垄 zhùlǒng 〈农业〉ridging
筑路 zhùlù road making; roadbuilding:～拌料机 roadmixer /～工人 roadman /～石料 roadstone /～机 roadbuilder /～机械 road machine
筑室道谋 zhùshì-dàomóu seek guidance from every passerby as to how to build one's house — have no idea or plan of one's own and fail to accomplish anything:此事应当机立断,岂可～,久议不决? How can we keep consulting others and put off a decision on the matter which brooks no delay?
筑室返耕 zhùshì-fǎngēng retire and return to the countryside
筑梯田 zhù tītián 〈农业〉terracing:～农具 terracer

铸(鑄) zhù cast; found:铜～的古钟 bronze bell /浇～ casting; pouring
铸币 zhùbì coin; specie
铸币厂 zhùbìchǎng mint
铸币权 zhùbìquán mintage
铸成大错 zhùchéng-dàcuò 〈书面〉commit a gross error; make a serious blunder:他屡错不改,遂～。Refusing to correct repeated mistakes he ended up in committing an awful blunder.
铸床 zhùchuáng 〈冶金〉casting bed; pig bed
铸错 zhùcuò make a blunder; commit a serious error:以贪心～ serious error caused by one's greed
铸锭 zhùdìng 〈冶金〉ingot casting
铸钢 zhùgāng 〈冶金〉cast steel
铸工 zhùgōng 〈冶金〉❶ foundry work: ～车间 foundry (shop); casting shop /～鼓风机 foundry fan /～铲 casting shovel ❷ foundry worker; founder; moulder
铸管 zhùguǎn 〈冶金〉cast tube
铸锅 zhùguō 〈冶金〉skillet
铸焊 zhùhàn 〈冶金〉cast joint; cast-weld; cast solder:～件 cast-weld assembly /～结构 cast-weld construction
铸件 zhùjiàn 〈冶金〉cast; casting; foundry goods; founding:干砂～ dry sand casting /压～ die casting /冷硬～ chill (*or* chilled) casting /～清理 casting clean-up /～清理机 casting cleaning machine
铸坑 zhùkēng 〈冶金〉foundry pit
铸口 zhùkǒu 〈冶金〉casting nozzle
铸铝 zhùlǚ 〈冶金〉aluminium casting; cast aluminium
铸模 zhùmú *also*“铸型” casting mould
铸排机 zhùpáijī 〈印刷〉composing machine; typesetting machine
铸坯 zhùpī 〈冶金〉casting blank
铸石 zhùshí cast stone; molten-rock casting; stone casting
铸铁 zhùtiě ❶ iron casting ❷ cast iron:球墨～ nodular cast iron
铸铜 zhùtóng 〈冶金〉cast brass; cast copper:～合金 casting copper alloy
铸型 zhùxíng *also*“铸模” casting mould
铸造 zhùzào casting; founding:蜡模～ investment casting; lost wax casting /无砂～ sandless casting /～车间 casting shop; foundry (shop) /～一座青铜雕像 cast a statue in bronze
铸造厂 zhùzàochǎng foundry
铸字 zhùzì 〈印刷〉typefounding; typecasting:～工场 typefoundry /～工人 typefounder; linotyper /～机 typecasting machine; caster /～模 cast type

zhuā

檛(檛、簻) zhuā 〈书面〉horsewhip

挝(撾) zhuā ❶〈书面〉strike; beat (a drum):～鼓 beat a drum ❷ *see*“抓” zhuā
see also wō

抓 zhuā ❶ seize; clutch; grab; grasp: ～钱 grab money; raise money /～要点 grasp the main points /～机遇 seize a good opportunity/～某人的把柄 try to get hold of sth. with which to discredit sb.; try to catch sb. tripping /～事物的本质 grasp the essence /～住一点小事大做文章 seize on a trifle and make an issue of it; make a fuss over sth. trivial; make a mountain out of a molehill /听到有声音,他一把～起枪。He snatched up his gun at the sound. /她摔倒时一下子～住我的胳膊。She seized hold of my arm as she fell. ❷ scratch: ～痒 scratch an itch; relieve the itching /小心这只猫,它会～人! Beware of the cat: it'll scratch! ❸ arrest; catch; press-gang:小偷当场被～获。The thief was caught red-handed. /诈骗犯被～起来了。The swindler was arrested (*or* taken into custody). ❹ lay stress on; stress:～主要矛盾 identify and tackle the principal contradiction /～职工福利 pay special attention to the welfare of workers and staff members /～苗头 watch out for the first signs (*or* the symptoms of a trend) /讲话要～重点。You should focus on the essential points in your speech. ❺ in charge of; responsible for:她是～人事的。She is in charge of personnel matters. ❻ vie for (work):～紧把麦子割完 rush in harvesting the wheat /三～两～就把工作～完了。The work will be done in no time if everyone tries to lend a hand. ❼ grip or hold attention:他们的演出很能～住观众。Their performance enthralled the audience.
抓辫子 zhuā biànzi grab by the queue — seize on sb.'s faults or errors for one's own advantage; capitalize on sb.'s vulnerable point:别叫人家抓住辫子。Don't let them catch you in the wrong. /这些人抓住马先生的辫子屡敲竹杠。These people kept blackmailing Mr. Ma because they had (*or* got) something on him. /你说话失礼,叫他们抓住了辫子。Your rude remarks gave them a handle against you.
抓膘 zhuābiāo fatten (pigs, cattle, etc.)
抓兵 zhuābīng 〈旧语〉press-gang conscripts
抓捕 zhuābǔ arrest; catch; apprehend:因抢劫银行被～ be arrested for robbing a bank
抓不起来 zhuābuqǐlai ❶ too soft to be held or lifted:面和得太软,～。The dough is too soft to take shape. ❷ fail to manage; be unable to do:这项工作他～。He is not competent for the job.
抓茬儿 zhuāchár 〈方言〉find fault; pick holes; nitpick:他总抓我的茬儿。He is always finding fault with (*or* picking on) me.
抓差 zhuāchāi get sb. to do a particular job; press sb. into service:人手不够,只好临时抓你的差了。As we are short of hands, we have to get you to do the work for the time being.

抓大放小 zhuādà-fàngxiǎo (policy in SOE reform) focus on the restructuring of large enterprises and give a free hand to small ones

抓大头 zhuā dàtóu *also* "拿大头" ná dàtóu 〈口语〉draw lots as to who should stand treat or take the largest share of the expense of a dinner

抓点 zhuādiǎn concentrate on work at selected units: ～带面 promote work in an entire area by drawing experience from selected units

抓丁 zhuādīng *see* "抓壮丁"

抓斗 zhuādǒu 〈机械〉grab; grab bucket; clamshell; clamshell bucket: 双瓣式～ two-jaw grab /～吊车 clamshell (-equipped) crane; grab(bing) crane /～挖泥船 grab boat /～挖泥机 grab dredger; grapple dredger; clamshell dredger /～式挖土机 clamshell excavator /～式装载机 grab-type loader; clam-type loader

抓赌 zhuādǔ catch those engaged in gambling; arrest gamblers

抓耳挠腮 zhuā'ěr-náosāi ❶ tweak one's ears and scratch one's cheeks; scratch one's head; be anxious: 急得他～，不知如何是好。He scratched his head out of anxiety and was at a loss what to do. ❷ be beside oneself with joy: 听得这个喜讯，他～，心花怒放。On hearing the good news he was wild with joy.

抓饭 zhuāfàn (food of the Uygur or other minority nationalities) rice cooked with mutton, carrots, raisins, etc. and eaten with hands

抓夫 zhuāfū *also* "抓伕" press-gang; press people into service

抓哏 zhuāgén (of a clown in an opera or a cross talk performer) improvise lines to amuse the audience

抓工夫 zhuā gōngfu find time (to do sth.); make good use of every minute: ～帮妈妈干点儿家务 find time to help one's mother with the housework

抓钩 zhuāgōu grab hook; grabs

抓官差 zhuā guānchāi 〈旧语〉press sb. into service; make sb. do a job without pay

抓获 zhuāhuò catch; seize; arrest; capture: 罪犯已～归案。The criminal has been arrested and brought to justice.

抓髻 zhuāji *also* "髽髻" zhuāji wear hair in two buns

抓尖儿 zhuājiānr 〈方言〉try to be the first to do sth. in order to show off: 大家都还没有开始呢，你抓什么尖儿? Nobody has started yet. Why do you jump the gun?

抓尖儿卖快 zhuājiānr-màikuài go out of one's way to ingratiate oneself: 她生性机灵，又好～。She is smart and takes every opportunity to curry favour with people.

抓紧 zhuājǐn keep a firm grasp on; pay close attention to; lose no time in doing sth.: ～时间 make the best use of one's time /～基础理论的研究 pay close attention to the study of basic theories /～有利时机 seize a golden opportunity /～权力不放 cling to one's power /～执行合作项目 act promptly to implement cooperation projects /～制定改革方案 lose no time in working out a programme for reform /这伤须～治疗。The wound needs an early and speedy treatment.

抓阄儿 zhuājiūr draw or cast lots: 我们只好～决定谁先休息了。We had to draw lots as to who should be the first to take a rest.

抓举 zhuājǔ 〈体育〉snatch: 他的～成绩超过了亚运会记录。His snatch record is better than that of the Asian Games.

抓具 zhuājù 〈机械〉grab handle; gripping apparatus

抓空子 zhuā kòngzi *see* "抓工夫"

抓两头，带中间 zhuā liǎngtóu, dài zhōngjiān grasp the two ends to bring along the middle — sustain the advanced and help the backward so as to spur the vast majority on

抓挠儿 zhuānáor 〈方言〉(of a baby) stretch and flex its fingers

抓挠 zhuānao 〈方言〉❶ scratch: 蚊子咬过的地方很痒，但你不能～。A mosquito bite itches, but you must not scratch it. ❷ make a mess of sth.; muddle things up: 我的打字机，你们别乱～。Don't mess about (*or* tamper) with my typewriter. ❸ come to blows; exchange blows; fight: 这两个男孩吵着吵着就～起来了。The two quarrelling boys came to blows. ❹ do a job in a hasty and disorderly manner; be in a rush and a muddle: 他一会儿～这，一会儿～那，结果什么也没做好。He rushed now through this and now through that without doing anything satisfactorily. ❺ earn; make (money): 想办法～几个钱儿 find some ways of making money ❻ sth. one can use or sb. one can rely on: 儿子要不走，她还有个～儿。If her son were here, she would have someone to fall back on. ❼ way to handle a problem, etc.: 看得出他已没～儿了。Obviously he is at his wit's end.

抓扒子 zhuā pázi 〈方言〉*see* "抓瞎"

抓拍 zhuāpāi take a snapshot of; take a candid photograph

抓破 zhuāpò scratch or claw someone so as to injure

抓破脸 zhuāpòliǎn *also* "撕破脸" sīpòliǎn 〈口语〉come out clawing and scratching; have no consideration for sb.'s face or feelings; offend sb. openly; shed all pretences of cordiality: ～跟他们干 challenge (*or* attack) them openly /～跟他说 tell him bluntly

抓取装置 zhuāqǔ zhuāngzhì 〈机械〉gripping device

抓权 zhuāquán grab power: 在公司里拼命～ make all efforts to seize control of the firm

抓人 zhuārén arrest; apprehend; take into custody

抓手 zhuāshou 〈方言〉handle (of a door, drawer, window, etc.)

抓瞎 zhuāxiā 〈口语〉be at a loss what to do; be in a rush and muddle; be thrown off balance: 事先做好准备，就不会临时～了。You won't find yourself at a loss (as to) how to act if you make good preparations beforehand.

抓岩机 zhuāyánjī 〈矿业〉grab loader; grab: ～绞车 grab hoist

抓药 zhuāyào ❶ (of a pharmacy) fill or make up a prescription (of Chinese herbal medicine) ❷ have a prescription (of Chinese herbal medicine) filled or made up

抓早儿 zhuāzǎor as early as possible; promptly: 你还是～出发吧，免得误了车。You'd better start out right away (*or* as soon as possible) so as not to miss the train.

抓周 zhuāzhōu (old Chinese custom) grabbing test on a child's first birthday anniversary (in which the parents place an assortment of articles on the table for him to choose from as a test of his inclinations and capabilities in later life)

抓爪 zhuāzhuǎ 〈机械〉grabhook: ～进给机构 gripper-feed mechanism /～机构 gripper mechanism

抓砖器 zhuāzhuānqì 〈建筑〉brick grab

抓壮丁 zhuā zhuàngdīng 〈旧语〉press-gang able-bodied men; press-gang conscripts

抓总儿 zhuāzǒngr 〈口语〉assume overall command or responsibility

髽 zhuā

髽髻 zhuāji *also* "抓髻" zhuāji two knots or rolls of hair worn on both sides of the head by women; bun; chignon; knot: 这姑娘头上梳了两个～。The girl tied her hair in two buns.

髽髻夫妻 zhuāji fūqī husband and wife by the first marriage

髽鬏 zhuājiu *see* "髽髻"

zhuǎ

爪

zhuǎ claw; talon; paw: 利～ sharp claws /前～ front paws /后～ hind paw

see also zhǎo

爪尖儿 zhuǎjiānr pig's trotters; pettitoes

爪儿 zhuǎr 〈口语〉❶ paw of a small animal: 狗～ dog's paws ❷ foot of a utensil: 这种锅有三个～。The pan stands on three feet.

爪式起重机 zhuǎshì qǐzhòngjī claw crane

爪子 zhuǎzi 〈口语〉claw; paw; talon: 鸡～ chicken's feet /鹰～ eagle's talons /他差点儿被熊～抓着。He barely escaped being pawed by the bear. /猫在用～撕扯书呢。The cat is tearing the book with its claws.

zhuāi

拽[1]

zhuāi 〈方言〉fling; cast; throw; hurl: 把球～给我。Fling me the ball. *or* Throw the ball to me. /他把客人～在一边儿不理了。He left the guest out in the cold.

拽[2]

zhuāi 〈方言〉injured in the arm: 他摔～了。He had a fall and injured his arm.

see also zhuài

zhuǎi

转(轉)

zhuǎi lard one's speech with literary allusions;

Z

use flowery language：他好～一番。He used a lot of ornate phrases in his speech.
see also zhuǎn；zhuàn
转文 zhuǎiwén also zhuǎnwén talk like a book
跩 zhuǎi 〈方言〉waddle：鸭子一～一～地走到塘边。The ducks waddled to the pond. /那胖子一～一～地进了屋。The stout man waddled into the room.

zhuài

拽(揶) zhuài pull; drag; haul：～他的袖子 pull him by the sleeve /生拉硬～ drag sb. along against his will /硬～他去看足球赛 haul him (or drag him off) to the football match
see also zhuāi

zhuān

专(專、❶❷❸耑) zhuān ❶ concentrate on; specialize in：～挑别人毛病 be fond of nitpicking /他的毛病是心不～。The trouble with him is that he can't concentrate. /痢特灵～治痢疾。Furazolidone is a specific for dysentery. ❷ expert：一～多能 be expert in one subject and good at many; be a versatile person as well as a specialist /又红又～ be both red and expert; be both politically conscious and professionally competent ❸ have a monopoly of; monopolize：这部计算机由他～用。This computer is exclusively for him. ❹ (Zhuān) a surname
专案 zhuān'àn special case for investigation; major case：～组 special group for the examination of a case; group for handling a special case /～人员 persons engaged in investigating a special case /～材料 material relating to a special case; dossier /～处理 to be handled as a special case /他的问题已立了～。His problem has been made a special case for investigation.
专差 zhuānchāi ❶ special mission or errand：他～去昆明进行调查。He went to Kunming on a special mission of inquiry. ❷ person sent on a special mission
专长 zhuāncháng special skill; specialized knowledge; speciality; expertise：发挥各人～ give full play to everyone's professional knowledge or skill /学有～ have sound scholarship; be expert in a special field of study /儿童文学是她的～。Children's literature is her speciality.
专场 zhuānchǎng ❶ special performance; show intended for a special audience：学生～ show (intended) for students ❷ show of particular variety：杂技～ acrobatic show
专车 zhuānchē ❶ special purpose vehicle, train or car：夏季北京至秦皇岛的旅游往返～ special summer tourist train between Beijing and Qinhuangdao ❷ car exclusively used by a person or an organization：这是部长的～。This is the car for the minister only.
专诚 zhuānchéng for a special purpose; specially：～拜访 pay a special call on (or visit to) sb. /～求教 visit sb. specially for counsel
专程 zhuānchéng special trip：外交部副部长～赴沈阳迎接贵宾。The Vice-Minister of Foreign Affairs made a special trip to Shenyang to welcome the distinguished guests.
专宠 zhuānchǒng monopolize the favour (of a ruler, leader. etc.)
专电 zhuāndiàn special dispatch or telegram：新华社记者由东京发来的～ special dispatch sent by the Xinhua correspondent from Tokyo
专断 zhuānduàn make arbitrary decisions; act peremptorily：他～的行动引起同事们的反感。His arbitrary actions caused great resentment among his colleagues.
专访 zhuānfǎng ❶ special interview：对这些科学家，我做过多次～。I've had many special interviews with these scientists. ❷ special report on or coverage of such an interview：这篇～写得很好。This special report is well-written.
专攻 zhuāngōng specialize in; be a specialist of：他～声乐。He specializes in vocal music.
专柜 zhuānguì counter (in a store) where commodities of a particular kind or products of a particular locality are sold：医药～ medicine counter /杭州丝绸～ counter for silk made in Hangzhou
专号 zhuānhào special issue (of a periodical)：美国研究～ special issue on American studies
专横 zhuānhèng tyrannical; imperious; peremptory; domineering：～跋扈 arrogant and despotic /他对下级～霸道。He domineers (or rides roughshod) over his subordinates.
专机 zhuānjī ❶ special plane; specially chartered plane：乘～赴英 fly to Britain by special plane ❷ plane for a particular person：总统～ special plane for the president; presidential plane
专集 zhuānjí ❶ collection of works by one author; collected works：老舍～ collected works of Lao She ❷ anthology; collection：英国文学～ anthology of English literature /国际评论～ collection of papers on international affairs
专辑 zhuānjí album：音乐～ music album /她已经出了五张个人～了。She has already published five albums.
专家 zhuānjiā expert; specialist：儿科～ specialist in children's diseases; paediatrist; paediatrician /农作物～ crop expert /法律～ legal expert /～意见 expert opinion /～小组 panel of experts; expert group /～会议 conference of experts /～治国 technocracy /～治国论者 technocrat
专家系统 zhuānjiā xìtǒng 〈计算机〉expert system
专刊 zhuānkān ❶ special issue or column：《光明日报》的"文学遗产"～ *Guangming Daily*'s Literary Legacy column ❷ monograph：美学研究～ monograph on aesthetics
专科 zhuānkē ❶ speciality; special field of study：～词典 dictionary for a special field ❷ college for professional training; vocational training school：～毕业 graduate from a professional training college
专科学校 zhuānkē xuéxiào college for professional training; professional or vocational training school
专科医生 zhuānkē yīshēng (medical) specialist
专控 zhuānkòng (commodities) specially controlled by the state：～商品 controlled commodities
专款 zhuānkuǎn fund earmarked for a special purpose; special fund：为灾区拨出～ appropriate special funds for a disaster area /科研～ scientific research funds; funds earmarked for scientific research /～专用 fund for specified purpose only
专栏 zhuānlán special column："经济研究"～ "Economic Studies" column /开辟一个社交新闻～ open a society column
专栏作家 zhuānlán zuòjiā columnist
专力 zhuānlì concentrate (on doing sth.)：你可以～解决这个技术难题，其他事情我们包了。You can concentrate on solving this difficult technical problem and leave everything else to us.
专利 zhuānlì patent：申请～ apply for a patent /获得一项发明～ get (or obtain) a patent for an invention /拥有一项～ hold a patent /～制造的照相机 cameras made under patent /～保护 patent protection /～技术 patented technology /～产品 patented product
专利法 zhuānlìfǎ patent law
专利局 zhuānlìjú patent office
专利品 zhuānlìpǐn patent; patented article
专利权 zhuānlìquán patent right; patent
专利人 zhuānlìrén patentee
专利证 zhuānlìzhèng letters patent; *literse patentes*
专列 zhuānliè (short for 专用列车) special train：国家元首～ special train for the head of state /春运～ additional train service during the Spring Festival period
专卖 zhuānmài monopoly; exclusive control of the trade in some commodity
专卖店 zhuānmàidiàn exclusive agency; franchised store：福特汽车～ exclusive agency for the sale of Ford cars
专卖权 zhuānmàiquán exclusive right to sell sth.：政府拥有烟草～。The government holds a monopoly on tobacco.
专美 zhuānměi 〈书面〉enjoy a good reputation alone; enjoy high prestige exclusively (in a profession, field of study, etc.)：青年演员努力提高演技，不让上代艺人～于前。Young actors and actresses strive to improve their acting (or thespian skill) so as to be on a par with the older generation.
专门 zhuānmén ❶ special; specialized：～研究人类学 specialize in anthropology /～为老年人提供的保健食品 health food specially provided for old people /～人材 people with professional skill; professional talent /～知识 specialized knowledge; expertise; technical know-how /～机构 special (or specialized) agency; special organ /～术语 technical terms; nomenclature /这课本是～为初学者编写的。The textbook is intended for beginners. ❷ 〈方言〉frequently; habitually：～会讲风凉话 be given to making sarcastic comments /他～爱打听小道消息。He is a habitual inquirer after grapevine news.

专门家 zhuānménjiā expert; specialist
专门人民法院 zhuānmén rénmín fǎyuàn special people's court
专门人民检察院 zhuānmén rénmín jiǎncháyuàn special people's procuratorate
专名 zhuānmíng 〈语言〉proper noun
专名号 zhuānmínghào underline, used under names of people, places, organizations, etc.
专区 zhuānqū (changed to 地区 in 1975) subprovincial administrative region; prefecture:承德～ Chengde Prefecture
专权 zhuānquán monopolize power:～误国。Monopoly of power would ruin the country.
专人 zhuānrén person specially assigned for a task or job:材料是～送去的。The materials were sent by a special messenger./已有～负责公关工作。Someone has been put in charge of public relations.
专任 zhuānrèn full-time; regular:～工会主席 full-time chairman of the trade union
专擅 zhuānshàn 〈书面〉usurp authority; act presumptuously:独行～ act without authorization from one's superior; act arbitrarily
专神 zhuānshén be engrossed; focus one's attention:～贯注 be wholly absorbed (*or* immersed) in
专史 zhuānshǐ specialized history such as that of philosophy, literature, economics, etc.
专使 zhuānshǐ special envoy
专书 zhuānshū book on a special subject; monograph:这是一本研究我国货币沿革的～。This is a monograph on the development of the currency in our country.
专属 zhuānshǔ exclusive:～经济区 exclusive economic zone /～渔区 exclusive fishing zone /～渔权 exclusive fishery right /～区 exclusive area /～权利 exclusive right /～主权 exclusive sovereignty /～职权 exclusive competence /～权利要求 exclusive claim /～管辖权 exclusive jurisdiction
专署 zhuānshǔ (short for 专员公署) prefectural commissioner's office
专题 zhuāntí special subject or topic:～报告 report (*or* lecture) on a special topic (*or* subject) /～报道 special coverage /～讨论 seminar /～研究 monographic study /～著作 monograph; treatise /～纲要 schematic outline /～性世界会议 *ad hoc* world conference
专文 zhuānwén article on a special subject; monograph:本报就环保问题发了几篇～。The newspaper carried several articles on environmental protection.
专席 zhuānxí seat provided specially for sb.:来宾～ seats for visitors /车上有孕妇～。In the bus there are seats reserved for the pregnant.
专线 zhuānxiàn ❶ special railway line ❷ special telephone line; private line; leased line
专项 zhuānxiàng special item:～训练 specialized training; training in a special field /～审计制度 separate item auditing system
专心 zhuānxīn concentrate on; be engrossed:～地看着黑板 look at the blackboard attentively /运动员们练得非常～。The athletes trained with great concentration. /你应当～于工作。You should devote your attention to your work. /她读书太～了,连敲门声都没听见。She was so absorbed in reading (*or* wrapped up in her book) that she didn't hear the knock on the door.
专心致志 zhuānxīn-zhìzhì single-minded; completely absorbed:～于中国哲学研究 devote oneself to the study of Chinese philosophy /～地攻读博士学位 work with great concentration for a doctorate
专修 zhuānxiū specialize in:～生物学 specialize in biology /财会～班 special finance and accounting class
专修科 zhuānxiūkē special (training) course
专业 zhuānyè ❶ special field of study; specialized subject; speciality; discipline:～设置 specialities offered /你准备报考那所大学的什么～? Which programme of that university are you planning to apply for? ❷ specialized trade or profession; special vocation or line:～技术 professional skill /～知识 professional (*or* vocational) knowledge /～教育 vocational education /～队伍 professional contingent /～人员 personnel in a specific field; professional /城市青年～人员 Yuppie (Young Urban Professional) /～承包 responsibility contracts on specialities ❸ professional:～作家 writer by profession
专业村 zhuānyècūn specialized village; village engaged in one particular undertaking
专业队 zhuānyèduì specialized working team
专业户 zhuānyèhù household specialized in a particular economic undertaking; specialized household
专业化 zhuānyèhuà specialize:～程度 level of specialization
专业课 zhuānyèkè specialized course
专业学校 zhuānyè xuéxiào vocational school
专一 zhuānyī concentrating on one aim or purpose; single-minded:心思～(give sth.) undivided attention; (with) concentrated attention /爱情～ be constant (*or* faithful) in love /～于史论著述 be wholeheartedly engaged in writing books on history
专意 zhuānyì for a special purpose; specially; particularly:我们～访问了几个厂子,了解技术革新的情况。We visited a few factories specially to find out their technical innovations.
专用 zhuānyòng special purpose; special:～贷款 loan for a stipulated (*or* special) purpose /～磨床 special purpose grinder /～计算机 special purpose computer /～联动机床 special power-pack set machine /～设备 special hardware / ～列车 special train
专用网 zhuānyòngwǎng private network
专有 zhuānyǒu belonging to sb. or sth. alone; not shared with others; exclusive:～权 exclusive right /～名词 proper noun
专员 zhuānyuán ❶ prefectural commissioner ❷ assistant director; (administrative) commissioner; attaché:使馆文化～ cultural attaché of an embassy /联合国难民事务高级～ UN High Commissioner for Refugees /高级～公署 high commission; high commissioner's office (of British Commonwealth countries) ❸ person specially assigned for a job
专员公署 zhuānyuán gōngshǔ *also* "专署" prefectural commissioner's office
专约 zhuānyuē convention
专责 zhuānzé specific responsibility:工作人员各有～。Each employee is charged with specific responsibilities. /此事由你负～。You are in sole charge of the matter.
专政 zhuānzhèng dictatorship:对…实行～ exercise dictatorship over /实行人民民主～的国家 country which practises the people's democratic dictatorship /法西斯～ fascist dictatorship /～对象 object (*or* target) of dictatorship /～工具 instrument of dictatorship
专政机关 zhuānzhèng jīguān organ of dictatorship
专职 zhuānzhí ❶ sole duty; specific responsibility ❷ full-time:～教员 full-time teacher /～人员 full-time personnel
专指 zhuānzhǐ with special reference to
专制 zhuānzhì ❶ autocracy ❷ autocratic; despotic:封建君主～制度 absolute feudal monarchy /君主～ autocratic (*or* absolute) monarchy /～帝王 autocratic monarch; despotic emperor /～君主 autocrat /家长～ arbitrary rule by a patriarch
专制政府 zhuānzhì zhèngfǔ autocratic government
专制政体 zhuānzhì zhèngtǐ autocracy
专制主义 zhuānzhìzhǔyì despotism:～者 despot; autocrat
专挚 zhuānzhì sincere and single-minded
专注 zhuānzhù focus on; be absorbed in; devote oneself to:神情～ with concentrated attention /他～于学习。He is thoroughly engrossed in his studies.
专著 zhuānzhù monograph; treatise:他最近出版了一部形式逻辑学～。He recently published a monograph on formal logic.

砖(塼、甎、塼)

zhuān ❶ brick:青～ blue brick /耐火～ fire (*or* refractory) bricks /烧～ bake (*or* make, *or* burn) brick /砌～ lay bricks /窑洞内壁都砌上了～。The inside of the cave was bricked over. ❷ brick-like thing:冰～ brick of ice cream /煤～ brick-shaped briquet
砖茶 zhuānchá *also* "茶砖" brick tea
砖厂 zhuānchǎng brickfield; brickyard:～工人 brickmaker
砖雕 zhuāndiāo brick carving; brick engraving
砖缝 zhuānfèng brickwork joint
砖工 zhuāngōng 〈建筑〉bricklaying; brickwork; brick setting
砖红壤 zhuānhóngrǎng laterite
砖红壤性土 zhuānhóngrǎngxìngtǔ *also* "砖红土" lateritic soil; laterite
砖墁地 zhuānmàndì brick-paved floor or ground
砖模 zhuānmú brick die
砖木结构 zhuānmù jiégòu post and panel structure
砖坯 zhuānpī unfired brick
砖铺路面 zhuānpū lùmiàn brick paving
砖石工程 zhuānshí gōngchéng masonry
砖石结构 zhuānshí jiégòu 〈建筑〉brick construction; brick ma-

sonry construction
砖头 zhuāntóu fragment of a brick：～瓦块 fragments of bricks and tiles；rubble；debris
砖头 zhuāntou 〈方言〉brick
砖砚 zhuānyàn inkslab made of ancient brick
砖窑 zhuānyáo brickkiln

肫(膞) zhuān 〈方言〉gizzard：鸡～ chicken's gizzard

颛 zhuān 〈书面〉❶ ignorant；benighted ❷ see "专" zhuān
颛蒙 zhuānméng 〈书面〉benighted：～不化 unenlightened
颛孙 Zhuānsūn a surname
颛顼 Zhuānxū name of a legendary emperor of ancient times

zhuǎn

转(轉) zhuǎn ❶ turn；shift；change；transform：向右～ turn to the right；right face；right turn /逆～ take a turn for the worse；become worse；deteriorate /好～ take a turn for the better；improve /星移斗～ change in the positions of the stars；passage of time /～怒为喜 one's anger gives way to delight /～亏为盈 turn loss into gain；show a turn from loss to profit /我们好不容易才使比赛～败为胜。We just managed to pull the game out of the fire. /风向由北～西。The wind changed (round) from northerly (*or* north) to westerly (*or* west). /天气由雨～阴。The weather changed from rain to overcast. /如果同样的事发生在你身上，你就会～喜为忧了。If the same thing ever happens to you, you'll laugh on the other side of your face. /她～过头来和我打招呼。She greeted me over her shoulder. ❷ pass on；forward；transfer：请把包裹～给他。Please pass the parcel on to him. /我负责将这本书～寄到新地址。I'll forward the book to the new address. /到达汽车终点站后，乘客们～乘了渡轮。The passengers were transferred to a ferry at the bus terminus.
see also zhuǎi；zhuàn
转氨酶 zhuǎn'ānméi transaminase；transaminase enzymes；aminotransferase enzymes：谷丙～ glutamic-pyruvic transaminase (*or* GPT)
转包 zhuǎnbāo contract out to sb. else the contracted project one has undertaken；subcontract：他们是从另一家工程队～这项工程的。They have sub-contracted this project from another construction brigade.
转背 zhuǎnbèi 〈方言〉turn；turn round；face about：他一声不吭，～就走了。He turned and left without a word.
转变 zhuǎnbiàn change；transform：～思想 change one's ideology；transform one's thinking /～态度 change one's attitude (*or* outlook) /从落后的农业国～为先进的工业国 change from a backward agricultural country into an advanced industrial country /虽经多次教育，但他仍无～。He remained unrepentant in spite of repeated persuasion. /发电机将机械能～为电能。A dynamo transforms mechanical energy into electricity.
转播 zhuǎnbō (of radio or TV broadcast) relay：各地方台都～中央电视台的"新闻联播"节目。All local TV stations relay the "National Network" news broadcast from the Central TV Station. /中央电视台将从首都体育馆对这场篮球赛作实况～。The CCTV will televise the basketball match live from the Capital Gymnasium.
转播车 zhuǎnbōchē broadcast van；OB (outside broadcast) van
转播台 zhuǎnbōtái relay station
转侧 zhuǎncè 〈书面〉❶ move to another place；shift：～看花 move to the other side to look at the flowers ❷ toss about (in bed)；toss and turn：～达旦 lie tossing and turning all night /他在床上～许久，方才入睡。He tossed about in bed for quite a while before falling asleep.
转产 zhuǎnchǎn (of an enterprise, etc.) discontinue the production of its original commodities and divert to that of other commodities；convert production from one commodity to another；change the line of production
转车 zhuǎnchē change buses or trains；transfer to another bus or train：在北京～去沈阳 transfer at Beijing to a train going to Shenyang；change trains at Beijing for Shenyang
转储 zhuǎnchǔ 〈自控〉dump：磁鼓信息～ drum dump /快速～ snapshot dump /信息～ change dump
转船 zhuǎnchuán change to another ship；transship：我们在青岛～去上海。We changed to another ship at Qingdao for Shanghai.
转达 zhuǎndá pass on；convey；forward；communicate：～问候 give sb. one's regards /一定要把这个口信～给他。Be sure to pass on (*or* convey) the message to him. /我已把你的意见～给有关方面。I have told the competent authorities (*or* the parties concerned) about your suggestions.
转道 zhuǎndào go by way of；make a detour；via：～香港飞往台北 fly to Taibei via (*or* by way of) Hong Kong
转递 zhuǎndì *see* "转交"
转调 zhuǎndiào ❶ *also* "变调" biàndiào；"移调" yídiào 〈音乐〉 modulation：音乐由这里从 E 调转到 G 调。Here the music modulates from E to G. ❷ transfer from one unit to another
转动 zhuǎndòng turn；move；rotate；turn round and round：～手臂 flail one's arm /～膝关节 flex one's knee joint /～眼珠 goggle (*or* roll, *or* rotate) one's eyes /她～了两下身子，觉得比先前好点儿。She limbered herself up and felt a bit better than before.
see also zhuàndòng
转舵 zhuǎnduò turn the steering wheel or handle：转左(右)舵！Port (Starboard) the helm! /～迎风！Luff the helm! *or* Up with the helm! /～背风！Down with the helm! /他看风向不对，马上～。Finding the wind was blowing in the wrong direction, he trimmed his sails accordingly.
转发 zhuǎnfā ❶ transmit；dispatch：把中央的文件～到下属各单位 disseminate the document of the Party Central Committee to all the subordinate organizations ❷ *see* "转载" ❸ relay；transmit：～通信卫星电视信号 transmit the television signal received from the communication satellite
转发器 zhuǎnfāqì transponder
转发中心 zhǎnfā zhōngxīn head-end
转法 zhuǎnfǎ 〈军事〉facing
转干 zhuǎngàn (of a worker) become a cadre or public servant
转告 zhuǎngào pass on a message；convey；transmit：我有话要～你。I have a message for you. /你们的决定他已～我了。He's told me your decision.
转关系 zhuǎn guānxi transfer the registration (of one's Party or League membership from one unit to another, of one's permanent residence from one place to another, etc.)：转户口关系 report to the local authorities for change of domicile /转党的组织关系 transfer the registration of one's Party membership from one unit to another
转轨 zhuǎnguǐ ❶ change tracks ❷ change (the existing structure, etc.)：从劳动密集型向技术密集型～ change from labour-intensive to technology-intensive production /～经济 economy in transition；transition economy
转行 zhuǎnháng ❶ change one's profession or occupation：当了几年中学教员，又～去经商。He became a businessman after teaching in a middle school for a few years. ❷ change from one line to the next (in writing, typing, printing, etc.)
转化 zhuǎnhuà change；turn；transform：互相～ transform oneself into one's opposite /向有利的方面～ change for the better；take a favourable turn /把坏事～为好事 turn bad things (*or* bane) into good things (*or* boon)
转圜 zhuǎnhuán ❶ save or retrieve (a situation)：事情已难以～。Little can be done to save the situation. ❷ mediate；reconcile：从中～ mediate among the various parties
转换 zhuǎnhuàn ❶ switch；change；transform：～频道 switch (over) to another channel /～一个角度来研究这问题 examine the matter from a different (*or* another) angle /别～话题。Don't change the subject of conversation (*or* switch the talk to another subject). ❷〈电工〉cut-over：～电路 switching circuit /～器 electropeter ❸〈自控〉conversion：数字模拟～ digital-analog conversion /～程序 conversion program /～器 converter
转换开关 zhuǎnhuàn kāiguān switch；switch unit；transfer lever；transfer switch；changeover switch
转换语法 zhuǎnhuàn yǔfǎ 〈语言〉transformational grammar
转会 zhuǎnhuì 〈体育〉transfer to another (sports) club
转祸为福 zhuǎnhuòwéifú turn misfortune into good fortune；change from adversity to prosperity
转机 zhuǎnjī turn for the better；favourable turn：事情有了～。The situation has taken a turn for the better. /医生说妈的病情难有～。The doctor said that Mother's condition was not likely to improve. /家庭经济状况有～。The family is getting better-off.

转基因 zhuǎnjīyīn transgenic: ~山羊 transgenic goat

转基因食品 zhuǎnjīyīn shípǐn genetically-engineered plant and food; genetically-altered food; Frankenfood

转嫁 zhuǎnjià ❶ (of a woman) marry again; remarry ❷ shift; transfer: ~罪责 lay the blame upon sb. else / ~经济危机 shift an economic crisis on to others / 你们不能把公司的经济损失~给用户。You mustn't let consumers bear the financial losses of your company.

转交 zhuǎnjiāo pass on; send (in) care of; transmit: 我受托把这本书~给你。I was asked to deliver this book to you. / 来信请由王石教授~。Please address my mail care of (*or* c/o) Professor Wang Shi.

转角 zhuǎnjiǎo street corner; corner: 我在大街的~处等你。I shall wait for you at the street corner.

转接 zhuǎnjiē 〈通信〉 transfer; transit; switch through; switch: ~电路 built-up circuit; switching network / ~电键 transfer key / ~交换台 through (*or* transfer) switchboard; transfer board / ~器 adapter; switchboard

转借 zhuǎnjiè ❶ lend a borrowed thing: 你那本书我又~给他了。I've lent him the book I borrowed from you. ❷ let other people use one's ID card, etc.: 借书证不得~他人。The library card is not transferable.

转矩 zhuǎnjù torque; torque moment; torsion: ~电动机 torque motor

转剧 zhuǎnjù aggravate; intensify: 前沿战斗~。A fiercer battle is raging at the front. *or* The fighting is getting more intense at the front. / 病势~。The patient's condition deteriorated (*or* worsened).

转科 zhuǎnkē ❶ (of a patient) change from one department of a hospital to another for treatment ❷ (of a college student) transfer from one department to another; change one's major

转口 zhuǎnkǒu ❶ transit: ~货物 transit goods / ~税 transit duty (*or* dues) / 这批货物在香港~。Hong Kong is the entrepôt for these goods. ❷ 〈方言〉 withdraw or modify one's previous remarks; correct oneself; change one's tone: 你自己说的话, 怎么可以~不认账? How can you go back on your word?

转口港 zhuǎnkǒugǎng transit port; entrepôt

转口贸易 zhuǎnkǒu màoyì entrepôt trade; transit trade; switch trade

转亏为盈 zhuǎnkuīwéiyíng show a turn from loss to profit

转隶 zhuǎnlì 〈军事〉 (during a battle) transfer troops or arms from one unit to another

转脸 zhuǎnliǎn ❶ turn one's face ❷ in the twinkling of an eye; in no time; in an instant: 这孩子~就没影儿了。The child disappeared in a wink. / 他是个~不认人的人。He is the kind of person who'll turn against you in a flash.

转捩点 zhuǎnlièdiǎn turning point

转录 zhuǎnlù make a recording of another recording; re-record; copy; 〈信息〉 dump: ~器 transcriber / 纸带~器 paper tape transcriber / 卡片~器 card transcriber / 我要将这首歌~到你们的带子上。I shall copy this song onto your tapes.

转卖 zhuǎnmài resell: 这房子不~。The house is not for resale.

转年 zhuǎnnián ❶ coming of a new year: 时间过得真快, 眼看又~了。Time flies and a new year is coming soon. ❷ 〈方言〉 following year: 他的病~春天才好利落。He did not fully recover from his illness until the following spring. ❸ 〈方言〉 coming year; next year: 这件事咱们~再说。Let's discuss the matter next year.

转念 zhuǎnniàn think better of; change one's opinion after rethinking: 她刚想与他吵, 但一~, 又忍住了。She was about to quarrel with him when she thought better of it. / 他刚想告诉她这一秘密, 但一~, 觉得还是谨慎为好。He was just going to tell her the secret when, on second thoughts, he felt it better to remain cautious.

转蓬 zhuǎnpéng ❶ sway of bitter fleabane in the wind ❷ 〈比喻〉 of uncertain whereabouts; wandering; adrift: 此身如~, 漂泊不定。I am wandering all the time, finding no shelter anywhere.

转染 zhuǎnrǎn 〈医学〉 transfection

转让 zhuǎnràng transfer the ownership of; transfer; make over: 技术~ technology transfer; technological transaction / 股票~ stock transfer / ~收款权 factoring / 可~票据 transferable instrument / 可~股票 transferable shares / 可~信用证 transferable (*or* assignable) letter of credit / 把房子~给孤儿院 make over the house to the orphanage

转让人 zhuǎnràngrén 〈法律〉 assignor

转入 zhuǎnrù change over to; switch to; shift to: ~地下 go underground / ~正常 back to normal / 由战略防御~战略进攻 switch (*or* shift) from the strategic defensive to the strategic offensive / 现在~下一项议程。Let's proceed (*or* move on) to the next item on the agenda now. / 我们别扯题外话了, 还是~正题吧。Let's cut short this digression and get down to brass tacks.

转身 zhuǎnshēn ❶ (of a person) turn; turn round; face about: 他~离开了屋子。He turned and left the room. ❷ in no time; in a wink: 说好了的事他~就不认账。He can break his promise in the twinkling of an eye.

转生 zhuǎnshēng *also* "转世" 〈佛教〉 reincarnation; transmigration

转世 zhuǎnshì 〈佛教〉 ❶ *also* "转生" reincarnation; transmigration ❷ (in Tibetan Buddhism) system of succession to grand lama, either the Dalai or the Panchen, by direct divine reincarnation (upon the death of either, his spirit is believed to pass into the body of some infant just born, and an exacting series of tests and divinations is needed to determine the right boy, who is then carefully trained for the post)

转世灵童 zhuǎnshì língtóng (in Tibetan Buddhism) reincarnated soul boy; soul boy: 班禅~寻访小组 group for locating the reincarnated soul boy of the Panchen Lama

转手 zhuǎnshǒu ❶ do sth. through a third party; (ask sb. to) pass on: 这张收据是你让我~交给他的。You told me to give him this receipt. ❷ resell: 这批货物他一~就赚了一万多。He resold the goods at a profit of over 10,000 *yuan*.

转述 zhuǎnshù tell or report sth. as told by another; retell: 他向我~了你们的意见。He told me your suggestion.

转瞬 zhuǎnshùn in the twinkling of an eye; in a twinkle; in a flash: ~之间, 暴风雨骤起。In the bat of an eye, a heavy storm came down upon us. / 春节~就要到了。The Spring Festival is coming soon. *or* The Spring Festival will be here before you know it.

转送 zhuǎnsòng ❶ *see* "转交" ❷ make a present of what one has received as a gift: 这是小王送我的, 现在~给你。This is a present from Xiao Wang. Now I'd like to give it to you.

转肽酶 zhuǎntàiméi 〈生化〉 transpeptidase

转糖酶 zhuǎntángméi 〈生化〉 transglycosylase

转体 zhuǎntǐ 〈体育〉 turn; twist: ~跳 turning leap / ~跳水 twist dive / ~180度 make a 180-degree turn / ~三周 triple turn

转天 zhuǎntiān 〈方言〉 ❶ following day: 头天许下的诺言, ~就兑现。The promise made on the first day was carried out on the second. ❷ some other day; another day: 今天太忙, ~再去看他。As I am too busy today, I shall go to see him some other time.

转头 zhuǎntóu ❶ turn round; turn about; make a U-turn: ~望望四周 turn to look around / 路太窄, 卡车没法儿~。The road is too narrow for the truck to turn around. ❷ repent one's error; be repentant: 你再不~, 不会有好结果的。You'll come to no good end if you don't mend your ways.

转托 zhuǎntuō entrust sb. with a task which one is asked by others to perform: 我已~大姐替你办这件事。I've asked my eldest sister to do it for you.

转弯 zhuǎnwān ❶ make a turn; turn: 去动物园应向右~。You must turn right to get to the zoo. / 银行一~就到。The bank is just round the corner. ❷ speak in a roundabout way: 他脾气直, 说话从来不~儿。He is straightforward and always speaks his mind plainly. ❸ change one's view; change one's stand: 给他们~的时间 give them enough time to change their minds / 对他要有耐心, 不能指望他一下子就能转过弯子来。Be patient with him; you can't expect to bring him round to your views right away.

转弯抹角 zhuǎnwān-mòjiǎo ❶ be full of twists and turns; zigzag: 这条路~的, 可真难走。The road is full of twists and turns, which makes heavy going. / 汽车~地开进了这个小村子。The bus took a tortuous route before getting into the small village. ❷ beat about the bush; speak without coming to the main point: 有话就痛快说, 别~的。Say what you want to, and don't beat about the bush. / 他们是直说直办, 没有~做文章。They were straightforward in all dealings and avoided circuitous rhetoric.

转弯子 zhuǎn wānzi *see* "转弯❷"

see also zhuàn wānzi

转危为安 zhuǎnwēiwéi'ān turn danger into safety; pull through a crisis: 祖母上周病势严重, 但现在已~。Grandmother was very ill last week but she has turned the corner now. / 他是个幸运儿, 似乎总是能~。He is a lucky fellow; he always seems to land on his feet. / 该国

Z

的经济形势已～。The country has tided over the economic crisis.
转文 zhuǎnwén also zhuǎiwén lard one's speech with literary allusions; talk like a book
转徙 zhuǎnxǐ move from place to place; wander:流离～ be a vagrant
转系 zhuǎnxì (of a college student) transfer to another department
转向 zhuǎnxiàng ❶ change direction:～装置 steering gear /风～了。The wind changed its direction. ❷ change one's political orientation
see also zhuànxiàng
转向架 zhuǎnxiàngjià 〈铁路〉bogie
转学 zhuǎnxué (of a student) transfer to another school:～生 transfer student
转眼 zhuǎnyǎn in the twinkling of an eye; in an instant; in a trice; soon:才一～他就跑得没影儿了。He ran out of sight (or disappeared) in a trice. /～就是冬天了。Winter is coming on (or fast approaching). /～三年过去了。Three years elapsed before we were aware of it (or before we knew it).
转业 zhuǎnyè (of military personnel) be transferred to civilian work:～军人 military person transferred to civilian work
转移 zhuǎnyí ❶ shift; transfer; divert; evacuate:～视线 distract (or divert) sb.'s attention /～重点 shift focus on to sth. or sb. else /把伤病员～到后方 evacuate the sick and wounded to the rear /主权～ transfer of sovereignty /债务～ debt transference /在洪水到来之前把粮食～到安全地点。The grain had been moved to a safe place before the flood came. ❷ change; shift; transform:～风俗 change the customs /～话题 shift the conversation to other topics; guide the conversation onto other subjects; switch the conversation into another line /他的兴趣～了。His interests have changed. /矛盾是客观存在,不以人的意志为～的。Contradictions are an objective reality independent of man's will. ❸〈医学〉metastasis:癌～ metastasis of a carcinoma /～癌 metastatic carcinoma /～瘤 metastases /～灶 metastases ❹〈生化〉transfer:～酶 transferase
转移性触痛 zhuǎnyíxìng chùtòng 〈医学〉shifting tenderness
转义 zhuǎnyì 〈语言〉transferred meaning; figurative sense
转译 zhuǎnyì translate sth. (into a third language) from a translated version:这本小说原文是西班牙文,中译本是根据英译本～的。The novel was originally in Spanish, but the Chinese version was based on its English translation.
转引 zhuǎnyǐn quote from a secondary source:～自《人民日报》新年社论 quoted from a quotation in the New Year editorial of the *People's Daily*
转院 zhuǎnyuàn (of a patient) transfer to another hospital
转运 zhuǎnyùn ❶ have a turn or change of luck; luck turns in one's favour:他盼望着～的一天。He is longing for (or looking forward to) the day when luck turns in his favour. ❷ transfer; transport; forward; transship:～公司 transport company; forwarding agency /～站 transfer post; staging post /～营 transit camp /～候机处 transit
转运起重机 zhuǎnyùn qǐzhòngjī 〈机械〉transport crane
转韵 zhuǎnyùn also "换韵" huànyùn (of traditional poetry) change in the rhyme
转载 zhuǎnzǎi reprint sth. that has been published elsewhere; reprint; carry:全文～ reprint (an article) in full /本报～此文,略有删节。The article was carried in our newspaper in a slightly abridged form.
转载 zhuǎnzài transship
转赠 zhuǎnzèng make a present of sth. given to one
转战 zhuǎnzhàn fight in one place after another:～南北 fight the enemy north and south
转账 zhuǎnzhàng transfer accounts:～支票 check only for account/～凭单 transfer document /～机构 transfer mechanism
转折 zhuǎnzhé ❶ turn or shift in the course of events:戏剧性的～ dramatic turn /海湾局势出现了新的～。The situation in the gulf region took a new turn. ❷ transition (of an essay)
转折点 zhuǎnzhédiǎn also "转捩点" turning point:1942 年是抗日战争的一个重要～。The year 1942 marked an important turning point in the War of Resistance Against Japanese Aggression.
转辙器 zhuǎnzhéqì 〈铁路〉switch
转正 zhuǎnzhèng ❶ (of a probationary member of the Communist Party of China) become a full member after completion of the probationary period ❷ (of a temporary worker) be put on the regular payroll; become a regular worker
转注 zhuǎnzhù 〈语言〉mutually explanatory or synonymous characters such as 老 (old age) and 考 (long life, aged) — one of the six categories of Chinese characters (六书)
转租 zhuǎnzū sublet; sublease:她暑假把房子～给了别人。She sublet her house during the summer vacation.

zhuàn

转(轉) zhuàn ❶ rotate; revolve; spin:地球既自～又绕太阳公～。The earth revolves round the sun as well as on its own axis. /陀螺～得飞快。The top is spinning very fast. ❷ turn round; move about:他绕着湖～了两圈。He walked twice round the lake. /出去～～好吗? Do you feel like a stroll? /人们的眼睛跟着这孩子～。All the attention gyrated around the child. ❸〈量词〉revolution:这台发动机每分钟六千～。The engine turns over at 6,000 revolutions per minute (or at 6,000 rpm).
see also zhuǎi, zhuǎn
转笔刀 zhuànbǐdāo pencil sharpener
转臂 zhuànbì 〈机械〉swiveling jib; swivel jib:～起重机 derrick crane; jibcrane /～式挖沟机 jib-type ditcher /～式装载机 jib-type loader; rotating loader
转碟 zhuàndié 〈杂技〉plate-spinning
转动 zhuàndòng turn; revolve; rotate; spin:绕轴心～ revolve round the axle centre /顺时针方向～ clockwise rotation /在锁眼中～钥匙 turn the key in the lock /轮子～灵不灵? Does the wheel turn freely? /水龙头转不动。The tap's stuck. or The tap is stiff; it won't turn on.
see also zhuǎndòng
转动惯量 zhuàndòng guànliàng moment of inertia
转动能量 zhuàndòng néngliàng rotational energy
转缸式发动机 zhuàngāngshì fādòngjī 〈机械〉rotary engine; revolving cylinder engine
转鼓 zhuàngǔ 〈建筑〉rotary drum; revolving drum:～搅拌机 rotary-drum mixer; rotary speed mixer
转筋 zhuànjīn 〈中医〉spasm of the gastrocnemius muscles; cramp:那个游泳的人腿～了。The swimmer was seized with a cramp in his leg.
转经筒 zhuànjīngtǒng prayer wheel
转铃 zhuànlíng a kind of bicycle bell which spins as it rings
转炉 zhuànlú 〈冶金〉converter:碱性～ converter of basic lining /酸性～ converter of acid lining; Bessemer converter /酸性～钢 Bessemer; Bessemer pig; Bessemer steel /～钢 converter steel; pneumatic steel /～铜 converter copper /～炼钢 converting; pneumatic steelmaking /～炼钢法 converter process; converting process
转轮手枪 zhuànlún shǒuqiāng revolver
转门 zhuànmén revolving door
转磨 zhuànmò 〈方言〉❶ move round a millstone; grind sth. on a millstone ❷〈比喻〉keep walking to and fro or around out of anxiety
转盘 zhuànpán ❶ rotary table; rotor disc; swivel; turntable:～接触器〈化工〉rotary-disc contactor; rotary-disc extactor; rotary contact disc /～压砖机 turntable press /～装煤车 rotary table charging car ❷〈体育〉giant stride;〈杂技〉disc-spinning ❸〈交通〉rotary; roundabout; (US) traffic circle
转盘式磁带存储器 zhuànpánshì cídài cúnchǔqì 〈计算机〉carousel memory
转盘速度 zhuànpán sùdù rotary speed
转圈 zhuànquān ❶ revolve; spin; rotate ❷〈方言〉speak in a roundabout way:～骂人 abuse sb. in an indirect way; attack sb. by innuendo ❸〈方言〉round; around; nearby:～儿家都跟他家沾亲。Several families in the neighbourhood are related to his.
转日莲 zhuànrìlián 〈方言〉sunflower
转数 zhuànshù 〈机械〉revolution:每分钟～为一千五 1,500 revolutions per minute (or 1,500 rpm) /额定～ rated revolution
转速 zhuànsù rotation speed; rotative velosity:砂轮～很快。The grinding wheel turns very fast.
转速比 zhuànsùbǐ drive ratio; ratio of transmission; transmission ratio; transmitting ratio
转速表 zhuànsùbiǎo revolution counter
转速计 zhuànsùjì tachometer

转塔 zhuàntǎ 〈机械〉turret: ～车床 turret lathe; capstan lathe /～六角孔冲床 turret punch press /～式铣床 turret miller /～式压力机 turret press

转台 zhuàntái ❶ revolving stage ❷ Lazy Susan ❸ revolving table: ～磨床 rotary grinding machine /～铣床 rotary milling machine

转梯 zhuàntī spiral staircase

转筒 zhuàntǒng 〈机械〉revolving drum; rotating bowl: ～混合机 rotating drum mixer /～筛 rotating (*or* rotary) cage; revolving screen; trummel /～式搅拌机 revolving drum mixer /～式洗涤器 revolving drum washer

转弯子 zhuàn wānzi beat about the bush; speak in a roundabout way: 这人说话爱～。He is not a straight forward person.
see also zhuǎn wānzi

转向 zhuànxiàng lose one's bearings; get lost; be confused: 在树林里转了向 get lost in the woods /这么一大堆数字把我搞得晕头～。In all this mass of figures I've lost my bearings. *or* I got totally confused with all this mass of figures.
see also zhuǎnxiàng

转腰子 zhuàn yāozi 〈方言〉❶ walk back and forth with worry and anxiety ❷ speak in circumlocution: 你别跟我～，我喜欢直来直去。Don't beat about the bush. I prefer outspokenness.

转窑 zhuànyáo revolving tubular kiln

转椅 zhuànyǐ ❶ swivel chair; revolving chair ❷ set of seats on a platform made to revolve by pushing, on which children ride for fun; merry-go-round

转悠 zhuànyou *also* "转游"〈口语〉❶ turn; roll; move from side to side: 他眼珠子盯着我直～。He rolled his eyes at me. ❷ take a leisurely walk; stroll; saunter: 她常上街～，浏览商店橱窗。She often goes windowshopping along the streets.

转轴 zhuànzhóu ❶ revolution axis; axle ❷〈方言〉〈比喻〉definite view: 心里有根～儿 have a definite view of one's own; know one's mind

转子 zhuànzǐ 〈机械〉rotor; rotator: ～泵 rotary pump; impeller pump /～发动机〈汽车〉Wankel engine; epitrochoidal engine; rotor motor

啭(囀) zhuàn

〈书面〉(of birds) twitter; chirp; sing: 莺啼燕～ chirp (*or* singing) of the oriole and twitter of the swallow

传(傳) zhuàn

❶ commentaries on classics: 经～ Confucian classics and commentaries on them ❷ biography: 列～ biographies (in ancient Chinese history books) /评～ critical biography /自～ autobiography /外～ anecdotal biography; unauthorized biography /别～ supplementary biography /小～ profile; biographical sketch /为他立～ write his biography ❸ novel or story written in historical style:《水浒～》*Water Margin* or *Heroes of the Marshes* /《水浒后～》*Sequel to Water Margin* or *An After Story of Water Margin*
see also chuán

传记 zhuànjì biography: ～文学 biographical literature /名人～ biographies of famous people; who's who

传略 zhuànlüè brief biography; biographical sketch:《孙中山～》*A Brief Biography of Sun Yat-sen*

传舍 zhuànshè way station; houses of a post (where formerly couriers changed horses or rested)

传赞 zhuànzàn commentaries by the author at the end of each biography of an ancient biographical history book

赚 zhuàn

❶ make a profit; gain: 他从这笔买卖中净～五千元。He netted 5,000 *yuan* from the deal. ❷ profit: 这桩买卖没～儿。This is an unprofitable deal. ❸〈方言〉earn: 舒适的生活要靠辛勤的劳动去～。A comfortable life has to be earned by hard work.
see also zuàn

赚钱 zhuànqián make money; net a profit: 他炒股票赚了大钱。He made a fortune by speculation in shares.

赚头 zhuàntou 〈口语〉profit: 卖水果比卖菜有～。Selling fruit is more profitable than selling vegetables.

赚外快 zhuàn wàikuài moonlight

瑑 zhuàn

〈书面〉jade carvings in relief

篆 zhuàn

❶ seal character (a style of Chinese calligraphy, often used on seals): 小～ ancient style of calligraphy, adopted in the Qin Dynasty for the purpose of standardizing the script ❷ write seal characters: ～额 write seal characters on the top part of a tablet ❸ seal: 接～ receive the seals; take over a government post /摄～ hold (an office) in an acting capacity

篆刻 zhuànkè seal cutting

篆书 zhuànshū seal character (a style of Chinese calligraphy, often used on seals)

篆字 zhuànzì *see* "篆书"

谍 zhuàn

see "撰" zhuàn

撰 zhuàn

write; compose: 为报刊～稿 contribute to newspapers and magazines

撰集 zhuànjí 〈书面〉write; compose; edit

撰述 zhuànshù ❶ write; compose ❷ writings; books: 他在通俗历史小说方面的～甚多。He's written many popular historical novels.

撰文 zhuànwén write an article or essay

撰写 zhuànxiě write; compose: ～书评 write a book review

撰著 zhuànzhù write; compose

馔 zhuàn

〈书面〉food: 肴～ sumptuous courses at a banquet /美～ delicious food; delicacies /盛～享宾 treat one's guests to a sumptuous dinner

zhuāng

妆(妝、粧) zhuāng

❶ make up; wear makeup: 梳～ dress one's hair and apply makeup /淡～ (wear) light makeup ❷ woman's personal adornments or ornaments: 卸～ remove one's makeup and costume ❸ trousseau; dowry

妆扮 zhuāngbàn *see* "装扮" zhuāngbàn

妆点 zhuāngdiǎn *see* "装点" zhuāngdiǎn

妆奁 zhuānglián ❶ dressing case ❷ trousseau; dowry: 具办～ prepare the dowry

妆饰 zhuāngshì adorn; embellish; dress up; deck out: 一身阔小姐的～ be dressed up like a lady

妆梳 zhuāngshū dress one's hair and apply makeup

妆台 zhuāngtái dressing table

妆新 zhuāngxīn 〈方言〉❶ arrange things (such as clothes, bedding, etc.) in a bridal chamber ❷ clothes and bedding for newlyweds

装[1](裝) zhuāng

❶ dress up; attire; deck; act: 化～ (of actors) make up; disguise oneself /女扮男～ woman in man's disguise /男扮女～ in drag /珠玉～ be decked up with jewels ❷ clothing; dress; suit; outfit: 冬～ winter outfit /男～ men's wear (*or* clothing) /学生～ students' uniform /工～裤 overalls /西～ Western-style suit /戏～ stage costume /时～ fashionable dress; latest fashion ❸ outfit for a journey; luggage: 治～ buy clothes (*or* have clothes made) for a journey; buy things for travel /轻～旅行 travel light ❹ stage makeup and costume: 上～ dress and make up (for a theatrical performance) /卸～ remove (*or* take off) stage makeup and costume ❺ pretend; feign; fake; make believe: ～出一副吃惊的样子 assume a look of surprise /～出大人样 put on (*or* assume) an air of a grown-up /不懂～懂 pretend to know what one doesn't /别在我面前～穷叫苦。Don't make a poor mouth to me.

装[2](裝) zhuāng

❶ load; pack; fill; hold: ～车 load a truck (*or* train, *or* cart) /把油箱～满 fill up the tank (with petrol) /碗柜里～满了无用的东西。The cupboard is full of rubbish. /这箱子～不下这么多衣服。The suitcase won't hold so many clothes. ❷ install; fit; assemble: 在门上～保险锁 fit a safety lock on the door /～电话 have a telephone installed /～收音机 assemble a radio /这电扇拆开后他～不起来了。He couldn't put the electric fan together after it had been taken apart. ❸ binding; bookbinding: 平～ paperbound; paperback /精～ hard-cover; hardback /特精～本 de luxe binding; costly binding /线～本 thread-bound edition

装版 zhuāngbǎn 〈印刷〉lock up：～顺序 plating sequence /～台 imposing stone

装扮 zhuāngbàn ❶ dress up；attire；deck out；play the role of：～入时 be fashionably attired /～新娘 dress up the bride /整条大街都用彩旗和鲜花～起来了。The whole street was decked out in bunting and flowers. ❷ make up：她～好了，准备上场。She had finished making herself up and was ready to appear on the stage. /他善于～反面人物。He is good at acting the part of the villain. ❸ disguise；masquerade；pretend：她～出开心的样子以掩盖自己的悲痛。She disguised her sorrow beneath a cheerful appearance. /他想～成局外人。He tried to make believe that he was an outsider.

装备 zhuāngbèi ❶ equip；furnish；fit out：用先进的机床～起来 be equipped with sophisticated machine tools /这艘军舰上～有大口径炮。The warship is fitted with large-calibre guns. ❷ equipment；outfit；installation：滑雪旅行用的全套～ complete outfit for a skiing trip /先进的军事～ advanced military equipment /野营～ camp equipage；camping outfit /～精良 well-equipped /我们厂全是国产～。Our factory is fitted out with complete sets of Chinese-made equipment.

装备部 zhuāngbèibù 〈军事〉armament department：总～ General Armament Department (of the PLA) /省军区～部长 director of the Armament Department of the Provincial Army Command

装裱 zhuāngbiǎo mount (a picture, etc.)

装病 zhuāngbìng malinger；feign illness：～泡假 shun work on pretence of illness

装舱 zhuāngcāng stow (cargo) in the hold (of a ship)

装船 zhuāngchuán load a cargo into the hold：抓紧时间～ speed up the shipment

装弹 zhuāngdàn 〈军事〉loading；weapon loading；ammunition loading；ram：自动～ automatic loading /～机 ammunition loader

装点 zhuāngdiǎn decorate；adorn；dress；deck：～江山 beautify the landscape /鲜花把广场～得分外绚丽。The square was gaily decorated with flowers. /～此关山，今朝更好看。Now adorn hill and pass And make them doubly fair.

装订 zhuāngdìng binding；bookbinding：硬面～ hard-bound /布面～ cloth-bound /皮面～ bound in leather /无线～ perfect binding；threadless binding /～成册 bind in a volume；bind together into book form /用订书机把这些油印活页材料～起来 staple the mimeographed sheets together /～工人 bookbinder

装订车间 zhuāngdìng chējiān bookbindery；bindery

装订机 zhuāngdìngjī bookbinding machine；binding machine

装疯卖傻 zhuāngfēng-màishǎ feign madness and act like an idiot；play the fool：你是当真，还是～？Are you serious or are you just acting the fool?

装裹 zhuāngguo ❶ wrap (a corpse) in a shroud；dress a corpse ❷ shroud；burial suit

装糊涂 zhuāng hútu pretend not to know；sham ignorance；act stupid：少～！Stop acting stupid! /你用不着～！这事你比谁都清楚。Don't pretend；you know this better than anybody else.

装潢 zhuānghuáng ❶ mount (a picture, etc.)；decorate；adorn ❷ decoration；packaging；mounting：～别致的客厅 uniquely decorated parlour /～讲究的工艺品 tastefully packaged handicraft articles /未加～的食品 no-frills foods

装潢门面 zhuānghuáng ménmiàn put up a facade；keep up appearances；put up a front；do window dressing：被帝国主义势力用来～ be used as a facade by imperialist forces

装幌子 zhuāng huǎngzi use sth. as mere window dressing；put up a show

装货 zhuānghuò load cargo：～费 loading charges /～容量 shipping capacity；loading capacity

装货单 zhuānghuòdān shipping order；loading list

装货港 zhuānghuògǎng port of shipment；port of loading

装机容量 zhuāngjī róngliàng 〈电学〉installed capacity

装甲 zhuāngjiǎ ❶ armoured：～飞机 armoured aeroplane /～汽车 armoured automobile；armoured car；armoured motor (*or* motor car) ❷ plate armour

装甲兵 zhuāngjiǎbīng armoured force or troops

装甲车 zhuāngjiǎchē armoured car or vehicle

装甲登陆车 zhuāngjiǎ dēnglùchē armoured landing vehicle

装甲舰 zhuāngjiǎjiàn tinclad；ironclad

装甲师 zhuāngjiǎshī armoured division

装甲输送车 zhuāngjiǎ shūsòngchē armoured carrier

装甲巡逻车 zhuāngjiǎ xúnluóchē armoured scout；armoured scout car or vehicle

装假 zhuāngjiǎ pretend；feign；sham；dissimulate：她是～，并不是真高兴。She is not really happy but only shamming.

装架 zhuāngjià restoration of unearthed animal skeletons

装具 zhuāngjù supplies and gear of an army

装老 zhuānglǎo 〈方言〉〈婉词〉dress the corpse of a senior

装殓 zhuāngliàn dress and lay a corpse in a coffin

装料 zhuāngliào ❶ feed (a machine)：～传送机 feeder conveyor ❷ 〈冶金〉loading；charging：～槽 charge chute /～车 charging lorry /～机构 charge mechanism /～破碎机 feeder-breaker /～台 charge level；charging area；charging floor；loading platform

装聋作哑 zhuānglóng-zuòyǎ pretend to be deaf and dumb；act as a dummy；feign ignorance：我看他是在～。I think he is pretending ignorance. /你为什么～不吭声？Why do you act deaf and dumb?

装门面 zhuāng ménmian put up a facade or front；do window dressing；maintain an outward show：他的慷慨只是用来装装门面的。His generosity is merely window dressing. /仅仅为了～而那样花钱是愚蠢的。It's silly to spend so much money just to keep up appearances. /我不信小温能读那么些书，摆在那里不过是装装门面而已。I don't think Xiao Wen can read all those books；they are merely for show.

装模作样 zhuāngmú-zuòyàng behave affectedly；put on a show；attitudinize：我看她并非真疼，只不过～罢了。I don't think she is really in pain；she's just putting it on. /她～地应酬客人，既为讨大家的称赞，也为在祥子面前露一手儿。She gave herself airs as a hostess, not only to win the approval of the guests but also to impress Xiangzi.

装配 zhuāngpèi 〈机械〉assemble；fit；fit together：把部件～到机器上 fit a part to the machine /～车间 assembling (*or* assembly) plant；assembling (*or* assembly) shop；assembling department /～工 assembler；fitter /～机 assembly machine /～件 assemblage；assembly parts；assembly unit /～图 assembly drawing

装配式动力反应堆 zhuāngpèishì dònglì fǎnyìngduī package power reactor

装配线 zhuāngpèixiàn assembly or assembling line

装瓶 zhuāngpíng bottling：～车间 bottling department /～机 bottling machine；bottle filler；bottle filling machine

装腔作势 zhuāngqiāng-zuòshì strike a pose；be affected or pretentious：他的同事都不喜欢他，因为他老是～。His colleagues all disliked him because he is in the habit of giving himself airs. /那演员～地大引莎士比亚的话。The actor, striking an attitude, quoted Shakespeare copiously. /他这人毫不～。There are no frills about him. /你别想～吓唬人。Don't think you can overawe us by striking a pose.

装傻 zhuāngshǎ pretend ignorance；play the fool

装傻充愣 zhuāngshǎ-chōnglèng *also* "装傻充呆"〈方言〉pretend ignorance；feign stupidity：这是在～，其实他比谁都明白。He is pretending to be stupid and is in fact smarter than all of us.

装设 zhuāngshè install；fit：～路灯 install road lamps

装神弄鬼 zhuāngshén-nòngguǐ ❶ disguise oneself as a ghost or deity (to deceive people) ❷ be deliberately mystifying；cast a mist before sb.'s eyes：他～糊弄人。He played a sleight of hand to fool people.

装饰 zhuāngshì decorate；adorn；ornament；trick out：用画～大厅 decorate a hall with paintings /仅仅为了～ for mere ornament /室内～ interior decoration /建筑～ architectural adornment /～图案 decorative pattern /这房子～得富丽堂皇。The house is lavishly adorned (*or* ornately decorated). /她衣着朴素，不加任何～。She was dressed simply, with no ornamentation.

装饰布 zhuāngshìbù upholstery fabrics

装饰品 zhuāngshìpǐn ornament；decoration

装饰音 zhuāngshìyīn 〈音乐〉grace note；grace；ornament

装束 zhuāngshù ❶ dress；clothes；attire：～朴素大方 be simply and tastefully attired /她一身学生～。She is dressed like a student. /看她的～，可能是农村姑娘。Judging from her dress, she is probably a country girl. ❷ 〈书面〉pack for a journey：～停当 have one's travelling outfit ready

装死 zhuāngsǐ feign death；sham dead；play possum

装蒜 zhuāngsuàn 〈口语〉pretend not to know；fake ignorance：你甭～了！这种事，除了你，谁能干得出来？Don't pretend! (*or* Quit pretending!) Who could have ever done such a thing except you?

装孙子 zhuāng sūnzi 〈口语〉❶ assume a pitiable look：你刚才还趾高气扬，怎么这会儿～了？Why all this cringing now? You were so cocky only a moment ago. ❷ *see* "装蒜"

装填 zhuāngtián load；ram：～机 loader /自动～机 power loader；

Z

automatic rammer; loader rammer /～手 ammunition loader
装桶 zhuāngtǒng cask filling:～机 cask filling machine
装箱 zhuāngxiāng box; case:～待运 be cased up for transport /～机 casing machine /～烧结〈冶金〉pack-sintering /～渗碳〈冶金〉pack-hardening; pack carburizing /～退火〈冶金〉box annealing
装相 zhuāngxiàng behave affectedly; put on an act:在行家面前你装什么相! Stop showing off before the expert.
装卸 zhuāngxiè ❶ load and unload:～货物 load and unload goods; load and unload a truck, train, ship, etc. /文明～ careful loading and discharge; handle goods with care /野蛮～ careless loading and discharge; careless operation ❷ assemble and disassemble:他会～缝纫机。He can take a sewing machine apart and put it back again.
装卸工 zhuāngxiègōng loader; docker; longshoreman; stevedore
装卸码头 zhuāngxiè mǎtou shipping dock
装卸时间 zhuāngxiè shíjiān 〈航海〉lay day
装修 zhuāngxiū fix up; fit up (a house, etc.):～铺面 give a shop a face-lift; fit up the front of a shop /～室内 fit up the interior of a house
装佯 zhuāngyáng 〈方言〉pretend; feign; make believe:他是～,还是真不知道此事? Is he really ignorant of this or simply pretending?
装洋蒜 zhuāng yángsuàn *also* "装蒜" feign ignorance; pretend:你知道得很清楚,不用～。You know all about it and needn't pretend not to.
装样子 zhuāng yàngzi put on an act; keep up appearances:搞面试只是～而已。The interview was just for appearances. /她的友好表示不过是～罢了。Her show of friendship was only acting.
装窑 zhuāngyáo kiln placing
装药 zhuāngyào 〈军事〉powder charge; filling
装运 zhuāngyùn load and transport:导弹～车 missile loader; missile-transporter loader /～车 loader-transporter
装载 zhuāngzài loading:～量 loading capacity /～设备 loading plant; loading system; loading device /～推土两用机 loader-dozer /～了满满一卡车煤。The truck was fully loaded with coal.
装帧 zhuāngzhēn binding and layout (of a book, magazine, etc.):～新颖 novelly bound
装置 zhuāngzhì ❶ install; equip; fit:～天线 install an antenna /在电话上～窃听器 fit a tapping device (*or* a bug) on the telephone ❷ installation; equipment; device:安全～ safety device /雷达～ radar installation /自控～ automatic control arrangement /自动化～ automatic device /防护～ protective equipment /减震～ damping device
装作 zhuāngzuò pretend; disguise as:～不懂 pretend not to understand; feign ignorance /～算命的 disguise oneself as a fortune-teller

庄[1]（莊）

zhuāng ❶ village:李家～ Lijiazhuang Village ❷ manor; estate:田～ country estate ❸ place of business:茶～ tea shop /钱～ old-fashioned Chinese private bank /布～ cloth store /饭～ restaurant ❹ (in gambling) person who holds the bank; banker:谁做～? Who is banking (*or* is the banker)? ❺ (Zhuāng) a surname

庄[2]（莊）

zhuāng serious; sober; solemn; grave:端～ dignified /亦～亦谐 serious and facetious at the same time; serio-comic
庄户 zhuānghù peasant household:～人 peasant; farmer
庄家 zhuāngjia banker (in gambling)
庄稼 zhuāngjia crops:种～ grow crops /收割～ get in (*or* harvest) crops
庄稼地 zhuāngjiadì cropland; farmland; fields
庄稼汉 zhuāngjiahàn farmer; peasant
庄稼活儿 zhuāngjiahuór farm work
庄稼人 zhuāngjiarén farmer; peasant
庄稼院 zhuāngjiayuàn 〈方言〉peasant household
庄稼主 zhuāngjiazhǔ 〈方言〉peasant; farmer
庄静 zhuāngjìng (of a woman) quiet and dignified
庄客 zhuāngkè 〈旧语〉❶ labourers hired by landlords; tenant-peasant; tenant farmer ❷ purchasing agents and salesmen of stores, factories, etc.
庄票 zhuāngpiào securities issued by old-fashioned Chinese private banks which can be exchanged for cash
庄亲 zhuāngqīn 〈方言〉local people; villagers; folks; fellow villagers or townspeople
庄肃 zhuāngsù serious; grave; earnest
庄田 zhuāngtián ❶ land rented out by the imperial family, high officials, monasteries, etc. to tenant-peasants; land estate ❷ fields; farmland; cropland
庄头 zhuāngtóu ❶ edge of a village ❷〈旧语〉person hired by a landlord to manage his country estate; estate manager
庄严 zhuāngyán solemn; stately; dignified; imposing:～宣告 solemnly declare /宏伟～的纪念碑 stately and imposing monument /神色～ grave expression /～的殿堂 temple hall filled with a sombre silence
庄园 zhuāngyuán manor; estate
庄院 zhuāngyuàn large country houses with courtyards
庄重 zhuāngzhòng serious; grave; solemn; sober:举止～ be dignified in one's bearing /语气～ in a solemn tone
庄子 Zhuāngzǐ ❶ Zhuangzi (formerly translated as Chuang-tzu, c. 369-286 BC), Chinese philosopher and writer of the Warring States Period ❷ *Zhuangzi* or *Book of Master Zhuang*, a Taoist classic by Zhuangzi and his followers
庄子 zhuāngzi ❶ village; hamlet ❷ country estate

桩（樁）

zhuāng ❶ stake; pile; post:界～ boundary marker; boundary post /木～ wooden stake /打～ drive piles ❷〈量词〉:一～丑闻 a scandal /一～错案 a mishandled case; a miscarriage of justice /了却一～心事 take a load off one's mind
桩砦 zhuāngzhài 〈军事〉post obstacles
桩子 zhuāngzi stake; pile; post

zhuǎng

奘

zhuǎng 〈方言〉big and thick; thickset; stout; robust:他长得又高又～。He is tall and burly. *or* He is of great stature.
see also zàng

zhuàng

撞

zhuàng ❶ bump against; knock down; crash; collide:～了个满怀 bump into sb. /把门～开 ram the door open /头～在墙上 bump one's head against a wall /我走路～在路灯杆子上,头上起了个大包。I got this big bump on the head by walking into a lamppost. /飞机～在山坡上坠毁了。The plane crashed on a hillside. /他的车失去了控制,～在树上。He lost control of his car and ran it into a tree. /汽车～人了。A car knocked somebody down. ❷ meet by chance; run into; come across:我在市场～见李太太了。I ran across Mrs. Li in the market. /今儿个真是～鬼了,干什么都不顺利。What bad luck! Nothing is going on well today. ❸ probe; try:～运气 try one's luck ❹ barge; dash; rush:横冲直～ barge around; dash about madly; push one's way by shoving or bumping
撞车 zhuàngchē ❶ collision of vehicles:昨天两辆卡车在这儿～了。Two trucks collided (with each other) here yesterday. ❷ clash; contradict:这两个会～了,我只能参加一个。As the two meetings are to be held at the same time, I can only attend one of them. ❸ (of literary works, etc.) repeat each other; resemble each other:有时电影、电视几家同时抢一个剧目,造成～现象。Sometimes several movie or television studios vie for the same programme, causing a plethora of the same item.
撞冻 zhuàngdòng 〈气象〉accretion
撞击 zhuàngjī collide; strike; dash against:汹涌的波涛～着船帮。Surging waves swashed against the side of the ship. /悔恨～着他的心灵。His heart ached with deep regret.
撞见 zhuàngjiàn meet by chance; run across; bump into:我在回家的路上～小王了。I ran into Xiao Wang on my way home. /小偷作案时被他～了。He caught the thief redhanded. /我～这男孩抽烟了。I caught the boy smoking a cigarette.
撞客 zhuàngkè 〈迷信〉encounter an evil spirit, which causes a coma or disease
撞木钟 zhuàng mùzhōng ❶〈方言〉meet with a rebuff; run into snags ❷ do sth. useless; waste one's energy ❸ (often used in the early vernacular) swindle; cheat

撞骗 zhuàngpiàn look about for a chance to swindle; cheat:招摇～ swindle and bluff; deceive and beguile

撞墙 zhuàngqiáng ❶ bump against a wall ❷ encounter an obstacle; suffer a setback:他请求总工程师取消这个项目,但～了。He ran into a brick wall when he asked the chief engineer to cancel the project.

撞锁 zhuàngsuǒ ❶ spring lock ❷〈口语〉find that sb. is not in:昨天去拜访一位朋友,真不巧,～了。I went to visit a friend yesterday but found the door locked (*or* he was not in).

撞针 zhuàngzhēn 〈军事〉firing pin

幢 zhuàng 〈方言〉〈量词〉*for buildings*:一～五层楼房 a five-storeyed building
see also chuáng

僮 Zhuàng old form for 壮[2] Zhuàng

戆 zhuàng 〈书面〉blunt and tactless; simple and honest:性～ straightforward and honest
see also gàng

戆直 zhuàngzhí 〈书面〉blunt and tactless; simple and honest

壮[1](壯) zhuàng ❶ having great strength; strong; robust:身体健～ be powerfully built; be physically strong; have a strong physique ❷ magnificent; splendid; grand:气～山河 full of power and grandeur; magnificent /豪言～语 proud words ❸ strengthen; improve; make better:～军威 add to military prowess /～声势 lend impetus and strength; enhance fame and influence ❹〈中医〉〈量词〉:一～ burning of one moxa cone in moxibustion

壮[2](壯) Zhuàng Zhuang, the minority nationality in the Guangxi Zhuang Autonomous Region

壮大 zhuàngdà ❶ become strong; strengthen; expand:～进步力量 expand the progressive forces /～经济实力 increase or enhance the economic power /我们的力量不断～。Our forces are growing steadily. ❷ strong; robust:四肢～ strong limbs; strong arms and legs

壮胆 zhuàngdǎn do or say sth. intended to fill sb. with courage; boost sb.'s courage; embolden:这番话壮了他的胆。He was emboldened by the words./他说他一只手就能打败那恶棍,但我们知道他不过是在给自己～。He said he could beat the bully with one hand tied behind his back, but we knew that he was just whistling in the dark.

壮丁 zhuàngdīng 〈旧语〉able-bodied man (subject to conscription):抓～ press-gang able-bodied men; press-gang conscripts

壮歌 zhuànggē folk songs of the Zhuang nationality, the text of which usually consists of four lines, each containing five or seven characters

壮疙瘩 zhuànggēda 〈方言〉acne

壮工 zhuànggōng unskilled labourer

壮观 zhuàngguān magnificent sight; grand spectacle:尼亚加拉瀑布的～ grandeur of Niagara Falls /泰山的日出景象蔚为～。The sunrise on (*or* observed from the top of) Mount Tai is a magnificent sight.

壮怀 zhuànghuái 〈书面〉great aspirations; lofty ideals:仰天长啸,～激烈 look up to heaven and utter a long cry, with sublime aspirations unrealized

壮健 zhuàngjiàn healthy and strong; powerful; robust

壮锦 zhuàngjǐn Zhuang brocade

壮举 zhuàngjǔ magnificent feat; great exploit; act of heroism:空前伟大的～ unprecedentedly great undertaking /大无畏的～ feat of great daring

壮阔 zhuàngkuò immense; magnificent; grand:规模～ of a grand scale /～无比的海洋 vast (*or* limitless) expanse of the ocean /波澜～ surging forward with great momentum; unfolding on a magnificent scale

壮劳力 zhuàngláolì ❶ strong labour power ❷ able-bodied adult:兄弟俩都是～。The two brothers are both able-bodied labourers.

壮丽 zhuànglì majestic; magnificent; splendid; glorious:～的事业 glorious undertaking /～的诗篇 splendid poem /这座建筑宏伟～。This building is magnificent. /披上银装的山峰更显～。The snow-covered mountains look even more majestic. /我从未感到过祖国的山河是如此～可爱。I have never been so struck by the splendour and beauty of the mountains and rivers of our country.

壮烈 zhuàngliè heroic; brave and noble-minded:～牺牲 die a hero's death; die a martyr; lay down one's life for a worthy cause

壮美 zhuàngměi beautiful and magnificent

壮门面 zhuàng ménmian lend impressiveness or grandeur (to a scene):他打算邀请当地所有名流来参加婚礼,以～。He intends to add (*or* lend) lustre to the wedding ceremony by inviting all the local celebrities.

壮苗 zhuàngmiáo strong sprout

壮年 zhuàngnián in one's thirties or forties:他正当～。He is in the prime of life.

壮士 zhuàngshì heroic man; hero; warrior

壮实 zhuàngshi strong and vigorous; sturdy; robust:他身体～。He is healthy and robust. /他～得像头牛。He is as strong as a horse.

壮硕 zhuàngshuò big and strong; husky; robust

壮图 zhuàngtú great plans; grand prospects:大展～ carry out a grand plan

壮伟 zhuàngwěi magnificent; full of grandeur:～的山峰 magnificent mountain peaks

壮戏 zhuàngxì one of the operas of the Zhuang nationality which evolved from the Zhuang folk songs and is popular in the Guangxi Zhuang Autonomous Region and areas in Yunnan inhabited by the Zhuang people

壮心 zhuàngxīn *see*"壮志"

壮行 zhuàngxíng (give a big send-off, etc.) to enable sb. to depart in style

壮阳 zhuàngyáng 〈中医〉invigorate *yang* (vital function) by administering warm-nature drugs to promote the kidney function for increasing virility and sexual potency of the male:～药剂 aphrodisiac

壮志 zhuàngzhì noble ideals; high aspirations:胸怀～ entertain great ambitions; cherish lofty aspiration

壮志凌云 zhuàngzhì-língyún with lofty or soaring aspirations

壮志未酬 zhuàngzhì-wèichóu with one's noble ambitions unfulfilled; with one's lofty aspirations unrealized:～空悲切 fail to realize one's aspirations and feel deeply grieved

壮族 Zhuàngzú Zhuang or Chuang nationality, distributed over the Guangxi Zhuang Autonomous Region, Yunnan and Guangdong

状(狀) zhuàng ❶ shape; form; appearance:呈衰老～ old and feeble; senile; decrepit /奇形怪～ of grotesque (*or* fantastic) shapes;strange-shaped ❷ state of affairs;condition:症～ symptom /现～ status quo;present state /原～ status quo ante;original state /罪～ crimes ❸ describe; depict:不可名～ indescribable; beyond description; beyond words /写景～物 describe both scenery and objects ❹ account; record:报功～ written account of sb.'s meritorious service ❺ written complaint; lawsuit:告～ lodge a complaint; file a suit (against sb.); charge sb. with ❻ certificate:奖～ certificate of commendation /委任～ certificate of appointment; commission

状词 zhuàngcí written complaint; indictment

状况 zhuàngkuàng condition; situation; state; state of affairs:生活～ living conditions /社会～ conditions of society /婚姻～ marital status /经济～ (a person's) financial situation; (a country's) economic situation /交通拥挤～ congested state of traffic /健康～好 in good health; in shape /健康～不好 in poor health; out of shape /恢复到战前～ return to pre-war conditions /不允许这种～继续存在 not allow this state of affairs to exist any longer

状貌 zhuàngmào looks; appearance; form:兄弟俩～很相似。The two brothers look very much alike (*or* are as like as two peas).

状态 zhuàngtài state;condition:紧急～ state of emergency /落后～ backward conditions; backward state /无政府～ anarchy /临界～〈物理〉critical condition; critical state /处于半清醒～ be in a semiconscious condition /处于昏迷～ be in a comatose (*or* an unconscious) condition; be in a coma /处于最佳竞技～ be in top condition (*or* great form)

状态图 zhuàngtàitú 〈冶金〉state diagram

状语 zhuàngyǔ 〈语言〉adverbial modifier; adverbial

状元 zhuàngyuan ❶ Number One Scholar, title conferred on the person who came out first in the highest imperial examination ❷ very best (in any field); top-notch:他是高考中的文科～。He came out first (*or* got the first place) in the college-entrance examination instituted for students of liberal arts. /行行出～。Every profession produces its own leading authority. *or* Every trade has its master.

状元红 Zhuàngyuanhóng *Zhuangyuanhong*, a kind of high-quality rice wine produced in Shaoxing (绍兴), Zhejiang
状纸 zhuàngzhǐ ❶ official form for filing a complaint ❷ *see* "状子"
状子 zhuàngzi written complaint; indictment: 呈上～ submit one's written complaint; lodge a complaint

zhuī

隹 zhuī (in ancient books) bird with a short tail
椎 zhuī vertebra: 腰～ lumbar vertebra / 脊～ vertebra / 颈～ cervical vertebra / 胸～ thoracic vertebra; dorsal vertebra
see also chuí
椎弓裂 zhuīgōngliè 〈医学〉 spondyloschisis
椎骨 zhuīgǔ 〈生理〉 vertebra: ～切除术 vertebrectomy
椎间盘 zhuījiānpán 〈生理〉 intervertebral disc; disciintervertebrales
椎间盘突出症 zhuījiānpán tūchūzhèng 〈医学〉 herniated disc; protruded disc; slipped disc
椎间盘造影术 zhuījiānpán zàoyǐngshù 〈医学〉 discography
椎间韧带 zhuījiān rèndài ligamenta intervertebralia
椎间体 zhuījiāntǐ intercentrum
锥 zhuī ❶ awl: ～尖儿 point of an awl ❷ awl-like thing; cone: 圆～体 cone ❸ bore; drill: ～个眼儿 make a hole with an awl ❹ 〈数学〉 cone
锥齿鲨 zhuīchǐshā 〈动物〉 ragged-tooth shark; brown shark
锥虫病 zhuīchóngbìng trypanosomiasis
锥处囊中 zhuīchǔ-nángzhōng awl in bag, whose point will stick out sooner or later — real talent will not remain obscure for long
锥刀之末 zhuīdāozhīmò negligible profits: 他连～也不愿放过。He won't let go of even the smallest gains.
锥度 zhuīdù 〈机械〉 ❶ taper; coning: ～规 taper gauge ❷ taper ratio
锥孔 zhuīkǒng bore-hole
锥栗 zhuīlì 〈植物〉 chinquapin
锥面 zhuīmiàn 〈数学〉 cone; conical surface
锥探 zhuītàn probe the stratum with an awl-shaped tool
锥形 zhuīxíng 〈机械〉 taper; cone; pyramid
锥形波束 zhuīxíng bōshù 〈电子〉 conical beam
锥形阀 zhuīxíngfá cone valve
锥指 zhuīzhǐ 〈书面〉 point an awl at the ground; 〈比喻〉 of tunnel vision; with a very limited outlook
锥子 zhuīzi awl
骓 zhuī 〈书面〉 horse with white and black hair
追 zhuī ❶ chase; pursue; run after; catch up with: ～逃犯 chase (*or* give chase to) an escaped criminal / 紧～不舍 be in hot pursuit; be hot on sb.'s trail / 你～我赶 try to overtake each other (in friendly emulation) / 把比分～到九比十 close the margin to 9-10; catch up and bring the score to 9-10 / 快去～你妈，她忘带月票了。Run after your mother; she's forgotten her monthly ticket. ❷ trace; look into; try to find out: ～～失败根源 trace the root cause of the failure / 警察抓住线索一～到底，终于抓住了罪犯。The police followed home (*or* through) the clue and finally caught the culprit ❸ seek; go after; woo: ～名逐利 go after (*or* seek) fame and wealth / 他一直在～这位姑娘，但没～上。He has been running after (*or* courting) the girl but with no success. ❹ bring back to mind; recall; reminisce: ～念过去的美好时光 reminisce about (*or* recall) the good old days; be nostalgic for the past / ～忆往昔 recall the past ❺ posthumously; retroactively: ～授战斗英雄称号 be posthumously awarded the title of Combat Hero
追奔逐北 zhuībēn-zhúběi *also* "追亡逐北" pursue a routed enemy force: 我军～，直抵江边。Our army pursued the fleeing enemy to the river.
追本溯源 zhuīběn-sùyuán *also* "追本穷源" trace back to the source; get at the root of the matter; get to the bottom of: 做学问必须有～的精神。In scholarly research, one must be thorough and have an inquiring mind. / 对所学的词汇，他爱～。He likes to trace the origin of the words he learns.
追逼 zhuībī ❶ pursue closely (a fleeing enemy); hot on sb.'s trail: 乘胜～ follow up a victory with hot pursuit ❷ press for (repayment); extort (a confession): ～债款 dun sb. for money; press sb. for payment of debts / ～口供 extort a confession
追兵 zhuībīng pursuing troops: 摆脱～ shake off the pursuing enemy forces
追补 zhuībǔ ❶ add to (the original amount): ～拨款 allocate more funds ❷ compensate or make up afterwards: 不可～的遗憾 everlasting remorse; eternal regret
追捕 zhuībǔ pursue and capture: ～凶犯 pursue and capture the murderer / 那动物逃脱了猎人的～。The prey escaped the hunter.
追查 zhuīchá investigate; find out; look into; trace: ～谣言 trace a rumour to its source / ～飞机失事原因 investigate (*or* look into) the causes of an air-crash / ～偷税漏税分子 find out the tax-evader (*or* tax-dodger)
追偿 zhuīcháng recovery: ～损失 recover losses
追偿费 zhuīchángfèi recovery fee
追悼 zhuīdào mourn over a person's death: ～死者 mourn for (*or* over) the dead / ～词 memorial speech
追悼会 zhuīdàohuì memorial meeting
追访 zhuīfǎng press sb. for an interview
追肥 zhuīféi 〈农业〉 top-dressing; top application: 给棉田施～ top-dress the cotton fields / 棉花打尖以后要～。Cotton should be fertilized after topping.
追风 zhuīfēng ❶ 〈中医〉 cure diseases caused by chills with medicinal herbs ❷ follow the fashion or trend
追风逐电 zhuīfēng-zhúdiàn chase wind and pursue lightning — very swift: 火车～般地前进。The train was running at full speed.
追封 zhuīfēng 〈旧语〉 present sb. with a posthumous honour or title: 死后～为武侯 be honoured with the title of "Martial Marquis" after death
追赶 zhuīgǎn run after; chase; pursue: ～潮流 follow the trend; try to be in the swim / 拼命～ in full chase / 如果你抓紧，能很快～上他。You will soon catch him up if you hurry. / 小男孩绕着房子～他的伙伴。The little boy chased his playmate round the house. / 他领先其他运动员约十米，直到终点，也没人～上他。He was about ten metres ahead of the other runners and held the lead till the finish. / 敌人被～得走投无路。The enemy was driven into a tight corner.
追根 zhuīgēn get to the root of a matter: 这孩子什么都爱～。The child has a habit of getting to the bottom of things.
追根究底 zhuīgēn-jiūdǐ *also* "追根刨底"; "追根问底" get to the bottom of sth.; go into the whys and wherefores of sth.: 这事一定得～。We must get to the root of the matter. / 他经常～地打听别人的隐私。He often noses into other people's private affairs.
追光 zhuīguāng spotlight
追怀 zhuīhuái reminisce; recall: ～往事 call to mind one's past
追还 zhuīhuán *see* "追回"
追回 zhuīhuí recover: ～赃款 recover stolen (*or* embezzled) money / 悬赏重金～失窃的财物 offer a handsome reward for the recovery of stolen property
追悔 zhuīhuǐ repentance; regret; remorse: ～不已 be seized with remorse; feel endless remorse / ～莫及 too late to repent (*or* regret); show tardy repentance
追击 zhuījī pursue and attack; follow up: ～敌舰 pursue and attack enemy warships / 乘胜～ follow up a victory with hot pursuit / 摆脱了敌人的～ throw off the pursuing enemy
追缉 zhuījī track down (an escaped criminal)
追记 zhuījì ❶ award or cite posthumously: ～一等功 be posthumously awarded a Merit Citation Class I ❷ write down afterwards or from memory: ～会上发言的主要内容 note down the gist of the speeches at the meeting retrospectively ❸ sth. written down from memory; retrospective account
追加 zhuījiā add to (the original amount); supplement: ～预算 supplement a budget; make a supplementary budget / ～经费 allocate additional funds / ～基建投资 appropriate more funds for capital construction
追加成本 zhuījiā chéngběn additional cost
追加订货 zhuījiā dìnghuò supplementary order; additional order
追加契约 zhuījiā qìyuē add-on contract
追加书 zhuījiāshū supplemental bill

Z

追加税 zhuījiāshuì additional tax
追歼 zhuījiān pursue and annihilate：～逃敌 pursue and wipe out the fleeing enemy
追剿 zhuījiǎo pursue and exterminate：～队 pursuit detachment
追缴 zhuījiǎo cause to disgorge or surrender ill-gotten gains; recover：～赃物 recover stolen property
追究 zhuījiū look into; find out; get to the root of (a matter, etc.)：～失火原因 look into (*or* investigate) the cause of a fire /～刑事责任 ascertain criminal responsibility (for an accident, etc.) /对肇事者必须～。The offenders must be held to account (*or* must be held responsible for what they have done). /对不知情者概不～。No action will be taken against those ignorant of the facts of the case.
追名逐利 zhuīmíng-zhúlì crave for fame and fortune：他一生～，到头来却落了一场空。He spent his whole life pursuing fame and fortune which never came.
追念 zhuīniàn recall; reminisce：～英雄的业绩 reminisce about someone's heroic deeds /～故人 recall one's old friends
追蹑 zhuīniè 〈书面〉follow; track; trace; follow the trail of
追陪 zhuīpéi follow and accompany (sb.)
追求 zhuīqiú ❶ seek; pursue; go after：～利润 seek profits /～名誉地位 hanker after (*or* be after) fame and position /～真理 be in pursuit of truth; pursue truth /单纯～数量 concentrate on quantity alone; lay stress on quantity at the expense of quality /片面～产值 go exclusively after output value /盲目～高指标 blindly chase high targets ❷ woo; court; chase; run after：她有众多～者。She has a host of wooers (*or* admirers). /他执著地～那姑娘。He paid assiduous court to the girl.
追认 zhuīrèn ❶ subsequently confirm; recognize retroactively：～一项决议 subsequently endorse a resolution ❷ admit or confer after death：～为共产党员 be posthumously admitted as a member of the Communist Party
追述 zhuīshù tell about the past; recount what has happened：她向青年朋友们～当年的经历。She was relating her past experience to her young friends.
追思 zhuīsī recall; reminisce; look back on：她时常～往事。She often falls into a reverie about the past.
追诉 zhuīsù 〈法律〉prosecute：～权 power to prosecute /～时效 limitation of prosecution
追溯 zhuīsù ❶ trace back to; date from：～佛教在中国的历史 trace the history of Buddhism in China /我们两国人民之间的友好交往可以～到唐代。The friendly exchanges between our two peoples date back to the Tang Dynasty. /这个传说可以～到远古时代。The legend goes (*or* can be traced) back to remote antiquity. ❷ retrospective：～效力 retroactive effect /～解释 retroactive interpretation /～适用 retroactive application
追溯法 zhuīsùfǎ retrospective law; retroactive law
追溯力 zhuīsùlì 〈法律〉retroactivity
追随 zhuīsuí follow; adhere to：～潮流 follow new trends /～左右 follow sb. closely /～者 follower; adherent /他赢得了大批～者。He gained a large following.
追索 zhuīsuǒ ❶ seek and probe：他一生～真理，至死不悔。He has no regrets about pursuing truth all his life. ❷ demand repayment：他去镇上～一笔旧账。He went to the town to recover (*or* collect) an old debt.
追讨 zhuītǎo demand payment (of an old debt); dun
追亡逐北 zhuīwáng-zhúběi *see* "追奔逐北"
追尾 zhuīwěi bump into the rear (of the car in front)：保持车距，严防～。Avoid bumping by keeping a safe distance from the car ahead.
追问 zhuīwèn inquire about; question closely; examine minutely：～下落 inquire about sb.'s whereabouts /他们～那位候选人对这个问题的看法。They questioned the candidate closely on his views about the matter. /警察～他肇事的原因。The police interrogated him trying to find out the causes of the accident.
追想 zhuīxiǎng recall; recollect; reminisce
追星族 zhuīxīngzú movie star fan; pop music star fan; groupie
追叙 zhuīxù ❶ tell about the past; recount what has happened：～他们两家上代的交情 recount the friendship between the two families during the last generation ❷ narration of earlier episodes or events; flashback：采用～的手法 apply the technique of flashback
追寻 zhuīxún pursue; search; trace：～梦境 search for a dreamland /考察队员～着印地安人的足迹向西行进。The explorers followed the trail of the Indians and advanced westward.
追询 zhuīxún *see* "追问"
追忆 zhuīyì call to mind; recollect; recall; look back：～幸福的童年，不胜怀念 recall with nostalgia one's happy childhood /这本书使我～起许多愉快的往事。The book brought many happy recollections to my mind. /～往事，历历在目。As I look back, scenes of the past leap up vividly before my eyes. *or* The past events are still fresh in my memory. /年代太久，难以～。As it happened ages ago, I can't call it to mind (*or* I've lost all recollection of it).
追赃 zhuīzāng recover (*or* order the return of) stolen goods or money embezzled, etc.; make sb. disgorge the spoils
追赠 zhuīzèng confer (an honoury position or a title) posthumously
追债 zhuīzhài demand payment of a debt
追逐 zhuīzhú ❶ chase; pursue：～猎物 pursue one's prey /孩子们在花园里～嬉戏。The children are chasing one another in the garden. ❷ seek; quest; go after：～高额利润 seek exorbitant profits /～名利 hanker after fame and gain
追逐赛 zhuīzhúsài 〈体育〉(in cycling) pursuit race：个人～ individual pursuit race /团体～ team pursuit race
追踪 zhuīzōng track; trace; trail：警察正在～凶犯。The police are on the trail (*or* track) of the murderer.

zhuì

惴 zhuì 〈书面〉be anxious and afraid：～恐 be anxious and frightened
惴栗 zhuìlì 〈书面〉shake with fear
惴惴不安 zhuìzhuì-bù'ān 〈书面〉anxious and fearful; alarmed and on tenterhooks; ill at ease：即便是偶尔的抛头露面，她也会感到～。She was even alarmed about the prospect of being in the limelight on rare occasions.

赘 zhuì ❶ superfluous; tautological; redundant：冗～ verbose; diffuse /冗词～句 superfluous wording /不待～言。Any further remarks on the matter would seem superfluous. ❷ (of a man) go to live in the household of one's in-laws upon marriage; (of the bride's parents) gain a son-in-law in such a manner：入～张家 go and live with the Zhangs after marrying their daughter /招～养老女婿 get a son-in-law to live in one's house and take care of one in old age ❸ 〈方言〉be a drag on; be burdensome; be cumbersome：这些孩子实在～人。These children are really burdensome.
赘词 zhuìcí unnecessary words; superfluity; redundancy
赘瘤 zhuìliú anything superfluous or useless; superfluity; redundancy
赘述 zhuìshù give unnecessary details; be repetitious：毋庸～ there is no need to go into details
赘婿 zhuìxù son-in-law who lives in the home of his wife's parents
赘芽 zhuìyá sterile shoot
赘言 zhuìyán ❶ say more than is needed, be superfluous：不必～。No further details are called for. ❷ superfluous words
赘疣 zhuìyóu ❶ wart ❷ anything superfluous or useless; superfluity：多此一笔，反成～。Adding one more touch is like putting a fifth wheel to the coach.
赘余 zhuìyú superfluous; redundant：～之词 redundant expressions

膇 zhuì 〈书面〉(of foot) swelling

缒 zhuì let down (with a rope)：把篮子从阳台上～下来。Let the basket down from the balcony by a rope.

醊 zhuì 〈书面〉hold a memorial ceremony for

缀 zhuì ❶ sew; stitch; mend：补～ patch; mend /把衬衫扣子～上 sew (*or* stitch) buttons on to a shirt /～上几针 put in a few stitches ❷ put words together correctly; compose; write：～字成句，～句成文 put words together to make a sentence and sentences together to make an essay ❸ embellish; adorn; decorate：点～ embellish; ornament; adorn /～满繁星的天空 sky studded with stars /头上

～满珠翠 wear a lot of pearl and jade ornaments in one's hair
缀合 zhuìhé join together; put together:把这些珠子～起来 string the beads together
缀辑 zhuìjí edit; compile:把资料～成书 compile materials into a book
缀头 zhuìtou 〈方言〉small bundle of straw, etc. for silkworms to spin cocoons in
缀文 zhuìwén write an article; compose an essay

坠(墜) zhuì ❶ fall; tumble; drop:～马 fall off a horse; take a toss /摇摇欲～ on the verge of collapse; tottering /起飞不久,飞机便～入沙漠中。The plane crashed into the desert shortly after take-off. ❷ weigh down; droop:下～ strain (at stool) /沉甸甸下～的稻穗儿 drooping ears of rice /累累果实把树枝～得弯弯的。Heavy fruit weighed the branches down. *or* Branches were borne down with the weight of the fruit. ❸ weight; hanging object:扇～儿 pendant of a fan /铅～ plummet /耳～ ear pendant
坠地 zhuìdì 〈书面〉(of a child) be born:呱呱～ be born crying (*or* with a cry)
坠胡 zhuìhú *see* "坠琴"
坠毁 zhuìhuǐ (of a plane, etc.) fall and smash; crash:客机～,无一人生还。The passenger plane crashed with no survivors at all.
坠角 zhuìjiǎo corner seal, a seal in one of the lower corners of a Chinese traditional painting
坠楼 zhuìlóu jump off a building (to kill oneself):～自杀 commit suicide by jumping off a building
坠落 zhuìluò fall; drop:从悬崖上～下来 drop off a cliff /看见一颗流星划过天空～下来。A meteor was seen darting through the sky.
坠琴 zhuìqín *also* "坠子";"坠胡";"二弦" èrxián *zhuiqin*, stringed instrument shaped like *sanxian* (3-stringed Chinese guitar), which is used in ballad singing popular in Henan Province
坠胎 zhuìtāi *also* "堕胎" duòtāi (have an) abortion: ～药 abortive
坠腿 zhuìtuǐ 〈方言〉hold sb. back; be a drag on sb.; encumber:家里有五个孩子～,她很少出门。Encumbered with five children at home, she seldom goes out.
坠子 zhuìzi ❶〈方言〉weight; plummet; pendant ❷〈方言〉ear pendant ❸ *also* "河南坠子" Hénán zhuìzi ballad singing to the accompaniment of the *zhuiqin*, popular in Henan Province ❹ *see* "坠琴"

zhūn

谆 zhūn sincerely; earnestly and tirelessly: ～嘱 advise (*or* enjoin) earnestly
谆谆 zhūnzhūn earnestly and ceaselessly:～教诲 earnestly instruct /～告诫 repeatedly admonish; enjoin assiduously /～善诱 teach and guide untiringly /言者～,听者藐藐。Earnest words of admonition fell on deaf ears.

屯 zhūn
see also tún
屯邅 zhūnzhān 〈书面〉*see* "迍邅" zhūnzhān

窀 zhūn
窀穸 zhūnxī 〈书面〉grave; tomb

迍 zhūn
迍邅 zhūnzhān *also* "屯邅" zhūnzhān 〈书面〉❶ be at a standstill; make no progress ❷ fail to achieve one's ambition

肫[1] zhūn 〈书面〉sincere; earnest; genuine:～挚 sincere

肫[2] zhūn gizzard (of a fowl):鸡～ chicken gizzard

衠 zhūn 〈方言〉pure; untainted

zhǔn

准[1] zhǔn allow; permit; approve; grant:批～ approve; ratify /获～ obtain (*or* get) permission /～假一月 grant sb. a month's leave /不～入内! No admittance! /学生不～去这种地方。Students are not allowed to go to places like this. /他父母不～他与这些人混在一起。His parents forbid him to mix with these people.

准[2](準) zhǔn ❶ standard; norm; criterion; yardstick: 生活水～ living standard /评选标～ criterion for the selection /不合乎标～ not up to the norm /用高标～要求自己 set high demands on oneself /以文件为～ take the document as the standard (*or* criterion) ❷ in line with; follow:～此办理 be handled in the same manner ❸ accurate; exact; precise:瞄～ aim at /枪打得很～ (be a) crack at shooting; crack shot; sharpshooter /投篮很～ accurate shooting (in basketball) /放之四海而皆～ valid everywhere; universally applicable /我的表走得很～。My watch keeps very good time. /他的话说不～。His words are not reliable. ❹ definitely; surely; certainly:这办法～行。You bet this will work. *or* This will definitely work. /他不～能去。He may be able to go. /明天的会我～参加。I'll certainly go to the meeting tomorrow. ❺ quasi-; para-: ～战争状态 quasi-state of war /～中立地位 quasi-neutral status /～国际法 quasi-international law /～国际协定 quasi-international agreement /～司法团体 quasi-judicial body /～契约性义务 quasi-contractual obligation /～光波〈物理〉quasi-optical waves /～单色光〈物理〉quasi-monochromatic light /～军事组织 paramilitary organization /～国家实体 *entité paraétatique*
准保 zhǔnbǎo certainly; undoubtedly; for sure:这已校对三次,～没错儿了。This has been proofread three times. You can be sure there is no mistake. /他～不来了。I am certain he won't come. /别担心,我们～按时送到。Don't worry. We'll guarantee delivery on time.
准饱和 zhǔnbǎohé 〈化学〉quasi-saturation
准备 zhǔnbèi ❶ prepare; get ready:～午饭 prepare lunch /为婚礼作～ make preparations for the wedding /搜集资料为实验作～ collect material in preparation for the experiment /作好思想～ be mentally prepared /作两手～ prepare for both eventualities /不打无～之仗 fight no war unprepared /～阶段 preparatory stage /～工作 preparatory work; homework/午餐已经～好了。The lunch is ready. /我已做好旅行的充分～。I am all set for the journey. ❷ think; intend; plan:我今天不～讲了。I don't think I'll take the floor today. /她～把这本书译成中文。She plans to translate the book into Chinese. /他们～去巴黎度假。They intend to go to Paris for the holidays.
准备程序 zhǔnbèi chéngxù preparatory procedure
准备活动 zhǔnbèi huódòng 〈体育〉warming-up (exercise); limbering-up (exercise)
准备金 zhǔnbèijīn reserve (fund); reserves; provisions
准博士 zhǔnbóshì all but dissertation (ABD)
准导体 zhǔndǎotǐ 〈物理〉quasi-conductor
准得 zhǔnděi *see* "准保"
准定 zhǔndìng *see* "准保"
准点 zhǔndiǎn on the dot; on time:我们～开车。Our car will leave on time. /你瞧,我～到啦。Look, I arrived on the dot.
准分子激光器 zhǔnfēnzǐ jīguāngqì excimer laser
准噶尔盆地 Zhǔngá'ěr Péndì Junggar Basin or Dzungharian Basin in northern Xinjiang
准稿子 zhǔngǎozi certain; positive; sure:什么时候动工,还没～呢。It is still uncertain when construction will begin.
准核国家 zhǔnhéguójiā near-nuclear state
准话 zhǔnhuà definite information:这活儿几天能完,你得给个～。Give me the date when you can finish the job. *or* Tell me how many days exactly you'll need for the job.
准会员 zhǔnhuìyuán associated member
准货币 zhǔnhuòbì near money; quasi-money
准将 zhǔnjiàng (UK army and marines) brigadier; (UK air force) air commodore; (UK navy) commodore; (US army, air force, and marines) brigadier general; (US navy, coast guard) rear admiral lower grade
准金属 zhǔnjīnshǔ metalloid
准静止锋 zhǔnjìngzhǐfēng 〈气象〉quasi-stationary front
准绝缘子 zhǔnjuéyuánzǐ 〈物理〉quasi-insulator
准军事部队 zhǔnjūnshì bùduì paramilitary force
准科学 zhǔnkēxué parascience
准粒子 zhǔnlìzǐ quasi-particle
准男爵 zhǔnnánjué baronet
准平面 zhǔnpíngmiàn 〈数学〉directrix plane

准平原 zhǔnpíngyuán 〈地质〉paraplain

准谱儿 zhǔnpǔr certainty; sure thing：下午干什么，现在还没个～。We are not certain yet what to do in the afternoon.

准情 zhǔnqíng grant sb.'s request; agree to do sb. a favour：看在老朋友的面子上，我就准了他这个情。As you are my old friend, I agree to grant him the favour for your sake.

准球面 zhǔnqiúmiàn 〈数学〉director sphere

准确 zhǔnquè accurate; precise; exact：计算～ be precise in calculation／观察～ be accurate in one's observation／～度 degree of accuracy; accuracy／他发音不～。His pronunciation is inaccurate.／谁能～无误地解释这一现象？Who can explain the phenomenon with unerring accuracy?／他的回答～无误。His answer is exactly right.／你必须～地测量这一长度。You must measure the length by rule and line.

准儿 zhǔnr 〈口语〉certain; sure; positive：心里没～ feel uncertain／心里有～ know what one is doing; feel sure; be quite positive about／没～他今天不来了。Perhaps he won't come today.／他能否信守诺言，你有～吗？Can you count on his keeping the promise?／不管别人怎样说，对他，我心里有～。Whatever other people may say, I have no doubt of his reliability.／他能成不能成没～。The chances of his success are anybody's guess.

准绳 zhǔnshéng criterion; norm; yardstick：社会生活须有一定的道德作～。There should be certain moral standards in public life.

准时 zhǔnshí punctual; on time; on schedule：～开会 punctual start to the meeting; meeting held on time／尽管下雨，他们还是～到达。They arrived on the dot in spite of the rain.／列车～进站。The train pulled into the station at the scheduled time (*or* on schedule).

准所有权 zhǔnsuǒyǒuquán quasi-proprietary right

准同步 zhǔntóngbù 〈物理〉quasi-synchronization

准头 zhǔntou 〈口语〉accuracy (in speech, marksmanship, etc.); precision：枪法有～ shoot well; shoot with great accuracy; be a good shot; be an expert marksman; be a crack shot／这孩子说话没个～。You can't depend on what the child says.

准卫星 zhǔnwèixīng 〈航天〉satelloid

准尉 zhǔnwèi warrant officer：一级～ (UK armed forces) warrant officer, class I; (US army and air force) chief warrant officer; (US navy) commissioned warrant officer／二级～ (UK armed forces) warrant officer, class II; (US army and air force) warrant officer, junior grade; (US navy) warrant officer

准线 zhǔnxiàn 〈数学〉directrix (pl. directrices or directrixes)

准新娘 zhǔnxīnniáng intended; fiancée

准信 zhǔnxìn definite and reliable information; accurate information：你哪天能来，给我个～。Let me know exactly when you can come.

准星 zhǔnxīng ❶ zero point on a steelyard;〈比喻〉(often used in the negative) definite ideas：说话没～。His words are not reliable. ❷ front sight (of a gun)：校正～ adjust the front sight or align the sights (of a gun); sight

准行 zhǔnxíng 〈口语〉it's a sure-fire success：这件事让他干～。He'll surely do a good job of it.／你去找他帮忙，～。If you go and ask him for help, he won't say no.

准许 zhǔnxǔ grant; allow; permit：～他的要求 grant his request／～她回家探亲 allow her to go home to visit her family／要求～参加短训班 ask for permission to take a short-term course／得到～延期交学期论文 get (*or* be granted) an extension on one's term paper

准予 zhǔnyǔ (of documentary usage) grant; approve; permit; allow：～放行 allow sb. to pass／～请假一周 grant a week's leave of absence

准原子 zhǔnyuánzǐ 〈物理〉quasiatom

准圆 zhǔnyuán 〈数学〉director circle

准则 zhǔnzé norm; standard; code; criterion：道德～ moral code; morality／社会行为～ social norms／国际行为～ standard of international conduct／外交～ diplomatic norms／国际法的起码～ elementary requirements of international law／国际关系基本～ basic norms of international relations; basic norms guiding international relations／新闻道德～ code of newspaper ethics

准直 zhǔnzhí 〈物理〉collimation：～透镜 collimating lens／～光束 collimated beam／～仪 collimator

准子公司 zhǔnzǐgōngsī quasi-subsidary

准自动化 zhǔnzìdònghuà quasi-automatic

准租金 zhǔnzūjīn quasi-rent

埻

zhǔn 〈书面〉bull's eye (of a target)

zhuō

棁

zhuō 〈书面〉short post on a roof beam

捉

zhuō ❶ clutch; hold firmly; grab; grasp：～住他的手臂 grab him by the arm／～笔赋诗 pick up a brush (*or* pen) to write a poem ❷ catch; seize; capture：生擒活～ capture sb. alive／贼喊～贼 thief crying "stop thief"; robber acting like a cop／我们～到一个探子。We caught a spy.／他企图逃跑，被我一把～住。When he tried to run away, I got him by the neck.

捉刀 zhuōdāo write (an article, etc.) for someone else; ghost-write：请人～ ask sb. to write for one

捉刀人 zhuōdāorén ghost-writer

捉对 zhuōduì in pairs：～厮杀 fight in pairs

捉奸 zhuōjiān catch sb. committing adultery; catch adulterers in the act：捉贼见赃，～见双。For robbery find the loot, for adultery catch the pair. *or* Show the loot to prove a theft, catch both lovers to prove a tryst.

捉襟见肘 zhuōjīn-jiànzhǒu pull together one's lapels to conceal the raggedness only to expose one's elbows — have too many things to take care of (*or* too many difficulties to cope with) at the same time; be in straitened circumstances：知识贫乏，写起文章来难免～。One can hardly avoid paucity of ideas if he has little knowledge of what he is writing about.／那年头，生活经常入不敷出，～。In those years, life was hard and we were often unable to make both ends meet.

捉迷藏 zhuō mícáng ❶ hide-and-seek; blindman's bluff ❷ play hide-and-seek; beat about the bush; hedge：有话你就直说，别跟我～。Get straight to the point (*or* Be frank with me). Don't hum and haw.

捉摸 zhuōmō (often used in the negative) ascertain; conjecture; fathom; predict：～不定 difficult to conjecture; unpredictable; elusive／我～不透他的来意。I cannot figure out why he is coming.／究竟发生了什么事，真让人难以～。It was hard to make head or tail of what was happening.

捉拿 zhuōná arrest; apprehend; catch：～凶手 arrest a murderer／把劫匪～归案 bring the robbers to justice

捉弄 zhuōnòng tease; make fun or a fool of; play pranks on：他可不是你能～的那种人。He is not the sort of man you can put something over on.／愚人节时，人们经常互相～。On April Fools' Day people often play pranks on each other.／她特爱～人。She is a real teaser.／他遭到同事的～。He was made fun of by his colleagues.／不许你再～我。You shall not play me that trick twice.

拙

zhuō ❶ clumsy; awkward; unskilful; dull：眼～ slow to sight and react／手～ be all thumbs／勤以补～ make up for lack of skill with industry／～于言辞 inarticulate; unable to communicate one's ideas adequately ❷ 〈谦词〉my：～译 my translation

拙笨 zhuōbèn clumsy; awkward; dull：口齿～ clumsy of speech／他做针线活～得很。He is very awkward with a needle.

拙笔 zhuōbǐ 〈谦词〉my (poor) writing, painting, or calligraphy

拙稿 zhuōgǎo 〈谦词〉my (poor) manuscript

拙见 zhuōjiàn 〈谦词〉my (humble) opinion：谨献～。Here I offer my humble opinion.

拙荆 zhuōjīng 〈旧词〉my (humble) wife

拙劣 zhuōliè clumsy and inferior：～手法 inferior tactics; clumsy trick／文笔～ poor (*or* bad) writing／～表演 clumsy (*or* poor) performance; bad show

拙朴 zhuōpǔ plain and unadorned：形式～ simple form

拙涩 zhuōsè (of writing) clumsy and obscure

拙政园 Zhuōzhèngyuán Humble Administrator's Garden in Suzhou (苏州), Jiangsu Province

拙直 zhuōzhí honest and straightforward：～的乡下人 simple and straightforward country folk

拙著 zhuōzhù 〈谦词〉my writing

拙嘴笨舌 zhuōzuǐ-bènshé *also*"拙嘴笨腮" be inarticulate; be clumsy in expressing oneself：他说话～。He is clumsy in speaking. *or* He does not shine in conversation.

拙作 zhuōzuò 〈谦词〉my works

焯 zhuō 〈书面〉clear; obvious; evident: ～见 penetrating view (*or* insight)
see also chāo

桌 zhuō ❶ table; desk: 谈判～ negotiating table / 课～ desk / 书～ writing desk; desk / 办公～ (office) desk / 餐～ dining table / 八仙～ old-fashioned square table for eight persons ❷ 〈量词〉*of a feast table, etc.*: 摆一～盛筵 set an abundant table / 两～酒菜 two tables of wine and dishes / 一～～的佳肴 tablefuls (*or* tables) of excellent food / 有五～客人 have five tables of guests / 客人八人一～。The guests sat eight to a table.

桌案 zhuō'àn 〈方言〉(writing) desk
桌布 zhuōbù tablecloth: 铺～ spread a tablecloth
桌菜 zhuōcài half-prepared dishes of meat, fish, vegetables, etc. for a table of guests, which are sold in the market
桌灯 zhuōdēng desk lamp
桌面 zhuōmiàn top of a table; tabletop
桌面出版系统 zhuōmiàn chūbǎn xìtǒng desktop publishing
桌面儿上 zhuōmiànrshang on the table; aboveboard; in public: 把问题都摆到～来 put all the cards on the table; bring problems out into the open / ～的话 appropriate remarks
桌披 zhuōpī *also* "桌裙"; "桌帷" piece of square cloth hanging in front of a desk as decoration
桌椅板凳 zhuōyǐ-bǎndèng tables, chairs and benches — ordinary household furniture
桌子 zhuōzi table; desk
桌子山 Zhuōzishān *also* "卓子山" Zhuózishān Mount Zhuozi in Inner Mongolia, a mesa consisting mainly of crystal slates and sandstones

倬 zhuō 〈书面〉striking; marked; great

镨 zhuō 〈方言〉dig the ground or dig out stubbles (of grain) with a pick
镨钩 zhuōgou 〈方言〉pick; pickaxe

zhuó

着[1] zhuó ❶ wear (clothes); be dressed: 穿红～绿 be dressed in red and green — be gaily dressed / 衣～时髦 be fashionably (*or* stylishly) dressed / 吃～不愁 need not worry about food and clothing; there is plenty to eat and wear ❷ touch; contact: 不～边际 irrelevant; not to the point; wide of the mark; neither here nor there / 附～ adhere to ❸ attach; apply; use: 不～痕迹 leave no trace / 无从～力 not know where to apply one's strength ❹ whereabouts; assured source: 衣食无～ have nothing to eat and wear / 遍寻无～ nowhere to be found; whereabouts unknown / 经费有～了么? Are the funds available?

着[2] zhuó ❶ send; dispatch: 请～人前去联系。Please send someone to contact them. ❷ 〈旧语〉*of documentary usage, indicating an imperative tone of voice*: ～即缉拿凶手。The criminal must be arrested immediately.
see also zhāo; zháo; zhe

着笔 zhuóbǐ set pen to paper; begin to write or paint: 不知从何处～ not know where to begin the writing or painting / 难于～ find it difficult to put it in writing
着花 zhuóhuā 〈书面〉put forth or shoot out buds; bud
着劲儿 zhuójìnr exert all one's strength; make great efforts: 他～拉了我一把。He gave me a tug. / 我这么抬桌子不～。I can't very well use my strength in this position to lift the table.
着力 zhuólì make an effort; exert oneself: ～描写 take great pains to describe sb. or sth.; concentrate one's efforts on depicting sb. or sth. / 无从～ fail to see where to direct one's efforts / ～不多 not make much of an effort / 我当～完成此项任务。I shall put my shoulder to the wheel to accomplish the task.
着陆 zhuólù land; touch down: 安全～ safe landing / 紧急～ emergency landing / 可用～距离 landing distance available / ～滑跑距离 landing run
着陆舱 zhuólùcāng landing module
着陆场 zhuólùchǎng landing field; landing ground
着陆灯 zhuólùdēng landing light
着陆方向标 zhuólù fāngxiàngbiāo landing direction indicator
着陆接地 zhuólù jiēdì touchdown
着落 zhuóluò ❶ whereabouts: 走失的孩子已经有～了。The lost child has been found. ❷ assured source: 研究基金仍无～。We still don't know where to get the research funds. ❸ fall on; rest with: 这任务就～在你身上了。The task has fallen on you. ❹ lay; (often used in the early vernacular) settle: ～停当 properly laid; settled
着墨 zhuómò describe in writing; paint: 画中山峰～太浅。The ink applied to the mountain peaks in the painting is not strong enough. / 小说中这个人物～不多, 却令人感到真实生动。Although only sketchily depicted in the novel, the character is true to life.
着棋 zhuóqí 〈方言〉play chess
着色 zhuósè apply colour; colour: ～法 colouring / ～剂 colouring agent; colouring material / 他在给画～。He is colouring a picture.
着生 zhuóshēng (of an organism) be parasitic on
着实 zhuóshí ❶ indeed; really; truly: 此事～难办。This is indeed a sticky business (*or* a hard nut to crack). / 为了这个晚会, 他们～准备了一番。They really put in a lot of time preparing for the party. ❷ sharply; severely: ～数落了他一顿 give him a good scolding (*or* dressing-down); reprove him sharply
着手 zhuóshǒu put one's hand to; set about; begin: ～写报告 set about preparing the report / ～编教材 undertake the preparation of textbooks / 从调查事实～ start with finding out the facts / 你们怎样～修复这座寺庙? How will you go about restoring the temple? / 既然你已～做这项工作, 就应当把它做好。Now that you've put your hand to the work, you should make a good job of it.
着手成春 zhuóshǒu-chéngchūn *also* "妙手回春" miàoshǒu-huíchūn effect a miraculous cure and bring the dying back to life
着先鞭 zhuó xiānbiān go before; take the lead: 我们要抓紧注册这个商标, 不要让别人着了先鞭。We must register this trade mark ahead of others.
着想 zhuóxiǎng consider; think about: 为他人～ have other people's interests at heart / 他得为自己的前途～。He had to think about his own future. / 从长远利益～, 我们必须这样办。For the sake of our long-term interest, we must do so. / 她是为你～才劝你放弃这个计划的。It was for your good that she advised you to give up the plan.
着眼 zhuóyǎn have sth. in mind; view from the angle of; take as the basis: ～于未来 have one's eyes on the future / ～于人民 have the people in mind / ～于人材培养 aim at the training of professional people / 从大处～, 小处着手 keep the general goal in view (*or* bear larger interests in mind) while going about solving the practical problems / 他在建房时主要～于建筑风格上的美。He constructed the house with an eye to architectural beauty. / 两国领导人～于21世纪, 就发展两国关系作出了具有远见卓识的决策。The leaders of both countries have made farsighted policy decisions with a view to furthering their relations in the 21st century.
着眼点 zhuóyǎndiǎn focus of attention; point of departure: 考虑问题的～ one's focus of attention in considering the problem
着意 zhuóyì ❶ spare no pains; exert oneself; strive: ～领会 strive to understand / ～准备 take great pains with the preparation for / 这篇小说～于主要人物的刻画。This novel concentrates on the depiction of main characters. ❷ take seriously; mind: 他听了这话也不～。He didn't seem to mind much what has been said.
着重 zhuózhòng stress; emphasize; underline: ～指出 point out emphatically; emphasize / ～解决住房问题 make a special effort to solve the housing problem / ～强调体制改革的重要性 stress the importance of structural reform / 他～谈了过去一年的一些主要事件。He highlighted some of the main events of the past year. / 我想～谈一谈这个问题。I would like to address this question in some detail. *or* I would like to dwell on this subject at some length.
着重号 zhuózhònghào mark of emphasis (as in "贵在坚持")
着装 zhuózhuāng ❶ put on (clothes, headgear, etc.) ～完毕 finish dressing oneself; be dressed / 他一向～考究。He is always a smart dresser. / ～要适宜。One should dress for the occasion. ❷ clothing, headgear and footwear

鷟 zhuó *see* "鸑鷟" yuèzhuó

Z

诼 zhuó 〈书面〉slander; calumny; defamation:谣～ rumourmongering and mudslinging

琢 zhuó chisel; cut; carve:用玛瑙～成的饰品 carved agate ornaments /玉不～,不成器 if jade is not cut and polished, it cannot be made into anything — one cannot become useful without being educated; the best horse needs breaking in and the aptest child needs teaching
see also zuó

琢磨 zhuómó ❶ carve and polish (jade, etc.):把汉白玉～成一尊塑像 carve white marble into a statue ❷ (of literary works) polish; refine:这篇文章还需要～一下。The article still needs polishing.
see also zuómo

椓 zhuó castration (a torture in ancient China)

啄 zhuó peck:鸟儿从树干中～食小虫。The bird pecked insects from the trunk of a tree.

啄花鸟 zhuóhuāniǎo flowerpecker
啄木鸟 zhuómùniǎo *also* "䴕" liè woodpecker

浊(濁) zhuó ❶ muddy; murky; turbid:～水 turbid water /污～ filthy; dirty /原清则流清,原～则流～。Clear water flows from a clear source, muddy water from a muddy source. ❷ (of voices) deep and thick:说话～声～气 speak in a deep, raucous voice ❸ chaotic; confused; disorderly

浊点 zhuódiǎn 〈化学〉cloud point
浊度 zhuódù 〈化学〉turbidity /～测定 turbidimetric analysis; turbidimetry /～分析 turbidimetric analysis
浊浪 zhuólàng muddy waves:～排空 tall muddy waves
浊流 zhuóliú ❶ muddy stream:滚滚～ rolling muddy stream; roily waters ❷〈书面〉〈比喻〉base person; vile character; villain ❸〈比喻〉forces of darkness and decadence
浊世 zhuóshì ❶〈书面〉corrupted world; turbulent times:那年月政治腐败,军阀混战,真是名符其实的～。Those were really chaotic times with political corruption and tangled warfare among warlords. ❷〈佛教〉mortal world
浊水溪 Zhuóshuǐxī Zhuoshui River, the longest river (about 170 km) in Taiwan, China
浊物 zhuówù mundane creature; ignoramus
浊音 zhuóyīn 〈语言〉voiced sound:浊辅音 voiced consonants
浊油 zhuóyóu roily oil
浊重 zhuózhòng deep and thick; heavy:～的鼻音 thick nasal voice; deep nasal sound

镯(鐲) zhuó bracelet:手～ bracelet /玉～ jade bracelet

镯子 zhuózi bracelet:银～ silver bracelet

浞 zhuó drench:浑身都被雨～湿了 be drenched (*or* soaked) through with rain; be drenched from head to foot with rain

灼 zhuó ❶ burn; sear; scorch:烧～ burn ❷ bright; shining; luminous:事已彰～,无所复疑。This is already evident and beyond any doubt.

灼急 zhuójí anxious; worried
灼见 zhuójiàn penetrating insight; profound idea:真知～ profound knowledge and penetrating insight; wise judgment
灼烤 zhuókǎo bake; scorch; scald:大地在太阳的～下裂了缝。The land cracked under the scalding sun.
灼亮 zhuóliàng bright; brilliant
灼然 zhuórán very clear; obvious; evident:～可见 as plain as daylight
灼热 zhuórè scorching hot:～的感情 fervour; passion
灼伤 zhuóshāng burn:腿部二度～ second-degree burn on the leg /小男孩玩火把手～了。The little boy burnt his hand playing with fire.
灼灼 zhuózhuó 〈书面〉brilliant; dazzling; shining:若日出之～ as brilliant as the rising sun

酌 zhuó ❶ pour out (wine); drink:自斟自～ drink alone; enjoy a glass of wine all by oneself /对～ (two people) have a drink together ❷〈书面〉meal with wine or spirits:小～ light meal /菲～ simple meal /便～ informal dinner ❸ weigh and consider; mull over; use one's discretion:商～ discuss and think over; deliberate /字斟句～ weigh one's words /以上几点意见,请～予答复。Please consider the above points and favour us with a reply.

酌办 zhuóbàn do as one thinks fit; act according to one's judgment:这件事,请～。Please deal with (*or* handle) the matter at your discretion.
酌处 zhuóchǔ use one's own discretion:请～。I leave it to your discretion.
酌定 zhuódìng make a decision as one sees fit; use one's discretion:～对策 work out counter measures to deal with the matter
酌定法 zhuódìngfǎ *jus dispositivum* (dispositive law or flexible law)
酌量 zhuóliang give due consideration; use one's judgment:礼品由你～购买吧。Buy the presents at your discretion.
酌情 zhuóqíng take into consideration the circumstances; use one's discretion:～处理 settle a matter as one sees fit; deal with matters on the merits of each case; act at one's discretion /对灾区～给予救助 provide relief to disaster areas according to the damage done in each place /我已将此事交由王先生～处理。I have left the matter to Mr. Wang's discretion.
酌予 zhuóyǔ grant (a subsidy, etc.) according to the conditions of the grantee

斫 zhuó cut; chop; hack:～柴 cut fireword /～树 hack (*or* cut, *or* chop) down a tree

斮 zhuó 〈书面〉chop; cut

斲 zhuó 〈书面〉chop; hack; cut:～木为舟 make a boat out of a tree truck; make a dugout canoe

斲鼻 zhuóbí with exceptional skill
斲轮老手 zhuólún-lǎoshǒu expert wheelwright; old hand; very experienced man; past master
斲丧 zhuósàng 〈书面〉destroy one's health or sap one's vitality, esp. by dissipation

缴 zhuó 〈书面〉raw silk string tied to an arrow for shooting birds
see also jiǎo

濯 zhuó 〈书面〉wash:～足 wash one's feet

濯濯 zhuózhuó 〈书面〉(of mountains) bare; bald; denuded:～童山 bare (*or* treeless) hills
濯足节 Zhuózújié 〈基督教〉Maundy Thursday, the Thursday before Easter observed in commemoration of the Last Supper

擢 zhuó 〈书面〉❶ pull out; extract ❷ advance in rank; raise; promote:拔～ select; promote

擢发难数 zhuófà-nánshǔ (of crimes) be as countless as the hairs on a head; be innumerable:毒枭罪行累累,～。This drug baron has committed countless heinous crimes.
擢升 zhuóshēng 〈书面〉promote; raise (in position or rank):～他为经理 promote him to (the position of the) manager
擢用 zhuóyòng 〈书面〉promote:～人才 promote qualified (*or* capable) personnel

卓 zhuó ❶ tall and upright:群峰～立。Ranges of mountains stand upright. ❷ remarkable; outstanding; eminent:成绩～然 achieve outstanding (*or* remarkable) results ❸ (Zhuó) a surname

卓拔 zhuóbá outstanding; eminent:～的才能 outstanding ability (*or* talent)
卓别麟 Zhuóbiélín Charles Spencer Chaplin (1889-1977), English film actor and director
卓尔不群 zhuó'ěr-bùqún rise above the common herd; stand head and shoulders above all others; be pre-eminent; be outstanding:论才识,他在同代人中～。In ability and insight he towers above his contemporaries. *or* He is gifted with talent and insight far beyond his contemporaries.
卓见 zhuójiàn excellent views; brilliant idea:对这类事,她确有～。

Z

She really has some excellent ideas in such matters.

卓绝 zhuójué unsurpassed; outstanding; extreme; of the highest degree:艰苦～的斗争 extremely hard and bitter struggle; most arduous struggle /英勇～的事迹 extremely brave exploits

卓立 zhuólì stand upright; stand erect:～于世界 stand upright in the world

卓荦 zhuóluò *also* "卓跞"〈书面〉unsurpassed; outstanding:～冠群 tower above the rest; eminent among one's contemporaries

卓跞 zhuóluò *see* "卓荦"

卓然 zhuórán outstanding; remarkable:功勋～ with outstanding achievements to one's credit

卓识 zhuóshí outstanding insight; judicious judgment; sagacity:远见～ foresight and vision (*or* sagacity); foresightedness /有～的政治家 politician with vision

卓特 zhuótè *see* "卓异"

卓午 zhuówǔ 〈书面〉high noon

卓异 zhuóyì outstanding; remarkable; unique; out of the ordinary:～的风貌 splendid and unique view /成绩～ achieve remarkable results

卓有成效 zhuóyǒu-chéngxiào highly effective; very fruitful:～的努力 fruitful efforts /农村改革～。Very good results have been attained in rural reform. *or* The reform in rural areas has proved highly successful.

卓越 zhuóyuè outstanding; pre-eminent; remarkable; brilliant:～的才能 superior (*or* remarkable) ability /～的成就 splendid achievements /～的科学家 brilliant (*or* distinguished) scientist /作出～的贡献 make outstanding (*or* singular, *or* extraordinary) contributions /他是青年教师的～代表。He is a pre-eminent representative of the young teachers.

卓著 zhuózhù distinguished; illustrious; eminent:政绩～ outstanding (*or* signal) service in one's political career /战功～ shine with military exploits; render meritorious (*or* illustrious) military service

著[1]

zhuó *see* "着[1]" zhuó

著[2]

zhuó *see* "着[2]" zhuó

see also zhe; zhù

茁

zhuó grow vigorously

茁实 zhuóshi 〈方言〉healthy and strong; robust; sturdy:一条～的汉子 a sturdy man

茁长 zhuózhǎng grow vigorously; grow luxuriantly:两岸茅竹～。Bamboos grow luxuriantly on both banks.

茁壮 zhuózhuàng vigorous; sturdy:～的小树 sturdy young tree /～生长的小麦 wheat growing vigorously (*or* well) /老师的辛勤劳动使得孩子们能够～成长。The hard work of the teachers enabled the healthy and vigorous growth of the children.

zī

粢

zī sacrificial grain in ancient times

see also cí

趑(趦)

zī

趑趄 zījū 〈书面〉❶ walk with difficulty; plough one's way; lumber along ❷ hesitate to advance; falter:～不前 hesitate to act or choose one's course; hang back /～却顾 look back and hesitate to advance

咨

zī ❶ consult; seek ad-vice; take counsel:～问 seek advice; consult /事无大小,悉以～之,然后实行。Whether in matters of major or minor importance, you should take counsel from him before taking action. ❷ *see* "～文"

咨访 zīfǎng 〈书面〉go to solicit the opinion of; consult:～贤能 take counsel from the virtuous and capable

咨嗟 zījiē 〈书面〉❶ sigh; heave a sigh ❷ gasp in admiration; marvel at; highly praise

咨文 zīwén ❶〈旧语〉official communication (between government offices of equal rank) ❷ report delivered by the head of a government on state affairs:国情～(US) State of the Union Message /预算～(US) budget message

咨询 zīxún consult; seek advice; hold counsel with:提供健康～ give counsel on how to keep fit /进行法律～ seek legal advice /～民意 consult the people /～服务 consultancy /～小组 advisory panel /～意见 advisory opinion /～机构 advisory body /～委员会 advisory committee (*or* council, *or* commission); consultative committee

咨询业 zīxúnyè consultancy service

谘

zī *see* "咨❶" zī

资[1]

zī ❶ fund; money; expenses; capital:工～ pay; wages; salary /外～ foreign (*or* oversea) capital /邮～ postage /合～ joint venture /～不抵债 unable to pay one's debt with all his assets; insolvent /劳～双方 labour and capital /集～办厂 raise funds to set up a factory ❷ help; subsidize; support:～以万金 provide with huge subsidies /此乃天～我也。God is helping me. ❸ serve; provide; supply:可～借鉴 can serve as an example /以～参考 for your reference /广泛报道,以～鼓励 give wide publicity by way of encouragement ❹ (Zī) a surname

资[2]

zī ❶ natural ability; endowment; aptitude:天～聪颖 be endowed with remarkable talents; be of brilliant natural endowments ❷ qualifications; seniority; record of service:年～ years of service; seniority /～深元老 senior statesmen /论～排辈 give top priority to seniority (in the selection of cadres); promotion goes by seniority /～浅齿少 of a young age and with little work experience

资本 zīběn ❶ capital:官僚～ bureaucrat-capital (capital assets of bureaucrat-capitalists) /垄断～ monopoly capital /不变～ constant capital / 可变～ variable capital /固定～ fixed capital /流动～ circulating (*or* current, *or* floating) capital; working (*or* liquid, *or* fluid) capital /金融～ financial capital /生产～ productive (*or* production) capital /信用～ credit capital /股份～ joint-stock capital /借贷～ loan capital /货币～ money capital /外国～ foreign capital /过剩～ surplus capital /～过剩 overcapitalization /～积累 accumulation of capital /～收益 capital gains (*or* income, *or* revenue) /～输出 export of capital; capital export /～投入 capital input /～投资 capital investment /～外流 outflow of capital /～转移 capital transfer /～增值 increase in capital /～循环 rotation of capital /～周转 turnover of capital /～的有机构成 organic composition of capital /～集中 centralization of capital /～密集程度 capital intensity /该公司拥有～五百万元。The company has a capital of 5 million *yuan*. ❷ sth. to capitalize on:捞取政治～ gain political capital; make political capital out of /讨价还价的～ bargaining chip (*or* counters) /把集体成果作为个人名利的～ capitalize on the achievements of the team for personal fame and gain

资本成本 zīběn chéngběn cost of capital

资本承诺 zīběn chéngnuò capital commitment

资本帝国主义 zīběn dìguózhǔyì capitalist-imperialism

资本化 zīběnhuà capitalisation

资本货物 zīběn huòwù capital goods

资本家 zīběnjiā capitalist:大～ mammoth capitalist /产业～ industrial capitalist /商业～ merchant capitalist /货币～ money capitalist /借贷～ loaning capitalist /垄断～ monopoly capitalist /不法～ law-breaking capitalist /～代理人 agent of a capitalist /～阶级 capitalist class

资本论 Zīběnlùn *Das Kapital* (works in three volumes completed in 1867, 1885 and 1894 by Karl Marx with the 2nd and 3rd volumes edited by Friedrich Engels)

资本密集工业 zīběn mìjí gōngyè capital intensive industry

资本市场 zīběn shìchǎng capital market:～价值总额 market capitalisation

资本收益率 zīběn shōuyìlǜ return on capital

资本收益税 zīběn shōuyìshuì capital gains tax

资本税 zīběnshuì capital tax

资本系数 zīběn xìshù capital coefficient

资本账户 zīběn zhànghù capital account:～不可兑换 capital account inconvertibility

资本主义 zīběnzhǔyì capitalism:国家垄断～ state monopoly capitalism /自由～ laissez-faire (*or* non-monopoly) capitalism /官僚～ bureaucrat-capitalism /产业～ industrial capitalism /金融～ financial

capitalism /商业~ commercial capitalism /~社会 capitalist society /~制度 capitalist system /~私有制 capitalist private ownership /~道路 capitalist road /~残余势力 remnant capitalist forces /~复辟 capitalist restoration /~计划经济 capitalist planned economy /~经济成分 capitalist sector of the economy /~经营思想 capitalist ideas in management; ideas characterizing capitalist management /~商品经济 capitalist commodity economy /~市场经济 capitalist market economy /~前生产方式 pre-capitalist modes of production /~生产方式 capitalist mode of production /~世界货币体系 capitalist world monetary system /~农业 capitalist farming /~自发势力 spontaneous capitalist forces

资本主义总危机 zīběnzhǔyì zǒngwēijī general crisis of capitalism

资本准备金 zīběn zhǔnbèijīn capital reserves

资材 zīcái materials and equipment:调剂~ redistribute goods and materials

资财 zīcái capital and goods; assets:年终清点~ make a year-end inventory of the assets (of a factory, etc.) /调拨~ allocate and transfer goods and funds

资产 zīchǎn ❶ property; estate:巨额~ large property /世袭~ hereditary property ❷ capital fund; capital ❸〈经济〉assets:固定~ fixed assets /流动~ liquid assets /短期~ short-lived assets /有形~ tangible assets /~冻结 freezing of assets /~比率 asset ratio /~总额 general assets /~决算 assets settlement /~结构 assets structure /~估价 assets valuation /~和负债 assets and liabilities

资产剥离 zīchǎn bōlí asset-stripping

资产重组 zīchǎn chóngzǔ reorganization of assets

资产负债表 zīchǎn fùzhàibiǎo statement of assets and liabilities; balance sheet

资产阶级 zīchǎnjiējí capitalist class; bourgeoisie:官僚~ bureaucrat-capitalist class /民族~ national bourgeoisie /买办~ comprador bourgeoisie /小~ petty bourgeoisie /~分子 bourgeois element /~民主 bourgeois democracy /~民族主义分子 bourgeois nationalist elements /~化 become bourgeoisified /~世界观 bourgeois world outlook /~思潮 bourgeois trend /~思想 bourgeois ideas (*or* ideology)

资产阶级革命 zīchǎnjiējí gémìng bourgeois revolution

资产阶级个人主义 zīchǎnjiējí gèrénzhǔyì bourgeois individualism

资产阶级和平主义 zīchǎnjiējí hépíngzhǔyì bourgeois pacifism

资产阶级民主革命 zīchǎnjiējí mínzhǔ gémìng bourgeois-democratic revolution

资产阶级权利 zīchǎnjiējí quánlì bourgeois right

资产阶级专政 zīchǎnjiējí zhuānzhèng dictatorship of the bourgeoisie

资产阶级自由化 zīchǎnjiējí zìyóuhuà bourgeois liberalization or liberalism

资产账户 zīchǎn zhànghù asset account

资敌 zīdí aid or support the enemy

资方 zīfāng owner of a private enterprise; capital:~人员 capitalists and their representatives /~代理人 agent of a capitalist

资费 zīfèi expenses; costs

资斧 zīfǔ 〈书面〉travelling expenses; travel costs:~无着 have no money to pay one's travelling expenses

资格 zīgé ❶ qualifications:就业~ job qualification /投票~ qualification for voting /有~ be qualified; have the requisite qualifications /取消考试~ be disqualified from the examination /丧失俱乐部会员~ lose or forfeit one's membership in a club /有~领取养老金 be entitled to a pension /没~参加校足球队 not eligible for the school football team /获得当教师的~ obtain the qualifications for teaching; become a certified teacher /他太年轻,没有~当主席。His youth disqualified him from becoming president. *or* He is too young to be qualified for presidency. /你有什么~指责我? What right have you to criticize me? ❷ seniority:老~的政治家 senior statesman /老~的工会主席 trade union chairman of long standing /摆老~ flaunt one's seniority; put on the airs of veterans

资格审查委员会 zīgé shěnchá wěiyuánhuì credentials committee

资格证书 zīgé zhèngshū credentials

资金 zījīn ❶ fund:科研~ funds for scientific research /发展农业的~ funds for developing agriculture /储备~ reserve funds /周转~ working (*or* circulating, *or* revolving) funds /~周转 cash flow /~短缺 be short of funds /筹措~ raise funds for /提供~ financing ❷ capital:开一个小饭馆用不了多少~。Not much capital is needed for starting a small restaurant. /店铺经营不善,~亏损严重。The business suffered a great loss due to poor management.

资力 zīlì ❶ financial strength:~雄厚 awash with capital; financially powerful /~匮乏 be short of capital ❷ talent and ability:搞这项科研,我的~不够。I am not competent for this research project.

资历 zīlì qualifications; record of service; seniority:~不足 lack in qualifications and experience /晋升应当根据~还是根据实绩? Should promotion go by seniority or by merit? /他做外交工作的~很深。He has credentials of long diplomatic service. /做管理工作,他~很浅。He had very little previous experience in management.

资料 zīliào ❶ means:生活~ means of livelihood (*or* subsistence); consumer goods /生产~ means of production; capital goods ❷ data; material; information:统计~ statistical data /研究~ research material /文献~ documents; literature /~处理 data processing /~室 reference room

资遣 zīqiǎn give money and send home or back to one's own country; dismiss sb. with severance pay

资深 zīshēn senior:~教授 senior professor

资送 zīsòng give material assistance; provide with goods and materials:他对我多有~。He has offered me generous assistance.

资望 zīwàng seniority and prestige:~很高的外交家 prestigious senior diplomat

资信可靠 zīxìn kěkào safe to give credit to; creditworthy

资信情况 zīxìn qíngkuàng credit position

资性 zīxìng *see* "资质"

资讯战 zīxùnzhàn 〈军事〉information warfare

资用 zīyòng 〈物理〉available:~功率 available power /~电子 available electron

资用荷载 zīyòng hèzài 〈物理〉working load

资源 zīyuán natural resources; resources:水力~丰富 abound (*or* be rich) in water-power resources /木材~枯竭 exhausted timber resources /开发~ tap (*or* exploit, *or* develop) natural resources /保护~ conserve resources /爱护人力~ treasure manpower (*or* human) resources /充分利用我们的风景~ make the most of our scenic resources /地下~ hidden resources /煤炭~ resources in coal /旅游~ tourist resources /农业~ farm resources /智力~ intellectual resources /未开采的~ undeveloped (*or* untapped) resources /未利用的~ idle resources /~勘探 prospecting of resources; resource survey /~利用 resource utilization

资政 zīzhèng senior advisor; (Singapore) senior minister

资治通鉴 Zīzhì Tōngjiàn *Zi Zhi Tong Jian* or *Historical Events Retold as a Mirror for Government*, first chronological general history of China (from 403 BC to 959 AD), written by Sima Guang (司马光, 1019-1086) of the Northern Song Dynasty

资质 zīzhì natural endowments; aptitude; intelligence:~超群 of extraordinary endowments /~愚鲁 be foolish and rash by nature /不能否认~对人的成长所起的作用。It is undeniable that natural endowments play a role in the making of a man.

资助 zīzhù give financial aid; aid financially; subsidize:从物质上给予~ give material assistance to /受过他~的人不少。Quite a few people have received financial aid from him.

姿

zī ❶ looks; countenance; appearance:雄~ majestic looks; heroic posture /风~ charming appearance; graceful bearing ❷ gesture; carriage; bearing; posture:坐~ sitting (*or* seated) posture; in a sitting position /舞~ dancer's posture and movements /绰约多~ graceful carriage /蒲柳之~ fragile frame; frail beauty

姿控陀螺 zīkòng tuóluó 〈航空〉attitude gyro

姿媚 zīmèi 〈书面〉charming carriage:~可人 lovely and charming

姿容 zīróng looks; appearance:~俏丽 good-looking; attractive; pretty

姿色 zīsè (of a woman) good looks:~出众 extraordinary beauty /颇有几分~ be rather good-looking /她的美貌令许多~欠佳的人羡慕不已。Her beauty made her the envy of many less lavishly endowed.

姿势 zīshì gesture; posture; carriage:站立或躺着的~ standing or recumbent posture /跪或蹲的~ kneeling or squatting posture /笔直的~ erect carriage (*or* posture) /滑稽的~ antic gestures; antics /保持这种~ maintain (*or* hold) the pose /~正确有助于保持健康。Good (*or* Correct) posture helps you keep fit. /他摆好~与老师合影。He posed for a photograph with his teacher.

姿首 zīshǒu 〈书面〉good looks (with heavy, jet-black hair)

姿态 zītài ❶ posture; bearing; deportment; carriage:~优美潇洒 have a graceful (*or* elegant) carriage /说话时的~ one's deportment

(*or* demeanour) while speaking /～各异的泥塑 clay figures in various postures /保持威严庄重的～ preserve one's grave and dignified bearing ❷ attitude; pose; gesture:保持低～ maintain (*or* cut) a low profile /采取高～ keep a high profile; show magnanimity; exercise forbearance; be tolerant /作出～ make gestures; strike a pose (*or* posture) /作出强硬～ take a strong posture; show intransigence /摆出一副矫揉造作的～ make an affected pose /以调停者的～出现 assume the role of a mediator /他的宽宏大度不过是一种～。His easy generosity was a mere pose.

兹(茲) zī 〈书面〉❶ this:念～在～ always remember this; bear this in mind ❷ now; at present:自～以后 from now on /～将获奖人员名单公布如下。Below is a list of the prize-winners. /为庆祝"五·一"国际劳动节,～定于五月一日上午在中山公园举行游园活动。To mark the International Labour Day, celebrations will be held in Dr. Sun Yat-sen Memorial Park on the morning of May 1. ❸ year:不待来～ before next year /今～美禾,来～美麦。Strong seedlings this year, a fine crop of wheat next year.
see also cí

兹事体大 zīshì-tǐdà 〈书面〉this is a serious matter indeed; this is no small matter:创办一所大学,～,有关方面尚在考虑中。As the establishment of a university is no small matter, it is still under consideration by the authorities concerned.

滋[1] zī ❶ grow; multiply; breed:繁～ multiply profusely /～茂 (of plants) grow vigorously; thrive ❷ more:贪取～甚 be more corrupt than ever /积货～多,蓄怨～厚。The more wealth one piles up (*or* accumulates, *or* amasses), the greater enmity he incurs.

滋[2] zī 〈方言〉spurt; spout; burst:水管裂了,～得到处都是水。The pipe had a crack and water spurted all over the place (*or* everywhere). /动脉切断了,血直往外～。Blood was spouting from the severed artery.

滋补 zībǔ nourishing; nutritious:～药 tonic /～食品 nourishing food; nourishment /～身体 build up one's health (with nourishing food or tonics) /西洋参的～功效不凡。American ginseng has a good tonic effect.

滋蔓 zīmàn 〈书面〉grow and spread; grow fast:池中水草～。Waterweeds grew and spread quickly in the pond.

滋蔓难图 zīmàn-nántú 〈书面〉difficult to deal with dangerous forces that grow insidiously; hard to cope with a fast-spreading evil

滋毛儿 zīmáor *also* "髭毛儿" zīmáor ❶ fly into a temper; get angry ❷ make trouble; create a disturbance

滋扰 zīrǎo harass; stir up trouble:聚众～ gather a crowd to create a disturbance

滋润 zīrùn ❶ moist; humid:空气～ moist air /～的秀发 silken (*or* sleek) hair ❷ moisten:～皮肤 soften (*or* moisten) one's skin /河水～着两岸的田地。The river provides moisture for the fields on both sides. ❸ 〈方言〉well-off; comfortable:日子过得很～ lead a very comfortable life

滋生 zīshēng ❶ *also* "孳生" zīshēng breed; propagate; grow; multiply:防止蚊蝇～ prevent the breeding (*or* multiplication) of flies and mosquitoes /春天是万物～的季节。Spring is the season when all lives begin to waken and grow. ❷ bring; cause; create; provoke:～祸患 bring disaster (*or* misfortune) /～事端 create (*or* stir up) trouble; raise a disturbance /双方之间～了爱慕之情。Love grew up between them.

滋事 zīshì make trouble; provoke a dispute:酗酒～ kick up a row when one is in drink (*or* is drunk); make trouble under the influence of alcohol

滋味 zīwèi taste; savour; flavour:苦涩的～ bitter and puckery flavour /品尝菜肴的～ taste (*or* have a taste of) the dishes /心中不是～ feel upset (*or* bad) /吃得有滋有味 eat with great relish /她感冒了,吃东西没～。The cold dulled her appetite. /那是我第一次尝到寄人篱下的～。That was my first taste of life under another's roof.

滋芽 zīyá 〈方言〉sprout; germinate

滋养 zīyǎng ❶ nourish:～病体 take nourishment (and rest) to regain one's health (*or* to recuperate) /仅靠药物～,身体壮不起来。You can't rely on tonics alone to build up your strength. ❷ nutriment; nourishment:吸收～ assimilate nutriment

滋养品 zīyǎngpǐn nourishing food; nutriment; nourishment

滋阴 zīyīn 〈中医〉method of treating *yin* deficiency by reinforcing body fluid and nourishing the blood

滋育 zīyù cultivate and nourish:太阳的光和热,～着万物生长。Everything on earth draws nourishment from the light and heat of the sun.

滋长 zīzhǎng grow; develop; engender:～骄傲情绪 become conceited /防止～官僚主义作风 guard against bureaucratism /如果"一切向钱看"的思想得以～蔓延,后果必将十分严重。If the idea of "putting money above everything else" is allowed to grow unchecked, grave consequences will definitely ensue.

滋殖 zīzhí multiply; breed; propagate:植物～。Plants grow.

嗞 zī *see* "吱" zī

嗞啦 zīlā *also* "嗞喇" 〈象声〉hissing sound (made as when sth. is put in hot oil); sputter; sizzle:热油锅里的鱼～直响。The fish are sizzling in the hot frying pan.

嵫 zī *see* "崦嵫" Yānzī

镃 zī

镃镇 zījī *also* "镃基" 〈书面〉big hoe

孳 zī multiply; propagate:～衍 grow and multiply

孳乳 zīrǔ 〈书面〉❶ (of mammals) breed; multiply; propagate ❷ derive:探索文字变化～的轨迹 trace the derivation of characters

孳生 zīshēng multiply; breed; propagate:～地 breeding ground /夏季是蚊蝇～的季节。Mosquitoes and flies breed in summer.

孳孳 zīzī *see* "孜孜" zīzī

吱 zī 〈象声〉❶ squeak:老鼠在墙角～～叫。The mouse squeaked in the corner. /这门铰链不上油就嘎～作响。The door hinge will squeak if you don't oil it. ❷ (of small birds) chirp; cheep; peep
see also zhī

吱声 zīshēng 〈方言〉utter a sound; speak:这孩子一直没～。The child remained silent (kept his mouth shut). /问他半天,他就是不～。We kept questioning him for quite a while but couldn't get a peep out of him. /她一声也不敢吱。She dared not utter a word.

鼒 zī 〈书面〉tripod tapering off towards the top

訾 zī ❶ 〈书面〉*see* "赀 ❶" zī ❷ (Zī) a surname
see also zǐ

髭 zī moustache

髭蟾 zīchán *also* "胡子蛙" húziwā 〈动物〉*Vibrissaphora boringii*

髭毛儿 zīmáor *also* "滋毛儿" zīmáor 〈方言〉❶ flare up; lose one's temper:他一听这话就～了。He blew up when hearing this. ❷ make trouble; create a disturbance:流氓们再也不敢～了。The gansters no longer dared to make any trouble.

髭须 zīxū moustache; whiskers:～皆白 grey beard

龇(呲) zī 〈口语〉bare; show

龇牙咧嘴 zīyá-liězuǐ ❶ show one's teeth; look ferocious:凶手挥动菜刀,～地扑向警察。The murderer, brandishing the knife, sprang desperately on the policeman. ❷ contort one's face in agony; grimace with pain; make a wry face:他疼得～。His face contorted in a grimace at the pain. *or* He grimaced with pain. /她～地尝着酸葡萄。She tasted the sour grapes with a wry expression on her face.

赀 zī ❶ reckon; calculate; estimate:所费不～ incur a considerable expense /一日所损不～ cause enormous (*or* great) losses within a day ❷ fund; money; expenses

觜 zī one of the twenty-eight constellations (二十八宿) in ancient Chinese astronomy (consisting of three stars in Orion)
see also zuǐ

孜 zī

孜孜 zīzī *also* "孳孳" zīzī diligent; industrious; studious; hard-working:对学业～以求 study hard; work assiduously to acquire knowledge /～不怠地工作 work diligently and indefatigably; work with indefatigable zeal
孜孜不倦 zīzī-bùjuàn diligently; industriously; assiduously; indefatigably:～地学习 be assiduous (*or* diligent) in one's studies; study with remarkable diligence
孜孜矻矻 zīzī-kūkū 〈书面〉diligent; industrious:～的学者生涯 life of a diligent and serious scholar

仔

zī
see also zǎi; zǐ
仔肩 zījiān 〈书面〉official responsibilities

菑

zī ❶〈古语〉newly cultivated land ❷〈书面〉weeding

辎

zī ancient covered wagon
辎重 zīzhòng 〈军事〉impedimenta; baggage and other supplies of an army:～车辆 vehicles carrying the supplies and gear of an army

锱

zī ancient unit of weight, equal to one fourth of a *liang* (两)
锱铢 zīzhū small amount of money; farthing; trifle
锱铢必较 zīzhū-bìjiào haggle over every penny; dispute over trivialities:何必～? Why quibble over these trifles? /这个吝啬鬼对钱向来是～的。The miser haggles over every penny.

鲻

zī 〈动物〉mullet

缁

zī 〈书面〉black:～衣 black coat
缁黄 zīhuáng black and yellow — Buddhist monk and Taoist priest
缁素 zīsù black and white — monk and layman

zǐ

滓

zǐ ❶ sediment; dregs; lees:渣～ dregs ❷ muddy; dirty:垢～ dirt

梓

zǐ ❶〈植物〉Chinese catalpa (*Catalpa ovata*) ❷ cut blocks for printing:付～ send to the printers
梓宫 zǐgōng coffin for an emperor or empress, often made of Chinese catalpa wood
梓里 zǐlǐ 〈书面〉hometown; native place:荣归～ return to one's native place with honour
梓童 zǐtóng (often used in old novels and operas) term used by an emperor to address the empress
梓行 zǐxíng blockprinting; printing; publishing

訾

zǐ 〈书面〉slander; smear; calumniate:～毁 vilify; defame
see also zī
訾议 zǐyì discuss the failings of others; find fault with; disparage:竞相～ (of a number of people) hurl criticisms at sb.

呰

zǐ 〈书面〉❶ *see* "訾" zǐ ❷ *see* "呰" zǐ

呰

zǐ
呰窳 zǐyǔ 〈书面〉laziness

紫

zǐ ❶ purple; violet ❷ (Zǐ) a surname
紫菜 zǐcài 〈植物〉laver; *Porphyra*:甘～ *Porphyra tenera* / 条斑～ *Porphyra yezoensis* / 坛～ *Porphyra haitanensis*
紫菜苔 zǐcàitái 〈植物〉*Brassica chinensis* var. *purpurea*
紫草 zǐcǎo Asian puccoon; Chinese gromwell (*Lithosopermum erythrorrhizon*)
紫草茸 zǐcǎoróng 〈中药〉shellac; lac
紫癜 zǐdiàn 〈医学〉purpura
紫貂 zǐdiāo *also* "黑貂" hēidiāo 〈动物〉sable:～皮大衣 sable coat
紫丁香 zǐdīngxiāng (early) lilac (*Syringa oblata*)
紫绀 zǐgàn 〈医学〉cyanosis
紫光阁 Zǐguānggé Hall of Purple Light in Zhongnanhai (中南海), Beijing
紫毫 zǐháo writing brush made of dark purple rabbit's hair
紫河车 zǐhéchē 〈中药〉dried human placenta
紫红 zǐhóng purplish red
紫花 zǐhuā light reddish brown
紫花布 zǐhuābù nankeen
紫花地丁 zǐhuā dìdīng *also* "地丁"〈植物〉Chinese violet (*Viola philippica*)
紫花苜蓿 zǐhuā mùxu *also* "紫苜蓿";"苜蓿" mùxu alfalfa (*Medicago sativa*)
紫胶 zǐjiāo shellac; lac
紫胶虫 zǐjiāochóng lac insect (*Laccifer lacca*)
紫金山 Zǐjīnshān Mount Zijin (in the eastern suburb of Nanjing, where China's biggest observatory is situated)
紫金牛 zǐjīnniú 〈植物〉Japanese ardisia (*Ardisia japonica*)
紫堇 zǐjǐn 〈植物〉corydalis (*Corydalis edulis*)
紫禁城 Zǐjìnchéng Forbidden City (in Beijing)
紫荆 zǐjīng 〈植物〉Chinese redbud (*Cercis chinensis*)
紫荆花 zǐjīnghuā bauhinia (flower of the Chinese redbud):香港特别行政区的区旗是五星花蕊的～红旗。The regional flag of the Hong Kong Special Administrative Region is a red flag with a bauhinia highlighted by five star-tipped stamens.
紫晶 zǐjīng *see* "紫石英"
紫羚羊 zǐlíngyáng bongo
紫罗兰 zǐluólán 〈植物〉violet; common stock (*Matthiola incana*)
紫露草 zǐlùcǎo tradescantia
紫霉素 zǐméisù 〈生化〉viomycin
紫茉莉 zǐmòli *also* "草茉莉" cǎomòli 〈植物〉four-o'clock (*Mirabilis jalapa*)
紫薸 zǐpiáo 〈植物〉*Azolla imbricata*
紫萍 zǐpíng *also* "浮萍" fúpíng duckweed (*Spirodela polyrrhiza*)
紫气 zǐqì 〈旧语〉auspicious atmosphere indicating the arrival of an emperor, a sage, or the appearance of treasure:～东来 the purple air comes from the east — a propitious omen appears
紫砂 zǐshā boccaro ware:～壶 boccaro teapot
紫杉 zǐshān 〈植物〉(Japanese) yew (*Taxus cuspidata*)
紫参 zǐshēn *also* "石见穿" shíjiànchuān 〈中药〉Chinese salvia (*Salvia chinensis*) (not including the subterranean part)
紫石英 zǐshíyīng *also* "紫水晶";"紫晶" amethyst
紫树 zǐshù tupelo
紫苏 zǐsū 〈植物〉purple perilla (*Perilla frutescens* var. *crispa*):～油 perilla oil
紫穗槐 zǐsuìhuái 〈植物〉false indigo (*Amorpha fruiticosa*)
紫檀 zǐtán 〈植物〉red sandlewood; padauk (*Pterocarpus indicus*):～家具 sandlewood furniture; padauk furniture
紫糖 zǐtáng *also* "紫棠";"紫膛" (of complexion) swarthy touched with red:～脸 dark red face
紫藤 zǐténg 〈植物〉Chinese wistaria (*Wistaria sinensis*)
紫铜 zǐtóng *also* "红铜" hóngtóng red copper
紫外天文学 zǐwài tiānwénxué ultraviolet astronomy
紫外线 zǐwàixiàn *also* "紫外光"〈物理〉ultraviolet ray:～灯 ultraviolet lamp /～辐射损伤 ultraviolet radiation injury
紫菀 zǐwǎn 〈植物〉aster (*Aster tataricus*)
紫葳 zǐwēi *also* "凌霄花" língxiāohuā Chinese trumpet creeper (*Campsis grandiflora*)
紫薇 zǐwēi 〈植物〉crape myrtle (*Lagerstroemia indica*)
紫雪 zǐxuě *also* "紫雪丹"〈中药〉purplish red powder made from rhinoceros horn, antelope horn, gypsum, musk and so on, which has a febrifugal and resuscitating effect
紫药水 zǐyàoshuǐ *also* "龙胆紫" lóngdǎnzǐ 〈药学〉gentian violet
紫云英 zǐyúnyīng *also* "红花草" hónghuācǎo 〈植物〉Chinese milk vetch (*Astragalus sinicus*)
紫芝 zǐzhī 〈中药〉type of gill fungus similar to glossy ganoderma
紫竹 zǐzhú *also* "黑竹" hēizhú 〈植物〉black bamboo (*Phyllostachys nigra*):～手杖 walking stick made of black bamboo
紫竹院公园 Zǐzhúyuàn Gōngyuán Purple Bamboo Park, Beijing

笫

zǐ 〈书面〉mat made of thin bamboo strips:床～ bed mat

秭 zǐ 〈古语〉billion (as in the UK and Germany); thousand billion or trillion (as in the US and France)

姊 zǐ elder sister; sister

姊妹 zǐmèi elder and younger sisters; sisters:三～ three sisters

姊妹城 zǐmèichéng *also* "姊妹市" sister city relationship; twinning of cities; twin cities:上海与旧金山结成了～。Shanghai is twinned with San Francisco.

姊妹船 zǐmèichuán boats or ships of the same design; sister ship

姊妹花 zǐmèihuā two sisters

姊妹篇 zǐmèipiān companion volume or piece

子[1] zǐ ❶ son; child:长～ eldest son /独～ only son /爱～ one's darling (*or* beloved) son /母以～贵。The mother basks in her son's glory. /母～候车室 waiting room (as in a railway station) for mothers with babies ❷ person:男～ male person; man /女～ female person; woman /弟～ disciple /学～ student ❸ ancient title of respect for a learned or virtuous man or a man in general:孔～ Confucius /孟～ Mencius /荀～ Master Xun /夫～ master ❹ (in ancient times) you:以～之矛,攻～之盾 pierce your shield with your own spear — beat sb. with his own weapon; refute sb. with his own argument ❺ "philosophy", the third traditional category of Chinese writings, as distinct from "Confucian classics" (经), "history" (史), and "belles-lettres" (集) ❻ seed:油菜～儿 rapeseed /南瓜～儿 pumpkin seed /结～儿 bear seed; go to seed ❼ egg:鸭～儿 duck's egg /鱼～ roe ❽ young; small; tender: *see* "～鸡"; "～姜" ❾ subsidiary: *see* "～公司" ❿ sth. small and hard:石头～儿 small stone; pebble /算盘～儿 abacus bead /枪～儿 bullet ⓫ copper coin; copper:半个～儿都不值 not worth half a copper; worthless /手头只剩两个小～儿了 have only two coppers left /一个～儿也不给你。I won't give you a single penny. ⓬〈量词〉:一～毛线 a hank of knitting wool /一～挂面 a bundle of fine dried noodles ⓭ (Zǐ) a surname

子[2] zǐ viscount

子[3] zǐ first of the twelve Earthly Branches

子 zi ❶ *used after a noun, adjective or verb as a noun suffix*:桌～ table; desk /窗～ window /刀～ knife; sword /矮～ short person; shorty; dwarf /胖～ fat person; fatty /傻～ foolish person; fool /垫～ mat; cushion /筷～ chopsticks /推～ hair-clippers; barber's clippers ❷ *used after a classifier as a suffix*:忙了一阵～ be busily occupied (*or* busy) for some time /这档～事可不能含糊。We must not be careless in handling this matter. /她一下～就认出了他。She recognized him at first glance.

子部 zǐbù *also* "丙部" bǐngbù "philosophy", third of the four traditional categories of Chinese writings, which contains works by the exponents of the various schools of thought other than confucianism from the Spring and Autumn Period onwards

子潮 zǐcháo high tide coming in during the period from 11 p.m. to 1 a.m.

子城 zǐchéng extension of the old city; satellite town

子程序 zǐchéngxù 〈计算机〉subroutine; subprogram:～库 subroutine library /子～ sub-subroutine

子丑寅卯 zǐ-chǒu-yín-mǎo ❶ first four of the twelve Earthly Branches ❷〈比喻〉proper arrangement of ideas (in speech, etc.); reason; argument:她叨叨了半天,也没说出个～来。She talked a lot but failed to come up with any convincing argument (*or* but made you none the wiser).

子畜 zǐchù *also* "仔畜" zǐchù young animal; newborn animal

子代 zǐdài 〈生物〉filial generation:第一～ first filial generation

子代换 zǐdàihuàn subsubstitution

子弹 zǐdàn bullet; cartridge:手枪～ pistol bullet /汽枪～ airgun pellet /练习～ dummy cartridge /橡皮～ rubber bullet /～壳 cartridge case /～带 cartridge belt; bandoleer /～箱 cartridge box

子导弹 zǐdǎodàn 〈军事〉submissile

子堤 zǐdī *see* "子埝"

子弟 zǐdì sons and younger brothers; younger generation; children; juniors:农家～ sons and daughters of peasants or farmers /职工～ children of the workers and staff (of a factory, etc.) /纨绔～ profligate sons of the rich; dandies

子弟兵 zǐdìbīng army made up of the sons of the people; people's own army:工农～ army of the workers and peasants

子弟书 zǐdìshū *zidishu*, stories told to the accompaniment of a drum, similar to *dagu* (大鼓) and originated by the descendants of the "Eight Banners" (八旗) of the Man nationality in the Qing Dynasty

子房 zǐfáng 〈植物〉ovary

子妇 zǐfù 〈书面〉❶ son and daughter-in-law ❷ daughter-in-law

子公司 zǐgōngsī subcompany; subsidiaries:外国～ foreign affiliates

子宫 zǐgōng 〈生理〉uterus; womb

子宫癌 zǐgōng'ái hysterocarcinoma; metrocarcinoma

子宫肌瘤 zǐgōngjīliú hysteromyoma:～切除术 hysteromyomectomy

子宫节育环 zǐgōng jiéyùhuán intrauterine contraceptive device

子宫颈 zǐgōngjǐng cervix (of womb); cervix uteri:～癌 carcinoma of cervix uterus /～糜烂 cervical erosion /～炎 cervicitis

子宫镜 zǐgōngjìng hysteroscope; uteroscope:～检 hysteroscopy; metroscopy

子宫扩张术 zǐgōng kuòzhāngshù metreurysis

子宫帽 zǐgōngmào cervical cap

子宫内膜 zǐgōng nèimó endometrium:～炎 endometritis

子宫切除术 zǐgōng qiēchúshù uterectomy

子宫脱垂 zǐgōng tuōchuí metreptosis; prolapse of uterus

子宫外孕 zǐgōng wàiyùn ectopic or extrauterine pregnancy

子宫纤维瘤 zǐgōng xiānwéiliú metrofibroma

子宫炎 zǐgōngyán metritis

子规 zǐguī 〈动物〉cuckoo

子鸡 zǐjī *also* "仔鸡" zǐjī chick

子姜 zǐjiāng tender ginger

子金 zǐjīn interest

子爵 zǐjué viscount:～夫人 viscountess

子爵号 Zǐjuéhào Viscount (a kind of civilian passenger aircraft made in the UK)

子空间 zǐkōngjiān subspace

子口 zǐkou opening or mouth (of a bottle, jar, jug, box, etc.)

子粒 zǐlì *also* "籽粒" zǐlì 〈农业〉seed; grain; kernel; bean:～饱满 full grains

子棉 zǐmián *also* "籽棉" zǐmián unginned cotton

子母弹 zǐmǔdàn 〈军事〉cluster bomb unit

子母机 zǐmǔjī 〈军事〉composite aircraft

子母扣儿 zǐmǔkòur *also* "摁扣儿" ènkòur snap fastener; press-stud; popper

子母绿 zǐmǔlǜ emerald

子母钟 zǐmǔzhōng secondary and primary clock

子目 zǐmù specific item; subtitle

子囊 zǐnáng 〈植物〉ascus

子埝 zǐniàn *also* "子堤" reinforcement on top of a dyke during a flood

子女 zǐnǚ sons and daughters; children:独生～ only child /独生～家庭 single-child family

子时 zǐshí period of the day from 11 p.m. to 1 a.m.

子实 zǐshí 〈农业〉seed; grain; kernel; bean

子兽 zǐshòu *also* "仔兽" zǐshòu newborn animal; young animal

子书 zǐshū works of ancient philosophers other than those of Confucius, which belong to the third traditional category of Chinese writings
see also "子部"

子嗣 zǐsì son; male offspring:有乏～之虞 fear that one will have no son

子孙 zǐsūn children and children's children; descendants:～万代 generation after generation /炎黄～ descendants of Yandi and Huangdi — Chinese people

子孙饽饽 zǐsūn bōbo 〈旧语〉small dumplings at a wedding feast specially prepared for the bride and bridegroom

子孙后代 zǐsūn-hòudài descendants; posterity; generations to come:为～造福 benefit future generations

子孙满堂 zǐsūn-mǎntáng family of many children (which was considered a blessing in the past):这位六十年不见的朋友,如今已是～了。The friend, whom I haven't seen for sixty years, is now surrounded by children and grandchildren.

子卫星 zǐwèixīng 〈天文〉hitch-hiker satellite; subsatellite
子午莲 zǐwǔlián 〈植物〉*also* "睡莲" shuìlián water lily
子午卯酉 zǐwǔ-mǎoyǒu ❶ entire process; complete picture：他们都是死心眼儿，非要问个～不可。They were all very stubborn and insisted on hearing the whole story (*or* on getting to the bottom of the matter). ❷ *see* "子丑寅卯❷" ❸ achievement; fruit; positive result：他在外多年，也没混出个～来。He has been away from home for many years without any achievement to his credit.
子午线 zǐwǔxiàn 〈天文〉〈测绘〉〈地理〉meridian (line)：本初～prime (*or* first) meridian
子午仪 zǐwǔyí 〈天文〉meridian instrument
子息 zǐxī ❶ *see* "子嗣" ❷ 〈书面〉interest
子系统 zǐxìtǒng subsystem
子细 zǐxì *see* "仔细" zǐxì
子弦 zǐxián fine silk strings of such musical instruments as *pipa* (琵琶, 4-stringed Chinese lute), *sanxian* (三弦, 3-stringed Chinese guitar), etc.
子痫 zǐxián 〈医学〉eclampsia
子虚 zǐxū 〈书面〉fictitious; unreal; imaginary
子虚乌有 zǐxū-wūyǒu groundless; baseless; unreal; non-existent：这都是些～的事情，千万不要相信。All this is sheer fiction. Never believe it.
子婿 zǐxù 〈书面〉son-in-law
子药 zǐyào bullets and gunpowder; ammunition
子叶 zǐyè 〈植物〉cotyledon
子夜 zǐyè midnight
子音 zǐyīn 〈语言〉consonant
子瘖 zǐyīn 〈中医〉hoarseness or voicelessness during pregnancy
子鱼 zǐyú *also* "仔鱼" zǐyú; "稚鱼" zhìyú newborn fish
子侄 zǐzhí sons and nephews
子猪 zǐzhū *also* "仔猪" zǐzhū; "苗猪" miáozhū piglet; shoat

籽 zǐ seed：葵花～ sunflower seed /菜～ vegetable seed
籽粒 zǐlì *see* "子粒" zǐlì
籽棉 zǐmián *also* "子棉" zǐmián unginned cotton
籽实 zǐshí *see* "子实" zǐshí
籽种 zǐzhǒng 〈方言〉seed

耔 zǐ 〈书面〉hill up; earth up

虸 zǐ
虸蚄 zǐfāng 〈方言〉armyworm

仔 zǐ (of domestic animals or fowl) young：～鸭 duckling
see also zǎi; zī
仔畜 zǐchù *also* "子畜" zǐchù young animal; newborn animal; suckling
仔鸡 zǐjī *also* "子鸡" zǐjī chick
仔密 zǐmì (of fabric or knitwear) closely woven or knitted; of a close texture：袜子织得很～。The socks are tightly knit.
仔兽 zǐshòu *also* "子兽" zǐshòu young animal
仔细 zǐxì *also* "子细" zǐxì ❶ careful; meticulous; attentive：～观察 observe carefully /～听她发言 listen attentively to her statement /～询问 close questioning /～考虑工人们的建议 give a careful consideration to the suggestions of the workers /～研究这项新计划 pore over the new scheme; make an in-depth study of the new scheme /～活儿 job requiring meticulous care or fine workmanship; skilled work ❷ look out; take care; watch out：～你妈骂你。Be careful, or you'll get a scolding from your mother. /～小偷儿! Look out for thieves (*or* pickpockets)! /路很滑，走路～点儿。Watch your step! The road is very slippery. ❸ 〈方言〉frugal; thrifty; economical：日子过得～ be frugal of one's expenses; live with frugality
仔鱼 zǐyú *also* "稚鱼" zhìyú; "子鱼" zǐyú fry; fingerling
仔猪 zǐzhū *also* "子猪" zǐzhū pigling; shoat

zì

字 zì ❶ word; character：汉～ Chinese character /常用～ everyday words /象形文～ hieroglyph /识～ learn to read and write ❷ pronunciation (of a word or character)：吐～清楚 pronounce every word clearly; have clear articulation (*or* enunciation) ❸ form of a written or printed character; style of handwriting：草～ Chinese characters written in the cursive hand; cursive hand; grass character /篆～ seal character /美术～ artistic calligraphy; art lettering /斜体～ italics; italicized word /颜体～ style of calligraphy of Yan Zhenqing (颜真卿) ❹ scripts; writings; calligraphy：碑上的～是苏轼的手笔。The inscription on the tablet is in Su Shi's handwriting (*or* calligraphy). /我请这位书法家给写了几个～。I asked the calligrapher to write me a few characters. /他不仅藏画，也藏～。He not only collects paintings but also scripts. ❺ wording：咬文嚼～ pay excessive attention to wording; talk pedantically; juggle with words like a pedant ❻ receipt; voucher; written pledge：立～为凭 give a written pledge /见～付款 pay the deliverer when you receive the letter ❼ another name derived from the meaning of one's original name：杜甫～子美。Du Fu styled himself Zimei. ❽ 〈俗语〉number shown on an electric meter, water meter, etc.：这个月水表走了十五个～。As shown on the meter fifteen tons of water has been used this month. /这种冰箱可费～了。This refrigerator is energy-consuming. ❾ 〈书面〉(of a girl) be betrothed or engaged：许～于人 be betrothed /待～闺中 not betrothed yet
字典 zìdiǎn dictionary：查～ consult a dictionary /《康熙～》*Kangxi Dictionary* /活～ living dictionary; walking dictionary
字典纸 zìdiǎnzhǐ India paper
字调 zìdiào *also* "声调" shēngdiào 〈语言〉tones of Chinese characters
see also "四声" sìshēng
字段 zìduàn 〈信息〉field
字符 zìfú 〈信息〉character：～块 character block /～组 character set /～串 character string /～识别 character reading (*or* recognition) /～移入 character shift in /～发生器 character generator /～编码表 character code table
字幅 zìfú vertical or horizontal scroll of calligraphy
字号 zìhao ❶ name of a shop：这家商店是什么～? What's the name of this shop? ❷ shop：京城的老～ old, reputable shop in Beijing ❸ characters used to designate particular groups of persons or things
字盒 zìhé 〈印刷〉(type) mould
字画 zìhuà calligraphy and painting：他收藏了不少古人～。He's collected quite a few ancient scripts (*or* writings) and paintings.
字汇 zìhuì vocabulary; glossary; lexicon; wordbook
字迹 zìjì handwriting; writing：～清楚 clear handwriting /～潦草 sloppy handwriting; rude calligraphy /他的～，难以辨认。His writing is difficult to read (*or* is almost illegible).
字节 zìjié 〈信息〉byte
字句 zìjù words and expressions; writing：～顺畅 (make) easy and smooth reading; coherent and smooth writing /～不通 ungrammatical and incoherent writing
字据 zìjù written pledge such as receipt, IOU, contract, etc.：你立个～，我借给你五百元。I'll lend you 500 *yuan* if you write me an IOU.
字卷 zìjuàn calligraphy scroll
字里行间 zìlǐ-hángjiān between the lines; by implication：从～可以看出，他有一种愤愤不平的情绪。If you read between the lines you'll find he is seething with indignation.
字码儿 zìmǎr numeral：中文～ Chinese numerals /阿拉伯～ Arabic numerals
字谜 zìmí riddle about a character or word; riddle：猜～ answer (*or* read, *or* guess) a riddle about a word /纵横填～ crossword puzzle
字面 zìmiàn literal：～上的解释 literal interpretation /从～上看，他似乎很愿意这样做。Taken literally, he seems quite willing to do so.
字模 zìmú *also* "铜模" tóngmú 〈印刷〉(type) matrix：冲压～ punched matrix /～合金 matrix alloy
字母 zìmǔ ❶ letters of an alphabet; letter：汉语拼音～ Chinese phonetic alphabet /拉丁～ Latin alphabet; Roman alphabet /大写～ capital letter /小写～ small letter /按～顺序排列 be arranged in the order of the alphabet or in alphabetical order; be arranged alphabetically ❷ character representing an initial consonant (of a Chinese syllable)
字母表 zìmǔbiǎo alphabet
字幕 zìmù captions (of films; videos, etc.); subtitles：有英文～的中国影片 Chinese film with English subtitles (*or* captions) /影片中所

有的唱词都配上了～。All the songs in the film have been captioned.
字盘 zìpán 〈印刷〉case:大写～ upper case /小写～ lower case /～式计算机 dialing set computer
字书 zìshū wordbook; lexicon; dictionary
字顺索引 zìshùn suǒyǐn alphabetical register; alphabetical index
字体 zìtǐ ❶ form of a written or printed character; typeface; script ❷ style of calligraphy ❸ handwriting; writing:～工整 neat handwriting
字条 zìtiáo brief note:他没留下个～什么的吗? Didn't he leave a brief note or something?
字帖儿 zìtiěr brief note; notice:墙上贴着各种～。There are various notices on the wall.
字帖 zìtiè copybook (for calligraphy); models of calligraphy:临摹～ practise calligraphy after a master sheet
字形 zìxíng character pattern; font:标准～ standard font
字眼 zìyǎn turn of expression; wording; diction:抠～儿 find fault with the wording; be word-catching; be word-splitting /挑～儿 cavil at sb.'s choice of words; quibble /找不到合适的～来形容他激动的心情 have no suitable words to describe his excitement; his elation is beyond description
字样 zìyàng ❶ model of written characters ❷ printed or written words or expressions:扉页上有"赠给兰兰"～。On the title page are the words "To Lanlan".
字义 zìyì meaning of a word:讲解～ interpret or explain the meaning of a word
字音 zìyīn pronunciation of a word:注有～的课文 text marked with phonetic symbols
字斟句酌 zìzhēn-jùzhuó pick one's words with great care; deliberate what words to use; weigh every word:～的文章 carefully worded essay /许久,他才～地说:"你也不是无可责怪的。" It was quite a while before he spoke in a deliberate tone, "You are not entirely free from blame either." /她写东西一向～。It was her wont to weigh every word before putting it in writing.
字正腔圆 zìzhèng-qiāngyuán (of opera singers) pronounce every word correctly and in a sweet, mellow voice:他的京戏唱得～。He is a perfect Beijing opera singer.
字纸 zìzhǐ wastepaper with characters written or printed on it
字纸篓 zìzhǐlǒu wastepaper basket
字字珠玑 zìzì-zhūjī every word a pearl; each word a gem; exquisite writing

牸

zì 〈方言〉female domestic animals:～牛 cow

恣

zì ❶ be self-indulgent; throw off all restraint:自～ indulge oneself; do as one pleases ❷ 〈方言〉comfortable; at ease:～得很 live comfortably; lead an easy life
恣情 zìqíng ❶ indulge oneself as much as one likes; enjoy to one's heart's content:～欢笑 laugh to one's heart's content ❷ wantonly; wilfully; at will:钱拿到手别～胡花。Don't squander away the money once you get it.
恣肆 zìsì 〈书面〉❶ unrestrained; wilful; self-indulgent:骄横～ arrogant and wilful ❷ (of speech, writing style, etc.) forceful and unrestrained; free and natural:文笔汪洋～ write in a free and unrestrained style
恣睢 zìsuī 〈书面〉reckless; wanton; unbridled:暴戾～ unbridled cruelty
恣行无忌 zìxíng-wújì act recklessly; be wilful and unscrupulously in action:一些贪污分子仍旧无视法律,～。Some corrupt people kept acting unscrupulously in defiance of the law.
恣意 zìyì wanton; unbridled; reckless; wilful:～践踏别国主权 wantonly trample on the sovereignty of other countries /～掠夺发展中国家的资源 wilfully plunder the resources of developing countries /他年轻时曾～作乐。He had his fling (*or* sowed his wild oats) when he was young.
恣意妄为 zìyì-wàngwéi behave unscrupulously; act wilfully
恣纵 zìzòng 〈书面〉unrestrained; self-indulgent; wanton:父母～ be indulged (*or* pampered) by one's parents

胾

zì 〈书面〉large chunk of meat

剚(倳)

zì 〈书面〉stab

眦(眥)

zì corner of the eye; canthus

胔

zì 〈书面〉putrid meat

自[1]

zì ❶ self; oneself; one's own:独～ all alone; by oneself /～顾 give consideration only to oneself; be selfregarding; be selfish /各～为政 each does things in his own way /监守～盗 steal what is entrusted to one's care; defalcate /不由～主 cannot help doing sth.; act involuntarily ❷ naturally; certainly; as a matter of course:～当悔改 will certainly repent one's sins (*or* mend one's ways) /是非～有公论。The public should be the best judge. /～当如此。It should be so as a matter of course. /久别重逢,～有乐趣。It naturally gave us great pleasure to meet each other after a long separation.

自[2]

zì from; since:～此以后 since then; from then on /～古以来 from time immemorial; since ancient times /～天而降 descend from heaven; come from nowhere /发～内心深处 from the heart of hearts /摘～《西游记》extracted from *Pilgrimage to the West* /有朋～远方来 have a friend coming from afar /～即日起生效 become effective (as) from this date; with effect from this date
自爱 zì'ài self-respect; proper respect for oneself:不知～ have no (sense of) self-respect
自傲 zì'ào ❶ arrogant; haughty:居功～ become arrogant because of one's meritorious service /他～起来时,颇令人讨厌。When he gets a bit above himself, he is really a nuisance. ❷ feel proud of; be filled with pride; take pride in:他觉得～的是他的科研成果给社会带来了大量财富。What he feels proud of is (*or* He prides himself on the fact) that the result of his scientific research has brought (about) great wealth to society.
自拔 zìbá rid oneself (of pain or evildoing); free or extricate oneself:越陷越深,无法～ get increasingly involved and be unable to extricate oneself
自拔来归 zìbá-láiguī enemy forces defect and come over to our side
自白 zìbái ❶ make clear one's meaning or position; vindicate oneself:无以～ cannot find a way to justify oneself ❷ confession
自白书 zìbáishū written confession
自报公议 zìbào-gōngyì assessing one's own merits and demerits and letting others discuss whether or not the assessment accords with facts; self-assessment and public discussion
自报家门 zìbào-jiāmén (of leading characters in traditional Chinese dramas) introduce oneself when appearing on the stage:他一进屋便向我～。He introduced himself to me the moment he entered the room.
自暴自弃 zìbào-zìqì give oneself up for lost; be self-abandoned:有些人因为工作成绩不突出而～。Some people lose confidence in themselves when they fail to make significant achievements in their work. /犯错误是难免的,但不能因此而～。One can hardly avoid making mistakes, but he should not give himself up as hopeless on this account.
自卑 zìbēi feel oneself inferior (to others); be self-abased:别～,你一点儿不比他们差。Don't look down upon yourself; you are just as good as they are.
自卑感 zìbēigǎn sense of inferiority; inferiority complex:希望你能克服～。I hope that you will free yourself from the sense of inferiority.
自备 zìbèi provide for oneself:～饮料的聚会 BYO (Bring Your Own) party /上这门课的同学必须～打字机。Students who attend this class must bring their own typewriters.
自变数 zìbiànshù *also* "自变量"〈数学〉independent variable
自便 zìbiàn suit oneself; do as one pleases; act at one's convenience:悉听～。Let everyone do as he pleases. /饮料、饭菜都上了,请大家～吧。Here are the drinks and dishes. Please help yourselves.
自播 zìbō 〈农业〉natural seeding; self-sowing:～作物 self-seed crop (*or* self-sown crop)
自不待言 zìbùdàiyán it goes without saying; it is self-evident; it is axiomatic:～,这条纪律人人都必须遵守。It goes without saying that everyone must observe this rule.
自不量力 zìbùliànglì overestimate oneself or one's strength; overrate oneself:他觉得一个人可以完成这个任务,真有点～。He over-

Z

estimated his own ability, thinking he could accomplish the task all by himself.

自裁 zìcái 〈书面〉commit suicide; kill oneself; take one's own life:引咎～ take the blame and commit suicide

自残 zìcán injure oneself; kill each other (in the same group):骨肉～ fratricidal fight

自惭 zìcán be ashamed of oneself:此事让我深感～。This made me feel guilty.

自惭形秽 zìcán-xínghuì have a sense of inferiority or inadequacy; feel ashamed of one's unworthiness; feel small:和她在一起,他总有～之感。He always feels unworthy of her company. /山鸡见到孔雀未免～。The pheasant feels rather ashamed of its ungainly appearance in the presence of the peacock.

自差 zìchā 〈电学〉autodyne:～电路 autodyne circuit / ～收音机 autodyne (radio receiver)

自查 zìchá make self-examination

自产自销 zìchǎn-zìxiāo produce and market on one's own; market one's own products:这些鲜菜都是近郊菜农～的。The farmers in the suburbs grow and sell all these vegetables.

自嘲 zìcháo laughing at oneself; self-ridicule

自沉 zìchén 〈书面〉commit suicide by throwing oneself into a river, well, etc.; drown oneself

自称 zìchēng style oneself; claim to be; profess:～为帝 proclaim oneself emperor /项羽～西楚霸王。Xiang Yu styled himself the Conqueror of Western Chu. /我问过她,但她～不知情。I asked her, but she professed ignorance. /此人～万事通。The man claimed to know all.

自成一家 zìchéng-yījiā *also* "自成一体" (in calligraphy, painting, sculpture, etc.) have a style of one's own; be unique in one's style:他画风独特,～。He has a style of his own in painting. *or* His style of painting is unique.

自成体系 zìchéng-tǐxì create a system of one's own; have one's own system:他的学说～。His theory has its own system.

自乘 zìchéng 〈数学〉involution; squaring:九～得八十一。The square of 9 is 81. *or* Nine squared is 81.

自持 zìchí keep one's desire or emotion under control; control oneself; exercise self-restraint:～力强 be self-collected /他激动异常,几乎难以～了。He was too excited to contain himself. *or* He could hardly contain himself for excitement.

自筹 zìchóu self-collected; locally-collected:～资金 self-collected funds; funds raised by oneself /地方和企业～的基本建设投资 capital construction investment in the form of funds collected by localities and enterprises themselves /为明年的发展规划～资金 self-finance next year's development programme

自出机杼 zìchū-jīzhù (of a piece of writing, etc.) be original in conception:其文～,别成一家。Original in conception, his writing has a distinctive style of its own.

自出心裁 zìchū-xīncái conceive an original idea; make a new departure:～的设计 novel and original design

自吹自擂 zìchuī-zìléi blow one's own trumpet or horn; brag:他这人～很在行。He is pretty good at blowing his own trumpet (*or* singing his own praises). /听他～,令人生厌。People get tired of his braggadocio. /你就改不掉这～的毛病吗? Will you ever quit bragging?

自从 zìcóng since:～五月以来,我就没收到他的信。I haven't heard from him since May. /～孩子入托以后,我可省心多了。Having the child in kindergarten saves me a lot of worry.

自打 zìdǎ 〈方言〉*see* "自从"

自大 zìdà self-important; arrogant; conceited:夜郎～ ludicrous conceit stemming from pure ignorance; sheer parochial arrogance

自大狂 zìdàkuáng megalomania

自导引 zìdǎoyǐn 〈军事〉homing:～导弹 homing missile; target seeker homer

自得 zìdé self-satisfied; complacent; contented:洋洋～ complacent; smug /悠然～ be carefree and content; contentedly take one's ease

自得其乐 zìdé-qílè be happy and content; be content with one's lot:只要有二两老酒,一碟小菜,老张头便可～地喝起来。Whenever he had two *liang* of liquor and a dish of pickles, Old Zhang would start drinking contentedly.

自动 zìdòng ❶ voluntary; of one's own accord:～加入 participate voluntarily /不会～退出历史舞台 will not step down from the stage of history of one's own free will /～投案 give oneself up to the police ❷ automatic; automated:～延长 (of a treaty, lease, etc.) be automatically prolonged (*or* extended) /～音量控制 automatic volume control /～调谐〈电子〉automatic tuning; autotune /～聚焦 automatic focus; autofocus; self-focusing /～装填炮 autoloading gun

自动报火警系统 zìdòng bàohuǒjǐng xìtǒng automatic fire detection system

自动报警器 zìdòng bàojǐngqì auto-alarm

自动编码 zìdòng biānmǎ 〈计算机〉autocoding; automatic coding:～器 autocoder /～语言 automatic coding language

自动变速器 zìdòng biànsùqì automatic transmission

自动步枪 zìdòng bùqiāng automatic rifle

自动程序 zìdòng chéngxù automatic sequence:～控制计算机 automatic sequence controlled computer (*or* calculator) /～设计 automatic programming /～设计机 automatic programming machine /～设计器 automatic program units /～装置 automatic sequencer

自动出纳机 zìdòng chūnàjī automatic teller machine (ATM)

自动词 zìdòngcí *also* "不及物动词" bùjíwù dòngcí intransitive verb

自动电话 zìdòng diànhuà 〈通信〉automatic telephone; dial service:～局 dial office /～机 dial telephone /～交换机 dial exchange /长途～网 automatic telephone trunk network /～系统 automatic telephone system; dial system

自动定时器 zìdòng dìngshíqì autotimer

自动对焦相机 zìdòng duìjiāo xiàngjī self-focusing camera; autofocusing camera

自动分类 zìdòng fēnlèi automatic sorting

自动扶梯 zìdòng fútī escalator

自动跟踪 zìdòng gēnzōng 〈自控〉automatic following; automatic tracking; autotrack:～分析数字计算机 automatic digital tracking analyzing computer /～控制 automatic following control /～器 autotracking unit /～装置 autotracker

自动化 zìdònghuà automation:使…～ automate; automatize /生产过程～ process automation /数字～ digital automation /数字计算机～ digital automatization /～过程 automation process /～理论 automatics /车辆检修～ automation of rolling stock inspection and repair /铁路编组站～ automation of a railway marshalling yard /～编译程序装置 autopiler compiler; autopiler /～仓库 autowarehouse /～程度 automaticity /～发电站 automatic generating station /～机械加工 automatic machining /～设计 automation design /～生产线 automatic production line

自动换梭织机 zìdòng huànsuō zhījī automatic shuttle-changing loom

自动机床 zìdòng jīchuáng 〈机械〉automatic machine

自动记录器 zìdòng jìlùqì pen-and-ink recorder

自动驾驶仪 zìdòng jiàshǐyí automatic pilot; autopilot

自动拣信机 zìdòng jiǎnxìnjī computerized mail sorter

自动检测系统 zìdòng jiǎncè xìtǒng automatic checkout system

自动绢网印花机 zìdòng juànwǎng yìnhuājī automatic screen printing machine

自动开关 zìdòng kāiguān auto-switch; automatic switch; recloser

自动控制 zìdòng kòngzhì automatic control; autocontrol:～机床 automatic control machine tool /～器 automatic controller /～装置 automatic control device

自动离职 zìdòng lízhí quit a job without permission; take French leave

自动免疫 zìdòng miǎnyì 〈医学〉active immunity

自动炮 zìdòngpào automatic gun

自动铅笔 zìdòng qiānbǐ propelling pencil

自动取款机 zìdòng qǔkuǎnjī *also* "自动柜员机" ATM; automated teller machine; automated teller; teller machine

自动伞 zìdòngsǎn automatic umbrella

自动刹车滑行装置 zìdòng shāchē huáxíng zhuāngzhì automatic skidding device

自动售货机 zìdòng shòuhuòjī vending machine; automat

自动数据收集系统 zìdòng shùjù shōují xìtǒng automated data acquisition system

自动饲喂机 zìdòng sìwèijī self-feeder

自动提示器 zìdòng tíshìqì autocue

自动同步 zìdòng tóngbù 〈电工〉automatic synchronization:～发电机 selsyn generator /～机 selsyn; synchro; synchro motor /～电动机 selsyn motor /～接收机 receiving selsyn

自动线 zìdòngxiàn transfer machine

自动寻的导弹 zìdòng xúndì dǎodàn homing missile

Z

自动饮水器 zìdòng yǐnshuǐqì 〈畜牧〉automatic drinking bowl
自动症 zìdòngzhèng 〈医学〉automatism:～患者 automaton
自动制图仪 zìdòng zhìtúyí autocartograph
自动装配 zìdòng zhuāngpèi 〈机械〉automatic assembly; self-erecting:～机 automatic assembly machine /～线 automatic (*or* automated) assembly line
自渎 zìdú self-abuse; masturbation
自发 zìfā spontaneous:～的积极性 automatic enthusiasm /～性罢工 wildcat strike /～资本主义倾向 spontaneous tendency towards capitalism /～性 spontaneity /这个学习小组是他们～组织起来的。They themselves launched this study group.
自发病 zìfābìng 〈医学〉idiogenesis; idiopathy; autopathy
自反 zìfǎn 〈书面〉self-questioning; self-examination:～无愧 feel no qualms upon self-examination; have a clear conscience
自返性 zìfǎnxìng 〈逻辑〉reflexivity
自肥 zìféi fatten oneself at other's expense; enrich oneself by misappropriating funds or material; feather one's nest:～私囊 line one's pockets with public funds or other people's money; embezzle
自费 zìfèi at one's own expense:～出国留学 go to study abroad at one's own expense /～医疗 pay for one's own medical care
自费生 zìfèishēng self-funded students
自焚 zìfén burning oneself to death; self-immolation:玩火～ those who play with fire will get burned (*or* will be consumed by fire)
自分 zìfèn 〈书面〉make a self-appraisal or assessment:～不足以当此重任 conclude after a self-appraisal that one is incapable of shouldering (*or* is not up to) such an important task
自封 zìfēng ❶ proclaim or style oneself:～的艺术家 self-styled (*or* self-appointed) artist /～为改革者 proclaim oneself a reformer ❷ confine oneself:故步～ be conservative and complacent; be satisfied with old practices; remain in a rut
自奉 zìfèng 〈书面〉provide the necessities of life for oneself:～极俭 lead an extremely simple life
自奉菲薄 zìfèng-fěibó content with bare necessities of life; hard-working and frugal
自负 zìfù ❶ hold oneself responsible:文责～。The author takes sole responsibility for his views. ❷ be conceited; be puffed up; pride oneself (on one's talent):他这人过于～。He thinks pretty well of himself. *or* He is rather conceited. /他对自己的酒量颇有些～。He prided himself on his capacity for liquor.
自负盈亏 zìfù yíng-kuī (of an enterprise) assume sole responsibility for its profits and losses; be held economically responsible:集体企业是～的。The collective enterprises are responsible for their own profits and losses.
自甘堕落 zìgān-duòluò wallow in degeneration; abandon oneself to vice; lead a degraded life without regret:此后,他便～,酗酒成性。After that, he degraded himself by taking to drinking. /人生旅途多坎坷,我辈岂能因此而～? Life is full of frustrations. How can we give ourselves up for lost just after one setback?
自感应 zìgǎnyìng 〈物理〉self-induction
自高自大 zìgāo-zìdà arrogant; conceited; self-important; full of vainglory:为人要谦虚,不可～。One should be modest, not haughty and conceited. /他这个人有点～。He has a somewhat swelled head.
自告奋勇 zìgào-fènyǒng volunteer to undertake (a difficult task); offer to do (sth. difficult):老汉～为我们带路。The old man volunteered to act as a guide for us.
自割 zìgē 〈动物〉autotomy
自个儿 zìgěr *also* "自各儿"〈方言〉oneself; by oneself:如果你们太忙,我～干。If you are too busy, I'll manage this myself. /他们都走了,只剩下我～。They have all gone and I am alone. /不要只顾～。Don't just think about yourself. *or* Don't be so selfish.
自耕农 zìgēngnóng owner-peasant; land-holding peasant
自供 zìgòng confess:据罪犯～ according to the culprit's confession
自供状 zìgòngzhuàng confession
自古 zìgǔ from time immemorial; since antiquity:文人相轻,～而然。From generation to generation scholars have tended to scorn each other. /～嫦娥爱少年。Young nymphs always prefer youth to age.
自顾不暇 zìgù-bùxiá be unable even to shift for oneself (much less look after others); have trouble even in taking care of oneself:他最近太忙,～,哪有时间去管别人的事! He's been busy enough with his own affairs. How can he find time to mind other people's business?

自汗 zìhàn 〈中医〉spontaneous perspiration or sweating
自豪 zìháo be proud of; take pride in:～感 sense of pride /我为有你这样的朋友而感到～。I feel proud to have (*or* pride myself on having) a friend like you. /她真为儿子的成就感到～。She took a genuine pride in her son's achievements. /他为自己的出身而～。He values himself on his birth. *or* He's proud of his birth.
自好 zìhào self-respect:洁身～ preserve one's moral integrity
自花不稔性 zìhuā bùrěnxìng 〈植物〉self-sterility
自花传粉 zìhuā chuánfěn 〈植物〉self-pollination
自画像 zìhuàxiàng self-portrait
自回归 zìhuíguī 〈数学〉autoregression
自毁 zìhuǐ 〈军事〉self-destruction:～装置 self-destruction equipment; destructor
自激 zìjī 〈电工〉self-excitation; self-feeding:～电动机 motor with self excitation /～放电 self-excited discharge
自己 zìjǐ ❶ oneself:～跟～过不去 be (too) hard on oneself /你不会～跟他说去? Can't you talk to him yourself? /我只能谈谈～的意见,别人可能有不同看法。I can only speak for myself; others may have different views. /怪我～不好,没把话说清楚。It was my own fault; I didn't make myself clear. /他们享受免费医疗,不必～花钱付医药费。They enjoy free medical care and needn't dip into their own purse for medical expenses. ❷ related to oneself; one's own:～学校 one's own school /～身上 in (*or* on) oneself /对～子女,尤其要严格。One should be particularty strict with one's own children.
自己人 zìjǐrén one of us; people of one's own circle; one's pal:别害怕,他是～。Don't be afraid. He is one of us. /～嘛,何必动武呢? We are all friends. Why start a fight against each other?
自己个儿 zìjigěr 〈方言〉oneself
自给 zìjǐ self-sufficient; self-supporting; self-contained:生产～ supply one's own needs by engaging in production /～生产 self-supplying production /～经济 self-supporting (*or* self-contained) economy/～企业 self-contained plant/～率 degree of self-sufficiency/该市肉蛋不能～。This city is not self-sufficient in meat and eggs. /老人无儿无女,靠种菜～。The childless old man makes a living by growing vegetables.
自给自足 zìjǐ-zìzú self-sufficiency; autarky:～的自然经济 self-sufficient natural economy
自记 zìjì self-recording:～气压计 self-recording barometer /～湿度计 self-recording hygrometer
自家 zìjiā 〈方言〉oneself:～姐妹 one's own sisters
自家人 zìjiārén 〈方言〉*see* "自己人"
自荐 zìjiàn offer oneself as a candidate for a position; recommend oneself for a job:毛遂～ volunteer one's services
自交 zìjiāo 〈植物〉〈动物〉self-fertilization
自矜 zìjīn 〈书面〉sing one's own praises; blow one's own trumpet
自尽 zìjìn commit suicide; kill oneself; take one's own life:悬梁～ hang oneself /服毒～ commit suicide by taking poison; kill oneself by poison
自禁 zìjìn (often used in the negative) restrain one's passion; contain oneself:情不～地大叫起来 cannot help crying out
自经 zìjīng 〈书面〉hang oneself
自刭 zìjǐng 〈书面〉kill oneself by cutting one's throat; cut one's own throat
自净 zìjìng 〈环保〉self-purification
自疚 zìjiù guilty conscience; compunction:她深感～。Her conscience pricked her. *or* She had a bad conscience. /你不为自己的差错感到～吗? Don't you feel guilty about your error?
自咎 zìjiù blame oneself; reproach oneself:我为没完成任务而～。I blame myself for failing to accomplish the task.
自救 zìjiù support oneself; work to save oneself:生产～ support oneself by engaging in production /团结～ unite for self-preservation
自居 zìjū consider oneself to be; call oneself; pose as:以功臣～ give oneself the airs of (*or* pose as) a hero /以文学界名家～ regard oneself as among literary celebrities /以老资格～ flaunt one's seniority /他以这方面的权威～。He sets up as an authority on the subject.
自决 zìjué self-determination:民族～权 right to national self-determination /此事你们有权～。You have the right to make your own decision on the matter.
自觉 zìjué ❶ realize; be aware of:他～理亏。He knew he was in the wrong. /他看得太入神,竟不～地念出了声。He was so absorbed in the book that he read it aloud without realizing it. ❷ on one's own initiative; consciously:～采取行动 act on one's own initiative /大家都

很～，不在这里抽烟。Everyone consciously refrains from smoking here.

自觉性 zìjuéxìng (level of political) consciousness

自觉症状 zìjué zhèngzhuàng subjective symptoms

自觉自愿 zìjué-zìyuàn of one's own volition; voluntarily; willingly：他这样做，完全是～的。He did it of his own free will.

自绝 zìjué alienate oneself：～于人民 isolate oneself from the people

自掘坟墓 zìjué-fénmù dig one's own grave; court one's own ruin：这些反动家伙的倒行逆施，无异于～。These reactionaries are simply seeking destruction by their perverse acts.

自控 zìkòng (short for 自动控制) automatic control

自苦 zìkǔ deny oneself; be hard on oneself; work too hard：君第行，毋～！Please go abroad, and don't be too hard on yourself! /要注意身体，别太～了。Pay attention to your health. Don't work your fingers to the bone.

自夸 zìkuā sing one's own praises; blow one's own trumpet; build oneself up：～其德 swagger about one's own virtues /他～为神枪手，其实枪法并不佳。He bragged of being a crack shot, but he was actually nothing of the sort. /不是～，论体力活，我比你强多了。I am not singing my own praises, but so far as physical labour goes, I am much better at it than you.

自郐以下 zìkuài-yǐxià except those above (*or* better than) Kuai, none is worth mentioning; except so-and-so, none of them is worth a dime：这些作品属于～。These writings are not worth reading.

自宽 zìkuān 〈书面〉 console or comfort oneself

自况 zìkuàng 〈书面〉 liken oneself to sb. else; compare oneself to another：以包公～ liken oneself to Bao Gong, justice incarnate

自愧不如 zìkuì-bùrú *also* "自愧弗如" feel inadequate; be ashamed of one's inferiority：看到老张的科研成果，我～。Seeing Lao Zhang's achievements in scientific research, I had to admit that he was head and shoulders above me.

自拉自唱 zìlā-zìchàng ❶ accompany one's own singing — do everything by oneself：这个店全靠他～，内外张罗。He ran the shop all by himself. /他习惯于抛开别人，～。He tends to run the whole show, ignoring all other people. ❷ blow one's own horn; second one's own motion：他如此～，自我标榜，令人作呕。He blew his own trumpet so loudly that everybody got sick of him.

自来 zìlái from the outset; in the first place; originally：这姑娘～伶俐乖巧。The girl is lovely and bright by nature.

自来红 zìláihóng be born red; be born revolutionary; be born into a revolutionary family

自来火 zìláihuǒ 〈方言〉 ❶ matches ❷ cigarette-lighter; lighter

自来水 zìláishuǐ running water; tap water：～管 water pipe

自来水笔 zìláishuǐbǐ fountain pen

自来水厂 zìláishuǐchǎng waterworks

自冷 zìlěng self-cooling：～式变压器〈电工〉 self-cooled transformer / ～电机 self-cooled machine

自理 zìlǐ ❶ provide for oneself：费用～ pay one's own expenses / 伙食～ make one's own eating arrangements ❷ take care of：她虽有残疾，但生活完全能～。She can well take care of herself in spite of her disability.

自力 zìlì depend on one's own strength：～制造 manufacture through one's own efforts

自力更生 zìlì-gēngshēng self-reliance; reliance on one's own efforts：独立自主，～ independence and self-reliance / ～为主，争取外援为辅的方针 policy of relying mainly on one's own efforts while seeking external assistance as an auxiliary; policy of enlisting foreign help as a supplement to one's own efforts /我们一贯主张～，艰苦奋斗。We have always stood for self-reliance and hard work.

自力霉素 zìlìméisù 〈药学〉 mitomycin C

自立 zìlì stand on one's own feet; earn one's own bread; be self-supporting：～于世界民族之林 stand proudly in the family of nations / 父母早逝使她小小年纪便～了。Her parents' early death made her stand on her own feet when she was still quite young. /别为你儿子担心，他已到了足以～的年龄了。Don't worry about your son; he is old enough to paddle his own canoe (*or* to fend for himself).

自立门户 zìlì-ménhù ❶ separate from one's family; live apart from one's family ❷ break away from (a larger group, organization, association, etc.)：这家刊物已～。The magazine is now independent (*or* independently run).

自励 zìlì 〈电工〉 self-excitation：～电动机 self-excited motor / ～电机 self-excited machine

自量 zìliàng rate one's own ability or strength：不知～ overrate one's abilities; fail to take a proper measure of oneself /这人太不～了。The man thinks too highly of himself. /我～能承担这项工作。I believe that I am capable of doing the job.

自料 zìliào ❶ materials supplied by customers ❷ expect; foresee; anticipate：他～此事难成。He anticipated that he would not succeed in the attempt.

自流 zìliú ❶ (of water, etc.) flow spontaneously; flow by itself：～排水 free-draining ❷ drift along; run or take its course; (of a person) do as one pleases：放任～ laissez-faire; let things drift along; let people act as they like ❸ artesian 〈地理〉：～泉 artesian spring

自流灌溉 zìliú guàngài 〈农业〉 gravity irrigation

自流井 zìliújǐng artesian well

自留 zìliú retain or reserve for one's own use：～山 private hilly land

自留畜 zìliúchù livestock for personal needs; privately owned livestock

自留地 zìliúdì plot of land for personal needs; family plot; private plot

自律 zìlǜ 〈书面〉 self-discipline：廉洁～ be incorruptible and self-disciplined

自卖自夸 zìmài-zìkuā praise one's own wares; be given to self-glorification; blow one's own horn：王婆卖瓜，～ ring one's own bell; there is nothing like leather

自满 zìmǎn self-satisfied; smug; complacent：骄傲～ conceited and self-satisfied; arrogant and complacent /我们取得了很大的成绩，但没理由～。We have achieved great successes, but we have no reason for complacency.

自民党 Zìmíndǎng Liberal Democratic Party (LDP), a major political party in Japan

自明 zìmíng self-evident; self-explanatory; clear as crystal：是非～，无庸置辩。It is indisputably clear who is right and who is wrong.

自鸣得意 zìmíng-déyì be very pleased with oneself; feel smug about; preen oneself：你没什么可以～的。You've got nothing to be smug about. /不要以奚落别人而～。Don't think it will be a feather in your cap to scoff at others.

自鸣钟 zìmíngzhōng striking clock; chime clock

自命 zìmìng claim; consider oneself; regard oneself as：～为现代派诗人 consider (*or* style) oneself a modernist poet; profess to be a modernist poet

自命不凡 zìmìng-bùfán consider oneself head and shoulders above the ordinary run; think no end of oneself; be self-important：他不过是个～的家伙。He is nothing but a stuffed shirt. /即使你赢了，也不必摆出那副～的样子。You needn't assume an air of importance like that, even if you've won.

自命清高 zìmìng-qīnggāo *also* "自鸣清高" profess to be above worldly considerations; claim to keep aloof from politics and material pursuits

自磨 zìmó self-sharpening：～刃式锄铲 self-sharpening blade / ～刃犁铧 self-sharpening ploughshare / ～钻头 self-sharpening bit

自谋出路 zìmóu-chūlù find one's own means of livelihood; search for jobs; seek employment：被公司辞退后，他只得～。After he was dismissed by the company, he had to find his own means of livelihood. /他失业了，正在～。He has lost his job and is looking for a new one.

自馁 zìněi lose heart; lose confidence; be disheartened：足球队首战失利，但队员们并不～。The football players were not discouraged by their team's defeat in the first game.

自捻纱 zìniǎnshā 〈纺织〉 self-twisted yarn

自耦变压器 zì'ǒu biànyāqì 〈电工〉 auto-transformer; autoconverter; autoformer; auto-jigger

自拍机 zìpāijī 〈摄影〉 self-timer

自喷井 zìpēnjǐng 〈石油〉 flowing well; gusher well

自喷期 zìpēnqī 〈石油〉 flush stage; flowing life

自皮移植术 zìpí yízhíshù 〈医学〉 dermato-autoplasty

自欺欺人 zìqī-qīrén deceiving onself as well as others; self-deception：～的借口 self-deceiving excuse /这是～之谈。This is a hoax, pure and simple. /你们这样做，不过是～，无济于事。You are but deceiving yourselves by such an act; it won't help solve the problem.

自弃 zìqì lose self-confidence and have no urge to make progress; give oneself up as lost：何必为小挫而～。You need not lose heart be-

cause of such a minor setback.

自谦 zìqiān modest; self-effacing: ～之词 self-depreciatory remarks

自遣 zìqiǎn divert oneself from melancholy, etc.; amuse oneself: 以书画～ amuse (*or* divert) oneself with painting and calligraphy

自谴 zìqiǎn self-reproach; self-condemnation: 为挫伤老友之心而～ blame oneself for hurting one's old friend

自戕 zìqiāng 〈书面〉commit suicide; kill oneself; take one's own life

自强 zìqiáng strive to become stronger: 男儿当～。A man should strive to improve himself constantly.

自强不息 zìqiáng-bùxī strive unceasingly to become stronger; work hard to improve oneself: 他身处逆境, 仍～。He was constantly striving even in adversity.

自轻自贱 zìqīng-zìjiàn lack self-confidence or self-respect; be self-contemptuous; belittle oneself: 人宜自尊, 不应～。One should have self-respect and must not unduly humble oneself.

自取灭亡 zìqǔ-mièwáng court or invite destruction; work for one's own doom: 这是他～。He has courted his own ruin. /这些侵略者只能是～。Those aggressors will only end up bringing destruction upon themselves.

自取其咎 zìqǔ-qíjiù bring reproach on oneself; have only oneself to blame: 你何必～? Why should you ask for it?

自然 zìrán ❶ natural world; nature: 征服～ conquer nature /大～ nature /～景观 natural scenery /～金 native gold ❷ naturally; in the natural course of events: ～损耗 ordinary wear and tear; normal loss /～减员 natural reduction of staff and workers /船到桥头～直。Everything will straighten out in the end. /别着急, 到时～会知道结果的。Don't worry. You'll get to know the results in due course. /除了一切听其～外, 我们别无他法。We can do nothing except let things run their course. ❸ of course; certainly; naturally: 第一次来, 有点拘束, 这是～的。Naturally, you feel a bit ill at ease as this is the first time you are here. /走了这么长路～精疲力尽。It is only natural to feel exhausted after such a long walk.

自然 zìran at ease; unaffected; natural: 表情很～ look quite unaffected /他的表演极其～。His acting was perfectly natural. /说话人的口气镇定～。The speaker was quite at ease. /你这像片照得不～。You don't look natural in the photo.

自然保护区 zìrán bǎohùqū natural reserve; nature preservation zone

自然辩证法 zìrán biànzhèngfǎ dialectics of nature

自然博物馆 zìrán bówùguǎn museum of natural history

自然崇拜 zìrán chóngbài 〈宗教〉nature worship

自然村 zìráncūn (as distinct from "administrative village", i.e. village as grass-roots administrative unit) natural village; hamlet

自然地理 zìrán dìlǐ physical geography

自然对数 zìrán duìshù 〈数学〉Napierian logarithm; natural logarithm

自然而然 zìrán'érrán naturally; spontaneously; of oneself: 现代化不是～实现的。Modernization does not come of itself. /彼此了解加深了, 两人之间～地产生了爱情。Love grew up between them as they got to know each other better.

自然法 zìránfǎ *jus naturae*; law of nature; natural law

自然光 zìránguāng natural light

自然规律 zìrán guīlǜ natural law; law of nature

自然环境 zìrán huánjìng natural environment

自然界 zìránjiè natural world; nature

自然金属 zìrán jīnshǔ native metal

自然经济 zìrán jīngjì natural economy

自然经济学 zìrán jīngjìxué physioeconomics, attributing varied economic behaviour to different physical environment

自然科学 zìrán kēxué natural science

自然类群 zìrán lèiqún 〈生物〉natural group

自然力 zìránlì natural forces

自然粮 zìránliáng unprocessed food grains

自然免疫 zìrán miǎnyì *also* "天然免疫" tiānrán miǎnyì natural immunity; innate immunity; native immunity

自然区域 zìrán qūyù natural region

自然权利 zìrán quánlì natural right

自然人 zìránrén 〈法律〉natural person

自然神 zìránshén 〈宗教〉natural god

自然神论 zìránshénlùn 〈哲学〉deism: ～者 deist

自然神学 zìránshénxué 〈宗教〉natural theology

自然生态体系 zìrán shēngtài tǐxì natural ecosystem

自然数 zìránshù 〈数学〉natural number

自然死亡 zìrán sǐwáng natural death

自然铜 zìrántóng native copper

自然物 zìránwù unprocessed thing

自然现象 zìrán xiànxiàng natural phenomenon

自然形态 zìrán xíngtài natural form

自然选择 zìrán xuǎnzé natural selection

自然循环 zìrán xúnhuán natural circuit: ～反应堆 natural circulation reactor /～干燥窑 (化工) natural circulation kiln /～锅炉 natural circulation boiler

自然元素 zìrán yuánsù native element

自然灾害 zìrán zāihài natural calamity or disaster

自然增长率 zìrán zēngzhǎnglǜ natural growth: 人口～ natural population growth

自然哲学 zìrán zhéxué philosophy of nature

自然主义 zìránzhǔyì naturalism

自然资源 zìrán zīyuán natural resources; natural wealth: ～保护技术 conservation technology /～保护专家 conservationist

自然宗教 zìrán zōngjiào 〈宗教〉nature religion

自燃 zìrán self-ignition; spontaneous ignition; spontaneous combustion: ～金属 (化学) pyrophoric metals

自认 zìrèn accept as inevitable; resign oneself to: ～倒霉 accept the bad luck without complaint (*or* as sth. unavoidable)

自认晦气 zìrèn-huìqi look upon a piece of bad luck with resignation; grin and bear it: 遇到这种倒霉事, 只好～了。We can do nothing but accept the bad luck with resignation.

自溶酶 zìróngméi 〈生化〉autoenzyme

自如 zìrú 〈书面〉smoothly; freely; with ease: 行动～ move about freely /应付～ handle a situation with ease /操作～ operate with facility /演员优美～的舞姿 dancer's smooth and graceful movements

自若 zìruò 〈书面〉self-possessed; composed; with composure: 神情～ appear calm and at ease /言笑～ talk and laugh imperturbably /坦然～ calm and confident; completely at ease /泰然～ behave with perfect composure; be self-possessed

自杀 zìshā commit suicide; kill oneself: 剖腹～ commit suicide by disembowelling; hara-kiri /～未遂 failing in one's attempt to commit suicide; attempted suicide

自杀学 zìshāxué suicidology

自伤 zìshāng ❶ be distressed; be sentimental: ～幼年丧母 be distressed about one's loss of mother in one's childhood ❷ 〈法律〉self-wounding; self-inflicted wound; self-injury

自上而下 zìshàng'érxià from top to bottom; from above: ～地进行整顿 carry out consolidation (*or* reorganization) from top to bottom /～的指令性计划 mandatory plans issued from superior departments

自身 zìshēn one's own; oneself: ～利益 one's own interests /我们～有没有错? Are we in the wrong ourselves?

自身免疫 zìshēn miǎnyì autoimmunity; autoimmunization

自身难保 zìshēn-nánbǎo cannot even protect oneself: 泥菩萨过河, ～ be like a clay idol fording a river — hardly able to save oneself (*or* to fend for oneself)

自生自灭 zìshēng-zìmiè (of a thing) emerge of itself and perish of itself; take its course: 任其～ let it run its course /这些花草, 无人管理, 年复一年, ～。These flowers and plants, which are in a state of neglect, come out and fade away year after year.

自食其果 zìshí-qíguǒ eat one's own bitter fruit; pay for one's own evil doings; reap what one has sown; sow the wind and reap the whirlwind: 这惯犯被判死刑, 是～。The hardened criminal got what he deserved when he was sentenced to death. /这个工厂由于管理不善, 浪费了大量资金, 现在要～了。This factory wasted much of the fund owing to mismanagement, so now it must pay the piper. /如果你再不改过, 总有一天要～的。If you don't mend your ways, you'll one day be made to pay for what you've done.

自食其力 zìshí-qílì earn one's own living; earn one's bread; live on one's own toil: ～的劳动者 working people earning their own living /你现在该学着～了。You should learn to live by your own labour now. /从现在起, 我可以～了。From now on I am on my own.

自食其言 zìshí-qíyán go back on one's word; break one's word: 如果我这样做, 那就是～了。If I should do it, I would act in bad faith.

自始至终 zìshǐ-zhìzhōng from beginning to end; from start to fin-

ish; all through:会上他～一言不发。He remained silent throughout the meeting. /我～都在场。I was present from beginning to end. /老师～都知道这件事。The teacher knew it all through. /晚会～充满着愉快的气氛。The party was permeated with a cheerful atmosphere from start to finish.

自视 zìshì consider or imagine oneself:～过高 think too highly of oneself; think too much of oneself; be self-important

自是 zìshì ❶ naturally; of course:他乡遇故知,～喜出望外。It was of course a delight for him to run into an old friend in an alien land. ❷ regard oneself as faultless; consider oneself always in the right:他既～又倔强。He is opinionated and obstinate.

自恃 zìshì 〈书面〉❶ over-confident and complacent:他为人～,目空一切。He is extremely conceited, considering everybody and everything beneath his notice. ❷ rely on; count on; depend on:～其能,不听人言 trust one's own ability and refuse to heed other's advice /～有后台 rely on sb.'s backing (*or* patronage); count on one's powerful connections

自适应 zìshìyìng self-adapting:～程序 self-adapting program /～计算机 self-adapting computer /～控制 adaptive control; self-adaptive /～通信 self-adjusting communication; self-optimizing communication

自首 zìshǒu ❶ (of a criminal) surrender oneself; give oneself up:投案～ surrender oneself to the police or judicial department /坦白～ give oneself up to the police and confess one's crime ❷ make a political recantation; capitulate to the enemy:～变节 recant and defect to the enemy

自首书 zìshǒushū confession

自赎 zìshú redeem oneself:以功～ render meritorious services to atone for one's crime; redeem oneself by performing commendable services

自述 zìshù give an account of oneself:～本人经历 give an account of one's experience /写了一篇～ write one's autobiography

自说自话 zìshuō-zìhuà 〈方言〉❶ act on one's own; go it alone; decide for oneself:他也不跟别人商量一下,就～干开了。He started working on his own without consulting with others. ❷ talk to oneself:他走路时常常～。He often thinks aloud while walking along.

自私 zìsī egoistic; selfish; self-centred:～心太重 too selfish /出于～的动机 act from egoistic (*or* selfish) motives

自私自利 zìsī-zìlì selfish; egoistic:～的人 self-seeker; selfish person /我们可不能这样～。We must not be so selfish.

自讼 zìsòng 〈书面〉reprove or reproach oneself:自此之后,他常怀～之心。Since then he has often had a guilty conscience.

自诉 zìsù 〈法律〉case prosecuted by an injured party without the participation of the public prosecutor; private prosecution

自诉人 zìsùrén 〈法律〉party initiating a private prosecution; private prosecutor

自讨苦吃 zìtǎokǔchī bring trouble upon oneself:你要去帮他们的忙,那是～。You are asking for trouble (*or* You'll only burn your fingers) if you try to help them. /你要是那么溺爱孩子,将来会～的。If you spoil the child like that, you are making (*or* preparing) a rod for your own back.

自讨没趣 zìtǎo-méiqù ask for a snub or rebuff:人家并不欢迎你,你何必～呢? They don't want you to go. Why should you offer them an opportunity to cold-shoulder you?

自体 zìtǐ autogenous

自体不育性 zìtǐ bùyùxìng 〈动物〉self-sterility

自体繁殖 zìtǐ fánzhí 〈生物〉autoreproduction

自体感染 zìtǐ gǎnrǎn 〈医学〉autoinfection

自体抗体 zìtǐ kàngtǐ autoantibody

自体免疫 zìtǐ miǎnyì autoimmunity

自体输血 zìtǐ shūxuè autoinfusion; autotransfusion

自体移植 zìtǐ yízhí autograft; autotransplantation

自调恒温器 zìtiáo héngwēnqì self-acting thermostat

自通风 zìtōngfēng self-ventilation:～电机 self-ventilation machine

自投罗网 zìtóu-luówǎng throw oneself into a trap; bite the hook:这次你是真的～了。This time you've really put your head in a noose. /现在我们来个"守株待兔",叫他们～。Now let's lay a snare and make them fall into it. /能否设法让这个罪犯～呢? Can we think of a way to lure the criminal (*or* make the criminal walk) into the trap?

自外 zìwài separate or alienate oneself from; be divorced from; stand on the opposing side of; side against:～于集体 cut oneself off (*or* be divorced) from the collective /～于人民 set oneself against the people

自卫 zìwèi defending oneself; self-defence:奋起～ rise in self-defence /～战争 war of self-defence /集体～ collective self-defence

自卫队 Zìwèiduì (Japan) Self-Defence Force:陆上～ Ground Self-Defence Force

自卫反击 zìwèi fǎnjī fight or strike back in self-defence:～战 counterattack in self-defence

自卫军 zìwèijūn self-defence corps

自卫权 zìwèiquán 〈法律〉right of self-defence:行使～ exercise the right of self-defence

自卫杀人 zìwèi shārén 〈法律〉homicide in self-defence; manslaughter in self-defence

自为阶级 zìwèijiējí class-for-itself

自慰 zìwèi console oneself:聊以～ just to console oneself /足以～ be enough to cheer oneself up

自刎 zìwěn commit suicide by cutting one's throat; cut one's throat:拔剑～ draw out one's sword and cut one's throat

自稳态 zìwěntài homeostasis

自问 zìwèn ❶ ask oneself; examine one's conscience:反躬～ examine oneself; examine (*or* search) one's conscience ❷ conclude after weighing a matter:我～对得起任何人。I don't remember ever doing anybody wrong. /我～是尽力了。I think I have spared no efforts. *or* I believe I've done my best.

自我 zìwǒ self; oneself:～意识 self-consciousness /今天早上你～感觉怎样? How do you find yourself this morning? /人人都有～消遣的办法。Everyone has some way to amuse himself.

自我安慰 zìwǒ ānwèi self-consolation

自我暗示 zìwǒ ànshì 〈心理〉self-suggestion

自我暴露 zìwǒ bàolù self-betrayal; self-exposure:这番话是他无知的～。These remarks were an exposure of his own ignorance.

自我辩解 zìwǒ biànjiě self-justification

自我标榜 zìwǒ biāobǎng blow one's own trumpet; sing one's own praise; glorify oneself

自我表现 zìwǒ biǎoxiàn self-expression; showing off:此人好～。He is a showy person.

自我吹嘘 zìwǒ chuīxū self-glorification:何必～? What's the use of all this bragging?

自我催眠 zìwǒ cuīmián autohypnosis

自我改造 zìwǒ gǎizào self-remoulding

自我观察 zìwǒ guānchá 〈心理〉self-observation

自我检查 zìwǒ jiǎnchá self-examination; self-criticism:他一再～,还是过不了关。He failed to win understanding despite repeated self-criticism.

自我教育 zìwǒ jiàoyù self-education

自我解嘲 zìwǒ jiěcháo find excuses to console oneself

自我介绍 zìwǒ jièshào self-introduction

自我批评 zìwǒ pīpíng self-criticism:批评与～ criticism and self-criticism

自我陶醉 zìwǒ táozuì intoxicated with narcissism; self-satisfaction

自我完善 zìwǒ wánshàn self-perfection

自我牺牲 zìwǒ xīshēng self-sacrifice

自我欣赏 zìwǒ xīnshǎng self-appreciation; self-admiration

自我作古 zìwǒ-zuògǔ be the first to do sth.; not rely on past precedents

自吸泵 zìxībèng self-priming pump

自习 zìxí (of students) study by oneself in scheduled or free time

自下而上 zìxià'érshàng from bottom to top; from the grass roots up:～、上下结合的指导性计划制度 system of guidance planning in which plans are drafted first at lower levels and then decided by higher and lower departments together

自相残杀 zìxiāng-cánshā seek to destroy each other among members of the same group; dog eats dog:兄弟～ fratricide

自相关 zìxiāngguān 〈自控〉autocorrelation:～器 autocorrelator /～式计算机 autocorrelogram computer

自相惊扰 zìxiāng-jīngrǎo cause alarm among one's own group, etc.; create disturbance within one's ranks:近日盛传要地震的谣言,人们以讹传讹,～。Rumours have been spreading recently about an earthquake and have caused great alarm among people.

自相矛盾 zìxiāng-máodùn contradict oneself; be self-contradictory; be inconsistent:你前后的态度～。You have been inconsistent in your attitude. /他说了些～的话。He made some contradictory re-

marks. /你不觉得他的发言～吗? Don't you think he contradicted himself in his speech?

自相水火 zìxiāng-shuǐhuǒ (of members of a family or persons within a group, party, etc.) incompatible as fire and water; at loggerheads with each other

自相鱼肉 zìxiāng-yúròu see "自相残杀"

自销 zìxiāo self-marketing; sales through one's own channels: 企业～ sales by enterprises on their own /自购～ buy and market all by oneself /～门市部 enterprise-operated shops

自小 zìxiǎo from childhood; as a child: ～儿养成早起的习惯 form (*or* develop) the habit of rising early as a child

自卸 zìxiè self-discharge: ～式矿车 self-clearing car; self-discharge car

自卸卡车 zìxiè kǎchē dump truck; tip lorry; tipper

自卸拖车 zìxiè tuōchē self-unloading wagon; dump carrier

自新 zìxīn turn over a new leaf; make a fresh start; begin life anew: 悔过～ repent one's errors and make a fresh start /翻然～ quickly wake up to one's errors and start a new life

自信 zìxìn be self-confident: ～心很强 have great confidence in oneself /过于～ be overconfident; be cocksure of oneself /缺乏～ lack self-confidence; have no confidence in oneself /我～能担任这项工作。I am sure I'll be able to do the work.

自行 zìxíng ❶ by oneself: ～处理 deal with (sth.) on one's own /～解决 solve by oneself /他们让科学家们～决定所需的研究设备。They allow the scientists to write their own ticket for the kind of research setup they want. ❷ of oneself; of one's own accord; of one's free will: ～消失 disappear of itself /他们会～撤军吗? Will they withdraw (*or* pull out) their troops of their own accord? ❸〈天文〉proper motion

自行车 zìxíngchē bicycle; bike: 女用～ lady's bicycle; bicycle for ladies /他会骑～吗? Can he ride a bicycle? /你今天骑～上学吗? Will you go to school by bike today? *or* Will you cycle to school today? /我推着～走回来的。I walked my bicycle back.

自行车把 zìxíngchēbǎ handlebars

自行车架 zìxíngchējià bicycle stand

自行车棚 zìxíngchēpéng bicycle shed

自行车赛 zìxíngchēsài cycle racing; cycling

自行车座 zìxíngchēzuò saddle; seat on a bicycle

自行火箭炮 zìxíng huǒjiànpào 〈军事〉self-propelled rocket launcher

自行火炮 zìxíng huǒpào 〈军事〉mechanized gun; self-propelled artillery; self-propelled gun

自行加榴炮 zìxíng jiāliúpào 〈军事〉self-propelled howitzer

自行其是 zìxíng-qíshì act as one thinks fit; go one's own way: 你不能总是～,最好听听别人的意见。You can't always go your own way. You'd better listen to what others have to say. /别～,要通过正常渠道提出你的申请。Don't take matters into your own hands; make your application through the usual channels.

自省 zìxǐng 〈书面〉examine oneself critically; examine one's thoughts and conduct: ～才力,不能胜任。I think my ability is not equal to the task.

自省程序 zìxǐng chéngxù 〈计算机〉introspective program

自修 zìxiū ❶ (of students) study by oneself; study individually ❷ study on one's own; study independently: ～两门外语 teach oneself two foreign languages

自许 zìxǔ ❶ praise oneself; build oneself up: 以善于经营～ pride oneself on being a good manager ❷ style oneself; claim to be: 他管我叫小曹,他～为大曹。He calls me Little Cao and himself Big Cao.

自诩 zìxǔ 〈书面〉praise oneself; boast; brag: 他以谈判能手～。He bragged that he was an expert negotiator. /这年轻人～为作家。The young man styled himself writer.

自序 zìxù *also* "自叙" ❶ author's preface; preface ❷ autobiographic note; brief account of one's life: 这部小说带有～性质。This is an autobiographical novel.

自选 zìxuǎn ❶〈体育〉free; optional: ～手枪五十米赛 free pistol 50m (shooting-match) ❷ (of a store, etc.) self-service

自选动作 zìxuǎn dòngzuò 〈体育〉optional exercise

自选商场 zìxuǎn shāngchǎng self-service market; supermarket

自炫 zìxuàn 〈书面〉sing one's own praises; crack oneself up; talk big: ～清高 boast of being above worldly considerations

自旋 zìxuán spin

自旋轴 zìxuánzhóu *also* "尾旋轴" wěixuánzhóu 〈航天〉spin axis (axis about which a space vehicle rotates to provide stability)

自学 zìxué study on one's own; study independently; teach oneself; go through self-schooling: ～会计课程 teach oneself accounting /～成才 become educated through self-study; be self-taught /培养～能力 foster (*or* cultivate) one's ability to study independently

自学考试 zìxué kǎoshì self-study examination

自学课本 zìxué kèběn teach-yourself books

自血疗法 zìxuè liáofǎ 〈医学〉autohemotherapy

自寻出路 zìxún-chūlù *also* "自谋出路" find a way out for oneself; find employment: 大学毕业后,他准备～。He plans to find a job for himself upon graduation from college.

自寻的鱼雷 zìxúndì yúléi 〈军事〉homing torpedo

自寻烦恼 zìxún-fánnǎo torture oneself with unpleasant thoughts; work oneself up for no reason at all; worry oneself needlessly; vex oneself: 我认为你这是～。I think you are tormenting yourself unnecessarily. /你成天担心家里会发生什么事情,这不是～吗? Aren't you borrowing trouble worrying about what's going to happen to your family?

自寻死路 zìxún-sǐlù bring about one's own destruction; take the road to one's doom: 你这样沉溺于赌博,不是～吗? Aren't you courting destruction by indulging in gambling like this?

自言自语 zìyán-zìyǔ speak one's thoughts aloud; talk to oneself; think aloud; soliloquize: 你～说些什么呀? What are you muttering to yourself? /她～道:"怎么办呢?" She thought aloud, "What's to be done?"

自养生物 zìyǎng shēngwù 〈生物〉autotroph

自养植物 zìyǎng zhíwù 〈植物〉autophyte; autotrophic plant

自贻伊戚 zìyí-yīqī *also* "自诒伊戚" bring trouble on oneself; court disaster

自已 zìyǐ (often used in the negative) able to control oneself: 兴奋之情不能～。He is too excited to control himself. *or* He is beside himself with excitement.

自以为得计 zì yǐwéi déjì 〈贬义〉be pleased with one's own scheming; be smug about one's stratagem; think oneself smart

自以为非 zìyǐwéifēi recognize or admit one's fallibility: 人要有一点～的精神。One should have the courage to admit one's own mistakes.

自以为是 zìyǐwéishì consider oneself always in the right; be cocksure and impervious to criticism; be opinionated: 科学的态度是实事求是,而不是～。The scientific approach is not to claim infallibility presumptuously but to seek truth from facts.

自缢 zìyì 〈书面〉hang oneself

自应 zìyīng of course; naturally: 这样重要的问题,～商讨解决。Such an important matter should, of course, be settled through discussion.

自用 zìyòng ❶ obstinately sticking to one's own opinions; opinionated; self-willed: 刚愎～ bigoted; opinionated /～则小。The self-willed tend to be narrow-minded. ❷ for private use; private; personal: ～汽车 private car /～药品 medicine for one's own use

自由 zìyóu ❶ freedom; liberty: 争取言论～ strive for freedom of speech /获得婚姻～ gain freedom of marriage /保障通商～ guarantee freedom of commerce /压制舆论～ suppress freedom of public opinion /限制通信～ abridge freedom of correspondence /侵犯宗教～ violate religious freedom /妨碍他的行动～ hamper his freedom of action /享受公民～权 enjoy civil liberties /个人～ personal liberty; individual freedom /学术～ academic freedom /新闻～ freedom of information /出版～ freedom of the press /集会、结社、游行、示威、罢工的～ freedom of assembly, association, procession, demonstration and the freedom to strike /宪法赋予的～ constitutional freedoms /四大～ the Four Freedoms (proclaimed by F.D. Roosevelt on 6 January 1941) — freedom of speech, freedom of worship, freedom from want, freedom from fear ❷〈哲学〉freedom: ～和必然 freedom and necessity ❸ free; unrestricted; unrestrained: ～参加 free to participate /～讨论 have a free exchange of views; hold free discussion /～选购 be free to buy; make free purchase /～发表意见 be at liberty to air one's views; express one's views unreservedly /～过境 free transit /～进入 free access /～买卖 free trading /～意志 free will

自由大气 zìyóu dàqì free atmosphere (500-1500 metres above ground)

自由电子 zìyóu diànzǐ free electron

自由兑换 zìyóu duìhuàn 〈经济〉convertibility: 可以～的货币 convertible currency /不能～的货币 inconvertible currency

Z

自由泛滥 zìyóu-fànlàn (of erroneous ideas) spread unchecked; run wild; run rampant
自由放任 zìyóu-fàngrèn letting things go their own way; allowing unrestrained freedom; laissez-faire:～的经济政策 laissez-faire economic policy
自由放任主义 zìyóu fàngrènzhǔyì laissez-faire
自由浮动 zìyóu fúdòng free floating
自由港 zìyóugǎng free (trade) port
自由公教会 Zìyóu Gōngjiàohuì 〈宗教〉Free Catholics
自由关税区 zìyóu guānshuìqū tariff-free zone
自由滑 zìyóuhuá 〈体育〉free skating
自由化 zìyóuhuà liberalization:资产阶级～ bourgeois liberalization (attempt to transform socialism into capitalism in the name of freedom)
自由汇率 zìyóu huìlǜ free exchange rate
自由基 zìyóujī 〈化学〉free radical
自由价格 zìyóu jiàgé free price
自由竞争 zìyóu jìngzhēng free competition
自由联想 zìyóu liánxiǎng 〈心理〉free or uncontrolled association
自由恋爱 zìyóu liàn'ài free choice of marriage partner; free courtship
自由落体 zìyóu luòtǐ free-falling body
自由落体运动 zìyóu luòtǐ yùndòng free fall
自由贸易 zìyóu màoyì free trade
自由民 zìyóumín freeman; freedman
自由能 zìyóunéng 〈物理〉free energy
自由女神像 Zìyóu Nǚshénxiàng (US) Statue of Liberty (inaugurated on 28 October 1886 in New York)
自由企业制度 zìyóu qǐyè zhìdù free-enterprise system
自由人 zìyóurén (in soccer) libero
自由散漫 zìyóu-sǎnmàn lax in discipline; slack:～的习气 slackness (in discipline) /学生们的～行为 indiscipline of the students /这孩子～惯了。The child is in the habit of going his own way (*or* doing what he likes).
自由诗 zìyóushī free verse; unorthodox verse
自由市场 zìyóu shìchǎng free market; open market
自由体操 zìyóu tǐcāo floor exercise; free exercise; free callisthenics
自由通货 zìyóu tōnghuò free currency
自由王国 zìyóu wángguó 〈哲学〉realm of freedom:人类的历史,就是一个不断地从必然王国向～发展的历史。The history of mankind is one of continuous development from the realm of necessity to the realm of freedom.
自由意志 zìyóu yìzhì free will
自由泳 zìyóuyǒng freestyle; crawl
自由职业 zìyóu zhíyè profession:～者 professional
自由主义 zìyóuzhǔyì liberalism; indiscipline; lack of principle or sense of organization:～倾向 liberalistic tendencies; tendencies to indiscipline /～者 liberalist
自由撰稿人 zìyóu zhuàngǎorén freelance; freelancer
自由资本主义 zìyóu zīběnzhǔyì laissez-faire capitalism; free capitalism; non-monopoly capitalism
自由资产阶级 zìyóu zīchǎnjiējí liberal bourgeoisie
自由自在 zìyóu-zìzài leisurely and carefree; happy-go-lucky; free and easy:～地生活 lead a free and easy life
自由组合规律 zìyóu zǔhé guīlǜ 〈生物〉law of independent assortment
自有公论 zìyǒu gōnglùn the people will pass a fair or just judgment
自有资金 zìyǒu zījīn self-possessed funds
自幼 zìyòu since childhood; from the cradle:这两个女孩～在一起长大。The two girls were brought up together from the cradle.
自娱 zìyú divert oneself; while away the time:作诗～ divert oneself by writing poems; write poems as a pastime
自育 zìyù 〈动物〉self-fertilization; self-fertilizing
自愈 zìyù 〈医学〉autotherapy
自圆其说 zìyuán-qíshuō make one's statement sound plausible; justify oneself:无法～ cannot offer an acceptable explanation (*or* a tenable argument) /你怎么～呢? How can you justify yourself? /这一解释不能～。This is a flimsy explanation.
自怨自艾 zìyuàn-zìyì be full of remorse and self-reproach:她虽然常常～,却又常常自满自足。Though she suffered frequent bouts of self-reproach, she was just as often quite happy with herself.
自愿 zìyuàn of one's own free will; voluntarily:～退出 opt out /本着～互利的原则 on the principle of voluntary participation and mutual benefit /～参加这项事业 volunteer for the undertaking /有谁～做这件事吗? Any volunteers?
自愿遣返 zìyuàn qiǎnfǎn voluntary repatriation
自在 zìzài free; untrammelled; unrestrained:逍遥～ leisurely and carefree; at liberty to enjoy oneself; free from trammels
自在 zìzai comfortable; at ease:觉得心里很不～ feel rather ill at ease /感觉身体不～ feel a bit under the weather; feel a little out of sorts /主人太热情好客,反而使我们感到不～。We didn't feel quite at home, as the host showered us with too much hospitality.
自在阶级 zìzàijiējí 〈哲学〉class-in-itself
自在之物 zìzài zhī wù 〈哲学〉thing-in-itself; *ding an sich*
自责 zìzé self-reproach; self-reproof:你不必为此～。You needn't blame yourself for that. /这种～与感激的心情,常常在我心中交错出现。I have been prey to alternate feelings of self-reproach and gratitude.
自找 zìzhǎo invite trouble; ask for it:～苦吃 be looking for trouble /～重担挑 volunteer to do difficult work /小刘总是～麻烦,说些不该说的话。Xiao Liu is always sticking his neck out by saying something he shouldn't say.
自斟自饮 zìzhēn-zìyǐn pour one's own wine:～,不亦乐乎? How pleasant it is to drink all by oneself!
自知之明 zìzhīzhīmíng self-knowledge; wisdom of knowing one's own limitations:此人太没有～了。The person has no self-knowledge at all. /人贵有～。A man's virtue lies in taking a proper measure of himself.
自治 zìzhì autonomy; self-government:高度～ high degree of autonomy /民族区域～ regional national autonomy /享有地方～权 enjoy local autonomy /～的权限 autonomous jurisdiction /～领土 autonomous territory /～区域 autonomous area /～实体 autonomous entity /～条例 autonomy statutes /二次大战以后,英国不得不同意它的许多殖民地～。After World War II, Britain was forced to grant many of its colonies autonomy.
自治国家 zìzhì guójiā autonomous state
自治机关 zìzhì jīguān organ of self-government
自治领 zìzhìlǐng self-governing dominion; dominion
自治区 zìzhìqū autonomous region
自治权 zìzhìquán autonomy; right to autonomy
自治省 Zìzhìshěng (Japan) Ministry of Home Affairs
自治系统 zìzhì xìtǒng autonomous system
自治县 zìzhìxiàn autonomous county
自治州 zìzhìzhōu autonomous prefecture
自制 zìzhì ❶ made by oneself; self-made:～的冰淇淋 self-made ice-cream /这些教具都是我们～的。These teaching aids are all made by ourselves. ❷ self-control; self-restraint; self-mastery:面对此情此景,他实在难以～。Seeing this, he could hardly contain (*or* restrain) himself.
自重 zìzhòng ❶ behave with dignity:请～点儿! Mind your conduct, please! ❷ 〈书面〉enhance one's influence or position:拥兵～ extend one's influence with military power ❸ dead weight:卡车～ dead weight of a truck
自主 zìzhǔ decide for oneself; be the master of one's own fate; keep the initiative in one's own hands:婚姻～ freedom of marriage /不由～ cannot help (doing sth.); (act) involuntarily /独立～地处理本国事务 independently handle the domestic affairs /独立～的和平外交政策 independent foreign policy of peace /一旦你和她结婚,你就再不能～了。You'll never be able to call your soul your own once you marry her.
自主教会 zìzhǔ jiàohuì 〈宗教〉autocephalous churches
自主权 zìzhǔquán power to make one's own decisions; decision-making power
自主神经 zìzhǔ shénjīng 〈生理〉autonomic nerve
自助 zìzhù self-service
自助餐 zìzhùcān buffet:～厅 automat; cafeteria
自助洗衣店 zìzhù xǐyīdiàn laundromat
自专 zìzhuān 〈书面〉act on one's own; act arbitrarily
自传 zìzhuàn autobiography:～体小说 autobiographical novel
自转 zìzhuàn 〈天文〉rotation:地球～一周是一天。The period of one complete rotation of the earth is a day.
自转轴 zìzhuànzhóu axis of rotation
自走式 zìzǒushì 〈农业〉self-propelled:～播种机 self-propelled

drill /～联合收获机 self-propelled combine; autoheader /～喷雾机 self-propelled sprayer /～收割装载机 self-propelled cutter loader /～挖掘机 self-propelled ditch digger

自足 zìzú ❶ self-sufficiency; autarky:～经济 self-sufficient economy ❷ self-satisfied; self-contented:骄傲～ smug and conceited

自尊 zìzūn self-respect; self-esteem; pride:伤了别人的～心 wound sb.'s self-esteem; hurt sb.'s pride /满足他人的～心 gratify (*or* satisfy) sb.'s pride /民族～心 national self-esteem /～感 sense of self-respect

自作聪明 zìzuò-cōngmíng fancy oneself smart; think oneself clever:他这人总是～,不听别人劝。He always considers himself clever and turns a deaf ear to other people's advice.

自作多情 zìzuò-duōqíng imagine oneself the favorite of one of the opposite sex:你这是～,那姑娘根本不爱你。You are just imagining yourself in love; the girl has no affection for you at all.

自作主张 zìzuò-zhǔzhāng act on one's own; decide for oneself; make a decision all alone:事情紧急,没时间商量,只好～了。As the matter is urgent and allows no time for consultation, I'll have to make a decision myself.

自作自受 zìzuò-zìshòu be hoist with one's own petard; lie in the bed one has made; stew in one's own juice:当初我警告你别开快车,你不听,出了事,这是你～。I warned you not to drive too fast, but you wouldn't listen and had an accident. As you've made your bed, now you have to lie on it. /若是出了问题,由他～。If he runs into trouble, he'll have brought it on himself.

渍 zì ❶ soak; steep; ret:汗水把白衬衣～黄了。The white shirt has yellowed with sweat. /凉干的菜浸～得慢。Dried vegetables steep slowly. ❷ floodwater on low-lying land; waterlogging:防涝排～ prevention of waterlogging and drainage of floodwater ❸ be soiled or stained (with grease, etc.):～满油泥的工作服 work clothes stained with grease /他的鞋上～满了泥。His shoes were caked with mud. /有了挡泥板,车上没～上一点儿烂泥。Fenders kept dirt off the car. ❹〈方言〉stain; smear; sludge:血～ bloodstain /墨～ ink stain; smears of ink /汗～ sweat stain /桶底的油～ sludge at the bottom of the tank

渍涝 zìlào waterlogging; floodwater in the fields:排除～ drain water from the fields

渍染 zìrǎn stain; contaminate; soil:血污～ be soiled with blood

渍水 zìshuǐ floodwater (on low-lying land, etc.):麦田里～ floodwater in the wheat fields /排干～ drain off the floodwater

zōng

宗[1] zōng ❶ ancestor:列祖列～ successive generations of ancestors /光～耀祖 bring honour to one's ancestors ❷ clan:同～ of the same clan /～兄～弟 brothers of the same clan ❸ faction; sect; school:正～ orthodox school /天台～ Tiantai Sect /禅～ *Chan* Sect; Zen Sect ❹ aim; purpose; objective:万变不离其～ remain essentially the same despite all apparent changes; all changes, no matter how varied, centre on one purpose /开～明义 make clear the purpose and main theme from the very beginning ❺ (in academic or artistic work) model on:他的唱腔～马派。His singing belongs to the Ma School. ❻ great master; example; model: *see* "～师" ❼〈量词〉:一～心事 a cause for worry /一～刑事案件 a criminal case /大～贷款 a large loan /大～生意 a big (*or* an immense) business /大～货物 a large quantity of goods ❽ (Zōng) a surname

宗[2] zōng 〈旧语〉*zong*, an old administrative unit in Tibet, roughly corresponding to the county

宗本 zōngběn 〈旧语〉official serving at the *zong* (an old administrative unit in Tibet) level, who was in charge of such administrative affairs as collecting taxes, etc.

宗祠 zōngcí ancestral hall or temple:王氏～ ancestral hall of the Wang clan

宗法 zōngfǎ ❶ patriarchal clan rules and regulations:～社会 patriarchal society /～制度 patriarchal clan system ❷ follow; model on; take as example:他的字～颜体。His handwriting is modelled on the calligraphic style of Yan Zhenqing. /其画历来为人所～。His paintings have always been taken as example by others.

宗匠 zōngjiàng 〈旧语〉(in academic or artistic work) great master:诗家以李、杜为～。Li Bai and Du Fu are regarded as great masters of Chinese poetry.

宗教 zōngjiào religion:放弃～信仰 renounce one's religion /皈依～ experience religion; embrace a religion /笃信～ profoundly religious /～自由 freedom (*or* liberty) of religion; religious freedom (*or* liberty) /～事业 religious undertaking

宗教法庭 zōngjiào fǎtíng the Inquisition (in medieval Europe)

宗教改革 zōngjiào gǎigé the Reformation; religious reform

宗教贡礼 zōngjiào gònglǐ ecclesiastical tributes

宗教画 zōngjiàohuà religious paintings of sacred subjects; icons

宗教戒律 zōngjiào jièlǜ religious taboos

宗教派别 zōngjiào pàibié religious sect; distinctions of religious creed

宗教信仰 zōngjiào xìnyǎng religious belief:～自由 freedom of religious belief; freedom of worship

宗教仪式 zōngjiào yíshì religious rites; ritual

宗筋 zōngjīn 〈中医〉penis

宗喀巴 Zōngkābā Tsong-kha-pa (1357-1419), founder of Gelugpa (格鲁派) or Yellow sect of Tibetan Buddhism

宗脉 zōngmài 〈中医〉confluence of channels

宗庙 zōngmiào ancestral temple or shrine of a ruling house:拜祭～ worship and offer sacrifices to one's ancestors at the ancestral shrine

宗派 zōngpài ❶ faction; sect:～斗争 factional strife /～活动 factional activities; sectarian activities /～分裂活动 factional splitting activities; sectarian and divisive activities /～林立 host of factions ❷〈书面〉branch of a clan:这个姓在江南江北都有～。People with this surname are scattered on either side of the Yangtze River.

宗派主义 zōngpàizhǔyì sectarianism; factionalism:～者 sectarian; factionalist

宗谱 zōngpǔ family tree; genealogical tree; genealogy:杨氏～ genealogy of the Yang family

宗亲 zōngqīn ❶ clansman ❷ brothers of the same mother

宗人 zōngrén clansman and clanswoman

宗社 zōngshè 〈书面〉❶ ancestral shrine of a ruling house and the gods of the land and of grain ❷ state; country

宗师 zōngshī master of great learning and integrity:一代～ leading scholar of his time /被尊为山水画的～ be respected as a great master of landscape painting

宗室 zōngshì ❶ imperial or royal clan ❷ imperial or royal clansman

宗祧 zōngtiāo 〈旧语〉❶ ancestral shrine ❷ pedigree; genealogy

宗仰 zōngyǎng 〈书面〉hold in esteem; be revered:远近～ be held in esteem far and near /国人～ be revered by one's countrymen

宗支 zōngzhī *also* "宗枝" ❶ lateral branch of a clan ❷ of the same clan

宗旨 zōngzhǐ aim; purpose:以振兴教育为～ aim at vitalizing education /办报的～ aim of running the newspaper /我们的～是竭诚为顾客服务。It is our purpose to serve the customers to the best of our ability.

宗主国 zōngzhǔguó suzerain (state); metropolitan state

宗主权 zōngzhǔquán suzerainty

宗族 zōngzú ❶ patriarchal clan:～关系 of the same clan /按～的辈分论,他俩是叔侄。They are uncle and nephew according to the seniority in the clan. ❷ clansman

棕(椶) zōng ❶ palm ❷ palm fibre; coir:～刷子 coir brush

棕绷 zōngbēng *also* "棕绷子" wooden bed frame strung with crisscross coir ropes

棕编 zōngbiān handicraft articles made of coir; coir-woven articles

棕黑 zōnghēi dark or chestnut brown; Spanish brown:～的脸 swarthy complexion

棕红 zōnghóng reddish brown

棕黄 zōnghuáng light or pale brown

棕榈 zōnglǘ palm

棕榈酒 zōnglǘjiǔ palm wine

棕榈栗 zōnglǘlì palm chestnut

棕榈酸 zōnglǘsuān palmitic acid; palmic acid

棕榈油 zōnglǘyóu palm oil; palm butter

棕毛 zōngmáo palm fibre; coir: ～蓑衣 palm rain cape
棕壤 zōngrǎng *also* "综色森林土" zōngsè sēnlíntǔ 〈农业〉 brown earth; brown forest soil
棕色 zōngsè brown
棕绳 zōngshéng coir rope
棕树 zōngshù palm
棕毯 zōngtǎn coir rug
棕箱 zōngxiāng wooden trunk or chest with a slipcover made of palm fibre
棕熊 zōngxióng 〈动物〉 brown bear
棕衣 zōngyī palm rain cape
棕鳟 zōngzūn brown trout; German brown trout (*Salmo truta*)

鬃 zōng hair (on the neck of a pig, horse, etc.): 马～ horse's mane /猪～ pig's bristles /红～烈马 spirited steed with a red mane
鬃狼 zōngláng maned wolf (*Chrysocyon brachyurus*)
鬃毛 zōngmáo hair (on the neck of a pig, horse, etc.)
鬃鼠 zōngshǔ maned rat; crested rat (*Lophismys imhausi*)
鬃刷 zōngshuā bristle brush

踪(蹤) zōng track; trail; trace; footprint: 追～ follow the trail of; track; trace /跟～ be on the track of; shadow /失～ be missing /行～ whereabouts; track /无影无～ vanish into thin air; disappear without a trace
踪迹 zōngjì trace; trail; track: 找到窃贼的～ get on the trail of the burglars /车轮在泥土上留下的～ tyre tracks in the mud /没有发现逃犯的任何～。No trace of the escaped criminal was found.
踪影 zōngyǐng trace; shadow; sign: 我找了她一上午，但到处不见她的～。I've been looking for her all morning, but she is nowhere to be found. /老汉目送着远去的列车，直到看不见～。The old man gazed after the departing train until it was out of sight.

腙 zōng 〈化学〉 hydrazone

综 zōng sum up; put together; combine: ～理万机 manage a myriad of affairs /错～复杂 intricate; complex
see also zèng
综观 zōngguān take an overall view; make a comprehensive survey: ～全局 take a look at (*or* size up) the overall situation
综合 zōnghé ❶ synthesize; summarize: 分析与～在座各位的意见 analyze and sum up (*or* synthesize) the opinions of all those present /这需要～起来考虑。This has to be taken as a whole. ❷ synthetical; comprehensive; multiple; composite: ～货船 composite vessel / ～经营 multipurpose (*or* diverse) economic undertakings
综合保险 zōnghé bǎoxiǎn comprehensive insurance; all risk insurance
综合报道 zōnghé bàodào news roundup; comprehensive or composite dispatch
综合报告 zōnghé bàogào comprehensive report; summing-up report; consolidated report
综合大学 zōnghé dàxué university; comprehensive university
综合规划 zōnghé guīhuà unified plan; comprehensive planning
综合国力 zōnghé guólì overall national strength
综合经济效益 zōnghé jīngjì xiàoyì overall economic efficiency or performance
综合考察 zōnghé kǎochá comprehensive survey
综合利用 zōnghé lìyòng comprehensive utilization; multipurpose use
综合模式 zōnghé móshì aggregative model
综合配套措施 zōnghé pèitào cuòshī comprehensive coordinated measures
综合平衡 zōnghé pínghéng (strike an) overall balance
综合商品指数 zōnghé shāngpǐn zhǐshù composite merchandise index number
综合商社 zōnghé shāngshè (Japan) *zaibatsu*
综合体制 zōnghé tǐzhì comprehensive institutional framework
综合信息系统 zōnghé xìnxī xìtǒng integrated information system
综合性工厂 zōnghéxìng gōngchǎng multiple-producing factory
综合业务数字网 zōnghé yèwù shùzìwǎng 〈信息〉 integrated services digital network (ISDN)
综合语 zōnghéyǔ 〈语言〉 synthetic language
综合预算 zōnghé yùsuàn united budget
综合征 zōnghézhēng *also* "综合病症" syndrome: 闭合性颅脑损伤～ closed head syndrome /颈神经～ cervical syndrome /心绞痛～ anginal syndrome; anginose syndrome
综合指标承包制 zōnghé zhǐbiāo chéngbāozhì contract system embracing all quotas
综合治理 zōnghé zhìlǐ comprehensive or coordinated measures for maintaining law and order; tackling a problem in a comprehensive way
综计 zōngjì sum up; add up: 这些问题～有五种类型。To sum up, these problems fall into five classes. /全文～九千字。The essay has 9,000 words altogether.
综括 zōngkuò summarize; sum up: ～起来说 to sum up; to state briefly; to put it in a nutshell
综述 zōngshù summarize; wrap up: 一周新闻～ roundup of the week's news /时事～ wrap-up of current affairs /商情～ comprehensive report on the business situation

纵(𡙡) zōng *see* "鸡纵" jīzōng
骔(騌) zōng horse's mane

zǒng

总(総、總) zǒng ❶ assemble; gather; put together; sum up: 汇～ collect; assemble; gather together /～在一起考虑 take everything into consideration /～起来说，该方法有三大优点。To summarize, the method has three strong points. ❷ general; overall; gross; total: ～成本 total cost; overall cost /～利润 gross profits /～需求量 aggregate demand /～收益 total revenue; gross income /～指数 combined index /～根源 root cause /～开关 master switch /抓～ assume overall responsibility ❸ chief; leading; general: ～代表 chief representative /～工长 general foreman; section chief /～调度 chief dispatcher ❹ without exception; always; invariably: 他～忘记带钥匙。He invariably forgets to take his keys. /我们～是步行去那儿。We always went there on foot. ❺ anyway; after all; eventually; sooner or later: 但他～还是你的父亲。But after all, he is your father. /只要你努力工作，～有一天会出成绩的。Just work hard, and you'll become accomplished one day. /你～会明白的。You'll understand it sooner or later. /人～是要死的。Death is inevitable. *or* We must go the way of all flesh. *or* Everyone must die. /你的梦想～会实现的。Your dream will eventually come true. ❻ at least; surely: 你～不会出卖我吧? Surely, you wouldn't betray me, would you? /你大学毕业，～该有十年了吧。It must have been ten years at least since you graduated from the university. /她～该给我个解释。She should at any rate give me an explanation.
总安装图 zǒng'ānzhuāngtú general assembly drawing
总罢工 zǒngbàgōng general strike
总办 zǒngbàn 〈旧语〉 director-general of an administrative bureau
总包合同 zǒngbāo hétong lump-sum contract
总包价 zǒngbāojià total contract value
总编辑 zǒngbiānjí editor-in-chief
总兵 zǒngbīng 〈旧语〉 commanding officer of garrison troops or of an area
总部 zǒngbù general headquarters: 联合国～ headquarters of the United Nations
总裁 zǒngcái ❶(in the Qing Dynasty) minister in charge of the imperial editing staff and the imperial civil service examination at the capital ❷ president (of a company or political party): 微软公司～ president of the Microsoft Co. / 自民党～ (Japan) President of the Liberal Democratic Party (LDP)
总参谋部 zǒngcānmóubù headquarters of the general staff
总参谋长 zǒngcānmóuzhǎng chief of the general staff
总产量 zǒngchǎnliàng total output
总产值 zǒngchǎnzhí total output value; gross output value
总称 zǒngchēng general term or reference: 舰艇是各种军用船只的～。Naval ships are a general reference to all the vessels for military use.
总成 zǒngchéng ❶ 〈机械〉 assembly; unit assemblage: 发动机～

engine (*or* motor) assembly ❷ *also* "总承" (often used in the early vernacular) help sb. to achieve his aim: ～我与她的婚事 help to bring about my marriage with her

总赤字 zǒngchìzì total deficit

总胆管 zǒngdǎnguǎn choledochus; ductus communis: ～切开术 choledochotomy /～炎 choledochitis

总得 zǒngděi must; have to; cannot but: 问题～解决。The problem must be solved. /无论如何, 你～答应他的这个要求。Anyway, you've got to grant his request. /他今天会上～说几句。He's bound to say something at today's meeting.

总店 zǒngdiàn head office (of a firm); main store (of a business): 新华书店～ main store of the Xinhua bookstores

总动员 zǒngdòngyuán ❶ general or total mobilization: 全国～ national mobilization ❷ call up all the forces to fulfil an urgent task: 为了按期交货, 我们来了个全厂～。We put all hands on the line in the factory in order to deliver the goods on time.

总督 zǒngdū ❶ governor-general (in the Qing Dynasty): 两广～ governor-general of Guangdong and Guangxi ❷ viceroy; governor (in British overseas possessions): 香港前～ former Governor of Hong Kong /印度前～ ex-viceroy of India ❸ governor-general (in some Commonwealth countries): 加拿大～ Governor-General of Canada

总队 zǒngduì army unit roughly corresponding to a regiment or division

总额 zǒng'é total (amount); gross amount: 工资～ total wages / 存款～ total deposits /销售或零售～ gross amount of wholesale or retail /上半年利润～达一百万元。The profit in the first half of the year reached a total of one million *yuan*.

总而言之 zǒng'éryánzhī in brief; in short; to sum up; to make a long story short: ～, 他是不想来。In a nutshell, he doesn't want to come. /～, 他们的经济情况并不坏。All in all, their financial condition is not bad. /说来说去, ～就是没钱。The money isn't there, and that's the long and short of it. /～, 这就是对你的论点的回答。This, in brief, is the answer to your argument.

总方针 zǒngfāngzhēn general policy; general principle: 对外贸易～ general policy of foreign trade /发展国民经济的～ general principles governing the development of the national economy

总纲 zǒnggāng general programme; general principles: 宪法～ general principles of the constitution /在章程的～中写明了本会的宗旨。The purposes of this association were spelt out clearly in the general programme of its charter.

总工程师 zǒnggōngchéngshī chief engineer

总工会 zǒnggōnghuì federation of trade unions: 中华全国～ All-China Federation of Trade Unions

总公司 zǒnggōngsī head office of a corporation; parent company; controlling corporation; head company

总功 zǒnggōng 〈物理〉 effective work plus idle work; total work

总攻 zǒnggōng 〈军事〉 general offensive: 向敌人发起～ launch a general offensive against the enemy

总供给 zǒnggōngjǐ aggregate supply

总共 zǒnggòng altogether; in all; *in toto*: 这个学校～有三千多学生。There are altogether over 3,000 students in the school. /她～养了三十头猪。She raised thirty pigs in all. /～有七人在场。All in all, there were seven people present.

总管 zǒngguǎn ❶ be in full charge of: ～生产 be in general charge of production ❷ person in full or general charge; manager: 企业～ manager of an enterprise ❸ 〈旧语〉 butler (of a rich family); chief steward

总归 zǒngguī eventually; anyhow; after all; at any rate: 这个难题～会得到解决的。This tough problem will eventually be solved. /他～还是你的兄弟, 别叫他丢面子了。Don't let him lose face; he is your brother after all.

总行 zǒngháng head office (of a bank, etc.)

总合 zǒnghé summing up; everything put together: 把各种现金～起来也不足一万元。The sum total of all available cash was less than 10,000 *yuan*.

总合幕僚会议 Zǒnghé Mùliáo Huìyì (Japan) Joint Staff Council

总和 zǒnghé whole; sum; total; sum total: 全年产量的～ output of the year taken as a whole /全年全市新建住宅面积的～为一百万平方米。The houses constructed this year in the city have a total residential space of one million square metres.

总和仪表 zǒnghé yíbiǎo 〈电工〉 summation instrument

总后方 zǒnghòufāng rear base where the general headquarters is located

总后勤部 zǒnghòuqínbù general logistics department: ～部长 director of the general logistics department

总汇 zǒnghuì ❶ (of streams) come or flow together: 湘、资、沅、澧四水～于洞庭湖。The Xiang, Zi, Yuan and Li rivers flow together into the Dongting Lake. ❷ confluence; concourse; compendium; aggregate: 力量的～ aggregation of strength /思想的～ confluence of ideas /《全唐诗》是唐代诗歌的～。*The Compendium of Tang Poems* is a complete collection of the poems of the Tang Dynasty.

总机 zǒngjī telephone exchange; switchboard

总机械师 zǒngjīxièshī chief mechanic

总集 zǒngjí anthology; collection of writings or poems by many authors or poets: 《诗经》是古代的一本诗歌～。*The Book of Songs* is an anthology of ancient poems.

总计 zǒngjì ❶ 〈数学〉 grand total ❷ total; amount to; add up to: 该书三个月～销售一万三千册。The book attained a gross sale of 13,000 copies in three months. /修理那些旧房子～花了八千元。The renovation of the old houses cost 8,000 *yuan* in all. /旅行开销～达五百元。The sum total of expenses for the trip was 500 *yuan*. /乐团在上海～演出十五场。While in Shanghai, the philharmonic orchestra altogether gave fifteen performances. /账单～达一百三十美元。The bill added up to $130.

总价 zǒngjià total price

总监 zǒngjiān inspector general; chief inspector: 税务～ Tax Inspector General /财务～ (of a company, etc) CFO (Chief Financial Officer)

总检察长 zǒngjiǎncházhǎng attorney general

总角 zǒngjiǎo 〈书面〉 child's hair twisted in a knot — childhood: ～学琴 learn to play the piano when a child

总角之交 zǒngjiǎozhījiāo childhood friend: 想不到这一对～竟成了死对头。No one could have thought that the two childhood friends would become deadly foes.

总结 zǒngjié ❶ sum up; summarize: ～经验教训 sum up one's experience and lessons /～上半年的工作情况 summarize the work of the first half of the year /～我们三年来的成绩 give a summation of our achievements in the past three years ❷ summary; summing-up; summation: 写～ write a summary /年终～ year-end summing-up of work

总结报告 zǒngjié bàogào final report; concluding report; summary report

总结会 zǒngjiéhuì summing-up meeting

总经济师 zǒngjīngjìshī chief economic manager; chief economic engineer

总经理 zǒngjīnglǐ general or executive manager; president: 大通银行～ president of Chase Manhattan Bank

总警监 zǒngjǐngjiān (highest Chinese police rank) General Police Commissioner: 副～ Deputy General Police Commissioner

总开关 zǒngkāiguān 〈电工〉 main switch; main supply switch; master cock; master switch

总会计师 zǒngkuàijìshī chief accountant; general accountant; treasurer

总括 zǒngkuò sum up; summarize: 对各方面的情况加以～ sum up all aspects of the situation

总览 zǒnglǎn overview: ～国际形势 make an overall survey of the international situation

总揽 zǒnglǎn assume overall responsibility; take full charge: ～大权 exercise overall authority; assume full power /以改革～全局 let reform take a dominant role; put reform at the centre of all our undertakings

总理 zǒnglǐ ❶ title of the head of the Chinese government: 中华人民共和国国务院～ Premier of the State Council of the People's Republic of China /国务院副～ vice-premier of the State Council ❷ title of the heads of government of certain countries: 法国～ Prime Minister of France /德国～ Chancellor of Germany /日本国～大臣 Prime Minister of Japan ❸ title of leaders of some political parties: 孙中山担任过中国国民党的～。Dr. Sun Yat-sen was once Chairman of the Chinese Nationalist Party. ❹ title of heads of institutions or corporations in former times: 分公司的～ general manager of a subsidiary company ❺ 〈书面〉 assume overall responsibility: ～其事 take full charge of the matter /～军务 be in charge of all the military affairs

总理府 zǒnglǐfǔ office of a prime minister

总理衙门 Zǒnglǐ Yámen (short for 总理各国事务衙门) *Zongli Yamen*, an office in charge of foreign affairs of the Qing Government set up on 20 Jan. 1861 and renamed Ministry of Foreign Affairs in 1901
总量控制 zǒngliàng kòngzhì control of overall supply and demand; control of the aggregates
总量平衡 zǒngliàng pínghéng overall balance
总领事 zǒnglǐngshì consul general
总领事馆 zǒnglǐngshìguǎn consulate-general: 中国驻纽约～ Consulate-General of the People's Republic of China in New York
总路线 zǒnglùxiàn general line: 社会主义建设～ general line for socialist construction
总论 zǒnglùn introduction
总目 zǒngmù catalogue; comprehensive table of contents: 大百科全书的～ general table of contents of the Encyclopedia
总能 zǒngnéng 〈物理〉 total energy
总配电盘 zǒngpèidiànpán 〈电工〉 main distribution board
总平面图 zǒngpíngmiàntú general layout; general arrangement plan
总评 zǒngpíng overall appraisal; general comment: ～成绩相当好。The results of the overall appraisal were fairly good.
总谱 zǒngpǔ 〈音乐〉 score
总其成 zǒngqíchéng assume responsibility for completing sth.: 各章由众人分写，最后由张教授～。The chapters were written by many authors, and Professor Zhang assumed the responsibility to put them together in a book.
总鳍鱼 zǒngqíyú crossopterygian
总任务 zǒngrènwù general task: 党在过渡时期的总路线和～ Party's general line and general task for the transition period
总设计 zǒngshèjì general design
总设计师 zǒngshèjìshī chief architect: 桥梁～ chief architect for bridges / 邓小平是中国改革开放政策的～。Deng Xiaoping is the chief architect of China's policy of reform and opening to the outside world.
总书记 zǒngshūjì general secretary; secretary-general: 中国共产党的～ General Secretary of the Communist Party of China
总数 zǒngshù total; sum total; aggregate: 工人～ aggregate (*or* total) number of workers / 观众～约十万人。The audience aggregated about a hundred thousand people. / 捐款～达百万元。Contributions totalled a million *yuan*.
总司令 zǒngsīlìng commander-in-chief: 三军～ commander-in-chief of the three armed forces
总司令部 zǒngsīlìngbù general headquarters
总算 zǒngsuàn ❶ at last; eventually; finally: 考大学三次落榜，今年～考上了。After failing the college entrance examination three times, he finally succeeded this year. / 连续刮了三天的大风～停了。The wind, which had blown hard for three days on end, at last stilled down (*or* subsided). ❷ all things considered; by and large; on the whole: 您需要的材料大部分都找到了，～没白跑这一趟。I found most of the materials you needed. It was worth the trip on the whole.
总损耗 zǒngsǔnhào total losses
总体 zǒngtǐ general; overall; total: 博览会给人的～印象 general impression of the international fair / ～设计 overall design; master design; gross design / ～经济计划 macroeconomic plan / ～市场 aggregate market; macromarket / ～销售 macromarketing / ～外交 total diplomacy / 我先谈谈下一阶段会谈的～设想。Let me set out our general idea on how the next round of talks should proceed.
总体战争 zǒngtǐ zhànzhēng *also* "总体战" total war; general war; total warfare
总统 zǒngtǒng president (of a republic): 竞选～ run for president / 任～期间 during one's presidency / ～候选人 presidential candidate / ～任期 presidential tenure / 当选～ president-elect; president designate / ～否决权 presidential veto / ～特赦 presidential clemency
总统府 zǒngtǒngfǔ presidential palace; residence and office of a president
总统选举 zǒngtǒng xuǎnjǔ presidential election
总统制 zǒngtǒngzhì presidential system: ～政体 presidential government
总统咨文 zǒngtǒng zīwén presidential message
总危机 zǒngwēijī general crisis
总务 zǒngwù ❶ general affairs; general services ❷ person in charge of general affairs
总务处 zǒngwùchù general affairs division
总务科 zǒngwùkē general affairs section: ～科长 chief of the general affairs section
总务司 zǒngwùsī general service department
总星系 zǒngxīngxì metagalaxy; hypergalaxy
总需求 zǒngxūqiú aggregate demand
总则 zǒngzé general principles; general rules
总闸门 zǒngzhámén 〈石油〉 master valve; master gate
总长 zǒngzhǎng ❶ 〈旧语〉 cabinet minister (China, 1912-1927): 财政～ finance minister / 外交～ foreign minister ❷ (short for 总参谋长) chief of the general staff
总账 zǒngzhàng general ledger; general account
总政治部 zǒngzhèngzhìbù general political department: ～主任 director of the general political department
总之 zǒngzhī generally speaking; in short; in brief: ～前途是光明的，道路是曲折的。In a word, the prospects are bright, although the road has twists and turns. / 这孩子聪明有礼，品行端正，～，值得夸奖。The child is bright, polite, and well-behaved. In short, he is quite praiseworthy.
总支 zǒngzhī general branch: 团～ general Youth League branch / 党～书记 secretary of the general Party branch
总值 zǒngzhí total value; gross value: 国民生产～ gross national product (GNP) / 工农业生产～ total (*or* gross) output value of industry and agriculture / 出口～ gross export value
总指挥 zǒngzhǐhuī ❶ commander-in-chief ❷ general director: 工地～ general director of the construction site / ～部 general headquarters
总指数 zǒngzhǐshù general index
总重 zǒngzhòng gross; gross load; gross weight
总装 zǒngzhuāng general assembly; final assembly
总装备部 Zǒngzhuāngbèibù General Armament Department (of the PLA)
总状花序 zǒngzhuàng huāxù 〈植物〉 raceme
总资产 zǒngzīchǎn total assets

偬(傯) zǒng *see* "倥偬" kǒngzǒng

zòng

粽(糉) zòng *see* "粽子"

粽子 zòngzi pyramid-shaped dumpling made of glutinous rice wrapped in bamboo or reed leaves (eaten during the Dragon Boat Festival on the fifth day of the fifth lunar month)

稯 zòng 〈方言〉 boar

疭(瘲) zòng *see* "瘛疭" chìzòng

纵[1](縱) zòng ❶ from north to south or vice versa: 京广铁路是～贯中国南北的大动脉。The Beijing-Guangzhou railway line is a great artery that extends from the north to the south of China. ❷ from the front to the back: ～深 depth ❸ vertical; longitudinal; lengthwise: *see* "～剖面" ❹ former troop unit corresponding to a corps

纵[2](縱) zòng ❶ release; set free; free: 七擒七～ capture and release seven times / 欲擒故～ allow sb. some latitude at first in order to keep a tighter rein on him afterwards; give sb. line enough ❷ indulge; let loose; pander: 恣～ self-indulgent; unrestrained; wanton / 骄～ arrogant and wilful / 娇～ pamper (a child); spoil ❸ jump up; leap: 他向上一～，单手投篮命中。He jumped up and shot the ball in with one hand.

纵[3](縱) zòng 〈书面〉 even if; even though; though: ～死不悔 refuse to repent even to the end of one's life

纵[4](縱) zòng 〈方言〉 wrinkle; crease; crumple: 这纸起～了。The paper got crumpled.

Z

纵波 zòngbō 〈物理〉longitudinal wave
纵步 zòngbù ❶ take long steps; stride:一路～而行 walk along in big strides ❷ jump; leap; bound:一个～跳出三米 leap three metres at one go.
纵敌贻患 zòngdí-yíhuàn court future troubles by setting one's enemy free
纵断面 zòngduànmiàn vertical section
纵队 zòngduì ❶ column; file:列成～ form a file /以～通过检阅台 file past the reviewing stands /成四路～行进 march in column of fours ❷ troop unit corresponding to a corps (of the People's Liberation Army during China's War of Liberation, 1946-1949)
纵隔 zònggé 〈生理〉mediastinum:～炎 mediastinitis
纵观 zòngguān take a panoramic or sweeping view of:～时事 take a panoramic view of current events
纵贯 zòngguàn vertical; from north to south or vice versa:大运河～冀、鲁、苏、浙四省。The Grand Canal flows southwards through the four provinces of Hebei, Shandong, Jiangsu and Zhejiang.
纵横 zònghéng ❶ vertically and horizontally; in length and breadth:～交错的高速公路 crisscross of highways /老泪～ (of an old person) be all tears /～填字谜 crossword puzzle /～法律关系 vertical-horizontal legal relations /这个镇子～十余里。The town is over ten *li* in length and breadth. /铁路～。The railways crisscross. ❷ with great ease; fluently; freely:笔意～ write fluently ❸ (of an army) move about freely and quickly; sweep through the length and breadth of:我军长驱直入，～数省。Our troops drove straight in, sweeping through several provinces.
纵横捭阖 zònghéng-bǎihé manoeuvre among various states or political groupings; artfully scheme:善于在谈判桌上～的外交老手 master diplomat skilled in manoeuvres at the negotiating table
纵横驰骋 zònghéng-chíchěng (of an army) move about freely and swiftly; sweep through vast areas:青年们可以在农村这个广阔的天地里～。Young people can give their talents full play in the vast area of the countryside.
纵横家 Zònghéngjiā Political Strategists (in the Warring States Period)
纵横交错 zònghéng-jiāocuò crisscross:～的战壕 crisscross trenches /江南水乡，河汉～。Rivers and other watercourses crisscross the provinces south of the Yangtze.
纵虎归山 zònghǔ-guīshān *also* "放虎归山" fànghǔ-guīshān let the tiger return to the mountain; set a tiger free — cause future calamity:这次不抓住他，就是～。We'll have no end of future trouble if we don't catch him this time.
纵火 zònghuǒ set fire (to houses, etc.); commit arson:～案 case of arson /～犯 arsonist
纵肌 zòngjī 〈生理〉longitudinalis
纵酒 zòngjiǔ drink to excess; be given or addicted to drinking:～解愁 drink one's sorrows away /～致死 drink oneself to death /那以后，他便开始～了。After that, he plunged headlong into heavy drinking.
纵览 zònglǎn look far and wide; make a comprehensive survey:～四周 look far into the surrounding area /～群书 read extensively; well-read /～古今 take a panoramic view of both ancient and modern times
纵梁 zòngliáng 〈航空〉longitudinal girder; longitudinal; longeron
纵令 zònglìng ❶ even if; even though ❷ connive; indulge; wink at:不能～坏人逃脱。You can't allow an evildoer to escape punishment.
纵论 zònglùn comment freely; discuss without restraint:～古今 make critical remarks on people or things past and present /～天下大事 comment freely on important world and domestic events
纵目 zòngmù look as far as the eye can see; look far ahead:～远眺 gaze into the distance
纵辔 zòngpèi give (a horse, etc.) the reins:～急追 let go (*or* loosen) one's rein in hot pursuit
纵剖面 zòngpōumiàn *also* "纵切面"; "纵断面" vertical section; longitudinal profile or section
纵切单轴自动车床 zòngqiē dānzhóu zìdòng chēchuáng 〈机械〉longitudinal automatic single spindle lathe
纵情 zòngqíng to one's heart's content; as much as one likes; give oneself over:～欢呼 cheer enthusiastically /～歌舞 sing and dance to one's heart's content; sing and dance heartily /～痛哭 weep one's fill /～取乐 give oneself over to pleasure and unbridled licence /～大笑 laugh a hearty laugh; split one's sides; give oneself over to laughter
纵然 zòngrán even though; even if; no matter whether:～他不支持，我们也要干到底。We'll stick to the end even if he refuses to support us.
纵容 zòngróng connive; indulge; wink at:～手下人干坏事 connive at one's subordinates' evildoing /～非法活动 wink at unlawful activities /父母亲不该～自己的孩子。Parents shouldn't pamper their children. /没有你的～，你儿子是不会犯罪的。Your son couldn't have committed the crime without your indulgence.
纵射 zòngshè 〈军事〉enfilade fire; enfilade
纵身 zòngshēn throw oneself (forward or upward); jump; leap:～扑向敌人 throw oneself on the enemy / 一～就过了壕沟 jump across a ditch at one try /他～上马，飞驰而去。He leaped onto a horse and galloped off.
纵深 zòngshēn 〈军事〉depth:向～推进 push in deep /沟壕错综交织，～达二、三里。The crisscrossed ditches and trenches are two or three *li* in depth.
纵声 zòngshēng at the top of one's voice; as loudly as one can:～大笑 burst out laughing; laugh outright (*or* loudly)
纵使 zòngshǐ even if; even though:他清晨坚持锻炼，～天寒地冻，也不间断。Persisting in early morning exercise, he went at it even in freezing weather.
纵视图 zòngshìtú longitudinal view
纵谈 zòngtán comment freely:～时事 talk freely about current affairs
纵眺 zòngtiào look far ahead:～黄山景色 look at Huangshan Mountain in the distance
纵向 zòngxiàng ❶ vertical; from top to bottom:～调查 longitudinal study /～协调 vertical coordination /～联合 vertical integration; vertical combination; perpendicular association; longitudinal association /中国的信贷资金基本上是实行～管理。The credit funds in China are basically administered vertically from top to bottom. ❷ from south to north:这条铁路是～的。This railway runs from the south to the north.
纵欲 zòngyù indulge in sensual pleasures; be given to sexual indulgence; give way to one's carnal desires
纵轴 zòngzhóu longitudinal axis
纵恣 zòngzì 〈书面〉self-indulgent; unrestrained
纵坐标 zòngzuòbiāo 〈数学〉ordinate

zōu

诹 zōu 〈书面〉consult; hold counsel with:谘～善道 seek counsel (*or* advice) as to how to administer a country
诹访 zōufǎng consult; ask advice of
诹吉 zōují 〈书面〉choose an auspicious date (for wedding, etc.) through consultation

鲰 zōu 〈书面〉❶ small fish; fry; fingerling ❷ tiny; small
鲰生 zōushēng 〈书面〉❶ mean or contemptible person ❷〈谦词〉my humble self; I

缬 zōu 〈书面〉dark red

陬 zōu 〈书面〉❶ corner:东南～ southeast corner ❷ foot of a hill

邹（鄒） Zōu ❶ name of a principality of the Zhou Dynasty in today's Zou County, Shandong Province ❷ a surname

驺（騶） zōu ❶〈旧语〉groom ❷ (Zōu) a surname
驺从 zōucóng 〈书面〉groom and attendant

zǒu

走 zǒu ❶ walk; go; follow:～进屋 go into the room /～向门口 make for the door /边～边唱 sing while walking /～下台阶 descend the steps /～上讲台 step onto the platform /累得实在～不动了

be too fatigued to walk any further /～自己工业发展的道路 follow one's own road of industrial development /～错路 take a wrong path; mistake a road; go astray /～老路 follow a set routine; move in a rut; stick to the old path /～出新路子 blaze a new trail; provide a new approach to /～一步看一步 take one step and look around before taking another — proceed without a plan or be very cautious in one's action /有理～遍天下。With justice on your side, you can travel anywhere unimpeded. /等她～远，他才说这话。He didn't say this until she was out of earshot. /这孩子刚学会～。The baby has just learned to toddle. /车两小时～了二百五十公里。Our car made 250 kilometres in two hours. ❷ run; rush about: 奔～相告 rush to spread the news /远～高飞 go far and fly high — go to distant places /飞沙～石 sand flying about and stones hurling through the air (as in a sandstorm) ❸ (of cars, boats, etc.) move; operate: 该你～棋了。It is your turn to make the next move. /我的表不～了。My watch has stopped. /船～得很慢。The boat was going very slowly. ❹ leave; be off; go away: 汽车刚～。The bus has just left. /他们搬～了。They have moved out. /别把字典拿～了。Don't take the dictionary away. ❺〈婉词〉go; die: 他这么年轻就～了，令人痛心。It is most painful that he died so young. ❻ (of friends and relatives) call on; pay a visit; visit: ～姥姥家 go and visit one's (maternal) grandmother /～亲访友 call on relatives and friends ❼ through; by; from: ～这个门到礼堂。Go to the auditorium through this door. /我们从上海到大连～水路。We travelled from Shanghai to Dalian by water. ❽ leak; reveal; let out: 车胎～气，慢慢瘪了。The tyre went flat because of a slow leak. /他说～了嘴。He made a slip of the tongue. *or* He gave away the secret. *or* He let the cat out of the bag. ❾ be different from the original; lose shape, flavour, etc.: 衣服～样了。The dress is no longer the shape it used to be. /这点心～味了。The cake has lost its flavour.

走八字 zǒu bāzì 〈方言〉have good luck; be in luck: 王大爷这几年～，诸事都顺遂。Everything has gone smoothly for Grandpa Wang in recent years because luck has come his way.

走板 zǒubǎn ❶ (in traditional Chinese operas) be off the beat: 他唱戏总～。He often went off the beat when singing Beijing opera. ❷ speak beside the point; wander from the subject; be wide of the mark: 你这话太～了。Your statement has strayed from the point. ❸ (of divers) warm up by walking on the plank

走背运 zǒu bèiyùn *also* "走背字儿" have bad luck; be out of luck; be down on one's luck; be off one's luck: 我如今～，事事不顺心。I am out of luck now, and everything went against my wish.

走笔 zǒubǐ 〈书面〉write swiftly

走避 zǒubì flee, escape: ～他乡 go into hiding in another place

走边 zǒubiān (of traditional opera actors in military plays) travel stealthily by night; walk lightly and cautiously

走镖 zǒubiāo 〈旧语〉act as an armed escort for a convoy

走步 zǒubù ❶ (in a basketball game) walk with the ball ❷〈方言〉walk: 刚会～的幼儿 infant who just learns to walk

走村串寨 zǒucūn-chuànzhài go from village to village: 挑着货郎担～ go from village to village, carrying goods on a shoulder pole

走刀量 zǒudāoliàng 〈机械〉feed

走道 zǒudào ❶ pavement; sidewalk ❷ path; walk; footpath: 楼内～宽敞。The building has wide corridors.

走道儿 zǒudàor 〈口语〉walk: 这孩子不满周岁就会～了。The baby learned to toddle before he was one year old.

走电 zǒudiàn leakage of electricity

走调儿 zǒudiàor out of tune; not at the correct musical pitch

走锭精纺机 zǒudìng jīngfǎngjī 〈纺织〉self-acting mule; self-actor

走动 zǒudòng ❶ move about; stretch one's legs: 来回～ walk to and fro /他病情好转，可以～了。His condition is improving, and he is able to get about now. /你不能老坐着，得～～。You must stretch your legs and not sit there all the time. ❷ socialize; visit each other: 他们虽是亲戚，可平常不大～。They rarely visit each other although they are relatives. /两家人过年过节才～～。The two families call on each other only on festive occasions.

走读 zǒudú attend a day school: ～学校 day school

走读生 zǒudúshēng day student; nonresident student

走肚子 zǒu dùzi 〈方言〉suffer from diarrhoea; have loose bowels: 他在外面吃了一顿午餐，回来就～。He suffered from loose bowels upon return from lunch somewhere.

走方郎中 zǒufāng lángzhōng *also* "走方医"〈方言〉doctor who rings a bell and goes from place to place to practise medicine; itinerant doctor

走访 zǒufǎng ❶ have an interview with; interview: 本报记者～了这位世界冠军的父母。Our reporter interviewed the parents of the world champion. ❷ go and see; pay a visit to; visit: ～亲友 visit relatives and friends

走风 zǒufēng disclose; let out; leak out: 此事绝密，千万不能～。This is top secret; not a word should be breathed.

走钢丝 zǒu gāngsī ❶〈杂技〉wire-walking; walking a tightrope: ～演员 wire-walker /表演～ perform on the tightrope ❷ walk on thin ice: 你这样做太危险，简直就是～。The way you did it was nothing short of tightrope walking.

走狗 zǒugǒu running dog; lackey; flunkey; stooge: 有时候～比主人还可恶。Sometimes, the lackey is more vicious than his master.

走关节 zǒu guānjié 〈旧语〉bribe (officials, etc.) secretly; offer secret bribes to: 他们走了关节，这件丑闻被压下了。The scandal was hushed up after they had greased the palms of some key officials.

走过场 zǒu guòchǎng ❶ actor or actress going from one end of the stage to the other without stopping ❷ make a gesture to give the impression of doing sth.; do sth. perfunctorily and superficially; go through the motions: 这项工作要注重实效，不能～。We should emphasize practical results of the work instead of reducing it to mere formality.

走合 zǒuhé (of a vehicle or machine) run in

走黑道 zǒu hēidào ❶ walk in an unlit street at night; walk in the dark at night ❷ be a burglar, a thief, etc.

走红 zǒuhóng *also* "走红运" ❶ be in luck; have good luck: 如今他正～，步步高升。Now he is just in luck and has been promoted quickly. ❷ in favour; in demand: 音像制品开始～。Audio-visual products are much in demand. /经纪人在沿海地区重新～。Brokers are again in favour in coastal areas.

走后门 zǒu hòumén get in by the back door; secure advantages through pull or influence; resort to backstairs influence; pull strings: 杜绝招工中的～现象 put an end to backdoor dealings in recruiting workers /他～给儿子找了个好工作。He pulled wires and got his son a good job.

走话 zǒuhuà 〈方言〉leak out a secret: 他嘴不严，爱～。He has a loose tongue and often lets out secrets.

走回头路 zǒu huítóulù turn back; backtrack; retrace one's steps: 历史绝不会～。History will never reverse its course.

走火 zǒuhuǒ ❶ (of firearms) discharge accidentally; go off half-cocked: 当心枪～! Be careful not to let the gun go off! ❷ go too far in what one says; put sth. too strongly; overstate: 他心直口快，说话常～。He wears his heart on his sleeve and often goes too far in what he says. ❸〈电学〉sparking: 这场火灾是由电线～引起的。The fire was caused by electric sparks from the wire. ❹ on fire: 他家～了。His house was aflame.

走极端 zǒu jíduān go to extremes: 她这人好～。She is inclined to go to extremes.

走江湖 zǒu jiānghu wander from place to place and earn a living by peddling, juggling, fortune-telling, etc.; live a vagrant's life

走鹃 zǒujuān roadrunner; chaparral cock

走口 zǒukǒu *also* "走嘴"〈方言〉slip of the tongue

走廊 zǒuláng corridor; passage; passageway: 河西～ Hexi (*or* Gansu) Corridor

走溜儿 zǒuliùr 〈方言〉walk back and forth or to and fro; go for a stroll: 急得他满屋子里～。He paced up and down the room anxiously.

走漏 zǒulòu ❶ *also* "走露" divulge; let out; leak out: ～消息 leak information; let out a secret /关于这事，你不要在你父亲面前～一点儿风声。Don't breathe a word of this to your father. /市长参与毒品走私的事，已经～了风声。There has been a leak about the mayor's involvement in drug trafficking. ❷ smuggling and tax evasion ❸ have things stolen in large quantities: 器材管理不严，颇有～。Much of the equipment was stolen, as it was not under close guard.

走路 zǒulù ❶ walk; go on foot: 我们到动物园是～去的。We went to the zoo on foot. /小孙子还不会～。My grandson cannot walk yet. ❷ get away; clear off; beat it: 叫他～，否则我就不客气了。Tell him to go chase himself or I'll make it hot for him.

走马 zǒumǎ ❶ gallop or trot along on horseback ❷ fine horse; steed: 将军有一匹好～。The general has a fine steed.

走马灯 zǒumǎdēng lantern with a revolving circle of paper-cut horses or other figures: 如此精巧的～，令人赞叹不已。There was

Z

much admiration for the fine workmanship of the revolving horse lanterns. /~似的更换内阁部长。The cabinet ministers were reshuffled as frequently as if they were on a merry-go-round.

走马疳 zǒumǎgān 〈医学〉noma; gangrenous stomatitis

走马换将 zǒumǎ-huànjiàng change of personnel:领导班子~后,工作有了起色。There has been some improvement in the work since the reshuffle of the leadership.

走马看花 zǒumǎ-kànhuā *also*"走马观花" look at flowers while riding on horseback — gain a superficial understanding through cursory observation:汽车只停一小时,我们只能~地看看风景。Our bus stopped over for only an hour, so we could just snatch a transient glance of the landscape. /学一年的世界史课程,只能是~地学点一般性东西而已。In a one-year course in world history, one can only skim the surface.

走马上任 zǒumǎ-shàngrèn take office; assume a post:新经理明天~。The new manager will assume office tomorrow.

走门路 zǒu ménlù *also*"走门子" gain one's end through pull, bribery, etc.:在这个地方,不~事儿就办不成。Nothing could get done here without buying one's way.

走南闯北 zǒunán-chuǎngběi journey north and south; travel extensively; be much travelled:他这人~,见多识广。He has travelled widely and is rich in experience.

走内线 zǒu nèixiàn seek sb.'s favour by approaching his family members (esp. wife) or confidant; go through private channels to achieve one's end:他是~才谋上这份差事的。He secured his present position by going through private channels.

走娘家 zǒu niángjia (of a married woman) go and visit her parents' home

走票 zǒupiào 〈旧语〉(of amateurs) act in a play; appear on the stage:她在戏班儿走过票。She once acted in a play as an amateur in a theatrical troupe.

走俏 zǒuqiào (of goods or commodities) sell well; be salable:国产名牌冰箱日渐~。Chinese-made brand-name refrigerators are selling better day by day.

走亲戚 zǒu qīnqi call on or visit relatives

走禽 zǒuqín cursores; cursorial birds

走人 zǒurén 〈口语〉(of a person) leave; depart; get away:咱们~,不等他了。Let's set out without him. /叫他卷铺盖~。Tell him to pack himself off.

走色 zǒushǎi lose colour; discolour; fade:这件衣服一洗就~。The coat discoloured after only one wash.

走扇 zǒushàn (of door or window leaves) out of shape and unable to close properly

走墒 zǒushāng loss of moisture in the soil; soil evaporation

走神儿 zǒushénr absent-minded; inattentive:她工作时常~。She is often absent-minded while working.

走绳 zǒushéng *also*"走索"〈杂技〉ropedancing; ropewalking; tightrope walking

走失 zǒushī ❶ get lost; wander away; stray; be missing:孩子在公园里~了。The child got lost in the park. /我家的猫~了。My cat has wandered away from home. ❷ alter or lose its original meaning:译文~了原意。The translation loses much of the original flavour.

走时 zǒushí ❶ (of clocks and watches) tick; keep time:这钟~不准。The clock does not keep good time. ❷ *also*"走运"〈方言〉be lucky

走事儿 zǒushìr 〈方言〉ponder on sth.; turn sth. over in one's mind:这人少言寡语,心里可是爱~。He is a thoughtful person (*or* likes to mull things over) despite his taciturnity.

走势 zǒushì ❶ trend; tendency:欧洲各国银行利率~继续下降。The interest rates of the banks of the various European countries continue to fall (*or* come down). ❷ direction; alignment:山谷的~ alignment of the valley

走兽 zǒushòu beast; quadruped; four-footed animal:飞禽~ birds and animals

走水 zǒushuǐ ❶ (of roof, kettle, bottle, etc.) leaking:房顶~了。The roof is leaking. ❷ flow:渠道~流畅。Water flows smoothly through the channel. ❸〈婉词〉catch fire; be on fire

走水 zǒushui 〈方言〉short streamer over the top of a screen or curtain

走私 zǒusī smuggle:~毒品 smuggle narcotic drugs /~贩私活动 smuggling and sale of smuggled goods /~集团 smuggling ring /~犯 smuggler

走索 zǒusuǒ *see*"走绳"

走题 zǒutí digress from the subject; stray from the point; be wide of the mark:发言请不要~。Please keep to the point. /她说走了题,向大家表示歉意。She apologized for the digression.

走投无路 zǒutóu-wúlù have no way out; be driven to a tight corner; be in an impasse; come to the end of one's tether:敌军精疲力尽,又缺乏给养,已到了~的境地。The enemy troops, exhausted and out of supplies, were at the end of their rope. /他长期失业,身无分文,真是~。He had long been out of work and broke and really had nowhere to turn.

走弯路 zǒu wānlù make a detour; follow a zigzag course; take a wrong path:我是走过一段弯路才接受教训的。I once took a wrong path and learned my lesson the hard way.

走味儿 zǒuwèir lose flavour:这东西~了,不能吃。The food must not be eaten, now that it has lost its flavour.

走下坡路 zǒu xiàpōlù go downhill; go from bad to worse; take a bad turn:这个一度兴旺发达的城市现在已~了。The once-prosperous city has now slid downhill (*or* is now on the decline).

走险 zǒuxiǎn run risks; take chances:被逼无奈,铤而~ risk danger in desperation

走乡随乡 zǒuxiāng-suíxiāng adopt local ways; when in Rome, do as the Romans do:~,随遇而安 settle for whatever comes one's way in an alien land /到了一个新地方,就得~。One has to follow the locals when in a new place.

走向 zǒuxiàng ❶ run; trend; alignment:海岸线~ trend of the coastline /山脉的~ run of a range of mountains /边界~ alignment of the boundary line /长江是东西~的河流。The Yangtze River flows from east to west. ❷〈地质〉strike; bearing:~断层 strike fault /~谷 strike valley /矿层~ seam strike ❸ move towards; head for; be on the way to:~深渊 move towards the abyss /~衰落 be on the decline /经济~衰退 head for economic recession /~成功之路 on the road to success /从胜利~胜利 advance (*or* march) from victory to victory

走相 zǒuxiàng lose one's former appearance; be altered in appearance; become deformed or misshapen:她生病以后,完全~了。Her ailment has changed her countenance beyond recognition.

走心 zǒuxīn 〈方言〉mindful; conscientious:学习先进技术不~不行。One has to be conscientious in learning advanced techniques.

走形 zǒuxíng be out of shape; be deformed; be misshapen:这衣柜~,门关不严。The wardrobe refused to close tight because it had gone out of shape.

走形式 zǒu xíngshì make a gesture to give the impression of doing sth.; do sth. as a mere formality; go through the motions:学先进可不能~。It just won't do to go through the motions in learning from the advanced workers.

走穴 zǒuxué (of performers) moonlight:他靠~发了财。He has become rich by moonlighting.

走眼 zǒuyǎn mistake for:我看走了眼,把次货当好货了。I mistook defective goods for quality goods.

走样 zǒuyàng lose shape; be out of form; deviate from the original model; be different from what is expected or intended:这鞋一穿就~了。The shoe goes out of form the moment you put it on. /你把作者的意思说~了。You misinterpreted the author's meaning.

走一步,看一步 zǒu yī bù, kàn yī bù move circumspectly; go about cautiously:这事儿咱们谁也没干过,只能~。As this is something none of us have done before, we must go about it with great caution.

走油 zǒuyóu (of oily food) go rancid

走运 zǒuyùn have a stroke of luck; be lucky:不~ have bad (*or* tough, *or* hard) luck; have ill fortune; be off one's luck /公司录用了我,真~! How fortunate I am to have been employed by the company! /他真~,有这么个好老师。He was lucky enough to have such a good teacher.

走账 zǒuzhàng charge to an account; enter or register in the ledger

走着瞧 zǒuzheqiáo wait and see:究竟谁对,咱们~! Let's wait and see who is right.

走资派 zǒuzīpài person in power taking the capitalist road or capitalist-roader (a political label often pinned on cadres by the Red Guards during the Cultural Revolution)

走字 zǒuzì 〈方言〉*see*"走运"

走卒 zǒuzú pawn; flunkey; stooge; cat's-paw
走嘴 zǒuzuǐ make a slip of the tongue; blurt sth. out; let slip an inadvertent remark: 那是他说走了嘴。That was a slip of the tongue on his part.

zòu

奏 zòu ❶ play; strike up; perform (on a musical instrument): ～国歌 play the national anthem /～迎宾曲 strike up a tune of welcome /吹～ play (wind instruments) /独～ (instrumental) solo /钢琴伴～ to the accompaniment of the piano /合～ (instrumental) ensemble /二重～ duet /三重～ trio /四重～ quartet /五重～ quintet /六重～ sextet /七重～ septet /八重～ octet /演～ performance of musical instrument ❷ achieve; attain; produce: 大～奇功 render outstanding service ❸ present a memorial to an emperor: 面～ memorialize the throne in person /启～ present a memorial to the emperor
奏案 zòu'àn desk where an emperor read over and made comments on the memorials presented to him
奏报 zòubào ❶ make a report to an emperor: 据实～ report to the emperor on the true state of affairs ❷ memorial to the throne
奏本 zòuběn ❶ present a memorial to the throne ❷ memorial to the throne
奏刀 zòudāo 〈书面〉 carve or cut with a knife
奏功 zòugōng achieve success; get the desired result: 措施得当，立即～。Immediate success was won as the measures were appropriate.
奏技 zòujì *also* "奏艺" 〈书面〉 (of artists in local drama, acrobats, dancers, singers, etc.) stage a performance
奏捷 zòujié win a battle; score a victory; be triumphant: ～归来 return in triumph; make a triumphal return
奏凯 zòukǎi win victory; be victorious; score a success; triumph: 足球队首战～。The football team won the first match.
奏鸣曲 zòumíngqǔ 〈音乐〉 sonata: 小～ sonatina /月光～ Moonlight Sonata
奏鸣曲式 zòumíngqǔshì sonata form
奏疏 zòushū memorial to the throne: 上一道～ present a memorial to the emperor
奏效 zòuxiào prove effective; achieve the intended result: 这个办法果然～。The method worked as expected. /我服这药～。The medicine proved quite efficacious after I took it. /他们试图通过斡旋实现停火，但未能～。They failed in their attempt to mediate a cease-fire.
奏议 zòuyì ❶ present a memorial to the throne ❷ general name for all memorials to the throne
奏乐 zòuyuè play music; strike up a tune: 乐队～。The band struck up a tune.
奏章 zòuzhāng memorial to the throne: 递上～ present a memorial to the emperor
奏折 zòuzhé memorial to the throne (as written on paper folded in accordion form)

揍 zòu ❶ 〈口语〉 beat; hit; strike: ～了他一巴掌 give him a slap /～了孩子一顿 beat the child up; give the child a sound beating /挨～ get a thrashing (*or* beating) ❷ 〈方言〉 break; smash: 小心莫把茶杯～了。Take care not to break the teacup. /我把瓶子给～了。I smashed the bottle.

zū

菹(葅) zū 〈书面〉 ❶ marshland ❷ pickled Chinese cabbage; Chinese sauerkraut ❸ cut or chop up (meat or vegetables) into very small pieces; mince; shred
菹醢 zūhǎi form of torture and execution in ancient China by which prisoners were chopped into minced meat

租 zū ❶ rent; hire; lease; charter: ～一套公寓 rent an apartment /按小时计算～自行车 hire a bicycle by the hour /～一块土地，为期十年 take a piece of land on a lease of ten years; lease a piece of land for ten years /学校为旅行包～了三辆大轿车。The school chartered three buses for the trip. ❷ rent out; let out; hire out; lease: 此房出～。House to let. /张先生以每月一千元把公寓套房～给我们。Mr. Zhang rents out the flat to us at 1,000 *yuan* a month. /该公司办理～车业务。The company hires out cars. /我把房间转～给了朋友。I sublet my room to a friend. ❸ rent: 房～ house rent /地～ land rent (to a landlord) /收～ collect rent ❹ 〈旧语〉 land tax: 交田～ pay land tax
租船 zūchuán 〈航海〉 chartering: ～代理 chartering agent /～合同 charter party; contract of affreightment/～运货 affreightment /～费 charterage /～费率 charter rate /～人 charterer /～市场 chartering market
租佃 zūdiàn (of a landlord) rent out land to tenants: ～关系 tenant-landlord relationship; tenancy relationship /～制度 tenancy system
租户 zūhù ❶ tenant (of a building or part of it); leaseholder; lessee ❷ hirer (of a thing)
租价 zūjià rent: 这座房子～便宜。This house rents cheaply.
租界 zūjiè land in a port city leased to and governed by an imperialist power under an unequal treaty; leased territory; concession; settlement: 法～ French Concession /旧上海的公共～ International Settlement in old Shanghai
租界法案 Zūjiè Fǎ'àn Lend-Lease Act (adopted in 1941 to enable the United States to supply its allies in World War II)
租借 zūjiè ❶ rent; hire; let; lease: ～了两间房 rent two rooms /～不动产 leased immovables /～人 lessee; leaseholder; tenant; hirer ❷ rent out; hire out; let out; lease: 他把一间屋～给我。He leased a room to me.
租借地 zūjièdì leased territory; leasehold
租金 zūjīn rent; rental: 昂贵的～ high rent /～收入 rental receipts; rental /那套三居室单元房月～是一千五百元。Rent for that three-room apartment is 1,500 *yuan* a month. /她常拖欠～。She was often back in (*or* often in arrears with) her rent.
租赁 zūlìn ❶ rent; hire; lease: 为演出～服装 rent costumes for a performance /～购买 lease-purchase /湿～ wet-lease (e.g. leasing a plane with its crew) /～权益保险 leasehold interest insurance ❷ rent out; hire out; lease: 这家公司向外～建筑机械。The company hires out construction machinery.
租赁公司 zūlìn gōngsī leasing company
租赁经营责任制 zūlìn jīngyíng zérènzhì responsibility system under which (usu. small state-owned) enterprises are managed (by a contractor or lessee) on lease
租赁贸易 zūlìn màoyì chartering and leasing trade
租赁业 zūlìnyè leasing trade
租米 zūmǐ 〈旧语〉 rice that tenant-peasants paid to the landlord as land rent
租钱 zūqian 〈口语〉 rent; rental
租让 zūràng concession: ～制 concession system /～合同 concession agreement /～合同承租人 concessionaire
租书处 zūshūchù book rental
租税 zūshuì 〈旧语〉 land tax and other levies
租用 zūyòng rent; hire: ～场地 hire a venue /～汽车 rent a car /～人 leaseholder; lessee; hirer; tenant
租用线路 zūyòng xiànlù 〈通信〉 leased line
租约 zūyuē lease: 续订～ renew the lease /把～期限延长两年 extend the lease for two years /我的～六月三十日到期。My lease expires on 30 June.
租债 zūzhài rent and debt
租栈 zūzhàn 〈旧语〉 agency set up by big landlord in town for collecting land rent from tenant-peasants
租子 zūzi 〈口语〉 land rent; ground rent; rent: 交～ pay rent /收～ collect rent

zú

卒[1] zú ❶ soldier; private: 兵～ soldiers; rank and file /无名小～ mere nobody /马前～ pawn; cat's-paw ❷ servant; attendant: 狱～ prison guard; turnkey /走～ lackey; underling; stooge ❸ pawn, one of the pieces in Chinese chess

卒[2] zú ❶ finish; end: 有始有～ begin well and end well /语～

而单于大怒。The *Chanyu* flared up on hearing these words. ❷ at last; in the end; finally:～成帝业。He finally won the imperial throne. ❸ die:暴～ die a violent death /生～年月不详。The dates of birth and death are unknown.
see also cù
卒岁 zúsuì 〈书面〉pass a year:聊以～ just to tide over the year /无衣无褐，何以～? How can we pass the winter without warm clothes?
卒业 zúyè 〈书面〉graduate; complete one's studies:～于清华大学 graduate from Tsinghua University
卒子 zúzi 〈旧语〉soldier

崒（崪） zú 〈书面〉steep; perilous

族 zú ❶ clan:亲～ members of the same clan; relatives /贵～ noble; aristocrat ❷ death penalty in ancient China, imposed on an offender and his whole family, or even the families of his mother and wife:～九族 execution of the whole clan relatives of an offender ❸ nationality; race; ethnic group:回～ Hui nationality /异～ different race or nation ❹ class or group of things or people with common features:水～ aquatic animals /猫～ cat tribe (*or* family); felines /语～ family of languages /芳～化合物〈化学〉aromatic compound; aromatic /工薪～ salaried people /追星～ star fans; star chasers
族产 zúchǎn clan property such as land, ancestral temple, etc.
族规 zúguī rules and regulations of a clan
族类 zúlèi of the same clan or class:非我～ not of my (*or* our) kind
族灭 zúmiè *also*"族诛"〈旧语〉execution of the whole clan relatives of the offender
族内婚 zúnèihūn endogamy
族谱 zúpǔ family tree; genealogical tree; genealogy
族亲 zúqīn clansman and clanswoman
族权 zúquán clan power; clan authority
族人 zúrén clansman
族田 zútián 〈旧语〉farmland owned by a clan
族外婚 zúwàihūn exogamy
族长 zúzhǎng clan elder; head of a clan
族尊 zúzūn clan elder; senior clansman

镞 zú 〈书面〉arrowhead:箭～ arrowhead

足[1] zú ❶ foot; leg:缠～ foot-binding /立～点 foothold; footing /顿～ stamp one's feet /驻～ stop; stay /画蛇添～ draw a snake and add feet to it — add sth. superfluous ❷ leg-shaped support of utensils or instruments:鼎～ leg of a tripod /三～凳 three-legged stool

足[2] zú ❶ adequate; sufficient; ample:干劲十～ be full of energy /资金不～ inadequate fund /心满意～ fully satisfied; to one's heart's content /丰衣～食 have plenty of food and clothing; be well-fed and well-clothed ❷ full; as much as:从这儿进城～有一天的路程。The town is a good day's trip from here. /这个包裹～有十斤重。This package weighs a full ten *jin*. ❸ (often used in the negative) as much or as many as necessary; enough; sufficient:何～挂齿 nothing to speak of; not worth mentioning /微不～道 insignificant; negligible
足板 zúbǎn 〈方言〉sole (of the foot)
足本 zúběn complete, unabridged edition
足秤 zúchèng (of weight) full measure:给得不～ give short measure
足尺 zúchǐ (of length or size) full measure
足赤 zúchì pure gold:金无～，人无完人。There is no pure gold in the world, nor is there a perfect man.
足底反射 zúdǐ fǎnshè 〈生理〉plantar reflex; sole reflex
足跟 zúgēn heel
足够 zúgòu ❶ adequate; enough; sufficient; ample:～吃一周的食物 food sufficient to last a week /二百元～我用的了。200 *yuan* will be ample for my needs. /他的薪水～养活一个四口之家。His salary is adequate to support a family of four. /车里有～六人坐的地方吗? Is there enough room for six people in the car? /我们要有～的思想准备。We must be fully prepared mentally. ❷ be satisfied; be content with one's lot:有您这句话就～了。I'm fully satisfied with what you said.
足关节炎 zúguānjiéyán 〈医学〉podarthritis
足迹 zújì footprint; footmark; trace; track:～遍全国 have been to every corner of the country /发现了熊的～ come across traces of bears /猎人认出了河岸上鹿的～。The hunter recognized the footprints of a deer on the river bank.
足见 zújiàn it serves or suffices to show; one can well imagine; obviously:他走不了了，～伤得不轻。He could hardly walk. Obviously, his wound was a serious one. /她考试成绩不错，～复习是花了功夫的。She did well in the exam, which shows she had put in much time at her revision.
足金 zújīn pure gold; solid gold
足力 zúlì strength of one's legs:～好 have strong legs
足球 zúqiú ❶ soccer; football:英国式～ soccer; association football /美国式～ American football /～运动员 footballer; football player /～队 football team; eleven /职业～运动员 professional soccer players /～教练员 football coach /全国～联赛 national football league matches /世界杯～赛 world cup football games /国际～联合会 Federation of International Football Associations (FIFA) /全国～协会 National Football Association /～场 field; pitch ❷ football (the ball used in playing soccer or American football)
足色 zúsè (gold or silver) of standard purity
足实 zúshi 〈方言〉❶ sufficient; adequate; abundant:力气很～ with exuberant strength ❷ full; plump:大花生粒粒～。The peanuts are quite plump.
足水肿 zúshuǐzhǒng podedema
足岁 zúsuì actual age; full years:这孩子今年四～。The child is fully four years old this year.
足坛 zútán football circles; world of soccer:～名将 famous football player
足下 zúxià respectful form of address between friends (used mostly in letters):烦～代劳。Will you please do this for me? /不知～有此雅兴否? I just wonder whether you are in the mood for this or not?
足兴 zúxìng 〈方言〉satisfied; contented:他吃了四碗饭还不～。Having finished four bowls of rice, he still felt he hadn't had enough.
足医 zúyī 〈医学〉chiropodist; podiatrist:～术 chiropody; podiatry; podology
足以 zúyǐ enough; ample; sufficient:我们战胜了强队，这～证明我们是一支不可轻视的力量。We've beaten a strong team, which amply proves that we are a force to be reckoned with. /他的话不～说明问题。His words fell short of clarifying the matter. *or* What he said was not enough to elucidate the matter. /这样凶残的罪犯，不杀不～平民愤。Only the execution of such a heinous criminal could assuage popular indignation.
足音 zúyīn (sound of) footsteps; footfall:杂乱的～ clatter of footsteps
足银 zúyín silver of standard purity
足月 zúyuè (of a foetus) born after the normal period of gestation; mature:孩子不～就降生了。The baby was born ahead of the full gestation period (*or* prematurely).
足智多谋 zúzhì-duōmóu wise and resourceful; shrewd and full of stratagems:他这人比姜太公还要～。He is more resourceful than Jiang Taigong (the legendary mastermind in ancient China).
足壮 zúzhuang 〈方言〉❶ robust; healthy and strong:这孩子挺～。The child is robust and healthy. ❷ sonorous; loud and clear:他的声音～。He has a sonorous voice.

zǔ

诅 zǔ ❶ curse; swear ❷ take an oath; vow:～盟 swear to form an alliance
诅骂 zǔmà curse; abuse; revile; blaspheme
诅咒 zǔzhòu curse; swear; imprecate; call down evil, misfortune, etc. upon sb.:咬牙切齿地～ curse between one's teeth /～那黑暗的旧社会 condemn the dark old society

祖 zǔ ❶ grandfather:外～父 maternal grandfather /叔～ grandfather's younger brother; granduncle ❷ ancestor:曾～ (paternal) great-grandfather /高～ (paternal) great-great-grandfather /始

~ remote ancestors ❸ founder (of a craft, religious sect, etc.); originator:鼻~ originator (of a tradition, school of thought, etc.); earliest ancestor ❹ (Zǔ) a surname

祖辈 zǔbèi forefathers; forebears; ancestors; ancestry

祖本 zǔběn original copy of a block-printed edition or first rubbing from a stone inscription

祖妣 zǔbǐ 〈书面〉one's deceased (paternal) grandmother

祖产 zǔchǎn property handed down from one's ancestors; ancestral estate:这座房子是他家仅有的~。The house is the only property that has descended from his ancestors.

祖冲之 Zǔ Chōngzhī Zu Chongzhi (formerly translated as Tsu Ch'ung-chih, 429-500), mathematician and astronomer of the Northern and Southern Dynasties

祖传 zǔchuán handed down from one's forefathers:~宝刀 treasure sword handed down from one's ancestors

祖传秘方 zǔchuán mìfāng secret recipe handed down in the family from generation to generation

祖代 zǔdài generation after generation; for generations:~务农 have worked on the land for generations

祖坟 zǔfén ancestral grave:祭扫~ pay one's respects and offer sacrifices to one's ancestors at the ancestral tomb

祖父 zǔfù (paternal) grandfather:外~ maternal grandfather

祖国 zǔguó motherland; fatherland; native land; homeland:歌唱~ sing praises of one's motherland /怀念~ long for one's homeland

祖国光复会 Zǔguó Guāngfùhuì Association for the Restoration of the Fatherland (a Korean united front against Japanese imperialism founded in May 1936 by Kim Il Sung)

祖籍 zǔjí original family home; ancestral home; land of one's forefathers:他的~是山东。He is of Shandong origin.

祖饯 zǔjiàn 〈书面〉give (a friend) a farewell dinner

祖居 zǔjū ❶ land of one's ancestors; ancestral home ❷ live (in a place) for generations:~南京 have lived in Nanjing for generations

祖考 zǔkǎo 〈书面〉❶ one's deceased grandfather ❷ ancestors; forefathers; forebears

祖鲁人 Zǔlǔrén Zulu, one of the Bantu peoples, now living mainly in South Africa's Natal Province; member of the Zulu tribe

祖鲁语 Zǔlǔyǔ Zulu (language)

祖率 zǔlǜ 〈数学〉approximate ratio of the circumference of a circle to its diameter as calculated by Zu Chongzhi (祖冲之), i.e. between 3.1415926 and 3.1415927

祖庙 zǔmiào ancestral temple

祖母 zǔmǔ (paternal) grandmother:外~ maternal grandmother

祖母绿 zǔmǔlǜ emerald

祖上 zǔshàng ancestors; forefathers; forebears:她~是从湖南搬来的。Her ancestors moved here from Hunan.

祖师 zǔshī *also* "祖师爷" ❶ founder of a school of learning, etc.:孔子是儒家的~。Confucius was the founder of the Confucian school. ❷ founder of a Buddhist or Taoist sect:佛教的~是释迦牟尼。The founder of Buddhism was Sakyamuni. ❸ originator of a superstitious sect or a secret society ❹ 〈旧语〉originator of a trade or profession:木匠历来尊鲁班为~。Carpenters all respectfully refer to Master Lu Ban as the founding father of their trade.

祖述 zǔshù 〈书面〉revere and follow the example of one's forefathers:仲尼~尧舜。Confucius followed in the ways of the ancient sages Yao and Shun.

祖孙 zǔ-sūn grandparent and grandchild

祖先 zǔxiān ❶ ancestors; ancestry; forefathers; forebears:炎帝和黄帝是中华民族传说中的共同祖先。Yandi and Huangdi are the legendary ancestors of the Chinese nation. ❷ ancient organisms from which present-day living things or beings are evolved:人类的~是类人猿。Men descended from apes.

祖业 zǔyè ❶ ancestral estate; property handed down from one's ancestors ❷ exploits performed by one's forefathers; great achievements of one's ancestors:光大~ build upon one's ancestral achievements

祖遗 zǔyí handed down from one's ancestors:~的房产 house property bequeathed by one's ancestors; ancestral house property

祖荫 zǔyìn 〈书面〉protection by one's ancestors

祖茔 zǔyíng 〈书面〉ancestral grave

祖制 zǔzhì 〈旧语〉system passed down by the ancestors of the emperor

祖宗 zǔzong ancestors; ancestry; forebears; forefathers:祭奠~ make sacrificial offerings to one's ancestors /祠堂里供奉着~的牌位。The memorial tablets of the forefathers were enshrined in the ancestral hall.

祖祖辈辈 zǔzǔ-bèibèi from generation to generation; generation after generation; for generations:他家~都是做工的。His family have been workers for generations. *or* He comes from a long line of workers.

俎

zǔ ❶ ancient utensils for sacrificial ox or sheep ❷ chopping block used in ancient times:置之~上 put it on the chopping block /刀~ butcher's knife and chopping block /人为刀~,我为鱼肉。They are the butcher's cleaver, we are the meat on their chopping block. ❸ (Zǔ) a surname

俎豆 zǔdòu ❶ sacrificial vessels; ritual vessels ❷ 〈书面〉sacrifices:~千秋 offer perennial sacrifices to one's ancestors

俎上肉 zǔshàngròu 〈书面〉meat on the chopping block — a helpless victim:这个国家当年是大国的~。This country was once helplessly subjected to the exploitation of big powers.

阻

zǔ block; impede; hinder; obstruct:梗~ block; hold back; obstruct /畅行无~ pass unobstructed; go through without hindrance /劝~无效 try in vain to talk sb. out of doing sth. (*or* to dissuade sb. from doing sth.) /艰难险~ hardships and obstacles /道~且长。The road is long and difficult. /这起事故使他工作受~。He was impeded in his work by the accident.

阻碍 zǔ'ài ❶ hinder; impede; block; obstruct:~经济的健康发展 obstruct the sound growth of the economy /~他的进步 hinder him in his progress /~交通 block (*or* hold up) the traffic /排除~两国关系正常化的障碍 remove the obstacles (standing) in the way of the normalization of relations between the two countries ❷ obstacle; hindrance; impediment:一切顺利,毫无~。Everything went off without a hitch. *or* Everything went on smoothly. *or* Everything went swimmingly.

阻挡 zǔdǎng stop; block; stem; obstruct:~列车 stop the train /~行人 block the way of pedestrians /~改革大潮 stem (*or* hold back) the general trend of reform /这种潮流是不可~的。The tide is irresistible.

阻挡犯规 zǔdǎng fànguī (in a basketball game) blocking

阻断 zǔduàn block; obstruct:~去路 block the way /~敌人的退路 cut off the enemy's retreat

阻遏 zǔ'è check; stop; stem:谁也~不住历史的进步。Nobody can arrest the progress of history.

阻隔 zǔgé cut off; separate:排除海峡两岸交往的人为~ remove the man-made impediments to exchanges across the Taiwan Straits

阻梗 zǔgěng 〈书面〉block; obstruct:交通~ traffic jam; road congestion

阻击 zǔjī 〈军事〉block; check; intercept:~战 blocking action /~阵地 blocking position /我军以少量兵力~来犯之敌。Our army used a small part of its forces to check the invading enemy troops.

阻截 zǔjié obstruct; intercept:沿途~ check the advance (of the enemy forces, etc.) along the way /我歼击机立即起飞~敌机。Our fighters took off immediately to intercept the enemy planes.

阻绝 zǔjué be blocked; be obstructed:音信~ be cut off entirely from the outside world

阻抗 zǔkàng 〈电学〉impedance:~匹配 impedance matching /~变化 impedance change /~参数 impedance parameter

阻拦 zǔlán stop; block; obstruct; bar the way:我们想走近点看看发生了什么事,但受到警察的~。We wanted to get closer to see what had happened, but were barred by the police. /他执意要走,我们最好别去~。As he is bent on going, we'd better not stop him.

阻力 zǔlì ❶ obstruction; hindrance; resistance:~相当大 meet with considerable resistance /改革的~ resistance to reform /冲破重重~ break through one obstruction after another ❷ 〈物理〉resistance; pullback; drag:空气~ air resistance /摩擦~ friction drag /~测量 drag measurement /~系数 drag coefficient; coefficient of resistance

阻力臂 zǔlìbì (formerly 重臂)〈物理〉distance between the point of resistance and the fulcrum while applying a lever

阻力点 zǔlìdiǎn (formerly 重点)〈物理〉point of resistance (at which a lever is applied at a weight, etc.)

阻难 zǔnàn put obstacles in sb.'s way; stand in the way; obstruct:无理~ obstruct for no reason at all /一再~ repeatedly bar

the way
阻挠 zǔnáo stand in the way; create obstacles; put a spoke in sb.'s wheel; obstruct: 百般～ create all sorts of obstacles; offer innumerable obstructions /～条约的履行 hinder the execution of the treaty /～经济的发展与社会的进步 stand in the way of economic and social progress
阻尼 zǔní 〈物理〉damping: ～波 damped wave /～振荡 damped oscillation /～电路 damping circuit; damper circuit; anti-bunt circuit
阻塞 zǔsè block; jam; obstruct; clog: 车辆～达两公里。Traffic was stacked (*or* jammed) up for two kilometres. /这条街上交通～足足四小时。Traffic in this street was held up for a good four hours.
阻塞振荡器 zǔsè zhèndàngqì blocking oscillator
阻抑 zǔyì stop; hold back; check
阻雨 zǔyǔ 〈书面〉be hampered by the rain: 归来途中～，只得在茶馆歇脚打尖。Caught in the rain on our way back, we had to stop at a teahouse for a rest and a cup of tea.
阻援 zǔyuán hold off or check enemy reinforcements
阻值 zǔzhí 〈物理〉numerical value of resistance
阻止 zǔzhǐ stop; check; prevent; hold back: ～这项计划实现 prevent the plan from being carried out /试图～历史车轮前进 try to hold back the wheel of history /～他们交往 bar them from associating with each other /他们这种轻率行动必须立即～。Their rash actions must be stopped at once. /只有人民团结一致，才能～侵略，挽救和平。Only a united people can check aggression and save peace.
阻止发盘 zǔzhǐ fāpán blocking offer (in negotiation)
阻滞 zǔzhì block; check; stem; stop: 心传导～ heart block /被～在马路上的车辆排成了长龙。Cars held up in the street formed a long queue.

组

zǔ ❶ organize; build; form: 另～一个乒乓球队 organize another table tennis team /改～ reorganize; reshuffle ❷ group; team: 分成三～讨论 be divided into three groups for discussion /互助～ mutual aid team /学习小～ study group /～长 group (*or* team) leader ❸〈量词〉set; series; battery; group: 一～纪念邮票 a set of commemorative stamps /一～特技镜头 a series of special effect shots (*or* trick shots) /四～人 four groups of people /两～电池 two batteries ❹ (of literary works) suite; series
组氨醛 zǔ'ānquán 〈生化〉histidinal
组氨酸 zǔ'ānsuān 〈生化〉histidine: ～酶 histidase
组胺 zǔ'àn *also* "组织胺"〈生化〉histamine: ～酶 histaminase
组办 zǔbàn organize: ～文艺演出 organize a theatrical performance
组编 zǔbiān compile; edit: ～一套国际问题资料 compile (*or* put together) a set of data on international issues
组成 zǔchéng form; constitute; compose; consist of: ～一个检查团 form an inspection team /美国是由五十个州～的。The United States comprises fifty states. /代表团由二十人～。The delegation consists of twenty members. /该计划由三部分～。The plan is made up of three parts. /每六人～一个小组。Every six persons constitute a group.
组成部分 zǔchéng bùfen component; component part; ingredient
组锉 zǔcuò assorted files
组蛋白 zǔdànbái 〈生化〉histone
组分 zǔfèn component (of a compound)
组稿 zǔgǎo (of editors) commission authors to write on specific topics; solicit contributions: 为这家杂志～ solicit contributions to the magazine
组歌 zǔgē 〈音乐〉suite of songs: 《长征～》*Suite of Songs on the Long March*
组阁 zǔgé ❶ form or set up a cabinet: 受命～ be authorized to form a cabinet ❷ form a leading body: 实行厂长责任制要由厂长～。In fulfilling his overall management responsibility, a factory manager is entitled to set up a leading body.
组合 zǔhé ❶ make up; constitute; combine; compose: ～法则 rules for forming combinations; rule of combination /～设计 unitized design /该执政党内的各派正在重新～。A realignment of forces is going on among the various factions of the ruling party. ❷ association; combination: 词组是词的～。A phrase is a combination of words. ❸〈数学〉combination
组合柜 zǔhéguì composite cabinet
组合机床 zǔhé jīchuáng *also* "组合车床"〈机械〉combination lathe; combined machine tool; combined lathe: 车铣～ combined lathe and mill /立卧铣～ combined vertical and horizontal milling machine /铣插～ combined milling and slotting machine
组合几何 zǔhé jǐhé combinational geometry
组合家具 zǔhé jiājù composite furniture; component furniture
组合价格 zǔhé jiàgé package price
组合结构 zǔhé jiégòu unit construction: ～系统 unit construction system
组合理论 zǔhé lǐlùn 〈数学〉combinatorial theory
组合体 zǔhétǐ 〈机械〉assembly
组合显示器 zǔhé xiǎnshìqì composite monitor
组合学 zǔhéxué 〈数学〉combinatorics
组合音响 zǔhé yīnxiǎng hi-fi stereo component system; hi-fi (set or equipment)
组合钻床 zǔhé zuànchuáng combination drilling machine
组画 zǔhuà series of paintings in the same form and on the same subject: 他正在创作有关《水浒》人物的～。He was working on a series of paintings of the characters in the *Heroes of the Marshes*.
组件 zǔjiàn module; package; construction unit: 计算机～ computer unit /微型～ micromodule; module /液压～ hydraulic package
组建 zǔjiàn form; establish; set up: 国务院各部、委机构的～ establishment of the various ministries and commissions under the State Council /～剧团 set up a theatrical troupe
组接 zǔjiē montage; film editing
组曲 zǔqǔ 〈音乐〉suite: 弦乐～ suite for strings
组诗 zǔshī series of poems
组式播种机 zǔshì bōzhǒngjī 〈农业〉gang seeder
组态 zǔtài 〈物理〉configuration: ～相互作用 configuration interaction
组团 zǔtuán form or organize a troupe or delegation: ～出访 organize a delegation for a foreign tour /运动员～参加运动会。Athletes shall participate in the sports meet in teams.
组织 zǔzhī ❶ organize; form: ～座谈会 organize a symposium /～领导班子 form a leading body /～货源 find new sources of goods /～劳力完成这项任务 organize a labour force for the task /～起来 get organized /～能力 organizational ability /～才干 organizational skills /～工作 organizational work /～委员 committee member in charge of organizational work /～委员会 organizing committee /～者 organizer /她把参观者～得很好。She conducted the visitors around in an orderly manner. ❷ system; coordination: 这篇文章的～严密。The essay is well organized. ❸〈纺织〉weave: 粗～ coarse weave / 密～ tight weave /平纹～ plain weave /斜纹～ twill weave /缎纹～ satin weave /～细密的棉布 cotton of fine and close texture ❹〈生理〉〈医学〉tissue: 皮下～ subcutaneous tissue /结缔～ connective tissue /神经～ nerve (*or* nervous) tissue ❺〈冶金〉structure: 显微～ microscopic structure ❻ organization; organized system: 各级党团～ Party and Youth League organizations at all levels /国际劳工～ International Labour Organization (ILO) /非政府～ non-governmental organization /学术～ academic societies /群众～ mass organizations /下级～ lower (*or* subordinate) organization /～处理 organizational measures; disciplinary measures /服从～分配 accept any job assigned by the authority (*or* Party organization) /～观念 sense of organization /～条例 organic rules /～原则 organizational principle /～制度 organizational system /～职能 organizational function /我们的～不纯。There are undesirable elements in our ranks.
组织胺 zǔzhī'àn *see* "组胺"
组织部 zǔzhībù Organization Department (of the Communist Party of China)
组织法 zǔzhīfǎ rules of organization; organic law; constituent act
组织关系 zǔzhī guānxi credentials showing membership in an organization; membership credentials or certificates
组织疗法 zǔzhī liáofǎ tissue therapy; histotherapy
组织瘤 zǔzhīliú 〈医学〉histioma; histoma
组织切片术 zǔzhī qiēpiànshù 〈医学〉histotomy
组织生活 zǔzhī shēnghuó regular activities or cell meetings of an organization
组织细胞 zǔzhī xìbāo 〈生理〉histiocyte; histocyte: ～瘤〈医学〉histiocytoma /～增多病 histiocytosis
组织学 zǔzhīxué 〈生理〉histology: 病理～ pathologic histology; histopathology /～家 histologist /～诊断 histodiagnosis
组织液 zǔzhīyè 〈生理〉tissue fluid
组钟 zǔzhōng bell chime
组装 zǔzhuāng assemble: ～图 assembly drawing /将零件～成部件 assemble parts into a unit /这些所谓进口家电差不多都是在国内～的。

Almost all the so-called imported household electrical appliances were assembled domestically (*or* inside China).
组装车间 zǔzhuāng chējiān assembly shop
组装程序 zǔzhuāng chéngxù assembly programme
组字游戏 zǔzì yóuxì crossword puzzle

zuān

蹤 zuān ❶ jump up ❷ dash forward; shoot across: 老鹰～云而上。The hawk darted up through the clouds.

钻(鑽) zuān ❶ drill; bore: 在门上～个眼儿 bore a hole through the door /～木取火 drill wood to make fire /这木头很容易～孔。The wood bores easily. ❷ get into; sneak into; make one's way into: ～进地窖 go down into the cellar /～到水里 disappear into the water /～进人群 be lost (*or* vanish) in the crowd /火车～过一个又一个山洞。The train passed through one tunnel after another. /飞机从云海中～了出来。The plane broke through the thick clouds. /～进我们内部的敌人比公开的敌人危险得多。Enemies who have wormed their way into (*or* sneaked into) our ranks are far more dangerous than those operating in the open. ❸ make a thorough study of; study intensively; dig into: ～书本 bury oneself in books; dig into books /～技术 perfect one's technical knowledge /他干一行～一行。He strives to be proficient in whatever he undertakes to do. ❹ curry favour with sb. in authority: 削尖脑袋～门路 try to secure personal gains by hook or by crook
see also zuàn
钻刺 zuāncì 〈书面〉❶ ridicule; satirize; pick faults and criticize: ～吹求 carp; make carping criticism ❷ ingratiate oneself with sb. in authority for personal gain: 夤缘～ try to advance one's career by currying favour with influential people
钻狗洞 zuān gǒudòng ❶〈旧语〉toady to or curry favour with powerful and influential people to secure personal gain: ～弄了个差使 secure a post by toadying to the powerful ❷ (sexual) promiscuity; carryings-on
钻故纸堆 zuān gùzhǐduī delve into musty old books; engross or immerse oneself in outdated writings: 国难当头, 怎么能去～呢? With the country in peril, how could one lose oneself in such outdated writings?
钻劲儿 zuānjìnr perseverance in learning; zest in probing into sth.: 他有一股子～, 学习进步很快。He is a man of great perseverance and has made rapid progress in his studies.
钻空子 zuān kòngzi take advantage of loopholes; exploit an advantage: 不要让他～。Don't let him exploit this loophole. /她说话不小心, 叫对方钻了空子。She made a slip of the tongue and gave the other side a handle against her. /我信了他的话, 让他钻了空子。I was taken in by his story. *or* I believed him and let him get away with it.
钻门子 zuān ménzi 〈口语〉fawn on those in influential positions; curry favour with the powerful and influential: ～得了个肥缺 gain a plum job by fawning on the powerful and influential
钻谋 zuānmóu *see* "钻营"
钻牛角尖 zuān niújiǎojiān *also* "钻牛角"; "钻牛犄角" ❶ waste time and effort trying to study an insignificant or insoluble problem; make small, unimportant distinctions; split hairs: 爱～ be fond of hairsplitting /我们不要～, 问题已经很清楚了。Let's not split hairs; the issue is perfectly clear. ❷ get oneself into a dead end or a blind alley
钻圈 zuānquān 〈杂技〉jumping or plunging through hoops
钻探 zuāntàn (exploration) drilling: ～石油 drill (*or* bore) for oil /近海～ offshore drilling /～设备 drilling equipment /～工 driller
钻探机 zuāntànjī drilling machine
钻天柳 zuāntiānliǔ 〈植物〉*Chosenia macrolepis*
钻天杨 zuāntiānyáng 〈植物〉lombardy poplar; black poplar (*Populus nigra* var. *italica*)
钻头觅缝 zuāntóu-mìfèng *also* "钻天觅缝" ❶ look for everywhere: ～找不到他。I've looked for him here, there, and everywhere but can't find him. ❷ leave no stone unturned to secure personal gain; try every possible means to make up to sb. in authority for personal advantage
钻心 zuānxīn ❶ (of pain) cutting; sharp; poignant; acute: 我的左脚痒得～。My left foot is itching like mad. ❷ worm one's way into: 采用～战术 adopt the tactic of sneaking into an organization and wreaking havoc
钻心虫 zuānxīnchóng *also* "蛀心虫" zhùxīnchóng borer
钻穴逾墙 zuānxué-yúqiáng peep through the hole and climb over the wall — illicit love affair between young man and woman
钻研 zuānyán make a careful study of; study intensively; dig into: ～业务 strive for professional proficiency; work hard to improve one's professional skill; dig into one's vocational work /～这一学说的各个方面 delve into (*or* study) all aspects of the theory
钻营 zuānyíng curry favour with or fawn on sb. in authority for personal gain; use pull to attain one's end: 千方百计～ stop at nothing to secure personal gain

zuǎn

纂(❷鬟) zuǎn ❶〈书面〉compile; edit: 编～字典 compile a dictionary ❷〈方言〉large knot or roll of hair worn at the back of the head by women; bun; chignon
纂辑 zuǎnjí sort out and edit: ～旧文 sift and edit piles of old texts
纂修 zuǎnxiū ❶ compile: ～《清史》compile the *History of the Qing Dynasty* ❷ inherit and develop: ～洪业 carry forward a great undertaking

缵 zuǎn 〈书面〉inherit

zuàn

攥 zuàn grip; grasp; clasp; hold: 手里～着一支钢笔 hold a pen in one's hand /～住她的胳膊 grasp her arm; grasp her by the arm /～拳 clench one's fist /～牢一点儿。Grip harder. /老太太紧紧～着钱包, 生怕被小偷抢走。The old woman clutched her purse tightly, fearing that a thief might snatch it.

赚 zuàn 〈方言〉deceive; hoax; fool; kid: 把她～到这里 hoax (*or* deceive) her into coming here /我整个儿让他给～了。I was completely taken in by him.
see also zhuàn
赚弄 zuànnong 〈方言〉cheat; kid: 你别～人! Stop kidding!

钻(鑽) zuàn ❶ drill; auger: 台～ bench drill /电～ electric drill /风～ air drill; pneumatic drill /手摇～ hand drill; drill ❷ diamond; jewel: 二十一～的手表 21-jewel watch ❸ bore; drill: 在板上～孔 bore a hole through the board /每隔五厘米～一个孔 drill holes five centimetres apart /我们深～二十米才找到水。We had to drill down twenty metres to find water.
see also zuān
钻床 zuànchuáng 〈机械〉drilling machine; driller: 龙门～ planer drilling machine /摇臂～ radial drill /立式～ upright drill /重型～ heavy-duty drill
钻杆 zuàngān 〈石油〉drill rod or pipe
钻机 zuànjī 〈石油〉(drilling) rig; drilling machine: 旋转～ rotary rig /套管～ casing drilling rig /～房 shanty /安装～ rig up /拆卸～ rig down
钻戒 zuànjiè diamond ring
钻井 zuànjǐng well drilling: ～采矿法 borehole mining /近海～ offshore drilling /构造～ core drilling /～船 oil rig; offshore drilling rig /～队 drilling crew (*or* team) /～工人 driller /～记录 drill log; boring log /～机 well drill
钻具 zuànjù 〈石油〉drilling tool; drilling rig
钻模 zuànmú 〈机械〉(drill) jig; drill plate: 分度～ indexing jig /～钻床 jig drill
钻石 zuànshí ❶ diamond: ～项链 diamond necklace ❷ jewel (used in a watch, etc.)
钻石婚 zuànshíhūn diamond wedding, the 60th or 75th wedding anniversary
钻塔 zuàntǎ 〈矿业〉boring tower; derrick
钻台 zuàntái drilling platform

钻铤 zuàntǐng 〈石油〉drill collar

钻头 zuàntóu bit (of a drill); drill bit: 装上～ brace a bit /卸下～ break out a bit /金刚石～ diamond drill /～进尺 footage per bit /～切削刃 drill edge /～卡在洞里了。The drill was stuck in the bore.

钻压 zuànyā 〈石油〉bit pressure; bit weight

zuī

朘 zuī 〈方言〉male genital organ; penis
see also juān

zuǐ

觜 zuǐ *see* "嘴" zuǐ
see also zī

嘴 zuǐ ❶ mouth: 樱桃小～ rosebud mouth /歪～ wry mouth /豁～ harelip /张～ open one's mouth /闭～ keep one's mouth shut /撅～ pout one's mouth (*or* lips) ❷ anything shaped or functioning like a mouth: 瓶～儿 mouth of a bottle /壶～ spout of a teapot /烟～儿 cigarette holder /喷～ spray nozzle; spray head ❸ speak; talk: ～不干净 have a foul mouth /多～多舌 long-tongued; talkative; given to gossip /堵他的～ tie his tongue; stop (*or* shut) his mouth /她这张～真厉害。She's really got a sharp tongue. /这事你就别插～了。You'd better not to cut (*or* butt) in on this matter.

嘴把式 zuǐbǎshi 〈方言〉mere talker

嘴巴 zuǐba ❶ *also* "嘴巴子" *often used in the following collocations*: 打～ slap sb.'s face; box sb.'s ears /挨了一个～ be slapped across one's face; get a box in the ears ❷ mouth: 张大～ open one's mouth wide

嘴笨 zuǐbèn not good at speech; inarticulate: 他～, 请多多包涵。He is rather clumsy of speech. Please excuse him.

嘴岔 zuǐchà *also* "嘴岔子" 〈方言〉corners of the mouth

嘴馋 zuǐchán fond of good food; gluttonous: 她一见到好吃的就～。Her mouth waters (*or* She drools) at the sight of good food.

嘴长 zuǐcháng 〈方言〉fond of gossip; gossipy

嘴敞 zuǐchǎng 〈方言〉have a loose tongue: ～存不住话 have a big mouth that can keep nothing in

嘴唇 zuǐchún lip: 厚～ thick lips /薄～ slim (*or* thin) lips /皲裂的～ chapped (*or* cracked) lips /咬～ bite one's lips /湿一下～ wet one's lips

嘴刁 zuǐdiāo ❶ be particular about food: 她从小～, 这不吃那不吃的。She has been rather choosy and picky about food since a child. ❷ 〈方言〉be a tricky talker: 这小鬼～, 差点儿被他骗了。That little trickster! I was almost taken in by his words.

嘴乖 zuǐguāi 〈口语〉(of children) clever and pleasant when speaking to elders; talking sweetly: 小姑娘～, 逗人喜欢。Always speaking sweetly, the little girl was a darling to everyone around.

嘴尖 zuǐjiān ❶ sharp-tongued; pungent in speech: 这姑娘～, 专爱损人。This sharp-tongued girl delights in making caustic remarks. ❷ have a keen sense of taste: 他～, 喝一口就知道是什么茶。He has a sharp taste and can tell the brand of the tea as soon as he drinks it. ❸ particular about food: 这孩子～, 不对口味的东西不吃。The child is rather choosy about food and eats only what suits his taste.

嘴角 zuǐjiǎo corners of the mouth: 她～露出一丝微笑。A faint smile came to her lips.

嘴紧 zuǐjǐn tight-lipped; close-mouthed; secretive: 他～, 靠得住。He is tight-lipped and reliable.

嘴啃泥 zuǐkěnní (fall) prostrate: 他脚底一绊, 摔了个～。He tripped and fell flat on his face. /那位摔跤运动员把对手摔了个～。The wrestler prostrated his opponent.

嘴快 zuǐkuài have a loose tongue; talk too freely: 你说话可小心点, 她～。Be careful when you speak; she is rather loose-tongued.

嘴懒 zuǐlǎn not disposed to talk; uncommunicative; taciturn: 他这人～, 半天没一句话。He is a man of few words.

嘴冷 zuǐlěng 〈方言〉speak without due consideration; rash in speech: 我这话可有点～, 请您原谅。Excuse (*or* Forgive) me for my blunt remarks.

嘴脸 zuǐliǎn 〈贬义〉looks; features; countenance: 成天没个好～ pull a long face all day long /揭露这些伪君子的丑恶～ expose the ugly features of these hypocrites /他那副～令人厌恶。The look on his face is disgusting.

嘴皮子 zuǐpízi 〈口语〉lips (of a glib talker): 耍～ talk glibly; be a slick talker /我可不是光耍耍～, 我是有诚意的。I am not sweet-talking; I am sincere. /那推销商的两片儿～能把死人说活了。That glib salesman is capable of making you believe the dead can talk (*or* selling freezers to Eskimos).

嘴贫 zuǐpín *also* "嘴频" talkative; garrulous; loquacious: 这小子～, 招人讨厌。The chap is shooting his mouth off and is quite a bore.

嘴勤 zuǐqín ready to greet and begin a chat with other people; ready of speech: 他为人热情, ～, 很有人缘。He is liked by everybody for his warm heartedness and sociability.

嘴软 zuǐruǎn unable to speak frankly after being bought over with small favours: 吃人的～。After being fêted one has one's mouth sealed.

嘴上没毛, 办事不牢 zuǐshang méi máo, bànshì bù láo a man too young to grow a beard is too green to trust; a man with downy lips is bound to make slips

嘴松 zuǐsōng loose-tongued; blabbing

嘴碎 zuǐsuì loquacious; talkative; garrulous: 老太太～, 见面就叨唠这事。The garrulous old lady began harping on this matter the moment she met me.

嘴损 zuǐsǔn 〈方言〉be sharp-tongued; be cutting in speech; have a bitter tongue: 你干嘛嘴这么损? Why did you make such scathing remarks?

嘴甜 zuǐtián ingratiating in speech; smooth-tongued; honey-mouthed; honey-lipped: 她～, 在厂里可吃得开了。Honey-lipped, she got on well with everybody in the factory.

嘴头 zuǐtóu *also* "嘴头子" 〈方言〉ability to talk: ～儿能说会道 have a glib tongue /～厉害 cutting in speech; sharp-tongued /他那～没人比得上。He is unrivalled (*or* unparalleled) in eloquence.

嘴稳 zuǐwěn close-mouthed; discreet in speech: 他们年轻, 嘴不稳。They were too young to hold their tongues.

嘴严 zuǐyán *see* "嘴紧"; "嘴稳"

嘴硬 zuǐyìng reluctant or unwilling to admit error or defeat: 你明明错了还～! How could you refuse to admit the error when you are obviously in the wrong? /你再～, 总还要面对现实吧。You may stick to your contrary opinions, but you have to face facts (*or* you can't fly in the face of facts).

嘴直 zuǐzhí outspoken; frank in speech: 我因为～得罪了不少人。My candour makes me a lot of enemies.

嘴子 zuǐzi 〈方言〉❶ anything shaped or functioning like a mouth: 茶壶～ spout of a teapot ❷ mouthpiece (of a wind instrument)

咀 zuǐ 〈俗语〉mouth
see also jǔ

zuì

醉 zuì ❶ drunk; intoxicated; inebriated; tipsy: 烂～如泥 be dead (*or* blind) drunk; be drunk as a fiddler (*or* a lord, *or* the devil) /把他灌～ drink him down /喝啤酒容易喝～吗? Is it easy to get drunk on beer? /～是醒时言。Sober thoughts become drunken words. ❷ be drunk with; indulge in: 被幸福所陶～ be drunk with happiness /沉～在家人团聚的欢乐之中 be intoxicated with (*or* by) the joy of a family reunion /美丽的夜色使她心～。She was enchanted by (*or* with) the beauty of the night. ❸ (of certain food or fruits) liquor-saturated; soaked or steeped in liquor: *see* "～虾"

醉笔 zuìbǐ 〈书面〉*see* "醉墨"

醉步 zuìbù staggering or tottering steps (of a drunkard)

醉鬼 zuìguǐ drunkard; sot; soak; inebriate: 他一拿到酒杯, 便成～。After one cup he drinks like the devil.

醉汉 zuìhàn drunkard; drunken man; drunk

醉红 zuìhóng crimson; deep-red: 秋来枫叶～。As autumn sets in, maple leaves turn crimson.

醉话 zuìhuà remarks made under the influence of liquor

醉酒饱德 zuìjiǔ-bǎodé thank the host for his generous hospitality

醉猫儿 zuìmāor person walking unsteadily and acting abnormally under the influence of alcohol

醉墨 zuìmò 〈书面〉painting or calligraphy done under the influ-

ence of alcohol
醉拳 zuìquán drunkard boxing
醉人 zuìrén ❶ (of alcoholic drinks) make drunk; intoxicate:这种酒度数不高,可爱~。Though low in alcohol content, the liquor is very inebriating. ❷ intoxicate; enchant:春意~ enchanting springtime
醉生梦死 zuìshēng-mèngsǐ dream one's life away; lead a befuddled life:难道你就打算这样~地虚度年华? Are you going to dream your life away like this without doing anything useful?
醉态 zuìtài state of being drunk; drunkenness: ~可掬(be) the very picture of drunkenness
醉翁之意不在酒 zuìwēng zhī yì bù zài jiǔ the drinker's heart is not in the cup — have other things in mind; many kiss the baby for the nurse's sake:~,他来,恐怕不单单是为了探病吧? The drinker's heart is not in the cup. I'am afraid there must be some ulterior motives in his coming to visit the patient.
醉虾 zuìxiā (as a cold dish) liquor — soaked shrimp
醉乡 zuìxiāng daze (a drinker is in); drunken stupor: 不觉已入~ get tipsy without knowing it
醉蟹 zuìxiè (as a cold dish) liquor — saturated crab
醉心 zuìxīn be preoccupied with; be wrapped up in:~于科学研究 be engrossed in scientific research; be all wrapped up (*or* be absorbed) in one's scientific studies /~书画 be immersed in calligraphy and painting
醉醺醺 zuìxūnxūn drunk; intoxicated; sottish; tipsy:他喝得~地在家里骂人。He was calling every one names at home after he became drunk.
醉眼 zuìyǎn 〈书面〉 eyes showing the effect of drink: ~乜斜 drunken and with eyes half-closed
醉意 zuìyì signs or feeling of being drunk:~顿消 suddenly sober up /他已有三分~。He is a bit tipsy.
醉枣 zuìzǎo *also* "酒枣" jiǔzǎo liquor-saturated dates

晬

zuì 〈书面〉 child's first birthday

最

zuì ❶ most; least; best; to the highest or lowest degree: ~要紧 most crucial; most important /~便宜 cheapest; least expensive /~困难 most difficult; hardest /跑得~快 run the fastest; be the fastest runner /质量~差 of the poorest quality /时间~短 take the shortest time /~能说明问题 can best illustrate the point /作~坏打算 prepare for the worst /~完美的设计 perfect design /~优先考虑的事 top priority ❷ (used before a noun of orientation or of place) farthest to or nearest:~北边 farthest to the north; northernmost /~里头 innermost /~下层 nearest the bottom; at the very bottom; bottommost /~前线 nearest the front; forefront ❸ best; top; without any parallel:中华之~ best of China /世界之~ best of the world
最不发达 zuìbùfādá least developed:~地区 least developed area
最不发达国家 zuìbùfādá guójiā least developed country (LDC)
最初 zuìchū initial; first; earliest:~的文本 original (*or* earliest) text /~几天 on the first few days /~她不同意我的意见。At first, she didn't agree with me. /~我学习上有很多困难。In the beginning, I had a lot of difficulties in my studies.
最大 zuìdà largest; greatest; utmost; maximum: ~光荣 highest honour /~耻辱 deepest disgrace /~牺牲 greatest (*or* maximum) sacrifice /~的幸福 greatest happiness; supreme happiness /~的份额 lion's share /~限度的 fullest possible extent; maximum /尽~的努力 do one's utmost; try one's best /~功率 maximum power /~负载 peak load /~偿债能力 ultimate solvency /~生产能力 maximum productive capacity; peaking capacity
最大公约数 zuìdà gōngyuēshù *also* "最大公因子"〈数学〉 greatest common divisor
最低 zuìdī lowest; minimum:~工资 subsistence wages /~工资制度 minimum wage system /~要求 minimum (*or* essential) requirement /~生活水准 minimum (*or* absolute) standard of living
最低纲领 zuìdī gānglǐng minimum programme
最低价格 zuìdī jiàgé lowest price; bottom or floor price
最多 zuìduō at most; at best; maximum:第三组人数~。The third group has the most people. /我们~一小时走十里地。We made ten *li* an hour at most. /她~一天看五十页。She reads a maximum of fifty pages a day. /他们在北京~只能呆十天。They can stay in Beijing for ten days at the longest. /该校学生人数~时达到四千。The school's enrolment at its height reached 4,000. /今年该厂~只能生产去年产量的一半。At best the factory can produce only half as much as last year.
最高 zuìgāo highest; tallest; best; supreme:~水位 highest water level /~成就 greatest achievement /~纪录 best record /~法院 supreme court /~价 highest possible price; highest bid /~年度额 annual ceiling /~权威 supreme authority /~速度 maximum speed; top speed /~效率 peak efficiency /~学府 highest institute of learning /她是三人中~的。She is the tallest of the three.
最高点 zuìgāodiǎn 〈统计〉 peak
最高纲领 zuìgāo gānglǐng maximum programme
最高国家权力机关 zuìgāo guójiā quánlì jīguān highest organ of state authority
最高国务会议 zuìgāo guówù huìyì Supreme State Conference
最高级 zuìgāojí ❶ highest; top-level; summit:~的豪华旅馆 first-class luxury hotel /~会谈 top-level talks; summit talks /~外交会谈 summitry ❷〈语言〉 superlative degree
最高级会议 zuìgāojí huìyì summit conference or meeting
最高人民法院 Zuìgāo Rénmín Fǎyuàn Supreme People's Court: ~院长 President of the Supreme People's Court
最高人民检察院 Zuìgāo Rénmín Jiǎncháyuàn Supreme People's Procuratorate:~检察长 Procurator-General of the Supreme People's Procuratorate
最高苏维埃 Zuìgāo Sūwéi'āi Supreme Soviet, the highest legislative authority of the former Soviet Union
最高统帅 zuìgāo tǒngshuài supreme commander
最高限价 zuìgāo xiànjià ceiling price
最高刑罚 zuìgāo xíngfá 〈法律〉 maximum sentence
最广泛 zuìguǎngfàn broadest; fullest:结成~的统一战线 form (*or* establish) the broadest possible united front /~的民主 fullest democracy
最好 zuìhǎo ❶ best; top-notch; first-rate:学习成绩~ get the highest grades in school /~的管理人员 first-rate managerial personnel /~的服务 first-class (*or* best) service /~的方法 best method ❷ had better; had best; it would be best:你~三思而行。You'd better think twice (*or* thrice) before you act. /我们~让她自己做主。It would be best if we let her decide for herself. /我~还是先听听你的意见。I had best have your opinion first.
最后 zuìhòu lastly; finally; ultimately; eventually:~的但并非最不重要的 last but not the least /流尽~一滴血 shed the last drop of blood /~部分 finale; last part /~裁定 final ruling /~交货日期 end delivery date /~结果分析 end-point analysis /~润色 final polishing; put the finishing touches to /~定稿 finalize (a document, etc.) /~制品 final (*or* end) product /在~时刻出现了意想不到的困难。An unexpected difficulty cropped up at the last minute. /谁有~决定权? Who has the last (*or* final) say? /所有办法都已失败,~一着就是溜了。All attempts have failed; what now remains in the bottom of the bag is escape. /提案~被通过了。The proposal was eventually adopted. /~,他们总算抵达目的地。At length, they reached their destination. /~,我想谈谈青少年犯罪问题。Lastly, I'd like to touch on the problem of juvenile crime.
最后贷款人 zuìhòu dàikuǎnrén 〈金融〉 lender of last resort
最后审判 Zuìhòu Shěnpàn 〈宗教〉 Last Judgement
最后条款 zuìhòu tiáokuǎn final provisions; final articles or clauses
最后通牒 zuìhòu tōngdié *also* "哀的美敦书" āidìměidūnshū ultimatum:发出~ issue an ultimatum
最后晚餐 Zuìhòu Wǎncān 〈基督教〉 Last Supper
最后协定 zuìhòu xiédìng final agreement
最后宣言 zuìhòu xuānyán final declaration
最后议定书 zuìhòu yìdìngshū final protocol
最后议事录 zuìhòu yìshìlù *precés-verbal final*
最惠国 zuìhuìguó most-favoured-nation (MFN): ~地位 most-favoured-nation status /~条约 most-favoured-nation treaty /~条款 most-favoured-nation clause /~税率 most-favoured-nation rate
最惠国待遇 zuìhuìguó dàiyù (now usu. called 正常贸易关系) most-favoured-nation (MFN) treatment; MFN trading status:给予~ accord (a country) with the most-favoured-nation treatment
最佳 zuìjiā best; top; optimal; optimum:处于~竞技状态 be in top form /生物生存的~条件 optimum in which the organism lives /~运动员 top (*or* best) athlete (*or* sportsman, *or* sportswoman) /~口译人员 top-notch interpreter /~程序设计 optimum programming /~方案 optimization programme; optimum solution /~分配 optimum (*or* optimal) allocation /~工艺 optimum technology /~经营

规模 optimal size of business /～设计 optimal design /城市～规模 optimal city size
最佳数 zuìjiāshù 〈物理〉optimum number
最佳谐振 zuìjiā xiézhèn 〈物理〉optimum resonance
最简分数 zuìjiǎn fēnshù 〈数学〉fraction reduced to lowest terms
最近 zuìjìn ❶ lately; recently; of late; not long ago:～几个月 in the last (*or* past) few months /～的事件 recent event /～一期的《新闻周刊》latest issue of *Newsweek* /～她的身体好多了。Her health has improved considerably of late. /～下了不少雨。It has rained a lot recently. /他～有些反常。Lately, he has behaved somewhat abnormally. ❷ soon; in the near future:我～两三天要去广州出差。I'll go to Guangzhou on business in a couple of days.
最快存储 zuìkuài cúnchǔ 〈计算机〉minimal-access; minimum access:～编码 minimal access coding /～程序 minimal access program; minimal latency routine
最轻量级 zuìqīngliàngjí 〈体育〉bantamweight
最少 zuìshǎo fewest; least; at the least; minimum:人数～ fewest people /～付出 least expense /这双鞋～也值二百元。This pair of shoes costs 200 *yuan* at the least.
最为 zuìwéi (used before a disyllabic adjective or verb) most; least; best; to the highest or lowest degree:～重要 of the utmost importance /～典型的事例 most typical case /～简便 simplest and most convenient
最小二乘法 zuìxiǎo èrchéngfǎ 〈数学〉least square method; least squares
最小公倍数 zuìxiǎo gōngbèishù 〈数学〉least or lowest common multiple
最小公分母 zuìxiǎo gōngfēnmǔ 〈数学〉least or lowest common denominator
最小量订货策略 zuìxiǎoliàng dìnghuò cèlüè minimum order ploy (in negotiation)
最小致死量 zuìxiǎo zhìsǐliàng minimum lethal dose (MLD)
最优化 zuìyōuhuà 〈数学〉optimization:线性～ linear optimization /～理论 optimization theory
最终 zuìzhōng last; final; ultimate:～目的 ultimate aim /～的胜利 final victory /～成本 final (*or* ultimate) cost /她～还是原谅了弟弟的无知。At long last, she forgave her younger brother for his ignorance.
最终报价 zuìzhōng bàojià final offer
最终判决 zuìzhōng pànjué 〈法律〉conclusive judgment; final decision; final ruling; final verdict

蕞 zuì

蕞尔 zuì'ěr 〈书面〉(of an area) tiny; small:～小国 small country; tiny state

槜(檇) zuì

槜李 zuìlǐ a kind of plums, the most well-known of which are found in Tongxiang, Zhejiang Province

罪(辠) zuì

❶ guilt; offence; crime:犯～ commit a crime /无～ innocent; not guilty /有～ guilty; guilty of a crime /重～ felony; grave (*or* serious) crime /轻～ misdemeanour; minor crime; petty offence /治～ punish /赦～ pardon /判～ condemn; pass sentence /刑事～ penal offence /免于死～ exempt from capital punishment /～加一等 be doubly guilty /宣判无～ acquit sb. (of a crime); declare sb. innocent /重～轻判 pass a light sentence on a serious offender /立功赎～ atone for one's crime with meritorious deeds ❷ fault; failing; blame:归～于人 lay the blame on others; shift the blame on to others /赔～ apologize /恕～ excuse sb. /是我之～。It's my fault. *or* I'm to blame. ❸ suffering; hardship; pain:受～ suffer; have a hard time; be in pain ❹ put the blame on; blame:怪～ blame sb. /见～ take offence
罪案 zuì'àn details of a criminal case; case:核实～ verify the details of a criminal case
罪不容诛 zuìbùróngzhū even death cannot atone for the offence; commit heinous crimes which even capital punishment cannot expiate:这国贼,实在是～。Death is too good for this traitor.
罪大恶极 zuìdà-èjí be guilty of the most atrocious crimes:这个抢劫杀人犯实属～。The murderous bandit is guilty of towering crimes.
罪恶 zuì'è crime; guilt; evil:～累累 be guilty of innumerable crimes; have a long criminal record /～弥天 be guilty of monstrous (*or* fiendish) crimes; one's crimes and evil deeds reach to the heavens /这帮盗匪～滔天! The crimes of these brigands reach the sky!
罪恶昭彰 zuì'è-zhāozhāng notorious crimes:这个人～,应予严惩。The man must be severely punished for the flagrant crimes he has committed.
罪犯 zuìfàn criminal; offender; culprit:刑事～ criminal offender; criminal /战争～ war criminal /在押～ criminal in custody; prisoner /被通缉的～ wanted criminal /～引渡 extradition of criminal
罪该万死 zuìgāiwànsǐ be guilty of a crime for which one deserves ten thousand deaths; be guilty of a crime for which even death is too light a punishment
罪过 zuìguo ❶ fault; offence; sin:饶恕～ condone (*or* forgive) an offence /这不是他的～,是家庭的～。This is not his fault, but his family's. /孩子有什么～,要这样粗暴对待他? What sin has the child committed to deserve such rough treatment? ❷〈谦词〉thanks, but this is really too much of an honour:让你这样破费,真是～! It gives me a guilty conscience to let you go to such expense.
罪己 zuìjǐ ❶ accept the blame oneself; blame oneself (for the mistake, etc.) ❷ (of a ruler) take the blame for misgovernment or natural disasters:下～诏 issue an imperial penitential edict
罪迹 zuìjì crime; guilt; offence:～昭彰 be guilty of flagrant crimes
罪咎 zuìjiù slip; fault; offence:多有～ have done many things wrong
罪款 zuìkuǎn charges as listed in an indictment
罪魁 zuìkuí chief criminal or culprit; chief offender; archcriminal
罪魁祸首 zuìkuí-huòshǒu archcriminal; chief culprit:分裂祖国的～ chief culprit responsible for splitting (up) the country
罪戾 zuìlì 〈书面〉sin; offence; crime
罪名 zuìmíng accusation; charge:以间谍～被捕 be arrested on an espionage charge /洗刷～ clear oneself of guilt /罗织～ frame a case (*or* trump up a charge) against sb.
罪莫大焉 zuìmòdàyān there is no crime greater than this; it's a towering crime indeed
罪孽 zuìniè wrongdoing that brings retribution; serious fault; sin:洗清自己的～ wash away one's sin /他自感此生～深重。He sensed that his life had been steeped in iniquity.
罪愆 zuìqiān 〈书面〉fault; guilt; offence; sin:她觉得自己负有～。She felt guilty.
罪情 zuìqíng facts about a crime or offence:～严重 grave (*or* serious) crime; flagrant offence
罪人 zuìrén guilty person; sinner; offender; criminal:千古～ person standing condemned through the ages; person held up to infamy through the ages; man of eternal guilt; eternal villain /历史～ person condemned by history; greatest or most infamous crook of all times /民族的～ traitor to one's nation
罪刑 zuìxíng crime and due punishment:宣判～ decide on a criminal case
罪行 zuìxíng crime; guilt; offence:犯下滔天～ commit towering (*or* heinous, *or* diabolical) crimes /揭露他的～ expose his guilt /交待全部～ make a full confession (*or* make a clean breast) of one's crimes /～较轻 minor offence
罪业 zuìyè 〈佛教〉one's sins in karma:前生～ karmic sins
罪尤 zuìyóu 〈书面〉fault; offence; sin:无端获～ be blamed for no reason at all; be unjustly blamed
罪有应得 zuìyǒuyīngdé the punishment fits the crime; receive well-deserved punishment:他被判极刑,实在是～。He was given a capital punishment which he rightly deserved.
罪责 zuìzé ❶ responsibility for an offence; culpability:推卸～ shirk responsibility for an offence /～难逃 can hardly get away with one's culpability; will not escape punishment for one's crime (*or* offence) ❷〈书面〉penal punishment:免于～ be exempt from punishment
罪证 zuìzhèng evidence of a crime; proof of one's guilt:～确凿 conclusive (*or* ironclad) proof of one's guilt
罪状 zuìzhuàng charge in an indictment; fact about a crime; crime:列举被告五条～ list five charges against the accused /历数这伙流氓的～ enumerate the crimes of the hoodlums

zūn

尊[1] zūn

❶ of a senior generation; senior; elder:～卑有序

proper regard for precedence (*or* priority in place or rank); proper order of seniority /位～ be in high position ❷ esteem; respect; honour; venerate: ～老爱幼 respect the old and cherish the young /～德乐道 honour virtue and keep to (*or* abide by) moral principles /～他为师 look up to him as one's teacher /～而不敬 show courtesy but no respect ❸〈敬词〉your: 令～ your father /请教～姓大名? May I know your name, please? ❹〈量词〉: 一～石膏像 a plaster figure (*or* statue) /二十～大炮 twenty artillery pieces

尊[2] zūn *also* "樽" zūn ancient wine vessel

尊称 zūnchēng ❶ address sb. respectfully: 人们～他为夏老。People respectfully called him the venerable Xia. ❷ respectful form of address; honorific title: 杨老是人们对他的～。The venerable Yang is an honorific way people address him.

尊崇 zūnchóng esteem; revere; venerate: 极受～的美国问题权威 highly respected authority on American studies /老年人在部落里受到～。Old age is revered in the tribe.

尊奉 zūnfèng 〈书面〉❶ worship; revere: ～古训 revere ancient teachings ❷ respect and carry out: ～上峰旨意 respectfully carry out the orders of one's superiors

尊服 zūnfú esteem; admire: 内心～ admire from the bottom of one's heart

尊甫 zūnfǔ 〈书面〉〈敬词〉your father

尊府 zūnfǔ 〈敬词〉❶ your residence ❷〈书面〉your father

尊公 zūngōng 〈书面〉〈敬词〉❶ your father ❷ form of address between friends

尊贵 zūnguì honourable; respectable; respected: ～的来宾 honoured (*or* distinguished) guests

尊号 zūnhào honorific title for the emperor or the empress

尊驾 zūnjià 〈敬词〉your good self: 恭候～光临。We request the pleasure of your company. *or* Your presence is cordially requested.

尊敬 zūnjìng ❶ respect; revere; esteem; honour: 赢得世人的～ win the respect of the world /深受～ be held in great esteem (*or* honour) /令人～ deserve (*or* be worthy of) respect /～长辈 be respectful to one's elders ❷ honourable; respectable; respected; distinguished: ～的来宾们 distinguished guests /～的总理阁下 Your Excellency Mr. Prime Minister

尊命 zūnmìng 〈敬词〉your wish; your command

尊亲 zūnqīn ❶ one's parents, grandparents and other relatives of older generations ❷〈敬词〉your relatives

尊荣 zūnróng dignity and honour: 安享～ enjoy dignity and prestige

尊容 zūnróng (often used to show contempt) sb.'s looks or appearance: 瞧你那副～! See what a spectacle you are!

尊尚 zūnshàng uphold; advocate; stand up for: ～节俭 advocate thrift (*or* frugality)

尊师 zūnshī ❶ respect one's teacher ❷〈旧语〉respectful form of address used to call a Taoist priest

尊师爱生 zūnshī-àishēng respect the teacher and cherish the student; students respect teachers and teachers cherish students

尊师重道 zūnshī-zhòngdào honour the teacher and respect truth

尊堂 zūntáng 〈书面〉〈敬词〉your mother

尊翁 zūnwēng 〈书面〉〈敬词〉your father

尊严 zūnyán dignity; integrity; honour: 民族～ national dignity /保持自己的～ keep or maintain one's integrity /失去了做人的～ be unworthy of human dignity /尊重法制的～ respect the sanctity (*or* inviolability) of the legal system

尊意 zūnyì 〈敬词〉your opinion: 不知～如何? What's your opinion? *or* What do you think of it?

尊长 zūnzhǎng elders and betters: 敬重～ hold one's elders and betters in esteem /目无～ with no regard for one's elders and betters

尊重 zūnzhòng ❶ respect; revere; value; esteem: ～老人 respect the elderly /～工人的劳动 value the workers' labour /～知识, ～人才 esteem knowledge and talent / ～生命 cherish life /你该多～别人的感情。You should have more consideration for other people's feelings. ❷ set store by; recognize: ～经济规律 set store by (*or* recognize) economic laws /～事实 face the facts /互相～主权和领土完整 mutual respect for sovereignty and territorial integrity ❸ (of behaviour) dignified; serious: 请你放～些! Behave yourself, please!

遵 zūn abide by; adhere to; observe; follow: ～纪守法 observe law and discipline; abide by the law and observe discipline /谨～师命 strictly comply with the wishes of one's master /～令而行 act according to orders

遵办 zūnbàn act in compliance with instructions; do as ordered

遵从 zūncóng follow; comply with; conform to; defer to: ～领导的指示 in compliance with the directives of the leadership /～法院的判决 accept the verdict of the court /～党的政策 conform to the Party's policy /～师友的劝告 follow the advice of one's teacher and friends /～人民的意愿 in deference to the wishes of the people /～道德准则 adhere to moral principles

遵奉 zūnfèng 〈书面〉follow; comply with; act on

遵命 zūnmìng 〈敬词〉obey your command; comply with your wish; do whatever you say: ～照办 will act on your instructions

遵守 zūnshǒu abide by; observe; comply with; honour: ～诺言 keep (*or* be true to) one's promise; honour one's commitment /～操作规程 conform to the operational procedures /～交通规则 observe traffic rules /～国际关系准则 adhere to the norms (*or* principles) governing international relations /～国际协议 honour (*or* comply with) international agreements /双方必须～契约。Both parties must live up to (*or* abide by) the contract.

遵行 zūnxíng act on; abide by; follow: 制订法律, 上下～ enact laws which must be abided by at all levels /军令必须～。Military orders must be carried out.

遵循 zūnxún follow; observe; adhere to; abide by: ～党的路线 follow the Party's line /～联合国宪章的宗旨和原则 keep to the aim and principles set out in the Charter of the United Nations /我们所～的基本方针 fundamental policy we are pursuing /这个法规出台后, 大家便有所～了。Once this piece of legislation is promulgated, everyone will have something to go by.

遵依 zūnyī *see* "遵照"

遵义会议 Zūnyì Huìyì Zunyi Meeting (the historic meeting held in Zunyi, Guizhou Province in January 1935, which spelt the end of the domination of the "Left" opportunist line in the Party Central Committee and established Chairman Mao's leadership in the whole Party)

遵照 zūnzhào comply with; conform to; act in compliance with: ～上级指示 in compliance with the instructions from above /～法律 in conformity with the law /～以往惯例 according to the established practice /～社会习俗 conform to the customs of society

樽(罇) zūn wine vessel used in ancient times: ～中有美酒。There is mellow wine in the cup.

樽俎 zūnzǔ feast; banquet: 折冲～ outmanoeuvre the enemy at the negotiating table; carry on diplomatic negotiations successfully; conduct diplomatic negotiations

鳟 zūn trout: 虹～ rainbow trout

zǔn

撙 zǔn save: ～钱买房 save up to buy a house

撙节 zǔnjié practise economy; save; retrench: ～用度 retrench; cut down expenses

zùn

捘 zùn 〈书面〉press with one's finger: ～其腕 press his wrist with the fingers

zuō

嘬 zuō 〈方言〉suck: 让她～一口 let her have a suck /～奶的婴儿 baby sucking at its mother's breast

see also chuài

嘬瘪子 zuō biězi 〈方言〉be embarrassed; feel awkward: 他的英语不大灵光, 一动嘴, 那就算～了。His English is rather poor. He would be nonplussed if he is asked to speak.

嘬牙花子 zuō yáhuāzi 〈方言〉be worried and embarrassed: 他急得

直～。He is out of his wits with worry.

作 zuō workshop：五行八～ all walks of life；all trades and crafts /石～ stonemasons' workshop /洗衣～ laundry；cleaner's
see also zuò

作场 zuōchǎng 〈方言〉workshop

作坊 zuōfang workshop：木工～ carpenters' workshop /纺织品～ workshop for making textiles

zuó

捽 zuó 〈方言〉seize；hold tight：～住他的胳膊不放 catch hold of his arm and not let go

琢 zuó
see also zhuó

琢磨 zuómo turn sth. over in one's mind；mull over；ponder：～出个弥补损失的办法 figure out a way to make up for the loss /反复～ turn sth. over and over in one's mind；mull over sth. /谁也～不透他的意思。Nobody could fathom what he meant. /这事儿真费～。The matter indeed requires a good deal of thinking. /这问题我～不止一天了。I've pondered over the problem for a long time.
see also zhuómó

昨 zuó ❶ yesterday ❷ in the past；formerly

昨非 zuófēi 〈书面〉past mistakes：觉今是而～。I realize I am right now, but I was wrong in the past.

昨儿 zuór *also*"昨儿个"〈方言〉yesterday

昨日 zuórì yesterday

昨天 zuótiān yesterday：直到～，我才看完这本书。I didn't finish the book until yesterday.

昨晚 zuówǎn yesterday evening；last night：～忙到深夜。I worked late last night.

昨叶何草 zuóyèhécǎo *also*"瓦松"wǎsōng 〈植物〉*Orostachys fimbriatus*

昨夜 zuóyè last night

筰(筰) zuó rope made of thin bamboo strips

筰桥 zuóqiáo bamboo bridge

zuǒ

左 zuǒ ❶ left；left side：靠～行 keep to the left /向～拐弯 turn left；turn to the left；take a turn to the left /你和他谈没用，他就是听也只是～耳朵进右耳朵出罢了。It's no use talking to him, for your words will only go in at one ear and out at the other. ❷ east：山～ areas east of the Taihang Mountains, specifically Shandong /江～ areas south of the lower reaches of the Yangtze River east of Wuhu and Nanjing ❸ eccentric；heretical；unorthodox：*see*"～脾气" ❹ wrong；erroneous；incorrect：想～了 get it wrong；be mistaken /他说～了。What he said is incorrect. ❺ contrary；opposite；different：他们观点相～。They hold different views. *or* They are at variance. ❻ progressive；revolutionary；the left：～翼 left wing ❼ "left" deviation：思想极～ be ultra-left in one's thinking /宁～勿右 would rather be "left" than "right" /他比他的前任更～。He is further "left" than his predecessor. ❽〈书面〉*see*"佐"zuǒ ❾ (Zuǒ) a surname

左膀右臂 zuǒbǎng-yòubì right-hand man；capable aide or lieutenant

左边锋 zuǒbiānfēng (in a football game) outside left；left wing

左边 zuǒbian left；left (*or* left-hand) side：商店～是邮局。On the left side of the store is the post office.

左不过 zuǒbuguò 〈方言〉❶ anyhow；anyway；in any case；at any rate：他说来说去，～是不同意呗。He put it this way and that, but anyway what he meant is that he didn't agree. ❷ merely；only；just：这连衣裙式样不错，～贵点儿。The dress is quite stylish, only that it's a bit too expensive.

左侧 zuǒcè *see*"左边"

左道旁门 zuǒdào-pángmén *also*"旁门左道"❶ heretical sect；heterodox school：他们把不同意自己观点的人一律斥之为～。They denounced all those who don't agree with them as heretics. ❷ heresy；heterodoxy；unorthodoxy

左舵 zuǒduò 〈航海〉left standard rudder；left rudder：～十五度！Port fifteen degrees!

左锋 zuǒfēng (in a basketball game) left forward

左顾右盼 zuǒgù-yòupàn glance right and left；cast one's glances about；look around：这姑娘初进大城市，在街上～，对什么都感到新鲜。The girl, being in a big city for the first time, looked all around the street where everything was novel to her. /他爬出地道口，～地寻视着。He got out of the tunnel and surveyed the scene closely from left to right.

左后卫 zuǒhòuwèi (in a football game) left back

左强 zuǒjiàng (often found in the early vernacular) stubborn；dogged；pig-headed；crotchety：性子～ be cantankerous

左近 zuǒjìn in the neighbourhood；round the corner；nearby：～有书店吗？Is there a book store in the vicinity? /这工厂～有家旅馆。There is a hotel near the factory.

左邻右舍 zuǒlín-yòushè next-door neighbours；neighbours

左轮 zuǒlún revolver

左面 zuǒmiàn left or left-hand side：楼～有一个停车场。There is a parking lot on the left of the building.

左内锋 zuǒnèifēng (in a football game) inside left

左派 zuǒpài the left；left wing；leftist：～政党 parties of the left /～势力 left forces；forces of the left /～报纸 newspaper on the left /执政党的～ left wing of the ruling party /投～的票 vote left /《共产主义运动中的"～"幼稚病》"*Left-Wing*" *Communism, an Infantile Disorder*

左脾气 zuǒpíqi eccentric or queer temperament：他这人～。He is a person of eccentric temperament. *or* He's an odd ball.

左撇子 zuǒpiězi left-handed person；left-hander；lefty；southpaw

左迁 zuǒqiān 〈书面〉demote：～岭南 be demoted to a post south of the Five Ridges (the area covering Guangdong and Guangxi)

左前卫 zuǒqiánwèi (in a football game) left halfback；left half

左倾 zuǒqīng ❶ left-leaning；progressive；inclined towards the revolution：～进步刊物 left-leaning, progressive magazine ❷ "left" deviation：～思想 left-deviationist thinking /～错误 left-deviationist mistakes；"left" mistakes /～空谈 "left" phrase-mongering

左倾关门主义 zuǒqīng guānménzhǔyì "left" closed-doorism

左倾机会主义 zuǒqīng jīhuìzhǔyì "left" opportunism

左倾盲动主义 zuǒqīng mángdòngzhǔyì "left" putschist tendency

左倾冒险主义 zuǒqīng màoxiǎnzhǔyì "left" adventurism

左倾排外主义 zuǒqīng páiwàizhǔyì "left" exclusiveness

左券 zuǒquàn ❶〈古语〉contract or agreement written on two (the left and the right) bamboo slips with each of the two parties keeping one of them and the holder of the left slip having the right to demand payment ❷ confidence in success：稳操～ be sure to win

左嗓子 zuǒsǎngzi ❶ out-of-tune voice ❷ person who sings in such a voice：我是～，一唱就跑调。When I sing, I always get out of tune.

左手 zuǒshǒu ❶ left hand ❷ *see*"左首"

左首 zuǒshǒu *also*"左手" left-hand side：她～坐着一位老大爷。An old man sat on her left.

左思右想 zuǒsī-yòuxiǎng think sth. over from different angles；turn sth. over in one's mind；ponder：～，不得其解 think sth. over and over again but fail to understand it

左袒 zuǒtǎn 〈书面〉side with；be partial to：裁判不应该～。A referee should be impartial.

左提右挈 zuǒtí-yòuqiè ❶ help and support each other；give mutual assistance ❷ help in this way and that；do one's best to assist：我能有今天，也是靠老先生～。My achievement today would not have been possible without the help of the old master.

左图右史 zuǒtú-yòushǐ have a large collection of books

左舷 zuǒxián 〈航海〉port

左性子 zuǒxìngzi ❶ stubborn；bigoted；pig-headed；wilful：这人有些～，怕不大好商量。He is an opinionated man, not easy to talk to. ❷ person of obdurate temperament

左旋糖 zuǒxuántáng 〈生化〉fructose；laevulose

左翼 zuǒyì ❶〈军事〉left wing；left flank：敌军从～向我们发起了进攻。The enemy troops attacked us on the left flank. ❷ left wing；the left：～分子 left-winger /～作家 left-wing writer/～文艺运动 left-wing movement in art and literature /工党～ left wing of the Party

Labour

左翼作家联盟 Zuǒyì Zuòjiā Liánméng League of Leftist Writers (organized in 1930)

左右 zuǒyòu ❶ left and right sides：～邻居 neighbours /～摇摆 vacillate now to the left and now to the right; waver between the left and right /入口～各站着一名卫兵。Two guards stood on both sides of the entrance. ❷ those in close attendance; attendants; retinue：屏退～ order one's attendants to leave /恩及～ bestow favour upon those around one ❸ control; manipulate; influence：～政局 be master of the political scene (*or* situation) /为人所～ be under the sway (*or* thumb) of sb.; fall under sb.'s influence /他不是别人能～得了的人。He is not somebody who is easily manipulated by others. /中国独立制定外交政策，不受任何人～。China formulates its foreign policy independently, free from any outside control. ❹ (used after a numeral) around; or so：六十人～ some sixty people /七十元～ approximately 70 *yuan* /十天～ ten days or so /三点～ around three o'clock ❺〈方言〉anyway; anyhow; in any event; in any case：这活儿～得有人干，就让我干吧。Since someone has got to do the work anyway, let me do it.

左…右… zuǒ…yòu… *used to emphasize repetition of the same action*：左盘右算 calculate carefully; turn over everything in one's mind /左等右等 wait and wait; wait for an unconscionable time /左砍右劈 cut and slash right and left /左也不是，右也不是，这老太太真难伺候。I've tried a hundred and one ways to gratify the old lady but without success; she is really hard to please.

左右逢源 zuǒyòu-féngyuán ❶ be able to achieve success one way or another; get things done easily：他人头很熟，所以办起事来～。He has a network of friends here, so he always gets things done. ❷ gain advantage from both sides; do things in a slick way：他做事～，很有手腕。He is quite skilled at using artifices and finds favour with both sides.

左右开弓 zuǒyòu-kāigōng shoot first with one hand, then with the other; shoot first to one side, then to the other; use first one hand and then the other in quick succession; hit with both hands：～的网球运动员 ambidextrous tennis player /～地打了他几个耳光 slap him in the face with both hands; box his ears right and left /他手持双枪，～，百发百中。He is a crack shot, shooting with both hands.

左右手 zuǒyòushǒu right-hand man; chief aide; valuable assistant

左右袒 zuǒyòutǎn *see*"左袒"

左右为难 zuǒ-yòu wéinán between two fires; between the devil and the deep blue sea; in a dilemma; in an awkward predicament：双方都不愿接受这一方案，这使市长～。Neither side would accept the proposal so that the mayor found himself between two fires. /王先生～，不知是帮张家还是帮李家。Mr. Wang was in a dilemma whether to help the Zhang family or the Li family. /下一步该怎么办，我感到～。I was in a quandary about what to do next.

左证 zuǒzhèng *see*"佐证" zuǒzhèng

左支右绌 zuǒzhī-yòuchù not have enough money to cover the expenses; unable to cope with a situation; be in straitened circumstances; be hard up

左传 Zuǒzhuàn *also*"春秋左氏传" Chūnqiū Zuǒshìzhuàn;"左氏春秋" *Zuo Zhuan*, first chronological history covering the period from 722 BC to 464 BC, presumably illustrating *The Spring and Autumn Annals*, and attributed to Zuoqiu Ming (左丘明) official historian of the State of Lu (鲁), but generally believed to have been completed in the early Warring States Period

左宗棠 Zuǒ Zōngtáng Zuo Zongtang (1812-1894), general of the Qing Dynasty who helped suppress the Taiping rebels

佐

zuǒ ❶ assist; help：～理国事 assist (a ruler) with state affairs /辅～ assist a ruler in governing a country ❷ assistant：僚～〈旧语〉assistant in a government office

佐餐 zuǒcān be eaten together (*or* go) with rice or bread：为～之佳品 go very well with rice or bread

佐贰 zuǒ'èr〈旧语〉deputy to the chief of an office, department, etc.

佐酒 zuǒjiǔ ❶〈书面〉drink with sb.; accompany sb. in drinking ❷ go with wine or liquor：～佳肴 dishes that go very well with liquor

佐理 zuǒlǐ〈书面〉assist：～军务 assist sb. with military affairs

佐料 zuǒliào condiments; seasoning

佐命 zuǒmìng〈书面〉person who assists a ruler in winning state power

佐藤荣作 Zuǒténgróngzuò Sato Eisaku (1901-1975), Japanese Prime Minister (1964-1972)

佐药 zuǒyào〈医学〉adjuvant

佐证 zuǒzhèng *also*"左证" zuǒzhèng evidence; proof：～确凿 conclusive (*or* irrefutable) evidence; indubitable (*or* indisputable) proof; absolute proof

佐治亚 Zuǒzhìyà Georgia, a southeastern state of the United States, bordering on the Atlantic

撮

zuǒ〈量词〉*used for a bunch of hair*：一～白毛 a tuft of white hair

see also cuō

撮子 zuǒzi〈口语〉tuft (of hair)：一～头发 a tuft (*or* wisp, *or* lock) of hair

zuò

坐

zuò ❶ sit; be seated; take a seat：端～ sit upright; sit up straight /～正 sit properly /～着出神 sit brooding /～得住 (manage to) sit still; be calm and collected /请～！ Please be seated. /有空就来～～。Drop in if you have time. ❷ travel by (bus, train, plane, etc.)：～船去大连 go to Dalian by boat; embark (on a ship) for Dalian /～飞机去南京 go to Nanjing by air ❸ (of a building) have its back towards：这幢大楼～西朝东。This building faces east. ❹ put (a kettle, pot, pan, etc.) on a fire：把这壶水～上 put the kettle of water on the fire ❺ seat; place ❻ (of guns, etc.) recoil; kick; kick back ❼ (of a building) sink; sag; subside：这座塔向后～了。This tower is beginning to slope backwards. ❽ (of fruit, melon, gourd, etc.) bear fruit：*see*"～果" ❾ be punished：连～ be punished for being related to or friendly with sb. who has committed an offence /反～ sentence the accuser to the punishment facing the person he falsely accused ❿ result in a disease; develop into a disease：～下了腰疼病 gradually get lumbago ⓫〈书面〉because of; owing to; on account of：～此解职 be given the sack on this account ⓬ for no reason at all; without cause or reason：惊砂～飞 dust flew without wind

坐班 zuòbān have office hours：大学老师与中小学老师不同，一般不～。University teachers are different from primary and secondary school teachers in that they do not have stipulated office hours.

坐标 zuòbiāo ❶〈数学〉coordinate：点～ point coordination /线～ line coordination /～系 coordinate system /～仪 coordinatograph /～轴 coordinate axis (*or* axes) /横～轴 axes of abscissa /纵～轴 axes of ordinate ❷〈测绘〉coordinate：～测量机 coordinate measuring machine /～测量仪 coordinate measuring apparatus (*or* instrument) /～绘图机 coordinate plotter ❸〈机械〉coordinate：～磨床 jig grinder; jig grinding machine /～镗床 coordinate setting boring machine; jig-borer; jig-boring machine /～钻床 coordinate setting drilling machine; jig drill

坐不住 zuòbuzhù restless; fidgety：这孩子学习不好，因为他老～。This boy doesn't do well in school for he simply can't sit still for any length of time. /这办公室的工作～可不行。Those who don't have the patience to stay behind an office desk won't be suitable for the job. /听了这话，他有些～了。He began to fidget at the remarks.

坐草 zuòcǎo *also*"坐月子"〈书面〉confinement in childbirth

坐禅 zuòchán〈佛教〉sit in meditation：～悟道 sit in meditation and apprehend the Buddhist doctrine

坐场诗 zuòchǎngshī *also*"定场诗" dìngchǎngshī (in traditional opera) poetry that opens the play

坐吃山空 zuòchī-shānkōng sit idle and eat, and one will dissipate one's entire fortune; remain idle and eat away a whole fortune; spend without earning：似这般～，今后怎么办？What will you live on in the future if you just sit idle like this and eat up all your property?

坐次 zuòcì *also*"座次" zuòcì seating arrangement; seating order：排～ arrange the seating order /～表 seating chart

坐大 zuòdà be left to grow in strength unhindered：地方势力日渐～。The local forces grew stronger with each passing day.

坐待 zuòdài sit back and wait：我们不能就这样～灭亡。We cannot just face destruction lying down.

坐等 zuòděng sit back and wait：～其成 sit back waiting for success with folded arms /～时机 sit tight and wait for an opportunity /

不付出辛勤的劳动，～成功是不可能的。Success won't come of itself but belongs only to the hardworking.

坐地 zuòdì ❶ stay in the same place; be fixed at a certain place: ～营业 have a fixed place for business /～日行八万里，巡天遥看一千河。Motionless, by earth I travelled eighty thousand *li* a day, Surveying the sky I see a myriad Milky Ways from afar. ❷ on the spot: 货物～转手 resell the goods right on the spot

坐地分赃 zuòdì-fēnzāng (of a ringleader, criminal, booty harbourer, etc.) take a share of the spoils without participating personally in the robbery; divide or split the loot

坐地虎 zuòdìhǔ local tyrant or bully; local villain

坐地户 zuòdìhù 〈方言〉 local family who has lived there for generations

坐垫 zuòdiàn cushion

坐定 zuòdìng ❶〈书面〉 be seated; sit down ❷〈方言〉 be destined: 今年的饥荒算是～了。We are destined to suffer from famine this year.

坐蔸 zuòdōu 〈农业〉 wilting and tardy growth of rice seedlings usually caused by low water temperature, lack of fertilizer, etc.

坐而论道 zuò'érlùndào sit back and indulge in empty talk; be a phrase-monger

坐根儿 zuògēnr 〈方言〉 at all; just; simply: 她～就不喜欢这孩子。She doesn't like the child at all.

坐功 zuògōng 〈道教〉 practice of sitting in meditation

坐骨 zuògǔ 〈生理〉 ischium

坐骨神经 zuògǔ shénjīng ischial nerve; sciatic nerve: ～痛 ischialgia; sciatica

坐观成败 zuòguān-chéngbài sit and watch a fight on the sidelines; wait to see what will come of another's venture; look on coldly: 他们决定暂且按兵不动，～。They decided to take no action for the time being and see which way the wind blows. *or* They refrained from throwing in their troops yet and waited to see the result of the battle.

坐馆 zuòguǎn 〈旧语〉❶ be a tutor in a private school ❷ serve as an assistant to a ranking official or general

坐柜 zuòguì ❶ a kind of horizontal cabinet on which people can sit ❷〈方言〉 serve at the counter

坐果 zuòguǒ bear fruit: 西红柿在低于五摄氏度时坐不了果。Tomatoes won't bear fruit at a temperature below 5℃.

坐化 zuòhuà 〈佛教〉(of a monk) die sitting cross-legged

坐家女 zuòjiānǚ 〈方言〉 unmarried girl; maiden

坐监 zuòjiān *also* "坐监狱" be imprisoned; be in jail; be put behind bars

坐江山 zuò jiāngshān rule the country

坐劲 zuòjìn ❶ give full support or firm backing to: 他倒是很给我们～。He really gave us strong backing. ❷ (of guns, etc.) recoil; kick back: 步枪的～ kick of the rifle

坐禁闭 zuò jìnbì be placed in confinement (as a disciplinary measure)

坐井观天 zuòjǐng-guāntiān observe the sky from the bottom of a well — have a very narrow view or limited outlook: 不进行深入的调查研究，～，难免要犯主观主义的错误。If we just "look at the sky from the bottom of a well" instead of making a thorough investigation and study, we are bound to err on the side of subjectivism.

坐具 zuòjù thing to sit on; seat

坐科 zuòkē receive professional training at an old-type opera school: ～学艺 take professional training to be an opera singer

坐困 zuòkùn confined; shut up; fenced in; walled in: ～孤城 be confined to an isolated town

坐困愁城 zuòkùn-chóuchéng be walled in by one's own worries; be weighed down with cares

坐蜡 zuòlà 〈方言〉 be put in a tight spot; land in a predicament: 这事儿我干不了，别让我～。This job is beyond my ability, so please don't get me into hot water.

坐牢 zuòláo be in jail; be imprisoned: 他因谋杀罪正在～呢。He is doing time for murder now. /法官至少要判他坐五年牢。The judge will put him behind bars for at least five years. *or* The judge will at least sentence him to a five-year imprisonment.

坐冷板凳 zuò lěngbǎndèng ❶ hold an unimportant post and be ignored: 我这是个～的差事。Mine is a job nobody takes any notice of. ❷ be kept waiting long for an appointment or audience with a VIP; be given the cold shoulder: 尽管王先生好耐性，却也感到～的滋味了。For all his patience Mr. Wang was beginning to feel he had been left to cool his heels too long.

坐力 zuòlì 〈军事〉 recoil; kick: 无后～炮 recoilless gun

坐立不安 zuòlì-bù'ān be restless whether sitting or standing; be fidgety; be on pins and needles; be on tenterhooks: 这事搞得他～。It gave him the fidgets. /奶奶急得～。Grandmother became quite restless from anxiety. /你今天～，有什么不对劲吗？You have ants in your pants today. Is there anything wrong?

坐落 zuòluò (of a building, etc.) be established in a place; be situated; be located: 我们学校～于市西郊。Our school is located in the western suburbs of the city.

坐坡 zuòpō 〈方言〉❶ lean back and refuse to step forward: 这孩子直打～，不肯走。The child leaned back and refused to go. ❷ slip back ideologically; retrogress

坐骑 zuòqí horse for riding on; one's personal mount

坐鞧 zuòqiū *also* "后鞧" hòuqiū leather strap round the rump of a shaft-horse

坐蓐 zuòrù 〈书面〉 confinement in childbirth; lying-in

坐山雕 zuòshāndiāo 〈动物〉 cinereous vulture

坐山观虎斗 zuò shān guān hǔ dòu sit atop the mountain to watch the tigers fight — watch in safety while others fight, and reap the spoils when both sides are exhausted: 见到两家大打出手，他倒乐得来个～，瞅准机会，从中渔利。He was quite content to let the two sides fight it out, while watching safely from the sidelines and waiting for an opportunity to profit from their conflict (*or* at their expense).

坐商 zuòshāng tradesman (as opposed to itinerant merchant); shopkeeper

坐失 zuòshī take no action and lose (a good chance)

坐失良机 zuòshī-liángjī let slip a golden opportunity: 在这场谈判中，他们行动迟缓，～。In this negotiation they acted too slowly and let the golden opportunity slip through their fingers.

坐实 zuòshí ❶ clear and certain; definite: 已经～他是敌人的奸细。It's certain that he is an enemy spy. ❷ verify; confirm: ～罪名 prove a charge

坐食 zuòshí 〈书面〉 eat bread without working for it; not live by the sweat of one's brow

坐视 zuòshì sit by and watch; look on with folded arms: ～不管 sit back and look on unconcerned; sit by and remain indifferent; look on with arms folded

坐视不救 zuòshì-bùjiù sit back and watch without going to the rescue; sit idly by without lending a helping hand: 邻省有饥荒，我们哪能～？Our neighbouring province is suffering from a famine. How can we sit by and look on unconcerned?

坐收渔利 zuòshōu-yúlì *also* "坐收渔人之利" reap advantages from both parties to a conflict without lifting a finger; profit from others' tussle; reap third party profit: 你们争斗，让他～，有什么好处呢？What's the good of letting him benefit from the fight between you?

坐守 zuòshǒu defend tenaciously; defend to the last; make a last-ditch defence

坐索 zuòsuǒ *also* "坐讨" wait at a debtor's home to demand payment of a debt; dun sb. for the payment of a debt at his home

坐胎 zuòtāi pregnant; with child; expecting

坐探 zuòtàn enemy agent planted within one's own ranks; mole

坐堂 zuòtáng ❶〈旧语〉(of magistrates) sit in court ❷〈佛教〉 sit in meditation in the meditation room ❸ (of a shop assistant) serve at the counter ❹〈方言〉(of a doctor) be invited by a Chinese pharmacy to see patients (*or* practise medicine) at the pharmacy

坐天下 zuò tiānxià rule the country; be masters of the country: 打天下不易，～更难。It's hard to seize state power and still harder to keep it.

坐桶 zuòtǒng commode; nightstool; closestool

坐位 zuòwei *also* "座位" zuòwèi ❶ place to sit; place; seat: 排～ make seating arrangements /前排～ front-row seat /这家电影院有一千五百个～。The cinema has a seating capacity of 1,500. *or* The cinema seats 1,500. /请给我留个～。Please reserve a seat for me. ❷ thing to sit on; chair or stool; seat: 给我搬个～来。Get (*or* Bring, *or* Fetch) me a seat.

坐卧不宁 zuòwò-bùníng *also* "坐卧不安" unable to sit or sleep at ease; be on tenterhooks; be agitated: 王太太为女儿的事牵肠挂肚，～。Mrs. Wang's concern about her daughter gave her no rest (*or* no end of worries).

坐误 zuòwù lose or let slip (an excellent opportunity):因循～ procrastinate until it is too late

坐席 zuòxí ❶ take one's seat at a banquet table; attend a banquet:请他去～ invite him to a banquet; invite him to dinner ❷ dinner seat

坐享其成 zuòxiǎng-qíchéng sit idle and enjoy the fruits of others' work; feed on the fruits of others' labour; reap where one has not sown:饭菜都是她做的,我是～。She cooked the dishes, and all I did was to enjoy the food.

坐像 zuòxiàng statue of a person in a seated or sitting posture

坐药 zuòyào 〈中医〉suppository

坐夜 zuòyè stay up overnight:～守岁 stay up on New Year's Eve /～守灵 stay up by the coffin to guard the spirit of the dead

坐以待毙 zuòyǐdàibì anticipate certain death without putting up a struggle; resign oneself to death; await one's doom:他们都觉得与其～,不如拼死抵抗。They all felt that to put up a last-ditch fight was better than to await death and do nothing.

坐以待旦 zuòyǐdàidàn sit up and wait for daybreak; remain awake till dawn

坐月子 zuò yuèzi 〈口语〉confinement in childbirth; lying-in:伺候妻子～ attend upon (*or* look after) one's wife while she is in confinement after giving birth to a child (*or* during the month of lying-in after she gives birth to a child)

坐赃 zuòzāng ❶〈方言〉plant stolen or banned goods on sb.; frame sb. ❷〈书面〉commit the crime of corruption

坐镇 zuòzhèn (of a commander) personally attend to garrison duty; assume personal command:～太原 take command of Taiyuan defence personally; assume personal command in Taiyuan

坐支 zuòzhī (of an enterprise) direct cash payment from its earnings with the permission of the bank

坐庄 zuòzhuāng ❶ be a resident buyer of a business firm ❷ be the banker or dealer (in a gambling game):你这是第三圈儿～了。This is the third time you are banker.

坐罪 zuòzuì 〈书面〉sentence; condemn

座(❶坐)

zuò ❶ seat; place:让～儿 offer one's seat to sb. /到主席台就～ take one's seat on the rostrum /雅～儿 private room (in a restaurant, etc.) /孕妇专～儿 seat specially reserved (*or* seat meant) for pregnant women /满～ have a full house; be packed /请入～。Please be seated. ❷ stand; base; pedestal:灯～儿 pedestal of a reading lamp /钟～儿 clock stand /茶杯～儿 coaster /雕像～儿 pedestal for (*or* base of) a statue ❸〈天文〉constellation:天琴～ Lyra /小熊～ Ursa Minor /大熊～ Ursa Major; Great Bear ❹〈旧语〉〈敬词〉form of address to high-ranking officials:省～ Your Excellency Mr. Governor /此事须请军～裁定。This has to be left to His Excellency the Army Commander for final decision. ❺〈量词〉*used of large and solid thing*:一～城堡 a castle /两～摩天大楼 two skyscrapers /一～水库 a reservoir /一～大理石雕像 a statue in marble

座舱 zuòcāng 〈航空〉❶ cabin:飞机～ aircraft cabin ❷ (of a fighter) cockpit

座舱盖 zuòcānggài canopy; cockpit canopy; hood; cockpit hood

座车 zuòchē passenger train or car; railway carriage:硬席～ hard-seat passenger train

座次 zuòcì *see* "坐次" zuòcì

座号 zuòhào number of the seat; seat number

座机 zuòjī private plane

座儿 zuòr (of a cinema, restaurant, etc.) patron; (of a rickshaw, pedicab, etc.) passenger:拉～ have passengers (of a vehicle) /这出戏很上～。The opera is a box-office success.

座上客 zuòshàngkè guest of honour; honoured guest

座师 zuòshī *also* "座主"〈旧语〉respectful form of address to the chief examiner used by a successful candidate in the imperial examinations at the provincial or the highest level

座谈 zuòtán have an informal discussion:～当前形势 have an informal discussion on the present situation

座谈会 zuòtánhuì forum; symposium; informal discussion:关于核能利用的～ symposium on the utilization of nuclear energy /文艺～ forum on art and literature /参加～ participate in a discussion /组织～ organize a discussion or a forum

座头 zuòtou 〈方言〉place to sit; seat

座位 zuòwei *see* "坐位" zuòwèi

座无虚席 zuòwúxūxí have a full (*or* packed) house; be packed:电影院里～。The cinema had a full house. /八百多个座位的礼堂内,真是～。Of the eight hundred or so seats in the auditorium, not a single one was unoccupied.

座椅 zuòyǐ 〈交通〉seat:朝后～ aft-facing seat; rearward-facing seat /朝前～ forward-facing seat

座右铭 zuòyòumíng motto; maxim:他的～是"知难而进"。His motto is "Advance in the face of difficulties".

座钟 zuòzhōng desk clock

座子 zuòzi ❶ stand; base; pedestal ❷ saddle (of a bicycle, motorcycle, etc.):把自行车～升高 raise the seat of the bicycle

唑

zuò *see* "咔唑" kǎzuò; "噻唑" sāizuò

怍

zuò 〈书面〉feel ashamed:深感愧～ feel deeply ashamed

祚

zuò 〈书面〉❶ good fortune; blessing:门衰～薄 the family is on the decline and its fortune running out ❷ throne:帝～ throne /践～ ascend the throne; accede to the throne

柞

zuò oak (*Quercus*)

柞蚕 zuòcán tussah

柞蚕丝 zuòcánsī tussah silk

柞栎 zuòlì 〈植物〉toothed oak

柞树 zuòshù *see* "柞栎"

柞丝绸 zuòsīchóu tussah silk; pongee

酢

zuò 〈书面〉(of a guest) propose a toast to the host:酬～ exchange of toasts

see also cù

作

zuò ❶ rise; get up:日出而～ get up at sunrise /振～ bestir oneself; brace up; cheer up /一鼓～气 press on to the finish without letup /枪声大～。Heavy fighting broke out. /鞭炮鼓乐并～。Firecrackers and the band joined in the ensemble. ❷ do; make:耕～ till; cultivate; farm /操～ operate /～假账 falsify accounts /～调查 investigate /～斗争 wage a struggle; fight against; combat /～功课 do one's homework /～报告 deliver a speech; give a talk; make a report /～结论 reach a conclusion; pass a verdict /无恶不～ commit every crime imaginable /～出最后裁定 give a final ruling /～长期打算 plan on a long-term basis ❸ write; compose:写～ write /～文章 write an essay (*or* article) /善于～画 be good at painting; paint well /～诗 compose (*or* write) a poem ❹ writings; work:杰～ masterpiece /原～ original work /不朽之～ monumental work; immortal writings /成名之～ work that makes one's name /归天之～ swan song ❺ pretend; feign; affect:装～一无所知 feign ignorance /装模～样 behave affectedly; put on an act /故～惊讶 put on a show of surprise; pretend surprise /装聋～哑 pretentd not to hear and see ❻ take sb. or sth. for; regard as; consider to be:把她当～亲闺女 treat her as one's own daughter /认贼～父 take the foe for one's father /过期～废 be invalidated after a specified date ❼ act as; be; become:～向导 act as a guide /～表率 serve as an example ❽ feel; have:浑身～痒 itch all over

see also zuō

作案 zuò'àn commit a crime or an offence; carry out criminal activities:～多起 commit many crimes /～时被捕 catch sb. redhanded; catch sb. in the act; catch sb. at it /这个抢劫银行团伙主要在这一带～。The gang of bank robbers mainly operated in this neighbourhood.

作罢 zuòbà drop; cancel; relinquish; give up:既然成功的希望不大,此事只好～。Since there was little hope of success, the matter had to be dropped.

作保 zuòbǎo be sb.'s guarantor; stand surety for sb.; go bail for sb.; sponsor sb.:找人～ find surety /这孩子品行没问题,我可以～。I can be guarantee for the child's good behaviour.

作报 zuòbào 〈方言〉(of telegraph or radio operator) transmit and receive messages by radio, telegraphy, etc.

作弊 zuòbì practise fraud; cheat:考试～ cheat in an examination

作壁上观 zuòbìshàngguān watch others fight from the rampart; stay behind the breastworks and watch others battle; be an onlooker:这场冲突背景复杂,你我慎勿介入,且～。As the background to the conflict is rather complicated, let's take care not to get involved but

stand by and watch for a while.

作别 zuòbié 〈书面〉bid farewell; say adieu; take one's leave:～家人,登途南下 take leave of one's family and start off on a journey to the south

作成 zuòchéng 〈方言〉help (sb. to achieve his aim):～这门亲事 help arrange the marriage

作词 zuòcí write words (for a song):由一位著名诗人～ words by a famous poet

作答 zuòdá answer; reply:考虑好了再～ reply after thinking it over /问了两次他也不～。He was asked twice but did not give any answer.

作大 zuòdà (often used in the early vernacular) put on airs

作抖 zuòdǒu 〈方言〉tremble; shiver; shake; shudder:吓得全身～ tremble all over with fear

作对 zuòduì ❶ set oneself against; be antagonistic to; oppose:你要与我～到几时? How long are you going to set yourself against me? /她害怕和你～。She is afraid to oppose you. ❷ make a pair; join in a marriage:成双～ in pairs

作恶 zuò'è do evil:～未遂 do not succeed in one's evildoing /你这是～自毙。You are courting your own destruction with your evil deeds.

作恶多端 zuò'è-duōduān do all sorts of evil; perpetrate numerous crimes; be steeped in iniquity

作伐 zuòfá 〈书面〉act as matchmaker or go-between

作法 zuòfǎ ❶〈旧语〉(as of a Taoist priest) resort to magic arts ❷ technique of writing; art of composition:应用文～ technique of practical writing ❸ way of doing things; course of action; practice; approach:普遍的～ common practice /特殊的～ special approach /惯常的～ usual way of doing things; usual practice /采取一种大家都能接受的～ adopt a method acceptable to all /你这种～行不通。Your present course of action will get you nowhere. *or* Your present approach won't work. /我们对你方的不友好～深表遗憾。We deeply regret your unfriendly act.

作法自毙 zuòfǎ-zìbì make a law only to fall foul of it oneself; be hoist with one's own petard; stew in one's own juice

作废 zuòfèi become invalid; be annulled or invalidated:使合同～ nullify (*or* cancel) a contract /宣布条约～ declare a treaty null and void /～的护照 invalid passport /逾期～ become invalid upon expiration

作风 zuòfēng style; style of work; way:生活～ way of life; life style /工作～ style of work; work (*or* working) style /家长～ high-handed way of dealing with people; patriarchal behaviour /杜绝官僚主义～ put an end to a bureaucratic style of work /提倡实事求是的～ advocate a practical and realistic way of doing things /端正思想～ correct (*or* rectify) one's thinking and attitude /～正派 be honest and upright; be open and aboveboard

作复 zuòfù write back; write in reply:迟未～,歉甚。I'm sorry I have not been able to reply earlier.

作梗 zuògěng obstruct; hinder; impede; create difficulties:没想到他会从中～。We had not expected he would create difficulties for us.

作古 zuògǔ 〈书面〉〈婉词〉pass away; depart this life:遽然～ pass away suddenly

作古正经 zuògǔ-zhèngjīng 〈方言〉in all seriousness; in dead earnest:他板着脸,～地说话。He put on a stern expression and spoke in a serious tone.

作怪 zuòguài make mischief; stir up trouble:兴妖～ conjure up a host of demons to create trouble; make trouble /私心杂念在她头脑中～。She is possessed (*or* obsessed) with selfish ideas.

作害 zuòhài 〈方言〉damage; make havoc of; spoil:别让猪～庄稼。Don't let the pigs damage crops.

作耗 zuòhào 〈方言〉make trouble; be mischievous:生事～ make trouble and create problems

作合 zuòhé make a match; act as go-between or matchmaker:多谢你从中～。Thank you very much for making the match.

作家 zuòjiā writer:专业～ professional writer /喜剧～ comic playwright /多产～ prolific (*or* productive) author /无名的～ obscure writer /著名～ prominent writer

作家协会 zuòjiā xiéhuì writers' association

作假 zuòjiǎ ❶ counterfeit; falsify; adulterate:这家商店常在烟酒中～。The wine and cigarettes sold in this store are often adulterated. ❷ cheat; play tricks; feign ignorance:～骗人 play tricks on sb. ❸ behave affectedly; be unnatural:想吃就吃,不必这么忸忸怩怩地～。Eat it if you want. Don't try to affect coyness like this.

作价 zuòjià fix a price for sth.; appraise; evaluate:七成新的自行车只～六十元 appraise a 70%-new bicycle at only 60 *yuan* /旧家具～变卖 sell old furniture at a reduced price /把这些固定资产～归公 transfer these fixed assets to public ownership with compensation to owners /你给这把旧椅子作个价吧。Will you price this old chair?

作奸犯科 zuòjiān-fànkē perpetrate crimes in defiance of the law; commit offences against law and discipline:不论是谁,只要～,就应惩罚。Whoever transgresses against the law must be punished.

作茧自缚 zuòjiǎn-zìfù spin a cocoon around oneself — get enmeshed in a web of one's own spinning; fall into a pit of one's own digging; put a noose around one's own neck:拒绝与外国进行经济贸易交流的作法实际上是～。Closing our country to international economic exchange and trade is in effect working against our own interests.

作件 zuòjiàn *also* "工件" gōngjiàn; "制件" zhìjiàn workpiece; work

作践 zuòjian (often pronounced zuójian in spoken Chinese) ❶ spoil; ruin; waste:～粮食 waste grain /你为了工作～自己的身体,这可不明智。It's not sensible to wear yourself down with overwork. ❷ run sb. down; humiliate; insult:你这不是故意～人吗? Didn't you say that just to run me down? ❸ violate (a woman)

作劲 zuòjìn 〈方言〉❶ exert oneself physically; make an effort; try hard:～干活 work hard ❷ shore up; bolster up; support:他真给咱们～。He went all out to back us up.

作客 zuòkè 〈书面〉sojourn:～异乡 sojourn in a strange place (*or* in an alien land)

作客思想 zuòkè sīxiǎng guest mentality; feeling of not belonging; consciousness of being an outsider:你去了村里,就是村里人了,不要有～。When you go to the village, you are one of them. You musn't behave like a guest.

作困兽斗 zuòkùnshòudòu put up a desperate fight like beasts at bay (*or* cornered beasts)

作乐 zuòlè make merry; have a good time; enjoy oneself; experience pleasure:寻欢～ seek pleasure and make merry; indulge in merry-making /苦中～ seek joy amidst hardship (*or* sorrow)

see also zuòyuè

作冷 zuòlěng feel a chill; take cold

作脸 zuòliǎn 〈方言〉win honour or glory for; try to bring credit to:给父母～ win honour for one's parents /替母校～ win credit for one's alma mater

作料 zuòliao (often pronounced zuóliao in spoken Chinese) condiments; seasoning

作乱 zuòluàn stage a rebellion; incite a revolt:犯上～ rebel against the authority /聚众～ gather a crowd and incite them to rebellion

作美 zuòměi (often used in the negative) (of weather, etc.) help; cooperate; support:老天爷不～,下了一天瓢泼大雨。As heaven wasn't cooperative, the rain came down in buckets all day.

作幕 zuòmù 〈旧语〉serve as an assistant to an official or as a member of his staff

作难 zuònán embarrass; make things difficult for sb.:对不起,让你～了。I'm sorry to have put you in this awkward situation.

作难 zuònàn 〈书面〉rise in revolt; start an uprising:乘机～ seize the chance to rise in rebellion

作鸟兽散 zuòniǎoshòusàn flee in every direction like startled birds and animals; flee helter-skelter

作孽 zuòniè do evil; commit a sin:这样对待孩子真是～! It is sinful to treat the child like this.

作弄 zuònòng (often pronounced zuōnòng in spoken Chinese) make a fool of; poke fun at; play tricks on; tease:受到～ be made a fool of /我叔叔就爱～人,总拿我们开玩笑。My uncle is a big tease, always making fun of us.

作呕 zuò'ǒu feel sick or nausea; feel like vomiting:令人～的气味 sickening smell /令人～的奉承 fulsome flattery /他这种行为令人～。His conduct is disgusting.

作派 zuòpai ❶ (in Chinese operas) acting ❷ style; manner; air:我看不惯她那种傲慢的～。I was repelled by her haughty air.

作陪 zuòpéi help entertain the guest of honour; be invited to keep the chief guest company at a banquet:他今晚宴请外宾,请你来～。You are invited to be present at the banquet he gives in honour of foreign guests tonight.

作品 zuòpǐn works (of art and literature): 老舍的～ works by Lao She / 油画～ painting in oils / 中国古典文学～ Chinese literary classics

作畦 zuòqí 〈农业〉 bedding: ～机 bedder

作情 zuòqing *also* "做情" zuòqing 〈方言〉 ❶ admire; hold in esteem: 他办事没人不～的。Everyone admires his way of handling things. ❷ do sb. a favour; send gifts: 他拿别人的东西去～。He made a gift of something belonging to somebody else. ❸ intercede; mediate: 双方都不肯说价钱, 只好由我～了。As neither party would make a price offer, I had to step in and set a figure for them. ❹ feel grateful; appreciate (kindness, favour, etc.): 只要你是真心, 人家会～。They will appreciate your kindness so long as you are sincere. ❺ behave in an affected way; make a pretence; strike a pose: 瞧他那～劲儿的, 真让人讨厌。That affected manner of his is really sickening.

作曲 zuòqǔ write music; compose: 谷建芬～ music by Gu Jianfen

作曲家 zuòqǔjiā composer

作人 zuòrén ❶ conduct oneself; behave; get along with people ❷ 〈书面〉 foster or train useful personnel; nurture talent

作如是观 zuòrúshìguān view the matter in this light; this is how I look at the matter

作色 zuòsè show signs of anger; get angry: 勃然～ flush with rage

作势 zuòshì strike a pose; assume a posture; attitudinize

作手 zuòshǒu 〈书面〉 writer

作数 zuòshù be valid; count; hold: 我说话向来～。I always mean what I say. / 班长的决定依然～。The monitor's decision still holds. / 酒后的话, 作不得数。What he said in drink should not be taken too seriously. / 过时的文件不～了。This document is expired and doesn't count any more (*or* is no longer valid).

作耍 zuòshuǎ 〈方言〉 ❶ play a joke on sb.; poke fun at sb.: 别跟他～。Don't make fun of him. ❷ play; have fun: 这种事不是～的, 弄不好要倒霉。It's no joking matter and will get you into big trouble if handled improperly.

作死 zuòsǐ (often pronounced zuōsǐ in spoken Chinese) seek death; invite destruction; court trouble: 车开得这么快, 你～呀! Are you tired of life that you drive so fast?

作速 zuòsù losing no time; quickly; at once: ～处理 deal with (sth.) at once

作算 zuòsuàn 〈方言〉 ❶ even if; even though: ～他今天下午能来, 我也见不到他了。Even if he can come this afternoon, I won't be able to see him. ❷ *see* "作数"

作祟 zuòsuì ❶ (of ghosts, spirits, etc.) haunt ❷ do mischief; create trouble; exercise evil influence: 这都是个人权利欲望～。All this trouble is caused by the lust for power and gain.

作态 zuòtài affect; put on a pose; strike an attitude: 惺惺～ be affected / 我讨厌她的忸怩～。Her affectations annoy me.

作田 zuòtián 〈方言〉 till the land; farm: ～人 farmer; peasant

作痛 zuòtòng ache; pain: 背部隐隐～ have a dull pain in one's back / 周身～ be aching all over

作威作福 zuòwēi-zuòfú ride roughshod over others; tyrannically abuse one's power; lord it over the people; play the tyrant: 他～的日子眼见要完蛋了。The days of his tyranny are numbered.

作为 zuòwéi ❶ conduct; action; act; deed: 不良～ bad conduct / 一看就知道是他的～。It's obvious that he did it. ❷ accomplish; do sth. worthwhile: 有所～ be able to display one's talent and do well in life / 无所～ attempt nothing and accomplish nothing / 只要勤奋努力, 任何岗位上都可以大有～。As long as you are hardworking, you can achieve a lot at any post. ❸ regard as; treat as; take for: ～挡箭牌 use sth. as an excuse (*or* a pretext, *or* a shield) / 以外国经验～借鉴 draw on the experience of foreign countries; make use of foreign experience for reference / 把他～靠山 look upon him as one's prop (*or* patron) / 把跑步～保持健康的最好方法 regard jogging as the best way to keep fit ❹ as: ～一个学生, 首先得把学习搞好。As a student, you must first of all study well (*or* make a success of your study).

作伪 zuòwěi fake (works of art and literature, cultural relics, etc.); make an imitation; forge; counterfeit

作文 zuòwén ❶ (of students) write a composition ❷ composition: ～讲评 comment on students' compositions

作文章 zuò wénzhāng *also* "做文章" zuò wénzhāng ❶ write an essay ❷ make an issue of

作务 zuòwù 〈方言〉 manage; attend to; take care of: ～庄稼 attend to the crops

作物 zuòwù crop: 经济～ cash (*or* money) crops / 粮食～ grain crops / 油料～ oil-bearing crops / 早熟～ early ripening crops / 越冬～ overwintering crops / 低产～ low-yielding crop / ～布局 crop pattern

作物微气象学 zuòwù wēiqìxiàngxué crop micrometeorology

作息 zuòxī work and rest: 按时～ work and rest according to schedule

作息时间表 zuòxī shíjiānbiǎo daily schedule; timetable; work schedule

作响 zuòxiǎng make a sound; sound: 门开时生锈的铰链嘎吱～。The rusty hinges squeaked when the door opened. / 牛拉大车走起来嘎吱～。The oxcart creaked along.

作想 zuòxiǎng 〈方言〉 consider; mull over: 我不知道他是怎么～的。I don't know what is in his mind.

作协 zuòxié (short for 作家协会) writers' association

作兴 zuòxing 〈方言〉 ❶ (often used in the negative) there is reason to; it's permissible (*or* justifiable) to: 可不～胡说八道! None of your nonsense! *or* You mustn't talk nonsense! ❷ maybe; perhaps; possibly: 她～不来了。She may not come. ❸ it's a common practice; be prevalent

作学问 zuò xuéwen *also* "做学问" zuò xuéwen do scholarly research

作眼 zuòyǎn *also* "做眼" zuòyǎn be a scout

作痒 zuòyǎng have an itch; itch: 头皮～ feel itchy in one's scalp

作业 zuòyè ❶ school assignment: 家庭～ homework / 数学～ assignment in mathematics / 课堂～ assignment to be done in class / 做～ do one's assignment (*or* homework) / 批改～ correct students' papers ❷ work; task; operation; production: 高空～ work high above the ground / 深海～ deep sea operation / 野外～ field work / ～班 work team / ～项目 events in operation / ～计划 production plan / ～进度 progress of operation / ～量 quantity of work / ～线 production line; operating line / ～区 operation area

作揖 zuòyī (often pronounced zuōyī in spoken Chinese) make a bow with hands folded in front: 打躬～ fold the hands and make deep bows; make obeisance

作艺 zuòyì 〈旧语〉 (of actors or artists in local drama, storytelling, acrobatics, etc.) stage a performance

作俑 zuòyǒng 〈书面〉 ❶ 〈旧语〉 make a tomb figure or figurine ❷ originate an immoral or bad practice
see also "始作俑者" shǐzuòyǒngzhě

作用 zuòyòng ❶ affect; act on; produce an effect on: ～范围 sphere of action / 反～力 reacting force / 在这种社会环境的～下, 他终于变好了。Affected by (*or* Under the influence of) such a social environment, he at last changed for the better (*or* turned into a decent man). ❷ action: 光合～ photosynthesis / 同化～ assimilation / 化学～ chemical action / ～与反～ action and reaction ❸ effect: 惯性～ inertial effect / 产生副～ produce (*or* have) side effects / 这饮料有提神～。The drink has a refreshing effect (*or* is refreshing). / 你这样做只能起到反～。What you did would only have the opposite effect (*or* would only be counterproductive). / 惩罚对她不起～。Punishment has no effect on her. / 他的话不起～。His words fell on deaf ears. ❹ role; function: 肾脏的～ function of the kidneys / 起积极～ play a positive role / 起形容词的～ function as adjectives / 这开关不起～。The switch doesn't work. ❺ intention; motive: 他那样说是另有～。He had ulterior motives in saying that.

作用力 zuòyònglì 〈物理〉 acting force

作乐 zuòyuè ❶ compose or write music ❷ play music
see also zuòlè

作战 zuòzhàn fight a battle; fight; conduct operations: 并肩～ fight side by side / 连续～ consecutive operations / ～部署 operational preparations / ～地图 battle (*or* operation) map / ～方案 battle plan; line of action / ～方法 method of fighting; tactics in operations / ～方针 concept of operations; operational principles; operational policy / ～间隙 break in the fighting; interval between wars / 实际～经验 practical experience in fighting / ～区域 theatre of war / ～指挥部 operational headquarters

作者 zuòzhě author; writer: ～不详 by an anonymous author; authorship unknown / ～赠 with the compliments of the author / 《子夜》的～是茅盾。*Midnight* was written by Mao Dun.

作证 zuòzhèng ❶ be used as proof or evidence ❷ testify; give evidence; give testimony; bear witness: 传某人～ summon sb. to testify (in court); call sb. to witness; call sb. in evidence / 在法庭～ bear witness in a law court / 在参议院～ give testimony before the senate / 作伪证 give false evidence; bear false witness / 他的朋友为他

～。His friend testified for him. /这事我可以～。I can give evidence on the matter.

作中 zuòzhōng act as a middleman; be an intermediary:此事由范先生～。Mr. Fan will act as the middleman for the matter.

作准 zuòzhǔn ❶ *see* "作数" ❷ valid; authentic:～文本 authentic text /这份合同经双方签字并得到公证后才能～。This contract will be valid only after the signatures are notarized.

胙 zuò 〈古语〉sacrificial meat:宗庙之～ sacrificial meat in an ancestral shrine

阼 zuò 〈古语〉flight of steps on the eastern side of a hall where the host stands to welcome his guests

做(作) zuò ❶ make; manufacture; produce:～鞋 make shoes /上衣～得瘦了点。The coat is (*or* was made) a bit too tight. /家具是杉木～的。The furniture is made of Chinese fir. ❷ write; compose:～一篇文章 write an article /～字典 compile a dictionary ❸ do; act; undertake; engage in:～零活儿 do odd jobs /～好后勤工作 do a good job of logistic support /从点滴的事情～起 start with little things /照多数人的意见～ act upon the views of the majority /～前人没有～过的事情 be engaged in a cause never undertaken by one's forefathers (*or* before) /她～得太过分了。She's gone too far. /说得好不如～得好。Action speaks louder than words. /你能～～他的工作,让他给我们贷款吗? Can you work on (*or* persuade) him to give us a loan? /我们已对双方～了大量工作。We've made tremendous efforts to bring the two parties together. ❹ hold a family celebration:为孙女～生日 celebrate one's granddaughter's birthday; hold (*or* throw) a birthday party for one's granddaughter ❺ be; become:～老实人 be an honest person /给主席～翻译 act as an interpreter for the chairman; interpret for the chairman /～哥哥的应爱护弟妹。Being the elder brother, one should take good care of the younger ones. ❻ be used as; serve as:用这条裙子～样品 use this skirt as a model /这雨伞也可以～拐杖。The umbrella can serve as a walking stick. ❼ form or contract a relationship:～朋友 make friends (with sb.); become friends /～对头 set oneself against sb.; be hostile to sb. ❽ pretend; feign; make believe; do sth. for appearance sake:他的谦虚不过是～～样子的。His modesty is all put on. *or* He is just being modest. /她一点儿没吃,只是放了点儿在盘子里～～样子。She didn't take any of the food, but just put a bit on the plate for appearance sake (*or* for the sake of appearance).

做爱 zuò'ài make love; have sex; go to bed with sb.

做伴 zuòbàn keep sb. company:人老了要有个人～。When one gets old, company is much needed. /有你～,我很高兴。I am very glad to have your company.

做操 zuòcāo do gymnastics; do exercises; do workout; work out

做大 zuòdà *also* "作大" zuòdà (often used in the early vernacular) put on airs; assume airs

做到 zuòdào accomplish; attain; achieve:～投资少,见效快 ensure quicker results with less investment /～仁至义尽 display the greatest magnanimity towards; show the utmost tolerance and patience towards /说到～ be as good as one's word; be true to one's promise; one's word is one's bond /他能～,你为什么做不到? If he can do it, why can't you?

做东 zuòdōng play the host; act as host to sb.; host sb.:今天我～,请你们吃西餐。I'll play the host today and treat you to Western-style food. /这次我～。This is my treat.

做法 zuòfǎ *also* "作法" zuòfǎ way of doing or making a thing; practice:习惯～ habitual (*or* conventional) practice /这个玩具～简单。It is easy to make the toy.

做饭 zuòfàn do the cooking; prepare a meal:生火～ start a fire to cook a meal /给他找个～的。Find a cook for him. /你们家谁～? Who does the cooking in your home?

Z

做工 zuògōng ❶ have a job; work:母亲在街道工厂～。Mother works in a neighbourhood workshop. ❷ *see* "做功" ❸ workmanship:～低劣 of poor (*or* inferior) workmanship /～很细 of excellent (*or* fine) workmanship ❹ charge for the making of sth.:这件连衣裙～二十元。The charge for the tailoring of this dress is 20 *yuan*.

做工夫 zuò gōngfu *also* "做功夫" ❶ (of actors, acrobats, etc.) practise their skill; put in time and energy in the improvement of their skill:在创作上～ concentrate one's efforts on creative work ❷ 〈方言〉work; do manual labour:我给他家做过工夫。I once worked in his house.

做公的 zuògōngde (often used in the early vernacular) runner or bailiff in a feudal *yamen*

做功 zuògōng *also* "做工"〈戏剧〉acting; stage business; business:擅长～ be good at acting

做官 zuòguān hold an official position; be an official:～当老爷 act as bureaucrats and overlords (*or* as bureaucratic overlords) /～儿的应该了解民情。Those in office should acquaint themselves with (*or* understand, *or* have a good grasp of) the condition and feelings of the people.

做鬼 zuòguǐ play tricks; practise deceit; be up to mischief:提防他暗中～。Beware of his tricks.

做鬼脸 zuò guǐliǎn make a wry face; make or pull faces; make grimaces:她尝了口酸葡萄,对我做了个鬼脸。She tasted the sour grapes and made a face at me. /那小男孩冲着小伙伴～嘲笑人家。The little boy thumbed his nose at his playmate.

做好人 zuò hǎorén try to be a good chap or fellow; get along with others often making no distinction between right and wrong

做好做歹 zuòhǎo-zuòdǎi ❶ try every possible way to persuade sb.:我们～地劝他跟我们走。We tried every possible means to persuade him to go with us. ❷ no matter in what way; anyhow:他们～地给他松了绑,把他放了。They untied him anyhow and set him free.

做活局子 zuò huójúzi gang up to cheat or trap sb.

做活儿 zuòhuór do manual labour; work:整年价～ toil all the year round

做绝 zuòjué push to the outside limit; leave no room or leeway for manoeuvre; allow no latitude:把事情～ push things to the extreme; leave oneself no avenue of retreat; pass the point of no return /坏事～ perpetrate every kind of villainy

做客 zuòkè be a guest:昨天我到老师家～了。I was a guest at my teacher's yesterday. /欢迎你来我家～。You are welcome to my house.

做礼拜 zuò lǐbài 〈基督教〉go to church; be at church; worship

做脸 zuòliǎn *also* "作脸" zuòliǎn win honour or glory (for sb.); do credit (to sb.)

做买卖 zuò mǎimai buy and sell; do business:做了一笔买卖 conclude a deal /～的 businessman; merchant; trader

做满月 zuò mǎnyuè hold a dinner party when a baby is one month old

做媒 zuòméi be a matchmaker or go-between:为他俩～ act as a matchmaker for them

做梦 zuòmèng ❶ have a dream; dream:老～ dream a lot /做恶梦 have a nightmare /她～也没想到会有这么好的机会。She never dreamt that such good opportunity would knock on her door (*or* come her way). ❷ daydream; have a pipe dream:你想要这个位子,做什么梦! You want this position? You must be daydreaming!

做派 zuòpai *see* "做功"

做亲 zuòqīn ❶ become related by marriage ❷ be united in marriage; get married

做情 zuòqing *see* "作情" zuòqing

做圈套 zuò quāntào set a trap or snare; set out to trap sb.:他们做好圈套,让我们钻了进去。They set the trap for us, and we walked right into it.

做人 zuòrén ❶ behave; conduct oneself; get along with people:懂得～处世的道理 know how to conduct oneself in society /不会～ not know how to behave tactfully in society ❷ be a person of integrity:重新～ turn over a new leaf

做人家 zuò rénjiā 〈方言〉thrifty; frugal:她平时不乱花钱,非常会～。She spends money cautiously and is rather thrifty.

做人情 zuò rénqíng do sb. a special favour:做个顺水人情 do sb. a favour at little cost to oneself /可别把我的书拿去～。Don't you make a gift of my books!

做生活 zuò shēnghuó 〈方言〉do manual labour; work; toil

做生日 zuò shēngri celebrate one's birthday:给朋友～ celebrate one's friend's birthday

做生意 zuò shēngyi do business; be engaged in trade:～的 businessman; trader; merchant /～要有本钱。You've got to have capital to start a business. /他做了多年生意了。He's engaged in trade for years. /这老头儿从不做亏本生意。The old man never sells at a loss.

做声 zuòshēng make a sound (as when speaking, etc.):别～! Hush! *or* Keep quiet! /叫我左右为难,～不得。I found myself in an

awkward predicament (*or* I was put on the spot), not knowing what to say.

做事 zuòshì ❶ do a deed; handle affairs; act: 做好事 do a good deed / 做家务事 do housework; do household chores / 热心为老百姓～ earnestly serve the ordinary people / 她～向来认真负责。She is conscientious in everything she does. / 叫你儿子别去做那傻事。Tell your son not to make an ass of himself over that matter. / ～不能不计后果。One must not act without considering the consequences. ❷ work; be employed; have a job: 我姐姐在银行～。My elder sister works in a bank.

做手 zuòshǒu 〈方言〉❶ raise one's hand to strike; hit out: 他～未免狠一点儿。He hit a bit too hard. ❷ deft hands ❸ manpower; hand; worker: 吃饭的人多，～少。We have many mouths to feed but few hands to work.

做手脚 zuò shǒujiǎo juggle things; rig a situation or job: 很明显，这事他做了手脚。It's obvious that he rigged it.

做寿 zuòshòu celebrate a birthday (usu. of an elderly person); give a birthday party: 我们昨天为祖母～了。We held a party to celebrate my grandmother's birthday yesterday.

做文章 zuò wénzhāng ❶ write an essay ❷ make an issue of; make a fuss over; try to capitalize on: 做表面文章 put on a show; be flashy and without substance / 别以为你可以利用我的失误～。Don't think you can capitalize on my mistake. / 一点儿小事，她就大～。She made a fuss about a trifling matter. / 他想抓住这件事～。He tried to seize upon the matter and make an issue of it.

做戏 zuòxì ❶ act in a play ❷ put on a show; play-act: 逢场～ join in sth. merely for fun without taking it seriously; act in the spirit of the occasion / 你别在我面前～! Don't you try to put on a show in front of me!

做小 zuòxiǎo be sb.'s concubine

做学问 zuò xuéwen do academic work; engage in scholarly research: 他是～的人，不懂交际。He is a scholar and no good at socializing.

做眼 zuòyǎn (often used in the early vernacular) be a scout

做眼色 zuò yǎnsè 〈方言〉close and open one eye as a signal; tip sb. the wink; wink at sb.: 她在一旁～，让他别说了。She winked at him, signalling that he should shut up.

做样子 zuò yàngzi make a show; go through the motions; do sth. for the sake of appearance: 她这只不过是做做样子而已，表示她有诚心。She was merely making a show of her sincerity.

做一天和尚撞一天钟 zuò yī tiān héshang zhuàng yī tiān zhōng *also* "当一天和尚撞一天钟" go on tolling the bell as long as one is a monk — do the least that is expected of one; do one's job perfunctorily: 采取～的态度 adopt a come-day-go-day attitude

做贼心虚 zuòzéi-xīnxū have a guilty conscience: 他们一再推委搪塞，正暴露他们～。In repeatedly trying to give us the run-around, they betrayed their own guilty conscience.

做张做智 zuòzhāng-zuòzhì (often used in the early vernacular) strike a pose; behave affectedly; attitudinize

做针线 zuò zhēnxian do needlework; sew: 坐在火炉旁～ sit sewing by the fire

做主 zuòzhǔ *also* "作主" zuòzhǔ ❶ decide; have the final say: 她的事我可做不了主。I am in no position to decide for her. *or* It's not up to me to make decision for her. / 家里的事他只能做一半主。He has only half the say in his family. / 这事是她自己～办的。She did it on her own responsibility. / 婚姻大事应由她自己～。She has the right to marry the man of her choice. *or* She is free to choose the man she wishes to marry. ❷ back up; uphold; support: 有厂长给你～呢，放手干吧! Go ahead boldly with your work, as you have the factory director to back you up.

做作 zuòzuo unnatural; affected; artificial: 举止～ be affected in manner; have artificial manners / 表情～ wear an unnatural expression / 女主角的表演太～。The leading lady's acting is overdone. / 他的～令人厌恶。His affectations are disgusting.

Z

西文字母开头的词语
Words or Expressions Beginning with Western Letters

α 粒子　*also* "阿尔法粒子" α particle; alpha particle
α 射线　*also* "阿尔法射线" α (particle) ray; alpha ray
α 衰变　α-decay (often accompanied by radiation)
β 粒子　*also* "贝塔粒子" β particle; beta particle
β 射线　*also* "贝塔射线" β ray; beta ray
β 衰变　β-decay
γ 刀　*also* "伽马刀"〈医学〉gamma knife
γ 射线　*also* "伽马射线" γ ray; gamma ray: ～源〈天文〉gamma ray source
A 型血　blood type A
A 种股票　(shortened as A 股) A-share, renminbi-valued share issued for Chinese natural and artificial persons only and purchased or sold domestically
AA 制　Dutch treat; going Dutch
AB 角　two actors or actresses who alternate in the role of a play
AB 型血　blood type AB
AB 制　system in which two actors or actresses alternate in the role of a play
ABC 武器　atomic, bacteriological and chemical weapons
APS 胶卷　APS (advanced photo system) film
APS 照相机　APS (advanced photo system) camera
ATM 机　*also* "自动取款机"; "自动柜员机" automated teller machine; ATM
B 超　ultrasonic diagnosis B; ultrasonic diagnostic apparatus B: 做～ undergo ultrasonic diagnosis B
B 夸克　beauty quark, a drug
B 型血　blood type B
B 种股票　*also* "人民币特种股票" (shortened as B 股) B-share, a renminbi-valued share issued for oversea investors and purchased or sold in hard currencies at stock exchanges in Shanghai (上海) and Shenzhen (深圳)
BP 机　*also* "寻呼机"; "呼机" beeper; pager
C 值　DNA content
CC 系　〈历史〉CC Faction (a faction of the Kuomintang, 1928-1949, headed by Ch'en Kuo-fu 陈果夫 and Ch'en Li-fu 陈立夫, with the Central Club as its venue, the initials standing for both the Ch'ens and the Central Club)
CD 机　CD (compact disk) player
CT 机　CT (computerized tomography) apparatus
CT 扫描　computerized tomography
DNA 基因图　DNA (deoxyribonucleic acid) profile: ～测定 DNA profiling
DNA 芯片　*also* "基因芯片"〈医学〉DNA chip (for diagnosing hereditary and infectious diseases)
DNA 指纹　DNA fingerprint: ～鉴定 DNA fingerprinting
DVD 机　DVD (digital video disk) player
F-1 赛车　Formula One racing (car); F-1 racing
H 种股票　(shortened as H 股) H-share, a special renminbi-valued share issued by state-owned Chinese corporations to raise funds in Hong Kong and traded in hard currencies
IC 卡　IC card
IP 电话　Internet phone; IP
IP 卡　IP (Internet phone) card
ISO 9000 系列标准　ISO (International Standards Organization) 9000 Serial Standards (for quality control), adopted in 1987
IT 产业　*also* "信息技术产业" IT (information technology) industry
K 金　carat gold: 14～ 14 carat gold (58.3% gold)/18～ 18 carat gold (75% gold)/24～ 24 carat gold (100% gold)
Ma 数　*also* "马赫数" Mach number
n 型半导体　negative semiconductor; N-semiconductor
O 型血　blood type O
p 型半导体　positive semiconductor; P-semiconductor
PC 机　*also* "个人电脑" PC; personal computer
pH 计　*also* "酸度计" pH meter (for measuring the concentration of hydrogen ions in solutions)
pH 值　pH value; pH
PTC 陶瓷　PTC (positive temperature coefficient) porcelain
SOS 儿童村　special philanthropic institution for taking in and looking after orphans
SPF 动物　*also* "无特定病原动物" SPF animal
T 恤衫　T-shirt
VCD 机　VCD (video compact disk) player
X 光　*also* "X 射线"; "爱克斯光" X-ray
X 射线源　X-ray source; X-ray burster

附 录

Appendices

1. 中国历史年代简表

A Brief Chronology of Chinese History

<table>
<tr><td colspan="2" rowspan="5">五帝时代
Period of the Five Legendary Rulers
c.2600 BC － 1600 BC</td><td colspan="2">黄帝 Huangdi (Yellow Emperor)</td></tr>
<tr><td colspan="2">颛顼 Zhuanxu</td></tr>
<tr><td colspan="2">帝喾 Diku (Emperor Ku)</td></tr>
<tr><td colspan="2">唐尧 Yao of Tang</td></tr>
<tr><td colspan="2">虞舜 Shun of Yu</td></tr>
<tr><td colspan="2">夏 Xia Dynasty</td><td colspan="2">c.2100 BC － c.1600 BC</td></tr>
<tr><td colspan="2">商 Shang Dynasty</td><td colspan="2">c.1600 BC － c.1100 BC</td></tr>
<tr><td colspan="2">西周 Western Zhou Dynasty</td><td colspan="2">c.1100 BC － c.771 BC</td></tr>
<tr><td rowspan="2">东周
Eastern Zhou Dynasty
770 BC － 256 BC</td><td>春秋
Spring and Autumn Period</td><td colspan="2">770 BC － 476 BC</td></tr>
<tr><td>战国 Warring States Period</td><td colspan="2">475 BC － 221 BC</td></tr>
<tr><td colspan="2">秦 Qin Dynasty</td><td colspan="2">221 BC － 206 BC</td></tr>
<tr><td rowspan="2">汉 Han Dynasty
206 BC － 220 AD</td><td>西汉 Western Han</td><td colspan="2">206 BC － 25 AD</td></tr>
<tr><td>东汉 Eastern Han</td><td colspan="2">25 － 220</td></tr>
<tr><td rowspan="3">三国 Three Kingdoms
220 － 280</td><td>魏 Wei</td><td colspan="2">220 － 265</td></tr>
<tr><td>蜀汉 Shu Han</td><td colspan="2">221 － 263</td></tr>
<tr><td>吴 Wu</td><td colspan="2">222 － 280</td></tr>
<tr><td rowspan="2">晋 Jin Dynasty
265 － 420</td><td>西晋 Western Jin</td><td colspan="2">265 － 316</td></tr>
<tr><td>东晋 Eastern Jin</td><td colspan="2">317 － 420</td></tr>
<tr><td rowspan="9">南北朝
Northern and
Southern Dynasties
386 － 589</td><td rowspan="4">南朝 Southern Dynasties</td><td>宋 Song</td><td>420 － 479</td></tr>
<tr><td>齐 Qi</td><td>479 － 502</td></tr>
<tr><td>梁 Liang</td><td>502 － 557</td></tr>
<tr><td>陈 Chen</td><td>557 － 589</td></tr>
<tr><td rowspan="5">北朝 Northern Dynasties</td><td>北魏 Northern Wei</td><td>386 － 534</td></tr>
<tr><td>东魏 Eastern Wei</td><td>534 － 550</td></tr>
<tr><td>北齐 Northern Qi</td><td>550 － 577</td></tr>
<tr><td>西魏 Western Wei</td><td>535 － 556</td></tr>
<tr><td>北周 Northern Zhou</td><td>557 － 581</td></tr>
<tr><td colspan="2">隋 Sui Dynasty</td><td colspan="2">581 － 618</td></tr>
<tr><td colspan="2">唐 Tang Dynasty</td><td colspan="2">618 － 907</td></tr>
</table>

<table>
<tr><td rowspan="16">五代十国
Five Dynasties and
Ten States</td><td rowspan="5">五　代
Five Dynasties
907 - 960</td><td>后梁 Later Liang</td><td>907 - 923</td></tr>
<tr><td>后唐 Later Tang</td><td>923 - 936</td></tr>
<tr><td>后晋 Later Jin</td><td>936 - 946</td></tr>
<tr><td>后汉 Later Han</td><td>947 - 950</td></tr>
<tr><td>后周 Later Zhou</td><td>951 - 960</td></tr>
<tr><td rowspan="11">十　国
Ten States
902 - 979</td><td>北汉 Northern Han</td><td>951 - 979</td></tr>
<tr><td>吴 Wu</td><td>902 - 937</td></tr>
<tr><td>南唐 Southern Tang</td><td>937 - 975</td></tr>
<tr><td>吴越 Wuyue</td><td>907 - 978</td></tr>
<tr><td>闽 Min</td><td>909 - 945</td></tr>
<tr><td>南汉 Southern Han</td><td>917 - 971</td></tr>
<tr><td>楚 Chu</td><td>927 - 951</td></tr>
<tr><td>荆南(又称“南平”)
Jingnan (also Nanping)</td><td>924 - 963</td></tr>
<tr><td>前蜀 Former Shu</td><td>907 - 925</td></tr>
<tr><td>后蜀 Later Shu</td><td>934 - 965</td></tr>
<tr><td rowspan="2">宋 Song Dynasty
960 - 1279</td><td>北宋 Northern Song</td><td colspan="2">960 - 1127</td></tr>
<tr><td>南宋 Southern Song</td><td colspan="2">1127 - 1279</td></tr>
<tr><td colspan="2">辽 Liao (or Qidan, or Chitan)</td><td colspan="2">916 - 1125</td></tr>
<tr><td colspan="2">金 Jin</td><td colspan="2">1115 - 1234</td></tr>
<tr><td colspan="2">西夏 Xixia (or Tangut)</td><td colspan="2">1038 - 1227</td></tr>
<tr><td colspan="2">元 Yuan Dynasty</td><td colspan="2">1279 - 1368 (est. 1206)</td></tr>
<tr><td colspan="2">明 Ming Dynasty</td><td colspan="2">1368 - 1644</td></tr>
<tr><td colspan="2">清 Qing Dynasty</td><td colspan="2">1644 - 1911 (est. 1616)</td></tr>
<tr><td colspan="2">中华民国 Republic of China</td><td colspan="2">1912 - 1949</td></tr>
<tr><td colspan="2">中华人民共和国 the People's Republic of China</td><td colspan="2">1949 -</td></tr>
</table>

2. 中国各民族
Ethnic Groups in China

中 文 in Chinese	汉语拼音 in Pinyin	英 文 in English	中 文 in Chinese	汉语拼音 in Pinyin	英 文 in English
阿昌族	Achang	Achang	傈僳族	Lisu	Lisu
白 族	Bai	Bai	珞巴族	Luoba	Lhoba
保安族	Bao'an	Bonan	满 族	Man	Manchu
布朗族	Bulang	Blang	毛南族	Maonan	Maonan
布依族	Buyi	Bouyei	门巴族	Menba	Monba
朝鲜族	Chaoxian	Korean	蒙古族	Menggu	Mongol
达斡尔族	Dawo'er	Daur	苗 族	Miao	Miao
傣 族	Dai	Dai	仫佬族	Mulao	Mulam
德昂族	De'ang	De'ang	纳西族	Naxi	Naxi
东乡族	Dongxiang	Dongxiang	怒 族	Nu	Nu
侗 族	Dong	Dong	普米族	Pumi	Primi
独龙族	Dulong	Derung	羌 族	Qiang	Qiang
俄罗斯族	Eluosi	Russian	撒拉族	Sala	Salar
鄂伦春族	Elunchun	Oroqen	畲 族	She	She
鄂温克族	Ewenke	Ewenki	水 族	Shui	Sui
高山族	Gaoshan	Gaoshan	塔吉克族	Tajike	Tajik
仡佬族	Gelao	Gelao	塔塔尔族	Tata'er	Tatar
哈尼族	Hani	Hani	土 族	Tu	Tu
哈萨克族	Hasake	Kazak	土家族	Tujia	Tujia
汉 族	Han	Han	佤 族	Wa	Va
赫哲族	Hezhe	Hezhen	维吾尔族	Weiwu'er	Uygur
回 族	Hui	Hui	乌孜别克族	Wuzibieke	Uzbek
基诺族	Jinuo	Jino	锡伯族	Xibo	Xibe
京 族	Jing	Gin	彝 族	Yi	Yi
景颇族	Jingpo	Jingpo	瑶 族	Yao	Yao
柯尔克孜族	Ke'erkezi	Kirgiz	裕固族	Yugu	Yugur
拉祜族	Lahu	Lahu	藏 族	Zang	Tibetan
黎 族	Li	Li	壮 族	Zhuang	Zhuang

3. 亲属关系
Family Relationships

(1) 赵新的家 Zhao Xin's Family

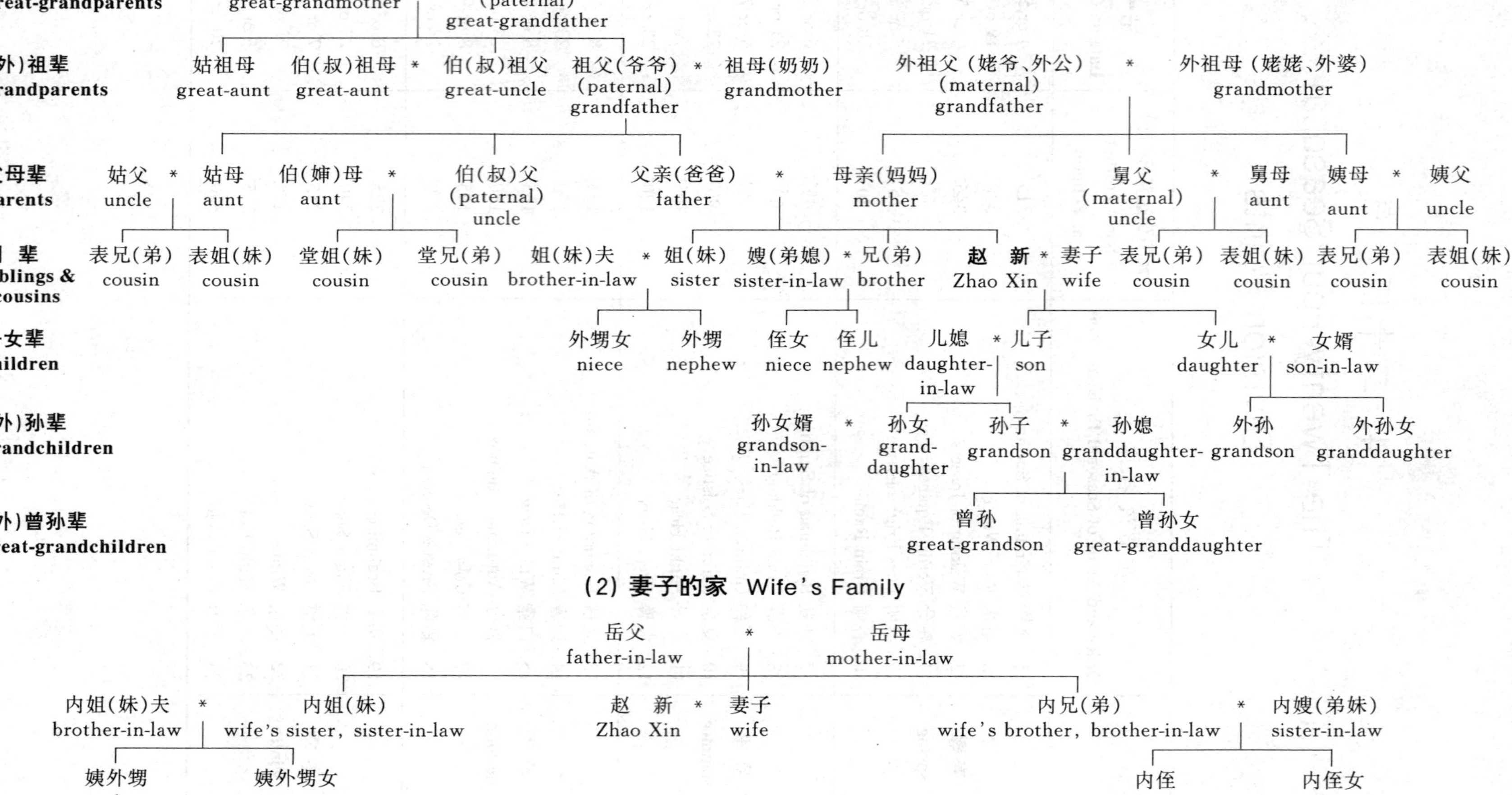

(2) 妻子的家 Wife's Family

注：* = 嫁娶 married to

附录

4. 二十四节气

The Twenty-Four Seasonal Division Points

	节 气 名、序 Order and Name of Seasonal Division Point	太阳到达黄经(度) Sun's Position at Ecliptic	节气的公历日期 Date on Gregorian Calendar
春季 spring	1. 立春 Beginning of Spring	315°	4 or 5 February
	2. 雨水 Rain Water	330°	19 or 20 February
	3. 惊蛰 Waking of Insects	345°	6 or 5 March
	4. 春分 Vernal Equinox	0°	21 or 20 March
	5. 清明 Pure Brightness	15°	5 or 6 April
	6. 谷雨 Grain Rain	30°	20 or 21 April
夏季 summer	7. 立夏 Beginning of Summer	45°	6 or 5 May
	8. 小满 Grain Budding	60°	21 or 22 May
	9. 芒种 Grain in Ear	75°	6 or 7 June
	10. 夏至 Summer Solstice	90°	22 or 21 June
	11. 小暑 Slight Heat	105°	7 or 8 July
	12. 大暑 Great Heat	120°	23 or 24 July
秋季 autumn	13. 立秋 Beginning of Autumn	135°	8 or 7 August
	14. 处暑 Limit of Heat	150°	23 or 24 August
	15. 白露 White Dew	165°	8 or 7 September
	16. 秋分 Autumnal Equinox	180°	23 or 24 September
	17. 寒露 Cold Dew	195°	8 or 9 October
	18. 霜降 Frost's Descent	210°	24 or 23 October
冬季 winter	19. 立冬 Beginning of Winter	225°	8 or 7 November
	20. 小雪 Slight Snow	240°	23 or 22 November
	21. 大雪 Great Snow	255°	7 or 8 December
	22. 冬至 Winter Solstice	270°	22 or 23 December
	23. 小寒 Slight Cold	285°	6 or 5 January
	24. 大寒 Great Cold	300°	20 or 21 January

5. 天干地支
(*tiangan dizhi*)
Heavenly Stems and Earthly Branches

天　干　(*tiangan*) **Heavenly Stem**	相　应　元　素 **Corresponding Element**	相　应　星　宿 **Corresponding Star**
甲(*jia*) Heavenly Stem One	木 wood	木星 Jupiter
乙(*yi*) Heavenly Stem Two		
丙(*bing*) Heavenly Stem Three	火 fire	火星 Mars
丁(*ding*) Heavenly Stem Four		
戊(*wu*) Heavenly Stem Five	土 earth	土星 Saturn
己(*ji*) Heavenly Stem Six		
庚(*geng*) Heavenly Stem Seven	金 metal	金星 Venus
辛(*xin*) Heavenly Stem Eight		
壬(*ren*) Heavenly Stem Nine	水 water	水星 Mercury
癸(*gui*) Heavenly Stem Ten		

地　支　(*dizhi*) **Earthly Branch**	生　肖 **Symbolic Animal**	相应时间 **Corresponding Hours**
子(*zi*) Earthly Branch One	鼠 Rat	11:00 p.m.-1:00 a.m.
丑(*chou*) Earthly Branch Two	牛 Ox	1:00-3:00 a.m.
寅(*yin*) Earthly Branch Three	虎 Tiger	3:00-5:00 a.m.
卯(*mao*) Earthly Branch Four	兔 Rabbit	5:00-7:00 a.m.
辰(*chen*) Earthly Branch Five	龙 Dragon	7:00-9:00 a.m.
巳(*si*) Earthly Branch Six	蛇 Snake	9:00-11:00 a.m.
午(*wu*) Earthly Branch Seven	马 Horse	11:00 a.m.-1:00 p.m.
未(*wei*) Earthly Branch Eight	羊 Sheep	1:00-3:00 p.m.
申(*shen*) Earthly Branch Nine	猴 Monkey	3:00-5:00 p.m.
酉(*you*) Earthly Branch Ten	鸡 Rooster	5:00-7:00 p.m.
戌(*xu*) Earthly Branch Eleven	狗 Dog	7:00-9:00 p.m.
亥(*hai*) Earthly Branch Twelve	猪 Pig	9:00-11:00 p.m.

6. 甲子纪年*

60年顺序 Order of Year in Cycle	1	2	3	4	5
干支名称 Combination of Heavenly Stem with Earthly Branch	甲　子 Heavenly Stem 1 Earthly Branch 1	乙　丑 Heavenly Stem 2 Earthly Branch 2	丙　寅 Heavenly Stem 3 Earthly Branch 3	丁　卯 Heavenly Stem 4 Earthly Branch 4	戊　辰 Heavenly Stem 5 Earthly Branch 5
汉语拼音 Pinyin	*jiazi*	*yichou*	*bingyin*	*dingmao*	*wuchen*
公历纪年 Corresponding Gregorian Year	1924 1984	1925 1985	1926 1986	1927 1987	1928 1988
60年顺序 Order of Year in Cycle	13	14	15	16	17
干支名称 Combination of Heavenly Stem with Earthly Branch	丙　子 Heavenly Stem 3 Earthly Branch 1	丁　丑 Heavenly Stem 4 Earthly Branch 2	戊　寅 Heavenly Stem 5 Earthly Branch 3	己　卯 Heavenly Stem 6 Earthly Branch 4	庚　辰 Heavenly Stem 7 Earthly Branch 5
汉语拼音 Pinyin	*bingzi*	*dingchou*	*wuyin*	*jimao*	*gengchen*
公历纪年 Corresponding Gregorian Year	1936 1996	1937 1997	1938 1998	1939 1999	1940 2000
60年顺序 Order of Year in Cycle	25	26	27	28	29
干支名称 Combination of Heavenly Stem with Earthly Branch	戊　子 Heavenly Stem 5 Earthly Branch 1	己　丑 Heavenly Stem 6 Earthly Branch 2	庚　寅 Heavenly Stem 7 Earthly Branch 3	辛　卯 Heavenly Stem 8 Earthly Branch 4	壬　辰 Heavenly Stem 9 Earthly Branch 5
汉语拼音 Pinyin	*wuzi*	*jichou*	*gengyin*	*xinmao*	*renchen*
公历纪年 Corresponding Gregorian Year	1948 2008	1949 2009	1950 2010	1951 2011	1952 2012
60年顺序 Order of Year in Cycle	37	38	39	40	41
干支名称 Combination of Heavenly Stem with Earthly Branch	庚　子 Heavenly Stem 7 Earthly Branch 1	辛　丑 Heavenly Stem 8 Earthly Branch 2	壬　寅 Heavenly Stem 9 Earthly Branch 3	癸　卯 Heavenly Stem 10 Earthly Branch 4	甲　辰 Heavenly Stem 1 Earthly Branch 5
汉语拼音 Pinyin	*gengzi*	*xinchou*	*renyin*	*guimao*	*jiachen*
公历纪年 Corresponding Gregorian Year	1960 2020	1961 2021	1962 2022	1963 2023	1964 2024
60年顺序 Order of Year in Cycle	49	50	51	52	53
干支名称 Combination of Heavenly Stem with Earthly Branch	壬　子 Heavenly Stem 9 Earthly Branch 1	癸　丑 Heavenly Stem 10 Earthly Branch 2	甲　寅 Heavenly Stem 1 Earthly Branch 3	乙　卯 Heavenly Stem 2 Earthly Branch 4	丙　辰 Heavenly Stem 3 Earthly Branch 5
汉语拼音 Pinyin	*renzi*	*guichou*	*jiayin*	*yimao*	*bingchen*
公历纪年 Corresponding Gregorian Year	1972 2032	1973 2033	1974 2034	1975 2035	1976 2036
生　肖** Symbolic Animal	鼠 Rat	牛 Ox	虎 Tiger	兔 Rabbit	龙 Dragon

注：* **甲子纪年**：中国农历纪年法。以干支依次相配，如甲子、乙丑、丙寅等，自甲子至癸亥，每组代表一年，其数凡六十（如表所示），称"六十甲子"。本甲子纪年表取两个周期（1924-1983，1984-2043），以示其周而复始，循环使用之妙。只要知道公历某年的干支名称，即可往前后推算得知各年的干支名称，反之亦然。

The Sixty-Year Jia-Zi Cycle, used to indicate the sequence of years in traditional Chinese calendar and historical chronology, combines each of the 10 Heavenly Stems with one of the 12 Earthly Branches to refer to a given year, until a total of 60 combinations representing 60 years are formed (as shown in the above chart). The pattern repeats itself *ad infinitum*. The above Jia-Zi Cycle is represented as corresponding to two 60-year periods of the Gregorian calendar (i.e. 1924-1983, 1984-2043), to illustrate its infinite repetitions. Thus, whenever a Gregorian

Sixty-Year Jia-Zi Cycle—
Traditional Chinese Chronology

6	7	8	9	10	11	12
己 巳 Heavenly Stem 6 Earthly Branch 6	庚 午 Heavenly Stem 7 Earthly Branch 7	辛 未 Heavenly Stem 8 Earthly Branch 8	壬 申 Heavenly Stem 9 Earthly Branch 9	癸 酉 Heavenly Stem 10 Earthly Branch 10	甲 戌 Heavenly Stem 1 Earthly Branch 11	乙 亥 Heavenly Stem 2 Earthly Branch 12
jisi	*gengwu*	*xinwei*	*renshen*	*guiyou*	*jiaxu*	*yihai*
1929 1989	1930 1990	1931 1991	1932 1992	1933 1993	1934 1994	1935 1995
18	19	20	21	22	23	24
辛 巳 Heavenly Stem 8 Earthly Branch 6	壬 午 Heavenly Stem 9 Earthly Branch 7	癸 未 Heavenly Stem 10 Earthly Branch 8	甲 申 Heavenly Stem 1 Earthly Branch 9	乙 酉 Heavenly Stem 2 Earthly Branch 10	丙 戌 Heavenly Stem 3 Earthly Branch 11	丁 亥 Heavenly Stem 4 Earthly Branch 12
xinsi	*renwu*	*guiwei*	*jiashen*	*yiyou*	*bingxu*	*dinghai*
1941 2001	1942 2002	1943 2003	1944 2004	1945 2005	1946 2006	1947 2007
30	31	32	33	34	35	36
癸 巳 Heavenly Stem 10 Earthly Branch 6	甲 午 Heavenly Stem 1 Earthly Branch 7	乙 未 Heavenly Stem 2 Earthly Branch 8	丙 申 Heavenly Stem 3 Earthly Branch 9	丁 酉 Heavenly Stem 4 Earthly Branch 10	戊 戌 Heavenly Stem 5 Earthly Branch 11	己 亥 Heavenly Stem 6 Earthly Branch 12
guisi	*jiawu*	*yiwei*	*bingshen*	*dingyou*	*wuxu*	*jihai*
1953 2013	1954 2014	1955 2015	1956 2016	1957 2017	1958 2018	1959 2019
42	43	44	45	46	47	48
乙 巳 Heavenly Stem 2 Earthly Branch 6	丙 午 Heavenly Stem 3 Earthly Branch 7	丁 未 Heavenly Stem 4 Earthly Branch 8	戊 申 Heavenly Stem 5 Earthly Branch 9	己 酉 Heavenly Stem 6 Earthly Branch 10	庚 戌 Heavenly Stem 7 Earthly Branch 11	辛 亥 Heavenly Stem 8 Earthly Branch 12
yisi	*bingwu*	*dingwei*	*wushen*	*jiyou*	*gengxu*	*xinhai*
1965 2025	1966 2026	1967 2027	1968 2028	1969 2029	1970 2030	1971 2031
54	55	56	57	58	59	60
丁 巳 Heavenly Stem 4 Earthly Branch 6	戊 午 Heavenly Stem 5 Earthly Branch 7	己 未 Heavenly Stem 6 Earthly Branch 8	庚 申 Heavenly Stem 7 Earthly Branch 9	辛 酉 Heavenly Stem 8 Earthly Branch 10	壬 戌 Heavenly Stem 9 Earthly Branch 11	癸 亥 Heavenly Stem 10 Earthly Branch 12
dingsi	*wuwu*	*jiwei*	*gengshen*	*xinyou*	*renxu*	*guihai*
1977 2037	1978 2038	1979 2039	1980 2040	1981 2041	1982 2042	1983 2043
蛇 Snake	马 Horse	羊 Sheep	猴 Monkey	鸡 Rooster	狗 Dog	猪 Pig

year is confirmed to correspond to a certain combination in this cycle, or vice versa, e.g. 1900＝庚子 (*gengzi*), it is immediately known that 1901 corresponds to 辛丑 (*xinchou*), 1899 to 己亥 (*jihai*) . . . and the rest of the cycle may be inferred.

** **生肖**:12 生肖与 12 地支依次相应。60 甲子之中,12 地支重复出现 5 次,与之相应的 12 生肖亦重复 5 次,但在本表中,12 生肖只在末行列出,以省篇幅。

Symbolic Animals: As the 12 symbolic animals match the 12 Earthly Branches as shown in the chart, so they correspond to each of the five groups of the Branches in the 60-year Cycle and repeat themselves five times accordingly, across the 12 columns, although they are listed only at the bottom of the chart to save space.

7. 中国法定假日和主要传统节日
Official Holidays and Main Traditional Festivals in China

法定假日 *	**Official Holidays ***
元旦	New Year's Day (1 January, 1 day off)
春节	*see next table*
国际劳动妇女节	International Working Women's Day (8 March, $\frac{1}{2}$ day off for women)
国际劳动节	International Labour Day (1 May, 3 days off)
中国青年节	Chinese Youth Day (4 May, $\frac{1}{2}$ day off for youths of and above 14)
国际儿童节	International Children's Day (1 June, 1 day off for those below 14)
中国人民解放军建军节	Army Day (Anniversary of the Founding of the Chinese People's Liberation Army, 1 August, $\frac{1}{2}$ day off for those in active service)
国庆节	National Day (1 October, 3 days off)
传统节日	**Traditional Festivals**
春节	Spring Festival (*or* Chinese New Year's Day, 1st of the first lunar month, 3 days off)
元宵节	Lantern Festival (15th of the first lunar month, marking the end of the Chinese New Year celebrations with a display of colourful lanterns and eating of *yuan-xiao*)
清明节	Pure Brightness Festival (marking the 5th seasonal division point and usually falling on the 5th or 6th of April, a traditional festival for commemorating the dead)
端午节	Dragon Boat Festival (5th of the fifth lunar month, celebrated by eating *zongzi* and holding dragon boat races)
中秋节	Mid-Autumn Festival (15th of the eighth lunar month, a traditional festival for family reunion, celebrated by eating moon cakes and enjoying the full moon)
重阳节	Double Ninth Festival (9th of the ninth lunar month, celebrated by climbing heights to enjoy nature and honouring elderly people)

* 自 1999 年 9 月 21 日生效。

Effective as from 21 September, 1999.

8. 中国民族乐器
Chinese Musical Instruments

中文名称 **Name in Chinese**	英文名称 **Name in English**	解释 **Description**
板胡	*banhu*	two-stringed bowed instrument with a thin wooden soundboard
梆子	*bangzi*	wooden clappers used in accompaniment for certain local operas
编钟	*bianzhong* or chime bells	ancient percussion instrument consisting of a set of copper bells (often 24 or 32), each giving forth a different note when struck
钹	*bo* or cymbals	pair of round brass plates struck together to produce a clanging sound
笛子	*dizi*	bamboo flute
冬不拉	*dongbula* or *dombira*	plucked stringed instrument, used by the ethnic Kazak people
二胡	*erhu*	two-stringed bowed instrument, slightly lower in tone than *jinghu*; two-stringed fiddle
古琴	*guqin*	seven-stringed plucked instrument; Chinese zither
鼓	*gu* or drum	
笳	*jia*	Tatar reed flute used in ancient times
伽倻琴	*jiayeqin* or *kayago*	twelve-stringed (possibly 13 to 18-stringed, or even 21-stringed) plucked instrument, used by the ethnic Korean people
京胡	*jinghu*	two-stringed bowed instrument specially used for Beijing opera; Beijing opera fiddle
箜篌	*konghou*	plucked stringed instrument used in ancient times
柳琴	*liuqin*	plucked stringed instrument, similar to *pipa* in shape
芦笙	*lusheng*	reed-pipe (wind instrument), used by the ethnic Miao, Yao or Dong peoples
锣	*luo* or gong	
马头琴	*matouqin* or *morin hort*	two-stringed bowed instrument with a scroll carved in the shape of a horse's head, used by the ethnic Mongolian people
木鱼	*muyu* or wooden fish	wooden percussion instrument used to beat rhythm
琵琶	*pipa* or balloon guitar	four-stringed plucked instrument with a fretted fingerboard
羌笛	*qiangdi*	double-piped wind instrument invented by the ancient Qiang ethnic group
磬	*qing* or chime stone	rectangular ancient percussion instrument made of stone or jade, hung from a rack and struck with a wooden hammer (played either as a single instrument or in a set)
热瓦甫	*rewafu* or *rawap*	plucked stringed instrument, used by the ethnic Uygur people

阮咸(阮)	*ruanxian*	four- or three-stringed plucked instrument, an ancient variety of *pipa*
三弦	*sanxian*	three-stringed plucked instrument; three-stringed guitar
瑟	*se*	16- or 25-stringed plucked instrument
笙	*sheng*	bamboo pipe (wind instrument)
唢呐	*suona*	woodwind instrument with seven holes on top and one on the backside
箫	*xiao*	vertical bamboo flute
埙	*xun*	egg-shaped ancient wind instrument made of clay pottery with one to six holes on it
扬琴	*yangqin* or dulcimer	metal-stringed instrument played with two hammers
腰鼓	*yaogu* or waist drum	used in folk dancing
竽	*yu*	reed pipe wind instrument used in ancient times
月琴	*yueqin*	four-stringed moon-shaped instrument; four-stringed mandolin
筝	*zheng*	21- or 25-stringed plucked instrument
竹板	*zhuban*	wooden or bamboo clappers; Chinese castanets

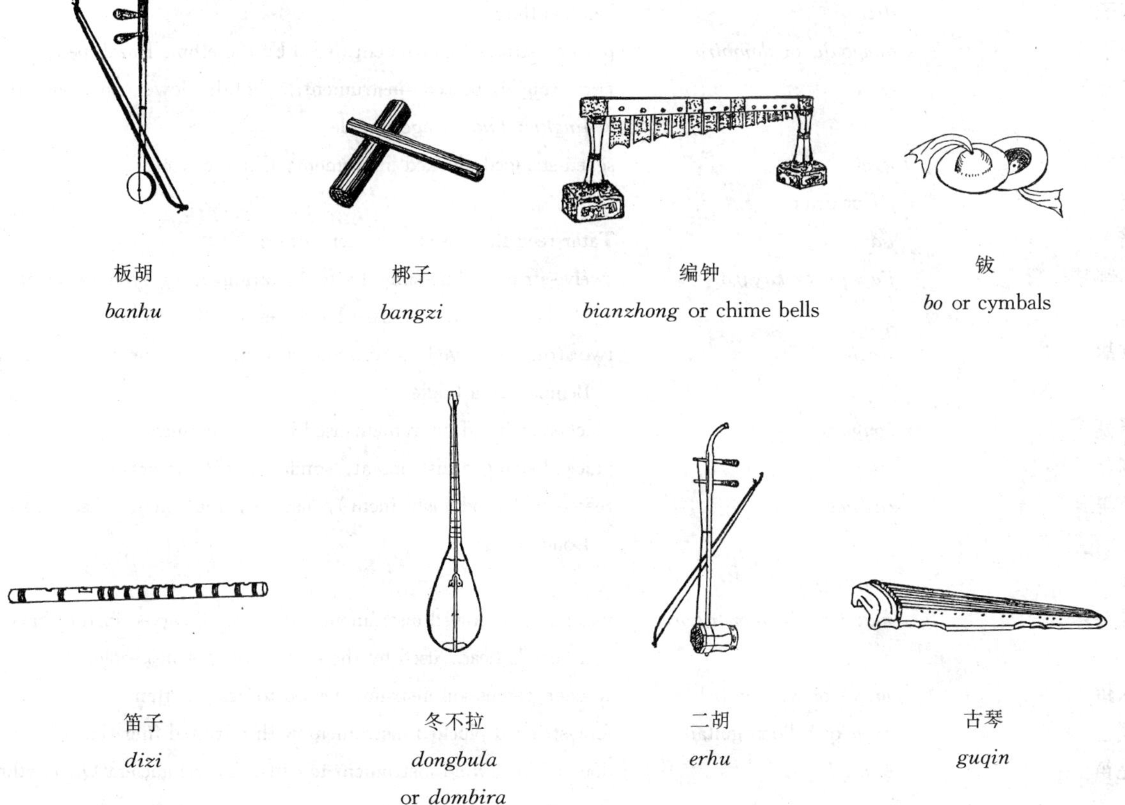

板胡 *banhu*

梆子 *bangzi*

编钟 *bianzhong* or chime bells

钹 *bo* or cymbals

笛子 *dizi*

冬不拉 *dongbula* or *dombira*

二胡 *erhu*

古琴 *guqin*

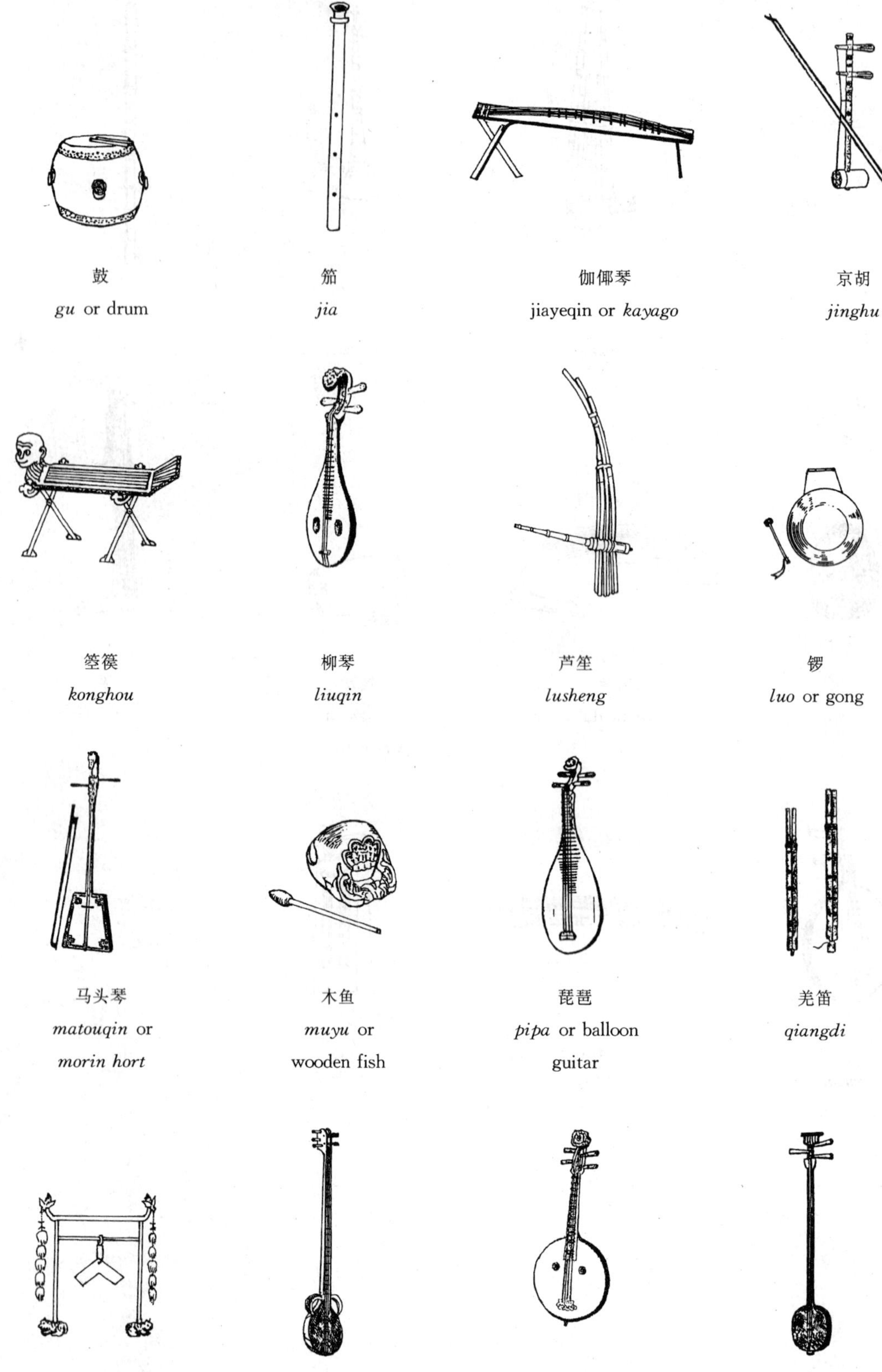

鼓
gu or drum

笳
jia

伽倻琴
jiayeqin or *kayago*

京胡
jinghu

箜篌
konghou

柳琴
liuqin

芦笙
lusheng

锣
luo or gong

马头琴
matouqin or
morin hort

木鱼
muyu or
wooden fish

琵琶
pipa or balloon
guitar

羌笛
qiangdi

磬
qing or
chime stone

热瓦甫
rewafu
or *rawap*

阮咸(阮)
ruanxian

三弦
sanxian

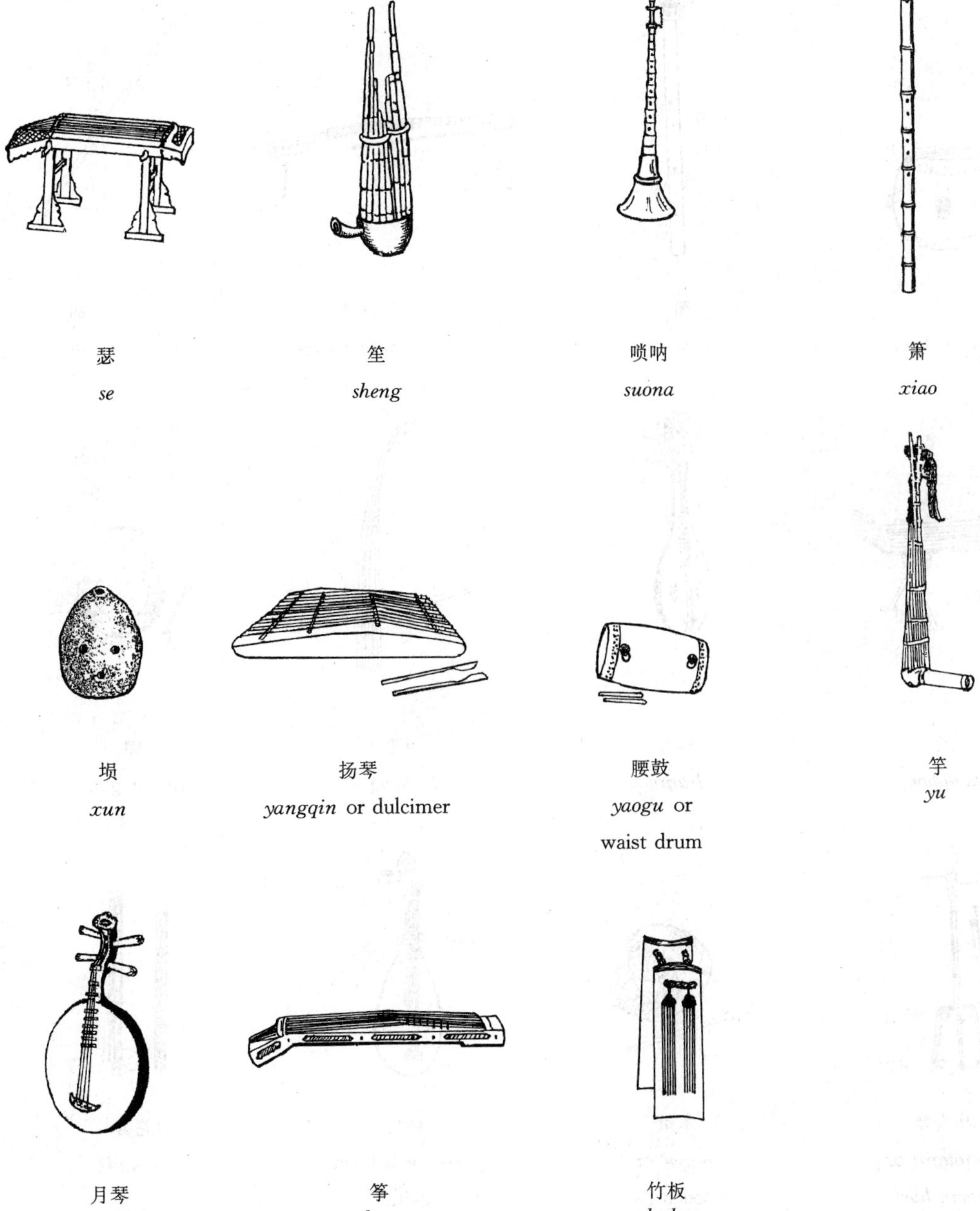

瑟
se

笙
sheng

唢呐
suona

箫
xiao

埙
xun

扬琴
yangqin or dulcimer

腰鼓
yaogu or
waist drum

竽
yu

月琴
yueqin

筝
zheng

竹板
zhuban

(插图由李谋源绘制。Illustrated by Li Mouyuan.)

9. 针灸穴位表

Acupuncture Points

经名 Meridian	穴位 Point	拼音 Pinyin	旧式拼音 Former Transcription	穴位 Point	拼音 Pinyin	旧式拼音 Former Transcription
手太阴肺经 The Arm Greater Yin Lungs Meridian	中府	Zhongfu	Chungfu	列缺	Lieque	Liechueh
	云门	Yunmen	Yunmen	经渠	Jingqu	Chingchu
	天府	Tianfu	Tienfu	太渊	Taiyuan	Taiyuan
	侠白	Xiabai	Hsiapai	鱼际	Yuji	Yuchi
	尺泽	Chize	Chitse	少商	Shaoshang	Shaoshang
	孔最	Kongzui	Kungtsui			
手阳明大肠经 The Arm Sunlight Yang Large Intestine Meridian	商阳	Shangyang	Shangyang	曲尺	Quchi	Chuchih
	二间	Erjian	Erhchien	肘髎	Zhouliao	Chouliao
	三间	Sanjian	Sanchien	五里	Wuli	Wuli
	合谷	Hegu	Hoku	臂臑	Binao	Pinao
	阳溪	Yangxi	Yanghsi	肩髃	Jianyu	Chienyu
	偏历	Pianli	Pienli	巨骨	Jugu	Chuku
	温溜	Wenliu	Wenliu	天鼎	Tianding	Tienting
	下廉	Xialian	Hsialien	扶突	Futu	Futu
	上廉	Shanglian	Shanglien	和髎	Heliao	Holiao
	三里	Sanli	Sanli	迎香	Yingxiang	Yingsiang
足阳明胃经 The Leg Sunlight Yang Stomach Meridian	承泣	Chengqi	Chengchi	滑肉门	Huaroumen	Huajoumen
	四白	Sibai	Szupai	天枢	Tianshu	Tienshu
	巨髎	Juliao	Chuliao	外陵	Wailing	Wailing
	地仓	Dicang	Titsang	大巨	Daju	Tachu
	大迎	Daying	Taying	水道	Shuidao	Shuitao
	颊车	Jiache	Chiache	归来	Guilai	Kuilai
	下关	Xiaguan	Hsiakuan	气冲	Qichong	Chichung
	头维	Touwei	Touwei	髀关	Piguan	Pikuan
	人迎	Renying	Jenying	伏兔	Futu	Futu
	水突	Shuitu	Shuitu	阴市	Yinshi	Yinshih
	气舍	Qishe	Chishe	梁丘	Liangqiu	Liangchiu
	缺盆	Quepen	Chuehpen	犊鼻	Dubi	Tupi
	气户	Qihu	Chihu	足三里	Zusanli	Tsusanli
	库房	Kufang	Kufang	上巨虚	Shangjuxu	Shangchuhsu
	屋翳	Wuyi	Wuyi	条口	Tiaokou	Tiaokou
	膺窗	Yingchuang	Yingchuang	下巨虚	Xiajuxu	Hsiachuhsu
	乳中	Ruzhong	Juchung	丰隆	Fenglong	Fenglung
	乳根	Rugen	Juken	解溪	Jiexi	Chiehhsi
	不容	Burong	Puyung	冲阳	Chongyang	Chungyang
	承满	Chengman	Chengman	陷谷	Xiangu	Hsienku
	梁门	Liangmen	Lianmen	内庭	Neiting	Neiting
	关门	Guanmen	Kuanmen	厉兑	Lidui	Litui
	太乙	Taiyi	Taiyi			

经 名 Meridian	穴 位 Point	拼 音 Pinyin	旧式拼音 Former Transcription	穴 位 Point	拼 音 Pinyin	旧式拼音 Former Transcription
足太阴脾经 The Leg Greater Yin Spleen Meridian	隐白	Yinbai	Yinpai	冲门	Chongmen	Chungmen
	大都	Dadu	Tatu	府舍	Fushe	Fushe
	太白	Taibai	Taipai	腹结	Fujie	Fuchieh
	公孙	Gongsun	Kungsun	大横	Daheng	Taheng
	商丘	Shangqiu	Shangchiu	腹哀	Fu'ai	Fuai
	三阴交	Sanyinjiao	Sanyinchiao	食窦	Shidou	Shihtou
	漏谷	Lougu	Louku	天谿	Tianxi	Tienhsi
	地机	Diji	Tichi	胸乡	Xiongxiang	Hsiunghsiang
	阴陵泉	Yinlingquan	Yinlingchuan	周荣	Zhourong	Chouyung
	血海	Xuehai	Hsuehhai	大包	Dabao	Tapao
	箕门	Jimen	Chimen			
手少阴心经 The Arm Lesser Yin Heart Meridian	极泉	Jiquan	Chichuan	阴郄	Yinxi	Yinhsi
	青灵	Qingling	Chingling	神门	Shenmen	Shenmen
	少海	Shaohai	Shaohai	少府	Shaofu	Shaofu
	灵道	Lingdao	Lingtao	少冲	Shaochong	Shaochung
	通里	Tongli	Tungli			
手太阳小肠经 The Arm Greater Yang Small Intestine Meridian	少泽	Shaoze	Shaotse	天宗	Tianzong	Tientsung
	前谷	Qiangu	Chienku	秉风	Bingfeng	Pingfeng
	后溪	Houxi	Houhsi	曲垣	Quyuan	Chuyuan
	腕骨	Wangu	Wanku	肩外腧	Jianwaishu	Chienwaishu
	阳谷	Yanggu	Yangku	肩中腧	Jianzhongshu	Chienchungshu
	养老	Yanglao	Yanglao	天窗	Tianchuang	Tienchuang
	支正	Zhizheng	Chihcheng	天容	Tianrong	Tienyung
	小海	Xiaohai	Hsiaohai	颧髎	Quanliao	Chuanliao
	肩贞	Jianzhen	Chienchen	听宫	Tinggong	Tingkung
	臑腧	Naoshu	Naoshu			
足太阳膀胱经 The Leg Greater Yang Bladder Meridian	睛明	Jingming	Chingming	肺腧	Feishu	Feishu
	攒竹	Zanzhu	Tsanchu	厥阴腧	Jueyinshu	Chuehyinshu
	眉冲	Meichong	Meichung	心腧	Xinshu	Hsinshu
	曲差	Qucha	Chucha	督腧	Dushu	Tushu
	五处	Wuchu	Wuchu	膈腧	Geshu	Keshu
	承光	Chengguang	Chengkuang	肝腧	Ganshu	Kanshu
	通天	Tongtian	Tungtien	胆腧	Danshu	Tanshu
	络却	Luoque	Lochueh	脾腧	Pishu	Pishu
	玉枕	Yuzhen	Yuchen	胃腧	Weishu	Weishu
	天柱	Tianzhu	Tienchu	三交腧	Sanjiaoshu	Sanchiaoshu
	大杼	Dazhu	Tachu	肾腧	Shenshu	Shenshu
	风门	Fengmen	Fengmen	气海腧	Qihaishu	Chihaishu

经名 Meridian	穴位 Point	拼音 Pinyin	旧式拼音 Former Transcription	穴位 Point	拼音 Pinyin	旧式拼音 Former Transcription
足太阳膀胱经（续） The Leg Greater Yang Bladder Meridian (continued)	大肠腧	Dachangshu	Tachangshu	志室	Zhishi	Chishih
	关元腧	Guanyuanshu	Kuanyuanshu	胞肓	Baohuang	Paohuang
	小肠腧	Xiaochangshu	Hsiaochangshu	秩边	Zhibian	Chihpien
	膀胱腧	Pangguangshu	Pangkuangshu	承扶	Chengfu	Chengfu
	中膂腧	Zhonglüshu	Chunglushu	殷门	Yinmen	Yinmen
	白环腧	Baihuanshu	Paihuanshu	浮郄	Fuxi	Fuhsi
	上髎	Shangliao	Shangliao	委阳	Weiyang	Weiyang
	次髎	Ciliao	Tzuliao	委中	Weizhong	Weichung
	中髎	Zhongliao	Chungliao	合阳	Heyang	Hoyang
	下髎	Xialiao	Hsialiao	承筋	Chengjin	Chengchin
	会阳	Huiyang	Huiyang	承山	Chengshan	Chengshan
	附分	Fufen	Fufen	飞扬	Feiyang	Feiyang
	魄户	Pohu	Pohu	跗阳	Fuyang	Fuyang
	膏肓	Gaohuang	Kaohuang	昆仑	Kunlun	Kunlun
	神堂	Shentang	Shentang	仆参	Pushen	Pushen
	譩譆	Yixi	Yihsi	申脉	Shenmai	Shenmo
	膈关	Geguan	Kekuan	金门	Jinmen	Chinmen
	魂门	Hunmen	Hunmen	京骨	Jinggu	Chingku
	阳纲	Yanggang	Yangkang	束骨	Shugu	Shuku
	意舍	Yishe	Yishe	通谷	Tonggu	Tungku
	胃仓	Weicang	Weitsang	至阴	Zhiyin	Chihyin
	肓门	Huangmen	Huangmen			
足少阴肾经 The Leg Lesser Yin Kidneys Meridian	涌泉	Yongquan	Yungchuan	中注	Zhongzhu	Chungchu
	然谷	Rangu	Janku	肓腧	Huangshu	Huangshu
	太溪	Taixi	Taihsi	商曲	Shangqu	Shangchu
	大钟	Dazhong	Tachung	石关	Shiguan	Shihkuan
	水泉	Shuiquan	Shuichuan	阴都	Yindu	Yintu
	照海	Zhaohai	Chaohai	通谷	Tonggu	Yungku
	复溜	Fuliu	Fuliu	幽门	Youmen	Yumen
	交信	Jiaoxin	Chiaochsin	步廊	Bulang	Pulang
	筑宾	Zhubin	Chupin	神封	Shenfeng	Shenfeng
	阴骨	Yingu	Yinku	灵墟	Lingxu	Linghsu
	横骨	Henggu	Hengku	神藏	Shencang	Shentsang
	大赫	Dahe	Taheh	彧中	Yuzhong	Yuchung
	气穴	Qixue	Chihsueh	腧府	Shufu	Shufu
	四满	Siman	Szuman			
手厥阴心包经 The Arm Absolute Yin Pericardium Meridian	天池	Tianchi	Tienchih	内关	Neiguan	Neikuan
	天泉	Tianquan	Tienchuan	大陵	Daling	Taling
	曲泽	Quze	Chutse	劳宫	Laogong	Laokung
	郄门	Ximen	Hsimen	中冲	Zhongchong	Chungchung
	间使	Jianshi	Chienshih			

附录

经名 Meridian	穴位 Point	拼音 Pinyin	旧式拼音 Former Transcription	穴位 Point	拼音 Pinyin	旧式拼音 Former Transcription
手少阳三焦经 The Arm Lesser Yang Triple Warmer Meridian	关冲	Guanchong	Kuanchung	臑会	Naohui	Naohui
	液门	Yemen	Yemen	肩髎	Jianliao	Chienliao
	中渚	Zhongzhu	Chungchu	天髎	Tianliao	Tienliao
	阳池	Yangchi	Yangchih	天牖	Tianyou	Tienyu
	外关	Waiguan	Waikuan	翳风	Yifeng	Yifeng
	支沟	Zhigou	Chihkou	瘈脉	Qimai	Chihmo
	会宗	Huizong	Huitsung	颅息	Luxi	Lusi
	三阳络	Sanyangluo	Sanyanglo	角孙	Jiaosun	Chuehsun
	四渎	Sidu	Szutu	耳门	Ermen	Erhmen
	天井	Tianjing	Tienching	和髎	Heliao	Holiao
	清冷渊	Qinglengyuan	Chinglengyuan	丝竹空	Sizhukong	Ssuchukung
	消泺	Xiaole	Hsiaolo			
足少阳胆经 The Leg Lesser Yang Gall-Bladder Meridian	瞳子髎	Tongziliao	Tuntzuliao	辄筋	Zhejin	Chechin
	听会	Tinghui	Tinghui	日月	Riyue	Jihyueh
	上关	Shangguan	Shangkuan	京门	Jingmen	Chingmen
	颔厌	Hanyan	Hanyen	带脉	Daimai	Taimo
	悬颅	Xuanlu	Hsuanlu	五枢	Wushu	Wushu
	悬厘	Xuanli	Hsuanli	维道	Weidao	Weitao
	曲鬓	Qubin	Chupin	居髎	Juliao	Chuliao
	率谷	Shuaigu	Shuaiku	环跳	Huantiao	Huantiao
	天冲	Tianchong	Tienchung	风市	Fengshi	Fengshih
	浮白	Fubai	Fupai	中渎	Zhongdu	Chungtu
	窍阴	Qiaoyin	Chiaoyin	膝阳关	Xiyangguan	Hsiyangkuan
	完骨	Wangu	Wanku	阳陵泉	Yang-Lingquan	Yanglingchuan
	本神	Benshen	Penshen	阳交	Yangjiao	Yangchiao
	阳白	Yangbai	Yangpai	外丘	Waiqiu	Waichiu
	临泣	Linqi	Linchi	光明	Guangming	Kuangming
	目窗	Muchuang	Muchuang	阳辅	Yangfu	Yangfu
	正营	Zhengying	Chengying	悬钟	Xuanzhong	Hsuanchung
	承灵	Chengling	Chengling	丘墟	Qiuxu	Chiuhsu
	脑空	Naokong	Naokung	足临泣	Zulinqi	Tsulinchi
	风池	Fengchi	Fengchih	地五会	Diwuhui	Tiwuhui
	肩井	Jianjing	Chienchin	侠溪	Xiaxi	Hsiahsi
	渊液	Yuanye	Yuanyeh	足窍阴	Zuqiaoyin	Tsuchiaoyin
足厥阴肝经 The Leg Absolute Yin Liver Meridian	大敦	Dadun	Tatun	曲泉	Ququan	Chuchuan
	行间	Xingjian	Hsingchien	阴包	Yinbao	Yinpao
	太冲	Taichong	Taichung	五里	Wuli	Wuli
	中封	Zhongfeng	Chungfeng	阴廉	Yinlian	Yinlien
	蠡沟	Ligou	Likou	急脉	Jimai	Chimo
	中都	Zhongdu	Chungtu	章门	Zhangmen	Changmen
	膝关	Xiguan	Hsikuan	期门	Qimen	Chimen

经 名 Meridian	穴 位 Point	拼 音 Pinyin	旧式拼音 Former Transcription	穴 位 Point	拼 音 Pinyin	旧式拼音 Former Transcription
督 脉 The Governing Vessel	龈 交	Yinjiao	Yinchiao	大 椎	Dazhui	Tachui
	兑 端	Duiduan	Tuituan	陶 道	Taodao	Taotao
	水 沟	Shuigou	Shuikou	身 柱	Shenzhu	Shenchu
	素 髎	Suliao	Suliao	神 道	Shendao	Shentao
	神 庭	Shenting	Shenting	灵 台	Lingtai	Lingtai
	上 星	Shangxing	Shanghsing	至 阳	Zhiyang	Chihyang
	囟 会	Xinhui	Hsinhui	筋 缩	Jinsuo	Chinso
	前 顶	Qianding	Chienting	中 枢	Zhongshu	Chungshu
	百 会	Baihui	Paihui	脊 中	Jizhong	Chichung
	后 顶	Houding	Houting	悬 枢	Xuanshu	Hsuanshu
	强 间	Qiangjian	Chiangchien	命 门	Mingmen	Mingmen
	脑 户	Naohu	Naohu	阳 关	Yangguan	Yangkuan
	风 府	Fengfu	Fengfu	腰 腧	Yaoshu	Yaoshu
	哑 门	Yamen	Yamen	长 强	Changqiang	Changchiang
任 脉 The Vessel of Conception	承 浆	Chengjiang	Chengchiang	中 脘	Zhongwan	Chungwan
	廉 泉	Lianquan	Lienchuan	建 里	Jianli	Chienli
	天 突	Tiantu	Tientu	下 脘	Xiawan	Hsiawan
	璇 玑	Xuanji	Hsuanchi	水 分	Shuifen	Shuifen
	华 盖	Huagai	Huakai	神 阙	Shenque	Shenchueh
	紫 宫	Zigong	Tzukung	阴 交	Yinjiao	Yinchiao
	玉 堂	Yutang	Yutang	气 海	Qihai	Chihai
	膻 中	Shanzhong	Shanchung	石 门	Shimen	Shihmen
	中 庭	Zhongting	Chungting	关 元	Guanyuan	Kuanyuan
	鸠 尾	Jiuwei	Chiuwei	中 极	Zhongji	Chungchi
	巨 阙	Juque	Chuchueh	曲 骨	Qugu	Chuku
	上 脘	Shangwan	Shangwan	会 阴	Huiyin	Huiyin

其他六脉 Six Other Vessels

脉 名 Vessel	拼 音 Pinyin
冲 脉	Chongmai
带 脉	Daimai
阴维脉	Yinweimai
阳维脉	Yangweimai
阴跻脉	Yinqiaomai
阳跻脉	Yangqiaomai

10. 中国行政区划和主要地名
Administrative Divisions and Major Place Names in China

直　辖　市
Municipalities Directly under the Central Government

北京(京)　Beijing (Jing)
上海(沪)　Shanghai (Hu)
天津(津)　Tianjin (Jin)
重庆(渝)　Chongqing (Yu)

省、自治区及主要城市
Provinces, Autonomous Regions and Major Cities

河北省(冀)　**Hebei Province (Ji)**
*石家庄　Shijiazhuang
邯　郸　Handan
邢　台　Xingtai
保　定　Baoding
张家口　Zhangjiakou
承　德　Chengde
唐　山　Tangshan
秦皇岛　Qinhuangdao
沧　州　Cangzhou
廊　坊　Langfang
衡　水　Hengshui

山西省(晋)　**Shanxi Province (Jin)**
*太　原　Taiyuan
大　同　Datong
阳　泉　Yangquan
长　治　Changzhi
晋　城　Jincheng
榆　次　Yuci
临　汾　Linfen
运　城　Yuncheng

忻　州	Xinzhou
侯　马	Houma

内蒙古自治区(内蒙古)	**Nei Mongol (or Inner Mongolia) Autonomous Region (Nei Mongol)**
*呼和浩特	Hohhot
包　头	Baotou
乌　海	Wuhai
赤　峰	Chifeng
满洲里	Manzhouli
集　宁	Jining
锡林浩特	Xilinhot
海拉尔	Hailar
通　辽	Tongliao
东　胜	Dongsheng
临　河	Linhe
乌兰浩特	Ulanhot
二连浩特	Erenhot

辽宁省(辽)	**Liaoning Province (Liao)**
*沈　阳	Shenyang
大　连	Dalian
鞍　山	Anshan
抚　顺	Fushun
本　溪	Benxi
丹　东	Dandong
锦　州	Jinzhou
营　口	Yingkou
盘　锦	Panjin
阜　新	Fuxin
辽　阳	Liaoyang
铁　岭	Tieling
朝　阳	Chaoyang

吉林省(吉)	**Jilin Province (Ji)**
*长　春	Changchun
吉　林	Jilin
四　平	Siping
辽　源	Liaoyuan
通　化	Tonghua
延　吉	Yanji

黑龙江省(黑)	**Heilongjiang Province (Hei)**
*哈尔滨	Ha'erbin
齐齐哈尔	Qiqiha'er
鹤　岗	Hegang

双鸭山	Shuangyashan
鸡　西	Jixi
大　庆	Daqing
伊　春	Yichun
牡丹江	Mudanjiang
佳木斯	Jiamusi
七台河	Qitaihe
绥　化	Suihua
黑　河	Heihe
江苏省(苏)	**Jiangsu Province (Su)**
*南　京	Nanjing
徐　州	Xuzhou
连云港	Lianyungang
淮　阴	Huaiyin
盐　城	Yancheng
扬　州	Yangzhou
南　通	Nantong
镇　江	Zhenjiang
常　州	Changzhou
无　锡	Wuxi
苏　州	Suzhou
浙江省(浙)	**Zhejiang Province (Zhe)**
*杭　州	Hangzhou
宁　波	Ningbo
温　州	Wenzhou
嘉　兴	Jiaxing
湖　州	Huzhou
绍　兴	Shaoxing
金　华	Jinhua
衢　州	Quzhou
舟　山	Zhoushan
安徽省(皖)	**Anhui Province (Wan)**
*合　肥	Hefei
淮　南	Huainan
淮　北	Huaibei
芜　湖	Wuhu
铜　陵	Tongling
蚌　埠	Bengbu
马鞍山	Ma'anshan
安　庆	Anqing
黄　山	Huangshan

福建省(闽)	**Fujian Province (Min)**
*福　州	Fuzhou
厦　门	Xiamen
三　明	Sanming
莆　田	Putian
泉　州	Quanzhou
漳　州	Zhangzhou
南　平	Nanping
江西省(赣)	**Jiangxi Province (Gan)**
*南　昌	Nanchang
九　江	Jiujiang
景德镇	Jingdezhen
萍　乡	Pingxiang
新　余	Xinyu
鹰　潭	Yingtan
赣　州	Ganzhou
上　饶	Shangrao
瑞　金	Ruijin
山东省(鲁)	**Shandong Province (Lu)**
*济　南	Jinan
青　岛	Qingdao
淄　博	Zibo
枣　庄	Zaozhuang
东　营	Dongying
潍　坊	Weifang
烟　台	Yantai
威　海	Weihai
济　宁	Jining
泰　安	Tai'an
日　照	Rizhao
曲　阜	Qufu
河南省(豫)	**Henan Province (Yu)**
*郑　州	Zhengzhou
开　封	Kaifeng
洛　阳	Luoyang
平顶山	Pingdingshan
焦　作	Jiaozuo
鹤　壁	Hebi
新　乡	Xinxiang
安　阳	Anyang
濮　阳	Puyang
信　阳	Xinyang

南　阳	Nanyang
许　昌	Xuchang
漯　河	Luohe
三门峡	Sanmenxia
湖北省(鄂)	**Hubei Province (E)**
*武　汉	Wuhan
黄　石	Huangshi
襄　樊	Xiangfan
十　堰	Shiyan
宜　昌	Yichang
荆　州	Jingzhou
鄂　州	Ezhou
湖南省(湘)	**Hunan Province (Xiang)**
*长　沙	Changsha
株　洲	Zhuzhou
湘　潭	Xiangtan
衡　阳	Hengyang
邵　阳	Shaoyang
岳　阳	Yueyang
常　德	Changde
张家界	Zhangjiajie
广东省(粤)	**Guangdong Province (Yue)**
*广　州	Guangzhou
深　圳	Shenzhen
珠　海	Zhuhai
汕　头	Shantou
揭　阳	Jieyang
潮　州	Chaozhou
韶　关	Shaoguan
河　源	Heyuan
梅　州	Meizhou
惠　州	Huizhou
汕　尾	Shanwei
东　莞	Dongguan
中　山	Zhongshan
江　门	Jiangmen
佛　山	Foshan
阳　江	Yangjiang
湛　江	Zhanjiang
茂　名	Maoming
肇　庆	Zhaoqing
清　远	Qingyuan

广西壮族自治区(桂)	Guangxi Zhuang Autonomous Region (Gui)
*南　宁	Nanning
百　色	Baise
柳　州	Liuzhou
桂　林	Guilin
凭　祥	Pingxiang
梧　州	Wuzhou
北　海	Beihai
海南省(琼)	**Hainan Province (Qiong)**
*海　口	Haikou
三　亚	Sanya
四川省(川或蜀)	**Sichuan Province (Chuan or Shu)**
*成　都	Chengdu
自　贡	Zigong
攀枝花	Panzhihua
泸　州	Luzhou
德　阳	Deyang
绵　阳	Mianyang
广　元	Guangyuan
遂　宁	Suining
内　江	Neijiang
乐　山	Leshan
南　充	Nanchong
宜　宾	Yibin
贵州省(黔或贵)	**Guizhou Province (Qian or Gui)**
*贵　阳	Guiyang
六盘水	Liupanshui
遵　义	Zunyi
安　顺	Anshun
云南省(滇或云)	**Yunnan Province (Dian or Yun)**
*昆　明	Kunming
东　川	Dongchuan
西双版纳	Xishuangbanna
大　理	Dali
个　旧	Gejiu
西藏自治区(藏)	**Xizang (or Tibet) Autonomous Region (Zang)**
*拉　萨	Lhasa
那　曲	Naqu
昌　都	Changdu

日喀则	Xigaze (or Shigatze)
江　孜	Gyangze

陕西省(陕或秦)	**Shaanxi Province (Shan or Qin)**
*西　安	Xi'an
铜　川	Tongchuan
宝　鸡	Baoji
咸　阳	Xianyang
延　安	Yan'an
汉　中	Hanzhong

甘肃省(甘或陇)	**Gansu Province (Gan or Long)**
*兰　州	Lanzhou
金　昌	Jinchang
白　银	Baiyin
天　水	Tianshui
嘉峪关	Jiayuguan
敦　煌	Dunhuang
玉　门	Yumen

青海省(青)	**Qinghai Province (Qing)**
*西　宁	Xining
格尔木	Golmud
玉　树	Yushu

宁夏回族自治区(宁)	**Ningxia Hui Autonomous Region (Ning)**
*银　川	Yinchuan
石嘴山	Shizuishan
青铜峡	Qingtongxia

新疆维吾尔自治区(新)	**Xinjiang Uygur Autonomous Region (Xin)**
*乌鲁木齐	Ürümqi
克拉玛依	Karamay
哈　密	Hami (or Kumul)
吐鲁番	Turpan
喀　什	Kashi (or Kaxgar)
石河子	Shihezi

台湾省(台)	**Taiwan Province (Tai)**
*台　北	Taipei
高　雄	Kaohsiung
基　隆	Chilung (or Keelung)
台　中	Taichung
台　南	Tainan
新　竹	Hsinchu
嘉　义	Chia-i

特别行政区
Special Administrative Regions

香港(港) **Hong Kong Special Administrative Region (HKSAR)**
澳门(澳) **Macao Special Administrative Region (MSAR)**

* 省会或自治区首府。
Provincial or regional capitals.

11. 中国国家机构、政协、政党和人民团体
China's State Organs, CPPCC, Political Parties and People's Organizations

中国国家机关　China's State Organs

1.	**全国人民代表大会**	**National People's Congress (NPC)**
	主席团	Presidium
	常务委员会	Standing Committee
	办公厅	General Office
	秘书处	Secretariat
	代表资格审查委员会	Credentials Committee
	提案审查委员会	Motions Examination Committee
	民族委员会	Ethnic Affairs Committee
	法律委员会	Law Committee
	财政经济委员会	Finance and Economy Committee
	外事委员会	Foreign Affairs Committee
	教育、科学、文化和卫生委员会	Education, Science, Culture and Public Health Committee
	内务司法委员会	Committee for Internal and Judicial Affairs
	华侨委员会	Overseas Chinese Affairs Committee
	法制工作委员会	Commission of Legislative Affairs
	特定问题调查委员会	Committee of Inquiry into Specific Questions
	宪法修改委员会	Committee for Revision of the Constitution
2.	**中华人民共和国主席**	**President of the People's Republic of China**
3.	**中央军事委员会**	**Central Military Commission**
4.	**最高人民法院**	**Supreme People's Court**
5.	**最高人民检察院**	**Supreme People's Procuratorate**
6.	**国务院**	**State Council**
	(1)　国务院部委	**Ministries and Commissions Directly under the State Council**
	外交部	Ministry of Foreign Affairs
	国防部	Ministry of National Defence
	国家发展计划委员会	State Development Planning Commission

国家经济贸易委员会	State Economic and Trade Commission
教育部	Ministry of Education
科学技术部	Ministry of Science and Technology
国防科学技术工业委员会	Commission of Science, Technology and Industry for National Defence
国家民族事务委员会	State Ethnic Affairs Commission
公安部	Ministry of Public Security
国家安全部	Ministry of State Security
监察部	Ministry of Supervision
民政部	Ministry of Civil Affairs
司法部	Ministry of Justice
财政部	Ministry of Finance
人事部	Ministry of Personnel
劳动和社会保障部	Ministry of Labour and Social Security
国土资源部	Ministry of Land and Resources
建设部	Ministry of Construction
铁道部	Ministry of Railways
交通部	Ministry of Communications
信息产业部	Ministry of Information Industry
水利部	Ministry of Water Resources
农业部	Ministry of Agriculture
对外贸易经济合作部	Ministry of Foreign Trade and Economic Cooperation
文化部	Ministry of Culture
卫生部	Ministry of Public Health
国家计划生育委员会	State Family Planning Commission
中国人民银行	People's Bank of China
国家审计署	State Auditing Administration

(2) **国务院办事机构** **Offices under the State Council**

国务院办公厅	General Office of the State Council
侨务办公室	Office of Overseas Chinese Affairs
港澳事务办公室	Hong Kong and Macao Affairs Office
台湾事务办公室	Taiwan Affairs Office
法制办公室	Office of Legislative Affairs
经济体制改革办公室	Office for Economic Restructuring
国务院研究室	Research Office of the State Council
新闻办公室	Information Office

(3) **国务院直属机构** **Departments Directly under the State Council**

海关总署	General Administration of Customs
国家税务总局	State Taxation Administration
国家环境保护总局	State Environmental Protection Administration
中国民用航空总局	Civil Aviation Administration of China (CAAC)
国家广播电影电视总局	State Administration of Radio, Film and Television
国家体育总局	State Physical Culture Administration

国家统计局	State Statistics Bureau
国家工商行政管理局	State Administration of Industry and Commerce
新闻出版署	Press and Publication Administration
国家版权局	State Copyright Bureau
国家林业局	State Forestry Bureau
国家质量技术监督局	State Bureau of Quality and Technical Supervision
国家药品监督管理局	State Drug Administration (SDA)
国家知识产权局	State Intellectual Property Office (SIPO)
国家旅游局	National Tourism Administration
国家宗教事务局	State Bureau of Religious Affairs
国务院参事室	Counsellors' Office of the State Council
国务院机关事务管理局	Government Offices Administration of the State Council
(4) 国务院直属事业单位	**Institutions Directly under the State Council**
新华通讯社	Xinhua News Agency
中国科学院	Chinese Academy of Sciences
中国社会科学院	Chinese Academy of Social Sciences
中国工程院	Chinese Academy of Engineering
国务院发展研究中心	Development Research Centre of the State Council
国家行政学院	National School of Administration
中国地震局	China Seismological Bureau
中国气象局	China Meteorological Bureau
中国证券监督管理委员会	China Securities Regulatory Commission (CSRC)
(5) 部委管理的国家局	**State Bureaux Administered by Ministries or Commissions**
国家粮食储备局(国家发展计划委员会)	State Bureau of Grain Reserve (under the State Development Planning Commission)
国家国内贸易局	State Bureau of Internal Trade
国家煤炭工业局	State Bureau of Coal Industry
国家机械工业局	State Bureau of Machine-Building Industry
国家冶金工业局	State Bureau of Metallurgical Industry
国家石油和化学工业局	State Bureau of Petroleum and Chemical Industries
国家轻工业局	State Bureau of Light Industry
国家纺织工业局	State Bureau of Textile Industry
国家建筑材料工业局	State Bureau of Building Materials Industry
国家烟草专卖局	State Tobacco Monopoly Bureau
国家有色金属工业局	State Bureau of Nonferrous Metal Industry
(以上由国家经贸委管理)	(all under the State Economic and Trade Commission)
国家外国专家局(人事部)	State Bureau of Foreign Experts Affairs (under the Ministry of Personnel)
国家海洋局(国土资源部)	State Oceanic Administration (under the Ministry of Land and Resources)
国家测绘局(国土资源部)	State Bureau of Surveying and Mapping (ditto)
国家邮政局(信息产业部)	State Post Bureau (under the Ministry of Information Industry)
国家文物局(文化部)	State Cultural Relics Bureau (under the Ministry of Culture)

国家中医药管理局(卫生部)	State Administration of Traditional Chinese Medicine (under the Ministry of Public Health)
国家外汇管理局(中国人民银行总行)	State Administration of Foreign Exchange (under the People's Bank of China)
国家出入境检验检疫局(海关总署)	State Administration for Entry-Exit Inspection and Quarantine (under the General Administration of Customs)

中国人民政治协商会议及其机构
The Chinese People's Political Consultative Conference (CPPCC) and Its Structure

中国人民政治协商会议全国委员会	**National Committee of the CPPCC**
中国人民政治协商会议全国委员会常务委员会	**Standing Committee of the National Committee of the CPPCC**
中国人民政治协商会议全国委员会办公厅	General Office of the CPPCC National Committee
专门委员会	Special Committees
提案委员会	Committee for Handling Proposals
经济委员会	Committee for Economic Affairs
人口资源环境委员会	Committee of Population, Resources and Environment
教科文卫体委员会	Committee of Education, Science, Culture, Health and Sports
社会和法制委员会	Committee for Social and Legal Affairs
民族和宗教委员会	Committee for Ethnic and Religious Affairs
文史资料委员会	Committee of Cultural and Historical Data
港澳台侨委员会	Committee for Liaison with Hong Kong, Macao, Taiwan and Overseas Chinese
外事委员会	Committee of Foreign Affairs
中国人民政治协商委员会地方委员会	CPPCC Local Committees

中国政党 Chinese Parties

中文名称 Name in Chinese	中文简称 Abbreviation	英文名称 Name in English
* 中国共产党	中共	Communist Party of China (CPC)
中国国民党革命委员会	民革	Revolutionary Committee of the Chinese Kuomintang
中国民主同盟	民盟	China Democratic League
中国民主建国会	民建	China Democratic National Construction Association
中国民主促进会	民进	China Association for Promoting Democracy
中国农工民主党		Chinese Peasants and Workers Democratic Party
中国致公党		China Zhi Gong Dang
九三学社		Jiu San Society
台湾民主自治同盟	台盟	Taiwan Democratic Self-Government League

附录

* 中国共产党组织机构 Structure of the CPC

中国共产党中央委员会	Central Committee of the Communist Party of China (CCCPC)
中央政治局	Political Bureau of the Central Committee of the CPC
中央政治局常务委员会	Standing Committee of the Political Bureau of the CPC
中央书记处	Secretariat of the Central Committee of the CPC
中央军事委员会	Central Military Commission of the CPC
中央纪律检查委员会	Central Commission for Discipline Inspection of the CPC
中央办公厅	General Office, CCCPC
中央组织部	Organization Department, CCCPC
中央宣传部	Publicity Department, CCCPC
中央统一战线部	United Front Work Department, CCCPC
中央对外联络部	International Liaison Department, CCCPC
中央政法委员会	Committee of Political and Legislative Affairs, CCCPC
中央政策研究室	Policy Research Office, CCCPC
中央直属机关工作委员会	Work Committee for Offices Directly under the CCCPC
中央国家机关工作委员会	State Organs Work Committee of the CPC
中央台湾工作办公室	Taiwan Affairs Office, CCCPC
中央对外宣传办公室	International Communication Office, CCCPC
中央党校	Party School of the CPC
中央党史研究室	Party History Research Centre, CCCPC
中央文献研究室	Party Literature Research Centre, CCCPC
中央编译局	Compilation and Translation Bureau, CCCPC
中央外文出版发行事业局	China Foreign Languages Publishing and Distribution Administration
中央档案馆	Archives Bureau, CCCPC

人民团体 People's Organizations

测绘学会	Society of Geodesy, Photogrammetry and Cartography
地震学会	Seismological Society
国际金融学会	International Finance Society
国际战略问题学会	Institute for International Strategic Studies
海洋学会	Society of Oceanography
科普学会	Popular Science Society
全国少年儿童文化艺术委员会	National Council on Cultural and Art Work for Children
全国少年儿童工作协调委员会	National Children's Work Coordination Committee
全国史学会	China Society of History
宋庆龄基金会	Soong Ching Ling Foundation
中国奥林匹克委员会	Chinese Olympic Committee
中国笔会中心	Chinese Pen Centre
中国标准化协会	China Association for Standardization

中国残疾人福利基金会	China Welfare Fund for the Handicapped
中国出版协会	Chinese Publishers Association
中国道教协会	Chinese Taoist Association
中国电视艺术家协会	Chinese Television Artists Association
中国电影家协会	China Film Association
中国法律咨询中心	Chinese Legal Consultancy Centre
中国法学会	China Law Society
中国翻译工作者协会	Translators Association of China
中国佛教协会	Chinese Buddhists Association
中国福利会	China Welfare Institute
中国歌剧研究会	Chinese Opera Research Institute
中国共产主义青年团	Communist Youth League of China
中国国际法学会	Chinese Society of International Law
中国国际交流协会	Association for International Understanding of China
中国红十字会总会	Red Cross Society of China
中国会计学会	Chinese Accounting Society
中国基督教"三自"爱国运动委员会	Three-Self Patriotic Movement Committee of the Protestant Churches of China
中国基督教协会	China Christian Council
中国计量测试学会	Chinese Society for Measurement
中国金融学会	Chinese Monetary Society
中国考古协会	Archaeological Society of China
中国科学技术史学会	Chinese Society of Science and Technology History
中国科学技术协会	China Science and Technology Association
中国联合国教科文组织全国委员会	National Commission of the People's Republic of China for UNESCO
中国联合国协会	United Nations Association of the People's Republic of China
中国美术家协会	Chinese Artists Association
中国民间文艺家协会	China Society for the Study of Folk Literature and Art
中国企业管理协会	China Enterprise Management Association
中国曲艺家协会	Chinese Ballad Singers Association
中国人民保卫儿童全国委员会	Chinese People's National Committee for Defence of Children
中国人民对外友好协会	Chinese People's Association for Friendship with Foreign Countries
中国少年儿童基金会	Children's Foundation of China
中国少年先锋队	China Young Pioneers
中国摄影家协会	Chinese Photographers Society
中国书法家协会	Chinese Calligraphers Association
中国天主教爱国会	Chinese Patriotic Catholic Association
中国天主教教务委员会	National Administrative Commission of the Chinese Catholic Church
中国天主教主教团	Chinese Catholic Bishops College
中国文学艺术界联合会	China Federation of Literary and Art Circles
中国舞蹈家协会	Chinese Dancers Association
中国戏剧家协会	Chinese Dramatists Association
中国伊斯兰教协会	Chinese Islamic Association
中国音乐家协会	Chinese Musicians Association
中国杂技艺术家协会	Chinese Acrobats Association

中国政法学会	China Society of Political Science and Law
中国作家协会	Chinese Writers Association
中华全国妇女联合会	All-China Women's Federation
中华全国工商联合会	All-China Federation of Industry and Commerce
中华全国归国华侨联合会	All-China Federation of Returned Overseas Chinese
中华全国青年联合会	All-China Youth Federation
中华全国世界语联合会	All-China Esperanto League
中华全国台湾同胞联谊会	All-China Federation of Taiwan Compatriots
中华全国体育总会	All-China Sports Federation
中华全国新闻工作者协会	All-China Journalists' Association
中华全国总工会	All-China Federation of Trade Unions
中华医学会	Chinese Medical Association

12. 香港特别行政区政府和其他机构
Government and Other Institutions of HKSAR

一、香港特别行政区政府机构图
Organization Chart of the Government of the Hong Kong Special Administrative Region

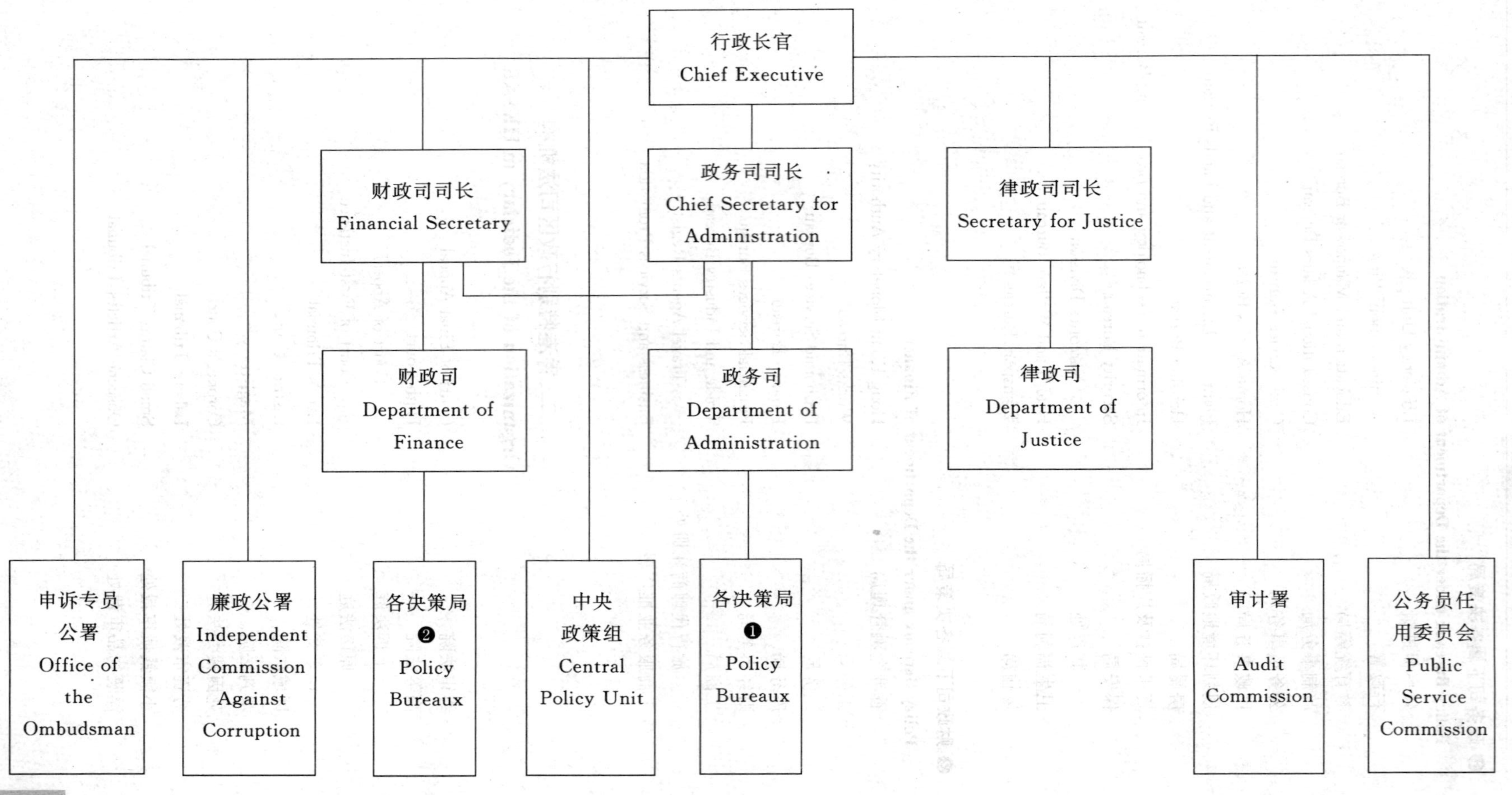

附录

❶ 政务司下属各决策局
Policy Bureaux under the Department of Administration

效率促进组	Efficiency Unit
行政署	Administration Wing
教育统筹局	Education and Manpower Bureau
政制事务局	Constitutional Affairs Bureau
公务员事务局	Civil Service Bureau
民政事务局	Home Affairs Bureau
规划环境地政局	Planning, Environment and Lands Bureau
房屋局	Housing Bureau
资讯科技及广播局	Information Technology and Broadcasting Bureau
保安局	Security Bureau
禁毒处	Narcotics Division
卫生福利局	Health and Welfare Bureau
运输局	Transport Bureau

❷ 财政司下属各决策局
Policy Bureaux under the Department of Finance

香港金融管理局	Hong Kong Monetary Authority
工务局	Works Bureau
经济局	Economic Services Bureau
库务局	Finance Bureau
财经事务局	Financial Services Bureau
工商局	Trade and Industry Bureau
旅行代理商注册处	Travel Agents Registry
工商服务业推广署	Business and Services Promotion Unit

二、香港特别行政区司法机构
Organization of the Judiciary in HKSAR

终审法院	Court of Final Appeal
高等法院	High Court
上诉法庭	Court of Appeal
原讼法庭	Court of First Instance
土地审裁处	Lands Tribunal
区域法院	District Court
裁判法院	Magistracy
死因裁判法庭	Coroner's Court
劳资审裁处	Labour Tribunal
小额钱债审裁处	Small Claims Tribunal
淫亵物品审裁处	Obscene Articles Tribunal

三、行政会议、立法会及其他有关机构
Executive Council, Legislative Council and Related Councils or Boards

行政会议	Executive Council
立 法 会	Legislative Council
临时市政局	Provisional Urban Council
临时区域市政局	Provisional Regional Council
临时区议会	Provisional District Board

附：首任香港特别行政区主要官员和终审法院大法官(1997 年 7 月 1 日起生效)
Principal Officials of the HKSAR Government and the Chief Justice of the Court of Final Appeal as from 1 July, 1997

行政长官	董建华
Chief Executive	TUNG Chee-hwa
政务司司长	陈方安生
Administrative Secretary	CHAN Anson
财政司司长	曾荫权
Financial Secretary	TSANG Am-kuen, Donald
律政司司长	梁爱诗
Secretary of Justice	LEUNG Oi-sie, Elsie
公务员事务局局长	林焕光
Secretary for the Civil Service	LAM Woon-kwong
保安局局长	黎庆宁
Secretary for Security	LAI Hing-ling, Peter
教育统筹局局长	王永平
Secretary for Education & Manpower	WONG Wing-ping, Joseph
卫生福利局局长	霍罗兆贞
Secretary for Health & Welfare	FOK LO Shiu-ching, Katherine
规划环境地政局局长	梁宝荣
Secretary for Planning, Environment & Lands	LEUNG Po-wing, Bowen
文康广播局局长	周德熙
Secretary for Recreation & Culture	CHAU Tak-hay
运输局局长	萧炯柱
Secretary for Transport	SIU Kwing-chue, Gordon
民政事务局局长	孙明扬
Secretary for Home Affairs	SUEN Ming-yeung, Michael
政制事务局局长	吴荣奎
Secretary for Electoral Affairs	NG Wing-fui, Nicholas
经济局局长	叶澍堃
Secretary for Economic Service	IP Shu-kwan, Stephen
库务局局长	邝其志

Secretary for Treasury	KWONG Ki-chi
财经事务局局长	许仕仁
Secretary for Financial Services	HUI Si-yan, Rafael
工商局局长	俞宗怡
Secretary for Trade & Industry	YUE Chung-yee, Denise
工务局局长	邝汉生
Secretary for Works	KWONG Hon-sang, Benedict
房屋局局长	黄星华
Secretary for Housing	WONG Shing-wah, Dominic
廉政专员	任关佩英
Commissioner Against Corruption	YAM KWAN Pui-ying, Lily
审计署署长	陈彦达
Director of Audit	CHAN Yin-tat, Dominic
警务处处长	许淇安
Commissioner of Police	HUI Ki-on, Eddie
海关关长	李树辉
Commissioner of Customs & Excise	LI Shu-fai, Lawrence

* * * *

终审法院大法官	李国能
Chief Justice of the Court of Final Appeal	LI Kwok-nang, Andrew

13. 澳门特别行政区政府和其他机构
Government and Other Institutions of MSAR

一、澳门特别行政区政府机构图
Organization Chart of the Government of the Macao Special Administrative Region

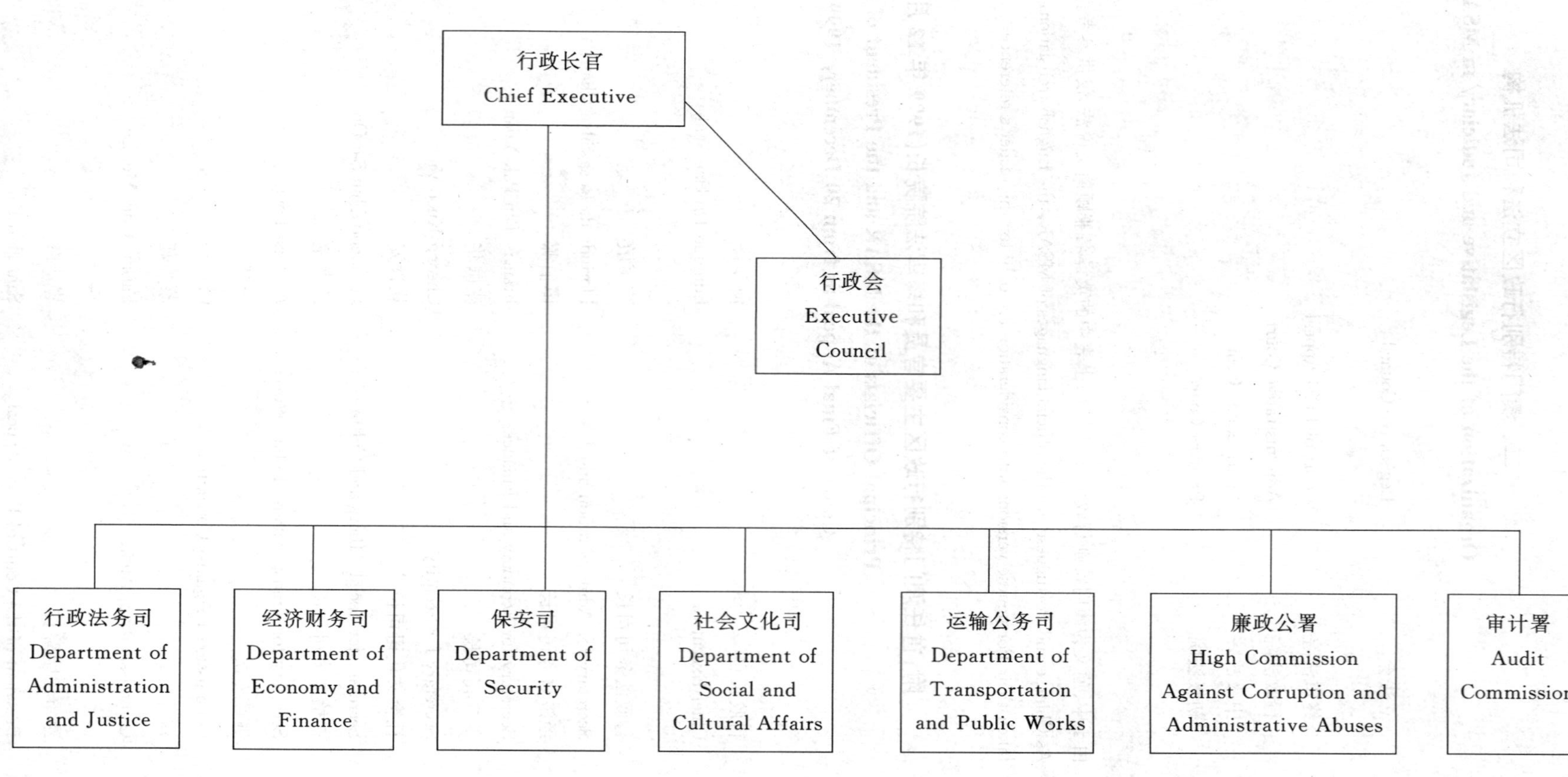

二、澳门特别行政区立法和司法机构

Organization of the Legislative and Judiciary in MSAR

立法会	Legislative Council
* * * *	
终审法院	Court of Final Appeal
行政法院	Administrative Court
中级法院	Intermediate Court
初级法院	Primary Court

由于中、葡文为澳门特别行政区官方文字，上表中的英译名兼顾葡文说法，仅供参考。

As Chinese and Portuguese are the official languages of MSAR, the English translations in the above charts which have taken their Portuguese versions into consideration are only for the reader's reference.

附：首任澳门特别行政区主要官员和终审法院院长（1999 年 12 月 20 日起生效）

Principal Officials of the MSAR and the President of the Court of Final Appeal as from 20 December, 1999

行政长官	何厚铧
Chief Executive	Edmund Ho Hau Wah
行政法务司司长	陈丽敏
Secretary for Administration and Justice	Florinda da Rosa Silva Chan
经济财务司司长	谭伯源
Secretary for Economy and Finance	Francis Tan Pak Yuan
保安司司长	张国华
Secretary for Security	Cheong Kuoc Va
社会文化司司长	崔世安
Secretary for Social Affairs and Culture	Fernando Chui Sai On
运输工务司司长	欧文龙
Secretary for Transports and Public Works	Ao Man Long
廉政专员	张裕
Commissioner Against Corruption	Cheong U
审计长	蔡美莉
Commissioner of Audit	Fatima Chio Mei Lei
* * * *	
终审法院院长	岑浩辉
President of the Court of Final Appeal	Sam Hou Fai

14. 中国武装力量构成和中国人民解放军编制

Composition of China's Armed Forces and Organization of the Chinese People's Liberation Army (PLA)

一、中国武装力量构成

Composition of China's Armed Forces

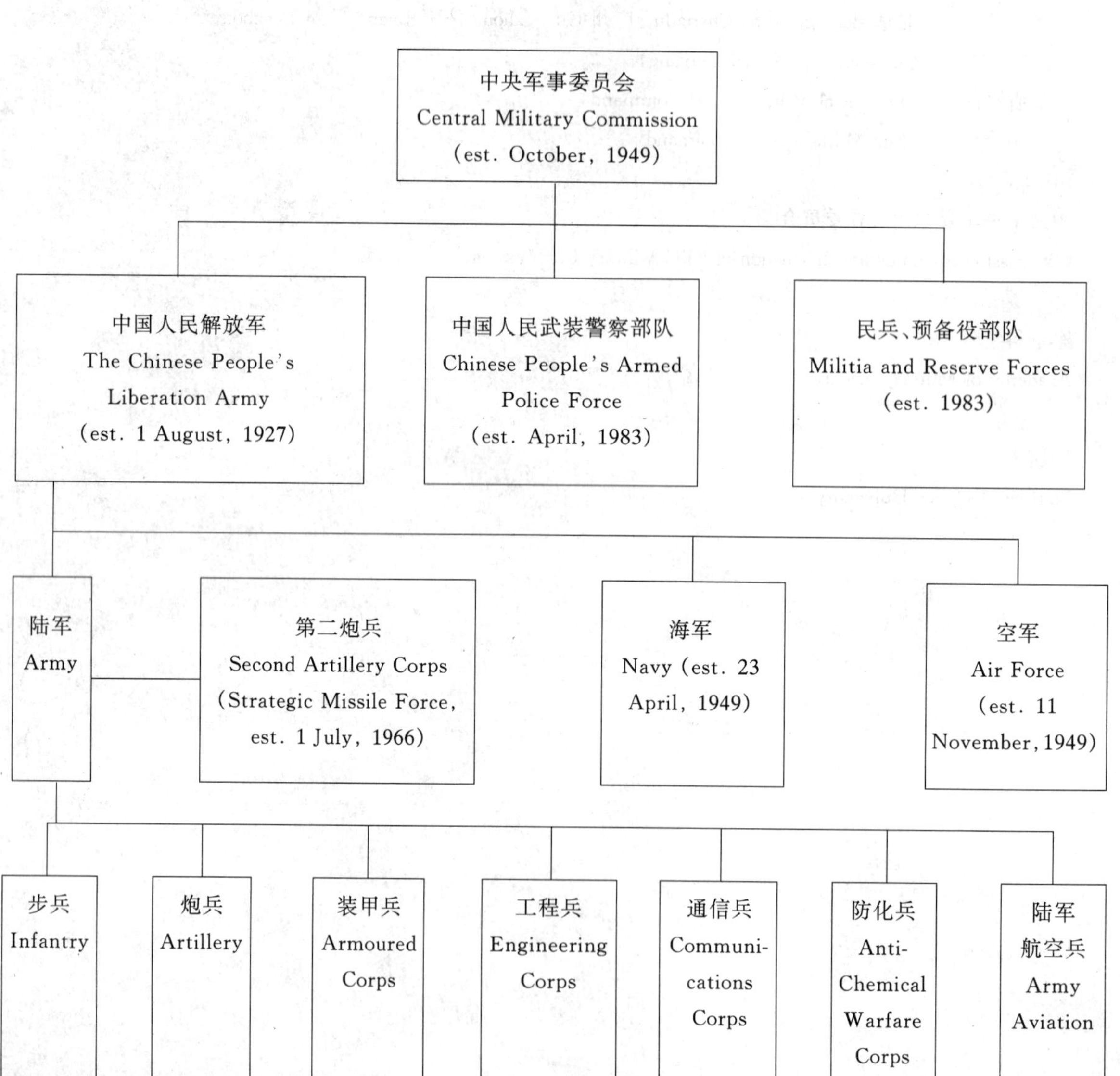

二、中国人民解放军编制

Organization of the Chinese People's Liberation Army

中国人民解放军总部

General Headquarters of the Chinese People's Liberation Army (PLA)

总参谋部　Headquarters of the General Staff

总政治部　General Political Department

总后勤部　General Logistics Department

总装备部　General Armament Department

总部下属之地方指挥系统

Local Levels of Command under the General Headquarters

军区　Military Area Command

(北京 Beijing, 成都 Chengdu, 广州 Guangzhou, 济南 Jinan, 兰州 Lanzhou, 南京 Nanjing, 沈阳 Shenyang)

省军区　Provincial Military Area Command

军分区　Sub-Military Area Command

中共中央军委纪律检查委员会

Commission for Discipline Inspection of CPC Military Commission

军事科学院

Academy of Military Sciences

国防大学

National Defence University

15. 中国军衔与英、美军衔对照表
Ranks in the Chinese, US and UK Armed Forces

陆军 Army

中国军衔 Rank in Chinese Armed Forces	美国军衔 Rank in US Armed Forces	英国军衔 Rank in UK Armed Forces
	General of the Army(五星上将)	Field Marshal(陆军元帅)
一级上将* General First Class		
上将 General	General	General
中将 Lieutenant General	Lieutenant General	Lieutenant General
少将 Major General	Major General	Major General
	Brigadier General (准将)	Brigadier (准将)
大校 Senior Colonel		
上校 Colonel	Colonel	Colonel
中校 Lieutenant Colonel	Lieutenant Colonel	Lieutenant Colonel
少校 Major	Major	Major
上尉 Captain	Captain	Captain
中尉 First Lieutenant	First Lieutenant	Lieutenant
少尉 Second Lieutenant	Second Lieutenant**	Second Lieutenant**
军士长 Master Sergeant	Command Sergeant Major**	
专业军士 Specialist Sergeant		
上士 Sergeant, First Class	Staff Sergeant	Staff Sergeant
中士 Sergeant	Sergeant	Sergeant
下士 Corporal	Corporal	Corporal
上等兵 Private, First Class	Private, First Class (一等兵)	Lance Corporal (一等兵)
列兵 Private	Private (二等兵) Basic Private (三等兵)	Private (二等兵) Recruit (新兵)

* 1955年中国首次颁布军官军衔时,还包括元帅(Marshal)、大将(Senior General)和大尉(Senior Captain),但无一级上将。

** 英美军制少尉以下设有准尉(Warrant Officer, etc.),而美国军士长在Command Sergeant Major以下还有数级,均与中国军衔不对应,此处略去。空、海军也有此种情况,从略。

海军 Navy

中国军衔 Rank in Chinese Armed Forces	美国军衔 Rank in US Armed Forces	英国军衔 Rank in UK Armed Forces
	Fleet Admiral (五星上将)	Admiral of the Fleet (海军元帅)
一级上将 * Admiral, First Class		
上　将 Admiral	Admiral	Admiral
中　将 Vice Admiral	Vice Admiral	Vice Admiral
少　将 Rear Admiral	Rear Admiral	Rear Admiral
	Commodore (准将)	Commodore (准将)
大　校 Senior Captain		
上　校 Captain	Captain	Captain
中　校 Commander	Commander	Commander
少　校 Lieutenant Commander	Lieutenant Commander	Lieutenant Commander
上　尉 Lieutenant	Lieutenant	Lieutenant
中　尉 Lieutenant, Junior Grade	Lieutenant, Junior Grade	Sub-Lieutenant
少　尉 Ensign	Ensign	Acting Sub-Lieutenant
军士长 Chief Petty Officer	Master Chief Petty Officer	Fleet Chief Petty Officer (舰队上士)
专业军士 Specialist Petty Officer		
上　士 Petty Officer, First Class	Petty Officer, First Class	Chief Petty Officer
中　士 Petty Officer, Second Class	Petty Officer, Second Class	Petty Officer, First Class
下　士 Petty Officer, Third Class	Petty Officer, Third Class	Petty Officer, Second Class
上等兵 Seaman, First Class	Seaman, First Class (一等兵)	Leading Seaman(上等水兵) Able Seaman(一等水兵)
列　兵 Seaman, Second Class	Seaman Apprentice(二等兵) Seaman Recruit(三等兵)	Ordinary Seaman (二等水兵) Junior Seaman (新兵)

* 1955年中国首次颁布军衔时还包括海军大将(Senior Admiral)、海军大尉(Senior Lieutenant),但无一级上将。

空军 Air Force

中国军衔 Rank in Chinese Armed Forces	美国军衔 Rank in US Armed Forces	英国军衔 Rank in UK Armed Forces
	General of the Air Force (五星上将)	Marshal of the Royal Air Force (皇家空军元帅)
一级上将 * General, First Class		
上 将 General	General	Air Chief Marshal
中 将 Lieutenant General	Lieutenant General	Air Marshal
少 将 Major General	Major General	Air Vice Marshal
	Brigadier General (准将)	Air Commodore (准将)
大 校 Senior Colonel		
上 校 Colonel	Colonel	Group Captain
中 校 Lieutenant Colonel	Lieutenant Colonel	Wing Commander
少 校 Major	Major	Squadron Leader
上 尉 Captain	Captain	Flight Lieutenant
中 尉 First Lieutenant	First Lieutenant	Flying Officer
少 尉 Second Lieutenant	Second Lieutenant	Pilot Officer
军士长 Master Sergeant	Chief Master Sergeant	
专业军士 Specialist Sergeant		Technician * * (技术军士)
上 士 Technical Sergeant	Technical Sergeant	Flight Sergeant
中 士 Staff Sergeant	Staff Sergeant	Sergeant
下 士 Sergeant	Sergeant	Corporal
上等兵 Airman, First Class	Airman, First Class (一等兵)	Senior Aircraftsman (一等兵)
列 兵 Airman, Second Class	Airman, Second Class (二等兵) Airman Basic (三等兵)	Leading Aircraftsman(二等兵) Aircraftsman (新兵)

* 1955 年中国首次颁布军衔时无一级上将,而有空军大尉(Senior Captain)。

* * 英空军中技术军士有两级:总技术军士(Chief Technician),在上士之下,中士之上;初级技术军士(Junior Technician)则在下士之下,上等兵之上。

附录

16. 中国人民警察警衔

Police Ranks in China

总 警 监	General Police Commissioner
副总警监	Deputy General Police Commissioner
一级警监	Police Commissioner, Class I
二级警监	Police Commissioner, Class II
三级警监	Police Commissioner, Class III
一级警督	Police Supervisor, Class I
二级警督	Police Supervisor, Class II
三级警督	Police Supervisor, Class III
一级警司	Police Superintendent, Class I
二级警司	Police Superintendent, Class II
三级警司	Police Superintendent, Class III
一级警员	Police Constable, Class I
二级警员	Police Constable, Class II

17. 中国法定计量单位及换算表
China's Weights and Measures with Conversion Tables

(中国采用公制为度量衡法定单位。
China follows the metric system for weights and measures.)

I. 长度单位表 Units of Linear Measure

公制 metric system	符号 symbol	市制 traditional Chinese system	英制 British system
千米(公里) (kilometre) =1000 米	km	2 市里(*li*)	0.6214 英里(mile)
米(公尺) (metre) =10 分米	m	3 市尺(*chi*)	3.2808 英尺(foot;ft); 1.0936 码(yard;yd)
分米(公寸) (decimetre) =0.1 米	dm	3 市寸(*cun*)	0.32808 英尺(foot;ft); 0.10936 码 (yard;yd)
厘米(公分) (centimetre) =0.01 米	cm	3 市分(*fen*)	0.3937 英寸(inch;in)
毫米(公厘) (millimetre) =0.001 米	mm	3 市厘(*li*)	
微米(公微) (micrometre; micron) $=10^{-6}$米	μm		
纳米 (nanometre) = millionth m $=10^{-9}$米	nm		

注:1 海里(nautical mile; nmi) = 1.85 公里 = 3.704 市里 = 1.15 英里

II. 面积单位表 Units of Area Measure

公制 metric system	符号 symbol	市制 traditional Chinese system	英美制 British-American system
平方千米 (平方公里) (square kilometre)	km^2	4 平方市里(*li*^{2}); 1500 市亩(*mu*)	0.3861 平方英里(sq mi;mi^2); 100 公顷(hectare;ha); 247.1 英亩(acre)
平方米 (square metre) =100 平方分米	m^2	9 平方市尺(*chi*^{2})	10.7639 平方英尺(sq ft; ft^2); 1.1960 平方码(sq yd;yd^2)
平方分米 (square decimetre) =0.01 平方米 =100 平方厘米	dm^2	0.09 平方市尺(*chi*^{2})	0.107639 平方英尺(sq ft;ft^2); 0.01196 平方码(sq yd;yd^2)
平方厘米 (square centimetre) =0.0001 平方米 =0.01 平方分米 =100 平方毫米	cm^2		
平方毫米 (square millimetre)	mm^2		
公顷 (hectare) =100 公亩(are) =10000 平方米	ha	15 亩(*mu*)	2.47 英亩 (acre)

注:1 亩 (*mu*) = 60 平方丈(*zhang*^{2}) = 0.1644 英亩(acre) = 0.0667 公顷(hectare;ha)

III. 体积单位表 Units of Cubic Measure

公制 metric system	符号 symbol	市制 traditional Chinese system	英美制 British-American system
立方米 (cubic metre) =1000 立方分米	m^3	27 立方市尺(*chi*^{3})	35.3147 立方英尺(cubic foot;ft^3); 1.308 立方码(cubic yard;yd^3)
立方分米 (cubic decimetre) =0.001 立方米 =1000 立方厘米	dm^3	0.027 立方市尺(*chi*^{3})	0.0353147 立方英尺(ft^3); 0.001308 立方码(yd^3)
立方厘米 (cubic centimetre) =0.000001 立方米 =0.001 立方分米 =1000 立方毫米	cm^3		
立方毫米 (cubic millimetre) =0.001 立方厘米	mm^3		

IV. 容积单位表 Units of Capacity Measure

公制 metric system	符号 symbol	市制 traditional Chinese system	英美制 British-American system
升(liter) =10 分升	L(l)	1 市升(*sheng*)	1.7598 品脱(pint) 0.22 加仑(gallon, UK)
分升(decilitre) =0.1 升 =10 厘升	dL(dl)	1 市合(*gě*)	0.17598 品脱(pint) 0.022 加仑(gallon, UK)
厘升(centilitre) =0.01 升 =10 毫升	cL(cl)		
毫升(millilitre); 西西(cc) =0.001 升	mL(ml)		

V. 重量单位表 Units of Weight

公制 metric system	符号 symbol	市制 traditional Chinese system	英美制 British-American system
吨(metric ton; tonne) =1000 公斤	t	2000 市斤(*jin*)	0.9842 长吨(long ton, UK); 1.1023 短吨(short ton, US)
千克(公斤) (kilogramme) =1000 克	kg	2 市斤(*jin*)	2.2046 磅(pound)
克(gram) =10 分克	g	2 市分	15.4324 格令(grain) 0.035 盎司(ounce;oz)
分克(decigram) =0.0001 千克 =0.1 克	dg		
厘克(centigram) =0.00001 千克 =0.1 分克	cg		
毫克(milligram) =0.000001 千克 =0.1 厘克	mg		

VI. 英美制计量单位换算表

Conversion Tables from the British-American to the Metrical & Traditional Chinese System

1) 长度单位 Units of Length

1 英里(mi) = 1.609 千米(公里) (km) = 3.218 市里(*li*) = 0.869 海里(nmi)
1 码(yd) = 3 英尺(ft;foot) = 0.9144 米 = 2.7432 市尺(*chi*)
1 英尺(ft) = 0.305 米(m) = 0.914 市尺(*chi*)

2) 面积单位 Units of Area

1 英亩(acre) = 6.070 市亩(*mu*) = 0.405 公顷(ha)
1 平方码(yd^2) = 0.8361 平方公尺 (m^2)
1 平方英尺(ft^2) = 0.835 平方市尺(chi^2) = 0.0939 平方公尺(m^2)

3) 重量单位 Units of Weight

1 磅(pound) = 0.45359 千克(公斤)(kg) = 0.90719 市斤(*jin*)
长吨(long ton) = 1016.05 千克(公斤)(kg) = 2032.09 市斤(*jin*)
短吨(short ton) = 907.185 千克(公斤)(kg) = 1814.37 市斤(*jin*)

4) 容量单位 Units of Capacity Measure

1 加仑 (gallon, UK) = 4 夸脱(quart) = 8 品脱(pint) = 4.5461 升(L) = 4.5461 市升(*sheng*)
1 品脱 (pint, US) = 0.10409 加仑(gal) = 0.5 夸脱(quart) = 0.47317 升(L) = 0.47317 市升(*sheng*)

18. 联合国系统

The United Nations

联合国主要机构

Principal Organs of the United Nations

中文名称 Name in Chinese	中文简称 Chinese Abbreviation	英文名称 Name in English	英文简称 English Abbreviation
联合国大会	大会	General Assembly	GA
安全理事会	安理会	Security Council	SC
经济及社会理事会	经社理事会	Economic and Social Council	ECOSOC
托管理事会		Trusteeship Council	
国际法院		International Court of Justice	
秘书处		Secretariat	

联合国系统的组织及专门机构
Organizations and Specialized Agencies under the United Nations

政府间组织及专门机构
Inter-Governmental Organizations and Specialized Agencies

中文名称 Name in Chinese	中文简称 Chinese Abbreviation	英文名称 Name in English	英文简称 English Abbreviation
国际电信联盟	国际电联	International Telecommunication Union	ITU
国际复兴开发银行（世界银行）	复兴开发银行；世行	International Bank for Reconstruction and Development (World Bank)	IBRD
国际海事组织	海事组织	International Maritime Organization	IMO
国际货币基金组织	货币基金	International Monetary Fund	IMF
国际金融公司		International Finance Corporation	IFC
国际开发协会		International Development Association	IDA
国际劳工组织	劳工组织	International Labour Organization	ILO
国际民用航空组织	民航组织	International Civil Aviation Organization	ICAO
联合国教育、科学及文化组织	教科文组织	United Nations Educational, Scientific and Cultural Organization	UNESCO
联合国粮食及农业组织	粮农组织	Food and Agriculture Organization of the United Nations	FAO
世界气象组织	气象组织	World Meteorological Organization	WMO
世界卫生组织	卫生组织	World Health Organization	WHO
万国邮政联盟	万国邮联	Universal Postal Union	UPU

其他组织及专门机构

Other Organizations and Specialized Agencies

中文名称 Name in Chinese	中文简称 Chinese Abbreviation	英文名称 Name in English	英文简称 English Abbreviation
国际麻醉品管理局		International Narcotics Control Board	INCB
国际农业发展基金	农发基金	International Fund for Agricultural Development	IFAD
国际提高妇女地位研究所		International Research and Training Institute for the Advancement of Women	
联合国巴勒斯坦和解委员会		United Nations Conciliation Commission for Palestine	UNCCP
联合国巴勒斯坦难民救济组织		United Nations Relief for Palestine Refugees	UNRPR
联合国裁军会议		United Nations Conference on Disarmament	UNCD
联合国裁军审议委员会		United Nations Disarmament Commission	UNDC
联合国裁军中心		United Nations Center for Disarmament	
联合国大学		United Nations University	UNU
联合国地区经济委员会		United Nations Regional Economic Commission	
联合国儿童基金会		United Nations Children Fund	UNICEF
联合国非殖民化特别委员会		United Nations Special Committee on Decolonization	
联合国非洲经济委员会		United Nations Economic Commission for Africa	UNECA
联合国妇女地位委员会		United Nations Commission on the Status of Women	
联合国工业发展组织	工发组织	United Nations Industrial Development Organization	UNIDO

中文名称 Name in Chinese	中文简称 Chinese Abbreviation	英文名称 Name in English	英文简称 English Abbreviation
联合国脱离接触观察员部队		United Nations Disengagement Observer Force	UNDOF
联合国国际法委员会		United Nations International Law Commission	UNILC
联合国国际贸易法委员会		United Nations Commission on International Trade Law	UNCITRAL
联合国国际刑事管辖问题委员会		United Nations Committee on International Criminal Jurisdiction	
联合国环境规划署	环境署	United Nations Environment Programme	UNEP
联合国环境基金		United Nations Environment Fund	UNEF
联合国环境与发展大会	环发大会	United Nations Conference on Environment and Development	UNCED
联合国货币金融会议		United Nations Monetary and Financial Conference	
联合国禁毒中心		United Nations Fund for Drug Abuse Control	UNFDAC
联合国经济发展特别基金		Special United Nations' Fund for Economic Development	SUNFED
联合国经济发展总署		United Nations Economic Development Administration	UNEDA
联合国经济合作行动计划署		United Nations Action Programme for Economic Cooperation	
联合国开发公司		United Nations Development Corporation	UNDC
联合国救灾协调专员办事处		Office of United Nations Disaster Relief Co-ordinator	UNDRO
联合国开发计划署	开发署	United Nations Development Programme	UNDP

附录

中文名称 Name in Chinese	中文简称 Chinese Abbreviation	英文名称 Name in English	英文简称 English Abbreviation
联合国跨国公司委员会		United Nations Economic Commission on Transnational Corporations	
联合国跨国公司中心		United Nations Centre on Transnational Corporations	UNCTC
联合国拉丁美洲经济委员会		United Nations Economic Commission for Latin America	UNECLA
联合国麻醉品管制署	禁毒署	United Nations International Drug Control Programme	UNIDCP
联合国贸易促进中心		Trade Promotion Centre of the United Nations	UNTPC
联合国贸易和发展会议	贸发会议	United Nations Conference on Trade and Development	UNCTAD
联合国贸易与发展理事会		United Nations Trade and Development Board	UNTDB
联合国难民事务高级专员办事处		Office of the United Nations High Commissioner for Refugees	UNHCR
联合国区域发展中心		United Nations Centre for Regional Development	UNCRD
联合国人口活动基金	人口基金	United Nations Fund for Population Activities	UNFPA
联合国人口奖委员会		Committee for the United Nations Population Award	
联合国人口委员会		Population Commission of the United Nations	
联合国人类环境会议		United Nations Conference on the Human Environment	
联合国人类住区会议		United Nations Conference on Human Settlement	
联合国人类住区中心		Centre for Human Settlements	HABITAT
联合国人权委员会		United Nations Commission on Human Rights	

附录

中文名称 Name in Chinese	中文简称 Chinese Abbreviation	英文名称 Name in English	英文简称 English Abbreviation
联合国人权中心		United Nations Centre for Human Rights	
联合国善后救济总署	救济总署	United Nations Relief and Rehabilitation Administration	UNRRA
联合国社会发展和人道主义事务中心		United Nations Centre for Social Development and Humanitarian Affairs	UNCSDHA
联合国社会发展首脑会议		World Summit for Social Development	Social Summit
联合国社会发展研究所		United Nations Research Institute for Social Development	UNRISD
联合国特别基金		United Nations Special Fund	
联合国停战监督组织		United Nations Truce Supervision Organization	UNTSO
联合国统计局		United Nations Statistical Office	
联合国宪章问题委员会		Committee on the Charter of the United Nations	
联合国协会世界联合会		World Federation of United Nations Associations	WFUNA
联合国行政法庭		United Nations Administrative Tribunal	
联合国行政和预算问题咨询委员会		UN Advisory Committee on Administrative and Budgetary Questions	UNACABQ
联合国训练研究所	训研所	United Nations Institute for Training and Research	UNITAR
联合国亚洲及太平洋经济和社会委员会	亚太经社委员会	United Nations Economic and Social Commission for Asia and the Pacific	ESCAP
联合国印度巴基斯坦委员会		United Nations Commission for India and Pakistan	UNCIP
联合国预防和控制犯罪委员会		United Nations Committee on Crime Prevention and Control	

中文名称 Name in Chinese	中文简称 Chinese Abbreviation	英文名称 Name in English	英文简称 English Abbreviation
联合国殖民主义问题特别委员会		United Nations Special Committee on Colonialism	
联合国周转基金		United Nations Revolving Fund	
联合国资本开发基金		United Nations Capital Development Fund	UNCDF
世界粮食理事会	粮食理事会	World Food Council	WFC
世界知识产权组织		World Intellectual Property Organization	WIPO

附录

19. 其他国际与区域组织

Other International and Regional Organizations

阿拉伯共同市场　Arab Common Market (ACM)
阿拉伯国家联盟(阿盟)　League of Arab States (Arab League; LAS)
阿拉伯货币基金组织　Arab Monetary Fund (AMF)
阿拉伯经济统一委员会　Council of Arab Economic Unity (CAEU)
阿拉伯联盟教科文组织　Arab League Educational, Cultural and Scientific Organization (ALECSO)
阿拉伯马格里布联盟　Union du Maghreb Arabe (UMA); Union of the Arab Maghreb
阿拉伯石油输出国组织　Organization of Arab Petroleum Exporting Countries (OAPEC)
安第斯共同市场　Andean Common Market (ANCOM)
安第斯共同体　Andean Community
安第斯条约组织　Andean Pact Organization (APO); Pacto Andino (PA)
八国集团　Group of Eight (G8)
巴黎俱乐部　Paris Club (Group of Ten)
巴黎联盟(国际保护工业产权联盟)　Paris Convention (International Union for the Protection of Industrial Property)
巴黎统筹委员会(巴统)　Coordinating Committee on Export Control (COCOM); Coordinating Committee for Export to Communist Countries
北大西洋公约组织(北约)　North Atlantic Treaty Organization (NATO)
北大西洋合作理事会　North Atlantic Cooperation Council
北美自由贸易区　North American Free Trade Area (NAFTA)
北南核控制联合委员会　North-South Nuclear Joint Committee
北欧理事会　Nordic Council
北欧邮政联盟　Nordic Postal Union (NPU)
北太平洋海洋科学组织　North Pacific Marine Science Organization (PICES)
伯尔尼(国际保护文学艺术作品)联盟　Berne Union (for the Protection of Literary and Artistic Works)
不结盟运动　Non-Aligned Movement (NAM)
朝鲜半岛能源开发组织　Korean Peninsula Energy Development Organization (KEDO)
船长协会国际联合会　International Federation of Shipmasters' Associations (IFSMA)
促进种族平等公民协会　Citizens' Association for Racial Equality
大陆架界限委员会　Commission on the Limits of the Continental Shelf
大气科学委员会　Commission of Atmospheric Sciences (CAS)
大气污染管制委员会　Air Pollution Control Commission (APCC)
大气污染控制管理局　Air Pollution Control Administration (APCA)
大赦国际　Amnesty International
大西洋自由贸易区　Atlantic Free Trade Area (AFTA)
第三世界科学院　Academy of Sciences for the Third World
东非共同体　East African Community (EAC)
东加勒比共同市场　East Caribbean Common Market (ECCM)

东加勒比组织 Organization of the Eastern Caribbean States

东盟各国议会组织 ASEAN Inter-Parliamentary Organization

东盟自由贸易区 ASEAN Free Trade Area (AFTA)

东南非共同市场 Common Market for Eastern and Southern Africa (COMESA)

东南亚国家联盟(东盟) Association of Southeast Asian Nations (ASEAN)

发展工业产权和有关权利合作常设委员会 Permanent Committee for Development Cooperation Related to Industrial Property

发展中国家间经济合作委员会 Committee on Economic Cooperation Among Developing Countries

发展著作权和邻接权利合作常设委员会 Permanent Committee for Development Related to Copyright and Neighboring Rights

法语国家首脑会议 Somet de la francophonie; Summit of Francophone Countries

反对原子弹氢弹会议 Conference Against Atomic and Hydrogen Bombs

泛非电信联盟 Pan-African Telecommunication Union (PATU)

泛非妇女组织 Organization Panafricaine des Femmes (OPF); Pan-African Women's Organization (PAWO)

防止空气污染协会国际联合会 International Union of Air Pollution Prevention Associations (IUAPPA)

防止歧视和保护少数小组委员会 Sub-Commission on Prevention of Discrimination and Protection of Minorities

防止外层空间军备竞赛特设委员会 Ad Hoc Committee on the Prevention of Arms Race in Outer Space

非殖民化委员会(24 国委员会) Commission on Decolonization (Committee of 24)

非洲、加勒比和太平洋地区国家集团(非加太集团) Group of African, Caribbean and Pacific Region Countries (ACP Group)

非洲经济共同体 African Economic Community

非洲人权和民族权委员会 African Committee on Human and People's Rights

非洲统一组织(非统组织) Organization of African Unity (OAU)

非洲邮政联盟 African Postal Union (APU)

扶轮社国际 Rotary International

各国议会联盟 Inter-Parliamentary Union (IPU)

国际奥林匹克委员会 International Olympic Committee (IOC)

国际版权协会 International Copyright Society

国际保护工业产权联盟(即巴黎联盟) International Union for the Protection of Industrial Property (Paris Union)

国际保护工业产权协会 International Association for the Protection of Industrial Property (IAPIP)

国际保护知识产权联合局 United International Bureau for the Protection of Intellectual Property (BIRPI)

国际保护自然与自然资源联盟 International Union for Conservation of Nature and Natural Resources (IUCN)

国际笔会(国际诗人、剧作家、编辑、散文作家和小说家协会) International PEN (International Association of Poets, Playwrights, Editors, Essayists and Novelists)

国际标准化组织 International Standardization Organization (ISO)

国际标准协会 International Standard Association (ISA)

国际材料物理中心 International Center for Materials Physics (ICMP)

国际船东协会 International Shipping Federation (ISF)

国际船级社协会 International Association of Classification Societies (IACS)

国际纯粹和应用化学联盟 International Union of Pure and Applied Chemistry (IUPAC)

国际纯粹和应用生物物理学联盟 International Union of Pure and Applied Biophysics (IUPAB)

国际大坝委员会 International Commission on Large Dams (ICOLD)

国际大学生体育联合会 Fédération Internationale du Sport Universitaire (FISU)

国际地球科学信息网络集团 Consortium for International Earth Science Information Network (CIESIN)

国际地球学联盟 International Geographical Union (IGU)

附录

国际地震中心 International Seismological Centre (ISC)
国际地质大会 International Geological Congress (IGC)
国际地质科学联盟 International Union of Geological Sciences (IUGS)
国际冻土协会 International Permafrost Association (IPA)
国际独立油船东协会 International Association of Independent Tanker Owners (INTERTANKO)
国际度量衡局 International Bureau of Weight and Measurements (IBWM)
国际儿童福利联合会 International Union for Child Welfare (IUCW)
国际法官联合会 International Union of Judges
国际法协会 International Law Association
国际法学家委员会 International Commission of Jurists (ICJ)
国际法学协会 International Association of Legal Science (IALS)
国际纺织学会 International Textile Institute (ITI)
国际辐射防护协会 International Radiation Protection Association (IRPA)
国际妇女同盟 International Alliance of Women (IAW)
国际妇女协会 International Women Society
国际港口协会 International Association of Ports and Harbours (IAPH)
国际公务员协会联合会 Federation of International Civil Servants Associations (FICSA)
国际公务员制度委员会 International Civil Service Commission (ICSC)
国际古生物协会 International Palaeontological Association (IPA)
国际雇主组织 International Organization of Employers (IOE)
国际广播协会 International Association of Broadcasting (IAB)
国际海道测量组织 International Hydrographic Organization (IHO)
国际海底管理局 International Sea-Bed Authority
国际海事卫星组织 International Maritime Satellite Organization (INMARSAT)
国际海运联盟 International Shipping Federation
国际航标协会 International Association of Lighthouse Authorities (IALA)
国际航空科学理事会 International Council of Aeronautical Sciences (ICAS)
国际航空联合会 Aeronautic International Federation (FAI)
国际航空运输协会 International Air Transport Association (IATA)
国际航运会议常设协会 Permanent International Association of Navigation Congresses (PIANC)
国际航运协会 International Chamber of Shipping
国际和平利用原子能会议 International Conference on the Peaceful Use of Atomic Energy
国际和平学会 International Peace Academy (IPA)
国际核数据委员会 International Nuclear Data Committee (INDC)
国际红十字 International Red Cross (IRC)
国际环境法理事会 International Council of Environmental Law
国际环境事务研究所 International Institute for Environmental Affairs
国际计划生育联合会 International Planned Parenthood Federation (IPPF)
国际建筑师协会 International Union of Architects (IUA)
国际救济联合会 International Relief Union (IRU)
国际军事体育理事会 International Military Sports Council (IMSC)
国际开发委员会 Commission on International Development (CID)
国际科学基金会 International Foundation of Sciences (IFS)
国际科学联盟理事会 International Council of Scientific Unions (ICSU)
国际空间研究委员会 International Committee on Space Research (ICSR)

国际空运协会 International Air Transport Association (IATA)
国际理论和应用力学联盟 International Union of Theoretical and Applied Mechanics
国际理论物理中心 International Centre for Theoretical Physics (ICTP)
国际律师协会 International Bar Association (IBA)
国际毛纺组织 International Wool Textile Organization (IWTO)
国际民主妇女联合会 Women's International Democratic Federation (WIDF)
国际难民组织 International Refugee Organization (IRO)
国际能源机构 International Energy Agency (IEA)
国际欧亚科学院 International Academy for Europe and Asia (IAEA)
国际清算银行 Bank for International Settlements (BIS)
国际人口问题科学研究联合会 International Union for the Scientific Study of Population (IUSSP)
国际人权法院 International Court of Human Rights
国际人权联合会 International Federation of Human Rights
国际人与生物圈保护区网络 International Man and Biosphere Reserve Network
国际商会 International Chamber of Commerce (ICC)
国际商事仲裁协会 International Commercial Arbitration Association
国际商业仲裁协会 International Council for Commercial Arbitration
国际生态学协会 International Association for Ecology
国际生物化学与分子生物学联盟 International Union of Biochemistry and Molecular Biology (IUBMB)
国际生物科学联合会 International Union of Biological Sciences (IUBS)
国际圣经协会 International Bible Society (IBS)
国际世界语协会 Universala Esperanto-Asocio ; Universal Esperanto Association (UEA)
国际数学联盟 International Mathematical Union (IMU)
国际水资源协会 International Water Resources Association (IWRA)
国际丝绸协会 International Silk Association (ISA)
国际体操联合会 Fédération Internationale de Gymnastique (FIG); International Federation of Gymnastics
国际天文学联合会 International Astronomical Union (IAU)
国际通讯卫星组织 International Telecommunications Satellite Organization (INTELSAT)
国际投资银行 International Investment Bank (IIB)
国际土壤协会 International Society of Soil Science (ISSS)
国际细胞生物学联合会 International Federation for Cell Biology (IFCB)
国际心理科学联盟 International Union of Psychological Science
国际新闻工作者协会 International Federation of Journalists
国际信息和文献联合会 International Federation for Information and Documentation
国际刑法协会 International Association of Penal Law (IAPL)
国际刑警组织 International Criminal Police Organization (INTERPOL;ICPO)
国际刑事学会 International Association of Criminal Science
国际宣教协会 International Missionary Council (IMC)
国际学生联合会 International Union of Students (IUS)
国际移民组织 International Organization for Migration (IOM)
国际遗传学联合会 International Genetics Federation (IGF)
国际译联 International Federation of Translators
国际音乐理事会 International Music Council (IMC)
国际应用心理学协会 International Association of Applied Psychology (IAAP)
国际有线发行联盟 International Alliance for Distribution by Cable

国际宇航科学院　International Academy of Astronautics (IAA)
国际植物生理学家协会　International Association for Plant Physiologists (IAPP)
国际自动控制联合会　International Federation of Automatic Control (IFAC)
国际自由工会联合会(自由工联)　International Confederation of Free Trade Unions (ICFTU)
国际足球联合会　International Football Federation (FIFA)
海湾(阿拉伯国家)合作委员会　Cooperation Council for the Arab States of the Gulf;Gulf Cooperation Council (GCC)
海洋研究科学委员会　Scientific Committee on Oceanic Research (SCOR)
海洋研究气象委员会　Commission on Maritime Meteorology (CMM)
海洋资源研究咨询委员会　Advisory Committee on Marine Resources Research
和平利用外层空间委员会　Committee of Peaceful Uses of Outer Space
和平利用原子能国际会议咨询委员会　Advisory Committee of the International Conference on the Peaceful Uses of Atomic Energy
和平利用原子能委员会　Committee on the Use of Atomic Energy for Peaceful Purposes (CUAEPP)
红十字会与红新月会国际联合会　International Federation of Red Cross and Red Crescent Societies (IFRCS)
环境问题科学委员会　Scientific Committee on Problems of the Environment (SCOPE)
环境与发展国际研究中心(环发中心)　Centre for International Research of Environment and Development (CIRED)
环太平洋论坛　Pacific Rim Forum (PRF)
基督教会联合会　World Council of Churches (WCC)
基督教女青年会　Young Women's Christian Association (YWCA)
基督教青年会　Young Men's Christian Association (YMCA)
计划生育-世界人口组织　Planned Parenthood-World Population
加勒比共同体和共同市场　Caribbean Community and Common Market (CARICOM)
经济合作与发展组织(经合组织)　Organization for Economic Cooperation and Development (OECD)
孔塔多拉集团　Contadora Group
拉丁美洲共同市场　Latin American Common Market (LACM)
拉丁美洲和加勒比禁止核武器组织　Organization for the Prohibition of Nuclear Weapons in Latin America and the Caribbean
拉丁美洲货币同盟　Latin American Monetary Union
拉丁美洲经济体系　Latin American Economic System (LAES)
拉丁美洲经济委员会　Economic Commission of Latin America(ECLA)
拉丁美洲开发金融机构协会　Latin American Association of Development of Financing Institutions
拉丁美洲能源组织　Latin American Energy Organization (OLAE)
拉丁美洲社会学会　Association of Latin American Sociology (ALAS)
拉丁美洲协调特别委员会　Special Committee on Latin American Coordination
拉丁美洲一体化协会　Latin American Integration Association (LAIA)
拉丁美洲自由贸易区　Latin American Free Trade Area (LAFTA)
拉丁美洲自由贸易市场　Latin American Free Trade Market
拉丁美洲自由贸易协会　Latin American Free Trade Association
联合国协会世界联合会　World Federation of United Nations Associations (WFUNA)
伦敦核供应国俱乐部　London Suppliers' Club
马格里布联盟　Union du Maghreb (UMA)
美洲出口贸易促进中心　Inter-American Export Promotion Centre
美洲储蓄和贷款银行　Inter-American Savings and Loans Bank
美洲国家间人权委员会　Inter-American Commission on Human Rights
美洲国家组织　Organization of American States (OAS)

美洲经济及社会理事会 Inter-American Economic and Social Council
美洲开发银行 Inter-American Development Bank
美洲人权委员会 Inter-American Commission on Human Rights (IACHR)
南北协调委员会 North-South Coordinating Committee
南部非洲发展共同体 Southern African Development Community (SADC)
南部非洲关税同盟 Southern African Customs Union (SACU)
南方共同市场 South Common Market
南南会议 South-South Conference
南太平洋论坛 South Pacific Forum (SPF)
南亚区域合作联盟 South Asian Association for Regional Cooperation (SAARC)
欧洲安全与合作组织(欧安组织,原欧洲安全与合作会议) Organization for Security and Cooperation in Europe (OSCE, formerly known as Conference on Security and Cooperation in Europe)
欧洲裁军会议 Conference on Disarmament in Europe (CDE)
欧洲复兴开发银行 European Bank of Reconstruction and Development
欧洲经济合作组织 Organization for European Economic Cooperation (OEEC)
欧洲联盟(欧盟) European Union (EU)
欧洲人权法院 European Court of Human Rights
欧洲人权委员会 European Commission of Human Rights
欧洲原子能委员会 European Atomic Commission (EAC)
欧洲原子能学会 European Atomic Energy Society (EAES)
欧洲自由贸易联盟 European Free Trade Association (EFTA)
七国集团 Group of Seven (G7)
七十七国集团 Group of 77
区域合作发展组织 Regional Cooperation Organization for Development (RCOD)
三边委员会(日美欧委员会) Trilateral Commission of Japan, North America and Europe (TC)
社会党国际 Socialist International
石油输出国组织(欧佩克) Organization of Petroleum Exporting Countries (OPEC)
世界残疾人组织理事会 Council of World Organizations Interested in the Handicapped (CWOIH)
世界动物保护联合会 World Federation for the Protection of Animals
世界佛教徒联谊会 World Fellowship of Buddhists (WFB)
世界工会联合会(世界工联) World Federation of Trade Unions (WFTU)
世界海关组织 World Customs Organization
世界和平理事会 World Peace Council (WPC)
世界基督教联合会 World Council of Churches (WCC)
世界教师工会协进会 World Federation of Teachers' Unions
世界科学工作者联合会 World Federation of Scientific Workers (WFSW)
世界劳工联合会 World Confederation of Labour (WCL)
世界旅游组织 World Tourism Organization (WTO)
世界贸易组织 World Trade Organization (WTO)
世界穆斯林大会 World Muslim Congress
世界穆斯林联盟 Muslim World League (MWL)
世界青年大会 World Assembly of Youth (WAY)
世界人权大会 World Conference on Human Rights
世界野生动物基金会 World Wildlife Fund (WWF)
世界伊斯兰大会 World Islamic Congress

世界医学协会 World Medical Association
世界艺术与科学学会 World Academy of Art and Science
世界犹太人大会 World Jewish Congress
世界幼儿教育组织 World Organization for Early Children's Education
世界针灸学会联合会 World Federation of Acupuncture and Moxibustion Societies
世界自然保护联盟 World Conservation Union
世界宗教和平大会 World Conference on Religion and Peace (WCRP)
太平洋经济合作理事会 Pacific Economic Cooperation Council (PECC)
西方七国首脑会议 Seven-Nation Economic Summit; Group of Seven Summit (G7 Summit)
西非国家经济共同体 Economic Community of West African States (ECOWAS)
西欧联盟 Western European Union (WEU)
亚大邮联 Asian-Oceanic Postal Union (AOPU;UPAO)
亚非法律协商委员会 Asian-African Legal Consultative Committee (AALCC)
亚非会议 Asian-African Conference
亚非拉人民团结组织 Organization of Solidarity of the Peoples of Africa, Asia and Latin America (OSPAALA)
亚非人民团结组织 Afro-Asian People's Solidarity Organization (AAPSO)
亚非新闻工作者协会 Afro-Asian Journalists' Association (AAJA)
亚欧合作理事会 Council for Asia-Europe Cooperation (CAEC)
亚欧环境技术中心 Asia-Europe Environmental Technology Center
亚太安全合作理事会 Council on Security Cooperation in Asia and Pacific Region (CSCAP)
亚太经合组织 Asia-Pacific Economic Cooperation (APEC)
亚太空间技术与应用多边合作会议 Asia-Pacific Conference on Multilateral Cooperation in Space Technology and Applications (APC-MCSTA Conference)
亚洲大洋洲邮政联盟 Asian-Oceanic Postal Union (AOPU; UPAO)
亚洲化学学会联合会 Federation of Asian Chemical Societies (FACS)
亚洲环境问题协会 Asian Environmental Society (AES)
亚洲基督教会议 Christian Conference of Asia (CCA)
亚洲及太平洋和平与裁军区域中心 Regional Centre for Peace and Disarmament in Asia and the Pacific
亚洲及太平洋理事会 Asian and Pacific Council (ASPAC)
亚洲开发银行 Asian Development Bank (ADB)
亚洲科学联合会 Federation of Asian Scientific Academies and Societies
亚洲青年理事会 Asian Youth Council (AYC)
亚洲生产力组织 Asian Productivity Organization
亚洲太平洋广播联盟(亚广联) Asian-Pacific Broadcasting Union (ABU)
亚洲-太平洋通讯社组织 Organization of Asia-Pacific News Agencies (OANA)
亚洲-太平洋邮政联盟 Asian-Pacific Postal Union
亚洲遥感协会 Asian Association on Remote Sensing (AARS)
伊斯兰会议组织 Organization of the Islamic Conference (OIC)
伊斯兰教事务最高理事会 Supreme Council for Islamic Affairs
印度洋特设委员会 Ad Hoc Committee on the Indian Ocean
英联邦 British Commonwealth of Nations (Commonwealth)
中非国家经济共同体 Economic Community of Central African States (CEEAC)
中非国家联盟 Union of Central African States (UEAC)
中美洲共同市场 Central American Common Market
中美洲国家组织 Organization of Central American States

20. 世界各国家、地区、首都或首府及货币 Countries, Regions and Their Capitals and Currencies

亚洲 Asia

国家、地区 Country, Region	首都、首府 Capital	货币 Currency
阿富汗伊斯兰国 the Islamic State of Afghanistan	喀布尔 Kabul	阿富汗尼 Afghani (Af)
阿拉伯联合酋长国 the United Arab Emirates	阿布扎比 Abu Dhabi	迪拉姆 Dirham (Dh)
阿拉伯叙利亚共和国 the Syrian Arab Republic	大马士革 Damascus	叙利亚镑 Syrian Pound
阿曼苏丹国 the Sultanate of Oman	马斯喀特 Muscat	阿曼里亚尔 Rial Omani (RO)
阿塞拜疆共和国 Azerbaijani Republic	巴库 Baku	马纳特 Manat
巴基斯坦伊斯兰共和国 the Islamic Republic of Pakistan	伊斯兰堡 Islamabad	巴基斯坦卢比 Pakistan Rupee
巴勒斯坦 Palestine	耶路撒冷 * Jerusalem	
巴林国 the State of Bahrain	麦纳麦 Manama	巴林第纳尔 Bahrain Dinar (BD)
不丹王国 the Kingdom of Bhutan	廷布 Thimphu	努尔特鲁姆 Ngultrum (Nu)
朝鲜民主主义人民共和国 the Democratic People's Republic of Korea	平壤 Pyongyang	朝鲜元 Won
大韩民国 the Republic of Korea	汉城 Seoul	韩元 Won
菲律宾共和国 the Republic of the Philippines	马尼拉 Manila	菲律宾比索 Philippine Peso
格鲁吉亚共和国 the Republic of Georgia	第比里斯 Tbilisi	拉里 Lari
哈萨克斯坦共和国 the Republic of Kazakhstan	阿斯塔纳 Astana	坚戈 Tanga
吉尔吉斯共和国 Kyrghyz Republic	比什凯克 Bishkek	索姆 Som

附录

柬埔寨王国 the Kingdom of Cambodia	金边 Phnom Penh	瑞尔 Riel
卡塔尔国 the State of Qatar	多哈 Doha	卡塔尔里亚尔 Qatar Riyal (QR)
科威特国 the State of Kuwait	科威特城 Kuwait City	科威特第纳尔 Kuwait Dinar (KD)
老挝人民民主共和国 the Lao People's Democratic Republic	万象 Vientiane	基普 Kip
黎巴嫩共和国 the Republic of Lebanon	贝鲁特 Beirut	黎巴嫩镑 Lebanese Pound (￡L)
马尔代夫共和国 the Republic of Maldives	马累 Male	拉菲亚 Rufiyaa
马来西亚 Malaysia	吉隆坡 Kuala Lumpur	林吉特 Ringgit
蒙古国 the State of Mongolia	乌兰巴托 Ulan Bator	图格里克 Tugrik
孟加拉人民共和国 the People's Republic of Bangladesh	达卡 Dhaka	塔卡 Taka
缅甸联邦 the Union of Myanmar	仰光 Yangon	缅元 Kyat
尼泊尔王国 the Kingdom of Nepal	加德满都 Kathmandu	尼泊尔卢比 Nepalese Rupee (NR)
日本国 Japan	东京 Tokyo	日元 Yen
塞浦路斯共和国 the Republic of Cyprus	尼科西亚 Nicosia	塞浦路斯镑 Cyprus Pound (Cyprus ￡)
沙特阿拉伯王国 the Kingdom of Saudi Arabia	利雅得 Riyadh	沙特里亚尔 Saudi Riyal
斯里兰卡民主社会主义共和国 the Democratic Socialist Republic of Sri Lanka	科伦坡 Colombo	斯里兰卡卢比 Sri Lanka Rupee
塔吉克斯坦共和国 the Republic of Tadzhikistan	杜尚别 Dushanbe	塔吉克卢布 Tajik Rouble (Ruble)
泰王国 the Kingdom of Thailand	曼谷 Bangkok	铢 Baht
土耳其共和国 the Republic of Turkey	安卡拉 Ankara	土耳其里拉 Turkish Lira (TL)
土库曼斯坦 Turkmenistan	阿什哈巴德 Ashkhabad	马纳特 Manat
文莱达鲁萨兰国 Negara Brunei Darussalam	斯里巴加湾市 Bandar Seri Begawan	文莱元 Brunei Dollar (Br $)
乌兹别克斯坦共和国 the Republic of Uzbekistan	塔什干 Tashkent	苏姆 Sum
锡金 Sikkim	甘托克 Gangtok	印度卢比 Indian Rupee

附录

新加坡共和国 the Republic of Singapore	新加坡城 Singapore City	新加坡元 Singapore Dollar (S$)
亚美尼亚共和国 the Republic of Armenia	埃里温 Yerevan	德拉姆 Dram
也门共和国 the Republic of Yemen	萨那 Sana'a	里亚尔 Rial
伊拉克共和国 the Republic of Iraq	巴格达 Baghdad	伊拉克第纳尔 Iraqi Dinar (ID)
伊朗伊斯兰共和国 the Islamic Republic of Iran	德黑兰 Tehran	里亚尔 Rial
以色列国 the State of Israel	耶路撒冷 * Jerusalem	谢克尔 Shekel
印度共和国 the Republic of India	新德里 New Delhi	卢比 Rupee
印度尼西亚共和国 the Republic of Indonesia	雅加达 Jakarta	印尼盾 Indonesia Rupiah (Rp)
约旦哈希姆王国 the Hashemite Kingdom of Jordan	安曼 Amman	约旦第纳尔 Jordanian Dinar (JD)
越南社会主义共和国 the Socialist Republic of Viet Nam	河内 Hanoi	越盾 Dong
中华人民共和国 the People's Republic of China	北京 Beijing	人民币元 Renminbi Yuan (RMB)

* 巴、以有争议。Disputed by Palestine and Israel.

非洲 Africa

阿尔及利亚民主人民共和国 the Democratic People's Republic of Algeria	阿尔及尔 Algiers	阿尔及利亚第纳尔 Algerian Dinar (AD)
阿拉伯埃及共和国 the Arab Republic of Egypt	开罗 Cairo	埃及镑 Egyptian Pound
埃塞俄比亚联邦民主共和国 the Federal Democratic Republic of Ethiopia	亚的斯亚贝巴 Addis Ababa	比尔 Birr
安哥拉共和国 the Republic of Angola	罗安达 Luanda	新宽扎 New Kwanza
贝宁共和国 the Republic of Benin	波多诺伏 Porto-Novo	非洲法郎 African Franc (FA)
博茨瓦纳共和国 the Republic of Botswana	哈博罗内 Gaborone	普拉 Pula (P)
布基纳法索 Burkina Faso	瓦加杜古 Ouagadougou	非洲法郎 African Franc
布隆迪共和国 the Republic of Burundi	布琼布拉 Bujumbura	布隆迪法郎 Burundi Franc (Fbu)
赤道几内亚共和国 the Republic of Equatorial Guinea	马拉博 Malabo	非洲法郎 African Franc (FA)

附录

多哥共和国 the Republic of Togo	洛美 Lomé	非洲法郎 African Franc (FA)
厄立特里亚国 Eritrea	阿斯马拉 Asmara	比尔 Birr
佛得角共和国 the Republic of Cape Verde	普拉亚 Praia	埃斯库多 Escudo (Esc)
冈比亚共和国 the Republic of Gambia	班珠尔 Banjul	达拉西 Dalasi
刚果民主共和国 the Democratic Republic of Congo	金沙萨 Kinshasa	刚果法郎 Congolese Franc
刚果共和国 the Republic of the Congo	布拉柴维尔 Brazzaville	非洲法郎 African Franc (FA)
吉布提共和国 the Republic of Djibouti	吉布提市 Djibouti	吉布提法郎 Djibouti Franc (DF)
几内亚共和国 the Republic of Guinea	科纳克里 Conakry	几内亚法郎 Guinea Franc (GF)
几内亚比绍共和国 the Republic of Guinea-Bissau	比绍 Bissau	比索 Peso
加纳共和国 the Republic of Ghana	阿克拉 Accra	塞迪 Cedi
加蓬共和国 the Republic of Gabon	利伯维尔 Libreville	非洲法郎 African Franc (FA)
津巴布韦共和国 the Republic of Zimbabwe	哈拉雷 Harare	津巴布韦元 Zimbabwe Dollar (Z$)
喀麦隆共和国 the Republic of Cameroon	雅温得 Yaoundé	非洲法郎 African Franc (FA)
科摩罗伊斯兰联邦共和国 the Islamic Federal Republic of Comoros	莫罗尼 Moroni	科摩罗法郎 Comoros Franc
科特迪瓦共和国 the Republic of Cote d'Ivoire	亚穆苏克罗 Yamoussoukro	非洲法郎 African Franc (FA)
肯尼亚共和国 the Republic of Kenya	内罗比 Nairobi	肯尼亚镑 Kenya Pound (K£)
莱索托王国 the Kingdom of Lesotho	马塞卢 Maseru	洛蒂 Loti
利比里亚共和国 the Republic of Liberia	蒙罗维亚 Monrovia	利比里亚元 Liberian Dollar (L$)
大阿拉伯利比亚人民社会主义民众国 the Great Socialist People's Libyan Arab Jamahiriya (Libya)	的黎波里 Tripoli	利比亚第纳尔 Libyan Dinar (LD)
留尼汪岛 Réunion	圣旦尼 Saint-Denis	法国法郎 French Franc
卢旺达共和国 the Republic of Rwanda	基加利 Kigali	卢旺达法郎 Rwanda Franc
马达加斯加共和国 the Republic of Madagascar	塔那那利佛 Antananarivo	马达加斯加法郎 Madagascar Franc

马拉维共和国 the Republic of Malawi	利隆圭 Lilongwe	马拉维克瓦查 Malawi Kwacha (K)
马里共和国 the Republic of Mali	巴马科 Bamako	非洲法郎 African Franc (FA)
马约特岛(法) Mayotte (French)	扎乌兹 Dzaoudzi	法国法郎 French Franc
毛里求斯共和国 the Republic of Mauritius	路易港 Port Louis	毛里求斯卢比 Mauritius Rupee
毛里塔尼亚伊斯兰共和国 the Islamic Republic of Mauritania	努瓦克肖特 Nouakchott	乌吉亚 Ouguiya
摩洛哥王国 the Kingdom of Morocco	拉巴特 Rabat	迪拉姆 Dirham
莫桑比克共和国 the Republic of Mozambique	马普托 Maputo	梅蒂卡尔 Metical
纳米比亚共和国 the Republic of Namibia	温得和克 Windhoek	纳米比亚元 Namibia Dollar
南非共和国 the Republic of South Africa	比勒陀利亚 Pretoria	兰特 Rand (R)
尼日尔共和国 the Republic of Niger	尼亚美 Niamey	非洲法郎 African Franc (FA)
尼日利亚联邦共和国 the Federal Republic of Nigeria	阿布贾 Abuja	奈拉 Naira (N)
塞拉利昂共和国 the Republic of Sierra Leone	弗里敦 Freetown	利昂 Leone (L)
塞内加尔共和国 the Republic of Senegal	达喀尔 Dakar	非洲法郎 African Franc (FA)
塞舌尔共和国 the Republic of Seychelles	维多利亚 Victoria	塞舌尔卢比 Seychelles Rupee
圣多美和普林西比民主共和国 the Democratic Republic of São Tomé and Principe	圣多美 São Tomé	多布拉 Dobra (Db)
圣赫拉拿岛(英) St. Helena (UK)	詹姆斯敦 Jamestown	圣赫拉拿镑 St. Helena Pound
斯威士兰王国 the Kingdom of Swaziland	姆巴巴纳 Mbabane	埃马兰吉尼 Emalangeni
苏丹共和国 the Republic of Sudan	喀土穆 Khartoum	苏丹镑 Sudanese Pound
索马里共和国 the Somali Republic	摩加迪沙 Mogadishu	索马里先令 Somali Shilling (So. Sh.)
坦桑尼亚联合共和国 the United Republic of Tanzania	达累斯萨拉姆 Dar es Salaam	坦桑尼亚先令 Tanzania Shilling
突尼斯共和国 the Republic of Tunisia	突尼斯 Tunis	突尼斯第纳尔 Tunisian Dinar (TD)
乌干达共和国 the Republic of Uganda	坎帕拉 Kampala	乌干达先令 Uganda Shilling

西撒哈拉 West Sahara	阿尤恩 Lá Youne	
赞比亚共和国 the Republic of Zambia	卢萨卡 Lusaka	克瓦查 Kwacha
乍得共和国 the Republic of Chad	恩贾梅纳 N'Djamena	非洲法郎 African Franc (FA)
中非共和国 the Central African Republic	班吉 Bangui	非洲法郎 African Franc (FA)

欧洲 Europe

阿尔巴尼亚共和国 the Republic of Albania	地拉那 Tirana	列克 Lek
爱尔兰共和国 the Republic of Ireland (Eire)	都柏林 Dublin	爱尔兰镑 Irish Pound (I£)
爱沙尼亚共和国 the Republic of Estonia	塔林 Tallinn	爱沙尼亚克朗 Estonian Kroon
安道尔公国 the Principality of Andorra	安道尔城 Andorra la Vella	西班牙比塞塔和法国法郎 Spanish Peseta & Franc
奥地利共和国 the Republic of Austria	维也纳 Vienna	奥地利先令 Austrian Schilling
白俄罗斯共和国 the Republic of Belarus	明斯克 Minsk	白俄罗斯卢布 Belarus Rouble
保加利亚共和国 the Republic of Bulgaria	索菲亚 Sofia	列弗 Lev
比利时王国 the Kingdom of Belgium	布鲁塞尔 Brussels	比利时法郎 Franc Belge (FB)
冰岛共和国 the Republic of Iceland	雷克雅未克 Reykjavik	冰岛克朗 Icelandic Krona (IKr)
波兰共和国 the Republic of Poland	华沙 Warsaw	兹罗提 Zloty (ZL)
波斯尼亚和黑塞哥维那共和国 the Republic of Bosnia and Herzegovina	萨拉热窝 Sarajevo	第纳尔 Dinar
大不列颠及北爱尔兰联合王国 the United Kingdom of Great Britain and Northern Ireland	伦敦 London	英镑 Pound Sterling (£)
丹麦王国 the Kingdom of Denmark	哥本哈根 Copenhagen	丹麦克朗 Danish Krone (DKr)
德意志联邦共和国 the Federal Republic of Germany	柏林 Berlin	德意志马克 Deutsche Mark (DM)
俄罗斯联邦 the Russian Federation	莫斯科 Moscow	卢布 Rouble (Ruble)
法兰西共和国 the Republic of France	巴黎 Paris	法郎 Franc

法罗群岛(丹) the Faeroe Islands (Danish)	曹斯哈恩 Torshavon	法罗克朗 Faeroe Krone
梵蒂冈城国 the Vatican City State	梵蒂冈城 the Vatican City	意大利里拉 Italian Lira
芬兰共和国 the Republic of Finland	赫尔辛基 Helsinki	芬兰马克 Finnish Markka (FIM)
格陵兰(丹) Greenland (Danish)	戈德霍普 Godthaab	丹麦克朗 Danish Krone (DKr)
荷兰王国 the Kingdom of the Netherlands	阿姆斯特丹 Amsterdam	荷兰盾 Guilder or Florin (Fl)
捷克共和国 the Czech Republic	布拉格 Prague	捷克克朗 Czech Crown
克罗地亚共和国 the Republic of Croatia	萨格勒布 Zagreb	库纳 Kuna
拉脱维亚共和国 the Republic of Latvia	里加 Riga	拉特 Lat
立陶宛共和国 the Republic of Lithuania	维尔纽斯 Vilnius	利塔斯 Litas (Lt)
列支敦士登公国 the Principality of Liechtenstein	瓦杜兹 Vaduz	瑞士法郎 Swiss Franc (SF)
卢森堡大公国 the Grand Duchy of Luxembourg	卢森堡 Luxembourg	卢森堡法郎 Franc Luxembourgeois
罗马尼亚 Romania	布加勒斯特 Bucharest	摩尔多瓦列伊 Moldovian Leu
马耳他共和国 the Republic of Malta	瓦莱塔 Valletta	马耳他里拉 Malta Lira (LM)
马其顿共和国 the Republic of Macedonia	斯科普里 Skopje	代纳尔 Denar
摩尔多瓦共和国 the Republic of Moldova	基希讷乌 Kishinev	摩尔多瓦列伊 Moldovian Leu
摩纳哥公国 the Principality of Monaco	摩纳哥 Monaco-Ville	法国法郎 French Franc
南斯拉夫联盟共和国 the Federal Republic of Yugoslavia	贝尔格莱德 Belgrade	第纳尔 Dinar
挪威王国 the Kingdom of Norway	奥斯陆 Oslo	挪威克朗 Norwegian Krone
葡萄牙共和国 the Portuguese Republic	里斯本 Lisbon	埃斯库多 Escudo
瑞典王国 the Kingdom of Sweden	斯德哥尔摩 Stockholm	瑞典克朗 Swedish Krona
瑞士联邦 the Confederation of Switzerland	伯尔尼 Bern(e)	瑞士法郎 Swiss Franc
圣马力诺共和国 the Republic of San Marino	圣马力诺 San Marino	意大利里拉 Italian Lira

附录

斯洛伐克共和国 the Slovak Republic	布拉迪斯拉发 Bratislava	克朗 Slovak Crown
斯洛文尼亚共和国 the Republic of Slovenia	卢布尔雅那 Ljubljana	托拉尔 Tolar
乌克兰 Ukraine	基辅 Kyiv (Kiev)	格里夫纳 Hryvina
西班牙王国 the Kingdom of Spain	马德里 Madrid	比塞塔 Peseta
希腊共和国 the Hellenic Republic (or the Republic of Greece)	雅典 Athens	德拉克马 Drachma
匈牙利共和国 the Republic of Hungary	布达佩斯 Budapest	福林 Forint
意大利共和国 the Italian Republic	罗马 Rome	里拉 Lira
直布罗陀 (英,西) Gibraltar (UK, Spanish)	直布罗陀城 the City of Gibraltar	直布罗陀镑和比塞塔 Pound & Peseta

美洲 Americas

阿根廷共和国 the Republic of Argentina	布宜诺斯艾利斯 Buenos Aires	比索 Peso
阿鲁巴 (荷) Aruba (Dutch)	奥兰也斯特德 Oranjestad	阿鲁巴弗罗林 Aruban Florin (AFI)
安圭拉 (英) Anguilla (UK)	瓦利 Valley	东加勒比元 East Caribbean Dollar (EC$)
安提瓜和巴布达 Antigua and Barbuda	圣约翰 St. John's	东加勒比元 East Caribbean Dollar (EC$)
巴巴多斯 Barbados	布里奇敦 Bridgetown	巴巴多斯元 Barbados Dollar
巴哈马联邦 the Commonwealth of the Bahamas	拿骚 Nassau	巴哈马元 Bahamian Dollar (B$)
巴拉圭共和国 the Republic of Paraguay	亚松森 Asuncion	瓜拉尼 Guarani (G)
巴拿马共和国 the Republic of Panama	巴拿马城 Panama City	巴波亚 Balboa (B)
巴西联邦共和国 the Federative Republic of Brazil	巴西利亚 Brasilia	雷亚尔 Real
百慕大群岛 (英) the Bermuda Islands (UK)	哈密尔顿 Hamilton	百慕大元 Bermuda Dollar (B$)
秘鲁共和国 the Republic of Peru	利马 Lima	新索尔 New Sol
波多黎各自由邦 (美) the Commonwealth of Puerto Rico (US)	圣胡安 San Juan	美元 US Dollar ($)

玻利维亚共和国 the Republic of Bolivia	苏克雷 Sucre	玻利维亚诺 Boliviano (B)
伯利兹 Belize	贝尔莫潘 Belmopan	伯利兹元 Belizean Dollar (BZ $)
多米尼加共和国 the Dominican Republic	圣多明各 Santo Domingo	比索 Peso
多米尼克联邦 the Commonwealth of Dominica	罗索 Roseau	东加勒比元 East Caribbean Dollar (EC $)
厄瓜多尔共和国 the Republic of Ecuador	基多 Quito	苏克雷 Sucre
哥伦比亚共和国 the Republic of Colombia	圣菲波哥大 Santa Fe Bogota	比索 Peso
哥斯达黎加共和国 the Republic of Costa Rica	圣何塞 San José	科朗 Colón
格林纳达 Grenada	圣乔治 St. George's	东加勒比元 East Caribbean Dollar (EC $)
古巴共和国 the Republic of Cuba	哈瓦那 La Havana	比索 Peso
瓜德罗普 (法) Guadeloupe (French)	巴斯特尔 Basse-Terre	法国法郎 French Franc
圭亚那合作共和国 the Cooperative Republic of Guyana	乔治敦 Georgetown	圭亚那元 Guyana Dollar
圭亚那 (法) Guyana (French)	卡宴 Cayenne	法国法郎 French Franc
海地共和国 the Republic of Haiti	太子港 Port-au-Prince	古德 Gourde
荷属安的列斯 Netherlands Antilles	威廉斯塔德 Willemstad	荷属安的列斯盾 Netherlands Antilles Guilder or Florin
洪都拉斯共和国 the Republic of Honduras	特古西加尔巴 Tegucigalpa	伦皮拉 Lempira
加拿大 Canada	渥太华 Ottawa	加拿大元 Canadian Dollar (C $)
开曼群岛 (英) Cayman Islands (UK)	乔治敦 Georgetown	开曼元 Cayman Dollar
马尔维纳斯群岛 (福克兰群岛) Malvinas Islands (Falkland Islands)	斯坦利港 Stanley	福克兰镑 Falkland Pound
马提尼克 (法) Martinique (French)	法兰西堡 Fort-de-France	法国法郎 French Franc
美利坚合众国 the United States of America	华盛顿特区 Washington D. C.	美元 US Dollar (US $)

美属维尔京群岛 the Virgin Islands of the United States	夏洛特阿马利亚 Charlotte Amalie	美元 US Dollar
蒙特塞拉特（英） Montserrat (UK)	普利茅斯 Plymouth	东加勒比元 East Caribbean Dollar (EC)
墨西哥合众国 the United States of Mexico	墨西哥城 Mexico City	比索 Peso
尼加拉瓜共和国 the Republic of Nicaragua	马那瓜 Managua	科多巴 Córdoba
萨尔瓦多共和国 the Republic of El Salvador	圣萨尔瓦多 San Salvador	科郎 Colón
圣克里斯托弗和尼维斯联邦 the Federation of St. Christopher and Nevis	巴斯特尔 Basseterre	东加勒比元 East Caribbean Dollar (EC)
圣卢西亚 St. Lucia	卡斯特里 Castries	东加勒比元 East Caribbean Dollar (EC)
圣皮埃尔和密克隆群岛 St. Pierre & Miquelon Islands	圣皮埃尔 St. Pierre	法国法郎 French Franc
圣文森特和格林纳丁斯 St. Vincent & the Grenadines	金斯敦 Kingstown	东加勒比元 East Caribbean Dollar (EC)
苏里南共和国 the Republic of Suriname	帕拉马里博 Paramaribo	苏里南盾或弗罗林 Surinam Guilder or Florin
特克斯和凯科斯群岛（英） Turks and Caicos Islands (UK)	科伯恩城 Cockburn Town	美元 US Dollar
特立尼达和多巴哥共和国 the Republic of Trinidad & Tobago	西班牙港 Port of Spain	特立尼达和多巴哥元 Trinidad & Tobago Dollar
危地马拉共和国 the Republic of Guatemala	危地马拉城 Guatemala City	格查尔 Quetzal
委内瑞拉共和国 the Republic of Venezuela	加拉加斯 Caracas	玻利瓦尔 Bolivar
乌拉圭东岸共和国 the Oriental Republic of Uruguay	蒙得维的亚 Montevideo	新比索 New Peso
牙买加 Jamaica	金斯敦 Kingstown	牙买加元 Jamaican Dollar (J $)
英属维尔京群岛 the British Virgin Islands	罗德城 Road Town	美元 US Dollar
智利共和国 the Republic of Chile	圣地亚哥 Santiago	比索 Peso

大洋洲及太平洋岛屿 Oceania and the Pacific Islands

澳大利亚联邦 the Commonwealth of Australia	堪培拉 Canberra	澳大利亚元 Australian Dollar ($ A)

巴布亚新几内亚独立国 the Independent State of Papua New Guinea	莫尔兹比港 Port Moresby	基纳 Kina (K)
北马里亚纳联合邦 (美) the Commonwealth of the Northern Marianas (US)	塞班岛 Saipan Island	美元 US Dollar
东萨摩亚 (美) Eastern Samoa (US)	帕果帕果 Pago-Pago	美元 US Dollar
法属波利尼西亚 French Polynesia	帕皮提 Papeete	太平洋法郎 Pacific Franc
斐济群岛共和国 the Republic of the Fiji Islands	苏瓦 Suva	斐济元 Fiji Dollar ($ F)
关岛 (美) Guam (US)	阿加尼亚 Agana	美元 US Dollar
豪兰、贝克和贾维斯岛 (美) Howland, Baker and Jarvis Islands (US)		美元 US Dollar
基里巴斯共和国 the Republic of Kiribati	塔拉瓦 Tarawa	澳大利亚元 Australian Dollar($ A)
库克群岛 (新) the Cook Islands (New Zealand)	阿瓦鲁阿 Avarua	新西兰元 New Zealand Dollar ($ NZ)
马绍尔群岛共和国 the Republic of the Marshall Islands	马朱罗 Majuro	美元 US Dollar
密克罗尼西亚联邦 the Federated States of Micronesia	波纳佩 Ponape	美元 US Dollar
瑙鲁共和国 the Republic of Nauru	亚伦区 Yaren District	澳大利亚元 Australian Dollar ($ A)
纽埃 (新) Niue (New Zealand)	阿洛菲 Alofi	新西兰元 New Zealand Dollar ($ NZ)
诺福克岛 (澳) Norfolk Island (Australian)	金斯敦 Kingstown	澳元 Australian Dollar ($ A)
帕劳共和国 the Republic of Palau	科罗尔 Koror	美元 US Dollar
皮特开恩群岛 (英) Pitcairn Islands Groups (UK)	亚当斯敦 Adamstown	新西兰元 New Zealand Dollar
萨摩亚独立国 the Independent State of Samoa	阿皮亚 Apia	塔拉 Tala
新喀里多尼亚(法) New Caledonia (French)	努美阿 Noumea	太平洋法郎 Pacific Franc
所罗门群岛 Solomon Islands	霍尼亚拉 Honiara	所罗门群岛元 Solomon Dollar
汤加王国 the Kingdom of Tonga	努库阿洛法 Nukualofa	潘加 Pa'anga
图瓦卢 Tuvalu	富纳富提 Funafuti	澳元和图瓦卢硬币 Australian or Tuvaluan Dollars
托克劳 (新) Tokelau (New Zealand)		新西兰元 New Zealand Dollar

瓦利斯和富图纳群岛（法） Wallis and Futuna Islands (French)	马塔乌图 Mata-Utu	太平洋法郎 Pacific Franc
瓦努阿图共和国 the Republic of Vanuatu	维拉港 Port Vila	瓦图 Vatu
威克岛（美） Wake Island (US)		美元 US Dollar
新西兰 New Zealand	惠灵顿 Wellington	新西兰元 New Zealand Dollar ($ NZ)
约翰斯顿岛（美） Johnston Atoll (US)		美元 US Dollar
中途岛（美） Midway Islands (US)		美元 US Dollar

21. 元素周期表

Periodic Table of Elements

24 Cr 铬 ge chromium 51.9961(6)

- 24 → 原子序数 atomic number
- Cr → 元素符号 symbol
- 铬 ge → 元素中文名称与拼音 name in Chinese & Pinyin
- chromium → 英文名称 name in English
- 51.9961(6) → 原子量** atomic weight

族 Family / 周期 Period	IA	IIA	IIIB	IVB	VB	VIB	VIIB	VIII			IB	IIB	IIIA	IVA	VA	VIA	VIIA	O
1	1 H 氢 qing hydrogen 1.00794(7)																	2 He 氦 hai helium 4.002602(2)
2	3 Li 锂 li lithium 6.941(2)	4 Be 铍 pi beryllium 9.0121823(3)											5 B 硼 peng boron 10.811(5)	6 C 碳 tan carbon 12.011	7 N 氮 dan nitrogen 14.006747(7)	8 O 氧 yang oxygen 15.9994(3)	9 F 氟 fu fluorine 18.9984032(9)	10 Ne 氖 nai neon 20.1797(6)
3	11 Na 钠 na sodium 22.989768(6)	12 Mg 镁 mei magnesium 24.3050(6)											13 Al 铝 lü aluminium 26.981539(5)	14 Si 硅 gui silicon 28.0855(3)	15 P 磷 lin phosphorus 30.973762(4)	16 S 硫 liu sulphur 32.066(6)	17 Cl 氯 lü chlorine 35.4527(9)	18 Ar 氩 ya argon 39.948
4	19 K 钾 jia potassium 39.0983	20 Ca 钙 gai calcium 40.078(4)	21 Sc 钪 kang scandium 44.955910(9)	22 Ti 钛 tai titanium 47.88(3)	23 V 钒 fan vanadium 50.9415	24 Cr 铬 ge chromium 51.9961(6)	25 Mn 锰 meng manganese 54.93805(1)	26 Fe 铁 tie iron 55.847(3)	27 Co 钴 gu cobalt 58.93320(1)	28 Ni 镍 nie nickel 58.69	29 Cu 铜 tong copper 63.546(3)	30 Zn 锌 xin zinc 65.39(2)	31 Ga 镓 jia gallium 69.723(4)	32 Ge 锗 zhe germanium 72.61(2)	33 As 砷 shen arsenic 74.92159(2)	34 Se 硒 xi selenium 78.96(3)	35 Br 溴 xiu bromine 79.904	36 Kr 氪 ke krypton 83.80
5	37 Rb 铷 ru rubidium 85.4678(3)	38 Sr 锶 si strontium 87.62	39 Y 钇 yi yttrium 88.90585(2)	40 Zr 锆 gao zirconium 91.224(2)	41 Nb 铌 ni niobium 92.90638(2)	42 Mo 钼 mu molybdenum 95.94	43 Tc 锝 de technetium [98]	44 Ru 钌 liao ruthenium 101.07(2)	45 Rh 铑 lao rhodium 102.90550(3)	46 Pd 钯 ba palladium 106.42	47 Ag 银 yin silver 107.8682(2)	48 Cd 镉 ge cadmium 112.411(8)	49 In 铟 yin indium 114.82	50 Sn 锡 xi tin 118.710(7)	51 Sb 锑 ti antimony 121.75(3)	52 Te 碲 di tellurium 127.60(3)	53 I 碘 dian iodine 126.90447(3)	54 Xe 氙 xian xenon 131.29(2)
6	55 Cs 铯 se cesium 132.90543(5)	56 Ba 钡 bei barium 137.327(7)	57—71 La—Lu 镧系 lanxi La group	72 Hf 铪 ha hafnium 178.49(2)	73 Ta 钽 tan tantalum 180.9479	74 W 钨 wu tungsten 183.85(3)	75 Re 铼 lai rhenium 186.207	76 Os 锇 e osmium 190.2	77 Ir 铱 yi iridium 192.22(3)	78 Pt 铂 bo platinum 195.08(3)	79 Au 金 jin gold 196.96654(3)	80 Hg 汞 gong mercury 200.59(3)	81 Tl 铊 ta thallium 204.3833(2)	82 Pb 铅 qian lead 207.2	83 Bi 铋 bi bismuth 208.98037(3)	84 Po 钋 po polonium [209.210]	85 At 砹 ai astatine [210]	86 Rn 氡 dong radon [222]
7	87 Fr 钫 fang francium [223]	88 Ra 镭 lei radium 226.0254	89—103 Ac—Lr 锕系 axi Ac group	104 Rf * 𬬻 lu rutherfordi-um [261]	105 Db * 𬭊 du dubnium [262]	106 Sg * 𬭳 xi seaborgium [263]	107 Bh * 𬭛 bo bohrium [262]	108 Hs * 𬭶 hei hassium [265]	109 Mt * 鿏 mai meitnerium [266]									

57—71 La—Lu 镧系 lanxi La group	57 La 镧 lan lanthanum 138.9055(2)	58 Ce 铈 shi cerium 140.115(4)	59 Pr 镨 pu praseodymi-um 140.90765(3)	60 Nd 钕 nü neodymium 144.24(3)	61 Pm * 钷 po promethium [147]	62 Sm 钐 shan samarium 150.36(3)	63 Eu 铕 you europium 151.965(9)	64 Gd 钆 ga gadolinium 157.25(3)	65 Tb 铽 te terbium 158.92534(3)	66 Dy 镝 di dysprosium 162.50(3)	67 Ho 钬 huo holmium 164.93032(3)	68 Er 铒 er erbium 167.26(3)	69 Tm 铥 diu thulium 168.93421(3)	70 Yb 镱 yi ytterbium 173.04(3)	71 Lu 镥 lu lutetium 174.967
89—103 Ac—Lr 锕系 axi Ac group	89 Ac 锕 a actinium 227.0278	90 Th 钍 tu thorium 232.0381	91 Pa 镤 pu protactinium 231.0359	92 U 铀 you uranium 238.0289	93 Np 镎 na neptunium 237.0482	94 Pu 钚 bu plutonium [244]	95 Am * 镅 mei americium [243]	96 Cm * 锔 ju curium [247]	97 Bk * 锫 pei berkelium [247]	98 Cf * 锎 kai californium [251]	99 Es * 锿 ai einsteinium [252]	100 Fm * 镄 fei fermium [257]	101 Md * 钔 men mendelevium [258]	102 No * 锘 nuo nobelium [259]	103 Lr * 铹 lao lawrencium [260]

注*的为人造元素
Those marked with * are man-made elements.

** 原子量均采用国际标准数，末位数的准确度注于其后的圆括弧内，未加注者，准确度至±1。原子量置于方括弧内者为最稳定同位素的质量。
Here listed are internationally acknowledged data on the atomic weights of the elements, with the accuracy of the last digit of each figure noted in round brackets and those of the unnoted figures accurate up to ±1. Data of atomic weight listed in square brackets indicate the most stable isotope of a given element.

*** 截至1998年底
updated as by the end of 1998

22. 中国地质年表
A Geologic Time Scale of China

宙 Eon	代 Era	纪 Period	世 Epoch	生物发展阶段 Development of Organisms	距今时间 (百万年) Time (Ma BP)
显生宙(PH) Phanerozoic	新生代(Kz) Cenozoic	第四纪(Q) Quaternary	全新世(Q_H) Holocene	现代人类出现。 *Homo sapiens sapiens* appear.	(0.01)
			更新世(Q_P) Pleistocene	生物绝大部分与现在类似。智人出现。 Most organisms are similar to those of today. *Homo sapiens* appear.	2.48*, 1.64**
		新第三纪(N) Neogene	上新世(N_2) Pliocene	生物面貌与现在接近，哺乳类形体变大。直立人出现。 Organisms are close to those of today. Mammals become larger. *Homo erectus* appear.	5.3(4.8)
			中新世(N_1) Miocene	类人猿出现。 Anthropoids appear.	23.3
		老第三纪(E) Paleogene	渐新世(E_3) Oligocene	哺乳类迅速发展，被子植物繁盛。 Mammals develop rapidly. Angiosperms prosper.	36.5
			始新世(E_2) Eocene		53.0(57.8)
			古新世(E_1) Paleocene		65
	中生代(Mz) Mesozoic	白垩纪(K) Cretaceous		被子植物出现，末期恐龙等大批生物绝灭。 Angiosperms appear. Dinosaurs and large numbers of organisms become extinct.	135(140)
		侏罗纪(J) Jurassic		鸟类出现，爬行类及苏铁等裸子植物繁盛。 Birds appear. Reptiles and gymnosperms such as *Cycas revoluta*.	205
		三叠纪(T) Triassic		哺乳类出现。 Mammals appear.	250
	古生代(Pz) Paleozoic	二叠纪(P) Permian		无脊椎动物和裸子植物发展。 Invertebrates and gymnosperms develop.	290
		石炭纪(C) Carboniferous		爬行类出现，蕨类植物繁盛。 Reptiles appear. Pteridophytes prosper.	355
		泥盆纪(D) Devonian		昆虫、原始鱼类、蕨类和原始裸子植物出现。 Insects, primordial fishes, pteridophytes and primordial gymnosperms appear.	410
		志留纪(S) Silurian		原始鱼类、原始陆生植物出现。 Primordial fishes and terrestrial plants appear.	439
		奥陶纪(O) Ordovician		无颌类脊椎动物出现，海生藻类发育。 Jawless vertebrates appear. Marine algae develop.	510
		寒武纪(C) Cambrian		小壳动物出现，藻类、三叶虫开始繁盛。 Small-valve animals appear. Algae and trilobito begin to prosper.	570

宙 Eon	代 Era	纪 Period	世 Epoch	生物发展阶段 Development of Organisms	距今时间 (百万年) Time (Ma BP)
元古宙(PT) Proterozoic	新元古代(Pt_3) Neoproterozoic	震旦纪(Z) Sinian		藻类、细菌繁盛,软躯体无脊椎动物出现。 Algae and bacteria prosper. Soft-bodied invertebrates appear.	570
		青白口纪(Qb) Qingbaikouian			800
	中元古代(Pt_2) Mesoproterozoic	蓟县纪(Jx) Jixianian			1000
		长城纪(Chc) Changchengian			1400
	古元古代(Pt_1) Paleoproterozoic	滹沱纪(Ht) Hutuoian			1800
		未名 unnamed			
太古宙(AR) Archaean	新太古代(Ar_2) Neoarchaean	五台纪(Wt) Wutaian		晚期有细菌和蓝藻出现。 Bacteria and blue green algae appear later in the period.	2500
		阜平纪(Fp) Fupingian			
	古太古代(Ar_1) Paleoarchaean	迁西纪(Qx) Qianxian			3100
冥古宙(HD) Hadean					3850(4000)

* 中国陆相标准。Terrestrial facies standard of China.
** 欧洲海相标准。Marine facies standard of Europe.

附录

23. 汉语拼音方案

Phonetic Chinese Alphabet

（1957 年 11 月 1 日国务院全体会议第 60 次会议通过）

（1958 年 2 月 11 日第一届全国人民代表大会第五次会议批准）

一、字母表

字母	Aa	Bb	Cc	Dd	Ee	Ff	Gg
名称	ㄚ	ㄅㄝ	ㄘㄝ	ㄉㄝ	ㄜ	ㄝㄈ	ㄍㄝ
	Hh	Ii	Jj	Kk	Ll	Mm	Nn
	ㄏㄚ	ㄧ	ㄐㄧㄝ	ㄎㄝ	ㄝㄌ	ㄝㄇ	ㄋㄝ
	Oo	Pp	Qq	Rr	Ss	Tt	Uu
	ㄛ	ㄆㄝ	ㄑㄧㄡ	ㄚㄦ	ㄝㄙ	ㄊㄝ	ㄨ
	Vv	Ww	Xx	Yy	Zz		
	ㄪㄝ	ㄨㄚ	ㄒㄧ	ㄧㄚ	ㄗㄝ		

v 只用来拼写外来语、少数民族语言和方言。

字母的手写体依照拉丁字母的一般书写习惯。

二、声母表

b	p	m	f	d	t	n	l
ㄅ玻	ㄆ坡	ㄇ摸	ㄈ佛	ㄉ得	ㄊ特	ㄋ讷	ㄌ勒
g	k	h		j	q	x	
ㄍ哥	ㄎ科	ㄏ喝		ㄐ基	ㄑ欺	ㄒ希	
zh	ch	sh	r	z	c	s	
ㄓ知	ㄔ蚩	ㄕ诗	ㄖ日	ㄗ资	ㄘ雌	ㄙ思	

在给汉字注音的时候，为了使拼式简短，zh ch sh 可以省作 ẑ ĉ ŝ。

三、韵母表

	i ㄧ 衣	u ㄨ 乌	ü ㄩ 迂
a ㄚ 啊	ia ㄧㄚ 呀	ua ㄨㄚ 蛙	
o ㄛ 喔		uo ㄨㄛ 窝	
e ㄜ 鹅	ie ㄧㄝ 耶		üe ㄩㄝ 约
ai ㄞ 哀		uai ㄨㄞ 歪	
ei ㄟ 欸		uei ㄨㄟ 威	
ao ㄠ 熬	iao ㄧㄠ 腰		
ou ㄡ 欧	iou ㄧㄡ 忧		
an ㄢ 安	ian ㄧㄢ 烟	uan ㄨㄢ 弯	üan ㄩㄢ 冤
en ㄣ 恩	in ㄧㄣ 因	uen ㄨㄣ 温	ün ㄩㄣ 晕
ang ㄤ 昂	iang ㄧㄤ 央	uang ㄨㄤ 汪	
eng ㄥ 亨的韵母	ing ㄧㄥ 英	ueng ㄨㄥ 翁	
ong （ㄨㄥ）轰的韵母	iong ㄩㄥ 雍		

(1) “知、蚩、诗、日、资、雌、思”等七个音节的韵母用 i，即：知、蚩、诗、日、资、雌、思等字拼作 zhi, chi, shi, ri, zi, ci, si。

(2) 韵母ㄦ写成 er，用做韵尾的时候写成 r。例如：“儿童”拼作 ertong，“花儿”拼作 huar。

(3) 韵母ㄝ单用的时候写成 ê。

(4) i 行的韵母，前面没有声母的时候，写成 yi（衣），ya（呀），ye（耶），yao（腰），you（忧），yan（烟），yin（因），yang（央），ying（英），yong（雍）。

u 行的韵母，前面没有声母的时候，写成 wu（乌），wa（蛙），wo（窝），wai（歪），wei（威），wan（弯），wen（温），wang（汪），weng（翁）。

ü 行的韵母，前面没有声母的时候，写成 yu（迂），yue（约），yuan（冤），yun（晕）；ü 上两点省略。

ü 行的韵母跟声母 j, q, x 拼的时候，写成 ju（居），qu（区），xu（虚），ü 上两点也省略；但是跟声母 n, l 拼的时候，仍然写成 nü（女），lü（吕）。

(5) iou, uei, uen 前面加声母的时候，写成 iu, ui, un，例如 niu（牛），gui（归），lun（论）。

(6) 在给汉字注音的时候，为了使拼式简短，ng 可以省作 ŋ。

四、声调符号

阴平	阳平	上声	去声
ˉ	ˊ	ˇ	ˋ

声调符号标在音节的主要母音上，轻声不标。例如：

妈 mā	麻 má	马 mǎ	骂 mà	吗 ma
（阴平）	（阳平）	（上声）	（去声）	（轻声）

五、隔音符号

a, o, e 开头的音节连接在其他音节后面的时候，如果音节的界限发生混淆，用隔音符号（'）隔开，例如：pi'ao（皮袄）。

24. 汉字繁简体字对照表

Original and Simplified Chinese Characters

说　明

一、本表收录了1986年经国务院批准重新发表的《简化汉字总表》中的全部简化字和它们的繁体字，也包括总表《附录》中所列的39个正体字和它们的异体字。

二、本词典正文所收其他单字，凡可以按照《简化字总表》的有关规定类推简化的，本词典均已简化。

三、《简化字总表》规定的简化偏旁为：讠〔言〕、饣〔食〕、𠃓〔昜〕、纟〔糸〕、𰃮〔臤〕、𦍌〔𤇾〕、𭕄〔臨〕、只〔戠〕、钅〔金〕、𭕄〔𦥯〕、𰆊〔睪〕、𢀖〔巠〕、亦〔䜌〕、呙〔咼〕。其中"讠、饣、纟、钅"一般只用于左偏旁。

四、字后标△的为可作简化偏旁用的简化字，字前标＊的为异体字。

六至七画

＊〔兇〕凶
〔車〕车△
〔夾〕夹△
〔貝〕贝△
〔見〕见△
＊〔牠〕它
＊〔佈〕布
＊〔佔〕占
〔壯〕壮
〔妝〕妆
＊〔災〕灾

八画

〔衹〕只
〔長〕长△
〔亞〕亚△
〔軋〕轧
〔東〕东△
〔兩〕两△
〔協〕协
〔來〕来△
〔戔〕戋△
＊〔昇〕升
〔門〕门△
〔岡〕冈△
〔侖〕仑△
〔兒〕儿
＊〔牀〕床
〔狀〕状
〔糾〕纠

九画

【丶】

〔訂〕订
〔計〕计
〔訃〕讣
〔軍〕军

【一】

〔剋〕克
〔軌〕轨
〔庫〕库
〔頁〕页△
〔郟〕郏
〔剄〕刭
〔勁〕劲

【丨】

〔貞〕贞
〔則〕则
〔鬥〕闩
〔迴〕回

【丿】

〔俠〕侠
〔係〕系
〔鳧〕凫
〔帥〕帅
〔後〕后
〔釓〕钆
〔釔〕钇
〔負〕负
〔風〕风△

【乛】

〔陣〕阵
〔韋〕韦△
〔陝〕陕
＊〔陞〕升
〔陘〕陉
〔飛〕飞
〔紆〕纡
〔紅〕红
〔紂〕纣
〔紈〕纨
〔級〕级
〔約〕约
〔紇〕纥
〔紀〕纪
〔紉〕纫

十画

【丶】

〔訐〕讦
〔訌〕讧
〔討〕讨
〔訕〕讪
〔訖〕讫
〔訓〕训
〔這〕这
〔訊〕讯
〔記〕记
〔凍〕冻
〔畝〕亩
〔庫〕库
〔浹〕浃
〔涇〕泾

【一】

〔馬〕马△
〔挾〕挟
＊〔紥〕扎
〔貢〕贡
〔華〕华△
〔莢〕荚
〔莖〕茎
〔莧〕苋
〔莊〕庄
〔軒〕轩
〔連〕连
〔軔〕轫
〔劃〕划

【丨】

〔鬥〕斗⑤
〔時〕时△
〔畢〕毕△
〔財〕财
〔覎〕觃
〔閃〕闪
〔唄〕呗
〔員〕员
〔豈〕岂△
〔峽〕峡
〔峴〕岘
〔剛〕刚
〔剮〕剐

【丿】

〔氣〕气△
〔郵〕邮
〔倀〕伥
〔倆〕俩
〔條〕条△
〔們〕们
〔個〕个
〔倫〕伦
〔隻〕只
〔島〕岛
〔烏〕乌△
〔師〕师
〔徑〕径
〔釘〕钉
〔針〕针
〔釗〕钊
〔釙〕钋
〔釕〕钌
〔殺〕杀△
〔倉〕仓△
〔脅〕胁
〔狹〕狭
〔狽〕狈
〔芻〕刍△
＊〔脈〕脉

【乛】

〔書〕书
〔陸〕陆
〔陳〕陈
〔孫〕孙△
〔陰〕阴△
〔務〕务
〔紜〕纭
〔純〕纯
〔紕〕纰
〔紗〕纱
〔納〕纳
〔紝〕纴
〔紛〕纷
〔紙〕纸
〔紋〕纹
〔紡〕纺
〔紖〕纼
〔紐〕纽
〔紓〕纾

十一画

【丶】

〔詎〕讵
〔訝〕讶
〔訥〕讷
〔許〕许
〔訛〕讹
〔訢〕䜣
〔訩〕讻
〔訟〕讼
〔設〕设
〔訪〕访
〔訣〕诀
〔産〕产△
〔牽〕牵
〔烴〕烃
＊〔淚〕泪
〔淶〕涞
〔淺〕浅
〔渦〕涡
〔淪〕沦
〔悵〕怅
〔鄆〕郓
〔啓〕启
〔視〕视

【一】

〔責〕责
〔現〕现
〔匭〕匦
〔規〕规

〔殼〕壳△
〔埡〕垭
*〔掛〕挂
〔掗〕挜
〔捨〕舍
〔捫〕扪
〔掆〕㧏
〔堝〕埚
〔頂〕顶
〔掄〕抡
〔執〕执△
〔捲〕卷
〔掃〕扫
〔堊〕垩
〔萊〕莱
〔萵〕莴
*〔剳〕札
〔乾〕干①
〔梘〕枧
*〔紮〕扎
〔軛〕轭
〔斬〕斩
〔軟〕软
〔專〕专△
〔區〕区△
〔堅〕坚
〔帶〕带
*〔脣〕唇
〔厠〕厕
〔硃〕朱
〔麥〕麦△
〔頃〕顷

【丨】

〔鹵〕卤△
〔處〕处
〔敗〕败
〔販〕贩
〔貶〕贬
〔啞〕哑
〔閉〕闭
〔問〕问
〔婁〕娄△
〔啢〕唡
〔國〕国△
〔喎〕㖞
〔帳〕帐
〔崬〕岽
〔崍〕崃
〔崗〕岗
*〔崐〕昆
*〔崑〕昆
*〔異〕异
〔圇〕囵
〔過〕过△

【丿】

〔氫〕氢
〔動〕动△
〔偵〕侦
〔側〕侧
〔貨〕货
〔進〕进△
〔梟〕枭
〔鳥〕鸟△
〔偉〕伟
〔徠〕徕
〔術〕术
〔從〕从△
〔釷〕钍
〔釬〕钎
〔釧〕钏
〔釤〕钐
〔釣〕钓
〔釩〕钒
〔釹〕钕
〔釵〕钗
〔貪〕贪
〔覓〕觅
〔飥〕饦
〔貧〕贫
〔脛〕胫
*〔週〕周
〔魚〕鱼△

【乛】

〔將〕将△
〔晝〕昼
〔張〕张
〔階〕阶
〔陽〕阳
〔隊〕队△
〔婭〕娅
〔媧〕娲
〔婦〕妇
〔習〕习
〔參〕参△
〔紺〕绀
〔紲〕绁
〔紱〕绂
〔組〕组
〔紳〕绅
〔紬〕䌷
〔細〕细
〔終〕终
〔絆〕绊
〔紼〕绋
〔絀〕绌
〔紹〕绍
〔紿〕绐
〔貫〕贯
〔鄉〕乡△

十二画

【丶】

*〔註〕注
〔詁〕诂
〔訶〕诃
〔評〕评
〔詛〕诅
〔詗〕诇
〔詐〕诈
〔訴〕诉
〔診〕诊
〔詆〕诋
〔詞〕词
〔詘〕诎
〔詔〕诏
〔詒〕诒
〔馮〕冯
〔痙〕痉
*〔棄〕弃
〔勞〕劳
〔湞〕浈
〔測〕测
〔湯〕汤
〔淵〕渊
〔渢〕沨
〔渾〕浑
*〔湧〕涌
〔愜〕惬
〔惻〕恻
〔惲〕恽
〔惱〕恼
〔運〕运
〔補〕补
〔禍〕祸

【一】

〔貳〕贰
〔預〕预
〔堯〕尧△
〔揀〕拣
〔馭〕驭
〔項〕项
〔賁〕贲
〔場〕场
〔揚〕扬
〔塊〕块
〔達〕达△
〔報〕报
〔揮〕挥
〔壺〕壶
〔惡〕恶
〔葉〕叶
〔貰〕贳
〔萬〕万△
〔葷〕荤
〔喪〕丧
〔葦〕苇
〔葒〕荭
〔葤〕荮
〔棖〕枨
〔棟〕栋
〔棧〕栈
*〔棲〕栖
〔棡〕㭎
〔極〕极
〔軲〕轱
〔軻〕轲
〔軸〕轴
〔軼〕轶
〔軤〕轷
〔軫〕轸
〔軺〕轺
〔畫〕画△
〔腎〕肾
〔棗〕枣
〔硨〕砗
〔硤〕硖
〔硯〕砚
〔殘〕残
〔雲〕云△

【丨】

〔覘〕觇
〔睏〕困
〔貼〕贴
〔貺〕贶
〔貯〕贮
〔貽〕贻
〔閏〕闰
〔開〕开
〔閑〕闲
〔間〕间
〔閔〕闵
〔悶〕闷
〔貴〕贵
〔鄖〕郧
〔勛〕勋
〔單〕单△
〔喲〕哟
〔買〕买△
〔剴〕剀
〔凱〕凯
〔幀〕帧
〔嵐〕岚
〔幃〕帏
〔圍〕围

【丿】

〔無〕无△
〔氬〕氩
〔喬〕乔△
〔筆〕笔△
*〔筍〕笋
〔備〕备△
〔貸〕贷
*〔傑〕杰
〔順〕顺
〔傖〕伧
〔㑳〕㑇
〔傢〕家
〔鄔〕邬
〔衆〕众
〔復〕复
〔須〕须
〔鈃〕钘
〔鈣〕钙
〔鈈〕钚
〔鈦〕钛
*〔鉅〕巨
〔釾〕铘
〔鈍〕钝
〔鈔〕钞
〔鈉〕钠
〔鈐〕钤
〔欽〕钦
〔鈞〕钧
〔鈎〕钩
〔鈧〕钪
〔鈁〕钫
〔鈥〕钬
〔鈄〕钭
〔鈕〕钮
〔鈀〕钯
〔傘〕伞
〔爺〕爷
〔創〕创
〔飩〕饨
〔飪〕饪
〔飫〕饫
〔飭〕饬
〔飯〕饭
〔飲〕饮
〔爲〕为△
〔脹〕胀
〔腖〕胨
〔腡〕脶
〔勝〕胜
〔猶〕犹△
〔貿〕贸
〔鄒〕邹

【乛】

〔尋〕寻△
〔費〕费
〔違〕违
〔韌〕韧
〔隕〕陨
〔賀〕贺
〔發〕发△
〔綁〕绑
〔絨〕绒
〔結〕结
〔絝〕绔
〔絰〕绖
〔絎〕绗
〔給〕给
〔絢〕绚
〔絳〕绛
〔絡〕络
〔絞〕绞
〔統〕统
〔絶〕绝
〔絲〕丝
〔幾〕几△

十三画

【丶】

〔詎〕讵
〔誄〕诔
〔試〕试
〔詿〕诖
〔詩〕诗
〔詰〕诘
〔誇〕夸
〔詼〕诙
〔誠〕诚
〔誅〕诛
〔話〕话
〔誕〕诞
〔詬〕诟
〔詮〕诠
〔詭〕诡
〔詢〕询
〔詣〕诣
〔諍〕诤
〔該〕该
〔詳〕详
〔詫〕诧
〔詡〕诩
〔裏〕里
〔準〕准
〔頏〕颃
〔資〕资
〔羥〕羟
〔義〕义△
〔煉〕炼
〔煩〕烦
〔煬〕炀
〔塋〕茔
〔煢〕茕
〔煒〕炜
〔遞〕递
〔溝〕沟
〔漣〕涟
〔滅〕灭
〔溳〕涢
〔滌〕涤
〔溮〕浉
〔塗〕涂
〔滄〕沧
〔愷〕恺
〔愾〕忾
〔愴〕怆
〔㥮〕㤘
〔窩〕窝
〔禎〕祯
〔禕〕祎

【一】

〔頊〕顼
〔琿〕珲
〔瑋〕玮
〔頑〕顽
〔載〕载
〔馱〕驮
〔馴〕驯
〔馳〕驰
〔塒〕埘
〔塤〕埙
〔損〕损
〔遠〕远
〔塏〕垲
〔勢〕势
〔搶〕抢
〔搗〕捣

〔蘚〕藓
〔鶘〕鹕
〔飄〕飘
〔櫪〕枥
〔櫨〕栌
〔櫸〕榉
〔礬〕矾
〔麵〕面
〔櫬〕榇
〔櫳〕栊
〔礫〕砾

【丨】

〔鹹〕咸
〔鹺〕鹾
〔齟〕龃
〔齡〕龄
〔齣〕出
〔齙〕龅
〔齠〕龆
〔獻〕献△
〔黨〕党△
〔懸〕悬
〔鶪〕䴗
〔罌〕罂
〔贍〕赡
〔闥〕闼
〔闡〕阐
〔鶡〕鹖
〔曨〕昽
〔蠣〕蛎
〔蠐〕蛴
〔蠑〕蝾
〔嚶〕嘤
〔鶚〕鹗
〔髏〕髅
〔鶻〕鹘

【丿】

〔犧〕牺
〔鶖〕鹙
〔籌〕筹
〔籃〕篮
〔譽〕誉
〔覺〕觉
〔嚳〕喾
〔衊〕蔑
〔艦〕舰
〔鐃〕铙
〔鐝〕镢
〔鐐〕镣
〔鏷〕镤
〔鐦〕锎
〔鐧〕锏
〔鐓〕镦
〔鐘〕钟
〔鐥〕𫓹
〔鐠〕镨
〔鐒〕铹
〔鏹〕镪
〔鐨〕镄
〔鐙〕镫
〔鏺〕钹
〔釋〕释
〔饒〕饶
〔饊〕馓
〔饋〕馈
〔饌〕馔
〔饑〕饥
〔臚〕胪
〔朧〕胧
〔騰〕腾
〔鰆〕䲠
〔鰈〕鲽
〔鰂〕鲗
〔鰛〕鳁
〔鰓〕鳃
〔鰐〕鳄
〔鰍〕鳅
〔鰒〕鳆
〔鰉〕鳇
〔鰌〕䲡
〔鯿〕鳊
〔獮〕狝
〔觸〕触

【乛】

〔鶥〕鹛
〔鶩〕鹜
〔纊〕纩
〔繽〕缤
〔繼〕继
〔饗〕飨
〔響〕响

二十一画

【丶】

〔癩〕癞
〔癧〕疬
〔癮〕瘾
〔斕〕斓
〔辯〕辩
〔礱〕砻
〔鶼〕鹣
〔爛〕烂
〔鶯〕莺
〔灄〕滠
〔灃〕沣
〔灕〕漓
〔懾〕慑
〔懼〕惧
〔竈〕灶
〔顧〕顾
〔襯〕衬
〔鶴〕鹤

【一】

〔䎱〕䎬
〔瓔〕璎
〔鰲〕鳌
〔攝〕摄
〔騾〕骡
〔驅〕驱
〔驃〕骠
〔驄〕骢
〔驂〕骖
〔㩳〕㧐
〔攛〕撺
〔韃〕鞑
〔鞽〕鞒
〔歡〕欢
〔權〕权
〔櫻〕樱
〔欄〕栏
〔轟〕轰
〔覽〕览
〔酈〕郦
〔飆〕飙
〔殲〕歼

【丨】

〔齜〕龇
〔齦〕龈
〔[illegible]〕[illegible]
〔贐〕赆
〔囁〕嗫
〔囈〕呓
〔闢〕辟
〔囀〕啭
〔顥〕颢
〔躊〕踌
〔躋〕跻
〔躑〕踯
〔躍〕跃
〔纍〕累
〔蠟〕蜡
〔囂〕嚣
〔巋〕岿
〔髒〕脏

【丿】

〔儺〕傩
〔儷〕俪
〔儼〕俨
〔鷉〕䴘
〔鐵〕铁
〔鑊〕镬
〔鐳〕镭
〔鐺〕铛
〔鐸〕铎
〔鐶〕镮
〔鐲〕镯
〔鐮〕镰
〔鐿〕镱
*〔鏽〕锈
〔鶺〕鹡
〔鷂〕鹞
〔鷄〕鸡
〔鶬〕鸧
〔臟〕脏
〔臞〕臞
〔鰭〕鳍
〔鰱〕鲢
〔鰣〕鲥
〔鰨〕鳎
〔鰥〕鳏
〔鰷〕鲦
〔鰟〕鳑
〔鰜〕鳒

【乛】

〔屬〕属△
〔纈〕缬
〔續〕续
〔纏〕缠

二十二画

【丶】

〔讀〕读
〔讅〕谉
〔巒〕峦
〔彎〕弯
〔孿〕孪
〔孌〕娈
〔顫〕颤
〔鷓〕鹧
〔癭〕瘿
〔癬〕癣
〔聾〕聋
〔龔〕龚
〔襲〕袭
〔灘〕滩
〔灑〕洒
〔竊〕窃

【一】

〔鬚〕须
〔驍〕骁
〔驕〕骄
〔攤〕摊
〔覿〕觌
〔攢〕攒
〔鷙〕鸷
〔聽〕听
〔蘿〕萝
〔驚〕惊
〔轢〕轹
〔鷗〕鸥
〔鑒〕鉴
〔邐〕逦
〔鷖〕鹥
〔霽〕霁

【丨】

〔齬〕龉
〔齪〕龊
〔鱉〕鳖
〔贖〕赎
〔躚〕跹
〔躓〕踬
〔蠨〕蟏
〔囌〕苏
〔囉〕啰
〔囒〕㘓
〔囅〕冁
〔巔〕巅
*〔巖〕岩
〔邏〕逻
〔體〕体

【丿】

〔罎〕坛
〔籜〕箨
〔籟〕籁
〔籙〕箓
〔籠〕笼
〔鰵〕鳘
〔儻〕傥
〔艫〕舻
〔鑄〕铸
〔鑌〕镔
〔鑔〕镲
〔龕〕龛
〔糴〕籴
〔鰳〕鳓
〔鰹〕鲣
〔鰾〕鳔
〔鱈〕鳕
〔鰻〕鳗
〔鱅〕鳙
〔鰼〕鳛
〔玀〕猡

【乛】

〔鷚〕鹨
〔轡〕辔

二十三画

【丶】

〔讌〕䜩
〔欒〕栾
〔攣〕挛
〔變〕变
〔戀〕恋
〔鷲〕鹫
〔癰〕痈
〔齏〕齑
〔讋〕詟

【一】

〔瓚〕瓒
〔驛〕驿
〔驗〕验
〔攪〕搅
〔欏〕椤
〔轤〕轳
〔靨〕靥
〔魘〕魇
〔饜〕餍
〔鷯〕鹩
〔靆〕叇
〔顬〕颥

【丨】

〔曬〕晒
〔鷳〕鹇
〔顯〕显
〔蠱〕蛊
〔髖〕髋
〔髕〕髌

【丿】

〔籤〕签
〔讎〕雠①
〔鷦〕鹪
〔黴〕霉
〔鑠〕铄
〔鑕〕锧
〔鑥〕镥
〔鑣〕镳
〔鑞〕镴
〔臢〕臜
〔鱖〕鳜
〔鱔〕鳝
〔鱗〕鳞
〔鱒〕鳟
〔鱘〕鲟

【乛】

〔鷸〕鹬
〔纓〕缨
〔纖〕纤
〔纔〕才
〔鷥〕鸶

二十四画

【丶】

〔讕〕谰
〔讖〕谶
〔讒〕谗
〔讓〕让
〔鸇〕鹯
〔鷹〕鹰
〔癱〕瘫
〔癲〕癫
〔贛〕赣
〔灝〕灏

【一】

〔鬢〕鬓
〔攬〕揽
〔驟〕骤
〔壩〕坝
〔韆〕千
〔觀〕观
〔鹽〕盐
〔釀〕酿
〔靂〕雳
〔靈〕灵△
〔靄〕霭
〔蠶〕蚕

【丨】

〔艷〕艳
〔顰〕颦
〔齲〕龋
〔齷〕龌
〔鹼〕硷
〔贜〕赃
〔鷺〕鹭
〔囑〕嘱
〔羈〕羁

【丿】

〔籩〕笾
〔籬〕篱
〔籪〕簖
〔黌〕黉

附录

〔鱟〕鲎
〔鱧〕鳢
〔鱠〕鲙
〔鱣〕鳣

【㇇】

〔鸊〕䴙

二十五画

【丶】

〔蠻〕蛮
〔臠〕脔
〔廳〕厅
〔灣〕湾

【一】

〔韉〕鞯
〔欖〕榄
〔靉〕叆

【丨】

〔顱〕颅
〔躡〕蹑
〔躥〕蹿
〔鼉〕鼍

【丿】

〔籮〕箩
〔鑭〕镧
〔鑰〕钥
〔鑲〕镶
〔饞〕馋
〔鱨〕鲿
〔鱭〕鲚

【㇇】

〔糶〕粜
〔纘〕缵

二十六画

〔灤〕滦
〔驥〕骥
〔驢〕驴
〔趲〕趱
〔顴〕颧
〔黶〕黡
〔釃〕酾
〔釅〕酽
〔矚〕瞩
〔躪〕躏
〔躦〕躜
〔釁〕衅
〔鑷〕镊
〔鑹〕镩

二十七画

〔讞〕谳
〔讜〕谠
〔鑾〕銮
〔灧〕滟
〔鬮〕阄
〔驤〕骧
〔顳〕颞
〔鸕〕鸬
〔黷〕黩
〔鑼〕锣
〔鑽〕钻
〔鱸〕鲈
〔纜〕缆

二十八画至三十二画

〔戇〕戆
〔鸛〕鹳
〔欞〕棂
〔鑿〕凿
〔鸚〕鹦
〔钂〕镋
〔钁〕䦆
〔驪〕骊
〔鬱〕郁
〔鸞〕鸾
〔鸝〕鹂
〔饢〕馕
〔鱺〕鲡
〔籲〕吁

注释:

① 乾坤、乾隆的乾读 qián(前),不简化。

② 读 me 轻声。读 yāo(夭)的么应作幺(么本字)。吆应作吆。麽读 mó(摩)时不简化,如幺麽小丑。

③ 在折和摺意义可能混淆时,摺仍用摺。

④ 作多解的夥不简化。

⑤ 鬥字头的字,一般也写作門字头,如鬧、鬮、鬩写作閙、𨶹、閲。因此,这些鬥字头的字可简化作门字头。但鬥争的鬥应简作斗。

⑥ 宫商角徵羽的徵读 zhǐ(止),不简化。

⑦ 在余和馀意义可能混淆时,仍作馀。如文言句“馀年无多”。

⑧ 藉口、凭藉的藉简化作借,慰藉、狼藉等的藉仍用藉。

⑨ 瞭:读 liǎo(了解)时,仍简作了,读 liào(瞭望)时作瞭,不简作了。

⑩ 四川省酆都县已改丰都县。姓酆的酆不简化作邦。

⑪ 雠:用于校雠、雠定、仇雠等。表示仇恨、仇敌义时用仇。

图书在版编目(CIP)数据

新时代汉英大词典/吴景荣,程镇球主编。－北京:商务印书馆,2000
ISBN 7－100－02717－9

I.新… II.①吴… ②程… III.①英语－词典 ②对照词典－汉、英 IV.H316

中国版本图书馆 CIP 数据核字 (1998) 第 21325 号

XĪNSHÍDÀI HÀNYĪNG DÀCÍDIǍN
新时代汉英大词典
吴景荣 程镇球 主编

商务印书馆出版
(北京王府井大街36号 邮政编码100710)
商务印书馆发行
北京景煌激光照排有限公司排版
河北三河市艺苑印刷厂印刷
ISBN 7－100－02717－9/H·699

2000年8月第1版 开本 787×1092 1/16
2001年7月北京第4次印刷 印张 138 3/4 插页 1
印数 10 000 册

定价: 185.00 元

目　录

Table of Contents

“九五”国家重点图书出版规划项目

主　　编：吴景荣　程镇球
顾　　问：潘绍中　刘丽媛　袁士槟
副主编（以姓氏笔画为序）：
任小萍（兼执行）　邹明榕　张益庭
陈敦荃（汉语）　金　莉　秦亚青
常明玉　褚广友
英语顾问：William N. Moss
Glenn A. Van Haitsma
编　　委（以姓氏笔画为序）：
万春香　马义禄　王　立　王妙琴
王　燕　杨雪燕　何　群　宋爱群
姚毓华　熊海龙　薛如林
编　　务：刘雪美　杜秀霞（校对）
电脑输入：许大力　袁慧燕　崔　峙

NEW AGE CHINESE-ENGLISH DICTIONARY

新时代汉英大词典

吴景荣 程镇球 主编

商务印书馆

THE COMMERCIAL PRESS

2001年·北京

CW00689317